MARTINDALE-HUBBELL® LAW DIRECTORY

VOLUME 5

IDAHO, ILLINOIS
INDIANA, IOWA

LexisNexis®

121 Chanlon Road, New Providence, NJ 07974 • Phone: 1-800-526-4902
Email: info@martindale.com • www.martindale.com • www.lawyers.com

Published by LexisNexis® Martindale-Hubbell®

John Roney, Senior Vice President, Operations, Customer Support, & Technology
Marty Falle, Vice President, Sales
Joe Douress, Vice President, Business Development
Philip Evans, Vice President, Chief Financial Officer
Dean Hollister, Vice President, Database Production
Carlton Dyce, Senior Director, Customer Experience

For additional help or explanation, please call Martindale-Hubbell
Customer Service at 1-800-526-4902, or in New Jersey at 908-464-6800.

International Standard Book Number: 1-56160-690-1 (Set)

Printed and bound in the United States of America
by R.R. Donnelley
Chicago, Illinois and Willard, Ohio

ISBN 1-56160-690-1

9 781561 606900

IMPORTANT NOTICES

Martindale-Hubbell® has used its best efforts in collecting and preparing material for inclusion in the **Martindale-Hubbell Law Directory** but cannot warrant that the information herein is complete or accurate, and does not assume, and hereby disclaims, any liability to any person for any loss or damage caused by errors or omissions in the **Martindale-Hubbell Law Directory** whether such errors or omissions result from negligence, accident or any other cause.

Lawyers providing information regarding themselves and their law firms for inclusion in the **Martindale-Hubbell Law Directory** are responsible for both the accuracy of the information submitted and compliance with local law and bar regulations.

Some lawyers and law firms are omitted from the **Martindale-Hubbell Law Directory** by request while others are omitted because adequate information is not available.

The Martindale-Hubbell Peer Review Ratings contained in this Directory are intended primarily for the use of lawyers and law firms in the practice of their profession. They may not be used in any advertisement or for any commercial, political or other purpose. Peer Review Ratings may be referenced in printed lawyer-to-lawyer communications (such as law firm brochures), professional announcements, and legal directories targeted to lawyers and law firms. For more information on requirements for acknowledgements, please see Guidelines for Using Your Martindale-Hubbell Peer Review Rating on page XV, or visit www.martindale.com/ratings.

Omission of individual lawyer Peer Review Ratings should not be construed as unfavorable since Martindale-Hubbell does not undertake to develop ratings for every lawyer. In addition, certain lawyers have requested their Peer Review Ratings not be published while in other instances, definitive information has yet to be developed.

FOREWORD

We are pleased to present the 2006 edition of the **Martindale-Hubbell® Law Directory**, the world's leading guide to the legal profession since 1868.

What began as a two-volume register of recommended lawyers has evolved into a global network of over one million legal practitioners, firms, alliances, and services. Today Martindale-Hubbell's 17 volumes offer uniquely authoritative practice profiles and professional biographies of virtually every lawyer and law firm in the United States, along with extensive coverage of the international legal community in over 165 countries — from Albania to Zimbabwe.

The classic print edition represents but a single component of the Martindale-Hubbell Legal Network, a multimedia legal research and networking tool. Spanning the full array of fast-access digital formats, the **Law Directory** is also available via the *Martindale-Hubbell Lawyer Locator* at *martindale.com®* and *lawyers.com*SM, on CD-ROM, and online through LexisNexis®.

To help the lawyers and firms represented in our database unlock new opportunities for practice development, our growing network of strategic alliance partners within the legal, business, and consumer spheres offers prominent access to *martindale.com* and its consumer-facing counterpart, *lawyers.com*. Our Internet partners range from professional sites such as CNN.com and law.com to high-traffic consumer destinations including Google, Yahoo!, SuperPages and MSN, which reach over 85% of Internet users. Together, these alliance partners attract over 100 million unique visitors each month, delivering a vast universe of potential clients.

To ensure the most up-to-date information on lawyers and law firms is made available in our directories, we recently launched the *Client Service Center*. This online updating tool allows law firms to securely make changes to their Martindale-Hubbell listing whenever they have new information to share, including staff changes, new practice areas, updated contact information and recent awards.

We are also continuing to enhance and expand our Web marketing tools, designed to help law firms grow their practices via the Internet. *Custom Web Sites* and *Search Placement Pro* maximize a firm's Internet presence through sophisticated graphics, creative content, and improved ranking in the results of major search engines. City, county, state and nationwide *Sponsorships* on *lawyers.com* are also available in specific practice areas to increase visibility and drive targeted prospects to a firm's credentials.

Another initiative, *The Advantage Program*, is a unique portfolio of client development opportunities that includes speaking engagements at well-respected conferences; publication in *Counsel to Counsel* magazine and in *Legal Articles* on *martindale.com*; the opportunity to co-host a Counsel to Counsel forum; expanded practice area and industry *Group Profiles* and *Diversity Profiles* on our proprietary Web sites.

In addition, we are pleased to announce that we've re-launched *Experts & Services* on *martindale.com*. The new *Experts & Services* — available from links via *martindale.com's* home page or directly at www.martindale.com/resources — is the Internet's most comprehensive directory of resources available to attorneys. It includes extensive information on experts, consultants, investigators, court reporters, and many other legal-service providers.

While technological advances will no doubt further enhance the practice of law and our own offering of services, nothing will change Martindale-Hubbell's fundamental partnership with the legal profession: a commitment to enhance the visibility and working efficiency of every firm and individual attorney.

Carlton Dyce
Senior Director, Customer Experience

TABLE OF CONTENTS

TABLE OF CONTENTS — *continued*

LEGAL ADVISORY BOARD

The Advisory Board's mission is to ensure that LexisNexis and Martindale-Hubbell are responsive to the constantly changing needs of the legal profession. In response to these needs, the Board entertains new strategies and concepts developed by the company, and provides impartial and candid points of view. The following lawyers selected from the private, corporate, academic and international sectors of the profession comprise the 2005-2006 Board.

DENNIS W. ARCHER of Dickinson Wright PLLC; Detroit, Michigan. Mr. Archer is the former Mayor of the City of Detroit, (1994-2001) and a former Associate Justice of the Michigan Supreme Court (1986-1990). He is the past President of the Wolverine Bar Association, the National Bar Association and the State Bar of Michigan. Mr. Archer is the past President of the National League of Cities, past President of the National Conference of Democratic Mayors and a past member of the Board of Trustees of the United States Conference of Mayors and Board of Directors of the National Conference of Black Mayors. He currently serves on the American Bar Association's Board of Governors. He was President of the American Bar Association-August 2002 to August 2003, the first person of color to be so honored. He also serves as Chairman of Dickinson Wright PLLC.

MARTHA W. BARNETT of Holland & Knight, Tallahassee, Florida. Ms. Barnett is a former Chair of the House of Delegates of the American Bar Association, the first woman lawyer to be so honored, and has served on the ABA's Board of Governors. She was elected President of the American Bar Association, serving as such from July 2000 to August 2001. Ms. Barnett now serves as Chair of Holland & Knight.

ROBERT H. BERNSTEIN joined Reed Smith in January 2005. Mr. Bernstein heads the Firm's Labor & Employment Global Marketing Team, strengthening the Firm's offering to its national and international corporate clients. During the past 23 years, Mr. Bernstein has developed an extensive labor and employment practice, exclusively representing multinational and domestic corporations nationwide, with an emphasis in employment litigation. Mr. Bernstein lectures and writes extensively throughout the United States and overseas concerning a wide array of employment law issues. In 1982, Mr. Bernstein earned his J.D. from Georgetown University Law Center; in 1979, he received his B.S.F.S., with distinction, from the Georgetown University School of Foreign Service. Mr. Bernstein is admitted to the New Jersey Bar, the U.S. Court of Appeals for the Third Circuit, and the U.S. District Court for the District of New Jersey. He is a member of the Labor Law Section and Litigation Section of the American Bar Association.

BENJAMIN R. CIVILETTI of Venable, Baetjer, Howard & Civiletti, Washington, D.C. and Baltimore, Maryland. Mr. Civiletti is a former Attorney General of the United States under President Carter, 1979-1981. He is the former Chairman of the ABA Litigation Section and has been a member of the ABA House of Delegates since 1991. He also serves as the ABA Representative to the United Nations. He is the former Chairman of Venable. Mr. Civiletti is a Fellow of the American College of Trial Lawyers and the American Law Institute.

THOMAS R. CURTIN of Graham, Curtin & Sheridan, A Professional Association, Morristown, New Jersey. Mr. Curtin is a Life Fellow of the American Bar Foundation. He is a past President of the Morris County Bar Association (1978-1979), the New Jersey State Bar Foundation (1986-1988), the New Jersey State Bar Association (1993-1994), and the Notre Dame Law Foundation (2000-2001). He is a former Chairman of the New Jersey Commission on Professionalism in the Law (1996-1998). He is a member of the American Bar Association House of Delegates, serving as the New Jersey State Delegate, and the Sports Lawyers Association. He is currently a member of the Notre Dame Law School Advisory Council and has been on the Board of Directors for the National Football Foundation and College Hall of Fame since 2002.

THOMAS G. HEINTZMAN, O.C., Q.C., is a trial and appellant counsel practicing with the law firm of McCarthy Tétrault, Toronto, Ontario. He is a Bencher of the Law Society of Upper Canada and an Officer of the Order of Canada. Mr. Heintzman is a Fellow of the International Academy of Trial Lawyers, and the American College of Trial Lawyers and the Chair of its Canadian Competitions Committee.

DOUGLAS B. HENDERSON is the Founding and Senior Partner of Finnegan, Henderson, Farabow, Garrett & Dunner, Washington, D.C. Mr. Henderson is a Member of the Advisory Council of the United States Court of Federal Claims, and a Member of the Board of the Federal Circuit Bar Association. He was formerly Chairman of the Patent Division and Member of Council of the Section of Intellectual Property Law of the American Bar Association. He was the Founder of the Federal Circuit Bar Association, a co-founder of the U.S. Court of Federal Claims Bar Association, and a co-founder of the ITC Trial Lawyers Association.

PATRICK E. HOBBS, Dean of Seton Hall University School of Law, first joined the faculty of Seton Hall in 1990. He teaches in the area of taxation and has taught Federal Income Taxation, Corporate Taxation and Business Planning, and Law and Literature. In 1995, he became the Associate Dean for Finance. In 1999, he became the Law School's seventh Dean. Dean Hobbs graduated magna cum laude from Seton Hall University with a B.S. in Accounting. He received his J.D. from the University of North Carolina at Chapel Hill, and earned his LL.M. from New York University. Dean Hobbs was recently appointed a Commissioner on the New Jersey State Commission of Investigation by former Governor James McGreevy. He has chaired the American Bar Association, Section of Legal Education and Admissions to the Bar, Law School Development Committee since 2002, and was also recently appointed to serve on the American Bar Association Standards Review Committee. He also serves as a member of the boards of the Newark Alliance, LexisNexis, Newark Beth Israel Medical Center, the New Jersey Commission of Professionalism, and the New Jersey Institute for Continuing Legal Education. In 2004, he served as Chair of the Newark, New Jersey Mayor's Blue Ribbon Commission on the Downtown Core Redevelopment.

THOMAS J. KLITGAARD, formerly Senior Vice President and General Counsel of Sega of America, Inc., is now a partner with Dillingham & Murphy, San Francisco. He is a former Chairman of the California State Bar's Committee on the Maintenance of Professional Competence. He is a member of the panel of technology arbitrators of the American Arbitration Association in New York and a member of the Advisory Board of the Southwestern Legal Foundation in Dallas. He is currently the chairman of a graduate business management program in Shanghai, China.

RALPH I. LANCASTER, JR. of Pierce Atwood, Portland, Maine has served as Independent Counsel, In Re Herman, by appointment of the Special Division of the D.C. Court of Appeals. He previously served as Counsel for the United States before the International Court of Justice in a case concerning delimitation of the Maritime Boundary in the Gulf of Maine and as Special Master by appointment of the United States Supreme Court in State of New Jersey vs. State of Nebraska and again as Special Master in State of Virginia vs. State of Maryland. Mr. Lancaster began his legal career as a law clerk to the Honorable Edward T. Gignoux. He is a Past-President of the Maine State Bar Association and a former member of the House of Delegates of the American Bar Association. He served as Chair of the Standing Committee on Federal Judiciary of the ABA. He is a Fellow of the American College of Trial Lawyers and served as its President, 1989-1990. He is engaged in civil and criminal trial practice.

JUDY PERRY MARTINEZ of Northrop Grumman Corp., New Orleans, Louisiana. Ms. Martinez has been on the Board of Directors of the American Judicature Society, (1991-1998) and the Elmo B. Hunter Center for Judicial Excellence, (1994-1997). She is a Lifetime Fellow of the Louisiana Bar Foundation and a Fellow of the American Bar Foundation. She is a Member of the New Orleans, Louisiana State (Chairperson of the Minority Involvement and Professionalism and Quality of Life Committee, 1992-1993) and American (Member of the Executive Committee, 1998-1999; Board of Governors, 1996-1999; Standing Committee on Federal Judiciary (2000-2003); Commission on Women in the Profession, 1991-1994; ABA Nominating Committee, 1993-1996;

LEGAL ADVISORY BOARD — *continued*

Chair: Young Lawyers Division, 1990-1991; Chair Commission on Domestic Violence, 1999—; Member: Executive Council, Young Lawyers Division, 1986-1996; Special Advisor, Standing Committee on the Federal Judiciary, 1994-1995; Division Delegate, 1991-1996 and Delegate-at-Large, 1999—, ABA House of Delegates; Young Lawyers Division Liason to the ABA Section of Litigation, 1991-1993); Bar Associations and also the Association for Women Attorneys.

JERALYN E. MERRITT is a criminal defense lawyer in private practice in Colorado. Her practice is limited to criminal defense and related forfeitures, with an emphasis on complex federal drug and white collar crimes. Ms. Merritt served as Treasurer and Secretary and on the Board of Directors of the National Association of Criminal Defense Lawyers, from 1996 through 2004. She was a member of the governing council of the American Bar Association's Criminal Justice Section from 2000 through 2004. She is an elected fellow of the American Board of Criminal Lawyers and a past member of its Board of Governors. Ms. Merritt has testified before both Congress and the United States Sentencing Commission on drug sentencing laws. She is the co-author of a text on the Patriot Act, published by Lexis Publishing. She lectures nationally on a variety of criminal defense topics, and since 1996, has provided insightful legal analysis for MSNBC, Fox News, CNN, Court TV and other television and radio networks. From 2000 to 2003, she was a Lecturer-In-Law at Denver University's College of Law teaching "Wrongful Convictions" and "Criminal Defense." In 1996 and 1997, she served as one of the principal trial lawyers for Timothy McVeigh in the Oklahoma City Bombing Case. She is the founder and creator of two award winning websites, CrimeLynx.com, and TalkLeft: The Politics of Crime (TalkLeft.com), a weblog for legal professionals, journalists and the public.

PAUL F. MICKEY, JR. is a partner in Steptoe & Johnson LLP of Washington, D.C. Prior to joining Steptoe & Johnson LLP, Mr. Mickey was with Pillsbury Winthrop Shaw Pittman LLP where he founded the firm's employment law practice and led it for a decade prior to assuming a full-time management role. He has served as Chair of the D.C. Bar's Subcommittee on Individual Employment Rights, handled several noted employment cases, and argued successfully before the U.S. Supreme Court. Mr. Mickey often serves as an arbitrator in cases involving contract, commercial, workplace, and environmental disputes, and is a member of the CPR Panels of Distinguished Neutrals. He received his A.B. degree, summa cum laude, from Princeton University in 1971, and in 1974 he was awarded his J.D. degree from the University of Virginia Law School, where he served as Articles Editor of the Virginia Law Review. His professional background includes serving as law clerk to the Hon. George E. MacKininnon, U.S. Court of Appeals for the District of Columbia Circuit, 1974-1977; as Attorney-Advisor in the Office of Legal Advisor, U.S. Department of State, 1975-1977; and as Vice President-General Counsel, 1979-1983, and Executive Vice President - Law and Public Affairs, 1983-1985, of the National Railroad Passenger Corp. ("Amtrak"). He is a Fellow of the College of Law Practice Management.

WILLIAM G. PAUL of Crowe & Dunlevy, Oklahoma City, Oklahoma. Mr. Paul is the former Senior Vice President & General Counsel, Phillips Petroleum Company, Bartlesville, Oklahoma. In 1999, he was elected President of the American Bar Association, to serve as such from August 1999 to July 2000. He has served as President for both the Oklahoma State Bar Association and National Conference of Bar Presidents. Mr. Paul has been a Member of the American Bar Association, House of Delegates since 1975 and is a Fellow in the American College of Trial Lawyers.

FERNANDO POMBO, Founder and Senior Partner of Gomez-Acebo & Pombo, Madrid, Spain, has contributed to and authored several publications in the field of international business law. Currently, he is Vice-President of the International Bar Association. Mr. Pombo has been a visiting professor at the Institute on International Legal Studies in Salzburg, Austria since 1985. He is also a former President of LES International and a member of the Spanish Arbitration Court. He is fluent in Spanish, English, French and German.

WM. REECE SMITH, JR. of Tampa, Florida, is the senior member of Carlton, Fields, Ward, Emmanuel, Smith & Cutler, P.A. A Rhodes Scholar at Oxford University, England, he was later President of The Florida Bar (1972-73), the American Bar Association (1980-81), and the International Bar Association (1988-90). He is a Fellow of the American College of Trial Lawyers and the International Academy of Trial Lawyers and serves on the Council of the American Law Institute. He received the American Bar Association's Gold Medal for "exceptionally distinguished service to the cause of American Jurisprudence."

STEVEN T. WALTHER of Walther, Key, Maupin, Oats, Cox & LeGoy of Reno, Nevada, is a Trustee of The National Judicial College, former President of the Boalt Hall Alumni Association, University of California, Berkeley, Immediate past Chair of The Fellows of the American Bar Foundation, and a member of the Executive Board of the ABA Central and East European Law Initiative. Mr. Walther previously served as a member of the Board of Governors of the ABA, President of the State Bar of Nevada, Chair of the Board of Trustees of The Nevada Law Foundation, Chair of the ABA Standing Committee on World Order Under Law, and Chair of the ABA Section on International Activities. Mr. Walther has also served as the ABA representative to the United Nations. Mr. Walther has a degree in Russian and has lectured extensively on rule of law, international and human rights issues, both in the United States and Russia.

WALTER H. WHITE, JR. is a Founding Partner of White, Savelieva, LLP London, England. Mr. White previously has served as a Partner of Steptoe & Johnson L.L.P. in Washington, D.C. and as the Managing Director of its Moscow office. Mr. White is a former Commissioner of Securities for the State of Wisconsin 1988-1991. He has served as a member of the ABA House of Delegates, as the Chair of the Section of Individual Rights and Responsibilities and as chair of the Young Lawyers Division. Mr. White has also been a member of the State Bar of Wisconsin Board of Governors, on the Board of the Milwaukee Foundation and is currently a Board member of the Central-Asian-American Enterprise Fund by appointment of former President Clinton. He also currently serves as a member of the American Bar Association Board of Governors.

LONNIE J. WILLIAMS, JR. is a Partner of Quarles & Brady LLP, Phoenix, Arizona. Mr. Williams has served as Past President of the Maricopa County Bar Association and as a Past Delegate of the American Bar Association. He is also a Member of the National Bar Association and the Arizona Women Lawyers Association and currently serves as President for the National Conference of Bar Presidents. Mr. Williams was inducted as a Fellow into the American College of Trial Lawyers and the American Bar Foundation. He has been listed in the *Best Lawyers in America* since 1995.

USER GUIDE

The **Martindale-Hubbell® Law Directory** now consists of:

- twelve numbered U.S. volumes (burgundy spine accent). Each volume consists of three main sections, which have been separated for easy access: Practice Profiles on blue pages, Professional Biographies on white pages and Experts & Services on white pages following the divider tab. Included in Volume 1 are listings for the Corporate Law Departments and in Volume 12 are Law School listings. In each Section, headings are provided at the top of each page to indicate the section being referenced and to provide a guide to the listings on that page.
- two volumes of the **Martindale-Hubbell International Law Directory** (blue spine accent), containing listings for lawyers and firms in over 165 countries (including sections for Canada and U.S. lawyers with international interests).
- one **Martindale-Hubbell Law Digest** for the U.S. (black spine accent).
- one **Martindale-Hubbell International Law Digest** (black spine accent).
- one **Martindale-Hubbell Directory of Experts & Legal Services** (Buyer's Guide), a national directory of service providers to the legal industry.

Guam, Northern Mariana Islands, Puerto Rico, U.S. Pacific Territories and the U.S. Virgin Islands can be found both at the end of the U.S. volumes (Volume 12) and in the appropriate sections of the **Martindale-Hubbell International Law Directory** (see Table of Contents).

EXPLANATORY NOTES AND SYMBOLS

Dates following a name, i.e., "'31 '57," indicate the year of birth and the year of first admission to the Bar.

"C." or "L." followed by a numeral indicates the college or law school attended; first degree, if known, is shown following the number. See Index of Colleges, Universities and Law Schools in prefatory section.

Individual alphabetical listings, which are published without charge or other obligation, include lawyers admitted and located at a particular place, as well as others who are not admitted to the Bar of that jurisdiction. In the case of the latter, nonadmission is shown, as is the state of first admission. *It is always possible that a lawyer has been admitted subsequent to the insertion of a listing.* Confirmation of individual state admission can be obtained by writing the admitting authority of the jurisdiction or the lawyer.

"*" following the name of a place in the United States or Canada indicates a county seat. *Population* figures following the name of the place are the most recent available.

"[Lobe,B.&R.]" indicates a lawyer is in the primary firm management of Lobe, Bryant & Rogers; such as member, partner, managing partner, principal, shareholder, senior partner, marketing partner, hiring partner or director; or is an employee of an office operating as a legal professional association, company, corporation or other legal entity, unless otherwise disclosed.

"[Ⓐ Hane,M.&H.]" indicates a lawyer is employed as a junior partner, senior attorney, senior associate or similar position by the office shown.

"[Ⓒ Shipley&S.]" indicates a lawyer has the relationship of Counsel or Of Counsel, senior or special counsel with the office shown.

"[Ⓢ Snell,S.C.&B.]" indicates a lawyer is employed as a staff or contract attorney by the office shown.

"***PRACTICE AREAS***" appearing near the end of a lawyer's professional biography indicates the area(s) of practice to which he or she devotes a significant portion of professional time. In each case, the information has been supplied by the attorney and constitutes a "representation" by the lawyer and does not imply official approval or certification by any state authority.

All "officially recognized" specialties are indicated with language that identifies the approving or certifying authority. Such programs are now in existence in Arizona, Arkansas, California, Connecticut, Florida, Georgia, Idaho, Indiana, Louisiana, Michigan, Minnesota, New Jersey, New Mexico, North Carolina, Ohio, Pennslyvania, South Carolina, Tennessee, Texas and Ontario, Canada.

Title of public office, company name, government agency, educational institution, etc., with which a lawyer is connected is shown in his or her listing.

Professional Companies, Corporations or Associations: Chartered, Associated, P.C., P.A., S.C., Inc., Ltd., etc. following the name of an individual lawyer or law firm means that such office is operating as a Professional Company, Corporation or Association under the laws of that jurisdiction.

"‡" indicates one who devotes all or the greater part of one's time to the affairs of a single client, or is retired, semi-retired or semi-active, or principally engaged in activities other than the practice of law.

"⊙" indicates a lawyer maintains law offices at more than one place.

"★" indicates a lawyer is with the Armed Forces.

"(Pat.)" indicates lawyers who are registered to practice before the U.S. Patent and Trademark Office and who devote a considerable portion of time or duties to Patent, Trademark and other related matters.

"Ⓣ" indicates the Peer Review Rating was established in an admitting jurisdiction other than where the attorney is currently listed.

"BR" indicates a subscriber to the **Martindale-Hubbell® Bar Register of Preeminent Lawyers™**.

SECTION DESCRIPTIONS

PRACTICE PROFILES (BLUE PAGES)

This section contains rosters for the Bars of the United States. Listings of United States Government Lawyers located in Washington, D.C. are grouped by departments, agencies and commissions, etc. and follow the regular listings for that city in Volume 3.

This Section is alphabetically arranged by state, by city or town, and then by name of attorney or law firm. Contact information for state bar associations appears on the first page of each state.

Listings for individual attorneys include the following information, when available: name, Peer Review Rating (if any), year of birth, first year of admission to the Bar, college attended, first degree received, law school attended, first degree received, and where the attorney practices.

A typical individual attorney listing follows:

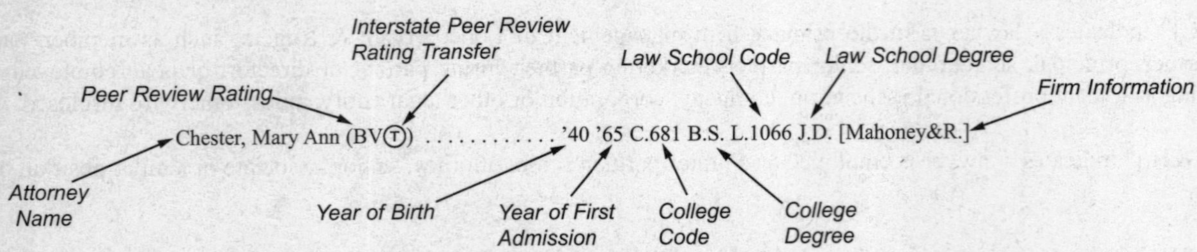

Law firm listings provide name, address and rating information, where available.

A typical law firm listing will appear as follows:

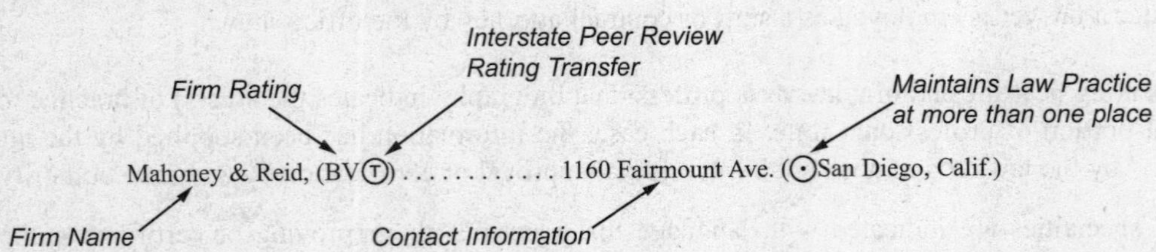

Practice Profiles listings for subscribing attorneys and law firms appear in boldface type and include name, Peer Review Rating (if available), address, firm personnel, statement of practice, representative clients, references, and language proficiency as well as other pertinent information.

Typical Subscriber Full Practice Profiles follow:

Firm Subscriber:

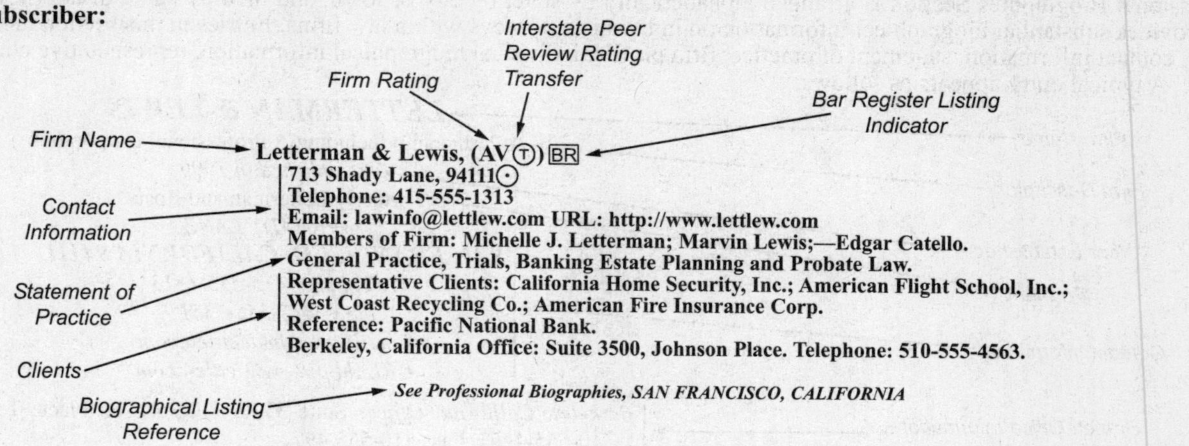

Firm — members, associates, etc.:

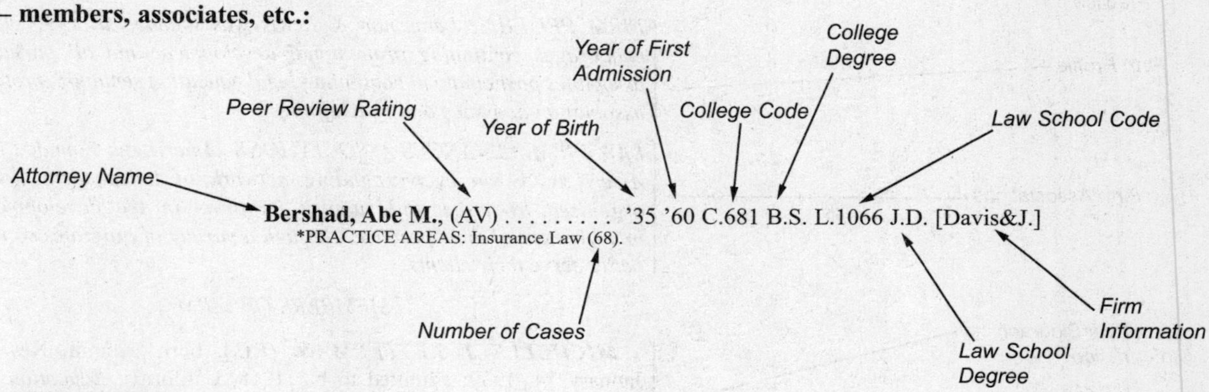

Individual subscriber:

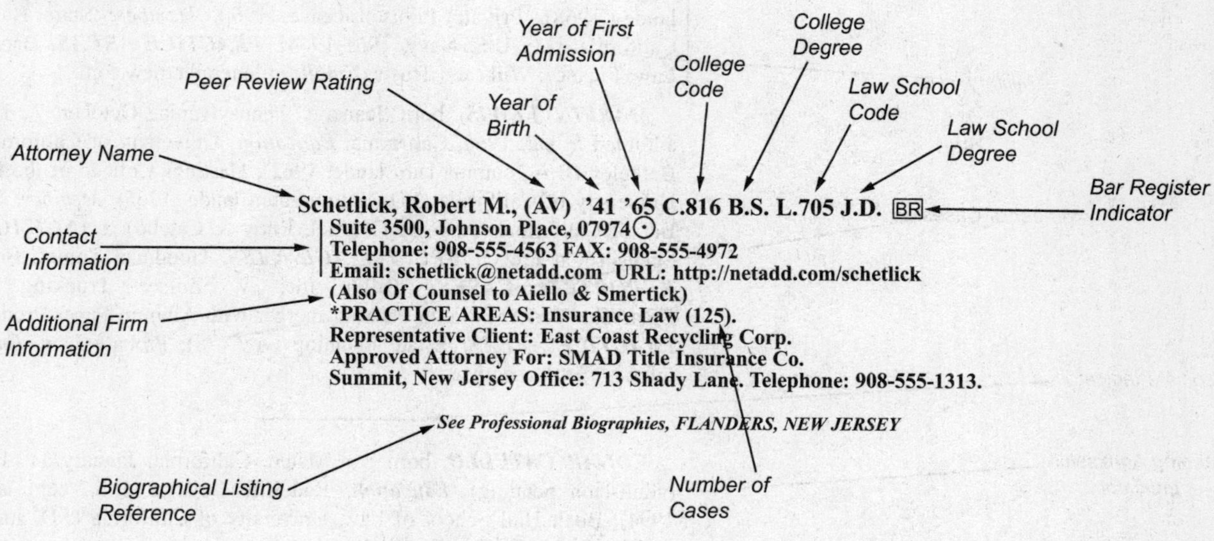

PATENT AND TRADEMARK PRACTICE PROFILES (BLUE PAGES)

This Section contains the names of subscribing lawyers registered to practice Patent Law and those who practice Trademark Law before the United States Patent and Trademark Office and who devote a considerable portion of their practice or duties to this field of law. It is arranged in the same manner as the Practice Profiles Section.

USER GUIDE: SECTION DESCRIPTIONS — *continued*

PROFESSIONAL BIOGRAPHIES (WHITE PAGES)

The Professional Biographies Section is arranged alphabetically by state, by city or town, and then by name of attorney or law firm. It provides substantial biographical information on individual attorneys within law firms. Entries in this section include the firm name, contact information, statement of practice, firm profile, individual biographical information, representative clients and references. A typical entry appears as follows:

Firm Name

LETTERMAN & LEWIS

Firm Descriptor

A Partnership including A Professional Corporation

Year Established

Established in 1990

Formerly

Formerly Letterman and Rosta

Contact Information

731 SHADY LANE

SAN FRANCISCO, CALIFORNIA 94111

Telephone: 415-555-1313

FAX: 415-555-7351

Email: lawinfo@lettlew.com

URL: http://www.lettlew.com

Branch Office Information

Berkeley, California Office: Suite 3500, 110 Johnson Place. Telephone: 510-555-4563. Fax: 510-555-4972.

Statement of Practice

General Practice, Trials, Banking, Finance, Wills, Trusts, Estate Planning and Probate Law.

Firm Profile

FIRM PROFILE: Letterman & Lewis was founded in 1990. The firm encourages continuing professional development and all partners and associates participate in continuing legal education seminars, professional association activities and civic affairs.

Firm Associations

LAW FIRM ALLIANCES/ASSOCIATIONS: ***AmeriLaw:*** *Founded in 1981, AmeriLaw is an ever-expanding network of independent law firms organized to assist and support its firms in the development and improvement of their practices through a variety of programs so they can better serve their clients.*

MEMBERS OF FIRM

Individual Biographical Information

MICHELLE J. LETTERMAN, (P.C.), born Summit, New Jersey, January 14, 1939; admitted to bar 1968, California. *Education:* United States Naval Academy (B.S., 1960); Harvard University (J.D., summa cum laude, 1968). Private Pilots License, 1960. *Member:* State Bar of California. [Lt., U.S. Navy, 1961-1964]. ***PRACTICE AREAS:*** Banking Law; Finance; Wills and Trusts. ***Email:*** mjletter@lettlew.com

Military

MARVIN LEWIS, born Jeanette, Pennsylvania, October 7, 1940; admitted to bar, 1965, California. *Education:* University of California at Berkeley (B.A., summa cum laude, 1962); Hastings College of the Law, University of California (J.D., summa cum laude, 1965). *Member:* State Bar of California. (Also Of Counsel, Rudy & Catello). ***LANGUAGES:*** Spanish and French. ***SPECIAL AGENCIES:*** Goodman Zoning Board. ***REPORTED CASES:*** Bilko Inc. v. Zotser Trucking Co. ***TRANSACTIONS:*** Aiello Packing merger with Alboum Paper Products. ***PRACTICE AREAS:*** Estate Planning Law (78); Probate Law. ***Email:*** mlewis@lettlew.com

Number of Cases

Associate Indicator

Pending Admission Indicator

EDGAR CATELLO, born San Mateo, California, January 11, 1972; (admission pending). *Education:* Radcliffe College (B.S., cum laude, 1994); Boalt Hall School of Law, University of California (J.D. summa cum laude, 1998). ***Email:*** ecatello@lettlew.com

LEGAL SUPPORT PERSONNEL

Individual Email Address

KATHLEEN VEGA, born Summit, New Jersey, August 22, 1962. *Education:* Rutgers University (B.A., 1984). Certified Paralegal, New Jersey, 1984. *Member:* National Association of Paralegals. (Paralegal). ***PRACTICE AREAS:*** Estates.

Clients

REPRESENTATIVE CLIENTS: California Home Security, Inc.; American Flight School, Inc.; West Coast Recycling Co.; American Fire Insurance Corp.
REFERENCE: Pacific National Bank.

CORPORATE LAW DEPARTMENTS (WHITE PAGES)

Corporate Law Department representations reside in Volume 1. They are arranged alphabetically by name and present information about corporations and corporate attorneys. Typical information supplied includes name, company profile, office location(s) and type of business.

LAW SCHOOLS (WHITE PAGES)

The Law School Section, in Volume 12, profiles the academic programs, special course offerings and teaching staff of participating schools. Non-participating schools are also identified.

For each school, the data may include: school name, address, telephone and fax numbers; a substantial profile including ABA approval information, history, academic character, resources, special programs and activities of the institution; the names, titles and direct dial numbers of key contacts; and a roster of full-time faculty with biographical summary information. This Section is arranged alphabetically by law school name.

School Name → ***JOHN A. JAMES SCHOOL OF LAW***

Contact Information →

214 HOYT AVENUE
HONOLULU, HAWAII 98621
Telephone: (808) 555-9038
Fax: (808) 555-0983
Email: law@jaj.edu
URL: http://www.jaj.law.edu

ABA Approval Information → **ABA Approved Since 1994**

School Profile →

The John A. James School of Law is a privately funded institution with a highly diversified student body, representing over 40 countries. Founded in 1988, it quickly achieved a reputation as one of the top universities specializing in the area of environmental law. With close connections to several firms on the North American and Asian continents, the School of Law provides its students with the opportunity to experience law as practiced on both sides of the Pacific. Sixty full-time faculty members represent 35 law schools across the globe; holding a total of 40 advanced degrees in law and 18 Ph.D. degrees.

Key Contacts →

Dean: John Posta (808) 555-5649
Admissions Officer: Tracey Hutchinson (808) 555-6218
Director of Library Services: Robert Berry (808) 555-6214
Placement Officer: Harriett Ko (808) 555-8281

FULL TIME FACULTY

Faculty Sketch →

ARTHUR JAMES, born Newark, New Jersey, June 30, 1957; admitted to bar 1982, New Jersey. Education: Drew University (B.A., 1978; M.A. 1984); Harvard University (J.D., 1982); Yale University (LL.M., 1985; J.S.D. 1989). Professor and a Director of the Environmental Law Center. *Courses:* Environmental Liability, Water Rights, Torts.

STATE BAR ASSOCIATION PROFILES

State Bar Association Profiles can now be found at *www.martindale.com*. These profiles include a bar profile, mission statements of the association, names of officers, directors, and key staff personnel, as well as membership and program information.

EXPERTS & SERVICES (WHITE PAGES)

Experts & Services provides information on businesses and professionals serving the legal community. This section is arranged alphabetically by state, city or town, category of service provided, and company name. Typical information in the company listing includes contact information, company profile, office locations and services provided.

DIRECTORY OF EXPERTS & SERVICES (BUYER'S GUIDE)

The Directory of Experts & Services (Buyer's Guide) is a print directory that's provided (at no additional cost) as part of each Martindale-Hubbell subscription. This directory is a national consolidation of the thousands of Experts & Services listings contained in the Martindale-Hubbell Law Directories (see above) and places them in one, easy to use desk reference.

USER AIDS

In the front matter, sections are provided to aid in the use of the Directory. "Explanatory Notes and Symbols," found on page IX, provides a guide to the various symbols and notations which are utilized in the individual entries. The "Index of Colleges, Universities, and Law Schools," found on page XVII, provides a comprehensive guide to numeric codes which are used in Practice Profiles listings to indicate academic institutions and law schools attended by individual attorneys.

Page numbers in the 2006 **Martindale-Hubbell® Law Directory** are constructed in the format XXYYYZ, where XX is the state, province or international grouping, YYY is a consecutive page numbering, and Z is a code denoting section.

Pages listing attorneys under the U.S. Government use the abbreviation "GV", the Law School Section uses the abbreviation "LS", and the Corporate Section uses the abbreviation "C". For International Volumes, the following group abbreviations are used:

EU	Europe	NA	North America
AS	Asia	CB	The Caribbean
AU	Australasia	CS	Central & South America
AF	Middle East & Africa		

Z may be one of the following:

P	Practice Profiles	T	Patent & Trademark
B	Professional Biographies	S	Experts and Services

For additional help or explanation, please call Martindale-Hubbell Customer Service at 1-800-526-4902, or in New Jersey at 908-464-6800.

LEXISNEXIS MARTINDALE-HUBBELL PEER REVIEW RATINGS

The first Martindale books were published in 1868, the principal one being *Martindale's United States Law Directory* and later *Martindale's American Law Directory*.

In 1930, the publishing rights to *Hubbell's Legal Directory* were purchased by the Martindale Company and ever since has been known as the **Martindale-Hubbell® Law Directory**.

Legal Ability and General Ethical Standards Ratings have appeared in the Directory for over 100 years. Martindale-Hubbell strives to publish fair and accurate Peer Review Ratings for as many lawyers as possible, subscribers and non-subscribers alike. While the vast majority of rating reviews are initiated by the Company, an inquiry will be undertaken upon request. When forwarding legal matters, lawyers in private practice and in corporate law departments rely with confidence on the accuracy of the Peer Review Ratings published.

Legal Ability Ratings are: "C" (from Good to High), "B" (from High to Very High), "A" (from Very High to Preeminent).

General Ethical Standards Rating is: "V" (Very High).

Unless a Peer Review Rating is established in both categories, no rating will be published.

Over 115,000 rating reviews are undertaken each year. Of those, approximately 80% are done at our own initiative. An additional 20% are conducted by request and through the efforts of our Field Staff.

Martindale-Hubbell develops its Peer Review Ratings for individual lawyers by soliciting confidential opinions from members of the Bar, including those who themselves have ratings and those who do not. In addition, members of the U.S. Judiciary are queried. We encourage all lawyers to participate in the process. Greater participation assures the continued accuracy of the system. Respondents to written questionnaires and personal interviews are asked to base their opinions on the following:

LEGAL ABILITY RATING

Based on the standard of ability for the area where the lawyer practices, it takes into consideration experience, nature of practice and qualifications relevant to the profession. Where a lawyer's practice is limited or specialized, rating opinions are made on the basis of performance in those Fields of Law.

GENERAL ETHICAL STANDARDS RATING

Embraces faithful adherence to professional standards of conduct and ethics of the legal profession, professional reliability and diligence, and standards relevant to the attorney's discharge of his or her professional responsibilities.

Legal Ability and General Ethical Standards Ratings appearing in the Directory reflect strictly confidential opinions and responses to professionally developed surveys and adhere to meticulously monitored research principles and practices. Martindale-Hubbell does not make any independent evaluation of lawyers. Rather, it depends exclusively upon the opinions of its confidential sources.

FIRM RATING

Generally, a law firm will be accorded the rating of its highest-rated principal.

In some instances, lawyers may be asked to submit names of lawyers and judges with whom they have had professional experience. Inquiries are then directed to those sources in addition to sources developed by Martindale-Hubbell.

Field Representatives of Martindale-Hubbell visit tens of thousands of law offices on an annual basis. They make oral rating inquiries during these calls and submit written reports. However, a formal rating review must occur before any Peer Review Rating is established, advanced, lowered or withdrawn.

Martindale-Hubbell does not undertake developing ratings for every listed lawyer. The absence of a rating should not be construed as unfavorable since some lawyers have requested their Peer Review Ratings not be published while in other instances definitive information has not yet been completely developed.

LEXISNEXIS MARTINDALE-HUBBELL PEER REVIEW RATINGS — *continued*

Peer Review Ratings are published for lawyers in the United States, the U.S. Virgin Islands, Northern Mariana Islands and Canada.

No subscription or listing in the **Martindale-Hubbell® Law Directory** is ever solicited or accepted on the promise of publication of a particular Peer Review Rating. No preferential consideration is ever given to any lawyer or law firm.

As a general rule, Peer Review Ratings are transferable within state boundaries. Ratings may be transferred inter-state/inter-province, with the Ⓣ symbol indicating the rating was established in another jurisdiction.

It is our policy to conduct regular periodic reviews of all Peer Review Ratings to insure their accuracy. Where supporting opinions dictate, appropriate action (such as deleting, raising or lowering a rating) is taken.

There is never any payment made to lawyers and judges who participate in rating reviews. The process is a cooperative service to the Bar. It has always been Martindale-Hubbell policy to treat all phases of the rating review process as absolutely confidential. Sources contacted participate with that understanding, and under no circumstances will any review materials ever be released.

Peer Review Ratings are intended primarily for the use of lawyers in the practice of their profession. Specific guidelines for particular uses of a Peer Review Rating or the Peer Review Rated icon can be found on the Martindale-Hubbell Peer Review Ratings website at www.martindale.com/ratings or can be requested in writing from:

LexisNexis Martindale-Hubbell
Peer Review Rating Services
121 Chanlon Road
New Providence, NJ 07974

Or via Email: ratings@martindale.com

In addition to the previously permitted uses of the Peer Review Ratings, rated lawyers are now also permitted to more widely and prominently display the Peer Review Rated icon:

LexisNexis®
Martindale-Hubbell®
Peer Review Rated
For Ethical Standards and Legal Ability

Peer Review Rated attorneys can display the icon in multiple media consistent with the original purpose of facilitating lawyer-to-lawyer referrals and also to announce to a wider audience that they have been rated by their peers. As with the other permitted uses of the Peer Review Ratings, lawyers must use the icon in compliance with the requirements of their local and state bars.

If you would like to publish your Peer Review Rating in a format not mentioned in the detailed Usage Guidelines, prior written permission from LexisNexis Martindale-Hubbell Peer Review Rating Services must be obtained.

Note: Please review Important Notices located on page III.

Index of Colleges, Universities and Law Schools

This list is a guide to the numeric school codes found in Practice Profiles Section entries. Institutions which no longer exist, junior colleges, correspondence schools or colleges with very small enrollments are not included. Such unlisted schools are indicated by the numeric code "999".

01. Acadia University
Wolfville, NS
02. Alberta, University of
Edmonton, AB
03. Bishop's University
Lennoxville, QU
04. British Columbia, Law Society of
Vancouver, BC
05. British Columbia, University of
Vancouver, BC
06. Dalhousie University
Halifax, NS
07. King's College, University of
Halifax, NS
08. Laval University
Quebec, QU
09. Concordia University
Formerly Loyola College
Montreal, QU
010. MacDonald College
Ste. A. de Bellevue, QU
011. Manitoba, University of
Winnipeg, MB
012. McGill University
Montreal, QU
013. McMaster University
Hamilton, ON
014. Montreal, University of
Montreal, QU
015. Mount Allison University
Sackville, NB
016. New Brunswick, University of
Fredericton, NB
017. Nova Scotia College of Agriculture
Truro, NS
018. Ottawa, University of
Ottawa, ON
019. Queen's University
Kingston, ON
020. St. Dunstan's University
Charlottetown, PE
021. St. Francis Xavier University
Antigonish, NS
022. St. Joseph's University
St. Joseph, NB
023. Ste. Marie, College of
Montreal, QU
024. Saskatchewan, University of
Saskatoon, SK
025. Toronto, University of
Toronto, ON
026. Upper Canada, Law Society of
Toronto, ON
027. Victoria University
Toronto, ON
028. Western Ontario, University of
London, ON
029. Osgoode Hall
Toronto, ON
030. Assumption University
Windsor, ON
031. Windsor, University of
Windsor, ON
032. Royal Military College
Kingston, ON
033. Wilfrid Laurier University
Formerly Waterloo Lutheran University
Waterloo, ON
034. Carleton University
Ottawa, ON
035. York University
Toronto, ON
036. Memorial University of Newfoundland
St. John's, NF
037. Calgary, University of
Calgary, AB
038. Waterloo, University of
Formerly Waterloo University
Waterloo, ON
039. Victoria, University of
Victoria, BC
040. Guelph, University of
Guelph, ON
041. Concordia University
Formerly (Sir) George Williams University
Montreal, QU
042. St. Marys University
Halifax, NS
043. Simon Fraser University
Burnaby, BC
044. Lethbridge, University of
Lethbridge, AB
045. Winnipeg, University of
Winnipeg, MB
046. Moncton, University of
Moncton, NB
047. St. Thomas University
Fredericton, NB
048. Regina, University of
Regina, SK
049. Brandon University
Brandon, MB
050. Cambridge University
Cambridge, England
051. Oxford University
Oxford, England
052. Heidelberg University
Baden, Germany
054. London, University of
London, England
055. Paris, University of
Formerly Sorbonne University
Paris, France
056. Rome, University of
Rome, Italy
057. Vienna, University of
Vienna, Austria
058. Trinity College, University of Dublin
Dublin, Ireland
059. Edinburgh University
Edinburgh, Scotland
060. Munich, University of
Munich, Germany
062. National University of Ireland, Dublin
Dublin, Ireland
063. Royal Military Academy
Sandhurst, England
064. Santo Thomas, University of
Manila, Philippines
065. Durham, University of
Durham, England
066. Manuel L. Quezon University
Manila, Philippines
067. Stockholm, University of
Stockholm, Sweden
068. Queen's University, The
Belfast, Northern Ireland
080. Lakehead University
Thunder Bay, ON
081. Brock University
St. Catharines, ON
082. Prince Edward Island, University of
Charlottetown, PE
083. Laurentian University of Sudbury
Sudbury, ON
084. Trent University
Peterborough, ON
085. Quebec, University of
Sainte Foy, Montreal, Trois-Rivieres, Chicoutimi, Hull and Rimouski, QU
086. Sherbrooke, University of
Sherbrooke, QU
087. Quebec Bar Law School
Montreal, QU
1. Abilene Christian University
Abilene, TX
3. Adams State College
Alamosa, CO
4. Adelphi University
Garden City, NY
5. Adrian College
Adrian, MI
6. Agnes Scott College
Decatur, GA
7. Akron University Law School
Akron, OH
8. Akron, University of
Formerly Buchtel College
Akron, OH
9. Montevallo, University of
Formerly Alabama College
Montevallo, AL
10. Auburn University
Formerly Alabama Polytechnic Institute
Auburn and Montgomery, AL
11. North Alabama, University of
Formerly Alabama State Teachers College
Florence, AL
12. Jacksonville State University
Formerly Alabama State Teachers College
Jacksonville, AL
13. West Alabama, The University of
Formerly Livingston University
Livingston, AL
14. Alabama State University
Formerly Montgomery State College
Montgomery, AL
15. Troy State University
Formerly Alabama State Teachers CollegeTroy, AL
16. Alabama, University of
Birmingham, Huntsville and Tuscaloosa, AL
17. Alaska, University of
Fairbanks, Anchorage and Juneau, AK
18. Albany College
Portland, OR
19. Albertus Magnus College
New Haven, CT
20. Albion College
Albion, MI
21. Albright College
Reading, PA
22. Alcorn A. & M. College
Alcorn, MS
23. Alderson-Broaddus College
Philippi, WV
24. Alfred University
Alfred, NY
25. Allegheny College
Meadville, PA
26. Allen University
Columbia, SC
27. Alma College
Alma, MI
28. American International College
Springfield, MA
29. American University
Los Angeles, CA
30. American University
Washington, DC
See Also No. 904
31. Amherst College
Amherst, MA
32. Andrew Jackson University
Nashville, TN

142. Chattanooga College of Law
Chattanooga, TN
143. Tennessee at Chattanooga, University of
Formerly Chattanooga, University of
Chattanooga, TN
144. Chicago Law School
Formerly Midland University
Chicago, IL
145. Chicago, University of
Chicago, IL
146. Chicago-Kent College of Law, Illinois
Institute of Technology
Chicago, IL
147. California State University, Chico
Formerly Chico State College
Chico, CA
148. Chicora College
Columbia, SC
149. Chowan College
Murfreesboro, NC
150. Cincinnati, University of
Cincinnati, OH
151. Cincinnati Y.M.C.A. Schools
Cincinnati, OH
152. Citadel, The
Charleston, SC
153. Claflin College
Orangeburg, SC
154. Claremont McKenna College
Claremont, CA
155. Clark Atlanta University
Atlanta, GA
156. Clark University
Worcester, MA
157. Clarke College
Dubuque, IA
158. Clarkson University
Formerly Clarkson College of
Technology
Potsdam, NY
159. Cleary College
Ypsilanti, MI
160. Clemson University
Clemson, SC
161. Cleveland State University
Cleveland, OH
162. Coe College
Formerly Western College
Cedar Rapids, IA
163. Coker College
Hartsville, SC
164. Colby College
Waterville, ME
165. Colgate University
Hamilton, NY
166. Holy Names College
Formerly College of the Holy Names
Oakland, CA
167. College Misericordia
Dallas, PA
168. College of the Ozarks
Clarksville, AR
169. Pacific, University of the
Formerly College of the Pacific
Stockton, CA
See Also No. 464
170. Colorado College
Colorado Springs, CO
171. Colorado School of Mines
Golden, CO
172. Colorado State University
Formerly Colorado A. & M. College
Fort Collins, CO
173. Northern Colorado, University of
Formerly Colorado State College
Greeley, CO
174. Colorado at Boulder, University of
Boulder, CO
176. Columbia College
Columbia, SC
177. Loras College
Formerly Columbia College of
Dubuque
Dubuque, IA
178. Columbia University
New York, NY
179. Capital University
Formerly Columbus College of Law
Columbus, OH
See Also No. 117
180. Columbus School of Law of The Catholic
University of America
Washington, DC
See Also No. 128
181. Concord College
Athens, WV
182. Concordia College
Moorehead, MN
183. Connecticut College
New London, CT
184. Connecticut, University of
Storrs and Hartford, CT
185. Converse College
Spartanburg, SC
186. Cooper Union
New York, NY
187. Cornell College
Mount Vernon, IA
188. Cornell University
Ithaca, NY
189. Cotner College
Lincoln, NE
190. Creighton University
Omaha, NE
191. Culver-Stockton College
Canton, MO
192. Cumberland School of Law of Samford
University
Formerly part of Cumberland
University (now Cumberland College
of Tennessee, at Lebanon, TN)
Birmingham, AL
193. Dakota Wesleyan University
Mitchell, SD
194. Dana College
Blair, NE
195. Daniel Baker College
Brownwood, TX
196. Daniel W. Voorhees Law School
Terre Haute, IN
197. Dartmouth College
Hanover, NH
198. Davidson College
Davidson, NC
199. Davis & Elkins College
Elkins, WV
200. Dayton Law School
Dayton, OH
201. Dayton, University of
Dayton, OH
202. Decorah College for Women
Decorah, IA
203. Defiance College
Defiance, OH
204. Delaware State College
Dover, DE
205. Delaware, University of
Newark, DE
206. Delta State College
Cleveland, MS
207. Denison University
Granville, OH
208. Denver, University of
Denver, CO
209. DePaul University
Chicago, IL
210. DePauw University
Greencastle, IN
211. Des Moines College of Law
Des Moines, IA
212. Wayne University
Formerly Detroit City Law School
Detroit, MI
213. Michigan State University College of
Law
Formerly Michigan State University
Detroit College of Law
Detroit, MI
214. Detroit Institute of Technology
Detroit, MI
215. Detroit Mercy, University of
Formerly University of Detroit
Detroit, MI
216. Dickinson College
Carlisle, PA
217. Dillard University
New Orleans, LA
218. Doane College
Crete, NE
219. Dominican College of San Rafael
San Rafael, CA
220. St. Mary's Dominican College
Formerly Dominican College
New Orleans, LA
221. Drake University
Des Moines, IA
222. Drew University
Formerly Brothers College
Madison, NJ
223. Drexel University
Philadelphia, PA
224. Dropsie University
Philadelphia, PA
225. Drury College
Springfield, MO
226. Dubuque, University of
Dubuque, IA
227. Duchesne College
Omaha, NE
228. Duke University
Durham, NC
229. Duquesne University
Pittsburgh, PA
230. D'Youville College
Buffalo, NY
231. Earlham College
Richmond, IN
232. East Carolina University
Greenville, NC
233. Texas A&M University-Commerce
Formerly East Texas State University
Commerce, TX
234. Eastern Illinois University
Charleston, IL
235. Eastern Kentucky University
Formerly Kentucky Normal College
Richmond, KY
236. Eastern Nazarene College
Quincy, MA
237. Elizabethtown College
Elizabethtown, PA
238. Elmhurst College
Elmhurst, IL
239. Elmira College
Elmira, NY
240. Elon College
Elon College, NC
241. Emerson College
Boston, MA
242. Emmanuel College
Boston, MA
243. Andrews University
Formerly Emmanuel Missionary
College
Berrien Springs, MI
244. Emory and Henry College
Emory, VA
245. Emory University School of Law
Formerly Lamar School of Law
Atlanta, GA
246. Emporia, College of
Emporia, KS
247. Erskine College
Due West, SC
248. Eureka College
Eureka, IL
249. Evansville, University of
Evansville, IN
250. Fairmont State College
Fairmont, WV

362. Stetson University
Formerly John B. Stetson University
De Land and St. Petersburg, FL
363. John Carroll University
Formerly St. Ignatius College
Cleveland, OH
364. Kletzing College
Formerly John Fletcher College
University Park, IA
365. John Marshall Law School
Chicago, IL
366. John Randolph Neal College of Law
Knoxville, TN
367. Johns Hopkins University
Baltimore, MD
368. Johnson Bible College
Kimberlin Heights, TN
369. Johnson C. Smith University
Formerly Biddle University
Charlotte, NC
370. Jones Law School
Montgomery, AL
371. Judson College
Marion, AL
372. Juniata College
Huntingdon, PA
373. Kalamazoo College
Kalamazoo, MI
374. Kansas City School of Law
Part of University of Missouri at Kansas City
Kansas City, MO
375. Kansas State University
Formerly Kansas State College of Agriculture and Applied Science
Manhattan, KS
376. Emporia State University
Formerly Kansas State College
Emporia, KS
377. Pittsburg State University
Formerly Kansas State College
Pittsburg, KS
378. Kansas, University of
Lawrence, KS
379. Kansas Wesleyan University
Salina, KS
380. Keene State College
Keene, NH
381. Kent State University
Kent, OH
382. Kentucky State University
Frankfort, KY
383. Kentucky, University of
Lexington, KY
384. Kentucky Wesleyan College
Owensboro, KY
385. Kenyon College
Gambier, OH
386. Keuka College
Keuka Park, NY
387. King College
Bristol, TN
388. Knox College
Galesburg, IL
389. Knoxville College
Knoxville, TN
390. Lafayette College
Easton, PA
391. LaGrange College
LaGrange, GA
392. Lake Erie College
Painesville, OH
393. Lake Forest College
Lake Forest, IL
394. Lambuth College
Jackson, TN
395. Lander College
Greenwood, SC
396. Lane College
Jackson, TN
397. LaSalle University
Philadelphia, PA
398. La Verne, University of
La Verne, CA
399. Lawrence University
Appleton, WI
400. Lebanon Valley College
Annville, PA
401. Lehigh University
Bethlehem, PA
402. Leland College
Baker, LA
403. Le Moyne-Owen College
Memphis, TN
404. Lenoir-Rhyne College
Hickory, NC
405. Illinois Institute of Technology
Formerly Lewis Institute
Chicago, IL
See Also No. 46
406. Limestone College
Gaffney, SC
407. Lincoln College of Indiana
Indianapolis, IN
408. Lincoln College of Law
Bakersfield, CA
409. Lincoln Memorial University
Harrogate, TN
410. Lincoln University
Jefferson City, MO
411. Lincoln University
Lincoln University, PA
412. Lindenwood University
Formerly The Lindenwood Colleges
St. Charles, MO
413. Linfield College
McMinnville, OR
414. Livingstone College
Salisbury, NC
415. Long Island University, C.W. Post Campus of
Brookville, NY
416. Loretto Heights College
Denver, CO
417. Louisiana College
Pineville, LA
418. Louisiana Tech University
Formerly Louisiana Polytechnic Institute
Ruston, LA
419. Northwestern State University
Formerly Louisiana State Normal College
Natchitoches, LA
420. Louisiana State University
Baton Rouge, LA
421. Louisville, University of
Louisville, KY
422. Lowell Technological Institute
Part of University of Lowell
Lowell, MA
423. Loyola College
Baltimore, MD
424. Loyola University
Chicago, IL
425. Loyola University
New Orleans, LA
426. Loyola Marymount University
Los Angeles, CA
427. Luther College
Decorah, IA
428. Lynchburg College
Lynchburg, VA
429. Macalester College
St. Paul, MN
430. MacMurray College
Jacksonville, IL
431. Maine, University of
Orono, Farmington, Fort Kent, Machias and Presque Isle, ME
432. Manchester College
N. Manchester, IN
433. Manhattan College
Riverdale, NY
434. Marietta College
Marietta, OH
435. Marion College
Marion, IN
436. Marquette University
Milwaukee, WI
437. Marshall University
Huntington, WV
438. Mary Baldwin College
Staunton, VA
439. Mary Hardin-Baylor College
Belton, TX
440. Mary Manse College
Toledo, OH
441. Marygrove College
Detroit, MI
442. Maryland College for Women
Lutherville, MD
443. Frostburg State College
Formerly Maryland State Teachers College
Frostburg, MD
444. Salisbury State University
Formerly Maryland State Teachers College
Salisbury, MD
445. Towson State University
Formerly Maryland State Teachers College
Towson, MD
446. Maryland, University of
Baltimore and College Park, MD
447. Marylhurst College
Oswego, OR
448. Marymount College of Kansas
Salina, KS
449. Marymount College
Tarrytown, NY
450. Maryville College
St. Louis, MO
451. Maryville College
Maryville, TN
452. Marywood College
Scranton, PA
453. Massachusetts Institute of Technology
Cambridge, MA
454. Massachusetts, University of
Amherst and Boston, MA
455. Bridgewater State College
Formerly Massachusetts State College
Bridgewater, MA
456. Fitchburg State College
Formerly Massachusetts State College
Fitchburg, MA
457. Framingham State College
Formerly Massachusetts State College
Framingham, MA
458. Hyannis State College
Formerly Massachusetts State College
Hyannis, MA
459. Massachusetts Lowell, University of
Formerly Massachusetts State College
Lowell, MA
460. North Adams State College
Formerly Massachusetts State College
North Adams, MA
461. Salem State College
Formerly Massachusetts State College
Salem, MA
462. Westfield State College
Formerly Massachusetts State College
Westfield, MA
463. Worcester State College
Formerly Massachusetts State College
Worcester, MA
464. McGeorge School of Law
Part of University of the Pacific
Sacramento, CA
465. McKendree College
Lebanon, IL
466. McMurry College
Abilene, TX
467. McPherson College
McPherson, KS
468. Rutgers University
Formerly Mercer Beasley School of Law
Newark, NJ
See Also No. 705

469. Mercer University
Macon, GA
470. Mercyhurst College
Erie, PA
471. Meredith College
Raleigh, NC
472. Miami, University of
Coral Gables, FL
473. Miami University
Oxford, OH
474. Michigan Technological University
Houghton, MI
475. Michigan State University
East Lansing, MI
476. Eastern Michigan University
Formerly Michigan State Normal College
Ypsilanti, MI
477. Michigan, University of
Ann Arbor, Dearborn and Flint, MI
478. Middlebury College
Middlebury, VT
479. Middlesex University
Waltham, MA
480. Midland Lutheran College
Formerly Fremont College
Fremont, NE
481. Miles College
Birmingham, AL
482. Milligan College
Milligan College, TN
483. Mills College
Oakland, CA
484. Millsaps College
Jackson, MS
485. Milton College
Milton, WI
486. Milwaukee-Downer College
Milwaukee, WI
487. William Mitchell College of Law
Formerly Minnesota College of Law
Minneapolis, MN
See Also No. 1035
488. Bemidji State University
Bemidji, MN
489. Minnesota Duluth, University of
Duluth, MN
490. Mankato State University
Formerly Minnesota State Teachers College
Mankato, MN
491. Moorhead State University
Formerly Minnesota State Teachers College
Moorhead, MN
492. St. Cloud State University
Formerly Minnesota State Teachers College
St. Cloud, MN
493. Winona State University
Formerly Minnesota State Teachers College
Winona, MN
494. Minnesota, University of
Minneapolis and St. Paul, MN
495. Mission House College & Theological Seminary
Plymouth, WI
496. Mississippi College
Clinton, MS
497. Mississippi State University
State College, MS
498. Mississippi University for Women
Columbus, MS
499. Mississippi, University of Southern
Hattiesburg, MS
500. Mississippi, University of
University, MS
(Also maintains branch campuses at Oxford, Jackson, Southaven and Tupelo, MS)
501. William Carey College
Formerly Mississippi Woman's College
Hattiesburg, MS
502. Missouri, University of
Columbia, Rolla, St. Louis and Kansas City, MO
503. Missouri Valley College
Marshall, MO
504. Monmouth College
Monmouth, IL
505. Montana College of Mineral Science and Technology
Butte, MT
506. Montana State University
Bozeman, MT
507. Western Montana College
Formerly Montana State Normal College
Dillon, MT
508. Montana, University of
Formerly Montana State University
Missoula, MT
509. Moravian College & Theological Seminary
Bethlehem, PA
510. Morehead State University
Morehead, KY
511. Morehouse College
Atlanta, GA
512. Morgan State University
Baltimore, MD
513. Morningside College
Formerly University of Northwest
Sioux City, IA
514. Morris Brown College
Atlanta, GA
515. Morris College
Sumter, SC
516. Charleston, University of
Formerly Morris Harvey College
Charleston, WV
517. Mount Angel Seminary
St. Benedict, OR
518. Mount Holyoke College
South Hadley, MA
519. Mount Mary College
Milwaukee, WI
520. Mount Mercy College
Grand Rapids, MI
521. Carlow College
Formerly Mount Mercy College
Pittsburgh, PA
522. Chestnut Hill College
Formerly Mount St. Joseph College
Chestnut Hill, PA
523. Mount St. Joseph-on the Ohio, College of
Mount St. Joseph, OH
524. Mount St. Mary's College
Emmitsburg, MD
525. Mount St. Mary's College
Los Angeles, CA
526. Mount St. Scholastica College
Atchison, KS
527. Mount St. Vincent, College of
Riverdale, NY
528. Mount Union College
Alliance, OH
529. Muhlenberg College
Allentown, PA
530. Mundelein College
Chicago, IL
531. Murray State University
Murray, KY
532. Muskingum College
New Concord, OH
533. Tennessee State University
Formerly Nashville Agricultural Normal Institute
Nashville, TN
See Also No. 1220
534. Nassau College
Hempstead, NY
535. Nasson College
Springvale, ME
536. National College of Education
Formerly Pestalozzi Froebel Teachers College
Evanston, IL
537. George Washington University
Formerly National University
Washington, DC
See Also No. 273
538. Nazareth College
Louisville, KY
539. Nazareth College
Nazareth, MI
540. Nazareth College of Rochester
Rochester, NY
541. Nebraska Central College
Central City, NE
542. Chadron State College
Formerly Nebraska State Teachers College
Chadron, NE
543. Nebraska at Kearney, University of
Formerly Nebraska State Teachers College
Kearney, NE
544. Peru State College
Formerly Nebraska State Teachers College
Peru, NE
545. Wayne State College
Formerly Nebraska State Teachers College
Wayne, NE
546. Nebraska at Lincoln, University of
Lincoln, NE
547. Nebraska Wesleyan University
Lincoln, NE
549. Nevada, University of
Reno and Las Vegas, NV
550. New Hampshire, University of
Durham, NH
551. Douglass College of Rutgers University
Formerly New Jersey College for Women
New Brunswick, NJ
See Also No. 705
552. Rutgers University
Formerly New Jersey Law School
Newark, NJ
See Also No. 705
553. Kean College of New Jersey
Formerly New Jersey State College
Union, NJ
555. Montclair State University
Formerly New Jersey State College
Upper Montclair, NJ
556. New Mexico State University
Formerly New Mexico College of A. & M. Arts
University Park, NM
557. New Mexico Highlands University
Las Vegas, NM
558. New Mexico Institute of Mining & Technology
Socorro, NM
559. Western New Mexico University
Formerly New Mexico Western College
Silver City, NM
560. New Mexico, University of
Albuquerque, NM
561. West Virginia Institute of Technology
Formerly New River State College
Montgomery, WV
562. New Rochelle, College of
New Rochelle, NY
563. New York, City College of the City University of
New York, NY
564. New York Law School
New York, NY
565. New York College of Environmental Science & Forestry, State University of
Formerly New York State College of Forestry
Syracuse, NY
566. New York State College for Teachers
Albany, NY

567. New York at Buffalo, State University of
Formerly New York State Teachers College
Buffalo, NY
See Also No. 107
568. New York Teachers College
New York, NY
569. New York University
New York, NY
570. New Jersey Institute of Technology
Formerly Newark College of Engineering
Newark, NJ
571. Rutgers University
Formerly Newark, University of
Newark, NJ
See Also No. 705
572. Newberry College
Newberry, SC
573. Niagara University
Niagara University, NY
574. North Carolina Central University
Durham, NC
575. North Carolina at Chapel Hill, University of
Chapel Hill, NC
576. North Carolina State University
Raleigh, NC
577. North Carolina, University of,
Greensboro, N.C.
Greensboro, NC
578. North Central College
Naperville, IL
579. North Dakota State University
Formerly North Dakota Agricultural College
Fargo, ND
580. North Dakota State Normal & Industrial College
Part of University of North Dakota
Ellendale, ND
581. Dickinson State College
Formerly North Dakota State College
Dickinson, ND
582. Mayville State College
Formerly North Dakota State College
Mayville, ND
583. Valley City State University
Formerly North Dakota State College
Valley City, ND
584. Minot State University
Formerly Dakota Northwestern University
Minot, ND
585. North Dakota, University of
Grand Forks, ND
586. North Texas, University of
Formerly North Texas State University
Denton, TX
587. Truman State University
Formerly Northeast Missouri State University
Kirksville, MO
588. Northeastern University
Boston, MA
589. Northern Illinois University
DeKalb and Glen Ellyn, IL
590. Northern State College
Aberdeen, SD
591. Northern Michigan University
Marquette, MI
592. Northland College
Ashland, WI
593. Northwest Missouri State University
Maryville, MO
594. Northwest Nazarene College
Nampa, ID
595. Northwestern College
Watertown, WI
596. Lewis & Clark Law School
Formerly Northwestern School of Law
Portland, OR
597. Northwestern University
Evanston, IL
598. Norwich University
Northfield, VT
599. Notre Dame College
South Euclid, OH
600. Notre Dame of Maryland, College of
Baltimore, MD
601. Notre Dame College of Staten Island
Part of St. Johns University
Staten Island, NY
See Also No. 724
602. Notre Dame, University of
Notre Dame, IN
603. Oakland City College
Oakland City, IN
604. Oberlin College
Oberlin, OH
605. Occidental College
Los Angeles, CA
606. Oglethorpe University
Atlanta, GA
607. Ohio Northern University
Ada, OH
608. Ohio State University, The
Columbus, OH
609. Athenaeum of Ohio, The
Formerly Ohio Teachers College
Cincinnati, OH
610. Ohio University
Athens, OH
611. Ohio Wesleyan University
Delaware, OH
612. Oklahoma State University
Formerly Oklahoma A. & M. College
Stillwater, OK
613. Oklahoma Baptist University
Shawnee, OK
614. Central State University
Formerly Oklahoma Central State Teachers College
Edmond, OK
See Also No. 1147
615. Oklahoma City University School of Law
Formerly Oklahoma City College of Law
Oklahoma City, OK
616. Oklahoma City University
Formerly Epworth University
Oklahoma City, OK
617. Science and Arts of Oklahoma, University of
Formerly Oklahoma College of Liberal Arts
Chickasha, OK
618. East Central Oklahoma State University
Formerly Oklahoma East Central State College
Ada, OK
619. Northeastern State University
Tahlequah, OK
620. Northwestern Oklahoma State University
Formerly Oklahoma Northwestern State College
Alva, OK
621. Southeastern Oklahoma State University
Formerly Oklahoma Southeastern State College
Durant, OK
622. Southwestern Oklahoma State University
Formerly Oklahoma Southwestern Institute of Technology
Weatherford, OK
623. Oklahoma, University of
Norman, OK
624. Olivet Nazarene College
Kankakee, IL
625. Olivet College
Olivet, MI
626. Omaha Law School, Inc., University of
Omaha, NE
627. Nebraska at Omaha, University of
Formerly Omaha, Municipal University of
Omaha, NE
628. Oregon State University
Corvallis, OR
629. Oregon, University of
Eugene, OR
630. Ottawa University
Ottawa, KS
631. Otterbein College
Westerville, OH
632. Ouachita Baptist University
Arkadelphia, AR
633. Elms College
Formerly Our Lady of the Elms, College of
Chicopee, MA
634. Our Lady of the Lake University
San Antonio, TX
635. George Fox College
Formerly Pacific College
Newberg, OR
636. Pacific Union College
Angwin, CA
637. Pacific University
Forest Grove, OR
638. Paine College
Augusta, GA
639. Oklahoma Panhandle State University of Agriculture and Applied Sciences
Formerly Panhandle State College
Goodwell, OK
640. Park College
Parkville, MO
641. Parsons College
Fairfield, IA
642. Pasadena College
Pasadena, CA
643. Chatham College
Formerly Pennsylvania College for Women
Pittsburgh, PA
644. Widener University
Formerly Pennsylvania Military College
Chester, PA and Wilmington, DE
See Also No. 1338
645. Pennsylvania State University
University Park, PA
646. Bloomsburg University of Pennsylvania
Formerly Pennsylvania State Teachers College
Bloomsburg, PA
647. California University of Pennsylvania
Formerly Pennsylvania State Teachers College
California, PA
648. Clarion University of Pennsylvania
Formerly Pennsylvania State Teachers College
Clarion, PA
649. East Stroudsburg University
Formerly Pennsylvania State Teachers College
E. Stroudsburg, PA
650. Edinboro University of Pennsylvania
Formerly Pennsylvania State Teachers College
Edinboro, PA
651. Indiana University of Pennsylvania
Formerly Pennsylvania State Teachers College
Indiana, PA
652. Kutztown University
Formerly Pennsylvania State Teachers College
Kutztown, PA
653. Lock Haven University of Pennsylvania
Formerly Pennsylvania State Teachers College
Lock Haven, PA
654. Mansfield University
Formerly Pennsylvania State Teachers College
Mansfield, PA
655. Millersville University of Pennsylvania
Formerly Pennsylvania State Teachers College
Millersville, PA

762. San Antonio Public School of Law
San Antonio, TX
763. San Diego State University
San Diego, CA
764. Lone Mountain College
Formerly San Francisco College for Women
San Francisco, CA
765. San Francisco Law School
San Francisco, CA
766. San Francisco State University
Formerly California State University
San Francisco, CA
767. San Francisco, University of
Formerly St. Ignatius College
San Francisco, CA
768. San Jose State University
San Jose, CA
769. California at Santa Barbara, University of
Formerly Santa Barbara State College
Santa Barbara, CA
770. Santa Clara University
Formerly Santa Clara, University of
Santa Clara, CA
771. Sarah Lawrence College
Bronxville, NY
772. Scarritt College for Christian Workers
Nashville, TN
773. Scripps College
Claremont, CA
774. Seattle Pacific University
Seattle, WA
775. Selma University
Selma, AL
776. Seton Hall University
South Orange & Newark, NJ
777. Seton Hill College
Greensburg, PA
778. Shaw University
Raleigh, NC
779. Shepherd College
Shepherdstown, WV
780. Shorter College
Formerly Shorter-Flipper-Curry College
N. Little Rock, AR
781. Shorter College
Rome, GA
782. Shurtleff College
Alton, IL
783. Simmons College
Boston, MA
784. Simpson College
Indianola, IA
785. Sioux Falls College
Sioux Falls, SD
786. Sisters' College of Cleveland
Cleveland, OH
787. Skidmore College
Saratoga Springs, NY
788. Smith College
Northampton, MA
789. South Carolina State College
Orangeburg, SC
790. South Carolina, University of
Columbia, SC
791. South Dakota State University
Brookings, SD
792. South Dakota School of Mines and Technology
Rapid City, SD
793. South Dakota, University of
Vermillion, SD
794. Georgia Teachers College
Formerly South Georgia Teachers College
Collegeboro, GA
795. Rutgers University
Formerly South Jersey, College of
Camden, NJ
See Also No. 1292
796. South Texas College of Law
Houston, TX
797. South, University of the
Sewanee, TN
798. Southeast Missouri State University
Cape Girardeau, MO
799. Southeastern University
Washington, DC
800. Southern California, University of
Los Angeles, CA
801. Southern Illinois University
Carbondale and Edwardsville, IL
802. Southern Methodist University
Dallas, TX
803. Southern University
Baton Rouge, LA
804. Missouri State University
Formerly Southwest Missouri State University
Springfield, MO
805. Texas State University-San Marcos
Formerly Southwest Texas State University
San Marcos, TX
806. Rhodes College
Formerly Southwestern at Memphis
Memphis, TN
807. Southwestern College
Winfield, KS
808. Southwestern Louisiana, University of
Lafayette, LA
809. Southwestern University School of Law
Los Angeles, CA
810. Southwestern University
Georgetown, TX
811. Spelman College
Atlanta, GA
812. Spring Hill College
Spring Hill, AL
813. Stanford University
Stanford, CA
814. Stephen F. Austin State University
Nacogdoches, TX
815. Sterling College
Sterling, KS
816. Stevens Institute of Technology
Hoboken, NJ
817. Wisconsin-Stout, University of
Formerly Stout State College
Menomonie, WI
818. Suffolk University
Boston, MA
819. Sul Ross State University
Alpine, TX
820. Susquehanna University
Selinsgrove, PA
821. Swarthmore College
Swarthmore, PA
822. Sweet Briar College
Sweet Briar, VA
823. Syracuse University
Syracuse, NY
824. Talladega College
Talladega, AL
825. Tampa, University of
Tampa, FL
826. Tarkio College
Tarkio, MO
827. Taylor University
Upland, IN
828. Teachers College of the City of Boston
Boston, MA
829. Central Connecticut State College
Formerly Teachers College of Connecticut, The
New Britain, CT
830. Teachers College of Kansas City
Kansas City, MO
831. Temple University
Philadelphia, PA
832. Tennessee State University
Formerly Tennessee A. & I. State University
Nashville, TN
833. Tennessee College for Women
Murfreesboro, TN
834. Tennessee Technological University
Formerly Tennessee Polytechnic Institute
Cookeville, TN
835. East Tennessee State University
Formerly Tennessee State Teachers College
Johnson City, TN
836. Memphis, University of
Formerly Memphis State University
Memphis, TN
See Also No. 1015
837. Middle Tennessee State University
Formerly Tennessee State Teachers College
Murfreesboro, TN
838. Tennessee at Knoxville, University of
Knoxville, TN
839. Texas A & M University
College Station, TX
840. Texas Christian University
Fort Worth, TX
841. Texas College
Tyler, TX
842. Texas Arts & Industries University
Kingsville, TX
843. Texas at El Paso, University of
Formerly Texas, College of Mines & Metallurgy
El Paso, TX
844. Texas Woman's University
Formerly Texas State College for Women
Denton, TX
845. Texas Tech University
Lubbock, TX
846. Texas at Austin, University of
Austin, TX
847. Texas Wesleyan University
Fort Worth, TX
848. Thiel College
Greenville, PA
849. Huston-Tillotson College
Formerly Tillotson College
Austin, TX
See Also No. 1037
850. Toledo Teachers College
Toledo, OH
851. Toledo, University of
Toledo, OH
852. Tougaloo College
Tougaloo, MS
853. Transylvania University
Lexington, KY
854. Tri-State University
Angola, IN
855. Trinity College
Hartford, CT
856. Trinity College
Washington, DC
857. Trinity College
Sioux City, IA
858. Trinity College
Burlington, VT
859. Trinity University
San Antonio, TX
860. Tufts University
Medford, MA
861. Tulane University
New Orleans, LA
862. Tulsa, University of
Tulsa, OK
863. Tusculum College
Greeneville, TN
864. Tuskegee University
Tuskegee, AL
865. Union College
Barbourville, KY
866. Union College
Lincoln, NE
867. Union College
Schenectady, NY
868. Union University
Jackson, TN

869. United States Coast Guard Academy
New London, CT
870. United States Military Academy
West Point, NY
871. United States Naval Academy
Annapolis, MD
872. Upper Iowa University
Fayette, IA
873. Upsala College
East Orange, NJ
874. Ursinus College
Collegeville, PA
875. Ursuline College
New Orleans, LA
876. Ursuline College
Cleveland, OH
877. Utah State University
Formerly Utah State Agricultural College
Logan, UT
878. Utah, University of
Salt Lake City, UT
879. Valparaiso University
Formerly Northern Indiana Law School
Valparaiso, IN
880. Vanderbilt University
Nashville, TN
881. Vassar College
Poughkeepsie, NY
882. Vermont, University of
Burlington, VT
883. Villa Maria College
Erie, PA
884. Villanova University
Villanova, PA
885. Virginia Military Institute
Lexington, VA
886. Virginia Polytechnic Institute and State University
Blacksburg, VA
887. Virginia State University
Petersburg (Ettrick), VA
888. Radford University
Formerly Virginia State Teachers College
East Radford, VA
889. Longwood College
Formerly Virginia State Teachers College
Farmville, VA
890. Mary Washington College
Formerly Virginia State Teachers College
Fredericksburg, VA
892. Virginia Union University
Richmond, VA
893. Virginia, University of
Charlottesville, VA
894. Wabash College
Crawfordsville, IN
895. Wagner College
Staten Island, NY
896. Wake Forest University
Winston-Salem, NC
897. Walla Walla College
College Place, WA
898. Wartburg College
Waverly, IA
899. Wartburg Theological Seminary
Dubuque, IA
900. Washburn University of Topeka
Topeka, KS
901. Washington & Jefferson College
Washington, PA
902. Washington & Lee University
Lexington, VA
903. Washington College
Chestertown, MD
904. Washington College of Law
(of American University)
Washington, DC
See Also No. 30
905. Columbia Union College
Formerly Washington Missionary College
Takoma Park, DC
906. Washington State University
Pullman, WA
907. Western Washington University
Formerly Washington State Normal School
Bellingham, WA
908. Eastern Washington University
Formerly Washington State Normal School
Cheney, WA
909. Central Washington University
Formerly Washington State Normal School
Ellensburg, WA
910. Washington University
St. Louis, MO
911. Washington, University of
Seattle, WA
912. Wayne State University
Detroit, MI
913. Waynesburg College
Waynesburg, PA
914. Wellesley College
Wellesley, MA
915. Wells College
Aurora, NY
916. Wesley College
Grand Forks, ND
917. Wesleyan College
Macon, GA
918. Wesleyan University
Middletown, CT
919. West Baden College
West Baden, IN
920. West Liberty State College
W. Liberty, WV
921. West Texas State University
Canyon, TX
922. West Virginia State College
Institute, WV
923. West Virginia University
Morgantown, WV
924. West Virginia Wesleyan College
Buckhannon, WV
925. Western Carolina University
Cullowhee, NC
926. Western College
Oxford, OH
927. Western Illinois University
Macomb, IL
928. McDaniel College
Formerly Western Maryland College
Westminster, MD
929. Western Kentucky University
Formerly Western Kentucky State College
Bowling Green, KY
930. Case Western Reserve University
Formerly Western Reserve University
Cleveland, OH
931. Western State College of Colorado
Gunnison, CO
932. Western Michigan University
Kalamazoo, MI
933. Westmar College
Formerly Western Union College
Le Mars, IA
934. Westminster College
Fulton, MO
935. Westminster College
New Wilmington, PA
937. Wheaton College
Wheaton, IL
938. Wheaton College
Norton, MA
939. Whitman College
Walla Walla, WA
940. Whittier College
Whittier, CA
941. Whitworth College
Spokane, WA
942. Wichita State University
Wichita, KS
943. Wilberforce University
Wilberforce, OH
944. Wiley College
Marshall, TX
945. William & Mary, College of
Williamsburg, VA
946. William Jennings Bryan College
Dayton, TN
947. William Jewell College
Liberty, MO
948. William McKinley School of Law
Canton, OH
949. William Penn College
Oskaloosa, IA
950. Willamette University
Salem, OR
951. Williams College
Williamstown, MA
952. Wilmington College
Wilmington, OH
953. North Carolina at Wilmington, University of
Formerly Wilmington College
Wilmington, NC
954. Wilson College
Chambersburg, PA
955. Winston-Salem State University
Winston-Salem, NC
956. Winthrop College
Rock Hill, SC
957. Wisconsin-Eau Claire, University of
Eau Claire, WI
958. Wisconsin-La Crosse, University of
La Crosse, WI
959. Wisconsin-Milwaukee, University of
Milwaukee, WI
960. Wisconsin-Oshkosh, University of
Oshkosh, WI
961. Wisconsin-Platteville, University of
Platteville, WI
962. Wisconsin-River Falls, University of
River Falls, WI
963. Wisconsin-Stevens Point, University of
Stevens Point, WI
964. Wisconsin-Superior, University of
Superior, WI
965. Wisconsin-Whitewater, University of
Whitewater, WI
966. Wisconsin-Madison, University of
Madison, WI
967. Wittenberg University
Springfield, OH
968. Wofford College
Spartanburg, SC
969. Woodrow Wilson College of Law
Formerly Kilbride Law School
Atlanta, GA
970. Wooster, College of
Wooster, OH
971. Worcester Polytechnic Institute
Worcester, MA
972. Wyoming, University of
Laramie, WY
973. Xavier University
Cincinnati, OH
974. Xavier University of Louisiana
New Orleans, LA
975. Y.M.C.A. Schools
Houston, TX
976. Yale University
New Haven, CT
977. Yankton College
Yankton, SD
978. Yeshiva University
New York, NY
979. York College
York, NE
980. Youngstown State University
Youngstown, OH
981. LaSalle Extension University
Chicago, IL
982. Albany Law School of Union University
Albany, NY

983. San Antonio, University of
San Antonio, TX
984. Blue Ridge College
New Windsor, MD
985. Briar Cliff College
Sioux City, IA
986. Missouri at Kansas City, University of
Formerly University of Kansas City
Kansas City, MO
987. Sulpician Seminary of the Northwest
Formerly St. Edward's Seminary
Seattle, WA
988. Seattle University
Seattle, WA
989. Cleveland-Marshall College of Law
Formerly John Marshall Law School
Cleveland, OH
See Also No. 1003
990. Pepperdine University
Los Angeles, Malibu, Anaheim and
Santa Ana, CA
991. Barat College
Lake Forest, IL
992. Anderson College
Anderson, IN
993. St. Mary's College
Orchard Lake, MI
994. Queens College of the City University of
New York
Flushing, NY
995. Alfred Holbrook College
Manchester, OH
996. Lincoln College of Law
Springfield, IL
997. Seton Hall University
Formerly John Marshall Law School
Jersey City, NJ
See Also No. 776
998. Houston Law School
Houston, TX
999. Unlisted colleges, etc., see prefatory
notice
1000. John Marshall Law School
Atlanta, GA
1001. Pacific Coast University
Los Angeles, CA
1002. Baltimore School of Law, University of
Formerly Mt. Vernon School of Law
Baltimore, MD
1003. Cleveland-Marshall College of Law
Part of Cleveland State University
Cleveland, OH
1004. St. Mary of the Plains College
Dodge City, KS
1005. Southern Law University
Part of Memphis State University
Memphis, TN
1006. College of St. Francis Xavier
New York, NY
1007. American Extension School of Law
Chicago, IL
1008. Blackstone School of Law
Carrollton, TX
1009. Brooklyn Law School
Brooklyn, NY
1010. Alabama Agricultural & Mechanical
University
Formerly State Agricultural and
Mechanical Institute
Normal, AL
1011. Fayetteville State University
Fayetteville, NC
1012. Eastern New Mexico University
Portales, NM
1014. Robert H. Terrell Law School
Washington, DC
1015. Memphis State University
Memphis, TN
1016. Roosevelt University
Chicago, IL
1017. Dickinson School of Law of the
Pennsylvania State University
Carlisle, PA
1018. William Mitchell College of Law
Formerly Minneapolis-Minnesota
College of Law
Minneapolis, MN
See Also No. 1035
1019. Hofstra University
Hempstead, NY
1020. Portland University Law School
part of University of Maine
Portland, ME
See Also No. 431
1021. Siena College
Formerly St. Bernardine of Siena
College
Loudonville, NY
1022. New England School of Law
Formerly Calvin Coolidge College
Boston, MA
See Also No. 1202
1023. Central State University
Wilberforce, OH
1024. St. Joseph's College
Rensselaer, IN
1025. Jersey City State College
Formerly New Jersey State College
Jersey City, NJ
1026. Lincoln University
San Francisco, San Jose and
Sacramento, CA
1027. United States Merchant Marine Academy
Kings Point, NY
1028. Wilkes University
Wilkes-Barre, PA
1029. Bridgeport, University of
Bridgeport, CT
1030. Fairfield University
Fairfield, CT
1031. Le Moyne College
Syracuse, NY
1032. Idaho State University
Formerly Idaho State College
Pocatello, ID
1033. Hartford, University of
Formerly Hillyer College
Hartford, CT
1034. Christian Brothers College
Memphis, TN
1035. William Mitchell College of Law
St. Paul, MN
1036. Brandeis University
Waltham, MA
1037. Huston-Tillotson College
Austin, TX
1038. Jacksonville University
Jacksonville, FL
1039. North Georgia College
Dahlonega, GA
1040. Pace University
New York, Pleasantville and White
Plains, NY
1041. Iona College
New Rochelle, NY
1042. California State University, Long Beach
Formerly Long Beach State University
Long Beach, CA
1043. California State University, Los Angeles
Formerly Los Angeles State College
of Applied Arts and Sciences
Los Angeles, CA
See Also No. 1097
1044. New York at Albany, State University of
Albany, NY
1045. Nashville School of Law
Nashville, TN
1046. Fairleigh Dickinson University
Madison, Rutherford and Teaneck, NJ
1047. Lycoming College
Williamsport, PA
1048. Western New England College
Springfield, MA
1049. San Diego, University of
San Diego, CA
1050. Midwestern State University
Wichita Falls, TX
1051. Lewis and Clark College
Portland, OR
1052. Houston Baptist University
Houston, TX
1053. Messiah College
Grantham, PA
1054. Tennessee Wesleyan College
Athens, TN
1055. Southeastern Louisiana College
Hammond, LA
1056. Portland State University
Portland, OR
1057. Merrimack College
North Andover, MA
1058. Pacific Lutheran University
Tacoma, WA
1059. Georgia State University
Atlanta, GA
1060. California State University, Sacramento
Formerly Sacramento State College
Sacramento, CA
1061. Lamar University
Beaumont, TX
1062. Gannon University
Erie, PA
1063. Georgia Southern College
Statesboro, GA
1064. Lipscomb University
Formerly David Lipscomb College
Nashville, TN
1065. Hastings College of the Law, University
of California
San Francisco, CA
1066. Boalt Hall School of Law, University of
California
Berkeley, CA
1067. California School of Law, Davis,
University of
Davis, CA
1068. California School of Law, Los Angeles,
University of
Los Angeles, CA
1069. Chaminade University of Honolulu
Honolulu, HI
1070. United States Air Force Academy
Colorado Springs, CO
1071. Southern Oregon State College
Ashland, OR
1072. Alliance College
Cambridge Springs, PA
1073. California State University, Hayward
Hayward, CA
1074. California Polytechnic State University
San Luis Obispo, CA
1075. California State Polytechnic University
Pomona, CA
1076. Orange State College
Fullerton, CA
1077. California State University, Northridge
Formerly San Fernando Valley State
College
Northridge, CA
1078. Sonoma State University
Rohnert Park, CA
1079. California State University, Stanislaus
Formerly Stanislaus State College
Turlock, CA
1080. Northeast Louisiana University
Monroe, LA
1081. Austin Peay State University
Clarksville, TN
1082. Quincy University
Quincy, IL
1083. Old Dominion University
Norfolk, VA
1084. Northern Montana College
Havre, MT
1085. Weber State College
Ogden, UT
1086. Florida Atlantic University
Boca Raton, FL
1087. Catholic University of Puerto Rico
Ponce, PR
1088. Inter-American University of Puerto Rico
San Juan, PR

1089. McNeese State University
Lake Charles, LA
1090. Virginia Commonwealth University
Formerly Richmond Professional Institute
Richmond, VA
1091. South Alabama, University of
Mobile, AL
1092. Princess Anne State College
Princess Anne, MD
1093. Utica College of Syracuse University
Utica, NY
1094. Southern Arkansas University
Formerly Southern State College
Magnolia, AR
1095. La Verne College of Law, University of
Formerly San Fernando Valley, University of
Sepulveda, CA
1096. Angelo State University
Formerly San Angelo State University
San Angelo, TX
1097. California State University, Los Angeles
Formerly Los Angeles State College
Los Angeles, CA
1098. Louisiana State University at Alexandria
Alexandria, LA
1099. New Orleans, University of
Formerly Louisiana State University of New Orleans
New Orleans, LA
1100. Shimer College
Waukegan, IL
1101. Blackburn College
Carlinville, IL
1102. Southern Connecticut State College
New Haven, CT
1103. Western Connecticut State University
Danbury, CT
1104. Eastern Oregon College
La Grande, OR
1105. Dallas, University of
Irving, TX
1106. North Park College
Chicago, IL
1107. Assumption College
Worcester, MA
1108. Monmouth University
West Long Branch, NJ
1109. California State University, Fullerton
Fullerton, CA
1110. California State University, San Bernardino
San Bernardino, CA
1111. South Florida, University of
Tampa, FL
1112. Urbana College
Urbana, OH
1113. King's College
Wilkes Barre, PA
1114. Van Norman University
Los Angeles, CA
1115. Wheeling Jesuit University
Formerly Wheeling Jesuit College
Wheeling, WV
1116. Rowan University
Formerly Glassboro State College
Glassboro, NJ
1117. Pepperdine University School of Law
Formerly Orange University College of Law
Malibu, CA
1118. Thomas More College
Formerly Villa Madonna College
Covington, KY
1119. Indiana University School of Law - Bloomington
Bloomington, IN
1120. Westminster College
Salt Lake City, UT
1121. Aquinas College
Grand Rapids, MI
1122. St. John Fisher College
Rochester, NY
1123. Goddard College
Plainfield, VT
1124. Eastern Mennonite College
Harrisonburg, VA
1125. Arkansas Tech University
Formerly Arkansas Polytechnic University
Russellville, AR
1126. Belmont Abbey College
Belmont, NC
1127. California College of Law
Hollywood and West Covina, CA
1128. North Carolina at Charlotte, University of
Charlotte, NC
1129. Mars Hill College
Mars Hill, NC
1130. St. Andrews Presbyterian College
Laurinburg, NC
1131. California State University, Dominguez Hills
Dominguez Hills, CA
1132. Humphreys College
Stockton, CA
1133. New York Institute of Technology
New York, NY
1134. Bentley College
Waltham, MA
1135. Marymount-Manhattan College
New York, NY
1136. West Los Angeles, University of
Culver City, CA
1137. Western State University
Fullerton, CA
1138. Baruch College of the City University of New York
New York, NY
1139. John Jay College of Criminal Justice of the City University of New York
New York, NY
1140. College of Staten Island of the City University of New York
Formerly Richmond College of the City University of New York
Staten Island, NY
1141. York College of the City University of New York
Queens, NY
1142. Texas at Arlington, University of
Arlington, TX
1143. Albuquerque, University of
Albuquerque, NM
1144. Bethel College
St. Paul, MN
1145. Bryant College
Smithfield, RI
1146. Santa Fe, College of
Santa Fe, NM
1147. Central Oklahoma, University of
Formerly Central State University
Edmond, OK
1148. Whittier College School of Law
Formerly Beverly College of Law
Los Angeles, CA
1149. Boston State College
Boston, MA
1150. Bellarmine College
Formerly Bellarmine Ursuline College
Louisville, KY
1151. Lewis University
Lockport, IL
1152. South Bay University
Harbor City, CA
1153. John F. Kennedy University
Walnut Creek, CA
1154. Oakland University
Rochester, MI
1155. Babson College
Babson Park, MA
1156. New Haven, University of
West Haven, CT
1157. St. Joseph College
East Chicago, IN
1158. St. Thomas University
Formerly Biscayne College
Miami, FL
1159. Indiana Institute of Technology
Fort Wayne, IN
1160. Herbert H. Lehman College of the City University of New York
Bronx, NY
1161. Northern Kentucky University
Highland Heights, KY
1162. Antioch School of Law
Washington, DC
1163. Loma Linda University
Formerly La Sierra College
Loma Linda, CA
1164. Colorado at Colorado Springs, University of
Colorado Springs, CO
1165. Colorado at Denver, University of
Denver, CO
1166. Nicholls State University
Thibodaux, LA
1167. Harvey Mudd College
Claremont, CA
1168. Pitzer College
Claremont, CA
1169. California at Santa Cruz, University of
Santa Cruz, CA
1170. Franklin Pierce College
Rindge, NH
1171. Wisconsin-Green Bay, University of
Green Bay, WI
1172. Wisconsin-Parkside, University of
Kenosha, WI
1173. Southeastern Massachusetts University
North Dartmouth, MA
1174. William Paterson College of New Jersey
Wayne, NJ
1175. Central Florida, University of
Formerly Florida Technological University
Orlando, FL
1176. West Florida, University of
Pensacola, FL
1177. Grambling State University
Grambling, LA
1178. City University of New York School of Law, Queens College
Flushing, NY
1179. Northrop University
Inglewood, CA
1180. Bloomfield College
Bloomfield, NJ
1181. Western Oregon State College
Formerly Oregon College of Education
Monmouth, OR
1182. Benedictine College
Atchison, KS
1183. Northeastern Illinois University
Chicago, IL
1185. Southern College of Seventh-Day Adventists
Formerly Southern Missionary College
Collegedale, TN
1186. Ventura College of Law
Ventura, CA
1187. Thomas M. Cooley Law School
Lansing, MI
1188. United States International University
Formerly California Western University
San Diego, CA
1189. San Joaquin, College of Law
Fresno, CA
1190. Glendale University
Glendale, CA
1191. Chicago State University
Chicago, IL
1192. Dowling College
Oakdale, NY
1193. Boise State University
Boise, ID
1194. Vermont Law School
South Royalton, VT
1195. Covenant College
Lookout Mountain, TN

1196. Southern Colorado, University of
Pueblo, CO
1197. Armstrong College
Berkeley, CA
1198. Citrus Belt Law School
Riverside, CA
1199. Cabrini College
Radnor, PA
1200. Stonehill College
North Easton, MA
1201. Metropolitan State College
Denver, CO
1202. New England School of Law
Boston, MA
1203. St. Mary's College of Maryland
St. Mary's City, MD
1204. Tennessee at Martin, University of
Martin, TN
1205. Tennessee at Memphis, University of
Memphis, TN
1206. Nova Southeastern University
Formerly Nova University
Fort Lauderdale, FL
1207. Minnesota Morris, University of
Morris, MN
1208. Wright State University
Dayton, OH
1209. George Mason University School of Law
Formerly International School of Law
Arlington, VA
1210. Florida Institute of Technology
Melbourne, FL
1211. Sacred Heart University
Bridgeport, CT
1212. California State College, Bakersfield
Bakersfield, CA
1213. Rochester Institute of Technology
Rochester, NY
1214. Stockton State College
Pomona, NJ
1215. Simon's Rock of Bard College
Great Barrington, MA
1216. Marian College
Indianapolis, IN
1217. Lawrence Technological University
Southfield, MI
1218. Franklin Pierce Law Center
Formerly part of Franklin Pierce
College
Concord, NH
1219. Pan American University
Edinburg, TX
1220. Tennessee at Nashville, University of
Formerly Nashville Agricultural
Normal Institute
Nashville, TN
1221. Woodland University
Van Nuys, CA
1222. Florida International University
Miami, FL
1223. West Georgia College
Carrollton, GA
1224. Valley University College of Law
North Hollywood, CA
1225. Irvine University
Irvine, CA
1226. Monterey College of Law
Monterey, CA
1227. Empire College School of Law
Santa Rosa, CA
1228. Campbell University
Buies Creek, NC
1229. General Motors Institute
Flint, MI
1230. New College of California
San Francisco, CA
1231. San Mateo Law School
San Mateo, CA
1232. Azusa Pacific University
Azusa, CA
1233. Briarcliff College
Briarcliff Manor, NY
1234. Potomac School of Law
Washington, DC
1235. Eastern Montana College
Billings, MT
1236. Eckerd College
St. Petersburg, FL
1237. Louisiana State University at Shreveport
Shreveport, LA
1238. Peoples College of Law
Los Angeles, CA
1239. Westmont College
Santa Barbara, CA
1240. American College of Law
Anaheim, CA
1241. National University
Formerly Cabrillo Pacific University
San Diego, CA
1242. United States Naval Postgraduate School
Monterey, CA
1243. Arkansas at Little Rock, University of
Formerly Little Rock University
Little Rock, AR
1244. St. Bernard College
St. Bernard, AL
1245. Phoenix, University of
Phoenix, AZ
1246. Woodbury University
Los Angeles, CA
1247. Sangamon State University
Springfield, IL
1248. Southern Maine, University of
Portland, ME
1249. Saginaw Valley College
University Center, MI
1250. California Maritime Academy
Vallejo, CA
1251. Los Angeles College of Law
Los Angeles, CA
1252. Quinnipiac University
Hamden, CT
1253. California Lutheran University
Formerly California Lutheran College
Thousand Oaks, CA
1254. Menlo College
Menlo Park, CA
1255. Black Hills State College
Spearfish, SD
1256. St. Patrick's College
Mountain View, CA
1257. Mid-America Nazarene College
Olathe, KS
1258. St. John's College
Camarillo, CA
1259. Biola University
La Mirada, CA
1260. Walsh College
Canton, OH
1261. Cheyney State College
Cheyney, PA
1262. Fort Lewis College
Durango, CO
1263. St. John's Seminary
Brighton, MA
1264. Colorado Women's College
Denver, CO
1265. Grand Valley State University
Allendale, MI
1266. Marist College
Poughkeepsie, NY
1267. Augusta College
Augusta, GA
1268. St. Thomas, University of
Houston, TX
1269. Ramapo College
Mahwah, NJ
1270. Texas Lutheran College
Seguin, TX
1271. Texas at Dallas, University of
Richardson, TX
1272. Texas of the Permian Basin, University of
Odessa, TX
1273. Texas at San Antonio, University of
San Antonio, TX
1274. Texas at Tyler, University of
Tyler, TX
1275. New College of the University of South
Florida
Sarasota, FL
1276. Armstrong Atlantic State University
Formerly Armstrong State College
Savannah, GA
1277. Augusta Law School
Augusta, GA
1278. Barry College
Miami Shores, FL
1279. Benjamin Franklin University
Washington, DC
1280. District of Columbia, University of the
Washington, DC
1281. Graceland College
Lamoni, IA
1282. Georgia Southwestern College
Americus, GA
1283. Kansas Newman College
Formerly Sacred Heart College
Wichita, KS
1284. Corpus Christi State University
Corpus Christi, TX
1285. Lake Superior State College
Sault Ste. Marie, MI
1286. Norfolk State University
Norfolk, VA
1287. North Florida, University of
Jacksonville, FL
1288. Oral Roberts University
Tulsa, OK
1289. Savannah State College
Savannah, GA
1290. Saint Leo College
Saint Leo, FL
1291. Webster College
St. Louis, MO
1292. Rutgers University Law School
Camden, NJ
Note: There are two separate Law Schools. One at Newark, NJ (No. 705) and one at Camden, NJ (No. 1292)
1293. Berklee College of Music
Boston, MA
1294. Maine, University of, School of Law
Portland, ME
1295. Dunbarton College of the Holy Cross
Washington, DC
1296. Allentown College of St. Francis De
Sales
Formerly St. Francis De Sales
Center Valley, PA
1297. Avila College
Kansas City, MO
1298. Bennett College
Greensboro, NC
1299. Brescia College
Owensboro, KY
1300. Cameron University
Lawton, OK
1301. Columbus College
Columbus, GA
1302. Cumberland College
Williamsburg, KY
1303. Curry College
Milton, MA
1304. Dordt College
Sioux Center, IA
1305. Eastern College
St. Davids, PA
1306. Great Falls, University of
Great Falls, MT
1307. Hampshire College
Amherst, MA
1308. Massachusetts Maritime Academy
Buzzards Bay, MA
1309. Methodist College
Fayetteville, NC
1310. Missouri Southern State College
Joplin, MO
1311. Missouri Western State College
St. Joseph, MO
1312. New England College
Henniker, NH

1313. New School for Social Research
New York, NY
1314. Ozarks, School of the
Point Lookout, MO
1315. Oklahoma Christian College
Oklahoma City, OK
1316. Philadelphia College of Textiles and Science
Philadelphia, PA
1317. Pembroke State University
Pembroke, NC
1318. Pfeiffer College
Misenheimer, NC
1319. Pikeville College
Pikeville, KY
1320. St. Johns College
Santa Fe, NM
1321. Southwest Baptist University
Bolivar, MO
1322. Stephens College
Columbia, MO
1323. Steubenville, University of
Steubenville, OH
1324. Southern Utah University
Formerly Southern Utah State College
Cedar City, UT
1325. Touro College Jacob D. Fuchsberg Law Center
New York, NY
1326. York College of Pennsylvania
York, PA
1327. Trevecca Nazarene College
Nashville, TN
1328. Baptist College at Charleston
Charleston, SC
1329. Christopher Newport College
Formerly Christopher Newport College of the College of William and Mary
Newport News, VA
1330. Castleton State College
Castleton, VT
1331. Evergreen State College, The
Olympia, WA
1332. Tarleton State University
Stephenville, TX
1333. Embry-Riddle Aeronautical University
Daytona Beach, FL
1334. Guam, University of
Agana, GU
1335. Brigham Young University
Laie, HI
1336. Southern California Institute of Law
Santa Barbara and Ventura, CA
1337. Texas at Galveston, University of
Galveston, TX
1338. Widener University
Including Widener University School of Law, formerly Delaware Law School
Chester, PA and Wilmington, DE
1339. Regent University
Formerly CBN University
Virginia Beach, VA
1340. Salmon P. Chase College of Law
Highland Heights, KY
1341. Texas at Houston, University of
Houston, TX
1342. Southwest State University
Marshall, MN
1343. Caldwell College
Caldwell, NJ
1344. Oakland College of Law
Oakland, CA
1345. Wiggins, Norman A., School of Law
Formerly Campbell University School of Law
Buies Creek, NC
1346. Prescott College
Prescott, AZ
1347. Missouri at St. Louis, University of
St. Louis, MO
1348. Northwestern College
Orange City, IA
1349. New York at Binghamton, State University of
Binghamton, NY
1350. New York at Stony Brook, State University of
Stony Brook, NY
1351. Simon Greenleaf School of Law
Anaheim, CA
1352. Alverno College
Milwaukee, WI
1353. Long Island University, Brooklyn Campus of
Brooklyn, NY
1354. Monterey Institute of International Studies
Monterey, CA
1355. San Francisco Law School, University of
San Francisco, CA
1356. George Mason University
Formerly George Mason College of The University of Virginia
Fairfax, VA
1537. Istanbul University
Istanbul, Turkey
1357. Touro College
New York, NY
1358. Seattle University School of Law
Formerly University of Puget Sound School of Law
Tacoma, WA
1359. Evangel College
Springfield, MO
1360. Roger Williams University School of Law
Bristol, RI
1362. Langston University
Langston, OK
1363. Texas Wesleyan University School of Law
Irving, TX
1364. District of Columbia School of Law
Washington, DC
1365. Emory University
Atlanta, GA
1366. California Southern Law School
Riverside, CA
1367. Siena Heights College
Adrian, MI
1369. James Madison University
Harrisonburg, VA
1370. Thomas Jefferson School of Law
San Diego, CA
1371. New York College at Cortland, State University of
Cortland, NY
1372. New York College at Geneseo, State University of
Geneseo, NY
1373. New York College at New Paltz, State University of
New Paltz, NY
1374. New York College at Oneonta, State University of
Oneonta, NY
1375. California, Berkeley, University of
Berkeley, CA
1376. College of New Jersey, The
Formerly Trenton State College
Trenton, NJ
1377. Valdosta State University
Valdosta, GA
1378. North Carolina Agricultural & Technical State University
Greensboro, NC
1379. Chapman University School of Law
Anaheim, CA
1380. New York College at Purchase, State University of
Purchase, NY
1381. New York College at Brockport, State University of
Brockport, NY
1382. Queensland, University of
Brisbane, Australia
1383. Madras, University of
Chennai, India
1384. National University of Ireland, Galway
Galway, Ireland
1385. New York College at Potsdam, State University of
Potsdam, NY
1386. Appalachian School of Law
Grundy, VA
1387. National Law School of India
Bangalore, India
1388. Virginia Wesleyan College
Norfolk, VA
1389. Massachusetts School of Law
Andover, MA
1390. Alfred Adler Institute of San Francisco
San Francisco, CA
1391. Franciscan University of Steubenville
Steubenville, OH
1392. Francaise Alliance USA
Paris, France
1393. Thunderbird American Graduate School of International Management
Glendale, AZ
1394. American University in Cairo
Cairo, Egypt
1395. Anna Maria College
Paxton, MA
1396. Associated Mennonite Biblical Seminary
Elkhart, IN
1397. Bangalore University
Bangalore, India
1398. Benjamin N. Cardozo School of Law, Yeshiva University
New York, NY
1399. Cairo University
Cairo, Egypt
1400. Concordia University
Irvine, CA
1401. Canadian Mennonite University
Winnipeg, Manitoba
1402. Catholic University of Argentina
Buenos Aires, Argentina
1403. Central Bible College
Springfield, MO
1404. Chadwick University
Birmingham, AL
1405. City Colleges of Chicago
Chicago, IL
1406. City College of San Francisco
San Francisco, CA
1407. College for Financial Planning
Denver, CO
1408. College of Law, London, The
London, England
1409. College of Saint Mary
Omaha, NE
1410. Denver, College of Law, University of
Denver, CO
1411. Columbia Pacific University
Novato, CA
1412. Curtis Institute of Music, The
Philadelphia, PA
1413. Czech Technical University
Prague, Czechlovakia
1414. Daemen College
Amherst, NY
1415. Delft University of Technology
Delft, Netherlands
1416. Delhi, The University of
Delhi, India
1417. Finch University of Health Sciences/The Chicago Medical School
1418. Flagler College
St. Augustine, FL
1419. Francis Marion University
Florence, SC
1420. Freed-Hardeman University
Henderson, TN
1421. Fresno Pacific College
Fresno, CA
1422. Fuller Theological Seminary
Pasadena, CA
1423. Frankfurt, University of
Frankfurt, Germany

1424. Institute of Political Studies, Paris
Paris, France
1425. Institute for Advanced Studies
Geneva, Switzerland
1426. Sophia University
Tokyo, Japan
1427. Johannes Gutenberg University
Mainz, Germany
1428. Johnson State College
Westbury, VT
1429. Kemper Military School & College
Boonville, MO
1430. Kennesaw State University
Kennesaw, GA
1431. Kennedy-Western University
Cheyenne, WY
1432. Lehman College of the City University of New York
Bronx, NY
1433. Lesley College
Cambridge, MA
1434. Lourdes College
Sylvania, OH
1435. Catholic University of Louvain
Louvain-la-Neuve, Belgium
1436. Manhattan School of Music
New York, NY
1437. Massachusetts College of Pharmacy & Health Sciences
Boston, MA
1438. Mennonite Brethren Biblical Seminary
Fresno, CA
1439. Missouri at Columbia, School of Law, University of
Columbia, MO
1440. Molloy College
Rockville, NY
1441. National Chung Hsing University
Taiwan, China
1442. National Law Center for Inter-American Free Trade
Tucson, AZ
1443. National University of Mexico
Mexico City, Mexico
1444. National War College
Washington, DC
1445. New York Medical College
Valhalla, NY
1446. Pacific School of Religion
Berkeley, CA
1447. Parsons School of Design
New York, NY
1448. Polytechnic School of Engineering
Milan, Italy
1449. Rivier College
Nashua, NH
1450. Royal Academy of Arts
London, England
1451. Seoul National University
Seoul, Korea
1452. Shenandoah University
Winchester, VA
1453. Smith Institute
London, England
1454. Southwestern Michigan College
Dowagaic, MI
1455. Spring Garden College
Philadelphia, PA
1456. St. Petersburg State Institute of Technology
St. Petersburg, Russia
1457. New York at Fredonia, State University of
Fredonia, NY
1458. New York at Oswego, State University of
Oswego, NY
1459. New York, Brooklyn College of Medicine, State University of
Brooklyn, NY
1460. New York, Institute of Technology at Utica/Rome, State University of
Utica/Rome, NY
1461. Teheran, University of
Teheran, Iran
1462. National Judicial College, The
Reno, NV
1463. Texas Southern University, Thurgood Marshall School of Law
Houston, TX
1464. Defense Language Institute, The
Monterey, CA
1465. Union Theological Seminary
New York, NY
1466. Bordeaux, University of
Bordeaux, France
1467. Universidad Iberoamericana
La Cruz, Mexico
1468. Amsterdam, University of
Amsterdam, Netherlands
1469. Birmingham, University of
Birmingham, England
1470. Bristol, University of
Bristol, England
1471. Catholic University of Brussels
Brussels, Belgium
1472. Canterbury, University of
Canterbury, New Zealand
1473. Costa Rica, University of
Moravia, Costa Rica
1474. East Anglia, University of
East Anglia, England
1475. Exeter, University of
Exeter, England
1476. Geneva, University of
Geneva, Switzerland
1477. Grenoble, University of
Grenoble, France
1478. Hannover, University of
Hannover, Germany
1479. Keele, University of
Keele, England
1480. Kent at Canterbury, University of
Canterbury, England
1481. Manchester, University of
Manchester, England
1482. New South Wales, University of
New South Wales, Australia
1483. Newcastle-upon-Tyne, University of
Newcastle-upon-Tyne, England
1484. Northern California, University of
Petaluma, CA
1485. Panama, University of
Panama, Rep. of Panama
1486. San Carlos, University of
University City, Guatemala
1487. Santa Monica College
Santa Monica, CA
1488. Sheffield, University of
Sheffield, England
1489. National University of Singapore
Singapore, Singapore
1490. Sydney, University of
Sydney, Australia
1491. Vrije Universiteit
Amsterdam, Netherlands
1492. Valley Forge Military Academy and College
Wayne, PA
1493. Zurich, University of
Zurich, Switzerland
1494. California at Los Angeles, University of
Los Angeles, CA
1495. Henry W. Bloch School of Business & Public Administration, University of Missouri
Los Angeles, CA
1496. European University
Amsterdam, Netherlands
1497. Nevada Mackay School of Mines, University of
Reno, NV
1498. Havana, University of
Havana, Cuba
1499. Rio Grande University
Rio Grande, OH
1500. Rhode Island School of Design
Providence, RI
1502. Ryerson Polytechnic University
Toronto, Canada
1503. Paul H. Nitze School of Advanced International Studies
Washington, DC
1504. California at Sacramento, University of
Sacramento, CA
1505. New York at Stony Brook, State University of
Stony Brook, NY
1506. Thayer School of Engineering at Darmouth College
Hanover, NH
1507. New York at Brockport, State University of
Brockport, NY
1508. Denver, Graduate School of International Studies, University of
Denver, CO
1509. Richmond, T.C. Williams School of Law, University of
Richmond, VA
1510. Long Island University, Southampton College
Southampton, NY
1511. St. Paul's College
Lawrenceville, VA
1512. Strayer University
Washington, DC
1513. Hague Academy of International Law, The
The Hague, Netherlands
1514. Naval Justice School
Newport, RI
1515. Glasgow, University of
Glasgow, Scotland
1516. Madrid, University of
Madrid, Spain
1517. Americas, University of the
Mexico City, Mexico
1518. Witwatersrand, University of the
Johannesburg, South Africa
1519. Webb Institute
Glen Cove, NY
1520. Southern New England School of Law
North Dartmouth, MA
1521. Leicester, University of
Leicester, England
1522. Loyola Law School
Los Angeles, CA
1523. Katholieke Universiteit Leuven
Leuven, Belgium
1524. Belmont University
Nashville, TN
1525. Universidad Nacional de Mexico
Mexico City, Mexico
1526. Florida Coastal School of Law
Jacksonville, FL
1527. British-American University School of Law
Santa Ana, CA
1528. Florida Metropolitan University
Tampa, FL
1529. New York College at Buffalo, State University of
Buffalo, NY
1530. Hebrew University of Jerusalem, The
Jerusalem, Israel
1531. Southern New Hampshire University
Manchester, NH
1532. Thomas Aquinas College
Santa Paula, CA
1533. Copenhagen, University of
Copenhagen, Denmark
1534. Basel, University of
Basel, Switzerland
1535. Bern, University of
Bern, Switzerland
1536. Tokyo, The University of
Tokyo, Japan
1538. Athens, University of
Athens, Greece
1539. Ner Israel Rabbinical College
Baltimore, MD
1540. London School of Economics and Political Science
London, England

1541. Pittsburgh School of Law, University of
Pittsburgh, PA
1542. Buenos Aires, University of
Buenos Aires, Argentina
1543. Hamburg, University of
Hamburg, Germany
1544. Malaya, University of
Kuala Lumpur, Malaysia
1545. Uppsala University
Uppsala, Sweden
1546. Lund University
Lund, Sweden
1547. Leeds Metropolitan University
Leeds, England
1548. Ghana, University of
Accra, Ghana
1549. Waseda University
Tokyo, Japan
1550. Buckingham, University of
Buckingham, England
1551. Monash University
Melbourne, Victoria, Australia
1552. Mount Mercy College
Cedar Rapids, IA
1553. William S. Boyd School of Law
Las Vegas, NV
1554. Salve Regina University
Newport, RI
1555. Eastern Oregon University
La Grande, OR
1556. Cornell University Law School
Ithaca, NY
1557. Rutgers College
New Brunswick, NJ
1558. Ave Maria School of Law
Ann Arbor, MI
1559. Philadelphia Biblical University
Langhorne, PA
1560. Barry University School of Law
Orlando, FL
1561. Lancaster University
Lancaster, England
1562. Paul Tulane College
New Orleans, LA
1563. St. Francis University
Loretto, PA
1564. Point Park University
Pittsburgh, PA
1565. Harvard Law School
Cambridge, MA
1566. William Howard Taft University
Santa Ana, CA
1567. Trinity Law School
Santa Ana, CA
1568. Liberty University
Formerly Lynchburg Baptist College
Lynchburg, VA
1569. New York at Plattsburgh, State
University of
Plattsburgh, NY
1570. Moody Bible Institute
Chicago, IL
1571. St. Thomas School of Law
Minneapolis, MN
1572. Charleston Southern University
Charleston, SC
1573. Grand Canyon University
Phoenix, AZ
1574. California State University, Bakersfield
Bakersfield, CA
1575. Tel Aviv University
Ramat Aviv, Tel Aviv, Israel
1576. Colby-Sawyer College
New London, NH
1577. Mercy College
Bronx, Dobbs Ferry, Manhattan,
White Plains and Yorktown, NY
1578. Charter Oak State College
New Britain, CT
1579. New York College at Old Westbury,
State University of
Old Westbury, NY
1580. New York, Maritime College, State
University of
Throggs Neck, NY
1581. Florida Memorial University
Miami Gardens, FL
1582. Albany State University
Albany, GA
4210. Louis D. Brandeis School of Law,
University of Louisville
Louisville, KY

PRACTICE PROFILES BAR ROSTER

IDAHO, ILLINOIS
INDIANA, IOWA

IDAHO

CAPITAL: BOISE

Idaho State Bar
P.O. Box 895
Boise, Idaho 83701
Telephone: 208-334-4500
Fax: 208-334-4515

Index of Towns and Cities Listed by County

*Indicates County Seat

Ada County
* Boise
Eagle
Meridian

Adams County
Council
Indian Valley

Bannock County
Fort Hall
* Pocatello

Bear Lake County
Montpelier
* Paris

Benewah County
Plummer
* St. Maries

Bingham County
* Blackfoot
Fort Hall

Blaine County
* Hailey
Ketchum
Sun Valley

Boise County
Banks
* Idaho City

Bonner County
Hope
Priest River
Sagle
* Sandpoint

Bonneville County
* Idaho Falls

Boundary County
* Bonners Ferry
Moyie Springs
Porthill

Butte County
* Arco

Camas County
* Fairfield

Canyon County
* Caldwell
Middleton
Nampa
Parma

Caribou County
* Soda Springs

Cassia County
* Burley

Clearwater County
* Orofino

Custer County
* Challis

Elmore County
* Mountain Home

Franklin County
Clifton
* Preston

Fremont County
Ashton
Newdale
* St. Anthony

Gem County
* Emmett

Gooding County
* Gooding
Wendell

Idaho County
* Grangeville
Kooskia

Jefferson County
* Rigby

Jerome County
* Jerome

Kootenai County
Athol
* Coeur d'Alene
Hayden
Hayden Lake
Post Falls
Rathdrum
Worley

Latah County
Juliaetta
Kendrick
* Moscow

Lemhi County
* Salmon

Lewis County
Craigmont
* Nez Perce

Lincoln County
* Shoshone

Madison County
* Rexburg

Minidoka County
* Burley
* Rupert

Nez Perce County
Lapwai
* Lewiston

Oneida County
* Malad City

Owyhee County
Homedale
* Murphy

Payette County
Fruitland
New Plymouth
* Payette

Power County
* American Falls

Shoshone County
Kellogg
* Wallace

Teton County
* Driggs
Victor

Twin Falls County
Buhl
Filer
* Twin Falls

Valley County
* Cascade
McCall

Washington County
Cambridge
* Weiser

AMERICAN FALLS, * 4,111, *Power Co.*

Beebe, Mark A. ... '48 '74 C.1193 B.A. L.336 J.D. Mag. J.
Eliasen, Lyle D. ... '44 '68 C&L.336 B.S., J.D. 202 Idaho St.
Glarborg, James E., (CV) ... '46 '78 C&L.336 B.S., J.D. 714 Hutchinson
Laggis, Paul S., (BV) ... '62 '92 C&L.336 B.A., J.D. P.O. Box 419

ARCO, * 1,016, *Butte Co.*

Carlson, William G. ... '37 '66 C&L.336 B.S., J.D. Mag. J.
Savage, Ralph, (BV) ... '60 '88 C.877 B.S.M.S. L.101 J.D. 326 W. Grand Ave.

ASHTON, 1,114, *Fremont Co.*

Purcell, Donald H. ... '26 '50 C.999 L.336 LL.B. P.O. Box 855‡

ATHOL, 676, *Kootenai Co.*

Richman, Harvey, (AV) ... '39 '64 C&L.472 B.A., LL.B. 19643 E. Perimeter Road

BANKS, 50, *Boise Co.*

Weidman, Arnold ... '12 '44 C&L.378 B.S., LL.B. P.O. Box 11‡

BLACKFOOT, * 10,419, *Bingham Co.*

Acevedo, Daniel R., (BV) ... '64 '91 C.877 B.A. L.276 J.D. [D.R.Acevedo]
Acevedo, Daniel R., P.C., (BV) ... 298 W. Bridge
Andrew, J. Scott, (BV) ... '67 '93 C&L.336 B.A., J.D. Pros. Atty.
Baker, Dwight E., (AV) ... '41 '71 C.966 B.S. L.336 J.D. [Baker&H.]
Baker & Harris, (AV) ... 199 W. Bridge

Beard St. Clair Gaffney McNamara Calder PA
(See Idaho Falls)

Beebe, Arnold T. ... '21 '49 C.334 L.336 LL.B. Ret. Dist. J.
Blaser, Stephen J., (BV) ... '49 '76 C.999 A.D. L.336 J.D. [Blaser,S.&H.]
Blaser, Sorensen & Hansen, Chartered, (BV) ... 285 North West Main
Brower, Robert C. ... '45 '74 C.1032 B.A. L.336 J.D. Mag.
Campbell, Cindy L., (BV) ... '60 '85 C.101 B.A. L.336 J.D. P.O. Box 853
Cannon, David M., (CV) ... '69 '95 C.101 B.A. L.878 J.D. [Moss,C.R.C.]
Castleton, Trevor L., (BV) ... '69 '98 C.1192 B.S. L.336 J.D. [Moss,C.R.C.]
Dutt, Philip L. '49 '82 C.575 B.A. L.477 J.D.
(adm. in CO; not adm. in ID) 190 E. Bannock‡
Esplin, DaLon, (BV) ... '51 '78 C&L.101 B.A., J.D. [Esplin P.]
Esplin Packer Law Office, (BV) ... 186 E. Judicial
Ferrin, Michael K. ... '40 '73 C.877 B.S. L.336 J.D. 156 W. Judicial St.‡
Hansen, Scott Hillam, (BV) ... '58 '87 C&L.101 B.A., J.D. [Blaser,S.&H.]
Harris, Jared M., (BV) ... '62 '91 C.877 B.S. L.101 J.D. [Baker&H.]
Herndon, James C. ... '41 '66 C&L.336 B.A., J.D. Dist. J.
Larsen, Reid K., (BV) ... '32 '74 C.1032 B.B.A. L.336 J.D. 157 N. Broadway
Lloyd, Bryce C. ... '— '03 C.1032 B.A. L.336 J.D. [Lloyd]
Lloyd Law Office ... 408 W. 280 North
Martsch, James L. ... '42 '67 C.877 B.S. L.336 J.D. Mag.

Merrill & Merrill, Chartered
(See Pocatello)

Moss, Cannon, Romrell, Castleton, P.A., (BV) ... 75 East Judicial Street
Murdoch, Manuel Travis ... '71 '01 C.877 B.A. L.336 J.D. [Parmenter]
Oleson, Justine B. ... '75 '01 C&L.336 B.S., J.D. P.O. Box 1047
Packer, Thomas W., (BV) ... '52 '82 C.877 B.S. L.878 J.D. 186 E. Judicial
Parmenter, David N., (CV) ... '51 '79 C.101 B.A. L.336 J.D. [Parmenter]
Parmenter Law Office, (CV) ... 53 S. Shilling
Peterson, Kevin Charles ... '58 '89 C.877 L.1032 J.D. [K.Peterson]
Peterson, Kevin ... 154 S. Oak
Romrell, Jason Michael, (BV) ... '70 '98 C.1032 B.S. L.336 J.D. [Moss,C.R.C.]
Simpson, Darren B., (BV) ... '63 '95 C.877 B.S. L.336 J.D. Dep. Prosecutor
Sorensen, Murray Jim, (BV) ... '48 '75 C.101 B.S. L.336 J.D. [Blaser,S.&H.]
Stufflebeam, Dwain H. ... '32 '56 C&L.508 B.A., LL.B. CEO, First American Title Co.
Williams, Dean ... '25 '56 C.877 L.878 J.D. 53 S. Shilling St.‡

BOISE, * 185,787, *Ada Co.*

Aaserud, Eric '— '92 C.907 B.A. L.1358 J.D.
(adm. in WA; not adm. in ID) [Ⓐ Perkins C.]
Adkins, Kara K. '51 '02 C&L.508 B.A., J.D.
(adm. in UT; not adm. in ID) Corp. Staff Atty., Washington Group Intl., Inc.
Ahrens, Edward D., (AV) ... '46 '71 C&L.336 B.A., J.D. [Ahrens&D.]
Ahrens & DeAngeli, P.L.L.C., (AV) ... P.O. Box 6561 (⊙Seattle, WA)
Aiken, Conrad J. ... '44 '69 C.967 A.B. L.228 J.D. [Racine O.N.B.&B.]
Alderman, James B. ... '74 '01 C.335 B.A. L.336 J.D. [Batt&F.]
Aldridge, Robert L., (BV) ... '45 '70 C.336 B.A. L.910 J.D. [R.L.Aldridge]
Aldridge, Robert L., Chartered, (BV) ... 1209 North Eighth Street
Alegria, Joseph John, II ... '62 '87 C.950 B.A. L.564 J.D. 4715 N. Anchor Way
Alkire, Steven E., (BV) ... '54 '87 C.1193 B.B.A. L.285 J.D. [Alkire]
Alkire & Co., PLLC, (BV) ... 205 N. Tenth Street
Allen, Gary G., (BV) ... '61 '87 C.197 A.B. L.813 J.D. [Givens P.]
Allyn, Kathleen P. '50 '79 C.681 B.A. L.145 J.D.
Dep. Admr., State Dept. of Health & Welfare
Andersen, Steven B., (AV) ... '52 '80 C&L.101 B.A., J.D. [Holland&H.]
Anderson, Larry D. ... '49 '76 C.589 B.S. L.209 J.D. Dir., Litig., Albertson's, Inc.
Anderson, Peter R. ... '60 '85 C.939 B.A. L.477 J.D. Atty. Gen. Off.
Anderson, Richard J.T., (BV) ... '30 '54 C&L.336 B.A., LL.B. [Anderson]
Anderson, Robert A., (AV) ... '51 '77 C.878 B.S. L.174 J.D. [Anderson,J.&H.]

Anderson, Julian & Hull, (AV) BR
C.W. Moore Plaza, 250 South 5th Street, Suite 700, P.O. Box 7426, 83707-7426
Telephone: 208-344-5800 Fax: 208-344-5510 URL: http://www.andersonjhlaw.com
Email: ajhlaw@ajhlaw.com URL: http://www.ajhlaw.com
Members of Firm: Robert A. Anderson; Brian K. Julian; Alan K. Hull; Chris H. Hansen; Phillip J. Collaer; Michael P. Stefanic II; Amy G. White. Associates: Randall L. Schmitz; Justin P. Aylsworth; Paul J. Stark; Matthew O. Pappas; Brian J. Coffey; Todd M. Joyner; Glenda M. Talbutt; Rachael M. O'Bar. Of Counsel: Kenneth D. Nyman.
Insurance Defense, Education Law, Worker's Compensation, Complex Commercial Litigation, Construction Law, Real Estate, Professional Liability, Personal Injury Defense, Employment Law, Defense of Governmental Entities, Civil Rights, Insurance Coverage Disputes, Automobile Insurance, Fire Insurance, ERISA Litigation, Products Liability, Commercial Transactions, Trial Practice, Appellate Practice, Alternative Dispute Resolution, Immigration and Naturalization, Environmental Litigation, and Natural Resources Litigation.

See Professional Biographies, BOISE, IDAHO

Anderson Law Offices, (BV) ... 207 North 3rd
Angstman, T.J., (CV) ... '68 '98 C.1193 B.A. L.336 J.D. [Angstman]
Angstman Law, PLLC, (CV) ... 3649 N. Lakeharbor Lane
Apel, Edwin (Win) V., Jr., (AV) '49 '77
C.976 B.A. L.336 J.D. V.P.-Risk Mgmt., Washington Grp. Intl., Inc.
Arkoosh, John C. '50 '78 C.602 A.B. L.336 J.D.
Adm. Law. J., Hearings & Appeals, Soc. Sec. Adm.
Armbruster, Ryan P., (AV) ... '51 '76 C.98 B.A. L.208 J.D. [Elam&B.]
Armstrong, Shelley W., (BV) ... '68 '93 C&L.336 B.A., J.D. Dep. Pros. Atty.
Arnold, Dean B. ... '69 '03 C.906 B.A. L.336 J.D. [Ⓐ Holland&H.]
Arnold, Elaine A. '65 '93 C.911 B.A. L.336 J.D.
Assoc. Gen. Coun., Blue Cross of Idaho Health Serv., Inc.
Arnold, Rebecca W., (BV) ... '— '87 C.531 B.S. L.910 J.D. Sr. Atty., Albertson's, Inc.
Arnold, Steven P., (AV) '55 '88 C&L.326 B.S., J.D.
Chf. Coun., Tech. Lic., Micron Technology, Inc. (Pat.)
Arnold, William H. '46 '73
C.1236 B.A. L.477 J.D. V.P., Real Estate Law, Albertson's, Inc.
Ashby, D. John '76 '05 C.1193 B.A. L.37 J.D.
(adm. in AZ; not adm. in ID) [Ⓐ Hawley T.E.&H.]
Ashmore, David A. '68 '95 C.309 A.B. L.893 J.D.
(adm. in DC; not adm. in ID)
Assoc. Gen. Coun., Litig. & Antitrust, Micron Technology, Inc.
Augustine, Paul J., (BV) ... '66 '92 C.299 B.A. L.107 J.D. 2627 W. Idaho St.
Aylsworth, Justin P. ... '71 '97 C.1193 B.S. L.285 J.D. [Ⓐ Anderson,J.&H.]
Babbitt, Gary D., (AV) ... '46 '73 C.335 B.A. L.145 J.D. [Hawley T.E.&H.]
Baca, Anthony '60 '92 C.801 B.S.E.E. L.36 J.D.
(adm. in AZ; not adm. in ID; Pat.) Sr. Coun., Hewlett-Packard Co.
Bailey, Eric Stephen, (CV) ... '58 '91 C.210 B.A. L.336 J.D. [Bowen&B.]
Bailey, Ransom J. ... '71 '02 C.939 B.A. L.336 J.D. [Ⓐ Moore S.B.&T.]
Baird, Denise C., (BV) ... '56 '85 C.694 B.A. L.336 J.D. Sr. Coun., Hewlett-Packard Co.
Baird, Joseph H., (AV) ... '54 '81 C.165 A.B. L.893 J.D. [Baird H.Q.]
Baird Hanson Quinn LLP, (AV) ... 2117 Hillway Drive (⊙Boulder, CO; Hous., TX)
Baker, Teresa A., (CV) ... '70 '96 C.1193 B.A. L.336 J.D. Dep. Pros. Atty.
Bakes, Robert E., (AV) ... '32 '56 C&L.336 B.A., J.D. [Ⓒ Moffatt T.B.R.&F.]
Baldner, Michael E. ... '68 '94 C.1193 B.A. L.336 J.D. [Ⓐ Meuleman M.]
Balkins, A. James, III, (AV) '52 '79 C.897 B.A. L.950 J.D.
V.P., Corp. Planning & Dev., Boise Cascade Corporation
Ball, James K., (BV) ... '70 '97 C.1193 B.S. L.336 J.D. [Manweiler,M.B.&B.]
Ball, Robert R., (BV) ... '58 '84 C.112 B.A. L.990 J.D. 916 Wyndemere Drive
Ballard, Brian L., (AV) ... '50 '80 C.1193 B.A. L.336 J.D. [Hawley T.E.&H.]
Ballard, David G., (BV) ... '53 '80 C.1193 B.A. L.336 J.D. [Bosch,D.&B.]
Banducci, Thomas A., (AV) ... '54 '79 C.813 A.B. L.1065 J.D. [Greener B.S.]
Banks, Robert K. ... '49 '80 C.1070 B.S. L.36 J.D. Sr. V.P., Real Estate, Albertson's, Inc.
Bantz, Judith Barkan ... '— '82 C.766 B.A. L.1065 J.D. 1421 E Bannock St
Barber, David J., (BV) ... '49 '74 C&L.1067 B.A., J.D. Atty. Gen. Off.
Barbour, Kelly T. '74 '01 C.335 B.A. L.893 J.D.
(adm. in TX; not adm. in ID) [Ⓐ Givens P.]
Barchas, Rudolf D. ... '43 '69 C.33 B.A. L.1065 J.D. 803 Locust St.‡
Barker, Albert P., (AV) ... '54 '81 C.976 B.A. L.945 J.D. [Barker R.&S.]
Barker, Mitchell R., (CV) ... '58 '85 C.878 B.A. L.336 J.D. 6550 Emerald, Suite 108

Barker Rosholt & Simpson LLP, (AV)
205 North 10th Street, Suite 520, P.O. Box 2139, 83701-2139 ⊙
Telephone: 208-336-0700 Facsimile: 208-344-6034
Email: brs@idahowaters.com URL: http://www.idaho-waters.com
Albert P. Barker; John K. Simpson.
Natural Resources, Water, Environmental, Construction and Commercial Litigation.
Twin Falls, Idaho Office: 113 Main Avenue West, Suite 303, 83301. Telephone: 208-733-0700. Facsimile: 208-735-2444.

See Professional Biographies, BOISE, IDAHO

Barnum, Randall S., (CV) ... '69 '99 C.112 B.A. L.950 J.D. 222 North 13th Street
Barrera, Benson ... '80 '05 C.878 B.S. L.1049 J.D. [Ⓐ Holland&H.]
Barrett, John W., (AV) ... '31 '59 C&L.336 B.S., LL.B. [Moffatt T.B.R.&F.]
Bartlett, Michael J., (BV) ... '69 '96 C.950 B.S. L.336 J.D. [Nevin,B.&M.]
Baskin, Nancy A. ... '61 '91 C&L.336 B.S., J.D. Law Clk., U.S. Dist. Ct. J.
Baskin, Thomas P., III, (AV) ... '56 '81 C&L.336 B.S., J.D. [Moore,B.&P.]
Batt, William J., (AV) ... '50 '82 C.335 B.S. L.336 J.D. [Batt&F.]

Batt & Fisher, LLP, (AV)
A Limited Liability Partnership
U.S. Bank Plaza, Suite 500, 101 South Capitol Boulevard, P.O. Box 1308, 83701
Telephone: 208-331-1000 Fax: 208-331-2400
URL: http://www.battfisher.com
Members of Firm: William J. Batt; Melville W. Fisher, II; David B. Lincoln; Jeffrey W. Pusch; John R. Hammond, Jr.; James B. Alderman.
Business Transactions, Civil Trial and Appellate Practice before State and Federal Courts and Administrative Agencies, Arbitration and Mediation regarding all types of Business and Commercial Disputes, Antitrust, Banking, Lending, Communications, Computers and Software, Construction, Corporations, Partnerships and Other Entities, Estate Planning, Trusts, Health Care, Insurance, Intellectual Property, Legislative and Regulatory, Mergers and Acquisitions, Probate, Guardianships, Conservatorships, Project and Venture Capital Financing, Public Contracts, Public Utilities, Real Estate, Securities, Taxation.

See Professional Biographies, BOISE, IDAHO

Bauer, Charles B., (BV) ... '53 '79 C.675 B.A. L.336 J.D. [Bauer&F.]
Bauer, Jonathan R. ... '72 '02 C.910 B.A. L.1398 J.D. [Ⓐ Meuleman M.]

Bauer & French, (BV)
733 North Seventh Street, P.O. Box 2730, 83701-2730
Telephone: 208-383-0090 Fax: 208-383-0412
URL: http://www.bauerandfrench.com
Members of Firm: Charles B. Bauer; Randal J. French.
Trial and Appellate Practice. Family Law, Divorce, Interstate Child Custody, Community Property Law. Commercial, Bankruptcy, Real Estate.

See Professional Biographies, BOISE, IDAHO

Baugh, James R., (BV) ... '52 '77 C.878 B.S. L.336 J.D. 4477 Emerald St.
Baughman, Jeanne C. '58 '03 C.169 B.A. L.999 J.D.
Litigation Atty., Washington Group Intl., Inc.
Bauman, Jon M., (BV) ... '53 '82 C.878 B.A. L.336 J.D. [Ⓐ Elam&B.]
Baxter, Garrick L. '— '00 C.628 B.S. L.1051 J.D.
(adm. in OR; not adm. in ID) Atty. Gen. Off.
Beane, Stephen W., (BV) ... '51 '76 C.878 B.S. L.336 J.D. 2112 Mirtimer Dr.
Beaton, Kevin J., (BV) ... '57 '84 C.93 B.A. L.273 J.D. [Stoel R.]
Beckstrom, Bradley R., (AV) '63 '89
C&L.101 B.A., J.D. Dir., Real Estate Law, Albertson's, Inc.
Beehner-Kane, Barbara, (BV) ... '56 '82 C&L.336 B.A., J.D. [Ⓐ Huntley P.]
Beeman, Josephine P., (AV) ... '47 '75 C.813 B.A. L.629 J.D. [Beeman&Assoc.]
Beeman & Associates, P.C., (AV) ... 409 West Jefferson Street
Beer, Stephen L., (AV) ... '46 '72 C&L.336 B.S., J.D. [Beer&C.]
Beer & Cain, (AV) ... 302 W. Idaho
Beeson, Christopher J., (AV) ... '50 '80 C&L.336 B.S., J.D. [Givens P.]
Belnap, Wm. Lyman, (BV) ... '48 '78 C&L.101 B.A., J.D. [Belnap C.D.]
Belnap Curtis Drozda, PLLC, (BV) ... 1401 Shoreline Dr.
Belodoff, Howard A. '52 '78
C.999 B.A. L.336 J.D. Assoc. Dir., Idaho Legal Aid Servs., Inc.

Beltramo, Robert J. .... '48 '74 C&L.767 B.A., J.D. 5605 Marcliffe Ave.
Bengoechea, Shane O., (BV) .... '56 '82 C.1193 B.A. L.285 J.D. [Bengoechea,W.]
Bengoechea, Walther Law Offices, PLLC, (BV) .... 671 E. Riverpark Lane, Suite 130
Benjamin, Dennis, (AV) .... '57 '84 C&L.911 B.A., J.D. [Nevin,B.&M.]
Bennett, Robt. W. .... '21 '50 C.275 L.608 J.D. Ret. Mag. J.
Berenter, Steven W., (AV) .... '54 '80 C.813 B.A. L.911 J.D. [Hawley T.E.&H.]
Bergesen, Richard A. .... '64 '93 C.629 B.S. L.336 J.D. 300 Main St.
Bergquist, Kenneth G. .... '22 '51 L.336 LL.B. P.O. Box 1775
Berlin, Robert L. '55 '81 C.629 B.A. L.285 J.D.
Assoc. Gen. Coun., Washington Grp. Intl., Inc.
Bernstein, G. Philip, (BV) .... '49 '75 C.1044 B.A. L.862 J.D. 2308 N. Cole Road, Suite C
Berringer, Howard G. .... '37 '75 C.999 L.345 LL.B. Asst. City Atty.
Bethke, Brian .... '57 '94 C.378 B.A. L.285 J.D. Dir., Bus. Law, Albertson's, Inc.
Bevis, James A., (AV) .... '48 '74 C.174 B.S. L.336 J.D. [Bevis,C.&J.]

Bevis, Cameron & Johnson, P.A., (AV) [BB]
Suite 220, 960 Broadway Avenue, P.O. Box 827, 83706-3667
Telephone: 208-345-1040 Fax: 208-345-0365
Email: mjohnson@bevislaw.com URL: http://www.bevislaw.com
James A. Bevis; Michael R. Johnson;—Krista Dawn Thiry.
General Trial and Appellate Practice before State and Federal Courts. Personal Injury, Family Law, Business, Corporation, Real Estate and Military Law.
Representative Clients: State of Idaho Military Division; Idaho Credit Union League; Capital Educators Federal Credit Union; Boise U.S. Employees Federal Credit Union; Idaho Concrete Company.
Reference: U.S. Bank.
See Professional Biographies, BOISE, IDAHO

Bianchi, Carl F. .... '43 '69 C.299 B.A. L.228 J.D. Idaho State Legis.
Bieter, Christopher M. .... '56 '83 C&L.336 B.A., J.D. Dist. J.
Bilow, Robert L., (AV) .... '43 '70 C.674 A.B. L.911 J.D. 2277 N. Longview Place‡
Bistline, Bruce S., (BV) .... '51 '76 C.170 B.A. L.336 J.D. [Gordon]
Bithell, Walter H., (AV) .... '42 '68 C&L.336 B.S., J.D. [Holland&H.]
Bixby, Michael B. '43 '69 C&L.477 B.A., J.D.
(adm. in DC; not adm. in ID) Boise State Univ.
Bjorkman, Eric R. .... '44 '83 C.1078 B.A. L.336 J.D. 3065 S. Crabapple Lane‡
Bjorkman, Eric R., Jr., (BV) .... '70 '97 C.197 A.B. L.336 J.D. [A] Perkins C.]
Bjorkman, Kristin E. .... '75 '03 C.594 B.S. L.336 J.D. [A] Hawley T.E.&H.]
Blackburn, Rex, (AV) .... '55 '80 C.335 B.A. L.1065 J.D. [Blackburn&J.]

Blackburn & Jones LLP, (AV) [BB]
1673 W. Shoreline Drive, Suite 200, P.O. Box 7808, 83707-7808
Telephone: 208-489-8989 Fax: 208-489-8988
URL: http://www.blackburnjoneslaw.com
Members of the Firm: Rex Blackburn; Bruce C. Jones; Patrick E. Mahoney;—Eric B. Swartz; Daniel L. Glynn.
Civil Trial and Appellate Practice, Products Liability, Personal Injury, Transportation, Aviation, Corporate, Labor, Employment, Public Utilities, Administrative Law.
See Professional Biographies, BOISE, IDAHO

Blancaflor, Dawn C. .... '68 '94 C.112 B.A. L.285 J.D. 1111 West Jefferson Street
Blanton, J. Charles, (AV) .... '26 '51 C&L.336 J.D. [A] Hall,F.O.&B.]
Blount, Ralph Reed, (CV) .... '62 '99 C.1193 B.A. L.336 J.D. Atty. Gen. Office
Boardman, Richard C., (AV) .... '51 '82 C.1032 B.A. L.336 J.D. [Perkins C.]
Bock, Les, (BV) .... '49 '79 C.112 B.A. L.1065 J.D. [Bosch,D.&B.]
Bock, P. Maureen .... '56 '91 C.1109 B.A. L.45 J.D. State Industrial Comm.
Bohn, Brent R. '66 '91 C.112 B.A. L.426 J.D.
(adm. in CA; not adm. in ID) Dir., Labor Rel., CA Off., Albertson's, Inc.
Bohn, Matthew R. .... '72 '99 C&L.336 B.S., J.D. [A] Cosho H.]
Boice, Paul A. .... '70 '01 C.878 B.S. L.336 J.D. [A] Meuleman M.]
Bolinder, Clint R., (CV) ...... '70 '97 C.1193 B.B.A. L.336 J.D. 913 W. River St., Ste. 430
Bond, Brook B. '— '89 C.112 B.S. L.1049 J.D.
(adm. in CA; not adm. in ID) [A] Perkins C.]
Borger, Kevin Scot .... '61 '86 C.594 B.A. L.900 J.D. Pros. Attys. Off.
Bosch, Allan R., (AV) .... '54 '79 C.585 B.S.B.A. L.190 J.D. [Bosch,D.&B.]

Bosch, Daw & Ballard, Chartered, (AV)
9th and Idaho Center, 225 North 9th Street, Suite 210, 83702
Telephone: 208-344-8990 Telecopier: 208-344-9140
Email: dbdb@dbdb.com URL: http://www.dbdb.com
Allan R. Bosch; C. A. Daw; David G. Ballard; Les Bock.
Commercial and Business Law including Real Estate, Employee Benefit Plans, Estate Planning, Taxation, Litigation, Transportation, Immigration, Bankruptcy and Health, Law and Taxation of Nonprofit Organizations.
See Professional Biographies, BOISE, IDAHO

Bowen, James D. .... '75 '03 C.101 B.S. L.285 J.D. [A] Holland&H.]
Bowen, Jo-Ann Leigh '63 '88 C&L.184 B.A., J.D.
Dep. Atty. Gen., Human Rights Comm.
Bowen, R. Daniel, (AV) .... '53 '80 C&L.336 B.A., J.D. [Bowen&B.]
Bowen & Bailey, L.L.P., (AV) .... 350 North Ninth Street, Suite 302
Bower, Greg H., (AV) .... '49 '74 C.336 B.S. L.878 J.D. Pros. Atty.
Bowler, Bruce, (BV) .... '11 '38 C&L.336 LL.B. 1111 Shaw Mountain Rd.
Bowman, Steven C., (BV) .... '60 '91 C.1032 B.A. L.336 J.D. [Holland&H.]
Boyd, Paul M., (AV) .... '49 '82 C.813 A.B. L.276 J.D. [Stoel R.]
Boyd, Peter J., (AV) '19 '49 C.906 B.A. L.911 LL.B.
199 N. Capitol Boulevard, Suite 500
Boyle, Brian L. .... '— '00 [A] Cosho H.]
Boyle, Larry M. .... '43 '73 C.101 B.S. L.336 J.D. U.S. Mag. J.
Bradbury, Stephen A., (AV) .... '55 '81 C.336 B.S. L.1051 J.D. 1015 W. Hays St.
Brady, Michael G., (AV) .... '46 '70 C&L.336 B.A., J.D. [Brady]
Brady Law, Chartered, (AV) .... 9300 Overland Road
Brailsford, Amanda K., (BV) .... '67 '93 C&L.336 B.A., J.D. [Holland&H.]
Braley, Kevin C. .... '66 '98 C.791 B.S.E.E. L.793 J.D. [A] Holland&H.]
Brantley, Charles B. '— '93 C.846 B.S. L.365 J.D.
(adm. in IL; not adm. in ID; Pat.) Sr. Pat. Coun., Micron Technology, Inc.
Brassey, Andrew C., (AV) .... '52 '77 C&L.336 B.S., J.D. [Brassey,W.C.&G.]
Brassey, Carol Lynn, (AV) .... '52 '78 C.685 B.A. L.629 J.D. Dep. Atty. Gen.
Brassey, John Michael, (AV) '46 '71
C&L.336 B.S., J.D. [Hopkins R.C.H.&H.] (©Idaho Falls)

Brassey, Wetherell, Crawford & Garrett, L.L.P., (AV) [BB]
203 W. Main Street, P.O. Box 1009, 83701-1009
Telephone: 208-344-7300 Facsimile: 208-344-7077
Email: bwcm@brassey.net URL: http://www.bwcmlaw.com
Andrew C. Brassey; Robert T. Wetherell; J. Nick Crawford; Nancy Jo Garrett;—John McEvoy Howell; Ellen S. Elliott; Christopher P. Graham; Clinton S. Coddington.
General Civil and Trial Practice, Appeals, Insurance Defense, Business Defense, Defense of Governmental Entities, Trucking Law, Medical Malpractice, DEF, Environmental, Civil Rights, Commercial, Real Estate, Employment, Personnel, Agriculture, and Products Liability.
Representative Clients: Safeco Insurance Cos.; Industrial Indemnity Co.; Transamerica Insurance Group; Fireman's Fund Insurance Co.; Royal Insurance Co.; Lumbermans Mutual Insurance Co.; American Motorists Insurance Co.; Northwestern National Insurance Co.; Reliance Insurance Co.; Insurance Company of North America.
See Professional Biographies, BOISE, IDAHO

Breen, M. Sean, (CV) .... '63 '92 C.1032 B.A. L.336 J.D. [Manweiler,M.B.&B.]
Breitsameter, George W., (BV) .... '55 '81 C.927 L.801 J.D. Asst. U.S. Atty.
Broadbent, Rebecca A., (BV) .... '66 '89 C.1193 B.A. L.1335 J.D. [Finch&B.]
Brooks, Joseph B. '21 '49 C&L.546 B.A., J.D.
(adm. in NE; not adm. in ID) 4948 N. Point Pl.‡
Brooks, Susan Corisis, (CV) .... '61 '90 C.1193 B.B.A. L.911 J.D. 1005 N. 9th St., Ste. 11

Brooks, Kimberly D.
(See Nampa)

Brown, Christian D., (BV) ...... '58 '89 C.906 B.A. L.336 J.D. 2399 South Orchard Street
Brown, Clifford L., (BV) .... '63 '90 C&L.336 B.S., J.D. [Holzer,E.&H.]
Brown, Leslie S. .... '— '97 C.678 B.A. L.464 J.D. [A] Quane S.]
Brown, Stephen C., (AV) .... '46 '74 C.813 B.A. L.336 J.D. [Ellis,B.&S.]
Bruce, James E., Jr., (AV) '20 '48
C.670 B.A. L.336 LL.B. Pres. & CEO, Idaho Power Co.
Buffington, M. Dean '40 '70
C.335 B.A. L.950 J.D. Exec. V.P., First Sec. Bk. of Idaho, N.A.
Burch, James W., (AV©) '54 '83 C.377 B.A. L.659 J.D.
Expert Counsel, Albertson's, Inc.
Burgoyne, Grant T., (BV) .... '53 '88 C.336 B.A. L.378 J.D. [Mauk&B.]
Burke, Carl P., (AV) .... '24 '50 C&L.813 B.A., LL.M. [©] Greener B.S.]
Burke, Christopher C., (AV) .... '50 '77 C.813 B.A. L.336 J.D. [Greener B.S.]
Burke, John J., (BV) .... '55 '92 C.1085 B.S. L.878 J.D. [Hall,F.O.&B.]
Burkett, F. Michael, Jr., (BV) .... '48 '79 C.1070 B.S. L.336 J.D. [Huntley P.]
Burleigh, Richard B., (BV) .... '62 '89 C.174 B.A. L.629 J.D. Atty., Albertson's, Inc.
Burns, Phillip O., (BV) .... '53 '81 C&L.336 B.A., J.D. Mng. Staff Atty., Idaho Power Co.
Burns, Robert B., (AV) .... '52 '82 C.1193 L.813 J.D. [Moffatt T.B.R.&F.]
Burri, Laura E., (BV) .... '— '86 C.594 B.A. L.336 J.D. [Ringert C.]
Burrow, Alan G. '56 '81 C.484 B.A. L.259 J.D.
(adm. in FL; not adm. in ID) Asst. U.S. Atty., U.S. Atty.'s Off.
Bush, Cheri L. .... '48 '84 C.1193 B.A. L.259 J.D. Ref., Idaho Indus. Comm.
Bush, John A., (AV) .... '61 '88 C&L.336 B.S., J.D. [Comstock&B.]
Bush, Sheila G., (CV) '58 '83 C.645 B.A. L.273 J.D.
Asst. Gen. Coun., J.R. Simplot Co.
Butler, JoAnn C., (AV) .... '51 '87 C.107 B.S. L.146 J.D. [Spink B.]
Butler, Paul B., (BV) .... '57 '89 C.1235 B.A. L.1051 J.D. 1011 Miller Street
Buttars, Rodney T., (CV) ..... '50 '87 C.1193 B.B.A. L.336 J.D. 1101 W. River, Suite 110
Butterfield, Kathleen .... '55 '90 C.813 A.B. L.629 J.D. Jud. Law Clk. to U.S. Dist. Ct.
Buxton, Susan E., (BV) .... '63 '89 C.939 B.A. L.336 J.D. [Moore S.B.&T.]
Byron, Gregory A. .... '69 '98 C.1193 B.S. L.336 J.D. [A] Thornton B.]
Bywater, Stephen A., (BV) .... '50 '76 C&L.878 B.A., J.D. 6311 E. Gateway Ct.
Cain, Dennis L., (BV) .... '47 '74 C&L.336 B.S., J.D. [Beer&C.]
Callister, Marion J. .... '21 '51 C&L.878 B.S., J.D. U.S. Sr. Dist. J.
Camacho Mendoza, Natalie .... '63 '91 C.1032 B.A. L.900 J.D. [Camacho M.]

Camacho Mendoza Law Office
623 W. Hays Street, 83702
Telephone: 208-342-2960 Fax: 208-345-0050
Email: camacho@cableone.net
Member of Firm: Natalie Camacho Mendoza.
Workers' Compensation, Immigration, Indian Law.
See Professional Biographies, BOISE, IDAHO

Cameron, Alan D., II, (AV) .... '46 '76 C&L.336 B.A., J.D. P.O. Box 827
Cameron, Kelly A. '67 '95 C.101 B.A. L.902 J.D.
(adm. in MD; not adm. in ID) [A] Perkins C.]
Campbell, Scott L., (AV) .... '52 '78 C.939 B.A. L.336 J.D. [Moffatt T.B.R.&F.]
Cantrill, David W., (AV) .... '42 '70 C.1032 B.A. L.336 J.D. [Cantrill,S.S.&K.]

Cantrill, Skinner, Sullivan & King, LLP, (AV) [BB]
1423 Tyrell Lane, P.O. Box 359, 83701
Telephone: 208-344-8035 Fax: 208-345-7212
Email: cssklaw@cssklaw.com
Members of Firm: David W. Cantrill; Gardner W. Skinner, Jr.; Willis E. Sullivan, III (1941-2001); John L. King; Robert D. Lewis; Clinton O. Casey; Dean C. Sorensen. Associate: Steven J. Meade.
Insurance Defense, Workers Compensation, Corporate and Real Estate Law, Criminal Law, Domestic Relations. Trial and Appellate Practice.
Representative Clients: Safeco Insurance Companies; Prudential Property and Casualty Insurance Co.; State Insurance Fund; Farmers Insurance Co.; Cincinnati Insurance Co.; Nature Conservancy; Independent School District of Boise City; Hartford Insurance Group; Mutual of Enumclaw Insurance Co.
Reference: Key Bank.
See Professional Biographies, BOISE, IDAHO

Cardon, Andrea L., (CV) '65 '92 C.906 B.S. L.336 J.D.
355 West Myrtle Street, Suite 103, P.O. Box 2633, 83701
Telephone: 208-384-0011 Fax: 208-344-7100
Email: cardon5747@aol.com URL: http://www.andrealcardonlaw.com
Construction Contracts and Social Security Disability.
See Professional Biographies, BOISE, IDAHO

Carlson, James D., (BV) .... '55 '82 C&L.336 B.S., J.D. P.O. Box 83720

Carnahan, Debrha J., (BV) '52 '78 C&L.336 B.S., J.D.
101 South Capitol Boulevard, Suite 400, P.O. Box 2125, 83701
Telephone: 208-338-1420 Facsimile: 208-338-0762
Email: debrha@carnahanlawoffice.com
Family Law, Probate, Child Custody and Domestic Relations.
See Professional Biographies, BOISE, IDAHO

Carty, Stuart W., (BV) .... '44 '74 C&L.838 B.A, J.D. [Carty L.]

Carty Law, P.A., (BV)
380 South 4th Street Suite 102, 83702
Telephone: 208-342-3501 Fax: 208-342-3548 URL: http://www.carty-law.com URL: http://www.cartylaw.us
URL: http://www.cartylaw.net
Stuart W. Carty.
Personal Injury, Medical Malpractice, Products Liability, Trucking Liability, Mediation, Arbitration, Torts, Insurance Bad Faith, Slip and Fall, Dog Bites, Wrongful Death, Airplane Accidents, Automobile Accidents, Brain Injury, Spinal Injury, Truck Accidents.
See Professional Biographies, BOISE, IDAHO

Case, Syrena T. '70 '00 C.821 B.A. L.309 J.D.
(adm. in CA; not adm. in ID) 550 West Fort Street
Casey, Clinton O., (BV) .... '63 '90 C.336 B.S. L.767 J.D. [Cantrill,S.S.&K.]
Casey, Karen A. '66 '91 C.188 B.S. L.245 J.D.
(adm. in NJ; not adm. in ID) Dir., Human Resources & Labor Rel., Albertson's, Inc.
Castaneda, Janet L. '56 '83
C.763 B.A. L.1494 J.D. Dir., Real Estate Law, Albertson's, Inc.
Castleton, Bruce .... '— '04 C.336 B.A. L.101 J.D. [A] Naylor&H.]
Chalfant, Charles L., (BV) .... '26 '52 C.939 A.B. L.336 LL.B. 2921 Arran Ct.
Chalfant, Frank E., Jr., (AV) .... '23 '51 C.335 B.S. L.336 LL.B. 2675 W. Main St.
Chaloupka, Susan K., (BV) .... '49 '78 C.112 B.A. L.336 J.D. 1117 N. 19th St.

Chandler, Thomas B., (AV) ....'54 '79 C.813 B.A. L.145 J.D. [Hawley T.E.&H.]
Channer, David A., (AV) '57 '85
C&L.101 B.S., J.D. Chf. Corp. Coun., Micron Technology, Inc.
Charbonneau, Jennifer .... '62 '89 C.174 B.A. L.629 J.D. Law Clk., U.S. Bkrptcy J.
Charrier, Aaron C. ....'71 '03 C.1193 B.A. L.221 J.D. [Ⓐ Hawley T.E.&H.]
Chasan, Andrew M., (AV) ....'50 '77 C.611 B.A. L.930 J.D. [Chasan&W.]

Chasan & Walton, L.L.C., (AV)
1459 Tyrell Lane, P.O. Box 1069, 83701
Telephone: 208-345-3760 Fax: 208-345-0288
URL: http://www.chasanwalton.com
Members of Firm: Andrew M. Chasan; Timothy C. Walton.
Personal Injury, Wrongful Death, Interstate Trucking Litigation, Insurance Bad Faith, Products Liability, Mediation, Medical Malpractice.
See Professional Biographies, BOISE, IDAHO

Chen, Kevin M. ....'70 '97 C.1193 B.A. L.878 J.D. [Ahrens&D.]
Chess, Laura A. ....'75 '00 C.941 B.A. L.336 J.D. [Ⓐ Kane&T.]
Chou, Jeremy C. ....'70 '97 C.69 B.A. L.904 J.D. Atty. Gen. Off.
Christensen, Donald Craig '62 '91 C.800 B.S. L.1065 J.D.
(adm. in CA; not adm. in ID) Amresco Coml. Fin., Inc.
Christensen, Glenna M., (AV) ....'43 '78 C.877 B.A. L.101 J.D. [Moffatt T.B.R.&F.]
Christenson, Jeffrey R., (AV) ....'— '76 C.610 B.S.J. L.607 J.D. [Ringert C.]
Christian, Michael R. ....'65 '90 C.597 B.A. L.911 J.D. 737 N. 7th St.

Christian, Ron, Attorney at Law, (CV) '60 '91 C.112 B.S. L.101 J.D.
671 E. Riverpark Lane, Suite 130, 83706
Telephone: 208-322-6448; 208-424-7985 URL: http://www.ronchristianlaw.com
Email: rchristian@ronchristianlaw.com URL: http://www.ronchristianlawfirm.com
Family Law, Adoptions, Alimony, Child Support, Custody, Divorce, Domestic Violence, Separation Agreements, Visitation Rights, Grandparents Rights, Restraining Orders, Criminal Law, Drugs Crimes, Drunk Driving, Felonies, Misdemeanors, Business Litigation and Transactions, Corporations, Limited Liability Companies, Employment Litigation, Real Estate Transactions and Litigation.
See Professional Biographies, BOISE, IDAHO

Churchill, Winston H., (AV) ....'29 '56 C&L.336 B.S., LL.B. 555 W. Bannock St.
Claiborne, David P. ....'78 '02 C.1193 B.A. L.950 J.D. [Ⓐ Ringert C.]
Clark, Charles R., (BV) '50 '82
C.67 B.S. L.1202 J.D. 225 North 9th Street, Suite 210 (Pat.)
Clark, Christopher W., (BV) ....'56 '81 C.608 B.S. L.150 J.D. Dep. Atty Gen.
Clark, D. Blair, (AV) ....'— '71 C&L.336 B.S., J.D. [Ringert C.]
Clark, Merlyn W., (AV) ....'37 '64 C&L.336 J.D. [Hawley T.E.&H.]
Cleere, Scott R. ...... '69 '00 C.101 B.S. L.336 J.D. [Cleere] & [Ⓐ Technology L.G., LLC]
Cleere Law Office, PLLC .... 4199 Oxbow Way
Cloninger, Coite E. ....'15 '45 L.180 LL.B. 397 Silver City Dr.‡
Cloonan, Joan M. ....'40 '74 C.1031 B.S. L.259 J.D. V.P., J.R. Simplot Co.
Cockerille, Roger E., (BV) ....'65 '93 C.312 B.A. L.972 J.D. Asst. City. Atty.
Coddington, Clinton S. ....'74 '00 C.93 B.A. L.1049 J.D. [Ⓐ Brassey,W.C.&G.]
Coffey, Brian J. ....'70 '96 C&L.1049 B.A., J.D. [Ⓐ Anderson,J.&H.]
Coffin, Terry E., (AV) ....'46 '72 C&L.336 B.A., J.D. Off. of Atty. Gen.
Colaianni, Cary B., (BV) '60 '86
C.1032 B.A. L.336 J.D. City Atty., Boise City Atty's Off.
Colborn, James W. ....'68 '95 C.906 B.A. L.950 J.D. [Ⓐ Neal&U.]
Cole, Charles F., (AV) ....'49 '82 C.188 B.A. L.446 J.D. Albertson's, Inc.
Cole, William C., (BV) ....'64 '91 C.35 B.S. L.1049 J.D. [Givens P.]
Coleman, Nancy R. '57 '99 C.878 B.S. L.508 J.D.
(adm. in MT; not adm. in ID) 3440 Victory View Dr.
Collaer, Phillip J., (BV) ....'56 '85 C.336 B.S. L.285 J.D. [Anderson,J.&H.]
Collins, Christian D. ....'68 '99 C.1193 B.A. L.336 J.D. [Ⓐ Westberg,M.&C.]
Collins, Patrick V., (AV) ....'55 '80 C.791 B.S. L.813 J.D. [Hawley T.E.&H.]
Collins, William D., (AV) .... '39 '65 C&L.336 B.S.Ch.E., LL.B. [Westberg,M.&C.]
Comstock, Chris D. ....'— '02 C.1193 B.A. L.336 J.D. [Ⓐ Hall,F.O.&B.]
Comstock, David E., (AV) ....'54 '79 C.336 B.S. L.285 J.D. [Comstock&B.]

Comstock & Bush, (AV)
199 N. Capitol Boulevard, Suite 500, P.O. Box 2774, 83701-2774
Telephone: 208-344-7700 Telecopier: 208-344-7721
URL: http://www.comstockandbush.com
David E. Comstock; John A. Bush.
Accident and Personal Injury Law, Wrongful Death, Head Injuries, Insurance Bad Faith Law, Medical Malpractice Law, Aviation Law, Employment Law, Product Liability Law.
See Professional Biographies, BOISE, IDAHO

Connolly, John P., (AV) ....'51 '77 C.363 B.A. L.215 J.D. 134 South 5th St.
Cooper, David P. '58 '87 C.436 B.S.Chem. L.966 J.D.
(adm. in WI; not adm. in ID; Pat.) [Kolisch H.] (ⓞPort., OR)
Cooper, Lea C., (BV) ....'55 '86 C.629 B.A. L.37 J.D. 3227 Morris Hill Rd.
Copple, E. Don, (AV) ....'42 '66 C&L.336 B.A., J.D. [Davison,C.C.&C.]
Copple, Terry C., (AV) ....'52 '76 C&L.336 B.A., J.D. [Davison,C.C.&C.]
Cosho Humphrey, LLP, (AV) .... 800 Park Boulevard, Suite 790
Coster, Kimberly A., (BV) .... '61 '87 C&L.629 B.A., J.D. Dep. Atty. Gen.
Coston, Ronald D. ....'47 '81 C.1032 B.A. L.336 J.D. Coun., State Ins. Fund
Coulter, Charles D., (BV) ....'38 '70 C.413 B.S. L.336 J.D. 1002 N. 8th St.
Cox, Jon R., (BV) ....'63 '92 C.1193 B.S. L.336 J.D. [Davison,C.C.&C.]
Cozakos, Shelly, (CV) ....'68 '96 C&L.336 B.S., J.D. [Ⓐ Perkins C.]
Crane, Tracy Jack ....'74 '03 C.1032 B.S. L.336 J.D. [Ⓐ Holland&H.]
Crawford, J. Nick, (AV) ....'58 '84 C&L.336 B.S., J.D. [Brassey,W.C.&G.]
Crawford, Katherine B., (BV) ....'57 '90 C.1356 B.A. L.878 J.D. Dep. Atty. Gen.
Creamer, Michael C., (BV) ....'57 '89 C.172 B.S. L.174 J.D. [Givens P.]
Croner, John F., (CV) ....'44 '71 C&L.336 B.A., J.D. 1215 West Hays Street
Crossland, Julia A. .... '60 '86 C.112 B.A. L.273 J.D. Law Clk., Idaho Supm. Ct.

Cummings, Richard A., (AV) '48 '75 C.597 B.A. L.546 J.D.
999 Main Street, P.O. Box 1545, 83701-1545
Telephone: 208-367-0722 Fax: 208-367-0892
Email: cummingsricharda@qwest.net URL: http://www.racummings.com
Business Law, Commercial Litigation, Real Estate Law, Estate Planning, Tax Planning, Wills, Trusts and Estates, Wills and Probate, Family Trusts, Living Trust, Off-Shore Trusts, Wealth Preservation, Fiduciary Law, Tax Controversies.
See Professional Biographies, BOISE, IDAHO

Cunningham, Heather A., (BV) ..... '70 '96 C.317 B.A. L.990 J.D. [Ⓐ Davison,C.C.&C.]
Cunnington, Christie Woodward .... '72 '97 C.628 B.S. L.629 J.D. Atty. Gen. Off.
Curtis, R. Wade ....'48 '73 [Belnap C.D.]
Dale, Candy Wagahoff, (AV) ....'56 '82 C.335 B.S. L.336 J.D. [Hall,F.O.&B.]
Dale, James C., (AV) ....'56 '82 C.454 B.A. L.336 J.D. [Ⓒ Stoel R.]
Danehy, Maryellen ....'58 '85 C.1031 B.A. L.823 J.D. State Treasurer's Off.
Daniel, David M. '50 '78 C.813 B.A. L.1026 J.D.
(adm. in CA; not adm. in ID) 2816 Malibu Rd.‡

Daubney, James S. '55 '83 C.112 M.B.A. L.1065 J.D.
(adm. in CA; not adm. in ID) IRS, US Treas.
Davis, Gary L., (CV) ....'57 '90 C.1193 B.B.A. L.336 J.D. 3914 State St.
Davis, J. Layne, (BV) ..... '66 '94 C.1193 B.A. L.878 J.D. 200 North 4th Street, Suite 302
Davis, James J., (AV) ....'53 '78 C.1193 B.A. L.336 J.D. 406 W. Franklin St.
Davis, Jarrod G. ....'69 '97 C.285 B.B.Ad. L.629 J.D. 877 Main St., Suite 1000
Davis, Lon F. ....'35 '59 C&L.336 B.A., LL.B. State Supm. Ct.
Davis, Lynnette M., (CV) ....'67 '96 C.911 B.A. L.285 J.D. [Ⓐ Hawley T.E.&H.]
Davis, Reagan G. ....'64 '91 C&L.336 B.S., J.D. 3016 S. Longleaf Avenue

Davison, Copple, Copple & Cox, (AV)
199 North Capitol Boulevard, Suite 600, P.O. Box 1583, 83702
Telephone: 208-342-3658 Fax: 208-386-9428
Email: edcopple@davisoncopple.com URL: http://www.davisoncopple.com
Members of Firm: W. Howard Davison (1878-1964); Frank H. Davison (1907-1984); Robert H. Copple (1919-1995); E. Don Copple; Terry C. Copple; Jon R. Cox. Associates: Heather A. Cunningham; Jay M. Gustavsen; Edward J. Guerricabeitia; Cynthia L. Yee-Wallace.
General Civil and Trial Practice, Litigation, Commercial Banking, Real Estate, Title Insurance, Corporation, Antitrust, Eminent Domain, Condemnation and Inverse Condemnation, Probate, Estate Planning, Family Law, Personal Injury, Products Liability, Insurance Bad Faith, Land Use Planning and Shopping Center Law.
References: West One Bank; Washington Federal Savings and Loan Assn.
See Professional Biographies, BOISE, IDAHO

Daw, C. A., (AV) ....'53 '79 C&L.336 B.S.Ch.E., J.D. [Bosch,D.&B.]
Day, Daniel S. .... '63 '90 C&L.878 B.A., J.D. Coun., Albertson's, Inc.
DeAngeli, Darin A., (AV) ....'64 '91 C.1193 B.S. L.629 J.D. [Ahrens&D.]
DeAngelo, Michael ....'42 '67 C&L.831 B.S., J.D. Dep. Atty. Gen.
deGlee, James C., (AV) ....'— '84 C&L.878 B.S., J.D. [Moffatt T.B.R.&F.]
Delana, Sumner ....'19 '49 C&L.336 B.S., LL.B. 203 Summit Ridge‡
DeLange, Brett T., (BV) '57 '84 C.101 B.A. L.911 J.D.
Off. Atty. Gen., Chief, Consumer Protect. Unit
DeMeester, Mark A. ......'— '88 C.037 B.P.E. L.101 J.D. Sr. Coun., Hewlett Packard Co.
Derbidge, Warren S., (BV) ....'43 '68 C.1032 B.A. L.336 J.D. Idaho Legal Aid
Derr, Allen, (AV) .... '28 '59 C&L.336 B.A., J.D. Suite 8, Ground Floor 200 N. 3rd Street
Desler, Peter .... '47 '72 C.676 B.A. L.945 J.D. Princ., Boise Arbitration/Mediation Servs.
De Voe, Jeffrey A. ....'65 '94 C.1193 B.B.A. L.950 J.D. 8645 West Franklin Road
Dewoody, Jeanette Alice ......'51 '77 C.385 A.B. L.836 J.D. Idaho Legal Aid Servs., Inc.
Dickinson, Rob G. ....'64 '95 C.612 B.S. L.744 J.D. 8645 W. Franklin Road
Diddle, Samuel A., (BV) ....'65 '90 C.473 B.S. L.575 J.D. [Eberle,B.K.T.M.&J.]
DiLuglio, Raymond A. '40 '65 C&L.724 B.B.A., J.D.
(adm. in NY; not adm. in ID) U.S. Dept. of Interior
Dingel, Lori A., (BV) ....'69 '94 C&L.336 B.S., J.D. [Orndorff]
Dingel, M. Allyn, Jr., (AV) ....'36 '61 C.336 B.A. L.569 LL.B. [Elam&B.]
Dingel, Michael M., (CV) '69 '96 C&L.336 B.S., J.D.
Assoc. Gen. Coun., OfficeMax Incorporated (ⓞItasca, IL)
Dinger, Daniel Richard ....'74 '01 C&L.101 B.A., J.D. Co. Pros. Atty.
Dixon, Bradley J. ....'75 '00 C.1193 B.S L.950 J.D. [Ⓐ Stoel R.]
Dobler, Clifford I. ....'11 '41 C&L.336 B.S., J.D. 4450 Foothill Rd.‡
Dockstader, Kim J., (AV) ....'64 '90 C.877 B.S. L.878 J.D. [Dockstader]

Dockstader Law Office, (AV)
199 North Capitol Boulevard Suite 302, 83702
Telephone: 208-338-5000 Fax: 208-336-4980
Email: kdockstader@kdockstaderlaw.com URL: http://www.dockstaderlaw.com
Kim J. Dockstader.
Labor and Employment, Employment Litigation, Civil Litigation.
See Professional Biographies, BOISE, IDAHO

Dominick, Bobbi Killian, (AV) ....'55 '82 C.1193 B.A. L.336 J.D. [Ⓒ Gjording&F.]
Dominick, Thomas B., (AV) ....'56 '82 C.1032 B.S. L.336 J.D. [Hoagland,D.&H.]
Donesley, Brian N., (BV) ....'48 '78 C.813 B.A. L.336 J.D. 604 North 16th Street
Donnelly, Thomas J. .... '59 '84 C&L.190 B.A., J.D. V.P., Claims, Great West Cas. Co.
Doolittle, Michael J., (BV) .... '— '82 C.1193 B.B.A. L.336 J.D. [Doolittle L.]
Doolittle Law, Chartered, (BV) ....300 W. Myrtle Street, Suite 102
Dougherty, Peg M. ....'58 '99 C.173 B.A. L.336 J.D. [Ⓐ Howard L.&K.P.]
Dredge, Richard Kim, Law Offices of, (BV) '49 '81
C.878 B.S. L.336 J.D. 6550 West Emerald, Suite 108
Drozda, Robert L. "Bob", (BV) ....'54 '80 C.627 B.S.B.A. L.190 J.D. [Drozda]

Drozda Law Offices, PLLC, (BV)
P.O. Box 6370, 83707
Telephone: 208-344-9355 Fax: 208-386-9944
Email: drozdar1@drozdalaw.com URL: http://www.drozdalaw.com
Robert L. "Bob" Drozda.
Estate Planning, Taxation, Entity Formation, Operation and Dissolution, Business, Real Estate.
See Professional Biographies, BOISE, IDAHO

Dryden, William G., (AV) ....'53 '78 C.813 B.A. L.950 J.D. [Elam&B.]
Duke, Keely E., (CV) ....'74 '99 C.120 B.A. L.950 J.D. [Ⓐ Hall,F.O.&B.]
Dunlop, William N. '30 '54 C&L.911 B.A., LL.B.
(adm. in WA; not adm. in ID) 732 Santa Paula Pl.‡
Duren, Kyle D., (CV) ....'70 '98 C&L.336 B.S., J.D. [Ⓐ Brady]
Dvorak, Thomas E., (BV) ....'67 '94 C.1193 B.A. L.336 J.D. [Givens P.]
Dwelle, Karin ....'77 '03 C.939 B.A. L.336 J.D. [Ⓐ Hall,F.O.&B.]
Dykas, Frank J., (AV) ....'46 '75 C.1156 B.S. L.972 J.D. [Dykas,S.&N.] (See Pat. Sect.)

Dykas, Shaver & Nipper, LLP, (AV)
P.O. Box 877, 83701
Telephone: 208-345-1122 Fax: 208-345-8370 Toll Free: 1-877-611-1122
Email: info@dykaslaw.com URL: http://www.dykaslaw.com
Frank J. Dykas; Robert L. Shaver; Stephen M. Nipper;—Derek H. Maughan.
Intellectual Property, Patent, Trademark, including National and International Filing, Copyright, Contracts, Unfair Competition, Trade Secrets, Licensing, Litigation and Related Matters.
See Professional Biographies, BOISE, IDAHO

Dykstra, Jason G., (CVⓉ) ....'69 '95 C&L.508 B.S., J.D. [Ⓐ Sasser&I.]
Early, Darrell G., (BV) ....'67 '92 C.908 B.A. L.336 J.D. P.O. Box 1617
Eaton, Donald J. ....'37 '65 C&L.770 B.S., LL.B. 1513 Claremont

Eberle, Berlin, Kading, Turnbow, McKlveen & Jones, Chartered, (AV)
Capitol Park Plaza, 300 North Sixth Street, P.O. Box 1368, 83701-1368
Telephone: 208-344-8535 Facsimile: 208-344-8542
Email: jbc@eberle.com URL: http://www.eberle.com
J. Louis Eberle (1890-1964); T. H. Eberle (1922-1977); James L. Berlin (1926-2000); R. M. Turnbow; William J. McKlveen; Warren Eugene Jones; Thomas R. Linville; Joseph H. Uberuaga, II; Neil D. McFeeley; Stanley J. Tharp; Samuel A. Diddle;—Peter W. Ware, Jr.; Stephen J. Olson; Corey J. Rippee; Richard W. Stover. Of Counsel: R. B. Kading, Jr.
Personal Injury, Products Liability, Toxic Torts, Professional Liability, Aviation, Construction, Lender Liability, Commercial and Business Litigation, Insurance Bad Faith Defense, Healthcare, Workers Compensation, Corporations and Partnerships, Antitrust, Corporate Finance and Securities, Securities Litigation and Arbitration, Mergers, Acquisitions, Tender Offers, and other Business Transactions, Copyright and Trademark, Banking and Creditor's Rights, Bankruptcy, Real Estate Finance and Development, Land Use, Taxation, Estate Planning and Employee Benefits, Governmental Relations (Administrative, Regulatory, Legislative), Securities and Insurance Regulation, Environment, Energy, Water Rights, Natural Resources and Agriculture Law.

(This Listing Continued)

Eberle, Berlin, Kading, Turnbow, McKlveen & Jones, Chartered (Continued)
Representative Clients: Key Bank of Idaho; Key Bank Nat'l Assn.; Key Corp Leasing Ltd.; Agri Beef Co.; Cessna Aircraft Co.; Energy Release Products Corp.; Ada County Highway Dist.
See Professional Biographies, BOISE, IDAHO

Echols, Ted M. .... '27 '53 C&L.911 B.S., LL.B. 10093 Secretariat St.‡
Eddie, William Michael, II .... '72 '98 C.112 B.S. L.1051 J.D. P.O. Box 1612
Edwards, John L.T., (BV) .... '62 '90 C.336 B.A. L.1049 J.D. [Holzer,E.&H.]
Eidam, Bradford S., (AV) .... '56 '82 C&L.336 B.S., J.D. 1505 Tyrell Lane
Eiden, Max A., (AV) .... '42 '66 C&L.336 LL.B. [🄲 Jones G.H.F.&E.]
Eiguren, Roy Lewis, (AV) .... '52 '78 C&L.336 B.S., J.D. [Givens P.]
Eismann, Daniel T. .... '47 '76 C&L.336 B.A., J.D. Mag.

Elam & Burke, A Professional Association, (AV)
251 E. Front Street, Suite 300, P.O. Box 1539, 83702
Telephone: 208-343-5454 Telecopier: 208-384-5844
Email: eblaw@elamburke.com URL: http://www.elamburke.com
Members of Firm: Laurel E. Elam (1888-1974); Carl A. Burke (1898-1961); M. Allyn Dingel, Jr.; John Magel; James D. LaRue; Ryan P. Armbruster; William G. Dryden; James A. Ford; Jeffrey A. Thomson; Loren C. Ipsen; Joshua S. Evett. Associates: Jon M. Bauman; Matthew L. Walters; W. Ben Slaughter III; Soo Y. Kang; Joseph N. Pirtle. Of Counsel: R. Michael Southcombe; Mack A. Redford.
Administrative Litigation, Appellate Practice, Arbitration, Automobile Insurance Defense, Aviation Defense, Bankruptcy, Banks and Banking, Business Law, Casinos and Gambling, Class Action Defense, Commercial Law, Commercial Transactions, Construction Law, Contracts, Corporate Law, Environmental Litigation, Federal Civil Practice, Fire Insurance Defense, General Liability Defense, Insurance Bad Faith Defense, Intellectual Property; Local Government Law, Mediation, Municipal Law, Products Liability Defense, Real Estate, Self Insured Defense, Ski Area Liability, State Government Law, Torts, Trusts and Estates, Wills.
Representative Clients: State Farm Insurance Companies; Farmers Insurance Companies; Thompson Creek Mining; Employers Reinsurance Corp.; Capital City Development Corp.; Philadelphia Ins. Co.; The Hartford; University of Idaho Foundation.
See Professional Biographies, BOISE, IDAHO

Elia, Michael J., Law Office of, (AV) '62 '87 C.285 B.A. L.911 J.D.
1199 Shoreline Lane, Suite 308, 83702
Telephone: 208-331-9800 Fax: 208-331-9805
Email: melia@mjelawpc.com URL: http://www.mjelawfirmpc.com
Insurance, Personal Injury, Insurance Defense, Business Litigation, General Practice.
See Professional Biographies, BOISE, IDAHO

Elkin, Vicky J. .... '73 '99 C&L.336 B.A., J.D. [🄰 Jones G.H.F.&E.]
Eller, Terry K., (BV) '53 '84 C.966 B.A. L.336 J.D.
V.P. Intl.; & Assoc. Gen. Coun., Washington Grp. Intl., Inc.
Ellers, Debra K., (BV) '59 '86 C.838 B.A. L.893 J.D.
Sr. Asst. Gen. Coun., Micron Technology, Inc.
Elliott, Ellen S. .... '75 '03 C.628 M.P.H. L.464 J.D. [🄰 Brassey,W.C.&G.]
Elliott, John M. '63 '89 C.187 B.S.S. L.300 J.D.
(adm. in MN; not adm. in ID) All American Publishing
Elliott, Kathleen Jean .... '63 '90 C.336 B.S. L.174 J.D. 912 N. 8th St.
Elliott, Kenneth M., (BV) '54 '80
C.508 B.A. L.1051 J.D. Dir., Real Estate Law, Albertson's, Inc.
Ellis, Allen B., (AV) .... '38 '66 C&L.813 A.B., LL.B. [Ellis,B.&S.]
Ellis, Brown & Sheils, Chartered, (AV) .... 707 North 8th
Ellsworth, Maurice O., (BV) .... '48 '75 C&L.36 B.S., J.D. [🄲 Perry L.]

Ellsworth Kallas & Talboy, P.L.L.C., (BV)
The Greyhawk Building, 2402 West Jefferson Street, 83702
Telephone: 208-336-1843 Fax: 208-345-8945
Email: rwt@greyhawklaw.com URL: http://www.greyhawk-law.com
Robert W. Talboy.
General Civil and Criminal Practice, Trials, Insurance, Business, Real Estate, Collections, Workers Compensation, Probate, Estate Planning and Mediation, Water Law, Wills.
See Professional Biographies, BOISE, IDAHO

Ennis, Robert J., (AV) .... '38 '66 C&L.770 B.S.C., J.D. 4477 Emerald St.
Ericson, Carlton R., (BV) .... '56 '87 C&L.101 B.A., J.D. [🄰 Naylor&H.]
Eustermann, John M. .... '65 '95 C.602 B.A. L.1358 J.D. [🄰 Holland&H.]
Evans, Blaine F., (AV) .... '23 '50 C.336 B.A. L.309 LL.B. [🄲 Evans K.]

Evans Keane LLP, (AV)
1405 West Main Street, 83702 ⊙
Telephone: 208-384-1800 Facsimile: 208-345-3514
Email: firm@evanskeane.com URL: http://www.evanskeane.com
Members of Firm: Jed W. Manwaring; James D. Hovren; David W. Gratton;—David M. Swartley; Jeremy P. Pisca (Resident, Boise Office); Victor S. Villegas; Judy L. Geier. Of Counsel: Blaine F. Evans. Kellogg Office: James P. Keane (1925-1988); Charles L. A. Cox.
General Trial and Appellate Practice, Products Liability, Personal Injury Law, Corporate, Real Property, Banking, Employment, Labor, Mining, Public Utilities, Legislative and Administrative.
Representative Clients: Albertson's Inc.; American Trucking Associations, Inc.; Edward Jones & Company; E.I. du Pont de Nemours and Company; Ford Motor Co.; GlaxoSmithKline; Hoffman & LaRoche; Hyundai; IDACorp (Idaho Power); Phillip Morris
Kellogg, Idaho Office: 111 Main Street, P.O. Box 659. Telephone: 208-784-1105.
See Professional Biographies, BOISE, IDAHO

Evett, Joshua S., (BV) .... '65 '97 C.429 B.A. L.1065 J.D. [Elam&B.]
Fanning, Patrick W. .... '44 '70 C.988 B.S. L.767 J.D. Dep. Atty. Gen.
Farley, Donald J., (AV) .... '48 '73 C&L.336 B.A., J.D. [Hall,F.O.&B.]
Farris, S. Bryce, (CV) .... '— '97 C.335 B.A. L.336 J.D. [🄰 Ringert C.]
Faucher, Robert A., (AV) .... '62 '88 C.976 B.A. L.309 J.D. [Holland&H.]
Fawcett, Charles W., (BV) .... '46 '71 C.112 B.A. L.1066 J.D. [Skinner F.]
Fearnside, Timothy P., (CV) .... '67 '96 C.97 B.A. L.285 J.D. [🄰 Givens P.]
Feeny, Mary E. .... '44 '77 C.911 B.ED. L.285 J.D. Dep. Atty. Gen.
Feldman, Murray D., (BV) .... '— '89 C.112 B.S. L.1066 J.D. [Holland&H.]

Fenwick & West LLP
877 West Main Street, Suite 706, 83702 ⊙
Telephone: 208-331-0700 Fax: 208-331-7723
URL: http://www.fenwick.com
Partner: Robert A. Freedman (Resident). Associate: Ilana Simone Rubel (Resident).
General Practice. Corporate, Securities, Mergers and Acquisitions, Executive Compensation and Employee Benefits, Intellectual Property, Patent, Trademark and Copyright, Science and Technology Transactions, Life Sciences and High Technology Law, Litigation and Alternative Dispute Resolution, Antitrust and Trade Regulation, Privacy and Security, Trade Secrets, Employment and Labor Law, Domestic and International Taxation, and Venture Capital.
San Francisco, California Office: 275 Battery Street, Suite 1600. Telephone: 415-875-2300. Fax: 415-281-1350.
Mountain View, California Office: Silicon Valley Center, 801 California Street. Telephone: 650-988-8500. Fax: 650-938-5200.
See Professional Biographies, BOISE, IDAHO

Fereday, Jeffrey C., (AV) .... '49 '80 C.178 A.B. L.596 J.D. [Givens P.]
Ferry, William M. '56 '93 C.431 B.S. L.629 J.D.
Off. of Field Solr., U.S. Dept. of Interior
Fery, J. Brent .... '58 '85 C.813 B.A. L.285 J.D. V.P., First Sec. Bk. of Idaho, N.A.
Fica, Michael J. .... '68 '97 C.1032 B.S. L.276 J.D. Asst. U.S. Atty.
Fields, Richard C., (AV) .... '31 '64 C.309 A.B. L.208 J.D. [Moffatt T.B.R.&F.]
Filicetti, Joseph P., (BV) .... '61 '87 C.906 B.A. L.336 J.D. [Filicetti]
Filicetti Law Office, A Professional Association, (BV) .... 5987 West State Street, Suite B
Finch, Michelle R., (BV) .... '60 '85 C.1235 B.S.B.A. L.285 J.D. [Finch&B.]

Finch & Broadbent, P.A., (BV)
103 West Idaho Street, 83702
Mailing Address: P.O. Box 1296, Boise, ID 83701
Telephone: 208-385-0800 Fax: 208-389-2186
Email: fandblaw@finchbroadbent.com URL: http://www.finchbroadbentlaw.com
Michelle R. Finch; Rebecca A. Broadbent;—Brooke A. O'Neil.
Adoption, Child Custody, Corporate Law, Divorce, Elder Law, Family Law, General Practice, Guardianship and Conservatorship, Insurance Bad Faith, Insurance Law, Interstate Trucking Litigation, Mediation, Medical Malpractice, Personal Injury, Probate, Wills, Trusts and Estates, Wrongful Death.
See Professional Biographies, BOISE, IDAHO

Fischenich, Brian Thomas .... '74 '04 C.401 B.A. L.276 J.D. [🄰 Holland&H.]
Fisher, Melville W., II, (AV) .... '52 '77 C.336 B.S. L.208 J.D. [Batt&F.]
Flake, Joel A. .... '76 '03 C.101 B.A. L.477 J.D. Staff Atty., U.S. Dist. Ct. of Idaho
Flanagan, Michael J., (BV) .... '52 '81 C&L.629 B.S., J.D. [M.J.Flanagan]
Flanagan, Michael J., P.A., (BV) .... 338 E. Bannock
Fleming, Hoyt A., III '64 '94 C.880 B.E. L.802 J.D.
(adm. in TX; not adm. in ID) Sr. Intell. Prop. Coun., Micron Electronics, Inc.
Fleming, Linda D. .... '53 '93 C.907 B.A. L.1358 J.D. Atty. Gens. Office
Foote, Thomas R. '54 '79 C&L.8 B.S., J.D.
(adm. in OH; not adm. in ID) V.P. - Tax, Washington Grp. Intl., Inc.
Ford, James A., (AV) .... '60 '85 C.508 B.S. L.336 J.D. [Elam&B.]
Foster, Byron V., (AV) .... '47 '81 C.1262 B.A. L.336 J.D. 199 North Capitol Boulevard
Fouser, Trudy Hanson, (AV) .... '55 '81 C.1059 B.A. L.336 J.D. [Gjording&F.]
Fransen, Curt A., (BV) .... '57 '83 C.112 B.A. L.1065 J.D. Dep. Atty. Gen.
Fredland, Allan L. '21 '68 C.608 L.426 J.D.
(adm. in CA; not adm. in ID) 4024 Delmonte Dr.‡
Fredricks, Randall C., (BV) .... '37 '63 C&L.336 LL.B. 2220 Heights Dr.
Freedman, Robert A. .... '66 '93 C.95 A.B. L.813 J.D. [Fenwick&W.]
French, Randal J., (BV) .... '55 '83 C.1193 B.B.A. L.336 J.D. [Bauer&F.]
French, Stephen W., (BV) .... '50 '82 C.804 B.S. L.285 J.D. [S.W.French]
French, Stephen W., Chartered, (BV) .... 2304 N. Cole Rd., Ste. A
Frost, Thomas C., (BV) .... '37 '65 C.942 B.B.A. L.900 J.D. Legal Coun., State Supm. Ct.
Fuhrman, William A., (AV) .... '54 '82 C.1193 B.A. L.336 J.D. [Jones G.H.F.&E.]
Furey, Patrick D., (BV) .... '54 '79 C&L.336 B.A., J.D. 301 E. Brook Hollow Drive
Furey, Sherman F., III, (BV) .... '55 '81 C&L.336 B.S., J.D. Dep. Atty. Gen.
Furey, Sherman F., Jr., (AV) .... '19 '47 C&L.336 B.A., J.D. 5795 N. Lilybrook Way‡

Gabbert, Myron Dan, J.D. P.A.
(See McCall)

Gabel, Roger L., (BV) .... '53 '85 C&L.585 B.S.B.A., J.D. Dep. Atty. Gen.
Gadda, David G., (AV) .... '47 '73 C.629 B.S. L.1066 J.D. 1111 West Jefferson Street
Gallagher, Irene F. .... '71 '96 C.145 B.A. L.339 J.D. [Holland&H.] (⊙Denver, CO)
Gannon, John L., (BV) .... '50 '76 C.112 B.A. L.1065 J.D. P.O. Box 5624
Gardiner, Nathan F. .... '— '90 Idaho Power Company (Legal Department)
Garrett, Nancy Jo, (BV) .... '49 '89 C.1032 B.S. L.336 J.D. [Brassey,W.C.&G.]
Gass, Elbert E., (BV) .... '19 '53 C&L.190 LL.B. 733 N. 7th St.
Gass, Timothy J., (BV) .... '55 '79 C&L.190 B.S.B.A., J.D. [Gass]
Gass Law Offices, (BV) .... 733 North 7th Street
Gates, Robert R. .... '51 '76 C.659 B.A. L.930 J.D. Dep. Atty. Gen.
Geddes, Anthony Ray .... '66 '97 C.243 B.A. L.1194 J.D. Off. of the Co. Pub. Def.
Gee, Gavin M., (AV) .... '49 '77 C.1335 B.A. L.336 J.D. State Dept. of Fin. Dir.
Geier, Judy L. .... '60 '02 C.30 M.A. L.336 J.D. [🄰 Evans K.]
Geile, Patrick J. .... '— '04 [🄰 Cosho H.]
Gere, Roderick D., (CV) .... '47 '75 C.107 B.A. L.229 J.D. P.O. Box 1683
Geston, Mark S., (AV) .... '46 '71 C.385 A.B. L.569 J.D. [🄲 Stoel R.]
Gibala, Dennis, (BV) .... '47 '75 C.124 B.S. L.800 J.D. [Skinner F.]
Gill, C. Clayton, (BV) .... '69 '94 C.880 B.A. L.861 J.D. [Moffatt T.B.R.&F.]
Gillespie, James R., (AV) .... '39 '64 C&L.878 B.S., J.D. [J.R.Gillespie]

Gillespie, James R., P.A., (AV) 🅱🅱
300 West Myrtle, Suite 100, 83702
Telephone: 208-344-8400 Fax: 208-344-7100
URL: http://www.jamesrgillespie.com
James R. Gillespie.
General Practice. Business, Commercial Real Estate, Agricultural, Natural Resources Law, Environment and Construction Law, Mediation and Arbitration.
See Professional Biographies, BOISE, IDAHO

Gilmore, Michael S. .... '49 '74 C.453 S.B. L.336 J.D. Dep. Atty. Gen.
Gines, Ralph J. .... '33 '66 C.101 B.S. L.273 J.D. [R.J.Gines]
Gines, Ralph J., P.A. .... 1705 North Cole Road
Givens, Raymond D., (AV) .... '17 '41 C&L.336 B.A., J.D. [🄲 Givens P.]

Givens Pursley LLP, (AV) 🅱🅱
601 W. Bannock St., 83702
Telephone: 208-388-1200 Fax: 208-388-1300
Email: info@givenspursley.com URL: http://www.givenspursley.com
Members of Firm: Kenneth L. Pursley; L. Edward Miller; Christopher J. Beeson; Kenneth R. McClure; Jeffrey C. Fereday; Conley E. Ward; Patrick J. Miller; David R. Lombardi (Certified Civil Trial Specialist by Idaho Trial Lawyers Association); Christopher H. Meyer; Roy Lewis Eiguren; W. Hugh O'Riordan; Gary G. Allen; Michael C. Creamer; Judson B. Montgomery; Debora K. Kristensen; Kelly Greene McConnell; Robert B. White; Karl T. Klein; Thomas E. Dvorak; Steven J. Hippler; William C. Cole; Kimberly D. Maloney; Angela K. Nelson; Deborah E. Nelson. Associates: Emily MacMaster; Timothy P. Fearnside; John M. Marshall; Cynthia A. Melillo; H. Barton Thomas; Franklin G. Lee; Bradley V. Sneed; D. David Lorello, Jr.; Anne C. Kunkel; Michael C. Orr; Kelly T. Barbour (Not admitted in ID); Jeremy G. Ladle; John Wilkinson (Will) Varin. Of Counsel: Raymond D. Givens; James A. McClure.
Business, Commercial, Mergers and Acquisitions, Communications and Media, Employment, Environmental, Water, Public Lands and Natural Resources, Financial Transactions, Securitization, Structured Finance, Banking, Credit Recovery and Bankruptcy, Public Policy, Health Care and Hospital, Intellectual Property, Real Estate, Real Estate Financing and Land Use, Securities and Bonds, Tax and Estate Planning, Trial and Appellate Litigation, Telecommunications, Energy, Utilities and Regulatory Affairs.
See Professional Biographies, BOISE, IDAHO

Gjording, Jack S., (AV) .... '39 '66 C&L.336 B.S., J.D. [Gjording&F.]

Gjording & Fouser, PLLC, (AV)
509 West Hays Street, P.O. Box 2837, 83701
Telephone: 208-336-9777 Facsimile: 208-336-9177
Email: jgjording@g-g.com URL: http://www.g-f-law.com
Members: Jack S. Gjording; Trudy Hanson Fouser. Associate: Elaine Herrick Lee. Of Counsel: Bobbi Killian Dominick.
Insurance Defense, Medical Malpractice Defense, Employment and Commercial Litigation.
See Professional Biographies, BOISE, IDAHO

Gledhill, Stephen J., (AV) .... '52 '79 C.335 B.A. L.336 J.D. [Jones G.H.F.&E.]
Glivar, Daniel J. .... '67 '92 C.770 B.S. L.602 J.D. [Holland&H.]
Glynn, Daniel L. .... '69 '95 C.939 B.S. L.285 J.D. [🄰 Blackburn&J.]
Goddard, Stephen V., (BV) .... '37 '76 C.612 Ph.D. L.300 J.D. Dep. Atty. Gen.

Goergen, Brad A. ... '72 '02 C.1181 B.S. L.911 J.D. [[A] Holland&H.]
Goicoechea, Jerry J., (BV) ... '49 '76 C&L.336 B.A., J.D. [Goicoechea]
Goicoechea Law Offices, Chartered, (BV) ... 200 North 23rd Street
Goodenough, Fred C., (BV) '49 '77
C.846 B.A. L.336 J.D. Dep. Secy. of State, Secy. State Off.
Goodenough, Jeanne T., (BV) ... '49 '78 C.846 B.A. L.336 J.D. Atty. Gen. Off.
Goodrum, Forrest R., (BV(T)) '41 '71 C.1128 B.A. L.705 J.D.
(adm. in NJ; not adm. in ID) [Penland M.G.]
Goodsell, Bradford D., (CV) ... '57 '85 C.101 B.S. L.336 J.D. Dep. Atty. Gen.
Goodson, Richard F., (AV) ... '49 '74 C&L.285 B.B.A., J.D. [Hawley T.E.&H.]
Gordon, Daniel J., (BV) ... '73 '99 C.112 B.S. L.1067 J.D. [[A] Greener B.S.]
Gordon, Philip, (BV) ... '43 '77 C.951 B.A. L.336 J.D. [Gordon]
Gordon, R. "Bruce" '43 '71
C.101 B.A. L.878 J.D. Dir., Lit. & Pharmacy Law, Albertson's, Inc.
Gordon Law Offices, Chartered, (BV) ... 623 W. Hays Street
Goss, David D., (AV) ... '47 '73 C&L.336 B.S., J.D. [[C] Risch G.I.G]
Goss, Geoffrey E., (BV) ... '71 '99 C&L.285 B.A., J.D. [Risch G.I.G.]
Gould, Jon C. ... '— '04 C.147 B.S. L.336 J.D. [[A] Ringert C.]
Gourley, Kimbell D., (BV) ... '59 '86 C.670 B.B.A. L.336 J.D. [Jones G.H.F.&E.]
Gowland, Karen E., (AV) ... '59 '84 C&L.336 B.S., J.D. 1111 West Jefferson Street
Gowland, Kimbal L., (AV) ... '59 '84 C&L.336 B.S., J.D. [Meuleman M.]
Graham, Christopher P. ... '72 '00 C.1193 B.A. L.336 J.D. [[A] Brassey,W.C.&G.]
Graham, Susan M., (BV) ... '46 '77 C.188 B.S. L.336 J.D. [S.Graham]
Graham, Susan, Inc, Law Offices, (BV) ... 960 Broadway Ave., Ste. 460
Grant, Louis W., III ... '54 '91 C.880 B.E. L.861 J.D. Sr. Staff Atty., Albertson's, Inc.
Gratton, David W., (AV) ... '60 '85 C.1193 B.A. L.336 J.D. [Evans K.]
Gray, John G., Jr. ... '19 '51 C.770 B.C.S. L.336 LL.B. P.O. Box 5322
Gray, Krista ... '71 '99 C.1193 B.A. L.336 J.D. [[A] Howard L.&K.P.]
Greathouse, Cecil R. ... '11 '50 C.336 B.S. L.911 LL.B. 1611 Bway. Ave.
Greener, Richard H., (AV) ... '42 '68 C.911 B.A. L.336 J.D. [Greener B.S.]

Greener Banducci Shoemaker P.A., (AV)
The Carnegie Building, 815 West Washington Street, 83702
Telephone: 208-319-2600 Fax: 208-319-2601
Email: TBanducci@greenerlaw.com URL: http://www.greenerlaw.com
Richard H. Greener; Thomas A. Banducci; Fredric V. Shoemaker; Christopher C. Burke; Erik F. Stidham; Jon T. Simmons; Wade L. Woodard;—Curtis D. McKenzie; LaDawn Marsters; Daniel J. Gordon; G. Rey Reinhardt, IV; Matthew E. Hedberg; Scott E. Randolph. Of Counsel: Carl P. Burke; William C. Tharp.
General Civil Trial Practice including Commercial Litigation, Securities, Real Estate, Product Liability, Construction, Eminent Domain, Employment, and Personal Injury, Insurance, Intellectual Property. The firm also has substantial expertise in class actions.
See Professional Biographies, BOISE, IDAHO

Greenfield, John F., (AV) ... '43 '74 C.988 B.A. L.336 J.D. [J.F.Greenfield]

Greenfield, John F., P.A., (AV)
242 North 8th Street, Suite 220, P.O. Box 854, 83701
Telephone: 208-345-0380 Fax: 208-345-0422
URL: http://www.johnfgreenfield.com
John F. Greenfield;—Darin G. Monroe.
Workers' Compensation, Personal Injury, and Labor Law.
See Professional Biographies, BOISE, IDAHO

Griffard, Leo N., Jr., (AV(T)) ... '52 '83 C&L.734 A.B., J.D. [Griffard]
Griffard Law Offices, (AV(T)) ... 413 West Jefferson, Suite 4
Guerricabeitia, Edward J. ... '72 '00 C.878 B.S. L.336 J.D. [[A] Davison,C.C.&C.]
Guilfoy, Joanna L. ... '61 '90 C.321 B.A. L.1292 J.D. Atty. Gen. Off.
Gunn, John W., (CV) ... '20 '49 C.668 L.336 LL.B. 2502 W. Idaho St.
Gustavel, Matthew J., (BV) ... '67 '93 C&L.336 B.S., J.D. [Risch G.I.G]
Gustavsen, Jay M., (BV) ... '68 '97 C.112 B.A. L.336 J.D. [[A] Davison,C.C.&C.]
Guth, Joel H., (AV(T)) '57 '83 C.112 B.A. L.1068 J.D.
(adm. in CA; not adm. in ID) Dir., Real Estate Law, Albertson's, Inc.
Gwartney, Tore Beal, (BV) ... '59 '93 C.1193 B.A. L.336 J.D. [Cosho H.]
Hackney, Gar, (AV) ... '49 '76 C.878 B.A. L.336 J.D. [G.Hackney]

Hackney, Gar, P.L.L.C., (AV)
500 W. Bannock, 83702
Telephone: 208-342-7600 Fax: 208-342-6553
Email: hackney@spro.net URL: http://www.ghackney.com
Gar Hackney.
Criminal Law, Driving Under the Influence, Domestic Violence, Sexual Assault, Drug Crimes, Burglary, Search and Seizure, White Collar Crime, Federal Crimes, State and Felony Misdemeanor, Petty Theft, Personal Injury, Automobile Accidents, Bicycle Accidents, Pedestrian Accidents.
See Professional Biographies, BOISE, IDAHO

Haff, Eric L., (BV) ... '50 '75 C&L.336 B.A., J.D. [Hyde,W.&H.]
Hales, Roger J., (BV) ... '61 '87 C&L.336 B.S., J.D. [Naylor&H.]
Hall, Richard E., (AV) ... '44 '70 C.336 B.A. L.309 J.D. [Hall,F.O.&B.]
Hall, Roderick R. ... '64 '95 C&L.336 B.S., J.D. P.O. Box 2181

Hall, Farley, Oberrecht & Blanton, P.A., (AV) [BB]
Key Financial Center, 702 West Idaho Street, Suite 700, P.O. Box 1271, 83701-1271
Telephone: 208-395-8500 Facsimile: 208-395-8585
Email: contact@hallfarley.com URL: http://www.hallfarley.com
Richard E. Hall; Donald J. Farley; Phillip S. Oberrecht; Raymond D. Powers; Candy Wagahoff Dale; J. Kevin West; Bart W. Harwood; John J. Burke; Kevin J. Scanlan; Tamsen L. Leachman;—J. Charles Blanton; Keely E. Duke; James S. Thomson, II; Scott R. Learned; Bryan A. Nickels; Matthew J. Ryden; Brent T. Wilson; Chris D. Comstock; Jill M. Twedt; Jennifer A. Swartz; Karin Dwelle.
Litigation, Insurance Defense, Medical Malpractice and Professional Liability, Employment Law, Labor Relations, Products Liability, Construction, Health and Hospital, Corporation, Commercial, Banking, Real Estate, Legislative Counseling, Bankruptcy, Appellate Law, Administrative Agencies, Agricultural, Municipal, Estate Planning and Probate.
References: Boise State University; Farm Bureau Mutual Insurance Company of Idaho; Medical Insurance Exchange of California; The St. Paul Cos.
See Professional Biographies, BOISE, IDAHO

Hamlin, Robert G., (AV) ... '46 '73 C.1060 B.A. L.336 J.D. [[C] Naylor&H.]
Hammerquist, David, (BV) ... '— '83 C&L.336 B.S., J.D. [Ringert C.]
Hammond, John R., Jr. ... '69 '96 C&L.336 B.S., J.D. [Batt&F.]
Hampton, Teresa A. ... '60 '87 C&L.336 B.S., J.D. P.O. Box 1352
Hancock, Nicole C. ... '73 '04 C.1181 B.S. L.950 J.D. [[A] Stoel R.]
Hanks, Stephen G., (BV) ... '50 '78 C.101 B.S. L.336 J.D. 720 Park Blvd.
Hansen, Chris H., (AV) ... '57 '83 C.1193 B.B.A. L.336 J.D. [Anderson,J.&H.]
Hansen, James D. ... '59 '85 C.945 B.A. L.336 J.D. Boise State Univ.
Hansen, John R., Jr., (BV) ... '30 '57 C.101 B.A. L.1068 J.D. 12035 Ginger Creek Dr.
Hansen, Kindra L., (BV) '63 '94 C.906 B.A. L.336 J.D.
Assoc. Gen. Coun., OfficeMax Incorporated (©Itasca, IL)
Hansen, Timothy L. ... '51 '86 C.477 B.A. L.336 J.D. Mag.
Hardee, Daniel R., (BV) ... '68 '93 C.335 B.A. L.336 J.D. 737 N. 7th
Hardesty, Stephen C., (BV) ... '62 '87 C.231 B.A. L.1067 J.D. [Hawley T.E.&H.]
Hardin, Roseanne ... '47 '84 C&L.336 B.S., J.D. Dept. of Health & Welfare
Hargrave, Franki Jean ... '— '98 [[A] Cosho H.]
Harmon, E. Scott ... '53 '84 C.1193 B.B.A. L.950 J.D. Dep. Atty. Gen.
Harrigfeld, William G., (BV) ... '57 '88 C.1058 B.A. L.336 J.D. 222 North 13th Street
Harrington, Patrick, (BV) ... '60 '85 C&L.336 B.S., J.D. Staff Atty., Idaho Power Co.
Harris, Jim C., (BV) ... '46 '74 C.336 B.A. L.950 J.D. P.O. Box 9345
Harrison, Matthew R., (BV) ... '63 '91 C.878 B.S. L.336 J.D. [Holzer,E.&H.]
Hart, Trevor L., (CV) ... '67 '98 C&L.101 B.A., J.D. [[A] Perry L.]
Harty, John T. ... '42 '67 C&L.602 B.A., J.D. 1020 Main Street
Harty, Maureen A. ... '44 '78 C.741 B.A. L.1137 J.D. 1020 Main Street
Harwood, Bart W., (AV) ... '42 '66 L.336 LL.B. [Hall,F.O.&B.]
Harwood, Gregory B., (BV) '67 '94
C.597 B.A. L.336 J.D. Asst. Gen. Coun., Micron Technology, Inc.
Hawley, Jess B., Jr., (AV) ... '14 '40 C.602 A.B. L.276 J.D. [Hawley T.E.&H.]
Hawley, John T., Jr., (AV) ... '53 '80 C.336 B.S. L.285 J.D. [Hawley]
Hawley Law Office, (AV) ... 202 N. 9th St.

Hawley Troxell Ennis & Hawley LLP, (AV)
877 Main Street, Suite 1000, P.O. Box 1617, 83702 ⊙
Telephone: 208-344-6000 Facsimile: 208-342-3829
Email: info@hteh.com URL: http://www.hawleytroxell.com
Members of Firm: Paul B. Ennis (1916-1982); Robert I. Troxell (1908-1998); John T. Hawley (P.A.) (1920-1999); Jess B. Hawley, Jr. (Retired); Thomas A. Miller; Craig L. Meadows; Joseph D. McCollum, Jr.; Gary D. Babbitt; Richard F. Goodson; Merlyn W. Clark; Eugene A. Ritti; John F. Kurtz, Jr.; Richard G. Smith; Nicholas G. Miller; Steven W. Berenter; Kenneth C. Howell; Patrick V. Collins; Michael M. Stoddard; Brian L. Ballard; Brad P. Miller; Thomas B. Chandler; Stephen C. Hardesty; Kim C. Stanger; Richard A. Riley; Sheila R. Schwager; Thomas J. Mortell; Steven F. Schossberger. Of Counsel: Kate Kelly; John McGown, Jr. Associates: Lynnette M. Davis; Paula Landholm Kluksdal; Timothy W. Tyree; Geoffrey M. Wardle; Jason D. Scott; Janine P. Reynard; Robert F. Thomas; Brian C. Larsen; Michelle Burke Points; Sara C. 'Danielle' Quade; Aaron C. Charrier; John K. Olson; William E. Wardwell; D. John Ashby (Not admitted in ID); Kristin E. Bjorkman; Dylan Lawrence.
General Civil Trial and Appellate Practice before all State and Federal Courts and Administrative Agencies. Alternative Dispute Resolution, Antitrust, Aviation, Banking, Bankruptcy and Creditor Rights, Communications, Construction, Copyright, Corporate, Education, Employee Benefits, Environmental, ERISA, Trusts and Estates, Finance, Health Care and Hospital, Insurance, Intellectual Property, Labor and Employment, Legislative, Media, Mergers and Acquisitions, Mining, Natural Resources, Probate, Products Liability, Public Contract, Public Finance, Public Utility, Qualified and Nonqualified Deferred Compensation, Real Estate, Securities, Taxation, Technology and Science, Trademark and Workers' Compensation Law.
Representative Clients: Albertson's, Inc.; First Security Bank; J. R. Simplot Co.; Morrison-Knudsen Corp.; Union Pacific Corp.
Ketchum, Idaho Office: 540 Second Avenue North, P.O. Box 297. Telephone: 208-726-1700. Facsimile: 208-726-9743.
Pocatello, Idaho Office: 333 South Main Street, P.O. Box 100. Telephone: 208-233-0845. Facsimile: 208-233-1304.
Reno, Nevada Office: 6490 S. McCarran, Suite 4. Telephone: 775-829-9944. Facsimile: 775-829-2627.
See Professional Biographies, BOISE, IDAHO

Hayes, Bill '42 '68 C&L.378 B.S., J.D.
(adm. in KS; not adm. in ID) I.R.S.
Hayes, Le Roy H. ... '52 '77 C.1032 B.B.A. L.878 J.D. Touche Ross & Co.
Hedberg, Matthew E. ... '74 '02 C.336 B.S. L.911 J.D. [[A] Greener B.S.]
Heffner, Kirstin ... '65 '90 C&L.623 B.B.A., J.D. [[A]]
Hendrickson, Martin C., (CV) ... '71 '98 C.336 B.S. L.845 J.D. [[A] Moore,B.&P.]
Henken, Marla S. ... '66 '95 C.478 B.A. L.1194 J.D. [[A] Stoel R.]
Henretty, Brian "D", (BV) '60 '88
C.101 B.S. L.1066 J.D. Asst. Gen. Coun., Micron Technology, Inc.
Hepworth, J. Charles, (AV) ... '56 '81 C.813 B.A. L.1065 J.D. [Hepworth,L.&J.]

Hepworth, Lezamiz & Janis, Chartered, (AV)
537 West Bannock, P.O. Box 2582, 83701-2582 ⊙
Telephone: 208-343-7510 Fax: 208-342-2927
Email: hlhboise@aol.com URL: http://www.hljlawyers.com
J. Charles Hepworth (Resident); John J. Janis (Resident);—John W. Kluksdal (Resident).
General Civil and Trial Practice in State and Federal Courts. Automobile Liability, Personal Injury, Medical Malpractice, Negligence, Products Liability, Business and Commercial Law, Corporations, Real Estate, Banking, Probate and Estate Planning, Appellate Practice.
Representative Clients: Twin Falls County Mutual Insurance Co. (Property & Fire Insurance); Glenn Dale Ranches, Inc. (Farming & Ranching).
Reference: Key Bank of Idaho, N.A. (Twin Falls branch).
Twin Falls, Idaho Office: 133 Shoshone Street North, P.O. Box 389. Telephone: 208-734-7510. Fax: 208-734-4115.
See Professional Biographies, BOISE, IDAHO

Herrington, Charles D., (AV) '53 '78 C.477 B.A. L.284 J.D.
Sr. Asst. Gen. Coun., Micron Technology, Inc.
Herzfeld, Alan, (AV) ... '47 '83 C.174 B.A. L.336 J.D. [Herzfeld&P.]
Herzfeld & Piotrowski, LLP, (AV) ... 713 West Franklin
Hess, Jeffery L. ... '49 '92 C.906 B.A. L.336 J.D. Law Clk., Supm. Ct. Jus.
Hess, Scott D., (AV) ... '53 '78 C.629 B.A. L.378 J.D. [Jones G.H.F.&E.]
Heuser, Peter E., (AV) ... '49 '76 C.1027 B.S. L.966 J.D. [Kolisch H.] (Pat.) ⊙
Hicks, Francis H., (AV) ... '24 '49 C&L.602 LL.B. [[C] Hoagland,D.&H.]
Hicks, George G., (BV) ... '54 '80 C&L.336 B.S., J.D. Asst. City Atty. [Hoagland,D.&H.]
Hicks, Gregory L. ... '58 '85 C&L.285 B.A., J.D. Touche Ross & Co.
Hicks, Matthew M. ... '70 '96 C.69 B.A. L.602 J.D. [[A] Holland&H.]
Higer, Dale G., (AV) ... '41 '66 C.911 B.A. L.309 J.D. [[C] Stoel R.]
Hill, Leonard ... '44 '74 C.112 B.A. L.464 J.D. Dept. of Transportation
Hill, Randolph J., (AV) '55 '82 C.273 B.A. L.276 J.D.
Assoc. Gen. Coun., Washington Group International, Inc.
Hill, Teresa A. ... '— '00 C.1193 B.A. L.878 J.D. [[A] Stoel R.]
Himberger, Richard D., (BV) ... '54 '89 C.101 B.A. L.950 J.D. [Himberger]

Himberger Law Offices, Chtd., (BV)
575 East Parkcenter Boulevard, Suite 100, 83706
Telephone: 208-336-8442 Fax: 208-336-1690
Email: info@himbergerlaw.com URL: http://www.himbergerlaw.com
Richard D. Himberger.
Commercial Law, Business Litigation, Government Contracts, Lien and Bond Claims, Mediation, Arbitration, Construction Law, Creditors Rights, Bankruptcy, Collections, Foreclosures, Land Use, Commercial Development, Residential Development, Zoning, Real Estate, Alternative Dispute Resolution, Mediation and Arbitration, Eminent Domain, Government Contracts, Mergers, Acquisitions, Real Property, Easements, Lien and Board Claims.
See Professional Biographies, BOISE, IDAHO

Hinton, John B., (BV) ... '62 '87 C.838 B.A. L.629 J.D. P.O. Box 2702
Hippler, Steven J., (BV) ... '66 '91 C.1193 B.A. L.877 J.D. [Givens P.]
Hoagland, Samuel A., (BV) ... '53 '82 C.1032 B.S. L.336 J.D. [Hoagland,D.&H.]
Hoagland, Dominick & Hicks, PLLC, (AV) ... 1471 Shoreline Drive, Suite 100
Hobson, Mary S., (AV) ... '50 '77 C.906 B.A. L.336 J.D. [Stoel R.]
Hockberger, John J., Jr., (BV) ... '51 '78 C.309 A.B. L.1067 J.D. U.S. Dept. of Interior
Hodge, Robert B. ... '24 '51 L.336 LL.B. Intermountain Gas Co.
Hodge, Ronald S. ... '52 '78 C.1193 B.B.A. L.336 J.D. Idaho Medical Assn.
Hofstetter, Dana L., (BV) ... '57 '88 C.674 B.S.E. L.1066 J.D. [Hofstetter]
Hofstetter Law Office, LLC, (BV) ... 608 West Franklin Street

Hoidal, Ernest A., (AV) '49 '74 C.767 B.S. L.336 J.D.
960 Broadway Avenue, Suite 220, 83706
Telephone: 208-342-4647 Facsimile: 208-342-0027
Email: eahoidal@hoidallaw.com URL: http://www.lawyers.com/hoidal

(This Listing Continued)

Hoidal, Ernest A. (Continued)

General Civil and Trial Practice, Immigration and Naturalization Law, Business and Corporate Law, Family, Insurance/Negligence Defense, Personal Injury (Plaintiff's) and Probate Law.
See Professional Biographies, BOISE, IDAHO

Holcombe, Judith K., (BV) .... '42 '68 C.112 B.A. L.336 J.D. 2310 West State Street
Holland, Joseph W., (BV) .... '52 '89 C.877 B.S. L.336 J.D. [Korfanta&H.] (Pat.)

Holland & Hart LLP, (AV)
U.S. Bank Plaza, Suite 1400, 101 South Capitol Boulevard, P.O. Box 2527, 83701 ⊙
Telephone: 208-342-5000 Telecopier: 208-343-8869
Email: info@hollandhart.com URL: http://www.hollandhart.com
Members: Walter H. Bithell; J. Frederick Mack; Larry E. Prince; B. Newal Squyres; Steven B. Andersen; Linda B. Jones; Murray D. Feldman; Robert A. Faucher; Daniel J. Glivar; Steven C. Bowman; Amanda K. Brailsford; Irene F. Gallagher. Of Counsel: Ted C. Murdock; William G. Myers, III; Wendy Thomas Wendrowski; Mary V. York. Associates: Dean B. Arnold; Benson Barrera; James D. Bowen; Kevin C. Braley; Tracy Jack Crane; John M. Eustermann; Brian Thomas Fischenich; Brad A. Goergen; Matthew M. Hicks; Pamela Simmons Howland; Tobi J. Mott; Maureen G. Ryan; Nicole Snyder.
Alternative Dispute Resolution, Antitrust, Appellate, Banking and Finance, Bankruptcy, Business Transactions, Class Actions, Commercial Litigation, Construction Law, Contracts, Copyrights, Corporate Law, E-Commerce, Emerging Business, Employee Benefits, Endangered Species, Energy, Environmental, Estate Planning and Administration, Finance, Healthcare and Hospitals, Immigration, Indian Law, Intellectual Property, International, Labor and Employment, Legislative, Litigation, Medical Malpractice, Mergers, Acquisitions and Divestitures, Natural Resources, Oil/Gas and Minerals, Patents, Product Liability, Professional Liability, Public Land, Public Utilities and Energy Regulation, Personal Injury, Real Estate, Securities, Tax, Technology and Trade Regulation, Telecommunications, Torts and Insurance, Toxic Torts, Trade Secrets, Trademarks, Trusts and Estates, Venture Capital, Water, Wealth Transfer, White Collar Crime.
Regional Offices:
Denver, Colorado
Denver Tech Center, Greenwood Village, Colorado
Aspen, Colorado
Boulder, Colorado
Colorado Springs, Colorado
Billings, Montana
Salt Lake City, Utah
Cheyenne, Wyoming
Jackson, Wyoming
Santa Fe, New Mexico
Washington, D.C.
See Professional Biographies, BOISE, IDAHO

Holleran, John W., (AV) .... '54 '79 C&L.285 B.A., J.D. 1111 West Jefferson Street
Holt, McPherson, Jr. .... '21 '50 C.951 B.A. L.145 J.D. 1837 N. 19th St.‡
Holzer, Kurt D., (BV) .... '61 '92 C.999 B.A. L.878 J.D. [Murphy,H.&V.]
Holzer, Edwards & Harrison, Chtd., (BV) .... 1516 W. Hays
Honsinger, Charles L. .... '— '95 C.35 B.S. L.1051 J.D. [Ringert C.]

Hopkins Roden Crockett Hansen & Hoopes, PLLC, (AV)
802 West Bannock, Suite 900, P.O. Box 2110, 83701-2110 ⊙
Telephone: 208-336-7930 Fax: 208-336-9154
Email: BoiseLaw@hrchh.com URL: http://www.hrchh.com
Resident Partners: William C. Roden; John Michael Brassey (Resident). Of Counsel: Bruce L. Thomas.
General Civil, Trial and Appellate Practice before all State and Federal Courts and Administrative Agencies, Administrative Law, Agricultural Law, Alcoholic Beverages, Banking Law, Bankruptcy, Business Law, Civil Rights, Contracts, Construction Law, Corporate Law, Criminal Law, Debtor and Creditor, Election, Campaign and Political Law, Eminent Domain, Employment Law, Family Law, Government, Insurance, Health Care, Hospital Law, Immigration Law, Natural Resources, Negligence, Personal Injury (plaintiffs and defense), Real Estate, Social Security, Taxation, Trusts and Estates, Utility Law, Wills and Probate, Workers' Compensation Law, and Zoning, Planning and Land Use.
Idaho Falls, Idaho Office: 428 Park Avenue, P.O. Box 51219, 83405-1219. Telephone: 208-523-4445. Fax: 208-523-4474.
Washington, D.C. Office: 8 East Street, S.E., 20003. Telephone: 202-546-0361. Fax: 202-546-6294.
See Professional Biographies, BOISE, IDAHO

Horton, Joel D. .... '59 '85 C.911 B.A. L.336 J.D. Dist. J.
Houst, Henry E., Jr., (BV) .... '50 '77 C.911 B.A. L.950 J.D. [Houst]
Houst Law Office, (BV) .... 913 W. River St., Ste. 440
Hovren, James D., (AV) .... '57 '85 C.335 B.A. L.911 J.D. [Evans K.]
Howard, John P., (AV) .... '48 '73 C.336 B.S. L.911 J.D. [Howard L.&K.P.]

Howard Lopez & Kelly PLLC, (AV)
702 West Idaho Street, P.O. Box 856, 83701-0856
Telephone: 208-342-4300 Fax: 208-342-4344
URL: http://www.idahodefense.com
John P. Howard; Thomas H. Lopez; Michael E. Kelly. Associates: Randall Curtis Probasco; Lou Piccioni; Peg M. Dougherty; Krista Gray.
Construction Litigation, Commercial Litigation, Environmental Litigation, Insurance Defense, Insurance Coverage, Products Liability, Professional Malpractice Defense and Subrogation Law.
See Professional Biographies, BOISE, IDAHO

Howe, Jeffrey G., (AV) .... '47 '74 C.31 B.A. L.336 J.D. Asst. U.S. Trustee
Howell, Donald L. .... '51 '85 C.473 A.B. L.336 J.D. Idaho Atty. Gen.
Howell, John McEvoy .... '74 '01 C.723 B.A. L.336 J.D. [Ⓐ Brassey,W.C.&G.]
Howell, Kenneth C., (AV) .... '60 '84 C.335 B.A. L.336 J.D. [Hawley T.E.&H.]
Howland, Pamela Simmons .... '70 '00 C.506 B.S. L.285 J.D. [Ⓐ Holland&H.]
Hull, Alan K., (AV) .... '47 '73 C&L.336 B.S., J.D. [Anderson,J.&H.]
Humphrey, Michael C. '49 '82 C.208 B.S.E.E. L.336 J.D.
Assoc. Gen. Coun., Washington Grp. Intl, Inc.
Hunter, Larry C., (AV) .... '46 '76 C.309 A.B. L.597 J.D. [Moffatt T.B.R.&F.]
Huntley, Christopher F., (BV) .... '65 '94 C.336 B.A. L.30 J.D. [Huntley P.]
Huntley, Robert C., Jr., (AV) .... '32 '59 C&L.336 B.A., J.D. [Huntley P.]
Huntley Park, LLP, (AV) .... 250 South 5th Street, Suite 660
Husch, Gerald T., (AV) .... '51 '78 C&L.221 B.A., J.D. [Moffatt T.B.R.&F.]
Huskey, Dari M. .... '— '02 C.101 B.A. L.336 J.D [Ⓐ Quane S.]
Hyde, David W., (BV) .... '44 '69 C&L.336 B.A., J.D. [Hyde,W.&H.]
Hyde, Wetherell & Haff, P.L.L.C., (AV) .... 1199 W. Main St.
Ide, Britt E. .... '71 '99 C.608 B.S. L.878 J.D. 1111 West Jefferson Street
Imhoff, Joseph M., Jr., (AV) .... '19 '50 C.670 A.B. L.878 LL.B. 1001 W. Idaho St.‡
Inglis, Patrick J., (BV) .... '60 '86 C.911 B.A. L.336 J.D. [Sasser&I.]
Insinger, R. John, (AV) .... '47 '74 C.174 B.A. L.336 J.D. [Risch G.I.G.]
Ipsen, Loren C., (AV) .... '50 '75 C.309 B.A. L.1065 J.D. [Elam&B.]
Irish, Debra Young, (BV) '52 '90
C.1193 B.B.A. L.336 J.D. 355 West Myrtle Street, Suite 103
James, W. Craig, (BV) .... '44 '76 C.164 B.A. L.285 J.D. [Mauk&B.]
Janis, John J., (AV) .... '53 '86 C.553 B.S. L.336 J.D. [Hepworth,L.&J.]
Jankowski, Richard W., (CV) .... '71 '96 C.1169 B.A. L.1065 J.D. P.O. Box 1518
Jaynes, Blair D. .... '43 '77 C.878 B.S. L.101 J.D. 4040 Guard St.★
Jenkins, E. Kenneth, III '58 '91 C.506 B.A. L.276 J.D.
(adm. in HI; not adm. in ID) Boise Police Dept.
Jensen, Berne K. .... '22 '50 C&L.336 B.S., LL.B. 3120 Hillcrest Lane‡
Jensen, David S., (BV) .... '62 '90 C.118 L.494 J.D. [Moffatt T.B.R.&F.]

Jensen, Donald F. '53 '85 C.1056 B.S. L.1051 J.D.
(adm. in OR; not adm. in ID) I.R.S.
Johnson, Byron J. .... '37 '62 C&L.309 A.B., LL.B. Ret. Supm. Ct. Jus.‡
Johnson, Joshua D. .... '71 '97 C.1071 B.S. L.365 J.D. [Ⓐ Racine O.N.B.&B.]
Johnson, Michael E. .... '46 '75 C.1193 B.A. L.1068 J.D. Comr., State Tax Comm.
Johnson, Michael R., (BV) .... '64 '93 C.1193 B.B.A. L.336 J.D. [Bevis,C.&J.]
Johnson, Russell L., (CV) .... '65 '93 C.877 B.A. L.999 J.D. 7235 Emerald Street
Johnson, Sam, (BV) .... '66 '93 C&L.336 B.S., J.D. [Johnson&M.]
Johnson, Wyatt B., (CV) .... '72 '98 C.906 B.A. L.596 J.D. [Ⓐ Angstman]

Johnson & Monteleone, LLP, (BV)
405 South 8th Street, Suite 250, 83702
Telephone: 208-331-2100 Fax: 208-947-2424
Email: jason@treasurevalleylawyers.com URL: http://www.treasurevalleylawyers.com
Sam Johnson; Jason R.N. Monteleone.
Personal Injury, Employment Law, Automobile Accidents and Injuries, Head Injury, Dog Bites, Wrongful Termination, Slip and Fall.
See Professional Biographies, BOISE, IDAHO

Jones, Bruce C., (AV) .... '53 '82 C.335 B.A. L.1065 J.D. [Blackburn&J.]
Jones, Jim, & Associates, (AV) ...... '42 '67 C.629 B.A. L.597 J.D. 1275 Shoreline Drive
Jones, Joseph B., (BV) .... '— '81 C.1042 B.S. L.285 J.D. Dep. Atty. Gen.
Jones, Linda B., (BV) .... '50 '86 C.768 B.A. L.1066 J.D. [Holland&H.]
Jones, Michael R., (BV) .... '52 '77 C&L.285 B.B.A., J.D. Dep. Atty. Gen.
Jones, Rory R., (BV) .... '55 '82 C&L.336 B.S., LL.B. [Jones G.H.F.&E.]
Jones, Terrence S., (CV) .... '— '98 C.1193 B.A. L.336 J.D. [Quane S.]
Jones, Thomas J., III, (BV) ...... '29 '54 C.602 B.S.C. L.336 LL.B. 1611 W. Jefferson St.
Jones, Warren Eugene, (AV) .... '43 '68 C.335 B.A. L.145 J.D. [Eberle,B.K.T.M.&J.]

Jones Gledhill Hess Fuhrman & Eiden, P.A., (AV) BB
225 N. Ninth Street, Suite 820, P.O. Box 1097, 83701
Telephone: 208-331-1170 Fax: 208-331-1529
Email: jg@idalaw.com URL: http://www.idalaw.com
Rory R. Jones; Stephen J. Gledhill; Scott D. Hess; William A. Fuhrman; Derrick J. O'Neill; Scott A. Tschirgi; Kimbell D. Gourley; David M. Penny; Terri R. Yost;—Ellen N. Smith; Vicky J. Elkin. Of Counsel: Max A. Eiden.
Civil and Business Litigation, Employment Law, Family Law, Commercial Litigation and Appeals, Insurance Coverage and Defense, Business and Finance, Construction Law, Real Property, Estate Planning and Tax Law.
See Professional Biographies, BOISE, IDAHO

Jones-Mesler, Lisa A. '60 '89 C.475 B.S. L.1325 J.D.
(adm. in MI; not adm. in ID) Sr. Staff Atty., Chambers of J. Mikel H. Williams
Joyce, T. Steve, (AV) .... '48 '76 C&L.285 B.B.A., J.D. 1419 W. Washington
Joyner, Todd M. .... '62 '91 C.877 B.S. L.1335 J.D. [Ⓐ Anderson,J.&H.]
Judd, Linda, (AV) .... '39 '70 C&L.336 B.A., J.D. 5647 South Caper Place
Julian, Brian K., (AV) .... '54 '79 C.877 B.S. L.336 J.D. [Anderson,J.&H.]
Jurries, Jill S. .... '75 '01 C.774 B.A. L.1117 J.D. 222 N. 13th
Kading, R. B., Jr., (AV) .... '30 '58 C.629 B.S. L.336 LL.B. [⊡ Eberle,B.K.T.M.&J.]
Kane, Michael, (AV) .... '52 '80 C.1032 B.A. L.336 J.D. [Kane&T.]

Kane & Tobiason, LLP, (AV)
A Limited Liability Partnership
Blue Heron Building, 1087 West River Street Suite 100, 83702
Mailing Address: P.O. Box 2865, Boise, ID 83701-2865
Telephone: 208-342-4545 Fax: 208-342-2323
Michael Kane (Certified as Criminal Trial Specialist by the Idaho Trial Lawyers Association); Steven J. Tobiason. Associate: Laura A. Chess.
Tort Litigation, Insurance Related Issues, Administrative and Governmental Relations.
See Professional Biographies, BOISE, IDAHO

Kang, Soo Y. .... '76 '03 C.1193 B.A. L.336 J.D. [Ⓐ Elam&B.]
Kaplan, David J. '68 '96 C.339 B.S.E.E. L.770 J.D.
(adm. in CA; not adm. in ID)
Assoc. Gen. Coun., Pat. Litig. & Lic., Micron Technology, Inc.
Kaufman, James P., (BV) .... '— '73 C&L.336 B.A., J.D. [Ringert C.]
Kaufmann, Angela Schaer, (BV) .... '69 '96 C.1058 B.A. L.336 J.D. [Moffatt T.B.R.&F.]
Kelly, Kate .... '57 '92 C.1209 B.A. L.878 J.D. [⊡ Hawley T.E.&H.]
Kelly, Michael E., (AV) .... '58 '89 C.885 B.A. L.1040 J.D. [Howard L.&K.P.]
Kennedy, Shane Aiden .... '75 '01 C.939 B.A. L.336 J.D. Law Clk.
Kidwell, Wayne L. .... '38 '64 C&L.336 B.A., J.D. Supm. Ct. J.
King, John L., (AV) .... '42 '67 C&L.629 B.A., J.D. [Cantrill,S.S.&K.]
Kirkendall, Lawrence E., (BV) .... '56 '86 C&L.336 B.S., J.D. [Kirkendall]
Kirkendall Law Office, (BV) .... 3535 Dewey Street
Kiser, Alfred C. .... '22 '50 C&L.336 B.A., LL.B. 2435 Mountain View Dr.‡
Kiser, Jerry A., (BV) .... '56 '87 C.1120 B.S. L.336 J.D. 620 W. Hays St.
Klein, Erika Katherine, (CV) .... '71 '97 C&L.629 B.A., J.D. Pros. Atty. Off.
Klein, Karl T. .... '67 '94 C.112 B.A. L.260 J.D. [Givens P.]
Klein, R. Wayne .... '56 '82 C.878 B.A. L.273 J.D. Sec. Admr., Dept. of Fin.
Kline, Barton L., (BV) .... '47 '73 C.547 B.S. L.336 J.D. Staff Atty., Idaho Power Co.
Klocke, Julie N. '55 '80 C.491 B.A. L.494 J.D.
(adm. in MN; not adm. in ID) 4946 N. Contour Way‡
Kluksdal, John W., (BV) .... '72 '97 C.335 B.A. L.336 J.D. [Ⓐ Hepworth,L.&J.]
Kluksdal, Paula Landholm, (BV) .... '72 '97 C.335 B.A. L.336 J.D. [Ⓐ Hawley T.E.&H.]
Knipe, Quentin M., (AV) .... '64 '89 C.1051 B.S. L.911 J.D. [Stoel R.]
Knotts, David W., (BV) .... '— '86 C.347 B.A. L.629 J.D. [Quane S.]
Koch, Francis G. (Fran) '57 '85
C.300 B.A. L.1035 J.D. Gen. Coun., H&W Computer Systems, Inc.
Kolisch Hartwell, P.C., A Professional Corporation, (AV)
101 S. Capitol Blvd. (Pat.) (⊙Palo Alto, CA; Port., OR)
Korfanta, Craig M., (BV) .... '61 '93 C.1193 B.S. L.336 J.D. [Korfanta&H.] (Pat.)
Korfanta & Holland, P.C., (BV) .... 802 W. Bannock, Ste. 305 (Pat.)
Koshuta, Cheryl R. .... '54 '79 C.878 B.A. L.911 J.D. Dept. of Health & Welfare
Kozakiewicz, Vincent J. .... '54 '83 C.506 B.S. L.508 J.D. City J.
Kraft, Steve R. .... '65 '93 C.1193 B.S. L.1358 J.D. [Ⓐ Moore,B.&P.]
Krema, C. Nicholas, (BV) .... '56 '84 C.338 B.S. L.221 J.D. Atty. Gen.
Kristensen, Debora K., (AV) .... '65 '90 C.1375 B.A. L.770 J.D. [Givens P.]
Krogh, A. Lynne .... '58 '84 C.172 B.A. L.174 J.D. Mag. J.
Kronberg, Lisa J., (BV) '60 '89 C.506 B.S. L.508 J.D.
Envir. Res. Div. Envir. Quality Sec.
Kulchak, J. Michael, (CV) .... '56 '90 C.1193 B.A. L.336 J.D. [⊡ Perry L.]
Kunkel, Anne C. .... '75 '01 C.383 B.A. L.596 J.D. [⊡ Givens P.]
Kurtz, John F., Jr., (AV) .... '51 '78 C.1077 B.S. L.426 J.D. [Hawley T.E.&H.]
Kuster, Kellie D. .... '69 '03 C&L.336 B.A., J.D. [Ahrens&D.]
Kyte, Robert E. .... '53 '90 C.897 B.A. L.596 J.D. [Skinner F.]
Ladle, Jeremy G. .... '76 '04 C.335 B.A. L.336 J.D. [Ⓐ Givens P.]
Lakey, Todd .... '— '93 C.101 B.S. L.1051 J.D. [⊡ Moore S.B.&T.]
Langfield, Kathryn T., (BV) .... '56 '83 C.172 B.S. L.336 J.D. 3100 S. Vista Ave., Ste. 200
Lansing, Karen L. .... '50 '78 C.336 B.A. L.911 J.D. Ct. of App. J., ID Ct. of App.
Larimer, Linda A. '62 '87 C.228 B.A. L.976 J.D.
(adm. in MA; not adm. in ID) 2189 White Pine Pl.‡

Larsen, Brian C. .... '73 '01 C.877 B.S. L.174 J.D. [Ⓐ Hawley T.E.&H.]
Larsen, David W. .... '69 '97 C&L.101 B.S., J.D. Albertson's, Inc. (⊙Boise)
Larsen, David W. .... '69 '97 C&L.101 B.S., J.D. [Larsen] (⊙Boise)
Larsen Law Offices .... 250 Park Center Boulevard
LaRue, James D., (AV) .... '46 '75 C&L.336 B.A., J.D. [Elam&B.]
Lawrence, Dylan .... '75 '02 C&L.846 B.B.A., J.D. [Ⓐ Hawley T.E.&H.]
Leachman, Tamsen L. .... '64 '93 C.908 B.A. L.336 J.D. [Hall,F.O.&B.]
Learned, Scott R. .... '76 '01 C.939 B.A. L.276 J.D. [Ⓐ Hall,F.O.&B.]
Leaverton, Jack D., (BV) '48 '78 C&L.336 B.S., J.D.
Assoc. Coun., LandAmerica Financial Group, Inc.
Lee, David J., (BV) .... '58 '89 C.339 B.S. L.508 J.D. Idaho State Insurs. Fund
Lee, Elaine Herrick .... '73 '00 C.976 B.A. L.336 J.D. [Ⓐ Gjording&F.]
Lee, Franklin G. .... '70 '99 C&L.336 B.S., J.D. [Ⓐ Givens P.]
Lee, Jerold W., (CV) .... '61 '95 C.911 B.A. L.336 J.D. Dep. Atty. Gen.
Leroy, David H., (AV) .... '47 '71 C&L.336 B.S., J.D. 1130 East State Street
Levy, Paul E. .... '50 '76 C.978 B.A. L.276 J.D. [Levy]
Levy Law Offices .... 582 E. Boise Ave.
Lewis, Robert D., (AV) .... '53 '81 C.174 B.A. L.336 J.D. [Cantrill,S.S.&K.]
Lewis, Roderic W., (BV) '55 '83 C.101 B.A. L.178 J.D.
V.P. of Legal Affs., Gen. Coun. & Corp. Sec., Micron Technology, Inc.
Lezamiz, Margaret M., (BV) .... '56 '83 C.335 B.A. L.336 J.D. [Schroeder&L.]
Lierz, Richard K., (BV) '57 '84
C&L.336 B.A., J.D. Gen. Coun., Franklin Building Supply Co.
Lincoln, David B., (AV) .... '45 '71 C.336 B.A. L.1065 J.D. [Batt&F.]
Lindquist, Kim R., (BV) .... '52 '79 C&L.101 B.A., J.D. U.S. Atty.'s Off.
Linville, Thomas R., (AV) .... '51 '76 C&L.336 B.S., J.D. [Eberle,B.K.T.M.&J.]
Litster, William J. .... '54 '85 C.101 B.A. L.336 J.D. [Litster I.]
Litster Injury Lawyers .... 6550 Emerald, Suite 108
Lloyd, Brent F., (BV) .... '52 '80 C.112 B.A. L.336 J.D. Pres. & CEO, Futura Corp.
Lodge, Edward J. .... '33 '62 C.335 B.A. L.336 J.D. U.S. Dist. J.
Lojek, Donald W., (AV) .... '40 '72 C.116 B.A. L.208 J.D. [Lojek]

Lojek Law Offices, Chartered, (AV)
1199 West Main Street, P.O. Box 1712, 83701
Telephone: 208-343-7733 Facsimile: 208-389-1294
Email: lojeklaw@aol.com
Donald W. Lojek.
General and Civil Trial Practice, Aviation, Business, Commercial, Corporate, Employment, Healthcare, Insurance, Medical, Products Liability and Transportation.
Representative Clients: Argonaut Insurance Co.; Aviation Office of America; Bergen Brunswig Drug Co.; Boise State University; Design Professional Insurance Co.; First Security Bank of Idaho, N.A.
References: First Security Bank; Westone Bank.

See Professional Biographies, BOISE, IDAHO

Lombardi, David R., (AV) .... '49 '76 C.813 B.A. L.770 J.D. [Givens P.]
Longeteig, Iver J., (BV) .... '41 '65 C&L.336 B.A., J.D. [I.J.Longeteig]
Longeteig, Iver J., P.A., (BV) .... 817 West Franklin Street, Suite B100
Lopez, Thomas H., (AV) .... '51 '86 C.477 B.S. L.336 J.D. [Howard L.&K.P.]
Lord, Stephen J., (BV) .... '54 '80 C.335 B.A. L.950 J.D. 800 West State St.
Lorello, D. David, Jr. .... '69 '00 C.908 B.A. L.285 J.D. [Ⓐ Givens P.]
Loza, Emile .... '— '03 C.612 B.S. L.273 J.D. [Technology]
Ludwig, Scot M., Law Offices of, (BV) '59 '86 C.1193 B.A. L.336 J.D.
209 W. Main St.
Ludwigson, Sandra B. .... '53 '78 C.37 B.A. L.221 J.D. Idaho Legal Aid Servs., Inc.
Luker, Lynn M., (AV) .... '53 '80 C.112 A.B. L.336 J.D. [L.M.Luker]
Luker, Lynn M., P.A., (AV) .... 1010 N. Orchard St., Ste. 4
Lundgreen, Scott, (BV) .... '63 '93 C.878 B.A. L.950 J.D. 7235 Emerald, Ste. C
Lutze, Peter C. .... '46 '77 C.879 B.A. L.966 J.D. 4280 Bristol St.
Lynch, James B., (AV) .... '32 '57 C&L.336 B.A., LL.B. [Lynch&Assoc.]
Lynch, Katherine M., (BV) .... '65 '95 C&L.336 B.S., J.D. [Ⓐ Lynch&Assoc.]
Lynch, Michael L. '51 '81 C.1061 B.S. L.326 J.D.
Chf. Pat. Coun., Micron Technology, Inc. (Pat.)

Lynch & Associates, P.L.L.C., (AV) BR
1412 West Idaho Street, Suite 200, P.O. Box 739, 83701
Telephone: 208-331-5088 Fax: 208-331-0088
Email: lynchlaw@qwest.net URL: http://www.lynch-lawfirm.com
James B. Lynch;—Katherine M. Lynch.
General Civil Trial and Appellate Practice including Negligence, Product Liability and Professional Liability Litigation in the areas of Insurance Coverage, Insurance Defense, Commercial Litigation and Collections, Construction, Employment and Managed Health Care, General Liability Defense, Trusts and Estates, Wills, Probate, Self Insured Law.

See Professional Biographies, BOISE, IDAHO

Lynn, John, (AV) .... '45 '73 C.475 B.S. L.477 J.D. 500 West Bannock
Lyon, Frederick C. .... '39 '64 C&L.336 B.S., J.D. Clk., Idaho Supm. Ct. & Ct. of App.
Lyons, A. L., (BV) .... '28 '56 C&L.813 A.B., J.D. P.O. Box 2574
Lyons, James F. .... '38 '68 C.813 A.B. L.336 J.D. 830 Ridenbaugh St.‡
MacAllister, William H. '21 '56
C.216 A.B. L.1017 LL.B. 5769 North Marcliffe Avenue (Pat.)
Mack, J. Frederick, (AV) .... '46 '73 C&L.336 B.A., J.D. [Holland&H.]
Mack, John F. .... '— '73 C&L.336 B.A., J.D. 101 S. Capitol Boulevard
MacMaster, Emily .... '59 '95 C.1077 B.A. L.112 J.D. [Ⓐ Givens P.]
Madigan, Patrick D., (CV) .... '62 '92 C.678 B.A. L.629 J.D. Atty., Albertson's, Inc.
Magel, John, (AV) .... '38 '64 C.336 B.S. L.1066 LL.B. [Elam&B.]
Mahoney, Jennifer Reid, (BV) .... '— '95 C.112 B.A. L.336 J.D. [Ⓐ Ringert C.]
Mahoney, Patrick E., (CV) .... '70 '95 C.911 B.A. L.336 J.D. [Blackburn&J.]
Mallet, Joseph D., (CV) .... '68 '98 C&L.336 B.A., J.D. [Filicetti]
Malmgren, Richard E. '58 '89 C.101 B.A. L.178 J.D.
Sr. Asst. Gen. Coun., Micron Technology, Inc.
Maloney, Kevin T. '— '94
C.339 B.A. L.602 J.D. Asst. U.S. Atty., U.S. Atty. Off., Dist. of ID
Maloney, Kimberly D., (BV) .... '69 '94 C.347 B.S. L.602 J.D. [Givens P.]
Mann, Lori K., (CV) .... '59 '85 C.1193 B.A. L.336 J.D. Dep. Atty. Gen.
Manwaring, Jed W., (BV) .... '54 '83 C.101 B.A. L.336 J.D. [Evans K.]
Manweiler, David D., (AV) .... '61 '86 C.174 B.A. L.336 J.D. [Manweiler,M.B.&B.]
Manweiler, Kay C., (BV) .... '53 '83 C&L.336 B.S., J.D. Dep. Atty. Gen.
Manweiler, Mark H., (AV) .... '58 '83 C.174 B.A. L.336 J.D. [Manweiler,M.B.&B.]

Manweiler, Manweiler, Breen & Ball, PLLC, (AV)
290 Bobwhite Court, Suite 300, P.O. Box 937, 83701-0937
Telephone: 208-424-9100 Facsimile: 208-424-3100
Email: markm@mmbb-law.com URL: http://www.mmbb-law.com
Mark H. Manweiler; David D. Manweiler; M. Sean Breen; James K. Ball. Of Counsel: Howard I. Manweiler (1931-2001).
General Trial and Appellate Practice before State and Federal Courts. Business Law, Criminal Law, Family Law, Insurance, Personal Injury and Workers Compensation.

See Professional Biographies, BOISE, IDAHO

Marchbanks, Brent ...... '50 '75 C.910 B.A. L.950 J.D. Coalition of Adv. for the Disabled
Marcus, Barry, (BV) .... '41 '67 C&L.813 A.B., LL.B. 737 N. 7th St.
Marcus, Claude V., (AV) .... '10 '34 C&L.336 LL.B. 737 N. 7th St.
Marcus, Craig, (AV) .... '39 '63 C&L.336 J.D. 737 N. 7th St.
Marcus, Jenifer K. .... '64 '90 C.878 B.A. L.911 J.D. Atty., Albertson's, Inc.
Marcus, Trent B. .... '66 '96 C.1193 B.A. L.336 J.D. 737 N. 7th St.
Marsh, Andrew C. '59 '85 C.347 B.A. L.228 J.D.
(adm. in IN; not adm. in ID) 942 West Myrtle Street
Marshall, John M. .... '72 '97 C&L.174 B.A., J.D. [Ⓐ Givens P.]
Marshall, Nicholas S. .... '70 '97 C.678 B.A. L.336 J.D. [Ⓐ Thornton B.]
Marsters, LaDawn .... '65 '97 C.1193 B.S. L.336 J.D. [Ⓐ Greener B.S.]
Martens, Jared B. .... '74 '01 C.1193 B.A. L.208 J.D. [Martens]

Martens Law Office, PLLC
Eighth Street Marketplace, 404 S. 8th Street, Suite 300, 83702
Telephone: 208-322-9488 Fax: 208-322-3360
Email: info@martenslawoffice.com URL: http://www.martenslawoffices.com
Jared B. Martens.
Bankruptcy, Personal Bankruptcy, Commercial Bankruptcy, Criminal Law, DUI, DWI, Drug Crimes, White Collar Crimes, Felonies, Fraud and Deceit, Juvenile Law, Misdemeanors, Family Law, Divorce, Custody and Visitation, Adoption, Alimony, Spousal Support, Children's Rights, Guardianship, Conservatorship, Wills, Trusts, Estate, Probate.

See Professional Biographies, BOISE, IDAHO

Martin, A. René Fitzpatrick, (BV) .... '48 '84 C.1193 B.A. L.336 J.D. Atty. Gen. Off.
Martin, James L., (AV) .... '64 '90 C.1193 B.S. L.336 J.D. [Moffatt T.B.R.&F.]
Massoth, Elisa G. .... '71 '97 C.1193 B.A. L.336 J.D. P.O. Box 500
Matthews, Ellison M., (AV) .... '38 '65 C&L.336 B.S., LL.B. [Matthews]

Matthews Law Offices, (AV)
413 West Jefferson, Suite 4, P.O. Box 1988, 83701
Telephone: 208-336-1433 Fax: 208-336-9133
Email: matlaw@aol.com URL: http://www.lawyers.com/matthewslawoffices
Ellison M. Matthews (Certified as Criminal Trial Specialist by the Idaho Trial Lawyers Association).
General Civil and Criminal Trial Practice. Personal Injury Litigation and Appeals. Federal and State.
Reference: Wells Fargo Bank, N.A.

See Professional Biographies, BOISE, IDAHO

Maughan, Derek H. ...... '71 '01 C.101 B.S. L.336 J.D. [Ⓐ Dykas,S.&N.] (See Pat. Sect.)
Mauk, William L., (AV) .... '47 '75 C.800 B.A. L.1162 J.D. [Mauk&B.]

Mauk & Burgoyne, (AV)
515 South 6th Street, P.O. Box 1743, 83701-1743
Telephone: 208-345-2654 Facsimile: 208-345-3319
Email: maukburgoyne@rmci.net URL: http://www.lawyers.com/m&b-law
Members of Firm: William L. Mauk; Grant T. Burgoyne; W. Craig James.
Litigation, Labor and Employment Law, Personal Injury, Commercial Law, Insurance, Health Care, Government Law, Administrative Law.

See Professional Biographies, BOISE, IDAHO

Maulin, Stephanie A. .... '53 '92 C.813 B.A. L.336 J.D. Dep. of Corr.
Mayes, Robert C. '48 '79 C.871 B.S. L.169 J.D.
(adm. in IA; not adm. in ID) 11413 Chinden Blvd.
Maynard, Robert A., (AV) .... '53 '81 C.886 B.S. L.477 J.D. [Perkins C.]
McAllister, Bruce R., (AV) .... '— '80 C&L.494 B.A., J.D. [Quane S.]
McAnaney, David P., (BV) .... '54 '85 C.999 B.A. L.464 J.D. [McAnaney P.&Assoc.]
McAnaney & Associates PLLC, (BV) .... 1101 W. River St., Ste. 100
McBride, Mark C. '— '04 C.101 B.S. L.878 J.D.
(adm. in UT; not adm. in ID) [Ⓐ Ahrens&D.]
McCabe, Thomas J., (AV) .... '46 '80 C.397 B.A. L.336 J.D. [Westberg,M.&C.]
McCall, Samia E. '— '02 C.893 B.A. L.30
(adm. in VA; not adm. in ID) [Ⓐ Stoel R.]
McClure, James A., (BV) .... '24 '50 C&L.336 J.D. [Ⓒ Givens P.]
McClure, Kenneth R., (AV) .... '54 '80 C.945 B.A. L.336 J.D. [Givens P.]
McColl, Brian F., (AV) .... '47 '78 C.028 B.A. L.64 J.D. [Wilson M.&R.]
McColl, Matthew F. .... '— '99 C.335 B.A. L.878 J.D. [Ⓐ Quane S.]
McCollum, Joseph D., Jr., (AV) ...... '45 '70 C.336 B.S. L.1065 J.D. [Hawley T.E.&H.]
McConnell, Geoffrey J., (BV) .... '59 '86 C.105 B.A. L.464 J.D. [Meuleman M.]
McConnell, Kelly Greene, (BV) .... '— '89 C.1060 B.S. L.464 J.D. [Givens P.]

McCurdy, William A., (AV) '49 '74 C&L.336 B.A., J.D.
702 W. Idaho, Suite 1000, 83702-8911
Telephone: 208-947-7250 Fax: 208-947-5910
Email: wam@mccurdylaw.com
Litigation.

See Professional Biographies, BOISE, IDAHO

McCutcheon, Sue G., (BV) '56 '90
C.773 B.A. L.966 J.D. Corporate Attorney, Novartis Seeds, Inc.
McDaniel, James R. '59 '89 C.645 B.S.M.E. L.1209 J.D.
(adm. in VA; not adm. in ID; Pat.) Sr. Coun., Hewlett-Packard Co.
McDevitt, Chas. F., (AV) .... '32 '56 C.1032 L.336 J.D. [McDevitt&M.]

McDevitt & Miller, LLP, (AV)
420 West Bannock Street, P.O. Box 2564-83701, 83702
Telephone: 208-343-7500 Telecopy: 208-336-6912 Email: chas@mcdevitt-miller.com
Email: joe@mcdevitt-miller.com URL: http://www.mcdevitt-millerlaw.com
Dean J. Miller; Chas. F. McDevitt.
Business Law, Public Utility Law, Administrative Law, Litigation, Water Law, Family Law, Franchising.

See Professional Biographies, BOISE, IDAHO

McFadden, John J., (BV) .... '57 '88 C.336 B.S.C.E. L.950 J.D. [Ⓒ Moore S.B.&T.]
McFeeley, Neil D., (BV) .... '49 '86 C.846 B.A. L.228 J.D. [Eberle,B.K.T.M.&J.]
McGown, John, Jr., (AV) ...... '49 '75 C.383 B.S.Acct. L.174 J.D. [Ⓒ Hawley T.E.&H.]
McGreaham, Michael W. .... '53 '94 C.101 B.S. L.285 J.D. [Moffatt T.B.R.&F.]
McHugh, Candice M. '72 '98 C.285 B.A. L.208 J.D.
Dep. Atty. Gen., Nat. Resources Div.
McIntyre, Krista K., (AV) .... '64 '89 C.880 B.A. L.472 J.D. [Stoel R.]
McIntyre, Michael D., (AV) '57 '84 C.976 B.A. L.208 J.D.
Sr. Asst. Gen. Coun., Micron Technology, Inc.
McKay, Scott, (AV) .... '63 '91 C.941 B.A. L.285 J.D. [Nevin,B.&M.]
McKee, D. Duff, (AV) .... '39 '64 C&L.336 B.S., J.D. Dist. Ct. Judge‡
McKenzie, Curtis D. .... '69 '95 C.594 B.S. L.276 J.D. [Ⓐ Greener B.S.]
McKinney, Jack H., (CV) .... '69 '98 C&L.336 B.S., J.D. [Ormiston&M.]
McKlveen, William J., (AV) .... '43 '68 C.293 B.A. L.846 J.D. [Eberle,B.K.T.M.&J.]
McLaughlin, Michael R. .... '50 '77 C&L.336 B.A., J.D. 200 West Front Street
McLennan, Michael E. '64 '90 C.800 B.S. L.94 J.D.
(adm. in OR; not adm. in ID) FBI
McMillan, H. Knox, (BV) .... '64 '89 C.16 B.A. L.902 J.D. 1111 West Jefferson Street
McMillan, Susan A., (CVⓉ) '64 '89
C.473 B.A. L.902 J.D. Dir., Real Estate Law, Albertson's, Inc.
McNeill, John R. .... '47 '77 C.174 B.A. L.208 J.D. 350 N. Mitchell (83704)
McQuade-Grisham, Sharon L. .... '43 '87 C.1193 M.B.A. L.336 J.D. Law Clk. to Dist. Ct.
Meade, Steven J. .... '62 '00 C.1193 B.S. L.336 J.D. [Ⓐ Cantrill,S.S.&K.]
Meadows, Craig L., (AV) .... '40 '66 C.172 B.S. L.336 J.D. [Hawley T.E.&H.]

Meek, Robert M. .... '54 '80 C.923 B.S. L.893 J.D. 1111 West Jefferson Street

Meienhofer, John, (BV) '64 '92 C.95 B.A. L.629 J.D.
300 West Myrtle Street, Suite 200, 83702
Telephone: 208-343-3600 Fax: 208-344-7100
Email: meienhofer@earthlink.net URL: http://www.meienhofer.com
Federal and State Drugs and Narcotics, Land Use, Criminal Defense, DUI, Theft, White Collar Crime, Embezzlement, Civil Forfeiture, Personal Injury, Divorce, Child Custody, Domestic Violence Protection Orders, Social Security Disability, Corporate Law, Wills.
See Professional Biographies, BOISE, IDAHO

Meier, Joseph M., (AV) .... '59 '84 C.629 B.A. L.950 J.D. [Cosho H.]
Meier, L. Victoria .... '62 '00 C.446 B.S. L.336 J.D. 300 North Sixth St.
Melillo, Cynthia A., (CV) .... '62 '98 C.800 B.A. L.37 J.D. [Givens P.]
Mellon, Richard C., Jr., (AV) '44 '73
C.500 B.A. L.838 J.D. Claim Atty., State Farm Mut. Auto. Ins. Co.
Melville, James W. '14 '39 C&L.145 B.A., J.D.
(adm. in NE; not adm. in ID) 1130 Allumbaugh St.‡
Melville, Jason D., (CV) ....'69 '97 C.101 B.A. L.845 J.D. [McAnaney P.&Assoc.]
Mendes, Ronald T. '46 '73 C&L.209 B.A., J.D.
(adm. in IL; not adm. in ID) Dir., Regulatory Compl., Albertson's, Inc.
Merrick, Gale M., (BV) ....'39 '68 C.1032 B.A. L.336 J.D. 737 N. 7th St.
Merrill, Milford S. ....'13 '39 C&L.878 J.D. 1004 Lewis‡
Mesler, Lisa Jones '60 '89 C.475 B.S. L.1325 J.D.
Staff Atty. to the Fed. J., U.S. Dist. Ct., Dist. of ID
Metcalf, David L. ....'54 '79 C.112 A.B. L.1068 J.D. Law Clk to Dist. Ct. J.
Meuleman, Wayne V. (AV) .... '48 '72 C&L.336 B.S., J.D. [Meuleman M.]

Meuleman Mollerup LLP, (AV)
University Plaza, 960 Broadway Avenue, Suite 500, 83706
Telephone: 208-342-6066 Fax: 208-336-9712
Email: firm@lawidaho.com URL: http://www.lawidaho.com
Members of Firm: Wayne V Meuleman; Kimbal L. Gowland; Richard W. Mollerup; Geoffrey J. McConnell; Jeff R. Sykes; Arnold L. Wagner. Associates: Paul A. Boice; Richard L. Stacey, Jr.; Jonathan R. Bauer; Michael E. Baldner.
Construction Law, Real Estate Law, Business Law.
Representative Clients: Earthtech Inc.; Kaiser Engineers & Constructors, Inc.; Albertsons, Inc.
See Professional Biographies, BOISE, IDAHO

Meyer, Christopher H., (AV) ....'52 '81 C&L.477 A.B., J.D. [Givens P.]
Meyer, Karen .... '59 '86 C.228 B.A. L.861 J.D. 3443 S. Millspur Way‡
Miller, Barbara J. .... '43 '77 C.927 B.A. L.336 J.D. Sr. V.P., SRP Healthcare, Inc.
Miller, Brad P., (AV) .... '61 '86 C&L.336 B.S., J.D. [Hawley T.E.&H.]
Miller, Celeste, (BV) .... '49 '80 C.549 B.S. L.336 J.D. Asst. U. S. Atty.
Miller, Daniel A., (BV) .... '60 '86 C.172 B.A. L.336 J.D. 209 W. Main St.
Miller, Dean J., (AV) .... '48 '76 C.770 B.A. L.336 J.D. [McDevitt&M.]
Miller, J. Lynn, (CV) '61 '86 C.679 B.A. L.336 J.D.
Foreclosure Specialist, Transnation Title & Escrow, Inc.‡
Miller, John A., (BV) .... '63 '94 C.1073 B.A. L.464 J.D. 200 N. 4th St., Ste. 302
Miller, L. Edward, (AV) .... '52 '77 C.335 B.A. L.336 J.D. [Givens P.]
Miller, Nicholas G., (AV) .... '50 '77 C&L.813 A.B., J.D. [Hawley T.E.&H.]
Miller, Patrick J., (AV) .... '59 '84 C&L.336 B.A., J.D. [Givens P.]
Miller, Robert L., (BV) .... '43 '67 C&L.629 B.S., J.D. 2700 West Airport Way
Miller, Thomas A., (AV) .... '30 '56 C&L.336 B.A., J.D. [Hawley T.E.&H.]
Minder, Carolyn M. .... '54 '85 C.1193 B.A. L.336 J.D. Dist. J.
Minnick, Walter C. .... '42 '69 C.939 B.A. L.309 J.D. 815 Park Blvd.
Mitchell, Donald '39 '66 C.112 B.S. L.1065 J.D.
(adm. in CA; and limited adm. in ID) 1552 Lenz Lane
Mitchell, Hans A., (BV) ....'— '96 C.629 B.A. L.950 J.D. [Quane S.]
Mitchell, Robert C. '40 '66 C.187 B.A. L.145 J.D.
V.P. & Div. Coun., LandAmerica Financial Group, Inc.
Moen, Monica, (BV) '52 '97 C.350 B.S. L.352 J.D.
Atty., Idaho Power Company (Legal Department)

Moffatt Thomas Barrett Rock & Fields, Chartered, (AV)
101 South Capitol Boulevard, 10th Floor, P.O. Box 829, 83701 ⊙
Telephone: 208-345-2000 FAX: 208-385-5384
URL: http://www.moffatt.com
Willis C. Moffatt (1907-1980); John W. Barrett; R. B. Rock; Richard C. Fields; John S. Simko; John C. Ward; Larry C. Hunter; Randall A. Peterman; Mark S. Prusynski; Stephen R. Thomas; Glenna M. Christensen; Gerald T. Husch; Scott L. Campbell; Robert B. Burns; Michael E. Thomas; Patricia M. Olsson; James C. deGlee; Michael O. Roe; David S. Jensen; James L. Martin; C. Clayton Gill; Angela Schaer Kaufmann; Michael W. McGreaham. Of Counsel: Eugene C. Thomas; Morgan W. Richards, Jr.; Robert E. Bakes.
General Civil, Trial and Appellate Practice. Administrative Law, Alternative Dispute Resolution, Antitrust and Trade Regulation, Aviation, Bankruptcy, Banks and Banking, Business Law, Commercial Real Estate, Construction Law, Contracts, Corporate Law, Debtor and Creditor, Disabilities, Employee Benefits, Environmental Law, Finance, Government Relations, Health Care, Hospital Law, Insurance Defense, Intellectual Property, Labor and Employment Law, Leases and Leasing, Litigation, Medical Malpractice, Mergers, Acquisitions and Divestitures, Mortgages, Nonprofit and Charitable Organizations, Partnership Law, Probate, Products Liability, Professional Liability, Public Utility Law, Real Estate, Regulatory Law, Securities, Taxation, Torts, Trusts and Estates, Water Law, Worker's Compensation.
Idaho Falls, Idaho Office: 420 Memorial Drive, P.O. Box 51505, 83405. Telephone: 208-522-6700. Fax: 208-522-5111.
Pocatello, Idaho Office: 412 West Center, Suite 2000, P.O. Box 817, 83204. Telephone: 208-233-2001. Fax: 208-232-0150.
Twin Falls, Idaho Office: 621 N. College Road, Suite 103, P.O. Box 5483, 83303-5483. Telephone 208-734-7500. Fax: 208-734-7508.
See Professional Biographies, BOISE, IDAHO

Mollerup, Richard W., (BV) .... '48 '93 C.1193 B.B.A. L.336 J.D. [Meuleman M.]
Monroe, Darin G. .... '— '01 C.1032 B.S. L.336 J.D. [J.F.Greenfield]
Monteleone, Jason R.N., (BV) .... '69 '98 C.216 B.A. L.900 J.D. [Johnson&M.]
Montgomery, Gary L., (AV) ... '42 '71 C.101 B.S. L.878 J.D. 12466 W. Ramblin Rose Dr.
Montgomery, Judson B., (BV) .... '67 '93 C.228 B.A. L.602 J.D. [Givens P.]
Montgomery, Robert C., (BV) .... '47 '75 C.101 B.A. L.336 J.D. [R.C.Montgomery]
Montgomery, Robert C., Chtd., (BV) ....2160 S. Twin Rapid Way
Moody, Robert C., (BV) '50 '85 C.1193 B.A. L.336 J.D.
Regional Couns., Great West Casualty Company
Moore, Michael C., (AV) .... '42 '68 C.197 B.A. L.336 J.D. [Moore S.B.&T.]
Moore, Michael W., (AV) .... '51 '76 C&L.336 B.A., J.D. [Moore,B.&P.]

Moore, Baskin & Parker, (AV)
Washington Federal Plaza, 1001 West Idaho Street, Suite 400, P.O. Box 6756, 83707
Telephone: 208-336-6900 Facsimile: 208-336-7031
Members of Firm: Michael W. Moore; Thomas P. Baskin, III; Paige Alan Parker. Associates: Martin C. Hendrickson; Steve R. Kraft.
General Civil Trial and Appellate Practice. Aviation, Insurance, Civil Rights, Governmental Liability, Construction, Employment, Negligence, Product Liability, Professional Liability and Workers Compensation Law.
Representative Clients: Travelers Insurance Co./Aetna Casualty & Surety, Co.; Capitol Indemnity Co.; Clarendon Insurance Co.; Crawford & Co.; Empire Fire & Marine Insurance Co.; Fireman's Fund Insurance Cos.; Idaho Counties Reciprocal Management Program; Idaho State Insurance Fund; Insurance Company of the West; Protective Insurance Co.
See Professional Biographies, BOISE, IDAHO

Moore Smith Buxton & Turcke, Chartered, (AV)
225 North 9th, Suite 420, 83702 ⊙
Telephone: 208-331-1800 Fax: 208-331-1202
Email: info@msbtlaw.com URL: http://www.msbtlaw.com
Susan E. Buxton; Michael C. Moore; Paul A. Turcke; Bruce Smith;—Christopher E. Yorgason; Tammy A. Zokan; Ransom J. Bailey. Of Counsel: Todd Lakey; John J. McFadden.
Business, Employment, Environmental, General Municipal Law, Mining, Municipal Bond, Natural Resource, Public Utility, Land Use, Telecommunications, Water Law, General Civil Trial and Appellate Practice in State and Federal Courts and before Various Federal and State Administrative Tribunals.
Nampa, Idaho Office: 17 12th Avenue South, Burns and Fox Building, 83651. Telephone: 208-466-1300.
See Professional Biographies, BOISE, IDAHO

Morey, Charles E. '38 '70 C.112 A.B. L.1065 J.D.
(adm. in CA; not adm. in ID) Dir., Land & Develop., J.R. Simplot Company
Morfitt, Michael G., (BV) '44 '69
C&L.336 B.S., J.D. Dist. Coun., U.S. Small Bus. Admin.
Morris, Stewart A., (BV) .... '44 '69 C&L.336 B.S., J.D. 1020 Main St.
Morris, Thomas C., (BV) .... '55 '82 C&L.101 B.S., J.D. 1101 W. River St., Ste. 100
Mortell, Thomas J., (CV) .... '66 '94 C&L.101 B.S., J.D. [Hawley T.E.&H.]
Morton, Alan L. .... '55 '83 C.101 B.A. L.336 J.D. [Morton]
Morton Law Offices, Chartered ....P.O. Box 420
Moss, Jeffrey M. '64 '92 C&L.101 B.S., J.D.
Asst. Gen. Coun., Micron Technology, Inc.
Moss, Thomas E., (AV) .... '37 '65 C&L.336 B.A., J.D. U.S. Atty. Off.
Mossman, Hugh V., (BV) ....'46 '71 C&L.352 B.A., J.D. [Mossman]
Mossman Law Office, (BV) ....611 W. Hays
Mott, Tobi J. ....'74 '02 C.1120 B.A. L.174 J.D. [Holland&H.]
Munson, Joseph S., (AV) .... '48 '74 C&L.336 B.A., J.D. 1111 West Jefferson Street
Munson, Thomas V., (BV) ....'52 '81 C.1193 B.S. L.336 J.D. [Penland M.G.]
Munther, Merrily, (AV) .... '46 '76 C.911 B.A. L.336 J.D. [Penland M.G.]
Murdock, Ted C., (CV) ....'68 '96 C.1193 B.B.A. L.336 J.D. [Holland&H.]
Murphy, Holzer & Vaughan, LLC, (BV) ....1516 W. Hays St.
Murray, Leslie G. '42 '84 C&L.336 B.S., J.D.
Sr. Coun., Intell. Prop. Sect., Hewlett-Packard Co. (Pat.)
Musgrove, Sheryl L. .... '60 '95 C&L.336 B.S., J.D. [Nevin,B.&M.]
Myers, Terry L., (AV) ....'55 '80 C.1032 B.A. L.336 J.D. Chf. J., U.S. Bkrptcy.
Myers, William G., III, (BV) ....'55 '81 C.945 A.B. L.208 J.D. [Holland&H.]
Myrick, Amber R. ....'68 '95 C&L.285 B.B.A., J.D. 1101 W River St Ste 340
Myshin, Amil N. .... '46 '71 C.901 B.A. L.273 J.D. Sr. Trial Atty, Pub. Def.
Naugle, Cathy, (BV) .... '49 '80 C.36 B.S. L.336 J.D. [Naugle]
Naugle Law Offices, (BV) .... 1109 Main, Suite 450
Naylor, Kirtlan G., (BV) .... '58 '86 C&L.101 B.A., J.D. [Naylor&H.]

Naylor & Hales, P.C., (BV)
1199 North Shoreline Lane, Suite 200, P.O. Box 9496, 83707
Telephone: 208-383-9511 Fax: 208-383-9516
Kirtlan G. Naylor; Roger J. Hales:—Carlton R. Ericson; Colleen D. Zahn; Bruce Castleton. Of Counsel: Robert G. Hamlin.
Corporate Law, Banking, Real Estate, Employment, Commercial Litigation, Business Law, Civil Rights, Litigation, Estate Planning, Insurance Defense, Administrative Law, Contract Law, Wills, Trusts, Intellectual Property Law, Technology Licensing, Landlord and Tenant Law, Education Law, Adoptions, Municipality Defense, Construction Law, Finance, Product Liability, Collections, Mergers and Acquisitions, Transactions, Sexual Harassment, Discrimination, Wrongful Termination, Government Law, Law Enforcement, Personal Injury.
See Professional Biographies, BOISE, IDAHO

Neal, Gary L., (BV) .... '60 '94 C.57 B.A. L.629 J.D. [Neal&U.]
Neal, Ramona Schwehr, (BV) '66 '93
C.1193 B.A. L.629 J.D. Coun., Hewlett-Packard Co.

Neal & Uhl, PLLC, (BV)
1101 West River Street, Suite 110, P.O. Box 1926, 83701
Telephone: 208-343-5931 Fax: 208-343-5807 URL: http://www.IdahoRealEstateLaw.com
Email: info@idahorealestatelaw.com URL: http://www.nealuhl.com
Gary L. Neal; Holger Uhl;—Robert E. Rice; James W. Colborn.
Business Law, Real Estate, Commercial Law, E-Commerce, Community Association Law, Landlord and Tenant Law, Fair Housing and Bankruptcy.
Representative Clients: Capstead Mortgage; Temple-Inland Mortgage Corp.; Ocwen Federal Bank; Young Electric Sign Company (YESCO); Boise Cascade Employees Credit Union; G.E. Capital Mortgage Services; Colliers International.
References: Idaho Association of Realtors; Idaho Apartment Owners Assoc.
See Professional Biographies, BOISE, IDAHO

Neill, James M. ....'55 '81 C.31 B.A. Eng. L.569 J.D. [J.M.Neill]
Neill, James M., P.C. ....223 N. 6th Street, Suite 410
Nelson, Angela K., (CV) .... '70 '95 C.95 B.A. L.861 J.D. [Givens P.]
Nelson, Deborah E., (CV) .... '72 '97 C.806 B.A. L.596 J.D. [Givens P.]
Nelson, Kent E., (BV) ....'55 '84 C&L.336 B.S., J.D. Dep. Atty. Gen.
Nelson, Thomas G. ....'36 '62 C&L.336 J.D. U.S. Sr. Cir. J.‡
Nelson, Wilbur T., (BV) ....'40 '69 C&L.336 B.S., J.D. 8917 Springhurst
Neville, Thomas F. .... '46 '77 C.871 B.S. L.770 J.D. Dist. J.
Neville, Timothy D. ....'52 '91 C.309 B.A. L.1194 J.D. [Huntley P.]
Nevin, David Z., (AV) ....'49 '79 C.172 B.A. L.336 J.D. [Nevin,B.&M.]

Nevin, Benjamin & McKay, LLP, (AV)
303 West Bannock Street, P.O. Box 2772, 83701
Telephone: 208-343-1000 Fax: 208-345-8274
URL: http://www.nbmlaw.com
Members of Firm: David Z. Nevin (Certified as a Criminal Trial Specialist by the Idaho Trial Lawyers Association); Dennis Benjamin; Scott McKay; Michael J. Bartlett;—Deborah Whipple; Sheryl L. Musgrove.
Criminal Defense, Personal Injury and Civil Litigation.
See Professional Biographies, BOISE, IDAHO

Newby, Jane M., (BV) .... '50 '78 C&L.966 B.A., J.D. Dep. Atty. Gen.
Newell, Janice D. ....'38 '84 C&L.285 B.A., J.D. I.R.S.
Newhouse, M. Neal, (AV) .... '37 '61 C&L.336 LL.B. 1117 Kimberley Ln.
Nicholas, Brian D., (BV) ....'58 '86 C.1032 B.A. L.336 J.D. Dep. Atty. Gen.
Nicholas, Christine E., (AV) '60 '85 C.454 B.B.A. L.336 J.D.
Assoc. Gen. Coun. & Asst. Secy., J.R. Simplot Co.
Nickels, Bryan A. ....'— '01 C.336 B.A. L.93 J.D. [Hall,F.O.&B.]
Nipper, Stephen M., (BV) '72 '98 C.999 B.S. L.801 J.D.
[Dykas,S.&N.] (See Pat. Sect.)
Noack, Harold Q., Jr., (BV) .... '31 '60 C.112 B.A. L.1065 LL.B. [H.Q.Noack,Jr.]

Noack, Harold Q., Jr., P.A., (BV)
733 North 7th Street, P.O. Box 875, 83702
Telephone: 208-336-9292 Fax: 208-336-6701
Email: pete@noacklaw.com URL: http://www.noacklaw.com
Harold Q. Noack, Jr.
Creditor and Debtor Bankruptcy, General Civil, Trial and Appellate Practice. Commercial, Corporation, Family Law, Divorce, Alimony, Child Support, Real Estate, Construction Law, Elder Law, Wills and Probate.

(This Listing Continued)

Noack, Harold Q., Jr., P.A. (Continued)
Reference: West One Bank, Idaho, N.A.
See Professional Biographies, BOISE, IDAHO

Noble, Ritchard S. '51 '86 C.1060 B.A. L.336 J.D. 1624 Lenz Lane
Nona, Jeffery E., (BV) '65 '93 C.112 A.B. L.336 J.D. 302 West Idaho
Numbers, Audrey, (BV) '53 '93 C.740 M.A. L.336 J.D. [Numbers]

Numbers Law Office, (BV)
611 West Hayes, 83703
Telephone: 208-424-0800 Fax: 208-343-5791
Email: audreyn@numberslaw.com URL: http://www.numberslawfirm.com
Audrey Numbers.
Family Law, Divorce, Custody, Child Support, Adoption, Guardianship, Conservatorship.
See Professional Biographies, BOISE, IDAHO

Nyman, Kenneth D., (AV) '48 '75 C.336 B.A. L.309 J.D. [Ⓒ Anderson,J.&H.]
O'Bar, Rachael M. '67 '98 C.1176 B.A. L.192 J.D. [Ⓐ Anderson,J.&H.]
Oberrecht, Phillip S., (AV) '48 '76 C&L.608 B.A., J.D. [Hall,F.O.&B.]
Ocker, Kirsten A. '64 '91 C.446 B.A. L.336 J.D. [Ⓐ Huntley P.]
Olsen, Steven LaMar, (BV) '58 '86 C&L.101 B.A., J.D. [Huntley P.]
Olson, John K. '69 '04 C.101 B.A. L.846 J.D. [Ⓐ Hawley T.E.&H.]
Olson, Stephen J., (BV) '61 '89 C.769 B.A. L.208 J.D. [Ⓐ Eberle,B.K.T.M.&J.]
Olsson, Carl Eric, (AV) '47 '83 C.385 B.A. L.146 J.D. Dep. Atty. Gen.
Olsson, Patricia M., (AV) '54 '83 C.1275 L.146 J.D. [Moffatt T.B.R.&F.]
O'Neil, Brooke A. '71 '97 C.1169 B.A. L.770 J.D. [Ⓐ Finch&B.]
O'Neill, Derrick J., (BV) '64 '89 C.336 B.S. L.878 J.D. [Jones G.H.F.&E.]
Onnen, Robert E., (BV) '47 '74 C&L.352 B.A., J.D. 8151 W. Rifleman Street
O'Riordan, Kaye L., (AV) '49 '73 C&L.37 B.A., J.D.
V.P. & Corp. Sec., Albertson's, Inc.
O'Riordan, W. Hugh, (AV) '47 '78 C&L.37 B.A., J.D. [Givens P.]
Ormiston, Steven R., (AV) '57 '84 C.475 B.S.M.E. L.336 J.D. [Ormiston&M.] (Pat.)
Ormiston & McKinney, P.L.L.C., (AV) 802 W. Bannock Street, Suite 400 (Pat.)
Ormseth, Kris, (BV) '61 '92 C.813 B.A. L.1066 J.D. [Stoel R.]
Orndorff, Owen H., (BV) '46 '74 C.475 B.A. L.597 J.D. [Orndorff]

Orndorff Law Offices, (BV)
1087 West River Street, Suite 230, 83702
Telephone: 208-343-8880 Telecopy: 208-345-0314
Email: orndorfflaw@aol.com
Owen H. Orndorff; Lori A. Dingel. Of Counsel: R. Lee Roberts (Not admitted in ID).
Business Law, Estate Planning and Probate, Real Estate Law, Power Project Development.
See Professional Biographies, BOISE, IDAHO

Orr, Michael C. '57 '01 C.475 B.S. L.629 J.D. [Ⓐ Givens P.]
Orton, Thorpe P., (BV) '66 '92 C.1193 B.S. L.285 J.D. Dep. Chf. of Staff
Oths, Michael J., (BV) '57 '82 C.201 B.A. L.629 J.D. Coun., Idaho State Bar
Owen, Patrick H., (BV) '52 '78 C.966 B.S. L.188 J.D. Dep. Pros. Atty.
Palmer, Jacque L., (AV) '— '86 C&L.336 B.S., J.D. [Ⓒ Perkins C.]
Pappas, Jim D. '52 '77 C.1032 B.A. L.336 J.D. U.S. Bkrptcy. J.
Pappas, Matthew O. '75 '00 C&L.336 B.S., J.D. [Ⓐ Anderson,J.&H.]
Parham, George, (BV) '50 '84 C.112 B.A. L.61 J.D.
Chf. Legal Coun., Idaho St. Ins. Fund
Park, Susan E. '62 '90 C.174 B.A. L.336 J.D. 250 S. 5th St.‡
Park, W. Anthony, (AV) '34 '63 C&L.336 B.A., J.D. [Ⓒ Huntley P.]
Parker, Paige Alan, (BV) '47 '86 C.906 B.A. L.336 J.D. [Moore,B.&P.]
Parkinson, Ward, (BV) '45 '97 C.877 B.S.E.E. L.146 J.D. 300 Main St., Ste. 111
Parry, Richard D., (BV) '52 '80 C.1077 B.A. L.101 J.D.
(adm. in OH; not adm. in ID)
Sr. V.P. & Gen. Coun., Washington Group International, Inc.
Partridge, Olivia Lowe '47 '83 C.766 B.A. L.284 J.D. 3565 Gekeler Lane
Paschke, John F. '72 '97 C.339 B.S.E.E. L.309 J.D.
(adm. in IL; not adm. in ID)
Assoc. Gen. Coun., Pat. Lit. & Lic., Micron Technology, Inc.
Pasley, R. Scott, (BV) '51 '76 C.335 B.A. L.336 J.D.
Asst. Gen. Coun., J.R. Simplot Co.
Patterson, George C., (BV) '51 '92 C.1079 B.A. L.1065 J.D. [Patterson]
Patterson Law Offices, (BV) 410 South Orchard Street, Suite 136
Pearson, Victor D. '24 '50 C&L.508 B.A., LL.B.
(adm. in MT; not adm. in ID) 2604 Redway Rd.‡
Pedersen, Kenneth J., (AV) '51 '82 C.46 B.S. L.209 J.D. [Pedersen] (Pat.)
Pedersen & Company, PLLC, (AV) 1410 North 28th Street (Pat.)
Penland, Paul S., (BV) '49 '76 C.802 B.A. L.69 J.D. [Penland M.G.]

Penland Munther Goodrum, Chartered, (AV)
1161 West River Street, Suite 260, P.O. Box 199, 83701
Telephone: 208-344-4566 Fax: 208-344-9836 URL: http://www.PMGAttorneys.com
Email: general@PMGAttorneys.com URL: http://www.pmea-lawfirm.com
Paul S. Penland; Merrily Munther; Forrest R. Goodrum (Not admitted in ID);—Thomas V. Munson; Skip Sperry.
Reference: Key Bank of Idaho.
See Professional Biographies, BOISE, IDAHO

Penny, David M., (BV) '60 '86 C.1193 B.B.A. L.285 J.D. [Jones G.H.F.&E.]
Perison, Mark D., (CV) '67 '93 C.112 B.A. L.336 J.D. [Ⓐ W.R.Snyder&Assoc.]
Perkins, David S., (BV) '— '91 C.878 B.S. L.336 J.D. [Quane S.]

Perkins Coie LLP, (AV)
251 East Front Street, Suite 400, 83702-7310 ⊙
Telephone: 208-343-3434 Facsimile: 208-343-3232
Email: perkins@perkinscoie.com URL: http://www.perkinscoie.com
Partners: Richard C. Boardman; Robert A. Maynard. Of Counsel: Jacque L. Palmer; Melanie Rubocki. Associates: Eric Aaserud (Not admitted in ID); Brook B. Bond (Not admitted in ID); Eric R. Bjorkman, Jr.; Kelly A. Cameron (Not admitted in ID); Shelly Cozakos; Christine M. Salmi.
General Civil Trial and Appellate Practice in Federal and State Courts and before various Federal and State Administrative Tribunals. Administrative; Antitrust and Trade Regulation; Aviation and Aerospace; Banks and Banking; Bankruptcy; Biotechnology; Business Law; Corporate Law; Employee Benefits; Energy; Environmental; Estate Planning; Federal Indian Law; Franchising; General Litigation; Government Contracts; Government Relations; Immigration; Intellectual Property; International Trade; International Law; Internet and Electronic Commerce; Labor and Employment; Land Use; Life Sciences; Mergers, Acquisitions and Divestitures; Municipal/Public Finance; Natural Resources; Nonprofit and Charitable Organizations; Probate; Patents; Product Liability; Project Finance; Political Law; Public Utility; Real Estate; School Law; Securities Law and Litigation; Taxation; Technology; Telecommunications; Toxic Torts; Trademarks and Copyrights; Venture Capital and Investment Funds; Water Rights; White-Collar Criminal Representation; Workers' Compensation.
Other Offices: Anchorage, Alaska; Bellevue, Washington; Chicago, Illinois; Denver, Colorado; Los Angeles, California; Menlo Park, California; Olympia, Washington; Phoenix, Arizona; Portland, Oregon; San Francisco, California; Seattle, Washington; Washington, D.C.
Reviser of the Washington Law Digest for this Directory.
See Professional Biographies, BOISE, IDAHO

Perry, Mark B., (BV) '54 '84 C.1042 B.S. L.37 J.D. [Perry L.]
Perry Law, P.C., (BV) 2627 W. Idaho Street
Pershing, Laura M. '32 '61 C.679 B.S. L.345 J.D.
(adm. in IN; not adm. in ID) P.O. Box 1725‡
Peterman, Randall A., (AV) '51 '77 C.594 B.A. L.911 J.D. [Moffatt T.B.R.&F.]
Peterson, Carsten A. '— '01 C.877 B.S. L.336 J.D. [Ⓐ Quane S.]
Peterson, Herbert J. '18 '45 C&L.378 A.B., LL.B.
(adm. in KS; not adm. in ID) 2923 Gretchen Way‡
Phillips, Robert L. '65 '95 C.877 B.A. L.101 J.D. Pres., Hawkins-Smith Mgmt., Inc.
Pica, Derek A., (BV) '61 '86 C.336 B.S. L.878 J.D. [D.A.Pica]

Pica, Derek A., P.L.L.C., (BV)
199 N. Capitol Boulevard, Suite 302, 83702
Telephone: 208-336-4144 Fax: 208-336-4980 URL: http://www.picalaw.com
Email: derekpica@msn.com URL: http://www.picalawfirm.com
Derek A. Pica.
Divorce, Child Custody, Real Estate, Probate, Contracts, Personal Injury.
See Professional Biographies, BOISE, IDAHO

Piccioni, Lou, (BV) '66 '92 C.712 B.A. L.972 J.D. [Ⓐ Howard L.&K.P.]
Piotrowski, James Marshall '67 '94 C.363 b.A. L.930 J.D. [Herzfeld&P.]
Pirtle, Joseph N. '78 '04 C&L.336 B.S., J.D. [Ⓐ Elam&B.]
Pisca, Jeremy P., (BV) '73 '99 C.1193 B.A. L.336 J.D. [Ⓐ Evans K.]
Points, Michelle Burke '70 '00 C.629 B.A. L.285 J.D. [Ⓐ Hawley T.E.&H.]
Poole, Bradley B., (Chartered), (BV) '47 '74 C.101 B.A. L.336 J.D. [B.B.Poole]
Poole, Bradley B., Chartered, (BV) 1110 North Five Mile Road
Pooser, Christopher, (BV) '69 '96 C.277 B.S. L.861 J.D. [Ⓐ Stoel R.]
Pope, William G. '— '97 C&L.101 B.A., J.D. [Ⓐ Quane S.]
Poplack, Richard A. '44 '71 C.154 B.A. L.1066 J.D. I.R.S.
Poppen, Joel L. '63 '92 C.339 B.S. L.228 J.D.
(adm. in AZ; not adm. in ID) Dir. of Litig., Micron Technology, Inc.
Powers, Michael E., (BV) '48 '74 C.1032 B.B.A. L.336 J.D. Ref., State Indus. Comm.
Powers, Raymond D., (BV) '56 '81 C.24 B.A. L.607 J.D. [Hall,F.O.&B.]
Powers, Sharon D., (AV) '68 '93 C.844 B.A. L.900 J.D. [Ahrens&D.]
Price, Steven B., (BV) '62 '94 C.878 B.S. L.336 J.D. 5960 N. Rothmans Ave.
Prince, Larry E., (AV) '50 '75 C.1193 B.A. L.1065 J.D. [Holland&H.]
Pritchett, M. Jed, Jr. '29 '59 C.101 B.S. L.878 J.D. 250 Parkcenter Blvd.‡
Probasco, Randall Curtis '69 '00 C.1193 B.A. L.336 J.D. [Ⓐ Howard L.&K.P.]
Prusynski, Mark S., (AV) '53 '78 C.375 B.S. L.352 J.D. [Moffatt T.B.R.&F.]
Purnell, David R. '56 '83 C&L.101 B.A., J.D. [Purnell]
Purnell Law Offices 1661 West Shoreline Drive Suite 204
Pursley, Kenneth L., (AV) '40 '65 C.188 B.A. L.145 J.D. [Givens P.]
Pusch, Jeffrey W., (BV) '64 '92 C.668 B.A. L.93 J.D. [Batt&F.]
Quade, Sara C. 'Danielle' '76 '01 C&L.336 B.A., J.D. [Ⓐ Hawley T.E.&H.]
Quane, Jeremiah A., (AV) '— '62 C&L.336 B.A., LL.B. [Quane S.]

Quane Smith LLP, (AV) BR
U.S. Bank Plaza, 16th Floor, P.O. Box 519, 83701-0519 ⊙
Telephone: 208-345-8600 Facsimile: 208-345-8660
Email: info@quanesmith.net URL: http://www.quanesmith.net
Members of Firm: Jeremiah A. Quane; E.B. Smith (1896-1975); Bruce R. McAllister; Randall R. Adams (Resident, Coeur d'Alene Office); Richard L. Stubbs; Donald F. Carey (Resident, Idaho Falls Office); David W. Knotts; David S. Perkins; Michael L. Haman (Resident, Coeur d'Alene Office); Tyra H. Stubbs; Terrence S. Jones. Associates: Leslie S. Brown; Robert D. Williams (Resident, Idaho Falls Office); Hans A. Mitchell; Matthew F. McColl; William G. Pope; Dari M. Huskey; Jennifer D. Gaffaney (Resident, Coeur d'Alene Office); Carsten A. Peterson; Jennifer L. Gorman (Resident, Coeur d'Alene Office); Carole I. Wesenberg (Resident, Idaho Falls Office); Brad S. Richardson.
Insurance, Insurance Defense, Litigation, Accountants Liability, Advertising and Marketing, Agents and Brokers Liability, Agricultural Law, Airplane Crashes, Alcoholic Beverages, Alternative Dispute Resolution, Americans with Disabilities Act Defense, Appellate Practice, Architects and Engineers Liability, Arson and Insurance Fraud, Asbestos Defense, Automobile Insurance, Aviation, Brain Injury, Business Law, Casualty Insurance Defense, Catastrophic Injury, Civil Practice, Commercial Insurance, Commercial Law, Complex and Multi-District Litigation, Computers and Software, Construction Accidents, Construction Defects, Construction Law, Contracts, Corporate Law, Design Professionals Liability, Drug and Medical Device Defense, Education Law, Employer Liability, Environmental Law, ERISA Litigation, Extra Contractual Insurance Defense, Federal Practice, Fire Insurance, Firearms Litigation, Food Products Liability, Fraud and Deceit, Government, Hazardous Waste Liability, Head Injury, Health Care, Health Insurance Defense, Insurance Bad Faith Defense, Labor and Employment, Legal Malpractice Defense, Libel, Slander and Defamation, Life Insurance Defense, Manufacturers Liability, Medical Malpractice, Natural Resources, Negligence, Nursing Home Litigation, Personal Injury, Pesticide Litigation, Physicians Licensing, Pollution, Premises Liability, Products Liability, Professional Discipline, Professional Liability, Propane Products Liability, Property Damage Defense, Property Insurance, Real Estate, Recreational Products Liability, School Board Defense, Sexual Harassment Defense, Slip and Fall, Spinal Injury, Subrogation, Torts, Toxic Torts, Transportation, Transportation Law, Workers Compensation, Wrongful Death and Wrongful Termination Defense.
Representative Clients: Continental National American Group; Crum & Forster Group; Fireman's Fund Insurance Cos.; Greyhound Lines, Inc.; Unitrin Insurance Companies; Interstate Insurance Group; National Casualty Insurance Company.
Coeur d'Alene, Idaho Office: 2020 Lakewood Drive, Suite 312, P.O. Box 1758. Telephone: 208-664-9281. Facsimile: 208-664-5380.
Idaho Falls, Idaho Office: 2325 West Broadway, Suite B. Telephone: 208-529-0000. Facsimile: 208-529-0005.
See Professional Biographies, BOISE, IDAHO

Racine Olson Nye Budge & Bailey , Chartered, (AV)
101 South Capitol Boulevard, U.S. Bank Plaza, Suite 208, 83702 ⊙
Telephone: 208-395-0011 Fax: 208-433-0167
Email: cja@racinelaw.net URL: http://www.racinelaw.net
Conrad J. Aiken (Resident);—Lisa R. Tanner (Resident); Joshua D. Johnson (Resident).
Litigation, Probate, Real Estate, Corporation, Insurance and Utility Law. Creditor's Bankruptcy.
Pocatello, Idaho Office: 201 East Center, P.O. Box 1391, 83201-1391. Telephone: 208-232-6101. Fax: 208-232-6109.
See Professional Biographies, BOISE, IDAHO

Rader, Dale A. '19 '51 C.628 L.767 LL.B.
(adm. in OR; not adm. in ID) 1687 E. Silverspot Lane‡
Ramey, Fred L., (BV) '48 '74 C&L.336 B.S., J.D. [F.L.Ramey]
Ramey, Fred L., P.A., (BV) 815 Park Boulevard, Suite 270
Ramirez, Victor A. '58 '84 C.475 B.A. L.285 J.D.
(adm. in WA; not adm. in ID) Chief Coun., I.R.S.
Randolph, Scott E. '77 '03 C.628 B.S. L.846 J.D. [Ⓐ Greener B.S.]
Rasmussen, Lisa B. '63 '94 C&L.101 B.A., J.D. [Wilson M.&R.]
Rassier, Phillip J., (BV) '47 '75 C&L.336 B.S., J.D. Dep. Atty. Gen.
Rayhill, Philip Richard '57 '85 C.478 B.A. L.336 J.D. Law Clk., U.S. Dist. J.
Reardon, Michael J., (BV) '57 '85 C.999 B.A. L.336 J.D. [Reardon]
Reardon Law Offices, (BV) 913 W. River St., Ste. 420
Redford, Hugh '12 '34 C&L.336 LL.B. 838 Warm Springs Ave.‡
Redford, Mack A., (AV) '37 '67 C&L.336 B.S., J.D. [Ⓒ Elam&B.]
Reichelt, Jason D., (BV) '71 '96 C.629 B.A. L.188 J.D. Dep. Co. Pros.
Reid, James G., (BV) '— '71 C&L.336 B.S., J.D. [Ringert C.]
Reilly-Pirnic, Heather C., (BV) '— '96 C.1193 B.A. L.336 J.D. Dep. Pros. Atty.
Reinhardt, G. Rey, IV '76 '00 C&L.336 B.S., J.D. [Ⓐ Greener B.S.]
Reuling, Michael F. '46 '71 C.118 B.A. L.477 J.D. Albertson's, Inc.
Reynard, Janine P. '66 '99 C.651 B.S. L.285 J.D. [Ⓐ Hawley T.E.&H.]
Reynoldson, Lauren Maiers, (BV) '71 '98 C.911 B.A. L.285 J.D. [Ⓐ Spink B.]

Rice, Edward W. '11 '38 C&L.378 B.S., J.D.
(adm. in KS; not adm. in ID) Pres. & CEO, Doctors Bus. Bur., Inc.‡
Rice, Robert E., (BV) . . . '72 '98 C.335 B.A. L.336 J.D. [🄰 Neal&U.]
Richards, Morgan W., Jr., (AV) . . . '47 '76 C.172 B.A. L.336 J.D. [🄲 Moffatt T.B.R.&F.]
Richardson, Brad S. . . . '— '05 C.101 B.A. L.336 J.D. [🄰 Quane S.]
Richardson, Harry D., (BV) . . . '51 '76 C.629 B.S. L.336 J.D. 413 W. Jefferson
Riley, Richard A., (AV) . . . '50 '77 C.197 B.A. L.208 J.D. [Hawley T.E.&H.]
Ringert, William F., (AV) . . . '— '62 C.336 B.S. L.802 LL.B. [🄲 Ringert C.]

Ringert Clark, Chartered, (AV)
455 South Third Street, 83702
Telephone: 208-342-4591 Fax: 208-342-4657
Email: reception@ringertclark.com URL: http://www.ringertclark.com
Laura E. Burri; Jeffrey R. Christenson; D. Blair Clark; David Hammerquist; Charles L. Honsinger; James P. Kaufman; James G. Reid; Daniel V. Steenson. Associates: Jennifer Reid Mahoney; S. Bryce Farris; David P. Claiborne; Jon C. Gould. Of Counsel: William F. Ringert; Allyn L. Sweeney.
General and Civil Trial Practice, Administrative, Agricultural, Bankruptcy, Appeals, Condemnation, Corporation, Insurance, Family Law, Insurance Defense, Legislative, Negligence, Personal Injury, Probate, Real Estate, Tort, Water, Environmental and Workers Compensation Law.
Hammett, Idaho Office: P.O. Box 105, 83627. Telephone: 208-366-7993. Fax: 208-366-7994.
See Professional Biographies, BOISE, IDAHO

Rippee, Corey J. . . . '77 '03 C&L.336 B.S., J.D. [🄰 Eberle,B.K.T.M.&J.]
Risch, James E., (AV) . . . '43 '68 C&L.336 B.S., J.D. [Risch G.I.G.]
Risch Goss Insinger Gustavel, (AV) . . . 407 West Jefferson Street
Ritti, Eugene A., (AV) . . . '48 '73 C.884 A.B. L.228 J.D. [Hawley T.E.&H.]
Roath, Paul D. '— '01 C.560 B.S. L.273 J.D.
(adm. in DC; not adm. in ID; Pat.) [🄲 Technology]
Roats, Richard T., (BV) . . . '64 '90 C.506 B.A. L.950 J.D. 9300 Overland Road
Roberts, Barbara J. . . . '43 '75 C.1056 B.S. L.596 J.D. 1701 N. 21st St.‡
Roberts, R. Lee '41 '78 C.800 B.S. L.1137 J.D.
(adm. in CA; not adm. in ID) [🄲 Orndorff]
Robinson, Sharla D. . . . '70 '97 C.1193 B.A. L.336 J.D. State Indus. Comm.
Rock, R. B., (AV) . . . '38 '65 C.999 B.A. L.336 LL.B. [Moffatt T.B.R.&F.]
Roden, William C., (AV) . . . '29 '53 C&L.336 B.A., LL.B. [Hopkins R.C.H.&H.]
Rodriguez, Joanne P., (BV) . . . '53 '78 C.770 B.S. L.1067 J.D. Asst. U.S. Atty.
Roe, Michael O. . . . '64 '89 C.336 B.A. L.178 J.D. [Moffatt T.B.R.&F.]
Roosevelt, Theodore Steven '47 '88 C.878 M.D. L.1137 J.D.
(adm. in CA; not adm. in ID) 6324 N. Buckley Pl.
Rose, Dana H. . . . '62 '93 C.1375 B.S. L.174 J.D. [🄰 Beeman&Assoc.]
Rossman, Eric S., (BV) . . . '66 '92 C.1193 B.B.A. L.336 J.D. [Rossman]
Rossman Law Group, (BV) . . . 737 N. 7th St.
Rowan, Paul G. . . . '58 '84 C.335 B.A. L.950 J.D. Albertson's, Inc.
Rubel, Ilana Simone . . . '— '97 C.276 B.A. L.309 J.D. [🄰 Fenwick&W.]
Rubin, S. Richard, (AVⓉ) '45 '69 C&L.352 B.A., J.D.
Sr. Trial Atty., Fed. Defenders Off.
Rubocki, Melanie . . . '— '97 C.659 B.S.,B.A. L.602 J.D. [🄲 Perkins C.]
Runft, John L., (AV) . . . '37 '65 C.335 B.A. L.145 J.D. [Runft&S.]
Runft, Karl J. . . . '75 '02 C.145 B.A. L.966 J.D. [Runft&S.]

Runft & Steele Law Offices, PLLC, (AV) 🅱🅱
1020 West Main Street, Suite 400, 83702-5745
Telephone: 208-333-8506 Fax: 208-343-3246 URL: http://www.runftlaw.com
Email: jlrunft@runftlaw.com URL: http://www.lawyers.com/runftlaw.com
John L. Runft; Jon M. Steele; Karl J. Runft.
General Civil and Trial Practice in all Courts with emphasis on Business, Corporate, Contract, Administrative Law; Business Litigation, Bad Faith Insurance Defense.
See Professional Biographies, BOISE, IDAHO

Rutherford, Richard Stephen, (BV) . . . '69 '96 C.1032 B.S. L.336 J.D. Asst. City Atty.
Ryan, Maureen G. . . . '79 '04 C&L.285 B.A., J.D. [🄰 Holland&H.]
Ryden, Matthew J. . . . '68 '02 C.770 B.S.C. L.336 J.D. [🄰 Hall,F.O.&B.]
Sahlberg, John T., (AV) . . . '53 '81 C.309 A.B. L.276 J.D. Boise Cascade Corp.
Saldin, Thomas R., (AV) '46 '74
C.118 B.A. L.150 J.D. Exec. V.P. & Gen. Coun., Albertson's, Inc.
Salladay, G. Lance, (AV) . . . '51 '76 C&L.336 B.S., J.D. 222 N. 13th St., Ste. 250
Sallaz, Dennis J., (BV) . . . '40 '65 C&L.336 LL.B. [Sallaz]
Sallaz Law Offices, Chtd., (BV) . . . 1000 S. Roosevelt
Salmi, Christine M. . . . '67 '97 C.338 B.A. L.336 J.D. [🄰 Perkins C.]
Samuelsen, David R., (BV) . . . '32 '63 C&L.336 LL.B. 1611 W. Jefferson St.
Samuelson, Paul W., (BV) . . . '61 '89 C.182 B.A. L.336 J.D. Staff Atty., Albertson's, Inc.
Sanchez, Ernesto G. '45 '73
C.1032 B.B.A. L.336 J.D. Exec. Dir., Idaho Legal Aid Servs., Inc.
Sandmeyer, Gregory J. . . . '57 '83 C&L.1193 B.S.Ed., J.D. 2902 S. Swallowtail Ln.
Sarti, Janine . . . '— '88 C.413 B.A. L.285 J.D. St. Luke's Reg. Med. Ctr., Ltd.
Sasser, David, (AV) '49 '83
C.1279 B.C.S. L.464 J.D. 3100 South Vista Avenue, Suite 200
Sasser, M. Michael, (AV) . . . '48 '74 C.446 B.A. L.336 J.D. [Sasser&I.]

Sasser & Inglis, P.C., (AV)
3100 South Vista Avenue, Suite 200, 83705
Telephone: 208-344-8474 Fax: 208-344-8479
Email: si@sasseringlis.com URL: http://www.sasseringlis.com
M. Michael Sasser; Patrick J. Inglis;—Clay M. Shockley; Jason G. Dykstra; Andrew E. Schepp.
General Civil, Trial and Appellate Practice. Business and Corporate Practice, Civil Rights, Construction, Domestic, Employment, Environmental, Governmental, Insurance, Labor, Negligence, Personal Injury, Products Liability, Professional Liability, Real Estate Law and Transportation.
Representative Clients: Alcoa; Allstate Insurance Co.; American Agency Life Insurance Co.; American Family Life Insurance Co.; American Hardware Mutual Insurance Co.; Amex Life Assurance Co.; Attorney Liability Protection Society, Inc.; Beneficial Finance Co.; Boise Air Service; CNA Insurance Cos.
See Professional Biographies, BOISE, IDAHO

Scanlan, James E., (BV) . . . '40 '65 C.629 B.S. L.336 J.D. P.O. Box 8956
Scanlan, Kevin J., (BV) . . . '70 '96 C.121 B.B.A. L.1358 J.D. [Hall,F.O.&B.]
Scanlin, Steven F., (BV) . . . '45 '84 C.999 B.S.Ed. L.336 J.D. [Scanlin]
Scanlin Law Offices, (BV) . . . P.O. Box 2631
Schepp, Andrew E. . . . '71 '00 C.931 B.A. L.336 J.D. [🄰 Sasser&I.]
Schild, Raymond D., (BV) . . . '52 '82 C&L.209 B.A., J.D. 6550 Emerald, Suite 108
Schindele, Michael L., (BV) . . . '49 '75 C.1193 B.A. L.336 J.D. 1475 W. Hays St., Ste. A
Schmidt, Richard A. . . . '45 '78 C.768 B.A. L.765 J.D. Mag., 4th Dist. Ct.
Schmitz, Randall L. . . . '70 '99 C&L.950 B.S., J.D. [🄰 Anderson,J.&H.]
Schossberger, Steven F., (BV) . . . '70 '95 C.990 B.A. L.767 J.D. [Hawley T.E.&H.]
Schroeder, Gerald F. . . . '39 '65 C.335 B.A. L.309 J.D. Supm. Ct. Jus.
Schroeder, John T., (BV) . . . '56 '81 C.1058 B.A. L.336 J.D. [Schroeder&L.]
Schroeder, W. Alan, (AV) . . . '61 '86 C.1058 B.B.A. L.678 J.D. [Schroeder&L.]

Schroeder & Lezamiz, Law Offices, L.L.P., (AV)
447 West Myrtle, P.O. Box 267, 83701
Telephone: 208-384-1627 Fax: 208-384-1833
URL: http://www.schroederlezamiz.com
Members of Firm: John T. Schroeder; Margaret M. Lezamiz; W. Alan Schroeder.
(This Listing Continued)

Schroeder & Lezamiz, Law Offices, L.L.P. (Continued)
Public Land Law, Civil Litigation, Family Law, Bankruptcy (Creditors), Probate and Wills, Real Estate, Plaintiff's Personal Injury and Workmens Compensation, Timber Trespass.
See Professional Biographies, BOISE, IDAHO

Schuster, Steven J. . . . '53 '85 C.339 B.S. L.629 J.D. Dep. Atty Gen
Schwager, Sheila R., (BV) . . . '69 '94 C&L.336 B.S., J.D. [Hawley T.E.&H.]
Schwartzman, Alan M. . . . '41 '67 C.976 B.A. L.813 LL.B. Idaho Court of Appeals
Scoggin, Andrew J. '62 '89 C&L.101 B.A., J.D.
(adm. in CA; not adm. in ID) V.P., Human Resources & Labor Rel., Albertson's, Inc.
Scott, Jason D., (CV) . . . '72 '97 C.1032 B.B.A. L.228 J.D. [🄰 Hawley T.E.&H.]
Scott, Larry D., (BV) . . . '51 '77 C.1193 B.A. L.336 J.D. 500 W. Bannock St.
Scrivner, Wes L., (AV) '52 '78
C.1193 B.B.A. L.336 J.D. Asst. Gen. Coun., J.R. Simplot Co.
Sebby, Kenneth M., (BV) '47 '73 C.123 B.A. L.546 J.D.
U.S. Dept. of Interior, Solr. Off.
Seibert, Kail Q. . . . '49 '88 C.684 B.S.B.A. L.1049 J.D. [K.Q.Seibert]
Seibert, Kail Q., P.L.L.C. . . . P.O. Box 6473
Seiniger, Julie Marsh, (BV) . . . '57 '82 C.679 B.S. L.273 J.D. [Seiniger]
Seiniger, William Breck, Jr., (AV) . . . '47 '79 C.454 B.A. L.336 J.D. [Seiniger] ⊙
Seiniger Law Office, (BV) . . . 942 Myrtle St.

Seiniger Law Offices, (AV)
942 West Myrtle, 83702 ⊙
Telephone: 208-345-1000 Fax: 208-345-4700
Email: wbs@seinigerlaw.com URL: http://www.seinigerlaw.com
William Breck Seiniger, Jr.
Personal Injury, Workers Compensation, Employment Discrimination and Harassment, Business Torts, Insurance Disputes.
Seattle, Washington Office: 601 Union Street, Suite 4200, 98101. Telephone: 208-345-1000. Fax: 208-345-1000.
See Professional Biographies, BOISE, IDAHO

Semanko, Norman M., (BV) . . . '66 '93 C.336 B.S. L.276 J.D. 205 N. 10th Street
Setzke, Raymond W., (BV) . . . '46 '76 C&L.260 B.S., J.D. [Setzke]
Setzke Law Office, (BV) . . . 1487 West Hayes
Shah, Faisal '60 '87 C.174 B.S. L.767 J.D.
(adm. in CA; not adm. in ID) Chmn., Mark Monitor
Sharp, Lincoln V., Jr., (AV) '52 '79
C.235 B.A. L.1161 J.D. V.P., Real Estate Law, Albertson's, Inc.
Shaver, Robert L., (BV) '50 '95 C.1079 B.A. L.336 J.D.
[Dykas,S.&N.] (See Pat. Sect.)
Sheehan, Karen O. . . . '66 '95 C.105 B.A. L.273 J.D. [🄰 McAnaney P.&Assoc.]
Sheils, Max M., Jr., (AV) . . . '50 '75 C.285 B.B.A. L.1032 J.D. [Ellis,B.&S.]
Shepard, Ann K., (BV) . . . '58 '89 C.1193 B.B.A. L.336 J.D. 200 N. 4th St., Ste. 302
Shockley, Clay M., (CV) . . . '62 '93 C.1193 B.A. L.336 J.D. [🄰 Sasser&I.]
Shoemaker, Fredric V., (AV) . . . '48 '74 C&L.546 B.S., J.D. [Greener B.S.]
Shoufler, Bret W., (BV) . . . '67 '95 C&L.336 J.D. [🄰]
Shurtliff, M. Karl, (BV) . . . '39 '68 C.1032 B.A. L.336 J.D. P.O. Box 1652
Silva, Karen L., (CV) . . . '58 '99 C.1193 B.A. L.336 J.D. [Silva]
Silva Law Office, (CV) . . . 380 S. 4th Street, Suite 203
Simboli, Christopher '62 '97 C.034 B.A. L.215 J.D.
Sr. Tech. Lic. Coun., Micron Technology, Inc.
Simko, John S., (AV) . . . '39 '66 C&L.336 B.A., J.D. [Moffatt T.B.R.&F.]
Simmons, Jon T., (BV) . . . '68 '94 C.1032 B.B.A. L.336 J.D. [Greener B.S.]
Simmons, Lane R. '59 '93 C.101 B.S. L.336 J.D.
Sr. Coun., Hewlett-Packard Co. (Pat.)
Simons, Clay G., Jr. '28 '57 L.809 LL.B.
(adm. in CA; not adm. in ID) Pres., Sioux Veneer Panel Co.
Simpson, John K., (BV) . . . '57 '90 C.336 B.S. L.1051 J.D. [Barker R.&S.]
Sims, John Rex, Jr., (AVⓉ) '50 '75 C&L.502 B.A., J.D.
(adm. in MO; not adm. in ID) Gen. Coun., Albertsons
Sinclair, J. Walter, (AV) . . . '53 '78 C.813 B.A. L.336 J.D. [Stoel R.]

Sirhall, Lawrence G., Jr., (BV) '58 '84 C.336 B.A. L.602 J.D.
Imperial Plaza, 200 North 3rd, Suite 8, 83702
Telephone: 208-342-2444 Fax: 208-342-2676
Email: sirhalllaw@aol.com URL: http://www.sirhalllaw.com
Personal Injury, Tax, Criminal Tax Defense, Real Estate, Adoption, Neck and Back Injuries, Slip and Fall, Car Accidents.
See Professional Biographies, BOISE, IDAHO

Sisson, Peter C., (BV) . . . '59 '88 C.861 B.A. L.910 J.D. 605 E. Highland View
Skinner, David Rupert, (BV) . . . '53 '86 C.1193 B.A. L.336 J.D. 6098 Tonkin Dr.
Skinner, Gardner W., Jr., (AV) . . . '44 '70 C.770 B.A. L.336 J.D. [Cantrill,S.S.&K.]
Skinner, Richard A., (AV) . . . '45 '70 C.813 B.A. L.145 J.D. [Skinner F.]
Skinner Fawcett, (AV) . . . 515 South 6th Street
Slaughter, W. Ben, III, (CV) . . . '74 '00 C.878 B.S. L.336 J.D. [🄰 Elam&B.]
Slaughter, Wayne B., Jr., (AV) '44 '70
C.686 B.A. L.208 J.D. Asst. Gen. Coun., J.R. Simplot Co.
Sleeper, Bradley J. '51 '76 C.602 B.A. L.494 J.D.
(adm. in MN; not adm. in ID) Prof. of Bus. Law, Boise State Univ.
Sloan, Eric R. . . . '72 '01 C.635 B.A. L.285 J.D. [Sloan]
Sloan Law Office, PLLC . . . 1020 Main Street, Suite 210
Smith, Bruce, (AV) . . . '50 '85 C.10 B.S. L.336 J.D. [Moore S.B.&T.]
Smith, Clay R., (AVⓉ) . . . '48 '75 C.893 B.A. L.208 J.D. Solr., State Atty. Gen. Off.
Smith, Ellen N. . . . '74 '99 C&L.336 B.S., J.D. [🄰 Jones G.H.F.&E.]
Smith, Lawrence G., (BV) . . . '55 '86 C.1193 B.A. L.228 J.D. Pub. Def.
Smith, Margery W., Law Office of, (BVⓉ) '39 '80
C.298 B.A. L.184 J.D. 500 West Bannock Street
Smith, Marsha H. . . . '50 '80 C.1032 B.S. L.911 J.D. Comr., Pub. Util. Comm.
Smith, Ray E., (BV) . . . '54 '81 C.112 A.B. L.767 J.D. 515 S.6th St.
Smith, Richard G., (AV) . . . '52 '79 C.336 B.A. L.276 J.D. [Hawley T.E.&H.]
Smith, Tyler D., (BV) . . . '— '94 C.335 B.A. L.950 J.D. 2402 W. Jefferson St.
Smith, Vernon K. . . . '46 '71 C.285 B.A. L.336 J.D. 1900 Main St.
Smylie, Robert E., (AV) . . . '14 '41 C.335 A.B. L.273 J.D. Gov.
Sneed, Bradley V. . . . '71 '99 C.475 B.S. L.596 J.D. [🄰 Givens P.]
Snyder, Nicole . . . '75 '01 C.1049 B.A. L.477 J.D. [🄰 Holland&H.]
Snyder, William R., (AV) . . . '46 '72 C&L.336 B.S., J.D. [W.R.Snyder&Assoc.]
Snyder, William R., & Associates, P.A., (AV) . . . 520 West Franklin Street, Upper Level
Solis, Beatrice E. '60 '88 C.93 B.A. L.813 J.D.
Sr. Asst. Gen. Coun., Micron Technology, Inc.
Sorensen, Dean C., (CV) . . . '72 '99 C.878 B.S. L.336 J.D. [Cantrill,S.S.&K.]
Southcombe, R. Michael, (AV) . . . '35 '62 C&L.336 B.A., LL.B. [🄲 Elam&B.]
Spangler, Theodore V., Jr., (BV) . . . '45 '70 L.336 J.D. ID Atty. Gen. Off.
Sperry, Skip . . . '66 '93 C.336 B.S. L.190 J.D. [🄰 Penland M.G.]
Spink, Michael T., (AV) . . . '50 '78 C.813 B.A. L.208 J.D. [Spink B.]

Spink Butler, LLP, (AV)
251 East Front Street, Suite 200, P.O. Box 639, 83701
Telephone: 208-388-1000 Fax: 208-388-1001
Email: contact@sb-attorneys.com URL: http://www.sb-attorneys.com
Michael T. Spink; JoAnn C. Butler;—Lauren Maiers Reynoldson.
Commercial Real Estate, Zoning, Planning and Land Use, Business Law, Commercial Litigation.
See Professional Biographies, BOISE, IDAHO

Spurling, David E., (AV) '58 '84 C.335 B.A. L.336 J.D. Asst. Gen. Coun., J.R. Simplot Co.
Squyres, B. Newal, (AV) '46 '72 C&L.845 B.A., J.D. [Holland&H.]
Stacey, Richard L., Jr. '70 '03 C.1193 B.A. L.878 J.D. [(A) Meuleman M.]
Stahman, Myrna A. I., (BV) '46 '74 C.494 B.A. L.336 J.D. Dep. Atty. Gen.
Stahman, Robert W., (BV) '44 '73 C.1207 B.A. L.336 J.D. V.P., Gen. Coun. & Secy., Idaho Power Co.
Stanger, Kim C., (BV) '62 '90 C&L.101 B.A., J.D. [Hawley T.E.&H.]
Stark, Paul J., (CV) '70 '99 C.1193 B.A. L.45 J.D. [(A) Anderson,J.&H.]
Stecher, David J. '47 '75 C.813 A.B. L.1188 J.D. 1020 W. Main St., Ste. 400
Steele, Carolyn S., (CV) '43 '82 C&L.101 B.A., J.D. 4456 Quail Point Ct.
Steele, Jon M., (BV) '50 '76 C.352 B.A. L.221 J.D. [Runft&S.]
Steenkolk, Tony J., (AV) '60 '90 C.629 B.S. L.950 J.D. 1111 West Jefferson Street
Steenson, Daniel V., (BV) '— '91 C.747 B.A. L.174 J.D. [Ringert C.]
Stefanic, Michael P., II, (BV) '63 '89 C.190 B.A. L.336 J.D. [Anderson,J.&H.]
Sticklen, Kathryn A., (AV) '46 '76 C&L.878 B.A., J.D. 200 West Front Street
Stidham, Erik F., (BV) '64 '91 C.36 B.A. L.893 J.D. [Greener B.S.]
Stoddard, Michael M., (BV) '59 '85 C.605 A.B. L.880 J.D. [Hawley T.E.&H.]

Stoel Rives LLP, (AV)
101 S. Capitol Boulevard Suite 1900, 83702-5958 ⊙
Telephone: 208-389-9000 Facsimile: 208-389-9040
URL: http://www.stoel.com
Resident Members: Kevin J. Beaton; Paul M. Boyd; Mary S. Hobson; Quentin M. Knipe; Krista K. McIntyre; Kris Ormseth; J. Walter Sinclair. Resident Associates: Bradley J. Dixon; Nicole C. Hancock; Marla S. Henken; Teresa A. Hill; Christopher Pooser; Gregory C. Tollefson; Samia E. McCall (Not admitted in ID). Of Counsel: Mark S. Geston; James C. Dale; Dale G. Higer.
General Practice and Litigation in State and Federal Courts; Corporate Transactions; Finance; Securities; Labor and Employment Law; Construction; Products Liability; Real Estate and Development; Environmental; State and Local Taxation; Federal Taxation; Trusts and Estates; Banking; Commercial Law; Bankruptcy and Secured Lending; Legislative Affairs.
Portland, Oregon Office: Suite 2600, 900 S.W. Fifth Avenue. Telephone: 503-224-3380.
Seattle, Washington Office: Suite 3600, One Union Square, 600 University. Telephone: 206-624-0900.
Vancouver, Washington Office: Suite 725, 805 Broadway. Telephone: 360-699-5900.
Salt Lake City, Utah Office: Suite 1100, One Utah Center, 201 South Main Street. Telephone: 801-328-3131.
San Francisco, California Office: 111 Sutter Street, Suite 700. Telephone: 415-617-8900.
Sacramento, California Office: 770 L Street, Suite 800. Telephone: 916-447-0700.
Tahoe City, California Office: 3000 N. Lake Boulevard, Suite 1, P.O. Box 7336. Telephone: 530-583-2116.
Fresno, California Office: 1233 W. Shaw Avenue, Suite 103. Telephone: 559-228-9900.
See Professional Biographies, BOISE, IDAHO

Stoppello, Frank W., (AV) '43 '69 C&L.336 B.S., J.D. 620 W. Hays St.
Storti, P. Craig, (AV) '46 '72 C.336 B.S. L.1065 J.D. V.P., Litigation & Claims, Washington Group International, Inc.
Stout, Chas. S. '06 '31 L.878 J.D. 707 Michael St.‡
Stover, Richard W. '74 '03 C.335 B.A. L.336 J.D. [(A) Eberle,B.K.T.M.&J.]
Stoy, Michael S., Law Offices of, (CV) '46 '87 C.1193 B.A. L.336 J.D. 222 N. 13th Street
Strand, Ivan '35 '59 C&L.813 A.B., J.D. 815 Park Blvd.‡
Street, Paul S., (AV) '48 '73 C.335 B.A. L.911 J.D. Sr. VP, Chf. Adm. Offr., Gen. Coun. & Corp. Secy., Building Materials Holding Corp.
Strickling, Douglas K., (BV) '57 '84 C.285 B.A. L.336 J.D. Dep. City Atty.
Strong, Clive J., (AV) '52 '78 C&L.336 B.S., J.D. Dep. Atty. Gen.
Strother, Jeffrey A., (BV) '50 '75 C.976 B.A. L.174 J.D. [Strother]
Strother Law Office, (BV) 200 North Fourth, Suite 30
Stubbs, Richard L., (AV) '— '84 C.118 B.A. L.596 J.D. [Quane S.]
Stubbs, Tyra H., (BV) '— '84 C.118 B.A. L.1051 J.D. [Quane S.]
Stukel, John D. '64 '92 C.477 B.B.A. L.1066 J.D. Asst. Gen. Coun., Micron Technology, Inc.
Stutzman, Weldon B., (BV) '56 '84 C.1193 B.A. L.336 J.D. Dept. of Health & Welfare
Suarez, Stephen A. '69 '94 C.628 B.S. L.629 J.D. Assoc. Gen. Coun., Micron Technology, Inc.
Sullins, Tony '66 '92 C.798 B.S. L.972 J.D. (adm. in WY; not adm. in ID) U.S. Dept. of Interior, Off. of Solr.
Sutton, John Eric, (BV) '46 '77 C.336 B.A. L.192 J.D. [J.E.Sutton&Assoc.]
Sutton, J.E., and Associates, (BV) 420 West Idaho Street
Swainston, Paul C. '66 '96 C.101 B.A. L.285 J.D. 6550 W. Emerald, Ste. 108
Swanstrom, Roger '30 '56 C&L.336 B.A., LL.B. (Ret.) Ct. of App. J.‡
Swartley, David M. '70 '98 C.678 B.A. L.336 J.D. [(A) Evans K.]
Swartz, Eric B. '73 '01 C.877 B.S. L.862 J.D. [(A) Blackburn&J.]
Swartz, Jennifer A. '75 '01 C.623 B.A. L.862 J.D. [(A) Hall,F.O.&B.]
Sweeney, Allyn L., (AV) '— '80 C.1193 B.A. L.336 J.D. [(C) Ringert C.]
Swinehart, Thomas H. '48 '75 C.1066 B.A. L.770 J.D. Dep. Atty. Gen.
Sykes, Jeff R., (BV) '67 '94 C.147 B.A. L.285 J.D. [Meuleman M.]
Talboy, Frank L., (BV) '48 '78 C.734 A.B. L.190 J.D. 200 S. Villa Pl.
Talboy, Robert W., (BV) '59 '86 C.1193 B.A. L.336 J.D. [Ellsworth K.&T.]
Talbutt, Glenda M. '63 '97 C.790 B.S. L.629 J.D. [(A) Anderson,J.&H.]
Tanner, Lisa R. '79 '03 L.999 J.D. [(A) Racine O.N.B.&B.]
Tappen, Diane M. '59 '84 C&L.336 B.S., J.D. 818 La Cassia Drive
Taylor, Craig G., (BV) '56 '84 C&L.101 B.S., J.D. Assoc. Gen. Coun. & Corp. Secy., Washington Grp. Intl., Inc.

Technology Law Group, LLC
3355 North Five Mile Road, Suite 333, 83713
Telephone: 208-939-4472 Fax: 208-939-5755
Email: info@technologylawgroup.com URL: http://www.technologylawgroup.com
Emile Loza. Associate: Scott R. Cleere. Special Counsel: Paul D. Roath (Not admitted in ID).
Languages: Chinese, Korean, Japanese, Spanish, German, French and English.
Intellectual Property Licensing, International Business Transactions and Trade, Intellectual Property, Internet and E-Commerce.
See Professional Biographies, BOISE, IDAHO

Temple, Rondee '68 '99 C&L.336 B.A., J.D. Law Clk.
Tharp, Stanley J., (BV) '61 '88 C.1032 B.A. L.336 J.D. [Eberle,B.K.T.M.&J.]
Tharp, William C., (AVⓉ) '48 '73 C&L.950 B.A., J.D. [(C) Greener B.S.]
Thiel, W. John, Jr., (BV) '61 '89 C&L.336 B.A., J.D. P.O. Box 1634
Thiry, Krista Dawn, (CV) '75 '00 C&L.336 B.S., J.D. [(A) Bevis,C.&J.]
Thomas, Bruce L., (AV) '48 '74 C.939 B.A. L.208 J.D. [(C) Hopkins R.C.H.&H.]
Thomas, Eugene C., (AV) '31 '54 C&L.178 A.B., J.D. [(C) Moffatt T.B.R.&F.]
Thomas, Evelyn B. '46 '78 C.043 B.A. L.629 J.D. Dep. Atty. Gen.
Thomas, H. Barton '65 '98 C.699 A.B. L.1051 J.D. [(A) Givens P.]
Thomas, Lynn E., (AV) '38 '69 C.1032 B.A. L.273 J.D. 2143 Rockridge Way
Thomas, Michael E., (BV) '52 '83 C.976 B.A. L.336 J.D. [Moffatt T.B.R.&F.]
Thomas, Robert F., (CV) '67 '98 C&L.336 B.S., J.D. [(A) Hawley T.E.&H.]
Thomas, Stephen R., (BV) '53 '78 C.976 A.B. L.178 J.D. [Moffatt T.B.R.&F.]
Thomas, William H., (BV) '44 '77 C.966 B.A. L.1051 J.D. [Huntley P.]
Thompson, James R. '48 '76 C.594 B.A. L.336 J.D. Staff Atty., Idaho Power Co.
Thompson, P. Mark, (AV) '51 '76 C.610 A.B. L.597 J.D. Assoc. Gen. Coun., J.R. Simplot Co.
Thompson, Paul Mark '51 '76 C.610 A.B. L.597 J.D. P.O. Box 27
Thomson, James S., II, (CV) '68 '96 C.260 B.A. L.836 J.D. [(A) Hall,F.O.&B.]
Thomson, Jeffrey A., (AV) '59 '85 C&L.336 B.S., J.D. [Elam&B.]
Thornton, D. John, (AV) '46 '73 C&L.336 B.S., J.D. [Thornton B.]
Thornton Byron, LLP, (AV) 1101 W. River St., Ste 340
Thorpe, Geoffrey L., (BV) '55 '80 C.154 B.A. L.1066 J.D. P.O. Box 36
Tingey, Brent C., (BV) '63 '90 C&L.101 B.A., J.D. Staff Atty., Albertson's, Inc.
Tobiason, Steven J., (BV) '51 '79 C.172 B.A. L.336 J.D. [Kane&T.]
Todd, John B. '54 '80 C.352 B.L.A. L.1187 J.D. 1487 W. Hays St.
Tollefson, Gregory C., (CV) '71 '97 C.336 B.A. L.1065 J.D. [(A) Stoel R.]
Toothman, Richard D., (BV) '46 '74 C.197 A.B. L.336 J.D. Pub. Def. Off.
Toryanski, Kim Wherry '62 '82 C.1175 B.A. L.260 J.D. 512 W Bannock St A
Trabert, Robert L., (BV) '37 '68 C.1032 B.A. L.336 J.D. Chief Legal Coun., Dept. of Trans.
Tracy, Daniel K. '61 '87 C.338 B.A. L.989 J.D. (adm. in IL; not adm. in ID) Dir., Labor Rel., IL Off., Albertson's, Inc.
Trott, Stephen S. '39 '66 C.918 B.A. L.309 LL.B. 550 W. Fort St., Ste. 667‡
Trout, Linda Copple '51 '77 C&L.336 B.A., J.D. Supm. Ct. Jus.
Tschirgi, Scott A., (BV) '58 '90 C.506 B.A. L.950 J.D. [Jones G.H.F.&E.]
Turcke, Paul A., (BV) '65 '93 C.939 B.A. L.336 J.D. [Moore S.B.&T.]
Turnbow, R. M., (AV) '36 '60 C&L.336 B.A., LL.B. [Eberle,B.K.T.M.&J.]
Tway, Faber F. '12 '35 C.335 L.608 J.D. 713 Harcourt Rd.‡
Twedt, Jill M. '— '02 C.335 B.A. L.336 J.D. [(A) Hall,F.O.&B.]
Tyree, Mary W. '71 '97 C.740 B.A. L.950 J.D. City Atty. Off
Tyree, Timothy W., (CV) '70 '97 C.1193 B.A. L.950 J.D. [(A) Hawley T.E.&H.]
Uberuaga, Joseph H., II, (AV) '52 '78 C&L.285 B.A., J.D. [Eberle,B.K.T.M.&J.]
Uhl, Holger, (BV) '63 '93 C.335 B.A. L.950 J.D. [Neal&U.]
Uhling, Terry Tomas, (AV) '55 '80 C.906 B.A. L.546 J.D. Sr. V.P., Secy. & Gen. Coun., J.R. Simplot Co.
Underwood, James S., Jr., (BV) '38 '71 C.362 B.A. L.259 J.D. [J.S.Underwood,Jr.]
Underwood, James S., Jr., A Professional Association, (BV) 605 West Franklin Street
Uranga, Jean R., (AV) '49 '75 C.907 B.A. L.950 J.D. [Uranga&U.]
Uranga, Louis L., (AV) '50 '75 C.335 B.S. L.950 J.D. [Uranga&U.]
Uranga & Uranga, (AV) 714 North 5th Street
Vance, Tracy V., (BV) '67 '96 C&L.878 B.A., J.D. In-House Sr. Counsel, Hawkins Companies
Varin, John Wilkinson (Will) '78 '04 C.635 B.S. L.1065 J.D. [(A) Givens P.]
Vaughn, David, (BV) '42 '73 C.101 B.A. L.1065 J.D. U.S. Dept. of Agric.
Vehlow, John '46 '75 C.846 B.A. L.744 J.D. Mag. J.
Villegas, Lori Ann '73 '98 C&L.285 B.A., J.D. Subrogation Couns., Great West Casualty Company
Villegas, Victor S. '72 '99 C.549 B.A. L.285 J.D. [(A) Evans K.]
Visser, Richard, (BV) '51 '90 C.112 B.A. L.336 J.D. Libr., Idaho State Law Library
von Tagen, William A., (AV) '55 '80 C.508 B.A. L.336 J.D. Atty. Gen. Off.
Wagner, Arnold L., (CV) '72 '97 C.907 B.A. L.911 J.D. [Meuleman M.]
Waldner, Cydni Jo '71 '97 C.309 B.A. L.508 J.D. 1111 West Jefferson Street
Walker, Thomas G., Jr. '45 '76 C.276 B.S. L.336 J.D. [Cosho H.]

Wallace, Robert A., (BV) '50 '76 C.112 B.A. L.1065 J.D.
815 Park Boulevard, Suite 130, 83712
Telephone: 208-342-0100 Fax: 208-343-2069 URL: http://www.rwallacelaw.com
Email: lawyer@idahocrimlaw.com URL: http://www.idahocrimlaw.com
Languages: Espanol.
Criminal Defense, DWI, Drug Crimes, Felonies, Misdemeanors, Traffic Violations, Juvenile, Plaintiffs' Personal Injury, Collections.
See Professional Biographies, BOISE, IDAHO

Walter, Thomas J. '51 '76 C&L.424 B.A., J.D. (adm. in IL; not adm. in ID) V.P., Labor Rel., IL Off., Albertson's, Inc.
Walters, Jesse R., Jr. '38 '63 C&L.336 B.A., LL.B. 451 W. State St.‡
Walters, Matthew L. '75 '02 C.508 B.A. L.336 J.D. [(A) Elam&B.]
Walther, Bret A., (BV) '60 '93 C.161 B.S. L.94 J.D. [Bengoechea,W.]
Walton, Timothy C., (AV) '51 '77 C.879 B.A. L.336 J.D. [Chasan&W.]
Ward, Conley E., (BV) '47 '74 C.178 B.A. L.174 J.D. [Givens P.]
Ward, John C., (AV) '41 '67 C.1032 B.A. L.336 J.D. [Moffatt T.B.R.&F.]
Wardle, Geoffrey M., (CV) '68 '96 C.878 B.A. L.930 J.D. [(A) Hawley T.E.&H.]
Wardwell, William E. '78 '04 C.280 B.B.A. L.228 J.D. [(A) Hawley T.E.&H.]
Ware, Peter W., Jr. '66 '94 C.37 B.A. L.950 J.D. [(A) Eberle,B.K.T.M.&J.]
Wasden, Lawrence G., (AV) '57 '85 C.101 B.A. L.336 J.D. P.O. Box 83720
Watkins, Thomas P. '59 '85 C.560 B.A. L.336 J.D. Dist. J.
Weaver, James C. '44 '70 C&L.336 B.A., J.D. P.O. Box 2597
Webb, Julie A. '— '79 C.602 B.A. L.365 J.D. (adm. in IL; not adm. in ID) Dir., Real Estate Law, IL Off., Albertson's, Inc.
Weeks, Larry F., (BV) '43 '78 C&L.336 B.A., J.D. 2308 North Cole Road, Suite C
Weiser, Hermine E., (BV) '46 '94 C.629 L.999 J.D. Risk Mgmt. Atty., Washington Grp. Intl., Inc.
Weissenberger, Bradley R. '69 '98 L.350 J.D. (adm. in IL; not adm. in ID) Tech. Lic. Coun., Micron Technology, Inc.
Welsh, Stanley W., (AV) '46 '76 C.285 B.A. L.336 J.D. [Cosho H.]
Wendrowski, Wendy Thomas '63 '91 C&L.945 B.A., J.D. [(C) Holland&H.]
West, J. Kevin, (AV) '58 '84 C&L.101 B.A., J.D. [Hall,F.O.&B.]
Westberg, Paul L. (Larry), (AV) '43 '68 C&L.336 B.S., J.D. [Westberg,M.&C.]

Westberg, McCabe & Collins, Chartered, (AV)
The Tullis Building, 516 West Franklin Street, Lower Level, P.O. Box 2836, 83701-2836
Telephone: 208-336-5200 Fax: 208-336-2121
URL: http://www.wmclaw-firm.com
Paul L. (Larry) Westberg; Thomas J. McCabe; William D. Collins. Associate: Christian D. Collins.
General Practice, Real Estate, Probate, Estate Planning, Federal and State Court Civil Litigation, Criminal Defense, White Collar Crimes, Administrative, Business and Corporate Law, Government Contract, Water Rights and Mining Law.
See Professional Biographies, BOISE, IDAHO

Westergard, W. David, (AV) '61 '88 C&L.101 B.S., J.D. (adm. in TX; not adm. in ID; Pat.) Chf. Coun., Pat. Litig. & Lic, Micron Technology, Inc.
Weston, Richard E., (BV) '35 '62 C&L.336 B.A., LL.B. [Weston]
Weston Law Offices, (BV) 413 W. Jefferson
Wetherell, Michael E., (AV) '45 '72 C.336 B.S. L.273 J.D. [Hyde,W.&H.]
Wetherell, Robert T., (AV) '58 '83 C.723 B.A. L.336 J.D. [Brassey,W.C.&G.]
Whelan, William S. '59 '86 C.976 B.A. L.629 J.D. Idaho Conser. League

Whipple, Deborah ......'58 '84 C.770 B.S. L.911 J.D. [Ⓐ Nevin,B.&M.]
White, Amy G., (BV) ......'67 '92 C.645 B.S. L.464 J.D. [Anderson,J.&H.]
White, Robert B., (CV) ......'63 '92 C&L.336 B.S., J.D. [Givens P.]
Widman, Thomas D., (CV) ......'61 '89 C&L.336 B.S., J.D. 202 N. 9th St.
Wigle, W. Scott, (AV) ......'54 '81 C.1193 B.A. L.336 J.D. [Bowen&B.]
Wilde, Anne B. ......'70 '95 C&L.336 B.S., J.D. Labor Rel. Rep., Albertson's, Inc.
Williams, Daniel E., (BV) ......'62 '88 C.976 B.A. L.477 J.D. [Huntley P.]
Williams, H. Brent ......'— '95 C.502 B.A. L.734 J.D. [Ⓐ Brady]
Williams, Linda J. ......'49 '80 C.112 B.A. L.336 J.D. Idaho Legal Aid Servs., Inc.
Williams, Marcia E. '56 '90 C.37 B.A. L.608 J.D.
(adm. in CO; not adm. in ID)
V.P., Diversity & Employ. Law, AZ Off., Albertson's, Inc.‡
Williams, Mikel H. ......'46 '69 C&L.336 LL.B. U.S. Mag. J.
Williams, Robert J., (BV) ......'54 '84 C.1109 B.A. L.336 J.D. 1401 Shoreline Dr., Ste. 2
Williams, Ronald L., (AV) ......'53 '79 C.336 B.S. L.596 J.D. 1015 West Hays Street
Williamson, Darla S. ......'46 '72 C.950 B.A. L.336 J.D. Fourth Judicial District Ct.
Wilper, Ronald J., (BV) ......'54 '88 C.1193 B.A. L.336 J.D. Dist. J.
Wilson, Brent T. ......'— '02 C.877 B.S. L.950 J.D. [Ⓐ Hall,F.O.&B.]
Wilson, Jeffrey M., (AV) ......'49 '74 C.208 B.S.B.A. L.607 J.D. [Wilson M.&R.]
Wilson, Jon R. ......'55 '82 C.375 B.S. L.900 J.D. 4614 Emerald St.

Wilson McColl & Rasmussen, (AV)
420 Washington Street, P.O. Box 1544, 83701
Telephone: 208-345-9100 FAX: 208-384-0442
Email: jeff@wilsonmccoll.com URL: http://www.wilsonmccoll.com
Jeffrey M. Wilson; Brian F. McColl; Lisa B. Rasmussen.
General Civil Practice, Bankruptcy, Real Property, Insurance, Commercial Litigation, Agricultural, Farm, Family Law, Personal Injury, Estate, Probate, Commercial Transactions, Collections, Communications and Media Law, Professional Liability, Creditors Rights, Business Law, Trials.
Representative Clients: A & J Construction, Inc.; Communication Workers of America, Local # 8103; Employer Re-Insurance.Pure-gro Company; Engineered Structures, Inc.; Higgins and Rutledge Insurance Co., Inc.; Jess W. Swan Insurance Agency; John H. Crowther, Inc.; Transamerica Commercial Finance Corp.

See Professional Biographies, BOISE, IDAHO

Winer, Rachel Jane ......'73 '98 C.1369 B.A. L.596 J.D. United Vision for Idaho
Winmill, B. Lynn ......'52 '77 C.1032 B.A. L.309 J.D. Dist. Ct. J., U.S. Dist. Ct.
Wishney, David E., (AV) ......'49 '77 C&L.336 B.S., J.D. 300 W. Myrtle, Suite 200
Wohlers, Everett T. '46 '76 C.870 B.S. L.846 J.D.
Dir., Research & Market Develop., Natl. Info. Consortium
Wolf, Colette F., (CV) ......'62 '91 C.1278 B.S. L.1206 J.D. 1111 West Jefferson Street
Woodard, Wade L. ......'70 '97 C&L.101 B.A., J.D. [Greener B.S.]
Woychick, Nicholas J., (BV) ......'59 '88 C.1193 B.A. L.336 J.D. 877 Main St., Suite 1000
Woychick, Stephen T., (BV) ......'62 '90 C.1193 B.A. L.494 J.D. 350 North Ninth
Wreggelsworth, Robert A., (BV) ......'60 '89 C&L.336 B.S., J.D. 623 W. Hayes
Wyman, Jon N. ......'39 '64 C&L.911 B.A., LL.B. 2401 Regan Ave.‡
Wynkoop, David E., (BV) ......'53 '79 C.1193 B.A. L.911 J.D. Gen. Coun.
Yee-Wallace, Cynthia L. ......'78 '03 C&L.336 B.S., J.D. [Ⓐ Davison,C.C.&C.]
Yorgason, Christopher E. ......'69 '98 C&L.101 B.S., J.D. [Ⓐ Moore S.B.&T.]
York, Mary V., (BV) ......'68 '94 C.285 B.A. L.336 J.D. [Ⓒ Holland&H.]
Yost, Terri R., (CV) ......'72 '98 C.800 B.A. L.336 J.D. [Jones G.H.F.&E.]
Young, Gray Anthony, (BV) '49 '81
C.174 B.A. L.208 J.D. Assoc. Gen. Coun., J.R. Simplot Co.
Young, Merlin S. ......'18 '46 C.939 A.B. L.800 LL.B. Ret. U.S. Bkrptcy. J.
Youngstrom, Robert C. ......'35 '60 C&L.336 B.S., J.D. Chf. Ref., Industrial Comm.
Ysursa, Benito T. ......'49 '74 C.285 A.B. L.734 J.D. Chf. Dep. Secy. of State
Zahn, Colleen D., (CV) ......'— '00 C&L.336 B.S., J.D. [Ⓐ Naylor&H.]
Zaleha, Bernard Daley, (BV) ......'57 '88 C.1110 B.A. L.1051 J.D. 2119 N. 33rd Street
Zokan, Tammy A. ......'70 '96 C.963 B.S. L.336 J.D. [Ⓐ Moore S.B.&T.]

BONNERS FERRY, * 2,515, *Boundary Co.*

Gabourie, Fred W., Sr. ......'22 '65 C.426 B.S. L.809 J.D. P.O. Box 1269
Harden, Quentin F. ......'45 '72 C&L.336 B.S., J.D. Mag. J.
McGuire, Thomas K., (AVⓉ) ......'32 '66 C.112 B.A. L.1066 LL.B. P.O. Box 328
Shelton, Talbot, Jr. ......'42 '74 C.813 A.B. L.902 LL.B. P.O. Box 207‡
Wilson, Peter B., (AV) ......'25 '53 C&L.336 B.A., LL.B. 205 Kottenai AVe.‡

BUHL, 3,985, *Twin Falls Co.*

Felton, Michael Harland, (BV) ......'64 '90 C&L.336 B.S., J.D. [Felton&F.]
Felton, Michael Hoyt, (AV) ......'40 '65 C&L.336 B.S., J.D. [Felton&F.]
Felton & Felton, (AV) ......1020 Main Professional Ctr.

BURLEY, * 8,702, *Cassia & Minidoka Cos.*

Annest, James ......'27 '60 C.293 B.A. P.O. Box 686
Barrus, Alfred E., (BV) ......'47 '74 C.101 B.A. L.336 J.D. 1918 Overland Ave.
Bradley, John A., (BV) ......'51 '78 C.37 B.S. L.990 J.D. [Bradley]
Bradley Law Office, (BV) ......210 E. 5th St. N., Ste. 1
Byington, Dennis R., (BV) ......'49 '82 C.101 B.A. L.336 J.D. [Byington]
Byington Law Office, Chartered, (BV) ......111 W. 15th St.
Carlson, Monte B. ......'43 '70 C.101 B.A. L.878 J.D. Dist. J.
Chisholm, Donald J., (AV) ......'41 '67 C.670 B.B.A. L.767 LL.B. 223 E. Main St.
Fletcher, William Kent, (AV) ......'54 '78 C.877 B.A. L.878 J.D. [Fletcher]
Fletcher Law Office, (AV) ......1200 Overland Avenue
Holloway, Roy C. ......'47 '72 C.1032 B.A. L.336 J.D. Mag. J.

Ling, Robinson & Walker
(See Rupert)

Loveland, Lance Ardel, (CV) ......'70 '98 C.1324 B.A. L.336 J.D. [Ⓐ Parsons,S.&S.]
Parsons, William A., (AV) ......'32 '58 C&L.336 B.S., LL.B. [Parsons,S.&S.]
Parsons, Smith & Stone, LLP, (AV) ......137 West 13th Street
Smith, Richard K., (AV) ......'29 '58 C&L.336 B.A., LL.B. [Parsons,S.&S.]
Smyser, Howard D., (BV) ......'53 '79 C.508 B.S. L.902 J.D. Mag. J.
Snow, Peter G., (AV) ......'32 '59 C&L.336 B.S., LL.B. 1534 Overland Ave.
Stone, Randolph C., (AV) ......'48 '76 C.172 B.S. L.546 J.D. [Parsons,S.&S.]
Tuft, Steven A., (BV) ......'47 '74 C.101 B.A. L.878 J.D. P.O. Box 759
Whipple, Douglas R., (BV) ......'53 '80 C.877 B.S. L.990 J.D. [Whipple]
Whipple Law Office, Chrtd., (BV) ......2300 Overland Ave.

CALDWELL, * 25,967, *Canyon Co.*

Abernathy, Deborah L. ......'52 '85 C&L.629 B.A., J.D. P.O. Box 1116

Bauer & French
(See Boise)

Bevis, Cameron & Johnson, P.A.
(See Boise)

Brassey, Wetherell, Crawford & Garrett, L.L.P.
(See Boise)

Brauner, Wm. J., (AV) ......'32 '56 C.335 B.A. L.336 J.D. [W.J.Brauner]
Brauner, Wm. J., P.A., (AV) ......P.O. Box 1078

Cardon, Andrea L.
(See Boise)

Cherin, A. Marvin ......'35 '60 C.477 A.B. L.893 LL.B. Mag. J.

Christian, Ron, Attorney at Law
(See Boise)

Clapp, Sandra L., Associates, P.A.
(See Eagle)

Cross, John Milton, Jr. ......'47 '80 C.429 B.A. L.1194 J.D. Idaho Legal Aid Servs.
DeFord, Julie Adams ......'67 '97 C&L.101 B.A., J.D. 1001 Blaine Street
Dodge, Shari A., (CV) ......'63 '96 C.1193 B.A. L.336 J.D. Dep. Co. Pros.
Doolittle, Jim R. ......'28 '59 C.336 L.69 LL.B. Ret. Dist. J.
Downen, Donald E., (BV) ......'31 '59 C&L.336 B.S., LL.B. [Gigray,M.&D.]
Drescher, Stephen W. ......'49 '74 C.927 B.A. L.734 J.D. Dist. J.
Duggan, Michael E., (CV) ......'57 '86 C.594 B.A. L.336 J.D. Idaho Legal Aid Servs., Inc.

Evans Keane LLP
(See Boise)

Ford, Bradly S. ......'54 '79 C.335 B.A. L.336 J.D. Mag.
Fouser, Scott E., (BV) ......'56 '82 C.101 B.A. L.336 J.D. [Wiebe&F.]
Gigray, William F., Jr., (AV) ......'16 '40 C&L.336 B.A., LL.B. [Gigray,M.&D.]
Gigray, Miller & Downen, (AV) ......9th & Dearborn Sts.

Gillespie, James R., P.A.
(See Boise)

Gjording & Fouser, PLLC
(See Boise)

Goff, Dennis E. ......'50 '75 C.335 B.A. L.336 J.D. Dist. J.

Hackney, Gar, P.L.L.C.
(See Boise)

Harris, Richard L., (CV) ......'44 '71 C.101 B.A. L.336 J.D. 1023 Arthur
Hoff, Renae ......'51 '81 C.335 B.A. L.809 J.D. Dist. J.
Hurst, John L. ......'45 '73 C.350 B.A. L.846 J.D. 1014 Blaine‡
Johnson, Erik Smalley ......'63 '92 C.95 B.A. L.178 J.D. Dir., Idaho Legal Aid Servs., Inc.
Jones, Dennis R. ......'45 '73 C&L.336 B.A., J.D. V.P., J.R. Simplot Co.

Kane & Tobiason, LLP
(See Boise)

Kerrick, David E., (BV) ......'51 '80 C.911 B.A. L.336 J.D. 1001 Blaine Street
Kotyk, Frank P. ......'51 '80 C.475 B.A. L.336 J.D. Mag J., 3rd Jud. Dist.
Lovan, Gregg E., (BV) ......'49 '75 C.629 B.S. L.336 J.D. [Lovan&R.]
Lovan & Roker, P.A., (BV) ......717 South Kimball Avenue
Malone, Alan D. ......'65 '93 C.911 B.A. L.950 J.D. 11299 Bass Ln.

Manweiler, Manweiler, Breen & Ball, PLLC
(See Boise)

McWilliams, Ron ......'70 '02 C.1193 B.A. L.285 J.D. [Ⓐ Ronald P.R.]
Morfitt, James C. ......'41 '66 C&L.336 B.A., J.D. Dist. J.
Murphy, Michaelina B., (CV) ......'67 '94 C.911 B.A. L.336 J.D. [Murphy]
Murphy Law Office, (CV) ......117 S. 9th Ave., Ste. 7

Noack, Harold Q., Jr., P.A.
(See Boise)

Rainey, Ronald P., (AV) ......'38 '64 C.1032 B.S. L.336 LL.B. [Ronald P.R.]
Rettig, Herbert W., (AV) ......'28 '57 C.378 B.S. L.336 LL.B. [Rettig&R.]
Rettig & Rosenberry, (AV) ......1024 Belmont St.
Rocker, Matthew J., (BV) ......'64 '94 C.1032 B.S. L.336 J.D. [Lovan&R.]
Ronald P. Rainey, P.A., (AV) ......110 N. 9th Ave.
Rosenberry, Richard ......'21 '52 C.610 B.S. L.972 LL.B. [Rettig&R.] ‡
Runsvold, James M., (CV) ......'46 '82 C&L.336 B.S., J.D. 712 Albany
Saari, Charles L., (BV) ......'44 '72 C.569 B.S. L.608 J.D. Dep. Pros. Atty.
Schiller, James A. ......'57 '82 C&L.336 B.S., J.D. Mag.
Spears, Scott D., (CV) ......'60 '90 C.1193 B.A. L.336 J.D. Dep. Pros. Atty.
Tilley, Robert P. ......'63 '02 C.1193 B.A. L.560 J.D. 702 E. Chicago, Ste. 100
Weston, Gerald L. ......'36 '62 C&L.336 B.A., LL.B. Dist. J.
Whitney, David L., (AV) ......'39 '66 C.877 B.S. L.878 J.D. [Ronald P.R.]
Wiebe, Klaus, (BV) ......'42 '68 C.909 L.336 LL.B. [Wiebe&F.]
Wiebe & Fouser, P.A., (BV) ......702 East Chicago
Yost, C. Robert, (BV) ......'20 '50 C.335 B.A. L.336 LL.B. 1128 E. Linden Street
Young, David L., (CV) ......'52 '87 C.1193 B.B.A. L.336 J.D. Pros. Atty.

CAMBRIDGE, 374, *Washington Co.*

Hughes, Jerry S. ......'47 '75 C&L.336 B.S., J.D. P.O. Box 217‡

CASCADE, * 997, *Valley Co.*

Craig, James Edward Monroe, (CV) ......'76 '99 C&L.336 B.S., J.D. P.O. Box 1350
Hower, Ward E., (CV) ......'21 '49 C&L.813 A.B., LL.B. Mayor
Pierce, Michael G. ......'47 '72 C.336 B.A. L.629 J.D. 121 S. Main
Remaklus, Robert H., (BV) ......'23 '48 L.336 LL.B. [R.H.Remaklus]
Remaklus, Robert H., P.A., (BV) ......104 W. Casade St.

CHALLIS, * 909, *Custer Co.*

Bennetts, James R., (AV) ......'34 '63 C.1032 B.A. L.336 LL.B. 1231 S. Main
Furey, Jack B. ......'20 '48 C&L.336 LL.B. P.O. Box 280‡
Lee, G. Michael, (BV) ......'43 '73 C.593 B.S. L.1068 J.D. P.O. Box 1010
Roos, Charles L. ......'47 '73 C.941 B.A. L.950 J.D. Mag.

CLIFTON, 228, *Franklin Co.*

Smart, Wayne C. '45 '75 C&L.878 B.S., J.D.
(adm. in UT; not adm. in ID) Rte. 1, Box 159‡

COEUR D'ALENE, * 34,514, *Kootenai Co.*

Adams, Randall R., (BV) ......'— '83 C.800 B.A. L.336 J.D. [Quane S.]
Amaro, Rami, (BV) ......'68 '96 C.1331 B.A. L.150 J.D. [Amaro]

Amaro Law Office, (BV)
1875 North Lakewood Drive, Suite 102, 83814
Telephone: 208-667-4002 Facsimile: 208-667-9992
Email: contact@amarolaw.com URL: http://www.amaro-law.com
Rami Amaro. Associates: Joshua Leonard; Adam H. Green.
General Practice, Mediation.

See Professional Biographies, COEUR D'ALENE, IDAHO

Amendola, Gary I., (CV) ......'50 '79 C.174 B.A. L.285 J.D. [Walker R.A.A.&D.P.]
Andersen, C. Matthew, (AV) '49 '76
C.350 B.S. L.285 J.D. [Winston&C.] (ⓞSpokane, WA)

Andersen, Clayton G. ....'49 '77 C.335 B.A. L.836 J.D. [Walker R.A.A.&D.P.]
Anderson, Bruce A., (BV) .... '56 '85 C.908 B.A. L.336 J.D. [Elsaesser J.A.M.E.&M.] ⊙
Anson, Edward J., (BV) ....'51 '77 C.903 B.A. L.285 J.D. [Witherspoon,K.D.&T.]
Appleton, William M., (BV) ....'47 '76 C.494 B.A. L.285 J.D. 924 Sherman Ave.
Arney, Pat W. ....'27 '54 C&L.911 B.A., J.D. 607 S. 11th St.‡
Ayers, Stephen M., Attorney at Law, (BV) '46 '74
C&L.336 B.S., J.D. 1424 Sherman Ave., Ste. 100
Baughman, Richard L., (CV) ....'61 '91 C&L.336 B.S., J.D. Pros. Atty. Off.
Bean, Charles F., Law Offices of, (BV) '48 '76
C.1032 B.A. L.285 J.D. 2005 Ironwood Parkway, Suite 201
Beaudoin, Courtney R. '75 '00 C.770 B.A. L.285 J.D.
[▣ Winston&C.] (⊙Spokane, WA)
Bell, Steve F., (CV) ....'46 '71 C.336 B.S. L.508 J.D. 3102 Buckskin Rd.
Bennett, Kerwin C., Law Offices of, (CV) '49 '85
C.1061 B.S. L.285 J.D. 601 E. Sherman Ave., Ste. 2
Bignall, Bliss O., Jr., (BV) ....'26 '53 C.276 B.S. L.273 J.D. 408 Sherman Ave.
Black, Barry M., (CV) ....'57 '86 C&L.426 B.A., J.D. Dep. Pros. Atty.

Boyd, William F., (AV) '39 '65 C.628 B.S. L.336 LL.B.
601 Sherman Avenue Suite One, 83814
Telephone: 208-665-0666 Fax: 208-665-0864
Email: WBOYD1@GTE.NET
General Practice including Business, Environmental, Employee and Labor Issues, Mining Law, Probate, Civil Litigation and Appeals in all Courts.
See Professional Biographies, COEUR D'ALENE, IDAHO

Briseno, Janet A. ....'— '98 C.999 B.S. L.336 J.D. [Briseno]
Briseno Law Offices, P.C. ....2005 Ironwood Parkway, Suite 115
Brown, R. Romer, (BV) ....'42 '68 C.628 B.S. L.208 J.D. [Brown,J.&R.]
Brown, W. Baxter ....'42 '67 C&L.911 B.A., J.D. 118 N. 7th St.‡

Brown, Justh, & Romero, PLLC, (BV)
627 Government Way, P.O. Box 1148, 83816-1148
Telephone: 208-664-2191 Fax: 208-664-2193 1-888-302-9101
Email: brnjusth@my180.net URL: http://www.lawyers.com/cdalawyers
Members of Firm: R. Romer Brown; Carolyn Justh; Robert R. Romero, Jr.
General Civil Practice. Commercial and Residential Real Estate, Estate Planning, Business, Wills, Trusts, Probate. Collections over $1500.
Representative Clients: CBS Collections Inc.; Stock Building Supply West Inc.
References: Mountain West Savings Bank, Coeur d' Alene, Idaho.
See Professional Biographies, COEUR D'ALENE, IDAHO

Burke, Janell Seitz, (CV) ....'40 '83 C.335 B.A. L.285 J.D. Law Clk., Dist. Ct.
Burke, Muriel M. ....'64 '02 C.909 B.A. L.285 J.D. 1859 N. Lakewood Dr., Ste. 104
Cafferty, John A. ....'70 '97 C.1193 B.A. L.336 J.D. Kootenai County
Callahan, Kimmer W., (CV) ....'70 '95 C.336 B.S. L.285 J.D. [Callahan&Assoc.]

Callahan & Associates, Chtd., (CV)
1103 Best Avenue, P.O. Box 2226, 83816
Telephone: 208-664-9228 Fax: 208-664-5369
Email: kwc@idahoestatelaw.com URL: http://www.idahoestatelaw.com
Kimmer W. Callahan.
Living Trusts, Estate Planning, Probate, Elder Law, Guardianship & Conservatorship, Asset Protection Planning, Wills, Estate & Gift Taxation, Generation Skipping Tax, Trusts, Living Wills, Advanced Directives, Charitable Trusts and Foundations.
Reference: Idaho Trust Company, Coeur d'Alene, Idaho.
Other Offices: Sandpoint, Idaho Office: Telephone: 208-265-4506.
See Professional Biographies, COEUR D'ALENE, IDAHO

Campbell, Susan V., (CV) '46 '78
C.972 B.A. L.336 J.D. Asst. V.P. & Gen. Coun., Northern State Bk.
Carey, Marla S., (BVⓣ) ....'70 '97 C.36 B.A. L.285 J.D. [Huppin E.A.&P.] ⊙
Carter, Lisette F., (BVⓣ) ....'67 '93 C.508 B.A. L.950 J.D. [Evans,C.&L.] ⊙
Child, Jeffrey A., (BV) ....'56 '80 C.339 B.A. L.174 J.D. [Child&F.]
Child & Fisher, (BV) ....212 S. 11TH St.
Clemmons, Amy C., (BV) ....'66 '93 C.1262 B.A. L.285 J.D. [Evans,C.&L.] ⊙
Cody, Sandra G. ....'51 '95 C.101 B.S. L.285 J.D. [S.Cody]
Cody, Sandra, Attorney at Law .... 408 E Sherman Ave., Ste. 307
Combo, James F., (BV) ....'56 '83 C.413 B.A. L.336 J.D. [▣ C.F.Bean]
Conrad, George D., (CV) ....'55 '82 C.549 B.A. L.285 J.D. [Conrad,G.D.]
Conrad, George D., P.A., (CV) .... 2120 Northwest Blvd., Ste. C
Coulter, Everett B., Jr., (BV) ....'49 '76 C.1051 B.A. L.285 J.D. [Evans,C.&L.] ⊙
Crandall, Jeffery J., (CV) ....'57 '85 C.101 B.S. L.464 J.D. [Crandall L.&Assoc.]
Crandall & Associates, P.C., Attorneys at Law, (CV) ...... 1620 Northwest Blvd., Ste. 300
Cronin, Patrick J. .... '58 '98 C.763 B.S. L.285 J.D. [Winston&C.] (⊙Spokane, WA)
Crowe, James B. ....'31 '96 C.586 B.A. L.285 J.D. 301 First St., Suite 920‡
Cusack, Mary W. ....'59 '97 C.336 B.S. L.285 J.D. [▣ M.E.Wallace&Assoc.]
Daggett, David K. '64 '98 C.112 B.A. L.285 J.D.
(adm. in WA; not adm. in ID) [▣ Preston G.&E.] (⊙Spokane, WA)
Dal Pra, Merrilee A. Parr, (CV) ...... '59 '97 C.259 B.S. L.285 J.D. 2005 Ironwood Pkwy
Daugharty, Paul W., (CV) ....'63 '91 C.336 B.S. L.285 J.D. 110 Wallace Avenue
Davis, David J., (BVⓣ) '44 '90 C.1042 L.769 J.D.
(adm. in CA; not adm. in ID) 6184 N. 17th St.
Davis, Dennis M., (BV) ....'51 '77 C&L.336 B.S., J.D. [Witherspoon,K.D.&T.]
Dean, Charles R., Jr., (AVⓣ) ....'49 '74 C.207 B.A. L.910 J.D. Dean & Kolts
Decker, Gregory L., (BVⓣ) ....'51 '76 C.908 B.A. L.999 J.D. 315 E. Locust Ave.
Delfino, Patrick F., (BVⓣ) .... '49 '86 C.112 B.A. L.285 J.D. [Huppin E.A.&P.] ⊙
Dodson, Charles M., (BV) .... '49 '77 C.908 B.A. L.285 J.D. 1424 Sherman Ave.
Dolan, Philip E., (BV) ....'19 '47 C&L.285 B.A., LL.B. [Dolan&J.]
Dolan & Jacobsen, (BV) .... 118 N. 7th St., Suite B2
Ducharme, David R., (CV) .... '47 '81 C.763 B.A. L.336 J.D. 2020 Lakewood Dr.
Ealy, Michael A. ....'66 '97 C&L.336 B.S., J.D. [▣ Ramsden&L.]
Eash, David E., (BVⓣ) .... '48 '76 C.911 B.A. L.285 J.D. [Huppin E.A.&P.] ⊙
Eismann, Samuel, (AV) ....'37 '64 C&L.336 LL.B. 1424 E. Sherman Ave.
Ellingsen, Mark A., (CV) ....'66 '92 C.939 B.A. L.950 J.D. [Witherspoon,K.D.&T.]
Elliott, Cindy, (BV) .... '49 '89 C.1235 B.S. L.285 J.D. [Elsaesser J.A.M.E.&M.] ⊙
Elsaesser, Ford, (AV) ...... '51 '78 C.1123 B.S. L.336 J.D. [Elsaesser J.A.M.E.&M.] ⊙

Elsaesser Jarzabek Anderson Marks Elliott & McHugh, Chartered, (AV)
1400 Northwood Center Court, Suite C, 83814 ⊙
Telephone: 208-667-2900 Fax: 208-667-2150
Ford Elsaesser; Joseph E. Jarzabek; Bruce A. Anderson; Doug B. Marks; Cindy Elliott; Barry McHugh.
General Civil Trial Practice in all Courts and Agencies. Bankruptcy, Commercial, Creditor's Rights, Estate Planning, Labor, Personal Injury, Planning and Zoning, Probate, Public Utility, Real Estate, Social Security, Taxation, Workers Compensation Law and Family Law.
Sandpoint Office: Lake Plaza Building, 123 South Third Street, P.O. Box 1049, Sandpoint, Idaho, 83864. Telephone: 208-263-8517. Facsimile: 208-263-0759.
See Professional Biographies, COEUR D'ALENE, IDAHO

Erbland, Peter C., (AV) ....'52 '79 C.712 B.A. L.285 J.D. [Paine,H.C.B.&M.]

Esposito, George & Campbell, PLLC
(See Spokane)

Evans, Hugh O., (AVⓣ) ....'44 '75 C.911 B.A. L.285 J.D. [▣ Evans,C.&L.] ⊙

Evans, Craven & Lackie, P.S., (AVⓣ)
1424 Sherman Avenue Eastlake Professional Suites, #300, 83814 ⊙
Telephone: 208-667-8276
Gregory M. Kane; Michael E. McFarland Jr.; Amy C. Clemmons; Lisette F. Carter; Everett B. Coulter, Jr.; Jon D. Floyd; James F. Topliff; Heather C. Yakely. Of Counsel: Hugh O. Evans.
General Civil Trial and Appellate Practice. Professional Liability, Workman's Compensation, Personal Injury, Insurance Defense, Criminal, Municipal and Governmental, Zoning, Land Use, Environmental and Administrative Law, Wills, Trusts and Probate, Corporate and Personal Tax.
Spokane, Washington Office: 818 West Riverside Avenue, Suite 250. Telephone: 509-455-5200. Fax: 509-455-3632.
See Professional Biographies, COEUR D'ALENE, IDAHO

Fasnacht, Robert J., (BV) ....'57 '86 C&L.336 B.S., J.D. [R.J.Fasnacht]
Fasnacht, Robert J., P.C., (BV) .... 850 W. Ironwood Drive, Suite 101
Feltman, Richard C., (AV) ....'44 '69 C.209 B.A. L.365 J.D. [Feltman,G.G.&Z.] ⊙
Feltman, Gebhardt, Greer & Zeimantz, P.S., (AV)
1200 Ironwood, Suite 303 (⊙Spokane, WA)
Fisher, Heidi L., (BV) ....'55 '80 C.967 B.A. L.174 J.D. [Child&F.]
Fladwed, Thor E. ....'15 '45 C.300 A.B. L.981 LL.B. 1520 St. Maries Ave.‡
Flammia, Sue Solomon, (BV) ....'43 '78 C.336 B.S. L.285 J.D. [Flammia&S.]
Flammia & Solomon, (BV) ....317 Wallace Ave.
Flood, Monica M. ....'66 '94 C.550 B.A. L.1035 J.D. 105 N. 4th, Ste. 206
Floyd, Jon D., (BVⓣ) ....'68 '93 C.906 B.A. L.285 J.D. [Evans,C.&L.] ⊙
Follevaag, Carl A., (BV) ....'54 '85 C.685 B.A. L.336 J.D. Idaho Legal Aid Services
Friedlander, Penny E. ....'50 '90 L.336 J.D. 250 Northwest Boulevard
Fulgham, Mischelle R., (BV) '— '92
C.454 B.A. L.1048 J.D. [Lukins&A.] (⊙Spokane, WA)
Fullwiler, Ruth S., (CV) .... '46 '91 C.336 B.S. L.285 J.D. 1322 Kathleen Av., Ste. 2
Gaffaney, Jennifer D. ....'— '02 C&L.285 B.A., J.D. [▣ Quane S.]
Galbavy, John N. '59 '89 C.171 B.S. L.208 J.D.
Asst. Secy. & Corp. Coun., HECLA Mining Co.
Garbrecht, Louis, (BV) ....'49 '75 C.911 B.A. L.208 J.D. 1400 E. Sherman Ave.
Gebhardt, Frank J., (AVⓣ) ....'47 '72 C.285 B.B.A. L.602 J.D. [Feltman,G.G.&Z.] ⊙
Gissel, Norman L., (BV) .... '40 '70 C&L.336 B.A., J.D. 1424 E. Sherman Ave.
Gorman, Jennifer L. ....'— '03 C.375 B.S. L.900 J.D. [▣ Quane S.]
Graham, Suzanna L. .... '64 '92 C.628 B.S. L.336 J.D. 1034 N. 3rd St., Suite 9
Green, Adam H. ....'79 '04 C&L.336 B.A., J.D. [▣ Amaro]
Greer, Robert F., (BVⓣ) .... '58 '86 C.629 B.S. L.285 J.D. [Feltman,G.G.&Z.] ⊙
Gridley, Michael C. ....'56 '82 C.132 B.A. L.602 J.D. City Atty.
Grosch, Kim J., (CV) ....'50 '77 C.112 B.A. L.1068 J.D. [K.Grosch]
Grosch, Kim, Office, (CV) ....410 Sherman Ave.
Guin, John H., (BVⓣ) ... '72 '97 C.911 B.S. L.629 J.D. [Winston&C.] (⊙Spokane, WA)
Hague, Michael B., (BV) ....'60 '86 C&L.336 B.S., J.D. [Paine,H.C.B.&M.]
Hague, Wendy Marie, (BV) ....'64 '90 C.336 B.S. L.285 J.D. Asst. City Atty.

Hall, Farley, Oberrecht & Blanton, P.A.
(See Boise)

Haman, Gary M. ....'38 '66 C&L.336 B.S., J.D. Dist. J.‡
Haman, Michael L. ....'— '94 C&L.336 B.S., J.D. [Quane S.]
Hannon, James P. '49 '76 L.809 J.D.
(adm. in CA; not adm. in ID) 3204 17th St.‡
Hannon, Terrance W. ....'30 '72 L.809 J.D. P.O. Box 637‡
Harris, Terrance R. ....'63 '91 C.908 B.A. L.285 J.D. [▣ Ramsden&L.]
Harrison, Paula R. ....'41 '98 C.628 B.A. L.336 J.D. 250 NW Boulevard
Hazel, Joel P., (CV) ....'67 '94 C.285 B.A. L.336 J.D. [Witherspoon,K.D.&T.]
Holmes, Lisa A., (CV) ....'60 '92 C.1245 B.A. L.336 J.D. [Holmes]
Holmes Law Office, (CV) .... 2115 Sherman Ave., Ste. 107
Hosack, Charles W., (AV) ....'46 '72 C.629 B.A. L.174 J.D. Dist. J.
Howard, Kenneth B., Jr., (AV) ....'43 '71 C.999 B.S.M.E. L.912 J.D. [K.B.Howard]
Howard, Michael T. ......'69 '99 C&L.336 B.S., J.D. [▣ Winston&C.] (⊙Spokane, WA)

Howard, Kenneth B., P.A., (AV)
Attorney at Law
250 Northwest Boulevard, Suite 107A, P.O. Box 2528, 83816-2528
Telephone: 208-676-8890 Fax: 208-676-0981
Email: ken@kbhoward.com URL: http://www.kbhoward.com
Kenneth B. Howard, Jr.
Personal Injury, Product Liability, Insurance, Medical Malpractice, Contracts/Torts, Insurance Bad Faith, Automobile Accidents.
See Professional Biographies, COEUR D'ALENE, IDAHO

Huppin Ewing Anderson & Paul, P.S., (BVⓣ)
2101 Lakewood Drive, Suite 236, 83814 ⊙
Telephone: 208-667-7990 Fax: 509-838-4906
Email: lawyers@huppinlaw.com URL: http://www.huppinlaw.com
Irving "Buddy" Paul; Patrick F. Delfino; David E. Eash; Brad E. Smith; Marla S. Carey;—Constance H. Shields.
General Civil and Trial Practice. Aviation, Bankruptcy, Business and Commercial, Condemnation, Construction, Corporations, Creditor-Debtor Relations, Employment Law, Environmental Law, Estate Planning, Family Law, Insurance, Insurance Defense, Medical Malpractice Defense, Personal Injury, Probate, Real Property and Land Use, Taxation, and Criminal Law.
Reference: U.S. Bank-Spokane Main Branch.
Spokane, Washington Office: 221 North Wall Street, Suite 500. Telephone: 509-838-4261. Fax: 509-838-4906.
See Professional Biographies, COEUR D'ALENE, IDAHO

Ingalls, James W., (AV) ....'25 '51 C&L.336 LL.B. 2501 E. Sherman Ave.‡
Jacobsen, Kenneth T., (BV) ....'48 '74 C.908 B.A. L.285 J.D. [Dolan&J.]
James, Leander (Lee) L., IV, (BV) .... '60 '93 C.770 B.A. L.336 J.D. [▣ Owens,J.V.&W.]
Jarzabek, Joseph E., (BV) ......'54 '80 C.35 B.S. L.336 J.D. [Elsaesser J.A.M.E.&M.] ⊙

Johnson Law Group
(See Spokane, Washington)

Jones, Jeffrey A., (BV) ....'50 '78 C&L.259 B.A., J.D. City Atty.
Jovick, Fonda L. '72 '04 C&L.285 B.A., J.D.
(adm. in WA; not adm. in ID) [▣ Paine,H.C.B.&M.]
Justh, Carolyn, (BV) ....'47 '76 C.594 B.A. L.336 J.D. [Brown,J.&R.]
Kane, Gregory M., (AVⓣ) ....'51 '80 C.589 B.A. L.285 J.D. [Evans,C.&L.] ⊙

Keefe, King & Bowman, P.S.
(See Spokane, Washington)

Kelso, Starr, (CV) ....'51 '79 C.336 B.S. L.285 J.D. [Kelso]
Kelso Law Office, (CV) ....P.O. Box 1312
Keyes, J. Michael, (BVⓣ) '71 '98
C.426 B.M. L.285 J.D. [▣ Preston G.&E.] (⊙Spokane, WA)
Keyes, Theresa Lynn, (CVⓣ) '69 '95 C.911 B.A. L.285 J.D.
(adm. in WA; not adm. in ID) [▣ Preston G.&E.] (⊙Spokane, WA)
Kimball, Charles H., (BV) ....'16 '40 C&L.378 B.A., LL.B. P.O. Box 687
Kochansky, Richard W. ....'44 '70 408 E. Sherman Ave., Ste. 309
Kuck, Richard Keating, (CV) ....'62 '88 C&L.336 B.S., J.D. 408 E. Sherman Ave.
Lawlor, Edward John ....'66 '93 C.285 B.B.A. L.190 J.D. P.O. Box 1925
Layman, John R., (BVⓣ) ....'58 '83 C.906 B.A. L.285 J.D. [Layman,L.&R.] ⊙

Layman, Layman & Robinson, PLLP, (BVⓉ)
110 Wallace Avenue, 83814 ⊙
Telephone: 208-665-7270 Fax: 208-665-7290 URL: http://www.braininjurylaw.net
Email: info@laymanlawfirm.com URL: http://www.laymanlawfirm.com
John R. Layman.
General Civil and Trial Practice, Banking, Creditor's Rights, Real Estate, Commercial, Personal Injury, Brain Injury and Aquatic Injury, Products Liability, Insurance, Corporate, Antitrust, Securities Litigation.
Representative Clients: Avis Rent A Car; Continental Insurance Co.; Western Union Insurance Company of Calgary.
Seattle, Washington Office: 316 Occidental Avenue S., Suite 500, 98104. Telephone: 206-340-1314. Fax: 206-292-1790.
Spokane, Washington Office: 601 South Division, 99202. Telephone: 509-455-8883. Fax: 509-624-2902.
See Professional Biographies, COEUR D'ALENE, IDAHO

Leonard, Joshua ....'75 '05 C.1209 B.A. L.285 J.D. [Ⓐ Amaro]
Loats, Frederick G., (BV) ....'51 '77 C.352 B.A. L.1292 J.D. 111 N. 2nd St.
Lockwood, Edward Christopher ....'53 '88 2115 Sherman Ave., Ste. 109
Long, Brian D., (CV) ....'64 '91 C&L.336 B.S., J.D. 1034 North 3rd Street

Lukins & Annis, P.S., (AV)
Suite 102 Coeur d'Alene North, 250 Northwest Boulevard, 83814-2971 ⊙
Telephone: 208-667-0517 Telecopier: 208-664-4125
Email: info@lukins.com URL: http://www.lukins.com
Mischelle R. Fulgham; Richard Wayne Sweney (Resident); Edward F. Wroe (Resident). Associates: Michael G. Schmidt; Peter J. Smith, IV.
Antitrust, Banking and Bankruptcy, Business and Personal Injury, Litigation, Financing, Federal and State Tax, Commercial, Corporations and Partnerships, Franchise, Labor and Employment Law, Environmental Law, Estate Planning and Probate, Real Property, Insurance, Pension and Profit Sharing, Securities, Hospital and Health Care, Construction Law, Government Contracts, Class Action, Professional Malpractice, and Workers Compensation.
Representative Clients: Beneficial Mortgage Co.; FirstBank Northwest; Knudtsen Chevrolet Co.; Mountain West Bank; Old Republic National Title Insurance; U.S. Bancorp; West Fargo Bank.
Spokane, Washington Office: 1600 Washington Trust Financial Center, West 717 Sprague Avenue. Telephone: 509-455-9555. Telecopier: 509-747-2323.
Moses Lake, Washington Office: 1405 South Pioneer Way. Telephone: 509-765-9555. Telecopier: 509-765-4265.
See Professional Biographies, COEUR D'ALENE, IDAHO

Luster, John Patrick ....'52 '77 C.1110 B.A. L.285 J.D. Mag. J.
Lynch, J. Christopher, (BVⓉ) '61 '87
C&L.911 B.S.C.E., J.D. [Preston G.&E.] (⊙Spokane, WA)
Lyons, Marc A., (BV) ....'54 '83 C&L.336 B.S., J.D. [Ramsden&L.]
Madsen, Henry D., (CV) ....'60 '91 C&L.336 B.S., J.D. Dep. Pros. Atty.
Magnuson, John F., (BV) '61 '88
C.309 A.B. L.602 J.D. 1250 Northwood Center Court, Suite A
Marano, Eugene A. ....'44 '76 C&L.285 B.A., J.D. Mag. J.
Marfice, Douglas S., (BV) ....'64 '89 C&L.546 B.A., J.D. [Ramsden&L.]
Marks, Doug B. ....'69 '97 C&L.101 B.S., J.D. [Elsaesser J.A.M.E.&M.] ⊙
Mason, Jerry D., (BV) ....'48 '85 C.337 B.S. L.336 J.D. City Atty.
McCabe, Paul D. ....'37 '62 C&L.336 B.A., LL.B. Mag.
McDaniel, Mary E. '26 '68 C.473 B.S. L.809 LL.B.
(adm. in CA; not adm. in ID) 3865 W. Blalock Dr.‡
McFarland, Michael B., (CV) '45 '80 C.336 B.A. L.273 J.D.
421 E. Coeur d'Alene Ave.
McFarland, Michael E., Jr., (BVⓉ) ....'66 '93 C.911 B.A. L.285 J.D. [Evans,C.&L.] ⊙
McFarland, William D. ....'21 '48 C.285 L.336 LL.B. 816 Sherman Ave.‡
McGinn, Brian T., (BVⓉ) '68 '94 C&L.285 B.A., J.D.
[Winston&C.] (⊙Spokane, WA)
McHugh, Barry ....'58 '87 C.1193 B.S. L.336 J.D. [Elsaesser J.A.M.E.&M.] ⊙
Mein, Joseph I., (CV) ....'— '79 C.545 B.S. L.285 J.D. 401 Sherman Ave., Ste. 201
Miller, E. L., (AV) ....'22 '49 C.851 L.336 LL.B. [Paine,H.C.B.&M.]
Miller, Patrick E., (BV) ....'50 '75 C.950 B.A. L.336 J.D. [Paine,H.C.B.&M.]
Mitchell, John T. ....'58 '85 C&L.336 B.S., J.D. Dist. J.
Molenaar, Dennis L. '48 '80 C&L.585 B.A., J.D.
(adm. in ND; not adm. in ID) 3807 Buckskin Rd.‡
Murock, Tamara W. ....'— '96 C&L.285 B.A., J.D. [Ⓐ Winston&C.] (⊙Spokane, WA)
Nagel, Herbert, (AV) ....'31 '55 C&L.336 LL.B. 111 N. 2nd St.‡
Nass, Scot D., (BV) ....'61 '92 C.950 B.A. L.336 J.D. [Paine,H.C.B.&M.]
Nicely, William A. '30 '60 C.674 A.B. L.309 LL.B.
(adm. in NY; not adm. in ID) Chmn. of the Bd. & CEO, Callahan Mining Corp.
Nixon, W. W., (BV) ....'32 '57 C&L.336 B.A., LL.B. 409 Coeur d'Alene Ave.
O'Brien, John J. '31 '57 C.426 B.S. L.767 LL.B.
(adm. in CA; not adm. in ID) E-6303 Mullan Trial Rd.‡
Odegaard, Craig D., (CV) '59 '90 C.999 B.S. L.336 J.D.
2115 Sherman Avenue, Suite 104
Ormsby, Michael C., (AVⓉ) '57 '81
C&L.285 B.A., J.D. [Preston G.&E.] (⊙Spokane, WA)
Owens, R. Bruce, (AV) ....'45 '73 C.101 B.A. L.36 J.D. [Owens,J.V.&W.]
Owens, James, Vernon & Weeks, P.A., (AV) ....1875 N. Lakewood Drive

Paine, Hamblen, Coffin, Brooke & Miller LLP, (AV)
701 Front Avenue, #101, P.O. Box E, 83816-0328 ⊙
Telephone: 208-664-8115 Facsimile: 208-664-6338
Email: info@painehamblen.com URL: http://www.painehamblen.com
Members of Firm: E. L. Miller; Patrick E. Miller; Ausey H. Robnett III; Janet D. Robnett; Peter C. Erbland; Michael B. Hague; Scot D. Nass. Associates: Fonda L. Jovick (Not admitted in ID); Tyler Wirick.
General Civil and Trial Practice, Complex Litigation, Insurance Defense, Insurance Coverage, Professional Liability, Product Liability, Negligence Defense, Workers Compensation, Employment Law, Commercial Litigation, Corporate, Real Estate, Zoning, Planning and Land Use, Hospital and Healthcare Law, Railroad Law, Probate, Family Law and Criminal Law.
Spokane, Washington Office: 717 West Sprague Avenue, Suite 1200. Telephone: 509-455-6000.
Spokane Valley, Washington Office: 12209 East Mission Avenue. Telephone: 509-777-1087.
Kennewick, Washington Office: 7025 West Grandridge Boulevard, Suite A. Telephone: 509-735-1542.
See Professional Biographies, COEUR D'ALENE, IDAHO

Palmer, Michael G., (CV) ....'70 '96 C&L.336 B.S., J.D. [M.G.Palmer]
Palmer, Michael G., P.L.L.C., (CV) ....105 North 4th Street, Suite 208
Parisot, Albert H., Jr. ....'28 '63 C.1032 B.S. L.336 LL.B. Mag.
Paul, Irving "Buddy", (BVⓉ) ....'47 '74 C.597 B.A. L.477 J.D. [Huppin E.A.&P.] ⊙
Phillips, Cameron, (BV) ....'48 '78 C.475 B.A. L.1187 J.D. [C.Phillips]
Phillips, Cameron, P.A., (BV) ....924 Sherman Avenue
Potter, Douglas G., (CV) ....'54 '80 C.112 B.A. L.61 J.D. 114 Lakeview Dr.

Preston Gates & Ellis LLP, (AVⓉ)
1200 Ironwood Drive, Suite 315, 83814 ⊙
Telephone: 208-677-1839 Facsimile: 208-765-2494
Email: info@prestongates.com URL: http://www.prestongates.com
Partners: J. Christopher Lynch; Michael C. Ormsby; Todd Reuter (Also at Spokane, Washington Office). Associates: David K. Daggett (Not admitted in ID; Also at Spokane, Washington Office); J. Michael Keyes (Also at Spokane, Washington Office); Theresa Lynn Keyes (Not admitted in ID; Also at Spokane, Washington Office); Peter G. Scott.
Languages: Chinese, French, German, Japanese, Korean, Russian, Spanish and Taiwanese.

(This Listing Continued)

Preston Gates & Ellis LLP (Continued)
General Practice. Administrative, Affordable Housing, Americans with Disabilities Act, Bankruptcy Litigation, Business Transactions and Business Planning, Business Reorganization and Bankruptcy, Commercial Transactions and Litigation, Construction, Corporate, Corporate Financing, Creditors' Rights, Emerging Business, Employment, Environmental, Forest Products and Timber, Governmental Relations, Insurance, Intellectual Property and Technology Law (domestic and international, includes copyrights, trademarks, trade secrets, licensing and internet/e-commerce); International Business Transactions, Internet/E-Commerce Law, Labor, Land Use, Leasing, Legislative, Litigation, Mergers and Acquisitions, Municipal (general and finance), Natural Resources, Probate, Products Liability, Public Law, Real Estate, Real Estate Financing and Leasing, Securities, Solid Waste, Tax, Telecommunications, Uniform Commercial Code, Utilities and Transportation Law.
Anchorage, Alaska Office: 420 L Street, Suite 400, 99501-1937. Telephone: 907-276-1969. Facsimile: 907-276-1365.
Washington, D.C. Office: Preston Gates Ellis & Rouvelas Meeds LLP, 1735 New York Avenue, N.W., Suite 500, 20006-5209. Telephone: 202-628-1700. Facsimile: 202-331-1024.
Irvine, California Office: 1900 Main Street, Suite 600, 92614-7319. Telephone: 949-253-0900. Facsimile: 949-253-0902.
Portland, Oregon Office: 222 S.W. Columbia Street, 1400 KOIN Tower, 97201-6632. Telephone: 503-228-3200. Facsimile: 503-248-9085.
San Francisco, California Office: 55 Second Street, Suite 1700, 94105. Telephone: 415-882-8200. Facsimile: 415-882-8220.
Seattle, Washington Office: 925 Fourth Avenue, Suite 2900, 98104-1158. Telephone: 206-623-7580. Facsimile: 206-623-7022.
Spokane, Washington Office: 601 West Riverside Drive, Suite 1400, 99201-0636. Telephone: 509-624-2100. Facsimile: 509-456-0146.
Beijing, China Office: Preston Gates & Ellis, Suite 1003, Tower E3, Oriental Plaza, No. 1 East Chang An Avenue. Telephone: +86 10 8518 8528. Facsimile: +86 10 8518 9299.
Hong Kong Office: Preston Gates & Ellis, 35th Floor, Two International Finance Centre, 8 Finance Street, Central, Hong Kong. Telephone: 852-2511-5100. Facsimile: 852-2511-9515.
Taipei, Taiwan Office: Preston Gates & Ellis, 2/F, No. 131, Min Sheng E. Rd., Sec. 3. Telephone:+886 (2) 2717 6657. Facsimile:+886 (2) 2712-8264.
See Professional Biographies, COEUR D'ALENE, IDAHO

Prohaska, Daniel W. ....'56 '82 C&L.336 B.A., J.D. Idaho Trust Company

Quane Smith LLP, (AV)
2020 Lakewood Drive, Suite 312, P.O. Box 1758, 83816-1758 ⊙
Telephone: 208-664-9281 Facsimile: 208-664-5380
Email: info@quanesmith.net URL: http://www.quanesmith.net
Randall R. Adams; Michael L. Haman;—Jennifer D. Gaffaney (Resident); Jennifer L. Gorman (Resident).
Insurance, Insurance Defense, Litigation, Accountants Liability, Advertising and Marketing, Agents and Brokers Liability, Agricultural Law, Alcoholic Beverages, Alternative Dispute Resolution, Architects and Engineers Liability, Arson and Insurance Fraud, Asbestos Defense, Brain Injury, Business Law, Casualty Insurance Defense, Catastrophic Injury, Civil Practice, Commercial Law, Complex and Multi-District Litigation, Computers and Software, Construction Law, Contracts, Corporate Law, Design Professionals Liability, Drug and Medical Device Defense, Education Law, Employer Liability, Environmental Law, ERISA Litigation, Extra Contractual Insurance Defense, Federal Practice, Fire Insurance, Firearms Litigation, Food Products Liability, Fraud and Deceit, Government, Hazardous Waste Liability, Head Injury, Health Care, Insurance Bad Faith Defense, Labor and Employment, Legal Malpractice Defense, Libel, Slander and Defamation, Life Insurance Defense, Manufacturers Liability, Medical Malpractice, Natural Resources, Negligence, Personal Injury, Pesticide Litigation, Physicians Licensing, Pollution, Premises Liability, Products Liability, Professional Discipline, Professional Liability, Propane Products Liability, Property Damage Defense, Real Estate, Recreational Products Liability, School Board Defense, Slip and Fall, Spinal Injury, Subrogation, Torts, Toxic Torts, Transportation, Workers Compensation and Wrongful Death.
Boise, Idaho Office: U.S. Bank Plaza, 16th Floor. P.O. Box 519. Telephone: 208-345-8600. Facsimile: 208-345-8660.
Idaho Falls, Idaho Office: 2325 West Broadway, Suite B. Telephone: 208-529-0000. Facsimile: 208-529-0005.
See Professional Biographies, COEUR D'ALENE, IDAHO

Raeon, James Alan ....'52 '78 C.999 B.A. L.117 J.D. 1424 Sherman Ave., Ste. 300
Ramsden, Michael E., (AV) ....'52 '79 C.911 B.A. L.336 J.D. [Ramsden&L.]

Ramsden & Lyons, (AV)
618 North 4th Street, P.O. Box 1336, 83816-1336
Telephone: 208-664-5818 Fax: 208-664-5884
Email: firm@ramsdenlyons.com URL: http://www.ramsdenlyons.com
Michael E. Ramsden; Marc A. Lyons; Douglas S. Marfice. Associates: Michael A. Ealy; Jedediah J. Whitaker; Terrance R. Harris.
General Civil Trial and Appellate Practice. Insurance Defense, Eminent Domain/Condemnation, Arbitration, Mediation, Class Action Defense, Business Formation, Insurance Bad Faith, Land Use, Professional Liability, Product Liability, Negligence, Construction, Real Estate, Environmental, Error and Omission Defense, Governmental Liability, Worker Compensation and Employment Law.
See Professional Biographies, COEUR D'ALENE, IDAHO

Reed, Scott W., (AV) '28 '55 C.674 A.B. L.813 LL.B. [BB]
401 Front Street, P.O. Box A, 83816
Telephone: 208-664-2161 Fax: 208-765-5117
Email: scottwreed@imbris.com
General Civil and Trial Practice, Business and Commercial, Land Use and Environmental Law, Local Government Law.
Reference: Washington Trust Bank.
See Professional Biographies, COEUR D'ALENE, IDAHO

Reuter, Todd, (BVⓉ) '65 '91 C.911 B.A. L.1358 J.D.
[Preston G.&E.] (⊙Spokane, WA)
Rines, Stanton Parish, (CV) ....'49 '80 C&L.336 B.A., J.D. [Walker R.A.A.&D.P.]

Robinson, David K., Jr., (BV) '47 '75 C.1375 B.A. L.878 J.D.
2005 Ironwood Parkway, Suite 140, 83814
Telephone: 208-664-1414 Telecopier: 208-667-6603
Email: dkrjratty@icehouse.net URL: http://www.davidkrobinsonjr.com
General Practice. Divorce, Juvenile, Visitation, Support, Paternity, Family, Interstate Child Custody, Adoption, Mediation, Enforcement of Foreign Judgments, Criminal, Personal Injury, Negligence, Auto Accidents, Slip and Fall, General and Child Support Collections over $1,000.
Reference: US Bank.
See Professional Biographies, COEUR D'ALENE, IDAHO

Robnett, Ausey H., III, (BV) ....'53 '79 C.678 B.A. L.596 J.D. [Paine,H.C.B.&M.]
Robnett, Janet D., (BV) ....'55 '80 C.678 B.A. L.629 J.D. [Paine,H.C.B.&M.]
Romero, Robert R., Jr. (CV) ....'— '96 C.147 B.S. L.336 J.D. [Brown,J.&R.]
Rude, Dan J., (BV) ....'53 '80 C&L.336 B.A., J.D. P.O. Box 1453
Schmidt, Michael G. ....'— '03 C.1085 B.A. L.336 J.D. [Ⓐ Lukins&A.] (⊙Spokane, WA)
Scott, Peter G. ....'— '99 C.454 B.S. L.596 J.D. [Ⓐ Preston G.&E.] (⊙Spokane, WA)
Servick, Susan K., (BV) ....'58 '85 C.1193 B.A. L.336 J.D. 1250 Ironwood Dr., Ste. 303
Sheroke, Charles, (CV) ....'48 '74 C.665 B.A. L.446 J.D. Idaho Legal Aid Servs., Inc.
Shields, Constance H. ....'56 '01 C.347 B.S. L.285 J.D. [Ⓐ Huppin E.A.&P.] ⊙
Simpson, Benjamin R. ....'49 '84 C.147 B.A. L.285 J.D. Mag.
Smith, Brad E., (BVⓉ) ....'60 '86 C&L.911 B.A., J.D. [Huppin E.A.&P.] ⊙
Smith, Erik Paul, (CV) ....'66 '94 C.774 B.A. L.334 J.D. [E.P.Smith]
Smith, Ian D., (CV) ....'63 '93 C.1193 B.S. L.336 J.D. 608 Northwest Blvd., Ste. 101
Smith, Karen M. ....'69 '03 C.586 B.S.A.A. L.259 J.D. [K.M.Smith]
Smith, Peter J., IV ....'— '04 C.897 B.B.A. L.1117 J.D. [Ⓐ Lukins&A.]
Smith, Sidney E. ....'14 '42 C.494 L.174 J.D. 250 Northwest Blvd.‡
Smith, Erik P., P.C., (CV) ....607 Lakeside Avenue
Smith, Karen M., PLLC ....500 N. Government Way, Ste. 600

Snead, Charles D., Jr. '32 '60 C.401 B.S. L.893 LL.B.
(adm. in VA; not adm. in ID) Chmn. of the Bd. & Pres., Callahan Mining Corp.
Solomon, S.E. Anne, (BV) ... '51 '78 C.813 B.A. L.336 J.D. [Flammia&S.]
Sterett, Richard Reese ... '72 '99 C.628 B.A. L.285 J.D. 710 E. Mullan Avenue
Stoddard, Bradley J., (BV) ... '58 '83 C&L.336 B.A., J.D. 110 Wallace Ave.
Stricklin, Nancy, (BV) ... '46 '89 C.1032 B.S. L.336 J.D. 250 Northwest Boulevard
Stricklin, Timothy W., (CV) ... '48 '89 C.1060 B.S. L.336 J.D. P.O. Box 1545
Sweney, Richard Wayne, (AV) ... '— '74 C.223 B.S. L.446 J.D. [Lukins&A.]
Tarnasky, William G. ... '36 '89 C.585 M.S. L.285 J.D. 1106 Ironwood Dr.
Topliff, James F., (BVⓉ) ... '52 '81 C.477 B.A. L.285 J.D. [Evans,C.&L.] ⊙
Towles, James G., (AV) ... '21 '48 C&L.336 B.S., J.D. 4300 Blue Creek Bay Rd.‡

Trigg Law Firm, P.C.
(See Kalispell, Montana)

Vance, Lawrence H., Jr., (BVⓉ) '50 '76 C&L.285 B.B.A., J.D.
(adm. in WA; not adm. in ID) [Winston&C.] (⊙Spokane, WA)
Vasseur, Thomas M., (BV) ... '44 '71 C.906 L.336 J.D. 409 Coeur d'Alene Ave.
Verbillis, Michael J., (AV) ... '45 '71 C.17 B.A. L.336 J.D. [M.J.Verbillis]
Verbillis, Michael J., P.A., (AV) ... 111 N. 2nd St.
Vernon, Craig K., (BV) ... '68 '96 C.101 B.S.B.A. L.336 J.D. [Owens,J.V.&W.]
Waite, Kevin J., (BV) ... '52 '81 C.388 B.A. L.966 J.D. [K.J.Waite]

Waite, Kevin J., P.C., (BV)
Old City Hall, 424 Sherman Avenue, Suite 106, 83814
Telephone: 208-667-8553 Fax: 208-667-8630 URL: http://www.waitelaw.com URL: http://www.waitelawoffice.com URL: http://www.waite-law.com URL: http://www.waitelawfirm.com
Email: kevinjwaite@aol.com URL: http://www.waitelaw.com
Kevin J. Waite.
Family Law, Divorce, Child Custody, Child Support, Criminal Defense, Driving While Intoxicated, Drug Crimes, Parole and Probation and Civil Litigation.
See Professional Biographies, COEUR D'ALENE, IDAHO

Walker, Glen E., (BV) ... '44 '76 C&L.260 B.S., J.D. [Walker R.A.A.&D.P.]
Walker Rines Amendola Andersen & Doty PLLC, (BV) ... 702 N. 4th St., Ste. 200
Wallace, Marc E., (AV) ... '49 '77 C.911 B.A. L.285 J.D. [M.E.Wallace&Assoc.]
Wallace, Richard P., (BV) '44 '71 C.939 B.A. L.336 J.D.
1875 N. Lakewood Dr., Ste. 202

Wallace, Marc E., & Associates, P.A., (AV)
2370 N. Merritt Creek Loop, Suite 1, 83814
Telephone: 208-667-2264 Fax: 208-667-2419
Marc E. Wallace;—Mary W. Cusack.
Trusts and Estates, Probate.
See Professional Biographies, COEUR D'ALENE, IDAHO

Wasserman, Alan M., (BV) '52 '77
C.188 B.A. L.659 J.D. Mng. Atty., Idaho Legal Aid Servs., Inc.
Watson, Roland, (CV) ... '50 '84 C.508 B.A. L.285 J.D. [Watson L.]
Watson Law, (CV) ... 408 Sherman Ave.
Weeks, Susan P., (BV) ... '60 '90 C&L.336 B.S., J.D. [Owens,J.V.&W.]
Wetzel, Dana L. Rayborn, (BV) ... '51 '82 C.1032 B.S. L.336 J.D. [Wetzel&W.]
Wetzel, Steven C., (BV) ... '51 '82 C.1032 B.A. L.336 J.D. [Wetzel&W.]

Wetzel & Wetzel, P.L.L.C., (BV)
1322 Kathleen Avenue Suite 2, 83815-8339
Telephone: 208-667-3400 Fax: 208-664-6741
Email: wetzel@imbris.com
Steven C. Wetzel; Dana L. Rayborn Wetzel.
Commercial Litigation, Civil Litigation, Municipal Law, Real Estate Development, Land Use Regulation, Business Organization, Personal Injury, Probate, Construction Law, Employment Discrimination, Bad Faith, Banking Law, Municipal Bonds and Bankruptcy.
See Professional Biographies, COEUR D'ALENE, IDAHO

Wheeler, Dennis E. '42 '67 C&L.336 B.S., J.D.
Chmn., Pres. & CEO, Coeur d'Alene Mines Corp.
Whelan, John Patrick ... '53 '82 C.1042 B.S. L.1137 J.D. 103 N. 4th
Whitaker, Jedediah J. ... '70 '99 C.1193 B.B.A. L.285 J.D. [▣ Ramsden&L.]
Whitehead, Richard G., (CV) ... '55 '82 C.1032 B.A. L.336 J.D. P.O. Box 1319
Wick, Ann T. '79 '04 C&L.285 B.A., J.D.
(adm. in OR; not adm. in ID) Law Clk.
Williams, Meriwether D. (Mike), (AVⓉ) '49 '78
C.575 B.A. L.285 J.D. [Winston&C.] (⊙Spokane, WA)

Winston & Cashatt, Lawyers, A Professional Service Corporation, (AV)
250 Northwest Boulevard, Suite 107A, 83814 ⊙
Telephone: 208-667-2103 Fax: 208-765-2121
Email: info@winstoncashatt.com URL: http://www.winstoncashatt.com
Meriwether D. (Mike) Williams; C. Matthew Andersen; John H. Guin; Brian T. McGinn; Patrick J. Cronin; Lawrence H. Vance, Jr. (Not admitted in ID);—Tamara W. Murock; Michael T. Howard; Courtney R. Beaudoin.
General and Trial Practice including Construction, Insurance, Alternative Dispute Resolution, Corporate, Accident and Personal Injury, Municipalities, Banking, Land Use Development, Criminal Defense, Employment and Labor, Environmental, Commercial Litigation, Taxation, Antitrust and Trade Regulation, Public and Governmental Contracts, Worker's Compensation, Immigration and Bankruptcy.
Spokane, Washington Office: Bank of America Financial Center, 601 W. Riverside, Suite 1900. Telephone: 509-838-6131. Fax: 509-838-1416.
Seattle, Washington Office: 1620 Fourth Avenue, Suite 200. Telephone: 425-486-0170. Fax: 425-486-0431.
See Professional Biographies, COEUR D'ALENE, IDAHO

Wirick, Tyler ... '72 '05 C.1085 B.S. L.627 J.D. [▣ Paine,H.C.B.&M.]

Witherspoon, Kelley, Davenport & Toole, P.S., (BV)
The Spokesman Review Building, Suite 401, 608 Northwest Boulevard, 83814-2146 ⊙
Telephone: 208-667-4000 Fax: 208-667-8470
Email: info@wkdtlaw.com URL: http://www.wkdtlaw.com
Edward J. Anson (Resident); Dennis M. Davis (Resident); Mark A. Ellingsen (Resident); Joel P. Hazel.
General Civil and Trial Practice. Antitrust, Banking, Business, Commercial, Construction, Corporate Employment, Environmental, Estate Planning, Government Relations, Health Law, Insurance Defense, Mining, Medical, Personal Injury, Probate, Media, Real Estate Land Use, Securities and Taxation Law.
Spokane, Washington Office: 1100 U.S. Bank Building. 422 West Riverside. Telephone: 509-624-5265. FAX: 509-458-2728.
See Professional Biographies, COEUR D'ALENE, IDAHO

Work, Shannon D. ... '57 '88 C.1193 B.A. L.629 J.D. Idaho Legeal Aid Servs.
Wroe, Edward F., (AV) ... '— '73 C.674 B.S.E. L.813 J.D. [Lukins&A.]
Wytychak, Michael, III, (BV) ... '53 '84 C.668 B.A. L.285 J.D. 314 E. Garden
Yakely, Heather C., (BVⓉ) ... '71 '99 C&L.285 B.A., J.D. [▣ Evans,C.&L.] ⊙

COUNCIL, 816, *Adams Co.*

Gabbert, Myron Dan, (AV) ... '43 '67 C.98 B.A. L.339 J.D. [M.D.Gabbert] ⊙

Gabbert, Myron Dan, J.D. P.A., (AV)
P.O. Box 546, 83612 ⊙
Telephone: 208-253-6896 Fax: 208-253-4880
Email: gabbert@frontiernet.net URL: http://www.lawyers.com/gabbertlaw

(This Listing Continued)

Gabbert, Myron Dan, J.D. P.A. (Continued)
Myron Dan Gabbert.
Languages: German; Spanish.
General and Trial, Banking, Business, Commercial, Corporate, Insurance Defense, Real Estate, Wills, Trusts, Probate and Estate Planning.
Representative Clients: Amerigas; Argonaut Insurance Co.; Bergen Brunswig Drug Co.; Clark Real Estate; Commonwealth Land Title Ins. Co.; Meadowcreek Property Owners; McCall Veterinary Clinic; Red Lion Inns; Reliance Group; Rogers Electric; South Coast Lumber Co.
McCall, Idaho Office: Yacht Club Building, P.O. Box 2349, 83638. Telephone: 208-634-2200. Fax: 208-634-2200. Email: gabbert@frontiernet.net.
See Professional Biographies, MCCALL, IDAHO

CRAIGMONT, 542, *Lewis Co.*

Longeteig, Wilfrid W., (CV) ... '42 '66 C&L.336 B.S., J.D. 120 W. Main St.

DRIGGS, * 1,100, *Teton Co.*

Bonney, Stephanie Jaymes ... '69 '99 C.205 B.S. L.174 J.D. [Pike&S.] ⊙
Johnson, Neil, (BV) ... '45 '75 C.36 B.S. L.809 J.D. P.O. Box 546
Lewis-Frazee, Judith A. ... '44 '75 C.665 B.S. L.1002 J.D. [▣ Pike&S.] ⊙
Lowery, Laura Estay, (CV) ... '57 '85 Teton Co. Pros. Atty.
Martin, James H. '46 '79 C.37 B.S. L.1137 J.D.
(adm. in CA; not adm. in ID) P.O. Box 677
Miller, Mark J., (CV) ... '61 '92 C.1193 B.A. L.336 J.D. [Pike&S.] ⊙
Pike, Edward W., (AV) ... '24 '50 C&L.878 B.S., LL.B. [Pike&S.] (⊙Idaho Falls)
Pike & Smith, P.A., (AV) ... 10 Ashley Avenue, Suite 206 (⊙Idaho Falls)
Runyan, Cody H., (CV) ... '— '80 L.972 J.D 91 E. Little Ave.
Smith, Franklin N. '41 '65 C.1085 L.878 J.D.
[Pike&S.] (⊙Idaho Falls, ID; Salt Lake City, UT)
Woelk, Galen, (BV) ... '69 '98 C.795 B.A. L.972 J.D. P.O. Box 533

EAGLE, 11,085, *Ada Co.*

Bauer & French
(See Boise)

Brunetti, Louis L. ... '49 '74 C.816 B.E. L.229 J.D. P.O. Box 1240

Cardon, Andrea L.
(See Boise)

Charney, Dennis M., (CV) ... '65 '92 C&L.1193 B.A.S., J.D. [Charney]
Charney Law Office, (CV) ... 951 E. Plaza Dr., Ste. 140
Chatlin, Kimberly A. ... '66 '92 C&L.101 B.A., J.D. [Trafton,C.&O.] ⊙
Clapp, Sandra L., (BV) ... '66 '91 C&L.336 B.A., J.D. [S.L.Clapp&Assoc.]

Clapp, Sandra L., Associates, P.A., (BV)
1025 S. Bridgeway Place, Suite 180, P.O. Box 2660, 83616
Telephone: 208-938-2660 Fax: 208-938-2674
URL: http://www.clapp-legal.com
Sandra L. Clapp.
Trusts and Estates, Business Transactions, Property Law.
See Professional Biographies, EAGLE, IDAHO

Estate Planning Legal Consultants, PLLC, (BV) ... 1036 East Iron Eagle Drive, Suite 105
Jones, Rodney C., (AVⓉ) '50 '76 C.383 B.B.A. L.245 J.D.
(adm. in GA; not adm. in ID) V.P. & Gen. Coun., Conagra Foods/Lamb-Weston, Inc.
Kole, Patrick J., (BV) ... '52 '76 C.477 A.B. L.208 J.D. V.P.
Maile, Thomas G., IV, (CV) ... '52 '79 C.1044 B.A. L.208 J.D. 380 W. State
Marikos, Joanna A. ... '61 '99 C.285 B.S. L.950 J.D. [Marikos L.]
Marikos Law, P.C. ... 99 E. State
Martelle, Martin J. ... '47 '77 C.1078 B.A. L.1153 J.D. [Martelle]
Martelle Law Offices, P.A. ... 82 E. State
Milam, Ben R. '63 '88 C.668 B.A. L.800 J.D.
(adm. in CA; not adm. in ID) P.O. Box 1059
Moulton, Webb T. ... '67 '04 C.549 B.A. L.336 J.D. Gen. Counsel, Emerald Finance

Noack, Harold Q., Jr., P.A.
(See Boise)

Peters, Barry, (BV) ... '51 '77 C.112 B.A. L.1197 J.D. [B.Peters]
Peters, Barry, P.A., (BV) ... 101 Eagle Glen Lane
Richardson, Peter J., (AV) ... '56 '84 C.1193 B.A. L.767 J.D. 99 E. State St.
Schrader, Jeffrey L. '62 '88 C.879 B.S.B.A. L.602 J.D.
(adm. in TX; not adm. in ID) 3375 S. Pasa Tiempo Pl.
Shook, Julie H., (BVⓉ) '68 '94
C&L.623 B.A., J.D. [▣ Trafton,C.&O.] (⊙Las Vegas, NV)
Stellmon, John M., (BV) ... '57 '84 C&L.336 B.A., J.D. 1509 N. Dragonfly Place
Trafton, Mark E., (CVⓉ) ... '65 '97 C&L.1049 B.B.A., J.D. [Trafton,C.&O.] ⊙
Trafton, Chatlin & Olsen, Ltd., (CVⓉ) ... 2367 N Stonecrest Pl. (⊙Las Vegas, NV)
Wight, Mark E., (BV) ... '58 '85 C.877 B.A./B.S. L.101 J.D. [Estate P.C.]
Wright, Mark E., (CVⓉ) '51 '78 C.1266 B.A. L.724 J.D.
(adm. in NY; not adm. in ID) 1036 East Iron Eagle Drive

EMMETT, * 5,490, *Gem Co.*

Bjorkman, Ron, (AV) ... '48 '75 C.101 B.S. L.336 J.D. [H.R.Bjorkman]
Bjorkman, H. Ronald, (AV) ... 109 N. Hayes
Gorrono, Louie, (AV) ... '19 '49 C&L.336 B.S., LL.B. 105 N. Hayes Avenue
Linville, Richard K., (BV) ... '55 '82 C.813 B.A. L.911 J.D. Pros. Atty.
Petrie, Gordon W. ... '48 '76 C.1032 B.A. L.336 J.D. Mag.
Varie, Douglas R., (BV) ... '63 '89 C.678 B.A. L.228 J.D. Pros. Atty.

FAIRFIELD, * 371, *Camas Co.*

Nichols, Frank Wilson, (CV) ... '51 '90 C.909 B.A. L.336 J.D. Pros. Atty.
Varin, John F. ... '46 '71 C&L.336 B.S., J.D. U.S. Maj.
White, Margaret P. ... '43 '78 C&L.336 B.S., J.D. Pros. Atty.

FILER, 1,620, *Twin Falls Co.*

Decker, Fred D., (AV) ... '40 '66 C&L.336 B.S., J.D. 4202 N. 2100 E.‡
Fields, James R. ... '43 '73 C&L.336 B.S., J.D. 4200 North 2317 East

FORT HALL, 3,193, *Bannock & Bingham Cos.*

Wolfley, Jeanette '55 '83 C.494 B.A. L.560 J.D.
(adm. in CO; not adm. in ID) P.O. Box 306‡

FRUITLAND, 3,805, *Payette Co.*

Kofoed, Glenn L., (BV) ... '40 '74 C.101 B.S. L.336 J.D. Treasure Valley Prof. Bldg.
Lee, Glenn M., (BV) ... '45 '75 C.1193 B.B.A. L.336 J.D. 1511 N. Whitley Drive

Yturri Rose, LLP
(See Ontario, Oregon)

GOODING, * 3,384, *Gooding Co.*

Arkoosh, C. Tom, (AV) ... '51 '78 C.309 B.A. L.336 J.D. [Arkoosh]
Arkoosh Law Office, Chtd., (AV) ... 301 Main St.

Becker, Phillip M. .... '35 '62 C&L.285 J.D. 712 3rd Ave.
Booth, Theodore R. '62 '99 C&L.878 BA, JD
(adm. in UT; not adm. in ID) [🅰 Arkoosh]
Brown, Philip A., (BV) ....'55 '88 C.1193 B.B.A. L.336 J.D. Pros. Atty.
Cassidy, Kevin P. ....'55 '87 C.190 B.A. L.546 J.D. Mag. J.
Cushman, Thomas R. ....'46 '77 C.1176 B.A. L.260 J.D. Mag.
Hobdey, Craig, (CV) ....'51 '84 C.1032 B.B.A. L.336 J.D. [Hobdey&H.]
Hobdey & Hobdey, (AV) ....125 Fifth Ave., W.
Kiiha, Jay J. ....'72 '02 C.878 B.S. L.589 J.D. [🅰 Arkoosh]
Nelson, Lynn R. ....'47 '83 C.878 B.A. L.336 J.D. Pros. Atty.
Swenson, Severt, Jr., (BV) ....'40 '66 C.136 B.A. L.336 LL.B. 122 4th Ave. W.
Wood, Roderick Barry ....'51 '76 C.972 B.S. L.336 J.D. Dist. J.

GRANGEVILLE, * 3,226, *Idaho Co.*

Albers, Dennis L., (BV) ....'47 '72 C&L.336 B.S., J.D. P.O. Box 314

Creason, Moore & Dokken, PLLC
(See Lewiston)

Dee, MacGregor, Fales & MacGregor, L.L.P., (AV) .... 416 West Main Street
Fales, Daren W., (CV) ....'62 '87 C.1193 B.A. L.629 J.D. [D.Fales]
Fales, Daren, Law Offices, PLLC, (CV) .... 204 W. North St.
FitzMaurice, Gregory, (BV) ....'53 '78 C.37 B.S. L.336 J.D. [G.Fitzmaurice]
FitzMaurice, Gregory, P.A., (BV) .... 200 S. College St.
Griffin, Michael J. ....'48 '77 C.791 B.S. L.336 J.D. Mag.
Luplow, Dale L. ....'44 '71 C.959 B.S. L.966 J.D. 409 E. South St.
MacGregor, Kirk Angus, (BV) ....'60 '89 C.908 B.A. L.336 J.D. [Dee,M.F.&M.]
MacGregor, Wayne C., Jr., (AV) ....'25 '52 C&L.336 J.D. [Dee,M.F.&M.]
Olds, Scott ....'64 '91 C.585 B.A. L.336 J.D. [Olds]
Olds, Victoria A. ....'66 '91 C.340 B.A. L.336 J.D. [Olds]
Olds Law Offices, P.A. .... 204 N. Meadow
Payne, Jeff Paul, (BV) ....'61 '88 C.336 B.S. L.508 J.D. 114 S. Idaho
Payne, Terri Lynn, (CV) ....'58 '88 C.506 B.S. L.508 J.D. 821 Washington Ave.
Reinhardt, George ....'50 '75 C&L.336 J.D. Dist. J.
Spencer, Jane E., (CV) ....'53 '96 C.335 B.S. L.336 J.D. [🅰 G.Fitzmaurice]

HAILEY, * 6,200, *Blaine Co.*

Alban, Daniel ....'45 '73 C&L.37 B.S., J.D. 201 2nd Ave., S.‡
Bartlett, Robert W., II ....'33 '67 C.976 B.A. L.1065 J.D. P.O. Box 3334‡
Baxter, K. Ellen, (BV) ....'55 '81 C.939 B.A. L.911 J.D. [Roark]

Benoit, Alexander, Harwood, High & Valdez, L.L.P.
(See Twin Falls)

Chapman, John S., (AV) ....'36 '62 C.336 B.A. L.813 J.D. P.O. Box 3950
Donovan, Michael F., (BV) ....'51 '77 C&L.878 B.A., J.D. 940 Buckhorn Dr.
Dunlap, Tracy, (BV) ....'60 '87 C.915 B.A. L.878 J.D. [Hogue&D.]
Elgee, Robert J. ....'50 '76 C&L.336 B.S., J.D. Mag.
Haemmerle, Jennifer L. Kroos, (BV) '63 '89 C&L.336 B.S., J.D.
400 S. Main St., Ste. 102
Hogue, Terry G., (AV) ....'44 '72 C.267 A.B. L.1065 J.D. [Hogue&D.] ⊙
Hogue & Dunlap, LLP, (AV) .... 16 W. Croy (⊙Ketchum)
Kantor, Robert A. '43 '69 C.174 B.A. L.802 J.D.
(adm. in CA; not adm. in ID) Rokan Partrero
Kramer, Douglas D. ....'25 '51 C&L.336 B.A., LL.B. Ret. Dist. J.
Kraynick, Michael J. ....'56 '82 C.174 B.A. L.724 J.D. [M.J.Kraynick]
Kraynick, Michael J., P.L.L.C. .... 318 East Spruce Street

Lawson & Laski, PLLC
(See Ketchum)

May, James J. ....'25 '52 C&L.336 B.A., J.D. Dist. Ct. J.

Parnes, Andrew
(See Ketchum)

Phillips, James W., (BV) ....'47 '73 C.911 B.A. L.273 J.D. [Roark]
Rivers, Kathleen E. ....'54 '84 C.1044 B.A. L.629 J.D. 409 N. Main‡
The Roark Law Firm, LLP, (BV) .... 409 N. Main St.

HAYDEN, 9,159, *Kootenai Co.*

English, James M., (BV) '44 '73 C&L.336 B.S., J.D.
Pres. & Corp. Coun., Idaho Forest Industries Inc.
Koler, Duncan B. ....'58 '85 C.906 B.A. L.61 J.D. [D.B.Koler]
Koler, Duncan B., A P.C., Law Offices of .... 7687 E. Gem Shores Rd.
Poorman, Scott L., (CV) ....'63 '93 C.330 B.S. L.336 J.D. 8886 N. Government Way

HAYDEN LAKE, 494, *Kootenai Co.*

Covington, Robert E., III, (CV) '53 '78 C.309 B.A. L.880 J.D.
8884 N. Government Way
Kolts, Kathlene Landgraf '52 '86 C.932 B.S. L.770 J.D.
(adm. in CA; not adm. in ID) [Kolts&K.]
Kolts, Raymond G., (AVⓉ) '40 '67 C.1097 L.426 J.D.
(adm. in CA; not adm. in ID) [Kolts&K.]
Kolts & Kolts, (AVⓉ) .... 1510 Pebble Stone Court
Sims, William F., (BV) ....'43 '75 C&L.285 B.A., J.D. 10584 Lake View Drive
Williams, Jerome '12 '34 C&L.285 LL.B.
(adm. in WA; not adm. in ID) 2959 Ponderosa Lane‡
Zanetti, Rebecca A. ....'69 '99 C.990 B.A. L.336 J.D. P.O. Box 2875

HOMEDALE, 2,528, *Owyhee Co.*

Grober, Dan C., (CV) ....'48 '86 C.234 B.A. L.336 J.D. [Grober&H.]
Grober & Hart, Lawyers, (CV) .... 122 West Idaho Avenue
Hart, Lois W. ....'55 '88 C&L.336 B.G.S., J.D. [Grober&H.]

HOPE, 99, *Bonner Co.*

O'Hare, Timothy J. ....'49 '75 C&L.508 B.S., J.D. P.O. Box 329

IDAHO CITY, * 458, *Boise Co.*

Gardunia, Theresa, (BV) ....'63 '96 C.1193 B.B.A. L.336 J.D. Co. Atty.
Young, Patricia G. ....'46 '77 C.611 B.A. L.336 J.D. Mag. J.

IDAHO FALLS, * 50,730, *Bonneville Co.*

Adams, Fred M., (BV) ....'55 '79 C.1032 B.A. L.336 J.D. P.O. Box 2377
Allen, Jared W. ....'70 '98 C.101 B.A. L.336 J.D. [Beard S.C.G.M.C.]
Anderson, Gregory S. ....'45 '76 C.336 B.S. L.477 J.D. Dist. J.
Anderson, Marty R. ....'70 '99 C&L.336 B.S., J.D. [🅰 Ehardt,S.&T.]
Anderson Nelson Hall Smith, P.A., (AV) .... 490 Memorial Drive
Archibald, Lane R., Law Office of, (BV) ....'48 '78 C.101 B.S. L.678 J.D. 470 B St.
Arnold, James C., (CV) ....'58 '87 C.1193 B.A. L.336 J.D. 390 N. Capitol
Auman, Eva M. '54 '90 C&L.502 B.E.S., J.D.
(adm. in MO; not adm. in ID) Dept. of Energy, Off. of Chf. Coun.
Avery, John O., (CV) ....'51 '85 C.101 B.S. L.336 J.D. [Cooper,A.&L.]
Banks, Jeffery W., (BV) ....'63 '95 C.101 B.S. L.336 J.D. [Anderson N.H.S.]
Barrott, Tyrie Alan, (BV) '62 '92 C.101 B.S. L.221 J.D.
Asst. Gen. Coun., Melaleuca, Inc.
Bates, Jay F., (BV) ....'25 '56 L.336 J.D. 210 Tendoy Dr.
Beard, Winston V., (AV) ....'41 '67 C.101 L.878 J.D. [Beard S.C.G.M.C.]

Beard St. Clair Gaffney McNamara Calder PA, (AV) BR
2105 Coronado Street, 83404-7495
Telephone: 208-523-5171 Fax: 208-529-9732
Email: law@idahofallslaw.com URL: http://www.lawyers.com/idahofallslaw
Winston V. Beard; John G. St. Clair; Michael D. Gaffney; Harlow J. McNamara; Gregory C. Calder; Jarin O. Hammer; Jared W. Allen;—Chad A. Campos; Kari Marie Campos; Jeffrey D. Brunson.
Agricultural Law, Acquisitions, Americans with Disabilities Act, Antitrust, Arbitration, Asset Protection, Automobile Accidents, Automobile Insurance, Banking Law, Breach of Contract, Business Law, Buying and Selling Businesses, Charitable Giving, Collections, Commercial Insurance, Commercial Law, Commercial Real Estate, Computers and Software, Condominiums, Construction Law, Contested Wills, Contracts, Copyrights, Corporations, Creditors Rights, Crop Damage and Chemical Applications, Debtor and Creditor, Discrimination, Distribution and Distributorships, Divorce with significant assets, Elder Care, Elder Law, Employment Discrimination, Employment Law, Estate Planning, Estate and Gift Taxation, Family Business Law, Family and Medical Leave Act, Farm and Ranch Law, Fire Loss, Food, Drug and Cosmetic Law, Franchises and Franchising, Foreclosures, General Trial and Appellate Practice, Guardianship, Harassment, Health Care, Health Insurance, Income Taxation, Insurance, Insurance Bad Faith, Investments, Landlord and Tenant Law, Leasing, Liens, Life and Health Insurance, Limited Liability Company Law, Litigation, Long-term Care, Mechanics Liens, Mediation, Medical Malpractice and Malpractice Defense, Medicare and Medicaid, Minority Business Law, Mortgages, Multilevel Sales, Nonprofit and Charitable Organizations, Nursing Homes, PACA, Partnerships, Pension and Benefits, Personal Injury, Post Mortem Administration of Trusts and Estates, Products Liabilities, Professional Malpractice, Property Tax, Professional Practices, Property Insurance, Railroad Accidents, Real Estate, Sexual Abuse, Slip and Fall, Small Business Law, Social Security, Social Security Disability, Taxation, Torts, Trademarks, Trade Secrets, Trust and Estates, Valuations, Warranties, Wills and Probate, Workers Compensation, Wrongful Death, Wrongful Termination, Zoning, Planning and Land Use.
Representative Clients: Furnished Upon Request.
See Professional Biographies, IDAHO FALLS, IDAHO

Birch, Barton J. ....'74 '01 C.1032 B.A. L.336 J.D. 428 Park Avenue
Blower, Earl ....'52 '79 C.877 B.S. L.878 J.D. Mag. J.
Bonney, Stephanie Jaymes ....'69 '99 C.205 B.S. L.174 J.D. [Pike&S.] ⊙
Bowen, Dwight R., (CV) ....'43 '69 C.101 B.S. L.336 J.D. 520 3rd St.
Bowen, Travis L., (BVⓉ) '52 '80 C&L.101 B.A., J.D.
(adm. in UT; not adm. in ID) [T.Bowen] ⊙
Bowen, Travis, P.C., (BVⓉ)
1906 Jennie Lee Drive, Suite 100 (⊙Salt Lake City, St. George, UT)
Bowhan, Brett R. '51 '84 C.174 B.A. L.208 J.D.
(adm. in CO; not adm. in ID)
Dept. Chf. Coun., U.S. Dept. of Energy, Chf. Coun. ID Opers. Off.
Brady, Jerry M. '36 '63 C.602 B.A. L.1066 LL.B.
(adm. in CA; not adm. in ID) Pres., Post Company, The
Brandstetter, Dean C., (BV) ....'57 '82 C&L.336 B.S., J.D. [Cox,O.&B.]
Brassey, John Michael, (AV) '46 '71 C&L.336 B.S., J.D.
[Hopkins R.C.H.&H.] (⊙Boise)
Brown, Steven K., (AV) ....'55 '85 C&L.336 B.S., J.D. [Hopkins R.C.H.&H.]
Browning, Allen H., (CV) ....'54 '83 C.605 B.A. L.546 J.D. 2281 Trivet
Brunson, Jeffrey D. ....'77 '04 C.101 B.S. L.336 J.D. [🅰 Beard S.C.G.M.C.]
Calder, Gregory C., (BV) ....'66 '95 C.101 B.S. L.336 J.D. [Beard S.C.G.M.C.]
Campos, Chad A., (CV) ....'71 '00 C.101 B.A. L.336 J.D. [🅰 Beard S.C.G.M.C.]
Campos, Kari Marie, (CV) ....'69 '00 C.1032 B.S. L.101 J.D. [🅰 Beard S.C.G.M.C.]
Carey, Donald F., (BV) ....'57 '91 C.999 B.A. L.972 J.D. [Quane S.]
Carr, Steven E., (BV) ....'57 '84 C.877 B.A. L.36 J.D. [Fuller&C.]
Casper, Thel W., (BV) ....'64 '93 C.101 B.S. L.1066 J.D. [Holden,K.H.&C.]
Casperson, DeAnne ....'— '99 C.877 B.S. L.986 J.D. [🅰 Holden,K.H.&C.]
Christian, Stephen R. '56 '88
C.612 B.S.M.E. L.1218 J.D. 2525 North Fremont Avenue (Pat.)
Combo, John X., (BV) ....'22 '50 C.505 B.S. L.276 J.D. [🅲 Woolf,C.&T.]
Combo, William P., (BV) ....'53 '79 C.335 B.A. L.336 J.D. [Woolf,C.&T.]
Cook, Linda J. ....'44 '73 C.101 B.S. L.336 J.D. Mag. J.
Cooper, R. Fred, (BV) ....'57 '85 C.101 B.S. L.336 J.D. [Cooper,A.&L.]
Cooper, Avery & Lee, P.A., (BV) ....770 S. Woodruff
Cox, Roger D., (BV) ....'38 '67 C.101 B.S. L.273 J.D. [Cox,O.&B.]

Cox, Ohman & Brandstetter, Chartered, (AV)
510 D Street, P.O. Box 51600, 83405
Telephone: 208-522-8606 Fax: 208-522-8618
Email: cobjmo@ida.net URL: http://www.coblaw.com
Roger D. Cox; John M. Ohman (Certified as Civil Trial Specialist by the Idaho Trial Lawyers Association); Dean C. Brandstetter.
General Civil and Criminal Trial, Appellate and Administrative Practice in State and Federal Courts. Social Security, Workmen's Compensation and Corporation. Personal Injury, Insurance, Family Law, Divorce, Child Support, Child Custody, Automobile Accidents and Injuries, Wrongful Death, Head Injury, Criminal Law.
See Professional Biographies, IDAHO FALLS, IDAHO

Crapo, Michael D., (AV) ....'51 '77 C.101 B.A. L.309 J.D. U.S. Sen.
Crockett, Gregory L., (AV) ....'49 '74 C&L.336 B.S., J.D. [Hopkins R.C.H.&H.]
Cutler, John E., (BV) ....'62 '90 C&L.101 B.S., J.D. [Cutler]
Cutler Law Office, P.A., (BV) ....482 Constitution Wy., Ste. 109
Dalling, Dean, (Chartered), (AV) ....'53 '81 C&L.101 B.S., J.D. [Dalling&D.]
Dalling, William R., (Chartered), (BV) ....'51 '78 C&L.101 B.S., J.D. [Dalling&D.]
Dalling & Dalling, (AV) ....525 Park Avenue, Suite 2D
Davis, Bart M., (AV) ....'55 '81 C.101 B.A. L.336 J.D. 696 S. Bellin Rd.
Decker, Karl R., (BV) ....'54 '85 C&L.101 B.A., J.D. [Holden,K.H.&C.]
Dennert, Wiley R., (CV) ....'71 '00 C&L.101 B.A., J.D. [🅰 Anderson N.H.S.]

Dockstader Law Office
(See Boise)

Driscoll, Buster J. ....'77 '04 C&L.1335 B.A., J.D. [🅰 McGrath,M.&S.]
Duffin, M. Patrick ....'68 '96 C.101 B.A. L.336 J.D. 525 9th St.
Ehardt, Gregory J. ....'70 '98 C.101 B.A. L.862 J.D. [Ehardt,S.&T.]

Ehardt, Smith & Torgesen, (BV)
2235 East 25th Street, Suite 290, 83404
Telephone: 208-542-9292 Fax: 208-552-2518
Gregory J. Ehardt; Samuel R. Torgesen; Curtis Reed Smith;—Marty R. Anderson.
Business, Corporate, Estate Planning, Wills and Trusts, Real Estate, Taxation, Probate, Bankruptcy, Real Property, Criminal Defense, Family Law, Litigation, Juvenile Law.
See Professional Biographies, IDAHO FALLS, IDAHO

Erikson, Todd R., (BV) ....'64 '91 C&L.101 B.A., J.D. 525 Park Avenue
Eskelson, Scott P., (AV) ....'53 '79 C.877 B.S. L.878 J.D. [Martin&E.]

Faler, William D., (BV) ... '47 '72 C&L.378 B.A., J.D. [Holden,K.H.&C.]
Farnam, Robert E., (AV) ... '45 '69 C&L.336 B.S., J.D. [Holden,K.H.&C.]
Fetzer, Mark S. '50 '79 C.383 B.A. L.208 J.D.
(adm. in CO; not adm. in ID) Portage Environmental, Inc.
Follett, Robert Marinus, (BV) ... '61 '88 C&L.878 B.A., J.D. [A Holden,K.H.&C.]
Foster, Kent W., (AV) ... '41 '68 C&L.878 B.A., J.D. [Holden,K.H.&C.]
Fuller, Mark R., (BV) ... '54 '81 C&L.101 B.S., J.D. [Fuller&C.]
Fuller & Carr, (BV) ... 410 Memoril Drive, Suite 201
Gaffney, Michael D., (AV) ... '52 '86 C.686 B.S. L.336 J.D. [Beard S.C.G.M.C.]
Gardner, Steven A., (BV) ... '52 '80 C.101 B.A. L.285 J.D. 1428 E. 17th St.
Goodson, W. Gary '35 '66 C.101 B.S. L.273 J.D.
(adm. in TX; not adm. in ID; Pat.) Lockheed Martin ITC
Grimes, Kevin D., (BV) ... '60 '85 C.170 B.A. L.802 J.D. [Grimes&R.]
Grimes & Reese, P.L.L.C., (BV) ... 1270 S. Woodruff Ave.
Groberg, Joseph H., Law Office of ... '42 '71 C.101 B.A. L.145 J.D. 1605 S. Woodruff St.
Hahn, Fred Joseph, (AV) ... '33 '58 C.120 B.A. L.276 J.D. [© Holden,K.H.&C.]
Hahn, Frederick J., III, (BV) ... '63 '90 C&L.336 B.A., J.D. [Holden,K.H.&C.]
Hall, Blake G., (BV) ... '53 '79 C.101 B.A. L.273 J.D. [Anderson N.H.S.]
Hall, Scott R., (BV) ... '59 '86 C.101 B.S. L.336 J.D. [Anderson N.H.S.]
Hall, Stephen D., (BV) ... '52 '79 C&L.101 B.A., J.D. [Petersen,M.&H.]

Hall, Farley, Oberrecht & Blanton, P.A.
(See Boise)

Hammer, Jarin O., (CV) ... '67 '97 C.101 B.S. L.336 J.D. [Beard S.C.G.M.C.]
Hansen, John D., (AV) ... '33 '59 C&L.336 B.S., LL.B. [Hopkins R.C.H.&H.]
Harris, Donald L., (AV) ... '47 '76 C.112 B.A. L.101 J.D. [Holden,K.H.&C.]
Harris, Robert L. ... '77 '04 C.877 B.S. L.336 J.D. [A Holden,K.H.&C.]
Hart, Stephen S., (BV) ... '52 '76 C&L.878 B.S., J.D. [Hart&K.]
Hart & Kohler, (BV) ... 482 Constitution Way
Hartnett, Ronald J. '43 '81 C.871 B.S. L.472 J.D.
Proj. Atty., Engineering and Construction Grp.
Hertzler, Tim '59 '00 L.378 J.D.
(adm. in MT; not adm. in ID) 225 S. Ridge Ave.
Hinman, Michael H., (BV) '50 '77
C.454 B.A. L.336 J.D. Mng. Atty., Idaho Legal Aid Servs., Inc.

Holden, Kidwell, Hahn & Crapo, P.L.L.C., (AV)
1000 Riverwalk Drive, Suite 200, P.O. Box 50130, 83405
Telephone: 208-523-0620 Telefax: 208-523-9518
Email: hkhc@holdenlegal.com
Members of Firm and Associates: Arthur W. Holden (1877-1967); Robert Bonnifield Holden (1911-1971); Terry L. Crapo (1939-1982); William Sutherland Holden (1907-1988); Kent W. Foster; Robert E. Farnam; William D. Faler; Charles A. Homer; Gary Lane Meikle; Donald L. Harris; Dale W. Storer; Marie T. Tyler; Frederick J. Hahn, III; Karl R. Decker; Thel W. Casper; Shan B. Perry;—Robert Marinus Follett; Amelia A. Sheets; DeAnne Casperson; Robert L. Harris. Of Counsel: Fred Joseph Hahn.
General and Trial Practice. Banking, Corporation, Taxation, Insurance, Real Estate, Condemnation, Trust and Probate, Bankruptcy, Creditors Rights, Negligence, Products Liability, Water Rights, Labor and Construction, Education, Estate Planning, Local Government, Planning and Zoning, Employee Benefits and Pension.
Representative Clients: The Equitable Life Assurance Society of the U. S. (Commercial, Farm & City Loans); The Post Register; West One Bank Idaho N.A.; School District #91; John Hancock Mutual Life Insurance Co.; KIFI TV; Melaleuca, Inc.
See Professional Biographies, IDAHO FALLS, IDAHO

Holman, James D., (BV) ... '51 '78 C.597 B.A. L.546 J.D. [Thomsen&S.]
Homer, Charles A., (AV) ... '49 '74 C.101 B.A. L.336 J.D. [Holden,K.H.&C.]
Hoopes, D. Fredrick, (AV) ... '40 '73 C.101 B.S. L.845 J.D. [Hopkins R.C.H.&H.]
Hopkins, C. Timothy, (AV) ... '36 '64 C.813 A.B. L.273 J.D. [Hopkins R.C.H.&H.]

Hopkins Roden Crockett Hansen & Hoopes, PLLC, (AV) BB
428 Park Avenue, P.O. Box 51219, 83405-1219 ⊙
Telephone: 208-523-4445 Fax: 208-523-4474
Email: IFLaw@hrchh.com URL: http://www.hrchh.com
Members of Firm: C. Timothy Hopkins; William C. Roden (Resident, Boise Office); Gregory L. Crockett; John D. Hansen; D. Fredrick Hoopes; John Michael Brassey (Resident, Boise, Idaho Office); Lary S. Larson; Paul B. Rippel; Steven K. Brown; David H. Shipman; Lance J. Schuster. Of Counsel: Bruce L. Thomas (Resident, Boise Office); Orval Hansen (Resident, Washington, D.C. Office); George L. Denison (Resident, Washington, D.C. Office).
General Civil, Trial and Appellate Practice before all State and Federal Courts and Administrative Agencies, Administrative Law, Agricultural Law, Alcoholic Beverages, Banking Law, Bankruptcy, Business Law, Civil Rights, Contracts, Construction Law, Corporate Law, Criminal Law, Debtor and Creditor, Election, Campaign and Political Law, Eminent Domain, Employment Law, Family Law, Government, Insurance, Health Care, Hospital Law, Immigration Law, Natural Resources, Negligence, Personal Injury (plaintiffs and defense), Real Estate, Social Security, Taxation, Trusts and Estates, Utility Law, Wills and Probate, Workers' Compensation Law, and Zoning, Planning and Land Use.
Boise, Idaho Office: 802 West Bannock, Suite 900, P.O. Box 2110, 83701-2110. Telephone: 208-336-7930. Fax: 208-336-9154. Email: BoiseLaw@hrchh.com.
Washington, D.C. Office: 8 East Street, S.E., 20003. Telephone: 202-546-0361. Fax: 202-546-6294.
See Professional Biographies, IDAHO FALLS, IDAHO

Jenkins, Gordon W. ... '45 '76 C.101 B.S. L.426 J.D. 2388 Eastview Dr.
Johnson, David A., (BV) ... '58 '85 C.101 B.S. L.336 J.D. [Wright W.&J.]
Just, Charles C., (BV) ... '49 '76 C&L.336 B.A., J.D. [Just]

Just Law Office, (BV)
381 Shoup Avenue, Suite 211, P.O. Box 50271, 83405
Telephone: 208-523-9106; Toll Free: 800-923-9106 Fax: 208-523-9146
Email: cjust@justlawidaho.com URL: http://www.justlawidaho.com
Charles C. Just.
Languages: English and Spanish.
Real Estate, Foreclosures, Bankruptcy, Deeds-in-Lieu, Evictions, Document Preparation, Title Packages, Centralized Statewide Reconveyances, REO Services, REO Closings, Real Estate Litigation.
See Professional Biographies, IDAHO FALLS, IDAHO

Kohler, Jay A., (BV) ... '47 '75 C.101 B.S. L.336 J.D. [Hart&K.]
Larson, Lary S., (BV) ... '53 '80 C.575 B.A. L.101 J.D. [Hopkins R.C.H.&H.]
Lee, Royce B., (BV) ... '47 '74 C&L.878 B.A., J.D. [Cooper,A.&L.]
Lewis-Frazee, Judith A. ... '44 '75 C.665 B.S. L.1002 J.D. [© Pike&S.] ⊙
Linton, Bruce A. '36 '65 C&L.37 B.F.A., LL.B.
(adm. in AZ; not adm. in ID) 120 E. 16th St.‡
Love, Dennis A., (BV) '47 '85 C.101 B.S. L.336 J.D.
V.P., Gen. Coun. & Secy., CH2M-WG Idaho, LLC
Luke, Colin W. ... '50 '80 C&L.101 B.S., J.D. Mag. J.
Madsen, Stephen Kent ... '72 '01 C.101 B.A. L.336 J.D. RS&I, Inc.
Marotz, Scott, (AV) ... '55 '81 C.1193 B.A. L.336 J.D. [Marotz]
Marotz Law Office, (AV) ... P.O. Box 52147
Martin, Simon S., (BV) '45 '71 C&L.336 B.A., J.D.
Sr. Staff Coun., U.S. Dept. of Energy
Martin, Stephen E., (AV) ... '47 '72 C&L.597 B.A., J.D. [Martin&E.]

Martin & Eskelson, P.L.L.C., (AV)
425 South Holmes Avenue, P.O. Box 3189, 83403-3189
Telephone: 208-523-6644 Fax: 208-522-0791
URL: http://www.stephenemartinlaw.com
(This Listing Continued)

Martin & Eskelson, P.L.L.C. (Continued)
Stephen E. Martin; Scott P. Eskelson.
Estate Planning, Federal Taxation, Real Estate, Probate, Business Law, Estate and Gift Taxation.
See Professional Biographies, IDAHO FALLS, IDAHO

Mason, Kimball W., (BV) ... '54 '81 C.101 B.S. L.336 J.D. City Pros.
McBride, Michael R., (BV) ... '55 '83 C.101 B.A. L.336 J.D. 1495 E. 17th St.
McCrady, Allen D. '28 '53 C.145 Ph.B. L.665 LL.B.
(adm. in PA; not adm. in ID) 1110 Monaghan Ct.‡
McGrath, Stephen J., (AV) ... '46 '73 C.352 B.A. L.336 J.D. [McGrath,M.&S.]

McGrath, Meacham & Smith, PLLC, (AV)
414 Shoup Avenue, P.O. Box 50731, 83405
Telephone: 208-524-0731 Fax: 208-529-4166
Email: info@eidaholaw.com URL: http://www.lawyers.com/eidaholaw
Members of Firm: Stephen J. McGrath; Gregory P. Meacham; Bryan D. Smith. Associate: Buster J. Driscoll.
General Civil Practice, Banking, Insurance Defense, Business, Real Estate, Worker's Compensation, Products Liability, Commercial, Personal Injury, Trusts and Estates, Wills and Probate, Creditor Bankruptcy, Municipal Law.
See Professional Biographies, IDAHO FALLS, IDAHO

McKnight, Mary M. ... '60 '89 C.627 B.A. L.190 J.D. Coun., U.S. Dept. of Energy
McNamara, Harlow J., (BV) ... '42 '70 C.101 B.S. L.273 J.D. [Beard S.C.G.M.C.]
Meacham, Gregory P., (BV) ... '46 '74 C.877 B.S. L.336 J.D. [McGrath,M.&S.]
Meikle, Gary Lane, (AV) ... '50 '77 C&L.101 B.A., J.D. [Holden,K.H.&C.]
Meikle, Stephen A., (CV) ... '57 '82 C.1032 B.B.A. L.336 J.D. Assoc. Coun., Valley Bk.

Merrill & Merrill, Chartered
(See Pocatello)

Milam, Beth E. ... '50 '80 C.174 B.A. L.190 J.D. 1949 Malibu‡
Miller, Mark J., (CV) ... '61 '92 C.1193 B.A. L.336 J.D. [Pike&S.] ⊙

Moffatt Thomas Barrett Rock & Fields, Chartered, (AV)
420 Memorial Drive, P.O. Box 51505, 83405 ⊙
Telephone: 208-522-6700 Fax: 208-522-5111
URL: http://www.moffatt.com
Bradley J. Williams; Lee Radford.
General Civil, Trial and Appellate Practice. Administrative Law, Alternative Dispute Resolution, Antitrust and Trade Regulation, Aviation, Bankruptcy, Banks and Banking, Business Law, Commercial Real Estate, Construction Law, Contracts, Corporate Law, Debtor and Creditor, Disabilities, Employee Benefits, Environmental Law, Finance, Government Relations, Health Care, Hospital Law, Insurance Defense, Intellectual Property, Labor and Employment Law, Leases and Leasing, Litigation, Medical Malpractice, Mergers, Acquisitions and Divestitures, Mortgages, Nonprofit and Charitable Organizations, Partnership Law, Probate, Products Liability, Professional Liability, Public Utility Law, Real Estate, Regulatory Law, Securities, Taxation, Torts, Trusts and Estates, Water Law, Worker's Compensation.
Boise, Idaho Office: 101 South Capitol Boulevard, 10th Floor, P.O. Box 829, 83701. Telephone: 208-345-2000. Fax: 208-385-5384.
Pocatello, Idaho Office: 412 West Center, Suite 2000, P.O. Box 817, 83204. Telephone: 208-233-2001. Fax: 208-232-0150.
Twin Falls, Idaho Office: 621 N. College Road, Suite 103, P.O. Box 5483, 83303-5483. Telephone: 208-734-7500. Fax: 208-734-7508.
See Professional Biographies, IDAHO FALLS, IDAHO

Monson, Nancy J. ... '64 '96 C.101 B.A. L.61 J.D. 1386 Saint Clair Rd.
Moriarty, Katherine S., (BV) ... '52 '91 C.878 B.A. L.336 J.D. 428 Park Avenue
Moss, Reed L., (AV) ... '30 '60 C.101 B.A. L.273 J.D. [© Petersen,M.&H.]
Nalder, G. Lance, (BV) ... '56 '85 C.101 B.S. L.336 J.D. [Nalder]
Nalder Law Office PC, (BV) ... 301 A St.
Nelson, Douglas R., (AV) ... '49 '73 C.101 L.878 J.D. [Anderson N.H.S.]
North-Shaul, Penelope ... '67 '94 C&L.336 B.A., J.D. [A Pike&S.]
O'Brien, Anne Bedinghaus, (CV) '56 '84
C.339 B.A. L.146 J.D. Idaho Legal Aid Servs., Inc.
Ohman, John M., (AV) ... '48 '72 C&L.190 B.S.B.A., J.D. [Cox,O.&B.]
Olson, William D., (AV) '33 '59
C.1032 B.A. L.910 J.D. [Racine,O.N.B.&B.] (⊙Pocatello)
Parry, Steven R., (BV) ... '59 '87 C&L.101 B.S., J.D. [Anderson N.H.S.]
Perry, Shan B., (BV) ... '69 '96 C.336 B.A. L.878 J.D. [Holden,K.H.&C.]
Petersen, Dennis R., (BV) ... '48 '80 C.1073 B.A. L.862 J.D. 390 N. Capitol
Petersen, George C., Jr., (AV) ... '24 '50 C&L.878 J.D. [Petersen,M.&H.]

Petersen, Moss & Hall, (AV)
485 E Street, 83401
Telephone: 208-523-4650 FAX: 208-524-3391
Members of Firm: George C. Petersen, Jr.; Stephen D. Hall. Of Counsel: Reed L. Moss.
General Civil and Trial Practice in all State and Federal Courts and Administrative Agencies. Corporation, Partnership, Business, Personal Injury, Real Estate, Employment. Insurance, Estate Planning, Probate, Taxation and Construction.
Representative Client: State Farm Insurance Cos.
See Professional Biographies, IDAHO FALLS, IDAHO

Pike, Edward W., (AV) ... '24 '50 C&L.878 B.S., LL.B. [E.W.Pike] (⊙Driggs)
Pike, Edward W., P.A., (AV) ... P.O. Box 2949
Pike & Smith, P.A., (AV) ... 151 North Ridge Avenue, Suite 210 (⊙Driggs)

Quane Smith LLP, (AV)
2325 West Broadway, Suite B, 83402 ⊙
Telephone: 208-529-0000 Facsimile: 208-529-0005
Email: info@quanesmith.net URL: http://www.quanesmith.net
Donald F. Carey;—Robert D. Williams; Carole I. Wesenberg (Resident).
Insurance, Insurance Defense, Litigation, Accountants Liability, Advertising and Marketing, Agents and Brokers Liability, Agricultural Law, Alcoholic Beverages, Alternative Dispute Resolution, Architects and Engineers Liability, Arson and Insurance Fraud, Asbestos Defense, Brain Injury, Business Law, Casualty Insurance Defense, Catastrophic Injury, Civil Practice, Commercial Law, Complex and Multi-District Litigation, Computers and Software, Construction Law, Contracts, Corporate Law, Design Professionals Liability, Drug and Medical Device Defense, Education Law, Employer Liability, Environmental Law, ERISA Litigation, Extra Contractual Insurance Defense, Federal Practice, Fire Insurance, Firearms Litigation, Food Products Liability, Fraud and Deceit, Government, Hazardous Waste Liability, Head Injury, Health Care, Insurance Bad Faith Defense, Labor and Employment, Legal Malpractice Defense, Libel, Slander and Defamation, Life Insurance Defense, Manufacturers Liability, Medical Malpractice, Natural Resources, Negligence, Personal Injury, Pesticide Litigation, Physicians Licensing, Pollution, Premises Liability, Products Liability, Professional Discipline, Professional Liability, Propane Products Liability, Property Damage Defense, Real Estate, Recreational Products Liability, School Board Defense, Slip and Fall, Spinal Injury, Subrogation, Torts, Toxic Torts, Transportation, Workers Compensation and Wrongful Death.
Boise, Idaho Office: U.S. Bank Plaza, 16th Floor, P.O. Box 519. Telephone: 208-345-8600. Facsimile: 208-345-8660.
Coeur d'Alene, Idaho Office: 2020 Lakewood Drive, Suite 312, P.O. Box 1758. Telephone: 208-664-9281. Facsimile: 208-664-5380.
See Professional Biographies, IDAHO FALLS, IDAHO

Racine, Olson, Nye, Budge & Bailey , Chartered, (AV)
477 Shoup Avenue, Suite 203A (⊙Boise, Pocatello)
Radford, Lee, (BV) ... '63 '89 C&L.101 B.A., J.D. [Moffatt T.B.R.&F.]
Radin, John L., (BV) ... '51 '76 C.112 B.A. L.767 J.D. [Radin&W.]
Radin & Webb, (BV) ... 520 D St.

Reese, Spencer, (BV) ....'60 '86 C.170 B.A. L.910 J.D. [Grimes&R.]
Reeves, Reginald R. ....'27 '52 C.1378 B.S. L.336 J.D. 690 Cambridge
Richards, Steven A., (BV) ....'65 '95 C.335 B.A. L.1358 J.D. 1270 S. Woodruff Ave.
Rippel, Paul B., (BV) ....'52 '81 C&L.336 B.S., J.D. [Hopkins R.C.H.&H.]
Roberts, Delwin W., (BV) ....'53 '83 C.101 B.S. L.336 J.D. 1945 E. 17th St.
St. Clair, John G., (BV) ....'45 '70 C&L.336 B.S., J.D. [Beard S.C.G.M.C.]
St. Clair, Richard T. ....'47 '72 C&L.336 B.S., J.D. Dist. J.
Schuster, Lance J. ....'67 '96 C.101 B.A. L.336 J.D. [Hopkins R.C.H.&H.]
Seamons, Justin R., (BV) ....'62 '88 C&L.101 B.A., J.D. 525 Park Avenue, Suite 2A
Sharp, John M., (AV) ....'16 '47 C&L.878 LL.B. 490 Memorial Dr.
Sheets, Amelia A. ....'— '99 C.112 B.A. L.1370 J.D. [Ⓐ Holden,K.H.&C.]
Sheppard, Kenneth J., (BV) .... '57 '84 C.101 B.S. L.813 J.D. Gen. Coun., Melaleuca, Inc.
Shindurling, Jon J., (BV) ....'47 '77 C.36 B.A. L.336 J.D. Dist. J.
Shipman, David H., (BV) ....'60 '86 C.339 B.S. L.597 J.D. [Hopkins R.C.H.&H.]
Simmons, John G., (BV) ....'59 '84 C&L.101 B.S., J.D. 796 Memorial Dr.
Smirch, James McCord ....'70 '96 C.629 B.A. L.972 J.D. Law Clk., Co. Ct.
Smith, Bryan D., (AV) ....'62 '89 C.101 B.A. L.464 J.D. [McGrath,M.&S.]
Smith, Curtis Reed, (BV) ....'65 '94 C.1032 B.S. L.336 J.D. [Ehardt,S.&T.]
Smith, Franklin N. '41 '65 C.1085 L.878 J.D.
[Pike&S.] & [Ⓒ Van Cott,B.,C.&M.] (⊙Driggs, ID; Salt Lake City, UT)
Smith, Marvin M., (AV) ....'52 '78 C.877 B.S. L.101 J.D. [Anderson N.H.S.]
Smith, Mary Ann H. '56 '81 C.893 B.A. L.178 J.D.
(adm. in WA; not adm. in ID) 781 Cedar Ridge Dr.‡
Sorenson, Gayle A., (AV) ....'52 '78 C&L.336 B.S., J.D. 5203 S. 11 E.
Spilker, H. Larry ....'33 '68 C&L.878 B.S., J.D. 5858 E. 21st St.
Stephens, Alan C., (AV) ....'51 '78 C.101 B.A. L.336 J.D. [Thomsen&S.]
Storer, Dale W., (AV) ....'50 '77 C&L.101 B.S., J.D. [Holden,K.H.&C.]
Stucki, Marvin R. ....'47 '75 C.101 B.S. L.336 J.D. [M.Stucki]
Stucki, Marvin ....520 Legion Dr.
Sturm, Teresa L., (BV) ....'54 '80 C&L.878 B.A., J.D. 428 Park Avenue
Swafford, Jack D. ....'40 '71 C.1032 B.B.A. L.336 J.D. 4383 E. 49th S.‡
Telford, Stephen H., (BV) ....'55 '85 C.101 B.S. L.336 J.D. [Thomsen&S.]
Thompson, Stevan H., (BV) ....'56 '82 C&L.336 B.A., J.D. [Woolf,C.&T.]
Thomsen, Curt R., (AV) ....'52 '77 C.36 B.S. L.336 J.D. [Thomsen&S.]
Thomsen and Stephens, P.A., (AV) ....2635 Channing Way
Throckmorton, Ralph R. '46 '71 C&L.352 B.B.A., J.D.
(adm. in IA; not adm. in ID) Chf. Coun., U.S. Dept. of Energy, State Opers. Off.
Tingey, Joel E., (BV) ....'55 '83 C&L.101 B.A., J.D. [Anderson N.H.S.]
Tolson, Aaron John ....'68 '02 C.1335 B.S. L.623 J.D. [Ⓐ Wright W.&J.]
Torgesen, Samuel R. ....'71 '02 C.101 B.A. L.464 J.D. [Ehardt,S.&T.]
Transtrum, Terrel F. ....'58 '87 C.101 B.S. L.336 J.D. Melaleuca, Inc.
Tucker, Brian Thomas, (BV) ....'68 '95 C.1032 B.A. L.336 J.D. [Anderson N.H.S.]
Tyler, Marie T., (BV) ....'39 '87 C.1032 B.A. L.336 J.D. [Holden,K.H.&C.]
Voshell, Jack G., (P.A.), (BV) ....'20 '49 C&L.900 B.A., LL.B. Pros. Atty.
Ward, Jeffery Kurt, (CV) ....'56 '83 C.1193 B.B.A. L.336 J.D. [J.K.Ward]
Ward, Jeffery K., (CV) ....149 N. Placer Ave.
Watkins, Dane H., Jr. ....'70 '99 C&L.101 B.A., J.D. Pros. Off.
Webb, Russell E., III, (BV) ....'48 '75 C.165 A.B. L.276 J.D. [Radin&W.]
Weinpel, Marc J., Law Office of, (BV) '49 '74
C&L.190 B.A., J.D. 482 Constitution Way, Ste. B4
Wesenberg, Carole I. ....'— '00 C.506 B.S. L.801 J.D. [Ⓐ Quane S.]
Wheiler, J. Michael, (AV) ....'56 '85 C.877 B.S. L.336 J.D. [Thomsen&S.]
Whittington, Kent E. ....'50 '78 C.101 B.S. L.336 J.D. 1820 E. 17th St., Suite 340
Whyte, Michael J., (CV) ....'66 '93 C.120 B.A. L.190 J.D. [Thomsen&S.]
Whyte, Tammie D., (BV) ....'65 '92 C.1262 B.A. L.190 J.D. [Ⓐ Woolf,C.&T.]
Whyte, Thomas C., (AV) ....'29 '54 C&L.190 B.S.C., LL.B. 2971 Stone Haven Cr.‡
Williams, Bradley J., (BV) ....'60 '89 C.1032 B.A. L.336 J.D. [Moffatt T.B.R.&F.]
Williams, Robert D. ....'— '94 C.966 B.S. L.336 J.D. [Ⓐ Quane S.]
Wood, T. Jason, (BV) ....'68 '94 C.101 B.A. L.336 J.D. [Thomsen&S.]
Wood, Theodore V. ....'42 '72 C.813 B.S. L.336 J.D. Dist. J.
Woolf, Aaron J. ....'72 '98 C.1032 B.B.A. L.336 J.D. [Ⓐ Woolf,C.&T.]
Woolf, Combo & Thompson, (BV) ....408 Shoup Avenue
Wright, Roger B., (BV) ....'40 '65 C&L.336 B.A., J.D. [Wright W.&J.]
Wright, Steven J., (BV) ....'63 '90 C&L.101 B.S., J.D. [Wright W.&J.]
Wright Wright & Johnson, PLLC, (BV) ....477 Shoup Avenue, Suite 109

INDIAN VALLEY, 60, *Adams Co.*

Ellis, Alan E. '44 '72 C.112 A.B. L.770 J.D.
(adm. in CA; not adm. in ID) Ret. Ct. J.

JEROME, * 7,780, *Jerome Co.*

Borresen, Thomas H. ....'49 '75 C&L.336 B.A., J.D. Mag. J.
Butler, John K. ....'52 '80 C.1077 B.A. L.1137 J.D. Dist. J.
Fredericksen, Eugene D., (BV) '41 '69 C&L.336 B.S., J.D.
[Ⓒ Fredericksen,W.M.&L.] ‡

Fredericksen, Williams, Meservy & Lothspeich, LLP, (AV)
117 South Adams Street, P.O. Box 168, 83338
Telephone: 208-324-2303 FAX: 208-324-3135
Email: fwmattys@cableone.net
Members of Firm: Robert E. Williams, III; James C. Meservy; Frank M. Rettig (1903-1987); John B. Lothspeich. Of Counsel: Eugene D. Fredericksen (Retired).
General Civil and Trial Practice. Business, Real Estate, Agriculture, Probate, Estate Planning, Family Law, Personal Injury, Workers Compensation, Wrongful Death, Municipal Law, Administrative Law.
Representative Clients: City of Jerome; Hazelton Housing Authority; City of Hazelton; KART Broadcasting Co.; Arlo G. Lott Trucking, Inc.; Giltner Inc. (Trucking); South Central Idaho Solid Waste District; Rich Thompson Trucking, Inc.; Ridley's Food Corporation; Shoshone School District; City of Eden.
Reference: D.L. Evans Bank, Jerome, Idaho.

Higer, Nathan W. ....'44 '69 C&L.911 B.A., J.D. Dist. J.
Horgan, John L., (BV) ....'55 '83 C&L.336 B.Mus., J.D. Co. Pros. Atty.
Lammers, Rockne K., (BV) ....'57 '83 C.335 B.A. L.336 J.D. P.O. Box 591
Lothspeich, John B., (BV) ....'65 '91 C&L.336 B.S., J.D. [Fredericksen,W.M.&L.]
Meservy, James C., (BV) ....'53 '79 C&L.336 B.S., J.D. [Fredericksen,W.M.&L.]
Shaud, Russell C. ....'19 '51 C.216 L.336 LL.B. Ret. Mag.
Shull, Luverne Eugene, (CV) ....'55 '96 C.1193 B.S. L.336 J.D. P.O. Box 544
Skeen, Jannece-Marie ....'— '98 C.1032 B.S. L.336 J.D. 608 2nd Ave. E.
Williams, Robert E., III, (AV) ... '46 '74 C.101 B.A. L.597 J.D. [Fredericksen,W.M.&L.]

JULIAETTA, 609, *Latah Co.*

Curtin, Jack L., (CV) ....'42 '73 C.628 B.S. L.336 J.D. P.O. Box 380
Rishling, Steve A., Attorney at Law, (CV) ....'55 '89 C&L.336 B.S., J.D. P.O. Box 260

KELLOGG, 2,395, *Shoshone Co.*

Cox, Charles L. A., (BV) ....'52 '81 C.931 B.A. L.352 J.D. [Evans K.]

Evans Keane LLP, (AV)
111 Main Street, P.O. Box 659, 83837 ⊙
Telephone: 208-784-1105 Facsimile: 208-783-7601
Email: ccox@usamedia.tv
James P. Keane (1925-1988); Charles L. A. Cox.
General Trial and Appellate Practice, Corporation, Mining, Labor, Banking, Real Property, Insurance, Products Liability, Workers Compensation Law, Environmental Law, Personal Injury.
Representative Clients: Beamis Oil Co.; City of Kellogg; City of Wardner; Coeur d'Alene Mines Corp.; Hecla Mining Co.; Kellogg School District No. 391; Silver Mountain Corp.; Coeur Silver Valley, Inc.; Sidney Resources Corporation.
Boise, Idaho Office: 1405 W. Main Street, P.O. Box 959. Telephone: 208-384-1800

See Professional Biographies, KELLOGG, IDAHO

Peacock, Michael F., (BV) .... '48 '78 C&L.336 B.S., J.D. 123 McKinley Ave.
Russell, William J., (BV) ....'51 '76 C.378 B.A. L.208 J.D. Pintlar Corp.

KENDRICK, 395, *Latah Co.*

Jacobs, Hugh Garret .... '47 '73 C.800 B.A. L.770 J.D. 1647 Cedar Ridge Rd.‡

KETCHUM, 3,003, *Blaine Co.*

Aanestad, Douglas J., (AV) ....'48 '74 C.813 A.B. L.1065 J.D. [Speck&A.]
Barsotti, Brian, (BV) .... '53 '78 C.602 B.A. L.310 J.D. P.O. Box 370

Benoit, Alexander, Harwood, High & Valdez, L.L.P., (AV)
160 Second Street East, Suite 218, P.O. Box 2246, 83340 ⊙
Telephone: 208-726-4900 Fax: 208-726-3101
Email: benoitlaw@benoitlaw.com URL: http://www.benoitlaw.com
Robert M. Harwood.
General Civil Trial Practice. Business Corporation, Partnership, Wills, Estate Planning, Probate, Municipal, Banking, Insurance Defense, Real Estate, Environmental, Agriculture, Real Estate Transactions, Real Estate Litigation, Residential Real Estate and Commercial Real Estate, Product Liability Defense, Professional Liability Defense, Criminal Defense.
Twin Falls, Idaho Office: 126 Second Avenue North. Telephone: 208-733-5463. Fax: 208-734-1438.

See Professional Biographies, KETCHUM, IDAHO

Bernstein, Cushner & Kimmell, P.C. .... P.O. Box 1527 (⊙Boston, MA)
Campion, Thomas B. ....'42 '72 C.197 A.B. L.174 J.D. P.O. Box 538‡
Clark, Erin Farrell .... '67 '93 C.893 B.A. L.1065 J.D. [Ⓐ Lawson&L.]
Clayton, Steven E. ....'48 '72 C.877 B.S. L.336 J.D. 206 East Ave.‡
Cohen, Earl R. '37 '62 C.112 B.A. L.800 LL.B.
(adm. in CA; not adm. in ID) P.O. Box 2938‡
Collier, Bruce J., (AV) ....'49 '74 C.1193 B.A. L.878 J.D. [Kneeland,K.C.&L.]
Crabtree, J. Stephen, (BV) ....'47 '72 C&L.800 B.A., J.D. P.O. Box 1623
Crist, Roger E. ....'39 '65 C&L.813 B.A., LL.B. 204 Spruce Ave., N.
Dolan, Daniel M., (BV) '54 '80 C.350 B.S. L.285 J.D.
160 Second Street East, Suite 202
Donohoe, Kevin E., Law Office of, (BV) '52 '80
C.112 B.A. L.1065 J.D. 128 Saddle Rd., Ste. 103

Elkins, Brian E., (BV) '55 '83 C&L.336 B.S., J.D.
Bitterroot Square Professional Building, 208 Spruce Avenue North, P.O. Box 766, 83340
Telephone: 208-726-4338 Facsimile: 208-726-9328
URL: http://www.lawyers.com/elkinslaw
Criminal Defense, DUI, General Litigation and Appellate Practice.

See Professional Biographies, KETCHUM, IDAHO

Eshman, Jill W. ....'61 '86 C.800 B.S. L.426 J.D. [Ⓐ Lawson&L.]
Fallowfield, Robert I., (BV) .... '47 '76 L.336 J.D. [Luboviski,W.F.&W.]
Fjeld, Kirstin K. ....'74 '03 [Ⓐ Woolley&P.]
Gariepy, Richard N. ....'43 '74 C.1107 B.A. L.1049 J.D. P.O. Box 3869
Grabow, John C. ....'56 '81 C&L.477 B.A., J.D. P.O. Box 6880
Harwood, Robert M., (AV) ....'46 '71 C&L.336 B.A., J.D. [Benoit,A.H.H.&V.]

Hawley Troxell Ennis & Hawley LLP, (AV)
540 Second Avenue North, P.O. Box 297, 83340 ⊙
Telephone: 208-726-1700 Facsimile: 208-726-9743
Email: info@hteh.com URL: http://www.hawleytroxell.com
Member of Firm: Rand L. Peebles. Associate: Adam Bruno King.
General Civil Trial and Appellate Practice before all State and Federal Courts and Administrative Agencies. Alternative Dispute Resolution, Antitrust, Aviation, Banking, Bankruptcy and Creditor Rights, Communications, Construction, Copyright, Corporate, Education, Employee Benefits, Environmental, ERISA, Trusts and Estates, Finance, Health Care and Hospital, Insurance, Intellectual Property, Labor and Employment, Legislative, Media, Mergers and Acquisitions, Mining, Natural Resources, Probate, Products Liability, Public Contract, Public Finance, Public Utility, Qualified and Nonqualified Deferred Compensation, Real Estate, Securities, Taxation, Technology and Science, Trademark and Workers' Compensation Law.
Boise, Idaho Office: Suite 1000, 877 Main Street. Telephone: 208-344-6000. Facsimile: 208-342-3829.
Pocatello, Idaho Office: 333 South Main Street, P.O. Box 100. Telephone: 208-233-0845. Facsimile: 208-233-1304.
Reno, Nevada Office: 6490 S. McCarran, Suite 4. Telephone: 775-829-9944. Facsimile: 775-829-2627.

See Professional Biographies, KETCHUM, IDAHO

Himberger Law Offices, Chtd.
(See Boise)

Hogue, Terry G., (AV) ....'44 '72 C.267 A.B. L.1065 J.D. [Hogue&D.] ⊙
Hogue & Dunlap, LLP, (AV) .... 120 East Ave. (⊙Hailey)
Kantor, Sandra F. '46 '69 C.846 B.B.A. L.802 J.D.
(adm. in TX; not adm. in ID) P.O. Box 610‡
Kennedy, James L., Jr., (AV) .....'41 '66 C.228 A.B. L.893 LL.B. 340 Second Street East
King, Adam Bruno, (BV) ....'61 '89 C.112 B.A. L.1065 J.D. [Ⓐ Hawley T.E.&H.]
Kneeland, G.R., (AV) ....'18 '49 C.909 B.S. L.911 LL.B. [Ⓒ Kneeland,K.C.&L.]

Kneeland, Korb, Collier & Legg, (AV)
Kneeland Professional Building, 128 Saddle Road, Suite 103, P.O. Box 249, 83340
Telephone: 208-726-9311 Telecopier: 208-726-4515
Email: kneeland@cox-internet.com
Members of Firm: Robert Korb, III; Bruce J. Collier; Ann Legg. Of Counsel: G.R. Kneeland.
General Civil Practice. Trials. Appellate, Condominium, Business and Corporation, Probate and Estate, Zoning, Real Estate, Family and Municipal Law.
Reference: First Security Bank of Idaho, N. A.

See Professional Biographies, KETCHUM, IDAHO

Korb, Robert, III, (BV) .... '44 '72 C.174 B.A. L.208 J.D. [Kneeland,K.C.&L.]
Kronenberg, Debra, Attorney at Law, (BVⓉ) '52 '81
C.696 B.A. L.1051 J.D. P.O. Box 1286
Kunick, Leslie Thullen .... '60 '88 C.908 B.A. L.285 J.D. City Atty.
Laggis, Stratton P., (AV) ....'35 '68 C.336 B.A. L.793 J.D. 128 Saddle Rd.
Laski, James R., (BV) ....'66 '95 C.321 B.A. L.1338 J.D. [Lawson&L.]
Lawson, Edward A., (AV) .... '50 '75 C.767 A.B. L.1065 J.D. [Lawson&L.]

Lawson & Laski, PLLC, (AV)
675 Sun Valley Road, Suite A, P.O. Box 3310, 83340
Telephone: 208-725-0055 Fax: 208-725-0076
URL: http://www.lawyers.com/lawsonlaski
Edward A. Lawson; James R. Laski;—Erin Farrell Clark; Jill W. Eshman.

(This Listing Continued)

Lawson & Laski, PLLC (Continued)

Real Estate, Business Organizations, Civil Litigation, Contracts, Securities, Commercial Law.

See Professional Biographies, KETCHUM, IDAHO

Legg, Ann, (BV) .... '52 '80 C.1193 B.A. L.336 J.D. [Kneeland,K.C.&L.]
Luboviski, Barry J., (BV) .... '43 '76 C.763 B.A. L.336 J.D. [Luboviski,W.F.&W.]
Luboviski, Wygle, Fallowfield & Williamson, P.A., (BV) .... 460 Sun Valley Rd.
Mills, Wallace W., Attorney at Law '44 '74 C.309 A.B. L.790 J.D.
220 2nd Ave., Ste. 101
Monson, Dana R., (CV) .... '70 '97 C.475 B.A. L.1358 J.D. P.O. Box 2984
O'Toole, Erin M. .... '70 '96 C.1030 B.A. L.818 J.D. [Ⓐ Bernstein,C.&K.]
Parker-Bass, Harriet '48 '76 C.477 B.A. L.284 J.D.
(adm. in CA; not adm. in ID) P.O. Box 3970‡

Parnes, Andrew, (AVⓉ) '46 '78 C.951 B.A. L.1066 J.D.
160 2nd Street East, Suite 216, P.O. Box 5988, 83340
Telephone: 208-726-1010 Facsimile: 208-726-1187
Email: aparnes@mindspring.com
Criminal Trial and Appellate Practice in all State and Federal Courts. Habeas Corpus, DUI, Felonies, Misdemeanors, Homicide, Juvenile, Traffic Violations and Drug Crimes.

See Professional Biographies, KETCHUM, IDAHO

Peebles, Rand L., (BV) .... '46 '73 C.312 B.A. L.767 J.D. [Hawley T.E.&H.]
Pogue, Michael D. .... '— '97 C.112 B.A. L.767 J.D. [Woolley&P.]
Praggastis, Thomas C., (BV) .... '51 '77 C&L.878 B.A., J.D. P.O. Box 6090
Ranill, William Lee .... '51 '90 C.878 B.S. L.61 J.D. P.O. Box 3689
Ritzau, Lee P., (CV) .... '64 '95 C.602 B.A. L.336 J.D. P.O. Box 2400
Seiller, John A., Attorney at Law .... '66 '92 C.473 B.A. L.608 J.D. P.O. Box 6090
Simon, Edward, (BV) .... '46 '78 C.645 B.A. L.564 J.D. 500 S. Main St., Ste. 205
Speck, James P., (AV) .... '45 '76 C.197 B.A. L.174 J.D. [Speck&A.]

Speck & Aanestad, A Professional Corporation, (AV)
120 East Avenue, P.O. Box 987, 83340
Telephone: 208-726-4421 Fax: 208-726-0752
Email: sandalaw@mindspring.com
James P. Speck; Douglas J. Aanestad.
Business Transactions, Civil Litigation, Real Estate, Estate Planning, Probate, Water and Family Law.
Representative Client: First Security Bank of Idaho, N.A.

See Professional Biographies, KETCHUM, IDAHO

Thompson, Stephen D., (CV) .... '62 '88 C.911 B.A. L.950 J.D. 120 East Avenue
Williamson, Ned, (BV) .... '55 '83 C.1262 B.S. L.336 J.D. [Luboviski,W.F.&W.]
Woolley, Cynthia J. .... '58 '92 C.773 B.A. L.597 J.D. [Woolley&P.]
Woolley & Pogue, PLLC .... 180 First St. W., Ste. 107
Wygle, Janet C., (BV) .... '50 '76 C.911 B.A. L.174 J.D. [Luboviski,W.F.&W.]

KOOSKIA, 692, *Idaho Co.*

Harris, Mildred '34 '81 C.569 B.A. L.1230 J.D.
(adm. in CA; not adm. in ID) R.R. 1‡
Hoyt, Wesley W., (AVⓉ) .... '49 '72 C.174 B.A. L.208 J.D. Hc 66 Box 313A

LAPWAI, 1,134, *Nez Perce Co.*

Eichstaedt, Richard K. .... '73 '97 C.300 B.A. L.596 J.D. Nez Perce Tribe
Gudgell, K. Heidi '48 '89 C&L.336 B.S., J.D.
Staff Atty., The Legal Coun. Off., NezPerce Tribal Exec. Commitee
Smith, Rob Roy .... '76 '00 C.321 B.A. L.596 J.D. P.O. Box 305

LEWISTON, * 30,904, *Nez Perce Co.*

Aherin, Darrel W., (AV) .... '46 '73 C.999 B.A. L.336 J.D. [Aherin,R.&A.]

Aherin, Rice & Anegon, A Professional Association, (AV)
1212 Idaho Street, Drawer 698, 83501
Telephone: 208-746-3646 Fax: 208-746-3650
Email: araoffice@valley-internet.net URL: http://www.aralawoffice.com
Darrel W. Aherin; Stephen C. Rice; Anthony C. Anegon.
Language: English.
Personal Injury, Auto Accidents, Wrongful Death, Products Liability, Automobile Negligence, Insurance Bad Faith, Medical and Legal Negligence, Workers Compensation, Criminal Defense, Libel and Slander, Condemnation, General Litigation including Domestic Relations, Contracts and Commercial Law, Probate, Real Property, Estate Planning, Employment and Environmental Law.

See Professional Biographies, LEWISTON, IDAHO

Anderson, Kenneth L., (BV) .... '38 '78 C.846 B.A. L.336 J.D. 504 Main St.
Anegon, Anthony C., (BV) .... '57 '82 C.477 A.B. L.336 J.D. [Aherin,R.&A.]
Ater, Derrick A., (CV) .... '48 '90 C&L.336 B.A., J.D. [Ⓐ Randall,B.&C.]
Berger-Schneider, Nancy F. '— '02 C.131 B.S. L.336 J.D.
Nez Perce Co. I.D. Pros. Off.
Blake, Wynne M., (AV) .... '22 '48 C&L.336 LL.B. [Ⓒ Randall,B.&C.]
Blewett, Ron T., (AV) .... '57 '82 C&L.336 B.S., J.D. [Clark&F.]
Bradbury, John H. .... '36 '65 C.336 B.A. L.477 LL.B. Dist. J.
Brower, Robert L., (BV) .... '43 '73 C&L.336 B.S., J.D. [Jones,B.&C.]
Brown, Charles A., (BV) .... '52 '77 C.999 B.S. L.336 J.D. 324 Main
Brown, Robert P., (AV) .... '40 '64 C&L.336 B.A., LL.B. [Clements,B.&M.]
Brudie, Jeff M., (BV) '59 '84 C&L.336 B.S.C.E., J.D.
Gen. Coun. & V.P., Legal Servs., Regence Group
Burton, Edward G. .... '40 '66 C.674 A.B. L.309 LL.B. P.O. Box 243
Calhoun, Todd B. '45 '71 C&L.802 B.A., J.D.
(adm. in TX; not adm. in ID) Potlatch Corp.
Callery, Thomas W., (BV) .... '53 '78 C.335 B.A. L.336 J.D. [Jones,B.&C.]
Cannon, Ned A., (BV) .... '52 '78 C.941 B.A. L.336 J.D. [Smith&C.]
Carr, William J. .... '75 '03 C.594 B.S. L.336 J.D. [Ⓐ Clark&F.]
Caylor, Steven E. M. '51 '85 C.347 B.A. L.879 J.D.
(adm. in IN; not adm. in ID) Trial Ct. Admr., Nez Perce Co. Courthouse
Chapman, Scott M., (BV) .... '56 '85 C.629 B.S. L.336 J.D. [Randall,B.&C.]
Church, John A. .... '41 '66 C.629 B.S. L.336 J.D. 2501 17th St.
Clark, Paul T., (AV) .... '45 '70 C.594 B.A. L.336 J.D. [Clark&F.]

Clark and Feeney, (AV)
The Train Station, Suite 201, 13th and Main, P.O. Box 285, 83501
Telephone: 208-743-9516; 1-800-865-9516 Fax: 208-746-9160 URL: http://www.clarkandfeeneylaw.com
Email: cflaw@lewiston.com URL: http://www.clarkandfeeney.com
Paul T. Clark; Thomas W. Feeney; Ron T. Blewett; Rube G. Junes (Not admitted in ID); Douglas L. Mushlitz; Charles M. Stroschein; Connie W. Taylor; Scott D. Gallina. Associates: Tina L. Kernan; Jonathan D. Hally; William J. Carr.
Trial Practice, Personal Injury, Corporation, Commercial, Construction, Surety, Real Property, Probate, Domestic Relations, General Practice, Criminal Law, Bankruptcy.
Representative Client: Port of Lewiston.

See Professional Biographies, LEWISTON, IDAHO

Clearwater Law Offices, (CV) .... 1301 G St.

Clements, Brown & McNichols, P.A., (AV)
321 13th Street, P.O. Box 1510, 83501
Telephone: 208-743-6538 FAX: 208-746-0753
URL: http://www.clbrmc.com

(This Listing Continued)

Clements, Brown & McNichols, P.A. (Continued)

V. R. Clements (1896-1982); Philip E. Peterson (1922-2003); Robert P. Brown; Michael E. McNichols; Bentley G. Stromberg; Eric K. Peterson; Sonyalee R. Nutsch.
Civil Trial and Appellate Practice. Banking, Corporation, Education Law, Health Care Law, Estate Planning, Real Estate, Probate, Products Liability, Insurance Defense, Surety, Workers Compensation Law and Employment Law.
Reference: FirstBank Northwest.

See Professional Biographies, LEWISTON, IDAHO

Cochnauer, Amé Q., (CV) .... '54 '97 C.1051 B.S. L.336 J.D. Dep. Pros. Atty.
Cox, Steve R., (AV) .... '46 '73 C&L.336 B.S., J.D. [Randall,B.&C.]
Creason, Theodore O., (AV) .... '48 '73 C&L.336 B.A., J.D. [Creason,M.&D.]

Creason, Moore & Dokken, PLLC, (AV) [BR]
Lewiston Professional Building, 1219 Idaho Street, Drawer 835, 83501
Telephone: 208-743-1516 Fax: 208-746-2231 URL: http://www.cmd-law.com
Email: cmd@cmd-law.com URL: http://www.creasonmdlaw.com
Members of Firm: Daniel W. O'Connell (1928-1988); Marcus J. Ware (1904-1996); Theodore O. Creason; Christopher J. Moore; David E. Dokken; Tod D. Geidl.
General Civil Practice, Insurance Defense, Appeals, Business Organizations, Commercial, Real Property, Probate and Estate Planning, Tax Law, Personal Injury, Criminal Defense, Auto Accident, Head Injury.
Representative Clients: Nationwide Insurance Co.; Horace Mann Insurance Co.; Valley Medical Center/Children's Clinic, Inc.

See Professional Biographies, LEWISTON, IDAHO

Dokken, David E., (BV) .... '54 '82 C&L.336 B.A., J.D. [Creason,M.&D.]
Eddy, Loren J., Law Office, (CV) .... '56 '81 C.697 B.A. L.770 J.D. 524 Bryden Ave.
Feeney, Thomas W., (BV) .... '22 '50 L.336 LL.B. [Clark&F.]
Fitzgerald, William J., (CV) .... '51 '76 C&L.336 B.A., J.D. 504 Main St., Ste. 480
Forsman, William F. '50 '88 C.907 B.A. L.911 J.D.
(adm. in WA; not adm. in ID) 1200 Waha Rd.‡
Gallina, Scott D., (BV) .... '63 '90 C.906 B.A. L.336 J.D. [Clark&F.]
Geidl, Tod D. .... '73 '98 C&L.336 B.S., J.D. [Creason,M.&D.]
Givens, James W., (BV) .... '21 '50 C&L.208 B.S., LL.B. 1026 F St.
Grow, James Wesley, Jr., (CV) .... '56 '87 C.1051 B.A. L.336 J.D. [J.W.Grow,Jr.]
Grow, James W., Jr., PLLC, Law Office of, (CV) .... 1301 G St.
Gustafson, Laura N. '45 '93 C.999 B.A. L.336 J.D.
(adm. in NV; not adm. in ID) State Atty.
Haley, Ralph H. .... '26 '56 C&L.336 B.S., LL.B. Ret. Mag.

Hall, Farley, Oberrecht & Blanton, P.A.
(See Boise)

Hally, Jonathan D., (BV) .... '66 '94 C.1193 B.B.A. L.336 J.D. [Ⓐ Clark&F.]
Havens, Mark M. '60 '87
C.285 A.B. L.597 J.D. Dir., Community Rel., Lewiston School Dist.
Jones, Garry W., (BV) .... '45 '69 C&L.336 B.S., J.D. [Jones,B.&C.]
Jones, William J., (BV) .... '20 '48 C&L.336 LL.B. [Ⓒ Jones,B.&C.]
Jones, Brower & Callery, P.L.L.C., (BV) .... 1304 Idaho Street
Junes, Rube G., (CV) '44 '84 C&L.336 B.S., J.D.
(adm. in WA; not adm. in ID) [Clark&F.]

Keeton & Tait, (AV)
312 Miller Street, 83501
Telephone: 208-743-6231 Fax: 208-746-0962 URL: http://www.ktlaw.org
Email: lewlawus@lewiston.com URL: http://www.keeton-tait.com
Members of Firm: Paul C. Keeton (1913-2005); John Reid Tait. Associate: Ken Everett Nagy.
General Practice, Workers Compensation, Personal Injury, Criminal Defense, Probate, Real Estate, Family Law, Housing and Employment Discrimination, Indian Law, Appellate Practice.

See Professional Biographies, LEWISTON, IDAHO

Kernan, Tina L., (BV) .... '66 '93 C&L.336 B.A., J.D. [Ⓐ Clark&F.]
Kerrick, Carl B. .... '55 '83 C.629 B.S. L.336 J.D. Mag. J.
Knowlton & Miles, PLLC, (BV) .... 312 Seventeenth Street

Libey, Ensley, Esser & Nelson, PLLC
(See Colfax, Washington)

Litteneker, Edwin L., (BV) .... '51 '78 C&L.336 B.A., J.D. P.O. Box 1225
Maynard, John H. .... '21 '52 C&L.285 LL.B. Ret. Dist. J.
McCann, William Vern, Jr., (BV) .... '43 '69 C&L.336 B.S., J.D. 1027 Bryden Ave.
McCarthy, Bob J. .... '54 '88 C.120 B.A. L.508 J.D. Idaho Legal Aid Servs.
McGeoghegan, Earl Leon, (CV) .... '44 '87 C.990 B.A. L.336 J.D. [Clearwater]
McNichols, Michael E., (AV) .... '39 '63 C&L.336 B.A., LL.B. [Clements,B.&M.]
Miles, Manderson L., (BV) .... '47 '73 C.623 B.S. L.336 J.D. [Knowlton&M.]
Miller, Milan E., Law Offices of, (CV) ... '40 '90 C&L.336 B.S.E.E., J.D. 502 Thain Road
Moore, Christopher J., (BV) .... '52 '89 C&L.336 B.S., J.D. [Creason,M.&D.]
Mushlitz, Douglas L., (BV) .... '59 '85 C.1032 B.B.A. L.336 J.D. [Clark&F.]
Nagy, Ken Everett, (CV) .... '64 '00 C.1292 B.A. L.336 J.D. [Ⓐ Keeton&T.]
Nutsch, Sonyalee R., (CV) .... '75 '00 C.999 B.S. L.336 J.D. [Clements,B.&M.]
Peterson, Eric K., (BV) .... '55 '87 C.494 Ph.D. L.336 J.D. [Clements,B.&M.]
Radakovich, Danny J., (CV) .... '50 '76 C.1196 B.S. L.336 J.D. 1624 G St.
Ramalingam, Sunil, (BV) .... '62 '97 C.1060 B.A. L.336 J.D. Dep. Pros.

Ramsden & Lyons
(See Coeur d'Alene)

Randall, Blake & Cox, P.A., (AV)
1106 Idaho Street, P.O. Box 446, 83501
Telephone: 208-743-1234 Telefax: 208-743-1266
Email: david@rbcox.com URL: http://www.rbclaw.com
Steve R. Cox; David R. Risley; Kerry A. Wagner; Scott M. Chapman;—Derrick A. Ater; April A. Smith. Of Counsel: Russell S. Randall (1908-2004); Wynne M. Blake.
General Practice, Agricultural Law, Bankruptcy, Business Law, Contracts, Criminal Law, Debtor and Creditor Law. Employment Law, Family Law, Domestic Relations, Personal Injury, Products Liability, Real Estate, Taxation, Trusts and Estates, Estate Planning, Wills, Probate, Workers Compensation, Zoning, Planning and Land Use.

See Professional Biographies, LEWISTON, IDAHO

Rapaich, Eli, (AV) .... '25 '54 C&L.336 B.A., LL.B. 1040 Powers Ave.
Rice, Stephen C., (AV) .... '45 '75 C.1032 B.S. L.336 J.D. [Aherin,R.&A.]
Richardson, Todd Samuel, (CV) .... '64 '98 1301 G Street
Risley, David R., (BV) .... '50 '75 C.413 B.A. L.336 J.D. [Randall,B.&C.]
Roberts, Don L., (BV) .... '49 '76 C.878 B.A. L.336 J.D. City Atty.
Robinson, Randall W., (BV) ..... '52 '79 C&L.339 B.A., J.D. Idaho Legal Aid Servs., Inc.
Schilling, Ron .... '43 '71 C&L.336 J.D. Dist. J.
Seib, Michael J. .... '66 '95 C&L.336 B.S., J.D. Dep. Co. Pros.
Shropshire, Jamie C., (CV) .... '48 '83 C.1051 B.S. L.770 J.D. Pros. Atty.
Smith, April A. .... '79 '04 C&L.336 B.A., J.D. [Ⓐ Randall,B.&C.]
Smith, Jerry V., (AV) .... '24 '50 C&L.336 LL.B. [Smith&C.]

Smith & Cannon, (AV) [BR]
508 Eighth Street, 83501
Telephone: 208-743-9428 Fax: 208-746-8421
Email: s-claw@lewiston.com URL: http://www.smithandcannon.com

(This Listing Continued)

Smith & Cannon (Continued)

Members of Firm: Jerry V. Smith; Ned A. Cannon.
General Trial Practice. Personal Injury, Aviation, Automobile Accidents and Injuries, Wrongful Death, Family Law, Divorce, Child Custody, Child Support, Alternative Dispute Resolution, Insurance, Probate Law, Workers Compensation Claims, Arbitration and Mediation.
Representative Client: Aetna Casualty & Surety Co.
See Professional Biographies, LEWISTON, IDAHO

Spickler, Daniel L., (BV) '48 '82 C.629 B.S. L.336 J.D. V.P. & Gen. Coun., AIA Servs. Corp.
Spilker, Marcy J., (BV) '59 '86 C&L.336 B.S., J.D. Dep. Atty. Gen.
Stedman, Kristine Louise '52 '94 C&L.336 B.S., J.D. Pro Family Legislative Network
Stromberg, Bentley G., (BV) '61 '87 C&L.336 B.A., J.D. [Clements,B.&M.]
Stroschein, Charles M., (CV) '58 '83 C.285 B.A. L.734 J.D. [Clark&F.]
Tait, John Reid, (AV) '46 '74 C.178 B.A. L.880 J.D. [Keeton&T.]
Taylor, Connie W., (BV) '54 '93 C.999 B.S. L.336 J.D. [Clark&F.]
Taylor, R. John '49 '76 C.101 B.S. L.902 J.D. Chmn. of the Bd., AIA Servs. Corp.
Van Idour, Robert J., (CV) '56 '80 C&L.336 B.S., J.D. 504 Main St., Ste. 480
Wagner, Kerry A., (BV) '58 '83 C&L.336 B.S., J.D. [Randall,B.&C.]
Weeks, Patricia '67 '93 C.1193 B.S. L.336 J.D. NezPerce Co.
Wullenwaber, Dean, (AV) '48 '79 C.605 B.A. L.336 J.D. [Wullenwaber]

Wullenwaber Law Firm, (AV)
703 8th Street, P.O. Box 452, 83501
Telephone: 208-743-8981 Fax: 208-743-9442
Email: dwlawfirm@cableone.net
Dean Wullenwaber.
Personal Injury Litigation, Insurance Law, Product Liability, Civil Litigation, Workers Compensation, Criminal Law.
See Professional Biographies, LEWISTON, IDAHO

Young, Craig Marvin '68 '96 C.1193 B.A. L.336 J.D. P.O. Box 287

MALAD CITY, * 2,158, *Oneida Co.*

Crowther, J. Wesley '29 '57 C.877 B.S. L.273 J.D. Mag. J.

McCALL, 2,005, *Valley Co.*

Boomer, Henry R., (BV) '49 '75 C&L.336 B.A., J.D. P.O. Box 5
Gabbert, Myron Dan, (AV) '43 '67 C.98 B.A. L.339 J.D. [M.D.Gabbert] ⊙

Gabbert, Myron Dan, J.D. P.A., (AV)
Yacht Club Building, P.O. Box 2349, 83638 ⊙
Telephone: 208-634-2200 Fax: 208-634-2200
Email: gabbert@frontiernet.net URL: http://www.lawyers.com/gabbertlaw
Myron Dan Gabbert.
Languages: German; Spanish.
General and Trial, Banking, Business, Commercial, Corporate, Insurance Defense, Real Estate, Wills, Trusts, Probate and Estate Planning.
Representative Clients: Amerigas; Argonaut Insurance Co.; Bergen Brunswig Drug Co.; Clark Real Estate; Commonwealth Land Title Ins. Co.; Meadowcreek Property Owners; McCall Veterinary Clinic; Red Lion Inns; Reliance Group; Rogers Electric; South Coast Lumber Co.
Council, Idaho Office: P.O. Box 546, 83612. Telephone: 208-253-6896. Fax: 208-253-4880. Email: gabbert@frontiernet.net.
See Professional Biographies, MCCALL, IDAHO

Killen, William M., (AV) '38 '76 C.813 B.S.E.E. L.336 J.D. [W.M.Killen]
Killen, William M., P.A., (AV) 200 Park Street
McMahan, Brian L., (BV) '55 '86 C&L.101 B.S., J.D. 706 N. 1st St.
Millemann, Steven J. '50 '75 C.629 B.S. L.800 J.D. [Millemann&P.]
Millemann & Pittenger, (BV) 706 N. 1st St.
Pemberton, Amy N. '64 '93 C.906 B.S. L.911 J.D. (adm. in WA; not adm. in ID) 706 N. 1st
Pittenger, Gregory C., (BV) '50 '75 C&L.285 B.A., J.D. [Millemann&P.]
Thompson, James A. '26 '53 C&L.424 B.S.S.S., LL.B. (adm. in NM; not adm. in ID) 204 N. 3rd St.‡
Wilcox, Todd J., (AV) '54 '81 C.813 A.B. L.336 J.D. P.O. Box 947

MERIDIAN, 34,919, *Ada Co.*

Adelson, Robert M. '71 '97 C.1365 B.A. L.1059 J.D. [Ⓐ Trout,W.&N.]
Baker, Geoffrey M., (BV) '70 '96 C.945 B.A. L.336 J.D. P.O. Box 7777
Becker, Robert J. '51 '83 C.1032 B.S. L.1051 J.D. Sr. Assoc. Gen. Coun., Blue Cross of Idaho, Health Service, Inc.
Bickel, Dwight F. '31 '57 C&L.339 B.S., J.D. 2935 W. Ann Street
Bolinder, Erik J., (CV) '66 '95 C.101 B.A. L.910 J.D. DBSI Grp. of Cos.
Borton, Joseph W., (BV) '71 '97 C.629 B.S. L.336 J.D. [Foley,F.B.&S.]
Butikofer, Paul '64 '94 C.1193 B.A. L.336 J.D. [Thompson,A.&B.]
Cartwright, W. Corey, (CV) '56 '85 C&L.878 B.A., J.D. Dep. Atty. Gen.
Catlett, Charlotte Wereb '59 '88 C.347 B.S. L.1003 J.D. (adm. in OH; not adm. in ID; Pat.) P.O. Box 1147
Denton, Mary K. '56 '82 C.605 B.A. L.36 J.D. Business Legal Consulting
Ellison, Mark A., (BV) '48 '76 C&L.101 B.S., J.D. DBSI
Fitzgerald, John O., (P.A.), (AV) '39 '65 C&L.336 B.S., J.D. P.O. Box 427
Foley, Howard R., (AV) '46 '71 C&L.336 B.S., J.D. [Foley,F.B.&S.]
Foley, Freeman, Borton & Stern, Chartered, (AV) 77 East Idaho
Freeman, Mark S., (BV) '56 '83 C.27 B.S. L.851 J.D. [Foley,F.B.&S.]
Gooding, R. Thomas '33 '58 C&L.950 B.A., LL.B. (adm. in OR; not adm. in ID) 6630 N. Can Ada Rd.
Hay, Charles L. '45 '74 C.813 B.A. L.336 LL.B. 5925 N. Serenity Lane
Henson, Ryan P. '74 '02 C.336 B.S. L.585 J.D. 1396 E. Doberman Street
Krueck, David T. '71 '00 C.766 B.A. L.336 J.D. [Ⓐ Trout,W.&N.]
Madsen, Roger B. '47 '76 C.906 B.A. L.101 J.D. 465 W Kodiak Dr.
Mallea, Kenneth L., (AV) '52 '78 C.285 B.A. L.911 J.D. [Mallea]

Mallea Law Offices, (AV)
78 S.W. 5th Avenue, 83642-2923
Mailing Address: P.O. Box 857, Meridian, ID 83680-0857
Telephone: 208-888-2790 Fax: 208-888-2789
Email: KLM@MalleaLaw.com
Kenneth L. Mallea.
General Practice, Business Law, Wills, Trusts and Probate, Civil Litigation, Workers Compensation Defense, Education Law, Real Estate.
See Professional Biographies, MERIDIAN, IDAHO

Mimura, Susan L., (BV) '— '83 C.1193 B.S. L.336 J.D. 1404 N. Main St., Ste. 100
Nary, William L. M., (BV) '60 '85 C.335 B.A. L.336 J.D. Dep. City Atty., Meridian
Nemec, Aaron H., (BV) '68 '94 C&L.336 B.S., J.D. [Trout,W.&N.]
Niland, Theresa C. '62 '98 C.1042 B.S. L.1049 J.D. Staff Atty., Blue Cross of Idaho, Health Service, Inc.
Penton, A. Denise, (CV) '— '96 C&L.336 B.S., J.D. 211 S. Pine Ave., Ste., 102
Sherer, Stephen T., (CV) '51 '86 C.597 B.A. L.336 J.D. 730 E. 1st. St.
Shockley, Rob H., (BV) '67 '93 C.1193 B.A. L.336 J.D. [Ⓐ Trout,W.&N.]
Smith, Dale '42 '77 C.336 B.S. L.285 J.D. 3695 N. Legacy Common Ave.
Smith, William L. '73 '00 C&L.336 B.S., J.D. [Ⓐ Trout,W.&N.]
Stern, Frances R., (BV) '69 '94 C.629 B.A. L.950 J.D. [Foley,F.B.&S.]
Thompson, Kristen R., (AV) '52 '89 C.454 B.A. L.336 J.D. [Thompson]
Thompson, Ashcraft & Butikofer, L.L.P. 55 S.W. 5th Ave., Ste. 150
Thompson Law Firm, (AV) 55 S.W. Fifth Ave., Ste. 150
Trout, Kim J., (BV) '54 '79 C&L.336 B.S., J.D. [Trout,W.&N.]

Trout, Weeks & Nemec, PLLC, (BV)
3067 E. Copper Point Drive, 83642
Telephone: 208-376-4461 Fax: 208-376-4481 URL: http://www.trout-law.com
URL: http://www.lawyers.com/twnpllc
Kim J. Trout; Steven R. Weeks; Aaron H. Nemec;—William L. Smith; David T. Krueck; Rob H. Shockley; Robert M. Adelson.
Construction, Commercial Litigation, Business Litigation, Business Formation, Real Estate Development, Agribusiness, Buying and Selling of Businesses, Energy/Cogeneration, Bankruptcy and Appeals.
See Professional Biographies, MERIDIAN, IDAHO

Weeks, Steven R., (BV) '65 '93 C.37 B.A. L.336 J.D. [Trout,W.&N.]

MIDDLETON, 2,978, *Canyon Co.*

DeMeyer, Gary D., (BV) '51 '76 C&L.336 B.A., J.D. Dist. J.

MONTPELIER, 2,785, *Bear Lake Co.*

Helm, Ardee, Jr. '43 '69 C.347 B.S. L.345 J.D. 720 Washington St.
Jones, Roger L., (CV) '55 '83 C&L.101 B.S., J.D. 484 Washington
Wuthrich, Steve A., (CV) '54 '85 C.878 B.S. L.336 J.D. [S.A.Wuthrich]
Wuthrich, Steve A., PA, (CV) 1011 Washington St., Ste. 102

MOSCOW, * 21,291, *Latah Co.*

Agidius, Paul C., (CV) '51 '84 C&L.336 B.S., J.D. 312 S. Washington

Aherin, Rice & Anegon, A Professional Association
(See Lewiston)

Anderson, William E., (A Sole Proprietorship), (BV) '36 '67 C&L.336 B.S., J.D. [Anderson&W.]
Anderson and Walker, (BV) 1208 Alturas Drive
Barker, D. Ray, (BV) '46 '71 C&L.336 B.S.Econ., J.D. 204 E. First St.
Beard, D. Benjamin '54 '82 C.150 B.A. L.930 J.D. (adm. in OH; not adm. in ID) Prof. of Law, Univ. of Idaho
Bengtson, John H. '31 '55 C&L.336 LL.B. Ret. Dist. J.
Bowles, Allen V., (BV) '38 '71 212 E. 6th St.
Brandt, Elizabeth Barker '57 '82 C.970 B.A. L.930 J.D. (adm. in OH; not adm. in ID) Univ. of ID Law Sch.
Case, Lisa '57 '84 C.112 B.A. L.1068 J.D. (adm. in CA; not adm. in ID) [Ⓐ D.M.Palmatier]
Clark, Paul Lawrence '64 '01 C.37 B.A. L.336 J.D. 309 E. 2nd St.

Clark and Feeney
(See Lewiston)

Costello, Patrick D. '49 '77 C.378 B.A. L.94 J.D. Visiting Assoc. Prof., Univ. of Idaho Coll. of Law

Creason, Moore & Dokken, PLLC
(See Lewiston)

Curley, Michael E., (AVⓉ) '46 '75 C&L.986 B.A., J.D. 1913 East E St.
Dwelle, Anne Zier, (CV) '48 '88 C.118 B.A. L.336 J.D. [Wakefield&D.]
Eckmann, Robin M., (BV) '62 '86 C.906 B.A. L.336 J.D. Latah Co. Pros. Attorney's Off.
Ewers, Jennifer A., (CV) '63 '90 C.988 B.A. L.911 J.D. 609 S. Washington
Fife, Randall D., (AVⓉ) '55 '83 C.877 B.A. L.802 J.D. City Atty.
Franklin, Neil E. '44 '74 C.629 B.S. L.284 J.D. Prof. of Law, Univ. of Idaho College of Law
Graham, Charles L., (BV) '52 '88 C.877 B.S. L.336 J.D. [Landeck,W.J.&G.]
Grant, Douglas L. '40 '67 C.352 B.A. L.174 J.D. Prof. of Law, Univ. of Idaho

Gresback, Tim, (BV) '60 '87 C.747 B.A. L.1162 J.D.
312 South Washington, P.O. Box 9696, 83843
Telephone: 208-882-2222 Fax: 208-892-3535
Email: gresslaw@turbonet.com URL: http://www.gresbacklaw.com
Criminal Defense, Personal Injury, Car Crashes, Wrongful Death, Brain Injury, Civil Rights.
See Professional Biographies, MOSCOW, IDAHO

Guss, Andrea '63 '00 C.560 B.S. L.336 J.D. [Ⓐ D.M.Palmatier]
Henderson, Joann P. '42 '73 C&L.336 B.A., J.D. (adm. in WA; not adm. in ID) Prof. of Law, Univ. of Idaho
Herrington, William L., (BV) '44 '75 C.906 B.A. L.629 J.D. [W.L.Herrington]
Herrington, William L., P.A., (BV) 410 S. Jefferson
Hess, Danielle A. '67 '92 C.685 B.A. L.911 J.D. P.O. Box 443158
Judge, John C. '55 '84 C.112 B.A. L.336 J.D. [Landeck,W.J.&G.]

Keeton & Tait
(See Lewiston)

Kovis, Charles Eugene, (BV) '51 '93 C.629 B.S. L.336 J.D. [C.Kovis]
Kovis, Charles, Law Office, (BV) 312 Seventeenth St.
Landeck, Ronald J., (BV) '45 '69 C.674 A.B. L.597 J.D. [Landeck,W.J.&G.]
Landeck, Westberg, Judge & Graham, P.A., (BV) 414 S. Jefferson
Lewis, D. Craig '44 '69 C.597 B.S.B.A. L.976 LL.B. Prof. of Law, Univ. of Idaho

Libey, Ensley, Esser & Nelson, PLLC
(See Colfax, Washington)

Lillard, Monique C. '57 '83 C.813 B.A. L.1068 J.D. (adm. in CA; not adm. in ID) Univ. of Idaho Sch. of Law
Liston-Wakefield, Robert, (CV) '36 '92 C.112 A.B. L.336 J.D. [Wakefield&D.]
Magyar, Robert M., (CV) '49 '74 C.98 B.S. L.879 J.D. 530 S. Asbury St.
Mickelsen, J. Carl, (CV) '47 '92 C.1056 B.A. L.336 J.D. Staff Atty., CO-AD, Inc.
Miller, Cynthia L. '58 '98 C.112 B.S. L.336 J.D. [Miller,S.&Assoc.]
Miller, Smith-Hill & Associates 109 South Washington
Monson, Mark T., (CV) '73 '00 C.36 B.S. L.336 J.D. [Ⓐ Mosman]
Mosman, Roy E., (BV) '32 '60 C.336 B.S. L.629 LL.B. [Ⓒ Mosman]
Mosman, Wynn R., (BV) '64 '92 C.878 B.A. L.336 J.D. [Mosman]

Mosman Law Offices, (BV)
803 South Jefferson Street, P.O. Box 8456, 83843
Telephone: 208-882-0588 Fax: 208-882-0589
URL: http://www.mosmanlaw.com
Of Counsel: Roy E. Mosman. Member of Firm: Wynn R. Mosman. Associate: Mark T. Monson.
General Practice, Litigation, Personal Injury, Automobile Accidents, Wrongful Death, Criminal Law, Family Law, Divorce, Child Custody, Probate, Wills, Trusts, Estate Planning, Real Estate.
See Professional Biographies, MOSCOW, IDAHO

Nickels, Donald L. '42 '89 C.804 B.A. L.336 J.D. 1312 Lande Ln.
Norton, John Howard, (BV) '53 '79 109 S. Washington

5 C.112 A.B. L.464 J.D. 317 North Lincoln St.‡
426 J.D. 530 South Asbury Street, Suite 5 (Pat.)
71 '98 C.906 B.A. L.336 J.D. [Ⓐ Anderson&W.]
'52 '01 C&L.336 B.S., J.D. [Ⓐ D.M.Palmatier]
.... '43 '91 C.612 B.S. L.336 J.D. 1026 E. 3rd
.... '42 '91 C.645 B.S. L.336 J.D. 1026 E. 3rd
C&L.813 B.A., J.D. 609 S. Washington, Ste. 206

.....'58 '84 C&L.336 B.S., J.D. P.O. Box 8972

(adm. in NY; not adm. in ID) Univ. of Idaho
.... '53 '79 C.1193 B.A. L.336 J.D. [Siebe]
..............................202 E. Second St.
J.D.
DC; not adm. in ID) Univ. of Idaho Coll. of Law

L.336 J.D.
(adm. in WA; not adm. in ID) [Miller,S.&Assoc.]
.... '53 '82 C.939 B.A. L.336 J.D. Dist. J.
'01 C.999 B.S. L.336 J.D. [Ⓐ Landeck,W.J.&G.]
........'58 '93 C.906 B.A. L.336 J.D. [B.D.Thie]
.... 212 E. 6th St.
.'54 '81 C.436 B.A. L.336 J.D. P.O. Box 9071
.... '56 '80 C.877 B.S. L.336 J.D. Pros. Atty.
... '39 '64 C.906 B.A. L.336 J.D. P.O. Box 8477
B., LL.B.
adm. in ID) Dean & Prof. of Law, Univ.of Idaho
..........................609 S. Washington, Ste 206
tion), (BV) '48 '73
C&L.336 B.S., J.D. [Anderson&W.]
'41 '66 C.1066 L.336 LL.B. 2477 W. Twin Rd.‡
... '44 '70 C.188 B.A. L.178 J.D. Univ. of Idaho
'52 '78 C&L.336 B.S., J.D. [Landeck,W.J.&G.]
'65 '97 C.446 B.A. L.336 J.D. 424 S. Van Buren
C.604 B.A. L.336 J.D. Univ. Coun., Univ. of Idaho

Elmore Co.

........'69 '96 C.629 B.A. L.1188 J.D. Pros. Off.
.'68 '96 C.594 B.A. L.336 J.D. 160 N. 3rd E. St.
......'60 '87 C.1193 B.A. L.336 J.D. [Egusquiza]
....700 N. 3rd E.
'62 '89 C.174 B.S. L.336 J.D. 150 S. 4th E., Ste. 5
..........'47 '72 C&L.546 B.A., J.D. [Hall,F.&W.]
. '13 '37 C.1032 S.B. L.878 LL.B. [Ⓒ Hall,F.&W.]

4

W. Ward; Brian B. Peterson. Of Counsel: Perce Hall.
w, Business Law, Real Estate, Personal Injury, Trucking,
Wrongful Death, Slip and Fall, Probate, Family Law,
Support, Custody, Bankruptcy, Estate Planning, Agricul-

phies, MOUNTAIN HOME, IDAHO

.... '49 '80 C.999 B.A. L.326 J.D. Co. Pros.
....'74 '00 C&L.336 B.A., J.D. 190 South 4th East
... '74 '05 C.1193 B.B.A. L.336 J.D. [Hall,F.&W.]
.... '58 '86 C.1193 B.S. L.336 J.D. [Ratliff]
..................................290 South Second East
.... '31 '59 C&L.336 B.S., LL.B. Dist. J.
'67
C.1032 B.A. L.336 J.D. 4900 N.E. 18th Avenue
.............'43 '68 C.1032 B.A. L.336 J.D. Mag.
..........'62 '91 C.101 B.S. L.336 J.D. [Hall,F.&W.]

dary Co.

........'37 '79 C.336 B.S. L.285 J.D. P.O. Box 412

.............'53 '83 C.602 B.B.A. L.336 J.D. Mag.

.........'47 '77 C.594 B.A. L.336 J.D. 1224 1st St., S.

1085 B.S. L.878 J.D. Shilo Automatic Sprinklers, Inc.
..................'64 '93 C&L.101 B.S., J.D. [Bailey]
.... 504 11th Ave. South
...............................'74 '01 [Ⓐ Hamilton,M.&H.]
.... '46 '75 C.877 L.1026 LL.B. Pub. Def.

B.A. L.802 J.D.
50, 83687
4030 URL: http://www.kbrookslaw.com
p://www.lawyers.com/kimberlydbrooks
ns, Child Custody, Child Support, Adoptions, Guardianship,
ts, Domestic Violence, Alimony.
l Biographies, NAMPA, IDAHO

.... '48 '75 C.594 A.B. L.336 J.D. P.O. Box 846
'— '99 C.1193 B.S. L.336 J.D. [White P.]
'63 '90 C&L.336 Comm., J.D. [Eismann]
'24 '49 C&L.629 B.S., LL.B. [Eismann]
.................................3016 Caldwell Boulevard

, (CV) '51 '78 C.950 B.S. L.285 J.D.
P.O. Box 1029
'— '92 C.335 B.A. L.336 J.D. [White P.]
'72 '97 C.335 B.A. L.336 J.D. City Pros.
'70 '01 C.1051 B.A. L.950 J.D. 2600 E. Powerline Rd.

Frazer, Bradlee R., (AV) '61 '88
C.101 B.S. L.1065 J.D. Deputy Gen. Coun., MPC Computers, LLC
Gigray, William F., III, (BV) .... '— '73 C&L.336 B.A., J.D. [White P.]
Gillespie, James R., P.A.
(See Boise)
Gjording & Fouser, PLLC
(See Boise)
Greener Banducci Shoemaker P.A.
(See Boise)
Hackney, Gar, P.L.L.C.
(See Boise)
Hallam, T. Guy, Jr. .... '— '99 C.838 B.A. L.596 J.D. [White P.]
Hamilton, Carl D., (AV) .... '41 '66 C&L.336 B.S., J.D. [Hamilton,M.&H.]
Hamilton, Michaelson & Hilty, LLP, (AV) ....1303 - 12th Ave. Rd.
Hansen, Brian T. '63 '90 C.101 B.A. L.893 J.D.
(adm. in UT; not adm. in ID) VP, Legal, Gen. Couns., MicronPC, LLC
Hilty, Mark R. ....'69 '95 C.594 B.A. L.950 J.D. [Hamilton,M.&H.]
Johnson, Dennis L., (BV) '54 '79
C.594 B.A. L.336 J.D. United Heritage Mut. Life Ins. Co.
Johnson & Monteleone, LLP
(See Boise)
Lakey, Todd .... '— '93 C.101 B.S. L.1051 J.D. [Ⓒ Moore S.B.&T.]
Leavell, Stephen K. ....'50 '76 C.594 A.B. L.285 J.D. 716 W. Benton Ave.
Lew, Gary H., (CV) .... '49 '75 C&L.336 B.S., J.D. 503 11th Ave., S.
McDevitt & Miller, LLP
(See Boise)
Medema, Alexa M. ....'71 '97 C.1210 B.S. L.988 J.D. [Ⓐ Hamilton,M.&H.]
Meienhofer, John
(See Boise)
Michaelson, Terry, (BV) .... '50 '77 C&L.36 B.S., J.D. [Hamilton,M.&H.]
Moore, Larry D. ....'42 '92 C&L.101 B.A., J.D. 5700 E. Franklin Rd.
Moore Smith Buxton & Turcke, Chartered, (AV) .... 17 12th Avenue South (⊙Boise)
Morrow, William A., (BV) .... '— '79 C.381 B.A. L.336 J.D. [White P.]
Nichols, William F., (BV) .... '— '80 C.413 B.A. L.629 J.D. [White P.]
Noack, Harold Q., Jr., P.A.
(See Boise)
Nye, Christopher S., (BV) .... '— '82 C&L.378 B.A., J.D. [White P.]
Owen, Richard S. ....'51 '81 C.1051 B.A. L.596 J.D. P.O. Box 278
Pearsall, Joel K. '58 '83 C.594 B.A. L.950 J.D.
V.P. Finan. Affs. & Gen. Coun., N.W. Nazarene Univ.
Peterson, Philip A., (BV) ....'— '79 C&L.336 B.S., J.D. [White P.]
Pica, Derek A., P.L.L.C.
(See Boise)
Rossman, Todd A. .... '— '89 C.1193 B.A. L.285 J.D. [White P.]
Schiller, Edwin G., (BV) .... '48 '74 C&L.336 B.S., J.D. [Schiller&S.]
Schiller & Schiller, Chartered, (BV) .... 1202 1st Street South
Seiniger Law Offices
(See Boise)
Shaw, Steve F. '32 '60 C&L.623 B.A., LL.B.
(adm. in OK; not adm. in ID) 525 Burk Lane‡
Shepherd, Ronald R. ....'74 '02 [Ⓐ Hamilton,M.&H.]
Sirhall, Lawrence G., Jr.
(See Boise)
Stark, Stephen, (CV) ....'49 '90 C&L.336 B.A., J.D. 1019 Second Street South
Turner, David A. ....'53 '79 C&L.546 B.S., J.D. West One Bk., Idaho
Verner, Reese E. Ugene ....'41 '66 C.999 B.A. L.37 J.D. [R.E.Verner]
Verner, Reese E. .... 1303 12th Ave. S.
Walker, Bryan K., (CV) ....'64 '94 C.714 B.S.S. L.326 J.D. [Ⓐ Hamilton,M.&H.]
Wallace, Robert A.
(See Boise)
Wellman, William H., (BV) ....'52 '79 C.473 B.A. L.923 J.D. P.O. Box 453
White, Kenneth F., (BV) ....'38 '68 C.335 B.A. L.950 J.D. 703 2nd St. S.
White, Terrence R., (AV) .... '— '71 C&L.336 B.A., J.D. [White P.]

White Peterson, P.A., (AV)
5700 East Franklin Road, Suite 200, 83687-7901
Telephone: 208-466-9272 Facsimile: 208-466-4405
Email: contact@whitepeterson.com URL: http://www.whitepeterson.com
Terrence R. White; Philip A. Peterson; William A. Morrow; William F. Gigray III; Christopher S. Nye; Todd A. Rossman; Julie Klein Fischer; William F. Nichols; Kevin E. Dinius; T. Guy Hallam, Jr.
Trusts and Estates, Wills, Guardianship and Conservatorship, Probate, Business Law, Contracts, Debtor and Creditor, Corporate Law, Taxation, Partnership Law, Labor and Employment, Employee Benefits, Real Estate, Leases and Leasing, Mortgages, Municipal Law, Civil Rights, Zoning, Planning and Land Use, Eminent Domain, Environmental Law, Workers Compensation, Litigation, Personal Injury, Medical Malpractice, Collections, Agricultural Law, Family Law, Torts, Products Liability, Education Law, Nonprofit and Charitable Organizations, Civil Practice, General Practice.
Representative Client: Nampa Radiologists, P.A.
See Professional Biographies, NAMPA, IDAHO

Yost, William F., (BV) ....'39 '69 C.473 B.A. L.336 J.D. [Yost]
Yost Law Office, (BV) ....4 Ogden Avenue
Young, R. H. ....'16 '48 C.335 A.B. L.273 LL.B. 624 3rd St., S.‡
Yu, Victoria C. '69 '95 C.112 B.A. L.1065 J.D. Counsel, Micron Electronics, Inc.

NEWDALE, 377, *Fremont Co.*

Walters, W. Jeffrey ....'48 '78 C.101 B.S. L.273 J.D. Pres., Walters Produce Inc.

NEW PLYMOUTH, 1,313, *Payette Co.*

Batt, Stephen C. ....'40 '66 C&L.336 B.S., J.D. 4060 N.W. 1st Ave.‡
Felton, Warren J. .... '28 '54 C&L.336 LL.B. 5053 Hwy. 72‡
Moscrip, Douglas D. '38 '65 C&L.878 B.S., J.D.
(adm. in CA; not adm. in ID) P.O. Box 128‡

NEZ PERCE, * 453, *Lewis Co.*

Calhoun, Stephen L. ....'45 '75 C&L.336 B.S., J.D. Mag.

OROFINO, * 3,247, *Clearwater Co.*

Cox, Dale O., (BV) ....'38 '63 C.318 A.B. L.477 J.D. P.O. Box 666
Creason, Moore & Dokken, PLLC
(See Lewiston)
Swayne, John A., (BV) ....'45 '76 C&L.336 B.A., J.D. Pros. Atty.

Tyler, Eric Clayne, (CV) ....'69 '95 C&L.336 B.S., J.D. P.O. Box

PARIS, * 581, *Bear Lake Co.*

Brower, Lynn ....'55 '83 C.567 B.S. L.336 J.D. M

PARMA, 1,771, *Canyon Co.*

Nielsen, Rod Pace ....'57 '87 C.101 B.S. L.336 J.D. Pace & Nielson Farms,

PAYETTE, * 7,054, *Payette Co.*

Dillon, William B., III ....'50 '78 C&L.546 B.A., J.D. Mag.Ju
Faulks, Matthew W. ....'64 '01 C&L.336 B.S., J.D. Co. Pros.
Gatchel, John K., (BV) ....'31 '63 C.347 B.A. L.1119 LL.B. Pub. I
Osborn, Bert L., (BV) ....'50 '75 C.939 B.A. L.336 J.D. 26 South 9th St
Posey, David L. ....'42 '73 C.506 B.S. L.845 J.D. P.O. Bo
Rouillard, Rebecca Ann '57 '85 C.1312 B.A. L.1137 J.D.
(adm. in CA; not adm. in ID) 1521 6th Ave.,
Welch, Dwaine L., (BV) ....'26 '53 C&L.336 B.S., LL.B. P.O. Box 3

PLUMMER, 990, *Benewah Co.*

Cowley, Constance '54 '79 C.597 B.A. L.378 J.D.
(adm. in KS; not adm. in ID) Rte. 1, Box 60A

POCATELLO, * 51,466, *Bannock Co.*

Aikin, Leland M., II ....'50 '78 C&L.36 B.S., J.D. 270 Thurston St
Alexander, David E., (CV) ....'61 '91 C.859 B.S. L.910 J.D. [Racine O.N.B.&B
Anderson, Gus C. ....'09 '34 C&L.336 A.B., LL.B. 1180 Sage D
Bacon, William F., (CV) ....'56 '81 C.597 B.A. L.336 J.D. 1600 Arlingto
Bailey, John A., Jr., (BV) ....'54 '80 C.1032 B.S. L.336 J.D. [Racine O.N.B.&B.
Balfour, Douglas J., (BV) ....'52 '77 C.1032 B.A. L.273 J.D. [D.Balfour
Balfour, Douglas, (BV) .... 230 W. Lewi

Beard St. Clair Gaffney McNamara Calder PA
(See Idaho Falls)

Becker, William W., (BV) ....'21 '49 L.966 J.D. P.O. Box 1725
Belzer, Frederick F., (BV) ....'47 '80 C.745 B.A. L.1202 J.D. 850 East Center
Berrett, Edward J. ....'28 '55 C.1032 B.S. L.878 J.D. 1335 E. Center St.
Bistline, Beverly B. ....'22 '55 C.336 B.A. L.878 J.D. 808 N. 8th Ave.‡
Bohrer, William C. ....'50 '80 C.813 B.A. L.1065 J.D. Lumber Dealers Supply, Inc.
Box, Gaylen L. ....'51 '78 C.1032 B.A. L.336 J.D. Mag.
Brown, Mitchell W., (BV) ....'61 '90 C.877 B.S. L.336 J.D. [Racine O.N.B.&B.]
Brown, Ruby Y., (Mrs.) ....'11 '49 746 E. Center St.,#4‡
Budge, Randall C., (AV) ....'51 '76 C.877 B.S. L.336 J.D. [Racine O.N.B.&B.]
Burnett, Howard D., (AV) ....'50 '78 C.309 B.A. L.659 J.D. [Hawley T.E.&H.]
Bush, Ronald E. ....'56 '83 C.336 B.A. L.273 J.D. Dist. J.
Bybee, D. Kirk, (BV) ....'55 '81 C.1032 B.S. L.336 J.D. [Bybee]
Bybee, Duane A., (AV) ....'25 '53 C.1032 B.A. L.900 J.D. 3828 Blue Grouse‡
Bybee Law Office Chartered, (BV) .... 850 E. Center
Byington, Jonathon ....'77 '04 C.877 B.S. L.336 J.D. [A Racine O.N.B.&B.]
Carnaroli, Rudolph E. (Rick), (BV) ....'58 '85 C.637 B.A. L.950 J.D. Chf. Civil Dep.
Carter, E.W. "Skip", (CV) ....'59 '90 C.178 B.A. L.862 J.D. [A Cooper&L.]
Cather, C. Edward, III ....'68 '99 C.1335 B.S. L.893 J.D. [Merrill&M.]
Cheney, Brian J. ....'73 '04 C&L.101 M.S., J.D. [A Dial,M.&R.]
Christensen, Craig W., (AV) ....'51 '77 C.1032 B.B.A. L.336 J.D. [C.W.Christensen]
Christensen, Kay M., (BV) '55 '84
C.878 B.S. L.336 J.D. Paralegal Instructor, Idaho State Univ.

Christensen, Craig W., Chartered, (AV)
414 South Garfield, P.O. Box 130, 83204-0130
Telephone: 208-234-9353 Fax: 208-234-9357
Email: cwcc@ida.net URL: http://www.cwc-law.com
Craig W. Christensen.
Litigation, Banking, Bankruptcy, Personal Bankruptcy, Chapters 7, 11, 12, 13, Commercial, Corporations, Creditor's Rights, Real Estate Law.
See Professional Biographies, POCATELLO, IDAHO

Christon, Lisa M., (CV) ....'64 '92 C.999 B.A. L.607 J.D. [A Racine O.N.B.&B.]
Clark, Mark B. ....'20 '50 C&L.878 B.S., J.D. 575 Marlu‡
Clark, Thomas W., (BV) ....'56 '83 C.101 B.S. L.336 J.D. [Merrill&M.]
Cooper, Gary L., (AV) .... '50 '75 C&L.336 B.S., J.D. [Cooper&L.]

Cooper & Larsen, (AV) BR
151 North 3rd Avenue, Suite 210, P.O. Box 4229, 83205-4229
Telephone: 208-235-1145 Fax: 208-235-1182
Email: gary@cooper-larsen.com URL: http://www.cooper-larsen.com
Gary L. Cooper; Reed W. Larsen. Of Counsel: Ron Kerl. Associates: M. Anthony Sasser; E.W. "Skip" Carter; James D. Ruchti; Marvin K. Smith.
Trial Practice, Appellate Practice, Personal Injury, Insurance Defense, Federal Employers Liability Act (FELA); Railroad Litigation, Workers Compensation, Agricultural Claims, Products Liability, Commercial Law, Indian Law.
Representative Clients: Albertsons; Allstate; Federated; Farmers; Hartford; Orion Auto; Safeco; Bowen Petroleum; Pixton Oil; Guy Nielson Co.
See Professional Biographies, POCATELLO, IDAHO

Cox, Ohman & Brandstetter, Chartered
(See Idaho Falls)

Cunningham, Amy ....'63 '94 C.967 B.A. L.1187 J.D. Co-Ad Inc.
Dance, Gary T., (AV) ....'46 '73 C.1193 B.A. L.950 J.D. [Moffatt T.B.R.&F.]
Dial, Thomas F., (AV) ....'38 '67 C.1032 B.A. L.336 J.D. [Dial,M.&R.]

Dial, May & Rammell, Chartered, (AV) BR
216 W. Whitman, P.O. Box 370, 83204-0370
Telephone: 208-233-0132 Facsimile: 208-234-2961
Email: dmr@dats.com URL: http://www.dialmayrammell-law.com
Thomas F. Dial; Gregory C. May; Bron M. Rammell; Aaron N. Thompson;—Brian J. Cheney.
General Civil and Criminal Practice. Workers Compensation, Commercial, Corporation, Creditor, Real Estate, Bankruptcy, Immigration, Litigation, Family, Personal Injury, Head Injury, Trucking Accidents, Wrongful Death, and Estate and Probate Law.
See Professional Biographies, POCATELLO, IDAHO

Dunn, Stephen S., (BV) ....'50 '77 C&L.101 B.S., J.D. [Merrill&M.]
Dykman, Douglas K. ....'54 '89 C.1032 L.336 J.D. [Dykman]
Dykman Law Office .... P.O. Box 4981
EchoHawk, Paul C. ....'71 '98 C&L.1335 B.S., J.D. [EchoHawk]
EchoHawk Law Offices ....151 N. 4th Ave., Ste. A

Ehardt, Smith & Torgesen
(See Idaho Falls)

Eldredge, Robert O., Jr., (CV) ....'50 '78 C.1032 B.S. L.336 J.D. 1347 E. Clark St.
Ellis, Justin R. ....'79 '04 C.1032 B.A. L.508 J.D. [A Racine O.N.B.&B.]
Erickson, Lane V. ....'70 '99 C.1032 B.A. L.336 J.D. [Racine O.N.B.&B.]
Ferris, Nancy A., (BV) ....'55 '79 C.216 A.B. L.607 J.D. Chf. Dep. City Atty.
Gabiola, Julian E. ....'71 '96 C&L.336 B.A., J.D. [Moffatt T.B.R.&F.]

Nuhn, Theresa A. ....'56 '8
Palmatier, Duncan M. '57 '85
C.999 B.A. L.
Pattinson, Michael J., (CV) ....
Peterson, Gary E. ....
Pike, Linda, (CV) ....
Pike, Robert B. ....
Porter, John R. ....'46 '73

Randall, Blake & Cox, P.A.
(See Lewiston)

Riedner, Gary J., (BV) ....
Schurtman, Monica Ann '— '91

Siebe, James E., (BV) ....
Siebe Law Office, (BV) ....
Smith, Arthur D. '42 '68 C.877 B.S. L.273
(adm. in

Smith & Cannon
(See Lewiston)

Smith-Hill, Janice L. '49 '01 C.112 Ph.D.

Stegner, John R. ....'74
Stewart, Trapper ....
Thie, Brian Dean, (CV) ....
Thie, Brian D., (CV) ....
Thompson, Frances H., (BV) ....
Thompson, William W., Jr., (BV) ....
Utzman, Glen G., (CV) ....
Vincenti, Sheldon A. '38 '63 C&L.309 A.
(adm. in UT; no

Wakefield & Dwelle, (CV) ....
Walker, John W., (A Professional Corpora

Warren, Jon G. ....
Wegman, Jerry L. ....
Westberg, James L., (BV) ....
Whitney, Thomas W., (BV) ....
Yuan, Georgia, (BV) ....'53 '85

MOUNTAIN HOME, * 11,143,

Bazzoli, Aaron J. ....
Clark, Jay P., Law Office of, (CV) ....
Egusquiza, Mitchell L., (CV) ....
Egusquiza Law Office, (CV) ....
Epis, David C. ....
Friedly, Jay R., (AV) ....
Hall, Perce, (AV) ....

Hall, Friedly & Ward, (AV)
340 East Second North, 83647
Telephone: 208-587-4412 Fax: 208-587-31
Email: hfwlaw@adelphia.net
Members of Firm: Jay R. Friedly; Robert
General and Trial Practice. Corporate La
Automobile, and Construction Accidents
Divorce, Domestic Relations, Adoptions,
tural and Appellate Work.
See Professional Biogra

Layher, Barbara J. ....
Leatham, Deena Anne ....
Peterson, Brian B. ....
Ratliff, Terry S. ....
Ratliff Law Offices, Chartered ....
Rowett, Robert M. ....
Schlender, E. Lee, Chartered, (BV) '42

Sellman, John R. ....
Ward, Robert W., (BV) ....

MOYIE SPRINGS, 656, *Boun*

Lopez, Camilo M. ....

MURPHY, * 150, *Owyhee Co*

Ryan, Thomas J. ....

NAMPA, 51,867, *Canyon Co.*

Alban, Richard L., (BV) ....
Arslanian, James L., (BVⓉ) '60 '90
C.
Bailey, B. Todd, (BV) ....
Bailey Law Group, P.C., (BV) ....
Bean, Eric J. ....
Bishop, VanNoy G. ....

Brooks, Kimberly D. '71 '99 C.767
5700 East Franklin Road, Suite 2
Telephone: 208-442-7489 Fax: 208-468-
Email: kim@kbrookslaw.com URL: ht
Family Law, Divorce, Domestic Relatio
Visitation Rights, Separation Agreeme
See Profession

Cardon, Andrea L.
(See Boise)

Clark, Mark L., (BV) ....
Dinius, Kevin E. ....
Eismann, Debra L., (CV) ....
Eismann, Richard B., (AV) ....
Eismann Law Offices, (AV) ....

Elia, Michael J., Law Office of
(See Boise)

Farber, Randolph E., Attorney at Law

Fischer, Julie Klein, (CV) ....
Fleming, Timothy L., (BV) ....
Flores-Brewer, Dina Marie ....

Beck, Joel A. .... '73 '02 C.878 B.A. L.336 J.D. [A Hepworth,L.&J.]
Beeks, Paul M., (BV) .... '39 '63 C&L.585 B.A., J.D. [Smith&B.]
Bennett, Golden R. .... '27 '52 L.336 LL.B. 1302 Fremont Dr.

Benoit, Alexander, Harwood, High & Valdez, L.L.P., (AV)
126 Second Avenue North, P.O. Box 366, 83303-0366 ⊙
Telephone: 208-733-5463 Fax: 208-734-1438
Email: benoitlaw@benoitlaw.com URL: http://www.benoitlaw.com
Members of Firm: Harry Benoit (1893-1966); Edward L. Benoit (1921-1998); J. Robert Alexander; Robert M. Harwood (Resident, Ketchum Office); Thomas B. High, P.A.; Anthony M. Valdez. Associate: Nicholas M. Staley.
General Civil Trial Practice. Business Corporation, Partnership, Wills, Estate Planning, Probate, Municipal, Banking, Insurance Defense, Real Estate, Environmental, Agriculture, Real Estate Transactions, Real Estate Litigation, Residential Real Estate and Commercial Real Estate, Product Liability Defense, Professional Liability Defense, Criminal Defense.
Counsel for: College of Southern Idaho; Independent Meat Co.; Twin Falls Highway District.
Local Counsel for: Mutual of Enumclaw Insurance; AIG; Zurich Insurance; ALPS; Chubb Insurance; Farmers Alliance Mutual; Miller Group; Continental Western Insurance; State Farm Insurance.
Ketchum, Idaho Office: 160 Second Street East, Suite 218. Telephone: 208-726-4900. Fax: 208-726-3101.

See Professional Biographies, TWIN FALLS, IDAHO

Berry, L. Clyel, (BV) .... '49 '76 C.906 B.A. L.336 J.D. [L.C.Berry]
Berry, L. Clyel, (Chartered), (BV) .... Wells Fargo Bank Building

Bevis, Cameron & Johnson, P.A.
(See Boise)

Bilyeu, Brigette, (BV) ....'57 '88 C.309 A.B. L.336 J.D. Spec. Mas.
Bingham, Loren D., (CV) .... '51 '92 C.101 B.A. L.336 J.D. 219 Third Avenue East

Brassey, Wetherell, Crawford & Garrett, L.L.P.
(See Boise)

Brizee, Jennifer Kauth, (BV) .... '66 '94 C.971 B.A. L.336 J.D. [A Tolman]
Brody, Robyn Maddox, (BV) ....'70 '97 C&L.208 B.A., J.D. [Hepworth,L.&J.]
Brown, Patrick D., (BV) ....'60 '91 C.208 B.S. L.678 J.D. 104 Lincoln
Browning, Bart D., (BV) .... '57 '85 C&L.101 B.S., J.D. [May,S.&B.]
Brumbach, Charles P. ....'45 '71 C.335 B.A. L.7 J.D. Mag.
Burdick, Roger S. ....'47 '74 C.174 B.S. L.336 LL.B. Dist. J.
Burton, J. Riley ....'39 '65 C.629 B.S. L.950 J.D. 127 Pierce‡
Campbell, Calvin H., (CV) ....'65 '92 C.1193 B.A. L.336 J.D. [A Fuller]

Carty Law, P.A.
(See Boise)

Cluff, Benjamin J., (BV) ....'69 '00 C.101 B.S. L.336 J.D. [Hepworth,L.&J.]
Coleman, David A., (BV) ....'67 '98 C.101 B.A. L.336 J.D. [Coleman,R.&R.]
Coleman, John R., (AV) ....'33 '57 C.1032 B.S. L.336 J.D. [Coleman,R.&R.]
Coleman, Ritchie & Robertson, (AV) .... 156 2nd Ave. W.
DeHaan, Harry C., (CV) .... '45 '75 C.475 B.S. L.802 J.D. 335 Blue Lakes Blvd. N.
Detweiler, George C. .... '43 '68 C.273 B.A. L.276 J.D. 189 Lincoln St.‡
Doerr, John A., (AV) .... '33 '58 C&L.585 B.A., LL.B. 1031 Eastland Drive
Dunlap, M. Lynn ....'51 '84 C.911 B.A. L.336 J.D. P.O. Box 2754
Eaton, Curtis H., (BV) '45 '74
C.813 B.A. L.336 J.D. V.P. & Bd. Mbr., First Sec. Bk. of Idaho
Fassett, Stephanie A., (BV) .... '68 '94 C&L.336 B.S., J.D. [Fassett]
Fassett Law Office, (BV) ....160 Main Avenue North

Finch & Broadbent, P.A.
(See Boise)

Fitzgerald, John O., II, (BV) ....'63 '90 C&L.336 B.S., J.D. [Moffatt T.B.R.&F.]
Fuller, Greg J., (CV) ....'42 '73 C.112 A.B. L.1065 J.D. [Fuller]
Fuller Law Offices, (CV) .... 161 Main Ave., W.

Givens Pursley LLP
(See Boise)

Glenn, James D., Jr., (Chtd.) ....'34 '60 C&L.878 J.D. 127 2nd St., W.

Greener Banducci Shoemaker P.A.
(See Boise)

Greenwood, Richard D., (BV) ....'50 '77 C.358 B.A. L.585 J.D. P.O. Box 5737
Guerry, Mark J., (BV) .... '59 '91 C.1193 B.A. L.336 J.D. [Webb,W.&G.]

Hall, Farley, Oberrecht & Blanton, P.A.
(See Boise)

Hepworth, John C., (AV) .... '27 '52 C&L.878 B.S., LL.B. [Hepworth,L.&J.]

Hepworth, Lezamiz & Janis, Chartered, (AV)
133 Shoshone Street North, P.O. Box 389, 83303-0389 ⊙
Telephone: 208-734-7510 Fax: 208-734-4115
Email: hepworth@spro.net URL: http://www.hljlawyers.com
John C. Hepworth; John T. Lezamiz; J. Charles Hepworth (Resident, Boise Office); John J. Janis (Resident, Boise Office); Robyn Maddox Brody; Benjamin J. Cluff;—John W. Kluksdal (Resident, Boise Office); Joel A. Beck. Of Counsel: William L. Nungester.
General Civil and Trial Practice in State and Federal Courts, Automobile Liability, Personal Injury, Medical Malpractice Probate and Estate Planning, Appellate Practice.
Representative Clients: Twin Falls County Mutual Insurance Co. (Property & Fire Insurance); Glenn Dale Ranches, Inc. (Farming & Ranching).
Reference: Key Bank of Idaho, N.A. (Twin Falls branch).
Boise, Idaho Office: 537 West Bannock, P.O. Box 2582. Telephone: 208-343-7510. Fax: 208-342-2927.

See Professional Biographies, TWIN FALLS, IDAHO

High, Thomas B., P.A., (AV) .... '52 '79 C.878 B.S. L.336 J.D. [Benoit,A.H.H.&V.]
Hohnhorst, John C., (AV) .... '52 '78 C&L.336 B.S., J.D. Dist. Ct. J.
Hollifield, William R., (AV) ....'44 '69 C&L.336 B.A., J.D. [Hollifield]

Hollifield Law Office, (AV)
249 Third Avenue East, P.O. Box 66, 83303-0066
Telephone: 208-734-5610; 800-296-5610 FAX: 208-734-8077
Email: bill@hollifieldlawoffice.com
William R. Hollifield.
Civil and Criminal Trial Practice. Mediation, Bankruptcy (Creditor-Trustee), Commercial, Real Estate, Personal Injury, Automobile Accidents and Injuries, Wrongful Death, Head Injury, and DUI Defense.

See Professional Biographies, TWIN FALLS, IDAHO

Hutchinson, Keith E., (BV) ....'52 '82 C.629 B.S. L.336 J.D. 104 Lincoln
Kershaw, Thomas D., Jr., (BV) ....'54 '81 C&L.101 B.A., J.D. [T.D.Kershaw,Jr.]
Kershaw, Thomas D., Jr., p.c., (BV) .... 184 Second Street West
Kornblum, Fran R., (CV) ....'59 '91 C.963 B.S. L.508 J.D. 102 Main Ave., S.
Kvanvig, Russell G., (AV) ....'47 '75 C.491 B.A. L.585 J.D. [Stephan,K.S.&T.]
Langley, William J. ....'17 '47 C&L.336 B.A., LL.B. 109 Larkspur Dr.‡
Lezamiz, John T., (AV) ....'52 '77 C.335 B.A. L.336 J.D. [Hepworth,L.&J.]
Martens, Tara, (BV) ....'72 '98 C.1193 B.B.A. L.861 J.D. [A Tolman]
May, J. Dee, (BV) ....'50 '75 C&L.336 B.A., J.D. [May,S.&B.]
May, J. Justin ....'72 '98 C.336 B.S. L.1032 J.D. [A May,S.&B.]
May, Sudweeks & Browning, LLP, (BV) .... 516 Second Street East

McCarthy, Michael F., (BV) '58 '85 C.931 B.A. L.336 J.D.
Idaho Legal Aid Services, Inc.
McDevitt, Eileen A., Law Office, (BV) '55 '85 C&L.336 B.S., J.D.
752 Falls View Drive
Meehl, Daniel B. ....'40 '66 C&L.813 B.A., LL.B. Dist. J.‡
Meyerhoeffer, Christopher L., (CV) ... '60 '94 C.1193 B.S. L.336 J.D. 1060 Plainview Dr,

Moffatt Thomas Barrett Rock & Fields, Chartered, (AV)
621 N. College Road, Suite 103, P.O. Box 5483, 83303-5483 ⊙
Telephone: 208-734-7500 FAX: 208-734-7508
Email: jof@moffatt.com URL: http://www.moffatt.com
John O. Fitzgerald, II.
General Civil, Trial and Appellate Practice. Administrative Law, Alternative Dispute Resolution, Antitrust and Trade Regulation, Aviation, Bankruptcy, Banks and Banking, Business Law, Commercial Real Estate, Construction Law, Contracts, Corporate Law, Debtor and Creditor, Disabilities, Employee Benefits, Environmental Law, Finance, Government Relations, Health Care, Hospital Law, Insurance Defense, Intellectual Property, Labor and Employment Law, Leases and Leasing, Litigation, Medical Malpractice, Mergers, Acquisitions and Divestitures, Mortgages, Nonprofit and Charitable Organizations, Partnership Law, Probate, Products Liability, Professional Liability, Public Utility Law, Real Estate, Regulatory Law, Securities, Taxation, Torts, Trusts and Estates, Water Law, Worker's Compensation.
Boise, Idaho Office: 101 South Capitol Boulevard, 10th Floor, P.O. Box 829, 83701. Telephone: 208-345-2000. Fax: 208-385-5384.
Idaho Falls, Idaho Office: 420 Memorial Drive, P.O. Box 51505, 83405. Telephone: 208-522-6700. Fax: 208-522-5111.
Pocatello, Idaho Office: 412 West Center, Suite 2000, P.O. Box 817, 83204. Telephone: 208-233-2001. Fax: 208-232-0150.

See Professional Biographies, TWIN FALLS, IDAHO

Nielson, Brent Bradford .... '79 '05 C&L.101 B.A., J.D. [A Roy,N.B.&P.]
Nielson, Brent H., (Chrtd), (AV) ....'54 '81 C.101 B.A. L.878 J.D. [Roy,N.B.&P.]
Nolan, Thomas A., (CV) .... '31 '83 C.1183 B.A. L.424 J.D. 397 Blue Lakes Blvd., N.
Nungester, William L., (AV) ......'34 '60 C.1032 B.S. L.336 LL.B. [C Hepworth,L.&J.]
Olson, John A., (BV) ....'65 '90 C.174 B.S. L.596 J.D. Chf. Dep. Pub. Def.
Parker, Penelope, (BV) ....'50 '83 C&L.878 B.S., J.D. 2034 Addison Ave. E.
Peterson, Steven D., (AV) ..... '54 '86 C.1032 B.B.A. L.336 J.D. 163 2nd Ave. W., Ste. 1
Pike, Emil F., Jr., (CV) ....'32 '63 C.906 B.A. L.336 LL.B. [E.F.Pike Jr.]

Pike, Emil F., Jr., P.A., (CV)
Magic Valley Bank Building, 3rd Floor, 83303
Telephone: 208-734-9960 Fax: 208-734-9960
Emil F. Pike, Jr.
General Civil Trial Practice. Personal Injury, Probate, Workmen's Compensation and Commercial Law. Domestic Relations.
Reference: Wells Fargo Bank (Twin Falls Branch).

Platts, Seth Craig, (CV) .... '70 '96 C&L.336 B.A., J.D. [Roy,N.B.&P.]
Rayborn, Robert E., (AV) ....'31 '56 C&L.813 B.A., J.D. [Rayborn&R.]
Rayborn and Rayborn, (AV) ....112 Shoshone Street East
Redman, R. Michael ....'45 '75 C.999 A.B. L.150 J.D. Mag.
Ritchie, John S., (BV) ....'48 '75 C.197 A.B. L.336 J.D. [Coleman,R.&R.]
Robertson, J. Evan, (AV) ....'43 '75 C.312 B.A. L.336 J.D. [Rosholt,R.&T.]
Robertson, Thomas M., (AV) ....'45 '84 C.674 A.B. L.339 J.D. [Coleman,R.&R.]
Rolig, Jeffrey E., (BV) ....'48 '77 C.939 B.A. L.336 J.D. [J.E.Rolig]

Rolig, Jeffrey E., P.C., (BV)
139 River Vista Place, Suite 104, P.O. Box 5455, 83303-5455
Telephone: 208-733-0075 Fax: 208-733-0717
Email: jrolig@roliglaw.com URL: http://www.jroliglaw.com
Jeffrey E. Rolig.
Agricultural Creditors Rights, Bankruptcy Collections, Creditor Bankruptcy, Commercial Foreclosure, Business Formation, Business Litigation, Business Transactions, Commercial Collections, Secured Collections, Unsecured Collections, Commercial Transactions, Contract Litigation, Commercial Contracts, Evictions, Real Estate Contracts, Real Estate Foreclosures.

See Professional Biographies, TWIN FALLS, IDAHO

Rosholt, John A., (AV) ....'37 '64 C&L.336 B.A., LL.B. [Barker R.&S.]
Rosholt, Robertson & Tucker, Chartered, (AV) ....142 Third Ave., N.
Roy, Susan P., (Chrtd), (AV) ....'48 '76 C.147 B.A. L.1065 J.D. [Roy,N.B.&P.]

Roy, Nielson, Barini-García & Platts, (AV)
A Partnership of Professional Corporations
780 Eastland Drive, Suite 1, P.O. Box 487, 83303-0487
Telephone: 208-734-4450 FAX: 208-734-4452
Members of Firm: Susan P. Roy (Chrtd); Brent H. Nielson (Chrtd); Lisa Barini-García (Chrtd); Seth Craig Platts. Associate: Brent Bradford Nielson.
General Civil Trial Practice. Personal Injury, Commercial Banking, Corporation, Family, Insurance, Probate, Real Estate, Workers Compensation, Bankruptcy Law, Criminal Defense Law and Immigration.
Representative Clients: First Security Bank of Idaho; Twin Falls Truck and Equipment; Agri Credit Acceptance Corp.; Randy Hansen Chevrolet; Rock Creek Trading, Inc.; Gern Linen & Supply.

See Professional Biographies, TWIN FALLS, IDAHO

Sinclair, Paula Brown, Attorney at Law, (BV) '46 '81
C.966 B.A. L.802 J.D. P.O. Box 2322
Skabronski, Jill C., (CV) .... '71 '96 C.120 B.S. L.285 J.D. Dep. Pros. Atty.
Smith, Granville B. '14 '57 C.707 B.S. L.809 LL.B.
(adm. in CA; not adm. in ID) 1961 Falls Ave., E.‡
Smith, Leon Edward, (AV) '37 '66
C.375 B.S. L.900 J.D. Chmn., State Transp. Bd. [Smith&B.]
Smith, Paul T., (BV) .... '41 '72 C.999 B.S. L.61 J.D. P.O. Box 1941
Smith & Beeks, P.L.L.C., (AV) .... 210 Sixth Ave., E.
Staley, Nicholas M. .... '76 '03 C.1032 B.A. L.336 J.D. [A Benoit,A.H.H.&V.]
Stephan, Robert W., (AV) .... '17 '49 C.813 A.B. L.336 LL.B. [Stephan,K.S.&T.] ‡
Stephan, Kvanvig, Stone & Trainor, (AV) ....102 Main Avenue South
Stoker, Jeff, (BV) ....'46 '74 C.101 B.A. L.336 J.D. [J.Stoker]
Stoker, Jeff, Chartered, (BV) .... 733 Addison
Stone, Laird B., (BV) .... '53 '79 C&L.336 B.S., J.D. [Stephan,K.S.&T.]
Sudweeks, Jay D., (BV) .... '40 '69 C.101 B.S. L.878 J.D. [May,S.&B.]
Taylor, G. Kent, (BV) ....'43 '70 C&L.336 B.S., J.D. 401 2nd St. N.
Tolman, Steven K., (AV) .... '46 '75 C.101 B.A. L.336 J.D. [Tolman]

Tolman Law Office P.C., (AV)
132 3rd Avenue East, P.O. Box 1276, 83303
Telephone: 208-733-5566 Fax: 208-733-5444
Email: STolman@TolmanLaw.com URL: http://www.lawyers.com/tolmanlawoffice
Steven K. Tolman. Associates: Jennifer Kauth Brizee; Tara Martens.
General Civil, Trial and Appellate Practice. Medical Malpractice and Professional Liability, Commercial, Real Estate, Employment Law, Insurance Law, Agricultural and Appellate Law.

See Professional Biographies, TWIN FALLS, IDAHO

Trainor, Kevin F., (BV) ....'44 '75 C.197 A.B. L.336 J.D. [Stephan,K.S.&T.]
Turner, Harry B., (BV) .... '27 '54 C&L.336 B.A., LL.B. 102 Main Ave., S.
Valdez, Anthony M., (BV) ....'68 '94 C.1262 B.A. L.174 J.D. [Benoit,A.H.H.&V.]
Voorhees, Dennis S., (BV) .... '51 '78 C.375 B.A. L.336 J.D. 112 Shoshone St E
Wakefield, Jacqueline, (BV) .... '56 '81 C.585 B.S. L.336 J.D. [Wonderlich&W.]
Webb, Curtis R., (Chartered), (BV) ....'58 '84 C.877 B.A. L.101 J.D. [Webb,W.&G.]

Webb, Lloyd J., (Chartered), (AV) ....'31 '55 C.101 L.878 LL.B. [Webb,W.&G.]

Webb, Webb & Guerry, (AV)
155 Second Avenue North, P.O. Box 1768, 83303-1768
Telephone: 208-734-1616 Fax: 208-734-5769 URL: http://www.curtiswebb.net
Email: crwebb@mindspring.com URL: http://www.vaccineinjurycompensation.com
Members of Firm: Lloyd J. Webb (Chartered); Curtis R. Webb (Chartered); Mark J. Guerry.
General Civil Trial Practice. Vaccine Injury Compensation, Personal Injury, Legal Malpractice, Products Liability, Immigration, Land Use and Family Law..
Reference: First Security Bank of Idaho, N.A., Twin Falls, Idaho Branch.
See Professional Biographies, TWIN FALLS, IDAHO

Wildman, Eric J., (BV) '63 '94 C.878 B.S. L.336 J.D.
The Snake River Basin Adjudication
Williams, Tim J., (BV) ....'62 '88 C.1193 B.S. L.336 J.D. 401 2nd St N Ste 101
Wonderlich, Fritz A., (BV) ....'53 '80 C.878 B.S. L.336 J.D. [Wonderlich&W.]
Wonderlich & Wakefield, (BV) .... P.O. Box 1812
Wright, Charles F. ....'74 '99 C.674 B.A. L.309 J.D. [C.F.Wright]
Wright, Charles F., P.A. ....P.O. Box 226

VICTOR, 840, *Teton Co.*

Harvey, Pamela T. '68 '02 C.259 B.S. L.1252 J.D.
(adm. in CT; not adm. in ID) 197 Highland Way

WALLACE, * 1,010, *Shoshone Co.*

Branstetter, Michael K., (BV) ....'53 '79 C.336 B.S. L.285 J.D. [Hull&B.]
Cossel, John O., (BV) ....'45 '72 C&L.336 B.S., J.D. Pros. Atty.
Gibler, Fred M. ....'50 '76 C&L.336 B.S., J.D. Dist. Ct. J.

Hull & Branstetter Chartered, (BV)
416 River Street, P.O. Box 709, 83873
Telephone: 208-752-1154 Fax: 208-752-0951
H.J. Hull (1888-1975); Alden Hull (1919-1984); Piatt Hull (1914-1992); Michael K. Branstetter.

(This Listing Continued)

Hull & Branstetter Chartered (Continued)

General Civil and Trial Practice. Personal Injury, Corporation, Mining, Probate, Real Estate, Workers Compensation, Municipal, Negligence, Insurance Law and Planning and Zoning.
References: West One Bank, Wallace Branch; Bank of America, Osburn Branch.
See Professional Biographies, WALLACE, IDAHO

Kosonen, Craig C. ....'36 '61 C&L.336 B.A., LL.B. Dist. J.
Lumsden, L. Scott '57 '90 L.1339 J.D.
(adm. in OR; not adm. in ID) Dist. Ct.
Magnuson, Richard G. ....'27 '51 C&L.336 LL.B. Ret. Dist. J.
McGee, Daniel J., (BV) ....'56 '84 C.336 B.S. L.285 J.D. 700 Bank St.
Watson, Barry E., (BV) ....'52 '77 C.397 B.A. L.8 J.D. Mag.

WEISER, * 5,343, *Washington Co.*

Bokides, Nicholas T., (BV) ....'52 '79 C&L.174 B.S.M.E., J.D. 131 W. Main
Culet, Gregory M. ....'51 '78 C&L.336 B.A., J.D. Mag. Div. of Dist. Ct. J.
Felton, Timothy L., (CV) ....'52 '77 C&L.336 B.S., J.D. Pub. Def.
Fuller, Wayne P. ....'32 '57 C&L.813 B.A., LL.B. P.O. Box 148‡
Kroll, Charles R., (BV) ....'50 '76 C&L.336 B.A., J.D. Pros. Atty.
Masingill, R. Brad ....'51 '77 C.1085 B.S. L.285 J.D. 27 W. Commercial
Norris, Gilbert C. ....'18 '46 C.939 B.A. L.336 LL.B. Ret. Dist. J.
Walker, Lary C., (BV) ....'39 '70 C.101 B.A. L.336 J.D. 232 E. Main St.

WENDELL, 2,338, *Gooding Co.*

Kroeger, Paul R., (CV) ....'49 '81 C.494 B.A. L.336 J.D. 112 W Main

WORLEY, 182, *Kootenai Co.*

Barrett, Kathleen B. '42 '90 C.483 B.A. L.878 J.D.
(adm. in UT; not adm. in ID) 7550 W. Ben Point Rd.‡

ILLINOIS

CAPITAL: SPRINGFIELD

Illinois State Bar Association
Bar Center (Headquarters)
Springfield, Illinois 62701-1779
Telephone: 217-525-1760
Fax: 217-525-0712

Index of Towns and Cities Listed by County

*Indicates County Seat

Adams County
Liberty
* Quincy

Alexander County
* Cairo

Bond County
* Greenville

Boone County
* Belvidere
Caledonia
Loves Park
Poplar Grove

Brown County
* Mount Sterling

Bureau County
De Pue
Ohio
* Princeton
Spring Valley

Calhoun County
* Hardin

Carroll County
Lanark
Milledgeville
* Mount Carroll
Savanna

Cass County
Beardstown
* Virginia

Champaign County
Champaign
Fisher
Homer
Mahomet
Rantoul
Tolono
* Urbana

Christian County
Assumption
Pana
* Taylorville

Clark County
Casey
* Marshall

Clay County
Flora
* Louisville

Clinton County
Breese
* Carlyle
Centralia
Trenton

Coles County
* Charleston
Mattoon

Cook County
Alsip
Arlington Heights
Barrington
Barrington Hills
Bartlett
Bedford Park
Bellwood
Bensenville
Berkeley
Berwyn
Blue Island
Bridgeview
Broadview
Brookfield
Buffalo Grove
Burbank
Burnham
Burr Ridge
Calumet City
* Chicago
Chicago Heights
Chicago Ridge
Cicero
Country Club Hills
Countryside
Crestwood
Deerfield
Des Plaines
Dixmoor
Dolton
Elgin
Elk Grove Village
Elmwood Park
Evanston
Evergreen Park
Flossmoor
Forest Park
Franklin Park
Glencoe
Glenview
Glenwood
Golf
Hanover Park
Harvey
Harwood Heights
Hazel Crest
Hickory Hills
Hillside
Hines
Hinsdale
Hoffman Estates
Homewood
Hubbard Woods
Indian Head Park
Inverness
Justice
Kenilworth
La Grange
La Grange Park
Lansing
Lemont
Lincolnwood
Lyons
Markham
Matteson
Maywood
Melrose Park
Midlothian
Morton Grove

Cook Co.—*Continued*
Mount Prospect
Niles
Norridge
Northbrook
Northfield
Northlake
North Riverside
Oak Forest
Oak Lawn
Oak Park
Olympia Fields
Orland Hills
Orland Park
Palatine
Palos Heights
Palos Hills
Palos Park
Park Forest
Park Ridge
Posen
Prospect Heights
Richton Park
Riverdale
River Forest
River Grove
Riverside
Rolling Meadows
Roselle
Rosemont
Sauk Village
Schaumburg
Schiller Park
Skokie
South Barrington
South Chicago Heights
South Holland
Steger
Streamwood
Summit
Tinley Park
University Park
Westchester
Western Springs
Wheeling
Willow Springs
Wilmette
Winnetka
Worth

Crawford County
Oblong
* Robinson

Cumberland County
Neoga
* Toledo

DeKalb County
Cortland
DeKalb
Genoa
Hinckley
Maple Park
Sandwich
Shabbona
Somonauk
* Sycamore
Waterman

DeWitt County
* Clinton
Farmer City

Douglas County
Arcola
Arthur
* Tuscola
Villa Grove

DuPage County
Addison
Argonne
Aurora
Bartlett
Bensenville
Bloomingdale
Burr Ridge
Carol Stream
Clarendon Hills
Darien
Downers Grove
Elk Grove Village
Elmhurst
Glendale Heights
Glen Ellyn
Hanover Park
Hinsdale
Itasca
Lisle
Lombard
Medinah
Naperville
Oak Brook
Oakbrook Terrace
Roselle
St. Charles
Schaumburg
Villa Park
Warrenville
Wayne
West Chicago
Westmont
* Wheaton
Willowbrook
Winfield
Wood Dale
Woodridge

Edgar County
* Paris

Edwards County
* Albion
Grayville

Effingham County
Altamont
* Effingham
Teutopolis

Fayette County
St. Elmo
* Vandalia

Ford County
Gibson City
Kempton
* Paxton

Franklin County
* Benton
Sesser
West Frankfort

Fulton County
Canton
Farmington
* Lewistown

Gallatin County
* Shawneetown

Greene County
* Carrollton
White Hall

Grundy County
Channahon
Coal City
Minooka
* Morris

Hamilton County
* McLeansboro

Hancock County
* Carthage
Hamilton
Nauvoo

Hardin County
* Elizabethtown

Henderson County
* Oquawka
Stronghurst

Henry County
Alpha
Annawan
* Cambridge
Coal Valley
Galva
Geneseo
Kewanee
Lynn Center
Orion
Woodhull

Iroquois County
Ashkum
Cissna Park
Clifton
Milford
Onarga
Sheldon
* Watseka

Jackson County
Carbondale
Elkville
Grand Tower
Makanda
* Murphysboro

Jasper County
* Newton

Jefferson County
Centralia
* Mount Vernon

Jersey County
Brighton
Elsah
* Jerseyville

Jo Daviess County
East Dubuque
Elizabeth
* Galena
Stockton
Warren

Johnson County
* Vienna

Kane County
Algonquin
Aurora
Barrington Hills
Batavia
Carpentersville
Dundee
East Dundee
Elburn
Elgin
* Geneva
Hampshire
Huntley
Lafox
Maple Park
Montgomery
Mooseheart
North Aurora
St. Charles
South Elgin
Wayne
West Dundee

Kankakee County
Aroma Park
Bourbonnais
Bradley
* Kankakee
Manteno
Momence

Kendall County
Aurora
Joliet
Montgomery
Newark
Oswego
Plano
* Yorkville

Knox County
* Galesburg
Knoxville
Oneida

Lake County
Antioch
Bannockburn
Barrington
Barrington Hills
Buffalo Grove
Deerfield
Fox Lake
Fox River Grove
Grayslake
Great Lakes
Gurnee
Hawthorn Woods
Highland Park
Highwood
Indian Creek
Ingleside
Island Lake
Kildeer
Lake Barrington

Lake Co.—*Continued*
Lake Bluff
Lake Forest
Lake Villa
Lake Zurich
Libertyville
Lincolnshire
Lindenhurst
Long Grove
Mundelein
North Barrington
North Chicago
Prairie View
Riverwoods
Round Lake
Round Lake Beach
Tower Lakes
Vernon Hills
Wadsworth
Wauconda
* Waukegan
Wheeling
Winthrop Harbor
Zion

La Salle County
Earlville
Grand Ridge
La Salle
Leland
Marseilles
Mendota
Oglesby
* Ottawa
Peru
Somonauk
Streator
Tonica

Lawrence County
Bridgeport
* Lawrenceville

Lee County
Amboy
Ashton
* Dixon

Livingston County
Chatsworth
Dwight
Fairbury
* Pontiac
Streator

Logan County
* Lincoln

Macon County
* Decatur
Maroa
Mount Zion

Macoupin County
Benld
Brighton
Bunker Hill
* Carlinville
Gillespie
Staunton
Virden

Madison County
Alton
Bethalto
Collinsville
East Alton
* Edwardsville
Glen Carbon
Godfrey
Granite City
Hamel
Highland
Madison

Madison Co.—*Continued*
Maryville
Troy
Wood River

Marion County
Centralia
* Salem

Marshall County
Henry
* Lacon
Toluca
Wenona

Mason County
* Havana
Mason City

Massac County
* Metropolis

McDonough County
Blandinsville
Bushnell
* Macomb

McHenry County
Alden
Algonquin
Barrington Hills
Cary
Crystal Lake
Fox River Grove
Harvard
Hebron
Huntley
Island Lake
Lake In The Hills
Marengo
McHenry
Richmond
Spring Grove
Wonder Lake
* Woodstock

McLean County
* Bloomington
Chenoa
Gridley
Heyworth
LeRoy
Normal

Menard County
* Petersburg

Mercer County
* Aledo
Seaton
Sugar Grove

Monroe County
Columbia
* Waterloo

Montgomery County
Farmersville
* Hillsboro
Litchfield
Nokomis
Raymond
Taylor Springs

Morgan County
* Jacksonville

Moultrie County
Arthur
Bethany
* Sullivan

Ogle County
Byron
Forreston
Mount Morris
* Oregon
Polo
Rochelle

Peoria County
Bartonville
Chillicothe
Dunlap
Elmwood
Hanna City
Mapleton
* Peoria
Peoria Heights
Princeville
* West Peoria

Perry County
Du Quoin
* Pinckneyville

Piatt County
Cerro Gordo
Hammond
* Monticello

Pike County
* Pittsfield

Pope County
* Golconda

Pulaski County
Karnak
* Mound City

Putnam County
Granville
* Hennepin
Standard

Randolph County
* Chester
Red Bud
Sparta

Richland County
* Olney

Rock Island County
Coal Valley
East Moline
Milan
Moline
* Rock Island
Silvis

St. Clair County
* Belleville
Cahokia
Caseyville
Collinsville
Dupo
East St. Louis
Fairview Heights
Freeburg
Lebanon
Marissa
Mascoutah
O'Fallon
Smithton
Swansea

Saline County
Eldorado
Galatia
* Harrisburg
Raleigh

Sangamon County
Chatham
New Berlin
Pawnee
Pleasant Plains
Rochester
Sherman
* Springfield
Virden
Williamsville

Schuyler County
* Rushville

Scott County
* Winchester

Shelby County
Findlay
Moweaqua
* Shelbyville

Stark County
Speer
* Toulon
Wyoming

Stephenson County
Cedarville
* Freeport
Lena

Tazewell County
Creve Coeur
Delavan
East Peoria
Mackinaw
Morton
* Pekin
Tremont
Washington

Union County
Anna
Dongola
* Jonesboro

Vermilion County
* Danville
Georgetown
Hoopeston

Wabash County
* Mount Carmel

Warren County
* Monmouth
Roseville

Washington County
Ashley
Centralia
* Nashville
Okawville

Wayne County
* Fairfield

White County
* Carmi
Grayville
Norris City

Whiteside County
Erie
Fulton
* Morrison
Prophetstown
Rock Falls
Sterling

*Indicates County Seat

Maguire & Kress, P.C., (AV) BB
1414 E. Center, P.O. Box 4758, 83205-4758
Telephone: 208-232-5167 Fax: 208-232-5181; URL: http://www.maguire-kress.com
URL: http://www.maguirekress.com
David H. Maguire; David R. Kress;—David K. Penrod.
Business and Commercial Litigation, Personal Injury Claims, Product Liability Claims, Business and Corporation Matters, Insurance Defense, Insurance Coverage Disputes, Construction Claims, Environmental Law, Agricultural Claims, Domestic Relations, Criminal Law, Probate.
Representative Clients: Farmers Insurance Group (Truck Exchange); Commercial General Union Group, North Pacific, Hawkeye; State Farm Insurance Company; Mutual Services Insurance Company; Scottsdale Insurance; Certain Underwriters Lloyd's of London; Western Surety; Clarendon Insurance Group; St. Paul-Travelers Insurance.
See Professional Biographies, POCATELLO, IDAHO

Manning, D. James, Jr., (AV) ....'42 '67 C&L.336 J.D. [Moffatt T.B.R.&F.]
May, Gregory C., (BV) ....'49 '77 C.878 B.S. L.336 J.D. [Dial,M.&R.]
McDermott, Patricia L., (BV) ....'38 '61 C.1032 B.A. L.273 J.D. [McDermott&Z.]
McDermott, Peter D. ....'39 '68 C.1032 B.A. L.336 J.D. Dist. J.
McDermott & Zollinger, Chartered, (AV) ....136 S. 4th
McDougall, Dan C. ....'42 '73 C.1061 B.S. L.862 J.D. Mag.
McDougall, Isaac ....'29 '52 C.336 B.A. L.188 LL.B. 600 E. Oak‡
Merkley, Douglas K., (CV) ....'55 '84 C.1032 B.A. L.336 J.D. 353 N. 4th
Merrill, Wesley F., (AV) ....'19 '49 C.878 B.A. L.309 J.D. [Merrill&M.] ‡

Merrill & Merrill, Chartered, (AV) BB
Key Bank Building, P.O. Box 991, 83204
Telephone: 208-232-2286 Fax: 208-232-2499
Email: mmlaw@merrillandmerrill.com
A. L. Merrill (1886-1961); R. D. Merrill (1893-1972); Wesley F. Merrill (Retired); Dave R. Gallafent; Stephen S. Dunn; David C. Nye; Kent L. Hawkins; Thomas W. Clark; Thomas J. Lyons; Brendon C. Taylor; Kent A. Higgins; C. Edward Cather, III.
General Civil Practice. Trials and Appeals in all State and Federal Courts. Probate, Real Estate, Insurance Law, Negligence, Corporate, Estate Planning, Education Law, Taxation, Hospital Law, Workers Compensation and Public Utility Law.
Representative Clients: Key Bank of Idaho; Portneuf Medical Center; The Travelers Insurance Co.; Aetna Casualty & Surety Co.; Hartford Accident & Indemnity Co.; Equitable Life Assurance Society; Pacific Corp.; Porteneuf-Marsh Valley Canal Co.; Farm Bureau Mutual Insurance Co. of Idaho; Pocatello School District.
Reviser of the Idaho Law Digest for this Directory.
See Professional Biographies, POCATELLO, IDAHO

Meyers, M. Jay, (BV) ....'49 '74 C.1032 B.B.A. L.336 J.D. [Meyers,T.&L.]
Meyers, Thomsen & Larson, PLLP, (BV) ....300 North 7th Ave.

Moffatt Thomas Barrett Rock & Fields, Chartered, (AV)
412 West Center, Suite 2000, P.O. Box 817, 83204-0817 ⊙
Telephone: 208-233-2001 Fax: 208-232-0150
URL: http://www.moffatt.com
Gary T. Dance; D. James Manning, Jr.; David P. Gardner; Julian E. Gabiola.
General Civil, Trial and Appellate Practice. Administrative Law, Alternative Dispute Resolution, Antitrust and Trade Regulation, Aviation, Bankruptcy, Banks and Banking, Business Law, Commercial Real Estate, Construction Law, Contracts, Corporate Law, Debtor and Creditor, Disabilities, Employee Benefits, Environmental Law, Finance, Government Relations, Health Care, Hospital Law, Insurance Defense, Intellectual Property, Labor and Employment Law, Leases and Leasing, Litigation, Medical Malpractice, Mergers, Acquisitions and Divestitures, Mortgages, Nonprofit and Charitable Organizations, Partnership Law, Probate, Products Liability, Professional Liability, Public Utility Law, Real Estate, Regulatory Law, Securities, Taxation, Torts, Trusts and Estates, Water Law, Worker's Compensation.
Boise, Idaho Office: 101 South Capitol Boulevard, 10th Floor, P.O. Box 829, 83701. Telephone: 208-345-2000. Fax: 208-385-5384.
Idaho Falls, Idaho Office: 420 Memorial Drive, P.O. Box 51505, 83405. Telephone: 208-522-6700. Fax: 208-522-5111.
Twin Falls, Idaho Office: 621 N. College Road, Suite 103, P.O. Box 5483, 83303-5483. Telephone 208-734-7500. Fax: 208-734-7508.
See Professional Biographies, POCATELLO, IDAHO

Morgan, M. Brent, (BV) ....'45 '79 C.284 M.B.A. L.101 J.D. [M.B.Morgan]
Morgan, M. Brent, PC, (BV) ....1106 East Center Street
Muhonen, Stephen J. ....'71 '03 C.1032 B.A. L.336 J.D. [Ⓐ Racine O.N.B.&B.]
Murray, Bryan K. ....'56 '83 C.1032 B.A. L.336 J.D. Mag. J.
Neilsen, Michael B., (BV) ....'52 '85 C.101 L.336 J.D. 365 Roosevelt

Nielson, Nick L., (CV) '58 '88 C&L.101 B.A., J.D.
120 North 12th Avenue, Suite 2, P.O. Box 6159, 83201
Telephone: 208-232-1735 Fax: 208-232-0048
Email: nielson1199@aol.com URL: http://www.nicknielsonlaw.com
Insurance Bad Faith, Products Liability, Personal Injury, Automobile Accidents, Business, Employment, Sexual Harassment, Wrongful Termination, Discrimination, Contracts, Family Law, Divorce, Child Custody, Child Support, Adoption, Wills and Probate.
See Professional Biographies, POCATELLO, IDAHO

Nye, David C., (BV) ....'58 '86 C&L.101 B.A., J.D. [Merrill&M.]
Nye, W. Marcus W., (AV) ....'45 '74 C.309 A.B. L.336 J.D. [Racine O.N.B.&B.]
Oliver, Arthur P. ....'25 '50 C.1032 B.A. L.900 LL.B. Ret. Dist. J.
Olley, Dennis W., (BV) ....'51 '76 C.316 A.B. L.790 J.D. [Olley]
Olley Law Office, Chartered, (BV) ....P.O. Box 400
Olsen, Eric L., (BV) ....'65 '93 C.101 B.S. L.336 J.D. [Racine O.N.B.&B.]
Olson, Gerald W., (AV) ....'25 '53 C.1032 B.A. L.900 J.D. City Atty. Emeritus
Olson, Wendy J. '64 '90 C.221 B.A. L.813 J.D.
(adm. in CA; not adm. in ID) Off. of U.S. Atty.
Olson, William D., (AV) '33 '59
C.1032 B.A. L.910 J.D. [Racine O.N.B.&B.] (⊙Idaho Falls)
Palmer, P. Bruce ....'50 '80 C.101 B.A. L.336 J.D. P.O. Box 306
Parris, Zachary G. ....'57 '01 C.1032 B.S. L.336 J.D. Pub. Def. Off.
Penrod, David K. ....'73 '03 C.1032 B.S. L.336 J.D. [Ⓐ Maguire&K.]
Petersen, Mark R. ....'76 '05 C.101 B.S. L.336 J.D. 1106 E. Center
Petersen, Richard D., (BV) '49 '77 C&L.101 B.S., J.D.
Gen. Coun., Farm Bureau Mut. Ins. Co. of Idaho
Phoenix, E. Chilton, (AV) ....'21 '50 C.336 B.A. L.813 J.D. 255 Hewlett‡
Pincock, Garth S. ....'27 '67 C.999 B.S. L.30 J.D. Acting Trial Court Admin.
Porter, Roger S. '43 '69 C.101 B.A. L.37 J.D.
(adm. in AZ; not adm. in ID) L.D.S. Institute of Religion
Racine, Louis F., Jr., (AV) ....'17 '40 C&L.336 B.A., J.D. [Racine O.N.B.&B.]

Racine Olson Nye Budge & Bailey , Chartered, (AV) BB
201 East Center, P.O. Box 1391, 83201-1391 ⊙
Telephone: 208-232-6101 Fax: 208-232-6109
Email: racine@racinelaw.net URL: http://www.racineolson.com
Louis F. Racine, Jr.; William D. Olson; W. Marcus W. Nye; Randall C. Budge; John A. Bailey, Jr.; John R. Goodell; John B. Ingelstrom; Daniel C. Green; Brent O. Roche; Kirk B. Hadley; Fred J. Lewis; Mitchell W. Brown; Eric L. Olsen;—Conrad J. Aiken (Resident, Boise Office); Richard A. Hearn; David E. Alexander; Lane V. Erickson;—Lisa M. Christon; Patrick N. George; Scott J. Smith; Lisa A. Wood; Stephen J. Muhonen; Brent L. Whiting; Lisa R. Tanner (Resident, Boise Office); Justin R. Ellis (Resident); Joshua D. Johnson (Resident, Boise Office); Jonathon Byington.
Litigation, Probate, Real Estate, Corporation, Insurance, Banking, Commercial and Utility Law. Creditor's Rights and Creditor's Bankruptcy.
Boise, Idaho Office: 101 South Capitol Boulevard, U.S. Bank Plaza, Suite 208, 83702. Telephone: 208-395-0011. Fax: 208-433-0167.

(This Listing Continued)

Racine Olson Nye Budge & Bailey , Chartered (Continued)
Idaho Falls, Idaho Office: 477 Shoup Avenue, Suite 203A, 83402. Telephone: 208-528-6101. Fax: 208-528-6109.
See Professional Biographies, POCATELLO, IDAHO

Rammell, Bron M., (CV) ....'63 '92 C.101 B.A. L.950 J.D. [Dial,M.&R.]
Reece, Norman G., Jr., (CV) ....'60 '89 C.1032 B.A. L.101 J.D. [N.G.Reece]
Reece, Norman G., P.C., (CV) ....151 N. 3rd Ave., Ste. 309
Reynolds, Kent V., (CV) ....'55 '87 C.1032 B.A. L.336 J.D. Dep. Pub. Def.
Richert, Steven V., (BV) ....'54 '79 C.336 B.S. L.950 J.D. [Service,G.&K.]
Robison, Jack H., (BV) ....'51 '77 C.1032 B.A. L.336 J.D. [Jones]
Roche, Brent O., (BV) ....'55 '80 C.1032 B.A. L.911 J.D. [Racine O.N.B.&B.]
Ruchti, James D. ....'69 '01 C.870 B.S. L.336 J.D. [Ⓐ Cooper&L.]
Sasser, M. Anthony ....'71 '99 C.101 B.A. L.336 J.D. [Ⓐ Cooper&L.]
Service, Archie W., (AV) ....'26 '53 C.813 B.S. L.336 LL.B. [Service,G.&K.]
Service, Gasser & Kerl, (AV) ....2043 East Center Street
Small, E. Brent ....'40 '84 C.878 B.S. L.285 J.D. 300 North 7th Avenue
Smith, Marvin K. ....'76 '04 C.1193 B.A. L.336 J.D. [Ⓐ Cooper&L.]
Smith, N. Randy ....'49 '77 C&L.101 B.S., J.D. Co. J.
Smith, Scott J. ....'69 '99 C.101 B.S. L.336 J.D. [Ⓐ Racine O.N.B.&B.]
Soulliere, Dacia, (CV) ....'64 '91 C.1032 B.A. L.174 J.D. World Mktg. Alliance
Southworth, George A., (CV) ....'53 '81 C.1032 B.A. L.878 J.D. 824 E. Center
Souza, John C., (CV) ....'46 '76 C&L.37 B.A., J.D. P.O. Box 6359
Spinner, James A., (BV) ....'59 '85 C.877 B.S. L.336 J.D. [Service,G.&K.]
Taylor, Brendon C. ....'71 '99 C.1032 B.S. L.900 J.D. [Merrill&M.]
Thompson, Aaron N. ....'75 '00 C.63 B.S. L.972 J.D. [Dial,M.&R.]
Thomsen, Steven A., (BV) ....'48 '77 C.1032 B.A. L.285 J.D. [Meyers,T.&L.]
Tranmer, A. Dean, (BV) ....'55 '81 C.1032 B.A. L.336 J.D. Legal Dept., City of Pocatello
Vance, Richard D., (CV) ....'58 '90 C.967 B.A. L.336 J.D. 845 W. Center St.
White, Boyd B., II ....'43 '77 C&L.101 B.S., J.D. Mag. J.
Whiting, Brent L. ....'71 '02 C.1032 B.A. L.508 J.D. [Ⓐ Racine O.N.B.&B.]
Wood, Lisa A. ....'66 '01 C.1032 B.S. L.1187 J.D. [Ⓐ Racine O.N.B.&B.]
Yost, Kent L. ....'46 '77 C.101 B.S. L.836 J.D. P.O. Box 4987
Zollinger, Keith A., (AV) ....'50 '75 C.101 B.S. L.336 J.D. [McDermott&Z.]
Zundel, Frederick G., (BV) '48 '83
C.112 B.A. L.101 J.D. Mng. Atty., Idaho Legal Aid Servs., Inc.

PORTHILL, 126, *Boundary Co.*

Gardiner, Ada ....'43 '69 C.112 B.A. L.800 J.D. HCR 60

POST FALLS, 17,247, *Kootenai Co.*

Albi, Fred A. '40 '65 C.686 B.A. L.208 J.D.
(adm. in CO; not adm. in ID) 2620 North Sand Trap Way
Duncan, Freeman B., (BV) ....'46 '73 C&L.972 B.S., J.D. P.O. Box 1629
Gabourie, Fred W., Jr., (CV) ....'47 '75 C.336 B.S. L.426 J.D. 810 N. Spokane St.
Gardner, Buford M., Jr., (BVⓉ) '41 '65 C.43 B.S. L.45 LL.B.
(adm. in AR; not adm. in ID) 802 S. Osprey Dr.
Goodson, Carlotta J. (Lottie) '35 '88 C.1075 B.S. L.1137 J.D.
(adm. in CA; not adm. in ID) 310 S. Ross Point Rd.
Hatfield, Guy E. '34 '63 C.98 B.S. L.1049 J.D.
(adm. in CA; not adm. in ID) 5676 E. Seltice Blvd.‡
Hughes, Richard A. ....'40 '73 C&L.336 B.A., J.D. 402 S. Forest Glen Boulevard
Lempesis, Charles B., (AV) ....'51 '80 C.112 B.A. L.285 J.D. W. 201 7th Ave.
Rupp, Theodore L., (CV) ....'48 '81 C&L.336 B.S., J.D. Dep. Pros.
Wobker, Thomas F. ....'44 '81 C&L.378 B.S., J.D. 1606 E. Plaza Drive

PRESTON, * 4,682, *Franklin Co.*

Castleton, Lowell D., (BV) ....'44 '75 C.101 B.A. L.878 J.D. Mag.
Fuller, Steven R., Law Offices, (BV) ....'53 '82 C.877 B.A. L.101 J.D. 24 N. State St.
McKenzie, Jay R., Attorney at Law, (BV) '45 '81 C&L.101 B.A., J.D.
102 N. State, St. 1

PRIEST RIVER, 1,560, *Bonner Co.*

Cogswell, Dar, (AV) ....'27 '53 C&L.336 LL.B. [Cooke,L.S.C.&E.] ‡
Cooke, Thomas E., (AV) ....'42 '70 C.678 A.B. L.336 J.D. [Cooke,L.S.C.&E.]
Cooke, Lamanna, Smith, Cogswell & Elliott, Chartered, (AV) ..............P.O. Box 789
Lamanna, Nick M., (AV) ....'40 '73 C&L.285 B.A., J.D. [Cooke,L.S.C.&E.]

RATHDRUM, 4,816, *Kootenai Co.*

Mitchell, Thomas A., (AV) ....'30 '53 C&L.336 LL.B. 14524 N. Arbor St.
Pigman, Gary H., (CV) ....'38 '73 C.506 B.S. L.596 J.D. 825 Bingham St.
Schulze, J. Warren, (CVⓉ) '59 '87 C.182 B.A. L.300 J.D.
(adm. in MN; not adm. in ID) 10670 N. Church Road

REXBURG, * 17,257, *Madison Co.*

Andrus, G. Rich, (AV) ....'44 '71 C.101 B.A. L.629 J.D. [Rigby,T.A.R.&M.]
Andrus, Reed E., (BV) ....'68 '94 C&L.101 B.A., J.D. [Rigby,T.A.R.&M.] (Pat.)
Barton, Breck H., (BV) ....'49 '76 C.878 B.S. L.101 J.D. [B.Barton&Assoc.]
Barton, Breck, & Associates, P.A., (BV) ....70 North Center, Suite 2

Beard St. Clair Gaffney McNamara Calder PA
(See Idaho Falls)

Dummar, Dan ....'73 '01 C.1032 B.A. L.336 J.D. 49 Professional Plz.
DuPree, Billy Glenn, Jr., (BV) ....'52 '80 C&L.101 B.S., J.D. [B.DuPree,Jr.]
DuPree, Billy, Jr., (BV) ....58 E. 1st N.
Eames, W. Brent, (BV) ....'40 '68 C.101 B.S. L.273 J.D. 41 Prof. Plaza
Evans, Troy D. ....'74 '01 C.1193 B.B.A. L.336 J.D. P.O. Box 609
Forbush, H. S. ....'21 '49 C&L.336 B.A., LL.B. Ret. Mag.
Forsberg, William R., (BV) ....'51 '79 C.906 B.A. L.101 J.D. 49 Professional Plz.
Hancock, J. D. ....'43 '70 C.101 B.A. L.629 J.D. [Smith&H.]
Hurley, Casey Ann ....'74 '99 C.101 B.A. L.896 J.D. Faculty, Brigham Young U.
Lee, E. Scott ....'58 '84 C.878 B.A. L.336 J.D. [E.S.Lee]
Lee, E. Scott, P.C. ....115 East Main Street
Moeller, Gregory W., (BV) ....'63 '90 C&L.101 B.A., J.D. [Rigby,T.A.R.&M.]
Moss, Brent J. ....'44 '71 C.101 B.S. L.878 J.D. Dist. J.
Porter, W. Charles '46 '77
C.101 B.S. L.426 J.D. Pres., Porter's Book & Variety, Inc. (Pat.)
Rammell, Mark S. ....'58 '86 C.101 B.A. L.950 J.D. P.O. Box 389
Rigby, Jerry R., (AV) ....'51 '79 C&L.101 B.A., J.D. [Rigby,T.A.R.&M.]
Rigby, Ray W., (AV) ....'23 '50 C&L.336 B.A., LL.B. [Rigby,T.A.R.&M.]

Rigby, Thatcher, Andrus, Rigby & Moeller, Chartered, (AV) BB
25 North Second East, P.O. Box 250, 83440
Telephone: 208-356-3633 Fax: 208-356-0768
Email: rexlaw@rigby-thatcher.com
Ray W. Rigby; Gordon S. Thatcher; G. Rich Andrus; Jerry R. Rigby; Michael S. Kam (1954-2001); Gregory W. Moeller; Reed E. Andrus.

(This Listing Continued)

Rigby, Thatcher, Andrus, Rigby & Moeller, Chartered (Continued)

General Practice, Trials, Negligence, Personal Injury, Probate, Commercial, Real Estate, Workers Compensation, Corporate, Estate Planning, Utility, Water Rights Law and Appeals.
Attorneys for: North Fork Reservoir Co.; Class "A" School Districts 321 & 322; Fall River, Raft River and Lost River Electric Cooperatives; Ultimate Director, Inc.; Madison Cooperative Association, Inc.; W.R. Henderson Construction, Inc.; Committee of Nine of Water District 01.
Representative Clients: Taylor Chevrolet Co.; Madison Cooperative Assn., Inc.; Valley Bank (Headquarter Office).

See Professional Biographies, REXBURG, IDAHO

Romney, Joseph B. ....'35 '63 C&L.878 Ph.D., J.D. 53 South Mill Hollow Road
Smith & Hancock ....30 S. 2nd W.
Thatcher, Gordon S., (AV) ....'31 '58 C.999 B.S. L.273 J.D. [Rigby,T.A.R.&M.]
Thomson, Dale P., (BV) ....'50 '80 C&L.101 B.A., J.D. [Thomson]

Thomson Law Offices, Chartered, A Professional Corporation, (BV)
115 East Main Street, P.O. Box 609, 83440
Telephone: 208-356-9000 Fax: 208-356-9336
Email: thomson@nstep.net
Dale P. Thomson.
Collections, Foreclosures, Creditor Law, Real Estate, Mortgages, Family Law, Business Law, Criminal Law, Wills, Probate.

See Professional Biographies, REXBURG, IDAHO

Young, Grant L. ....'25 '49 C.112 L.336 LL.B. Dist. J.
Zollinger, Stephen Porter, (CV) ....'61 '90 C&L.878 B.S., J.D. City Pros. Atty.

RIGBY, * 2,998, *Jefferson Co.*

Clark, Stephen J., (BV) ....'54 '82 C.112 B.A. L.336 J.D. Chf. Dep. Pros. [Dunn&C.]
Crowley, Robert L., Jr., (BV) ....'50 '77 C.101 B.S. L.336 J.D. [R.L.Crowley,Jr.]
Crowley, Robert L., Jr., Chartered, (BV) ....102 N. Clark St.
Dunn, Robin D., (BV) ....'55 '82 C.101 B.S. L.336 J.D. Pros. Atty. [Dunn&C.]
Dunn & Clark, P.A., (BV) ....115 N. Clark
Grover, Blair J., (AV) ....'40 '68 C.877 B.S. L.273 J.D. 215 Farnsworth Way
Kennedy, Michael B. ....'48 '73 C&L.336 B.S., J.D. Mag.

Rigby, Thatcher, Andrus, Rigby & Moeller, Chartered
(See Rexburg)

RUPERT, * 5,645, *Minidoka Co.*

Anthon, Kelly Arthur ....'74 '02 C.101 B.A. L.336 J.D. [Ⓐ Ling,R.&W.]
Bollar, Rick L., (BV) ....'52 '86 C.1032 B.A. L.336 J.D. [Goodman&B.]
Cole, Stanley G., (CV) ....'44 '78 C.258 B.S. L.500 J.D. 7th & F St.
Creason, Charles H., Jr., (BV) '52 '78 C&L.336 B.S., J.D.
Gen. Mgr. & Pres., Project Mut. Tel. Coop Assoc., Inc.
Duff, Larry R., (AV) ....'36 '62 C.1032 B.S. L.950 J.D. Mag. J.
Goodman, Alan C., (BV) ....'56 '81 C.878 B.S. L.336 J.D. [Goodman&B.]
Goodman, William T., (AV) ....'29 '54 C&L.336 LL.B. [Goodman&B.]
Goodman & Bollar, Chartered, (AV) ....717 7th Street
Hart, J. William ....'40 '66 C&L.336 B.S., J.D. Dist. J.
Ling, Roger D., (AV) ....'33 '64 C.1032 B.S. L.950 LL.B. [Ⓒ Ling,R.&W.]

Ling, Robinson & Walker, (AV)
615 H Street, P.O. Box 396, 83350
Telephone: 208-436-4717 Fax: 208-436-6804
Members of Firm: Brent T. Robinson; Jason David Walker. Associate: Kelly Arthur Anthon. Of Counsel: Roger D. Ling.
General Civil Trial Practice, Bankruptcy Law, Water Rights, Appellate Practice, Agricultural, Family, Negligence, Real Estate Law, Estate Planning, Probate, Personal Injury and Criminal Law.
Representative Clients: A & B Irrigation District; Falls Irrigation District; Aberdeen-Springfield Canal Co.; Joint School District No. 331; Minidoka, Cassia, Jerome and Lincoln Counties.

See Professional Biographies, RUPERT, IDAHO

Newman, Gara B., (CV) ....'55 '82 C.336 B.A. L.285 J.D. Pros. Atty.
Pena, Raymundo G. ....'58 '84 C.605 B.A. L.770 J.D. [Pena]
Pena Law Offices ....724 8th St.
Robinson, Brent T., (AV) ....'49 '76 C.101 B.A. L.336 J.D. [Ling,R.&W.]
Walker, Jason David, (CV) ....'67 '98 C.101 B.S. L.336 J.D. [Ling,R.&W.]

SAGLE, —, *Bonner Co.*

Lyons, Hardy C. ....'23 '49 C&L.336 LL.B. Ret. Mag.

ST. ANTHONY, * 3,342, *Fremont Co.*

Dewey, Judith M. ....'42 '96 C.684 B.A. L.336 J.D. 1450 E. 400 N.
Hossner, W. Lynn, (BV) ....'39 '65 C.336 B.A. L.273 LL.B. 109 N. 2nd W.
Sahl, Nels T. ....'12 '51 C.585 B.S. L.336 LL.B. 625 E. 4th N.‡
Walker, Keith M. ....'51 '77 C.101 B.A. L.336 J.D. Mag. J.

ST. MARIES, * 2,652, *Benewah Co.*

Britton, Jack B., (CV) ....'30 '80 C.1242 B.S. L.336 J.D. Pros. Atty.
Christensen, Richard S., (BV) ....'56 '82 C.172 B.A. L.336 J.D. [Christensen&D.]
Christensen & Doman, PC, (BV) ....907 Main Ave.
Doman, Andrew P., (BV) ....'54 '88 C&L.923 B.S., J.D. [Christensen&D.]
Hutchinson, Peter J., (CV) ....'46 '73 C&L.336 B.S., J.D. P.O. Box 597
McFadden, Patrick R. ....'56 '84 C&L.336 B.S.Bus., J.D. Mag.
McFadden, Richard L., (AV) ....'27 '51 C&L.336 LL.B. 622 College Ave.
Morris, Thomas C., (AV) ....'28 '59 C.112 B.A. L.1065 J.D. 722 Main Ave.

Morris and Wolff, P.A., (BV)
722 Main Avenue, 83861
Telephone: 208-245-2523 Fax: 208-245-4392
Nancy A. Wolff.
Commercial and Corporate, Real Estate, Natural Resource and Environmental Law, Probate, Civil Litigation, Business Law.

See Professional Biographies, ST. MARIES, IDAHO

Park, Jerrold E., (BV) ....'21 '51 C.208 B.A. L.966 LL.B. [Park&R.]
Park & Rogers, Chartered, Law Offices of, (BV) ....720 College Ave.
Payne, Douglas Paul, (BV) ....'57 '93 C.3 B.A. L.336 J.D. Co. Pros., Pros. Atty. Off.
Rogers, David B., (BV) ....'47 '77 C.768 B.A. L.336 J.D. [Park&R.]
Wolff, Nancy A., (BV) ....'52 '82 C.208 B.A. L.336 J.D. [Morris&W.]

SALMON, * 3,122, *Lemhi Co.*

Jordan, Clark L. ....'57 '87 C.1032 B.S. L.285 J.D. [Jordan]
Jordan Law Office ....P.O. Box 1015
McKinney, John S., (BV) ....'42 '72 C.1032 B.S. L.336 J.D. 1015 Main St.
Meyers, Jerry R. ....'46 '86 C.101 B.S. L.336 J.D. Mag. J.
Slavin, Milton A., (BV) ....'45 '73 C&L.336 B.S., LL.B. Co. Pros.
Smith, Jordan P., (AV) ....'46 '75 C&L.336 B.A., J.D. 807 Main St.
Snook, Frederick H. ....'46 '71 C.507 B.S. L.336 J.D. Mag. J.

SANDPOINT, * 6,835, *Bonner Co.*

Anderson, Bruce A., (BV) ....'56 '85 C.908 B.A. L.336 J.D. [Elsaesser J.A.M.E.&M.] ⊙
Berg, William M. ....'44 '95 C.629 B.S. L.1358 J.D. [W.M.Berg]
Berg, William M., PC ....316 N. 2nd Ave.
Buchanan, Barbara, (BV) ....'58 '83 C&L.336 B.A., J.D. Mag. J.

Callahan & Associates, Chtd.
(See Coeur d' Alene)

Cottrell, Jonathan W., Law Office of ....'47 '71 C.336 L.878 J.D. P.O. Box 874
Diehl, James Theodore, (BV) ....'54 '86 C.508 B.A. L.285 J.D. 106 W. Superior St.
Dullea, Catherine L. ....'50 '95 C.1494 B.A. L.336 J.D. [C.Dullea]
Dullea, Catherine, PC ....101 N. 4th Ave., Ste. 204
Elliott, Cindy, (BV) ....'49 '89 C.1235 B.S. L.285 J.D. [Elsaesser J.A.M.E.&M.] ⊙
Elsaesser, Ford, (AV) ....'51 '78 C.1123 B.S. L.336 J.D. [Elsaesser J.A.M.E.&M.] ⊙

Elsaesser Jarzabek Anderson Marks Elliott & McHugh, Chartered, (AV)
Lake Plaza Building, Third & Lake Streets, P.O. Box 1049, 83864 ⊙
Telephone: 208-263-8517 Fax: 208-263-0759
Ford Elsaesser; Joseph E. Jarzabek; Bruce A. Anderson; Doug B. Marks; Cindy Elliott; Barry McHugh;—Taeya Howell.
General Civil Trial Practice in all Courts and Agencies. Bankruptcy, Commercial, Creditor's Rights, Estate Planning, Labor, Personal Injury, Planning and Zoning, Probate, Public Utility, Real Estate, Social Security, Taxation, Workers Compensation Law and Family Law.
Coeur d'Alene, Idaho Office: 1400 Northwood Center Court, Suite C, 83814. Telephone: 208-667-2900. Facsimile: 208-667-2150.

See Professional Biographies, SANDPOINT, IDAHO

Elstun, Claire ....'58 '91 C.273 B.A. L.260 J.D. P.O. Box 1781
Featherston, Brent Clayton, (BV) ....'65 '92 C.897 B.A. L.678 J.D. [Featherston]
Featherston, Jeremy Paul ....'72 '01 C.897 B.S.B. L.336 J.D. 113 S. 2nd Ave.
Featherston Law Firm, (BV) ....113 S. 2nd Ave.
Greene, Bruce H., (CV) ....'50 '75 C&L.336 B.A., J.D. 320 N. 2nd Ave.
Greene, Raymond T., Jr., (BV) ....'19 '47 L.336 LL.B. [R.T.Greene,Jr.]
Greene, Raymond T., Jr., P.A., (BV) ....320 N. 2nd Ave.
Grewal, Savi ....'50 '85 C&L.1137 B.A., J.D. 123 S. Third Ave.
Hanlon, Roger M., (BV) ....'49 '74 C.259 B.S. L.362 J.D. 1104 Birch St.
Howell, Taeya ....'78 '03 C.906 B.A. L.101 J.D. [Ⓐ Elsaesser J.A.M.E.&M.]
Hunt, James E. ....'27 '52 C&L.336 LL.B. P.O. Box 1486‡
Jarzabek, Joseph E., (BV) ......'54 '80 C.35 B.S. L.336 J.D. [Elsaesser J.A.M.E.&M.] ⊙
Jenkins, Janet, (CV) ....'41 '82 C.1071 B.S. L.285 J.D. 706 Superior St.
Jensen, Terry L., (BV) ....'49 '76 C&L.336 B.A., J.D. P.O. Box 1382
Marks, Doug B. ....'69 '97 C&L.101 B.S., J.D. [Elsaesser J.A.M.E.&M.] ⊙
McHugh, Barry ....'58 '87 C.1193 B.S. L.336 J.D. [Elsaesser J.A.M.E.&M.] ⊙
Michaud, James R. ....'45 '75 C.629 B.S. L.285 J.D. Dist. J.
Mills, Charlton, (BV) ....'45 '76 C.1155 B.S.B.A. L.285 J.D. P.O. Box 814
Nisbet, Hugh Kenneth, Jr., (BVⓉ) ....'43 '95 C.450 B.A. L.615 J.D. Pub. Def.
Palmer, Fred R., (BV) ....'46 '75 C.911 B.A. L.285 LL.B. 106 W. Superior St.
Paulsen, James H., (BV) ....'42 '68 C.188 A.B. L.494 J.D. 110 S. 3rd
Powell, Bryce W., (CV) ....'70 '97 C&L.336 B.S., J.D. 318 Pine St.

Ramsden & Lyons
(See Coeur d'Alene)

Robertson, Isabella, (CVⓉ) ....'51 '93 C.1073 B.A. L.336 J.D. [Robertson]
Robertson Law Office, PC, (CVⓉ) ....P.O. Box 1637
Robinson, Philip H., (BV) ....'46 '70 C&L.336 B.S.Bus., J.D. Co. Pros. Atty.
Rosenthal, Michael, (BV) ....'57 '86 C.908 B.A. L.45 J.D. Dep. Pros. Atty.
Smith, Stephen F., (BV) ....'52 '77 C&L.336 B.S., J.D. [S.F.Smith]
Smith, Stephen F., Attorney at Law, Chartered, (BV) ....102 W. Superior
Swanstrom, Don L. ....'44 '69 C&L.336 B.S., J.D. Mag.
Verby, Steven C., (AV) ....'50 '76 C.429 B.A. L.336 J.D. [S.C.Verby]
Verby, Steven C., Atty. at Law, P.A., A Prof. Corp., (AV) ....113 N. 2nd Ave.
Vitalie, Carl L. '37 '66 C&L.800 Phar.D., J.D.
(adm. in VA; not adm. in ID) 2000 Gold Creek Rd.‡

Waite, Kevin J., P.C.
(See Coeur d'Alene)

Wruck, Sandra J. ....'42 '71 C.112 B.A. L.284 J.D. 113 S. 2nd Ave.

SHOSHONE, * 1,398, *Lincoln Co.*

Ingram, Mark A., (BV) ....'55 '82 C.309 B.A. L.930 J.D. 210 W. C Street
Melanson, John M. ....'47 '81 C.1032 B.B.A. L.336 J.D. Mag. J.

SODA SPRINGS, * 3,381, *Caribou Co.*

Christensen, John A. ....'54 '89 C&L.336 B.A., J.D. Law Clk. to Dist. J.
Harding, Don L. ....'37 '72 C&L.273 B.A., J.D. Dist. J.
Hart, Ronald M. ....'43 '76 C.101 B.S. L.336 J.D. Mag.
Kingsford, Edward ....'50 '74 C&L.336 B.S., J.D. 160 S. Main St.★

Merrill & Merrill, Chartered
(See Pocatello)

Nelson, Clyde G., (BV) ....'43 '68 C&L.336 B.A., J.D. 172 S. Main St.
Smith, Dell W. ....'17 '51 C.336 B.S. L.878 LL.B. 159 S. Main St.‡
Smith, Dustin W. ....'71 '99 C.101 B.A. L.336 J.D. 240 S. Main St.
Transtrum, Wallace M. ....'30 '57 C.877 B.S. L.336 LL.B. Dist. J.

SUN VALLEY, 1,427, *Blaine Co.*

Augustus, Bruce '36 '67 C.188 B.M.E. L.1068 J.D.
(adm. in CA; not adm. in ID) P.O. Box 450‡
Daily, Robert F. '21 '49 C.976 B.A. L.597 J.D.
(adm. in IL; not adm. in ID) P.O. Box 1677‡
Dunbar, William F. '29 '61 C.999 A.B. L.800 J.D.
(adm. in CA; not adm. in ID) P.O. Box 1810‡

Hall, Farley, Oberrecht & Blanton, P.A.
(See Boise)

Morrison, Robert H., (AVⓉ) '39 '65 C.800 B.S. L.1065 J.D.
(adm. in CA; not adm. in ID) P.O. Box 2529‡
Wolf, Thomas E. '39 '67 C&L.285 B.A., J.D.
(adm. in OR; not adm. in ID) P.O. Box 2390‡

TWIN FALLS, * 34,469, *Twin Falls Co.*

Alexander, J. Robert, (AV) ....'40 '64 C&L.336 B.A., LL.B. [Benoit,A.H.H.&V.]
Ashby, Wells B., (BV) ....'69 '97 C&L.174 B.A., J.D. P.O. Box 126
Baird, James T., (BV) ....'47 '73 C.1032 B.A. L.878 J.D. Atty. Gen. Off.
Barini-Garcia, Lisa, (Chrtd), (BV) ......'60 '88 C.1350 B.A. L.1162 J.D. [Roy,N.B.&P.]

Barker Rosholt & Simpson LLP, (AV)
113 Main Avenue West, Suite 303, 83301 ⊙
Telephone: 208-733-0700 Facsimile: 208-735-2444
URL: http://www.idaho-waters.com
John A. Rosholt (Resident).
Natural Resources, Water, Environmental, Construction and Commercial Litigation.
Boise, Idaho Office: 205 North 10th Street, Suite 520, P.O. Box 2139, 83701-2139. Telephone: 208-336-0700. Facsimile: 208-344-6034.

See Professional Biographies, TWIN FALLS, IDAHO

Will County
- Aurora
- Bolingbrook
- Channahon
- Crete
- Frankfort
- * Joliet
- Lockport
- Manhattan
- Minooka
- Mokena
- Monee
- Naperville
- New Lenox
- Park Forest
- Peotone
- Plainfield
- Romeoville
- Shorewood
- Steger
- Tinley Park
- University Park
- Wilmington

Williamson County
- Carterville
- Herrin
- * Marion

Winnebago County
- Cherry Valley
- Durand
- Loves Park
- Pecatonica
- * Rockford
- Rockton
- Roscoe
- South Beloit

Woodford County
- El Paso
- * Eureka
- Metamora
- Minonk
- Peoria Heights

*Indicates County Seat

ADDISON, 35,914, *DuPage Co.*

Axley, William R., Law Office of, (BV) '— '83 C.201 B.S. L.365 J.D. 45 N. Addison Rd.
Bono, Nicole, Law Office of '70 '95 C.238 B.S. L.209 J.D. 1001 W. Lake St.
Brechin, John H., (BV) '48 '75 C.597 B.A. L.424 J.D. 619 S. Addison Rd.
Carbon, John P., Jr. '49 '75 C.201 B.S. L.209 J.D. 45 N. Addison Rd.
Christiansen, Nicole Roth '69 '94 C&L.879 B.S., J.D. Atty., The Pampered Chef
Colucci, Vito A. '42 '70 C.209 B.A. L.365 J.D. 1237 W. Byron Ave.
Connors, Charles W. B. '37 '67 C.339 B.S. L.209 J.D. CEO, Magneco/Metrel, Inc.
Davis, Michael J. '53 '82 C.602 B.A. L.880 J.D. [Kofkin,S.S.&D.]
Drenk, Douglas '48 '76 C.589 B.A. L.209 J.D. 619 S. Addison Rd.
Duff, Dann, (CV) '47 '72 C&L.221 B.S., J.D. 240 East Lake Street, Suite 301
Ferrara, Alex N. '44 '75 C.1150 B.A. L.424 J.D. 848 Westgate Dr.
Gailan, Theodore '52 '83 C.393 B.A. L.365 J.D. [Gailan&N.]

Gailan & Najera, P.C.
1690 W. Lake Street, 60101-1833
Telephone: 630-467-0400 Fax: 630-467-0500
Email: gailan@mcleodusa.net URL: http://www.theodoregailan.com
Theodore Gailan; Maria Gloria Najera.
Criminal Defense, Family Law, Divorce, Child Custody, Adoption, Grandparents Rights, Domestic Violence, Visitation Rights, Child Support, Criminal Law, Driving While Intoxicated, Drug Crimes, Juvenile Crimes, Parole and Probation, Traffic Violations, White Collar Crimes.
See Professional Biographies, ADDISON, ILLINOIS

Kaske, William E. '24 '50 C.209 L.146 J.D 3N 601 Central Ct.‡
Kinnan, Jerry W. '41 '84 C.352 B.B.A. L.146 J.D. 1112 Old Fence Rd.
Kofkin, Scott J. '56 '83 C.339 B.S. L.146 J.D. [Kofkin,S.S.&D.]
Kofkin, Springer, Scheinbaum & Davis, P.C., (BV) 611 S. Addison Road
Landman, Catherine R. '— '88 C.276 B.S. Sr. V.P. & Gen Coun., The Pampered Chef
Lovelace, Mark L. '63 '89 C.424 B.B.A. L.365 J.D. Quality Fabricators, Inc.
McGarr, William G., (AV) '57 '83 C.339 B.A. L.424 J.D. 101 S. Addison Rd., Ste. B
Najera, Maria Gloria '52 '87 [Gailan&N.]
Niederer, Donald '31 '57 C.839 M.E. L.146 LL.B. Krack Corp.
Pauls, Robert J. '49 '76 C.339 B.A. L.365 J.D. 619 S. Addison Rd.
Raczka, James K. '56 '81 C.209 B.S.C. L.365 J.D. 722 N. 10th Ave.
Raymond, E. James '49 '74 C.347 B.S. L.146 J.D. 45 N. Addison Rd.

Reese, Jay M. '50 '75 C&L.339 B.A., J.D.
286 W. Fullerton, 60101-3767
Telephone: 630-628-0773 Fax: 630-628-3652
Email: lawofficeofjmreese@sbcglobal.net URL: http://www.jayreeselaw.com
Criminal Law, Personal Injury, Family Law, Real Estate, Bankruptcy, Wills, Probate, General Practice.
See Professional Biographies, ADDISON, ILLINOIS

Scheinbaum, Marc C., (BV) '47 '81 C.46 B.S. L.209 J.D. [Kofkin,S.S.&D.]
Springer, Thomas E. '62 '91 C.679 B.A. L.209 J.D. [Kofkin,S.S.&D.]
Stringini, Robert F. '49 '74 C.209 B.A. L.365 J.D. 45 N. Addison Rd.

ALBION, * 1,933, *Edwards Co.*

Crisel, Jerry, (BV) '49 '74 C&L.339 B.A., J.D. 16 E. Elm St.
Fieber, Samuel L. '59 '97 C.339 B.S. L.801 J.D. 7 North 5th Street
Frankland, David K. '48 '73 C.801 B.A. L.502 J.D. Cir. Ct. J.
Lundmark, John I. '30 '55 C.210 B.A. L.145 J.D. [M.J.Nead]
Nead, Morris J. '68 '97 C.291 B.A. L.1339 J.D. 29 North 5th Street

Rhine, Ernest & Vargo
(See Mount Carmel)

Saxe, W. Bruce '28 '55 C&L.502 A.B., LL.B. Ret. Cir. J.

ALDEN, 1,304, *McHenry Co.*

Epst, Bradley I. '42 '75 C.46 B.S. L.146 J.D. P.O. Box 123

ALEDO, * 3,681, *Mercer Co.*

Appleton, Mark A., (BV) '52 '79 C.57 B.A. L.146 J.D. [Appleton] (Pat.)
Appleton Law Offices P.C., (BV) 129 East Main Street (Pat.)
Berglund, Thomas C. '52 '77 C.707 B.A. L.734 J.D. Assoc. Cir. J.
Bredberg, Karl A., (BV) '51 '78 C&L.339 A.B., J.D. [K.Bredberg]
Bredberg, Karl, Law Office, (BV) 2020 S.E. 3rd St.
Conway, James G., Jr. '46 '80 C.707 B.A. L.1049 J.D. Cir. J.
Herr, Michael J. '54 '80 C.597 B.S. L.339 J.D. State's Atty.
Mesich, James J., (BV) '49 '74 C.339 B.A. L.424 J.D. State of Ill. Asso. Judge
Rillie, Robert J. '41 '76 C.597 Ch.E. L.146 J.D. City Atty.
Shoemaker, Dwight L., (BV) '43 '68 C.339 B.S. L.910 J.D. 403 S.E. 2nd Avenue
Zwicker, David E. '47 '73 C.339 B.S. L.597 J.D. 115 E. Main St.

ALGONQUIN, 23,276, *Kane & McHenry Cos.*

Barney, Joshua S., (BV) '56 '85 C.147 B.S. L.112 J.D. [J.S.Barney&Assoc.] ⊙
Barney, J. S., and Associates, Ltd., (BV) 2403 Harnish Drive (⊙Barrington)
Field, A. Joseph '43 '73 C.801 B.S. L.1136 J.D. P.O. Box 7787
Ford, Stephen E., (AV) '52 '77 C.1349 B.A. L.365 J.D. [Ford]

Ford Law Firm, (AV)
409 South Main Street, 60102
Telephone: 847-854-9800 Fax: 847-854-9809
Email: fordfirm1@comcast.net
Stephen E. Ford.
Employer Liability, Construction Accidents, Product Liability, School District Liability, Municipal Liability, Dram Shop, Civil Rights Litigation, Premises Liability.
See Professional Biographies, ALGONQUIN, ILLINOIS

Hammerlund, Jeffrey B., Attorney and Counselor at Law '56 '81 C.338 B.A. L.801 J.D. 309 N. Main St.
Kenski, Robert Richard '— '52 C&L.910 A.B., J.D. 2004 Clematis Dr.‡

Michling Hofmann Vinton Plaza & Wick, P.C.
(See Woodstock)

Miller, Anne Bartos '58 '99 C&L.209 B.A., J.D. 907 Scott St.
Morrissey, Daniel C. '66 '91 C.93 A.B. L.312 J.D. (adm. in HI; not adm. in IL) Algonquin State BK., N.A.
Perrone, Mathew R. P., Jr., (BV) '43 '70 C.339 B.S. L.128 J.D. [Perrone,M.R.P.] (Pat.)

Perrone, Mathew R. P., (BV)
210 S. Main Street, 60102-2639
Telephone: 847-658-5140 Fax: 847-658-1088
Email: matperon@mc.net
Mathew R. P. Perrone, Jr.
Patents, Trademarks, Copyrights, Intellectual Property, Real Estate, Wills.
See Professional Biographies, ALGONQUIN, ILLINOIS

Schulze, Jeffrey E. '51 '76 C.339 B.A. L.146 J.D. [J.E.Schulze]
Schulze, Jeffrey E., PC 1142 Main St.
Slater, R. Winston '48 '80 C.46 B.S.E.E. L.146 J.D. 109 N. Main St. (Pat.)
Stanis, Beverly E., Law Offices of '53 '77 C.1101 B.A. L.424 J.D. 3681 Grayhawk Drive
Sthay, Gerald P. '55 '92 C.679 B.S. L.365 J.D. 9 Steven Ct.
Stone, David G. '23 '50 C.504 B.A. L.146 LL.B. 9707 Arthur Dr.

Travis, Richard E., Law Offices of
(See Elgin)

ALPHA, 753, *Henry Co.*

Steele, R. Philip, (BV) '42 '71 C.1159 B.S.E.E. L.862 J.D. 110 W. "D" St.

ALSIP, 19,725, *Cook Co.*

Kohan, Virginia Casey '23 '77 C.367 B.S. L.659 J.D. (adm. in PA; not adm. in IL) 11501 Villa Ct.‡
Kopeny, James A. '44 '96 C.152 B.A. L.365 J.D. Linderlake Corp.
Legg, James S. '56 '81 C.880 B.A. L.1119 J.D. V.P & Gen Coun., Griffith Laboratories, Inc.
Mescall, Thomas J. '47 '73 C.1143 B.A. L.365 J.D. 4300 W. 119th Place
Snow, Lendol D., (AV) '19 '60 C.918 L.146 LL.B. 4245 W. 123rd St.‡

ALTAMONT, 2,296, *Effingham Co.*

Wright, Charles M. '12 '36 C&L.910 B.S., J.D. 3 W. Jackson St.‡

ALTON, 30,496, *Madison Co.*

Alfeld, Philip B., (BV) '53 '81 C.339 B.S. L.801 J.D. [Schrempf,B.K.&D.]
Ammann, John J. '58 '84 C.801 B.A. L.734 J.D. Land of Lincoln Legal Assistance
Anderson, Harry '65 '90 211 E. Elm
Andre, Patrick F., Law Offices of '64 '89 C.339 B.S. L.734 J.D. 510 E. 6th St.
Bader, Gail Donnelly, (BV) '54 '79 C.136 B.S. L.910 J.D. 1600 Wash.
Barron, Lee W., (AV) '54 '87 C.675 B.A. L.910 J.D. [L.W.Barron]
Barron, Lee W., P.C., (AV) 305 State St.
Bartylak, Joseph R. '24 '47 L.910 LL.B. Exec. Dir., Land of Lincoln Legal Assist. Found., Inc.
Berkel, Michele Lynne '67 '93 C&L.910 B.A., J.D. 510 E. 6th
Bjorseth, Scott D., (BV) '64 '90 C.502 B.J. L.801 J.D. [Hoagland,F.S.&P.]
Blaine, Kevin F., (BV) '49 '75 C.339 B.S. L.910 J.D. [Schrempf,B.K.&D.]
Bohne, Edward D. '56 '87 C.927 B.A. L.910 J.D. 2915 Gilbert Lane‡
Cagle, Carol L. '61 '85 C.880 B.A. L.734 J.D. [Cagle]
Cagle, Richard A. '25 '53 C&L.339 B.A., LL.B. 1720 Main St.
Cagle Law Office 1720 Main St.
Cole, Laura A. '69 '95 C.801 B.A. L.910 J.D. [Talbert&Assoc.]
Darr, Lanny H., II, (BV) '64 '90 C.801 B.A. L.734 J.D. [Schrempf,B.K.&D.]
Daugherty, Jack '67 '95 C.338 B.S. L.734 J.D. 707 Berkshire Blvd.
Diaz, Theodore E., (BV) '24 '54 C.782 A.B. L.734 J.D. P.O. Box 492
Durr, Malcolm D., (BV) '17 '40 C&L.339 B.A., J.D. 307 Henry St.
Eastman, C. Dana, Jr., (AV) '35 '63 C.339 B.S. L.880 J.D. [Thomas,M.E.&E.]
Edelmann, Thomas K. '44 '69 C.262 A.B. L.910 J.D. (adm. in MO; not adm. in IL) 100 E. 12th St.
Edmonds, J. Robert, (CV) '64 '91 C.801 B.S. L.339 J.D. 3517 College Ave.
Emons, Clifford C., (BV) '53 '78 C&L.339 B.S., J.D. [Smith,M.E.&S.]
Erthal, Gregory Paul, (BV) '62 '87 C.98 B.A. L.734 J.D. [Thomas,M.E.&E.]
Evola, Robert J. '72 '97 C.108 B.A. L.801 J.D. [Wise&J.]
Falb, Thomas O., (BV) '48 '74 C&L.339 A.B., J.D. [Williamson,W.G.F.&G.]
Fischer, R. Michael '38 '65 C&L.734 B.S., J.D. 1001 McPherson Ave.
Fitzgerald, R. Emmett, (AV) '26 '52 C&L.602 A.B., J.D. [Hoagland,F.S.&P.]
Flavin, Robert S., (BV⊕) '50 '81 C.1182 B.A. L.734 J.D. [Wiseman,H.M.H.V.E.&S.]
Forbes, Robert S., (BV) '55 '80 C.178 B.A. L.910 J.D. 305 State St.
Garcia, Anne K. '80 '05 C.602 B.A. L.861 J.D. [Hoagland,F.S.&P.]
Glisson, Michael P., (CV) '71 '96 C.340 B.S. L.879 J.D. [Williamson,W.G.F.&G.]
Glisson, Richard C. '62 '87 C.210 B.S. L.801 J.D. 630 E. Bway
Godfrey, Charles B., (AV) '21 '48 C&L.477 B.A., J.D. 531 Summit St.‡
Gouy, Jean T. '60 '85 C&L.734 B.A., J.D. P.O. Box 336
Greenwood, Arthur L., (BV) '42 '67 C.801 B.S. L.347 J.D. Asst. State's Atty. & Township Atty.
Greider, Deborah S. '50 '79 C.1505 B.A. L.339 J.D. [T.E.Kennedy,III]
Griffith, Roland W., Jr., (BV) '23 '51 C.339 B.S. L.597 J.D. P.O. Box 532
Groshong, Donald E., (BV) '47 '72 C.338 B.A. L.339 J.D. [Williamson,W.G.F.&G.]
Grounds, David K., (BV) '49 '76 C.801 B.A. L.146 J.D. 2960 Shady Pl.

Harper, Julie '66 '02 C.801 B.A. L.734 J.D.
612 Belle Street, Suite 101, 62002
Telephone: 618-462-5299 Fax: 618-462-5311
Email: julieharperlaw@cbnstl.com URL: http://www.julieharperlaw.com
Traffic, DWI, Bankruptcy, Estate Planning, Real Estate, Contracts, Wills, Probate, Trusts, General Practice, Criminal, Buying and Selling Homes, Guardianships, Automobile Accidents, Adoptions.
See Professional Biographies, ALTON, ILLINOIS

Heflin, Janet R. Sheley, (BV) '66 '91 C.261 B.A. L.734 J.D [Thomas,M.E.&E.]
Heil, James R., (BV) '35 '61 C&L.339 A.B., J.D. [J.Heil]
Heil, James, (BV) 816 E. 5th St.
Hesi, David O., (BV) '52 '77 C.806 B.A. L.910 J.D. [Wiseman,H.M.H.V.E.&S.]
Hoagland, Karl K., Jr., (AV) '33 '58 C.659 B.A. L.339 LL.B. [Hoagland,F.S.&P.]
Hoagland, William H., (BV) '40 '65 C.477 B.A. L.339 LL.B. [Hoagland,F.S.&P.]

Hoagland, Fitzgerald, Smith & Pranaitis, (AV)
401 Market Street, P.O. Box 130, 62002
Telephone: 618-465-7745 Telecopier: 618-465-3744
Email: hfsp@il-mo-lawfirm.com URL: http://www.il-mo-lawfirm.com
Members of Firm: William H. Hoagland; R. Emmett Fitzgerald; Donald L. Smith; Alphonse J. Pranaitis; Stephen J. Maassen; Scott D. Bjorseth. Associate: Anne K. Garcia. Of Counsel: Karl K. Hoagland, Jr.
General Practice and Trials in all Federal and State Courts. Insurance, Litigation, Negligence, Product Liability, Malpractice, Employment Discrimination, Corporate, Banking, Probate, Trusts, Estates, Labor Relations, Tax Law, Workers Compensation, Commercial Transactions, Real Estate, Governmental, Bankruptcies and Foreclosures.
Representative Clients: Jefferson Smurfit Corporation (U.S.); Millers First Insurance Companies; Mississippi Lime Company.
Reference: Magna Bank.
See Professional Biographies, ALTON, ILLINOIS

Hoefert, Joseph E., (BV) '59 '84 C.357 B.A. L.190 J.D. [Hoefert&P.]
Hoefert & Perica, P.C., (BV) 1600 Washington
Hubbs, Earl W., (CV) '57 '87 C&L.801 B.S., J.D. 3517 College Ave.
Hunt, Bradford E. '57 '82 C.859 B.A. L.734 J.D. 604 E. Bway.
Julian, John Barry '50 '95 C.801 B.A. L.734 J.D. [Wise&J.]
Kelly, Matthew W., (BV) '60 '85 C.910 B.S.B.A. L.801 J.D. [Schrempf,B.K.&D.]
Kennedy, Thomas E., III, (BV) '45 '71 C.918 B.A. L.339 J.D. [T.E.Kennedy,III]

Kennedy, Thomas E., III, L.C., Law Offices of, (BV)
2745 East Broadway, Suite 101, 62002
Telephone: 618-474-5326 Fax: 618-474-5331
Email: tkennedy@ezl.com
Thomas E. Kennedy, III; Deborah S. Greider.
Disability Rights, Civil Rights, Constitutional Law, School Law, Elder Law, Probate, Estate Planning, Trusts and Estates, Wills, Social Security Disability.
See Professional Biographies, ALTON, ILLINOIS

Larson, Robert D., (BV) .... '44 '69 C&L.339 B.A., J.D. 307 Henry St.
Long, J. Thomas, (BV) .... '50 '77 C.234 B.S. L.802 J.D. 219 Piasa St.
Maassen, Stephen J., (BV) .... '51 '77 C.132 B.A. L.879 J.D. [Hoagland,F.S.&P.]
Matthews, Charles D., V '56 '83 C&L.880 B.A., J.D.
(adm. in MO; not adm. in IL) Pres., Crown Optical
McGivern, Gerald J., (BV) '37 '65 C.363 B.S.S. L.365 LL.B.
[Wiseman,H.M.H.V.E.&S.]
Mendenhall, Douglas R., (BV) .... '51 '77 C&L.339 B.A., J.D. 510 E. 6th
Metz, Nelson F., Jr., (BV) .... '46 '82 C&L.801 B.A., J.D. Asst. State Atty.
Meyer, S. Russell, (BV) .... '45 '76 C&L.801 B.S., J.D. [Meyer,D.S.&W.]
Meyer, Dos Santos & Wood, P.C., (BV) .... 2010 State St.
Moorman, G. Edward, (BV) .... '37 '63 C.976 B.A. L.145 J.D. 510 E. 6th St.
Mormino, Samuel A., Jr, (BV) '62 '87 C.502 B.A. L.801 J.D.
[Wiseman,H.M.H.V.E.&S.]
Mottaz, Ronald C., (AV) .... '31 '56 C.210 B.A. L.339 J.D. [Thomas,M.E.&E.]
Mottaz, Steven N., (BV) .... '40 '65 C&L.339 B.S., J.D. [Thomas,M.E.&E.]
Napp, Allan L., (CV) .... '65 '91 C.502 B.S. L.734 J.D. [Ⓐ Schrempf,B.K.&D.]
Perica, Bob L., (BV) .... '51 '83 C.927 B.S. L.801 J.D. [Hoefert&P.]
Pranaitis, Alphonse J., (AV) .... '48 '75 C.339 B.S. L.734 J.D. [Hoagland,F.S.&P.]
Roberts, Jeffrey D., (BV) .... '60 '86 C.337 B.A. L.339 J.D. Assoc. Gen. Coun.
Rothert, Anthony E. '70 '96 C&L.734 M.S.W., J.D.
Legal Advocacy Service, Ill. Guardianship & Advoc. Comm.
Ryan, Robert E., (BV) .... '23 '53 C&L.734 LL.B. 1st Nat. Bank Bldg., Ste. 302
St. Peters, Robert B., (BV) .... '49 '74 C&L.734 B.A., J.D. 322 State St.
Saville, Richard L., Jr. .... '64 '89 C&L.502 A.B., J.D. [Ⓐ Wise&J.]
Schlafly, John F. .... '50 '80 C.910 B.S.E.E. L.472 J.D. P.O. Box 495
Schrempf, James E., (BV) .... '52 '76 C.801 B.A. L.339 J.D. [Schrempf,B.K.&D.]
Schrempf, Blaine, Kelly & Darr, Ltd., (BV) .... Suite 415, 307 Henry St.
Schultz, Scott W. .... '69 '94 C.339 B.S. L.862 J.D. 3517 College Ave.
Selby, Steven W., (CV) .... '64 '89 C.234 B.A. L.589 J.D. [Smith,M.E.&S.]
Shaikewitz, Richard P., (BV) '38 '62 C.597 B.S. L.910 LL.B.
[Wiseman,H.M.H.V.E.&S.]
Sholar, John .... '58 '98 C.1290 B.A. L.801 J.D. 288 Buckmaster Lane, Suite B
Sinclair, James S., (AV) .... '49 '77 C.339 A.B. L.910 J.D. [Stobbs&S.]
Smith, Donald L., (AV) .... '38 '62 C&L.339 B.S., LL.B. [Hoagland,F.S.&P.]
Smith, Marshall H., (BV) .... '21 '49 C.782 L.910 LL.B. [Smith,M.E.&S.]
Smith, Mendenhall, Emons & Selby, (BV) .... 510 E. 6th St.
Stillwell, Raymond S., (BV) '49 '73
C.340 B.S. L.880 J.D. 112 W. Homer Adams Parkway
Stobbs, John Dale, (AV) .... '32 '56 C&L.734 B.S., J.D. [Stobbs&S.]
Stobbs, John Dale, II, (AV) .... '64 '92 C&L.734 B.A., J.D. 307 Henry St., Suite 211
Stobbs, Stephen A., (CV) .... '68 '94 C.734 B.A. L.1187 J.D. [Stobbs&S.]
Stobbs and Sinclair, Ltd. Law Offices, (AV) .... 500 Bond St.
Struif, L. James, (BV) .... '31 '60 C.597 B.S. L.339 J.D. [Struif]
Struif, Scott, (CV) .... '55 '81 C&L.801 B.A., J.D. 2900 Homer Adams Pkwy.
Struif Law Office, The, (BV) .... 2900 Adams Pkwy.
Talbert, Hugh M., (AV) .... '37 '62 C&L.910 A.B., LL.B. [Talbert&Assoc.] ⊙

Talbert & Associates, P.C., (AV)
630 East Broadway, P.O. Box 800, 62002 ⊙
Telephone: 618-465-1000; 1-800-465-1529 Fax: 618-465-1506
Email: talbertlawfirm@charter.net URL: http://www.talbertlawfirm.com
Hugh M. Talbert;—Laura A. Cole.
Practice Limited to Personal Injury for Plaintiff. Maritime, Federal Employers Liability Act (Railroad), Malpractice, Products Liability, all types of Negligence and Workers' Compensation.
St. Louis, Missouri Office: 10 Branford Drive, 63132. Telephone: 314-231-5305.
See Professional Biographies, ALTON, ILLINOIS

Thomas, W.H., (AV) .... '13 '36 C&L.597 B.S., J.D. [Thomas,M.E.&E.]
Thomas, Mottaz, Eastman & Erthal, (AV) .... 2520 State Street
Vitali, Richard L. .... '54 '81 C.1292 B.A. L.1117 J.D. Assoc., Argosy Gaming Co.
Wahl, David C., (BV) .... '38 '70 C&L.910 A.B., J.D. [Wiseman,H.M.H.V.E.&S.]
Wallace, Neal J. .... '68 '96 C.130 B.A. L.201 J.D. 5224 Wickway Drive
Webster, John C., (BV) .... '44 '70 C.321 B.S. L.734 J.D. [Williamson,W.G.F.&G.]
Williamson, James T., (BV) .... '37 '61 C.934 L.910 J.D. [Williamson,W.G.F.&G.]
Williamson, Webster, Groshong, Falb & Glisson, (BV) .... 510 E. 6th Street
Wise & Julian P.C. .... 3555 College Avenue
Wiseman, Hesi, Mormino, Hubbs, Velloff, Edmonds & Snider, P.C., (BV)
3517 College Ave.
Wood, Leslie A. .... '67 '98 C.339 B.S. L.801 J.D. [Meyer,D.S.&W.]
Wyss, Emert L., Jr., (BV) .... '41 '66 C.602 B.A. L.734 J.D. [Wyss]
Wyss Law Offices, (BV) .... 1600 Washington Ave.

AMBOY, 2,561, *Lee Co.*

Dixon, Henry S., (AV) .... '34 '63 C.602 B.A. L.365 J.D. 238 E. Main St. (⊙Dixon)
Walter, Louis P., Jr. .... '28 '54 C.734 B.S. L.276 J.D. 15 W. Wasson Rd.‡

ANNA, 5,136, *Union Co.*

Ballard, William B., Jr, (CV) .... '43 '70 C.801 L.352 LL.B. 500 S. Main St.
Boie, Wesley L., (BV) .... '36 '74 C.801 B.A. L.836 J.D. 105 B Transcraft Dr.
Karnes, Penelope S. .... '57 '85 C&L.801 B.S., J.D. Guardianship & Advocacy Comm.
Murray, Richard D., Jr., (BV) .... '56 '82 C.901 B.S. L.801 J.D. 200 S. St.
Rose, Kenneth D., (CV) .... '44 '80 C&L.801 B.A., J.D. 200 South St.
Shapiro, Fred L. .... '47 '73 C.801 B.A. L.472 J.D. P.O. Box 684
Trambley, D. Brian .... '67 '93 C.801 B.A. L.356 J.D. Co. Pub. Def.
Westphal, Rudolph J., (BV) .... '30 '52 C&L.209 J.D. 303 W. High St.

ANNAWAN, 802, *Henry Co.*

Stewart, William E., (BV) .... '34 '64 C.339 B.S. L.276 J.D. Village Atty. (⊙Kewanee)

ANTIOCH, 8,788, *Lake Co.*

Bates, Amy C., Law Office of, (CV) .... '66 '93 C.966 B.A. L.365 J.D. 397 Lake St.
Brown, Christopher V. '40 '65 C.103 A.B. L.976 LL.B.
(adm. in CT; not adm. in IL) 1216 Edgewater Lane
Clark, Kenneth M. .... '38 '65 C.209 B.A. L.339 LL.B. [K.M.Clark]
Clark, Kenneth M., PC .... 425 Lake St.
DeMartini, Raymond D., (AV) .... '49 '75 C.383 B.A. L.365 J.D. [Gantar&D.]
Fremgen, Thomas E. .... '41 '75 C.742 B.S. L.365 J.D. 42553 N. Linden Lane
Galley, John R. .... '40 '84 C.197 B.A. L.146 J.D. 505 Orchard Street
Gantar, Michael W., (BV) .... '47 '73 C.424 B.A. L.146 J.D. [Gantar&D.]
Gantar & DeMartini, (AV) .... 382 Lake St.
Gideon, Helen M. .... '71 '03 C.58 B.S. L.589 J.D. 1474 Main St.
Gissel, Eric S. '70 '98 C.746 B.B.A. L.966 J.D.
(adm. in WI; not adm. in IL) 683 Needlegrass Pkwy.
Heyl, Erica L. .... '65 '92 C&L.966 B.A., J.D. [E.Heyl]
Heyl, Erica, PC .... 397 Lake St.

Idlas, Paul R., Law Office of
(See Grayslake)

Inglis, Lawrence D. .... '35 '60 C&L.339 B.S., J.D. App. Ct. J.‡
Jacobs, Edward C., (BV) .... '15 '40 C&L.424 A.B., J.D. 425 Lake St.
Jelinek, Julie .... '— '01 C.176 B.A. L.1000 J.D. 425 Lake St.
Lumber, F. James, (BV) .... '35 '64 C.436 B.S. L.477 LL.B. 397 Lake St.
Lynch, Andrew C., (BV) .... '42 '67 C.1157 B.A. L.597 J.D. 397 Lake St.
Sarmont, Richard L. .... '39 '62 C.339 B.S. L.365 J.D. 23565 W. Beach Grove Road‡

ARCOLA, 2,678, *Douglas Co.*

Petty, Mark T., (BV) .... '47 '74 C.234 B.S. L.339 J.D. [M.T.Petty]
Petty, Mark T., P.C., Law Office of, (BV) .... 111-113 E. Main St.

ARGONNE, —, *DuPage Co.*

Albrecht, John M. .... '33 '60 C.966 B.S. L.276 J.D. U.S. Dept. of Energy
Anderson, Thomas G. '43 '74
C.350 B.S.A.E. L.862 J.D. Asst. Chf. Pat. Coun., U.S. Dept. of Energy
Baines, Thomas B., (BVⓉ) '38 '81 C.623 B.B.A. L.862 J.D.
Argonne National Laboratory (Legal Department)
Churm, Arthur A. .... '33 '64 C.679 B.E.E. L.209 J.D. 9700 S. Cass Ave.‡
Cordell, Helen S. .... '43 '76 C.753 B.A. L.209 J.D. Sr. Atty., Argonne Natl. Lab.
Davis, Tyrone .... '58 '88 C.671 L.209 J.D. U.S. Dept. of Energy (Pat.)
Dvorscak, Mark P. '56 '83 C.679 B.S. L.879 J.D.
(adm. in IN; not adm. in IL; Pat.) Asst. Chf. Coun.
Fisher, Robert J. '44 '70 C&L.966 B.S., J.D.
(adm. in WI; not adm. in IL; Pat.) U.S. Dept. of Energy
Fuerstenberg, James P. .... '— '80 C.339 B.S. L.209 J.D. U.S. Dept. of Energy
Glenn, Hugh W. '37 '67 C&L.260 B.C.H.E., J.D.
(adm. in FL; not adm. in IL; Pat.) Asst. Chf., U.S. Dept. of Energy
Haffenden, Rebecca A. '53 '79 C.339 B.A. L.818 J.D.
Argonne National Laboratory (Legal Department)
Hilliard, Mark D., (BV) '55 '81 C.980 B.E. L.8 J.D.
Chf. Patent Coun., Argonne National Laboratory (Legal Department) (Pat.)
Lally, Brian J. .... '75 '01 C.893 B.A. L.347 J.D. Pat. Atty. (Pat.)
Langguth, Mark A. '65 '93 C.350 B.I.E. L.352 J.D.
Sr. Atty., Univ. of Chicago, Argonne Natl. Laboratory, Intell. Prop. (Pat.)
Lerner, Ken .... '56 '82 C.339 B.A. L.477 J.D. Argonne Natl. Lab.
Lubben, George .... '29 '55 C&L.424 B.S., J.D. Sr. Atty., Argonne Natl. Lab.‡
Luck, William D. '50 '75 C.966 B.A. L.309 J.D.
(adm. in MA; not adm. in IL) Asst. Gen. Coun., Argonne Natl. Lab.
McMahon, Kimberly J. .... '68 '93 C.385 B.A. L.910 J.D. U.S. Dept. of Energy
Miller, Lynn L. '— '94 C.338 B.S. L.146 J.D.
Sr. Atty. - Labor, Argonne Natl. Laboratory
Park, Daniel D. .... '— '92 C.870 B.S. L.424 J.D. U.S. Dept. of Energy
Prouty, Vicki L. .... '51 '80 C&L.150 B.S., J.D. Asst. Chf. Coun.
Quinn, Carol A. .... '47 '76 Dir., Human Resources, Argonne Natl. Lab.‡
Silbergleid, Steven A. '46 '71 C.994 B.A. L.724 J.D.
(adm. in NY; not adm. in IL) Dep. Chf. Coun., U.S. Dept. of Energy
Smith, Bradley W. .... '46 '90 C.576 B.S. L.146 J.D. Pat. Atty., U.S. Dept. of Energy (Pat.)
Tanzman, Edward A. .... '52 '76 C.145 A.B. L.276 J.D. Argonne Natl. Lab.
Uretsky, Jack L. .... '24 '75 C.453 B.S. L.145 J.D. 9700 Cass Avenue, Building 362
Wojciechowski, Gregory M. '49 '87
C&L.424 B.A., J.D. Sr. Atty., Argonne Natl. Laboratory
Zameic, Joseph N. .... '25 '76 C.399 B.S. L.146 J.D. 9800 S. Cass Ave.
Zilberstein, Arthur .... '40 '65 C.659 B.A. L.145 J.D. 9700 S. Cass Ave.‡

ARLINGTON HEIGHTS, 76,031, *Cook Co.*

Ackeret, Christopher N. .... '78 '03 C.424 B.S. L.146 J.D. [Ⓐ Stitt,K.D.A.&G.]
Adler, Charles E. .... '52 '77 C.339 B.A. L.1000 J.D. [Adler]

Adler Law Offices, Ltd.
9 North Vale, Suite 102, 60005
Telephone: 847-394-0100 Fax: 847-394-0500
Email: ca@adlerltd.com URL: http://www.adlerltdlaw.com
Charles E. Adler.
Personal Injury, Automobile Accidents, Medical Malpractice, Products Liability, Wrongful Death.
See Professional Biographies, ARLINGTON HEIGHTS, ILLINOIS

Agenlian, Murad .... '27 '64 C.999 B.A. L.365 LL.B. 1336 N. Vail St.‡
Ahern, Thomas J. .... '48 '75 C.363 B.A. L.209 J.D. [T.J.Ahern]
Ahern, Thomas J., P.C. .... 102 N. Evergreen, Ste. 220

Anderson & Associates, P.C.
(See Schaumburg)

Andress, Peter .... '31 '60 C.46 B.S. L.209 J.D. 1123 Carlyle Court‡
Aretos, Michael G. .... '63 '89 C.317 B.A. L.365 J.D. [Stitt,K.D.A.&G.]
Barr, Adam R. .... '61 '86 C.659 B.A. L.229 J.D. 402 S. Belmont‡
Barth, Max M. .... '10 '34 C&L.145 Ph.B., J.D. 1405 E. Central Rd.‡

Berger, Newmark & Fenchel P.C.
(See Chicago, Illinois)

Biestek, John P., Jr. .... '35 '64 C&L.424 B.S., J.D. [J.P.Biestek&Assoc.]
Biestek, Kimberly C. .... '57 '92 C.238 B.S. L.46 J.D. 115 N. Arlington Hts. Rd.
Biestek, Scott A. .... '57 '89 C.238 B.A. L.146 J.D. 115 N. Arlington Hgts. Rd.
Biestek, John P., and Associates, Ltd. .... 115 N. Arlington Heights Rd.
Biosca, Richard E. .... '72 '00 C.339 B.A. L.209 J.D. [Ⓐ Stitt,K.D.A.&G.]
Bixby, Roger A., (AV) .... '48 '74 C.347 B.S. L.145 J.D. P.O. Box 1637
Blomquist, Ernest R., III, (AV) .... '46 '73 C.927 B.A. L.146 J.D. 750 W. Northwest Hwy.
Braiman, Jeffrey S. .... '52 '77 C.221 B.A. L.365 J.D. 4256 N. Arlington Heights Rd.
Brickman, Heather .... '65 '91 C.340 B.A. L.339 J.D. 3030 Salt Creek Lane
Brown, Philip W. .... '48 '74 C.589 B.S. L.146 J.D. 750 W. Northwest Hwy.
Bryer, Paul R. .... '45 '76 C.339 B.A. L.209 J.D. 603 McKinley Ave., Ste. 3N

Budin Law Offices
(See Chicago)

Buehler, E. Marvin, (AV) .... '19 '43 C&L.597 B.S., J.D. 615 N. Haddow St.‡
Busch, James R. .... '60 '85 C&L.801 B.A., J.D. 120 W. Eastman St., Ste. 101
Camp, Ralph C. .... '37 '66 C.679 B.S. L.424 J.D. 702 E. Appletree Ln.
Campbell, Adra Farriss .... '49 '87 C.260 B.A. L.365 J.D. 115 S. Wilke Rd.

Carroll, Raymond J., (AV) '25 '49 C.473 L.209 LL.B. 205 W. Clarendon St.‡
Cassling, Sally '51 '77 C&L.145 A.B., J.D. 822 S. Bristol Lane
Champaneri, Anil R. '42 '77 State of Ill, Dept. of Employ. Sec.
Chelberg, Bruce S. '34 '58 C&L.339 B.S., LL.B. 18 N. Wilshire
Christofalos, Athena '75 '00 C.339 B.A. L.146 J.D. [A Hodges,L.E.R.&K.]
Clohessy, Vanessa V. '65 '91 C.347 B.A. L.146 J.D. 3030 Salt Creek Lane, Suite 202
Conlon, Stevie D., (AV) '57 '86 C&L.424 B.B.A., J.D.
1102 East Northwest Highway 2A
Corbett, Robt. G. '18 '42 C&L.145 B.A., J.D. 806 Lynden Ln.‡
Coventry, Dale E. '43 '75 C.399 B.A. L.424 J.D. 2630 E. Bel Aire Dr.
Daday, Stephen G. '55 '80 C.602 B.A. L.365 J.D. [Stitt,K.D.A.&G.]
Daleiden, Norbert A., (AV) '42 '68 C&L.597 B.S., J.D. [Daleiden&T.]

Daleiden & Tremaine, Ltd., (AV)
2815 North Douglas Avenue, 60004
Telephone: 847-577-7438 Fax: 847-577-7458
Norbert A. Daleiden; Arthur J. Tremaine.
General Practice, Corporate, Tax, Employee Benefits, Estate Planning, Probate, Real Estate, Litigation, Elder Law.
See Professional Biographies, ARLINGTON HEIGHTS, ILLINOIS

DeWald, Lee F. '58 '83 C.473 B.A. L.365 J.D. [Riebandt&D.]
Dickler, Marshall N. '39 '69 C.339 B.S.E.E. L.365 J.D. [M.N.Dickler] (Pat.)
Dickler, Marshall N., Ltd. 85 W. Algonquin Rd. (Pat.)
Dini, Cynthia '64 '90 C.339 B.A. L.209 J.D. 1241 N. Mitchell Avenue
Drost, George T. '46 '72 C.57 A.B. L.209 J.D. [Drost,K.&M.]
Drost, John A. '09 '61 L.365 LL.B. [© Drost,K.&M.]
Drost, Kivlahan & McMahon, Ltd. 11 South Dunton Avenue
Duda, Thomas W., (BV) '47 '73 C.602 A.B. L.597 J.D. 3125 Wilkes Rd. (⊙Chicago)
Dunn, Lisa L. '74 '94 C.339 B.A. L.209 J.D. 4256 N. Arlington Heights
Eisen, Gerald '40 '64 C.339 B.S. L.209 LL.B. 2355 S. Arlington Heights Rd.
Eisenhammer, Stanley B. '49 '73 C.910 A.B. L.339 J.D. [Hodges,L.E.R.&K.]
Elliott, Joanne P., (BV) '60 '84 C.347 B.S. L.365 J.D. 2355 S. Arlington Heights Rd.
Elliott, Michael J., (BV) '59 '84 C.679 B.S. L.424 J.D. 2355 S. Arlington Hts. Rd.
Elsener, George M., (AV) '41 '67 C.20 B.A. L.477 J.D. 730 S. Beverly Ln.
Farrington, Lisa A. '63 '89 C.66 B.A. L.145 J.D.
Staff Atty., Village of Arlington Heights
Farwell, Cyril A. '25 '53 C.209 B.S. L.365 LL.B. [Farwell,F.&P.]
Farwell, Joseph C. '64 '92 C.436 B.S. L.365 J.D. [Farwell,F.&P.]
Farwell, Farwell & Peters, PC 8 West Campbell Street, 2nd Floor
Filvaroff, Amy R. '61 '88 C.103 B.A. L.846 J.D.
(adm. in TX; not adm. in IL) Sr. Coun., Motorola Inc.
Florio, Anthony L. '43 '67 C.339 B.S. L.424 J.D. 855 E. Golf Rd.
Friedman, Scott B. '59 '84 C.339 B.A. L.365 J.D. 120 W. Eastman, Ste. 300
Gabbard, Tonya Zdon, (AVⓣ) '69 '96 C.1144 B.A. L.1018 J.D.
(adm. in MN; not adm. in IL) Family Center for Elder Law

Gabe, Caryl Jacobs, & Associates, Inc., Law Offices of
(See South Barrington)

Gasey, Carolyn Eckert '66 '92 C.339 B.S. L.365 J.D. 202 S. Dunton Ave.
Giampietro, Wayne B., (AV) '42 '66 C.679 B.A. L.597 J.D. [Stitt,K.D.A.&G.]

Glasgow, Thomas, Ltd., The Law Offices of
(See Schaumburg)

Glenn, Robert J., (AV) '47 '75 C.339 B.S. L.46 J.D. 114 N. Kaspar
Glink, Martin L. '52 '77 C.339 B.S. L.146 J.D. 3345 N. Arlington Hgts. Rd.
Goble, Wayne H., Jr. '45 '70 C&L.209 B.S.C., J.D. Asst. V.P., NBD Bank
Gottlieb, Jeffrey H. '43 '68 C.339 B.S. L.209 J.D. 1650 N. Arlington Hgts. Rd.
Gottner, Robert E. '18 '41 C&L.597 B.S., J.D. 609 W. George St.‡
Grabowski, John B. '28 '78 C.209 B.S.C. L.589 J.D. 14 N. Dryden Ave.
Grayson, Denise M. '52 '84 C.1082 B.A. L.146 J.D. 1013 N. Kaspar Ave.‡
Gurgiolo, Donnalyn M. '73 '99 C.578 B.A. L.365 J.D. 121 South Wilke Road
Hackbart, Rolland R. '44 '81 C.966 B.S.E.E. L.146 J.D.
Intell. Property Coun., GTSS, Motorola, Inc. (Pat.)
Hammerslag, Steven S. '61 '92 C.339 B.S.E.E. L.365 J.D.
Pres., S & J Products Intl., Inc.
Harrison, Peter B., (AV) '30 '56 C.209 B.S.C. L.602 J.D. 3800 N. Wilke Rd.
Hart, John K. '14 '40 C&L.623 A.B., LL.B.
(adm. in OK; not adm. in IL) 1020 Watling Rd.‡
Hattenbach, Jonathan A. '56 '81 C.951 B.A. L.276 J.D. Sr. Coun., Motorola, Inc.
Hester, Todd Brian '62 '01 C.589 B.A. L.146 J.D. 626 South Newbury Place
Hodges, Therese Linden '51 '77 C.430 B.A. L.339 J.D. [Hodges,L.E.R.&K.]
Hodges, Loizzi, Eisenhammer, Rodick & Kohn 3030 W. Salt Creek Ln., Ste. 202
Hoffman, Kathleen K. '68 '96 C.436 B.S. L.365 J.D.
Asst. Coun., Allstate Insurance Co.

Judson, Douglas A. '51 '76 C.339 B.A. L.365 J.D.
132 West Northwest Highway, 60004
Telephone: 847-577-5800 Fax: 847-577-5869
Email: lawofc@judson.com URL: http://www.lawyers.com/judsonlaw
Criminal Defense, Driving While Intoxicated, Divorce.
See Professional Biographies, ARLINGTON HEIGHTS, ILLINOIS

Julius, Joseph R. '49 '81 C.339 B.S. L.209 J.D. 116 S. Arlington Heights Rd., Ste. 203
Jung, Peter '— '85 C&L.209 B.S., J.D. NBD Tr. Co. of Ill.
Kalkas, George N. '08 '34 C.970 B.A. L.930 LL.B.
(adm. in OH; not adm. in IL) 220 E. Brittany Ct.
Kane, Terrence D. '42 '72 C&L.209 B.A., J.D. 505 E. Golf Rd.
Kantor, John A. '66 '91 C.209 B.S. L.146 J.D. 2825 N. Arlington Heights Rd.
Karm, Guy M. '47 '82 C.1183 B.A. L.365 J.D. 750 W. Northwest Hwy.
Katz, Jeffrey S. '56 '81 C&L.339 B.A., J.D. V.P., CNA Insurance Cos.
Kavenik, Frank E. '50 '75
C.46 B.S.E.E. L.146 J.D. Pres., Midwest Broadcast Assocs., Ltd.
Kessler, Nathan N., (AV) '18 '40 L.209 LL.B. 3265 N. Arlington Heights Rd.‡
Kessler, Stuart M. '50 '76 C.679 B.S. L.365 J.D. [S.M.Kessler]
Kessler, Stuart M., P.C. 3255 N. Arlington Rd., Ste. 501
Kivlahan, Thomas W. '61 '86 C.276 A.B. L.145 J.D. [Drost,K.&M.]
Klein, Joseph J. '57 '83 C.339 B.S. L.146 J.D. [Stitt,K.D.A.&G.] ⊙
Klein, Thomas M. '21 '48 L.209 LL.B. [© Stitt,K.D.A.&G.]

Klest Law Firm
(See Schaumburg)

Kohn, Robert A. '54 '79 C&L.910 B.A., J.D. [Hodges,L.E.R.&K.]
Koloms, Harvey X., (BV) '32 '58 C.597 L.209 J.D. 59 W Seegers Rd
Kozlov, Scott A. '67 '94 C.234 B.A. L.879 J.D. 11 S. Dunton Ave.
Kramer, Gerald L. '35 '59 C.1016 L.597 LL.B. 1405 E. Central Rd.
Krent, Nancy Fredman '57 '83 C&L.477 B.A., J.D. 3030 Salt Creek Ln., Ste. 202
Larmee, Donald H. '12 '38 C&L.477 B.S.E., J.D.
(adm. in NY; not adm. in IL) 30 Regency Dr. E.‡

Leahy, Edward H. '24 '49 C&L.209 A.B., J.D. 2739 N. Patton Ave.
Lebovitz, Michael '49 '74 C.959 B.A. L.209 J.D. [M.Lebovitz]
Lebovitz, Michael, Ltd. 1500 W. Shure Dr., Ste. 245
Levinson, Alfred L. '43 '67 C.424 L.209 J.D. 3325 N. Arlington Heights Rd.
Levon, Joseph Paul '— '93 C.339 B.A. L.146 J.D. 215 N. Arlington Hgts. Rd., Ste. 100
Lind, Cary A. '48 '73 C.1036 B.A. L.597 J.D. [C.A.Lind]
Lind, Cary A., P.C. 121 S. Wilke Rd.
Lins, Harold A. '23 '52 C&L.966 B.B.A., LL.B.
(adm. in WI; not adm. in IL) 818 Catino St.‡
Lockwood, C. Russell '22 '50 C&L.546 B.S., J.D. 626 N. Carlyle Lane‡
Lohmeier, William J., Law Offices of '64 '92 C.352 B.S. L.910 J.D. 418 S. Evergreen
Lohrentz, Carlton W. '45 '70 C&L.879 B.S., J.D. [C.W.Lohrentz&Assoc.]
Lohrentz, Carlton W., & Associates 1655 N. Arlington Hgts. Rd.
Loizzi, Michael A., Jr. '51 '79 C.927 B.A. L.146 J.D. [Hodges,L.E.R.&K.]
Lyons, John J. '05 '30 C.424 L.602 LL.B. 1250 W. Central Rd.‡
Maas, E. Jerome '41 '83 C.424 B.S. L.589 J.D. Oakton College
MacNeil, Rosa M. '— '85 C.999 B.S. L.365 J.D. 8 W. Emerson
Magnus, Karl H. '57 '98 C.1016 B.G.S. L.365 J.D. 121 S. Wilke, Ste. 407
Maramba, Ignacio D., (BV) '68 '93 C&L.424 B.A., J.D. [Maramba&Assoc.]

Maramba & Associates, LLC, (BV)
121 South Wilke Road, Suite 101, 60005
Telephone: 847-255-3222 Fax: 847-255-4119
Email: idm@idmaramba.com URL: http://www.idmaramba.com
Member of Firm: Ignacio D. Maramba.
Business Law, Chancery Practice, Corporate Litigation, Civil Litigation, Complex Litigation, Defense Litigation, Federal Litigation, Administrative Litigation, Business Enterprises, Business Litigation, Closely Held Business Law, Real Estate Litigation, Veterans Rights, Military Law, Wills, Commercial Collections, Post Judgment Collections, Closely Held Corporations.
See Professional Biographies, ARLINGTON HEIGHTS, ILLINOIS

Marcus, Kenneth E., (AV) '44 '69 C.174 B.A. L.424 J.D.
Corp. Coun., American Financial Management, Inc.
Massucci, Raymond R., (AV) '43 '70 C.221 B.S.B.A. L.365 J.D.
750 W. Northwest Hwy.
Mathias, Sidney H. '44 '68 C.1016 B.S. L.209 J.D. [S.H.Mathias]
Mathias, Sidney H., P.C., Law Offices of 4256 N. Arlington Hgts. Rd.
Maxwell, Catherine M., (BVⓣ) '65 '92 C.812 B.S. L.347 J.D.
(adm. in IN; not adm. in IL) 1433 N. Vail Ave.
Mazurek, LeRoy F. '19 '51 L.365 LL.B. 1515 E. Central, Apt. 122-C‡
McCabe, James B. '40 '69 C.602 B.A. L.329 J.D. 121 South Wilke
McCabe, James L. '31 '54 L.209 J.D. 9 N Vail Ave Ste 102
McCarty, Richard C. '54 '80 C.597 B.A. L.421 J.D. 2045 S. Arlington Heights Rd.
McClellan, Thomas E. '46 '79 C.473 B.A. L.146 J.D. [A Drost,K.&M.]
McGarr, Maureen A. '27 '77 C.700 B.A. L.146 J.D. 1937 Charter Point Dr.‡
McGrath, Peter J. '28 '53 C&L.209 B.S., J.D. 121 S. Wilke Rd.
McMahon, Patrick M. '66 '93 C.347 B.S. L.365 J.D. [Drost,K.&M.]
McQuillan, Thomas J. '45 '82 C.338 B.A. L.209 J.D. 16 S. Evanston
Mesoloras, Helen '79 '04 C&L.209 B.A., J.D. 3345 N. Arlington He, Ste. D
Miller, Eric J. '79 '04 C.966 B.A. L.365 J.D. [A Farwell,F.&P.]
Miller, Richard P., Law Office of '41 '73 C.103 B.A. L.146 J.D. 515 E Golf Road
Miller, Ross A. '24 '53 C&L.209 B.S.C., J.D. 2045 S. Arlington Hgts. Rd.
Miroballi, Daniel V. '39 '66 C.424 B.B.A. L.209 J.D. 2340 S. Arlington Heights Rd.
Moore, Bruce L., P.C., (AV) '20 '49 C.627 A.B. L.477 J.D. 345 S. Windsor Dr.‡
Moran, Michael J., & Associates '53 '80 C.339 B.A. L.365 J.D.
121 S. Wilke Rd., Ste. 201

Morgan, Wendy R., The Law Firm of '55 '81 C.424 B.A. L.146 J.D.
1845 East Rand Road Suite 211, 60004 ⊙
Telephone: 847-259-5700 1-800-WRMORGAN Fax: 847-259-6560 URL: http://www.wendymorgan.com
Email: WRM@lawyer.com URL: http://www.lawyers.com/wendyrmorgan
Family Law, Divorce, Child Custody, Interstate Custody, Adoptions, Child Support, Paternity, Premarital Agreements, Domestic Violence, Visitation Rights, Adoption Law, Domestic Violence, Visitation Rights.
See Professional Biographies, ARLINGTON HEIGHTS, ILLINOIS

Morris, Jeffrey M. '47 '73 C.339 B.S.G.E. L.910 J.D. [J.M.Morris]
Morris, Jeffrey Michael, Ltd. 4256 N. Arlington Heights Rd.
Moskovic, Alex '67 '93 C.338 B.S. L.879 J.D. [Moskovic&Assoc.]
Moskovic, Joanne S. '69 '94 C.57 B.A. L.879 J.D. [A Moskovic&Assoc.]

Moskovic & Associates
120 West Eastman Street, Suite 207, 60004
Telephone: 847-797-1300 Fax: 847-797-1350 URL: http://www.moskoviclaw.com
Email: attorneys@moskoviclaw.com URL: http://www.lawyers.com/moskovic&assoc
Alex Moskovic. Associate: Joanne S. Moskovic.
Language: Spanish.
Civil Practice, Litigation, Commercial Law, Contracts, Personal Injury, Medical Malpractice, Divorce, Child Support, Child Custody, Visitation Rights, Family Law, Collections.
See Professional Biographies, ARLINGTON HEIGHTS, ILLINOIS

Moss, Gayla L., (BVⓣ) '60 '85 C&L.101 B.S., J.D.
(adm. in AZ; not adm. in IL) Motorola Inc.
Murray, James M. '44 '70 C.339 L.209 J.D. 11 E. Miner St.
Murray, Stephen R. '43 '74 C.232 B.S.B.A. L.365 J.D. 637 E. Golf Rd., Ste. 209
Nelson, Richard A., (AV) '35 '62 C.694 A.B. L.146 J.D. [R.A.Nelson&Assoc.]
Nelson, Ronald J. '41 '77 C.477 B.S. L.365 J.D. 750 W. Northwest Hwy.

Nelson, Richard A., & Associates, P.C., (AV)
A Professional Corporation
11 South Dunton Avenue, 60005
Telephone: 847-788-0055 Fax: 847-577-3897
Email: ranelson1@earthlink.net URL: http://www.lawyers.com/ranelsonlaw
Richard A. Nelson.
Estate Planning Law, Living Trusts, Probate Administration Law, Closely Held Corporations, Business Estate Planning, Commercial Real Estate Sales, Civil Litigation.
See Professional Biographies, ARLINGTON HEIGHTS, ILLINOIS

Newberg, B. Alan '46 '73 C.504 B.A. L.365 J.D.
3295 N. Arlington Heights Rd., Ste. 113
Newland, Charles T. '62 '88 C.339 B.S. L.365 J.D. [Newland,N.&N.] ⊙
Newland, Gary A. '68 '93 C&L.424 B.S., J.D. [Newland,N.&N.] ⊙
Newland, Stephen S. '66 '91 C.339 B.A. L.209 J.D. [Newland,N.&N.] ⊙

Newland, Newland & Newland
121 S. Wilke Road, Suite 101, 60005 ⊙
Telephone: 708-797-8000 Fax: 708-797-9090
Email: newlandglaw@aol.com
Gary A. Newland; Charles T. Newland; Stephen S. Newland.
Real Estate; Personal Injury.
See Professional Biographies, ARLINGTON HEIGHTS, ILLINOIS

North, William D., (AV) '30 '59 C.339 B.S. L.309 J.D. 22 N. Regenoy Dr., E.‡

O'Brien, James R. '40 '80 C.473 A.B. L.209 J.D.
Sr. V.P., Arlington Fed. Svgs. & Loan
O'Brien, John G. .... '46 '72 C.602 B.A. L.424 J.D. 2340 S. Arlington Heights Rd.
O'Donoghue, Timothy .... '25 '55 C.209 L.365 J.D. 121 South Wilke
O'Donoghue, Timothy J. .... '65 '92 C.363 B.A. L.1000 J.D. [Stitt,K.D.A.&G.]
Olson, Mark D. .... '43 '66 C.582 B.A. L.879 J.D. [© Stitt,K.D.A.&G.]
Pappas, Samuel L. .... '64 '89 C.597 B.A. L.910 J.D. 712 S. Yale Ave.

Paynter, Bruce D., The Law Offices of, (AV) '51 '76 C&L.597 B.A., J.D.
3345 North Arlington Heights Road, Suite G, 60004
Telephone: 847-392-1212 Fax: 847-392-1222
Email: paynterlaw@earthlink.net URL: http://www.paynterlaw.com
Criminal Law, Felonies, Misdemeanors, Drug Offenses, Driving While Intoxicated, Assaults, Weapons Charges, Drivers License Suspension, Traffic Violations, Sex Offenses, Personal Injury, Automobile Accidents, Motorcycle Accidents, Trucking Accidents, Wrongful Death, Real Estate Transactions, Buying and Selling Real Estate.
See Professional Biographies, ARLINGTON HEIGHTS, ILLINOIS

Pearson, Kerry W. .... '52 '77 C.801 B.A. L.221 J.D. 1216 E. Central Rd.

Perkins, Leonard F., & Associates '46 '74 C.966 B.B.A. L.276 J.D.
1139 North Ridge Avenue, 60004
Telephone: 847-577-0757 Fax: 847-577-0754
Email: lenperkins@comcast.net URL: http://www.lawyers.com/lenperkins
General Business Law, State Taxation, Intellectual Property and Unclaimed Property, Corporations, Business Enterprises; Business Start-Ups, Promotion Law.
See Professional Biographies, ARLINGTON HEIGHTS, ILLINOIS

Perkins, Y. Jacqueline '46 '81 C.1139 B.C.J. L.564 J.D.
1655 N. Arlington Heights Road, Suite 102E, 60004
Telephone: 847-394-8121 Fax: 847-394-1775
Family Law, Criminal, Murder, Homicide, Drug Crimes, Wrongful Felonies, Misdemeanors, Sex Assault, Police Misconduct, Divorce, Child Support, Domestic Violence.
See Professional Biographies, ARLINGTON HEIGHTS, ILLINOIS

Perlis, Steven C. .... '48 '74 C.352 A.B. L.546 J.D. [S.C.Perlis&Assoc.]
Perlis, Steven C., & Associates, P.C., Elder Law Office of
3345 N. Arlington Heights Rd., Ste. D
Perry, Stanley A. ....'29 '53 C.999 L.209 J.D. Sr. V.P. & Tr. Offr., NBD Tr. Co. of Ill.
Peters, A. Allen .... '32 '60 C.221 B.A. L.365 LL.B. 202 E. Wing St.
Peters, Angela E. .... '51 '85 C.339 B.A. L.146 J.D. 3800 North Wilke Street
Peters, Jeffrey A. ....'57 '82 C.339 B.S. L.209 J.D. [Farwell,F.&P.]
Petritis, Danielle Marie ....'— '94 C.339 B.S. L.436 J.D. State Farm
Pittas, John F. .... '32 '60 C.602 A.B. L.276 J.D. Laporte, Inc.
Poile, Henry J. .... '23 '49 C.209 L.424 LL.B. Honeywell Inc.
Post, Ira A. .... '48 '75 C&L.209 B.S., J.D. 125 S. Wilke Rd.‡
Pyshos, Basil N. .... '19 '43 C.999 L.209 LL.B. 825 E. Golf Rd.
Ralph, Alice M. .... '42 '88 C.665 M.A. L.209 J.D. 3030 Salt Creek Lane
Reilley, James W. '43 '69 C.424 B.S. L.365 J.D.
2015 S. Arlington Heights Rd., Ste. 119
Riebandt, James J. .... '50 '75 C.602 A.B. L.209 J.D. [Riebandt&D.]
Riebandt & DeWald, P.C. ....1237 S. Arlington Heights Road
Rigby, Shannon Barry .... '70 '01 C.870 B.S. L.589 J.D. [Ⓐ Stitt,K.D.A.&G.]
Riley, James E. .... '19 '63 C.339 B.S. L.209 J.D. 502 W. Fairview St.
Robin, Daniel K. .... '50 '77 C.347 B.A. L.146 J.D. [D.K.Robin]

Robin, Daniel K., LTD
121 S. Wilke Road, Suite 201, 60005
Telephone: 847-670-9100 Fax: 847-398-8377
Email: danatlaw@aol.com URL: http://www.danrobin.com
Daniel K. Robin.
Bankruptcy, Chapter 7, Chapter 13, Divorce, Family Law, Child Support, Separation, Pre-nuptial Agreements, Equitable Distribution, Driving While Intoxicated, Traffic Violations, Criminal Law, Wills and Trusts, Estate Planning, Asset Protection.
See Professional Biographies, ARLINGTON HEIGHTS, ILLINOIS

Rodick, S. Bennet .... '54 '78 C.597 B.A. L.910 J.D. [Hodges,L.E.R.&K.]
Rogers, Jonathan N. .... '61 '97 C.339 B.A. L.209 J.D. [Ⓐ Stitt,K.D.A.&G.]
Rogers, Steven M. ....'51 '76 C.339 B.S. L.365 J.D. 3375 F N. Arlington Heights Rd.
Rooney, Randi Shanley ....'60 '87 C&L.280 B.S.Ed., J.D. 2525 S. Clearbrook Dr.
Rothmann, Michael ....'70 '96 C.1345 B.A. L.146 J.D. 3345 North Arlington Heights
Rowley, Marshall G. ....'14 '53 C&L.424 J.D. 1225 Luther Lane
Sabin, Robert J. '24 '49 C.999 L.209 LL.B.
(adm. in MI; not adm. in IL) 822 S. Bristol Ln.‡
Sabin, Robert J., Jr. .... '50 '80 C.234 B.A. L.589 J.D. 855 E. Golf Road
Saternus, Christopher M. ....'50 '77 C&L.209 B.S.C., J.D. 102 W. Emerson St.
Schlickman, Eugene F., (AV) ....'29 '56 C.177 B.A. L.276 J.D. 85 W. Algonquin Rd.
Schlott, Mary C. ....'32 '74 C.350 B.S. L.365 J.D. [M.C.Schlott]
Schlott, Mary C., P.C. .... 423 S. Windsor Dr.
Schneider, Keith .... '58 '83 C.274 B.A. L.146 J.D. 1620 W. No.W. Highway
Schwartz, Robert ....'44 '75 C.339 B.S. L.209 J.D. 3116 N. Volz Dr., W. (Pat.)
Scotillo, Nancy S. ....'49 '75 [© Stitt,K.D.A.&G.]
Segalla, Jody Mackenzie .... '62 '87 C.352 B.A. L.424 J.D. [Ⓐ Drost,K.&M.]
Sexner, Mitchell Scott .... '61 '86 C.597 B.A. L.146 J.D. [M.S.Sexner]
Sexner, Mitchell S. ....8 E. Northwest Hwy., Ste. B
Sharp, Anne A. .... '47 '72 C.518 A.B. L.1017 J.D. 1342 N. Race Ave.
Sheridan, Charles R. .... '63 '92 C.339 B.S. L.146 J.D. 3030 Salt Creek Lane
Sherwell, Jonathan N. .... '62 '89 C&L.424 B.A., J.D. 750 W. Northwest Highway
Siebert, James C., Law Offices of '56 '81
C.339 B.S.A.S. L.209 J.D. 3325 N. Arlington Heights Rd., Ste. 500
Simon, Barry E. .... '49 '76 C.339 B.S. L.424 J.D. [B.E.Simon]
Simon, Barry E., P.C. .... 1320 E. Eton Dr.
Skowron, David R. ....'68 '94 C.352 B.A. L.365 J.D. 2355 S. Arlington Heights Rd.
Smoller, Olivia Dan ....'43 '98 C.339 B.A. L.365 J.D. 3243 Daniels Court
Soto, Catalina ....'59 '90 C.209 B.A. L.424 J.D. 2160 N. Coldspring Rd.
Srodes, Paul G. .... '44 '76 C.474 B.S.E.E. L.424 J.D. 1725 E. Peachtree Dr.
Starck, Andrew P. .... '46 '72 C.1 B.S. L.846 J.D. 1145 N. Harvard Ave.

Stelk, Roger W., Law Offices of '61 '87 C.339 B.A. L.365 J.D.
1500 W. Shure Drive, Suite 245, 60004
Telephone: 847-506-7330 Fax: 847-506-7331 URL: http://www.stelklaw.com
Email: rwstelk@aol.com URL: http://www.stelklawfirm.com
Family Law, Divorce, Real Estate, Buying and Selling a Home, Civil Litigation.
See Professional Biographies, ARLINGTON HEIGHTS, ILLINOIS

Stitt, Klein, Daday, Aretos & Giampietro, LLC, (AV)
121 S. Wilke Road, Suite 500, 60005 ⊙
Telephone: 847-590-8700 Fax: 847-590-9825
URL: http://www.skdaglaw.com
Members of Firm: LeMoine D. Stitt, Jr. (1926-1997); Joseph J. Klein; Stephen G. Daday; Michael G. Aretos; Wayne B. Giampietro; Timothy J. O'Donoghue. Associates: Jonathan N. Rogers; Richard E. Biosca; Christopher N. Ackeret; Shannon Barry Rigby. Of Counsel: Thomas M. Klein; Nancy S. Scotillo; Mark D. Olson.
(This Listing Continued)

Stitt, Klein, Daday, Aretos & Giampietro, LLC (Continued)
Litigation, Employment Litigation, Business Litigation, Intellectual Property Litigation, Commercial Litigation, Personal Injury Litigation, Divorce, Family Law, Estate Planning, Foreclosure, Civil Rights Litigation and Real Estate.
Chicago, Illinois Office: 300 W. Adams Street, Suite 350, 60602. Telephone: 312-853-3485.
See Professional Biographies, ARLINGTON HEIGHTS, ILLINOIS

Stoller, Robert C. .... '49 '75 C.339 B.A. L.616 J.D. 121 S. Wilke Rd.
Swanson, Daniel ....'— '91 C.597 B.S. L.589 J.D. 115 N. Arlington Heights Rd.
Teichman, Harvey L. ....'50 '76 C.994 B.A. L.365 J.D. 11 N. Arlington Heights Rd.
Tennant, Stephen C. .... '45 '76 C.966 B.A. L.365 J.D. 2305 E. Miner St.
Thomas, Richard D. .... '47 '73 C.210 B.A. L.1119 J.D. 1655 N. Arlington Hgts. Rd.

Thomas, Robert S. '— '84 C.347 B.A. L.1003 J.D.
1655 North Arlington Heights Road Suite 300 West, 60004
Telephone: 847-392-5893 Fax: 847-392-5894
Email: rstlaw2000@yahoo.com URL: http://www.arlingtonheightslawyers.com
Bankruptcy, Chapter 7, Personal Bankruptcy, Collections, Residential and Commercial Real Estate, Buying and Selling a Home, Zoning and Land Use, Family Law, Divorce, Adoption, Child Custody, Child Support, Wills and Probate, Trusts and Estates, Estate Planning, Asset Protection, Contracts, Breach of Contract.
See Professional Biographies, ARLINGTON HEIGHTS, ILLINOIS

Trainor, Sonja H. ....'71 '96 C.910 B.A. L.339 J.D. [Hodges,L.E.R.&K.]
Tremaine, Arthur J., (AV) .... '48 '77 C.228 B.A. L.209 J.D. [Daleiden&T.]
Tucker, Bowen H., (AV) ....'38 '63 C.103 L.477 J.D. 107 West Nayes St.‡
Vincent, Elizabeth Reiling ....'73 '99 C.597 B.A. L.145 J.D. 3030 Salt Creek Lane
Vojta, John C. .... '56 '82 C.589 B.A. L.209 J.D. [Vojta&L.]
Vojta & Lagattuta, P.C. .... 121 S. Wilke Rd.
Volden, John E. '16 '47 C&L.494 B.B.A., J.D.
(adm. in MN; not adm. in IL) 1527 N. Douglas Ave.‡
Ward, Robin R. .... '58 '83 C.347 B.A. L.209 J.D. Asst. Vil. Atty.
Weber, J. Bradley ......'59 '86 C.36 B.S. L.1187 J.D. Pres., Weber Marking Systems Inc.
Weber, Joseph A. .... '32 '56 C.221 B.A. L.597 LL.B. Weber Marking Systems Inc.
Wilhelm, Margaret M. .... '13 '38 C&L.424 Ph.B., J.D. 1506 E. Hawthorne St.‡
Wittmeyer, Ronald F., Jr. ... '55 '82 C.801 B.A. L.589 J.D. 1635 N. Arlington Heights Rd.
Wolf, Ilene M. ....'44 '75 C.597 B.S. L.365 J.D. [I.M.Wolf]
Wolf, Stuart H. .... '48 '73 C.352 B.A. L.880 J.D. 3345 N. Arlington Heights Rd., Ste. G
Wolf, Ilene M., PC ....121 S. Wilke Rd., Ste. 407
Wypych, Patricia Lynn '60 '86 C.136 B.S.W. L.1187 J.D.
2340 S. Arlington Heights Road
Yedor, William W. .... '56 '82 C.339 B.A. L.477 J.D. 2465 E. Town Blvd.
Young, Russell J. ....'67 '97 C.768 B.A. L.966 J.D. [Ⓐ Riebandt&D.]
Young, Thomas, Law Firm
(See Palatine)
Zweiban, Neil S., Law Firm of '55 '82
C.966 B.S. L.801 J.D. 3295 N. Arlington Heights Rd., Ste. 113

AROMA PARK, 821, *Kankakee Co.*

Shapiro, Jerome C., (BV) .... '53 '79 C.589 B.A. L.221 J.D. 501 Lowe Road

ARTHUR, 2,112, *Douglas & Moultrie Cos.*

Casteel, Keith W., (BV) .... '50 '75 C.679 B.S.I.E. L.339 J.D. [Samuels,M.S.J.&S.] ⊙
Crossman, Robert M., (CV) ....'52 '77 C.234 B.A. L.801 J.D. 225 S. Vine St.
Jurgens, James B. ..... '41 '67 C.597 B.S.B.A. L.339 J.D. Leg. Coun., State Bank of Arthur
Samuels, Miller, Schroeder, Jackson & Sly, LLP, (AV)
131 B South Vine Street (⊙Decatur)

ASHKUM, 650, *Iroquois Co.*

Snyder, Nicolette J. '59 '84 C.959 B.S. L.966 J.D.
(adm. in WI; not adm. in IL) R.R. 2‡

ASHLEY, 583, *Washington Co.*

Calautti, Susan M. '49 '85 C&L.801 B.A., J.D.
Gen. Coun., Technical Systems Grp., Inc.

ASHTON, 1,042, *Lee Co.*

Keller, J. Richard, (AV) ....'24 '50 C&L.339 B.S., LL.B. [Keller] ⊙
Keller Law Office, (AV) ....P.O. Box 127 (⊙Dixon)

ASSUMPTION, 1,244, *Christian Co.*

La Charite, George J. .... '14 '46 C.597 B.S. L.996 201 N. Chestnut‡

AURORA, 142,990, *DuPage, Kane, Kendall & Will Cos.*

Aguinaga, Deanna L. .... '68 '95 C.999 B.A. L.589 J.D. [D.Aguinaga]
Aguinaga, Deanna, Attorney at Law .... 45 W. Downer Pl.
Alschuler, Sam, (AV) ....'13 '35 C.966 A.B. L.145 J.D. 60 E. Downer Pl.
Alschuler, Simantz & Hem, L.L.C., (BV) ....1961 West Downer Place
Amoni, Larry M., (AV) ....'51 '77 C.339 B.A. L.146 J.D. [Amoni]
Amoni Law Offices, P.C., (AV) ....One North Constitution Drive
Anderson, Kathleen A. ....'58 '85 C.339 B.A. L.209 J.D. 2112 W. Galena Blvd.
Andersson, Steven A., (BV) ....'64 '92 C&L.589 B.A., J.D. [Mickey,W.W.R.&A.]
Anfinson, Carol L. .... '45 '70 C&L.339 B.S., J.D. [© B.A.Brown]
Ariano, Hardy, Nyuli, Johnson, Richmond & Goettel, P.C.
(See Elgin)
Atwell, Charles H., Jr., (BV) ....'44 '74 C.641 B.S. L.365 J.D. 111 W. Downer Pl.
Banas, Theresa M. ....'49 '78 C.145 B.A. L.209 J.D. 3 S. 505 Norris Rd.
Banbury, John C., (BV) ....'44 '68 C.589 B.S. L.424 J.D. [Banbury,D.&E.]
Banbury, Davis and Erschen, P.C., (BV) ....122 West Downer Place
Bieber, Gretta E. .... '52 '87 C.927 B.S. L.425 J.D. [Ⓐ Alschuler,S.&H.]
Blomberg, Randolph K., Law Offices of '51 '76
C.578 B.A. L.145 J.D. 260 S. Highland Ave.
Bloom, Marvin I., (BV) ....'53 '78 C.352 B.A. L.424 J.D. 546 West Galena Boulevard
Bode, Joseph D. .... '50 '80 C.58 B.S. L.589 J.D. 518 Hankes Ave.
Brent, Mark D., The Law Office of, (CV) '66 '91
C&L.339 B.A., J.D. 2000 W. Galena Blvd., Ste. 200
Brenton, Roberta C. ....'50 '89 C.1097 B.S. L.1015 J.D. 2799 Carriage Way‡
Brim, Phyllis T. Turner '64 '93 C.46 B.S.Ch.E. L.150 J.D.
870 N. Commons Drive (Pat.)
Brouch, Robert F., (BV) ....'61 '86 C.338 B.S. L.589 J.D. [Dreyer,F.S.F.&S.]

Brown, Bruce A., Law Office of, (BV) '46 '73 C&L.339 B.A., J.D.
2000 West Galena, Suite 201, 60506
Telephone: 630-897-2800 Fax: 630-897-2876
Email: bbrown@bablegal.com
Of Counsel: Carol L. Anfinson.
Corporate Law, Banks and Banking, Business Law, Construction Law, Commercial Real Estate, Real Estate, Mortgages, Contracts, Contested Estates, Litigation.
See Professional Biographies, AURORA, ILLINOIS

Brown, Valerie Dee '62 '88 C.927 B.S. L.339 J.D.
Asst. Corp. Coun., Mun. City of Aurora
Bruckner, Sandra Petras, (BV) .... '61 '86 C.339 B.S. L.589 J.D. 54 W. Downer Pl.

Brundage, Stephen A.
(See Wheaton)

Burnell, Wilson D., (AV) .... '16 '39 C&L.339 LL.B. [⊡ Truemper,H.&T.]
Cassell, Martin L., (BV) .... '44 '70 C.894 B.A. L.339 J.D. [M.L.Cassell]
Cassell, Martin L., Ltd., (BV) .... 330 N. Broadway
Castagnoli, Susan G. .... '53 '79 C.504 B.A. L.589 J.D. [S.G.Castagnoli] ⊙

Castagnoli, Susan G., P.C., Law Offices of
1444 North Farnsworth Avenue, Suite 107, 60505 ⊙
Telephone: 630-717-1594; TT4-630-566-5222 Fax: 630-717-1596
Email: susancastagnoli@scastagnolilaw.com URL: http://www.castagnolilaw.com
Susan G. Castagnoli.
Languages: Sign Language.
Bankruptcy, Commercial Bankruptcy, Consumer Bankruptcy, Foreclosures, Debt Management, Family, Divorce, Divorce Planning, Premarital Agreements, Custody, Adoptions, Child Support, Real Estate, Financial Planning, Wills and Probate, Estate Planning, Trusts and Estates, Equine Law.
Naperville, Illinois Office: 1119 North Washington Street, 60563. Telephone: 630-717-1594. Fax: 630-717-1596.
See Professional Biographies, AURORA, ILLINOIS

Castelli, John B., (CV) .... '48 '89 C&L.589 B.S., J.D. 816 S. Spencer St.
Chase, Michelle T. .... '62 '87 C&L.209 B.A., J.D. 116 Newberry Ct.
Cheatham, James E., (BV) .... '23 '51 C.337 B.A. L.221 LL.B. 301 W. Galena Blvd.
Cibulskis, Julie L., (BV) .... '73 '98 C.190 B.A. L.776 J.D. [Lindner,S.&R.]
Clark, Denise M. .... '61 '87 C.436 B.A. L.574 J.D. Gen. Coun., Hereiu Funds
Coaxum, Donna Bunch ..... '63 '92 C.679 B.S. L.966 J.D. Sen. Coun., OSI Industries, Inc.
Cook, Vincent S., (BV) .... '55 '82 C.339 B.A. L.365 J.D. 403 W. Galena Blvd.
Craig, Theodore J., (CV) .... '47 '75 C.927 B.S. L.365 J.D. 1133 N. Farnsworth Ave.
Cruz, Rene .... '— '95 C.152 B.S. L.589 J.D. 151 S. Lincoln Ave.
Davis, Noel C., (BV) .... '41 '67 C.207 B.A. L.930 J.D. [Banbury,D.&E.]
De Hart, Gordon F., (CV) .... '28 '57 C.1016 L.339 LL.B. 203 S. Calumet Ave.
Dickinson, Donald R., (BV) .... '40 '70 C.1100 B.A. L.365 J.D. 440 W. Galena Blvd.
Dickson, Frederick H., (AV) .... '38 '64 C&L.339 B.S., LL.B. [Dickson&H.]

Dickson & Hasenbalg, (AV)
2000 West Galena Boulevard Suite 305, 60506-4360
Telephone: 630-859-3300 Fax: 630-859-3375
Email: chasenbalg@d-hlaw.com URL: http://www.d-hlaw.com
Members of Firm: Frederick H. Dickson; Craig D. Hasenbalg. Associates: Jean C. Francissen; Andrew G. White. Of Counsel: Calvin B. Thelin.
Language: English.
Corporate Law, Business Law, Taxation, Trusts and Estates, Commercial Real Estate, Litigation, General Civil and Trial Practice.
Representative Client: The Merchants National Bank of Aurora.
See Professional Biographies, AURORA, ILLINOIS

Dillon, Timothy C., (AV) '62 '89 C.436 B.A. L.46 J.D.
Vice President, Secretary & General Counsel, Succcessories

Dommermuth, Brestal, Cobine and West, Ltd., (AV)
Old Second National Bank Building, 111 West Downer Place, Suite 300, 60506 ⊙
Telephone: 630-892-5700
Email: PLP@DBCW.com
John F. Philipchuck.
General Civil Practice. Personal Injury, Worker's Compensation, Corporate, Banking, Municipal, Zoning and Development, Real Estate, Family and Probate Law, Litigation, Federal and State Taxation, Commercial Collection.
Naperville, Illinois Office: 123 Water Street. Telephone: 630-355-5800.
See Professional Biographies, AURORA, ILLINOIS

Doyle, Julie Lynn .... '59 '89 C.679 B.S. L.365 J.D. 330 N. Broadway Ave.
Dreyer, John E., (AV) .... '29 '53 C.424 B.S. L.209 J.D. [⊡ Dreyer,F.S.F.&S.]

Dreyer, Foote, Streit, Furgason and Slocum, A Professional Association, (AV) BB
1999 W. Downer Place, 60506-4384
Telephone: 630-897-8764 FAX: 630-897-1735
Email: info@dreyerfoote.com URL: http://www.dreyerfoote.com
William J. Foote; Thomas J. Streit; Richard M. Furgason; Richard C. Slocum; Paul T. Patricoski; Robert F. Brouch; Jonathan B. Shanower;—Michael W. Huseman; Jackie L. Jalley. Of Counsel: John E. Dreyer.
Civil and Criminal Trial and Appellate Practice in all State and Federal Courts. Business Planning, Commercial, Corporate, Estate Planning, Wills, Probate, Trusts and Estates, Elder Law, Family Law, Healthcare, Insurance and Insurance Defense, Labor, Municipal, Personal Injury, Probate, Real Estate, State and Federal Taxation, Adoption, Child Support, Child Custody, Divorce, Domestic Violence, DWI, Automobile Accidents, Wrongful Death, Buying and Selling a Home, Landlord/Tenant, Construction, Bankruptcy, Guardianships, Collections, Buying and Selling a Business, Business Enterprises, Franchise, Closely Held Business, Limited Liability, Partnerships, Small Business, Contracts, Lawsuits, Starting a Business, Zoning.
Representative Clients: Old Second National Bank; Aurora Eye Clinic; Aurora Pediatric Clinic; Rush Copley Medical Center; Industrial Motor Service, Inc.; R.D. Marcley, Inc.; Aurora Fast Freight, Inc.; Mid-States Express, Inc.; United Express System, Inc.; Fox Valley Machining Co., Inc.
See Professional Biographies, AURORA, ILLINOIS

Dykema Gossett PLLC, (AV)
2 Hankes Road, 60506 ⊙
Telephone: 630-844-2200 Fax: 630-844-2277
URL: http://www.dykema.com
Member of Firm: Bruce L. Goldsmith.
Antitrust and Trade Regulation, Automotive, Banking and Financial Services, Bankruptcy, Biotechnology and Life Sciences, Casino Gaming, Class Action Defense, Computer and Software Law, Construction, Consumer Financial Services, Corporate Finance, E-Commerce, Emerging Business and Technology, Employee Benefits, Entertainment and Sports, Environmental Law, Family Law, Franchise Law and Regulation, Government Contracts, Government Policy and Practice, HealthCare, Indian Law, Insurance, Intellectual Property, International Law, Labor and Employment, Litigation and Dispute Resolution, Mergers and Acquisitions, Products Liability Defense, Public Finance, Real Estate, Retail Law, Securities, Taxation and Estates, Trade Associations.
Ann Arbor, Michigan Office: 2723 South State Street, Suite 400, 48104. Telephone: 734-214-7660. Fax: 734-214-7696.
Bloomfield Hills, Michigan Office: 39577 Woodward Avenue, Suite 300, 48304-2820. Telephone: 248-203-0700. Fax: 248-203-0763.
Chicago, Illinois Office: 10 South Wacker Drive, Suite 2300. Telephone: 312-876-1700. Fax: 312-876-1155.
Detroit, Michigan Office: 400 Renaissance Center, 48243-1668. Telephone: 313-568-6800. Fax: 313-568-6545.
Grand Rapids, Michigan Office: Suite 700, 300 Ottawa Avenue, N.W., 49503-2306. Telephone: 616-776-7500. Fax: 616-776-7573.
Joliet, Illinois Office: 111 North Ottawa Street. Telephone: 815-727-4511. Facsimile: 815-727-1586.
Lansing, Michigan Office: 124 W. Allegan Street, Suite 800, 48933-1742. Telephone: 517-374-9100. Fax: 517-374-9191.
Lisle, Illinois Office: 4200 Commerce Court, Suite 300. Telephone: 630-245-0400. Facsimile: 630-245-0140.
Los Angeles, California Office: 333 South Grand Avenue, Suite 2100, 90071. Telephone: 213-457-1800. Fax: 213-457-1850.
Washington, D.C. Office: Franklin Square, Suite 300 West, 1300 I Street, N.W., 20005-3353. Telephone: 202-906-8600. Fax: 202-906-8669.
See Professional Biographies, AURORA, ILLINOIS

Edwards, James R., (BV) .... '34 '58 C.999 L.365 LL.B. [Edwards,J.&O.]
Edwards, Jordan & O'Connor, (BV) .... 6 W. Downer Pl.
Evers, Jeffrey W. .... '59 '87 C.339 B.A. L.365 J.D. 902 Waverly Ct.
Flaherty, Patrick M., (AV) .... '51 '78 C.209 B.A. L.589 J.D. [Thompson,L.F.&M.]
Foote, William J., (AV) .... '32 '58 C&L.309 A.B., LL.B. [Dreyer,F.S.F.&S.]
Fradkin, Jeffery H. '59 '84 C&L.910 A.B., J.D.
Sr. Coun., OSI Industries Inc. (Legal Department)
Francissen, Jean C. .... '66 '92 C.339 B.S. L.1065 J.D. [Ⓐ Dickson&H.]
Frieders, Dean M. .... '79 '04 C.578 B.A. L.146 J.D. [Ⓐ Mickey,W.W.R.&A.]
Fuchs, Ernest P. .... '66 '99 C.871 B.S. L.589 J.D. 921 Wellington Cir.
Funkey, Michael C., (AV) .... '45 '70 C.425 B.A. L.209 J.D. [M.C.Funkey]

Funkey, Michael C., P.C., Law Offices of, (AV)
2111 Plum Street, Suite 301, 60506
Telephone: 630-897-4284 FAX: 630-897-4220
URL: http://www.michaelcfunkeypc.com
Michael C. Funkey.
General Practice, Civil Litigation, Contested Litigation, and Trials and Appeals in all civil matters including Automobile Accidents, Slip and Fall, Dog Bites, Wrongful Death, Products Liability, Divorce, Child Custody, Child Support, Proceedings involving Orders of Protection, Family Law Matters, Personal Injury, Eminent Domain, Real Estate, Juvenile Law, Municipal and Election Law, Wills, Probate, Trusts and Estates, Estate Planning, DUI, Trials and Appeals in Misdemeanor and Criminal Matters.
See Professional Biographies, AURORA, ILLINOIS

Furgason, Richard M., (AV) .... '49 '74 C.209 B.A. L.602 J.D. [Dreyer,F.S.F.&S.]
Goldsmith, Bruce L., (AV) ...... '45 '71 C.597 B.A. L.145 J.D. [Dykema G.P.] (⊙Lisle)
Goldsmith, Zalmon S., (AV) .... '15 '38 C&L.145 A.B., J.D. 1600 West Downer Place‡
Goodin, Ben A. .... '41 '68 C.934 B.A. L.734 J.D. [B.A.Goodin&Assoc.]
Goodin, Ben A., & Associates, P.C. .... 330 North Broadway Ave.
Griffin, Eugene G. .... '34 '58 C&L.602 B.S., LL.B. 444 W. Galena Blvd.
Hallsby, Susan M. '61 '90 C.252 B.S.B.A. L.851 J.D.
Sr. Coun., OSI Industries Inc. (Legal Department)
Harris, Gretchen M. .... '75 '05 C.966 B.S. L.424 J.D. [Ⓐ Whitt L.]
Hasenbalg, Craig D., (CV) .... '68 '93 C&L.112 B.A., J.D. [Dickson&H.]
Heady, Terrance W., (CV) .... '68 '96 C.1175 B.A. L.589 J.D. [Ⓐ Lindner,S.&R.]
Heimsoth, Mark E., (BV) .... '49 '78 C.182 B.A. L.879 J.D. 563 W. Galena Blvd.
Hem, Ronald M., (BV) .... '49 '75 C.927 B.B.A. L.365 J.D. [Alschuler,S.&H.]
Herman, Matthew J., (CV) .... '70 '96 C.205 B.S. L.365 J.D. [Kinnally,K.L.H.&H.]
Hill, Herbert .... '40 '69 C.872 B.A. L.365 J.D. 31 W. Downer Pl.
Hodge, Gerald K., (BV) .... '59 '84 C.57 B.A. L.879 J.D. [Kinnally,K.L.H.&H.]
Hollingsworth, Christopher G. ... '72 '98 C.339 B.A. L.589 J.D. 1700 N. Farnsworth Ave.
Hollingsworth, Dewey G., (BV) .... '46 '77 C.339 B.A. L.146 J.D. [Truemper,H.&T.]
Holloway, Lisa Colleen .... '75 '02 C.477 B.A. L.770 J.D. 417 Jamestown Ct.
Holzrichter, Linda M., (CV) .... '58 '91 C.339 B.S. L.146 J.D. 16 S. Locust St.
Hughes, Gordon R., Jr., (CV) .... '47 '75 C.966 B.A. L.365 J.D. 320 E. Indian Tr.
Hurrell, Dianne Lenert .... '59 '89 C.190 B.S.N. L.589 J.D. 38 Windwood Dr.
Hurt, Gary B. .... '41 '68 C.473 B.S. L.339 J.D. 440 W. Galena Blvd.
Huseman, Michael W. .... '77 '03 C.1024 B.A. L.589 J.D. [Ⓐ Dreyer,F.S.F.&S.]
Jalley, Jackie L. .... '— '02 C.339 B.A. L.589 J.D. [Ⓐ Dreyer,F.S.F.&S.]
Johnson, Jay .... '65 '98 C.383 B.A. L.365 J.D. [Ⓐ C.Woodruff&Assoc.] ⊙
Jordan, Darrell L., (BV) .... '51 '76 C.927 B.S. L.339 J.D. [Edwards,J.&O.]
Joy, Walter W. .... '57 '87 546 West Galena Boulevard
Joyner, Wade R. .... '64 '88 C.679 B.A. L.823 J.D. [⊡ Lowe&S.] (⊙Plano)
Kachelhoffer, Scott S. .... '58 '91 C.388 B.A. L.46 J.D. 554 Kingsway Dr. (⊙Chicago)
Kadden, Steven L., (BV) .... '50 '76 C.910 B.A. L.861 J.D. 1st Asst. Corp. Coun.
Kane, Christopher A. ...... '65 '96 C.879 B.A. L.365 J.D. Asst. V.P., Chicago Motor Club
Khan, Ned C. .... '66 '91 C.339 B.S. L.347 J.D. 31 W. Downer Place
King, Jason D. .... '72 '99 C&L.589 B.S., J.D. 122 W. Downer Pl.
King, Lincoln M. .... '77 '03 C.234 B.A. L.589 J.D. [Ruddy,M.&K.]
Kinnally, Patrick M., (AV) .... '50 '80 C.424 B.A. L.365 J.D. [Kinnally,K.L.H.&H.]

Kinnally, Krentz, Loran, Hodge & Herman, P.C., (AV) BB
2114 Deerpath Road, P.O. Box 5030, 60506
Telephone: 630-907-0909 Fax: 630-907-0913 URL: http://www.kklhhlaw.com
Email: pkinnally@kklhhlaw.com URL: http://www.lawyers.com/kklhhlaw
Patrick M. Kinnally; Paul G. Krentz; Joseph C. Loran; Gerald K. Hodge; Matthew J. Herman;—Diana M. Law. Of Counsel: William C. Murphy.
Language: Spanish.
General Practice. Civil Trial Practice, Personal Injury, Auto Accidents, Worker's Compensation, Corporate Law, Immigration and Naturalization, Business Law, Estate Planning, Trusts, Estates and Probate, Municipal and Zoning Law, Education Law, Environmental and Eminent Domain.
See Professional Biographies, AURORA, ILLINOIS

Klenke, Daniel F., (BV) '55 '81 C.339 B.A. L.910 J.D.
563 West Galena Boulevard, 60506-3854
Telephone: 630-896-1020 Fax: 630-892-7184
Email: dfklaw@sbcglobal.net URL: http://www.dfklawfirm.com
Alternative Dispute Resolution, Business, Commercial, Employment, Discrimination, Wrongful Termination, Administrative, Family Law, Divorce, Adoption, Real Estate and Litigation, Buying and Selling, Municipal Law, Child Custody, Child Support, Grandparent Rights, Step-parent.
See Professional Biographies, AURORA, ILLINOIS

Krentz, Paul G., (AV) .... '58 '83 C&L.879 B.S., J.D. [Kinnally,K.L.H.&H.]
Kriaris, Karyn .... '56 '89 2697 S. Carriage Way‡
Lamont, John M., (AV) .... '40 '65 C&L.602 A.B., LL.B. [Thompson,L.F.&M.]
Larsen, Richard G., (BV) .... '59 '86 C.58 B.A. L.589 J.D. [Myler,R.&M.]
Law, Diana M. .... '78 '04 C.288 B.A. L.589 J.D. [Ⓐ Kinnally,K.L.H.&H.]
Lawrence, Norman R., (BV) .... '38 '62 C&L.339 B.S., J.D. 7 West Windsor Court
Lee, Douglas E., Law Offices of, (CV) '62 '90 C.339 B.S. L.146 J.D.
2297 Lakeside Dr.
Leslie-Burr, Sharon K. .... '49 '90 L.221 J.D. Chicago Title Insurance Co.
Leszcynski, Laurence T. .... '52 '78 C.190 B.A. L.285 J.D. 67 E. Downer Pl.
Lindner, George P., (AV) .... '40 '65 C&L.174 B.A., LL.B. [Lindner,S.&R.]

Lindner, Speers & Reuland, P.C., (AV)
54 West Downer Place, P.O. Box 5055, 60507
Telephone: 630-892-8109 Fax: 630-892-8151
Email: Help@auroralawfirm.com URL: http://www.auroralawfirm.com
George P. Lindner; Robert L. Speers; Timothy J. Reuland; Julie L. Cibulskis;—Terrance W. Heady; Jonathan G. Pfleeger.
The firm represents persons injured by vehicles, trains, aircraft, doctors, hospitals, and products, as well as victims of sexual harassment, police misconduct, and all forms of employment discrimination. The firm also represents persons and businesses in disputes between business entities and business owners, and litigates will contests and zoning disputes.
See Professional Biographies, AURORA, ILLINOIS

Lipsman, William S. '49 '74 C.597 B.A. L.309 J.D.
Exec. V.P., Gen. Coun. & Secy., OSI Industries Inc.
Loats, J. Timothy, Law Offices of, (BV) '54 '78
C.274 B.A. L.602 J.D. 346 North Lake Street
Loran, Joseph C., (AV) .... '59 '85 C.103 B.A. L.424 J.D. [Kinnally,K.L.H.&H.]
Lovelace, Joseph D., Law Offices of ...... '66 '96 C.578 B.A. L.209 J.D. 67 E. Downer Pl

Lowe, Ralph E., (AV) ....'31 '56 C.210 B.A. L.339 LL.B. [Lowe&S.]

Lowe and Steinmetz, Ltd., (AV)
407 West Galena Boulevard, P.O. Box 1625, 60507-1625
Telephone: 630-897-0900 FAX: 630-897-9500
URL: http://www.lslegal.net
Ralph E. Lowe; Herbert C. Steinmetz, Jr. Of Counsel: Wade R. Joyner.
Real Estate Law, Civil Litigation, Corporate Law, Trusts and Estates, Syndications and Tax Law, Wills and Probate, Contracts, Business Law.
Reference: The Old Second National Bank of Aurora, Illinois.

See Professional Biographies, AURORA, ILLINOIS

Marquardt, Lynda S. ....'72 '97 C.350 B.S. L.352 J.D. 2880 Carlsbad Circle
Masur, Wolodymyr Mark, (BV) ....'64 '89 C.339 B.A. L.365 J.D. [Thompson,L.F.&M.]

McCaffery, Joseph P., Attorney at Law '65 '91 C.201 B.A. L.209 J.D.
2210 Sandburg Drive, 60506
Telephone: 630-801-8691 Fax: 630-896-2638
Email: jpmlaw@coyad.net URL: http://www.josephmccaffery.com
Criminal Litigation, White Collar, Felonies, Misdemeanors, Civil Defense, Legal Malpractice Defense, Insurance Defense, Medical Malpractice, Personal Injury, Divorce, Wills and Trusts, Real Estate Transactions, Banking, Securities, Corporate and Commercial Litigation.

See Professional Biographies, AURORA, ILLINOIS

McCleary, Scott Fitzgerald .... '62 '87 C.578 B.A. L.597 J.D. Asst. Corp. Coun.
Mc Tavish, G. Alexander, (BV) ....'52 '77 C.705 B.A. L.339 J.D. [Myler,R.&M.]
McWethy, Edward J., (AV) ....'25 '52 C.388 A.B. L.339 LL.B. 60 E. Downer Pl.
Mickey, Gary K., (AV) ....'39 '66 C.340 A.B. L.339 LL.B. [Mickey,W.W.R.&A.]

Mickey, Wilson, Weiler, Renzi & Andersson, P.C., (AV) [BR]
2111 Plum Street, 2nd Floor, P.O. Box 787, 60507-0787
Telephone: 630-801-9699 Fax: 630-801-9715 URL: http://www.mickeywilson.com
Email: office@mickeywilson.com URL: http://www.lawyers.com/mwwr
Gary K. Mickey; Peter K. Wilson, Jr.; Bernard K. Weiler; Constance Burnett Renzi; Steven A. Andersson;—Dean M. Frieders.
State and Federal Civil Practice. Trials and Appeals. Personal Injury, Corporation Law, Probate, Estate Planning, Real Estate, Workers Compensation, School Law, Aviation Law and Elder Law.

See Professional Biographies, AURORA, ILLINOIS

Middleton, Margaret R., (Mrs.) ....'15 '61 C&L.339 B.S.Ed., J.D. 111 W. Park Ave.‡
Milroy, John P. .... '49 '77 C.597 B.A. L.208 J.D. [Ruddy,M.&K.]
Morelli, Fred M., Jr., (AV) .... '41 '66 C&L.602 B.A., J.D. P.O. Box 1416
Murphy, J. Robert, (AV) ....'23 '49 C&L.309 LL.B. [Murphy&M.]
Murphy, James R., (BV) ....'51 '81 C.339 B.A. L.801 J.D. [Murphy&M.]
Murphy, William C., (AV) ....'20 '49 C&L.309 S.B., J.D. [C Kinnally,K.L.H.&H.]
Murphy & Murphy, P.C., (AV) ....111 W. Downer Pl., Ste. 400
Myler, Charles J., (AV) ....'31 '55 C.128 A.B. L.276 J.D. [Myler,R.&M.]
Myler, Ruddy & Mc Tavish, (AV) ....111 W. Downer Place
Neary, Mark J. '63 '89 C&L.352 B.A., J.D.
(adm. in IA; not adm. in IL) 546 West Galena Boulevard
Nelson, Robert E., Law Office of, (BV) '46 '72
C.210 B.A. L.339 J.D. 30 S. Stolp Ave., Ste. 402
Niermann, Kurt A. ....'65 '91 C&L.339 B.A., J.D. [A Presbrey&Assoc.]
Nolan, Roger W., Jr. '31 '56 C&L.602 B.S., LL.B.
(adm. in IA; not adm. in IL; Pat.) 1225 Corporate Boulevard‡
Notation-Rhoades, Anna J. ....'68 '93 C.66 B.A. L.146 J.D. JWReproductions, Inc.
Nowak, Gregory J. '61 '89 C.339 B.S. L.209 J.D.
Vice President, General Counsel & Corporate Sect'y, Succcessories
Ochsenschlager, Irving J., (BV) ....'42 '68 C.37 B.S.B.A. L.879 J.D. 519 W. Galena Blvd.
O'Connor, Robert J., (BV) ....'44 '69 C.339 A.B. L.602 J.D. [Edwards,J.&O.]
Olson, Robert T. ....'22 '50 C&L.966 J.D. 1024 Cypress Dr.
O' Neal, Ronald D., Jr. '66 '96
C.257 B.A. L.608 J.D. Asst. Corp. Coun., City of Aurora Law Dept.
Palermo, Mario C. ....'71 '96 C.93 B.A. L.146 J.D. [A C.Woodruff&Assoc.] ⊙
Patel, Dharma '71 '97 C.893 B.A. L.692 J.D.
International Union Welfare-Pension Funds
Patricoski, Paul T., (BV) ....'55 '81 C.757 B.S. L.602 J.D. [Dreyer,F.S.F.&S.]
Peterka, Edward R. ....'68 '94 C&L.339 B.A., J.D. [A Amoni]
Petersen, Charles E., (BV) ....'50 '77 C.98 B.S. L.365 J.D. [A Presbrey&Assoc.]
Peterson, Max G., (BV) ....'39 '64 C&L.352 B.A., J.D. 444 W. Galena Blvd.
Petesch, Richard T., (BV) ....'56 '83 C.58 B.A. L.365 J.D. [A Whitt L.]
Pfleeger, Jonathan G. ....'77 '03 C.207 B.A. L.608 J.D. [A Lindner,S.&R.]
Philipchuck, John F., (BV) ... '46 '78 C.963 B.S. L.365 J.D. [Dommermuth,B.C.&W.] ⊙
Piccony, Gary G., (BV) '46 '74
C.927 B.B. L.209 J.D. 1700 North Farnsworth Avenue, Suite 25
Porro, Michelle D. ....'69 '95 C.927 B.S. L.790 J.D. [A Presbrey&Assoc.]
Poulakidas, Michael J., The Law Office of '72 '98 C.578 B.A. L.1187 J.D.
346 N. Lake St.
Presbrey, Kim Edward, (AV) ....'51 '77 C.597 B.A. L.880 J.D. [Presbrey&Assoc.]
Presbrey & Associates, P.C., (AV) ....821 W. Galena Blvd.
Puscas, Victor E., Jr., (CV) ....'66 '94 C.338 B.S. L.365 J.D. 546 W. Galena Blvd.
Putnam, Ralph C., Jr., (AV) ....'15 '41 C.197 B.A. L.309 LL.B. 60 E. Downer Pl.
Reed, Daniel A. ....'57 '83 C.801 B.S. L.339 J.D. [A Alschuler,S.&H.]
Renzi, Constance Burnett, (BV) .....'62 '86 C.338 B.S. L.339 J.D. [Mickey,W.W.R.&A.]
Reuland, Timothy J., (AV) ....'48 '73 C.424 B.A. L.597 J.D. [Lindner,S.&R.]
Richards, G. William, (BV) '33 '57 C&L.339 A.B., LL.B.
Comr., Aurora Election Comm.
Ries, Stacey Ann ....'68 '97 C.966 B.S.N. L.209 J.D. 2000 Ogden Avenue
Ruddy, C. John, (AV) ....'50 '77 C.208 B.A. L.365 J.D. [Ruddy,M.&K.]
Ruddy, Clarence J., (AV) ....'05 '27 C&L.602 J.D. [C Myler,R.&M.] ‡
Ruddy, Philip C., (AV) ....'41 '66 C&L.602 A.B., J.D. [Myler,R.&M.]

Ruddy, Milroy & King, (AV)
Farnsworth Commons Office Center, 1700 North Farnsworth Avenue, Suite 12, 60505-1512
Telephone: 630-820-0333 Fax: 630-820-0594 URL: http://www.ruddyvmlaw.com
Email: rvlawfirm@aol.com URL: http://www.rvmlawfirm.com
Members of Firm: C. John Ruddy; John P. Milroy; Lincoln M. King.
Bankruptcy, Commercial Litigation, Family Law, Import-Export Law, Secured Transactions, Lender Liability.

See Professional Biographies, AURORA, ILLINOIS

Sachs, Jeffrey W. ....'46 '73 C.645 B.S. L.831 J.D. 2400 Inverness Ct.
Schanlaber, William C., (AV) ....'38 '64 C&L.45 J.D. [C Schanlaber&R.]
Schanlaber & Reed, A Professional Corporation ....1961 W. Downer Place
Self, Bruce A., (BV) ....'47 '76 C.339 B.S. L.365 J.D. [B.A.Self&Assoc.]
Self, Bruce A., & Associates, Ltd., (BV) ....408 N. Lake St.
Shanower, Jonathan B., (BV) .... '62 '89 C.578 B.A. L.607 J.D. [Dreyer,F.S.F.&S.]
Shea, Mark C. ....'70 '96 C.624 B.A. L.589 J.D. [A R.E.Nelson]
Simantz, Donald J., (BV) ....'48 '75 C.602 B.B.A. L.365 J.D. [Alschuler,S.&H.]
Slocum, Richard C., (BV) ....'50 '76 C.927 B.A. L.221 J.D. [Dreyer,F.S.F.&S.]
Smutzer, Jeniffer Anne .... '76 '01 C.338 B.S. L.589 J.D. 151 S. Lincoln Ave.

Solomon, Richard R., (BV) ....'41 '66 C.339 B.S. L.209 J.D. 320 E. Indian Trail
Speers, Robert L., (AV) .... '45 '72 C.350 B.S. L.339 J.D. [Lindner,S.&R.]
Steinmetz, Herbert C., Jr., (AV) .... '42 '68 C.1024 B.A. L.339 J.D. [Lowe&S.]
Stiles, Stanley R., (BV) ....'16 '48 C.578 B.S. L.597 J.D. 122 W. Downer Place
Streit, Edward F., Jr., (BV) ....'35 '61 C.339 L.424 LL.B. 2000 W. Galena
Streit, Thomas J., (AV) ....'40 '65 C.436 A.B. L.477 LL.B. [Dreyer,F.S.F.&S.]
Thelin, Calvin B., (AV) ....'29 '58 C.165 A.B. L.597 J.D. [C Dickson&H.]
Thompson, Charles F., Jr., (AV) ....'37 '62 C.118 B.A. L.145 J.D. [Thompson,L.F.&M.]

Thompson, Lamont, Flaherty & Masur, A Professional Corporation, (AV)
1281 North Farnsworth Avenue, 60505-2011
Telephone: 630-851-6500 Fax: 630-851-6523
Email: info@tlfmlaw.com URL: http://www.tlfmlaw.com
Charles F. Thompson, Jr.; John M. Lamont; Patrick M. Flaherty; Wolodymyr Mark Masur.
Practice limited to Personal Injury Litigation, including General Negligence, Automobile Accidents, Medical Malpractice, Product Liability, Wrongful Death and Workers Compensation, Transportation, Negligence, Slip and Fall, Dog Bites, Sexual Abuse. Serving all clients in DuPage, Kane, Kendall, DeKalb, Will and Cook Counties.

See Professional Biographies, AURORA, ILLINOIS

Titiner, Steven D., (CV) ....'62 '87 C.347 B.A. L.339 J.D. [Truemper,H.&T.]
Todas, Richard ....'46 '78 C.339 B.A. L.365 J.D. Mayor's Off.
Truemper, William J., (BV) ....'48 '77 C.58 B.A. L.365 J.D. [Truemper,H.&T.]
Truemper, Hollingsworth & Titiner, (BV) ....1700 N. Farnsworth Ave.
Turner-Brim, Phyllis T. '64 '93
C.46 B.S.CHE. L.150 J.D. 870 North Commons Drive (Pat.)
Vago, Louis N. ....'25 '55 C&L.209 LL.B. 1054 Church Rd.

Vaught, Kathleen, P.C.
(See Wheaton)

Venuti, Daniel E., (BV) ....'64 '89 C.424 B.S. L.46 J.D. [A B.A.Self&Assoc.]
Voiland, Joseph R., (BV) ....'52 '77 C.906 B.A. L.424 J.D. 346 N. Lake St.
Voland, Richard E., (AV) ....'16 '41 C&L.309 B.S., LL.B. 1400 Southlawn Pl.
Weber, Theodore V. ....'— '93 C.589 P.O. Box 2432
Weiland, Charles H., (AV) ....'21 '49 C.367 A.B. L.309 LL.B. 211 S. Fourth St.‡
Weiler, Bernard K., (BV) ....'53 '78 C&L.424 B.A., J.D. [Mickey,W.W.R.&A.]
Weiler, Wayne F., (BV) .... '48 '73 C.177 B.A. L.602 J.D. 1700 N. Farnsworth Ave.
White, Andrew G. ....'79 '04 C.339 B.S. L.607 J.D. [A Dickson&H.]
Whitt, Joshua S. ....'77 '03 C.234 B.A. L.117 J.D. [A Whitt L.]
Whitt, Stuart L., (AV) .... '52 '77 C.58 B.A. L.424 J.D. [Whitt L.]

Whitt Law, (AV)
105 East Galena Boulevard, 8th Floor, 60505-3338
Telephone: 630-897-8875 Fax: 630-897-1258 URL: http://www.lawyers.com/stuartlwhitt
Email: swhitt@whittlaw.com URL: http://www.whittlaw.com
Stuart L. Whitt. Associates: Richard T. Petesch; Joshua S. Whitt; Gretchen M. Harris.
Education Law, Municipal Law, Tax Law.

See Professional Biographies, AURORA, ILLINOIS

Wienold, John, & Associates, (AV) '51 '76
C&L.802 B.A., J.D. One North Constitution Drive
Wilson, Peter K., Jr., (AV) ....'42 '67 C&L.879 B.A., J.D. [Mickey,W.W.R.&A.]
Woodruff, Casey (Kenneth) ....'62 '90 C.339 B.A. L.146 J.D. [C.Woodruff&Assoc.] ⊙
Woodruff, Kenneth Crane ...... '62 '90 C.339 B.A. L.146 J.D. 75 Executive Dr., Ste. 105

Woodruff, Casey, & Associates
Millennium Park Plaza, 75 Executive Drive, Suite 105, 60504 ⊙
Telephone: 630-585-2320 Fax: 630-585-2327
Email: cwoodruff@woodrufflawyers.com URL: http://www.cwoodrufflaw.com
Casey (Kenneth) Woodruff. Associates: Jay Johnson; Mario C. Palermo.
Language: Spanish.
Workers Compensation, Personal Injury, Automobile Accidents, Social Security, Medical Malpractice, Products Liability.
Chicago, Illinois Office: 155 N. Michigan Avenue, Suite 500, 60601. Telephone: 630-585-2320. Toll Free: 1-866-891-9211. Fax: 630-585-2327.

See Professional Biographies, AURORA, ILLINOIS

BANNOCKBURN, 1,388, *Lake Co.*

Alexander, Rosemary Ryan '48 '79 C.424 B.A. L.802 J.D.
2201 Waukegan Rd., Ste. S-100

Berger Schatz, (AV)
A Partnership including Professional Corporations
2333 Waukegan Road, Suite 260, 60015 ⊙
Telephone: 847-405-9500 Fax: 847-405-9563
Email: info@ksbfamilylaw.com URL: http://www.ksbfamilylaw.com
Mary J. Clark (Resident); Debbie K. Lerner (Resident); Jason G. Adess (Resident, Chicago Office); Amanda B. Clayman (Resident, Chicago Office); P. André Katz (Resident, Chicago Office); David H. Levy (P.C.) (Resident, Chicago Office); Michael S. Sabath (Resident, Chicago Office); Tracey A. Wertman (Resident, Chicago Office); Barry A. Schatz (P.C.) (Resident, Chicago Office); Michael J. Berger (P.C.) (Resident, Chicago Office); Andrew D. Eichner (Resident, Chicago Office); Leon I. Finkel (Resident, Chicago Office); Norman Ruber (Resident, Chicago Office);—Joshua E. Hornaday (Resident); Marcelle R. Kott (Resident, Chicago Office); Margaret E. Keane (Resident, Chicago Office); Sharon Steinberg Mobley (Resident, Chicago Office); Kristina L. Jarvis (Resident, Chicago Office); Catherine M. Dunn (Resident, Chicago Office); Brian J. Blitz (Resident, Chicago Office); Laurence B. Hirsch (Resident, Chicago Office); Karen Rose Krehbiel (Resident, Chicago Office); Melinda C. Rogers (Resident, Chicago Office).
Matrimonial, Family, Domestic Relations Law, Trial and Appellate Practice: Including Divorce, Child Custody, Child Support, Paternity, Spousal Support and Visitation Rights.
Chicago, Illinois Office: 161 North Clark Street, Suite 2800. Telephone: 312-782-3456. Fax: 312-782-8463.

See Professional Biographies, BANNOCKBURN, ILLINOIS

Chance, Michael W. '47 '77 C.1016 B.S.B.A. L.365 J.D.
Princ. Mgmt. Consultant, Raymond F. Mikus & Assoc.‡
Clark, Donald C., Jr., (AV) '54 '79 C.951 B.A. L.1292 J.D.
2333 Waukegan Rd., Ste. 160
Clark, Mary J., (AV) ....'54 '79 [Berger S.]
Condon, Robert E. '61 '86
C.145 B.A. L.209 J.D. Gen. Coun., Mellon First United Leasing
Corvino, John P. ....'56 '85 C.347 B.S. L.209 J.D. Gen. Coun., CRL Industries, Inc.
Gaitan, Kathleen Loula '59 '85
C.340 B.A. L.209 J.D. Casualty Claim Mgr., Allstate Ins. Co.
Goldstein, Ilene Beth, (BV) '60 '85 C.339 B.S. L.146 J.D.
2345 Waukegan Rd., Ste. 150
Halpern, Marlene R. ....'63 '88 C&L.339 B.A., J.D. 2345 Waukegan Rd., Ste. 150
Holloway, Jennifer S. ....'59 '89 C&L.352 B.A., J.D. [A D.C.Clark,Jr.]
Hornaday, Joshua E. ....'74 '00 C.504 B.A. L.352 J.D. [A Berger S.]
Karlin, Larry M. ....'49 '74 C.352 B.A. L.146 J.D. Concession Enterprises
Katz, Stephen H., (AV) .....'41 '66 C&L.339 A.B., J.D. 2345 Waukegan Road, Suite 150
Lerner, Debbie K. ....'— '92 C.763 B.A. L.436 J.D. [Berger S.]
Quigley, James M. ....'66 '92 C.966 B.A. L.209 J.D. [Quigley&Assoc.] (⊙Chicago)
Quigley & Associates, P.C., Law Offices of
2275 Half Day Road, Suite 350 (⊙Chicago)

Wyshnytzky, Orlana E. ...... '58 '85 C.339 B.A. L.365 J.D. 2525 Waukegan Rd., Ste. 265

BARRINGTON, 10,168, *Cook & Lake Cos.*

Adams, Dwight C., & Associates ....'45 '68 C.303 B.A. L.146 J.D. 138 W. Station
Allen, Bradford S., (AV) ....'34 '60 C.867 A.B. L.982 J.D. 240 Castle Ct. (Pat.)
Anderson, Mark V. '55 '81 C.339 B.S. L.365 J.D.
Gen. Coun. & Asst. to Pres., CTI Industries Corp.
Arthur, Joan E. ....'69 '94 323 W. Main St.
Barney, Joshua S., (BV) .... '56 '85 C.147 B.S. L.112 J.D. [J.S.Barney&Assoc.] ⊙
Barney, J. S., and Associates, Ltd., (BV) ....323 West Main Street (⊙Algonquin)
Bateman, James P. ....'52 '77 C.589 B.S. L.339 J.D. [J.P.Bateman]
Bateman, James P., Ltd., The Law Offices of .... 600 Hart Rd., Ste. 260
Bauders, Heidi L. ....'— '94 C.150 B.A. L.851 J.D. [Gallitano&O.]
Benson, John A. ....'51 '79 C.339 B.S. L.365 J.D. Pres., First Colonial Bk., N.W.
Boehm, Garrett L. .... '— '74 C.675 B.A. L.146 J.D. 201 W. Main St.
Bohacz, Steven J. ....'49 '84 C.424 B.A. L.365 J.D. 27009 W. Lake Shore Dr.
Botsford, Stephen F. ......'50 '75 C&L.602 B.B.A., J.D. Pres., Turnberry Financial Group
Brady, Lawrence M. ....'60 '86 C.436 B.A. L.424 J.D. 21062 Crestview Dr.
Brodnan, David S. ....'42 '67 C.424 B.S. L.276 J.D. GE Reinsurance Corp.
Brownson, Robert S. .....'55 '81 C.339 B.S. L.424 J.D. Pres. & CEO, Rubloff Dev. Corp.
Burchfield, Thomas E., (AV) '35 '61 C.473 B.S. L.1119 LL.B.
711 Woodbridge Ct.-LBS
Bush, Anna Markley ....'49 '77 C&L.879 B.A., J.D. [Bush&H.]
Bush & Heise ....18-3 E. Dundee Rd.
Buttitta, Angela M., The Law Office of ..... '76 '05 C.473 B.S. L.365 J.D. P.O. Box 3275
Caner, E. David, Law Offices of '60 '99 C.1097 B.A. L.1187 J.D.
442 Ela Street, Suite 3N
Cannon, Eric E. ... '67 '05 C.665 B.A. L.1338 J.D. Claims Coun., GE Insurance Solutions
Caprini, Elizabeth J. ....'55 '80 C.383 B.A. L.880 J.D. [Hanson P.N.]
Cohen, Vicki ....'51 '80 C.932 B.S. L.1187 J.D. 3230 Frances Lane
Connolly, Catherine Anne ....'66 '93 C.436 B.A. L.128 J.D. 528 S. Grove Ave.
Cross, Patricia Foy ....'51 '76 C.945 A.B. L.823 J.D. Loyola Univ. Law School
Culver, Richard W. ....'36 '65 C.597 B.S. L.209 LL.B. [R.W.Culver]
Culver, Richard W., Ltd. .... 18-4 E. Dundee Road
Curielli, John Peter ....'46 '73 C&L.209 B.S.C., J.D. [J.P.Curielli]
Curielli, Peter John, Law Offices of '73 '00
C&L.209 B.S., J.D. 126 S. Northwest Highway
Curielli, John Peter, PC, Law Office of ....126 S. Northwest Hwy.
Cushwa, David J. ....'55 '80 C.436 B.S.C.E. L.209 J.D. P.O. Box 3633
Daugherty, Fred H., (AV) ....'24 '49 C&L.383 B.A., LL.B. 776C Oak Hill Rd.‡
DeBoer, Rita E. ....'53 '80 C.773 B.A. L.1068 J.D. 1024 Oakland Dr.
Dienstag, Gary E., (AV) ....'45 '69 C.966 B.S. L.424 J.D. [Springer,C.&D.] ⊙
Duffy, Brendan P. '— '89 C.276 B.A. L.61 J.D.
(adm. in CA; not adm. in IL) P.O. Box 490‡
Fernandez, Miguel A. ....'78 '03 C.260 B.A. L.145 J.D. [Ⓐ Hanson P.N.]
Finch, Deborah K. .... '50 '85 C.475 B.A. L.365 J.D. 20779 N. Deer Lake Dr.
Fish, Robert B. ....'70 '96 C.475 B.S. L.494 J.D. [Ⓐ Hanson P.N.]
Fitzpatrick, William J. ....'43 '73 C.339 B.A. L.424 J.D. 341 E. Lincoln Ave.
Foy, George B. ....'21 '50 C&L.209 LL.B. 350 Westwood Dr.
Freeman, Terrence J. ....'59 '84 C.424 B.B.A. L.365 J.D. 117 S. Cook Street
Frommeyer, Daniel T. ....'55 '85 C.966 B.B.A. L.365 J.D. 400 E. Main St.
Gallitano, Dennis J., (AV) ....'— '84 C.597 B.A. L.209 J.D. [Gallitano&O.]

Gallitano & O'Connor LLP, (AV)
257 E. Main Street, Suite 300, 60010
Telephone: 224-633-5000 Fax: 224-633-5006
URL: http://www.gallitanoocconnor.com
Members of Firm: Dennis J. Gallitano; Karen J. O'Connor; Marcus D. Lawlor; Heidi L. Bauders.
Information Technology, Corporate Law, telecommunications Law, Health Care, Technology Law, Technology Licensing, Outsourcing.
See Professional Biographies, BARRINGTON, ILLINOIS

Gilbert, Ralph J. ....'29 '61 C.871 B.S. L.276 J.D. 48 Hawthorne Lane

Goddard, Alexandra M., Law Offices of '48 '73 C.350 B.S. L.546 J.D.
18-3 East Dundee Road, Suite 202, 60010
Telephone: 847-382-3995 Fax: 847-382-4038
Email: agodatty@aol.com URL: http://www.alexandragoddard.com
Family Law, Adoptions, Child Custody, Child Support, Divorce, Domestic Violence, Premarital Agreements, Spousal Support, Visitation Rights, Prenuptial Agreements, Guardianships, Unmarried Couples, Real Estate, Buying or Selling a Home, Estate Planning, Corporate Law.
See Professional Biographies, BARRINGTON, ILLINOIS

Gordon, Thomas J. '67 '98 C.1269 B.A. L.999 J.D.
(adm. in MA; not adm. in IL) Sr. Atty., Recon Optical, Inc.
Graves, Lee C. .... '58 '83 C&L.190 B.S.B.A., J.D. 721 Walnut Rd.‡
Greenfield, Pamela ....'69 '96 C.1044 B.S. L.107 J.D. [Ⓐ Hanson P.N.]
Hall, Martin S. ....'51 '76 C.197 B.S. L.597 J.D. 21116 N. 24th St.
Halvorsen, Jack R., (AV) .... '23 '50 C&L.597 B.S., J.D. 523-B Woodview Road (Pat.)
Hannon, Bonnie Spaccarelli .... '42 '80 C.530 B.A. L.94 J.D. [B.S.Hannon]
Hannon, Bonnie Spaccarelli, P.C., Law Offices of .... 18-5 East Dundee Road
Hansen, Julian R., (BV) .... '27 '52 C&L.145 J.D. 497 White Oak Lane
Hanson, Keith A. .... '53 '76 C&L.966 B.S., J.D. [Hanson P.N.]

Hanson Peters Nye
1301 South Grove Avenue, Suite 200, 60010
Telephone: 847-277-9988 Fax: 847-277-7339
Members of Firm: Keith A. Hanson; Victor C. Peters; Anastasia Markakis Nye; Nancy K. Tordai; Lynne Reinders Miller; Elizabeth J. Caprini. Associates: Julianne Piotrowski Nery; Jeremy M. Moen; Robert B. Fish; Pamela Greenfield; Renee C. Robak; Joanne M. Snow; Anne K. Lewis; Richard B. Wicka; Miguel A. Fernandez; Matthew T. Hoover; Natelle M. Wick; Farhan Younus; Alison K. Landeck; Michelle L. Stone; Zhanna Rondel; Charles J. Madden, III. Of Counsel: David A. Wilford.
Commercial Litigation and Arbitration, Insurance Coverage, Complex Insurance Litigation, Complex Professional Liability Coverage.
See Professional Biographies, BARRINGTON, ILLINOIS

Harley, J. Michael '60 '85 C.269 B.A. L.880 J.D.
(adm. in TN; not adm. in IL) CEO, GrowthPhases, LLC
Heise, Brian L. ....'50 '77 C&L.879 B.A., J.D. [Bush&H.]
Hill, David K. ....'40 '65 C.674 B.A. L.597 J.D. 2008 Abbotsford Rd.
Hollensteiner, James A. ....'31 '65 C.210 B.A. L.146 J.D. 186 Kimberly Rd.‡
Hoover, Matthew T. ....'78 '03 C&L.339 B.A.S., J.D. [Ⓐ Hanson P.N.]
Horton, Jeanne M. '53 '80 C&L.597 B.A., J.D.
Gen. Coun., Auto Fin. Servs., GE Capital Corp.

Hudson Cook, LLP
111 North Avenue, Suite 11, 60010 ⊙
Telephone: 847-277-7039 Fax: 847-277-7243
Email: contact@hudco.com URL: http://www.hudco.com
Elena A. Lovoy.
Consumer Financial Services.
Linthicum, Maryland Office: 971 Corporate Boulevard, Suite 301, 21090-2232. Telephone: 410-684-3200. Fax: 410-684-2001.

(This Listing Continued)

Hudson Cook, LLP (Continued)
El Segundo, California Office: 2301 Rosecrans Avenue, Suite 2175, 90245. Telephone: 310-536-9099. Fax: 310-536-7644.
Charlottesville, Virginia Office: 301 E. Market Street, 22902. Telephone: 434-220-9310. Fax: 434-220-9311.
New Haven, Connecticut Office: Building One, Unit 7, Third Floor, 85 Willow Street, 06511. Telephone: 203-776-1911. Fax: 203-776-1922.
Clifton Park, New York Office: 636 Plank Road, Suite 107, 12065. Telephone: 518-383-9440. Fax: 518-383-9401.
Washington, D.C. Office: 1900 M Street NW, Suite 700, 20036. Telephone: 202-223-6930. Fax: 202-223-6935
See Professional Biographies, BARRINGTON, ILLINOIS

Iatarola, Anthony ....'58 '85 C.37 B.S.B.A. L.284 J.D. 22 E. Dundee Rd., Ste. 23
Johnson, Gloria Michelotti, (AV) ..... '47 '71 C.209 B.S. L.597 J.D. 410 Waterford Lane‡
Johnson, Terrence M. ....'49 '74 C&L.424 B.A., J.D. 400 E. Main St.
Juffernbruch, Daniel W. ....'63 '91 C.339 B.S.E.E. L.273 J.D. [Patents&L.] (Pat.)
Julian, John N., III ....'66 '92 C.339 B.A. L.209 J.D. 331 E. Russell St.
Karahalios, Peter G. ....'50 '76 C.339 B.A. L.146 J.D. [Karahalios&K.]
Karahalios, Vasiliki Aliki ....'58 '89 C.339 B.A. L.1187 J.D. [Karahalios&K.]
Karahalios & Karahalios, Law Offices of ....23 Polo Dr.
Keegan, Thomas A., (AV) ....'08 '33 C.602 A.B. L.309 J.D. 108 Brinker Rd.‡
Kelleher, Andrew J., Jr. ....'67 '95 C.209 B.S. L.365 J.D. 231 W. Main St.
Kuehn, Robert O. ....'43 '69 C.1106 B.A. L.424 J.D. 102 N. Cook St. (⊙Chicago)
Kuehn, William R. ....'70 '95 C.197 B.A. L.146 J.D. 102 N. Cook St. (⊙Chicago)
Landeck, Alison K. ....'76 '01 C.339 B.S. L.146 J.D. [Ⓐ Hanson P.N.]
LaSusa, Samuel A., (AV) ....'30 '55 C&L.209 J.D. 2093 Rand Rd.
Lawlor, Marcus D. ....'— '97 C.339 B.A. L.734 J.D. [Gallitano&O.]
Lessman, Robert E., (BV) '47 '72
C.746 B.A. L.424 J.D. Gen. Coun., Pepper Construction Co.
Lewis, Anne K. ....'64 '89 C.813 B.A. L.145 J.D. [Ⓐ Hanson P.N.]
Light, Wade B. ....'63 '89 C.347 B.S. L.339 J.D. 220 Honeylake Ct.
Lovoy, Elena A. ....'62 '87 C&L.16 B.S., J.D. [Hudson C.]
Madden, Charles J., III ....'70 '04 C.339 B.A. L.424 J.D. [Ⓐ Hanson P.N.]
McLaughlin, Thomas P. ....'42 '66 C&L.424 B.S., J.D. 711 Bent Ridge Lane
Melone, Robert J. ....'42 '74 C.1070 B.S. L.209 J.D. 507 W. Old Northwest St.
Meroni, Charles F., Jr., (AV) '— '60
C.170 A.B. L.365 J.D. [Meroni&M.] (See Pat. Sect.)

Meroni & Meroni, P.C., (AV)
5 Bellwood Drive, P.O. Box 309, 60011
Telephone: 847-304-1500 Telefax: 847-382-5478
Email: meronilaw@ameritech.net URL: http://www.meronilaw.com
Charles F. Meroni, Sr. (1905-1986); Charles F. Meroni, Jr.;—Christopher J. Scott. Of Counsel: Jim Xu.
Patent, Trademark, Copyright, Licensing and Related Intellectual Property Law.
See Professional Biographies, BARRINGTON, ILLINOIS

Miller, Jay L., (AV) '42 '67
C.187 B.A. L.339 J.D. 217 South Northwest Highway, Suite 200
Miller, Lynne Reinders ....'68 '93 C.436 B.A. L.910 J.D. [Hanson P.N.]
Moen, Jeremy M. ....'75 '00 C.339 B.A. L.146 J.D. [Ⓐ Hanson P.N.]
Mormino, Anthony J. '65 '95 C.36 B.A. L.30 J.D.
V.P. & Asst. Gen. Coun., GE Employers Reinsurance Corp.
Mrozinski, Walter J. .....'46 '77 C.424 B.B.A. L.209 J.D. Sr. Trial Atty., Allstate Ins. Co.
Mueller, Richard N. ....'43 '69 C.999 B.A. L.146 J.D. 202 S. Cook St.
Nery, Julianne Piotrowski ....'73 '98 C.597 B.S. L.1040 J.D. [Ⓐ Hanson P.N.]
Neuffer, Helen M. ....'11 '39 C.597 L.365 J.D. Rte. 7, Box 145‡
Nye, Anastasia Markakis ....'62 '87 C.477 B.A. L.608 J.D. [Hanson P.N.]
O'Connor, Karen J., (AV) ....'— '90 C.927 B.B. L.597 J.D. [Gallitano&O.]
O'Leary, Thomas M. '50 '76 C.746 B.A. L.209 J.D.
Exec. V.P., Gen. Coun. & CFO, The Pepper Cos.
Patents and Licensing, LLC ....28 Barrington Bourne (Pat.)
Peithman, Robert C. '50 '86 C.228 B.A. L.986 J.D.
1250 South Grove Avenue, Suite 200

Perrelli, Anthony
(See Deerfield)

Peters, Victor C. ....'56 '82 C&L.352 B.A., J.D. [Hanson P.N.]
Peterson, Maria P. ....'62 '89 C.424 B.S. L.365 J.D. 125 Carriage Rd.
Plank, Laura S. ....'— '86 C.209 B.A. L.365 J.D. Coun., Orius Corp.
Pokorski, Patricia J. ....'54 '81 C&L.339 B.A., J.D. 612 Concord Pl.
Polachek, R. Steven ....'41 '65 C.162 B.A. L.597 J.D. 18-3 E. Dundee Rd.
Polachek, Susan ....'56 '01 C.1016 B.S. L.365 J.D. 18-3 E. Dundee Rd.
Polasek, Ronald L. ....'46 '74 C&L.846 B.A., J.D. General Counsel, Recon/Optical, Inc.
Poplar, Susan L. .... '49 '94 C.393 B.A. L.365 J.D. [S.Poplar]
Poplar, Susan, Law Office of ....330 E. Main St., Ste. 207
Potter, James .... '47 '72 C.578 B.A. L.146 J.D. [J.Potter]
Potter, James, Ltd. ....200 Applebee St., Ste. 201
Present, Wendy D. ....'69 '95 C.339 B.A. L.209 J.D. GE Employers Reins. Corp.
Przybylski, Michael William ....'72 '98 C.1183 B.S. L.209 J.D. [Przybylski&Assoc.]
Przybylski & Associates, Ltd. ....117 S. Cook Street, Suite 360
Reeves, Charles W. '52 '80 C.221 B.A. L.174 J.D.
(adm. in CO; not adm. in IL) Exec. V.P., Jack Nicklaus Develop. Corp.
Robak, Renee C. ....'76 '00 C.339 B.S. L.146 J.D. [Ⓐ Hanson P.N.]
Rondel, Zhanna ....'77 '04 C.959 B.B.A. L.966 J.D. [Ⓐ Hanson P.N.]
Root, Gregory Brian ....'69 '97 C.802 B.A. L.424 J.D. Sr. V.P., CodeMap
Schlemmer, Carla K. ....'40 '63 C&L.339 B.A., LL.B. 250 Steelechase Rd.
Scott, Christopher J. .....'— '00 C.1157 B.A. L.209 J.D. [Ⓐ Meroni&M.] (See Pat. Sect.)
Shechtman, Irwin R. '42 '67 C.339 B.S. L.309 LL.B.
Partner, American Mobile Home Commission
Shim, Kie-Young .... '31 '63 C.226 B.A. L.597 J.D. 2000 S. Braymore Dr.
Simek, Ervin J. ....'15 '50 C.46 B.S. L.365 LL.B. P.O. Box 625‡
Smith, Roger L. '46 '71 C&L.339 B.S., J.D.
General Counsel & Secretary, Gidwitz Private Holdings
Snow, Joanne M. ....'59 '99 C.999 B.S. L.365 J.D. [Ⓐ Hanson P.N.]
Solberg, Emily Claire ....'66 '90 C.1036 B.A. L.880 J.D. 20530 Deerpath‡
Spada, Deborah D. ....'48 '75 C.991 B.A. L.365 J.D. 4 S. Wynstone Dr., N. Barrington
Spak, Lorin M. ....'41 '66 C.339 B.S. L.209 J.D. 59 Hawthorne Rd.
Springer, Edward M., (AV) ....'42 '67 C.339 A.B. L.209 J.D. [Springer,C.&D.] ⊙

Springer, Casey & Dienstag, P.C., (AV)
509 West Old Northwest Highway, 60010 ⊙
Telephone: 847-382-9797 847-382-4213
Email: SCDCHGO@global.net
Edward M. Springer; Gary E. Dienstag.
General Practice. Civil Trial and Appellate Litigation in State and Federal Courts. Insurance Defense and Coverage Litigation. Administrative Agencies. Corporation, Estate Planning and Probate, Federal Taxation, Matrimonial, Municipal and Real Estate Law.

(This Listing Continued)

Springer, Casey & Dienstag, P.C. (Continued)

Chicago, Illinois Office: 100 West Monroe Street 60603. Telephone: 312-372-0800. Fax: 312-372-0842.

See Professional Biographies, BARRINGTON, ILLINOIS

Steenburg, Thomas N. '49 '78
C.309 A.B. L.184 J.D. CEO, Duff & Phelps Investment Mgmt. Co.‡
Steencken, Rachelle L. '73 '01 C.1349 B.A. L.823 J.D.
1301 South Grove Ave., Suite 160
Stone, Michelle L. ....'79 '04 C.340 B.A. L.280 J.D. [Ⓐ Hanson P.N.]
Summers, Nancy Ann, Attorney at Law '64 '93
C.20 B.A. L.365 J.D. 145 W. Main St., Ste. 6
Svenson, Judith M. .... '— '91 C.700 B.A. L.589 217 S. Northwest Hwy.
Tordai, Nancy K. ....'57 '82 C.145 B.A. L.424 J.D. [Hanson P.N.]
Uscian, Paula M., (AV) '55 '79 C.597 B.S. L.424 J.D.
Senior Associate Attorney, Baker Robbins & Company
Vandenburgh, Beverly A. .... '30 '58 C.597 B.S. L.209 J.D. 400 E. Main St.‡
Viets, Hamilton P. '17 '41 C&L.966 B.A., J.D.
(adm. in WI; not adm. in IL) 110 Hunt Trail‡
Von Heimburg, Petra ....'53 '95 C.415 B.S. L.365 J.D. [VonHeimburg,P.]
Von Heimburg, Petra, P.C. ....P.O. Box 725
Wasem, Peter A. ....'57 '82 C.221 B.A. L.365 J.D. 522 S. Northwest Hwy.
Wick, Natelle M. ....'78 '03 C.424 B.S. L.352 J.D. [Ⓐ Hanson P.N.]
Wicka, Richard B. ....'74 '02 C&L.966 B.S., J.D. [Ⓐ Hanson P.N.]
Wilford, David A. ....'68 '93 C.352 B.B.A. L.190 J.D. [Ⓒ Hanson P.N.]
Wyatt, J. Frank ....'22 '49 C.10 B.S. L.276 J.D. 200 Applebee St.
Xu, Jim ....'71 '98 C.1000 LL.M. L.209 J.D. [Ⓒ Meroni&M.]
Younus, Farhan ....'69 '95 C.339 B.A. L.352 J.D. [Ⓐ Hanson P.N.]

BARRINGTON HILLS, 3,915, *Cook, Kane, Lake & McHenry Cos.*

Beaubien, Mark H., Jr. ....'42 '68 C&L.597 B.A., J.D. 4 Acorn Ln.‡
Grubner, Steven M. ......'58 '83 C.477 B.A. L.365 J.D. Independent Coun., HH Financial
Ktsanes, Basil D. ....'39 '68 C.597 B.A. L.421 J.D. Rt. 5, 312 Algonquin Rd.

BARTLETT, 36,706, *Cook & DuPage Cos.*

Franson, Kenneth ....'26 '55 L.146 J.D. 148 Jodi Lane
Harbst, John W., (BV) ......'47 '84 C.1016 B.G.S. L.365 J.D. 1180 Litchfield Lane (Pat.)
Hauslein, Richard E. ....'29 '56 C.597 B.S. L.209 J.D. 300 E. Devon St.
Kelly, Michael E. ....'55 '83 C.1151 B.A. L.146 J.D. 118 W. Bartlett Ave., Ste. 1
Krupp, Robert Jon ....'56 '83 C.1151 B.A. L.146 J.D. [R.J.Krupp]
Krupp, Robert J, P.C., Law Offices of ....990 South Bartlett Rd.

Martucci, Gregory J., P.C., Law Office of
(See Roselle)

Nolan, Dennis M. ....'63 '89 C.720 B.A. L.365 J.D. [D.M.Nolan]
Nolan, Dennis M., Law Office of, P.C. .... 449 Giles Court
Travis, Charles M. ....'41 '71 C.1108 B.S. L.585 J.D. 726 Hackberry Court

BARTONVILLE, 6,310, *Peoria Co.*

Tilton, Kevin W., (BV) ....'54 '79 C.98 B.S. L.424 J.D. Bartonville, Sq., 1359 W. Garfield

BATAVIA, 23,866, *Kane Co.*

Babcock, Joel E. '29 '53 C&L.546 B.S., J.D.
(adm. in NE; not adm. in IL) 2nd V.P., Gen. Reins. Corp.‡
Beck, Ralph S., (BV) ....'43 '66 C&L.339 B.S., LL.B. 228 E. Wilson

Benson, Mair & Gosselin, (BV)
133 South Batavia Avenue, P.O. Box 129, 60510-0129
Telephone: 630-879-1560 Facsimile: 630-879-9473
Members of Firm: John W. Gosselin; Gabrielle A. Gosselin; Thomas W. Gosselin.
Real Estate, Estate Planning, Probate, Business, Personal Injury, Civil Litigation, Family Law, Taxation, Collections, Wills and Workers Compensation.
Attorneys for: Shumway Foundry, Inc.

See Professional Biographies, BATAVIA, ILLINOIS

Bina, Robert I., (BV) ....'40 '70 C&L.424 B.A., J.D. [Youssi,Y.&B.]
Blake, Michael W., (BV) ....'55 '81 C.927 B.S. L.365 J.D. 510 S. Batavia Ave.
Bristow, Paul R. ....'70 '96 C.339 B.S. L.966 J.D. [Ⓐ Markuson&N.]
Budilovsky, John A., Jr. ....'52 '82 C.238 B.S. L.146 J.D. P.O. Box 901
Burke, Thomas J., (BV) ....'28 '57 C.120 A.B. L.424 J.D. 331 Woodland Hill Rd.
Busch, Kevin T., (BV) ....'58 '85 C.234 B.A. L.365 J.D. 428 S. Batavia Ave.
Cadwell, James W. ....'20 '48 C&L.339 A.B., LL.B. 937 S. Raddant Rd.‡
Colton, Kathleen, Law Offices of, (BV) ....'— '89 C&L.339 J.D. 226 S. Batavia Ave.
Comstock, Douglas F. ....'25 '55 C.424 B.S.C. L.209 J.D. 363 N. Lincoln St.‡
Covey, Bradley S. ....'61 '92 C.801 B.S. L.589 J.D. [Covey]
Covey Law Firm, P.C. ....232 South Batavia Avenue
Davoust, Melody Brasel, (BV) ....'51 '83 C.393 B.A. L.146 J.D. 715 Hunter Dr.
Donat, Anthony F., (BV) ....'15 '46 C.337 A.B. L.273 LL.B. [Donat&D.]
Donat, Peter M., (BV) ....'46 '74 C&L.339 A.B., J.D. [Donat&D.]
Donat, Walter J., (BV) ....'48 '73 C.339 B.A. L.879 J.D. [Donat&D.]
Donat & Donat, (BV) ....150 W. Houston St.
Drendel, Gilbert X., Jr., (AV) ....'36 '61 C.187 A.B. L.309 J.D. [Drendel&D.]
Drendel, Kevin G., (BV) ....'59 '91 C.187 B.S.S. L.589 J.D. [Drendel&D.]

Drendel & Drendel, A Professional Corporation, (AV) BB
201 Houston Street, Suite 300, 60510
Telephone: 630-406-5440 Fax: 630-406-6179
Email: dandd@batavialaw.com URL: http://www.lawyers.com/drendeltatnall
Gilbert X. Drendel, Jr.; Kevin G. Drendel;—Carolyn Jansons.
Family Law, Real Estate Development, Zoning, Sales and Acquisitions, Corporate, Business, Planning Sales and Acquisitions, Estate and Trust Planning and Administration, Commercial and other Civil Litigation, Banking and Collection Law, Trials and Appeals in all State Courts and Mediation Services, Municipal Law and Local Government Law.
Reference: Old Second National Bank of Aurora, Aurora, Illinois.

See Professional Biographies, BATAVIA, ILLINOIS

Engelhardt, Jennifer L. ....'56 '81 C.347 B.A. L.893 J.D. 445 Church Street‡
Fornek, Brian M. ....'63 '90 C.927 B.S. L.146 J.D. 201 Houston St., Ste. 300
Giampoli, Frank J., Law Office, (BV) '50 '74 C.339 B.A. L.734 J.D.
428 S. Batavia Ave.
Glisson, William E. ....'45 '73 C.747 B.A. L.51 LL.B. 321 E. Wilson St.
Gosselin, Gabrielle A., (CV) ....'58 '95 C.273 B.A. L.146 J.D. [Benson,M.&G.]
Gosselin, John W., (BV) ....'34 '59 C.72 B.A. L.145 J.D. [Benson,M.&G.]
Gosselin, Thomas W. ....'69 '01 C.694 B.A. L.365 J.D. [Benson,M.&G.]
Hoffman, Thomas J., Law Office of, (BV) ...'56 '81 C.98 B.S. L.365 J.D. 870 Ryan Court
Hogan, Judy L., (BV) ....'— '84 C.274 B.S.W. L.615 J.D. [J.L.Hogan]
Hogan, Judy L., P.C., (BV) ....34 N. Island Ave., Ste. F
Hubbard, Donald K. ....'50 '91 C.927 B.S. L.365 J.D. 29 N. River St.
Jansons, Carolyn ....'74 '01 C&L.589 B.S., J.D. [Ⓐ Drendel&D.]
Larson, Van A. ....'52 '78 C.221 B.A. L.365 J.D. [V.A.Larson]
Larson, Van A., P.C. ....233 W. Wilson St.
Markuson, Grant R. ....'62 '90 C.339 B.S. L.209 J.D. [Markuson&N.]
Markuson & Neufeld, LLC ....15 E. Wilson St., Ste. 22 (⊙Princeton, NJ)
Mayer, Frederick H. '10 '46 L.569 LL.B.
(adm. in NY; not adm. in IL) 700 W. Fabyan Pkwy.‡
McCracken, Thomas G., (AV) .....'25 '51 C&L.352 B.S., J.D. 201 Houston St., Ste. 300‡
McGrath, William R., (BV) ....'50 '77 C.602 B.A. L.365 J.D. 100 N. Island Ave.
McKay, Thomas, Jr. ....'20 '45 C.705 A.B. L.569 LL.B. Prarie State Legal Servs.
Mogensen, Andrea M. ....'66 '90 C&L.966 B.S., J.D. Prairie State Legal Servs.
Moore, Amber S. ....'70 '96 C&L.589 B.A., J.D. 201 Houston Street
Muldoon, Peter O. ....'62 '89 C.436 B.A. L.1187 J.D. 340 Houston Street
Nealis, Richard J., (AV) ....'52 '79 C.339 B.S. L.589 J.D. 510 S. Batavia Ave.
Neptune, Tyler G., Jr., Law Offices of, (BV) '48 '80 C.429 B.A. L.365 J.D.
387 Mill St.
Paradis, Suzanne Lisinski ....'69 '97 C.378 B.S. L.209 J.D. 346 Meadowrue Ln.
Pick, Steven L. '65 '92 C&L.477 A.B., J.D.
Staff Atty., Prairie State Legal Services, Inc.
Searl, Cathy L. (Youssi), (BV) ....'59 '84 C.58 B.A. L.209 J.D. [Youssi,Y.&B.]
Softcheck, John E. ....'22 '49 C&L.424 A.B., LL.B. P.O. Box 500‡
Stanek, John George ....'54 '80 C.57 L.146 J.D. [J.G.Stanek]
Stanek, John G., Attorney at Law ....800 Hanson St.
Strnad, Robt. G. ....'17 '44 1219 Thrun Dr.‡
Tassi, Nancy Paluch ....'67 '01 C.338 B.S. L.365 J.D. 519 Bailey Drive‡
Thompson, Juul H. ....'45 '73 C.145 B.A. L.339 J.D. 105 Hamlet St.
Traut, Donald L. ....'47 '76 C.502 B.S. L.878 J.D. 2844 Weaver Ln. (Pat.)
Youssi, Francis E., (AV) ....'23 '50 C.58 B.S. L.209 J.D. [Youssi,Y.&B.]

Youssi, Youssi & Bina, Ltd., (AV) BB
Batavia Professional Building, 150 Houston Street, P.O. Box 490, 60510-1953
Telephone: 630-879-5777 Fax: 630-879-0736
Email: yyb3@dls.net
Francis E. Youssi; Cathy L. (Youssi) Searl; Robert I. Bina.
Probate, Estate Planning, Real Estate, Corporate, Municipal, Taxation and General Practice.
Representative Clients: Available Upon Request.
Attorneys for: Feece Oil Co.; Eagle Concrete; Three Fires Council No. 127, Boy Scouts of America; Smith and Richardson Manuf. Co.
References: Harris Bank, Batavia; Fifth Third Bank, Batavia; Chicago Title.

BEARDSTOWN, 5,766, *Cass Co.*

Brannan, Thomas J., (AV) ....'43 '73 C.339 B.S. L.1119 J.D. [McClure,M.&B.] ⊙
Endres, John M. ....'41 '68 C.210 B.A. L.365 J.D. Pub. Def.
McClure, George S., (AV) ....'47 '75 C&L.339 B.S., J.D. [McClure,M.&B.] ⊙
McClure, L. Milton, (AV) ....'41 '66 C&L.339 B.S., J.D. [McClure,M.&B.] ⊙
McClure, Milton, (AV) ....'14 '39 C&L.339 A.B., J.D. [McClure,M.&B.] ‡

McClure, McClure & Brannan, (AV)
113 State Street, P.O. Box 170, 62618-0170 ⊙
Telephone: 217-323-2212 Fax: 217-323-5522
Email: mbhlaw@casscomm.com
Members of Firm: Milton McClure (Retired); L. Milton McClure; Thomas J. Brannan; George S. McClure. Associate: Luke Thomas.
General Civil and Trial Practice in all State and Federal Courts. Probate, Real Estate, Corporation, Drainage and Tax Law, Workers Compensation.
Representative Clients: First National Bank of Beardstown; Beardstown Community Park District; First State Bank of Beardstown; Beardstown Savings, s.b.; Sanitary District of Beardstown; City of Beardstown; Village of Ashland.
Virginia, Illinois Office: South Side Square, P.O. Box 48. Telephone: 217-452-3037. FAX: 217-452-3040.

Thomas, Luke ....'75 '02 C.339 B.A. L.801 J.D. [Ⓐ McClure,M.&B.]

BEDFORD PARK, 566, *Cook Co.*

Ach, Samuel W. '61 '87 C.31 B.A. L.145 J.D.
Sr. V.P., Gen. Coun. & Secy., CHEMCENTRAL Corporation (Legal Department)
Brennan, Daniel H., Jr. '56 '81 C&L.209 B.A., J.D.
Staff Atty., CHEMCENTRAL Corp.
Carpio, J. Graham ....'54 '78 C.339 B.A. L.477 J.D. CHEMCENTRAL Corp.
Heyl, John Michael '66 '94 C.436 B.A. L.209 J.D.
V.P. Corp. Claim., American Agencies Holdings, Inc.
Levy, Bruce T. ....'52 '84 C.94 B.S. L.209 J.D. V.P., M. Block & Sons, Inc.
Mulliken, William D. '39 '64
C.473 B.B.S. L.309 J.D. V.P. & Gen. Coun., CHEMCENTRAL Corp.
Trudeau, Roger J. '56 '81 C.960 B.A. L.300 J.D.
(adm. in MN; not adm, in IL) Real Estate Mgr., 3M Nat. Advertising Co.

BELLEVILLE, * 41,410, *St. Clair Co.*

Aguirre, Richard A. ....'45 '72 C.339 A.B. L.365 J.D. Assoc. Cir. J.
Allen, Bradley C. ....'67 '01 C.338 B.S. L.734 J.D. [Blake&A.]
Allen, John M. ....'74 '00 C&L.734 B.A., J.D. [Ⓐ Fox G.] ⊙
Alvey, Thomas W., Jr., (AV) ....'— '66 C.885 B.A. L.910 J.D. [Thompson C.]

Amelung, Wulff & Willenbrock, P.C., (AV)
P.O. Box 368, 62222 ⊙
Telephone: 618-233-9765
Email: info@awwstl.com URL: http://www.awwstl.com
Robert J. Wulff; Ronald D. Robinson;—Amber Lee Kempf; Peter M. Westhoff; David C. Berwin (Not admitted in IL).
General Trial and Appellate Practice in State and Federal Courts of Missouri and Illinois; Automobile Liability, Contract, Employment Discrimination, Environmental, General Liability, Insurance, Medical Malpractice, Premises Liability, Products Liability, Professional Liability, Errors and Omissions and Workers Compensation Law.
Representative Clients: American Family Insurance Group; Argonaut-Great Central Ins. Co.; Contintental Western Ins. Co.; Farm Bureau Town & Country Insurance Company of Missouri; Federated Mutual Ins. Co.; InterMed Ins. Co.; LaFarge Corp.; Sinclair Oil Co.; State Auto Mutual Ins. Co.; State Farm Ins. Co.
St. Louis, Missouri Office: 11th Floor, 705 Olive Street 63101. Telephone: 314-436-6757. Telecopier: 314-231-7305.

See Professional Biographies, BELLEVILLE, ILLINOIS

Anderson, Robert C. ....'53 '91 C.801 B.S. L.734 J.D. [Ⓐ Cates,K.B.&S.]
Andes, Diane E. '72 '98 C.502 B.S.B.A. L.734 J.D.
(adm. in MO; not adm. in IL) Appellate Law Clk.
Andorfer, Susan M. ....'61 '87 C.436 B.S. L.734 J.D. 111 W. Washington St., Ste. 200
Andrekanic, Robert D., (AV) ....'54 '79 C.397 B.A. L.734 J.D. [Gundlach,L.E.B.&R.] ⊙
Antoniou, Pamela C., (BV) ....'73 '99 C.1165 B.A. L.734 J.D. [Ⓐ D.E.Dusek]

Armstrong Teasdale LLP, (AV)
A Partnership including Professional Corporations
23 South First Street, 62220 ⊙
Telephone: 618-397-4411
Email: armstrongteasdale@armstrongteasdale.com URL: http://www.armstrongteasdale.com
Members of Firm: Ann E. Buckley; Susan Bradley Buse; Michael A. Chivell; Clark H. Cole; Glenn E. Davis; Richard W. Engel, Jr.; Raymond R. Fournie; David L. Going; David G. Loseman; John Talbot Sant, Jr.(P.C.); Mark D. Sophir (P.C.); Therese Rolufs Trelz; James J. Virtel; George M. von Stamwitz; Thomas B. Weaver (P.C.). Senior Counsel: Donald U. Beimdiek (P.C.).
General Civil Practice. Administrative Law, Agricultural Law, Alternative Dispute Resolution, Antitrust and Trade Regulation Law, Appellate Practice, Banking and Financial Services, Biotechnology/

(This Listing Continued)

Armstrong Teasdale LLP (Continued)

Life Sciences, Business Law, Civil Rights, Class Actions, Communications Law, Computer, Constitutional Law, Construction Law, Corporate Compliance and Governance, Corporate Law, Corporate Finance, Education Law, Eminent Domain, Employee Benefits, Employment and Labor, Energy, Entertainment & Sports, Environmental Law, Financial Restructuring, Reorganization and Bankruptcy, Distribution and Franchise, Government Contracts, Governmental Relations, Health Care, Immigration and Naturalization, Insurance Coverage/Reinsurance and Extracontractual Liability, International Law, International Trade, Internet Law, Investments, Litigation, Medical Malpractice, Mergers & Acquisitions, Natural Resources, Occupational Safety & Health Administration, Patent, Trademark and Intellectual Property, Pension and Executive Compensation, Personal Injury, Products Liability, Professional Liability, Public Law and Finance, Real Estate, Securities, Taxation, Technology and Science, Toxic Torts, Transportation, Trusts and Estates, White Collar Crime, Workers Compensation and Zoning, Planning & Land Use and Development.
St. Louis, Missouri Office: One Metropolitan Square, Suite 2600, 63102. Telephone: 314-621-5070. Facsimile: 314-621-5065.
Kansas City, Missouri Office: 2345 Grand Boulevard, Suite 2000, 64108. Telephone: 816-221-3420. Facsimile: 816-221-9786.
Jefferson City, Missouri Office: 3405 West Truman Blvd., Suite 210, 65109-5713. Telephone: 573-636-8394. Facsimile: 573-636-8457.
Springfield, Illinois Office: 3201 Pleasant Run, Suite A, P.O. Box 13317, 62791-3317. Telephone: 217-726-8200. Facsimile: 217-726-8300.
Washington, D.C. Office: 1747 Pennsylvania Avenue, N.W., Suite 300, 20006. Telephone: 202-454-2800. Facsimile: 202-454-2805.
Overland Park, Kansas Office: 7400 West 132nd Street, Suite 200, 66213.
Edwardsville, Illinois Office: 241 North Main Street, 62025. Telephone: 618-650-7087. Facsimile: 618-655-4004.
Henderson, Nevada Office: 701 North Green Valley Parkway, Suite 200, 89074. Telephone: 702-678-5070. Facsimile: 702-990-3003.
Sydney, Australia Office: C/Clayton Utz, Level 31, No. 1 O'Connell Street, Sidney, NSW 2000, Australia. Telephone: 61-29-262-6700. Facsimile: 61-29-262-3263.
New York, New York Office: 230 Park Avenue, Suite 2300, 10169. Telephone: 212-867-9500. Facsimile: 212-599-1759.
Shanghai, China Office: 1376 Nan Jing Xi Lu, Shanghai Center - Suite 718, Shanghai 200040, P.R. China. Telephone: 011-8621-6279-8808. Facsimilie: 011-8621-6279-8866.

See Professional Biographies, BELLEVILLE, ILLINOIS

Badgett, Melissa R., (BV) . . . . '70 '99 C.500 B.P.A. L.734 J.D. [🄰 Cates,K.B.&S.]
Badgley, Brad L., (AV) . . . . '52 '78 C.339 B.A. L.365 J.D. [B.L.Badgley]

Badgley, Brad L., Professional Corporation, (AV) BB
26 Public Square, 62220
Telephone: 618-235-1000 Fax: 618-235-1086
URL: http://www.bbadg.wld.com
Brad L. Badgley. Of Counsel: Christian E. Heiligenstein (Retired).
Negligence, Automobile, Products Liability, Medical Malpractice, Railroad, Marine, Workers Compensation and Labor Law.
References: Union Planters Corp.; Leader Funds; Banc Star One; Bank of O'Fallon.

See Professional Biographies, BELLEVILLE, ILLINOIS

Bailey, Curtis R., (BV) . . . . '66 '91 C.934 B.A. L.502 J.D. [Cates,K.B.&S.]
Baldock, Andrew P. '76 '02 C.340 B.A. L.273 J.D.
Asst. State Atty., St. Calir Co. State Atty. Off.
Bandy, James H., (AV) . . . . '19 '47 C&L.910 B.S., J.D. 33 Lindorf Dr.‡
Baricevic, John, (BV) . . . . '48 '78 C.711 B.S. L.801 J.D. Cty. Bd. Chmm.
Bartholomew, Joseph A., (AV) . . . . '58 '84 C&L.734 B.S., J.D. [Cook,S.Y.B.&B.]
Bartosiak, Teresa D. '69 '93 C.339 B.A. L.910 J.D.
[Sandberg,P.&v.] (⊙St. Louis, MO)
Bas, Jamie . . . . '77 '02 C.801 B.A. L.209 J.D. [🄰 Ripplinger&Z.]
Bas, Robert D. . . . . '76 '04 C.763 B.A. L.209 J.D. [🄰 Hinshaw&C.]
Bassett, Robert J., (BV) . . . . '61 '86 C.531 B.S. L.910 J.D. [Donovan,R.N.&J.]
Bates, Timothy J., (CV) . . . . '63 '88 C.606 B.A. L.910 J.D. 10 S. Jackson
Baum, Tracy L. . . . . '75 '00 C.337 B.A. L.734 J.D. [🄰 Cates,K.B.&S.]
Bauman, John D., (AV) . . . . '30 '57 C.798 B.A. L.910 J.D. P.O. Box 509‡
Bauman, Mark D., (BV) '59 '84 C.734 B.A. L.801 J.D.
[Hinshaw&C.] (⊙Edwardsville)
Bean, Kenneth W., (AVⓉ) '52 '77
C&L.910 A.B., J.D. [Sandberg,P.&v.] (⊙St. Louis, MO)
Becker, Robert E., (AV) . . . . '40 '65 C&L.734 B.S.C., J.D. 5111 W. Main St.
Beimdiek, Donald U., (P.C.), (AV) '28 '54
C&L.597 B.S., J.D. [🄲 Armstrong T.] (⊙St. Louis, MO)
Bement, Gary L., (BV) . . . . '56 '82 C&L.734 B.A., J.D. P.O. Box 23926
Benninger, Mary P. . . . . '77 '03 C.209 B.A. L.910 J.D. Asst. State's Atty.
Berry, William L., (AV) . . . . '48 '73 C.357 B.A. L.910 J.D. [Dunham,B.&L.] ⊙
Berwin, David C. '77 '03 C.734 B.A.
(adm. in MO; not adm. in IL) [🄰 Amelung,W.&W.] ⊙
Beske, Richard S., (BV) . . . . '36 '61 C.910 B.S. L.602 LL.B. P.O. Box 324
Bitzer, John L., (BV) . . . . '52 '79 C.339 B.A. L.365 J.D. [Dunham,B.&L.] ⊙
Blake, Edward J., Jr., (AV) . . . . '52 '78 C&L.734 B.S.B.A., J.D. [Blake&A.]

Blake & Allen, P.C., (AV)
Richland Executive Plaza II, Suite 100, 521 West Main Street, 62220
Telephone: 618-233-7900; 618-398-1000 Fax: 618-233-9490 URL: http://www.BlakeandAllen.com
Email: law@BlakeandAllen.com URL: http://www.blakeallenpc.com
Edward J. Blake, Jr.; Bradley C. Allen.
Estates and Trusts, Family Law, Divorce, Guardianships, Litigation, Real Estate Law, Tax Law, Business Law as well as General Practice.

See Professional Biographies, BELLEVILLE, ILLINOIS

Bloch, Barry S. '48 '74
C.221 B.S.B.A. L.597 J.D. Gen. Coun., Jaffe Lighting and Supply, Inc.
Bloesch, Calvin Paul, (CV) . . . . '53 '94 C.238 B.A. L.734 J.D. 12 Iowa Ave.
Bock, John A., Jr. . . . . '31 '58 C.812 L.910 J.D. 300 W. Wash. St.
Bock-Vavroch, Martha, (Mrs.) . . . . '29 '54 C&L.734 LL.B. 300 W. Wash. St.
Bode, Dale L., (AV) . . . . '45 '76 C.801 B.A. L.502 J.D. [Walker&W.] ⊙
Boggs, Beth C., (BVⓉ) . . . . '67 '91 C.999 B.A. L.801 J.D. [Boggs,B.&B.] ⊙

Boggs, Boggs & Bates, LLC, (AVⓉ)
23 South First Street, 62220-2029 ⊙
Telephone: 618-746-9540 Fax: 618-746-9541
Email: bbblawyers.com
Beth C. Boggs; Michael J. Lach.
Insurance Defense, Workers Compensation Defense. Professional Liability, Employment Law, Environmental, Insurance Coverage, Products Liability, Negligence Defense.
St. Louis, Missouri Office: 7912 Bonhomme, Suite 400, 63105-1912. Telephone: 314-726-2310. Fax: 314-726-2360.
Kansas City, Missouri Office: 1300 N.W. Jefferson Court, Kansas City, 64105. Telephone: 816-472-5599. Fax: 816-472-0870.
Collinsville, Illinois Office: 120 East Church Street, 62234. Telephone: 618-343-0031. Fax: 618-343-0177.

See Professional Biographies, BELLEVILLE, ILLINOIS

Bonaldi, Alfred R., (BV) . . . . '43 '70 C&L.339 B.S., J.D. [Bonaldi,C.&D.]
Bonaldi, Clinton and Davis, Ltd., (AV) . . . . . . 2900 Frank Scott Pkwy. W., Copper Bend S.
Bone, David H., (CV) . . . . '60 '87 C.339 B.S. L.734 J.D. [Kassly,B.E.&H.]
Bone, Maurice E., (AV) . . . . '24 '51 C&L.734 B.S., J.D. [Kassly,B.E.&H.]
Bonifield, Jerald J., (AV) . . . . '42 '77 C.801 B.A. L.910 J.D. [Bonifield&R.]
Bonifield & Rosenstengel, P.C., (AV) . . . . 16 E. Main St.
Bortz, Christopher B., (BV) . . . . '74 '00 C.679 B.A. L.734 J.D. [🄰 Neville,R.&W.]
Bott, Edward S., Jr., (AV) . . . . . . '55 '80 C.228 A.B. L.1048 J.D. [Greensfelder,H.&G.] ⊙
Boyle, Richard E., (AV) . . . . '37 '61 C&L.339 A.B., J.D. [Gundlach,L.E.B.&R.] ⊙
Boyne, Kevin, (BV) . . . . '54 '81 C.927 B.B. L.734 J.D. [K.Boyne]
Boyne, Kevin, P.C., (BV) . . . . 1803 N. Belt W.
Brauer, Mary Mansfield . . . . '52 '81 C.801 B.S. L.339 J.D. [Cook,S.Y.B.&B.]
Brennan, Edward F., Jr., (BV) . . . . '40 '68 C.801 B.S. L.734 J.D. [Brennan]
Brennan, Ryan E. . . . . '72 '98 C.934 B.A. L.734 J.D. [Brennan]
Brennan, Susan E., (BV) . . . . '66 '91 C.221 B.A. L.734 J.D. [Brennan]
Brennan Law Firm, The, P.C., (BV) . . . . 19 Bronze Pointe
Bronsky, A. J., (AV) . . . . '56 '81 C.734 B.A. L.910 J.D. [Brown&J.] (⊙St. Louis, MO)
Brousseau, Sean K. . . . . '71 '04 C.951 B.A. L.734 J.D. [🄰 Gundlach,L.E.B.&R.] ⊙
Brown, Terry N., (AV) . . . . '49 '74 C.174 A.B. L.734 J.D. [Brown&Assoc.]

Brown & Associates, (AV) BB
5520 West Main Street, 62226
Telephone: 618-236-2887 Fax: 618-236-2086
Email: terry@tbrownandassociates.com URL: http://www.lawyers.com/brown&associates
Terry N. Brown. Associate: Kevin T. Dawson.
Civil Litigation, Personal Injury, Medical Malpractice, Products Liability, Admiralty Law, Railroad Law and Commercial Law.
Representative Client: Transportation Communications Union.

See Professional Biographies, BELLEVILLE, ILLINOIS

Brown & James, P.C., (AV)
Richland Executive Plaza, Suite 200, 525 West Main, 62220-1502 ⊙
Telephone: 618-235-5590 Facsimile: 618-235-5591
Email: brownjames@bjpc.com URL: http://www.brownjames.com
John L. McMullin, III; A. J. Bronsky; Beth Kamp Veath; John P. Cunningham; Kenneth M. Burke;—Eutha F. Ochoa; Denise Baker Seal; Ericka D. McCaskill; Tara L. Morris; Lee J. Karge; Daniel G. Hasenstab; Elizabeth S. Phipps (Not admitted in IL); Anthony E. Dos Santos; Aaron J. Byram; Deanne R. Jockish (Not admitted in IL).
Civil Trials, Appeals and Arbitrations with respect to the following areas: Accountants Liability; Agents and Brokers Liability; Appellate; Arson Fraud Litigation; Business Litigation; Commercial Litigation; Computer Law; Construction Law; Consumer Law; Design Professional Liability; Employment Law; Environmental Law; Fire Subrogation; Health Care Liability; Insurance Law; Intellectual Property; Legal Professional Liability; Medical Malpractice Defense; Premises Liability; Product Liability; Technology Law; Transportation; Worker's Compensation.
Representative Clients: Allstate Insurance Co.; CNA Insurance; Chubb & Sons, Inc.; Great American Insurance Co.; Ryder Truck Rental, Inc.; St. Joe Minerals Corp.; Ralston Purina, Inc.; U.S.F. & G. Co.; Zurich-American Insurance Co.
St. Louis, Missouri Office: 1010 Market Street, 20th Floor. Telephone 314-421-3400. Facsimile: 314-421-3128.
Kansas City, Missouri Office: City Center Square, 1100 Main Street, Suite 1900. Telephone: 816-472-0800. Facsimile: 816-421-1183.
Springfield, Missouri Office: 300 John Q. Hammons Parkway, Suite 202. Telephone: 417-831-1412. Facsimile: 417-831-6062.

See Professional Biographies, BELLEVILLE, ILLINOIS

Bub, Michael E., (AVⓉ) '62 '87 C&L.734 B.S., J.D.
[Sandberg,P.&v.] (⊙St. Louis, MO)
Buckley, Ann E., (AVⓉ) '54 '78 C&L.734 A.B., J.D.
[Armstrong T.] (⊙St. Louis, MO)
Burger, Lowell G. . . . . '28 '55 C.465 L.880 LL.B. Union Planters Bank
Burke, James L. . . . . '68 '94 C.1082 B.A. L.602 J.D. [Burke&P.]
Burke, Kenneth M., (AV) . . . . '53 '91 C.1291 B.A. L.734 J.D. [Brown&J.]
Burke & Poirier Law Firm . . . . 424 S. High St.
Burr, Karen L. . . . . '54 '91 C.734 B.S. L.339 J.D. Asst. States Atty.

Burroughs, Hepler, Broom, MacDonald, Hebrank & True, LLP
(See Edwardsville)

Buse, Susan Bradley, (AV) '59 '85
C.910 B.A. L.893 J.D. [Armstrong T.] (⊙St. Louis, MO)
Butz, David R., II . . . . '77 '03 C.602 B.A. L.339 J.D. [🄰 Gundlach,L.E.B.&R.] ⊙
Byram, Aaron J. . . . . '72 '98 C.339 B.A. L.734 J.D. [🄰 Brown&J.]
Cagas, Christian . . . . '68 '02 C.339 B.S. L.734 J.D. [🄰 Walker&W.]
Cain, Jeffery A., (BV) . . . . '61 '86 C&L.734 B.S., J.D. [Freeark,H.M.D.W.C.&M.]
Cannady, Thomas B., (BV) . . . . '56 '84 C.801 B.S. L.734 J.D. 3005 W. Main St.
Caponi, Kirk A., (BV) . . . . '65 '90 C.337 B.A. L.734 J.D. [Williams,C.&Assoc.]

Carey, Jack, (AV) '42 '76 C.934 B.A. L.734 J.D.
23 South First Street, 62220-2029
Telephone: 618-234-2424 Fax: 618-234-2470
Email: jclaw@compu-type.net
Civil Litigation, Personal Injury, Labor, Criminal Defense.

See Professional Biographies, BELLEVILLE, ILLINOIS

Carr, Rex, (AV) . . . . '26 '50 C&L.339 A.B., J.D. [Rex C.] ⊙
Cates, Judy L., (AV) . . . . '52 '78 C.188 B.A. L.910 J.D. [Cates,K.B.&S.]

Cates, Kurowski, Bailey & Shultz, LLC, (AV)
24 Bronze Pointe (Swansea), 62226
Telephone: 618-277-5500 Fax: 618-277-6334 URL: http://www.kbslaw.net
Email: kbs@kbslaw.net URL: http://www.lawyers.com/kurowskibailey
Judy L. Cates; John J. Kurowski; Curtis R. Bailey; William D. Shultz, Jr.:—Melissa R. Badgett; Michael Wade Tackett; Lindsay A. Dibler; Robert C. Anderson; Steven A. Trefts; Jerome S. Warchol, Jr.; Tracy L. Baum; Candice C. Kusmer.
Civil Litigation Practice. Toxic Tort, Asbestos, Insurance, Bad Faith Claims, Insurance Defense, Employment Law, Family Law.

See Professional Biographies, BELLEVILLE, ILLINOIS

Cavataio, Lorraine Kay, (BV) . . . . '69 '95 C.378 B.S. L.910 J.D. [Mathis,M.R.&G.]
Chandler, Tamara R. . . . . '74 '01 C.999 B.S.N. L.801 J.D. [🄰 Dunham,B.&L.] ⊙
Chapkin, Paul J. . . . . '78 '03 C.734 B.A. L.986 J.D. [🄰 Neville,R.&W.]
Chivell, Michael A., (AVⓉ) '54 '83
C.340 B.A. L.352 J.D. [Armstrong T.] (⊙St. Louis, MO)
Christianson, Dean L., (BV) '57 '82
C.801 B.A. L.502 J.D. 74 Granvue Dr. (⊙St. Louis, MO)
Clark, Stephen R., (BV) . . . . '49 '74 C&L.734 B.A., J.D. [Courtney,C.&Assoc.]
Clayborne, James F., Jr., (BV) '63 '88
C.832 B.S. L.472 J.D. [Hinshaw&C.] (⊙Edwardsville)
Clinton, David W., (AV) . . . . '50 '75 C.339 B.A. L.734 J.D. [Bonaldi,C.&D.]
Cole, Clark H., (AVⓉ) '55 '80 C.420 B.A. L.502 J.D.
[Armstrong T.] (⊙Edwardsville, IL; St. Louis, MO)
Collins, Don Cary, Attorney at Law, (BV) '51 '76 C.338 B.A. L.801 J.D.
126 W. Main St.
Conner, Francis D., (BV) . . . . '17 '47 C&L.339 A.B., J.D [F.D.Conner]
Conner, Francis D., P.C., (BV) . . . . 5 Autumn Ln.
Connors, Neal A., (BV) . . . . '62 '89 C&L.339 B.A., J.D. [N.A.Connors]

Connors, Neal A., Law Firm, P.C., (BV)
422 South High Street, 62220
Telephone: 618-233-2466 Fax: 618-233-8447
Email: nconnors@peaknet.net

(This Listing Continued)

Connors, Neal A., Law Firm, P.C. (Continued)
Neal A. Connors.
Languages: French, Spanish and Japanese.
Immigration Law, Criminal Law, Business Law, Military and International Law.
See Professional Biographies, BELLEVILLE, ILLINOIS

Constance, Michael B., (AV) ... '41 '65 C.357 B.S. L.910 J.D. [Nester&C.]
Cook, Bruce N., (AV) ... '40 '66 C.801 L.339 J.D. [Cook,S.Y.B.&B.]
Cook, James C., (AV) ... '51 '76 C.339 B.A. L.424 J.D. [Walker&W.]
Cook, Michael C. ... '52 '78 C.967 B.A. L.477 J.D. 12 W. Lincoln St.
Cook, Shevlin, Ysursa, Brauer & Bartholomew, Ltd., (AV) ... 12 W. Lincoln Street
Corkery, Andrew C. ... '73 '00 C&L.734 B.A., J.D. [🄰 Gundlach,L.E.B.&R.] ⊙
Corray, Jason W. ... '73 '01 C.339 A.B. L.801 J.D. [🄰 Dunham,B.&L.] ⊙
Courtney, Charles W., Jr., (BV) ... '61 '86 C.801 B.S. L.910 J.D. [Courtney,C.&Assoc.]
Courtney, Clark & Associates P.C., (BV) ... 104 S. Charles St.
Crego, Robert O., (BV) ... '52 '82 C.801 B.A. L.365 J.D. 416 S. High St.
Cueto, Christopher F., (BV) ... '59 '86 7110 W. Main St.
Cummings, Robert E. ... '14 '39 C.502 L.424 LL.B. 208 Williamsburg Dr.‡
Cummings, Wayne L. ... '44 '74 C.734 B.S. L.421 J.D. 208 Williamsburg
Cunningham, John P., (AV) ... '61 '86 C.238 B.S. L.801 J.D. [Brown&J.]
Dahlmann, Donald J., (AV) ... '48 '73 C.801 B.A. L.734 J.D. [Walker&W.]
Daley, Madelyn J. ... '68 '99 C.339 B.A. L.801 J.D. 123 W. Main St.
Dauber, Ellen A. ... '60 '85 C.602 B.A. L.880 J.D. Co. J.
Davis, David C., (BV) ... '55 '83 C.902 B.A. L.734 J.D. [Bonaldi,C.&D.]
Davis, Glenn E., (AV) '56 '82 C.210 B.A. L.910 J.D.
[Armstrong T.] (⊙Edwardsville, IL; St. Louis, MO)
Davis, Warren W., (AVⓉ) '46 '71 C.910 A.B. L.94 J.D.
(adm. in MO; not adm. in IL) [Sandberg,P.&v.] (⊙St. Louis, MO)
Dawson, Kevin T. ... '79 '05 C.465 B.A. L.801 J.D. [🄰 Brown&Assoc.]
Denney, Brad S., (BV) ... '55 '83 C.98 B.A. L.809 J.D. 201 S. Jackson St.
Dennis, Ted W., (AV) ... '52 '78 C.337 A.B. L.801 J.D. [Freeark,H.M.D.W.C.&M.]
Derango, Ralph J., (BV) ... '37 '61 C.339 L.365 LL.B. 100 W. Main St.
Dexheimer, Karl D., (AV) ... '42 '67 C.357 B.A. L.910 J.D. [🄲 Greensfelder,H.&G.]
Dibble, Elizabeth J., (CV) ... '58 '83 C.430 B.S. L.801 J.D. Dir., Belleville Area Coll.
Dibler, Lindsay A., (BV) ... '60 '93 C.871 B.S. L.734 J.D. [🄰 Cates,K.B.&S.]
Dix, Barry D., (AV) ... '49 '74 C&L.910 A.B., J.D. 5111 West Main Street
Dixon, Scott, (BV) ... '53 '78 C.339 B.S. L.365 J.D. [Dixon&J.]

Dixon & Johnston, P.C., (AV)
103 West Main Street, 62220-1501
Telephone: 618-233-1103 1-800-733-2440 Fax: 618-233-9368
Email: johnjohnston@compu-type.net URL: http://www.dixonandjohnston.com
Members of Firm: Scott Dixon; John J. Johnston. Associate: Stanley R. Weller.
Family Law, Social Security Disability, Personal Injury, Bankruptcy, Mortgage Foreclosure.
See Professional Biographies, BELLEVILLE, ILLINOIS

Donelson, Michael E., (BV) '65 '99 C.801 B.S. L.734 J.D.
[🄰 Freeark,H.M.D.W.C.&M.]

Donovan, Rose, Nester & Joley, P.C., (AV)
8 East Washington Street, 62220
Telephone: 618-235-2020 Telecopier: 618-235-9632
Email: firm@ilmoattorneys.com
Dennis E. Rose; Michael J. Nester; Charles L. Joley; Robert J. Bassett; Kenneth M. Nussbaumer; Georgiann Oliver; Kristine McGee Mack;—Chi-yong Throckmartin.
Admiralty and Maritime Law, Alcoholic Beverages, Appellate Practice, Civil Practice, Civil Rights, Environmental Law, Estate Planning, Health Care Law, Hospitals, Insurance, Insurance Defense, Litigation, Medical Malpractice, Legal Malpractice, Negligence, Personal Injury, Premises Liability, Products Liability, Professional Liability, Railroads, Torts.
Representative Clients: State Farm Mutual Auto & Life Co.; Travelers Insurance Co.; Liberty Mutual Insurance Co.; Government Employees Insurance Co.; Great American Insurance Co.; Aetna Casualty & Surety Co.; Royal Globe Insurance Co.
See Professional Biographies, BELLEVILLE, ILLINOIS

Dos Santos, Anthony E. ... '71 '98 C.94 B.A. L.801 J.D. [🄰 Brown&J.]
Downey, Michael P., (BVⓉ) ... '70 '98 C.276 B.A. L.910 J.D. [🄰 Fox G.] ⊙
Ducey, C. Patout ... '50 '77 C.339 A.B. L.910 J.D. [Ducey&Assoc.]
Ducey, Cornelius T., Sr., (AV) ... '19 '49 C&L.602 LL.B. [🄲 Ducey&Assoc.] ⊙
Ducey & Associates, P.C. ... 20 Bronze Pointe (⊙St. Louis, MO)
Duebbert, Ronald R. ... '62 '90 C.801 B.A. L.339 J.D. [Duebbert]
Duebbert Law Office ... 100 S. Charles St., Ste. 2

Dunham, Boman & Leskera, (AV)
208 N. High, 62220 ⊙
Telephone: 618-235-7222 Telecopier: 618-236-2800
Email: dbl103@mvp.net
M.F. Oehmke (1887-1963); Wm. C. Dunham (1893-1975); Howard Boman (1917-1985); John W. Leskera; William L. Berry; Eric C. Young; John L. Bitzer. Associates: Jason W. Corray; Tamara R. Chandler; Harvey Taylor, Jr.; Kevin J. Newton.
General Civil Trial and Appellate Practice. Negligence and Products Liability, Medical Malpractice, Probate, Insurance, Family, Real Estate, Environmental, School, Criminal and Bankruptcy Law.
Attorneys for: Collinsville School District #10; Hanover Insurance Co.; Hartford Insurance Group; State Farm Insurance Cos.; Transamerica Insurance Group; The Travelers Indemnity Co.; Wausau Insurance Cos.; Nationwide Insurance Co.; RLI Insurance Group.
Collinsville Office: 300 West Clay Street. Telephone: 618-344-7734. Telecopier: 618-344-3853.
See Professional Biographies, BELLEVILLE, ILLINOIS

Dusek, Douglas E., (AV) ... '53 '78 C&L.734 A.B., J.D. 1601 11th Fairway Dr.
Eckert, Annette A. ... '51 '76 C.98 B.A. L.209 J.D. Assoc. Cir. J.
Eckert, Heidi L. ... '71 '99 C.1347 B.A. L.801 J.D. [🄰 Hinshaw&C.]
Ehlers, Carla J., (BV) ... '45 '86 C.801 M.S. L.910 J.D. 23 Public Sq.
Elliot, Julie Constance, (BV) ... '70 '00 C.210 B.A. L.734 J.D. [🄰 Hinshaw&C.]
Ellis, Jim D., (CV) ... '61 '95 C&L.801 B.S., J.D. [🄰 Freeark,H.M.D.W.C.&M.]
Engel, Richard W., Jr., (AVⓉ) '61 '87
C.734 B.S.B.A. L.502 J.D. [Armstrong T.] (⊙St. Louis, MO)
English, John M., (BV) ... '46 '74 C.711 A.B. L.734 J.D. [Kassly,B.E.&H.]
Enyart, William L., (AV) ... '49 '79 C&L.801 B.A., J.D. [Enyart&P.]

Enyart & Peebles, (AV) 🄱🄱
12 South Second Street, 62220
Telephone: 618-235-8300; 398-4505 Fax: 618-235-8673 Email: mspeebles_2000@yahoo.com
URL: http://www.lawyers.com/enyart&peebles
William L. Enyart; Mark S. Peebles.
Social Security Disability, Personal Injury, Military Law, Trial Practice, Administrative Law, Criminal Law, Probate, Municipal Law.
See Professional Biographies, BELLEVILLE, ILLINOIS

Epperson, Heidi, (BV) ... '70 '97 C.958 B.S. L.801 J.D. Asst. States Atty.
Epperson, Myles L., (CV) ... '70 '96 C.340 B.A. L.801 J.D. 2027 West Main St.
Erickson, Greg J. ... '67 '92 C.347 B.A. L.734 J.D. [Fox G.] ⊙
Evanko, Lyndon Philip, (BV) ... '56 '94 C.801 B.S. L.734 J.D. [L.P.Evanko]
Evanko, Lyndon P., P.C., (BV) ... 6464 W. Main St., Ste. A
Farthing, William D. ... '21 '50 C&L.339 8221 W. Main St.‡
Feder, Philip G., (BV) ... '29 '56 C&L.734 B.S., LL.B. 9 Vandor Ct. (⊙St. Louis, MO)
Ferguson, Connie S. ... '48 '80 C.801 B.S. L.734 J.D. Asst. Atty. Gen.
Ferguson, John M. ... '21 '49 L.910 J.D. 12 Oak Knoll‡
Ferrell, William H. ... '14 '38 C.339 A.B. L.309 LL.B. 26 Symonds Dr.‡
Fields, David Wayne '56 '85 C.1027 B.S. L.93 J.D.
(adm. in NY; not adm. in IL) 2867 Fairway Dr.
Fiss, Jan V. ... '42 '68 C.36 B.A. L.339 J.D. Assoc. Cir. J.
Fiss, Rhonda D., Law Office of, (BV) '52 '85 C&L.801 B.S., J.D.
22 South Illinois Street
Flynn, Patrick M., (BV) ... '44 '69 C&L.734 B.S., J.D. [Flynn&G.]
Flynn & Guymon, (BV) ... 23 Public Sq., Ste. 440
Fournie, Raymond R., (AV) '51 '79 C.339 B.S. L.734 J.D.
[Armstrong T.] (⊙Edwardsville, IL; St. Louis, MO)
Fowler, Katherine M. ... '74 '00 C.201 B.A. L.734 J.D. [🄰 Fox G.] ⊙
Fox, Ronald E., (AV) ... '55 '81 C.910 A.B. L.734 J.D. [Fox G.] ⊙

Fox Galvin, LLC, (AV)
5111 West Main Street, 62226 ⊙
Telephone: Toll Free: 866-588-7001
Ronald E. Fox; John E. Galvin; Thomas J. Smith; Suzanne P. Galvin; Greg J. Erickson; Jonathan H. Garside; Dana W. Tucker (Not admitted in IL). Associates: John M. Allen; Michael P. Downey; Katherine M. Fowler; Richard B. Korn; Ronda F. Williams; Reginald C. Johnson (Not admitted in IL). Of Counsel: Bart C. Sullivan.
Trial and Appellate Practice in State and Federal Courts. Areas of practice: Admiralty, Product Liability, Class Action, Insurance Coverage, Professional Liability, Employment Law, Commercial Law and Personal Injury.
St. Louis, Missouri Office: One Memorial Drive, 8th Floor, 63102. Telephone: 314-588-7000; 866-588-7001. Telecopier: 314-588-1965. URL: http://www.foxgalvin.com.
See Professional Biographies, BELLEVILLE, ILLINOIS

Freeark, Harvey, Mendillo, Dennis, Wuller, Cain & Murphy, P.C., (AV)
115 W. Washington St.
Friess, David H. ... '68 '99 C.470 B.S. L.365 J.D. [🄰 Gundlach,L.E.B.&R.] ⊙
Frisella, John Paul ... '69 '00 C.798 B.S. L.365 J.D. [J.P.Frisella] ⊙
Frisella, John P., L.L.C., The Law Offices of ... 23 South First Street (⊙St. Louis, MO)
Fuld, James Howard ... '55 '99 C.560 B.V.S. L.734 J.D. State Atty. Off.
Galvin, John E., (AVⓉ) ... '60 '86 C.436 B.A. L.910 J.D. [Fox G.] ⊙
Galvin, Suzanne P. ... '66 '91 C.802 B.A./B.B.A. L.352 J.D. [Fox G.] ⊙
Garnhart, Corrine M. ... '— '02 C.383 B.A. L.801 J.D. [🄰 Thompson C.]
Garrison, James R., (BV) ... '55 '82 C&L.339 B.S., J.D. [🄰 Gundlach,L.E.B.&R.] ⊙
Garside, Jonathan H. ... '65 '97 C.1375 B.A. L.910 J.D. [Fox G.] ⊙
Gatlin, William M., (BV) ... '56 '86 C.98 B.A. L.801 J.D. 31 Ramona Dr.
Gavin, William P., (AV) ... '55 '80 C&L.734 A.B., J.D. [Gavin]

Gavin Law Firm, (AV)
#17 Park Place Professional Centre, 62226
Telephone: 618-236-0100 Toll Free: 888-360-0100 Fax: 618-236-2684 URL: http://www.gavinlaw.com
Email: billg@gavinlaw.com URL: http://www.lawyers.com/gavinlaw
William P. Gavin; Rachel Marie Lewis.
Civil Trial Practice, consisting primarily of Personal Injury, Federal Employers Liability, Medical Malpractice, Admiralty, Products Liability, Occupational Disease, Environmental, Toxic Tort and Commercial Law in State and Federal Courts.
See Professional Biographies, BELLEVILLE, ILLINOIS

Generous, Teresa A., (AVⓉ) ... '56 '88 C.732 B.S. L.502 J.D. [Mathis,M.R.&G.] ⊙
Gilbert, John L., (AV) ... '50 '75 C.339 B.A. L.910 J.D. [Hinshaw&C.] (⊙Edwardsville)
Glass, Jeffrey R., (AV) ... '53 '78 C&L.734 B.A., J.D. [Hinshaw&C.] (⊙Edwardsville)
Gleeson, Andrew J. ... '59 '85 C.602 B.A. L.734 J.D. Assoc. Cir. J.
Going, David L., (AVⓉ) '58 '83
C.228 A.B. L.910 J.D. [Armstrong T.] (⊙St. Louis, MO)
Goldenhersh, Del A. ... '48 '73 C&L.910 B.A., J.D. [Goldenhersh&G.]
Goldenhersh, Jerold H., (BV) ... '48 '74 C&L.910 A.B., J.D. 9700 W. Main St.
Goldenhersh, Marvin W. ... '20 '42 C&L.910 B.S., J.D. [Goldenhersh&G.]
Goldenhersh, Richard P. ... '44 '69 C&L.910 A.B., J.D. Appl. J.
Goldenhersh & Goldenhersh, P.C. ... 6400 West Main Street
Gomric, James A. ... '69 '95 C&L.734 B.S., J.D. [O'Gara,G.&S.]
Gomric, Julia R., (BV) ... '70 '95 C.676 B.A. L.734 J.D. 6 East Washington Ave.
Goodwin, John M., Jr. ... '48 '74 C.801 B.A. L.734 J.D. Assoc. Cir. J.
Gossage, Roza ... '47 '71 C.339 B.A. L.209 J.D. 525 W. Main St., Ste. 130
Graber, Dennis J., (BV) '59 '84 C.337 B.A. L.801 J.D.
[Hinshaw&C.] (⊙Edwardsville)
Graham, J. Kenneth, III ... '70 '99 C.1147 B.A. L.734 J.D. [🄰 Walker&W.]
Grandy, Laura Koeneman, (AV) ... '58 '84 C.234 B.A. L.734 J.D. [Mathis,M.R.&G.]
Greenberg, Scott, (AVⓉ) '58 '83 C.L.502 B.S.B.A., J.D.
(adm. in MO; not adm. in IL) [Sandberg,P.&v.] (⊙St. Louis, MO)

Greensfelder, Hemker & Gale, P.C., (AV)
12 Wolf Creek Drive Suite 100 (Swansea), 62226 ⊙
Telephone: 618-257-7308 Telefax: 618-257-7353
Email: ghg@greensfelder.com URL: http://www.greensfelder.com
Edward S. Bott, Jr.; Thomas F. Hennessy, III (Resident); Cherie K. Macdonald (Resident); Joseph B. McDonnell (Resident); Garrett C. Reuter (Resident); William A. Schmitt (Resident); Donald K. Schoemaker (Resident); Russell K. Scott (Resident); George A. Uhl; L. Kevin Vick; Donald E. Weihl (Resident);—Dayna L. Johnson (Resident); Linda M. Kniepkamp (Resident); Michelle Rousseau (Resident); Emily C. Singley (Resident); David W. Ybarra (Resident). Of Counsel: Joseph R. Lowery (Resident); Karl D. Dexheimer (Resident).
Antitrust, Appellate Practice, Creditors' Rights and Bankruptcy, Communications and Television, Computer and High Technology, Construction, Corporate and Finance, Employee Benefits and Employment, Environmental, Food Processing and Distribution, General Trial Practice in all State and Federal Courts, Health Care, Immigration, Intellectual Property, International Business, Labor, Litigation, Manufacturing and Distribution, Probate and Estate Planning, Real Estate, Securities, Tax Exempt Financing, Taxation, Trade Secret.
St. Louis, Missouri Office: 2000 Equitable Building, 10 South Broadway. Telephone: 314-241-9090. Telefax: 314-241-8624.
See Professional Biographies, BELLEVILLE, ILLINOIS

Griesemer, Elizabeth ... '66 '91 C&L.734 B.S., J.D. Asst. State's Atty.
Grossmann, Louis C. ... '27 '52 C.339 B.S. L.734 LL.B. 376 Breckenridge Dr.

Gundlach, Lee, Eggmann, Boyle & Roessler LLC, (AV) 🄱🄱
5000 West Main Street, P.O. Box 23560, 62223-0560 ⊙
Telephone: 618-277-9000; East St. Louis: 271-8000 Telecopier: 618-277-4594
Email: info@gundlachlee.com URL: http://www.gundlachlee.com
Members: Norman J. Gundlach (1907-1996); Carl W. Lee; Robert E. Eggmann (1928-1986); Richard E. Boyle; Richard M. Roessler; Kenneth L. Halvachs; Thomas R. Peters; Charles J. Swartwout; Robert D. Andrekanic; Curtis R. Picou; Mark R. Kurz. Associates: Brad G. Pelc; James R. Garrison; Andrew C. Corkery; Todd R. McFarland; David B. Schneidewind; David R. Butz, II; David H. Friess; Sean K. Brousseau.
General Civil and Trial Litigation Practice, State and Federal Courts, Corporate and Insurance Litigation: Products Liability, Medical Malpractice, Professional Liability, Railroad, Automobile, Aviation, Admiralty, Life, Surety Bond, Cargo, Casualty, Commercial, Toxic Tort, Civil Rights, Fire and Construction.
Division Counsel for: NorfolkSouthern Railway Company.
Attorneys for: Canadian National/Illinois Central Railroad Company; Minnesota Mining & Manufacturing Company; Terminal Railroad Association of St. Louis; Mack Trucks, Inc; Raytheon Aircraft Company; Vought Aircraft Company; Liberty Mutual Insurance Company; Volvo Trucks North America, Inc.; Illinois State Medical Insurance Service; AIG.

(This Listing Continued)

Gundlach, Lee, Eggmann, Boyle & Roessler LLC (Continued)

St. Louis, Missouri Office: 1010 Market Street, Suite 1640. Telephone: 314-231-2084. Telecopier: 314-231-1960.

See Professional Biographies, BELLEVILLE, ILLINOIS

Guymon, David E., (BV) .... '47 '75 C.338 B.S. L.365 J.D. [Flynn&G.]
Haller, James J. .... '66 '93 C.118 B.A. L.910 J.D. [Mueller&H.] ⊙
Halvachs, Kenneth L., (BV) ..... '59 '84 C.338 B.S. L.339 J.D. [Gundlach,L.E.B.&R.] ⊙
Hamilton, Charles E., (AV) .... '34 '60 C&L.734 B.S., LL.B. [C.E.Hamilton]
Hamilton, Harriet Homsher, (BV) .... '56 '89 C&L.112 B.A., J.D. [Ⓐ Cook,S.Y.B.&B.]
Hamilton, Charles E., Ltd., (AV) .... 10 Persimmon Ridge
Hamman, K. Douglas, (BV) .... '47 '77 C.339 B.A. L.801 J.D. 627 Sycamore St.
Hammel, Jeffrey S., (AV) .... '55 '80 C.339 B.A. L.734 J.D. 23 S. 1st St.
Hanna, Myron A., (BV) .... '57 '81 C.465 B.A. L.339 J.D. [Hanna&V.]
Hanna & Volmert, LLC, (BV) .... 530 Fullerton Rd., Suite A
Harkins, John D., (AVⓉ) .... '61 '87 C.884 B.A. L.724 J.D. Gen. Coun., Allsup, Inc.
Harla, Harlan A., (AV) .... '— '85 C&L.801 B.S., J.D. [Thompson C.]
Harter, Gary R., (BV) .... '54 '79 C.879 B.A. L.345 J.D. [Harter&L.]
Harter & Larson, (BV) .... 201 S. Jackson St.
Harvey, Ted R., Jr., (AV) .... '43 '68 C&L.339 A.B., J.D. [Freeark,H.M.D.W.C.&M.]
Hasenstab, Daniel G. .... '75 '02 C&L.734 B.A., J.D. [Ⓐ Brown&J.]
Hatch, Mary Ann, (AV) .... '50 '78 C&L.734 B.S., J.D. [Herzog C.]
Hayes, Daniel J., Law Offices of, (BV) '50 '77
C.201 B.S. L.339 J.D. 3540 N. Belt W., Ste. A
Heiligenstein, Christian E., (AV) .... '29 '55 C&L.339 B.S., J.D. [Ⓒ B.L.Badgley] ‡
Hennessy, Thomas F., III, (BV) .... '50 '75 C&L.734 B.S., J.D. [Greensfelder,H.&G.]

Herzog Crebs LLP, (AV)
5111 West Main Street, 62226 ⊙
Telephone: 618-235-7656
Mary Ann Hatch.
General Civil Practice, including Trial and Appellate Practice in Federal and State Courts. Products Liability, General Corporate and Corporate Litigation, Insurance and Insurance Defense, Asbestos and Toxic Tort Litigation, Estate Planning, Probate and Trust, Real Estate, Construction Law, Taxation, Employment Law, Zoning.
St. Louis, Missouri Office: 515 North Sixth Street, 24th Floor, 63101. Telephone: 314-231-6700. Fax: 314-231-4656. Email: Webmaster@HerzogCrebs.com. Website: http://www.HerzogCrebs.com.

See Professional Biographies, BELLEVILLE, ILLINOIS

Hess, Frederick J., (AV) .... '41 '71 C.734 B.S. L.900 J.D. [Lewis,R.&F.]
Hickman, Charles F., (CV) .... '54 '85 C.43 B.S. L.45 J.D. 521 W. Main St., Ste. 100
Hillebrand, Joseph R., (BV) .... '64 '92 C.339 B.A. L.347 J.D. [Kassly,B.E.&H.]
Hillebrand, Robert J. .... '40 '65 C&L.339 A.B., LL.B. Assoc. Cir. J.

Hinshaw & Culbertson LLP, (AV) BR
Hinshaw & Culbertson LLP is an Illinois registered limited liability partnership that has elected to be governed by the Illinois Uniform Partnership Act (1997)
521 West Main Street Suite 300, P.O. Box 509, 62222-0509 ⊙
Telephone: 618-277-2400 Facsimile: 618-277-1144 Telex: 880248
Email: kfox@hinshawlaw.com URL: http://www.hinshawlaw.com
Partners: Mark D. Bauman (Also at Edwardsville, Illinois Office); James F. Clayborne, Jr.; John L. Gilbert; Jeffrey R. Glass; Dennis J. Graber; Jeffrey A. Kopis; Charles A. Pierce; Jeffrey T. Reel; John E. Sabo; Dawn A. Sallerson; Michael L. Wagner. Associates: Robert D. Bas; Heidi L. Eckert; Julie Constance Elliot; Chad A. Jennings; A. Randall Knopf; Madelyn J. Lamb.
Appellate, Banking & Financing, Bankruptcy & Creditors' Rights, Class Action Litigation, Civil Rights Defense, Commercial Litigation, Corporate, Construction Law, Director & Officer Liability, Employee Benefits, Environmental, Fidelity & Surety, General Liability Litigation, Government, Health Care, Insurance Coverage, Insurance and Reinsurance, Labor & Employment, Legal Malpractice, Medical Malpractice, Mergers & Acquisitions, Municipal Liability, Personal Injury Defense, Public Law, Products Liability Litigation, Professional Liability, Regulatory, Real Estate, School Law, Securities, Taxation, Transportation, White Collar Crime and Workers' Compensation Defense.
Other Office Locations: Chicago, Illinois; Appleton, Wisconsin; Boston, Massachusetts; Champaign, Illinois; Crystal Lake, Illinois; Edwardsville, Illinois; Fort Lauderdale, Florida; Jacksonville, Florida; Joliet, Illinois; Lisle, Illinois; Los Angeles, California; Miami, Florida; Milwaukee, Wisconsin; Minneapolis, Minnesota; New York, New York; Peoria, Illinois; Phoenix, Arizona; Portland, Oregon; Providence, Rhode Island; Rockford, Illinois; St. Louis, Missouri; San Francisco, California; Schererville, Indiana; Springfield, Illinois; Tampa, Florida; Waukegan, Illinois.

See Professional Biographies, BELLEVILLE, ILLINOIS

Hoerner, Kevin T., (BV) .... '62 '87 C.339 B.A. L.734 J.D. 5111 W. Main St.
Holdener, Sarah Elizabeth '76 '01 C&L.734 B.S., J.D.
(adm. in MO; not adm. in IL) Coun., Benchmark Title Co.
Hooks, Heath H. .... '— '93 C&L.801 BA., J.D. [Ⓐ Thompson C.]
Hunter, Thomas J. .... '66 '98 C.927 B.A. L.910 J.D. Appl. Ct. of IL, 5th Dist.
Hutnick, Melroy B., Law Office of ... '37 '62 C.910 B.S. L.502 J.D. 209 S. Jackson Street
Jacknewitz, Dennis J., (AV) .... '47 '74 C&L.734 B.S., J.D. [Jennings,J.&S.]
James, Ernest W. '31 '79 C.871 B.S. L.734 J.D.
(adm. in MO; not adm. in IL) 7416 Foley Drive
Jennings, Chad A. .... '75 '02 C.801 B.S. L.1000 J.D. [Ⓐ Hinshaw&C.]
Jennings, Robert L., (BV) .... '32 '63 C&L.734 J.D. [Jennings,J.&S.]
Jennings, Jacknewitz & Schrader, (AV) .... 720 W. Main Street, Suite 150
Jockish, Deanne R. '71 '04 C.801 B.S.N. L.734 J.D.
(adm. in MO; not adm. in IL) [Ⓐ Brown&J.]
Johnson, Dayna L., (BV) .... '50 '95 C.465 B.S. L.734 J.D. [Ⓐ Greensfelder,H.&G.] ⊙
Johnson, P. K., IV, (AV) .... '45 '71 C.339 B.A. L.146 J.D. [Johnson&J.]
Johnson, P. K., V, (BV) .... '70 '95 C.339 B.S. L.146 J.D. [Johnson&J.]
Johnson, Reginald C. '72 '98 C.502 B.S.M.E. L.425 J.D.
(adm. in LA; not adm. in IL) [Ⓐ Fox G.] ⊙

Johnson & Johnson, (AV)
11 South High, 62220
Telephone: 618-277-3600 Fax: 618-277-1184 Email: pkjiv@aol.com
Email: pkjIv@aol.com URL: http://www.lawyers.com/johnson&johnson
P. K. Johnson, Sr., III (1915-1997); P. K. Johnson, IV; P. K. Johnson, V.
General Civil Practice. Family Law and Divorce, Probate, Wills, Trust Law, Estate Planning, Real Estate, Personal Injury, Corporate Law, Banking Law.

See Professional Biographies, BELLEVILLE, ILLINOIS

Johnston, John J., (AV) .... '54 '79 C.378 B.S. L.339 J.D. [Dixon&J.]
Joley, Charles L., (BV) .... '58 '84 C&L.339 B.A., J.D. [Donovan,R.N.&J.]
Jones, Jodee Favre, (AV) .... '— '89 C.719 B.S. L.734 J.D. 121 E. Main St.
Jones, Thomas E., (AV) .... '— '79 C&L.801 B.S., J.D. [Thompson C.]
Juncker, Daniel K., (BV) .... '53 '78 C.338 B.S. L.739 J.D. [D.K.Juncker]
Juncker, Daniel K., P.C., (BV) .... 1803 N. Belt West
Kalish, James R., (BV) .... '43 '69 C.339 B.S. L.734 J.D. [Ⓐ Jennings,J.&S.]
Karge, Lee J. .... '71 '99 C.900 B.A. L.221 J.D. [Ⓐ Brown&J.]
Kasnetz, Andrew R., (AVⓉ) '56 '82
C.378 B.A. L.734 J.D. [Sandberg,P.&v.] (⊙St. Louis, MO)
Kassly, Bone, English & Hillebrand, P.C., (AV) .... 5111 West Main Street
Katz, Julie Keehner, (BV) .... '59 '84 C&L.339 B.A., J.D. 3005 W. Main St.
Katzman, Steven E., (BV) .... '47 '75 C.1036 B.A. L.734 J.D. [Katzman&Assoc.]
Katzman & Associates, (BV) .... 300 South Charles Street

Kaufhold, Kevin C., (BV) .... '55 '81 C.801 B.A. L.276 J.D. 5111 W. Main St.
Keefe, Thomas Q., Jr., (AV) .... '52 '78 C.93 B.A. L.734 J.D. [T.Q.Keefe,Jr.]
Keefe, Thomas Q., Jr., P.C., (AV) .... #6 Executive Woods Ct.
Keehner, Jim D., Ltd., (BV) .... '35 '59 C&L.339 B.A., LL.B. 508 S. Jackson
Kellogg, Steven E. .... '65 '96 C.225 B.A. L.734 J.D. 2129 W. Main St.
Keltner, Joan Bretsch .... '61 '87 C&L.801 B.A., J.D. App. Ct. Law Clk.
Kempf, Amber Lee .... '74 '02 C.1347 B.A. L.734 J.D. [Ⓐ Amelung,W.&W.] ⊙
Kernan, Stephen M. .... '47 '72 C.602 B.B.A. L.910 J.D. Chf. Cir. J.
Kerth, Samantha, (BV) .... '58 '88 C.734 B.S. L.801 J.D. 1 Cedar Point
Kievlan, Patricia H., (BV) .... '56 '95 C.378 B.S.W. L.734 J.D. 105 N. Illinois
Kionka, Edward J., (AV) '39 '62 C&L.339 B.S., J.D.
26 E. Washington Street, 2nd Floor
Kirkpatrick, Eric, (BV) .... '66 '91 C&L.801 B.S., J.D. [Ⓐ T.Q.Keefe,Jr.]
Klekner, Pamela Ann, (BV) .... '58 '83 C.136 B.A. L.734 J.D. 34 Signal Hill Blvd.
Kloess, Bernard J., (BV) .... '54 '83 C.801 B.S. L.734 J.D. 3540 N. Belt W.

Knapp, Ohl & Green
(See Edwardsville)

Kniepkamp, Linda M., (BV) ..... '59 '89 C.801 B.S. L.734 J.D. [Ⓐ Greensfelder,H.&G.]
Knopf, A. Randall .... '66 '92 C.861 B.A. L.1148 J.D. [Ⓐ Hinshaw&C.]
Kolker, Charles J., Jr., (BV) .... '40 '68 C&L.734 B.S., J.D. [Ⓒ C.J.Kolker,Jr.]
Kolker, Christopher Thomas, (BV) .... '66 '98 C.36 B.A. L.801 J.D. [C.J.Kolker,Jr.]
Kolker, Charles J., Jr., P.C., (BV) .... 9423 W. Main St.
Kopis, Jeffrey A. .... '64 '92 C.339 B.A. L.734 J.D. [Hinshaw&C.]
Korein, Sandor, (AV) .... '32 '56 C&L.910 A.B., LL.B. [Korein T.] ⊙

Korein Tillery, (AV)
10 Executive Woods Court, 62226 ⊙
Telephone: 618-277-1180 Telecopier: 618-222-6939
URL: http://www.koreintillery.com
Members of Firm: Sandor Korein; Stephen M. Tillery; Christine J. Moody. Associates: Lisa R. Kernan; Donald M. Flack; Christie Deaton; Stephen J. Telken; Aaron M. Zigler; Eugene Y. Barash. Of Counsel: Katherine J. Tillery.
Class Action, Securities Law, Environmental Law, Commercial Litigation, Pension and Profit Sharing, Railroad, Maritime, Medical Malpractice, Product Liability, Toxic Tort, General Negligence, Trial Practice.
St. Louis, Missouri Office: 701 Market Street, Suite 300, 63101-1820. Telephone: 314-241-4844. Telecopier: 314-241-3525.

See Professional Biographies, BELLEVILLE, ILLINOIS

Korn, Richard B. .... '70 '95 C.477 B.A. L.209 J.D. [Ⓐ Fox G.] ⊙
Kramer, John B. .... '10 '33 C&L.339 A.B., LL.B. 9500 W. Rte. 15‡
Krueger, Kevin P., (AVⓉ) '59 '85 C.502 A.B. L.910 J.D.
(adm. in MO; not adm. in IL) [Sandberg,P.&v.] (⊙St. Louis, MO)
Kuehn, Clyde L., (AV) .... '48 '73 C.339 B.S. L.383 J.D. 2027 W. Main St.
Kurowski, John J., (AV) .... '53 '78 C.424 B.A. L.734 J.D. [Cates,K.B.&S.]
Kurz, Mark R., (BV) .... '67 '92 C.436 B.A. L.339 J.D. [Gundlach,L.E.B.&R.] ⊙
Kusmer, Candice C. .... '76 '05 C.623 B.A. L.910 J.D. [Ⓐ Cates,K.B.&S.]
Lach, Michael J., (AVⓉ) '63 '89
C.338 B.S. L.801 J.D. [Boggs,B.&B.] (⊙St. Louis, MO)
Lamb, Madelyn J., (BV) .... '56 '81 C.339 B.A. L.734 J.D. [Ⓐ Hinshaw&C.]
Lang, Carl C., (AVⓉ) .... '46 '73 C.473 B.S. L.910 J.D. [Rosenblum,G.S.&Z.] ⊙
Lantz, Herbert J., Jr. .... '38 '70 C.871 B.S. L.339 J.D. 100 S. Charles St.
Larson, Nancy R., (BV) .... '54 '80 C.879 B.S. L.734 J.D. [Harter&L.]
LeChien, Elaine Louise, (BV) .... '61 '86 C&L.734 B.S., J.D. [LeChien&L.]
Lechien, Kara Leigh .... '73 '01 C.357 B.A. L.734 J.D. 120 West Main St., Ste. 110
LeChien, Robert P. .... '52 '76 C&L.801 B.S., J.D. Cir. J.
LeChien, Thomas A., (AV) .... '39 '67 C&L.734 B.A., J.D. [LeChien&L.]
LeChien & LeChien, Ltd., (AV) .... 120 West Main Street, Suite 110
Lee, Carl W., (AV) .... '27 '51 C&L.339 B.S., J.D. [Gundlach,L.E.B.&R.]
Leskera, John W., (AV) .... '31 '55 C&L.339 A.B., J.D. [Dunham,B.&L.] ⊙

Levenhagen, T. Fritz, (BV) '60 '86 C.801 B.A. L.734 J.D.
4495 North Illinois Street Suite E, 62226
Telephone: 618-235-2562 Toll Free: 877-235-2562 Fax: 618-235-2631
Email: fritz@levenhagen.com URL: http://www.levenhagen.com
Workers Compensation, , Automobile Accidents and Injuries, Products Liability, Wrongful Death, Personal Injury, Medical Malpractice and Premises Liability.

See Professional Biographies, BELLEVILLE, ILLINOIS

Lewis, Rachel Marie .... '— '03 C.339 B.A. L.801 J.D. [Gavin]

Lewis, Rice & Fingersh, (AV)
A Limited Liability Company
325 South High Street, 62220 ⊙
Telephone: 618-234-8636 Telecopier: 618-234-8671
Email: For attorney e-mails use: first initial of first name and last name @lewisrice.com e.g., jsmith@lewisrice.com URL: http://www.lewisrice.com
Resident Member: Frederick J. Hess. Associate: G. Ethan Skaggs.
General Civil Trial and Appellate Practice. Administrative, Admiralty, Agricultural Law, Antitrust, Banking, Bankruptcy, Business Law, Commercial, Corporation, Defamation, Divestitures, Employee Benefits, Environmental, Estate Planning, Health Care, High Technology, Insurance, Intellectual Property, Labor and Employment, Limited Liability Company, Media, Mergers and Acquisitions, Municipal, Not-for-Profit Institutions, Probate, Products Liability, Real Estate, Securities, Taxation, Toxic Torts, Zoning.
Kansas City, Missouri Office: 1010 Walnut, Suite 500. Telephone: 816-421-2500.
St. Louis, Missouri Office: 500 North Broadway, Suite 2000. Telephone: 314-444-7600.
Creve Coeur, Missouri Office: 555 North New Ballas Road, Suite 260. Telephone: 314-569-2262.
Overland Park, Kansas Office: 7015 College Boulevard, Suite 135. Telephone: 913-381-8898.
Washington, Missouri Office: 216 West Main, P.O. Box 1040. Telephone: 636-239-7747.
Jefferson City, Missouri Office: 221 East Capitol Avenue. Telephone: 573-893-7724.

See Professional Biographies, BELLEVILLE, ILLINOIS

Litzenburg, Deanna L., (BV) .... '74 '99 C.798 B.A. L.801 J.D. [Ⓐ Mathis,M.R.&G.]
Lopinot, Mary E., (BV) .... '62 '98 C.801 B.S.A. L.734 J.D. [Ⓐ Mathis,M.R.&G.]
Loseman, David G., (AVⓉ) '60 '85
C&L.339 B.A., J.D. [Armstrong T.] (⊙St. Louis, MO)

Lowe, Jeffrey J., P.C.
(See St. Louis, Missouri)

Lowery, Joseph R., (AV) .... '24 '50 C&L.339 B.S., J.D. [Ⓒ Greensfelder,H.&G.]
Lowery, Margaret J. .... '61 '87 C.802 B.A. L.862 J.D. Gen. Coun., Memorial Hospital
Maag, Edward G., (AV) .... '25 '50 C.473 B.S. L.910 J.D. 205 Southgate Drive
Macdonald, Cherie K., (BV) .... '61 '90 C.337 B.A. L.733 J.D. [Greensfelder,H.&G.]
Mack, Gary A., (BV) .... '63 '90 C.347 B.A. L.734 J.D. Asst. States Atty.
Mack, Kristine McGee, (BV) .... '66 '91 C&L.801 B.S., J.D. [Donovan,R.N.&J.]
Madigan, Kelli E., (CV) .... '70 '96 C&L.734 B.A., J.D. [Mathis,M.R.&G.]
Madigan, Patrick .... '71 '96 C&L.734 B.A., J.D. [Nester&C.]
Marifian, George E., (AV) .... '50 '77 C.910 B.S.B.A. L.734 J.D. [Mathis,M.R.&G.]
Marlen, Matthew J., (BV) .... '67 '92 C&L.339 B.A., J.D. 7012 W. Main St.
Martin, Anthony L., (AVⓉ) '52 '82
C.338 B.S. L.801 J.D. [Sandberg,P.&v.] (⊙St. Louis, MO)
Mathis, Patrick B., (AV) .... '52 '78 C.734 B.A. L.910 J.D. [Mathis,M.R.&G.]

Mathis, Marifian, Richter & Grandy, Ltd., (AV) BR
23 Public Square, Suite 300, P.O. Box 307, 62220 ⊙
Telephone: 618-234-9800; 314-421-2325 Fax: 618-234-9786
URL: http://www.mmrg.com
Patrick B. Mathis; George E. Marifian; Kevin J. Richter; Laura Koeneman Grandy; Kevin J. Stine; Mark J. Stegman; T. Bradford Waltrip; Mark S. Schuver; Kurt S. Schroeder; William J. Niehoff; Lorraine Kay Cavataio; Teresa A. Generous; Kelli E. Madigan; Bradley W. Small;—Mary E. Lopinot; Deanna L. Litzenburg; Joseph P. O'Keefe; Philip D. Speicher (Not admitted in IL).
Federal and State Tax Law and Controversy. Banking, Civil and Criminal Trial Practice. Tort and Commercial Litigation, Corporate, Business, ERISA Litigation, Employee Benefits, Real Estate, Probate, Estate Planning, Bankruptcy and Creditors Rights Law, Product Liability, Public Utilities, Medical Malpractice, Class Actions, Personal Injury, Wrongful Death, Employment Discrimination, Wrongful Discharge and Employment Law.
St. Louis, Missouri Office: 7751 Carondelet Avenue, Suite 500, 63105. Telephone: 314-421-2325. Fax: 314-727-3046.

See Professional Biographies, BELLEVILLE, ILLINOIS

McCarthy, Brian Thomas, (BV) ... '68 '93 C.363 B.S. L.734 J.D. [A Wimmer&S.]
McCaskill, Ericka D. ... '74 '01 C&L.801 B.A., J.D. [A Brown&J.]
McDonnell, Joseph B., (AV) ... '35 '60 C&L.734 B.S., LL.B. [Greensfelder,H.&G.]
McFarland, Todd R., (BV) '73 '00 C.1185 B.A. L.339 J.D. [A Gundlach,L.E.B.&R.] ⊙
McGlynn, James ... '29 '56 C&L.602 A.B., LL.B. [McGlynn&M.] ‡
McGlynn, Michael L., (BV) ... '59 '84 C.602 B.A. L.734 J.D. [McGlynn&M.]
McGlynn, Robert E., (AV) ... '26 '51 C&L.602 A.B., LL.B. [McGlynn&M.]
McGlynn, Stephen P., (BV) ... '62 '87 C.201 B.A. L.734 J.D. [McGlynn&M.]

McGlynn & McGlynn, (AV) BR
116 South Charles Street, 62220
Telephone: 618-234-8800; 314-381-5112 Telecopier: 618-234-8813
Email: mcglaw@htctech.net URL: http://www.lawyers.com/mcglynn&mcglynn
Members of Firm: Robert E. McGlynn; James McGlynn (Retired); Michael L. McGlynn; Stephen P. McGlynn.
General Civil and Trial Practice in Illinois, Missouri and the Federal Courts in the following areas: Torts, Admiralty (Jones Act), FELA, Medical Malpractice, Products Liability, and Workers Compensation. Also Election, Campaign and Political Law, Transportation Law and Transactions, Commercial Transactions, VCG & Warranty Litigation and Contracts, Government Law, Civil Rights.

See Professional Biographies, BELLEVILLE, ILLINOIS

McKechan, Douglas B. ... '59 '86 C.801 B.S. L.734 J.D. 5111 W. Main St.
McKee, Gregory J. ... '60 '91 C.1070 B.S. L.910 J.D. 115 N. Church St.

McMahon, Berger, Hanna, Linihan, Cody & McCarthy, A Professional Corporation
(See Collinsville)

McMullin, John L., III, (AV) '46 '72 C.910 B.S.B.A. L.502 J.D. [Brown&J.] (⊙St. Louis, MO)
McRoberts, James W., (BV) ... '36 '60 C.910 L.339 LL.B. Chapter 13 Trustee
Mellow, Mary Anne, (AVⓉ) '57 '82 C.228 B.A. L.910 J.D. [Sandberg,P.&v.] (⊙St. Louis, MO)
Mendillo, James R., (AV) ... '45 '72 C.1156 B.S. L.910 J.D. [Freeark,H.M.D.W.C.&M.]
Menges, Eugene C., (AV) ... '52 '77 C.93 B.S. L.734 J.D. 2027 W. Main St.
Metzger, Edward R., (CV) ... '38 '78 C.339 B.S.B.A. L.770 J.D. Assured Plumbing Co.
Meyer, Scott B., (BV) ... '55 '81 C.338 B.S. L.801 J.D. 416 S. High St.
Moore, Carolyn E. '55 '80 C.801 B.A. L.477 J.D. (adm. in CA; not adm. in IL) 356 Bunker Hill Rd.‡
Morris, Tara L., (BV) ... '70 '97 C&L.500 B.A., J.D. [A Brown&J.]
Mueller, William A., (BV) ... '59 '84 C.234 B.A. L.734 J.D. [Mueller&H.] ⊙
Mueller & Haller, LLC, Law Offices of, (BV) ... 7805 W. Main St. (⊙Glen Carbon)
Murphy, Michael P., (BV) '64 '89 C.190 B.S.B.A. L.502 J.D. [Freeark,H.M.D.W.C.&M.]
Murphy, Patricia S. ... '58 '93 C&L.801 B.A., J.D. 26 E. Washington Street
Muskopf, W. Jeffrey, (BV) ... '67 '93 C.934 B.A. L.802 J.D. [A Freeark,H.M.D.W.C.&M.]
Nelson, David C., (BV) ... '69 '94 C&L.228 B.S., J.D. [Nelson&N.]
Nelson, Robert C., (BV) ... '48 '73 C&L.339 B.S., J.D. [Nelson&N.]
Nelson & Nelson, P.C., (BV) ... 420 N. High Street
Nester, Alexander J., (BV) ... '32 '57 C.602 A.B. L.339 J.D. 123 W. Washington St.
Nester, David A., (BV) ... '60 '85 C.802 B.A. L.801 J.D. [Nester&C.]
Nester, Michael J., (AV) ... '48 '73 C&L.734 A.B., J.D. [Donovan,R.N.&J.]
Nester, Norbert Dean, (BV) ... '43 '69 L.734 J.D. 21 Coral Drive
Nester & Constance, P.C., (AV) ... 123 West Washington Street
Neville, Edward ... '20 '50 C&L.734 LL.B. 117 Lamoine Ln.‡
Neville, James E., (AV) ... '55 '80 C&L.734 B.S., J.D. [Neville,R.&W.]

Neville, Richards & Wuller, (AV) BR
5 Park Place, 62226
Telephone: 618-277-0900 Facsimile: 618-277-0970
URL: http://www.nrw-law.com
Members of Firm: James E. Neville; Timothy S. Richards; Robert G. Wuller, Jr. Associates: Matthew C. Zittel; Christopher B. Bortz; Paul J. Chapkin.
General Civil Trial and Appellate Practice, Personal Injury, Negligence, Products Liability, Premises Liability, Admiralty, Railroad, Medical and Legal Malpractice, Professional Negligence, Construction, Insurance Defense, Employment Law, Environmental, Municipal, Corporate, Real Estate and Probate Law.

See Professional Biographies, BELLEVILLE, ILLINOIS

Newton, Kevin J. ... '75 '04 C.339 B.A. L.734 J.D. [A Dunham,B.&L.] ⊙
Niehoff, William J., (BV) ... '60 '86 C.502 B.S.B.A. L.910 J.D. [Mathis,M.R.&G.]
Niemira, Stephen P., (AVⓉ) '67 '92 C&L.502 A.B., J.D. [Sandberg,P.&v.] (⊙St. Louis, MO)

Noonan, Thomas J., P.C.
(See St. Louis, Missouri)

Norman, John W. ... '57 '84 C.393 B.A. L.365 J.D. Asst. Pub. Def.
Nussbaumer, Kenneth M., (BV) ... '59 '88 C&L.801 B.A., J.D. [Donovan,R.N.&J.]
Ochoa, Eutha F., (BV) ... '52 '99 C.1291 B.S. L.734 J.D. [A Brown&J.]
Offergeld, Leslie, (BV) ... '62 '87 C.339 B.A. L.801 J.D. [A Walker&W.]
O'Gara, John J., Jr., (BV) ... '61 '87 C.1082 B.A. L.734 J.D. [O'Gara,G.&S.]

O'Gara, Gomric & Schultz, P.C., (BV)
6 East Washington Street, 62220
Telephone: 618-234-2788 Fax: 618-234-0670
Email: o'gara@compu-type.net URL: http://www.lawyers.com/ogaralaw
John J. O'Gara, Jr.; James A. Gomric; Todd M. Schultz.
Criminal Defense, Personal Injury Law. Capital Offenses, Murder, Felonies, Misdemeanors, Driving While Intoxicated, Traffic Violations, Automobile Accidents and Injuries, Federal Criminal, White Collar Crime.

See Professional Biographies, BELLEVILLE, ILLINOIS

O'Keefe, Joseph P. ... '71 '96 C&L.734 B.A., J.D. [A Mathis,M.R.&G.]
Oliver, Georgiann, (BV) ... '60 '86 C.801 B.S. L.910 J.D. [Donovan,R.N.&J.]
O'Malley, Edward Francis, (BV) ... '11 '39 C&L.602 B.C.S., J.D. 44 Glenview Dr.
O'Malley, Michael J. ... '53 '79 C.801 B.A. L.589 J.D. Cir. J.
Parham, James R., (AV) ... '21 '48 C.674 A.B. L.339 J.D. 525 West Main Street
Paulson, Alvin C., (BV) ... '60 '86 C.321 B.A. L.734 J.D. 5111 W. Main St.
Pawloski, John F., (BV) ... '71 '97 C.339 B.S. L.8 J.D. 300 S. Charles
Peebles, Mark S., (BV) ... '63 '94 C.103 A.B. L.734 J.D. [Enyart&P.]
Pelc, Brad G., (CV) ... '69 '94 C.339 B.A. L.999 J.D. [A Gundlach,L.E.B.&R.] ⊙
Perryman, Ted L., (AV) ... '52 '77 C.347 A.B. L.734 J.D. [Roberts,P.B.&M.] ⊙
Pessin, Sam S., (AV) ... '13 '37 C&L.339 A.B., J.D. 105 N. illinois
Peters, Thomas R., (BV) ... '60 '87 C.960 B.B.A. L.339 J.D. [Gundlach,L.E.B.&R.] ⊙
Phipps, Elizabeth S. '77 '03 C.339 B.S. L.861 J.D. (adm. in NC; not adm. in IL) [A Brown&J.]
Phoenix, G. Keith, (AV) '46 '74 C.801 B.A. L.734 J.D. [Sandberg,P.&v.] (⊙St. Louis, MO)
Picou, Curtis R., (BV) ... '63 '91 C&L.801 B.A., J.D. [Gundlach,L.E.B.&R.] ⊙
Pierce, Charles A., (BV) '66 '91 C.352 B.S. L.801 J.D. [Hinshaw&C.] (⊙Edwardsville)
Pine, Kathleen L., (AVⓉ) ... '57 '82 C.338 B.S. L.801 J.D. [Sandberg,P.&v.] ⊙
Pipher, Crystal M. ... '— '05 C.234 B.A. L.801 J.D. [A Thompson C.]
Pitzer, Michael J., (AV) ... '— '73 C&L.734 B.S., J.D. [Rabbitt,P.&S.] ⊙
Plattner, Frank T., (AV) ... '12 '37 C&L.339 B.A., LL.B. 110 Paddock Rd.‡
Poirier, Joseph M. ... '48 '78 C.763 B.S. L.365 J.D. [Burke&P.]
Polster, Lieder, Woodruff & Lucchesi, L.C., (BV) 2 Park Place (⊙St. Louis, MO; Basking Ridge, NJ)
Porter, James L., (AV) ... '52 '77 C.340 B.A. L.734 J.D. Chief Asst. Pub. Def.
Porter, Lisa Lindsay, (BV) ... '57 '82 C.465 B.A. L.734 J.D. Asst. States Atty.
Price, Keith D., (AVⓉ) '63 '89 C.339 B.S. L.69 J.D. [Sandberg,P.&v.] (⊙St. Louis, MO)
Quarenghi, John P. ... '65 '90 C.339 B.A. L.801 J.D. State's Atty. Off.

Rabbitt, Pitzer & Snodgrass, P.C., (AV)
23 South First Street, 62222-8336 ⊙
Telephone: 314-421-5545 Fax: 314-421-3144
Michael J. Pitzer.
General Civil Trial and Appellate Litigation in State and Federal Courts of Eastern Missouri and Southern Illinois, including Personal Injury Defense, Professional Liability (Medical, Legal Architectural and Engineering), Products Liability, Environmental, Construction, Employment, Fire and Marine and General Business Litigation.
St. Louis, Missouri Office: 100 South Fourth Street, Suite 400, 63102-1821. Telephone: 314-421-5545. Facsimile: 314-421-3144.

See Professional Biographies, BELLEVILLE, ILLINOIS

Radcliffe, James M. ... '48 '77 C.424 B.S. L.365 J.D. Assoc. Cir. J.
Randle, Ned W., (BV) ... '50 '91 C&L.734 B.S., J.D. [Polster,L.W.&L.] ⊙
Ransom, Brian L. ... '51 '76 C.465 B.A. L.734 J.D. 900 E. Main St.
Ratterree, Amy S., (CV) ... '67 '92 C.234 B.S. L.734 J.D. 23 S. 1st St.
Read, P. Michael, (BV) ... '52 '77 C.339 B.S. L.734 J.D. 114 E. Lincoln St.

Reed, Armstrong, Gorman, Mudge & Morrissey, Professional Corporation
(See Edwardsville)

Reel, Jeffrey T., (BV) ... '63 '91 C.801 B.S. L.1187 J.D. [Hinshaw&C.]
Reitz, Kurt E., (AV) ... '— '84 C&L.339 B.A., J.D. [Thompson C.]
Reuter, Garrett C., (BV) ... '47 '73 C.801 B.S. L.734 J.D. [Greensfelder,H.&G.]

Rex Carr Law Firm, LLC, The, (AV)
7012 W. Main Street, 62223 ⊙
Telephone: 618-397-9191 800-333-5297 URL: http://www.rexcarr.com
URL: http://www.lawyers.com/rexcarr
Rex Carr.
Railroad, Medical Malpractice, Product Liability, Toxic Torts, Nursing Home Negligence, General Negligence, Trial Practice, Workers Compensation, Class Actions, Complex Litigation, Automobile Litigation.
St. Louis, Missouri Office: 1 Metropolitan Square, 211 North Broadway, Suite 2970, 63102. Telephone: 1-800-333-5297.
East St. Louis, Illinois Office: 412 Missouri Avenue, 62201. Telephone: 618-274-0434. Fax: 618-274-8369.

See Professional Biographies, BELLEVILLE, ILLINOIS

Rhein, Eric M., (BV) ... '58 '83 C.927 B.S. L.802 J.D. [E.M.Rhein]
Rhein, Eric M., PC, (BV) ... 201 S. Jackson St.
Rice, Philip Robert, (BV) ... '58 '84 C.1111 B.S. L.362 J.D. [Rice]
Rice, Steven D. '— '03 C.769 B.A. L.284 J.D. (adm. in CA; not adm. in IL) Cir.J.
Rice Law Offices, Ltd. Inc., (BV) ... 110 E. Lincoln St.
Richards, Timothy S., (BV) ... '56 '82 C.57 A.B. L.801 J.D. [Neville,R.&W.]
Richter, Kevin J., (AV) ... '58 '83 C.801 B.S. L.734 J.D. [Mathis,M.R.&G.]
Ries, Jonathan, (AV) '48 '74 C.228 B.A. L.602 J.D. [Sandberg,P.&v.] (⊙St. Louis, MO)
Ripplinger, George R., Jr., (AV) ... '45 '70 C&L.339 B.A., J.D. [Ripplinger&Z.]

Ripplinger & Zimmer L.L.P., (AV)
2215 West Main Street, 62226
Telephone: 618-234-2440; 800-733-8333 Telecopier: 618-234-6728 URL: http://www.lawyers.com/ripplinger&associates
URL: http://georgeripplinger.wld.com
George R. Ripplinger, Jr.; Patricia A. Zimmer. Associate: Jamie Bas.
Legal Malpractice, Plaintiffs Personal Injury, Wrongful Death, Medical Malpractice, Products Liability.
A list of Representative Clients provided on request.
Reference: First Bank of Belleville, Illinois.

See Professional Biographies, BELLEVILLE, ILLINOIS

Roberts, Perryman, Bomkamp & Meives, P.C., (AV) ... 23 Public Sq. (⊙St. Louis, MO)
Robinson, Ronald D., (BV) ... '66 '92 C.234 B.S. L.734 J.D. [Amelung,W.&W.] ⊙
Roessler, Richard M., (AV) ... '39 '68 C.910 B.S. L.734 J.D. [Gundlach,L.E.B.&R.] ⊙
Rose, Dennis E., (AV) ... '47 '72 C&L.339 B.A., J.D. [Donovan,R.N.&J.]
Rosenblum, Goldenhersh, Silverstein & Zafft, P.C., (AVⓉ) 2 Park Pl. Professional Centre (⊙St. Louis, MO)
Rosenstengel, Jon E., (BV) ... '68 '93 C.339 B.S. L.801 J.D. [Bonifield&R.]
Rouse, Turner A., (BVⓉ) ... '55 '88 C.338 B.S. L.801 J.D. [Rouse]
Rouse Law Firm, The, (BVⓉ) ... 103 W. Main St., Ste. 1
Rousseau, Michelle ... '74 '01 C.836 B.A. L.801 J.D. [A Greensfelder,H.&G.]
Roustio, Richard Thomas, (BV) ... '56 '94 C.871 B.S. L.734 J.D. 123 W. Main St.
Ryseff, Carolyn B., (AVⓉ) ... '46 '78 C.347 B.A. L.424 J.D. Union Planters Bank
Sabo, John E., (BV) ... '57 '87 C.465 B.B.A. L.801 J.D. [Hinshaw&C.] (⊙Edwardsville)
Sallerson, Dawn A., (BV) '61 '86 C.739 B.A. L.734 J.D. [Hinshaw&C.] (⊙Edwardsville)
Samson, Donald M., (BV) ... '47 '74 C&L.326 B.A., J.D. 226 W. Main St., Ste. 102
Samuelson, Joseph, (AV) ... '53 '78 C.363 B.A. L.1151 J.D. [J.Samuelson]
Samuelson, Joseph, PC, (AV) ... 12 W. Lincoln St.
Sandberg, John S., (AV) '48 '72 C&L.502 A.B., J.D. [Sandberg,P.&v.] (⊙St. Louis, MO)

Sandberg, Phoenix & von Gontard, A Professional Corporation, (AV)
23 South 1st Street, 62220 ⊙
Telephone: 618-397-2721; 800-225-5529
Email: spvg.com URL: http://www.spvg.com

(This Listing Continued)

Sandberg, Phoenix & von Gontard, A Professional Corporation (Continued)

Shareholders: John S. Sandberg; G. Keith Phoenix; Peter von Gontard; Jonathan Ries; Kenneth W. Bean; Reed W. Sugg; Warren W. Davis (Not admitted in IL); Mary Anne Mellow; Kathleen L. Pine; Kevin P. Krueger (Not admitted in IL); Scott Greenberg (Not admitted in IL); Andrew R. Kasnetz; Rodney M. Sharp; Stephen M. Strum; Lyndon P. Sommer; Anthony L. Martin; Teresa D. Bartosiak; Keith D. Price; Anthony Soukenik; Michael E. Bub; Stephen P. Niemira.
Trial and Appellate Practice in Federal and State Courts, Product Liability, Health Law, Medical Malpractice Defense, Class Action Litigation, Employment Law, Banking, Commercial and Corporate Law, Admiralty, Aviation, Insurance, Bankruptcy and Reorganization, Estate Planning and Probate, Real Estate, Family Law.
St. Louis, Missouri Office: 15th Floor, One City Centre. Telephone: 314-231-3332. Telecopier: 314-241-7604.
Carbondale, Illinois Office: Westowne Centre, 2015 West Main, Suite G, 62901. Telephone: 618-351-7200. Toll Free: 866-351-5529. Fax: 618-351-7604.

See Professional Biographies, BELLEVILLE, ILLINOIS

Sant, John Talbot, Jr.(P.C.), (AV) '60 '85 C.674 A.B. L.880 J.D. [Armstrong T.] (⊙St. Louis, MO)
Schaefer, John W. '56 '82 C.201 B.S. L.734 J.D. (adm. in MO; not adm. in IL) 5 Wesley Dr.‡
Schaefer, Richard W., (BV) '50 '83 C.801 M.B.A. L.734 J.D. 6 E. Washington St.
Scherck, Roger L. '35 '59 C&L.910 A.B., J.D. 310 Julia Pl.
Schmitt, William A., (AV) '51 '76 C.927 B.A. L.734 J.D. [Greensfelder,H.&G.]
Schneidewind, David B. '75 '00 C&L.801 B.S., J.D. [Ⓐ Gundlach,L.E.B.&R.]
Schoemaker, Donald K., (BV) '63 '88 C.339 A.B. L.801 J.D. [Greensfelder,H.&G.]
Schooley, Renee E., (BV) '55 '85 C.338 B.S. L.734 J.D. Asst. Pub. Def.
Schooley, William W.
(See Granite City)
Schrader, Mark G., (BV) '55 '82 C.698 B.S.B.A. L.734 J.D. [Jennings,J.&S.]
Schroeder, Kurt S., (BV) '56 '85 C.801 B.S. L.910 J.D. [Mathis,M.R.&G.]
Schuessler, Kenneth J., (BV) '14 '39 C&L.339 A.B., J.D. 525 W. Main St.
Schultz, Raymond K. '62 '88 C&L.900 B.A., J.D. (adm. in MO; not adm. in IL) Asst. Gen. Coun., National Assn. of Govt. Employees
Schultz, Todd M. '74 '00 C.602 B.A. L.339 J.D. [Ⓐ O'Gara,G.&S.]
Schuver, Mark S., (BV) '59 '87 C&L.502 B.A., J.D. [Mathis,M.R.&G.]
Scott, James T., (BV) '65 '92 C.338 B.S. L.734 J.D. 8 E. Washington St.
Scott, Russell K., (AV) '49 '74 C.231 B.A. L.910 J.D. [Greensfelder,H.&G.]
Scrivner, Roger M. '44 '70 C.934 B.A. L.910 J.D. Cir. J.
Seal, Denise Baker, (BV) '73 '98 C.357 B.A. L.588 J.D. [Ⓐ Brown&J.]
Sharp, Rodney M., (AV) '60 '85 C&L.801 B.A., J.D. [Sandberg,P.&v.] (⊙St. Louis, MO)
Sheppard, Royce B., (BV) '21 '48 C&L.910 B.S.B.A., LL.B. 133 Country Club Acres
Shevlin, Dennis W., (BV) '47 '72 C.711 B.A. L.339 J.D. [Cook,S.Y.B.&B.]
Shevlin, Gregory L., (BV) '63 '88 C.1182 B.A. L.900 J.D. [Cook,S.Y.B.&B.]
Shultz, William D., Jr., (BV) '66 '91 C.1182 B.A. L.190 J.D. [Cates,K.B.&S.]
Singley, Emily C. '75 '00 C.69 B.M. L.339 J.D. [Ⓐ Greensfelder,H.&G.]
Skaggs, G. Ethan '66 '92 C.120 B.A. L.801 J.D. [Ⓐ Lewis,R.&F.]
Skinner, Gregory M., (BV) '60 '85 C.602 B.A. L.734 J.D. 4010 N. Illinois St.
Small, Bradley W., (CV) '55 '79 C.801 B.A. L.734 J.D. [Mathis,M.R.&G.]
Smith, Thomas J., (BV) '69 '93 C.502 B.S.B.A. L.734 J.D. [Fox G.] ⊙
Sommer, Lyndon P., (BVⓉ) '64 '92 C&L.801 B.S., J.D. [Sandberg,P.&v.] (⊙St. Louis, MO)
Sophir, Mark D., (P.C.), (AVⓉ) '59 '85 C&L.846 B.A., J.D. [Armstrong T.] (⊙St. Louis, MO)
Soraghan, Thomas C., (AVⓉ) '44 '73 C.502 A.B. L.910 J.D. Asst. Atty. Gen., Atty. Gen. Off.
Soukenik, Anthony, (AVⓉ) '60 '86 C&L.734 B.S.B.A., J.D. [Sandberg,P.&v.] (⊙St. Louis, MO)
Spaccarotella, Marie '— '04 C.477 B.A. L.910 J.D. [Ⓐ Thompson C.]
Speicher, Philip D. '78 '04 C.1257 B.A. L.910 J.D. (adm. in MO; not adm. in IL) [Ⓐ Mathis,M.R.&G.]
Spencer, Jon William '69 '94 C&L.502 B.S., J.D. 8 E. Washington St.
Sprague, Robert J., (BV) '44 '68 C&L.734 B.S., J.D. [Sprague&U.]
Sprague & Urban, (BV) 26 E. Washington St.
Starnes, William B. '72 '98 C.337 B.A. L.339 J.D. Asst. Pub. Def.
Stegman, Mark J., (AV) '57 '82 C.589 B.S. L.734 J.D. [Mathis,M.R.&G.]
Stegmeyer, Charles F. '15 '39 C.339 L.733 LL.B. [Stegmeyer&S.]
Stegmeyer, Charles H., Jr., (BV) '41 '66 C&L.910 B.S.B.A., J.D. [Stegmeyer&S.]
Stegmeyer & Stegmeyer, (BV) 100 S. Charles St.
Steinke, Marvin R. '47 '72 C&L.546 B.A., J.D. Pres. & Gen. Coun., Metro East Title Corp.
Stenger, Ralph T., (BV) '38 '64 C&L.734 B.S., J.D. 312 S. Illinois St.
Sterling, Richard W. '22 '50 C&L.339 B.S., LL.B. 1801 N. Belt W.
Stern, James M. '60 '86 C&L.339 B.S., J.D. Asst. State's Atty.
Stiehl, Harley '— '38 10 Narcissus St.‡
Stiehl, James P., (BV) '43 '67 C.801 B.A. L.910 J.D. 5 Executive Woods Ct.
Stiehl, William D., Jr., (BV) '52 '77 C.880 B.A. L.861 J.D. [Wimmer&S.]
Stine, Kevin J., (AV) '61 '87 C.801 B.S.B.A. L.910 J.D. [Mathis,M.R.&G.]
Storment, Paul M., III, (CV) '63 '91 C.388 B.A. L.734 J.D. [Storment]
Storment Law Office, (CV) 424 S. High St.
Striano-Bates, Lisa R. '64 '89 C.606 B.A. L.734 J.D. (adm. in MO; not adm. in IL) 10 S. Jackson St.‡
Strum, Stephen M., (AV) '63 '88 C.339 B.A. L.734 J.D. [Sandberg,P.&v.] (⊙St. Louis, MO)
Sturgeon, Paul Richard, (BV) '49 '74 C.801 B.A. L.500 J.D. 23 S. First St.
Stutsman, David B., (AV) '29 '53 C&L.339 B.S., LL.B. [Walker&W.]
Sugg, Reed W., (AVⓉ) '52 '78 C.269 B.A. L.880 J.D. [Sandberg,P.&v.] (⊙St. Louis, MO)
Sullivan, Bart C., (AV) '57 '87 C.383 B.B.A. L.734 J.D. [Ⓒ Fox G.] ⊙
Swartwout, Charles J., (BV) '60 '85 C.679 B.S. L.801 J.D. [Gundlach,L.E.B.&R.] ⊙
Tackett, Michael Wade '73 '00 C.1024 B.S. L.910 J.D. [Ⓐ Cates,K.B.&S.]
Taylor, Harvey, Jr. '77 '03 C&L.339 B.A., J.D. [Ⓐ Dunham,B.&L.]
Tedesco, Donald L., (BV) '31 '55 C&L.734 J.D. 211 S. Jackson St.
Teter, Jeanne M., (BV) '52 '83 C.339 B.S. L.801 J.D. Asst. Atty. Gen.
Thomas, Chas. F. '26 '51 C&L.352 B.A., J.D. 511 Springdale Dr.‡
Thompson, Richard W., (BV) '48 '94 C&L.734 B.A., J.D. 120 West Main, Suite 116
Thompson, Rodney W., (AV) '51 '76 C.234 B.S. L.910 J.D. 5111 W. Main St.

Thompson Coburn LLP, (AV)
525 West Main Street, 62222-0730 ⊙
Telephone: 618-277-4700; 314-271-1800 Telecopier: 618-236-3434 For attorney e-mail use: first initial of first name, last name@thompsoncoburn.com, e.g. aallred@thompsoncoburn.com
Email: info@thompsoncoburn.com URL: http://www.thompsoncoburn.com
Partners: Thomas W. Alvey, Jr.; Harlan A. Harla; Thomas E. Jones; Kurt E. Reitz. Associates: Corrine M. Garnhart; Heath H. Hooks; Crystal M. Pipher; Marie Spaccarotella; Erick E. VanDorn.
Admiralty, Appellate Litigation, Bankruptcy, Environmental, Government Contracts, Government, Health Care, Human Resources, Intellectual Property, Litigation, Municipal, Product Liability, Railroad, Real Estate, Toxic Tort.

(This Listing Continued)

Thompson Coburn LLP (Continued)

Representative Clients: General Motors Corp.; Harcros Pigments, Inc.; The Kilian Corp.; Norfolk Southern Corp.; Peabody Coal Co.
St. Louis, Missouri Office: One US Bank Plaza. Telephone: 314-552-6000. Telecopier: 314-552-7000.
Washington, D.C. Office: 1909 K Street N.W., Suite 600. Telephone: 202-585-6900. Telecopier: 202-585-6969.

See Professional Biographies, BELLEVILLE, ILLINOIS

Throckmartin, Chi-yong, (CV) '73 '98 C.338 B.S. L.801 J.D. [Ⓐ Donovan,R.N.&J.]
Tillery, Katherine J., (BV) '52 '77 C.337 B.A. L.734 J.D. [Ⓒ Korein T.]
Trefts, Steven A. '73 '99 C.999 B.S. L.190 J.D. [Ⓐ Cates,K.B.&S.]
Trelz, Therese Rolufs, (AV) '59 '87 C.893 B.A. L.734 J.D. [Armstrong T.] (⊙St. Louis, MO)
Tucker, Dana W. '63 '95 C.502 B.S. L.734 J.D. (adm. in MO; not adm. in IL) [Fox G.] ⊙
Uhl, George A., (BV) '54 '87 C.339 B.S. L.910 J.D. [Greensfelder,H.&G.] ⊙
Unger, Lucy T., (AVⓉ) '64 '89 C.435 B.A. L.910 J.D. [Williams V.&S.] (⊙St. Louis, MO)
Urban, Donald W., (BV) '53 '79 C.801 B.A. L.910 J.D. [Sprague&U.]
Vale, Thomas H. '57 '84 C.225 B.A. L.801 J.D. Asst. Atty. Gen.
VanDorn, Erick E. '— '98 C.234 B.S. L.339 J.D. [Ⓐ Thompson C.]
Vassen, P.C., (AV) 1801 North Belt West
Vassen, John A., (BV) '56 '85 C.801 B.S. L.734 J.D. [Ⓐ Vassen]
Vassen, John J., (AV) '33 '62 C.339 B.S. L.734 J.D. [Vassen]
Veath, Beth Kamp, (AV) '57 '83 C.339 B.S. L.801 J.D. [Brown&J.]
Vetter, Roger L., (BV) '45 '73 C.430 B.A. L.734 J.D. [R.L.Vetter]
Vetter, Roger L, P.C., (BV) 100 W. Main St.
Vick, Bruce S., (BV) '51 '76 C&L.734 B.A., J.D. P.O. Box 23631
Vick, L. Kevin, (AV) '63 '88 C&L.910 A.B., J.D. [Greensfelder,H.&G.] ⊙
Virtel, James J., (AV) '44 '69 C.177 B.A. L.734 J.D. [Armstrong T.] (⊙Edwardsville, IL; St. Louis, MO)
von Gontard, Peter, (AV) '48 '73 C&L.502 B.S., J.D. [Sandberg,P.&v.] (⊙St. Louis, MO)
von Stamwitz, George M., (AV) '57 '82 C.860 B.A. L.734 J.D. [Armstrong T.] (⊙St. Louis, MO)
Wagner, Michael L., (BV) '72 '97 C.339 B.S. L.734 J.D. [Hinshaw&C.]

Walker & Williams, Professional Corporation, (AV)
4343 West Main Street, 62226 ⊙
Telephone: 618-274-1000; 277-1000 Telecopier: 618-233-1637
Email: waw@wawpc.net URL: http://www.lawyers.com/walkerwilliams
Ralph D. Walker (1906-1988); Wayne P. Williams (1904-1990); John B. Gunn (1933-2001); David B. Stutsman; Donald J. Dahlmann; Dale L. Bode; James C. Cook; Paul P. Waller III;—Leslie Offergeld; Christian Cagas; J. Kenneth Graham, III.
General Trial and Appellate Practice in Federal and State Courts, including Automobile, Environmental, Civil Rights, Products Liability, Fire and Insurance Law, Railroad Defense, Governmental Liability, Professional Liability and Third Party Insurance Defense.
Representative Clients: Allstate Insurance Co.; Alton and Southern Railway Co.; Consolidated Rail Corp.; CSX Transportation, Inc.; Farmers Insurance Group; Firemen's Fund American Insurance Cos.; Madison Mutual Insurance Co.; St. Louis Southwestern Railway Co.; Scottsdale Insurance Co.; Union Pacific Railroad.

See Professional Biographies, BELLEVILLE, ILLINOIS

Waller, Paul P., III, (BV) '55 '80 C.602 B.A. L.734 J.D. [Walker&W.]
Waller, Paul P., Jr., (BV) '24 '49 C.802 L.734 J.D. 211 S. Jackson St.
Waltrip, T. Bradford, (BV) '55 '87 C.234 B.A. L.801 J.D. [Mathis,M.R.&G.]
Warchol, Jerome S., Jr. '79 '04 C&L.734 B.S., J.D. [Ⓐ Cates,K.B.&S.]
Weaver, Thomas B., (P.C.), (AV) '51 '78 C.228 B.A. L.734 J.D. [Armstrong T.] (⊙St. Louis, MO)
Weihl, Donald E., (AV) '37 '61 C&L.339 A.B., J.D. [Greensfelder,H.&G.]
Weilmuenster, J. Michael, (BV) '61 '87 C.880 B.A. L.734 J.D. 3201 W. Main Street
Welch, Julia Buser, (BV) '44 '91 C.734 B.S. L.339 J.D. 12 Persimmon Rdg.
Weller, Stanley R., (CV) '69 '98 C.966 B.S. L.801 J.D. [Ⓐ Dixon&J.]
Wells, Robert E., Jr., (AV) '49 '74 C.645 B.A. L.734 J.D. 105 N. Illinois
Westhoff, Peter M. '69 '02 C.1347 B.B.A. L.986 J.D. [Ⓐ Amelung,W.&W.] ⊙
Wharton, Milton S. '46 '75 C.801 B.S. L.209 J.D. Cir. J.
Wigginton, Stephen R., (BV) '63 '88 C.801 B.S. L.734 J.D. 3201 W. Main St.
Williams, James R., (BV) '65 '90 C&L.801 B.S., J.D. [Williams,C.&Assoc.]
Williams, Michael S., (BV) '48 '80 C&L.734 A.B., J.D. CO Div. of Admin. Hearing
Williams, Ronda F. '71 '02 C.302 B.S. L.734 J.D. [Ⓐ Fox G.] ⊙
Williams, Caponi & Associates, P.C., (BV) 30 East Main Street

Williams Venker & Sanders LLC, (AVⓉ)
23 South First Street, 62220 ⊙
Telephone: 314-345-5000 Fax: 314-345-5055 URL: http://www.lawyers.com/wvslaw
Email: wvs@wvslaw.com URL: http://www.wvslaw.com
Member of Firm: Lucy T. Unger.
Aviation, Business Litigation, Employment Discrimination Litigation, Environmental Litigation, FELA, Health Care Litigation, Insurance Defense, Labor and Employment, Maritime, Medical Malpractice Defense, Occupational Disease Litigation, Premises Liability Defense, Product Liability Defense, Railroad Litigation, Toxic Torts, Transportation Litigation.
St. Louis, Missouri Office: 10 South Broadway, Suite 1600, 63102. Phone: 314-345-5000. Fax: 314-345-5055.
Edwardsville, Illinois Office: 111 E. Vandalia Street, Suite 3, 62025. Phone: 618-659-9100. Fax: 618-659-9125.

See Professional Biographies, BELLEVILLE, ILLINOIS

Wilson, Susan Parnell, (BV) '50 '85 C.291 B.A. L.734 J.D.
14 South Second Street, 62220
Telephone: 618-235-1600 Fax: 618-235-1617
Email: susanwilsonlaw@norcom2000.com URL: http://www.susanpwilson.com
Child Custody, Child Support, Divorce, Family Law, Paternity.

See Professional Biographies, BELLEVILLE, ILLINOIS

Wiltsie, Timothy S., (CV) '63 '90 C.276 B.S.F.S. L.597 J.D.
120 West Main Street, Suite 207, 62220
Telephone: 618-235-5750 Fax: 618-257-9300
Email: wiltsielaw@peaknet.net URL: http://www.wiltsielaw.com
Civil Trial and Appellate Practice, Family Law, Divorce, Child Support, Child Custody, Business Litigation, Business Transactions, Real Estate, Personal Injury, Wills, Trusts and Estates.

See Professional Biographies, BELLEVILLE, ILLINOIS

Wimmer, Richard S., (BV) '46 '82 C.934 B.A. L.734 J.D. 163 Pineywoods Dr.
Wimmer, William L., III, (BV) '42 '70 C.934 B.A. L.734 J.D. [Wimmer&S.]
Wimmer & Stiehl, P.C., (BV) 2 Park Place Professional Centre
Wulff, Robert J., (AV) '61 '86 C.502 B.S.E.E. L.734 J.D. [Amelung,W.&W.] ⊙
Wuller, Ransom P., (BV) '54 '79 C&L.734 B.S.B.A., J.D. [Freeark,H.M.D.W.C.&M.]
Wuller, Robert G., Jr., (BV) '47 '72 C.602 A.B. L.734 J.D. [Neville,R.&W.]
Ybarra, David W. '71 '00 C.586 B.A. L.339 J.D. [Ⓐ Greensfelder,H.&G.]
Young, Eric C., (AV) '50 '75 C.1182 B.A. L.339 J.D. [Dunham,B.&L.] ⊙
Ysursa, Bernard J., (BV) '44 '68 C.602 A.B. L.734 J.D. [Cook,S.Y.B.&B.]
Zimmer, Patricia A., (BV) '53 '92 C&L.734 B.S., J.D. [Ripplinger&Z.]
Zittel, Matthew C., (CV) '71 '97 C.465 B.B.A L.801 J.D. [Ⓐ Neville,R.&W.]

BELLWOOD, 20,535, *Cook Co.*

Amenta, Mark Leonard .... '57 '83 C.234 B.A. L.221 J.D. [M.L.Amenta]
Amenta, Mark L. .... 413 N. Mannheim Rd., Ste. 4
Bruder, Elizabeth Martens .... '38 '80 C.238 B.A. L.365 J.D. 119 50th Ave.
Brunner, Joseph M. .... '56 '82 C.209 B.A. L.365 J.D. Corp. Coun., Sleepeck Printing Co.
Cacchillo, Michaelle Greco '70 '95
C.473 B.S. L.424 J.D. Shamrock Scientific Specialty Systems
Keller, George R. .... '11 '38 C.976 B.A. L.146 LL.B. 815 25th Ave.‡
Nannini, Kenneth J. .... '48 '78 4219 Saint Charles Rd.

BELVIDERE, * 20,820, *Boone Co.*

Abate & Smith
(See Rockford)

Babb, David R. .... '28 '60 C.72 B.S. L.145 J.D. 200 S. Main St.‡

Brody, Steven J., & Associates, LTD
(See Crystal Lake)

Cicero & France, A Professional Corporation
(See Rockford)

Conboy, Patrick M. .... '44 '69 C.589 B.A. L.339 J.D. United Auto Wkrs. Union

Cwynar, Daniel A.
(See Rockford)

Doherty, J. Mark, (BV) .... '56 '82 C.1247 B.A. L.339 J.D. 1901 Union Ave.

Franks, Gerkin & McKenna, P.C., The Law Firm of
(See Marengo)

Freek, William S. .... '19 '48 C&L.339 B.A., LL.B. 618 S. State St.
Grubb, Gerald F. .... '47 '75 C.589 B.S. L.365 J.D. Assoc. Cir. J.
Havrilesko, Michael K. .... '46 '78 C.647 B.A. L.365 J.D. [Havrilesko]
Havrilesko Law Office .... 1151 Barberry Lane
Hetzler, Stanley A., (BV) .... '39 '64 C&L.585 B.S.B.A., J.D. 130 S. State St.
Kennedy, J. Todd .... '45 '72 C.966 B.S. L.339 J.D. 601 N. Main St.
Larson, Donald B., (BV) .... '53 '87 C.338 B.S. L.589 J.D. [D.B.Larson]
Larson, Kyle I. E., (BV) .... '56 '81 C&L.339 B.A., J.D. 107 1st St.
Larson, Laurie W., Jr., (AV) .... '24 '50 C.337 B.A. L.477 LL.B. 94 Andrews Dr.‡
Larson, Donald B., P.C., (BV) .... 215 S. State St.
Lateer, James W. '48 '73 C&L.339 B.S., J.D.
(adm. in MN; not adm. in IL) St. Joseph's Hosp.
Loos, Deborah S., (CV) .... '53 '91 C.589 B.A. L.1187 J.D. [Loos,D.]
Loos, Deborah, (CV) .... 130 South State Street, Suite 210
Maville, John H., Law Office of, (BV) .... '42 '67 C&L.339 J.D. 600 South State Street
Norton, Daniel J. .... '43 '73 C.338 B.S. L.365 J.D. 601 S. State St.

O'Brien, Healy & Zuba
(See Rockford)

O'Sullivan, Dennis P., (CV) .... '43 '73 C.177 B.A. L.190 J.D. 618 S. State St.
Penniman, Alford R. .... '35 '59 C.118 B.A. L.145 J.D. Assoc. Cir. J.

Pollock, Meyers, Eicksteadt & Pulak, Ltd.
(See Marengo)

Popp, Charles G., (BV) .... '57 '87 C&L.589 B.S., J.D. [C.G.Popp]
Popp, Charles G., P.C., (BV) .... 215 S. State St.
Quittschreiber, Bradley J. .... '63 '94 C.927 L.1148 J.D. 215 S. State St.
Ramon, Lois Cannell, (BV) .... '49 '74 C.234 B.S. L.339 J.D. [Tobin&R.]

Rehberg, Curt P.
(See Crystal Lake)

Repay, Henry, Law Offices of, (CV) '63 '88 C&L.424 B.A., J.D.
405 1/2 South State Street, 61008-3706
Telephone: 815-547-3369 Fax: 815-544-5429
Email: repaylawfirm@ithink2.net URL: http://www.lawyers.com/repaylawfirm
General Practice, Real Estate, Commercial Real Estate, Residential Real Estate, Mortgages, Personal Bankruptcy, Consumer Bankruptcy, Debtor Bankruptcy, Chapter 7, Chapter 13, Nonprofit and Charitable Organizations, Guardianship, Adoptions.
See Professional Biographies, BELVIDERE, ILLINOIS

Russell, Roger T., (CV) .... '46 '76 C.801 B.A. L.796 J.D. State's Atty.
Sewell, Charles T., (CV) .... '48 '74 C.339 B.S. L.146 J.D. 215 S. State St.
Silver, Allen .... '27 '58 C.477 B.B.A. L.966 J.D. 405 1/2 S. State St.
Smith, Tricia .... '72 '97 C.98 B.A. L.352 J.D. 530 S. State St.‡

Szymanski Koroll Litigation Group, The
(See Rockford)

Tobin, Curtis R., II, (AV) .... '41 '65 C.340 B.S. L.339 J.D. [Tobin&R.]

Tobin & Ramon, (AV)
530 South State Street Suite 200, 61008
Telephone: 815-544-0316 Fax: 815-544-4398
Email: tobinramon@mwci.net
Members of Firm: Curtis R. Tobin, II; Lois Cannell Ramon.
General Practice. Business Litigation. Probate, School Law, Real Estate, Estate and Business Planning, Zoning and Family Law.
See Professional Biographies, BELVIDERE, ILLINOIS

BENLD, 1,604, *Macoupin Co.*

Denby, W. W., (AV) .... '31 '61 C.339 B.A. L.597 J.D. [Denby,M.B.&D.] (⊙Carlinville)
Denby, Meno, Bloomer & Denby, (AV) .... 209 E. Central (⊙Carlinville, Staunton)
Meno, J. Richard, (BV) .... '48 '73 C&L.734 B.S., J.D. [Denby,M.B.&D.] ⊙

BENSENVILLE, 20,703, *Cook & DuPage Cos.*

Bellgrau, Scott Eugene, Law Offices of '76 '00
C.339 B.A. L.910 J.D. 229 W. Grand Ave, Ste. X
Cohen, Alan .... '59 '84 C&L.472 B.B.A., J.D. Aaron Equip. Co.
Freeman, Thom J., III .... '45 '71 C.339 B.S. L.383 J.D. 145 S. Center St.
Fuentes-Smith, Myrna G. .... '— '91 C.339 B.A. L.352 J.D. 20 S. York Rd.
Garfinkel, Norman J. .... '27 '51 C.46 L.365 LL.B. 1100 Industrial Dr.
Glass, Michael Scott .... '72 '98 C.978 B.A. L.1398 J.D. Morre-Tec Midwest, Inc.
Green, Kenneth .... '54 '80 C.801 B.A. L.221 J.D. 877 Supreme Dr.
Hunt, Thomas C. .... '60 '85 C.424 B.A. L.365 J.D. 1035 S. York
Kaiser, Daniel J. .... '61 '86 C&L.424 B.A., J.D. 1035 S. York Rd.
Kiser, Thomas J. .... '59 '92 C.436 B.S. L.209 J.D. Gen. Coun., Lifelink Corp.
Kupisch, Lance W. .... '47 '75 C.338 B.A. L.862 J.D. 201 N. Church Rd.
Moran, William J. .... '27 '58 C.46 B.S. L.209 J.D. 755 Rte. 83
Morris, Dawn Marie .... '56 '81 C.339 B.A. L.209 J.D. 837 W. Green
Northrop, John L. .... '31 '75 C.209 M.B.A. L.597 J.D. 1021 Daniel Dr.
O'Connor, Cornelius J. .... '23 '58 C.436 B.S. L.424 J.D. 618 W. McLean Ct.‡
Odeh, Elaine .... '— '91 C.338 B.A. L.209 J.D. 16 East Green Street
Parrino, Jack L. .... '35 '61 C&L.209 B.A., J.D. 2 S. York Rd.

Prato & Associates, P.C.
(See Oak Brook)

Riley, William E. .... '22 '49 C.424 B.S. L.209 J.D. 128 Daniel Dr.
Scanlon, Brian Patrick .... '66 '01 C.927 B.S. L.365 J.D. 16 East Green Street
Sethna, Darius .... '73 '00 C.424 B.S. L.365 J.D. 1035 S. York Rd.
Smith, Myrna G. .... '62 '91 C.339 B.A. L.352 J.D. 2 S. York Road
Storto, Joseph P. .... '44 '72 C.424 B.B.A. L.146 J.D. 100 W. Green St.
Swanson, Leigh J. .... '55 '79 C.1101 B.A. L.146 J.D. 3N646 Oak Ln.★

BENTON, * 6,880, *Franklin Co.*

Barrett, Twomey, Broom, Hughes & Hoke, LLP
(See Carbondale)

Bonan, Donna L., (BV) .... '54 '81 C.337 B.A. L.801 J.D. 301 W. Main St.
Carr, Michael C., (BV) .... '51 '79 C&L.801 B.A., J.D. Asst. U.S. Atty.
Chullen, John L. .... '46 '86 C&L.801 B.S., J.D. 903 W. Washington St.
Coffel, Ron D., (BV) .... '62 '89 C.801 B.A. L.589 J.D. 502 West Public Square
Cox, A. Courtney, (AV) .... '52 '82 C.340 B.M. L.801 J.D. [Hart&H.]

Craig & Craig
(See Mount Vernon)

Desmond, Leo T. .... '50 '77 C.357 B.S. L.209 J.D. Assoc. Cir. J.

Feirich/Mager/Green/Ryan
(See Carbondale)

Foreman, James L. .... '27 '52 C&L.339 B.S., J.D. U.S. Dist. J.
Frazier, Connie J. .... '64 '93 C.340 B.S L.801 J.D. Law Clk.
Frazier, Philip M. .... '51 '80 C.339 B.S. L.801 J.D. U.S. Mag.
Garavalia, David B., (BV) .... '54 '80 C.339 B.A. L.801 J.D. [D.Garavalia]
Garavalia, David, (BV) .... 417 N. Main St.
Giacone, Ronald J., Law Office of, (BV) '44 '69
C.801 B.A. L.365 J.D. C.A. Jackson Bldg.
Gilbert, J. Phil .... '49 '74 C.339 B.S. L.424 J.D. U.S. Dist. J.
Hart, Murphy C., (BV) .... '57 '83 C.234 B.A. L.801 J.D. [Hart&H.]
Hart, Richard O., (AV) .... '27 '54 C.339 A.B. L.910 J.D. [Hart&H.]

Hart and Hart, (AV)
602 West Public Square, P.O. Box 937, 62812-0937
Telephone: 618-435-8123 Telecopier: 618-435-2962
URL: http://www.harthart.com
William H. Hart (1862-1941); William W. Hart (1894-1968); Marion M. Hart (1896-1964); William W. Hart, Jr. (1925-1996); Richard O. Hart; Murphy C. Hart; A. Courtney Cox.
General Trial and Appellate Practice in State and Federal Courts. Probate, Trust, Real Estate Deeds and Title Insurance, Bankruptcy (Creditors), Traffic, Banking, Business, Commercial and Corporation Law and Creditor Collections, Employment Law.
Representative Clients: State Bank of Whittington; Credit Bureau Systems, Inc.; Walgreen Co.; Asset Acceptance, LLC; Old National Bank; Canter-Jones Lumber.
See Professional Biographies, BENTON, ILLINOIS

Hickman, Joseph W., (BV) .... '17 '42 C.339 L.734 LL.B. 1407 N. DuQuoin Rd.
Hill, Robert S. .... '23 '49 C&L.339 B.S., J.D. Ret. Cir. J.
Hundley, John T., (AV) .... '48 '79 C.339 B.S. L.209 J.D. [T.Sharp] ⊙
Jenkins, Elmer, (AV) .... '20 '49 C&L.339 LL.B. 123 E. Main St.
Lacey, Pamela Sue, (BV) .... '53 '82 C&L.801 B.A., J.D. [P.Lacey]
Lacey, Pamela, Attorney at Law, (BV) .... 123 E. Main
Lewis, Loren P. .... '42 '67 C&L.339 B.A., J.D. Cir. J.
Lewis, Robert W., (AV) .... '49 '74 C.339 B.A. L.259 J.D. P.O. Box 485

McMahon, Berger, Hanna, Linihan, Cody & McCarthy, A Professional Corporation
(See Collinsville)

Meehan, William F., (BV) .... '30 '59 C.801 A.B. L.880 LL.B. 307 W. Webster St.
Miller, Robert L., (BV) .... '57 '83 C.597 B.A. L.339 J.D. 12172 State Hwy. 37
Owens, Evan L., (CV) .... '68 '93 C.339 B.A. L.734 J.D. 10353 North Main Street
Popit, Peter E., (BV) .... '51 '78 C.602 B.A. L.801 J.D. [Troutt P.&W.]
Quindry, Charles L. .... '40 '65 C.234 B.S. L.383 J.D. Cir. J.
Rowland, Michael A., (BV) .... '53 '82 C.465 B.A. L.801 J.D. Asst. State's Atty.
Sharp, Terrell Lee, (AV) .... '44 '73 C&L.339 B.S., J.D. [T.Sharp] ⊙

Sharp, Terry, P.C., Law Office of, (AV)
105 North Main Street, 62812 ⊙
Mailing Address: 1115 Harrison Street, P.O. Box 906, Mount Vernon, IL 62864
Telephone: 618-435-5109 Fax: 618-242-1170
Email: law@lotsharp.com URL: http://www.lawyers.com/tsharp
Terrell Lee Sharp; John T. Hundley.
Bankruptcy, Creditor's Rights, Commercial, Banking, Real Estate, Corporate, Probate and Estate Planning Law. No small collections.
Mount Vernon, Illinois Office: 1115 Harrison Street, P. O. Box 906. Telephone: 618-242-0246. Telecopier: 618-242-1170.
See Professional Biographies, BENTON, ILLINOIS

Stallman, Karen L. .... '56 '82 C.347 B.S. L.801 J.D. Law Clk. to U.S. Mag.
Troutt, Jeff, (AV) .... '39 '69 C.801 B.A. L.339 J.D. [Troutt P.&W.]

Troutt Popit & Warner, P.C., (AV)
105 North Main Street, P.O. Box 548, 62812
Telephone: 618-439-9427; 438-2200 Fax: 618-435-3916
Email: bentonlaw@onecliq.net URL: http://www.lawyers.com/trouttalexander
Jeff Troutt; Peter E. Popit; Edwina Daum Warner.
General Civil and Criminal Practice in all State and Federal Courts. Trials and Appeals. Personal Injury, Worker's Compensation, Criminal/Traffic Defense, Municipal Law, Probate Cases and Wills, Real Estate, Collections, Creditor Litigation, Adoptions, Family Law and Mediations.
See Professional Biographies, BENTON, ILLINOIS

Vantrease, E. Kyle .... '51 '76 C.388 B.A. L.146 J.D. Cir. J.
Warner, Edwina Daum, (BV) .... '48 '81 C.338 B.S. L.836 J.D. [Troutt P.&W.]

BERKELEY, 5,245, *Cook Co.*

Malin, Charles J. .... '17 '42 L.209 J.D. 5544 St. Charles Rd.
Zikic, Gordon .... '59 '84 C&L.209 B.A., J.D. 1501 Harding Ave.

BERWYN, 54,016, *Cook Co.*

Berkes, Eugene J. .... '56 '83 C.339 B.A. L.209 J.D. [E.Berkes]
Berkes, Eugene .... 6904 W. Cermak Rd.
Berkos, Michael J. .... '24 '50 L.146 LL.B. 6504 W. Cermak
Bosworth, Paula R. .... '50 '88 C&L.209 B.A., J.D. 1248 S. Maple Avenue
Boucek, George W. .... '12 '34 C.999 L.146 J.D. 6915 W. Cermak Rd.‡
Brown, Edward G. .... '52 '80 C.750 B.A. L.589 J.D. 1807 Harvey
Cheely, Robert A., Law Office .... '— '81 C.424 B.A. L.589 J.D. 6446 W. Cermak Rd.
Como, Robert Michael .... '60 '85 C.339 B.A. L.146 J.D. 1618 Kenilworth Ave.
DeRose, Louis .... '51 '90 C.679 B.S.M.E. L.365 J.D. 1434 Lombard Avenue
DeStefano, Robert Anthony .... '60 '88 C.339 B.A. L.365 J.D. [R.A.DeStefano&Assoc.]
DeStefano, Robert A., and Associates, P.C. .... 6547 Cermak Rd., Ste. LL1
Goergen, Jerome J. .... '55 '81 C.145 B.A. L.365 J.D. 3306 S. Grove
Gribben, Thomas E. .... '48 '75 C.326 B.B.A. L.365 J.D. [Lanzillotti,G.&M.]
Hummel, Paul M., (BV) .... '46 '80 C.339 B.S. L.365 J.D. 1423 S. Scoville Ave.

Jakala, Stanley H. ....'26 '57 C.424 A.B. L.597 J.D. 3219 Maple Ave.
Kempe, Enid L. ....'49 '78 C&L.209 B.A., J.D. 6915 W. Cermak Rd.
Kocurek, Richard A. ....'56 '81 C.209 B.S. L.365 J.D. 3239 S. Grove Ave.
Lanzillotti, Joseph J. ....'30 '58 C.707 B.A. L.209 J.D. Mayor [Lanzillotti,G.&M.]
Lanzillotti, Gribben & Marchuk ....3417 S. Harlem Ave.
Leuck, Matthias J. ....'44 '67 C.602 B.B.A. L.424 J.D. 2318 Elmwood Ave.
Liewald, Lisa H. ....'53 '87 C.700 B.A. L.146 J.D. 6904 W. Cermak Rd.
Lovero, Robert J. ....'55 '81 C.424 B.S. L.589 J.D. City Pros.
Marchuk, Robert C. ....'48 '74 C.504 B.A. L.424 J.D. [Lanzillotti,G.&M.]
McShane, John David ....'51 '87 C.339 B.A. L.365 J.D. [J.D.McShane]
McShane, John D. ....6904 W. Cermak
Naughton, John A. ....'47 '77 C.209 B.S.C. L.365 J.D. 6514 W. Cermak Rd.
Oplatka, William ....'10 '33 6921 Riverside Dr.‡
Ostendorp, Louis A. ....'20 '64 C&L.209 B.S., J.D. 3421 Maple Ave.‡
Pena, Rogelio ....'59 '85 C.339 B.A. L.365 J.D. 2337 S. Grove Ave.
Peters, Marshall F. ....'48 '75 C.424 B.A. L.365 J.D. 2709 Clinton Ave.
Petlak, Elliott E. ....'65 '90 C.128 B.A. L.209 J.D. 6717 31st St.

Prato & Associates, P.C.
(See Oak Brook)

Rock, Richard A. ....'52 '77 C.589 B.A. L.365 J.D. 7112 Cermak Rd., 2nd Fl.
Salerno, Alexander M. ....'61 '86 C.801 B.A. L.209 J.D. 6447 Cermak Rd., 2nd Fl.
Toman, John A. ....'41 '67 C.597 B.A. L.209 J.D. 6924 W. Cermak Rd.

Vitale, Michael J., The Law Offices of '50 '80 C.424 B.A. L.589 J.D.
6332 W. 26th Street, 60402
Telephone: 708-795-0055 Fax: 708-795-0059
Email: mvitale1@sbcglobal.net URL: http://www.michaelvitalelaw.com
Family Law, Child Support, Domestic Relations, Divorce, Criminal Law, Felonies, Driving While Intoxicated.
See Professional Biographies, BERWYN, ILLINOIS

Vlach, G. Robert ....'39 '86 C.209 B.S. L.146 J.D. 6904 W. Cermak Rd.
Zitnik, Edwin J. ....'22 '50 C&L.209 LL.B. 6735 Cermak Rd.

BETHALTO, 9,507, *Madison Co.*

Balsters, Kenneth E., (BV) ....'51 '77 C.339 B.S. L.801 J.D. [Balsters&H.]
Balsters and Hinrichs, (BV) ....476 S. Prairie
Grammer, Susan F. ....'50 '82 C.339 B.S. L.910 J.D. 2 Terminal Drive
Hinrichs, Timothy C., (CV) ....'52 '91 C.801 B.A. L.734 J.D. [Balsters&H.]
Virgin, David A. ....'50 '79 C&L.801 B.S., J.D. 202 South Walnut
Woelfel, John ....'60 '94 C.801 B.S. L.734 J.D. 516 Oak Street

BETHANY, 1,369, *Moultrie Co.*

Scott, A. Jay, (BV) ....'61 '86 C&L.339 A.B., J.D. 107 E. Main St.
Scott, Jacques W. ....'22 '51 C.234 B.S. L.339 J.D. 107 E. Main St.

BLANDINSVILLE, 762, *McDonough Co.*

Evans, Stephen G. ....'— '72 C.337 B.A. L.339 J.D. 2090 N. County Road 2900
Rogers, Susan K. ....'57 '81 C.927 B.S. L.339 J.D. R.R. 1★

BLOOMINGDALE, 21,675, *DuPage Co.*

Baugher, Leasa J. ....'63 '02 C.1183 B.S. L.365 J.D. [L.J.Baugher]

Baugher, Leasa J., Ltd., Law Offices of
125 East Lake Street, Suite 304, 60108
Telephone: 630-529-2050 Fax: 630-529-2051
Email: lbaugher@baugherlaw.com URL: http://www.baugherlaw.com
Leasa J. Baugher.
Estate Planning, Elder Law, Wills and Trusts, Powers of Attorney, Probate and Trust Administration, Real Estate, Employee Benefits (ERISA).
See Professional Biographies, BLOOMINGDALE, ILLINOIS

Cantore, Harold A., (BV) ....'06 '40 L.146 LL.B. [Cantore&C.]
Cantore, Harold A. ....'41 '70 [Cantore&C.]
Cantore, Preston H. ....'45 '70 C.927 B.A. L.339 J.D. [Cantore&C.]
Cantore & Cantore, (BV) ....56 Castle Rock Ln.
Civinelli, Ronald R., (AV) ....'42 '68 C.221 B.S. L.365 J.D. 181 S. Bloomingdale Rd.
Deneufbourg, Daniel J., (AV) '62 '87
C.734 B.S. L.209 J.D. Sr. Intell. Prop. Coun., CTS Corp. (Pat.)
Doerr, Richard F. ....'42 '73 C.707 B.A. L.910 J.D. 123 E. Lake St.
Eland, Terry P., (BV) ....'46 '73 C.679 B.S.I.E. L.424 J.D. 181 S. Bloomingdale Rd.
Fakes, Arthur, (AV) ....'45 '76 C.1183 B.A. L.209 J.D. [A.Fakes]
Fakes, Arthur, P.C., (AV) ....107 South Third Street, Suite Three
Giacobbe, Thomas M., Attorney at Law, (BV) '51 '79
C.750 B.A. L.1151 J.D. 181 S. Bloomingdale Rd., Ste. 103
Giagnorio, Joseph D., (BV) ....'52 '78 C&L.209 B.A., J.D. [Giagnorio&R.]
Giagnorio & Robertelli, Ltd., (AV) ....130 S. Bloomingdale Rd.
Gienko, James R. ....'47 '75 C.589 B.S. L.365 J.D. [J.R.Gienko&Assoc.]
Gienko, James R., and Associates, Ltd. ....121 Fairfield Way, Suite 100
Gourdin, Deborah T. '56 '81 C.602 B.A. L.280 J.D.
(adm. in SC; not adm. in IL) 1 Bloomingdale Pl.‡
Grady, Brian A., Law Offices of ....'67 '92 C&L.589 B.S., J.D. 125 S. Bloomingdale Rd.
Hovde, Michael D., Jr. ....'— '94 C&L.801 B.A., J.D. 107 3rd St., Ste. 3
Keller, John D. ....'42 '70 C.927 B.S. L.365 J.D. [J.D.Keller&Assoc.]
Keller, John D., & Associates, Ltd., (BV) ....125 S. Bloomingdale Ave.
Klein, Timothy J., Law Office ....'56 '81 C.182 B.A. L.209 J.D. 290 Springfield Dr.
Kola, Isuf ....'— '92 C.424 B.A. L.46 J.D. [Kola&M.]
Kola & Miceli, P.C. ....181 S. Bloomingdale Road, Suite 104
Lawrence, Larry S. ....'48 '82 C.339 B.S. L.209 J.D. 109 Fairfield Way, Ste. 304

Martucci, Gregory J., P.C., Law Office of
(See Roselle)

Mevorah, Steven H., & Associates '54 '79
C.1139 B.S. L.589 J.D. 123 E. Lake Street (☉Lombard)
Miceli, Vincent M. ....'— '95 C.98 B.S. L.1000 J.D. [Kola&M.]
Morrisroe, Michael J., (BV) ....'60 '86 C.424 B.A. L.209 J.D. [M.J.Morrisroe,Sr.]
Morrisroe, Michael J., Ltd., (BV) ....114 S. Bloomingdale Rd.
O'Connor, Robert J. ....'56 '89 C&L.589 B.S., J.D. 125 S. Crandon Court

Prescott, Warren, Law Offices of '51 '78 C.339 B.A. L.365 J.D.
181 S. Bloomingdale Road, Suite 103, 60108
Telephone: 630-924-8052 Fax: 630-924-8057
Email: prescott@lawyer.com URL: http://www.livingrevocabletrusts.com
Estate Planning, Probate and Wills, Real Estate.
See Professional Biographies, BLOOMINGDALE, ILLINOIS

Quinn, John M., (BV) ....'66 '93 C.879 B.S. L.209 J.D. [J.M.Quinn&Assoc.]

Quinn, John M., & Associates, Ltd., (BV)
125 South Bloomingdale Road, Suite 11, 60108-1216
Telephone: 630-529-2000 Toll Free: 877-NO-WALKIN Fax: 630-894-2528 URL: http://www.jmqlaw.com
Email: drive@jmqlaw.com URL: http://www.lawyers.com/jmqlaw

(This Listing Continued)

Quinn, John M., & Associates, Ltd. (Continued)
John M. Quinn.
Language: Spanish.
Drivers License Suspension, Administrative Hearings, Driving While Intoxicated, Criminal Law, Traffic Violations, Criminal Defense, Misdemeanors.
See Professional Biographies, BLOOMINGDALE, ILLINOIS

Robertelli, Vincent, (AV) ....'53 '78 C.1100 B.A. L.146 J.D. [Giagnorio&R.]
Schlosser, Bernard A. ....'49 '77 C.927 B.A. L.365 J.D. 181 S. Bloomingdale Rd., Ste. 103
Waghorne, John E., (BV) ....'31 '60 C.46 B.S. L.209 J.D. 201 E. Army Trail Rd.
Wicks, Robert D. ....'34 '70 C.1016 B.S.B.A. L.209 J.D. Sales Rep., West Publishing‡

BLOOMINGTON, * 64,808, *McLean Co.*

Aaberg, Richard E. '— '53 C&L.494 B.S., J.D.
(adm. in MN; not adm. in IL) 15 Lake Pointe Ct.‡
Abbott, Jeffrey T. ....'60 '88 C.340 B.A. L.910 J.D. [Ⓐ Johnson]
Alexander, Joelle Belinda ....'69 '01 C.98 B.A. L.801 J.D. Atty., State Farm Ins.
Allison, William A., (AV) ....'41 '65 C&L.339 B.A., J.D. [Allison&M.]
Allison & Mosby-Scott, (AV) ....202 North Prospect, Suite 204
Ambrose, Joseph M., (AV) ....'57 '82 C.339 B.S. L.1119 J.D. [Ⓒ Costigan&W.]
Anderson, James L., (AV) ....'36 '61 C&L.339 B.S., LL.B. [Anderson,H.Q.&S.]
Anderson, Harmon, Quick & Stumpf, (AV) ....1701 Towanda Avenue
Angles, Francisco ....'— '90 1102 Hollyridge Cir.
Ansbro, James M. ....'— '85 C.209 B.A. L.365 J.D. [Ⓐ Johnson]
Apfelbaum, Larry A., (BV) '61 '87 C.338 B.S. L.339 J.D.
[Ⓐ Kanoski&Assoc.] (☉Macomb, Peoria, Quincy, Rushville, Springfield)
Arkell, F. James, (BVⓉ) '62 '90 C&L.845 B.A., J.D.
(adm. in TX; not adm. in IL) [Ⓒ Dunn,W.A.&B.]
Arkell, Thomas J. ....'70 '97 C&L.602 B.A., J.D. [Dunn,W.A.&B.]
Armstrong, Lyndel K. ....'57 '82 C.340 B.S. L.801 J.D. 2201 Eastland Drive, Suite 3
Ashenfelter, John W. ....'62 '87 C.340 B.A. L.339 J.D. Coun., State Farm Ins. Cos.
Autry, Cecil J. '64 '97 C.326 B.A. L.347 J.D.
(adm. in TX; not adm. in IL) Asst. Coun., State Farm Ins. Co.
Bach, William S., (AV) ....'37 '62 C.611 B.A. L.477 J.D. [Ⓒ Costigan&W.]

Backman, Jonathan A., Law Office of, (BV) '62 '87 C&L.309 B.A., J.D.
117 North Center, 61701-1640
Telephone: 309-820-7420 Fax: 309-820-7430 URL: http://www.BackLawOffice.com
Email: jbackman@BackLawOffice.com URL: http://www.lawyers.com/backmanlaw
Trial Practice, Appellate Practice, Bankruptcy, Corporate Reorganization, Civil Rights, Criminal Defense and Employment Law.
See Professional Biographies, BLOOMINGTON, ILLINOIS

Bain, Florence, (BV) '42 '78 C.350 B.S. L.36 J.D.
[Ⓐ Kanoski&Assoc.] (☉Macomb, Peoria, Quincy, Rushville, Springfield)
Barger, Thomas M., III, (AV) ....'40 '65 C.597 B.S. L.209 J.D. [Livingston,B.B.&S.]
Barnhart, William F. '41 '81 C.172 B.A. L.174 J.D.
(adm. in NE; not adm. in IL) One State Farm Plaza
Barr, Cary B. ....'52 '80 C.339 B.A. L.365 J.D. V.P., Claims, Bliss-McKnight, Inc.
Barrientes, John Charles '44 '82 C.744 B.A. L.1136 J.D.
(adm. in CA; not adm. in IL) State Farm Ins. Co.
Bass, James D., (CV) ....'54 '81 C&L.879 B.S., J.D. 102 N. Center St.
Bates, Richard A. '61 '87 C&L.190 B.S.B.A., J.D.
(adm. in IN; not adm. in IL) One State Farm Plaza
Bauer, David E. '51 '80 C&L.508 B.S., J.D.
(adm. in MT; not adm. in IL) Asst. Coun., State Farm Ins. Cos.
Bernardi, Donald D. ....'51 '78 C.388 B.A. L.1048 J.D. Cir. J.
Bernstein, John T. '29 '54 C.150 B.A. L.309 J.D.
(adm. in OH; not adm. in IL) Coun., State Farm Mut. Auto. Ins. Co.
Berry, Erin L. ....'79 '04 C.338 B.A. L.502 J.D. [Ⓐ Hartweg,T.W.&S.]
Bliss, James I. ....'44 '67 C&L.339 B.S., J.D. Pres., Bliss-McKnight, Inc.
Borowski, Carrie L. ....'78 '03 C.338 B.A. L.339 J.D. [Ⓐ Costigan&W.]
Bowers, H. Paxton ....'43 '69 C.43 B.A. L.502 J.D. Asst. Corp. Coun.
Boyle, George D. ....'58 '90 C&L.339 B.A., J.D. Prairie State Legal Servs., Inc.
Bragg, Michael E. '47 '76 C&L.546 B.A., J.D.
(adm. in NE; not adm. in IL) Assoc. Gen. Coun., State Farm Ins. Co's.
Brandau, Herman '41 '65 C.339 B.A. L.424 J.D.
Assoc. Gen. Coun., State Farm Mut. Auto. Ins. Co.
Brandt, Peter W., (AV) ....'55 '83 C.339 B.A. L.801 J.D. [Livingston,B.B.&S.]
Brandt, Susan H., (BV) ....'50 '77 C.174 B.A. L.280 J.D. [Livingston,B.B.&S.]
Brandt, William R., (AV) ....'25 '50 C.871 L.145 J.D. [Ⓒ Livingston,B.B.&S.]
Bray, Harry C. '44 '75 C.277 B.S.I.E. L.64 J.D.
(adm. in MD; not adm. in IL) 3212 Leafy Ln.
Brown, Kevin S. ....'71 '96 C.338 B.S. L.352 J.D. Coun., State Farm Insurance Co.

Brown, Joel E., Attorney at Law
(See Peoria)

Brucker, Gene Carson ....'75 '01 C.338 B.S. L.1017 J.D. [Ⓐ Mueller&R.]
Brunner, Kim M. '49 '76 C.57 B.A. L.37 J.D.
Exec. V.P. & Gen. Coun., State Farm Ins. Co.
Brunson-Wheeler, Natalie Y. '63 '86 C.346 B.S. L.880 J.D.
(adm. in LA; not adm. in IL) One State Farm Plz., Ste. E5
Bugg, Todd E., (BV) ....'65 '90 C.340 B.A. L.339 J.D. [Dunn,W.A.&B.]
Butler, David W., (BV) ....'53 '80 C.338 B.S. L.801 J.D. 205 N. Main, Ste. 103
Byerly, Scott D. ....'54 '80 C.1101 B.S. L.879 J.D. Coun., State Farm Ins. Co.
Bykowski, Anthony ....'45 '71 C.352 B.A. L.477 J.D. Coun., State Farm Ins. Cos.
Cahill, Brian G. ....'72 '99 C.339 B.S. L.347 J.D. 1701 N. Towanda Ave.
Carlon, Cynthia A., (CV) ....'56 '93 C.338 B.S. L.801 J.D.
Carlon, John A., (CV) ....'29 '64 C.338 B.S.Ed. L.339 LL.B. 1110 E. Emerson St.
Carr, R. Stephen '41 '67 C.801 B.A. L.339 J.D.
Vice President & General Counsel, Growmark, Inc.
Carter, Robert J., (CV) ....'70 '96 C.801 B.A. L.616 J.D. [Ⓐ Johnson]
Cavanagh, James D.L. ....'54 '86 C.347 M.B.A. L.564 J.D. 1 State Farm Plaza
Cavanaugh, Mark J. ....'72 '97 C&L.339 B.S., J.D. Counsel, State Farm Ins. Cos.
Church, Timothy Douglas '67 '92
C.910 A.B. L.309 J.D. Coun., State Farm Mut. Auto. Ins. Co.
Cicero, Anthony R., (BVⓉ) '70 '95 C.966 B.S. L.201 J.D.
(adm. in OH; not adm. in IL) [Ⓐ Johnson] (☉Dayton, OH)
Ciesielski, Eric G. '67 '94 C.347 B.S. L.879 J.D.
(adm. in IN; not adm. in IL) State Farm Ins. Cos.
Clay, Jordan E., (BVⓉ) '61 '90 C&L.878 B.A., J.D.
(adm. in PA; not adm. in IL) State Farm Ins. Co.
Coffelt, Wayne P., (CV) ....'41 '74 C&L.862 B.A., J.D. [Fleming,M.&O.]
Corwin, Lisa R. ....'71 '97 C.373 B.A. L.339 J.D. [Walker&W.]
Costigan, J. Casey, (BV) ....'65 '91 C.347 B.A. L.1187 J.D. [Costigan&W.]
Costigan, William F., (AV) ....'26 '51 C&L.339 B.A., LL.B. [Ⓒ Costigan&W.]

Costigan & Wollrab, P.C., (AV)
308 East Washington Street, 61701
Telephone: 309-828-4310 Telecopier: 309-828-4325
URL: http://www.cwlawoffice.com
James C. Wollrab (1919-1989); Paul R. Welch (1936-2004); David C. Wochner; Robert W. Neirynck; Dawn L. Wall; Robert S. White; J. Casey Costigan;—Carrie L. Borowski; Brian L. Curtis; Dominic Salvati. Of Counsel: William F. Costigan; William S. Bach; Joseph M. Ambrose.
Civil and Criminal Litigation in Federal and State Courts, Banking and Finance Law, Business and Commercial Law, Corporate Law, Divorce and Family Law, Eminent Domain, Estate Planning and Probate, Insurance Law, Mergers and Acquisitions, Personal Injury Litigation, Real Estate and Worker's Compensation Law.
Representative Clients: Aetna Life & Casualty Farmland Insurance Group; Allstate Insurance Co.; CIGNA; CNA; Commercial Bag Co.; Firestone Tire & Rubber Co.; Freedom Oil Co.; Hartford Insurance Group; The Norfolk and Western Railroad; Pekin Insurance Co.
See Professional Biographies, BLOOMINGTON, ILLINOIS

Cox, A. Clay, (AV) ....'54 '79 C.502 B.S.B.A. L.339 J.D. [Hayes,H.M.&C.]
Crissman, Carol G. '37 '64 C.347 B.S.B.A. L.352 J.D.
(adm. in IA; not adm. in IL) [Anderson,H.Q.&S.]
Curtis, Brian L. ....'79 '04 C.465 B.B.A. L.801 J.D. [Ⓐ Costigan&W.]
Darner, Robert G. ....'51 '79 C.339 B.S. L.46 J.D. Country Mut. Ins. Co.
Davis, Dean M., (BV) '54 '79
C.340 B.A. L.221 J.D. Coun., State Farm Mut. Auto. Ins. Co.
Dearborn, Luther H. ....'41 '66 C&L.339 B.A., J.D. Chf. Cir. J.
DeCandio, Vincent J. ....'63 '89 C.1044 B.A. L.904 J.D. State Farm Ins. Co.
DeGenova-Carter, Catherine A., (CV) '71 '97 C.945 B.A. L.615 J.D.
1 State Farm Plaza
Dehn, Joseph Albert ....'70 '95 C.338 B.S. L.801 J.D. [J.Dehn]
Dehn, Joseph, Law Office of ....201 W. Olive St., Fl. 2
Deighan, Thomas M. ....'55 '80 C&L.339 A.B., J.D. Coun., State Farm Ins. Cos.
Deneen, Daniel G., (BV) ....'57 '82 C&L.339 B.S., J.D. [Deneen&D.]
Deneen & Deneen, (BV) ....202 South Eldorado Road, Suite A-1
De Pew, James R., (AV) ....'19 '48 C.338 B.E. L.339 J.D. [De Pew,G.&D.] ☉
De Pew, Russell E., (BV) ....'56 '82 C.338 B.A. L.285 J.D. 201 W. Olive St.
De Pew, Grimes & De Pew, (AV) ....201 W. Olive St. (☉Heyworth)
Dick, Geo. F., III ....'19 '47 C.174 B.S. L.339 LL.B. Pres., Peoples Bk.
Dirkes, Daniel F. '56 '82 C.1154 B.A. L.215 J.D.
(adm. in MI; not adm. in IL) State Farm Mut. Auto. Ins. Co.
Dirks, John A. ....'48 '74 C&L.339 B.A., J.D. Coun., State Farm Ins. Cos.
Dodds, Terry W. ....'74 '00 C.338 B.A. L.801 J.D. Asst. Pub. Def.
Dodson, Patrick D. ....'63 '91 C&L.546 B.B.A., J.D. State Farm Ins.
Dominy, Shawn R. '70 '97 C&L.608 B.A., J.D.
(adm. in OH; not adm. in IL) [Ⓐ Johnson]
Dorris, David V., (AV) ....'47 '73 C.1101 B.A. L.339 J.D. [Dorris]
Dorris Law Firm, P.C., (AV) ....207 West Jefferson, Suite 601
Downer, Elizabeth A. '64 '90
C.337 B.A. L.801 J.D. Asst. Coun., State Farm Mut. Auto. Ins. Co.
Dozier, Ronald C. ....'46 '73 C&L.339 B.A., J.D. Cir. J., 11th Jud. Cir., Ct. Litig.
Drazewski, Scott D. ....'57 '82 C.338 B.S. L.209 J.D. Assoc. Cir. J.
Drinan, Ronald J. ....'43 '74 C.338 B.S. L.339 J.D. Asst. Gen. Coun., State Farm Ins. Co.
Dunagan, Patrick E. '49 '75 C&L.16 B.A., J.D.
(adm. in AL; not adm. in IL) State Farm Mut. Auto. Ins. Co.
Dunn, David S., Law Office, (BV) ....'47 '76 C.338 B.S. L.365 J.D. 712 E. Empire St.
Dunn, Mark T., (AV) ....'45 '72 C&L.602 B.A., J.D. [Dunn,W.A.&B.]
Dunn, Richard T., (AV) ....'18 '47 C&L.339 A.B., J.D. [Ⓑ Dunn,W.A.&B.]

Dunn, Willard, Arkell & Bugg, (AV)
1001 North Main Street, Suite A, 61701
Mailing Address: P.O. Box 3488, Bloomington, IL 61702-3488
Telephone: 309-828-6241 Fax: 309-828-8321
Email: MTD@DunnLaw.com URL: http://www.DunnLaw.com
Members of Firm: Richard F. Dunn (1888-1963); Mark T. Dunn; Donald A. Willard; Thomas J. Arkell; Todd E. Bugg. Associate: Clayton J. Patterson. Of Counsel: Louis F. Ulbrich; Richard T. Dunn; F. James Arkell (Not admitted in IL).
General Civil Trial and Appellate Practice. General Practice, Litigation, Business Law, Business Litigation, Business Enterprises, Insurance, Intellectual Property, Licensing Agreements, Trade Secrets, Contracts, Commercial Law, Commercial Litigation, Civil Litigation, Copyright, Trademark, Bankruptcy, Banking Law, Corporate, Real Estate, Buying or Selling, Construction, Probate, Trusts and Estates, Municipal, University, Civil Rights, Immigration, Labor, Employment, Human Resources, Internet.
Representative Clients: Northeastern Illinois University; Southern Illinois University; Illinois State University; Western Illinois University; Chicago State University; Illinois Wesleyan University; University of Illinois at Urbana-Champaign; Bradley University; City of Bloomington; City of LeRoy.
See Professional Biographies, BLOOMINGTON, ILLINOIS

Echols, Margaret A. '61 '86
C.97 B.S. L.851 J.D. Asst. Coun., State Farm Mut. Auto. Ins. Co.
Eckols, Thomas A. '50 '75 C.352 B.A. L.339 J.D.
Coun. Corp. Law Dept., State Farm Mutual Auto Ins. Co.
Edmiston, Charles N., II, (BV) '54 '80 C.339 B.S. L.352 J.D.
[Ⓐ Kanoski&Assoc.] (☉Macomb, Peoria, Quincy, Rushville, Springfield)
Edwards, Pamela Kaye '65 '89
C.340 B.A. L.352 J.D. Counsel, State Farm Mut. Auto. Ins. Co.

Ehlers, Randall B., Law Office of, (BV) '48 '73 C&L.339 B.S., J.D.
103 North Main Street, 61701
Telephone: 309-827-8084 Fax: 309-828-6948 URL: http://www.ehlerslaw.com
Email: rehlers@ehlerslaw.com URL: http://www.lawyers.com/ehlerslaw
General Civil Practice. Trial Practice in State and Federal Courts. Family Law, Personal Injury, Real Estate, Municipal, Wills, Estate Administration, Small Business.
See Professional Biographies, BLOOMINGTON, ILLINOIS

Eidsmoe, Daniel C. '62 '88 C.427 B.A. L.352 J.D.
(adm. in IA; not adm. in IL) Claim Atty., Country Mut. Ins. Co.
Elterich, John P. '51 '76 C.659 B.S. L.669 J.D.
(adm. in OH; not adm. in IL) Invest. Coun., State Farm Ins. Co.
Enright, Elizabeth A. '55 '85
C.424 B.S.N. L.146 J.D. Claims Atty., Country Cos. Ins. Grp.
Erickson, Charles N. ....'65 '95 C.338 B.S. L.347 J.D. 306 North Center Street
Ervin, Brian C. ....'57 '83 C&L.801 B.A., J.D. Rept. of Decisions, Supm. Ct.
Evans, Ethan C. '46 '71 C.318 B.A. L.1119 J.D.
Assoc. Gen. Coun., State Farm Ins. Cos.
Fehr, Renee K. ....'65 '89 C.340 B.A. L.362 J.D. State Farm Ins. Co.
Feldman, Richard P. '52 '80 C.705 B.A. L.1003 J.D.
(adm. in NJ; not adm. in IL) Counsel, State Farm Ins. Cos.
Ferguson, Beth, (BVⓉ) ....'52 '84 C.338 B.A. L.910 J.D. [Ⓐ Wilber]
Fields, Jack Ceacil '49 '83 C.340 B.S. L.589 J.D.
Univ. Regr. & Asst. Dean, Ill. Wesleyan Univ.
Fiero, James G. '65 '91 C.170 B.A. L.145 J.D.
(adm. in CA; not adm. in IL) State Farm Mut. Auto. Ins. Co.
Finegan, James T., (BV) ....'49 '72 C.339 B.A. L.597 J.D. [Finegan]
Finegan Law Firm, (BV) ....111 W. Front St.
Fitzgerald, Kevin P. ....'56 '81 C.338 B.S. L.339 J.D. Assoc. Cir. J.
Fleming, Robert T., (AV) ....'23 '49 C.340 B.S. L.597 J.D. [Fleming,M.&O.]
Fleming, Messman & O'Connor, (AV) ....217 E. Washington St.
Flynn, George R., (BV) ....'44 '70 C.707 B.A. L.339 J.D. [G.R.Flynn]
Flynn, George R., P.C., (BV) ....102 S. East St., Suite 340
Foley, James T., (BV) ....'31 '58 C.602 A.B. L.209 J.D. [Ⓑ Livingston,B.B.&S.]
Foley, Rebecca Simmons, (BV) ....'69 '95 C.339 B.S. L.209 J.D. 207 W. Jefferson St.
Fosen, Nannette Castaneda '69 '96
C&L.339 B.A., J.D. Corp. Coun., State Farm Mut. Auto. Ins. Co.
Fox, Richard D. ....'63 '90 C.338 B.S. L.801 J.D. State Farm Mut. Auto. Ins. Co.
Fraker, Guy C., (AV) ....'38 '62 C&L.339 B.A., LL.B. [Guy C.F.]
Geosling, Gary '54 '81 C.963 B.S. L.300 J.D.
(adm. in MN; not adm. in IL) Asst. Claims Coun., State Farm Ins. Cos.
Gielow, G. Roger ....'43 '68 C&L.802 B.A., J.D. Invest. Coun., State Farm Ins. Cos.

Ginzkey, James P., (AV) '53 '79 C.339 B.S. L.744 J.D.
221 E. Washington, 61701
Telephone: 309-821-9707 Fax: 309-821-9708
Email: jim@jimginzkey.com URL: http://www.lawyers.com/jimginzkey
Personal Injury, Medical Malpractice, Products Liability.
See Professional Biographies, BLOOMINGTON, ILLINOIS

Glenn, Ronda D. Taylor, (BV) '61 '86 C.98 B.S. L.910 J.D.
115 West Jefferson, Suite 303A, 61701
Telephone: 309-827-3535 FAX: 309-828-2574
Family Law, Trial and Appellate Practice in State and Federal Courts, Divorce, Child Custody, Name Changes, Juvenile Law, Adoptions, Interstate and Intrastate Adoptions, Juvenile Abuse, Neglect and Delinquency Cases.
See Professional Biographies, BLOOMINGTON, ILLINOIS

Goebel, William M., (AV) ....'22 '49 C.337 A.B. L.477 J.D. 1001 N. Main St.
Goldrick, J. Brian ....'— '91 C.338 B.S. L.356 J.D. 111 West Front Street
Goodridge, John A. '70 '96 C.894 B.A. L.879 J.D.
(adm. in IN; not adm. in IL) [Ⓐ Johnson] (☉Evansville, IN)
Graden, William T., (BVⓉ) '58 '85 C&L.347 B.S., J.D.
(adm. in IN; not adm. in IL) State Farm Mut. Auto. Ins. Co.

Gramm, Chris, Attorney at Law '71 '01 C.338 B.A. L.589 J.D.
2422 E. Washington Street, Suite 101, 61704
Telephone: 309-275-6677 Fax: 309-663-6164
Email: chris@getgramm.com URL: http://www.lawyers.com/getgramm
Criminal Defense, DUI, Traffic Violations, Felonies, Misdemeanors, Drug Crimes, Sex Crimes, Real Estate, Wills, Trust and Estates and Immigration Law.
See Professional Biographies, BLOOMINGTON, ILLINOIS

Greenburg, J. Todd, (BV) '55 '80
C.1247 B.A. L.602 J.D. Corp. Coun., City of Bloomington
Greenleaf, John L., Jr., (CV) ....'53 '78 C.339 B.S. L.365 J.D. [Ⓐ Ostling&Assoc.]
Griffin, Teena ....'58 '84 C.927 B.S. L.339 J.D. First Asst. State's Atty.
Grimes, Bernard T., (AV) ....'11 '38 C.338 B.E. L.339 J.D. [Ⓑ De Pew,G.&D.]
Grimes, David R. '42 '69 C&L.339 A.B., J.D.
State Farm Investment Management Corp.
Groves, John R. ....'46 '76 C.293 A.B. L.734 J.D. Coun., State Farm Ins. Cos.
Grow, David P. .....'76 '02 C.101 B.A. L.494 J.D. State Farm Mutual Automobile Ins. Co.
Gustavson, Dennis M. ....'43 '85 C.340 B.S. L.339 J.D. 1323 W. Mulberry St.
Guy C. Franker, Law Office of, P.C., (AV) ....306 East Grove Street
Hackman, William Henry ....'44 '71 C.602 B.A. L.339 J.D. P.O. Box 3333
Hall, Blair A. '53 '78 C.547 B.A. L.546 J.D.
Exec. Liaison, State Farm Mut. Auto. Ins. Co.
Hall, Daniel S. ....'54 '84 C.927 B.A. L.339 J.D. Asst. Gen. Coun., Growmark, Inc.
Hammer, Don C., (AV) ....'45 '75 C.608 B.A. L.365 J.D. [Hayes,H.M.&C.]
Hansen, D. Thomas, (BVⓉ) '57 '82 C.47 B.S.Ed. L.421 J.D.
(adm. in KY; not adm. in IL) State Farm Mut. Auto. Ins. Co.
Harmon, Paul M., Jr., (BV) ....'42 '68 C.226 B.A. L.339 J.D. [Anderson,H.Q.&S.]
Harris, Thomas M., Jr., (BV) ....'63 '88 C.339 B.A. L.174 J.D. [Ⓐ J.Mirza&Assoc.] ☉
Hartweg, Darrell L., (AV) ....'42 '68 C&L.339 B.A., J.D. [Hartweg,T.W.&S.]

Hartweg, Turner, Wood & Simkins, P.C., (AV)
207 West Jefferson Street, Suite 400, P.O. Box 397, 61701-0397
Telephone: 309-827-0044 Telecopier: 309-829-0328
Email: HTWSLAW.COM
Darrell L. Hartweg; Ralph T. Turner; George C. Wood; Brenda H. Simkins;—Erin L. Berry.
Civil Practice in all Courts. Trials and Appeals in Personal Injury, Insurance, Commercial and Family Law. Estate Planning, Probate, Real Estate, Corporate, Commercial and Transactional Law.
Reference: Magna Bank of McLean County.
See Professional Biographies, BLOOMINGTON, ILLINOIS

Hayes, Merrick C., (AV) ....'37 '60 C&L.221 B.S., J.D. [Hayes,H.M.&C.]

Hayes, Hammer, Miles & Cox, LLP, (AV)
202 N. Center, 61701
Telephone: 309-828-7331 Fax: 309-827-7423
URL: http://www.hhmcg.com
Members of Firm: Merrick C. Hayes; Frank Miles; Don C. Hammer; A. Clay Cox.
General Civil Practice, Commercial, Corporate, Pension and Profit Sharing, Estate Planning, Real Estate, Probate, Taxation, Trust, Litigation, Family Law, Divorce, Adoption Law, Land Use, Zoning, Municipal, Alternative Dispute Resolution, Mediation, Collaborative Law.
See Professional Biographies, BLOOMINGTON, ILLINOIS

Hemenway, Christina S. '62 '94
C.804 B.A. L.502 J.D. Claims Atty., Country Mut. Ins. Co.
Hess, William J. '42 '67 C.201 B.A. L.150 J.D.
Invest. Coun., State Farm Mut. Auto. Ins. Co.
Hiestand, Jean C., (Mr.) '22 '49 C.611 B.A. L.309 LL.B.
(adm. in OH; not adm. in IL) One State Farm Plaza‡
Hightower, David E. '46 '74 C.420 B.A. L.846 J.D.
(adm. in TX; not adm. in IL) 1312 E. Empire St.
Hill, David L. '52 '77 C.340 B.A. L.339 J.D.
V.P. & Coun., State Farm Mut. Auto. Ins. Co.
Hill, Lee Ann S., (BV) ....'58 '97 C.338 B.S. L.801 J.D. [Ⓐ John W.Y.]
Hoekstra, John A., (CV) ....'58 '83 C.123 B.A. L.352 J.D. 201 W. Olive St.
Hoffman, Frank E., Law Offices of, (BV) '54 '80 C.234 B.A. L.801 J.D.
401 N. Main St.
Hogan, Roberta R. .....'59 '85 C.338 B.S. L.589 J.D. Claims Atty., Country Cos. Ins. Grp.
Holder, Dan W. ....'36 '63 C.801 B.A. L.793 LL.B. Pres., Holder Publishing Corp.
Holman, Kirk A., (BV) ....'61 '86 C.504 B.A. L.365 J.D. [Ⓐ Livingston,B.B.&S.]
Horton, Stephen L. ....'57 '83 C&L.339 B.A., J.D. Tax Coun., State Farm Ins. Cos.
Howard, Catherine L. ....'72 '97 C.340 B.A. L.879 J.D. State Farm Ins. Co.

Howard & Howard Attorneys, P.C.
(See Peoria)

Hoyt, Carolyn S. ....'42 '67 C.145 B.A. L.966 J.D. Asst. Rept., Ill. Supm. & Appl. Cts.

Hundman, Douglas J., (BV) '66 '92
C.338 B.S. L.1187 J.D. Claims Atty., Country Mut. Ins. Co.
Jackson, Cheryl '63 '90 C.502 B.A. L.339 J.D.
(adm. in MO; not adm. in IL) Asst. Coun., State Farm Ins. Cos.
Jackson, Jeffrey W., (BV) '52 '79 C.399 B.A. L.734 J.D.
Associate General Counsel, State Farm Mut. Auto. Ins. Co.
Jacob, Thomas N., (BV) '40 '66 C.546 A.B. L.597 J.D. 1701 Clearwater Ave.
Jacobs, Jennifer A. '63 '88 C&L.339 B.S., J.D. 201 W. Olive St.
Jaynes, Donald O. '48 '73 C&L.502 B.J., J.D.
Assoc. Gen. Coun., State Farm Mut. Auto. Ins. Co.
Jennings, Harold M. '40 '64 C&L.339 B.A., LL.B. [Jennings,S.&D.]
Jennings, Thomas A., (CV) '64 '92 C.338 B.S. L.16 J.D.
Jennings, Smalley & Davis, P.C. P.O. Box 3335
John W. Yoder Law Firm, (AV) 306 E. Grove St.
Johnson, Earle B. '14 '40 C&L.260 B.S., J.D. 1 State Farm Plaza‡
Johnson, Mark D. '— '92 C.338 B.A. L.589 J.D. [Johnson] ⊙

Johnson Law Group
61701 ⊙
Telephone: 309-827-3670 Fax: 309-827-3991
Email: johnson.law@verizon.net
Mark D. Johnson; Peter C. Samouris; P. Steven Maasz; Sean P. Hilgendorf. Associates: Thomas A. Sobecki; James M. Ansbro; Andy Scharf; Michael R. Puterbaugh (Not admitted in IL); Jeffrey T. Abbott; K. Robert Toy; Carl Jordan (Not admitted in IL); William F. McGinnis (Not admitted in IL); Jeffrey A. Kline; Matthew J. McQuaid; Michael T. Maddaloni (Not admitted in IL); Anthony R. Cicero (Not admitted in IL); Robert J. Carter; John A. Goodridge (Not admitted in IL); David A. Merchant, II (Not admitted in IL); Shawn R. Dominy (Not admitted in IL); Gregory Kaufman (Not admitted in IL); Douglas R. Smith; Andrew M. Liefer; Michael J. Rousseau.
Languages: Japanese and Greek.
Felonies, Murder, White Collar Crime, Drugs, Domestic Violence, DWI.
Okemos, Michigan Office: 3474 Alaiedon Parkway, 47764. Telephone: 877-333-2889.
Canton, Ohio Office: 4571 Stephen Circle N.W., 44718. Telephone: 877-333-2889.
South Bend, Indiana Office: 218 W. Washington Street, 46601. Telephone: 877-333-2889.
See Professional Biographies, BLOOMINGTON, ILLINOIS

Jordan, Carl '66 '94 C.302 B.A. L.966 J.D.
(adm. in WI; not adm. in IL) [Ⓐ Johnson]
Joslin, Roger '36 '61 C.473 B.S. L.339 LL.D. State Farm Mut. Auto. Ins. Co.
Kanoski, Ronald J., (BV) '47 '74 C.234 B.S. L.424 J.D. [Kanoski&Assoc.] ⊙
Kanoski & Associates, (BV)
237 E. Front St. (⊙Decatur, Macomb, Peoria, Quincy, Rushville, Springfield)
Kaufman, Gregory '— '97 C.608 B.A. L.607 J.D.
(adm. in OH; not adm. in IL) [Ⓐ Johnson]
Kelly, Andrew J. '74 '99 C.028 B.A. L.475 J.D. [Ⓐ Walker&W.]
Kelly, Terence B. '62 '89 C.652 B.A. L.352 J.D. [Thomson&W.]
Kelly, Timothy W., (AV) '53 '78 C&L.201 B.S., J.D. [Kelly]

Kelly Law Offices, P.C., (AV)
121 North Main Street 3rd Floor, 61701 ⊙
Telephone: 309-661-2558; Chicago and Toll Free: 866-727-6507 Fax: 309-662-7443
Email: tw.kelly@verizon.net URL: http://www.kellylawoffices.com
Timothy W. Kelly.
Personal Injury, Products Liability, Torts, Medical Malpractice, and Insurance cases in State and Federal Courts.
Chicago, Illinois Office: 222 N. Columbus Drive, Suite 408, 60601.
See Professional Biographies, BLOOMINGTON, ILLINOIS

Kennett, Christie Shih '70 '95 C.339 B.A. L.734 J.D. One State Farm Plaza
Kenney, Stuart D. '60 '87 C.177 B.A. L.209 J.D.
Counsel, State Farm Mut. Auto. Ins. Co.
Kersey, Martha S. '63 '89 C&L.339 B.A., J.D.
Claims Atty. I, Country Insurance & Financial Services
Kline, Jeffrey A. '— '92 C&L.589 B.A., J.D. [Ⓐ Johnson]
Klopp, Frank '33 '61 L.1035 L.L.B.
(adm. in MN; not adm. in IL) Coun., State Farm Ins. Cos.
Klosterboer, David C. '63 '90 C.839 B.S. L.796 J.D.
(adm. in TX; not adm. in IL) 1 State Farm Plz.‡
Knecht, James A. '44 '73 C.338 B.S. L.339 J.D. Appl. Ct. J.

Koepke & Hiltabrand, P.C.
(See Springfield)

Kording, Scott '79 '05 C.338 B.S. L.339 J.D. 102 S. E. St., Ste. 350
Kraft, Kathleen McDonald, (BV) '66 '91 C&L.339 B.A., J.D. [Thomson&W.]
Kraft, Mary Therese '65 '90 C.338 B.S. L.1119 J.D. Asst. Coun., State Farm Ins. Cos.
Kramp, Mark L. '49 '75 C.723 B.A. L.597 J.D. Coun., State Farm Ins. Cos.
Kurtock, John P. '25 '50 C.337 A.B. L.145 J.D. 2103 Hedgewood Dr.‡
Lapan, Roger D., (BV) '29 '58 C.338 B.S.Ed. L.597 J.D. 202 N. Prospect Rd.
Lawrence, William B., (AV) '28 '51 C.338 L.339 J.D. [Lawrence M.&O.]
Lawrence Moore and Ogar, (AV) 108 W. Monroe
Leach, Shelton B. '11 '37 C.340 A.B. L.339 LL.B. 2025 E. Lincoln‡
Ledgerwood, Thomas P., (AV) '43 '69 C.344 B.A. L.347 J.D.
(adm. in IN; not adm. in IL) State Farm Mut. Auto. Ins. Co.
Leifel, Danny J., (BV) '44 '74 C.338 B.S. L.339 J.D. [Anderson,H.Q.&S.]
Leighton, G. Timothy '59 '88 C.276 A.B. L.273 J.D. 802 N. Clinton St., Ste. 1
Lenz, Robert J., (AV) '36 '63 C&L.339 A.B., J.D. 205 N. Main
Lewis, Kristi G. '70 '00 C&L.801 B.M., J.D. 121 N. Main St., 4th fl.
Lewis, Ronald L., (BV) '66 '91 C.234 B.A. L.365 J.D. Co. Pub. Def. Off.
Liefer, Andrew M. '— '95 C&L.879 B.A., J.D. [Ⓐ Johnson]

Livingston, Barger, Brandt & Schroeder, (AV)
115 West Jefferson, Suite 400, P.O. Box 3457, 61702-3457 ⊙
Telephone: 309-828-5281 Fax: 309-827-3432
URL: http://www.lbbs.net
Herbert M. Livingston (1898-1987); Ralph Schroeder (1927-1991); Thomas M. Barger, Jr. (1912-1992). Of Counsel: William R. Brandt; James T. Foley. Members of Firm: William C. Wetzel; Thomas M. Barger III; Christopher L. Nyweide; Susan H. Brandt; Richard E. Stites; Peter W. Brandt; Thomas B. Borton (Resident, Champaign Office); Richard T. Marvel. Associates: Kirk A. Holman; Michael A. Wozniak; Kenneth S. Weiss (Resident, Champaign Office).
***Corporate, Business,* Business Litigation, Real Estate Transactions, Creditors' Rights, Employment Law EEOC, ERISA, Estate Planning, Partnerships, Joint Ventures, Estates and Probate. Insurance Litigation, Product Liability, Medical Negligence Defense, Pharmaceutical Litigation, Construction Disputes, Environmental Litigation, Financial Litigation, Employment, Health Care to Physicians and Hospitals, Professional Liability, Officer's and Director's Liability, Environmental Law, Administrative Agency Procedures, Governmental Law, General Counsel Representation, Eminent Domain, Land Use Law, Subdivision and Zoning.**
Representative Clients: Bloomington-Normal Airport Authority; Illinois Power Company; Northern Illinois Gas; Champion Federal Savings & Loan; Citizens Savings Bank; Aetna Casualty & Surety Co.; Kemper Insurance; Liberty Mutual Insurance Co.; Travelers Insurance Co.; American States Insurance.
Champaign, Illinois Office: 2506 Galen Drive, Suite 108. Telephone: 217-351-7479. Fax: 217-351-6870.
See Professional Biographies, BLOOMINGTON, ILLINOIS

Lucie, Mitchell K. '59 '85 C.123 B.A. L.339 J.D. Asst. Coun., State Farm Ins. Cos.
Luedtke, John R., (AV) '32 '56 C&L.339 B.A., LL.B. 218 Mays Dr.‡
Maas, Deborah Sue '72 '01 C.339 B.S. L.596 J.D. Staff Atty.
Maddaloni, Michael T. '— '95 C.829 B.A. L.1187 J.D.
(adm. in MI; not adm. in IL) [Ⓐ Johnson]
Malito, John Robert '73 '98 C.339 B.S. L.424 J.D. One State Farm Plaza
Markowitz, Robert, (BV) '26 '52 C&L.966 B.S., J.D. 326 Vista Dr.
Marron, Timothy W., (BVⓉ) '64 '92 C.791 S.D. L.546 J.D. 1 State Farm Plaza, B-3
Marvel, Richard T. '75 '01 C.340 B.A. L.734 J.D. [Livingston,B.B.&S.]
Mather, Robert O. '69 '95 C&L.585 B.B.A., J.D State Farm Insurance Co.
McCarron, Joseph A. '71 '96 C.57 B.A. L.602 J.D. [J.A.McCarron]
McCarron, Joseph A., P.C., Law Office of 306 N. Center Street
McCullagh, Mary K. '53 '78 C.187 B.A. L.339 J.D. 2808 Morningside Dr.‡
McDade, Robert J. '68 '93 C.800 A.B. L.276 J.D. 170K N Towanda Ave
McElvain, Mike, (AV) '47 '72 C&L.339 B.S., J.D. 234 E. Front St.
McGinnis, William F. '57 '92 C.381 B.A. L.7 J.D.
(adm. in OH; not adm. in IL) [Ⓐ Johnson]
McGlynn, Allen '65 '93 C.798 B.A. L.801 J.D. Atty., State Farm Mut. Auto. Ins. Co.
McGrath, Melissa M., (BV) '58 '91 C.338 B.S. L.801 J.D. [Thomson&W.]
McGraw, Richard W. '59 '89 C.608 B.S.B.A. L.851 J.D. Milwaukee Ins.
McKnight, Kerry B., (BVⓉ) '63 '89 C.469 B.A. L.902 J.D. Coun., State Farm Ins. Cos.
McNamee, Peter F. '27 '54 C&L.436 B.S., LL.B. 2107 Berrywood St.‡
McQuaid, Matthew J. '— '92 C.388 B.A. L.365 J.D. [Ⓐ Johnson]
Mecherle, Gregg R., (BV) '57 '82 C&L.339 B.S., J.D. Coun., State Farm Ins. Cos.
Meints, Paul A., (BV) '47 '74 C.927 B.B.A. L.879 J.D.
Sr. Staff Atty. Legal Servs., Country Cos., Financial Servs. Div.
Merchant, David A., II, (BVⓉ) '67 '96 C.477 B.A. L.213 J.D.
(adm. in MI; not adm. in IL) [Ⓐ Johnson]
Messman, C. Daniel, (AV) '28 '53 C.340 A.B. L.339 LL.B. [Fleming,M.&O.]
Miles, Frank, (AV) '46 '72 C&L.339 B.S., J.D. [Hayes,H.M.&C.]
Miller, Richard M. '38 '66 C.942 B.A. L.734 J.D. V.P., Tr., I.A.A. Tr. Co.
Miller, Scott '74 '00 C.134 B.S. L.1439 J.D. State Farm Ins. Co.
Miller, Todd C. '65 '90 C.210 B.A. L.365 J.D. 200 W. Front Street, Ste. 400-C
Mintel, Judith K. '48 '73 C&L.145 A.B., J.D. Assoc. Gen. Coun., State Farm Ins. Cos.
Mirza, Jerome, (AV) '37 '63 C.340 B.S. L.339 LL.B. [J.Mirza&Assoc.] ⊙

Mirza, Jerome, and Associates, Ltd., (AV)
705 East Washington Street, 61701 ⊙
Telephone: 309-827-8011 Facsimile: 309-829-8638
URL: http://www.mirzalawfirm.com
Jerome Mirza;—Thomas M. Harris, Jr.
Trial and Appellate Practice. Products Liability, Malpractice and Railroad Law.
Reference: National City Bank, Bloomington, Illinois.
Chicago, Illinois Office: Three First National Plaza. Telephone: 312-368-1903. Facsimile: 312-368-0528.
See Professional Biographies, BLOOMINGTON, ILLINOIS

Mitra, Keesha-Lu M. '65 '89
C.410 B.A. L.502 J.D. Asst. Coun., State Farm Mut. Auto. Ins. Co.
Montney, Wayne W. '56 '89 C&L.1051 B.S., J.D.
(adm. in OR; not adm. in IL) State Farm Ins. Co.
Moore, David M. '61 '87 C&L.352 B.B.A., J.D.
Counsel, State Farm Mut. Auto. Ins. Co.
Moore, Fred B., (BV) '45 '70 C.234 B.A. L.339 J.D. [Lawrence M.&O.]
Morel, John L., (AV) '— '65 C.927 B.A. L.339 J.D. [J.L.Morel]
Morel, John L., P.C., (AV) 235 East Front Street
Morgan, Richard W. '52 '77 C.339 B.A. L.221 J.D.
Sr. Staff Atty. Legal Servs., Country Cos., Financial Servs. Div.
Mosby-Scott, Michelle, (BV) '71 '95 C.234 B.A. L.801 J.D. [Allison&M.]
Mueller, William A., Jr., (BV) '45 '72 C&L.339 B.A.F., J.D. [Mueller&R.]

Mueller & Reece, LLC, (BV)
202 North Center Street, 61701
Telephone: 309-827-4055 Fax: 309-829-6742
URL: http://www.muellerreece.com
William A. Mueller, Jr.; Jay D. Reece;—Gene Carson Brucker.
Commercial Law, Civil and Commercial Litigation, Real Estate, Business Formations and Incorporations, Business Transactions, Personal Injury, Banking Law, Estate Planning, Trusts and Probate, Family Law.
See Professional Biographies, BLOOMINGTON, ILLINOIS

Napolitano, Neil '62 '87 C.1349 B.A. L.930 J.D. Country Mut. Ins. Co.
Neirynck, Robert W., (AV) '44 '69 C.339 A.B. L.602 J.D. [Costigan&W.]
Nelson, Lawrence J. '39 '66 C.375 B.S. L.900 J.D. Coun., State Farm Ins. Cos.
Newbold, Stephen A. '59 '84
C.338 B.S. L.339 J.D. Sr. Claims Atty., Country Mut. Ins. Co.
Novack, John R. '62 '87 C&L.339 B.S., J.D. 1701 N. Towanda Ave.
Nyweide, Christopher L., (BV) '51 '77 C.340 B.A. L.365 J.D. [Livingston,B.B.&S.]
O'Connor, Martin L., (BV) '40 '68 C.338 B.S. L.793 J.D. [Fleming,M.&O.]
O'Dell, Robert B., (BV) '46 '74
C.879 B.A. L.146 J.D. Champion Fed. Svgs. & Loan Assn.
O'Flaherty, Mark E. '58 '00 C&L.339 B.S.N.E., J.D. One State Farm Plaza (Pat.)
Ogar, Helen E., (BV) '60 '85 C&L.502 B.S., J.D. [Lawrence M.&O.]
Olivero, Kathy A., (CV) '56 '82 C.339 B.S. L.801 J.D.
[Ⓐ Kanoski&Assoc.] (⊙Macomb, Peoria, Quincy, Rushville, Springfield)
Olsen, Sverre M., Jr. '54 '80
C.450 B.A. L.734 J.D. Asst. Coun., State Farm Mut. Auto. Ins. Co.
O'Rourke, Michael J., (BV) '48 '79 102 S. East St., Ste. 200
Ostling, Lars Eric '47 '74 C.338 B.S. L.378 J.D. [Ostling&Assoc.]
Ostling & Associates 201 W. Olive Street
Patterson, Clayton J. '79 '04 C.339 B.A. L.234 J.D. [Ⓐ Dunn,W.A.&B.]
Pavey, Mitzi G. '65 '92 C&L.421 B.S.B.A., J.D.
(adm. in KY; not adm. in IL) 617 Bradley Dr.‡
Paxton, Anna M. '58 '83 C.477 B.A. L.208 J.D.
(adm. in CO; not adm. in IL) State Farm Mutual Automobile Ins. Co.
Porter, John R., Jr, (BV) '36 '78 C.604 A.B. L.339 J.D. 102 N. Center‡
Prall, G. Michael '47 '72 C&L.339 B.A., J.D. Cir. J.
Pratt, Catherine A., (BV) '55 '80 C.339 B.S. L.362 J.D. 415 N. Center St.
Prior, John G., Jr. '— '90 C.162 B.A. L.365 J.D. [Prior]

Prior Law Firm, The, P.C.
1210 Towanda Avenue, Suite 15, P.O. Box 5968, 61702-5968
Telephone: 309-827-4300 Fax: 309-827-4111
Email: johnprior@insightbb.com URL: http://www.thepriorlawfirm.com
John G. Prior, Jr.; Larry J. Spears.
Criminal Defense, Driving While Intoxicated, Traffic Violations, Juvenile Law, Family Law, Personal Injury, Collections and Insurance Subrogation.
See Professional Biographies, BLOOMINGTON, ILLINOIS

Prusak, Winne & Gorman, Ltd.
(See Peoria)

Puterbaugh, Michael R., (BVⓉ) '61 '88 C.528 B.A. L.930 J.D.
(adm. in OH; not adm. in IL) [Ⓐ Johnson] (⊙Canton, OH)

Quick, Jerry W., (BV) ....'44 '70 C&L.339 J.D. [Anderson,H.Q.&S.]
Quitschau, Drew R. .... '77 '02 C.297 B.A. L.45 J.D. [Ⓐ Thomson&W.]
Reece, Jay D., (BV) ....'60 '92 C.338 B.S. L.146 J.D. [Mueller&R.]
Reid, Suzann M. '65 '90 C.234 B.S. L.46 J.D.
Tax Coun., State Farm Mut. Auto. Ins. Co.
Remmes, Michael J. .... '62 '87 C.190 B.S.B.A. L.352 J.D. Tax Coun., State Farm Ins. Co.
Rennick, Tamarra Terese .... '65 '91 C.339 B.S. L.464 J.D. 1 State Farm Plz., Ste. B3
Reu, Rex L., Attorney at Law ....'54 '78 C&L.339 A.B., J.D. 111 W. Front St.
Reynard, Charles G., (BV) .... '46 '74 C.1024 B.A. L.424 J.D. State's Atty.
Reynolds, B. Gerald '43 '68 C&L.221 B.S., J.D.
V.P. & Corp. Gen. Coun., State Farm Ins. Co.
Ridge, David C. '57 '82 C.723 B.S. L.300 J.D.
(adm. in MN; not adm. in IL) State Farm Mut. Auto. Ins. Co.
Ritchie, Chad ....'— '02 C.340 B.A. L.801 J.D. 2401 E. Washington St.
Robb, Elizabeth A. ..... '55 '81 C.340 B.A. L.424 J.D. Assoc. Cir. J., McLean Co. Cir. Ct.
Rolley, E. William .... '30 '55 C&L.597 B.S., J.D. 102 North Center Street
Roth, Millicent M. '75 '02
C.302 B.S. L.365 J.D. Asst. Pub. Def., McLean Co. Pub. Def. Off.
Rottunda, Larry '52 '78 C.513 B.A. L.793 J.D.
(adm. in IA; not adm. in IL) Invest. Coun., State Farm Mut. Auto. Ins. Co.
Rousseau, Michael J. ....'— '01 C.502 B.A. L.801 J.D. [Ⓐ Johnson]
Ruud, Brenda Temke, (BV) .... '60 '87 C.338 B.S. L.801 J.D. 201 W. Olive St.
Ruud, Eric T., (BV) ....'53 '80 C.338 B.S. L.801 J.D. Chief Asst. States Atty.

Saaf, Adele M., (CV) '49 '96 C.881 B.A. L.1187 J.D.
121 North Main Street, 4th Floor, 61701
Telephone: 309-827-3700 Fax: 309-828-3536
Email: a.saaf@insightbb.com
Family Law, Wills, Living Trusts, Real Estate.
See Professional Biographies, BLOOMINGTON, ILLINOIS

Saint, Gale W., (AV) ....'36 '62 C&L.879 B.S., J.D.‡
Saint Law Group, P.C., (CV) ....115 W. Jefferson St., Ste. 400
Salvati, Dominic ....'76 '04 C.57 B.A. L.1000 J.D. [Ⓐ Costigan&W.]
Sanchez, Manuel "Manny", (AV) .... '47 '74 C.589 B.A. L.659 J.D. [Sanchez&D.] ⊙
Sanchez & Daniels, (AV) ....237 East Front Street (⊙Chicago, Wheaton)
Schaeffer, Rex L. .... '57 '84 C.338 B.S. L.500 J.D. State Farm Ins. Co.
Schaffer, Wendy H. '57 '86 C.340 B.S.N. L.209 J.D.
Claims Atty., Country Mut. Ins. Co.
Schaltegger, Eric H. .... '67 '93 C.352 B.S. L.365 J.D. State Farm Ins. Co.
Scharf, Andy ....'62 '88 C.339 B.S. L.146 J.D. [Ⓐ Johnson]
Schiller, Eugene F., Jr. '59 '84 C.205 B.A. L.776 J.D.
(adm. in NJ; not adm. in IL) State Farm Mut. Auto. Ins. Co.
Schillinger, Paul, (CV) ....'20 '47 C&L.597 B.S., J.D. 102 N. Center St.
Schnake, Jeffrey H. '61 '89 C.234 B.A. L.801 J.D.
Claims Atty. II, Country Mut. Ins. Co.
Schneider, S.S., (BV) ....'20 '50 C.248 B.A. L.174 J.D. 202 S. El Dorado Rd.
Schneider, Thomas M. .... '60 '88 C.210 B.A. L.608 J.D. Coun., State Farm Ins. Cos.
Schwulst, John P., (BV) ....'44 '71 C&L.260 B.A., J.D. 200 West Front Street
Semmler, Albert K., (BV) '42 '70
C.150 B.A. L.1340 J.D. Dir., Country Cos., Financial Servs. Div.
Shaffer, J. Scott '54 '81 C.197 B.A. L.930 J.D.
(adm. in OH; not adm. in IL) Coun., State Farm Ins. Cos.
Shah, Rajiv C. .... '69 '97 L.339 J.D. 14 Brownstone Ct.
Shay, Susan Knowles .... '62 '90 C.338 B.S. L.339 J.D. 1312 E. Empire St.
Shepherd, William G. .... '52 '77 C&L.546 B.A., J.D. Asst. Coun., State Farm Ins. Cos.
Shirk, James A. ....'44 '70 C.802 B.A. L.339 J.D. Mng. Dir., Beer Nuts, Inc.
Simkins, Brenda H., (BV) ....'69 '95 C&L.500 B.B.A., J.D. [Hartweg,T.W.&S.]
Simon, Thomas W., Law Office of ...... '45 '92 C.732 B.A. L.339 J.D. 416 Phoenix Ave.
Skelton, Steven, (BV) .... '49 '76 C.340 B.S. L.365 J.D. 301 S. Center St.
Smith, Douglas R. .... '57 '02 C&L.339 B.S., J.D. [Ⓐ Johnson]
Sobecki, Thomas A., (BVⓉ) '56 '81 C.851 B.A. L.597 J.D.
[Ⓐ Johnson] (⊙Toledo, OH)
Spears, Larry J. ....'53 '80 C&L.339 B.S., J.D. [Prior]
Spies, Roland .... '60 '89 C.338 B.S. L.339 J.D. State Farm Ins. Cos.
States, John P. '37 '62 C.477 B.B.A. L.966 LL.B.
Coun., State Farm Mut. Auto. Ins. Co.
Sternberg, Alan L., (BV) '45 '70 C.208 B.S.B.A. L.146 J.D.
Assoc. Gen. Coun., State Farm Mut. Auto. Ins. Co.
Stille, Barbara Kay .... '65 '90 C&L.734 B.A., J.D. 1701 Towanda Ave.
Stites, Richard E., (AV) ....'54 '79 C.339 A.B. L.1119 J.D. [Livingston,B.B.&S.]
Stockton, Stephen F. .... '47 '72 C&L.597 B.S., J.D. One State Farm Plaza
Stone, Jerry H. '26 '51 C&L.623 LL.B.
(adm. in OK; not adm. in IL) 509 E. University St.‡
Stonikas, William John .... '61 '86 C.602 B.A. L.365 J.D. 1 State Farm Plaza # B.-3
Strawn, Evan A., (CV) ....'32 '59 C.338 B.A. L.326 J.D. 604 N. Colton Ave.

Strodel, Robert C., Ltd.
(See Peoria)

Stuckey, Charles E., (BVⓉ) ....'55 '80 C.340 B.A. L.339 J.D. State Farm Ins. Co.
Stumpf, David B., (BV) ....'47 '75 C&L.339 B.S., J.D. [Anderson,H.Q.&S.]
Sullivan, Laura P. '47 '72 C.187 B.A. L.221 J.D.
(adm. in IA; not adm. in IL) V.P., Coun. & Secy., State Farm Ins. Co.
Swee, Jean A., (AV) ....'57 '86 C.475 B.A. L.1187 J.D. [Williams&S.]
Tannenbaum, David '52 '77 C.1350 B.A. L.446 J.D.
(adm. in MD; not adm. in IL) Coun., State Farm Ins. Cos.
Taylor, Mark J., (BVⓉ) '50 '79 C&L.101 B.A., J.D.
(adm. in ID; not adm. in IL) Coun., State Farm Ins. Cos.
Thielen, Brian P., (BV) ....'57 '83 C.338 B.S. L.801 J.D. 207 W. Jefferson St., Ste. 600
Thomson, W. Loren, (AV) .... '31 '59 C.339 B.S. L.421 J.D. 105 N. Center Street

Thomson & Weintraub, (AV)
105 North Center Street, P.O. Box 3577, 61702-3577
Telephone: 309-829-7069 Facsimile: 309-827-3458
URL: http://www.thomsonandweintraub.com
Members of Firm: Chester Thomson (1910-1977); Alan I. Weintraub; Kathleen McDonald Kraft; Gina L. Wood; Terence B. Kelly; Melissa M. McGrath. Associate: Drew R. Quitschau.
General Civil and Trial Practice in all State and Federal Courts. Personal Injury, Auto Accidents, Workers Compensation, Family Law, Divorce, Adoptions, Bankruptcy, Real Estate, Criminal Law, Probate and Corporate Law, Civil Rights, Discrimination Law, Employment Law, Labor Law, School Law, Immigration Law.
See Professional Biographies, BLOOMINGTON, ILLINOIS

Tompkins, Bruce H., (CVⓉ) '56 '81 C.339 B.S. L.629 J.D.
(adm. in OR; not adm. in IL) State Farm Mutual Automobile Insurance Co.
Toy, K. Robert ....'52 '77 C.608 B.A. [Ⓐ Johnson]
Tran, Susanna C. .... '70 '95 C.339 B.S. L.347 J.D. State Farm Ins. Co.
Traskell, Jake Paul .... '57 '91 C.413 B.A. L.596 J.D. P.O. Box 1747
Tuite, James R. ....'48 '73 C&L.665 B.A., J.D. State Farm Mut. Auto. Ins. Co.
Turner, Mercer, (BV) ....'52 '77 C&L.339 B.S., J.D. [M.Turner]
Turner, Ralph T., (AV) ....'46 '73 C.861 B.A. L.339 J.D. [Hartweg,T.W.&S.]

Turner Law Office
(See Springfield)

Turner, Mercer, P.C., The Law Office of, (BV) .... 1 Brickyard Drive
Ulbrich, Barbara Traub ....'57 '91 C&L.339 B.A., J.D. Coun., State Farm Ins. Co.
Ulbrich, Louis F., (BV) .... '28 '52 C.340 Ph.B. L.339 J.D. [Ⓒ Dunn,W.A.&B.]
Varney, Robert T., (CV) ....'61 '86 C&L.339 B.S., J.D. 121 N. Main St.
Vieley, Jack C. ....'41 '67 C&L.339 B.S., J.D. 121 N. Main Street
Vogel, Charles D. .... '54 '79 C.696 B.A. L.228 J.D. Coun., State Farm Ins. Cos.
Waldman, John J., (CV) '62 '88 C.801 B.A. L.339 J.D.
[Ⓐ Kanoski&Assoc.] (⊙Macomb, Peoria, Quincy, Rushville, Springfield)
Walker, Clark A., (BV) .... '63 '90 C.446 B.S. L.801 J.D. 120 N. Center St.
Walker, James G., (AV) ....'44 '68 C&L.339 B.S., J.D. [Walker&W.]

Walker & Wylder, LTD, (AV)
207 W. Jefferson Street, 61701
Telephone: 309-828-5044 Fax: 309-827-2742
Email: info@walkerwylder.com URL: http://www.walkerwylder.com
James G. Walker; James R. Wylder; Lisa R. Corwin;—Andrew J. Kelly.
Toxic Torts, Asbestos, Chrome, Personal Injury, Automobile Accidents, Wrongful Death, Medical Malpractice, Employment Wrongful Discharge, Worker's Compensation.
See Professional Biographies, BLOOMINGTON, ILLINOIS

Wall, Dawn L., (BV) ....'62 '87 C.384 B.S. L.801 J.D. [Costigan&W.]
Watkins, Robert L. .... '64 '89 C&L.339 B.S., J.D. Coun., State Farm Ins. Cos.
Weaver, Bradley M. '54 '82 C.1249 B.A. L.1187 J.D.
(adm. in MI; not adm. in IL) State Farm Mut. Auto. Ins. Co.
Weintraub, Alan I., (AV) .... '47 '72 C&L.339 B.A., J.D. [Thomson&W.]
Wellman, Catherine B. .... '61 '86 C.840 B.B.A. L.734 J.D. State Farm Mut. Auto. Ins. Co.
Wells, D. Mark '52 '77 C.305 B.A. L.16 J.D.
(adm. in AL; not adm. in IL) State Farm Mut. Auto. Ins. Co.
Weltman, Eitan, Law Office of, (BV) '53 '79
C.339 B.A. L.146 J.D. 802 N. Clinton St., Ste. A
Wetzel, William C., (AV) .... '39 '64 C.602 B.A. L.339 LL.B. [Livingston,B.B.&S.]
White, Robert S., (BV) ....'43 '85 C.388 A.B. L.801 J.D. [Costigan&W.]
Whitman, Kathy Smith ....'56 '85 C.932 B.B.A. L.280 J.D. [Anderson,H.Q.&S.]
Wilber, Donald L., (BV) .... '39 '64 C.357 B.S. L.339 LL.B. [Wilber]
Wilber, Kenneth L., (CV) .... '66 '91 C&L.801 B.A., J.D. [Wilber]
Wilber Law Firm, The, (BV) ....816 Eldorado Road, Suite 7

Wilcox, Donald W., Jr., (BV) '48 '76 C&L.339 B.S., J.D.
318 West Washington Street, 2nd Floor, 61701
Telephone: 309-827-7403 Fax: 309-827-9377
URL: http://www.lawyers.com/dwilcoxlaw
General Practice.

Wiley, James Bruce '54 '80 C.797 B.A. L.16 J.D.
Mgr. Legal Servs., Country Cos., Financial Servs. Div.
Willard, Donald A., (AV) ....'52 '78 C.339 B.S. L.904 J.D. [Dunn,W.A.&B.]
Williams, Louis D., (AV) ....'24 '50 C.340 Ph.B. L.339 LL.B. 1901 E. Taylor St.‡
Williams, Robert E., (AV) ....'37 '64 C.894 B.A. L.378 LL.B. [Williams&S.]
Williams, Steven R., (BV) ....'69 '95 C.210 B.A. L.879 J.D. [Ⓐ Williams&S.]
Williams & Swee, Ltd., (AV) ....2011 Fox Creek Road
Wilson, Michael J., (BV) ....'50 '75 C.338 B.S. L.339 J.D. 235 E. Front Street
Wisdom, James M. .... '72 '99 C.340 B.A. L.879 J.D. Coun., State Farm Corp.
Witte, W. Charles ....'41 '75 C.338 B.S. L.64 J.D. Resident Cir. J.
Wochner, David C., (AV) ....'39 '64 C.602 B.B.A. L.339 LL.B. [Costigan&W.]
Wood, George C., (BV) ....'64 '89 C.338 B.S. L.801 J.D. [Hartweg,T.W.&S.]
Wood, Gina L., (BV) ....'68 '94 C.338 B.S. L.365 J.D. [Thomson&W.]
Wozniak, Debra G. ..... '54 '80 C&L.546 B.A., J.D. Coun., State Farm Mut. Auto. Ins. Co.
Wozniak, Michael A. ....'59 '84 C.338 B.S. L.339 J.D. [Ⓐ Livingston,B.B.&S.] ⊙
Wylder, James R., (AV) .... '53 '78 C&L.339 A.B., J.D. [Walker&W.]
Yeagle, Gary M. ...... '47 '74 C&L.339 B.S., J.D. State Farm Mutual Automobile Ins. Co.
Yoder, J. Stephen, (BV) ....'59 '83 C.340 B.S. L.221 J.D. 306 E. Grove St.
Yoder, James W., Law Office, (AV) ...... '37 '60 C&L.221 B.A., J.D. 306 E. Grove Street
Yoder, John W., (AV) ....'26 '52 C.340 Ph.B. L.221 LL.B. [John W.Y.]
Yoder, John Wm., (BV) .... '56 '82 C.340 B.A. L.365 J.D. [John W.Y.]
Zagaroli, Mark A. '54 '80 C.1121 B.A. L.1187 J.D.
(adm. in MI; not adm. in IL) State Farm Mut. Auto. Ins. Co.
Zanoni, Leon J., (AV) ....'37 '64 C&L.878 B.S., J.D. 234 1/2 E. Front St.

BLUE ISLAND, 23,463, *Cook Co.*

Babb, Ronald D. ....'38 '73 C.339 B.A. L.597 J.D. 2250 W. 121st St.
Carey, Frank T., Jr., (BV) ....'45 '73 C.750 B.A. L.365 J.D. [Carey&C.]
Carey, Michael D., (BV) ....'53 '78 C.339 B.A. L.365 J.D. [Carey&C.]
Carey & Carey, (BV) ....13004 S. Western Ave.
Cross, Robert C. ....'21 '48 C&L.145 A.B., J.D. 12716 Maple Ave.
Horvath, Cary A. .... '51 '76 C.339 B.A. L.146 J.D. City Atty.
Keefe, Hope F. .... '31 '78 C.145 B.A. L.146 J.D. 2428 Vermont St.
Keefe, John T. .... '19 '48 C.1191 B.Ed. L.145 J.D. P.O. Box 266

Petersen, Cynthia L. '65 '97 C.1348 B.A. L.424 J.D.
12757 S. Western Avenue, Suite 201, 60406
Telephone: 708-388-2250 Fax: 708-388-2150
Email: attypetersen@sbcglobal.net URL: http://www.attypetersen.com
Divorce, Qualified Domestic Relations Order (QDRO), Paternity, Premarital Agreements, Child Support.
See Professional Biographies, BLUE ISLAND, ILLINOIS

Scannell, William F., (Ltd.) .... '23 '48 C&L.893 J.D. 12757 S. Western Ave.
Stroka, Albert A. '42 '70 C&L.209 B.A., J.D.
V.P. & Gen. Coun., Heritage Financial Servs.
Thomson, William H. '42 '67 C&L.339 A.B., J.D.
Sr. V.P. & Sr. Tr. Offr., First Natl. Bk. of Blue Island-Trust Dept.

BOLINGBROOK, 56,321, *Will Co.*

Anderson, Lara A. ....'67 '92 C&L.589 B.S., J.D. [Ⓐ Tressler,S.M.&P.]
Arrigo, James P. ....'60 '94 C.339 B.S. L.209 J.D. [Ⓐ Tressler,S.M.&P.]
Belsante, Michael '57 '83 C.354 B.A. L.201 J.D.
(adm. in NJ; not adm. in IL)
Senior Vice President & General Counsel, U.S. Water L.L.C.
Bloomberg, Steven P., (AV) ....'43 '69 C.966 B.S. L.209 J.D. [Tressler,S.M.&P.]
Boan, James, (CV) ....'51 '83 C.339 B.S. L.589 J.D. [Tressler,S.M.&P.]
Denkmann, Rex ....'43 '70 C.62 A.B. L.734 J.D. 684 W. Boughton Rd.
DiSabato, Daniel A. '42 '70
C.339 B.A. L.146 J.D. Admin. Law J., State Dept. of Employ. Sec.
Freeman, David J. ....'58 '83 C.276 A.B. L.1338 J.D. [Tressler,S.M.&P.]
Grabavoy, Denise ....'52 '77 C&L.221 B.A., J.D. 684 W. Boughton Rd.

Grabavoy, Marie ....'54 '79 C&L.424 A.B., J.D. 684 W. Boughton Rd.
Hedayat, Mazyar M. ....'66 '95 C.477 B.A. L.209 J.D. [M.Hedayat&Assoc.]

Hedayat, M., & Associates, P.C.
425 Quadrangle Drive, Suite 101, 60440
Telephone: 630-378-2200 Fax: 630-578-2878 URL: http://www.mha-law.com
Email: mmhedayat@mhu-law.com URL: http://www.lawyers.com/mhedayat
Mazyar M. Hedayat;—Andrew R. Kreamer.
Language: Farsi.
Commercial Litigation, Commercial Transactions, Construction Law and Mechanics Liens, Debtor and Creditor Law, Commercial and Personal Bankruptcy, Commercial and Residential Real Estate.
See Professional Biographies, BOLINGBROOK, ILLINOIS

Kennedy, Thomas A......................'20 '45 C.339 L.365 LL.B. 504 Kildeer #203‡
Kreamer, Andrew R. ....'— '02 C.162 L.862 J.D. [Ⓐ M.Hedayat&Assoc.]
Kusta, Edward D., (BV) ....'42 '69 C.589 B.S. L.146 J.D. [Kusta&B.]
Kusta & Boan, P.C., (BV) ....430 W. Boughton Rd.

Lynch, John J., Law Offices of
(See Woodridge)

Marchetti, George A. ....'48 '78 C.602 B.A. L.146 J.D. [Tressler,S.M.&P.]
McFarland-Taylor, Laura ....'60 '99 C.472 B.A. L.365 J.D. 1084 Four Seasons Lane
Meadowcroft, Reynar, Jr., (BV) '44 '72 C.210 B.A. L.930 J.D.
440 W. Boughton, Ste. 200

Mitchell, Bolden & Melton, P.C.
(See Joliet)

Moss, Barry L., (AV) ....'43 '68 C.98 B.S. L.597 J.D. [Tressler,S.M.&P.]

Moss and Bloomberg, Ltd.
(See Tressler, Soderstrom, Maloney & Priess)

Panega, David S. ....'52 '86 C.209 B.A. L.146 J.D. 5 Pennsbury Ct.
Pohlenz, Julius '68 '95 C.352 B.S.E. L.861 J.D.
Corp. Atty., Goss Graphic Systems, Inc.

Tressler, Soderstrom, Maloney & Priess, (AV)
305 West Briarcliff Road, Suite 201, 60440-0858 ⊙
Telephone: 630-759-0800 Telecopier: 630-759-8504
URL: http://www.tsmp.com
Resident Members: Barry L. Moss; Steven P. Bloomberg; George A. Marchetti; David J. Freeman; James Boan. Resident Associates: Lara A. Anderson; James P. Arrigo.
General Civil Litigation and Trial Practice, Insurance, Reinsurance, Litigation, Insurance Bad Faith, Appellate Practice, Business Litigation, Business Transactions, Class Action Defense, Commercial Litigation, Complex Litigation, Directors and Officers Liability, Construction Law, Architects and Engineers, Fidelity and Surety, Real Estate Litigation and Transactions, Alternative Dispute Resolution, Product Liability, Intellectual Property, Internet Law, Electronic Commerce, Environmental Law, Asbestos Litigation, Health Care, ERISA, Labor and Employment, Technology Law, Securities Litigation, Health Care, Bankruptcy, Advertising Law, Personal Injury, Trusts and Estates, Contracts, Professional Liability, Regulatory, White Collar Crime, Corporate Law, Mergers and Acquisitions, Commodities, Condominium and Common Interest Community Law, Municipal Law.
Chicago, Illinois Office: 233 Wacker Drive, Sears Tower, 22nd Floor, 60606. Telephone: 312-627-4000. Fax: 312-627-1717.
Wheaton, Illinois Office: 2100 Manchester Road, Suite 950, 60187. Telephone: 630-668-2800. Fax: 630-668-3003.
Newark, New Jersey Office: 744 Broad Street, Suite 1510, 07102. Telephone: 973-848-2900. Fax: 973-623-0405.
Los Angeles, California Office: 1901 Avenue of the Stars, Suite 450, 90067. Telephone: 310-203-4800. Fax: 310-203-4850.
Costa Mesa, California Office: 3070 Bristol Street, Suite 450, 92626. Telephone: 714-429-2900. Fax: 714-429-2901.
See Professional Biographies, BOLINGBROOK, ILLINOIS

Waldie, Kandy F. '61 '86 C.169 B.S. L.464 J.D.
(adm. in CA; not adm. in IL) Gen. Mgr., UNICARE
Zahour, Alonzo H. ....'49 '74 C.17 B.A. L.339 J.D. [A.Zahour]
Zahour, Alonzo .... 101 Royce Rd.

BOURBONNAIS, 15,256, *Kankakee Co.*

Biczinski, Ann L., Law Office of .... 4 St.47 S. Main, Ste. 1
Brasel, Tony L., (CV) ....'52 '78 C.679 B.A. L.221 J.D. 201 Park Place
Brezinski, Ann Lesley Burkey ......'59 '85 C.339 B.S. L.801 J.D. 447 S. Main St., Ste. 1
Brezinski, Ann Lesley Burkey ....'— '85 C.339 B.S. L.801 J.D. [A.L.Biczinski]
Brock, Walter D., (CV) ....'56 '84 C&L.589 B.S., J.D. P.O. Box 95
Collins, James P., (BV) ....'32 '63 C.339 L.365 LL.B. 1061 Bar L Lane
Engels, Patricia L. ....'26 '79 C.624 B.S. L.365 J.D. 33 Brittany Lane
Gerts, Ronald J., (BV) ....'46 '77 C.103 A.B. L.365 J.D. 735 Almar Parkway, Suite B
Higgins, Georganne R. '52 '77 C.675 B.A. L.608 J.D.
(adm. in OH; not adm. in IL) 2904 Chippewa Dr.
McClure, Thomas E., (AV) '54 '79 C.338 B.S. L.209 J.D.
18 Briarcliff Professional Center
Tetreault, Frederick P. ....'63 '94 C.624 B.A. L.339 J.D. 201 Park Pl.

BRADLEY, 12,784, *Kankakee Co.*

Chaplinski, Randall R., (BV) '54 '80
C.679 B.S. L.365 J.D. V.P. & Cheif. Trust Off., HomeStar
Regas, Gus R. ....'52 '79 C.339 B.A. L.365 J.D. 300 N. Kennedy Dr.

Smietanski, Alan F., (BV) '51 '76 C.339 B.A. L.365 J.D.
236 North Industrial Drive, 60915
Telephone: 815-935-2100 FAX: 815-935-2121
Email: afslaw@ameritech.net URL: http://www.afslawfirm.com
General Civil and Trial Practice. Corporate, Real Estate, Probate, Collections, Personal Injury, Municipal and Domestic Relations Law, Estate Planning, Wills, Probate, Trusts and Estates, Adoption Law, Child Custody, Child Support, Wrongful Death Automobile Accidents, Medical Malpractice.
See Professional Biographies, BRADLEY, ILLINOIS

BREESE, 4,048, *Clinton Co.*

Becker, William J. ....'50 '75 C.597 B.A. L.910 J.D. Assoc. Cir. J.
Donnewald, James H., (BV) ....'25 '51 C.734 L.996 LL.B. 1301 Apple Lane
Frutiger, Carma L. ....'63 '88 C.234 B.S. L.1187 J.D. 832 N. 10th St.
Granberg, Kurt M. ....'53 '80 C.339 B.A. L.146 J.D. 1301 Apple Lane
Schuette, P. Michael ....'49 '77 C.339 B.A. L.300 J.D. Schuette Stores, Inc.

BRIDGEPORT, 2,118, *Lawrence Co.*

Floyd, Lindsey D. ....'— '03 C.249 B.S. L.801 J.D. [Ⓐ J.D.Stout]

Stout, James D., Law Offices of, (BV) '— '74 C.801 B.A. L.339 J.D.
324 North Main Street, P.O. Box 8, 62417 ⊙
Telephone: 618-945-2911 Fax: 618-945-3941
Email: jds1@shawneelink.net URL: http://www.lawyers.com/stoutholtzhouser
Associate: Lindsey D. Floyd.
General Civil Practice. Trials. Corporation, Real Estate, Oil and Gas, Probate and Estate Planning Law.
§§.
Robinson, Illinois Office: 309 South Jefferson, P.O. Box 714, 62454. Telephone: 618-546-5404. Fax: 618-544-3659.
See Professional Biographies, BRIDGEPORT, ILLINOIS

BRIDGEVIEW, 15,335, *Cook Co.*

Barth, Michael A. ....'49 '79 C&L.589 B.A., J.D. Asst. Pub. Def.
Darragh, Thomas C. ....'33 '64 C.397 B.A. L.602 LL.B. Asst. Pub. Def.
Flaherty, John M. ....'21 '50 C&L.209 LL.B. Assoc. Cir. J.
Haleas, James W. ....'14 '47 C.137 L.365 LL.B. [Haleas&H.]
Haleas, Peter E. ....'30 '53 C&L.209 LL.B. [Haleas&H.] ‡
Haleas, Peter J. ....'59 '84 C.93 A.B. L.602 J.D. 7940 S. Harlem Ave.
Haleas & Haleas ....7940 S. Harlem St.
Krzanowski, Ralph J. ....'44 '73 C.766 B.A. L.1049 J.D. Co. Pub. Def. Off.
Laport, Frank L. ....'41 '66 C.238 B.A. L.209 J.D. 7421 W. 100th Pl.
Locke, Ronald P. ....'50 '80 C.103 A.B. L.446 J.D. Pub. Def. Off.
Martin, Patricia Manila ....'59 '86 C.478 B.S. L.589 J.D. Asst. Pub. Def.
Mash, Gordon S. ....'47 '72 C&L.209 B.A., J.D. Chf. Pub. Def.
McCurrie, Lester D. ....'30 '63 C&L.209 B.A., J.D. Cir. J.
McElligott, Joseph P. ....'53 '78 C.1151 B.A. L.146 J.D. Pub. Def.
McGinnis, Michael E., Jr. ....'53 '80 C.339 B.A. L.146 J.D. Asst. Pub. Def.
Meekins, Frank W. ....'43 '67 C.742 B.A. L.209 J.D. Supvr. J., Crim. Div.
Mraibie, Hanna ....'76 '01 C.339 B.S. L.209 J.D. 8550 S. Harlem Ave., Ste. F
Murray, Michael J. ....'34 '62 C.884 B.S.E. L.209 J.D. Assoc. Cir. J.
O'Donnell, Maria A. '62 '86
C.597 B.A. L.339 J.D. Compl. Offr., Bridgeview Bank & Trust Co.
Ronkowski, Edward E. ....'50 '74 C.326 B.S. L.209 J.D. Asst. States Atty.
Sherwin, Michael R. ....'46 '77 C.475 B.A. L.365 J.D. Asst. States Atty.
Silaides, Daniela ....'76 '02 C&L.209 B.A., J.D. Asst. U.S. Atty.
Snow, Susan ....'47 '73 C.339 B.A. L.146 J.D. Assoc. Cir. J.
Stoecker, Leonard E., II, (CV) '53 '83 C.339 B.A. L.61 J.D.
Assoc. Gen. Coun. & Dir., Prairie Material Sales, Inc.
Welter, Daniel G. ....'49 '76 C.424 A.B. L.146 J.D. Assoc. J.
Zogas, Paul M. ....'55 '82 C.477 A.B. L.209 J.D. 8929 S. Harlem Ave.

BRIGHTON, 2,270, *Jersey & Macoupin Cos.*

Albert-Fritz, Mary M., (BV) ......'54 '81 C.961 B.S. L.910 J.D. 401 North Maple Avenue
Watson, Robert L., (BV) ......'37 '63 C.357 B.S. L.339 J.D. 201 N. Main (⊙Bunker Hill)

BROADVIEW, 8,264, *Cook Co.*

Baer, Luke '50 '79 C.966 B.A. L.1035 J.D.
(adm. in MN; not adm. in IL) V.P., Gen. Coun. & Secy., Robert Bosch Corp.
Comstock, R. Warren, (AV) '39 '66 C&L.966 B.S.C.E., J.D.
Chf. Coun., Intell. Prop., Robert Bosch Corp. (Pat.)
Gordon, Sara '64 '91 C.477 B.S. L.424 J.D.
Asst.Gen.Coun., Indus.& Household Prods., Robert Bosch Corp.
Gorey, John J. ....'47 '81 C.363 B.A. L.589 J.D. [Winkler&G.]
Mullins, William J. ....'56 '83 C.436 B.A. L.365 J.D. Mullins Food Products
Ozga, Daniel T. '71 '99 C.339 B.A. L.209 J.D.
In-House Counsel, Prism Innovative Resources, Inc.
Perlow, S. James '45 '70 C.966 B.S. L.597 J.D.
Pres. & Gen. Coun., R. L. Perlow Steel Corp.
Stuart, Frederick A., (AVⓉ) '42 '73 C.938 A.B. L.245 J.D.
(adm. in GA; not adm. in IL) Chief Coun., Labor Rels. Employ., Robert Bosch Corp.
Thiess, Gregory G. '54 '79 C.209 B.A. L.215 J.D.
Asst. Gen. Coun., Robert Bosch Corp.
Torpats, John P. '28 '54 C.299 B.A. L.276 J.D.
(adm. in DC; not adm. in IL) Gen. Coun. & Corp. Coun., National Van Lines, Inc.
Winkler, Charles R., (AV) ....'35 '60 C.424 B.S. L.209 LL.B. [Winkler&G.]
Winkler & Gorey, Ltd., (AV) ....1903 W. Cermak Rd.

BROOKFIELD, 19,085, *Cook Co.*

Billik, Richard J. ....'28 '52 C.339 L.365 LL.B. 9043 W. 28th St.
Cregar, Wm. L. ....'24 '50 C.352 L.365 J.D. 3726 Prairie Ave.
Granado, John ....'45 '80 C.424 B.S. L.209 J.D. 3148 Sunnyside Ave.
Horn, William D. ....'51 '93 C.378 B.M.Ed. L.209 J.D. P.O. Box 326
James, Curtis A. ....'58 '85 C.209 B.A. L.146 J.D. Asst. State Atty.
Kanelos, Frank S. ....'16 '42 L.365 LL.B. 3726 Prairie Ave.
McCabe, James K. ....'51 '84 C.589 B.A. L.146 J.D. [McCabe&M.]
McCabe, Kathleen L. ....'55 '85 C.424 B.S. L.146 J.D. [McCabe&M.]
McCabe & McCabe ....8827 Ogden Avenue
Miranda, Daniel R. ....'47 '73 C.339 B.A. L.365 J.D. Assoc. Cir. J.
Mooney, Jos. C. ....'13 '50 C&L.209 LL.B. 4604 Prairie Ave.‡
Preston, John G. ....'21 '52 C.578 L.365 J.D. 3726 Prairie Ave.
Szymanski, Ronald J. ....'47 '77 C.339 B.A. L.365 J.D. Asst. Pub. Def.
Usher, Edward M. ....'70 '99 C.679 B.S. L.209 J.D. 9515 Southview Ave.

BUFFALO GROVE, 42,909, *Cook & Lake Cos.*

Adler Law Offices, Ltd.
(See Arlington Heights)

Ament, Neil S. ....'61 '88 C.966 B.A. L.365 J.D. 171 W. Fabish Dr.
Ament, Rickey J. ....'47 '72 C.339 A.B. L.209 J.D. 1110 W. Lake Cook Rd., Ste. 295
Bartell, Kerry T. ....'74 '98 C.597 B.S. L.146 J.D. [Ⓐ Kovitz S.N.]
Bazianos, William S. ....'66 '92 C.209 B.S. L.1187 J.D. [Ⓐ Kovitz S.N.]
Bell, Ronald L. ....'55 '80 C.393 B.A. L.365 J.D. [R.L.Bell&Assoc.]
Bell, Ronald L., & Associates, P.C. .... 1250 Barclay Blvd.
Bendoff, David M., (AV) ....'57 '84 C.36 B.S. L.365 J.D. [Kovitz S.N.]
Berkson, Norman N., (BV) ....'28 '57 C.1016 B.S.C. L.209 J.D. 540 Chebourg Ct.
Bermudez, Noe G. .... '65 '96 C.209 B.S. L.146 J.D. Coun., Siemens Bldg. Tech, Inc.
Bernstein, Howard ....'34 '59 C.339 B.S. L.209 J.D. 1110 Lake Cook Rd.
Bickley, John H., III, (AV) ....'52 '78 C.172 B.A. L.146 J.D. [Kovitz S.N.]
Blumenthal, Marc J. ....'51 '76 C.339 B.A. L.146 J.D. 355 W. Dundee Rd.
Boeh, Cynthia Adamson, (BVⓉ) '62 '87
C.490 B.A. L.494 J.D. Gen. Coun., Yanmar America Corp.
Bonaccorsi, Joseph P. ......'64 '89 C.597 B.S. L.424 J.D. Gen. Coun., OPTION Care, Inc.
Bouslog, Thomas D. .....'51 '82 C.339 B.S. L.209 J.D. 1110 W. Lake Cook Rd., Ste. 353
Brostoff, Ben C. ....'14 '41 L.209 LL.B. 225 Lake Blvd.‡
Cloer, Stewart L. '56 '82 L.574 J.D.
(adm. in NY; not adm. in IL) [Ⓒ Foster&K.]
Crost, Hillard ....'13 '38 C.597 L.424 LL.B. 241 Belaire Dr.
Danziger, Sebastian N. '64 '91
C.347 B.M. L.209 J.D. Assoc. Coun., Siemens Bldg. Tech. Inc.
Davis, Paul M. ....'34 '63 C.46 B.S. L.209 LL.B. 517 Cobblestone Ln.
DeNotto, Gerald F. '54 '80 C.339 B.A. L.424 J.D.
Sr. V.P. & Gen. Coun., Indeck Energy Servs., Inc.
Dentzer, John L. ....'37 '62 C&L.424 A.B., J.D. Applied Indus. Materials Corp.

Entman, Bruce R. ....'52 '78 C.339 B.S. L.146 J.D. 750 Lake Cook Rd., Ste. 495
Feldgreber, Robert, The Law Office of '60 '85
C.339 B.S. L.424 J.D. 100 Lexington Dr., Ste. 201
Finkle, Kenneth S. ....'38 '73 C.1016 B.S.B.A. L.365 J.D. 1401 W. Dundee Rd.
Firfer, Jodi I. ....'61 '86 C.339 B.S. L.597 J.D. 1010 N. Highland Grove Ct.
Foster, Timothy Michael '69 '02 C.999 B.S. L.229 J.D.
(adm. in PA; not adm. in IL) [Foster&K.]
Foster & Koop, LLC ....1250 Barclay Boulevard, Suite 200
Gilbert, Sherwin ....'43 '68 C.339 B.S. L.209 J.D. Indeck Energy Servs., Inc.
Glieberman, Sheldon L. ....'24 '50 C.1016 B.S. L.597 J.D. 101 Old Oak Dr.‡
Goldgehn, Seymour R., (AV) ....'24 '49 C.339 L.209 J.D. 364 Bentley Pl.‡
Golub, Martin H. ....'49 '75 C.339 B.A. L.209 J.D. 723 Pinehurst Ln.
Graham, Keith E. ....'56 '82 C.976 B.A. L.145 J.D. Coun., Siemens Bldg. Tech. Inc.
Grodner, Jay R., (BV) ....'52 '78 C.966 B.A. L.365 J.D. [J.R.Grodner&Assoc.] ⊙
Grodner, Jay R., & Associates, P.C., (BV)
1110 Lake Cook Rd., Ste. 190 (⊙Chicago, Highland Park)
Gross, Theodore M. ....'72 '97 C.339 B.A. L.209 J.D. 750 W. Lake Cook Rd.
Gumbiner, Gary M. ....'52 '79 C.589 M.S. L.424 J.D. 732 Marseilles Circle
Gunn, Joseph N. '52 '78 C.604 B.A. L.665 J.D.
Assoc. Coun., Siemens Bldg. Tech., Inc.
Heuberger, Michael A. ....'48 '77 C.1016 B.A. L.365 J.D. 1000 Deerfield Pkwy.
Hillsberg, Richard W., (AV) ....'41 '67 C.659 B.S. L.276 J.D. [Kovitz S.N.]
Hornstein, Diane G., (BVⓉ) '42 '85 C.102 B.A. L.1029 J.D.
(adm. in CT; not adm. in IL) 75 Woodstone Drive
Huff, Matthew R. ....'77 '02 C&L.597 B.A., J.D. 750 W. Lake Cook Rd., Ste. 350
Israelstam, Alfred W. ....'08 '34 C&L.145 Ph.B., J.D. [A.W.Israelstam]
Israelstam, Alfred W., P.C. ....1111 Lake Cook Rd.
Jablonski, Heather L. ....'69 '94 C.174 B.A. L.146 J.D. [Ⓐ Kovitz S.N.]
Jacobs, Rodney L. ....'38 '65 C&L.64 LL.B. 1516 Anderson Lane
Jacobson, Julie A. ....'70 '00 C.36 B.A. L.146 J.D. [Ⓐ Kovitz S.N.]
Jobe, Melissa A. '68 '96 C.910 B.A. L.339 J.D.
V.P. & Gen. Coun., Salespage Technologies, Inc.
Juster, Stefanie A., Attorney At Law ....'70 '99 C.910 B.A. L.365 J.D. 254 Windsor Drive
Kapustka, Ronald J. ....'63 '90 C.1183 B.S. L.365 J.D. [Kovitz S.N.]
Kaufman, Jay C. ....'53 '80 C&L.589 B.A., J.D. [J.C.Kaufman]
Kaufman, Jay C., P.C. ....P.O. Box 7809
Kay, John ....'67 '92 C.966 B.A. L.365 J.D. 750 Lake Cook Rd.
Kliff, Michael David ....'51 '86 C.339 B.S. L.365 J.D. 630 Pinehurst Ln.
Kogen, Robert B. ....'67 '92 C.339 B.A. L.209 J.D. [Kovitz S.N.]
Kole, Julius S. ....'53 '78 C.339 B.S. L.365 J.D. [J.Kole]
Kole, Julius, Law Office of .... 750 W. Lake Cook Rd., Ste. 135
Koop, Craig J. ....'67 '99 C&L.209 B.S., J.D. [Foster&K.]
Kopka, Robert J., (AV) ....'— '82 C.1036 B.A. L.209 J.D. [Kopka,P.D.&E.]
Kopka, Pinkus, Dolin & Eads, (AV)
100 Lexington Drive, Suite 100 (⊙Chgo., IL; Crown Point, Indpls., South Bend, IN; Farmington Hills, MI)
Kovitz, Alan D., (AV) ....'34 '58 C&L.597 B.S.L., J.D. [Kovitz S.N.] ⊙
Kovitz Shifrin Nesbit, A Professional Corporation, (AV)
750 Lake Cook Road, Suite 350 (⊙Chicago)
Krupnick, Scott ....'56 '81 C.338 B.S. L.424 J.D. 1274 N. Wellington Ct.

Kulinsky, Lois, & Associates, Ltd.
(See Wheeling)

Lipsky, Edward S. ....'50 '75 C.339 B.A. L.209 J.D. [E.S.Lipsky]
Lipsky, Edward S., P.C. ....355 W. Dundee Rd.
Lorber, Tamara Elvove ....'56 '81 C.966 B.B.A. L.146 J.D. 880 Port Clinton Ct. W.
Machtinger, Marc D. ....'69 '96 C.597 B.S. L.910 J.D. [M.D.Machtinger]
Machtinger, Marc D., Law Office of, Ltd. ....750 W. Lake Cook Rd., Ste. 350
Malfar, D. E., & Associates ....'55 '81 C.339 B.A. L.209 J.D. 1315 Devonshire Rd.
Mednick, Richard M. ....'47 '81 C.589 B.S.Ed. L.365 J.D. P.O. Box 7377
Moodhe, Matthew L. ....'66 '91 C.210 B.A. L.209 J.D. [Kovitz S.N.]
Morano, Christopher J. '65 '90 C.93 L.1019
V.P. & Gen. Coun., Essex Crane Rental Corp.
Nesbit, Robert P. ....'58 '84 C.210 B.A. L.802 J.D. [Kovitz S.N.]
Newman, Jeffrey C. ....'55 '80 C&L.339 B.S., J.D. 415 Marvins Way
Orth, Jason E. ....'68 '93 C.679 B.A. L.209 J.D. [Ⓐ Kovitz S.N.]
Ottenheimer, Lester A., III ....'55 '80 C.347 B.S. L.345 J.D. [Kovitz S.N.]
Park, Pamela J. ....'71 '96 C.350 B.S. L.146 J.D. [Ⓐ Kovitz S.N.]
Peake, Darryl L. ....'52 '80 C.801 B.S. L.365 J.D. Sr. Coun., Siemens Corp.

Pinzur, Cohen & Kerr, Ltd.
(See Long Grove)

Posey, John T. ....'24 '49 C.602 L.145 J.D. 154 S. Buffalo Grove Rd.‡
Powell, Michael H. ....'60 '85 C.589 B.S. L.146 J.D. 280 Blackthorn Dr.‡
Present, Jeffrey A. ....'68 '95 C.352 B.A. L.209 J.D. Forsythe Technology

Robins, Martin B., (AV) '— '80 C.659 B.S. L.309 J.D.
1110 Lake Cook Road, Suite 355, 60089
Telephone: 847-229-8710 Fax: 847-229-8839
Email: mrobins@mr-laws.com

See Professional Biographies, BUFFALO GROVE, ILLINOIS

Rubin, Brian, & Associates, The Law Offices of '50 '76
C.339 B.S. L.146 J.D. 1110 West Lake Cook Road, Suite 165
Schwartz, Marc K. ....'53 '79 C.216 B.A. L.365 J.D. [M.K.Schwartz]
Schwartz, Sheldon ....'44 '73 C.339 B.A. L.209 J.D. 750 W. Lake Cook Rd., Ste. 135
Schwartz, Marc K, & Associates ....314 N. McHenry Rd.
Shamash, Steven R. '— '89
C.350 B.A. L.146 J.D. Assoc. Coun., Siemens Bldg. Tech. Inc.
Shanker, Lisa K. ....'62 '87 C&L.339 B.S., J.D. [Ⓐ Kovitz S.N.]
Shifrin, Jordan I. ....'50 '77 C.339 B.A.M.A. L.365 J.D. [Kovitz S.N.]
Shpritz, Ryan H. ....'76 '01 C.339 B.A. L.146 J.D. [Ⓐ Kovitz S.N.]
Siegel, Larry A. ....'51 '76 C.966 B.A. L.861 J.D. [Ⓑ B.Rubin&Assoc.]
Silverberg, Diane J., (AV) ....'61 '86 C&L.966 B.A., J.D. [Kovitz S.N.]
Smith, Judith L. ....'60 '85 C.1365 B.A. L.146 J.D. [Ⓑ B.Rubin&Assoc.]
Smoller, Gerald J. ....'43 '68 C.339 B.A. L.146 J.D. [Kovitz S.N.]
Stanton, Stuart R. ....'60 '86 C.339 B.A. L.365 J.D. 75 Fabish Ct.
Stein, Andrew H. ....'59 '99 C.589 B.S. L.146 J.D. 17 E. Chevy Chase Dr.

Stelk, Roger W., Law Offices of
(See Arlington Heights)

Sternberg, Robert A., (AV) ....'48 '72 C.477 B.A. L.597 J.D. [Kovitz S.N.]
Stolman, Anne L. '66 '91 C.966 B.A. L.146 J.D.
Assoc. Coun., Siemens Building Technologies
Tarnoff, David ....'58 '83 C.339 B.S. L.273 J.D. 920 Chaucer Way
Wagner, Matthew C. ......'74 '00 C.801 B.S. L.365 J.D. Gen. Coun., CEM Insurance Co.
Walsh, Steven J. ....'64 '89 C.424 B.A. L.146 J.D. 750 Lake Cook Rd.
Ward, Michael W., (AV) ....'50 '76 C.602 B.A. L.146 J.D. [M.W.Ward]
Ward, Michael W., P.C., (AV) ....1608 Barclay Blvd.
Waskin, Alan R. '60 '85 C.339 B.A. L.800 J.D.
Assistant General Counsel, Indeck Energy Services, Inc.
Weis, Randi B. ....'65 '90 C.347 B.A. L.424 J.D. 2943 Whispering Oaks Dr.‡
Wiltse, Vincent E. '71 '00 C.477 B.S.E. L.912 J.D.
750 W. Lake Cook Rd., Ste. 350 (Pat.)
Zerman, Keith A. ....'56 '81 C.221 B.S.B.A. L.734 J.D. [Ⓐ Kovitz S.N.]
Zweifel, Rebecca L. ....'71 '96 C.597 B.S. L.209 J.D. [Ⓐ Kovitz S.N.]

BUNKER HILL, 1,722, *Macoupin Co.*

Watson, Robert L., (BV) ....'37 '63 C.357 B.S. L.339 J.D. 115 N. Wash. St. (⊙Brighton)

BURBANK, 27,902, *Cook Co.*

Abraham, Katherine ....'29 '65 C.339 B.A. L.146 J.D. 6355 W. 82nd Pl.
Borawski, Wayne C. ....'56 '84 C.589 B.S. L.146 J.D. 7801 Massasoit Ave.
Cainkar, Vincent ....'49 '74 C.734 A.B. L.209 J.D. 6215 W. 79th St., Ste. 2A
Foreman, John E. ....'29 '64 C.424 B.S. L.146 LL.B. 7149 W. 79th St.
Franowsky, Allan J. ....'45 '90 C.339 B.S. L.365 J.D. 6458 W. 87th St. (Pat.)
Kotz, James C. ....'61 '92 C.93 B.S. L.146 J.D. 5624 W. 79th St., 2nd Fl.

BURNHAM, 4,170, *Cook Co.*

Petrich, George M. ....'30 '61 14200 S. Burnham Ave.

BURR RIDGE, 10,408, *Cook & DuPage Cos.*

Alderman, Heather Higgins ....'60 '85 C.602 B.A. L.339 J.D. [Grasso D.]
Anthony, Evelyn Tsamtsouris ....'63 '89 C.860 B.A. L.1202 J.D. 302 Ambriance Drive
Bembinster, Gregory E. ....'40 '65 C.746 B.A. L.209 J.D. Financial Title Serv.
Brennan, James J., (AV) '50 '75 C.679 B.S. L.345 J.D.
Sr. V.P. & Gen. Coun., BankFinancial, F.S.B.
Brennan, William M. ....'64 '90 C.339 B.S. L.424 J.D. 835 McClintock Dr., Ste. 200
Buchenauer, Kristina E. ....'73 '99 C.966 B.B.A. L.339 J.D. [Ⓐ Goldstine,S.R.N.&H.]
Buikema, Paul R. ....'67 '92 C.114 B.A. L.880 J.D. [Goldstine,S.R.N.&H.]
Burke, Bernard J., Jr. ....'30 '54 C.602 B.S.C. L.209 J.D. 38 Red Oak Ct.
Constantino, Gregory J. ......'49 '73 C.424 B.A. L.209 J.D. 835 McClintock Dr., Ste. 200
Dixon, John F. ....'72 '97 C.339 B.S. L.365 J.D. 835 McClintock Dr., 2nd Fl.
Dose, Gregory L., (AV) ....'51 '79 C&L.494 B.A., J.D. 835 McClinton Dr., Ste. 200
Eilers, Robert E. ....'54 '80 C&L.421 B.A., J.D. 53 Tomlin Cir.‡
Eklund, Maria E. ....'59 '90 C.128 LL.B. L.477 J.D. 1333 Burr Ridge Pkwy.
Enlund, E. Stanley ....'17 '42 L.209 J.D. 403 Burr Ridge Club Dr.‡
Fletcher, James Elrod ....'21 '79 C.597 B.S. L.365 J.D. 10 Tartan Ridge Rd.
Gillespie, James F. ....'26 '51 C&L.209 LL.B. 362 Countryside Ct.
Goldstine, Robert D., (AV) ....'32 '56 C.597 B.S. L.339 J.D. [Goldstine,S.R.N.&H.]
Goldstine, Skrodzki, Russian, Nemec and Hoff, Ltd., (AV)
835 McClintock Dr., Ste. 200
Grace, Amy P. ....'71 '99 C.686 B.A. L.365 J.D. 15W030 N. Feontage Rd.
Grasso, Gary A., (AV) ....'51 '78 C.276 B.S.F.S. L.262 J.D. [Grasso D.]
Grasso Dunleavy, P.C., (AV) ....7020 County Line Rd., Suite 100
Haddad, Michael J., Law Offices of '48 '73
C.912 B.A. L.213 J.D. 455 S. Frontage Rd., Ste. 215
Healy, James David ....'57 '93 C.238 B.A. L.365 J.D. 835 McClintock Dr., Ste. 200
Hoff, Howard M. ....'57 '82 C.114 B.A. L.209 J.D. 835 McClintock Dr.
Hrabak, William H., Jr. ....'55 '81 C.608 B.S. L.851 J.D. 835 McClintock Dr., Ste. 200
Kash, Kimberly Marie ....'62 '92 BankFinancial, F.S.B.
King, Teresa A. ....'58 '88 C.589 B.S. L.365 J.D. M. Ramsey King Inc.
Lee, Michael ....'68 '94 C.197 A.B. L.597 J.D. 1 Sylvan Glen Cout
Levy, Robert L. ....'47 '73 C.210 B.A. L.209 J.D. 8104 Garfield
Matus, Seth D. ....'70 '96 C.705 B.A. L.174 J.D. 835 McClintock Drive
McNear, Sara A. ....'60 '94 C.477 B.A. L.475 J.D. 7600 S. County Line Rd., Ste. 1
Moody, Gregory J. ....'65 '91 C.1121 B.S.B.A. L.209 J.D. 15W030 N. Frontage Road
Nemec, Kenneth J., Jr. ....'54 '82 C.177 B.A. L.365 J.D. 835 McClindock Dr.,
Nogal, Richard J. ....'56 '81 C&L.597 B.A., J.D. [Goldstine,S.R.N.&H.]
Oldershaw, John B. ....'32 '91 C.424 B.S. L.365 J.D. 62 Huntington Court
Pavel, Erich O., III ....'54 '80 C.801 B.A. L.365 J.D. Legal Services Plan
Pecen, Diana K. ....'61 '97 C.347 B.A. L.879 J.D. 835 McClintock, 2nd Fl.
Perkowitz, William T. '54 '82 C.801 B.A. L.424 J.D.
(adm. in CA; not adm. in IL) 1102 Burr Ridge Club Dr.‡
Riley, John J. ....'56 '88 C.339 B.S. L.365 J.D. 7600 County Line Rd.
Riley, Richard Connor ....'47 '76 C.1151 B.A. L.365 J.D. 7600 S. County Line Rd.
Rothschild, Donald S. ....'48 '74 C.98 B.S. L.424 J.D. 835 McClintock Dr., Ste. 200
Russian, Thomas P. ....'46 '77 C.197 A.B. L.365 J.D. 835 McClintock Dr., Ste. 200
Schwartz, Randall R. '59 '84 C&L.190 B.S.B.A., J.D.
V.P. & Gen. Coun., Standard Fed. Bk. for Svgs.
Schwartzburt, Norman ....'48 '79 C.502 B.S. L.1151 J.D. 43 Hidden Lake Drive
Shugar, Gregory ....'72 '98 C.347 B.A. L.146 J.D. 835 McClintock Dr., Ste. 200
Spindler, George S. ....'38 '66 C.277 B.Ch.E. L.209 J.D. 803 Ambriance (Pat.)‡
Spitler, Sara L. ....'74 '99 C.967 B.A. L.597 J.D. 835 McClintock Dr., Ste. 200
Stratis, Michael S. ....'62 '88 C.20 B.A. L.215 J.D. 15W506 63rd Street
Strumillo, Donald R. ....'58 '83 C.1082 B.A. L.602 J.D. Co-Founder, AMS Direct, Inc.
Thanas, Thomas A., (AV) '54 '80
C.602 B.A. L.879 J.D. Sr. Atty., Harrah's Entertainment, Inc.
Weiss Brown, Heather ....'76 '03 C.741 B.A. L.201 J.D. 835 McClintock Dr., Ste. 200
Wetzel, Alison J. ....'76 '01 C&L.424 B.A., J.D. [Ⓐ Goldstine,S.R.N.&H.]
Wilen, Eric R. ....'69 '95 C.475 B.A. L.213 J.D. [Ⓐ Goldstine,S.R.N.&H.]
Ziemer, Charles O. ....'39 '64 C.679 B.S. L.1119 J.D. 4 Regent Court

BUSHNELL, 3,288, *McDonough Co.*

Bisbee, John H., (BV) ....'41 '68 C.174 B.A. L.208 J.D. 785 N. Dean St.
Holland, Brian P., (BV) ....'54 '79 C.504 B.A. L.339 J.D. [Holland&H.]
Holland, Stephen E., (BV) ....'51 '76 C.504 B.A. L.221 J.D. [Holland&H.]
Holland and Holland, (BV) ....W. Main at Hurst St.
Pierce, Craig F., (BV) ....'51 '80 C.927 B.A. L.589 J.D. [Pierce]
Pierce Law Offices, (BV) ....461 W. Main St.
Steelman, Michael G., (BV) '50 '79 C.927 B.A. L.1151 J.D.
Chmn. & CEO, Farmers & Merchants State Bk.

BYRON, 2,917, *Ogle Co.*

Albrecht, Kenneth Allen ....'61 '96 C.1164 B.A.P.S. L.801 J.D. 1058 Shadow Wood Drive
Gosdick, Robert W., (AV) '33 '58 C.602 B.A. L.597 J.D.
215 N. Union St. (⊙Rockford)

CAHOKIA, 16,391, *St. Clair Co.*

Barnett, John W. '44 '75 C.309 A.B. L.734 J.D.
(adm. in MO; not adm. in IL) 214 Hawkins Dr.‡

Forman, M. Barry, Law Office of .... '48 '75 C.1350 B.A. L.339 J.D. 3325 Mississippi

CAIRO, * 3,632, *Alexander Co.*

Clarke, Mark H., Chartered, (BV) ....'57 '82 C&L.339 B.S., J.D. Courthouse
Flummer, James A., Attorney at Law, (BV) '51 '75 C.801 B.S. L.339 J.D.
3305 Sycamore
Holland, John G., Jr., (BV) ....'54 '80 C.500 B.A. L.801 J.D. [Holland&H.]

Holland and Holland, (BV)
230 Eighth Street, P.O. Box 186, 62914
Telephone: 618-734-2800 Fax: 618-734-2801
Members of Firm: John G. Holland (1915-2004); John G. Holland, Jr.
Admiralty, Personal Injury and Civil Rights, Medical Malpractice, Products Liability. General Civil and Trial practice in all State and Federal Courts.
Representative Clients: Local Firms: First National Bank, N.A., Cairo, Il. Railroads: Illinois Central Railroad. Insurance Companies: The Home Insurance Co.; Liberty Mutual Insurance Co.; Wausau Insurance Companies; The Medical Protective Co.; Kentucky Farm Bureau Insurance Co.; Washington National Insurance Co.; Associated Aviation Underwriters.

Spomer, Dorothy W., (AV) ....'21 '43 C&L.339 B.S., J.D. 306 20th St.
Spomer, Stephen L. ....'49 '74 C&L.861 B.A., J.D. Cir. J.
Spomer, Waldemar C., (BV) ....'19 '51 C&L.546 B.S., J.D. 306-20th St.
Stark, Gary, (BV) ....'68 '94 C.801 B.A. L.356 J.D. 309 Division St.

CALEDONIA, 199, *Boone Co.*

Dunn, William Gerald, (BVⓉ) '24 '74 C.494 B.S. L.813 J.D.
(adm. in CA; not adm. in IL) 11870 Oakridge Rd.

CALUMET CITY, 39,071, *Cook Co.*

Becker, Fred M., (BV) ....'44 '72 C.1016 B.A. L.209 J.D. 136 Pulaski Rd.
Belzeski, Kathleen M. '59 '86
C.424 B.S. L.879 J.D. Staff Atty., UAW - Ford Legal Servs. Plan
Bloesch, Jeffrey M. ....'57 '81 C&L.339 A.B., J.D. 8 Elm St.★
Brown, Roger L. ...'53 '85 C.1016 B.S.B.A. L.209 J.D. 2100 Sibley Boulevard, Suite 105
Bullock, Monica Hyman ....'56 '81 C&L.597 B.A., J.D. UAW-Ford Legal Servs.
Casey, Michael P. ....'49 '75 C.339 B.S. L.209 J.D. 495 Burnham Ave.
Collins, Robert C., Jr. ....'51 '76 C.339 B.S. L.365 J.D. 850 Burnham Ave.
Dinwiddie, Candy F. ....'49 '80 C.347 B.A. L.345 J.D. UAW-Ford Legal Serv. Plan
Garmon, Julie A. ....'69 '95 C.679 B.A. L.879 J.D. 1461 Ring Rd.
Gately, Kathryn Elizabeth, (CVⓉ) ....'63 '95 C.477 A.B. L.879 J.D. 1579 Huntington Dr.
Gerrity, Paul F. ....'27 '53 C&L.209 A.B., J.D. Ret. Cir. J.
Green, Henry S. ....'35 '60 C&L.597 B.S., J.D. 80 River Oaks Plaza
Jeffers, John R. ....'15 '42 C.346 L.365 LL.B. 134 Pulaski Rd.
Kiefor, Louis V. ....'42 '70 C.589 B.S.Ed. L.146 J.D. 684 State Line Ave.
Lem, Darryl R. ....'34 '58 C&L.339 B.S., LL.B. 850 Burnham Ave.
Lipschultz, Robert N. ....'22 '50 C.966 L.365 J.D. 2100 Sibley Boulevard, Suite 200
McCoy, Theresa, Law Office of ....P.O. Box 18
McCoy-Woods, Theresa M. ....'55 '02 C&L.329 B.S.N., J.D. [T.McCoy]
Mirkov, Vincent S. ....'60 '86 C.347 B.A. L.365 J.D. 1579 Huntington Dr.
Narcisse, Chris G. ....'33 '76 C.1016 B.A. L.209 J.D. 1637 Downs Drive
Newell, Warren L., Jr. ....'43 '69 C.339 B.S. L.146 J.D. 134 Pulaski Rd.
Pelkey, John F. ....'51 '84 C.339 B.A. L.365 J.D. [Ⓐ G.R.Skubisz]

Pintas, William G., & Associates, Ltd.
(See Chicago)

Resney, Michael M. ....'45 '71 C&L.209 B.S., J.D. 850 Burnham Ave.
Schab, Thomas J. ....'57 '89 C.679 B.S.M.E. L.365 J.D. 247 Ruth Street (Pat.)
Seneczko, John P. '62 '93 C.339 B.A. L.879 J.D.
Asst. Gen. Coun., Guarantee Reserve Life Insurance Company (Legal Department)

Skubisz, Gregory R., (AV) '51 '79 C.1157 B.A. L.365 J.D.
1461 Ring Road, 60409
Telephone: 708-862-0101 Fax: 708-862-0202
URL: http://www.lawyers.com/gregoryrskubisz
Associate: John F. Pelkey.
Criminal, Personal Injury, General Civil Litigation, Family, Real Estate, Estate Planning and Probate, Driving Under Influence, Traffic and Felonies.
See Professional Biographies, CALUMET CITY, ILLINOIS

Williams, Ann Ellen ....'55 '85 C.338 B.S. L.146 J.D. U.S. Dept. of Labor. O.S.H.A.

CAMBRIDGE, * 2,124, *Henry Co.*

Braendle, James T., (BV) ....'34 '66 C.879 L.365 LL.B. [Ⓒ Telleen,H.S.&C.]

Brown and Ray
(See Geneseo)

Carmen, Bruce L., (AV) ....'58 '84 C&L.339 A.B., J.D. [Telleen,H.S.&C.]
Hanson, Jay M. ....'40 '66 C&L.336 B.S., J.D. Cir. J.
Horberg, Kurt J., (AV) ....'52 '77 C.57 B.A. L.365 J.D. [Telleen,H.S.&C.]

Montgomery, Thomas W., (BV) '45 '72 C&L.339 B.S., J.D.
127 North Prospect Street, P.O. Box 176, 61238-0176 ⊙
Telephone: 309-937-3313 Fax: 309-937-3314
Email: twmlaw@theinter.com
Criminal Law, Traffic Violations, Driving While Intoxicated, Real Estate, Estate Planning, Wills, Trusts, Probate, Family Law, Divorce, Adoption, Personal Injury, Child Support, General Practice.
See Professional Biographies, CAMBRIDGE, ILLINOIS

Noth, Scott Theron ....'72 '00 C.357 B.A. L.1339 J.D. State's Atty. Off.
Sanders, Grant D. ....'69 '95 C.747 B.A. L.221 J.D. 307 West Center Street
Smith, Scott M., (BV) ....'65 '92 C.339 B.S. L.589 J.D. [Telleen,H.S.&C.]
Telleen, Kenneth L., (AV) ....'10 '34 C&L.339 A.B., J.D. [Telleen,H.S.&C.] ‡

Telleen, Horberg, Smith & Carmen, P.C., (AV)
124 West Exchange Street, P.O. Box 179, 61238
Telephone: 309-937-3339 Fax: 309-937-2830
Email: attys@telleen.com URL: http://www.telleen.com
Leonard E. Telleen (1877-1966); Kenneth L. Telleen (Retired); Leonard W. Telleen (1911-1994); Kurt J. Horberg; Scott M. Smith; Bruce L. Carmen. Of Counsel: James T. Braendle.
General Practice, Probate, Trusts and Estates, Wills, Real Estate, Collections, Banks and Banking, Commercial Law, Bankruptcy, Business Law, Municipal Law, Taxation, Agricultural Law, Farm Drainage and Environmental Law, Personal Injury, Domestic Relations, General Civil and Criminal Litigation.
References: Bank Orion; Central Bank, Illinois; Farmers National Bank of Prophetstown.

Vandersnick, Larry S., (BV) ....'51 '77 C.339 B.A. L.365 J.D. States Atty.

CANTON, 15,288, *Fulton Co.*

Barnhart, Gary E., (AV) ....'47 '73 C.388 B.A. L.910 J.D. [Claudon,K.B.&B.]
Barra, Walter D., (CV) ....'52 '77 C.357 B.A. L.734 J.D. 21 Ingersoll Ct.
Bath, Kenneth L. ....'33 '68 C.388 A.B. L.365 J.D. Ret. Cir. J.‡
Beal, Bruce C., (BV) ....'50 '76 C.337 B.A. L.1048 J.D. [Claudon,K.B.&B.]

BryceDowney, LLC, (AV)
P.O. Box 100, 61520 ⊙
Telephone: 309-789-2839 Fax: 309-789-2840
URL: http://www.brycedowney.com

(This Listing Continued)

BryceDowney, LLC (Continued)

Dawn M. Tarter.
General Practice.
Chicago, Illinois Office: 200 North LaSalle Street, Suite 2700, 60601. Telephone: 312-377-1501. Fax: 312-377-1502.
See Professional Biographies, CANTON, ILLINOIS

Claudon, Chester J., (AV) ....'22 '48 C.945 B.A. L.893 J.D. [Ⓒ Claudon,K.B.&B.]
Claudon, Kost, Barnhart & Beal, Ltd., (AV) .... 121 West Elm Street (⊙Lewistown)
Elson, James J., Chtd., (AV) ....'31 '57 C&L.339 B.S., J.D. City Atty.‡
Evans, Michael E., (BV) ....'60 '85 C.339 B.S. L.801 J.D. [Froehling,W.&E.]
Froehling, Ralph, (AV) ....'28 '52 C&L.339 B.S., J.D. [Froehling,W.&E.]
Froehling, Weber & Evans, (AV) ....167 West Elm Street
Haynes, David L. ....'49 '84 L.801 J.D. V.P. & Tr. Offr., MidAmerica Natl. Bk.‡
Jochums, Justin G. ....'77 '02 C.801 B.A. L.879 J.D. [Ⓐ Claudon,K.B.&B.]
Kost, Keith K., (BVⓉ) '57 '81
C.191 B.S. L.801 J.D. [Ⓒ Claudon,K.B.&B.] (⊙Rhinelander, WI)
Kost, Oral C., (AV) ....'29 '53 C.504 A.B. L.339 J.D. [Claudon,K.B.&B.] ⊙
Malmgren, William H., (BV) ....'12 '52 C.393 B.A. L.339 LL.B. 369 N. Main St.
Maxwell, Susan M. ....'73 '00 C.927 L.16 J.D. [Ⓐ Froehling,W.&E.]
McCarthy, John J., (BV) ....'43 '70 C.321 B.S. L.339 J.D. 45 E. Side Sq. Ste. 301
Murphy, Francis P. ....'14 '49 C.339 B.S. L.209 J.D. Ret. Cir. J.‡
Neigel, Jeff L., (BV) ....'58 '86 C.801 B.A. L.378 J.D. 122 N. Ave. A
Scott, G. Albert ....'21 '49 C.894 A.B. L.339 LL.B. 55 Winegar Dr.‡
Tarter, Dawn M. ....'63 '94 C.72 B.A. L.146 J.D. [BryceDowney]
Van Sickle, James E. ....'31 '56 C.393 B.A. L.597 J.D. 2 N. Main St.‡
Walters, Christopher W., (CV) ....'72 '98 C.338 B.A./B.S. L.910 J.D. [Claudon,K.B.&B.]
Weber, Ronald J., (BV) ....'48 '73 C&L.339 B.S., J.D. [Froehling,W.&E.]

CARBONDALE, 20,681, *Jackson Co.*

Adams, Jill E., (CV) '52 '82 C.575 B.A. L.560 J.D.
Assoc. Prof., Southern Ill. Univ. School of Law
Anderson, Farrah L. ....'78 '02 C&L.801 B.A., J.D. [Ⓐ Rusin M.&F.]

Barrett, Twomey, Broom, Hughes & Hoke, LLP, (BV)
100 North Illinois Avenue, P.O. Box 3747, 62902-3747
Telephone: 618-457-0437 Facsimile: 618-457-0411
Email: mail@btbhw.com URL: http://www.lawyers.com/btbh&w
Members of Firm: William L. Broom III; Michael R. Twomey; Kenneth R. Hughes; Patricia A. Hoke. Associates: Craig R. Reeves; Patricia A. Small; Carey C. Gill; Sarah J. Taylor.
Banking, Estate Planning, Real Estate, Civil Trials and Appeals.
References: First National Bank and Trust Company Carbondale, Illinois; First Bank of Carbondale, Illinois.
See Professional Biographies, CARBONDALE, ILLINOIS

Basanta, W. Eugene '50 '75 C.951 B.A. L.383 J.D.
(adm. in KY; not adm. in IL) Prof., Southern Ill. Univ. Sch. of Law
Basko, Susan M. ....'55 '01 C.999 B.A. L.801 J.D. 1200 East Grand
Beard, Larry Lee ....'50 '87 C.502 L.801 J.D. [Beard]
Beard Law Firm, The ....812 W. Main St.
Beck, Robert E. '37 '60 C&L.494 B.S., LL.B.
(adm. in MN; not adm. in IL) Prof. of Law, Southern Ill. Univ.
Beyler, Keith H. '47 '74 C.674 A.B. L.145 J.D.
(adm. in CA; not adm. in IL) Prof., Southern Ill. Univ. Sch. of Law
Black, Katherine M. ....'— '89 L.801 J.D. P.O. Box 309
Boyer, Diann Basler ....'57 '82 C&L.801 B.A., J.D. [D.Boyer]
Boyer, Diann, Law Office of .... P.O. Box 3955
Brandon, Wm. Kent, (AV) ....'39 '65 C.801 B.A. L.597 J.D. [Brandon,S.&G.]

Brandon, Schmidt & Goffinet, (AV) BB
916 West Main Street, P.O. Box 3898, 62902-3898
Telephone: 618-549-0777 Telecopier: 618-457-4691
Email: inquiry@carbondalelaw.com URL: http://www.carbondalelaw.com
Members of Firm: Wm. Kent Brandon; Charles E. Schmidt; Jeffrey A. Goffinet. Associates: Kenton J. Owens; Aaron L. Wright.
General and Trial Practice. Insurance, Malpractice, Workers Compensation and Personal Injury Law.
Representative Clients: State Farm Insurance Co.; Pekin Insurance Co.; Illinois State Medical Insurance Services; The St. Paul Insurance Co.; Madison Mutual Insirance Co.; PICOM Insurance Co.; MetLife Insurance; Unitrin Insurance Company; RML Insurance; Liberty Mutual Group.
Reference: First National Bank of Carbondale.
See Professional Biographies, CARBONDALE, ILLINOIS

Britton, Thomas C. '48 '76 C&L.801 B.A., J.D.
Assoc. Dean; Assoc. Prof., So. Illinois Univ. Sch. of Law
Broom, William L., III, (BV) ....'47 '72 C&L.339 B.S., J.D. [Barrett,T.B.H.&H.]
Capps, Timothy, (CV) ....'— '89 C&L.801 B.A., J.D. [Capps&Assoc.]
Capps & Associates, (CV) .... P.O. Box 3279
Clemons, John R., (BV) ....'48 '75 C.352 B.A. L.209 J.D. 813 W. Main St.
Colvin, Barbara Jean ....'32 '81 C&L.801 B.A., J.D. 818 W. Main St.‡
Dahlen, Michael F., (BV) ....'49 '74 C.177 B.A. L.209 J.D. [Feirich M G R.]
Daly, John R. ....'67 '97 C&L.801 B.S., J.D. [Ⓐ Feirich M G R.]
Daly, Reona J. ....'69 '94 C.340 B.A. L.801 J.D. [Sandberg,P.&v.] (⊙St. Louis, MO)
Denny, Timothy D. ....'76 '04 C.248 B.S. L.589 J.D. [Ⓐ Rusin M.&F.]
Dominguez-Urban, Ileana '60 '86
C.674 A.B. L.597 J.D. Asst. Prof., Southern Ill. Univ. Sch. of Law
Dorsey, Edward '49 '93 C.339 B.B.A. L.801 J.D.
Assistant Dean, So. Illinois Univ. Sch. of Law
Duggan, James E. '61 '87 C.886 B.A. L.500 J.D.
(adm. in MS; not adm. in IL) Prof., Southern Ill. Univ.
Duhl, Gregory M., Law Offices of ....'69 '95 C.976 B.A. L.309 J.D. 15B Canary Rd.
Eaton, Carol L. ....'59 '84 C.801 B.S. L.339 J.D. 1114 N. Marion
Edelman, Elaine D. ....'49 '82 C.339 B.A. L.733 J.D. R.R. 4, Box 367‡
Erdman, Cheryl L. ....'68 '02 C.339 B.A. L.801 J.D. [Ⓐ Feirich M G R.]
Favreau, Carl L., (BV) ....'55 '81 C.801 B.A. L.339 J.D. 322 East Walnut

Feirich/Mager/Green/Ryan, (AV) BB
2001 West Main Street, P.O. Box 1570, 62903-1570
Telephone: 618-529-3000 Telecopier: 618-529-3008
Members of Firm: John K. Feirich (1909-1998); T. Richard Mager (1934-2002); Richard A. Green; John C. Ryan; Michael F. Dahlen; Kevin L. Mechler; Pieter N. Schmidt; John S. Rendleman, III; Gary B. Nelson; Edward E. Renshaw; Kara L. Jones; R. James Giacone, II. Associates: John R. Daly; Thomas R. Frenkel; Cheryl L. Erdman; William B. Levanti.
General Trial and Appellate Litigation, Business, Probate, Trust, Real Estate, Insurance Law, Worker's Compensation, Banking and Corporation Law, Intellectual Property and Healthcare Law.
Representative Clients: Country Mutual Insurance Co.; Sentry Insurance Co.; Great Central Insurance Co.; Consolidation Coal Co.; Heitman Properties, Ltd.; Southern Illinois Hospital Services; Electric Energy, Inc.; Gilster Mary Lee Corp.; Downstate National Banks.
See Professional Biographies, CARBONDALE, ILLINOIS

Feltman, Jeffrey M. ....'48 '96 C&L.801 B.A., J.D. Asst. Atty. Gen.
Frenkel, Thomas R. ....'53 '00 C&L.801 B.A., J.D. [Ⓐ Feirich M G R.]

Garner, Donald W. '43 '72 C.1142 B.A. L.846 J.D.
(adm. in TX; not adm. in IL) Prof., Southern Ill. Univ. Sch. of Law
Garner, R. Kathy '41 '77
C.629 B.A. L.801 J.D. Assoc. Prof., So. Illinois Univ. Sch. of Law
Garwin, Leo '18 '64 L.616 LL.B.
(adm. in OK; not adm. in IL) 35 Hillcrest Dr.‡
Giacone, R. James, II .... '73 '98 C.798 B.S. L.502 J.D. [Feirich M G R.]
Gilbert, Kimmel, Huffman, Prosser and Hewson, Ltd., (BV) ....102 Orchard Drive
Gill, Carey C. .... '76 '01 C.504 B.A. L.801 J.D. [Ⓐ Barrett,T.B.H.&H.]
Gill, L. Douglas ....'62 '98 C.234 B.A. L.801 J.D. [Gill]
Gill Law Firm ....239 S. Lewis Ln., Ste. B
Goffinet, Jeffrey A., (BV) .... '59 '84 C&L.801 B.A.B.S., J.D. [Brandon,S.&G.]
Green, Bill F., (AV) .... '22 '46 C.801 A.B. L.910 J.D. 2001 W. Main St.‡
Green, Richard A., (AV) .... '46 '72 C.801 B.A. L.339 J.D. [Feirich M G R.]
Gross, Leonard ...... '51 '77 C.1349 B.A. L.94 J.D. Prof., Southern Ill. Univ. Sch. of Law
Gruny, C. Richard ....'32 '59 C.337 A.B. L.339 J.D. 1104 Hill St.‡
Guernsey, Thomas F. '51 '76 C.477 B.A. L.912 J.D.
(adm. in NH; not adm. in IL) Dean, So. Illinois Univ. Sch. of Law
Habiger, Richard J. .... '41 '70 C.698 B.A. L.986 J.D. 802 W. Main St.
Haney, Thomas W. .... '37 '62 C.801 A.B. L.209 J.D. 133 Bobette Lane‡
Harders, R. Terrence '47 '75
C.339 B.A. L.893 J.D. Prof., Southern Illinois Univ Sch. of Law
Hayes, Michael J. '63 '89 C.188 B.S. L.893 J.D.
(adm. in NY; not adm. in IL) Assistant Prof., So. Illinois Univ. Sch. of Law
Hewson, Patrick J., (CV) .... '55 '86 C.339 B.S. L.801 J.D. [Gilbert,K.H.P.&H.]
Higgerson, Richard G. ....'45 '70 C.801 B.A. L.339 J.D. Coun., Southern Ill. Univ.
Hines, Charles C., Law Offices of, (BV) '32 '60 C.801 B.A. L.339 LL.B.
809 W. Main St.
Hogan, Dennis J. ....'29 '55 C.999 L.209 LL.B. 1003 Johnson St.‡
Hoke, Patricia A., (BV) ....'53 '91 C&L.801 B.S., J.D. [Barrett,T.B.H.&H.]
Holley, Raymond Neil ....'69 '97 C.338 B.S. L.801 J.D. 813 W. Main St.
Houdek, Frank G. '48 '74 C&L.112 B.A., J.D.
(adm. in CA; not adm. in IL)
Prof. of Law & Library Dir., So. Illinois University Sch. of Law
Howd, Jay B. .... '66 '92 C&L.801 B.S., J.D. Bkrptcy. Clinic

Howerton, Dorris & Stone
(See Marion)

Huffman, John W., (BV) ....'37 '64 C.234 B.S. L.339 LL.B. [Gilbert,K.H.P.&H.]
Hughes, Kenneth R., (BV) .... '48 '82 C.339 B.A. L.801 J.D. [Barrett,T.B.H.&H.]
Hughes, R. Courtney, (BV) ....'60 '85 C&L.801 J.D. [Hughes]
Hughes Law Firm, (BV) ....1317 W. Main

Hunter, Eugenia C., (BV) '41 '77 C&L.801 B.A., J.D.
905 West Cherry Street, 62901
Telephone: 618-457-0476 Fax: 618-457-0477
Email: ech99@msn.com
Bankruptcy, Real Estate, Wills and Trusts, Probate, Elder Law, Guardianship, Adoption, Expungements

See Professional Biographies, CARBONDALE, ILLINOIS

Jackson, Martine P. ....'67 '98 C.1040 B.B.A. L.801 J.D. 1405 W Main
Jackson, Tammi Noreen .... '72 '01 C&L.801 B.S., J.D. 1317 W Main St
Johnson, David C. '37 '61 C&L.585 B.S.B.A., J.D.
(adm. in ND; not adm. in IL) Prof. of Law, Southern Ill. Univ., Sch. of Law
Jones, Kara L. .... '69 '94 C.734 B.S.B.A. L.801 J.D. [Feirich M G R.]
Kelley, Patrick J. '43 '69 C.602 B.A. L.352 J.D.
Prof. of Law, Southern Ill. Univ. Sch. of Law
Kimmel, P. Michael, (BV) .... '46 '76 C.1070 B.S. L.339 J.D. [Gilbert,K.H.P.&H.]
Kyndberg, Kathleen A. .... '59 '97 C&L.801 B.A., J.D. 9914 S. Countyline Rd.
Langenstein, Michael A. ....'70 '97 C.339 B.A. L.986 J.D. In-House Coun., S. I. Securities
Lee, Mark R. '49 '74 C.976 B.A. L.846 J.D.
(adm. in TX; not adm. in IL) Prof., Southern Ill. Univ. Law Sch.
Levanti, William B. .... '76 '02 C.531 B.S. L.801 J.D. [Ⓐ Feirich M G R.]
Margolis, Thomas E. .... '65 '93 C.999 B.A. L.801 J.D. [Ⓐ Rusin M.&F.]
McAffee, Thomas B. '52 '79 C&L.878 B.S., J.D.
(adm. in CA; not adm. in IL) Prof. of Law, So. Illinois Univ. Sch. of Law
Mechler, Kevin L., (BV) ....'57 '82 C&L.801 B.S., J.D. [Feirich M G R.]
Medlin, Elmer J. .... '14 '37 C.801 L.146 LL.B. 809 W. Main St.‡
Miller, James Joseph .... '44 '91 C.234 B.S. L.801 J.D. P.O. Box 562‡
Miller, Timothy L. ....'57 '84 C&L.801 B.S., J.D. 2003 Norwood Dr.★

Mitchell & Mitchell
(See Marion)

Nelson, Gary B., (CV) .... '63 '91 C.352 B.A. L.801 J.D. [Feirich M G R.]
Noble-Allgire, Alice M. '57 '90 C&L.801 B.S., J.D.
Assistant Prof., So. Illinois Univ. Sch. of Law
O'Neill, Rebecca J. .... '63 '88 C&L.801 B.S., J.D. Southern Ill. Univ.
O'Neill, Treva H., (BV) ....'41 '81 C.304 B.A. L.801 J.D. [O'Neill&P.]
O'Neill and Proctor, (BV) ....818 W. Main St.
Owens, Kenton J. .... '71 '99 C.339 A.B. L.801 J.D. [Ⓐ Brandon,S.&G.]
Pine, Kathleen L., (AV⊕) ....'57 '82 C.338 B.S. L.801 J.D. [Sandberg,P.&v.] ⊙
Proctor, Janet C., (CV) ....'47 '92 C.59 B.A. L.801 J.D. [O'Neill&P.]
Prosser, Don E., (BV) .... '49 '75 C.210 B.A. L.347 J.D. [Gilbert,K.H.P.&H.]
Prosser, Everett, (BV) .... '16 '41 C.339 A.B. L.477 J.D. [Ⓒ Gilbert,K.H.P.&H.]
Reeves, Craig R., (BV) .... '58 '85 C&L.801 B.A., J.D. [Ⓐ Barrett,T.B.H.&H.]
Rendleman, John S., III, (CV) .... '58 '87 C&L.801 B.A., J.D. [Feirich M G R.]
Renshaw, Edward E., (CV) .... '56 '92 C.291 B.S. L.801 J.D. [Feirich M G R.]
Rhode, Shari R., (BV) .....'51 '76 C&L.801 B.S., J.D. Chf. Trial Atty., Southern Ill. Univ.
Robertson, Ralph J., Jr. '51 '76 C&L.502 A.B., J.D.
(adm. in MO; not adm. in IL) Prof., Southern IL Sch. of Law
Robinson, Cyril D. .... '24 '52 C.102 L.597 LL.B. 520 N. Michaels St.‡
Rudasill, Mary C., (BV) '49 '80 C.338 B.S. L.801 J.D.
Dir., Legal Clinic, Southern Ill. Univ. School of Law

Rusin Maciorowski & Friedman, Ltd., (AV)
239 South Lewis Lane, Suite A, 62901-3443 ⊙
Telephone: 618-351-8100 Fax: 618-351-8109
URL: http://www.rusinlaw.com
Timothy D. Denny; Thomas E. Margolis; Farrah L. Anderson.
Workers Compensation Law. Insurance Defense, Personal Injury, Products Liability, Auto and Trucking Liability, Structural Work Act, Commercial Litigation, Subrogation, Contract Insurance, Employment Discrimination. Wrongful Discharge.
Chicago, Illinois Office: Suite 1530, 10 South Riverside Plaza, 60606. Telephone: 312-454-5110. Fax: 312-454-6166.
Champaign, Illinois Office: 2506 Galen Drive, Suite 104, 61821-7047. Telephone: 217-351-1700. Fax: 217-351-1732.

See Professional Biographies, CARBONDALE, ILLINOIS

Ryan, John C., (BV) .... '51 '76 C.208 B.A. L.801 J.D. [Feirich M G R.]
Ryan, Marsha G. .... '50 '88 C.616 B.A. L.801 J.D. 120 N. Illinois Ave.

Sandberg, Phoenix & von Gontard, A Professional Corporation, (AV)
Westowne Centre, 2015 West Main, Suite G, 62901 ⊙
Telephone: 618-397-2721; 800-225-5529 Fax: 618-351-7604
Kathleen L. Pine; Reona J. Daly.
Trial and Appellate Practice in Federal and State Courts, Product Liability, Health Law, Medical Malpractice Defense, Class Action Litigation, Employment Law, Banking, Commercial and Corporate Law, Admiralty, Aviation, Insurance, Bankruptcy and Reorganization, Estate Planning and Probate, Real Estate, Family Law.
St. Louis, Missouri Office: 15th Floor, One City Centre. Telephone: 314-231-3332. Telecopier: 314-241-7604.
Belleville, Illinois Office: 23 South 1st Street. Telephone: 618-397-2721.

See Professional Biographies, CARBONDALE, ILLINOIS

Schmidt, Charles E., (AV) ....'52 '77 C&L.801 B.S., J.D. [Brandon,S.&G.]
Schmidt, Pieter N., (BV) .... '56 '88 C&L.801 B.A., J.D. [Feirich M G R.]
Schmitz, Suzanne J. .... '47 '81 C.720 B.A. L.734 J.D. So. Illinois Univ. Sch. of Law
Schroeder, William A. '43 '72 C&L.339 A.B., J.D.
(adm. in MA; not adm. in IL) Prof., Southern Ill. Univ. Law Sch.
Schulhof, Robert P., (BV) .... '38 '69 C.801 B.A. L.339 J.D. 1317 W. Main St.
Sherwood, William F., (AV) '50 '77
C.801 B.A. L.734 J.D. V.P. & Gen. Coun., Southern Ill. Healthcare
Small, Patricia A., (CV) ....'60 '88 C.627 B.S. L.546 J.D. [Ⓐ Barrett,T.B.H.&H.]
Smith, Webb, (CV) ....'58 '85 C&L.801 B.S., J.D. [Gilbert,K.H.P.&H.]
Spencer, M. Yvonne .... '58 '96 C&L.801 B.S., J.D. 913 South Oakland Avenue
Taylor, Sarah J. .... '74 '02 C&L.801 B.A., J.D. [Ⓐ Barrett,T.B.H.&H.]
Thomas, Jerry K. '54 '81 C.465 B.A. L.862 J.D.
Assoc. Dir., Institutional Advancement, Southern IL Univ.
Turk, Gene A., Jr. .... '58 '85 C.350 B.A. L.976 J.D. 511 W. Main St.
Twomey, Michael R., (BV) ....'54 '80 C&L.801 J.D. [Barrett,T.B.H.&H.]
Tyler, R. Stanley ....'29 '52 C.346 B.S. L.339 J.D. Southern Ill. Univ.
Vaughn, Brandon M. ....'73 '00 C&L.801 B.A., J.D. 812 W. Main St.
Veach, Gregory A., (CV) ....'50 '75 C.801 B.A. L.1049 J.D. [G.Veach]
Veach, Gregory, Law Offices of, (CV) ....3200 Fishback Rd.
Vieira, Norman '37 '63
C.178 A.B. L.145 J.D. Prof. of Law, So. Illinois Univ. Sch. of Law
Waters, Gola E. '29 '57 C.707 B.A. L.352 J.D.
(adm. in IA; not adm. in IL) Southern Ill. Univ.
Wendt, Laurel Anne '43 '78 C.347 B.A. L.345 J.D.
(adm. in IN; not adm. in IL) Southern Ill. Univ. Sch. of Law
Whitfield, Wenona Y. '49 '77
C.340 B.A. L.801 J.D. Assoc. Prof., So. Illinois Univ. Sch. of Law
Whittington, Rebecca, (CV) .... '— '83 C.801 B.A. L.910 J.D. 930 W. Walnut St.
Williams, Hugh R. ....'52 '03 C.338 B.S. L.801 J.D. [Williams]
Williams, Jeffrey Dale ....'71 '00 C.798 B.A. L.801 J.D. 310 E. Main Street
Williams Law Firm .... 611 East Park, Suite 117

Winters, Brewster, Crosby and Schafer LLC
(See Marion)

Wright, Aaron L. ....'— '03 C.999 B.A. L.801 J.D. [Ⓐ Brandon,S.&G.]
Zimmer, James R. .... '20 '50 C.801 L.910 J.D. 104 Hidden Trace Rd.‡

CARLINVILLE, * 5,685, *Macoupin Co.*

Bergen, Francis J. ....'18 '49 L.734 LL.B. Ret. Cir. J.
Bertinetti, Richard J., (BV) ....'51 '76 C.339 B.A. L.734 J.D. [Bertinetti&C.]
Bertinetti & Cain, (BV) .... 227 E. 1st So. St.
Bloomer, Paul W., (BV) ....'49 '77 C.210 B.A. L.339 J.D. [Denby,M.B.&D.]
Brandenburg-Rees, Jacqueline ... '51 '74 C.1087 B.A. L.209 J.D. [Brandenburg-Rees&R.]
Brandenburg-Rees & Rees, (BV) ....128 S. Broad St.
Brunton, Diane L. ....'47 '73 C.339 B.A. L.910 J.D. Assoc. Cir. J.
Cain, Brent A., (BV) ....'53 '78 C.234 B.A. L.607 J.D. [Bertinetti&C.]
Carmody, Thomas P. ....'32 '57 C.1101 A.B. L.602 J.D. Cir. J.
Clark, Larry F. ....'42 '72 C.504 B.A. L.208 J.D. 209 N. East St.
Denby, Thomas D., (BV) ....'63 '88 C.357 B.A. L.734 J.D. [Denby,M.B.&D.]
Denby, W. W., (AV) ....'31 '61 C.339 B.S. L.597 J.D. [Denby,M.B.&D.] (⊙Benld)
Denby, Meno, Bloomer & Denby, (AV) .... S.E. Corner of Square (⊙Benld, Staunton)
Dobbs, Stuart, (AV) .... '32 '59 C.339 B.A. L.597 J.D. 504 East First North Street
Goings, Douglas Richardson, (BV) '52 '79 C.884 B.A. L.910 J.D.
First Asst. States Atty.
Hebron, M. E. ....'19 '43 C&L.339 B.S., LL.B. [Hebron&H.] ‡
Hebron, William S., (BV) ....'48 '75 C.339 B.S. L.365 J.D. [Hebron&H.]
Hebron & Hebron, (BV) .... 516 N. Side Square
Kasten, Carl E., (AV) .... '44 '69 C.338 B.A. L.597 J.D. [Phelps,K.R.B.S.&M.]
Koval, Joseph P. ....'29 '55 C&L.339 B.S., LL.B. Cir. J.
Meno, J. Richard, (BV) .... '48 '73 C&L.734 B.S., J.D. [Denby,M.B.&D.] ⊙
Meyer, Joshua A. ....'75 '01 C.1101 B.A. L.734 J.D. [Phelps,K.R.B.S.&M.]

Moore, Kim L., Law Office of
(See Virden)

Phelps, Kasten, Ruyle, Burns, Sims & Meyer, P.C., (AV)
130 East Main Street, P.O. Box 587, 62626
Telephone: 217-854-3283 FAX: 217-854-9527
Email: pkrb@accunet.net URL: http://www.lawyers.com/pkrb
Edward R. Phelps (1904-1985); Thomas P. Burns (1952-2001); John W. Russell (Retired); Carl E. Kasten; Nancy L. Ruyle; Byron J. Sims; Joshua A. Meyer.
General Civil Practice in State and Federal Courts. Negligence, Wills and Trusts, Probate and Real Estate Law.
Representative Clients: Carlinville National Bank; Blackburn University; Area Diesel Service, Inc.; H & H Construction Services, Inc.

See Professional Biographies, CARLINVILLE, ILLINOIS

Rees, Edmond H., (BV) ....'42 '67 C.339 B.S. L.585 J.D. [Brandenburg-Rees&R.]
Russell, John W. .... '20 '50 C.393 A.B. L.597 J.D. [Phelps,K.R.B.S.&M.]
Ruyle, Nancy L., (BV) .... '59 '83 C.707 B.A. L.734 J.D. [Phelps,K.R.B.S.&M.]
Schwartz, Dennis L. .... '40 '66 C.357 B.S. L.910 J.D. [Ⓒ Denby,M.B.&D.]
Sims, Byron J., (CV) .... '65 '91 C.337 B.A. L.801 J.D. [Phelps,K.R.B.S.&M.]
Watson, Jennifer A. ....'70 '99 C.357 B.A. L.589 J.D. State's Atty's Off.

CARLYLE, * 3,474, *Clinton Co.*

Bergmann, Henry F., (CV) ....'53 '80 C.339 B.S. L.801 J.D. State's Atty.
Conrad, Norman L., (CV) .... '54 '84 C&L.801 B.S., J.D. 550 N. 2nd St., Ste. 201
Heiligenstein, Bernard G., (BV) ....'28 '60 C.801 L.734 J.D. [B.G.Heiligenstein]
Heiligenstein, Joseph B., (BV) ....'66 '91 C.36 B.A. L.734 J.D. [B.G.Heiligenstein]
Heiligenstein, Bernard G., Ltd., (BV) ....521 9th St.
Henken, Arthur G. ....'31 '66 C.602 B.A. L.734 J.D. Cir. J.
Hitpas, Patrick J. ....'47 '72 C.1024 B.S. L.734 J.D. Cir. J.
Hudspeth, John A., Jr. .... '58 '85 C.1247 B.A. L.01 J.D. 1190 18th St.
Kuiken, Richard A., (BV) ....'45 '70 C&L.339 A.B., J.D. 541 9th St.
Mehochko, Kenneth E., (BV) .... '46 '75 C&L.339 B.S., J.D. 1010 Franklin
Moran, Kathleen P. ....'50 '76 C.801 B.A. L.378 J.D. Cir. J.

Warren, William W. .... '26 '49 L.910 J.D. 511 9th St.‡

Wham & Wham
(See Centralia)

CARMI, * 5,422, *White Co.*

Conger & Elliott, Prof. Corp., (AV) ....304 East Robinson
Drone, Robert Michael, (AV) .... '52 '77 C.234 B.S. L.339 J.D. [Conger&E.]
Endicott, Wm. R., (BV) .... '25 '52 C.531 L.192 LL.B. [Endicott&F.]
Endicott & Finch, (AV) ....222 E. Main St.
Finch, Gary W., (AV) .... '42 '75 C.801 B.S. L.838 J.D. [Endicott&F.]

Jelliffe, Ferrell, Morris & Doerge
(See Harrisburg)

Lewis, Henry ....'26 '53 C.210 B.A. L.339 LL.B. 114 S. Walnut St.‡
Stanley, David L., (BV) ....'33 '57 C.339 L.880 LL.B. City Atty. [Stanley]
Stanley, John D., (BV) .... '62 '87 C.210 B.A. L.192 J.D. [Stanley]
Stanley Law Office, (BV) ....114 S. Walnut
Stewart, Gregory K., (BV) .... '61 '87 C.346 B.S. L.801 J.D. [Conger&E.]
Sutton, Thomas H. .... '48 '73 C&L.339 B.S.B.A., J.D. Cir. J.

CAROL STREAM, 40,438, *DuPage Co.*

Abarbanel, Eliot W. .... '49 '83 C.145 B.A. L.608 J.D. Prarie State Legal Servs.
Bardeleben, Heather L., Law Office of '72 '00
C.932 B.S. L.365 J.D. 780 W. Army Trail Rd., Ste. 147
Broecker, Howard W., (AV) ....'40 '66 C.578 L.146 J.D. [Johnson,W.B.W.&N.]
Butcher, Connie J., (CV) .... '60 '86 C.63 B.S. L.365 J.D. 350 S. Schmale Rd.
Cavanaugh, Annette Mildred ..... '64 '96 C.999 B.A. L.209 J.D. Prairie State Legal Servs.
Comiano, Philip A. ....'12 '42 C.597 B.S.L. L.365 J.D. 140 Windsor Park Dr.‡
Coyle, Carole J., (BV) .... '66 '91 C.339 B.A. L.209 J.D. Prairie State Legal Servs.
Darbo, Howard H., (AV) '09 '36 C.966 B.S.Ch.E. L.477 J.D.
120 Windsor Park Dr. (Pat.)‡
Handley, Robert, (AV) .... '52 '79 C.339 B.A. L.589 J.D. [Moroni&H.]
Holtermann, David T. .... '68 '94 C.436 B.A. L.911 J.D. Prairie State Legal Servs., Inc.
Jensen, John E. '28 '51 C&L.145 B.A., J.D.
CEO & Chmn. of the Bd., American States Insurance
Johnson, Thomas L., (AV) ...... '45 '74 C.477 B.G.S. L.209 J.D. [Ⓒ Johnson,W.B.W.&N.]
Johnson, Westra, Broecker, Whittaker & Newitt, P.C., (AV)
380 S. Schmale Rd., Ste. 102
Krause, Jack C. ....'29 '55 C&L.424 B.S., J.D. Amer. States Ins. Co.
Lee, Alfred S. ....'70 '96 C.197 B.A. L.602 J.D. [Ⓐ Johnson,W.B.W.&N.]
Lindsay, Walter H., Jr. '44 '69 C.228 A.B. L.477 J.D.
Pres. & CEO, Produce Reporter Co.
May, Markus .... '64 '91 C&L.174 B.S., J.D. [Ⓐ Johnson,W.B.W.&N.]

Mazza, Patrick, & Associates, (AV) '40 '67 C.602 A.B. L.209 J.D.
290 South Main Place, 60188-2476
Telephone: 630-933-9200 Fax: 630-933-9824
Email: schodera@mcminc.net
Construction, Commercial, Contract and Mechanics Lien Law. Trial Practice.
Chicago, Illinois Office: 33 N. La Salle, Suite 1800. By Appointment Only.
See Professional Biographies, CAROL STREAM, ILLINOIS

McNees, Robert A., (CV) .... '53 '78 C.205 B.A. L.597 J.D. 195 Hiawatha Dr.
Miller, Elsa .... '51 '91 C&L.589 B.A., J.D. Prairie State Legal Servs., Inc.
Moroni, James J. ....'48 '73 C.98 B.S. L.339 J.D. [Moroni&H.]
Moroni & Handley, (AV) ....373 S. Schmale St.
Myers, Laura .... '76 '01 C.339 B.A. L.352 J.D. Prairie State Legal Services
Newitt, Timothy B. ....'43 '75 C.937 B.A. L.276 J.D. [Johnson,W.B.W.&N.]
Pratscher, Peggy A. ....'52 '02 C.238 B.A. L.365 J.D. [P.A.Pratscher]
Pratscher, Peggy A., Ltd. ....335 E. Geneva Road, Suite 267
Quist, Patrick L. .... '66 '93 C.338 B.S. L.879 J.D. Asst. V.P., Chicago Title Ins. Co.
Radocha, Daniel J. .... '37 '62 C.436 B.S. L.424 J.D. 786 Stockbrige Drive
Romano, Rocco A. .... '38 '64 C.242 L.209 J.D. 706 Hickory Ln.
Schmidt, Melinda A., (BV) ....'67 '92 380 S. Schmule Rd., Suite 102
Sofferman, Elaine R. '67 '92
C.339 B.A. L.589 J.D. Staff Atty., Perry State Legal Servs. Inc.'
Susler, David G., (BV) .... '62 '87 C&L.339 B.A., J.D. Gen. Coun., AVG Automation
Westra, Donald F. '18 '54 C.446 B.S. L.744 LL.B.
(adm. in TX; not adm. in IL) [Ⓒ Johnson,W.B.W.&N.]
Westra, John J., (BV) ....'49 '75 C.937 B.A. L.607 J.D. [Johnson,W.B.W.&N.]
Whittaker, Donald S., (BV) ....'46 '79 C.827 A.B. L.209 J.D. [Johnson,W.B.W.&N.]
Wolowitz, David '49 '75 C&L.339 A.B., J.D.
Dir., Spec. Proj., Prairie State Legal Servs., Inc.

CARPENTERSVILLE, 30,586, *Kane Co.*

Costello, Stephen J., (BV) ....'58 '84 C.351 B.A. L.589 J.D. [Costello&C.]
Costello & Costello, P.C., (BV) ....19 N. Western Ave.
David, Bruce K., (BV) .... '47 '71 C.221 B.S.B.A. L.424 J.D. [David&Assoc.]
David & Associates, (BV) .... 231 W. Main St., Ste. 200
Geimer, Raymond R., (CV) '50 '80
C.589 B.S. L.365 J.D. 96 Kennedy Memorial Dr., Ste. 203
Kiss, James M., (BV) ....'49 '78 C.589 B.S. L.1151 J.D. [Kiss&R.]
Kiss & Ryan, Ltd., P.C., (BV) ....96 Kennedy Memorial Dr.
McNamara-Ripoli, Christine M. .... '62 '87 C.209 B.S. L.190 J.D. 3063 Shenandoah Drive
Ryan, Michael E., (BV) .... '50 '81 C.589 B.A. L.424 J.D. [Kiss&R.]

Travis, Richard E., Law Offices of
(See Elgin)

CARROLLTON, * 2,507, *Greene Co.*

Clough, Anne N. ....'76 '00 C.337 B.S. L.801 J.D. [Ⓐ McDonald,S.&C.]
Clough, Richard F., (BV) ....'45 '72 C.337 B.A. L.910 J.D. [McDonald,S.&C.]
Davis, Patrick C., (BV) ....'54 '80 C.338 B.S. L.339 J.D. [Ⓐ Gustine&T.]
Day, James W. ....'39 '63 C.430 B.A. L.339 LL.B. Cir. J.
Gillingham, Richard N., (BV) ....'59 '85 C.134 B.S. L.862 J.D. 220 6th St.
Gustine & Theivagt, Ltd., (BV) .... 620 N. Main Street
Hobson, Kenneth H. ....'58 '91 C.339 B.S. L.801 J.D. State's Atty.
McDonald, Strickland & Clough, (AV) ....524 N. Main St.
Strickland, Hugh A., (AV) .... '31 '60 C.388 A.B. L.146 J.D. [McDonald,S.&C.]
Theivagt, Charles E., (BV) ....'51 '76 C&L.801 B.S., J.D. [Gustine&T.]
Vogt, William G., (AV) ....'09 '34 C&L.910 B.S., J.D. [Vogt]
Vogt Law Offices, (AV) ....506 N. Courthouse Sq.

CARTERVILLE, 4,616, *Williamson Co.*

Eytalis, Edward C. ....'56 '84 C&L.801 B.S., J.D. [E.Eytalis]
Eytalis, Edward ....106 N. Division
Mitchell, Donald R. ....'26 '51 C&L.339 B.S., J.D. 405 Oakwood Dr.‡
Moore, James R., (BV) ....'53 '77 C&L.801 B.A., J.D. 100 N. Division St.
Olson, Bradley P. ....'70 '97 C.36 B.A. L.801 J.D. [B.Olson]
Olson, Bradley ....103 Quail Run

CARTHAGE, * 2,657, *Hancock Co.*

Ancelet, Albert V., (BV) ....'47 '75 C.338 B.S. L.146 J.D. 55 S. Adams St.
Clark, Rodney G., (BV) ....'65 '89 C.234 B.S. L.500 J.D. 55 S. Adams St.
Cook, Robert W. ....'43 '77 C.688 B.E.E. L.146 J.D. 520 Wabash St. (Pat.)
Glidden, John R., (AV) ....'36 '61 C.162 B.A. L.352 LL.B. [Hartzell,G.T.&H.] ⊙
Hartzell, Franklin M., (AV) ....'23 '50 C&L.339 B.S., LL.B. [Hartzell,G.T.&H.] ⊙
Hartzell, Thomas F., (AV) ....'59 '84 C.340 B.S. L.801 J.D. [Hartzell,G.T.&H.] ⊙

Hartzell, Glidden, Tucker and Hartzell, (AV) 🅱🅡
1852 as Ferris and Manier
Williams Building, P.O. Box 70, 62321 ⊙
Telephone: 217-357-3121 FAX: 217-357-2027
Email: firm@adams.net
Members of Firm: Homer H. Williams (1894-1965); Franklin M. Hartzell; John R. Glidden; Stanley L. Tucker; Thomas F. Hartzell.
General Civil Trial and Appellate Practice in all State and Federal Courts. Real Estate, Estate Planning and Probate, Trust, Banking Law, Taxation, Personal Injury, Family Law, Municipal Law and Agricultral Law.
Counsel for: Marine Bank and Trust; Bowen State Bank; City of Hamilton; City of Carthage; Memorial Hospital Assn.
Local Counsel for: State Farm Mutual Insurance Co.; The Prudential Insurance Company of America.
Macomb, Illinois Office: Old Bailey House, 100 South Campbell Street. Telephone: 309-833-3121.
See Professional Biographies, CARTHAGE, ILLINOIS

Naylor, Samuel, VI, (BV) ....'38 '73 C.339 B.A. L.365 J.D. States Atty.
Rasmussen, William Andrew ....'75 '00 C.249 L.1439 55 S. Adams
Ripple, Richard C. ....'34 '58 C&L.352 B.A., J.D. Ret. Cir. J.‡
Stewart, Max B. ....'21 '49 C.123 B.A. L.930 LL.B. Ret. Cir. J.
Stoverink, David F., (BV) ....'50 '77 C.177 B.A. L.502 J.D. Cir. J.
Tucker, Stanley L., (BV) ....'42 '70 C&L.339 B.S., J.D. [Hartzell,G.T.&H.] ⊙
Ufkes, LeRoy A. ....'23 '50 C.123 A.B. L.352 J.D. P.O. Box 459

CARY, 15,531, *McHenry Co.*

Armstrong, Bruce T. '49 '76 C.339 B.A. L.365 J.D.
Gen. Coun., Fox Valley Systems, Inc.
Binder, Walter J., Jr., (BV) ....'37 '73 C.597 B.S. L.146 J.D. 21 Northwest Hwy.
Gibbons, Monica H. ....'63 '90 C.813 A.B. L.602 J.D. 740 Big Sky Trail
Hartmann, Thomas W. '55 '84 C.1070 B.S. L.273 J.D.
Sr. V.P. & Gen. Coun., Orius Corp.
Holmes, Melvin C. ....'27 '51 C.118 B.A. L.477 LL.B. Cary Oaks Exec. Bldg.
Jaenicke, Steven William, (CV) ....'55 '82 C.589 B.A. L.146 J.D. [Jaenicke,S.W.]
Jaenicke, Steven W., (CV) ....21 Northwest Hwy.
Koelling, Peter M., (BVⓉ) ....'56 '85 C.859 B.A. L.744 J.D. 920 Crabtree Lane
Kuzniewski, Denise Mary, (BV) .... '67 '92 C.337 B.A. L.879 J.D. 121 W. Main St.
Larkin, Walter N. ....'20 '77 C.1027 B.S. L.1009 LL.B. P.O. Box 22
Lower, Jacqueline H. ....'— '82 C.209 B.A. L.424 J.D. [Sheehan&L.]
McCabe, Susan E., Law Office of ....'— '01 C.176 B.A. L.424 J.D. 350 High Road
Narusis, Bernard V., (BV) ....'29 '58 C.801 B.A. L.339 J.D. Vil. Atty. [Narusis&N.]
Narusis, Regina G. F., (BV) ....'36 '60 C&L.339 B.A., LL.B. [Narusis&N.]
Narusis & Narusis, (BV) ....213 W. Lake Shore Dr.
Pearson, Carolyn S. ....'55 '90 C.855 B.A. L.1000 J.D. 6 Jefferson Lane
Pietschmann, Candace, (CV) ....'— '89 C.1183 B.A. L.365 J.D. 10 Spring St.
Sheehan, Thomas M. ....'— '84 C.339 B.S. L.424 J.D. [Sheehan&L.]

Sheehan & Lower
6 Spring Street, 60013
Telephone: 847-516-3200; Toll Free: 800-RIDE LAW Fax: 847-516-3443
Email: ridelaw@aol.com
Members of Firm: Thomas M. Sheehan; Jacqueline H. Lower. Associate: Stephen J. Tasch.
Civil Trial Practice, Product Liability, Insurance Coverage, Defense of the Amusement Industry, Defense of Roller Skating Establishments, Aviation, Employment Discrimination and Employment Law.
See Professional Biographies, CARY, ILLINOIS

Tasch, Stephen J., (BV) ....'— '84 C.399 B.A. L.365 J.D. [Ⓐ Sheehan&L.]
Yost, Stephen R., (BV) ....'41 '66 C.339 B.S. L.146 J.D. 354 Crystal St. (US Rte. 14)

CASEY, 2,914, *Clark Co.*

Arbogast, Alane A. ....'64 '89 C.339 B.S. L.477 J.D. [Arbogast]
Arbogast, Daniel S., (BV) ....'52 '79 C.346 B.S. L.146 J.D. [Arbogast]
Arbogast Law Offices, P.C., (BV) ....110 East Main Street
Austin, William W., (AV) ....'45 '70 C&L.339 B.S., J.D. [Siemer,A.R.F.&T.] ⊙
Baird, Perry D. ....'61 '86 C.801 B.S.Acct. L.910 J.D. 2 S. Central
Fuhr, Ronald E., (BV) ....'54 '84 C.136 B.S. L.801 J.D. [Siemer,A.R.F.&T.] ⊙

Grant, James M., (BV) '50 '75 C.234 B.A. L.734 J.D.
101 North Central, 62420 ⊙
Telephone: 217-932-5885 Fax: 217-932-5889
Email: jmgrant@jamesmgrantlaw.com URL: http://www.lawyers.com/jamesmgrantlaw
Language: English.
Real Estate, Real Estate Title, Wills & Estates.
Charleston, Illinois Office: 611 6th Street, 61920. Telephone: 217-345-2510. Fax: 217-348-0082.
See Professional Biographies, CASEY, ILLINOIS

Resch, Marilyn B., (AV) ....'48 '73 C.970 B.A. L.347 J.D. [Siemer,A.R.F.&T.] ⊙
Siemer, Martin W., (CV) ....'67 '94 C.339 B.S. L.734 J.D. [Siemer,A.R.F.&T.] ⊙
Siemer, Q. Anthony, (BV) ....'44 '69 C.339 B.A. L.602 J.D. [Siemer,A.R.F.&T.] ⊙

Siemer, Austin, Resch, Fuhr & Totten, (AV)
14 North Central, Room 204, 62420 ⊙
Telephone: 217-932-2158 Fax: 217-932-2159
Email: psarf@joink.com
Members of Firm: Q. Anthony Siemer; William W. Austin; Marilyn B. Resch; Ronald E. Fuhr; William B. Totten; Martin W. Siemer.
General Civil Practice. Real Estate, Corporate, Estate Planning, Probate, Insurance Defense, Banking, Family Law, Children, Commercial, Collections, Criminal Defense, Personal Injury Law, Social Security Law, Oil and Gas Law. Trial and Appellate Practice in all Courts.
Effingham, Illinois Office: 307 North Third Street, P.O. Box 607. Telephone: 217-342-9291. Fax: 217-342-9295.
See Professional Biographies, EFFINGHAM, ILLINOIS

Totten, William B., (BV) ....'60 '91 C.970 B.A. L.347 J.D. [Siemer,A.R.F.&T.] ⊙

CASEYVILLE, 4,310, *St. Clair Co.*

Schmidt, James R. ....'45 '76 C.430 B.A. L.910 J.D. 218 W. Wash. St.‡
Settle, Susan M. ....'61 '86 C.1359 B.B.A. L.1288 J.D. [S.M.Settle]
Settle, Susan Marie, Law Office ....P.O. Box 718

CEDARVILLE, 751, *Stephenson Co.*

Law, Robt. D. ....'22 '54 C.339 B.S. L.966 LL.B. P.O. Box 65‡

CENTRALIA, 14,136, *Clinton, Jefferson, Marion & Washington Cos.*

Cary, Richard A., (AV) .... '44 '73 C.234 B.S. L.734 J.D. [Wham&W.]
Crain, William P., (AV) .... '39 '64 C.477 B.A. L.502 LL.B. [Crain,M.&Assoc.]

Crain, Miller & Associates, Ltd., (AV)
623 East Broadway, P.O. Box 867, 62801
Telephone: 618-532-4744 Telefax: 618-532-7648
Email: mmiller@crainmiller.com
William E. Hall (1913-1983); Robert M. Crain (1910-1985); James H. Cooksey (1943-1993); William P. Crain; Marvin G. Miller;—Brian C. Wernsman; Stewart A. Freeman.
Personal Injury, Workers Compensation, Taxation, Tax Exempt Organizations, Oil and Gas, Probate, Corporate, Health Care, Administrative Law, Federal Practice, Criminal, Civil and Criminal Trial Practice, Wills.

Daniels, Christopher B. .... '67 '93 C.234 B.A. L.801 J.D. [Daniels]
Daniels Law Office .... 134 S. Locust
Freeman, Stewart A. .... '— '93 C.339 B.A. L.190 J.D. [Ⓐ Crain,M.&Assoc.]
Hodson, Jones & Pennock, Ltd., (AV) .... 140 South Poplar
Jones, G. Scott, (BV) .... '55 '80 C.234 B.A. L.801 J.D. [Hodson,J.&P.]
Jones, Michael R., (BV) .... '47 '76 C.234 B.S. L.245 J.D. 217 S. Locust St.
Lackey, George C., (AV) .... '36 '61 C&L.339 B.A., J.D. [Lackey&S.]
Lackey, John D., (BV) .... '43 '67 C&L.339 B.A., J.D. [Lackey&S.]
Lackey & Stevenson, P.C., (AV) .... 331 E. Broadway
Mann, Ronald J. '48 '73 C&L.500 B.C.E., J.D.
(adm. in MS; not adm. in IL) V.P., A. C. Mann Inc.
Miller, Marvin G., (BV) .... '57 '83 C.57 B.A. L.146 J.D. [Crain,M.&Assoc.]
Noonan, Thomas J., (AVⓉ) .... '55 '80 C.502 B.A. L.823 J.D. [T.J.Noonan] ⊙
Noonan, Thomas J., P.C., (AVⓉ) .... 820 East Noleman (⊙St. Louis, MO)
Parker, Jack S. .... '46 '72 C.497 B.S. L.500 J.D. Drawer G
Pennock, Harold H., III .... '49 '82 C.894 A.B. L.801 J.D. Assoc. Cir. J.
Pennock, Harold H., Jr., (AV) .... '25 '50 C.894 B.A. L.477 J.D. [Hodson,J.&P.]
Price, Daniel R., (AV) .... '59 '84 C.339 B.S. L.801 J.D. [Wham&W.]
Price, Jennifer W., (BV) .... '55 '84 C.37 B.A. L.801 J.D. [Wham&W.]
Reed, Michael E., (BV) .... '53 '81 C.927 B.A. L.365 J.D. [M.Reed]
Reed, Michael, Law Office of, (BV) .... 423 S. Poplar St.
Smith, Janie F., (BV) .... '57 '83 C&L.502 B.J., J.D. [Ⓒ Wham&W.]
Stedelin, Mark W., (CV) .... '53 '78 C.531 B.A. L.339 J.D. 217 S. Locust St.
Stevenson, Joanne Turner, (CV) .... '64 '89 C.172 B.A. L.801 J.D. [Lackey&S.]
Stevenson, John A., (CV) .... '64 '89 C&L.801 B.S., J.D. [Lackey&S.]
Veltman, Eddie, Law Offices of, (AV) .... '51 '76 C.339 B.S. L.300 J.D. 310 S. Elm
Warner, Tom B. .... '40 '69 C.497 B.S. L.500 J.D. Tr. Off., Old Nat. Bk. of Centralia
Wernsman, Brian C. .... '61 '95 C.1291 B.A. L.734 J.D. [Ⓐ Crain,M.&Assoc.]
Wham, Fred L., Jr. .... '10 '33 C&L.339 B.S., LL.B. 40 Evergreen Dr.‡
Wham, James B., (AV) .... '18 '46 C&L.339 B.S., J.D. [Wham&W.]
Wham, William B., (AV) .... '22 '47 C&L.339 B.S., J.D. [Wham&W.] ‡

Wham & Wham, (AV)
212 East Broadway, 62801
Telephone: 618-532-5621 Fax: 618-532-5055
Email: whamlawyers@aol.com URL: http://www.lawyers.com/wham&wham
Charles Wham (1887-1963); John P. Wham (1902-1992); William B. Wham (Retired). Members of Firm: James B. Wham; Richard A. Cary; Jennifer W. Price; Daniel R. Price. Of Counsel: Janie F. Smith.
General Trial and Appellate Practice. Insurance Defense including Medical Malpractice, Automobile Accidents, Premises Liability, Products Liability, Personal Injury, Probate, Wrongful Discharge from Employment.
Counsel for: State Farm Mutual Insurance Cos.; Auto-Owners Insurance Co; MMI Cos; Met Life Auto and Home; St. Mary's.
See Professional Biographies, CENTRALIA, ILLINOIS

Wood, Joanetta Mondino, Law Office, (CV) '55 '78
C.991 B.A. L.146 J.D. 24 Edgewood Lane N.

CERRO GORDO, 1,436, *Piatt Co.*

Burger, Walter F., Jr., (BV) .... '24 '51 C&L.734 B.S., LL.B. P.O. Box 440 (⊙Decatur)
Clarkson, Lynn .... '45 '76 C.388 B.A. L.966 J.D. Pres., Clarkson Grain Co.

CHAMPAIGN, 67,518, *Champaign Co.*

Adams, Harold N. .... '70 '96 C&L.339 B.A., J.D. [Meyer C.]
Aeilts, Rick Wayne, (BV) .... '65 '95 C.798 B.A. L.801 J.D. [Ⓐ Erwin,M.&C.]
Aldeen, Donald R., (AV) .... '34 '62 C&L.339 B.A., J.D. [Meyer C.]
Allen, Andrew S. .... '65 '90 P.O. Box 3817

Allen & Korkowski & Associates
(See Rantoul)

Amjad, Steven A. .... '74 '01 C.734 B.S. L.339 J.D. [Ⓐ Meyer C.]
Anderson, Scott, Jr. .... '47 '73 C.340 B.A. L.208 J.D. 501 W. University Avenue
Ansel, Marc J., (AV) .... '49 '74 C&L.339 B.S., J.D. [Ansel&S.]

Ansel & Small, Ltd., Law Office of, (AV) 🅱🅱
41 East University Avenue, 61820
Mailing Address: P.O. Box 468, Champaign, IL 61824-0468
Telephone: 217-359-0200 Fax: 217-359-0888
Email: mjalaw@shout.net
Marc J. Ansel; Howard W. Small;—Stanley E. Freeman.
Business Law, Commercial Litigation, Intellectual Property, Personal Injury, Insurance Litigation, and Insurance Defense. Civil Litigation and Civil Trial Practice Appeals.
See Professional Biographies, CHAMPAIGN, ILLINOIS

Austin, Magalie Desroches '61 '95 C.724 B.S. L.861 J.D.
(adm. in LA; not adm. in IL) Univ. of IL Coll. of Law
Bae, Wonsun .... '74 '03 C.999 B.A. L.339 J.D. Staff Atty., Christie Clinic
Baechle, Daniel A., (CV) '51 '76 C&L.339 B.S., J.D.
State Dept. of Child. & Fam. Servs.
Baer, Ora J., II .... '45 '70 C&L.339 B.S., J.D. 810 W. Springfield, Ste. 201
Bailey, Barbara Ann, (BV) '45 '98
C.1044 B.S. L.801 J.D. Examining Atty., Chicago Title Ins. Co.
Bailie, David A., (AV) .... '48 '75 C.935 B.A. L.339 J.D. [Thomas,M.&H.]
Bainbridge, Stephen M. '58 '86 C.928 B.A. L.893 J.D.
(adm. in DC; not adm. in IL) Prof. of Law, Univ. of Ill. Coll. of Law
Banner, Delmar K. .... '45 '71 C&L.339 B.S., J.D. [Lietz,B.&F.]
Barbercheck, Catherine H., (BV) '53 '78 C.589 B.S. L.1151 J.D.
[Ⓐ L.E.Johnson&Assoc.]
Bartell, Jason S. .... '73 '98 C.339 B.S. L.801 J.D. [Dodd,M.&B.]
Bauer, Wendy Shields, (BV) .... '50 '89 C&L.339 B.S., J.D. [Nally H.&B.]

Beckett & Webber, P.C.
(See Urbana)

Bednar, Maggie .... '71 '03 C&L.801 B.S., B.A., J.D. [Ⓐ Dobbins,F.T.J.&P.]
Bell, George J. .... '50 '76 C.475 B.A. L.339 J.D. Assoc. Clinical Prof.
Bellington, Janice E. .... '54 '79 C.16 B.S. L.209 J.D. 2408 Windsor Pl.
Bergstrom, John C. .... '32 '61 C&L.339 A.B., LL.B. 44 E. Main‡
Beth, Kenneth N., (Ltd.), (BV) .... '43 '68 C&L.879 B.A., J.D. [Evans,F.B.&C.]
Beyers, Robert J., (BV) .... '47 '74 C&L.339 B.S., J.D. 2217 Georgetown Drive‡
Black, Todd J., (BV) .... '59 '86 C.339 B.S. L.365 J.D. [Meyer C.]
Borton, Thomas B. .... '63 '88 C.340 B.A. L.910 J.D. [Livingston,B.B.&S.]
Boyle, Elizabeth Hunt .... '56 '82 C.914 B.A. L.339 J.D. 3805 Deerfield Dr.
Boyle, Francis A. '50 '77 C.145 A.B. L.309 J.D.
(adm. in MA; not adm. in IL) Prof., Univ. of IL. Coll. of Law
Bramfeld, John F., (BV) .... '50 '77 C.801 B.S. L.339 J.D. 115 North Neil Street
Brandt, Michael K. '52 '79 C&L.339 A.B., J.D.
V.P. & Gen. Coun., Attys. Title Guaranty Fund, Inc.
Brazitis, George E. .... '30 '55 C&L.597 B.S., J.D. 2606 Coppertree Rd.‡
Brenner, Andrew S. .... '47 '01 C.102 B.A. L.339 J.D. [A.Brenner]
Brenner, Andrew .... 3115 Old Warson Rd.
Brinkmann, William J., (AV) .... '48 '74 C&L.339 B.S., J.D. [Thomas,M.&H.]
Brown, R. Michael, (BV) .... '48 '80 C.339 B.S. L.879 J.D. [Erwin,M.&C.]
Bullock, Ellyn J. .... '63 '94 C.145 B.A. L.339 J.D. [Nally H.&B.]
Buttress, Amanda M. '69 '94 C.118 B.A. L.629 J.D.
(adm. in OR; not adm. in IL) Asst. Prof., Univ. of Ill. Coll. of Law
Causeman, Craig J., (BV) .... '55 '80 C.339 A.B. L.801 J.D. [Thomas,M.&H.]
Chamley, Joseph P., (Ltd.), (BV) .... '69 '94 C&L.339 B.A., J.D. [Evans,F.B.&C.]
Chapin, Richard A., (AV) .... '53 '78 C&L.339 B.S., J.D. [Hinshaw&C.]
Clausen, L. John .... '77 '02 C.339 B.A. L.879 J.D. [Ⓐ Erwin,M.&C.]
Cole, Paul R., (BV) .... '45 '77 C.385 B.A. L.339 J.D. [Erwin,M.&C.]
Comstock, Angela D. .... '71 '96 C.339 B.S. L.734 J.D. 1802 Fox Dr.
Coobs, Evan D., (CV) .... '63 '89 C&L.352 B.B.A., J.D. [Meyer C.]
Cosimini, R. Mark .... '66 '92 C.597 B.A. L.589 J.D. [Rusin M.&F.]
Cottrell, James D., (BV) .... '55 '83 C.339 B.S. L.221 J.D. [Dobbins,F.T.J.&P.]
Cozad, Gregory D. .... '59 '85 C.347 B.S. L.602 J.D. 2500 Galen Dr.
Crawford, Anita C. .... '13 '53 C.339 B.S. L.996 LL.B. 707 W. Kirby Ave.‡
Curtis, Wesley W. '60 '86 C&L.339 B.S., J.D.
Sr. V.P., Commercial Banking, BankIllinois
Czys, Elizabeth Bedard '56 '81 C.145 B.A. L.597 J.D.
V.P. & Tr. Offr., First Busey Tr. & Invest. Co.
Dastrup, Benson G. .... '75 '03 C.101 B.A. L.145 J.D. In-House Coun., Wolfram Research
Davey, William J. '49 '74 C&L.477 B.A., J.D.
(adm. in MI; not adm. in IL) Prof. of Law, Univ. of Ill.
Davis, Jeffrey M. .... '70 '96 C&L.339 B.S., J.D. [Meyer C.]
Deering, Matt C., (CV) .... '68 '96 C.383 B.A. L.607 J.D. [Meyer C.]
Dempsey, Scott M. .... '68 '94 C.231 B.A. L.879 J.D. [Ⓐ Dodson P.&Assoc.]
Dicken, Jennifer E. .... '— '04 C&L.347 B.A., J.D. [Ⓐ Thomas,M.&H.]
Didier, Brooke A.M. .... '78 '03 C.504 B.A. L.339 J.D. [Ⓐ Meyer C.]
Dieker, James W., (BV) '55 '81 C.339 B.S. L.365 J.D.
Staff Atty., Attorneys' Title Guaranty Fund, Inc.
Ding, Walter, (CV) .... '66 '92 C.597 B.A. L.801 J.D. [Dodson P.&Assoc.]
Dobbins, D. Cameron, (AV) .... '41 '67 C&L.339 B.A., J.D. [Ⓒ Dobbins,F.T.J.&P.]

Dobbins, Fraker, Tennant, Joy & Perlstein, A Professional Corporation, (AV)
215 North Neil, 61820-4012
Telephone: 217-356-7233 Telecopier: 217-356-3548
Email: dftjp@dobbinslaw.com URL: http://www.dobbinslaw.com
Donald V. Dobbins (1913-1981); Todd M. Tennant (1954-1997); French L. Fraker (1914-2005); Richard M. Joy; Guy C. Hall; Renee L. Monfort; James D. Cottrell; Stephen J. LeSueur; Daniel P. Wurl;—Maggie Bednar. Of Counsel: Donald M. Tennant; Creed D. Tucker; D. Cameron Dobbins.
General Practice, Trial and Appellate Practice in State and Federal Courts. Health Care, Privacy Law, Real Estate, Corporate, Estate Planning, Probate, Insurance Defense, Alternative Dispute Resolution, Family, Personal Injury, Medical Malpractice, Professional Liability, Products Liability, Commercial Litigation, Workers Compensation, Municipal and Drainage and Levee Law.
See Professional Biographies, CHAMPAIGN, ILLINOIS

Dodd, Robert W., (BV) .... '38 '74 C.999 A.B. L.339 J.D. [Dodd,M.&B.]
Dodd, McClellan & Bartell, P.C., Law Offices of, (BV) .... 303 S. Mattis
Dodson, John D., (BV) .... '38 '66 C&L.339 B.A., J.D. [Dodson P.&Assoc.]
Dodson Piraino & Associates, (BV) .... 501 West University
Dubrick, Anton J., Law Offices of '51 '02 C.339 B.S. L.276 J.D.
1000 W. Kirby Avenue

Dunn, Willard, Arkell & Bugg
(See Bloomington)

Elder, John E., (CV) .... '40 '73 C.942 B.A. L.339 J.D. 208 East Springfield
Elder, John H., (AV) .... '47 '72 C.679 B.S.I.M. L.339 J.D. [Meyer C.]
Emmons, Keith E., (AV) .... '47 '74 C.801 B.A. L.424 J.D. [Meyer C.]
Engert, Lloyd S. .... '09 '34 C&L.339 B.S., J.D. 711 South Prospect‡
Epsteen, Ralph .... '52 '77 C.339 B.S. L.209 J.D. 706 S. Fair St.

Erwin, Martinkus & Cole, Ltd., (BV)
411 West University Avenue, P.O. Box 1098, 61824-1098
Telephone: 217-351-4040 Telecopier: 217-351-4314
Sam Erwin (1935-2002); James A. Martinkus; Paul R. Cole; Richard C. Kirby; Sarah B. Tinney; Jeffery B. Wampler; Lynne R. Feldman; R. Michael Brown; Wayne O. Smith; Jeffrey L. Hays;—Anne M. Martinkus; Mike McCormick; Brian Edward King; Rick Wayne Aeilts; L. John Clausen.
General Civil Trial and Appellate Practice. Business and Corporate Practice including Securities and Banking Law. Tort and Insurance Litigation. Medical Malpractice, Probate and Estate Planning, Real Estate, Family Law, Bankruptcy and Immigration and Naturalization.
Reference: Champaign National Bank.
See Professional Biographies, CHAMPAIGN, ILLINOIS

Evans, Bill J. .... '30 '66 C&L.502 B.S.Ch.E., J.D. 9 Stanford Pl.‡
Evans, James W., (Ltd.), (AV) .... '37 '62 C.72 B.A. L.339 LL.B. [Evans,F.B.&C.]

Evans, Froehlich, Beth & Chamley, (AV)
A Partnership including Professional Corporations
44 Main Street, P.O. Box 737, 61820
Telephone: 217-359-6494 Telecopier: 217-359-6468
URL: http://www.efbclaw.com
Members of Firm: James W. Evans (Ltd.); Kurt P. Froehlich (Ltd.); Kenneth N. Beth (Ltd.); Joseph P. Chamley (Ltd.).
General Practice. Real Estate, Banking, Bankruptcy and Collection Law. Corporate, State, Municipal and Public Authority Financing and Municipal Law, Taxation, Trust and Probate Law. Litigation in Federal and State Courts.
Reference: Champaign National Bank.
See Professional Biographies, CHAMPAIGN, ILLINOIS

Feinen, Deborah F., (CV) .... '67 '92 C.518 B.A. L.146 J.D. [Nally H.&B.]
Feldman, Lynne R., (BV) .... '47 '75 C.483 B.A. L.1065 J.D. [Erwin,M.&C.]
Fernandes, David A., (BV) '53 '88 C.862 B.S. L.339 J.D.
Trust Ofc., Hickory Point Bank
Fischer, Kristen H. .... '52 '77 C.57 B.A. L.339 J.D. 602 S.Ridgeway Avenue
Fisher, Gail R., (Mr.), (CV) .... '06 '33 C&L.339 A.B., LL.B. 1122 W. Armory Ave.‡
Fitzgerald, Patrick T. .... '63 '89 C&L.339 B.A., J.D. [Meyer C.]

Flynn, Palmer & Tague, (BV)
402 West Church Street, P.O. Box 1517, 61824-1517
Telephone: 217-352-5181 Telecopier: 217-352-7964
Email: fpt5law@aol.com

(This Listing Continued)

Flynn, Palmer & Tague (Continued)

Members of Firm: Michael J. Tague; Jerome P. Lyke; Robert E. Jacobson. Of Counsel: Charles L. Palmer.
General Civil Practice in State and Federal Courts. Trials and Appeals. Banking, Estate Planning and Probate, Personal Injury, Real Estate, Family and Taxation Law.
Representative Clients: Bituminous Insurance Co.; Standard Mutual Insurance Co.; Universal Underwriters Co.; BankChampaign N.A.; BankIllinois; Champaign Asphalt Co.; Champaign Board of Education; First Federal Savings Bank; Shelter Insurance Co.

See Professional Biographies, CHAMPAIGN, ILLINOIS

Ford, Kelly E., (BV) .... '63 '88 C.504 B.A. L.339 J.D. [Lietz,B.&F.]
Forrest, Clyde W., Jr. .... '34 '62 C&L.862 B.A., J.D. Prof., Univ. of Illinois
Frampton, George T. '17 '42 C&L.228 A.B., J.D.
Prof. Emeritus, Univ. of Ill. Coll. of Law
Freeland, Rusty W., (BV) .... '58 '85 C.339 B.A. L.910 J.D. [Meyer C.]
Freeman, Stanley E., (BV) .... '59 '88 C.339 B.A. L.801 J.D. [[A] Ansel&S.]
Freyfogle, Eric T. '52 '76 C.401 B.A. L.477 J.D.
(adm. in DC; not adm. in IL) Prof. of Law, Univ. of Ill.
Froehlich, Kurt P., (Ltd.), (AV) .... '43 '73 C&L.339 B.S., J.D. [Evans,F.B.&C.]
Funderburg, Rochelle A., (BV) .... '56 '81 C&L.339 B.A., J.D. [Meyer C.]
Funk, John W. .... '59 '86 C.197 A.B. L.880 J.D. Insurance Risk Managers, Ltd.
Gadau, John E., (BV) .... '42 '67 C.249 L.339 LL.B. [Zimmerly,G.S.&O.]
Gajda, Amy '61 '92 C.477 B.A. L.912 J.D.
(adm. in VA; not adm. in IL) 504 E. Pennsylvania Avenue
Gardner, Matt .... '69 '00 C.878 B.S. L.339 J.D. 504 East Pennsylvania Avenue
Geerdes, Cynthea E. .... '61 '87 C.114 B.A. L.569 J.D. Law Prof., Univ. of IL
Geiler, Lorna K., (AV) .... '— '86 C.338 B.S. L.339 J.D. [Meyer C.]
Gohl-Noice, Jeane M. .... '52 '84 C.846 B.A. L.339 J.D. 2511 Waterbury Pl.
Goldstein, William M., (BV) '44 '69
C&L.339 B.S., J.D. Pres. & CEO, CodeTek Studios, Inc.
Gordon, Thomas J. .... '41 '68 C&L.339 A.B., J.D. 502 W. Clark St.
Gorman, Jerry T., (BV) '52 '77 C.174 B.A. L.1119 J.D.
V.P.& Corp. Coun., Attys. Title Guaranty Fund, Inc.
Gorski, Mary G., (CV) .... '53 '79 C.424 A.B. L.339 J.D. Champaign Urbana Legal Clinic
Greaves, Burt, (AV) .... '15 '41 C&L.339 B.S. 805 W. Green‡
Green, Bianca T., (BV) .... '68 '94 C.339 B.S. L.801 J.D. [Thomas,M.&H.]
Green, James D., (BV) .... '61 '89 C.340 B.S. L.734 J.D. [[A] Thomas,M.&H.]
Grose, Jeremy David .... '74 '00 C.999 B.A. L.339 J.D. Student Legal Serv
Grosser, Frederic M. .... '43 '71 C.284 B.B.A. L.365 J.D. 811 W. Springfield Ave.
Gunsalus, C. Kristina .... '57 '84 C&L.339 A.B., J.D. Assoc. Provost, Univ. of Ill.
Haasis, Regina B., (BV) .... '54 '79 C&L.339 B.A., J.D. [Nally H.&B.]
Hackmann, Tamara K., (AV) .... '62 '95 C.502 B.S. L.477 J.D. [[A] Meyer C.]
Hall, Guy C., (BV) .... '58 '83 C.339 B.A. L.862 J.D. [Dobbins,F.T.J.&P.]

Hallihan Intellectual Property Law, Ltd.
(See Chicago)

Harden, Richard R., (AV) .... '58 '83 C.388 B.A. L.339 J.D. [Thomas,M.&H.]
Harrington, Daniel G., (AV) .... '57 '82 C.339 B.S. L.362 J.D. [Harrington&T.] ⊙
Harrington, Thomas E., (AV) .... '31 '55 C&L.339 B.S., J.D. [Harrington&T.] ⊙

Harrington & Tock, (AV)
Suite 601 Huntington Towers, 201 West Springfield Avenue, P.O. Box 1550, 61824-1550 ⊙
Telephone: 217-352-4167 Telecopier: 217-352-8707
URL: http://www.lawyers.com/harringtont&rlaw
Members of Firm: Earl C. Harrington (1895-1981); Louis A. Busch (1886-1946); Robert F. Busch (1914-1969); W. Kenneth Porter (1919-1996); J. C. Ermentrout (1912-1998); Thomas E. Harrington; Daniel G. Harrington; Jeffrey W. Tock. Of Counsel: Kip Randolph Pope; Chapin Rose.
General Practice. Business, Partnership Law, Small Business Law, Family Business Law, Business Formation, Commercial Litigation, Probate, Tax, Corporation, Real Estate, Eminent Domain and Drainage Law, Shopping Center Law, Commercial Leasing, Commercial Landlord and Tenant Law, Tax Planning, IRS Controversies, Trials, Appeals and Commercial Arbitration.
Delray Beach, Florida Office: 100 East Linton Boulevard, Suite 215B, 33486. Telephone: 561-279-1840. Fax: 561-279-7842.

See Professional Biographies, CHAMPAIGN, ILLINOIS

Harris, Marjorie A. .... '58 '84 C.103 Sc.B. L.477 J.D. [[A] Meyer C.]
Hatch, Andrew J. .... '74 '01 C.610 B.S. L.801 J.D. [[A] Hatch&M.]
Hatch, Lawrence R., (AV) .... '12 '37 C&L.339 B.S., LL.B. [Hatch&M.]
Hatch, William L., (BV) .... '42 '68 C.303 A.B. L.339 J.D. [Hatch]
Hatch Law Firm, (BV) .... 115 N. Neil St., Ste. 309
Hatch & McPheters, Lawyers, P.C., (AV) .... 115 North Neil Street
Haughey, Roger E., (AV) .... '28 '52 C.338 L.339 J.D. [Thomas,M.&H.]
Hays, Jeffrey L., (BV) .... '47 '93 C&L.339 B.S., J.D. [Erwin,M.&C.]
Hendren, Paul C., (AV) .... '42 '67 C&L.339 B.A., J.D. [Miller&H.]
Hendrix, Charles W., (AV) .... '19 '47 C&L.339 A.B., LL.B. 909 S. Foley St.‡
Henneman, Jane Hays, (BV) .... '55 '79 C&L.339 A.B., J.D. Downey Grp., Inc., The
Hensley, John B., (BV) .... '— '82 C.339 B.S. L.209 J.D. [Secrest W.]
Henss, Donald A. .... '30 '56 C&L.339 B.S., J.D. 1304 Old Farm Rd.‡

Hinshaw & Culbertson LLP, (AV)
Hinshaw & Culbertson LLP is an Illinois registered limited liability partnership that has elected to be governed by the Illinois Uniform Partnership Act (1997)
1802 Fox Drive, 61820 ⊙
Telephone: 217-352-1400 Facsimile: 217-352-1401 Telex: 880248
Email: kfox@hinshawlaw.com URL: http://www.hinshawlaw.com
Partner: Richard A. Chapin. Associate: Matthew M. Sebek.
Appellate, Banking & Financing, Bankruptcy & Creditors' Rights, Class Action Litigation, Civil Rights Defense, Commercial Litigation, Corporate, Construction Law, Director & Officer Liability, Employee Benefits, Environmental, Fidelity & Surety, General Liability Litigation, Government, Health Care, Insurance Coverage, Insurance and Reinsurance, Labor & Employment, Legal Malpractice, Medical Malpractice, Mergers & Acquisitions, Municipal Liability, Personal Injury Defense, Public Law, Products Liability Litigation, Professional Liability, Regulatory, Real Estate, School Law, Securities, Taxation, Transportation, White Collar Crime and Workers' Compensation Defense.
Other Office Locations: Chicago, Illinois; Appleton, Wisconsin; Belleville, Illinois; Boston, Massachusetts; Crystal Lake, Illinois; Edwardsville, Illinois; Fort Lauderdale, Florida; Jacksonville, Florida; Joliet, Illinois; Lisle, Illinois; Los Angeles, California; Miami, Florida; Milwaukee, Wisconsin; Minneapolis, Minnesota; New York, New York; Peoria, Illinois; Phoenix, Arizona; Portland, Oregon; Providence, Rhode Island; Rockford, Illinois; St. Louis, Missouri; San Francisco, California; Schererville, Indiana; Springfield, Illinois; Tampa, Florida; Waukegan, Illinois.

See Professional Biographies, CHAMPAIGN, ILLINOIS

Hodson, Thomas Z., (BV) '47 '75 C.597 B.S.B.A. L.339 J.D.
701 Devonshire Drive, C-21, 61820-7330
Telephone: 217-239-6652 Fax: 217-398-0413
Email: thodson@aol.com URL: http://www.lawyers.com/thodsonlaw
Commercial Law, Agricultural Law, Real Estate.

See Professional Biographies, CHAMPAIGN, ILLINOIS

Huddlestone, Cameron D. '18 '54 C.339 B.S. L.1005 LL.B.
(adm. in TN; not adm. in IL) Clifton, Gunderson & Co.
Hutchens, Robt. S. .... '13 '38 C&L.339 B.S., LL.B. 201 N. Neil St.‡
Irion, Frederick W. .... '22 '49 C&L.339 B.S., LL.B. [[A] L.E.Johnson&Assoc.]
Jacobson, Robert E. .... '71 '96 C.999 B.A. L.339 J.D. [Flynn,P.&T.]
Jahn, Francis J., (AV) .... '42 '67 C&L.339 B.A., J.D. [Meyer C.]
Jefferson, Timothy S., (BV) .... '61 '86 C.347 B.S. L.502 J.D. [Rawles,O.S.&K.]
Jensen, Harold L. .... '34 '63 C&L.339 B.S., LL.B. [[C] Hatch&M.]
Johnson, Lawrence E., (AV) ...... '37 '65 C.589 M.S. L.339 LL.B. [L.E.Johnson&Assoc.]
Johnson, Lawrence E., and Associates, P.C., (AV) .... 202 West Hill Street
Jones, Sharon Sue '43 '91 C.927 B.S. L.339 J.D.
Staff Atty., Land of Lincoln Legal Assistance Found.
Joy, Richard M., (AV) .... '43 '69 C.477 B.A. L.339 J.D. [Dobbins,F.T.J.&P.]
Kaplan, Richard L. '48 '76 C.347 B.S. L.976 J.D.
(adm. in TX; not adm. in IL) Prof. of Law, Univ. of IL Coll. of Law
Karlstrom, Paul E. .... '20 '51 C&L.339 B.S., J.D. 44 Main St., Ste. 514‡
Kennedy, Daniel B. .... '46 '79 C.901 B.A. L.665 J.D. One E. Main Plaza, Suite 217
Kepley, Brett A., (BV) .... '61 '86 C.339 B.A. L.589 J.D. [Rawles,O.S.&K.]
Kepley, Vance I., (AV) .... '24 '62 C&L.339 B.S., J.D. 501 West Church Street‡
King, Brian Edward .... '72 '00 C.338 B.S. L.589 J.D. [[A] Erwin,M.&C.]
Kinports, Kit '54 '82 C.103 A.B. L.659 J.D.
(adm. in DC; not adm. in IL) Prof. of Law, Univ. of Ill.
Kirby, Richard C., (BV) .... '48 '80 C.339 B.A. L.801 J.D. [Erwin,M.&C.]
Kordik, Ellen R. .... '55 '86 C.146 B.S. L.339 J.D. 504 E. Penn. Ave.
Krchak, David E., (BV) .... '50 '80 C&L.339 B.A., J.D. [Thomas,M.&H.]
Lafond, John D., (CV) '59 '86 C&L.339 A.B., J.D.
Sr. Staff Atty., Land of Lincoln Legal Assistance Found., Inc.
Lansing, Paul .... '47 '73 C.994 B.A. L.339 J.D. 350 Commerce Bldg., W.
Laugges, Linda L., (BV) '60 '87 C.338 B.S. L.339 J.D.
Corp. Compl. Mgr., Personal Care Insurance Co.
LeFebvre, Charles A., (CV) .... '69 '98 C&L.339 B.S., J.D. [[A] Thomas,M.&H.]
Lerner, Arthur M., (AV) .... '35 '59 C&L.339 A.B., LL.B. [Lerner]
Lerner, Scott A., (CV) .... '65 '92 C.966 B.A. L.339 J.D. [[A] Lerner]

Lerner Law Offices, (AV)
Huntington Towers, Suite 608, 201 West Springfield Avenue, P.O. Box 1340, 61824-1340
Telephone: 217-356-8381 Fax: 217-356-7739
Email: sherri@lerner-law.com
Arthur M. Lerner. Associate: Scott A. Lerner.
General Civil and Criminal Trial Practice in all Courts. Family, Matrimonial, Driving Under The Influence, Administrative, Personal Injury, Civil Rights & Constitutional Litigation, Civil and Criminal Appeals.

LeSueur, Stephen J., (BV) .... '55 '80 C.399 B.A. L.339 J.D. [Dobbins,F.T.J.&P.]
Lewis, Milton E. '38 '80 C.944 B.A. L.209 J.D.
V.P., Admin. Servs. & Legal Affs., Parkland Coll.
Lierman, Joseph H., (BV) .... '49 '74 C&L.339 B.S., J.D. 502 W. Clark St.
Lietz, Gary R., (BV) .... '51 '77 C.207 B.A. L.365 J.D. [Lietz,B.&F.]

Lietz, Banner & Ford, (BV)
1605 S. State Street, Suite 103, 61820-7264
Telephone: 217-353-4900 Facsimile: 217-353-4901
URL: http://www.lawyers.com/lbf
Members of firm: Gary R. Lietz; Delmar K. Banner; Kelly E. Ford.
Employment Law, Wills and Estates, Agricultural Law, Real Estate, General Litigation, Personal Injury, Securities.

See Professional Biographies, CHAMPAIGN, ILLINOIS

Limentato, Sam A., (CV) .... '69 '94 C.1288 B.A. L.339 J.D. [Torricelli&L.]
Lingle, Elizabeth A. .... '72 '97 C&L.801 B.A., J.D. Asst. Atty. Gen.
Lipton, Mark D., (AV) .... '47 '75 C.388 B.A. L.597 J.D. [Meyer C.]

Livingston, Barger, Brandt & Schroeder, (AV)
2506 Galen Drive, Suite 108, 61821 ⊙
Telephone: 217-351-7479 Fax: 217-351-6870
Member of Firm: Thomas B. Borton (Resident, Champaign Office). Associates: Michael A. Wozniak; Kenneth S. Weiss.
Corporate, Business, Business Litigation, Real Estate Transactions, Creditors' Rights, Employment Law EEOC, ERISA, Estate Planning, Partnerships, Joint Ventures, Estates and Probate. Insurance Litigation, Product Liability, Medical Negligence Defense, Pharmaceutical Litigation, Construction Disputes, Environmental Litigation, Financial Litigation, Employment, Health Care to Physicians and Hospitals, Professional Liability, Officer's and Director's Liability, Environmental Law, Administrative Agency Procedures, Governmental Law, General Counsel Representation, Eminent Domain, Land Use Law, Subdivision and Zoning.
Representative Clients: Bloomington-Normal Airport Authority; Illinois Power Company; Northern Illinois Gas; Champion Federal Savings & Loan; Citizens Savings Bank; Aetna Casualty & Surety Co.; Kemper Insurance; Liberty Mutual Insurance Co.; Travelers Insurance Co.; American States Insurance.
Bloomington, Illinois Office: 115 West Jefferson, Suite 400, P.O. Box 3457. Telephone: 309-828-5281. Fax: 309-827-3432.

See Professional Biographies, CHAMPAIGN, ILLINOIS

Lyke, Jerome P., (BV) .... '57 '82 C.602 B.A. L.339 J.D. [Flynn,P.&T.]

Maatuka, Shayla, Law Office of
(See Urbana)

Maggs, Peter B. '36 '62 C&L.309 A.B., J.D.
(adm. in DC; not adm. in IL) Prof. of Law, Univ. of Ill.
Maguire, Linda L. .... '52 '88 C&L.339 B.S., J.D. 303 South Mattis Ave.
Mamer, Stuart M., (AV) .... '21 '47 C&L.339 A.B., J.D. [Thomas,M.&H.]
Mann, Barbara J., (CV) ..... '62 '90 C.679 B.S. L.339 J.D. 41 E. University Ave., Ste. 2A
Marshall, Damian P. .... '— '04 C.597 B.S. L.339 J.D. [[A] Thomas,M.&H.]
Martinkus, Anne M., (CV) .... '67 '96 C.339 B.S. L.1187 J.D. [[A] Erwin,M.&C.]
Martinkus, James A., (BV) .... '50 '77 C.112 B.A. L.339 J.D. [Erwin,M.&C.]
McCormick, Mike .... '59 '84 C.339 B.S. L.801 J.D. [[A] Erwin,M.&C.]
McDonald, Ward F. .... '42 '69 C&L.339 B.S., J.D. [Meyer C.]
McGrath, Susan W., (CV) .... '56 '82 C&L.339 B.A., J.D. [[A] L.E.Johnson&Assoc.]
McMahon, John J., (CV) .... '56 '91 C.801 B.S. L.339 J.D. [Wilkie&M.]
McPheron, Rita Joanne .... '50 '88 C.234 B.S. L.339 J.D. Asst. Atty. Gen.
McPheters, Brian L., (AV) .... '45 '73 C.294 B.S. L.339 J.D. [Hatch&M.]
McWilliams, Valerie Dykstra '57 '82
C.999 A.B. L.339 J.D. Land of Lincoln Legal Assist. Found., Inc.
Mengler, Thomas M. '53 '81
C.118 B.A. L.846 J.D. Dean & Prof., Univ. of Illinois Coll. of Law
Merritt, Andrew L. '55 '81 C.999 B.A. L.178 J.D.
(adm. in GA; not adm. in IL) Asst. Prof. of Law, Univ. of Ill.
Meyer, David D. .... '61 '92 C&L.477 B.A., J.D. Asst. Prof., Univ. of IL Coll. of Law

Meyer Capel, A Professional Corporation, (AV) [BB]
306 West Church Street, P.O. Box 6750, 61826-6750
Telephone: 217-352-1800 Telecopier: 217-352-1083
Email: attorneys@meyercapel.com URL: http://www.meyercapel.com
James L. Capel, Jr. (1933-1991); Dennis K. Muncy; Francis J. Jahn; Donald R. Aldeen; David B. Sholem; John H. Elder; Mark D. Lipton; Tracy J. Nugent; Richard T. West; Rusty W. Freeland; Lorna K. Geiler; Patrick T. Fitzgerald; Todd J. Black; Joseph D. Murphy; James M. Mullady; William B. Moore; Evan D. Coobs; John J. Powers; Rochelle A. Funderburg; Jeffrey M. Davis; Keith E. Emmons; Matt C. Deering; Harold N. Adams; Ward F. McDonald;—Marjorie A. Harris; Rebecca E.P. Wade; Jenny H. Park; Brooke A.M. Didier; Steven A. Amjad; Tamara K. Hackmann; Scott E. Perkins. Of Counsel: Richard J. Winkel, Jr.

(This Listing Continued)

Meyer Capel, A Professional Corporation (Continued)

General Civil Litigation, Corporate Law, Business Law, Estate Planning, Estate Administration, Real Estate, Tax, Telecommunications and Public Utility, Intellectual Property Law, Labor and Employment Law (Management), Municipal Law, Family Law, Health Care Law, Personal Injury, Products Liability Law, Criminal Law, Social Security Disability, Software Licensing, Education Law.
Representative Clients: Main Street Bank & Trust Co.; Bell Foods, Inc.; Christie Clinic; Communications Management, Inc.; Intel Americas, Inc.; Midwest Television, Inc.; Parkland College.

See Professional Biographies, CHAMPAIGN, ILLINOIS

Midden, Mary Ann .... '53 '79 C.710 B.A. L.801 J.D. [Ⓐ Dodd,M.&B.]
Miely, Gregory J. .... '54 '81 C.645 B.S. L.365 J.D. 2408 Windsor Pl.
Mikva, Laurie I. ... '55 '84 C.72 B.A. L.569 J.D. Land of Lincoln Legal Asst. Found., Inc.
Miller, George S. .... '28 '56 C.597 B.S. L.309 J.D. [Ⓒ Thomas,M.&H.]
Miller, Harold A., (AV) .... '22 '50 C&L.339 B.S., J.D. [Miller&H.]
Miller, Marc R., (BV) .... '61 '87 C.309 B.A. L.589 J.D. [Miller&H.]

Miller & Hendren, (AV)
National City Bank Building, 30 Main Street, Second Floor, P.O. Box 980, 61824-0980
Telephone: 217-352-2171 Fax: 217-352-3839
Email: mhlawoffice@aol.com URL: http://www.mhlawoffice.com
Harold A. Miller; Paul C. Hendren; Marc R. Miller.
General Civil Practice, Probate, Trusts and Estate Planning. Real Estate. Business, Commercial and Corporate Law. Taxation. Municipal Law. School Law.
Representative Clients: Municipalities of Fisher, Gibson City, Homer, Philo, Sadoras, Savoy, Sidney, Tolono, and Village Grove Illinois; Public School Districts in Champaign County; Champaign County Mental Health Center; ABP Farm Trust; Microsystems; Campus Property Management.

Monfort, Renee L., (AV) .... '64 '90 C.531 B.S. L.362 J.D. [Dobbins,F.T.J.&P.]
Moore, William B. .... '56 '82 C.877 B.S. L.1068 J.D. [Meyer C.]
Morgan, Colleen M. .... '61 '87 C.670 B.A. L.276 J.D. Asst. Def.
Mullady, James M., (BV) .... '52 '91 C.338 B.S.M.S. L.347 J.D. [Meyer C.]
Muncy, Dennis K., (AV) .... '42 '67 C.597 B.S. L.339 J.D. [Meyer C.]
Murphy, Joseph D., (BV) .... '60 '86 C.93 B.A. L.904 J.D. [Meyer C.]
Nally, Traci E., (BV) .... '54 '82 C&L.339 B.A., J.D. [Nally H.&B.]
Nally Haasis & Bauer, P.C., (BV) .... 41 E. University Avenue, Suite 2A
Nordheden, John A. .... '53 '79 C&L.339 B.A., J.D. Clifton, Gunderson & Co.
Nowak, John E. .... '47 '71 C.436 A.B. L.339 J.D. Prof., Univ. Of IL Coll. of Law
Nugent, Tracy J., (BV) .... '56 '84 C&L.339 B.S., J.D. [Meyer C.]
O'Byrne, J. Michael, (AV) .... '25 '50 C&L.339 B.S., J.D. [Ⓒ Rawles,O.S.&K.]
O'Byrne, Stephen M., (BV) .... '50 '75 C&L.339 B.A., J.D. [Rawles,O.S.&K.]
Otto, John H., (BV) .... '46 '77 C.1124 B.A. L.477 J.D. [Zimmerly,G.S.&O.]
Pahre, Jennifer N., (AVⓉ) .... '— '86 C.813 B.A. L.426 J.D. [Secrest W.]
Palmer, Charles L., (AV) .... '31 '57 C&L.339 A.B., J.D. [Ⓒ Flynn,P.&T.]
Park, Jenny H. .... '73 '01 C.339 B.S. L.345 J.D. [Ⓐ Meyer C.]
Paterson, Richard W., (BV) .... '27 '53 C&L.339 B.S., J.D. 44 Main St.
Pelini, Gregory E., Law Office of, (CV) ..... '49 '76 C&L.339 A.B., J.D. 501 W. Church
Perkins, Scott E. .... '79 '04 C&L.339 B.S., J.D. [Ⓐ Meyer C.]
Perlstein, Mary A., (AV) .... '34 '75 C.597 B.S.B. L.339 J.D. 215 N. Neil St.
Peters, Gregory Hoerr .... '54 '81 C&L.339 B.S., J.D. Scheitlin-Peters Construction
Pfanner, James E. .... '56 '83 C.502 B.A. L.893 J.D. Prof. of Law, Univ. of Ill.

Phebus & Koester
(See Urbana)

Phipps, John T., (AV) .... '37 '65 C.210 B.A. L.339 J.D. [J.T.Phipps]

Phipps, John T., Law Offices, P.C., (AV)
303 Lincoln Building, 44 Main Street, P.O. Box 1220, 61824-1220
Telephone: 217-359-2929 Fax: 217-359-5329
URL: http://www.lawyers.com/johnphippslaw
John T. Phipps.
General Civil Trial Practice. Family, Personal Injury, Corporate, Banking, Paternity, Child Custody, Visitation, Divorce, Wills and Estate Planning, Domestic Relations, Probate, Elder Law, Traffic Defense, Business Fraud, White Collar Crimes, Mediation, Arbitration, Real Estate, Criminal Law, Domestic Violence, DUI.

See Professional Biographies, CHAMPAIGN, ILLINOIS

Piraino, Edwin, (CV) .... '42 '95 C.339 B.A. L.146 J.D. [Dodson P.&Assoc.]
Pope, Kip Randolph, (BV) .... '47 '74 C.339 A.B. L.1119 J.D. [Ⓒ Harrington&T.]
Powers, John J. .... '55 '80 C.339 B.S. L.477 J.D. [Meyer C.]
Prillaman, Terry S. '59 '84 C.234 B.A. L.801 J.D.
Sr. Mgr & Staff Atty., Attorneys' Title Guaranty Fund, Inc.
Puglisi, Bernard A., (CV) ..... '43 '75 C.299 B.A. L.365 J.D. 2106 W. Springfield Ave.
Ratcliffe, Bruce G., (CV) ..... '49 '83 C.801 B.A. L.209 J.D. 1200 W. Union Street
Rawles, Edward H., (AV) .... '45 '70 C.339 A.B. L.146 J.D. [Rawles,O.S.&K.]

Rawles, O'Byrne, Stanko & Kepley, P.C., (AV) BB
501 West Church Street, P.O. Box 800, 61824-0800
Telephone: 217-352-7661 Telecopier: 217-352-2169 URL: http://www.lawyers.com/rosklaw
URL: http://www.rosklaw.com
Edward H. Rawles; Stephen M. O'Byrne; Glenn A. Stanko; Brett A. Kepley; Timothy S. Jefferson.
Of Counsel: J. Michael O'Byrne.
General practice in all State and Federal Courts, Trials and Appeals, Personal Injury, Product Liability, Estate and Business Planning, Probate, Real Estate, Hospital and Health Law, Commercial Litigation, Insurance Defense, Malpractice, Criminal Law, Taxation, Domestic Relations, Employment Law, Bankruptcy, Worker's Compensation, and General Counseling.
Local Counsel For: American International Group; Black & Co.; Construction Industry Welfare Fund of Central Illinois; Frances Nelson Health Center; Fraternal Order of Police; New Hampshire Insurance Group; Pekin Insurance Co.; Provena Covenant Medical Center; ServiceMaster of Champaign; Unitrin Insurance Group.

See Professional Biographies, CHAMPAIGN, ILLINOIS

Reeves, John E., Law Offices of, (CV) .... '54 '80 C.339 B.S. L.589 J.D. 2500 Galen Drive
Reifsteck, Kenneth D., (CV) .... '65 '91 C.338 B.S. L.801 J.D. [Thomas,M.&H.]
Roberts, William M. .... '32 '70 C&L.339 B.S., J.D. [Ⓐ L.E.Johnson&Assoc.]
Rose, Chapin .... '73 '00 C&L.339 B.S., J.D. [Ⓒ Harrington&T.]
Rotunda, Ronald D. ..... '45 '71 C&L.309 A.B., J.D. Prof., Univ. of Ill. Coll. of Law
Royse, Mary Ann, Law Office, (CV) ... '67 '95 C.339 B.S. L.846 J.D. 1 E. Main, Ste. 218

Rusin Maciorowski & Friedman, Ltd., (AV)
2506 Galen Drive, Suite 104, 61821-7047 ⊙
Telephone: 217-351-1700 Fax: 217-351-1732
Email: mcosimini@rusinlaw.com URL: http://www.rusinlaw.com
R. Mark Cosimini;—Terry E. Schroeder (Resident, Champaign Office).
Workers Compensation Law. Insurance Defense, Personal Injury, Products Liability, Auto and Trucking Liability, Structural Work Act, Commercial Litigation, Subrogation, Contract Insurance, Employment Discrimination. Wrongful Discharge.
Chicago, Illinois Office: Suite 1530, 10 South Riverside Plaza, 60606. Telephone: 312-454-5110. Fax: 312-454-6166.
Carbondale, Illinois Office: 239 South Lewis Lane, Suite A, 62901-3443. Telephone: 618-351-8100. Fax: 618-351-8109.

See Professional Biographies, CHAMPAIGN, ILLINOIS

Sasek, John G. .... '61 '97 [Ⓐ L.E.Johnson&Assoc.]
Sebek, Matthew M. .... '75 '03 C.340 B.A. L.339 J.D. [Ⓐ Hinshaw&C.]

Secrest Wardle, (AVⓉ)
2919 Crossing Court, Suite 11, 61822 ⊙
Telephone: 217-378-8002 Fax: 217-378-8003
Email: info@secrestwardle.com URL: http://www.secrestwardle.com
John B. Hensley; Jennifer N. Pahre.
Appellate, Commercial and Business, Construction, Drug and Medical Device, Employment, Environmental and Toxic Tort, Governmental Litigation, Insurance Coverage, Intellectual Property/Advertising Injury, Motor Vehicle Litigation, Municipal, Premises Liabilty, Product Liability, Malpractice and Professional Liability.
Farmington Hills, Michigan Office: 30903 Northwestern Highway, P.O. Box 3040. Telephone: 248-851-9500. Telefacsimile: 248-851-2158.
Lansing, Michigan Office: 6639 Centurion Drive, Suite 130. Telephone: 517-886-1224. Facsimile: 517-886-9284.
Mount Clemens, Michigan Office: 94 Macomb Place. Telephone: 586-465-7180. Telefacsimile: 586-465-0673.
Grand Rapids, Michigan Office: 2025 E. Beltline, S. E., Suite 103. Telephone: 616-285-0143. Fax: 616-285-0145.

See Professional Biographies, CHAMPAIGN, ILLINOIS

Seegmiller, Trent T. .... '76 '03 C.101 B.S. L.339 J.D. 3121 Village Office
Selin, Paul E., (BV) .... '51 '77 C.339 B.A. L.190 J.D. [Zimmerly,G.S.&O.]
Sheffler, Stephen K., (BV) .... '51 '76 C.337 A.B. L.339 J.D. 501 W. Church St.
Shlens, Edmund N. .... '32 '58 C.347 B.S. L.339 LL.B. 701 Devonshire Dr.
Shoben, Elaine W. '48 '74 C.66 A.B. L.1065 J.D.
(adm. in CA; not adm. in IL) Univ. of Ill., College of Law
Sholem, David B., (AV) .... '53 '78 C.103 B.A. L.930 J.D. [Meyer C.]
Sinder, Carl J., (BV) .... '40 '64 C&L.339 B.S., J.D. 206 N. Randolph
Singleton, Alan R. .... '64 '91 C&L.339 B.S., J.D. [Singleton] (Pat.)

Singleton Law Firm, P.C.
One East Main, Suite 215, 61820
Telephone: 217-352-3900 Fax: 217-352-4900
URL: http://www.singletonlaw.pro
Alan R. Singleton.
Corporate Law, Securities, Intellectual Property, Patents, Real Estate, Health Care.

See Professional Biographies, CHAMPAIGN, ILLINOIS

Slack, Dan M., (BV) '56 '83 C&L.339 B.A., J.D.
Gen. Coun., State Universities Retirement Sys.
Slanker, Barbara Olsen, (CV) .... '34 '83 C.172 B.A. L.339 J.D. 206 N. Randolph
Small, Howard W., (AV) .... '48 '74 C.37 B.A. L.339 J.D. [Ansel&S.]
Smith, Wayne O., (BV) .... '62 '87 C.338 B.S. L.801 J.D. [Erwin,M.&C.]
Snyder, Tania Marie '71 '98 C&L.339 B.A., J.D.
Staff Atty., Attorneys' Title Guaranty Fund, Inc.
Spencer, Robert B. '46 '73 C.373 B.A. L.209 J.D.
Gen. Coun., Allied Title Services, Inc.
Spielman, Joseph M., III .... '47 '75 C.424 A.B. L.209 J.D. 307 W. Clark St.‡
Stanko, Glenn A., (AV) .... '49 '76 C.927 B.S. L.339 J.D. [Rawles,O.S.&K.]
Stavins, Frederick C., Jr., (BV) .... '49 '76 C.602 B.A. L.339 J.D. City Atty.
Stinson, Judith M. '64 '88 C&L.37 B.S., J.D.
(adm. in AZ; not adm. in IL) 504 E. Pennsylvania Ave.
Streeter, Harrison .... '26 '51 C&L.339 B.S., LL.B. 1807-C Lake Side Dr.‡
Sturmanis, John M., (CV) .... '67 '92 C&L.801 J.D. [Thomas,M.&H.]
Tabb, Charles Jordan '55 '80 C.880 B.A. L.893 J.D.
(adm. in TX; not adm. in IL) Prof. of Law, Univ. of Ill.
Tague, Michael J., (BV) .... '55 '80 C.96 B.A. L.339 J.D. [Flynn,P.&T.]
Tennant, Donald M., (AV) .... '31 '58 L.339 LL.B. [Ⓒ Dobbins,F.T.J.&P.]
Tepper, Edward P. .... '38 '62 C&L.339 B.S., LL.B. Tepper Elec. Supply Co.
Thomas, Lott H., (AV) .... '34 '62 C.210 B.A. L.339 J.D. [Thomas,M.&H.]
Thomas, Melissa A. .... '69 '94 C&L.339 B.S., J.D. [Thomas,M.&H.]

Thomas, Mamer & Haughey, LLP, (AV) BB
National City Bank Building, 30 E. Main Street, Suite 500, 61820-3629
Mailing Address: P.O. Box 560, Champaign, IL 61824-0560
Telephone: 217-351-1500 Fax: 217-355-0087; 217-351-2017 217-351-2169
Email: tmh@tmh-law.com URL: http://www.tmh-law.com
James G. Thomas (1901-1990). Members of Firm: Stuart M. Mamer; Roger E. Haughey; Lott H. Thomas; William J. Brinkmann; David A. Bailie; Craig J. Causeman; Richard R. Harden; David E. Krchak; Bruce E. Warren; John M. Sturmanis; Bianca T. Green; Kenneth D. Reifsteck; Melissa A. Thomas. Associates: Charles A. LeFebvre; Damian P. Marshall; James D. Green; Jennifer E. Dicken. Of Counsel: George S. Miller.
General Practice, Federal and State Trials, Probate, Trusts, Taxation, Real Estate, Business and Commercial Law, Insurance Defense, Employment and Employment Discrimination, Elder Law, Discrimination, Construction Accident, Adoptions, Premarital Agreements, Long Term Care, American with Disabilities Act, Family and Medical Leave Act, Sexual Harassment, Wrongful Termination, Medical practice, Automobile Accidents, Slip and Fall, Wrongful Death, Condominium Law, Landlord and Tenant Law, Residential Real Estate, Estate and Gift Taxation, Income Tax, Estate Litigation, Estate Planning, Guardianship and Conservatorship, Wills and Probate, Workers Compensation, Business Formation, Business Litigation, Buying and Selling of Business, Limited Liability Company Law, Partnership Law, Small Business Law, Construction Accidents, Breach of Contract, Employment Contracts, Personal Policies, Commercial Leasing, Commercial Real Estate, Landlord and Tenant Law.
Representative Clients: American States Insurance Co.; Auto Owners Insurance Co.; Bituminous Insurance Co.; Capitol Indemnity Co.; Cannon Cochran Management Services Inc.; Chicago Motor Insurance Co.; Ecomony Fire & Casualty Co.; Federated Insurance; Hanover Insurance Co.; Hartford Insurance Co.

See Professional Biographies, CHAMPAIGN, ILLINOIS

Tichenor, Christopher L. .... '73 '02 C.339 B.A. L.146 J.D. [Ⓐ Hatch&M.]
Tinney, Sarah B., (BV) .... '52 '77 C.112 B.A. L.339 J.D. [Erwin,M.&C.]
Tock, Jeffrey W., (BV) .... '48 '80 C.339 B.S. L.46 J.D. [Harrington&T.]
Torricelli, Kenneth R., (BV) .... '60 '85 C.339 B.A. L.801 J.D. [Torricelli&L.]
Torricelli & Limentato, (BV) .... 2504 Galen Drive, Suite 101
Trimpe, Robert T., (CV) .... '25 '56 C&L.276 B.S.S., J.D. 701 Devonshire Dr., C-32
Tucker, Creed D. .... '24 '55 C&L.339 B.S., LL.B. [Ⓒ Dobbins,F.T.J.&P.]

Tummelson Bryan & Knox
(See Urbana)

Waaler, Jack, (BV) .... '34 '59 C&L.339 B.A., LL.B. City Atty.
Wade, Rebecca E.P. .... '71 '98 C&L.339 B.A., J.D. [Ⓐ Meyer C.]
Wampler, Jeffery B., (BV) .... '61 '86 C.347 B.S. L.879 J.D. [Erwin,M.&C.]
Warren, Bruce E., (BV) .... '54 '86 C.339 B.A. L.801 J.D. [Thomas,M.&H.]
Watts, Robin Denise '66 '93 C.383 B.A. L.431 J.D.
Staff Atty., Attorneys' Title Guaranty Fund, Inc.
Weaver, S. Blake, Jr., (BV) .... '50 '75 C.339 B.S. L.734 J.D. 130 W. Main St.

Webber & Thies, P.C.
(See Urbana)

Weber, Mark A. .... '61 '86 C&L.339 B.S., J.D. Univ. of Ill. Coll. of Law
Weiss, Kenneth S. .... '49 '01 C.477 B.S. L.339 J.D. [Ⓐ Livingston,B.B.&S.]
Weith, Glenna J., (BV) .... '45 '84 C.338 B.S. L.339 J.D. [Weith]

Weith Law Office, (BV)
Suite 230, 116 North Chestnut Street, C-U Station, 61820
Telephone: 217-398-1200 Facsimile: 217-398-0078
Email: glennaweith@hotmail.com URL: http://www.lawyers.com/illinoisadoptionlaw

(This Listing Continued)

Weith Law Office (Continued)

Glenna J. Weith.
Adoption Law, Interstate Adoption, International Adoptions, Step-parent Adoptions, Grandparent Adoptions, Contested Adoptions, Guardianship, Surrogacy Law, Child Sexual Abuse, Child Abuse and Neglect, Childrens Rights, Child Advocacy, Assisted Reproductive Technology, Agency Adoptions, Child Support, Child Welfare, Termination of Parental Rights, Family Mediation, Foster Care, Divorce, Separation Agreements, Prenuptial Agreements, Post-Divorce Modification, Domestic Violence, Interstate Support, Parental Rights, Immigration Adoption Issues.
See Professional Biographies, CHAMPAIGN, ILLINOIS

West, Richard T., (AV) ... '44 '69 C&L.339 B.S., J.D. [Meyer C.]
Wilcoxen, David B. ... '64 '00 C&L.339 B.A., J.D. 2113 W. White
Wilkie, John M. (Jack), (CV) ... '58 '86 C.178 B.A. L.589 J.D. [Wilkie&M.]
Wilkie & McMahon, (CV) ... 1 E. Main St., Ste. 214
Wilson, Alexander M., (CV) ... '64 '90 C.604 B.A. L.801 J.D. Pub. Def.
Winkel, Richard J., Jr., (BV) ... '56 '82 C.339 B.A. L.209 J.D. [Ⓒ Meyer C.]
Wozniak, Michael A. ... '59 '84 C.338 B.S. L.339 J.D. [Ⓐ Livingston,B.B.&S.] ⊙
Wurl, Daniel P., (AV) ... '56 '81 C&L.339 B.A., J.D. [Dobbins,F.T.J.&P.]
Zanewicz, James R. '69 '97 C.138 B.S. L.861 J.D.
(adm. in KY; not adm. in IL; Pat.)
Tech. Transfer Specialist, Univ. of IL at Urbana-Champaign
Zimmerly, Philip C., (AV) ... '23 '49 C&L.339 B.S., LL.B. [Ⓒ Zimmerly,G.S.&O.]
Zimmerly, Gadau, Selin & Otto, (BV) ... 116 North Chestnut Street, Suite 200

CHANNAHON, 7,344, *Grundy & Will Cos.*

Wilson, Claire M., (CV) ... '53 '79 C.339 B.A. L.589 J.D. 25154 W. Channon Dr.
Zito-Nash, Judith Amy ... '69 '98 C.339 B.S. L.365 J.D. 26516 W. Melissa Drive

CHARLESTON, * 21,039, *Coles Co.*

Anderson, Jack H., (AV) ... '20 '42 C.234 L.209 Charleston Nat. Bk. Bldg.
Bays, Kirsten Crouse, (CV) ... '66 '91 C.234 L.910 J.D. [Crouse C.&B.]
Bower, Brian L., (BV) ... '58 '83 C.597 B.S.S. L.589 J.D. [Brainard]
Bower, J. Leeds, (AV) ... '31 '57 C&L.339 B.A., J.D. [Ⓒ Brainard]

Brainard Law Offices, The, (AV) BB
Brainard Building, 600 Jackson Avenue, 61920
Telephone: 217-345-3929 Fax: 217-345-6501
URL: http://www.brainardlaw.com
Members of Firm: H. Ogden Brainard (1905-1992); William A. Sunderman; Henry E. Kramer; Brian L. Bower; William J. Warmoth; Mark R. Karpus; Kristin L. Wilson. Of Counsel: J. Leeds Bower.
General Practice. Insurance Defense, Personal Injury, Products Liability, Probate, Trusts, Real Estate, Taxation, Municipal, Family and Health Law. Trials in all State and Federal Courts.
Representative Clients: Community Bank & Trust Savings Bank; Sarah Bush Lincoln Health Center; Firstar Bank; Neighborhood Bankshares; First Mid-IL Bank & Trust, N.A.
See Professional Biographies, CHARLESTON, ILLINOIS

Britton, Sean McCoy ... '71 '96 C.475 B.A. L.912 J.D. 609 Monroe
Brown, Robert E., (BV) ... '44 '81 C.754 B.A. L.1119 J.D. [Ⓐ R.Tulin]

Choate, Murray R., II, Attorney at Law '54 '79 C.197 B.A. L.880 J.D.
622 Jackson Avenue, 61920
Telephone: 217-345-4452 Fax: 217-348-7522
Email: rickchoate@choatelawyers.com URL: http://www.choatelawyers.com
Real Estate, Resort and Planned Community Development, Condominiums, Property Owners Associations, Interstate and International Real Estate Offerings, Regulated Real Estate Product Disclosure and Registration, Real Estate Brokerage, Real Estate Broker Licensing, Franchise Law, International Travel and Tourism, International Commerical Transactions, U.S.- Australia Free Trade Agreement Opportunities.
See Professional Biographies, CHARLESTON, ILLINOIS

Craig & Craig
(See Mattoon)

Crouse Cobb & Bays, (BV) ... 1513 University Dr. (⊙Collinsville)
Deters, Duane A. ... '71 '97 C.234 B.A. L.801 J.D. Asst. State's Atty.
Ebdon, Priscilla Ragle, (CV) ... '43 '77 C.1012 A.B. L.339 J.D. 517 7th Street
Edwards, Jerry L., (CV) ... '62 '87 C.234 B.A. L.801 J.D. 821 Monroe Avenue
Ferguson, C. Stephen, (BV) ... '57 '82 C.357 B.A. L.339 J.D. States Atty.
Gano, Kenneth R., Jr., (CV) ... '52 '80 C.234 B.A. L.589 J.D. 938 6th Street
Geisler, Kevin L., (CV) ... '— '96 C.267 B.S.B.A. L.734 J.D. [K.Geisler]
Geisler, Kevin, The Law Office of, (CV) ... 821 Monroe Ave.

Grant, James M., (BV) '50 '75 C.234 B.A. L.734 J.D.
611 6th Street, 61920 ⊙
Telephone: 217-345-2510 Fax: 217-348-0082
Email: jmgrant@jamesmgrantlaw.com URL: http://www.lawyers.com/jamesmgrantlaw
Language: English.
Real Estate, Real Estate Title, Wills & Estates.
Casey, Illinois Office: 101 North Central, 62420. Telephone: 217-932-5885. Fax: 217-932-5889.
See Professional Biographies, CHARLESTON, ILLINOIS

Heller, Holmes & Associates, P.C.
(See Mattoon)

Jacobs, Gary W. ... '52 '77 C.234 B.S. L.734 J.D. County J.
Karpus, Mark R., (BV) ... '60 '89 C.234 B.S. L.1187 J.D. [Brainard]
Komada, Paul C. ... '42 '67 C.238 B.A. L.146 J.D. 821 Monroe Avenue
Kramer, Henry E., (BV) ... '41 '65 C&L.339 J.D. [Brainard]
McPike, Cynthia L. ... '57 '86 C.260 B.S. L.365 J.D. Jud. Clk. for Cir. J.
Miller, Robert Lee, Law Office of ... '69 '98 C.234 B.A. L.836 J.D. P.O. Box 821
Righter, Dale A., (CV) ... '66 '91 C.234 B.S. L.734 J.D. 821 Monroe Avenue

Ryan, Bennett & Radloff
(See Mattoon)

Shick, Mitchell K., (BV) ... '61 '86 C.234 B.S. L.734 J.D. 821 Monroe Avenue
Smith, Rodney L., (BV) ... '65 '91 C.338 B.S. L.801 J.D. 622 Jackson Ave.
Sunderman, William A., (AV) ... '46 '72 C.234 B.S. L.339 J.D. [Brainard]
Swenson, Karen B. ... '63 '89 C.604 B.A. L.880 J.D. 15883 Sunnydale Drive
Tidwell, James Alvin ... '48 '85 C.613 B.A. L.421 J.D. Prof., Eastern Illinois University‡
Tulin, Ronald, (AV) ... '39 '68 C.339 B.S. L.209 J.D. [R.Tulin]
Tulin, Ronald, Ltd., (AV) ... 609 Monroe Ave.
Waller, Ashton C. ... '41 '70 C&L.597 B.A., J.D. Cir. J.
Warmoth, William J., (BV) ... '49 '74 C.234 B.S. L.339 J.D. [Brainard]
Wilson, Kristin L., (CV) ... '67 '91 C&L.190 B.A.B.A., J.D. [Brainard]

Winter-Black & Livesay, Law Offices of
(See Mattoon)

CHATHAM, 8,583, *Sangamon Co.*

Bordenkircher, Thomas E., (BV) ... '51 '77 C.339 B.A. L.796 J.D. P.O. Box 528
Kelly, James D., (BV) ... '47 '72 C.1151 B.A. L.339 J.D. [Presney,K.&P.] ⊙
Post, Alan R., Attorney and Mediator '48 '72 C&L.966 B.B.A., J.D.
841 Magnolia Drive
Presney, Kelly and Presney, (AV) ... 114 E. Walnut (⊙Springfield)
Solberg, Gerard A. ... '51 '85 C.494 B.A. L.209 J.D. 10 Charleston Ct.
Thomas, Alan Blake '72 '98
C&L.339 B.A., J.D. Coun. & COO, United Community Bancorp

CHATSWORTH, 1,186, *Livingston Co.*

Herr, James J., (BV) '30 '54
C&L.602 Ph.B., LL.B. Citizens Bank Bldg. (⊙Kempton, Pontiac)

CHENOA, 1,845, *McLean Co.*

Caughey, Robert R., (BV) ... '40 '66 C&L.339 B.S., J.D. [Caughey,L.&F.] ⊙
Caughey, Legner & Freehill, (BV) ... 213 Green St. (⊙Pontiac)
Freehill, John A., (BV) ... '48 '77 C.339 B.A. L.800 J.D. [Caughey,L.&F.] ⊙

CHERRY VALLEY, 2,191, *Winnebago Co.*

Smith, Ander ... '69 '96 C.57 B.A. L.339 J.D. Corp. Coun., Ringland-Johnson, Inc.

CHESTER, * 5,185, *Randolph Co.*

Arbeiter, Ronald W., (BV) ... '55 '80 C&L.801 B.A., J.D. [Schuwerk,B.&A.]
Brown, Richard A., (BV) ... '52 '77 C&L.801 B.S., J.D. [Schuwerk,B.&A.]

Brown & Associates
(See Belleville)

Fisher, Edward J., (AV) ... '43 '71 C.801 B.A. L.365 J.D. 1300 1/2 Swanwick St.
Flynn, Jerry D. ... '48 '74 C.337 B.A. L.734 J.D. Cir. J.
Fricke, Rayburn A., (BV) ... '39 '77 C.502 B.S. L.365 J.D. 1st Bk. Bldg. (⊙Red Bud)
Kerkhover, R. Jeffrey, (BV) ... '54 '80 C.798 B.S. L.801 J.D. 1300 1/2 Swanwick St.
Koeneman, D. Paul, (BV) ... '57 '82 C.347 B.A. L.345 J.D. [Koeneman&K.]
Koeneman, Don P., (AV) ... '34 '58 C&L.910 A.B., J.D. [Koeneman&K.]
Koeneman & Koeneman, (AV) ... 609 State Street
Levine, Steven J. '64 '92 C.188 B.A. L.976 J.D.
(adm. in NY; not adm. in IL) Equal Employ. Opportunity Comm.
Pinks, Tracy L. '70 '98 C.339 B.S. L.734 J.D.
(adm. in MO; not adm. in IL) 1300 1/2 Swanwick Street
Schuwerk, William A., (AV) ... '21 '48 C&L.734 J.D. [Ⓒ Schuwerk,B.&A.]
Schuwerk, William A., Jr. ... '48 '73 C.339 A.B. L.734 J.D. Cir. J.
Schuwerk, Brown & Arbeiter, (BV) ... First Bank Building, Suite 213
Smith, David R., Law Office, (BV) '52 '78
C&L.801 B.S., J.D. 1300 1/2 Swanwick, Ste. 211
Walker, Jeremy R. ... '78 '03 C&L.801 B.A., J.D. 1300 1/2 Swanwick, Ste. 203
Welge, Tracy Lynn ... '70 '98 C.339 B.S. L.734 J.D. 1300 1/2 Swanwick St.
Williamson, Darrell G., (BV) ... '51 '76 C&L.801 B.S., J.D. State's Atty.

CHICAGO, * 2,896,016, *Cook Co.*

Aaronson, Jeffrey B. ... '57 '83 C.910 A.B. L.339 J.D. [Bell,B.&L.]
Aaronson, Lawrence H. '65 '91
C.477 B.S.E.E. L.339 J.D. [McDonnell B.H.&B.] (See Pat. Sect.)
Abbell, Jos. J. ... '11 '34 C&L.145 Ph.B., J.D. 332 S. Michigan Ave.‡
Abbinante, Chris E. ... '72 '97 C.602 B.B.A. L.659 J.D. [Ⓐ Sidley A.B.&W.]
Abbott, Colleen C. ... '76 '01 C.473 B.A. L.424 J.D. 30 North La Salle Street, Suite 4300
Abbott, James E. ... '73 '98 C.339 B.S. L.146 J.D. [Bollinger,R.&G.]
Abbott, Kenneth W. '44 '69 C.188 B.A. L.309 J.D.
(adm. in MA; not adm. in IL) Prof. of Law, Northwestern Univ.
Abboud, Anthony L. ... '66 '94 C.118 B.A. L.352 J.D. [Wildman,H.A.&D.]
Abderholden, Edward C. ... '52 '74 C.311 B.A. L.910 J.D. [Momkus M.M.M.M.&S.]
Abell, Kenneth M. ... '73 '01 C.966 B.A. L.597 J.D. [Ⓐ Novack&M.]
Abella-Austriaco, Aurora N., (AV) '65 '91
C.202 B.S. L.209 J.D. 105 W. Adams, 31st Floor
Abellera, Philip M. ... '71 '99 C.339 B.A. L.365 J.D. [Ⓐ Cassiday,S.&G.]
Abelski, Sidney ... '46 '73 C.208 B.A. L.424 J.D. [Abelski&Assoc.]
Abelski & Associates Ltd. ... 180 N. Michigan, Ste. 1800
Abendroth, Thomas W., (AV) ... '— '84 C.694 B.A. L.597 J.D. [Schiff H.]
Abens, Linda C. ... '60 '88 C.123 B.A. L.146 J.D. [Ⓐ Kralovec&M.]
Aberman, Carolyn G. ... '70 '97 C.659 B.A. L.597 J.D. [Ⓐ Skadden,A.S.M.&F.]
Aberman, Jonathan E. ... '— '98 C.228 B.A. L.597 J.D. [Ⓒ Foley&L.]
Abern, Holby M. ... '77 '02 C.339 L.424 J.D. [Ⓐ Bell,B.&L.] (Pat.)
Abernathy, Michael J., (AV) ... '56 '82 C.750 B.A. L.209 J.D. [Bell,B.&L.]
Abington, Michelle Stevens ... '51 '82 C.597 B.S. L.365 J.D. 3624 S. King Dr.
Abinoja, Allan V. ... '76 '01 C.976 B.A. L.602 J.D. [Ⓐ Novack&M.]
Ables, Michael S. '60 '85 C.339 B.S. L.629 J.D.
Financial & Legal Advisor, Alion Science and Tech. Corp.
Abood, Mary Margaret '70 '95 C.741 B.A. L.365 J.D.
Assoc. Coun., MCI Worldcom Telecommunications, Inc.
Abraham, Enrique ... '74 '00 C&L.339 B.A., J.D. Jud. Clk.; Ct. of App
Abraham, K. Robin ... '— '01 C&L.966 B.A., J.D. [Ⓐ Mayer,B.R.&M.]
Abraham, Lawrence F. ... '47 '73 C.472 B.A. L.146 J.D. Astor Develop. Co.
Abraham, Mark E. ... '74 '99 C.424 B.A. L.273 J.D. [Ⓐ Gould&R.]
Abrahams, Amina ... '75 '02 C.951 B.A. L.477 J.D. [Ⓐ Perkins C.]
Abrahams, Darrow ... '73 '02 C&L.339 B.A. [Ⓐ Lovells]
Abrahams, Nadine C. ... '— '92 C.145 B.A. L.569 J.D. [Ⓐ Fisher&P.]
Abrahamson, Vicki Lafer, (AV) ... '53 '80 C&L.477 B.A., J.D. [Abrahamson V.&L.]

Abrahamson Vorachek & Levinson, (AV)
120 North La Salle Street, Suite 1050, 60602
Telephone: 312-263-2698 Facsimile: 312-419-6770
Email: attorneys@avmlaw.com URL: http://www.lawyers.com/avmlaw
Vicki Lafer Abrahamson; Darlene A. Vorachek; Roberta A. Levinson. Associate: Lori L. Deem.
Civil Rights, Employment Discrimination, Employees' Individual Rights, Equal Opportunity, Equal Employment, Labor (or Relations), Labor (Management or Employees) and Wage and Hour Law.
See Professional Biographies, CHICAGO, ILLINOIS

Abram, Thomas G., (AV) ... '48 '73 C.118 B.A. L.813 J.D. [Vedder,P.K.&K.]
Abramic, John L. '74 '01 C.46 B.S. L.146 J.D.
[Ⓐ McAndrews,H.&M.] (See Pat. Sect.)
Abramovitch, Tina J. ... '75 '02 C.012 L.209 J.D. 33 N. Dearborn St., Ste. 1910
Abramovitz, Lawrence A. ... '47 '73 C.1016 B.A. L.146 J.D. Asst. Corp. Coun.
Abrams, Andrew J. ... '75 '00 C.339 B.A. L.145 J.D. [Ⓐ Sugar,F.&F.]
Abrams, Bruce C. ... '61 '86 C.339 B.S. L.145 J.D. Pres., LR Develop. Co.
Abrams, Burton R. ... '11 '35 C.999 B.A. L.146 J.D. 111 W. Washington St.
Abrams, Gary D. ... '46 '77 C.352 B.S. L.209 J.D. [G.D.Abrams&Assoc.]
Abrams, Gregory P. ... '— '03 C.659 B.A. L.145 J.D. [Ⓐ Morgan,L.&B.]
Abrams, Hugh A., (AV) ... '60 '84 C&L.339 B.S.M.E., J.D. [Sidley A.B.&W.] (Pat.)
Abrams, Kathryn '58 '87 C.309 B.A. L.976 J.D.
(adm. in MA; not adm. in IL) Prof., Northwestern Univ. School of Law
Abrams, Lee N., (AV) ... '35 '57 C&L.477 A.B., J.D. [Mayer,B.R.&M.]
Abrams, Leonard O., (AV) ... '34 '60 C.339 B.A. L.209 J.D. [L.O.Abrams]
Abrams, Mark E. ... '61 '87 C.339 B.S. L.800 J.D. 75 E. Wacker Dr., Ste. 320
Abrams, Marlene R. ... '— '74 C.94 B.S. L.276 J.D. 3200 N. Lake Shore Drive
Abrams, Matthew K. ... '76 '01 C.477 B.A. L.146 J.D. [Ⓐ Cassiday,S.&G.]
Abrams, Sandra Gentner ... '48 '78 C.347 B.S. L.209 J.D. [G.D.Abrams&Assoc.]

Abrams, Sherwin D., (AV) .... '43 '67 C&L.597 B.A., J.D. [Abrams&C.]
Abrams & Chapman, (AV) .... 321 S. Plymouth Ct.
Abrams, Gary D. & Associates, Ltd. ....55 W. Monroe Street
Abrams, Leonard O., Law Offices of, A Prof. Corp., (AV) .... 75 E. Wacker Dr.
Abramsky, Randi Hammer ....'57 '81 C.187 B.S. L.659 J.D. Educ. Labor Rel. Bd.
Abramson, Elliott M. '39 '64 C.178 A.B. L.309 J.D.
(adm. in NY; not adm. in IL) Prof., DePaul Univ. Coll. of Law
Abramson, Floyd H., (AV) ....'31 '56 C.976 B.A. L.309 J.D. [Abramson&F.]
Abramson, Michael A. .... '— '74 C&L.209 B.A., J.D. [Arnstein&L.]

Abramson & Fox, (AV) BB
One East Wacker Drive, 60601
Telephone: 312-644-8500 Fax: 312-644-0798
Email: AandF1@aol.com URL: http://www.abramsonandfox.com
Members of Firm: Floyd H. Abramson; Donald P. Colleton; Joseph C. Grayson; Richard S. Hartford; Anthony P. Janik. Of Counsel: John J. Alioto; Renato L. Amponin; James L. Fox; Richard Hirschtritt; Malcolm S. Kamin; Juris Kins.
General Civil Trial and Appellate Practice, Commodity Futures, Federal and State Securities Registration and Regulation, Antitrust, Intellectual Property and Trademark Law, Employment Law, Health, Immigration, Commercial, Corporate, State and Federal Taxation and Real Estate, Banking, Finance, Estate Planning and Probate, Housing Discrimination, Bankruptcy and Reorganization.
See Professional Biographies, CHICAGO, ILLINOIS

Abrell, Matthias ...... '— '01 C.763 B.S. L.365 J.D. [A Marshall,G.&B.] (See Pat. Sect.)
Abt, Morton S. .... '23 '49 C&L.209 LL.B. 20 S. Clark St.
Abt, Ralph E. ....'60 '87 C.424 B.A. L.365 J.D. State Dept. of Pub. Aid
Abuel, Christine A. ......'79 '04 C.912 B.A. L.209 J.D. [A Fitch,E.T.&F.] (See Pat. Sect.)
Abuzir, Omar A. .... '71 '99 C.339 B.A. L.146 J.D. [A Azulay,H.&S.]
Acena, Ana L. '71 '01 C.145 B.A. L.188 J.D.
(adm. in NY; not adm. in IL) [A Wildman,H.A.&D.]
Acevedo, Arthur ....'60 '89 L.209 J.D. V.P./Gen. Coun., Marbo Inc.
Acevedo, Lisa J. ....'— '95 C.424 B.S. L.209 J.D. [Foley&L.]
Acharya, Narendra ....'67 '96 C.031 B.Comm. L.188 J.D. [A Baker&M.]
Achterhof, Kristin J. ....'65 '91 C.429 B.A. L.597 J.D. [Katten M.R.]
Acker, Ann E., (AV) ....'— '73 C.741 B.A. L.424 J.D. [Chapman&C.]
Acker, Laurence C., (AV) ....'51 '76 C.602 B.A. L.424 J.D. [Harrington,T.A.&H.]
Acker, Richard H. ....'— '97 C.103 B.A. L.145 J.D. Openlands Project
Ackerman, Allan A., (AV) ....'37 '61 C.145 L.365 J.D. [A.A.Ackerman]
Ackerman, David, (AV) ....'49 '74 C.674 A.B. L.1565 J.D. [Morgan,L.&B.]
Ackerman, Julie Brown ....'— '98 C.165 B.A. L.597 J.D. [C Banner&W.]
Ackerman, Julie M. Hood ....'70 '96 C.228 A.B. L.966 J.D. V.P. & Coun., RREEF
Ackerman, Kristine A. ....'— '98 C&L.966 B.A., J.D. [A Latham&W.]
Ackerman, Philip F. ....'68 '98 C.966 B.B.A. L.861 J.D. [A Sonnenschein N.&R.]

Ackerman, Allan A., P.C., (AV) BB
2000 North Clifton Avenue, 60614-4120
Telephone: 312-332-2891; 332-2863 Fax: 773-871-3304
Email: profaaa@aol.com URL: http://www.lawyers.com/allanaackerman
Allan A. Ackerman.
Criminal Trial and Appellate Practice.
See Professional Biographies, CHICAGO, ILLINOIS

Ackermann, Robert P. '52 '88 C.927 M.B.A. L.424 J.D.
V.P., Regulatory Servs., Cincinnati Stock Exch.
Ackerson, Fred M., (AV) ....'56 '80 C.299 B.A. L.145 J.D. [Wildman,H.A.&D.]
Acosta, Daniel ....'66 '93 C.674 A.B. L.813 J.D. [C Holland&K.]
Acosta, Sergio Enrique '60 '85 C.209 B.A. L.273 J.D.
(adm. in FL; not adm. in IL) 219 S. Dearborn St., 3rd Fl.
Acton, June C. ....'73 '99 C.679 B.A. L.209 J.D. Atty. Gen.'s Off.
Adair, Gary W. ....'47 '76 C.597 B.A. L.424 J.D. 900 W. Jackson, Ste. 5E
Adam, Samuel E., Attorney at Law ....'72 '98 C&L.966 B.A., J.D. 6133 S. Ellis
Adamczyk, Joseph P. ....'76 '01 C.209 B.S. L.424 J.D. [A Freeman,F.&S.]
Adamczyk, Robert S. ....'44 '69 C&L.209 B.A., J.D. Legal Assist. Found.
Adams, Barbara A. ....'58 '83 C.388 B.A. L.597 J.D. [Holland&K.]
Adams, Daniel R. ....'46 '74 C.145 B.S. L.146 J.D. 6332 1/2 Archer Ave.
Adams, David Charles ....'64 '91 C&L.339 B.A., J.D. [A Grund&L.]
Adams, David J., (AV) ....'44 '77 C.747 B.A. L.477 J.D. [Pfeiffer&A.]
Adams, Frank M., Jr. ....'68 '94 C.329 B.A. L.597 J.D. 5000 South Cornell Avenue
Adams, Hall, (AV) ....'62 '87 C.164 B.A. L.424 J.D. [H.Adams]
Adams, John B., (AV) ....'46 '73 C.352 B.B.A. L.146 J.D. [Roddy,L.&Z.]
Adams, John F., (AV) ....'— '77 C.674 A.B. [Schiff H.]
Adams, John P. ....'60 '86 C.879 B.S. L.607 J.D. [A Chuhak&T.]
Adams, John R. ....'44 '77 C.1074 B.S. L.597 J.D. [A Taylor,M.S.H.&M.]
Adams, Joseph S. ....'68 '92 C.145 B.A. L.188 J.D. [McDermott W.&E.]
Adams, Kathleen O'Connor ......'72 '99 C.221 B.S.B.A. L.209 J.D. [A Gardner C.&D.]
Adams, Kathy J. ....'49 '78 C.651 B.S. L.209 J.D. Asst. Coun, Ill. Racing Bd.
Adams, Lauren Girard ....'69 '99 C.787 B.A. L.597 J.D. 130 East Randolph Drive
Adams, Lisa E. '— '87 C.321 B.A. L.966 J.D.
Atty. Advsr., Dept. of Housing & Urban Develop.
Adams, Michael D. .....'73 '02 C.338 B.A. L.209 J.D. V.P., Diners Club International Ltd.
Adams, Philina N. '75 '02 C.477 B.A. L.339 J.D.
Asst. States Atty., Cook Co. State Atty.'s Off.
Adams, Thomas J., III '42 '68 C.197 B.S. L.597 J.D.
V.P. & Gen. Corp. Coun., Chicago Title Ins. Co.
Adams, Walter L., (AV) ....'31 '58 C.228 A.B. L.477 J.D. [C Schuyler,R.&Z.]
Adams, Ware ....'31 '57 C.976 B.A. L.597 J.D. 1560 N. Sandburg Ter.
Adams, Wiley S., (AV) '60 '86
C.57 A.B. L.966 J.D. Asst. Gen. Coun., Prudential Capital Grp.

Adams, Hall, LLC, Law Offices of, (AV)
77 West Wacker Drive, Suite 4800, 60601
Telephone: 312-606-8711 Fax: 312-444-9658 URL: http://www.adamslegal.net
Email: hall@adamslegal.net URL: http://halladams.com
Hall Adams.
Trial Practice, State and Federal Courts, Personal Injury, Catastrophic Injury, Automobile Accidents, Premise Liability, Professional Negligence, Wrongful Death, Consumer Fraud, Business Litigation.
See Professional Biographies, CHICAGO, ILLINOIS

Adamski, Gregory A., (AV) ....'48 '73 C.973 A.B. L.128 J.D. [Adamski&C.]

Adamski & Conti, (AV) BB
100 N. La Salle Street Suite 1520, 60602
Telephone: 312-332-7800 Fax: 312-332-7818; URL: http://www.adamskiandconti.com
Email: gaadamski@adamskiandconti.com URL: http://www.lawyers.com/adamski&conti
Members of Firm: Gregory A. Adamski; Karen Conti. Associates: Samantha R. Engel; Andrea M. Weiser.
Civil and Criminal Trial Practice in all State and Federal Courts.
See Professional Biographies, CHICAGO, ILLINOIS

Adamson, James ....'67 '94 C.339 B.A. L.146 J.D. [A Swanson,M.&B.]
Adamson, Kenneth N. ....'49 '79 C.339 B.A. L.146 J.D. 5100 W. Strong St.
Adams-Taylor, Shavaun .....'65 '95 C.293 B.A. L.365 J.D. 515 North State St., Ste. 2800
Adan, Sheila M. ....'62 '90 C.475 B.S. L.347 J.D. 500 W. Madison St.‡

Addis, David H., (AV) ....'28 '51 C.1016 L.424 J.D. [Spitzer,A.S.&E.]
Addis, David I., (AV) ....'63 '88 C.347 B.S. L.94 J.D. [Schuyler,R.&Z.]
Addis, Jeremy A. ....'63 '88 C.1036 B.A. L.339 J.D. 100 W. Monroe St.
Addison, Jennifer C. ....'74 '98 C.165 B.A. L.494 J.D. City of Chicago, Dept. of Law
Addison, Stephan W. ....'78 '04 C.1151 B.S. L.966 J.D. [A Seyfarth S.]
Adducci, James D., (AV) ....'51 '76 C.424 B.A. L.309 J.D. [Adducci,D.L.M.&B.]

Adducci, Dorf, Lehner, Mitchell & Blankenship, P.C., (AV)
150 North Michigan Avenue, Suite 2130, 60601-7524
Telephone: 312-781-2800 Facsimile: 312-781-2811
Email: mblankenship@adlmb.com URL: http://www.lawyers.com/adlmb
James D. Adducci; Michael C. Dorf; Paul E. Lehner; Randall L. Mitchell; Marshall L. Blankenship. Commercial Litigation, Complex Litigation, Intellectual Property Litigation, Securities and Commodities Litigation, Employment and Labor Counseling and Litigation, Insurance Law, Business Law, Commercial Transactions, Legislative and Government Relations.
See Professional Biographies, CHICAGO, ILLINOIS

Adduce, David S. ....'65 '90 C.339 B.A. L.209 J.D. [Kelly,O.M.D.&R.]
Addy, Meredith Martin, (AV) '68 '93
C.691 B.S.E.E. L.280 J.D. [Brinks H.G.&L.] (See Pat. Sect.)
Adedeji, Adedapo A. ....'73 '00 L.597 J.D. [A Barack F.K.P.&N.]
Adelman, Harry, (AV) ....'12 '36 C.339 B.A. L.145 J.S.D. 53 W. Jackson Blvd.
Adelman, Howard L., (AV) ....'52 '77 C.338 B.S. L.734 J.D. [Adelman&G.]
Adelman, Robert J. ....'74 '99 C.966 B.A. L.209 J.D. [A Levin,R.]
Adelman, Ronald S., (AV) ....'50 '75 C.339 B.S. L.146 J.D. 33 North La Salle Street
Adelman, Stanley J., (AV) ....'42 '67 C&L.966 B.S., J.D. [DLPiper R.G.C.U.]
Adelman, Steven H., (AV) ....'45 '70 C.966 B.S. L.209 J.D. [Lord,B.&B.]

Adelman & Gettleman, Ltd., (AV) BB
Suite 1050, 53 West Jackson Boulevard, 60604
Telephone: 312-435-1050 Fax: 312-435-1059
URL: http://www.adelmangettlemanlaw.com
Howard L. Adelman; Chad H. Gettleman; Henry B. Merens; Brad A. Berish; Mark A. Carter; Adam P. Silverman;—Nathan Q. Rugg; Stanley F. Orszula; Michael I. Feinberg.
Insolvency, Bankruptcy and Reorganization Law. General Civil and Trial Practice. Corporation, Commercial, Real Estate.
See Professional Biographies, CHICAGO, ILLINOIS

Adelson, Jeffrey M. ....'52 '77 C.1109 B.A. L.1137 J.D. [Adelson,T.&B.] ⊙
Adelson, Testan & Brundo
1450 E. American Lane, Suite 1400 (⊙Calabasas, Concord, Fresno, Glendale, Grover Beach, Long Beach, Oxnard, Sacra., San Bernardino, San Diego, San Fran., San Jose, Santa Ana, Santa Rosa, CA; Hartford, CT; Berkeley Heights, Princeton, NJ; Oklahoma City, OK; Austin, Dallas, Hous., TX)
Adelstein, Harvey M., (AV) ....'36 '61 C.385 A.B. L.930 LL.B. [Neal,G.&E.]
Ader, David Lincoln, (AV) ....'43 '67 C.339 B.A. L.597 J.D. [C Ancel,G.D.B.D.&R.]
Aderman, Richard E. ....'66 '92 C.918 B.A. L.145 J.D. [Shefsky&F.]
Adess, Jason G. ....'70 '95 C.446 B.A. L.209 J.D. [Berger S.]
Adiga, Shekar ....'— '03 C.429 B.A. L.910 J.D. [A Arnstein&L.]
Adkins, Tammy L. ....'70 '96 C&L.608 B.A., J.D. [A McGuirewoods]
Adkison, Larry E., (BV) ....'47 '77 C.578 B.A. L.365 J.D. 79 W. Monroe
Adleman, Maria Lourdes C. '67 '94
C.597 B.S. L.1194 J.D. Off. of Gen. Coun., Dept of HHS
Adler, Arthur B. ....'44 '72 C.339 B.A. L.209 J.D. [A.B.Adler&Assoc.]
Adler, Charles F., Jr. ....'43 '68 C.966 B.S. L.477 J.D. [Adler]
Adler, David M., & Associates '72 '97 C.347 B.A. L.209 J.D.
2 N. La Salle St., Ste. 1600
Adler, Ericka L. ....'71 '96 C.787 B.S. L.209 J.D. [Kamensky,R.H.&D.] ⊙
Adler, John W., (AV) .... '— '61 C&L.276 B.S., LL.B. [Adler,M.&M.]
Adler, Jos. I. ....'21 '48 C&L.145 A.B., J.D. 20 N. Clark St.
Adler, Marion B., (AV) ....'54 '82 C.478 A.B. L.145 J.D. [Rachlis D.D.&A.]
Adler, Arthur B., & Associates, Ltd. ....25 E. Washington St.
Adler Law Offices, Ltd. ....30 N. LaSalle St., Ste. 3440

Adler, Murphy & McQuillen, (AV)
One North La Salle Street Suite 2300, 60602
Telephone: 312-345-0700 Telefax: 312-345-9860
Email: amm-law.com URL: http://www.amm-law.com
Members of Firm: John W. Adler; James F. Murphy; Michael G. McQuillen; Lawrence S. Gosewisch; Kevin W. Murphy; Mark S. Susina; Eric A. Cunningham III; Thomas S. Flanigon; John M. Kelly; Paula LoMonaco Wegman. Associates: Nicholas C. Bart; T. Patrick Byrnes; Austin W. Bartlett; Sarah Jayne Condon; David J. Altschuler; Peter C. Kim; John G. McAuley; William F. Moore; Kerry Bute; Lisa A. Iadevaia.
Civil Litigation, Aviation and Space Law, Products Liability, Premises Liability, Professional Liability, Insurance Defense and Coverage Matters, Environmental and Toxic Tort Litigation, Construction Claims and Litigation.
See Professional Biographies, CHICAGO, ILLINOIS

Adrian, Michael J. ....'50 '78 C.363 B.A. L.365 J.D. Asst. Pub. Def.
Advani, Suresh T. ....'65 '92 C.339 B.S. L.597 J.D. [Sidley A.B.&W.]
Aeschleman, Heather ....'76 '01 C&L.339 B.A., J.D. [A Schwartz C.]
Aeschlimann, Wendy A. ....'— '98 C.94 B.A.B.A. L.146 J.D. [S Jones D.]
Agathen, Jean M. ....'53 '79 C.145 B.A. L.309 J.D. Legal Assist. Found.
Agay, David A. ....'— '98 C.668 B.A. L.477 J.D. [A Kirkland&E.]
Agin, Bruce D. ....'61 '86 C.477 B.A. L.1068 J.D. [Peck,S.&W.]
Agin, Richard G. ....'61 '88 C.674 A.B. L.597 J.D. [Gardner C.&D.]
Agin, Stephen L., (AV) ....'57 '83 C.578 B.A. L.209 J.D. [DLPiper R.G.C.U.]
Agnew, David M., (AV) ....'45 '72 C.477 B.A. L.339 J.D. [Lord,B.&B.]
Agnew, Joan T. ....'— '89 C&L.190 B.S.B.A., J.D. Asst. State Atty.
Agnew, Patrick J. ....'42 '66 C&L.209 J.D. [P.Agnew]
Agnew, Patrick ....1614 W. Nelson
Agosto, Euclides A., Jr., (BV) ....'50 '77 C.339 B.A. L.146 J.D. 2750 N. Ashland Ave.
Agran, Abraham ....'15 '45 C.597 B.S. L.209 J.D. 105 W. Madison St.‡
Agrawal, Rishi ....'73 '98 C.597 B.A. L.424 J.D. [A Eimer S.K.&S.]
Agrawala, Sanjay J. .....'68 '02 C.145 B.A. L.146 J.D. 155 North Harbor Drive, Suite 4810
Aguilar, Maggie ....'— '93 C.339 B.A. L.589 J.D. 33 N. Dearborn
A'Hearn, Kathryn ....'— '03 C.347 B.S. L.424 J.D. [A Michaels&M.]
Ahern, Ellen Therese ....'— '92 C.276 A.B. L.477 J.D. [Kirkland&E.]
Ahern, Gregory E., (AV) ....'44 '78 C.209 B.S. L.1151 J.D. [Kane,D.&H.]
Ahern, James D., (AV) ....'55 '89 C.436 B.A. L.365 J.D. [Cassiday,S.&G.]
Ahern, James J., (AV) ....'30 '55 C&L.424 B.S.C., J.D. 221 N. LaSalle, Ste. 2300
Ahern, John E. ....'51 '81 C.339 B.S. L.365 J.D. [J.E.Ahern]
Ahern, Mary L. ....'52 '83 C.309 A.B. L.209 J.D. 200 E. Randolph Dr.
Ahern, Patrick J., (BV) ....'59 '84 C.276 B.A. L.339 J.D. [Baker&M.]
Ahern, Thomas D., (AV) ....'15 '42 C&L.145 B.A., J.D. Asst. States Atty.
Ahern, John E., P.C. ....10829 S. Western Ave.
Ahler, James R. ....'70 '97 C.347 B.A. L.734 J.D. [A Scandaglia&R.]
Ahlgren, Richard A., (Ltd.) ....'27 '57 C.238 L.209 J.D. 4801 W. Peterson Ave.
Ahlgren, Robert D. ....'43 '68 C.999 B.A. L.424 J.D. 105 W. Madison
Ahlgrim, Kimberly L. ....'— '96 C.338 B.S. L.339 J.D. [A Chapman&C.]
Ahlm, Karl M. ....'71 '96 C.597 B.A. L.273 J.D. [A DLPiper R.G.C.U.]

Ahlman, Jodi L. '75 '00 C&L.352 B.A., J.D.
(adm. in IA; not adm. in IL) [A] Lovells]
Ahmad, Ameer I. '— '01 C&L.339 B.S., J.D. [A] Kirkland&E.]
Ahmadian, Kristin A. '— '04 C.323 B.A. L.365 J.D. [A] Hickey,M.&Assoc.]
Ahmed, Mona '69 '95 L.339 J.D. Asst. Reg. Coun., S.S.A.
Ahn, Cindy S. '— '98 C.339 B.S. L.904 J.D. [Kirkland&E.] (Pat.)
Ahn, Jennifer '— '95 C.104 A.B. L.424 J.D. IMIN Law Group, LLC
Ahn, Rachel C. '73 '99 C&L.309 B.A., J.D. Sr. Coun., Bank One Corp. (Law Dept.)
Ahrens, Terri '77 '02 C.597 B.A. L.339 J.D. [A] Gardner C.&D.]
Ahronheim, Anna M. '54 '85 C.477 B.M. L.339 J.D. Dep. Def., Post Conviction Unit
Aidasani, Maureen '76 '04 C.823 B.A. L.276 J.D. [A] Winston&S.]
Aiello, Anthony J., (BV) '61 '86 C.602 B.B.A. L.209 J.D. [Sidley A.B.&W.]
Aigner, Seth M. '— '02 C.967 B.A. L.93 J.D. [A] Katten M.R.]

Aimen, Julie B., (AV) '57 '84 C.966 B.A.S.W. L.146 J.D.
407 S. Dearborn Street Suite 1675, 60605
Telephone: 312-697-0022 Fax: 312-697-0812
Email: julie.aimen@juliebaimen.com URL: http://www.juliebaimen.com
Criminal Defense, Criminal Appellate Practice, Family Law. Child Custody, Child Support, Divorce, Domestic Violence, Spousal Support, Driving Under the Influence, Drug Crimes, Felonies, Homicides, Misdemeanors, Probation, Parole, Sexual Assault, Traffic Violations.
See Professional Biographies, CHICAGO, ILLINOIS

Aimonette, W. Gregory '— '98 C.210 B.A. L.589 J.D. [A] Clausen M.]
Ainger, Dennis R., (BV) '66 '91 C.589 B.A. L.339 J.D. [Schwartz C.]
Ainley, David Clyde '67 '94 C.679 B.S. L.365 J.D. [A] Davis F.Z.K.M.M.&R.]
Ainsworth, Diane '— '85 C.1044 B.A. L.597 J.D. [Ainsworth&Assoc.]

Ainsworth & Associates, P.C.
203 North La Salle Street, Suite 2100, 60601
Telephone: 312-984-0398 Fax: 847-556-0648
Email: funny21@prodigy.net URL: http://www.lawyers.com/ainsworthlaw
Diane Ainsworth. Of Counsel: Zedrick T. Braden, III.
Trusts and Estates, Estate Planning, Guardianship, Wills, Probate, Civil Rights, Criminal Law, Felonies, Misdemeanors, Contested Estates, Contested Wills, Estate Tax, Conservatorships, Heir Property, Land Trusts, Living Wills, Power of Attorney, Fiduciary Litigation, Breach of Contracts, Chancery, Complaint for Declaratory Judgment, Quiet Title, Joint Tenancy Accounts, Policy Brutality, Probate, Dependency, Wrongful Death, Spousal Awards, Minors Awards, Minors Estates, Minor Guardianships, Gift to Minors, Small Estate, Convenience Accounts, Criminal Appeals, Civil Appeals, Employment Discrimination, Race Discrimination, Sex Discrimination.
See Professional Biographies, CHICAGO, ILLINOIS

Aiossa, Frederick N. '48 '73 C.750 B.A. L.209 J.D. [Goldstein,A.&G.]
Airan, David M. '67 '93 C.436 B.S.E.E. L.597 J.D. [Leydig,V.&M.] (See Pat. Sect.)
Airdo, Michael A. '71 '96 C&L.209 B.A., J.D. [Cremer,K.S.&S.]
Aiston, Kevin C. '59 '84 C&L.861 J.D., J.D. [C] Fragomen,D.B.&L.]
Aizenberg, Gabriel '66 '96 C.1036 B.A. L.597 J.D. [A] Sidley A.B.&W.]
Aizenstein, Neal '63 '87 C.339 B.S. L.597 J.D. [Sonnenschein N.&R.]
Akins, Tanya L. '70 '05 C.589 B.S. L.209 J.D. [A] Beermann S.W.B.B.G.&L.]
Alamat, Lana '78 '05 C.999 B.A. L.910 J.D. [A] Winston&S.]
Alamuddin, Sari M. '68 '93 C.674 B.A. L.966 J.D. [Morgan,L.&B.]
Albanis, Pete V. '77 '02 C.145 B.A. L.209 J.D. [A] Tressler,S.M.&P.]
Albers, Daniel P., (AV) '— '83 C&L.339 B.S., J.D. [Barnes&T.] (See Pat. Sect.)
Albert, Charles G., (AV) '55 '79 C.674 A.B. L.309 J.D. [Albert,W.]
Albert, G. Peter, Jr., (AV) '— '93 C.474 B.S.E.E. L.365 J.D. [Foley&L.]
Albert, Jeffrey A., Law Offices of '69 '95
C.477 B.A. L.213 J.D. 205 W. Randolph St., Ste. 920

Albert, Whitehead, P.C., (AV) [BB]
10 North Dearborn Street, Suite 600, 60602
Telephone: 312-357-6300 Fax: 312-357-6219
URL: http://www.albertwhiteheadpc.com
Charles G. Albert; Stephanie S. Green; Patricia C. Holland; Laurie D. Jaffe; Gregory C. Whitehead; Johner T. Wilson III.
Corporate, Business, Creditors' Rights, Financial Services, Labor and Employment, Litigation, Municipal Finance and Real Estate.
See Professional Biographies, CHICAGO, ILLINOIS

Alberts, Barry S., (AV) '— '71 C.473 B.A. L.145 J.D. [Schiff H.]
Albertson, Annie L. '78 '03 C.813 B.A. L.597 J.D. [A] Pattishall,M.N.H.&G.]
Alberty, Allison L. '69 '94 C&L.608 B.S.B.A., J.D. Chicago Merc. Exch.
Albin, Maurice '23 '48 L.209 LL.B. [Albin&L.]
Albin & Landau 77 W. Wash. St.
Albrecht, Cathryn E. '58 '90 C.966 B.A. L.424 J.D. [Jackson L.]
Albrecht, Joseph W. '68 '00 C.589 B.S. L.365 J.D. [A] A.J.Madonia&Assoc.]
Albrecht, Thomas W., (AV) '54 '79 C.201 B.A. L.145 J.D. [Sidley A.B.&W.]
Albright, Christine L., (AV) '51 '76 C&L.477 B.A., J.D. [Winston&S.]
Albright, John M. '67 '95 C.277 B.S. L.880 J.D.
V.P., Leg. & Corp. Secy., Accenture HR Services, Inc.
Albritton, Douglas A. '— '95 C.338 B.S. L.339 J.D. [Freeborn&P.]
Albukerk, J. Nicolas '67 '93 C.319 B.A. L.124 J.D. 2552 S. Central Park
Alcala, Brian V. '— '97 C.602 B.B.A. L.597 J.D. [A] Ungaretti&H.]
Alcantar, Beth Anne '71 '95 C&L.339 B.A., J.D. [A] Johnson&N.]
Alcantara, Oscar L. '68 '93 C.309 A.B. L.477 J.D. [Goldberg,K.B.B.R.&M.]
Alderfer, Christina M. '— '02 C.216 B.A. L.424 J.D. [A] Williams M.&J.]
Alderman, Stephen M., (AV) '59 '84 C.475 B.A. L.339 J.D. [Garfield&M.]
Aldort, Joshua A. '70 '97 C.679 B.A. L.146 J.D. [A] Clausen M.]
Aldort, Julie Rodriguez '72 '99 C.154 B.A. L.477 J.D. [A] Butler R.S.&B.]
Aldrich, Lauri K. '67 '95 C.339 B.S. L.424 J.D. 411 W. Ontario St., #315‡
Aleemuddin, Yasir S. '73 '99 C.339 B.A. L.352 J.D. [A] BryceDowney]
Aleksy, Richard E., (AV) '45 '76 C.339 B.S. L.365 J.D. [Corti,F.&A.]
Alesia, Brian J. '70 '96 C.602 B.A. L.424 J.D. [Quinlan&C.]
Alevizos, Kyriakoula '74 '00 C.209 B.A. L.365 J.D. State's Atty.
Alex, James G. '33 '58 C&L.209 B.S.C., LL.B. 9714 S. Bell St.
Alex, James G. '41 '68 C.424 B.S. L.209 J.D. 100 W. Monroe Street, Suite 1312
Alex, John L., (AV) '36 '62
C&L.597 B.S.Ch.E., J.D. [Cook,A.M.M.C.&M.] (See Pat. Sect.)
Alex, Louis John '68 '01 C.188 B.S.B.A. L.276 J.D. [A] Cook,A.M.M.C.&M.]
Alexander, Bonnie L. '— '85 C.932 B.S. L.146 J.D.
431 South Dearborn Street, Suite 409
Alexander, Brian E. '51 '76 C.339 B.A. L.128 J.D. [Alexander,A.&Assoc.]
Alexander, Daniel S. '58 '89 C.37 B.S. L.145 J.D. [Alexander,A.&Assoc.]
Alexander, Deborah Rosenberg '55 '82 C.273 B.A. L.365 J.D. [Alexander,A.&Assoc.]
Alexander, George P. '— '02 C.597 B.A. L.569 J.D. [A] Kirkland&E.]
Alexander, George W., (AV) '28 '52 C&L.209 J.D. [G.W.Alexander]
Alexander, Ian Robert '70 '95 C.339 B.A. L.861 J.D. 640 N. LaSalle Street, Suite 556
Alexander, James A. '53 '78 C&L.976 B.A., J.D. Sr. V.P., Admn., Natl. Louis Univ.
Alexander, James L., (AV) '50 '78 C.697 B.A. L.910 J.D. [Alexander&A.]
Alexander, John H. '48 '74 C.339 B.A. L.209 J.D. [J.H.Alexander&Assoc.]
Alexander, Laura J. '— '00 C.906 B.S L.602 J.D. [A] Winston&S.]
Alexander, Lisa T. '72 '03 C.918 B.A. L.178 J.D. [A] Miner,B.&G.]
Alexander, Mary Rose, (BV) '— '89 C.112 B.A. L.178 J.D. [Latham&W.]
Alexander, Scott Michael '52 '77 C.337 B.A. L.146 J.D. [S.M.Alexander]
Alexander, Suzanne Milne '— '04 C.597 B.S. L.209 J.D. [A] Kirkland&E.]
Alexander, Vanessa V. '65 '91 C.347 B.A. L.146 J.D. Asst. Atty. Gen.
Alexander, William H. '02 '30 C.388 B.S. L.145 J.D. [Alexander&A.]
Alexander & Alexander, (AV) 79 W. Monroe St.
Alexander, Alexander & Associates 111 W. Washington St., Ste. 750
Alexander & Associates, Ltd. 33 N. LaSalle, Suite 3300
Alexander, George W., Ltd., (AV) 11 S. LaSalle St.
Alexander, John H., & Associates, LLC 100 West Monroe Street, Suite 2100
Alexander, Scott Michael, P.C. 111 W. Washington St.
Alexiades, John '49 '84 C.339 B.A. L.365 J.D. 205 W. Randolph St.
Alexis, Hilary I. '63 '92 C.813 A.B. L.597 J.D. Blue Cross and Blue Shield
Al-Farisi, Zaid '71 '97 C.602 B.A. L.145 J.D. [A] Baker&M.]
Alfert, Rebecca '69 '96 C&L.280 B.A., J.D. [A] Wildman,H.A.&D.]
Alfini, David J. '72 '00 C.569 B.A. L.1119 J.D. [A] Hinshaw&C.]
Alholm, Daniel G. '— '03 C.802 B.A. L.424 J.D. [A] Alholm,M.K.H.&O.]

Alholm, Monahan, Klauke, Hay & Oldenburg, L.L.C., (AV) [BB]
221 N. LaSalle, Suite 450, 60601
Telephone: 312-704-8444 Fax: 312-704-1352
Email: info@illinois-law.com URL: http://www.illinois-law.com
Anthony J. Alholm (1949-1999). Members of Firm: Peter A. Monahan; George F. Klauke, Jr.; Linda J. Hay; Anne Marie Oldenburg; Marc J. Cairo;—Melvin G. Hobbs; Lisa A. Trull; Adnan A. Arain; Daniel G. Alholm; Mark Dinos; Mary Hasse; Tammera E. Banasek; Lawrence R. Stolberg; Susan Ann Wagener. Of Counsel: Patricia M. Noonan.
Legal Malpractice, Medical Malpractice, Professional Licensure, Employment Litigation and Workers' Compensation.
See Professional Biographies, CHICAGO, ILLINOIS

Alioto, John J., (BV) '49 '74 C.190 B.A. L.146 J.D. [C] Abramson&F.]
Alipourian, Sarah '— '03 C.339 B.A. L.209 J.D. Asst. Atty Gen.
Aljinovic, Michele Antonia '61 '86 C.424 B.B.A. L.365 J.D. 77 W. Washington Street
Alkhouja, Cynthia H. '77 '02 C.424 B.A. L.146 J.D. [A] Pretzel&S.]
Allaband, Kendra M. '74 '99 C&L.424 B.A., J.D. [A] Gardner C.&D.]
Allan, Arthur R. '41 '76 C.339 A.B. L.146 J.D. Asst. State's Atty.
Allard, Jean, (AV) '24 '53 C.191 B.A. L.145 J.D. [Sonnenschein N.&R.] ‡
Allegretti, John M. '65 '95 C.339 B.A. L.1158 J.D. [A] Weis&D.]
Allen, Brian B. '51 '78 C.597 B.S. L.424 J.D.
Coun., National Automatic Merchandising Assn.
Allen, Claudia Harri, (AV) '60 '87 C.976 B.A. L.178 J.D. [Neal,G.&E.]
Allen, David M., (AV) '46 '72 C.951 B.A. L.145 J.D. [Schuyler,R.&Z.]
Allen, Gemma B., (AV) '48 '70 C.424 B.S. L.477 J.D. [Ladden&A.]
Allen, Henry S., Jr., (AV) '47 '74 C.910 A.B. L.188 J.D. [Holland&K.]
Allen, James '— '00 C.685 B.A. L.477 J.D.
(adm. in MI; not adm. in IL) [A] Kirkland&E.]
Allen, Jason S. '72 '97 C.861 B.A. L.365 J.D. [A] Menges&M.]
Allen, John E., (AV) '36 '64
C.347 B.S. L.1119 J.D. V. Chmn., Amli Residential Props. Tr.
Allen, John T., (AV) '39 '64 C.951 B.A. L.309 LL.B.
39 South La Salle Street, Suite 200
Allen, Jonathan F. '73 '02 C&L.966 B.B.A., J.D. [A] Jenner&B.]
Allen, Jordan B., (AV) '62 '87 C.339 B.S. L.597 J.D.
Exec. V.P. & Gen. Coun., American Classic Voyages Co.
Allen, Julie O'Donnell '58 '83 C.813 B.A. L.352 J.D. [Sidley A.B.&W.]
Allen, Keith E. '74 '00 C.511 B.A. L.477 J.D. [A] Mandell M.]
Allen, Kenneth B. '54 '85 C.112 B.A. L.1017 J.D. Talamo Court Reporters, Inc.
Allen, Kristen J. '— '02 C.502 B.J. L.339 J.D. [A] Kirkland&E.]
Allen, Kristy L. '— '96 C.103 A.B. L.477 J.D. [Schiff H.]
Allen, Michael H. '69 '95 C&L.339 B.A., J.D. [A] Bell J.&Q.]
Allen, Michael Scott '58 '83 C.339 B.S. L.188 J.D. V.P. & Gen. Coun., Telution, Inc.
Allen, Nora K. '52 '80 C.530 B.A. L.365 J.D. 3016 S. Lowe‡
Allen, Patrick J. '48 '74 C.234 B.A. L.976 J.D.
Vice President-Legal, & Asst. Gen. Coun., The Marmon Group, Inc.
Allen, Raymond '31 '60 205 W. Randolph St.
Allen, Richard B. '19 '47 C&L.339 B.S., LL.B. Intl. Assoc. of Def. Coun.
Allen, Ronald J. '48 '74 C.437 B.S. L.477 J.D. [C] Eimer S.K.&S.]
Allen, Shara D. '— '03 C.999 B.A. L.1000 J.D. [S.Allen]
Allen, Susan W. '48 '77 C.234 B.S.in Ed. L.146 J.D. Central Telephone Co.
Allen, Thomas D., (AV) '26 '52 C.597 B.S. L.477 J.D. [C] Wildman,H.A.&D.]
Allen, Tracy J. '70 '95 C.813 A.B. L.228 J.D. [A] Winston&S.]
Allen, William J. '— '02 C.339 B.S.E.E. L.209 J.D. [A] Banner&W.]
Allen, Shara, Ltd. 1757 W. 95th Street
Allen-Goldstein, Jennifer '— '03 C.475 B.A. L.46 J.D. [A] G.H.Smith]
Alley, Erika A. '— '02 C.967 B.A. L.146 J.D. [A] Foley&L.]
Allison, Brenda M. '76 '02 C.575 B.A. L.209 J.D. [A] Horwood M.&B.]
Allison, Grace, (AV) '46 '79 C.914 A.B. L.145 J.D. 50 S. La Salle St.
Allison, Margaret O. '45 '79 C.145 B.S. L.209 J.D. 2212 W. 116th Pl.
Allison, Matthew G. '68 '95 C.197 B.A. L.1066 J.D. [Baker&M.]
Allison, Rinda Y. '39 '92 C.518 B.A. L.146 J.D. [A] Klein,T.&J.]
Allison, Robert A. '71 '97 C.893 B.A. L.276 J.D. Sr. Atty., Technology Solutions Co.
Allison, Robert D., & Associates, (AV) '48 '74
C.207 B.A. L.597 J.D. 122 S. Michigan Ave., Ste. 1850
Allison, Stephen A. '57 '85 C&L.597 B.A., J.D. [Wildman,H.A.&D.]
Allison, Thomas D., (AV) '44 '69 C.674 A.B. L.976 J.D. [Allison,S.&K.]
Allison, Slutsky & Kennedy, P.C., (AV) 230 W. Monroe St., Ste. 2600
Allman, Thomas Young, (AV Ⓣ) '39 '65 C.150 B.S. L.976 J.D.
(adm. in OH; not adm. in IL) [C] Mayer,B.R.&M.]
Allswang, David B. '67 '94 C&L.94 B.S., J.D. [Duane M.]
Allswang, Tod H. '70 '01 C.378 B.A. L.365 J.D. 30 N. LaSalle St.
Allyn, Barbara L. '47 '78 C.597 B.A. L.365 J.D. 111 W. Washington St.
Alman, David Alan '71 '97 C&L.339 B.A., J.D. [Much S.F.D.A.&R.]
Almazan, Armando '51 '77 C.352 B.A. L.209 J.D. 3743 W. 26th St.‡
Almeida, C. Victoria, Law Offices of '56 '82 C.597 B.S. L.209 J.D. 100 E. Walton
Almeida, David S. '— '00 C.999 B.A. L.1556 J.D. [A] Gardner C.&D.]
Alop, Alan A. '46 '72 C.339 B.A. L.145 J.D.
Dep. Dir., Legal Assistance Found. of Chicago
Alper, Bruce R., (AV) '54 '78 C.339 B.A. L.94 J.D. [Vedder,P.K.&K.]
Alperin, Jeffrey Mark '68 '94 C&L.477 B.A., J.D. [A] Tressler,S.M.&P.]
Alpert, Sharyn Beth '65 '93 C.347 B.S. L.365 J.D. [A] Shaheen,N.S.F.&E.]
Alred, Mary T. '59 '84 C.679 B.S. L.424 J.D. V.P. & Sr. Tr. Admr., Bank One‡
Alroth, Deborah '71 '95 C.347 B.S. L.146 J.D. [A] Cirignani H.H.&L.]
Alschuler, Albert W. '40 '65 C&L.309 A.B., LL.B. Prof. of Law, Univ. of Chicago
Alshouse, Matthew C. '73 '99 C.228 A.B. L.477 J.D. [A] Daspin&A.]
Alshuler, John D. '47 '75 C.36 B.A. L.146 J.D. Spec. Asst. Atty. Gen., Dept. of Rev.
Alster, Caliste J., (AV) '28 '54 C.453 B.S. L.273 J.D.
105 W. Adams St., 36th Floor (Pat.)

Alsterda, John B. ... '60 '88 C.170 B.A. L.339 J.D. [Davis M.]
Alsterda, R. Scott, (AV) ... '— '80 C.95 B.A. L.365 J.D. [Ungaretti&H.]
Alt, Aaron Edward ... '71 '97 C.597 B.A. L.309 J.D. Sr. Corp. Coun., Sara Lee Corp
Alt, Christine Decke ... '73 '99 C&L.475 B.S., J.D. [🄰 Pedersen&H.]
Alt, David M. ... '75 '01 C.957 B.B.A. L.424 J.D. [🄰 Bates&C.]
Alt, Julane Brooks '53 '78 C.1154 B.A. L.912 J.D.
(adm. in MI; not adm. in IL) Assoc. Gen. Coun., Fannie Mae
Alt, Leo F., Law Offices of, (AV) ... '47 '73 C&L.209 B.A., J.D. 221 N. LaSalle St.
Altahawi, Sal ... '77 '03 C.363 B.S.B.A. L.209 J.D. [Hussain E.B.&F.]
Alter, Irwin C., (AV) ... '34 '58 C.339 B.S.M.E. L.209 J.D. [Alter&W.] (Pat.)
Alter, Jeffrey Marc ... '71 '99 C&L.424 B.S., J.D. [🄰 Anesi,O.R.N.&K.]

Alter and Weiss, (AV)
19 South LaSalle Street, Suite 1650, 60603
Telephone: 312-337-2100 Fax: 312-236-1365
Email: alterandweiss@yahoo.com URL: http://www.alterandweiss.com
Irwin C. Alter. Of Counsel: Phillip A. Weiss, retired; Nora A. Preece.
Patent, Trademark, Copyright, Unfair Competition and Related Antitrust Practice.
See Professional Biographies, CHICAGO, ILLINOIS

Altman, Barbara F. ... '47 '77 C.188 A.B. L.276 J.D. Asst. Reg. Coun., Dept. of HHS
Altman, Harry W. ... '24 '50 C.1016 L.146 LL.B. 20 N. Clark St.
Altman, Louis, (AV) '— '59 C.188 A.B. L.309 LL.B.
[🄲 Michael B.&F.] (See Pat. Sect.)
Altman, Paul S. ... '44 '69 C&L.339 A.B., J.D. [Pedersen&H.]
Altman, Ross J., (AV) ... '56 '82 C.477 B.S. L.273 J.D. [DLPiper R.G.C.U.]
Altman, Sidney S. ... '13 '40 C.597 L.209 LL.B. [S.J.Altman&Assoc.]
Altman, Stephanie F. '64 '89 C.293 B.A. L.424 J.D.
Legal Assistance Found. of Chicago
Altman, Sidney J., & Associates ... 6640 N. Clark St.
Altschul, Mark J. ... '74 '02 C.477 B.A. L.339 J.D. [🄰 McDermott W.&E.]
Altschuler, David J. ... '76 '02 C.910 B.A. L.880 J.D. [🄰 Adler,M.&M.]
Altschuler, Stuart, (AV) ... '54 '79 C.674 A.B. L.188 J.D. [Winston&S.]
Altshul, Jeffrey E., (AV) ... '56 '81 C.959 B.A. L.221 J.D. [🄲 Kaye S.]
Altshuler, Adi ... '— '93 C.999 LL.B. L.145 J.D. 357 East Chicago Ave.
Altur, Gayle A. '49 '79 C.719 B.A. L.209 J.D.
V.P - Natl. Bus. Develop., Stewart Title Guaranty Company
Alul, Andrew M. ... '— '00 C&L.734 B.A., J.D. [🄰 Schiff H.] (Pat.)
Alvarez, Alicia ... '58 '85 C.424 B.A. L.93 J.D. DePaul Univ. Coll. of Law
Alvarez, Anita M. ... '60 '86 C.424 B.S.E. L.146 J.D. Asst. State's Atty.
Alvarez, Fred L. ... '64 '89 C.339 B.A. L.424 J.D. [Lord,B.&B.]
Alvine, Eric ... '75 '01 C.210 B.A. L.365 J.D. [🄰 Worker,S.&H.]
Alwin, Janice A. ... '72 '02 C.589 B.S. L.209 J.D. [🄰 Shaw G.F.G.W.&T.]
Aly, Imron T. ... '— '99 C.228 B.S.E. L.276 J.D. [Kirkland&E.] (Pat.)
Amadon, Carolyn D. ... '— '99 C.69 B.A. L.424 J.D. [🄰 Barnes,R.&C.]
Amari, Katherine A. ... '— '00 C.589 B.A. L.365 J.D. State Atty. Off.
Amari, Leonard F., (AV) ... '42 '68 C.589 B.S. L.365 J.D. [Amari&L.]
Amari & Locallo, (AV) ... 734 N. Wells St.
Amarilio, Joseph Daniel, (BV) ... '52 '79 C.597 B.A. L.365 J.D. [🄰 Wolfe&E.]
Amash, John A. ... '76 '01 C.309 A.B. L.477 J.D. [🄰 Kirkland&E.]
Amati, Alan C. ... '59 '84 C.339 B.S. L.146 J.D. Dir., Legal Servs., Internet Systems Corp.
Amato, Ronald M. ... '69 '99 C.589 B.A. L.146 J.D. [🄰 Shaheen,N.S.F.&E.]
Amattey, William Horatius '61 '95 L.999 LL.B.
(adm. in NY; not adm. in IL) 619 S. Lasalle, Ste. 103
Amberg, John J. ... '— '99 C.339 B.S. L.145 J.D. [Kirkland&E.]
Ambrogi, John L., (BV) ... '65 '90 C&L.424 B.S., J.D. [Welsh&K.]
Ambrose, Gerald A. ... '47 '72 C.210 B.A. L.477 J.D. [Sidley A.B.&W.]
Ambrose, John C., (AV) ... '35 '59 C&L.424 B.S.C., J.D. [Ambrose&C.]
Ambrose, Robert J. ... '69 '97 C.436 B.A. L.365 J.D. [🄰 Meckler B.&T.]

Ambrose & Cushing, P.C., (AV)
221 North LaSalle Street, Suite 1748, 60601
Telephone: 312-726-1470 Fax: 312-726-3505
Email: bcolbert@ambrosecushing.com URL: http://www.ambrosecushinglaw.com
John C. Ambrose; F. John Cushing;—Thomas M. Cushing; Joseph F. Vitu, Jr.; Michael M. Cushing; James J. Ryan; Marilyn J. Martin.
Personal Injury, Medical Malpractice, Products Liability, Workers Compensation, Medical Negligence, Premises Liability, Automobile Accidents and Injuries, Slip and Fall, Spinal Injury, Wrongful Death, Construction Accidents and Commercial Litigation, Real Estate Law.
See Professional Biographies, CHICAGO, ILLINOIS

Ambutas, Algirdas P. ... '58 '83 C.932 B.A. L.209 J.D. 203 N. La Salle St., Suite 1800
Amend, James M., (P.C.), (AV) ... '— '67 C&L.477 B.S.E., J.D. [🄲 Kirkland&E.] (Pat.)
Ament, Joseph D., (AV) ... '36 '63 C.339 B.S. L.365 J.D. [Much S.F.D.A.&R.]
Americus, David S. ... '62 '88 C.589 B.S. L.365 J.D. [Gozdecki&D.]
Americus, Susan A. ... '60 '89 C.238 B.A. L.365 J.D. 39 S. LaSalle
Amert, Amanda S. ... '75 '00 C.951 B.A. L.228 J.D. [🄰 Jenner&B.]
Ames, Sarah A. A. ... '68 '97 L.16 J.D. [🄰 Thiedmann&E.]
Amin, Rakesh M. ... '67 '95 C.252 B.S. L.365 J.D. [Amin L.]

Amin Law
217 North Jefferson Street, 5th Floor, 60661
Telephone: 312-466-1033; 312-286-3925 Fax: 312-466-0808
URL: http://www.amin-law.com
Rakesh M. Amin. Associates: Christina Kolliniatis; Laura A. Chubb.
Administrative Law, Food and Drug Administration, Federal Trade Commission, US Customs, Drug Enforcement Agency, USDA and related Federal and State Attorney General Regulatory Compliance and Litigation matters; Food, Beverage, Drug, Pharmaceutical, Cosmetic, Dietary Supplement, Medical Device, Animal Feed and Biotechnology Law; Restaurant, Liquor and Wine Law, Organic and Proposition 65 Law; Advertising, Marketing and Direct Seller Law, Healthcare Law, Intellectual Property, Patent, Trademark, Copyright, Trade Secret, Licensing, Internet, Entertainment and Unfair Competition Law; Telemedicine and Internet Pharmacy Law; Compounding Pharmacy Law; Practice of Medicine Law; Practice of Pharmacy Law; Bioterrorism Act Law; Manufacturer and Distributor Agreements; Corporate Law and Contracts and Business Litigation.
See Professional Biographies, CHICAGO, ILLINOIS

Amini, Gilda, Law Office of ... '— '95 C&L.209 B.A., J.D. 477 N. Canal Street
Amir-Mokri, Mina ... '67 '94 C.145 B.A. L.339 J.D. [Sonnenschein N.&R.]
Ammendola, Marina E., (AV) ... '60 '89 C.700 B.A. L.146 J.D. [M.E.Ammendola]

Ammendola, Marina E., P.C., Law Offices of, (AV)
33 North LaSalle Street, Suite 900, 60602
Telephone: 312-220-9100 Fax: 312-220-9110
URL: http://www.lawyers.com/marinaammendola
Marina E. Ammendola.
Plaintiffs Personal Injury Law, Medical Malpractice Law.
See Professional Biographies, CHICAGO, ILLINOIS

Amos, Alan O., (AV) ... '37 '63 C&L.209 B.A., J.D. [A.O.Amos&Assoc.]

Amos, Alan O., & Associates, P.C., (AV)
Suite 3150, 180 North LaSalle Street, 60601
Telephone: 312-419-1300 Telecopier: 312-419-0302
Alan O. Amos. Of Counsel: Thomas H. Boerschinger.
(This Listing Continued)

Amos, Alan O., & Associates, P.C. (Continued)
Real Estate Law and Development, Probate and Estate Litigation.
Reference: Bank Leumi USA.
See Professional Biographies, CHICAGO, ILLINOIS

Ampil, Janice P. ... '70 '96 C.339 B.S. L.436 J.D. [🄰 S.B.Handelman]
Amponin, Renato L. ... '38 '63 C&L.999 LL.B. [🄲 Abramson&F.]
Amu, Lanre O. ... '61 '96 C.494 B.C.E. L.365 J.D. 407 S. Dearborn St., Ste. 1395
Amundsen, Glen E., (AV) ... '— '80 C.57 B.A. L.46 J.D. [O'Hagan,S.&A.]
An, Lisa M. ... '70 '97 C.339 B.A. L.30 J.D. [🄰 Mayer,B.R.&M.]
Anaclerio, Nicholas, (BV) ... '— '84 C.966 B.A. L.424 J.D. [Ungaretti&H.]
Anagnos, Basil C. ... '36 '63 [Angelos&A.]
Anagnost, Peter G., (AV) ... '35 '62 C.597 B.S.B.A. L.209 J.D. 11 S. La Salle St.
Anagnost, Themis J. ... '13 '41 C.145 A.B. L.46 J.D. 30 N. LaSalle St.
Anagnostopoulos, Lisa M. ... '— '97 C.98 B.A. L.209 J.D. [🄰 Chapman&C.]
Anastasiou, Paula S. ... '65 '92 C.910 B.A. L.146 J.D. Starbucks Coffee Co.
Anaszewicz, Sara L. ... '77 '04 C.879 B.A. L.146 J.D. [🄰 Horowitz&W.]
Anawis, Monique A. ... '— '01 C.103 B.A. L.209 J.D. 2650 Lakeview, Suite 809
Anaya, William J., (AV) ... '— '81 C.679 B.A. L.1119 J.D. [Arnstein&L.]
Ancel, Glink, Diamond, Bush, DiCianni & Rolek, (AV) ... 140 S. Dearborn St.
Andalman, Robert M., (AV) ... '66 '92 C.477 B.A. L.94 J.D. [Sonnenschein N.&R.]
Anderfuren, Jill, (BV) '— '90 C.597 B.S. L.146 J.D.
[🄰 Marshall,G.&B.] (See Pat. Sect.)
Anders, Daniel M. ... '75 '03 C.424 B.A. L.146 J.D. [🄰 Wiedner&M.]
Andersen, Edward S. '43 '71
C.1024 B.S. L.209 J.D. Claims Mangr., Chicago Title Ins. Co.
Andersen, Erik L. ... '68 '98 C.966 B.A. L.146 J.D. [🄰 Cassiday,S.&G.]
Andersen, Wayne R. ... '45 '70 C.309 B.A. L.339 J.D. U.S. Dist. J.
Anderson, Aimee B., (AV) ... '50 '84 C.1275 B.A. L.424 J.D. [Wildman,H.A.&D.]
Anderson, Amy L. ... '65 '90 C&L.339 B.A., J.D. [Brenner,F.M.&S.]
Anderson, Andy R. ... '59 '84 C.466 B.S. L.339 J.D. [🄲 Morgan,L.&B.]
Anderson, Arthur H., Jr. ... '— '70 C.860 A.B. L.145 J.D. [Tenney&B.]
Anderson, Brette Cecile ... '— '99 C.811 B.A. L.329 J.D. Dept. of Prof. Reg.
Anderson, Brian N. ... '76 '03 C.679 B.S. L.209 J.D. [🄰 Winston&S.]
Anderson, Charles E. ... '44 '77 C.589 B.S.E. L.209 J.D. 457 E. 41st St.
Anderson, Christine P. '61 '86 C.1183 B.A. L.146 J.D.
Atty. Regis. & Disciplinary Comm. of the Supm. Ct.
Anderson, Cory D. ... '74 '01 C.958 B.S. L.365 J.D. [🄰 Connelly R.&M.]
Anderson, Courtney L. ... '77 '02 C&L.659 B.A., J.D. [🄰 Mayer,B.R.&M.]
Anderson, Craig E., (AV) ... '47 '74 C.747 B.A. L.424 J.D. [Jacobson,B.&A.]
Anderson, David F. ... '25 20 North Clark Street, Suite 2200
Anderson, David H. ... '— '93 C.597 B.S. L.339 J.D. [Schiff H.]
Anderson, David L. '53 '79 C.937 B.A. L.273 J.D.
(adm. in OH; not adm. in IL) 400 E. Randolph 2705‡
Anderson, Diane M., (AV) ... '59 '83 C.424 B.B.A. L.178 J.D. [Neal,G.&E.]
Anderson, Douglas W. ... '67 '93 C.197 B.A. L.145 J.D. [Barack F.K.P.&N.]
Anderson, Edward T. '56 '84 C.209 B.A. L.365 J.D.
Dep. Reg. Dir., NASD Dispute Resolution, Inc.
Anderson, Eric D. ... '65 '92 C.259 B.S. L.1187 J.D. 134 N. La Salle St., Ste. 2116
Anderson, Francine ... '61 '89 C.424 B.S. L.365 J.D. Exec. Dir., Cook Co. Bar Assoc.
Anderson, Gina M. ... '65 '95 C.608 B.A. L.209 J.D. [Bell J.&Q.]
Anderson, J. Trent, (AV) ... '39 '65 C.679 B.S. L.893 LL.B. [Mayer,B.R.&M.]
Anderson, James Craig ... '61 '93 C.475 B.A. L.597 J.D. [Katten M.R.]
Anderson, James D. ... '72 '98 C.36 B.S. L.339 J.D. [Shefsky&F.]
Anderson, James L. ... '31 '67 C.424 A.B. L.911 J.D. Sr. V.P., Stein Roe & Farnham Inc.
Anderson, Jane F. ... '61 '86 C.393 B.A. L.424 J.D. 111 W. Washington St., Ste. 1100
Anderson, Jeffrey W. ... '66 '92 C.228 B.A. L.910 J.D. [🄰 Condon&C.]
Anderson, Jill C. ... '— '95 C.260 B.A. L.178 J.D. [Freeborn&P.]
Anderson, John C. ... '70 '99 C.338 B.S. L.365 J.D. [🄰 Kubasiak,F.R.&R.]
Anderson, John H., (AV) ... '50 '76 C.951 B.A. L.365 J.D. [Seyfarth S.]
Anderson, Jolen V. ... '78 '03 C&L.597 B.S., J.D. [🄰 Lord,B.&B.]
Anderson, Jonathan G. ... '53 '81 C.966 B.A. L.260 J.D. [Anderson&Assoc.] ⊙
Anderson, Karin ... '66 '02 C.309 B.A. L.209 J.D. [🄰 Matkov,S.M.&G.]
Anderson, Keith R. ... '— '82 C.210 B.A. L.273 J.D. [Gardner C.&D.]
Anderson, Kimball R., (AV) ... '52 '77 C&L.339 B.A., J.D. [Winston&S.]
Anderson, Kimberly J. ... '64 '98 C.238 B.S.B. L.365 J.D. [Anderson&B.]
Anderson, Kristine L. ... '— '91 C.1288 B.A. L.146 J.D. [🄲 Kirkland&E.]
Anderson, Margaret M., (AV) ... '55 '80 C.177 B.A. L.976 J.D. [Lord,B.&B.]
Anderson, Mark ... '77 '03 C&L.339 B.S., J.D. [🄰 Jenkens&G.]
Anderson, Mark R. ... '73 '99 C&L.347 B.A., J.D. [🄰 Fuchs&R.]
Anderson, Marla ... '— '00 C.197 A.B. L.424 J.D. [🄰 Gardner C.&D.]
Anderson, Matthew A. ... '76 '02 C.36 B.S.M.E. L.602 J.D. [🄰 McAndrews,H.&M.]
Anderson, Melissa A. ... '77 '02 C.352 B.A. L.146 J.D. [🄰 Cassiday,S.&G.]
Anderson, Michele C., (AV) ... '— '94 C.339 B.A. L.423 J.D. [🄰 Anderson,R.]
Anderson, Nancy D. '34 '65
C.838 B.S. L.365 J.D. V.P. & Tr. Coun., The Chicago Trust Co.
Anderson, Paul S. ... '52 '79 C.896 B.A. L.146 J.D. [Sonnenberg&A.]
Anderson, R. John ... '— '83 C&L.912 B.A., J.D. [Querrey&H.]
Anderson, Richard H. ... '52 '83 C.57 B.A. L.589 J.D. I.R.S.
Anderson, Richard H., (AV) '— '73
C.383 B.S.Ch.E. L.273 J.D. [Marshall,G.&B.] (See Pat. Sect.)
Anderson, Robert R., (AV) ... '59 '84 C.94 B.A. L.597 J.D. [Hughes S.P.R.&D.]
Anderson, Sarah Nicole ... '74 '00 C.340 B.A. L.339 J.D. Pub. Guardians Off.
Anderson, Scott L. ... '74 '99 C.187 B.A. L.424 J.D. [🄰 Pretzel&S.]
Anderson, Scott R. ... '— '93 C.57 B.A. L.424 J.D. [Chapman&C.]
Anderson, Shelli L. ... '72 '97 C&L.424 B.S., J.D. [Franczek S.]
Anderson, Theodore W., (AV) '26 '53
C.339 B.S.E.E. L.209 J.D. [🄲 Leydig,V.&M.] (See Pat. Sect.)
Anderson, Thomas K. ... '— '03 C&L.602 B.A., J.D. [🄰 Foley&L.]
Anderson, Tracy Houff '66 '91
C.347 B.S. L.424 J.D. Gen. Coun., Roy Houff Company, The
Anderson, Tricia L. ... '77 '03 C.597 B.A. L.910 J.D. [🄰 Wiedner&M.]
Anderson, William C., III, (AV) ... '— '75 C.276 A.B. L.884 J.D. [Anderson,R.]

Anderson & Associates, P.C.
166 W. Washington Street, Suite 640, 60602 ⊙
Telephone: 312-236-5599
Jonathan G. Anderson;—Robin M. Zandri; Andrea C. Lawrence; Christopher J. Maurer; Mia Do.
Family Law, Bankruptcy, Real Estate Litigation and Transactions, Estate Planning and Probate.
Wheaton Office: 400 S. County Farm Road, Suite 120, 60187. Telephone: 630-653-9400. Fax: 630-653-9450.
Schaumburg Office: 1701 East Woodfield Road, Suite 1050. Telephone: 847-995-9999. Fax: 847-995-0117.
See Professional Biographies, CHICAGO, ILLINOIS

Anderson & Boback
20 North Clark Street, Suite 1400, 60602
Telephone: 312-920-0870
Email: lawyers@illinoislawforyou.com URL: http://www.illinoislawforyou.com
Kimberly J. Anderson; Janice L. Boback.
Child Custody, Adoption, Divorce, Domestic Violence and Paternity. Criminal Defense.
See Professional Biographies, CHICAGO, ILLINOIS

Anderson Kill & Olick
230 West Monroe Street, Suite 2540, 60606 ⊙
Telephone: 312-201-9516 Fax: 312-201-8548; 312-201-9553
Email: AKO@andersonkill.com URL: http://www.andersonkill.com
James M. Davis; Paul R. Walker-Bright.
Litigation, Insurance Coverage (Exclusively for Policyholders), Environmental Law, Trial and Appellate.
New York, N.Y. Office: Anderson Kill & Olick, P.C., 1251 Avenue of the Americas. Telephone: 212-278-1000. Fax: 212-278-1733.
Washington, D.C. Office: Anderson Kill & Olick, L.L.P., 2100 M Street, N.W. Telephone: 202-218-0040. Fax: 202-218-0055.
Newark, New Jersey Office: Anderson Kill & Olick, P.C. One Gateway Center, Suite 901. Telephone: 973-642-5858. Fax: 973-621-6361.
Philadelphia, Pennsylvania Office: Anderson Kill & Olick, P.C., 1600 Market Street. Telephone: 215-568-4202. Fax: 215-568-4573.
Greenwich, Connecticut Office: Anderson Kill & Olick, P.C., Two Sound View Drive, Suite 100. Telephone: 202-622-7668. Fax: 202-622-0321.
See Professional Biographies, CHICAGO, ILLINOIS

Anderson, Rasor & Partners, LLP, (AV) .... 55 E. Monroe, Ste. 3650
Anderton, D. Chad .... '68 '95 C.477 B.A. L.800 J.D. [Ⓐ Littler M.]
Andes, Fredric P., (AV) .... '— '80 C.597 B.A. L.309 J.D. [Barnes&T.]

Andjelkovich, Peter, & Associates, (AV) '46 '80 C.339 B.S. L.989 J.D.
39 South La Salle Street, Suite 200, 60603
Telephone: 312-782-8345 Fax: 312-782-6517
Email: PAlaw@sbcglobal.net URL: http://www.lawyers.com/pandjelkovich
Associate: Bradley J. Wartman.
Personal Injury, Lottery Law, Commercial Litigation, Employment Litigation Defense, Executive Compensation and Severance, Wrongful Termination, ERISA, Civil Rights, Shareholder and Employee Disputes, Union/Labor Organizing Issues, Corporate Bankruptcy Modification Bargaining Agreements, White Collar Criminal Defense.
See Professional Biographies, CHICAGO, ILLINOIS

Andrade, Nancy C. .... '68 '94 C.424 A.B. L.128 J.D. Staff Atty., Chicago Legal Clinic
Andre, Gregory R., (BV) .... '60 '85 C.93 B.S. L.273 J.D. [Bell,B.&L.]
Andreasik, Andrew R. .... '66 '91 C.228 A.B. L.910 J.D. [Bell,B.&L.]
Andreoli, Thomas A. .... '63 '97 C.846 B.A. L.424 J.D. [Sonnenschein N.&R.]
Andreou, James .... '51 '78 C.339 B.A. L.146 J.D. Asst. States Atty.
Andreozzi, Bradley J. .... '58 '84 C.976 B.A. L.145 J.D. [Mayer,B.R.&M.]
Andreozzi, William G. .... '69 '02 C.589 B.S. L.365 J.D. Sr. Mng., BDO Seidman LLP
Andresen, Scott Alan .... '72 '99 C.339 B.A. L.879 J.D. [Andresen&Assoc.]
Andresen & Associates, PC .... 655 W. Irving Park Road, Suite 3812
Andrews, Amy Curtner .... '— '95 C.385 B.A. L.477 J.D. [Kirkland&E.]
Andrews, Don J. .... '58 '88 C.238 B.A. L.46 J.D. V.P. & Sr. Atty., Everen Securities, Inc.
Andrews, Lori B. .... '52 '78 C&L.976 B.A., J.D. Prof. of Law, Chicago Kent Coll. of Law
Andrews, Mark D. .... '72 '97 C.937 B.A. L.339 J.D. [Pugh,J.J.&Q.]
Andrews, Peggy Q. '40 '88
C.561 B.S. L.424 J.D. Asst. Reg. Coun., U.S. Envir. Protec. Agcy.
Andrews, Richard S. .... '— '87 C.274 B.A. L.146 J.D. NLRB
Andrews, Shauna L. .... '— '89 C.679 B.A. L.209 J.D. Ofc. of the State's Atty.
Andrews, Telly .... '72 '97 C.339 B.A. L.424 J.D. [Kaplan,v.&M.]
Andrews, Thomas J., (AV) .... '52 '77 C.908 B.A. L.477 J.D. [Johnson&B.]
Andrews, W. Anthony .... '66 '93 C.1151 B.A. L.209 J.D. [Norton,M.W.&D.] ⊙
Andrews, William P., Jr. .... '65 '91 C.679 B.A. L.347 J.D. General Counsel, Netco, Inc.
Andrin, Albert A. .... '28 '56 C.1016 B.A. L.146 LL.B. 670 N. Clark
Andringa, Dirk W. .... '— '93 C&L.339 B.A., J.D. [Schiff H.]
Andrioff, Joni L., (AV) .... '— '87 C.597 B.A. L.146 J.D. [Jones D.]
Andris, Matthew R. '— '00 C.482 B.A. L.569 J.D.
Two North LaSalle Street, Suite 2200
Androw, Mark R. .... '54 '79 C.569 B.F.A. L.209 J.D. 401 S. Superior‡
Andry, Armand L., Attorney At Law .... '49 '75 C.145 B.A. L.178 J.D. 7801 S. Reilly Ter.
Anekwe, Ali O. .... '— '03 C.801 B.A. L.477 J.D. [Ⓐ Chapman&C.]

Anesi, Ozmon, Rodin, Novak & Kohen, Ltd., (AV) BB
161 North Clark Street, 21st Floor, 60601
Telephone: 312-372-3822 Fax: 312-372-3833
URL: http://www.anesilaw.com
Nat P. Ozmon; Curt N. Rodin; Mark Novak; Bruce M. Kohen; Douglas A. Colby; Marc A. Taxman; Daniel V. O'Connor; David J. Comeau; Telly C. Nakos; John M. Popelka;—Alain Leval; John A. Salzeider; Martin J. Lucas; Mark Murnane; Steven A. Berman; Steven W. Burrows; Bradley Michael Arnold; Michael P. Hellman; Stephen J. Cummings; Jeffrey Marc Alter; Sean P. Murray; Jonathan Becket Schlack (Not admitted in IL); Jeffrey S. Jordan; James B. Hardy.
Civil Trial and Appellate Practice. Workers Compensation and Personal Injury Law. General Practice.
See Professional Biographies, CHICAGO, ILLINOIS

Angarola, Joann Tansey, (AV) .... '51 '77 C.477 B.S. L.424 J.D. [Ⓒ McGuirewoods]
Angel, Naomi R. .... '48 '87 C.112 B.A. L.209 J.D. [Ⓐ Howe&H.]
Angell, Thomas J., (AV) .... '53 '78 C.436 A.B. L.365 J.D. [Jacobs,B.O.S.&H.]
Angelos, Mychal P. .... '29 '51 C.424 L.145 J.D. [Angelos&A.]
Angelos & Anagnos, Ltd. .... 39 S. LaSalle St. Ste 805
Angelucci, Margaret .... '69 '94 C.475 B.A. L.209 J.D. [Asher,G.G.&D.]
Anglin, Shannon Skinner .... '— '01 C.925 B.A. L.861 J.D. [Ⓐ Sonnenschein N.&R.]
Angst, Gerald L., (AV) .... '50 '75 C&L.424 B.A., J.D. [Sidley A.B.&W.]
Angstadt, Janet M. '62 '90 C.747 B.A. L.209 J.D.
V.P. & Cap. Markets Compliance Coun., Everen Securities, Inc.
Anguizola, Roberto .... '73 '99 C&L.597 B.A., J.D. [Ⓐ Schwartz C.]

Ankin, Howard H., (BV) '68 '93 C.339 B.S. L.365 J.D.
200 N. LaSalle Street, Suite 1810, 60601
Telephone: 312-346-8780 Fax: 312-346-8681
Email: howard@ankinlaw.com URL: http://www.lawyers.com/hankin
Workers Compensation, Personal Injury, Automobile Accidents, Wrongful Death, Medical Malpractice, Slip and Fall, Dog Bites.
See Professional Biographies, CHICAGO, ILLINOIS

Annes, Andrew J., (AV) .... '56 '82 C.424 B.B.A. L.365 J.D. [Schenk,A.B.&T.]
Annes, Gary P. .... '70 '95 C.339 B.A. L.424 J.D. [Ⓐ J.M.Goldberg]
Annes, George Paul .... '39 '63 C.339 B.A. L.597 J.D. 134 N. La Salle St.

Annes, Scott M., Law Offices of
(See Park Ridge)

Annulis, Brian D., (BV) .... '66 '92 C.423 B.A. L.734 J.D. [Katten M.R.]
Annunziata, Craig R. .... '63 '92 C.209 B.S. L.365 J.D. [Fisher&P.]
Anos, George J., (AV) .... '26 '49 C.137 L.209 LL.B. [Ash,A.F.&L.]
Ansani, Robert C. .... '56 '99 C.37 B.A. L.365 LL.M. [Ⓐ Leff,C.&W.]

Anscomb, Brian Charles '74 '01
C.136 B.S. L.209 J.D. 1914 N. Milwaukee Avenue, 3rd Floor
Anscombe, Anthony J., (AV) .... '61 '88 C.976 B.A. L.893 J.D. [Sedgwick,D.M.&A.]
Anselmo, Frank M., Jr., (BV) .... '47 '72 C.339 B.S. L.209 J.D. [F.Anselmo]
Anselmo, Frank, (BV) .... 6424 W. Belmont Ave.
Ansley, Noelle .... '69 '00 C.381 B.F.A. L.365 J.D. [Ⓐ Weissberg&Assoc.]
Ansorge, Howard J. '47 '74 C&L.879 B.A., J.D.
Admin. Law J., U.S. Merit Systems Protec. Bd.
Anspach, Kenneth G., (AV) .... '52 '77 C.339 B.A. L.910 J.D. [Anspach&Assoc.]
Anspach, William N., Jr., (AV) .... '49 '74 C.477 B.A. L.339 J.D. [Much S.F.D.A.&R.]
Anspach & Associates, (AV) .... 8 S. Michigan Ave., Ste. 3400
Antas, Craig M. .... '60 '85 C.338 B.A. L.365 J.D. [Ellison,N.Z.&A.]
Antholt, Amanda C. .... '75 '02 C&L.958 B.A., J.D. 312 N. May Street
Anthony, Diana M. .... '75 '00 C.1085 B.A. L.36 J.D. Dept. of HHS
Anthony, Julie Maria '71 '98 C.597 B.S. L.378 J.D.
(adm. in KS; not adm. in IL) Golin/Harris Intl.
Anthony, Michael F., (AV) .... '50 '78 C.973 B.S. L.64 J.D. [McDermott W.&E.]
Anthony, William N. .... '17 '42 C.999 L.209 221 N. LaSalle St.
Antinossi, Matthew .... '— '99 C.47 B.A. L.608 J.D. [Ⓐ Kirkland&E.]
Anto, Christine V. .... '— '01 C.436 B.A. L.209 J.D. [Ⓐ O'Hagan,S.&A.]
Antognoli, Anthony E. .... '75 '00 C.339 B.S. L.424 J.D. [Ⓐ Hinshaw&C.]
Antolin, Joseph A. .... '54 '79 C.918 B.A. L.128 J.D. Legal Assist. Found. of Chicago
Antone, Debra R., (BV) .... '53 '81 C.339 B.B.A. L.365 J.D. 20 North Clark St., Ste. 2200
Antonio, Douglas J., (AV) .... '55 '80 C&L.446 B.S., J.D. [Duane M.]
Antonopoulos, James J. .... '— '03 C&L.339 B.S., J.D. [Ⓐ Kirkland&E.]
Antonovych, Boris R. .... '43 '69 C&L.339 B.A., J.D. 2232 W. Chicago Ave.
Antonow, Christopher S. '71 '98 C.385 B.A. L.424 J.D.
Legal Coun. & Dir., Guggenheim Capital, LLC, Legal Dept.
Apcel, Melissa A., (AV) '51 '77 C&L.597 B.A., J.D.
Gen. Coun., U.S. Soccer Federation
Apel, Steven R., (BV) .... '— '88 C.424 B.B.A. L.365 J.D. [Karbal,C.E.S.&D.]
Apicella, Kenneth C. .... '71 '99 C.589 B.S. L.209 J.D. [Ⓐ Ellison,N.Z.&A.]
Apichai, Naris '75 '01 C.910 B.S.B.A. L.597 J.D.
444 North Michigan Avenue, Suite 3600
Apolskis, Michael G. .... '67 '93 C.347 B.S. L.879 J.D. 333 W. Wacker Dr., Ste. 1050
Apostolides, George P. .... '— '95 C.674 A.B. L.597 J.D. [Arnstein&L.]
Appelbaum, Steven .... '64 '89 C.339 B.A. L.146 J.D. 233 S. Wacker Dr., Ste. 8000
Appell, Annette R. .... '61 '87 C.188 B.A. L.597 J.D. Northwestern Univ. School of Law
Appelt, Sharon Steberl .... '39 '87 C.207 B.A. L.146 J.D. 6033 N. Sheridan Rd.‡
Apple, Eric W. .... '69 '96 C.659 B.S. L.861 J.D. 222 N. LaSalle St.
Applebaum, Jacob .... '10 '33 C&L.209 LL.B. 2458 W. Berwyn St.
Applegate, Bennett P., (AV) .... '60 '85 C.473 B.S. L.424 J.D. [Applegate&T.]
Applegate, David L., (AV) .... '53 '78 C.976 B.A. L.145 J.D. [Williams M.&J.]
Applegate & Thorne-Thomsen, P.C., (AV) .... 322 S. Green St.
Aquilino, Vincent M., (AV) .... '— '73 C.209 B.A. L.597 J.D. [Ungaretti&H.]
Arado, Frank E. .... '70 '96 C.145 B.A. L.339 J.D. [Ⓒ Mayer,B.R.&M.]
Arado, John J., (AV) .... '42 '67 C.602 B.B.A. L.477 J.D. [Wildman,H.A.&D.]
Arain, Adnan A. .... '— '00 C.145 B.A. L.597 J.D. [Ⓐ Alholm,M.K.H.&O.]
Arain, Affan .... '76 '01 C.597 B.A. L.145 J.D. [Ⓐ Sidley A.B.&W.]
Arain, Monazza .... '76 '01 C.245 B.A. L.597 J.D. [Ⓐ Sperling&S.]
Arain, Nizam .... '74 '00 C.339 B.A. L.477 J.D. [Ⓐ Foran G.P.&P.]
Arango, Joseph A. .... '51 '77 C&L.273 B.A., J.D. Mgr., Health Care Serv. Corp.‡
Araujo, Mauricio .... '— '93 C.966 B.A. L.424 J.D. Sr. Staff Atty., Am. Fam. Ins. Grp.
Arbel, Rafi R. .... '68 '94 C.352 L.146 J.D. Acct. Rep., Westgroup, Inc.
Arbetter, Brian .... '66 '92 C.910 B.S. L.145 J.D. [Baker&M.]
Arbogast, Michael Robert '76 '02 C.209 B.S. L.309 J.D.
(adm. in MA; not adm. in IL) [Ⓐ Mayer,B.R.&M.]
Arbolino, Jennifer P. .... '51 '86 C.788 A.B. L.326 J.D. Contract Negotiator
Arbus, Mark A. '64 '89
C.589 B.S. L.365 J.D. Senior Atty, General Growth Properties, Inc.
Archer, George F., (AV) .... '24 '51 C.813 B.A. L.145 J.D. [Archer&Assoc.]
Archer, Richard D. '57 '82
C.477 B.A. L.1068 J.D. Sr. Coun., Bank One Corp. (Law Dept.)
Archer & Associates, Ltd., (AV) .... 205 North Michigan Avenue
Ardell, Nancy Fox '67 '96
C.210 B.A. L.146 J.D. Assoc. Gen. Coun., Rehab. Inst. of Chicago
Arden, Thomas P. .... '— '85 C.188 B.A. L.976 J.D. [Holland&K.]
Arend, Douglas E. .... '58 '83 C&L.477 B.A., J.D. [Henderson&L.] ⊙
Arendt, Richard J. .... '52 '77 C&L.424 B.S., J.D. 640 N. LaSalle St.
Arenson, Joseph L. .... '71 '98 C.659 B.S.E. L.597 J.D. 2 N. La Salle St.
Arfa, Arthur A. .... '47 '76 C.339 B.A. L.424 J.D. Supvr. R.R. Retire. Bd.
Arfa, Jack A. .... '50 '74 C.966 B.A. L.339 J.D. 77 W. Washington
Argentar, David S. .... '68 '93 C.112 B.A. L.597 J.D. [Chuhak&T.]
Arger, Harry N. .... '63 '88 C.399 A.B. L.910 J.D. [Dykema G.P.]
Argeros, Anthony G. .... '64 '90 C.338 B.S. L.209 J.D. [A.G.Argeros]

Argeros, Anthony G., L.L.C.
10 South La Salle Street, Suite 3300, 60603
Telephone: 312-332-1100 Fax: 312-332-0644 URL: http://www.argeroslaw.com
Email: aga@ArgerosLaw.com URL: http://www.anthonyargeros.com
Anthony G. Argeros.
Personal Injury, Wrongful Death, Products Liability, Diesel Exposure, Toxic Mold, Automobile Accidents, Medical Malpractice, Birth Trauma, Traumatic Head Injuries, Nursing Home Litigation, Workers' Compensation, Civil Litigation, Appellate Practice.
See Professional Biographies, CHICAGO, ILLINOIS

Argionis, George G. .... '— '96 C.424 B.A. L.146 J.D. [Ⓐ Karavidas]
Argionis, James G. .... '71 '95 C&L.424 B.A., J.D. [Ⓐ Meckler B.&T.]
Arias, Joseph F. .... '76 '02 [Ⓐ Jenner&B.]
Aridas, Thomas G. .... '71 '97 C.209 B.A. L.436 J.D. Staff Coun., IL Com. Comm.
Aries, Thomas L., (AV) .... '45 '72 C.473 B.S.B.A. L.1003 J.D. 1859 N. Dayton St.‡
Arkebauer, Evelyn C. .... '— '86 C.966 B.A. L.477 J.D. [Sachnoff&W.]
Arkebauer, J. Todd .... '— '88 C.477 B.A. L.608 J.D. [Sachnoff&W.]
Arkin, Charles A. .... '57 '00 C.339 B.S. L.146 J.D. General Electric Commerical Finance
Arkin, Daniel W., (BV) .... '55 '87 C.589 B.S. L.146 J.D. [Rusin M.&F.]
Arkin, Henry R. .... '45 '77 C.966 B.A. L.209 J.D. State Dept. of Professional Regul.
Arkiss, Earl .... '20 '48 C.477 A.B. L.424 J.D. Cir. J.
Arlan, Chloe .... '42 '69 C&L.209 B.A., J.D. V.P., Cole Taylor Bk.
Arlow, Allan J. .... '44 '69 C.477 B.A. L.276 J.D. V.P., Centel Communications Co.
Armagno, Dana Simaitis .... '67 '92 C.339 B.S. L.209 J.D. [Vedder,P.K.&K.]
Armbruster, James R. '47 '74
C.801 B.A. L.46 J.D. Claims Coun., Bankers Life & Cas. Co.
Armel, Bernard S., Attorney at Law '45 '76 C.693 B.S. L.146 J.D.
77 W. Washington St.
Armiros, Konstantinos, (AV) .... '— '77 C.966 B.A. L.94 J.D. [Arnstein&L.]
Armstrong, Candace D. .... '77 '04 C.608 B.A. L.879 J.D. 10 S. Dearborn
Armstrong, Edwin R., (AV) .... '21 '49 C.388 B.A. L.597 J.D. [Armstrong&D.]

Armstrong, Gregory C., (AV) .... '64 '88 C.388 B.A. L.209 J.D. [Armstrong&D.]
Armstrong, Robert E. .... '52 '77 C.339 B.A. L.678 J.D. 233 S. Wacker Dr., 98th Fl.
Armstrong, Stephen H. .... '— '80 C.604 B.A. L.966 J.D. [Ungaretti&H.]
Armstrong & Donnelly, Ltd., (AV) .... 77 W. Wash. St.
Arnburg, David M., (AV) .... '49 '74 C.350 B.S. L.273 J.D. [Gould&R.]
Arner, Leah F. .... '— '81 C.378 B.S. L.208 J.D. [Chapman&C.]
Arnett, Daniel J. .... '67 '94 C.477 B.A. L.209 J.D. [Ⓐ Tribler O.&M.]

Arnett Gaubert, LLP
311 South Wacker Drive Suite 5600, 60606 ⊙
Telephone: 312-922-0900 Facsimile: 312-922-2255
Email: info@aghalaw.com URL: http://www.aghalaw.com
Partner: Bart F. Higgins.
Civil and Commercial Litigation.
Dallas, Texas Office: 4650 Trammell Crow Center, 2001 Ross Avenue, 75201. Telephone: 214-760-0900. Facsimile: 214-760-0905.
Christiansted, St. Croix, Virgin Islands Office: Moore & Sopuch, P.C., 2108 Company Street, Lot 55-A, 2nd Floor, 00820-4936. Telephone: 340-773-4150. Facsimile: 340-778-7168.
See Professional Biographies, CHICAGO, ILLINOIS

Arnoff, Alisa B., (AV) .... '62 '88 C&L.424 A.B., J.D. 33 N. La Salle
Arnold, Bradley Michael .... '73 '98 C.352 B.A. L.365 J.D. [Ⓐ Anesi,O.R.N.&K.]
Arnold, David A. .... '55 '80 C.347 A.B. L.477 J.D. V.P., CIT Grp./ Credit Finance
Arnold, Helen P. .... '50 '97 C.1023 B.A. L.146 J.D. Asst. Pub. Def.
Arnold, Hugh B. .... '35 '61 L.209 LL.B. [Arnold&K.]
Arnold, Jeffrey C. .... '71 '97 C.323 B.A. L.146 J.D. [Ⓐ Fisher K.]
Arnold, Jeffrey M. .... '43 '68 C.72 B.S. L.365 J.D. Adm. Dir., Cir. Ct.
Arnold, Jeffrey S., (AV) '64 '89
C.93 A.B. L.145 J.D. V.P., Legal, Equity Office Properties Trust
Arnold, Katherine Streicher .... '61 '87 C.477 A.B. L.1119 J.D. [Ⓒ Tressler,S.M.&P.]
Arnold, Kathryn Kovitz, (AV) .... '65 '90 C.339 B.S. L.597 J.D. [Shefsky&F.]
Arnold, Margaret A., (AV) .... '43 '77 C.157 B.S. L.424 J.D. [Ⓒ Vedder,P.K.&K.]
Arnold, Nancy J. .... '45 '77 C.720 B.A. L.424 J.D. Chan. J.
Arnold, Patrick J., Jr., (AV) '66 '90
C.339 B.A. L.424 J.D. [McAndrews,H.&M.] (See Pat. Sect.)
Arnold, Paul F., (AVⓉ) '30 '56 C.347 B.S. L.1119 LL.B.
(adm. in IN; not adm. in IL) 2125 W. Agatite Ave.‡
Arnold, Robert P. .... '54 '86 C.339 B.A. L.589 J.D. [Lord,B.&B.]
Arnold, William O. .... '28 '51 C.145 L.209 LL.B. 6253 N. Sauganash
Arnold & Kadjan, (AV) .... 19 W. Jackson, 3rd Fl.

Arnold, White & Durkee
(See Howrey LLP, Washington, D.C.)

Arnoux, Matthew C. .... '60 '84 C.276 B.A. L.339 J.D. [Nadler,P.&M.]

Arnstein & Lehr LLP, (AV)
Suite 1200, 120 South Riverside Plaza, 60606-3910 ⊙
Telephone: 312-876-7100 Fax: 312-876-0288
Email: mail@arnstein.com URL: http://www.arnstein.com
Leo H. Arnstein (1906-1993). Members of Firm: Michael A. Abramson; William J. Anaya; George P. Apostolides; Konstantinos Armiros; Bruce H. Balonick; Brandon E. Bell; Roy L. Bernstein; William K. Blomquist; J. William Braithwaite; Robert D. Butters; Barry A. Chatz; James A. Chatz; Stephen R. Chesler; Colleen Adams Chindlund; Anna-Katrina S. Christakis; Robert T. Cichocki; Thomas P. Conley; Brian J. Cooke (Resident, West Palm Beach, Florida Office); Patrick J. Cotter; Steven L. Daniels (Resident, West Palm Beach and Boca Raton, Florida Offices); David C. Dunkin; Kenneth Edelman (Not admitted in IL); Mark E. Enright; Luis A. Espino (Resident, Miami, Florida Office); Willa A. Fearrington (Resident, West Palm Beach Office); Thadford A. Felton; Richard C. Gering; Allan Goldberg; Matthew J. Goldberg; James F. Gossett; John F. Grady; Lawrence E. Grelle; Maureen B. Grzeskiewicz; John C. Hanson, II (Resident, Miami, Florida Office); Nancy S. Harbottle (Resident, Hoffman Estates Office); R. Kymn Harp; Kurt J. Heinz; Richard K. Hellerman; David S. Horwitch; Phillip M. Hudson, III (Resident, Miami, Florida Office); Joel M. Hurwitz; Richard B. Ivans (Resident, Miami, Florida Office); Norman P. Jeddeloh; Michael N. Jonas (Resident, West Palm Beach, Florida Office); Scott H. Kapp; Barry R. Katz; Eugene J. Kelley, Jr.; Stephanie J. Kim; Arthur L. Klein; Kathleen M. Lach; Robert J. Lasky; Louis A. Lehr, Jr.; Neville M. Leslie (Resident, Miami, Florida Office); Samuel H. Levine; Patti S. Levinson; Steven N. Malitz; Alfredo J. Marquez-Sterling (Resident, Miami, Florida Office); Thomas F. McGuire; Robert E. McKenzie; Ronald D. Menaker; Mark F. Miller; Trev M. Minnaert; Hal R. Morris; Cynde Hirschtick Munzer; Christopher S. Naveja; William G. Nosek; Joe Ourth; R. Delacy Peters, Jr.; Jeffrey D. Pilgrim; Hilda Piloto (Resident, Miami, Florida Office); Philip L. Pomerance; Guy E. Quattlebaum (Resident, West Palm Beach, Florida Office); John L. Ropiequet; Jeffrey B. Shapiro (Resident, Miami, Florida Office); Jerold N. Siegan; A. Thomas Skallas; Edward A. Snyder; Jose D. Sosa (Resident, West Palm Beach, Florida Office); Walter J. Starck; Paul E. Starkman; Miriam R. Stein; David Sugar; Howard J. Swibel; Jay P. Tarshis; Robert J. Taylor; Jessica Tovrov; Harry N. Turk (Resident, Miami, Florida Office); John A. Turner (Resident, West Palm Beach, Florida Office); Michael R. Turoff; Robert I. Ury; Mary Cannon Veed; John T. Wagener; David S. Waxman; David S. Wayne; Raymond J. Werner; Dawn C. Wrona Eby; Thomas P. Yardley; Michael J. Zdeb. Special Counsel: Theresia E. Wolf-McKenzie. Associates: Shekar Adiga; Kevin Brenner; Ray H. Burgan; Kristina M. Candido (Not admitted in IL); Jenifer L. Caracciolo; Andrea J. Durkin; Jason C. Hill (Resident, West Palm Beach, Florida Office); Jason B. Hirsh; Erik L. Kantz; Sharilee Kempa; Laura L. Lau; Joy E. Levy; Martha K. Milia; Elizabeth M. Perry; Daniel I. Schlade; Irina Shelest; Harley Storrings (Resident, Miami, Florida Office); E. Jason Tremblay; Keli M. Videtto. Of Counsel: Joseph T. Ganzer (Resident, Milwaukee, Wisconsin Office); Michael J. Ganzer (Resident, Milwaukee, Wisconsin Office); Theodore J. Hodan (Resident, Milwaukee, Wisconsin Office); Stanley M. Lipnick; Martin Pico (Resident, Miami, Florida Office); David T. Rallo; L. Trent Stinson (Resident, Miami, Florida Office); Patrick A. Tuite.
General Practice, including Litigation in State and Federal, Trial and Appellate Courts, Products Litigation, Medical Malpractice, Litigation Management, Business Transactions, Real Estate, Employee Benefits, Creditors' Rights and Bankruptcy, Criminal Law, Commercial Finance, Commercial Litigation, Not-for-Profit Corporations, Estate Planning, Trust Administration and Probate, Taxation, Employment, Consumer Credit, Securities Law, Transportation Law, International Law, Insurance Law, Local Government, Intellectual Property, Environmental Law, Health Care and Practice before Federal and State Administrative Bodies.
West Palm Beach, Florida Office: 515 North Flagler Drive, Suite 600, 33401-4323. Telephone: 561-833-9800. Fax: 561-655-5551.
Boca Raton, Florida Office: 2424 North Federal Highway, Suite 462, 33431. Telephone: 561-322-6900. Fax: 561-322-6940.
Miami, Florida Office: Miami Center, 201 South Biscayne Boulevard, Fourth Floor, 33131. Telephone: 305-374-3330. Fax: 305-374-4744.
Tampa, Florida Office: 300 South Hyde Park Avenue, Suite 180, 33606. Telephone: 813-259-9964. Fax: 813-259-9724.
Hoffman Estates, Illinois Office: 2800 West Higgins Road, Suite 425, 60195-5224. Telephone: 847-843-2900. Fax: 847-843-3355.
Milwaukee, Wisconsin Office: 7161 North Port Washington Road, 53217. Telephone: 414-351-2440. Fax: 414-352-6901.
See Professional Biographies, CHICAGO, ILLINOIS

Aron, Charles J. .... '46 '72 C.339 B.A. L.209 J.D. 19 W. Jackson Blvd.
Aron, Elise S. .... '57 '83 C.352 B.A. L.146 J.D. Alden Management Services Inc.
Aron, Harry B. .... '19 '47 C&L.209 LL.B. Assoc. Cir. Ct. J.‡
Aron, Leonard V. '52 '80 C.150 B.A. L.1340 J.D.
(adm. in OH; not adm. in IL) Postal Inspec., U.S. Postal Inspection Serv.
Aronberg, Ronald J., (AV) ...... '32 '57 C.597 B.S. L.145 J.D. [Ⓒ Aronberg G.D.&G.] ‡

Aronberg Goldgehn Davis & Garmisa, (AV) ▣
Suite 3000 One IBM Plaza, 60611 ⊙
Telephone: 312-828-9600 Telecopier: 312-828-9635
Email: agdg@agdglaw.com URL: http://www.agdglaw.com
Members of Firm: Christopher J. Bannon; Eric M. Brown; Howard J. Fishman; Jay A. Frank; William J. Garmisa; Paul A. Gilman; Mitchell S. Goldgehn; James S. Jarvis; Elizabeth Olen Lazzara;

(This Listing Continued)

Aronberg Goldgehn Davis & Garmisa (Continued)
Nathan H. Lichtenstein; Mitchell J. Melamed; Henry M. Morris; John M. Riccione; Ned S. Robertson; David H. Sachs; Bernard A. Schlifke; William J. Serritella, Jr.; Robert N. Sodikoff; Blooma Stark; Andrew S. Williams. Of Counsel: Ronald J. Aronberg (Retired); Melvin A. Blum; Joel C. Levin; Steven H. Nemerovski; William P. Rosenthal (1923-2004); Charles E. Zeitlin (Retired). Associates: Andrea Aycinena; Lisa J. Brodsky; David C. Goldstein; Elvis D. Gonzalez; Paul A. Greenberg; Mary Vidal Hays; Jennifer Papahronis; Christina B. Perez.
Corporate, Banking and General Business Practice. Insurance Coverage, General Civil, Insurance Defense, Products Liability, Trial and Appellate Practice in all Courts. Real Estate Transactions, Estate Planning and Probate, Federal Taxation, Employee Benefits, Domestic Relations, Employment, Trademark, Copyright and Unfair Competition, Health Care and Government Relations.
Schaumburg, Illinois Office: 10 North Martingale Road, Fourth Floor, 60173. Telephone: 847-985-4060.
See Professional Biographies, CHICAGO, ILLINOIS

Aronovitz, Cory .... '68 '93 C.529 B.A. L.365 J.D. [Casino]
Aronson, Richard J., (AV) .... '39 '64 C.659 B.Econ. L.477 J.D. [Fitzgerald&C.]

Aronson, Robert H., (AV) '35 '58 C&L.597 B.S.L., J.D. ▣
Suite 714, 100 West Monroe Street, 60603
Telephone: 312-372-7123 FAX: 312-372-1247
Email: rharonson35@yahoo.com URL: http://www.lawyers.com/robertharonson
General Criminal Trial and Appellate Practice in all State and Federal Courts.
See Professional Biographies, CHICAGO, ILLINOIS

Aronson, Simon H., (AV) .... '43 '73 C&L.145 B.A., J.D. [Ⓒ Lord,B.&B.]
Aronson, Virginia L., (AV) .... '47 '75 C&L.145 B.A., J.D. [Sidley A.B.&W.]
Arpaia, James A. .... '53 '91 C.339 B.S. L.146 J.D. [Vedder,P.K.&K.]
Arranz, John P. .... '78 '03 C&L.966 B.A., J.D. [Ⓐ Swanson,M.&B.]
Arrigo, Sheryl M. .... '— '96 C.589 B.S.N. L.209 J.D. [Ⓐ Donohue B.M.&S.]
Arrotti-Carter, Cynthia .... '76 '03 C.861 B.S. L.424 J.D. [Ⓐ Bollinger,R.&G.]
Arroyo, Laurice Z.B. .... '70 '96 C&L.477 B.B.A., J.D. [Ⓐ Sidley A.B.&W.]
Arroyo, Robert E., (AV) .... '48 '74 C.801 B.S. L.365 J.D. [Jackson L.]
Arthur, James K. '31 '57 C&L.597 B.S.B.A., J.D.
V.P. & Treas., Certified Reporting Co.
Arthur, Thomas, (AV) .... '30 '58 C.299 B.A. L.597 J.D. [Ⓒ Gardner C.&D.]
Artoe, L. Robert .... '37 '74 C.911 B.A. L.365 J.D. 424C E. North Water St.
Artwick, Frederic J., (AV) .... '44 '70 C.309 A.B. L.145 J.D. [Sidley A.B.&W.]
Arvanitis, Nicholas James .... '62 '88 C.424 B.A L.209 J.D. [N.J.Arvanitis]
Arvanitis, Nicholas J., P.C. .... 900 W. Jackson Blvd., Ste. 5 East
Arvey, Howard, (AV) .... '21 '48 C&L.597 B.S., J.D. [Ⓒ Wildman,H.A.&D.]
Asaro, Lenny D. .... '— '95 C.990 B.S. L.365 J.D. [Ⓐ Neal&L.]
Asbahi, Mazen .... '— '00 C.477 B.A. L.597 J.D. [Ⓐ Goldberg,K.B.B.R.&M.]
Asbille, Robert C. '48 '76
C.293 B.A. L.597 J.D. Spec. Asst. Atty. Gen., State Dept. of Rev.
Aschenbrenner, Richelle L. .... '69 '94 C.602 B.B.A. L.424 J.D. [McGuirewoods]
Ascher, Michael R. .... '69 '95 C.228 B.A. L.1068 J.D. Brookdale Living Communities
Ash, Barry, (AV) .... '61 '87 C.347 B.S. L.146 J.D. [Ash,A.F.&L.]
Ash, Joseph, (AV) .... '27 '49 C.339 L.209 LL.B. [Ash,A.F.&L.]

Ash, Anos, Freedman & Logan, L.L.C., (AV)
Suite 1211, 77 West Washington Street, 60602
Telephone: 312-346-1390 Fax: 312-346-7847
Members of Firm: George J. Anos (Retired); Joseph Ash; Lawrence M. Freedman; Bruce T. Logan; Barry Ash.
General Trial Practice. Products Liability, Malpractice, Probate, Corporate, Zoning, Municipal, Real Estate and Condominium Law.
See Professional Biographies, CHICAGO, ILLINOIS

Ashbell, Theodore Shelly .... '38 '79 C.910 M.D. L.424 J.D. 990 N. Lake Shore Dr.
Ashby, Lorraine .... '45 '63 C.1055 B.A. L.209 J.D. 10336 S. Western Ave.
Ashcraft, Anna B. .... '55 '81 C.597 B.A. L.145 J.D. Cook Co. Bd., Pres. Off.

Ashcraft & Ashcraft, Ltd.
Two Prudential Plaza, 180 North Stetson Avenue Suite 5510, 60601
Telephone: 312-819-4010 Telecopier: 312-819-4009
URL: http://www.lawyers.com/ashcraft&ashcraft
Rufus Dawes Beach (1903-1989); Charles H. G. Kimball (1909-1997); Charles F. Moles; Randall C. Romei.
Trust and Estates, Wills and Probate, Estate Planning, Elder Law, Trust Administration, Liquidity Planning, Asset Protection, Taxation, Tax Planning, Business Law, Contract Law, Corporate Law, Real Estate, Commercial Real Estate, Residential Real Estate, Buying and Selling a Home, Condominium Law.
See Professional Biographies, CHICAGO, ILLINOIS

Ashen, Deborah S. .... '61 '89 C.36 B.S. L.209 J.D. [D.S.Ashen]

Ashen, Deborah S., Ltd., The Law Offices of
217 North Jefferson Street, Suite 600, 60661
Telephone: 312-655-0800 Fax: 312-655-0801
Email: dsa@ashenlaw.com
Deborah S. Ashen.
Equipment Leasing, Finance, Commercial Litigation, Collection Litigation and Real Estate.
See Professional Biographies, CHICAGO, ILLINOIS

Ashenden, John R., (AV) '52 '79
C.36 B.A. L.589 J.D. 33 North La Salle Street, Suite 2600

Asher, Gittler, Greenfield & D'Alba, Ltd., (AV)
200 West Jackson Boulevard, Suite 1900, 60606
Telephone: 312-263-1500 Fax: 312-263-1520
Email: firm@ulaw.com
Lester Asher (1910-1990); Michael C. Greenfield; Marvin Gittler; Joel A. D'Alba; Robert B. Greenberg; Leonard J. Elberts; Barry G. Collins; Patricia A. Collins; Margaret Angelucci;—Ryan A. Hagerty; Librado Arreola Vega; Michele Cotrupe. Of Counsel: Stephen J. Feinberg.
Labor Relations, Employment and Employee Benefit Law, General Trial Practice in all Courts.
See Professional Biographies, CHICAGO, ILLINOIS

Ashford-Nolan, Cynthia .... '65 '91 C.339 B.A. L.325 J.D. Asst. States Atty.
Ashley, Anthony J., (AV) .... '66 '92 C.473 B.S. L.209 J.D. [Vedder,P.K.&K.]
Ashley, Carol R. .... '68 '94 C.597 B.A. L.966 J.D. [Futterman&H.]
Ashley, Daniel J., (BV) .... '52 '77 C&L.339 A.B., J.D. [Ⓒ Laner,M.D.B.L.&T.]
Ashley, James W., (AV) .... '23 '48 C.262 L.597 J.D. 227 W. Monroe St.
Ashley, James W., Jr., (AV) .... '49 '79 C.170 B.A. L.208 J.D. [Lord,B.&B.]
Ashley, Philip S. '48 '76 C.697 B.A. L.862 J.D.
Assoc. Prof., DePaul Univ. Coll of Law
Ashley, Richard W. '43 '68 C.597 B.A. L.966 J.D.
(adm. in WI; not adm. in IL) McKinsey & Co.
Ashley, Richard W., III .... '66 '93 C.823 B.A. L.365 J.D. [DLPiper R.G.C.U.]
Ashman, Gary D. .... '51 '76 C.339 B.A. L.209 J.D. 150 N. Wacker Dr., Ste. 3000
Ashman, Kenneth J., (AV) .... '61 '90 C.36 B.A.E. L.94 J.D. [Ashman] ⊙
Ashman, Martin C. .... '31 '53 L.209 LL.B. Dist. Mag. J.

Ashman Law Offices, LLC, (AV)
161 North Clark Street Suite 3575, 60601 ⊙
Telephone: 312-596-1700 Facsimile: 312-873-3800
Email: info@ashmanlawoffices.com URL: http://www.ashmanlawoffices.com

(This Listing Continued)

Ashman Law Offices, LLC (Continued)

Kenneth J. Ashman;—Neal D. Kitterlin.
Business, Corporate and Commercial Litigation, Securities Litigation, Class Actions, Internet Law, Insurance Litigation, Employment Litigation, Civil Rights, Intellectual Property Litigation, Corporate Counseling, and Foreign Corrupt Practices Act Litigation and Counseling.
New York, New York Office: 270 Madison Avenue, Suite 1203, 10016. Telephone: 212-581-9700. Facsimile: 312-873-3800. URL: http://www.AshmanLawOffices.com.
Riverwoods, Illinois Office: 2801 Orange Brace Road, 60015. Telephone: 847-444-1366. Facsimile: 312-873-3800.

See Professional Biographies, CHICAGO, ILLINOIS

Ashmore, Laura N. ....'69 '94 C&L.209 B.F.A., J.D. [[A] Lake,T.&D.]
Ashton, Kathryn B. ....'72 '99 C.221 B.A. L.146 J.D. [[A] Sonnenschein N.&R.]
Askounis, Homer J. ....'23 '50 C.145 B.S. L.597 J.D. [H.J.Askounis]
Askounis, Thomas V., (AV) ....'51 '75 C.597 B.A. L.880 J.D. [Askounis&B.]

Askounis & Borst, P.C., (AV)
303 East Wacker Drive, Suite 1000, 60601
Telephone: 312-861-7100 Facsimile: 312-861-0022
Email: attorneys@askborst.com URL: http://www.askborst.com:
Thomas V. Askounis; Vincent T. Borst; Daniel L. Collins; D. Alexander Darcy;—Kenneth D. Peters; Dennis A. Dressler; Jennifer L. Jerzy; D. Ann Coker; C. Randall Woolley, II; Debra Rose Devassy. Of Counsel: Kenneth B. Drost.
General Practice. Commercial Litigation, Commercial Transactions, Bankruptcy Workouts and Litigation, Intellectual Property, Franchise Law, Telecommunications, Commercial Finance/Commercial Equipment Leasing, Corporate Law.

See Professional Biographies, CHICAGO, ILLINOIS

Askounis, Homer J., P.C. ....2460 Estes Ave.
Askow, Irwin J., (AV) ....'— '38 C&L.145 A.B., J.D. [[C] Tenney&B.]
Asmussen, James R. ....'63 '89 C.884 B.S.A. L.339 J.D. [Shefsky&F.]
Asonye, Uche O. ....'— '92 C.209 B.Sc. L.424 J.D. [Asonye&Assoc.]

Asonye & Associates
11 South La Salle Street, Suite 2140, 60603
Telephone: 312-795-9110 Fax: 312-795-9114
Email: uche@aa-law.com URL: http://www.aa-law.com
Uche O. Asonye. Associate: Mark Pando.
Languages: Polish, Spanish.
Employment Law, Immigration Law, Workers Compensation and Civil Rights.

See Professional Biographies, CHICAGO, ILLINOIS

Aspen, Jessica M. '72 '97 C.881 B.A. L.597 J.D.
Asst. Gen. Coun., Exelon Business Services Co.
Aspen, Marvin E. ....'34 '58 C.424 B.S.L. L.597 LL.B. U.S. Dist. J.
Aspengren, Alfred E. ....'39 '64 C.357 B.A. L.145 J.D. 4510 N. Hermitage
Asperger, Jeffrey J., (AV) ....'52 '79 C.381 B.A. L.365 J.D. [Asperger&Assoc.]

Asperger Associates, LLC, (AV)
303 East Wacker Drive, Suite 1000, 60601
Telephone: 312-856-9901 Fax: 312-856-9905
Email: jasperger@asplaw.net
Jeffrey J. Asperger;—Kelly A. Saindon; Daile V. Grigaitis; Antonia Hays.
Construction Products Liability, Complex and Multi-District Litigation, Commercial Torts, Admiralty and Maritime Law, Construction Liability, Negligence, Personal Injury, Products Liability, Torts, Insurance and Mold Litigation.

See Professional Biographies, CHICAGO, ILLINOIS

Assmus, Richard M. ....'73 '98 C.145 B.S. L.477 J.D. [[A] Mayer,B.R.&M.]
Ast, Heather Marie ....'74 '00 C.477 B.A. L.146 J.D. IL Dept. of Prof. Reg.
Astle, Richard W., (AV) ....'55 '80 C.659 B.S. L.276 J.D. [Sidley A.B.&W.]
Atcherson, Sophia J. ....'70 '97 C.347 B.A. L.1119 J.D. Asst. App. Def.
Atchison, David L. ....'51 '76 C.338 B.S. L.801 J.D. 333 W. Wacker Dr.
Athanas, Josef S., (AV) ....'— '91 C.347 B.S. L.145 J.D. [Latham&W.]
Athas, Christopher ....'73 '00 C.691 B.A. L.145 J.D. [[A] Skadden,A.S.M.&F.]
Athas, Gus J. ....'36 '65 C.339 B.S. L.424 J.D. [Stamos&T.]
Athas, Leo J., (AV) ....'43 '73 C.339 B.S. L.146 J.D. [Hinshaw&C.] (⊙Lisle)
Atique, Shuaib A. '— '03 C.339 B.S. L.477 J.D.
(adm. in CA; not adm. in IL) [[A] Kirkland&E.]
Atkin, Jennifer A. ....'77 '04 C.174 B.A. L.1410 J.D. [[A] Landon&W.]
Atkin, Julie M. Hassett ....'69 '96 C.608 B.A. L.117 J.D. Asst. States Atty.
Atkins, Jacqueline T. ....'47 '73 C&L.339 B.A., J.D. JMB Institutional Realty Corp.

Atkinson & Atkinson
(See Evanston)

Atkins-Trimnell, Katherine Louise ....'60 '94 C.57 B.A. L.945 J.D. Cir. Ct. Staff Atty.
Atlas, David S., (AV) ....'54 '79 C.339 B.A. L.146 J.D. [[A] Patton&R.]
Atsaves, Louis G., (AV) ....'55 '79 C.339 B.A. L.1151 J.D. [L.G.Atsaves] ⊙
Atsaves, Louis G., Ltd., (AV) ....200 West Jackson Boulevard (⊙Zion)
Attermeyer, Dorothy M. ....'42 '67 C&L.209 B.A., J.D. Assoc. Reg. Coun., EPA
Atwood, Stetson F. ....'67 '94 C.823 B.A. L.190 J.D. [[A] Donohue B.M.&S.]
Atz, Kimberly A. ....'70 '96 C.36 L.365 Cook Co. Mandatory Arbitration
Aubel, Leo G., (AV) ....'60 '86 C.119 B.F.A. L.146 J.D. [Deutsch,L.&E.]
Aubin, Kristine ....'71 '97 C&L.966 B.A., J.D. [[A] Connelly S.H.]
Aubry, Alison R. '— '03 C.339 B.S. L.1565 J.D.
(adm. in MA; not adm. in IL) [[A] Kirkland&E.]
Audette, Brian A. ....'74 '02 C.103 B.A. L.424 J.D. [[A] DLPiper R.G.C.U.]
Audley, David T. B. ....'— '85 C&L.966 B.S., J.D. [Chapman&C.]
Auerbach, Gary L., (AV) ....'42 '68 C.347 B.S. L.477 J.D. [Weinberg R.]
Auerbach, Marshall J., (AV) ....'32 '55 C.339 L.365 J.D. [M.J.Auerbach&Assoc.]
Auerbach, Melissa J., (AV) ....'55 '80 C.976 B.A. L.309 J.D. [Cornfield&F.]
Auerbach, Nicole Nehama ....'66 '93 C.966 B.A. L.209 J.D. [Katten M.R.]

Auerbach, Marshall J., & Associates, Ltd., (AV) [BR]
30 North LaSalle Street, Suite 3400, 60602
Telephone: 312-853-3300 Fax: 312-853-1043
URL: http://www.auerbachlawoffice.com
Marshall J. Auerbach.
Family, Domestic Relations, Divorce, Matrimonial. General Civil Practice.

See Professional Biographies, CHICAGO, ILLINOIS

Aufmann, Arthur W., (AV) ....'57 '82 C.927 B.B.A. L.424 J.D. [E.T.Joyce&Assoc.]
Aufrecht, David B., Attorney at Law '70 '95
C.347 B.S. L.910 J.D. 65 E. Wacker Pl., Ste. 1700
Augspurger, Thomas J. '67 '92 C.178 B.A. L.912 J.D.
(adm. in MI; not adm. in IL) [[A] McDermott W.&E.]
August, Brett A., (AV) ....'52 '77 C.339 B.A. L.976 J.D. [Pattishall,M.N.H.&G.]
Augustine, Algis K. ....'44 '72 C.602 A.B. L.339 J.D. [Augustine,K.&L.]
Augustine, Andrea M. ....'— '97 C&L.339 B.S., J.D. [[C] Foley&L.] (Pat.)
Augustine, Anthony J., Jr. ....'45 '73 C&L.339 B.S., J.D. [Levy&A.]
Augustine, Karen ....'80 '04 C&L.424 B.A., J.D. [[A] Davis F.Z.K.M.M.&R.]
Augustine, Kern and Levens, Ltd.
218 N. Jefferson Street, Suite 202 (⊙Bridgewater, Marlton, NJ; Lake Success, NY)

Augustus, Sue L. '55 '82 C.602 B.A. L.146 J.D.
Assoc. Dir., SSI Coalition for a Responsible Safety Net‡
Augustyn, James E. ....'51 '85 C.276 B.S.F.S. L.365 J.D. 4021 C. W. 63rd St.
Augustyn, John M., (AV) '59 '87 C.146 B.S. L.424 J.D.
[Leydig,V.&M.] (See Pat. Sect.)
Augustynski, Adam J. ....'65 '90 C.309 A.B. L.597 J.D. 5850 W. Bryn Mawr Ave.
Aukstik, Dennis J., (AV) ....'56 '82 C&L.424 B.S., J.D. [[A] Daley&G.]
Aune, Katie R. ....'— '01 C.352 B.A. L.494 J.D. [[A] Sachnoff&W.]
Auricchio, Vincent Michael ....'71 '97 C.880 B.S. L.209 J.D. [[A] McKay,N.T.D.&K.]
Aurichio, Louis J., (AV) ....'61 '89 C.165 B.A. L.597 J.D. [Butler R.S.&B.]
Auslander, Merwin B. ....'31 '56 C&L.339 B.A., LL.B. 111 W. Wash.
Auslander, Sheila E. ....'72 '97 C.145 B.A. L.383 J.D. Amer. Bar Assn.
Auslander, Stewart J. ....'78 '03 C.339 B.S. [[A] Schiller,D.&F.]
Austin, Brent R. ....'64 '89 C.1494 B.A. L.1066 J.D. [Wildman,H.A.&D.]
Austin, Cathy Kiselyak ....'54 '80 C.453 S.B. L.976 J.D. [Gardner C.&D.]
Austin, Daniel G. ....'72 '02 C.424 B.B.A. L.146 J.D. 1021 West Adams
Austin, David W. ....'65 '01 C.446 B.A. L.1000 J.D. [[A] Jenner&B.]
Austin, Edward J. ....'70 '96 C.347 B.A. L.424 J.D. [McNamara&A.]
Austin, Henry W., Jr., (CV(T)) '55 '80 C&L.846 B.A., J.D.
200 N. LaSalle St., Ste. 2850
Austin, Jenny ....'78 '03 C&L.910 B.S., J.D. [[A] Baker&M.]
Austin, Margaret C. '72 '98 C.1049 B.B.A. L.424 J.D.
Asst. Corp. Secy., Chicago Merchantile Exchange Inc.
Austin, Robert B., (AV) ....'66 C.207 B.A. L.145 J.D. [Anderson,R.]
Austin, Ronald, Jr. ....'71 '97 C.257 B.S. L.339 J.D. [[A] Brothers&T.]
Austin, Stacey ....'— '04 C.597 B.S. L.1565 J.D. [[A] Winston&S.]
Austriaco, Aurora ....'65 '91 C&L.209 B.S., J.D. [[C] Peck,B.A.&M.] ⊙
Auten, Anne C. ....'70 '95 C.659 B.A. L.477 J.D. [DLPiper R.G.C.U.]
Auten, Stephen R. ....'71 '97 C.339 B.S. L.146 J.D. [[A] Leydig,V.&M.] (See Pat. Sect.)
Auton, Sean D. ....'70 '95 C&L.477 B.A., J.D. [[A] FagelHaber]
Autry, Nicholas J. '70 '02 C.347 B.S. L.1119 J.D.
Asst. V.P./ Claims Coun., Chicago Title Ins. Co.
AuYeung, Geoff ....'— '01 L.339 J.D. [[A] Katten M.R.]
AuYeung, ManChit ....'— '01 C.999 B.S. L.339 J.D. [[A] Latham&W.]
Aven, Jonathan M. ....'70 '95 C.339 B.A. L.365 J.D. [J.Aven]
Aven, Jonathan, Law Office of ....180 N. Michigan Ave., Ste. 2105
Avery, Cameron S., (AV) ....'38 '63 C.674 B.S.E. L.309 J.D. [Bell,B.&L.]
Avery, Ellen M. ....'75 '00 C.602 B.A. L.146 J.D. [[A] Shefsky&F.]
Avery, Mary Katherine, (BV) ....'68 '93 C.477 B.A. L.424 J.D. [Avery C.K.]
Avery, Robert Dean, (AV(T)) ....'— '71 C.597 B.A. L.178 J.D. [Jones D.]

Avery Camerlingo Kill, LLC, (BV)
218 North Jefferson, Suite 200, 60661
Telephone: 312-648-9707 Fax: 312-648-9713
Members of Firm: Mary Katherine Avery; Pepi Camerlingo; Annemarie E. Kill.
Family Law including Divorce, Child Custody, Child Support, Visitation Rights, Spousal Support (Alimony), Maintenance, Adoptions, Step Parent Adoptions, Marital Property Settlements, Modifications of Decree, Name Changes, Separation Agreements, Qualified Domestic Relations Orders (QDRO'S), Paternity, Guardianship, Employment Law including Wrongful Termination, Sexual and Racial Discrimination/Harassment, Age Discrimination, Disability Discrimination, Whistleblower Litigation, Family and Medical Leave Act, Retaliatory Discharge.

See Professional Biographies, CHICAGO, ILLINOIS

Avgerinos, Nick James, (AV) '56 '81
C.378 B.A. L.221 J.D. [Capron&A.] (⊙Des Moines, IA)
Avila, Frank B. ....'70 '00 C.326 B.A. L.209 J.D. [Avila,T.]
Avila, Tomic LLC ....227 W. Monroe, Suite 2000
Aviles, Eduardo ....'— '04 C.339 B.A. L.477 J.D. [[A] Chapman&C.]
Avramovich, Michael Paul ....'52 '97 C.1106 B.A. L.365 J.D. [Avramovich&Assoc.]
Avramovich & Associates, P.C. ....70 W. Madison St., Ste. 1400
Avrushin, Adam Michael ....'72 '00 C.912 B.A. L.930 J.D. Off of the Pub. Guardian
Awick, Darryl L. ....'59 '95 C.338 B.S. L.365 J.D. [[A] Pretzel&S.]
Awodiran, Babatunde O. '68 '93
(adm. in NY; not adm. in IL) Assoc. Atty., Wm. Wrigley Jr. Co.
Axel, Bradley J. ....'71 '96 C.966 B.A. L.365 J.D. [Torshen,S.G.D.&A.]
Axelrod, David A., (AV) ....'57 '83 C.475 B.A. L.904 J.D. [D.A.Axelrod&Assoc.]
Axelrod, Gary E. ....'— '97 C&L.339 B.S., J.D. [Kirkland&E.]
Axelrod, Sidney H. ....'30 '52 C&L.209 LL.B. 70 W. Madison St.

Axelrod, David A., & Associates, P.C., (AV)
20 South Clark, Suite 2200, 60603
Telephone: 312-782-4600 Fax: 312-782-3015
Email: daa@axelrodpc.com URL: http://www.axelrodpc.com
David A. Axelrod;—Robert A. Cohen; Stacey L. Leinheiser; H. David Roseth.
Commercial Litigation, Professional Negligence, Fraud Litigation.

See Professional Biographies, CHICAGO, ILLINOIS

Axelrod, Goodman, Steiner & Bazelon, (AV) [BR]
39 South LaSalle Street, Suite 920, 60603
Telephone: 312-236-9375 Fax: 312-236-2877
Email: jhs1@worldnet.att.net URL: http://www.trans-law.com
David Axelrod (1910-1976); Joel H. Steiner; Paul A. Gajewski.
Civil and Appellate Litigation, Transportation Law. Administrative, Real Estate, Business, Insurance Defense.

See Professional Biographies, CHICAGO, ILLINOIS

Axelrood, Larry G. ....'60 '85 C.346 B.S. L.146 J.D. 53 W. Jackson Blvd.
Axelsen, Jennifer Hahn ....'69 '93 C.339 B.S. L.209 J.D. [[A] M.H.Erde&Assoc.]
Ayala, Dolores ....'— '96 C.910 B.A. L.209 J.D. [[A] Schuyler,R.&Z.]
Aycinena, Andrea ....'— '03 C.473 B.A. L.209 J.D. [[A] Aronberg G.D.&G.]
Ayres, James J. ....'54 '84 C.339 B.A. L.209 J.D. [[C] Novoselsky]
Ayres, Stephen R., (BV) ....'59 '84 C.210 B.A. L.339 J.D. [Cheely,O.&A.]
Ayyagari, Swati '75 '01 C.339 B.S. L.209 J.D.
Compliance Dir., Rush University Medical Center
Azeris, Ivar R., (BV) ....'48 '74 C.339 B.A. L.93 J.D. [Clausen M.]
Azulay, Daniel, (AV) ....'44 '73 C.1016 B.A. L.146 J.D. [Azulay,H.&S.]
Azulay, Heidi J. ....'74 '00 C.966 B.A. L.146 J.D. [[A] DLPiper R.G.C.U.]
Azulay, Ira ....'70 '96 C.477 A.B. L.94 J.D. [Azulay,H.&S.]
Azulay, Y. Judd, (AV) ....'47 '74 C.472 B.S. L.192 J.D. [Azulay,H.&S.] (Pat.)
Azulay, Horn & Seiden, LLC, (AV)
205 N. Michigan Ave., 40th Fl. (Pat.) (⊙Chgo., Palos Hills, IL; New York, NY)
Azulay, Horn & Seiden, LLC, Law Offices of, (AV)
5757 N. Lincoln Avenue, Suite 20 (⊙Chgo., Palos Hills, IL; New York, NY)
Baal, Robert B., (AV) ....'46 '73 C.973 B.S. L.209 LL.D. [Baal&O.]
Baal & O'Connor, (AV) ....221 N. LaSalle St.
Baarsma, William F. ....'70 '03 C.678 B.A. L.597 J.D. [[A] Katten M.R.]
Babbitt, Ellen M., (AV) ....'55 '81 C.880 B.A. L.597 J.D. [Babbitt&M.]
Babbitt, Floyd, (AV) ....'41 '73 C.1106 B.A. L.146 J.D. [FagelHaber]
Babbitt, Robert P. ....'52 '78 C.339 B.S. L.1051 J.D. 6121 N. Northwest Hwy., Ste. 104

Babbitt & Melton LLP, (AV) BB
332 South Michigan Avenue, Suite 710, 60604
Telephone: 312-427-5555 Fax: 312-427-5556
URL: http://www.babbittandmelton.com
Partners of Firm: Ellen M. Babbitt; Bruce W. Melton; Peter G. Land. Associates: Zachary B. Silverstein; Steven J. Winger; Brian C. Boardman.
College and University Law, Labor and Employment Law, Appellate Practice, Counseling, and Complex Commercial Litigation.
See Professional Biographies, CHICAGO, ILLINOIS

Babbo, Heidi L. ....'67 '97 C.475 B.A. L.424 J.D. Off. of Pub. Guard.
Babel, Sabina ....'— '04 C.477 B.A. L.472 J.D. [A Weldon-Linne&V.]
Babetch, Daniel I. ....'— '93 C.378 B.A. L.989 J.D. [Scott,H.&B.]
Babiarz, Richard S. '35 '59
C&L.209 B.S.C., J.D. V.P. & Sr. Assoc. Coun., Ticor Title Ins. Co.
Babych, Douglas W. ....'42 '70 C.424 B.S.B.A. L.146 J.D. 5231 N. Harlem
Bacastow, Daniel J. ....'— '82 C.668 B.A. L.597 J.D. [C Jones D.]
Baccash, Michael F., (AV) ....'48 '73 C.674 A.B. L.145 J.D. [Sarnoff&B.]
Bacchiocchi, Gianluca G. ....'71 '99 C.477 B.A. L.569 J.D. [A Mayer,B.R.&M.]
Bach, Joanne C. ....'66 '00 C.958 L.209 Standard Parking Corp.
Bacher, Michelle ....'77 '02 C&L.424 B.A., J.D. [A Bollinger,R.&G.]
Bachert-Bedford, Sharon K. ....'46 '86 C.719 B.S. L.365 J.D. Asst. State's Atty.
Bachta, Paul R., Attorney at Law '52 '83
C&L.209 B.S., J.D. 1741 W. Chicago Ave., Ste. 2F
Bachtell, Vanessa A. ....'74 '99 C.37 B.A. L.597 J.D. [A Goldberg,K.B.B.R.&M.]
Bachus, Dean C. ....'— '04 C.352 B.A. L.145 J.D. [A Kirkland&E.]
Bacigalupo, Richard J. '49 '75 C.436 A.B. L.273 J.D.
Exec. Dir., Regional Transp. Auth.
Backus, Asilia S. ....'76 '02 C&L.597 B.A., J.D. [A Littler M.]
Bacon, Andrea G. ....'— '79 C.339 B.A. L.597 J.D. [Chapman&C.]
Bacon, J. Douglas, (AV) ....'— '83 C&L.846 B.B.A., J.D. [Latham&W.]
Bacon, Rebecca Weinstein ....'72 '97 C.1494 B.A. L.178 J.D. [Bartlit B.H.P.&S.]
BaCote, Jeffrey E. ....'74 '04 C.228 A.B. L.145 J.D. [A McDermott W.&E.]
Baddley, David W. ....'— '98 C.277 B.S. L.260 J.D. [A Greenberg T.]
Bade, Donna L. ....'52 '98 C.323 B.A. L.365 J.D. [A Sandler,T.&R.]
Badel, Julie, (AV) ....'46 '77 C.999 B.A. L.209 J.D. [Epstein B.&G.]
Baden, Cheri L. ....'— '03 C.121 B.S. L.879 J.D. [A Clausen M.]
Bader, Laura E. ....'66 '97 C.145 B.A. L.846 J.D. [Mayer,B.R.&M.]
Badger, Kyle C. ....'68 '95 C.339 B.A. L.276 J.D. [A McDermott W.&E.]
Badger, Richard I., Jr. '43 '73
C.882 B.A. L.144 J.D. Asst. Dean, Univ. of Chicago Law Sch.
Badgley, Robert A., (AV) ....'65 '91 C.339 B.A. L.145 J.D. [Lord,B.&B.]
Badia-Tavas, M. Mercedes ....'64 '93 10 S. La Salle, Ste. 3500
Badyna, Marek H. ....'62 '03 L.145 J.D. [A Jenner&B.]
Bae, Samuel S. ....'71 '99 C.36 B.A. L.365 J.D. [Bae&B.]
Bae & Bae, P.C. ....39 S. Lasalle Street
Baer, Barbara J. ....'— '84 C.966 B.A. L.209 J.D. Unisys
Baer, Janet S., (AV) ....'— '82 C.966 B.A. L.209 J.D. [Kirkland&E.]
Baer, Jerome I. ....'36 '65 C.659 B.S. L.209 J.D. 123 N. Wacker Dr.
Baer, John R. F., (AV) ....'41 '66 C&L.339 B.A., J.D. [Sonnenschein N.&R.]
Baer, Kurt D. ....'48 '81 C.399 B.A. L.46 J.D. [Clausen M.]
Baer, Steven K. ....'60 '86 C.339 B.S. L.146 J.D. 2602 N. Wayne Ave.‡
Baerson, Steven L., (AV) ....'67 '92 C.347 B.S. L.188 J.D. [Williams&B.]
Baffa, David S. ....'69 '95 C.674 A.B. L.146 J.D. [Seyfarth S.]
Bagan, Grant A. ....'53 '79 C.861 B.A. L.339 J.D. [McDermott W.&E.]
Bagato, Shannon K. ....'76 '02 C.436 B.A. L.365 J.D. Gen. Atty., TTX Company
Bagdon, Bonnie F. ....'51 '86 C.966 B.S. L.273 J.D. Asst. Corp. Coun.
Baggett, Donna M. Banik '52 '83
C.999 B.S. L.209 J.D. Personnel Servs. Dir., S & C Elec. Co.
Baggot, Michael R. ....'69 '96 C.352 B.S. L.365 J.D. 205 W. Randolph St., 19th Fl.
Bagley, Mark R. ....'73 '99 C.309 A.B. L.145 J.D. [A Olson&H.] (See Pat. Sect.)
Bagnall, Scott ....'52 '86 C.209 B.S. L.424 J.D. [S.Bagnall&Assoc.]
Bagnall, Scott, & Associates, P.C. ....100 North LaSalle Street, Suite 1500
Bahcall, Miriam G. ....'58 '85 C.966 B.S. L.145 J.D. [Morgan,L.&B.]
Bahe-Jachna, Ruth A. ....'— '89 C.898 B.A. L.597 J.D. [Greenberg T.]
Bahrmasel, Harry A. ....'10 '34 L.146 LL.B. 123 W. Madison St.
Bahrmasel, Steven J. ....'46 '71 C.339 B.S. L.209 J.D. 123 W. Madison St., Ste. 1500
Baier, Jay A., (AV) ....'32 '57 C.602 A.B. L.597 J.D. [J.A.Baier]
Baier, Jay A., Ltd., (AV) ....200 S. Michigan Ave.
Baig, Michael S. ....'— '99 C&L.477 A.B., J.D. [A Foley&L.]
Bailen, John R., (BV) ....'51 '78 C.339 B.S. L.209 J.D. 120 N. LaSalle St., Ste. 1900
Bailey, Anthony William ....'61 '90 C.188 B.A. L.276 J.D. 222 N. La Salle St.
Bailey, B. Carlton, Jr. ....'41 '70 C&L.469 B.A., J.D. Admin. Law J., S.S.A.
Bailey, Brian T., (BV) ....'64 '89 C.190 B.A. L.424 J.D. [Bailey&B.]
Bailey, Edna S. ....'75 '00 L.339 LL.M. [A Wilson E.M.E.&D.]
Bailey, Gregory S. ....'71 '98 C.174 B.A. L.221 J.D. [A Skadden,A.S.M.&F.]
Bailey, Heather A. ....'70 '01 C.97 B.A. L.365 J.D. [A Connelly S.H.]
Bailey, Holly A. ....'76 '02 C.27 B.A. L.146 J.D. [A Madden,J.M.&S.]
Bailey, Jack Michael ....'55 '83 C.927 B.A. L.146 J.D. Asst. States Atty.
Bailey, James M. ....'34 '58 C&L.424 B.S., J.D. [C Bailey&B.]
Bailey, Julie D. ....'— '98 C.999 B.S. L.221 J.D. [A Latham&W.]
Bailey, Julie Line, (AV) ....'65 '90 C.190 B.A. L.597 J.D. [Bailey&B.]
Bailey, Michael G. ....'— '81 C.813 A.B. L.145 J.D. [Foley&L.]
Bailey, Robert C., (AV) ....'35 '60 C&L.424 J.D. [Bailey B.N.]
Bailey, Robert M. ....'30 '55 C.821 B.A. L.597 J.D. 225 N. Mich. Ave.
Bailey, Robert S., (AV) ....'31 '56 C.918 A.B. L.145 J.D. 53 W. Jackson Blvd.

Bailey & Bailey, (AV)
20 N. Clark Street, Suite 3600, 60602
Telephone: 312-252-2800 Fax: 312-372-0511
URL: http://www.baileyandbaileylaw.com
Brian T. Bailey; Julie Line Bailey. Of Counsel: James M. Bailey.
Civil Litigation and Appellate Practice, Business Litigation, Breach of Contract, Labor and Employment, Employment Discrimination, Sexual Harassment, Wrongful Termination, Civil Rights, Pension and Profit Sharing, Insurance Law, Personal Injury, Automobile Accidents, Libel, Slander and Defamation, Consumer Law Defense.
See Professional Biographies, CHICAGO, ILLINOIS

Bailey Borlack Nadelhoffer LLC, (AV)
135 South La Salle Street, Suite 3950, 60603
Telephone: 312-629-2700 Facsimile: 312-629-0174
Email: bbn@bbn-law.com URL: http://www.bbn-law.com
Robert C. Bailey; Alan R. Borlack; Richard D. Cohler; Sarah Nadelhoffer; Kenneth S. Perlman.
Commercial Real Estate, Landlord and Tenant Law, Real Estate Sales, Real Estate Acquisitions, Real Estate Secured Lending, Real Estate Development, Construction Law, Zoning Law, Corporate Law, Commercial Law, Business Law, Commercial Litigation, Business Litigation, Complex Litigation, Arbitration, Civil Litigation, Alternative Dispute Resolution, Mergers, Acquisitions and Divestitures.
See Professional Biographies, CHICAGO, ILLINOIS

Bailey-Perry, Heather Anne ....'70 '01 C.97 B.A.C. L.365 J.D. 150 S. Wacker Dr.

Baim, Darrin S. ....'70 '98 C.339 B.S. L.424 J.D. [A Field&G.]
Baim, Michael S. ....'65 '90 C.339 B.S. L.146 J.D. 30 N. LaSalle, Ste. 1520
Baim, Stacy A. ....'— '98 C&L.477 B.S.E., J.D. [A Jones D.] (See Pat. Sect.)
Baime, Colleen E. ....'68 '93 C.27 B.A. L.813 J.D. [McDermott W.&E.]
Baime, Kenneth E., (BV) ....'69 '93 C.339 B.S. L.813 J.D. [Baime&B.]
Baime, Stephen G., (AV) ....'43 '66 C&L.339 A.B., J.D. [Baime&B.]
Baime & Baime, (AV) ....200 N. LaSalle St., Ste. 2340
Bain, Alan E. ....'49 '73 C.339 B.A. L.424 J.D. 4500 W. Berteau Ave.
Bain, Douglas G., (AV⓪) '49 '74 C&L.893 B.A., J.D.
(adm. in CA; not adm. in IL) Sr. V.P. & Gen. Coun., The Boeing Co.
Bainbridge, Harry B. ....'25 '56 C.388 B.A. L.365 J.D. [C Pancratz,R.&S.] ⊙‡
Baird, Frederick R., II ....'49 '84 C.347 B.M. L.424 J.D. State Dept. of Employ. Sec.
Baird, James, (AV) ....'43 '68 C.475 B.A. L.966 J.D. [Seyfarth S.]
Baird, Michael S., (AV) '52 '77 C.966 B.A. L.146 J.D.
200 W. Jackson Blvd., Ste. 1050
Baird, Russell M., (AV) ....'16 '41 C.145 A.B. L.309 LL.B. One 1st. National Plz.‡
Bakakos, Peter ....'26 '51 L.365 LL.B. Cir. J.
Bakal, Scott J., (AV) ....'60 '85 C.976 B.S. L.309 J.D. [Neal,G.&E.]
Baker, Bennett J., (BV) ....'54 '78 C.174 B.A. L.365 J.D. [A Goldberg,W.&C.]
Baker, Bruce, (AV) ....'48 '77 C.367 B.A. L.145 J.D. [Baker&M.]
Baker, Bruce Jay, (AV) ....'54 '79 C.339 B.S. L.911 J.D. [C Barack F.K.P.&N.]
Baker, C. Steven '54 '81 C.503 B.A. L.352 J.D.
(adm. in IA; not adm. in IL) Dir., Midwest Region
Baker, Cynthia A. ....'— '90 C.1154 B.G.S. L.477 J.D. [Chapman&C.]
Baker, Daniel W. ....'— '95 C.31 B.A. L.145 J.D. [Chapman&C.]
Baker, Darren C. ....'— '98 C.225 B.A. L.597 J.D. [Schiff H.]
Baker, David A., (AV) ....'54 '79 C.339 B.A. L.424 J.D. [McDermott W.&E.]
Baker, Drew E. ....'49 '75 C.390 A.B. L.365 J.D. [A S.Kahn]
Baker, Eileen E. ....'73 '98 C.339 B.S. L.146 J.D. [A Meckler B.&T.]
Baker, Helen N. ....'— '90 C.103 A.B. L.345 J.D. [Freeborn&P.]
Baker, James E. S., (AV) ....'12 '36 C&L.597 A.B., J.D. One 1st National Plz.‡
Baker, Jenny C. ....'— '01 C.836 B.A. L.477 J.D. [A Latham&W.]
Baker, Jeremy S. ....'76 '02 C.769 B.A. L.861 J.D. [A Cozen O.]
Baker, Katharine K. '62 '90 C.681 B.A. L.145 J.D.
Assoc. Prof. of Law, Chicago Kent College of Law
Baker, Kenneth ....'29 '52 C.339 L.365 LL.B. 211 W. Wacker Dr., 17th Fl.
Baker, Nicholas P. ....'79 '05 C.338 B.A. L.365 J.D. [N.Baker]
Baker, Pamela, (AV) ....'51 '76 C.788 A.B. L.966 J.D. [Sonnenschein N.&R.]
Baker, Richard C. ....'53 '80 C.937 B.A. L.424 J.D. [Mauck&B.]
Baker, Robert M. ....'18 '48 C.966 B.A. L.597 J.D. 79 W. Monroe St.
Baker, Robert S., (AV) ....'56 '81 C.337 B.A. L.879 J.D. [Baker&E.]
Baker, Roger L. ....'53 '81 C.339 B.S. L.365 J.D. Sr. Staff Atty., Amer. Fam. Ins. Grp.
Baker, Sean M. ....'66 '94 C.1042 B.A. L.365 J.D. [Seidman]
Baker, Suzanne Goldstein '53 '78 C.339 B.A. L.146 J.D.
Vice. Pres., Invest. Prop. Exchange Services, Inc.
Baker, Thomas A., (AV) ....'48 '74 C.436 B.A. L.145 J.D. [Vedder,P.K.&K.]
Baker, Warren von Credo, (AV) ....'48 '75 C.659 B.S. L.365 J.D. [Gardner C.&D.]
Baker and Enright, (AV) ....33 W. Jackson Blvd., 3rd Fl.
Baker & McKenzie LLP, (AV)
130 East Randolph Drive (Pat.) (⊙Palo Alto, San Diego, San Fran., CA; Wash., DC; Miami, FL; New York, NY; Dallas, Hous., TX; Calgary, AB; Toronto, ON; Melbourne, Victoria, Sydney, New South Wales, Australia; Vienna, Austria; Baku, Azerbaijan; Antwerp, Brussels, Belgium; Brasilia, Porto Alegre, Rio de Janeiro, Sao Paulo, Brazil; Beijing, Hong Kong, Shanghai, China; Prague, Czech Republic; Cairo, Egypt; London, England; Paris, France; Berlin, Dusseldorf, Frankfurt/Main, Munich, Germany; Budapest, Hungary; Jakarta, Indonesia; Bologna, Milan, Rome, Italy; Tokyo, Japan; Almaty, Kazakhstan; Kuala Lumpur, Malaysia; Amsterdam, Netherlands; Metro Manila, Philippines; Warsaw, Poland; Moscow, St. Petersburg, Russia; Riyadh, Saudi Arabia; Singapore, Singapore; Barcelona, Madrid, Spain; Stockholm, Sweden; Geneva, Zurich, Switzerland; Taipei, Taiwan; Bangkok, Thailand; Kyiv (Kiev),Ukraine;Hanoi,Ho Chi Minh City,Vietnam)
Baker, Nicholas ....30 N. LaSalle, Ste. 2340
Bakke, Ilya A. ....'— '02 C.938 B.A. L.339 J.D. [A Barnes,R.&C.]
Bakker, Jeffrey J. ....'68 '97 C.504 B.A. L.339 J.D. [Neal,G.&E.]
Balac, Drew ....'69 '97 C.145 B.A. L.146 J.D. [A Weldon-Linne&V.]
Balachandran, Madhavaro ....'38 '73 C.999 B.A. L.365 J.D. 207 E. Ohio St., PMB 120‡
Balan, Violeta I. ....'— '04 C.393 B.A. L.365 J.D. [A Mayer,B.R.&M.]
Balanoff, M. Jane ....'54 '83 C.145 B.A. L.209 J.D. 10100 S. Ewing Ave.
Balanoff, Miriam D. ....'— '63 C&L.145 B.A., J.D. 10101 Ewing Ave.
Balanoff, Robert ....'56 '82 L.209 J.D. 10100 Ewing Ave.
Balasa, Donald A. '52 '77 C&L.597 B.A., J.D.
Exec. Dir. & Legal Coun., Amer. Assn. of Med. Assts.
Balassa, Gabor ....'— '97 C&L.178 B.A., J.D. [Kirkland&E.]
Balasubramanian, Vandhana ....'72 '00 C.918 B.A. L.347 J.D. 10 South Dearborn St.
Balchunas, Z. John ....'56 '83 C.339 B.A. L.146 J.D. 150 S. Wacker Dr.
Balder, Linnea M. ....'38 '72 C.597 B.S. L.365 J.D. Prob. Admr.
Baldi, Joseph A., (BV) ....'49 '77 C.927 B.A. L.209 J.D. [J.A.Baldi&Assoc.]

Baldi, Joseph A., & Associates, P.C., (BV)
19 South LaSalle Street Suite 1500, 60603
Telephone: 312-726-8150 Fax: 312-332-4629
Email: jabaldi@ameritech.net
Joseph A. Baldi;—Elizabeth C. Berg; Donna B. Wallace.
Bankruptcy, Insolvency, Creditors' Rights, Workouts.
See Professional Biographies, CHICAGO, ILLINOIS

Baldini-Potermin, Maria T. ....'— '97 C.201 B.A. L.494 J.D. [A S.D.Pollock&Assoc.]
Baldwin, Alison Jameen ....'70 '00 C.679 B.S. L.146 J.D. [McDonnell B.H.&B.]
Baldwin, Keith Shaylan ....'73 '01 C.209 B.A. L.424 J.D. [A Levin G.]
Baldwin, Kevin W. ....'77 '02 C.339 B.S. L.424 J.D. 812 N. Dearborn St.
Baldwin, Robert D. ....'33 '63 C.388 A.B. L.339 J.D. Asst. V.P., Chicago Title & Tr. Co.
Baldwin, Sharon ....'44 '75 C.475 B.A. L.145 J.D. Asst. Corp. Coun., City Law Dept.
Baldwin, Shaun McParland, (AV) ....'54 '80 C.589 B.S. L.365 J.D. [Tressler,S.M.&P.]
Balesteri, Joseph W., (AV) ....'70 '95 C.347 B.S. L.209 J.D. [A Power R.&S.]
Balesteri, Peggy M. ....'71 '96 C.475 B.A. L.209 J.D. [Winston&S.]
Balfour, Michelle B. ....'74 '01 C.579 B.A. L.209 J.D. [A Merlo K.B.&G.]
Balice, Anthony N. ....'73 '00 C.339 B.A. L.209 J.D. [A Merlo K.B.&G.]
Baliunas, Kathleen Bowers, (AV) ....'45 '73 C.424 B.S. L.209 J.D. 9054 S. Bell Ave.
Balkin, Charles R., (AV) '41 '66
C.339 B.S. L.209 LL.B. 111 West Washington St, Ste. 1505
Balko, John J. '26 '52 C.339 L.209 J.D.
Sr. V.P. & Tr. Offr., Chicago City Bk. & Tr. Co.
Ball, Frederick R. ....'64 '96 C.174 B.A. L.188 J.D. [Duane M.]
Ball, James T., (BV) ....'56 '82 C.608 B.S. L.930 J.D. 120 S. LaSalle St., Ste. 1500
Ball, John R. '44 '71 C.1365 A.B. L.228 J.D.
(adm. in NC; not adm. in IL) 2100 W. Harrison St.

Ball, Joseph A. .... '71 '97 C.108 B.A. L.904 J.D. 180 N. LaSalle Street
Ballantine, Frank D., (AV) ....'— '85 C.311 B.A. L.477 J.D. [Sachnoff&W.]
Ballard, David T. .... '— '01 L.146 J.D. [[A] Barnes&T.]
Ballard, Mark J., (BV) ....'58 '83 C&L.424 A.B., J.D. 39 S. LaSalle St.
Ballard, Rena A. ....'60 '96 C.206 B.M. L.209 J.D. [[A] Pretzel&S.]
Ballard, Shelley B. .... '57 '87 C.880 B.S. L.597 J.D. [Ballard,D.B.&H.]
Ballard, Desai, Bush-Joseph & Horwich .... 221 N. LaSalle St., Ste. 1136
Ballinger, J. David ....'70 '95 C.112 B.A. L.209 J.D. [[A] Horwood M.&B.]
Ballis, Jon A. .... '— '94 C.401 B.A. L.1565 J.D. [Kirkland&E.]
Ballmer, Jody A. ....'65 '92 C.916 B.S. L.494 J.D. [Littler M.]
Ballou, Carmin D. ....'73 '02 C.937 L.190 J.D. [[A] Skadden,A.S.M.&F.]
Balog, James P., (AV) ....'— '83 C.339 B.S. L.365 J.D. [O'Hagan,S.&A.]
Balonick, Barney H. ....'69 '97 C.98 B.S. L.146 J.D. 3rd Fl, 415 N Lasalle St
Balonick, Bruce H., (AV) ....'— '74 C.208 B.S.B.A. L.146 J.D. [Arnstein&L.]
Balonick, Farrel J. ....'37 '63 C.1016 B.S.B.A. L.146 LL.B. [Balonick&B.]
Balonick & Bloch .... 221 N. LaSalle St.
Balough, Richard C., (AV) '47 '76
C.347 A.B. L.365 J.D. 53 West Jackson Boulevard, Suite 956
Balow, Geraldine M. ....'55 '85 C.530 B.A. L.146 J.D. [[A] Maciorowski,S.&U.]
Balsam, Hugh S. .... '59 '95 C.399 B.A. L.365 J.D. [Lord,B.&B.]
Balsley-Cross, Margaret B. '49 '86
C.966 B.A. L.597 J.D. Asst. Gen. Coun., Exelon Bus. Servs. Co.
Balson, Ronald H. ....'44 '72 C.861 B.A. L.209 J.D. [Hill G.&B.]
Baltz, Thomas E. .... '62 '89 C&L.347 B.A., J.D. [[A] N.I.Grey]
Baluk, Robert R. ....'57 '85 C.927 B.B. L.365 Gen. Coun., Guarantee Tr. Life Ins. Co.
Balys, Daniel D. ....'64 '98 C.573 B.A. L.209 J.D. Equity Off. Props. Trust
Bambrick, J. Gerard, Jr. ....'45 '72 C&L.602 B.A., J.D. [Nyhan,P.B.K.&L.]
Banasek, Tammera E. ....'— '93 C.589 B.A. L.365 J.D. [[A] Alholm,M.K.H.&O.]
Banasik, Kevin A. ....'— '96 C.436 B.A. L.309 J.D. [Winston&S.]
Banciu, Louis James .... '43 '70 C.477 B.S.Ch.E. L.213 J.D. [© Donohue B.M.&S.]
Bandes, Corey .... '60 '86 C.1044 B.A. L.365 J.D. 19 S. LaSalle Street, Suite 707
Banghart, Steven F., (AV) ....'52 '83 C.475 B.A. L.1187 J.D. [Katten M.R.]
Bang-Thompson, Hyeyoung ....'72 '00 C.145 B.A. L.101 J.D. Natl. Labor Rel. Bd.
Bangura, Lucia Paula ....'67 '01 C.597 B.S. L.365 J.D. Dept. of Homeland Sec.
Baniak, Michael H., (AV) '55 '80 C.201 B.S. L.1119 J.D.
[Baniak P.&G.] (See Pat. Sect.)

Baniak Pine & Gannon, (AV) [BB]
150 North Wacker Drive, Suite 1200, 60606
Telephone: 312-673-0360 Fax: 312-673-0361
URL: http://www.bpglaw.com
Members of Firm: Michael H. Baniak; Jeffrey A. Pine; Michael D. Gannon; Christina L. Brown; Charles C. Valauskas; Charles C. Kinne. Associates: Allison Dudley; Christopher E. Haigh (Not admitted in IL); Andrew F. Pratt; Anuj K. Wadhwa; William F. Ward, III. Counsel: Gary E. Hood.
Intellectual Property, Patent, Trademark, Copyright and Trade Secret Law, Litigation, Licensing.
See Professional Biographies, CHICAGO, ILLINOIS

Baniassadi, Mohammad ....'58 '91 C.999 L.L.B. L.597 J.D. 180 N. LaSalle St.
Banich, Terence G., II ....'74 '99 C.1049 B.A. L.424 J.D. [[A] Jenner&B.]
Baniewicz, Evelyn G. ....'49 '84 C.209 B.A. L.597 J.D. 69 W. Washington St., 15th Fl.
Bank, John S. ......'59 '84 C.477 B.B.A. L.1068 J.D. Exec. V.P., Phoenix Elec. Mfg. Co.
Bank, Jonathan F., (AV①) '43 '68 C.623 B.B.A. L.190 J.D.
(adm. in NE; not adm. in IL) [© Lord,B.&B.] (⊙L.A., CA)
Bankendorf, Elliott C. ....'45 '69 C.209 B.S.C. L.339 J.D. [Welsh&K.]
Banks, Joseph J. ....'52 '84 C.209 B.A. L.365 J.D. Corp. Coun., Crown Products, Inc.
Banks, Samuel V. P., (AV) ....'35 '61 L.209 J.D. 221 N. LaSalle St., Rm. 3800
Banks, Sheldon L., (AV) ......'40 '65 C.1016 B.S.B.A. L.365 J.D. 77 W. Washington St.

Banks-Golub, Mark A. '61 '89 C.393 B.A. L.146 J.D.
10 South La Salle Street Suite 3500, 60603-1025
Telephone: 312-781-9310 Fax: 312-781-9312
Email: mark.banks-golub@banks-golub.com URL: http://www.banks-golub.com
Business Law, Real Estate, Taxation, Trusts and Estates, Wills and Probate.
See Professional Biographies, CHICAGO, ILLINOIS

Banner, Mark T., (AV) .....'— '79 C.679 B.A. L.365 J.D. [Banner&W.] (See Pat. Sect.)

Banner & Witcoff, Ltd., (AV)
Established In 1920 - Predecessor Parent
Ten South Wacker Drive, Suite 3000, 60606-7407 ⊙
Telephone: 312-463-5000 Facsimile: 312-463-5001
Email: info@bannerwitcoff.com URL: http://www.bannerwitcoff.com
Mark T. Banner; Matthew P. Becker; Joseph J. Berghammer; Aimee Boss Kolz; Scott A. Burow; James V. Callahan; Marc S. Cooperman; Allen E. Hoover; Timothy C. Meece; Charles Miller; Janice V. Mitrius; Jon O. Nelson; Binal J. Patel; Thomas K. Pratt; Christopher J. Renk; Robert H. Resis; Rebecca P. Rokos; Charles W. Shifley; Jason Shull; Richard Stockton; J. Pieter van Es. Of Counsel: Julie Brown Ackerman; Sheldon W. Witcoff. Associates: William J. Allen; Justin Busch; Jeffrey M. Cox; Ted L. Field; Shawn P. Gorman; Michael J. Harris; Wendell W. Harris; William J. Klein; Erik S. Maurer; Phoebe K. Phillips.
Intellectual Property including Procurement of Patents, Trademarks, Copyrights, Trade Secrets, Counseling & Opinions, Unfair Competition, Interferences, Licensing, Antitrust and International Trade Matters. Litigation including Trials and Appeals in Federal and State Courts and International Trade Commission.
Washington, D.C. Office: 1001 G Street, N.W., Suite 1100. Telephone: 202-824-3000. Facsimile: 202-824-3001.
Boston, Massachusetts Office: 28 State Street, 28th Floor. Telephone: 617-720-9600. Fax: 617-720-9601.
Portland, Oregon Office: 601 SW Second Avenue, Suite 1900. Telephone: 503-425-6800. Fax: 503-425-6801.
See Professional Biographies, CHICAGO, ILLINOIS

Bannister, Leroy W., Jr. .... '48 '73 C.475 B.A. L.893 J.D. 6815 S. Paxton Ave., Unit A
Bannister, Shelley A. ....'52 '78 C.927 B.A. L.424 J.D. Prof., Northeastern Ill. Univ.
Bannon, Christopher J. ....'62 '87 C.339 B.A. L.424 J.D. [Aronberg G.D.&G.]
Bannon, John A. ....'— '91 C.893 B.A. L.145 J.D. [Schiff H.]
Banoff, Sheldon I., (P.C.), (AV) ....'49 '74 C.339 B.S. L.145 J.D. [Katten M.R.]
Banovetz, Mark T. .... '67 '92 C.589 B.A. L.209 J.D. [Tressler,S.M.&P.]
Baptista, Robert C., Jr., (AV) .... '48 '82 C.937 B.A. L.339 J.D. [Mayer,B.R.&M.]
Barack, Peter J., (AV) ....'43 '70 C.674 A.B. L.309 J.D. [Barack F.K.P.&N.]

Barack Ferrazzano Kirschbaum Perlman & Nagelberg LLP, (AV)
Suite 2700, 333 West Wacker Drive, 60606
Telephone: 312-984-3100 Telecopier: 312-984-3150 Cable: "BFKLAW"
URL: http://www.bfkpn.com
Partners of Firm: Douglas W. Anderson; Peter J. Barack; William J. Barrett; Mark J. Beaubien; Mark S. Bernstein; Sarah M. Bernstein; Suzanne Bessette-Smith; Edwin S. del Hierro; Daniel L. Dominguez; Dennis A. Ferrazzano; John E. Freechack; David E. Gordon; Marc M. Jacobs; Howard J. Kirschbaum; Amy Listick Koenig; Alexander Lourie; Lynne D. Mapes-Riordan; Malcolm McCaleb, Jr.; Elliot I. Molk; David H. Nadoff; Howard A. Nagelberg; Christine K. Nichols; Richard S. Nikchevich; Donald L. Norman, Jr.; Randall L. Oyler; Thomas H. Page; Charles H. Perlman; W. Scott Porterfield; Julie K. Rademaker; Ray G. Rezner; John W. Roberts; Kimberly J. Robinson; Bryan Segal; David R. Selmer; Jeffrey S. Shamberg; Robert E. Shapiro; Wendi E. Sloane; Karol K. Sparks (Not admitted in IL); Katherine S. Sprenger; Gretchen Anne Trofa; William E. Turner II; James R. Vogler; Dennis R. Wendte;—Adedapo A. Adedeji; Jeremy Todd Bunnow; Karyn L. Doerfler; Brett Feinberg; Robert M. Fleetwood; Annaliese F. Fleming; John M. Geiringer; T. Randall

(This Listing Continued)

Barack Ferrazzano Kirschbaum Perlman & Nagelberg LLP (Continued)
Graeb; Andrew R. Grossmann; Michael R. Hall; Randy J. Heinig; Jackson Hwu; Shermin Izadpanah; Peter B. Jurgeleit; Myriam Benhamou Kaplan; Joseph D. Lambert; Heather J. Macklin; Bradley W. Marzullo; George R. Mesires; Gillian E. Munitz (Not admitted in IL); Jessica M. Perez (Not admitted in IL); Charles E. Picton III; Jeffrey S. Rinkov; J.D. Rubin; Janelle M. Savage; Andrea L. Sill; Roger H. Stetson; Catherine M. Thomson; Judith A. Van Hoose; Melissa M. Villalobos; David M. Wiese; Steven J. Yatvin. Of Counsel: Bruce Jay Baker; Gayle Yeatman Fisher; Joshua S. Kanter; Judith K. Muncy; Beth S. Rubin.
Real Estate, Corporate, Banking, Savings and Loan, Financial Services, International Business, Secured Lending, Securities, Employee Benefits and Executive Compensation, Litigation, Tax and Proprietary Rights.
See Professional Biographies, CHICAGO, ILLINOIS

Barakat, Dean ....'73 '98 C.910 B.A. L.209 J.D. [[A] Nyhan,P.B.K.&L.]
Baran, Cynthia Storer '64 '95 C.210 B.A. L.1119 J.D.
Sr. Atty., Midwest Reg. Off., U.S. Secs. & Exch. Comm.
Baran, Jeralyn H. .... '62 '90 C.436 B.A. L.339 J.D. [Chuhak&T.]
Baran, William B. '61 '86 C.477 B.A. L.904 J.D.
V.P.- Compliance Coun., Everen Securities, Inc.
Barancik, Alysa M. .... '— '00 C.188 B.S. L.424 J.D. [[A] Seyfarth S.]
Baranyk, Alexandra D. .... '— '01 C.1016 B.A. L.210 J.D. 55 E. Monroe, Ste. 3484
Baratta, Joseph ....'69 '95 C.209 B.A. L.365 J.D. Executives' Club of Chicago
Baratta, Robert M., Jr. ....'— '90 C&L.276 A.B., J.D. [Freeborn&P.]
Baraz, Marshall J. ....'24 '50 L.146 J.D 25 E. Washington St.
Barba, Robert A. ....'66 '92 C.174 B.A. L.146 J.D. 100 W. Randolph St., 12th Fl.
Barbahen, Paul W. ....'58 '84 C.209 B.S.C. L.365 J.D. 151 N. Michigan Ave., Ste. 816
Barbakoff, Lee R., (AV) ....'46 '72 C.339 B.S. L.209 J.D. [L.R.Barbakoff&Assoc.]
Barbakoff, Lee R., & Associates, P.C., (AV) ....Suite 200, One West Superior
Barber, Christopher J., (AV) .... '— '86 C.608 B.S.B.A. L.500 J.D. [Gardner C.&D.]
Barber, James S., (AV) ....'46 '77 C&L.209 B.A., J.D. [Clausen M.]
Barber, Robert W. ....'44 '76 C.1016 B.A. L.146 J.D. Asst. Corp. Coun.
Barber, Vaughn J. ....'— '81 L.209 J.D. City Bd. of Educ.
Barbosa, Raymond ....'54 '80 C.262 B.A. L.569 J.D. [Barbosa] & [© Huff&G.]
Barbosa Law Group, P.C. ....10 South LaSalle Street, Suite 3500
Barclay, Jeffrey D. .... '64 '96 C.424 B.A. L.209 J.D. [[A] Tressler,S.M.&P.]
Barclay, Lester L. ....'59 '85 C.604 A.B. L.930 J.D. 39 S. LaSalle St.
Bardelas, Emily J. ....'— '04 C.347 B.A. L.957 J.D. [[A] Querrey&H.]
Barden, Larry A., (AV) ....'56 '82 C.473 B.S. L.902 J.D. [Sidley A.B.&W.]
Bardo, Stacy M. ....'75 '00 C.597 B.S. L.424 J.D. [Consumer,A.]
Bardwell, Marjorie R. '52 '76 C.999 B.A. L.436 J.D.
V.P. & Sr. Underwriting Coun., Chicago Title Ins. Co.
Bareck, Philip, (BV) ....'66 '91 C.339 B.S. L.46 J.D. 77 W. Washington St., 20th Fl.
Barella, Derek G. ....'69 '94 C.63 B.S. L.347 J.D. [Winston&S.]
Barengolts, Phillip ....'76 '01 C.103 Sc.B. L.309 J.D. [[A] Pattishall,M.N.H.&G.]
Barezky, Bonny S. '46 '72 C&L.597 B.S.B.A., J.D.
Chf. U.S. Admin. Law J., Off. of Hearings & App.
Barezky, Lawrence R., (AV) '— '63
C.1016 B.S.B.A. L.597 J.D. [Beermann S.W.B.B.G.&L.] ⊙
Bargfrede, Charles Allen ....'74 '99 C&L.846 B.A., J.D. Corp. Coun., Orbitz LLC
Bargher, Craig M. ....'68 '93 C.103 A.B. L.209 J.D. [[A] Chittenden,M.&N.]
Bargiel, Paul J., (AV) .... '43 '72 C.1151 B.A. L.365 J.D. [P.J.Bargiel]

Bargiel, Paul J., P.C., (AV)
100 West Monroe, Suite 902, 60603
Telephone: 312-263-0888 Fax: 312-236-1065
Email: monsuite@aol.com
Paul J. Bargiel.
General Civil Appellate Practice, Family, Divorce, Child Custody, Commercial, Personal Injury and Medical Malpractice.
See Professional Biographies, CHICAGO, ILLINOIS

Bargione, Christopher, (AV) ....'58 '83 C.724 B.A. L.365 J.D. [Collins&B.]
Barhorst, Stacie E. .... '70 '00 C.350 B.M. L.221 J.D. [Barhorst&Assoc.]
Barhorst & Associates, P.C. ....2000 West Haddon, Suite 210
Barich, Joseph M. '72 '98 C.339 B.S.E.E. L.93 J.D.
[McAndrews,H.&M.] (See Pat. Sect.)
Barich, Valerie C. ....'— '00 C.338 B.S. L.209 J.D. [[A] Horwitz,H.&Assoc.]
Barinholtz, Alan, (AV) ....'51 '80 C.608 B.A. L.424 J.D. [A.Barinholtz]
Barinholtz, Mark H. .... '46 '80 C.966 B.A. L.424 J.D. [Barinholtz,M.H.]
Barinholtz, Alan, P.C., Law Offices of, (AV) .... 55 West Monroe Street Suite 3330

Barinholtz, Mark H., P.C.
Suite 3330, 55 West Monroe Street, 60603
Telephone: 312-977-0121 FAX: 312-977-0733
URL: http://www.mhbpc.com
Mark H. Barinholtz.
General Civil Litigation. Business, Corporate and Commercial Law. Arts and Entertainment including Copyright, Trademark, Communications and Related Matters.

Barish, David M., (AV) ....'57 '83 C.597 B.S. L.209 J.D. [Katz,F.E.E.&J.]
Barker, Derek M. ....'65 '91 C.424 B.S. L.365 J.D. [[A] Stellato&S.]
Barker, Justin A. ....'— '01 C&L.101 B.A., J.D. [[A] Kirkland&E.]
Barker, Patricia J., (AV) ....'— '89 C.720 B.A. L.424 J.D. [Anderson,R.]
Barker, Stephanie ....'— '04 C.197 A.B. L.477 J.D. [[A] Latham&W.]
Barker, William T., (AV) ....'47 '75 C.475 B.A. L.1066 J.D. [Sonnenschein N.&R.]
Barkidjija, John M. '63 '88 C.178 B.A. L.569 J.D.
(adm. in NY; not adm. in IL) First V.P., Corus Bank, N.A.
Barkley, Alison, (AV) ....'49 '77 C.339 B.S. L.209 J.D. [Schuyler,R.&Z.] ⊙
Barkoff, Aaron F. '71 '02 C.399 B.A. L.145 J.D.
[[A] McDonnell B.H.&B.] (See Pat. Sect.)
Barliant, Ronald ....'45 '69 C.1016 B.A. L.813 J.D. [Goldberg,K.B.B.R.&M.]
Barloga, Susanne Michele ....'75 '00 C.136 B.S. L.209 J.D. State's Atty. Off.
Barlow, Aaron A., (AV) ....'63 '89 C.453 B.S.Ch.E. L.145 J.D. [Jenner&B.] (Pat.)
Barlow, John C. '56 '84
C.234 B.S. L.365 J.D. Assoc. V.P., NASD Dispute Resolution, Inc.

Barlow, Kobata & Denis
222 S. Riverside Plaza, 60606 ⊙
Telephone: 312-648-5570 Fax: 312-648-9697
Email: bkdlaw@bkd-law.com
Members of Firm: Marty Denis; Daniel R. Madock. Associate: Bethany A. Hilbert. Of Counsel: Lawrence M. Cohen.
Management Labor, Employment Discrimination Litigation.
Los Angeles, California Office: 2049 Century Park East, Suite 2270, 90067. Telephone: 310-277-7556. Fax: 310-277-2982.
See Professional Biographies, CHICAGO, ILLINOIS

Barna, Martin F. ....'80 '05 C.228 A.B. L.477 J.D. [[A] Gardner C.&D.]
Barnard, Morton John, (AV) .... '05 '27 C&L.145 Ph.B., J.D. 208 South LaSalle Street
Barnard, Ronald L., (BV) ....'35 '58 C.339 L.597 J.D. [Barnard&M.]
Barnard & McCollam, Ltd., (BV) .... 33 N. LaSalle St.
Barner, Rachel F. ....'70 '98 C.145 A.B. L.209 J.D. [[A] Littler M.]

Barner, Sharon R., (AV) ... '— '82 C.823 B.S.B.A. L.477 J.D. [Foley&L.]
Barnes, Angela E. L. ... '— '94 C.914 B.A. L.178 J.D. [Barnes&B.]
Barnes, Earl J., (AV) ... '35 '61 C&L.209 B.A., J.D. [Barnes&B.]
Barnes, Earl J., II, (BV) ... '64 '89 C.393 B.A. L.477 J.D. [Ⓒ Gardner C.&D.]
Barnes, James G., (AV) ... '40 '67 C.976 B.A. L.477 J.D. [Ⓒ Baker&M.]
Barnes, James T. ... '63 '93 C.30 B.A. L.215 J.D. 431 S. Dearborn St., Ste. 506
Barnes, Sara K. ... '— '04 C.475 B.A. L.209 J.D. [Ⓐ Bollinger,R.&G.]
Barnes, Timothy A. ... '67 '96 C.473 B.A. L.608 J.D. [Ⓒ LeBoeuf,L.G.&M.]
Barnes, William M., Jr. ... '69 '99 C&L.597 B.A., J.D. [Ⓐ Wildman,H.A.&D.]
Barnes & Barnes, (AV) ... 401 N. Michigan Ave., Ste. 775

Barnes, Richardson & Colburn, (AV)
303 East Wacker Drive Suite 1100, 60601 ⊙
Telephone: 312-565-2000 Facsimile: 312-565-1782
Email: barnes@brc-chi.com URL: http://www.barnesrichardson.com
Resident Members of Firm: Robert E. Burke; Donald J. Unger; Brian F. Walsh; Kazumune V. Kano; Lawrence M. Friedman; David G. Forgue. Non-Resident Members of Firm: James S. O'Kelly (N.Y.); Matthew T. McGrath (D.C.); Sandra Liss Friedman (N.Y.); Frederic D. Van Arnam, Jr. (N.Y.); Alan Goggins (N.Y.). Resident Associates: Carolyn D. Amadon; Ilya A. Bakke; Louisa Vassileva Carney; Diane A. MacDonald; Christine H. Martinez; William J. Murphy; Nikolay A. Ouzounov.
Customs and International Trade Law, Administrative Law. General Federal Litigation and Appellate Practice.
New York, New York Office: 475 Park Avenue South, 10016. Telephone: 212-725-0200.
Washington, D.C. Office: 1420 New York Avenue, N.W., Suite 700, 20005. Telephone: 202-628-4700.

See Professional Biographies, CHICAGO, ILLINOIS

Barnes & Thornburg LLP, (AV) [BR]
One North Wacker Drive, Suite 4400, 60606-2833 ⊙
Telephone: 312-357-1313 FAX: 312-759-5646
URL: http://www.btlaw.com
Partners: Sidney G. Saltz; Larry D. Blust; Dennis M. McWilliams; Lee T. Polk; William M. Lee, Jr.; Paula Cozzi Goedert; Glenn W. Ohlson; David C. Brezina; William M. McErlean; David G. Edwards; Daniel P. Albers; Deborah L. Thorne; Charles J. Schultz; Donald J. McNeil; Thomas J. Donovan; Jeffrey R. Gray; Mark E. Rust; Bradley B. Falkof; Alice O. Martin; Grant H. Peters; Fredric P. Andes; Mari Yamamoto Regnier; Timothy J. Engling; James B. Conte; Howard B. Rockman; Peter J. Shakula; Scott T. Longman; Carolyn S. Hesse; Melissa A. Vallone; Marc S. Silver; David R. Schenk. Of Counsel: Stephen M. Fatum; Michael J. Mueller; Erika K. Powers; Norma W. Zeitler; Jason M. Cain; Gerald S. Geren; Darren C. Collier; John W. Morse; Mark J. McAndrew. Associates: Jonathan P. Froemel; Ellen L. Luepke; Mark A. Hagedorn; Mark J. Nahnsen; Charla L. Hausler; Kevin C. Driscoll, Jr.; Vladimir Khodosh; David T. Ballard; Kelly M. Bellinger; Brad E. Rago; Jeremy B. Lewin; Wesley W. Broquard; Evan J. Haim; Marc E. Darnell; Pascale J. Bishop; John P. Wappel; James E. Michel; Douglas M. Oldham.
Acquisitions and Divestitures, Ad Valorem Tax, Administrative Law, Affirmative Action, Agriculture Law, Americans with Disabilities Act, Antidumping, Antitrust, Antitrust and Trade Regulation, Appellate Practice, Attorney Grievances, Automotive Warranty Law, Aviation and Aerospace, Aviation Law, Banking Law, Banking Regulations, Bankruptcy, Bankruptcy Reorganization, Banks and Banking, Biochemical Patents, Biomedical Products Liability, Biomedical Technology, Biotechnology Patent Prosecution, Bond Law, Brain Injury, Breach of Warranty, Brown Fields Redevelopment, Business Immigration, Business Law, Business Litigation, Business Planning, Business Regulatory and Administrative, Business Start-ups, Business Succession Planning, Business Taxation, Business Torts, Business Transactions, Business Transfers, Buying and Selling of Businesses, Cable TV, Cargo Claims, Charitable Trusts and Foundations, Chemical Intellectual Property, Chemical Patent Prosecution, Chemical Patents, Chemical Products Liability, Civil Appeals, Civil Litigation, Civil Practice, Civil RICO, Class Action Defense, Clean Air Act, Clean Water Act, Closely Held Business Estate Planning, Closely Held Businesses, Closely Held Business Law, Closely Held Corporations, Collective Bargaining, Commercial Bankruptcy, Commercial Finance Law, Commercial Law, Commercial Leasing and Financing, Commercial Litigation, Commercial Conveyancing, Commercial Real Estate, Commercial Real Estate Acquisition, Commercial Real Estate Development, Commercial Real Estate Finance, Commercial Transactions, Commodities Fraud, Communications and Media, Complex Commercial Litigation, Complex Litigation, Computer and Software Patents, Computer Law, Computers and Software, Conflicts of Interest, Construction Labor Law, Construction Law, Consumer Credit, Contract Litigation, Cooperatives, Copyrights, Corporate Finance, Corporate Formation, Corporate Law, Corporate Taxation, Corporate Tax Planning, Countervailing Duties, Covenants Not To Compete, Creditors Rights, Creditors Rights in Bankruptcy, Criminal Defense, Criminal Law, Criminal Tax Audits, Customs Law, Dealer and Distributor Termination, Debt and Equity Finance, Decedents Estates, Defense Litigation, Design Patents, Disability Insurance Defense, Discrimination, Distribution, Drug and Medical Device Defense, Economic Development, Education Law, Elder Law, Election, Campaign and Political Law, Electric Power, Electric Utilities, Electrical Intellectual Property, Electrical Patents, Electro-mechanical Patents, Electronic Commerce, Electronic Patents, Eminent Domain, Employee Benefits, Employee Stock Ownership Plans, Employment Defense, Employment Discrimination, Employment Law, Employment Litigation, Energy, Energy Contracts, Energy Regulation, Environmental Administrative Law, Environmental Cleanup, Environmental Compliance, Environmental Criminal Defense, Environmental Law, Environmental Litigation, Environmental Permitting, Environmental Real Estate, Environmental Regulation, Environmental Risk Management, Equal Employment Opportunity Law, ERISA Litigation, Estate Administration, Estate and Gift Taxation, Estate Planning, Estate Planning and Taxation, Estate Planning and Administration, Estate Planning and Probate, Estate Planning for Parents of Handicapped Children, Estate Planning for Unmarried Individuals, Executive Compensation, Executive Severance Contracts, Export Regulation, Fair Employment Practices, Family and Medical Leave Act, Family Business Successions, Family Wealth Transfer, Federal and State Administrative Regulatory Practice, Federal and State Legislative Practice, Federal Civil Litigation, Federal Civil Practice, Federal Criminal Law, Federal Estate and Gift Taxation, Federal Litigation, Federal Tax Controversies, Federal Taxation, Fiduciary Income Tax, Finance, Financial Transactions, First Party Insurance, Foreign Investment in the United States, Freight Claims, Freight Loss and Damage, Gaming Law, Gaming Licensing, Gas Utilities, General Litigation, Government, Government Affairs, Government Agency Practice, Government Contracts, Government Investigations, Government Relations, Groundwater Contamination, Hazardous Materials and Substances, Hazardous Waste, Hazardous Waste Liability, Head Injury, Health Care, Health Care Corporate Law, Health Care Contracts, Health Care Fraud, Health Care Licensing, Health Care Litigation, Health Care Mergers and Acquisitions, Health Care Regulation, Health Care Reimbursement, Health Law, Heavy Equipment Products Liability, Immigration Law, Industrial Revenue Bond Law, Inheritance Tax, Initial Public Offerings, Insurance, Insurance Bad Faith, Insurance Coverage, Insurance Litigation, Insurance Regulation, Integrated Health Care Delivery Systems, Intellectual Property, Intellectual Property General Prosecution, Intellectual Property Infringement, Intellectual Property Licensing, Intellectual Property Litigation, Intellectual Property Procurement, Intellectual Property Protection, Intellectual Property Rights, International Business Law, International Intellectual Property, International Law, International Patents, International Trade, International Transportation Law, Internet Law, Internet Trademark Law, Joint Ventures, Labor and Employment, Labor Arbitration, Labor Law, Labor Relations, Land Use, Lease Law, Leasing, Legal Ethics and Professional Responsibility, Legal Malpractice Defense, Legislative Practice, Licensing, Life Insurance Defense, Limited Liability Company Law, Limited Partnerships, Liquor Licensing, Litigation, Loans, Lobbying, Local Government Law, Logistics, Long Term Care, Managed Care, Managed Care Contracts, Management Employment Law, Management Labor Law, Manufacturers Liability, Maritime Regulations, Mechanical Intellectual Property, Mechanical Patents, Media Law, Mediation, Medical Antitrust, Medical Intellectual Property, Medical Patents, Mental Health Law, Mergers, Acquisitions and Divestitures, Mergers and Acquisitions, Mineral Taxation, Molecular Biology Patents, Motor Carrier Law, Motor Carrier Regulation, Multi-Employer Pensions, Municipal Bonds, Municipal Bonds Taxation, Municipal Finance, Municipal Law, Municipal Leasing, Municipal Redevelopment, Municipal Securities, Municipal Taxation, National Labor Relations Act, Neurolaw, Nonprofit and Charitable Organizations, Nonprofit Organizations Law, North American Free Trade Agreement, Occupational Safety and Health, OSHA, Partnership Law, Partnership Taxation, Patent Infringement, Patent Interference Practice, Patent Litigation, Patent Prosecution, Patents, PCT Legal Export, Personal Injury, Personal Injury Defense, Pesticide Litigation, Pharmaceutical Intellectual Property, Pharmaceutical Patents, Physician Contracts, Physician Practices, Planning and Land Use, Power Line Contact Injury, Probate, Probate Litigation, Products Liability, Products Liability Defense, Professional Liability, Property Law, Property Tax, Property Tax Abatement, Property Tax Appeals, Psychological Injury, Public Finance, Public Sector Labor Relations, Public Utility Law, Railroad Law, Real Estate, Real Estate Acquisitions, Real Estate Contracts, Real Estate Development, Real Estate Finance, Real Estate Licensing, Real Estate Secured Lending, Real Estate Title Insurance, Real Property, Real Property Acquisitions, Real Property Finance, Reorganizations, Resource Conservation and Recovery Act (RCRA), Retirement Benefit Plans, School Law, Securities, Securities Litigation, Securitization, Semiconductor Technology, Sexual Harassment, Small Business Corpora-

(This Listing Continued)

Barnes & Thornburg LLP (Continued)

tions, State Government Law, State Tax Controversies, State Taxation, Structured Finance, Succession Planning, Superfund, Tax Controversies, Tax Exempt Finance, Tax Exempt Organizations, Tax Increment Finance, Tax Law, Tax Litigation, Taxation, Technology and Science, Technology Law, Technology Licensing, Technology Transfers, Telecommunications Competition, Telecommunications Law, Theft of Trade Secrets, Title VII Discrimination, Title IX Discrimination, Tort Defense, Toxic Exposure, Toxic Tort Class Actions, Toxic Torts, Toxic Tort Defense, Trade Dress, Trade Secrets, Trademark Litigation, Trademarks, Trademark Prosecution, Trademark Protection, Trademark Registration, Transportation, Transportation Safety, Trial Practice, Trusts and Estates, Unfair Competition, Unfair Trade, Uniform Commercial Codes, Union Contract Negotiations, Union Elections, Utilities, Utility Law, Wage and Hour Law, WARN Act, Water Pollution, Water Quality, Water Utilities, Wetland Regulation, White Collar Crime, White Collar Criminal Defense, Wills, Workers Compensation, Workouts, World Trade Organization, Wrongful Death, Wrongful Termination, Wrongful Termination Defense, Zoning, Planning and Land Use.
Representative Clients: Argonne National Laboratory; Chicago Football, LLC; Citizens Commercial Leasing Corporation; Commonwealth Edison Company; Greater Cincinnati Cardiovascular Consultants, Inc.; Harley-Davidson Motor Company; International Facilities Group, LLC.; Marchesan Implementos E. Maquinas Agricoles Tatu SA; West Virginia Physicians Management Services; Whirlpool Corporation.
Indianapolis, Indiana Office: 11 South Meridian Street, 46204. Telephone: 317-236-1313. FAX: 317-231-7433.
Fort Wayne, Indiana Office: 600 One Summit Square, 46802. Telephone: 260-423-9440. FAX: 260-424-8316.
South Bend, Indiana Office: 600 1st Source Bank Center, 100 North Michigan, 46601-1632. Telephone: 574-233-1171. FAX: 574-237-1125.
Elkhart, Indiana Office: 121 West Franklin Street, Suite 200, 46516. Telephone: 574-293-0681. FAX: 574-296-2535.
Washington, D.C. Office: Suite 900, 750 17th Street, N.W., 20006. Telephone: 202-289-1313. FAX: 202-289-1330.
Grand Rapids, Michigan Office: 300 Ottawa Avenue, N.W., Suite 500, 49503. Telephone: 616-742-3930. FAX: 616-742-3999.

See Professional Biographies, CHICAGO, ILLINOIS

Barnett, Charles Rayburn, III ... '60 '01 C.339 B.S. L.589 J.D. [Ⓒ Nolan]
Barnett, Harvey J., (AV) ... '43 '67 C.339 B.A. L.597 J.D. [Ⓒ Sperling&S.]
Barnett, Scott B. ... '— '94 C&L.339 B.S., J.D. [Freeborn&P.]
Barnett, Theresa A. ... '52 '81 C.742 B.A. L.424 J.D. Dep. Gen. Coun., Corp., Metra
Barnett, William A., Law Offices of, (AV) '16 '41
C&L.424 LL.B. 134 N. La Salle St., Ste. 300
Barnett, Zachary K. ... '76 '02 C.238 B.S. L.597 J.D. [Ⓐ Mayer,B.R.&M.]
Barney, Kevin L., (AV) ... '58 '85 C.101 B.A. L.339 J.D. [Kutak R.]
Barnickol, Karl R. ... '71 '97 C.276 A.B. L.910 J.D. [Ⓐ Katten M.R.]
Barnickol, Laura Ann ... '73 '00 C.276 B.A. L.910 J.D. 205 W. Monroe
Barnicle, Brigid Moira ... '71 '99 C.473 B.A. L.608 J.D. Nat'l. Labor Relations Bd.
Barnicle, Terrence M. ... '43 '68 C.424 B.S. L.597 J.D. [Klein,T.&J.]
Barnow, Ben, (AV) ... '44 '69 C.966 B.B.A. L.477 J.D. [Barnow&Assoc.]

Barnow and Associates, P.C., (AV)
One North LaSalle Street, Suite 4600, 60602
Telephone: 312-621-2000 Fax: 312-641-5504
Email: b.barnow@barnowlaw.com
William T. McNeill (1907-1983); Ben Barnow;—Sharon A. Harris.
General Civil Practice in all Courts. Civil Action Litigation, Class Actions.

See Professional Biographies, CHICAGO, ILLINOIS

Baron, Diane M. ... '53 '84 C&L.597 B.S., J.D. [Clausen M.]
Baron, Steven L. ... '62 '88 C.494 B.A. L.966 J.D. [Mandell M.]
Baron, Walter R. ... '23 '58 C.597 B.S.B.A. L.424 J.D. 400 E. Randolph St.
Barone, Michael P., (AV) ... '46 '74 C.742 B.A. L.365 J.D. [Fishman,F.&S.]
Barone, Russell S. '29 '64 C.424 B.S. L.209 J.D.
Admin. Law J., Off. of Hearings And App., Soc. Sec. Admin.
Baroni, Peter ... '66 '96 C.210 B.A. L.329 J.D. 321 S. Plymouth Court
Barr, Courtney Engelbrecht ... '77 '02 C.602 B.A. L.597 J.D. [Ⓐ Winston&S.]
Barr, D. Daniel, (AV) ... '43 '68 C.597 B.A. L.966 J.D. 222 Merchandise Mart Plaza
Barr, Martin P., (AV) ... '51 '85 C.339 B.A. L.424 J.D. 225 W. Washington St.
Barr, Richard J., Jr., (AV) ... '49 '76 C.801 B.S. L.146 J.D. [Lannon,L.&B.]
Barr, William L., Jr., (AV) ... '48 '76 C.103 A.B. L.365 J.D. [Hilfman,M.&B.]
Barrett, Brian William ... '74 '99 C.473 B.A. L.893 J.D. [Ⓐ Seyfarth S.]
Barrett, Jennifer A. ... '64 '92 C.66 B.A. L.145 J.D. [Ⓒ Sonnenschein N.&R.]
Barrett, Michael P., (AV) ... '— '75 C&L.339 B.A., J.D. [Chapman&C.]
Barrett, Peter ... '31 '56 C.659 B.S. L.597 J.D. Stein Roe & Farnham Inc.
Barrett, Richard A., Jr., (AV) ... '51 '76 C.602 B.S. L.276 J.D. [Cassiday,S.&G.]
Barrett, Robert M., (AV) ... '56 '81 C&L.623 B.S., J.D. [Bell,B.&L.] (Pat.)
Barrett, Roger W., (AV) ... '15 '40 C.674 A.B. L.597 J.D. [Ⓒ Mayer,B.R.&M.]
Barrett, Ronit C. ... '75 '99 C.112 B.A. L.893 J.D. [Ⓐ Eimer S.K.&S.]
Barrett, William Henry, (AV) ... '53 '80 C.309 A.B. L.424 J.D. [Connelly S.H.]
Barrett, William J., (AV) ... '58 '85 C.475 B.A. L.800 J.D. [Barack F.K.P.&N.]
Barrido, Brian Joseph ... '73 '01 C&L.339 B.S., J.D. Asst. Pub. Def.
Barrish, Jonathan E., (BV) ... '— '92 C.597 B.A. L.424 J.D. [Litchfield C.]
Barrish, Kenneth J., (BV) ... '— '90 C.339 B.A. L.209 J.D. [Litchfield C.]
Barritt, David S. ... '— '81 C.210 B.A. L.1119 J.D. [Chapman&C.]
Barrocas, David S. ... '77 '02 C.724 B.A. L.339 J.D. Cook Co. State's Atty's Off.
Barron, Bernadette M. ... '55 '90 C.912 B.S. L.569 LL.M. 8 South Michigan Avenue
Barron, Blake A. ... '— '03 C.170 B.A. L.436 J.D. [Ⓐ Daley&M.]
Barron, Edward ... '56 '82 C.339 B.A. L.589 J.D. Asst. State's Atty.
Barron, Harold S., (AV) '36 '61
C&L.477 B.A., J.D. 980 North Michigan Avenue, Suite 1400
Barron, Howard R., (AV) ... '— '53 C.145 Ph.B. L.976 LL.B. [Ⓒ Schiff H.]
Barron, Timothy J. ... '62 '90 C.350 B.S.M.E. L.770 J.D. [Jenner&B.] (Pat.)
Barron, Troy R. ... '73 '99 C.894 B.A. L.862 J.D. Legal Coun., ICG Commerce
Barrow, Peter H., (AV) ... '50 '76 C.910 B.A. L.823 J.D. [Neal,G.&E.]
Barry, Alan L., (AV) ... '56 '81 C.339 B.S.Biol. L.146 J.D. [Bell,B.&L.] (Pat.)
Barry, Amanda T. ... '74 '01 C&L.477 B.S., J.D. [Ⓐ Mayer,B.R.&M.] (Pat.)
Barry, Angela M. ... '— '04 C.914 B.A. L.597 J.D. [Ⓐ Jenner&B.]
Barry, Carroll A., (BV) ... '— '80 C.274 B.S. L.589 J.D. [Feinberg&B.] ⊙
Barry, David R., Jr., (AV) ... '56 '81 C.746 B.A. L.597 J.D. [Corboy&D.]
Barry, James R. ... '60 '85 C&L.210 B.S.C., J.D. [Mayer,B.R.&M.]
Barry, Mary R. ... '65 '94 C&L.339 B.A., J.D. [Mayer,B.R.&M.]
Barry, Michael E. ... '53 '78 C.309 B.A. L.602 J.D. [Gardner C.&D.]
Barry, Norman J., Jr., (AV) ... '50 '75 C&L.602 B.A., J.D. [Donohue B.M.&S.]
Barry, Richard E. .. '48 '75 C.999 B.A. L.365 J.D. V.P. & Dep. Gen. Coun., AON Corp.
Bart, Nicholas C. ... '— '98 C.234 B.A. L.436 J.D. [Ⓐ Adler,M.&M.]
Bart, Susan T., (AV) ... '61 '85 C.293 B.A. L.477 J.D. [Sidley A.B.&W.]
Bartell, Carey L. ... '— '98 C.918 B.A. L.145 J.D. [Sachnoff&W.]
Barth, Christopher R., (BV) ... '65 '91 C.352 B.B.A. L.209 J.D. [Lord,B.&B.]
Barthel, Renee C. '73 '01
C.260 B.S.ENE L.146 J.D. [Ⓐ Cook,A.M.M.C.&M.] (See Pat. Sect.)
Barthel, Ted J. ... '64 '00 C.120 B.A. L.209 J.D. [Ⓐ Bell,B.&L.] (Pat.)
Bartholomew, David L. '55 '80
C.234 B.A. L.801 J.D. Chief Dep. Dir., Ofc. of Secy. of State
Bartholomy, Erin P. ... '— '93 C&L.602 B.A., J.D. [Chapman&C.]

Bartholow, Steven A. '48 '73 C.352 B.A. L.972 J.D.
(adm. in WY; not adm. in IL) Gen. Coun., U.S. R.R. Retirement Bd.
Bartizal, Joyce B. '65 '91 C.597 B.A. L.146 J.D. Staff Atty., Cir. Ct. of Cook Co.
Bartkowicz, Ronald F. '40 '65 C.209 B.S. L.424 J.D. Cir.J.
Bartlett, Austin W. '— '00 C&L.589 B.S., J.D. [Adler,M.&M.]
Bartlett, James, (AV) '44 '74 C.1183 B.A. L.365 J.D. [Stellato&S.]
Bartlett, Shannon P. '77 '03 C.910 B.A. L.209 J.D. [Jenner&B.]
Bartlett-Svehla, Dorothy '53 '88 C.927 B.A. L.146 J.D. 4801 W. Peterson Ave.
Bartley, James P. '— '05 C.340 B.A. L.1000 J.D. [Kirkland&E.]
Bartley, James P. '47 '76 C.424 B.S. L.365 J.D. [Klein,T.&J.]
Bartlit, Fred H., Jr. (P.C.), (AV) '32 '60 C.870 B.S. L.339 LL.B.
[Bartlit B.H.P.&S.] ⊙

Bartlit Beck Herman Palenchar & Scott LLP, (AV)
Courthouse Place, 54 West Hubbard Street, 60610 ⊙
Telephone: 312-494-4400 Facsimile: 312-494-4440
Email: bartlit-beck.com URL: http://www.bartlit-beck.com
Partners: Fred H. Bartlit, Jr. (P.C.); Philip S. Beck; Sidney N. Herman; Mark E. Ferguson; Rebecca Weinstein Bacon; Peter B. Bensinger, Jr.; Steven E. Derringer; Sean W. Gallagher; Andrew L. Goldman; Jeffrey A. Hall; James B. Heaton, III; Adam L. Hoeflich; Tarek Ismail; Christopher D. Landgraff; Mark L. Levine; Chris Lind; Mark S. Ouweleen; Andre M. Pauka; Jason L. Peltz; Elizabeth L. Thompson; Michael J. Valaik. Associates: Allison W. Freedman; Hamilton H. Hill; Carrie A. Jablonski; J. Scott McBride; Steven J. Nachtwey; Andrew K. Polovin; Reeghan Raffals (Not admitted in IL); Paul J. Skiermont; Brian C. Swanson; Jill R. Trumbull-Harris. Of Counsel: Mary Szews Moore.
General Civil and Trial Practice in all Courts and Corporate Transactional Practice.
Denver, Colorado Office: 1899 Wynkoop Street. Telephone: 303-592-3100. Facsimile: 303-592-3140.
See Professional Biographies, CHICAGO, ILLINOIS

Bartoli, Christopher M. '71 '96 C&L.602 B.S., J.D. [Baker&M.]
Bartolotta, Ross W. '69 '94 C.339 B.A. L.589 J.D. [Swanson,M.&B.] (⊙Lisle)
Barton, Frank W. '17 '38 L.1015 LL.B. 515 N. State St.
Barton, Gregory L. '59 '87 C.602 B.S. L.145 J.D. [Mayer,B.R.&M.]
Bartos, Sara '63 '01 C.339 B.S.E.E. L.1000 J.D. [McAndrews,H.&M.]
Baruch, Hurd, (AV) '37 '60 C.299 B.A. L.976 LL.B. [Winston&S.] ‡
Barzano, William J., Jr. '48 '74 C.424 B.S. L.146 J.D. Asst. Atty. Gen.
Bascos, Alfonso S. '35 '59 C&L.662 M.A., LL.B. 120 W. Madison
Baseer, Naser '— '03 L.146 J.D. [Holland&K.]
Baseman, Lois J. '47 '79 C.546 B.S.B.A. L.910 J.D. Sr., V.P., Bank of America, N.A.
Bashford, Rodney C. '67 '99 C.123 B.A. L.424 J.D. [Williams M.&J.]
Bashwiner, Steven L., (P.C.), (AV) '41 '66 C.321 A.B. L.145 J.D. [Katten M.R.]
Basil, Matt D. '73 '97 C.339 B.S. L.424 J.D. [Jenner&B.]
Basil, Michael W. '68 '95 C.477 B.A. L.734 J.D. [Clausen M.]
Basile, Joseph P. '54 '79 C.734 B.S.B.A. L.365 J.D. [Rusin M.&F.]
Basile, Mark Glenn '65 '97 C.338 B.S. L.365 J.D. [M.G.Basile]
Basile, Mark G., Law Office of 180 N. LaSalle St. Ste. 1408
Basinger, Matthew R. '78 '03 C.610 B.S. L.1003 J.D. [S.E.Loggans&Assoc.]
Basinski, Stanley E. '25 '51 6151 N. Milwaukee

Baskes, Daniel L., (BV) '65 '90 C.293 B.A. L.339 J.D.
300 West Adams Street, Suite 529, 60606
Telephone: 312-236-2696 Fax: 312-236-2699
Email: dbaskes@yahoo.com URL: http://www.lawyers.com/dbaskes
Real Estate, Commercial Real Estate, Residential Real Estate, Condominium Law, Commercial Leasing.
See Professional Biographies, CHICAGO, ILLINOIS

Baskes, Roger S. '35 '59 C.339 B.S. L.309 J.D. 980 N. Michigan Ave.‡
Baskin, Isadore '12 '34 C.999 A.A. L.209 LL.B. [Baskin&B.]
Baskin, Louis '08 '35 C.137 A.A. L.365 LL.B. [Baskin&B.]
Baskin, Sheldon L. '37 '63 C.674 A.B. L.309 J.D. 222 N. LaSalle St.
Baskin & Baskin 133 W. Randolph
Baskin, Server, Berke & Weinstein, (AV) 20 N. Wacker Dr., Ste. 1745
Bass, David R. '69 '96 C.910 A.B. L.365 J.D. [FagelHaber]
Bass, Renée F., (BV) '46 '77 C&L.209 B.S., J.D. [R.F.Bass]
Bass, Richard Ivan, (AV) '36 '61 C.209 B.S.C. L.426 J.D. [R.I.Bass&Assoc.]
Bass, William K. '55 '89 C.569 B.F.A. L.851 J.D. [Pasulka&W.]
Bass, Yale P. '35 '59 C&L.597 B.S.L., LL.B. 188 W. Randolph St.
Bass, Renée F., Ltd., (BV) 180 North LaSalle Street, Suite 1919
Bass, Richard I., & Associates, Ltd., (AV) 180 North LaSalle Street, Suite 2101
Bassi, Carrie E. '— '03 C.276 B.S. L.893 J.D. [Jones D.]
Bassi, Kathleen C. '— '85 C.927 B.A. L.589 J.D. [Schiff H.]
Basso, Thomas C. '67 '99 C.597 B.A. L.146 J.D. [Bell,B.&L.]
Bastedo, Emily Todd '— '03 C.602 B.A. L.209 J.D. [Chapman&C.]
Bateman, Emily Ann '74 '03 C.966 B.A. L.477 J.D. [Lord,B.&B.]
Bateman, Paul E., (AV) '56 '80 C.338 B.S. L.477 J.D. [Littler M.]
Bateman, Sylvia L. '56 '80 C.339 B.S. L.477 J.D. Asst. Gen. Coun., Exelon Corp.
Bates, Benjamin Will '— '02 C&L.878 B.A., J.D. [Kirkland&E.]
Bates, Robert J., Jr., (AV) '51 '78 C.339 B.A. L.597 J.D. [Bates&C.]
Bates, William, Jr. '54 '89 C.339 B.A. L.365 J.D. Seaway National Bank of Chicago
Bates & Carey, (AV) 191 N. Wacker Dr., Ste. 2400
Batler, Michael D. '43 '69 C.1016 B.S.B.A. L.209 J.D. [Kamensky,R.H.&D.] ⊙
Batson, Kevin L. '— '01 C.896 B.A. L.477 J.D. [McDermott W.&E.]
Batt, Allison A. '74 '00 C.221 B.A. L.209 J.D. [Magnani&B.]
Battaglia, Erica Lewis '70 '96 C.473 B.A. L.209 J.D. [Sedgwick,D.M.&A.]
Batterson, Donald E. '66 '94 C.589 B.S. L.245 J.D. [Jenner&B.]
Battin, Catherine A. '71 '99 C.393 B.A. L.209 J.D. [Handler,T.&D.]
Battista, Thomas M. '57 '83 C.927 B.A. L.424 J.D.
Coun. to Chrmn., U.S. Railroad Retirement Bd.
Battle, Kenneth M. '73 '99 C.339 B.A. L.124 J.D. [Brenner,F.M.&S.]
Battoglia, Robert L. '47 '76 C.602 B.A. L.862 J.D.
(adm. in OK; not adm. in IL) Lexis-Nexis, Inc.
Bauch, Paul M., (BV) '58 '83 C.932 B.S. L.472 J.D. [Bauch&M.]
Bauch, Reva S. C. '58 '84 C.112 B.A. L.472 J.D.
(adm. in NJ; not adm. in IL) Regional Atty., FDIC
Bauch & Michaels, (BV) 53 W. Jackson Boulevard, Suite 1115
Baue, Vicki J. '58 '97 C.16 B.S. L.347 J.D. 3170 N. Sheridan Road, Suite 902
Bauer, Constance L. '60 '86 C.1365 B.A. L.477 J.D. 3450 N. Lake Shore Dr.‡
Bauer, Julie A., (AV) '60 '85 C.893 B.A. L.339 J.D. [Winston&S.]
Bauer, Louise '66 '94 C.145 B.A. L.424 J.D. Admr., Jane Addams Hull House
Bauer, Ronald G. '47 '72 C.994 B.A. L.309 J.D.
(adm. in NY; not adm. in IL) Sr. Tax Coun., BP America Inc.
Bauer, Steven C. '76 '04 C.339 B.A. L.146 J.D. [Holland&K.]
Bauer, Tracy E. '48 '86 C&L.424 B.A., J.D.
Asst. Reg. Coun., Off. of Thrift Supervision
Bauer, William J. '26 '51 C.238 B.A. L.209 J.D. U.S. Sr. Cir. J.‡
Bauerle, Diana C. '74 '00 C.260 B.A. L.424 J.D. 332 S. Michigan Ave., Ste. 1428
Bauerschmidt, Robert A. '65 '90 C.477 A.B. L.339 J.D. [Goldberg&F.]
Baugh, David A., (AV) '54 '79 C.280 B.B.A. L.838 J.D. [Mora,B.W.&U.] ⊙
Baugh, Jennifer L. '— '04 C.228 A.B. L.352 J.D. [Wildman,H.A.&D.]
Baugher, Peter V., (AV) '48 '74 C.674 A.B. L.976 J.D. [Schopf&W.]
Baughman, Michael J. '64 '89 C.578 B.A. L.424 J.D. 333 W. Wacker Dr., Ste. 900
Baum, Bernard M., (AV) '36 '60 C&L.597 B.S.L., J.D. [Baum S.A.&N.]
Baum, Charles M. '68 '95 C.209 B.S. L.365 J.D. [Schwartz C.]
Baum, David M. '54 '79 C.72 B.A. L.146 J.D. [Reibman,H.B.H.&O.]
Baum, David N. '41 '64 C.339 B.S. L.209 J.D. 821 W. VanBuren
Baum, Jonathan K., (AV) '57 '82 C.309 A.B. L.145 J.D. [Katten M.R.]
Baum, Michael J. '— '02 C.846 B.B.A. L.424 J.D. [Greenberg T.]
Baum, Richard W., (AV) '43 '71 C.321 A.B. L.146 J.D. [Baum,R.&M.]
Baum, Stephen Lowell '41 '66 C.339 B.S. L.472 J.D. 738 N Wells St.
Baum, Ruffolo & Marzal, Ltd., (AV) 33 N. La Salle Street
Baum Sigman Auerbach & Neuman, Ltd., (AV) 200 West Adams Street Suite 2200
Bauman, Janet E. '66 '94 C.813 A.B. L.145 J.D. [Sidley A.B.&W.]
Baumann, Deidre '68 '92 C&L.339 B.S., J.D. [Baumann,S.&L.]
Baumann, Jennifer J. '— '03 C&L.477 B.A., J.D. [DLPiper R.G.C.U.]
Baumann, Timothy R. '63 '95
C.350 B.S.E.E. L.339 J.D. [Fitch,E.T.&F.] (See Pat. Sect.)
Baumann, Shuldiner & Lee, (BV) 3700 Three First National Plaza
Baumgaertner, Martin W. '48 '74 C.221 B.A. L.879 J.D.
Chief Adm. J., U.S. Merit Systems Protection Bd.
Baumgart, Fran '44 '72 C.742 B.A. L.365 J.D. [Baumgert,J.&Assoc.]
Baumgartner, William H., Jr., (AV) '55 '79 C.145 A.B. L.309 J.D. [Sidley A.B.&W.]
Baumgert, Jones and Associates 520L W. Erie St.
Bautista, Andrew '— '03 C.178 B.A. L.813 J.D. [Kirkland&E.]
Bautista, Christine S. '— '03 C.145 B.A. L.446 J.D. [Gardner C.&D.]
Bautista, Natalie A. '75 '02 C.475 B.A. L.146 J.D. [Hughes S.P.R.&D.]
Bawden, Heather '— '02 C.339 B.A. L.309 J.D. [Kirkland&E.]
Bawolek, Valerie A. '52 '77 C.589 B.A. L.146 J.D. Admin. Law J., Dept. of Rev.
Baxendale, Scott E. '— '96 C.930 B.S. L.365 J.D. [Marshall,G.&B.] (See Pat. Sect.)
Baxendale, Valerie Lynne '— '02 C.347 B.A. L.209 J.D. 25 East Erie Street
Bayer, Jas. W. '26 '53 C.210 A.B. L.597 J.D. 312 W. Randolph St.
Bayer, Thomas P. '58 '83 C&L.209 B.A., J.D. [Klein,T.&J.]
Bayles, James E., Jr. '64 '91 C.145 B.A. L.1066 J.D. [Morgan,L.&B.]
Bayles, Leslie Allen '63 '00 C.136 B.S. L.424 J.D. [Vedder,P.K.&K.]
Bayo, Julia M. Antonsen '75 '02 C.446 B.A. L.146 J.D. Asst. Pub. Def.
Bays, Gregory C. '67 '95 C.477 B.S.M.E. L.930 J.D. [Leydig,V.&M.] (See Pat. Sect.)
Bayster, Raymond J. '20 '49 C.137 L.209 LL.B.
Exec. Dir., Ill. State Medical Ctr. Comm.
Bazelon, Edward G., (AV) '25 '51 C.477 L.597 LL.B. 39 S. La Salle St.
Bazianos, Patrice A. '72 '99 C&L.424 B.S., J.D. [Bell,B.&L.]
Bea, David, Law Office of '— '97 L.209 J.D. 19 S. LaSalle St., Ste. 1203
Beach, Virginia L. '68 '96 C.696 B.A. L.209 J.D. [Donohue B.M.&S.]
Beal, John '45 '73 C&L.145 B.A., J.D. 53 W. Jackson Blvd.
Beal, Scott D. '62 '94 C.1111 B.A. L.425 J.D. [Boudreau&B.]
Beall, Ingrid L., (AV) '26 '56 C&L.145 A.B., J.D. 130 E. Randolph Dr.
Beall, L. Scott '67 '03 C.339 B.S. L.705 J.D. [Leydig,V.&M.]
Beals, Bart E. '66 '00 C.46 B.A. L.329 J.D. 233 East Erie
Beans, William W. '58 '88 C&L.589 B.S., J.D. Admin. Law J., Dept. of Employ. Sec.
Bear, Frank A. '74 '03 C.339 B.S. L.209 J.D. [Seyfarth S.]
Beard, James L., (AV) '54 '80 C.339 B.A. L.46 J.D. [DLPiper R.G.C.U.]
Beard, Paul '37 '64 C&L.352 B.A., LL.B. Asst. Pub. Guard.
Beard, Rhonda Scott '72 '99 C.893 B.A. L.1119 J.D. 30 N. LaSalle St.
Beard, Stephen W. '71 '99 C.339 B.A. L.1119 J.D.
Asst. Gen. Coun., Heidrick & Struggles International, Inc.
Bearrows, Thomas R., (AV) '57 '83 C&L.339 A.B., J.D. Gen. Coun., Univ. of Illinois
Beasley, Brendan S. '— '02 C.253 B.A. L.659 J.D. [Latham&W.]
Beasley, Tena Gaston '58 '89 C.98 B.M.E. L.365 J.D. Asst. Co. Pub. Def.
Beatty, William G., (AV) '53 '78 C.57 B.A. L.146 J.D. [Johnson&B.]
Beatus, Bruce A. '57 '81 C.1365 B.A. L.245 J.D. Gen. Coun., Caylon Financial Inc.
Beaubien, Mark J. '67 '94 C.188 A.B. L.597 J.D. [Barack F.K.P.&N.]
Beauchamp, Bobb A., III '71 '97
C.475 B.A. L.477 J.D. Asst. Reg. Coun., U.S. Envir. Protec. Agcy.
Beaulieu, Robert Neil '51 '78 C.209 B.A. L.365 J.D. [Beaulieu]

Beaulieu Law Offices
5339 West Belmont, 60641
Telephone: 773-545-9339 Fax: 773-545-8819
URL: http://www.beaulieulawfirm.com
Member of Firm: Robert Neil Beaulieu. Associate: Elaine A. Llerena. Of Counsel: Rory D. Cassidy.
Languages: English, Spanish.
Real Property Law, Commercial Litigation, Personal Injury.
See Professional Biographies, CHICAGO, ILLINOIS

Beavers, Emilie M. '78 '04 C.293 B.A. L.178 J.D. [Mayer,B.R.&M.]
Becherer, Robert E. '56 '88
C.855 B.A. L.477 J.D. Gen. Atty., R. R. Donnelley & Sons Co.
Bechly, Cary Ann '14 '38 C&L.339 B.A., LL.B. 5550 S. South Shore Dr.‡
Beck, Elizabeth Rowntree '68 '95 C&L.910 B.A., J.D. [DLPiper R.G.C.U.]
Beck, Geo. A., (AV) '26 '54 C.209 L.365 LL.B. 5487 N. Milwaukee Ave.
Beck, Kristina M. '76 '01 C.36 B.A. L.365 J.D. [Cremer,K.S.&S.] (Pat.)
Beck, Nancy M. '50 '75 C.174 B.A. L.209 J.D. Resident V.P., Chic. Title & Tr. Co.
Beck, Norman K. '70 '95 C.605 A.B. L.910 J.D. [Winston&S.]
Beck, Philip S., (AV) '51 '77 C.966 B.A. L.94 J.D. [Bartlit B.H.P.&S.]
Becka, Daniel J. '62 '88 C.930 B.S. L.659 J.D. [M.M.Cherry&Assoc.]
Becker, Alan I., (AV) '46 '70 C.188 A.B. L.976 LL.B. [Litchfield C.]
Becker, Alvin R., (AV) '— '62 C.1016 B.A. L.209 J.D. [Beermann S.W.B.G.&L.]
Becker, Anne S. '77 '05 C.210 B.A L.477 J.D. [McDermott W.&E.]
Becker, Cassandra A. '79 '04 C.339 B.A. L.597 J.D.
Staff Atty., Enforce., U.S. Secs. & Exch. Comm.
Becker, Colleen A. '72 '99 C.339 B.A. L.365 J.D. 2338 S. Indiana Avenue
Becker, David '— '00 C.696 B.A. L.209 J.D. [Freeborn&P.]
Becker, Donald M. '19 '47 C.145 M.B.A. L.209 J.D. 134 N. LaSalle St.‡
Becker, Glenn I. '61 '86 C.477 B.A. L.339 J.D. [Seyfarth S.]
Becker, Jeffrey A. '57 '83 C.178 A.B. L.477 J.D. Dir. & Sr. Coun., CNA
Becker, Jeffrey J. '68 '96 C.446 B.S. L.339 J.D. Accenture LLP
Becker, Jeffrey S. '— '04 C.340 B.A. L.209 J.D. [Kozacky&W.]
Becker, Laurence P. '— '97 C.823 B.S. L.365 J.D. [Masuda,F.E.&M.]
Becker, Mark R. '74 '00 C.597 B.S. L.352 J.D. [Conway&W.]
Becker, Mary Ann '— '02 C.597 B.A. L.209 J.D. [Sachnoff&W.]
Becker, Mary E. '45 '80 C.424 B.S. L.145 J.D. Prof., Univ. of Chicago Sch. of Law
Becker, Matthew P. '— '98 C.679 B.S. L.597 J.D. [Banner&W.] (See Pat. Sect.)
Becker, Robert J. '25 '55 C.436 L.365 LL.B. 330 S. Wells St.
Becker, Scott '64 '89 C.339 B.S. L.309 J.D. [McGuirewoods]
Becker, Theodore M., (AV) '49 '75 C.910 A.B. L.597 J.D. [Morgan,L.&B.]
Becker, Wesley N. '— '83 C.172 B.S. L.145 J.D. [Foley&L.]

Becker, William L. .... '43 '69 C.311 B.A. L.910 J.D. [Ⓒ Laner,M.D.B.L.&T.]
Becker, William W., (AVⓉ) '43 '68 C.197 A.B. L.309 LL.B.
(adm. in MA; not adm. in IL) [W.W.Becker]
Becker, William W., Chartered, Law Offices of, (AVⓉ) .... 175 N. State St.
Beckert, Anne M., (BV) .... '60 '85 C.475 B.A. L.912 J.D. [A.Beckert]
Beckert, A., at Law, LLC, (BV) .... 3222 N. Kenmore Ave., 3rd Fl.
Beckett, Michael A. .... '73 '04 C.339 B.S. L.910 J.D. [Ⓐ Bell,B.&L.]
Beckman, Henry P. .... '34 '66 C.424 L.365 J.D. 221 N. LaSalle St.
Beckman, Marvin E. '30 '60 C&L.911 B.A., LL.B.
V.P. & Assoc. Gen. Coun., Moody Bible Institute
Beckman, Vincent H., III '44 '74 C.602 B.A. L.597 J.D.
Supervisory Atty., Legal Assistance Found. of Chicago
Beckstrom, John H. .... '32 '59 C&L.352 B.A., J.D. Prof. of Law, N.W. Univ.
Beckwith, Amy C. .... '72 '98 C.597 B.S. L.273 J.D. [Ⓐ McDermott W.&E.]
Bedard, Peter J. .... '69 '94 C.884 B.A. L.472 J.D. [Ⓐ Stein,R.&H.]
Bedell, Gregory A., (AV) .... '60 '85 C.145 A.B. L.1019 J.D. 20 S. Clark St., Ste. 2301
Bedell, Stephen P., (AV) .... '— '80 C.973 H.A.B. L.597 J.D. [Foley&L.]
Bednarek, Lucy B. .... '74 '99 C.424 B.A. L.347 J.D. [Ⓐ Ancel,G.D.B.D.&R.]
Bedore, Robert A., (AV) .... '54 '80 C&L.209 B.S., J.D. [Neal,G.&E.]
Beederman, Asher J. .... '49 '74 C.339 B.A. L.209 J.D. [A.J.Bederman]
Beederman, Daniel E. .... '52 '78 C.339 B.A. L.209 J.D. [Schoenberg,F.N.&R.]
Beederman, Asher J., Ltd. .... 11 S. LaSalle St., Ste. 1900
Beem, Marc O., (AV) .... '48 '75 C.674 A.B. L.145 J.D. [Miller S.&H.]
Beem, Richard P., (AV) .... '54 '85 C.350 B.S.Ch. E. L.326 J.D. [Beem] (Pat.)

Beem Patent Law Firm, (AV)
53 West Jackson Boulevard, Suite 1352, 60604-3787
Telephone: 312-201-0011 Fax: 312-201-0022
Email: patents@beemlaw.com URL: http://www.beemlaw.com
Richard P. Beem; Roger J. French;—Michael T. Griggs; Grace I. Liu.
Patents, Patent Law, Opinions, Litigation, Appellate Practice, Intellectual Property.
See Professional Biographies, CHICAGO, ILLINOIS

Beemer, Courtney M. .... '— '01 C.276 B.S.F.S. L.145 J.D. [Ⓐ Jenner&B.]
Beemer, Michael G., (AV) .... '37 '63 C.951 A.B. L.309 LL.B. [Ⓒ Vedder,P.K.&K.]
Been, Carol Anne, (AV) .... '55 '83 C&L.339 B.S., J.D. [Sonnenschein N.&R.]
Beerly, Gustav E., Jr. .... '14 '42 C.393 B.A. L.365 LL.B. 2 N. La Salle St.‡
Beerman, Deborah .... '— '03 C.966 B.A. L.339 J.D. [Ⓐ McGuirewoods]
Beermann, Miles N., (AV) .... '— '58 C.339 L.209 J.D. [Beermann S.W.B.B.G.&L.]

Beermann Swerdlove Woloshin Barezky Becker Genin & London, (AV) BR
161 North Clark Street, Suite 2600, 60601-3221 ⊙
Telephone: 312-621-9700 Telefax: 312-621-0909
Email: info@beermannlaw.com URL: http://www.beermannlaw.com
Members of Firm: Lawrence R. Barezky; Alvin R. Becker; Miles N. Beermann; Lyle S. Genin; Pamela J. Hutul; Herbert A. Kessel; Howard A. London; William Woloshin; Deane B. Brown; Howard C. Emmerman; Roger A. Rubin; James M. Quigley. Associates: Julie P. Brett; Maribeth Olenski; Jacqueline J. Torshen; Katherine A. Grosh; Martin W. Burzawa; William A. Zolla, II; Bradley T. Cheskes; Stefania Pialis; Charles Phillips; Rhonda E. deFreitas; Shana L. Vitek; Katarinna McBride; Tanya L. Akins. Of Counsel: Nathan B. Swerdlove.
Commercial, Insurance and Banking Litigation. Family (Divorce; Adoption), General Civil Trial and Appellate, Corporate, Real Estate and Condominium, Estate Planning and Probate, Personal Injury, Negligence, Plaintiff's Trial Law, Tort, Insurance, Business, Products Liability, and Business Organization and Transactions.
Highland Park, Illinois Office: 1700 Greenbay Road, 60035.
See Professional Biographies, CHICAGO, ILLINOIS

Beery, Dawn M. .... '72 '98 C.347 B.A. L.597 J.D. [Ⓐ Kelley D.&W.]
Beery, John B. .... '74 '98 C.197 A.B. L.597 J.D. [Ⓐ Gould&R.]
Beggs, Andrea J., (AV) '56 '81 C&L.477 B.S., J.D.
Sr. Assoc. Gen. Coun., Bank One Corp. (Law Dept.)
Beggs, Tracy C., (AV) .... '— '80 C&L.477 B.A., J.D. [Litchfield C.]
Begley, Heather A. .... '— '03 C.339 B.S. L.209 J.D. [Ⓐ Clifford]
Begley, Walter P. .... '— '84 C.347 B.A. L.602 J.D. [Chapman&C.]
Begy, Fred C., III, (AV) .... '47 '73 C.1111 B.A. L.602 J.D. [Chuhak&T.]
Behar, José J. .... '65 '90 C.477 A.B. L.597 J.D. [Hughes S.P.R.&D.]
Behm, Allyson R. .... '77 '01 C.504 B.A. L.94 J.D. [Ⓐ Dykema G.P.]
Behn, Michael I. .... '61 '87 C.197 A.B. L.588 J.D. [Futterman&H.]
Behrens, George J. .... '57 '82 C.602 B.A. L.597 J.D. 134 N. LaSalle St.
Beierwaltes, Mark G. .... '58 '85 C.424 B.B.A. L.146 J.D. Price Waterhouse
Beihoffer, Denise Boklach '59 '93 C.612 B.S. L.623 J.D.
V.P., Legal, Equity Residential
Beiler, Benjamin, (AV) .... '47 '72 C.966 B.A. L.178 J.D. C.O.O., PCM
Beilfuss, Robert P. .... '57 '84 C.589 B.S. L.209 J.D. [Ⓐ Davis&C.]
Beilinson, David E. '75 '01 C.378 B.G.S. L.146 J.D.
Asst. V.P. & Asst. Gen. Coun., ABN AMRO Inc.
Beinstein, Debra .... '— '91 C.477 B.A. L.145 J.D. [Ⓒ Kirkland&E.]
Beirne, Michael T. .... '66 '95 C.93 B.A. L.146 J.D. [Quinlan&C.]
Beirne, Noreen Geralyn .... '— '00 C.424 B.A. L.146 J.D. 550 N. Kingsbury St., Apt. 407
Beiser, Robert S., (AV) .... '47 '76 C.475 B.A.B.S. L.146 J.D. [Vedder,P.K.&K.] (Pat.)
Beiting, Melissa R. .... '— '04 C.602 B.A. L.276 J.D. [Ⓐ Jones D.]
Beker, David E. .... '— '03 C.597 B.A. L.424 J.D. [Ⓐ Schwartz C.]
Bekman, Svetlana V. .... '— '96 C.103 B.A. L.597 J.D. [Schiff H.]
Belanger, Anne M. .... '— '93 C.30 B.A. L.424 J.D. [Querrey&H.]
Belcastro, Jacquelyne M. '66 '91
C.339 A.B. L.597 J.D. Asst. V.P. & Asst. Gen. Coun., CNA
Belcher, Benjamin B. .... '72 '01 C.136 B.S. L.339 J.D. [Ⓐ Iwan C.H.H.&V.]
Belcove, Ira J., (AV) .... '63 '87 C.178 B.A. L.145 J.D. [Butler R.S.&B.]
Belgrade, Steven B., (AV) .... '50 '75 C&L.424 B.A., J.D. [Belgrade&O.]

Belgrade and O'Donnell, A Professional Corporation, (AV) BR
20 North Wacker Drive, Suite 1900, 60606
Telephone: 312-422-1700 Facsimile: 312-422-1717 URL: http://www.belgradeodonnell.com
URL: http://www.bodpc.com
URL: http://www.belgradeodonnelllaw.com
Steven B. Belgrade; John A. O'Donnell; George M. Velcich; Patrick J. Cullinan;—Richard P. Girzadas; James Saranteas; Brian A. Corby; John C. Coyne; Kathryn Rives Band.
Civil Trial and Appellate Practice. Tort and Commercial Law including General Negligence, Admiralty, Transportation, Insurance Defense, Insurance Coverage, Construction Injuries, Products Liability, Professional Malpractice and Environmental Insurance Litigation.
See Professional Biographies, CHICAGO, ILLINOIS

Belkin, Elizabeth H., (AV) .... '46 '79 C.339 B.A. L.146 J.D. [Ⓒ DLPiper R.G.C.U.]
Belkin, Gary G. .... '44 '69 C&L.339 B.S., J.D. 55 W. Monroe St., Ste. 3300
Bell, Alan M. .... '63 '91 C&L.602 B.B.A., J.D. [Charity&Assoc.]
Bell, Brandon E. .... '— '96 C.604 B.A. L.966 J.D. [Arnstein&L.]
Bell, Brian W., (AV) .... '52 '77 C.347 B.A. L.345 J.D. [Swanson,M.&B.]
Bell, Brigitte Schmidt, (AV) .... '48 '79 C.821 B.A. L.145 J.D. [B.S.Bell] ⊙
Bell, Bruce E. .... '57 '82 C.339 B.S. L.424 J.D. [Schoenberg,F.N.&R.]
Bell, Cheryl A. '60 '84 C&L.260 B.A., J.D.
(adm. in FL; not adm. in IL) Off. of the U.S. Atty.
Bell, Diane E. .... '78 '03 C.910 B.A. L.145 J.D. [Ⓐ Bell,B.&L.]

Bell, Eileen L. .... '58 '84 C.910 B.A. L.597 J.D. Asst. Corp. Coun.
Bell, Emilie Suzanne .... '75 '00 C.1439 B.A. L.209 J.D. [Hardt&S.]
Bell, Ira, (AV) .... '35 '60 C.597 B.A. L.145 J.D. [Bell&P.]
Bell, Joel M., (AV) .... '49 '75 C.95 B.A. L.365 J.D. 221 N. La Salle ST.
Bell, John W., (AV) .... '46 '71 C.597 B.A. L.424 J.D. [Johnson&B.]
Bell, Jordan .... '37 '62 C&L.209 B.S., J.D. 820 N. Orleans St.
Bell, Joshua C. .... '74 '99 C.338 B.S. L.365 J.D. [Ⓐ Brenner,F.M.&S.]
Bell, Laertes T. .... '32 '63 C.339 L.146 5302 S. Cornell St.
Bell, Louis Michael .... '— '78 C.674 A.B. L.145 J.D. [Griffith&J.]
Bell, Melissa Ann .... '76 '01 C.910 B.A. L.209 J.D. [Ⓐ D.DiMaggio]
Bell, Peter G., Law Offices of, (AV) '48 '75
C.118 B.A. L.365 J.D. 20 N. Clark St., Ste. 501
Bell, Richard S. .... '43 '87 C.597 B.A. L.976 J.D. [Mauck&B.]
Bell, Robert, Jr. '47 '77 C.597 B.A. L.146 J.D.
Dir., Govt. Affs. & Sr. Corp. Coun., USG Corp.
Bell, Robert S., Jr. .... '49 '79 C.430 B.A. L.365 J.D. [Cosby,O.&B.]
Bell, Stephen B., (AV) .... '44 '69 C.937 A.B. L.309 J.D. [Goldberg,K.B.B.R.&M.]
Bell, Theodore B. .... '66 '93 C.477 B.A. L.215 J.D. [Kowalczyk&B.]
Bell, Walter W., (AV) .... '47 '71 C&L.597 B.A., J.D. [Bell J.&Q.]

Bell, Boyd & Lloyd LLC, (AV)
70 West Madison Street Suite 3100, 60602 ⊙
Telephone: 312-372-1121 FAX: 312-827-8000
Email: attorneys@bellboyd.com URL: http://www.bellboyd.com
Members of Firm: Jeffrey B. Aaronson; Michael J. Abernathy; Gregory R. Andre; Andrew R. Andreasik; Cameron S. Avery; Robert M. Barrett; Alan L. Barry; Patrick S. Belville; Nancy E. Bertoglio (Chief Operating Officer); Robert J. Best; Donald J. Bingle; John H. Bitner; John C. Blew; Christopher A. Bloom; Randy A. Bridgeman; Robert Raymond Brown; William G. Brown; Terrence E. Budny; Thomas R. Carey; Lisa A. Carroll; Pawel Chudzicki; James W. Collins; Randy J. Curato; James P. Daley; Lee A. Daniels; John S. Delnero; William F. Dolan; Raymond H. Drymalski; Juliette Gregory Duara; Steven E. Ducommun; Erik F. Dyhrkopp; Paul H. Dykstra; Lawrence A. Eiben; Lawrence C. Eppley; Nicholas J. Etten; Jerry K. Fellows; Nicola Fiordalisi; Sanford R. Gail; Stanley J. Garber; Lawrence M. Gavin; Carol A. Genis; Alan P. Goldberg; Graham C. Grady; Victor E. Grimm; Sana Hakim; Merrick D. Hatcher; Bonita L. Hatchett; Daniel J. Hayes; Michael J. Hayes, Sr.; Thomas Z. Hayward, Jr.; David F. Heroy; Francis J. Higgins; Patricia S. Hofstra; Thomas C. Homburger; Gregory W. Hummel; Thomas F. Joyce; Thor W. Ketzback; Bryan E. Keyt; Mark Thomas Kindelin; Steven M. Kowal; Jeffrey R. Ladd; Daniel J. Lawler; Josh M. Leavitt; John F. Lemker, Jr.; Irving B. Levinson; Bruce E. Lithgow; Carmen H. Lonstein; Francis X. Lyons; Lawrence M. Mages; Patrick J. Maloney; Brian E. Martin; Michael E. Martínez; Adam H. Masia; Jane K. McCahill; John T. McCarthy (Chairman); Kevin J. McCarthy; S. Patrick McKey; D. Mark McMillan; Carrie C. McNally; Scott M. Mendel; Paul T. Metzger; John P. (Pete) Morrison; Robert M. Moye; Sandra K. Newman; David M. Novak; Kimberly D. Novotny; Michael K. Ohm; Stephen J. O'Neil; Michael R. Osterhoff; Amy G. O'Toole; Michael L. Owen; Kenneth A. Peterson, Jr.; Paulita A. Pike; William S. Price; Kenneth E. Rechtoris; Paula Wilson Render; John T. Roache; John W. Rotunno; Peter G. Rush; David M. Saltiel; Patricia Kane Schmidt; Gregory J. Schroedter; John P. Scotellaro; Michael Sennett; Alan M. Serwer; Richard L. Sevcik; Peter M. Sfikas; Robert V. Shannon; Thomas C. Shields; David C. Sienko; Woon-Wah Siu; Stanley P. Sklar; Renato L. Smith; Cornelius J. Tanis; Pamela L. Taylor; Sandra L. Waldier; John Craig Walker; Paul J. Walsen; Neal H. Weinfield; Donald S. Weiss; Robert L. Wiesenthal; Richard O. Wood; Feng Xue. Of Counsel: Laird Bell (1910-1965); James D. Benak; Mark H. Berens; Stanton H. Berlin; Darrell S. Boyd (1919-1971); Alan R. Brodie; George M. Burditt; William G. Burns (1907-1988); Richard L. Curry (Retired); Paul F. Donahue; R. James Gormley (1921-2001); William N. Haddad (1903-2001); William B. Hanley (1933-2005); Dolores K. Hanna; Warren C. Haskin (Retired); J. William Hayton (1926-1994); Frank K. Heap; James P. Hemmer; Rollin C. Huggins, Jr.; Glen A. Lloyd (1931-1975); Alice S. Lonoff; Charles T. Martin; Charles T. Price; James T. Rhind; Allen R. Smart; Daniel P. Ward (1918-1995); Jack M. Whitney, II (1922-1995). Associates: Holby M. Abern; Ted J. Barthel; Thomas C. Basso; Patrice A. Bazianos; Michael A. Beckett; Diane E. Bell; Timothy W. Boarini; Heather A. Boice; Carol Cachey; Christopher I. Cedillo; Robert W. Connors; Bradley E. Davis; Amy S. Dolgin; Ania Domagala-Pierga; Steven Domanowski; Mary M. Donners; Kara A. Elgersma; Jason A. Engel; Nicholas I. Fink; John M. Fitzgerald; Maura Forde O'Meara; Jeffrey S. Gardner; James F. Goedken; Robert M. Gould; Edward M. Graham; Joel C. Griswold; Anis H. Ha; Douglas J. Hatlestad; Veena K. Jain; Dawn L. Johnson; Deanna L. Keysor; David Kim; Marcus M. Lee; Jeana R. Lervick; Colleen D. Lundgren; Cynthia S. Mangiaforte; Karl L. Marschel; Eric P. Martin; Andrew P.R. McDermott; Maria A. Mendoza; Abram I. Moore; Sanjay K. Murthy; Sean R. Odendahl; Curt A. Paison; Kevin Y. Pak; Todd E. Pentecost; Alicia A. Perla; Jeffrey T. Petersen; Courtney Ratzburg; Frances P. Reynolds; Matthew T. Ridsdale; Daniel G. Rosenberg; Michael J. Roth, Jr.; Wendy J. Sawyer; Sarah E. Schaefer; Adam R. Schaeffer; James R. Schueller; Laura E. Simpson; Gregory P. Sitrick; Wallace C. Solberg; Kathryn Starshak; Saren K. Sudel; John Susoreny; Aaron K. Tantleff; John E. "Jay" Truty; Brent W. Vincent; Karen E. Walther; Brooke P. Weinstein; Trayne S. Wheeler; Allyson L. Wilcox; Joseph C. Wylie, II; Peter Zura (Not admitted in IL).
General Practice. Corporate and Securities Law; Litigation; Antitrust; Trade Regulation; Intellectual Property; Labor and Employment Law; Employee Benefits; Environmental Law; Real Estate; Healthcare Law; Food, Drug and Device Law; Business Taxation; Personal Tax and Estate Planning; Banking and Financial Services; Insurance Law; Bankruptcy and Business Reorganization; Investment Management and Financial Markets; Communications Law; Government Contracts, Construction Law.
Washington, D.C. Office: Bell Boyd & Lloyd, PLLC, 1615 L Street, N.W., Suite 1200. Telephone: 202-466-6300. Fax: 202-463-0678.
See Professional Biographies, CHICAGO, ILLINOIS

Bell, Brigitte Schmidt, P.C., (AV)
53 West Jackson Boulevard, Suite 702, 60604 ⊙
Telephone: 312-360-1124 Fax: 312-360-1126; Email: mediators@BSBPC.com
Email: lawyers@BSBPC.com URL: http://www.mediate.com/brigittebell
Brigitte Schmidt Bell.
Family, Domestic Relations, Matrimonial, Adoption and Mediation Law, Mediation of Family, Adoption, Employment and Business issues, Collaborative Law.
Evanston, Illinois Office: 500 Davis Street, Suite 1006, 60201.
Lake Forest, Illinois Office: One Westminster Place, 60045.(By appt. only).
See Professional Biographies, CHICAGO, ILLINOIS

Bell Jones & Quinlisk, (AV)
200 West Adams Street Suite 2600, 60606-5233
Telephone: 312-425-2700 Fax: 312-960-9560
Walter W. Bell; Jerry D. Jones; John J. Quinlisk; Gina M. Anderson. Associate: Michael H. Allen. Of Counsel: Kent Chandler, Jr.
Estate Planning, Estate and Trust Administration, Taxation, Employee Benefits, Tax Exempt Organizations, Real Estate, Corporate and Business Matters, Insurance Law, Civil Litigation.
See Professional Biographies, CHICAGO, ILLINOIS

Bell & Pensyl, (AV)
111 W. Washington Street, Suite 1640, 60602
Telephone: 312-580-1940 Fax: 312-580-1943
Ira Bell; Claire E. Pensyl.
Business, Corporate, Real Estate and Employment.
See Professional Biographies, CHICAGO, ILLINOIS

Bellah, Kenneth D., Law Offices, (AV) '55 '80 C.57 B.A. L.146 J.D.
222 South Riverside Plaza Suite 1410, 60606 ⊙
Telephone: 312-648-9878 Fax: 312-648-0438
Email: kenbellah@aol.com
Estate Planning, Estate Administration, Real Estate, Commercial Litigation, Corporate Law.
Palos Heights, Illinois Office: 12750 South Harlem Avenue, 60463. Telephone: 708-448-1520.
Sanderson, Texas Office: 119 West Oak Street, P.O. Box 175, 79848. Telephone: 915-345-2914. Fax: 915-345-2926.
See Professional Biographies, CHICAGO, ILLINOIS

Bellande, Louis E., Jr., (AV) .... '42 '67 C.57 L.209 LL.B. [Bellande&S.]
Bellande & Sargis Law Group, LLP, (AV) .... 19 S. LaSalle St., Ste. 1203

Beller, Bernard ... '19 '48 C.339 B.A. L.146 LL.B. 3930 Pine Grove
Beller, Scott M., & Associates, (BV) '50 '77
C.339 B.A. L.146 J.D. 208 South LaSalle Street, Suite 1400
Bellinger, Kelly M. ... '— '01 C.880 B.A. L.602 J.D. [Ⓐ Barnes&T.]
Bellis, Nancy K., (AV) '56 '82 C.976 B.A. L.893 J.D.
V.P., Gen. Coun. & Sec., DiamondCluster International, Inc.
Bellows, Carole Kamin ... '35 '60 C.339 B.A. L.597 J.D. Cir. J.
Bellows, Joel J., (AV) ... '39 '65 C.145 B.A. L.365 J.D. [Bellows&B.] ⊙
Bellows, Laurel G., (AV) ... '48 '74 C.659 B.A. L.424 J.D. [Bellows&B.] ⊙

Bellows and Bellows, A Professional Corporation, (AV) BB
209 South LaSalle Street, Suite 800, 60604 ⊙
Telephone: 312-332-3340 Fax: 312-332-1190
Joel J. Bellows; Laurel G. Bellows;—Christopher L. Gallinari; Leslie P. Poole; Helen Bloch; Gretchen L. Gradinger; Connie S. Pike.
Administrative Law, Advertising/Marketing; Aged and Aging; Business Law, Civil Practice, Class Actions, Commercial Law, Commodities, Contracts, Copyrights, Corporate Law, Family Law, General Practice, Labor and Employment Litigation, Partnership Law, Intellectual Property, Securities Law, Real Estate, Taxation, Torts, Trusts and Estates, Wills.
Los Angeles, California Office: 601 South Figueroa Street, 27th Floor. Telephone: 213-485-1555.
See Professional Biographies, CHICAGO, ILLINOIS

Belofsky, Douglas M., (AV) ... '61 '86 C.145 B.A. L.910 J.D. [Belofsky&B.]
Belofsky, Sheldon ... '27 '52 C&L.145 B.A., J.D. 29 S. LaSalle St.
Belofsky & Belofsky, P.C., (AV) ... 33 N. Dearborn St.
Belom, John F. ... '56 '82 C.209 B.A. L.365 J.D. 410 S. Clark St.
Belongia, Heidi L. ... '— '02 C.436 B.A. L.209 J.D. [Ⓐ Foley&L.]
Belongia, Mark D. ... '72 '99 C.221 B.S.B.A. L.209 J.D. [Ⓐ Wolin&R.]
Belshaw, Carol J. ... '35 '82 C.999 B.Ed. L.365 J.D. John Marshall Law School
Belsher, Geoffrey S. '66 '92 C.043 B.A. L.029 LL.B.
(adm. in BC; not adm. in IL) [Blake,C.&G.]
Belsley, Michael D. ... '— '96 C&L.597 B.A., J.D. [Kirkland&E.]
Belstner, Raymond Edward ... '41 '67 L.339 J.D. Atty., Metra
Belush, Thomas A., (AV) ... '64 '91 C.679 B.S.M.E. L.1119 J.D. [Gardner C.&D.] (Pat.)
Belvedere, Josette, (BV) ... '46 '82 C.424 B.S. L.597 J.D. 1312 N. LaSalle St.
Belville, Patrick S. ... '70 '95 C.338 B.S. L.145 J.D. [Bell,B.&L.]
Belvis, Glen P., (AV) ... '58 '85 C.602 B.S. L.209 J.D. [Brinks H.G.&L.] (See Pat. Sect.)
Belyn, Pamela Mitchell ... '— '99 C.329 B.B.A. L.930 J.D. [Ⓐ Harris K.&G.]
Belz, Edwin J., (AV) ... '36 '61 C.757 B.A. L.209 J.D. 4407 N. Elston Ave.
Benak, James D. ... '54 '80 C.627 B.S. L.190 J.D. [Ⓒ Bell,B.&L.]
Bencivenga, Holly Ann ... '74 '99 C.575 B.A. L.30 J.D. [Ⓐ Lake,T.&D.]
Bender, Alan H. ... '45 '69 C.102 B.A. L.339 J.D. 1 N. LaSalle St., Ste. 2600
Bender, Gerald C. ... '37 '69 C.1016 B.S.B.A. L.365 J.D. 2801 R.J. Daley Center
Bender, Joseph E. ... '68 '93 C.339 B.A. L.436 J.D. [Wildman,H.A.&D.]
Bender, Michael Ian ... '65 '91 C.339 B.A. L.365 J.D. [Nadler,P.&M.]
Bender, Sarah C. ... '71 '99 C.98 B.A. L.339 J.D. [Ⓒ Neal,G.&E.]
Bendersky, Jordan ... '70 '96 C.172 B.A. L.823 J.D. [Hussain E.B.&F.]
Bendersky, Wendy L. ... '67 '93 C.597 B.A. L.273 J.D. [Neal,G.&E.]
Bendix, Richard M., Jr., (AV) ... '50 '75 C&L.477 B.A., J.D. [Schwartz C.]
Ben-Dov, David J. ... '72 '98 C.339 B.A. L.146 J.D. [Ⓒ Deutsch,L.&E.]
Benedek, Ann Lowry ... '54 '79 C.597 B.A. L.209 J.D. Asst. States Atty.
Benegas, David F. ... '35 '66 C.999 B.S. L.209 J.D. 5339 W. Wilson Ave.
Benes, Edward G. ... '73 '04 C.679 B.S.C.E. L.424 J.D. [Benes S.&K.]
Benes, Julie E. ... '76 '04 C.94 B.S.B.A. L.146 J.D. [Ⓐ Johnson&B.]
Benes Staudacher and Krantz, LLC ... 1242 S. Federal, Ste. C
Benford, Harry C., III, (AV) ... '37 '63 C.665 B.A. L.309 LL.B. [Schuyler,R.&Z.]
Bengel, Lauralyn G. ... '— '86 C.210 B.A. L.910 J.D. [Schiff H.]
Benham, William T. '48 '73 C.945 B.A. L.861 J.D.
(adm. in DC; not adm. in IL) V.P., Amoco Production Co.
Beninati, Francis A., (AV) ... '47 '72 C.228 A.B. L.893 J.D. [Krasnow S.C.]
Beninato, Dennis J. ... '68 '93 C.339 B.A. L.365 J.D. [Ⓐ Amari&L.]
Ben-Isvy, Lisa H. ... '68 '93 C.477 B.A. L.597 J.D. [Ⓐ Much S.F.D.A.&R.]
Ben-Isvy, Michael L. ... '68 '93 C.477 B.A. L.597 J.D. [DLPiper R.G.C.U.]
Benjamin, Anna L. ... '— '04 L.600 [Ⓐ Ungaretti&H.]
Benjamin, Corey A. ... '73 '99 C.378 B.A. L.365 J.D. 180 N. LaSalle, Ste. 2600
Benjamin, Fred I. ... '40 '65 C.1016 B.A. L.209 LL.B. 180 N. La Salle St.
Benjamin, J. Kevin ... '64 '89 C.966 B.A. L.146 J.D. [Benjamin]
Benjamin, Lawrence M. ... '62 '87 C.597 B.A. L.145 J.D. [Neal,G.&E.]
Benjamin, Marc A., (BV) ... '— '89 C.966 B.A. L.309 J.D. [Pircher,N.&M.]
Benjamin Legal Services, P.C. ... 130 S. Jefferson St., Ste. 501
Benn, Marvin N., (AV) ... '44 '72 C&L.339 B.S.E.E., J.D. [Much S.F.D.A.&R.] (Pat.)
Bennett, Anne A. ... '— '91 C&L.347 B.A., J.D. Dir. Internal Audit
Bennett, Barry M., (AV) ... '54 '80 C.477 A.B. L.309 J.D. [Dowd,B.&B.]
Bennett, Camille E. ... '— '94 C.914 B.A. L.145 J.D. [Ⓒ Sonnenschein N.&R.]
Bennett, Christopher P. ... '— '99 C&L.502 B.A., J.D. [Ⓐ Latham&W.]
Bennett, David E., (AV) ... '44 '69 C.209 B.A. L.597 J.D. [Vedder,P.K.&K.]
Bennett, David M., (BV) ... '64 '89 C.679 B.A. L.146 J.D. [Pretzel&S.]
Bennett, David R. ... '71 '97 C.886 B.S.M.E. L.945 J.D. [Jenner&B.] (Pat.)
Bennett, Eric ... '— '01 C.589 B.S. L.597 J.D. [Ⓐ Kirkland&E.]
Bennett, Eugene L. ... '43 '68 C.276 A.B. L.597 J.D. 55 W. Monroe St., Ste. 500
Bennett, George O. ... '58 '85 C.597 B.A. L.802 J.D. V.P. & Secy., Bennett Brothers, Inc.
Bennett, Kathryn C. ... '79 '04 C.103 B.A. L.597 J.D. [Ⓐ Baker&M.]
Bennett, Kelly Q. ... '69 '98 C.959 B.A. L.146 J.D. [Ciardelli&C.]
Bennett, Mark W. ... '64 '92 C&L.209 B.A., J.D. [Laner,M.D.B.L.&T.]
Bennett, Michael C. ... '65 '93 C.801 B.A. L.209 J.D. Asst. Def., St. App. Def. Office
Bennett, Michael P., (AV) ... '59 '89 C.602 B.A. L.424 J.D. [Wildman,H.A.&D.]
Bennett, Nancy J. '50 '78 C.1064 B.A. L.365 J.D.
Chief of Pros., Dept. of Prof. Regulation
Bennett, Paul E., II ... '— '02 C.574 B.A. L.352 J.D. [Ⓐ Neal&L.]
Bennett, R. Clay, (AV) ... '49 '75 C.976 B.A. L.861 J.D. [Ⓒ Lord,B.&B.]
Bennett, Robert W. ... '41 '66 C&L.309 B.A., LL.B. Prof. of Law, Northwestern Univ.
Bennett, Russell O., (AV) ... '15 '39 C.623 A.B. L.309 LL.B. One 1st National Plz.‡
Bennett, Ryan Blaine ... '— '00 C.475 B.A. L.602 J.D. [Ⓐ Kirkland&E.]
Bennett, Zula L. ... '43 '76 C.801 B.S. L.209 J.D. 111 E. Chestnut St.‡
Bennington, Thomas F., Jr. ... '62 '87 C.578 B.A. L.209 J.D. [Chuhak&T.]
Benodin, Ellen C. '41 '86 C.145 B.A. L.424 J.D.
Chf. Asst. Corp. Coun., Contracts & Aviation Div.
Benoit, Dexter G. ... '— '05 C.473 B.A. L.339 J.D. Two North LaSalle Street, Suite 2200
Bensinger, Charles N., III ... '— '97 C.98 B.S. L.910 J.D. [Ⓐ Jones D.]
Bensinger, Ethan E., (AV) ... '49 '76 C.339 B.A.S. L.146 J.D. [Ⓒ Fragomen,D.B.&L.]
Bensinger, Peter B., Jr., (AV) ... '58 '89 C.813 A.B. L.569 J.D. [Bartlit B.H.P.&S.]
Bensinger, Sarah R. ... '62 '92 C.976 B.A. L.112 J.D. 3618 N. Fremont‡
Bensinger, V. Brette ... '77 '05 C.597 B.A. L.146 J.D. [Ⓐ Hinshaw&C.]
Benson, David F. ... '— '03 C.880 B.S. L.146 J.D. [Ⓐ Katten M.R.]
Benson, Gary S., (BV) ... '51 '77 C.589 B.S. L.146 J.D. 2615 N. Sheffield
Benson, George W., (AV) ... '48 '73 C.951 B.A. L.309 J.D. [McDermott W.&E.]

Benson, Joel W., (AV) '49 '78
C.477 B.S.E.E. L.276 J.D. [Brinks H.G.&L.] (See Pat. Sect.)
Benson, Katherine M. ... '— '03 C.201 B.A. L.209 J.D. [Ⓐ LaBarge,C.&L.]
Benson, Kristen M. ... '73 '97 C.602 B.B.A. L.893 J.D. [Ⓐ Sidley A.B.&W.]
Benson, Stephen P. ... '70 '05 C.477 B.S. L.209 J.D. [Ⓐ Welsh&K.]
Bentivenga, Scott C., (AV) ... '63 '88 C.602 B.A. L.424 J.D. [Bollinger,R.&G.]
Bentley, Jason S. ... '73 '03 C.879 B.A. L.209 J.D. [Ⓐ Hinshaw&C.]
Bentley, Peter J. H., (AV) ... '34 '66 C.050 B.A. 130 East Randolph Drive‡
Benton, Christy J. ... '70 '95 C.475 B.A. L.215 J.D. [Ⓐ Segal M.S.&M.]
Benton, Grandon P. ... '63 '01 C.383 B.A. L.146 J.D. 542 S. Dearborn St., Ste. 1260
Benton, Jennifer Wendell ... '— '02 C.308 B.S.N. L.209 J.D. [Ⓐ Anderson,R.]
Benton-Powers, Susan M., (AV) ... '52 '82 C.502 B.A. L.94 J.D. [Winston&S.]
Bentsen, Ronald Eric ... '60 '92 C.339 B.S.C.E. L.424 J.D. [Ⓐ Morris&S.]
Benway, Stephanie A. ... '74 '99 C.966 B.A L.146 J.D. [Ⓐ Ancel,G.D.B.D.&R.]
Benz, Mary Patricia, (AV) ... '51 '78 C.339 B.A. L.597 J.D. [Winston&S.]
Benz, Michael T., (AV) ... '— '86 C.339 B.A. L.424 J.D. [Chapman&C.]
Benz, Thomas R., (AV) ... '21 '49 C&L.424 LL.B. 10315 S. Seeley Ave.‡
Benzon, Melissa L. ... '74 '01 C.209 B.A. L.597 J.D. [Ⓐ Freeborn&P.]
Beranek, Kurt G., (AV) ... '49 '75 C.340 B.S. L.365 J.D. [Fraterrigo,B.F.&K.]
Berbas, George Peter ... '— '02 C&L.209 B.A., J.D. 180 N. La Salle Street, Suite 1800
Berberian, H. Nicholas, (AV) ... '52 '78 C.385 A.B. L.145 J.D. [Neal,G.&E.]
Berc, Harold T., (AV) ... '14 '37 C.597 L.209 LL.B. [H.T.Berc] ‡
Berc, Harold T., P.C., (AV) ... 2960 N. Lake Shore Dr., Ste. 1703
Berckmueller, Fritz E. ... '75 '00 C.902 B.A. L.145 J.D. [Ⓐ Katten M.R.]
Berdahl, Ann L. ... '— '00 C.966 B.A. L.494 J.D. [Ⓐ Karavidas]
Berdelle, James J., (BV) ... '58 '83 C&L.802 B.B.A., J.D. [Bullaro&C.]
Berdelle, Richard L., Jr., (AV) ... '53 '78 C.473 B.S. L.436 J.D. [R.L.Berdelle,Jr.]

Berdelle, Richard L., Jr., P.C., (AV)
The Rookery Building, 209 South LaSalle Street, Suite 501, 60604-1447
Telephone: 312-726-0400 Fax: 312-726-0401
Email: dberdelle@sbcglobal.net URL: http://www.berdellelaw.com
Richard L. Berdelle, Jr.
Medical Malpracticing including: Surgical and Physician Malpractice, Obstetric Malpractice, Hospital Malpractice, Birth Defects and Birth Trauma. Plaintiff Personal Injury including: Automobile Accidents, Trucking Accidents, Motorcycle Accidents, Head Injuries, Catastrophic Accidents and Wrongful Death.
See Professional Biographies, CHICAGO, ILLINOIS

Berek, David A. '64 '99 C.209 B.S. L.365 J.D.
Family CFO, Frye Louis Capital Management, Inc.
Beremski, Ognyan (Oggie) ... '70 '00 C.399 B.A. L.424 J.D. [Ⓐ McAndrews,H.&M.]
Berends, Scott ... '78 '03 C&L.339 B.S., J.D. [Ⓐ Patterson]
Berendt, Gerald E. '47 '72 C&L.790 A.B., J.D.
(adm. in SC; not adm. in IL) Prof., The John Marshall Law Sch.
Berendt, Michael H. ... '76 '01 C.1044 B.A. L.365 J.D. [Ⓐ Wessels&P.]
Berens, Brian F. ... '28 '58 C.1016 A.B. L.146 J.D. 8 S. Mich. Ave.
Berens, Mark H., (AV) ... '28 '51 C&L.602 B.S.C., J.D. [Ⓒ Bell,B.&L.]
Berens, Raymond M., (AV) '59 '84
C.339 B.A. L.477 J.D. Gen. Coun., Wilson Sporting Goods Co.
Berenstein, Greg L. ... '— '85 C&L.352 B.A., J.D. [Sachnoff&W.]
Berent, James M. '53 '79 C.339 B.S. L.365 J.D.
Metro. Water Reclamation Dist. of Greater Chicago
Berenz, Philip J., Law Offices of Philip J. Berenz '70 '00 C.679 B.S L.1119 J.D.
350 North LaSalle Street, Suite 900 (⊙Chicago)
Berenz, Philip J., Law Offices of Philip J. Berenz '70 '00
C.679 B.S L.1119 J.D. [Ⓒ Crowley&L.] (⊙Chicago)
Berenzweig, Jack C., (AV) '42 '68
C.188 B.E.E. L.30 J.D. [Brinks H.G.&L.] (See Pat. Sect.)
Bereyso, Mark J., (AV) ... '57 '85 [Ⓒ Huff&G.]
Berg, Anne Kathryn ... '68 '94 C&L.339 B.S., J.D. [Ⓒ Schwartz C.]
Berg, Dennis A. ... '64 '89 C.339 B.A. L.209 J.D. [Keating,K.P.&B.]
Berg, Elizabeth C. ... '58 '89 C.103 B.A. L.424 J.D. [Ⓐ J.A.Baldi&Assoc.]
Berg, Eric, (AV) ... '65 '92 C.976 B.A. L.597 J.D. [DLPiper R.G.C.U.]
Berg, Jean Scholl '50 '82 C.679 B.A. L.602 J.D.
(adm. in IN; not adm. in IL) U.S. Postal Serv.
Berg, Joan T. ... '65 '92 C.424 B.S. L.146 J.D. [Schain,B.R.&C.]
Berg, John Anton ... '71 '98 C.473 B.A. L.424 J.D. [Ⓐ Connelly S.H.]
Berg, Kenneth F., (AV) ... '54 '79 C.910 A.B. L.93 J.D. [Ulmer&B.]
Berg, Royal F. ... '51 '84 C.98 B.S. L.365 J.D. Travelers & Immigrants Aid
Berg, Thomas C. '50 '75 C.145 B.A. L.209 J.D.
V.P., Gen. Coun. & Secy., Amsted Industries (Legal Department)
Bergal, Mark G., (CV) ... '63 '91 C.966 B.S. L.146 J.D. 33 N. Lasalle St.
Bergamino, Anthony, Jr. ... '63 '88 C.1044 B.A. L.145 J.D. [Bronson&K.]
Bergen, Amy Lewis ... '63 '95 C.477 B.A. L.362 J.D. 1060 W. Fry St.
Bergen, Charles S., (AV) ... '55 '81 C&L.309 A.B., J.D. [Grippo&E.]
Berger, Adam M. ... '71 '99 C.910 B.A. L.424 J.D. [Ⓐ Mangan,L.G.&L.]
Berger, Carrie L. ... '72 '97 C&L.597 B.A., J.D. [Ⓐ Stein,R.&H.]
Berger, Helaine L. ... '56 '81 50 W. Washington Street
Berger, Michael J., (P.C.), (AV) ... '49 '73 C.1016 B.A. L.146 J.D. [Berger S.]
Berger, Norman B., (AV) ... '56 '81 C.966 B.A. L.209 J.D. [Varga B.L.H.&C.]
Berger, Paula Kaplan ... '52 '76 C.502 B.J. L.209 J.D. [Neal,G.&E.]
Berger, Philip M. ... '53 '79 C.659 B.A. L.477 J.D. 3506 N. Janssen Ave.‡
Berger, Robert I., (AV) ... '— '75 C.339 B.A. L.597 J.D. [Schiff H.]
Berger, Robert M., (AV) ... '42 '66 C.477 A.B. L.145 J.D. [Ⓒ Krasnow S.C.]
Berger, Sidney R. '51 '75 C.1016 B.S.B.A. L.146 J.D.
70 West Madison Street Suite 3700
Berger, Stephen L., (AV) ... '45 '70 C.339 B.A. L.146 J.D. [Neal,G.&E.]

Berger, Newmark & Fenchel P.C., (AV) BB
303 West Madison Street, 23rd Floor, 60606-3308 ⊙
Telephone: 312-782-5050 Fax: 312-782-6491
William B. Berger (1892-1974); Lawrence S. Newmark (1905-1986); Marvin S. Fenchel (1917-2003); Philip Cowan; John M. Cytron; Frank T. Davenport; Barry D. Elman; Lawrence M. Elman; Alan Garland; Lynn Lucchese-Soto; Howard Marks; Wendy M. Reutebuch; Julius H. Shapiro. Of Counsel: Sidney E. Morrison; Jeffrey T. Saltz; Avrum H. Dannen.
Civil Trial and Appellate Practice in all State and Federal Courts. Corporate, Real Estate, Banking, Estate Planning, Probate, Labor and Employment Law, Pension and Taxation Law, Bankruptcy and Bankruptcy Avoidance Law, Mechanics Lien and Construction Law.

Berger Schatz, (AV) BB
A Partnership including Professional Corporations
161 North Clark Street, Suite 2800, 60601 ⊙
Telephone: 312-782-3456 Fax: 312-782-8463
Email: info@bergerschatz.com URL: http://www.bergerschatz.com
Members of Firm: Jason G. Adess; Michael J. Berger (P.C.); Mary J. Clark (Resident Partner-in-Charge, Bannockburn Office); Amanda B. Clayman; Michael S. Cohen (1954-2004); Andrew D. Eichner; Leon I. Finkel; P. André Katz; Debbie K. Lerner (Resident, Bannockburn Office); David H. Levy (P.C.); Norman Ruber; Michael S. Sabath; Barry A. Schatz (P.C.); Tracey A. Wertman;—Brian J. Blitz; Catherine M. Dunn; Laurence B. Hirsch; Joshua E. Hornaday (Resident, Bannockburn

(This Listing Continued)

Berger Schatz (Continued)

Office); Kristina L. Jarvis; Margaret E. Keane; Marcelle R. Kott; Karen Rose Krehbiel; Sharon Steinberg Mobley; Melinda C. Rogers; Dina Warner.
Matrimonial, Family, Domestic Relations Law, Trial and Appellate Practice: Including Divorce, Child Custody, Child Support, Paternity, Spousal Support and Visitation Rights.
Lake County Office: 2333 Waukegan Road, Suite 260, Bannockburn, Illinois 60015. Telephone: 847-405-9500. Fax: 847-405-9563.

See Professional Biographies, CHICAGO, ILLINOIS

Berger Zerman, Beth Ann .... '64 '93 C.352 B.B.A. L.146 J.D. [Bollinger,R.&G.]
Berger-White, Juliet V. .... '73 '99 C.966 B.S. L.597 J.D. [Hughes S.P.R.&D.]
Bergetz, Carl T. .... '69 '96 C.813 B.A. L.339 J.D. [Robinson C.&C.]
Berghammer, Joseph J. ..... '— '95 C.453 B.S. L.976 J.D. [Banner&W.] (See Pat. Sect.)
Berghoff, Ethan A. .... '72 '97 C.575 B.A. L.276 J.D. [Baker&M.]
Berghoff, John C. ...... '10 '40 C.145 Ph.B. L.146 LL.B. 8770 S. Longwood Dr.‡
Berghoff, John C., Jr., (AV) .... '41 '66 C&L.597 B.S., J.D. [Mayer,B.R.&M.]
Berghoff, Paul H., (AV) '56 '81
C.399 B.A. L.477 J.D. [McDonnell B.H.&B.] (See Pat. Sect.)
Berghoff, Robert A. .... '37 '63 C.597 B.A. L.145 J.D. 134 N. LaSalle St.
Bergin, John P., (AV) .... '67 '92 C&L.424 B.A., J.D. [Braun S.L.B.&M.]
Bergman, Jeffrey H. .... '— '86 C.145 A.B. L.966 J.D. [Sachnoff&W.]
Bergman, Robin L. '62 '87 C.339 B.A. L.94 J.D.
Sr. V.P. & Asst. Gen. Coun., Information Res., Inc.
Bergmann, Edward W., (AV) .... '41 '66 C.597 B.S. L.188 J.D. [Seyfarth S.]
Bergmann, Matthew F. .... '69 '94 C&L.477 B.B.A., J.D. [Winston&S.]
Bergmann, Michael G. '75 '02
C.128 B.A L.209 J.D. Staff Atty., Chicago Volunteer Legal Srvs.
Bergmann, Paul T. '53 '85 C.339 B.S. L.365 J.D.
Sr. Vice Pres., Prairie States Adminstrative Services Inc
Bergner, Mark A. .... '— '99 C.502 B.S.E.E. L.734 J.D. [Schiff H.] (Pat.)
Bergren, Holly .... '71 '96 C.339 B.S. L.424 J.D. 222 N. La Salle St.
Bergstrom, Robert W., (AV) '18 '40
C.145 M.B.A. L.146 J.D. 111 E. Chestnut St., Apt. 49C
Beringer, Benjamin P., (AV) ...... '65 '90 C.894 B.A. L.347 J.D. [Cirignani H.H.&L.]
Berish, Brad A., (AV) .... '62 '89 C.347 B.S. L.275 J.D. [Adelman&G.]
Berish, Christina M. .... '78 '03 C&L.477 B.A., J.D. [FagelHaber]
Berk, Keith H., (AV) .... '58 '83 C&L.339 B.S., J.D. [Horwood M.&B.]
Berk, Michael .... '70 '97 C&L.309 A.B., J.D. Venture Capital Frontenac Co.
Berk, Peter T. .... '— '97 C.477 B.A. L.597 J.D. [Sachnoff&W.]
Berke, Benitta .... '53 '77 C.472 B.B.A. L.46 J.D. 36 Randolph Street
Berke, Michael A. '— '79
C.367 B.A. L.339 J.D. U.S. Dept. of Housing & Urban Develop.
Berke, Perry M., (AV) .... '31 '55 C&L.597 B.S., LL.B. [Baskin,S.B.&W.]
Berke, Ralph L. .... '50 '74 C.937 B.A. L.597 J.D. [Garofalo,S.H.&S.]
Berkeley, Jill B., (AV) .... '— '75 C.477 B.A. L.597 J.D. [Schiff H.]
Berkeley, Stephen S., (BV) .... '70 '95 C.299 B.A. L.146 J.D. [Neal,G.&E.]
Berkley, Lonni E. .... '60 '83 C.174 B.A. L.597 J.D. [McGuirewoods]
Berkoff, Adam T. .... '69 '94 C.966 B.A. L.436 J.D. [DLPiper R.G.C.U.]
Berkoff, Mark A., (AV) .... '61 '87 C.966 B.A. L.145 J.D. [DLPiper R.G.C.U.]
Berkowitz, Diane L. .... '59 '87 C&L.424 B.A., J.D. IRS, Ofc. of the Dist. Coun.
Berkowitz, Melanie H. .... '71 '96 C.659 B.A. L.569 J.D. [Seyfarth S.]
Berks, Stuart .... '41 '66 C&L.209 B.A., J.D. [Deutsch,L.&E.]
Berkshire, Alan G. '60 '86 C.477 B.S. L.178 J.D.
Sr.V.P. & Gen. Coun., John Nuveen & Co., Inc.
Berkson, Dennis A., (AV) .... '47 '72 C.966 B.A. L.273 J.D. 180 N. LaSalle St., Ste. 1925
Berkson, Jerome .... '18 '42 C.597 L.209 LL.B. 230 W. Monroe St.
Berkson, Stuart M., (AV) .... '55 '80 C.339 B.A. L.309 J.D. [McDermott W.&E.]
Berland, Abel E. .... '15 '38 L.209 J.D. Vice Chmn., Rubloff Inc.
Berland, Jamie Lyn .... '73 '98 C&L.966 B.A., J.D. Law Clk., Cir. Ct. of Cook Co.
Berland, Richard B. .... '43 '68 C.339 B.A. L.209 J.D. Cir. J.
Berlanga, Felicitas .... '52 '80 C.338 B.A. L.209 J.D. NLRB
Berliant, Jerry B. .... '42 '70 C.966 B.S. L.209 J.D. Leg. Sec. Srv.
Berlin, Eric P. .... '— '93 C.197 B.A. L.966 J.D. [Jones D.]
Berlin, Gerald L. .... '58 '84 C.610 B.S. L.209 J.D. [Berlin&Assoc.]
Berlin, Randy Lamm, Law Offices of '— '91
C.393 A.B. L.424 J.D. 111 N. Canal St., Ste. 300
Berlin, Stanton H., (AV) .... '34 '59 C&L.477 B.B.A., J.D. [Bell,B.&L.]
Berlin, Steven I. .... '59 '84 C.31 B.A. L.597 J.D. City of Chicago, Bd. of Ethics

Berlin & Associates
222 North Columbus Drive Suite 4102, 60601
Telephone: 312-297-9000 Fax: 312-297-9000
Email: berlinlaw@sbcglobal.net URL: http://www.berlinlawfirm.com
Gerald L. Berlin.
General Practice and Real Estate.

See Professional Biographies, CHICAGO, ILLINOIS

Berlinsky, Jay S., (AV) .... '44 '69 C.597 B.A. L.813 J.D. [Schwartz C.]
Berman, Arthur L., (AV) ...... '35 '58 C.339 B.S. L.597 J.D. Dir. Labor Mediation Servs.
Berman, Arthur M., (AV) .... '39 '64 C.339 B.S. L.209 J.D. [Kirsh&B.]
Berman, Bennett I. .... '18 '46 C.339 B.S. L.309 LL.B. 135 S. La Salle St.
Berman, Cary Mark .... '62 '89 C.1106 B.A. L.365 J.D. Asst. Pub. Def.
Berman, Debbie L., (AV) .... '66 '90 C.1036 A.B. L.309 J.D. [Jenner&B.]
Berman, Edwin M. .... '28 '52 C.472 L.209 LL.B. Cir. J.
Berman, Jane S. .... '— '87 C&L.339 B.S., J.D. [Chapman&C.] (Pat.)
Berman, Jeffrey A. .... '62 '87 C&L.339 B.S., J.D. [Meckler B.&T.]
Berman, Julian L., (AV) .... '— '48 C&L.966 Ph.B., LL.B. [Michael B.&F.]
Berman, Marvin D., (AV) .... '31 '55 C&L.339 B.S., J.D. [Kiesler&B.]
Berman, Michael H., (AV) .... '45 '69 C.424 B.S. L.365 J.D. [M.H.Berman]
Berman, Mitchell D. .... '56 '81 C.910 B.A. L.146 J.D. V.P., The Carlyle Grp. Ltd.
Berman, Myles D., (AV) .... '— '83 C.339 A.B. L.597 J.D. [Foley&L.]
Berman, Peter J., (AV) .... '46 '74 C.966 B.A. L.209 J.D. [P.J.Berman]
Berman, Steven A. .... '69 '94 C.98 B.S. L.146 J.D. [Anesi,O.R.N.&K.]
Berman, Stuart L. .... '71 '98 C.67 B.A. L.146 J.D. [McKay,N.T.D.&K.]

Berman, Michael H., P.C., (AV)
180 North LaSalle Street, Suite 2108, 60601
Telephone: 312-726-0531 Fax: 312-726-4928
Email: mhbermanpc@yahoo.com
Michael H. Berman.
Personal Injury, Torts, Medical Malpractice, Professional Liability, Automobile Accidents, Wrongful Death, Premises Liability, Civil Litigation.

See Professional Biographies, CHICAGO, ILLINOIS

Berman, Peter J., Ltd., (AV)
Suite 1000 332 South Michigan Avenue, 60604-4398
Telephone: 312-408-1114 Fax: 312-408-1936
Email: pberman@pbermanlaw.com URL: http://www.pbermanlaw.com
Peter J. Berman.

(This Listing Continued)

Berman, Peter J., Ltd. (Continued)

Business Litigation, Securities Arbitration, Broker-Dealer Arbitration, Commodities Arbitration, Federal Civil Practice, Shareholder Disputes, Trial Practice, Civil Appeals, Employment Litigation, Commercial Litigation.

See Professional Biographies, CHICAGO, ILLINOIS

Berman Sandler, Leatrice .... '— '05 C.477 B.A. L.424 J.D. [McDermott W.&E.]
Bern, David S. .... '08 '47 L.209 J.D. 309 W. Washington‡
Bernard, Catherine A. .... '71 '02 C.813 B.A. L.569 J.D. [Mayer,B.R.&M.]
Bernard, Christopher J., (BV) '51 '76 C.612 B.A. L.862 J.D.
(adm. in OK; not adm. in IL)
Lead Coun. Power Team & Assoc. Gen. Coun., Exelon Corp.
Bernard, Debra Rae .... '58 '85 C.339 B.A. L.146 J.D. [Mayer,B.R.&M.]
Bernardi, Richard L. .... '54 '80 C.436 B.A. L.365 J.D. 130 E. Randolph St.
Bernardini, Charles R., (AV) .... '— '72 C&L.339 B.S., J.D. [Ungaretti&H.]
Bernat, John P. .... '52 '79 C.46 B.s. L.146 J.D. Rush-Presbyterian-St. Luke's Medical
Bernath, Kristen J. .... '72 '97 C.645 B.A. L.209 J.D. State Dept. of Human Rights
Bernauer, Beatrix .... '71 '97 C.766 B.A. L.424 J.D. Sr. Coun., Grant Thornton, LLP
Berndt, Caroll A. .... '56 '02 C.999 L.365 J.D. 19 South La Salle St., Ste. 450
Berndt, William B. .... '74 '99 C.347 B.A. L.477 J.D. [Schopf&W.]
Berner, Robert L., Jr., (AV) .... '31 '56 C.602 A.B. L.309 LL.B. [Baker&M.]
Bernet, Richard G. '62 '89
C.234 B.S. L.209 J.D. Asst. Gen. Coun., Exelon Bus. Servs. Co.
Bernick, Alan J. .... '36 '64 L.209 LL.B. 5500 S. Sawyer Ave.
Bernick, David M., (P.C.), (AV) .... '— '78 C&L.145 B.A., J.D. [Kirkland&E.]
Bernick, Reuben A., (AV) .... '51 '77 C.145 A.B. L.309 J.D. [Mandel,L.&S.]
Bernik, Joseph M. .... '24 '60 C.339 B.S. L.146 J.D. 227 E. Delaware Pl.‡
Berning, Larry D., (AV) .... '40 '68 C.347 A.B. L.1119 J.D. [Sidley A.B.&W.]
Bernover, Alan M. .... '— '01 C.502 B.A. L.472 J.D. [Litchfield C.]
Bernstein, Alan J. .... '55 '81 C.96 B.A. L.365 J.D. 10 S. La Salle St.
Bernstein, Amy J. .... '53 '77 C.659 B.A. L.767 J.D. 111 W. Monroe Street
Bernstein, Arnold .... '50 '77 C.589 B.S. L.365 J.D. 39 S. La Salle, Suite 2802
Bernstein, Charles B. .... '41 '65 C.145 A.B. L.209 J.D. 10 S. La Salle St., Ste. 1400
Bernstein, Eugene H., (AV) '45 '70
C.339 B.S. L.597 J.D. Asst. Gen. Coun., Exelon Corp.
Bernstein, H. Bruce, (AV) .... '43 '68 C.188 A.B. L.309 J.D. [Sidley A.B.&W.]
Bernstein, Howard L., (AV) .... '43 '68 C&L.846 B.B.A., J.D. [Neal,G.&E.]
Bernstein, Irwin S. .... '57 '81 C.339 B.S. L.597 J.D. Gelber Mgt.
Bernstein, Isadore M. .... '14 '41 C.999 L.146 LL.B. 6315 S. Central Ave.
Bernstein, Jack N. .... '— '95 C.245 B.A. L.365 J.D. [Kirkland&E.]
Bernstein, Joseph L. ..... '36 '64 C.973 B.S.B.A. L.209 J.D. Misc. Warehousemen's Union
Bernstein, Joseph T. .... '78 '03 C&L.477 B.S., J.D. [Wallenstein W.&R.]
Bernstein, Joshua .... '70 '02 C.959 B.A. L.209 J.D. [Statman,H.S.&E.]
Bernstein, Louis D. .... '58 '84 C.347 B.A. L.1019 J.D. [Gould&R.]
Bernstein, Mark S. .... '63 '88 C.399 B.S. L.477 J.D. [Barack F.K.P.&N.]
Bernstein, Matthew Ian, (BV) '64 '93 C.37 B.A. L.146 J.D.
Asst. Prof. of Clinical Ed., Chicago-Kent College of Law
Bernstein, Moria A. .... '— '96 C.209 B.S. L.146 J.D. 30 N. Lasalle St., Fl. 29
Bernstein, Philip J., (AV) ...... '64 '89 C.966 B.B.A. L.209 J.D. [R.M.Bernstein&Assoc.]
Bernstein, Ralph M., & Associates, (AV) '30 '56
C.734 B.S.C. L.209 J.D. 208 South LaSalle, Suite 1400
Bernstein, Robert T. .... '69 '95 C.188 B.S. L.966 J.D. [Laner,M.D.B.L.&T.]
Bernstein, Roy L. .... '— '83 C.966 B.A. L.273 J.D. [Arnstein&L.]
Bernstein, Sarah M. .... '66 '91 C.30 B.A. L.597 J.D. [Barack F.K.P.&N.]
Bernstein, Stuart, (AV) .... '19 '47 C&L.145 A.B., J.D. [Mayer,B.R.&M.]
Berntsen, Denis A., (AV) '47 '72
C&L.339 B.S.E.E., J.D. [McDonnell B.H.&B.] (See Pat. Sect.)
Beroukas, Evdoxia .... '59 '88 C.597 B.S.J. L.209 J.D. 1472 W. Balmoral Ave.
Berra, Louis M. '42 '77 C&L.215 M.B.A., J.D.
(adm. in MI; not adm. in IL) U.S. Dept. H.U.D.‡
Berres, Daneen Fitzpatrick .... '75 '00 C.436 B.A. L.209 J.D. [Tressler,S.M.&P.]
Berrington, Howard M., (AV) .... '53 '78 C.339 B.A. L.209 J.D. [FagelHaber]
Berrones, Luis A. .... '57 '83 C&L.209 B.A., J.D. [Gardner C.&D.]
Berry, Alan M., (P.C.), (AV) .... '44 '69 C.966 B.S. L.94 J.D. [Katten M.R.]
Berry, Daryl R. .... '54 '78 C.511 B.A. L.1119 J.D. 2609 W. 79th St.
Berry, Ilona M. ...... '56 '80 C.98 B.A. L.339 J.D. Sr. Coun., Bank One Corp. (Law Dept.)
Berry, J. Dale .... '43 '70 C.475 B.A. L.477 J.D. [Cornfield&F.]
Berry, Jeffrey D. .... '— '80 C.150 B.B.A. L.276 J.D. [Chapman&C.]
Berry, John M. .... '46 '74 C.589 B.S. in Ed. L.146 J.D. Asst. States Atty.
Berry, Richard M. .... '45 '74 C.645 B.A. L.1009 J.D. American Dental Assn.
Berry, Tracy W. '61 '92 C.1120 B.S. L.802 J.D.
(adm. in TX; not adm. in IL) Dep. Gen. Coun., Grant Thornton, LLP
Bers, Alan B., (AV) ..... '47 '73 C&L.339 B.A., J.D. 200 North La Salle Street, Suite 2750
Bersson, Shalom D. .... '76 '02 C.978 B.S. L.146 J.D. [Nadler,P.&M.]
Bertagnolli, Leslie A., (AV) .... '48 '79 C.338 B.A. L.339 J.D. [Baker&M.]
Berten, David P. .... '64 '89 C.893 B.C.P. L.966 J.D. [Competition L.]
Bertocchi, Joel D. .... '57 '83 C&L.966 B.A., J.D. [Mayer,B.R.&M.]
Bertoglio, Brad R. .... '73 '00 C.339 B.S.E.E. L.146 J.D. [Greenberg T.] (Pat.)
Bertoglio, Nancy E., (BV) .... '48 '73 C.879 B.A. L.424 J.D. [Bell,B.&L.]
Bertoldi, Jessica .... '69 '94 C.945 B.A. L.818 J.D. Goldman Sachs & Co.
Bertram, Darren .... '73 '98 C&L.339 B.S., J.D. [FagelHaber]
Bertsch, Gregory J. .... '71 '00 C.424 B.B.A. L.209 J.D. [Handler,T.&D.]
Bertsche, J. Paul .... '53 '86 C.338 B.A. L.209 J.D. 4545 W. Berteau
Bertucci, Donald T., (AV) ...... '43 '67 C.424 B.S. L.209 J.D. 30 W. Monroe St., Ste. 710
Bertucci, Robert W. .... '56 '83 C.393 B.A. L.146 J.D. Cir.J.
Berz, Marvin S., (AV) .... '23 '48 C.208 L.209 LL.B. 111 W. Washington
Berzon, David B., (AV) .... '59 '84 C.861 B.S. L.904 J.D. [Levenfeld P.]
Berzon, Vera, (CV) .... '40 '90 L.365 J.D. 180 N. La Salle St.
Besecker, Cynthia L. .... '— '95 C.209 B.A. L.1000 J.D. [O'Hagan,S.&A.]
Besler, Paula Meyer .... '64 '89 C.339 B.S. L.424 J.D. [Pretzel&S.]
Besner, Eric A. '69 '97 C.1494 B.A. L.659 J.D.
(adm. in CA; not adm. in IL)
V.P., Acquisitions & Bus. Affs., Home Vision Entertainment, Inc. (Legal Department)
Bess, Michael D. .... '70 '95 C.477 B.A. L.339 J.D. [Winston&S.]
Bessette-Smith, Suzanne, (AV) .... '56 '80 C.578 B.A. L.339 J.D. [Barack F.K.P.&N.]
Best, Edward S., (AV) .... '61 '86 C.339 A.B. L.424 J.D. [Mayer,B.R.&M.]
Best, James F., (AV) .... '49 '74 C&L.221 B.S., J.D. [Best,V.&H.]
Best, Peter J. .... '29 '51 6668 N. Leoti Ave.
Best, Robert J., (AV) .... '50 '75 C.597 B.A. L.209 J.D. [Bell,B.&L.]

Best, Vanderlaan & Harrington, (AV)
25 E. Washington Street, Suite 210, 60602
Telephone: 312-819-1100 Fax: 312-819-8062
Email: bvh@bestfirm.com URL: http://www.bestfirm.com
Members of Firm: James F. Best; Lori A. Vanderlaan; Alison M. Harrington.

(This Listing Continued)

Best, Vanderlaan & Harrington (Continued)

General Liability Defense, Insurance Coverage, Medical Malpractice Defense, Employment Discrimination Defense, Insurance Coverage.
Wheaton, Illinois Office: 2100 Manchester Road, Suite 1420, 60187. Telephone: 630-752-8000. Fax: 630-752-8763.

Besunder, Eric J. .... '77 '02 C.339 B.A. L.146 J.D. 451 W. Wrightwood, #409
Betar, Samuel J., (AV) .... '28 '55 C&L.352 B.A., LL.B. 19 W. Jackson Blvd.
Betar, Samuel J., III .... '56 '83 C.93 B.A. L.424 J.D. Cir. J.
Beth, Phillip .... '73 '98 C&L.879 B.A., J.D. [Ⓐ Meckler B.&T.]
Beth-Halachmy, Sharon .... '68 '96 C.154 B.A. L.339 J.D. [Ⓐ Funkhouser V.L.&D.]

Betke, James E., (AV) '40 '66 C.323 B.A. L.145 J.D.
161 North Clark Street, Suite 4950, 60601-3238
Telephone: 312-346-5050 Fax: 312-332-0515
Email: jebetke@imsif.com
Commercial Litigation, Insurance Law, Arbitration, Class Actions, Insurance Coverage, Professional Liability.
See Professional Biographies, CHICAGO, ILLINOIS

Betman, Ronald S., (BV) ....'61 '86 C&L.477 B.B.A., J.D. [Winston&S.]
Bettasso, Kathryn A., (BV) ....'58 '83 C.741 B.A. L.424 J.D. 1450 North Astor Street
Bettman, Suzanne S., (AV) '64 '89 C.597 B.A. L.339 J.D.
Sr. V.P. & Gen. Coun., R. R. Donnelley & Sons Company (Legal Department)
Bettman, William J. .... '63 '92 C.597 B.A. L.424 J.D. [Vedder,P.K.&K.]
Beuk, Jelena .... '72 '97 C&L.209 B.A., J.D. Law Clk., App. Ct.
Beutel, Ernest W., M.D. .... '46 '86 C&L.424 B.S., J.D. [Ⓒ Taxman&H.]
Beutler, Erica .... '— '00 C.976 B.A. L.597 J.D. [Ⓒ Kirkland&E.]
Beutler, Stacy T. .... '71 '96 C.879 B.A. L.209 J.D. [Ⓐ Horowitz&W.]
Beveridge, Charles P., Jr. '— '96
C.801 B.A. L.339 J.D. Staff Atty., U.S. Ct. of Appeals, Seventh Cir.
Bevilacqua, Lisa ....'71 '98 C.475 B.S. L.146 J.D. Assoc. Atty. [Bevilacqua&R.]
Bevilacqua & Rzepczynski, P.C. ....175 West Jackson, Suite 750
Beyer, Carrie A. .... '77 '04 C.350 B.S. L.339 J.D. [Ⓐ Gardner C.&D.]
Beyer, James R. ....'59 '84 C.210 B.A. L.146 J.D. Counsel, Accenture
Beyer, Joshua J. ....'72 '99 C.723 B.A. L.365 J.D. [Ⓐ Colky&K.]
Beyer, Justin K. .... '79 '04 C.72 B.A. L.339 J.D. [Ⓐ Seyfarth S.]
Beyer, Stephan V. ....'43 '81 C.696 B.A. L.966 J.D. [Sidley A.B.&W.]
Bezark, Sean W., (AV) .... '65 '90 C.477 B.S. L.424 J.D. [Greenberg T.]
Bezman, Victor H., (P.C.), (AV) .... '41 '67 C.339 B.S. L.597 J.D. [Katten M.R.]
Bhandari, Aileen ....'72 '02 C.424 B.A. L.209 J.D. Cook Co. State's Atty.'s Off.
Bharam, Durga M. ....'65 '90 C.999 B.Comm L.597 J.D. [Tressler,S.M.&P.]
Bharathi, Sowmya .... '77 '04 C.145 B.A. L.146 J.D. [Ⓐ Quarles&B.]
Bhatt, Vivek G. ....'74 '00 C.339 B.S. L.1148 J.D. [Ⓐ Mayer,B.R.&M.]
Bhavnani, Ajay Chandru .... '75 '00 C.696 B.A. L.209 J.D. 111 W. Washington
Bhosale, Parag P. ....'76 '02 C.910 B.A. L.472 J.D. [Ⓐ S.D.Gertler&Assoc.]
Bialka, Walter S. ....'16 '44 C.999 L.365 LL.B. 3530 W. 71st Pl.
Bianca, Salvatore ....'— '03 C.1142 B.A. L.144 J.D. [Ⓐ Kirkland&E.]
Bianchi, Michele A. '67 '99 C.1183 B.A. L.209 J.D.
Dir. of Legal Servs., Catholic Charities of the Archdiocese of Chicago
Bianchin, Sheri L. ....'60 '92 C.558 B.S. L.146 J.D. 77 W. Jackson
Bianco, Brian C. '77 '03 C&L.339 B.S.E.E., J.D.
[Ⓐ McAndrews,H.&M.] (See Pat. Sect.)
Biasetti, Jon ....'62 '87 C&L.93 B.A., J.D. [Lord,B.&B.]
Bibby, John F., Jr. .... '— '89 C&L.966 B.A., J.D. [Jones D.]
Biberman, Serge .... '71 '95 C&L.597 B.A., J.D. [Enterprise]
Bibko, Edward A. ....'66 '95 C.882 B.S. L.823 J.D. [Ⓐ Baker&M.]
Bichkoff, Brian .... '76 '01 C.339 B.A. L.146 J.D. [Hardt&S.]
Bickel, David M. ....'65 '01 C.1183 B.A. L.365 J.D. 3641 N. Pulaski Road
Bickel, Roger H., (AV) ....'— '89 C.347 B.A. L.424 J.D. [Freeborn&P.] ⊙
Bickel, Todd A. ....'69 '94 C.608 B.A. L.575 J.D. [Wildman,H.A.&D.]
Bidwill, James E. .... '44 '75 C.339 B.A. L.424 J.D. Chic. Transit Auth.
Biebel, Christine M. ....'70 '95 C.473 B.A. L.276 J.D. [O'Keefe,L.&H.]
Biebel, Paul P., Jr. ....'42 '67 C.436 A.B. L.276 J.D. Cir. Ct. J.
Bieber, Scott, (AV) ....'— '79 C.659 B.A. L.145 J.D. [Schiff H.]
Biedar, Sherry L. .... '62 '89 C.37 B.A. L.365 J.D. Asst. State's Atty.
Biederman, Daniel J. ....'57 '86 C.209 B.S. L.365 J.D. [Grotefeld&D.]
Biederman, Jerry H., (AV) .... '46 '71 C.813 B.A. L.145 J.D. [Neal,G.&E.]
Biederman, William, (AV) ....'50 '76 C.910 B.A. L.94 J.D. [Weinberg R.]
Biek, John A. ....'61 '87 C.976 B.S. L.276 J.D. [McDermott W.&E.]
Biel, Zoe G. ....'70 '99 C.966 B.A. L.365 J.D. [Klise&B.]
Bielawski, Alan P., (AV) ....'53 '78 C.276 B.A. L.893 J.D. [Sidley A.B.&W.]
Bielawski, Diane Dillon '55 '80
C.597 B.A. L.339 J.D. Gen. Atty., R. R. Donnelley & Sons Co.
Bien, Melissa M. .... '74 '01 C&L.124 B.A., J.D. [Ⓐ McGuirewoods]
Bienen, Leigh B. ....'38 '75 C.188 B.A. L.705 J.D. Northwestern Univ.
Bieniek, Michael E. ....'58 '89 C.597 B.A. L.145 J.D. [Mayer,B.R.&M.]
Bier, Jason Jay ....'74 '01 C.347 B.S. L.1040 J.D. [Bier&G.]
Bier & Gutstein, LLC .... 111 West Washington Street, Suite 1900
Bierhals, Bobbi J. ....'— '01 C.659 B.A. L.309 J.D. [Ⓐ McDermott W.&E.]
Bierig, Jack R., (AV) ....'47 '72 C.1036 A.B. L.309 J.D. [Sidley A.B.&W.]
Biery, James B. ....'— '93 C.145 B.A. L.966 J.D. [Ⓐ Sidley A.B.&W.]
Biery, Shawn R. ....'71 '01 C.506 B.S. L.1370 J.D. [Ⓐ Keefe&Assoc.]
Bieschke, Walter B. ....'24 '51 C&L.602 A.B., LL.B. Cir. J.
Biesenthal, Bethany Kaye ....'79 '04 C.966 B.A. L.1000 J.D. [Ⓐ Jenner&B.]
Biesiada, John M. '56 '81 C&L.339 B.A., J.D.
Asst. V.P. & Underwriting Coun., Greater Ill. Title Co.
Biesiada, Mark A. ....'73 '00 C.338 B.S. L.1000 J.D. [Ⓐ Levenfeld P.]
Bigane, Virginia M., (AV) ....'58 '85 C.201 B.A. L.424 J.D. Asst. States Atty.
Biggam, Charles M. ....'— '96 C.684 B.A. L.146 J.D. [Ⓐ Chapman&C.]
Biggane, Patrick J. ....'60 '87 C.436 B.S. L.365 J.D. 9924 Walden Pkwy.
Biggs, James D. ....'38 '69 C&L.966 B.S., J.D. Legal Assist. Found. of Chic.
Biggs, John W., Jr. .... '13 '55 C.1016 L.146 12142 S. State St.
Bigoness, James Joseph ....'— '82 C.1024 B.S. L.209 J.D. [Clausen M.]
Bijak, *Bonnie Bernadette* ....'58 '87 C.234 B.A. L.365 J.D. [Ⓐ Worker,S.&H.]
Bila, William P. ....'62 '88 C&L.339 A.B., J.D. [Walker W.M.]
Bilaisis, Vilija A. .... '55 '84 C.339 B.A. L.597 J.D. Asst. U.S. Atty.
Bilal, Karris A. ....'70 '00 C.927 B.A. L.365 J.D. Tax Atty., BP America Inc.
Bilas, Laura L., (AV) .... '— '85 C.879 B.A. L.494 J.D. [Foley&L.]
Bilek, Rhett S. ....'— '83 C.499 B.S. L.365 J.D. Supv. Atty.
Bilimoria, Neville M. ....'70 '94 C&L.597 B.A., J.D. [Duane M.]
Billhorn, John W., (BV) ....'60 '87 C.340 B.A. L.365 J.D. [W.J.Sneckenberg&Assoc.]
Billik, Richard J., Jr. .... '52 '77 C&L.802 B.A., J.D. Cir. J.
Billingsley, Frances Newberry .... '54 '79 C.860 B.A. L.94 J.D. 5620 Kimbark‡
Billows, Tracy M. ....'— '01 C.209 B.A. L.146 J.D. [Ⓐ Seyfarth S.]
Bills, Matthew A. ....'77 '02 C.927 B.B. L.339 J.D. [Ⓐ Winston&S.]
Bilotti, Deborah L. ....'65 '91 C.105 B.A. L.128 J.D. 77 W. Wacker Dr., Ste. 3100

Bilshausen, Ehren V. .... '77 '02 C.209 B.S. L.365 J.D. [Ⓐ Cassiday,S.&G.]
Bilsky, Moses '23 '50 C&L.421 LL.B.
(adm. in KY; not adm. in IL) 161 E. Chicago Ave.‡
Bilton, Dean H., (AV) .... '37 '60 C.37 L.209 LL.B. [Flanagan //B.]
Bilton, Paula L. '46 '99 C&L.209 B.A., J.D.
Mgr. & Owner, The Rate Search Company LLC
Bilut, Mark A. .... '70 '95 C.339 B.S. L.823 J.D. [McDermott W.&E.]
Bilyk, Thomas D. ....'58 '83 C.201 B.A. L.424 J.D. Asst. States Atty.
Bina, Jessica L. .... '— '04 C.477 B.A. L.597 J.D. [Ⓐ Kirkland&E.]
Binder, Mary Beattie '57 '85
C.966 B.A. L.209 J.D. Sr. Portfolio Coun., General Growth Prop.
Binder, Mary S. ... '53 '88 C.700 B.A. L.146 J.D. Sr. Coun., Bank One Corp. (Law Dept.)
Binder, Paul K. ....'53 '80 C.700 B.A. L.146 J.D. 4165 N. Lincoln Ave.
Binder, Wendy C., (AV) ....'48 '72 C.966 B.A. L.145 J.D. 111 W. Monroe St.‡
Bindi, David E., (BV) .... '56 '81 C.338 B.S. L.209 J.D. Asst. Atty. Gen.
Bingham, Donald E. ....'— '98 C.1106 B.A. L.1066 J.D. [Ⓐ Sidley A.B.&W.]
Bingle, Donald J. .... '54 '79 C&L.145 A.B., J.D. [Bell,B.&L.]
Bingle, Robert J., (AV) .... '51 '81 C.602 B.A. L.424 J.D. [Corboy&D.]
Binnig, Christian F., (AV) .... '61 '86 C.893 B.A. L.477 J.D. [Mayer,B.R.&M.]
Binns, Duane D. .... '52 '81 C.475 B.A. L.424 J.D. Sr. Tax Atty., Quaker Oats Corp.
Bira, Patrick G. '59 '85 C.698 B.S.B.A. L.734 J.D.
Asst. to the Pres. & Risk Mgr., St. Marys of Nazareth Hospital Ctr.
Bird, Daniel C., Jr. .... '47 '77 C.870 B.S. L.893 J.D. [Winston&S.]
Bird, Gregory J., (AV) .... '60 '86 C.388 B.A. L.339 J.D. [Williams M.&J.]
Bird, Tina M. .... '71 '96 C&L.260 B.S., J.D. [FagelHaber]
Birkeland, Cathy A. ....'— '97 C.197 B.A. L.597 J.D. [Ⓐ Latham&W.]
Birkenstein, David B. ....'30 '60 C.597 B.S. L.424 J.D. 10 S. Riverside Plz.
Birks, David C. ....'62 '93 C.475 B.A. L.602 J.D. [Crowley B.&K.]
Birman, Joel D. ....'45 '81 C.339 B.S. L.1048 J.D. Asst. Corp. Coun.
Birmingham, Jon A. ....'75 '00 C.597 B.S. L.339 J.D. [Ⓐ Fitch,E.T.&F.]
Birnbaum, Jacalyn .... '51 '92 C.273 B.A. L.209 J.D. [Nadler,P.&M.]
Birnbaum, Peter J. '57 '83 C.352 B.A. L.146 J.D.
Pres. & CEO, Attorney's Title Guaranty Fund Inc.
Birndorf, Beryl A., (AV) ....'22 '50 C.597 B.S. L.477 J.D. [Birndorf&B.]
Birndorf, Robert M., (AV) ....'53 '78 C.597 B.S.S. L.1049 J.D. [Birndorf&B.]
Birndorf, Theodore, and Associates, (AV) '32 '59
C.597 B.S. L.365 LL.B. 33 N. La Salle St., Ste. 3200

Birndorf & Birndorf, (AV)
200 West Madison Street, Suite 2040, 60606-3416
Telephone: 312-201-9300 Fax: 312-984-1047
Email: rbirndorf@cs.com
Members of Firm: Beryl A. Birndorf; Robert M. Birndorf. Of Counsel: Howard B. Prossnitz; Robert F. Miller.
Business Litigation, General Corporate and Employment Law, Probate, Trust and Estate Planning and Class Actions.

Biro, Louis L., (AV) ....'19 '48 221 N. LaSalle St.
Bisbikis, John G. ....'66 '92 C&L.339 B.S.G.E., J.D. [McDermott W.&E.] (Pat.)
Bisceglia, Joseph G., (AV) .... '49 '73 C.339 B.A. L.209 J.D. [Jenner&B.]
Bischoff, Jerry David .... '58 '87 C.966 B.A. State's Atty. Off.
Bischoff, Mark P., (AV) ....'47 '74 C.339 B.A. L.1049 J.D. [Bischoff]

Bischoff Partners, LLC, (AV)
217 North Jefferson Street, Suite 600, 60661
Telephone: 312-466-9100 Facsimile: 312-466-1186
Mark P. Bischoff; Thomas J. Swabowski (1951-1999);—Monica A. Forte; Ted A. Koester; Scott A. Weinstein.
Corporate Law, Business Law, Transactional, Secured Transactions, Federal and State Civil Trial Practice, Commercial and Residential Real Estate, Estate Planning and Estate Administration, Zoning & Land Use.
UBS Financial Services, Inc.; St. Mark's Missionary Baptist Church; Al Piemonte Automobile Dealerships; The Art Institute of Chicago; Freedom Mortgage Team, Inc.
See Professional Biographies, CHICAGO, ILLINOIS

Bisgeier, Stephen J., (AV) .... '43 '69 C.112 B.S. L.1066 J.D. [Miller S.&H.]
Bish, Suzanne M. ....'69 '97 C&L.608 B.S.B.A., J.D. [Ⓐ Sidley A.B.&W.]
Bishof, John Stephan, Jr. ....'48 '75 C.339 B.S. L.424 J.D. [J.Bishof]
Bishof, John, P.C., Law Office of .... 77 W. Washington St., Ste. 1910
Bishop, Martin J. ....'— '99 C.1086 B.A. L.94 J.D. [Ⓐ Foley&L.]
Bishop, Pascale J. ....'— '01 C.502 B.A. L.477 J.D. [Ⓐ Barnes&T.]
Bishop, Ronald T., (AV) ....'31 '63 C.424 L.365 LL.B. [Garretson&S.]
Bishop, Timothy S. ....'58 '88 C.051 B.A. L.597 J.D. [Mayer,B.R.&M.]
Biswurm, Robert J. ....'45 '78 C.339 B.S. L.1151 J.D. [R.J.Biswurm&Assoc.]
Biswurm, Robert J. & Associates ....123 W. Madison St., Suite 1200
Bitner, John H., (AV) ....'40 '64 C.597 B.A. L.178 J.D. [Bell,B.&L.]
Bitterly, Kelley A. ....'78 '03 C.602 B.A. L.93 J.D. [Ⓐ Daar&V.]
Bitterman, Patrick J., (AV) ....'65 '90 C.339 B.A. L.597 J.D. [Quarles&B.]
Bixby, Frank L., (AV) ....'28 '53 C.309 A.B. L.966 LL.B. [Ⓒ Sidley A.B.&W.]
Bixby, Thomas D. .... '— '00 C.309 A.B. L.502 J.D. [Ⓒ Neal,G.&E.]
Bixler, Diana Lee .... '52 '81 C.802 B.A. L.564 J.D. [Pattishall,M.N.H.&G.]
Bixler, Holden ....'— '02 C.339 B.A. L.1119 J.D. [Ⓒ Kirkland&E.]
Bixler, John Donovan, (AV) ...... '33 '59 C.347 B.S. L.1119 LL.B. 1515 N. Astor #16C‡
Bizot, John E. '62 '88 C.259 B.A. L.178 J.D.
(adm. in FL; not adm. in IL) Asst. Reg. Coun., Dept. of HHS
Bjork, Nicole L. ....'78 '04 C.966 B.A. L.552 J.D. [Ⓐ Swanson,M.&B.]
Blacha, Monika M. ....'74 '99 C.424 B.A. L.597 J.D. [Ⓐ Winston&S.]
Black, A. Samuel ....'64 '92 C.339 A.B. L.589 J.D. 3519 North Sheffield Avenue, Apt. 1S
Black, Beth A. ....'— '99 C.589 B.S. L.365 J.D. [Ⓐ Morgan,L.&B.]
Black, Brian T. .... '60 '89 C.339 B.S. L.910 J.D. [Winston&S.]
Black, Dennis B., (AV) .... '44 '68 C.188 A.B. L.309 J.D. [Goldberg,K.B.B.R.&M.]
Black, Gregory W. .... '61 '91 C.339 B.A. L.477 J.D. [Ⓐ Lord,B.&B.]
Black, John E., Jr. ....'58 '83 C.337 A.B. L.339 J.D. [Boundas S.W.&B.]
Black, Michael W. .... '— '87 C&L.339 B.S., J.D. [Ungaretti&H.]
Black, Milton, (AV) ....'45 '72 C.339 B.A. L.209 J.D. [M.Black&Assoc.]
Black, Nandia P. ....'58 '84 C.597 B.S. L.602 J.D. 2824 W. Diversey Avenue
Black, Milton, & Associates, Ltd., (AV) ....33 North La Salle Street, Suite 2412
Blackburn, Harry A. ....'47 '79 C.1034 B.A. L.589 J.D. Ill. State Dept. of Educ.
Blackburn, Julie E. ....'54 '80 C.27 B.A. L.879 J.D. Sr. Tax Atty., Quaker Oats Corp.
Blackburn, Lucille A. ....'73 '03 C.339 B.A. L.365 J.D. [Ⓐ Greene&L.]
Blackburn, Rachael ....'78 '02 C.339 B.A. L.966 J.D. [Ⓐ Lovells]
Blackman, Charles E., Jr. ....'— '74 C.363 A.B. L.424 J.D. [Querrey&H.]
Blackman, Gary L., (BV) ....'59 '84 C.339 B.S. L.209 J.D. [Levenfeld P.]
Blackman, Irving L. ....'27 '55 C.597 L.365 LL.B. 300 S. Riverside
Blackman, Jana Cohen, (AV) ....'62 '87 C.597 B.A. L.145 J.D. [Sonnenschein N.&R.]
Blackman, Marc S. ....'— '96 C.477 B.S. L.273 J.D. [Ⓐ Jones D.] (See Pat. Sect.)
Blackman, Philip M., (AV) ..... '62 '87 C.477 B.A. L.145 J.D. [Goldberg,K.B.B.R.&M.]
Blackman, Rodney J. .....'36 '60 C.477 B.A. L.309 J.D. Prof., De Paul Univ. Coll. of Law

Blackstone, Raiford A., Jr., (AV) '43 '70
C.150 B.S.E.E. L.424 J.D. [Trexler,B.G.B.&M.] (See Pat. Sect.)
Blackstone, Shane W. '74 '00 C.879 B.S. L.424 J.D. [🄰 Lord,B.&B.]
Blackwell, Michelle A. '65 '90 C.339 B.A. L.145 J.D. [🄰 Worsek&V.]
Blackwell, Victor '56 '91 C.339 B.A. L.424 J.D. Chief Adm. of Prosecutions
Blackwood, Elizabeth Anne '— '05 C.575 B.A. L.477 J.D. [🄰 Schiff H.]
Blaeser, Lisa '— '02 C.112 B.A. L.597 J.D. [🄰 Baker&M.]
Blagg, Jennifer Lynne '69 '00 C.315 B.A. L.45 J.D. State Appl. Def.
Blaida, Derek Anthony '76 '01 C.602 B.A. L.209 J.D. Asst. to Mayor, City of Chicago
Blair, Charles G. '69 '04 C.589 B.S. L.365 J.D. [🄰 Schenk,A.B.&T.]
Blair, Chester L. E., (AV) '28 '59 C.1191 B.Ed. L.365 LL.B. 310 S. Michigan Ave.
Blair, Deanna R. '72 '01 C.1331 B.A. L.1051 J.D. [🄰 Longwell]
Blair, Kimberly E. '75 '00 C.339 B.A. L.880 J.D. [🄰 Ross,D.&B.]
Blair, Lauren '69 '94 C.188 B.A. L.146 J.D. [🄰 Pedersen&H.]
Blair, Michael T. '62 '90 C.172 B.S. L.365 J.D. [Mayer,B.R.&M.]
Blake, Coleen A. '54 '92 C.339 B.S.E.E. L.424 J.D. [🄰 Johnson&Assoc.]
Blake, George P., (AV) '34 '61 C.602 B.S. L.145 J.D. [Vedder,P.K.&K.]
Blake, Jos. A., Jr. '21 '49 C&L.209 LL.B. 6969 N. Ridge St.‡

Blake, Cassels & Graydon (U.S.) LLP, (AV)
181 West Madison Street, Suite 3610, 60602-4645 ⊙
Telephone: 312-739-3610 Facsimile: 312-739-3611
Email: chicago@blakes.com URL: http://www.blakes.com
Partner: Geoffrey S. Belsher (Not admitted in IL).
Alternate Dispute Resolution, Aviation, Business, China Practice, Class Actions (Class Action), Commodity Tax and Trade, Communications, Competition and Trade, Constitutional and Charter of Rights, Construction, Corporate Governance, Criminal, Electronic Commerce (E-commerce), Energy, Environmental, Estates and Trusts, Financial Services, First Nations Law (Aboriginal Law), Forestry, Franchising, Gaming, Health, Hospitality and Tourism, Immigration, Information Technology, Insurance, Intellectual Property, International, Labour and Employment, Linguistics, Litigation, Marketing and Advertising, Media, Mergers and Acquisitions, Mining, Municipal and Planning, Oil and Gas, Outsourcing, Pension and Employee Benefits (Pensions), Privacy, Procurement, Product Liability (Products Liability), Real Estate, Research, Restructuring and Insolvency, Securities, Sports and Entertainment, Structured Finance, Tax Litigation and Controversy Resolution, Tax (Taxation).
The Firm maintains other offices in: Montréal, Québec; Toronto, Ottawa, Ontario; Calgary, Alberta; Vancouver, British Columbia; New York, New York; London, England and Beijing, China.
See Professional Biographies, CHICAGO, ILLINOIS

Blakemore, Jerry D. '54 '82 C.674 B.A. L.365 J.D. [Sales,G.G.&B.]
Blakemore, Thomas F., (BV) '50 '78 C&L.339 B.S., J.D. [Winston&S.]
Blakley, Allison C., (AV) '56 '82 C.112 B.S. L.629 J.D. [Sonnenschein N.&R.]
Blanc, Steven D., (AV🅣) '58 '87 C.352 B.B.A. L.767 J.D.
311 W. Superior St., Ste. 525
Blanchard, Eric D. '73 '99 C.93 B.A. L.966 J.D. [🄰 Walker W.M.]
Blanchard, Jonathan M., Ph.D. '66 '00 C.138 B.S. L.383 J.D. [Evan] (Pat.)
Blanchard, Patrick M. '63 '90 C.424 B.A. L.365 J.D. State Atty's Off.
Blanchard, Thomas N. '— '01 C.597 B.A. L.477 J.D. [🄰 Kirkland&E.]
Blanchard, Wenyu Ho '73 '99 C&L.93 B.A., J.D. [🄰 Sonnenschein N.&R.]
Blanchard, William B. '46 '73 C.801 B.S. L.209 J.D. Reg. Mgr.
Blanchet, Joel A. '— '98 C.116 B.A. L.339 J.D. [🄰 Ungaretti&H.]
Blandin, Stephan David, (AV) '61 '86 C&L.209 B.A., J.D. [Romanucci&B.]
Blankenship, Marshall L. '61 '86 C.602 B.A. L.339 J.D. [Adducci,D.L.M.&B.]
Blankfield, Barry R. '64 '90 C.221 B.S.B.A. L.910 J.D. [🄰 Mayer,B.R.&M.]
Blankshain, Michael R., (AV) '56 '81 C.674 A.B. L.339 J.D. [Wildman,H.A.&D.]
Blasi, John J., (AV) '43 '67 C&L.602 B.B.A., J.D. [Dykema G.P.]
Blatchford, John T. '— '91 C&L.861 B.A., J.D.
(adm. in NY; not adm. in IL) [Vedder,P.K.&K.]
Blatchford, Kevin F. '61 '86 C.27 B.A. L.309 J.D. [Sidley A.B.&W.]
Blatnick, Samuel '— '03 C.276 B.S. L.145 J.D. [🄰 Kirkland&E.]
Blatt, Elaine S. '— '51 C&L.597 B.S., J.D. [🄲 Blatt,H.L.&M.]
Blatt, Lauren W. '75 '01 C.1365 B.A. L.245 J.D. [🄰 Meckler B.&T.]
Blatt, Richard L. '40 '68 C.339 B.A. L.447 J.D. [Cozen O.]
Blatt, Robert S., (AV) '30 '52 C&L.145 Ph.B., J.D. [Weinberg R.]
Blatt, Hasenmiller, Leibsker & Moore, (BV) 211 Landmark Dr., Ste. E-5
Blatter, William J. '64 '88 C&L.472 B.B.A., J.D. 4732 N. Lincoln Ave.
Blattner, Kellie '68 '98 C.209 B.S. L.146 J.D. [🄰 Winston&S.]
Blau, Leslie A., (AV) '— '73 C.478 B.A. L.178 J.D. [Blau&B.]

Blau & Bonavich, (AV)
140 South Dearborn Street, Suite 1610, 60603-5202
Telephone: 312-443-1600 Fax: 312-443-1665
Email: lesblau@aol.com URL: http://www.blauandbonavich.com
Leslie A. Blau; Peter R. Bonavich (Retired).
Civil and Commercial Litigation, Commodity Futures Litigation, Securities Litigation, Employment Litigation.
See Professional Biographies, CHICAGO, ILLINOIS

Blaylock, Gwendolyn C. '54 '84 C.66 B.A. L.597 J.D.
(adm. in NY; not adm. in IL) Sr. Atty., F.D.I.C.
Blazejowski, Robert J. '74 '01 C.347 B.S. L.365 J.D. [🄰 Jenner&B.]
Bledsoe, Henry, Jr. '21 '53 C.436 L.365 LL.B. 8235 Sangamon St.
Bleiman, Andrew P. '73 '98 C.846 B.A. L.146 J.D. [🄰 DLPiper R.G.C.U.]
Bleiweis, Jeffrey I. '53 '79 C.1036 B.A. L.93 J.D. CJA & Assoc. Inc.

Bleiweis, Shell J., Law Offices of, (AV) '50 '82 C.801 B.A. L.597 J.D.
321 South Plymouth Court, Suite 1200, 60604
Telephone: 312-360-8782 Fax: 312-360-9212
Email: sbleiweiss@shell-bleiweiss.com URL: http://www.shell-bleiweiss.com
Environmental Law, Occupational Safety and Health, OSHA, Chemical Regulation, Alternative Dispute Resolution, Litigation.
Barrington, Illinois Office: 25840 Indian Trail Road, 60010. Telephone: 312-360-8782.
See Professional Biographies, CHICAGO, ILLINOIS

Blenke, John W., Jr. '55 '80 C.494 B.A. L.209 J.D.
Exec. V.P. & Corp. Gen. Coun., TransUnion LLC
Blenko, James Crawford '68 '01 C.674 A.B. L.145 J.D. 10 South Dearborn Street
Blenner, Stuart J. '46 '71 C.184 B.A. L.421 J.D. U.S. Postal Serv.
Blesoff, Marc S., (BV) '49 '84 C.95 B.A. L.180 J.D. Asst. Pub. Def.
Blessen, Richard P. '61 '86 C.879 B.A. L.339 J.D. [Gardner C.&D.]
Bletsas, Charles C. '— '95 C.477 B.A. L.912 J.D. [🄰 Anderson,R.]
Blew, John C., (AV) '41 '66 C.197 A.B. L.309 J.D. [Bell,B.&L.]
Bley, Gail Potysman '52 '79 C.36 B.S. L.146 J.D. [Gould&R.]
Blickenstaff, David C. '— '94 C.674 A.B. L.597 J.D. [Schiff H.]
Bligh, William J. '70 '98 C&L.602 B.A., J.D. 676 N. Lasalle St., Ste. 329
Blim, John M. '58 '94 C&L.597 B.A., J.D. [Blim&E.]
Blim & Edelson, LLC 53 W. Jackson Blvd., Ste. 1642
Blitstein, Lori P. '65 '92 C.1086 B.B.A. L.165 J.D. 77 W. Washington, Ste. 719
Blitstein, Sherwood E. '61 '86 C.966 B.A. L.228 J.D. Centrum Properties
Blitz, Brian J. '77 '02 C.846 B.A. L.339 J.D. [🄰 Berger S.]
Bloch, Helen '73 '98 C.978 B.A. L.146 J.D. [🄰 Bellows&B.]
Bloch, Jon-Thomas '— '04 C.893 B.S. L.145 J.D. [🄰 Jones D.]
Bloch, Norman L. '39 '64 C.902 L.209 LL.B. [Balonick&B.]
Bloch, Robert E., (AV) '57 '84 C.881 A.B. L.597 J.D. [Dowd,B.&B.]
Blocher, Nelson David '49 '93 C.937 B.A. L.365 J.D. 3 First National Plz., Ste. 2100
Block, Alan F. '59 '89 C.339 B.S. L.365 J.D. [Block&L.]

Block, Alvin W., & Associates, (AV) '30 '56 C.1016 B.S.C. L.365 J.D.
33 North La Salle Street, Suite 3000, 60602
Telephone: 312-346-5656 Fax: 312-78 BLOCK URL: http://www.chicagolawyers.com
Email: attorneys@chicagolawyers.com URL: http://www.lawyers.com/chicagolawyers
Associates: Bernard N. Block; Jerome E. Boyle.
Federal and State Civil, Trial and Appellate Practice, Trials, Corporate, Business, Contracts, Breach of Contract, Insurance, Catastrophic Injury, Automobile Accidents, Commercial Insurance, Insurance Bad Faith, Life and Health Insurance, Property Insurance, Chancery and Class Actions, Personal Injury, Airplane Crash Litigation, Railroad Accidents, Sexual Abuse, Construction Accidents, Product Liability, Consumer, Civil Rights, Wrongful Death, Probate, Wills, Trust and Estates, Asset Protection, Contested Wills, Guardianship, Real Estate, Commercial Real Estate, Condominium, Cooperative Housing, Landlord and Tenant Mortgages, Commercial, Commercial Banking, Buying and Selling Business, Family Business, Limited Liability Company, Minority Business, Partnership, Professional Practices and Small Business Law.
Reference: American National Bank & Trust Company of Chicago., Illinois.
See Professional Biographies, CHICAGO, ILLINOIS

Block, Bernard N. '57 '85 C.221 B.S. L.365 J.D. [🄰 A.W.Block]
Block, J. Randolph '53 '78 C.674 A.B. L.145 J.D.
Asst. Prof., DePaul Univ. Sch. of Law
Block, Jack L., (AV) '— '73 C.910 A.B. L.276 J.D. [Sachnoff&W.]
Block, Kenneth L. '54 '81 C.339 B.S. L.365 J.D. [Weiss&B.]
Block, Lawrence, (P.C.), (AV) '— '59 C&L.597 B.S., J.D. [Schiff H.]
Block, Neal J., (AV) '42 '68 C.339 B.S. L.145 J.D. [Baker&M.]
Block, Robert H. '51 '79 C.589 B.S. L.146 J.D. 730 N. LaSalle St.
Block, Stanley B., (AV) '33 '57 C.597 B.S. L.145 J.D. [Vedder,P.K.&K.]
Block, Steven A. '74 '99 C&L.597 B.S., J.D. [🄰 Butler R.S.&B.]
Block & Landsman Eleven South LaSalle Street, Suite 1600
Blocker, Mark B. '64 '88 C.145 B.A. L.309 J.D. [Sidley A.B.&W.]
Blockovich, Brian '69 '94
C.339 B.S. L.424 J.D. Pres. & Gen. Coun., Chicago Clearing Corp.
Bloedorn, Gregory S. '— '04 C.1556 B.A. L.339 J.D. [🄰 Chapman&C.]
Blomquist, William K. '— '72 C&L.976 B.A., J.D. [Arnstein&L.]
Blonder, Steven P., (AV) '67 '93 C.477 B.A. L.145 J.D. [Much S.F.D.A.&R.]
Bloom, Christopher A., (AV) '51 '75 C.385 B.A. L.1119 J.D. [Bell,B.&L.]
Bloom, Jacob '11 '34 C&L.145 Ph.B., J.D. 35 E. Wacker Dr., Suite 1750‡
Bloom, Jennifer Morrison '74 '04 C.477 B.A. L.146 J.D. [🄰 Schain,B.R.&C.]
Bloom, JoAnne Gazarek '48 '76 C.339 B.A. L.424 J.D.
V.P., Reg. Strategies, Commonwealth Edison Co.
Bloom, Jonathan James '— '90 C.1183 B.S. L.146 J.D. 233 S. Wacker Drive
Bloom, Kenneth M., (AV) '63 '88 C.339 B.S. L.146 J.D. [Peck,B.A.&M.] ⊙
Bloom, Robert A. '38 '63 C.659 B.S. L.884 LL.B. [🄲 Mayer,B.R.&M.]
Bloom, Sara E. '73 '01 C.881 B.A. L.904 J.D. State Atty.'s Off.
Bloom, Wendy L. '— '93 C.659 B.A. L.309 J.D. [Kirkland&E.]
Bloomer, Andrew B., (AV) '— '92 C.309 A.B. L.966 J.D. [Kirkland&E.]
Bloomquist, Todd M. '74 '99 C.162 B.A. L.352 J.D. [🄰 Winston&S.]
Blough, Kevin C. '63 '96 C.893 B.A. L.146 J.D.
In-house Coun., American Dental Assoc.
Blouin, Daniel M., (AV) '63 '88 C.679 B.S. L.424 J.D. [Seyfarth S.]
Blount, Michael E. '49 '74 C.846 B.A. L.326 J.D. [Seyfarth S.]
Blue, Jagady '75 '01 C.631 B.A. L.209 J.D. [🄰 Bollinger,R.&G.]
Bluestein, Louis H. '25 '51 C.209 L.146 LL.B. 330 S. Wells
Bluestone, David H. '74 '99
C.339 B.S.E.E. L.597 J.D. [🄰 Brinks H.G.&L.] (See Pat. Sect.)
Blum, Alan A. '53 '78 C.339 B.A. L.589 LL.B. [🄲 K.B.Moll&Assoc.]
Blum, David C. '68 '97 C.37 B.S.B.A. L.1000 J.D. [🄰 Vedder,P.K.&K.]
Blum, John D. '48 '74 C.116 B.A. L.602 J.D.
(adm. in PA; not adm. in IL)
Prof. and Assoc. Dean, Loyola Univ. of Chicago Sch. of Law
Blum, Joshua '72 '01 C.339 B.S. L.209 J.D. The CBC Group
Blum, Melvin A., (AV) '32 '57 C.477 B.A. L.597 J.D. [🄲 Aronberg G.D.&G.]
Blum, Milton '29 '52 C&L.597 B.S., J.D. 188 W. Randolph St.
Blum, Rachel M. '— '95 C.477 B.A. L.309 J.D. [🄰 Sidley A.B.&W.]
Blum, Selwyn '28 '53 C.339 B.A. L.209 J.D. 123 W. Madison St.
Blum, Steven T. '52 '78 C.339 B.S. L.365 J.D. 130 E. Randolph St., Fl. 1500
Blumberg, G. John '37 '64 C.309 B.A. L.705 LL.B. [🄲 Levenfeld P.] (Pat.)
Blumberg, Jeffrey R. '69 '00 C.813 B.A. L.146 J.D. [🄰 Gardner C.&D.]
Blume, Anne L. '63 '91 C.475 B.A. L.365 J.D. [Meckler B.&T.]
Blume, Benjamin A. '— '89 C.388 B.A. L.424 J.D. [O'Hagan,S.&A.]
Blume, Paul C., Sr. '29 '57 C&L.424 B.S.C., J.D. [🄲 Lord,B.&B.]
Blumenfeld, Barry E. '42 '67 C.1016 B.S.B.A. L.209 J.D. 3424 W. 26th St.
Blumenfeld, David, (Ltd.) '35 '66 C.339 B.S. L.365 J.D. 134 N. LaSalle St.
Blumenfeld, Edgar A., (Ltd.) '26 '50 C.1016 L.365 J.D. 134 N. LaSalle St.
Blumenshine, Scott A., (BV) '62 '87 C.352 B.S. L.46 J.D. [Meyer&B.]
Blumenthal, Amy M., (BV) '56 '85 C.696 B.S. L.273 J.D. [Gould&R.]
Blumenthal, Grant '71 '96 C.473 B.S. L.365 J.D. [Tamari&B.]
Blumenthal, Jeffrey S., (AV) '54 '79 C.659 B.A. L.146 J.D. 33 N. Dearborn, Ste. 800
Blumenthal, Katharine E. '46 '84 C.668 B.A L.1000 J.D. [Stahl C.C.]

Blumenthal, Marc N., Law Office of '53 '81 C&L.861 B.A., J.D.
19 South LaSalle Street, Suite 1500, 60603
Telephone: 312-641-0616 Fax: 312-332-4629
Email: mnblawyer@cs.com URL: http://www.blumenthalfranchiselaw.com
Franchise Law, Start-Up Franchisors and Franchisees, Leasing, Licensing, Trademarks, Trademark Information, Copyrights, Breach of Contract, Corporate Law, Business Formations, Business Transactions, Litigation, Arbitration.
See Professional Biographies, CHICAGO, ILLINOIS

Blumenthal, Michael L. '57 '82 C.589 B.S. L.146 J.D. 77 W. Washington St.
Blumenthal, Steven H., (AV) '53 '78 C.966 B.A. L.910 J.D. [Much S.F.D.A.&R.]
Blumer, Joel A. '63 '96 C.424 B.S. L.209 J.D.
Legal Servs. Offr. & Coun., Harris Trust and Savings Bank
Blust, Larry D., (AV) '— '68 C&L.339 B.S., J.D. [Barnes&T.]
Boardman, Brian C. '76 '03 C.597 B.S. L.813 J.D. [🄰 Babbitt&M.]
Boarini, Timothy W. '79 '04 C.478 B.A. L.352 J.D. [🄰 Bell,B.&L.]
Boback, Janice L. '61 '98 C.339 B.S. L.365 J.D. [Anderson&B.]
Bobb, Patricia C., (AV) '47 '72 C.1146 B.A. L.602 J.D. [🄲 Propes&K.]
Bobber, Peter C., (BV) '68 '94 C&L.339 B.S., J.D. [🄰 Lewis,D.&H.]
Bobbitt, Ronald A., (AV) '53 '79 C.339 B.S. L.1162 J.D. [Bobbitt&Assoc.]
Bobbitt & Associates, (AV) 155 N. Michigan Avenue, Suite 500
Boberg, Wayne D., (AV) '52 '78 C.347 B.S. L.1119 J.D. [Winston&S.]
Boblick, Shelby S., (BV) '52 '81 C.788 A.B. L.210 J.D. 2 N. Riverside Plaza
Bobo, Stephen T., (AV) '— '81 C.880 B.A. L.273 J.D. [Sachnoff&W.]
Bobrick, Edward A. '35 '64 C.339 B.S. L.209 J.D. 219 S. Dearborn St., Ste. 1822‡
Bobrow, Myla Denise '56 '81 C.339 B.A. L.46 J.D. Sears, Roebuck & Co.

Boch, Brian R. .... '70 '95 C.339 A.B. L.597 J.D. [Jenner&B.]
Bock, Joel H., (AV) '52 '77
C.477 B.S. L.1119 J.D. [Cook,A.M.M.C.&M.] (See Pat. Sect.)
Bock, Phillip A. .... '67 '94 C.57 B.A. L.893 J.D. [Diab&B.]
Bockelman, J. Richard, (AV) .... '25 '51 C.597 B.S. L.145 J.D. 1212 N. Lake Shore Drive
Bodach, L. Barrett, (AV) .... '43 '68 C.602 B.A. L.424 J.D. [Heineke,B.&B.]
Boddy, Elizabeth J. .... '55 '92 C.57 B.A. L.589 J.D. [[C] Shefsky&F.]
Bode, Dawn E. .... '61 '88 Corp. Coun. Off.
Bode, Jeannette R. .... '31 '58 C.339 B.A. L.365 J.D. 7706 W. Touhy Ave.
Bodenstab, Richard G. .... '19 '50 C&L.879 B.A., J.D. 79 W. Monroe St.
Bodenstein, Ira, (AV) .... '54 '80 C.264 B.A. L.472 J.D. U.S. Trustee
Boeckman, LaDonna L. .... '73 '98 C&L.221 B.A., J.D. [[A] Iwan C.H.H.&V.]
Boege, Kathleen M. '66 '91 C.597 B.A. L.494 J.D.
Assoc. Gen. Coun., Chicago Stock Exchange, Inc.
Boeglin, Brian J. .... '66 '90 C&L.347 B.S., J.D. Price Waterhouse
Boehm, Garrett L., Jr. .... '74 '99 C.999 B.A. L.146 J.D. [[A] Johnson&B.]
Boehm, Heather Rae Klear .. '73 '00 C.475 B.A. L.146 J.D. Off. of Cook Co. Pub. Guard.
Boehm, Jack E., Jr. .... '56 '82 C.602 B.B.A. L.365 J.D. [Fisk K.K.&R.]
Boehnen, Daniel A., (AV) '50 '76
C.602 B.S.Ch.E. L.188 J.D. [McDonnell B.H.&B.] (See Pat. Sect.)
Boehrer, Charles B., (AV) .... '59 '85 C.966 B.B.A. L.477 J.D. [Winston&S.]
Boelter, John P. .... '— '02 C&L.494 B.A., J.D. [[A] Mayer,B.R.&M.]
Boerschinger, Thomas H. .... '37 '63 C&L.209 LL.B. [[C] A.O.Amos&Assoc.]
Boersma, Brian J. .... '71 '02 C.145 B.A. L.424 J.D. Asst. State's Atty.
Boffa, Michael J. .... '— '04 C.1556 B.S. L.424 J.D. [[A] Schiff H.]
Bogaard, Jonathan H., (AV) .... '57 '81 C&L.352 B.B.A., J.D. [Vedder,P.K.&K.]
Bogart, Mark I. .... '57 '87 C.161 B.A. L.930 J.D. [Vedder,P.K.&K.]

Bogart, Susan, (AV) '52 '78 C.477 B.A. L.424 J.D.
30 North La Salle Street Suite 2900, 60602
Telephone: 312-263-0900 Fax: 312-263-5013
URL: http://www.lawyers.com/bogart
Civil and Criminal Litigation. Labor and Employment Litigation, Counseling and Executive Coaching-Public and Private Sector, Representation of Officers and Directors, White Collar Federal Criminal Defense, Civil and Criminal Civil Rights and Privacy Litigation, Business Litigation, Representation of Private Parties in Disputes with Governmental and other Regulatory Authorities.
See Professional Biographies, CHICAGO, ILLINOIS

Bogda-Cleveland, Hedi E. '70 '97 C.747 B.A. L.585 J.D.
(adm. in MN; not adm. in IL) Asst. Reg. Coun., U.S. Environ. Protec. Agcy.
Boggs, Catherine J. '54 '82 C&L.208 B.A., J.D.
(adm. in CO; not adm. in IL) [Baker&M.]
Boggs, Craig .... '63 '88 C&L.339 B.S., J.D. [Perkins C.]
Boggs, Roy E., Jr. '46 '76 C.309 A.B. L.1066 J.D.
(adm. in CA; not adm. in IL) Intl. Catholic Migration Comm.
Bognar, Erin J. .... '71 '99 C.347 B.A. L.734 J.D. [[A] Lake,T.&D.]
Bogner, William E. .... '44 '75 C.57 B.A. L.597 J.D. I.R.S.
Bogo-Ernst, Debra L. .... '— '00 C&L.339 B.A., J.D. [[A] Mayer,B.R.&M.]
Bogucki, Edw. A. .... '23 '51 C&L.209 LL.B. 5487 N. Milwaukee Ave.
Bogusz, Richard P. .... '27 '53 C&L.209 LL.B. 2 N. LaSalle St.
Bohan, David C., (AV) .... '— '78 C.597 B.A. L.309 J.D. [Sachnoff&W.]
Boharic, Robert V. .... '45 '73 C.363 A.B. L.339 J.D. Cir. J.
Bohland, Catherine Marie .... '62 '00 C.378 B.S. L.424 J.D. 1340 S. Michigan
Bohlen, Jonathan A. .... '69 '98 C.145 B.A. L.597 J.D. [[A] Wildman,H.A.&D.]
Bohn, Joseph P. .... '38 '77 C.569 B.A. L.146 J.D. Interstate Com. Comm.
Boho, Dan L., (AV) .... '52 '77 C&L.424 B.A., J.D. [Hinshaw&C.]
Boice, Heather A. .... '73 '00 C.679 B.S.E.E. L.365 J.D [[A] Bell,B.&L.]
Boies, Wilber H., (P.C.), (AV) .... '44 '68 C.103 A.B. L.145 J.D. [McDermott W.&E.]
Boigues, Manuel A. '78 '02 C.1183 B.S. L.339 J.D.
Asst. Corp. Coun., City of Chicago, Dept. of Law, Comm. and Policy Lit. Div.
Bolan, Michael Buckley, Law Offices of '41 '66
C.174 B.S. L.424 J.D. 53 W. Jackson Blvd.
Boland, Edmund P., (AV) .... '42 '67 C.750 B.A. L.424 J.D. [Carey,F.W.&B.]
Boland, James J. .... '— '95 C.145 B.A. L.597 J.D. [Kirkland&E.]
Boland, Michael J. .... '— '85 C.424 B.A. L.597 J.D. [Holland&K.]
Bolander, Eric D. .... '69 '02 C.352 B.S. L.339 J.D. [[A] Funkhouser V.L.&D.]
Boldingh, Mary Jo .... '57 '91 C.424 A.B. L.146 J.D. [Kelley D.&W.] (Pat.)
Boleky, Thomas F., (AV) .... '63 '93 C.812 B.S. L.209 J.D. [[A] Corboy&D.]
Bolerjack, Bradley James .... '— '01 C.393 B.A. L.424 J.D. [[A] Sachnoff&W.]
Boley, John N. .... '35 '62 C.674 B.A. L.976 LL.B. 190 S. La Salle St.‡
Boley O'Keefe, MaryAnne .... '75 '00 C.602 B.A. L.209 J.D. [[A] Bates&C.]
Bolger, Kevin P., (BV) .... '50 '76 C.209 B.S. L.146 J.D. 150 N. Wacker Dr., Ste. 2460
Bolger, Michael William .... '64 '89 C.602 B.A. L.209 J.D. Asst. State's Atty.
Bolin, Alenna K. .... '58 '91 C.589 B.A. L.1067 J.D. [[A] F.N.Trevino]
Bolin, Britta J. .... '60 '92 C.424 B.S. L.209 J.D. Coun., Mansur & Co.
Boling, Andrew J. .... '58 '84 C.57 B.A. L.339 J.D. [Baker&M.]
Boling, Deborah K., (BV) .... '59 '84 C&L.145 B.A., J.D. [Winston&S.]
Bolkema, Gerald K. .... '54 '89 C.114 B.A. L.145 J.D. [Baker&M.]
Boller, Harvey R. .... '43 '68 C.1349 B.A. L.188 J.D. 1762F W. Thome
Bollinger, Barry G., (AV) .... '43 '73 C&L.966 B.S., J.D. [Bollinger,R.&G.]
Bollinger, Chris L. .... '— '93 C&L.477 B.S.E.E., J.D. [Schiff H.]

Bollinger, Ruberry & Garvey, (AV)
500 West Madison Street, 23rd Floor, 60661
Telephone: 312-466-8000 Fax: 312-466-8001
Partners of Firm: Barry G. Bollinger; Edward F. Ruberry; Maurice J. Garvey; Jeremiah P. Connolly; Nicholas A. Riewer; Mark F. Wolfe; Jeffrey A. Goldwater; Francis R. Petrek, Jr.; William J. Rogers; John M. Stalmack; Michael S. Knippen; Bryan G. Schumann; Robert J. Franco, II; Robert M. Collins; Darcy Lynn Ibach; Clay H. Phillips; Amy L. Miner; Scott C. Bentivenga; Michael T. Walsh; John J. Moroney, IV; George J. Manos; Carol L. Johnson; Luisa F. Trujillo; John P. Sullivan; Michelle M. Bracke; Robert W. Brunner; Robert Allen Chaney; James Michael Eastham; Richard M. Kuntz; Alison L. Miner; Mitchell D. Rose; Krista R. Frick; Karie J. Valentino; Martin P. Head; Michael P. Latz; Ruth Goldwater McCoy; Vincent P. Tomkiewicz; Perry M. Shorris; James E. Abbott; John J. Riewer. Of Counsel: Beth Ann Berger Zerman; David W. Kane; James A. Lupo, Jr.;—Cynthia Arrotti-Carter; Michelle Bacher; Sara K. Barnes; Jagady Blue; Walter Leonard Brown III; Christopher G. Buenik; Jayne Megan Cadice; Diane Karp Ehrhart; Ahmed El-Ganzouri; W. Grant Farrar; Janet A. Flynn; Jordan E. Frank; James M. Freeman; Gregory V. Ginex; Gena Gruss; Charles A. Hafner; Michael S. Haggerty; Michael L. Hahn; Katherine L. Hartley; Sarah E. Heidenreich; Rachel Kiley; Carla P. Larned; David A. Larson; Sarah E. Lopez; Marc E. McCallister; Alison Milnamow; Amanu M. Nwaomah; Adewale A. Oduye; Tanya Poth; Zachary M. Raimi; Sharon Rice; Aaron J. Shuler; Lisa Smuckler; Rostyslaw J. Smyk; Kelly Link Stoltz; Richard P. Tauras; Lisa Thaviu; Brett L. Warning; Jeffrey I. Young.
Insurance Coverage Analysis and Litigation, Bad Faith, Declaratory Actions, Toxic Tort Defense, Commercial Litigation, Construction Litigation, Product Liability, Insurance Defense, Transportation, Medical Malpractice, Rental Car Industry, Construction, School and Municipal Liability, Environmental Law, Director's and Officer's Liability.
See Professional Biographies, CHICAGO, ILLINOIS

Bollow, Richard C. .... '45 '70 C.103 A.B. L.339 J.D. [Quinlan&C.]

Bolon, Laurence J., (AV) '44 '69 C.339 B.S. L.365 J.D.
19 South La Salle Street, Suite 1500, 60603
Telephone: 312-782-1272 Fax: 312-782-9870
URL: http://www.bolonlaw.com
Family Law, Divorce, Child Custody, Child Support, Visitation Rights, Criminal Law, Federal Criminal Law, White Collar Crime, Bank Fraud, Electronic Fraud, Felonies, Drug Offenses, Driving While Intoxicated, Civil Litigation, Business and Probate Litigation.
See Professional Biographies, CHICAGO, ILLINOIS

Bolotin, William J., (AV) .... '58 '83 C.602 B.B.A. L.339 J.D. [Doyle&B.]
Bolton, Richard L. .... '43 '81 C&L.209 B.S.C., J.D. [Ginsparg,B.&Assoc.]
Bom, Kathleen A. .... '56 '86 C.589 B.M. L.146 J.D. Asst. State's Atty.
Bomar, Valarie Tatem .... '69 '97 C.811 B.S. L.477 J.D. [Sonnenschein N.&R.]
Bomchill, Fern C., (AV) .... '48 '72 C.477 B.A. L.145 J.D. [Mayer,B.R.&M.]
Bonacci, Maria Salcedo .... '— '90 C.112 B.A. L.1066 J.D. Sears Tower
Bonaccorsi, Mary Clare .... '— '89 C.165 B.A. L.597 J.D. [Bryan C.]
Bonadies, Paul N., (BV) .... '66 '91 C.602 B.A. L.209 J.D. [Dahl&B.]
Bonaguro, Lester A. .... '37 '61 C&L.424 J.D. Cir. J.
Bonami, E. Andre .... '51 '76 C.589 B.S. L.146 J.D. Sr. Tax Atty., BP America Inc.
Bonanno, Steven R. .... '66 '92 C.24 B.A. L.365 J.D. [Hinshaw&C.]
Bonavich, Peter R. .... '— '70 C.170 B.A. L.145 J.D. [Blau&B.] ‡
Bond, R. Douglass .... '54 '90 C.478 B.A. L.477 J.D. [Butler R.S.&B.]
Bond, Shea Lita '73 '99 C.1375 B.A. L.365 J.D.
Asst. Regional Coun., Soc. Sec. Admin.
Bonebrake, James G. .... '65 '90 C.210 B.A. L.597 J.D. [Friedman&B.]
Bonebrake, Stephen J. .... '— '92 C.210 B.A. L.424 J.D. [Schiff H.]
Bonem, Stuart J. .... '28 '50 C&L.339 B.A., LL.B. 400 E. Ohio St.
Bonifacic, Frank M., (AV) '42 '67
C.973 A.B. L.424 J.D. 111 W. Washington St., Ste. 1850
Bonifield, Gregory D. .... '74 '00 C.315 B.A. L.1375 J.D. [[A] Jenner&B.]
Bonjour, Bruce A. .... '49 '76 C.20 B.A. L.273 J.D. [Perkins C.]
Bonn, Michael, (AV) .... '45 '73 C.976 B.A. L.309 J.D. [Johnson&C.]
Bonneau, Steven M. .... '71 '98 C.93 B.A. L.201 J.D. [[A] Handler,T.&D.]
Bonner, Bethany N. .... '— '03 C.475 B.A. L.276 J.D. [[A] Katten M.R.]
Bonthala, Satish .... '68 '92 C&L.352 BBA, J.D. Claim Atty., AIG
Boodell, Thomas J., Jr., (AV) .... '35 '64 C.674 A.B. L.309 J.D. [Boodell D.&S.]

Boodell Domanskis & Saipe, LLC, (AV)
205 N. Michigan Avenue, Suite 4307, 60601
Telephone: 312-938-4070 Fax: 312-540-1162
URL: http://www.boodlaw.com
Thomas J. Boodell, Jr.; Alexander R. Domanskis; Gary Scott Saipe. Associates: Jae Choi Kim; Dainius R. Dumbrys.
Business Law, Real Estate, International Law, Dispute Resolution, Trusts and Estates, Wills and Probate, Asset Protection, Finance, Banking Law, Corporate Law, Immigration.
See Professional Biographies, CHICAGO, ILLINOIS

Booden, Michael R. '61 '86 C.589 B.S. L.365 J.D.
Sr. Assoc. Gen. Coun., American Bar Association
Booker, John R. .... '63 '93 C.446 B.A. L.801 J.D. [[A] Weltman,W.&R.]
Booker, Mark S. .... '68 '99 C.1365 B.A. L.309 J.D. Dept. of HHS
Boomgarden, Michael W. .... '55 '83 C.961 B.S. L.93 J.D. 209 S. Lasalle St., Ste. 600
Boon, David M. '66 '93 C.787 B.A. L.982 J.D.
Financial Advisor, UBS Financial Services, Inc.
Boonstra, Richard D. .... '57 '83 C.114 B.A. L.365 J.D. [Hoogendoorn&T.]
Boorstein, Ronald L., (AV) '35 '60 C.477 A.B. L.309 J.D.
Chmn. of the Bd., Pres. & CEO, Storage Equity Concepts, Inc.
Booth, Cathleen A. .... '74 '00 C.607 B.S. L.851 J.D. [[A] Katten M.R.]
Booth, Fenton C. .... '61 '87 C.112 B.A. L.424 J.D. Partner, Ogden Partners, Inc.
Booth, Jason L. .... '72 '98 C.98 B.S. L.309 J.D. [[A] Winston&S.]
Booth, William S. .... '69 '00 C.234 B.A. L.209 J.D. [[A] Eimer S.K.&S.]
Bootzin, Joel H. .... '67 '96 C.999 B.S. L.146 J.D. [[A] Fitch,E.T.&F.] (See Pat. Sect.)
Bora, Peter G., (AV) .... '62 '89 C.338 B.S. L.365 J.D. [Clausen M.]
Borcia, James K. .... '64 '89 C.589 B.S. L.146 J.D. [Tressler,S.M.&P.]
Borde, Howard, (AV) .... '29 '52 C&L.221 B.A., LL.B. 415 N. LaSalle St.
Bordelon, Richard L. .... '49 '75 C.910 A.B. L.597 J.D. 50 S. La Salle St.
Borden, Katherine .... '79 '04 C.105 B.A. L.424 J.D. [[A] Winston&S.]
Borders, Joseph J. .... '59 '93 C&L.209 B.S., J.D. [Walker W.M.]
Borders, Michael C., (AV) .... '55 '81 C&L.602 B.B.A., J.D. [Dykema G.P.]
Borders, Thomas C., (AV) .... '48 '74 C.734 B.A. L.276 J.D. [McDermott W.&E.]
Borders, William A. .... '69 '03 C.25 B.A. L.146 J.D. [[A] DLPiper R.G.C.U.]
Bordewick, Carrie .... '— '00 C.597 B.S.J. L.228 J.D. [[A] Latham&W.]
Bordo, Julie M. .... '63 '91 C.477 B.A. L.146 J.D. Illinois Legal Resch.
Borenstein, Judith A., (AV) '48 '83
C.966 M.S. L.597 J.D. Gen. Coun., Swedish Covenant Hospital
Borenstein, William E., (AV) .... '48 '73 C.966 B.A. L.424 J.D. [[C] Burman&M.]
Borg, Emily E. .... '73 '00 C.475 B.A. L.209 J.D. [[A] Wiedner&M.]
Borg, Karen Minkoff .... '66 '95 C.228 B.A. L.146 J.D. [[A] Butler R.S.&B.]
Boris, Andrew S. .... '67 '96 C.93 B.A. L.209 J.D. [Tressler,S.M.&P.]
Borkan, Steven Blair, (BV) .... '59 '86 C.338 B.S. L.365 J.D. [Stellato&S.]
Borkon, David J. '78 '03 C.597 B.A. L.552 J.D.
(adm. in NJ; not adm. in IL) [[A] Vedder,P.K.&K.]
Borlack, Alan R., (AV) .... '47 '72 C.477 B.A. L.309 J.D. [Bailey B.N.]
Borman, Deborah L. .... '61 '89 C.94 B.S. L.209 J.D. Off. of Atty. Gen.
Bormes, James X., (AV) .... '62 '88 C&L.734 B.A., J.D. [J.X.Bormes]

Bormes, James X., P.C., Law Office of, (AV)
8 South Michigan Avenue, 60603
Telephone: 312-201-0575 Fax: 312-332-0600
James X. Bormes.
Construction Law, Construction Defects, Mechanics Liens, Consumer Law, Consumer Fraud, Business Law, Business Litigation, Breach of Contract, Employment Contracts, Landlord and Tenant Law, Securities Fraud.
See Professional Biographies, CHICAGO, ILLINOIS

Bornstein, Bruce H. .... '52 '77 C.174 B.S. L.1194 J.D. [Freedman&B.]
Bornstein, Deborah H., (AV) .... '53 '78 C.75 B.A. L.145 J.D. [Williams M.&J.]
Bornstein, Maureen .... '53 '78 C.436 B.A. L.209 J.D. Commerce Clearing House, Inc.
Boron, Andrew E. .... '73 '98 C.966 B.A. L.146 J.D. Dir, Gov. Relations, CNA
Boros-Stepen, Daphana L. .... '66 '94 C.477 B.A. L.309 J.D. Dept. of HHS
Borovsky, Herbert L., (AV) '31 '56
C.197 A.B. L.597 J.D. 111 East Wacker Drive, Suite 1325‡

Borovsky & Ehrlich, (AV)
111 East Wacker Drive, Suite 1325, 60601
Telephone: 312-861-0800 Fax: 312-819-0948
Lawrence D. Ehrlich; Julian D. Schreiber; Thomas Canafax, Jr.;—Jacquelyn C. Haynes; Ari M. Trubitt; Donald J. Mock; Samuel Z. Goldfarb; Shellé E. Riley; Jack R. Levin; John O. Walsh.

(This Listing Continued)

Borovsky & Ehrlich (Continued)

Labor Relations and Equal Opportunity Law. Labor Antitrust Law. Occupational Safety and Health Law. Pension and Employee Benefit Law. Related Trial and Appellate Practice, Matrimonial Law, Real Estate, Bankruptcy, Criminal Defense, Personal Injury, Civil Litigation, Consumer, Immigration.

See Professional Biographies, CHICAGO, ILLINOIS

Borsand, Steven F., (AV) '— '91 C.477 B.S. L.309 J.D.
VP, Intell. Prop., Trading Technologies (Pat.)
Borsos, Mark A. '77 '02 C&L.477 B.S., J.D. [Ⓐ Fitch,E.T.&F.]
Borst, Vincent T., (AV) '58 '86 C.838 B.S.M.E. L.365 J.D. [Askounis&B.]
Borstein, Scott R., (BV) '63 '88 C.473 B.A. L.276 J.D. [Wildman,H.A.&D.]
Borth, Paul R. '63 '95 C.589 B.A. L.365 J.D. 19 S. La Salle St., Ste. 800
Borun, Michael F., (AV) '— '70 C.145 B.S. L.424 J.D.
[Marshall,G.&B.] (See Pat. Sect.)
Boruszak, Bruce L., (AV) '57 '82 C.339 B.S. L.477 J.D. [Wildman,H.A.&D.]
Borzym, Alice Donna '51 '80 C.597 Ph.B. L.209 J.D.
6650 N. Northwest Hwy., Ste. 204
Bosco, Anthony J. '28 '56 C.1016 A.B. L.209 J.D. Ret. Cir. J.
Bosco, Ronald T. '33 '58 C.714 B.A. L.209 J.D. Chf. Atty., Chicago Transit Auth.
Bossen, Roy M., (BV) '51 '79 C.94 B.L.S. L.734 J.D. [Hinshaw&C.]
Bossov, Adam E., Law Offices of '67 '93
C.339 B.A. L.146 J.D. 846 W. Ainslie, Suite R-3
Bostjancich, John '47 '77 C.118 B.A. L.424 J.D. [Smart&B.]
Boston, Roy L. '50 '85 C.347 B.S. L.809 J.D. Commerce Commission
Bostwick, Jarrett T. '73 '98 C.273 B.A. L.285 J.D. [Ⓐ Gardner C.&D.]
Bosworth, Kenneth W., (AV) '75 C.589 B.S. L.365 J.D. [Horwood M.&B.]
Bosy, George S., (AV) '52 '77 C.339 B.S. L.597 J.D. [Jenner&B.] (Pat.)
Botana, James F. '63 '92 C.1191 B.S. L.209 J.D. [Jackson L.]
Botica, Matthew J., (AV) '51 '75 C.93 A.B. L.309 J.D. [Winston&S.]
Botkin, Abbey Mark, Law Offices of, (CV) '53 '80
C.339 B.A. L.209 J.D. 111 West Washington Street
Botkin, Carol B., (Mrs.) '27 '52 C.1016 B.A. L.421 LL.B. 5808 N. St. Louis Ave.‡
Bots, Theodore R. '69 '94 C.589 B.S. L.221 J.D. [McDermott W.&E.]

Botti, Marinaccio & DeLongis, Ltd.
(See Oak Brook)

Bottomlee, Thomas W. '62 '95 C.347 B.S. L.597 J.D. [Mayer,B.R.&M.]
Boudreau, Alan R., (AV) '53 '79 C.1151 B.A. L.589 J.D. [Boudreau&B.]
Boudreau, Jessica Marie '75 '03 C.960 B.S. L.1049 J.D. [Ⓐ Schain,B.R.&C.]
Boudreau & Beal, P.C., (AV) 33 North Dearborn Street, Suite 815
Bouer, Robert '25 '81 C.339 B.S. L.424 J.D. St. Joseph Hosp.
Bouldon, Allyson '62 '92 C.197 A.B. L.145 J.D. Coun., Americas, Wm Wrigley Jr. Co.
Boulos, Nader R. '— '94 C.813 A.B. L.477 J.D. [Kirkland&E.]
Boulton, Stephen F. '58 '83 C.659 B.A. L.930 J.D. [Cantwell&C.]
Bouma, Robert E., (AV) '38 '62 C.162 B.A. L.352 J.D. [McDermott W.&E.]
Boundas, Theodore A., (AV) '38 '64
C.884 A.B. L.309 LL.B. [Boundas S.W.&B.] (©London, England)

Boundas Skarzynski Walsh & Black LLC, (AV)
200 East Randolph Drive, Suite 7200, 60601-7719 ©
Telephone: 312-946-4200 Fax: 312-946-4272
URL: http://www.bswb.com
Principals: Theodore A. Boundas; Peter F. Lovato, III; John E. Black, Jr.; David T. Burrowes; Michael J. Rosen; R. Nathan Randall; Teri Lee Ferro; Ellen D. Jenkins. Of Counsel: Regina K. McCabe; Norbert J. Wegerzyn. Associates: Patrick W. Carlson; Amanda F. Fayne; David A. Shedd; Thomas M. Sheffield; Brian A. White.
Insurance, Reinsurance, Commercial Litigation, Arbitration, Counseling, Directors and Officers Liability, E-Commerce, Internet, Technology, Employment Liability, Environmental Liability, Fidelity Insurance, Fiduciary Liability, Financial Insurance, Financial Institution Liability, Mutual Fund Liability, Finite Risk, Alternative Risk Transfer Products, Insurance Company Professional Liability, Insurance Regulation, Intellectual Property, Trademarks, Patents, Copyrights, Managed Care Liability, Health Care Liability, Municipal, School Board, Non-Profit Liability, Products Liability, Professional Liability, Securities Liability, Specialty Lines Insurance, Commercial Lines Insurance, Personal Lines Insurance, Alternative Dispute Resolution, Appellate Litigation, Corporate Governance, Corporate Compliance, Privacy Compliance.
New York, New York Office: One Battery Park Plaza, 22nd Floor, 10004. Telephone: 212-820-7750. Fax: 212-820-7740; 820-7788.
London, England Office: 37-39 Lime Street, EC3M 7AY. Telephone: +011-44-020-7929-5588. Fax: +011-44-020-7929-5999.

See Professional Biographies, CHICAGO, ILLINOIS

Bourgeois, Adam '29 '51 C.974 B.A. L.424 LL.B. 53 West Jackson Boulevard
Bourke, John J. '— '91 C.339 B.S. L.424 J.D. Sr. Coun., Aon Corp.
Bouxsein, Dennis G. '— '86 C.747 B.A. L.339 J.D. [Ungaretti&H.]
Bouzeos, Darcy L. '60 '85 C.378 B.S. L.365 J.D. [Jacobs&Assoc.]
Bove, Patricia A. '53 '88 C.999 B.A. L.146 J.D. Law Clk., Appl. Ct.
Bovia, Lester G., Jr. '73 '98 C&L.339 B.S., J.D. [Ⓐ Winston&S.]
Bowe, William J. '42 '67 C.976 B.A. L.145 J.D.
Exec.V.P., Gen. Coun. & Secy., Encyclopaedia Britannica, Inc.
Bowen, Stephen S., (AV) '— '72 C.894 B.A. L.145 J.D. [Latham&W.]
Bowen, Terry R. '68 '97 C.383 B.A. L.209 J.D. [Ⓐ R.T.Napier&Assoc.]
Bower, Albert M. '— '01 C.1070 B.S. L.339 J.D. [Ⓐ Wildman,H.A.&D.]
Bower, Bruce L., (AV) '33 '60 C.339 B.A. L.477 J.D. [Winston&S.]
Bower, Eileen King, (AV) '64 '88 C&L.424 B.A., J.D. [Ross,D.&B.]
Bower, Glen L. '49 '74 C.801 B.A. L.146 J.D. Chm., U.S. R.R. Ret. Bd.
Bower, Robert A., (AV) '55 '85 C.108 B.S. L.424 J.D. [Tucker B.R.&M.]
Bower, Theodore D. '26 '57 C.502 B.S. L.209 LL.B. Sears, Roebuck & Co.
Bowers, James L., Jr. '50 '77 C.339 B.A. L.209 J.D. U.S. Dept. of Labor
Bowers, Kellye '— '98 C.383 B.A. L.347 J.D.
(adm. in OH; not adm. in IL) [Ⓐ Katten M.R.]
Bowes, Karen J., (BV) '56 '80 C&L.500 B.A., J.D. [Rinella&R.]
Bowhay, James H. '59 '87 C.293 B.A. L.339 J.D. [Ⓐ Figliulo&S.]
Bowler, Denise Kirkowski '75 '00 C.602 B.A. L.477 J.D. [Ⓐ Jenner&B.]
Bowles, Clyde O., Jr., (AV) '27 '51 C.597 B.S. L.976 J.D. [Ⓒ Dykema G.P.]
Bowley, John R. '— '01 C.608 B.A. L.1000 J.D [Ⓐ Crisham&K.]
Bowly, Devereux, Jr. '42 '69 C.46 B.S. L.966 J.D. Legal Assistance Found.
Bowman, Cynthia Grant '45 '82
C.821 B.A. L.597 J.D. Prof., Northwestern Univ. Sch. of Law
Bowman, George A., Jr. '17 '43 C.966 L.436 J.D.
(adm. in WI; not adm. in IL) U.S. Admin. Law J., Soc. Sec. Admin.
Bowman, Jerome K., (AV) '63 '88 C.734 B.A. L.339 J.D. Asst. Gen. Coun.
Bowman, Jill Hubbard '62 '98 C.101 B.S. L.477 J.D. [Ⓐ Brinks H.G.&L.]
Bowman, John T., Jr., (AV) '45 '76 C.823 B.S. L.801 J.D. [Bowman&C.]
Bowman, Kristi L. '76 '01 C.221 B.A. L.228 J.D. [Ⓐ Franczek S.]
Bowman, Locke E., III, (AV) '54 '82
C.309 A.B. L.145 J.D. Legal Dir., The MacArthur Justice Ctr.
Bowman, Phillip B., (AV) '36 '61 C.674 B.S.E. L.477 J.D. [Defrees&F.]
Bowman & Corday, Ltd., (AV) 20 N. Clark, Ste. 500
Bowman, Heintz, Boscia & Vician, A Professional Corporation, (BV①)
134 N. La Salle St., Ste. 1200 (©Indpls., Merrillville, IN)
Box, John R. '56 '81 C.339 B.A. L.1066 J.D. [Sidley A.B.&W.]
Boxerman, Marc Jay '68 '93 C.188 B.A. L.145 J.D. Pub. Def.
Boxerman, Michael J. '69 '95 C.597 B.A. L.910 J.D. [Marcus,P.&C.]
Boyaris, Karen L. '55 '78 C.1191 B.A. L.477 J.D. Deloitte & Touche
Boyce, Donald S., Jr. '72 '04 C.734 B.A. L.602 J.D. [Ⓐ Jenner&B.]
Boyce, Michael D. '54 '86 C.424 B.A. L.209 J.D. Asst. State's Atty.
Boychuck, Stanley V., (AV) '51 '79 C.424 B.A. L.365 J.D. [Swanson,M.&B.]
Boyd, Brian Y. '75 '02 C.198 B.A. L.424 J.D. [Ⓐ Williams M.&J.]
Boyd, Craig T., (AV) '47 '73 C.103 Sc.B.Engin. L.597 J.D. [Butler R.S.&B.]
Boyd, Eric E., (AV) '59 '86 C.597 B.S. L.1119 J.D. [Seyfarth S.]
Boyd, William Stewart '52 '81 C.339 B.S. L.589 J.D. Richard J. Daly Center, Ste. 1605
Boye, Deborah T., (AV①) '— '80 C.45 B.A. L.602 J.D. [Chapman&C.]
Boye, Lee A. '— '61 C&L.339 B.A., LL.B. [Ⓒ Chapman&C.]
Boyer, Ardwin Eugene, (BV) '52 '80 C.112 B.A. L.1049 J.D. 20 N. Clark St., Ste. 800
Boyer, Bruce A. '60 '86 C.197 B.A. L.597 J.D. Northwestern Univ. School of Law
Boyer, Cory M. '77 '02 C.475 B.A. L.365 J.D. 205 W. Randolph, Ste. 1040
Boyer, Heather L. '— '03 C.338 L.361 JD. [Ⓐ Hennessy&R.]
Boyer, Kristin Morgan '56 '82 C.429 B.A. L.494 J.D. 20 N. Clark St., Ste. 800
Boye-Williams, Patricia '76 '03 C.188 B.S. L.146 J.D. [Ⓐ Jenner&B.]
Boykin, Barry C. '53 '84 C.424 B.A. L.209 J.D.
Staff Atty., Austin Christian Law Center
Boykins, Michael L. '65 '90 C&L.966 B.S., J.D. [McDermott W.&E.]
Boylan, Robert T. '70 '95 C.477 B.A. L.94 J.D. [Foran G.P.&P.]
Boylan, Thomas P., (AV) '61 '86 C.339 B.A. L.424 J.D. [Cassiday,S.&G.]
Boyle, Cassandra L. '— '97 C.839 B.B.A. L.309 J.D. [Ⓐ Jones D.]
Boyle, Cecil F., Jr., (AV①) '48 '77 C.475 B.S. L.215 J.D. [C.F.Boyle,Jr.]
Boyle, Charles A., (AV) '41 '66 C&L.425 B.A., J.D. [C.A.Boyle&Assoc.]
Boyle, Dao L. '— '99 C.339 B.A. L.597 J.D. Two North LaSalle Street, Suite 2200
Boyle, Eugene A., (AV) '61 '86 C.399 B.A. L.910 J.D. [Neal,G.&E.]
Boyle, Gregory M. '71 '97 C.118 B.A. L.309 J.D. [Jenner&B.]
Boyle, Iwona K. '66 '91 C&L.209 B.A., J.D. 222 N. LaSalle St.
Boyle, James P. '63 '88 C.321 B.A. L.146 J.D. 221 N. LaSalle St.
Boyle, Jerome E., (AV) '56 '83 C.424 B.A. L.339 J.D. [Ⓐ A.W.Block]
Boyle, Kevin V. '67 '92 C.602 B.A. L.989 J.D. [Swanson,M.&B.]
Boyle, Mark H., (AV) '64 '89 C.602 B.A. L.424 J.D. [Donohue B.M.&S.]
Boyle, Richard J. '35 '62 C&L.352 B.S.C., J.D.
(adm. in IA; not adm. in IL) 55 W. Monroe Street, Suite 700
Boyle, C. F., Jr., Law Office of, (AV①) 1313 N. Ritchie Ct., Ste. 1702
Boyle, Charles A., & Associates, Ltd., (AV) 11 East Adams Street, Suite 1600
Boyles, Magda '— '03 C.823 B.S. L.597 J.D. [Ⓐ Schwartz C.]

Boynovska, Tzvetelina T., Law Office of '67 '97 C.999 L.424 J.D.
1834 West North Avenue, Suite 1-SE, 60622
Telephone: 773-342-8671 Fax: 773-342-8680
Email: tboynovska@yahoo.com URL: http://www.lawyers.com/tboynovska
Languages: Bulgarian and Russian.
Immigration, Family Law, Divorce, Residential Real Estate.

See Professional Biographies, CHICAGO, ILLINOIS

Boynton, Julie A. '52 '94 C.927 B.S. L.365 J.D. [Ⓐ F.L.Ingram]
Bozek, Laura L. '66 '91 C.1044 B.S. L.188 J.D. 180 N. Stetson Ave.
Bozeman, Alzetta L. '71 '98 C.811 B.A. L.365 J.D. Asst. States Atty.
Bozic, Marnie N. '77 '03 C.69 B.A. L.339 J.D. [Ⓐ Walker W.M.]
Bozic, Martha A. '71 '97 C&L.424 B.A., J.D. 1964 W. Lawrence Ave.
Bozick, Gary W., (AV) '49 '74 C.589 B.S. L.209 J.D. 77 W. Wash. St.
Bozych, Paul, (BV) '63 '88 C.339 A.B. L.209 J.D. [Clausen M.]
Brabeck, Jean M. '56 '81 C.602 B.A. L.880 J.D. 2422 W. Morse Ave.
Brace, Frederic F., Law Firm of, Jr., (AV) '34 '59 C&L.477 A.B., J.D. 2 N. LaSalle St.
Bracke, Michelle M. '66 '94 C.597 B.G.S. L.424 J.D. [Bollinger,R.&G.]
Bracy, Delars J. '23 '52 C.999 L.989 7719 S. Vernon
Bracy, Lorenzo E. '52 '76 C.339 B.A. L.365 J.D. 900 N. Michigan Ave., Ste. 1900
Braden, Everette A. '32 '69 C.597 B.S. L.365 LL.B.,J.D Appl. Ct. Jus.
Braden, Zedrick T., III '56 '85 C.138 B.A. L.1463 J.D. [Ⓒ Ainsworth&Assoc.]
Bradford, Darryl M., (AV) '55 '80
C.293 B.A. L.145 J.D. V.P. & Assoc. Gen. Coun., Com Ed Exelon
Bradford, David J., (AV) '52 '76 C.475 B.A. L.145 J.D. [Jenner&B.]
Bradford, David J. '71 '97 C.427 B.A. L.365 J.D. [Ⓐ Lord,B.&B.]
Bradford, Dina A. '75 '00 C.597 B.A. L.424 J.D. [Krasnow S.C.]
Bradford, Mark A. '79 '04 C&L.339 B.S., J.D. [Ⓐ Lord,B.&B.]
Bradley, Byron K. '48 '83 C.209 B.A. L.365 J.D. [Bradley&B.]
Bradley, Craig C. '58 '83 C.238 B.S. L.1119 J.D. [Katten M.R.]
Bradley, Edward J., (AV) '13 '39 C.999 L.209 J.D. [Bradley&B.]
Bradley, Edward J., Jr., (AV) '39 '64 C&L.597 B.A., J.D. [Bradley&B.]
Bradley, Galen A. '— '95 C.234 B.S. L.879 J.D. [Querrey&H.] (©Merrillville, IN)
Bradley, Thomas '57 '88 C.145 B.A. L.365 J.D. [Laner,M.D.B.L.&T.]
Bradley & Bradley, (AV) 29 S. La Salle St. Ste. 950
Bradley & Burke, Ltd. 10345 S. Western Ave.
Bradley-Coar, Alfreda '63 '91 C&L.659 B.A., J.D.
Gen. Coun., Coregis Ins. Co., Employers Reinsurance Corp.
Bradshaw, Elizabeth M. '66 '94 C.321 L.145 J.D. [LeBoeuf,L.G.&M.]
Bradwish, LeRoy L. '35 '72 C.193 B.A. L.424 J.D. 175 E. Delaware
Brady, Alpha '61 '86 C.238 B.S. L.597 J.D. Spec. Asst. to the Pres., Amer. Bar Assn.
Brady, Francis M., (AV) '— '81 C.339 B.A. L.424 J.D. [Brady,C.&M.]
Brady, Jill M. '75 '03 C&L.477 B.A., J.D. [Ⓐ Eimer S.K.&S.]
Brady, Joan E. '67 '92 C.475 B.A. L.608 J.D. [Ⓐ Kerns,P.F.&P.]
Brady, Lauren E. '76 '03 C.145 B.A. L.966 J.D. [Ⓐ Polsky&Assoc.]
Brady, Orla M. '74 '01 L.1202 J.D. [Ⓐ Nolan]
Brady, Patrick '— '01 C.966 B.A. L.424 J.D. [Ⓐ Mayer,B.R.&M.]
Brady, Patrick E. '54 '83 C.597 B.A. L.365 J.D. [McGuirewoods]
Brady, Paul E. '63 '99 C.927 B.S. L.365 J.D. [Ⓐ Johnson&B.] (©Waukegan)
Brady, Sean R. '67 '00 C.339 B.S. L.146 J.D. IL Com. Comm.
Brady, Tanya '— '99 C.999 B.C.L. L.209 J.D. [Ⓐ Kirkland&E.]
Brady, Terrence R. '58 '85 C.197 A.B. L.602 J.D. [Winston&S.]
Brady, Thos. J. '13 '52 C.597 L.365 LL.B. U.S. Vets. Adm.
Brady, Thos. P. '20 '50 C.262 B.S. L.209 J.D. 3227 W. 83rd Pl.
Brady, Connolly & Masuda, P.C., (AV) 1 North La Salle Street, Suite 1000 (©Normal)
Braendel, Addison D. '64 '92 C.831 B.A. L.145 J.D. [Mayer,B.R.&M.]
Brafman, Stuart M. '35 '60 C.966 L.767 LL.B.
(adm. in WI; not adm. in IL) 161 Chicago Ave.‡
Bragança, Celiza P. '— '92 C&L.145 B.A., J.D. [Ⓐ Sperling&S.]
Bragg, O. Randolph '48 '73 C.250 B.S. L.923 J.D. [Horwitz,H.&Assoc.]
Bragga, Terri Barton '— '98 C.880 B.A. L.608 J.D.
(adm. in OH; not adm. in IL) [Ⓐ Zulkie]
Brahin, Lynn Hirschfeld '63 '89 C.966 B.S.J. L.365 J.D. Staff Atty., State Appl. Ct.

Braidwood, George Christopher '70 '95
C&L.477 B.S.E.E., J.D. [Ⓐ Marshall,G.&B.] (See Pat. Sect.)
Brainerd, Scott A. '55 '82 C.823 B.A. L.597 J.D. [S.A.Brainerd]
Brainerd, Scott A., Ltd. 1941 N. Mohawk St.
Braithwaite, J. William, (AV) '— '56
C.184 B.A. L.178 LL.B. [Arnstein&L.] (⊙Hoffman Estates)
Braitman, Barry H., (BV) '48 '74 C&L.966 B.A., J.D. Sr. V.P. & Gen. Coun., RREEF
Bramlette, Robert C., Jr. '49 '75 C.602 B.B.A. L.597 J.D. [BryceDowney]
Bramnik, Robert P., (AV) '49 '74 C.563 B.A. L.1009 J.D. [Duane M.]
Bramson, Melvin R. '29 '53 C.339 L.209 J.D. 734 N. La Salle St.
Branch, Roderick O. '— '03 C.840 B.A. L.1565 J.D.
(adm. in NY; not adm. in IL) [Ⓐ Latham&W.]
Brand, Mark A., (AV) '— '79 C.182 B.A. L.602 J.D. [Sachnoff&W.]
Brand, Russell '47 '70 22 W. Monroe, Ste. 1800
Brand-Ballard, Jeffrey '69 '96 C.881 A.B. L.477 J.D. 120 N. La Salle St., Ste. 1050
Brandenburg, John R. '41 '72 C&L.424 B.B.A., J.D. [J.R.Brandenburg&Assoc.]
Brandenburg, John R., & Associates, Ltd. 20 N. Wacker Dr.
Brandfonbrener, Eric D. '61 '87 C.309 A.B. L.477 J.D. [Perkins C.]
Branding, Frederick H., (AV) '44 '73 C.221 B.A. L.146 J.D. [McGuirewoods]
Brandon, Karen N. '65 '00 C.1103 B.S. L.30 J.D. [Ⓒ Ogletree,D.N.S.&S.]
Brandonisio, Michelina '78 '04 C.209 B.A. L.365 J.D. Assoc. Counsel, Alpha Thought
Brandow, Michael K., (CV) '53 '81 C.98 B.A. L.365 J.D. [Ⓐ Brady,C.&M.]
Brandstrader, Thomas C., (AV) '49 '79 C.763 B.A. L.1137 J.D.
53 West Jackson Boulevard, Suite 615 (⊙Northfield)
Brandt, Arthur F. '64 '90 C.477 A.B. L.215 J.D. [Bates&C.]
Brandt, Stephen M., (BV Ⓣ) '49 '78 C.145 A.B. L.1119 J.D. [Dymkar&B.]
Brandwein, Bruce E. '51 '78 C.589 B.A. L.1151 J.D. 20 S. Clark, Ste. 410
Brandys, Roy R., (BV Ⓣ) '57 '85 C.388 B.A. L.896 J.D. [Childress D.G.]
Branigan, Terence P. '53 '84 C.755 B.A. L.309 J.D.
(adm. in MN; not adm. in IL) Asst. Reg. Coun., U.S. Environmental Agcy.‡
Branit, James R. '61 '85 C&L.146 B.A., J.D. [Bullaro&C.]
Brankin, Patrick T. '70 '95 C.234 B.A. L.425 J.D. [Schain,B.R.&C.]
Brannigan, Thomas E., Sr., (AV) '39 '63 C&L.602 A.B., LL.B. [Smith,H.B.&B.]
Bransfield, John P. '69 '94 C.602 B.A. L.365 J.D. 1 N Lasalle St Ste 2046
Bransfield, Stephanie C. '60 '85 C.453 S.B. L.145 J.D. Corp. Coun., BorgWarner Inc.
Bransfield, Thomas D. '67 '92 C.93 B.A. L.424 J.D. [J.F.Bransfield]
Bransfield, Jeremiah F., Partnership 1 N. La Salle St., Ste. 2046
Bransley, Robert A., (AV) '30 '61 C&L.424 B.Sc., J.D. 8 S. Michigan Blvd.
Brant, George H. '43 '68
C.347 B.A. L.1119 J.D. Sr. Trial Coun., Union Pacific Railroad Co.
Brashler, Thomas R. '56 '81 C.477 B.A. L.273 J.D. [Stahl&B.]
Brass, Mary M. '50 '84 C.999 B.S. L.365 J.D.
Supvr. of Attys., Cook Co. Pub. Guardian's Ofc.
Brasser, Bradley C. '— '00 C.597 B.A. L.74 J.D. [Ⓐ Jones D.]
Bratton, Ann Renee '59 '84
C.1322 B.A. L.802 J.D. State Clean Energy Community Found.
Braun, Bruce R. '63 '91 C.311 B.A. L.893 J.D. [Winston&S.]
Braun, Mark A., (AV) '25 '50 C.436 L.424 J.D. [Braun S.L.B.&M.]
Braun, Michael A., (AV) '46 '72 C.976 B.A. L.145 J.D. 33 N. Dearborn St.
Braun, Michael F., (AV) '56 '81 C&L.339 B.A., J.D. [Schuyler,R.&Z.]
Braun, Michele J. '59 '84 C.1044 B.A. L.365 J.D. [Ⓒ Duane M.]
Braun, Robert A. '70 '97 C.602 B.A. L.966 J.D. [Ⓐ Brenner,F.M.&S.]
Braun, Scott D. '71 '97 C.966 B.A. L.910 J.D. [Ⓐ Sedgwick,D.M.&A.]
Braun, Traci M. '70 '98 C&L.966 B.A., J.D. [Jenner&B.]
Braun, W. David, (AV) '50 '75 C.339 B.A. L.602 J.D. [Gardner C.&D.]

Braun Strobel Lorenz Bergin & Millman, P.C., (AV)
33 North La Salle Street Suite 2800, 60602
Telephone: 312-726-3877 FAX: 312-332-0039
Email: info@bslbm.com URL: http://www.bslbm.com
Francis J. Lynch (1921-2000); Mark A. Braun; John A. Strobel; Peter J. Lorenz; John P. Bergin; Craig Millman.
General Civil and Trial Practice. State and Federal Workers Compensation Law. Litigation and Appellate Practice.
Representative Clients: 21st Century Insurance; ESIS; BP; Employers Claim Service; Gallagher Bassett Services; General Casualty; Loyola University Health System; Liberty Mutual; General Casualty; Siemens.
See Professional Biographies, CHICAGO, ILLINOIS

Braverman, Eric '75 '03 C&L.976 B.A., J.D.
(adm. in NY; not adm. in IL) Aon Corporation
Braverman, Wayne R., (BV) '59 '87 C.589 B.S. L.146 J.D. 200 N. La Salle St.
Brayman, Paul M., (AV) '40 '70 C.813 B.A. L.339 J.D. [P.Brayman]
Brayman, Paul, (AV) 727 S. Dearborn St., Ste. 712
Brazen, Lionel I. '28 '50 C&L.339 B.S., J.D. 188 W. Randolph St.
Brazil-Breashears, Karen '44 '79 C.1191 B.Sc. L.209 J.D. 5352 S. Drexel Ave.
Breakstone, Donald S., (AV) '45 '70 C.477 B.A. L.309 J.D.
Sr. V.P. & Gen. Coun., Attorneys' Liability Assurance Society, Inc.
Bream, James M. '— '86 C.966 B.A. L.494 J.D. [Querrey&H.]
Bredin, Ann Marie '74 '98 C&L.597 B.S., J.D. [Ⓐ DLPiper R.G.C.U.]
Breems, Timothy S. '61 '85 C.209 B.S. L.424 J.D. [Ruff,W.&R.]
Breen, James M., (AV) '— '68 C.718 B.A. L.127 J.D. [Chapman&C.]
Breen, John M. '63 '88 C.602 B.A. L.309 J.D. Asst. Prof., Loyola Univ. Sch. of Law
Breen, Joseph F. '71 '01 C.719 B.A. L.365 J.D. [Ⓐ R.L.Prusak]
Breen, Lisa C. '67 '92 C.589 B.A. L.146 J.D. [Ⓒ Meckler B.&T.]
Breen, Nathan J. '74 '99 C.209 B.A. L.365 J.D. [Ⓐ Howe&H.]
Breen, Neil T. '44 '70 C.436 A.B. L.190 J.D.
(adm. in NE; not adm. in IL) Sr. Vip., Law Bulletin Publishing Co.
Breen, Thomas M., and Associates, (AV) '47 '72
C.602 A.B. L.424 J.D. 53 W. Jackson Blvd., Ste. 1460
Breen-Greco, Ann '— '85 C.999 B.A. L.146 J.D. 4123 N. Maplewood
Bregenzer, Michael P. '— '94 C.602 B.A. L.339 J.D. [Kirkland&E.]
Brehm, L. Andrew, (AV) '54 '79 C.602 B.A. L.477 J.D. [Schuyler,R.&Z.]
Breisblatt, Robert B., (AV) '48 '72 C.259 B.A. L.228 J.D. [Welsh&K.]
Breit, Lauren Hennessey '— '00 C.188 B.A. L.597 J.D. [Ⓒ Kirkland&E.] (Pat.)
Breitenstein, Laurie K. '62 '88
C.502 B.A. L.477 J.D. Sr. Coun., Bank One Corp. (Law Dept.)
Breitung, Barrett A. '61 '97 C.378 B.A. L.1365 J.D. [Ⓐ Lord,B.&B.]
Brejcha, Barrie L., (AV) '60 '85 C.597 B.A. L.424 J.D. [Baker&M.]
Brejcha, Thomas '43 '69 C.602 A.B. L.569 J.D. 29 S. La Salle St.
Brejcha, William D. '48 '73 C.602 B.A. L.424 J.D. [Scopelitis,G.L.&H.]
Bremer, Catherine Ward '49 '89 C&L.209 B.S.N., J.D. 218 N. Jefferson St., Ste. 201
Bremer, Jason A. '— '99 C.966 B.A. L.352 J.D. [Ⓐ Foley&L.]
Bremer, Scott A. '50 '75 C.747 B.A. L.597 J.D. [Pugh,J.J.&Q.]
Brend, Jeffrey W., (BV) '57 '84 C.589 B.S. L.365 J.D. [Levin&B.]
Brenman, Lawrence H., (AV) '57 '82 C.174 B.S. L.208 J.D. [Much S.F.D.A.&R.]
Brennan, Bevin M. '— '00 C.951 B.A. L.1565 J.D. [Ⓐ Perkins C.]
Brennan, Daniel S. '65 '90 C.602 B.A. L.273 J.D. [DLPiper R.G.C.U.]
Brennan, Danolda J. '41 '74 C.227 B.A. L.365 J.D. Carnegie Mtge. Co.
Brennan, John F. '59 '84 [Ⓒ Huff&G.]
Brennan, Margaret A. '62 '87 C.339 B.A. L.146 J.D. Richard J. Daley Ctr., Rm. 400
Brennan, Mark M., (BV) '67 '93 C.209 B.A. L.424 J.D. [Cassiday,S.&G.]
Brennan, Michael G., (AV) '52 '79 C.602 B.A. L.209 J.D. [DLPiper R.G.C.U.]
Brennan, Michael J., (AV) '52 '77 C&L.209 B.A., J.D. [Kane,D.&H.]
Brennan, Noelle C. '65 '95 C.112 B.A. L.209 J.D. EEOC
Brennan, Peter J. '59 '85 C&L.276 B.A., J.D. [Jenner&B.]
Brennan, Richard J., (AV) '36 '62 C&L.424 B.S., J.D. 35 W. Wacker Dr.‡
Brennan, Richard S., (AV) '38 '65
C.674 A.B. L.477 J.D. [Mayer,B.R.&M.] (⊙Racine, WI)
Brennan, Stephanie A. '— '03 C.197 B.A. L.976 J.D. [Ⓐ Kirkland&E.]
Brenneman, Steven L., (AV) '59 '85 C.288 B.A. L.477 J.D. [Matkov,S.M.&G.]
Brenner, David M. '30 '54 C.597 B.S. L.145 J.D. Corp. Supply Co., Inc.
Brenner, Kevin '— '02 C.966 B.A. L.146 J.D. [Ⓐ Arnstein&L.]
Brenner, Sheldon A., (AV) '44 '69 C&L.209 B.S., J.D. [Brenner,F.M.&S.]

Brenner, Ford, Monroe & Scott, Ltd., (AV)
33 North Dearborn Street, Suite 300, 60602-3102 ⊙
Telephone: 312-781-1970 Fax: 312-781-9202
URL: http://www.brennerlawfirm.com
Amy L. Anderson; Sheldon A. Brenner; Scott R. Britton; James W. Ford; Stephen A. Kolodziej; Teresa R. Maher; Randall C. Monroe; Mary Kay Scott. Associates: Kenneth M. Battle; Joshua C. Bell; Robert A. Braun; Katherine Amy Lemon; Melissa A. Lynott; Fred A. Nickl; Eydie R. Perry; Eric Alan Rywalski; Lanny VanDaele.
Insurance Defense, Personal Injury, Medical Malpractice, Construction Law, Product Liability, Uninsured/Underinsured Motorist Arbitrations and Litigation of Contested Coverage Issues.
See Professional Biographies, CHICAGO, ILLINOIS

Brenner, Leonard J., Ltd.
(See Northbrook)

Brennock, Michael W. '51 '77 C.209 B.S.A. L.365 J.D. Asst. Pub. Def.
Brennwald, James Quinn '57 '86 C.477 B.A. L.424 J.D. Asst. Corp. Coun.
Brent, David J. '45 '75 C.339 B.A. L.209 J.D. Amer. Bar Assn.
Brent, Nancy J. '— '81 C.883 B.S. L.424 J.D. 5445 N. Sheridan Rd.
Breseman, Kristi M. '73 '01 C.475 B.A. L.365 J.D. 120 S. LaSalle
Bresler, Martin B., (AV) '41 '66 C.339 B.A. L.209 J.D. [Bresler&H.]
Bresler & Harvick, Ltd., (AV) 33 North Dearborn Street, Suite 1300
Breslin, Kevin P., (AV) '54 '80 C.339 L.424 J.D. [Weinberg R.]

Breslin, Warren J., Law Offices
(See Schaumburg)

Bressler, Barbara B. '50 '80 C.494 B.S. L.209 J.D. DePaul Univ. Coll. of Law
Bressler, Michael A., II '73 '03 C.843 B.B.A. L.1410 J.D. [Coghlan K.C.]
Bressler Rose, Felice, (AV) '— '91 C.477 B.A. L.339 J.D. [Schiff H.]
Bretscher, John T. '58 '99 C.145 B.A. L.146 J.D. [Ⓐ Leydig,V.&M.] (⊙Rockford)
Brett, Julie P., (BV) '— '87 C.860 B.A. L.107 J.D. [Ⓐ Beermann S.W.B.B.G.&L.]
Brett, Matthew '— '03 C.228 A.B. L.1565 J.D. [Ⓐ Schiff H.]
Brett, Thomas F., II '— '78 C.602 B.B.A. L.831 J.D. [Ungaretti&H.]
Breuer, Jennifer R. '66 '95 C.918 B.A. L.597 J.D. [Gardner C.&D.]
Brewe, Helen K. '48 '85 C.339 B.S. L.146 J.D. V.P., Gen. Reins. Corp.
Brewer, Eileen Mary '52 '87 C.1031 B.A. L.309 J.D. 118 N. Clark St., 547 Co. Bldg.
Brewer, Tommy '— '76 C.951 B.A. L.597 J.D. 175 West Jackson Boulevard, Suite 646
Brewick, Irene Sheridan '51 '83 C.523 B.A. L.424 J.D. [Ⓒ Williams&B.]
Brewin, Katherine S. '47 '77 C.696 B.A. L.1340 J.D. Tr. Offr., La Salle Bk., N.A.‡
Brewster, Philip S. '— '97 C.823 B.A. L.93 J.D.
(adm. in MA; not adm. in IL) [Ⓐ McGuirewoods]
Brewster, William '66 '92 C.339 B.A. L.365 J.D. [Ⓐ Brady,C.&M.]
Breyer, Amy A. '64 '00 C.94 B.S.B.A. L.597 J.D. [A.A.Breyer]
Breyer, Amy A., The Law Offices of, LLC 33 N. LaSalle St., Ste. 2020
Brezina, David C., (AV) '— '78 C.187 B.S.S. L.146 J.D. [Barnes&T.] (See Pat. Sect.)
Brezina, John C. '30 '53 C.352 B.A. L.146 LL.B. [Brezina&B.] (Pat.)
Brezina & Buckingham, P.C. 47 W. Polk St., Ste. 333 (Pat.)
Briars, Eugene J. '31 '57 C&L.209 B.S.C., J.D. 5130 S. Archer Ave.
Brice, Roger T., (AV) '48 '73 C.209 A.B. L.145 J.D. [Sonnenschein N.&R.]
Brice, Susan '70 '95 C.597 B.S.J. L.276 J.D. [Mayer,B.R.&M.]
Bricker, Lew R.C. '— '91 C&L.339 B.A., J.D. [O'Hagan,S.&A.]
Brickman, Jeffrey M. '51 '76 C.339 B.A. L.209 J.D. [Cohon R.&R.]
Bridewell, David A., (AV) '09 '33 C.797 A.B. L.273 J.D. 135 S. La Salle St.‡
Bridge, Robert D. '64 '96 C.999 B.A. L.209 J.D.
Assoc. Gen. Coun. & Asst. Corp. Secy., TruServ Corp.
Bridgeman, Randy A. '67 '92 C.602 B.A. L.477 J.D. [Bell,B.&L.]
Bridgman, Thomas F., (AV) '33 '58 C.363 B.S. L.424 J.D. 130 E. Randolph Dr.
Bries, Maria A. '73 '98 C.352 B.B.A. L.569 J.D. [Ⓐ Mayer,B.R.&M.]
Brieske, Terri L. '66 '98 C.339 B.A. L.597 J.D. [Ⓐ Holland&K.]
Bright, Steven '55 '80 C.597 B.S. L.209 J.D. [Levenfeld P.] ⊙
Brill, Aaron P. '28 '53 C.1016 A.B. L.209 J.D. 180 N. LaSalle St.
Brill, Ralph L. '35 '60 C&L.339 B.A., J.D. Prof. of Law, Chicago-Kent College of Law
Brill, Robert J. '67 '92 C.602 B.S.M.E. L.436 J.D. 300 W Washington St # 1200
Brim, Scott W. '76 '02 C.201 B.S.E.E. L.339 J.D. [Ⓐ Brinks H.G.&L.] (See Pat. Sect.)
Brimeyer, Benjamin L. '— '01 C.597 B.S. L.494 J.D. [Ⓐ Sachnoff&W.]
Brinckerhoff, Philip G., (AV) '58 '85 C.436 A.B. L.734 J.D. [Garofalo,S.H.&S.]
Brink, Timothy W. '65 '91 C&L.477 B.S.E., J.D. [Lord,B.&B.]
Brinkley, Marissa Cashy '70 '96 L.424 J.D. [Ⓐ Holland&K.]
Brinkley, Timothy A., (CV) '67 '96 C.927 B.A. L.424 J.D. [Ⓐ Holland&K.]
Brinkmeier, Alan J., (AV) '54 '84 C.238 B.A. L.209 J.D. [Merlo K.B.&G.]
Brinks, Henry L., (AV) '24 '51 C.937 A.B. L.273 J.D.
[Brinks H.G.&L.] (See Pat. Sect.)

Brinks Hofer Gilson & Lione, A Professional Corporation, (AV) BB
NBC Tower, Suite 3600, 455 North Cityfront Plaza Drive, 60611-5599 ⊙
Telephone: 312-321-4200 Facsimile: 312-321-4299
Email: iplaw@usebrinks.com URL: http://www.usebrinks.com
Henry L. Brinks; Roy E. Hofer; Richard G. Lione; Jerome Gilson; Jack C. Berenzweig; Jerold A. Jacover; Gary M. Ropski; Joel W. Benson; John K. Lucas; Raymond W. Green; Cynthia A. Homan; James R. Sobieraj; Richard A. Kaplan; Steven P. Shurtz; Jeffery M. Duncan; Jeffery A. Handelman; Harold V. Johnson; Rodney A. Daniel; Glen P. Belvis; Thomas J. Filarski; William H. Frankel; Gustavo Siller, Jr.; James P. Naughton; Timothy Q. Delaney; Ralph J. Gabric; Bradley G. Lane; G. Peter Nichols; Michael E. Milz; Dominic P. Zanfardino; Robert S. Mallin; William F. Prendergast; John C. Freeman; David S. Fleming; Laura Beth Miller; Michael P. Chu; Meredith Martin Addy; Kent E. Genin; Craig A. Summerfield; Philip A. Jones; Marc V. Richards; John T. Gabrielides; Andrew D. Stover; Joseph V. Norvell; K. Shannon Mrksich; Jason C. White; Thomas M. Williams; Joseph F. Hetz; John G. Rauch; Mark H. Remus; Tadashi Horie; Jonathan E. Retsky; James A. Collins; Vineet Gauri; Thomas L. Holt; James L. Katz. Counsel: Mary M. Squyres; Amir N. Penn; Donald J. Silvert; Jeffrey H. Canfield; J. William Dockrey; Christopher A. Harkins; Janet A. Pioli; Robert B. Polit;—Howard S. Michael; Scott J. Slavick; Vincent J. Gnoffo; Richard E. Stanley, Jr.; David H. Bluestone; Christopher M. Dolan; Charles M. McMahon; Nicholas G. de la Torre; David W. Okey; Joseph W. Flerlage; Anastasia Heffner; Jeffry M. Nichols; Justin B. Rand; Lizabeth K. Vitellaro; Timothy P. Lucier; Elisa M. Valenzona; William D. Jackson; A. John Murray, Ph.D.; C. Noel Kaman; Daymon L. Ruttenberg; Sean P. Springman; Mircea A. Tipescu; Scott W. Brim;

(This Listing Continued)

Brinks Hofer Gilson & Lione, A Professional Corporation (Continued)

Amanda M. Miller; Benjamin B. Cotton; Heidi A. Dare; Robert G. Pluta; Jennifer A. Prioleau; Raymond R. Ricordati, III; Samuel E. Shehadeh; Joseph A. Yosick; Jill Hubbard Bowman; Anthony P. Curtis; Timothy J. Le Duc; John F. Nethery; Stephanie J. Felicetty; Brian A. Garcia; Miyoung Shin; Yolanda M. King; Nilay S. Dalal; Andrea L. Evensen; Julie L. Leichtman; David P. Lindner; Stephen Conrad Smith; Scott A. Timmerman; Jason M. Wejnert; Raynarldo K. Whitty (Not admitted in IL); Thomas J. Wrona; Bratislav Stankovic (Not admitted in IL); Michael K. Hendershot; Jay Burgett; Rochelle Claerbaut; Josh Garfield; Jeffrey A. Marx; Douglas A. Oguss; Heather N. Schafer; Jason W. Schigelone; Richard D. Watkins (Not admitted in IL); Rickard K. DeMille. Indianapolis Shareholder: A. James Richardson (Managing Attorney, Indianapolis Office). Indianapolis Of Counsel: David H. Badger. Indianapolis Counsel: Lawrence A. Steward. Indianapolis Associates: Sanders N. Hillis; Nicholas M. Boivin; Michael E. Wever. Ann Arbor Shareholders: David D. Murray (Senior Partner, Ann Arbor Office); Steven L. Oberholtzer; Eric J. Sosenko. Ann Arbor Counsel: Margaret Dobrowitsky. Ann Arbor Associates: Raymond J. Vivacqua; Dan L. Thompson; Lawrence G. Almeda; Michael N. Spink; John M. Card; Robert K. Fergan (Not admitted in IL); Jon H. Beaupre; John A. Lingl; James K. Cleland.
Languages: Arabic, Croatian, French, German, Greek, Hebrew, Japanese, Korean, Latvian, Macedonian, Polish, Romanian, Russian, Serbian and Spanish.
Patent, Trademark, Copyright, Trade Secret and Internet Work, Unfair Competition, Technology and Licensing Agreements, Intellectual Asset Management and Intellectual Property Litigation.
Indianapolis, Indiana Office: One Indiana Square, Suite 1600. Telephone: 317-636-0886. Facsimile: 317-634-6701.
Ann Arbor, Michigan Office: 524 South Main Street, Suite 200. Telephone: 734-302-6000. Facsimile: 734-994-6331.
Arlington, Virginia Office: 2001 Jefferson Davis Highway, Suite 208. Telephone: 703-415-0303. Facsimile: 703-415-0304.

See Professional Biographies, CHICAGO, ILLINOIS

Brinton, Howard T., (AV) '36 '61
C.966 B.A. L.309 J.D. 2506 North Clark Street, Suite 313
Briski, Andrea L. .... '73 '04 C.879 B.A. L.146 J.D. [Ⓐ Holland&K.]
Briskman, Arnold, (BV) .... '47 '72 C.339 B.A. L.209 J.D. [Briskman&B.]
Briskman, Robert I., (AV) .... '42 '68 C.339 B.A.S. L.146 J.D. [Briskman&B.]
Briskman & Briskman, (AV) .... 40 W. Hubbard
Brisky, Whitman H., (AV) .... '50 '75 C.188 B.A. L.597 J.D. [Mauck&B.]
Bristol, Douglas, (AV) '43 '69
C.966 B.S. L.339 J.D. 321 South Plymouth Court, Suite 1525
Brittain, Max G., Jr., (AV) .... '— '76 C.98 B.S. L.424 J.D. [Schiff H.]
Britton, Harold F. .... '31 '61 C&L.597 B.S., J.D. 5414 N. Magnolia Ave.‡
Britton, Homer C. .... '37 '77 C.339 L.209 J.D. [H.C.Britton]
Britton, Scott R., (AV) .... '60 '85 C.357 B.A. L.339 J.D. [Brenner,F.M.&S.]
Britton, Homer C., Ltd. .... 7847 S. Crandon Ave.
Brizgys, Vincent L. .... '54 '79 C.339 B.A. L.146 J.D. 188 W. Randolph St.
Brizzolara, Charles A., (AV) .... '29 '59 C.393 B.A. L.146 J.D. [Ⓒ Kane,C.&M.]
Bro, Ruth Hill .... '62 '94 C.597 B.A. L.145 J.D. [Baker&M.]
Broaddus, Mark, (BV) .... '63 '91 C.383 B.A. L.421 J.D. [Chuhak&T.]
Broberg, Jason S. '76 '02 C.182 B.A. L.585 J.D.
Assoc. Div. Claims Coun., Stewart Title Guaranty Company
Brocato, Joseph Benedict .... '67 '92 C.424 B.A. L.597 J.D. [Pedersen&H.]
Broccolo, Bernadette M., (AV) .... '55 '80 C.93 B.A. L.602 J.D. [McDermott W.&E.]
Broda, Jennifer Quinn .... '72 '00 C.388 B.A. L.424 J.D. [Ⓐ Sedgwick,D.M.&A.]
Brode, George, Jr., (AV) .... '38 '63 C.659 B.S. L.597 J.D. [G.Brode Jr.]
Brode, George, Jr., Ltd., (AV) .... 505 N. Lake Shore Dr.
Broderick, Brenda N. .... '— '97 C.741 B.A. L.46 J.D. [Ⓐ Ungaretti&H.]
Broderick, Edward M., III '47 '74 C.708 B.A. L.724 J.D.
(adm. in NY; not adm. in IL) Dir. & Sr. Coun., CNA Property & Casualty Oper.
Broderick, Thomas C., (AV) '50 '76
C&L.602 A.B., J.D. Reg. Mng. Atty., St. Paul Travelers
Brodey, Jami L. .... '71 '98 C.659 B.S. L.597 J.D. [Goldberg,K.B.B.R.&M.]
Brodhay, Stephen Y., (AV) .... '48 '73 C&L.597 B.A., J.D. Juv. Ct. J., Cook Co. Juv. Ct.
Brodie, Alan R. .... '30 '54 C.685 B.A. L.145 J.D. [Ⓒ Bell,B.&L.]
Brodkey, Hugh A. .... '32 '54 C&L.145 A.B., J.D. 3150 N. Lake Shore Dr., Ste. 24D
Brodkin, Martin F. .... '14 '39 L.146 J.D. Cir. J.
Brodsky, Jeffrey H., (AV) .... '56 '81 C&L.597 B.A., J.D. 525 W. Monroe St., Suite 1600
Brodsky, Joel A., (BV) .... '57 '82 C.221 B.A. L.209 J.D. [Brodsky&O.]
Brodsky, Joel A. .... '70 '95 C.347 B.A. L.339 J.D. [Ⓐ Quarles&B.]
Brodsky, Lawrence B., (AV) .... '34 '61 C&L.209 A.B., J.D. [Rieff S.&K.]
Brodsky, Lisa J. .... '61 '86 C.429 B.A. L.424 J.D. [Ⓐ Aronberg G.D.&G.]

Brodsky & Odeh, (BV)
8 South Michigan Avenue, 32nd Floor, 60603
Telephone: 312-701-3000 Fax: 312-701-3088
Email: brodsky-odeh@sbcglobal.net URL: http://www.brodskyodeh.com
Members of Firm: Joel A. Brodsky; Reem H. Odeh.
Languages: English, Arabic.
Criminal Defense, Commercial Litigation, Immigration Law, Family Law and Real Estate Law.

See Professional Biographies, CHICAGO, ILLINOIS

Brody, Amy D. .... '— '00 C.249 B.S. L.1119 J.D. [Ⓐ Rakoczy M.M.S.]
Brody, Evelyn '55 '81 C.976 B.A. L.276 J.D.
(adm. in DC; not adm. in IL) Asst. Prof. of Law, Chicago-Kent Coll. of Law
Brody, Fred M. .... '48 '76 C.339 B.S. L.46 J.D. 3108 W. Sherwin Ave.
Brody, Michael L., (AV) .... '52 '79 C.918 B.A. L.145 J.D. [Winston&S.]
Brody, Michael T., (AV) .... '58 '83 C.966 B.S. L.145 J.D. [Jenner&B.]
Brody, Robert S. .... '28 '53 C.1016 L.146 LL.B. [R.S.Brody]
Brody, Stuart M. .... '65 '90 C.339 B.S. L.424 J.D. [W.J.Sneckenberg&Assoc.]
Brody, Susan L. .... '53 '79 C.608 B.S. L.46 J.D. Asst. Prof., John Marshall Law School
Brody, Robert S., Ltd. .... 30 N. La Salle Street, Suite 2040
Brogan, Lisa Sopata .... '63 '87 C&L.597 B.A., J.D. [Baker&M.]
Brogan, Michael E. .... '— '00 C.352 B.A. L.424 J.D. [Ⓐ Mayer,B.R.&M.]
Brohman, Michael B., (AV) .... '54 '79 C.339 B.A. L.597 J.D. [Kamensky,R.H.&D.] ⊙
Bromberg, Stacey C. .... '72 '97 C.339 B.A. L.146 J.D. [Ⓐ Chuhak&T.]
Bromden, Lawrence E. .... '69 '00 C.696 B.A. L.146 J.D. [Bromden&D.]
Bromden & Dizon .... 3000 S. Archer Avenue, Suite 2B
Bromet, Rebecca Pratt .... '73 '02 C.112 A.B. L.880 J.D. [Ⓐ Seyfarth S.]
Bromley, Richard, (AV) .... '— '68 C&L.352 B.A., J.D. [Foley&L.]
Bronner, David A. .... '— '73 C.569 B.A. L.145 J.D. [Ungaretti&H.]
Bronska, Laurence R. .... '62 '87 C.477 B.B.A. L.94 J.D. [DLPiper R.G.C.U.]
Bronson, Daniel R., (AV) .... '59 '84 C&L.477 A.B., J.D. [Bronson&K.]

Bronson & Kahn LLC, (AV)
150 North Wacker Drive, Suite 1400, 60606
Telephone: 312-553-1700 FAX: 312-553-1733 URL: http://www.bronson-kahn.com
URL: http://www.lawyers.com/bronson&kahn
Daniel R. Bronson; Harlan D. Kahn; Marc W. O'Brien; Anthony Bergamino, Jr.; John A. Strye.
Real Estate, Real Estate Development, Condominium Law, Residential Real Estate Development, Commercial Leasing, Shopping Center Leasing, Construction Contracts, Construction Law, Office Leasing, Corporate Finance, Contracts, Real Estate Finance, Business and Corporate Law, Business Acquisitions, Business Divestitures, Commercial Loans, Commercial Finance, Private Placement, Estate Planning, Trust and Probate Administration, Tax, and Commercial Litigation.

See Professional Biographies, CHICAGO, ILLINOIS

Bronstein, Philip L. .... '52 '76 C.927 B.A. L.146 J.D. 2202 R. J. Daley Center

Bronte, Patricia A., (AV) .... '57 '87 C.499 B.M. L.597 J.D. [Jenner&B.]
Brookman, Robert K., (AV) .... '42 '70 C.477 A.B. L.174 J.D. [Schenk,A.B.&T.]
Brooks, Donald J. .... '32 '56 C.339 L.209 J.D. 188 W. Randolph St.
Brooks, Edwin E., (BV) .... '— '86 C.27 B.A. L.209 J.D. [Gardner C.&D.]
Brooks, John T., (AV) .... '— '89 C&L.339 B.S., J.D. [Foley&L.]
Brooks, Malcolm H. .... '55 '80 C.591 B.S. L.477 J.D. [Holland&K.]
Brooks, Melvin .... '59 '85 C.350 B.A. L.352 J.D. [J.D.Montgomery&Assoc.]
Brooks, Michael L. .... '62 '88 C.373 B.A. L.477 J.D. [Ⓒ Kerns,P.F.&P.]
Brooks, Nancy K. '60 '86 C.602 B.B.A. L.228 J.D.
V.P., Gen. Coun. & Secy., Board of Trade Clearing Corp.
Brooks, Rodney H. .... '53 '80 C.1177 B.A. L.597 J.D. 8945 S. Chappel Ave.
Brooks, Terrence J. '53 '80
C.339 B.S. L.966 J.D. Dir., Div. for Legal Servs., Amer. Bar Assn.
Brooks, Thomas D. .... '64 '95 C.976 B.A. L.597 J.D. [Sperling&S.]
Brooks, William E., & Associates '47 '77
C.337 B.A. L.352 J.D. 200 S. Michigan Avenue, Suite 1240

Brooks, Adams and Tarulis
(See Naperville)

Brookstein, Mark D. .... '— '01 C.966 B.A. L.146 J.D. [Ⓐ Mayer,B.R.&M.]
Brookstone, Arnold F. .... '30 '53 C.339 B.S. L.209 J.D. 8700 Sears Tower
Brophy, Thomas J., (AV) .... '43 '68 C.750 B.A. L.146 J.D. 30 N. La Salle St.
Broquard, Wesley W. .... '76 '02 C.339 B.A. L.209 J.D. [Ⓐ Barnes&T.]
Brosius, Edward J., (AV) '49 '76 C.602 B.S.E.E. L.209 J.D.
Asst. Gen. Coun., Tech. Affs., Amsted Industries (Legal Department) (Pat.)
Brosnahan, Mary M. .... '61 '86 C.339 B.A. L.209 J.D. Asst. State's Atty.
Brosnan, John F. '60 '85
C.145 B.A. L.146 J.D. Staff Coun., Admin. Law J., Labor Rel. Bd.
Brosnan, Kathleen A., (AV) .... '60 '85 C.388 B.A. L.339 J.D. [Ⓒ Fedota C.]
Bross, John A. .... '39 '65 C&L.309 A.B., LL.B. 50 S. La Salle St.‡
Brossman, Larry A. '33 '58 C.659 B.S. L.309 LL.B.
(adm. in PA; not adm. in IL) Duff & Phelps, Inc.
Brosterhous, Patricia, (AV) .... '50 '83 C.1375 B.A. L.424 J.D. [P.Brosterhous]

Brosterhous, Patricia, Ltd., (AV)
One North LaSalle Street Suite 1350, 60602
Telephone: 312-629-9629 Fax: 630-434-2844
Email: TRUSTLAW@AMERITECH.NET
Patricia Brosterhous.
Trusts and Estates, Estate Planning and Estate Administration.

See Professional Biographies, CHICAGO, ILLINOIS

Brothers, Alan W., (AV) .... '46 '73 C.208 B.A. L.174 J.D. [Brothers&T.]
Brothers & Thompson, P.C., (AV) .... 100 W. Monroe Street
Brotine, Barry C. .... '— '04 C.339 B.A. L.146 J.D. [Ⓐ Querrey&H.]
Brotman, Kenn .... '70 '95 C.472 B.S. L.589 J.D. [Ⓐ Kelley D.&W.]
Brotto, Christina .... '69 '95 C.424 [FagelHaber] (⊙Chicago)
Broucek, Karen A. .... '54 '79 C.1151 B.A. L.209 J.D. [Neal,G.&E.]
Broussard, John E. .... '66 '97 C.999 B.A. L.365 J.D. [Ⓐ Kralovec&M.]
Browdy, Brian L. .... '69 '96 C.597 B.A. L.209 J.D. [Horwood M.&B.]
Browdy, Michelle H., (AV) .... '— '90 C.674 B.S.E. L.976 J.D. [Kirkland&E.]
Browdy, Scott A. .... '66 '91 C.893 B.A. L.597 J.D. [Neal,G.&E.]
Brown, Alan C., (AV) .... '56 '81 C.473 B.A. L.145 J.D. [Neal,G.&E.]
Brown, Barbara F. .... '54 '02 C.1281 B.S.N. L.502 J.D. [Ⓐ Cassiday,S.&G.]
Brown, Bartram S. '52 '77 C.309 B.A. L.178 J.D.
(adm. in CA; not adm. in IL)
Asst. Prof. of Law, IL Instit. of Tech., Chicago-Kent Coll. of Law
Brown, Burton A., (BV) .... '48 '75 C.107 B.S. L.300 J.D. 205 W. Wacker Dr.
Brown, Carolyn J., (AV) .... '36 '68 C.98 B.S. L.597 J.D. [C.J.Brown&Assoc.]
Brown, Christina L. .... '65 '91 C.5 B.S. L.851 J.D. [Baniak P.&G.] (See Pat. Sect.)
Brown, Christopher A. '— '01 C.494 B.A. L.273 J.D.
(adm. in VA; not adm. in IL) [Ⓐ Sonnenschein N.&R.]
Brown, Colleen A. .... '74 '99 C.339 B.S. L.209 J.D. [Ⓐ Clausen M.]
Brown, Cornelius P. .... '53 '78 C.602 A.B. L.209 J.D. [Cohon R.&R.]
Brown, David D. .... '73 '98 C.880 B.A. L.339 J.D. [Ⓐ Meckler B.&T.]
Brown, David R. .... '— '00 C.339 B.A. L.146 J.D. [Ⓐ Gould&R.]
Brown, David T. .... '77 '02 C&L.352 B.B.A., J.D. [Ⓐ Cremer,K.S.&S.]
Brown, David T., (AV) .... '60 '86 C.339 B.S. L.424 J.D. [Much S.F.D.A.&R.]
Brown, Deane B., (AV) .... '— '90 C.367 B.A. L.94 J.D. [Beermann S.W.B.B.G.&L.]
Brown, Donald A. .... '50 '79 C.1191 B.S. L.209 J.D. 10603 S. Claremont Ave.
Brown, Donald J., Jr., (AV) .... '48 '73 C.363 A.B. L.424 J.D. [Donohue B.M.&S.]
Brown, Donald N., (AV) .... '33 '58 C.937 A.B. L.597 J.D. 180 North Stetson Avenue
Brown, Douglas M., (AV) .... '54 '88 C.107 B.A. L.365 J.D. [Brown]
Brown, Elizabeth A.S., (BV) '— '79 C.1106 B.A. L.145 J.D.
Asst. Gen. Coun., Moody Bible Institute (Legal Department)
Brown, Eric M. .... '66 '91 C.221 B.A. L.823 J.D. [Aronberg G.D.&G.]
Brown, Evan D. .... '74 '01 C.894 B.A. L.208 J.D. [Ⓐ Davis M.]
Brown, Gerald F. .... '— '97 C.309 A.B. L.145 J.D. [Ⓐ Mayer,B.R.&M.]
Brown, Geraldine Soat .... '50 '75 C.201 B.A. L.145 J.D. Mag.
Brown, Gregory K., (AV) .... '51 '76 C.383 B.S. L.339 J.D. [Gardner C.&D.]
Brown, Hal M., (AV) .... '42 '67 C&L.597 B.S.B.A., J.D. [DLPiper R.G.C.U.]
Brown, Harmon A., (AV) .... '— '79 C.112 A.B. L.1068 J.D. [Schiff H.]
Brown, James E. .... '— '83 C.608 B.A. L.145 J.D. [Schiff H.]
Brown, James J. .... '35 '58 C.221 L.209 LL.B. 651 W. Washington Blvd.
Brown, Jay M. .... '32 '55 C.339 L.146 LL.B. 141 W. Jackson Blvd.
Brown, Jeffrey A. .... '52 '79 C.107 B.A. L.273 J.D. [Fisk K.K.&R.]
Brown, Jeffrey H. .... '— '94 C.477 B.A. L.966 J.D. 401 N. Michigan Ave.
Brown, Jeffrey M., (BV) .... '61 '86 C.475 B.A. L.209 J.D. 180 N. La Salle St.
Brown, Jeffrey M. .... '59 '86 C.1307 L.424 J.D. [Ⓐ Novoselsky]
Brown, Jerry D. .... '63 '92 C.145 A.B. L.494 J.D. [Ⓒ Gonzalez,S.&H.]
Brown, Jessica E. .... '74 '99 C.604 B.A. L.477 J.D. [Ⓐ Mayer,B.R.&M.]
Brown, Joel F., (AV) .... '67 '92 C.918 B.A. L.569 J.D. [Goldberg,K.B.B.R.&M.]
Brown, John T. .... '61 '86 C.339 B.A. L.893 J.D. [Wildman,H.A.&D.]
Brown, Jon Michael, Jr. .... '70 '95 C.602 B.B.A. L.597 J.D. [Winston&S.]
Brown, Joseph '— '98 C&L.494 B.A., J.D.
(adm. in WI; not adm. in IL) [Ⓐ Crowley&L.]
Brown, Joseph C. '30 '56 C&L.966 B.S., J.D.
(adm. in WI; not adm. in IL) U.S. Dept. of Labor
Brown, Julie '68 '93 C.347 B.S. L.365 J.D.
Intell. Prop. Coun., Playboy Enterprises, Inc. (Law Department)
Brown, Julie Elena '58 '83 C&L.966 B.A., J.D.
Bus. & Professional People for the Pub. Interest
Brown, Kevin P. .... '56 '83 C&L.966 B.A., J.D. [Ⓐ Rieck&C.]
Brown, Kristen E. .... '64 '98 C.999 B.A. L.597 J.D. [Ⓐ Butler R.S.&B.]
Brown, Lindsey F. .... '— '01 C.362 B.A. L.146 J.D. [Ⓐ FagelHaber]
Brown, Lisa A. .... '— '95 C.918 B.A. L.145 J.D. [Schiff H.]
Brown, Mark A. .... '67 '94 C.339 B.A. L.146 J.D. [Ⓐ Lane&L.]

Brown, Marshall J. ... '— '99 C&L.477 B.S.E., J.D. [Ⓐ Foley&L.] (Pat.)
Brown, Marshall K. ... '44 '79 C.472 B.B.A. L.365 J.D. [Robbins,S.&P.]
Brown, Mary Elizabeth ... '— '99 C&L.190 B.S., J.D. [Ⓐ Gardner C.&D.] (Pat.)
Brown, Matthew S., (AV) ... '55 '78 C.183 B.A. L.276 J.D. [Katten M.R.]
Brown, Max D., (AV) '46 '75 C.352 B.A. L.209 J.D.
Gen. Coun. & V.P., Rush Presbyterian St. Luke's Med. Ctr.
Brown, Melanie M. ... '70 '97 C.893 B.A. L.902 J.D. [Ⓐ Sedgwick,D.M.&A.]
Brown, Melissa C. ... '— '97 C.1265 B.A. L.602 J.D. [Ⓒ Foley&L.]
Brown, Merilyn D. ... '54 '90 C.927 B.S. L.365 J.D. The John Marshall Law Sch.
Brown, Michael Dempsey ... '74 '99 C.72 B.A. L.146 J.D. 118 N. Clark St.
Brown, Michael I. ... '42 '67 C&L.339 B.S., J.D. [M.I.Brown]
Brown, Myra J., (AV) ... '50 '74 C.221 B.A. L.209 J.D. [McCullough,C.&L.]
Brown, Nancy J., (BV) ... '53 '81 C.210 B.A. L.339 J.D. Northern Trust Corporation
Brown, Narcisse A., (Mr.), (AV) '19 '50 C&L.145 M.A., J.D.
180 N La Salle St, Ste 2700
Brown, Nelson Anthony '45 '79 C.475 B.A. L.1187 J.D.
Sr. Coun., Chicago Park District
Brown, Nicole Rudman ... '69 '96 C.589 B.S. L.424 J.D. [Daspin&A.]
Brown, Patricia M. ... '61 '87 C&L.209 B.A., J.D. Asst. Pub. Guard.
Brown, Paul F. '64 '92 C.878 B.A. L.597 J.D.
V.P., Dep. Gen. Coun. & Asst. Corp. Secy., BlueCross BlueShield Association
Brown, Paul L., (AV) ... '39 '66 C.504 B.A. L.477 J.D. [Emrich&D.] (See Pat. Sect.)
Brown, Paul S. '— '01 C.339 B.S. L.597 J.D.
(adm. in CA; not adm. in IL) [Ⓐ Kirkland&E.]
Brown, Penny ... '48 '80 C.1016 B.A. L.146 J.D. [Much S.F.D.A.&R.]
Brown, Rachel S. ... '74 '00 C.477 B.A. L.424 J.D. [Ⓐ Katten M.R.]
Brown, Ralph E., (AV) ... '29 '56 C.339 B.A. L.145 J.D. [Schuyler,R.&Z.]
Brown, Richard M., (AV) ... '45 '70 C.910 A.B. L.597 J.D. [Sonnenschein N.&R.]
Brown, Robert H., (AV) ... '47 '72 C.597 B.S.J. L.477 J.D. [Laner,M.D.B.L.&T.]
Brown, Robert Raymond ... '68 '93 C.880 B.A. L.145 J.D. [Bell,B.&L.]
Brown, Ronald M. ... '34 '58 C.145 A.B. L.146 LL.B. 100 W. Monroe St.
Brown, Rowine Hayes '13 '63 C.339 B.S. L.146 J.D.
Adjunct Prof. of Law, Chgo.-Kent College of Law‡
Brown, Ryan T. ... '— '99 C&L.339 B.A., J.D. [Ⓐ Mandell M.]
Brown, Samuel S., (Ltd.) ... '16 '40 C.137 L.146 LL.B. 8 S. Michigan Ave., Suite 801
Brown, Sarah M. ... '78 '04 C.475 B.A. L.477 J.D. [Ⓐ Vedder,P.K.&K.]
Brown, Scott J., (AV) ... '64 '91 C.597 B.A. L.94 J.D. [Cassiday,S.&G.]
Brown, Steven S., (AV) ... '48 '73 C&L.502 B.S.B.A., J.D. [Martin,B.&S.]
Brown, Steven W. ... '60 '85 C&L.879 B.S.B.A., J.D. V.P. & Coun., Ticor Title Ins. Co.
Brown, Susanna M. ... '66 '91 C.385 B.A. L.608 J.D. [Ⓐ Shefsky&F.]
Brown, Thomas P. ... '56 '83 C.228 A.B. L.597 J.D. [Sidley A.B.&W.]
Brown, Victor ... '27 '64 C.347 A.B. L.365 LL.B. Legal Aid Bur.‡
Brown, Walter Leonard, III ... '68 '02 C.401 B.Sc. L.112 J.D. [Bollinger,R.&G.]
Brown, William G. ... '42 '69 C.674 B.A. L.309 LL.B. [Bell,B.&L.]
Brown, Willis E. ... '47 '78 C.589 B.S. L.209 J.D. [W.E.Brown]
Brown, Carolyn J., P.C., (AV) ... 155 Harbor Dr., Unit 3312
Brown Law Offices, (AV) ... 222 N. La Salle St., Ste. 200

Brown, Marc L., The Law Offices of
(See Park Ridge)

Brown, Michael I., Ltd. ... 1332 N. Halsted Street
Brown, Willis E., Ltd ... 120 W. Madison St., Ste. 825
Browne, Kristi L. ... '63 '87 C.793 B.A. L.597 J.D. [Ⓐ L.Walner&Assoc.]
Browne, Maureen Elizabeth ... '74 '04 C.602 B.A. L.128 J.D. [Ⓐ Holland&K.]
Browne, Robert E., (AV) ... '45 '71 C.602 B.S.C.E. L.966 J.D. [Neal,G.&E.] (Pat.)
Browne, Robert E., Jr. ... '70 '97 C.602 B.A. L.436 J.D. [Ⓐ Meckler B.&T.]
Browne, Thomas L., (AV) ... '49 '74 C.597 B.A. L.365 J.D. [Hinshaw&C.]
Browne, Vincent B. ... '72 '97 C.210 B.A. L.209 J.D. [Ⓐ Harrington,T.A.&H.]
Brownridge-Tucker, Byrdie ... '— '78 C&L.339 B.A., J.D. 20 N. Wacker Dr., Ste. 1040
Broxterman, Eric L. '73 '02 C.124 B.S. L.597 J.D.
(adm. in OH; not adm. in IL) [Ⓐ Winston&S.]
Broyles, Beth Ann ... '69 '98 C.589 B.A. L.146 J.D. [Broyles]

Broyles Law Office
3435 N. Sheffield, Suite 206, 60657
Telephone: 773-348-3101 Fax: 773-348-3181 URL: http://www.broyleslawoffice.com
Email: beth@broyleslawoffice.com URL: http://www.lawyers.com/broyleslawoffice
Beth Ann Broyles.
Immigration Law, Employer Rights, Investors Visas, Immigration and Naturalization Law.
See Professional Biographies, CHICAGO, ILLINOIS

Brozek, Jerome S. ... '52 '77 C.145 B.A. L.146 J.D. 2121 W. Morse Ave.
Brubaker, Warren E. ... '43 '71 C.165 B.A. L.597 J.D. 770 N. Halsted St.
Bruce, Devon C., (AV) ... '69 '93 C&L.339 B.A., J.D. [Ⓐ Power R.&S.]
Bruce, Jason W. ... '63 '88 C.893 B.A. L.813 J.D. 1525 E. 53rd St.
Bruce Zogbaum, Julie ... '76 '01 C.473 B.A. L.424 J.D. [Ⓐ Stamos&T.]
Bruck, Michael C., (AV) ... '62 '88 C.679 B.S. L.209 J.D. [Crisham&K.]
Bruckert, George L., Jr. ... '22 '52 C.475 B.A. L.966 LL.B. 100 N. La Salle St., 23rd Fl.
Brueckel, Becky, (BV) ... '— '77 C.976 B.A. L.94 J.D. [Ⓒ Chapman&C.]
Bruen, Richard F., Jr. ... '67 '97 C.589 B.S. L.209 J.D. [Ⓐ FagelHaber]
Bruer, Elizabeth A. ... '77 '02 C.339 B.S. L.424 J.D. [Ⓐ Swanson,M.&B.]
Brugess, George T. ... '55 '81 C.339 B.A. L.209 J.D. Chgo. NW Transp.
Bruks, Patrick J. ... '68 '94 C.602 B.A. L.339 J.D. [Burke,W.M.&S.]
Brunell, Alan R. ... '47 '74 C.589 B.S. L.365 J.D. Asst. States Atty.
Bruner, Stephen C., (AV) ... '41 '67 C.976 B.A. L.309 LL.B. [Winston&S.]
Brunner, Robert W. ... '61 '90 C&L.339 B.A., J.D. [Bollinger,R.&G.]
Brunner, Susan Davis ... '55 '85 C.145 B.A. L.424 J.D. State Attys. Off.
Bruno, Klint ... '73 '99 C.589 B.A. L.365 J.D. [Ⓐ Ellison,N.Z.&A.]
Bruno, Leah R. ... '74 '99 C.597 B.A. L.209 J.D. [Ⓐ Sonnenschein N.&R.]
Bruns, Jeffrey M. ... '74 '99 C&L.966 B.B.A., J.D. [Ⓐ Mayer,B.R.&M.]
Bruozas, Anthony J. ... '— '90 C.339 B.S. L.424 J.D. [Masuda,F.E.&M.]
Brusslan, Dan, (AV) ... '26 '50 C.339 B.S. L.146 J.D. [Fischel&K.]
Brusslan, James D., (AV) ... '57 '82 C.860 B.S. L.1068 J.D. [Ⓒ Levenfeld P.]
Brusstar, Thomas A., (AV) ... '64 '89 C&L.477 A.B., J.D. [Sedgwick,D.M.&A.]
Bruton, Michael G., (AV) ... '60 '85 C&L.602 B.A., J.D. [Ross,D.&B.]
Bryan, Mitchell ... '56 '82 C.339 B.A. L.910 J.D. [Levenfeld P.]
Bryan, Saskia Nora ... '— '98 C.999 B.A. L.597 J.D. [Ⓐ Levin G.]
Bryan, Thomas A. '58 '85 C.1350 B.A. L.564 J.D.
(adm. in NY; not adm. in IL) 843 W. Adams St., Apt. 611

Bryan Cave LLP, (AV)
161 North Clark Street, Suite 4800, 60601-3206 ⊙
Telephone: 312-602-5000 Facsimile: 312-602-5050
URL: http://www.bryancave.com
Partners: Mary Clare Bonaccorsi; Jules I. Crystal; Alan J. Dixon; Donald E. Figliulo; D. Scott Hargadon; Scott Hodes; Mary Margaret Moore; Jeffrey W. Morof (Not admitted in IL); Christian M. Poland; Brian A. Sher; Steven R. Smith; William J. Wortel. Of Counsel: Timothy C. Klenk; James M. Staulcup, Jr. Counsel: Monica A. Carroll; Tammie G. Krauskopf; Paul A. Lutter. Associates:

(This Listing Continued)

Bryan Cave LLP (Continued)

Craig D. Jeffrey; Erin F. Martin; Shonda K. Maupin (Not admitted in IL); Mark A. Paskar; Rodney Perry; Christy E. Phanthavong; Dmitry Shifrin; Caroline S. Soodek; William F. Zieske.
Agency and Distributorships, Agricultural Law, Alternative Dispute Resolution, Antitrust and Trade Regulation, Appellate Practice, Aviation and Aerospace, Bankruptcy, Banks and Banking, Biotechnology, Class Actions, Commercial Real Estate, Complex and Multi-District Litigation, Construction Law, Copyrights, Eminent Domain, Employee Benefits, Environmental Law, Finance, Franchises and Franchising, Government Contracts, Health Care, Insurance, Insurance Defense, Intellectual Property, International Law, International Trade, Labor and Employment, Litigation, Merger, Acquisitions and Divestitures, Nonprofit and Charitable Organizations, Patents, Products Liability, Public Finance, Real Estate, Regulatory Law, Securities, Taxation, Trademarks, Trusts and Estates, White Collar Crime, Zoning, Planning and Land Use.
Representative Clients: Financial & Insurance: Commerce Banks (St. Louis area); Edward D. Jones & Co.; Stifel, Nicolaus & Company, Incorporated; Industrial: Anheuser-Busch Companies, Inc.; Brown Group, Inc.; Emerson Electric Co.; McDonnell Douglas Corp. Others: The Pulitzer Publishing Co. (St. Louis Post-Dispatch); AT&T
St. Louis, Missouri Office: One Metropolitan Square, 211 North Broadway, Suite 3600, 63102-2750. Telephone: (314) 259-2000. Facsimile: (314) 259-2020.
Washington, D.C. Office: 700 Thirteenth Street, N.W., 20005-3960. Telephone: (202) 508-6000. Facsimile: (202) 508-6200.
New York, N.Y. Office: 1290 Avenue of the Americas, 10104-3300. Telephone: (212) 541-2000. Facsimile: (212) 541-4630.
Kansas City, Missouri Office: 3500 One Kansas City Place, 1200 Main Street, 64105-2100. Telephone: (816) 374-3200. Facsimile: (816) 374-3300.
Leawood, Kansas Office: 4707 W. 135th Street, Suite 210, 66224-9800. Telephone: (913) 338-7700. Facsimile: (913) 338-7777.
Jefferson City, Missouri Office: 221 Bolivar Street, 65101-1574. Telephone: (573) 556-6620. Facsimile: (573) 556-6630.
Phoenix, Arizona Office: Two North Central Avenue, Suite 2200, 85004-4406. Telephone: (602) 364-7000. Facsimile: (602) 364-7070.
Santa Monica, California Office: 120 Broadway, Suite 300, 90401-2386. Telephone: (310) 576-2100. Facsimile: (310) 576-2200.
Irvine, California Office: 2020 Main Street, Suite 600, 92614-8226. Telephone: (949) 223-7000. Facsimile: (949) 223-7100.
London, England Office: 33 Cannon Street, EC4M 5TE. Telephone: 44-20-7246-5800. Facsimile: 44-20-7246-5858.
Khaldiya, Kuwait Office: Mashora Advocates & Legal Consultants, Al Mashora Tower, Second Floor, Abu Bakar Siddiq Street, P.O. Box 17469, 72455. Telephone: 965-240-4470. Facsimile: 965-242-4047.
Hong Kong Office: Suite 1109, Gloucester Tower, The Landmark, 11 Pedder Street, Central Hong Kong. Telephone: 852-2522-2821. Facsimile: 852-2522-3830.
Shanghai 200040, People's Republic of China Office: Suite 448, Shanghai Centre, 1376 Nan Jing West Road. Telephone: 8621-6279-8166. Facsimile: 8621-6279-8165.
See Professional Biographies, CHICAGO, ILLINOIS

Bryant, Clarence ... '28 '56 C.1016 B.A. L.146 LL.B.,J.D Cir. J.
Bryant, David A., (AV) ... '68 '96 C.966 B.A. L.365 J.D. [Daley,D.&B.]
Bryant, David J., (BV) ... '61 '87 C.339 B.S. L.597 J.D. [Katten M.R.]
Bryant, David R., (AV) ... '39 '65 C.424 B.S. L.597 J.D. [Ⓒ Daley,D.&B.]
Bryant, L. Edward, Jr., (AV) ... '41 '67 C&L.597 B.S., J.D. [Gardner C.&D.]
Bryant, Mary C., (AV) '50 '77
C.339 B.A. L.424 J.D. Asst. Atty., Chicago Bd. of Education
Bryant, Matthew S. ... '— '05 C.659 B.A. L.597 J.D. [Ⓐ Kirkland&E.]
Bryant, Ottie Andre ... '— '77 C.832 B.S. L.209 J.D. Chf. Atty., Chicago Transit Auth.
Bryant, Robt. E. ... '10 '41 C.137 B.A. L.146 J.D. 3651 S. Mich. Ave.‡
Bryant, Timothy R. M. ... '64 '89 C&L.597 B.A., J.D. [McDermott W.&E.]
Bryant, W. Matthew ... '— '95 C.145 B.A. L.424 J.D. [Ⓐ BryceDowney]
Bryce, Geoffrey A. ... '49 '81 C.851 B.B.A. L.365 J.D. [BryceDowney]

BryceDowney, LLC, (AV)
200 North LaSalle Street, Suite 2700, 60601 ⊙
Telephone: 312-377-1501 Fax: 312-377-1502
URL: http://www.brycedowney.com
Geoffrey A. Bryce; Storrs W. Downey; Richard W. Lenkov; Dawn M. Cassie; Jeanne M. Hoffmann; Terrence J. Madden; Robert C. Bramlette, Jr.;—Yasir S. Aleemuddin; W. Matthew Bryant; Jennifer B. Cromheecke; Samantha H. Horwitz; Yvonne M. Kato; Martha A. Niles; Christopher M. Puckelwartz; Frank C. Rowland; Ioana Salajanu; Tyanika L. Saunders; Caroline Watson; Jennifer Van Blargan. Of Counsel: Philip W. Engle (Not admitted in IL).
General Practice.
Central Illinois Office: P.O. Box 100, Canton, Illinois, 61520. Telephone: 309-789-2839. Fax: 309-789-2840.
See Professional Biographies, CHICAGO, ILLINOIS

Bryceland, Linda A. ... '54 '86 C.339 B.A. L.209 J.D. [Ⓒ Novoselsky]
Bryer, Andrea S. ... '50 '79 C.339 B.A. L.209 J.D. [Cohon R.&R.]
Brymesser, J. David ... '50 '90 C.902 B.A. L.910 J.D. 111 W. Monroe Street
Brynn, Anne E. C. ... '70 '02 C.882 B.A. L.339 J.D. [Ⓐ Seyfarth S.]
Bryson, Cheryl Blackwell, (AV) ... '50 '77 C.512 B.A. L.608 J.D. [Duane M.]
Brzeczek, Richard J., (BV) ... '42 '72 C.424 B.S. L.365 J.D. [R.J.Brzeczek]
Brzeczek, Richard J., Ltd., (BV) ... 4801 West Peterson Avenue, Suite 614
Bub, Paula Sue ... '73 '00 C.57 B.A. L.221 J.D. Off of the Pub. Guardian
Bubar, Daniel Philip ... '79 '04 C.827 B.A. L.602 J.D. [Ⓐ McGuirewoods]
Bucaro, Thomas ... '52 '78 C.209 B.A. L.365 J.D. 53 W. Jackson Blvd.
Buccino, Sharon M. ... '— '87 C.436 B.S. L.424 J.D. [Ⓐ Hoogendoorn&T.]
Buch, Jerome F. ... '56 '82 C.424 B.B.A. L.209 J.D. [Seyfarth S.]
Bucha, Sandra L. ... '54 '80 C.813 B.A. L.347 J.D. 150 N. Wacker Dr.
Buchanan, Alfred L. ... '59 '90 C&L.383 B.A., J.D. [Michaels&M.]
Buchanan, David M. ... '— '00 C&L.101 B.A., J.D. [Ⓐ Latham&W.]
Buchanan, David P. ... '63 '92 C.839 B.A. L.221 J.D. [Ⓐ J.M.Goldberg]
Buchanan, Richard A., (AV) ... '51 '76 C.98 B.A. L.424 J.D. [Clausen M.]
Buchband, Richard D. '63 '89
C.674 A.B. L.178 J.D. V.P., Sr. Corp. Coun. & Secy., Orbitz LLC
Bucheit, John E. ... '73 '98 C.221 B.A. L.352 J.D. [Ⓐ Grippo&E.]
Buchele, Thomas C., (BV) '60 '86 C.340 B.A. L.339 J.D.
Staff Atty., Environment Law and Policy Center of Midwest
Buchholz, Charles, (BV) ... '43 '77 C.339 B.A. L.365 J.D. Asst. Pub. Def.
Buchholz, James Thomas ... '61 '86 C&L.209 B.A., J.D. 200 E. Randolph St., Fl. 21
Buchko, Christopher J. ... '69 '04 C.813 B.S. L.770 J.D. [Ⓐ McAndrews,H.&M.]
Buchler, Kathleen A. '60 '88 C.347 B.S. L.1119 J.D.
Asst. V.P. - Legal, Equity Residential
Buchman, Joshua T., (AV) ... '60 '86 C.207 B.A. L.597 J.D. [McDermott W.&E.]
Buchmiller, Ginger M. ... '64 '91 C.174 B.S. L.424 J.D. Asst. State's Atty.
Buck, Erich S. ... '— '01 C.597 B.A L.352 J.D. [Ⓐ Sachnoff&W.]
Buck, John A., II ... '44 '73 C.602 B.A. L.846 J.D. The John Buck Co.
Buck, Jonathan '— '02 C.678 B.A. L.477 J.D.
(adm. in WA; not adm. in IL) [Ⓐ Perkins C.]
Buck, Thomas L. ... '57 '83 C.880 B.A. L.209 J.D. [Magnani&B.]
Buck, Willis R., Jr. ... '52 '85 C.915 B.A. L.145 J.D. [Sidley A.B.&W.]
Buckingham, Milton K. ... '67 '92 C.37 B.A. L.339 J.D. [Winston&S.]
Buckley, Christopher W. '70 '97
C&L.339 B.A., J.D. Asst. Appl. Def., Off. of the State Pub. Def.
Buckley, Danette J. ... '55 '88 C.339 B.S.N. L.209 J.D. CNA Plaza
Buckley, Gabrielle M., (AV) ... '56 '81 C.530 B.A. L.209 J.D. [Vedder,P.K.&K.]
Buckley, John P., (AV) ... '— '85 C&L.477 B.A., J.D. [Ungaretti&H.]

Buckley, Timothy S. '54 '81 C.339 B.A. L.365 J.D. [Defrees&F.]
Buckley, William R. '61 '86 C.72 B.A. L.879 J.D.
Sr. Coun., Bank One Corp. (Law Dept.)
Bucklo, Elaine E. '44 '73 C.734 A.B. L.597 J.D. U.S. Dist. J.
Buckman, Joseph D. '52 '90 C.477 B.A. L.213 J.D. Gen. Atty., SBC Services, Inc.
Buckner, David R. '59 '85 C&L.339 B.A., J.D. Ernst & Young
Bucko, Michael J. '25 '52 C&L.209 B.S., J.D. 3601 N. Pulaski Rd.
Buda, Jenna L. '75 '01 C.347 B.A. L.209 J.D. [A Sedgwick,D.M.&A.]
Buday, Robert T., (AV) '— '91 C&L.1119 B.S., J.D. [Kirkland&E.]
Budelier, Mason L. '— '04 C.350 B.A. L.146 J.D. [A Querrey&H.]
Budin, Evan Jay '78 '04 C.475 B.S. L.1000 J.D. [A Jenner&B.]
Budin, John Joseph '56 '85 C.1183 B.A. L.209 J.D. [Budin]

Budin Law Offices
One North La Salle Street Suite 1560, 60602
Telephone: 312-377-0700 Fax: 312-377-0707
Email: budinlaw@aol.com URL: http://www.budinlaw.com
John Joseph Budin.
Language: Spanish; Arabic.
Automobile Accidents, Catastrophic Accidents and Injuries, Head Trauma, Spinal Cord Injuries, Construction Site Accidents, Work Related Injuries.
See Professional Biographies, CHICAGO, ILLINOIS

Budinger, Sandhya C. '— '90 C&L.597 B.A., J.D. [C Latham&W.]
Budny, Terrence E., (AV) '50 '76 C.93 A.B. L.145 J.D. [Bell,B.&L.]
Budorick, Daniel E. '59 '86 C.339 B.S. L.352 J.D. [A Hedlund&H.]
Budzik, Jeffrey J. '— '04 C.209 B.S. L.472 J.D. [A Handler,T.&D.]
Budzinski, Henry A. '23 '50 C&L.424 Ph.B., J.D. Cir. J.
Buechle, Kurt T. '74 '02 C.311 B.S. L.1119 J.D. [A Leydig,V.&M.] (See Pat. Sect.)
Buechler, Stacia A. '77 '02 C.108 B.A. L.146 J.D. [A Connelly R.&M.]
Buehler, Sara L. '— '81
C.118 B.A. L.424 J.D. V.P. & Sr. Coun., Citicorp Diners Club Inc.
Buehler, Stephen E. '51 '77 C.697 B.S.I.E. L.910 J.D. Price Waterhouse
Buehler, Terrence, Law Offices of, (AV) '55 '81 C.118 B.A. L.424 J.D.
19 S. La Salle St.
Buell, Ardin P. '49 '76 C.597 B.A. L.209 J.D.
Sr.Coun., ABN-AMRO North America, Inc. (Legal Department)
Buell, Joseph P., (AV) '46 '74 C.589 B.A. L.365 J.D. 79 W. Monroe St.
Buenik, Christopher G. '72 '01 C.966 B.A. L.365 J.D. [A Bollinger,R.&G.]
Buetow, David R. '70 '95 C&L.339 B.A., J.D. [Fuchs&R.]
Bufalino, Angelo J., (AV) '54 '79 C.602 B.S.E.E. L.424 J.D. [Vedder,P.K.&K.] (Pat.)
Buffa, Thomas A. '50 '75 C.477 B.A. L.912 J.D. 1447 W. Olive Ave.
Buffardi, Louis P. '43 '68 C.424 L.209 LL.B. Asst. State's Atty.
Buffen, David L., (AV) '44 '72 C.801 B.A. L.209 J.D. [Rittenberg,B.&G.]
Bufton, J. Kelly, (AV) '56 '80 C.813 B.A. L.145 J.D. [Seyfarth S.]
Bugan, Ana R. '69 '02 C.385 A.B. L.1565 J.D. [A Jenner&B.]
Buglass, Georgia A. '54 '80 C.966 B.A. L.188 J.D. Cook Co. States Atty. Off.
Bugos, Kevin M. '72 '97 C.602 B.A. L.146 J.D. [A McKay,N.T.D.&K.]
Bukata, Laura '72 '97 C.347 B.A. L.879 J.D. Chicago Legal Clinic
Bukata, Marta C. '48 '82 C.999 L.879 J.D. Dep. Dir., Chicago Legal Clinic
Bularzik, Jane F. '48 '76 C.720 B.A. L.339 J.D. Legal Coun., IL Dept. of Corrs.
Bulger, Brian W., (AV) '51 '77 C&L.276 A.B., J.D. [Meckler B.&T.]
Bulger, Richard F. '68 '93 C.210 B.A. L.347 J.D. [Mayer,B.R.&M.]
Bulkeley, Lewis E., (AV) '16 '41 C.477 B.A. L.597 J.D. 55 W. Monroe St.
Bull, Holly W. '— '97 C.205 B.S. L.352 J.D. [C Kirkland&E.]
Bull, Robert E., (BV) '66 '91 C.966 B.A. L.46 J.D. [A Sidley A.B.&W.]
Bullaro, John J., Jr., (AV) '41 '70 C.801 B.S. L.424 J.D. [Bullaro&C.]
Bullaro & Carton, P.C., (AV) 200 North LaSalle Street, Suite 2500 (©Munster, IN)
Bullat, G. Nicholas '43 '91 C.999 B.A. L.146 J.D.
V.P. & Coun., Harris Tr. & Svgs. Bk.
Bullock, Amy E. '76 '03 C.98 B.S. L.339 J.D. [A Quinlan&C.]
Bullwinkel, George E., (AV) '36 '64
C.188 B.M.E. L.309 LL.B. [Bullwinkel] (See Pat. Sect.)

Bullwinkel Partners, Ltd., (AV)
19 South La Salle Street, Suite 1300, 60603-1493
Telephone: 312-201-0777 Fax: 312-201-0737
URL: http://www.bullwinkel.com
George E. Bullwinkel; Constantine D. Kasson.
General Practice, Litigation, Intellectual Property, Patents, Entrepreneurial Law.
See Professional Biographies, CHICAGO, ILLINOIS

Bulman, Nicole M. '— '04 C.201 B.E.E. L.424 J.D. [A Gardner C.&D.]
Bulmer, Peter R., (AV) '59 '86 C.602 B.A. L.190 J.D. [Jackson L.]
Bunge, Adam R. '77 '03 C.585 B.A. L.589 J.D. [A Karbal,C.E.S.&D.]
Bunge, Jonathan '— '90 C.674 A.B. L.145 J.D. [Kirkland&E.]
Bunge, Jonathan G., (AV) '36 '61 C.674 A.B. L.309 J.D. [J.G.Bunge] & [C Davis&C.]
Bunge, Jonathan G., P.C., Law Offices of, (AV) 3014 North Racine Avenue
Bunn, Jeffrey H., (BV) '53 '80 C.910 B.A. L.365 J.D. [Weinberg R.]
Bunnow, Jeremy Todd '74 '99 C&L.966 B.A., J.D. [A Barack F.K.P.&N.]
Bunyak, Steven C., III '69 '94 C.976 B.A. L.93 J.D.
(adm. in MA; not adm. in IL) Proj. Coord., Museum in the Classroom
Buranosky, Thomas, (AV) '63 '88 C.976 B.A. L.145 J.D. [Gardner C.&D.]
Burau, Dean M. '— '98 [A Winston&S.]
Burban, Peter, The Law Offices of '51 '79 C.1191 B.S. L.1151 J.D.
6509 S. Kedzie Ave.
Burbank, Rosalind A. '43 '79 C.339 B.S. L.209 J.D. [C G.W.Watt&Assoc.]
Burch, Anthony '72 '03 C.511 B.A. L.966 J.D. [Burch&Assoc.]
Burch, William R. '56 '94 C.339 B.A. L.365 J.D.
Staff Coun., Commonwealth Edison Co.
Burch, Wm. E. '25 '51 C.911 L.285 LL.B.
(adm. in WA; not adm. in IL) Pres., Fred S. James & Co.
Burch & Associates 1430 N. Western
Burciaga, Eloy '51 '75 C.209 B.A. L.597 J.D. 111 W. Wash.
Burd, Bradley M. '77 '02 C.473 B.S. L.150 J.D. [A Cremer,K.S.&S.]
Burda, John A. '55 '86 C.475 B.A. L.589 J.D. Sr. Atty., Chicago Board of Trade
Burdelik, Thomas L. '59 '84 C.578 B.A. L.365 J.D. [T.L.Burdelik&Assoc.]
Burdelik, Thomas L. & Associates 123 W. Madison, 19th Fl.
Burden, Ernie '— '00 C.443 B.S. L.1000 J.D. [A Querrey&H.]
Burden, Mark M., (AV) '67 '92 C.188 B.A. L.146 J.D. [Donohue B.M.&S.]
Burdett, James C. '57 '90 C.97 B.A. L.1003 J.D.
(adm. in OH; not adm. in IL)
V.P., Assoc Coun. & Asst. Secy, APCOA/Standard Parking, Inc.
Burditt, Deborah J. '53 '80 C.339 B.A. L.597 J.D. 70 W. Madison St.
Burditt, George M., (AV) '22 '49 C&L.309 B.A., J.D. [C Bell,B.&L.]
Buresh, James F. '42 '69 C&L.208 B.S.B.A., J.D. Sears, Roebuck & Co.
Burfeind, William F., III '45 '76
C.879 B.S. L.365 J.D. Exec. V.P., Consumer Credit Ins. Assn.

Burgan, Jeffrey B., (AV) '55 '90
C.701 B.S.Ch.E. L.425 J.D. [Leydig,V.&M.] (See Pat. Sect.)
Burgan, Ray H. '— '02 C.347 B.S. L.146 J.D. [A Arnstein&L.]
Burgdoerfer, Jerry J., (BV) '58 '84 C.347 B.S. L.1119 J.D. [Jenner&B.]
Burgener, Julie L. '70 '99 C.589 B.A. L.339 J.D. [A Ross,D.&B.]
Burger, Jeffrey A. '— '79 C.390 A.B. L.1119 J.D. [Chapman&C.]
Burger, Joan H. '45 '85 C.210 B.A. L.424 J.D. [Meites,M.B.&M.] ‡
Burger, Julie A. '— '00 C.340 B.A. L.146 J.D. [A Gardner C.&D.]
Burgeson, Jack A. '24 '52 C&L.966 B.S., LL.B. 221 N. LaSalle St.‡
Burgett, George L., (AV) '44 '69 C.436 B.A. L.602 J.D. [Lord,B.&B.]
Burgett, Jay '77 '05 C.339 B.S. L.146 J.D. [A Brinks H.G.&L.]
Burghardt, Alyssa C. '74 '00 C.914 B.A. L.597 J.D. [A Seyfarth S.]
Burke, Anne M. '44 '83 C.209 B.A. L.146 J.D. Spec. Coun., Child Welfare Servs.
Burke, Arnold L., (AV) '31 '54 C.347 A.B. L.1119 J.D. 180 N. LaSalle St.
Burke, Carol A. '51 '76 C.788 B.A. L.273 J.D.
Exec. V.P. & Gen. Coun., Chicago Board of Trade
Burke, Curtis S. '63 '88 C.338 B.A. L.209 J.D. [C.S.Burke]
Burke, Denise Mary '66 '92 C.446 B.S. L.802 J.D.
(adm. in TX; not adm. in IL) Staff Coun., Americans United for Life
Burke, Dennis J. '49 '75 C.742 B.A. L.365 J.D. Cook Co. Cir. Ct.
Burke, Edmund J., (AV) '27 '51 C&L.602 A.B., J.D. 77 W. Washington St.
Burke, Edward J., (AV) '34 '61 C.999 B.A. L.602 J.D. [Burke B.&P.]
Burke, Edward M., (AV) '43 '68 C&L.209 B.A., J.D. 225 W. Washington St.
Burke, Fiona A. '— '01 C.999 BCL L.424 J.D. [A Schiff H.]
Burke, James E. '45 '74 C.339 B.A. L.209 J.D. Asst. Pub. Def.
Burke, James J. '48 '79 C.201 B.A. L.146 J.D. [Bradley&B.]
Burke, Jennifer A. '70 '95 C.276 B.S. L.146 J.D. [Jenner&B.]
Burke, Jennifer S. '72 '97 C.201 B.A. L.347 J.D. [Cassiday,S.&G.]
Burke, John D., (AV) '65 '90 C.393 B.A. L.146 J.D. [Ice M.]
Burke, John T., (AV) '25 '53 C.424 Ph.B. L.365 J.D. 55 W. Van Buren St.
Burke, Kathleen M. '64 '89 C&L.602 B.A., J.D. 10100 S. Washtenaw
Burke, Kevin G., (AV) '54 '79 C.436 B.A. L.146 J.D. [Burke,M.&W.]
Burke, Kevin Joseph, (AV) '56 '83 C.93 B.A. L.1202 J.D. [Hinshaw&C.]
Burke, Kevin P., (AV) '59 '84 C.161 B.A. L.209 J.D. [Smith,H.B.&B.]
Burke, Marianne B. '40 '67 C.339 B.A. L.209 J.D. Asst. Pub. Def.
Burke, Matthew B. '— '03 C.893 B.A. L.597 J.D. [A Mayer,B.R.&M.]
Burke, Michael J. '63 '90 C.436 B.A. L.128 J.D.
Assoc. Gen. Coun., Midway Games Inc.
Burke, Michelle C. '52 '83 C.393 B.A. L.309 J.D. [McDermott W.&E.]
Burke, Nancy A. '— '87 C&L.602 B.B.A., J.D. [Chapman&C.]
Burke, Richard F., Jr., (AV) '53 '78 C.424 B.S. L.209 J.D. [Clifford]
Burke, Richard W., (AV) '33 '59 C.602 A.B. L.145 J.D. [Burke,W.M.&S.]
Burke, Robert E., (AV) '42 '66 C&L.436 B.S., J.D. [Barnes,R.&C.]
Burke, Robert M., (AV) '36 '64 C.812 B.S. L.209 J.D. [Heineke,B.&B.]
Burke, Robert M., (AV) '58 '84 C&L.339 B.S., J.D. [Johnson&B.]
Burke, Robert M., Jr., (BV) '63 '88 C.339 B.S. L.209 J.D. [A Heineke,B.&B.]
Burke, Sean C., (BV) '64 '89 C.321 A.B. L.339 J.D. 33 N. La Salle St., Ste. 2000
Burke, Stephen M. '67 '93 C.103 B.A. L.424 J.D. [Foran,O.&B.]
Burke, Terrence P. '48 '84 C.873 B.A. L.326 J.D. 5249 N. Liano
Burke, Thomas F., (AV) '56 '83 C.339 B.S. L.365 J.D. 53 W. Jackson Blvd., Ste. 1441
Burke, William R. '— '03 C.339 B.A. L.178 J.D. [A Kirkland&E.]
Burke Burns & Pinelli, Ltd., (AV) 70 W. Madison St., Ste. 4300
Burke, Curtis S., P.C. 218 North Jefferson Street, Suite 401
Burke, Mahoney & Wise, L.L.C., (AV) 161 North Clark Street Suite 2240

Burke, Warren, MacKay & Serritella, P.C., (AV)
22nd Floor-IBM Plaza, 330 North Wabash Avenue, 60611-3607
Telephone: 312-840-7000 Facsimile: 312-840-7900
Email: info@burkelaw.com URL: http://www.burkelaw.com
Patrick J. Bruks; Richard W. Burke; Barbara Condit Canning; Patricia B. Carlson; John A. Darrow; Stephanie H. Denby; Jay S. Dobrutsky; Robert J. Emanuel; James C. Geoly; Terry D. Jeffrey; William H. Kelly, Jr.; Martin K. LaPointe; Edward J. Lesniak; Ira M. Levin; George J. Lynch; Karen K. MacKay; Christopher R. Manning; Michael J. Martin; Stephen R. Meinertzhagen; Frederic A. Mendelsohn; Jonathan W. Michael; Thomas W. Murphy; LeAnn Pedersen Pope; Kenneth H. Richman; Gerard D. Ring; Kevin J. Ryan; Martin P. Ryan; James A. Serritella; Terrence W. Stein; John P. Stephens; Mark O. Stern; Michael S. Virgil; Stephen C. Voris; Douglas E. Wambach; Jeffrey D. Warren; Gregory M. Winters; Melanie L. Witt;—Nora E. Flaherty; John G. Fogarty, Jr.; Rebecca Heinz Huston; Kristin J. Lemmon; Andrew S. Paine; Christopher J. Schafer; Bradley I. Schecter; Brett D. Smith; Kimberly A. Smith; Danielle J. Szukala; Joseph E. von Meier; Christina M. Yeager.
General Corporate and Business Matters including Real Estate, Eminent Domain, Financial Institutions, Mortgage Banking, Debtor-Creditor Relations, Bankruptcy, Automotive Franchises and Dealerships, Civil Practice in all State and Federal Courts. Litigation, including Complex and Class Action Defense, Securities, Mergers and Acquisitions, Health Care, Religious, Non-Profit, Educational and Social Services Organizations, Public Finance, Municipal Law, Employment and Labor, ERISA/Employee Benefits, Taxation, Estate Planning, Probate and Trust.
See Professional Biographies, CHICAGO, ILLINOIS

Burkett, Rebecca M. '71 '96 C.966 B.A. L.146 J.D. 120 N. La Salle St., 26th Fl.
Burkey, Lee M., (AV) '14 '44
C.339 A.B. L.365 J.D. 200 West Jackson Boulevard, Suite 1900
Burkhardt, Catherine M. '71 '93 C.945 B.S. L.893 J.D. [DLPiper R.G.C.U.]
Burkhardt, Kyle R. '70 '97 C.477 B.A. L.365 J.D. [Cassiday,S.&G.]
Burkholder, Samuel P. '58 '94 C.288 B.A. L.831 J.D.
(adm. in NJ; not adm. in IL; See Pat. Sect.) [Fitch,E.T.&F.]
Burkland, Mark E., (AV) '57 '82 C&L.339 B.S., J.D. [Holland&K.]
Burkland, Miriam Leskovar, (AV) '56 '81 C&L.339 B.A., J.D. [Defrees&F.]
Burks, L. Lee, Jr. '39 '70 C.966 B.S. L.146 J.D. 155 N. Michigan Ave.
Burky, Christopher M. '70 '96 C&L.424 B.A., J.D. [Neal,G.&E.]
Burleson, Melinda S. '69 '98 C.823 B.A. L.146 J.D. [A Baum S.A.&N.]
Burley, John L. '42 '67 C&L.966 B.S., J.D. Asst. U.S. Atty.
Burlingame, Jason '— '97 C&L.145 B.A., J.D. [A Perkins C.]
Burlingham, Rebecca A., (AV) '54 '86 C.339 B.A. L.209 J.D. Asst. Atty. Gen.
Burman, Craig A., Attorney at Law '46 '74
C.1183 B.A. L.146 J.D. 155 N. Harbor Dr., Ste. 6
Burman, Cynthia N. '54 '85 C.97 B.S. L.424 J.D. Sr. Coun., Hartmarx Corp.
Burman, Lisa M. '— '89 C.424 B.S. L.46 J.D. [Hinshaw&C.]
Burman, Marshall L. '29 '54 C.597 B.S. L.976 LL.B. [C Wildman,H.A.&D.]
Burman & Manning, (AV) 190 South La Salle Street, Suite 1700
Burn, Denise S. '— '84 C&L.597 B.A., J.D. [Katten M.R.]
Burnes, Edward M. '53 '77 C.339 B.S. L.46 J.D. 125 South Wacker Drive, Suite 1700
Burnette, Edwin A. '50 '77 C.871 B.S. L.209 J.D. Pub. Def.
Burney, Thomas R., (AV) '50 '77 C.966 B.A. L.424 J.D. [Schain,B.&C.]
Burnham, Daniel J. '67 '95 C.339 B.S.M.E. L.734 J.D. [Jenkens&G.] (Pat.)
Burns, Barbara Ann '44 '86 C.589 B.S. L.365 J.D. 5462 S. Cornell Ave., Apt. 1
Burns, Brendan M. '77 '02 C.966 B.B.A. L.190 J.D. [A Pretzel&S.]
Burns, Charles P. '55 '81 C.973 B.A. L.424 J.D. Asst. State's Atty.
Burns, Daniel J. '41 '83 C.363 A.B. L.1003 J.D.
Sr. V.P., Coffou-Kanzer Associates, Inc.

Burns, James A., Jr. ... '55 '80 C&L.477 A.B., J.D. [Katten M.R.]
Burns, Jeffrey S. ... '68 '93 C.473 B.A. L.365 J.D. [Crowley B.&K.]
Burns, Joseph M., (AV) ... '54 '79 C&L.424 A.B., J.D. [Jacobs,B.O.S.&H.]
Burns, Kristen S. ... '73 '98 C.116 B.A. L.209 J.D. [Ⓐ Tressler,S.M.&P.]
Burns, Lori R. ... '55 '79 C.112 A.B. L.477 J.D. 30 S. Wacker Dr.‡
Burns, Mark W. ... '45 '71 C.429 B.A. L.494 J.D. [Applegate&T.]
Burns, Mary Elizabeth ... '40 '84 C.741 B.A. L.597 J.D. Cook Co. Off. of the Pub. Guard.
Burns, Mary Patricia, (AV) ... '56 '81 C.602 B.A. L.424 J.D. [Burke B.&P.]
Burns, Michael Wm. ... '61 '91 C&L.339 B.S., J.D. 1130 W. Dearborn, Ste. 2307
Burns, Patrick G., (AV) ... '50 '78 C.339 B.S.E.E. L.46 J.D. [Greer,B.&C.] (Pat.)
Burns, Robert Emmett, (AV) '33 '58
C.321 B.S. L.976 LL.B. Prof., DePaul Univ. Coll. of Law
Burns, Robert P. ... '47 '74 C.262 A.B. L.145 J.D. Northwestern Univ. Sch. of Law
Burns, Robert S. ... '21 '47 C.502 A.B. L.309 LL.B. 3150 Sheridan Rd.‡
Burns, Robert W. ... '26 '52 C.177 L.602 LL.B. Fed. Trade Comm.
Burns, Scott F. ... '71 '96 C.339 B.A. L.424 J.D. [Holland&K.]
Burns, Terrence M., (AV) ... '54 '78 C.424 B.A. L.209 J.D. [Dykema G.P.]
Burns, Timothy W. ... '63 '91 C.1085 B.A. L.1439 J.D. [Neal,G.&E.]
Burnton, Cal R., (AV) ... '56 '81 C.966 B.B.A. L.436 J.D. [Wildman,H.A.&D.]
Burow, Scott A. ... '— '97 C.966 B.S.M.E. L.365 J.D. [Banner&W.] (See Pat. Sect.)
Burr, Edward R. ... '31 '58 C.339 B.A. L.597 J.D. Cir. J.
Burris, Roland W. ... '37 '64 C.801 B.A. L.329 LL.B. [Ⓒ Burris,W.S.&T.]
Burris, Roland W., II ... '57 '98 C.329 B.B.A. L.597 J.D. [Burris,W.S.&T.]
Burris, Wright, Slaughter & Tom, LLC, (AV) ... 35 East Wacker Drive, Suite 500
Burrowes, David T. ... '60 '86 C.112 B.A. L.880 J.D. [Boundas S.W.&B.]
Burrows, Steven W. ... '73 '98 C.340 B.A. L.146 J.D. [Ⓐ Anesi,O.R.N.&K.]
Burstein, Michael D. ... '72 '97 C.813 A.B. L.597 J.D. [Ⓐ Much S.F.D.A.&R.]
Burt, Antony S., (AV) ... '— '83 C.228 B.A. L.597 J.D. [Schiff H.]
Burt, Mark E. ... '57 '83 C.339 B.S. L.146 J.D. [Wolin&R.]
Burt, Marshall J. ... '56 '88 C.385 B.A. L.146 J.D. 77 W. Washington Street
Burt, Scott W., (AV) ... '— '91 C.174 B.A. L.208 J.D. [Jones D.]
Burtker, John C., (AV) ... '25 '51 C.221 L.146 LL.B. [Steinberg,B.&G.]
Burtker, Robert S., (AV) ... '55 '81 C.339 B.A. L.146 J.D. [Cassiday,S.&G.]
Burton, Alfred G. ... '52 '80 C.674 A.B. L.734 J.D. Adm. Law Off. of Hearing & Appl. J.
Burton, Anne M. ... '70 '97 C.788 B.A. L.347 J.D. [Ⓐ Edelman,C.&L.]
Burton, Bradford A. ... '57 '84 C.207 B.A. L.365 J.D. [Ⓒ Cassiday,S.&G.]
Burton, James Ralph ... '57 '91 C.793 B.A. L.365 J.D. Guardian Ad Litem
Burton, Jeremy T. ... '73 '01 C.424 B.A. L.966 J.D. [Ⓒ Cremer,K.S.&S.]
Burton, Justin Russell ... '74 '00 L.146 J.D. 20 N. Clark, Ste. 725
Burton, Staci A. ... '— '98 C.339 B.S. L.910 J.D. [Ⓐ Freeborn&P.]
Burton, Thomas J. ... '62 '00 C.502 B.S.E.E. L.734 J.D. [Ⓐ Sonnenschein N.&R.]
Burtzos, Stephanie M. Funteas ... '— '80 C.339 B.A. L.589 J.D. Asst. States Atty.
Burzawa, Martin W. ... '— '02 C.424 B.A. L.146 J.D. [Ⓐ Beermann S.W.B.B.G.&L.]
Busch, Alfred B., (AV) ... '15 '40 C.339 L.365 LL.B. 105 W. Madison St.
Busch, Justin ... '— '04 C.477 B.S.E. L.597 J.D. [Ⓐ Banner&W.]
Busch, Mary Ellen, (AV) ... '— '88 C.927 B.S. L.209 J.D. [Anderson,R.]
Buscher, Cass R. '72 '97 C.145 B.A. L.477 J.D.
Coun., Attorney Registration and Disciplinary Commission
Buser, Scott T. ... '76 '01 C.477 B.B.A. L.245 J.D. [Ⓐ Seyfarth S.]
Bush, Bernetta D. '46 '77
C.589 B.A.M.A. L.209 J.D. Asst. Legal Advisor, Ill. State Bd. of Educ.
Bush, Crystal Pruess ... '55 '79 C.976 B.A. L.309 J.D. [Gardner C.&D.]
Bush, Robert K., (AV) ... '52 '77 C.945 B.A. L.94 J.D. [Ancel,G.D.B.D.&R.]
Bush, Thomas F., Jr. ... '54 '79 C.197 A.B. L.145 J.D. [Lovells]
Bushell, Andrew '69 '95 C.188 B.A. L.1292 J.D.
Principal, Cornerstone Capital Holdings
Bush-Joseph, Victoria L., (AV) ... '55 '82 C&L.424 B.A., J.D. [Ⓒ Ballard,D.B.&H.]
Bushofsky, Jeffrey J. ... '69 '94 C.260 B.A. L.145 J.D. [Ⓐ McDermott W.&E.]
Busse, C. William, (AV) ... '27 '51 L.365 LL.B. [Busse&B.]
Busse, C. William, Jr., (BV) ... '53 '82 C.927 B.A. L.365 J.D. [Busse&B.]
Busse, Kent V. ... '43 '84 C.145 A.B. L.146 J.D. 1660 W. 104 St.‡

Busse & Busse, P.C., (AV)
20 North Wacker Drive, Suite 1860, 60606-2902
Telephone: 312-750-1212 Fax: 312-750-1211
URL: http://www.bussepc.com
C. William Busse; C. William Busse, Jr.; Edward K. Grassé;—Todd W. Hunnewell; Robert Wilder; Kenneth M. Lubinski; Courtney Dashiell; Michael Radak.
Insurance Defense, Automobile, Premises Liability, Insurance Coverage Litigation, Construction Litigation, Fire and Arson and Products Liability.

Bussman, Donald H. ... '25 '51 C&L.145 Ph.B., J.D. 860 N. Dewitt Pl.
Bustamante, Fernando M. ... '58 '83 C.589 B.S. L.209 J.D. [Ⓐ Patton&R.]
Bustamante, Peter V., (AV) '53 '81
C.589 B.S. L.209 J.D. One North La Salle Street Suite 2300
Butcher, Bryan T. ... '75 '00 C.1024 B.S. L.1000 J.D. [Ⓐ Iwan C.H.H.&V.]
Bute, Kerry ... '81 '05 C.473 B.A. L.589 J.D. [Ⓐ Adler,M.&M.]
Buten, Gerald L. ... '49 '76 C&L.150 B.A., J.D. F.B.I.
Butera, August R. '59 '85 C&L.209 B.S., J.D.
Corp. Coun., Attys. Title Guaranty Fund, Inc.
Butler, Adrienne ... '51 '04 C.103 A.B. L.424 J.D. [Ⓐ Kamensky,R.H.&D.]
Butler, Alison M. ... '72 '98 C.696 B.A. L.477 J.D. [Ⓐ Mayer,B.R.&M.]
Butler, Benjamin C. ... '— '04 C.1310 B.S.B.A. L.966 J.D. [Ⓐ Schiff H.]
Butler, Christopher ... '— '89 C.659 B.A. L.262 J.D. [Kirkland&E.]
Butler, Frank L., (AV) ... '37 '65 C&L.424 B.S., J.D. [Ⓒ Butler R.S.&B.]
Butler, J. Karen ... '54 '78 C.623 B.A. L.339 J.D. 858 W. Armitage Ave.
Butler, Jerome M. ... '44 '69 C.254 B.A. L.178 J.D. Chicago Transit Auth.
Butler, John Wm., Jr., (AV) ... '56 '80 C.674 B.A. L.477 J.D. [Skadden,A.S.M.&F.]
Butler, Lisa M. ... '71 '97 C.475 B.A. L.329 J.D. Asst. Coun., Johnson Publishing Co.
Butler, Michael P. ... '70 '94 C.691 B.A. L.339 J.D. [Ⓐ Epstein B.&G.]
Butler, William J., (AV) ... '60 '87 C.210 B.A. L.597 J.D. [McDermott W.&E.]

Butler Rubin Saltarelli & Boyd LLP, (AV)
70 West Madison Street, Suite 1800, 60602
Telephone: 312-444-9660 Fax: 312-444-9287
Email: info@butlerrubin.com URL: http://www.butlerrubin.com
Partners: Louis J. Aurichio; Ira J. Belcove; R. Douglass Bond; Craig T. Boyd; Randi L. Ellias; Kirk T. Hartley; David I. Herbst; Robert N. Hermes; Patrick J. Lamb; Catherine E. Lamsens; James A. Morsch; Kevin J. O'Brien; James I. Rubin; Gerald G. Saltarelli; Teresa Snider; Michael A. Stick; Harold C. Wheeler. Senior Counsel: Julie P. Shelton. Of Counsel: Frank L. Butler; Barbara J. Putta. Associates: Julie Rodriguez Aldort; Steven A. Block; Karen Minkoff Borg; Kristen E. Brown; Jason S. Dubner; Elizabeth Awe Hafkey; Amy B. Kelley; Brian E. Koncius; Noah B. Miller (Not admitted in IL); Kevin J. Mueller; Joseph P. Noonan, III; Mark A. Schwartz; John David Winters.
Complex Commercial Litigation, including Trial, Appellate and Administrative Proceedings. Insurance Coverage and Reinsurance Arbitration and Litigation, Employment, Antitrust, Franchise and Distribution, Intellectual Property Litigation, Securities Litigation, and Products Liability and Class Action, Legacy Liability Litigation and Mass Tort. Corporate and Business Matters, including Finance, Venture Capital, Mergers and Acquisitions, Contracts, Executive Employment Law, Separation Agreements, Real Estate and Land Use.

See Professional Biographies, CHICAGO, ILLINOIS

Butman, David C. ... '70 '98 C.966 B.S. L.146 J.D. [Ⓐ Lord,B.&B.]
Butovich, Nicholas D. ... '74 '02 C.93 B.A. L.424 J.D. [Ⓐ Sedgwick,D.M.&A.]
Butscher, Joseph M. ... '75 '00 C.1151 B.S. L.602 J.D. [McAndrews,H.&M.]
Butt, Edward T., Jr., (AV) '47 '71 C.399 B.A. L.477 J.D.
[Ⓒ Swanson,M.&B.] (⊙Lisle)
Buttell, Chadwick I., (BV) ... '68 '93 C.597 B.A. L.146 J.D. [Patzik,F.&S.]
Butterman, Mark B. ... '54 '80 C.293 B.A. L.424 J.D. [Schwartz C.]
Butters, Robert D. ... '— '77 C.855 B.A. L.880 J.D. [Arnstein&L.]
Buttita, John J., (AV) ... '54 '79 C&L.209 B.S., J.D. [Jenner&B.]
Butvilas, Aurelius, Law Offices of '62 '99
L.879 J.D. 135 South La Salle Street, Suite 2300
Butzen, David Richard ... '61 '86 C.932 B.A. L.424 J.D. Asst. State's Atty.
Buyer, Bruce M. ... '38 '62 L.146 J.D. 20 N. Clark St., Ste. 2200
Buzanowski, Walter L. ... '78 '04 C.477 B.A. L.209 J.D. [Ⓐ Kaplan,v.&M.]
Buzard, George D., III ... '53 '78 C&L.339 B.S., J.D. [Peck,S.&W.]
Buzzard, Nancy Ann ... '65 '02 C.1287 B.A. L.146 J.D. 20 S. Clark St.
Byck, Paul Mitchell ... '65 '90 C.475 B.A. L.209 J.D. [Kreiter,B.&Assoc.]
Bycraft, John T. ... '66 '92 C.770 B.S. L.602 J.D. [Ⓐ Mayer,B.R.&M.]
Byman, Robert L., (AV) ... '45 '70 C&L.339 B.A., J.D. [Jenner&B.]
Bynan, Gregory J. ... '66 '92 C.473 L.966 J.D. [Winston&S.]
Bynoe, Peter C. B., (AV) ... '51 '82 C&L.309 B.A., J.D. [DLPiper R.G.C.U.]
Byrd, Jennifer M. ... '— '94 C.345 B.A. L.436 J.D. [Ⓐ Colky&K.]
Byrd, Nicole R. ... '70 '98 C.679 B.A. L.602 J.D. [Ⓐ Mayer,B.R.&M.]

Byrne, Catherine M. '60 '87 C&L.190 B.A., J.D.
77 West Washington Street, Suite 1711, 60602
Telephone: 312-332-5100 Fax: 312-332-5105
Email: catherinebyrne@ameritech.net URL: http://www.cbyrnefamilylaw.com
Family Law including Child Custody, Child Support, Divorce, Domestic Violence, Premarital Agreement, Removal, Orders of Protection and Spousal Support.

See Professional Biographies, CHICAGO, ILLINOIS

Byrne, Kathy ... '— '88 C.741 B.A. L.424 J.D. [Ⓐ Cooney&C.]
Byrne, Kevin J. ... '— '81 C.424 B.A. L.597 J.D. [Schiff H.]
Byrne, Kevin T. ... '59 '85 C&L.209 B.A., J.D. Asst. State Atty.
Byrne, Lawrence W., (BV) ... '62 '92 C.190 B.S. L.365 J.D. [Pedersen&H.]
Byrne, Margaret ... '51 '82 C.530 B.A. L.146 J.D. 4669 N. Manor
Byrne, Margaret O. ... '62 '89 C.1016 B.S.B.A. L.209 J.D. [Swanson,M.&B.]
Byrne, Nora A. '— '99 L.424 J.D.
Assoc. Gen. Coun., Rush Presbyterian St. Luke's Med. Ctr.
Byrne, Paul M. ... '48 '84 C.424 B.S. L.339 J.D. Asst. Corp. Coun.

Byrne, Michael T.
(See Clarendon Hills)

Byrnes, Megan A. ... '— '02 C.221 B.A. L.818 J.D. [Ⓐ Querrey&H.]
Byrnes, T. Patrick ... '— '99 C.339 B.A. L.209 J.D. [Ⓐ Adler,M.&M.]
Byron, Earl T. ... '33 '57 C&L.209 B.S.C., J.D. 111 W. Monroe St.
Byrum, Charles L., (AV) ... '44 '69 C.210 B.A. L.597 J.D. [Gardner C.&D.]
Byvoets, Simone ... '55 '93 C.679 B.S.E.E. L.209 J.D. Asst. Gen. Coun., Exelon Corp.
Cabonargi, Michael M. '71 '00 C.473 B.A. L.339 J.D.
Atty. Div. of Enforce., U.S. Secs. & Exch. Comm.
Cabrera, Joel ... '65 '95 C.424 B.A. L.209 J.D. Dir., Legal Affairs
Caccamo, Matthew J. ... '— '04 C.602 B.A. L.1565 J.D. [Ⓐ Wildman,H.A.&D.]
Cacciatore, Joseph P. ... '58 '84 C&L.209 B.S., J.D. 527 S. Wells St.
Cacciatore, Victor J., (AV) ... '30 '58 C&L.209 B.S., J.D. 527 South Wells Street
Caccomo, Helen Szaropa ... '52 '80 C&L.209 B.A., J.D. [Ⓐ Kusper&R.]
Cachey, Carol ... '57 '83 C.477 A.B. L.424 J.D. [Ⓐ Bell,B.&L.]
Cadice, Jayne Megan ... '78 '03 C.602 B.A. L.424 J.D. [Ⓐ Bollinger,R.&G.]
Cadigan, William J. ... '64 '93 C.234 B.A. L.365 J.D. [W.J.Cadigan]

Cadigan, William J., P.C., Law Office of
180 N. Wacker Drive, Suite 600, 60606
Telephone: 312-279-0520 Fax: 312-946-0470
Email: wcadigan@cadiganlaw.net
William J. Cadigan.
Health Care, Corporate Law, Government.

See Professional Biographies, CHICAGO, ILLINOIS

Cafcas, Thomas H., Jr. ... '— '73 C.823 A.B. L.46 J.D. [Childress D.G.]
Caffarelli, Alejandro ... '70 '96 C.477 B.A. L.494 J.D. [Caffarelli&S.]
Caffarelli & Siegel Ltd. ... 180 North Stetson Avenue, Suite 3150
Cagan, Brett N. ... '70 '97 C.347 B.S. L.879 J.D. [Ⓐ Sugar,F.&F.]
Cage, Patrick B. ... '— '84 C.338 B.S. L.607 J.D. [O'Hagan,S.&A.]
Cagney, Mary Ellen, (AV) ... '— '76 C.93 B.A. L.209 J.D. [Levin&P.]
Cagney, William P., III, (AVⓉ) ... '42 '67 C&L.276 A.B., J.D. [W.P.Cagney,III] ⊙
Cagney, William P., III, P.A., (AVⓉ) ... 100 W. Monroe St. (⊙Delray Beach, FL)
Cahan, James N., (AV) ... '51 '76 C&L.273 B.A., J.D. [Sidley A.B.&W.]
Cahen, Daniel ... '21 '51 C.1016 A.B. L.209 J.D. 105 W. Madison St.
Cahill, Cathy F. ... '58 '87 C.475 B.A. L.365 J.D. V.P. & Coun., Harris Tr. & Svgs. Bk.
Cahill, Christine ... '75 '00 C.424 B.A. L.209 J.D. Staff Atty., Amer. Fam. Ins. Grp.
Cahill, Christopher ... '61 '96 C.339 A.B. L.477 J.D. [Ⓐ Schwartz C.]
Cahill, Robert ... '36 '66 C&L.424 B.S., J.D. Illinois Appellate Ct.
Cahill, William T., (AV) ... '47 '73 C.177 B.A. L.339 J.D. [Perkins C.]
Cahn, Stanley M. '31 '55 C.165 B.A. L.309 LL.B.
Assoc. Gen. Coun., claims, Chicago Title Ins. Co.
Cahnmann, Leonard ... '46 '74 C.339 B.S. L.209 J.D. Aardvark Financial
Cahr, Darren S., (AV) ... '68 '93 C&L.597 B.A., J.D. [Gardner C.&D.]
Cain, Barry S., (AV) ... '42 '67 C.347 B.S. L.597 J.D. The Metzler Group‡
Cain, Jason M. ... '— '94 C.338 B.S. L.1338 J.D. [Ⓒ Barnes&T.]
Cain, Patricia S., (AV) ... '53 '77 C.276 A.B. L.597 J.D. [Neal,G.&E.]
Cainkar, Louis F., (Ltd.) ... '11 '37 C&L.209 LL.B. 134 N. LaSalle St.
Caira, Christopher M. ... '71 '98 C.597 B.A. L.365 J.D. 225 W. Washington, Ste. 1701
Cairo, Louis C., (AV) ... '58 '83 C.436 B.A. L.424 J.D. [Goldberg,W.&C.]
Cairo, Marc J., (BV) ... '— '95 C.339 B.A. L.209 J.D. [Alholm,M.K.H.&O.]
Caison, Crystal L. ... '64 '01 C.999 B.A. L.365 J.D. 100 W. Randolph Street
Calabrese, Jeffrey C. ... '— '02 C.839 B.A. L.809 J.D. [Ⓐ Cozen O.]
Calabro, Regina W. ... '65 '93 C.838 B.S. L.209 J.D. [Michael B.&F.]
Caldwell, James E. ... '29 '59 C.665 A.B. L.329 J.D. 69 W. Washington
Caldwell, Samantha E. ... '— '99 C.768 B.A. L.201 J.D. Coun., Aon Corporation
Caldwell-Stone, Deborah ... '— '96 C.161 B.A. L.146 J.D. Amer. Libr. Assn.
Calhoun, Michael J. '67 '00 C.352 B.A. L.424 J.D.
Assoc. Gen. Coun., UBS Global Asset Management (America) Inc.
Calicchia, David J. ... '71 '99 C.145 B.A. L.569 J.D. [Ⓐ Katten M.R.]
Calihan, Patrick J. ... '51 '76 C.436 B.A. L.424 J.D. Asst. State's Atty.
Caliri, Robert R. ... '46 '73 C.188 A.B. L.575 J.D. [Emrich&D.] (See Pat. Sect.)
Calisoff, Adam Scott ... '69 '94 C&L.800 B.S., J.D. [Wildman,H.A.&D.]
Caliva, Michael J. ... '20 '64 C&L.209 LL.B. 7157 N. East Prairie Rd.‡
Calkins, Troy M. ... '— '91 C.475 B.A. L.477 J.D. [Gardner C.&D.]
Callaghan, Gerald P., (AV) ... '— '79 C&L.339 B.A., J.D. [Freeborn&P.]

Callahan, David K., (BV) .... '— '91 C.145 A.B. L.477 J.D. [Kirkland&E.]
Callahan, Dennis J. ....'53 '79 C.750 B.A. L.209 J.D. [D.J.Callahan&Assoc.]
Callahan, James V., (AV) '— '59
C.602 B.S.M.E. L.424 J.D. [Banner&W.] (See Pat. Sect.)
Callahan, John M. .... '68 '94 C.602 B.A. L.1049 J.D. [McDermott W.&E.]
Callahan, Laura Marie ....'69 '95 C.436 B.A. L.365 J.D. [Ⓐ Dykema G.P.]
Callahan, Mary Ann ....'55 '83 C.602 B.A. L.365 J.D. Asst. States Atty.
Callahan, Michael R., (AV) ....'53 '79 C.589 B.A. L.209 J.D. [Katten M.R.]
Callahan, Robert J., Law Office of '66 '94
C.339 B.A. L.146 J.D. 53 W. Jackson, Ste. 1460
Callahan, Shannon ....'— '04 C.477 B.A. L.424 J.D. [Ⓐ Morgan,L.&B.]
Callahan, Timothy P., (AV) ....'63 '88 C&L.477 B.A., J.D. [Mayer,B.R.&M.]

Callahan, Dennis J., & Associates P.C.
4801 West Peterson Avenue, 60646
Telephone: 773-481-5386 Fax: 773-481-5387
Email: Dennisjcallahan@aol.com URL: http://www.lawyers.com/callahan
Dennis J. Callahan.
Domestic Relations, Divorce, Family, Separation, Child Support, Child Custody, Paternity, Adoption, Guardianship, Personal Injury, Workers Compensation, Slip and Fall, Wrongful Death, Product Liability, Premises Liability, Railroad Accidents, Bus Accidents, Motorcycle Accidents, Automobile Accidents, Construction Accidents, Real Estate, Wills, Estate Planning, Criminal, Driving While Intoxicated, Drug Crimes, Felonies and General Practice, Commercial Litigation, Collection Litigation, Modifications, Mediation.
See Professional Biographies, CHICAGO, ILLINOIS

Callan, Joan S., (BV) .... '61 '87 C.741 B.A. L.966 J.D. [Mandell M.]
Callard, George D. '63 '92 C.867 B.A. L.930 J.D.
Sr. Coun., SBC Communications, Inc.
Callen, Jason W. .... '— '03 C.902 B.A. L.145 J.D. [Ⓐ Kirkland&E.]
Caloger, Philip D. ....'13 '37 C&L.597 B.S., LL.B. 3000 N. Sheridan
Calvert, Donna L. ....'59 '85 C.352 B.A. L.209 J.D. Soc. Sec. Admn.
Calvert, Louise M. ....'52 '78 C.209 B.A. L.365 J.D. Asst. Atty. Gen.
Calvert, Wendy D. ....'66 '99 C.436 B.A. L.966 J.D. 225 W. Washington, Ste. 1400
Camarena, Gloria M. ....'73 '99 C.339 B.S. L.365 J.D. 3449 S. Leavitt
Camarra, Joseph A., (AV) ....'46 '70 C.1021 B.A. L.602 J.D. [Cassiday,S.&G.]
Cambria, David G. '— '95 C.1122 B.A. L.201 J.D.
(adm. in OH; not adm. in IL) West Grp.
Camden, Jennifer L. ....'76 '02 C.801 B.S. L.602 J.D. [Ⓐ Connelly S.H.]
Camerlingo, Pepi, (CV) ....'69 '95 C.627 B.S. L.209 J.D. [Avery C.K.]
Camero, Mark A. ....'74 '02 C.589 B.S. L.209 J.D. [Ⓐ Vedder,P.K.&K.]
Cameron, Clinton E. .... '65 '91 C&L.477 A.B., J.D. [Ross,D.&B.]
Camilo-siracusa, Fior .... '61 '90 C.424 B.B.A. L.365 J.D. Special Asst. States Atty.
Caminiti, Michael Joseph .... '57 '82 C.602 B.B.A. L.209 J.D. [Caminiti&C.]
Caminiti, Peter David .... '59 '85 C.475 B.A. L.209 J.D. [Caminiti&C.]
Caminiti & Caminiti ....29 South La Salle, Suite 400
Camp, Kathryn Page '51 '78
C.323 B.A. L.146 J.D. Assoc. Gen. Coun., National Futures Assn.
Campagna, Marc R. .... '— '02 C.339 B.A. L.209 J.D. [Ciardelli&C.]
Campanale, Anthony C. ....'55 '80 C.602 B.A. L.209 J.D. [Marcus,P.&C.]
Campanario, Nick '76 '01 C.494 B.A. L.569 J.D.
(adm. in MN; not adm. in IL) [Ⓐ Skadden,A.S.M.&F.]
Campanella, Martin J., (AV) ....'— '71 C.339 B.S. L.309 J.D. [Holland&K.]
Campbell, Alyssa M. .... '62 '87 C.1111 B.A. L.260 J.D. [Williams M.&J.]
Campbell, Andrew D. ....'74 '99 C.477 B.A. L.424 J.D. [Ⓐ Novack&M.]
Campbell, Calvin C. .... '24 '51 C.329 A.B. L.145 J.D. Appl. Ct. J.
Campbell, John G., (AV) ....'32 '61 C.674 A.B. L.309 LL.B. [McCullough,C.&L.]
Campbell, John P., Jr. .... '72 '99 C.339 B.A. L.146 J.D. [Ⓐ Keefe&Assoc.]
Campbell, John W., Jr. .... '74 '01 C.475 B.S. L.209 J.D. [Ⓐ Schenk,A.B.&T.]
Campbell, Kevin, (AV) .... '56 '82 C.207 B.A. L.94 J.D. [LaBarge,C.&L.]
Campbell, Mark T., Law Offices of '58 '83
C&L.339 B.A., J.D. 53 W. Jackson Blvd., Ste. 727
Campbell, Melissa A. '69 '94 C.339 B.S. L.209 J.D.
Assoc. Gen. Coun., True North Communications, Inc. (Legal Department)
Campbell, Richard A., (AV) ....'56 '83 C&L.339 B.S., J.D. [Mayer,B.R.&M.]
Campbell, Richard J., Jr. .... '— '96 C.813 A.B. L.597 J.D. [Kirkland&E.]
Campbell, Richard P., (AV) .... '40 '66 C.597 B.S. L.309 LL.B. [Ⓒ Freeman,F.&S.]
Campbell, Terence H. .... '67 '95 C.602 B.B.A. L.597 J.D. [Ⓐ Cotsirilos,T.&S.]
Campbell, Thomas L. .... '— '95 C.145 B.A. L.146 J.D. [Kirkland&E.]
Campbell, Tracy A. ....'— '99 C.976 B.A. L.339 J.D. [Ⓐ Schiff H.]
Campbell, William J., Jr., (AV) ..... '48 '73 C.145 B.A. L.477 J.D. [DLPiper R.G.C.U.]
Campbell-O'Conor, Jill R. ....'63 '91 C.399 B.A. L.365 J.D. 4114 N. Damen Ave.
Canade, Terrence P. .... '62 '87 C.107 B.A. L.597 J.D. [Lord,B.&B.]
Canafax, Thomas, Jr. .... '36 '60 C&L.623 B.A., LL.B. [Borovsky&E.]
Canais Gris, Susana '76 '00 L.999 J.D.
(adm. in Spain; not adm. in IL) Atty., Wm. Wrigley Jr. Co.
Canavan, James Jeffrey .... '52 '81 C.339 B.A. L.597 J.D. Chicago Trans. Auth.
Cancila, Joseph A., Jr. .... '— '86 C.201 B.A. L.145 J.D. [Schiff H.]
Cancio, Marcos G. .... '78 '03 C.74 B.A. L.424 J.D. [Ⓐ Tressler,S.M.&P.]
Candia, Eileen M. .... '69 '99 C.1564 B.A. L.831 J.D. [Ⓐ Mayer,B.R.&M.]
Candido, Kristina M. '— '99 C.454 B.A. L.1206 J.D.
(adm. in FL; not adm. in IL) [Ⓐ Arnstein&L.] (⊙West Palm Beach, FL)
Canel, James H., (AV) .... '44 '68 C.910 L.209 J.D. [J.H.Canel&Assoc.] (⊙Waukegan)
Canel, Robert L., (AV) .... '51 '75 C.339 L.209 J.D. First Amer. Title Co.
Canel, Scott I., (AV) .....'56 '80 C&L.813 B.A., J.D. 10 South La Salle Street, Suite 3440

Canel, Davis & King, (AV)
10 South La Salle Street, Suite 3400, 60603
Telephone: 312-372-4142 Fax: 312-372-6737
URL: http://www.cdk-law.com
Members of Firm: Stephen D. Davis; Peter M. King; William H. Jones.
Trial and Appellate Practice, Commercial Litigation, Civil Rights, Environmental Law, Business Law, Construction Law, Contracts, Copyrights.
See Professional Biographies, CHICAGO, ILLINOIS

Canel, James H., Ltd., & Associates, (AV) .... 10 S. La Salle St., Ste. 3420
Canela, Alfonso .... '— '02 C&L.145 B.A., J.D. [Ⓐ Winston&S.]
Canela, Terrence F. ....'70 '01 C.569 B.A. L.209 J.D. Appraisal Institute
Canepa, Thomas V. ... '60 '88 C.966 B.A. L.365 J.D. 415 North La Salle Street, Suite 603
Canfield, Jeffrey H. '63 '93
C.474 B.S.E.E. L.365 J.D. [Ⓒ Brinks H.G.&L.] (See Pat. Sect.)
Canganelli, Michael Antonio .... '51 '82 C.74 B.A. L.146 J.D. P.O. Box 2121
Canham, Thomas R. '58 '83 C.477 B.A. L.209 J.D.
(adm. in AZ; not adm. in IL) [Ⓒ Cogan&M.]
Canmann, David L. ....'55 '80 C.347 B.S.L. L.1119 J.D. 111 W. Washington Street
Canna, Matthew J. ....'— '03 C.602 B.S. L.146 J.D. [Ⓐ Hinshaw&C.]
Canning, Barbara Condit .... '62 '88 C.477 B.A. L.424 J.D. [Burke,W.M.&S.]
Cannizzaro, Cindy .... '55 '83 C.339 B.A. L.146 J.D. 39 S. LaSalle St.
Cannizzaro, Sam F., (BV) ....'59 '84 C&L.424 B.A., J.D. [Nadler,P.&M.]

Cannon, Daniel E., (AV) ....'51 '81 C.966 B.A. L.365 J.D. [Ⓐ Kusper&R.]
Cannon, Jack ....'63 '93 C.424 B.A. L.1000 J.D. [Ⓐ Healy]
Cannon, Meridith G. .... '— '00 C.477 B.A. L.424 J.D. [Ⓐ Quarles&B.]
Cannon, Michael R. .... '69 '00 C.846 B.A. L.424 J.D. [Ⓒ Ogletree,D.N.S.&S.]
Cano, Lourdes M. ....'76 '01 C.339 B.S. L.665 J.D. [Ⓐ Mayer,B.R.&M.]
Cantarelli, Pat ....'47 '84 C.999 B.S.R.S. L.365 J.D. 7550 W. Belmont Ave.
Canter, David S. .... '23 '59 C.145 B.A. L.365 LL.B. Ill. Com. Comm.
Canter, Edith F. ....'58 '84 C.674 A.B. L.94 J.D. 122 S. Michigan Ave., Ste. 1850
Cantor, Rachel '— '03 C.976 B.S. L.145 J.D.
(adm. in NY; not adm. in IL) [Ⓐ Kirkland&E.]
Cantwell, Peter A., (AV) .... '50 '74 C&L.910 A.B., J.D. [Cantwell&C.]

Cantwell & Cantwell, (AV)
Suite 2850, Thirty North La Salle Street, 60602
Telephone: 312-372-3000 Fax: 312-346-8300
Peter A. Cantwell; Paul H. Scheuerlein; Stephen F. Boulton. Associates: Telly Stefaneas; Michael J. Cronin; Robert D. LaPorte. Of Counsel: Robert E. Cantwell, III (1925-1995); L. Yager Cantwell (1918-2000).
Civil and Trial Practice. Litigation, Securities, Commodities and Securities Regulation, Commercial and Real Estate, Family Law, Estate Planning, Banking, Corporate Law, Creditors Rights and Bankruptcy.
See Professional Biographies, CHICAGO, ILLINOIS

Canty, Dawn M. ....'64 '89 C.145 A.B. L.477 J.D. [Katten M.R.]
Canty, Steve C. .... '— '96 C.339 B.A. L.209 J.D. [Johnson&B.] (⊙Waukegan)
Capitani, Joseph S., (AV) ....'61 '87 C.597 B.A. L.424 J.D. [Madden,J.M.&S.]
Capitel, Irving S. ......'41 '71 C.1016 B.S. L.365 J.D. Better Business Bureau of Chicago
Capizzi, David H. ....'77 '03 C.347 B.S. L.1000 J.D. [Ⓐ Norton,M.W.&D.]
Capizzi, Robert L. ....'59 '84 C&L.107 B.S., J.D. [Perkins C.]
Caplan, Denise B. .... '58 '83 C.339 B.B.A. L.145 J.D. [Goldberg,K.B.B.R.&M.]
Caplan, Fred M. ....'31 '55 C.339 B.s. L.597 J.D. 29 S. La Salle St.
Caplan, Gary S., (AV) ....'— '88 C.339 B.A. L.597 J.D. [Sachnoff&W.]
Caplan, Herbert Lee, (AV) ....'31 '57 C&L.145 A.B., J.D. Asst. Corp. Coun.
Caplan, Kathleen McHenry .... '44 '79 C.966 B.S. L.365 J.D. Ill. Com. Comm.
Caplan, Mitchell H. .... '29 '56 C.1016 L.209 LL.B. 29 E. Madison St., Suite 910
Caplan, Suzanne Evita ....'60 '89 C.577 B.F.A. L.146 J.D. Pub. Guardian
Caplice, John G. ....'62 '96 C.602 B.A. L.209 J.D. K-Plus Consulting
Caplice, William F. .... '23 '47 C&L.209 B.S., J.D. 435 N. Michigan, 3rd Fl.‡
Caplis, Kevin J., (AV) ....'— '73 C.339 B.A. L.209 J.D. [Querrey&H.]
Capone, John ....'— '04 C&L.597 B.A., J.D. [Ⓐ Schiff H.]
Cappas, Craig A. ....'— '93 C.477 B.A. L.365 J.D. [O'Hagan,S.&A.]
Capper, Jean Marie ....'55 '80 C.399 B.A. L.146 J.D. 1701 W. Granville‡
Cappetta, Anthony G. ....'36 '61 C.602 B.S. L.209 J.D. 5858 W. Roosevelt Rd.
Cappiello, Maria L. ....'— '04 C.999 B.A. L.801 J.D. [Ⓐ Hennessy&R.]
Capra, Susan A., (AV) .... '60 '90 C&L.209 B.S.N., J.D. [Clifford]
Capraro, Ben .... '75 '02 L.209 J.D. [Ⓐ Kane,C.&M.]
Caprez, Molly A. ....'— '03 C.436 B.A. L.966 J.D. [Ⓐ O'Hagan,S.&A.]
Caprez, Timothy B. ....'78 '03 C.966 B.A. L.424 J.D. [Ⓐ Hogan M.]
Capron, Daniel F., (AV) .... '56 '81 C.339 B.A. L.1119 J.D. [Capron&A.]
Capron, Mary Anne H., (AV) ....'— '82 C.339 B.A. L.209 J.D. [Hennessy&R.]
Capron & Avgerinos, P.C., (AV) .... 30 N. LaSalle St.
Capt, Patricia E. ....'66 '93 C.744 B.S. L.209 J.D. [Carpenter&C.]
Capua, Robert M. ....'62 '88 C&L.209 B.A., J.D. [Ⓒ Connelly R.&M.]
Caputo, Nicholas A. .... '76 '01 C.884 B.S. L.146 J.D. [Ⓐ Segal M.S.&M.]
Caputo, William P., (AV) .... '51 '82 C.589 B.S. L.209 J.D. [Nilson,S.G.&C.]
Caracci, Patricia M.B. ....'— '96 C.363 B.A. L.209 J.D. [Ⓐ Karbal,C.E.S.&D.]
Caracciolo, Jenifer L. ....'— '03 C.1142 B.A. L.146 J.D. [Ⓐ Arnstein&L.]
Caraher, Kevin P. .... '56 '81 C.399 B.A. L.597 J.D. [Cozen O.]
Carani, Christopher V. '73 '99
C.436 B.S.I.E. L.145 J.D. [McAndrews,H.&M.] (See Pat. Sect.)
Caras, Dean J. .... '— '85 C.30 B.A. L.802 J.D. [D.Caras&Assoc.]

Caras, Dean, & Associates
320 W. Illinois Street, Suite 2216, 60610
Telephone: 312-494-1500 Fax: 312-822-0955
Email: dean.caras@deanjcaras.com URL: http://www.deanjcaras.com
Dean J. Caras.
Personal Injury, Catastrophic Injuries, Birth Trauma, Automobile Accidents, Railroad Accidents, Slip and Fall, Wrongful Death, Workers Compensation and Products Liability.
See Professional Biographies, CHICAGO, ILLINOIS

Caraska, Marc Anthony '62 '91 C.1060 B.S. L.464 J.D.
(adm. in CA; not adm. in IL) [Ⓐ Pfeiffer&A.]
Caravelli, Alia M. ...'73 '01 C.339 B.A. L.146 J.D. 5701 North Sheridan Road, Suite 12K
Caravello, Gabriel A. .... '77 '03 C.691 B.A. L.145 J.D. [Ⓐ Hubert&F.]
Caravette, E. Christopher ....'60 '85 C.197 A.B. L.209 J.D. [Caravette&Assoc.]
Caravette & Associates, P.C. ....19 S. LaSalle St., Ste. 450
Carballo, Anthony J. .... '— '86 C.177 B.A. L.146 J.D. [Freeborn&P.]
Carberry, Craig R. '60 '86 C.393 B.A. L.365 J.D.
Sr. Atty., Northern Trust Corporation
Carberry, Mark T. '56 '82 C.602 B.A. L.879 J.D.
Corporate Vice President, UBS Financial Services Inc.
Carbonara, Richard M., (AV) ....'57 '85 C&L.424 B.S., J.D. [Kane,C.&M.]
Carden, Nathaniel ....'74 '99 C.276 B.S. L.145 J.D. [Ⓐ Mayer,B.R.&M.]
Carden, S. Richard '67 '99
C.861 B.S.E. L.910 J.D. [McDonnell B.H.&B.] (See Pat. Sect.)
Carder, Brad A. .... '64 '91 C.424 B.A. L.209 J.D. 20 N. Clark St., Ste. 2350

Cardinal Law Group, Ltd., (AV)
720 South Dearborn Street, Suite 503, 60605 ⊙
Telephone: 847-905-7111 Fax: 847-905-7113 URL: http://www.cardinallawgroup.com/lawyers/cook/
Email: info@cardinallawgroup.com URL: http://www.cardinallawgroup.com
Frank C. Nicholas.
Technology and Intellectual Property Law Including U.S. and International Patents, Patent Preparation, Patent Prosecution, Patent Litigation, Intellectual Property Licensing, Intellectual Property Litigation, Trademark, Copyright, Trade Dress, Trade Secret, Unfair Competition, Antitrust, Cyberlaw, Biotech, Mechanical, Electrical, Computer and Software Patents.
Evanston, Illinois Office: 1603 Orrington Avenue, 60201. Telephone: 847-905-7111. Fax: 847-905-7113. URL: http://www.cardinallawgroup.com
See Professional Biographies, CHICAGO, ILLINOIS

Cardonick, Andrew R. .... '67 '93 C.645 B.S. L.145 J.D. [Goldberg,K.B.B.R.&M.]
Cardoso, Marcelo Maranhao '61 '97 C.659 B.A. L.861 J.D.
(adm. in NY; not adm. in IL) Nazar Collections
Carey, Anthony, (AV) ....'43 '69 C.602 B.A. L.209 J.D. [Carey,F.W.&B.]
Carey, Anthony C. '73 '00 C.475 B.A. L.209 J.D.
53 West Jackson Boulevard, Suite 1460
Carey, James P. .... '43 '70 C.321 B.S. L.145 J.D. Prof., Loyola Univ. Sch. of Law
Carey, James R., (AV) ....'—'89 C.436 B.A. L.424 J.D. [Levin&S.]
Carey, Jeffrey M. ....'53 '83 C.1116 B.A. L.902 J.D. [Ⓒ George W.H.]

Carey, Margaret A., (BV) '64 '91 C.93 B.A. L.209 J.D. Asst. Corp. Coun.
Carey, Peter B., (AV) '44 '69 C.602 A.B. L.424 J.D. [P.Carey]
Carey, R. Peter, (AV) '48 '73 C&L.339 B.A., J.D. [Mandel,L.&S.]
Carey, Scott L., (AV) '52 '82 C.965 B.B.A. L.365 J.D. [Bates&C.]
Carey, Thomas F., (AV) '32 '59 C.602 B.B.A. L.597 J.D. [Carey,F.W.&B.]
Carey, Thomas R. '60 '90 C.1154 B.S. L.146 J.D. [Bell,B.&L.]
Carey, Timothy J. '51 '80 C&L.602 B.A., J.D. [Gardner C.&D.]

Carey, Filter, White & Boland, (AV)
33 West Jackson Boulevard, Fifth Floor, 60604
Telephone: 312-939-4300 Fax: 312-939-4285
Members of Firm: Robert F. Carey (1904-1980); Thomas F. Carey; Edward M. White; Edmund P. Boland; Anthony Carey; F. Kevin Murnighan; Michael E. White; Michael J. Murray; Patrick S. Filter (1915-1999).
General, Banking, Corporation, Real Estate, Probate Practice. Construction, Estate Planning, Horse Racing.
See Professional Biographies, CHICAGO, ILLINOIS

Carey, Peter, (AV) 11 S. LaSalle St., Ste. 1600
Cargie, Thomas '62 '92 C.338 B.S. L.424 J.D. Chicago Bd. of Trade
Carifa, Cyri K. '70 '97 C.174 B.A. L.146 J.D. Corp. Coun., Encyclopaedia Britannica
Carini, Joseph B., III, (AV) '63 '88 C.436 B.A. L.365 J.D. [Johnson&B.]
Carl, Greta Fell, (AV) '43 '85 C.103 A.B. L.146 J.D. [Carl&H.]
Carl and Hiza, (AV) 1807 W. Sunnyside Avenue, Suite 2B
Carletti, Amy '79 '04 C.424 B.S. L.276 J.D. [[A] McDermott W.&E.]
Carlin, Dennis J., (AV) '41 '67 C.966 B.B.A. L.209 J.D. [Gardner C.&D.]
Carlin, Sarah R. '66 '91 C.966 B.A. L.146 J.D. Chicago Bd. of Educa.
Carlins, David J. '63 '88 [J.M.Carlins&Assoc.]
Carlins, Joel M. '35 '60 C.339 B.S. L.209 J.D. [J.M.Carlins&Assoc.]
Carlins, Joel M., & Associates, Ltd 1 W. Superior, Ste. 200
Carlos, Christopher J. '73 '00 C.770 B.S. L.424 J.D. [[A] Johnson&B.]
Carlson, Briggitte Marie '— '01 C.880 B.A. L.597 J.D. [[A] Sachnoff&W.]
Carlson, Carol '61 '85 C.238 B.A. L.424 J.D. Roosevelt Univ.
Carlson, Caroline E. '72 '99 C.165 B.S. L.209 [[A] McKay,N.T.D.&K.]
Carlson, Catherine L. '78 '03 C.1322 B.A. L.146 J.D. [[A] Gunty&M.]
Carlson, David R. '49 '84 C.602 B.B.A. L.209 J.D. [Mora,B.W.&U.]
Carlson, Deborah W. '57 '84 C.477 B.A. L.209 J.D. Legal Dept., U.S. Postal Serv.
Carlson, Douglas R., (AV) '45 '69 C.504 B.A. L.597 J.D. [Wildman,H.A.&D.]
Carlson, James F., (AV) '44 '71 C.352 B.B.A. L.146 J.D. [J.Carlson]
Carlson, James M. '— '99 C.475 B.A. L.477 J.D. [[A] Ungaretti&H.]
Carlson, James R. '45 '72 C.339 B.A. L.146 J.D. Asst. States Atty. [J.R.Carlson]
Carlson, Janet R. '55 '87 C.221 B.A. L.208 J.D. U.S. EPA
Carlson, Jennifer J. '75 '04 C.57 B.A. L.597 J.D. [[A] Skadden,A.S.M.&F.]
Carlson, Jon D. '41 '69 C&L.477 B.A., J.D. Exec. V.P., Yacktman Asset Mgmt. Co.
Carlson, Jon G., (AV) '43 '67 C&L.339 A.B., J.D. [[C] Mullen&K.] (⊙Edwardsville)
Carlson, Keith G., (AV) '— '84 C.1154 B.A. L.912 J.D. 218 N. Jefferson Street
Carlson, Kent R., (AV) '59 '84 C.209 B.A. L.365 J.D. 53 W. Jackson Blvd.
Carlson, Kurt M. '65 '90 C.475 B.A. L.1187 J.D. [Tishler&W.]
Carlson, Margaret O'Donnell '52 '85 C.679 B.A. L.146 J.D. Amer. Bar Assn.
Carlson, Patricia B. '53 '80 C.674 A.B. L.597 J.D. [Burke,W.M.&S.]
Carlson, Patrick W. '68 '94 C.585 B.A. L.146 J.D. [[A] Boundas S.W.&B.]
Carlson, Paul R., (AV Ⓣ) '46 '75 C&L.911 B.A., J.D.
(adm. in WA; not adm. in IL) Coun., The Boeing Co.
Carlson, Peter H. '66 '91 C.93 B.A. L.146 J.D. [Hinshaw&C.]
Carlson, Peter M. '55 '84 C.36 B.S. L.365 J.D. Ill. Liquor Control Comm.
Carlson, Scott A. '65 '95 C.339 B.S. L.801 J.D. [Seyfarth S.]
Carlson, Stephen C., (AV) '51 '77 C.674 A.B. L.976 J.D. [Sidley A.B.&W.]
Carlson, Steven G. '79 '04 C.1365 B.A. L.966 J.D. [[A] Johnson&B.]
Carlson, Susan Feingold, (AV) '59 '84 C.103 A.B. L.880 J.D. [Neal,G.&E.]
Carlson, Walter C., (AV) '53 '78 C.976 B.A. L.309 J.D. [Sidley A.B.&W.]
Carlson, James, Law Office, (AV) 212 N. Canal St., Ste. 300
Carlson, James R., Ltd. 7601 W Montrose Ave
Carman, Paul D., (AV) '— '86 C.379 B.A. L.597 J.D. [Chapman&C.]
Carmel, Marc J. '— '00 C.477 B.B.A. L.309 J.D. [[A] Kirkland&E.]
Carmel, Melvin M. '12 '37 C&L.502 B.A., LL.B. 2960 N. Lake Shore Dr.‡
Carmichael, Christopher W. '74 '02 C.424 B.A. L.209 J.D. [[A] Holland&K.]
Carmody, Matthew F. '— '00 C.339 B.S. L.209 J.D. [[A] DLPiper R.G.C.U.]
Carnahan, J. Aron '71 '97 C&L.339 B.S.M.E., J.D. [Welsh&K.] (See Pat. Sect.)
Carney, Louisa Vassileva '77 '02 C.999 B.A. L.45 J.D. [[A] Barnes,R.&C.]
Carney, Sean William '78 '03 C.413 B.A. L.209 J.D. 2441 N. Drake Ave., 2nd Fl.
Carney, Thomas P., Jr. '— '72 C.602 B.A. L.424 J.D. [[C] Querrey&H.]
Carnie, Brian R. '68 '95 C.589 B.S. L.930 J.D. [[A] Wildman,H.A.&D.]
Carnow, Mark H. '74 '01 C.597 B.A. L.339 J.D. [[A] Grippo&E.]
Carol, Colleen J. '74 '99 C.477 B.A. L.209 J.D. Nat'l Labor Rel. Brd.
Caroline, Jolynn C. '— '02 C&L.339 B.S., J.D. [[A] Ungaretti&H.]
Caron, Constants & Wilson, (BV) 33 W. Monroe St., Suite 1530 (⊙Rutherford, NJ)
Caronis, James '— '99 C.339 B.A. L.146 J.D. [[A] O'Hagan,S.&A.]
Carothers, John B., III '— '75 C.207 B.A. L.910 J.D. [[C] Jones D.]
Carpenter, David A. '62 '88 C.339 B.A. L.209 J.D. [Mayer,B.R.&M.]
Carpenter, David W., (AV) '50 '75 C.976 B.A. L.94 J.D. [Sidley A.B.&W.]
Carpenter, Eldeen M. '— '81 C.436 B.S. L.209 J.D.
Prog. Admr., Div for Professional Educ., Amer. Bar Assn.
Carpenter, Molly '64 '90 C.347 B.A. L.597 J.D.
Sr. Assoc. Coun. & Gen. Coun., Bank One Corp. (Law Dept.)
Carpenter, Robert T. '67 '92 C.260 B.A. L.209 J.D. [Carpenter&C.]

Carpenter & Capt, Chtd.
53 West Jackson Boulevard, Suite 1752, 60604
Telephone: 312-803-5110 Fax: 312-803-5112 URL: http://www.lawyers.com/cncchtd
Email: c&clawyers@carpenterandcapt.com URL: http://www.carpenterandcapt.com
Robert T. Carpenter; Patricia E. Capt;—John W. Mug.
The firm's immigration practice includes representation on family-based and work-based visas, all non-immigrant visas, and asylum applications. We also practice plaintiff's personal injury including auto and truck accidents, slip and falls, construction-related accidents, and wrongful death actions, real estate and probate law.
See Professional Biographies, CHICAGO, ILLINOIS

Carper, Nancy '51 '76 C.932 B.A. L.879 J.D. [Carper&R.]
Carper & Rubesh 407 S. Dearborn
Carpintero, Diana Amparo '69 '01 C.697 B.A. L.365 J.D. 19 S. LaSalle Street
Carponelli, Stephen P., (AV) '47 '72 C.221 B.S. L.365 J.D. [Carponelli&K.]

Carponelli & Krug, (AV) [BB]
230 W. Monroe Street, Suite 250, 60606
Telephone: 312-372-2707 Fax: 312-641-6174
Email: eastonlaw@aol.com URL: http://www.carponellikrug.com
Stephen P. Carponelli; Robert F. Krug, Jr.;—Brian M. Ozog; Raymond M. Rudnick; Don F. Taylor.
General Practice. Civil and Criminal Trial and Appellate Practice in all Courts. Antitrust, Hospital, Commercial, Corporate, Personal Injury, Workers Compensation, Estate Planning, Real Property

(This Listing Continued)

Carponelli & Krug (Continued)
Law, Trade Secrets, Trademark and Copyright Law, Dissolution, Professional Negligence, Environmental and Various Business and Real Estate Transactions.
See Professional Biographies, CHICAGO, ILLINOIS

Carr, Christopher P. '— '98 C.477 B.A. L.209 J.D. [[A] Garofalo,S.H.&S.]
Carr, Claude E. '30 '57 C&L.597 B.S.L., LL.B.
Prof. of Law, John Marshall Sch. of Law
Carr, Corinne Pavlis '69 '94 C.741 B.A. L.602 J.D. [[A] DLPiper R.G.C.U.]
Carr, Davis, (AV) '56 '79 C.1091 B.A. L.16 J.D.
(adm. in AL; not adm. in IL) Sr. V.P., CNA Insurance Co.
Carr, Donald A., (AV) '23 '50 C&L.209 B.S., J.D. 100 W. Monroe
Carr, Ian '— '91 C.050 B.A. L.424 J.D. 220 East Walton Pl.‡
Carr, James R., (AV) '57 '85 C&L.602 B.A., J.D. [Holland&K.]
Carr, John T., (AV) '44 '72 C.424 B.S. L.209 J.D. 100 W. Monroe St., Ste. 2100
Carr, Romy Elisabeth '77 '02 C.578 B.A. L.1494 J.D. [[A] Winston&S.]
Carr, Walter S., (AV) '45 '70 C.659 B.S. L.145 J.D. V.P. & Secy., Miami Corp.
Carra, Richard '50 '75 C.207 B.A. L.665 J.D. The Program Co.
Carrabotta, David A., (AV) '60 '85 C&L.209 B.S., J.D. 180 N. La Salle St., Ste. 2900
Carrabotta, Jos. M., (AV) '26 '51 C&L.209 J.D. 180 N. LaSalle St.
Carrabotta, Peter S. '59 '84 C.209 B.S. L.365 J.D. 180 N. LaSalle St.
Carreira, Hortensia S. '71 '01 C.309 A.B. L.145 J.D. [[A] Winston&S.]
Carrel, Mitchell A. '68 '94 C.473 B.S. L.213 J.D. [Vedder,P.K.&K.]
Carren, Jeffrey P., (AV) '46 '73 C.339 A.B. L.597 J.D. [Laner,M.D.B.L.&T.]
Carrigan, Catherine S. '77 '02 C.880 B.S. L.477 J.D. [[A] Goldberg,K.B.B.R.&M.]
Carriglio, Jack J., (AV) '51 '78 C.339 B.A. L.146 J.D. [Meckler B.&T.]
Carrillo, Don '53 '78 C.589 B.A. L.1119 J.D. 218 N. Jefferson
Carrillo, Michael A. '69 '96 C.679 B.S. L.339 J.D. [Neal,G.&E.] (Pat.)
Carris, James F. '62 '87 BP Chemicals Co.
Carroll, Christopher R. '— '03
C&L.339 B.S., J.D. [[A] McAndrews,H.&M.] (See Pat. Sect.)
Carroll, Clement J., Jr. '47 '72 C.602 B.A. L.424 J.D. [Sinar K.M.&F.]
Carroll, Gwen V., (AV) '54 '80 C.276 B.S. L.209 J.D. [G.V.Carroll]
Carroll, Howard W., (AV) '42 '67
C.1016 B.S.B.A. L.209 J.D. [[C] Kamensky,R.H.&D.] ⊙
Carroll, James E. '56 '82 C.177 B.A. L.597 J.D. [O'Keefe,L.&H.]
Carroll, James J., (AV) '48 '72
C&L.209 B.S., J.D. Tr. Coun., Northern Trust Corporation
Carroll, James R., (AV) '46 '78 C.1106 B.A. L.365 J.D. [Quinlan&C.]
Carroll, Jane Skelley, (BV) '56 '85 C.157 B.A. L.424 J.D. 651 W. Washington St.
Carroll, John, Jr. '71 '99 C.363 B.S. L.424 J.D. Asst. State's Atty.
Carroll, John S. '45 '72 C.177 B.A. L.339 J.D. [Carroll,H.&C.]
Carroll, Lisa A. '67 '98 C.339 B.S. L.365 J.D. [Bell,B.&L.]
Carroll, Mark '63 '89 C.436 B.A. L.597 J.D. Hull Trading
Carroll, Martin B. '63 '89 C.339 B.A. L.477 J.D. [Fox,H.S.L.&C.]
Carroll, Monica A. '— '79 C.339 B.A. L.309 J.D. [[C] Bryan C.]
Carroll, Patricia M. '52 '82 C.530 B.A. L.365 J.D. Asst. Corp. Coun.
Carroll, Paul W. '62 '87 C.339 B.A. L.209 J.D. [Gould&R.]
Carroll, Ralph T. '24 '51 C&L.424 Ph.B., J.D. 6049 W. Belmont Ave.
Carroll, Raymond P. '37 '63 C&L.424 B.S., J.D. 79 W. Monroe St.
Carroll, Timothy G., P.C., (AV) '47 '75 C.424 B.S. L.339 J.D. 70 W. Madison St.
Carroll, Timothy J. '71 '99 C.719 B.A. L.209 J.D. [[A] Vedder,P.K.&K.]
Carroll, Timothy W. '51 '76 C&L.190 B.A., J.D.
(adm. in NE; not adm. in IL) V.P., Employers Reinsurance Corp.
Carroll, William K. '27 '72
C.999 Ph.D. L.597 J.D. Prof. of Law, John Marshall Law School

Carroll, Gwen Veronica, Ltd., The Law Offices of, (AV) [BB]
53 West Jackson Boulevard Suite 205, 60604
Telephone: 312-939-4000 Fax: 312-939-4100
Email: gvcarroll@gvc-law.com URL: http://www.gvc-law.com
Gwen V. Carroll.
Labor and Employment Law.
See Professional Biographies, CHICAGO, ILLINOIS

Carroll, Hartigan & Cerney, Ltd., (AV)
30 North La Salle Street Suite 1200, 60602
Telephone: 312-236-3575 Fax: 312-236-3584
Email: info@chc-law.com URL: http://www.chc-law.com
John M. Hartigan; John S. Carroll; J. Timothy Cerney; Mary K. Hartigan; Carol Sharpe McMahan; Philip E. Old. Of Counsel: David M. Hartigan.
Commercial Transactions, Business Law, Banks and Banking, Civil Litigation, Insurance, Trusts and Estates, Probate, Real Estate, Nonprofit Organization Law.
Representative Clients: Thrall Enterprises, Inc.; Nazdar Co.; Peerless Investment Co.; Thomas W. Dower Foundation; Ryder International Corp.; B.B.C. Fasteners, Inc.; Nebiolo Machine, S.P.A.
References: American National Bank & Trust Co. of Chicago; Southwest Financial Bank & Trust Co.
See Professional Biographies, CHICAGO, ILLINOIS

Carsella, Michael B. '52 '80 C.424 B.A. L.276 J.D. Lasalle Bus. Credit, LLC
Carsello, Robert C. '52 '79 C&L.602 B.A., J.D. Pres., Speaker Resource Ctr.
Carson, June Wallace '64 '89 C.597 B.S.J. L.966 J.D. U.S.E.E.O.
Carson, Robert A. '55 '80 C.339 B.S. L.228 J.D. [Gould&R.]
Carstensen, Paula M. '54 '81 C.208 B.A. L.46 J.D. [[A] Clausen M.]
Carter, Adam C. '76 '01 C.57 B.A. L.339 J.D. [[A] Iwan C.H.H.&V.]
Carter, Courtney D. '66 '97 C.446 B.S. L.589 J.D. [[A] Rosenfeld H.S.&F.]
Carter, Daniel R. '55 '84 C.339 B.A. L.146 J.D. Asst. State Atty.
Carter, Edward C., III '53 '78 C.46 B.S. L.146 J.D. Spec. Asst. Atty. Gen.
Carter, Garrett C. '78 '03 C.475 B.A. L.424 J.D. [[A] Connelly R.&M.]
Carter, Mark A., (BV) '63 '88 C&L.339 B.S., J.D. [Adelman&G.]
Carter, Michael D., Jr. '— '97 C.801 B.S. L.146 J.D. [[A] Horwitz,H.&Assoc.]
Carter, Nicala R. '54 '84 C.518 B.A. L.597 J.D. Hyatt Legal Servs.
Carter, Philip V. '22 '49 C.347 L.209 LL.B. [Seyfarth S.] ‡
Carter, Robert L., (BV) '53 '81 C.801 B.S. L.365 J.D. [[A] McGuirewoods]
Carter, Stephanie E. '64 '94 C.339 B.S.E.E. L.209 J.D. [[A] Kelley D.&W.]
Carter, Terry J. '67 '92 19 S. La Salle St.
Carter, William Kent '72 '97 C.339 B.A. L.801 J.D. [[A] FagelHaber]
Carton, Laurence A., (AV) '18 '47 C.674 A.B. L.145 J.D. 321 N. Clark St.‡
Carton, Thomas A., (AV) '53 '78 C.57 B.A. L.46 J.D. [Bullaro&C.] ⊙
Caruso, Carmen D., (AV) '58 '83 C.436 B.A. L.424 J.D. [Schwartz C.]
Caruso, F. Willis '33 '62 C&L.597 B.S., J.D. Prof.
Caruso, John G. '— '92 C.846 B.A. L.209 J.D. [Daspin&A.]
Carvajal, Arthur G. '62 '89 C.744 B.A. L.602 J.D.
Sr. Leg. Editor, Dearborn Financial Services‡
Carvalho, David N. '54 '80 C&L.309 A.B., J.D. Dir., Illinois Dept. of Public Health
Carver, John W. '64 '90 C.801 B.A. L.352 J.D. [Tressler,S.M.&P.]
Carver Reid, Letissa '73 '98 C.477 B.A. L.1119 J.D. [[A] Sonnenschein N.&R.]
Carwile, Linda J. '— '02 C.421 B.S. L.345 J.D. [[A] Karbal,C.E.S.&D.]
Casanova, Deborah A. '66 '00 C.714 B.L.A. L.966 J.D.
(adm. in WI; not adm. in IL) Soc. Sec. Admin.

Casas, Carla M. ... '75 '02 C.243 B.A. L.260 J.D. [[A] McGuirewoods]
Casazza, Candice K. ... '54 '79 C.207 B.A. L.424 J.D. 601 W. Randolph St., 2nd Fl.
Casazza, Lawrence J., (AV) ... '46 '72 C.473 B.A. L.424 J.D. [Vedder,P.K.&K.]
Casciari, Mark, (AV) ... '— '79 C.112 B.A. L.94 J.D. [Seyfarth S.]
Casciato, Joseph N., (AV) ... '49 '74 C.424 B.A. L.209 J.D. [Rusin M.&F.]
Cascino, Michael P. ... '54 '79 C.352 B.A. L.424 J.D. 220 S. Ashland Ave.
Case, James L. ... '55 '80 C.840 B.A. L.910 J.D. The City Real Estate Services Corp.
Case, Kristin M. ... '75 '00 C.134 B.S. L.502 J.D. [[A] P.N.Kahan&Assoc.]
Case, M. Dudley, IV ... '49 '78 C.930 B.A. L.589 J.D. IRS (Estate Tax)‡
Case, Nancy Ann ... '— '02 C.1287 B.A. L.146 J.D. [[C] Ogletree,D.N.S.&S.]
Case, Robert O., (AV) ... '— '49 C.103 A.B. L.178 LL.B. [[C] Holland&K.]
Casello, Philip F. ... '11 '35 C.339 L.424 LL.B. [Reum&C.]
Caserio, James J. ... '71 '96 C.597 B.A. L.477 J.D. [[A] Greenberg T.]
Casey, B. John ... '— '00 C.276 B.A. L.144 J.D. [[A] Latham&W.]
Casey, Catherine J. ... '67 '93 C.674 B.A. L.276 J.D. [DLPiper R.G.C.U.]
Casey, Donald E., (AV) ... '24 '57 C.197 A.B. L.424 J.D. [Springer,C.&D.]
Casey, James A. ... '— '95 C.932 B.B.A. L.365 J.D. [Mayer,B.R.&M.]
Casey, John T. ... '72 '98 C.234 B.A. L.365 J.D. Off. of the Chf. J., Cir. Ct.
Casey, Judith Lauth ... '59 '84 C.734 A.B. L.597 J.D. 2300 N. Greenview Ave.
Casey, Kevin M. ... '— '04 C&L.209 B.A., J.D. [[A] Querrey&H.]
Casey, Matthias E. ... '39 '71 C&L.209 B.Ph., J.D. Chgo. Police Dept.
Casey, Michael V., (AV) ... '52 '81 C.959 B.A. L.209 J.D. [Varga B.L.H.&C.]
Casey, Patrick A. ... '54 '01 C.209 B.A. L.365 J.D. [P.Casey]
Casey, Patrick S. ... '59 '84 C&L.597 B.A., J.D. [Sidley A.B.&W.]
Casey, Phillip A. ... '62 '87 C.338 B.S. L.1000 J.D. [Sonnenschein N.&R.]
Casey, Robert P., (AV) ... '51 '76 C.708 B.A. L.209 J.D. [Ogletree,D.N.S.&S.]
Casey, Timothy R., (AV) ... '56 '81 C.363 B.A. L.365 J.D. [Gardner C.&D.]
Casey, William T. '63 '92 C.602 B.S. L.477 J.D.
Associate Counsel, MCI Telecommunications Corporation
Casey, Patrick, P.C., Law Offices of ... 70 W. Madison Avenue
Cash, Matthew E. ... '67 '93 C.882 B.A. L.209 J.D. Atty, General Growth Prop.
Cashion, John Bernard, (AV) '37 '63 C.602 B.B.A. L.597 J.D.
33 N. LaSalle St., 25th Fl.
Cashman, Anamaria E. '68 '93
C.436 B.A. L.966 J.D. Intell. Prop. Coun., Playboy Enterprises
Cashman, John G. '31 '57 C.586 B.A. L.846 LL.B.
(adm. in TX; not adm. in IL) Sears, Roebuck & Co.
Cashman, Joseph Patrick ... '70 '98 C.475 B.A. L.861 J.D. AT&T, Law & Gov't Affairs
Casiello, Albert M. ... '43 '73 C.424 B.A. L.365 J.D. Asst. Pub. Def.
Casieri, Vincent M. ... '66 '92 C.367 B.A. L.424 J.D. [Schueler,D.&C.]
Casimer, Gregory P. ... '62 '99 C.679 B.S.C.E. L.209 J.D. [[A] Niro,S.H.&N.]
Casino Law Group, The ... 1234 East Hyde Park Boulevard, Suite 2
Casmere, Edward M. ... '— '01 C.338 B.S. L.365 J.D. [[A] Schiff H.]
Cass, Neil E., (AV) ... '52 '77 C.678 B.A. L.352 J.D. [Duane M.]
Cass, R. Michael '45 '74 C.645 B.A. L.831 J.D.
(adm. in NY; not adm. in IL) [R.M.Cass&Assoc.]
Cass, Russell E. ... '68 '95 C.112 B.S. L.273 J.D. [[A] Sidley A.B.&W.] (Pat.)
Cass Associates, R. M. ... P.O. Box 543460
Cassano, Lawrence C., (BV) ... '63 '88 C.98 B.S. L.365 J.D. [Ritter&C.]
Cassel, Danielle Meltzer ... '70 '96 C.976 B.A. L.309 J.D. [DLPiper R.G.C.U.]
Cassiday, John D., (AV) ... '37 '62 C.597 A.B. L.893 LL.B. [[C] Cassiday,S.&G.]

Cassiday, Schade & Gloor, LLP, (AV)
20 North Wacker Drive, Suite 1040, 60606-2903 ⊙
Telephone: 312-641-3100 Fax: 312-444-1669
URL: http://www.cassiday.com
Members of Firm: James D. Ahern; Richard A. Barrett, Jr.; Marc F. Benjoya (Libertyville and Rockford Offices); Thomas P. Boylan; Mark M. Brennan; Scott J. Brown; Jennifer S. Burke; Kyle R. Burkhardt; Robert S. Burtker; Joseph A. Camarra; Susan E. Seiwert Conner; Michael J. Cucco; John R. Davis (Resident, Libertyville Office); James A. Foster; William J. Furey; Catherine L. Garvey; Joseph A. Giannelli; D. Patterson Gloor; Jean M. Golden; John D. Hackett; Michael J. Hennig; Brian J. Hickey (Resident, Naperville Office); Patricia J. Hogan; Richard C. Huettel; Christopher R. Kearns; James W. Kopriva; Kathleen M. McCabe; Michael J. Morrissey; William W. Ranard (Also at Rockford, Illinois Office); John J. Reid (Resident, Libertyville Office); Kimberly L. Robinson; Bradford D. Roth; Patricia A. Ryan; Jeffrey R. Sandler; Rudolf G. Schade, Jr.; Brian A. Schroeder; Therese S. Seeley (Resident, Naperville Office); John N. Seibel; A. Jeffrey Seidman; Stephanie R. Stomberg; Douglas S. Strohm (Resident, Naperville Office); David C. Van Dyke; Maria L. Vertuno; Bruce M. Wall; Sally J. Zimmerman (Also at Rockford, Illinois Office). Associates: Philip M. Abellera; Matthew K. Abrams; Erik L. Andersen; Melissa A. Anderson; James A. Berglund (Resident, Libertyville Office); Ehren V. Bilshausen; Jennifer A. Bollow (Resident, Naperville Office); Barbara F. Brown; Brook M. Carey (Resident, Naperville Office); Julie A. Flaherty-Cheatham; Stacey A. Cischke; Kimberly A. Craft; Mary C. Crawford; Thomas G. Cronin; Alexandra L. Dames; Andrew M. DeLuca; Stephen P. Ellenbecker; Denise P. Erlich; Ronald D. Fiet (Also at Rockford Office); Andrew T. Fleishman; Jamie H. Goldstein; Patrick E. Halliday; Trisha M. Hart; Jeffrey A. Hesser; James B. Hiller; Jamie L. Hull; Paul T. Kleppetsch; Brandon J. Kroft; Brian F. Lansu; Robin B. Levin (Resident, Libertyville Office); Thomas M. Lombardo; Anthony J. Longo; Gina M. Lukowski; Michael T. Lynch; Sara F. Marzullo; Yaro M. Melnyk; Jonathan P. Mincieli (Resident, Naperville Office); Donna L. Moore; Nathan I. Neff; Henry Ortiz; Tanya Park; Jori L. Polisner; Jennifer T. Rhoades; J. Hayes Ryan; Mark A. Sansone (Resident, Naperville Office); Lynde Selden, III; Steven M. Shear; Otto J. Shragal; Trisha K. Tesmer; Christine L. Trimarco; Tiffanie B. Tucker; Lisa Velez; Matthew H. Weller; Christopher M. Welling; Daniel E. Wiesch (Resident, Libertyville Office); Shantel D. Wood-Bill. Of Counsel: Bradford A. Burton; John D. Cassiday; Sharon T. Doherty; William M. Dunn; Donald F. Ivansek; Sandra E. Kupelian; Constance R. O'Neill; Tami J. Reding-Brubaker (Resident, Libertyville, Illinois Office); Deborah M. Sheridan; Julie A. Teuscher.
General Practice. Civil Trial Practice, Civil Appellate Practice, Insurance Coverage, Environmental, Medical and Professional Malpractice, Products Liability, Structural Work Act, Railroad, Employment, Corporate and Health Care Law, Commercial Litigation, Construction, Workers Compensation, Intellectual Property, Municipalities, Transportation, Patent Law.
A list of Representative Clients will be made available upon request.
Libertyville, Illinois Office: 1870 West Winchester Road, Suite 148, 60048-5353. Telephone: 847-932-6922. Fax: 847-932-6947.
Naperville, Illinois Office: 1230 East Diehl Road, Suite 202, 60563-9362. Telephone: 630-328-2970. Fax: 630-328-2979.
Rockford, Illinois Office: 120 West State Street, Suite 401, 61101-1159. Telephone: 815-962-8301. Fax: 815-962-8401.

See Professional Biographies, CHICAGO, ILLINOIS

Cassidy, Christopher C. ... '69 '94 C.309 B.A. L.1194 J.D. [[A] Pretzel&S.]
Cassidy, Jeremiah J. '60 '91 C.178 B.A. L.276 J.D.
(adm. in NY; not adm. in IL) Merit Sys. Protection Bd.
Cassidy, John C. ... '60 '86 C.210 B.A. L.424 J.D. [Sudekum,C.&S.]
Cassidy, John J. '46 '74 C&L.893 B.A., J.D.
(adm. in VA; not adm. in IL) Ill. Com. Comm.
Cassidy, Micaela M. ... '66 '92 C.238 B.S. L.146 J.D. [Nyhan,P.B.K.&L.]
Cassidy, Patrick C. ... '65 '97 C.694 B.A. L.46 J.D. 150 S. Wacker Dr., Ste. 2400
Cassidy, Rory D. ... '50 '78 C.884 B.A. L.365 J.D. [[C] Beaulieu]
Cassidy, Tracy S. ... '— '03 C.801 B.A. L.146 J.D. [[A] Winston&S.]
Cassie, Dawn M., (BV) ... '56 '81 C.188 B.A. L.424 J.D. [BryceDowney]
Cassil, Donald W. '54 '82
C.46 B.S.Ch.E. L.146 J.D. Dir., Design Engg., Sherwin-Williams Co.
Cassin, Stephen J., (BV) ... '53 '84 C.871 B.S. L.477 J.D. [Much S.F.D.A.&R.] (Pat.)
Cassioppi Tran, Huan D. ... '64 '01 C.352 B.A. L.424 J.D. [[A] Flanagan //B.]

Cassling, Donald R., (AV) ... '50 '77 C.228 A.B. L.145 J.D. [Jenner&B.]
Castaldi, Gregory G. '58 '83
C.424 B.B.A. L.365 J.D. 5521 N. Cumberland Ave., Ste. 1109
Castañeda, John Anthony ... '63 '92 C.145 A.B. L.477 J.D. 2502 N. Clark St.
Castaneda, John J., (AV) ... '61 '87 C.424 B.A. L.494 J.D. [[A] Corti,F.&A.]
Castanes, John C. ... '25 '51 L.365 LL.B. 33 N. Dearborn St.‡
Castanes, Theodore J. ... '59 '85 C.293 B.A. L.146 J.D. [Kavathas&C.]
Castellino, Michael J. ... '68 '94 C&L.602 B.A., J.D. [[A] Wildman,H.A.&D.]
Castillo, Ceely Anne ... '73 '99 C.1439 B.A. L.174 J.D. Co. Atty. Off.
Castillo, Denise C. ... '73 '99 C.210 B.A. L.93 J.D. [[A] DLPiper R.G.C.U.]
Castillo, J. Edward ... '71 '96 C.578 B.A. L.966 J.D. Natl. Labor Rel. Bd.
Castillo, Nicole L. ... '— '00 C.477 B.A. L.209 J.D. [[A] Neal&L.]
Castillo, Ruben ... '54 '79 C.424 B.A. L.597 J.D. U.S. Dist. J.
Castro, Chad M., (AV) ... '— '84 C&L.424 B.S., J.D. [Anderson,R.]
Castro, Martin R., (BV) ... '63 '88 C.209 B.A. L.477 J.D. [Sonnenschein N.&R.]
Castrogiovanni, Philip J. ... '71 '01 C.112 B.A. L.602 J.D. [[A] McDermott W.&E.]
Caswell, Benson T. ... '45 '74 C.431 B.S. L.145 J.D. Sr. V.P., Ponder & Co.
Caswell, Daniel P. ... '58 '83 C.57 B.A. L.597 J.D. CNA Ins. Co.
Catlett, Steven T., (AV) ... '— '86 C.659 B.S. L.178 J.D. [Jones D.]
Caudell, Susan Campbell '— '05 C.104 A.B. L.145
(adm. in NY; not adm. in IL) [[A] Kirkland&E.]
Caufield, Charles F. ... '36 '62 C&L.424 B.Sc., J.D. [[C] McCracken,W.d.&H.]
Cauley, Thomas K., Jr. ... '56 '83 C.602 B.B.A. L.339 J.D. [Sidley A.B.&W.]
Cavallo, Anthony A. ... '65 '90 C.597 B.A. L.339 J.D. [[A] Henderson&L.]
Cavallo, Charles A., III ... '— '05 C.339 B.S. L.597 J.D. [[A] McGuirewoods]
Cavallo, Giovanna '72 '97
C.103 A.B. L.146 J.D. Comptr. of Currency, U.S. Treasury Dept.
Cavan, Christopher M. '64 '92
C.597 B.S.M.E. L.424 J.D. [McDonnell B.H.&B.] (See Pat. Sect.)
Cavan, Marc A. ... '— '98 C.228 B.S. L.309 J.D. [[A] Sidley A.B.&W.]
Cavanagh, Stacey ... '— '95 C.93 B.A. L.146 J.D. [Ungaretti&H.]
Cavanagh, Timothy J., (AV) ... '62 '87 C.363 B.A. L.146 J.D. [Lloyd&C.]
Cavanaugh, Irene D., (BV) ... '51 '86 C.879 B.A. L.365 J.D. Asst. Pub. Def.
Cavanaugh, John J., (AV) ... '27 '56 C&L.276 B.S., J.D. 135 S. La Salle St. (Pat.)‡
Cavanaugh, Joseph ... '49 '77 C.1247 B.A. L.801 J.D. Asst. States Atty.
Cavanaugh, Michael K., (P.C.) ... '— '60 C.190 B.S.B.A. L.276 J.D. [[C] Foley&L.]
Cavendish, Jeanne ... '64 '89 C.352 B.A. Asst. State's Atty.
Cavins, Mark K., (AV) ... '47 '75 C.339 B.S. L.365 J.D. Asst. States Atty.
Cawley, Jean M. '60 '85 C.352 B.B.A. L.209 J.D.
Dir. & Spec. Coun., The Options Clearing Corp.
Cawley, Kevin J. ... '58 '84 C.339 B.S. L.209 J.D. Asst. State Atty.
Cawley, Michael G. ... '60 '86 C&L.424 B.S., J.D. Asst. State Atty.
Cazares, Jorge V., (BV) ... '63 '90 C.976 B.S. L.424 J.D. [Pugh,J.J.&Q.]
Cazeau, Rosemarie E., (AV) '— '84
C.331 B.S.N. L.209 J.D. Chf. Asst. Atty. Gen., Envir. Bur.

Cece, Frank, Jr. '64 '91 C.424 B.A. L.365 J.D.
53 West Jackson Boulevard Suite 1460, 60604
Telephone: 312-922-0400 Fax: 312-362-9907
Email: frank@cecelaw.com URL: http://www.cecelaw.net
Criminal Defense, Federal Crimes, Felonies, Misdemeanors and Traffic including DUI, Battery, Domestic, Drugs, Possession, Theft, Forgery, Burglary, Robbery, Criminal Sexual Assault, Reckless Homicide, Murder, Probation Violations, Bond Hearings, Preliminary Hearings, Personal Injury, Automobile Accidents, Wrongful Death, Construction Accidents, Truck Accidents.

See Professional Biographies, CHICAGO, ILLINOIS

Cedarbaum, Daniel G. ... '— '84 C&L.309 A.B., J.D. [[C] Levin&S.] ⊙
Cederoth, Richard A., (AV) ... '58 '83 C.98 B.S.E.E. L.339 J.D. [Sidley A.B.&W.] (Pat.)
Cedillo, Christopher I. ... '70 '01 C.475 B.A. L.597 J.D. [[A] Bell,B.&L.]
Ceko, Theresa C. ... '59 '85 C.145 B.A. L.209 J.D. Loyola Univ. Community Law Ctr.
Cella, Paul Patrick ... '77 '02 C.473 B.A. L.209 J.D. [[A] Cremer,K.S.&S.]
Cellini, Beatrice L. ... '40 '84 C.347 B.A. L.365 J.D. 1340 N. Astor
Cellini, Robert C. ... '42 '66 C.347 B.S. L.209 J.D. Sr. V.P., Bank One, Chicago, N.A.
Cellitti, David T. ... '74 '00 C.339 B.A. L.1051 J.D. [[A] Dykema G.P.]
Cena, Timothy M. ... '53 '81 C.750 B.S. L.365 J.D. State Dept. of Ins.
Cenar, Kara Eve Foster ... '63 '88 C&L.424 B.B.A., J.D. [Welsh&K.]
Cenar, Richard G., Jr. '61 '86 C.363 B.A. L.424 J.D.
Asst. State's Atty., Supvr. Child Protection Unit
Cenkus, Richard A. '67 '94 C.999 B.A. L.209 J.D.
Asst. Gen. Coun., Cushman & Wakefield of IL, Inc.
Centella, Jill ... '68 '93 C&L.339 B.S., J.D. Sr. Coun., Bank One Corp. (Law Dept.)
Centeno, H. Brian ... '— '95 C.339 B.S. L.188 J.D. [Sachnoff&W.]
Centracchio, Nicole ... '— '00 C.393 B.S. L.1000 J.D. [Reed,C.&Z.]
Centracchio, Nicole L. ... '73 '00 C.393 B.A. L.365 J.D. [Goldstein&L.]
Cepenas, Gintaras P. ... '52 '77 C.339 B.A. L.966 J.D. 6436 S. Pulaski Rd.
Cepuritis, Talivaldis, (AV) '35 '65 C.477 B.S.E. L.569 J.D.
[Olson&H.] (See Pat. Sect.)
Cera, Carol A. ... '60 '90 C.602 B.B.A. L.424 J.D. Asst. Atty. Gen., Civil Appeals Div.
Cerda, Clarissa ... '64 '93 C.309 A.B. L.477 J.D. [[C] Sonnenschein N.&R.]
Cerda, David ... '27 '55 C.339 B.S. L.209 J.D. Appl. Ct. Jus.‡
Cerney, J. Timothy, (AV) ... '53 '79 C&L.352 B.S., J.D. [Carroll,H.&C.]
Cerniglia, Sam J., (AV) ... '46 '72 C.755 B.S. L.436 J.D. [Roddy,L.&Z.]
Cernius, Rimas F. ... '51 '76 C&L.145 B.A., J.D. Asst. State's Atty.
Cernivivo, Diane, (BV) ... '57 '83 C&L.209 B.A., J.D. 20 S. Clark St.
Cervantes, Carole M. ... '42 '80 C.339 B.S. L.365 J.D. Savcedo Pub. School
Cervantes, Marc Anthony ... '75 '01 C.347 B.A. L.734 J.D. [[A] Worker,S.&H.]
Cervantes, Pedro ... '78 '03 C.57 B.A. L.339 J.D. [[A] Mangan,L.G.&L.]
Cerven, Jennifer M. ... '— '96 C.597 B.S. L.339 J.D. [Schiff H.]
Cervera, Samuel P. ... '75 '02 C&L.209 B.A., J.D. Cook Co. State Atty. Off.
Cesaretti, Carol A. ... '71 '97 C.36 B.A. L.221 J.D. [[A] Brady,C.&M.]
Cesario, Cheryl D. ... '49 '81 C.436 A.B. L.365 J.D. Asst. State's Atty.
Cesario, Wayne V. ... '51 '91 C.927 B.B.A. L.146 J.D. 111 W. Washington St.
Chabraja, Michael A. ... '67 '92 C.210 B.A. L.339 J.D. [McGuirewoods]
Chacon, Zacarias R. ... '56 '81 C&L.846 B.A., J.D. [Cozen O.]
Chadha, Paul ... '74 '02 C.209 B.A. L.597 J.D. [[A] Baker&M.]
Chadwick, Jeffrey A. ... '76 '01 C.894 B.A. L.1119 J.D. [[A] Katten M.R.]
Chadwick, Keith A. ... '64 '89 C.234 B.S. L.146 J.D. [[A] Garfield&M.]
Chadwick, Sturgis E., III, (CV) ... '57 '84 C.801 B.A. L.365 J.D. [Chadwick&L.]

Chadwick & Lakerdas, Law Offices of, (CV)
5300 South Shore Drive Suite 100, 60615
Telephone: 773-955-1088 Fax: 773-955-9511 URL: http://www.chadwicklakerdaslaw.com
URL: http://www.chadwicklakerdas.com
Members of Firm: Sturgis E. Chadwick, III; James G. Lakerdas. Associate: Michael G. Kelly.

(This Listing Continued)

Chadwick & Lakerdas, Law Offices of (Continued)

Criminal Law, Driving While Intoxicated, Drug Crimes, Felonies, Homicide, Juvenile Law, Misdemeanors, Parole and Probation, Sexual Assault, Traffic Violations, Personal Injury, Airplane Crash Litigation, Automobile Accidents, Dog Bites, Railroad Accidents, Sexual Abuse, Slip and Fall, Wrongful Death.

See Professional Biographies, CHICAGO, ILLINOIS

Chae, Sonia U. .... '63 '88 C.197 B.A. L.705 J.D. Secs. & Exch. Comm.
Chae, Susan K. ....'67 '92 C.424 B.A. L.365 J.D. [Sanchez&D.]
Chael, Mark L. ... '59 '01 C.679 B.S. L.365 J.D. [Ⓐ McDonnell B.H.&B.] (See Pat. Sect.)
Chaet, H. Joshua ....'65 '91 C.347 B.A. L.365 J.D. 30 N. LaSalle St.
Chafetz, Barry R., (AV) ....'46 '72 C&L.339 B.A., J.D. [Corboy&D.]
Chafey, Diana ....'— '94 C.36 B.A. L.879 J.D. [Ⓐ DLPiper R.G.C.U.]
Chaiken, David .... '51 '77 C.339 B.A. L.678 J.D. 111 W. Washington Street
Chait, Leland H. ....'59 '89 C&L.145 B.A., J.D. [McGuirewoods]
Chaja, Michael F. ....'22 '49 C.209 B.A. L.597 J.D. 2142 W. 18th Pl.
Chakos, Gus W. ....'23 '51 C.209 L.365 LL.B. 2731 W. Touhy Ave.
Chalfen, Marc J., (BV) ....'51 '76 C.339 B.A. L.910 J.D. [Ⓐ Kelly,O.M.D.&R.]
Chalfie, Edward J., (AV) .... '48 '78 C.453 B.S. L.424 J.D. [Ⓐ Ladas&P.] (See Pat. Sect.)
Challacombe, Joanna L. .... '63 '89 C.475 B.A. L.477 J.D. 120 W. Madison St.
Challenger, Mark L. .... '58 '88 C.273 B.A. L.597 J.D. 5800 Sears Tower
Chalmers, Caryn L. .... '69 '94 C.846 B.S. L.597 J.D. [Sonnenschein N.&R.]
Chalmers, Douglas M. ....'62 '89 C.385 B.A. L.146 J.D. [D.M.Chalmers]
Chalmers, Douglas M, P.C., Law Offices of .... 77 West Wacker Dr., Ste 4800
Chaloemtiarana, Thad .... '— '96 C.645 B.A. L.309 J.D. [Pattishall,M.N.H.&G.]
Chaloff, Miriam B. ...... '58 '84 C.1044 B.S. L.1009 J.D. Staff Atty., Westport Ins. Corp.
Chalstrom, Ann C. ....'72 '97 C.340 B.A. L.339 J.D. [Ⓐ Clausen M.]
Chalut, Erik W. ....'— '99 C.475 B.A. L.477 J.D. [Ⓐ Kirkland&E.]
Chamberlain, Kimellen A. .... '62 '92 C.424 B.S. L.365 J.D. Asst. State's Atty.
Champagne, Kathleen Holper ....'— '96 C.339 B.A. L.146 J.D. [Ungaretti&H.]
Champagne, Oliver W. R., Jr. '52 '77 C.31 B.A. L.208 J.D.
(adm. in CO; not adm. in IL) Gen. Coun., GE Capital Railcar Servs. Corp.
Chan, Denise M. ....'72 '98 C.597 B.A. L.339 J.D. [Ⓒ Funkhouser V.L.&D.]
Chan, Peter Ka Ming '65 '91 C.276 B.A. L.597 J.D.
Assist. Reg. Dir., U.S. Secs. and Exchange Comm.
Chan, Ping P. ....'53 '94 C.1378 B.S. L.209 J.D. [P.P.Chan&Assoc.]
Chan, Phillip P., & Associates .... 215 W. 23rd St.
Chandler, James J. .... '75 '00 C.259 B.S. L.424 J.D. [Ⓐ Worker,S.&H.]
Chandler, Kent, Jr., (AV) .... '20 '49 C.976 B.A. L.477 J.D. [Ⓒ Bell J.&Q.]
Chandler, Malcolm A., (AV) '23 '49 C&L.309 A.B., LL.B.
135 S. La Salle St., Ste. 1960
Chandler, Paul .... '65 '95 C&L.477 B.S.E.E., J.D. [Ⓒ Mayer,B.R.&M.] (Pat.)
Chandran, Tarun J. ....'— '03 C&L.477 B.A., J.D. [Ⓐ Kirkland&E.]
Chandrasekaran, Uma .... '78 '04 C.788 B.A. L.339 J.D. 150 S. Wacker, Ste. 2400
Chanen, Franklin A., (AV) ....'33 '57 C&L.597 B.B.A., J.D. One 1st. National Plz.‡
Chanen, Stuart J., (AV) ....'59 '86 C.1036 B.A. L.597 J.D. [Katten M.R.]
Chaney, Robert Allen .... '46 '81 C.339 B.A. L.365 J.D. [Bollinger,R.&G.]
Chang, Dayna .... '65 '03 C.912 B.A. L.146 J.D. [D.W.Chang] ⊙
Chang, Edmond E. .... '70 '94 C.477 B.S.E. L.597 J.D. [Ⓐ Sidley A.B.&W.]
Chang, Gina M. ....'74 '99 C.597 B.S. L.424 J.D. [Ⓐ Wildman,H.A.&D.]
Chang, Y. Kurt .... '57 '95 C.966 Ph.D. L.597 J.D. [Leydig,V.&M.] (See Pat. Sect.)

Chang, Dayna Wheatley, LLC
Suite 640, 166 W. Washington Street, 60602 ⊙
Telephone: 312-236-9911 Fax: 312-236-9500
Email: daynachg@aol.com
Dayna Chang.
Immigration Law, Mediation, Employment Law, Discrimination, Sexual Harassment, Wrongful Termination, Family Law, Real Estate.
Troy, Michigan Office: 100 Big Beaver Road, Suite 200, 48084. Telephone: 248-680-8408. Fax: 248-680-6699.

See Professional Biographies, CHICAGO, ILLINOIS

Chapa, Lawrence J. '67 '94 C&L.339 B.S.E.E., J.D.
500 W. Madison St., Suite 3800 (Pat.)
Chapa, Ruben R., (BV) .... '68 '93 C.339 B.A. L.209 J.D. U.S. Dept. of Labor
Chapekis, A. Frederick, (AV) .... '52 '77 C.347 B.A. L.146 J.D. [Chapekis,M.&C.]
Chapekis, Kristina M. .... '51 '76 C&L.879 B.A., J.D. [Chapekis,M.&C.]
Chapekis, Marcus & Chapekis, (AV) ....11 S. LaSalle St.
Chapelle, Ellen ....'66 '91 C&L.477 B.A., J.D. [Ⓒ Kubasiak,F.R.&R.]
Chapin, Thomas P. .... '56 '89 C.1183 B.A. L.146 J.D. Asst. Pub. Def.
Chapin, William Barton, IV '60 '86 C.957 B.A. L.365 J.D.
Staff Coun., Travelers Property Casualty Corporation
Chaplik, Ira '61 '86 C&L.339 B.S., J.D.
Exec. V. P. & Gen. Coun., Equity Group Investments, LLC
Chapman, Carl F. ....'19 '49 C&L.339 B.S., LL.B. Univ. of Chicago
Chapman, Catherine M. .... '65 '90 C.436 B.A. L.209 J.D. [Baum S.A.&N.]
Chapman, Howard S., (AV) '41 '68 C&L.339 B.S., J.D.
Prof. & Assoc. Dean, Chicago-Kent College of Law
Chapman, James P., (AV) ....'29 '54 C.174 B.A. L.309 LL.B. [J.P.Chapman&Assoc.]
Chapman, Jill M. '58 '85 C.114 B.A. L.912 J.D.
Dir. of Comp. & Benefits, Montgomery Ward, LLC
Chapman, John S., (AV) ....'40 '66 C.976 B.A. L.309 LL.B. [Lord,B.&B.]
Chapman, Richard H., (AV) ....'57 '82 C.339 B.A. L.424 J.D. [FagelHaber]
Chapman, Robert A. ....'60 '85 C.112 B.A. L.1066 J.D. [Chapman&S.]
Chapman, Robert B. .... '— '69 C.347 A.B. L.1119 J.D. [Ⓒ FagelHaber]
Chapman, Terry G., (AV) ....'52 '76 C.659 B.S. L.597 J.D. [Abrams&C.]

Chapman and Cutler LLP, (AV)
111 West Monroe Street, 60603 ⊙
Telephone: 312-845-3000 Fax: 312-701-2361
Email: postmaster@chapman.com URL: http://www.chapman.com
Ann E. Acker; Scott R. Anderson; Leah F. Arner; David T. B. Audley; Andrea G. Bacon; Cynthia A. Baker; Daniel W. Baker; Michael P. Barrett; David S. Barritt; Erin P. Bartholomy; Walter P. Begley; Michael T. Benz; Jeffrey D. Berry; Deborah T. Boye; James M. Breen; Jeffrey A. Burger; Nancy A. Burke; Paul D. Carman; Theodore S. Chapman (1877-1943); David J. Cholst; Steven L. Clark; Jeffrey G. Close; Marla Chernof Cohen; Rafael L. Cook; Richard A. Cosgrove; Robert M. Criswell; John R. Crossan; David S. Crossett; Patricia M. Curtner; Henry E. Cutler (1879-1959); Stathy Darcy; Daniel J. Favero; Eric F. Fess; J. Richard Fisher, Jr.; Felice R. Foundos; August J. Francis; Marc P. Franson; Brian D. Free; Steven G. Frost; Lynda K. Given; Ronald J. Hacker; Heather L. Hansche; Steven G. Hastings; Kyle W. Henderson; William C. Hermann; John C. Hitt, Jr.; Douglas R. Hoffman; Van E. Holkeboer; Charles S. Hughes; R. William Hunter; Charles L. Jarik; Daniel L. Johnson; Christian T. Jones; Gregory A. Klamrzynski; Richard F. Klein; Mark J. Kneedy; Jonathan A. Koff; Paul C. Kosin; Kelly K. Kost; Darrell R. Larsen, Jr.; Thomas C. Lee; Matthew R. Lewin; William M. Libit; Frederick V. Lochbihler; Robert E. Lockner; James E. Luebchow; David A. Lullo; Neil R. Mann; Steven C. Mason; Michael G. McGee; Timothy V. McGree; Terry A. McIlroy; Timothy P. Mohan; Robert C. Nash; James R. Nelson; Robert W. Ollis, Jr.; Lisa A. Olsen; Terence T. O'Meara; Edward J. Pelican; Stacy K. Pike; Gary R. Polega; Mark D. Rasmussen; James R. Richardson; Dianne E. Rist; Eric M. Roberson; Ronald E. Rokosz; Anthony R. Rosso; Suzanne M. Russell; Robert J. Schneider; David I. Schrodt; Susan Shallenberger; Suzanne L. Shier; Edward V. Sommer; James E. Spiotto; James R. Theiss, Jr.; Carol K. Thompson; Franklin H. Top III; M. John Trofa; Robert G. Tucker; William F.

(This Listing Continued)

Chapman and Cutler LLP (Continued)

Tueting; Christopher F. Walrath; Morrison C. Warren; Lawrence E. White; Karl T. Williams; Steven N. Wohl; Richard A. Wohlleber; David E. Worsley; Anthony D. Yager;—Kimberly L. Ahlgrim; Lisa M. Anagnostopoulos; Ali O. Anekwe; Eduardo Aviles; Emily Todd Bastedo; Jane S. Berman; Charles M. Biggam III; Gregory S. Bloedorn; S. Todd Cubbage; Keith M. Cyzen; Jennifer A. DeVriendt; Richard J. DiLallo; Walter L. Draney; Aaron J. Efta; Brent L. Feller; David M. Field; Todd E. Freier; Scott R. Fryzel; Rose E. Gallagher; Maria Clara Garcia; T. Kellan Grant; H. Richard Hagen; James Heiser; Jane C. Hong; Thomas F. Howard; Charles J. Kolin; Colleen A. Kushner; David J. LaSota; Willie F. Lewis, Jr.; Lorelle L. Lindo; Phillip Lodato; Joseph P. Lombardo; Jil L. Martin; John J. Martin; Laura L. McKinney; Jane E. Nagle; Nathan H.B. Odem; Amy L. Olshansky; Scott H. Olson; Mark R. O'Meara; Peggy Joyce Osterman; Mark A. Partin; David M. Pederson; Christopher A. Pesch; Michael D. Robson; Matthew B. Schmanski; Ryan T. Schultz (Not admitted in IL); Shelly A. Scinto; Jordan M. Sickman; Julia J. Singh; Stephen Todd Sipe; Timothy A. Stratton; James P. Sullivan; Tara Wagner Tilbury; Jeffrey L. Troxclair; Rebecca Wallenfelsz; Lisa M. Weier; Glenn E. Weinstein; Andrew L. Wool; Kerry E. Zarley. Of Counsel: Lee A. Boye; Becky Brueckel; F. B. Hubachek, Jr.; Charles A. Kelly; Barbara C. Klabacha; Robert V. Lewis; Eileen Strang; Kenneth J. Vaughan; Daniel W. Weil. Senior Counsel: Susan E. Rollins.
General Practice. Corporate, State, Municipal and Public Authority Financing. Corporation Law and Corporate Financing, Securities, Intellectual Property, Public Utilities, Real Estate, Banking, Lease Financing, Asset Securitization, State and Federal Taxation, Estate Planning, Trust and Probate Law. Bankruptcy Law. Practice before State and Federal Administrative and Regulatory Agencies. Litigation in Federal and State Courts.
San Francisco, California Office: 26th Floor, 595 Market Street, 94105. Telephone: 415-541-0500. Fax: 415-541-0506.
Salt Lake City, Utah Office: One Utah Center, Suite 2000, 201 South Main Street, 84111. Telephone: 801-533-0066. Fax: 801-533-9595.

See Professional Biographies, CHICAGO, ILLINOIS

Chapman, James P., and Associates, Ltd., (AV) .....140 South Dearborn Street, Suite 1400

Chapman & Spingola, LLP
77 West Wacker Drive, Suite 4800, 60601
Telephone: 312-630-9202 Facsimile: 312-630-9233 Email: rchapman@chapmanspingola.com
Email: pspingola@chapmanspingola.com
Members of Firm: Robert A. Chapman; Peter M. Spingola.
Civil Trial and Appellate Practice including General Commercial, Complex Commercial, Intellectual Property Litigation, Plaintiff's Personal Injury, Professional Liability, Transactional and Counseling Matters relating to Intellectual Property.

See Professional Biographies, CHICAGO, ILLINOIS

Charfoos, Aaron D. ....'— '02 C&L.597 B.A., J.D. [Ⓐ Kirkland&E.]
Charity, Elvin E., (AV) ....'53 '79 C.976 B.A. L.309 J.D. [Charity&Assoc.]

Charity & Associates, P.C., (AV)
20 North Clark Street, Suite 700, 60602
Telephone: 312-849-9000 Fax: 312-849-9001
URL: http://www.charityandassociates.com
Elvin E. Charity; Alan M. Bell;—Timothy K. Hinchman.
Real Estate, Corporate and Public Finance.
Representative Clients: Bank of America, FSB; Boulevard Realty Services Corp.; Chicago Park District; City of Chicago; Harris Trust and Savings Bank; National Black MBA Association; Sears Logistics Services, Inc.; Sears, Roebuck and Co.; Seaway National Bank of Chicago.

See Professional Biographies, CHICAGO, ILLINOIS

Charkow, Jeffrey B., (AV) ....'66 '93 C.966 B.A. L.910 J.D. [Stein,R.&H.]
Charles, David R. .... '66 '91 C&L.339 B.A., J.D. Legal Coun., General Growth Prop.
Charles, Patricia E. .... '72 '99 C.846 B.S. L.880 J.D. [Ⓐ Swanson,M.&B.]
Charles, Susan .... '70 '00 C.94 B.A. L.345 J.D. [Ⓐ Mayer,B.R.&M.]
Charnes, Clint B. ....'72 '01 C.1119 B.A. L.879 J.D. [Ⓐ Hinshaw&C.]
Charney, Stuart A. '60 '86 C.999 B.S. L.1325 J.D.
(adm. in NY; not adm. in IL) G.D. Searle & Co.
Charone, Sheldon M., (AV) ....'25 '50 C.145 B.A. L.209 LL.B. 225 W. Washington‡
Chase, Christine R. ....'70 '96 C.352 B.A. L.188 J.D. [Ⓐ Winston&S.]
Chaskin, Catherine F. ....'61 '90 C&L.597 B.S., J.D. 30 South Wacker Drive
Chaskin, Kit ....'— '90 C&L.597 B.S., J.D. [Sachnoff&W.]
Chathas, Alice L. ....'52 '75 C&L.209 B.A., J.D. Asst. States Atty.
Chatz, Barry A., (BV) ....'— '87 C.966 B.A. L.209 J.D. [Arnstein&L.]
Chatz, James A. ....'— '58 C&L.597 B.Sc., LL.B. [Arnstein&L.]
Chatz, John K. ....'59 '85 C.860 B.A. L.209 J.D. Co. Clk. Off., Cir. Ct.
Chaudhry, Urmila, MD ....'— '99 C.999 B.A. L.209 J.D. [Ⓒ Goldberg&F.]
Chaveriat, John W. .... '30 '55 C&L.597 B.S., J.D. 77 W. Wash.
Chavez, Lisa M. ....'66 '96 C.707 B.A. L.146 J.D. Atty., Northern Trust Corporation
Chaviano, Hugo, (AV) ....'52 '79 C.705 B.A. L.597 J.D. [Sanchez&D.]
Chavie, Ann M. .... '71 '98 C.914 B.A. L.597 J.D. [Ⓐ Baker&M.]
Cheely, Daniel J., (AV) ....'49 '74 C.674 A.B. L.309 J.D. [Cheely,O.&A.]
Cheely, O'Flaherty & Ayres, Attorneys at Law, (AV) .... 19 S. LaSalle St., Ste. 1203
Cheesbrough, Laura A. .... '— '91 C.589 B.A. L.436 J.D. Asst. Pub. Guard.
Chefitz, Joel G., (AV) ....'51 '76 C&L.94 A.B., J.D. [Howrey]
Cheifetz, Robert D. ....'66 '92 C.1036 B.A. L.145 J.D. [Sperling&S.]
Chejfec, Charles ....'— '96 C.966 B.A. L.365 J.D. [Katten M.R.]
Chelstrom, Jeffrey A. ....'69 '03 C.350 B.S. L.1018 J.D. [Ⓐ Fitch,E.T.&F.]
Chemers, Robert Marc, (AV) .... '51 '76 C.800 B.A. L.345 J.D. [Pretzel&S.]
Chen, Alan Keith .... '60 '85 C.930 B.A. L.813 J.D. American Civil Liberties Union of Ill.
Chen, Angie A. ....'69 '00 C&L.477 A.B., J.D. [Ⓒ Sperling&S.]
Chen, Hsing-Hua Pam ....'— '01 C&L.339 B.S., J.D. [Ⓐ Sachnoff&W.]
Cheney, Carole A. ....'— '91 C.339 B.S. L.597 J.D. [Kirkland&E.]
Cheng, Amy .... '71 '97 C.477 B.A. L.904 J.D. [Ⓐ DLPiper R.G.C.U.]
Cheng, Wen-Shin ....'71 '96 C.339 L.945 J.D. [Tressler,S.M.&P.]
Chenoweth, Christian .... '75 '02 C.999 L.209 J.D. 747 N. Sedgwick St., Apt. 1S
Cher, David E. '57 '82 C.145 B.A. L.1565 J.D.
(adm. in CA; not adm. in IL) [Ⓒ DLPiper R.G.C.U.]
Cherf, Kelly McCloskey ....'64 '90 C.602 B.A. L.537 J.D. [Hogan M.]
Cherian, Limo T. ....'69 '92 C.436 B.A. L.276 J.D. [Hogan M.]
Cherie, Jules R., (AV) ....'49 '75 C.123 B.A. L.146 J.D. [Jules R.C.]
Cherie Jules R., LTD., (AV) ....77 West Washington Street Suite 1704
Cherin, Steven ....'49 '75 C.1016 B.S.B.A. L.365 J.D. [Pyes&C.]
Cherkasov, Bernard ....'— '04 C&L.477 B.A., J.D. [Ⓐ McGuirewoods]
Chern, Kevin W. ....'— '93 C&L.339 B.S., J.D. [Legal H.]
Chernawsky, Paul M. .... '72 '97 C.339 B.A. L.209 J.D. Dir., Fast Track Demolition
Cherner, Paul J., (AV) ....'43 '68 C.831 B.S. L.966 J.D. [Hinshaw&C.]
Cherney, Burton E. ....'45 '72 C.1016 B.S. L.209 J.D. 3280 N. Calif. Ave.
Cherney, David T., (AV) .... '50 '82 C.339 B.S. L.209 J.D. [Stein&C.] ⊙
Cherney, James A., (AV) ....'— '73 C.860 B.A. L.178 J.D. [Latham&W.]
Chernoff, David S., (AV) '39 '63 C&L.145 B.A., J.D.
Assoc. Gen. Coun., John D. & Catherine T. MacArthur Found.
Cherry, Allen W. .... '52 '77 C.339 B.A. L.597 J.D. Legal Assist. Found. of Chic.
Cherry, Daniel R., (AV) ...... '48 '76 C.453 B.S. L.309 J.D. [Welsh&K.] (See Pat. Sect.)
Cherry, Joan S., (AV) ....'49 '74 C.393 B.A. L.424 J.D. [Johnson&C.]
Cherry, Joan Tess, (AV) .... '53 '78 C.339 B.A. L.597 J.D. Dept. of Pub. Aid
Cherry, Myron M., (AV) .... '39 '62 C&L.597 B.S.L., LL.B. [M.M.Cherry&Assoc.]

Cherry, Myron M., & Associates, LLC, (AV)
30 North La Salle Street, Suite 2300, 60602-2504
Telephone: 312-372-2100 Telecopier: 312-853-0279
Email: mcherry@cherry-law.com
Myron M. Cherry. Associates: Daniel J. Becka; Jacie Zolna. Of Counsel: Cary N. Goldberg.
Trial and Appellate Practice in all State and Federal Courts. Business, Commercial, Entertainment, Antitrust, Contract, Copyright, Environmental and Administrative Law.
See Professional Biographies, CHICAGO, ILLINOIS

Cherskov, Michael J., (AV) '58 '88
C.450 B.A. L.145 J.D. [Cherskov&F.] (See Pat. Sect.)

Cherskov & Flaynik, (AV)
The Civic Opera Building, 20 North Wacker Drive, Suite 1447, 60606
Telephone: 312-621-1330 Telefax: 312-621-0088
Email: mail@cherskov.com
Members of Firm: Donald G. Flaynik, Jr.; Michael J. Cherskov. Of Counsel: Charles Nissim-Sabat, Ph.D.
Intellectual Property and Technology Related Law including Patents, Trademarks, Trade Secrets, Copyrights, Unfair Competition, Entertainment and Related Litigation.
See Professional Biographies, CHICAGO, ILLINOIS

Chertkow, Glenn, (AV) ....'40 '67 C.339 B.S. L.209 J.D. 1525 E. 53rd St.
Chertow, Sheldon, (AV) .... '33 '60 C.209 B.S.C. L.597 J.D. 30 N. La Salle St.‡
Cheskes, Bradley T. ....'69 '95 C.378 B.A. L.1000 J.D. [Ⓐ Beermann S.W.B.B.G.&L.]
Chesler, Irving A. ....'26 '75 C.339 B.S. L.209 J.D. Asst. Corp. Coun.
Chesler, Lawrence D. '37 '62 C.696 B.A. L.107 J.D.
(adm. in NY; not adm. in IL) 222 Merchandise Mart Plaza
Chesler, Stephen R., (AV) ....'— '66 C.293 B.A. L.597 J.D. [Arnstein&L.]
Chesley, Richard A., (BVⓉ) .... '— '85 C.597 B.A. L.150 J.D. [Jones D.]
Chess, Eva L. '— '85 C.575 B.A. L.893 J.D.
(adm. in VA; not adm. in IL) 50 E. Bellevue Pl.
Chester, Mark V., (AV) ....'52 '77 C.1365 B.A. L.597 J.D. [Johnson&C.]
Chestnut, John W., (AV) .... '40 '65 C.602 B.S.E. L.597 J.D. [Ⓒ Greer,B.&C.] (Pat.)
Chevere, Gloria '52 '81 C.1183 B.A. L.365 J.D.
Sr. Dep. Exec. Dir., Chgo Transit Auth.
Chevlin, Paul J. ....'66 '95 C.870 B.S. L.192 J.D. Asst. States Atty.
Chez, Lawrence A. ....'21 '52 C.597 B.S.C. L.209 J.D. 141 W. Jackson Blvd.
Chhay, Ly S. .... '78 '03 C.597 B.A. L.146 J.D. [Ⓐ Cinnamon M.]
Chial, Eric M. .... '64 '91 C.475 B.A. L.477 J.D. 3839 N. Hamilton Avenue
Chiaviello, Philip S., (AV) ....'56 '83 C.1269 B.A. L.365 J.D. [Conway&C.]

Chicago Internet Attorneys, (BV)
105 West Madison, Suite 1300, 60602
Telephone: 312-782-6463 Fax: 312-855-1177
Dennis J. Kellogg.
Personal Injury, Spinal Cord Injury, Automobile Accidents, Wrongful Death, Products Liability, Medical Malpractice, Corporate, Business, Real Estate, Criminal and Civil Litigation.
See Professional Biographies, CHICAGO, ILLINOIS

Chicago Mediation LLC ....70 W. Madison, Ste. 1400 #14025A
Chicago Women at Law, Ltd. .... 33 W. Jackson Blvd., Ste. 220
Chico, Gery J., (AV) ....'56 '85 C.339 B.A. L.424 J.D. [Chico&N.]
Chico & Nunes, LLP, Law Offices, (AV) ....651 W. Washington Blvd., Ste. 202
Chiero, Michael J. ....'— '93 C.477 B.A. L.365 J.D. [Rinella&R.]
Chiganos, Terry C., (AV) ....'49 '75 C.589 B.A. L.209 J.D. 53 W. Jackson Blvd.
Childers, Charlotte A. ....'42 '75 C.339 B.A. L.209 J.D. Contl. Ill. Nat. Bk. & Tr. Co.
Childers, Christine L. ....'70 '02 C.549 B.S. L.879 J.D. [Ⓐ Jenner&B.]
Childers, J. Richard, (AV) ....'39 '67 C.801 B.A. L.339 J.D. [Fedota C.]
Childers, John A., (AV) ....'55 '80 C&L.597 B.A., J.D. [Johnson&B.]
Childers, Michael A., (AV) ....'54 '89 C.209 B.S.C. L.365 J.D. [Childers,W.&W.]
Childers, Williams & Windham, (AV) ....25 E. Washington Street
Childress, Michael, (AV) ....'55 '81 C.436 B.A. L.365 J.D. [Childress D.G.]
Childress Duffy Goldblatt, LTD., (AV) ....515 N. State Street, Suite 2200
Childs, Linton J. ....'63 '88 C&L.309 A.B., J.D. [Sidley A.B.&W.]
Childs, Lisa C. ....'— '97 C.691 B.A. L.424 J.D. [Michael B.&F.] (See Pat. Sect.)
Childs, Melissa A. ....'72 '00 C.802 B.A. L.209 J.D. Asst. U.S. Atty., Northern Dist.
Chill, Max, (AV) ....'12 '35 C&L.145 Ph.B., J.D. [Chill,C.&R.]
Chill, Chill & Radtke, P.C., (AV) .... 20 N. Clark Street
Chilton, Larry J., (AV) ....'57 '83 C.339 B.A. L.146 J.D. 150 S. Wacker Dr., Ste. 2400
Chimes, Marilyn J. ....'56 '99 C.475 B.S. L.146 J.D. [Ⓐ Jenner&B.] (Pat.)
Chin, Edward G. H., (AVⓉ) '47 '78 C.569 B.E. L.262 J.D.
(adm. in NY; not adm. in IL; Pat.) [Winston&S.] (⊙New York, NY)
Chindlund, Colleen Adams ....'— '99 C.260 B.S. L.365 J.D. [Arnstein&L.]
Chinlund, Gregory J. '— '96 C.350 B.A. L.589 J.D.
[Ⓐ Marshall,G.&B.] (See Pat. Sect.)
Chiola, Thomas R. ....'52 '77 C.338 B.S. L.339 J.D. Cir. J.
Chiss, Adam R. ....'— '00 C.966 B.A. L.339 J.D. [Ⓐ Sachnoff&W.]
Chiss, Rachel Gena ....'74 '00 C.910 B.A. L.597 J.D. [Ⓐ Goldberg,K.B.B.R.&M.]

Chitkowski Law Offices
(See Lisle)

Chittenden, William A., III, (AV) .....'57 '82 C.339 B.S. L.802 J.D. [Chittenden,M.&N.]

Chittenden, Murday & Novotny, LLC, (AV)
303 West Madison Street, Suite 1400, 60606
Telephone: 312-281-3600 Fax: 312-281-3678
William A. Chittenden, III; Elizabeth Gwynn Doolin; Joseph J. Hasman; Sean Patrick MacCarthy; Donald A. Murday; David J. Novotny; David F. Schmidt;—Craig M. Bargher; Michael Brian Galibois; Matthew W. Gasaway; Joseph R. Jeffery; Jennifer S. Stegmaier; Julie Freund Wall; Georgia L. Joyce; Jennifer L. Noland; Morgan J. Milner. Of Counsel: Donald B. Leventhal.
Appellate Practice, Business and Commercial Litigation, Business and Corporate Law, Class Action Defense, Employee Benefits Law, Employment and Labor Law, Insurance Tax Litigation, Life, Health & Disability Insurance Law, Managed Health Care Law, Medical Malpractice Defense, Product Liability Law, Securities Litigation and Arbitration.
See Professional Biographies, CHICAGO, ILLINOIS

Chivilo, James P. '75 '00 C.750 B.A. L.1000 J.D.
[Ⓐ Holland&K.] (⊙Oakbrook Terrace)
Chizewer, David J. .... '66 '91 C.668 B.A. L.145 J.D. [Goldberg,K.B.B.R.&M.]
Chmiel, Jessica E. ....'76 '03 C.965 B.A. L.209 J.D. [Ⓐ Seyfarth S.]
Cho, James R. ....'74 '99 C.477 B.A. L.494 J.D. [Ⓐ Seyfarth S.]
Cho, Michael H. '67 '93 C.339 B.S. L.424 J.D.
Sr. Coun., Bank One Corporation (Law Dept.)
Cho, Richard J. ....'73 '98 C.339 B.S. L.188 J.D. Asst. Atty. Gen.
Choate, Antoinette ....'79 '04 C.145 A.B. L.424 J.D. [Ⓐ F.N.Trevino]
Choate, Michael J. ....'59 '89 C.424 B.B.A. L.146 J.D. [Shefsky&F.]

Choate, Murray R., II, Attorney at Law
(See Charleston)

Chodorow, Gary, (BV) ....'67 '93 C.228 B.A. L.112 J.D. [Ⓒ Hughes S.P.R.&D.]
Choi, Jean ....'68 '94 C.145 A.B. L.424 J.D. [Wagreich&C.]
Choi, Paul L. ....'64 '89 C&L.309 A.B., J.D. [Sidley A.B.&W.]

Choi, Soo ....'75 '02 C.228 B.A. L.1556 J.D. [Ⓐ Much S.F.D.A.&R.]
Choi, Yukyong ....'73 '01 C.569 B.A. L.424 J.D. [Ⓐ Meckler B.&T.]
Cholst, David J. ....'— '83 C.309 A.B. L.145 J.D. [Chapman&C.]
Chomiak, Sarah Norem ....'— '02 C.339 B.A. L.209 J.D. [Ⓐ Seyfarth S.]
Chomicz, Thomas E., (AV) ....'41 '69 C.755 B.A. L.494 J.D. [Quarles&B.]
Chong, Casarine H. ....'— '03 C.668 B.A. L.597 J.D. [Ⓐ Mayer,B.R.&M.]
Chorlé, Erhard R. ....'55 '84 C.209 B.S. L.365 J.D. [Shefsky&F.]
Chorowsky, Ilan J. ....'70 '96 C&L.966 B.A., J.D. [Freed&W.]
Chorvat, Timothy J., (AV) ....'61 '86 C.597 B.A. L.477 J.D. [Jenner&B.]
Chorzempa, David J. ....'68 '93 C.679 B.A. L.602 J.D. AT&T Corp.
Choslovsky, William, (AV) ....'— '94 C.339 B.S. L.309 J.D. [Ⓐ DLPiper R.G.C.U.]
Choudhry, Amina S. ....'79 '04 C.602 B.A. L.124 J.D. [Ⓐ Segal M.S.&M.]
Chowhan, Samir Zia ....'73 '01 C.347 B.A. L.146 J.D. [Ⓐ Hughes S.P.R.&D.]
Choy, Renee C. ....'79 '05 C.597 B.A. L.146 J.D. [Ⓐ Hinshaw&C.]
Christakis, Anna-Katrina S. ....'— '97 C.188 B.A. L.966 J.D. [Arnstein&L.]
Christenholz, Steven J. ....'69 '94 C.339 B.S. L.209 J.D. [DLPiper R.G.C.U.]
Christensen, Amelia ....'76 '04 C.602 B.A. L.365 J.D. [Ⓐ Merlo K.B.&G.]
Christensen, Janelle K., (BV) ....'66 '93 C.174 B.F.A. L.472 J.D. [Tressler,S.M.&P.]
Christensen, Jon P. ...... '48 '89 C.966 B.S.E.E. L.365 J.D. [Welsh&K.] (See Pat. Sect.)
Christensen, Mark E., (AV) .... '56 '82 C.937 B.A. L.597 J.D. [Christensen&E.] ⊙
Christensen, Thomas A. ....'65 '93 C.238 B.A. L.879 J.D. [Kessler,K.&C.]

Christensen & Ehret, LLP, (AV) BR
222 West Adams Street 21st Floor, 60606 ⊙
Telephone: 312-634-1014 Facsimile: 312-634-1018
Email: law@christensenehret.com URL: http://www.christensenehret.com
Members of Firm: Mark E. Christensen (Also at Pasadena, California Office); John B. Ehret; Jack C. Hsu (Also at Pasadena, California Office); Eric D. Stubenvoll. Associates: Katherine A. Jones; Mimi Y. Kim; Kirsten Radler Waack. Of Counsel: Jay M. Smyser (1933-2003); William G. Oldford, Jr.
Admiralty and Maritime Law, Appellate Practice, Commercial Litigation, Construction Liability, Excess and Reinsurance, Insurance Coverage, Products Liability, Professional Malpractice, Transportation, Trial Practice.
Pasadena, California Office: 55 South Lake Avenue, Suite 560, 91101. Telephone: 626-793-7526. Facsimile: 626-793-7744.
See Professional Biographies, CHICAGO, ILLINOIS

Christenson, Deidre Ane ....'67 '00 C.1106 B.A. L.424 J.D. [Ⓐ Nyhan,P.B.K.&L.]
Christian, David C., II ....'— '98 C.698 B.S.B.A. L.945 J.D. [McDermott W.&E.]
Christian, John M., (AV) ....'48 '74 C.674 A.B. L.477 J.D. [Perkins C.]
Christiana, Timothy F. '55 '85
C.1024 B.S. L.209 J.D. 200 South Wacker Drive, 31st Floor
Christiansen, Amy B. '77 '01 C.30 B.A. L.146 J.D.
Staff Atty., United Neighborhod Organization
Christie, Margaret A., (AV) ....'54 '78 C.611 B.A. L.597 J.D. [Field&G.]
Christie, R. Lee, (AV) ....'— '84 C.340 B.A. L.309 J.D. [Foley&L.]
Christie, Robert ....'48 '95 C.375 B.S.C.S. L.209 J.D. [Henderson&L.]
Christlieb, David L. ....'77 '03 C.388 B.A. L.339 J.D. [Ⓐ Littler M.]
Christman, James A., (AV) ....'48 '73 C.210 B.A. L.910 J.D. [Wildman,H.A.&D.]
Christoff, Richard W. ... '50 '78 C.339 A.B. L.424 J.D. 10thS.Dearbornst.SUITEIL1-1243
Christopher, John W. ....'65 '92 C&L.477 B.A., J.D. [Winston&S.]
Christopher, Richard A., (BV) '48 '73
C.597 B.A. L.950 J.D. Dep. Chf. Coun., Dept. of Transp.
Christopoulos, Dimitrios G. ....'67 '92 C.424 B.A. L.365 J.D. [Webster W.C.]
Christus, Daniel N., (AV) '51 '80
C&L.966 B.S.Ch.E., J.D. [Wallenstein W.&R.] (See Pat. Sect.)
Christy, Jennifer Neviaser ....'50 '83 C.966 B.A. L.209 J.D. 1747 W. Carmen Ave.
Chroman, Melissa B. '68 '95 C.347 B.A. L.339 J.D.
Atty., Regis. and Disciplinary Comm.
Chrones, Jeffery G. ....'— '93 C.347 B.A. L.1187 J.D. [Ⓐ Johnson&B.]
Chronis, Paul E. ....'64 '89 C.339 B.A. L.597 J.D. [McDermott W.&E.]
Chronopoulos, Stacy P. ....'70 '97 C.473 B.A. L.209 J.D. [Pedersen&H.]
Chronowski, Louis S., Jr. ....'68 '99 C.679 B.S. L.146 J.D. [Ⓐ Seyfarth S.]
Chrystal, John J., (AV) .... '28 '55 C.46 B.S. L.424 J.D. 224 S. Michigan Ave. (Pat.)
Chu, Michael P., (AV) '67 '92
C.339 B.S.M.E. L.945 J.D. [Brinks H.G.&L.] (See Pat. Sect.)
Chua, Barbara C. ....'69 '96 C&L.209 B.S., J.D. 35 Monroe St., Ste. 3950
Chubb, Laura A. ....'77 '03 C.880 B.A. L.345 J.D. [Ⓐ Amin L.]
Chudacoff, Mark R. '60 '85
C.861 B.A. L.424 J.D. Pres., Midwest Truck & Auto Parts, Inc.
Chudoba, Brandi L. ....'— '04 C.597 B.S. L.339 J.D. [Ⓐ Kirkland&E.]
Chudzicki, Pawel ....'71 '98 C.976 B.A. L.424 J.D. [Bell,B.&L.]
Chugh, Sujata Barai .... '— '03 C.674 B.A. L.309 J.D. [Ⓐ Mayer,B.R.&M.]

Chuhak & Tecson, P.C., (AV)
30 South Wacker Drive, 26th Floor, 60606-7413
Telephone: 312-444-9300 FAX: 312-444-9027
URL: http://www.chuhak.com
Thomas S. Chuhak (1920-1995);—David S. Argentar; Jeralyn H. Baran; Fred C. Begy, III; Thomas F. Bennington, Jr.; Mark Broaddus; William F. DeYoung; John P. Fadden; Barry A. Feinberg; Mitchell S. Feinberg; Dennis A. Ferraro; Cary S. Fleischer; Valerie J. Freireich; Daniel J. Fumagalli; James B. Gottlieb; Albert L. Grasso; Joshua S. Hyman; Terrell J. Isselhard; Edwin I. Josephson; Arnold E. Karolewski; Loretto M. Kennedy; Stephen M. Margolin; James R. Pranger; Edward C. Richard; Alan B. Ronson; Lisa A. Rothstein; Donald J. Russ, Jr.; Steven M. Scholl; Gary J. Stern; Tracy E. Stevenson; Andrew P. Tecson; David J. Tecson; Mitchell D. Weinstein; Alan S. Wernick; Bari D. Wood; Joseph A. Zarlengo;—John P. Adams; Stacey C. Bromberg; Carri A. Conlon; Dimitra A. Dallas; Rudy A. Figueroa Jr.; Jeanne M. Kerkstra; Daniel F. Marren; David B. Shiner; David C. Strosnider; Matthew Thompson; Molly A. Ward; Kendall E. Woods. Of Counsel: Lawrence E. Glick; Laura A. Josephson Bernat; Joseph O. Rubinelli; Joseph A. Tecson.
Corporate, Employee Benefits, Estate Planning, General Business, Health Care, Litigation, Appellate Practice, Municipal, Probate, Real Estate, Taxation and Medical Malpractice.
See Professional Biographies, CHICAGO, ILLINOIS

Chun, Robert T. .... '51 '76 C.339 B.A. L.209 J.D. Northern Tr. Co.
Chung, Jin-Ho .... '71 '97 C&L.477 B.A., J.D. [Ⓐ Schuyler,R.&Z.]
Chung, Pei Yuan ....'76 '04 C.228 L.145 J.D. [Ⓐ Winston&S.]
Chung, Suzanne Kim ....'73 '00 C.339 B.A. L.209 J.D. 200 W. Adams
Chung, Unbo ....'71 '97 C.604 B.A. L.424 J.D. Asst. States Atty.
Chupack, Edward A. '54 '80
C.589 B.A. L.365 J.D. Reg. Coun., Equity Office Properties Trust
Church, John C. ....'46 '78 C.98 B.S. L.146 J.D. [Ⓒ Swanson,M.&B.]
Church, Thomas G. .... '40 '65 C.424 B.B.A. L.597 J.D. 231 S. LaSalle Street
Churgin, Ira ....'42 '72 C.145 B.A. L.209 J.D. Asst. Pub. Def.
Churilla, Paul W. '65 '00 C.475 B.S. L.596 J.D.
(adm. in OR; not adm. in IL; See Pat. Sect.) [McDonnell B.H.&B.]
Churm, Catherine E. ....'58 '84 C.347 B.A. L.209 J.D. States Atty.'s Ofc.
Ciambrone, Rosanne, (AV) ....'63 '88 C.477 B.A. L.602 J.D. [Duane M.]
Ciancio, Donna D. ....'66 '92 C.679 B.A. L.146 J.D. [Ⓐ Kiesler&B.]
Ciancio, Ronald J. '41 '66
C.602 A.B. L.597 J.D. V.P., Gen. Coun. & Secy., GATX Corp.
Cianciolo, Marylu ....'63 '87 C.208 B.A. L.879 J.D. [M.Cianciolo]

Cianciolo, Marylu, Law Offices of
823 South Western Avenue, 60612
Telephone: 312-455-1940 Fax: 312-455-0183 URL: http://www.ciancialolaw.com
Email: mcianciolo@ciancialolaw.com URL: http://www.lawyers.com/fraudaudit
Marylu Cianciolo. Associate: Bernadette C. McGuire (Not admitted in IL).
Family Immigration, Employment Immigration and Visas, Labor Certifications and Permanent Residency, Deportation, Asylum, Health Care Law including, Health Care Fraud, Health Care Licensing, Reimbursement, Medicare and Medicaid, Alternative Health Care Delivery Systems, Home Health Care, Long Term Care, Managed Care, Medical Ethics, Physical Therapist Licensing, Nursing Home Regulations, Physicians Contracts and Licensing. Business Immigration, Employment Immigration and Visas, Labor Certifications and Permanent Visas.
See Professional Biographies, CHICAGO, ILLINOIS

Ciancuillo, David A. ... '71 '97 C.36 B.S. L.424 J.D. [Mayer,B.R.&M.]
Ciardelli, Victor F. ... '34 '60 C&L.209 B.S., LL.B. [Ciardelli&C.]

Ciardelli and Cummings, (AV)
19 West Jackson Boulevard Suite 300, 60604
Telephone: 312-346-2522 Fax: 312-922-0631
URL: http://www.lawcicu.com
Members of Firm: Victor F. Ciardelli; Patrick M. Cummings; Kelly Q. Bennett; Marc R. Campagna. Criminal Law, Personal Injury, Medical Malpractice, Products Liability.
See Professional Biographies, CHICAGO, ILLINOIS

Ciastko, Paul J. '— '92 C&L.190 B.S., J.D.
Two Prudential Plaza, 180 North Stetson, Suite 3100
Cibella, Rosario, (AV) '57 '82 C.602 B.A. L.209 J.D.
30 North La Salle Street, Suite 4300
Cicero, Frank, Jr., (P.C.), (AV) ... '— '65 C.937 A.B. L.145 J.D. [Kirkland&E.]
Cicero, Joseph B. '38 '64 C.339 A.B. L.145 J.D.
Coun., Central States Joint Bd., AFL-CIO
Cichocki, Robert T. ... '— '76 C.912 B.A. L.365 J.D. [Arnstein&L.]
Cichon, Gary Joseph ... '46 '71 C.177 B.A. L.209 J.D. Stewart Title Guaranty Company
Cichorski, Arthur F., (AV) ... '34 '59 C.339 B.S. L.365 LL.B. [Davis&C.]
Ciesielski, David L. ... '— '03 C.679 B.S.E.E. L.347 J.D. [Ⓐ McDonnell B.H.&B.]
Cigelnik, Patricia A. ... '64 '92 C.338 B.S. L.424 J.D. [Ⓐ Orum&R.]
Cilfone, Patricia L. '— '91 C.845 B.A. L.846 J.D.
(adm. in TX; not adm. in IL) Dept. of Health & Human Servs.
Cimino, Thomas P., Jr. ... '62 '87 C&L.424 B.A., J.D. [Vedder,P.K.&K.]
Cimo, Robert G. ... '72 '00 C.145 B.A. L.276 J.D. [Ⓐ McDermott W.&E.]
Cimpoes, Sorinel ... '70 '01 C.46 B.S. L.146 J.D. [Ⓐ Jenkens&G.] (Pat.)
Cin, Bennett D. ... '61 '88 C.424 B.B.A. L.146 J.D. [Cin&W.]
Cin & Wagner ... 55 W. Monroe Street, Suite 2410
Cinnamon, Christopher C. ... '— '93 C.951 B.A. L.477 J.D. [Cinnamon M.]
Cinnamon Mueller ... 307 North Michigan Avenue, Suite 1020
Cinquino, Celeste P., (AV) ... '45 '86 C.589 B.A. L.146 J.D. [Righeimer M.&C.]
Cinquino, Leo N., (AV) ... '47 '73 C.589 B.S. L.424 J.D. [Righeimer M.&C.]
Ciombor, Roderick C. ... '45 '71 C.424 B.S. L.365 J.D. 6204 W. 63rd St.
Cios, Kostas ... '73 '00 C.597 B.A. L.209 J.D. 200 W. Jackson Blvd.
Ciotti, Martin J. '47 '73
C.966 B.B.A. L.425 J.D. Legal Coun., Tenneco Automotive Retail
Cipolla, Carl J. ... '22 '49 C.339 A.B. L.209 J.D. Assoc. Cir. J.
Cipolla, Marisa T. ... '76 '01 C.597 B.A. L.146 J.D. [Ⓐ Peck,B.A.&M.]
Ciprian, John H., Jr. ... '67 '93 C.473 B.A. L.209 J.D. 8501 W. Higgins, Ste. 440
Cipriano, Douglas A. ... '64 '92 C.145 A.B. L.424 J.D. [Ⓐ Gardiner K.&W.]
Cipriano, Lisa M. ... '70 '95 C.477 B.A. L.597 J.D. [Ⓐ Eimer S.K.&S.]
Cirignani, William A. ... '60 '88 C.424 B.B.A. L.597 J.D. [Cirignani H.H.&L.]

Cirignani Heller Harman & Lynch LLP, (AV)
Suite 2600, 150 South Wacker Drive, 60606
Telephone: 312-346-8700 Facsimile: 312-346-5180
Email: info@cirignani.com URL: http://www.cirignani.com
Stanley J. Heller; James C. Harman; William A. Cirignani; Daniel Lynch. Associates: Deborah Alroth; Benjamin P. Beringer; Scott C. Patton.
Medical Malpractice, Wrongful Death, Cerebral Palsy, ERBS Palsy, Brain Damage, Anesthesia Injury, Improper Medication, Operating Room Death, Misdiagnosis, Birth Injuries, Retardation, Surgical Error, Medical Product Failure, Nursing Errors, Hospital Negligence, Head and Spinal Injuries, Automobile Accidents, Truck Accidents, Construction Accidents, Product Liability, Labor and Employment Litigation, Commercial Litigation, Insurance Coverage, Torts. Litigation.
See Professional Biographies, CHICAGO, ILLINOIS

Cirincione, James F. ... '— '03 C.165 B.A. L.880 J.D. [Ⓐ Foley&L.]
Cischke, Stacey A. ... '75 '00 C.475 B.A. L.424 J.D. [Ⓐ Cassiday,S.&G.]
Cisek, Mark Alan ... '72 '97 C&L.339 B.A., J.D. [Ⓐ Baum S.A.&N.]
Ciszewski, Steven J. ... '73 '98 C&L.339 BA., J.D. [Ⓐ Novack&M.]
Citera, Francis A., (AV) ... '58 '83 C.178 B.A. L.472 J.D. [Greenberg T.]
Citro, Yael M. ... '— '01 C.477 B.A. L.659 J.D. [Ⓐ Latham&W.]
Citron, Bernard I., (AV) ... '57 '82 C.339 B.A.S. L.365 J.D. [Schain,B.R.&C.]
Citron, Jerome D. ... '48 '73 22 W. Monroe
Claerbaut, Rochelle ... '— '05 C.339 B.A. L.273 J.D. [Ⓐ Brinks H.G.&L.]
Clair, Edward E. ... '72 '99 C.436 B.S.E.E. L.46 J.D. [Fitch,E.T.&F.] (See Pat. Sect.)
Clair, Scott ... '— '03 C.436 B.A. L.339 J.D. [Ⓐ Kirkland&E.]
Clancy, Edward ... '— '87 C.339 B.S. L.146 J.D. [Ungaretti&H.]
Clancy, Kevin J. ... '68 '93 C&L.339 B.A., J.D. [Ⓐ Sonnenschein N.&R.]
Clancy, Michael R. ... '63 '89 C.352 B.A. L.339 J.D. Asst. State's Atty.
Clancy, Thomas A., (AV) ... '47 '73 C.424 B.S. L.1119 J.D. [Clancy&S.]
Clancy & Stevens, (AV) ... 29 South La Salle Street
Clapham, Ronald J. ... '50 '80 C.1154 B.A. L.215 J.D. 333 W. Wacker Dr.
Clapp, Abigail A. ... '74 '99 C.347 B.A. L.1119 J.D. [Ⓐ Greenberg T.]
Clar, Scott R., (AV) ... '57 '82 C.339 B.A. L.146 J.D. [Crane,H.S.W.&C.]
Claricoates, Gregory J., (BV) '46 '75
C.339 B.S. L.424 J.D. Claims Coun., Chicago Title Ins. Co.
Clark, Alfred M., III, (AVⓉ) '54 '81 C.813 A.B. L.426 J.D.
(adm. in CA; not adm. in IL) [Lord,B.&B.] (⊙L.A., CA)
Clark, Amber M. ... '67 '99 C.174 B.A. L.209 J.D. [Ⓐ Rusin M.&F.]
Clark, Brent I., (BV) ... '61 '86 C.385 B.A. L.893 J.D. [Seyfarth S.]
Clark, Cameron Blake ... '68 '00 C.338 B.S. L.146 J.D. [Ⓐ A.G.Rubin]
Clark, Chad E. ... '74 '01 C.226 B.S. L.352 J.D. [Ⓐ Wildman,H.A.&D.]
Clark, Christopher R. ... '— '96 C.674 A.B. L.145 J.D. [Sachnoff&W.]
Clark, David L. ... '48 '75 C.477 B.A. L.209 J.D. 11 S. LaSalle St., Ste. 1020
Clark, Debra S., (AV) ... '55 '79 C.802 B.B.A. L.846 J.D. [Ⓒ Sonnenschein N.&R.]
Clark, Gary R. ... '— '97 C.597 B.A. L.910 J.D. [Quarles&B.]
Clark, James A., (AV) ... '— '77 C.473 B.A.B.S. L.930 J.D. [Ⓒ Schiff H.]
Clark, James E., (AV) ... '48 '76 C.103 A.B. L.145 J.D. [Sidley A.B.&W.]
Clark, Jeffrey C., (AV) ... '65 '91 C.851 B.A. L.608 J.D. [McGuirewoods]
Clark, Jeffrey L., (AV) '53 '79 C.679 B.S. L.801 J.D.
[Wood,P.K.C.&M.] (See Pat. Sect.)
Clark, Katherine M. ... '70 '97 C.602 B.A. L.145 J.D. [Mayer,B.R.&M.]
Clark, Lance E. ... '70 '98 C.999 B.A. L.339 J.D. [Clark&J.]
Clark, Martez M. ... '— '03 C.340 B.A. L.813 J.D. [Ⓐ Jenner&B.]
Clark, Michael A., (AV) ... '54 '79 C.340 B.A. L.309 J.D. [Sidley A.B.&W.]
Clark, Peter A. ... '61 '90 C.252 B.A. L.880 J.D. [McDermott W.&E.]
Clark, R. Theodore, Jr., (AV) ... '40 '65 C.823 B.A. L.477 J.D. [Seyfarth S.]
Clark, Randall F. '54 '81 C.1151 B.A. L.365 J.D.
Sr. V.P. & Gen. Coun., Merchandise Mart Properties, Inc.
Clark, Ronald J. ... '42 '67 C&L.608 B.S., J.D. 221 N. La Salle St.
Clark, Shannon L. ... '69 '95 C&L.347 B.A., J.D. [Ⓐ Gould&R.]
Clark, Steven L., (AV) ... '— '68 C.347 B.A. L.145 J.D. [Chapman&C.]
Clark, Violet M., (AV) ... '57 '83 C.103 B.A. L.188 J.D. [Laner,M.D.B.L.&T.]
Clark, William G. ... '24 '47 C.424 L.209 J.D. Ret. Supm. Ct. Jus.‡
Clark, William G., Jr., (AV) ... '49 '77 C.424 B.A. L.209 J.D. [W.G.Clark,Jr.&Assoc.]

Clark & Johnson, LLC
446 North Wells Street, Suite 340, 60610
Telephone: 312-593-2009 Fax: 312-416-0312
Lance E. Clark; Tige C. Johnson.
Corporate Law, Commercial Real Estate, Business Litigation, Mergers and Acquistions, International Law.
See Professional Biographies, CHICAGO, ILLINOIS

Clark, William G., Jr., & Associates, LTD., (AV)
350 N. La Salle Street, Suite 800, 60610
Telephone: 312-329-0830 Fax: 312-329-1830
Email: wmclarkjrassoc@aol.com URL: http://www.williamgclarkjrassociates.com
William G. Clark, Jr.;—Lisa Marie Zahn.
Family Law, Divorce, Support, Custody, Prenuptial Agreements.
See Professional Biographies, CHICAGO, ILLINOIS

Clarke, Carol R. ... '55 '81 C&L.659 B.A., J.D. 6700 W. North Ave.
Clarke, Cecilia M. ... '60 '87 C.103 A.B. L.276 J.D. [Ⓒ Fedota C.]
Clarke, James L. ... '— '88 C.338 B.S. L.365 J.D. [Hennessy&R.]
Clarke, Michael A. ... '61 '87 C.339 B.S. L.209 J.D. [Pretzel&S.]
Clarke, Michael T. ... '58 '85 C.676 B.S. L.209 J.D. [Kralovec&M.]
Clarke, Peter D. ... '— '75 C.477 B.B.A. L.1119 J.D. [Jones D.]
Clarke, Robert H. ... '77 '03 C&L.966 B.S., J.D [Ⓐ Jenner&B.]
Clarke, William Case ... '— '74 C&L.209 B.A., J.D. [Ⓒ Levenfeld P.]
Clarke-Smith, Jennifer ... '— '03 C.679 B.A. L.180 J.D. [Ⓒ Kirkland&E.]
Claudio, Carlos ... '69 '02 C&L.209 B.A., J.D. Cook Co. State's Atty.
Claus, Marcie R. ... '— '83 C.37 B.F.A. L.365 J.D. Hearing Offr., Juv. Ct.

Clausen Miller P.C., (AV)
10 South La Salle Street Suite 1600, 60603-1098 ⊙
Telephone: 312-855-1010 Fax: 312-606-7777
Email: info@clausen.com URL: http://www.clausen.com
Ivar R. Azeris; Kurt D. Baer; James S. Barber; Diane M. Baron; Michael W. Basil; James Joseph Bigoness; Peter G. Bora; Paul Bozych; Richard A. Buchanan; Susan J. Condon; Margaret Hupp Fahey; Dennis D. Fitzpatrick; Robert E. Gilmartin III; Michael R. Grimm, Sr.; Thomas S. Gozdziak; John T. Groark; Susan N. K. Gummow; William J. Hacker; MaryLu Hahn; David M. Heilmann; Harvey R. Herman; Celeste A. Hill; James M. Hoey; Richard G. Howser; John M. Hynes; Tracey A. Jordan; Cole S. Kain; Richard M. Kaplan; Edward M. Kay; Kimbley A. Kearney; Melinda S. Kollross; Ilene M. Korey; Stephen D. Marcus; Randall I. Marmor; Barbara I. Michaelides; Erin E. Moran; Richard L. Murphy; Melissa A. Murphy-Petros; Steven N. Novosad; Sonia V. Odarczenko; Margaret J. Orbon; Edward J. Ozog; Mark D. Paulson; Amy Rich Paulus; William P. Pistorius; Dean S. Rauchwerger; Robert L. Reifenberg; Brian J. Riordan; Paul Scott Ritchie; Dominick W. Savaiano; K. Clark Schirle; Scott L. Schmookler; Gilbert J. Schroeder; Martin C. Sener; James F. Smith; Mary F. Stafford; Richard Wm Strawbridge; James R. Swinehart; Michelle R. Valencic; Sava Alexander Vojcanin; Debra B. Walker; Gordon K. Walton; Robert E. Wilens; Kirk Zapp; Mark W. Zimmerman. Of Counsel: James T. Ferrini; Francis A. Heroux; James O. Nolan; Harry L. Wilson. Senior Associate: William J. Floriano II;—W. Gregory Aimonette; Joshua A. Aldort; Cheri L. Baden; Colleen A. Brown; Paula M. Carstensen; Ann C. Chalstrom; James W. Davidson; Brian E. DeVilling; Rodd E. Elges; Michael S. Errera; Paul V. Esposito; Colleen M. Feeney; Keith G. Flanagan (Not admitted in IL); George K. Flynn; Lisa N. Fontana; Shannon M. Geier; Kathleen A. Johnson; Shawn K. Jones; Kelly A. Jorgensen; Paul D. Kerpan; Janine E. Kutylo; C. Kyle Lang; Mindy M. Medley; Todd M. Murphy; Salvatore A. Pellegrino; Agelo L. Reppas; Ellen G. Robinson; David J. Roe; Betsy R. Rosenberg; Tiffany J. Tracy; Anthony P. Ulm; Maria Z. Vathis; Amy L. Witt; Kenneth R. Wysocki.
Admiralty, Appellate, Banking and Secured Lending, Business/Corporate, Construction, Employment, Environmental/OSHA, Fidelity and Surety, First-Party Property, Insurance Coverage, Intellectual Property, International Law, Liability Defense, Medical Malpractice, Mold, Municipal Liability, Premises Liability, Products Liability, Professional Liability, Subrogation, Transportation.
References: The First National Bank of Chicago; La Salle National Bank.
Wheaton, Illinois Office: Building C, Suite 1700, 2100 Manchester Road, 60187-2402. Telephone: 630-668-9100. Fax: 630-668-9169.
European Affiliated Law Firm—Clausen Miller Europe: Tetaud-Lambard-Jami & Associés, 83, boulevard Raspail, 75006, Paris, France. Telephone: +33.1.45.48.62.63. Fax: +33.1.45.48.42.57. Studio Legale Corapi, Via Flaminia, 318 00196- Roma. Telephone: 39.06.32.18.563. Fax: 39.06.32.00.992. van Cutsem-Wittamer-Marnef & Partners, Avenue Louise 137/1, B-1050 Brussels, Belgium. Telephone: +32-2-543-02-00. Fax: +32-2-538-13-78.
European Affiliated Law Firm—Clausen Miller, L.L.P.: 148 Leadenhall Street, London, EC3V 4QT England. Telephone: +44.20.7648.8460. Fax: +44.20.7648.8461.
New York, N.Y. Office: One Chase Manhattan Plaza, 10005. Telephone: 212-805-3900. Fax: 212-805-3939.
Parsippany, New Jersey Office: One Gatehall Drive, Suite 203, 07054. Telephone: 973-401-0470. Fax: 973-401-0513.
Irvine, California Office: 2040 Main Street, Suite 500, 92614. Telephone: 949-474-3100. Fax: 949-474-3190.
See Professional Biographies, CHICAGO, ILLINOIS

Clausing, Marilee, (AV) ... '— '85 C.436 B.S.N. L.209 J.D. [Anderson,R.]
Clauss, Michele Lomax ... '70 '00 C.911 B.A. L.145 J.D. [Ⓐ Sinar K.M.&F.]
Clay, Joan D. ... '70 '04 C.424 B.A. L.215 J.D. 1945 S. Halsted, Ste. 309
Clay, John E., (AV) ... '21 '49 C.118 A.B. L.309 J.D. 190 S. La Salle St.
Clay, Lisa L. ... '69 '02 C.879 B.A. L.352 J.D. [Ⓐ McGuirewoods]
Clay-Clark, LaGuina ... '— '92 C.999 B.A. L.365 J.D. 1940 E. 87th St., Ste. 5
Clayman, Amanda B. ... '71 '96 C.478 B.A. L.597 J.D. [Berger S.]
Clayter, Richard L. ... '22 '57 C.209 A.B. L.424 J.D. 7248 S. Crandon
Clayton, Fay, (AV) ... '46 '78 C.1275 B.A. L.146 J.D. [Robinson C.&C.]
Clayton, Michelle W. '66 '01 C.682 B.A. L.146 J.D.
Leg. Coun., National Conf. of Comm. on Uniform State Laws
Clayton-Pedersen, Sonja K. ... '76 '01 C.806 B.A. L.880 J.D. [Ⓐ Katten M.R.]
Cleary, David D., (AV) ... '62 '88 C.36 B.S. L.209 J.D. [McDermott W.&E.]
Cleary, Gerald V., III ... '— '89 C.339 B.A. L.424 J.D. [O'Hagan,S.&A.]
Cleary, Michael J., (CV) '63 '89
C&L.339 B.A., J.D. St. of IL, Dept. of Financial Institutions
Cleary, Peter Stephen ... '55 '81 C.209 B.S.C. L.365 J.D. [Cleary,P.S.]
Cleary, Robert F., (BV) ... '56 '81 C.145 A.B. L.209 J.D. Asst. States Atty.
Cleary, Stephen L. ... '52 '80 C.339 A.B. L.589 J.D. 1725 N. Nordica Ave.
Cleary, Terese McKenna ... '67 '95 C.339 B.S. L.365 J.D. Coun., CNA
Cleary, Thomas M. ... '46 '73 C.424 B.B.A. L.339 J.D. Sr. V.P., Bank of America Illinois
Cleary, Peter S. ... 8542 S. Pulaski
Cleland, Kelly ... '71 '97 C.303 B.A. L.1119 J.D. Asst. Atty. Gen.
Clemens, Richard G. ... '40 '65 C&L.893 B.A., J.D. [Sidley A.B.&W.]
Clement, James W., (AV) '15 '41
C.339 A.B. L.597 J.D. 120 S. Riverside Plz., 22nd Fl. (Pat.)
Clement, John A. '56 '85 C.339 B.S. L.597 J.D.
Mng. Dir., JMB Institutional Realty Corp.
Clemente, Matthew A. ... '— '98 C.589 B.S. L.339 J.D. [Ⓐ Sidley A.B.&W.]

Clementi, Paul J., (AV) .... '66 '91 C.339 B.A. L.436 J.D. [Hinshaw&C.]
Clements, Robt H. .... '17 '41 C&L.339 B.S., J.D. 19 S. LaSalle‡
Clerkin, John J., (AV) .... '24 '47 C.424 L.597 J.D. 321 N. Clark St.
Cleveland, Gabriela F. .... '61 '90 C.66 B.A. L.659 J.D. Asst. Chf. Coun.
Cleveland, Herbert E. .... '31 '60 C&L.424 B.A., LL.B. 4407 N. Elston Ave.
Cleveland, Jean .... '64 '96 C.825 B.S. L.436 J.D. [A Donohue B.M.&S.]
Cleveland, Matthew J. .... '72 '98 C.678 B.A. L.365 J.D. [A Hogan M.]
Cleveland, Michael G., (AV) .... '49 '74 C.424 B.A. L.145 J.D. [Vedder,P.K.&K.]
Cleven, Dane H. .... '52 '77 C.597 B.A. L.424 J.D. Pres., Community Svgs. Bk.
Clichowski, Jennifer S. .... '— '00 C&L.339 B.A., J.D. [A Edelman,C.&L.]
Clifford, Ernest L. .... '69 '95 C.927 B.A. L.589 J.D. [A Fisher K.]
Clifford, John W., (AV) .... '53 '80 C&L.424 B.A., J.D. [J.F.Clifford&Assoc.]
Clifford, Mary C. .... '74 '03 C.716 B.A. L.910 J.D. [A Merlo K.B.&G.]
Clifford, Robert A., (AV) .... '51 '76 C&L.209 B.S.C., J.D. [Clifford]
Clifford, Roger L. .... '36 '63 C.393 B.A. L.597 J.D. V.P., Boulevard Bk. N.A.
Clifford, Shawn P., (AV) .... '58 '84 C.93 B.A. L.1049 J.D. [Hinshaw&C.]
Clifford, Walter G. .... '56 '84 C.424 B.A. L.365 J.D. [J.F.Clifford&Assoc.]
Clifford, Jack F., and Associates, Ltd., (AV) .... Suite 1668 221 North La Salle Street

Clifford Law Offices, P.C., (AV) BB
120 North La Salle Street, 31st Floor, 60602
Telephone: 312-899-9090; 1-800-899-0410 Fax: 312-251-1160
Email: info@CliffordLaw.com URL: http://www.cliffordlaw.com
Robert A. Clifford; Keith A. Hebeisen; Kevin P. Durkin; Thomas K. Prindable; Robert P. Walsh, Jr.; Susan A. Capra; Jeffrey J. Kroll; Richard F. Burke, Jr.; Robert A. Strelecky; Pamela S. Menaker; Michael S. Krzak; Timothy S. Tomasik; John T. Karnezis;—Brian Thomas Nash; Katherine L. Dzik; J. Ryan Potts; Craig J. Squillace; Heather A. Begley; Shannon M. McNulty; Matthew L. Willens; Brian Shallcross; Vivian T. Tarver. Of Counsel: Robert P. Sheridan.
Airplane Crash Litigation, Aviation Accidents, Aviation Litigation (Commercial and General), Health Care, Helicopter Crash Litigation, Commercial Litigation, Construction Accidents, Construction Liability, Construction Litigation, Consumer Litigation, Consumer Protection, Nursing Home Litigation, Nursing Home Liability, Nursing Home Negligence, Patients Rights, Hospital Negligence, Complex Litigation, Trial Practice, Birth Trauma, Medical Negligence, Nursing Negligence, Nursing Malpractice, Accidents, Automobile Accidents and Injuries, Automobile Negligence, Brain Injury, Head Injury, Motor Vehicle Accidents and Injuries, Railroad Accidents and Injuries, Truck Accidents, Plaintiff's Personal Injury Litigation, Wrongful Death, Medical Malpractice, Transportation, Product Liability, Premises Liability, Vehicular Accident Law.
See Professional Biographies, CHICAGO, ILLINOIS

Clinite, Barbara J., (BV) '47 '79
C.57 B.A. L.424 J.D. 120 West Madison Street, Suite 1212
Clinton, Edward X., (AV) .... '30 '53 C.209 L.365 J.D. [E.X.Clinton]
Clinton, Edward X., Jr. .... '67 '91 C.145 A.B. L.309 J.D. [A E.X.Clinton]

Clinton, Edward X., P.C., (AV)
19 South La Salle Street, Suite 1300, 60603
Telephone: 312-357-1515 Fax: 312-201-0737
Edward X. Clinton;—Edward X. Clinton, Jr.
Business Practice including Corporate, Securities, Real Estate and Litigation.

Clise, Brian Sommer '72 '99 C.228 B.S.E. L.910 J.D.
[A Fitch,E.T.&F.] (See Pat. Sect.)
Clisham, Patrick A. .... '70 '02 C.589 B.A. L.209 J.D. [A Shaw G.F.G.W.&T.]
Close, Deirdre Ann .... '68 '95 C.424 B.A. L.1158 J.D. [A R.J.Prendergast]
Close, Jeffrey G. .... '— '94 C.209 B.A. L.597 J.D. [Chapman&C.]
Closen, Michael L. .... '49 '74 C.98 B.S. L.339 J.D. Prof., John Marshall Law Sch.
Cloud, Jared R. .... '— '95 C&L.145 A.B., J.D. [Winston&S.]
Clough, David, P.C. .... '62 '01 C.679 B.S. L.1000 J.D. 55 West Monroe, Suite 3950
Clough, David W., (BV) .... '52 '93 C.37 B.S. L.146 J.D. [Howrey] (Pat.)
Clough, Joyce F. .... '64 '93 C.597 B.S.I.E L.209 J.D. [Walker W.M.]
Clousson, Jerry P. .... '32 '56 C&L.923 B.A., J.D. [C Lowis&G.]
Cloutier, Christina J. .... '72 '97 C&L.347 B.A., J.D. [A Ancel,G.D.B.D.&R.]
Cloutier, Kevin M. .... '72 '99 C.299 B.A. L.347 J.D. [A Winston&S.]
Cloyd, Sally Fitch '48 '83 C&L.879 B.A., J.D.
Asst.Gen Coun., DiamondCluster International, Inc.
Clukey, Beth A. .... '66 '92 C.578 B.A. L.365 J.D. [A Jacobs,B.O.S.&H.]
Clune, James R., (AV) .... '53 '78 C.602 B.A. L.362 J.D. [Garofalo,S.H.&S.]
Coalier, Amanda C. '73 '03 C.597 B.A. L.146 J.D.
(adm. in NY; not adm. in IL) Tax Offr., ABN-AMRO N. America, Inc.
Coar, David H. .... '43 '69 C.823 B.A. L.424 J.D. U.S. Dist. J.
Coar, Kamau A. .... '— '03 C.367 B.A. L.228 J.D. [A Ungaretti&H.]
Cobalovic, Julie .... '— '00 C.589 B.A. L.209 J.D. [A Edelman,C.&L.]
Cobb, Amy L. .... '— '01 C.623 B.A. L.146 J.D. [A Jones D.]
Cobb, Kendric M. .... '— '04 C&L.339 B.A., J.D. [A Winston&S.]
Cobb, Richard A. .... '43 '74 C.910 B.S. L.424 J.D. 1217 W. Oakdale‡
Cobb, Ronald W., Jr. .... '58 '83 C.340 B.A. L.209 J.D. 221 N. LaSalle St.
Coberly, Linda T. .... '67 '96 C.674 A.B. L.477 J.D. [Winston&S.]
Coblentz, Peter D. .... '53 '78 C.339 B.A. L.424 J.D. [Rosenthal,M.C.]
Coblitz, Marta, (AV) .... '— '78 C.477 B.A. L.930 J.D. 225 West Washington, Suite 1014
Cochran, Christine M. '77 '03 C.145 A.B. L.910 J.D.
[A Leydig,V.&M.] (See Pat. Sect.)
Cochran, Gregory L., (AV) .... '— '80 C&L.477 B.A., J.D. [McKenna S.]
Cochran, Richard J. .... '— '67 C&L.424 B.S., J.D. [Tenney&B.]
Cockrell, Geoffrey C. .... '70 '97 C.937 B.A. L.602 J.D. [Wildman,H.A.&D.]
Cockrill, Ann T. '53 '80 C.911 B.A. L.285 J.D.
(adm. in WA; not adm. in IL) Coun., The Boeing Co.
Coco, Nathan F. .... '70 '96 C&L.352 B.S., J.D. [A McDermott W.&E.]
Code, Michael A., (AV) .... '61 '89 C.57 B.A. L.950 J.D. [Lowis&G.]
Cody, Mark A. .... '— '96 C.197 B.A. L.724 J.D. [A Jones D.]
Coe, Lynn Leland, (AV) .... '— '76 C.918 B.A. L.309 J.D. [Jones D.]
Coe, Matthew J. '63 '88 C.906 B.A. L.1065 J.D.
(adm. in WA; not adm. in IL) V.P. & Assoc. Gen. Coun., Hyatt Hotels Corp.
Coen, Richard L. .... '41 '66 C&L.339 B.S., J.D. Contl. Bk. N.A.
Coenen, Kevin J. .... '— '97 C.502 B.S.B.A. L.608 J.D. [Kirkland&E.]
Coffey, John J., III, (AV) .... '36 '61 C.742 B.A. L.602 J.D. [Rothschild,B.&M.]
Coffey, Karen S., (BV) .... '70 '98 C.475 B.A. L.146 J.D. [Coffey&Assoc.]
Coffey, Michael P. .... '66 '94 C.602 B.B.A. L.1209 J.D. Dir. & Coun. III, CNA
Coffey, Patrick S., (AV) .... '58 '84 C.966 B.A. L.146 J.D. [Gardner C.&D.]
Coffey, Thomas P., (AV) .... '44 '69 C.177 B.A. L.209 J.D. 54 West Hubbard Street
Coffey & Associates, LLC, (BV) .... 2114 W. Potomac, Suite 1C

Coffield, Michael W., & Associates, (AV) '40 '67 C.197 A.B. L.477 J.D.
77 West Wacker Drive Suite 4800, 60601
Telephone: 312-444-9696 Fax: 312-444-9658
Email: mike@bigdoglaw.com
Litigation includes both Civil and Criminal Antitrust, RICO, Environmental, Labor, Products Liability, Trademark and Copyright, Constitutional and First Amendment Litigation, Admiralty, Tax, Bankruptcy, Wills and Trust Litigation, Corporate Internal Investigations.
See Professional Biographies, CHICAGO, ILLINOIS

Coffman, Amos J., Jr. .... '40 '65 C.309 A.B. L.477 J.D. [C Kurlander&G.]
Coffman, Christine A. .... '57 '91 C.347 B.S. L.209 J.D. 2 N. LaSalle St., Ste. 700
Coffman, Danielle A. R. .... '75 '01 C.378 B.A. L.966 J.D. [A Winston&S.]
Coffman, Edward M. .... '— '01 C&L.966 B.A., J.D. [S Winston&S.]
Cogan, Deborah Bleich, (AV) .... '57 '85 C.976 B.A. L.893 J.D. [C Cogan&M.]
Cogan, Jules G., (AV) .... '— '62 C.339 B.A. L.597 J.D. [C Sachnoff&W.]
Cogan, Michael P., (AV) .... '56 '81 C.339 B.A. L.365 J.D. [Cogan&M.]

Cogan & McNabola, P.C., (AV) BB
55 West Wacker Drive, 9th Floor, 60601
Telephone: 312-629-2900; 800-704-2900 Fax: 312-629-2916 URL: http://www.cogandmcnabola.com
Email: info@coganmcnabola.com URL: http://www.cogan-mcnabola.com
Members of Firm: Mark E. McNabola; Michael P. Cogan; Edward W. McNabola;—James P. Navarre; John M. Power; Jody B. Pravecek; Adria East Mossing; Patti L. Tuttle. Of Counsel: Thomas R. Canham (Not admitted in IL); Deborah Bleich Cogan.
Personal Injury, Medical Malpractice, Products Liability, Professional Negligence.
See Professional Biographies, CHICAGO, ILLINOIS

Coggins, James Jason .... '70 '97 C.966 B.A. L.146 J.D. [A Wiedner&M.]
Coghlan, Barbara J. .... '61 '88 C.339 B.A. L.209 J.D. [Coghlan K.C.]
Coghlan, Dennis M. .... '67 '94 C&L.339 B.A., J.D. [A Sidley A.B.&W.]
Coghlan, James L., (AV) .... '32 '55 C.276 L.209 LL.B. [Coghlan K.C.]
Coghlan, Mark J. .... '57 '84 C.339 B.A. L.209 J.D. [Coghlan K.C.]
Coghlan, Matthew Edward .... '62 '87 C&L.339 B.A., J.D. Cir. Judge
Coghlan, Susan H. .... '68 '93 C.339 B.S. L.209 J.D. [Coghlan K.C.]

Coghlan Kukankos Cook LLC, (AV)
55 West Wacker Drive, Suite 1210, 60601-1612
Telephone: 312-357-9200 Fax: 312-357-0961
Members of Firm: John P. Coghlan (1903-1968); James L. Coghlan; John A. Kukankos; Barbara J. Coghlan; Elizabeth A. Longo; Francis E. Stepnowski; Susan H. Coghlan; Mark J. Coghlan; Catherine C. Cook; Michael A. Bressler, II;—Kristine A. Mueller.
Civil Trial and Appellate Practice in State and Federal Courts. Administrative Law and Procedure, ERISA Compliance and Litigation; Pension, Labor, Employment, Commercial Litigation, Trade Secrets, Antitrust, Health Care, Employee Benefit Plan Design and Subrogation, Real Estate and Corporate.
Reference: JPMorgan Chase Bank, N.A.
See Professional Biographies, CHICAGO, ILLINOIS

Cohan, Cynthia A. .... '66 '91 C.910 B.A. L.188 J.D. Law Clk., U.S. Dist. Ct.
Cohan, Richard S. .... '35 '59 C.339 L.209 J.D. 542 S. Dearborn St.
Cohen, Aaron, (AV) .... '28 '56 C&L.339 B.S., LL.B. [Leff,C.&W.]
Cohen, Andrew J. '60 '85 C.188 B.S. L.569 J.D.
Sr. Atty., Legal Assistance Found. of Chicago
Cohen, Barbara E. .... '50 '84 C.813 B.A. L.966 J.D. 190 S. LaSalle St.
Cohen, Barney I. .... '51 '76 C.339 B.A. L.209 J.D. Rush-Presbyterian/St. Lukes Med. Ctr.
Cohen, Benjamin H., (AV) .... '38 '63 C.145 B.A. L.597 J.D. [Schwartzberg,B.&C.]
Cohen, Brian Adam .... '78 '03 C.339 B.A. L.597 J.D. [A DLPiper R.G.C.U.]
Cohen, Dale M., (AV) '58 '83
C.823 B.A. L.597 J.D. Editor, Opers./Sr. Coun., Tribune Co.
Cohen, David E. .... '54 '86 C.589 B.S. L.365 J.D. 205 W. Wacker Dr.
Cohen, David P. .... '— '98 C.339 B.A. L.1066 J.D. [A Katten M.R.]
Cohen, Edward A. .... '— '81 C.1044 B.S. L.365 J.D. [Karbal,C.E.S.&D.]
Cohen, Elizabeth J. .... '54 '79 C.66 B.A. L.178 J.D. Asst. Editor, Amer. Bar. Assn.
Cohen, Eric C., (AV) .... '48 '74 C.124 B.S. L.472 J.D. [Katten M.R.] (Pat.)
Cohen, Eric D. .... '55 '93 C.107 B.S.E.E. L.201 J.D. [Welsh&K.] (See Pat. Sect.)
Cohen, Eric J. '51 '83 C.1349 B.A. L.209 J.D.
Assoc. Reg. Coun., U.S. Environ. Protection Agcy.
Cohen, Etahn M. .... '52 '84 C.976 B.A. L.145 J.D. [Sugar,F.&F.]
Cohen, Ethan Michael Morley .... '64 '91 C.293 B.A. L.597 J.D. U.S. E.E.O.C.
Cohen, Frank R., (AV) .... '39 '66 C.339 L.365 J.D. [Deutsch,L.&E.]
Cohen, Frederick H., (AV) .... '— '90 C.339 B.A. L.145 J.D. [Goldberg,K.B.B.R.&M.]
Cohen, Fredric A. .... '60 '88 C.999 B.S.Sc. L.209 J.D. [DLPiper R.G.C.U.]
Cohen, Garry W. '52 '78 C.477 B.A. L.145 J.D.
Exec. V.P., Mesirow Real Estate Investments, Inc.
Cohen, Howard M., (AV) .... '44 '69 C.477 A.B. L.597 J.D. [Cohen,G.&R.]
Cohen, Irwin .... '30 '60 C.339 B.S. L.209 J.D. Cir. J.
Cohen, Jacqueline Miller .... '61 '87 C.347 B.A. L.597 J.D. Northwestern Mem. Hosp.
Cohen, Jerilyn S. '44 '81 C.477 A.B. L.597 J.D.
Legal Advocate, Advocacy Services, Jewish Federation of Metro. Chicago
Cohen, Jonathan A. .... '53 '81 C.604 A.B. L.145 J.D. [C DLPiper R.G.C.U.]
Cohen, Joseph L. .... '77 '02 C.98 B.S. L.902 J.D. [A Much S.F.D.A.&R.]
Cohen, Larry D. .... '— '78 C.1016 B.S. L.365 J.D. 180 N. LaSalle St.
Cohen, Larry H. .... '45 '71 C.339 B.A. L.146 J.D. Pres., Accurate Perforating Co.
Cohen, Lawrence M., (AV) .... '35 '60 C.477 B.B.A. L.145 J.D. [C Barlow,K.&D.]
Cohen, Leslee Moss .... '67 '93 C.477 B.A. L.569 J.D. [Much S.F.D.A.&R.]
Cohen, Linsey N. .... '73 '98 C.339 B.A. L.424 J.D. [A Schain,B.R.&C.]
Cohen, Loren S. .... '67 '92 C.339 B.A. L.209 J.D. [C Wilson E.M.E.&D.]
Cohen, Louis S., (AV) .... '56 '81 C.813 B.A. L.597 J.D. [DLPiper R.G.C.U.]
Cohen, Mara E. .... '74 '00 C.347 B.A. L.365 J.D. [A Gunty&M.]
Cohen, Marla Chernof .... '— '77 C.597 B.A. L.424 J.D. [Chapman&C.]
Cohen, Matthew David .... '55 '81 C.293 B.A. L.494 J.D. 225 W. Washington, Ste. 2300
Cohen, Melanie Rovner, (AV) .... '44 '77 C.1036 A.B. L.209 J.D. [Quarles&B.]
Cohen, Michael B. .... '40 '67 C.473 B.A. L.966 LL.B. 35 E. Wacker Dr., Ste. 595
Cohen, Michael C. .... '67 '98 C.477 A.B. L.146 J.D. 4039 North Maplewood Ave.
Cohen, Michael J., (BV) .... '49 '75 C.352 B.A. L.209 J.D. Bd. of Ed. Law Dept.
Cohen, Michael J., Ltd., (AV) .... '54 '81 C.659 B.S. L.146 J.D. [Levun,G.&C.] ⊙
Cohen, Michael P. .... '43 '71 C.1016 B.S.B.A. L.339 J.D. 435 W. Erie
Cohen, Miles V. .... '73 '97 C&L.339 B.S., J.D. [A Scott&K.]

Cohen, Neil H., (AV) '50 '76 C.30 B.A. L.472 J.D.
2000 North Clifton Avenue, 60614
Telephone: 773-871-4814 24 hours Telephone: 312-246-1734 Fax: 773-871-3304
Email: slim2@prodigy.net URL: http://www.lawyers.com/neilcohenlaw
State and Federal Criminal and Civil Trial Practice. White Collar Crime, Capital Litigation, Homicide, Felonies, Driving While Intoxicated, Traffic Violations, Misdemeanors, Criminal Appeals, RICO Defense and Commercial Law.
See Professional Biographies, CHICAGO, ILLINOIS

Cohen, Richard M. .... '64 '91 C.597 B.S.J. L.146 J.D. [A Leff,C.&W.]
Cohen, Robert A. .... '59 '85 C.112 A.B. L.1066 J.D. [A D.A.Axelrod&Assoc.]
Cohen, Robert R., (AV) .... '62 '86 C.446 B.S. L.145 J.D. [Frankel&C.]
Cohen, Ronald A. .... '51 '78 C.1111 B.A. L.365 J.D. [C Kusper&R.]
Cohen, Samuel S. .... '50 '98 C.453 B.S. L.597 J.D. Two North LaSalle Street, Suite 2200
Cohen, Samuel T. .... '15 '36 L.146 J.D. 20 N. Clark St.
Cohen, Scott M. .... '71 '96 120 W. Madison, 10th Fl.
Cohen, Seymour, (AV) .... '17 '41 C.347 B.S. L.1119 J.D. [C Laner,M.D.B.L.&T.]
Cohen, Sheldon B. .... '49 '74 C.339 B.S. L.209 J.D. 4000 W. Fillmore St.
Cohen, Stephen A. .... '48 '73 C.976 B.A. L.145 J.D. [A Marks,M.&K.]
Cohen, Stephen B., (AV) .... '39 '65 C.309 A.B. L.880 J.D. [Kelly,O.M.D.&R.] ⊙
Cohen, Steven H., (AV) .... '53 '79 C.72 B.A. L.597 J.D. [Cohen]

Cohen, Stuart J. '69 '96 C.705 B.A. L.94 J.D.
(adm. in NY; not adm. in IL) V.P. & Assoc. Gen. Coun., Nuveen Investments
Cohen, William G. .... '43 '77 C.209 B.S. L.365 J.D. 1700 N. North Pk. Ave.
Cohen, Grossman & Rosenson, LLC, (AV) .... 233 N. Michigan Ave., Ste. 1720
Cohen Law Group, P.C., (AV) .... 55 West Wacker Drive, Suite 801

Cohen, Milstein, Hausfeld & Toll, P.L.L.C.
39 South LaSalle Street, Suite 308, 60603 ⊙
Telephone: 312-357-0370 Fax: 312-357-0369
URL: http://www.cmht.com
General Civil Trial and Appellate Practice in State and Federal Courts. Antitrust and Unfair Trade Practices, Securities, Civil Rights and Employment Law, Consumer Product Liability, Franchising, Mass Torts, and Toxic Tort Litigation. Complex, Multi-District and Class Action Litigation.
Washington, D.C. Office: 1100 New York Avenue, N.W., Suite 500 West, 20005-3964. Telephone: 202-408-4600. Facsimile: 202-408-4699. Email: lawinfo@cmht.com. URL: http: //www.cmht.com.
New York, New York Office: 150 East 52nd Street, 30th Floor, 10019-6004. Telephone: 212-838-7797. Fax: 212-838-7745.
Philadelphia, Pennsylvania Office: One South Broad Street, Suite 1850, 19107. Telephone: 215-825-4010. Fax: 215-825-4001.
See Professional Biographies, CHICAGO, ILLINOIS

Cohler, Richard D. .... '42 '70 C.1016 B.S. L.339 J.D. [Bailey B.N.]
Cohn, Bradley L. .... '68 '94 C.228 B.A. L.477 J.D. [Pattishall,M.N.H.&G.]
Cohn, Charles A. .... '58 '83 C.597 B.S.J. L.209 J.D. [Cohn&C.]
Cohn, Erwin .... '28 '50 C&L.339 B.A., LL.B. [Cohn&C.]
Cohn, Frederick F., (Ltd.) .... '38 '62 C&L.145 B.A., J.D. 601 S. La Salle St.
Cohn, Lawrence J. .... '42 '66 C.477 L.209 LL.B. Weisner Realty, Inc.
Cohn, Louis J., (AV) .... '30 '55 C.339 L.145 J.D. [Cohn,L.R.S.&G.]
Cohn, Martin .... '35 '58 C.209 B.S.C. L.597 J.D. 116 S. Mich. Ave.
Cohn, Matthew C. .... '71 '01 C.105 B.S. L.146 J.D. [Ⓐ Meckler B.&T.]
Cohn, Mindy D. .... '75 '00 C.966 B.A. L.930 J.D. [Ⓐ Winston&S.]
Cohn, Stuart A. .... '52 '80 C&L.145 B.A., J.D. [Ⓒ J.S.Rothman&Assoc.]
Cohn, Zane M. .... '43 '67 C.339 B.S. L.309 J.D. [Z.M.Cohn&Assoc.]
Cohn & Cohn .... 77 West Washington Street, Suite 1422
Cohn, Lambert, Ryan, Schneider & Gray, Ltd., Law Offices of, (AV)
205 W. Randolph St., Ste. 1700
Cohn, Zane M., & Associates, P.C. .... 150 N. Michigan Ave., Ste. 3300
Cohon, Morton H. .... '27 '51 C.339 L.365 LL.B. 134 N. LaSalle St.

Cohon Raizes & Regal LLP, (AV)
Suite 1860, 208 South La Salle Street, 60604
Telephone: 312-726-2252 Telecopier: 312-726-0609 URL: http://www.lawyers.com/cohonraizes
Email: crrlaw@CohonRaizes.com URL: http://www.CohonRaizes.com
Members of Firm: Jack A. Cohon (1905-1981); Gerald D. Chiss (1941-1990); Maurice P. Raizes; Harry S. Wolin; Jeffrey M. Brickman; Bruce J. Waldman; Cornelius P. Brown; Andrea S. Bryer; J. Michael Williams; Carrie A. Dolan;—Cheryl A. Perry.
General Civil and Trial Practice in all State and Federal Courts. Corporation, Bankruptcy, Creditors Rights, Secured Transactions, Antitrust, Probate, Estate Planning, Wills and Trusts, Real Estate, Health Care, Employee Benefits, Family Law, Divorce, Federal Tax and Appellate Practice.
See Professional Biographies, CHICAGO, ILLINOIS

Coin, Angela M. '70 '95
C.575 B.A. L.597 J.D. Dir., Northwestern Community Law Clinic
Coker, D. Ann .... '72 '02 C.597 B.A. L.209 J.D. [Ⓐ Askounis&B.]
Coladarci, Anne Margaret .... '57 '94 C.183 B.A. L.209 J.D. 5626 N. Virginia Ave.
Coladarci, John A. .... '63 '90 C.385 A.B. L.910 J.D. 155 N. Michigan, Ste. 636
Coladipietro, Franco A. .... '68 '90 C.589 B.S. L.365 J.D. [Amari&L.]
Colantino, Emily A. .... '— '03 C.597 B.A. L.846 J.D. [Ⓐ Jones D.]
Colbert, John D., & Associates .....'— '91 C.999 B.C.C. L.365 J.D. 2724 N. Lincoln Ave.
Colbert, Thomas F. .... '30 '63 C.812 B.S. L.365 J.D. 33 N. Dearborn St.
Colby, Bernard G., (AV) .... '12 '40 C.145 Ph.B. L.209 J.D. 175 E. Delaware Pl.‡
Colby, Douglas A., (AV) .... '57 '82 C.589 B.S. L.365 J.D. [Anesi,O.R.N.&K.]
Cole, Alexandra R., (AV) .... '55 '79 C.209 B.A. L.145 J.D. [Perkins C.]
Cole, Bernadette, (CVⓉ) .... '52 '78 C.597 B.S. L.145 J.D. 1255 N. Clark St.
Cole, Charles H., (AV) .... '52 '77 C.46 B.S. L.365 J.D. [Schuyler,R.&Z.]
Cole, Constance W. .... '49 '77 C&L.597 B.A., J.D. Asst. Prof., DePaul Univ. Coll. of Law
Cole, Daniel C. .... '69 '94 C&L.339 B.S., J.D. A.V.P., Equity Residential
Cole, David M. '65 '92 C&L.101 B.A., J.D.
Branch Chf., Div. of Enforce., U.S. Secs. & Exch. Comm.
Cole, Deborah B. .... '51 '96 C.98 B.S. L.146 J.D. [D.B.Cole]
Cole, Franklin A. .... '26 '50 C.339 B.S. L.597 J.D. 54 W. Hubbard St.‡
Cole, Jeanne M. .... '59 '86 C.6 B.A. L.880 J.D. Univ. of Chicago Physician's Group
Cole, Jeffrey N. '65 '93 C.112 B.A. L.809 J.D.
(adm. in CO; not adm. in IL) U.S. Mag.
Cole, Jillian S. .... '77 '03 C.1036 B.A. L.124 J.D. Asst. Atty. Gen
Cole, Joseph J. '65 '91 C.311 B.A. L.30 J.D.
(adm. in DC; not adm. in IL) 444 W. Fullerton Pkwy.‡
Cole, Laura J. .... '— '98 C.260 B.S., B.A. L.309 J.D. [Ⓐ Sidley A.B.&W.]
Cole, Melvin J. .... '33 '57 C.339 B.S. L.209 J.D. 132 E. Delaware Pl.
Cole, Samuel B. .... '73 '98 C.691 B.A. L.309 J.D. Asst. U.S. Atty.
Cole, T. David .... '67 '92 C&L.339 B.S., J.D. Public Guardian of Cook Co.
Cole, Thomas A., (AV) .... '48 '75 C.367 A.B. L.145 J.D. [Sidley A.B.&W.]
Cole, Deborah B., LLP .... 1525 E. 53rd St., Ste. 400
Coleman, Andrew N. .... '73 '98 C.473 B.A. L.880 J.D. [Ⓐ Patton&R.]
Coleman, Brigid A. '76 '02 C.741 B.A. L.910 J.D.
Asst. Pub. Guard., Cook Co. Off. of the Pub. Guard.
Coleman, Donald .... '— '92 C.589 B.S. L.146 J.D. 2056 N. Hoyne
Coleman, Elizabeth Abbene .... '67 '96 C.339 B.S. L.424 J.D. [Jenner&B.]
Coleman, Jill Ann, (AV) .... '55 '80 C&L.477 B.A., J.D. [Neal,G.&E.]
Coleman, John M., (AV) .... '49 '77 C.973 A.B. L.365 J.D. [Coleman&O.]
Coleman, John T., (AV) .... '41 '66 C.602 B.S. L.424 J.D. [Donohue B.M.&S.]
Coleman, Khara .... '— '03 C&L.910 A.B., J.D. [Ⓐ Kirkland&E.]
Coleman, Maureen A. .... '44 '88 C.719 B.S. L.424 J.D. [Tressler,S.M.&P.]
Coleman, Michael L. .... '46 '73 C.025 B.A. L.861 J.D. [Baker&M.]
Coleman, Robert F., (AV) .... '44 '69 C&L.209 B.S., J.D. [R.F.Coleman&Assoc.]
Coleman, Sharon Johnson ....'— '84 C.589 B.A. L.910 J.D. 2001 Richard J. Daley Center
Coleman, Tracie V. .... '69 '01 C.339 B.A. L.365 J.D. [Ⓐ Johnson&B.]
Coleman & O'Halloran, Ltd., (AV) .... 111 W. Washington St.

Coleman, Robert F., & Associates, (AV) 🅱🅱
77 West Wacker Drive Suite 4800, 60601
Telephone: 312-444-1000 Telecopier: 312-444-1028
Email: rcoleman@colemanlawfirm.com URL: http://www.colemanlawfirm.com
Principal: Robert F. Coleman. Associates: Kenneth P. Ross; Eugene J. Schiltz; Jerry S. Menge; Sean B. Crotty; Cassandra A. Crotty; Elizabeth E. Richert; Ryan S. Zeller. Of Counsel: Steven R. Jakubowski.
Complex Business Litigation and Appellate Practice in all Courts. Legal Malpractice, Class Actions, Commercial, Labor and Employment, Intellectual Property, Professional Liability, Civil Rights, Antitrust and Insurance Law.
See Professional Biographies, CHICAGO, ILLINOIS

Coles, Lawrence A., Jr., (AV) .... '29 '57 C&L.966 B.S., J.D. [Ⓒ Holland&K.]

Colky, Scott C., (AV) .... '52 '77 C.339 B.A. L.424 J.D. [Colky&K.]

Colky & Kirsh, Ltd., (AV)
1 North La Salle Street, Suite 3100, 60602
Telephone: 312-558-9700 Fax: 312-558-9899
Email: scolky@colkyandkirsh.com URL: http://www.colkyandkirsh.com
Scott C. Colky; Matthew A. Kirsh;—Joshua J. Beyer; Jennifer M. Byrd; Alison G. Turoff; Amy M. Kesselring.
Family Law, Child Custody, Divorce, Post Divorce Litigation, Adoptions, Postnuptial Agreements, Paternity, Surrogacy, Premarital Agreements, Grandparents Rights and Litigation.
See Professional Biographies, CHICAGO, ILLINOIS

Collado, Victoria R. .... '64 '90 C.228 A.B. L.846 J.D. [Ⓒ Mayer,B.R.&M.]
Collen, John, (AV) .... '54 '80 C.197 A.B. L.276 J.D. [Duane M.]
Collen, Sheldon O., (AV) .... '22 '49 C.118 B.A. L.145 J.D. [S.O.Collen]
Collen, Sheldon O., P.C., (AV) .... 3750 Lake Shore Dr.
Collens, Lewis M. ....'38 '66 C.339 B.S. L.145 J.D. Pres., Ill. Institute of Technology
Colleton, Donald P. .... '42 '67 C.276 A.B. L.569 LL.B. [Abramson&F.]
Collias, Philip J., Jr. .... '50 '78 C.165 B.A. L.365 J.D. 168 N. Sangamon St.
Collier, Darren C. .... '— '00 C.347 B.A. L.117 J.D. [Ⓒ Barnes&T.]
Collier, Kristen Werries .... '71 '00 C&L.339 B.A., J.D. [Ⓐ Novack&M.]
Collier, Paul David .... '— '99 C&L.339 B.S., J.D. [Kirkland&E.]
Collin, Christian Scott .... '72 '01 C.477 B.A. L.209 J.D. [C.S.Collin]
Collin, Christian S., Law Office of .... 25 E. Washington
Collings, William N. .... '29 '53 C&L.597 B.S., J.D. Chicago Title Ins. Co.
Collins, Amy J. .... '76 '01 C&L.893 B.A., J.D. [Ⓐ Grippo&E.]
Collins, Ann Finley, (BV) .... '46 '85 C.112 B.A. L.146 J.D. Asst. Pub. Def.
Collins, Barry G., (AV) .... '48 '80 C.999 B.A. L.365 J.D. [Asher,G.G.&D.]
Collins, Brian M., Law Offices of, (AV) '47 '75
C.589 B.A. L.146 J.D. 70 W. Hubbard St., Ste. 302
Collins, Brian P. .... '76 '02 C.436 B.S. L.339 J.D. [Ⓐ Pedersen&H.]
Collins, Christopher T. .... '74 '02 C.602 B.A. L.146 J.D. [Ⓐ Vedder,P.K.&K.]
Collins, Daniel L. .... '69 '98 C.602 B.B.A. L.436 J.D. 11329 S. Talman
Collins, Daniel L. .... '45 '91 C.381 B.S. L.365 J.D. [Askounis&B.]
Collins, Diana G. ....'43 '91 C.238 B.S. L.146 J.D. Chf. Trial Clk., State Com. Comm.
Collins, George B., (AV) .... '31 '53 C.38 B.S. L.45 LL.B. [Collins&B.]
Collins, Gerald J., (AV) .... '45 '72 C.339 B.S. L.209 J.D. 100 W. Monroe
Collins, Harold E. .... '36 '61 C&L.339 B.S., LL.B. [Collins&C.]
Collins, James A. .... '— '97 C.961 B.S.E.E. L.436 J.D. [Brinks H.G.&L.] (See Pat. Sect.)
Collins, James T. .... '31 '72 C.209 B.A. L.365 J.D. V.P., Tr. Offr. & Secy., Aetna Bk.
Collins, James W., (AV) .... '42 '68 C.436 A.B. L.424 J.D. [Bell,B.&L.]
Collins, John J. .... '30 '55 C.999 L.209 LL.B. 134 N. LaSalle St.
Collins, John P., (AV) '64 '89
C.339 B.S. L.145 J.D. 332 South Michigan Avenue, Suite 605
Collins, Joseph E. .... '69 '96 C.424 B.A. L.146 J.D. [Ⓐ DLPiper R.G.C.U.]
Collins, Joseph P., (AV) .... '50 '75 C.321 A.B. L.569 J.D. [Mayer,B.R.&M.]
Collins, Kathleen J. '— '91 C.705 B.A. L.1338 J.D.
[Ⓐ Litchfield C.] (⊙Cherry Hill, NJ)
Collins, Michael R. .... '61 '86 C.477 B.B.A. L.209 J.D. [Collins&C.]
Collins, Patricia A., (AV) .... '— '78 C.434 B.A. L.209 J.D. [Asher,G.G.&D.]
Collins, Richard D. '49 '79 C.861 B.A. L.999 J.D.
(adm. in DC; not adm. in IL) Ongen-Portland World Concrete Supp. & Mfg.
Collins, Robert M., (AV) .... '58 '83 C.339 B.A. L.146 J.D. [Bollinger,R.&G.]
Collins, Sara M. .... '77 '02 C.339 B.S. L.146 J.D. [Ⓐ Azulay,H,&S.]

Collins & Bargione, (AV)
One North LaSalle Street Suite 2235, 60602
Telephone: 312-372-7813 Fax: 312-372-7840
Email: email@cb-law.com
Members of Firm: George B. Collins; Christopher Bargione; Adrian M. Vuckovich. Associate: James J. Lessmeister. Of Counsel: Theresa Gronkiewicz.
General Trial and Appellate Practice in all State and Federal Courts. Corporate, Criminal and Civil RICO, Criminal, Professional Discipline, Securities, Probate, Medical Malpractice, Banking Law and Federal Practice.
Counsel for: Water Tower Trust & Savings Bank; Chatham Corporation.
See Professional Biographies, CHICAGO, ILLINOIS

Collins & Collins .... 332 S. Michigan Ave.
Collins-Stapleton, Sean W. .... '73 '02 C.723 B.A. L.339 J.D. State App. Def. Off.
Colliton, James W. ...'44 '74 C.813 A.B. L.1065 J.D. Prof., DePaul Univ. College of Law
Collopy, Kevin .... '68 '98 C.46 B.S.A.E. L.146 J.D. [Ⓐ P.I.Drake&Assoc.]
Collora, Philip J. '45 '76 C.205 B.S. L.477 J.D.
Dir. & Coun., Deutsche Bank Americas
Colman, Jeffrey D., (AV) .... '47 '73 C.966 B.A. L.813 J.D. [Jenner&B.]
Colmar, Craig P., (AV) .... '52 '77 C&L.597 B.A., J.D. [Johnson&C.]
Colňn-Navarro, Fernando '52 '82
C.723 B.A. L.494 J.D. Mexican-Amer. Legal Def. & Educ. Fund
Colson, William P., (AV) ...... '37 '62 C.363 B.S.B.A. L.597 J.D. [Firm of Finkel,M.&C.]
Colton, Gary S., Jr., ... '54 '80 C.138 B.A. L.608 J.D. [Mayer,B.R.&M.]
Colvin, D. Kathryn .... '71 '98 C.741 B.A. L.424 J.D. [Ⓐ Vedder,P.K.&K.]
Colvin, Jeffrey .... '— '03 C.966 B.A. L.145 J.D. [Ⓐ Schiff H.]
Colvin, Jennifer .... '75 '01 C.436 B.A. L.209 J.D. [Ⓐ Cremer,K.S.&S.]
Colwell, Paul A. .... '61 '87 C.585 B.S.B.A. L.494 J.D. Sr. Tax Atty., BP America Inc.
Colwell, Paul A., Jr. .... '32 '57 C.188 B.S. L.705 LL.B. 200 East Randolph Drive
Combest, Christopher ....'60 '94 C&L.976 B.A., J.D. [Quarles&B.]
Combs, Cathleen M. .... '48 '76 C.339 B.S. L.424 J.D. [Edelman,C.&L.]
Combs, Katherine K. '50 '75 C.597 B.A. L.923 J.D.
(adm. in WV; not adm. in IL) V.P., Dep. Gen. Coun. & Corp. Secy., Exelon Corp.
Combs, Lynn M. .... '66 '95 C&L.966 B.A., J.D. [Ⓐ Nyhan,P.B.K.&L.]
Comeau, David J., (AV) .... '55 '81 C.473 B.A. L.365 J.D. [Anesi,O.R.N.&K.]
Comella, Michelle M. '66 '04
C.741 B.A. L.424 J.D. Staff Atty., Giuliani Capital Advisors LLC
Comella, Philip L. .... '55 '83 C.72 B.A. L.273 J.D. [Seyfarth S.]
Comer, Kristin L. .... '— '01 C.210 B.A. L.597 J.D. [McDermott W.&E.]
Comerford, Harry G. .... '21 '47 C&L.209 B.A., J.D. [Ⓒ Schwartz C.]
Comerford, James R. .... '— '02 C.260 B.S. L.365 J.D. [Ⓐ Daley,D.&B.]
Comfort, Robert J., (AV) .... '60 '86 C.770 B.A. L.602 J.D. [Johnson&B.]
Comin, Barry A., (AV) .... '52 '77 C.597 B.A. L.910 J.D. [Weinberg R.]
Comiskey, Joan E. .... '54 '97 C.209 B.S. L.46 J.D. [Mandel,L.&S.]
Comiskey, Michael P., (AV) .... '48 '75 C.602 B.A. L.309 J.D. [Lord,B.&B.]
Compall, Timothy G. '61 '91 C.339 B.S. L.365 J.D.
Associate Commercial Counsel, MCI Telecommunications Corporation
Compernolle, Paul J., (AV) .... '52 '78 C.976 B.A. L.339 J.D. [McDermott W.&E.]
Competition Law Group LLC, (AV) .... 120 South State Street Suite 300 (Pat.)
Comstock, Thomas .... '— '02 C.436 B.S. L.1000 J.D. [Ⓐ Querrey&H.]
Conapinski, Leonard D. .... '— '05 C.602 B.A. L.597 J.D. [Ⓐ McAndrews,H.&M.]
Concannon, Michael P., (AV) .... '58 '85 C.602 B.A. L.365 J.D. 10 S. LaSalle Street
Conde, Jean L., (BV) .... '55 '95 C.1183 B.A. L.424 J.D. [J.Conde]
Conde, Jean, P.C., Law Offices of, (BV) .... 35 E. Wacker Dr., Ste. 650

Condon, Dennis B. '— '91 C.424 B.A. L.146 J.D. [Ⓐ Karbal,C.E.S.&D.]
Condon, Mark E., (AV) '47 '72 C&L.436 B.A., J.D. [Condon&C.]
Condon, Michelle F. '69 '02 C.339 L.1000 J.D. State Atty.'s Off.
Condon, Sarah Jayne '— '00 C.339 B.A. L.424 J.D. [Ⓐ Adler,M.&M.]
Condon, Susan J., (AV) '— '77 C.339 B.S. L.209 J.D. [Clausen M.]
Condon & Cook, (AV) 745 N. Dearborn St.
Conforti, Gregory D., (AV) '63 '88 C.162 B.A. L.896 J.D. [Johnson&B.]
Conforti, Joe '33 '61 C.209 L.365 300 W. Washington St.
Conger, Edwin H., (AV) '— '57 C.477 A.B. L.309 LL.B. [Tenney&B.]
Conklin, John B., (AV) '52 '78 C&L.930 B.S.E.E., J.D.
[Leydig,V.&M.] (See Pat. Sect.)
Conklin, Thomas, Jr. '64 '96 C.145 B.A. L.424 J.D. [Conklin&C.]
Conklin, Thomas W., (AV) '38 '64 C.976 B.A. L.145 J.D. [Conklin&C.]
Conklin & Conklin, LLC, (AV) 53 West Jackson Boulevard, Suite 1150
Conlan, James F. '63 '88 C&L.352 B.S., J.D. [Sidley A.B.&W.]
Conley, Donald W., (AV) '27 '53 C&L.309 A.B., LL.B. [D.W.Conley]
Conley, Robert A. '76 '04 C.436 B.S. L.209 J.D. [Ⓐ Niro,S.H.&N.]
Conley, Robt. M. '17 '56 C&L.209 LL.B. 5967 N. Oconto Ave.
Conley, Ronald W. '50 '76 C.798 B.S. L.502 J.D.
Supvr., Peer Review Legal Servs., Dept. of Pub. Aid
Conley, Thomas P., (AV) '— '80 C.118 B.A. L.209 J.D. [Arnstein&L.]
Conley, Donald W., P.C., (AV) 875 N. Michigan Ave.
Conlin, Christina '— '98 C.966 B.A. L.424 J.D. [Ⓐ Gould&R.]
Conlin, Martha E. '71 '96 C.741 B.A. L.597 J.D. [Cozen O.]
Conlin, R. Dean '45 '75 C.339 A.B. L.309 J.D. [Lord,B.&B.]
Conlon, Alison C. '— '00 C.976 B.A. L.228 J.D. [Ⓐ Wildman,H.A.&D.]
Conlon, Carri A. '71 '98 C.932 B.S. L.644 J.D. [Ⓐ Chuhak&T.]
Conlon, Denis J. '35 '61 C&L.424 B.S.C., J.D. [Ⓒ Martin,B.&S.]
Conlon, Erica J. '69 '97 C.910 A.B. L.339 J.D. [Ⓐ Sidley A.B.&W.]
Conlon, John L., (AV) '40 '64 C.1024 B.A. L.276 J.D. [Schwartz C.]
Conlon, Lisa Plunkett '— '98 C.597 B.A. L.477 J.D. [Ⓐ Latham&W.]
Conlon, Robert P., (AV) '60 '85 C.790 B.S. L.209 J.D. [Walker W.M.]
Conlon, Suzanne B. '41 '68 C.530 B.A. L.424 J.D. Sr. U.S. Dist. J.
Conlon, William F., (AV) '45 '70 C.347 A.B. L.339 J.D. [Sidley A.B.&W.]
Conn, Leanne W. '79 '04 C.801 B.S. L.365 J.D. [Ⓐ Swanson,M.&B.]
Connah, Stephanie Michele '76 '01
C.973 B.A. L.209 J.D. Asst. Atty. Gen., IL Atty. Gen.'s Off.
Connell, Colleen K. '55 '80 C.579 B.A. L.352 J.D. Dir., Productive Rights Proj., ACLU
Connell, Dana S., (AV) '56 '82 C.207 B.A. L.902 J.D. [Littler M.]
Connell, Daniel J. '73 '00 C.339 L.A.S. L.209 J.D. [Ⓐ Prusik S.D.&K.]
Connell, Deirdre E. '66 '90 C.187 B.A. L.352 J.D. [Jenner&B.]
Connell, Eugene F., (AV) '12 '40 L.831 LL.B. 10540 S. Western Ave.
Connelly, Dawn R. '75 '00 C.260 B.A. L.146 J.D. [Ⓐ McDermott W.&E.]
Connelly, Matthew Patrick, (AV) '70 '95 C.927 B.S. L.365 J.D. [Connelly R.&M.]
Connelly, Michael E., (AV) '48 '74 C.238 B.A. L.365 J.D. [M.Connelly]
Connelly, Michael P., (AV) '41 '66 C&L.424 B.S., J.D. [Connelly R.&M.]
Connelly, P. Kevin, (AV) '50 '75 C.276 B.S.F.S. L.424 J.D. [Connelly S.H.]
Connelly, Vincent J., (AV) '50 '75 C.602 B.A. L.145 J.D. [Mayer,B.R.&M.]
Connelly, William J. '54 '83 C&L.209 B.A., J.D. [Hinshaw&C.]
Connelly, Michael, Law Offices, (AV) 910 W. Jackson Blvd.

Connelly Roberts & McGivney LLC, (AV)
One North Franklin Street, Suite 1200, 60606-3421
Telephone: 312-251-9600 Fax: 312-251-9601
Email: info@crmlaw.com URL: http://www.crmlaw.com
Michael P. Connelly; Michael S. Roberts; Catherine McGivney; Matthew Patrick Connelly; Thomas R. Rakowski; Terry M. Schlade; William E. Snyder; Raymond E. Stachnik;—Cory D. Anderson; Stacia A. Buechler; Garrett C. Carter; John D. Fitzpatrick; Sara D. Lund; Steven J. Scott. Of Counsel: Robert M. Capua.
Commercial Litigation, Corporate Transactions, Mergers and Acquisitions, Securities, Technology Law, Licensing, Intellectual Property, Commercial Real Estate, Healthcare, Antitrust, Professional Liability, Product Liability, Employment Disputes, Transportation, Rail and Aviation Law, Insurance and Reinsurance Disputes, Construction Defect Litigation, Copyright and Trademark Law, and Employment Litigation.
See Professional Biographies, CHICAGO, ILLINOIS

Connelly Sheehan Harris, (AV)
150 South Wacker Drive, Suite 1600, 60606
Telephone: 312-372-1969 Fax: 312-372-1968
URL: http://www.csh-law.com
Partners: P. Kevin Connelly; Michael J. Sheehan; Martin Harris; Rachel B. Cowen; William Henry Barrett; Allison Zousmer Stein. Associates: Kristine Aubin; Heather A. Bailey; John Anton Berg; Jennifer L. Camden; Kevin V. Dunphy; Zachary C. Jackson; Kyle D. Kickhaefer (Not admitted in IL); Terence P. Smith; Brian Edward Spang; Ellen D. Stuart (Not admitted in IL); Jacqueline J. Wade.
Labor and Employment Law. Litigation.
Representative Clients: American International Group, Inc.; Mars, Inc.; Maryville Academy; Metropolitan Life Insurance Cos.; National Automatic Merchandising Assn.; The Quaker Oats Co.; VWR Scientific.
See Professional Biographies, CHICAGO, ILLINOIS

Connelly-Warren, Catherine, (AV) '67 '91 C.477 A.B. L.602 J.D. [Tressler,S.M.&P.]
Conner, Susan E. Seiwert, (AV) '59 '84 C.297 B.A. L.424 J.D. [Cassiday,S.&G.]
Connolly, J. Erik '74 '99 C&L.597 B.A., J.D. [Ⓐ Winston&S.]
Connolly, Jennifer Fountain '72 '98 C.145 A.B. L.208 J.D. [Ⓐ Wexler]
Connolly, Jeremiah P., (AV) '54 '79 C.424 B.S. L.209 J.D. [Bollinger,R.&G.]
Connolly, John P., (AV) '— '84 C.424 B.A. L.209 J.D. [Brady,C.&M.]
Connolly, Mary S. '53 '79 C.477 B.A. L.215 J.D.
(adm. in MI; not adm. in IL) Argonaut Ins. Co.
Connolly, Terese '— '04 C.234 B.A. L.146 J.D. [Ⓐ Littler M.]
Connolly, Thomas M. '60 '89 C.121 B.S. L.209 J.D. [Ⓐ McDermott W.&E.]
Connor, Andrew H., (AV) '48 '79 C&L.145 A.B., J.D. [Schwartz C.]
Connor, Harry D. '18 '43 C&L.209 B.S., J.D. 10149 S. Oakley Ave.
Connor, Joan Webster '33 '59 C.381 B.A. L.273 LL.B. 150 N. Michigan Ave.
Connor, P. Phillips '33 '59 C.124 B.S.E.E. L.273 J.D. 233 S. Wacker Dr. (Pat.)
Connor, Robert J. '52 '79 C&L.209 B.S., J.D.
Act. Gen. Coun., Dept. of Mental Health & Dev. Dis.
Connor, Sean P. '70 '97 C.338 B.S. L.365 J.D. 2 N. La Salle, Ste. 1100
Connor Ranalli, Clare, (AV) '60 '86 C.339 B.A. L.209 J.D. [Hinshaw&C.]
Connors, Brian R. '64 '91 C.454 B.A. L.93 J.D.
Sr. Coun. & V.P., Merrill Lynch Bus. Financial Servs., Inc.
Connors, Christopher P. '73 '99 C.339 B.A. L.424 J.D. [Ⓐ Skadden,A.S.M.&F.]
Connors, Nicole R. '70 '99 C.339 B.A. L.424 J.D. 815 W. Van Buren, Ste. 215
Connors, Robert W. '67 '00 C.679 B.S. L.424 J.D. [Ⓐ Bell,B.&L.]
Conover, Douglas '56 '81 C.347 B.A. L.209 J.D. [Rieck&C.]
Conrad, Christopher T. '73 '98 C.475 B.A. L.209 J.D. [Ⓐ Kaplan,v.&M.]
Conrad, Mark W. '53 '79 C.123 B.A. L.365 J.D. [Ⓐ Norton,M.W.&D.]
Conroy, Jill P. '77 '04 C.1030 B.A. L.424 J.D. [Ⓐ Daley&G.]
Conroyd, Walter F. '20 '47 C.424 B.S.C. L.209 J.D. Loyola Univ.
Considine, Christopher T. '69 '99 C.436 B.A. L.424 J.D. [Ⓒ Tamari&B.]

Constantine, Zinder & Pallis Ste., 2900, 33 N. La Salle St.
Consumer Advocacy Center, The, P.C. 180 West Washington, Suite 700
Conte, James B., (CV) '— '93 C.339 B.S. L.112 J.D. [Barnes&T.] (See Pat. Sect.)
Conti, Guy '76 '01 C.93 B.A. L.602 J.D. [Ⓐ Condon&C.]
Conti, Karen, (AV) '62 '86 C.589 B.A. L.339 J.D. [Adamski&C.]
Conti, Matthew J., Law Offices, (AV) '60 '87
C.932 C.A.S. L.365 J.D. 218 N. Jefferson St., Ste. 201
Conti, Michael J. '71 '97 C.339 B.S. L.589 J.D. 107 W. Van Buren St.
Contis, David J. '58 '85 C&L.209 B.S., J.D. Sr. V.P., Equity Properties & Develop. Co.
Contorer, Jay '35 '59 C&L.597 B.A., J.D. 2626 W. Touhy Ave.‡
Contreras, Colleen Danaher '70 '95
C.602 B.A. L.424 J.D. Litig. Coun., Aon Corporation
Contreras, Robert A. '69 '96 C.347 B.S. L.424 J.D.
Assoc. Gen. Coun. & Sr. V.P., Deerfield Capital Mgmt. LLC
Convery, James J., (AV) '56 '81 C&L.209 B.S.C., J.D. [Laner,M.D.B.L.&T.]
Conviser, Richard J. '38 '63
C.112 B.S. L.1066 LL.B. Prof. of Law, Chicago-Kent College of Law
Conway, Bernard J. '16 '50 C&L.424 LL.B. 155 Harbor Dr.‡
Conway, Camille B., (AV) '61 '89 C.1106 B.A. L.597 J.D. [Schuyler,R.&Z.]
Conway, James M., (AV) '55 '82 C.424 B.B.A. L.365 J.D. Asst. U.S. Atty.
Conway, Kevin J., (AV) '51 '76 C&L.424 A.B., J.D. [Cooney&C.]
Conway, Linda B. '60 '85 C.276 A.B. L.602 J.D. 501 N. Sacramento Boulevard
Conway, Michael F., (AV) '52 '80 C.276 B.S.F.S. L.589 J.D. [Conway&C.]
Conway, Michael M., (AV) '— '73 C.597 B.S. L.976 J.D. [Foley&L.]
Conway, Michael P. '64 '89 C.339 A.B. L.145 J.D. [Grippo&E.]
Conway, Michael R., Jr. '64 '93 C.750 B.A. L.339 J.D. 180 N. La Salle St., Ste. 3850
Conway, Teresa M. '35 '60 C&L.597 B.A., J.D. CNA Plaza
Conway, Timothy R., (AV) '56 '80 C.209 B.A. L.597 J.D. [Conway&M.]

Conway & Chiaviello, Ltd., (AV)
77 West Washington Boulevard Suite 1601, 60602
Telephone: 312-782-3553 Fax: 312-782-3552
Email: conchiltd@yahoo.com
Michael F. Conway; Philip S. Chiaviello;—Todd P. Klein; Paul Gamboa.
Language: Spanish.
Personal Injury and Workers Compensation.
See Professional Biographies, CHICAGO, ILLINOIS

Conway & Mrowiec, (AV)
20 South Clark, Suite 750, 60603
Telephone: 312-658-1100 Fax: 312-658-1201
URL: http://www.cmcontractors.com
Members of Firm: Timothy R. Conway; John S. Mrowiec; Edward B. Keidan. Associates: Kenneth A. Cripe; Mark R. Becker; Brian W. Morris.
Construction, Mechanics Liens, Arbitration, Government Contracts, Insurance, Complex Litigation and Construction Related Bankruptcy.
See Professional Biographies, CHICAGO, ILLINOIS

Cook, Adrienne '59 '91 C.231 B.A. L.1119 J.D. Dir., American Bar Association
Cook, Alan J. '45 '73 C.339 B.A. L.424 J.D. 1 E. Superior St.
Cook, Annette J. '47 '85
C.999 B.A. L.146 J.D. Assoc. Dir., Ctr. for CLE, Amer. Bar Assn.
Cook, Brian J. '57 '91 C.999 B.S. L.209 J.D. V. P., Human Res., USG Corp.
Cook, Catherine C. '34 '74 C.424 B.A. L.273 J.D. [Coghlan K.C.]
Cook, Charles E. '19 '51 L.1003 J.D.
(adm. in OH; not adm. in IL) S.E.C.
Cook, Daniel A. '78 '04 C.118 B.A. L.352 J.D. [Ⓐ Mayer,B.R.&M.]
Cook, David M. '76 '02 C.339 B.A. L.209 J.D. 33 N. LaSalle St., Ste. 2300
Cook, Granger, Jr., (AV) '26 '55
C.597 B.S.E.E. L.477 J.D. [Cook,A.M.M.C.&M.] (See Pat. Sect.)
Cook, Jamie Lynn '75 '01 C.473 B.A. L.365 J.D. Law Clk.
Cook, John A., (AV) '21 '47 C&L.145 B.A., J.D. [J.A.Cook]
Cook, Kim Edward '50 '75 C.623 B.A. L.569 LL.M. Sr. Coun.
Cook, Margaret Katharine '75 '00 C.880 B.A. L.209 J.D. 3023 N. Clark St.
Cook, Mercer '30 '57 C.31 B.A. L.145 J.D. 1700 E. 56th St.‡
Cook, Patricia Cronin, (AV) '56 '84 C.339 B.S. L.809 J.D. [Cronin,P.&C.]
Cook, Rafael L. '— '83 C.611 B.A. L.1565 J.D. [Chapman&C.]
Cook, Rufus L. '36 '59 C.824 A.B. L.145 J.D. 1625 East 74th Street
Cook, Vincent P., (AV) '49 '75 C&L.424 B.A., J.D. [Condon&C.]
Cook, William J., (AV) '53 '79 C&L.424 B.A., J.D. 711 S. Dearborn St.
Cook, William J., (AV) '46 '73 C&L.190 A.B., J.D. [Wildman,H.A.&D.]

Cook, Alex, McFarron, Manzo, Cummings & Mehler, (AV)
200 West Adams, Suite 2850, 60606
Telephone: 312-236-8500 Fax: 312-236-8176
Email: firm@cammcm.com URL: http://www.cammcm.com
Granger Cook, Jr.; John L. Alex; Daniel M. Riess; Eugene M. Cummings; James S. Pristelski; Gary W. McFarron; Raymond M. Mehler; Edward D. Manzo; Joel H. Bock; Stephen B. Heller; David Lesht; Andrew G. Kolomayets; Mark J. Murphy; Michael J. McGee; David Michael Mundt. Associates: Renee C. Barthel; Louis John Alex; Michael D. Zaronias; Panasarn Aim Jirut; Paul Raya; Joseph R. Freund; Betsy J. Levstik. Of Counsel: Fred S. Lockwood (P.C.); William H. Magidson; Daniel C. McEachran; Edward M. Keating.
Patent, Trademark, Copyright and Unfair Competition Law, Intellectual Property Practice.
See Professional Biographies, CHICAGO, ILLINOIS

Cook, John August, P.C., (AV)
111 West Washington Street, Suite 1900, 60602-2713
Telephone: 312-807-4812 FAX: 312-807-4858
Email: jacookpc@aol.com
John A. Cook.
The General Practice of Law including, Privately Held Corporations, Probate, Trust and Estate Planning, Federal Taxation, and Business Litigation in all Courts.

Cooke, Gary E., II '62 '88 C.597 B.A. L.910 J.D. 333 N. Michigan Avenue
Cooke, Kevann M., (BV) '60 '86
C.674 B.A. L.813 J.D. V.P., Secy. & Chf. Compl. Offr., Aon Corp.
Cooke, Leon R. '41 '67 C.1016 B.S.B.A. L.209 LL.B. 11 South La Salle St.
Cooke, Patrick G. '67 '95 C&L.602 B.A., J.D. [Ⓐ Patzik,F.&S.]
Cooley, Dennis M., (BV) '46 '72 C.424 B.B.A. L.146 J.D. [D.Cooley]
Cooley, Dennis, Law Offices of, (BV) 155 N. Michigan Ave., Ste. 716
Coon, Karen E. '72 '97 C.475 B.A. L.477 J.D. [Ⓐ Wiedner&M.]
Coon, Linda S. '51 '89 C.430 B.A. L.424 J.D. 53 W. Jackson Blvd., Ste. 304
Coonan, James M. '— '73 C&L.966 J.D. [Masuda,F.E.&M.]
Cooney, Daniel P. '52 '77 C.188 A.B. L.145 J.D.
Dep. Gen. Coun., Bank One Corp. (Law Dept.)
Cooney, John D., (AV) '54 '79 C.276 B.A. L.424 J.D. [Cooney&C.]
Cooney, Loretta Weber '52 '77 C.339 B.A. L.424 J.D. Chicago Transit Auth.
Cooney, Robert J., Jr., (AV) '52 '78 C.93 B.A. L.424 J.D. [Cooney&C.]
Cooney and Conway, Law Offices, (AV) 30th Floor 120 North LaSalle Street
Coons, Gordon R., (AV) '39 '65
C.350 B.S.Ch.E. L.276 J.D. [Leydig,V.&M.] (See Pat. Sect.)
Cooper, Ada S. '60 '85 C.31 B.A. L.309 J.D. 1624A N. Mahawk St.‡

Cooper, Alexis Andrews '— '98 C.339 B.S. L.424 J.D. [Ⓐ Schiff H.]
Cooper, Christine G. '47 '76 C.700 B.A. L.209 J.D. Loyola Law School
Cooper, Edward L. '31 '55 C.339 L.146 J.D. [Ⓒ Kiesler&B.]
Cooper, Eric P. '48 '82 C.831 B.A. L.424 J.D. Mgr., Compensation, Inland Steel Co.‡
Cooper, Gerald F., Jr., (AV) '54 '80 C.473 A.B. L.209 J.D. [Scopelitis,G.L.&H.]
Cooper, Joel T. '— '81 C.679 B.A. L.209 J.D. [Freeborn&P.]
Cooper, John E. '26 '60 C.339 B.S. L.209 J.D. 333 W. Wacker Dr.
Cooper, Jonathan M. '68 '94 C.477 B.S. L.597 J.D. [Goldberg,K.B.B.R.&M.]
Cooper, Larissa '— '03 L.893 J.D. [Ⓐ Winston&S.]
Cooper, Peter E. '59 '85 C.188 B.A. L.569 J.D. [Lawrence,K.S.&U.]
Cooper, Sheila O'Connell '58 '85
C.446 B.A. L.802 J.D. Apt. 5502, 474 N. Lake Shore Drive
Cooper-Finkle, Andrea '— '77
C.1016 B.A. L.221 J.D. Div. Coun., American Medical Association
Cooperman, Marc S., (AV) '— '89 C&L.339 B.S., J.D. [Banner&W.] (See Pat. Sect.)
Coorlas, Peter S., (AV) '49 '74 C.352 B.B.A. L.209 J.D. Asst. State's Atty.
Cope, Carrie E. '59 '91 C.927 B.A. L.201 J.D. [Tressler,S.M.&P.]
Cope, Ronald S., (AV) '— '64 C&L.145 B.A., J.D. [Michael B.&F.]
Copeland, Edward J., (AV) '— '59 C.118 B.A. L.597 J.D. [Schuyler,R.&Z.]
Copeland, Richard Z. '47 '72 C.966 B.B.A. L.273 J.D. Asst. State's Atty.
Copeland, Sheldon I. '33 '57 L.209 LL.B. [Ⓒ Copeland,F.&F.]
Copeland, Finn and Fieri, LTD. 180 North La Salle Street, Suite 2507
Copland, David A. '68 '96 C.855 B.A. L.94 J.D. [Ⓐ Wildman,H.A.&D.]
Copland, Lisa A. '72 '97 C.674 A.B. L.597 J.D. [L.A.Copland]

Copland, Lisa A., P.C.
2600 S. Michigan Avenue, Suite 405, 60616
Telephone: 312-881-9225 Fax: 312-881-9226
Email: Coplandlaw@aol.com URL: http://www.lawyers.com/coplandlaw
Lisa A. Copland.
Family Law, Divorce, Adoptions, Child Custody, Child Support, Domestic Violence, Premarital Agreements, Spousal Support, Visitation Rights, Juvenile Law, Wills.
See Professional Biographies, CHICAGO, ILLINOIS

Copp, Kimberly M. '71 '97 C.473 B.S. L.365 J.D. [Shefsky&F.]
Coppa, Karen M. '59 '85 C.783 B.A. L.861 J.D. Chicago Law Dept.
Coppin, Michael D. '64 '97 C.339 B.A. L.146 J.D. [Ⓐ Mayer,B.R.&M.]

Corbett, John J., & Associates, (AV) '53 '80 C.801 B.S. L.589 J.D.
33 North La Salle Street, 60602
Telephone: 312-558-1900 Telefax: 312-750-0632
Email: john.corbett@corbettlawoffices.com URL: http://www.corbettlawoffices.com
Associate: Paul L. Jacobs.
Personal Injury, Medical Malpractice, Products Liability, Negligence, Construction Accidents, Wrongful Death and Automobile Accidents, Nursing Home Litigation, Airplane Crash Litigation, Maritime Personal Injury, Railroad Accidents, Police Misconduct, Sexual Harassment.
See Professional Biographies, CHICAGO, ILLINOIS

Corbin, William E. '55 '80 C.93 B.S. L.477 J.D. [Perkins C.]
Corboy, Philip H., (AV) '24 '49 L.424 J.D. [Corboy&D.]
Corboy, Philip Harnett, Jr., (AV) '50 '78 C.884 B.S. L.209 J.D. [Corboy&D.]

Corboy & Demetrio, P.C., (AV)
33 North Dearborn Street 21st Floor, 60602
Telephone: 312-346-3191 FAX: 312-346-5562 TDD: 312-236-3191
Email: phc9@corboydemetrio.com URL: http://www.corboydemetrio.com
Philip H. Corboy; Thomas A. Demetrio; Philip Harnett Corboy, Jr.;—Robert J. Bingle; Francis Patrick Murphy; Susan J. Schwartz; René A. Torrado, Jr.; Michael K. Demetrio; Shawn S. Kasserman; Barry R. Chafetz; Daniel M. Kotin; David R. Barry Jr.;—Thomas F. Boleky; William T. Gibbs; Daniel S. Kirschner; Kenneth T. Lumb; Douglas Petrovic; Margaret M. Power; Edward G. Willer; Michelle M. Kohut; Michael J. Mathew.
Plaintiff's Personal Injury and Wrongful Death Litigation, with an emphasis on Commercial and General Aviation, Professional and Hospital Negligence, FELA, Product Liability, Premises, Construction, Vehicular, Railroad and Commercial Litigation.
Reference: LaSalle Bank N.A., Chicago, Illinois.
See Professional Biographies, CHICAGO, ILLINOIS

Corby, Brian A. '76 '03 C.93 B.S. L.424 J.D. [Ⓐ Belgrade&O.]
Corby, Francis M., (AV) '16 '42 C&L.424 A.B. 77 W. Washington St.
Corcoran, Theresa A. '— '89 C.339 B.A. L.46 J.D. 332 S. Michigan Avenue
Corday, Amy B. '59 '86 C.860 B.A. L.910 J.D.
Staff Attorney, CCC Information Services, Inc.
Corday, Lane Allan, (AV) '54 '80 C&L.339 B.S., J.D. [Bowman&C.]
Cordes, Kelly '77 '04 C.338 B.S. L.209 J.D. [Ⓢ Winston&S.]
Cordill, Stephen R. '56 '81 C.347 B.S. L.602 J.D. Touche Ross & Co.
Core, Julia M. '56 '83 C.57 B.A. L.861 J.D. [Ⓐ N.R.Novak]
Corey, Elizabeth L., (AV) '— '82 C.108 A.B. L.564 J.D. [Foley&L.]
Corey, Harold '09 '38 L.365 LL.B. 655 W. Irving Pk. Rd.
Corkery, John E. '43 '67 C.734 B.S. L.597 J.D.
Prof. of Law and Assoc. Dean, John Marshall Law Sch.
Corn, Albert A. '11 '34 L.144 LL.B. 221 N. LaSalle St.
Cornblath, Glen R. '58 '83 C.597 B.A. L.659 J.D. [Krasnow S.C.]
Cornell, Catherine H. '— '02 Staff Atty., Legal Assistance Found. of Metro. Chicago
Cornell, Kimberly J. '— '97 C.174 B.A. L.966 J.D. [Pedersen&H.]
Cornell, Theodore E., III, (AV) '49 '75 C.602 A.B. L.597 J.D. [Seyfarth S.]
Cornell, Trent P. '71 '97 C.966 B.A. L.602 J.D. 55 W. Monroe St., Ste. 500
Cornfield, Gilbert A., (AV) '31 '54 C&L.145 B.A., J.D. [Cornfield&F.]
Cornfield, Michael J. '55 '80 C.338 B.A. L.365 J.D. 6153 N. Milwaukee Ave.

Cornfield and Feldman, (AV)
25 East Washington Street, Suite 1400, 60602
Telephone: 312-236-7800 FAX: 312-236-6686
Members of Firm: Arnold E. Charnin (1933-1978); Melissa J. Auerbach; J. Dale Berry; Gilbert A. Cornfield; Gilbert Feldman; David M. Goldberg; Barbara J. Hillman; Jacob Pomeranz; Robert A. Seltzer; Richard J. Tupper; Jim M. Vainikos; Stephen A. Yokich;—Gail E. Mrozowski; Peter C. Swanson. Of Counsel: Broudy Simons.
Labor Relations, Employment and Employee Benefit Law. General Practice. Workers Compensation. Trials. Appellate Practice.
See Professional Biographies, CHICAGO, ILLINOIS

Corns, Carole A. '63 '91 C.347 B.S. L.477 J.D. [Pugh,J.J.&Q.]
Cornwell, Barbara E. L. '60 '86
C&L.734 B.A., J.D. Sen. Atty, General Growth Properties, Inc.
Cornwell, Joel R. '53 '84 C.229 B.A. L.734 J.D. John Marshall Law Sch.
Corotis, Ashley H. '77 '02 C.608 B.A. L.209 J.D. 205 W. Wacker, Ste. 1220
Corrado, Philip C., Jr., (BV) '26 '58 L.209 LL.B. 8130 Catherine St.
Corrado, Regine W. '61 '91 C.999 L.464 LL.M. [Baker&M.]
Corré, Jacob I. '59 '86 C.145 A.B. L.976 J.D. [Jenner&B.]
Correa, Mario, Law Offices of '— '97
C.339 B.A. L.424 J.D. 1045 W. Belmont Ave., Ste. 200
Corrigan, James A., (AV) '45 '71 C.424 B.B.A. L.365 J.D. [J.A.Corrigan]
Corrigan, John C. '67 '94 C.97 B.A. L.209 J.D. [Ⓒ Dykema G.P.]

Corrigan, James A., Ltd., (AV)
39 South La Salle, Suite 610, 60603
Telephone: 312-853-2771 Fax: 312-853-3180
Email: jacorr@aol.com
James A. Corrigan.
Personal Injury, Negligence, Products Liability and Workers Compensation Law. Civil Trial Practice in all State and Federal Courts.
See Professional Biographies, CHICAGO, ILLINOIS

Corsiglia, Christina Karcher '62 '86 C.293 B.A. L.880 J.D. [Winston&S.]
Corso, Jeffrey D. '64 '89 C.339 B.A. L.802 J.D. [Ⓐ Rock F.]
Cortesi, Kenneth J., (AV) '42 '72 C.339 B.S. L.209 J.D.
Chf. Atty., Chicago Transit Auth.
Cortez, Elizabeth S. '72 '01 C.339 B.A. L.365 J.D. U.S. Govt., Nat. Labor Rel. Bd.
Corti, Peter D., (AV) '45 '71 C.415 B.S. L.209 J.D. [Corti,F.&A.]
Corti, Freeman and Aleksy, (AV) 180 N. La Salle St., Ste. 2910
Corwin, Frances '18 '41 C&L.145 A.B., J.D. Legal Aid Bur.
Corwin, Sherman P., (AV) '17 '41 C&L.145 A.B., J.D. 233 S. Wacker Dr.
Cosby, Richard W., (AV) '42 '68 C.575 B.A. L.339 J.D. [Cosby,O.&B.]
Cosby, Oltman & Bell, P.C., (AV) 77 W. Washington St.
Cosentino, Patricia L. '57 '85 C.339 B.S. L.365 J.D.
V.P. Fin. Admn., Heartland Alliance for Human Needs & Human Rights
Cosgrave, Carmel M., (AV) '— '80 C.1016 B.A. L.424 J.D. [O'Hagan,S.&A.]
Cosgrove, Ellen M. '62 '92 C.518 B.A. L.145 J.D.
(adm. in NY; not adm. in IL) Dean, Univ. of Chicago Law School
Cosgrove, Richard A., (AV) '— '77 C.162 B.A. L.352 J.D. [Chapman&C.]
Costa, Mark A. '56 '82 C.276 B.S. L.339 J.D. [Kelly,O.M.D.&R.]
Costanzo, David P. '64 '92 C.659 B.S. L.477 J.D. Lazard Frerest Co.
Costas, Pamela G. '65 '90 C.339 B.S. L.477 J.D.
Asst. Gen. Coun, Loyola University of Chicago
Costello, Colleen '75 '01 C.679 B.A. L.424 J.D. [Ⓐ Cremer,K.S.&S.]
Costello, James J. '34 '75 C.424 B.S. L.365 J.D. Asst. States Atty.
Costello, James Paul, (AV) '53 '78 C.339 B.A. L.209 J.D. [J.P.Costello]
Costello, John F., Jr. '75 '03 C.1082 B.S. L.365 J.D. [Ⓐ Jenner&B.]
Costello, John W., (AV) '47 '72 C.363 B.S. L.209 J.D. [Wildman,H.A.&D.]
Costello, Robert L. '59 '89 C.589 B.A. L.424 J.D. Ill. State Labor Rel. Board
Costello, T. Brent '52 '78 C.976 B.A. L.276 J.D.
(adm. in NY; not adm. in IL) [Ⓐ McBreen&K.]
Costello, James Paul, Ltd., (AV) 150 N. Wacker Dr.
Costigan, Matthew D. '70 '98 C&L.597 B.A., J.D. [Ⓐ Winston&S.]
Costin, Rosemary '62 '89 C.720 B.A. L.339 J.D. Asst. Pub. Def.
Coston, James E. '55 '80 C.597 B.A. L.209 J.D. [Coston&R.]
Coston & Rademacher 105 W. Adams, Suite 1400
Cotiguala, Jack A., (AV) '51 '79 C.339 B.S. L.146 J.D. [J.Cotiguala]
Cotiguala, Jack, (AV) 431 S. Dearborn St., Apt. 606
Cotillas, Eduardo M. '56 '85 L.424 J.D. [Pugh,J.J.&Q.]
Cotrupe, Michele '75 '00 C.886 B.A. L.209 J.D. [Ⓐ Asher,G.G.&D.]
Cotsirilos, George J., (AV) '20 '42 C&L.145 B.A., LL.B. [Cotsirilos,T.&S.]

Cotsirilos, Tighe & Streicker, Ltd., (AV)
Suite 600, 33 North Dearborn Street, 60602
Telephone: 312-263-0345 Facsimile: 312-263-4670
George J. Cotsirilos; John Powers Crowley (1936-1989); Ann C. Tighe; James R. Streicker; Theodore T. Poulos;—Terence H. Campbell; Tyson K. Harper. Of Counsel: Prentice H. Marshall (1926-2004).
White Collar Criminal Trial and Appellate Practice, Complex Civil Litigation, Administrative Enforcement Actions, Corporate Investigations.
See Professional Biographies, CHICAGO, ILLINOIS

Cotter, Anne B. '62 '87 C.424 B.A. L.339 J.D. V.P. & Gen. Coun., Bejco Development
Cotter, Carrie W. '— '98 C.228 B.A. L.347 J.D. [Ⓐ Sidley A.B.&W.]
Cotter, Dennis J., (BV) '— '85 C.602 B.B.A. L.209 J.D. [O'Hagan,S.&A.]
Cotter, Elizabeth J. '77 '03 C.475 B.A. L.1065 J.D. [Ⓐ Sedgwick,D.M.&A.]
Cotter, Patrick J., (AV) '— '83 C.338 B.S. L.569 J.D. [Arnstein&L.]
Cottier, Derek L. '55 '84 C.732 B.A. L.477 J.D. [Schwartz C.]
Cotton, Benjamin B. '76 '02
C.701 B.S.M.E. L.365 J.D. [Ⓐ Brinks H.G.&L.] (See Pat. Sect.)
Cotton, Deborah L. '53 '81 C.589 B.A. L.339 J.D. [Ⓢ Sidley A.B.&W.]
Cotton, Eugene, (AV) '14 '36 C.563 B.S.S. L.178 LL.B. 5050 S. Lake Shore Dr.
Couch, James R., Jr. '43 '73 C.589 B.S. L.209 J.D. [J.Couch&Assoc.]
Couch, James, & Associates 77 W. Washington St., Ste. 1712
Coughlan, James B. '— '89 C.98 B.S. L.209 J.D. [Kirkland&E.]
Coughlan, Kenneth L. '40 '67 C.602 B.A. L.597 J.D. [Kelly,O.M.D.&R.]
Coughlin, Joseph E., (AV) '42 '67 C.383 B.S. L.309 LL.B. [Lord,B.&B.]
Coughlin, Laurence L., (AV) '55 '82 C.339 B.S. L.209 J.D. [Coughlin&G.]
Coughlin, Terrance J., (AV) '48 '77 C.792 B.S. L.146 J.D. 39 S. LaSalle St. (Pat.)
Coughlin & Geleerd, LLP, (AV) 30 North LaSalle Street, Suite 3400
Coukos, Stephen J. '70 '95 C.103 B.A. L.347 J.D. [Ⓐ Levin&P.]
Coulson, William R., (AV) '47 '72 C.197 A.B. L.339 J.D. [Gold&C.]
Coult, John H. '39 '66 C.645 B.S.E.E. L.273 LL.B. 1129 W. Wellington Avenue (Pat.)
Courter, Ann C. '55 '81 C.352 B.A. L.976 J.D. Legal Assist. Found. of Chgo.
Courtheoux, Suzanne M. '— '04 C.976 B.A. L.145 J.D. [Ⓐ Jenner&B.]
Cousineau, Helen M. '64 '95 C.1109 B.A. L.94 J.D.
(adm. in NY; not adm. in IL) Sr. Mgr., Deloitte & Touche LLP‡
Cousino, Darrah Desmond '— '82
C.608 B.A. L.209 J.D. Asst. V.P., AMA Insurance Agency, Inc.
Cousins, Ertharin '57 '82 C.339 B.A. L.280 J.D. 8541 S. Cottage Grove
Cousins, William, Jr., (AV) '27 '53 C.339 B.A. L.309 LL.B. Jus., Appl. Ct.
Couture, Timothy R. '68 '93 C.339 B.A. L.209 J.D. [Ⓐ Johnson&B.]
Cover, Melissa L. '78 '03 C.339 B.A. L.910 J.D. [Ⓐ Kelly,O.M.D.&R.]
Covey, J. Tyson '65 '91 C.1267 A.B. L.339 J.D. [Mayer,B.R.&M.]

Covington, George M.
(See Lake Forest)

Covy, Karen A., (BV) '— '84 C.932 B.A. L.602 J.D.
180 North LaSalle Street Suite 2424
Cowan, Kristen '— '02 C.674 B.S.E. L.597 J.D. [Ⓐ Winston&S.]
Cowan, Philip '39 '62 C.339 B.A. L.209 J.D. [Berger,N.&F.]
Cowart, Marina Lark '77 '02 C.385 B.A. L.424 J.D. Illinois App. Ct.
Cowell, Susan E. '— '00 C.957 B.S. L.146 J.D. [Ⓐ Mayer,B.R.&M.]
Cowen, Rachel B. '— '93 C.234 B.A. L.146 J.D. [Connelly S.H.]
Cowen, Richard A., (AV) '34 '59 C&L.597 B.S., J.D. [Stahl C.C.]
Cowin, Merle Teitelbaum '54 '78 C.608 B.A. L.597 J.D. [DLPiper R.G.C.U.]
Cox, Jacqueline P. '— '75 C.188 B.A. L.94 J.D. Cook Co. Cir. Ct.
Cox, Jeffrey M. '— '91 C.347 B.A. L.1119 J.D. [Ⓐ Banner&W.]
Cox, John F. '70 '95 C.347 B.A. L.145 J.D. [Jenner&B.]
Cox, Julia Diamond '71 '95 C.339 B.S. L.145 J.D. [McDermott W.&E.]
Cox, Lisa H. '— '00 C&L.339 B.S., J.D. [Ⓐ Kirkland&E.]
Cox, Michael A. '72 '99 C.221 B.A. L.339 J.D. [Ⓐ Seyfarth S.]

Cox, Michael John .... '66 '92 C.932 B.S. L.209 J.D. [Goldberg&G.]

Cox, Pamela L. .... '— '00 C.347 B.S. L.602 J.D. [[A] Marshall,G.&B.] (See Pat. Sect.)

Cox, Robert W. '37 '62 C&L.602 B.S., J.D.
(adm. in IN; not adm. in IL) 130 E. Randolph Dr.‡

Coy, Robert W. .... '42 '69 C.221 B.S.B.A. L.1119 J.D. I.R.S.

Coyle, Lynn .... '64 '91 C.424 B.A. L.339 J.D. Travelers & Immigrants Aid

Coyle, N. Paul .... '68 '94 C.209 B.S. L.365 J.D. [Gardner C.&D.]

Coyne, Daniel W., (AV) .... '46 '71 C.436 B.A. L.309 J.D. [O'Keefe,L.&H.]

Coyne, John C. .... '66 '98 C.363 B.A. L.989 J.D. [[A] Belgrade&O.]

Coyne, Joseph F., (AV) .... '43 '69 C.339 B.S. L.309 J.D. [Ephraim&Assoc.]

Coyne, Raymond M. '57 '85 C.339 B.A. L.209 J.D.
Sr. Coun., U.S. Cellular Corporation

Cozen O'Connor, A Professional Corporation, (AV) [BR]
222 South Riverside Plaza, Suite 1500, 60606 ⊙
Telephone: 312-382-3100 Fax: 312-382-8910
Email: postmaster@cozen.com URL: http://www.cozen.com
Firm Members in Chicago: Richard L. Blatt; Kevin P. Caraher; Zacarias R. Chacon; Martha E. Conlin; Larry R. Eaton; Jay M. Goldstein (Not admitted in IL); Tia C. Glass; Robert W. Hammesfahr; Gregory D. Hopp; Josh M. Kantrow; Bruce M. Lichtcsien; Joseph G. Lyons; Anthony J. Morrone; Catherine A.T. Nelson; Lori S. Nugent; Marc A. Polansky; Margaret A. Reetz; Leena Soni; James I. Tarman, Jr.; Matthew T. Walsh. Firm Associates in Chicago: Jeremy S. Baker; Jeffrey C. Calabrese; D. Christine Ducat; S. Ellyn Farley; John E. Flaherty; Maya Hoffman; Keith E. Horton; Daniel R. Johnson; Christopher H. Murphy; Theodore W. Pannkoke; Beth A. Stroup.
Advertising Liability/Personal Injury, Alternative Dispute Resolution, Agent/Broker Liability, Antitrust and Unfair Competition, Appellate Practice, Arbitration and Alternative Dispute Resolution, Arson and Fraud, Aviation Litigation, Bad Faith Litigation, Bankruptcy, Insolvency and Restructuring, Business Torts, Cargo Losses, Class Actions, Multi-District Litigation and Other Consolidated Claims, Commercial General Liability, Commercial Litigaion, Construction Law and Litigation, Construction Liability, Corporate and Partnership Law, Corporate Planning, Crisis Management, Cross Border Transactions, Directors' and Officers' Liability, E-Commerce, Internet and Cyber-Peril Insurance, Emerging Business and Venture Capital, Employee Benefits and Executive Compensation, Employment, Labor and Employee Benefits, Environmental Coverage, Environmental Litigation, Estate Planning and Administration, Excess and Surplus Lines, Family Law, Fidelity and Surety, Financial Services, Health Law, Health Care Malpractice, Insurance Corporate and Regulatory Law, Intellectual Property, Intellectual Property Litigation, International Tax and Estate Planning, Labor and Employment, Life, Health and Disability Maritime Law, Medical Device and Drug Litigation, Mergers and Acquisitions, Personal Lines, Privacy Law and Regulation, Private Wealth Services, Products Liability, Professional Liability, Property Insurance, Public and Project Finance, Public Utilities and Energy, Punitive Damages, Real Estate, Real Estate Litigation, Reinsurance, Securities, Securities Litigation and Civil RICO, Security and Premises Liability, Tax, Tax Litigation, Toxic and Other Mass Torts, White Collar Crime.
Philadelphia, Pennsylvania Office: 1900 Market Street, 19103. Telephones: 215-665-2000; 800-523-2900. Fax: 215-665-2013.
Charlotte, North Carolina Office: One First Union Center, Suite 2100, 301 S. College Street, 28202. Telephones: 704-376-3400; 800-762-3575. Fax: 704-334-3351.
Dallas, Texas Office: 2300 BankOne Center, 1717 Main Street, 75201. Telephones: 214-462-3000; 800-448-1207. Fax: 214-462-3299.
New York, N.Y. Offices: 45 Broadway Atrium, 16th Floor, 10006. Telephones: 212-509-9400; 800-437-7040. Fax: 212-509-9492. Midtown Office: 909 Third Avenue, 17th Floor, 10022. Telephones: 212-509-9400; 800-437-7040. Fax: 212-207-4938.
West Conshohocken, Pennsylvania Office: 200 Four Falls Corporate Center, Suite 400, P.O. Box 800, 19428. Telephone: 610-941-5400; 800-379-0695. Fax: 610-941-0711.
San Diego, California Office: Suite 1610, 501 West Broadway, 92101. Telephones: 619-234-1700; 800-782-3366. Fax: 619-234-7831.
Los Angeles, California Office: 777 South Figueroa Street, Suite 2850, 90017. Telephones: 213-892-7900; 800-563-1027. Fax: 213-892-7999.
Seattle, Washington Office: Suite 5200, Washington Mutual Tower, 1201 Third Avenue, 98101. Telephones: 206-340-1000; 800-423-1950. Fax: 206-621-8783.
Newark, New Jersey Office: One Newark Center, Suite 1900, 07102. Telephone: 973-286-1200; 888-200-9521. Fax: 973-242-2121.
Atlanta, Georgia Office: Suite 2200, SunTrust Plaza, 303 Peachtree Street, N.E., 30308. Telephones: 404-572-2000; 800-890-1393. Fax: 404-572-2199.
London, England Office: Fountain House, 130 Fenchurch Street, London EC3M 5DJ. Telephone: 011-44-20-7864-2000. Fax: 011-44-20-7864-2013.
Wilmington, Delaware Office: Chase Manhattan Centre, 1201 North Market Street, Suite 1400, 19801. Telephone: 302-295-2000; 888-207-2440. Fax: 302-295-2013.
Las Vegas, Nevada Office (Affiliated with the Law Offices of J. Goldberg & D. Grossman): 601 South Rancho, Suite 20, 89106. Telephone: 800-782-3366.
San Francisco, California Office: 425 California Street, Suite 2400, 94104-2203. Telephone: 415-617-6100; 800-818-0165. Fax: 415-617-6101.
Washington, D.C. Office: 1667 K Street, NW, 20006. Telephone: 202-912-4800; 800-540-1355. Fax: 202-912-4830.
Cherry Hill, New Jersey Office: LibertyView, Suite 300, 457 Haddonfield Road, P.O. Box 5459, 08002-2220. Telephone: 856-910-5000; 800-989-0499. Fax: 856-910-5075.
Wichita, Kansas Office: 8415 E. 21st Street, Suite 220, 67206. Telephone: 316-609-3380. Fax: 316-634-3837.
Denver, Colorado Office: 707 17th Street, Suite 3100, 80202. Telephone: 303-292-9080. Fax: 303-292-9650.
Trenton, New Jersey Office: 144-B West State Street, 08608. Telephone: 609-989-8620.
Houston, Texas Office: 1 Houston Center, 1221 McKinney Street, Suite 2900, 77010. Telephone: 800-448-8502; 832-214-3900. Fax: 832-214-3905.
Toronto, Ontario Office: One Queen Street East, Suite 2000, M5C 2W5. Telephone: 416-361-2000. Fax: 416-361-1405.
Santa Fe, New Mexico Office: 125 Lincoln Avenue, Suite 400, 87501. Telephones: 505-820-3346; 866-231-0144. Fax: 505-820-3347.

See Professional Biographies, CHICAGO, ILLINOIS

Cozza, Richard S. .... '69 '03 C.589 B.S. L.1000 J.D. [[A] McDermott W.&E.]

Cozzi, Eileen B. .... '72 '97 C.424 BB.A. L.209 J.D. [[A] Schoenberg,F.N.&R.]

Cozzi, Robert J., (BV) .... '54 '81 C.339 B.S. L.209 J.D. 20 N. Clark St.

Cozzola, Richard T. .... '52 '80 C&L.424 B.A., J.D. Loyola Univ.

Craane, Paul C. .... '— '93 C.339 B.S.M.E. L.589 J.D. [Marshall,G.&B.] (See Pat. Sect.)

Crabb, David L. '39 '77 C.299 A.B. L.145 J.D.
(adm. in MA; not adm. in IL)
Sr. Dir. for Develop. & Asst. Gen. Coun., Univ. of Chicago

Crabtree, Juli K. .... '60 '85 C.624 B.A. L.597 J.D. 2011 W. Bradley Pl.

Craddock, J. Patrick, (AV) .... '34 '68 C.602 B.S. L.365 J.D. [Stride,C.&S.]

Craddock, Michael J. .... '67 '94 C.363 B.A. L.1187 J.D. [[A] Stride,C.&S.]

Craft, C. Edward .... '74 '00 C.477 B.A. L.339 J.D. [[A] Merlo K.B.&G.]

Craft, Jason M. .... '75 '01 C.475 B.A. L.209 J.D. [[A] Tressler,S.M.&P.]

Craft, Kimberly A. .... '76 '01 C.475 B.A. L.424 J.D. [[A] Cassiday,S.&G.]

Craft, Melodie K. .... '75 '00 C.645 B.A. L.339 J.D. [[A] Littler M.]

Craig, Richard M. .... '67 '92 C.352 B.A. L.424 J.D. 30 North La Salle Street, Suite 3900

Craig, Thomas M. .... '55 '83 C.801 B.A. L.767 J.D. [Kamenear K.S.&C.]

Crain, Lawrence J., (AV) .... '53 '83 C.339 B.S. L.424 J.D. [Greer,B.&C.] (Pat.)

Craine, Arnold H. .... '28 '52 C&L.339 A.B., LL.B. 221 N. LaSalle St.

Cramarosso, Michael A. .... '60 '85 C.209 B.A. L.228 J.D. [Shefsky&F.]

Cramer, Jordan M. .... '68 '93 C.339 B.S. L.146 J.D. [Levenfeld P.]

Cramer, Michael H., (AV) .... '— '88 C&L.477 B.A., J.D. [Ogletree,D.N.S.&S.]

Crane, Anne Janet .... '— '82 C.1183 B.A. L.589 J.D. 4250 N. Marine Dr., Ste. 532

Crane, Charlotte .... '51 '77 C.681 A.B. L.477 J.D. Prof. of Law, Northwestern Univ.

Crane, Edward M., (AV) .... '57 '82 C&L.209 B.S.C., J.D. [Skadden,A.S.M.&F.]

Crane, Eugene, (AV) .... '30 '54 C.1016 L.146 LL.B. [Crane,H.S.W.&C.]

Crane, Karen S. .... '54 '82 C.338 B.S. L.146 J.D. V.P., JMB Ins. Agcy.‡

Crane, Ken, (AV) .... '— '86 C&L.339 B.S., J.D. [Perkins C.]

Crane, Lauren R. .... '76 '99 C.473 B.A. L.146 J.D. Two North LaSalle Street, Suite 2200

Crane, Michael E., (AV) .... '40 '68 [Crane&N.]

Crane, Phillip Mark .... '59 '84 C.679 B.A. L.1119 J.D. [Segal M.S.&M.]

Crane, Heyman, Simon, Welch & Clar, (AV) .... 135 S. LaSalle St.

Crane and Norcross, (AV) .... 2 N. La Salle St.

Cranley, Grace Winkler .... '64 '93 C.339 B.A. L.146 J.D. [Leo&W.]

Craven, David J., (AV) .... '58 '85 C.352 B.A. L.273 J.D. [Riggle&C.]

Craven, George W., (AV) .... '51 '76 C.602 B.A. L.309 J.D. [Mayer,B.R.&M.]

Craven, Harold L. .... '28 '51 C&L.209 LL.B. 208 S La Salle St. Ste

Craven, Jack S. .... '63 '88 C.347 B.A. L.999 J.D. 188 W. Randolph St.‡

Craven, John P. '24 '85 L.273 J.D.
(adm. in HI; not adm. in IL) [[C] Riggle&C.]

Craven, Michael C. .... '57 '84 C.589 B.S. L.365 J.D. 208 South LaSalle Street Suite 1400

Craven, Donald M., P.C.
(See Springfield)

Crawford, Amy C. .... '74 '00 C.602 B.A. L.352 J.D. [[A] Scandaglia&R.]

Crawford, Bradley W. '66 '03
C.339 B.S. L.146 J.D. [[A] McDonnell B.H.&B.] (See Pat. Sect.)

Crawford, Christopher S. .... '— '99 C.339 B.S. L.221 J.D. [[A] Hennessy&R.]

Crawford, David H. .... '56 '86 C.339 B.A. L.276 J.D. 2 N. Riverside Plaza

Crawford, Dewey B., (AV) .... '— '67 C.197 A.B. L.477 J.D. [Foley&L.]

Crawford, John D. .... '24 '51 C.424 A.B. L.276 J.D. U.S. RR Retirement Bd.

Crawford, Mary C. .... '69 '98 C.494 B.A. L.1117 J.D. [[A] Cassiday,S.&G.]

Crawford, Sandra .... '— '89 C.209 B.A. L.365 J.D. [Feingold&C.]

Crawford, Thomas M. .... '— '92 C.352 B.S. L.1187 J.D. [Litchfield C.]

Crawley, James P. .... '64 '89 C.424 B.A. L.734 J.D. [J.Crawley&Assoc.]

Crawley, Thomas W. '44 '75 C&L.838 B.S., J.D.
(adm. in TN; not adm. in IL) U.S. Dept. of Health & Human Servs.

Crawley, James, & Associates, Ltd.
2 North La Salle Street, Suite 1776, 60602
Telephone: 312-750-1300 Toll Free: 1-866-324-2896 Fax: 312-873-3705
Email: info@312law.com URL: http://www.312law.com
James P. Crawley.
Plaintiff's Personal Injury Liability, Medical Malpractice, Birth Trauma, Aviation Liability, Product Liability, Premises Liability, Construction Accidents, Wrongful Death, Vehicular Accident Law, Appellate Practice, ADR, Professional Liability, Torts; Toxic Torts, Workers Compensation.

See Professional Biographies, CHICAGO, ILLINOIS

Cray, Daniel K., (AV) .... '56 '81 C.338 B.S. L.339 J.D. [Iwan C.H.H.&V.] ⊙

Creagan, David J., Jr., (AV) .... '28 '53 C&L.424 LL.B. [Lewis,O.&F.]

Creagh, David R., (AV) .... '59 '85 C&L.602 B.A., J.D. [Hinshaw&C.]

Creamer, Robert A., (AV) '41 '67 C.597 B.A. L.309 LL.B.
V.P. Loss Prevention Coun., Attorneys' Liability Assurance Society, Inc.

Creamer, Terrence T. .... '58 '90 C.589 B.S. L.46 J.D. [Franczek S.]

Creed, Daniel J. .... '48 '75 C.801 B.S. L.146 J.D. Amer. Dental Assn.

Creed, Philip A., (AV) .... '37 '70 C.927 B.A. L.209 J.D. [McCarthy&L.]

Creel, B. Wayne .... '76 '03 C.880 B.A. L.424 J.D. [[A] Schwartz C.]

Creen, James V., (BV) .... '33 '62 C.339 B.S. L.209 J.D. 188 W. Randolph St, Ste. 1300

Creevy, Robert X. '62 '94 C.321 B.A. L.424 J.D.
Vice President, The Northern Trust Co.

Crement, Anthony J., (AV) .... '44 '69 C.1024 B.A. L.309 J.D. [Franczek S.]

Cremer, William J., (AV) .... '56 '81 C.1151 B.A. L.300 J.D. [Cremer,K.S.&S.]

Cremer, Kopon, Shaughnessy & Spina, LLC, (AV)
180 North LaSalle Street, Suite 3300, 60601
Telephone: 312-726-3800 Fax: 312-726-3818
URL: http://www.ckslaw.com
William J. Cremer; Andrew Kopon, Jr.; Brian P. Shaughnessy; Francis A. Spina; Edmund J. Siegert; Gary T. Jansen; John P. Lynch, Jr.; Thomas R. Pender; Michael A. Airdo; Brian A. O'Gallagher; Kimberly A. Ross;—Kristina M. Beck; David T. Brown; Bradley M. Burd; Jeremy T. Burton; Paul Patrick Cella; Jennifer Colvin; Colleen Costello; Stacy Dolan Fulco; Kevin Georgerian; Timothy E. Hoerman; Mario M. Iveljic; Gregory James McKenna; Matthew W. Miller; Nicole D. Milos; Jacob C. Murov; Shanon Shumpert; Matthew Tibble; Dennis N. Ventura; Heather Watterson; Joshua D. Yeager.
Complex Civil Litigation Defense, including Product Liability, Construction Law, Insurance Coverage, Commercial Litigation, Drug and Medical Device Litigation, Employment Law, Toxic Torts, Commercial Real Estate, University and College Law and all aspects of Trial and Appellate work in both State and Federal Courts.

See Professional Biographies, CHICAGO, ILLINOIS

Cremieux, Richard J., (AV) .... '47 '76 C&L.424 B.A., J.D. [Baker&M.]

Cremin, Patrick Christopher, Jr. '57 '85 C&L.767 B.A., J.D.
200 N. LaSalle St., Ste. 2050

Cremin, Susan E., (AV) .... '47 '77 C.881 A.B. L.597 J.D. [Winston&S.]

Crenshaw, Mayron R. .... '23 '55 C.597 L.410 LL.B. 6326 S. Cottage Grove

Creppel, Morgan Gary '67 '01 C.659 B.A. L.602 J.D.
Asst. State's Atty., Cook Co. State's Atty.' Off.

Cressey, Bryan C. .... '49 '76 C.911 B.A. L.309 J.D. First Chicago Inves. Corp.

Crews, Halbert O., (AV) .... '11 '34 C&L.339 A.B., LL.B. Ste., 3000, One IBM Plaza

Crews, Kenneth D. .... '66 '93 C.659 B.S.E. L.145 J.D. [Goodsmith G.&U.]

Crick, Glen D. .... '48 '78 C.1151 B.A. L.146 J.D. [G.D.Crick]

Crick, Glen D., Ltd., Law Offices of .... 205 W. Wacker Dr., Ste. 1220

Crider, Dale R., (P.C.) '47 '72
C&L.352 B.B.A., J.D. Asst. V.P. & Asst. Gen. Coun., CNA

Crifase, Steven A., (AV) .... '57 '82 C.221 B.S.B.A. L.424 J.D. [S.A.Crifase]

Crifase, Steven A., Ltd., (AV)
8 South Michigan Suite 2000, 60203
Telephone: 312-855-0511 FAX: 312-855-0537
Email: crifase@aol.com URL: http://www.stevencrifase.com
Steven A. Crifase.
Personal Injury including Auto Negligence, Medical Negligence, Products Liability and Worker's Compensation.
Reference: American National Bank.

See Professional Biographies, CHICAGO, ILLINOIS

Crihfield, Philip J., (AV) .... '45 '71 C.679 B.S. L.365 J.D. [Sidley A.B.&W.] (Pat.)

Crillé, Karen Michels .... '49 '80 C.477 B.A. L.365 J.D. Asst. Atty. Gen.

Crimmins, Paul M. .... '63 '89 C&L.424 B.S., J.D. [Mayer,B.R.&M.]

Cripe, Andrew B. .... '73 '97 C.494 B.A. L.424 J.D. [Hinshaw&C.]

Cripe, Kenneth A. .... '67 '99 C.338 B.S. L.209 J.D. [[A] Conway&M.]

Crisham, Catherine L. .... '74 '00 C.602 B.A. L.276 J.D. [[A] Winston&S.]

Crisham, Catherine M., (AV) .... '66 '91 C.321 B.A. L.424 J.D. [Bates&C.]

Crisham, Thomas M., (AV) .... '39 '65 C&L.424 B.B.A., J.D. [Crisham&K.]

Crisham & Kubes, Ltd., (AV) [BR]
30 North LaSalle Street, Suite 2800, 60602
Telephone: 312-327-2500 Fax: 312-327-2450
URL: http://www.crishamlaw.com
Thomas M. Crisham; Jeffrey T. Kubes; Michael C. Bruck; John P. O'Malley; Daniel L. Stanner; Edward Fitzsimmons Dunne; Jean M. Prendergast;—Thomas W. Mulcahy; David J. Sullivan; John R. Bowley; Michael J. Faley; John P. Lynch; Jamie L. Ross; John E. Newton; Kathleen J. Doyle.

(This Listing Continued)

Crisham & Kubes, Ltd. (Continued)

General Civil Trial Practice, Complex Litigation, Commercial Law, Construction Law, Professional Liability, Environmental Litigation, Product Liability, Insurance/Reinsurance Coverage and Litigation, Labor and Employment, ERISA Litigation, Constitutional and Local Government Law, Appellate Law, Alternative Dispute Resolution, Intellectual Property Law, Trademark, Copyright, Unfair Competition, and Trade Secret Litigation.

See Professional Biographies, CHICAGO, ILLINOIS

Crispino, Joseph M. '43 '68 C.589 B.S. L.146 J.D. 6914 W. North Ave.
Criswell, Jacqueline A., (AV) '56 '81 C.937 B.M. L.209 J.D. [Tressler,S.M.&P.]
Criswell, Robert M. '— '94 C.966 B.A. L.209 J.D. [Chapman&C.]
Crivlare, Laura '60 '85 C.209 B.S. L.146 J.D. Admin. Law J., State Dept. of Employ. Sec.
Criz, Jesse A. '73 '98 C.339 B.S. L.424 J.D. [Ⓐ DLPiper R.G.C.U.]
Croak, Thomas M. '38 '92 C&L.209 M.S., J.D. 2233 N Kenmore Ave
Croghan, Richard '65 '90 C.201 B.S.B.A. L.424 J.D. Ernst & Young
Cromheecke, Jennifer B. '66 '94 C.197 A.B. L.861 J.D. [Ⓐ BryceDowney]
Cromley, J. Timothy '50 '92 C.339 B.S. L.365 J.D. 6617 W. Henderson St.
Crone, Douglas C., (AV) '54 '79 C.339 B.A. L.597 J.D. [Tribler O.&M.]
Cronin, Barbara A. '46 '82 C.339 B.A. L.209 J.D. [Gardner C.&D.]
Cronin, John J., (AV) '49 '76 C.363 B.A. L.146 J.D. [Cronin,P.&C.]
Cronin, Kathleen M. '63 '89 C.93 B.A. L.597 J.D. Gen. Coun. & Corp. Secy., Chicago Mercantile Exch. Inc.
Cronin, Michael J. '61 '89 C.309 B.A. L.597 J.D. [Ⓐ Cantwell&C.]
Cronin, Michael K. '68 '97 C.999 B.A. L.365 J.D. Broadwing Communications LLC
Cronin, Robert E., (AV) '25 '50 C.742 B.S. L.146 J.D. One 1st Nat. Plaza
Cronin, Thomas C. '64 '90 C.309 B.A. L.145 J.D. [Cummins&C.]
Cronin, Thomas G. '78 '04 C.473 B.A. L.424 J.D. [Ⓐ Cassiday,S.&G.]

Cronin, Peters & Cook, P.C., (AV)
221 North La Salle Street, Suite 1454, 60601
Telephone: 312-372-1872 Fax: 312-372-1733
Email: cpcworkcomp@aol.com URL: http://www.lawyers.com/candplaw
Thomas G. Cronin (1920-1999); Kenneth D. Peters; John J. Cronin; Patricia Cronin Cook.
Workers Compensation, Social Security Disability.
Reference: American National Bank and Trust Company of Chicago, Illinois.

See Professional Biographies, CHICAGO, ILLINOIS

Cronson, Robert G. '24 '51 C.197 A.B. L.145 J.D. Auditor Gen.
Crooks, Kendal A., (AV) '24 '52 C&L.424 J.D. 33 N. Dearborn St.‡
Crooks, Wilbur E. '40 '78 C&L.209 J.D. Cir. J.
Crosby, John B. '47 '72 C.910 A.B. L.608 J.D. (adm. in MO; not adm. in IL) American Ostepathic Ass'n.
Cross, Charles W., (AV) '48 '77 C.705 A.B. L.365 J.D. [Fitzgerald&C.]
Cross, Chester J. '31 '63 C.597 L.339 LL.B. P.O. Box 30339
Cross, Jeffery M., (AV) '— '75 C.339 B.A. L.823 J.D. [Freeborn&P.]
Cross, LeRoy, Jr. '54 '81 C.399 B.A. L.209 J.D. [L.Cross]
Cross, Robert P., IV '61 '87 C.209 B.A. L.896 J.D. 1255 N. Asland Ave., Ste. 2
Cross, LeRoy, Law Offices of 33 N. Dearborn St., Ste. 801A
Crossan, John R., (AV) '— '74 C.893 B.S. L.145 J.D. [Chapman&C.] (Pat.)
Crossett, David S., (AV) '— '80 C&L.602 B.A., J.D. [Chapman&C.]
Crossley, Lisa D. '61 '93 C.882 B.A. L.128 J.D. (adm. in PA; not adm. in IL) V. P.; Dir. of Compliance, John Nuveen & Co., Inc.
Crossman, David A., (BV) '41 '78 C.210 B.A. L.339 J.D. 433 Briar Pl.
Crossman, Fred L., Jr. '50 '83 C.197 A.B. L.209 LL.B. 1400 N. State Pkwy.
Croteau, Guy V. '52 '87 C.339 B.A. L.365 J.D. [Immigration]
Crotty, Cassandra A. '72 '98 C.347 B.A.J. L.209 J.D. [Ⓐ R.F.Coleman&Assoc.]
Crotty, James T., (AV) '41 '73 C.339 B.S. L.365 J.D. 20 N. Clark St.
Crotty, Jerome F., (AV) '47 '75 C.801 B.S. L.365 J.D. [Rieck&C.]
Crotty, Sean B. '72 '97 C.347 B.A. L.209 J.D. [Ⓐ R.F.Coleman&Assoc.]
Crouch, Dennis D. '75 '03 C.674 B.S.E. L.145 J.D. [Ⓐ McDonnell B.H.&B.]
Crouch, Franklin M., (AV) '20 '50 C.692 B.S.Physics L.146 J.D. 4600 One IBM Plaza (Pat.)
Crout Ziegler, Amy M. '74 '02 C&L.209 B.S., J.D. [Ⓐ Wallenstein W.&R.]
Crouvisier, Vanessa N. '74 '00 C.145 B.A. L.124 J.D. Jud. Law Clk.
Crow, Keith S., (P.C.) '— '86 C.976 B.S. L.145 J.D. [Kirkland&E.]
Crow, Leeann Marie '75 '01 C.475 B.A. L.424 J.D. [Ⓐ J.J.Roche&Assoc.]
Crowder, Elizabeth '58 '84 C.339 B.A. L.146 J.D. U.S. Dept. of HUD
Crowe, Brian L., (AV) '39 '64 C.177 B.A. L.424 J.D. [Shefsky&F.]
Crowe, Donald R. '46 '71 C.589 B.S.Ed. L.339 J.D. [Mahoney,C.&G.]
Crowe, Jack '60 '89 C.93 B.A. L.424 J.D. [Winston&S.]
Crowl, Matthew C. '62 '89 C.221 B.A. L.145 J.D. Law Clk., U.S. Dist. J.
Crowley, Brendan S. '78 '05 C.339 B.S. L.209 J.D. [Ⓐ Pretzel&S.]
Crowley, Brian P. '72 '97 C.472 B.A. L.339 J.D. [Ⓐ Franczek S.]
Crowley, Cathleen G. '— '03 C.686 B.A. L.1000 J.D. [Ⓐ Karbal,C.E.S.&D.]
Crowley, James M. '57 '82 C.589 B.A. L.209 J.D. [Crowley&L.]
Crowley, Michael J. '51 '79 C.339 B.A. L.46 J.D. Assoc. Gen. Coun., National Futures Assn.
Crowley, Suzanne Marie, (AV) '61 '87 C.589 B.S. L.365 J.D. [Ⓐ Pretzel&S.]
Crowley, Walter L. '40 '64 C&L.339 B.S., LL.B. Pres. & CEO, GIC Capital Mkts., Inc.
Crowley, Wilbert F., Jr., (AV) '40 '65 C.321 B.S. L.477 J.D. [Stahl C.C.]

Crowley Barrett & Karaba, Ltd., (AV) BB
Suite 2310 Two First National Plaza, 20 South Clark Street, 60603
Telephone: 312-726-2468 Fax: 312-726-2741
URL: http://www.cbklaw.com
Members of Firm: Alan Rauh Orschel; Gregory M. White; Charles W. Siragusa; Thomas F. Karaba; Scott D.H. Redman; Jeffrey S. Burns; David C. Birks; Bruno W. Tabis, Jr.; Paul F. Markoff, IV; Karl G. Leinberger; Andrew Nicholas Plasz.
Acquisitions, Divestitures and Mergers, Banking and Corporate, Business Law, Commercial Litigation, Real Estate, Domestic Relations, Probate and Estate Planning Law. General Practice.

See Professional Biographies, CHICAGO, ILLINOIS

Crowley & Lamb, P.C., Law Offices, (BV)
350 North La Salle Street Suite 900, 60610
Telephone: 312-670-6900 Fax: 312-467-5926
URL: http://www.crowleylamb.com
James M. Crowley; Patrick D. Lamb;—William J. Hurley, III; Francis J. Pendergast, III; Joseph Brown (Not admitted in IL); Christopher S. Fowler; Adela C. Lucchesi. Of Counsel: Philip J. Berenz, Law Offices of Philip J. Berenz.
Commercial and Residential Real Estate Acquisition, Development, Contracts, Financing, Litigation and Dispute Resolution, Commercial Litigation, Banking Law.

See Professional Biographies, CHICAGO, ILLINOIS

Crown, James S. '53 '80 C.1307 B.S. L.813 J.D. 222 N. La Salle St.‡
Cruger, James R. '61 '86 C.177 B.A. L.597 J.D. [Perkins C.]
Crull, Jan, Jr. '54 '90 C.06 B.A. L.861 J.D. Coun., SandCru, Inc.
Crumbaugh, David G., (AV) '— '76 C.338 B.S. L.339 J.D. [Latham&W.]
Crumley, Dana Fattore '66 '01 C.597 B.A. L.424 J.D. [Ⓐ Franczek S.]
Crummy, James G. '43 '78 C.424 B.A. L.589 J.D. 155 N. Michigan Avenue, 6th Floor
Crusor, Richard G., Jr. '54 '80 C.589 B.A. L.879 J.D. 201 W. 94th St.★

Cruz, Michael T. '— '97 C.339 B.S.E.E. L.477 J.D. (adm. in CA; not adm. in IL; See Pat. Sect.) [Ⓐ McAndrews,H.&M.]
Cruz, Rachel N. '79 '04 C.103 B.A. L.273 J.D. (adm. in VA; not adm. in IL) [Ⓐ Tabet D.&R.]
Cruz, Scott '77 '02 C.436 B.S. L.339 J.D. [Ⓐ Franczek S.]
Cryar, Mary K. '— '96 C&L.420 B.A., J.D. [Ⓐ Johnson&B.]
Crystal, Debra I. '— '86 C.339 B.A. L.365 J.D. [H.L.Walner&Assoc.]
Crystal, Frederick H. '48 '74 C.98 B.S. L.146 J.D. [Crystal,H.&W.]
Crystal, Jules I., (AV) '— '71 C&L.477 B.A., J.D. [Bryan C.]
Crystal, Heytow & Warnick, P.C., (AV) 111 West Washington Street Suite 1350
Csar, Michael F., (AV) '50 '77 C&L.976 B.A., J.D. [Gardner C.&D.]
Csicsila, Erika, L. '— '05 C&L.477 B.A., J.D. [Ⓐ Schiff H.]
Cubbage, S. Todd '— '93 C.612 B.S. L.862 J.D. [Ⓐ Chapman&C.]
Cubia, Gil R. '— '97 C.477 B.B.A. L.347 J.D. [Ⓐ Pugh,J.J.&Q.]
Cucco, Michael J., (AV) '59 '86 C.207 B.A. L.424 J.D. [Cassiday,S.&G.]
Cuchna, Ronald J., (AV) '47 '72 C.602 B.B.A. L.209 J.D. Union Pacific Railroad Co.
Cuculich, Jennifer L. '78 '03 C.93 B.A. L.424 J.D. [Ⓢ Winston&S.]
Cudahy, Richard D. '26 '55 C.870 B.S. L.976 J.D. Sr. Cir. J., U.S. Ct. of App.‡
Cudnowski, David P. '59 '86 C.694 B.A. L.209 J.D. [D.P.Cudnowski]
Cudnowski, David P., Ltd. 330 North Wabash Avenue, Suite 2604
Cuevas, Carlos J. '54 '82 C&L.209 B.A., J.D. Admin. Law J., Human Rights Comm.
Cuevas, Philip F. '70 '00 C.338 B.S. L.365 J.D. [Ⓐ Dowd&D.] (⊙Highland, IN)
Culbertson, Craig R., (AV) '55 '80 C.198 B.A. L.424 J.D. [McGuirewoods]
Culbertson, Timothy C. '61 '95 C.1293 B.Mus. L.146 J.D. [Ⓐ Mora,B.W.&U.]
Cull, Noreen H. '70 '95 C.424 B.S. L.146 J.D. [Ⓐ Gardner C.&D.]
Cullan, Daniel M. '45 '71 C&L.999 B.A., J.D. (adm. in NE; not adm. in IL) [Ⓒ Lane&L.]
Cullen, Christopher J. '67 '95 C.747 B.A. L.494 J.D. [Ⓐ Winston&S.]
Cullen, Daniel F. '72 '98 C.1349 B.A. L.30 J.D. [Ⓐ Baker&M.]
Cullen, Edward J., Jr. '47 '72 C.1041 B.A. L.884 J.D. (adm. in PA; not adm. in IL) V.P. & Dep. Gen. Coun, Exelon Corp.
Cullen, Gary P. '60 '85 C.339 B.A. L.178 J.D. [Skadden,A.S.M.&F.]
Cullen, George J., (AV) '35 '60 C&L.424 B.S., J.D. 35 E. Wacker Dr.
Cullen, Jeanne M. '70 '97 C.424 B.B.A. L.146 J.D. [Ⓐ Perkins C.]
Cullerton, John J., (AV) '48 '74 C&L.424 B.A., J.D. [FagelHaber]
Cullerton, Patrick J. '64 '90 C.234 B.A. L.424 J.D. [FagelHaber]
Cullinan, Patrick J. '59 '86 C.424 B.A. L.365 J.D. [Belgrade&O.]
Cullinan, Sean P. '64 '92 C.424 B.A. L.365 J.D. Ill. Dept. of Rev.
Cullis, John A. '— '00 C.028 B.A. L.215 J.D. Two North LaSalle Street, Suite 2200
Cullison, Brooks Andrews '55 '00 C.291 B.A. L.365 J.D. [Cullison&C.]
Cullison, Laura D. '69 '99 C.376 B.A. L.627 J.D. [Ⓐ Skadden,A.S.M.&F.]
Cullison, Tania Garcia '62 '00 C.1183 B.S. L.365 J.D. [Cullison&C.]
Cullison & Cullison, P.C. 6160 N. Cicero, Suite 226
Cullom, Brenda F. '74 '01 C.500 B.A. L.365 J.D. [Ⓐ Thompson&T.]
Cullotta, Peter, (BV) '65 '90 C.338 B.S. L.365 J.D. 33 N. Dearborn St., Ste. 2400

Culpepper, David A. '47 '78 C.563 B.B.A. L.597 J.D.
77 West Washington Street, Suite 1708, 60602
Telephone: 312-939-0779 Fax: 312-939-0875
Email: steaks2@aol.com URL: http://www.davidculpepper.com
Bankruptcy, Personal Injury, Wrongful Death, Automobile Accidents, Truck Accidents, Negligence, Probate, Chapter 7, Foreclosures, Domestic Relations, Family Law, Divorce, Adoptions.

See Professional Biographies, CHICAGO, ILLINOIS

Culver, Carter C. '61 '89 C.477 B.B.A. L.597 J.D. Assoc. Gen. Coun., Exelon Corp.
Culver, John A. '— '88 C.475 B.A. L.602 J.D. [McKenna S.]
Culver, Marianne W., (AV) '61 '90 C.976 B.A. L.145 J.D. Coun., The Boeing Co.
Cummings, Amory '— '77 C.976 B.A. L.477 J.D. [Ⓒ Freeborn&P.]
Cummings, Andrea J. '67 '95 C.94 B.A.B.S. L.893 J.D. [Ⓐ Sidley A.B.&W.]
Cummings, Daniel, (AV) '50 '75 C.103 A.B. L.569 J.D. [Rothschild,B.&M.]
Cummings, Eugene M., (AV) '41 '70 C.597 B.S.E.E. L.424 J.D. [Cook,A.M.M.C.&M.] (See Pat. Sect.)
Cummings, Jeffrey I. '62 '87 C.475 B.A. L.597 J.D. [Miner,B.&G.]
Cummings, Kent J. '61 '93 C.431 B.A. L.424 J.D. [Hinshaw&C.]
Cummings, Patrick M., (AV) '55 '80 C.363 B.A. L.365 J.D. [Ciardelli&C.]
Cummings, Richard C., Jr. '53 '78 C.861 B.A. L.146 J.D. [Ⓒ Mayer,B.R.&M.]
Cummings, Stephen J. '69 '98 C.145 B.A. L.424 J.D. [Ⓐ Anesi,O.R.N.&K.]
Cummins, John J. '66 '92 C&L.209 B.A., J.D. [Cummins&H.]
Cummins, Robert P., (AV) '33 '62 C.679 B.S.E.E. L.209 J.D. [Cummins&C.]

Cummins & Cronin, LLC, (AV)
77 West Wacker Drive, Suite 4800, 60601
Telephone: 312-578-0500 Fax: 312-578-1234
Robert P. Cummins; Thomas C. Cronin.
Trial Practice.

See Professional Biographies, CHICAGO, ILLINOIS

Cummins & Hession, P.C.
415 North LaSalle Street, Suite 603, 60610-4509
Telephone: 312-464-9840 Fax: 312-464-9845
Email: jcummins@cumminshession.com URL: http://www.cumminshession.com
John J. Cummins; Christopher D. Hession.
Corporate Law: including Mergers and Acquisitions, Venture Financing, Shareholder Agreements, Buy-Sell Contracts, Licensing, Franchising, Joint Ventures, Labor and Employment and Real Estate; Business Litigation and Counseling: Prosecution and Defense of Contractual, Statutory and Common Law Claims, including Business Contract Matters, Labor and Employment, Non-Competition Agreements, Severance Agreements, Restrictive Covenant Disputes and Risk Avoidance Counseling; Intellectual Property: including Analysis, Protection, Licensing and Sale of Patents, Trademarks, Copyrights and Trade Secrets; Counseling regarding Infringement and Theft.

See Professional Biographies, CHICAGO, ILLINOIS

Cundiff, James H. '69 '95 C&L.801 B.S., J.D. [McDermott W.&E.]
Cunningham, Brian G. '69 '96 C.339 B.A. L.365 J.D. [Ellison,N.Z.&A.]
Cunningham, Daniel J. '66 '91 C.352 B.A. L.209 J.D. [Tressler,S.M.&P.]
Cunningham, Jeanine M. '— '92 C.660 B.A. L.1000 J.D. [Ⓐ Peck,B.A.&M.]
Cunningham, Jeanne M. '73 '98 C.880 B.A. L.209 J.D. 3500 Three First National Plaza
Cunningham, Katherine M. '— '99 C.951 B.A. L.597 J.D. [Ⓐ Kirkland&E.]
Cunningham, Kathleen T. '— '02 C.209 B.A. L.339 J.D. [Ⓐ FagelHaber]
Cunningham, Ken '68 '96 C&L.880 B.A., J.D. Sr. Coun., Grant Thornton
Cunningham, M. Jason '70 '99 C.349 L.999 J.D. [Ⓐ Sonnenberg&A.]
Cunningham, Michael J. '62 '90 C&L.347 B.S., J.D. [Hinshaw&C.]
Cunningham, Robert J., (AV) '42 '67 C.546 B.A. L.569 J.D. [Baker&M.]
Cunningham, Thomas J., (AV) '68 '93 C.36 B.S. L.209 J.D. [Lord,B.&B.]
Cunningham, Thomas P., Jr. '38 '67 C.755 L.209 LL.B. Cunningham Grain Co.
Cunningham, Tiffany P. '— '02 C.453 S.B. L.309 J.D. [Ⓐ Kirkland&E.]
Cunningham III, Eric A. '— '92 C.880 B.A. L.910 J.D. [Adler,M.&M.]
Cupkovic, Walter D., (AV) '52 '79 C.597 B.A. L.424 J.D. [FagelHaber]
Curato, Randy J., (AV) '58 '84 C.706 B.A. L.602 J.D. [Bell,B.&L.]
Curciarello, Gerry V. '51 '87 C.884 B.S. L.209 J.D. Chf. Fin. Offr., Landau & Heyman
Curcio, Joseph R., (AV) '31 '56 C.209 L.365 LL.B. 161 North Clark Street, Suite 2550

Curkovic, David I. ... '77 '01 C&L.477 B.A., J.D. [Ⓐ Ross,D.&B.]
Curler, Kate ... '69 '00 C.213 B.A. L.770 J.D. [Ⓐ L.L.Veon]
Curley, Alan F. ... '58 '75 C.861 B.A. L.365 J.D. [Robinson C.&C.]
Curley, C. Philip, (AV) ... '54 '79 C.597 B.A. L.273 J.D. [Robinson C.&C.]
Curley, Robert E., (AV) ... '35 '59 C.597 B.S. L.602 LL.B. [Mayer,B.R.&M.]
Curran, Barbara A. '28 '53 C.454 B.A. L.184 LL.B.
(adm. in CT; not adm. in IL) Resch. Fellow, Emeritus, Amer. Bar Found.
Curran, Kris E., (BV) ... '— '84 C.98 B.A. L.228 J.D. [Ungaretti&H.]
Curran, M. Prial ... '14 '39 C&L.602 A.B., LL.B. 200 W. Adams St.‡
Curran, Mark C. ... '24 '50 C.707 B.S. L.597 J.D. One 1st. National Plz.‡
Curran, Scott M. ... '76 '01 C.339 B.A. L.146 J.D. [Ⓐ Patzik,F.&S.]
Curran, Stephen J. ... '63 '90 C.763 B.A. L.276 J.D. House Coun., Boeing Co.
Currie, David P. ... '36 '63 C.145 A.B. L.309 LL.B. Prof. of Law, Univ. of Chicago
Currin, Margaret E. ... '61 '89 C.145 B.A. L.564 J.D. Asst. Pub. Guard.
Curry, Bryan E. ... '72 '98 C.477 B.A. L.210 J.D. [Ⓐ Bullaro&C.]
Curry, David S., (AV) ... '51 '83 C.347 B.A. L.345 J.D. [Mayer,B.R.&M.]
Curry, John J., Jr. ... '53 '78 C.597 B.A. L.880 J.D. [Nasharr&S.]
Curry, Richard L. ... '29 '55 C.1024 L.209 LL.B. [Ⓒ Bell,B.&L.] ‡
Curry, Susan J. ... '64 '89 C.116 B.A. L.602 J.D. 5246 N. Glenwood Ave.
Curth, Daniel C. ... '— '95 C.475 B.A. L.477 J.D. [Freeborn&P.]
Curtin, James K. ... '35 '70 C.1191 B.Ed. L.365 J.D. 300 N. State St.
Curtin, James S. '37 '70 C&L.229 B.A., J.D.
(adm. in PA; not adm. in IL) Assoc. Prof. of Law, Loyola Univ.
Curtin, Timothy F. ... '57 '82 C.602 B.B.A. L.966 J.D. Deloitte Haskins & Sells
Curtis, Anthony P. '66 '03
C.453 B.S.E.E. L.424 J.D. [Ⓐ Brinks H.G.&L.] (See Pat. Sect.)
Curtis, Diane M. ... '56 '81 C.608 B.S. L.188 J.D. Roosevelt University
Curtis, James L. ... '65 '90 C.20 B.A. L.424 J.D. [Seyfarth S.]
Curtis, Tanya L. ... '65 '91 C.347 B.A. L.893 J.D. [Katten M.R.]
Curtner, Patricia M., (AV) ... '— '79 C&L.477 B.A., J.D. [Chapman&C.]
Curzio, Daniel M. '55 '87 C.994 B.A. L.564 J.D.
(adm. in NJ; not adm. in IL) 181 W. Madison, 42nd Fl.
Cusack, Dennis C., (AV) ... '58 '85 C.723 B.A. L.602 J.D. [Johnson&B.]
Cusack, John T., (AV) ... '35 '60 C.602 A.B. L.477 J.D. [Gardner C.&D.]
Cusack, John T. J., (AV) ... '58 '84 C.222 B.A. L.273 J.D. [DLPiper R.G.C.U.]
Cusack, Mary H. ... '78 '05 C.436 B.A. L.424 J.D. [Ⓐ Pretzel&S.]
Cusack, Robert E. ... '17 '42 C.145 A.B. L.477 J.D. Cir. J.
Cushing, F. John, (AV) ... '51 '76 C&L.424 B.A., J.D. [Ambrose&C.]
Cushing, Michael M. ... '78 '03 C.201 B.A. L.424 J.D. [Ⓐ Ambrose&C.]
Cushing, Thomas M. ... '61 '88 C.602 B.A. L.424 J.D. [Ⓐ Ambrose&C.]
Cushman, Robert S., (AV) ... '03 '29 C.210 A.B. L.309 LL.B. 77 W. Wacker Dr.
Cusic, Jeffery ... '65 '90 C.894 A.B. L.659 J.D. Off. of the Gen. Coun., US Dept. of HHS
Cutlan, Dawn M. ... '74 '00 C.209 B.A. L.339 J.D. [Ⓐ McGuirewoods]
Cutler, Brecken Joy ... '— '03 C.473 B.A. L.339 J.D. [Ⓐ Ungaretti&H.]
Cutler, David P. ... '54 '79 C&L.880 B.A., J.D. [McGowan&H.] ⊙
Cutler, John C. ... '30 '59 C.197 A.B. L.146 LL.B. Contl. Ill. Nat. Bk. & Tr. Co. of Chic.
Cutri, Gianni L. ... '— '00 C&L.339 B.S.M.E., J.D. [Ⓐ Kirkland&E.]
Cutshall, Richard ... '79 '04 C.494 B.A. L.424 J.D. [Ⓐ Seyfarth S.]
Cutter, David F. ... '— '95 C.477 B.G.S. L.180 J.D. [Ⓐ Ross,D.&B.]
Cwik, David L., (AV) ... '54 '79 C.597 B.A. L.602 J.D. 6968 W. North Ave., 2nd Fl.
Cwik, Joseph E. ... '69 '95 C.339 B.S.C.E. L.365 J.D. [Welsh&K.] (See Pat. Sect.)
Cybak, Robert ... '48 '72 C.339 B.A. L.209 J.D. [Simpson&C.]
Cygal, Everett J. ... '— '93 C.145 A.B. L.597 J.D. [Schiff H.]
Cygan, Stanley J., Jr. ... '49 '74 C.339 B.A. L.424 J.D. Ill. Dept. of Employ. Sec.
Cyhan, Adrian R. ... '— '00 C.602 B.S. L.477 J.D. [Ⓒ Foley&L.] (Pat.)
Cyr, David A. ... '73 '03 C&L.424 B.A., J.D. [Ⓐ Johnson&B.]
Cyranoski, Steven E. ... '— '92 C.339 B.S. L.884 J.D. [Freeborn&P.]
Cyrluk, Jonathan M. ... '67 '92 C&L.339 B.A., J.D. [Stetler&D.]
Cytron, John M. ... '47 '72 C.976 B.A. L.309 J.D. [Berger,N.&F.]
Cyze, Donald A. ... '55 '80 C.1082 B.S. L.879 J.D. 3304 W. 111th Street
Cyzen, Keith M. ... '— '97 C.339 B.S. L.209 J.D. [Ⓐ Chapman&C.]
Czaja, Stanley C. ... '50 '79 C.339 B.A. L.209 J.D. [S.Czaja&Assoc.]
Czaja, Stanley, The Law Offices of, and Associates ... 6121 N. Northwest Hwy., Ste. 104
Czaplicki, Tatiana D. ... '72 '01 C.209 B.A. L.1187 J.D. The Court Co., State Atty. Off.
Czarobski, Gerald R., Law Office Of '54 '79
C.177 B.A. L.365 J.D. 3501 E. 106th St., Ste. 208
Czech, Marie Qunlivan, (AV) ... '55 '81 C.339 B.A. L.602 J.D. Asst. States Atty.Cook Cty
Czyzycki, Alice D. ... '— '03 C.124 B.S. L.597 J.D. [Ⓐ Gardner C.&D.]
Daane, Peter J. ... '64 '96 C.960 B.S. L.209 J.D. [Johnson&C.]
Daar, Henry R. ... '55 '80 C.339 B.S. L.424 J.D. [Daar&V.]

Daar & Vanek, P.C., (AV)
225 W. Washington Street, 18th Floor, 60606
Telephone: 312-224-1500 Telecopier: 312-224-1510
URL: http://www.DAARVANEK.com
Henry R. Daar; Joseph M. Vanek; Thomas A. Vickers; Angela C. Wilcox;—David P. Germaine; Kelley A. Bitterly; Jeffrey R. Moran, Jr.
Corporate Litigation and transaction practice. Insurance Law, Policyholder Representation and Uninsured Loss Recovery, Antitrust, Intellectual Property, Brand Review and Protection.
See Professional Biographies, CHICAGO, ILLINOIS

Dabill, David John ... '59 '84 C.585 B.S.B.A. L.494 J.D. 910 N. Lake Shore Dr.‡
Dabis, Faten N. ... '73 '99 C.679 B.A. L.209 J.D. 333 West Wacker Drive, Suite 500
Dable, Timothy J. ... '68 '93 C.477 B.S. L.910 J.D. [Winston&S.]
Dabrowski, Stephen H. ... '60 '85 C.597 B.A. L.809 J.D. 208 S. La Salle St., Ste. 1231
DAC Partners ... 75 East Wacker Drive, Suite 400 (⊙Lagos, Nigeria)
Dachis, Robert H. ... '53 '83 C.494 B.A. L.424 J.D. 4215 N. Sheridan Rd.
Dadabo, Daniel ... '— '80 C.209 B.A. L.424 J.D. SSA
Dadabo, Marguerite P. ... '51 '80 C.697 B.A. L.424 J.D. U.S. Railroad Retire. Bd.
Daddino, Christopher M., (AV) ... '66 '91 C.473 B.A. L.424 J.D. [McKay,N.T.D.&K.]
Daffada, James V. ... '60 '88 C.840 B.B.A. L.365 J.D. [Goodrich&D.]
Daggett, Thomas W., (AV) ... '51 '76 C&L.339 M.S., J.D. [Daggett]

Daggett Law Firm, (AV)
Chicago Title Tower, Suite 4950, 161 N. Clark Street, 60601
Telephone: 312-960-1600 Fax: 312-332-0515
Email: TWDaggett@Comcast.net
Thomas W. Daggett.
Environmental Law, Brownfields Redevelopment, Litigation, Toxic Torts, Chemical Regulation.
See Professional Biographies, CHICAGO, ILLINOIS

Dahl, April M. ... '77 '03 C&L.602 B.A., J.D. [Ⓐ Hinshaw&C.]
Dahl, James E., (AV) ... '49 '74 C&L.602 B.A., J.D. [Dahl&B.]
Dahl, Laura A. ... '— '99 C.260 B.A. L.602 J.D. [Ⓢ Jones D.]
Dahl, Patrick ... '77 '02 C&L.602 B.A., J.D. [Ⓐ Dahl&B.]
Dahl, Walter P., (AV) ... '22 '48 C.575 L.597 LL.B. [Ⓒ Dahl&B.]

Dahl & Bonadies, (AV) BB
225 West Washington Street, Suite 1640, 60606
Telephone: 312-641-3245 Fax: 312-641-1662
Email: dahlfirm@dahlfirm.com URL: http://www.dahlfirm.com
James E. Dahl; Paul N. Bonadies. Associates: Richard Joseph Murphy; Patrick Dahl. Of Counsel: Walter P. Dahl.
Civil Litigation. Alternative Dispute Resolution. Probate and Civil Rights.
See Professional Biographies, CHICAGO, ILLINOIS

Dahlgren, Gregory R. A. ... '57 '82 C.339 B.S. L.659 J.D. [DLPiper R.G.C.U.]
Dahlin, Bryna ... '75 '01 C&L.339 B.S., J.D. [Ⓐ Winston&S.]
Dahlin, Jay P. ... '76 '01 C&L.339 B.A., J.D. [Ⓐ Schiller,D.&F.]
Dahlquist, David ... '76 '01 C.339 B.A. L.209 J.D. [Ⓐ Winston&S.]
Dahlstrom, Patrick V. ... '55 '88 C.973 A.B. L.904 J.D. [Pomerantz H.B.G.&G.] ⊙
Dahm, Albert J., (AVⓉ) '58 '83 C.973 B.S.B.A. L.345 J.D.
(adm. in IN; not adm. in IL) [Dahm&E.] ⊙
Dahm, Martha M. ... '59 '84 C.465 B.B.A. L.623 J.D. Staff Atty., U.S. Trustee's Off.

Dahm & Elvin, LLP, (AVⓉ)
161 North Clark Street, Suite 1750, 60601 ⊙
Telephone: 312-683-3900 Fax: 312-683-3911
URL: http://www.dahmandelvin.com
Albert J. Dahm (Not admitted in IL); Michael S. Elvin; Matthew S. Elvin;—Sandy L. Morris; T. Monique Jones. Of Counsel: Andrew M. Spangler.
Drug & Medical Device Litigation, Product Liability, Class Action Defense, Federal Civil Litigation, Complex and Multi-District Litigation, Business Litigation.
Fort Wayne Office: 9604 Coldwater Road, Suite 201, 46825. Telephone: 260-497-6000. Fax: 260-497-6019.
See Professional Biographies, CHICAGO, ILLINOIS

Dailey, Sean P. ... '74 '02 C.276 B.S. L.880 J.D. [Ⓐ Mayer,B.R.&M.]
Dajani, Mona E. ... '— '96 C.339 B.A. L.424 J.D. [Ⓐ Sonnenschein N.&R.]
Dakoff, Howard S. ... '70 '96 C.966 B.S. L.365 J.D. [Levenfeld P.]
Dalal, Mirut P. ... '69 '97 C&L.846 B.S., J.D. [McAndrews,H.&M.] (See Pat. Sect.)
Dalal, Nilay S. ... '79 '04 C&L.608 B.S., J.D. [Ⓐ Brinks H.G.&L.]
D'Alba, Joel A., (AV) ... '44 '71 C.910 A.B. L.339 J.D. [Asher,G.G.&D.]
Dale, Kareem A. ... '73 '99 C&L.339 B.A., J.D. [Ⓐ Winston&S.]
Dale, Lance C. ... '63 '90 C.338 B.S. L.149 J.D. 641 W. Lake St., Ste. 303
Dale, Richard M. ... '51 '76 C&L.339 B.S., J.D. [Dale,J.&G.]
Dale, Jacobs & Gensburg, P.C. ... 155 N. Wacker Dr.
Dalebroux, Jeffrey M. ... '51 '76 C.436 A.B. L.276 J.D. [Dykema G.P.]

Daleiden & Tremaine, Ltd.
(See Arlington Heights)

Dalenberg, Heidi ... '— '89 C.339 B.A. L.424 J.D. [Schiff H.]
D'Alessio, Gary A. '54 '80 C.884 B.S.B.A. L.861 J.D.
Pres., Chicago Legal Search, Ltd.‡
Daley, Frederick J., Jr. ... '48 '73 C.472 B.A. L.1202 J.D. [Daley,D.&B.]
Daley, James P., (AV) ... '48 '74 C&L.209 B.S., J.D. [Bell,B.&L.]
Daley, James P., (AV) ... '27 '55 C&L.209 J.D. [Daley&M.]
Daley, John J., III, (AV) ... '56 '81 C.602 B.A. L.209 J.D. [Prusik S.D.&K.]
Daley, Louise L. ... '58 '85 C.519 B.A. L.209 J.D. [Ⓐ Prusik S.D.&K.]
Daley, Michael, (AV) ... '43 '68 C.424 L.209 LL.B. [Daley&G.]
Daley, Michael J., (AV) ... '55 '80 C.208 B.A. L.424 J.D. [Nisen&E.]
Daley, Richard J., (AV) ... '35 '60 C.597 B.S. L.209 J.D. [Pierce,D.B.O.&M.]
Daley, Richard M., (AV) ... '42 '69 C&L.209 B.A., J.D. Mayor
Daley, Susan, (AV) ... '59 '81 C.184 B.A. L.309 J.D. [Perkins C.]

Daley, DeBofsky & Bryant, (AV)
1 North LaSalle Street, Suite 3800, 60602
Telephone: 312-372-5200 Fax: 312-372-2778 URL: http://www.ddbchicago.com
Email: info@ddbchicago.com URL: http://www.lawyers.com/ddbchicago
Members of Firm: Frederick J. Daley, Jr.; Mark D. DeBofsky; David A. Bryant. Associates: Marcie E. Goldbloom; James R. Comerford. Of Counsel: David R. Bryant.
Social Security Disability including, Denial of Claims, Disability Insurance, Life and Health Insurance, ERISA, Employee Benefits, Employment Discrimination.
See Professional Biographies, CHICAGO, ILLINOIS

Daley and George, Ltd., (AV)
Two First National Plaza, 20 South Clark, Suite 400, 60603-1903
Telephone: 312-726-8797 Fax: 312-726-8819
Michael Daley; John J. George;—Dennis J. Aukstik; Robert T. Oleszkiewicz; Chris A. Leach; Richard A. Toth; Kathleen A. Duncan; Jill P. Conroy.
General Civil, Trial and Appellate Practice in all Courts. Corporate, Probate, Labor, Real Estate, Land Development, Zoning, Land Use, Eminent Domain, Estate Planning, Welfare and Pension Funds, Employment and Discrimination Law.
See Professional Biographies, CHICAGO, ILLINOIS

Daley & Mohan, P.C., (AV)
150 North Wacker Drive, Suite 1550, 60606
Telephone: 312-422-9999 Fax: 312-201-9368
Email: info@daleymohan.com URL: http://www.daleymohan.com
James P. Daley; Raymond H. Groble III; Daniel J. Mohan; Bernard Roccanova; Sean M. Sullivan; Mary L. Kandyba;—Christopher R. Karsten; Daniel Marko; Blake A. Barron. Of Counsel: Elizabeth West Speidel.
General Corporate, Commercial Litigation, Casualty and Products Liability Litigation, Labor, Real Estate, Bankruptcy, Creditor's Rights.
See Professional Biographies, CHICAGO, ILLINOIS

Dalianis, Ares G., (AV) ... '64 '90 C&L.339 A.B., J.D. [Franczek S.]
Dalianis, Constandina Kallos '66 '91 C.910 B.A. L.245 J.D.
Assoc. Reg. Coun., U.S. EPA
Dalinka, Alan S., (AV) ... '68 '93 C&L.597 B.S., J.D. [DLPiper R.G.C.U.]
Dalinka, Joel S. ... '70 '96 C.339 B.S. L.597 J.D. [Ⓐ FagelHaber]
Dalla Santa, Cassie '51 '88 C.959 B.S. L.46 J.D.
Asst. Staff Coun., Amer. Bar Assn., Legal Servs. Div.
Dalla Valle, Mark A., (AV) '— '89 C.999 B.S.E.E. L.1522 J.D.
[Vedder,P.K.&K.] (Pat.)
Dallas, Dimitra A. ... '78 '02 C.339 B.S. L.146 J.D. [Ⓐ Chuhak&T.]
Dallas, Steven ... '50 '76 C&L.424 B.S., J.D. [Regas,F.&D.]
Dallas, William D. ... '60 '84 C.494 B.A. L.209 J.D. [Ⓐ Regas,F.&D.]
Dallavo, Christopher J. ... '66 '92 C.602 B.A. L.424 J.D. [Schueler,D.&C.]
Dalley, Joshua N. ... '77 '04 C.896 B.A. L.957 J.D. [Ⓐ Seyfarth S.]
Dalrymple, Lawrence D ... '55 '88 C.145 B.S. L.209 J.D. [Copeland,F.&F.]
Dalton, John D., (AV) ... '62 '87 C.340 B.A. L.365 J.D. [Merlo K.B.&G.]
Daluga, William G., Jr., (AV) ... '51 '81 C.339 B.S. L.424 J.D. [Nisen&E.]
Daly, Eugene M. ... '47 '72 C.927 B.A. L.339 J.D. State Bd. of Education
Daly, James F. '34 '60 C&L.276 B.S., J.D.
(adm. in CT; not adm. in IL) 1150 N. Lake Shore Dr.
Daly, James R., (AV) ... '— '82 C.608 B.A. L.930 J.D. [Jones D.]
Daly, Joel T., (AV) ... '34 '88 C.976 B.A. L.146 J.D. 190 N. State Street
Daly, John K. ... '63 '94 C.560 B.A. L.1065 J.D. [Ⓒ Meckler B.&T.]

Dam, Kenneth W. '32 '59 C.378 B.S. L.145 J.D.
(adm. in NY; not adm. in IL) Prof., Univ. of Chicago Law Sch.
Damashek, Ronald A., (AV) .... '57 '82 C.597 B.A. L.276 J.D. [Stahl&B.]
D'Amato, Anthony '37 '63 C.188 A.B. L.309 J.D.
(adm. in NY; not adm. in IL) Prof. of Law, Northwestern Univ.
Dames, Alexandra L. .... '— '00 C.911 B.F.A. L.424 J.D. [🄰 Cassiday,S.&G.]
Dames, John, (AV) .... '46 '71 C.910 B.A. L.424 J.D. [Drinker B.&R.]
Damholt, Sandra C. '52 '78 C&L.623 B.B.A., J.D.
(adm. in OK; not adm. in IL)
V.P. & Dep. Gen. Coun., Federal Home Loan Bk. of Chicago
Dami, Paul A. '64 '90 C.477 B.B.A. L.902 J.D.
(adm. in NY; not adm. in IL) Ernst & Young, LL.P.
D'Amore, Stephen V. .... '69 '94 C.424 B.A. L.209 J.D. [Winston&S.]
Damsma, Lynne M. Reardon .... '70 '95 C.610 B.S. L.8 J.D. [McKay,N.T.D.&K.]
Dan, Jeffrey C. .... '71 '97 C.339 B.S. L.209 J.D. [🄰 Crane,H.S.W.&C.]
Danahy, Mary J., (AV) .... '— '81 C.339 B.A. L.209 J.D. Asst. Pub. Def.

D'Ancona & Pflaum LLC
(See Seyfarth Shaw LLP)

Dandelles, Stefan R. .... '73 '98 C.966 B.A. L.352 J.D. [🄰 Wilson E.M.E.&D.]
Danek, Gregory C. .... '69 '97 C.339 B.A. L.1187 J.D. Asst. Pub. Def.
Danekas, Steven E., (AV) .... '55 '81 C.589 B.S. L.339 J.D. [Swanson,M.&B.]
Dang-Vu, Khoi .... '73 '00 C.477 A.B. L.910 J.D. [🄰 Leahy,E.&F.]
Daniel, David O., III .... '47 '72 C.228 B.A. L.597 J.D. 777 N. Michigan Ave.
Daniel, Eva S. .... '69 '95 C.477 B.B.A. L.347 J.D. [🄰 Sidley A.B.&W.]
Daniel, Kris, (AV) .... '53 '78 C.276 B.A. L.209 J.D. [Lamendella&D.]
Daniel, Michael B. '— '05 C&L.477 B.B.A., J.D.
(adm. in PA; not adm. in IL) [🄰 Kirkland&E.]
Daniel, Robert C. '47 '77 C.267 B.S. L.990 J.D.
(adm. in CA; not adm. in IL) U.S. Dept. of Jus.
Daniel, Rodney A., (AV) '54 '85 C.679 B.S. L.339 J.D.
[Brinks H.G.&L.] (See Pat. Sect.)
Danielewicz, Michael J., (CV) .... '67 '93 C.884 B.A. L.1187 J.D. [🄰 Keefe&Assoc.]
Daniels, Genevieve M. .... '68 '93 C.424 B.A. L.597 J.D. [🄰 Katten M.R.]
Daniels, Jill Beda .... '73 '99 C.750 B.A. L.424 J.D. [🄰 McLennon&Assoc.]
Daniels, John D., (AV) .... '39 '64 C.674 A.B. L.145 J.D. [Sanchez&D.]
Daniels, Lee A., (AV) .... '42 '67 C.352 B.A. L.365 J.D. [Bell,B.&L.]
Daniels, Peter G. .... '69 '98 C.347 B.A. L.424 J.D. [🄰 Walker W.M.]
Daniels, William L. .... '46 '71 C.36 B.A. L.424 J.D. 1541 N. Honore‡
Dannen, Avrum H., (AV) .... '35 '61 C.339 B.S. L.209 LL.B. [🄲 Berger,N.&F.]
Danyluk, Kristen M. .... '— '04 C.1556 B.A. L.477 J.D. [🄰 Katten M.R.]
Darch, Douglas A., (AV) .... '51 '80 C.277 B.S. L.575 J.D. [Seyfarth S.]
D'Arco, John M. .... '70 '98 C.339 B.A. L.365 J.D. [Lake,T.&D.]
Darcy, D. Alexander .... '65 '93 C.299 B.A. L.910 J.D. [Askounis&B.]
Darcy, Daniel Philip .... '47 '82 C&L.424 B.S., J.D. Asst. State Atty.
Darcy, Stathy .... '— '91 C.339 B.S.B.A L.1117 J.D. [Chapman&C.]
Darden, Loletta L. .... '— '91 C.679 B.S. L.818 J.D. [Sachnoff&W.] (Pat.)
Dardick, Christina M. .... '65 '95 C.209 B.A. L.146 J.D. [🄰 L.L.Veon]
Dare, Heidi A. .... '— '02 C.20 B.A. L.912 J.D. [🄰 Brinks H.G.&L.] (See Pat. Sect.)
Dargis, Robert J., (AV) .... '53 '82 C.589 B.S. L.424 J.D. [🄰 R.F.Mallen&Assoc.]
Darke, C. Elizabeth '69 '98 C.823 B.A. L.107 J.D.
(adm. in NY; not adm. in IL) [Schwartz C.]
Darke, Richard P. .... '71 '98 C.932 B.A. L.477 J.D. [🄰 Duane M.]
Darke, Sean F. .... '76 '05 C.1385 B.A. L.213 J.D. [🄰 Wessels&P.]
Darling, David J. ..... '56 '88 C.340 B.A. L.365 J.D. 30 North La Salle Street, Suite 4300
Darling, Leslie M. .... '— '97 C.98 B.S. L.209 J.D. [Ungaretti&H.]
Darmstadter, Seth E. .... '79 '05 C.29 B.A. L.146 J.D. [🄰 Meckler B.&T.]
Darnell, Marc E. .... '— '02 C.945 B.A. L.124 J.D. [🄰 Barnes&T.]
Darrah, John W. .... '38 '69 C&L.424 B.S., J.D. U.S. Dist. J.
Darrow, John A. .... '65 '90 C.602 B.A. L.276 J.D. [Burke,W.M.&S.]
Dart, Robert J. .... '79 '04 C.228 A.B. L.145 J.D. [🄰 Jenner&B.]
Daryanani, Raj .... '61 '96 C.145 B.A. L.659 J.D. V.P., ABN Amro Bk. N.V.
Das, Anjali C. .... '— '93 C.145 B.A. L.602 J.D. [Wilson E.M.E.&D.]
Dasari, Veda Praveen .... '— '02 C.679 B.S. L.879 J.D. [🄰 T.J.Scully,III&Assoc.]
Dash, James M., (AV) .... '59 '85 C.424 B.A. L.326 J.D. [Much S.F.D.A.&R.]
Dashiell, Courtney .... '78 '03 C.477 B.A. L.851 J.D. [🄰 Busse&B.]
Dashiell, James R., (AV) .... '47 '72 C&L.477 B.A., J.D. [Dashiell]

Dashiell Law Offices, LLC, (AV)
70 West Madison, Suite 1400, 60602
Telephone: 312-214-3329 Fax: 312-214-3328
Email: jrdashlaw@yahoo.com
James R. Dashiell.
Casualty Defense Law, Employment Practice, Commercial Litigation.
See Professional Biographies, CHICAGO, ILLINOIS

Dashow, Jules, (AV) .... '09 '32 C&L.339 A.B., J.D. 10 S. Wacker Dr.
Daskal, Frona C. .... '38 '80 C.145 B.A. L.424 J.D. Pres., The Mediation Grp.
Daskal, Robert H. .... '41 '65 C&L.477 B.B.A., J.D. 55 W. Delaware Pl.
Daspin, D. Albert .... '— '87 C.473 B.A. L.347 J.D. [Daspin&A.]

Daspin & Aument, LLP, (AV)
10 South Riverside Plaza Suite 1220, 60606 ⊙
Telephone: 312-258-1600 Fax: 312-258-1955
URL: http://www.daspinaument.com
Members of Firm: Robert C. Aument (Resident, Oak Brook Office); Nicole Rudman Brown; D. Albert Daspin; John G. Caruso; James H. Marshall; Jefferson Perkins (Resident, Oak Brook Office); Howard S. Thompson. Associates: Matthew C. Alshouse; Maria Toliopoulos; Dawn K. Luck; Cody Salter. Of Counsel: John T. Huntington (Resident, Oak Brook Office).
Real Estate, Commercial Real Estate Development, Estate Planning, Business Succession Planning, Tax Planning, Trust Administration, Estate Administration, Corporate Law and Financial Services Law. Intellectual Property including Patents, Trademarks, Copyrights and Computer Law.
Oak Brook Office: 210 W. 22nd Street, Suite 102, 60523. Telephone: 630-928-0430. Fax: 630-928-0392.
See Professional Biographies, CHICAGO, ILLINOIS

Dasso, James D. .... '— '87 C.629 B.S. L.477 J.D. [Foley&L.]
Dasso, William J., (AV) '50 '76
C.602 A.B. L.209 J.D. Coun., Old Republic International Corp.
Date, Winifred H., (AV) .... '— '76 C.788 B.A. L.597 J.D. V.P., Northern Trust Co.
Dates, Lindsey D. .... '— '03 C&L.339 B.A., J.D. [🄰 Jones D.]
D'Attomo, John J. .... '— '93 C.424 B.S. L.365 J.D. [🄰 Gardner C.&D.]
Daubach, James L. .... '37 '63 C&L.424 B.S.B.A., J.D. 415 N. La Salle St.
Daubard, Catherine A. '50 '85
C&L.339 B.S.W., J.D. Dep. Gen. Coun., American Bar Assn.
Dauchot, Luke L., (AVⓉ) .... '— '86 C&L.930 B.A., J.D. [Kirkland&E.] (ⓒL.A., CA)

Daudell, David, The Law Offices of '63 '92 C.424 L.1000 J.D.
30 N. LaSalle Street Suite 2340, 60602
Telephone: 312-701-0012 Fax: 312-701-9056
URL: http://www.daudelllaw.com

(This Listing Continued)

Daudell, David, The Law Offices of (Continued)
Adoption Law, Bankruptcy, Business Organization, Contracts, Criminal Law, Driving While Intoxicated, Divorce, Family Law, Gaming Law, Landlord and Tenant Law, Medical Malpractice, Motor Vehicle Accidents and Injuries, Personal Injury, Probate, Estate Administration, Real Estate, White Collar Crime, Wills, Litigation.
See Professional Biographies, CHICAGO, ILLINOIS

Daugerdas, Paul M. .... '50 '74 C&L.209 B.S.C., J.D. [🄲 Jenkens&G.]
Dault, Brian C. .... '77 '04 C.475 B.A. L.209 J.D. 20 W. Kinzie, Suite 1300
Daun, Sherry J. .... '77 '03 C.963 B.S. L.145 J.D. [🄰 Hubert&F.]
D'Aunno, Lisa E. '56 '84 C.602 A.B. L.477 J.D.
(adm. in CA; not adm. in IL) State Dept. of Children & Family Servs.‡
Davenport, Frank T. .... '57 '93 C.378 B.A. L.365 J.D. [Berger,N.&F.]
Davenport, Loretta Hopkins .... '56 '85 C.914 B.A. L.597 J.D. Asst. States Atty.
Davenport, Rebecca C. .... '71 '04 C&L.589 B.S., J.D. [🄰 Mayer,B.R.&M.]
Davenport, William B., (AV) .... '24 '50 C&L.339 A.B., J.D. 1 IBM Plaza
Davey, John P. .... '39 '62 C&L.145 A.B., J.D. [🄲 Gerstner&G.]
David, Andrew B., (AV) .... '54 '79 C.170 B.A. L.597 J.D. [Sugar,F.&F.]
David, Angelique Athiena .... '— '02 C.124 B.A. L.597 J.D. [🄰 Lord,B.&B.]
David, Celia Yerger, (AV) '52 '79 C.999 B.A. L.597 J.D.
V.P., Procurement, Commonwealth Edison Co.
David, Jay M. .... '27 '55 C.1016 B.S. L.209 LL.B. 2733 W. Jerome
David, Oscar A. .... '62 '87 C.273 B.A. L.145 J.D. [Winston&S.]
David, Patricia Pierce .... '64 '89 C.597 B.A. L.36 J.D. I.R.S.
David, Scott L. .... '55 '79 C.589 B.A. L.910 J.D. [Much S.F.D.A.&R.]
Davidova, Lyudmila '78 '04 C.1171 B.A. L.424 J.D.
Assoc. Atty., Wm. Wrigley Jr. Co.
Davids, Monique J. .... '— '98 C.454 B.A. L.424 J.D. City Dept. of Consumer Servs.
Davidson, Darryl R., (AV) .... '59 '83 C&L.339 B.A., J.D. [McGuirewoods]
Davidson, Deborah S. .... '— '98 C.862 B.A. L.910 J.D. [🄰 Morgan,L.&B.]
Davidson, Douglas G. .... '42 '69 C&L.424 B.S., J.D. 6413 N. Kinzua
Davidson, Elizabeth A. .... '65 '97 C.339 B.S. L.383 J.D. [Jenner&B.]
Davidson, James W. .... '— '03 C.63 B.S. L.424 [🄰 Clausen M.]
Davidson, Jeffrey O. .... '61 '87 C.932 B.S. L.477 J.D. [🄰 Baker&M.]
Davidson, Joshua D. .... '66 '93 C.878 B.A. L.597 J.D. [Varga B.L.H.&C.]

Davidson, Keith L., & Associates, (AV) '42 '68 C.339 A.B. L.424 J.D.
30 North La Salle Street, Suite 3516, 60602
Telephone: 312-419-0544 Fax: 312-419-0758
Email: KLDLAW@ix.netcom.com
Product Liability, Medical Malpractice Law, Personal Injury Law, Tort Law and Wrongful Death Law.
See Professional Biographies, CHICAGO, ILLINOIS

Davidson, Lawrence I., (AV) .... '49 '75 C.339 B.S. L.365 J.D. [Duane M.]
Davidson, Mark S. .... '— '82 C.477 B.A. L.339 J.D. 1 N. LaSalle, Ste. 2400
Davidson, Mitchell, (AV) .... '44 '70 C.1016 B.A. L.146 J.D. [Lewis,D.&H.]
Davidson, Robert G., (AV) .... '48 '74 C.966 B.A. L.1119 J.D. [Schwartz C.]
Davidson, Sheldon, (AV) .... '— '62 C&L.209 B.S.in Com., J.D. [🄲 Pedersen&H.]
Davidson, Stanley J., (AV) .... '46 '71 C.339 B.A. L.425 J.D. [Hinshaw&C.]
Davidson, Steven R. .... '52 '77 C.477 A.B. L.309 J.D. [Sonnenschein N.&R.]
Davie, Barrett C. .... '74 '01 C.861 B.A. L.146 J.D. CEO, Ad Community, LLC
Davies, Susan M. '64 '92 C.976 B.S. L.145 J.D.
(adm. in PA; not adm. in IL) One 1st Nat. Plaza‡
Davila, Nino R. .... '56 '92 C.999 B.A. L.900 J.D. 4244 W. North Ave.
Davis, Alan T. .... '52 '79 C.221 B.A. L.146 J.D. Off. of the State's Atty.
Davis, Anne Megan .... '49 '76 C.741 B.A. L.846 J.D. [Johnson,J.S.G.&D.]
Davis, Barbara J. .... '54 '79 C.339 B.A. L.424 J.D. Asst. States Atty.
Davis, Bernard .... '26 '50 C&L.221 B.A., LL.B. 205 W. Randolph St.
Davis, Beth Anne .... '66 '91 1350 N. Wells Street, Suite F316
Davis, Bradley E. .... '66 '02 C.665 B.S. L.209 J.D. [🄰 Bell,B.&L.]
Davis, Brian E. .... '— '98 C.63 B.S. L.1017 J.D. [Kirkland&E.]
Davis, Candace P. ... '54 '80 C.339 B.S.W. L.597 J.D. Dir., Qualified Plans, Amoco Corp.
Davis, Celeste Harriet .... '62 '87 C.679 B.A. L.1340 J.D. U.S. E.E.O.C.
Davis, Champ W., Jr., (AV) .... '40 '66 C&L.339 B.S., J.D. [Davis M.]
Davis, Charles A., Jr. .... '45 '74 C.1191 B.S. L.209 J.D. 5433 S. Drexel
Davis, Christopher S. .... '50 '74 C.801 B.A. L.8 J.D. [🄲 Greene&L.]
Davis, David J. .... '66 '90 C.339 B.S.E. L.228 J.D. [Baker&M.]
Davis, Donn M. .... '62 '88 C.473 B.S. L.477 J.D. Pres., Tribune Ventures
Davis, Elizabeth A. .... '— '03 C&L.352 B.A., J.D. [🄰 Ungaretti&H.]
Davis, Geoffrey M. .... '64 '92 C.966 B.B.A. L.94 J.D. [Jenner&B.]
Davis, Gregory M. .... '— '97 C.477 B.A. L.966 J.D. [Seyfarth S.]
Davis, Gregory S. '61 '87 C.347 B.A. L.94 J.D.
V.P., Gen. Coun. & Secy., La Petite Academy, Inc.
Davis, Herbert J. .... '35 '62 C.393 A.B. L.209 J.D. 1758 N. Park Ave.‡
Davis, Howard A., (AV) .... '55 '80 C.339 B.S. L.46 J.D. [Shefsky&F.]
Davis, Jack R. .... '30 '60 C.597 L.365 LL.B. 205 West Wacker Drive, Suite 717
Davis, James M. .... '— '95 C.911 B.A. L.146 J.D. [Anderson K.&O.]
Davis, Janet R., (AV) .... '55 '80 C&L.477 B.S.A., J.D. [Meckler B.&T.]
Davis, Jeffery S. .... '77 '02 C&L.339 B.S., J.D. [🄰 Sonnenschein N.&R.]
Davis, Jeffrey C. .... '61 '87 C.37 B.S. L.424 J.D. [Vedder,P.K.&K.]
Davis, Jeffrey L. ... '59 '85 C.228 A.B. L.145 J.D. Sr. Coun., Bank One Corp. (Law Dept.)
Davis, Joel Richard '68 '94 C.221 B.A. L.365 J.D.
Asst. V.P. - Legal, Equity Residential
Davis, Joseph E., (AV) .... '36 '60 C&L.597 B.S.L., J.D. 300 W. Wash.
Davis, Julie G. .... '68 '93 C.339 B.A. L.602 J.D. One North Wacker Drive
Davis, Keith Eugene .... '57 '82 C&L.801 B.A., J.D. [K.E.Davis]
Davis, Leslie D. .... '71 '95 C&L.352 B.A., J.D. [Sonnenschein N.&R.]
Davis, Marjorie Fink .... '67 '99 C.228 B.A. L.424 J.D. Lexis-Nexis
Davis, Mark R., (AV) .... '53 '79 C.560 B.A. L.209 J.D. [O'Keefe,L.&H.]
Davis, Mark S. .... '54 '79 C.347 B.S. L.345 J.D. Lake Pontchartrain Basin Found.
Davis, M.C. .... '58 '92 C.347 B.A. L.365 J.D. 55 W. Monroe St.
Davis, Michael W., (AV) .... '50 '75 C.1349 B.A. L.597 J.D. 10 S. Dearborn St.
Davis, Michele L. '73 '99 C.575 B.S.B.A. L.93 J.D.
Two North LaSalle Street, Suite 2200
Davis, Muller, (P.C.), (AV) ...... '35 '60 C.976 B.A. L.309 J.D. [Davis F.Z.K.M.M.&R.]
Davis, Patrick B. .. '39 '63 C.627 B.A. L.190 LL.B. V.P. & Dist. Exec., Bank of Montreal
Davis, Peter M. .... '50 '75 C.597 B.A. L.309 J.D. 633 N. St. Clair St.
Davis, R. Heath .... '42 '68 C.894 A.B. L.365 J.D. 134 N. La Salle St., Ste. 2116
Davis, Rachel .... '63 '97 C.629 B.A. L.365 J.D. Asst. States Atty.
Davis, Robert C., III .... '— '99 C.228 A.B. L.280 J.D. [Kirkland&E.]
Davis, Robert P. .... '48 '73 C.108 B.S. L.893 J.D. 111 W. Monroe St.‡
Davis, Ronald S. .... '33 '58 C&L.597 B.S.B.A., J.D. Cir.J.
Davis, Sally L. '66 '91 C.608 B.A. L.94 J.D.
V.P. & Assoc. Gen. Coun., True North Communications, Inc. (Legal Department)
Davis, Scott J., (AV) .... '52 '76 C.976 B.A. L.309 J.D. [Mayer,B.R.&M.]
Davis, Sharon Kennedy .... '42 '77 C.254 B.A. L.209 J.D. Ill. Com. Comm.

Davis, Shelia Cochran ....'56 '86 C.72 B.A. L.245 J.D. Asst. State Atty.
Davis, Sheri Drucker ....'— '01 C&L.597 B.S.J., J.D. [A] Mayer,B.R.&M.]
Davis, Stephen D. ....'56 '82 C.502 B.A. L.477 J.D. [Canel,D.&K.]
Davis, Theresa L. ....'66 '94 C.966 B.A. L.146 J.D. [Katten M.R.]
Davis, W. Kenneth, Jr., (AV) ....'61 '90 C.145 A.B. L.209 J.D. [Katten M.R.]
Davis, William A., II, (BVⓉ) '46 '74 C.674 A.B. L.976 J.D.
(adm. in CA; not adm. in IL) Chf. Regulatory Coun., Central Region, AT&T Corp.

Davis & Campbell L.L.C., (AV)
161 N. Clark, Suite 4700, 60601 ⊙
Telephone: 312-523-2120; 773-404-5900 Fax: 312-523-2121; 773-404-6232
Email: jgbunge@dcamplaw.com URL: http://www.dcamplaw.com
Of Counsel: Jonathan G. Bunge.
Management Labor Law, Corporate Law, Trial Practice, Employee Benefits, Mergers and Acquisitions, Employer Rights, Local Government Rights, Employment Law, Commercial Law, Commercial Litigation, Complex Litigation, Intellectual Property, Securities Regulation, Antitrust, Immigration and Naturalization, Real Estate, Zoning Planning and Land Use, Tax Law, Estate Planning, Probate.
Home Office of Jonathan G. Bunge: 3014 North Racine Avenue, Chicago, Illinois, 60657. Telephone: 773-404-5900. Fax: 773-404-6232.
Peoria, Illinois Office: 401 Main Street, Suite 1600, 61602-1241 Telephone: 309-673-1681. Telecopier: 309-673-1690.
Washington, D.C. Office: 1828 L Street, N.W., Suite 660, 20036. Telephone: 202-293-5690. Fax: 202-296-5706.
See Professional Biographies, CHICAGO, ILLINOIS

Davis & Cichorski, (AV) .... 30 North La Salle Street Suite 2124

Davis Friedman Zavett Kane MacRae Marcus & Rubens LLP, (AV) BB
A Limited Liability Partnership including Professional Corporations
135 South La Salle Street, 36th Floor, 60603
Telephone: 312-782-2220 Fax: 312-782-0464
Email: info@davisfriedman.com URL: http://www.davisfriedman.com
Members of Firm: Benjamin B. Davis (1946-1965); William C. Boyden (1946-1965); Muller Davis (P.C.); Errol Zavett; Larry R. Kane (P.C.); Dorene Marcus; James L. Rubens; Joshua T. Friedman; Robert D. Segal; Doris Schumacher McMorrow. Associates: Muriel Kuhs; Jody Meyer Yazici; David Clyde Ainley; Zorka Ristanovic; Karen Augustine. Of Counsel: James T. Friedman (P.C.); Roderick E. MacRae.
Family Law. Trial and Appellate Practice, Divorce, Child Custody, Spousal Support, Pre- and Post-Marital Agreements, Alimony, Paternity.
See Professional Biographies, CHICAGO, ILLINOIS

Davis, Keith E., Law Office of .... 1525 E. 53rd St., Ste. 516-11

Davis McGrath LLC, (AV)
125 South Wacker Drive, Suite 1700, 60606
Telephone: 312-332-3033 Fax: 312-332-6376
URL: http://www.davismcgrath.com
David C. Bogan (1946-1995); Champ W. Davis, Jr.; Marsha K. Hoover; Gini S. Marziani; William T. McGrath; John B. Alsterda;—Barbara J. Mulvanny; Jodi L. Flynn; Kevin A. Thompson; Evan D. Brown; Boris Umansky. Of Counsel: Teresa F. Frisbie; Celeste Ebers Kralovec; Gerald J. Mannix; Margaret F. Woulfe.
Commercial Litigation and Alternative Dispute Resolution, Business Transactions, Intellectual Property, Trademark, Copyright, Trade Secret, Entertainment Law, Computer Law, Real Estate Litigation and Transactions, Antitrust, Employment Law, Trade Associations, Creditors' Rights.
See Professional Biographies, CHICAGO, ILLINOIS

Davis Shedd, Erin ....'75 '03 C.806 B.A. L.910 J.D. [A] McDermott W.&E.]
Davisson, Timothy P. '56 '82
C.234 B.A. L.365 J.D. Sen. Coun., Smurfit-Stone Container Corp.
Davlantes, Harry P. ....'18 '50 C.424 B.S.C. L.365 LL.B. 2048 W. Platt Blvd.
Davy, Thomas M., (AV) ....'46 '71 C.424 A.B. L.209 J.D. Asst. State's Atty.
Dawes, Theodore E. '33 '63
C.679 B.S. L.209 LL.B. 175 West Jackson Boulevard, Suite 1600‡
Dawn, Susan ....'59 '86 C.339 B.A. L.365 J.D. 3 1st Natl. Plz., Ste. 610
Dawson, Blair L. ....'77 '02 C.436 B.A. L.146 J.D. [A] Meckler B.&T.]
Dawson, Daniel P., (BV) ....'63 '88 C.602 B.A. L.424 J.D. [Nisen&E.]
Dawson, Dawn H. ....'— '01 C.836 B.S. L.339 J.D. [A] Kirkland&E.]
Dawson, Susan L. ....'72 '00 C.610 B.S.C. L.424 J.D. [A] Marks,M.&K.]
Day, J. K. MacKendree '42 '70 C.105 A.B. L.273 LL.B.
(adm. in DC; not adm. in IL)
Vice President Human Resources, AKZO Nobel Chemicals Inc.
Dayal, Anjali ....'65 '92 C.145 B.A. L.823 J.D. [McBreen&K.]
De, Sampreeti ....'72 '00 C.339 B.S. L.424 J.D. [A] Katten M.R.]
Deady, Patrick E., (AV) ....'— '77 C.436 B.A. L.424 J.D. [Hogan M.]
Dean, Jeffrey H. ....'— '92 C.145 A.B. L.309 J.D, [Marshall,G.&B.] (See Pat. Sect.)
Dean, Kent D. ....'69 '99 C.338 B.S. L.209 J.D. Co. Pub. Def.
Deane, Kathleen M., (AV) '55 '80
C.741 B.A. L.602 J.D. V.P. & Sen. Coun., Harris Tr. & Svgs. Bk.
DeAngelis, Eugene A. ....'76 '04 C.309 A.B. L.597 J.D. [A] Skadden,A.S.M.&F.]
DeAngelo, Paula K. '67 '93 C&L.352 B.S., J.D.
Asst. Gen. Coun., Loyola University of Chicago
DeAno, James L., (AV) ....'56 '81 C.927 B.A. L.365 J.D. [Norton,M.W.&D.] ⊙
Dearing, Sarah H. ....'75 '00 C.388 B.A. L.477 J.D. [A] Lord,B.&B.]
Debboli, Stephen C. ....'50 '76 [Serpico,N.&N.]
deBeers, Kimberly A. ....'66 '95 C.659 B.A. L.861 J.D. [Skadden,A.S.M.&F.]
Debelak, William F. ....'14 '47 C.339 B.S. L.146 LL.B. The Quaker Oats Co.
Debicki, Agnieska E. Kowalska ....'74 '01 C.424 B.A. L.209 J.D. [Debicki,A.E.]
Debicki, Agnieska E., & Associates, LTD .... 7064 W. Belmont Ave.
DeBlase, Paul M. ....'70 '02 C.347 B.A. L.365 J.D. [A] Ellison,N.Z.&A.]
DeBlasio, Antonio ....'69 '94 C.679 B.A. L.365 J.D. [Gardner C.&D.]
DeBlaze, Sara B. ....'69 '99 C.932 B.B.A. L.146 J.D. Coun., Aon Corporation
DeBofsky, Mark D., (AV) ....'56 '80 C.477 B.A. L.339 J.D. [Daley,D.&B.]
DeBolt, Laura Carroll ....'78 '03 C.741 B.S. L.597 J.D. [A] Vedder,P.K.&K.]
Deboni, Frank Nicholas ....'75 '00 C.57 B.A. L.146 J.D. [A] Ellison,N.Z.&A.]
DeBruin, Jessica ....'75 '00 C.339 B.S. L.569 J.D. [A] Goldberg,K.B.B.R.&M.]
Decarlo, Anita ....'— '98 L.365 J.D. 210 W. Illinois St.
DeCarlo, Vito D., (AV) ....'32 '61 C.973 B.S. in B.A. L.365 J.D. [DeCarlo,G.&D.]
DeCarlo, William S. ....'50 '77 C.659 B.S. L.276 J.D. [Sidley A.B.&W.]
DeCarlo, Greenfield & DeCarlo, P.C., (AV) .... 210 W. Illinois Ave.
DeCaro, Dennis J. ....'60 '95 C.260 B.A. L.365 J.D. [Kupets&D.]
Decator, Eric R., (BV) ....'57 '83 C.477 B.A. L.174 J.D. [Sonnenschein N.&R.]
Decatorsmith, Jonathan P. ....'61 '86 C.339 B.A. L.174 J.D. 565 W. Adams, Ste. 600
DeCelles, David H. ....'— '05 C.597 B.A. L.145 J.D. [A] Kirkland&E.]
DeChazal, Claire D. ....'55 '81 C.188 B.A. L.477 J.D. Asst. Reg. Coun., Dept. of HHS
Dechene, James C., (AV) ....'53 '79 C.770 B.S. L.477 J.D. [Sidley A.B.&W.]
De Cherrie, Robert T. ....'34 '69 C.209 B.S.C. L.146 J.D. 105 W. Adams‡
Dechter, Eugene E. ....'35 '60 L.146 LL.B. 120 W. Madison
Decker, Alice E. ....'— '04 C.821 B.A. L.597 J.D. [A] Latham&W.]
Decker, Deborah E. ....'72 '98 C.578 B.A. L.966 J.D. [Tabet D.&R.]
Decker, Jarett B. '65 '90 C.945 B.A. L.477 J.D.
Sr. Trial Coun., Chicago, M.R.O., S.E.C.
Decker, John F. ....'44 '73 C.177 B.A. L.190 J.D. Prof., DePaul Univ. College of Law
Decker, Robert S., (AV) ....'24 '51 C.477 L.365 LL.B. 4337 S. Kildare Ave.‡
Decker, Ronald O. ....'32 '59 C.821 B.A. L.145 J.D. 3450 N. Lake Shore Dr.
Decker, Steven R., (AV) '52 '77 C.339 B.A. L.209 J.D.
708 N. Dearborn Street 4th Floor
Decker, Thomas D., (AV) ....'34 '63 C.393 B.A. L.597 J.D. [T.D.Decker&Assoc.]

Decker, Thomas D., and Associates, Ltd., (AV)
Suite 1500, 321 S. Plymouth Court, 60604
Telephone: 312-922-4180 Fax: 312-922-4184
Email: deckerlawoffice@ameritech.net
Thomas D. Decker.
Civil and Criminal Trial and Appellate Practice.
See Professional Biographies, CHICAGO, ILLINOIS

DeCoster, Barbara M., (AV) '48 '78 C.273 B.A. L.352 J.D.
4801 West Peterson, Suite 412, 60646
Telephone: 773-286-3800 Fax: 773-286-3504
Email: bdecoster@yahoo.com URL: http://www.lawyers.com/bdecoster
Litigation in State and Federal Courts. Collections, Commercial and Contract, Negligence, Personal Injury, Automobile Accidents, Slip and Fall, Dog Bites, Probate, Trusts, Real Estate, Products Liability, Professional Negligence, Dental Malpractice.
See Professional Biographies, CHICAGO, ILLINOIS

Decyk, Roxanne J. '52 '77 C.339 A.B. L.436 J.D.
(adm. in WI; not adm. in IL) Navistar Intl. Corp.
Dedmond, Lisa Ann ....'56 '85 C.589 B.A. L.146 J.D. Asst. Pub. Def., Cook Co.
Dedrick, Katherine Smith, (AV) ....'57 '83 C.36 B.S. L.146 J.D. [Levenfeld P.]
Dee, Terrence J. ....'— '92 C.918 B.A. L.910 J.D. [Kirkland&E.]
Dee, Thomas F., (AV) ....'24 '54 C.424 L.209 LL.B. [T.F.Dee]
Dee, Thomas R. ....'61 '93 C.700 B.A. L.365 J.D. [Vedder,P.K.&K.]
Dee, Thomas F., Ltd., (AV) ....77 W. Washington St.
Deeb, Daniel J., (BVⓉ) ....'— '96 C.999 B.S. L.1119 J.D. [C] Schiff H.]
Deely, Sheila H. ....'70 '96 C.679 B.A. L.146 J.D. [Gardner C.&D.]
Deely, Stephen G. ....'61 '88 C.999 B.A. L.146 J.D. Regent Properties
Deem, Lori L. ....'72 '98 C.973 B.A. L.424 J.D. [A] Abrahamson V.&L.]
Dees, Richard L., (AV) ....'55 '80 C.801 B.S. L.339 J.D. [McDermott W.&E.]
Deffet, Timothy J. ....'73 '98 C.184 B.A. L.365 J.D. [A] MacCabe&M.]

Defrees & Fiske, (AV) BB
Suite 1100, 200 South Michigan Avenue, 60604
Telephone: 312-372-4000 Fax: 312-939-5617
Email: defrees@defrees.com URL: http://www.defrees.com
Members of Firm: Donald Defrees (1915-1968); Kenneth M. Fiske (1928-1978); Gregory E. Norwell; Timothy J. Riordan; Henry J. Underwood; Kenneth A. von Kluck; Leslie Recht (Ms.); W. Michael Seidel; Miriam Leskovar Burkland; Charles A. Semmelhack; Michael J. Powers; Timothy S. Buckley; Phillip B. Bowman; L. Judson Todhunter; Scott M. Levin. Associates: Douglas C. Giese; Jennifer Paganessi Fisher; Steven Wiser; Melanie C. Leonard. Of Counsel: Edward J. Griffin; John W. Hupp; William P. Steinbrecher; Marvin S. Helfand.
General Practice including Business, Corporate Law, Finance, Mergers and Acquisitions, Public and Unregulated Utilities and Energy, Taxation, Employment Benefits, Labor and Employment Law, General Civil Litigation, Appellate Practice, Copyright and Trademark and Unfair Competition, Non Profit and Tax Exempt Organizations, Trade Association, Health Care and Hospital Law, Wills and Probate, Trusts and Estates, Real Estate Law, Construction Law and Environmental Law, Bankruptcy and Reorganizations, Creditors Rights, Music Law, Intellectual Property, Telecommunications.
See Professional Biographies, CHICAGO, ILLINOIS

deFreitas, Rhonda E. .....'63 '94 C.1222 B.A. L.424 J.D. [A] Beermann S.W.B.B.G.&L.]
Degen, Charlene '— '76 C.966 B.A. L.209 J.D.
Econ. Develop. Admn., Dept. of Comm.
Degnan, Daniel R. ....'66 '95 C.742 B.A. L.424 J.D. 1st Dep. Treas. & Asst. CFO
DeGraff, Steven ....'66 '91 C.477 B.A. L.209 J.D. [Weinberg R.]
DeGrand, Karen Kies ....'60 '85 C&L.339 B.S., J.D. [Donohue B.M.&S.]
DeGrand, Luke, (AV) ....'60 '85 C&L.339 B.A., J.D. [L.DeGrand&Assoc.]

DeGrand, Luke, & Associates, P.C., (AV) BB
20 North Clark Street, Suite 1450, 60602
Telephone: 312-236-9200 Fax: 312-236-9201
URL: http://www.lukedegrand.com
Luke DeGrand;—Tracey L. Wolfe.
Civil Litigation, including Employment and Commercial Law.
See Professional Biographies, CHICAGO, ILLINOIS

deGrasse, Kathleen M. ....'64 '98 C.424 B.S. L.365 J.D. 6137 N. Elston Ave.
deGrasse, Rocco J., (AV) ....'59 '84 C.602 B.A. L.879 J.D. KPMG Peat Marwick
DeGroff, Christopher J. ....'70 '96 C&L.347 B.A., J.D. [Seyfarth S.]
DeHaan, Ronald M., (AV) ....'42 '67 C.597 B.A. L.339 J.D. [Kelly,O.M.D.&R.]
DeHayes, Karina H. ....'73 '98 C.477 B.A. L.424 J.D. [Tabet D.&R.]
Dehgan, Alex '— '95 C.228 B.S. L.1065 J.D.
(adm. in CA; not adm. in IL) Univ. of Chicago
Dehner, Rachael E. '— '04 C.966 B.A. L.1398 J.D.
(adm. in NY; not adm. in IL) [A] Jones D.]
Dehnke, Joshua P. ....'— '04 C.502 B.A. L.846 J.D. [A] Latham&W.]
de Hoyos, Debora, (AV) ....'53 '78 C.914 B.A. L.309 J.D. [Mayer,B.R.&M.]
Deibert, Katherine ....'79 '04 C.352 B.A. L.494 J.D. [A] Mayer,B.R.&M.]
Deignan, Robert E., (AV) ....'38 '66 C.352 B.A. L.365 LL.B. [C] Baker&M.]
Deis, J. Gregory ....'75 '03 C.436 B.S. L.339 J.D. [A] Mayer,B.R.&M.]
Deitch, I. Walter ....'45 '69 C.145 A.B. L.966 J.D. [Dykema G.P.]
DeJesus, Pedro, Jr. '66 '99 C.1016 B.A. L.597 J.D.
V.P. & Corp. Coun., Information Resources, Inc.
DeJong, Alvin W. ....'31 '58 C&L.352 B.A., J.D. 122 S. Michigan Ave.
De Jong, David J., (AV) ....'51 '80 C.999 L.597 J.D. [D.J.DeJong&Assoc.]
De Jong, Jeffrey P., (AV) '58 '85 C.429 B.A. L.910 J.D.
Sr. Claims Coun., Attorneys' Liability Assurance Society, Inc. A Risk Retention Group
DeJong, Kyle ....'79 '04 C.114 B.A. L.477 J.D. [A] Winston&S.]
DeJong, Lauren E. ....'— '94 C.323 B.A. L.597 J.D. [Schuyler,R.&Z.]
DeJong, Ralph E. ....'57 '82 C.114 B.A. L.602 J.D. [McDermott W.&E.]
De Jong, David J., & Associates, Ltd., (AV) .... 20 N. Clark St., Ste. 2700
DeJonker, Jason J. ....'74 '00 C&L.339 B.A., J.D. [A] McDermott W.&E.]
De Koven, Herman J., (AV) ....'12 '36 C&L.145 B.A., J.D. [C] Laner,M.D.B.L.&T.]
DeKoven, Ronald .....'— '68 C.813 B.A. L.145 J.D. [C] Jenner&B.] (⊙London, England)
Del Aguila, Paul ....'75 '01 C.112 B.A. L.339 J.D. [A] Greenberg T.]
Delaney, Aimee E. ....'73 '98 C.352 B.A. L.424 J.D. [Hinshaw&C.]
Delaney, Damien P. ....'77 '03 C.945 B.A. L.902 J.D. [A] Jenner&B.]
Delaney, Daniel J. ....'64 '89 C.339 B.A. L.145 J.D. [Mayer,B.R.&M.]
Delaney, Martin A., III ....'54 '79 C.696 B.A. L.902 J.D. 19 S. La Salle St., Ste. 450
Delaney, Pamela Michele ....'70 '96 C.741 B.A. L.1338 J.D. Asst. Pub. Guardian
Delaney, Timothy Q., (AV) '60 '88
C.339 B.S. L.273 J.D. [Brinks H.G.&L.] (See Pat. Sect.)
De La Rosa, Andrew ....'52 '81 C.347 B.A. L.145 J.D. [Morris,R.&D.] ⊙
DeLascio, John E. ....'— '91 C.209 B.A. L.365 J.D. [Meckler B.&T.]
de la Torre, Jasmine ....'72 '98 C&L.339 B.A., J.D. [A] Harris K.&G.]
de la Torre, Nicholas G. ....'73 '99 C.645 B.A. L.94 J.D. [A] Brinks H.G.&L.]
de LaVan, Joseph M. ....'34 '61 C&L.597 B.S., J.D. [McCracken,W.d.&H.]

Del Campo, Joseph A. .... '46 '73 C.424 B.B.A. L.365 J.D. 5438 W. Belmont Ave.
Del Campo, Rafael A. .... '21 '52 C.209 L.365 J.D. 100 N. LaSalle St.
Delelio, James D. .... '58 '86 C.209 B.A. L.365 J.D. Corp. Coun., Oracle Corp.
Deleo, Daniel J. .... '68 '99 C.335 B.A. L.209 J.D. [🄰 Price T.R.]
DeLeon, John R., (AV) .... '51 '77 C.339 B.A. L.209 J.D. 53 W. Jackson
Delgado, Marta .... '— '96 C.597 B.A. L.966 J.D. [🄰 S.D.Pollock&Assoc.]
Del Genio, Edward D. '42 '68
C.755 B.A. L.146 J.D. Dir., Arbitration, United Air Lines, Inc.
Del Giudice, Richard A., (AV) .... '59 '85 C.472 B.B.A. L.209 J.D. [Gozdecki&D.]
del Hierro, Edwin S., (AV) .... '62 '86 C.424 B.B.A. L.339 J.D. [Barack F.K.P.&N.]
DeLisio, Therese B. .... '55 '84 C.716 B.A. L.724 J.D. 1401 W. Gregory St., Apt. 2E
Della Maria, Joseph P., Jr., (AV) .... '40 '66 C&L.602 A.B., J.D. [Rothschild,B.&M.]
Dellsy, Harlan M., (AV) .... '48 '72 C.124 B.S. L.145 J.D. Commonwealth Edison Co.
Delman, Byron S., (AV) .... '37 '61 C&L.597 B.A., J.D. [DLPiper R.G.C.U.]

Delmenico, Ronald R., (AV) '38 '76 L.999
30 North LaSalle Street, Suite 3400, 60602
Telephone: 312-641-5311 Fax: 312-641-5520
Email: delmenico@aol.com URL: http://www.lawyers.com/delmenicolaw
Corporate Law, Business Law, Real Property, Commercial Law and International Law.
See Professional Biographies, CHICAGO, ILLINOIS

Delnero, John S., (AV) .... '61 '87 C&L.209 B.A., J.D. [Bell,B.&L.]
DeLoriea, Dale A. .... '50 '75 C.1100 A.B. L.424 J.D. 7334 W. Rascher Ave.
Delort, Mathias W. .... '61 '85 C.209 B.S. L.365 J.D. [Robbins,S.N.L.&T.]
Delott, Avery, (AV) .... '47 '72 C.339 B.S. L.597 J.D. [Kamensky,R.H.&D.] ⊙
Delph, Angela J. .... '72 '03 C&L.339 B.A., J.D. [🄰 Katten M.R.]
Del Principe, Donna, (BV) '— '80 C.339 B.A. L.365 J.D.
Asst. Univ. Coun., Univ. of Illinois at Chicago
DeLuca, Andrew M. .... '73 '98 C.602 B.A. L.880 J.D. [🄰 Cassidy,S.&G.]
DeLung, Harry L., Jr., (AV) .... '— '68 C.575 A.B. L.245 J.D. [🄲 Freeborn&P.]
de Lyon, Jennifer L. .... '— '04 C.705 B.S. L.1194 J.D. [🄰 Gardner C.&D.]
DeMaertelaere, Philip P. .... '68 '94 C.597 B.A. L.146 J.D. [🄲 Regas,F.&D.]
DeMarco, Daniel J. .... '39 '64 C.339 A.B. L.209 J.D. 680 N. Lake Shore Dr.
DeMarino, Kimberly Ann '74 '00
C.339 B.A. L.146 J.D. Claims Spec., Westport Insurance Corp.
DeMars, Allan J., (BV) .... '48 '72 C.339 B.A. L.209 J.D. [Spiegel&D.]
DeMarte, Luke W. ....'— '99 C.502 B.A. L.339 J.D. 401 N. Michigan Avenue, Suite 1900
Demas, Thomas L. .... '50 '78 C.339 B.S. L.365 J.D. Asst. Pub. Def.
DeMay, Jennifer D. .... '73 '98 C.339 B.A. L.424 J.D. Coun., Archdiocese of Chicago
Dembo, Harold S., (AV) .... '54 '79 C.339 B.S. L.597 J.D. [Weinberg R.]
de'Medici, Bruce E., (BV) ..... '54 '80 C.477 B.A. L.912 J.D. [Mandell M.] (⊙Oak Park)
De Ment, Christopher T. .... '72 '98 C.837 B.A. L.966 J.D. [🄰 Quarles&B.]
Demeros, Georgia Loukas .... '72 '98 C.424 B.B.A. L.146 J.D. [🄰 FagelHaber]
Demetrio, Michael K., (AV) .... '54 '79 C.602 B.B.A. L.146 J.D. [Corboy&D.]
Demetrio, Thomas A., (AV) .... '47 '73 C.602 B.A. L.146 J.D. [Corboy&D.]
DeMille, Rickard K. .... '76 '05 C.101 B.S. L.339 J.D. [🄰 Brinks H.G.&L.]
Demitro, Steve .... '62 '99 C.999 B.A. L.365 J.D. 221 N. La Salle St., Ste. 2100
Demnicki, Michael R. .... '68 '97 C.424 B.S. L.734 J.D. [🄰 Vedder,P.K.&K.]
Demos, Barbara M. .... '60 '92 C.339 B.A. L.146 J.D. 4746 N. Milwaukee Ave.
Demos, James .... '33 '61 C.339 L.365 J.D. 300 W. Washington St.‡
DeMoss, Jon W. .....'47 '72 C&L.339 B.S., J.D. Pres. & CEO, ISBA Mutual Insurance Co.
DeMott, Christine M. .... '73 '00 C.602 B.B.A. L.228 J.D. [🄰 Skadden,A.S.M.&F.]
deMoulpied, John C. .... '— '03 C.880 B.A. L.145 J.D. [🄰 Schiff H.]
Dempsey, Eóin M. .... '81 '05 C&L.339 A.B., J.D. [🄰 Ross,D.&B.]
Dempsey, Frederick R., (BV) .... '56 '89 C.424 A.B. L.597 J.D. [Gould&R.]
Dempsey, Gerard E. .... '40 '65 C.973 A.B. L.309 LL.B. [Klein,T.&J.]
Dempsey, John D., (AV) .... '26 '55 C&L.209 B.S.C., J.D. One N. LaSalle St.
Dempsey, Maire .... '77 '02 C.741 B.A. L.339 J.D. [🄰 Garretson&S.]
DeNardo, James P., (AV) .... '— '67 C&L.209 B.A., J.D. [McKenna S.]
Denberg, Kenneth H., (AV) .... '35 '59 C.339 B.A. L.209 J.D. [🄲 Michael B.&F.]
Denby, Robert L. '64 '89 C.145 B.A. L.477 J.D.
Sr. Claims Coun., Attorney's Liability Assurance Society, Inc.
Denby, Stephanie H., (AV) .... '62 '88 C.145 B.A. L.477 J.D. [Burke,W.M.&S.]
Dencer, Deborah L. .... '78 '03 C.57 B.A. L.146 J.D. [🄰 L.L.Veon]
Deneen, Sarah J. .... '75 '01 C.679 B.S. L.365 J.D. [🄰 Hedlund&H.]
Denenberg, Howard M., (AV) .... '34 '59 C.597 B.S. L.339 J.D. [Much S.F.D.A.&R.]
Dengel, Paul E., (AV) .... '— '79 C.674 A.B. L.893 J.D. [Schiff H.]
Denham, Paul A. .... '77 '04 C.273 B.A. L.597 J.D. [🄰 Franczek S.]
Denis, Marty .... '47 '70 C.339 B.A. L.597 J.D. [Barlow,K.&D.]
Denison, JoAnne M. .... '57 '85 C.339 B.S.M.E. L.347 J.D. [Denison&Assoc.]
Denison & Assocs., PC .... 212 W. Washington St., Apt. 2004
Denlow, Morton .... '47 '70 C.910 A.B. L.597 J.D. Mag. J.
Dennerline, Rhett R., (AV) ....'64 '89 C.679 B.S.A.A.E. L.477 J.D. [Competition L.] (Pat.)
Dennerline, Richard R., (BV) .... '— '89 C.679 B.S.I.E. L.477 J.D. [🄲 Freeborn&P.]
Denney, Emily A. .... '— '01 C.477 B.A. L.424 J.D. [🄰 Cinnamon M.]
Dennison, William J., II .... '77 '02 C.187 B.A. L.597 J.D. Asst. State Atty.
Denniston, James R. '60 '86 C.477 B.A. L.424 J.D.
Sr. Atty., Law & Pub. Policy Dept., MCI Worldcom, Inc.
Denniston, John L., (AV) .... '22 '51 C.602 B.A. L.477 J.D. [Morgan,L.D.&J.]
Dennor, Jill C. .... '— '98 C&L.339 A.B., J.D. Law Clk.
Dent, Barbara A. '— '82 C.4 B.S. L.276 J.D.
V.P., Sr. Atty., Leo Burnett Worldwide, Inc.
Dent, Robyn L. .... '69 '97 C.1375 B.A. L.201 J.D. 180 N. LaSalle St.
Dent, Thomas G., (AV) .... '42 '70 C.339 L.209 LL.B. [Seyfarth S.]
Denton, Deborah J. '50 '87 C&L.838 B.A., J.D.
(adm. in TN; not adm. in IL) F.D.I.C.
Denvir, Robert F., (AV) .... '45 '71 C.602 B.B.A. L.209 J.D. [Winston&S.]
Deodhar, Neal S. .... '61 '88 C.429 B.A. L.904 J.D. [🄰 Jacobs,B.O.S.&H.]
De Olazabal, Jazmin Irene .... '74 '00 C.94 B.A. L.128 J.D. 28 N. Clark
DePaul, Tina L. .... '78 '03 C.98 B.S. L.365 J.D. [🄰 Maciorowski,S.&U.]
Depcik, Alan M. .... '43 '70 120 W. Madison
DePinto, Jessica T. .... '69 '96 C.966 B.A. L.146 J.D. [🄰 Hodes,K.&P.]
Depke, Robert J. '62 '92 C.339 B.S.E.E. L.424 J.D.
[Trexler,B.G.B.&M.] (See Pat. Sect.)
Depke, S. Robert, (BV) .... '29 '58 C&L.424 B.S., J.D. [🄰 Dowd&D.]
DePriest, Jennifer Yule .... '— '00 C.347 B.A. L.424 J.D. [🄰 Sachnoff&W.]
Deptula, Mark A. .... '74 '99 C.260 B.A. L.1000 J.D. [🄰 Lord,B.&B.]
Deptula, Melissa Giovanini .... '72 '99 C.597 B.A. L.365 J.D. [🄰 Pretzel&S.]
Derbis, Joseph R. '72 '98 C.903 B.A. L.602 J.D.
(adm. in MD; not adm. in IL) Two North LaSalle Street, Suite 2200
Derechin, Daniel P. .... '— '01 C.264 B.A. L.276 J.D. [🄰 O'Hagan,S.&A.]
de Resendiz, Susan Barnes, (AVⓉ) '47 '74 C&L.608 B.A., J.D.
(adm. in OH; not adm. in IL) [🄲 Gardner C.&D.]
DeRoberts, David N. '60 '95 C.608 B.F.A. L.1003 J.D.
V.P. & Asst. Gen. Coun., JP Morgan Chase Bank N.A., Prop. Exch.

DeRose, Louis E., Jr. .... '46 '74 Asst. States Atty.
Derouin, Laura A. .... '69 '95 C.339 B.S. L.276 J.D. [🄰 Holland&K.]
Derringer, Steven E. .... '69 '97 C.477 B.A. L.976 J.D. [Bartlit B.H.P.&S.]
Dershow, Jeremy L. .... '75 '02 C.475 B.A. L.146 J.D. [🄰 J.C.Wunsch]
Der-Yeghiayan, Samuel .... '52 '78 C.999 B.A. L.1218 J.D. Dist. J.
Desai, Jason P. .... '— '01 C.813 A.B. L.309 J.D. [🄰 Kirkland&E.]
Desai, Neal S. .... '73 '99 C.477 B.A. L.146 J.D. U.S. Dept. of Labor
Desai, Nidhi S. .... '72 '97 C.910 B.A. L.424 J.D. [Ballard,D.B.&H.]
Desai, Sonal P. .... '79 '04 C.1182 B.A. L.597 J.D. [🄰 Gould&R.]
Desai, Sonia A. .... '73 '98 C&L.339 B.S., J.D. [🄰 Dykema G.P.]
DeSalvo, Scott David .... '69 '98 C&L.209 B.A., J.D. [🄰 M.L.Karno&Assoc.]

DeSanto, Morgan & Mittelman, An Assoc. of Prof. Corps.
(See Libertyville)

DeShano, Kimberly M. .... '74 '99 C.473 B.A. L.930 J.D. [🄰 Greenberg T.]
Desharnais, Kevin G. .... '66 '93 C.188 B.S. L.1040 J.D. [🄲 Mayer,B.R.&M.]
Desideri, Lawrence R., (AV) .... '58 '83 C.589 B.S. L.339 J.D. [Winston&S.]
Des Jardins, Leonard A. ...... '28 '56 L.209 J.D. Eight South Michigan Avenue, Suite 3400
Des Laurier, Victor A. .... '65 '93 C.589 B.S. L.209 J.D. [FagelHaber]
Desmond, Michael K., (BV) .... '61 '92 C.589 B.S. L.989 J.D. [Figliulo&S.]
Desmond, Thomas P., (AV) .... '56 '81 C.602 B.B.A. L.597 J.D. [Vedder,P.K.&K.]
Desnet, Holly E., (CV) .... '55 '85 C.801 B.S. L.365 J.D. Asst. States Atty.‡
D'Esposito, Julian C., Jr., (AV) .... '44 '69 C.424 B.S. L.597 J.D. [Mayer,B.R.&M.]
Despotes, Andrea M. .... '69 '95 C.813 A.B. L.309 J.D. [Neal,G.&E.]
Despres, Leon M., (AV) .... '08 '29 C&L.145 Ph.B., J.D. [Despres,S.&G.]
Despres, Schwartz & Geoghegan, (AV) .... Suite 711, 77 West Washington Street
Desser, Jennifer .... '70 '97 C.477 B.A. L.146 J.D. [Neal,G.&E.]
De Stefano, John V. .... '44 '68 C.209 A.B. L.365 J.D. 4829 N. Sunrise Ln.
Detjen, Mary L. '49 '74 C.475 B.A. L.966 J.D.
(adm. in WI; not adm. in IL) Merit Systems Protection Bd.
Detuno, Joseph E., (AV) .... '31 '54 C&L.209 LL.B. [Roddy,L.&Z.]
Deuel, Patti Olson, (AV) .... '59 '85 C.589 B.A. L.365 J.D. [Kiesler&B.]
Deutsch, Adam B. .... '70 '96 C.552 B.A. L.569 J.D. [Eimer S.K.&S.]
Deutsch, Earl A., (AV) .... '24 '50 C.339 L.365 J.D. [Deutsch,L.&E.]
Deutsch, Michael E. .... '45 '69 C.339 B.A. L.597 J.D. [People's]
Deutsch, Stuart L. .... '45 '72 C.477 B.A. L.976 J.D. Chicago-Kent College of Law

Deutsch, Levy & Engel, Chartered, (AV)
225 West Washington Street Suite 1700, 60606 ⊙
Telephone: 312-346-1460 Fax: 312-346-1859
Email: Lawyers@dlec.com URL: http://www.dlec.com
Earl A. Deutsch; Paul M. Levy; Terry L. Engel; Frank R. Cohen; Jerry I. Rudman; Michael J. Devine; Stuart Berks; Kenneth W. Funk; Phillip J. Zisook; Dennis E. Frisby; Joel A. Stein; Alvin J. Helfgot; James E. O'Halloran, III; Aaron B. Zarkowsky; Leo G. Aubel;—Karen Kavanagh Mack; Moyenda Mutharika Knapp; David J. Ben-Dov; Lee E. Farbman. Counsel: Marshall D. Krolick; Arthur J. Sabin.
General Civil and Trial Practice in all State and Federal Courts. Corporation, Probate, Publishing and Libel Defense, Real Estate, Real Estate Taxation, Estate Planning, Deferred Compensation Planning, Taxation Law and Trademark and Copyright Law. Eminent Domain/Condemnation.
See Professional Biographies, CHICAGO, ILLINOIS

Deutschman, Jeffrey Scott .... '61 '88 C.966 B.A. L.61 J.D. 77 W. Washington St.
DeValk, Carrie L. .... '68 '93 C.971 A.B. L.339 J.D. [🄰 Goodsmith G.&U.]
Devane, Mark F., (AV) .... '51 '83 C.871 B.S. L.339 J.D. [🄲 Menges&M.]
Devaney, Joseph L., III .... '75 '01 C.473 B.A. L.94 J.D. [🄰 Winston&S.]
Devassy, Debra Rose .... '79 '04 C&L.339 B.A., J.D. [🄰 Askounis&B.]
Devata, Pamela Quigley .... '76 '01 C.910 B.A. L.146 J.D. [🄰 Seyfarth S.]
De Vault, Sharon L. .... '63 '90 C.145 B.A. L.338 J.D. [🄲 Mayer,B.R.&M.]
Devereux, Aimee M. ..... '63 '88 C.93 B.A. L.424 J.D. 2600 N. Southport Ave., Suite 119
Devereux, Clarke P. ..... '62 '87 C.93 B.A. L.424 J.D. [🄲 Durkin&R.] (⊙San Fran., CA)
Devereux, Mary Patricia .... '58 '84 C.93 B.A. L.424 J.D. Asst. State's Atty. Off.
Devereux, Matthew J. .... '70 '96 C.602 B.A. L.209 J.D. [🄰 Tressler,S.M.&P.]
Devience, Alexander, Jr., (Ltd.) '38 '68
C.446 B.A. L.424 J.D. Assoc. Prof. of Bus. Law, DePaul Univ.
DeVilling, Brian E. .... '— '02 C.477 B.A. L.424 J.D. [🄰 Clausen M.]
Devine, Denise M. .... '67 '94 C.172 B.S. L.209 J.D. [Katten M.R.]
Devine, Elizabeth A. .... '67 '95 C.209 B.S. L.178 J.D. [🄲 Skadden,A.S.M.&F.]
DeVine, John K. .... '64 '93 C.478 B.A. L.365 J.D. 20 N. Wacker Dr., Ste. 1040
Devine, Matthew R. .... '67 '04 C.352 B.A. L.424 J.D. [🄰 Jenner&B.]
Devine, Michael J., (AV) .... '52 '78 C.363 B.S.B.A. L.365 J.D. [Deutsch,L.&E.] ⊙
Devine, Richard A., (AV) .... '43 '68 C.424 B.A. L.597 J.D. Off. of State's Atty.
DeVito, Albert S. .... '52 '78 C.597 B.A. L.365 J.D. [Sudekum,C.&S.]
Devitt, Donald W., (AV) .... '59 '84 C&L.424 B.A., J.D. [🄲 Scopelitis,G.L.&H.]
Devitt, William E. .... '— '95 C.602 B.S.E.E. L.128 J.D. [Kirkland&E.]
Devlin, Donald M., (AV) .... '46 '74 C.72 B.A. L.502 J.D. 69 W. Washington
Devlin, Mary M. '45 '85 C.339 B.A. L.146 J.D.
Reg. Coun., Ctr. for Professional Responsibility, Amer. Bar Assn .
Devlin, Rosemary Ann .... '56 '81 C.228 A.B. L.94 J.D. 3100 N. Lake Shore Dr.
DeVriendt, Charles J., (AV) .... '46 '76 C.1024 B.A. L.209 J.D. [Fitzgerald&C.]
DeVriendt, Jennifer A. .... '— '02 C.352 L.146 J.D. [🄰 Chapman&C.]
De Vries, James H., (AV) '32 '61 C.174 B.S. L.477 J.D.
Exec. Vice President, Secretary & General Coun., Quixote Corporation
DeVries, Laurence J., & Associates ...... '60 '85 C.114 B.A. L.597 J.D. [DeVries&Assoc.]
De Vries, Melissa Hoogendoorn .... '69 '94 C.114 B.A. L.339 J.D. [🄰 Hoogendoorn&T.]
DeVries and Associates .... 566 W. Adams, Ste. 600
DeWitt, Douglas M. .... '74 '01 C.608 B.S. L.339 J.D. [🄰 Iwan C.H.H.&V.]
DeWitt, Kelly D. .... '75 '00 C&L.339 B.S., J.D. [🄰 Holland&K.]
DeWolfe, Elena M. .... '69 '95 C.112 B.A. L.597 J.D. Sr. Atty., IBM Corp.
DeWolfe, John C., Jr., (AV) .... '13 '39 C.339 B.A. L.966 J.D. 135 S. LaSalle St.
DeWolfe, Ruthanne K. .... '33 '76 C.597 B.A. L.209 J.D. Legal Asst. Found. of Chicago
Deyne, Herbert G. .... '24 '54 C.677 L.145 J.D. 3224 W. N. St.
De Yoe, David P. .... '48 '73 C.477 B.A. L.813 J.D. [🄲 McDermott W.&E.]
DeYoung, William F., (AV) .... '53 '80 C.597 B.S. L.339 J.D. [Chuhak&T.]
De Zelar, James M. .... '42 '70 C.608 B.S. L.150 J.D. [Robbins,S.&P.]
Diab, Malik R. .... '68 '93 C.597 B.A. L.339 J.D. [Diab&B.]
Diab & Bock .... 20 N. Wacker Drive, Suite 1741
Diacou, Nicholas H., (AV) '46 '72
C.424 B.A. L.209 J.D. Asst. V.P., CNAGlobal Specialty Lines
Diamant, Laura Jo .... '57 '87 C.910 B.A. L.146 J.D. State Attys. Off.
Diamantopoulos-Burgis, Tina '70 '94
C.436 B.A. L.597 J.D. Branch Chief, Chicago, M.R.O., S.E.C.
Diamond, Dale A. .... '59 '91 C.112 B.A. L.365 J.D. Institute Ins. Co.
Diamond, David N. .... '70 '97 C.966 B.A. L.910 J.D. Pres., Broadview, Inc.
Diamond, Eugene C. .... '52 '79 C.602 A.B. L.734 J.D. Holy Cross Hospital
Diamond, Jennifer L. Smrstik .... '72 '02 C.696 B.A. L.424 J.D. Trial Atty.
Diamond, Paul R., (AV) .... '55 '80 C&L.339 B.S., J.D. [Wildman,H.A.&D.]
Diamond, Shari S. .... '47 '85 C.477 B.A. L.145 J.D. Amer. Bar Found.
Diamond, Stephen B., (AV) .... '43 '68 C.309 A.B. L.477 J.D. [Schad,D.&S.]

Diamond, Stewart H., (AV) .... '41 '63 C&L.145 B.A., J.D. [Ancel,G.D.B.D.&R.]
Diamond, Terrance L. .... '— '79 C.339 B.A. L.945 J.D. [Ⓐ Neal&L.]
Diamond-Falk, Nathan, Law Offices of, (BV) '49 '74
C.477 B.A. L.209 J.D. 820 West Jackson Boulevard Suite 310
DiAndrea-Iversen, Laura, (BV) '— '88 C.589 B.S. L.365 J.D.
134 N. La Salle, Ste. 1020
Dibble, Kelly King .... '60 '88 C.914 B.A. L.309 J.D. Hyatt Develop. Corp.
DiBella, Mia Grace .... '— '01 C.165 B.A. L.597 J.D. [Ⓐ Latham&W.]
Di Camillo, Joseph G., (AV) .... '65 '90 C.597 B.A. L.424 J.D. [Ⓐ G.E.W.Kelter,Jr.]
DiCarlantonio, Pamela S. .... '64 '96 C.446 B.S. L.339 J.D. [Ⓐ Sugar,F.&F.]
DiCastri, Damon .... '68 '94 C.966 B.B.A. L.597 J.D. [Winston&S.]
DiCerbo, Louis P. ...... '59 '85 C.299 A.B. L.94 J.D. Asst. Gen. Coun., Bank of America
DiCerbo, Ronald A. .... '68 '00 C.999 B.S. L.1000 J.D. [McAndrews,H.&M.]
DiCianni, Thomas G. .... '54 '80 C.339 B.A. L.209 J.D. [Ancel,G.D.B.D.&R.]
Dick, Richard E., (AV) .... '46 '73 C.146 B.S.I.E. L.424 J.D. [Ⓒ Greenberg T.] (Pat.)
Dicker, Steven Michael .... '55 '80 C.1044 B.A. L.365 J.D. 134 N. La Salle St.
Dickerson, Anne E. .... '58 '86 C.959 B.F.A. L.209 J.D. [Ⓐ Gould&R.]
Dickerson, Chris L. .... '62 '98 C.871 B.S. L.966 J.D. [Ⓐ Skadden,A.S.M.&F.]
Dickett, Diane M. .... '61 '85 C.209 B.S. L.339 J.D. Asst. State's Atty.
Dickett, Gust W., (AV) .... '33 '60 C.339 B.S. L.209 J.D. [Ⓒ Regas,F.&D.]
Dickett, James E. .... '66 '91 C.339 B.S. L.597 J.D. State Dept. of Rev.
Dickett, William G., (BV) .... '64 '89 C.339 B.S. L.597 J.D. [Sidley A.B.&W.]
Dickie, Dean A., (AV) .... '— '69 C.597 B.A. L.276 J.D. [Dykema G.P.]
Dickinson, Christopher C. .... '60 '88 C&L.966 B.A., J.D. [Jenner&B.]
Dickler, Michael G. .... '74 '99 C&L.477 B.A, J.D. [Ⓐ Sperling&S.]
Dickman, Bruce A., Law Office of '46 '76
C.1016 B.A. L.365 J.D. 134 N. LaSalle St., Ste. 2222
Dickman, John M. .... '65 '92 C.352 B.B.A. L.424 J.D. [Winston&S.]
Dickman, Michael J. .... '60 '90 C.1016 B.S.B.A. L.209 J.D. Cir. J.
Dicks, Dennis D. .... '46 '72 C.966 B.A. L.46 J.D. 221 N. LaSalle St.
Dickson, William M., (AV) .... '26 '51 C&L.602 A.B., LL.B. Ill. Com. Comm. Comr.
Dickstein, Beth J. .... '63 '88 C.339 B.S. L.659 J.D. [Sidley A.B.&W.]
Di Cola, Elizabeth A. .... '59 '94 C.339 B.S. L.1066 J.D. Pub. Guard. Off.
DiCrescenzo, Nick .... '— '97 C&L.145 B.A., J.D. [Kirkland&E.]
Di Domenico, Michael G. .... '77 '03 C.209 B.A. L.365 J.D. [Ⓐ Lake,T.&D.]
Dieckman, Kathleen A. '— '92 C.473 B.A. L.200 J.D.
(adm. in OH; not adm. in IL) [Ⓐ Meyer&B.]
Diedrich, Michael C. .... '72 '98 C.424 B.A. L.146 J.D. 2 N. LaSalle St.
Diehl, Chad A. .... '— '03 L.424 J.D. [Ⓐ Katten M.R.]
Diehl, Robert S., Jr. .... '25 '51 C.209 L.365 LL.B. 6870 N. Wildwood St.‡
Diehl, Robert W. .... '64 '97 C.172 B.S. L.1000 J.D. [Ⓐ Seyfarth S.] (Pat.)
Diemer, Bryan P. .... '72 '99 C.339 A.B. L.146 J.D. [Ⓐ Baum S.A.&N.]
Dienner, John A., III, (AV) .... '45 '72 C.210 A.B. L.365 J.D. [Kubasiak,F.R.&R.]
Dienstag, Gary E., (AV) .... '45 '69 C.966 B.S. L.424 J.D. [Springer,C.&D.] ⊙
Dierkes, Michael T. .... '— '01 C.145 A.B. L.339 J.D. [Ⓐ Kirkland&E.]
Dierks, Marieluise H. .... '27 '54 C.597 B.S. L.365 LL.B. 1721 N. Kedvale Ave.
Dierstein, M. Lois .... '25 '57 C.597 B.S. L.209 J.D. Asst. Corp. Coun.
Dieterichs, Alison A. .... '74 '03 C.966 B.A. L.146 J.D. [Ⓐ Jenner&B.]
Diethelm, Hallie A. .... '— '99 C&L.608 B.A., J.D. [Ⓐ Ungaretti&H.]
Dietrich, Ronald R. .... '57 '82 C.597 B.A. L.424 J.D. [Ⓒ Mayer,B.R.&M.]
Dietz, Catherine M. .... '— '04 C.602 B.A. L.597 J.D. [Ⓐ Jones D.]
Dietz, Gerald T. .... '69 '99 C.339 B.A. L.1000 J.D. [Ⓐ Ancel,G.D.B.D.&R.]
Diffin, Ed .... '78 '03 C.827 B.A. L.145 J.D. [Ⓐ Lovells]

Di Franco & Associates, P.C.
(See Park Ridge)

DiFronzo, Michael A. '— '94 C.506 B.S. L.508 J.D.
(adm. in MT; not adm. in IL) [McDermott W.&E.]
DiGiannantonio, Michael P. .... '78 '04 C&L.477 B.A., J.D. [Ⓐ Winston&S.]
DIGiovanni, Frank R. .... '22 '80 C.424 B.S. L.146 J.D. 4405 W. Marquette Rd.‡
DiGiovanni, Nick J., (AV) .... '55 '80 C.802 B.B.A. L.602 J.D. [Lord,B.&B.]
Di Giulio, Barbara .... '59 '84 C.597 B.A. L.339 J.D. Fed. Trade Comm.
Digrino, Mariah F. .... '78 '04 C.927 B.A. L.339 J.D. [Ⓐ DLPiper R.G.C.U.]
Dijohn, John .... '— '01 C.209 B.A. L.146 J.D. [Ⓐ Littler M.]
DiLallo, Richard J. .... '— '01 C.589 B.A. L.146 J.D [Ⓐ Chapman&C.]
Dilbeck, Delbert N. '32 '59 C.169 L.770 LL.B.
(adm. in CA; not adm. in IL) Dept. of Jus.
Di Leonardi, Robert J., (AV) .... '34 '59 C.597 B.S. L.209 J.D. 56 W. Schiller
Dilgart, Sally L. .... '49 '77 C.207 B.A. L.608 J.D. Asst. Atty. Gen.
Dillard, Carol C. .... '57 '83 C.339 B.S. L.209 J.D. 175 West Jackson, Suite 1600
Dillard, Jeffery D. .... '60 '89 C.257 B.S. L.46 J.D. [Dillard&N.]
Dillard, Kirk W. .... '55 '83 C.927 B.A. L.209 J.D. State Sen. [Lord,B.&B.]
Dillard & Noel .... 25 East Washington Street, Suite 1206
Dillenbeck, John L. .... '76 '01 C.475 B.A. L.146 J.D. [Ⓐ Segal M.S.&M.]
Dillenbeck, Melissa Skylas .... '75 '01 C.597 B.A. L.146 J.D. [Ⓐ Gardner C.&D.]
Dillon, David C. .... '43 '75 C.209 B.S. L.146 J.D. [Dillon&N.]
Dillon, Elizabeth .... '— '95 C.475 B.A. L.365 J.D. [Ⓐ O'Hagan,S.&A.]
Dillon, John B. .... '23 '53 L.209 J.D. [Ⓒ Kessler,K.&C.]
Dillon, Thomas A., Jr. .... '28 '54 C&L.424 Ph.B. Ill. Indus. Comm.
Dillon, Thomas J., (AV) .... '54 '79 C.145 B.A. L.597 J.D. [McFadden&D.]
Dillon, Tracey A. ...... '73 '98 C.679 B.S. L.589 J.D. 200 North LaSalle Street, Suite 2700
Dillon, William A. .... '25 '58 C.999 B.E. L.365 LL.B. Inland Steel Co.
Dillon, William S., (AV) .... '16 '46 C&L.424 LL.B. 431 S. Dearborn St.
Dillon Kotz, Jennifer L. .... '69 '98 C.105 B.A. L.424 J.D. [Ⓐ Schiller,D.&F.]
Dillon & Nash, Ltd., (BV) .... 111 W. Washington St.
DiLoreto, Frank L. .... '56 '83 C.339 B.A. L.365 J.D. Sr. Atty., F.D.I.C.
DiLoreto, Martin A., Jr. .... '— '97 C.475 B.A. L.477 J.D. [Kirkland&E.]
Dim, Martin L. .... '49 '74 C.477 B.A. L.597 J.D. 333 N. Canal St.

DiMaggio, Debra, Law Offices of '58 '83 C&L.209 B.S., J.D.
161 North Clark Street, Suite 4700, 60601
Telephone: 312-364-0404 Facsimile: 312-364-0250 URL: http://www.setufree.net
Email: deb@dimaggio-law.com URL: http://www.lawyers.com/dimaggiolaw
—Leslie J. Fineberg; Melissa Ann Bell.
Family Law, including all phases of Matrimonial Litigation, Divorce Litigation, Divorce Taxation, Financial Law and Finances, Financial Discovery and Analysis, Tax Considerations and Retirement Benefits, Business Valuation, Corporate Holdings and Stock Plans, Negotiation and Mediation, Joint Parenting Agreements, Enforcement & Modification of Judgments, Disproportionate Awards, Custody and Visitation, Pre-nuptial and Post-nuptial Agreements, Parentage Actions, Adoption, UCCJA, Same-Sex Unions, Entertainment and Residential Real Estate.
See Professional Biographies, CHICAGO, ILLINOIS

Dimitrief, Alex, (AV) ... '— '85 C.976 B.A. L.309 J.D. [Kirkland&E.] (⊙New York, NY)
Dimond, Thomas W. .... '58 '90 C.339 B.S. L.145 J.D. [Mayer,B.R.&M.]
DiMonte, Karen Fisher, (BV) .... '57 '85 C.966 B.A. L.209 J.D. 1515 W. Roscoe

Di Monte & Lizak
(See Park Ridge)

DiNardo, Lawrence C., (AV) .... '— '74 C&L.602 B.A., J.D. [Jones D.]
DiNardo, Richard L. .... '67 '93 C.436 B.A. L.879 J.D. [Ⓐ Pedersen&H.]
Dingerson, Daniel A. .... '— '04 C.477 B.A. L.1068 J.D. [Ⓐ Foley&L.]
Dinizulu, Yao O. .... '72 '97 C.257 B.A. L.339 J.D. 205 W. Randolph St.
Dinkel, Norman J., Jr. .... '44 '69 C.393 B.A. L.424 J.D. Pres., Dinkel's Bakery Inc.
Dinos, Mark .... '— '02 C.999 B.S. L.365 J.D. [Ⓐ Alholm,M.K.H.&O.]
Dinwoodie, Graeme B. .... '66 '89 L.999 LL.B. 565 W. Adams St.
Diomedi, Gina M. .... '69 '01 C.477 B.A. L.424 J.D. [Ⓐ Mayer,B.R.&M.]
DiPentima, Matthew R. .... '75 '03 C.93 B.A. L.597 J.D. [Ⓐ Jenner&B.]
DiPiero, Vincent F. .... '54 '79 C.338 B.S. L.365 J.D. 61 W. Superior St.
DiRago, Joseph B. .... '— '04 C.221 B.A. L.339 J.D. [Ⓐ Katten M.R.]
Dirkin, Jennifer M., (AV) '60 '85
C&L.339 B.A., J.D. Sr. Atty., Northern Trust Corporation
Dirmantas, Darius R. .... '68 '00 C.1308 B.S. L.424 J.D. [Ⓐ Komie&Assoc.]
DiSanto, Carrie J. .... '71 '96 C.57 B.A. L.602 J.D. [Ⓐ Baker&M.]
Discipio, Francis J., (AV) .... '61 '88 C.338 B.S. L.1029 J.D. [F.J.Discipio] ⊙
Discipio, Francis J., Ltd., (AV) .... 111 West Washington Street, Suite 1259 (⊙Oak Brook)
Dishman, Neil H. .... '78 '03 C.303 B.A. L.477 J.D. 320 West Ohio Street, Suite 500
Di Silvestro, Robert F. .... '32 '56 C&L.424 B.S.C., J.D. 5231 N. Harlem Ave.
Di Silvestro, Robert J., (AV) .... '60 '85 C.597 B.A. L.602 J.D. 5231 N. Harlem Ave.
DiSilvestro, Stephen P. .... '63 '89 C.602 B.B.A. L.209 J.D. 5231 N. Harlem Ave.
DiStefano, Joann .... '52 '78 C.205 B.A. L.365 J.D. 6704 W. Thorndale
Ditelberg, Joshua L. .... '66 '91 C.659 B.A. L.477 J.D. [Seyfarth S.]
Ditkowsky, Kenneth K. .... '36 '61 C.145 B.S. L.424 J.D. [Ditkowsky&C.]
Ditkowsky & Contorer .... 2626 W. Touhy Ave.
DiVarco, Sandra M. .... '71 '02 C.339 B.S.N. L.424 J.D. [Ⓐ McDermott W.&E.]
Diver, Michael J. .... '69 '96 C.105 B.A. L.596 J.D. [Ⓐ Katten M.R.]
DiVincenzo, Anthony S., (AV) '52 '76
C.424 B.A. L.597 J.D. [DiVincenzo S.S.] (⊙Skokie)
DiVincenzo Schoenfield Swartzman, (AV) .... 33 N. La Salle St., Suite 2900
Divis, Timothy E. '54 '80 C&L.546 B.A., J.D.
(adm. in NE; not adm. in IL) Fed. Deposit Ins. Corp.
DiVito, Gino L. .... '37 '63 C&L.424 J.D. [Tabet D.&R.]
Diwan, Mohammed A. .... '— '04 C.477 B.A. L.228 J.D. [Ⓐ Wildman,H.A.&D.]
Dixler, Kevin Lawrence, (CV) .... '— '93 C.339 B.S. L.365 J.D. 28 E. Jackson Blvd.
Dixon, Alan J. '— '49 C.339 B.S. L.910 LL.B.
[Bryan C.] (⊙Wash., DC; St. Louis, MO)
Dixon, Elise .... '65 '92 C.243 B.B.A. L.597 J.D. 39 S. LaSalle St.
Dixon, John T. .... '21 '50 C.803 L.365 J.D. [Power&D.] ‡
Dixon, Karen M. .... '72 '97 C.546 B.A. L.146 J.D. [Meckler B.&T.]
Dixon, Robert W. .... '75 '01 C.352 B.B.A. L.221 J.D. [Ⓐ Vedder,P.K.&K.]
Dixon, Sherrie Rosen .... '55 '79 C.597 B.S. L.424 J.D. The Northern Tr. Co.
Dixon, Steven R. .... '74 '02 C.851 B.A. L.309 J.D. [Ⓐ Baker&M.]
Dixon, Stewart S., (AV) .... '30 '57 C.976 B.A. L.477 J.D. [Wildman,H.A.&D.]
Dizik, Victoria .... '79 '04 C.1036 B.A. L.209 J.D. [Ⓐ Meckler B.&T.]
Dizon, Gilbert R. .... '68 '96 C.347 B.A. L.1187 J.D. [Bromden&D.]
Djordjevic, Nada .... '70 '02 C.293 B.A. L.339 J.D. [Ⓐ Jenner&B.]
Djurisic, Paul I. .... '65 '92 C.339 B.A. L.209 J.D. [P.Djurisic]
Djurisic, Sheni H. .... '70 '95 C.424 B.S. L.146 J.D. [Ⓐ Weldon-Linne&V.]
Djurisic, Paul, Law Offices of .... 105 W. Madison St., Ste. 1200

DLA Piper Rudnick Gray Cary US LLP, (AV)
203 North La Salle Street, Suite 1900, 60601-1293 ⊙
Telephone: 312-368-4000 FAX: 312-236-7516
URL: http://www.dlapiper.com
Partners: Stanley J. Adelman; Stephen L. Agin; Ross J. Altman; Richard W. Ashley III; Anne C. Auten; James L. Beard; Michael L. Ben-Isvy; Eric Berg; Adam T. Berkoff; Mark A. Berkoff; Daniel S. Brennan; Michael G. Brennan; Laurence R. Bronska; Hal M. Brown; Catherine M. Burkhardt; Peter C. B. Bynoe; William J. Campbell, Jr.; Catherine J. Casey; Danielle Meltzer Cassel; Steven J. Christenholz; Fredric A. Cohen; Louis S. Cohen; Merle Teitelbaum Cowin; John T. J. Cusack; Gregory R. A. Dahlgren; Alan S. Dalinka; Byron S. Delman; Peter J. Donoghue; Brian K. Doyle; Mary Kay Gara Dreyfus; Janice L. Duban; Elizabeth R. Bacon Ehlers; Steven E. Ehrlich; Michael H. Elam; Lesli L. Mann Falk; Mark I. Feldman; Lawrence J. Fey; Michael B. Fischer; Harold W. Francke; Elizabeth H. Friedgut; William M. Gantz; Deborah L. Gersh; Mark A. Gershon; Thomas F. Geselbracht; Allen J. Ginsburg (P.C.); David Glickstein; Larry S. Goldberg; Edward S. Goldman; Robert H. Goldman; Stephen M. Gordon; Shepard Gould; Ross Green; David V. Hall; Errol R. Halperin; Timothy S. Harris; Gregory W. Hayes; Stuart Hershman; John H. Heuberger; Jennifer D. Homer; Paul Homer (P.C.); Leroy G. Inskeep; Samuel B. Isaacson; J. Kenneth Joung; Howard E. Kane; Jason N. Kaplan; C. Olivia Keating; Sandra Y. Kellman; Michael L. Kenaga; Jonathan D. King; Richard F. Klawiter; Robert W. Kleinman; Ian S. Kopelman (Chair, Employee Benefits and Executive Compensation Group); Michael P. Kuppersmith; Stephen A. Landsman; Ty D. Laurie; Norman M. Leon; Jason W. Levin; Peter A. Levy; Susan Grob Lichtenfeld; Janet A. Lindeman; Roger L. Longtin (P.C.); Gerald B. Lurie; David G. Lynch; Robert S. Markin; Christina L. Martini; Adrianne C. Mazura; Andrew W. McCune; Sally J. McDonald; Keith W. Medansky; David E. Mendelsohn; Lee I. Miller; Nicholas R. Minear; David N. Missner; Alison M. Mitchell; Anita T. Molano; Richard J. Morey; Portia Owen Morrison; Sonya D. Naar; David M. Neff; Theodore J. Novak (P.C.); Michael C. O'Neil; Jeffrey N. Owen; Anne M. Pachciarek; Marilyn A. Pearson (Not admitted in IL); James M. Phipps; Dov J. Pinchot; Ruth A. Pivar; George T. Plumb; Harold B. Pomerantz; Michael S. Poulos; Dennis J. Powers; William L. Rawson; David L. Reifman; James D. Roberts; Lawrence A. Robins (P.C.); Peter B. Ross; Lewis G. Rudnick; William A. Rudnick; James P. Ryther; Vincent A. Sanchez; Kenneth L. Schmetterer; Renee M. Schoenberg; Stephen W. Schwab; Andrew P. Scott; Randal J. Selig; Paul W. Shadle; Joseph W. Sheyka; Donald A. Shindler; David B. Sickle; Seymour F. Simon; Michael L. Sklar; Perry J. Snyderman; Morton M. Steinberg; Samuel B. Stempel; Kelly L. Stonebraker; Alexander Terras; Monica L. Thompson (P.C.); Bedell A. Tippins; Christopher J. Townsend; John Verhey; Richard A. Wendy; Dennis E. Wieczorek; Mark R. Williams; Dennis M. Wilson; Lawrence A. Wojcik; Theodore I. Yi; Mark D. Yura; Alison N. Zirn; William A. Zolla. Senior Counsel: Charles L. Edwards; Richard S. Homer; Carol S. Lepman. Of Counsel: Elizabeth H. Belkin; David E. Cher (Not admitted in IL); Jonathan A. Cohen; Rasha Elganzouri; Caryn S. Englander; Tracy L. Farley; Marc I. Fenton; Reynaldo Preston Glover; Lisa Goyer; David T. Hejna; Robert G. Hertel; Karen Litscher Johnson; Christina King Loundy; Charles Lynn Lowder; Michele G. Magner; Susan M. Pedersen; Patricia M. Relosky; David J. Richter; Lester Rosen; Paul D. Rudnick; Marc Seidler; Janet L. Tracy; Julius Y. Yacker. Associates: Karl M. Ahlm; Brian A. Audette; Heidi J. Azulay; Jennifer J. Baumann; Elizabeth Rowntree Beck; Andrew P. Bleiman; William A. Borders; Ann Marie Bredin; Matthew F. Carmody; Corinne Pavlis Carr; Denise C. Castillo; Diana Chafey; Amy Cheng; William Choslovsky; Brian Adam Cohen; Joseph E. Collins; Jesse A. Criz; Mariah F. Digrino; Jesse W. Dodson; C. Craig Dolly, Jr.; Gina L. Durham; Patrice D'Ziire; Peter M. Ellis; Timothy M. Enright; David J. Feinberg; Jeffrey M. Friedman; Paula Davis Friedman; Michael S. Gershowitz; Leah D. Gidron; Joshua M. Glazov; Emily S. Gottlieb; Gregg Seth Graines; Deborah M. Gutfeld; Krista S. Hallberg; Albert E. Hartmann; Robert T. Heffernan; Jonathan R. Helton; R. Matthew Hiller; John A. Hughes; Steven V. Hunter; Christina Hwang; Douglas W. Hyman; Unmaish Jindal; Richard Blake Johnston; Amanda Jones; Michael Kasdin; Alice A. Kelly (Not admitted in IL); Robyn Koyner; Erin Krejci; Jason Krellner; Vildana Kujundjic; Peter Gibbons Lawrence; Robert J. LeDuc; Sang-yul Lee; Sal A. Lele; Jamie Lockhart (Not admitted in IL); Gillian D. Madsen; Michele K. Malis; Katherine F. Marzo; Val D. Mathelier; Spiridoula Mavrothalasitis; Michael D. McCullough; Colleen E. McManus; Karla Mitchell; Lauren Jill Murov; Aileen T. Murphy; Nicole Ciszak Murphy; Mattathias H. Oberman; Micah R. Onixt; Kimberlie Pearlman; Ann Pille; Grace Y. Poe; Carl H. Poedtke, III; Kalyna A. Procyk; Marianne Raimondi; Alexandra D. Rose; Suzanne Karbarz Rovner; Terry I. Ryan; Thomas W. Ryan; Andrew J. Sannes; Maria Scherer; Jennifer L. Schilling; Judith L. Schuch; Raj N. Shah; Chad Shifrin; John P. Siemsen; David E. Singer; Erica S. Sitkoff; Christopher N. Skey; Coree Smith; Kathleen E. Stendahl; Darrell W. Taylor; Patrick Daley Thompson; Vasilios Toliopoulos; Kelli A. Toronyi; Julia A. Turk; Jared M. Warner; Joycelynn Watkins-Asiyanbi; Karen

(This Listing Continued)

DLA Piper Rudnick Gray Cary US LLP (Continued)

S. Way; Megan Webster; Sarah A. Weersing; Kenneth I. Weiner; Kurt A. Winiecki; Christy M. Young; Myla Barefield Young. Attorneys: Michelle D. Kane; Mia P. Jiganti; Linda Urbanik Johnson; Amy L. Kurland.
Advertising, Promotion and Trade Practices; Aerospace and Defense; Antitrust and Trade Regulation; Aviation; Bankruptcy and Business Reorganization; Biosciences; Business and Technology; Class Action Litigation; Communications; Construction; Copyrights; Corporate Governance and Protective Practices; Corporate and Securities; Domain Name Practice; Drug and Medical Device; Electronic Commerce and Privacy; Employee Benefits and Executive Compensation; Energy; Environmental; Federal Affairs and Legislative; Finance; Finance, Financial Services and Bankruptcy; Franchise and Distribution; Franchise and Distribution-International; Franchise and Distribution-Litigation; Franchise and Distribution-Technology; Government Contracts; Government Controversies; Governmental Affairs, Land Use and Development; HIPAA Privacy and Security; Health Care; Homeland Security; Information Technology; Insurance and Reinsurance; Insurance and Surety Litigation; Intellectual Property; International Commerce and Litigation; Iraq Reconstruction; Labor and Employment Law; Leasing; Legislative Financial Services; Litigation; Lodging and Timeshare; Medical Malpractice Defense; Mergers and Acquisitions; Multifamily Housing and Community Development Law; Nonprofit Organizations; Outsourcing; Patent Litigation; Patent Prosecution; Pesticide; Private Client Services; Product Liability and Toxic Torts; Professional Liability; Project Finance; Public Finance; REITs and Real Estate Securitization; Real Estate; Real Estate Finance; Securities Litigation; Sports Facilities Development; State Legislation and Public Policy; Tax; Tax Policy and Legislation; Technology Transfer; Trademark Litigation; Trademarks; Transportation; Venture Capital and Emerging Companies; White Collar; Workout Experience.
Annapolis, Maryland Office: 60 West Street, Suite 401, 21401-2434. Telephone: 443-482-3830. FAX: 443-482-3848.
Baltimore, Maryland Office (Downtown): 111 South Calvert Street, Suite 1950, 21202-6174. Telephone: 410-580-3000. FAX: 410-580-3665.
Baltimore, Maryland Office (Mt. Washington): 6225 Smith Avenue, 21209-3600. Telephone: 410-580-3000. FAX: 410-580-3001.
Boston, Massachusetts Office: One International Place, 21st Floor, 02110-2613. Telephone: 617-406-6000. FAX: 617-406-6100.
Dallas, Texas Office: 1717 Main Street, Suite 4600, 75201-4605. Telephone: 214-743-4500. FAX: 214-743-4545.
Easton, Maryland Office: 117 Bay Street, 21601-2703. Telephone: 410-820-4460. FAX: 410-820- 4463.
Edison, New Jersey Office: Piper Rudnick LLP, A New Jersey Limited Liability Partnership, Robert A. Assuncao, Managing Partner, 379 Thornall Street, Eighth Floor, 08837-2226. Telephone: 732-590-1850. FAX: 732-590-1860.
La Jolla, California Office: 1200 Prospect Street, Suite 575, 92037. Telephone: 858-638-6806. Fax: 858-456-3075.
Las Vegas, Nevada Office: Hughes Center, 3960 Howard Hughes Parkway, Suite 400, 89109. Telephone: 702-737-3433. FAX: 702-737-1612.
Los Angeles, California Office (Century City): 1999 Avenue of the Stars, Fourth Floor, 90067-6022. Telephone: 310-595-3000. FAX: 310-595-3300.
Los Angeles, California Office (Downtown): 550 South Hope Street, Suite 2300, 90071-2631. Telephone: 213-330-7700. FAX: 213-330-7701.
New York, New York Office: 1251 Avenue of the Americas, 10020-1104. Telephone: 212-835-6000. FAX: 212-835-6001.
Paris, France Office: Cariddi, Mee, Rue, Association d'Avocats au Barreau de Paris, Correspondants de Piper Rudnick LLP, 12 rue de la Paix, 75002 Paris, France. Telephone: +33-1 42.61.57.71. FAX: +33-1 42.61.79.21.
Philadelphia, Pennsylvania Office: One Liberty Place, 1650 Market Street, Suite 4900, 19103. Telephone: 215-656-3300. FAX: 215-656-3301.
Raleigh, North Carolina Office: Six Forks Center I, 4700 Six Forks Road, Suite 200, 27609. Telephone: 919-786-2000. FAX: 919-786-2200.
Reston, Virginia Office: 1775 Wiehle Avenue, Suite 400, 20190-5159. Telephone: 703-773-4000. FAX: 703-773-5000.
San Francisco, California Office: 333 Market Street, Suite 3200, 94105-2150. Telephone: 415-659-7000. FAX: 415-659-7300.
Tampa, Florida Office: 101 East Kennedy Boulevard, Suite 2000, 33602-5149. Telephone: 813-229-2111. FAX: 813-229-1447.
Washington, District of Columbia Office: 1200 Nineteenth Street, NW, Main Reception on 7th Floor, 20036-2412. Telephone: 202-861-3900. FAX: 202-223-2085.
See Professional Biographies, CHICAGO, ILLINOIS

Dlugie, David R. . . . '60 '86 C&L.339 B.S., J.D. [Katten M.R.]
Dmitrieva, Irina Y. . . . '73 '03 [Ⓐ Jenner&B.]
Dmitrovich, Veda '— '87
C.339 B.S. L.424 J.D. Pro Bono Prog. Dir., Chicago Legal Clinic
Dmyterko, Michael Philip . . . '48 '74 C.46 B.S. L.424 J.D. Commonwealth Edison Co.
Do, Mia . . . '— '04 C.339 B.A. L.146 J.D. [Ⓐ Anderson&Assoc.] ⊙
Do, Paul C. . . . '— '03 C.1375 B.A. L.1066 J.D. [Ⓐ Pugh,J.J.&Q.]
Dobben, Brian L. . . . '59 '84 C.879 B.A. L.228 J.D. [Hoogendoorn&T.]
Dobbins, Cindy . . . '72 '04 C.679 B.A. L.365 J.D. [Ⓐ LaBarge,C.&L.]
Dobbins, Edward F. (Bud), (AV) . . . '46 '73 C.676 B.A. L.724 J.D. [Fischel&K.]
Dobbs, Kenneth Paul . . . '47 '92 C.1043 B.S. L.146 J.D. [Dobbs&H.]

Dobbs and Hutchison
Dearborn Station, Suite M-2, 47 West Polk Street, 60605
Telephone: 312-461-9800 Fax: 312-461-9008
Email: roghutch@prodigy.net URL: http://www.dobbsandhutchison.com
Members of Firm: Kenneth Paul Dobbs; Roger S. Hutchison.
Personal Injury, Automobile Accidents, Trucking Accidents, Motorcycle Accidents, Head Trauma, Spinal Cord Injuries, Premises Liability, Wrongful Death, Social Security, Social Security Disability Benefits, Children's Benefits.
See Professional Biographies, CHICAGO, ILLINOIS

Dobie, W. Gordon, (AV) . . . '59 '86 C.94 B.A. L.910 J.D. [Winston&S.]
Dobkin, Laurence B., (AV) . . . '62 '87 C&L.339 B.S., J.D. [Greenberg T.]
Dobreff, David Albert . . . '71 '97 C.477 B.A. L.912 J.D. 401 S. LaSalle, Ste. 70
Dobrer, Jean . . . '54 '81 C.66 B.A. L.569 J.D. Asst. Corp. Coun., City of Chicago
Dobrusin, Charles E., (AV) . . . '— '79 C.1036 B.A. L.569 J.D. [Sachnoff&W.]
Dobrutsky, Jay S. . . . '57 '96 C.94 B.A. L.424 J.D. [Burke,W.M.&S.]
Dockery, Elfreda . . . '— '89 C.1060 B.A. L.1035 J.D. 25 E. Washington Street Suite 1224
Dockrey, J. William '53 '96 C.793 B.S. L.365 J.D.
[Ⓒ Brinks H.G.&L.] (See Pat. Sect.)
Docks, Adam M. . . . '79 '04 C.477 B.A. L.245 J.D. [Ⓐ Katten M.R.]
Docksey, J. Ross, (AV) . . . '51 '81 C.870 B.S. L.494 J.D. [Sonnenschein N.&R.]
Dockterman, Michael, (AV) . . . '54 '78 C.976 B.A. L.228 J.D. [Wildman,H.A.&D.]
Docter, Stephen H. '64 '99 C.424 B.A. L.365 J.D.
[McDonnell B.H.&B.] (See Pat. Sect.)
Dodd, Angela D. '64 '89 C.350 B.A. L.966 J.D.
Sr. Bankruptcy Coun., Chicago, M.R.O., S.E.C.
Dodd, Shirley D. '46 '77 C&L.801 B.A., J.D.
Dir., Policy Advocacy, Amer. Medical Assn.
Dodge, Stephanie Lee . . . '68 '93 C&L.339 B.S., J.D. [Gardner C.&D.]
Dodier, Grace M. . . . '59 '87 C.178 A.B. L.309 J.D. Instructor, Northwestern Univ.
Dodson, Jesse W. . . . '76 '03 C.174 B.S. L.597 J.D. [Ⓐ DLPiper R.G.C.U.]
Dodson, Paulette Rennalls '63 '87
C.563 B.A. L.188 J.D. Asst. Gen. Coun./Publishing, Tribune Co.
Doehring, Amy G. . . . '73 '00 C.813 B.A. L.424 J.D. [Ⓐ McDermott W.&E.]
Doell, Thomas J. . . . '46 '75 C.1024 B.A. L.146 J.D. [Galliani&D.]
Doellinger, Chad J. . . . '— '01 C.352 B.S. L.976 J.D. [Ⓐ Pattishall,M.N.H.&G.]
Doerfler, Karyn L. . . . '71 '98 C.209 B.S. L.597 J.D. [Ⓐ Barack F.K.P.&N.]
Doermer, Richard D., (AV) . . . '51 '77 C.602 B.A. L.365 J.D. [R.Doermer]
Doermer, Richard, Ltd, (AV) . . . 415 N. LaSalle St., Ste. 500
Doernhoefer, Gary R. '57 '84 C.293 B.A. L.145 J.D.
Vice President & General Counsel, Orbitz, LLC
Doerrer, John A., II . . . '55 '89 C.209 B.A. L.46 J.D. 121 N. LaSalle
Doerries, Michael F., (AV) . . . '59 '85 C.339 B.S. L.146 J.D. [Wiedner&M.]
Doerschein, Paul W. . . . '— '97 C.339 B.A. L.146 J.D. [Ⓐ McGuirewoods]
Doetsch, Douglas A. . . . '57 '87 C.373 B.A. L.178 J.D. [Mayer,B.R.&M.]
Doheny, James J., Jr. . . . '56 '83 C.339 B.S. L.365 J.D. Chgo. Bd. of Trade
Doherty, David M. '73 '01 C&L.602 B.A., J.D.
Chicago Board Options Exchange, Incorporated
Doherty, Kevin W., (AV) . . . '53 '81 C.436 B.A. L.365 J.D. [Doherty&P.]
Doherty, Mary E., (AV) . . . '58 '86 L.424 J.D. Atty., State Dept. of Prof. Reg.
Doherty, Richard J. . . . '62 '94 C.589 B.A. L.365 J.D. [Ⓐ Horwitz,H.&Assoc.]
Doherty, Robert J., Jr., (AV) . . . '64 '89 C.339 B.A. L.209 J.D. [Ⓐ Roddy,L.&Z.]
Doherty, Sharon A. . . . '— '96 C.339 B.A. L.146 J.D. [Schiff H.]
Doherty, Sharon T., (BV) . . . '63 '87 C&L.190 B.S.B.A., J.D. [Ⓒ Cassiday,S.&G.]
Doherty & Progar LLC, (AV) . . . 200 West Adams Street, Suite 2220 (⊙Munster, IN)
Dohm, Dolores H. . . . '51 '76 C.339 B.A. L.145 J.D. SEC
Dohra, Michelle V. . . . '70 '95 C.1494 B.A. L.1067 J.D. [Ⓐ Mayer,B.R.&M.]
Dolan, Alice E., (AV) . . . '55 '81 C.436 B.A. L.365 J.D. [A.E.Dolan&Assoc.]
Dolan, Carrie A. . . . '69 '94 C.966 B.S. L.209 J.D. [Cohon R.&R.]
Dolan, Christopher M. . . . '70 '99 C.338 B.S. L.273 J.D. [Ⓐ Brinks H.G.&L.]
Dolan, Dennis . . . '— '95 C.602 B.S. L.912 J.D. [Ⓐ Litchfield C.]
Dolan, Kristen A. . . . '— '01 C.170 B.A. L.276 J.D. [Ⓐ Grippo&E.]
Dolan, Lawrence . . . '43 '68 C.209 B.S. L.365 J.D. Ill. Dept. of Public Aid
Dolan, Martin A., (AV) . . . '63 '88 C.742 B.A. L.494 J.D. [Dolan&S.]
Dolan, Mary S. . . . '63 '91 C.602 B.A. L.893 J.D. U.S. Postal Serv.
Dolan, Michael F., (AV) . . . '— '82 C.177 B.S. L.352 J.D. [Jones D.]
Dolan, Patrick D. . . . '64 '92 C&L.966 B.A., J.D. [P.D.Dolan]
Dolan, William F. . . . '57 '82 C&L.178 A.B., J.D. [Bell,B.&L.]

Dolan, Alice E., & Associates LLC, (AV)
321 South Plymouth Court-14th Floor, 60604
Telephone: 312-386-1600 Fax: 312-386-1616
Email: adolan@aedolanllc.com URL: http://www.aedolanllc.com
Alice E. Dolan.
Medical Malpractice, Personal Injury, Negligence, Products Liability.
See Professional Biographies, CHICAGO, ILLINOIS

Dolan, Patrick Daley, Law Office of
155 North Michigan Avenue, Suite 718, 60601
Telephone: 312-239-9336 Fax: 312-239-9337
Email: pddlaw@aol.com
Patrick D. Dolan.
Labor and Employment, Litigation, Civil Rights, Executive Severance and Employment Contracts, Civil Litigation, Business Litigation, Commercial Litigation.
See Professional Biographies, CHICAGO, ILLINOIS

Dolan & Shannon, A Professional Corporation, (AV)
10 South LaSalle Street, Suite 2104
Dolehide, Beth S. . . . '— '97 C.589 B.S. L.365 J.D. [Ⓐ Gurber,M.&N.]
Dolgin, Amy S. . . . '75 '00 C.145 B.A. L.597 J.D. [Ⓐ Bell,B.&L.]
Dolgin, Jay L., (AV) . . . '44 '69 C.966 B.S. L.209 J.D. [Dolgin&F.]

Dolgin & Fischer, LLC, (AV)
30 North LaSalle Street, Suite 4300, 60602-2516
Telephone: 312-705-2000 Fax: 312-705-2001
Members of Firm: Jay L. Dolgin; David J. Fischer. Of Counsel: John L. Wahlers.
Estate Planning, Tax Planning, Probate, Guardianship, Trust Administration, Corporate Law, Business Planning, Succession Planning, Commercial Litigation, Business Law, Contested Estates, Probate Litigation, Elder Law and Asset Protection.
See Professional Biographies, CHICAGO, ILLINOIS

Dolin, Kenneth R., (AV) . . . '55 '81 C.966 B.A. L.339 J.D. [Seyfarth S.]
Dolin, Stewart, (AV) . . . '— '77 C.339 B.A. L.424 J.D. [Sachnoff&W.]
Dolinko, Alan R., (AV) . . . '61 '86 C.339 B.S. L.209 J.D. [Robinson C.&C.]
Doll, John H. . . . '44 '80 C.114 B.A. L.146 J.D. [McLachlan,R.&D.]
Dollar, Dawn De Keyser '70 '95 C&L.347 B.A., J.D.
10 South La Salle Street Suite 1600
Dollear, Steve J. . . . '74 '02 C.436 B.S. L.424 J.D. [Ⓐ Katten M.R.]
Dolly, C. Craig, Jr. . . . '70 '01 C.880 B.A. L.1000 J.D. [Ⓐ DLPiper R.G.C.U.]
Dolph, Ada W. . . . '— '04 C.966 B.A. L.597 J.D. [Ⓐ Seyfarth S.]
Domagala-Pierga, Ania . . . '73 '99 C.424 B.A. L.146 J.D. [Ⓐ Bell,B.&L.]
Domagalski, Philip W., (AV) . . . '50 '75 C.927 B.A. L.365 J.D. [Kralovec&M.]
Doman, Michael P., (BV) '59 '84
C.339 B.S. L.146 J.D. 200 North LaSalle Street, Suite 2750
Domanico, Valarie Michelle '73 '01
C.383 B.S. L.365 J.D. Assoc., Deloitte & Touche, LLP
Domanowski, Steven . . . '77 '03 C.107 B.A. L.209 J.D. [Ⓐ Bell,B.&L.]
Domanskis, Alexander R., (AV) . . . '52 '77 C&L.477 A.B., J.D. [Boodell D.&S.]
Domaratius, Stephen W. . . . '52 '78 C.589 B.A. L.365 J.D. 100 W. Monroe St., Ste. 1701
Dombai, Les . . . '54 '78 C&L.209 B.A., J.D. 53 W. Jackson Blvd., Ste. 515
Dombai, Thomas J. '60 '85 C&L.209 B.A., J.D.
Chief Asst. Corp. Coun., City of Chicago Law Dept.
Dombrosky, Julie M., Law Offices of '— '99
C.352 B.A. L.880 J.D. 53 West Jackson Boulevard, Suite 560
Dombrow, Anthony E., (AV) . . . '45 '69 C&L.966 B.A., J.D. [Laner,M.D.B.L.&T.]
Dombrow, Joshua A. . . . '— '98 C.597 B.A. L.424 J.D. [Ⓐ Laner,M.D.B.L.&T.]
Dombrow, Kimberly F. . . . '76 '01 C&L.597 B.A., J.D. [Ⓐ Katten M.R.]
Dombrowski, Gerald M. . . . '— '92 C.339 B.A. L.146 J.D. [Sanchez&D.]
Dombrowski, Leo P., (BV) . . . '56 '90 C.339 B.A. L.146 J.D. [Wildman,H.A.&D.]
Dombrowski, Todd Richard . . . '74 '99 C.57 B.A. L.146 J.D. 28 North Clark St.
Domer, Peter H. . . . '59 '04 C.691 B.A. L.597 J.D. [Ⓐ Leydig,V.&M.]
Domeyer, Tamra S. . . . '67 '92 C&L.352 B.A., J.D. Exelon Corporation
Dominguez, Daniel L. . . . '72 '97 C.324 B.A. L.145 J.D. [Barack F.K.P.&N.]
Dominguez, Joseph, (BVⓉ) '62 '90 C.570 B.S.M.E. L.1292 J.D.
(adm. in PA; not adm. in IL) V.P. & Assoc. Gen. Coun., Exelon Corp.
Dominici, Letitia . . . '61 '87 C.339 B.A. L.365 J.D. Legal Advsr.
Domitrovic, Leah J. . . . '66 '91 C.602 B.A. L.145 J.D. [Katten M.R.]
Domjan, Todd E. . . . '— '00 C.602 B.A. L.990 J.D. [Ⓐ Morgan,L.&B.]

Dommermuth, Brestal, Cobine and West, Ltd.
(See Naperville)

Domol, Robert J. . . . '79 '04 C.475 B.A. L.209 J.D. [Ⓐ Levin,R.]
Domsky, Ronald Z. . . . '34 '57 C&L.966 B.B.A., J.D. Prof., John Marshall Law School
Don, Arthur, (AV) . . . '53 '78 C&L.597 B.S., J.D. [Seyfarth S.]
Donahoe, Nancy A. . . . '60 '86 C.475 B.A. L.146 J.D. State's Atty. Off.
Donahue, John A., (AV) . . . '55 '80 C.602 B.A. L.424 J.D. Sr. Corp. Coun., USG Corp.
Donahue, Kathleen M. . . . '58 '83 C.475 B.S. L.339 J.D. 414 N. Orleans
Donahue, Patricia, (BV) . . . '53 '83 C.97 B.A. L.209 J.D. Atty., National Futures Assn.
Donahue, Paul F., (AV) . . . '43 '76 C.454 B.A. L.1119 J.D. [Ⓒ Bell,B.&L.]

Donahue, Peter A. ....'68 '94 C.504 B.A. L.589 J.D. [Menges&M.]
Donahue & Partners LLP .... 233 South Wacker Drive (New York, NY)
Donaldson, Chris-Tia ....'— '03 C.309 A.B. L.1565 J.D. [Jenner&B.]
Donaldson, Paige ....'67 '93 C&L.347 B.A., J.D. [Sanchez&D.]
Donati, Peter F., (AV) ....'67 '92 C.188 B.S. L.477 J.D. [Levenfeld P.]
Donati, Victoria L. ....'67 '92 C.49 B.A L.930 J.D. [Neal,G.&E.]
Dondanville, John W., (AV) ....'37 '62 C.321 A.B. L.597 J.D. 130 E. Randolph Dr.‡
Dondanville, Patricia, (AV) ....'— '81 C.602 B.A. L.893 J.D. [Schiff H.]
Donegan, James G. ....'28 '57 C&L.209 B.A., J.D. Cir. J.
Donenberg, Barbara A. '58 '84 C.477 B.A. L.146 J.D.
Admin. Law J., Dept. of Pub. Aid
Dong, Zack Z. ....'57 '98 L.597 J.D. [Sonnenschein N.&R.]
Donham, Cary E., (AV) ....'49 '88 C.927 B.A. L.146 J.D. [Shefsky&F.]
Donham, Jennifer A. ....'64 '00 C.172 B.A. L.209 J.D. Spec. Dep. Receiver Off.

Donlevy, John D., (AV) '33 '57 C.597 B.S. L.145 J.D.
30 North La Salle Street, Suite 2040, 60602-2506
Telephone: 312-201-0227 Fax: 312-236-6906
Email: jdonlevy@core.com URL: http://www.lawyers.com/jdonlevy
Diversified Trial Practice in State and Federal Courts, concentrating on Criminal Cases, Business Litigation and some Personal Injury. Criminal Law specialties include DUI, Drug Cases and White Collar Crime.
See Professional Biographies, CHICAGO, ILLINOIS

Donley, John, (AV) ....'— '85 C.309 B.A. L.145 J.D. [Kirkland&E.]
Donnell, John P. ....'50 '85 C.911 B.A. L.365 J.D. [J.P.Donnell&Assoc.]
Donnell, Margaret M. ....'74 '99 C.36 B.S. L.365 J.D. [Fisher K.]
Donnell, J. Patrick, & Associates .... 79 W. Monroe St., Ste. 900
Donnellan, Edward J. ....'52 '82 C.339 B.S. L.365 J.D. 155 Harbor Dr.
Donnelley, Robert G. ....'38 '70 C.976 B.A. L.146 J.D. The First Natl. Bk. of Chgo.
Donnelly, Daniel J. '65 '90 C&L.589 B.S., J.D.
V.P & Sr. Claims Coun., Attorneys' Liability Assurance Society, Inc.
Donnelly, Daniel J. ....'60 '85 C.927 B.A. L.209 J.D. [Kralovec&M.]
Donnelly, James L., (AV) ....'— '58 C.602 A.B. L.209 LL.B. [Dykema G.P.] ‡
Donnelly, Julia A. ....'— '90 C.436 B.A. L.589 J.D. [Ogletree,D.N.S.&S.]
Donnelly, Katherine Hale '75 '01 C.94 B.A. L.588 J.D.
(adm. in MA; not adm. in IL) [Sonnenschein N.&R.]
Donnelly, Patrick G., (BV) ....'61 '86 C.436 A.B. L.209 J.D. [Riordan,D.L.&M.]
Donnelly, Rett F. ....'47 '72 C.347 A.B. L.602 J.D. V.P., Claims, Marxh USA, Inc.
Donnelly, Thomas V. ....'59 '86 C.705 B.A. L.209 J.D. 1st Municipal Dist., Rm. 1401
Donner, Ted A., (AV) ....'60 '90 C.1016 B.A. L.424 J.D. 203 North LaSalle Street
Donners, Mary M. ....'52 '84 C.424 B.A. L.365 J.D. [Bell,B.&L.]
Donnersberger, David R. ....'38 '72 C.712 B.A. L.209 J.D. Cir. Ct.
D'Onofrio, Patrick M. ....'— '02 C.602 B.B.A. L.424 J.D. [Jones D.]
Donofrio, Thomas D. ....'70 '95 C.145 B.A. L.910 J.D. [Merlo K.B.&G.]
Donoghue, George T., Jr., (AV) ....'13 '39 C&L.145 A.B., J.D. 230 W. Monroe St.

Donoghue, Gerald T., (AV) '51 '77 C.339 B.A. L.424 J.D.
20 North Clark Street, Suite 3600, 60602
Telephone: 312-332-3359 Fax: 312-419-6688
Email: gdonoghue@att.net URL: http://www.donoghue-law.com
Civil Trial and Appellate Practice, Auto Accidents and Injuries, Personal Injury, Medical Malpractice, Legal Malpractice, Wrongful Death, Workers Compensation, Products Liability and Premises Liability Law.
See Professional Biographies, CHICAGO, ILLINOIS

Donoghue, Lawrence M. ....'51 '78 C.276 A.B. L.424 J.D. United Air Lines
Donoghue, Mary T. ....'48 '80 C.801 B.S. L.424 J.D. F.D.I.C.
Donoghue, Peter J. ....'64 '91 C.276 B.A. L.228 J.D. [DLPiper R.G.C.U]
Donohoe, Jerome F., (AV) ....'39 '64 C.723 B.A. L.494 J.D. [Mayer,B.R.&M.]
Donohoe, Thomas H., (AV) ....'48 '74 C.477 A.B. L.966 J.D. [McDermott W.&E.]
Donohue, Mary Pat ....'57 '84 C.741 B.A. L.424 J.D. 175 W. Jackson Blvd., Ste. 1000
Donohue, Richard H., (AV) ....'50 '79 C.197 A.B. L.597 J.D. [Donohue B.M.&S.]
Donohue, William J. '50 '75 C.659 B.S. L.1017 J.D.
(adm. in PA; not adm. in IL) Assoc. Gen. Coun., Exelon Corporation
Donohue Brown Mathewson & Smyth, (AV) .... 140 S. Dearborn Street, Suite 700
Donovan, Edward A. ....'— '04 C.870 B.S. L.893 J.D. [Kirkland&E.]
Donovan, Edward V., Jr., (AV) ....'29 '51 C.424 A.B. L.597 J.D. [Henehan,D.&I.]
Donovan, James F. ....'57 '84 C&L.602 B.A., J.D. [Kralovec&M.]
Donovan, Jason R. ....'77 '02 C.597 B.M. L.966 J.D. [Merlo K.B.&G.]
Donovan, Joseph E. ....'69 '97 C&L.900 B.A., J.D. [Kelley D.&W.]
Donovan, Robert F., Jr. '42 '68
C&L.209 B.S.C., J.D. Labor Rel. Dept., Chicago Park Dist.
Donovan, Thomas J. ....'— '87 C.339 B.S.M.E. L.146 J.D. [Barnes&T.] (See Pat. Sect.)
Doody, Patrick C. ....'49 '78 C.209 B.S. L.146 J.D. [Field&G.]
Doody, Timothy G. ....'62 '94 C.339 B.S. L.209 J.D. [Weis&D.]
Doohan, Mary Elizabeth '50 '89 C.034 B.Sc. L.845 J.D.
V.P., Legal Affairs, Morton International, Inc., a Rohm & Haas Company
Doohan, Pauline E. ....'— '89 C.475 B.A. L.912 J.D. [Foley&L.]
Dooley, Daniel S. ....'73 '01 C.494 B.A. L.345 J.D. [Jenner&B.]
Dooley, Joseph M., III, (AV) ....'— '88 C.802 B.A.B.S. L.146 J.D. [J.M.Dooley,III]
Dooley, Nathan T. '69 '95 C.1142 B.A. L.188 J.D.
(adm. in TX; not adm. in IL) [Baker&M.]
Dooley, Thomas Leslie '59 '89 C.896 L.192 J.D.
(adm. in TN; not adm. in IL) Sr. Corp. Coun., Fruit of the Loom, Inc.

Dooley, Joseph M., III, P.C., Law Office of, (AV)
100 West Monroe Street - Suite 1900, 60603
Telephone: 312-236-7282 Fax: 312-346-6549
Email: dooleylaw@covad.net URL: http://www.josephmdooley.com
Joseph M. Dooley III.
Personal Injury, Catastrophic Injuries, Medical Malpractice, Products Liability, Wrongful Death, Automobile Accidents, Trucking Accidents, Birth Injury, Spinal Injury, Head Injury, Neurological Injuries, Construction Accidents, Railroad Accidents, Slip and Fall, Pedestrian Injuries, Litigation.
See Professional Biographies, CHICAGO, ILLINOIS

Doolin, Elizabeth Gwynn ....'66 '92 C.477 B.A. L.910 J.D. [Chittenden,M.&N.]
Doornweerd, Michael A. ....'70 '96 C.373 B.A. L.597 J.D. [Jenner&B.]
Doose, Barbara W. ....'— '87 C&L.339 B.A., J.D. Coun., The Boeing Co.
Doppelt, Diann L. ....'64 '89 C.339 B.S. L.424 J.D. Asst. State's Atty.
Doppelt, Jack C. ....'52 '77 C.293 B.A. L.145 J.D. WBBM-AM Newsradio
Doran, James W., (AV) ....'— '81 C.352 B.B.A. L.813 J.D. [Latham&W.]
Doran, Karen J. ....'71 '04 C.136 B.A. L.146 J.D. [Madduff M.&M.]
Doran, Philip A., (AV) ....'40 '66 C.363 A.B. L.597 J.D. 221 N. La Salle St., Ste. 2036
Doran, Shawna M. ....'— '05 C.74 B.A. L.145 J.D. [Gardner C.&D.]
Doran, William E. ....'— '88 C.694 B.A. L.966 J.D. [Sachnoff&W.]
Dorf, Michael C. ....'52 '76 C.145 B.A. L.178 J.D. [Adducci,D.L.M.&B.]
Dorff, Karen M., (AV) ....'54 '80 C.234 B.A. L.424 J.D. 30 N. LaSalle St.
Dorfman, Daniel A. ....'79 '05 C.446 B.A. L.597 J.D. [Howrey]
Dorfman, Harry B. ....'12 '36 C.999 L.146 LL.B. 205 W. Wacker Dr.
Dorfman, Isaiah S., (AV) ....'07 '31 C&L.145 Ph.B., J.D. [Laner,M.D.B.L.&T.]

Dorfman, Michael A. ....'73 '98 C.339 B.S. L.209 J.D. [Katten M.R.] (Pat.)
Dorian, Barbara Bucci '72 '98 C.475 B.A. L.912 J.D.
(adm. in MI; not adm. in IL) 150 S. Wacker Dr.‡
Doris, Carole R. ....'47 '76 C.530 B.A. L.209 J.D. Dept. of Pub. Advocacy
Dorkin, Eric ....'65 '98 C.1044 B.A. L.352 J.D. [Holland&K.]
Dorman, Donald D. ....'54 '91 C.500 B.A. L.477 J.D. 226 S. Wabash Ave.
Dorman, Gregg M. ....'— '84 C.339 B.A. L.424 J.D. [Seyfarth S.]
Dorman, Jeffrey L. ....'— '74 C.477 B.A. L.930 J.D. [Freeborn&P.]
Dorman, Keith A., (AV) ....'57 '82 C.57 B.A. L.339 J.D. [McGuirewoods]
Dorn, Alan S. ....'53 '77 C&L.339 B.A., J.D. Off. of the Gen. Coun., Dept. of HHS
Dorn, Bruce Farrel, & Associates, (AV) '49 '75 C.339 B.S. L.365 J.D.
120 N. LaSalle St.
Dorn, Douglas C. ....'67 '95 C.338 B.S. L.209 J.D. [J.M.Trapp&Assoc.]
Dorn, Jennifer ....'— '02 C&L.339 B.A., J.D. [Quarles&B.]
Dorn, Jerrold S. ....'51 '77 C.352 B.A. L.424 J.D. 309 W. Washington, Ste. 900
Dorr, James P., (AV) ....'44 '69 C.197 B.A. L.597 J.D. [Wildman,H.A.&D.]
Dorris, Thomas B. ....'41 '71 C.674 A.B. L.477 J.D. 53 W. Jackson Blvd.
Dorsey, William J. ....'73 '98 C.154 B.A. L.477 J.D. [Katten M.R.]
Dort, Kenneth K., (AV) ....'61 '86 C.813 A.B. L.145 J.D. [Gordon&G.L.]
Dosier, Mark L. ....'66 '91 C.339 B.S. L.145 J.D. [Sonnenschein N.&R.]
Doss, Michael P. ....'58 '89 C.629 B.A. L.659 J.D. [Sidley A.B.&W.]
Dossas, Vasilios (Bill) D., (AV) '52 '82
C.339 B.S. L.424 J.D. [Niro,S.H.&N.] (See Pat. Sect.)
Dougherty, Euguene E. ....'53 '84 C.589 B.A. L.424 J.D. Asst. Atty. Gen.
Dougherty, George R. ....'60 '87 C.821 B.A. L.597 J.D. [Grippo&E.]
Dougherty, James R. ....'76 '02 C.234 B.A. L.365 J.D. [Wilson E.M.E.&D.]
Dougherty, Maren J. '53 '79
C.293 B.A. L.352 J.D. Admin. Law J., Ill. Human Rights Comm.
Dougherty, Marybeth, (AV) ....'57 '82 C.602 B.A. L.209 J.D. [Wittenberg,D.&M.]
Doughty, Bruce W. ....'— '90 C.674 A.B. L.145 J.D. [Foley&L.]
Douglas, Carol M. ....'— '87 C&L.424 B.A., J.D. [Ungaretti&H.]
Douglas, Charles W., (AV) ....'48 '74 C.597 B.A. L.309 J.D. [Sidley A.B.&W.]
Douglas, Dana S. ....'76 '02 C.597 B.A. L.659 J.D. [Mayer,B.R.&M.]
Douglas, George E. ....'40 '65 C.197 A.B. L.966 LL.B. 1440 North Lake Shore Drive
Douglas, Loretta C. ....'43 '68 C&L.424 B.S., J.D. Cir. J.
Douglass, Christopher J. ....'77 '01 C.597 B.A. L.352 J.D. [Wildman,H.A.&D.]
Douglass, Ellen E., (AV) ....'53 '77 C.399 B.A. L.597 J.D. 53 W Jackson Blvd.
Douglass, Richard G. ....'74 '02 C.665 B.A. L.280 J.D. [Novack&M.]
Douglass, W. Andrew ....'73 '00 C.473 B.S. L.734 J.D. [Seyfarth S.]
Douglass, Wylie B. ....'42 '68 C.932 B.A. L.365 J.D. Warner Candy Co.
Doumanian, Greta M. ....'69 '96 C.659 B.A. L.209 J.D. Staff Atty., Chicago Legal Clinic
Dover, Jennifer ....'54 '85 C.477 B.A. L.309 J.D. Asst Atty. Gen.
Dow, Amy ....'73 '04 C.37 B.S. L.597 J.D. [Epstein B.&G.]
Dow, Denise Jarrett ....'51 '78 C.597 B.S. L.424 J.D. Sr. Coun., I.R.S., Off. of Chf. Coun.
Dow, Harmon B. ....'47 '72 C.475 B.A. L.145 J.D. Trial Atty., I.R.S.
Dow, Robert M., Jr. ....'65 '93 C.976 B.A. L.309 J.D. [Mayer,B.R.&M.]
Dowd, J. Peter, (AV) ....'43 '75 C.201 B.A. L.145 J.D. [Dowd,B.&B.]
Dowd, Joseph V., (AV) ....'22 '50 C&L.209 LL.B. [Dowd&D.]
Dowd, Patrick C., (AV) ....'58 '85 C.35 B.S. L.209 J.D. [Dowd&D.] (Fontana, WI)
Dowd, Thomas A. ....'37 '63 C&L.424 B.S.C., J.D. 1440 Lake Shore Dr.‡
Dowd, Bloch & Bennett, (AV) .... 8 S. Michigan Ave., Ste. 19

Dowd & Dowd, Ltd., (AV)
617 West Fulton Street, 60661
Telephone: 312-704-4400 Telecopier: 312-704-4500
URL: http://www.dowdanddowd.com
Joseph V. Dowd; Michael E. Dowd (1957-1996); Patrick C. Dowd; Robert J. Golden; Patrick J. Ruberry;—Philip F. Cuevas; S. Robert Depke; Jeannine Gilleran-Lunt; Jane E. Hughes; Thomas A. Jacobson; Matthew R. Link; Kimberly A. Maltby; Daniel L. Polsby; Peter Zavodnyik. Of Counsel: Richard H. Lucy; Sam L. Miller; Norman E. Samelson; Edmund A. Stephan, III; Pamela K. Harman.
General Civil Trial Practice, Negligence and Products Liability, Insurance Coverage Litigation, Workers' Compensation, Appellate Practice, Employment Law, Municipal Law, Transportation Law.
Representative Clients: AIG American International Companies; American Bankers Insurance Co.; AON Corp. (Combined); Clarendon National Insurance Co.; Gallagher Bassett Services, Inc.; Insurance Corp. of Hanover; Kentucky Farm Bureau Mutual Insurance Co.; Nationwide Insurance Enterprise; North American Risk Services; Schneider National Insurance Companies.
Fontana, Wisconsin Office: 632 Middleton, 53125. Telephone: 262-275-0057. Telecopier: 262-275-6786.
Highland, Indiana Office: 9721 Prairie Avenue, 46322. Telephone: 219-924-8122. Fax: 219-924-8125.
See Professional Biographies, CHICAGO, ILLINOIS

Dowdle, Richd. E. ....'26 '51 C.602 L.209 LL.B. Assoc. Cir. J. (Probate)
Dowling, Virginia M. '50 '83
C.597 B.S. L.209 J.D. Asst. Gen. Coun. & Secy., Ryerson Tull, Inc.
Dowling, William G., (BV) ....'55 '80 C.742 B.A. L.365 J.D. 19 South La Salle, Suite 450
Downer, Andrew N. ....'74 '03 L.597 J.D. [Pattishall,M.N.H.&G.]
Downes, Daniel J., (AV) ....'44 '73 C.339 L.424 J.D. [D.J.Downes]
Downes, Daniel J., P.C., Law Offices of, (AV) .... 111 W. Washington Street, Suite 1100
Downey, Edward F. ....'30 '58 C&L.276 B.S., J.D. 10336 S. Western Ave.
Downey, Sean M. ....'76 '04 C.210 B.A. L.1119 J.D. [Ulmer&B.]
Downey, Storrs W., (AV) ....'57 '82 C.694 A.B. L.221 J.D. [BryceDowney]
Downing, Robert A., (AV) ....'29 '56 C&L.966 B.S., J.D. [Ruff,W.&R.]
Downing, Scott P. ....'66 '91 C.339 B.A. L.145 J.D. [McGuirewoods]
Downs, Jeremy M. ....'75 '00 C.309 A.B. L.597 J.D. [Goldberg,K.B.B.R.&M.]
Downs, Maureen Creighton ....'54 '81 C.602 B.B.A. L.597 J.D. Northwest Indus., Inc.
Downs, Robert K., (AV) ....'— '65 L.362 J.D. [Downs]

Downs Law Offices, P.C., (AV)
150 North Wacker Drive Suite 1870, 60606
Telephone: 312-781-1963 Fax: 312-781-1962 URL: http://www.lawyers.com/downslaw
Email: Bob@Downslaw.com URL: http://www.downslaw.com
Robert K. Downs.
Family Law, Divorce, Child Custody, Adoption, Domestic Violence, Premarital Agreements, Child Support, Trusts and Estates, Wills, Probate, Elder Law, Guardianship and Real Estate.
See Professional Biographies, CHICAGO, ILLINOIS

Doy, Samuel J., (AV) ....'23 '54 C.597 B.S. L.209 J.D. [Kane,D.&H.] ‡
Doyle, Bernard F., Jr., (AV) ....'45 '71 C.424 B.S. L.597 J.D. [Doyle&B.]
Doyle, Brian K. ....'64 '93 C.388 B.A. L.424 J.D. [DLPiper R.G.C.U]
Doyle, Carol Evans ....'59 '89 C.645 B.S. L.1049 J.D. U.S. Customs Serv.‡
Doyle, David E. ....'— '87 [Huff&G.]
Doyle, David J. ....'69 '94 C.373 B.S. L.597 J.D. [Winston&S.]
Doyle, David L., (AV) ....'50 '75 C.373 B.S. L.245 J.D. [Vedder,P.K.&K.]
Doyle, Debra M. ....'— '00 C.802 B.S. L.602 J.D. [Jenner&B.]
Doyle, Diana Slyfield ....'— '96 C.597 B.S.J. L.145 J.D. [Latham&W.]
Doyle, George M. ....'64 '89 C.388 B.A. L.339 J.D. [Falk J.]
Doyle, Hugh J., (CV) ....'64 '91 C.602 B.B.A. L.424 J.D. [Taylor,M.S.H.&M.]
Doyle, J. Stuart ....'15 '82 C&L.209 Ph.B., J.D. 2031 W. Hunt Ave.
Doyle, John A., (AV) ....'24 '50 C&L.424 Ph.B., J.D. 221 N. LaSalle St.‡
Doyle, John R., (AV) ....'50 '76 C.734 B.A. L.209 J.D. [McDermott W.&E.]

Doyle, John T., (AV) '— '80 C&L.424 B.B.A., J.D.
10 South La Salle Street, Suite 3500, 60603-1002
Telephone: 312-332-5560; 708-352-8981 Fax: 312-332-5566 Efax: 708-575-8959
Email: jdoyle@doylelaw.com URL: http://www.lawyers.com/doylelawfirm
Business Law and Transactions, Corporate Law, Mergers and Acquisitions, and Information Technology Law and Transactions.
See Professional Biographies, CHICAGO, ILLINOIS

Doyle, Joseph E., (AV) . . . . '59 '85 C.339 B.A. L.494 J.D. [Mayer,B.R.&M.]
Doyle, Joseph R. . . . . '76 '03 C.648 B.S. L.1187 J.D. [Leeders&D.]
Doyle, Kathleen J. . . . .'79 '05 C.436 B.A. L.424 J.D. [A Crisham&K.]
Doyle, Kellyn M. . . . .'76 '01 C.339 B.A. L.209 J.D. Asst. States Atty.
Doyle, Linda M. '63 '93 C.728 B.S. L.477 J.D. [McDermott W.&E.]
Doyle, Martin . . . .'61 '88 C.742 B.A. L.365 J.D. V.P. & Gen. Coun., Lind Waldock & Co.
Doyle, Nancy J., (BV) . . . .'50 '75 C.339 B.A. L.424 J.D. [Kane,D.&H.]
Doyle, Patrick O. . . . .'61 '86 C.602 B.B.A. L.597 J.D. [Winston&S.]
Doyle, Paul R. '49 '84 C.339 B.S. L.146 J.D.
Admin. Law J., State Human Rights Comm.
Doyle, Thomas A., (AV) . . . . '56 '80 C.69 B.B.A. L.145 J.D. [Baker&M.]
Doyle, Thomas A. . . . . '65 '90 C.98 B.S. L.339 J.D. [Saunders&D.]
Doyle, William M., Jr., (AV) . . . . '49 '76 C.363 B.S. L.209 J.D. [Winston&S.]

Doyle & Bolotin, Ltd., A Professional Corporation, (AV)
Ten South La Salle Street Suite 3450, 60603
Telephone: 312-782-5600 Facsimile: 312-782-6660
Bernard F. Doyle, Jr.; William J. Bolotin.
Commodity Futures Regulation and Litigation, Managed Funds, Commodities and Securities Arbitration, Business Law.
See Professional Biographies, CHICAGO, ILLINOIS

Dozois, Laura K. . . . . '65 '97 C.473 B.S. L.146 J.D. Lexis-Nexis, Inc.
Drachler, David S. . . . . '77 '02 C.597 B.A. L.659 J.D. [A Jenner&B.]
Dragich, Stephen J., (AV) . . . . '— '83 C&L.339 B.S., J.D. [Schiff H.]
Dragutinovich, Zoran, (AV) . . . . '46 '83 C.1016 B.A. L.146 J.D. [Torshen,S.G.D.&A.]
Drake, James M., (AV) . . . .'61 '87 C.477 B.A. L.209 J.D. [FagelHaber]
Drake, Melody L. . . . . '77 '02 C.788 B.A. L.910 J.D. [A Donohue B.M.&S.]
Drake, Paul I. . . . .'69 '95 C.145 B.A. L.146 J.D. [P.I.Drake&Assoc.]
Drake, Robert B. . . . .'76 '02 C.31 B.A. L.910 J.D. 10 S. Dearborn St.
Drake, Stephen R., (BVⓉ) '— '96 C.335 B.A. L.950 J.D.
(adm. in ID; not adm. in IL) [Epstein B.&G.]
Drake, Paul I., & Associates, P.C. . . . . One North LaSalle Street, Suite 2300
Drane, Scott A. . . . . '55 '81 C.339 B.A. L.597 J.D. [Drane F.&L.]

Drane Freyer & Lapins, Limited, (AV)
150 North Wacker Drive, 8th Floor, 60606
Telephone: 312-827-7100 Fax: 312-827-7111
Scott A. Drane; Wendy Freyer; David A. Lapins.
General Practice, Real Estate Law including Acquisitions and Dispositions, Financing, Leasing, Annexation, Zoning, Land Use, Land Development, and Property Management; Corporate and Securities Law, Venture Capital, Business Acquisitions, Sales and Divestitures, Technology Businesses, Litigation.
See Professional Biographies, CHICAGO, ILLINOIS

Draney, Walter L. . . . . '— '99 C&L.339 B.S., J.D. [A Chapman&C.]
Dranias, Nicholas C. . . . .'71 '96 C.94 B.A. L.424 J.D. 77 W. Washington St., Ste. 1020
Dranoff, David L., (AV) . . . . '55 '83 C.918 B.A. L.597 J.D. [Goldberg,K.B.B.R.&M.]
Drapatsky, Alexander . . . .'72 '97 C.339 B.A. L.146 J.D. [A Peck,B.A.&M.]
Draper, Ronald G., and Associates '50 '76 C&L.574 B.A., J.D.
220 S. State St., Ste. 1202
Draths, Thomas G., (AV) . . . .'52 '80 C.197 A.B. L.209 J.D. [Schuyler,R.&Z.]
Draus, Andrew J. . . . . . .'65 '91 C.589 B.S. L.209 J.D. 415 North La Salle Street, Suite 603
Dravillas, Kathleen . . . .'58 '86 C.339 B.A. L.209 J.D. Asst. Atty. Gen.
Drayer, Robin . . . .'62 '86 C.339 B.A. L.1162 J.D. Asst. Corp. Coun.
Drazdys, Vilia M., (BV) . . . . '68 '92 C.190 B.S. L.309 J.D. [Wildman,H.A.&D.]
Drazner, Richard J. . . . . '60 '85 C.209 B.S. L.365 J.D. Gen. Coun., Ritter & Co.
Draznin, Neal A. . . . . '59 '85 C.910 A.B. L.209 J.D. Pros. Atty
Dreger, Robert M. . . . .'57 '81 C&L.602 B.A., J.D. [Firm of R.M.Dreger]
Dreger, R. M., PC, Law Firm of . . . . 410 S. Michigan, Ste. 310
Dreher, Kevin . . . .'— '02 C.477 B.A. L.339 J.D. [A Morgan,L.&B.]
Drehkoff, W. Dennis, (AV) '46 '72 C.999 B.S. L.502 J.D.
[A Ladas&P.] (See Pat. Sect.)
Dreiser, Daniel L. . . . .'47 '84 C.176 B.A. L.365 J.D. Chf. Atty., Chicago Transit Auth.
Drennan, Thomas G. . . . . '76 '01 C.339 B.A. L.345 J.D. [A Tressler,S.M.&P.]
Drescher, Gregory P. . . . . '71 '97 C.776 B.S. L.309 J.D. NAVTEQ (Legal Dept.)
Dressler, Dennis A. . . . .'69 '97 C.804 B.S. L.734 J.D. [A Askounis&B.]
Drew, Bernard E., Jr. . . . .'42 '68 C.473 B.S. L.436 J.D. [C Tressler,S.M.&P.]
Drew, Daniel D. . . . . '60 '85 C&L.339 B.S., J.D. [Tribler O.&M.]
Drew, David Marc, (BV) . . . . .'51 '78 C&L.597 B.S., J.D. Gen. Coun., Drew Holdings Inc.
Drew, Sherry K. . . . .'47 '74 C.339 B.A. L.146 J.D. [McDowell&D.]
Drewke, Susan W., (AV) . . . . '58 '90 C.339 B.A. L.209 J.D. [Winston&S.]
Drewko, Margaret M. . . . . '— '83 C.1183 B.A. L.365 J.D. 6904 Talcott Ave.
Drexler, Ray F., (AV) . . . .'— '58 C&L.602 Ph.B., LL.B. [Dykema G.P.] ‡
Drexler, Thomas W., (BV) . . . .'50 '78 C.602 B.A. L.209 J.D. 77 W. Washington Street
Dreyer, Carl H., Jr. . . . .'76 '02 C.436 B.A. L.209 J.D. [A Momkus M.M.M.M.&S.]
Dreyfus, Larry M. . . . .'47 '79 C.37 B.S. L.365 J.D. 175 E. Delaware Pl., Rm. 4819
Dreyfus, Mary Kay Gara . . . . '65 '95 C.339 B.F.A. L.365 J.D. [DLPiper R.G.C.U.]
Dreznes, Laura M. . . . .'79 '04 C.201 B.A. L.339 J.D. [A Katten M.R.]
Dries, James J., (AVⓉ) . . . .'49 '74 C&L.436 B.A., J.D. [Baker&M.]

Drinker Biddle & Reath LLP, (AV)
A Pennsylvania Limited Liability Partnership
115 S. La Salle Street 23rd Floor, 60603-3862 ⊙
Telephone: 312-977-1510 Telefax: 312-977-1511 Cable Address: "Debemac"
URL: http://www.drinkerbiddle.com
Members of Firm: John Dames; David B. Sudzus. Associates: William V. Essig; Lara C. Otsuka; Stephanie J. Synol; B. Todd Vinson.
Products Liability, Toxic Torts, Environmental Litigation, Insurance Coverage, Antitrust, Intellectual Property, Commercial and Securities Litigation, Construction Litigation, Real Estate Litigation, Professional Error and Omissions, Employment Litigation and General Civil Litigation.
Philadelphia, Pennsylvania Office: One Logan Square, 18th & Cherry Streets. Telephone: 215-988-2700. Telefax: 215-988-2757. Cable Address: "Debemac."
Washington, D.C. Office: 1500 K Street, N.W., Suite 1100. Telephone: 202-842-8800. Telefax: 202-842-8465.
Wilmington, Delaware Office: 1100 N. Market Street, Suite 1000. Telephone: 302-467-4200. Fax: 302-467-4201.
Florham Park, New Jersey Office: 500 Campus Drive. Telephone: 973-360-1100. Fax: 973-360-9831.
Princeton, New Jersey Office: Suite 300, 105 College Road East. Telephone: 609-716-6500. Telefax: 609-799-7000.
Berwyn, Pennsylvania Office: Suite 300, 1000 Westlakes Drive. Telephone: 610-993-2200. Telefax: 610-993-8585.
San Francisco, California Office: 50 Fremont Street, 20th Floor. Telephone: 415-591-7500. Telefax: 415-591-7510.
Los Angeles, California Office: Wells Fargo Center, 333 South Grand Avenue. Telephone: 213-253-2300. Cable Address: "Debemac."

(This Listing Continued)

Drinker Biddle & Reath LLP (Continued)
New York, N.Y. Office: 140 Broadway, 39th Floor. Telephone: 212-248-3140. Fax: 212-248-3141.
See Professional Biographies, CHICAGO, ILLINOIS

Driscoll, Brian H. . . . . '61 '88 C.436 B.A. L.46 J.D. [A Wiedner&M.]
Driscoll, Joanne Rouzan . . . .'52 '78 C&L.209 B.S.C., J.D. [A K.M.Forde]
Driscoll, John J. . . . .'71 '97 C.339 B.S. L.365 J.D. [A S.M.Passen]
Driscoll, Kevin C., Jr. . . . . '— '00 C&L.339 A.B., J.D. [A Barnes&T.]
Driscoll, Patrick T., Jr., (AV) '42 '67 C.686 B.S. L.209 J.D.
Dep. State's Atty., State's Atty.'s Off. of Cook Co.
Drizin, Renata Jennifer . . . . '75 '02 C.424 B.S. L.146 J.D. 120 W. Madison, 10th Fl.
Drizin, Robert C., (BV) . . . .'60 '85 C.645 B.A. L.597 J.D. Asst. Pub. Def.
Drizin, Steven A. . . . .'61 '86 C.311 B.A. L.597 J.D. Northwestern Univ. Legal Clinic
Drizner, Paul S. . . . . '63 '88 C.339 B.S. L.424 J.D. [C Seyfarth S.]
Drobnak, Robert A. . . . . '— '00 C.98 B.S. L.659 J.D. [A Latham&W.]
Drobny, Dane . . . . '67 '93 C.165 B.A. L.910 J.D. [Winston&S.]
Drobny, Irving, (P.C.) . . . .'37 '62 C.339 L.365 LL.B. 4801 W. Peterson Ave.
Droeger, Jessica R. '64 '93 C.477 B.A. L.966 J.D.
V.P. & Asst. Gen. Coun., John Nuveen & Co., Inc.
Dronen, Keith G. '58 '84 C.597 B.A. L.146 J.D.
Financial Consultant, Smith Barney Inc.‡
Dropkin, Allen H. . . . .'30 '51 C&L.145 A.B., J.D. 100 N. LaSalle St.
Drost, Kenneth B., (AV) . . . .'53 '78 C.388 B.A. L.1065 J.D. [C Askounis&B.]
Drouillard, Jacob B. . . . . '— '04 C.201 B.S. L.477 J.D. [A Latham&W.]
Drozdzik, Ronald L., (AV) . . . .'— '75 C.388 B.A. L.146 J.D. [O'Hagan,S.&A.]
Drozt, Robert Allen . . . . '41 '79 C.339 B.S. L.365 J.D. 6953 N. Monon Ave.‡
Druck, Edward N. . . . . '65 '91 C.696 B.A. L.880 J.D. [Franczek S.]
Drucker, Fred L., (AV) . . . .'33 '58 C.221 B.A. L.209 J.D. 24 W. Chestnut‡
Drucker, Paul M. . . . . '73 '99 C.378 B.A. L.209 J.D. [A Mayer,B.R.&M.]
Drumke, Michael W. . . . .'— '91 C.860 B.A. L.966 J.D. [Schiff H.]
Drumm, Lawrence R. . . . . '69 '96 C.602 B.A. L.146 J.D. [Tishler&W.]
Drummond, Robert J., (BV) . . . . . '50 '79 C.424 B.A. L.209 J.D. [A B.R.Nevoral&Assoc.]

Drunken Driving Defense Lawyers of Illinois, Ltd., (AV)
One North La Salle Street Suite 4200, 60602-4011 ⊙
Telephone: 312-263-4422 Fax: 312-263-2803 URL: http://www. absolutely-100percent-not-guilty.com
URL: http://www.duidefense-law.com
Stephen M. Komie;—Darius R. Dirmantas; Elisabeth A. Ritter; Brian E. King; Sarah E. Toney. Of Counsel: Marc D. Wolfe.
Practice Limited to Criminal Defense, Driving While Intoxicated (DWI) and Other Offenses Arising Out of Operation of Motor Vehicles, Drug Crimes, Felonies, Homicide, Misdemeanors, Parole and Probation and Traffic Violations.
Waukegan, Illinois Office: 25 North County Street, 2nd Floor, 60085.
See Professional Biographies, CHICAGO, ILLINOIS

Drury, John Wesley . . . . '78 '04 C.436 B.A. L.597 J.D. [A Jenner&B.]
Drury, Larry D. . . . . '44 '70 C.339 B.S. L.365 J.D. 205 W. Randolph St., Ste. 1430
Drury, Shelby L. . . . . '73 '98 C.339 B.S. L.597 J.D. [A Novack&M.]
Drury, Sidney H. . . . . '30 '55 C.1016 B.A. L.597 J.D. 1550 N. Lake Shore Dr.
Drutchas, Grantland G. '61 '85
C.453 B.S.M.E. L.477 J.D. [McDonnell B.H.&B.] (See Pat. Sect.)
Dry, Fred Mark . . . . . .'48 '76 C.1183 B.A. L.365 J.D. 180 North LaSalle Street, Suite 1601
Drymalski, Raymond H., (AV) . . . . '36 '62 C.276 A.B. L.477 J.D. [Bell,B.&L.]
Drzewiecki, Jill Jennings . . . .'71 '97 C.616 B.S. L.424 J.D. [A Tressler,S.M.&P.]
D'Souza, Selma C. . . . .'65 '91 C.339 B.A. L.365 J.D. [Mondero D.&G.]

Duane Morris LLP, (AV) BR
227 West Monroe Street, Suite 3400, 60606 ⊙
Telephone: 312-499-6700 Fax: 312-499-6701
URL: http://www.duanemorris.com
Resident Partners: David B. Allswang; Douglas J. Antonio; Frederick R. Ball; Neville M. Bilimoria; Robert P. Bramnik; Cheryl Blackwell Bryson; Neil E. Cass; Rosanne Ciambrone; John Collen; Lawrence I. Davidson; Howard M. Hoffmann; Stanley R. Kaminski; Charles D. Katz (Not admitted in IL); David J. Kaufman; Brian P. Kerwin (Member, Chicago Office Management Committee, Duane Morris LLP); Daniel Kohn; Kenneth A. Latimer; Nicholas J. Lynn (Member, Chicago Office Management Committee, Duane Morris LLP); Joanne J. Matousek; Pamela J. Mills; Howard L. Mocerf; Vincent S. Oleszkiewicz; Michael A. Reiter; John T. Schriver, III; Larry Selander; Michael J. Silverman; Christopher B. Sullivan; Michael A. Witt; David B. Yelin (Partner-in-Charge, Chicago, Illinois Office, Duane Morris LLP; Member, Chicago Office Management Committee); Jon Zimring. Resident Associates: Richard P. Darke; Christopher P. Keleher; Dietrich A. Loos; Amy E. McCracken; Rachael G. Pontikes. Resident Special Counsel: Michele J. Braun; Dirk E. Ehlers.
Administrative Law, Accountants Liability, Admiralty and Maritime Law, Affordable Housing, Alternative Dispute Resolution, Antitrust and Trade Regulation, Appellate Practice, Architects and Engineers Liability, Aviation and Aerospace, Aerospace Law, Banks and Banking, Banking Litigation, Bankruptcy, Bankruptcy Chapter 11, Bankruptcy Reorganization, Business Development, Business Law, Business Litigation, Business Reorganization, Business Start-Ups, Business Taxation, Charitable Giving, Chemical Intellectual Property, Chemical Patent Prosecution, Civil Litigation, Civil Rights, Class Actions, Closely Held Business Law, Closely Held Corporations, COBRA, College and University Law, Commercial Law, Commercial Litigation, Commercial Real Estate, Complex Commercial Litigation, Computers and Software, Computer and Software Patents, Computer Law, Condominium Law, Construction Law, Construction Litigation, Consumer Law, Content Licensing, Copyrights, Copyright Infringement, Copyright Prosecution, Copyright Protection, Corporate Banking Law, Corporate Commercial Law, Corporate Finance, Corporate Law, Creditor Bankruptcy, Criminal Law, Customs Law, Debt Finance, Debtor and Creditor, Debtor and Creditor Rights, Debtor Bankruptcy, Deportation, Disability Benefits, Disability Insurance, Domain Names, E-Commerce, Education Law, Elder Law, Emerging Growth Companies, Eminent Domain, Employee Benefits, Employee Benefits Litigation, Employment Authorizations, Employment Discrimination, Employment Law, Employment Litigation, Energy, Energy Regulation, Environmental Law, Equipment Finance and Leasing, Equine Law, Equity Finance, ERISA, Estates and Asset Planning, Estate and Gift Taxation, Fair Housing, Family Law, Federal Income Tax, Fidelity and Surety, Fidelity and Surety Bonds, Finance, Financial Planning, Franchise and Franchising, Franchise Law, General Practice, Government, Government Investigations, Government Relations, Health Care, Health Care Compliance, Health Care Fraud, Health Maintenance Organizations, Homeowners Association Law, Housing Development, Housing Finance, Housing Law, Immigration and Naturalization, Immigration Law, Independent School Law, Information Technology, Initial Public Offerings, Insurance, Insurance Coverage, Insurance Defense, Insurance Litigation, Integrated Health Care Delivery, Intellectual Property, Intellectual Property Infringement, Intellectual Property Litigation, Intellectual Property Procurement, Intellectual Property Rights, International Energy Law, International Finance, International Law, International Taxation, International Trade, Internet Intellectual Property, Internet Law, Internet Patents, Joint Ventures, Labor and Employment, Land Use, Land Use Litigation, Leveraged Buyouts, Life and Health Insurance, Litigation, Local Government Law, Local Taxation, Low Income Housing, Managed Care, Managed Care Contracts, Mechanical Intellectual Property, Mediation, Medical Malpractice, Medicare and Medicaid, Mergers, Acquisitions and Divestitures, Mortgages, Municipal Bonds, Municipal Finance, Municipal Law, Natural Gas, Natural Resources, Nonprofit and Charitable Organizations, Oil and Gas Law, Partnership Law, Patents, Patent Licensing, Patent Prosecution, Personal Injury, Personal Injury Defense, Piracy, Political Asylum, Privatization, Private Foundations, Probate, Probate Litigation, Products Liability, Professional Liability, Professional Malpractice, Professional Negligence, Proxy Contests, Public Finance, Public Housing, Public Policy, Public School Law, Real Estate, Real Estate Acquisitions, Real Estate Development, Real Estate Litigation, Real Estate Tax Assessment, Regulatory Compliance, Regulatory Law, Reinsurance, Reorganization and Finance, RICO, Risk Management, Secured Creditors Rights, Securities, Securities Fraud, Securities Litigation, Securities Taxation and Telecommunications, Sexual Harassment, Shareholders Disputes, Shareholder Rights, Sports Law, State Government Law, Taxation, Torts, Toxic Torts, Trade Association Law, Trade Secrets, Trademarks, Trademark Licensing, Trademark Prosecution, Trademark Protection, Trusts and Estates, Unsecured Creditors

(This Listing Continued)

Duane Morris LLP (Continued)

Rights, Utility Law, Visas, Water Law, Water Rights, Web Site Development, White Collar Crime, Workers Compensation, Workouts, Wrongful Death, Zoning, Planning and Land Use.
Philadelphia, Pennsylvania Office: 30 South 17th Street. Telephone: 215-979-1000. Fax: 215-979-1020.
New York, New York Office: 380 Lexington Avenue. Telephone: 212-692-1000. Fax: 212-692-1020.
Los Angeles, California Office: 333 South Hope Street. Telephone: 213-229-2900. Fax: 213-229-2999.
London, England Office: Duane Morris, 4 Chiswell Street, 5th Floor, EC1Y 4UP. Telephone: +44 0 20 7786 2100. Fax: +44 0 20 7786 2101.
Washington, D.C. Office: 1667 K Street, N.W., Suite 700. Telephone: 202-776-7800. Fax: 202-776-7801.
San Francisco, California Office: One Market, Spear Tower, Suite 2000. Telephone: 415-371-2200. Fax: 415-371-2201.
Boston, Massachusetts Office: 470 Atlantic Avenue, Suite 500. Telephone: 617-9200. Fax: 617-598-9201.
Atlanta, Georgia Office: 1180 West Peachtree Street, Suite 700. Telephone: 404-253-6900. Fax: 404-253-6901.
Miami, Florida Office: 200 South Biscayne Boulevard, Suite 3400. Telephone: 305-960-2200. Fax: 305-960-2201
Wilmington, Delaware Office: 1100 North Market Street, Suite 1200. Telephone: 302-657-4900. Fax: 302-657-4901.
Harrisburg, Pennsylvania Office: 305 North Front Street, 5th Floor, P.O. Box 1003. Telephone: 717-237-5500. Fax: 717-232-4015.
Newark, New Jersey Office: 744 Broad Street, Suite 1200. Telephone: 973-424-2000. Fax: 973-424-2001.
Allentown, Pennsylvania Office: 968 Postal Road, Suite 200, P.O. Box 90400. Telephone: 610-266-3650. Fax: 610-266-3651.
Houston, Texas Office: 3200 Southwest Freeway, Suite 3150. Telephone: 713-402-3900. Fax: 713-402-3901.
Hamilton, New Jersey Office: 240 Princeton Avenue, Suite 150. Mailing Address: P.O. Box 5203, Princeton, NJ. Telephone: 609-631-2400. Fax: 609-631-2401.
San Diego, California Office: 101 West Broadway, Suite 900. Telephone: 619-744-2200. Fax: 619-744-2201.
Pittsburgh, Pennsylvania Office: 600 Grant Street, Suite 5010. Telephone: 412-497-1000. Fax: 412-497-1001.

See Professional Biographies, CHICAGO, ILLINOIS

Duara, Juliette Gregory .... '60 '95 C.939 B.A. L.145 J.D. [Bell,B.&L.]
Duarte, Allen .... '72 '97 C.276 B.S.F.S. L.569 J.D. City of Chicago, Corp. Coun. Off.
Dub, Allen W., (AV) .... '53 '78 C.273 B.A. L.1003 J.D. [Klein D.&H.] ⊙
Duban, Janice L., (AV) .... '51 '91 C.112 B.A. L.424 J.D. [DLPiper R.G.C.U.]
Dubbs, John W., III, (BV) .... '51 '76 C.339 B.S. L.597 J.D. [Hinshaw&C.]
Dube, Monte .... '56 '83 C.94 A.B. L.978 J.D. [McDermott W.&E.]
Dubin, Stuart B. .... '40 '65 C.1016 B.S. L.209 J.D. [S.B.Dubin&Assoc.]
Dubin, Stuart B., Ltd. & Associates .... 180 N. LaSalle St.
Dubner, Jason S. .... '70 '98 C.821 B.A. L.145 J.D. [🄰 Butler R.S.&B.]
Dubnow, Linda B. .... '63 '92 C.659 B.A. L.94 J.D. [McGuirewoods]
Dubovoy, Hugo .... '59 '83 L.999 J.D. [Baker&M.]
Dubovoy, Hugo, Jr. .... '79 '04 C.424 B.A. L.145 J.D. [🄰 Skadden,A.S.M.&F.]
Dubowsky, Martin J. .... '46 '70 C.477 A.B. L.145 J.D. 2235 N. Orchard Street
DuBrock, Daniel J. .... '59 '87 C.1151 B.A. L.365 J.D. [Weis&D.]
Duca, James F., II '58 '83 C.436 A.B. L.966 J.D.
(adm. in WI; not adm. in IL) Exec. V.P., Wealth Mgmt., Wintrust Financial Corp.
DuCanto, Joseph N., (AV) .... '27 '55 C.33 B.A. L.145 J.D. [Schiller,D.&F.]
Ducat, D. Christine .... '76 '03 C.215 B.A. L.831 J.D. [🄰 Cozen O.]
Ducayet, James W. .... '69 '96 C.145 B.A. L.569 J.D. [🄰 Sidley A.B.&W.]
Ducey, Kerry .... '— '01 C.602 B.A. L.880 J.D. [🄰 Latham&W.]
DuCharme, Nancy K. .... '54 '87 C.741 B.A. L.209 J.D. [🅂 Sidley A.B.&W.]
Duchowicz, Jerome J., (AV) .... '— '76 C.589 B.A. L.424 J.D. [O'Hagan,S.&A.]
Duckett, Theresa .... '75 '02 C.209 B.A. L.861 J.D. [🄰 Lord,B.&B.]
Duckstein, Norbert, (AV) .... '42 '74 C.229 B.A. L.146 J.D. 180 N. La Salle St., Ste. 2620
Duckworth, Kevin B., (AV) .... '59 '85 C.254 B.A. L.574 J.D. [Jenner&B.]
Ducommun, Steven E., (BV) .... '58 '86 C.221 B.S.B.A. L.188 J.D. [Bell,B.&L.]
Duczynski, John M., (AV) .... '48 '76 C&L.477 A.B., J.D. [🄰 Michaels&M.]
Duczynski, Margaret S. .... '50 '79 C&L.477 A.B., J.D. 340 W. Diversey
Duda, Kimberly A. .... '66 '94 C.475 B.A. L.215 J.D. 19 S. LaSalle St.
Duda, Robert R., Jr. .... '74 '99 C.201 B.A. L.209 J.D. [🄰 Smith O.&W.]
Duda, Thomas W., (BV) '47 '73 C.602 A.B. L.597 J.D.
39 S. LaSalle St., Ste. 408 (⊙Arlington Heights)
Dudek, Andrea M., (BV) .... '59 '84 C&L.339 B.S., J.D. 1 N Wacker Dr, # 1200
Dudek, Michael J., (P.C.) .... '44 '70 C&L.424 B.S., J.D. 703 S. Dearborn St.
Dudenas, Ruta G. .... '73 '01 C.339 B.A. L.424 J.D. Atty., Secs. and Exchange Comm.
Dudley, Allison .... '— '02 C.339 B.S.M.E. L.146 J.D. [🄰 Baniak P.&G.] (See Pat. Sect.)
Dudley, Ann Cleland .... '76 '01 C.347 B.A. L.477 J.D. Atty.
Dudley, Kelli '69 '03 C.346 B.A. L.1000 J.D.
Staff Atty; Supvr. of Chancery Advice Desk
Dudziak, Ralph P. .... '61 '86 C.57 B.A. L.880 J.D. [Mayer,B.R.&M.]
Dudzic, Paul F. .... '65 '91 C.1030 B.A. L.228 J.D. 5537 S. Hyde Pk. Blvd.‡
Dudzik, Christine A., (AV) .... '52 '88 C.589 B.S. L.146 J.D. [Howrey] (Pat.)
Duez, David J., (AV) .... '47 '73 C.357 B.S. L.339 J.D. [McDermott W.&E.]
Duff, Brian Barnett .... '30 '62 C.602 A.B. L.209 J.D. U.S. Sr. Dist. J.
Duff, F. Ellen, (AV) .... '55 '80 C.602 A.B. L.145 J.D. [Winston&S.]
Duff, Kevin B., (AV) .... '67 '92 C&L.276 A.B., J.D. [Rachlis D.D.&A.]
Duffee, Michael W., (AV) .... '52 '77 C.209 B.A. L.597 J.D. [Matkov,S.M.&G.]
Duffey, Lynne Plum, (BV) .... '59 '89 C.530 B.A. L.146 J.D. [🄰 Hofeld&S.]
Duffield, Charles A. .... '70 '00 C&L.339 B.S., J.D. [🄰 Sonnenschein N.&R.]
Duffield, Gwendolyn M. .... '74 '01 C.339 B.S. L.146 J.D. Asst. Pub. Guard.
Duffield, R. Bruce, (AV) .... '52 '76 C&L.101 B.A., J.D. [Lord,B.&B.]
Duffy, Daniel P., (BV) .... '65 '94 C&L.602 B.A., J.D. [Duffy&M.]
Duffy, David .... '52 '87 C.1192 B.S. L.209 J.D. 6142 N. Forest Glen Ave.
Duffy, J. David .... '— '94 C.862 B.A. L.1365 J.D. [Mandell M.]
Duffy, John J. .... '67 '94 C.352 B.A. L.424 J.D. [Donohue B.M.&S.]
Duffy, John M., (AV) .... '30 '54 C&L.424 B.S., J.D. [McCarthy D.]
Duffy, John R. .... '48 '73 C.602 B.A. L.339 J.D. Chicago Board of Education
Duffy, Joseph J., (AV) .... '51 '79 C.209 B.S.C. L.365 J.D. [Stetler&D.]
Duffy, Meggan F. .... '73 '98 C.339 B.S. L.424 J.D. [🄲 Marshall,G.&B.] (See Pat. Sect.)
Duffy, Michael, (AV) .... '51 '78 C.385 A.B. L.424 J.D. [Gardner C.&D.]
Duffy, Michael A. .... '— '00 C.93 A.B. L.597 J.D. [🄰 Kirkland&E.]
Duffy, Michael J., (AV) .... '60 '87 C.589 B.A. L.209 J.D. [Tressler,S.M.&P.]
Duffy, Michael W., (AV) .... '56 '81 C.602 B.A. L.424 J.D. [Childress D.G.]
Duffy, Patrick G. .... '56 '81 C.597 B.A. L.309 J.D. 7042 N. Ottawa Ave.
Duffy, Paul A. .... '— '92 C.238 B.S. L.209 J.D. [🄲 Freeborn&P.]
Duffy, Richard F. '47 '79 C.870 B.S. L.276 J.D.
V.P., Harcourt Brace Professional Educ. Grp., Inc.
Duffy, Thomas P., (AV) .... '50 '76 C.659 B.A. L.209 J.D. [Wildman,H.A.&D.]
Duffy, Thos. J. .... '19 '47 C.602 A.B. L.209 J.D. 10045 S. Bell Ave.
Duffy, Timothy A., (AV) .... '— '94 C.1164 B.A. L.145 J.D. [Kirkland&E.]
Duffy & Mundo, (BV) .... 208 W. Washington
Dufkis, Frank R. '66 '91 C&L.209 B.A., J.D.
Corp. Coun., Midwest Real Estate Invest. Co.
Dugan, Janet E. ... '64 '89 C.424 B.A. L.365 J.D. Hearing Offr., Dept. of Consumer Servs.
Dugan, John M. .... '55 '79 C&L.209 B.A., J.D. 6114 N. Tripp Ave.
Dugan, William F. .... '70 '95 C.339 B.A. L.602 J.D. [Seyfarth S.]
Dugard, Thomas M. .... '66 '91 C.602 B.B.A. L.813 J.D. [Matkov,S.M.&G.]
Duggan, David G., (AV) '51 '80 C.197 B.A. L.597 J.D.
140 South Dearborn, Suite 1610
Duggan, David G. .... '48 '81 C.424 A.B. L.365 J.D. [🄲 Susman&Assoc.]
Duggan, James M. .... '69 '94 C.339 B.S. L.209 M.B.A./J.D. [Handler,T.&D.]
Duggan, Michael J. .... '52 '82 C.1183 B.A. L.146 J.D. [Klein,T.&J.]
Duhart, Jake Jerome '51 '83 C.608 B.A. L.851 J.D.
(adm. in OH; not adm. in IL) 6007 N. Sheridan Rd.‡
Duk, Jennifer M. .... '72 '02 C.1260 B.S. L.424 J.D. [🄰 Leydig,V.&M.] (See Pat. Sect.)
Dumbrys, Dainius R. .... '77 '03 C.352 B.A. L.339 J.D. [🄰 Boodell D.&S.]
Dumezich, Daniel .... '59 '89 C.932 B.A. L.365 J.D. [Mayer,B.R.&M.]
Dunbar, David M. .... '60 '89 C.321 B.A. L.209 J.D. [Katten M.R.]
Dunbar, Emily J. .... '80 '05 C.352 B.A. L.589 J.D. 4746 N. Milwaukee
Duncan, Jeffery M., (AV) '56 '84 C&L.101 B.S., J.D.
[Brinks H.G.&L.] (See Pat. Sect.)
Duncan, John P.C., (AV) .... '49 '74 C.976 B.A. L.145 J.D. [Duncan a.&Assoc.]
Duncan, Kathleen A. .... '78 '03 C.108 B.A. L.365 J.D. [🄰 Daley&G.]
Duncan, Margaret M., (AV) .... '54 '81 C.973 B.S. L.424 J.D. [McDermott W.&E.] (Pat.)
Duncan Associates Attorneys and Counselors, P.C., (AV)
180 N. LaSalle Street, Suite 3850
Duncan-Brice, Jennifer .... '— '76 C.207 B.A. L.365 J.D. Cir. J.
Dunck, Shelley L. .... '64 '89 C.477 B.A. L.424 J.D. Assoc., Gunther Group LLC
Duncker, Conrad O. .... '46 '74 C.742 B.A. L.146 J.D. 258 W. 31st St.
Dunigan, E. Bryan, III, (AV) .... '46 '72 C&L.602 A.B., J.D. [🄲 Roddy,L.&Z.]
Dunitz, Nelson I. .... '34 '61 C&L.209 B.S., J.D. 39 S. LaSalle St.
Dunitz-Geiringer, Jennifer .... '71 '96 C.597 B.S. L.209 J.D. [🄰 Baum S.A.&N.]
Dunkin, David C. .... '— '85 C.339 B.A. L.424 J.D. [Arnstein&L.]
Dunleavy, Terence M. .... '57 '82 C.1151 B.A. L.589 J.D. [Vedder,P.K.&K.]
Dunlop, Douglas W. '46 '74 C.560 B.A. L.347 J.D.
(adm. in IN; not adm. in IL) Vice Chmn., Pure Energy Corp.
Dunlop, James C. .... '— '91 C.276 B.S. L.893 J.D. [🄲 Jones D.]
Dunlop, Karen O. .... '66 '92 C.276 B.A. L.893 J.D. [🄰 Sidley A.B.&W.]
Dunn, Amy S. '71 '03 C.1236 B.A. L.276 J.D.
(adm. in NY; not adm. in IL) [🄰 McDermott W.&E.]
Dunn, Barbara .... '66 '92 C.477 B.A. L.365 J.D. [Howe&H.] (⊙Ballwin, MO)
Dunn, Brian J. .... '— '03 C.477 B.A. L.597 J.D. [🄰 Mayer,B.R.&M.]
Dunn, Brian M. .... '74 '03 C.1111 B.A. L.276 J.D. [🄰 Novack&M.]
Dunn, Catherine M. .... '73 '99 C&L.477 B.A., J.D. [🄰 Berger S.]
Dunn, Colin H. .... '76 '02 C.473 B.A. L.424 J.D. Asst. State Atty.
Dunn, Damon E., (AV) .... '54 '81 C.970 B.A. L.146 J.D. [Funkhouser V.L.&D.]
Dunn, Deborah .... '— '95 C.878 B.A. L.101 J.D. [Kirkland&E.]
Dunn, Diedre S. '67 '92
C.602 B.A. L.150 J.D. Assoc. Gen. Coun., Natl. Equity Fund, Inc.
Dunn, Edwin R., (AV) .... '42 '67 C.602 B.A. L.597 J.D. [Baker&M.]
Dunn, Hillary Levitt .... '73 '99 C.966 B.A. L.597 J.D. [🄰 Goldberg,K.B.B.R.&M.]
Dunn, Jacqueline Riley '65 '92
C.1077 B.A. L.1065 J.D. U.S. Dist. Ct., Northern Dist. of IL
Dunn, Joseph E. '46 '88 C.93 A.B. L.818 J.D.
(adm. in MA; not adm. in IL) Asst. Reg. Coun., Soc. Sec. Admn.
Dunn, Marilyn P. .... '— '90 C.1168 B.A. L.378 J.D. [Sachnoff&W.]
Dunn, Matthew J., (AV) '58 '84
C.1101 B.A. L.602 J.D. Chf. Asst. Atty. Gen., Environ. Control Div.
Dunn, Thomas G., (AVⓉ) '46 '80 C.767 B.A. L.1026 J.D.
(adm. in CA; not adm. in IL) [Ellison,N.Z.&A.]
Dunn, William M. .... '67 '95 C.602 B.A. L.365 J.D. [🄲 Cassiday,S.&G.]
Dunne, Arthur L. .... '30 '58 C.477 B.A. L.597 J.D. Cir. J.
Dunne, Edward Fitzsimmons .... '68 '94 C.966 B.A. L.146 J.D. [Crisham&K.]
Dunne, Roderick T. .... '— '85 C.951 B.A. L.597 J.D. [Karbal,C.E.S.&D.]

Dunneback, James F., P.C.
(See Orland Park)

Dunning, Jeffrey P. .... '74 '98 C.339 B.S. L.910 J.D. [🄰 Greenberg T.] (Pat.)
Dunning, Ruth M., (AV) .... '57 '93 C.347 B.A. L.209 J.D. 53 W. Jackson Blvd., Ste. 750
Dunphy, Kevin V. .... '65 '96 C.339 B.A. L.424 J.D. [🄰 Connelly S.H.]
Dunsky, Lisa A. .... '63 '93 C.201 B.A. L.477 J.D. [🄲 Mayer,B.R.&M.]
Duplack, Ronald P. .... '54 '79 C.98 B.A. L.424 J.D. [Rieck&C.]
Dupont, Mark A. .... '61 '86 C.350 B.A. L.813 J.D. Law Clk., U.S. Ct. of App.
Dupree, James M., (AV) .... '43 '68 C.436 B.S. L.424 J.D. [Fitzgerald&C.]
Duprey, Anne .... '72 '99 C.385 B.A. L.902 J.D. [🄰 Seyfarth S.]
Duprey, Laura S. .... '— '01 C.399 B.A. L.339 J.D. Two North LaSalle Street, Suite 2200
Durava, Richard J. .... '32 '67 C&L.209 B.S., J.D. The Northern Tr. Co.
Durbin, Fletcher M., (AV) .... '50 '74 C.951 B.A. L.309 J.D. 1513 N. Western Ave.
Durbin, Mark L. .... '— '93 C.339 B.A. L.209 J.D. [Wildman,H.A.&D.]
Durbin, Paul D. .... '69 '94 C.439 B.A. L.339 J.D. [McGuirewoods]
Durchslag, M. L. .... '07 '30 C&L.145 Ph.B., J.D. 77 W. Wash. St.
Durchslag, Stephen P., (AV) .... '40 '66 C.966 B.S. L.309 LL.B. [Winston&S.]
Durham, Chas. J. .... '27 '55 C.339 L.209 LL.B. Ret. Cir. J.
Durham, Edwin L. .... '57 '90 C&L.339 A.B., J.D. [Rachlis D.D.&A.]
Durham, Gina L. .... '74 '99 C.597 B.A. L.209 J.D. [🄰 DLPiper R.G.C.U.]
Durham, Thomas C. .... '55 '80 C.187 B.A. L.569 J.D. [Mayer,B.R.&M.]
Duric, Nicholas M., Law Offices of '60 '85 C&L.424 B.B.A., J.D.
2101 W. Armitage Ave.
Durik, Curtis L. .... '73 '99 C.966 B.B.A. L.146 J.D. [🄰 Sarnoff&B.]
Durkin, Albert E., Jr., (AV) .... '52 '77 C.1151 B.A. L.209 J.D. [Miroballi,D.&R.]
Durkin, Andrea J. .... '— '01 C.339 B.A. L.146 J.D. [🄰 Arnstein&L.]
Durkin, Carrie A. .... '— '79 C.164 B.A. L.146 J.D. [Litchfield C.]
Durkin, John T. .... '26 '52 C.424 B.S. L.209 LL.B. 6762 N. Dowagiac‡
Durkin, Kevin P., (AV) .... '55 '80 C.339 B.S. L.209 J.D. [Clifford]
Durkin, Martin G., Jr. .... '62 '88 C.174 B.A. L.339 J.D. [Holland&K.]
Durkin, Melissa .... '71 '95 C.339 B.A. L.146 J.D. Asst. State's Atty.
Durkin, Michael J., (AV) .... '58 '83 C.339 B.S. L.209 J.D. [Harrison&H.]
Durkin, Patricia C., (BV) .... '64 '90 C.746 B.A. L.146 J.D. 120 N. La Salle St., 31st Fl.
Durkin, Thomas Anthony, (AV) .... '46 '73 C.602 A.B. L.767 J.D. [Durkin&R.]
Durkin, Thomas M., (AV) .... '53 '78 C.339 B.S. L.209 J.D. [Mayer,B.R.&M.]
Durkin, Thomas P. .... '43 '67 C&L.424 B.S., J.D. Cir. J.

Durkin & Roberts, (AV) BR
53 West Jackson Boulevard, Suite 615, 60604
Telephone: 312-913-9300 Fax: 312-913-9235
Email: admin@durkinroberts.com URL: http://www.lawyers.com/durkin&roberts
Thomas Anthony Durkin; Janis D. Roberts;—Mariah E. Moran. Of Counsel: Michael Buckley Bolan; Clarke P. Devereux.

(This Listing Continued)

Durkin & Roberts (Continued)

Criminal Trial, Appellate and Grand Jury Practice in all Federal and State Courts. International Extradition, Attorney Disciplinary Defense, Child Welfare and Juvenile Justice.

See Professional Biographies, CHICAGO, ILLINOIS

Durso, John J., (AV) ... '— '77 C.589 B.A. L.424 J.D. [Ungaretti&H.]
Dusberger, Roger H. ... '42 '66 C&L.339 B.S., J.D. [R.Dusberger]
Dusberger, Roger ... 140 S. Dearborn St., Ste. 411
Dusek, Brian J. ... '72 '98 C.494 B.A. L.209 J.D. [Ⓐ McCullough,C.&L.]
Dusek, Robin C. ... '73 '98 C.602 B.A. L.945 J.D. [Ⓐ Lovells]
Dusky, Maurice E. ... '64 '91 C.1062 B.S. L.365 J.D. 180 N. LaSalle St., Ste. 2910

Dussias, Dean S., (BV) '65 '91 C.424 B.A. L.365 J.D.
180 North LaSalle Street Suite 1800, 60601
Telephone: 312-263-9801 Fax: 312-855-0535
Email: esquire345@aol.com URL: http://www.lawyers.com/deandussias
Associate: Christopher S. Syregelas.
Divorce, Civil Litigation, Family Law Litigation.

See Professional Biographies, CHICAGO, ILLINOIS

Duster, Benj. C. ... '27 '55 C.339 M.B.A. L.209 J.D. 7459 S. Cottage Grove
Dustin, Andrew ... '— '03 C.145 B.A. L.477 J.D. [Ⓐ Kirkland&E.]
Dustman, Ann E. '67 '95 C.473 B.A. L.209 J.D.
(adm. in NY; not adm. in IL) [Ⓒ Seyfarth S.]
Duston, Thomas L., (AV) '— '87
C.178 B.A. L.1065 J.D. [Marshall,G.&B.] (See Pat. Sect.)
Dutenhaver, Katheryn M., (AV) '38 '72
C.578 A.B. L.209 J.D. Assoc. Prof. of Law, DePaul University
Dutterer, Dennis A., (BV) '44 '70
C.446 B.S. L.30 J.D. V.P. & CEO, Board of Trade Clearing Corp.
Dutton, Janna S., (AV) ... '53 '79 C.937 B.A. L.209 J.D. [J.Dutton&Assoc.]
Dutton, Thomas E., (AV) ... '— '87 C.352 B.A. L.178 J.D. [Greenberg T.]
Dutton, Janna, & Associates, P.C., (AV) ... One North LaSalle Street
DuVal, Thomas B., (AV) ... '36 '62 C.339 B.A. L.597 J.D. [Tinkoff,P.&D.]
Duve, Cherie '62 '92 C&L.352 B.S., J.D.
VP Assoc. Gen. Coun., Amalgamated Bank of Chicago (Legal Department)
Duwe, Brian W. ... '60 '87 C.197 B.A. L.145 J.D. [Skadden,A.S.M.&F.]
Duwe, Yasmina '63 '91 C.103 A.B. L.477 J.D.
First V.P. & Assoc. Gen. Coun., Equity Residential
Dvorak, George F., (P.C.), (AV) ... '24 '53 C.597 B.S.E.E. L.365 J.D. [Ⓒ Orum&R.] (Pat.)
Dvorak, Richard J. ... '70 '99 L.209 J.D. Pub. Def. Off.
Dvorken, Rachel, (AV) '61 '88 C.165 B.A. L.309 J.D.
Sen. Assoc. Gen. Coun., Northwestern Mem. Hosp.
Dwinn, Arnold H. ... '16 '39 C&L.209 LL.B. 55 W. Monroe St.
Dworkin, Bradley Saul, Law Offices of '64 '90
C.352 L.930 J.D. 134 N. LaSalle, Suite 1515
Dwyer, James G. '61 '88 C.93 B.A. L.976 J.D.
(adm. in NY; not adm. in IL) Chicago-Kent College of Law
Dwyer, James R., (AV) ... '— '80 C.602 B.A. L.1494 J.D. [LeBoeuf,L.G.&M.]
Dwyer, Patrick E., (AV) ... '40 '67 C.424 B.S. L.209 J.D. [Dwyer,M.&Assoc.]
Dwyer, Patrick Edward, III '73 '99 C.276 B.A. L.424 J.D.
City of Chicago Corp. Counsel
Dwyer, Paula M. ... '— '85 111 West Washington Street, Suite 942
Dwyer, Thomas J. ... '55 '81 C.746 B.B.A. L.209 J.D. 401 S. La Salle St., Ste. 606
Dwyer, William T., Jr., (AV) ... '47 '72 C.602 B.A. L.339 J.D. [O'Rourke,H.F.&D.]

Dwyer, McCarthy & Associates, Ltd., (AV)
39 South La Salle, Suite 610, 60603
Telephone: 312-782-7482 Fax: 312-782-7433
Email: pedts@aol.com URL: http://www.patrickedwyerandassociatesltd.com
Patrick E. Dwyer; James G. McCarthy;—William M. Wippold.
Auto Accidents, Construction Site Injuries, Product Liability, Dog Bites, Slip and Fall, Wrongful Death, Medical Malpractice, Construction Defects.

See Professional Biographies, CHICAGO, ILLINOIS

Dye, Marilynn J. '66 '99 C.597 B.A. L.365 J.D./LL.M.
Chicago Board of Education for the City of Chicago
Dygert, Diane V., (BV) ... '62 '87 C.188 B.S. L.477 J.D. [Seyfarth S.]
Dyhrkopp, Erik F. ... '65 '90 C.1099 B.A. L.597 J.D. [Bell,B.&L.]
Dykehouse, James B., (BV) ... '54 '85 C.31 B.A. L.597 J.D. [Ⓐ Seham S.M.&P.]

Dykema Gossett PLLC, (AV)
10 South Wacker Drive, Suite 2300, 60606 ⊙
Telephone: 312-876-1700 Fax: 312-876-1155
URL: http://www.dykema.com
Members of Firm: Harry N. Arger; John J. Blasi; Michael C. Borders; Terrence M. Burns; Jeffrey M. Daiebroux; I. Walter Deitch; Dean A. Dickie; Gwen M. Geraghty; Marc D. Ginsberg; Richard E. Gottlieb; Jodi L. Henninger; Glenn Z. Hering; Lee T. Hettinger; Thomas R. Hill; James H. Ihrke; Gregory J. Jordan; Terrence E. Kiwala; Charles A. LeMoine; John J. Mangan; Nick Marsico; Jerome I. Maynard; James W. McConkey; John M. McGarry; Paul A. Michalik; David L. Miller; Daniel M. Noland; Patricia Cari Nowak; Wayne F. Plaza; Marc A. Primack; Arthur F. Radke; Stephen D. Sayre; Michael F. Sexton; Ian M. Sherman; John M. Steed; Allan J. Sternstein; Janet A. Stiven; Robert K. Villa; Cheryl A. Warzynski; Mark W. Weisbard. Of Counsel: Clyde O. Bowles, Jr.; John C. Corrigan; John Alden Fritchey; Arthur I. Gould; Misty S. Gruber; Mark Lenz; Jay A. Lipe; Arnold A. Silvestri; Kathleen J. Swan; Stanley R. Weinberger. Retired Partners: James L. Donnelly; Ray F. Drexler; Jerome N. Groark; Timothy J. Groark; D. Glenn Ofsthun; Henry L. Pitts; John G. Poust. Associates: Allyson R. Behm; Laura Marie Callahan; David T. Cellitti; Sonia A. Desai; Evangelos J. Gegas; Jason L. Hopp; Rafi K. Jafri; Julie C. Keller; Justin T. Lange; Nahrin S. Marino; Tricia E. McVicker; Sharon A. Salinas; Peter J. Schmidt; Kathleen E. Surowiec; Rosa Tumialan; David A. Wheeler; Gregory M. Wright; Reneé L. Zipprich; Mark R. Zito. Staff Attorney: Margaret J. Rhiew.
Antitrust and Trade Regulation, Automotive, Banking and Financial Services, Bankruptcy, Biotechnology and Life Sciences, Casino Gaming, Class Action Defense, Computer and Software Law, Construction, Consumer Financial Services, Corporate Finance, E-Commerce, Emerging Business and Technology, Employee Benefits, Entertainment and Sports, Environmental Law, Family Law, Franchise Law and Regulation, Government Contracts, Government Policy and Practice, HealthCare, Indian Law, Insurance, Intellectual Property, International Law, Labor and Employment, Litigation and Dispute Resolution, Mergers and Acquisitions, Products Liability Defense, Public Finance, Real Estate, Retail Law, Securities, Taxation and Estates, Trade Associations.
***Ann Arbor, Michigan* Office: 2723 South State Street, Suite 400, 48104. Telephone: 734-214-7660. Fax: 734-214-7696.**
Aurora, Illinois Office: 2 Hankes Road. Telephone: 630-844-2200. Facsimile: 630-844-2277.
Bloomfield Hills, Michigan Office: 39577 Woodward Avenue, Suite 300, 48304-2820. Telephone: 248-203-0700. Fax: 248-203-0763.
Detroit, Michigan Office: 400 Renaissance Center, 48243-1668. Telephone: 313-568-6800. Fax: 313-568-6545.
Grand Rapids, Michigan Office: Suite 700, 300 Ottawa Avenue, N.W., 49503-2306. Telephone: 616-776-7500. Fax: 616-776-7573.
Joliet, Illinois Office: 111 North Ottawa Street. Telephone: 815-727-4511. Facsimile: 815-727-1586.
Lansing, Michigan Office: 124 W. Allegan Street, Suite 800, 48933-1742. Telephone: 517-374-9100. Fax: 517-374-9191.
Lisle, Illinois Office: 4200 Commerce Court, Suite 300. Telephone: 630-245-0400. Facsimile: 630-245-0140.
Los Angeles, California Office: 333 South Grand Avenue, Suite 2100, 90071. Telephone: 213-457-1800. Fax: 213-457-1850.

(This Listing Continued)

Dykema Gossett PLLC (Continued)

Washington, D.C. Office: Franklin Square, Suite 300 West, 1300 I Street, N.W., 20005-3353. Telephone: 202-906-8600. Fax: 202-906-8669.

See Professional Biographies, CHICAGO, ILLINOIS

Dykeman, Stephanie R. ... '— '04 C.966 B.A. L.1066 J.D. [Ⓐ Kirkland&E.]
Dyki, Steven R. ... '74 '99 C.136 B.S. L.209 J.D. [Ⓐ Rusin M.&F.]
Dykstra, Paul H., (AV) ... '43 '68 C.674 A.B. L.976 LL.B. [Bell,B.&L.]
Dym, Mark S., (AV) ... '57 '82 C.893 B.A. L.273 J.D. [Hughes S.P.R.&D.]
Dyme, Rochelle Secemsky, (AV) '55 '79 C.339 B.A. L.597 J.D.
[Funkhouser V.L.&D.]
Dymkar, Irene K., (BVⓉ) ... '51 '77 C.145 B.A. L.1119 J.D. [Dymkar&B.]
Dymkar & Brandt, (BVⓉ) ... 5907 W. Midway Park
Dyner, Morris G., (AV) ... '42 '67 C&L.145 B.A., J.D. [Fischel&K.]
Dziedziak, John F. ... '57 '82 C.98 B.S. L.209 J.D. [Williams&Ma.]

Dziezak Law Firm, P.C.
(See Hoffman Estates)

D'Ziire, Patrice ... '— '03 C.339 B.A. L.569 J.D. [Ⓐ DLPiper R.G.C.U.]
Dzik, Katherine L. ... '72 '00 C.999 B.S. L.209 J.D. [Ⓐ Clifford]
Eades, Deborah Bielicke '65 '90 C.502 B.S.B.A. L.910 J.D.
(adm. in MO; not adm. in IL) [Vedder,P.K.&K.]
Eadie-Daniels, L., (Mrs.) '49 '77
C.424 B.A. L.209 J.D. Asst. Coun., Chicago Transit Auth.
Eads, Ralph S. ... '44 '73 C.118 A.B. L.597 J.D. Exec. Dir., Tax Planning, Sara Lee Corp.
Eagle, Joan M., (AV) ... '39 '83 C.477 B.M. L.146 J.D. [Schwartz C.]
Eagle, Ross M. ... '66 '93 C.966 B.A. L.365 J.D. [Jester,K.&E.]
Eagle, Warren E., (AV) ... '37 '62 C.597 B.S. L.477 J.D. [Katz,F.E.E.&J.]
Eannace, John Jay ... '58 '82 C.927 B.S. L.365 J.D. Chf. Asst. State Atty.
Earl, Laura M. ... '02 C.347 B.A. L.597 J.D. [Ⓐ Jones D.]
Earle, David P., III ... '38 '62 C.951 A.B. L.145 J.D. 3 First National Plaza
Earley, Michael P. ... '— '03 C&L.602 B.A., J.D. [Ⓐ Jones D.]
Early, Bert H. ... '22 '49 C.228 A.B. L.309 LL.B. [Early C.&O.] ‡
Early, Michael W. '63 '88 C.473 B.A. L.228 J.D.
Assist. Gen. Coun., Chicago Underwriting Group, Inc.
Early, Scott E., (AV) ... '— '75 C.674 A.B. L.880 J.D. [Foley&L.]

Early Cochran & Olson, L.L.C.
One East Wacker Drive, Suite 2510, 60601
Telephone: 312-595-4200 Fax: 312-595-4209
URL: http://www.ecollc.com
B. Tucker Olson; Bruce R. LeMar (Not admitted in IL); Bert H. Early (Retired).
Nationwide executive search practice serving corporate and law firm clients on a retained basis in senior level lawyer recruitment. The practice includes law firm expansion consultation, corporate law department structure, audit and benchmark studies.

Earnest, David W. ... '51 '79 C.339 B.S. L.146 J.D. 1 N. LaSalle St., Ste. 1525
Easley, Brian W. ... '— '90 C.1105 B.A. L.477 J.D. [Jones D.]
Easterbrook, Frank H. '48 '75 C.821 B.A. L.145 J.D.
(adm. in DC; not adm. in IL) Cir. J.
Easterling, James T., (AV) ... '— '74 C.990 B.A. L.309 J.D. [Ungaretti&H.]
Eastham, James Michael ... '68 '94 C&L.339 B.S., J.D. [Bollinger,R.&G.]
Eastman, Molly ... '78 '04 C.94 B.A. L.910 J.D. [Ⓐ Seyfarth S.]
Easton, Lory Barsdate ... '62 '90 C&L.976 B.A., J.D. [Sidley A.B.&W.]
Eaton, David L. ... '— '78 C.477 B.A. L.339 J.D. [Kirkland&E.]
Eaton, J. Timothy, (AV) ... '— '77 C.473 B.A. L.801 J.D. [Ungaretti&H.]
Eaton, Jeffery G., (AV) '55 '80 C&L.383 B.A., J.D.
Asst. V.P. & Coun., United Ins. Co. of Amer.
Eaton, Larry R., (AV) ... '44 '68 C.927 B.A. L.477 J.D. [Cozen O.]
Eaton, Maja Campbell, (AV) ... '55 '84 C&L.352 B.A., J.D. [Sidley A.B.&W.]
Ebach, Hillary A. ... '63 '93 C&L.597 B.A., J.D. [Seyfarth S.]
Eberhard, Jeffrey S. ... '74 '02 C.165 B.A. L.597 J.D. [Ⓐ Jenner&B.]
Eberhard, Sarah H. ... '— '01 C.165 B.A. L.597 J.D. [Ⓐ Jones D.]
Ebert, Carl H., & Assoc. ... '20 '50 C.996 L.365 LL.B. 29 S La Salle St
Ebert, Regan D. ... '54 '79 C.339 B.S. L.365 J.D. 29 S. LaSalle St.
Ebner, Deborah K., Law Office of ... '56 '81 C.10 B.S. L.192 J.D. 11 East Adams Street
Ebner, Michael D. ... '73 '00 C.477 B.A. L.597 J.D. [Ⓐ Goldberg,K.B.B.R.&M.]
Ebzery, Bertram T., Law Offices of '51 '76
C.276 A.B. L.424 J.D. 321 N. Clark St., Ste. 2200
Eccleston, James J., (AV) ... '61 '87 C.145 A.B. L.818 J.D. [Shaheen,N.S.F.&E.]
Echlin, Bernard J., (AV) ... '18 '53 C&L.209 J.D. [Ⓒ Vedder,P.K.&K.]
Echols, Barack S. ... '— '99 C&L.145 B.A., J.D. [Kirkland&E.]
Echols, Heidi Christine Yernberg ... '73 '99 C.747 B.A. L.145 J.D. [Ⓐ McDermott W.&E.]
Eck, Daniel W. '68 '93 C.72 B.A. L.1119 J.D.
Legal Coun., Field Museum of Natural History

Eckberg, David '— '68 C.589 B.S. L.146 J.D.
39 South LaSalle Street, Suite 825, 60603
Telephone: 312-372-3448 Fax: 312-372-3099
Email: DavidEckberg@ameritech.net URL: http://www.davideckberg.com
Criminal Law, Driving While Intoxicated, Drug Crimes, Juvenile Crimes, Parole and Probation, Traffic Violations, White Collar Crime, Child Custody, Child Support, Divorce, Domestic Violence, Visitation Rights, Automobile Accidents, Sexual Abuse, Wrongful Death, Condemnation and Fast Track Demolition, Employment Law, Domestic Relations, Bankruptcy, Discrimination, Employee Benefits, Wrongful Termination.

See Professional Biographies, CHICAGO, ILLINOIS

Ecker, Lori D., (AV) ... '— '82 C.393 B.A. L.209 J.D. [L.D.Ecker]

Ecker, Lori D., PC, Law Office of, (AV)
180 North La Salle Street, Suite 2300, 60601
Telephone: 312-855-1880 Fax: 312-263-4609 URL: http://www.employmentlawyer.org
Email: loriecker@ameritech.net URL: http://www.lawyers.com/employee_rights
Lori D. Ecker.
Labor and Employment Law, Employment Contracts, Employment Arbitration, Employment Rights, Wrongful Termination Litigation, Family and Medical Leave Act, Sexual Harassment, Employment Discrimination and Americans with Disabilities Act.

See Professional Biographies, CHICAGO, ILLINOIS

Eckert, Jill Therese ... '77 '01 C.610 B.S. L.209 J.D. American Bar Association
Eckert, Ruth Ann '56 '92 C.229 B.S. L.209 J.D.
Asst. V.P. & Ass't Gen. Coun., CNA Property & Casualty Oper.

Eckhart Kolak LLC, (AV)
(Formerly Eckhart, McSwain, Silliman and Sears LLC)
55 West Monroe Street, Suite 1925, 60603
Telephone: 312-236-0646 Fax: 312-236-0105
Email: admin@eckhart.com URL: http://www.eckhart.com
Members of Firm: Percy B. Eckhart (1877-1969); Raymond P. Kolak; Angelo J. Loumbas; Jason S. Ornduff. Of Counsel: Roy W. Sears.
General Business Practice, including Corporate Law, Real Estate, Commercial Transactions, Litigation (State and Federal Courts), Federal Taxation, Probate, Estate Planning, Employment Law, and Not for Profit Corporations.

See Professional Biographies, CHICAGO, ILLINOIS

Eckhause, Melissa M. '73 '98 C.966 B.B.A. L.215 J.D.
(adm. in MI; not adm. in IL) [Ⓐ McDermott W.&E.]
Economos, Peter C., (AV) ....'44 '70 C.20 B.A. L.912 J.D. [Laser,P.S.F.&E.]
Economou, Dena, (AV) ....'— '91 C.424 B.B.A. L.146 J.D. [Karbal,C.E.S.&D.]
Eddington, Lisa M. ....'74 '99 C.339 B.S. L.597 J.D. [Ⓐ Jenner&B.]
Eddy, Donald F. ....'42 '76 C.339 L.424 J.D. [Ⓒ D.J.Downes]
Edelbrock, Jack ....'51 '89 C.339 B.S. L.46 J.D. [Ⓒ Mayer,B.R.&M.]
Edelman, Alvin, (AV) ....'16 '40 C&L.597 B.S.L., J.D. [Edelman&E.] ‡
Edelman, Bernard P. ....'60 '85 C.477 A.B. L.597 J.D. [F.A.Edelman]
Edelman, Daniel A., (AV) ....'54 '76 C.339 B.A. L.145 J.D. [Edelman,C.&L.]
Edelman, Frank A. ....'19 '42 C&L.597 B.S.L., J.D. [F.A.Edelman]
Edelman, Kenneth, (AVⓉ) '— '80 C.1505 B.A. L.724 J.D.
(adm. in NY; not adm. in IL) [Arnstein&L.] (☉Boca Raton, FL)
Edelman, Leon F., (AV) ....'51 '76 C.31 A.B. L.597 J.D. [Edelman&E.]
Edelman, Combs & Latturner, LLC, (AV) .... 120 South LaSalle Street

Edelman and Edelman, Chartered, (AV)
100 West Monroe Street, Suite 306, 60603-1902
Telephone: 312-372-3535 Fax: 312-372-3815
Email: ledelman48@yahoo.com URL: http://www.lawyers.com/edelmanandedelmanchtd
Leon Edelman (1888-1949); Alvin Edelman (Retired); Leon F. Edelman.
General Civil and Trial Practice. Probate, Estate Planning, Tax, Real Estate, Corporation, Medical Legal and Family Law, Domestic Relations, Divorce, Child Custody, Child Support.
See Professional Biographies, CHICAGO, ILLINOIS

Edelman, Frank A., Ltd. .... 77 West Washington Street, Suite 1514
Edelson, Jay ....'72 '97 C.1036 B.A. L.477 J.D. [Blim&E.]
Edelson, Leon I. ....'54 '88 C.347 B.A. L.276 J.D. [Levenfeld P.]
Edelson, Mitchell D. ....'28 '58 C.145 Ph.B. L.209 J.D. 39 S. LaSalle St.
Edelstein, Mark S. ....'61 '88 C.339 B.S. L.424 J.D. [Ⓐ Edelstein&E.]
Edelstein, Norman ....'31 '58 C&L.339 B.S., LL.B. [Edelstein&E.]
Edelstein, Sidney ....'25 '51 C.1016 L.146 LL.B. [Edelstein&E.]
Edelstein, Stuart T., (AV) ....'35 '59 C.118 B.A. L.597 J.D. [S.T.Edelstein]
Edelstein & Edelstein, P.C. .... 3825 W. Montrose Avenue
Edelstein, Stuart T., Ltd., (AV) .... 180 N. LaSalle St.
Edenfield, Scott M. ....'— '02 C.280 A.B. L.145 J.D. [Ⓐ Kirkland&E.]
Eder, Katherine J. ....'77 '04 C.755 B.A. L.209 J.D. [Ⓐ E.K.B.Siegel&Assoc.]
Edeus, Keith E., Jr. ....'— '98 C.999 B.S. L.589 J.D. [Ⓐ Ungaretti&H.]
Edfors, Hugh T. .... '46 '80 C.597 B.A. L.209 J.D. 1150 N. Lake Shore Dr., Ste. 18K
Edgeworth, Thomas M. ....'— '01 C.1041 B.A. L.477 J.D. [Ⓐ Kaye S.]
Edler, Robert W., (AV) '36 '62 C.210 B.A. L.813 LL.B.
[Thiedmann&E.] (☉Cin., OH)
Edlin, Gene K., (BV) ......'30 '62 C.309 A.B. L.424 J.D. 1 N. La Salle Street, Suite 2205
Edlund, Mitchell J. ....'67 '95 C.57 B.A. L.879 J.D. [Ⓐ Meckler B.&T.]
Edmonds, Laura Tallroth ....'— '96 C&L.966 B.A., J.D. [Masuda,F.E.&M.]
Edsey, David R. ....'— '93 C.209 B.A. L.424 J.D. [Ⓐ McDonald&M.]
Edstrom, Jane E. ....'55 '80 C.679 B.S. L.339 J.D. Mgr., Opers., Mary Walter, Inc.
Edwards, Alice Riedman '50 '88 C.645 B.S. L.665 J.D.
(adm. in PA; not adm. in IL) 50 South La Salle
Edwards, Charles L., (AV) ......'40 '65 C.966 B.B.A. L.145 J.D. [Ⓒ DLPiper R.G.C.U.]
Edwards, Christine A. ....'52 '83 C&L.446 B.A., J.D. [Winston&S.]
Edwards, D. R. ....'53 '85 C.923 B.F.A. L.597 J.D. [Ⓒ Goodsmith G.&U.]
Edwards, David G. ....'— '80 C.228 B.A. L.188 J.D. [Barnes&T.]
Edwards, Frank D. ....'52 '79 C.339 B.A. L.424 J.D. Asst. States Atty.
Edwards, Jamal M. ....'— '02 C.511 B.A. L.477 J.D. [Ⓐ Kirkland&E.]
Edwards, Martin S. '51 '77 C.347 B.A. L.30 J.D.
President, North Star Deferred Exchange Corp.
Edwards, Moranda C. ....'68 '96 C.576 B.S. L.574 J.D. Asst. Pub. Guard.
Edwards, Patrick J. ....'55 '80 C.385 B.A. L.209 J.D. 120 S. LaSalle St. IL1-1651
Edwards, Rebecca '76 '03 C&L.861 B.S., J.D.
(adm. in LA; not adm. in IL) [Ⓐ Levenfeld P.]
Efta, Aaron J. ....'— '04 C.494 B.A. L.477 J.D. [Ⓐ Chapman&C.]
Eftekhari, Ehsan ......'67 '99 C.424 B.A L.381 J.D. One North LaSalle Street, Suite 2600
Egan, Daniel R., (BV) ....'63 '88 C.602 B.A.G. L.427 J.D. [Rusin M.&F.]
Egan, Edward J. ....'23 '50 C&L.209 LL.B. 221 N. La Salle St., 25th Fl.
Egan, James F. ....'57 '88 C.339 B.A. L.1000 J.D. [Ⓐ Keefe&Assoc.]
Egan, John W. ....'— '77 C.973 A.B. L.597 J.D. [McKenna S.]
Egan, Julie Davis ....'— '95 C.867 B.A. L.150 J.D. [Ⓐ Statman,H.S.&E.]
Egan, Kevin J., (AV) ....'— '75 C.339 B.A. L.597 J.D. [Foley&L.]
Egan, Margaret C. ....'69 '96 C&L.602 B.A., J.D. Corp. Coun., Hyatt Hotels Corp.
Egan, Matthew J., (AV) ....'57 '82 C.339 B.A. L.424 J.D. [Pretzel&S.]
Egan, Michael Edward ....'67 '98 C.945 B.A. L.209 J.D. [Hussain E.B.&F.]
Egan, Michael T. ....'— '00 C.339 B.A. L.365 J.D. [Ⓐ Cooney&C.]
Egan, Robert A., (AV) ....'49 '75 C.339 B.S. L.209 J.D. [R.A.Egan]
Egan, Robert R., (AV) ......'48 '73 C&L.602 B.A., J.D. Dep. Chief, Co. Atty. Off.
Egan, Thomas P., (BV) ....'57 '87 C&L.209 B.S., J.D. [Scott&K.]
Egan, Robert A., P.C., (AV) ....203 North La Salle Street, Suite 2300
Eggers, Kathleen M. ....'69 '96 C.587 B.S. L.477 J.D. [Ⓐ Seyfarth S.]
Eggert, John C. ....'54 '82 C.209 B.A. L.365 J.D. [Ⓐ Hardt&S.]
Eggert, Russell R., (AV) ....'48 '73 C&L.339 A.B., J.D. [Mayer,B.R.&M.]
Eggertsen, Arly W. '46 '73 C&L.878 J.D.
(adm. in UT; not adm. in IL) NLRB
Eglit, Howard C. '42 '67
C.477 B.A. L.145 J.D. Prof. of Law, Chicago-Kent College of Law
Egolf, Vincent S. .... '73 '02 C.339 B.S. L.589 J.D. Atty., Wm. Wrigley Jr. Co. (Pat.)
Ehlenbach, Paul J. '57 '83 C.770 B.S. L.966 J.D.
VP. & Asst. Gen. Coun., Litigation, Boeing Company, The
Ehlers, Dirk E. ....'63 '88 C.188 B.A. L.145 J.D. [Ⓒ Duane M.]
Ehlers, Elizabeth R. Bacon, (AV) .... '— '89 C.970 B.A. L.424 J.D. [DLPiper R.G.C.U.]
Ehlman, Todd J. ....'66 '89 C.597 B.A. L.477 J.D. [Winston&S.]
Ehrenberg, Alan I., (AV) ....'49 '75 C.623 B.A. L.365 J.D. [Statman,H.S.&E.]
Ehrenberg, Dawn E. ....'— '87 C.1151 B.A. L.339 J.D. [McKenna S.]
Ehrenberg, Suzanne '54 '81
C.951 B.A. L.145 J.D. Chicago-Kent College of Law, Dean's Off.
Ehret, John B. ....'29 '58 C.188 B.M.E. L.597 J.D. [Christensen&E.]
Ehrhart, Diane Karp ....'41 '79 C.999 B.A. L.209 J.D. [Ⓐ Bollinger,R.&G.]
Ehrhart, Katheleen A. ....'— '00 C.339 B.S. L.145 J.D. [Ⓐ Kirkland&E.]
Ehrlich, Arthur R., (BV) ....'59 '84 C.94 B.A. L.209 J.D. [Goldman&E.]
Ehrlich, Burton S., (AV) ....'53 '78 C.1183 B.A. L.146 J.D. [Ⓐ Ladas&P.]
Ehrlich, John H. ....'58 '88 C&L.597 B.A., J.D. Chf. Corp. Coun., City Law Dept.
Ehrlich, Julie O. ....'— '89 C.477 A.B. L.912 J.D. 1522 W. Melrose St.
Ehrlich, Lawrence D., (AV) ....'29 '56 C.145 A.B. L.209 J.D. [Borovsky&E.]
Ehrlich, Sherwyn L. ....'20 '60 C.145 A.B. L.209 J.D. [Fernholz&E.]
Ehrlich, Steven E., (AV) ....'63 '90 C&L.339 B.S.Acct., J.D. [DLPiper R.G.C.U.]
Ehsan, Monique Laila ....'68 '96 C.659 B.A. L.861 J.D. Nazar Collections
Eiben, Lawrence A. ....'72 '97 C.599 B.B.A. L.424 J.D. [Bell,B.&L.]

Eich, Jeffrey W. ....'66 '91 C.339 B.A. L.597 J.D. Asst. Compl. Offr., Aon Corp.
Eichberger, Joseph M. ....'— '79 C.209 B.A. L.1151 J.D. [Ⓐ O'Hagan,S.&A.]
Eiche, Karen M. ....'69 '99 C.999 B.S. L.61 J.D. [Ⓐ Hinshaw&C.]
Eichenlaub, Frank J. ....'— '02 C.347 B.A. L.575 J.D. [Ⓐ Jenner&B.]
Eichhorn & Eichhorn
(See Hammond, Indiana)
Eichler, John F. ....'46 '72 C.210 B.S.C. L.46 J.D. 29 South LaSalle Street, Suite 825
Eichner, Andrew D., (BV) ....'55 '80 C.228 A.B. L.424 J.D. [Berger S.]
Eide, David A. ....'62 '88 C.145 B.A. L.608 J.D. 2 N. LaSalle St.
Eidelman, Michael M., (AV) ....'61 '88 C.477 B.S. L.209 J.D. [Vedder,P.K.&K.]
Eiden, Robert A. ....'44 '70 C&L.424 B.S., J.D. [Weinberg R.]
Eidukas, Theodore T. ....'— '94 C.57 B.A. L.597 J.D. [Ungaretti&H.]
Eilers, Karolyn A. .....'76 '02 C.339 B.A. L.352 J.D. U.S. Dept. of Jus., EOIR, Immig. Ct.
Eilers, Lisa S. ....'61 '89 C.951 B.A. L.597 J.D. 2300 N. Lincoln Park, W.‡
Eimer, Jonna Daleiden ....'73 '97 C.393 B.A. L.597 J.D. [Ⓐ Much S.F.D.A.&R.]
Eimer, Nathan P., (AV) ....'49 '73 C.339 A.B. L.597 J.D. [Eimer S.K.&S.]

Eimer Stahl Klevorn & Solberg LLP, (AV) Ⓑ
224 South Michigan Avenue, Suite 1100, 60604
Telephone: 312-660-7600 Fax: 312-692-1718
URL: http://www.eimerstahl.com
Nathan P. Eimer; David M. Stahl; Andrew G. Klevorn; Scott C. Solberg; Pamela R. Hanebutt; Lisa S. Meyer; Adam B. Deutsch; Vanessa G. Jacobsen. Of Counsel: Michael I. Miller; Ronald J. Allen; J. Cunyon Gordon;—Ronit C. Barrett; Christine M. Johnson; Linda P. Kurtos; Michelle K. Moritz; Jonathan M. Wier; Greg J. Weintraub; Rishi Agrawal; William S. Booth; Adam Oyebanji; Lisa M. Cipriano; Vanessa D. McClinton; Jill M. Brady; Ryan S. Hedges (Not admitted in IL).
Complex Commercial Litigation, Antitrust, Mergers & Acquisitions, Securities Fraud, Toxic Tort, Environmental Litigation, Civil Litigation and General Litigation.
See Professional Biographies, CHICAGO, ILLINOIS

Einstein, Jean M., (AV) ....'49 '77 C.477 B.A. L.150 J.D. [Gordon&E.]
Eisel, John L., (AV) ....'49 '74 C&L.339 B.S., J.D. [Wildman,H.A.&D.]
Eisen, David S., (AV) ....'56 '82 C.150 B.A. L.831 J.D. [Ⓒ Wilkow&W.]
Eisen, Robt. L. ....'25 '50 C&L.424 A.B., J.D. U.S. Bkrptcy. J.
Eisenberg, Andrew ....'71 '99 C.339 B.A. L.365 J.D. [Ⓐ Munday&N.]
Eisenberg, Arnee J., (AV) ....'49 '74 C&L.339 B.S., J.D. [Marks,M.&K.]
Eisenberg, Calvin, (AV) ....'38 '62 C.339 L.209 LL.B. [Eisenberg&J.]
Eisenberg, Marshall E., (AV) ....'45 '71 C&L.339 B.S., J.D. [Neal,G.&E.]
Eisenberg, Martin L. '50 '83 C.339 B.S. L.365 J.D.
ABN-AMRO North America, Inc. (Legal Department)
Eisenberg, Stephen P., (AV) ....'44 '69 C.910 B.A. L.209 J.D. [Leahy,E.&F.]
Eisenberg & Janger, (AV) .... 77 West Wacker Drive, 46th Floor
Eisenstein, Byron A. ....'33 '56 C&L.209 B.A., LL.B. 180 N. LaSalle St.
Eisenstein, Marci A., (AV) ....'— '79 C.681 B.A. L.569 J.D. [Schiff H.]
Eisenstein, Stanley, (AV) ....'46 '73 C&L.339 A.B., J.D. [Katz,F.E.E.&J.]
Eisin, Walter M., Jr. ....'42 '69 C.321 A.B. L.339 J.D. 2245 N. Seminary Ave.
Eisner, Rebecca S. ....'62 '89 C.608 B.A. L.477 J.D. [Mayer,B.R.&M.]
Eisner, Thomas S., Law Offices of, (BV) '44 '69
C&L.339 B.A., J.D. 205 W. Randolph St., Ste. 1040
Ekdahl, Jon N., (AV) '— '69
C&L.309 A.B., J.D. Gen. Coun., American Medical Association‡
Ekechukwu, Ebere ....'— '94 L.146 J.D. [E.N.Ekechukwu&Assoc.]
Ekechukwu, Ebere N., & Associates, P.C. .... 53 W. Jackson Blvd., Ste. 1440
Ekl, Tracy Lynn '76 '01 C.339 B.S. L.146 J.D.
Asst. State's Atty., Cook Co. State's Atty.
Eklund, Charles E., (AV) '27 '54
C&L.209 A.B., J.D. 175 West Jackson Boulevard, Suite 1600‡
Ekstrom, Brian D. ....'75 '02 C&L.352 B.B.A., J.D. [Ⓐ Hubbard&O.]
Elam, Michael H., (AV) ....'54 '80 C.429 B.A. L.1119 J.D. [DLPiper R.G.C.U.]
Elbaum, Daniel W. ....'71 '99 C&L.339 B.A., J.D. Asst. States Atty.
Elbert, Angela ....'71 '96 C.303 B.A. L.347 J.D. [Ⓒ Neal,G.&E.]
Elberts, Leonard J. ....'48 '74 C.424 B.A. L.209 J.D. [Asher,G.G.&D.]
Elden, Barry R., (AV) ....'46 '72 C.188 B.A. L.597 J.D. Asst. U.S. Atty.
Elden, Gary M., (AV) ....'44 '69 C.339 B.A. L.309 J.D. [Grippo&E.]
Elder, Diane G. ....'58 '83 C.112 A.B. L.800 J.D. [Wildman,H.A.&D.]
Elder, Donald E. ....'70 '98 C.494 B.A. L.1187 J.D. [Ⓐ Tressler,S.M.&P.]
Elder, Patrick J. ....'— '01 C.473 B.S. L.339 J.D. [Ⓐ Sachnoff&W.]
Eldridge, Brian H. ....'75 '02 C.378 B.A. L.1065 J.D. [Ⓐ Segal M.S.&M.]
Elegant, Jeffrey L., (AV) ....'54 '79 C.388 B.A. L.910 J.D. [Katten M.R.]
Elenius, Jon Eric, (BV) ....'62 '89 C&L.966 B.A., J.D. [Caron,C.&W.]
Elfenbaum, Ian J., (AV) ....'63 '88 C.112 B.A. L.1068 J.D. [Wolfe&E.]
El-Gabri, Hatem H. ....'51 '82 C&L.107 B.A., J.D. Reg. Coun., U.S. Small Bus. Adm.
El-Ganzouri, Ahmed ....'78 '03 C.347 B.S. L.146 J.D. [Ⓐ Bollinger,R.&G.]
Elganzouri, Rasha ....'71 '97 C.741 B.A. L.146 J.D. [Ⓒ DLPiper R.G.C.U.]
Elgersma, Kara A. ....'76 '00 C.378 B.A. L.276 J.D. [Ⓐ Bell,B.&L.]
Elges, Rodd E. ....'— '98 C.338 B.S. L.365 J.D. [Ⓐ Clausen M.]
Elgin, Ann C. ....'47 '80 C.477 B.A. L.424 J.D. 1000 North Lake Shore Drive
Elia, Michael G. ....'56 '82 C.974 A.B. L.734 J.D. 222 N. La Salle St., Ste. 1950
Eliasik, John S. ....'70 '99 C.966 B.A. L.1365 J.D. [Ⓐ Lipkin&H.]
Elinski, William W. ....'61 '98 C.550 B.S. L.1051 J.D. [Ⓐ Pretzel&S.]
Eliseuson, Anthony T. ....'75 '02 C.36 B.A. L.494 J.D. [Ⓐ Sonnenschein N.&R.]
Elkin, Laurie S. ....'63 '92 C.399 B.A. L.597 J.D. [Seliger&E.]
Elkins, Larry, (AV) ....'38 '64 C.20 A.B. L.309 LL.B. 111 W. Monroe St.‡
Elkins, Lindsy A. ....'77 '03 C.63 B.S. L.602 J.D. [Ⓐ Swanson,M.&B.]
Ellbogen, Andrew D., (AV) ....'— '88 C&L.352 B.A., J.D. [Kopka,P.D.&E.]
Elledge, Richard R., (AV) ....'34 '63 C.188 B.A. L.145 J.D. [Gould&R.]
Ellenbecker, Stephen P. ....'71 '02 C.965 B.S.E. L.146 J.D. [Ⓐ Cassiday,S.&G.]
Ellenberger, Lynn A. ....'65 '90 C.901 B.A. L.880 J.D. [Shefsky&F.]
Ellenby, Alan M. ....'57 '82 C.339 B.S. L.145 J.D. Ernst & Young LLP
Elli, Rebecca Chambers ....'69 '99 L.146 J.D. Third Coast Capital
Ellias, Randi L. ....'71 '96 C.264 B.A. L.597 J.D. [Butler R.S.&B.]
Ellin, Jennifer M. ....'67 '94 C.347 B.A. L.339 J.D. [Ⓒ Caron,C.&W.]
Elliott, Glynn J., Jr. ....'26 '51 C&L.424 Ph.B., J.D. Cir. J.
Elliott, Merle ......'78 '03 C.188 B.S. L.276 J.D. [Ⓐ McAndrews,H.&M.] (See Pat. Sect.)
Elliott, Susan ....'— '83 C.381 B.A. L.161 J.D. [Jones D.]
Elliott, Thomas C., Jr., (BV) '55 '81
C.210 B.A. L.146 J.D. [Wallenstein W.&R.] (See Pat. Sect.)
Ellis, Anne Spencer .....'52 '81 C.856 A.B. L.273 J.D. Editor, The Brief, Amer. Bar Assn.
Ellis, Arthur U., Law Offices of, (CV) '65 '93
C.145 A.B. L.94 J.D. 2149 W. Roscoe, Suite 1
Ellis, David W., (AV) ....'55 '81 C.31 B.A. L.93 J.D. [Baker&M.]
Ellis, Douglas M. ....'63 '88 C.107 B.A. L.309 J.D. [Neal,G.&E.]
Ellis, Garrettson, (AV) ....'35 '63 C.674 A.B. L.477 J.D. [Ⓒ Seyfarth S.] (Pat.)
Ellis, Lisa A. ....'74 '01 C.74 B.A.J. L.424 J.D. [Ⓐ Holland&K.]
Ellis, Morris W. ....'20 '51 L.365 LL.B. 134 N. LaSalle St.
Ellis, Peter M. ....'72 '98 C.477 B.A. L.608 J.D. [Ⓐ DLPiper R.G.C.U.]
Ellis, Robert B., (P.C.) ....'— '91 C&L.339 B.S., J.D. [Kirkland&E.]

Ellis, Robert E. . . . '33 '57 C&L.339 LL.B. [© Hinshaw&C.]
Ellis, Rose A., (AV) '55 '80 C.951 A.B. L.228 J.D.
Asst. Gen. Coun. &Corp. Secy., Northern Trust Corporation
Ellison, George C., (AV) . . . '54 '81 C.589 B.A. L.365 J.D. [Ellison,N.Z.&A.]
Ellison, Steven J., (AV) . . . '66 '91 C.350 B.S. L.494 J.D. [Sidley A.B.&W.]
Ellison, William D. . . . '51 '88 C.57 B.A. L.589 J.D. [Ⓐ Michaels&M.]
Ellison, Nielsen, Zehe & Antas, P.C., (AV) . . . 100 W. Monroe St., 18th Fl.
Ellman, James D. . . . '65 '91 C.352 B.B.A. L.146 J.D. [© Scopelitis,G.L.&H.]
Ellsworth, Anne M. . . . '67 '92 C.339 B.S. L.209 J.D. Coun., General Electric Co.
Elman, Barry D., (AV) . . . '30 '54 C.966 B.S. L.597 J.D. [Berger,N.&F.]
Elman, Dianne Clare . . . '56 '83 C.494 B.A. L.365 J.D. 1446 W. Jarvis
Elman, Lawrence M. . . . '58 '83 C.966 B.B.A. L.1119 J.D. [Berger,N.&F.]
Eloe, Timothy J. . . . '68 '01 C.965 B.B.A. L.345 J.D. [Ⓐ McDermott W.&E.]
Elovitz, Louis . . . '35 '61 C.339 L.209 LL.B. [Rotman&E.]
Elowe, Robin J. . . . '— '03 C.597 B.A. L.245 J.D. [Ⓐ Sachnoff&W.]
Elrod, Richard J. . . . '34 '59 C&L.597 B.A., J.D. Richard J. Daily Center
Elrod, Steven M., (AV) . . . '57 '82 C.861 B.A. L.597 J.D. [Holland&K.]
Elsberg, Alexander C. . . . '70 '96 C.881 B.A. L.124 J.D. [Ⓐ Fragomen,D.B.&L.]
Elsliger, Richard L. . . . '63 '89 C.025 B.A. L.801 J.D. [Ⓐ Kiesler&B.]
Elson, Alex, (AV) . . . '05 '28 C&L.145 Ph.B., J.D. 5550 South Shore Drive‡
Elson, John S. . . . '43 '67 C.309 A.B. L.145 J.D. Prof., Northwestern Univ. Sch. of Law
Elson, Sally T. '45 '74 C.788 B.A. L.424 J.D.
Coord., Fed. Ct. Prison Litig. Project, Legal Asst. Found. of Chicago
Elson, William B., (AV) . . . '14 '35 C&L.145 Ph.B., J.D. 3101 N. Sheridan Rd.‡
Elue, Vera . . . '— '98 L.424 J.D. City of Cgicago
Elvin, Matthew S. . . . '67 '92 C.105 B.A. L.1017 J.D. [Dahm&E.] ⊙
Elvin, Michael S., (CVⓉ) . . . '63 '88 C.105 B.S.B.A. L.597 J.D. [Dahm&E.] ⊙
Elward, Paul F. . . . '26 '52 C&L.424 A.B. Cir. J.
Elwin, J. William, Jr. '50 '75 C.208 B.A. L.597 J.D.
Assoc. Dean & Exec. Dir., Northwestern Univ. Sch. of Law
Elwood, Letticia L. . . . '71 '97 L.221 J.D. 10020 South Western Avenue
Elworth, Robert E. . . . '67 '92 C.546 B.A. L.190 J.D. [Ⓐ Price T.R.]

Emalfarb, Swan & Bain
(See Highland Park)

Emanuel, Robert J. . . . '69 '95 C.352 B.A. L.146 J.D. [Burke,W.M.&S.]
Emerick, Julie T., (BV) . . . '— '92 C.363 B.A. L.215 J.D. [J.T.Emerick]

Emerick, Julie T., Ltd., Law Offices of, (BV)
105 West Madison Street, Suite 2200, 60602
Telephone: 312-372-3380 Fax: 312-372-3392
Email: jtemerick@emigrate-immigrate.com URL: http://www.emigrate-immigrate.com
Julie T. Emerick.
Immigration and Naturalization Law.
See Professional Biographies, CHICAGO, ILLINOIS

Emerson, Carter W., (AV) . . . '— '72 C.473 B.S. L.597 J.D. [Kirkland&E.]
Emery, Ellen Kornichuk '56 '82 C.589 B.S. L.365 J.D.
140 S. Dearborn Street, Suite 600
Emeson, Brian S. . . . '75 '04 C.477 B.A. L.910 J.D. [Ⓐ Stowell&F.]
Emmerman, Howard C., (AV) '— '70
C.339 B.S. L.209 J.D. [Beermann S.W.B.B.G.&L.]
Emmerman, Ross D., (BV) . . . '62 '87 C.477 B.B.A. L.273 J.D. [Neal,G.&E.]
Emmitt, Tim J., (AV) . . . '40 '65 C.894 B.A. L.145 J.D. [Lewis,O.&F.]
Emmons, Francis J., (AV) . . . '— '77 C.436 B.S. L.597 J.D. [Ungaretti&H.]
Empson, Stacey Renee '69 '94 C&L.378 B.A., J.D.
(adm. in KS; not adm. in IL) 750 N. Rush St., Apt. 3201

Emrich & Dithmar LLC, (AV)
125 South Wacker Drive, Suite 2080, 60606-4401
Telephone: 312-663-9800 FAX: 312-663-9822
URL: http://www.emrichdithmar.com
Members of Firm: Paul L. Brown; James J. Hill; Harry M. Levy; Robert R. Caliri; Thomas E. Hill; Jonathan J. Krit.
Patent, Trademark, Copyright, and Unfair Competition Law. Trials and Appeals before Federal and State Courts and Governmental Agencies.
See Professional Biographies, CHICAGO, ILLINOIS

Emry, Debra A. . . . '62 '87 C.352 B.A. L.339 J.D. [McCullough,C.&L.]
Encher, Scott Edward . . . '71 '00 C.209 B.A. L.365 J.D. 33 N. LaSalle St.
Encinosa, Israel J. . . . '— '03 C.93 B.A. L.145 J.D. [Ⓐ Kirkland&E.]
Enders, Kimberly K., (AV) . . . '60 '85 C&L.339 B.S., J.D. [Spitzer,A.S.&E.]
Endres, Justin . . . '— '03 C.63 B.S. L.273 J.D. [Ⓐ Winston&S.]
Enerson, Wendy N. . . . '69 '00 C.339 B.A. L.597 J.D. [Ⓐ Sonnenschein N.&R.]
Engberg, Stephen N., (AV) . . . '41 '66 C.339 B.S. L.209 J.D. [S.Engberg&Assoc.]
Engberg, Stephen, & Associates, P.C., (AV) . . . 1 N. La Salle St., Ste. 1450
Engel, Allison M. . . . '71 '96 C.597 B.A. L.910 J.D. Law Clerk
Engel, Bruce M. . . . '57 '84 C&L.339 B.A., J.D. [Tressler,S.M.&P.]
Engel, Daniel A. '51 '78 C.910 B.A. L.339 J.D.
Sr. Assoc. Gen. Coun., Blue Cross Blue Shield Assn.

Engel, Donald F., (AV) '43 '86 C.209 B.A. L.424 J.D.
320 West Ohio Street, Suite 501, 60610
Telephone: 312-229-7900 Fax: 312-229-7901
Email: chicagolaw@uscounsel.com URL: http://www.uscounsel.com
Litigation, Real Estate, Bankruptcy, Corporate Finance, Business.
See Professional Biographies, CHICAGO, ILLINOIS

Engel, Jason A. . . . '74 '01 C&L.201 B.S., J.D. [Ⓐ Bell,B.&L.]
Engel, Lisa M. . . . '67 '92 C.339 B.S. L.575 J.D. Sr. Coun., Bank One Corp. (Law Dept.)
Engel, Ronald L., (AV) '38 '62 C.339 B.S.C.E. L.145 J.D.
203 N. La Salle St., Suite 1800
Engel, Samantha R. . . . '76 '01 C.477 B.A. L.145 J.D. [Ⓐ Adamski&C.]
Engel, Sheldon D. . . . '41 '66 C.339 B.S. L.597 J.D. 180 N. LaSalle St.
Engel, Terry L., (AV) . . . '44 '67 C.339 B.S. L.209 J.D. [Deutsch,L.&E.]
Engelberg, Allen B. . . . '60 '85 C.339 B.A. L.589 J.D. 140 S. Dearborn St., 14th Floor
Engelberg, Burt W. . . . '54 '79 C&L.339 B.S., J.D. [Engelberg&S.]
Engelberg & Smith, (AV) . . . 135 S. La Salle St., Ste. 2300
Engelhard, Patricia '47 '75 C.339 B.A. L.209 J.D.
Dir., Off. of Pres., American Bar Assn.
Engelhardt, Karen I., (BV) . . . '54 '81 C.910 B.A. L.1162 J.D. [Ⓐ Allison,S.&K.]
Engelland, Arthur E., Jr. . . . '31 '55 C.597 B.S. L.472 LL.B. 180 N. LaSalle St.
Englander, Caryn S. . . . '57 '84 C.966 B.S. L.597 J.D. [© DLPiper R.G.C.U.]
Engle, Andrew M. . . . '78 '04 C.339 B.S. L.209 J.D. [Ⓐ Lake,T.&D.]
Engle, Philip W. '55 '86 C.882 B.A. L.904 J.D.
(adm. in DC; not adm. in IL) [© BryceDowney] (⊙Marietta, GA)
Engle, Sasha M. . . . '72 '00 C.118 B.A. L.1119 J.D. [Ⓐ Gardner C.&D.]
Engling, Timothy J. . . . '— '95 C.870 B.S. L.146 J.D. [Barnes&T.] (See Pat. Sect.)
English, John D., (AV) . . . '— '76 C.221 B.A. L.424 J.D. [Ungaretti&H.]
Enright, John J. . . . '— '51 C&L.145 Ph.B., J.D. [© Horvath&L.]
Enright, Mark E., (AV) . . . '— '83 C.339 B.A. L.424 J.D. [Arnstein&L.]
Enright, Ruth V., (BV) . . . '62 '87 C.338 B.S. L.424 J.D. [Baker&E.]
Enright, Timothy M. . . . '71 '02 C.801 B.A. L.1000 J.D. [Ⓐ DLPiper R.G.C.U.]
Enriquez, Maria G., (AV) . . . '59 '85 C.339 B.S.W. L.209 J.D. [Bates&C.]
Enschedé, Andrew J. . . . '68 '94 C.860 B.A. L.365 J.D. [Greenberg T.]
Ensing, Donald A. . . . '72 '98 C.477 B.A. L.146 J.D. [Ⓐ McGuirewoods]
Enterprise Law Group, LLP . . . 70 W. Madison St., Ste. 740
Entertainment & Intellectual Property Group, The . . . 35 E. Wacker Dr., Ste. 1782

Entertainment Law Chicago, P.C.
6441 N. Bosworth Avenue, 3rd Floor, 60626
Telephone: 773-882-4912
Email: info@entertainmentlawchicago.com URL: http://www.entertainmentlawchicago.com
Donald R. Simon.
Entertainment Law, Entertainment Contracts, Motion Picture Production and Distribution, Music Copyright, Music Law, Music Licensing, Art Law, Publishing Law, Intellectual Property, Copyrights, Trademarks, Licensing Agreement.
See Professional Biographies, CHICAGO, ILLINOIS

Entertainment Law Office, The, P.C. . . . 208 S. LaSalle St.
Entin, Fredric J., (AV) . . . '— '72 C.966 B.A. L.209 J.D. [Foley&L.]
Entin, Robert E. . . . '74 '99 C.477 B.A. L.146 J.D. [Ⓐ Baum S.A.&N.]
Entin, Scott A. . . . '— '03 [Ⓐ Anderson,R.]
Entsminger, Daniel M. . . . '02 C.967 B.A. L.597 J.D. [Ⓐ Katten M.R.]

Entwistle & Cappucci LLC
123 N. Wacker Drive, Suite 1800, 60606 ⊙
Telephone: 312-474-7938 Facsimile: 312-474-7898
URL: http://www.entwistle-law.com
Craig E. Nelson (Resident); Richard E. Nawracaj.
General Corporate Practice, Commercial Litigation, Complex Business and Securities Litigation, Securities and Antitrust Class Action Litigation, Employment and Labor Law and Litigation, Insurance and Reinsurance Law and Litigation, Bankruptcy, Insolvency and Workouts, Executive Compensation, Estate Litigation and Administration, Commercial Transactions, Cyber Law and Intellectual Property and Product Liability Litigation.
Austin, Texas Office: 98 San Jacinto Boulevard, Suite 1300, 78701. Telephone: 512-703-5705. Facsimile: 512-476-5139.
Florham Park, New Jersey Office: 30 Columbia Turnpike, P.O. Box 95, 07982. Telephone: 973-236-0666. Facsimile: 973-236-9565.
New York, New York Office: 299 Park Avenue, 14th Floor, 10171. Telephone: 212-894-7200. Facsimile: 212-894-7272.
Tallahassee, Florida Office: 400 North Meridian Street, 32301. Telephone: 850-222-9886. Facsimile: 850-671-4402.
Washington D.C. Office: 1735 New York Avenue, NW, 20006. Telephone: 202-661-3960. Facsimile: 202-331-1024.
See Professional Biographies, CHICAGO, ILLINOIS

Eovaldi, Thomas L. . . . '40 '65 C&L.339 B.S., LL.B. Prof. of Law, Northwestern Univ.
Ephraim, Charles L. '52 '77
C.399 B.A. L.145 J.D. V.P. Develop., Hyatt International Corp.
Ephraim, David M. . . . '64 '90 C.659 B.S. L.339 J.D. [Ephraim&Assoc.]
Ephraim, Donald M., (AV) . . . '32 '55 C.209 B.S. L.145 J.D. [Ephraim&Assoc.]
Ephraim, Eliot S. . . . '67 '92 C.103 B.A. L.477 J.D. [Ephraim&Assoc.]
Ephraim & Associates, P.C., (AV) . . . 108 W. Grand Ave.
Episcope, Paul B., (AV) . . . '39 '69 C&L.209 B.Sc., J.D. [P.B.Episcope]
Episcope, Paul B., Ltd., (AV) . . . 77 West Washington Street, Suite 300
Epley, James D. . . . '48 '76 C.801 B.S. L.734 J.D. U.S. Dept. of Labor
Eppel, Theodore . . . '70 '97 C.477 B.A. L.347 J.D. [Ⓐ Monico,P.&S.]
Eppenstein, David E., Jr. . . . '48 '77 C.339 B.Arch. L.365 J.D. Asst. Pub. Def.‡
Eppley, Lawrence C., (AV) . . . '60 '85 C&L.339 B.S., J.D. [Bell,B.&L.]
Epstein, Ari R. '71 '97 C.197 B.S. L.930 J.D.
(adm. in OH; not adm. in IL) Legal Recruiter, The Affiliates
Epstein, Bennett L., (AV) . . . '— '75 C.477 B.A. L.910 J.D. [Foley&L.]
Epstein, Dan J. '47 '74 C.674 B.A. L.262 J.D.
Exec. V.P., Heitman Advisory Corporation
Epstein, Daniel N., (AV) . . . '38 '62 C.188 B.A. L.976 J.D. 222 N. La Salle St.
Epstein, David A., (AV) . . . '43 '68 C&L.339 B.S., J.D. [D.A.Epstein]
Epstein, David J. . . . '48 '74 C.112 B.S. L.94 J.D. 5490 South Shore Dr.
Epstein, Diana T. . . . '— '92 C.308 B.A. L.146 J.D. [Ⓐ Longwell]
Epstein, Elizabeth . . . '— '04 C.881 B.A. L.910 J.D. [Ⓐ Winston&S.]
Epstein, Eve C. . . . '49 '74 C&L.597 B.A., J.D. [Epstein&E.]
Epstein, Jack R., Law Offices, (CV) '65 '90
C.502 B.J. L.910 J.D. 4346 W. 26th St., Ste. 7000
Epstein, Jason R. '67 '97 C.1273 B.B.A. L.365 J.D.
134 North LaSalle Street, Suite 2222
Epstein, Mark B. . . . '46 '70 C.145 B.A. L.597 J.D. [Epstein&E.]
Epstein, Richard A. '43 '69 C.178 A.B. L.976 LL.B.
(adm. in CA; not adm. in IL) Prof., Univ. of Chic. Law Sch.
Epstein, Richard L. . . . '30 '55 C.31 A.B. L.976 LL.B. Amer. Hosp. Assn.
Epstein, Timothy Liam . . . '— '04 C.93 B.A. L.339 J.D. [Ⓐ O'Hagan,S.&A.]
Epstein, Wendy Netter . . . '— '03 C.339 B.A. L.1565 J.D. [Ⓐ Kirkland&E.]

Epstein Becker & Green, P.C., (AV)
150 North Michigan Avenue, Suite 420, 60601-7553 ⊙
Telephone: 312-499-1400 Facsimile: 312-845-1998
Email: martindale@ebglaw.com URL: http://www.ebglaw.com
Members of the Firm: Julie Badel; Stephen R. Drake (Not admitted in IL); Lola Miranda Hale; Paul C. Miltonberger; Diane J. Roma-Kutz; Michael T. Roumell; Peter A. Steinmeyer; Hans U. Stucki. Senior Attorneys: Michael P. Butler; Heather Fesko. Associates: Amy Dow; Catherine Katilius; Tanja Samardzija; Jason Schmidt.
General Practice. Corporation, Securities and Commercial Law. Banking, Antitrust. Health Care and Hospital Law. Management Labor Relations and Employee Benefits Law. Equal Employment Opportunity and Affirmative Action Law and Practice. Taxation, Insurance, Government Procurement, Municipal Finance, Real Estate, Political Activities, Legislation and Election Law. Arbitration, Administrative Proceedings, State and Federal Civil and Appellate Practice. Estate Planning and Estate and Trust Administration.
New York, N.Y. Office: 250 Park Avenue. Telephone: 212-351-4500.
Washington, D.C. Office: 1227 25th Street, N.W., Suite 700. Telephone: 202-861-0900.
San Francisco, California Office: One California Street, 26th Floor. Telephone: 415-398-3500.
Los Angeles, California Office: 1875 Century Park East, Suite 500. Telephone: 310-556-8861.
Dallas, Texas Office: Epstein Becker Green Wickliff & Hall, P.C., Lincoln Plaza, 500 North Akard Street, Suite 2700. Telephone: 214-397-4300.
Houston, Texas Office: Epstein Becker Green Wickliff & Hall, P.C., Wells Fargo Plaza, 1000 Louisiana, Suite 5400. Telephone: 713-750-3100.
Stamford, Connecticut Office: One Landmark Square, Suite 1800. Telephone: 203-348-3737.
Newark, New Jersey Office: Two Gateway Center, 12th Floor. Telephone: 973-642-1900.
Atlanta, Georgia Office: Resurgens Plaza, 945 East Paces Ferry Road, Suite 2700. Telephone: 404-923-9000.
Miami, Florida Office: Wachovia Financial Center, 200 South Biscayne Boulevard, Suite 2100. Telephone: 305-982-1520.
See Professional Biographies, CHICAGO, ILLINOIS

Epstein, David A., Ltd., (AV) . . . 30 North La Salle Street Suite 2900
Epstein & Epstein . . . 33 North Dearborn Street
Epting, Jacinta . . . '75 '00 C.238 B.A. L.339 J.D. [Ⓐ Wilson E.M.E.&D.]
Epton, Saul A., (AV) . . . '10 '32 C.477 L.365 LL.B. 444 N. Michigan Ave.‡

Erb, John C., (AV) .... '46 '76 C.215 A.B. L.146 J.D. [P.B.Episcope] ‡
Erbacci, Anthony G. .... '25 '52 C&L.209 A.B., LL.B. 1 E. Wacker Dr.
Ercoli, Karen M. '58 '83 C.1151 B.A. L.209 J.D.
Sr. Atty, General Growth Properties, Inc.
Erde, Michael H., (AV) .... '43 '69 C.910 B.S.B.A. L.339 J.D. [M.H.Erde&Assoc.]

Erde, Michael H., & Associates P.C., (AV)
4801 West Peterson Avenue Suite 412, 60646
Telephone: 773-286-3800 Toll Free: 866-378-3800 Fax: 773-286-3504 URL: http://www.erdelaw.com
Email: MHErde@aol.com URL: http://www.lawyers.com/erdelaw
Michael H. Erde;—Jennifer Hahn Axelsen.
Elder Law, Probate, Wills, Trusts and Estates, Guardianship, Asset Protection, Disabilities, Special Needs Trusts, Living Trusts.
See Professional Biographies, CHICAGO, ILLINOIS

Erdman, Michael H. ....'70 '96 C.910 B.S.B.A. L.94 J.D. [Teeple&L.]
Erdman, Todd L. .... '73 '98 C.98 B.S. L.209 J.D. [Harris K.&G.]
Erens, Brad B., (AV) .... '— '91 C.976 B.A. L.145 J.D. [Jones D.]
Erens, Jay, (AV) ....'— '59 C.976 B.A. L.309 LL.B. [Foley&L.]
Erens, Michael G., (AV) ....'44 '69 C.966 B.S. L.209 J.D. [Kamensky,R.H.&D.] ⊙
Erf, Stephen D., (AV) ....'53 '78 C.339 B.A. L.424 J.D. [McDermott W.&E.]
Erickson, Elizabeth .... '— '03 C.910 B.S.B.A. L.145 J.D. [Winston&S.]
Erickson, Heather D. .... '— '99 C.589 B.S. L.209 J.D. 333 West Wacker Drive, Suite 500
Erickson, Kathryn A. .... '66 '91 C.485 B.A. L.597 J.D. [Sugar,F.&F.]
Erie, David T. ....'— '84 C.228 A.B. L.145 J.D. [Kirkland&E.]
Erikson, Karen A. .... '67 '93 C.800 B.S. L.273 J.D. [Gardner C.&D.]
Erkonen, Samuel J. .... '63 '89 C.352 B.B.A. L.910 J.D. [Howe&H.]
Erlich, Barry A., (AV) .... '47 '71 C.1097 B.A. L.339 J.D. [Weinberg R.]
Erlich, Denise P. .... '64 '99 C.339 B.S. L.146 J.D. [Cassiday,S.&G.]
Erlich, Jason ....'74 '99 C.477 B.S. L.46 J.D. 135 S. LaSalle, Ste. 4102
Ernest, Roland P. ....'58 '83 C&L.209 B.S., J.D. 100 W. Monroe St., Ste. 1401
Erp, Michael B., (AV) .... '45 '71 C.269 B.A. L.893 J.D. [Katz,F.E.E.&J.]
Errera, Michael S. .... '73 '98 C.1365 B.A. L.362 J.D. [Clausen M.]
Ertel, Patrick D., (AV) '— '73
C.602 B.S.A.E. L.597 J.D. [Marshall,G.&B.] (See Pat. Sect.)
Ertler, Mark ....'67 '92 C.720 B.A. L.209 J.D. Asst. States Atty., Cook Co.
Erwin, Consuelo G. .... '— '03 C.338 B.S. L.339 J.D. [McAndrews,H.&M.]
Erwin, James A., (BV) .... '67 '92 C.393 B.A. L.209 J.D. [Erwin&Assoc.]
Erwin, Katherine A. '58 '83
C&L.477 B.B.A., J.D. Asst. Gen. Coun., John Nuveen & Co., Inc.
Erwin, Shari L. .... '66 '96 C&L.209 B.A., J.D. [Erwin&Assoc.]
Erwin & Associates, L.L.C., (BV) ....4048 North Hermitage Avenue (⊙Lombard)
Erzen, Mark D., (AV) ....'54 '80 C.475 B.S. L.477 J.D. [Karaganis,W.&M.]
Esayian, Lisa G., (AV) .... '— '91 C.674 A.B. L.597 J.D. [Kirkland&E.]
Esbrook, Christopher J. .... '— '04 C.424 B.B.A. L.339 J.D. [Kirkland&E.]
Escarciga, Laura M. ....'66 '97 C.813 B.A. L.146 J.D. Asst. Appl. Def.
Eshoo, Edward, Jr. ....'60 '85 C.388 B.A. L.365 J.D. [Childress D.G.]
Eskilson, John S., (AV) .... '— '64 C.103 A.B. L.145 J.D. [Tenney&B.]
Esko, Irwin W. .... '19 '49 C&L.209 Ph.B., J.D. 1530 N. Dearborn Pkwy.‡
Eslick, Dennis J. .... '36 '66 C.424 B.A. L.365 LL.B. 39 S. La Salle St.
Esparza, Jason E. .... '70 '01 C.339 B.A. L.365 J.D. Asst. Corp. Coun.
Espinosa, Joseph, Law Office of '73 '00
C.339 B.S. L.209 J.D. 500 N. Michigan Ave., Ste. 300
Esposito, Eugene '48 '75
C.588 B.S.B.A. L.365 J.D. Special Coun., PROactive Strategies Inc.
Esposito, Nicholas F., (BV) ....'49 '74 C.973 B.A. L.209 J.D. [Esposito&S.]
Esposito, Paul V., (AV) ....'50 '75 C.746 B.A. L.424 J.D. [Clausen M.]
Esposito & Schramm, (BV) .... 134 N. LaSalle St.
Esrick, Jerald P., (AV) .... '41 '67 C.597 B.A. L.309 J.D. [Wildman,H.A.&D.]
Esrig, Jerry A., (AV) .... '53 '78 C.597 B.A. L.145 J.D. [Zaideman&E.]
Essig, Christopher Blair .... '73 '00 C.473 B.A. L.608 J.D. [Winston&S.]
Essig, William V. ....'70 '96 C.976 B.A. L.597 J.D. [Drinker B.&R.]
Estacio, Kristine S. .... '— '00 C.339 B.A. L.1000 J.D. [O'Hagan,S.&A.]
Estaver, Phillip M. .... '49 '74 C.475 B.S. L.378 J.D. [Katten M.R.]
Ester, Elizabeth K. .... '57 '84 C.118 B.A. L.597 J.D. 5800 Sears Tower
Eterno, Jessica L. '70 '99 C.966 B.A. L.209 J.D.
Staff Atty., N.A. Co. for Life & Health Insurance
Etherington, David B. '57 '87 C.260 B.S.B.A. L.1059 J.D.
(adm. in GA; not adm. in IL) 10 S. LaSalle St.‡
Etherton, Regina Picone, (BV) ......'59 '84 C.802 B.A. L.424 J.D. [R.P.Etherton&Assoc.]
Etherton, Regina P., & Associates, LLC, (BV) ....303 W. Madison St., Ste. 1800
Ettelson, Bruce I. ....'— '89 C.659 B.S.E. L.145 J.D. [Kirkland&E.]
Ettelson, Jeanne Boxer .... '50 '83 C.732 B.A. L.145 J.D. 2350 N. Lincoln Park W.
Ettelson, Jerome L., (AV) ....'18 '41 C&L.597 B.S.L., J.D. 30 N. LaSalle St.
Etten, Nicholas J., (AV) .... '42 '67 C.602 A.B. L.424 J.D. [Bell,B.&L.]
Ettinger, Albert F. .... '54 '79 C&L.477 B.G.S., J.D. Envir. Law & Policy Ctr.
Ettinger, Joseph A., (AV) .... '31 '56 C&L.861 B.A., J.D. 134 N. LaSalle St., Ste. 1515
Etzkorn, John F., (AV) ....'48 '76 C.339 B.A. L.146 J.D. [Arnold&K.]
Eulgen, Lee J. ....'— '97 C.602 B.B.A. L.966 J.D. [Neal,G.&E.]

Evan Law Group, LLC
566 West Adams, Suite 350, 60661
Telephone: 312-876-1400 Fax: 978-268-8715
URL: http://www.evanlawfirmgroup.com
Member of the Firm: Paul E. Rauch, Ph.D.; Jonathan M. Blanchard, Ph.D.
Intellectual Property.
See Professional Biographies, CHICAGO, ILLINOIS

Evangelou, Angelo '70 '96 C.477 B.A. L.94 J.D.
Sr. Atty., Chicago Board Options Exchange, Incorporated
Evanich, Kevin R., (AV) .... '— '80 C.959 B.A. L.597 J.D. [Kirkland&E.]
Evanoff, Michael B. '46 '72 C.475 B.A. L.477 J.D.
(adm. in NY; not adm. in IL) Sr. V.P. and Gen. Coun., Hyatt Intl. Corp.
Evans, Arthur H., (AV) .... '49 '74 C.339 B.S. L.209 J.D. [Evans,L.S.&M.]
Evans, C. Thomas, Jr. ....'58 '86 C.138 B.A. L.602 J.D. Coun., Unitrin, Inc.
Evans, John V. .... '13 '37 C&L.209 J.D. Admin. Law J., Soc. Sec.
Evans, Monica Roth, (AV) '60 '86
C.209 B.A. L.46 J.D. Gen. Atty., R. R. Donnelley & Sons Co.
Evans, Roberta G. .... '38 '61 C.184 B.A. L.145 J.D. [Miller S.&H.]
Evans, Steven M. .... '— '89 C.679 B.S.E.E. L.347 J.D. [McGuirewoods] (Pat.)

Evans, Loewenstein, Shimanovsky & Moscardini, Ltd., (AV)
130 S. Jefferson Street, Suite 500, 60661
Telephone: 312-782-1850 Fax: 312-466-0819
URL: http://www.elsm.com
Arthur H. Evans; Daniel M. Loewenstein; David L. Shimanovsky; Frank A. Moscardini, Jr.;—Nora M. Hernandez.

(This Listing Continued)

Evans, Loewenstein, Shimanovsky & Moscardini, Ltd. (Continued)
General Practice. Corporate, Federal and State Taxation, Estate Planning and Probate, Real Estate, Litigation in State and Federal Courts, Partnerships, Tort and Personal Injury Law, Mechanics Liens, Employee Benefits, Family Law, Commercial Litigation, Insurance and Labor.
See Professional Biographies, CHICAGO, ILLINOIS

Eveland, William T. .... '— '05 C.11 B.S. L.424 J.D. [FagelHaber]
Eveleigh, Douglas M. .... '73 '98 C.94 B.S. L.365 J.D. [Mayer,B.R.&M.] (Pat.)
Even, Francis A., (AV) '20 '49
C.339 B.S.M.E. L.273 J.D. [Fitch,E.T.&F.] (See Pat. Sect.)
Evensen, Andrea L. ....'79 '04 C.679 B.S. L.1000 J.D. [Brinks H.G.&L.]
Evenson, Debra M. ....'42 '77 C.66 B.A. L.705 J.D. 1453 W. Addison (⊙New York, NY)
Everett, Robert Mitchell ....'75 '02 C.339 B.A. L.209 J.D. 161 N. Clark, Ste. 3575
Evers, Michael D. '64 '90 C.347 B.S. L.228 J.D.
(adm. in NJ; not adm. in IL) Gen. Coun., Evers Legal Search
Evers, Michael J., (AV) .... '56 '94 C.330 B.A. L.896 J.D. [Wolfe&E.]
Evert, James F. ..... '56 '82 C&L.494 B.S., J.D. Asst. Gen. Coun., Prudential Capital Grp.
Evins, Samuel L. .... '36 '59 C.339 L.209 LL.B. 188 W. Randolph St.
Ewell, Raymond W. .... '28 '56 C.339 B.A. L.145 J.D. 9415 S. State St.
Ewer, Phyllis A., (AV) .... '39 '82 C.347 B.A. L.597 J.D. [Sonnenschein N.&R.]
Ewert, Russell H. .... '35 '60 C&L.494 B.B.A., LL.B. Drexel Natl. Bk.
Ewing, Edward C. '68 '94
C.46 B.Arch. L.339 J.D. Prof. Liability Coun., Zurich Amer. Ins. Co.
Ewing, Michael D. ....'55 '79 C&L.347 A.B., J.D. Dean Witter Reynolds Inc.
Eygenhuysen, Robert H. A. ....'50 '76 C&L.1188 B.A., J.D. City Colleges of Chicago
Faber, Irving C. .... '45 '82 C.674 A.B. L.188 J.D. [Grippo&E.]
Fabian, Christian W. ....'68 '94 C.1154 B.S.E. L.215 J.D. [Mayer,B.R.&M.]
Fabian, Kellye L. .... '75 '00 C.339 B.A. L.209 J.D. [Freeborn&P.]
Fabian, M. C. Georgina '70 '01 L.999 J.D.
(adm. in NY; not adm. in IL) [Mayer,B.R.&M.]
Faccenda, Michael A. ....'70 '97 C&L.602 B.A., J.D. [Pretzel&S.]
Faccenda, Susan M. .... '62 '88 C&L.602 B.A., J.D. Sr. Atty., AT&T Corp.
Facchini, Gerard A. .... '34 '63 2 N. LaSalle St.
Facktor, Sheryl .... '62 '91 C.966 B.S. L.146 J.D. Renaissance Capital Grp., Inc.
Factor, Jill Sugar ....'— '86 C.910 B.S.B.A. L.597 J.D. [Jenner&B.]
Factor, Jody L. .... '58 '88 C.927 B.S. L.365 J.D. [Factor] (Pat.)
Factor, William J., (AV) .... '60 '91 C.145 A.B. L.209 J.D. [Seyfarth S.]
Factor & Partners, LLC ....1327 W. Washington Blvd. (Pat.)
Fadden, John P. .... '48 '73 C.645 B.A. L.276 J.D. [Chuhak&T.]
Fader, C. Eric .... '69 '98 C.98 B.S. L.209 J.D. [Horwood M.&B.]
Fagan, Timothy J. ....'— '89 C.436 B.A. L.424 J.D. [O'Hagan,S.&A.]
Fagel, Allen J., (AV) .... '38 '62 C.339 B.S. L.209 J.D. [FagelHaber]
Fagel, Brian D. .... '69 '94 C.813 A.B. L.145 J.D. [Goldberg,K.B.B.R.&M.]

FagelHaber LLC, (AV)
55 East Monroe Street, 40th Floor, 60603
Telephone: 312-346-7500 FAX: 312-580-2201
URL: http://www.fagelhaber.com
Members of Firm: Allen J. Fagel; Joel A. Haber; Floyd Babbitt; Dennis E. Quaid; Glen T. Keysor; Walter D. Cupkovic; John J. Cullerton; Richard H. Chapman; Howard M. Berrington; Norton N. Gold; James M. Drake; Victor A. Des Laurier; Edward L. Filer; Alan Jay Goldstein; Christina Brotto; Patrick J. Cullerton; Robert H. Lang; Arthur B. Sternberg; Barry L. Fischer; Gary E. Green; Tina M. Bird; Denean K. Sturino; Mark Maciasz. Associates: Sean D. Auton; David R. Bass; Christina M. Berish; Darren Bertram; Lindsey F. Brown; Richard F. Bruen, Jr.; William Kent Carter; Kathleen T. Cunningham; Joel S. Dalinka; Georgia Loukas Demeros; William T. Eveland; Thomas Bernard Golz; Clinton P. Hansen; Beth L. Hansher; Robert N. Kamensky; Susan M. Lorenc; James P. Moorhead; Lauren Newman; Michelle G. Novick; James L. Oakley; Jack L. Parrino; David M. Rownd; Jamie Brooke Schwartz; Adam C. Toosley. Of Counsel: James P. Chapman; Robert B. Chapman; Gordon H. Millner; Maynard B. Russell.
Bankruptcy, Reorganization and Creditors' Rights, Business Law, Commercial Finance and Secured Transactions, Construction Law, Corporate and Securities, Corporate Governance, E-Commerce, Employee Benefits and Executive Compensation, Employment Law, Environmental, Equipment Leasing, Finance and Structured Finance, Financial Institutions, Financial Services, Governmental Relations, Health Care, Insurance Regulation, Intellectual Property, Intellectual Property Litigation, Investment Management, Licensing and Distribution, Litigation and Dispute Resolution, Mergers and Acquisitions, Private Equity, Public Finance, Real Estate, Real Estate Development, Real Estate Finance, Real Estate Litigation, Real Estate Taxation, Securities, Tax Planning and Litigation, Taxation of Financial Products, Technology, Trusts and Estates, Taxation, Estate Planning and Wealth Preservation.
See Professional Biographies, CHICAGO, ILLINOIS

Fahey, Elizabeth .... '75 '00 C.602 B.A. L.597 J.D. [Baker&M.]
Fahey, Hallie Miller, (BV) ....'65 '90 C.108 B.S. L.339 J.D. [Ross,D.&B.]
Fahey, Margaret Hupp .... '61 '86 C.502 B.J. L.339 J.D. [Clausen M.]
Fahey, Thomas M., (AV) ....'— '80 C.966 B.S. L.209 J.D. [Ungaretti&H.]
Fahey, William R., (AV) .... '54 '80 C.927 B.A. L.365 J.D. [Cooney&C.]
Fahndrich, Fred P. .... '54 '84 C.209 B.S.C. L.365 J.D. 9618 S. Commercial Ave.
Fahner, Daniel T. ....'75 '00 C.477 B.A. L.597 J.D. [Greenberg T.]
Fahner, Tyrone C., (AV) .... '42 '68 C.477 B.A. L.912 J.D. [Mayer,B.R.&M.]
Fahrney, Brian J. .... '66 '92 C.966 B.B.A. L.597 J.D. [Sidley A.B.&W.]
Faier, James M. .... '60 '90 C.668 B.A. L.597 J.D. [Faier&F.]
Faier, Martin .... '30 '53 C&L.597 B.S., LL.B. [Faier&F.] (Pat.)
Faier, Melinda B. ....'— '87 C.309 A.B. L.813 J.D. [Faier&F.]
Faier & Faier, P.C. ....566 W. Adams St., Ste. 600 (Pat.)
Failor, Thomas R. .... '— '02 C.602 B.B.A. L.345 J.D. [Lord,B.&B.]
Fair, Lisa I. ....'59 '87 C.881 A.B. L.146 J.D. 20 N. Clark St.
Fair, Timothy .... '62 '87 C.388 B.A. L.352 J.D. Labor Coun., Tribune Co.
Fairbanks, William J., (AV) .... '52 '78 C.103 A.B. L.339 J.D. [Seyfarth S.]
Fairchild, Aren L. ....'— '95 C&L.477 A.B., J.D. [Freeborn&P.]
Fairchild, Jeffery N. '62 '97
C.339 B.S.M.E. L.365 J.D. [Wood,P.K.C.&M.] (See Pat. Sect.)
Fairchild, Thomas E. '12 '38 C.188 A.B. L.966 LL.B.
(adm. in WI; not adm. in IL) Sr. U.S. Ct. of App. J.‡
Fairhall, Thomas A., (AV) '59 '91
C.174 B.A. L.365 J.D. [McDonnell B.H.&B.] (See Pat. Sect.)
Fairman, Melanie K. .... '68 '94 C.273 B.A. L.424 J.D. [Monico,P.&S.]
Fait, Mary Jane Edelstein, (AV) '54 '80
C.339 B.A. L.188 J.D. [Wolf H.A.F.&H.] (⊙New York, NY)
Faklis, Nicholas J., (AV) .... '49 '75 C.339 B.A. L.209 J.D. 221 N. LaSalle St., #28
Faktor, Deborah A. .... '49 '89 C.209 B.A. L.146 J.D. [Polsky&Assoc.]
Falahee, Patrick J., Jr., The Law Offices of, (AV) '61 '86
C.209 B.S.C. L.365 J.D. 53 West Jackson Boulevard - Suite 541
Falasz, John M., Jr. (Ltd.), (AV) .... '31 '57 C.424 B.S. L.597 J.D. [Falasz&R.]
Falasz & Rakers, (AV) .... 20 N. Clark St.
Falbe, Lawrence W. ....'— '94 C.57 B.A. L.209 J.D. [Wildman,H.A.&D.]
Falconer, Michael J., (BV) .....'— '83 C.966 B.A. L.209 J.D. 35 E. Wacker Dr., Ste. 1750
Falconer, Peter J. '67 '92 C.183 B.A. L.597 J.D.
Asst. Gen. Coun., CCC Information Services Group Inc.
Faley, James P., Jr. .... '— '98 C.103 A.B. L.597 J.D. [Kirkland&E.]
Faley, Michael J. ....'76 '02 C.339 B.S. L.1000 J.D. [Crisham&K.]

Falk, Allan H. '38 '63 C.339 B.A. L.365 LL.B. 155 N. Michigan Ave.
Falk, Christopher R. '70 '95 C.56 B.A. L.477 J.D. Merrill Lynch-Investment Banking
Falk, Conrad E. '34 '61 C.1016 L.365 79 W. Monroe St.
Falk, Jessica R. '77 '03 C.339 B.A. L.477 J.D. [🄰 Nisen&E.]
Falk, Lesli L. Mann '66 '99 C.378 B.S. L.880 J.D. [DLPiper R.G.C.U.]
Falk, Michael G. '72 '98 C.597 B.A. L.339 J.D. [🄰 Winston&S.]
Falk, Paul T. '58 '85 C.436 B.S. L.365 J.D. [Falk J.]
Falk, R. Scott, P.C. '— '89 C&L.309 A.B., J.D. [Kirkland&E.]
Falk Johnson, LLC 20 S. Clark St., Ste. 1900
Falkenberg, Charles V., III, (BV) '61 '86 C.602 B.B.A. L.424 J.D. [🄰 Karlin&F.]
Falkenberg, Thomas F. '— '90 C&L.602 B.B.A., J.D. [O'Hagan,S.&A.]
Falkof, Bradley B. '— '78 C.103 B.A. L.597 J.D. [Barnes&T.]
Fallah, Melissa M. '76 '01 C.339 B.A.S. L.911 J.D. [🄰 Matushek,N.&S.]
Fallon, Geralyn M. '60 '87 C.424 A.B. L.365 J.D. Sears, Roebuck & Co.
Fallon, Steven P. '66 '95 C.801 B.S.E.E. [Greer,B.&C.] (Pat.)

Fallon-Houle, Nancy, P.C.
(See Downers Grove)

Falloon, Benjamin '75 '01 C.311 B.A. L.597 J.D. [🄰 Wilson E.M.E.&D.]
Falvey, John W. '39 '68 C.589 B.S. L.424 J.D. Sr. Corp. Coun., USG Corp.
Famparska, Valentina '64 '87 L.424 J.D. [🄰 Katten M.R.]
Fancsali, Beth L., (BVⓉ) '— '90 C.473 B.S. L.846 J.D. [Wildman,H.A.&D.]
Fandre, Scott '66 '91 C.98 B.A. L.589 J.D. Claims Coun., Chicago Title Ins. Co.
Fanning, David F. '74 '01 C.746 B.A. L.146 J.D. [🄰 Johnson&B.]
Fanning, Lori A. '63 '00 C.627 B.A. L.146 J.D. [🄰 Miller F.&C.]
Fanone, Anthony V. '47 '71 C.742 B.A. L.424 J.D.
Managing Trial Attorney, Nationwide Insurance Enterprise
Fanone, John R., (AV) '— '75 C.679 B.S.E.E. L.365 J.D. [🅂 Freeborn&P.]
Fanucchi, Charles A. '57 '84 C.339 B.A. L.365 J.D. [🄲 D.R.Fichera&Assoc.]
Farace, Anthony M. '67 '93 C.589 B.S. L.365 J.D. [Amari&L.]
Faraci, Dominick D. '38 '65 C&L.209 B.A., J.D. 203 North LaSalle Street, Suite 2350
Faraci, Rosanne J. '55 '81 C.338 B.S. L.365 J.D. [McDermott W.&E.]
Farah, Mariam A. '— '00 C.878 B.A. L.145 J.D. [🄰 Mayer,B.R.&M.]
Farah, Peter O. '75 '01 C&L.93 B.S., J.D. [🄰 Schwartz C.]
Farahvar, Paul A. '74 '99 C&L.339 B.A., J.D. 222 N. Lasalle St., Ste. 2150
Farber, Timothy S. '77 '03 C.502 B.S.B.A. L.910 J.D. [🄰 Lord,B.&B.]
Farbman, Lee E. '63 '99 C.951 B.A. L.597 J.D. [🄰 Deutsch,L.&E.]
Farbman, Ruth E. '35 '87 C.788 B.A. L.597 J.D. 2 E. Oak St., Suite 3604
Fardon, Zachary Thomas '66 '92 C&L.880 B.A., J.D.
(adm. in TN; not adm. in IL) Asst. U.S. Atty.
Fardy, Jennifer Kelly '70 '95 C.352 B.A. L.347 J.D. [Seyfarth S.]
Fardy, P. Stephen '69 '94 C&L.347 B.A., J.D. [Swanson,M.&B.]
Farenga, Andrew A. '30 '55 C&L.209 J.D. One IBM Plaza
Farenga, Cynthia R. '54 '79 C.597 B.S.J. L.146 J.D. 2939 W. Gregory St.
Fargo, David L., (AV) '27 '54 C&L.597 B.S., J.D. [🄲 Holland&K.] ‡
Fargo, Paul G. '27 '52 C&L.94 B.S., J.D. Legal Advsr. to Secy. of State
Farina, David J. '68 '95 C.999 B.A. L.989 J.D. [🄰 Iwan C.H.H.&V.]
Farina, James L., (AV) '54 '79 C.338 B.S. L.146 J.D. [Hoey&F.]
Farina, Philip J., (AV) '52 '76 C.1100 A.B. L.46 J.D. [Fasano&F.]
Faris, Bradley C. '— '00 C.473 B.A. L.309 J.D. [🄰 Latham&W.]
Faris, Geo. '— '48 C&L.145 Ph.B. U.S. Dept. of Labor
Faris, Michael J. '— '90 C.309 A.B. L.145 J.D. [🄰 Latham&W.]
Farkas, Alan L., (AV) '69 '93 C.208 B.A. L.910 J.D. [Madsen,F.&P.]
Farkas, Earl E. '65 '94 C.589 B.S. L.365 J.D. [Gozdecki&D.]
Farkas, Ronald L., (AV) '37 '62 C.1016 B.S.B.A. L.209 J.D. [R.L.Farkas]
Farkas, Ronald L., P.C., (AV) 77 W. Washington St.
Farley, S. Ellyn '72 '98 C.679 B.A. L.424 J.D. [🄰 Cozen O.]
Farley, Tracy L. '69 '95 C.597 B.A. L.339 J.D. [🄲 DLPiper R.G.C.U.]
Farley, William H., Jr., (AV) '50 '77 C&L.976 B.A., J.D. [Burris,W.S.&T.]
Farmer, Kathryn D., (AV) '58 '83 C&L.424 B.A., J.D. [Rosenfeld H.S.&F.]
Farnan, James Thomas '64 '89 C.234 B.A. L.365 J.D. 161 N. Clark St., Ste. 290

Farnell, Alan S. '48 '73 C.855 B.A. L.276 J.D.
10 South La Salle Street, Suite 3300, 60603
Telephone: 312-606-0655 Fax: 312-332-1811
Email: alan@farnelllaw.com URL: http://www.farnelllaw.com
Bankruptcy, Civil Litigation, Railroad Law, Railcar Law.
See Professional Biographies, CHICAGO, ILLINOIS

Farrar, W. Grant '70 '98 C.352 B.A. L.365 J.D. [🄰 Bollinger,R.&G.]
Farrell, Barbara Ann, (BVⓉ) '61 '90
C.128 B.A. L.982 J.D. Asst. V.P., Chicago Title Ins. Co.
Farrell, Christine Ryan '74 '00 C.347 B.A. L.209 J.D. Cabrini Grane Legal Aid Clinic
Farrell, Joseph S. '70 '95 C.436 B.S. L.365 J.D. [🄲 Levenfeld P.]
Farrell, Sarah R. '— '04 C.208 B.S. L.365 J.D. Two North LaSalle Street, Suite 2200
Farrell, William P., Jr. '68 '93 C.347 B.S. L.602 J.D. [Gardner C.&D.]
Fasano, Anthony A. '52 '79 C.98 B.S. L.209 J.D.
Sr. Coun., Bank One Corp. (Law Dept.)
Fasano, Barbara A., (BV) '38 '79 C.209 B.A. L.365 J.D. 53 W. Jackson Boulevard
Fasano, Joseph M., (AV) '24 '54 C.475 B.A. L.424 J.D. [Fasano&F.]
Fasano, Nancy A. '58 '84 C.339 B.S. L.209 J.D. [Weiss&B.]
Fasano & Farina, (AV) 33 N. Dearborn St., Ste. 1930
Fasciana, William O. '53 '81 C.339 B.A. L.365 J.D. 20 S. Clark, Ste. 2301
Fassnacht, Harold J., (AV) '55 '90
C.910 B.S.Ch.E. L.146 J.D. Ste 1600, 10 S Lasalle St (Pat.)
Fata, Anthony F. '73 '99 C.473 B.A. L.608 J.D. [🄰 Miller F.&C.]
Fatall, Michael G. '— '97 C.378 B.A. L.597 J.D. [Kirkland&E.]
Fattahian, Sage '74 '02 C.339 B.A. L.365 J.D. [🄰 Lewis,O.&F.]
Fatum, Stephen M., (BV) '— '85 C.321 B.A. L.245 J.D. [🄲 Barnes&T.]
Faught, James J. '49 '76 C.602 B.A. L.424 J.D. Assoc. Dean, Loyola Univ. Law Sch.
Faulkner, J. Todd '48 '77 C.674 A.B. L.209 J.D. [Franczek S.]
Faur, Cynthia A. '67 '93 C.477 B.A. L.145 J.D. [Sonnenschein N.&R.]
Favakeh, Stephen S. '64 '91 C.862 B.S. L.339 J.D. [Fitch,E.T.&F.] (See Pat. Sect.)
Favero, Daniel J. '— '89 C.1247 B.A. L.209 J.D. [Chapman&C.]

Favia, Michael V., (AV) '55 '82 C.424 B.A. L.365 J.D.
5045 North Harlem Avenue, 60656
Telephone: 773-631-4580 Fax: 773-631-7776
Email: Favia@lawyer.com URL: http://www.michaelfavia.com
(Also Of Counsel, Goldberg & Frankenstein, LLC).
Languages: Spanish, Polish and Italian.
Civil Litigation, Personal Injuries, Automobile Accidents, Medical Malpractice, Products Liability, Work Injuries, Health Law, Medicare and Medicaid Fraud, Medical and Health Related Regulatory Issues, Professional Licensure Matters.
See Professional Biographies, CHICAGO, ILLINOIS

Favoriti, Richard E., (AV) '43 '68
C.209 B.S. L.597 J.D. Dep. Gen. Coun., Energy, Ill. Com. Comm.
Fawkes, Thomas R. '— '02 C.424 B.A. L.597 J.D. [🄰 Freeborn&P.]

Fay, E. Garnet, (AV) '43 '68 C.597 B.S. L.146 J.D. [O'Brien,H.&F.]
Fayez, Omar J. '— '98 C.896 B.A. L.424 J.D. [🄰 Querrey&H.]
Fayhee, Michael R., (AV) '48 '73 C.339 B.S. L.477 J.D. [McDermott W.&E.]
Fayne, Amanda F. '77 '02 C.966 B.A. L.146 J.D. [🄰 Boundas S.W.&B.]
Fazio, Catherine E. '— '93 C.112 B.A. L.813 J.D. [Kirkland&E.]
Fazio, Christina '69 '95 C.424 140 South Dearborn Street, 14th Floor (ⓒChicago)
Fazio, Peter V., Jr., (AV) '— '64 C.321 A.B. L.477 J.D. [Schiff H.]
Feagley, Michael R., (AV) '45 '73 C.918 B.A. L.309 J.D. [Mayer,B.R.&M.]
Feaman, Scott N. '50 '89 C.589 B.S.Ed. L.365 J.D. 1836 W. Cuyler
Feder, Benjamin N. '76 '02 C.339 A.B. L.597 J.D. [🄰 Horwood M.&B.]
Feder, Lynn M. '69 '98 C.339 B.S. L.145 J.D. [🄰 Sidley A.B.&W.]
Feder, Scott B. '54 '87 C.339 B.S. L.146 J.D. [Lord,B.&B.]
Fedinets, Kenneth Alan, (BV) '54 '79 C&L.209 B.A., J.D. 53 W. Jackson Blvd.
Fedo, Stephen, (AV) '50 '81 C.429 B.A. L.145 J.D. [Neal,G.&E.]
Fedota, Mark C., (AV) '44 '69 C.424 A.B. L.276 J.D. [Fedota C.]

Fedota Childers, P.C., (AV)
Three First National Plaza, Suite 3900, 60602
Telephone: 312-236-5015 Fax: 312-236-8559
J. Richard Childers; Mark C. Fedota; Jason William Fura; Melissa L. Kerchner; John D. Kuhn; Ruwan C. Perera; David R. Schmidt; Paul D. Streicher; Christina S. Vasilatos; S. Ana Watson. Of Counsel: Kathleen A. Brosnan; Cecilia M. Clarke.
Insurance Defense, Excess and Reinsurance, Insurance Coverage, Medical Malpractice, Healthcare, Railroads, Product Liability, Professional Liability Insurance Coverage, Commercial Litigation, Family Law, Environmental, Business Law, Employment Law, Complex Litigation, General Civil Litigation, Directors and Officers Liability, Appellate Practice, Torts, Insurance Bad Faith International Dispute Resolution,
See Professional Biographies, CHICAGO, ILLINOIS

Fee, Kevin M., JR. '75 '02 C.1375 B.A. L.309 J.D. 10 S. Dearborn
Fee, Mary Carol '53 '79 C.602 B.A. L.597 J.D. 1448 N. Lake Shore Drive‡
Feehan, James J. '38 '66 C.830 B.S. L.209 J.D.
Sr. V.P. & Gen. Coun., Claims, Intercounty Title Company of Illinois
Feehan, Jared R. '75 '01 C.597 B.A. L.145 J.D. [🄰 Winston&S.]
Feeley, Cynthia Swiger, (AV) '50 '81 C.339 B.S. L.209 J.D. [Feeley&Assoc.]
Feeley, David J. '44 '71 C&L.424 A.B., J.D. 29 S. LaSalle St., Ste. 1210
Feeley, Kevin J. '65 '90 C.339 B.S. L.424 J.D. [McDermott W.&E.]

Feeley & Associates, P.C., (AV)
161 North Clark Street Suite 2500, 60601
Telephone: 312-541-1200 Fax: 312-541-1260
Email: feeleypc@aol.com
Cynthia Swiger Feeley.
Commercial Litigation, Creditors' Rights, Bankruptcy.
See Professional Biographies, CHICAGO, ILLINOIS

Feely, Elizabeth M., (BV) '62 '87 C.602 B.A. L.339 J.D. [E.M.Feely]
Feely, John G., III '47 '74 C.339 B.A. L.597 J.D. Asst. State's Atty.

Feely, Elizabeth M., P.C., (BV)
401 N. Michigan Avenue, Suite 1200, 60611
Telephone: 312-856-0306 Fax: 312-858-1812
Email: feelylaw@aol.com URL: http://www.feelylaw.com
Elizabeth M. Feely.
Family Law.
See Professional Biographies, CHICAGO, ILLINOIS

Feeney, Colleen M. '— '03 C.602 B.S. L.424 J.D. [🄰 Clausen M.]
Feeney, Daniel M. '69 '94 C.209 B.A. L.477 J.D. [Miller S.&H.]
Feerick, Maureen P. '59 '84 C&L.424 B.A., J.D. Asst. State Atty.
Feffer, Gary '57 '97 C&L.209 B.S.C., J.D. Chicago Police Dept., Off. of Legal Affairs
Fegan, Elizabeth Anne '71 '95 C.475 B.A. L.424 J.D. [Hagens B.S.S.]
Feibus, Susan G., (AV) '— '81 C.659 B.A. L.597 J.D. [Ungaretti&H.]
Feiereisel, Gary M., (AV) '55 '81 C&L.424 B.S.B.A., J.D. [Fraterrigo,B.F.&K.]
Feiertag, Terry Yale, (AV) '41 '67 C.95 B.A. L.145 J.D. [Mandel,L.&S.]
Feigelson, Aaron R. '69 '02 C.477 A.B. L.145 J.D. [🄰 Leydig,V.&M.] (See Pat. Sect.)
Feil, Clinton J., (AV) '46 '71 C&L.597 B.A., J.D. [Kiesler&B.]
Fein, David I., (BV) '67 '93 C.966 B.A. L.209 J.D. 550 W. Washington Blvd., Ste. 300
Fein, Roger G., (AV) '40 '65 C.112 B.S. L.597 J.D. 400 Richard J. Daley Center
Feinartz, David C., (BV) '53 '78 C.339 B.S. L.365 J.D. [Schaffner,R.&F.]
Feinberg, Barry A., (AV) '44 '71 C.209 B.A. L.365 J.D. [Chuhak&T.]
Feinberg, Brett '74 '99 C.477 B.A. L.597 J.D. [🄰 Barack F.K.P.&N.]
Feinberg, Daniel '74 '99 C.347 B.A. L.424 J.D. [🄰 Sonnenschein N.&R.]
Feinberg, David J. '— '03 C&L.597 B.A., J.D. [🄰 DLPiper R.G.C.U.]
Feinberg, Dennis M. '43 '69 C.823 B.S. L.209 J.D. 221 N. LaSalle St.
Feinberg, Joy M., (AV) '52 '77 C.339 B.A. L.209 J.D. [Feinberg&B.] ⊙
Feinberg, Michael I. '77 '04 C.1036 B.A. L.597 J.D. [🄰 Adelman&G.]
Feinberg, Mitchell S. '72 '97 C.477 B.A. L.597 J.D. [Chuhak&T.]
Feinberg, Rebecca B. '71 '98 C.393 B.A. L.424 J.D. [🄲 Lake,T.&D.]
Feinberg, Stephen J., (AV) '51 '75 C.339 B.S.E.E. L.145 J.D. [🄲 Asher,G.G.&D.]

Feinberg & Barry, P.C., (AV)
20 S. Clark Street, Suite 500, 60603 ⊙
Telephone: 312-444-1050 Fax: 312-444-1027
Email: joy@feinbergbarry.com URL: http://www.feinbergbarry.com
Joy M. Feinberg; Carroll A. Barry; David M. Goldman.
Practice Limited to Matrimonial, Family, Divorce Law Trial and Appellate Practice.
South Suburban Office: 14315 South 108th Avenue, Suite 222, Orland Park, Illinois. Telephone: 708-349-2050. Fax: 312-444-1027.
See Professional Biographies, CHICAGO, ILLINOIS

Feingold, Allan S., (AV) '39 '63 C&L.339 A.B., LL.B. [Feingold&C.]
Feingold, Jeffrey M. '50 '74 C.339 B.A. L.209 J.D. [Weltman,W.&R.]
Feingold, Richard I. '60 '86 C.339 B.A. L.424 J.D. 120 W. Madison Street
Feingold & Crawford, Law Offices of, (AV) 200 North La Salle Street, Suite 2750
Feinstein, Faye B., (AV) '53 '84 C.102 B.A. L.569 J.D. [Quarles&B.]
Feinstein, Fred I., (AV) '45 '70 C&L.209 B.S., J.D. [McDermott W.&E.]
Feinstein, Paul L., (AV) '55 '80 C.861 B.A. L.245 J.D. [P.L.Feinstein]

Feinstein, Paul L., Ltd., (AV) 🄱🅁
10 South LaSalle Street, Suite 1420, 60603-1078
Telephone: 312-346-6392 Fax: 312-346-0810
Email: pfeinlaw@aol.com URL: http://paulfeinstein.com
Paul L. Feinstein.
Family, Matrimonial, Divorce, Child Custody, Child Support, Visitation Rights, Family Law Appeals, Trials and Appellate Practice.
See Professional Biographies, CHICAGO, ILLINOIS

Feis, Brenda Hofman, (AV) '60 '85 C&L.228 B.A., J.D. [Seyfarth S.]
Feiwell, George S., (AV) '27 '53 C.162 L.352 LL.B. 10 S. LaSalle St.
Feld, Jonathan S., (AVⓉ) '52 '80 C.685 B.A. L.94 J.D. [Katten M.R.]
Feld, Neal '56 '89 C.339 B.S. L.1000 J.D. 500 North Michigan Avenue, Suite 300

Feldhaus, David M. '65 '93 C.793 B.S. L.378 J.D.
(adm. in SD; not adm. in IL)
V.P. & Dir. - Congressional & Media Rel., Federal Home Loan Bk. of Chicago
Feldkamp, Frederick L., (AVⓉ) ...'— '71 C&L.477 A.B., J.D. [Foley&L.]
Feldman, Avram I. ...'62 '88 C&L.477 B.B.A., J.D. [Neal,G.&E.]
Feldman, David I., (AV) ...'60 '85 C&L.339 B.A., J.D. [Feldman&H.]
Feldman, Edward W. ...'57 '84 C.339 B.A. L.309 J.D. [Miller S.&H.]
Feldman, Frederick M. '42 '68 C.1106 B.A. L.209 J.D.
Head Asst. Atty., Metro. Water Reclamation Dist. of Greater Chicago
Feldman, Gilbert, (AV) ...'31 '55 C&L.597 B.A., J.D. [Cornfield&F.]
Feldman, James H., (AV) ...'43 '69 C.860 B.A. L.339 J.D. [Jenner&B.]
Feldman, Jan, (AV) ...'52 '81 C.347 B.A. L.597 J.D. [Perkins C.]
Feldman, Jerome ...'31 '55 C.339 L.209 LL.B. [Feldman&H.]
Feldman, Joseph D. ...'42 '67 C&L.477 A.B., J.D. 1819 N. Orleans St.
Feldman, Mark I., (AV) ...'50 '74 C.339 B.S.I.E. L.276 J.D. [DLPiper R.G.C.U.] (Pat.)
Feldman, Melvin ...'31 '55 C&L.209 J.D. Assoc. Coun., Bankers Life & Cas. Co.
Feldman, Michel J., (AV) ...'43 '68 C&L.597 B.S.B.A., J.D. [Seyfarth S.]
Feldman, Steven E. ...'70 '95 C.597 B.S.M.Sc. L.273 J.D. [Welsh&K.] (See Pat. Sect.)
Feldman, Stewart L. '56 '81
C.339 B.S. L.589 J.D. Legal Coun., Ill. Liquor Control Comm.
Feldman & Halprin, (AV) ...226 South Wabash Avenue
Feldman-Gerber, Inna '73 '00
C.221 B.A. L.365 J.D. Sr. Assoc., Global Indirect Tax Services
Feldmeier, Robert C. ...'— '90 C.602 B.A. L.339 J.D. [Schiff H.]
Feldstein, Rachel E. ...'72 '97 C.477 B.A. L.424 J.D. [Much S.F.D.A.&R.]
Felice, Peter A. ...'51 '76 C.927 B.A. L.365 J.D. 1340 S. Michigan Ave., Ste. 701
Felicetty, Stephanie J. ...'74 '03 C.980 B.E. L.8 J.D. [[A] Brinks H.G.&L.]
Feliksik, James S., (BV) ...'55 '91 C.999 B.A. L.365 J.D. 1 N. La Salle St., Ste. 2600
Fell, David W. '62 '88 C.966 B.A. L.309 J.D.
V.P. & Assoc. Gen. Coun., Manufactured Home Communities, Inc.‡
Feller, Brent L. ...'— '98 C.878 B.A. L.508 J.D. [[A] Chapman&C.]
Feller, Lawrence J. ...'68 '94 C.477 B.B.A. L.339 J.D. [Horwood M.&B.]
Feller, Leonid ...'— '01 C.477 A.B. L.309 J.D. [[A] Kirkland&E.]
Fellman, Glenn M. ...'49 '75 C&L.597 B.A., J.D. Asst. Reg. Dir., Fed. Trade Comm.
Fellows, Gerard R. ...'72 '98 C.475 B.A. L.209 J.D. [[A] Gould&R.]
Fellows, Jerry K., (AV) ...'46 '71 C.966 B.A. L.494 J.D. [Bell,B.&L.]
Fels, Jerome L., (AV) ...'11 '33 C&L.597 B.A., J.D. 900 N. Lake Shore Dr.
Felsenthal, Steven A., (AV) ...'49 '74 C.339 A.B. L.309 J.D. [Sugar,F.&F.]
Felton, Thadford A. ...'— '94 C.207 B.A. L.146 J.D. [Arnstein&L.]
Felton-Elkins, Nancy ...'39 '81 C.914 A.B. L.893 J.D. V.P., The Northern Trust Co.
Fenchel, Joel H., (AV) ...'42 '66 C&L.597 B.S., J.D. [Fischel&K.]
Fencik, Joan M., (AV) '56 '81 C.477 B.A. L.912 J.D.
Assoc. Gen. Coun., Exelon Corp.
Fencl, Glenn F., (AV) ...'52 '80 C.339 B.A. L.146 J.D. [Johnson&B.]
Fender, Cheryl A. ...'— '04 C.260 B.A. L.597 J.D. Two North LaSalle Street, Suite 2200
Fennell, Mark A. ...'— '98 C.696 B.A. L.145 J.D. [Kirkland&E.]
Fenner, Kenneth A. ...'42 '74 C.145 B.A. L.146 J.D. U.S. Environ. Prot. Agcy.
Fenster, Scott J. ...'75 '99 C.339 B.A. L.477 J.D. Equity Residential Properties Trust
Fenton, Marc I., (BV) ...'53 '81 C.424 B.A. L.589 J.D. [[C] DLPiper R.G.C.U.]
Fenton, Richard L., (AV) ...'54 '78 C&L.145 B.A., J.D. [Sonnenschein N.&R.]
Fenton, Steven ...'52 '80 C.339 B.A. L.589 J.D. Sr. V.P. & Sr. Coun., LaSalle
Fentress, Chad A. ...'62 '87 C.347 B.A. L.345 J.D. Accenture
Fenu, Mario Pasquale ...'75 '01 C.999 L.464 J.D. 33 N. Dearborn, Suite 502
Ferak, Paul J. ...'— '00 C.589 B.A. L.146 J.D. [[A] Greenberg T.]
Ferak, Tracy Gregar ...'— '01 C.339 B.A. L.146 J.D. [[A] Sachnoff&W.]
Ferbend & Ferbend, Ltd., (AV) ...35 E. Wacker Dr., Ste. 1760
Ferber, Leonard A. ...'57 '83 C.477 A.B. L.659 J.D. [Katten M.R.]
Ferber, Rachel Best '60 '84 C.659 B.A. L.910 J.D.
V.P. & Asst. Gen. Coun., 360° Communications Co.
Ferencz, Glenn E., (AV) ...'50 '76 C.339 B.A. L.477 J.D. [Gardner C.&D.]
Ferencz, Robert A., (AV) ...'46 '73 C.339 B.S. L.477 J.D. [Sidley A.B.&W.]
Fergan, Robert K. '68 '03 C.1229 B.S.E.E. L.912 J.D.
(adm. in MI; not adm. in IL) [[A] Brinks H.G.&L.] (☉Ann Arbor, MI)
Fergemann, Brian D. ...'74 '99 C.475 B.D. L.893 J.D. [[A] Winston&S.]
Ferguson, Anthony B. ...'58 '83 C.393 B.A. L.831 J.D. [Miller&F.]
Ferguson, C. Douglas ...'71 '96 C&L.575 B.A., J.D. Asst. Reg. Coun.,U.S. Dept. of HHS
Ferguson, Douglas ...'71 '96 C&L.575 B.A., J.D. Dept. of HHS
Ferguson, James R., (AV) ...'— '76 C.347 B.A. L.597 J.D. [Mayer,B.R.&M.]
Ferguson, Kevin P. ...'— '99 C.894 A.B. L.477 J.F. [[A] Jones D.] (See Pat. Sect.)
Ferguson, Mark E., (AV) ...'58 '83 C.597 B.S.J. L.477 J.D. [Bartlit B.H.P.&S.]
Ferguson, Nathan E. ...'69 '00 C.145 B.A. L.146 J.D. [[A] Wildman,H.A.&D.]
Ferguson, Stanley L., (AV) '52 '78
C.597 B.A. L.94 J.D. V.P. & Assoc. Gen. Coun., USG Corp.
Ferguson, Thomas H. ...'71 '97 C.1083 B.S.B.A. L.201 J.D. [[A] Kelley D.&W.]
Ferguson, Tiffany M. '70 '96 C.339 B.A. L.352 J.D.
180 North La Salle Street, Suite 3400
Fern, Brian M. ...'71 '96 C.339 B.A. L.146 J.D. [[A] Skadden,A.S.M.&F.]
Fernandez, Carol A. ...'54 '89 C.326 B.B.A. L.37 J.D. Asst. Pub. Def.
Fernandez, Norma Iris ...'57 '88 C.339 B.A. L.424 J.D. 130 S. Jefferson St., Ste. 500
Fernandez, Robert L. ...'74 '99 C.209 B.A. L.597 J.D. [[A] Sonnenschein N.&R.]
Fernandez, Rossana P. '70 '97 C.339 B.A. L.146 J.D.
333 West Wacker Drive, Suite 500
Fernholz, Annette M. ...'— '97 C.477 B.A. L.146 J.D. [A.M.Fernholz]
Fernholz, Frank, (AV) ...'15 '42 C.339 B.S. L.146 LL.B. [Fernholz&E.]
Fernholz, Annette M., P.C., Law Offices of ...30 N. LaSalle Street, Suite 1210
Fernholz & Ehrlich, (AV) ...10 S. La Salle
Ferolie, Albert F., (AV) ...'61 '87 C.339 B.A. L.365 J.D. [Ferolie&S.]
Ferolie & Stephenson, P.C., (AV) ...218 N. Jefferson
Ferolo, James V. ...'67 '92 C.597 B.A. L.424 J.D. [Klein,T.&J.]
Ferraro, Dennis A., (AV) ...'46 '81 C.589 B.A. L.365 J.D. [Chuhak&T.]
Ferraro, Kenneth C. '45 '70 C.742 B.A. L.209 J.D.
V.P., Assoc. Gen. Coun. & Asst. Secy., Chicago Title Ins. Co.

Ferraro, Anthony B., The Law Offices of
(See Rosemont)

Ferrazzano, Dennis A., (AV) ...'46 '71 C.367 B.A. L.597 J.D. [Barack F.K.P.&N.]
Ferrell, Michael S. ...'— '02 C.839 B.B.A. L.424 J.D. [[A] Jones D.]
Ferrera, Isabelle F. ...'68 '95 C&L.966 B.A., J.D. U.S. Postal Serv.
Ferreti, George M. ...'69 '94 C.339 B.A. L.477 J.D. [Foran G.P.&P.]
Ferrini, James T., (AV) ...'38 '63 C&L.424 B.S., J.D. [[C] Clausen M.]

Ferris, Thompson & Zweig, Ltd.
(See Gurnee)

Ferro, Teri Lee ...'— '90 C.145 B.A. L.597 J.D. [Boundas S.W.&B.]
Ferry, Kathryn J. ...'50 '77 C&L.209 B.A., J.D. Vet. Admn.
Ferstel, Jas. L., (AV) ...'27 '50 C&L.602 B.S.C., J.D. 79 W. Monroe
Fertel, Martin ...'33 '58 C.339 B.S. L.209 LL.B. 230 W. Monroe
Fertik, Philip, Attorney at Law, (AV) '45 '81
C&L.145 A.B., J.D. 351 W. Hubbard St., Ste. 406
Fertman, Yelena ...'— '98 C.999 B.A. L.347 J.D [[A] Jones D.]
Fesko, Heather ...'— '96 C.210 B.A. L.1119 J.D. [[A] Epstein B.&G.]
Fess, Eric F. ...'— '78 C.802 B.B.A. L.339 J.D. [Chapman&C.]
Fessler, James W. ...'— '88 C.339 B.A. L.365 J.D. [O'Hagan,S.&A.]
Festenstein, Paul S. ...'54 '79 C.339 B.A. L.910 J.D. [Condon&C.]
Fetman, Corri D. ...'63 '88 C&L.209 B.A., J.D. 33 W. Jackson Blvd.
Fetzer, Brian C., (AV) ...'50 '75 C.973 B.S.B.A. L.597 J.D. [Johnson&B.]
Fetzer, Kelly A. ...'— '95 C.966 B.A. L.424 J.D. [[A] Gardner C.&D.]
Feuchtwang, Jonathan D. '65 '96 C.645 B.S. L.46 J.D.
In-House Coun., Zimmer Technology, Inc. (Pat.)
Feuer, David Z., (BV) ...'50 '76 C.966 B.A. L.208 J.D. 1 N. La Salle St., Ste. 2600
Fey, Lawrence J. ...'57 '86 C.145 B.A. L.910 J.D. [DLPiper R.G.C.U.]
Ficaro, Gina Marie ...'73 '02 C.347 B.A. L.209 J.D. Appl. Ct. J.; IL 1st Dist.
Ficaro, Michael A., (AV) ...'— '72 C&L.209 B.A., J.D. [Ungaretti&H.]
Fichera, Dominic R., (AV) ...'31 '62 C&L.209 B.S., LL.B. [D.R.Fichera&Assoc.]
Fichera, Dominic R., & Associates, (AV) ...415 N. La Salle Dr., Ste. 301
Fichera-Burke, Cristina A. ...'— '90 C.840 B.A. L.365 J.D. [[A] D.R.Fichera&Assoc.]
Fick, Jos. J. ...'18 '51 C.137 L.365 LL.B. 2334 N. Melvina
Fiedler, Anne ...'57 '82 C.802 B.A. L.846 J.D. 200 East Randolph Drive, Suite 7300
Fiegen, Jonathan Frawley ...'70 '96 [[A] Foran G.P.&P.]
Field, Bridget L. ...'64 '90 C.879 B.S. L.365 J.D. Asst. Atty. Gen.
Field, David B. ...'49 '77 C.597 B.S. L.365 J.D. Neuberger Berman LLC
Field, David M. ...'— '99 C&L.352 B.A., J.D. [[A] Chapman&C.]
Field, Eva, P.C. ...'47 '73 C.339 B.A. L.472 J.D. [E.Field]
Field, James A. ...'65 '91 C.347 B.S. L.245 J.D. [Field&G.]
Field, Kimberly A. ...'77 '02 C.340 B.A. L.424 J.D. [[A] Field&G.]
Field, Leslie E. ...'32 '58 C.309 B.A. L.597 J.D. 1450 N. Dayton St.
Field, Robert E., (AV) ...'45 '73 C.340 B.A. L.597 J.D. [Field&G.]
Field, Rodger C. ...'47 '75 C.95 B.A. L.1119 J.D. Reg. Coun. Off., U.S. EPA
Field, Ted L. ...'— '02 C.339 B.A. L.365 J.D. [[A] Banner&W.]
Field, Thomas R. ...'54 '80 C.477 B.A. L.597 J.D. [[C] Wildman,H.A.&D.]
Field, Eva, P.C. ...2038 N. Damen Ave.

Field & Golan LLP, (AV) [BB]
Three First National Plaza, 70 West Madison Street, Suite 1500, 60602-4206
Telephone: 312-263-2300 Fax: 312-263-0939
URL: http://www.fieldgolan.com
Members of Firm: Robert E. Field; Stephen L. Golan; Margaret A. Christie; Donna F. Hartl; Barbara L. Yong; David K. Schmitt; Margaret A. Gisch; Anthony R. Taglia. Associates: Darrin S. Baim; Kimberly A. Field; Owen P. Quinn; Liat R. Meisler; Michael J. Osty; Caren A. Lederer; Steven A. Marderosian; Jeffrey M. Glass. Of Counsel: Joan E. Maloney; Leonard W. Golan; Patrick C. Doody; John E. Vranicar.
Business, Real Estate, Creditor Rights, Banking, Mergers and Acquisitions, Commercial Litigation, Civil Trial, Real Estate Valuation Litigation, Probate and Tax Law.
See Professional Biographies, CHICAGO, ILLINOIS

Field and Goldberg, LLC
10 South LaSalle Street, Suite 2910, 60603
Telephone: 312-408-7200 Fax: 312-408-7201
Members of the Firm: James A. Field; Jay Russell Goldberg; Justin M. Newman; Robert Godnik; Elizabeth D. Jensen.
Real Estate, Real Estate Tax, Finance, Mortgage Foreclosure, Real Estate Litigation, Commercial Real Estate.
See Professional Biographies, CHICAGO, ILLINOIS

Fields, Barry E. ...'— '91 C.1150 B.A. L.145 J.D. [Kirkland&E.]
Fields, Jane F., (BV) ...'— '80 C.569 B.A. L.146 J.D. 70 W. Madison St.
Fields, Stephanie W. '65 '91 C&L.94 B.A., J.D.
(adm. in NY; not adm. in IL) Sr. V.P. & Gen. Coun., Classic Residence by Hyatt
Fierstein, Ira, (AV) ...'52 '77 C.339 B.S. L.597 J.D. [Seyfarth S.]
Fieseler, Robert W., (AV) '55 '84
C.688 B.S. L.424 J.D. [McAndrews,H.&M.] (See Pat. Sect.)
Fiesta, Ronald V. ...'76 '02 C.602 B.S. L.896 J.F. [[A] K.B.Moll&Assoc.]
Fiet, Ronald D. ...'66 '96 C.56 B.A. L.879 J.D. [[A] Cassiday,S.&G.] (☉Rockford)
Fieweger, James P. ...'63 '91 C.602 B.A. L.209 J.D. [Jenner&B.]
Fieweger, Michael J. ...'66 '94 C.602 B.A. L.597 J.D. [Baker&M.]
Fifer, Samuel, (AV) ...'50 '74 C.597 B.S. L.209 J.D. [Sonnenschein N.&R.]
Fiffer, James D., (AV) '53 '80 C.976 B.A. L.145 J.D.
S.V.P. & Assoc Gen. Coun., Equity Residential
Fifield, Sean C. ...'72 '97 C&L.477 B.S.E., J.D. [Lord,B.&B.]
Figler, Rebecca A. ...'76 '01 C.679 B.S. L.209 J.D. [[A] Smith O.&W.]
Figlioli, David, (AV) ...'55 '91 C.999 B.A. L.365 J.D. 150 N. Michigan Ave., Ste. 1100
Figliulo, Donald E. ...'— '78 C.742 B.A. L.146 J.D. [Bryan C.]
Figliulo, James R., (AV) ...'49 '75 C.742 B.A. L.37 J.D. [Figliulo&S.]
Figliulo, Sharon M. ...'— '01 C.742 B.A. L.424 J.D. [[A] Hinshaw&C.]

Figliulo & Silverman, P.C., (AV) [BB]
10 South La Salle Street, Suite 3600, 60603
Telephone: 312-251-4600 Fax: 312-251-4610
Email: law@fslegal.com URL: http://www.fslegal.com
James R. Figliulo; Peter A. Silverman; Carl A. Gigante; Marc S. Porter; James H. Bowhay; John J. Lynch; Jeff D. Harris; Michael K. Desmond; Stephen A. Viz;—Stephanie D. Jones; Gregory L. Stelzer; Colleen M. Schmiege; Michael T. Graham; Thomas D. Warman.
Trial and Appellate Practice in Federal and State Courts. Business and Corporate Litigation, Eminent Domain, Professional Liability, Bankruptcy, Construction, and Real Estate Related Litigation.
See Professional Biographies, CHICAGO, ILLINOIS

Figueroa, Rudy A., Jr. ...'73 '00 C.679 B.A. L.146 J.D. [[A] Chuhak&T.]
Figura, David A., (BV) ...'52 '79 C.339 B.A. L.1151 J.D. Asst. Pub. Def.
Figura, Stanley V. ...'61 '87 C&L.276 A.B., J.D. [Bates&C.]
Fijolek, William J. ...'55 '83 C.339 B.S. L.209 J.D. 141 W. Jackson
Fike, Lisa Eiserman ...'75 '00 C.610 B.A. L.339 J.D. City of Chgo., Dept. of Law
Filarski, Thomas J., (AV) '56 '86
C.424 B.A. L.209 J.D. [Brinks H.G.&L.] (See Pat. Sect.)
Filbin, Paul J. ...'71 '99 C.602 B.S.M.E. L.424 J.D. [[A] Leydig,V.&M.]
File, Katherine Gonser, (AV) ...'56 '81 C.879 B.S.W. L.912 J.D. [Pierce&Assoc.]
Filer, Edward L., (AV) ...'64 '91 C.477 B.A. L.966 J.D. [FagelHaber]
Filiaggi, Rita M. ...'— '97 C.910 L.146 J.D. [O'Hagan,S.&A.]
Filip, Mark R., (AV) ...'— '93 C.339 B.A. L.309 J.D. U.S. Dist. J.
Filipovic, Jamie L. ...'77 '03 C.477 B.A. L.209 J.D. [[A] Wilson E.M.E.&D.]
Filipowski, Steven C., (BV) ...'50 '75 C.723 B.A. L.424 J.D. [Shaheen,N.S.F.&E.]
Filippini, Victor P., Jr., (AV) ...'58 '83 C.309 A.B. L.477 J.D. [Holland&K.]
Filkins, James A. ...'54 '00 C.1089 B.A. L.209 J.D. City of Chicago, Dept. of Law
Filosa, John C. ...'58 '84 C.602 A.B. L.339 J.D. [Baker&M.]
Filpi, Robert A., (AV) ...'45 '70 C.309 B.A. L.597 J.D. [Stack&F.]
Finch, G. A., (AV) ...'55 '82 C.31 B.A. L.477 J.D. [Michael B.&F.]
Findlay, D. Cameron '59 '87
C.597 B.A. L.309 J.D. Exec. V.P. & Gen. Coun., Aon Corporation

Fine, Elizabeth L. ... '76 '04 C.1349 B.A. L.477 J.D. [A Jenner&B.]
Fine, Jeffrey A. ... '— '95 C.347 B.S. L.178 J.D. [Kirkland&E.]
Fine, Jennifer R. ... '74 '99 C.477 B.B.A. L.146 J.D. 111 N. Canal St.
Fine, Karen M. ... '— '95 C.976 B.A. L.178 J.D. [Kirkland&E.]
Fine, Lisa J. ... '76 '01 C.861 B.S. L.276 J.D. [A Mayer,B.R.&M.]
Fine, Louis R. ... '43 '68 C.339 B.A. L.209 J.D. 105 W. Madison St.
Fine, Mark H. ... '54 '79 C.339 B.A. L.209 J.D. Equity Off. Prop. Tr.
Fine, S. Richard, (AV) ... '25 '50 C&L.145 Ph.B., J.D. [C Michael B.&F.]
Fine, Steven H., Law Office of '69 '94
C.352 B.A. L.365 J.D. 53 W. Jackson Boulevard, Suite 1420
Fineberg, Leslie J. ... '— '91 C.30 B.A. L.472 J.D. [A D.DiMaggio]
Fineman, Marc E. ... '70 '96 C.705 B.S. L.365 J.D. [A Kegan&K.] (See Pat. Sect.)
Finestone, Elchanan ... '— '03 C.1357 B.A. L.569 J.D. [A Pircher,N.&M.]
Fingard, Richard A. ... '67 '96 C.339 B.S. L.146 J.D. Coun., Caylon Financial Inc.
Finger, Kevin D. ... '63 '93 C.602 B.S.E.E. L.424 J.D. [Greenberg T.]
Fingert, Nadine J. '60 '85 C.347 B.A. L.801 J.D.
Reg. Tax Coord., West Publishing Corp.
Fink, Allison A. ... '— '01 C.597 B.A. L.477 J.D. [A McDermott W.&E.]
Fink, Jerrold E. ... '— '71 C.112 B.A. L.309 J.D. [Masuda,F.E.&M.]
Fink, Karl R., (BV) ... '56 '81 C&L.477 B.S.E., J.D. [Fitch,E.T.&F.] (See Pat. Sect.)
Fink, Matthew J. ... '63 '89 C.478 B.A. L.597 J.D. [Bates&C.]
Fink, Nicholas I. ... '74 '99 C.999 D.E.S. L.597 J.D. [A Bell,B.&L.]
Fink, Robert D. ... '77 '02 C.350 B.S. L.146 J.D. 28 E. Jackson Blvd., Ste. 1004
Fink, Sam F. ... '10 '34 C.999 L.209 100 W. Monroe St.
Fink, Sheldon I., (AV) ... '30 '54 C&L.966 B.B.A., LL.B. [Sonnenschein N.&R.]
Fink, Tina L. ... '— '02 C.177 B.A. L.209 J.D. [A McKenna S.]
Fink, Wendy L., (BV) ... '65 '92 C.478 B.A. L.209 J.D. [A Baker&M.]
Finke, Jeffrey W., (AV) ... '50 '77 C.339 A.B. L.145 J.D. [C McCarthy&Assoc.]
Finke, Robert F., (AV) ... '41 '66 C.477 A.B. L.309 J.D. [Mayer,B.R.&M.]
Finkel, Leon I., (AV) ... '58 '83 C.589 B.S. L.424 J.D. [Berger S.]
Finkel, Noah A. ... '68 '94 C&L.477 B.A., J.D. [Seyfarth S.]
Finkel, Norman D. ... '31 '53 C&L.209 LL.B. [Firm of Finkel,M.&C.]
Finkel, Norman T., (AV) ... '57 '82 C&L.339 B.S., J.D. [Young,R.F.&S.]
Finkel, Martwick & Colson, Law Firm of, P.C., (AV) ... 203 N. LaSalle St.
Finkle, David H. ... '10 '32 L.209 LL.B. 20 N. Clark St.
Finkle, Lester W. ... '57 '82 C.339 B.A. L.209 J.D. Asst. Pub. Def.
Finkle, Stuart I. '42 '67 C.209 B.S.C. L.365 J.D.
V.P. & Nat'l Claims Cnsl, Stewart Title Guaranty Company
Finko, Andrew ... '— '92 C.339 B.S. L.365 J.D. [S Schiff H.]
Finley, Brian ... '66 '92 C&L.966 B.S., J.D. Asst. Pub. Guard.
Finley, L. Terrance Spencer ... '55 '84 C.477 B.A. L.1187 J.D. U.S. Postal Inspector Atty.
Finley, Patrick J., (BV) ... '56 '85 C.424 A.B. L.365 J.D. Asst. State's Atty.
Finley, Robert J. ... '73 '01 C.436 B.A. L.209 J.D. [A Hinshaw&C.]
Finn, Herbert H. ... '65 '91 C.339 B.S. L.209 J.D. [Greenberg T.] (Pat.)
Finn, Lawrence B., (BV) ... '61 '87 C.222 B.A. L.910 J.D. [A Levin&P.]
Finn, Thomas J. ... '57 '82 C.339 B.A. L.365 J.D. [Leahy,E.&F.]
Finnegan, Laura M. ... '— '92 C.722 B.A. L.146 J.D. [A Baum S.A.&N.]
Finnegan, Maurice E., III '— '03
C.477 B.S. L.339 J.D. Two North LaSalle Street, Suite 2200 (Pat.)
Finnegan, Sheila M., (AV) ... '60 '86 C.276 B.S.F.S. L.145 J.D. [Mayer,B.R.&M.]
Finnegan, Susan A. ... '— '99 C.20 B.A. L.146 J.D. [A C.C.Kendall]
Finnegan, Thomas J. '71 '96 C.589 B.S. L.146 J.D.
Sr. V.P., Sec., & Gen. Coun., Academic Capital Group, Inc.
Finnigan, Mindy A. ... '— '02 C.352 B.A. L.1119 J.D. [A Jones D.]
Finston, Albert L. ... '— '40 C&L.209 J.D. [C Tenney&B.]
Fintzen, Scott S. ... '68 '93 C.276 B.S.F.S. L.128 J.D. [Gaido&F.]
Fiordalisi, Nicola ... '62 '91 L.424 J.D. [Bell,B.&L.]
Fiore, Lidia ... '72 '99 C.424 B.S. L.597 J.D. 2304 N. Evergreen
Fiore, Richard Anthony ... '— '97 C&L.339 B.S., J.D. [Freeborn&P.]
Fiorentinos, Irene S. ... '— '84 C.610 B.S. L.597 J.D. [Jones D.]
Fioretto, Pasquale A. ... '65 '90 C&L.209 B.Sc., J.D. [Baum S.A.&N.]
Fioti, John L. ... '66 '91 C.238 B.S. L.209 J.D. Asst. State's Atty.
Firfer, Richard J., (AV) ... '43 '71 C&L.597 B.A., J.D. [Schwartz C.]
Fischel, Daniel R. ... '50 '77 C.188 B.A. L.145 J.D. Lexecon Inc.

Fischel & Kahn, Ltd., (AV)
190 South La Salle Street, Suite 2850, 60603-3412
Telephone: 312-726-0440 Fax: 312-726-1448
Frederic A. Fischel (1905-1956); Louis L. Kahn (1912-1965); Max Hess Weinberg (1936-1986); Dan Brusslan; Joel H. Fenchel; Morris G. Dyner; David W. Inlander; Robert W. Kaufman; Edward F. (Bud) Dobbins; Mark R. Rosenbaum; Peter J. Schmiedel; Ronald D. Menna, Jr.; Suzanne Glade; Deborah Jo Soehlig.
General Civil and Trial Practice. Corporation, Probate, Estate Planning, Tax, Insurance, Real Estate, Lending, Elder Law, Guardianships and Domestic Relations.
See Professional Biographies, CHICAGO, ILLINOIS

Fischer, Andrew M. ... '64 '89 C.813 B.A. L.597 J.D. Asst. V.P., LR Realty
Fischer, Ashley M. ... '74 '00 C.276 B.A. L.597 J.D. [A Gardner C.&D.]
Fischer, Barry L., (BV) ... '68 '93 C.597 B.A. L.477 J.D. [FagelHaber]
Fischer, David G. ... '55 '84 C.750 B.A. L.146 J.D. 69 W. Washinton St., Rm. 700
Fischer, David J., (AV) ... '50 '79 C.477 B.A. L.365 J.D. [Dolgin&F.]
Fischer, David J., (AV) ... '52 '77 C.976 B.A. L.94 J.D. [Wildman,H.A.&D.]
Fischer, Diane C. ... '53 '85 C.801 B.S. L.209 J.D. [Kane&F.]
Fischer, Fredric H., (AV) ... '42 '68 C.188 B.S. L.107 J.D. [Seyfarth S.]
Fischer, Jennifer L. ... '58 '92 C.694 B.A. L.365 J.D. Lexis-Nexis
Fischer, Matthew J. ... '— '94 C.339 B.S. L.477 J.D. [Schiff H.]
Fischer, Michael B., (AV) ... '49 '72 C.823 B.A. L.569 J.D. [DLPiper R.G.C.U.]
Fischer, Paul D. ... '43 '68 C&L.424 B.B.A., J.D. [C Shefsky&F.]
Fischer, Thomas K. ... '44 '75 C.347 B.A. L.424 J.D. Admin. L. J.
Fish, Amanda L. ... '77 '02 C.966 B.A. L.146 J.D. 77 West Wacker, 50th Fl.
Fishbein, Sue Ann, (AV) ... '50 '74 C.477 B.A. L.339 J.D. [Krasnow S.C.]
Fishel, Francine R., (BV) ... '51 '92 C.530 B.A. L.146 J.D. 180 N. LaSalle St.
Fisher, Ann H. '48 '77
C.477 B.A. L.912 J.D. Exec. Dir., AIDS Legal Council of Chicago‡
Fisher, Barry M. ... '44 '69 C.674 B.S.E. L.477 J.D. [Fisher&F.]
Fisher, Carlton D., (AV) ... '53 '78 C&L.339 B.A., J.D. [Hinshaw&C.]
Fisher, Christine Bay, (AV Ⓣ) ... '51 '81 C.797 B.A. L.260 J.D. [Sonnenschein N.&R.]
Fisher, Constance F. ... '47 '80 C.207 B.A. L.365 J.D. Asst. Prof., John Marshal Law Sch.
Fisher, Earl P., Jr. ... '55 '82 C.880 B.A. L.209 J.D. 5212 S. Dorchester Ave.‡
Fisher, Fred C. ... '— '02 C.473 B.S. L.597 J.D. [A Latham&W.]
Fisher, Gayle Yeatman ... '— '94 C&L.597 B.A., J.D. [C Barack F.K.P.&N.]
Fisher, Herbert H., (BV) ... '27 '52 C&L.966 B.A., LL.B. 200 North Dearborn
Fisher, Ian H. ... '69 '94 C.293 B.A. L.597 J.D. [Schopf&W.]
Fisher, J. Mark, (AV) ... '— '78 C.976 B.A. L.893 J.D. [Schiff H.]
Fisher, J. Richard, Jr. ... '— '71 C.608 B.A. L.597 J.D. [Chapman&C.]
Fisher, Jack ... '20 '47 C.999 L.209 LL.B. 221 N. LaSalle St.
Fisher, James Russell ... '42 '98 C.338 B.S. L.146 J.D. Law Clk.
Fisher, Jennifer Paganessi ... '— '95 C.823 B.S. L.146 J.D. [A Defrees&F.]
Fisher, Joseph G. ... '69 '97 C&L.339 B.S., J.D. [McDermott W.&E.]
Fisher, Kenneth H. ... '42 '67 C.966 B.B.A. L.597 J.D. [Fisher&F.]
Fisher, Laura Chase ... '68 '93 C.477 B.A. L.273 J.D. Tribune Co.
Fisher, Marc D. ... '65 '90 C.597 B.A. L.69 J.D. Lit. Coun., Aon Corporation
Fisher, Michael A. ... '42 '70 C.1016 B.A. L.146 J.D. 221 N. LaSalle St.
Fisher, Michael David ... '60 '87 C.112 B.A. L.209 J.D. 1 E. Wacker Dr.
Fisher, Paul E., (AV) ... '47 '73 C.697 B.A. L.477 J.D. [McGuirewoods]
Fisher, Paul S. ... '55 '80 C.602 B.A. L.145 J.D. VMS Realty, Inc.
Fisher, Robert A. ... '53 '79 C.339 B.A. L.1151 J.D. [R.A.Fisher]
Fisher, Scott J. ... '71 '96 C.608 B.A. L.146 J.D. [Gardner C.&D.]
Fisher, Steven B. ... '62 '87 C.339 B.S. L.146 J.D. [Fisher K.]
Fisher, Susan E. ... '52 '79 C.604 B.A. L.597 J.D. 2048 N. Kenmore St.
Fisher & Fisher ... 120 N. LaSalle St., Ste. 2520

Fisher Kanaris, P.C., (AV) BB
200 South Wacker Drive, 22nd Floor, 60606
Telephone: 312-474-1400 Telecopier: 312-474-1410
URL: http://www.FISHERKANARIS.com
Steven B. Fisher; David E. Heiss; Suanne P. Hirschhaut; Peter E. Kanaris; Marc F. Katalinic; Jon B. Masini; Lawrence D. Mason; Scott A. Ruksakiati; John R. Schleiter; Stephen A. Whelan;—Jeffrey C. Arnold; Ernest L. Clifford; Margaret M. Donnell; David L. Heaton; Cheryl L. Heiss; Robert J. Lentz; Aaron E. Lunt; Jefferson D. Patten; Kevin Michael Phillips; Kevin M. Pugliese; David M. Roach; John M. Schmidt; Steven C. Swanson; Michael A. Wax; Jonathan S. Weber.
A National Civil Litigation Practice with emphasis in First-Party Property and Third-Party Liability Insurance and Reinsurance, Subrogation-Loss Recovery, Professional Liability Defense, Construction Law, Warehouseman's Legal Liability Defense, Design Professional Contract Formation-Risk Management, Business and Commercial Litigation and Product Liability.
See Professional Biographies, CHICAGO, ILLINOIS

Fisher & Phillips LLP, (AV) BB
1000 Marquette Building, 140 South Dearborn Street, 60603 ⊙
Telephone: 312-346-8061 Fax: 312-346-3179
Email: fp@laborlawyers.com URL: http://www.laborlawyers.com
Members of Firm: Craig R. Annunziata; James F. Hendricks, Jr.; Jane M. McFetridge; Kevin S. Simon; Matt D. Strubbe. Of Counsel: Steve A. Miller; Joel W. Rice. Associates: Nadine C. Abrahams; Tany L. Jachimiak; Nesheba M. Kittling; Brian K. LaFratta.
Labor and Employment, Alternative Dispute Resolution, Arbitration, Business Immigration, Collective Bargaining, Employment Discrimination, Labor Relations, Mergers, Acquisitions and Divestitures, Sexual Harassment, Wage and Hour Law, Whistleblower Litigation, Wrongful Termination.
Atlanta, Georgia Office: 1500 Resurgens Plaza, 945 East Paces Ferry Road, 30326. Telephone: 404-231-1400. Fax: 404-240-4249.
Charlotte, North Carolina Office: Suite 2020, 227 West Trade Street, 28202. Telephone: 704-334-4565. Fax: 704-334-9774.
Columbia, South Carolina Office: Suite 1400, 1901 Main Street, 29201. Telephone: 803-255-0000. Fax: 803-255-0202.
Dallas, Texas Office: 4343 Thanksgiving Tower, 1601 Elm Street, 75201. Telephone: 214-220-9100. Fax: 214-220-9122.
Fort Lauderdale, Florida Office: Suite 800, 450 East Las Olas Boulevard, 33301. Telephone: 954-525-4800. Fax: 954-525-8739.
Irvine, California Office: Suite 400, 18400 Von Karman Avenue, 92612. Telephone: 949-851-2424. Fax: 949-851-0152.
Kansas City, Missouri Office: Suite 400, 104 West Ninth Street, 64105. Telephone: 816-842-8770. Fax: 816-842-8767.
Las Vegas, Nevada Office: Suite 650, 3993 Howard Hughes Parkway, 89109. Telephone: 702-252-3131. Fax: 702-252-7411.
New Orleans, Louisiana Office: Suite 3710, 201 St. Charles Avenue, 70170. Telephone: 504-522-3303. Fax: 504-529-3850.
Oakland, California Office: City Center Suite 200, 501 Fourteenth Street, 94612. Telephone: 510-763-4411. Fax: 510-763-4418.
Orlando, Florida Office: 1250 Lincoln Plaza, 300 South Orange Avenue, 32801. Telephone: 407-541-0888. Fax: 407-541-0887.
Portland, Oregon Office: Suite 1600, 1001 S.W. Fifth Avenue, 97204. Telephone: 503-242-4262. Fax: 503-242-4263.
San Diego, California Office: 4225 Executive Square, Suite 950, La Jolla, California, 92037. Telephone: 858-597-9600. Fax: 858-597-9601.
Somerset, New Jersey Office: Corporate Park III, Third Floor, 580 Howard Avenue, 08873. Telephone: 732-560-7100. Fax: 732-560-0788.
Tampa, Florida Office: Suite 2525, 401 East Jackson Street, 33602. Telephone: 813-769-7500. Fax: 813-769-7501.
See Professional Biographies, CHICAGO, ILLINOIS

Fisher, Robert A., Ltd. ... 20 S. Clark St., Ste. 700
Fishman, Gregory A. ... '— '98 C.608 B.A. L.930 J.D. [A Greenberg T.]
Fishman, Howard J. ... '68 '93 C.339 B.A. L.146 J.D. [Aronberg G.D.&G.]
Fishman, Jay B. ... '61 '88 C.347 B.S. L.365 J.D. Law Clk., Cir. Ct. J.
Fishman, Julius ... '08 '30 221 N. La Salle St.
Fishman, Michael T. ... '68 '95 C.608 B.A. L.1003 J.D. [Greenberg T.]
Fishman, Norman W., (BV) ... '36 '61 C&L.597 B.S., LL.B. 200 W. Madison St.
Fishman, Robert M., (AV) ... '53 '79 C.339 B.A. L.273 J.D. [Shaw G.F.G.W.&T.]
Fishman, Ronald S., (AV) ... '33 '57 C.339 B.A. L.597 LL.B. 25 E. Washington St.
Fishman, Seymour J. ... '34 '60 C.1016 B.A. L.209 LL.B. 1 N. LaSalle St.
Fishman, Stephanie A. '71 '01 C.823 B.A. L.912 J.D.
(adm. in MI; not adm. in IL) [A Gordon&G.L.]
Fishman, Fishman & Saltzberg, P.C., (AV) ... 221 N. La Salle St., Ste. 2036
Fisk, Michelle J. ... '— '00 C.27 B.A. L.209 J.D. [A Schiff H.]

Fisk Kart Katz and Regan, Ltd., (AV)
Suite 900, 77 West Washington Street, 60602
Telephone: 312-726-1833 FAX: 312-726-4622
URL: http://www.proptax.com
James P. Regan; Jack E. Boehm, Jr.; Jeffrey A. Brown; George J. Relias; William J. Seitz; Robert J. Tonos; Albert Fisk (1941-1964); Martin S. Katz (1946-2000). Of Counsel: Eugene Kart; Gilbert Kart.
Practice Limited to Property Taxation and Assessment Law. Ad Valorem Tax Law, Property Tax Law, Property Tax Appeals, Property Tax Assessments, Real Estate Taxation, Real Estate Tax Assessment, Tax Appeals.
Reference: American National Bank & Trust Co., Chicago.
See Professional Biographies, CHICAGO, ILLINOIS

Fister, Stephen T. ... '58 '84 C&L.209 B.S., J.D. 527 S. Wells St.
Fitch, Morgan L., Jr., (AV) '22 '49 C.46 B.S. L.477 J.D.
[Fitch,E.T.&F.] (See Pat. Sect.)

Fitch, Even, Tabin & Flannery, (AV) BB
120 South La Salle, Suite 1600, 60603 ⊙
Telephone: 312-577-7000 Fax: 312-577-7007
Email: email@fitcheven.com URL: http://www.fitcheven.com
Members of Firm: Morgan L. Fitch, Jr.; Francis A. Even; Julius Tabin; John F. Flannery; Robert B. Jones; James J. Schumann (Resident, San Diego, California Office); James J. Hamill; Timothy E. Levstik; Joseph E. Shipley; Kenneth H. Samples; Philip T. Petti; Joseph T. Nabor; Steven C. Schroer; Richard A. Kaba (Not admitted in IL); Karl R. Fink; Mark W. Hetzler; Timothy P. Maloney; James P. Krueger; Stephen S. Favakeh; Richard E. Wawrzyniak (Resident, San Diego, California Office); Steven G. Parmelee (Not admitted in IL; Resident at Omaha, Nebraska Office); Thomas F. Lebens; Kendrew H. Colton (Resident, Washington, D.C. Office); G. Paul Edgell (Resident, Washington, D.C. Office); Michael A. Sanzo, Ph.D. (Resident, Washington, D.C. Office); Scott J. Menghini (Resident, San Diego, California Office); Norman Kunitz (Resident, Washington, D.C. Office); Rudy I. Kratz; Ramon R. Hoch (Not admitted in IL; Also at Washington, D.C. Office); John D. Bauersfeld (Resident, Woodland Hills, California Office); Gary D. Mann (Resident, Woodland Hills, California Office); Edward E. Clair; John E. Lyhus; Samuel P. Burkholder (Not admitted in IL); David W. Maher, Ph.D.

(This Listing Continued)

Fitch, Even, Tabin & Flannery (Continued)

(Not admitted in IL); John J. Gresens. Of Counsel: George H. Spencer (Resident, Washington, D.C. Office);—Jon A. Birmingham; Steven M. Freeland (Resident, San Diego, California Office); Brian Sommer Clise; Martin R. Bader (Resident, San Diego, California Office); Mark A. Borsos; Timothy R. Baumann; Jeffrey A. Chelstrom; Nicholas T. Peters; Kenneth E. Plochinski; Grace Law O'Brien; Christine A. Abuel; Tara M. Reedy; Sarah M. Walkington; Joel H. Bootzin; Michael P. Furmanek; James M. Wakely.
Intellectual Property and Technology-Related Law including United States and International Patents, Trademarks, Trade Secret, Copyrights and Unfair Competition, Antitrust and International Trade Commission Causes and Related Litigation.
San Diego, California Office: 9276 Scranton Road, Suite 250, 92121. Telephone: 858-552-1311. Telecopier: 858-552-0095.
San Luis Obispo, California Office: 1010 Peach Street, 93406-0031. Telephone: 805-541-2800. Fax: 805-541-2802.
Washington, D.C. Office: Suite 1801 K Street, N.W., Suite 401L, 20006-1201. Telephone: 202-419-7000. Fax: 202-419-7007.
Boulder, Colorado Office: 1942 Broadway, Suite 213, 80302. Telephone: 303-402-6966. Fax: 303-402-6970.
Los Angeles, California Office: Warner Center Towers, Suite 780, 21800 Oxnard Street, Woodland Hills, California, 91367. Telephone: 818-715-7025. Fax: 818-715-7033.

See Professional Biographies, CHICAGO, ILLINOIS

Fitter, Seth B. '59 '85 C.1044 B.A. L.107 J.D.
(adm. in NY; not adm. in IL) 10 W. Jackson
Fitts, Ryan J. '74 '01 C.436 B.A. L.477 J.D. [Mayer,B.R.&M.]
Fitzell, Stephen P., (AV) '54 '82 C.602 B.B.A. L.424 J.D. [Sidley A.B.&W.]
Fitzgerald, Charles Francis '51 '81 C.339 B.A. L.365 J.D. [C.F.Fitzgerald]
Fitzgerald, Jennifer L. '— '95 C.800 B.S. L.424 J.D. [Freeborn&P.] (Pat.)
Fitzgerald, John M. '78 '04 C&L.145 B.A., J.D. [Bell,B.&L.]
Fitzgerald, John P., (AV) '56 '85 C.1151 B.A. L.365 J.D. [J.P.Fitzgerald]
Fitzgerald, Michele P. '69 '99 L.339 J.D. KPMG LLP
Fitzgerald, Robert E., Jr. '31 '59 C&L.209 B.S.C., J.D. 5850 N. Kostner Ave.
Fitzgerald, Thomas P. '54 '79 C&L.602 B.A., J.D. [Winston&S.]
Fitzgerald, Charles F., P.C. 10459 S. Kedzie Ave.
Fitzgerald & Cross, (AV) 33 W. Monroe St.
Fitzgerald, John P., Ltd., (AV) 10452 S. Kedzie Ave.
FitzGerald Meldrum, Nora '74 '00 C.276 B.A. L.477 J.D. [Franczek S.]
FitzGibbon, James T., (AV) '32 '60 C&L.424 B.S., J.D. [Vedder,P.K.&K.] (Pat.)
FitzGibbon, Thomas B. '79 '04 C.659 B.A. L.145 J.D. [McGuirewoods]
Fitzner, Linda K. '47 '78 C.1255 B.S. L.209 J.D. 5215 N. Moody
Fitzpatrick, Catherine L. '— '96 C.589 B.S. L.145 J.D. [Kirkland&E.]
Fitzpatrick, Cheryl B. '63 '89 C.801 B.S. L.146 J.D. Gen. Coun., Alaron Trading Corp.
Fitzpatrick, Collins T. '44 '69 C.436 A.B. L.309 J.D. Cir. Exec., 7th Cir. J. Coun.
Fitzpatrick, Dennis D., (BV) '64 '89 C.436 B.A. L.209 J.D. [Clausen M.]
Fitzpatrick, Edward C., (AV) '45 '73 C.352 B.A. L.309 J.D. [Lord,B.&B.]
Fitzpatrick, Elizabeth A. '55 '91 C.383 B.A. L.421 J.D.
(adm. in KY; not adm. in IL) 3 1st Nat. Plz.
Fitzpatrick, George F., Jr., (AV) '54 '83 C.679 B.A. L.209 J.D. [Swanson,M.&B.]
Fitzpatrick, John D. '74 '02 C.475 B.A. L.846 J.D. [Connelly R.&M.]
Fitzpatrick, Michael J. '76 '01
C.339 B.S. L.893 J.D. [McAndrews,H.&M.] (See Pat. Sect.)
Fitzpatrick, Peter, (AV) '06 '33 C.177 B.A. L.146 LL.B. 9923 S. Wood St.
Fitzpatrick, Richard H. '46 '73 C.210 B.A. L.910 J.D. 3500 Three First Nat. Plz.
Fitzpatrick, Samuel L. '40 '65 C.712 B.B.A. L.734 J.D.
Assoc. Gen. Coun., Unitrin, Inc.
FitzSimmons, Catherine '56 '85 C.215 B.Ch.E. L.326 J.D. 8510 W. Gregory St.
Fitzsimmons, Robert V., (AV) '59 '86 C.597 B.A. L.309 J.D. [Mayer,B.R.&M.]
Fitzsimmons, Roberts, Paine & Caruso, (AV)
135 S. La Salle St., Ste. 3705 (⊙Wheaton)
Fitzsimons, Kevin W. '— '91 601 W. Randolph St., 2nd Fl.
Fitzsimons, Thomas '65 '94 C.339 B.S. L.424 J.D. [Greer,B.&C.] (Pat.)
FitzSimons, Timothy P. '— '02 C.602 B.A. L.597 J.D. [Latham&W.]
Fix, Blake J. '— '01 C.378 B.A. L.602 J.D. [Gardner C.&D.]
Fizzell, J. Tobias '67 '97 C.339 B.A. L.424 J.D. Corp. Coun.
Flachsbart, William W. '67 '96 C.145 B.S. L.424 J.D. [Niro,S.H.&N.] (See Pat. Sect.)
Flack, Hope L. '56 '90 C.720 B.A. L.146 J.D.
V.P. Legal Compliance, Grosvenor Capital Management, L.P.
Flader, Richard L. '35 '80 C.597 B.S. L.589 J.D. 33 N. Dearborn St.
Fladung, Hans '47 '81 C.339 B.A. L.597 J.D. Asst. Atty. Gen.
Flahaven, Roger P., (AV) '55 '80 C.597 B.A. L.365 J.D. Asst. Atty. Gen.
Flaherty, Amy L. '— '01 C.1063 B.A. L.339 J.D. [Winston&S.]
Flaherty, John E. '— '91 C.339 B.A. L.424 J.D. [Cozen O.]
Flaherty, Megan A. '67 '03 C.473 B.S. L.146 J.D. [Katten M.R.]
Flaherty, Michael J., (AV) '58 '83 C.339 B.A. L.146 J.D. [Flaherty&J.]
Flaherty, Michael R. '46 '77 C.602 A.B. L.477 J.D. [Jackson L.]
Flaherty, Nora E. '76 '03 C.436 B.A. L.339 J.D. [Burke,W.M.&S.]
Flaherty, Thomas C. '— '99 C.339 B.S. L.879 J.D. [Hennessy&R.]

Flaherty & Jacobson, P.C., (AV) BR
134 North LaSalle Street Suite 1600, 60602
Telephone: 312-782-4700 Fax: 312-782-4725 URL: http://www.lawyers.com/fjlaw
Email: lawyers@fjlaw.com URL: http://www.fjlaw.com
Michael J. Flaherty; Richard J. Jacobson; Jeffrey S. Youngerman. Of Counsel: Stephen D. Sharp.
Business and Financial Tort, Legal Malpractice, Construction and Complex Commercial Litigation.

See Professional Biographies, CHICAGO, ILLINOIS

Flaherty-Cheatham, Julie A. '74 '99 C.209 B.S. L.146 J.D. [Cassiday,S.&G.]
Flaming, Todd H. '66 '93 C.426 B.A. L.145 J.D. [Schopf&W.]
Flamm, Matthew A., (AV) '53 '78 C.597 B.A. L.276 J.D. [Flamm&T.]

Flamm & Teibloom, Ltd., (AV)
20 North Clark Street, 22nd Floor, 60602
Telephone: 312-236-8400 Telecopier: 312-236-7660
Email: ft@flamm.com URL: http://www.flamm.com
Matthew A. Flamm; Joel D. Teibloom; John W. Stanko, Jr.;—Emmett R. McCarthy; Jose Moya; Natalie P. Nimerala. Of Counsel: Richard Orlikoff; William M. Laytin; Henry W. Kenoe (1907-1998); Arnold M. Flamm (1925-1998).
Organization, Acquisition, Representation and Sale of Businesses. Real Estate and Financial Transactions, Health Care Law and Regulation, Hospitals, Business, Real Estate and Insurance Litigation, Securities Law and Litigation, Antitrust and Trade Regulation, Federal, State and Local Taxation, Real Estate Tax Sale and Tax Deed Matters, Probate and Estate Planning.

See Professional Biographies, CHICAGO, ILLINOIS

Flanagan, Kathy M. '52 '79 C.999 B.A. L.365 J.D. Cir. J.
Flanagan, Kathy M. '68 '93 C&L.228 B.A., J.D. Cir. J.
Flanagan, Keith G. '73 '98 C.276 B.A. L.94 J.D.
(adm. in MA; not adm. in IL) [Clausen M.]
Flanagan, Lisa Najem '63 '90 C.607 B.A. L.146 J.D. CNA Plaza
Flanagan, Robert P. '65 '90 C.339 B.A. L.146 J.D. [Seyfarth S.]
Flanagan, Thomas D., (AV) '37 '63 C.424 B.S. L.146 J.D. [Flanagan //B.]
Flanagan, Thomas F. '53 '78 C&L.209 B.S.C., J.D.
V.P. & Dep. Gen. Coun., Natl. Equity Fund, Inc.

Flanagan / Bilton, (AV)
200 East Randolph Drive, Suite 6900, 60601
Telephone: 312-782-5000 Fax: 312-565-0821
URL: http://www.flanaganbilton.com
Members of Firm: Thomas D. Flanagan; Dean H. Bilton. Associate: Huan D. Cassioppi Tran.
National Practice Limited to Real Estate Taxation. Ad Valorem Tax Law. Personal Property Tax Law.

See Professional Biographies, CHICAGO, ILLINOIS

Flanigan, Stacy J. '— '02 C.425 B.A. L.146 J.D. [Winston&S.]
Flanigon, Thomas S. '— '93 C.174 B.A. L.362 J.D. [Adler,M.&M.]
Flannery, James P., Jr. '50 '76 C.46 B.A. L.365 J.D. Cir. J.
Flannery, John F., (AV) '28 '59
C.339 B.S.E.E. L.424 J.D. [Fitch,E.T.&F.] (See Pat. Sect.)
Flannigan, Ellen L. '59 '88 C.63 B.S. L.425 J.D. [Mora,B.W.&U.]
Flannigan, John Henry '52 '82 C.602 A.B. L.209 J.D. 4706 N. Kelso Ave.
Flannigan, Thomas W., Law Offices of '52 '83
C.93 B.A. L.209 J.D. 70 West Madison Street Suite 5330
Flatley, James L. '47 '76 C.746 B.A. L.365 J.D. [Seyfarth S.]
Flaum, Delilah B., (AV) '53 '80 C.276 B.S.F.S. L.146 J.D. [Mayer,B.R.&M.]
Flaum, Joel M. '36 '63 C.867 B.A. L.597 J.D. U.S. Cir. J., Ct. of App.
Flaum, Jonathan I. '65 '93 C.276 B.A. L.597 J.D. Navigant Consulting, Inc.
Flax, Karen Hilary '57 '84 C.1275 B.A. L.472 J.D. Asst. Gen. Coun., Tribune Co.
Flaxman, Kenneth D. '66 '93 C.188 B.S. L.146 J.D. [E.T.Joyce&Assoc.]
Flaxman, Kenneth N., (AV) '48 '72 C.563 B.E.E. L.146 J.D. [K.N.Flaxman]

Flaxman, Kenneth N., P.C., (AV)
Suite 1240, 200 South Michigan Avenue, 60604
Telephone: 312-427-3200 Fax: 312-427-3930
Email: knf@kenlaw.com URL: http://www.kenlaw.com
Kenneth N. Flaxman.
Civil Rights Law. Federal Civil Litigation (Trial and Appellate).

See Professional Biographies, CHICAGO, ILLINOIS

Flaynik, Donald G., Jr. '52 '80 C.339 B.S.E.E. L.146 J.D.
[Cherskov&F.] (See Pat. Sect.)
Flayton, Donald, (AV) '47 '72 C.665 B.A. L.597 J.D. [Wildman,H.A.&D.]
Fleck, Christopher R. '78 '04 C.210 B.A. L.879 J.D. [J.S.Rothman&Assoc.]
Fleetwood, Robert M. '72 '98 C.477 B.A. L.597 J.D. [Barack F.K.P.&N.]
Fleischaker, Joseph '36 '62 C.363 B.S. L.209 J.D. 4801 W. Peterson Ave.
Fleischer, Adam H. '68 '94 C&L.339 B.S., J.D. [Bates&C.]
Fleischer, Cary S., (AV) '50 '76 C.910 B.A. L.365 J.D. [Chuhak&T.]
Fleischer, Larry L. '42 '65 C.339 L.209 J.D. 205 W. Randolph
Fleischman, Bernard '11 '40 C.339 L.365 LL.B. 25 E. Washington
Fleischman, Marshall A. '37 '60 C.338 B.S. L.209 J.D. [Rubin&N.]
Fleischmann, Simon A. '75 '01 C.608 B.A. L.107 J.D. [Lord,B.&B.]
Fleisher, Jonathan B. '70 '95 C.823 B.S. L.209 J.D. [Karlin&F.]
Fleisher, Lynn D. '47 '86 C.102 B.A. L.912 J.D. [Sidley A.B.&W.]
Fleisher, Richard S., (AV) '37 '62 C.339 B.A. L.209 J.D. [Karlin&F.]
Fleisher, Ronald G., (AV) '39 '66 C.339 B.S. L.209 J.D. [Karlin&F.]
Fleishman, Andrew T. '68 '01 C.569 B.A. L.146 J.D.
[Cassiday,S.&G.] (⊙Libertyville)
Fleishmann, Jeffrey K. '68 '02 C.846 B.A. L.836 J.D.
(adm. in TN; not adm. in IL) [Goldberg,K.B.B.R.&M.]
Flemenbaum, Arieh M. '71 '96 C&L.861 B.A., J.D. [Griffith&J.]
Fleming, Annaliese F. '73 '99 C.966 B.A. L.597 J.D. [Barack F.K.P.&N.]
Fleming, David S. '55 '81 C.597 B.A. L.339 J.D. [Brinks H.G.&L.]
Fleming, Joan M. '33 '62 C.504 A.B. L.146 J.D. 300 N. State St.‡
Fleming, Laurel L. '59 '88
C.957 B.B.A. L.145 J.D. Northwestern Medical Faculty Found., Inc.
Fleming, P. Andrew, (AV) '58 '82 L.146 J.D. [Novack&M.]
Fleming, Susan '72 '01 Pros. Atty., Cook Co. State's Atty's Off.
Fleming, Susan G. '47 '79 C.966 B.A. L.365 J.D. Circuit Ct of Cook County
Flentye, Homer H. '10 '46 C&L.597 B.S.C., J.D. 7703 Sheridan Rd.
Flerlage, Joseph W. '— '00
C.339 B.S.E.E. L.209 J.D. [Brinks H.G.&L.] (See Pat. Sect.)
Flesch, James A., (Ltd.), (AV) '55 '80 C&L.339 B.S., J.D. [Gordon,G.F.&R.]
Fleske, Wendy A. '— '04 C.197 A.B. L.1066 J.D. [Kirkland&E.]
Flessner, Mark A., (AV) '54 '87 C.339 B.A. L.209 J.D. [Sonnenschein N.&R.]
Fletchall, Jennifer M. '78 '04 C.339 B.S. L.365 J.D. [Levin&B.]
Fletcher, Catherine L. '67 '94 C.966 B.S. L.1003 J.D. [Patterson]
Fletcher, James A., Law Office of '49 '74
C.597 B.S. L.813 J.D. 29 N. Wacker Dr., Ste. 920
Fletcher, James L., (AV) '43 '68 C.424 B.S. L.597 J.D. [Hinshaw&C.]
Fletcher, Kenneth L., (AV) '47 '76 C.339 B.A. L.146 J.D. Atty. Supvr., Pub. Def. Off.
Fletcher, Selvyn W. '72 '97 C.597 B.S. L.178 J.D. [Grippo&E.]
Fletcher, Tracey L. '62 '87 C&L.477 A.B., J.D. Coun., Edelman Publ Rel. Worldwide
Fliegel, Jason B. '74 '99 C.893 B.A. L.145 J.D. [Mayer,B.R.&M.]
Fligel Cochrane, Kristen E., (BV) '— '92 C.347 B.A. L.801 J.D. [Holland&K.]
Flight, James A. '66 '92 C&L.597 B.S.E.E., J.D. [Grossman&F.] (Pat.)
Flom, Barbara M., (AV) '56 '87 C.597 L.145 J.D. [Goldberg,K.B.B.R.&M.]
Flom, Erik B. '63 '98 C.323 B.S. L.597 J.D. [Welsh&K.] (See Pat. Sect.)
Flomenhoft, Michael A. '68 '94 C.352 B.A. L.339 J.D. [Winston&S.]
Flood, Brian T. '— '00 C.966 B.S. L.823 J.D. [O'Hagan,S.&A.]
Flood, Carie-Megan A. '78 '03 C.602 B.B.A. L.352 J.D. [Lord,B.&B.]
Flood, Mary Patricia '54 '82 C.959 B.S. L.209 J.D. [Sidley A.B.&W.]
Flood, Vincent P., Jr. '46 '75 C.363 B.S. L.146 J.D. Sr. Corp. Coun., USG Corp.
Flores, Kirk P. '58 '85 C&L.352 B.B.A., J.D.
Sr. V.P., ABN AMRO North America, Inc.
Flores, Noemi '— '00 C.309 A.B. L.178 J.D. [Gardner C.&D.]
Florey, Kenneth M. '67 '92 C.339 B.A. L.209 J.D. [Robbins,S.N.L.&T.]
Florian, Kurt W., Jr., (AV) '59 '84 C.145 A.B. L.228 J.D. [Katten M.R.]
Floriano, William J., II, (AV) '58 '83 C.602 B.A. L.424 J.D. [Clausen M.]
Florsheim, Steven C. '65 '91 C.976 B.A. L.477 J.D. [Sperling&S.]
Flosi, Lyndon M. '60 '85 C.209 B.A. L.365 J.D. [Hinshaw&C.]
Flowers, Kevin M. '— '97 C&L.608 B.S., J.D. [Marshall,G.&B.] (See Pat. Sect.)
Flowers, Maribeth, (BV) '57 '88 C.347 B.S. L.209 J.D. Asst. Corp. Coun.
Floyd, Mason N. '79 '04 C.210 B.A. L.1119 J.D. [Martin,B.&S.]
Floyd, Misti H. '77 '02 C.1081 B.S. L.146 J.D. [Swanson,M.&B.]
Fluxgold, Cindy G., (AV) '55 '79 C.339 B.A. L.46 J.D. [Goldstein&F.]
Flynn, Christopher W. '— '84 C.373 B.A. L.94 J.D. [Jones D.]
Flynn, David J., (AV) '— '90 C.927 B.A. L.210 J.D. [Querrey&H.]
Flynn, Edward John '64 '90
C.339 B.A. L.209 J.D. Staff Atty., Attys. Title Guaranty Fund, Inc.
Flynn, George K. '— '97 C.338 B.S. L.1187 J.D. [Clausen M.]
Flynn, James M. '67 '95 C.424 B.B.A. L.146 J.D.
Staff Atty., Chicago Board Options Exchange, Incorporated
Flynn, Janet A. '73 '99 C&L.602 B.A., J.D. [Bollinger,R.&G.]

Flynn, Jodi L. ....'66 '96 C.742 B.A. L.209 J.D. [Ⓐ Davis M.]
Flynn, John L., (AV) .... '30 '55 C&L.597 B.S.B.A., J.D. 180 N. LaSalle Street
Flynn, Karin Jagel .... '54 '82 C.881 A.B. L.30 J.D. [Vedder,P.K.&K.]

Flynn, Kevin M., & Associates, (AV) '53 '78 C.210 B.A. L.209 J.D.
77 West Wacker Drive Suite 4800, 60601
Telephone: 312-456-0240 Fax: 312-444-1028 URL: http://www.Kevinflynnlaw.com
Email: kevin@kmflynnlaw.com URL: http://www.Kevinflynnlaw.com
Trial Practice in all State and Federal Courts and all Alternative Dispute Resolution Forums. Substantive litigation experience includes Antitrust and Trade Regulation, Banking, Complex Business and Commercial, Chancery and Equity, Employment, Franchise, Information Technology, Real Estate, Litigation, Securities, Trade Secrets, White Collar Criminal, Arbitration and Mediation.
See Professional Biographies, CHICAGO, ILLINOIS

Flynn, Michael C. '55 '81 C.347 B.A. L.228 J.D.
(adm. in CA; not adm. in IL)
General Litigation Counsel, Chicago Title Insurance Company
Flynn, Peter, (AV) ....'42 '69 C.309 B.A. L.976 LL.B. Chancery Div.
Flynn, Susan Conley ....'— '94 C.1119 B.A. L.365 J.D. [Ⓒ Cohen,G.&R.]
Flynn, Thomas J., (AV) ....'41 '74 C.999 A.B. L.424 J.D. 190 S. LaSalle St.
Foale, William E. '57 '84 C.744 B.B.A. L.910 J.D.
Mng. Dir., Forensic & Investigative Servs., KPMF Peat Marwick, LLP
Fochler, Craig Steven ....'46 '71 C.388 B.A. L.597 J.D. [Wildman,H.A.&D.]
Foerster, Arthur F. .... '— '00 C.98 B.S. L.1494 J.D. [Ⓐ Latham&W.]
Fogarty, John G., Jr. ....'69 '99 C.597 B.S. L.146 J.D. [Ⓐ Burke,W.M.&S.]
Fogarty, Michael J., (AV) '43 '69
C&L.424 B.B.A., J.D. General Counsel, Tempel Steel Company
Fogel, Eric M. ....'55 '87 C.668 B.A. L.577 J.D. [Schuyler,R.&Z.]
Fogel, Joseph L. ....'— '86 C.112 B.A. L.209 J.D. [Freeborn&P.]
Fogel, Richard M., (AV) .... '55 '80 C.597 B.S. L.339 J.D. [Ⓒ Shaw G.F.G.W.&T.]
Fohrman, Donald W. .... '45 '70 C.339 B.S. L.424 J.D. [D.Fohrman&Assoc.]
Fohrman, Monica M. '49 '74 C.339 B.A. L.178 J.D.
Sr. V.P., Gen. Coun. & Secy., R. R. Donnelley & Sons Company (Legal Department)
Fohrman, Donald, & Associates .... 101 W. Grand, Ste. 500
Fokuo, Patricia J. ....'— '02 C.303 B.A. L.209 J.D. [Ⓐ Schiff H.]
Foley, Elizabeth Pfeiler, (AV) ....'60 '85 C.228 A.B. L.966 J.D. [Seyfarth S.]
Foley, Erin Dougherty ....'65 '99 C.436 B.S. L.146 J.D. [Ⓐ Littler M.]
Foley, F. James, Jr., (AV) .... '42 '67 C.276 B.S. L.424 J.D. [F.J.Foley,Jr.]
Foley, James R. .... '69 '95 C.339 B.S. L.365 J.D. [Trexler,B.G.B.&M.] (See Pat. Sect.)
Foley, John J. .... '48 '73 C.93 A.B. L.597 J.D. [Maurides&F.]
Foley, John M., (BV) ....'67 '92 C.339 B.S. L.209 J.D. [Spellmire&S.]
Foley, Katherine ....'66 '91 C.339 B.A. L.424 J.D. [Ⓐ Hinshaw&C.]
Foley, Kevin M., (AV) ....'— '72 [Ⓒ Ungaretti&H.]
Foley, Michael J. .... '53 '80 C.597 B.A. L.209 J.D. [Foley&F.]
Foley, Michael T. ....'67 '95 C.209 B.S. L.146 J.D. [Ⓐ Katten M.R.]
Foley, Scot J. '70 '04 C.1019 B.A. L.262 J.D.
(adm. in NY; not adm. in IL) [Ⓐ Vedder,P.K.&K.]
Foley, F. James, Jr., Chartered, (AV) ....221 N. La Salle St.
Foley & Foley ....9644 South Hamilton Avenue

Foley & Lardner LLP, (AV) BR
321 North Clark, Suite 2800, 60610 ⊙
Telephone: 312-832-4500 Fax: 312-832-4700
Email: webmaster@foley.com URL: http://www.foley.com
Partners: Lisa J. Acevedo; G. Peter Albert, Jr.; Michael G. Bailey; Sharon R. Barner; Wesley N. Becker; Stephen P. Bedell; Myles D. Berman; Laura L. Bilas; Richard Bromley; John T. Brooks; R. Lee Christie; Michael M. Conway; Elizabeth L. Corey; Dewey B. Crawford; James D. Dasso; Pauline E. Doohan; Bruce W. Doughty; Scott E. Early; Kevin J. Egan; Fredric J. Entin; Bennett L. Epstein; Jay Erens; Frederick L. Feldkamp; John N. Gavin; Diane Gianos; Jeanne M. Gills; Phillip M. Goldberg; George R. Goodman; David B. Goroff; Edward J. Green; Byron L. Gregory; Paul F. Hanzlik; James R. Hellige; Wm. Carlisle Herbert; Marianne Craigmile Holzhall; Heidi H. Jeffery; Dean M. Jeske; C. Richard Johnson; Bryan T. D. Jung; Glen H. Kanwit; Christopher N. Knight; Thomas P. Krebs; John R. Landis; John D. Lien; J. Craig Long; Mary Kay McCalla Martire; Edwin D. Mason; John W. McCaffrey; William J. McKenna, Jr.; William G. McMaster, Jr.; Gerald J. Neal; Gregory S. Norrod; Wayne F. Osoba; James D. Ossyra; John B. Palmer III; Kathleen R. Pasulka-Brown; Todd B. Pfister; Richard J. Phelan; Mark L. Prager; John P. Ratnaswamy; Michael D. Rechtin; Daniel S. Reinberg; E. Glenn Rippie; John L. Rogers, III; Charles P. Sheets; George T. Simon; Michael J. Small; Jeffrey A. Soble; Robert M. Stephenson; Kathryn M. Trkla; Robert J. Vechiola; William C. Weinsheimer; Tracy D. Williams; Michael H. Woolever (P.C.); John F. Zabriskie; Janet E. Zeigler; Christopher W. Zibart; Robert J. Zimmerman. Retired Partner: Stephen M. Slavin. Of Counsel: Michael K. Cavanaugh (P.C.); Sheldon Karon; Jay A. Steinberg; Helen L. Toal. Senior Counsel: Jonathan E. Aberman; Andrea M. Augustine; Melissa C. Brown; Adrian R. Cyhan; Cynthia A. Fonner; LaDale K. George; Steven Gerenraich; Jill L. Murch; Catherine B. Nelson; Richard L. Prebil; Gary S. Rovner; Lisa L. Tharpe; Dean M. Victor; Samantha E. Weissbluth; Ellen M. Wheeler. Special Counsel: Christine Gustafson; Miki V. Tesija. Associates: Erika A. Alley; Thomas K. Anderson; Michael S. Baig; Heidi L. Belongia; Martin J. Bishop; Jason A. Bremer; Marshall J. Brown; James F. Cirincione; Daniel A. Dingerson; Anders W. Franzon; Geoffrey S. Goodman; Jason J. Keener (Not admitted in IL); Kelly L. Koeppl; Joanne Lee; Joseph J. Lotus; Matthew E. Martin; Michael J. McMorrow; David A. Moore; Belinda S. Morgan; Sharon C. Nelson; Amy P. Purcell; David P. Resnick; Reagen C. Robbins Atwood; Michael S. Shapiro; Katherine Ann Siddon O'Brien; Jonathan R. Spivey; Nathaniel L. Strup; Mona Thakkar; Michael P. Tomlinson; Frances "Alexis" Tretter; Karl W. Von Drathen; Christopher J. Werner; Derek L. Wright.
General Practice. Bankruptcy and Insolvency, Domestic and International Patent, Trademark and Copyright, Corporate Law and Taxation, Corporate Securities, Broker/dealer matters, Commodities, Real Estate, Government Finance, Banking and Commercial Finance, Litigation, International and Health Law.
Los Angeles, California Office: 2029 Century Park East, 35th Floor. Telephone: 310-277-2223. Fax: 310-557-8475.
Palo Alto Office: 1530 Page Mill Road. Telephone: 650-856-3700. Facsimile: 650-856-3710.
Sacramento, California Office: 1215 K Street, Suite 1920. Telephone: 916-443-8005. Fax: 916-443-2240.
San Diego, California Office: 402 West Broadway, 23rd Floor. Telephone: 619-234-6655. Fax: 619-234-3510.
San Diego/North County, California Office: 11250 El Camino Real, Suite 200. Telephone: 858-847-6700. Facsimile: 858-792-6773.
San Francisco, California Office: One Maritime Plaza, Sixth Floor. Telephone: 415-434-4484. Fax: 415-434-4507.
Washington, D.C. Office: Washington Harbour, Suite 500, 3000 K Street, N.W. Telephone: 202-672-5300. Facsimile: 202-672-5399.
Jacksonville, Florida Office: One Independent Drive, Suite 1300. Telephone: 904-359-2000. Facsimile: 904-359-8700.
Orlando, Florida Office: Suite 1800, 111 North Orange Avenue, P.O. Box 2193. Telephone: 407-423-7656. Facsimile: 407-648-1743.
Tallahassee, Florida Office: 106 East College Avenue, Highpoint Center, Suite 900, P.O. Box 1819. Telephone: 850-222-6100. Facsimile: 850-561-6475.
Tampa, Florida Office: Suite 2700, 100 N. Tampa Street, P.O. Box 3391. Telephones: 813-229-2300; Pinellas County: 813-442-3296. Facsimile: 813-221-4210.
West Palm Beach, Florida Office: 777 South Flagler Drive, Suite 901, West Tower. Telephone: 561-655-5050. Facsimile: 561-655-6925.
Tokyo, Japan Office: JT Building 15F, 2-2-1 Toranomon Minato-ku, Tokyo, 105-0001. Telephone: +81 (03) 5114-8320. Facsimile: +81 (03) 5114-8321.
Detroit, Michigan Office: One Detroit Center, 500 Woodward Avenue, Suite 2700. Telephone: 313-234-7100. Fax: 313-234-2800.
New York, New York Office: 90 Park Avenue. Telephone: 212-682-7474. Facsimile: 212-687-2329; 212-490-3654.
Madison, Wisconsin Office: Verex Plaza, 150 East Gilman Street, P.O. Box 1497. Telephone: 608-257-5035. Facsimile: 608-258-4258.

(This Listing Continued)

Foley & Lardner LLP (Continued)
Milwaukee, Wisconsin Office: 777 East Wisconsin Avenue. Telephone: 414-271-2400. Facsimile: 414-297-4900.
Brussels, Belgium Office: Avenue de Cortenbergh, 118. Telephone: +011-32-2-639-2710. Facsimile: +011-32-2-646-0311.
Boston, Massachusetts Office: 111 Huntington Avenue. Telephone: 617-342-4000. Facsimile: 617-342-4001.
See Professional Biographies, CHICAGO, ILLINOIS

Folker, James K. ....'65 '96 C.705 B.S.M.E. L.146 J.D. [Ⓐ Greer,B.&C.] (Pat.)
Foltz, Patricia J., (AV) .... '— '82 C.33 B.S. L.209 J.D. [Anderson,R.]
Fondahn, Paul S. .... '— '04 C.880 B.A. L.178 J.D. [Ⓐ Kirkland&E.]
Fonner, Cynthia A. .... '— '92 C&L.1365 B.A., J.D. [Ⓒ Foley&L.]
Fontaine, Mary C. ....'56 '81 C.823 B.A. L.145 J.D. [Mayer,B.R.&M.]
Fontana, Lisa N. ....'— '02 C.473 B.A. L.424 J.D. [Ⓐ Clausen M.]
Fontoura, Lisa M. ....'71 '96 C.264 B.A. L.904 J.D. [Wildman,H.A.&D.]
Foody, Richard D. ....'54 '88 C.742 B.A. L.365 J.D. [Ⓐ Stellato&S.]
Foote, Edward L., (AV) ....'28 '55 C&L.309 A.B., LL.B. [Winston&S.]
Foote, Robert L., (AV) ....'14 '41 C.976 B.A. L.309 LL.B. 35 W. Wacker Dr.‡
Foradas, Michael P., (AV) .... '— '81 C.945 A.B. L.597 J.D. [Kirkland&E.]
Foran, John J., (AV) .... '52 '85 C.309 B.A. L.365 J.D. [Foran,O.&B.]
Foran, Michael L., (AV) ....'61 '85 C.165 B.A. L.424 J.D. [Foran G.P.&P.]
Foran, Thomas A., (AV) '24 '50
C.424 Ph.B. L.215 LL.B. Suite 3000, 30 North La Salle Street

Foran Glennon Palandech & Ponzi PC, (AV)
150 South Wacker Drive 11th Floor, 60606 ⊙
Telephone: 312-863-5000 Fax: 312-863-5099
URL: http://www.fgpp.com
Robert T. Boylan; George M. Ferreti; Michael L. Foran; James B. Glennon; Michael H. McColl; Mary C. O'Connor; Thomas B. Orlando; Douglas J. Palandech; Matthew S. Ponzi;—Brian T. Parsons; George Daniel Pilja; Ujjval K. Vyas; Jonathan Frawley Fiegen; Garrett P. Kern; John O'Grady; C. Zachary Ransel; Nizam Arain; Maura Yusof; Jason R. Williams. Of Counsel: Paul T. Lively. Senior Counsel: Kevin J. Glenn.
Civil Litigation, Property Insurance, Design Professional Liability, Construction Litigation, Products, Professional and Employment Liability, Bad Faith, Insurance Coverage Defense, Excess and Reinsurance, Subrogation and Liability Coverage.
Los Angeles, California Office: 12400 Wilshire Boulevard, 15th Floor, 90025. Telephone: 310-826-1810. Fax: 310-826-1821.
See Professional Biographies, CHICAGO, ILLINOIS

Foran, O'Toole & Burke LLC, (AV)
321 North Clark Street Suite 2450, 60610
Telephone: 312-644-1414 Facsimile: 312-644-1415
Email: attorneys@foblaw.com URL: http://www.foblaw.com
John J. Foran; Mark T. O'Toole; Stephen M. Burke.
Eminent Domain and Protection of Property Rights.
See Professional Biographies, CHICAGO, ILLINOIS

Forbes, Darrin S. .....'76 '01 C.589 B.S. L.339 J.D. Two North LaSalle Street, Suite 2200
Forbes, Steven H. ....'68 '97 C&L.966 B.B.A., J.D. [Ⓒ Skadden,A.S.M.&F.]
Forcade, Bill S., (AV) ....'46 '76 C.339 B.S. L.365 J.D. [Jenner&B.]
Ford, Derrick Maurice ....'61 '88 C.597 B.A. L.309 J.D. Northwestern Univ. Sch. of Law
Ford, Henry J., Jr. ....'77 '02 C.302 B.S. L.823 J.D. Staff Coun., BPI
Ford, James W. ....'49 '76 C&L.424 B.A., J.D. [Brenner,F.M.&S.]
Ford, Patricia Quinn ....'50 '78 C.352 B.A. L.424 J.D. [Ⓐ O'Keefe,L.&H.]
Ford, Robert C. '37 '63 C.228 A.B. L.16 J.D.
(adm. in AL; not adm. in IL) 941 W. Lawrence Ave.‡
Forde, Brian P. .... '71 '97 C.589 B.S. L.209 J.D. [Ⓐ O'Keefe,L.&H.]
Forde, Janice R. ....'43 '84 C.999 B.A. L.424 J.D. [Ⓐ K.M.Forde]
Forde, Kevin M., (AV) ....'38 '63 C.436 B.S. L.424 J.D. [K.M.Forde]
Forde, Michael K. ....'72 '96 C&L.276 A.B., J.D. [Mayer,B.R.&M.]

Forde, Kevin M., Ltd., (AV)
Suite 1100, 111 West Washington Street, 60602
Telephone: 312-641-1441 Fax: 312-641-1288
Kevin M. Forde;—Janice R. Forde; Kevin R. Malloy; Joanne Rouzan Driscoll; Melissa Guinta.
Trials and Appeals. Commercial Litigation, Constitutional Law, Class Actions, Business Torts, Products Liability, Antitrust, Securities Law, Chancery Practice, State and Local Taxation.
See Professional Biographies, CHICAGO, ILLINOIS

Forde O'Meara, Maura ....'76 '01 C.276 B.A. L.424 J.D. [Ⓐ Bell,B.&L.]
Fordyce, Gary K. '— '85 C.352 B.B.A. L.145 J.D.
Sr. Atty., ABN-AMRO North America, Inc. (Legal Department)
Foreman, Bradley H. ....'59 '85 C.477 B.A. L.365 J.D. [B.H.Foreman]
Foreman, Jerome ....'34 '62 C.1016 A.B. L.365 LL.B. [Foreman&F.]
Foreman, Lester D. ....'28 '53 C.1016 B.A. L.146 J.D. Cir. J.
Foreman, Bradley H., Law Offices of, P.C. .... 6914 W. North Ave.
Foreman & Foreman, Ltd. ....158 W. Erie St.
Forester, Aaron M. ....'— '04 C.939 B.A. L.597 J.D. [Ⓐ Schiff H.]
Forester, Laura E. ....'65 '91 C.945 B.A. L.146 J.D. Asst. State's Atty.
Forgue, David G. ....'71 '96 C&L.339 B.A., J.D. [Barnes,R.&C.]
Forkins, James M., (AV) ....'18 '47 C.215 Ph.B. L.477 J.D. 2306 N. Central Park‡
Formeller, Daniel R., (AV) .... '49 '76 C.339 B.A. L.209 J.D. [Tressler,S.M.&P.]
Formolo, Lisa M. ....'— '05 C&L.477 B.A., J.D. [Ⓐ Gardner C.&D.]
Formusa, S. Joseph, (AV) ....'32 '57 33 N. La Salle St.
Fornelli, Anthony J. ....'33 '60 2003 W. Grand Ave.
Forrer, Robert F., (AV) ....'45 '70 C.209 B.A. L.597 J.D. [Quarles&B.]
Forrester, J. Paul ....'53 '78 C&L.999 B.A., LL.B. [Mayer,B.R.&M.]
Fors, Judith E. ....'53 '78 C.597 B.A. L.424 J.D. [Ⓒ J.S.Ring&Assoc.]
Forsythe, Amy I. ....'67 '92 C.893 B.A. L.424 J.D. Sr. Coun., Bank One
Forsythe, Clarke D. ....'58 '83 C.25 B.A. L.879 J.D. Pres., Americans United for Life
Fort, Jeffrey C., (AV) ....'50 '75 C.504 B.A. L.597 J.D. [Sonnenschein N.&R.]
FortCamp, James R., (AV) ....'— '87 C&L.339 B.S., J.D. [Seyfarth S.]
Forte, Monica A. ....'66 '94 C.339 B.A. L.424 J.D. [Ⓐ Bischoff]
Forti, Michael A., (AV) ....'54 '80 C.273 B.A. L.597 J.D. Chf. Asst. Corp. Coun.
Fortini-Campell, Alan ....'54 '83 C.608 B.A. L.424 J.D. 69 W. Washington St.‡
Foss, Philip M. ....'42 '75 C.98 A.B. L.424 J.D. [Ⓒ Pfeiffer&A.]
Fossland, Jennifer M. ....'61 '88 C.957 B.A. L.966 J.D. 203 N. La Salle St., Suite 1800
Foster, Arthur L. ....'14 '38 C&L.424 J.D. 310 S. Michigan Ave.
Foster, Benjamin R. ....'66 '98 C.604 B.A. L.309 J.D. [Ⓐ Skadden,A.S.M.&F.]
Foster, David S., (AV) ....'— '85 C.674 A.B. L.976 J.D. [Latham&W.]
Foster, George W. ....'51 '82 C.339 B.A. L.424 J.D. Asst. Atty. Gen.
Foster, Howard W. ....'62 '89 C.1016 B.A. L.94 J.D. [Johnson&B.]
Foster, James A., (AV) ....'57 '83 C.477 B.A. L.339 J.D. [Cassiday,S.&G.]
Foster, James R. ....'30 '55 C.856 B.A. L.976 J.D. 401 N. Michigan Ave.
Foster, Lemuel L., Jr. ....'21 '49 C.563 B.S. L.178 LL.B. 1525 E. 53rd. St.‡
Foster, Leonard N., (AV) ....'31 '63 C.46 B.S. L.209 J.D. Asst. State's Atty.
Foster, Margaret Marie ....'— '88 C&L.45 B.A., J.D. [McKenna S.]
Foster, Michael D. ....'— '98 C.473 B.A. L.424 J.D. [Kirkland&E.]
Foster, Michele L. ....'— '99 C.763 B.A. L.424 J.D. [Ⓐ Freeborn&P.]

Foster, Nabil G. ..... '— '01 C.309 A.B. L.597 J.D. 180 North La Salle Street, Suite 3400
Foster, Richard B., III, (AV) .... '58 '84 C.597 B.S. L.339 J.D. [Donohue B.M.&S.]
Foster, Teree E., (AVⓉ) .... '47 '76 C.339 B.A. L.424 J.D. 25 E. Jackson, Rm. 931
Foudree, Bruce W. .... '47 '72 C&L.221 B.A., J.D. [Ⓒ Lord,B.&B.]
Foundos, Felice R. .... '— '90 C.424 B.B.A. L.602 J.D. [Chapman&C.]
Fournier, David B. .... '— '03 C.393 B.A. L.209 J.D. [Ⓐ Mayer,B.R.&M.] (Pat.)
Fournier, Julie .... '— '99 C.475 B.S. L.209 J.D. [Ⓐ Grotefeld&D.]
Fowerbaugh, Albert E., Jr. .... '64 '89 C.385 A.B. L.477 J.D. [Lord,B.&B.]
Fowkes, Scott W., (AV) .... '— '88 C.188 B.A. L.477 J.D. [Kirkland&E.]
Fowler, Christopher S. .... '— '03 C&L.190 B.A., J.D. [Ⓐ Crowley&L.]
Fowler, Don W., (AV) .... '44 '69 C.1365 B.A. L.145 J.D. [Lord,B.&B.]
Fowler, Jeffrey S., (AV) .... '59 '91 C.326 B.S. L.1000 J.D. [Laner,M.D.B.L.&T.]
Fowler, Philip J., (AV) .... '61 '86 C.602 B.A. L.424 J.D. [Hubert&F.]
Fowler, W. Craig, (AV) .... '52 '78 C.602 B.B.A. L.597 J.D. [O'Rourke,H.F.&D.]
Fowlkes, Norman T., III '47 '77 C.893 B.A. L.692 J.D.
(adm. in VA; not adm. in IL) Princ., Mellon, Inc.
Fox, Ariel A. .... '— '98 C.477 A.B. L.976 J.D. [Kirkland&E.]
Fox, Bruce A., (AV) .... '57 '81 C.339 B.S.B.A. L.477 J.D. [Neal,G.&E.]
Fox, Charles P. .... '61 '86 C.910 B.A. 20 N. Clark St., Ste. 1725
Fox, Corey D. .... '— '04 C.477 B.A. L.597 J.D. [Ⓐ Kirkland&E.]
Fox, David L. .... '61 '88 C.867 B.A. L.209 J.D. 4337 N. Claremont
Fox, David W. '59 '84 C&L.362 B.B.A., J.D.
(adm. in FL; not adm. in IL) Mgn. Editor
Fox, Dennis J. .... '30 '57 C&L.966 B.S., J.D. [Ⓒ Lord,B.&B.]
Fox, Elaine S., (AV) .... '— '75 C.597 B.S. L.146 J.D. [Seyfarth S.]
Fox, Etha Beatrice .... '14 '39 C.137 B.A. L.146 LL.B. 400 E. Randolph St.
Fox, Felicia M. .... '— '93 Staff Atty., NASD Dispute Resolution, Inc.
Fox, Gary J., (AV) .... '57 '84 C.1016 B.A. L.209 J.D. [Katten M.R.]
Fox, Gerard .... '52 '79 C.339 B.A. L.209 J.D. Asst. Gen. Coun., Peoples Energy Corp.
Fox, H. James, (AV) .... '43 '68 C.388 B.A. L.339 J.D. [Quarles&B.]
Fox, Horace, Jr., (AV) .... '48 '76 C.187 B.A. L.209 J.D. [Lehman&F.]
Fox, James F. '44 '74 C.436 B.A. L.339 J.D.
Reg. Coun. - Asia/Pacific, Rohm & Haas Co.
Fox, James L., (AV) .... '20 '56 C&L.424 B.S., J.D. [Ⓒ Abramson&F.]
Fox, Joseph P. .... '66 '95 C.339 B.S. L.146 J.D. [Ⓐ Greer,B.&C.] (Pat.)
Fox, Kathy Pinkstaff, (AV) .... '42 '79 C.210 B.A. L.597 J.D. [Wildman,H.A.&D.]
Fox, Michael E., (AV) .... '38 '62 C.339 B.S. L.309 J.D. [Fox,H.S.L.&C.]
Fox, Paul T., (AV) .... '53 '78 C&L.597 B.A., J.D. [Greenberg T.]
Fox, Ryan .... '— '04 C.477 L.S.A. L.339 J.D. [Ⓐ Henderson&L.]
Fox, Shayle P., (AV) .... '34 '57 C.339 B.S. L.209 J.D. [Holland&K.]
Fox, Sherryl Ann .... '44 '93 C.209 B.H.A. L.146 J.D. 69 West Washington
Fox, Terry A. .... '— '91 C.350 B.A. L.352 J.D. [McKenna S.]
Fox, Wendy D. '62 '87 C.477 B.A. L.910 J.D.
Atty. Advisor, U.S. Secs. and Exchange Comm.
Fox, William C., III .... '58 '83 C.103 A.B. L.209 J.D. General Growth Properties, Inc.

Fox, Hefter, Swibel, Levin & Carroll, LLP, (AV) BR
321 North Clark Street, Suite 3300, 60610
Telephone: 312-224-1200 Facsimile: 312-224-1201
URL: http://www.fhslc.com
Martin B. Carroll; Michael E. Fox; Roger B. Harris; Daniel S. Hefter; Joseph C. Huntzicker; Howard L. Kastel; Tracy E. Katz; Maria L. King; Laurie A. Levin; David J. Morris; William J. Peltin; Richard L. Sandler; Amanda A. Schwob; Yuri M. Shidenko (Not admitted in IL); David B. Singer; Lawrence B. Swibel; Dale B. Tauke; Robin L. Wolkoff.
Business Transactions, Business Litigation and Real Estate Practice.
See Professional Biographies, CHICAGO, ILLINOIS

Foye, Stephanie A. '59 '85 C.713 B.A. L.1035 J.D.
(adm. in MN; not adm. in IL) Aon Re Inc.
Fradin, Gerald E., (AV) .... '65 '90 C.339 A.B. L.659 J.D. [Sonnenschein N.&R.]
Fradin, Scott R. .... '64 '96 C.339 B.S. L.146 J.D. [Stein,R.&H.]
Fraenkel, Charles M. .... '48 '73 C.679 B.S. L.1119 J.D. [Leahy,E.&F.]

Fragomen, Del Rey, Bernsen & Loewy, LLP
200 West Jackson Boulevard, Suite 1800, 60606 ⊙
Telephone: 312-263-6101 Facsimile: 312-346-1970
URL: http://www.fragomen.com
Michael F. Turansick (Not admitted in IL). Associates: Jill M. Guzman; Shayda A. Safapour; Cynthia L. Shearn; Caterina P. Tassone; Alexander C. Elsberg; Anna Morzy; Isabel A. Kugler (Not admitted in IL); Robert W. Krug; Maria Veniaminova. Senior Counsel: Ethan E. Bensinger. Counsel: Kevin C. Aiston.
Immigration; Visas; I-9 Compliance; Export Control; U.S. and Global Immigration and Nationality Law.
New York, New York Office: 515 Madison Avenue. Telephone: 212-688-8555. Facsimile: 212-758-7215; 212-319-5236.
Washington, D.C. Office: 1212 New York Avenue, N.W., Suite 850. Telephone: 202-223-5515. Facsimile: 202-371-2898.
Coral Gables, Florida Office: 241 Sevilla Avenue, Suite 802. Telephone: 305-774-5800. Facsimile: 305-774-6666.
San Francisco, California Office: 100 Spear Street, 10th Floor. Telephone: 415-986-1446. Facsimile: 415-986-7964.
Los Angeles, California Office: 12121 Wilshire Boulevard, Suite 1001. Telephone: 310-820-3322. Facsimile: 310-820-2702.
Santa Clara, California Office: 2804 Mission College Boulevard, 2nd Floor. Telephone: 408-919-0600. Facsimile: 408-919-0615.
Irvine, California Office: 18401 Von Karman Avenue, Suite 255. Telephone: 949-261-0209. Facsimile: 949-261-2821.
San Diego, California Office: 11238 El Camino Real, Suite 100. Telephone: 858-793-1600. Facsimile: 858-793-1686.
Stamford, Connecticut Office: One Atlantic Street. Telephone: 203-352-1871. Facsimile: 203-352-1874.
Iselin, New Jersey Office: 99 Wood Avenue South. Telephone: 732-906-1230. Facsimile: 732-906-9190.
Troy, Michigan Office: 2301 West Big Beaver Road, Suite 225. Telephone: 248-649-5404. Facsimile: 248-649-5121.
Dallas, Texas Office: 5000 Quorum Drive, Suite 215. Telephone: 972-233-6646. Facsimile: 972-233-3134.
Boston, Massachusetts Office: 31 Milk Street, Suite 201. Telephone: 617-574-0400. Facsimile: 617-574-0450.
Brussels, Belgium Office: Rue Des Colonies 11 1000 Brussels, Belgium. Telephone: 32-2 517 61-23. Fax: 32-2 517-65-92.
Singapore Office: Centennial Tower, Level 21 3 Temasek Avenue, Singapore 039190. Telephone: 65 6549-7284. Facsimile: 65 6549-7284.
Affiliated Offices:
Fragomen Australia: Waterfront Place Level 16, 1 Eagle Street, Brisbane, QLD 4000 Australia. Telephone: 61 7 3257 5177. Fax: 61 7 3257 8009.
Fragomen Australia: 215 Spring Street, Melbourne, VIC 3001 Australia. Telephone: 61 3 8603 3607. Fax: 61 3 8603 6347.
Fragomen Australia: Level 24 6 O'Connell Street Sydney, NSW 2000 Australia. Telephone: 61 2 8224 8555. Fax: 61 2 8224 8500.
Fragomen Great Britain: 75 Cannon Street, London EC4N 5BN. Telephone: 44 0 870 735 1490. Fax: 44 0 207 556 7001.
Fragomen Hong Kong: 1811, Level 18 One International Finance Centre 1 Harbour View Street, Central Hong Kong. Telephone: 852 2166 8660. Fax: 852 2166 8841.
See Professional Biographies, CHICAGO, ILLINOIS

Frakes, Aron J. .... '76 '02 C.350 B.S. L.339 J.D. [Ⓐ McDermott W.&E.]
France, F. Dennis .... '32 '57 C.339 B.S. L.209 J.D. 77 W. Wash. St.
Francesconi, Guy W. '59 '90 C.1031 B.A. L.1009 J.D.
Gen. Coun., Merrill Lynch Bus. Financial Servs., Inc.
Franch, Richard T., (AV) .... '42 '67 C.602 B.A. L.145 J.D. [Jenner&B.]
Franchetti, Daniel R. '55 '85 C.1151 B.S. L.365 J.D.
Mng. Dir., American Express Tax and Bus. Servs.
Francis, August J. .... '— '94 C.209 B.S. L.146 J.D. [Chapman&C.]
Francis, Leila T. .... '71 '97 C.339 B.S. L.209 J.D. [Ⓐ Madden,J.M.&S.]
Francis, Michelle A.H. .... '— '98 C.339 B.S. L.145 J.D. [Kirkland&E.]
Francke, Harold W., (AV) .... '52 '79 C.145 B.A. L.339 J.D. [DLPiper R.G.C.U.]
Franco, Cecilio L., IV .... '72 '00 C.800 B.S. L.146 J.D. [Ⓐ Johnson&B.]
Franco, Jennifer .... '73 '00 C.31 B.A. L.597 J.D. Asst. Gen. Coun., Exelon corp.
Franco, Ofelia C. '52 '80 C.339 B.A. L.209 J.D.
U.S. Dept. of H.& U.D., Assoc.Reg.Coun.
Franco, Robert J., II, (AV) .... '57 '84 C.801 B.A. L.146 J.D. [Bollinger,R.&G.]
Francoeur, Jocelyn D. .... '71 '02 C.597 B.A. L.569 J.D. [Ⓐ McDermott W.&E.]
Francque, James A. .... '— '96 C.589 B.S. L.424 J.D. [Ⓐ Jones D.]
Franczek, James C., Jr., (AV) .... '46 '71 C.602 A.B. L.145 J.D. [Franczek S.]

Franczek Sullivan P.C., (AV)
300 South Wacker Drive Suite 3400, 60606-6785
Telephone: 312-986-0300 FAX: 312-986-9192
URL: http://www.franczek.com
Shelli L. Anderson; Terrence T. Creamer; Anthony J. Crement; Ares G. Dalianis; Edward N. Druck; J. Todd Faulkner; James C. Franczek, Jr.; Ronald J. Hein, Jr.; Michael J. Hernandez; Darcy L. Kriha; Lisa A. McGarrity; Paul A. Millichap; Jeremy C. Moritz; David P. Radelet; John A. Relias; Michael I. Richardson; Charles P. Rose; Sally J. Scott; William R. Sullivan, Jr.; Andrea R. Waintroob; Michael A. Warner, Jr.; Patricia J. Whitten; James J. Zuehl;—Kristi L. Bowman; Brian P. Crowley; Dana Fattore Crumley; Scott Cruz; Paul A. Denham; Nora FitzGerald Meldrum; Whitnie D. Hardy; Julie Heuberger Yura; Karen K. Hynes; Kyle B. Johansen; Pamela P. Jones; D. Sanders Lowery; Andrew A. Malahowski; Timothy P. McGrory; Jeffrey S. Nowak; Julia K. Oltmanns; Corinne S. O'Melia; Steven J. Pearlman; Thomas J. Posey; Lisa M. Spiegler; Dawn M. Spivey; Anne E. Wilson-Lokken. Of Counsel: Wesley A. Wildman; Respicio F. Vazquez.
Labor and Employment, Employment Discrimination, Labor Relations, Employment Litigation, Collective Bargaining, Equal Opportunity Law, Employee Benefits, OSHA, Education Law, Public Employment Relations.
See Professional Biographies, CHICAGO, ILLINOIS

Franczyk, John A. .... '59 '87 C.688 B.S.Che. L.597 J.D. [Hussain E.B.&F.]
Franek, David M. .... '54 '80 C.659 B.A. L.228 J.D. [Shefsky&F.]
Frangias, John .... '61 '96 C.209 B.A. L.365 J.D. Co. Pub. Def.
Frank, David L. .... '73 '98 C.339 B.A. L.365 J.D. 2 E. 8th St.
Frank, Emily M. .... '76 '02 C.734 B.S. L.910 J.D. [Ⓐ Jenner&B.]
Frank, Henry S., (AV) .... '32 '57 C.221 B.A. L.209 J.D. [Ⓒ Laser,P.S.F.&E.]
Frank, Irving .... '12 '36 C.339 L.209 LL.B. 175 W. Jackson Blvd.
Frank, J. William, III .... '46 '73 C.401 B.S.Ch.E. L.276 J.D. [McCracken&F.] (Pat.)
Frank, Jay A., (AV) .... '43 '69 C&L.339 B.S., J.D. [Aronberg G.D.&G.]
Frank, Jeffrey H., (BV) .... '52 '80 C.429 B.A. L.494 J.D. [Ⓒ Patzik,F.&S.]
Frank, Jordan E. .... '79 '04 C.339 B.S. L.365 J.D. [Bollinger,R.&G.]
Frank, Joseph D. .... '64 '93 C.118 B.A. L.145 J.D. [Frank/ G.]
Frank, Maurice A., (AV) .... '10 '33 L.209 LL.B. 20 E. Jackson
Frank, Miriam J. .... '52 '80 C.66 B.A. L.477 J.D. Major, Lindsey & Africa
Franke, Jay R., (AV) .... '49 '75 C.31 B.A. L.966 J.D. 215 W. Illinois St.
Frankel, David J. .... '71 '96 C.378 B.A. L.146 J.D. 203 N. LaSalle St., Ste. 2350
Frankel, Frederick S. '66 '97 C.1122 B.S. L.146 J.D.
Asst. Gen. Coun., Illinois Dept. of Human Services
Frankel, Hillel .... '57 '93 C.339 B.A. L.209 J.D. [Entertainment]
Frankel, Nicole A. .... '76 '03 C&L.966 B.A., J.D. [Ⓐ Vedder,P.K.&K.]
Frankel, Scott J. .... '59 '85 C.604 A.B. L.608 J.D. [Frankel&C.]
Frankel, Ted M. .... '— '03 C.674 A.B. L.597 J.D. [Ⓐ Kirkland&E.]
Frankel, William H., (AV) '55 '80
C&L.861 B.S.M.E., J.D. [Brinks H.G.&L.] (See Pat. Sect.)
Frankel & Cohen, (AV) .... 77 West Washington Street, Suite 1711
Frankenstein, Robert R. .... '43 '68 C.966 B.S. L.597 J.D. [Goldberg&F.]

Frank/Gecker LLP, (AV) BR
325 N. LaSalle Street, Suite 625, 60610
Telephone: 312-276-1400 Fax: 312-276-0035
URL: http://www.fgllp.com
Joseph D. Frank; Frances Gecker; Michael J. Golde. Senior Counsel: Micah R. Krohn. Associate: Zane L. Zielinski. Of Counsel: Dwight B. Palmer.
Bankruptcy Litigation and Appeals, Creditors Rights, Valuation Disputes, Workouts, Preferential and Fraudulent Transfers, Officer and Director Liability and Contested Plan Confirmation, Asbestos and Mass Tort Bankruptcies, Financial Transactions, Distressed Debt and Asset Sales and Acquisitions, Trustee and Trust Representation and Preferential Transfer Litigation.
See Professional Biographies, CHICAGO, ILLINOIS

Franklin, Brian L. .... '75 '01 C.511 B.A. L.178 J.D. [Ⓐ Winston&S.]
Franklin, Charles R., (AV) .... '54 '80 C.477 A.B. L.472 J.D. 55 W. Monroe St., Ste. 3600
Franklin, Christine C. .... '49 '80 C.999 B.A. L.1068 J.D. [Ⓒ Neal,G.&E.]
Franklin, Giles A. .... '44 '74 C.339 B.A. L.477 J.D. 2548 N. Kedzie Blvd.
Franklin, Jamie S. .... '69 '97 C.228 B.A. L.145 J.D. [Ⓐ Meites,M.B.&M.]
Franklin, Joseph P. .... '64 '92 C.894 B.A. L.659 J.D. [Winston&S.]
Franklin, Phyllis K. .... '— '00 C.94 B.S. L.146 J.D. [Ⓐ Sinar K.M.&F.]
Franklin, Richard M. .... '47 '73 C.966 B.A. L.178 J.D. [Baker&M.]
Franks, Daniel L., (BV) .... '50 '75 C.966 B.A. L.209 J.D. 120 S. Riverside Plz., Ste. 1150
Franks, Nancy L. .... '57 '82 C.607 B.A. L.602 J.D. 188 W. Randolph St.
Fransene, Sarah Lynne .... '76 '01 C.339 B.S. L.146 J.D. 3350 N. Kenmore
Franson, Marc P. .... '— '80 C&L.221 B.S.B.A., J.D. [Chapman&C.]
Franson, Marilyn D., C.P.A. '60 '86 C.425 B.A. L.597 J.D.
Ass't Controller, Tax Dept., Amsted Industries
Frantzen, Sandra A. '74 '99 C.350 B.S. L.145 J.D.
[McAndrews,H.&M.] (See Pat. Sect.)
Franz, Michael T. .... '— '96 C.477 B.A. L.213 J.D. [Ⓐ Freeborn&P.] ‡
Franzen, William R. .... '71 '96 C.339 B.A. L.823 J.D. [McDermott W.&E.]
Franzetti, Susan M., (AV) .... '54 '79 C.597 B.A. L.424 J.D. [Franzetti]
Franzetti Law Firm P.C., (AV) .... 10 South LaSalle St., Suite 3600
Franzon, Anders W. .... '— '03 C.105 B.A. L.339 J.D. [Ⓐ Foley&L.]
Fraser, William Dean '62 '87 C.612 B.S. L.623 J.D.
(adm. in OK; not adm. in IL) F.B.I.
Fratantoni, Sam J. .... '57 '82 C&L.424 B.S., J.D. [A.B.Adler&Assoc.]
Fraterrigo, Fredrick J., (AV) .... '40 '69 C&L.209 B.S., J.D. [Fraterrigo,B.F.&K.]
Fraterrigo, Gregory J. .... '69 '97 C&L.209 B.S., J.D. [Ⓐ Fraterrigo,B.F.&K.]
Fraterrigo, Beranek, Feiereisel & Kasbohm, P.A., (AV) .... 55 W. Monroe Street
Fraumann, Willard G., (P.C.), (AV) .... '73 C.477 A.B. L.309 J.D. [Kirkland&E.]
Frazel, Jerome A., Jr., (AV) .... '26 '50 C&L.602 LL.B. 222 North La Salle St.‡
Frazen, Mitchell H., (AV) .... '— '80 C.339 B.A. L.477 J.D. [Litchfield C.]
Frazer, Quin R., (AV) .... '45 '75 C.999 B.A. L.602 J.D. [Gardner C.&D.]
Frazier, Douglas Lee .... '46 '74 C.103 A.B. L.472 J.D. 19 S. La Salle St.

Frazier, Joan F. ... '53 '84 C.30 B.A. L.424 J.D. Asst. State's Atty.
Frazier, William D. ... '55 '80 C.901 B.A. L.309 J.D. Asst. Atty. Gen.
Frazin, Irwin L., (AV) ... '38 '64 C.339 B.A. L.597 J.D. 2536 S. California Ave.
Frazin, Julian J. ... '30 '56 C.1016 B.A. L.597 J.D. [Ⓒ Michael B.&F.]
Frazin-Weiner, Barbara '48 '74 C.145 B.A. L.209 J.D.
Chf. Coun., Dept. of Alcoholism & Substance Abuse
Fredd, Anne L., (AV) ... '— '73 C.98 B.A. L.597 J.D. [Neal&L.]
Frederick, Becky J. ... '57 '83 C.187 B.A. L.1119 J.D. Supt., Employment
Frederick, Nancy A. ... '63 '94 C.645 B.S. L.325 J.D. Asst. States Atty.
Frederick, Thomas J. ... '56 '84 C.475 B.A. L.477 J.D. [Winston&S.]
Fredian, Robert H. ... '58 '93 C.927 B.S. L.424 J.D. [Ⓐ Wiedner&M.]
Fredman, Barry G. ... '57 '84 C.1036 B.A. L.910 J.D. 221 N. LaSalle St.
Free, Brian D. ... '— '91 C.473 B.S. L.146 J.D. [Chapman&C.]
Freeborn, Michael D., (AV) ... '— '72 C.1070 B.S. L.345 J.D. [Freeborn&P.]
Freeborn, Paul K. ... '— '02 C.966 B.A. L.209 J.D. [Ⓐ Wildman,H.A.&D.]

Freeborn & Peters LLP, (AV)
311 South Wacker Drive Suite 3000, 60606-6677 ⊙
Telephone: 312-360-6000 Fax: 312-360-6520
URL: http://www.freebornpeters.com
Partners: Douglas A. Albritton; Jill C. Anderson; Helen N. Baker; Robert M. Baratta, Jr.; Scott B. Barnett; Roger H. Bickel; Gerald P. Callaghan; Anthony J. Carballo; Joel T. Cooper; Jeffery M. Cross; Daniel C. Curth; Steven E. Cyranoski; Jeffrey L. Dorman; Aren L. Fairchild; Richard Anthony Fiore; Jennifer L. Fitzgerald; Joseph L. Fogel; Michael D. Freeborn; Andrew L. Goldstein; Harley J. Goldstein; James S. Gray; David C. Gustman; Aaron L. Hammer; Edward J. Hannon; Steven M. Hartmann; William N. Howard; Robert W. Karr, Jr.; Michael J. Kelly; Kenneth K. Kneubuhler; Michael P. Kornak; William N. Krucks; John Z. Lee; Neal H. Levin; Richard B. Levy; Weston W. Marsh; Peter I. Mason; Jeffrey M. Mattson; Jeffrey J. Mayer; Robert A. McWilliams; Michael A. Moynihan; Brian P. Norton; Todd J. Ohlms; Jordan H. Peters; Joseph P. Roddy; William E. Russell; Michael J. Scotti III; John T. Shapiro; Richard T. Sikes, Jr.; Robert J. Sitkowski (Not admitted in IL); Hillard M. Sterling; John E. Stevens; John C. Stiefel; Kathryn C. Thomas; Richard J. Traub; Randall G. Vickery; Daniel J. Voelker; Charles E. Watson, II; Charles W. Webster; James M. Witz; Eugene F. Zelek, Jr.; Ann M. Zwick. Associates: David Becker; Melissa L. Benzon; Staci A. Burton; Kellye L. Fabian; Thomas R. Fawkes; Michele L. Foster; Michael T. Franz; Elizabeth T. Friedlander; John C. Hammerle; Jeffrey M. Hansen; Tonita M. Helton; John F. Jacobs; Marc H. Kallish; David L. Kane; Jacob D. Koering; Theodore J. Koerth; Hillary P. Krantz; Todd A. Labinsky; Eleni S. Lamperis; David M. Madden; Eric M. Madiar; Roger S. Malki; Tracy H. Michael; Catherine A. Miller; Jennifer L. Milos (Resident, Springfield Office); Kris R. Murphy; Andrew C. Nordahl; Raymond H. Pruchnicki; Verona M. Sandberg; Terrence J. Sheahan; Brian A. Smith; Joji Takada; David Ter Molen; Stephanie Towner; Susan E. Walsh; Garry L. Wills; Patrick J. Woytek; Jane D. Yanovsky; Sheila Zeller. Staff Attorney: John R. Fanone. Senior Counsel: Richard R. Dennerline; Kathleen L. Hobbins; William C. Holmes; Leland W. Hutchinson, Jr.; Michael A. Smith; William A. Spence. Of Counsel: Amory Cummings; Harry L. DeLung, Jr.; Paul A. Duffy; Paul A. Hybel; Andy V. Jonusaitis; Charles E. Kelly (Not admitted in IL).
Business Litigation, Securities Litigation, Complex Commercial Disputes, Insurance Coverage Litigation, Products Liability, Professional Malpractice, Corporate Counseling and Transactions, Alternative Dispute Resolution, Compliance with Regulations by Government Agencies, Employment Law, Labor Law, Mergers and Acquisitions, Antitrust and Trade Regulation, Commercial Real Estate Transactions, Estate Planning, Government Relations, Environmental Law, Health and Safety Law, Railroad Law.
Springfield, Illinois Office: 217 E. Monroe Street, Suite 202, 62701. Telephone: 217-535-1060. Fax: 217-535-1069.
See Professional Biographies, CHICAGO, ILLINOIS

Freechack, John E., (AV) ... '50 '75 C&L.597 B.A., J.D. [Barack F.K.P.&N.]
Freed, Eric D. ... '62 '92 C.154 B.S. L.339 J.D. [Freed&W.]
Freed, Martin J. ... '46 '71 C.597 B.A. L.145 J.D. 55 W. Monroe Street
Freed, Mayer G. ... '44 '71 C&L.178 A.B., J.D. Prof., Northwestern Univ. Law Sch.
Freed, Merrill A., (AV) ... '— '54 C&L.145 B.A., J.D. [Ⓒ Seyfarth S.] ‡
Freed, Michael J., (AV) ... '38 '63 C.659 B.S. L.145 J.D. [Much S.F.D.A.&R.]
Freed & Weiss LLC ... 111 West Washington Street, Suite 1331
Freedman, Allen R. ... '42 '67 C.339 B.S. L.597 J.D. 2 N. LaSalle St.
Freedman, Allison W. ... '71 '02 C.95 B.A. L.999 J.D. [Ⓐ Bartlit B.H.P.&S.]
Freedman, Douglas A. ... '— '85 C.932 B.S. L.597 J.D. [Latham&W.]
Freedman, Lawrence M., (AV) ... '43 '69 C.597 B.S. L.424 J.D. [Ash,A.F.&L.]
Freedman, Richard E. ... '41 '65 C&L.966 B.S., J.D. Title Offr., Chicago Title Ins. Co.
Freedman & Bornstein, P.C. ... 22 W. Monroe, Ste. 1504
Freehling, Paul E., (AV) ... '38 '62 C&L.309 A.B., LL.B. [Seyfarth S.]
Freel, Stacy S., (BV) ... '— '93 C.1365 B.A. L.424 J.D. [Karbal,C.E.S.&D.]
Freeman, Allen A. ... '15 '38 C&L.339 B.A., LL.B. Cir. J.
Freeman, Bernadette ... '46 '01 C.209 B.S. L.146 J.D. 801 South Plymouth Court
Freeman, Charles A., (AV) ... '38 '63 C.339 B.A. L.209 J.D. [Gardner C.&D.]
Freeman, Charles E. ... '33 '62 C.892 A.B. L.365 LL.B. Ill. Com. Comm.
Freeman, Glynna W., (AV) ... '45 '71 C.788 B.A. L.597 J.D. [Ⓒ Freeman,F.&S.]
Freeman, James M. ... '73 '00 C.339 B.A. L.209 J.D. [Ⓐ Bollinger,R.&G.]
Freeman, John C., (BV) '59 '90 C.339 B.S. L.273 J.D.
[Brinks H.G.&L.] (See Pat. Sect.)
Freeman, Kevin L. ... '69 '94 C.597 B.A. L.145 J.D. [Gardner C.&D.]
Freeman, Lee A., Jr., (AV) ... '40 '66 C&L.309 A.B., LL.B. [Freeman,F.&S.]
Freeman, Louis S., (AV) ... '40 '68 C.150 B.B.A. L.309 J.D. [Skadden,A.S.M.&F.]
Freeman, Lynda J. ... '60 '87 C.339 B.S. L.365 J.D. Off. of State's Atty.
Freeman, Marvin G., (AV) ... '24 '49 C.339 B.S. L.209 J.D. 401 N. Michigan Ave.
Freeman, Nicholas P. ... '65 '93 C.790 B.A. L.365 J.D. [Corti,F.&A.]
Freeman, Peter B. ... '44 '69 C.674 B.A. L.309 J.D. 2024 North Orleans Street
Freeman, Richard L., (AV) ... '32 '58 C.309 A.B. L.976 LL.B. [Ⓒ Michael B.&F.]
Freeman, Robert P. ... '30 '56 C&L.209 LL.B. Chicago Transit Authority
Freeman, Robert P. ... '62 '88 C.800 B.A. L.966 J.D. [Sidley A.B.&W.]
Freeman, Zachary J. ... '73 '03 C.674 A.B. L.597 J.D. [Ⓐ Miller S.&H.]

Freeman, Freeman & Salzman, P.C., (AV) BB
401 North Michigan Avenue, Suite 3200, 60611-4207
Telephone: 312-222-5100 Facsimile: 312-822-0870
Email: freeman@ffspc.com URL: http://www.ffspc.com
Lee A. Freeman (1909-1995); Lee A. Freeman, Jr.; Jerrold E. Salzman; John F. Kinney; James T. Malysiak; Phillip L. Stern;—Joseph P. Adamczyk; Kevin M. Jones. Of Counsel: Glynna W. Freeman; Richard P. Campbell.
Antitrust Litigation, Securities and Commodity Litigation, General Commercial Litigation and Employment Litigation.
See Professional Biographies, CHICAGO, ILLINOIS

Freer, Todd D. ... '51 '79 C.187 B.S.S. L.424 J.D. [Ⓒ Schiff H.]
Frei, Robert R., (AV) ... '23 '50 C.674 A.B. L.309 J.D. Bank One Plz.‡

Freibrun, Eric S., Ltd., Law Offices of
(See Northbrook)

Freiburg, James P. ... '50 '76 C.927 B.A. L.146 J.D. [Weil,F.&P.]
Freiburger, Richard ... '65 '91 C.477 A.B. L.823 J.D. 645 N. Michigan Ave., Ste. 800
Freidberg, David L. ... '69 '95 C.1273 B.B.A. L.744 J.D. [D.L.Freidberg]
Freidberg, David L., Law Offices of, P.C. ... 10 S. La Salle St., Ste. 3410
Freidheim, Elizabeth A. '40 '89 C.700 B.A. L.365 J.D.
Asst. Corp. Coun., City of Chicago
Freier, Todd E. ... '— '03 C.477 B.A. L.602 J.D. [Ⓐ Chapman&C.]
Freireich, Valerie J. ... '52 '77 C&L.339 B.S., J.D. [Chuhak&T.]

Freivogel, William, (AV) ... '40 '65 C&L.339 B.S., LL.B. 999 North Lake Shore Drive
Fremgen, William H. ... '32 '62 C.725 A.B. L.424 J.D. Home Fed. Svgs. & Loan Assn.
French, David W. ... '77 '02 C.209 B.S. L.365 J.D. [Ⓐ Vedder,P.K.&K.]
French, Dennis E. ... '54 '79 C.927 B.A. L.616 J.D. 55 West Wacker Drive
French, James A. ... '05 '31 C.145 Ph.B. L.146 LL.B. 6152 S. Evans Ave.‡
French, Jean M. ... '59 '86 C.339 B.S. L.365 J.D. [Ⓐ Gunty&M.]
French, Roger J., (AV) '47 '74 C.597 B.S.E.E. L.365 J.D.
53 West Jackson Boulevard, Suite 1352 (Pat.) (⊙Chicago)
French, Roger J., (AV) ... '— '74 C.597 B.S.E.E. L.365 J.D. [Beem] (Pat.) (⊙Chicago)
French, Timothy A., (AV) ... '59 '85 C.309 A.B. L.597 J.D. [Neal,G.&E.]
Freter, Paul L. ... '17 '48 C&L.339 B.S., J.D. [Ⓒ Lewis,O.&F.]
Frett, Eugene J., (AV) ... '52 '78 C.436 B.A. L.597 J.D. [Sperling&S.]
Fretzin, Lawrence G. ... '34 '59 C.339 B.S. L.209 J.D. 1 N. La Salle St.
Freud, Edward P. ... '49 '74 C&L.209 B.A., J.D. [Ruff,W.&R.]
Freund, Joseph R. ... '80 '04 C.339 B.S. L.209 J.D. [Ⓐ Cook,A.M.M.C.&M.]
Freund, Terry M. ... '26 '76 State Commerce Comm.
Freveletti, Jamie S. ... '59 '85 C.589 B.A. L.146 J.D. [Ⓒ Thiedmann&E.]
Frew, Stephen B., (AV) ... '51 '76 C.347 A.B. L.930 J.D. [Kiesler&B.]
Frey, Bertram C., (AV) '47 '74 C.311 B.A. L.910 J.D.
Dep. Reg. Coun., U.S. Environ. Protec. Agcy.
Frey, David A. ... '57 '95 C.871 B.S. L.365 J.D. [Ⓐ Gardner C.&D.] (Pat.)
Frey, John E., (BV) ... '51 '75 C.801 B.A. L.276 J.D. [Wildman,H.A.&D.]
Freyder, Robert G. ... '54 '81 C.72 B.A. L.424 J.D. [Ⓐ Gunty&M.]
Freyer, Wendy, (AV) ... '59 '85 C.788 A.B. L.597 J.D. [Drane F.&L.]
Frezados, Gregory A. ... '68 '94 C.478 B.A. L.861 J.D. [Harrison&H.]
Frezados, Peter G., (AV) ... '39 '70 C.801 B.A. L.734 J.D. [Regas,F.&D.]
Fricano, Peter ... '47 '73 C.424 B.A. L.146 J.D. 221 N. LaSalle St.
Frick, Krista R. ... '71 '96 C.1156 B.A. L.1019 J.D. [Bollinger,R.&G.]
Fricke, Raymond C. ... '— '90 C.597 B.A. L.209 J.D. [Ungaretti&H.]
Fried, Saundra N. ... '69 '94 C.260 B.A. L.124 J.D. [Ⓐ Sonnenschein N.&R.]
Friedberg, Michael R., (AV) ... '46 '71 C.597 B.A. L.145 J.D. [Sugar,F.&F.]
Friedel, Laura B. ... '— '98 C.910 A.B. L.145 J.D. [Ⓐ Schiff H.]
Friedes, Jennifer ... '69 '94 C.477 B.A. L.188 J.D. 3712 N. Paulina‡
Friedgut, Elizabeth H., (AV) ... '54 '81 C.478 B.A. L.910 J.D. [DLPiper R.G.C.U.]
Friedl, Marcia L. ... '53 '78 C.339 B.A. L.424 J.D. Asst. Atty. Gen.
Friedland, Jonathan P., (AV) ... '— '94 C.1044 B.S. L.659 J.D. [Kirkland&E.]
Friedland, Sidney ... '21 '50 C.597 B.S. L.209 J.D. 3750 Lake Shore Dr.‡
Friedland, Steven D., (AV) ... '— '88 C&L.339 B.A., J.D. [Schiff H.]
Friedlander, Elizabeth T. ... '— '99 C.880 B.S. L.424 J.D. [Ⓐ Freeborn&P.]
Friedlander, Gary Scott ... '59 '87 C.597 B.S. L.365 J.D. Sr. Atty., Trans Union LLC
Friedlander, Mark C., (AV) ... '— '82 C.477 B.A. L.309 J.D. [Schiff H.]
Friedlander, Robert L. ... '37 '68 C.103 B.S. L.146 J.D. 419 W. Webster Ave.‡
Friedler, Ellen B., (AV) ... '58 '83 C.966 B.A. L.309 J.D. [Neal,G.&E.]
Friedli, Helen R., (AV) ... '56 '80 C.679 B.S.I.M. L.1119 J.D. [McDermott W.&E.]
Friedman, Albert Brooks, (AV) ... '41 '64 L.209 LL.B. [A.B.Friedman]
Friedman, Arthur W., (AV) ... '43 '68 C.103 A.B. L.145 J.D. [Miller S.&H.]
Friedman, Benson K. ... '68 '94 C.145 B.S. L.477 J.D. [Ⓐ McDermott W.&E.]
Friedman, Bernard E. ... '35 '62 C.1016 B.S. L.209 J.D. 230 W. Monroe St.
Friedman, Brian A. ... '71 '97 C.352 B.B.A. L.146 J.D. 875 N. Michigan Ave.
Friedman, Brooke M. ... '79 '04 C.477 B.A. L.146 J.D. 30 N. LaSalle St., Ste. 4300
Friedman, Bruce M., (AV) ... '47 '72 C&L.477 B.B.A., J.D. [Laser,P.S.F.&E.]
Friedman, Dennis G. ... '47 '82 C.31 B.A. L.228 J.D. [Mayer,B.R.&M.]
Friedman, Eugene F. ... '40 '73 C.861 B.S. L.446 J.D. [E.F.Friedman] (Pat.)
Friedman, Gail Tuler ... '43 '79 C.339 B.S. L.146 J.D. 53 W. Jackson Blvd.
Friedman, Gary B., (BV) ... '46 '73 C.339 B.A. L.209 J.D. [G.B.Friedman]
Friedman, Gregory A., (AV) ... '47 '75 C.339 B.A. L.309 J.D. [Friedman&H.]

Friedman, Howard, (AV) '40 '64 C.347 B.S. L.597 J.D.
150 N. Wacker Drive, Suite 1400, 60606
Telephone: 312-553-1700 Fax: 312-553-1733
Corporate, Mergers and Acquisitions, Real Estate, International Transactions.
See Professional Biographies, CHICAGO, ILLINOIS

Friedman, Ira J., (AV) ... '31 '54 C.339 B.S. L.209 J.D. 30 N. LaSalle St.
Friedman, Irving M., (AV) ... '18 '47 C.563 A.B. L.569 LL.B. [Katz,F.E.E.&J.]
Friedman, James T., (P.C.), (AV) '36 '61 C&L.477 B.A., J.D.
[Ⓒ Davis F.Z.K.M.M.&R.]
Friedman, Jaqueline B. ... '— '86 L.146 J.D. [Ⓒ Goldberg&F.]
Friedman, Jason A. '— '99
C.966 B.B.A. L.276 J.D. VP, Project Develop., Friedman Properties
Friedman, Jeffrey A. ... '76 '03 C.597 B.A. L.209 J.D. [Ⓐ Entertainment]
Friedman, Jeffrey C. ... '72 '99 C.339 B.A. L.146 J.D. [Ⓐ Levenfeld P.]
Friedman, Jeffrey D. ... '66 '96 C.608 B.A. L.209 J.D. [Seyfarth S.]
Friedman, Jeffrey M. ... '— '00 C.477 B.A. L.146 J.D. [Ⓐ DLPiper R.G.C.U.]
Friedman, Jeffrey M. ... '62 '87 C&L.145 B.A., J.D. [K.B.Moll&Assoc.]
Friedman, Joel M., (AV) ... '49 '75 C.339 B.S. L.365 J.D. [Horwood M.&B.]
Friedman, John A. '49 '76
C.966 B.A. L.146 J.D. V.P. & Gen. Coun., Darco Enterprises, Inc.
Friedman, Jos. R. ... '14 '37 L.146 LL.B. 6080 N. Whipple
Friedman, Joshua T., (BV) ... '64 '91 C.473 B.A. L.910 J.D. [Davis F.Z.K.M.M.&R.]
Friedman, Julie H. ... '44 '70 C.788 B.A. L.276 J.D. [Ⓐ Miller S.&H.]
Friedman, Kara M. ... '67 '93 C.477 B.A. L.424 J.D. [McGuirewoods]
Friedman, Lawrence, (AV) ... '30 '58 C.339 L.365 J.D. [L.Friedman]
Friedman, Lawrence M., (AV) ... '63 '89 C.339 B.A. L.365 J.D. [Barnes,R.&C.]
Friedman, Lawrence M. ... '45 '70 C.339 B.A. L.608 J.D. [Lord,B.&B.]
Friedman, Leonard ... '48 '79 C.696 B.S.E.E. L.145 J.D. [Welsh&K.] (See Pat. Sect.)
Friedman, Linda Debra, (AV) ... '60 '85 C.174 B.A. L.209 J.D. [Stowell&F.]
Friedman, Mark S. ... '62 '87 C&L.339 B.S., J.D. [Sinar K.M.&F.]
Friedman, Martin J. ... '50 '76 C.72 B.A. L.904 J.D. Dearborn Wholesale Grocers, L.P.
Friedman, Matthew C. ... '65 '93 C.347 B.S. L.209 J.D. [Friedman&B.]

Friedman, Michael T., & Associates '67 '92 C.347 B.A. L.365 J.D.
155 North Michigan Avenue, Suite 600, 60601
Telephone: 312-616-8816 Fax: 312-938-8541
Email: mikefriedmanlaw@comcast.net URL: http://www.lawyers.com/injurylawyer
Personal Injury, Wrongful Death, Automobile Accidents, Slip and Fall, Workers' Compensation, Airline Accidents, Products Liability, Construction Accidents, Bus Accidents, Railroad Accidents, Dog Bites, Medical Malpractice, Brain and Spinal Injuries, Catastrophic Injuries, Pedestrian Injuries, Real Estate, Commercial Real Estate, Mechanics Liens, Zoning and Land Use, Buying and Selling a Home, Family Law, Divorce, Child Custody and Support, Adoptions.
See Professional Biographies, CHICAGO, ILLINOIS

Friedman, Mitchell Benjamin ... '73 '99 C.473 B.A. L.146 J.D. [Ⓐ Meyer&B.]
Friedman, Paula Davis ... '67 '94 C.401 B.A. L.64 J.D. [Ⓐ DLPiper R.G.C.U.]
Friedman, Peter M. ... '62 '90 C.25 B.A. L.904 J.D. [Holland&K.]
Friedman, Redina, & Associates '49 '77
C.339 B.A. L.209 J.D. 11 S. LaSalle St., Rm. 2600
Friedman, Renée M., (AV) ... '56 '80 C.597 B.A. L.910 J.D. [Katten M.R.]

Friedman, Richard C. . . . '48 '82 C&L.910 A.B., J.D. U.S. Trustees Off.
Friedman, Richard E., (AV) '29 '57
C.293 A.B. L.597 J.D. Suite 4620, 55 East Monroe Street
Friedman, Richard F., (AV) . . . '— '69 C.339 B.S. L.145 J.D. [Neal&L.]
Friedman, Robin C. . . . '57 '84 C&L.145 B.A., J.D. [Johnson&C.]
Friedman, Ronald M. . . . '53 '83 C.597 B.A. L.365 J.D. Quacker Oats Co.
Friedman, Roselyn L., (AV) . . . '— '77 C.665 B.S. L.424 J.D. [Sachnoff&W.]
Friedman, Ross H. . . . '— '01 C.339 B.S. L.145 J.D. [[A] Morgan,L.&B.]
Friedman, Shari L. . . . '— '86 C.339 B.S.W. L.209 J.D. [Marwedel,M.&R.]
Friedman, Stephen J., (AV) . . . '50 '75 C&L.339 A.B., J.D. [Rusin M.&F.]
Friedman, Victoria . . . '— '03 C.209 ClS L.365 J.D. [[A] McDonnell B.H.&B.]
Friedman, Albert Brooks, Ltd., (AV) . . . Suite 2401 33 North Dearborn Street

Friedman & Bonebrake, P.C.
150 N. Wacker Drive, Suite 2020, 60606
Telephone: 312-466-8200 Fax: 312-466-8238 URL: http://www.attorneyillinois.net
Email: friedman@attorneyillinois.net URL: http://www.lawyers.com/mattfriedman
Matthew C. Friedman; James G. Bonebrake.
Personal Injury; Automobile Accidents, Medical Malpractice, Products Liability, Workers Compensation, Toxic Torts and Insurance Coverage, Premises Liability, Wrongful Death, Consumer Fraud, Real Estate, Business Transactions.
See Professional Biographies, CHICAGO, ILLINOIS

Friedman, Eugene F., Ltd. . . . 53 W. Jackson Blvd. (Pat.)
Friedman, Gary B., Ltd., (BV) . . . 200 N. LaSalle St., Ste. 2750
Friedman & Holtz, P.C., (AV) . . . 11 E. Adams St., Ste. 1600
Friedman, Lawrence, P.C., (AV) . . . 19 S. LaSalle St., 10th Fl.
Friend, Barrie M. . . . '79 '04 C.477 B.A. L.276 J.D. [[A] Katten M.R.]
Friend, David M. . . . '56 '82 C.339 B.S. L.146 J.D. 605 W. Madison St.‡
Friend, Martin B. . . . '28 '52 C&L.209 J.D. 33 N. LaSalle St.
Frierdich, Bruce E. . . . '54 '82 C.959 B.A. L.190 J.D. Anderson Consulting
Friker, E. Kenneth . . . '41 '66 C.589 B.A. L.146 J.D. [Klein,T.&J.]
Frink, Anthony L. . . . '55 '82 C.976 B.A. L.146 J.D. [Holland&K.]
Frisbie, Teresa F., (AV) . . . '61 '86 C.339 B.A. L.424 J.D. [[B] Davis M.]
Frisby, Dennis E., (AV) . . . '54 '79 C&L.209 B.S.C., J.D. [Deutsch,L.&E.]
Frisch, Donald S., (AV) . . . '33 '57 C&L.209 J.D. 55 W. Monroe St., Ste. 1925
Frischer, Susan B. . . . '68 '96 C.339 B.A. L.365 J.D. [Frischer L.]
Frischer Law, P.C. . . . 4024 N. Milwaukee
Frischkorn, David M., (AV) '57 '89
C.112 B.S.Ch.E. L.209 J.D. [McDonnell B.H.&B.] (See Pat. Sect.)
Frisone, Nicholas J. . . . '58 '84 C.654 B.A. L.365 J.D. [Heller&F.]
Fritchey, John A., (AV) . . . '64 '89 C.477 A.B. L.597 J.D. [[B] Dykema G.P.]
Fritsch, Paula S. . . . '— '03 C.493 B.S. L.352 J.D. [[A] McDonnell B.H.&B.]
Fritsch, Ron . . . '39 '64 C.339 A.B. L.309 J.D. Legal Aid Bur.
Fritz, Daniel K. . . . '63 '88 C.597 B.A. L.339 J.D. [[A] Taylor,M.S.H.&M.]
Fritz, Jennifer . . . '72 '97 C.339 B.A. L.494 J.D. 500 West Madison Street, 23rd Floor
Fritz, Wendy L. . . . '71 '03 C.145 B.A. L.94 J.D. [[A] Jenner&B.]
Fritzshall, Robert S. . . . '28 '54 C.1016 L.365 J.D. 101 N. Wacker Dr.
Froehlich, Joseph N. '70 '96 C.1030 B.A. L.575 J.D.
(adm. in NJ; not adm. in IL) [[A] Lord,B.&B.] (⊙New York, NY)
Froehlke, Donald F. . . . '60 '94 C.602 B.A. L.146 J.D. [[A] Nisen&E.]
Froelich, Cezar M., (AV) . . . '46 '70 C&L.424 B.S., J.D. [Shefsky&F.]
Froemel, Jonathan P. . . . '— '96 C.910 B.A. L.339 J.D. [[A] Barnes&T.]
Frohling, Daniel D. . . . '57 '85 C&L.477 A.B., J.D. [Loeb&L.] (Pat.)
Froikin, Stephen D. . . . '51 '78 C.145 A.B. L.608 J.D. 2701 W. Jarvis Ave.

Froman, Michael S.
(See Skokie)

Fromm, Mark L., (AV) . . . '57 '82 C.339 B.A. L.146 J.D. 205 W. Randolph
Fross, Roger R., (AV) . . . '40 '65 C.210 B.A. L.145 J.D. [Lord,B.&B.]
Frost, Ciara Ryan . . . '64 '89 C.770 B.A. L.424 J.D. [Kerns,P.F.&P.]
Frost, Michael J., (AV) . . . '45 '71 C&L.424 B.S., J.D. 20 N. Clark St., Ste. 3600
Frost, Scott C. . . . '65 '90 C.1365 B.A. L.904 J.D. [Statman,H.S.&E.]
Frost, Stephen A. . . . '56 '81 C.350 B.S. L.352 J.D. [Pedersen&H.]
Frost, Steven G., (AV) . . . '— '83 C.174 B.A.,B.S. L.209 J.D. [Chapman&C.]
Frostic, Dennis L., (AV) . . . '43 '69 C&L.477 A.B., J.D. [McCullough,C.&L.]
Froum, Theodore E. . . . '— '98 C.1036 B.A. L.1398 J.D. [Levin&S.]
Froy, Michael M., (AV) . . . '59 '83 C.477 A.B. L.145 J.D. [Sonnenschein N.&R.]
Fruchter, Marcus D. . . . '74 '04 C.475 B.A. L.1191 J.D. [[A] Schopf&W.]
Fruchtman, Rebecca O'Neal, (AV⊤) . . '— '87 C&L.276 B.S.F.S., J.D. [[B] Kirkland&E.]
Fruehauf, Henry W. . . . '50 '76 C.597 B.A. L.365 J.D. 3525 W. Peterson Ave., Ste. 501
Fruth, Steven J., (AV) . . . '47 '76 C.801 B.A. L.365 J.D. 200 N. Lasalle St., Ste. 2000
Fry, John R. . . . '46 '76 C.1236 A.B. L.146 J.D. Chief Reg. Atty., U.S. Dept. of Educ.
Frye, Angela Bonfield . . . '— '97 C.597 B.A. L.146 J.D. [Kirkland&E.]
Frye, Patrick . . . '79 '04 C.577 B.A. L.1565 J.D. [[A] Ross,D.&B.]
Fryklund, Inge . . . '46 '79 C.1230 B.A. L.145 J.D. City Parking Admn.
Fryman, James Edward . . . '61 '89 C.473 B. Phi. L.608 J.D. Asst. Pub. Def.
Fryzel, Michael E., Law Offices of '45 '85
C.879 B.S.B.A. L.424 J.D. 100 W. Monroe St., Ste. 1900
Fryzel, Scott R. . . . '— '94 C.248 B.A. L.424 J.D. [[A] Chapman&C.]
Fuchs, Robert F., (AV) . . . '24 '48 C.966 L.309 LL.B. [[B] Fuchs&R.]
Fuchs, Stuart '46 '73 C&L.309 A.B., J.D.
(adm. in NY; not adm. in IL) V.P., Goldman, Sachs & Co.

Fuchs & Roselli, Ltd., (AV) [BB]
440 West Randolph Street, Suite 500, 60606-1507
Telephone: 312-651-2400 FAX: 312-651-2499
URL: http://www.frltd.com
John T. Roselli; Mark H. Schiff; Susan Ghelerter; Thomas W. Hayes; Steven M. Ruffalo; Michael T. O'Connor; Richard A. Harbaugh; Edward J. McGillen; Richard C. Perna; David R. Buetow; Terrence M. LaBant;—Mark R. Anderson; Alisa M. Levin; J. Matthew Pfeiffer; Jay E. Presser; James B. Toohey; John A. Tsoutsias; Joonho Yu. Of Counsel: Robert F. Fuchs; Paul Hansfield.
General Civil and Trial Appellate Practice. Corporation, Federal, State and Local Tax, Real Estate, Labor, Bankruptcy, Probate, Construction, Employee Benefits, Employment and Administrative Agency Law.
See Professional Biographies, CHICAGO, ILLINOIS

Fuechtman, David C. . . . '— '95 C.209 B.S. L.424 J.D. [Sachnoff&W.]
Fuentes, Celso, Jr. . . . '66 '02 C.339 B.A. L.146 J.D. 120 W. Madison St.
Fuentes, Lillian . . . '— '88 C.1376 B.A. L.705 J.D. 2750 N. Ashland Ave.
Fuglsang, Eric J. . . . '71 '97 C.238 B.S. L.209 J.D. [Quarles&B.]
Fuhrmann, Maria R. . . . '58 '84 C.209 B.A. L.146 J.D. Atty., U.S. Postal Serv.
Fukuda, Kozo . . . '24 '55 C.46 B.S. L.209 J.D. Fed. Trade Comm.
Fulbright, Shauna L. . . . '— '03 C&L.477 B.A., J.D. [[A] Mayer,B.R.&M.]
Fulco, Stacy Dolan . . . '71 '97 C.338 B.A. L.209 J.D. [[A] Cremer,K.S.&S.]
Fuller, David W. . . . '71 '00 C.747 B.A. L.494 J.D. [[A] Mayer,B.R.&M.]
Fuller, H. Laurance . . . '38 '65 C.188 B.Ch.E. L.209 J.D. Standard Oil Co. (Ind.)
Fuller, Jack W. . . . '46 '74 C.597 B.S. L.976 J.D. Pres. & Publisher, Chicago Tribune
Fuller, Nancy J. . . . '62 '91 C.339 B.S. L.145 J.D. Asst. Gen. Coun., Midway Games Inc.
Fulton, Brady J. . . . '70 '96 C.424 B.A. L.146 J.D. [Niro,S.H.&N.] (See Pat. Sect.)
Fulton, Deborah K. . . . '63 '88 C.393 B.A. L.309 J.D. Gen. Coun., Midway Games Inc.
Fulton, Ellen K. . . . '71 '00 C.802 B.S. L.145 J.D. [[A] Goodsmith G.&U.]

Fultz Law Offices
(See Springfield)

Fumagalli, Daniel J., (BV) . . . '57 '82 C.321 B.A. L.188 J.D. [Chuhak&T.]
Fumerton, Tara A. . . . '— '03 C&L.352 B.S., J.D. [[A] Jones D.]
Fumo, Michael R. . . . '30 '53 C.209 L.146 LL.B. 20 N. Clark St.
Funai, Bryan Y. . . . '— '81 C.589 B.S. L.1187 J.D. [Masuda,F.E.&M.] (⊙Schaumburg)
Funai, Masaru . . . '— '57 C.312 B.A. L.597 J.D. [Masuda,F.E.&M.] (⊙Schaumburg)
Funderburk, Raymond . . . '— '79 C&L.339 B.A., J.D. Cir. J.
Funk, Kenneth W. . . . '55 '82 C&L.209 B.A., J.D. [Deutsch,L.&E.]
Funkhouser, Wilson P., (AV) . . . '46 '73 C.976 B.A. L.145 J.D. [Funkhouser V.L.&D.]

Funkhouser Vegosen Liebman & Dunn Ltd., (AV)
(Formerly, Levin & Funkhouser, Ltd.)
55 West Monroe Street Suite 2410, 60603-5008
Telephone: 312-701-6800 Facsimile: 312-701-6801
Email: info@fvldlaw.com URL: http://www.fvldlaw.com
Damon E. Dunn; Rochelle Secemsky Dyme; Wilson P. Funkhouser; Daniel T. Graham; James F. Groth; Hal "Corky" Kessler; Vance L. Liebman; Glenn A. Rice; Jonathan Vegosen. Of Counsel: Denise M. Chan; Lawrence R. Levin;—Sharon Beth-Halachmy; Eric D. Bolander; Daniel M. Hinkle; Neil M. Rosenbaum; Dara Sahebjami.
General Corporate Practice. Corporate Litigation and White Collar Criminal Trial and Appellate Practice, Banking, Labor and Employee Relations, Business Planning, Commercial, Antitrust, Trade Regulation, Intellectual Property, Securities, Mergers and Acquisitions, Real Estate Development and Financing, Taxation, Mortgage Banking, Construction Law, Estate Planning and Probate Law, Civil Trial Practice.
See Professional Biographies, CHICAGO, ILLINOIS

Fuoco, Steven . . . '— '91 C.623 B.B.A. L.365 J.D. [[A] O'Hagan,S.&A.]
Fura, Jason William . . . '71 '98 C&L.472 B.B.A., J.D. [Fedota C.]
Fura, Shannon E. . . . '71 '04 C.34 B.A. L.146 J.D. [Sandler,T.&R.]
Furda, Gregory H., (AV) . . . '46 '75 C&L.424 B.A., J.D. [Sidley A.B.&W.]
Furer, Julie J. . . . '— '93 C.339 B.A. L.209 J.D. [Schiff H.]
Furey, Michael J. . . . '46 '78 C.742 B.A. L.209 J.D. Sr. V.P., The Northern Trust Company
Furey, William J., (AV) . . . '48 '73 C.589 B.S. L.209 J.D. [Cassiday,S.&G.]
Furlane, Mark E., (AV) . . . '49 '74 C.132 B.A. L.276 J.D. [Gardner C.&D.]
Furman, Ira J. '43 '87 C.331 B.A. L.128 J.D.
(adm. in NY; not adm. in IL) [[B] Rapoport]
Furmanek, Michael P. . . . '77 '03 C.477 B.S.M.E. L.209 J.D. [[A] Fitch,E.T.&F.]
Furniss, Robert F. . . . '55 '82 C.976 B.A. L.893 J.D. Labor Rel. Mgr.
Furrow, Timothy . . . '76 '02 C.347 B.A. L.352 J.D. [[A] Ross,D.&B.]
Furton, Matthew T. . . . '70 '95 C.477 B.A. L.347 J.D. [[B] Lord,B.&B.]
Fus, Steven Stanley . . . '59 '94 C.1222 B.S. L.284 J.D. Sr. Coun., United Airlines
Fusco, Anthony J., Jr. '48 '75
C.357 B.A. L.879 J.D. Assoc. Gen. Coun., Chicago Housing Auth.
Fusco, Daniel R., (AV) . . . '39 '64 C.602 B.S. L.424 J.D. [Rock F.]
Futterman, Craig B. . . . '66 '91 C.597 B.A. L.813 J.D. [[B] Futterman&H.]
Futterman, Ronald L., (AV) . . . '43 '67 C.966 B.B.A. L.597 J.D. [Futterman&H.]
Futterman & Howard, Chtd., (AV) . . . 122 South Michigan Avenue, Suite 1850
Fylstra, Raymond A., (AV) . . . '47 '72 C.323 B.A. L.597 J.D. [Kubasiak,F.R.&R.]
Fyock, Sheryl A. . . . '64 '90 C.221 B.A. L.378 J.D. [Latimer L.J.]
Gaan, Cary A. . . . '46 '72 C.339 B.A. L.146 J.D. Sr. V.P. & Sec., Bally Total Fitness Corp.
Gabbay, Alan . . . '53 '79 C.976 B.A. L.309 J.D. [[B] Sidley A.B.&W.]
Gaber, Kathleen M. '— '85 C.477 B.B.A. L.245 J.D.
[Masuda,F.E.&M.] (⊙Schaumburg)
Gable, Allen J. . . . '70 '96 C.477 B.A. L.213 J.D. [[A] Vedder,P.K.&K.]
Gabler, Paul W., (AV) . . . '31 '56 C.309 A.B. L.477 J.D. [[B] Schoenberg,F.N.&R.]
Gabric, Ralph J., (AV) . . . '62 '88 C.93 B.S. L.209 J.D. [Brinks H.G.&L.] (See Pat. Sect.)
Gabriel, Adriana R. . . . '77 '03 C.36 B.S. L.339 J.D. 150 S. Wacker Dr., Ste. 2400
Gabrielides, Harry E. . . . '22 '55 C.999 L.145 LL.M. 5711 N. Lincoln Ave.
Gabrielides, John T., (AV) '63 '88
C.339 B.A. L.209 J.D. [Brinks H.G.&L.] (See Pat. Sect.)
Gabrielson, Anthony S. . . . '75 '01 C.352 B.A. L.1565 J.D. [[A] Jenner&B.]
Gadia, Wigmor P. . . . '— '02 C.966 B.A. L.365 J.D. [W.Gadia]
Gadia, Wigmor, The Law Office of . . . 77 W. Washington, Suite 617
Gadowski, Melissa . . . '79 '04 C.788 A.B. L.145 J.D. [[A] Winston&S.]
Gaertner, Eric J. . . . '63 '88 C.602 B.A. L.339 J.D. Equity Office Properties Trust
Gaertner, Michael J., (AV) . . . '64 '89 C.363 B.S.B.A. L.945 J.D. [Lord,B.&B.]
Gaffke, Meredith A. . . . '79 '04 C.502 B.S. L.146 J.D. [[A] Swanson,M.&B.]
Gagala, Bruce M., (AV) . . . '52 '77 C.221 B.A. L.46 J.D. [Leydig,V.&M.] (See Pat. Sect.)
Gage, Mary Rose . . . '55 '80 C.424 B.A. L.597 J.D. Sr. Coun. B, Bk. of America
Gaggini, John Edmund, (AV) . . . '49 '75 C.388 A.B. L.209 J.D. [McDermott W.&E.]
Gagliardo, Joseph M., (AV) . . . '52 '77 C.209 B.S. L.365 J.D. [Laner,M.D.B.L.&T.]
Gaido, Peter A. . . . '64 '89 C.72 B.A. L.910 J.D. [Gaido&F.]
Gaido & Fintzen . . . 30 N. LaSalle, Suite 3010
Gail, Sanford R., (AV) . . . '43 '68 C.339 B.S. L.209 J.D. [Bell,B.&L.]
Gainer, Julienne Sorce . . . '49 '87 C.424 B.A. L.365 J.D. Northeastern Memorial Hospital
Gaines, John J., III, (AV) . . . '45 '70 C&L.276 A.B., J.D. [Huff&G.]
Gaines, Stephanie R. . . . '— '95 C.424 B.S. L.352 J.D. [Hinshaw&C.]
Gair, Chris C., (AV) . . . '59 '85 C.228 A.B. L.145 J.D. [Jenner&B.]
Gajewski, Paul A. . . . '60 '85 C.679 B.S. L.365 J.D. [Axelrod,G.S.&B.]
Gal, Robert P. . . . '71 '01 C.569 B.S. L.597 J.D. [[A] Skadden,A.S.M.&F.]
Galainena, M. David . . . '57 '83 C.861 B.A. L.602 J.D. [Winston&S.]
Galani, Ami J. . . . '— '04 C.207 B.A. L.910 J.D. [[A] Jenner&B.]
Galante, Paul A. '— '02 C.691 B.A L.724 J.D.
(adm. in NY; not adm. in IL) [[A] Mayer,B.R.&M.] (⊙New York, NY)
Galarnyk, John D. . . . '60 '85 C.966 B.A. L.365 J.D. [Galarnyk&Assoc.]

Galarnyk & Associates
70 W. Madison Street, Suite 2100, 60602-4253
Telephone: 312-441-5800 Fax: 312-853-1169
Email: jgalarnyk@galarnykandassociates.com
Member of Firm: John D. Galarnyk.
Business Law, Commercial, Contract, Employment, Unfair Competition, Securities, White Collar Defense, General Civil Litigation.
See Professional Biographies, CHICAGO, ILLINOIS

Galasek, John N. . . . '55 '83 C.339 B.A. L.365 J.D. 7550 W. Belmont Ave.
Galbreath, Scott E. . . . '61 '86 C.238 B.A. L.146 J.D. [Shaheen,N.S.F.&E.]
Gale, Charles J. . . . '54 '81 C.477 B.B.A. L.339 J.D. [C.J.Gale]
Gale, Gary K., (AV) . . . '54 '80 C.930 B.A. L.146 J.D. [[A] Maciorowski,S.&U.]
Gale, Joan E., (AV) . . . '— '79 C.347 A.B. L.209 J.D. [Seyfarth S.]
Gale, Jody S. . . . '— '99 C.20 B.A. L.930 J.D. [Kirkland&E.]
Gale, Michelle A. . . . '— '02 C.1157 B.S. L.1000 J.D. [[A] Mayer,B.R.&M.]
Gale, Todd A. . . . '— '87 C.475 B.A. L.602 J.D. [Kirkland&E.]
Gale, Charles J., P.C. . . . 208 S. La Salle St
Galhotra, Kulmeet S. . . . '66 '90 C.405 B.A. L.146 J.D. Asst. Pub. Def.
Galibois, Michael Brian . . . '74 '00 C.276 B.S.F.S L.602 J.D. [[A] Chittenden,M.&N.]

Galich, Andrew A., (AV) '31 '58 C&L.209 B.S.C., J.D. [Ⓐ B.R.Nevoral&Assoc.]
Galicia, Gilberto M. '48 '77 C.424 A.B. L.209 J.D. IL Wkrs. Comp. Comm.
Galin, Matthew A. '— '04 C.188 B.S. L.597 J.D. [Ⓐ Johnson&B.]
Galioto, Sarah N. '69 '96 C.339 B.A. L.146 J.D. [Sonnenschein N.&R.]
Galis, Mark R. '66 '91 C.602 B.S.M.E. L.273 J.D. [Greenberg T.] (Pat.)
Galivan, Daniel G. '62 '89 C.424 B.A. L.365 J.D. [Grotefeld&D.]
Galkin, Jeffrey M., (AV) '63 '89 C.339 B.S. L.597 J.D. [Neal,G.&E.]
Gall, John '70 '02 C.98 B.S. L.209 J.D. [Ⓐ Richardson,S.B.&M.]
Gallagher, Anne Stark '62 '88 C&L.966 B.A., J.D.
(adm. in WI; not adm. in IL) Daniel J. Edelman, Inc.
Gallagher, Daniel F., (AV) '— '73 C&L.339 B.A., J.D. [Querrey&H.]
Gallagher, Francis X. '14 '39 C.145 B.A. L.424 J.D. 6801 N. Hiawatha Ave.‡
Gallagher, Gregory J. '— '04 C.602 B.S.C.E. L.577 J.D. [Ⓐ Jones D.]
Gallagher, Gregory W. '— '97 C&L.339 B.S., J.D. [Kirkland&E.]
Gallagher, Jennifer A. '67 '97 C&L.477 B.A., J.D. [Ⓐ Lord,B.&B.]
Gallagher, John F. '45 '83 C.959 B.S. L.436 J.D.
(adm. in WI; not adm. in IL) Fed. Labor Rel. Bd.
Gallagher, Judee '47 '82 C.589 B.A. L.209 J.D. 53 W. Jackson Blvd., Ste. 915
Gallagher, Kevin C. '47 '76 C&L.602 B.A., J.D.
Sr. V.P., Gen. Coun. & Secy., 360° Communications Co.
Gallagher, Linda A. '52 '95 C.209 B.S. L.146 J.D. [Ⓐ Levenfeld P.]
Gallagher, Michael J. '53 '78 C.339 B.A. L.146 J.D. Appl. Ct. Jus. .
Gallagher, Priscilla F., (BV) '58 '84
C.578 B.A. L.424 J.D. [McAndrews,H.&M.] (See Pat. Sect.)
Gallagher, Rose E. '— '99 C&L.347 B.A., J.D. [Ⓐ Chapman&C.]
Gallagher, Sean A. '67 '93 C.339 B.A. L.209 J.D. Atty., Chicago Board of Trade
Gallagher, Sean W. '— '97 C&L.477 B.A., J.D. [Bartlit B.H.P.&S.]
Gallagher, Timothy M. '47 '77 C.755 B.A. L.365 J.D. 134 N. LaSalle St.
Galland, George F., Jr., (AV) '45 '73 C.674 A.B. L.145 J.D. [Miner,B.&G.]
Gallanis, Kathryn Ann, (AV) '60 '85
C.802 B.B.A. L.365 J.D. 120 N. LaSalle St., Ste. 1900
Gallant, Barbara A. '71 '02 C.591 B.S.N. L.1187 J.D. [Ⓐ Hinshaw&C.]
Gallas, Jack A. '26 '52 C&L.597 B.S., LL.B. Pres., LaSalle Natl. Tr., N.A.
Gallegos, Andrés J. '60 '93 C.499 B.S. L.733 J.D. [Mandel,L.&S.]
Gallegos, Wendy Dodson '71 '01 C.228 B.A. L.339 J.D. [Ⓐ Mayer,B.R.&M.]
Galler, Stephen F. '62 '89 C.659 B.A. L.597 J.D. 350 W. Hubbard, Ste. 301
Gallery, Jennifer G. '69 '94 C.352 B.S. L.209 J.D. [Ⓐ Siegel M.&S.]
Galliani, William R., (AV) '30 '55 C.999 L.146 J.D. [Galliani&D.]
Galliani & Doell, Ltd., (AV) 20 N. Clark St.,18th Fl.
Gallinari, Christopher L. '65 '91 C.222 B.A. L.569 J.D. [Ⓐ Bellows&B.]
Gallinson, Jennifer '76 '01 C.477 B.A. L.424 J.D. [Ⓐ Winston&S.]
Gallo, Claudia '74 '99 C.424 B.A. L.146 J.D. [Ⓐ Jenner&B.]
Gallo, Elena '75 '01 C.1505 B.S. L.1187 J.D. [Ⓐ Nisen&E.]
Gallo, John N., (AV) '60 '86 C.602 B.A. L.309 J.D. [Sidley A.B.&W.]
Gallo, Matthew J. '30 '59 C.555 B.S. L.569 LL.B. 200 E. Randolph Dr.
Gallopoulos, Gregory S., (AV) '59 '84 C&L.477 A.B., J.D. [Jenner&B.]
Galo, Matthew G. '— '98 C.602 B.A. L.597 J.D. [Schiff H.]
Galowich, David H., (AV) '60 '85 C.966 B.A. L.146 J.D. [Galowich&G.]
Galowich, Jeffrey A. '59 '84 C.339 B.S. L.1068 J.D. [Galowich&G.]
Galowich, Ronald H., (AV) '36 '59 C&L.339 B.S., J.D. [Galowich&G.]
Galowich & Galowich, (AV) 200 W. Madison St.
Galper, Howard D., (AV) '31 '55 C&L.976 A.B., LL.B. [Ⓒ Marks,M.&K.]
Galvan, Jaime '67 '95 C.145 B.A. L.365 J.D.
Atty. II, Chicago Board Options Exchange, Incorporated
Galvan, Luis '53 '79 C&L.209 B.A., J.D. Off. of Fed. Def.
Galvin, Emmett J., (AV) '17 '47 C&L.209 J.D. [Galvin,L.W.G.&S.]
Galvin, James R., P.C., (AV) '49 '78 C.591 B.S. L.209 J.D. [Galvin,L.W.G.&S.]
Galvin, Jeffrey C. '54 '88 C.927 B.S. L.365 J.D. 140 S. Dearborn Street, 14th Floor
Galvin, Kenneth J. '51 '85 C.801 B.S. L.146 J.D. Staff Atty. to Chief Cir. Ct. J.‡
Galvin, Lewis, Watson, Galvin & Seyring, (AV) 8501 W. Higgins Street, Suite 440
Gambino, Leonard J. '56 '90 C.930 B.A. L.365 J.D. [Schoenberg,F.N.&R.]
Gamboa, Paul '77 '04 C&L.339 B.A., J.D. [Ⓐ Conway&C.]
Gamboney, Patrick J. '53 '79 C.339 B.S. L.146 J.D.
City of Chicago, Dept. of Buildings
Gamburd, Nancy R. '58 '84 C.477 B.A. L.597 J.D. 566 West Adams, Suite 350
Gamperl, Paul R. '63 '97 C.339 B.A. L.209 J.D. [Ⓐ Tribler O.&M.]
Gamrath, Robert L., III '68 '94 C.347 B.S. L.365 J.D. [Quarles&B.]
Gamson, Edward P., (AV) '43 '78 C.855 B.S. L.365 J.D. [Welsh&K.] (See Pat. Sect.)
Ganan, Clifford I. '40 '65 C.339 B.S. L.209 J.D. [Ganan&S.]
Ganan & Shapiro, (AV) 210 W. Illinois St.
Gancer, Donald C., (AV) '— '57 C&L.436 B.S., LL.B. [Ⓒ Querrey&H.]
Gangemi, Columbus R., Jr., (AV) '47 '73 C&L.884 A.B., J.D. [Winston&S.]
Gania, Edwin T. '62 '93 C.013 B.Sc. L.273 J.D. 11 S. LaSalle St., Ste. 2800
Gannon, James R., (AV) '28 '58 C&L.215 Ph.B., LL.B. [Lewis,O.&F.]
Gannon, Michael D. '65 '91 C&L.436 B.S.E.E., J.D. [Baniak P.&G.] (See Pat. Sect.)
Gannon, Sean Robert '69 '97 C.475 B.A. L.1187 J.D. Chf. Coun. IRS Off.
Gans, Ira J. '51 '77 C.477 A.B. L.597 J.D. Hearing Ref., Ill. Dept. of Employ. Sec.
Gansberg, Jeffrey L. '71 '97 C.205 B.S. L.910 J.D. [Ⓐ Wildman,H.A.&D.]
Gantz, Neil P., (BV) '44 '71 C.1016 B.A. L.46 J.D. 105 West Madison Street, Suite 901
Gantz, Norman J., (AV) '47 '72 C.339 B.A. L.597 J.D. [Neal,G.&E.]
Gantz, William M. '64 '90 C.145 B.A. L.608 J.D. [DLPiper R.G.C.U.]
Garbaczewska, Justyna M. '78 '02 C&L.339 B.A., J.D. State Appl. Def. Off.
Garber, Samuel B. '34 '58 C&L.339 B.S., J.D.
Corp. Atty, General Growth Properties, Inc.
Garber, Sheldon C. '38 '64 C.339 L.365 J.D. Supvr. J., Cir. Ct., F.E.D. Sect.
Garber, Stanley J., (AV) '41 '73 C.94 A.B. L.424 J.D. [Bell,B.&L.]
Garbossa, John A. '49 '74 C.209 B.S.C. L.597 J.D. Exec. VP, U.S. Equities Realty, Inc.
Garbutt, J. Stuart, (AV) '45 '71 C.679 B.S.I.M. L.597 J.D. [Meckler B.&T.]
Garcha, Bonny '74 '99 C.339 B.A. L.424 J.D. [Ⓐ Tressler,S.M.&P.]
Garcia, Agustin G. '49 '79 C.339 B.A. L.209 J.D. [A.G.Garcia]
Garcia, Aurelio '64 '90 C.424 B.B.A. L.365 J.D. Asst. Corp. Coun., City of Chicago
Garcia, Brian A. '— '03 C.393 B.A. L.339 J.D. [Ⓐ Brinks H.G.&L.]
Garcia, Carrie M. '72 '97 C&L.477 B.A., J.D. Sr. Coun., Vantage Solutions LLC
Garcia, Christopher A. '59 '94 C.112 B.A. L.188 J.D. [Seyfarth S.]
Garcia, Cynthia E. '— '02 C.209 B.A. L.424 J.D. [Ⓐ Querrey&H.]
Garcia, Marcelino, III '72 '97 C.197 B.A. L.597 J.D. 2150 W. North Ave.
Garcia, Maria Clara '— '99 C.494 B.S. L.597 J.D. [Ⓐ Chapman&C.]
Garcia, Maria G. '62 '89 C&L.424 B.S., J.D. Gen Coun., Chicago Park District
Garcia, Paul R. '— '92 C.881 A.B. L.145 J.D. [Kirkland&E.]
Garcia, Richard J. '39 '73 C.589 B.S. L.365 J.D. 10400 S. Ewing
Garcia, Stephen E., (AV) '62 '87 C.475 B.A. L.477 J.D. [Kaye S.]
Garcia, Stephen L. '61 '87 C.339 B.S. L.602 J.D. Cook Co. State's Atty.
Garcia, Agustin G., PC 53 W. Jackson Blvd.
Garcia-Moreno, Pablo A. '56 '91 L.999 J.D. [Baker&M.]

Gard, Dawn E. '68 '93 C.93 B.A. L.477 J.D.
Asst. Gen. Coun., FMC Technologies, Inc.
Gard, Robert R. '52 '77 C.475 B.A. L.365 J.D. [Ⓐ Azulay,H.&S.]
Gardiner, Thomas G., (BV) '57 '81 C.339 B.S. L.597 J.D. [Gardiner K.&W.]
Gardiner Koch & Weisberg, (BV) 53 West Jackson Boulevard, Suite 950
Gardner, Amy M. '75 '02 C.427 B.A. L.145 J.D. [Ⓐ Skadden,A.S.M.&F.]
Gardner, Andrew M. '59 '86 C.145 B.A. L.209 J.D. [Vedder,P.K.&K.]
Gardner, Frank E. '52 '78 C&L.339 B.S., J.D.
V.P., Metro. Water Reclam. Dist. of Greater Chgo.
Gardner, Henry A., Jr. '12 '40 C.976 B.A. L.597 J.D. La Salle St. Press
Gardner, James K., (AV) '43 '68 C.679 B.A. L.1119 J.D. [Neal,G.&E.]
Gardner, Jeffrey S. '76 '03 C.608 B.S. L.276 J.D. [Ⓐ Bell,B.&L.]
Gardner, John Charles '77 '04 C.966 B.S. L.436 J.D. [Ⓐ McGuirewoods]
Gardner, Mary E. '— '98 C.315 B.A. L.831 J.D.
(adm. in MD; not adm. in IL) [Ⓐ McDermott W.&E.]
Gardner, Robert A., Jr., (AV) '20 '49 C.976 B.A. L.597 J.D. 321 N. Clark St.‡
Gardner, Sheldon '28 '54 C.145 A.B. L.146 J.D. Cir. J.
Gardner, Thomas F., (AV) '— '69 C.340 B.A. L.339 J.D. [Jones D.]
Gardner, Timothy J. '74 '00 C.511 B.A. L.424 J.D. [Gardner]

Gardner Carton & Douglas LLP, (AV) BB
191 North Wacker Drive, Suite 3700, 60606-1698 ⊙
Telephone: 312-569-1000 Facsimile: 312-569-3000
Email: gcdinfo@gcd.com URL: http://www.gcd.com
Partners of Firm: Henry A. Gardner (1883-1968); Alfred T. Carton (1884-1968); James H. Douglas, Jr. (1899-1988).
Richard G. Agin; Keith R. Anderson; Cathy Kiselyak Austin; Warren von Credo Baker; Christopher J. Barber; Michael E. Barry; Thomas A. Belush; Luis A. Berrones; Richard P. Blessen; W. David Braun; Jennifer R. Breuer; Edwin E. Brooks; Gregory K. Brown; L. Edward Bryant, Jr.; Thomas Buranosky; Crystal Pruess Bush; Charles L. Byrum; Darren S. Cahr; Troy M. Calkins; Timothy J. Carey; Dennis J. Carlin; Timothy R. Casey; Patrick S. Coffey; N. Paul Coyle; Barbara A. Cronin; Michael F. Csar; John T. Cusack; Antonio DeBlasio; Sheila H. Deely; Stephanie Lee Dodge; Michael Duffy; Karen A. Erikson; William P. Farrell, Jr.; Glenn E. Ferencz; Scott J. Fisher; Quin R. Frazer; Charles A. Freeman; Kevin L. Freeman; Mark E. Furlane; Gary W. Garner; Edwin A. Getz; D. Louis Glaser II; John P. Goebel; Joseph H. Greenberg; Terry M. Hackett; Roy M. Harsch; Valerie A. Haugh; Mark F. Hebbeln; Nancy L. Hendrickson; Laurie A. Holmes (Not admitted in IL); Kirk A. Hoopingarner; Gary W. Howell; Elissa L. Isaacs; Ira M. Kalina; Harold L. Kaplan; David N. Kay; Patrick J. Kelleher; Alan S. King; Brigitte T. Kocheny; Tina D. Kourasis; Mark A. Latham; Howard J. Levine; Susan J. Macaulay; Ruth I. Major; David M. Matteson; George C. McKann; Helen J. McSweeney; Michael E. Mermall; Joyce L. Meyer; Peter J. Meyer; Kathleen M. Murphy; Gordon B. Nash, Jr.; Mark D. Nelson; John K. Notz, Jr.; Stephen O'Donnell; Neil S. Olderman; Anita J. Ponder; Michael D. Rosenbaum; Kimberly K. Rubel; David A. Rubenstein; Jesse H. Ruiz; Brian C. Rupp; Barnett P. Ruttenberg; James L. Sawyer; David S. Schaffer; Kathleen Sheil Scheidt; Jeffrey M. Schwartz; Stephanie B. Shellenback; S Jonathan Silverman; John A. Simon; Timothy J. Stanton; Sanford M. Stein; Nancy L. Stern; K. Bruce Stickler; Richard M. Stock; Barry W. Sufrin; Douglas B. Swill; Liisa M. Thomas; Tracy L. Treger; Stephen A. Tsoris; Carol Hines Wacaser; Priscilla A. (Pam) Walter; John W. Watson III; Robert J. Wilczek; Elizabeth Anne Williams; David L. Wolfe; Richard W. Young; Alex W. Zabrosky; Howard P. Zweig. Of Counsel: Thomas Arthur; Earl J. Barnes II; Richard J. Kissel; Gordon Lang, Jr.; James J. McClure, Jr.; Peter H. Merlin; William L. Morrison; Geoffrey B. Shields; Gordon H. Smith; Steven M. Wagner. Counsel: Susan Barnes de Resendiz (Not admitted in IL); Carol Larcher; Mark S. Melickian; Michael P. Morrison; Katherine N. O'Connell. Associates: Kathleen O'Connor Adams; Terri Ahrens; Kelli Anne Alces; Kendra M. Allaband; David S. Almeida; Marla Anderson; Martin F. Barna; Christine S. Bautista; Carrie A. Beyer; Jeffrey R. Blumberg; Jarrett T. Bostwick; Mary Elizabeth Brown; Nicole M. Bulman; Julie A. Burger; Noreen H. Cull; Alice D. Czyzycki; John J. D'Attomo; Jennifer L. de Lyon; Melissa Skylas Dillenbeck; Shawna M. Doran; Sasha M. Engle; Kelly A. Fetzer; Ashley M. Fischer; Blake J. Fix; Noemi Flores; Lisa M. Formolo; David A. Frey; David P. Gearey; William L. Goldbeck; L. Robert Guenthner, III; Lawrence N. Hill; Scott M. Holmes; Jonathan E. Hyun; Alan A. Kelly; Ann M. Kim; Tina Kuska; Scott C. Lascari; Andrew D. McNair; Mina Mehta; Evan M. Meyers; Sarah Bassler Millar; David J. Moorhead; Steven J. Murawski; Douglas C. Murray; Nicole Murray; C. Brooks Newman; Michael A. Nicolas; Carrie E. O'Brien; Stephen R. Patterson; David W. Porteous; Kelly Powis; Tanvir A. Rahman; Rupal Raval; Howard J. Rosenburg; William R. Rucker; Heather Heath Ryan; Mary K. Samsa; Mark Schauerte; Arthur M. Scheller III; Daryl M. Schumacher; Wendy L. Seltzer; Lori L. Shannon; Steven S. Shonder; Annapurna Singh; David Neal Tanner; Laura Yates Taylor; Kevin Van Timmeren; Sally L. Venverloh; Virginia A. Walls; Krista L. Watson; Lionel W. Weaver; Andrew E. Weissman; John R. Wiktor; Richard A. Wulff. Contract Attorney: Beata K. Spuhler. Officer: Jacqueline M. Schimmel.
Corporate Law, Corporate Restructuring, Environmental, Financial Markets Litigation, Government Relations, Health Law, Hedge Funds, HR Law (Employee Benefits and Labor and Employment), Indian Tribal Governments, Intellectual Property, Litigation and Dispute Resolution, Real Estate, Taxation, Wealth Planning and Philanthropy.
Washington, D.C. Office: Suite 900, East Tower, 1301 K Street, N.W. 20005-3317. Telephone: 202-230-5000. Facsimile: 202-230-5300.
Milwaukee, Wisconsin Office: 777 East Wisconsin Avenue, Suite 2000, 53202-5319. Telephone: 414-221-6040. Facsimile: 414-224-1025.
Albany, New York Office: 321 Great Oaks Boulevard, 12203-5971. Telephone: 518-452-8787. Facsimile: 518-452-8767.
See Professional Biographies, CHICAGO, ILLINOIS

Gardner Legal, P.C.
53 W. Jackson Boulevard, Suite 1524, 60604
Telephone: 312-788-1008 Fax: 312-788-1088
Email: gardner@gardnerlegal.com
Timothy J. Gardner.
Personal Injury, Criminal Defense, Traffic Violations, Commercial Litigation.
See Professional Biographies, CHICAGO, ILLINOIS

Gardy, Rodger Lee, Jr. '71 '97 C&L.477 B.A., J.D. [Ⓐ Winston&S.]
Gareis, Patrick R. '65 '91 C.234 B.A. L.146 J.D. [Grotefeld&D.]
Gareis, Robert J. '36 '61 C.116 B.S. L.276 J.D. [Ⓒ Baker&M.]
Garelick, Jordan R. '47 '75 C.1016 B.A. L.146 J.D. Atty. Gens. Off.
Garetto, Janet M. '72 '97 C.597 B.A. L.424 J.D. [Jenkens&G.] (Pat.)
Garfield, Alan H., (AV) '49 '74 C.339 B.A. L.209 J.D. [Garfield&M.]
Garfield, James R. '52 '77 C.339 B.A. L.767 J.D. 1230 W. Norwood St.
Garfield, Josh '— '05 C.659 B.S.E. L.124 J.D. [Ⓐ Brinks H.G.&L.]

Garfield & Merel, Ltd., A Professional Corporation, (AV)
223 West Jackson Boulevard, Suite 1010, 60606-6908
Telephone: 312-583-1600 Telecopier: 312-583-1700
URL: http://www.garfield-merel.com
Richard A. Merel; Alan H. Garfield; Stephen M. Alderman;—Keith A. Chadwick; Gregory A. McCormick.
Real Estate, Business Law and Commercial Litigation.
See Professional Biographies, CHICAGO, ILLINOIS

Garfinkel, Paul E. '— '81 C.477 B.A. L.597 J.D. [Kopka,P.D.&E.]
Gargano, Jeffrey R. '64 '92 C.37 B.S. L.146 J.D. [Wallenstein W.&R.]
Gargula, Carl G. '51 '79
C.436 B.S.B.A. L.365 J.D. Mgr. of Planning, William Blair & Co.
Garipay, Kathryn E. '59 '86 C.550 B.A. L.678 J.D. [Olson&H.]
Garland, Alan '37 '62 C.1016 B.S. L.365 J.D. [Berger,N.&F.]
Garland, Amy Louise '75 '01 C.475 B.S. L.209 J.D. 33 N. Dearborn, Ste. 700
Garland, Kelly C. '77 '02 C.20 B.A. L.209 J.D. [Chicago W.]
Garmisa, William J., (AV) '43 '68 C.339 B.A. L.477 J.D. [Aronberg G.D.&G.]
Garner, Donald W., Jr. '71 '01 C&L.339 B.A., J.D. [LL.M]
Garner, Gary W. '62 '88 C.339 B.A. L.378 J.D. [Gardner C.&D.]
Garner, Lee P. '68 '95 C.575 B.A. L.597 J.D. [Ⓒ Skadden,A.S.M.&F.]

Garner, Lisa M. ... '64 '88 C.377 B.A. L.378 J.D. Harris Tr. & Svgs. Bk.
Garner, Sarah E. ... '— '03 C.399 B.A. L.966 J.D. Two North LaSalle Street, Suite 2200
Garofalo, John R., (AV) ... '40 '67 C.602 B.B.A. L.365 J.D. [Kiesler&B.]
Garofalo, Joseph A., (AV) ... '52 '77 C.1106 B.A. L.209 J.D. [Garofalo,S.H.&S.]
Garofalo, Laura Christine ... '77 '05 C.910 B.S.B.A. L.424 J.D. [Ⓐ Holland&K.]

Garofalo, Schreiber, Hart & Storm, Chartered, (AV)
55 West Wacker Drive, 10th Floor, 60601
Telephone: 312-670-2000 Facsimile: 312-419-1336
URL: http://www.gshslaw.com
Joseph A. Garofalo; Scott T. Schreiber; Bennett F. Hart; Derek A. Storm; Gregory P. Sujack; Philip G. Brinckerhoff; Steven R. Scarlati, Jr.; James R. Clune; Andrew L. Rane; Jeffrey C. Hart; Todd E. Wegman; Craig M. Scarpelli; Kevin James Reid; William R. Stanczak; David P. Hanson; Daniel L. Grant; Christopher P. Carr; Juan A. Rodriguez-Del Moral; Shawn F. Luedde; Ronak T. Joshi; Anita S. Oak. Of Counsel: Ralph L. Berke.
Insurance Defense Law, Employers' Liability, Workers Compensation-Defense, State and Federal, Trials and Appeals.

See Professional Biographies, CHICAGO, ILLINOIS

Garr, Anne R. ... '71 '97 C.30 B.A. L.734 J.D. [Lord,B.&B.]
Garretson, Melvin A., (BV) ... '17 '39 C&L.145 B.A., J.D. [Garretson&S.]
Garretson & Santora, Ltd., (AV) ... 2 N. LaSalle St., Ste. 1100
Garrett, Alan C., (AV) ... '34 '61 C.347 A.B. L.309 LL.B. 333 W. Wacker
Garrett, Frank B., III ... '60 '86 C.604 B.A. L.209 J.D. [Robbins,S.N.L.&T.]
Garrett, Matthew M. ... '75 '00 C.1082 B.S. L.339 J.D. [Ⓐ Wildman,H.A.&D.]
Garrett, Steffanie N. ... '— '91 C.788 A.B. L.945 J.D. [Holland&K.]
Garrett, Tina L. ... '56 '85 C.347 B.S. L.365 J.D. Asst. State's Atty.
Garrette, Thomas W., JR. ... '64 '98 C.209 B.A. L.365 J.D. 5130 South Archer Avenue
Garrison, Douglas S. ... '52 '78 C.966 B.A. L.345 J.D. Spec. Agent, FBI
Garrison, Julie A., (BV) ... '58 '82 C.879 B.A. L.209 J.D. [Ⓐ Maciorowski,S.&U.]
Garrity, Patrick J. ... '51 '91 C.927 B.S. L.365 J.D. 10142 S. Washtenaw Ave.
Garro, Robert K. '43 '68 C.504 B.A. L.228 J.D.
V.P. & Tr. Coun., Amer. Natl. Bk. & Tr. Co. of Chicago
Garry, Paul R., (AV) ... '52 '77 C.966 B.A. L.188 J.D. [Meckler B.&T.]
Garth, Bryant '49 '75 C.976 B.A. L.813 J.D.
(adm. in CA; not adm. in IL) Dir., Amer. Bar Found.
Gartin, Randell J. '71 '01 C.878 B.S. L.802 J.D.
(adm. in TX; not adm. in IL) [Ⓐ Skadden,A.S.M.&F.]
Gartner, Stewart I. ... '34 '58 C.339 B.S. L.597 J.D. 77 W. Washington
Garvey, Brian L. ... '44 '85 C.959 B.A., B.B.A. L.46 J.D. Asst. Exec. Vice Pres.
Garvey, Catherine L., (AV) ... '61 '90 C.339 B.S.N. L.209 J.D. [Cassiday,S.&G.]
Garvey, James V. ... '69 '94 C.770 B.S. L.602 J.D. [Vedder,P.K.&K.]
Garvey, Kenneth T., (AV) '46 '74 C.177 A.B. L.209 J.D.
1335 S. Prairie Ave., Unit 901
Garvey, Maurice J., (AV) ... '33 '60 C.1024 B.A. L.436 J.D. [Bollinger,R.&G.]
Garvey, Michael J., (AV) ... '53 '78 C.674 A.B. L.597 J.D. [Baker&M.]
Garvey, Patrick T. ... '63 '93 C.234 B.A. L.146 J.D. [Johnson&B.]
Garwin, Arthur H. '49 '74 C&L.339 B.S., J.D.
Coun., Ctr. for Prof. Responsibility, Amer. Bar Assn.
Garypie, Catherine J. '66 '91 C.299 B.A. L.146 J.D.
U.S. Envir. Protec. Agcy., Region 5 Off. of Reg. Coun.
Garza, Demetrio, JR. ... '71 '98 C.339 B.A. L.146 J.D. 4111 South Richmond Avenue
Garzino, Fred R. ... '— '98 C.221 B.A. L.209 J.D. Dept. of HHS
Gasaway, Matthew W. ... '75 '01 C.602 B.B.A. L.352 J.D. [Ⓐ Chittenden,M.&N.]
Gascoigne, Janice M. ... '49 '91 C.339 B.A. L.424 J.D. Admr., Jameson Realty Grp.
Gase, John L. ... '73 '99 C.475 B.S. L.273 J.D. [Ⓐ Leydig,V.&M.]
Gasey, Arthur A. ... '67 '92 C.602 B.S. L.365 J.D. [Niro,S.H.&N.] (See Pat. Sect.)
Gasior, Joseph J. ... '18 '42 C&L.145 B.A., J.D. 4814 S. Pulaski Rd.
Gasiorowski, John A. ... '61 '86 C.209 B.A. L.46 J.D. Asst. State Atty.
Gaskell, Judith A. ... '45 '80 C.118 B.A. L.209 J.D. Dir., DePaul Law Library
Gass, David A. ... '— '92 C.477 B.S. L.1066 J.D. [Marshall,G.&B.] (See Pat. Sect.)
Gass, Stanford E., (AV) ... '36 '61 C&L.477 B.A., LL.B. [Gass&L.] ⊙
Gass and Lewis, Ltd., (AV) ... Suite 340, 29 S. La Salle St. (⊙Northbrook)
Gassman, Barry ... '70 '96 C.347 B.S. L.365 J.D. 55 E. Monroe St., Ste. 2960
Gassman, Gary L. ... '68 '93 C.347 B.A. L.365 J.D. [Ⓐ Sedgwick,D.M.&A.]
Gastel, Laura ... '68 '03 C.118 B.A. L.209 J.D. Underwriting Consultant, CNA
Gattari, Patrick G. '62 '92 C.477 B.S. L.802 J.D.
[McDonnell B.H.&B.] (See Pat. Sect.)
Gattuso, Joseph P., (AV) ... '59 '90 C.339 B.A. L.209 J.D. [Ⓒ Shefsky&F.]
Gatz, John C. ... '68 '96 C.474 B.S.C.M. L.339 J.D. [Jenkens&G.] (Pat.)
Gatziolis, James J., (AV) ... '48 '74 C.339 B.S. L.146 J.D. [Quarles&B.]
Gatzulis, W. Jason ... '71 '99 C.424 B.A. L.1294 J.D. [Ⓐ Leahy&H.]
Gaughan, Francis I. ... '19 '53 C&L.424 Ph.B., J.D. 5415 N. Sheridan Rd.‡
Gaughan, Frank I., (BV) ... '50 '80 C.755 B.A. L.365 J.D. [Kane,D.&H.]
Gaughan, James P. ... '— '90 C.145 B.A. L.424 J.D. [Schiff H.]
Gaughan, Sharon L. ... '61 '85 C&L.424 B.S., J.D. Asst. States Atty.
Gault, Gordon F. ... '48 '74 C.339 B.S. L.424 J.D. 318 W. Adams., suite 1402
Gaur, Shanthi V. ... '70 '94 C&L.145 B.A., J.D. [Littler M.]
Gauri, Vineet ... '— '97 C.477 B.S. L.94 J.D. [Brinks H.G.&L.] (See Pat. Sect.)
Gaus, Beth W. ... '77 '02 C.197 A.B. L.597 J.D. Cir. Ct. Clk.
Gauza, Thaddeus S., (BV) ... '62 '87 C.424 A.B. L.228 J.D. 140 S. Dearborn St.
Gavin, Christopher Michael ... '71 '99 C.352 B.A. L.209 J.D. [Ⓐ Mayer,B.R.&M.]
Gavin, John N. ... '— '75 C.321 A.B. L.309 J.D. [Foley&L.]
Gavin, Lawrence M., (AV) ... '47 '72 C.999 A.B. L.477 J.D. [Bell,B.&L.]
Gavin, Linella Lim ... '73 '98 C.339 B.S. L.209 J.D. AIDS Legal Council of Chicago
Gavin, Steven J. ... '60 '85 C.976 B.A. L.813 J.D. [Winston&S.]
Gawne, Bernard, III ... '77 '04 C.339 B.S. L.146 J.D. [Ⓐ Segal M.S.&M.]
Gawryk, Terry R. ... '53 '79 C.339 B.A. L.365 J.D. 4964 N. Milwaukee Ave.
Gayed, Jeremy N. ... '— '04 C.937 B.S. L.602 J.D. [Ⓐ McAndrews,H.&M.]
Gayle, Richard L. ... '47 '72 C&L.209 B.S., J.D. [Robbins,S.&P.] ⊙
Gayles, Edw. R. ... '21 '50 C.339 L.365 LL.B. 6326 S. Cottage Grove St.
Gaylon, Alisa F. ... '72 '97 C.597 B.S. L.209 J.D. First Def. Legal Aid
Gaylord, Amy Moor ... '72 '97 C.188 B.S. L.339 J.D. [Ⓐ Katten M.R.]
Gaynor, Audrey L., (AV) ... '61 '88 C&L.477 B.A., J.D. [A.L.Gaynor&Assoc.]
Gaynor, Malcolm M., (AV) ... '35 '58 C&L.597 B.S.L., J.D. [Ⓒ Schwartz C.]

Gaynor, Audrey L., & Associates, P.C., (AV)
20 South Clark Street, Suite 1620, 60603
Telephone: 312-201-0030 Fax: 312-201-0608
Email: audreygaynor@earthlink.net URL: http://www.lawyers.com/gaynor
Audrey L. Gaynor;—George M. Sanders; Maureen A. Mitchel.
Family Law, Divorce, Paternity, Child Custody, Child Support, Domestic Violence, Premarital Agreements, Spousal Support.

See Professional Biographies, CHICAGO, ILLINOIS

Gaz, Jennifer I. ... '72 '97 C.339 B.A. L.209 J.D. [Ⓐ G.E.W.Kelter,Jr.]
Gaziano, Cara M. ... '66 '92 C.103 B.A. L.273 J.D. [Ⓐ M.A.Haber&Assoc.]
Gearen, John J., (AV) ... '43 '72 C.602 B.A. L.976 J.D. [Mayer,B.R.&M.]
Gearen, Thomas ... '56 '82 C.966 B.A. L.902 J.D. Asst. States Atty.
Gearey, David P. ... '— '05 C.293 B.A. L.145 J.D. [Ⓐ Gardner C.&D.]
Geary, Adrienne M., (AV) ... '41 '86 C.1191 B.Ed. L.365 J.D. 2650 W. 51st St.
Geary, Michael P., (CV) ... '— '95 C.473 B.A. L.896 J.D. [Hennessy&R.]
Gecht, Robert D. ... '51 '78 C.309 A.B. L.145 J.D. Pres., Albany Bk. Tr. Co., N.A.
Gecker, Frances, (AV) ... '53 '88 C.966 B.A. L.597 J.D. [Frank/ G.]
Gecker, James M., (AV) ... '47 '74 C.112 A.B. L.966 J.D. [Katten M.R.]
Geddes, Richard J. ... '48 '74 C.403 B.A. L.1065 J.D. [Sedgwick,D.M.&A.]
Gedville, Jennifer J. ... '71 '99 C.357 B.A. L.209 J.D. [Ⓐ Lavin&W.]
Geekie, Eugene J., Jr., (AV) ... '— '86 C&L.734 B.S.B.A., J.D. [Schiff H.]
Geer, Elaine ... '50 '77 C.1016 B.S. L.209 J.D. Asst. States Atty.
Geer, H. Stat ... '49 '74 C&L.383 B.A., J.D. 171 N. Clark St.
Geerdes-Lugo, Lynn ... '67 '97 C.221 B.A. L.352 J.D. [Ⓐ Meckler B.&T.]
Gegas, Evangelos J. ... '67 '99 C&L.608 B.A., J.D. [Ⓐ Dykema G.P.]
Gehant, Timothy ... '66 '91 C.339 B.A. L.209 J.D. Asst. Hearings Off.
Gehm, Gary F. '56 '89 C.339 B.S. L.365 J.D.
Asst. V.P., The First National Bk. of Chicago
Gehring, Durward J. (James), (BV) ... '52 '77 C.339 A.B. L.145 J.D. [Seyfarth S.]
Gehringer, Matthew J., (AV) ... '58 '83 C&L.477 B.B.A., J.D. [Perkins C.]
Geier, Andrew M. ... '— '00 C.746 B.A. L.424 J.D. [Ⓐ Schuyler,R.&Z.]
Geier, Shannon M. ... '— '02 C.746 B.A. L.424 J.D. [Ⓐ Clausen M.]
Geifman, Stephen I. '44 '69
C.910 B.S.B.A. L.276 J.D. Sr. Coun., Bank One Corp. (Law Dept.)
Geiger, Laura M. ... '— '99 C.339 B.A. L.146 J.D. [Ⓐ Morgan,L.&B.]
Geiger, Paul D. ... '67 '92 C.424 B.A. L.146 J.D. 29 S. La Salle St.
Geimer, Robert F., (AV) ... '65 '91 C.424 B.A. L.339 J.D. [Ⓐ P.J.Kenneally]
Geimer, Ronald F. ... '68 '93 C.597 B.A. L.339 J.D. [Schuyler,R.&Z.]
Geimer, Stephen D., (AV) '52 '77
C.339 B.S.M.E. L.424 J.D. [Wood,P.K.C.&M.] (See Pat. Sect.)
Geiringer, John M. ... '70 '96 C.30 B.A. L.209 J.D. [Ⓐ Barack F.K.P.&N.]
Geis, James A. ... '39 '67 C.597 B.S. L.365 J.D. 5647 S. Drexel Ave.
Geis, Norman, (AV) ... '25 '51 C&L.145 A.B., J.D. 208 S. La Salle St., Ste. 1100
Geis, Ruth S. ... '49 '75 C.783 B.A. L.93 J.D. 5647 S. Drexel
Geiser, William A., (AV) ... '56 '83 C.966 B.A. L.146 J.D. [Johnson&B.]
Geisler, Carol P. ... '— '03 C.879 B.A. L.1000 J.D. [Ⓐ Jones D.]
Geissler, Stephen M. ... '74 '00 C&L.339 B.S., J.D. [Ⓐ Jenner&B.]
Gekas, Constantine John (Chris), (AV) '46 '7• C.145 B.A. L.339 J.D.
[Gekas&Assoc.]
Gekas, John C. ... '— '03 C.477 B.A. L.893 J.D. [Ⓐ Kirkland&E.]

Gekas & Associates, Ltd., (AV) BR
11 South La Salle Street, Suite 1700, 60603
Telephone: 312-726-4501 Fax: 312-726-4505
Email: cjg@cjglaw.com URL: http://www.cjglaw.com
Constantine John (Chris) Gekas.
State and Federal Civil and Criminal Litigation, Trials and Appellate Practice, Securities, Commodities, Intellectual Property, Bankruptcy, Employment and Real Estate Law.

See Professional Biographies, CHICAGO, ILLINOIS

Gelb, Aaron R. ... '69 '95 C.145 B.A. L.846 J.D. [Ⓐ Vedder,P.K.&K.]
Gelb, Judith A., (AVⓉ) '35 '59 C.102 B.A. L.178 LL.B.
(adm. in NY; not adm. in IL) [Ⓒ Winston&S.] (⊙New York, NY)
Gelboim, Rick Y. ... '79 '04 C.823 B.S. L.910 J.D. [Ⓐ Jenner&B.]
Geleerd, Guy Delson, Jr., (BV) ... '64 '89 C.339 B.A. L.999 J.D. [Coughlin&G.]
Gellen, Pamela L., (AV) ... '51 '76 C.881 A.B. L.982 J.D. [Lewis&G.]
Geller, Jeremy L. ... '77 '02 C.966 B.S. L.365 J.D. [Ⓐ J.M.Trapp&Assoc.]
Gelman, Andrew R., (AV) ... '— '70 C.659 B.A. L.893 J.D. [Holland&K.]
Gelman, Arlene N. ... '— '94 C.339 B.A. L.94 J.D. [Sachnoff&W.]
Gelman, Bruce L. ... '68 '93 C.93 B.A. L.215 J.D. [Mayer,B.R.&M.]
Gelman, Marcia R. '54 '81 C.1036 B.A. L.94 J.D.
(adm. in DC; not adm. in IL) [Ⓐ Winston&S.]
Gelman, Peggy ... '— '82 C.597 B.A. L.424 J.D. 3550 N. Lake Shore Dr.
Gely, Rafael '61 '87 C.375 B.S. L.339 J.D.
Asst. Prof. of Law, Chicago-Kent College of Law
Geman, Kenneth Y. ... '40 '65 C.966 B.S. L.597 J.D. 33 N. LaSalle St.
Gembala, Bettina M. ... '47 '81 C.424 A.B. L.146 J.D. Assoc. Clk. for Ct. Opers.
Gembala, Francis A. ... '47 '72 C&L.424 A.B., J.D. [Nadler,P.&M.]
Gemmell, Thomas L. ... '62 '95 C.174 B.A. L.813 J.D. [Welsh&K.]
Gemperle, David E. ... '77 '03 C.94 B.A. L.339 J.D. [Ⓐ Nisen&E.]
Gemski, Carolann '66 '92 C.420 B.A. L.30 J.D.
Sr. Atty., U.S. Secs. and Exchange Comm.
Gendel, Paul ... '12 '39 C.137 L.146 LL.B. 77 W. Wash. St.
Genden, James K., (AV) ... '48 '75 C&L.309 B.A., J.D. [Torshen,S.G.D.&A.]
Genelly, David A., (AV) ... '52 '77 C.424 B.A. L.276 J.D. [Vanasco,G.&M.]
Genet, Russell J. ... '71 '98 C.679 B.S.E.E. L.146 J.D. [Ⓐ Jenkens&G.] (Pat.)
Gengler, Michael T. ... '44 '69 C.178 A.B. L.309 J.D. Sr. V.P. & Dep. Gen. Coun., CNA
Genin, Eric J. ... '71 '96 C.339 B.A. L.477 J.D. [Ⓐ Levenfeld P.]
Genin, Kent E. ... '66 '93 C.813 B.S.E.E. L.150 J.D. [Brinks H.G.&L.] (See Pat. Sect.)
Genin, Lyle S., (AV) ... '— '72 C.339 B.S. L.146 J.D. [Beermann S.W.B.B.G.&L.]
Genis, Carol A. ... '63 '88 C&L.597 B.A., J.D. [Bell,B.&L.]
Gens, Henry J. ... '17 '52 C.46 B.S.E.E. L.209 J.D. 8350 W. Addison Ave. (Pat.)‡
Gensburg, Lane M. ... '55 '81 C.1365 B.A. L.209 J.D. [Dale,J.&G.]
Gensburg, Matthew T., (AV) ... '58 '84 C.477 B.B.A. L.245 J.D. [Greenberg T.]
Genson, Edward M., (AV) ... '41 '65 C&L.597 B.A., J.D. [Genson&G.]
Genson, Laura Ruhl ... '72 '98 C.339 B.A. L.146 J.D. Gen. Coun., Ruhl Forensic, Inc.
Genson & Gillespie, (AV) ... 53 W. Jackson Blvd.
Gentleman, Joseph T. ... '— '98 C.597 B.A. L.365 J.D. 33 N. Dearborn St.
Gentner, Joshua D. ... '72 '97 C.347 B.A. L.597 J.D. [Vedder,P.K.&K.]
Gentry, Bradford S. '55 '82 C.821 B.A. L.309 J.D.
(adm. in MA; not adm. in IL) [Ⓐ Baker&M.]
Gentry, Patricia V. ... '55 '80 C.502 B.S. L.208 J.D. [Ⓒ Mayer,B.R.&M.]
Geocaris, Angelo ... '21 '48 642 N. Dearborn
Geoffrey, Lauren ... '— '04 C.477 B.A. L.1565 J.D. [Ⓐ Katten M.R.]
Geoghegan, J.T. Terence, (AV) ... '55 '93 C.999 B.A. L.365 J.D. [Healy]
Geoghegan, Thomas H., (AV) ... '49 '75 C&L.309 B.A., J.D. [Despres,S.&G.]
Geoly, James C., (AV) ... '60 '85 C.178 B.A. L.145 J.D. [Burke,W.M.&S.]
George, Arthur L. ... '56 '83 C.174 B.A. L.273 J.D. [Baker&M.]
George, Christopher N. '— '02
C&L.339 B.S., J.D. [Ⓐ McAndrews,H.&M.] (See Pat. Sect.)
George, John J., (AV) ... '40 '67 C.973 B.S. L.209 J.D. [Daley&G.]
George, John M., Jr. ... '47 '82 C.339 A.B. L.309 J.D. [Sidley A.B.&W.]
George, LaDale K. ... '— '91 C.378 B.A. L.597 J.D. [Ⓒ Foley&L.]
George, Peter R. ... '69 '97 C.477 B.A. L.597 J.D. [Ⓐ Baker&M.]
George Stewart, Ava M. ... '68 '03 C.597 B.A. L.339 J.D. [A.GeorgeStewart]
George Stewart, Ava, Law Office of ... 1400 N. Mohawk St., Ste. A
George W. Hamman, Law Offices of, (AV) ... 33 N. LaSalle St.,
Georgerian, Kevin ... '78 '04 C.692 B.A. L.902 J.D. [Ⓐ Cremer,K.S.&S.]

Golab, Richard G. ....'56 '90 C.475 B.F.A. L.209 J.D. [Schain,B.R.&C.]
Golan, Leonard W., (AV) ....'23 '48 C&L.597 B.S.L., J.D. [Ⓒ Field&G.]
Golan, Stephen L., (AV) ....'51 '78 C.154 B.A. L.597 J.D. [Field&G.]
Golant, Joseph H., (AVⓉ) ...'— '66 C.399 B.S. L.145 J.D. [Ⓒ Jones D.] (See Pat. Sect.)
Gold, Arthur S., (AV) ....'41 '65 C.339 B.A. L.597 J.D. [Gold&C.]
Gold, Brian J., (AV) ....'57 '82 C.473 A.B. L.276 J.D. [Sidley A.B.&W.]
Gold, Lawrence A., (AV) ....'46 '72 C.966 B.S. L.904 J.D. [Gomberg,S.G.&O.]
Gold, Michael L. ....'59 '84 C.339 B.S. L.365 J.D. [Sidley A.B.&W.]
Gold, Norbert L. ....'24 '51 C.597 B.A. L.365 LL.B. 5901 N. Cicero Ave.‡
Gold, Norton N., (AV) ....'34 '63 C.339 B.S. L.209 J.D. [FagelHaber]
Gold, Paul A. ....'33 '57 C.339 B.S. L.477 J.D. [P.A.Gold]
Gold, Rebecca L. ....'77 '03 C&L.910 B.A., J.D. Asst. Pub. Defender
Gold, Roger N. ....'45 '71 C.339 B.A. L.145 J.D. 77 W. Wacker Dr.
Gold, Stephen ....'59 '85 C.477 B.A. L.276 J.D. [Gordon&G.L.]
Gold & Coulson, (AV) .... 11 S. LaSalle Street
Gold, Paul A., Ltd. .... 33 N. Dearborn St., Ste. 1410
Goldbeck, William L. ....'58 '98 C.145 B.A. L.424 J.D. [Ⓐ Gardner C.&D.]
Goldberg, Alan D. ....'51 '76 C&L.339 B.A., J.D. Asst. Appl. Def.
Goldberg, Alan P. ....'64 '90 C.659 B.A. L.831 J.D. [Bell,B.&L.]
Goldberg, Allan, (AV) ....'— '70 C.560 B.A. L.424 J.D. [Arnstein&L.]
Goldberg, Allen S. ....'42 '67 C.339 B.S. L.209 J.D. Cir.J.
Goldberg, Andrew S. ....'70 '96 C.338 B.S. L.1068 J.D. [Laner,M.D.B.L.&T.]
Goldberg, Barry D., (AV) ....'40 '64 C&L.472 B.B.A., LL.B. [Goldberg&G.]
Goldberg, Barth H. ....'40 '64 C&L.472 B.B.A., LL.B. [Goldberg&G.]
Goldberg, Cary N. ....'59 '84 C.188 B.A. L.145 J.D. [Ⓒ M.M.Cherry&Assoc.]
Goldberg, Daniel ....'78 '03 C.976 B.A. L.145 J.D. 35 West Wacker Drive
Goldberg, David A. ....'68 '93 C.477 B.A. L.910 J.D. [Ⓐ Sidley A.B.&W.]
Goldberg, David M., (AV) ....'54 '80 C.597 B.A. L.365 J.D. [Cornfield&F.]
Goldberg, Debra B. ....'75 '00 C.910 B.A. L.273 J.D. [Ⓐ Kerns,P.F.&P.]
Goldberg, Gerald G. ....'42 '68 C&L.209 B.S., J.D. [Goldberg&F.]
Goldberg, James B. ....'— '99 C.209 B.A. L.365 J.D. [Ⓐ Goldberg&F.]
Goldberg, Jay Russell ....'54 '89 C.1111 B.A. L.424 J.D. [Field&G.]
Goldberg, Jeffrey M., (AV) ....'48 '74 C.98 B.S. L.365 J.D. [J.M.Goldberg]
Goldberg, Jerome F., (AV) ....'27 '51 C.339 L.597 J.D. 225 W. Washington St.
Goldberg, Jerry S. ....'51 '76 C.589 B.A. L.146 J.D. 10 S. LaSalle St.
Goldberg, Joseph L. ....'— '48 C.339 L.209 J.D. 77 W. Washington St., Ste. 1018
Goldberg, Keith A. ....'65 '91 C&L.339 B.S., J.D. 77 W. Washington St., Ste. 1018
Goldberg, Larry S. ....'47 '71 C.475 B.A. L.339 J.D. [DLPiper R.G.C.U.]
Goldberg, Linda V. ...'56 '84 C.966 B.A. L.597 J.D. Assoc. Gen. Coun., Shorebank Corp.
Goldberg, Matthew J. ....'— '01 C.352 B.B.A. L.146 J.D. [Arnstein&L.]
Goldberg, Michael B. ....'50 '74 [Goldberg,W.&C.]
Goldberg, Michael J. ....'76 '02 C.339 B.A. L.146 J.D. [Whiting]
Goldberg, Michael K. ....'67 '92 C&L.339 B.A., J.D. [Goldberg&F.]
Goldberg, Mitchell B. ....'74 '99 C&L.209 B.A., J.D. [Ⓐ Lawrence,K.S.&U.]
Goldberg, Phillip M., (AV) ....'— '83 C.347 B.A. L.209 J.D. [Foley&L.]
Goldberg, Robert B. ....'— '97 C.339 B.A. L.569 J.D. [Kirkland&E.]
Goldberg, Robert C. ....'48 '73 C.339 B.A. L.146 J.D. [Schoenberg,F.N.&R.]
Goldberg, Stephen B. ....'32 '61 C&L.309 A.B., LL.B. Prof. of Law, Northwestern Univ.
Goldberg, William I., (AV) ....'37 '62 C.31 B.A. L.309 J.D. [Seyfarth S.]
Goldberg & Frankenstein, LLC .... 222 S. Riverside Drive, Suite 810
Goldberg & Goldberg, (AV) .... 33 N. Dearborn Street

Goldberg, Jeffrey M., Law Offices, (AV)
20 North Clark Street, Suite 3100, 60602
Telephone: 312-236-4146 Fax: 312-236-5913 Fax: 1-800-564-1707
Email: firm@goldberglaw.com URL: http://www.goldberglaw.com
Jeffrey M. Goldberg;—Gary P. Annes; David P. Buchanan; Geoffrey G. Johnson; Megan E. Laser; Don M. Sowers, Jr.
Plaintiffs Personal Injury firm including Product Liability, Birth Injuries, Medical Malpractice, Aviation, Wrongful Death, Occupant Restraint and Seat Belt Accidents, F.E.L.A., Premises Liability, Class Action, Brain Injury.
See Professional Biographies, CHICAGO, ILLINOIS

Goldberg, Kohn, Bell, Black, Rosenbloom & Moritz, Ltd., (AV)
55 East Monroe Street, Suite 3700, 60603
Telephone: 312-201-4000 Telecopier: 312-332-2196
Email: info@goldbergkohn.com URL: http://www.goldbergkohn.com
Principals: Oscar L. Alcantara; Ronald Barliant; Stephen B. Bell; Dennis B. Black; Philip M. Blackman; Jami L. Brodey; Joel F. Brown; Denise B. Caplan; Andrew R. Cardonick; David J. Chizewer; Frederick H. Cohen; Jonathan M. Cooper; David L. Dranoff; Barbara M. Flom; Michael C. Hainen; Deborah Rzasnicki Hogan; Gerald L. Jenkins; Michael D. Karpeles; Frederic R. Klein; Randall L. Klein; Richard M. Kohn; Adam M. Laser; Steven A. Levy; Roger A. Lewis; William R. Loesch; Michael B. Manuel; David M. Mason; William C. Meyers; Terry F. Moritz; David E. Morrison; Gerald F. Munitz; Alice G. Owings; Keith G. Radner; James B. Rosenbloom; Gary N. Ruben; Daniel P. Shapiro; Keith A. Sigale; Alan P. Solow; Michael L. Sullivan; Carole K. Towne; Kenneth S. Ulrich; Matthew A.C. Zapf; Gary T. Zussman. Associates: Stacy S. Jakobe; Mazen Asbahi; Vanessa A. Bachtell; Catherine S. Carrigan; Rachel Gena Chiss; Jessica DeBruin; Jeremy M. Downs; Hillary Levitt Dunn; Michael D. Ebner; Brian D. Fagel; Jeffrey K. Fleishmann (Not admitted in IL); Alais L.M. Griffin; Allison G. Hammer; Caroline E. Hammond; Susan H. Kane; Dimitri G. Karcazes; Salvador K. Karottki; Jonathon J.H. Kim; Jon Eric Klinghoffer; Rachael R. Lape; Stephen Locher; James P. Madigan; Robert M. Oberlies; Kathryn A. Pamenter; Elan Peretz; John E. Peschke; Anne Marie Pisano; Shira Roth; Anne M. Sherry; Chante D. Spann; William A. Starshak; Marla Swartz; Andrew Torre; Jeanette K. Trudell (Not admitted in IL); Vanessa B.M. Vergara; Megan G. Walker; A. Colin Wexler. Of Counsel: Robin S. King; Joseph M. Martin.
Business Law, Business Litigation, Corporate, Commercial Finance, Asset-Based Finance, Real Estate, Creditor Bankruptcy, Workouts, Securities, Tax, Labor and Employment, Intellectual Property, Environmental Law.
See Professional Biographies, CHICAGO, ILLINOIS

Goldberg, Weisman & Cairo, Ltd., (AV) .... 1 E. Wacker Dr., Ste. 3400
Goldblatt, Ann D. '39 '65 C.681 B.A. L.309 LL.B.
(adm. in NY; not adm. in IL) 57 E. Bellevue Pl.‡
Goldblatt, Howard I. ....'62 '87 C.659 B.A. L.597 J.D. [O'Rourke,H.F.&D.]
Goldblatt, Joel N. ....'57 '82 C.813 B.A. L.209 J.D. [Childress D.G.]
Goldblatt, Stanford J., (AV) ....'39 '63 C&L.309 B.A., LL.B. [Winston&S.]
Goldblatt, Thomas C. ......'63 '88 C.339 B.S. L.145 J.D. Gen. Coun., Strombecker Corp.
Goldbloom, Marcie E. ....'61 '86 C.477 B.A. L.285 J.D. [Ⓐ Daley,D.&B.]
Golde, Michael J., (AV) ....'— '83 C.910 B.S.B.A. L.209 J.D. [Frank/ G.]
Golden, Bruce P. ....'43 '69 C.453 B.S. L.309 J.D. 4137 N. Hermitage
Golden, Gerald A., (AV) ....'45 '72 C.910 A.B. L.209 J.D. [Neal,G.&E.]
Golden, Howard S., (AV) ....'44 '69 C.347 B.S. L.209 J.D. [Robbins,S.&P.]
Golden, Jean M., (AV) ....'— '77 C.93 B.A. L.424 J.D. [Cassiday,S.&G.]
Golden, Kevin J., (AV) ....'66 '92 C&L.209 B.A., J.D. [Ⓐ Motherway&N.]
Golden, Robert J., (BV) ....'59 '86 C.339 B.A. L.365 J.D. [Dowd&D.]
Golden, Rosalyn M., (AV) ....'— '84 C.209 B.A. L.146 J.D. [O'Hagan,S.&A.]
Golden, Samuel D. '26 '49 C&L.145 A.B., J.D.
Assoc. Gen. Coun., The University of Chicago
Golden, Sarah J. ....'75 '02 C.436 B.A. L.345 J.D. [Ⓐ Seyfarth S.]

Goldenberg, Jay S., (AV) '38 '66 C.1100 B.A. L.365 J.D.
221 North La Salle Street, Suite 240, 60601
Telephone: 312-346-7899 Fax: 312-896-5047 URL: http://www.chicplan.com
Email: Attyjsg@chicplan.com URL: http://www.lawyers.com/chicplan
Probate, Trusts and Estates, Estate Planning and Wills, Elder Law, Living Trusts, Trust Planning, Asset Protection, Gift Tax, Family Limited Partnerships.
See Professional Biographies, CHICAGO, ILLINOIS

Goldenberg, Susan L., (AV) ....'62 '87 C.477 B.A. L.145 J.D. [Katten M.R.]
Goldfarb, Eugene L. '49 '80
C.1350 B.A. L.209 J.D. U.S. Dept. of Housing and Urban Develop.
Goldfarb, Renee G. ....'50 '75 C.94 B.A. L.339 J.D. Chief, Crim. App. Div.
Goldfarb, Samuel Z. ....'51 '75 C.339 B.A. L.424 J.D. [Ⓐ Borovsky&E.]
Goldfein, Charlotte R. ....'23 '59 C&L.209 LL.B. 77 W. Washington St.
Goldgar, A. Benjamin ....'57 '82 C.103 A.B. L.597 J.D. Bkrptcy. J.
Goldgehn, Mitchell S., (AV) ....'31 '53 L.209 J.D. [Aronberg G.D.&G.]
Goldhaber, Catherine E. Boyd ....'— '99 C.475 B.A. L.424 J.D. [Ⓐ Segal M.S.&M.]
Goldhaber, David M. ....'71 '97 C.679 B.A. L.424 J.D. [Ⓐ Sedgwick,D.M.&A.]
Golding, Richard N., (AV) ....'42 '67 C.98 L.146 J.D. [Ⓒ Weinberg R.]
Goldkind, Jeremy S. ....'— '04 C.339 B.S. L.352 J.D. [Ⓐ Wildman,H.A.&D.]
Goldman, Alan L. ....'63 '89 C.339 B.S. L.597 J.D. [Sidley A.B.&W.]
Goldman, Andrew L. ....'65 '95 C.477 B.A. L.597 J.D. [Bartlit B.H.P.&S.]
Goldman, Barry A. ....'48 '75 C.209 B.A. L.146 J.D. [Goldman&G.]
Goldman, David M., (AV) ....'49 '81 C.339 B.A. L.209 J.D. [Feinberg&B.]
Goldman, Edward S. ....'61 '86 C.477 B.B.A. L.145 J.D. [DLPiper R.G.C.U.]
Goldman, Emanuel ....'12 '39 C.145 Ph.B. L.209 J.D. 5000 S. East End Ave.‡
Goldman, Gerald A. ....'41 '66 C.339 B.S. L.209 J.D. 19 S. LaSalle St.
Goldman, Herbert C. ....'39 '64 C.339 B.S. L.597 J.D. [H.C.Goldman]
Goldman, Jeffrey A. ....'61 '92 C.959 B.A. L.145 J.D. [Ⓒ Mayer,B.R.&M.]
Goldman, Jeffrey S., (BV) ....'45 '70 C.103 A.B. L.145 J.D. [Sonnenschein N.&R.]
Goldman, Jonathan C. ....'67 '92 C.477 L.146 J.D. [Goldman&E.]
Goldman, Kenneth A. ....'67 '00 C.94 B.S. L.861 J.D. Assoc. Atty., RREEF
Goldman, Laurence L. '46 '71 C.477 B.A. L.597 J.D.
Sr. Assoc. Gen. Coun., Bank One Corp. (Law Dept.)
Goldman, Maxwell H. ....'11 '34 L.209 J.D. 19 S. LaSalle St.
Goldman, Norman E. ....'26 '53 C&L.145 B.A., J.D. 230 W. Monroe St.
Goldman, Robert G. ....'— '84 C.966 B.B.A. L.1068 J.D. [Latham&W.]
Goldman, Robert H., (AV) ....'45 '69 C&L.477 B.A., J.D. [DLPiper R.G.C.U.]
Goldman, Steven ....'43 '68 C.674 A.B. L.309 LL.B. 1301 N. Astor St.‡
Goldman, Varda A. ......'49 '74 C.597 B.A. L.209 J.D. V.P. & Gen. Coun., PCTEL, Inc.

Goldman & Ehrlich, (BV)
19 South LaSalle Street - Fifteenth Floor, 60603
Telephone: 312-332-6733 Facsimile: 312-332-4629
URL: http://www.goldmanandehrlich.com
Members of the Firm: Jonathan C. Goldman; Arthur R. Ehrlich.
Employment Law, Commercial Litigation, Discrimination, Disabled Access, Sexual Harassment, Wrongful Termination, Americans with Disabilities Act, Family and Medical Leave Act, Affirmative Action, Age Discrimination, Civil Service, Covenants Not To Compete.
See Professional Biographies, CHICAGO, ILLINOIS

Goldman & Grant .... 134 North LaSalle Street, Suite 1717
Goldman, Herbert C., P.C. .... 11 S. La Salle St., Ste. 1000
Goldner, Anthony M. ....'62 '94 C.966 B.A. L.146 J.D. [Ⓐ Wilson E.M.E.&D.]
Goldrick, Michael J. ....'52 '81 C.363 B.A. L.424 J.D. 10540 S. Western Ave.
Goldrick, Thomas A., (AV) ....'54 '80 C.339 B.S. L.146 J.D. [Mahoney,C.&G.]

Goldsmith, Marshall J., (AV) '40 '65 C.347 B.A. L.1119 J.D.
77 West Wacker Drive, Suite 3200, 60601 ⊙
Telephone: 312-346-6622 Toll Free: 877-346-6622 Fax: 312-346-1566 URL: http://www.mjgoldmithlaw.lawoffice.com
Email: goldsmithlaw@aol.com URL: http://www.lawyers.com/goldsmithlaw
Corporations, Tax, Real Estate, Estate Planning, Wills, Trusts and Probate Law, Commercial Real Estate, Elder Law, Asset Protection.
Highland, Indiana Office: 2546 45th Street, 46322. Telephone: 219-924-4101. Fax: 219-924-4104.
See Professional Biographies, CHICAGO, ILLINOIS

Goldsmith, Mitchell D., (AV) ....'53 '78 C.659 B.A. L.145 J.D. [Shefsky&F.]
Goldsmith, Ted G. ....'50 '87 C.910 A.B. L.209 J.D. Asst. Atty., Chicago Bd. of Educ.
Goldstein, Aaron B. ....'75 '00 C.339 B.A. L.352 J.D. Cook Cty Pub Defend Off
Goldstein, Alan Jay, (AV) ....'59 '84 C.339 B.A. L.209 J.D. [FagelHaber]
Goldstein, Andrew L., (AV) ....'— '84 C&L.339 B.S., J.D. [Freeborn&P.]
Goldstein, Arnold D., (BV) ....'38 '63 C.339 B.A. L.597 J.D. [Goldstein&L.]
Goldstein, Carla ....'55 '89 C.454 B.F.A. L.597 J.D. 111 E. Wachce Dr.
Goldstein, Charles R. ...'58 '84 C.188 B.A. L.339 J.D. Asst. Reg. Coun., Soc. Sec. Admn.
Goldstein, David C. ....'62 '93 C.1183 B.S. L.365 J.D. [Ⓐ Aronberg G.D.&G.]
Goldstein, David L., (AV) ....'50 '75 C.273 B.B.A. L.365 J.D. 35 E. Wacker Dr., Ste. 650
Goldstein, Elliott H. ....'38 '67 C&L.930 A.B., J.D. Ste 811, 39 S La Salle St
Goldstein, Harley J. ....'— '98 C.36 B.A. L.1398 J.D. [Freeborn&P.]
Goldstein, Jamie H. ...'79 '04 C.966 B.S. L.146 J.D. [Ⓐ Cassiday,S.&G.] (⊙Libertyville)
Goldstein, Jay M. '48 '73 C.831 B.B.A. L.884 J.D.
(adm. in PA; not adm. in IL) [Cozen O.]
Goldstein, Jeremy F. ....'71 '98 C.63 B.S. L.209 J.D. [Ⓐ McDonald&M.]
Goldstein, John A., (AV) ....'59 '84 C.910 A.B. L.597 J.D. [Harris K.&G.]
Goldstein, Kenneth A. ....'65 '90 C.352 B.B.A. L.365 J.D. [Horwood M.&B.]
Goldstein, Kenneth T. ....'68 '97 C.966 B.A. L.365 J.D. [Ⓐ Krislov&Assoc.]
Goldstein, Larry R. ....'48 '73 C.347 A.B. L.477 J.D. [McGuirewoods]
Goldstein, Laurie G., (P.C.) '49 '75 C.608 B.A. L.813 J.D.
525 W. Monroe St., Suite 1600
Goldstein, Lori A., (BV) ....'59 '84 C&L.339 BS., J.D. [Ⓒ Wildman,H.A.&D.]
Goldstein, Louis S., (AV) ....'43 '74 C.388 B.A. L.424 J.D. [Goldstein&F.]
Goldstein, Neal T., (AV) ....'62 '89 C.339 B.S. L.424 J.D. [Much S.F.D.A.&R.]
Goldstein, Paul E. ....'35 '62 C.339 B.S. L.976 LL.B. 4950 Chicago Beach Dr.‡
Goldstein, Ray J. ....'10 '31 C.339 B.S.L. L.597 J.D. Smith Barney Inc.
Goldstein, Scott Geoffrey ....'74 '00 C.388 B.A. L.589 J.D. [Ⓐ Lewis&G.]
Goldstein, Sidney J. ....'11 '34 C&L.209 B.S., J.D. 134 N. LaSalle St.‡
Goldstein, Aiossa & Good, Ltd. .... 150 N. Wacker Dr.
Goldstein & Fluxgold, Ltd., (AV) .... 33 North Dearborn Street
Goldstein & Lamb, P.C., (BV) .... 162 West Hubbard
Goldstick, Jerome ....'24 '51 C&L.597 B.S., J.D. 25 E. Wash. St.‡
Goldstick, Phillip C., & Assoc., Ltd., (BV) '31 '56 C.339 B.S. L.209 J.D.
20 N. Clark St.

Goldwasser, Richard M., (BV) '65 '91 C&L.339 A.B., J.D.
20 North Clark, Suite 1700, 60602
Telephone: 312-372-3300 Fax: 312-372-0531
Email: rmg@goldwasserlaw.com URL: http://www.goldwasserlaw.com
Commercial Litigation, Criminal Law, Appellate Practice.
See Professional Biographies, CHICAGO, ILLINOIS

Goldwater, Ben, (AV) ....'38 '64 C.597 B.S. L.146 J.D. 70 W. Madison St.

Goldwater, Jeffrey A. .... '59 '85 C.597 B.A. L.339 J.D. [Bollinger,R.&G.]
Goles, David S. '72 '98 C.30 B.A. L.589 J.D.
[🄰 Swanson,M.&B.] (⊙Libertyville, Waukegan)
Goletz, Christina N. .... '73 '03 C.659 B.A. L.597 J.D. 927 S. Bell, Suite 2
Golin, David Alan, (BV) .... '56 '81 C.477 B.A. L.276 J.D. [Gesas,P.&G.]
Golinkin, Scott G., (BV) .... '52 '84 C.597 B.M.E. L.209 J.D. [Reardon G.&R.]
Golko, Andrew A., Law Office of, (BV) '45 '75
C.339 B.S. L.365 J.D. 4141 N. Western Ave.
Gollwitzer, John A. .... '71 '04 C&L.339 B.A., J.D. [🄰 Swanson,M.&B.]
Golniewicz, Francis Xavier .... '20 '48 C&L.597 B.S., J.D. Ret. Assoc. Cir. J.
Golomb, Samuel J. .... '10 '43 C.608 B.S. L.424 J.D. 7033 N. Kedzie Ave.‡
Golota, Mariola A. .... '70 '98 C.700 B.A. L.424 J.D. [Golota&Assoc.]
Golota & Associates P.C. .... 5910 N. Milwaukee Ave., Ste. 100
Golson, Ari H. .... '71 '96 C.401 B.A. L.30 J.D. 1 E Wacker Drive
Golub, Beth T. .... '— '94 C.347 B.S. L.245 J.D. [Seyfarth S.]
Golub, Todd D. .... '67 '92 C.347 B.S. L.1119 J.D. [Baker&M.]
Golz, Thomas Bernard, (AV) .... '50 '87 C.339 B.S. L.209 J.D. [🄰 FagelHaber]
Gomberg, Arthur S. .... '13 '37 C.999 L.146 LL.B. 134 N. La Salle St.
Gomberg, Barry A., (BV) .... '45 '77 C.339 B.A. L.209 J.D. [B.A.Gomberg&Assoc.]
Gomberg, Robert M. .... '60 '86 C.172 B.A. L.146 J.D. [Gomberg,S.G.&O.]
Gomberg, Sheldon S., (AV) .... '41 '70 C.339 B.S. L.146 J.D. [A.S.Gomberg]
Gomberg, Steven P., (AV) .... '47 '73 C.98 B.S. L.209 J.D. [Levenfeld P.]
Gomberg, Arthur S., Law Offices of, A Professional Corporation, (AV)
134 N. La Salle St.
Gomberg, Barry A., & Associate, Ltd., (BV) .... 53 W. Jackson Blvd., Ste. 1350

Gomberg, Sharfman, Gold and Ostler, P.C., (AV)
208 South La Salle Street, Suite 1200, 60604
Telephone: 312-332-6194 FAX: 312-332-4083
Email: gsgo@gsgolaw.com URL: http://www.lawyers.com/gsgolaw
Of Counsel: Robert J. Sharfman. Partners: Lawrence A. Gold; Raymond J. Ostler; Robert M. Gomberg;—Kimberly A. Orel-Padjen; John J. Lydon; Maureseta T. Hawkins; John W. Rossiter.
General Corporation and business Matters, including Real Estate, Mortgage Banking, Debtor-Creditor Relations, Bankruptcy, General Practice in all State and Federal Courts, litigation, including Class Action Defense, Probate, Mortgages, Mortgage Foreclosure, Mechanic's Lien, Title Insurance, thrift Institution Regulations, Commercial Collections and Mortgage Broker Regulation.
Reference: MB Financial Bank.
See Professional Biographies, CHICAGO, ILLINOIS

Gómez, Verónica .... '69 '94 C.813 A.B. L.145 J.D. [Schopf&W.]
Gondek, Serena Jean .... '— '04 C.367 B.S. L.209 J.D. [🄰 Kirkland&E.] (Pat.)
Gonsalves, Stanislaus Andrew .... '63 '89 C.424 B.A. L.276 J.D. Asst. State Atty.
Gonsalves, Terance A. .... '67 '00 C.339 B.A. L.209 J.D. [🄰 Sonnenschein N.&R.]
Gonsky, Ronald M., (Ltd.) .... '36 '60 C.339 B.A. L.365 B.L. 821 W. Van Buren
Gont, William B. .... '70 '02 C.475 B.S.M.E. L.365 J.D. [🄰 McAndrews,H.&M.]
Gonzales, Thomas E. .... '72 '02 C.846 B.B.A. L.209 J.D. [🄰 Kiesler&B.]
Gonzalez, Carlos J. .... '58 '89 C.339 B.A. L.352 J.D. Asst. Pub. Def.
Gonzalez, Catherine T. .... '— '89 C.1183 B.A. L.146 J.D. [🄰 Ungaretti&H.]
Gonzalez, Dawn M. .... '69 '94 C.477 B.A. L.209 J.D. [Litchfield C.]
Gonzalez, Elvis D. .... '77 '03 C.339 B.S. L.424 J.D. [🄰 Aronberg G.D.&G.]
Gonzalez, Richard J. .... '53 '78 C.597 B.A. L.608 J.D. Chicago-Kent Coll. of Law

Gonzalez, Saggio & Harlan, L.L.P.
208 S. LaSalle Street, Suite 1460, 60604 ⊙
Telephone: 312-236-0475 Facsimile: 312-236-1750
Email: main@gshllp.com URL: http://www.gshllp.com
Elizabeth A. McDuffie (Not admitted in IL). Associate: Philip S. Holloway. Of Counsel: Emmitt C. House; Jerry D. Brown.
Business and Corporate Law, Civil Litigation, Insurance Defense Law, Equal Opportunities and Employment, School Law, Municipal Finance, Business and Commercial Litigation, Real Estate, Construction, Condemnation Law, Environmental, Taxation, Utilities Law, Trials and Appeals, Government Relations.
Representative Clients: Accenture; Alliant Energy; Bear, Stears & Co.; Chubb Insurance Company; City of Milwaukee; CNH Global N.V.; Darden Restaurants, Inc.; Denny's; Eastman Kodak Company; E.I. du Pont de Nemours and Company.
Milwaukee, Wisconsin Office: 225 East Michigan, 4th Floor, 53202. Telephone: 414-277-8500. Fax: 414-277-8521.
Indianapolis, Indiana Office: 201 North Illinois Street, Suite 1900, 46204. Telephone: 317-686-9800. Fax: 317-686-9821.
West Des Moines, Iowa Office: 1501 42nd Street, Suite 465, 50266. Telephone: 515-453-8509. Fax: 515-267-1408.
Cincinnati, Ohio Office: Carew Tower, 441 Vine Street, Suite 3615, 45202. Telephone: 513-651-3456. Fax: 513-651-3446.
See Professional Biographies, CHICAGO, ILLINOIS

Good, Kenneth J. .... '45 '72 C.477 A.B. L.424 J.D. [Goldstein,A.&G.]

Good, Neil H. '60 '86 C.589 B.S. L.146 J.D.
30 N. La Salle, Suite 3400, 60602 ⊙
Telephone: 312-629-1212
Email: neil@neilgood.com URL: http://www.neilgoodlawfirm.com
Social Security Disability, Personal Injury, Medical Malpractice, Plaintiffs Personal Injury.
Palatine, Illinois Office: 800 E. Northwest Highway, Suite 814, 60074. Telephone: 847-577-4476.
See Professional Biographies, CHICAGO, ILLINOIS

Good, Steven L., (AV) .... '56 '81 C.823 B.S. L.209 J.D. Pres., Sheldon Good & Co.
Goode, Irving H. .... '16 '39 C.597 L.209 LL.B. Sr. V.P., Stein and Company
Goode, Jodi Nicole .... '73 '99 C&L.966 B.A., J.D. 10 W. 35th. Street, Floor 4
Goode, Richard S. .... '66 '93 C&L.602 B.A., J.D. 721 N. LaSalle Street, 4th Floor‡
Goodemote, Pamela S. Trapp '52 '80
C.927 B.A.T.Ed. L.209 J.D. Soc. Sec. Admn./Hearings & Appeals
Goodfriend, Neal B., (AV) '53 '78
C.339 B.A. L.209 J.D. Senior Assistant Attorney General
Goodhart, Bruce J., (AV) .... '38 '63 C.165 B.A. L.597 J.D. 20 N. Clark St.
Goodin, J. Matthew .... '75 '01 C.894 B.A. L.910 J.D. [🄰 Lord,B.&B.]
Goodland, John S. '31 '57 C&L.966 B.B.A., J.D.
(adm. in WI; not adm. in IL) F.D.I.C.
Goodman, Adam B. .... '70 '95 C.691 B.A. L.145 J.D. [🄱 Lovells]
Goodman, Ann P., (AV) .... '57 '84 C.914 A.B. L.880 J.D. [McCullough,C.&L.]
Goodman, Bruce D., (AV) .... '49 '74 C.339 B.A. L.209 J.D. [Steinberg,P.&G.]
Goodman, David, (AV) .... '63 '89 C.1036 B.A. L.94 J.D. [Much S.F.D.A.&R.]
Goodman, Geoffrey S. .... '— '99 C.340 B.A. L.339 J.D. [🄰 Foley&L.]
Goodman, George R. .... '— '87 C.508 B.A. L.145 J.D. [Foley&L.]
Goodman, J. Chris .... '45 '75 22 W. Monroe St., Ste. 1800
Goodman, Jack .... '10 '33 C.966 L.597 135 S. La Salle St.
Goodman, Jennifer M. .... '78 '05 C.347 B.A. L.597 J.D. [🄰 Vedder,P.K.&K.]
Goodman, Jonathan S. .... '— '98 C.1365 B.A. L.966 J.D. [🄰 Wildman,H.A.&D.]
Goodman, Jordan M. .... '60 '85 C.347 B.S. L.339 J.D. [Horwood M.&B.]
Goodman, Karen R., (AV) .... '52 '77 C.339 B.S. L.424 J.D. [Shefsky&F.]
Goodman, Lawrence S., Ltd., (AV) '42 '67 C.966 B.B.A. L.339 J.D.
[Levun,G.&C.] ⊙
Goodman, Leonard C. .... '62 '89 C.118 B.A. L.597 J.D. 53 W. Jackson Blvd.
Goodman, M. Leonard .... '20 '43 C.477 L.146 LL.B. Dep. Chief Prob. Offr., Juv. Ct.
Goodman, Marcia E., (AV) .... '53 '80 C.477 A.B. L.309 J.D. [Mayer,B.R.&M.]
Goodman, Mark R. .... '56 '83 C.351 B.S. L.602 J.D. [Lord,B.&B.]
Goodman, Paul .... '66 '91 C.339 B.S. L.209 J.D. [Azulay,H.&S.]
Goodman, Shawn E. .... '68 '93 C.339 B.A. L.597 J.D. [Sabo&Z.]
Goodman, Steven S. '60 '87 C.145 B.A. L.276 J.D.
(adm. in PA; not adm. in IL) VP, Gen. Coun. & Sec., Hitachi Consulting Corp.
Goodman, Stuart L., (AV) .... '— '63 C.339 B.A. L.309 J.D. [Schiff H.]
Goodman, Susan .... '57 '83 C&L.602 B.B.A., J.D. Sr. Coun., A.T. Kearney, Inc.
Goodman, Tasneem K. .... '— '02 C&L.145 A.B., J.D. [🄰 Latham&W.]
Goodman, Zenia S. .... '21 '49 C.178 B.A. L.145 J.D. Industrial Comm.
Goodman, Zigmund S. .... '14 '40 L.146 LL.B. 3150 N. Lake Shore Dr.
Goodnow, Jannis E., (BV) .... '52 '85 C.388 B.A. L.209 J.D. [🄰 Walker W.M.]
Goodrich, David E. .... '60 '88 C.363 B.S. L.365 J.D. [Goodrich&D.]
Goodrich & Daffada .... 161 N. Clark St., Ste. 2500
Goodridge, James P. .... '50 '86 C.93 B.A. L.424 J.D. Law Libr., DePaul Univ.
Goodsir, David V. .... '— '91 C.477 B.A. L.424 J.D. [Neal,G.&E.]
GoodSmith, Kenneth S., (AV) .... '56 '81 C.276 B.A. L.597 J.D. [Goodsmith G.&U.]

Goodsmith Gregg & Unruh LLP, (AV)
105 West Adams Street, 26th Floor, 60603
Telephone: 312-322-1981 Fax: 312-322-0056
Email: ggu@ggulaw.com URL: http://www.ggulaw.com
Kenneth S. GoodSmith; David D. Gregg; Marilee C. Unruh; Linda S. Schurman; Kenneth D. Crews. Associates: Carrie L. DeValk; Ellen K. Fulton; Jennifer L. Hansen; Cameron R. Krieger; Keren L. Weiss. Of Counsel: D. R. Edwards; Gilbert E. Gildea, Jr.
Commercial Litigation, Employment Law, Real Estate and Finance, Mergers and Acquisitions, Corporate Law, Company Counseling.
See Professional Biographies, CHICAGO, ILLINOIS

Goodsnyder, Christopher M. .... '68 '93 C.339 B.A. L.209 J.D. 14 N. Peoria St., Ste. 2-C
Goodwill, Frederic C., II .... '— '92 C.454 B.A. L.1194 J.D. [🄰 O'Hagan,S.&A.]
Goodwin, Daniel P. .... '52 '81 C.569 B.A. L.309 J.D. [D.Goodwin]
Goodwin, Jean .... '59 '84 C.145 B.A. L.144 J.D. Legal Asst. Found. of Chicago
Goodwin, Louise M. .... '65 '93 C.1365 B.A. L.321 J.D. [🄰 Kerns,P.F.&P.]
Goodwin, Tara Leigh .... '66 '91 C.145 B.A. L.146 J.D. [Edelman,C.&L.]
Goodwin, Daniel .... 651 W. Washington Blvd., Ste. 500
Goodworth, Warren R. '— '02 C.877 B.A. L.823 J.D.
(adm. in MA; not adm. in IL) [🄰 Kirkland&E.]
Goossen, Dean H., (BV) '47 '74 C&L.178 B.A., J.D.
(adm. in NY; not adm. in IL) Corp. Secy., USG Corp.
Gootjes, Mary E. .... '58 '92 C.966 B.S. L.146 J.D. [🄰 Bates&C.]
Goran, Jay .... '14 '37 C.999 L.146 LL.B. 105 W. Madison
Gordon, Allen M. .... '26 '60 C&L.209 B.A., J.D. U.S. Railroad Retire. Bd.
Gordon, Amy M. .... '66 '91 C.645 B.S. L.1019 J.D. [McDermott W.&E.]
Gordon, Barry L. .... '42 '68 C.339 B.S. L.146 J.D. [B.L.Gordon&Assoc.]
Gordon, Belle Lind, (AV) .... '50 '75 C.339 B.S. L.424 J.D. [B.L.Gordon]
Gordon, Brad M. .... '71 '97 C.352 B.B.A. L.209 J.D. [Grotefeld&D.]
Gordon, Dale C. '48 '74 C.339 B.A. L.597 J.D.
VP & Gen. Coun., Wolters Kluwer U.S. Corp.
Gordon, Daniel D. .... '— '95 C&L.976 B.A., J.D. [Greenberg T.]
Gordon, David A. .... '73 '98 C.597 B.A. L.145 J.D. [🄰 Sidley A.B.&W.]
Gordon, David E., (AV) .... '65 '91 C&L.339 B.S., J.D. [Barack F.K.P.&N.]
Gordon, Deborah C. .... '69 '93 C&L.339 B.A., J.D. [Seyfarth S.]
Gordon, Debra G. '— '76 C.1036 B.A. L.597 J.D.
Immig. & Naturalization Serv., U.S. Dept. of Jus.
Gordon, Eugene W. .... '24 '49 C&L.597 J.D. V.P. & Secy., Adminco, Inc.
Gordon, George H., Jr. .... '32 '67 C.1031 B.S. L.146 J.D. 1349-B W. Cortez St.
Gordon, Gilbert .... '11 '33 C.424 L.146 LL.B. 5555 Sheridan Rd.
Gordon, Gilbert W. .... '49 '74 C.98 B.S. L.424 J.D. [Marks,M.&K.]
Gordon, Holly D. '73 '99 C.910 B.A. L.146 J.D.
Environ. Law Staff Atty., Chicago Legal Clinic
Gordon, J. Cunyon .... '52 '81 C.627 B.A. L.976 J.D. [🄱 Eimer S.K.&S.]
Gordon, James S., (Ltd.), (AV) .... '41 '65 C.260 B.A. L.976 LL.B. [Gordon,G.F.&R.]
Gordon, Jeanne E. Brown .... '— '36 L.597 J.D. Asst. States Atty.
Gordon, Joseph .... '32 '61 C.1016 B.A. L.597 J.D. Appl. Ct. Jus.
Gordon, Kathryn O. .... '71 '96 C.473 B.A. L.209 J.D. Off. of the Pub. Guard.
Gordon, Lawrence G. .... '61 '87 C.98 B.A. L.607 J.D. 180 N. La Salle St., Ste. 2310
Gordon, Leslye Chase .... '75 '00 C.597 B.A. L.1009 J.D. Pub. Guardian Off.
Gordon, Lisa I. .... '61 '88 C.103 A.B. L.424 J.D. 1240 N. Lake Shore Dr.‡
Gordon, Lois J. .... '37 '78 C&L.145 B.A., J.D. 1220 E. 48th St.
Gordon, Lori S. '57 '83 C.103 A.B. L.597 J.D.
Loss Prevention Coun., Attorneys' Liability Assurance Society, Inc.
Gordon, Margot, (AV) .... '— '89 C.112 B.A. L.145 J.D. [Levin&S.]
Gordon, Mark L., (AV) .... '51 '76 C.477 B.A. L.597 J.D. [Gordon&G.L.]
Gordon, Melissa J. .... '69 '94 C.846 B.S. L.405 J.D. [🄰 Mangan,L.G.&L.]
Gordon, Michael A. .... '66 '92 C.339 B.S. L.597 J.D. [🄰 Sidley A.B.&W.]
Gordon, Michaeline .... '60 '86 C.339 B.S. L.365 J.D. [M.Gordon] & [🄱 Shannon&Assoc.]
Gordon, Mitchell B. .... '75 '00 C.352 B.A. L.146 J.D. [🄰 Pasulka&W.]
Gordon, Morton A. .... '28 '51 C&L.339 B.S., LL.B. 25 E. Washington
Gordon, Phillip, (AV) .... '43 '69 C.1518 B.A. L.145 J.D. [Perkins C.]
Gordon, Raymond P., (AV) .... '49 '74 C.861 B.A. L.597 J.D. [Gordon&E.]
Gordon, Richard R. .... '77 '02 C.966 B.S. L.424 J.D. [🄰 Johnson&B.]
Gordon, Robert E. .... '37 '62 C.339 L.209 J.D. 180 N. La Salle St.
Gordon, Robert E., (AV) .... '54 '79 C.477 B.S. L.597 J.D. [Mayer,B.R.&M.]
Gordon, Robert M. '53 '83
C.339 A.B. L.597 J.D. Mgr., U.S. Tax Planning, BP America Inc.
Gordon, Samantha C. .... '70 '00 C.813 B.A. L.597 J.D. [🄰 McGuirewoods]
Gordon, Stephen M. .... '62 '88 C.475 B.A. L.477 J.D. [DLPiper R.G.C.U.]
Gordon, Theodora .... '23 '48 C.331 A.B. L.145 J.D. 8 S. Michigan Ave.
Gordon, Barry L., & Associates, Professional Corporation .... 205 West Randolph Street

Gordon, Belle Lind, P.C., Law Offices of, (AV)
33 North La Salle Street, Suite 900, 60602
Telephone: 312-443-9700 Fax: 312-443-9777
Email: blglawoffice@aol.com
Belle Lind Gordon.
Divorce, Domestic Relations, Family Law, Child Custody, Paternity and Adoption.
See Professional Biographies, CHICAGO, ILLINOIS

Gordon & Einstein, Ltd., (AV) 🄱
224 East Ontario, 60611
Telephone: 312-280-7766 Telecopier: 312-280-9599
URL: http://www.gordon-einstein.com
Raymond P. Gordon; Jean M. Einstein.
General Corporate, Business Mergers and Acquisitions. Real Estate and Finance Law.
See Professional Biographies, CHICAGO, ILLINOIS

Gordon, Glickman, Flesch & Rosenwein, (AV)
A Partnership of Professional Corporations
The Marquette Building, 140 South Dearborn Street, Suite 404, 60603
Telephone: 312-346-1080 Fax: 312-346-3708
URL: http://www.lawggf.com
James S. Gordon (Ltd.); Don E. Glickman (Ltd.); James A. Flesch (Ltd.); Thomas D. Rosenwein (Ltd.).
Trials and Appeals. Antitrust, Securities, Copyright and Commercial Litigation, Employment Law, Wrongful Discharge, Intellectual Property.
See Professional Biographies, CHICAGO, ILLINOIS

Gordon & Glickson LLC, (AV)
444 North Michigan Avenue, Suite 3600, 60611-3903
Telephone: 312-321-1700 FAX: 312-321-9324
Email: gg@ggtech.com URL: http://www.ggtech.com
Kenneth K. Dort; Scott L. Glickson; Stephen Gold; Mark L. Gordon; Michael T. Hepburn; Benjamin D. Kern; Janet Smerling LeVee; Thomas O. Levenberg; Philip P. McGuigan; Stuart Smith;—Stephanie A. Fishman (Not admitted in IL); James A. Kovacs; Derek A. Roach; Bradley A. Salmon; George R. Spatz.
Information Technology, Digital Strategies, Life Sciences, Computer Law, Online and Internet Law, Technology Licensing and Transactions, Outsourcing, Corporate and Securities, Finance, Venture Capital, Distribution, Marketing, Development, Intellectual Property, Multimedia and New Media, Telecommunications, Wireless, Commercial Law, Complex Commercial Litigation, Trials and Dispute Resolution.
See Professional Biographies, CHICAGO, ILLINOIS

Gordon, Michaeline, P.C. .... 8 S. Michigan Ave., Ste. 2600
Gordy, Susan K., (BV) '— '81 C.802 B.A. L.146 J.D.
LaSalle Bank Corp., Govt. Rel. Grp.
Gore, Jack H. .... '41 '69 L.146 J.D. 1118 N. State St.‡
Gore, Kenneth B., (Ltd.) .... '47 '71 C.339 L.209 J.D. 39 S. LaSalle St.
Gore, Lauren E. .... '56 '82 C.339 B.S. L.329 J.D. Sr. Staff Atty., I.R.S.
Gore, Scott A. .... '64 '89 C.347 B.S. L.930 J.D. [Laner,M.D.B.L.&T.]
Goreczny, Susan A. .... '59 '85 C.1151 B.A. L.365 J.D. 100 W. Monroe
Goren, Ralph M. .... '29 '52 L.145 J.D. 39 S. La Salle St.
Gorenberg, Kenneth M., (BV) .... '65 '90 C.659 B.A. L.145 J.D. [Wildman,H.A.&D.]
Gorey, Thomas M. .... '53 '78 C.339 B.A. L.209 J.D. Amer. Medical Assn.
Gorga, Nicholas B. .... '— '02 C.674 A.B. L.477 J.D. [Ⓐ Latham&W.]
Gorman, Claire E. .... '79 '04 C.436 B.A. L.209 J.D. [Ⓐ Nisen&E.]
Gorman, Eric J. .... '69 '95 C.145 A.B. L.477 J.D. [Ⓒ Skadden,A.S.M.&F.]
Gorman, Gregory X., (BV) .... '51 '77 C.339 B.A. L.146 J.D. [Gorman&G.]
Gorman, H. Candace, (AV) .... '54 '83 C.966 B.A. L.365 J.D. 542 S. Dearborn St.
Gorman, James E. .... '41 '80 C.1191 B.S. L.589 10644 S. Western
Gorman, James F. .... '26 '53 C&L.339 B.A., LL.B. 162 W. Grand Ave.‡
Gorman, Robert J., (AV) .... '15 '40 C.597 L.146 LL.B. [Gorman&G.] ‡
Gorman, Robert K. .... '48 '86 C.1191 B.A. L.365 J.D. 10540 S. Western Ave.
Gorman, Shawn P. .... '— '05 C.260 B.S.V.M. L.1218 J.D. [Ⓐ Banner&W.]
Gorman, Thomas G. .... '67 '93 C&L.602 B.A., J.D. 1 E Wacker Drive
Gorman and Gorman, (BV) .... 542 S. Dearborn St.
Gorny, Stephen T. .... '46 '76 C.424 B.S. L.209 J.D. Gen. Coun., Safer Found.
Gorodess, Dina .... '— '00 C.604 B.A. L.597 J.D. [Ⓐ Sonnenschein N.&R.]
Goroff, David B. .... '— '85 C.339 B.A. L.178 J.D. [Foley&L.]
Gorr, David D. .... '54 '79 C.1111 B.S. L.424 J.D. [Gorr,D.D.&Assoc.]
Gorr, David D. & Associates .... 205 W. Randolph St.
Gorrepati, Uday .... '— '05 C.976 B.A. L.1565 J.D. [Ⓐ Kirkland&E.]
Gorrie, Katie E. .... '76 '03 C.475 B.A. L.213 J.D. [Ⓐ Johnson&B.]
Goryl, John A. .... '43 '68 C&L.209 B.S., J.D. Harris Tr. & Savings Bk.
Goschi, Nicholas P., (AV) .... '25 '53 C&L.424 B.S., J.D. 135 S. LaSalle St.
Goschi, Peter E. .... '58 '83 C.424 B.S. L.365 J.D. 120 S. LaSalle St., Ste. 1720
Gosewisch, Lawrence S., (AV) .... '— '83 C.1151 B.A. L.209 J.D. [Adler,M.&M.]
Goshgarian, Jeanne T. .... '47 '77 C.1112 B.A. L.209 J.D. [Ⓐ Ancel,G.D.B.D.&R.]
Gosker, Erika .... '— '99 C&L.339 B.S., J.D. [Ⓐ Mayer,B.R.&M.]
Gosrisirikul, Vida .... '72 '97 C&L.339 B.S., J.D. [Mondero D.&G.]
Goss, Richard H., (AV) .... '35 '59 C.156 A.B. L.597 J.D. 111 W. Monroe St.
Gossett, James F. .... '— '76 C&L.597 B.S.J., J.D. [Arnstein&L.]
Gossman, Karen E. .... '79 '03 C&L.221 B.A., J.D. [Ⓐ Holland&K.]
Gotfryd, William T., (BV) .... '55 '80 C&L.424 B.S., J.D. [Ⓒ Susman,W.&W.]
Gottlick, John D. .... '40 '67 C.321 B.S. L.602 LL.B. 620 S. Laflin- Townhouse D‡
Gottlieb, Daniel .... '73 '99 C.477 B.A. L.597 J.D. [McDermott W.&E.]
Gottlieb, Emily S. .... '75 '00 C.477 B.A. L.424 J.D. [Ⓐ DLPiper R.G.C.U.]
Gottlieb, James B., (AV) .... '43 '68 C.473 B.A. L.597 J.D. [Chuhak&T.]
Gottlieb, Melvin R. .... '46 '74 C.339 B.S. L.209 J.D. 4801 W. Peterson, Ste. 412
Gottlieb, Richard E., (AV) .... '60 '86 C.880 B.A. L.107 J.D. [Dykema G.P.]
Gottschalk, Jeremy .... '79 '04 C.436 B.A. L.424 J.D. [Ⓐ Schwartz C.]
Gottschalk, Ronald E. .... '46 '73 C.339 B.A. L.424 J.D. U.S. Dept. of Agriculture
Gottschall, Joan B. .... '47 '73 C.788 B.A. L.813 J.D. U.S. Dist. J.
Gottshall, Julie L. .... '66 '91 C.188 B.S. L.273 J.D. [Katten M.R.]
Goudge, John A. .... '— '77 L.145 J.D. [Ⓐ Greene&L.]
Goudreau, Noël P. .... '69 '96 C.339 B.S. L.424 J.D. [Ⓐ Kubasiak,F.R.&R.]
Gough, Arnold G., Jr., (AV) .... '56 '81 C&L.602 B.B.A., J.D. [Winston&S.]
Gouinlock, Susan S. .... '63 '88 C.1365 B.A. L.597 J.D. [S.Gouinlock] ⊙
Gouinlock, Susan, Law Offices of, Ltd. .... 205 W. Wacker Drive (⊙Atlanta, GA)
Gould, Arthur I., (AV) .... '29 '56 C.339 B.S. L.597 J.D. [Ⓒ Dykema G.P.]
Gould, Emily B. .... '59 '87 C.221 B.A. L.424 J.D. 222 N. La Salle St.
Gould, Robert M. .... '58 '96 C.339 B.S. L.326 J.D. [Ⓐ Bell,B.&L.] (Pat.)
Gould, Ronald P. '66 '94 C.477 B.A. L.146 J.D.
Asst. Gen. Coun., Grant Thornton, LLP
Gould, Shepard, (AV) .... '56 '80 C&L.339 B.A., J.D. [DLPiper R.G.C.U.]
Gould, Thomas L. .... '30 '63 C.502 B.S. L.365 J.D. 6200 N. Mandell‡

Gould & Ratner, (AV)
222 North La Salle Street 8th Floor, 60601
Telephone: 312-236-3003 Fax: 312-236-3241
Email: info@gould-ratner.com URL: http://www.gould-ratner.com
Members of Firm: Gerald Ratner; Gerald A. Weber; Richard R. Elledge; Stephen P. Sandler; David M. Rubin; Thomas A. Korman; David M. Arnburg; John A. Washburn; John H. Mays; Ronald N. Mora; John S. Worthen; Gail Potysman Bley; Robert A. Carson; Fredric D. Tannenbaum; Edward A. Trio; *Louis D. Bernstein*; Amy M. Blumenthal; *Steven C. Gustafson*; Karin T. O'Connell; Brian B. Gilbert; Joseph M. Laub; Paul W. Carroll; Christopher J. Horvay; Frederick R. Dempsey; Theodore F. Kommers; Mark E. Leipold; David N. Michael; Jessica G. Lingertat. Of Counsel: Virginia M. Harding; Theodore M. Swain; Howard M. Turner;—Benjamin Z. Gould (1913-1986); Harold R. Schradzke (1892-1949); Henry Litvak (1920-1973); Fredrick G. Gould (1943-1982); Kathryn Smith Matkov (1954-1998); Terrence F. Netzky (1942-1999); Samuel Schlesinger (1913-2002); Harry M. Coven (1926-2004). Associates: Mark E. Abraham; John B. Beery; David R. Brown; Shannon L. Clark; Christina Conlin; Sonal P. Desai; Anne E. Dickerson; Gerard R. Fellows; Heather H. Manning (Not admitted in IL); Jill M. McNamara; Karen Osiecki Meehan; John J. Scharkey; Michelle L. Selig; Laura E. Smith; Shea D. Welch.
Family Business advisory and Planning, Entrepreneurial Business, Real Estate Law including Leasing, Annexation, Zoning, Land Development, Ground and Air Rights Leases, Condemnations, Property Taxes. Corporate and Securities Law. Business Acquisitions, Sales and Divestitures. Technology and E-Commerce Businesses. Mortgage Lending, Financing and Recapitalizations. Employment and Labor Law. ERISA and Employee Benefits. Bankruptcy, Workouts and Creditors Rights. Environmental Matters including Cost Recovery Actions and Allocations. Mining Law (stone, gravel, coal).

(This Listing Continued)

Gould & Ratner (Continued)
Telecommunications Law. Federal and State Taxation including Income Taxes, Sales and Use Taxes and Other Taxes, Tax Compliance. Charitable Giving, Estate Planning, Probate and Guardianships. Civil Litigation including Trial Practice and Appellate Practice. Admiralty Law. Administration Law including Black Lung. Government Regulation. Mechanics Lien Law. Member of Law Exchange International.
See Professional Biographies, CHICAGO, ILLINOIS

Goulding, Ronald K., (AV) .... '44 '68 C.1106 B.A. L.146 J.D. 134 N. La Salle St.
Gountanis, John H. .... '75 '00 C.424 B.A. L.146 J.D. US Dept. Just
Gourley, Sara J., (AV) .... '55 '80 C.694 A.B. L.339 J.D. [Sidley A.B.&W.]
Gournis, Dean .... '70 '95 C.393 B.A. L.339 J.D. [Kaplan P.&G.]
Gouveia, Gordon E. .... '79 '04 C.93 B.A. L.880 J.D. [Ⓐ Shaw G.F.G.W.&T.]
Goyer, Lisa .... '— '87 C.502 B.A. L.339 J.D. [Ⓒ DLPiper R.G.C.U.]
Gozdecki, Eugene E., (AV) .... '48 '76 C.339 B.A. L.365 J.D. [Gozdecki&D.]

Gozdecki & Del Giudice, LLP, (AV)
221 North La Salle Street, Suite 2200, 60601-1502
Telephone: 312-782-5010 Telecopier: 312-782-4324
Members of Firm: Eugene E. Gozdecki; Richard A. Del Giudice; David S. Americus; Earl E. Farkas; Carolyn A. Pykosz. Of Counsel: Joseph P. Mulhern; Clifford A. Harstad.
Business Litigation and Counseling, Civil and Complex Litigation, Corporate, Shareholder, Partner and Business Ownership Disputes, Commercial, Distributorship, Franchise, Agency, Labor and Employment, Real Estate, Construction, Mechanic's Liens, Foreclosures, Securities, Antitrust and Trade Regulation, Health Care, Local State and Federal Liquor Regulation and Appeals.
See Professional Biographies, CHICAGO, ILLINOIS

Gozdziak, Thomas S. .... '68 '95 C.98 B.S. L.365 J.D. [Clausen M.]
Grabavoy, Melanie .... '56 '84 C.589 B.A. L.365 J.D. 20 N. Clark St., Ste. 2450
Grabemann, Robert S. .... '61 '86 C.309 B.A. L.597 J.D. [Martin,B.&S.]
Graber, Brent J., (AV) .... '56 '81 C.352 B.B.A. L.477 J.D. [Meckler B.&T.]
Graber, Elizabeth A. .... '69 '93 C&L.424 B.S., J.D. 203 N. La Salle St., Suite 1800
Graber, Jonathan .... '— '02 C.932 B.B.A. L.424 J.D. [Ⓐ Katten M.R.]
Graber, Patrick M., (AV) .... '50 '79 C.679 B.S.A.E. L.602 J.D. [McCullough,C.&L.]
Graber Blazek, Anne .... '— '04 C.597 B.S. L.424 J.D. [Ⓐ Winston&S.]
Grabill, Jon G. .... '41 '69 C.589 B.S. L.424 J.D. 7339 W. Lunt St.‡
Grabowski, Marianne '58 '83
C.976 B.A. L.309 J.D. Assoc. Reg. Coun., Prudential Capital Grp.
Grace, Edward D. .... '42 '79 C.999 B.A. L.209 J.D. 8116 Niles Center Rd.‡
Gracey, Taras A. .... '69 '95 C.112 B.A. L.228 J.D. [Winston&S.]
Gracie, Elizabeth L. .... '57 '83 C&L.966 B.A., J.D. [O'Keefe,L.&H.]
Gradinger, Gretchen L. .... '76 '01 C.378 B.S. L.365 J.D. [Ⓐ Bellows&B.]
Grady, Graham C., (BV) .... '57 '84 C.339 B.A. L.597 J.D. [Bell,B.&L.]
Grady, John F. .... '29 '55 C&L.597 B.S., J.D. U.S. Sr. Dist. J.
Grady, John F. .... '— '96 C.352 B.A. L.597 J.D. [Arnstein&L.]
Grady, Patrick R. .... '49 '96 C.1069 B.A. L.365 J.D. [Wolf&W.]
Graeb, T. Randall .... '67 '00 C.273 B.A. L.597 J.D. [Ⓐ Barack F.K.P.&N.]
Graefe, Anthony S., (AV) .... '47 '81 C.321 B.A. L.597 J.D. [Graefe&H.]

Graefe & Hansen, Ltd., (AV) BB
55 West Monroe Street, Suite 3550, 60603
Telephone: 312-236-0177 Fax: 312-236-5517 Email: hansen@ghemployerlaw.com
Email: graefe@ghemployerlaw.com URL: http://www.ghemployerlaw.com
Anthony S. Graefe; Mark D. Hansen.
Management Labor Law, Employment Law, Employment Litigation, Wrongful Termination Defense, Labor Arbitration, Collective Bargaining, Labor Relations.
See Professional Biographies, CHICAGO, ILLINOIS

Graettinger, John S., Jr., (AVⓉ) ...... '49 '76 C.309 B.A. L.245 J.D. 53 W. Jackson Blvd.
Graettinger, Robert S. .... '55 '92 C.94 B.A.M.A. L.146 J.D. [Ⓒ R.S.Hoover&Assoc.]
Graff, Glenn A. .... '66 '91 C&L.339 A.B., J.D. [Applegate&T.]
Graff, M. Christine .... '69 '94 C.190 B.A. L.145 J.D. [Winston&S.]
Grage, Elmer C. .... '06 '34 C&L.145 Ph.B., J.D. The Decorators Supply Corp.
Graham, Brian M. .... '61 '97 C.209 B.A. L.146 J.D. [Ⓐ Shaw G.F.G.W.&T.]
Graham, Claudia M. '43 '88 C.700 B.A. L.424 J.D.
Claims Coun., Chicago Title Ins. Co.
Graham, Daniel T. .... '65 '90 C.177 B.A. L.352 J.D. [Funkhouser V.L.&D.]
Graham, Darrell J., (AV) .... '59 '85 C&L.477 B.A., J.D. [Ⓒ Perkins C.]
Graham, David F., (AV) .... '53 '78 C.311 B.A. L.145 J.D. [Sidley A.B.&W.]
Graham, Douglas A., (AV) '63 '88 C&L.477 A.B., J.D.
Asst. Gen. Coun., Exelon Corp.
Graham, Douglas W. .... '40 '69 C.1056 B.S. L.146 J.D. 29 S La Salle St # 330
Graham, Edward M. .... '59 '87 C.966 B.A. L.902 J.D. [Ⓐ Bell,B.&L.]
Graham, Eric E. .... '25 '57 C.784 A.B. L.145 J.D. 9415 S. State St.
Graham, John A., (BV) .... '64 '90 C.966 B.A. L.424 J.D. [Ⓐ Seyfarth S.]
Graham, Margaret E. .... '— '85 C.700 B.A. L.365 J.D. [Rieff S.&K.]
Graham, Melissa A. .... '69 '94 C.165 B.A. L.904 J.D. [Ⓐ McDermott W.&E.]
Graham, Michael R., (BV) '— '86
C.473 B.S. L.262 J.D. [Marshall,G.&B.] (See Pat. Sect.)
Graham, Michael T. .... '72 '03 C.339 B.S. L.145 J.D. [Ⓐ Figliulo&S.]
Graham, Michael T. .... '70 '95 C.339 A.B. L.879 J.D. [McDermott W.&E.]
Graham, Robert L., (AV) .... '48 '72 C.477 B.A. L.309 J.D. [Jenner&B.]
Grahl, Christine H. .... '68 '95 C.945 B.A. L.309 J.D. [Ⓐ Sidley A.B.&W.]
Graines, Gregg Seth .... '77 '02 C.966 B.A. L.146 J.D. [Ⓐ DLPiper R.G.C.U.]
Graines, Rebecca L. .... '— '02 C.477 B.A. L.146 J.D. [Ⓐ Jones D.]
Grais, Adam J. .... '68 '96 C.176 B.A. L.144 J.D. [Sugar,F.&F.]
Grais, Ronald B., (AV) .... '43 '68 C.188 A.B. L.145 J.D. [Schwartz C.]
Gralen, Mark E. '58 '84 C.880 B.A. L.339 J.D.
Sr. V.P., Member Servs., Attorneys' Liability Assurance Society, Inc.
Gram, William H. '37 '63 L.365 LL.B.
Sr. V.P., Gen. Coun. & Secy., Federal Reserve Bank of Chicago
Gramlich, Dean C., (AV) .... '53 '85 C&L.339 B.A., J.D. [McDermott W.&E.]
Grams, John F. .... '14 '39 C.597 L.209 LL.B. 1 First National Plaza
Granados Motley, Cinthia .... '— '03 C.424 B.A. L.209 J.D. [Ⓐ Wilson E.M.E.&D.]
Granchalek, Dale R. '47 '75
C.817 B.A. L.280 J.D. Sr. Coun., Bank One Corp. (Law Dept.)
Grandon, Jonathan M. .... '— '00 C.178 B.A. L.477 J.D. [Ⓐ Mayer,B.R.&M.]
Grandsart, Leonard M., The Law Office of '58 '00
C.1183 B.A. L.365 J.D. 5031 North Nordica
Graney, Edward T. .... '45 '73 C.145 B.S. L.365 J.D. 134 N. LaSalle St.
Granger, Lori L. .... '46 '92 C.33 B.A. L.146 J.D. 247 E. Chestnut St.

Granich, Jeffrey B. '66 '91 C.347 B.A. L.930 J.D.
53 W. Jackson Boulevard, Suite 840, 60604
Telephone: 312-939-9009 Pager: 312-490-4636 Fax: 312-939-9669
Email: coffee@xsite.net URL: http://www.granichlaw.com
Criminal Law, Civil Rights, DUI, Drug Crimes, Felonies, Homicides, Juvenile Law, Misdemeanors, Parole and Probation, Sexual Assault, Traffic Violations and Police Misconduct.
See Professional Biographies, CHICAGO, ILLINOIS

Grannan, Henry M., (AV) .... '36 '63 C.424 B.Sc. L.209 LL.B. [H.M.Grannan]

Grannan, Henry M., Chartered, (AV) … 601 W. Randolph, 2nd Fl.
Grant, Adam M. … '— '03 C.1168 B.A. L.597 J.D. [⊡ Katten M.R.]
Grant, Arnold E. … '57 '84 C.910 B.A. L.145 J.D. [McGuirewoods]
Grant, Burton F., (AV) … '38 '62 C&L.209 B.A., J.D. [Grant&G.] ⊙
Grant, Daniel L. … '— '02 C.338 B.S. L.209 J.D. [⊡ Garofalo,S.H.&S.]
Grant, Herman … '26 '52 C.274 L.365 [Goldman&G.]
Grant, Joan C., (AV) … '43 '80 C.477 B.A. L.209 J.D. [Grant&G.] ⊙
Grant, Jos. S. … '09 '33 L.209 J.D. 33 N. LaSalle St.‡
Grant, Maurice … '— '85 C.209 B.A. L.446 J.D. [Grant H.&S.]
Grant, Michael J., (AV) '49 '77 C.347 B.S.B.A. L.1119 J.D.
Managing Attorney, Zurich Financial Services Group
Grant, Michael J. … '75 '01 C.201 B.A. L.146 J.D. [⊡ Tabet D.&R.]
Grant, Robert N., (AV) … '30 '56 C.976 B.A. L.309 LL.B. [Sonnenschein N.&R.]
Grant, T. Kellan … '— '00 C.679 B.S. L.145 J.D. [⊡ Chapman&C.]
Grant, Tone N. '44 '69 C.976 B.A. L.880 J.D.
(adm. in TN; not adm. in IL) Pres. & Gen. Coun., Refco Grp. Ltd.

Grant and Grant, Professional Corporation, (AV)
30 North La Salle Street 29th Floor, 60602 ⊙
Telephone: 312-641-3600 Fax: 312-641-2723
Email: info@grantandgrant.com URL: http://www.lawyers.com/grantandgrantlaw
Louis Z. Grant (1907-1992); Burton F. Grant; Joan C. Grant.
Complex Family Law including Divorce, Dissolution of Marriage, Marital Property Distribution including Retirement Benefits, Spousal Support, Alimony, Maintenance, Child Custody, Visitation, Child Support, Domestic Violence, Paternity, all phases of Matrimonial Litigation, Post Divorce Modification, Premarital Agreements, Dissolution Agreements, Marital Settlement Agreements, Postmarital Agreements and Appeals.
Northbrook, Illinois Office: 707 Skokie Boulevard, Suite 600, 60062. Telephone: 847-291-4343. Fax: 312-641-2723.
See Professional Biographies, CHICAGO, ILLINOIS

Grant Holt & Schumann, LLC, (AV) … 30 N. LaSalle St., Ste. 3400
Grapsas, Diane Curry … '60 '85 C&L.424 B.S., J.D. Asst. Atty. Gen.
Grapsas, Nicholas G. … '61 '88 C&L.424 B.A., J.D. [Quinlan&C.]
Grass, Stuart E., (AV) … '46 '71 C&L.477 B.A., J.D. [Katten M.R.]
Grassé, Edward K. … '70 '98 C.589 B.S. L.146 J.D. [Busse&B.]
Grassmick, David … '— '02 C.893 B.A. L.339 J.D. [⊡ Kirkland&E.]
Grasso, Albert L., (AV) … '46 '73 C&L.276 B.S.F.S., J.D. [Chuhak&T.]
Grauer, Brenda L. … '68 '93 C.597 B.A. L.339 J.D. Legal Assistance Found. of Chicago
Graveline, Bradley C. … '65 '90 C.210 B.A. L.597 J.D. [Winston&S.]
Graver, David Arthur … '55 '00 C.1375 B.A. L.145 J.D. City of Chicago Law Dept.
Graves, Cheryl M. … '55 '84 C.118 B.A. L.146 J.D. Northwestern Univ. Sch. of Law
Graves, Robert J. … '— '84 C.340 B.A. L.339 J.D. [Jones D.]
Grawemeyer, Christine S. … '65 '90 C.477 B.B.A. L.912 J.D. Sr. Coun., United Airlines
Gray, Alan S. … '54 '81 C.994 B.A. L.365 J.D. Tax Mngr., Richardson Electronics, Ltd.‡
Gray, Amy Dickman … '68 '93 C.1375 B.A. L.1066 J.D. 430A W. Webster Ave.
Gray, Cynthia A. '55 '80
C.999 B.A. L.597 J.D. Dir., Ctr. for Jud. Con. Org. Amer. Jud. Soc.
Gray, David R. … '33 '58 C&L.339 A.B., LL.B. Fl 2820, 120 N La Salle St
Gray, James S., (AV) … '— '69 C.951 A.B. L.145 J.D. [Freeborn&P.]
Gray, Jeanne P. '47 '77 C.461 A.B. L.669 J.D.
Dir., Ctr. for Professional Responsibility, Amer. Bar Assn.
Gray, Jeffrey P., (AV) … '59 '84 C.347 B.A. L.597 J.D. [Wildman,H.A.&D.]
Gray, Jeffrey R. … '— '88 C.146 B.S.C.E. L.365 J.D. [Barnes&T.] (See Pat. Sect.)
Gray, Laura A. … '61 '86 C.207 B.A. L.146 J.D. Asst. State's Atty.
Gray, Lawrence A., (AV) … '49 '74 C.867 B.A. L.276 J.D. [Lord,B.&B.]
Gray, Maryon L. '48 '73 C.339 B.S. L.597 J.D.
Asst. Gen. Coun., Oil-Dri Corporation of America
Gray, Michael B. … '— '92 C.145 B.A. L.597 J.D. [Schwartz C.]
Gray, Michael J. … '— '92 C.477 B.A. L.597 J.D. [Jones D.]
Gray, Richard J., (AV) … '48 '74 C&L.477 A.B., J.D. [Jenner&B.]
Gray, Stephen F. … '55 '85 C.1016 B.A. L.146 J.D. [Cohn,L.R.S.&G.]
Gray, Steven J. … '57 '87 C.602 B.A. L.930 J.D. [Sonnenschein N.&R.]
Gray, Tania K. … '78 '04 C.473 B.S. L.365 J.D. [⊡ Nadler,P.&M.]

Gray & Idris, P.C., Law Offices of
(See Joilet)

Grayck, Marcus D. … '27 '52 C.102 A.B. L.309 LL.B. 130 Randolph Dr.
Grayson, Barbara … '— '01 C.502 B.A. L.309 J.D. [⊡ Mayer,B.R.&M.]
Grayson, Clarissa Cutler … '57 '99 C.846 B.F.A. L.365 J.D. 2008 W. Concord Pl. #2
Grayson, E. Lynn, (AV) … '61 '86 C.265 B.A. L.1119 J.D. [Jenner&B.]
Grayson, Joseph C. … '49 '76 C.966 B.A. L.365 J.D. [Abramson&F.]
Grazian, John L. … '60 '85 C.339 B.A. L.146 J.D. 6315 S. Central Ave.
Grazian, Leonard R. … '24 '50 C.46 B.S. L.365 J.D. Cir. Ct. J.
Graziani, Carrie L. … '75 '01 C.973 B.A. L.209 J.D. [⊡ Meckler B.&T.]
Grear, Joseph A., (AV) … '59 '84 C.338 B.S. L.339 J.D. [Stadheim&G.]
Grede, Frederick J. '52 '83 C.339 B.S. L.209 J.D.
Exec. V.P., Planning & Opers., Chicago Bd. of Trade‡
Green, Albert … '— '49 C&L.209 B.S., J.D. [Green&G.]
Green, Bryan J., (BV) … '59 '89 C.597 B.A. L.8 J.D. [Katten M.R.]
Green, Danielle … '61 '89 C.339 B.S. L.1051 J.D. U.S.E.P.A.
Green, Edward G. … '37 '61 C&L.597 A.B., J.D. 70 W. Burton Pl.‡
Green, Edward J. … '— '93 C&L.352 B.B.A., J.D. [Foley&L.]
Green, Gary E., (AV) … '— '88 C.424 B.A. L.1065 J.D. [FagelHaber]
Green, Jason J. … '76 '02 C.339 B.S. L.365 J.D. [⊡ Jenner&B.]
Green, John M. … '— '92 C.602 B.S. L.209 J.D. [Querrey&H.]
Green, Jonathan Clark, (AV) … '61 '86 C.178 B.A. L.46 J.D. [Green&G.]
Green, Jonathan T. … '52 '77 C.604 A.B. L.930 J.D. Harris Tr. & Svgs. Bk.
Green, Joni M. … '76 '01 C.645 B.S. L.424 J.D. [⊡ Stetler&D.]
Green, Lisa M. … '62 '87 C.222 B.A. L.831 J.D. [⊡ Bresler&H.]
Green, Marvin, (AV) … '25 '50 C&L.145 A.B., J.D. [⊡ McCullough,C.&L.]
Green, Raymond W., (AV) '40 '66 C&L.477 B.S., J.D.
[Brinks H.G.&L.] (See Pat. Sect.)
Green, Robert F., (AV) '49 '74
C.339 B.S.Chem. L.365 J.D. [Leydig,V.&M.] (See Pat. Sect.)
Green, Robert M., P.C., (AV) … '29 '56 C.339 B.S. L.145 J.D. [R.M.Green]
Green, Ross … '58 '84 C.309 B.A. L.145 J.D. [DLPiper R.G.C.U.]
Green, Stephanie S. … '65 '97 C.112 B.A. L.146 J.D. [Albert,W.]
Green, Thomas Joseph … '67 '93 C.234 B.A. L.339 J.D. Litig. Coun., Cingular Wireless
Green & Green, P.C., Law Offices of, (AV) … 350 North La Salle Street, Suite 800

Green & Kuchel, P.C.
(See Hammond, Indiana)

Green, Robert M., P.C., (AV) … 919 N. Michigan Ave.
Greenbaum, Jeffrey S. … '73 '99 C.347 B.A. L.209 J.D. 120 W. Madison
Greenbaum, Lewis, (AV) … '48 '74 C.569 B.A. L.276 J.D. [Katten M.R.]
Greenbaum, Myron E. … '39 '67 L.146 J.D. 79 W Monroe St, Ste 912
Greenbaum, Neil, (AV) … '— '55 C&L.597 B.S., J.D. [Sachnoff&W.]
Greenberg, Aaron S. … '58 '82 C.910 A.B. L.145 J.D. Clark Devon Hardware Co., Inc.
Greenberg, David C. … '66 '91 C.339 B.A. L.46 J.D. Sr. VP, Aon Service Corp.
Greenberg, Dolores H. … '37 '80 C.1016 B.G.S. L.146 J.D. 5855 N. Sheridan Rd.
Greenberg, Eric F. … '— '83 C.597 B.A. L.188 J.D. [⊡ Ungaretti&H.]
Greenberg, Joseph H. … '61 '88 C.910 B.A. L.309 J.D. [Gardner C.&D.]
Greenberg, Lorraine M., and Associates '52 '81
C.174 B.A. L.365 J.D. 20 E Jackson, Suite 800 (⊙Joliet, Lisle)
Greenberg, Mark I., (AV) … '65 '91 C.309 A.B. L.145 J.D. [Sidley A.B.&W.]
Greenberg, Paul A. … '69 '97 C.209 B.A. L.146 J.D. [⊡ Aronberg G.D.&G.]
Greenberg, Richard T., (AV) … '52 '77 C.597 B.A. L.569 J.D. [McGuirewoods]
Greenberg, Robert B., (AV) … '39 '64 C.1016 L.209 J.D. [Asher,G.G.&D.]
Greenberg, Samuel M. … '— '93 C.36 B.S. L.365 J.D. [Karbal,C.E.S.&D.]
Greenberg, Sanford N. '48 '90 C.674 A.B. L.273 J.D.
(adm. in MD; not adm. in IL)
Assoc. Prof. & Dir., Appellate Advocacy, Chicago-Kent Coll. of Law

Greenberg, Steven A., (AV) '60 '86 C.347 B.S. L.589 J.D.
820 West Jackson, Suite 310, 60607
Telephone: 312-879-9500 Fax: 312-993-1554
Email: greenberglaw@mac.com URL: http://www.sgreenberglaw.com
The defense of serious Federal and State Criminal Matters, Civil Rights, Injury, Appellate.
See Professional Biographies, CHICAGO, ILLINOIS

Greenberg, Freddi L.
(See Evanston)

Greenberg Traurig, LLP, (AV)
77 West Wacker Drive, Suite 2500, 60601 ⊙
Telephone: 312-456-8400 Facsimile: 312-456-8435
Email: info@gtlaw.com URL: http://www.gtlaw.com
Ruth A. Bahe-Jachna; Sean W. Bezark; Francis A. Citera; Laurence B. Dobkin; Thomas E. Dutton; Andrew J. Enschedé; Kevin D. Finger; Herbert H. Finn; Michael T. Fishman; Paul T. Fox; Mark R. Galis; Matthew T. Gensburg; John F. Gibbons; Daniel D. Gordon; Richard D. Harris; Gary R. Jarosik; Daniel L. Kraus; Charles B. Leuin; Peter H. Lieberman; Corey E. Light; Mark J. McCombs; Jane B. McCullough; Paul D. McGrady, Jr.; Gretchen N. Miller; Nancy A. Mitchell; Donna B. More; Paul K. Morton; Robert E. Neiman; Nancy A. Peterman; Rita Alliss Powers; E. Paul Quinn; James G. Richmond; Julia R. Sarron; Robert I. Schwimmer; Keith J. Shapiro; Howard E. Silverman; Richard A. Sirus; Douglas B. Teaney; Jeffrey S. Torosian; Randi L. Valerious. Of Counsel: Richard E. Dick; Amy C. Kurson; Myron Lieberman; Raymond S. McGaugh; David W. Schoenberg; Samuel K. Skinner; G. Ray Warner. Associates: David W. Baddley; Michael J. Baum; Brad R. Bertoglio; James J. Caserio; Abigail A. Clapp; Paul Del Aguila; Kimberly M. DeShano; Jeffrey P. Dunning; Daniel T. Fahner; Paul J. Ferak; Gregory A. Fishman; Eric G. Greenfield; Jordan Herzog; Howard K. Jeruchimowitz; Robert W. Lannan; Todd A. Mazur; Mary Kathryn McCreery; Ryan H. McLennan; Amit Mehta; Sherri Morissette; Jeffrey G. Mote; Cameron M. Nelson; Gregory E. Ostfeld; Matthew Prewitt; Edward M. Shin; Jeffrey L. Terry; Jason M. Toon; Andrew T. White; Collin B. Williams; André L. Zafrani; Arie Ben Zoller.
Administrative Law, Admiralty Law, Agricultural Law, Aircraft Finance and Leasing, Alternative Dispute Resolution, Americans with Disabilities Act, Antitrust, Appellate Practice, Arbitration, Aviation Law, Bankruptcy, Banks and Banking, Biotechnology, Broadcasting Law, Brownfields Redevelopment, Business Immigration, Business Law, Class Action Defense, Commercial Litigation, Communications Law, Constitutional Law, Construction Law, Consumer Finance, Copyrights, Corporate Governance, Corporate Law, Customs and International Trade, Education Law, Employee Benefits, Executive Compensation, Energy, Entertainment Law, Environmental Law, ERISA, FCC Licensing, FCC Regulation, Federal Government Law, Federal Legislative Law, Finance, Financial Institutions Law, Franchises and Franchising, Gaming Law, Government Affairs, Government Contracts, Governmental Law, Health Care, Immigration Law, Indians and Native Populations, Information Technology, Insurance Coverage, Intellectual Property, International Business Law, International Trade, Joint Ventures, Labor and Employment, Land Use, Legislative Practice, Litigation, Lobbying, Maritime Law, Mediation, Mergers, Acquisitions and Divestitures, Mining Law, Motion Pictures and Television, Multimedia Law, Music Law, Nonprofit and Charitable Organizations, Oil and Gas Law, Partnership Law, Patents, Privatization, Probate, Public Finance, Public Infrastructure, Public Utility Law, Railroad Law, Real Estate, Regulatory Law, Resorts and Leisure, Securities, Sports Law, Strategic Alliances, Structured Finance, Sweepstakes, Taxation, Telecommunications Law, Trade Regulation, Trademarks, Transportation, Trusts and Estates, White Collar Criminal Defense, Wills, Workouts, Zoning Law.
Miami, Florida Office: 1221 Brickell Avenue, 33131. Telephone: 305-579-0500. Facsimile: 305-579-0717.
Wilmington, Delaware Office: The Nemours Building, 1007 North Orange Street, Suite 1200, 19801. Telephone: 302-661-7000. Facsimile: 302-661-7360.
Albany, New York Office: 54 State Street, 6th Floor, 12207. Telephone: 518-449-7470. Facsimile: 518-689-3499.
New York, N.Y. Office: MetLife Building, 200 Park Avenue, 10166. Telephone: 212-801-9200. Facsimile: 212-801-6400.
Washington, D.C. Office: 800 Connecticut Avenue, N.W., Suite 500, 20006. Telephone: 202-331-3100. Facsimile: 202-331-3101.
Atlanta, Georgia Office: The Forum, 3290 Northside Parkway, Suite 400, 30327. Telephone: 678-553-2100. Facsimile: 678-553-2212.
Boston, Massachusetts Office: One International Place, 3rd Floor, 02110. Telephone: 617-310-6000. Facsimile: 617-310-6001.
McLean, Virginia Office: 1750 Tysons Boulevard, Suite 1200, 22102. Telephone: 703-749-1300. Facsimile: 703-749-1301.
Philadelphia, Pennsylvania Office: One Commerce Square, Suite 2700, 2001 Market Street, 19103. Telephone: 215-988-7800. Facsimile: 215-988-7801.
Phoenix, Arizona Office: 2375 East Camelback Road, Suite 700, 85016. Telephone: 602-445-8000. Facsimile: 602-445-8100.
Fort Lauderdale, Florida Office: 401 East Las Olas Boulevard, Suite 2000, 33301. Telephone: 954-765-0500. Facsimile: 954-765-1477.
West Palm Beach, Florida Office: 777 South Flagler Drive, Suite 300 East, 33401. Telephone: 561-650-7900. Facsimile: 561-655-6222.
Boca Raton, Florida Office: 5100 Town Center Circle, Suite 400, 33486. Telephone: 561-955-7600. Facsimile: 561-338-7099.
Other Boca Raton, Florida Office: 4800 North Federal Highway, Tower B, Suite 300, 33431. Telephone: 561-367-0430. Fax: 561-362-8803.
Orlando, Florida Office: 450 South Orange Avenue, Suite 650, 32801. Telephone: 407-420-1000. Facsimile: 407-420-5909.
Tallahassee, Florida Office: 101 East College Avenue, 32301. Telephone: 850-222-6891. Facsimile: 850-681-0207.
Denver, Colorado Office: The Tabor Center, 1200 17th Street, Suite 2400, 80202. Telephone: 303-572-6500. Facsimile: 303-572-6540.
East Palo Alto, California Office: 1900 University Avenue, 5th Floor, 94303. Telephone: 650-328-8500. Facsimile: 650-328-8508.
Costa Mesa, California Office: Center Tower, 650 Town Center Drive, Suite 1700, 92626. Telephone: 714-708-6500. Facsimile: 714-708-6501.
Sacramento, California Office: 1201 K Street, Suite 1100, 95814. Telephone: 916-442-1111. Facsimile: 916-448-1709.
Santa Monica, California Office: 2450 Colorado Avenue, Suite 400 East, 90404. Telephone: 310-586-7700. Facsimile: 310-586-7800.
Florham Park, New Jersey Office: 200 Campus Drive, P.O. Box 677, 07932. Telephone: 973-360-7900. Facsimile: 973-301-8410.
Dallas, Texas Office: 600 Three Galleria Tower, 13155 Noel Road, 75240. Telephone: 972-419-1250. Facsimile: 972-419-1251.
Other Dallas, Texas Office: 2200 Ross Avenue, Suite 4700E, 75201. Telephone: 972-419-9100. Facsimile: 972-419-9101.
Houston, Texas Office: 1000 Louisiana, Suite 1800, 77002. Telephone: 713-374-3500. Facsimile: 713-374-3505.
Las Vegas, Nevada Office: 3773 Howard Hughes Parkway, Suite 500 North, 89109. Telephone: 702-792-3773. Facsimile: 702-792-9002.
Zurich, Switzerland Office: Dufourstrasse 1, 8057. Telephone: +41 44 364 26 00. Facsimile: +41 44 364 27 13.
Amsterdam, Netherlands Office: Strawinskylaan 3127, 1077 ZX. Mailing Address: Post Office Box 75306, 1070 AH Amsterdam, Netherlands. Telephone: +31 20 30 17 300. Facsimile: +31 20 30 17 350.
See Professional Biographies, CHICAGO, ILLINOIS

Greenberger, James J. ....'— '83 C.311 B.A. L.477 J.D. [Sachnoff&W.]
Greenberger, Steven R. .... '54 '81 C.339 B.A. L.976 J.D. DePaul Univ.

Greenberger, Krauss & Tenenbaum
(See Schwartz Cooper Chartered)

Greenblatt, Jeffrey A. ....'66 '97 L.145 J.D. [Ⓐ Skadden,A.S.M.&F.]
Greenblatt, Lewis B., (AV) ....'— '69 C.473 B.A. L.339 J.D. [Sachnoff&W.]
Greenblatt, Ray H., (AV) .... '31 '56 C.659 B.S. L.309 J.D. 190 S. LaSalle St.‡
Greenblatt, Russell E., (P.C.), (AV) .... '52 '78 C.347 B.S. L.597 J.D. [Katten M.R.]
Greenburg, Barry H. .... '37 '63 C.339 A.B. L.209 LL.B. [Firm of B.H.Greenburg]
Greenburg, Joel H., (AV) .... '39 '63 C.339 L.209 J.D. [J.H.Greenburg]
Greenburg, Barry H., Law Firm of .... 180 N. LaSalle St., 3150
Greenburg, Joel H., Ltd., (AV) ....221 North La Salle Street, Suite 1050
Greene, Alan I., (AV) .... '45 '69 C.966 B.B.A. L.1565 J.D. [Hinshaw&C.]
Greene, Andrew R. .... '67 '94 C.473 B.A. L.597 J.D. [Sonnenschein N.&R.]
Greene, Francis R. ....'59 '00 C.367 B.A. L.597 J.D. [Ⓐ Edelman,C.&L.]

Greene, J. Clifford, Jr. '51 '94 C&L.300 B.S., B.S.
77 West Wacker Drive, Suite 3200, 60601
Telephone: 312-424-4002 Cell: 312-371-6501 Fax: 312-236-0336
Email: jcliffordgreene@msn.com URL: http://www.lawyers.com/greene
Employment Discrimination, Wrongful Termination, Civil Litigation, White Collar Crime, Employment Law, Entertainment Law, Appellate Practice, Criminal Defense, Criminal Appeals, Driving While Intoxicated, Drug Crimes, Felonies, Homicide, Juvenile Law, Misdemeanors, Parole and Probation, Sexual Assault, Automobile Accidents and Injuries, Slip and Fall, and Divorce.
See Professional Biographies, CHICAGO, ILLINOIS

Greene, James P., and Associates '— '95 C.1044 B.A. L.276 J.D.
75 East Wacker Drive, Suite 730, 60601
Telephone: 312-346-8077 Fax: 312-346-8066
Email: gglaweco@aol.com URL: http://www.jamesgreenelaw.com
Associate: Marthe C. Purmal.
Tax Law, Estate Planning, Elder Law, Asset Protection, Business Planning.
See Professional Biographies, CHICAGO, ILLINOIS

Greene, M. Howard .... '19 '51 C.597 L.365 J.D. 120 W. Madison
Greene, Martin P., (AV) .... '51 '77 C.339 B.A. L.145 J.D. [Greene&L.]
Greene, Mary Jo, (AV) .... '57 '83 C.700 B.A. L.424 J.D. [Doherty&P.]
Greene, Matthew A. '56 '82
C.373 B.A. L.477 J.D. Asst. Gen. Coun., Peoples Energy Corp.
Greene, Scott B., (AV) ....'53 '79 C.347 B.A. L.209 J.D. [Perkins C.]

Greene and Letts, (AV)
111 West Washington Street, Suite 1650, 60602
Telephone: 312-346-1100 Telefax: 312-346-4571
URL: http://www.greeneandletts.com
Members of Firm: Martin P. Greene; Eileen M. Letts; Allen P. Walker; Kevin T. Lee. Associates: John A. Goudge; Carl K. Turpin; Alfred M. Swanson, Jr.; Kathryn Woodward; Lucille A. Blackburn; Terry Miller; Byron M. Wardlaw; Riana N. Shipps. Special Counsel: Christopher S. Davis.
Practice before Federal and State Courts. Civil Litigation including Personal Injury Defense, Insurance and General Liability, Product Liability Defense, Employment, Commercial and Contract, Municipal Law, Real Estate, Finance and General Business Law.
See Professional Biographies, CHICAGO, ILLINOIS

Greenfield, Eric G. ....'78 '03 C&L.339 B.S., J.D. [Ⓐ Greenberg T.]
Greenfield, Frank M. .... '43 '68 C.1016 B.S.B.A. L.365 J.D. [F.M.Greenfield&Assoc.]
Greenfield, Michael C., (AV) .... '34 '57 C.339 B.A. L.597 J.D. [Asher,G.G.&D.]
Greenfield, Michael S. '60 '92
C.339 B.S. L.813 J.D. [McDonnell B.H.&B.] (See Pat. Sect.)
Greenfield, Richard O., (AV) ....'42 '68 C.209 L.424 J.D. [DeCarlo,G.&D.]
Greenfield, Frank M., & Associates, P.C. .... 200 W. Madison St., Ste. 710
Green-Kelly, Diane ....'54 '93 C.339 B.S. L.365 J.D. [Mayer,B.R.&M.]
Greeno, Christopher J. ....'— '98 C.804 B.S. L.597 J.D. [Kirkland&E.]
Greenough, Walter C., (AV) ....'— '75 C.31 B.A. L.145 J.D. [Schiff H.]
Greenspan, Jeffrey .... '77 '02 C.339 B.A. L.146 J.D. [Ⓐ Meckler B.&T.]
Greenspan, Julianna A. .... '71 '97 C.276 A.B. L.597 J.D. [Ⓐ Genson&G.]
Greenspon, Susan J. ....'— '89 C.966 B.A. L.424 J.D. [Kelley D.&W.]
Greenspoon, Robert P. ..... '70 '95 C.145 A.B. L.477 J.D. [Niro,S.H.&N.] (See Pat. Sect.)
Greenstein, David H. .... '37 '61 C&L.597 B.S.L., LL.B. 205 W. Randolph St.
Greenwald, David M., (AV) .... '61 '86 C.276 A.B. L.477 J.D. [Jenner&B.]
Greenwald, Edward M. .... '72 '00 C.273 B.A. L.30 J.D. 610 Canal St.
Greenwalt, Paul Edwin, III ....'— '92 C.221 B.S.B.A. L.352 J.D. [Schiff H.]
Greenwood, Kevin J. .... '56 '90 C.352 B.A. L.221 J.D. 221 N. La Salle St.
Greenwood, Vanessa L. .... '72 '97 C.879 B.A. L.209 J.D. [Ⓐ Sidley A.B.&W.]
Greer, Roger D., (AV) .... '41 '67 C&L.546 B.S.E.E., J.D. [Greer,B.&C.] (Pat.)
Greer, Burns & Crain, Ltd., (AV) ... 300 S. Wacker Dr., 25th Fl. (Pat.) (⊙San Diego, CA)
Greetis, Adam .... '72 '97 C.339 B.A. L.146 J.D. [Seyfarth S.]
Greetis, Kathleen Hughes .... '72 '97 C.879 B.A. L.146 J.D. Off. of Pub. Guard.
Gregg, David D. .... '56 '81 C.339 B.A. L.477 J.D. [Goodsmith G.&U.]
Gregg, Michael R., (AV) .... '59 '87 C.339 B.S. L.365 J.D. [Merlo K.B.&G.]
Gregg, Thomas J. .... '39 '64 C.309 A.B. L.597 J.D. 5852 N. St. John's Court‡
Gregorio, Antone F., (Ltd.), (AV) .... '22 '51 C.352 B.A. L.146 LL.B. 2 N. LaSalle St.
Gregorio, John F., (BV) .... '58 '83 2 N. LaSalle St., Ste. 1650
Gregory, Byron L., (AV) ....'— '69 C&L.597 B.A., J.D. [Foley&L.]
Gregory, Oliver W., Jr., (AV) .... '27 '53 C.999 L.365 LL.B. 222 N. La Salle St.‡
Gregory, Tom P. .... '67 '99 C.338 B.S. L.365 J.D. 5315 N. Delphia, Ste. 115
Gregus, Daniel R. '61 '86 C&L.339 B.S., J.D.
Assist. Reg. Dir., U.S. Secs. and Exchange Comm.
Gregus, Tara Leiby .... '62 '86 C.338 B.A. L.339 J.D. 140 Lawton Rd.
Greiman, Alan J. .... '31 '55 C&L.339 B.S., LL.B. App. Ct. Jus.
Greiman, Beau T. .... '69 '94 C&L.352 B.B.A., J.D. [Levenfeld P.]
Greiner, John T. '— '95 C&L.966 B.S., J.D.
(adm. in IN; not adm. in IL) U.S. Small Bus. Adm.
Greis, Jason .... '76 '05 C.1365 B.A. L.209 J.D. [Ⓐ Seyfarth S.]
Grelle, Lawrence E., (AV) '— '68
C.597 B.S. L.339 J.D. [Arnstein&L.] (⊙Hoffman Estates)
Grenvich, Richard S. .... '52 '78 C.339 B.A. L.589 J.D. Asst. Atty. Gen.
Gresens, John J. .... '59 '86 C.723 B.S. L.300 J.D. [Fitch,E.T.&F.] (See Pat. Sect.)
Gressel, Barbara Ann .... '— '99 C.473 B.A. L.424 J.D. City Atty.
Gresser, Lawrence T. '08 '34 C&L.724
(adm. in NY; not adm. in IL) 3550 N. Lake Shore Dr.‡
Greve, James T. '49 '83 C.339 B.A. L.365 J.D.
Off. of the Pub. Guardian Juv. Cook Co. Div.
Grey, Jordan A. .... '62 '87 C.339 B.A. L.659 J.D. [Ⓐ N.I.Grey]
Grey, Nathaniel I. .... '33 '57 C.1016 B.S. L.145 J.D. [N.I.Grey]
Grey, Nathaniel I., P.C. .... 11 S. La Salle St.
Grib, Philip J. .... '38 '63 C.973 A.B. L.145 J.D. 7958 W. Foster Ave.‡
Gridelli, Paul C., (AV) .... '51 '76 C.209 B.A. L.597 J.D. 53 West Jackson, Suite 1460
Grider, Amy L. .... '73 '04 C.112 B.A. L.145 J.D. [Ⓐ Seyfarth S.]
Grieger, John J., Jr. .... '64 '90 C.597 B.A. L.1049 J.D. [Ⓐ Weltman,W.&R.]
Grier, John R. .... '67 '93 C&L.352 B.B.A., J.D. [Winston&S.]

Griesmeyer, Christopher S. .... '73 '99 C.597 B.A. L.893 J.D. [Ⓐ Levenfeld P.]
Griffin, Alais L.M. .... '— '02 C.309 A.B. L.597 J.D. [Ⓐ Goldberg,K.B.B.&M.]
Griffin, Cecilia Hynes, (AV) .... '65 '90 C.602 B.A. L.424 J.D. [C.Griffin]
Griffin, David J. .... '38 '62 C.966 B.B.A. L.209 LL.B. 39 S. LaSalle St.
Griffin, Edward J., (AV) .... '32 '56 C&L.602 B.S., LL.B. [Ⓒ Defrees&F.]
Griffin, Eugene L., & Associates, (AV) '32 '59
C.999 B.A. L.424 J.D. 29 N. Wacker Dr., Ste. 650
Griffin, Gary L., (AV) .... '37 '61 C&L.209 J.D. [Ⓒ Riordan,D.L.&M.]
Griffin, Gary M., (AV) .... '50 '85 C.973 B.S.B.A. L.424 J.D. Asst. Atty. Gen.
Griffin, Hugh C., (AV) .... '43 '68 C.424 B.A. L.602 J.D. [Ⓒ Lord,B.&B.]
Griffin, James R. .... '71 '97 C.679 B.S.M.E. L.365 J.D. [Schain,B.R.&C.]
Griffin, Janessa M. .... '70 '00 C.602 B.A. L.146 J.D. [Ⓐ Seyfarth S.]
Griffin, John J. .... '33 '58 C.966 B.B.A. L.209 J.D. Ste 1005, 39 S La Salle St
Griffin, Lawrence J. .... '65 '91 C.188 B.A. L.209 J.D. [Ⓐ E.L.Griffin&Assoc.]
Griffin, Mary (Molly) A. '68 '94
C&L.602 B.A., J.D. Contract Coun., Interstate Insurance Group
Griffin, Matthew A. .... '69 '02 C.473 B.A. L.145 J.D. [Ⓐ Pattishall,M.N.H.&G.]
Griffin, Maxwell, Jr., (AV) .... '51 '80 C&L.602 A.B., J.D. [Goldstein&F.]
Griffin, Michael J. .... '31 '75 C.339 B.S. L.146 J.D. Coun., Cook Co. Hwy. Dept.
Griffin, Terrence J. .... '60 '85 C.339 B.A. L.365 J.D. 29 N. Wacker Dr.
Griffin, Thomas G., (AV) .... '61 '89 C&L.602 B.B.A., J.D. [Griffin]
Griffin, William D., III .... '51 '76 C.363 B.S.B.A. L.209 J.D. F.B.I.
Griffin, Wm. D. .... '24 '55 C.424 B.S.C. L.209 J.D. Asst. Atty. Gen.
Griffin, Cecilia, Law Office of, (AV) .... 1 N. La Salle St., Ste. 2475
Griffin Law Offices, LLC, (AV) .... 656 West Randolph Street, Suite 500W
Griffith, Christopher T. '59 '88
C.475 B.S.Ch.E. L.326 J.D. [Leydig,V.&M.] (See Pat. Sect.)
Griffith, Craig A. .... '58 '90 C.339 B.S. L.145 J.D. [Sidley A.B.&W.]
Griffith, D. Kendall, (P.C.), (AV) '33 '58
C&L.339 A.B., LL.B. 222 North La Salle Street‡
Griffith, James E. .... '74 '99 C.228 B.A. L.145 J.D. [McDermott W.&E.]
Griffith, Robert C. ....'— '02 C.118 B.A. L.345 J.D. [Ⓐ Jones D.]
Griffith, Robert H. ....'— '96 C.352 B.B.A. L.146 J.D. [Ungaretti&H.]

Griffith & Jacobson, LLC, (BV)
55 West Monroe Street, Suite 3550, 60603-5020
Telephone: 312-236-8110 Fax: 312-236-6724
URL: http://www.gjlaw.com
James D. Jacobson; Louis Michael Bell; Louis A. Rascia; James E. Mahoney. Associate: Arieh M. Flemenbaum.
Business Formation and Structuring, Finance, Commercial Contracts and Transactions, Mergers and Acquisitions, Buy-outs, Regulatory Matters, Succession Planning for Closely Held Businesses, Income, Sales, Use, Excise and Other Tax Issues, Estate Planning.
See Professional Biographies, CHICAGO, ILLINOIS

Griffiths, Margaret P., (BV) .... '66 '91 C.679 B.A. L.209 J.D. [Ⓒ Katten M.R.]
Grigaitis, Daile V. .... '71 '97 C.966 B.S. L.209 J.D. [Ⓐ Asperger&Assoc.]
Griggs, Michael T. ....'— '03 C.602 B.S. L.999 J.D. [Ⓐ Beem] (Pat.)
Grigoras, Alexandra ....'— '02 C&L.477 B.S., J.D. [Ⓐ Sachnoff&W.]
Grikis, Linas J. .... '68 '96 C.378 B.S. L.862 J.D. [McDermott W.&E.]
Grile, Kevin M. ..... '54 '80 C.597 B.A. L.273 J.D. Amer. Federation of Govt. Employees
Grimbau, Rochelle .... '46 '79 C.339 B.A. L.209 J.D. [Wilcox&G.]
Grimes, James R. '51 '77
C.98 B.A. L.300 J.D. Assoc. Coun., BlueCross BlueShield Assoc.
Grimes, John R. .... '31 '55 C&L.145 A.B., J.D. 2912 N. Commonwealth Ave.‡
Grimes, Roger M. '47 '75 C.197 B.A. L.838 J.D.
(adm. in TN; not adm. in IL) Assoc. Reg. Coun., U.S. EPA‡
Grimm, Michael R., Sr., (AV) .... '51 '78 C.339 B.A. L.365 J.D. [Clausen M.]
Grimm, Terry M., (AV) .... '42 '67 C.347 B.A. L.1119 J.D. [Winston&S.]
Grimm, Victor E., (AV) .... '37 '61 C.98 B.S. L.597 J.D. [Bell,B.&L.]
Grimm, W. Kirk .... '55 '80 C.597 B.A. L.813 J.D. [McGuirewoods]
Grimmer, Judith A. '63 '90 C.966 B.A. L.94 J.D.
Asst. Gen. Coun., BDO Seidman, LLP
Grip, Julia Packard '48 '74 C.339 B.A. L.146 J.D.
Admin. J., U.S. Merit Systems Protection Bd.
Gripman, David L. '65 '99 C.1016 B.A. L.365 J.D.
General Counsel, Chicago Mortgage Corporation
Grippando, Thomas J. .... '39 '63 C&L.209 B.A., J.D. Cook Co., Pub. Guardian
Grippo, Theodore W., (AV) .... '28 '52 C.276 B.S. L.597 J.D. [Grippo&E.]
Grippo, Theodore W., Jr. .... '53 '80 C.293 B.A. L.597 J.D. [Kurlander&G.]

Grippo & Elden LLC, (AV)
111 South Wacker Drive, 60606
Telephone: 312-704-7700 Fax: 312-558-1195; 312-263-7356
Email: info@grippoelden.com URL: http://www.grippoelden.com
Members of Firm: Theodore W. Grippo; Gary M. Elden; Philip C. Stahl; John R. McCambridge; Donald A. Vogelsang; Charles S. Bergen; Irving C. Faber; Gregory C. Jones; Lynn Hagman Murray; David E. Schoenfeld; Matthew I. Hafter; George R. Dougherty; Marc S. Lauerman; Michael P. Conway; Todd C. Jacobs; Patrick T. Nash; Matthew O. Sitzer; Gary M. Miller; Laura K. McNally. Associates: John E. Bucheit; Mark H. Carnow; Amy J. Collins; Kristen A. Dolan; Selvyn W. Fletcher; Jacob W. Harrell; Michael W. Kazan; Zubair A. Khan; Claudia M. Laurens; Jeffrey W. Luenz; Patrick R. Malone; Amanda H. McMurtrie; Sarah D. McTurnan; Brian J. Mowbray; Peter S. Roeser; Judy A. Smith; Maile H. Solis-Szukala; Robert D. Stonebraker; Mary L. Swietnicki; Andrew Szot. Senior Counsel: James P. Gitzlaff; Paul A. Sheldon.
General Practice.
See Professional Biographies, CHICAGO, ILLINOIS

Griseta, Joseph John .... '57 '82 C&L.424 B.B.A., J.D. 55 W. Wacker Dr., Ste. 702
Grissom, David W., Jr. '62 '94 C.475 B.A. L.215 J.D.
(adm. in MI; not adm. in IL) P.O. Box 7756‡
Griswold, Joel C. .... '77 '02 C.597 B.A. L.494 J.D. [Ⓐ Bell,B.&L.]
Groark, Jerome N., (AV) .... '— '61 C.602 B.S. L.209 J.D. [Dykema G.P.] ‡
Groark, John T., (AV) .... '51 '79 C.424 B.S. L.365 J.D. [Clausen M.]
Groark, Timothy J., (AV) ....'— '66 C.973 A.B. L.209 J.D. [Dykema G.P.] ‡
Groberg, Kurtas C. .... '75 '02 C.679 B.A. L.879 J.D. Asst. State Atty.
Groble, Donald G. .... '61 '89 C&L.602 B.A. L.365 J.D. 20 N. Clark St., Ste. 3600
Groble, George W., (AV) ...... '36 '60 C.602 B.B.A. L.424 J.D. 20 N. Clark St., Ste. 3600
Groble, Raymond H., III, (BV) .... '51 '86 C.209 B.A. L.339 J.D. [Daley&M.]
Groble, Raymond H., Jr., (AV) .... '18 '42 C.742 L.209 J.D. 33 W. Jackson Blvd.‡
Grode, Désirée Lee .... '58 '85 C.347 B.Mus. L.146 J.D. 1030 N. State St., Apt. 36B
Grodner, Jay R., (BV) .... '52 '78 C.966 B.A. L.365 J.D. [J.R.Grodner&Assoc.] ⊙
Grodner, Jay R., & Associates, P.C., (BV)
180 North LaSalle (⊙Buffalo Grove, Highland Park)
Grodsky, Eric S. .... '76 '02 C&L.966 B.B.A., J.D. [Ⓐ Maciorowski,S.&U.]
Groebe, Keith Walter, (AV) .... '— '79 C.339 B.A. L.209 J.D. [Masuda,F.E.&M.]
Groenendaal, Michael R. .... '65 '95 C.09 B.A. L.1187 J.D. 161 N. Clark, Suite 3100
Groenewold, Joel D. .... '— '96 C.879 B.A. L.424 J.D. [Kopka,P.D.&E.]
Groetken, Troy A. .... '70 '97 C&L.221 B.S., J.D. [McAndrews,H.&M.] (See Pat. Sect.)
Grogan, James J., (AV) '55 '80 C.1151 B.A. L.424 J.D.
Chf. Coun., Dept. of Atty. Regis. & Discip. Comm.

Grogan, William P., (AV) '49 '88 C&L.424 A.B., J.D. [🄲 Hinshaw&C.]
Grohne, Jack A. '35 '61 C.176 B.S. L.339 LL.B. Contl. Bk.
Groholski, Robert '75 '00 C&L.589 B.S., J.D. [🄰 Schwartz C.]
Gromacki, Joseph P. '65 '92 C.976 B.A. L.893 J.D. [Jenner&B.]
Groner, Julius '19 '47 C.424 Ph.D. L.209 J.D. 7141 North Kedzie Ave
Gronkiewicz, Edmund '39 '65 C&L.424 A.B., J.D. [Hinshaw&C.]
Gronkiewicz, Theresa, (AV) '56 '82 C.145 B.A. L.365 J.D. [🄲 Collins&B.]
Grosch, Julie F. '77 '03 C.339 B.A. L.146 J.D. [🄰 Varga B.L.H.&C.]
Grosh, Katherine A. '— '02 C.477 B.A. L.339 J.D. [🄰 Beermann S.W.B.B.G.&L.]
Gross, Gary E. '50 '75 C&L.339 B.S., J.D. Dir., Coopers & Lybrand‡
Gross, Irwin A. '38 '64 C.37 B.S. L.209 J.D. Coun., Combined Ins. Co. of Amer.
Gross, J. Arthur, (AV) '06 '32 C.339 B.S. L.209 J.D. 233 South Wacker Drive (Pat.)
Gross, J. Karl '72 '01 C.436 B.S.M.E. L.94 J.D. [🄰 Leydig,V.&M.]
Gross, Jennifer J. '— '02 C.477 B.A. L.209 J.D. [🄰 Querrey&H.]
Gross, Louise C. '52 '76 C.477 B.A. L.424 J.D. Assoc. Reg. Coun., U.S. EPA
Gross, Norman '45 '69 C.690 B.A. L.94 J.D.
(adm. in MA; not adm. in IL) Dir., Entrepreneurial Project, American Bar Assn.
Gross, Scott E. '59 '87 C.309 B.A. L.93 J.D. [Sidley A.B.&W.]
Gross, Vivien '— '73 C.588 B.A. L.347 J.D. Prof., Chicago Kent Law Sch.
Grossbart, John I. '54 '80 C&L.477 B.G.S., J.D. [Sonnenschein N.&R.]
Grossberg, David A., (AV) '— '76 C.112 A.B. L.145 J.D. [Schiff H.]
Grossman, Alan N. '49 '74 C.339 B.S. L.209 J.D. [Grossman]
Grossman, Arthur I., (AV) '14 '37 C&L.145 B.A., J.D. 111 E. Wacker Dr.
Grossman, Burton S. '25 '51 L.365 J.D. 2906 W. Peterson Ave.
Grossman, David '49 '77 C.339 B.A. L.146 J.D. Pinkerton Consulting & Investigations
Grossman, David A. '75 '00 C.691 B.A. L.569 J.D. [🄰 Mayer,B.R.&M.]
Grossman, Edward '57 '81 C.347 B.S. L.209 J.D. Exec. Dir., Chicago Legal Clinic
Grossman, Eric G. '58 '88 C.966 B.S. L.365 J.D. V.P. & Gen. Coun., Alpha Thought
Grossman, Geoffrey F., (AV) '35 '59 C.477 B.B.A. L.597 J.D. [Seyfarth S.]
Grossman, Gregory S. '— '03 C.339 B.S. L.273 J.D. [🄰 Katten M.R.]
Grossman, Harvey M. '47 '73 C.502 B.S. L.597 J.D. Legal Dir., ACLU
Grossman, Jeffrey C. '48 '73 C.659 B.A. L.262 J.D. 2835 N. Sheffield St., Suite 407
Grossman, Kay S. '46 '71 C.771 B.A. L.178 J.D. 2800 N. Lake Shore Dr.‡
Grossman, Lee F. '60 '86 C.339 B.S.C.E. L.365 J.D. [Grossman&F.]
Grossman, Michael A. '72 '98 C.347 B.A. L.209 J.D. [🄰 Cohen,G.&R.]
Grossman, Michael R. '69 '98 C.378 B.A. L.734 J.D. Co. Pub. Def. Off.
Grossman, Nathan M. '41 '69 C.339 B.S. L.209 J.D. [Cohen,G.&R.]
Grossman, Richard J. '50 '76 C.209 B.A. L.146 J.D. [Steinberg,B.&G.]
Grossman, Wendy A. '54 '80 C.326 B.A. L.564 J.D. 2930 N. Sheridan Road
Grossman & Flight, LLC 20 N. Wacker Drive Suite 4220 (Pat.)
Grossman Law Offices, P.C. 77 W. Wacker Dr., Ste. 3200
Grossmann, Andrew R. '75 '00 C.339 B.A. L.597 J.D. [🄰 Barack F.K.P.&N.]
Grossmann, Mark Richard '72 '97 C.966 B.B.A. L.424 J.D. [🄰 Katten M.R.]
Grossmark, Stephen T., (AV) '52 '77 C.339 B.A. L.910 J.D. [Tressler,S.M.&P.]
Groszek, Jennifer B. '77 '02 C.963 B.A. L.879 J.D. [🄰 Gunty&M.]
Groszek, Robert '74 '02 C.679 B.S. L.879 J.D. [Groszek]
Groszek Law Firm 3601 N. Pulaski Rd.
Grotberg, Karen F. R. '55 '85 C.373 B.A. L.597 J.D. [🄲 Mayer,B.R.&M.]
Grotefeld, Mark S., (BV) '56 '81 C.37 B.A. L.365 J.D. [Grotefeld&D.]
Grotefeld, William S., (AV) '18 '44 C.424 L.146 J.D. 100 West Monroe Street
Grotefeld, William S., (AV) '41 '71 C.238 A.B. L.365 J.D. [🄲 Grotefeld&D.]

Grotefeld & Denenberg, LLC, (BV)
105 West Adams Street, Suite 2300, 60603 ⊙
Telephone: 312-551-0200; 888-551-0700 Facsimile: 312-601-2402
Mark S. Grotefeld; Steve C. Silvey; Daniel G. Galivan; Brad M. Gordon; Lynn K. Weaver; Patrick R. Gareis; Daniel J. Biederman;—Julie Fournier; Megan E. Ritenour; Anooj M. Thakrar; Michael P. Swistak. Of Counsel: William S. Grotefeld.
Insurance Litigation, Subrogation, First and Third Party Defense, Insurance Coverage and General Civil Litigation.
Reference: Northern Trust.
Bingham Farms, Michigan Office: 30800 Telegraph Road, Suite 3858. Telephone: 248-727-7100. Facsimile: 248-593-5808.
San Francisco, California Office: 100 Spear Street, Suite 1850. Telephone: 415-344-9670. Facsimile: 415-989-2802.
Plantation, Florida Office: 8181 West Broward Boulevard, Suite 380, 33334. Telephone: 954-916-4780. Facsimile: 954-916-4785
Los Angeles, California Office: 199 Avenue of the Stars, Suite 1100 (Century Park), 90067. Telephone: 310-356-4683. Facsimile: 310-772-0631.
See Professional Biographies, CHICAGO, ILLINOIS

Groth, James F. '67 '92 C.966 B.B.A. L.597 J.D. [Funkhouser V.L.&D.]
Grotta & Moster, Ltd. 10020 S. Western Ave.
Groudine, Beverly V. '54 '80 C.860 B.A. L.569 J.D. Staff Counsel, Amer. Bar Assn.
Groulx, Heidi P. '67 '94 C.800 B.M. L.597 J.D. [🄰 Sidley A.B.&W.]
Groupe, Leonard M. '23 '50 C.145 L.146 J.D. 175 W. Jackson Blvd.
Grove, Angie M. '76 '01 C.473 B.A. L.209 J.D. [🄰 LaBarge,C.&L.]
Grskovich, Edward N. '29 '53 C&L.209 LL.B. VMS Realty, Inc.
Grubb, Brian '77 '04 C.1090 B.S. L.365 J.D. 217 North Jefferson Street, 5th Floor
Gruber, Erik D. '62 '88 C.94 B.A. L.339 J.D. [🄰 W.J.Harte]
Gruber, Misty S., (BV) '50 '78 C&L.37 B.S., J.D. [🄲 Dykema G.P.]
Grubner, Judith L., (AV) '51 '76 C.604 A.B. L.273 J.D.
[Michael B.&F.] (See Pat. Sect.)
Gruemmer, Brooks B. '— '90 C.602 B.B.A. L.477 J.D. [McDermott W.&E.]
Gruemmer, Kimberly Kelley '66 '91 C&L.352 B.A., J.D. Sr. Coun., CNA
Gruemmer, Paige Elise '63 '88 C.880 B.A. L.477 J.D. Sr. V.P., Heitman Financial LLC
Grund, David I., (AV) '47 '73 C&L.209 J.D. [Grund&L.]

Grund and Leavitt, P.C., (AV)
812 North Dearborn, 60610
Telephone: 312-640-0500 Fax: 312-640-8274
Email: info@grundlaw.com URL: http://www.grundlaw.com
David I. Grund; Lawrence S. Starkopf; Marvin J. Leavitt; Robert S. Kipnis; Michael Koenigsberger;—David Charles Adams; Alyssa Mogul.
Matrimonial Law including Domestic Relations, Divorce, Distribution of Property, Child Custody, Spousal Support, Visitation Rights, Appellate Practice.
See Professional Biographies, CHICAGO, ILLINOIS

Grundin, Robert E., (AV) '24 '51 C&L.597 B.S., J.D. 140 S. Dearborn St.
Grush, Eric H. '72 '98 C.477 B.S. L.659 J.D. [🄰 Sidley A.B.&W.]
Gruss, Gena '78 '00 C.339 B.A L.146 J.D. [Bollinger,R.&G.]
Gruss, Henry Phillip, (AV) '51 '77 C.209 B.A. L.365 J.D. [H.P.Gruss]
Gruss, Kristin M. '74 '99 C.477 B.A. L.365 J.D. [🄰 Donohue B.M.&S.]
Gruss, Henry Phillip, Ltd., (AV) Two North La Salle Street, Suite 1600
Gruszka, Peter T. '— '00 C.228 B.A. L.910 J.D. [🄰 Mayer,B.R.&M.]
Gryczan, Catherine C. '60 '85 C.339 B.S. L.861 J.D. [Schuyler,R.&Z.]
Gryniewicz, Victor M. '54 '79
C.424 B.A. L.209 J.D. U.S. Dept. of Jus., Off. of Inspec. Gen.
Gryzlo, Matthew J. '69 '97
C.339 B.S.M.E. L.365 J.D. [Wallenstein W.&R.] (See Pat. Sect.)

Grzeskiewicz, Maureen B. '— '99 C.436 B.A. L.209 J.D. [Arnstein&L.]
Grzyb, Anthony J. '60 '99 C.46 B.B.A. L.339 J.D. [🄰 Jenner&B.]
Grzymala, Mark B. '76 '01 C.339 B.A. L.146 J.D. [🄰 Rohlfing&O.]
Grzymek, Kenneth W. '49 '74 C&L.424 B.A., J.D. 6204 W. 63rd St.
Guadnolo, Rosemarie J., (AV) '46 '73 C.424 B.A. L.597 J.D. [Horvath&L.]
Guarisco, John W. '70 '95 C.813 B.A. L.339 J.D. [Neal,G.&E.]
Guarnieri, Kelly S. '60 '91 C.33 B.A. L.424 J.D. First Amer. Title Ins. Co.
Guberman, Daniel A. '55 '85
C.145 A.B. L.146 J.D. Dep. Gen. Coun., Ofc. of the Spec. Dep.
Gubin, Deborah J., & Associates, (AV) '49 '75
C.476 B.A. L.365 J.D. 605 West Madison Street, Suite 331
Guentert, Philip A. '58 '90 C.976 B.S. L.309 J.D.
(adm. in CA; not adm. in IL) Asst. U.S. Atty.
Guenther, Annette E. Gustafsson '62 '86 C.999 LL.M. L.146 J.D. [🄲 Thiedmann&E.]
Guenther, Robert S. '63 '89 C.893 B.A. L.910 J.D.
Asst. Reg. Coun., U.S. Environ. Protec. Agcy.
Guenthner, L. Robert, III '71 '99 C.201 B.S. L.910 J.D. [🄰 Gardner C.&D.]
Guerin, Donna Zak '60 '84 C&L.209 B.S.C., J.D. [Jenkens&G.]
Guerin, Roger J., (AV) '46 '71
C.602 A.B. L.339 J.D. Driehaus Enterprise Management, Inc.
Guerra, Michael '63 '88 C.424 B.B.A. L.365 J.D. [Sonnenschein N.&R.]
Guerrina, Britton B. '68 '99 C&L.145 B.A./M.A., J.D. [🄰 Mayer,B.R.&M.]
Gugenheim, Lynne '60 '85 C.597 B.A. L.846 J.D. Sr. V.P. & Dep. Gen. Coun., CNA
Guiao, Maria '— '02 C.276 B.S. L.436 J.D. [🄰 Winston&S.]
Guibord, Barbara B., (AV) '51 '77 C.183 B.A. L.262 J.D. [Guibord H.]

Guibord Homsy, LLP, (AV)
20 North Clark Street Suite 3200, 60602 ⊙
Telephone: 312-596-7777 Fax: 312-596-7788
URL: http://www.guibordhomsy.com
Barbara B. Guibord; Joseph G. Homsy. Associate: Douglas W. Michaud.
Environmental Law and Litigation, Brownsfields and Legacy Liability Restructuring, Commercial Litigation, Construction Law and Litigation, Corporate Finance and Transactions, Fund/Tax Expertise/Islamic Banking, International Practice, Policyholder Insurance Coverage Advice and Litigation, Toxic and Mass Tort.
New York, New York Office: 1350 Avenue of the Americas, Suite 3100, 10019. Telephone: 212-479-5620. Facsimile: 212-479-5621.
See Professional Biographies, CHICAGO, ILLINOIS

Guidice, Richard J. '40 '65 C&L.209 B.A., LL.B. 28 E. Jackson Blvd.
Guidubaldi, Mark D. '72 '97 C.473 B.S.B.A. L.93 J.D. [🄰 Katten M.R.]
Guild, Ronald J., (AV) '28 '56 C&L.339 B.S., LL.B. 55 W. Chestnut
Guilfoyle, Robert J. T., (AV) '36 '64 C.767 B.S. L.209 J.D. 200 N. LaSalle St.
Guin, David S. '62 '89 C&L.602 B.B.A., J.D. [McGuirewoods]
Guinta, Melissa '76 '01 C.473 B.A. L.424 J.D. [🄰 K.M.Forde]
Gulbrandsen, Margaret M. '78 '04 C.145 B.A. L.339 J.D. [🄰 Lord,B.&B.]
Guldberg, Christopher G. '65 '92 C.347 B.A. L.276 J.D. [🄰 Baker&M.]
Gulde, Matthew J. '— '00 C.602 B.S. L.846 J.D. [🄰 M.L.Rotert]
Gulino, Theodore '33 '57 C&L.424 B.S., J.D. 155 N. Michigan Ave.
Gulland, Michael S. '78 '04 C.893 B.A. L.597 J.D. [🄰 Jenner&B.]
Gullikson, Rosemary L.L. '52 '94 C.589 B.S. L.597 J.D. [Sonnenschein N.&R.]
Gumbiner, James Ellis, & Associates '48 '74
C&L.209 B.S., J.D. 180 North Michigan Avenue, Suite 2100
Gumina, James C., (AV) '59 '87
C.602 B.S. L.365 J.D. [McDonnell B.H.&B.] (See Pat. Sect.)
Gummow, Susan N. K. '— '91 C.69 B.B.A. L.420 J.D. [Clausen M.]
Gunn, Allan, (AV) '36 '61 C.118 B.A. L.569 J.D. [🄲 Matkov,S.M.&G.]
Gunn, Jeffrey W., (AV) '54 '84 C.424 B.A. L.209 J.D. [Morris&S.]
Gunn, Joshua A. '75 '00 C.338 B.S. L.145 J.D. [🄰 Sidley A.B.&W.]
Gunn, Kenneth A. '61 '88 C&L.339 B.S., J.D. Cook Co. Pub. Guard.
Gunn, Robert M., (AV) '27 '54 C.976 B.A. L.352 LL.B. [🄲 Wildman,H.A.&D.]
Gunnarsson, Helen Weidenheim '61 '85
C.597 B.S. L.339 J.D. Admin. Law J., IL. Human Rights Comm.
Gunter, Robert L., (AVⓉ) '45 '70
C.774 B.A. L.911 J.D. Gen. Coun., Moody Bible Institute
Gunther, Arthur D. '63 '90 C.339 B.S. L.1066 J.D. Pres., Gunther Group LLC
Gunty, Susan, (AV) '53 '80 C&L.424 B.A., J.D. [Gunty&M.]

Gunty & McCarthy, (AV)
150 South Wacker Drive, Suite 1025, 60606
Telephone: 312-541-0022 Facsimile: 312-541-0033
Susan Gunty; James P. McCarthy; Paul D. Van Lysebettens;—Stephen K. Milott; Robert G. Freyder; Jean M. French; Mary Ann O'Reilly; Catherine L. Carlson; Mara E. Cohen; Jeremy B. Harris; Jennifer B. Groszek; Sheryl E. Healy; Patricia M. Kelly; Scott D. Pfeiffer; Stephanie M. Thillens; James P. Kasper; Tamika D. Marshall. Of Counsel: Richard L. McLennan (Resident, St. Louis, MO Office).
Asbestos, Toxic Tort, Latex, Chemical Exposure, Repetitive Injury, Product Liability, Workers' Compensation, Insurance Coverage and Transportation Loss Litigation.
See Professional Biographies, CHICAGO, ILLINOIS

Guolee, Terrence F. '65 '91 C.966 B.A. L.209 J.D. [Querrey&H.]
Guon, Allen J. '70 '98 C.347 B.S.P.A. L.1119 J.D. [🄰 Shaw G.F.G.W.&T.]
Gupta, Ankur '71 '96 C.705 B.S. L.276 J.D. [🄰 Winston&S.]
Gupta, Paul R. '— '75 C.976 B.A. L.309 J.D.
(adm. in NY; not adm. in IL) [Mayer,B.R.&M.] (⊙New York, NY)
Gupta, Rashmi V. '— '01 C&L.494 B.S., J.D. [🄰 Marshall,G.&B.] (See Pat. Sect.)
Gupta, Raymond '70 '95 C.347 B.S. L.880 J.D. [Stamos&T.]
Gupta, Shilpi '69 '94 C.178 B.S. L.276 J.D. [🄲 Skadden,A.S.M.&F.]
Gupta, Valli V. '69 '97 C.602 B.A. L.436 J.D. [🄰 Levenfeld P.]
Gurak, Richard J. '65 '97 C.339 B.S. L.365 J.D. [🄰 Welsh&K.] (See Pat. Sect.)
Gurber, Kenneth, (AV) '46 '73 C.339 B.S. L.209 J.D. [Gurber,M.&N.]
Gurber, McAndrews & Norgle, LLC, (AV) 53 West Jackson Boulevard, Suite 301
Gurfinkel, Daniel M., (BV) '61 '87
C.339 B.S.C.E. L.1119 J.D. [🄰 Welsh&K.] (See Pat. Sect.)
Gurley, Helena E. '71 '96 C.436 B.A. L.629 J.D. Sr. Coun., Grant Thornton, LLP
Gurley, John C., (AV) '40 '65 C.589 B.S. L.966 LL.B. [Lord,B.&B.]
Gurvey, Gary A. '41 '70 C.339 B.S. L.209 J.D. 221 N. LaSalle St.
Gusman, Adam K. '76 '04 C.577 B.A. L.276 J.D. [🄰 Winston&S.]
Gussin, Zave H., (AV) '33 '56 C&L.145 B.A., J.D. 20 N. Clark St.
Gussis, Lloyd E., (AV) '47 '73 C.339 A.B. L.424 J.D. 2520 N. Lincoln Ave.
Gussis, Randy S., (AV) '48 '82 C.339 B.A. L.146 J.D. [Shaw G.F.G.W.&T.]
Gussis, Samuel '73 '99 C.197 A.B. L.339 J.D. [Shaw G.F.G.W.&T.]
Gust, Jennifer K. '71 '01 C.347 B.A. L.424 J.D. [🄰 Hinshaw&C.]
Gustafson, Christine '— '97 L.209 J.D. [🄲 Foley&L.]
Gustafson, Edw. R. '17 '41 C&L.145 B.A., J.D. Admin. Law J., Dept. of HHS, SSA
Gustafson, John W. '32 '56 C.742 L.424 J.D.,LL.B Cir. J.
Gustafson, Robert W. '66 '95
C.339 B.S.M.E. L.1000 J.D. Licensing Coun., Midway Games Inc. (Pat.)
Gustafson, Steven C. '61 '86 C.209 B.S. L.146 J.D. [Gould&R.]

Georges, Mara Stacy, (AV) '63 '88 C.602 B.A. L.424 J.D. Corp. Coun., City of Chicago, Dept. of Law, LLP
Georgevich, Christine M. '55 '92 C.339 B.S. L.424 J.D. Claims Coun., Chicago Title Ins. Co.
Geraci, Peter Francis .... '49 '74 C&L.209 B.A., J.D. 55 East Monroe Street
Gerage, Steven D., (BV) .... '64 '90 C.339 B.S. L.424 J.D. [Nadler,P.&M.]
Geraghty, Diane C. .... '43 '72 C.112 B.A. L.597 J.D. Prof., Loyola Univ. Sch. of Law
Geraghty, Gwen M., (BV) .... '68 '93 C.436 B.A. L.424 J.D. [Dykema G.P.]
Geraghty, Miriam N., (AV) .... '51 '77 C.881 B.A. L.209 J.D. [Kinoy,T.&G.]
Geraghty, Peter H. .... '55 '85 C.183 B.A. L.597 J.D. Dir., American Bar Association
Geraghty, Thomas .... '70 '97 C.724 B.A. L.976 J.D. [Ⓐ Mayer,B.R.&M.]
Geraghty, Thomas F. '44 '70 C.309 A.B. L.597 J.D. Assoc. Dean & Prof., Northwestern Univ.
Geraldson, Raymond I., (AV) .... '11 '35 C&L.966 A.B., J.D. [Seyfarth S.] ‡
Geraldson, Raymond I., Jr., (AV) '40 '65 C.210 B.A. L.597 J.D. [Pattishall,M.N.H.&G.]
Gerber, Brad S. .... '72 '97 C.339 B.A. L.146 J.D. [Ⓐ Laser,P.S.F.&E.]
Gerber, David J. '45 '73 C.855 B.A. L.145 J.D. (adm. in NY; not adm. in IL) Prof., ITT/Chicago-Kent College of Law
Gerber, Dean N., (AV) .... '59 '85 C.205 B.S. L.339 J.D. [Vedder,P.K.&K.]
Gerber, Robert G. .... '71 '98 C.347 B.A. L.365 J.D. [Neal,G.&E.]
Gerbosi, Paul F., (AV) .... '44 '69 C.597 B.S. L.424 J.D. [Nisen&E.]
Gerch, Edward L. .... '39 '63 C.339 B.S. L.597 J.D. Pres., Kingport Intl. Corp.
Gerdy, Harry .... '35 '66 C.1016 B.S.C. L.209 J.D. 2318 N. Lakewood Ave.
Geren, Gerald S., (AV) .... '— '66 [Ⓒ Barnes&T.] (See Pat. Sect.)
Geren, James B. '57 '98 C.560 B.A. L.608 J.D. (adm. in OH; not adm. in IL) Soc. Sec. Admn., Off. of Gen. Coun.
Gerenraich, Steven .... '— '96 C.477 B.A. L.339 J.D. [Ⓒ Foley&L.]
Gerhardstein, Michael C. .... '49 '85 C.750 B.A. L.365 J.D. Asst. State's Atty.
Gering, Charles M. .... '65 '92 C.597 B.A. L.347 J.D. [McDermott W.&E.]
Gering, Richard C., (AV) .... '— '77 C.602 B.A. L.597 J.D. [Arnstein&L.]
Gerlach, Charles L. .... '64 '91 C&L.309 A.B., J.D. Asst. Prof., John Marshall Law Sch.
Gerlach, Helmut E. .... '64 '97 C.445 B.A. L.446 J.D. [Ⓐ Baker&M.]
Gerlits, Francis J., (P.C.), (AV) .... '— '58 C.602 Ph.B. L.145 J.D. [Ⓒ Kirkland&E.]
Germaine, David P. .... '75 '01 C.363 B.A. L.209 J.D. [Ⓐ Daar&V.]
Germann, Hans J. .... '75 '01 C.118 L.862 J.D. [Ⓐ Mayer,B.R.&M.]
Gern, Ronald L., (AV) '58 '82 C.659 B.A.B.S. L.893 J.D. Sr. V.P. & Gen. Coun., General Growth Prop.
Gerner, Carol J., (AV) .... '— '81 C.860 B.A. L.910 J.D. [Ⓒ Sedgwick,D.M.&A.]
Gerner, Philip H., III .... '55 '80 C.732 B.A. L.910 J.D. [Robbins,S.N.L.&T.]
Geroulis, Nicholas .... '59 '87 C.339 B.A. L.365 J.D. [Martin&K.]
Geroulis, Patra S. .... '75 '00 C.209 B.S. L.602 J.D. [Ⓒ Ice M.]
Gerrie, Nancy S. .... '— '90 C.170 B.A. L.597 J.D. [McDermott W.&E.]
Gersh, Deborah L., (AV) .... '— '83 C.597 B.A. L.273 J.D. [DLPiper R.G.C.U.]
Gershenson, Bradley M. .... '63 '88 C.339 B.A. L.910 J.D. Pres., HealthUnits, Inc.
Gershenzon, Bruce W. .... '50 '75 C&L.339 B.S., J.D. 2033 N. Orleans St.
Gershon, Jeffrey M. .... '67 '96 C.37 B.A. L.1187 J.D. [Ⓐ Shaheen,N.S.F.&E.]
Gershon, Mark A., (AV) .... '61 '86 C&L.597 B.S., J.D. [DLPiper R.G.C.U.]
Gershon, Neil L. .... '53 '84 C.377 B.A. L.910 J.D. [Ⓐ R.Schey&Assoc.]
Gershowitz, Michael S. .... '71 '97 C.477 B.A. L.597 J.D. [Ⓐ DLPiper R.G.C.U.]
Gerson, Jerome H., (AV) .... '28 '51 C.339 L.146 J.D. 35 W. Wacker Dr.‡
Gerst, C. Graham .... '— '98 C.951 B.A. L.145 J.D. [Kirkland&E.]
Gerst, Christy S. .... '77 '01 C.910 B.A. L.339 J.D. [Ⓐ Wildman,H.A.&D.]
Gerstein, Allen H., (AV) '— '63 C.339 B.S. L.597 J.D. [Ⓒ Marshall,G.&B.] (See Pat. Sect.)
Gerstein, Avery Sheldon .... '57 '82 C.339 B.A. L.801 J.D. 711 W. Gordon Ter. Apt. 304
Gerstein, Mark D., (AV) .... '— '84 C.477 B.A. L.145 J.D. [Latham&W.]
Gerstein, Robert H., (AV) .... '— '59 C.339 A.B. L.145 J.D. [Holland&K.]
Gerstein, Robert M., (AV) '— '88 C&L.477 B.S.E., J.D. [Marshall,G.&B.] (See Pat. Sect.)
Gerstein, Sherwin A., and Associates '45 '69 C&L.209 B.A., J.D. 77 W. Washington St., Ste. 712
Gerstman, Gary D. .... '67 '92 C.813 A.B. L.309 J.D. [Ⓐ Sidley A.B.&W.]
Gerstman, George H., (AV) .... '39 '64 C.339 B.S.E.E. L.273 J.D. [Seyfarth S.] (Pat.)
Gerstman, Linda Ieleja '65 '90 C.297 B.A. L.494 J.D. Branch Chief, Chicago, M.R.O., S.E.C.
Gerstner, John W. .... '47 '73 C.162 B.A. L.424 J.D. [Gerstner&G.]
Gerstner, Mary Anne .... '48 '72 C&L.190 A.B., J.D. [Gerstner&G.]
Gerstner & Gerstner .... 53 W. Jackson Blvd.
Gertenrich, Alan J. .... '40 '67 C&L.339 B.S., J.D. Contl. Ill. Natl. Bk. & Tr. Co.
Gertler, Amy L. .... '57 '86 C.861 B.A. L.1000 J.D. [Nadler,P.&M.]
Gertler, Steven D., (BV) .... '54 '81 C.339 B.A. L.146 J.D. [S.D.Gertler&Assoc.]
Gertler, Steven D., & Associates, Ltd., Law Offices of, (BV) 188 W. Randolph St., Ste. 1518
Gertz, Elmer, (AV) .... '06 '30 C&L.145 Ph.B., J.D. 6249 N. Albany Ave.‡
Gertz, Scott William .... '68 '99 C.823 B.A L.146 J.D. [Ⓐ Jacobs,B.O.S.&H.]
Gertz, Theodore G., (AV) .... '36 '62 C.145 B.A. L.597 J.D. [Shefsky&F.]
Gervase, Megan E. '76 '01 C.339 B.A. L.146 J.D. (adm. in CA; not adm. in IL) [Ⓐ Winston&S.]
Gesas, Michael L., (AV) .... '55 '84 C.965 B.B.A. L.365 J.D. [Gesas,P.&G.]
Gesas, Pilati & Gesas, Ltd., (AV) .... 53 W. Jackson Blvd.
Geselbracht, Thomas F., (AV) .... '— '79 C.436 A.B. L.145 J.D. [DLPiper R.G.C.U.]
Gesicki, Glen J. .... '70 '04 L.209 J.D. [Ⓐ Kelley D.&W.] (Pat.)
Geslewitz, Irving M., (AV) .... '50 '76 C.705 B.A. L.145 J.D. [Much S.F.D.A.&R.]
Gessler, George W., (AV) '38 '63 C.894 B.A. L.145 J.D. 70 West Madison, Suite 4000‡
Gessner, Douglas C. .... '— '89 C.477 B.A. L.309 J.D. [Kirkland&E.]
Gestrin, Laura Leslie .... '73 '98 C.597 B.A. L.365 J.D. 135 S. LaSalle St., Ste. 2260
Gesualdo, Robert Raffaele .... '— '99 C.209 B.S. L.365 J.D. 4743 N. Delphia Avenue
Gettel, Nancy J. .... '76 '04 C.27 B.S. L.477 J.D. [Ⓐ Leydig,V.&M.]
Getter, Matthew M. .... '65 '92 C&L.659 B.S., J.D. Asst. U.S. Atty.
Gettleman, Chad H., (AV) .... '51 '76 C.339 B.S. L.436 J.D. [Adelman&G.]
Gettleman, Jeffrey W. .... '— '74 C.966 B.A. L.145 J.D. [Ⓐ Kirkland&E.]
Gettleman, Robert W., (AV) .... '43 '68 C.94 B.S.B.A. L.597 J.D. U.S. Dist. J.
Gettleson, Scott M. .... '67 '92 C.477 B.S.E. L.339 J.D. [Katten M.R.] (Pat.)
Getto, Chas. A. .... '18 '47 L.146 LL.B. 4941 N. Mozart
Getz, Bettina, (AV) .... '— '82 C.475 B.A. L.209 J.D. [Mayer,B.R.&M.]
Getz, Edwin A. .... '56 '85 C.118 B.A. L.910 J.D. [Gardner C.&D.]
Getzendanner, Vincent J., Jr., (AV) .... '42 '66 L.424 LL.B. [Madigan&G.]
Getzoff, William M., (AV) .... '47 '72 C.604 B.A. L.339 J.D. [Getzoff&G.]
Getzoff & Getzoff, (AV) .... Suite 650, 150 South Wacker
Geuther, Gregory K. .... '47 '74 C.37 B.S. L.365 J.D. 680 N. Lake Shore Dr.
Geverola, André M. .... '— '03 C.112 B.S. L.145 J.D. [Ⓐ Latham&W.]
Geyer, Jennifer S. .... '77 '02 C.477 B.S. L.851 J.D. Asst. State Atty.

Ghadimi, René .... '— '92 C.1350 B.A. L.145 J.D. [Katten M.R.]
Ghaowi, Zikar .... '73 '98 C.589 B.S. L.1158 J.D. 1231-1233 N. Ashland Ave.
Gharakhanian, Andre J. .... '77 '02 C.477 B.A. L.276 J.D. 190 S. LaSalle St.
Ghelerter, Susan, (BV) .... '55 '81 C.93 B.A. L.818 J.D. [Fuchs&R.]
Ghess, Benjamin, (AV) .... '— '80 C.98 B.S. L.339 J.D. [Ⓒ Neal&L.]
Ghezzi, June K. .... '— '83 C.1044 B.A. L.424 J.D. [Jones D.]
Ghezzi, Sheryl Rae **(See Lincolnwood)**
Ghilardi, Ronald S. .... '39 '63 C.750 B.A. L.365 J.D. 222 N. La Salle St.
Ghislandi, Anne C. .... '64 '99 C.145 B.A. L.209 J.D. Heller Financial, Inc.
Ghogomu, Puamuh T., II .... '— '04 C&L.339 B.S., J.D. [Ⓐ Littler M.]
Giacchetti, Cynthia, (AV) .... '52 '77 C.700 B.A. L.209 J.D. 53 W. Jackson Blvd
Giacomuzzi, Sylvia T. .... '62 '87 C&L.209 B.A., J.D. Cook Co. Public Guardian
Giagkou, Pamela M. '66 '02 C.473 B.A. L.365 J.D. P.M.G. Tradmark Consultants & Mkgt. Servs., Inc.
Giaimo, Frank P. .... '53 '79 C.970 B.A. L.1003 J.D. 19 W. Jackson Boulevard
Giamanco, Joseph P. .... '77 '02 C.208 B.A. L.209 J.D. [Ⓐ Stride,C.&S.]
Giangiorgi, Richard A., (AV) '39 '67 C.436 B.S.M.E. L.276 J.D. [Trexler,B.G.B.&M.] (See Pat. Sect.)
Giangrossi, David M., (CV) .... '52 '79 C.966 B.A. L.365 J.D. [Schuyler,R.&Z.]
Giannelli, Joseph A., (AV) .... '56 '82 C.424 B.A. L.365 J.D. [Cassiday,S.&G.]
Giannelli, Vincenza G. .... '58 '85 C.339 B.A. L.589 J.D. Coun., Chicago Title & Tr. Co.
Giannoulias, Alexander A. .... '76 '02 C.94 B.A. L.861 J.D. Corp. Coun., Broadway Bank
Giannoulias, Stavros S. .... '77 '02 C.473 B.A. L.146 J.D. [Ⓐ Horwood M.&B.]
Gianos, Diane .... '— '89 C.209 B.S. L.146 J.D. [Foley&L.]
Giardina, David C. .... '66 '94 C.69 B.A. L.145 J.D. [Ⓐ Sidley A.B.&W.]
Gibaitis, John A., Law Office of '37 '69 C.424 B.A. L.365 J.D. 6247 South Kedzie Avenue
Gibbons, Christopher J., (BV) .... '65 '92 C.966 B.A. L.424 J.D. [Nyhan,P.B.K.&L.]
Gibbons, Edward P., (BV) .... '63 '89 C.945 B.B.A. L.602 J.D. [Walker W.M.]
Gibbons, John F., (AV) .... '59 '85 C&L.602 B.A., J.D. [Greenberg T.]
Gibbons, Kathleen M. .... '58 '87 C.338 B.S. L.424 J.D. Chicago Board of Education
Gibbons, Paul C. .... '67 '97 C.971 B.S.E.E. L.818 J.D. [Niro,S.H.&N.] (See Pat. Sect.)
Gibbons, Thomas A. .... '54 '79 C.424 B.S. L.209 J.D. Asst. States Atty.
Gibbons, William J., (AV) .... '— '72 C&L.597 B.A., J.D. [Latham&W.]
Gibbs, Christopher M. .... '78 '04 C.966 B.A. L.1119 J.D. [Ⓐ Shefsky&F.]
Gibbs, Thomas E., (AV) .... '46 '72 C.602 B.A. L.424 J.D. 53 W. Jackson, Ste. 615
Gibbs, William T. .... '75 '04 C.602 B.A. L.146 J.D. [Ⓐ Corboy&D.]
Gibney, Kara K. .... '70 '95 C.162 B.A. L.221 J.D. [Ⓒ Mayer,B.R.&M.]
Gibson, Claire K. .... '74 '00 C.741 B.A. L.910 J.D. [Ⓐ Mayer,B.R.&M.]
Gibson, Donald J., Jr. .... '58 '83 C&L.424 B.A., J.D. [McGuirewoods]
Gibson, Jeremy A. .... '— '87 C.347 B.A. L.477 J.D. [Ⓒ Masuda,F.E.&M.]
Gibson, Keith L. .... '70 '96 C.347 B.A. L.209 J.D. [Johnson&B.]
Gibson, Margaret A., P.C. .... '— '89 C.477 B.A. L.597 J.D. [Kirkland&E.]
Gibson, Marlene A. .... '70 '95 C.477 B.A. L.209 J.D. Assoc. Coun., MCI WorldCom, Inc.
Gibson, Nancy S. '59 '85 C.860 B.S. L.597 J.D. Northwestern Univ. Legal Clinic (⊙Port., ME)
Gibson, Pamela V. '49 '78 C.999 B.A. L.831 J.D. (adm. in MA; not adm. in IL) Chf. Coun., I.R.S.
Gibson, Stephen W. .... '72 '99 C.37 B.A. L.208 J.D. P.O. Box 2379
Gidron, Leah D. .... '69 '96 C.112 B.A. L.597 J.D. [Ⓐ DLPiper R.G.C.U.]
Gierke, Scott N., (AV) .... '53 '81 C.339 B.S. L.46 J.D. [McDermott W.&E.]
Giese, Douglas C. .... '65 '97 C.589 B.S. L.146 J.D. [Ⓐ Defrees&F.]
Gieseke, Corinne J. .... '54 '79 C.339 B.S. L.424 J.D. Lt. Gov.
Gifford, Andrew R. .... '70 '98 C.174 B.A. L.477 J.D. [Lord,B.&B.]
Gifford, Geoffrey L., (AV) .... '46 '71 C.502 B.A. L.477 J.D. [Pavalon,G.L.&M.]
Gigante, Carl A., (AV) .... '57 '83 C&L.424 B.A., J.D. [Figliulo&S.]
Gigante, Richard, (AV) .... '33 '58 C.191 B.A. L.146 J.D. [R.Gigante]
Gigante, Richard, P.C., (AV) .... 221 N. LaSalle St.
Giglio, Anthony G. .... '60 '85 C.879 B.A. L.209 J.D. 2 N. Riverside Plaza
Gignac, James P. .... '— '05 C.20 B.A. L.1565 J.D. [Ⓐ Mayer,B.R.&M.]
Gignilliat & Hymen, P.C. **(See Northbrook)**
Gilbert, Alan S., (AV) .... '49 '75 C.674 A.B. L.145 J.D. [Sonnenschein N.&R.]
Gilbert, Brian B. .... '62 '87 C.339 B.S. L.228 J.D. [Gould&R.]
Gilbert, Gigi A. .... '63 '88 C.339 B.S. L.424 J.D. Asst. State's Atty.
Gilbert, Howard N., (AV) .... '28 '51 C.145 Ph.B. L.976 J.D. [Wildman,H.A.&D.]
Gilbert, Jay, (AV) .... '49 '75 C.347 B.A. L.1119 J.D. [Kutak R.]
Gilbert, Jeffrey B., (AV) .... '51 '76 C.597 B.A. L.309 J.D. [Johnson,J.S.G.&D.]
Gilbert, Jeffrey T., (AV) .... '— '80 C.910 B.A. L.597 J.D. [Sachnoff&W.]
Gilbert, Jennifer Schoen '75 '01 C.679 B.A. L.1119 J.D. Two North LaSalle Street, Suite 2200
Gilbert, Jerry H. .... '45 '72 C.793 B.S. L.851 J.D. 55 West Van Buren Street★
Gilbert, Michelle J. .... '61 '86 C.927 B.S. L.339 J.D. Legal Assistance
Gilbreth, David E. .... '63 '90 [Ⓐ B.L.Gordon&Assoc.]
Gilchrist, Kenneth L. .... '29 '57 C&L.585 Ph.B., J.D. V.P., Continental Bank
Gildea, Gilbert E., Jr. .... '44 '69 C.976 A.B. L.145 J.D. [Ⓒ Goodsmith G.&U.]
Gilden, Carol V. .... '56 '83 C.339 B.S. L.146 J.D. [Much S.F.D.A.&R.]
Gilden, Jairus M., (AV) .... '52 '82 C.976 B.A. L.276 J.D. [Karmel&G.]
Giles, Brooks .... '74 '99 C.145 B.A. L.228 J.D. [Ⓐ Katten M.R.]
Giles, David C. .... '— '01 C.821 B.A. L.602 J.D. [Ⓐ Schiff H.]
Gilfand, Alissa L. .... '75 '00 C.645 B.A. L.424 J.D. 435 N. Michigan Avenue
Gilford, Steven R., (AV) .... '52 '78 C.197 A.B. L.228 J.D. [Mayer,B.R.&M.]
Gilhooly, Edward D., (AV) '40 '68 C.446 B.S.Aero.E. L.128 J.D. 28 East Jackson Blvd., Suite 423 (Pat.)
Gilhooly, Mary C. .... '58 '83 C.339 B.S. L.424 J.D. Chicago Bd. Options Exchange
Giliberto, Louis J. .... '21 '47 C&L.209 LL.B. 6250 N. Leroy Avenue
Gill, Adam .... '— '03 C.790 B.A. L.1065 J.D. [Ⓐ Kirkland&E.]
Gill, Lawrence M., (AV) .... '— '68 C.734 A.B. L.477 J.D. [Schiff H.]
Gill, Michael J. .... '52 '77 C&L.597 B.A., J.D. [Mayer,B.R.&M.]
Gill, Michael Thomas, (BV) .... '72 '97 C.473 B.A. L.424 J.D. [Pfaff&G.]
Gillen, Gary R. .... '65 '91 C.436 L.365 J.D. [Wildman,H.A.&D.] (Pat.)
Gillen, Suzanne Favia, (BV) .... '61 '87 C.393 B.A. L.146 J.D. [Mangan,L.G.&L.] ⊙
Gilleran-Lunt, Jeannine .... '68 '93 C.339 B.F.A. L.146 J.D. [Ⓐ Dowd&D.]
Gillespie, Clarke M., III .... '61 '95 C.145 B.A. L.46 J.D. [Ⓐ Kubasiak,F.R.&R.]
Gillespie, Julie A. .... '— '96 C.446 B.A. L.228 J.D. [Mayer,B.R.&M.]
Gillespie, Peter J. .... '70 '97 C.597 B.A. L.276 J.D. [Ⓐ Baker&M.]
Gillespie, Terence P., (AV) .... '— '78 C.209 B.A. L.424 J.D. [Genson&G.]
Gillette, Merri Jo '57 '82 C.597 Ph.B. L.1017 J.D. (adm. in PA; not adm. in IL) Reg. Direct., Chicago, M.R.O., S.E.C.
Gillette, Pamela R. '54 '93 C.911 B.A. L.365 J.D. Asst. V.P. & Asst. Gen. Coun., CNA Property & Casualty Oper.
Gillies, Donald A., (AV) .... '31 '56 C.207 B.A. L.597 J.D. [Ⓒ Holland&K.] ‡
Gilligan, John W., III, (AV) .... '59 '86 C.121 B.A. L.146 J.D. [Stellato&S.]

Gilligan, Kathleen M., (AV) '61 '86 C.602 B.A. L.93 J.D. [Wildman,H.A.&D.]
Gilliom, Robyn R. '51 '81 C.502 B.G.S. L.276 J.D. Chf. Coun., I.R.S.
Gillis, Kenneth L. '36 '61 C.46 B.S. L.145 J.D. Cir. J.
Gillis, Susan Fox '43 '88 C.209 B.A. L.146 J.D. Cook Co. Cir. Ct. Assoc. J.
Gillman, J. Scott '64 '90 C.339 B.S. L.46 J.D. [Ⓐ Condon&C.]
Gillman, Patricia L., (BV) '47 '73 C.788 B.A. L.276 J.D. [Ⓒ Seyfarth S.]
Gillman, Steven L., (AV) '54 '80 C.188 B.S. L.477 J.D. [Holland&K.]
Gillogly, Daniel W., (AV) '49 '75 C.352 B.A. L.365 J.D. Asst. U.S. Atty.
Gills, Jeanne M. '— '94 C.475 B.S.E.E. L.145 J.D. [Foley&L.] (Pat.)
Gilman, Michael A. '56 '82 C.339 B.A. L.146 J.D. [O'Rourke,H.F.&D.]
Gilman, Paul A. '63 '89 C.339 B.A. L.424 J.D. [Aronberg G.D.&G.]
Gilman, Steven E. '55 '82 C.339 B.S. L.146 J.D. Ct. J.
Gilmartin, Charles A., (AV) '21 '51 C.209 L.146 LL.B. 10 S. La Salle St.
Gilmartin, Robert E., III, (AV) '50 '75 C.597 B.A. L.424 J.D. [Clausen M.]
Gilmer, Douglas Lee '59 '86 C.339 B.A. L.365 J.D.
Sr. Atty., Off. of Hearing & App., Soc. Sec. Adm
Gilson, Jerome, (AV) '31 '58 C.502 A.B. L.597 J.D. [Brinks H.G.&L.]
Gimbel, Barbara A. '73 '98 C.339 B.A. L.209 J.D. [Ⓐ Holland&K.]
Gimbel, Stuart M., (BV) '61 '86 C.597 B.S. L.893 J.D. [Kamensky,R.H.&D.] ⊙
Ginett, Laura J., (AV) '— '86 C.339 B.A. L.94 J.D. [Anderson,R.]
Ginex, Gregory V. '79 '04 C.424 B.A. L.146 J.D. [Ⓐ Bollinger,R.&G.]
Ging, Thomas F., (AV) '41 '66 C.363 A.B. L.276 J.D. [Hinshaw&C.]
Gingold, Scott H. '— '98 C.477 B.A. L.597 J.D. [Ⓐ Perkins C.]
Ginn, Bradley R. '60 '85 C.477 B.A. L.912 J.D. 1618 W. Diversey
Ginos, Robert A. '— '84 C.339 B.S. L.910 J.D. 10 South LaSalle Street, Suite 3300
Ginsberg, Allen L. '41 '67 C.339 B.S. L.209 J.D. 55 W. Monroe St.
Ginsberg, Gail C. '44 '73 C.103 B.A. L.904 J.D.
(adm. in VA; not adm. in IL) U.S. Environmental Protection Agency
Ginsberg, Lewis R., (AV) '32 '56 C&L.145 A.B., J.D. 5530 Kimbark Ave.‡
Ginsberg, Marc D., (AV) '51 '77 C.339 B.A. L.365 J.D. [Dykema G.P.]
Ginsberg, Robert E. '45 '69 C.103 A.B. L.30 J.D. U.S. Bkrptcy. J.
Ginsberg, Steven F., Law Offices of '65 '91
C.188 B.A. L.477 J.D. 300 W. Adams Street, Suite 505 (⊙Chicago)
Ginsberg, Steven "Sonny" F. '65 '91 C.188 B.A. L.477 J.D.
[Levenfeld P.] (⊙Chicago)
Ginsburg, Allen J., (P.C.), (AV) '44 '69 C&L.597 B.S., J.D. [DLPiper R.G.C.U.]
Ginsburg, Arnold H., (BV) '44 '74 C.424 B.S. L.146 J.D. 6177 S. Archer Ave.
Ginsburg, Joseph A., (AV) '— '69 C.1016 B.S. L.209 J.D. [Levin G.]
Ginsburg, Marvin E. '32 '56 C.1016 B.S.C. L.209 J.D. 77 W. Washington St.
Ginsburg, Seymour B. '34 '57 C&L.597 B.S., J.D. 20 N. Wacker Dr.
Ginsparg, Colman '33 '63 C.1016 B.S.C. L.146 J.D. [Ginsparg,B.&Assoc.]
Ginsparg, Bolton & Associates, Ltd. 79 West Monroe Street Suite 1119
Ginty, Patrick Sean '65 '94 C.339 B.S. L.146 J.D. [Ⓢ Winston&S.]
Giordano, Patrick N., (AV) '52 '79 C.860 B.A. L.1051 J.D. [Giordano&N.]

Giordano & Neilan, Ltd., (AV)
360 North Michigan Avenue, Suite 1005, 60601
Telephone: 312-580-5480 Fax: 312-580-5481 URL: http://www.dereglaw.com
Email: giordanoneilan@dereglaw.com URL: http://www.lawyers.com/giordano_law
Patrick N. Giordano; Paul G. Neilan. Of Counsel: Lawrence Weiss (Not admitted in IL). Associates: Arthur Z. Handelman; Christina A. Pusemp.
Energy and Telecommunications Law.
Representative Clients: John Buck Co.; Draper & Kramer; City of Chicago; Merchandise Mart; Central Illinois Light Co. (CILCO); Chicago Park District; QST Enterprises, Inc.; Building Owners and Managers Association of Chicago.
Reference: QST Enterprises, Inc.
See Professional Biographies, CHICAGO, ILLINOIS

Giovannini, Dennis A., (BV) '49 '75 C.209 B.A. L.365 J.D. [Giovannini&O.]
Giovannini & Olshansky, (BV) 605 West Madison Street, Suite 331
Girard, Ellen Marie '72 '02 C.879 B.A. L.146 J.D. [Ⓐ Quarles&B.]
Girard, Gwenn E. '70 '99 C.373 B.A. L.602 J.D. [Ⓐ Winston&S.]
Girardi, Joseph A. '46 '72 C.339 B.A. L.146 J.D. [Henderson&L.]
Girsch, Rebecca M. '74 '00 C.884 B.A. L.209 J.D. [Ⓐ Skadden,A.S.M.&F.]
Girzadas, Richard P. '65 '97 C.273 B.A. L.365 J.D. [Ⓐ Belgrade&O.]
Gisch, Margaret A. '65 '90 C.741 B.A. L.339 J.D. [Field&G.]
Gistenson, Steven H., (AV) '60 '86 C.339 B.A. L.365 J.D. [Schwartz C.]
Gitles, Gerald A., (AV) '31 '57 C.37 B.S. L.597 J.D. 1212 N. LaSalle St., #2701‡
Gitles, Jay A., (AV) '62 '87 C.477 A.B. L.597 J.D. [Seyfarth S.]
Gittler, Marvin, (AV) '38 '63 C.823 A.B. L.145 J.D. [Asher,G.G.&D.]
Gitzlaff, James P. '69 '95 C.679 B.A. L.339 J.D. [Ⓒ Grippo&E.]
Giudice, Daniel L. '59 '86 C&L.589 B.S., J.D. 218 North Jefferson Street Suite 202
Giusiana, Michele A., (BVⓉ) '56 '81 C.1044 B.A. L.276 J.D.
(adm. in DC; not adm. in IL) Coun., The Boeing Co.
Giusti, Jay R. '56 '81 C&L.276 B.A., J.D. [Ⓒ Kegan&K.]
Given, Jeffrey N. '56 '83 C.118 B.A. L.1119 J.D. XJD Corp.
Given, Lynda K., (AV) '— '80 C.473 A.B. L.608 J.D. [Chapman&C.]
Given, Ronald B. '52 '78 C.999 B.A. L.1119 J.D. [Mayer,B.R.&M.]
Givhan-Brewer, Darvionne J. '71 '97 C.339 B.S. L.365 J.D. Appl. Ct.
Gladden, James W., Jr., (AV) '40 '64 C.210 A.B. L.309 J.D. [Ⓒ Mayer,B.R.&M.]
Glade, Suzanne '59 '82 C.1098 L.861 J.D. [Ⓐ Fischel&K.]
Glader, Ralph N. '47 '78 C.674 A.B. L.209 J.D. [Ⓐ R.E.VanDemark]
Gladney, Jill J. '67 '91 C.502 B.S. L.145 J.D. [Knepper&G.]
Glantz, Robert W., (AV) '64 '89 C&L.339 B.S., J.D. [Shaw G.F.G.W.&T.]
Glaser, Albert B. '26 '48 C.145 L.94 LL.B. 2052 Lincoln Park W.‡
Glaser, D. Louis, II, (AV) '62 '89 C.210 B.A. L.424 J.D. [Gardner C.&D.]
Glaser, Deborah L. '69 '96 C.347 B.A. L.424 J.D. 140 S. Dearborn St., Ste. 420
Glass, Colleen M. '59 '95 C.1151 B.A. L.365 J.D. Cir. Ct. of Cook Co., 1st Mun. Dist.
Glass, Garret E. '69 '02 C.347 B.A. L.276 J.D. [Ⓐ Lord,B.&B.]
Glass, James L., Law Office of '52 '78
C.589 B.A. L.146 J.D. 77 W. Washington St., Ste. 812
Glass, Jeffrey M. '66 '91 C.339 B.S. L.145 J.D. [Ⓐ Field&G.]
Glass, Stanford L., (AV) '34 '60 C.339 B.A. L.309 J.D. 200 E. Deleware‡
Glass, Tia C. '71 '99 C.1024 B.S. L.365 J.D. [Cozen O.]
Glassberg, Donald A., (AV) '37 '68 C.477 B.B.A. L.209 J.D. [Levenfeld P.]
Glassgow, John A. '— '98 C.602 B.A. L.597 J.D. [Ⓐ Kirkland&E.]
Glassman, Eydie R. '66 '02 C.339 B.A. L.589 J.D. [Ⓐ Johnson&B.]
Glassman, Martin E. '48 '72 C.98 B.S. L.424 J.D. 55 W. Monroe St., Ste. 3330
Glasson, Eric Michael '71 '97 C.339 B.S. L.146 J.D. 205 W. Randolph St.
Glaub, Michael A., (BV) '59 '84 C.801 B.A. L.209 J.D. [Ⓐ Roddy,L.&Z.]
Glauberman, Kelly P. '— '98 C.309 A.B. L.597 J.D. [Ⓐ Jones D.]
Glauberman, Scott P. '72 '97 C.339 B.A. L.309 J.D. [Ⓐ Winston&S.]
Glaves, Robert A. '65 '91 C.966 B.A. L.365 J.D. 321 S. Plymouth Court
Glazer, Adam J., (AV) '64 '88 C.222 B.A. L.597 J.D. [Schoenberg,F.N.&R.]
Glazer, Barry '57 '82 C&L.339 B.S., J.D. [Robbins,S.&S.]
Glazier, Ilana '— '00 C.477 B.A. L.145 J.D. [Ⓐ Jones D.]
Glazier, Joshua M. '63 '88 C.477 B.B.A. L.309 J.D. Pres., Glazier Corp.
Glazov, Burton E. '38 '63 C.597 B.S. L.145 J.D. 900 N. Michigan Ave.‡
Glazov, Joshua M. '70 '95 C.273 B.A. L.472 J.D. [Ⓐ DLPiper R.G.C.U.]
Gleason, Edward W., (BV) '65 '90 C.436 B.A. L.46 J.D. [Keegan,L.L.&G.]
Gleason, Julie M. '71 '00 C.1434 B.A. L.851 J.D. [Ⓐ Gleason&M.]
Gleason, Kathryn '59 '87 C.399 B.A. L.966 J.D. Off. of U.S. Trustee
Gleason, Patrick M., (AV) '45 '73 C.145 B.S. L.365 J.D. Dir., Chicago Opers.
Gleason, Steven M. '53 '80 C.966 B.A. L.209 J.D. [Nilson,S.G.&C.]
Gleason, Troy L. '69 '02 C&L.851 B.A., J.D. [Gleason&M.]

Gleason & MacMaster, LLC
77 West Washington, Suite 1218, 60602
Telephone: 312-578-9530 Fax: 312-578-9524
URL: http://www.gleasonmacmasterlaw.com
Members of Firm: Troy L. Gleason; Sarah R. MacMaster. Associate: Julie M. Gleason.
Bankruptcy, Divorce, Real Estate, Driving While Intoxicated (DUI).
See Professional Biographies, CHICAGO, ILLINOIS

Gleicher, David W., (AV) '54 '80 C.978 B.A. L.145 J.D.
Asst. Def., State Appl. Def. Off.
Gleicher, Ilene '50 '79 C.208 B.A. L.146 J.D. 221 N. LaSalle St., 32nd Fl.
Glenn, Jeremy J. '72 '97 C.221 B.S.B.A. L.352 J.D. [Ⓐ Meckler B.&T.]
Glenn, Kevin J., (AV) '51 '79 C.602 B.B.A. L.1151 J.D. [Ⓒ Foran G.P.&P.]
Glennon, Caroline G. '69 '96 C.339 B.S. L.365 J.D. Asst. Pub. Def.
Glennon, James B. '63 '88 C.602 B.A. L.424 J.D. [Foran G.P.&P.]
Glennon, John E. '52 '77 C.597 B.A. L.602 J.D. Off. of the Gov.
Glewicz, William J. '59 '83 C.1183 B.A. L.209 J.D. Res. Develop. Mgr.
Glick, Heather L. '75 '01 C.112 B.A. L.879 J.D. [Ⓐ Ancel,G.D.B.D.&R.]
Glick, Lawrence E. '31 '54 C&L.472 B.B.A., J.D. [Ⓒ Chuhak&T.]
Glick, Marvin H., (AV) '37 '60 C.339 L.209 J.D. 208 S. La Salle St., Ste. 1650
Glick, Michael '65 '91 C.910 A.B. L.209 J.D. Asst. Atty. Gen.
Glick, Paul M., (AV) '48 '73 C.966 B.A. L.209 J.D. [P.M.Glick]
Glick, Robert D. '52 '77 C.339 B.A. L.209 J.D. Asst. Pub. Def.
Glick, Robert Dunn, (AV) '36 '62 C.659 B.S. L.145 J.D. [Schwartz C.]

Glick, Paul M., Chartered, (AV)
10 South LaSalle Street, Suite 1017, 60603
Telephone: 312-419-4770 Fax: 312-419-4771
Email: pmg@pglicklaw.com
Paul M. Glick.
Tax and Employee Benefits Law.
See Professional Biographies, CHICAGO, ILLINOIS

Glickman, Don E., (Ltd.), (AV) '47 '72 C.473 B.A. L.145 J.D. [Gordon,G.F.&R.]
Glickman, Sam '38 '63 C&L.209 J.D. 155 N. Michigan Ave.
Glickman, Stephen A. '61 '87 C.966 B.A. L.209 J.D. [S.A.Glickman]

Glickman, Stephen A., P.C.
225 West Washington Street Suite 2300, 60606
Telephone: 312-960-9550 Fax: 312-960-9555
Email: sagpc@aol.com
Stephen A. Glickman.
Employment Law, Employment Discrimination, Litigation, Sexual Harassment, Wrongful Termination, Separation Agreements, Executive Severance, Employment Contracts, Human Resources, Business Lawsuits, and General Commercial Litigation.
See Professional Biographies, CHICAGO, ILLINOIS

Glickson, Scott L., (AV) '50 '75 C.339 B.A. L.597 J.D. [Gordon&G.L.]
Glickstein, David, (AV) '41 '67 C.966 B.B.A. L.597 J.D. [DLPiper R.G.C.U.]
Glickstein, Jon L. '70 '96 C.165 B.A. L.597 J.D. Dir. Sales & Dev., VisaNow.com

Glieberman, Herbert A., & Associates, (AV) '— '54 C.1016 L.146 J.D.
19 South La Salle Street, Suite 600, 60603-1402
Telephone: 312-236-2879 Fax: 312-236-3417 URL: http//www.herbertgliebermandivorce.com
Email: hglieber@aol.com URL: http://www.lawyers.com/hglieber
Divorce Law, Family Law, Domestic Relations, Child Custody.
See Professional Biographies, CHICAGO, ILLINOIS

Glink, Shona B. '66 '91 C.860 B.A. L.339 J.D. [Meites,M.B.&M.]
Glisich, Gregory '53 '78 C.879 B.A. L.823 J.D. [Fitzgerald&C.]
Gliva, Raymond W. '38 '64 C.347 B.S. L.1119 J.D.
(adm. in IN; not adm. in IL) Hearings Officer, U.S. R.R. Retirement Bd.
Glockner, David A. '60 '85 C.145 B.A. L.813 J.D. Ofc. of the U.S. Atty.
Glockner, Stephen '62 '85 C.188 B.A. L.339 J.D. Asst. Corp. Coun.
Gloor, Carol L. '46 '81 C.1016 B.A. L.596 J.D. 6635 N. Glenwood
Gloor, D. Patterson, (AV) '41 '66 C.473 B.S. L.477 J.D. [Cassiday,S.&G.]
Glosniak, Ronald G. '50 '75 C&L.424 B.A., J.D. [Ⓐ Leff,C.&W.]
Gloss, Susan B. '79 '04 C.602 B.A. L.966 J.D. [Ⓐ Lord,B.&B.]
Glover, Jerry W. '49 '75 C&L.45 B.A., J.D.
Sr. Counsel, The Entertainment & Intellectual Property Group LLC
Glover, LaOuida '49 '93 C&L.339 B.S., J.D. 105 W. Madison St., Suite 700
Glover, Reynaldo Preston, (AV) '43 '70 C.254 B.A. L.309 LL.B.
[Ⓒ DLPiper R.G.C.U.]
Glusman, Jonathan R. '68 '04 C.72 B.A. L.910 J.D. [Ⓐ Lovells]
Glyman, Lynda '63 '88 C.339 B.A. L.209 J.D.
Resch. Atty., ABA Ctr. for Professional Responsibility
Glynn, John F. '49 '79 C&L.424 B.A., J.D. 6228 S. Kedvale
Glynn, William C. '49 '85 C.46 B.S. L.597 J.D. [Korshak,K.K.&S.]
Gnoffo, Vincent J. '69 '98 C.339 B.S.E.E. L.365 J.D.
[Ⓐ Brinks H.G.&L.] (See Pat. Sect.)
Gochanour, Gregory M. '61 '86 C.145 A.B. L.477 J.D. U.S. E.E.O.C.
Gochanour, Lynne A. '61 '87 C.373 B.A. L.477 J.D. [Vedder,P.K.&K.]
Goddard, Robert E. '45 '73
C.350 B.S. L.546 J.D. Claims Coun., Bankers Life & Cas. Co.
Godfrey, Richard C., (AV) '— '79 C.57 B.A. L.94 J.D. [Kirkland&E.]
Godfrey, Thomas J., Jr., (AV) '34 '57 C.602 A.B. L.309 LL.B. [Hoogendoorn&T.]
Godnik, Robert '— '92 C&L.339 B.S., J.D. [Field&G.]
Goebel, John P. '66 '91 C.478 B.A. L.309 J.D. [Gardner C.&D.]
Goedert, Paula Cozzi, (AV) '— '76 C.530 B.A. L.597 J.D. [Barnes&T.]
Goedert, Thomas W., (AV) '— '89 C.436 B.A. L.989 J.D. [Ⓐ Neal&L.]

Goedert, Huntington & DeBoer
(See Oak Park)

Goedken, James F. '66 '02 C.350 B.S. L.1000 J.D. [Ⓐ Bell,B.&L.] (Pat.)
Goel, Asheesh '— '95 C&L.339 B.S., J.D. Chief, Chicago, M.R.O., S.E.C.
Goering, Barbra, (AV) '52 '77 C&L.145 B.A., J.D. Atty., Miami Corp.
Goering, Gail M. '64 '90 C.83 B.A/B.S. L.145 J.D. [Lovells]
Goeser, James R. '45 '69 C.604 B.A. L.477 J.D.
(adm. in DC; not adm. in IL) Asst. Reg. Coun., Dept. of HHS
Goetz, Charles J. '68 '96 C.107 B.A. L.146 J.D. [Ⓐ Levenfeld P.]
Goggin, Michael J. '47 '74 C.966 B.A. L.365 J.D. Asst. State Atty.
Goitia, Jason J. '78 '03 C.260 B.A. L.145 J.D. [Ⓐ Mayer,B.R.&M.]
Goken, Jonathon W. '76 '02 C.338 B.S. L.365 J.D. [Ⓐ Johnson&B.]

Gustin, Gregory G. '57 '86 C.234 B.A. L.146 J.D. Atty., U.S. Dept. of Housing & Urban Devel.
Gustman, David C., (AV) .... '— '79 C.477 B.A. L.273 J.D. [Freeborn&P.]
Gutfeld, Deborah M. .... '76 '00 C.347 B.S. L.597 J.D. [Ⓐ DLPiper R.G.C.U.]
Guth, Glenn J., (AV) .... '52 '76 C.339 B.A. L.365 J.D. 161 N. Clark St., Ste. 2900
Guth, J. Eric .... '68 '97 C.674 A.B. L.966 J.D. [Ⓐ Winston&S.]
Guthman, Jack, (AV) .... '38 '63 C.597 B.A. L.976 LL.B. [Shefsky&F.]
Guthmann, Laurence I. .... '30 '55 C.659 B.S.E. L.472 LL.B. Supreme Finance Corp.
Guthrie, Jennifer L. .... '76 '01 C.473 B.A. L.424 J.D. [Ⓐ Hinshaw&C.]
Guthrie, Michael J. .... '50 '75 C&L.309 A.B., J.D. Johnson Products Co., Inc.
Guthrie, Richard Y. .... '44 '69 C.228 B.A. L.339 J.D. Sr. V.P., Amer. Nat. Bank
Gutierrez, Helen I. '72 '99 C&L.339 B.A., J.D. Nat'l Labor Rel. Bd., Region 13 - Chicago
Gutman, Jeffrey K., (CV) .... '62 '85 C.1183 B.S. L.146 J.D. 4018 N. Lincoln Ave.
Gutman, Phillip E., Jr. .... '57 '89 C.347 B.S. L.365 J.D. Merrill Lynch Capital Mkts.
Gutstein, Joshua Aaron .... '72 '98 C.477 B.A. L.904 J.D. [Bier&G.]
Gutstein, Solomon, (AV) .... '— '56 C&L.145 A.B., J.D. [Tenney&B.]
Gutterman, Allen B. .... '73 '98 C.966 B.A. L.365 J.D. [Ⓐ Katten M.R.]
Gutterman, Susan R. .... '56 '84 C.861 B.A. L.796 J.D. Jewish Family & Community Serv.
Guttman, Glenn S., (BV) .... '— '93 C.339 B.A. L.365 J.D. [Rieff S.&K.]
Gutzmer, Peter E., (AV) '53 '79 C.94 A.B. L.365 J.D. Sr. V.P., Gen. Coun. & Corp. Secy., Federal Home Loan Bk. of Chicago
Guynn, Kevin W., (AV) .... '52 '79 C.679 B.S.E. L.966 J.D. [Sonnenschein N.&R.] (Pat.)
Guzina, Bojan .... '76 '02 C.207 B.A. L.145 J.D. 10 South Dearborn
Guzman, Jill M. .... '70 '95 C.879 B.A. L.209 J.D. [Ⓐ Fragomen,D.B.&L.]
Guzzardo, John .... '72 '04 C.597 B.S. L.146 J.D. [Ⓐ Skadden,A.S.M.&F.]
Gylling, Jason .... '68 '95 C.339 B.A. L.209 J.D. [Ⓐ Erwin&Assoc.]
Gzesh, Irwin I., (AV) .... '54 '81 C.339 B.S. L.146 J.D. [Neal,G.&E.]
Gzesh, Morris A. .... '19 '42 C.137 L.209 LL.B. 11 S. LaSalle St.
Gzesh, Phillip .... '— '75 C&L.209 B.A., J.D. [Ⓒ Goldberg&F.]
Ha, Anis H. .... '78 '04 C.339 B.S. L.477 J.D. [Ⓐ Bell,B.&L.]
Haab, Eric A. .... '64 '89 C.477 A.B. L.309 J.D. [Lovells]
Haack, Cheryl L. .... '48 '94 C.352 B.A. L.365 J.D. [Ⓒ Seyfarth S.]
Haan, Jack L., (BV) .... '67 '92 C.323 B.A. L.904 J.D. [Shaheen,N.S.F.&E.]
Haarlow, John, Jr. .... '77 '04 C.674 A.B. L.339 J.D. [Ⓐ Jenner&B.]
Haarlow, John B., (AV) .... '46 '71 C.674 B.A. L.597 J.D. [Lord,B.&B.]
Haarsgaard, Karen .... '— '93 C.339 B.A. L.836 J.D. [Ⓐ Wolfe&E.]
Haas, Adolph L., (AV) .... '14 '37 L.209 J.D. 100 W. Monroe
Haas, B. Benjamin '69 '94 C.861 B.A. L.884 J.D. (adm. in PA; not adm. in IL) Exelon Corporation
Haas, Lawrence F. .... '61 '86 C.228 A.B. L.145 J.D. [Baker&M.]
Haas, Richard L. .... '69 '02 C.238 B.S. L.209 J.D. [Ⓐ Swanson,M.&B.]
Haas, Stephanie .... '73 '02 C&L.494 B.A., J.D. [Ⓐ Ross,D.&B.]
Haas, Trudy Elizabeth .... '65 '00 C.597 B.A. L.424 J.D. Chubb & Son
Haase, David K., (AV) .... '63 '89 C.118 B.A. L.309 J.D. [Jenner&B.]
Haase, Kerryann M. .... '69 '96 C.966 B.A. L.365 J.D. [Michael B.&F.]
Haber, Joel A., (AV) .... '43 '67 C.107 B.S. L.966 J.D. [FagelHaber]
Haber, Michael A., (BV) .... '52 '76 C.1016 B.A. L.209 J.D. [Kalcheim H.&K.]
Haber, Michael A. & Associates, P.C. .... 120 W. Madison St.
Haberkorn, Gerald .... '61 '87 C.210 B.A. L.365 J.D. [Lowis&G.]
Haberman, Morton J., (AV) '31 '55 C&L.597 B.S., J.D. 111 East Wacker Drive, Suite 2800
Habhab, Barbara J. .... '48 '90 C.352 B.A. L.659 J.D. Sr. Coun., CIT Group Inc.
Habicht, Patricia T. '49 '74 C.679 B.S. L.597 J.D. Sr. Assoc. Gen. Coun., Bank One Corp. (Law Dept.)
Hablutzel, Philip N. .... '35 '67 C.420 B.A. L.145 J.D. [Ⓒ Hablutzel&Assoc.]
Hablutzel & Associates .... 19 S. La Salle St.
Hachikian, Adam A. .... '79 '04 C.309 A.B. L.477 J.D. [Ⓐ Jenner&B.]
Hack, Randall A., (AV) .... '59 '84 C.602 B.A. L.477 J.D. [Lord,R.S.&B.]
Hackbarth, Alfred E., Jr. .... '31 '57 C.976 B.S. L.597 J.D. [Hackbarth&H.] ‡
Hackbarth, Philip M., (AV) .... '34 '60 C.197 A.B. L.477 J.D. 140 S. Dearborn
Hackbarth & Hudson, P.C. .... 20 N. Wacker Dr., Ste. 1520
Hacker, Ronald J. .... '— '88 C.339 B.A. L.352 J.D. [Chapman&C.]
Hacker, William J., (AV) .... '51 '76 C.209 B.S. L.365 J.D. [Clausen M.]
Hackett, David P., (AV) .... '53 '81 C.311 B.A. L.659 J.D. [Baker&M.]
Hackett, Dennis P. '— '02 C.757 B.A. L.209 J.D. [Ⓐ McAndrews,H.&M.] (See Pat. Sect.)
Hackett, John D. .... '62 '87 C.589 B.A. L.209 J.D. [Cassiday,S.&G.]
Hackett, Terry M. .... '65 '91 C.339 B.S. L.424 J.D. [Gardner C.&D.]
Hackney, Stephen C. .... '— '97 C.691 B.A. L.145 J.D. [Kirkland&E.]
Hackney, William Silas, III .... '72 '98 C.339 B.A. L.724 J.D. [Ⓐ Much S.F.D.A.&R.]
Hada, Rick L. '54 '82 C.388 B.A. L.879 J.D. Sr. V.P. & Grp. Sr. Coun., Fleet Business Credit Corp.
Haddad, Donna .... '70 '95 C&L.597 B.A., J.D. Council, Informat, IBM Corp.
Haddad, Mary Louise, (AV) .... '41 '76 C.705 B.A. L.597 J.D. [Ⓒ Schwartz C.]
Haddad, Ronald L. .... '40 '66 C.436 B.A. L.209 J.D. 100 West Monroe St.

Haddad, Susan Christine, (AV) '42 '77 C.393 B.A. L.365 J.D.
Suite 2100, Three First National Plaza, 70 West Madison Street, 60602
Telephone: 312-236-2298 FAX: 312-236-0089
Domestic Relations, Matrimonial, Family Law, Divorce.
See Professional Biographies, CHICAGO, ILLINOIS

Haddon, James T., (Ltd.), (AV) .... '41 '65 C.339 B.A. L.597 J.D. 111 E. Wacker Dr.
Haddox, Velisha L. .... '— '02 C.477 B.A. L.831 J.D. [Ⓐ Wildman,H.A.&D.]
Haderlein, Gerard D. .... '57 '82 C&L.209 B.S.C., J.D. 3413 N. Lincoln Ave.
Haderlein, John A. '60 '88 C.999 B.A. L.209 J.D. Sr. Bond. Coun., Ill. Develop. Finance Auth.
Haderlein, John F. .... '25 '50 C&L.209 LL.B. 3049 N. Ashland Ave.
Haderlein, Thomas M., (AV) '35 '60 C.209 B.S.C. L.276 J.D. 130 East Randolph Drive‡
Haennicke, Katherine L. .... '75 '00 C.388 B.A. L.365 J.D. [Ⓐ Tressler,S.M.&P.]
Hafertepe, James M. '69 '95 C.339 B.S.A.A.E. L.145 J.D. [McAndrews,H.&M.] (See Pat. Sect.)
Hafkey, Elizabeth Awe .... '71 '96 C&L.339 B.A., J.D. [Ⓐ Butler R.S.&B.]
Hafner, Charles A. .... '76 '01 C.597 B.A. L.1000 J.D. [Ⓐ Bollinger,R.&G.]
Hafron, Norman L., (AV) .... '38 '63 C.221 A.B. L.209 LL.B. [Rosenfeld H.S.&F.]
Haft, James G., (AV) .... '— '84 C.966 B.B.A. L.276 J.D. [Ⓒ Holland&K.]
Hafter, Matthew I. .... '61 '86 C&L.477 B.Mus.A., J.D. [Grippo&E.]
Hagan, Jeremy B.P. .... '77 '03 C.575 B.A. L.339 J.D. [Ⓐ McDermott W.&E.]
Hagan, John F., Jr. .... '— '96 C.145 B.A. L.569 J.D. [Kirkland&E.]
Hagedorn, Mark A. .... '— '98 C.679 B.S.Ch.E. L.347 J.D. [Ⓐ Barnes&T.]
Hagen, H. Richard .... '— '97 C.719 B.B.A. L.339 J.D. [Ⓐ Chapman&C.]

Hagens Berman Sobol Shapiro, LLP
60 West Randolph Street, Suite 200, 60601
Telephone: 312-762-9235 Facsimile: 312-762-9286
Email: info@hbsslaw.com URL: http://www.hbsslaw.com
Elizabeth Anne Fegan; Timothy A. Scott.
Exclusively Litigation including Securities, Antitrust, Consumer Fraud and Employment Discrimination, Environmental, Class and Derivative Actions in all State and Federal Courts, almost always for plaintiffs.
Seattle, Washington Office: 1301 Fifth Avenue, Suite 2900, 98101. Telephone: 206-623-7292. Facsimile: 206-623-0594.
Phoenix, Arizona Office: 2425 East Camelback Road, Suite 620, 85016. Telephone: 602-840-5900. Facsimile: 602-840-3012.
Los Angeles, California Office: 700 South Flower Street, Suite 2940, 90017-4101. Telephone: 213-330-7150. Facsimile: 213-330-7152.
Cambridge, Massachusetts Office: One Main Street, 4th Floor, 02142. Telephone: 617-482-3700. Facsimile: 617-482-3003.
See Professional Biographies, CHICAGO, ILLINOIS

Hagerty, Duane P. .... '66 '91 C.351 B.A. L.494 J.D. [Ⓒ Wildman,H.A.&D.]
Hagerty, Jack J., (AV) .... '58 '90 C.238 B.B.A. L.146 J.D. [Shefsky&F.]
Hagerty, Michael J., Law Office of '47 '82 C.363 A.B. L.209 J.D. Suite 210, 6321 North Avondale Ave
Hagerty, Ryan A. .... '76 '01 C.338 B.A. L.209 J.D. [Ⓐ Asher,G.G.&D.]
Haggerty, Barbara '— '87 C.339 B.A. L.966 J.D. (adm. in WI; not adm. in IL) Off. of the Thrift Supervision
Haggerty, Kathleen M. .... '61 '90 C.177 B.A. L.365 J.D. [Ⓐ Simpson&C.]
Haggerty, Michael '56 '82 C&L.602 A.B., J.D. Dep. Dir., Cty. of Chicago Bd. of Ethics.
Haggerty, Michael S. .... '78 '05 C.339 B.S. L.209 J.D. [Ⓐ Bollinger,R.&G.]
Hagler, James M., (BV) .... '50 '91 C.94 B.A. L.365 J.D. 19 South La Salle, Suite 450
Hagstrom, James A. .... '42 '77 C.312 B.A. L.365 J.D. 39 S. LaSalle St.
Hague, Gregg R., (AV) .... '57 '84 C.118 B.A. L.910 J.D. [Sperling&S.]
Hagy, James C., (AV) .... '— '78 C&L.930 B.A., J.D. [Jones D.]
Hahn, Arthur W., (AV) .... '44 '69 C.473 B.A. L.597 J.D. [Katten M.R.]
Hahn, Eva '71 '97 C.446 B.A. L.273 J.D. (adm. in MD; not adm. in IL) Asst. Reg. Coun., U.S. Envir. Protec. Agcy.
Hahn, Frederic L., (AV) .... '41 '66 C.188 A.B. L.309 J.D. [Mayer,B.R.&M.]
Hahn, MaryLu .... '49 '87 C.424 B.S. L.365 J.D. [Clausen M.]
Hahn, Michael L. .... '65 '95 C.589 B.A. L.424 J.D. [Ⓐ Bollinger,R.&G.]
Hai, Jill I. '63 '89 C.188 B.S. L.880 J.D. (adm. in MA; not adm. in IL) Labor & Employment Coun., Lechmere, Inc.
Haigh, Christopher E. '— '00 C.679 B.S.E. L.345 J.D. (adm. in IN; not adm. in IL; See Pat. Sect.) [Ⓐ Baniak P.&G.]
Haile, Debrai G. .... '71 '97 C.30 B.A. L.339 J.D. [Ⓐ Laner,M.D.B.L.&T.]
Haim, Evan J. .... '— '02 C.611 B.A. L.209 J.D. [Ⓐ Barnes&T.]
Hainen, Michael C. .... '72 '97 C.478 B.A. L.880 J.D. [Goldberg,K.B.B.R.&M.]
Hairrell, Cherish L. .... '66 '02 C.424 B.S. L.146 J.D. 200 East Randolph Drive, Suite 7300
Hairston, Scott W. .... '— '02 C.228 B.A. L.477 J.D. [Ⓐ Latham&W.]
Haiser, James A. .... '58 '88 C.339 B.A. L.365 J.D. [Ⓐ Martin&K.]
Hakim, Sana .... '70 '94 C.597 B.A. L.862 J.D. [Bell,B.&L.]
Halbleib, Brent W. .... '69 '94 C.502 B.A. L.910 J.D. [Ⓐ Rusin M.&F.]
Halbleib, John F. .... '53 '82 C.400 B.S. L.597 J.D. 190 South La Salle Street‡
Hale, Andrew M., (BV) .... '62 '87 C&L.339 B.A., J.D. [Ⓐ Rock F.]
Hale, David R. '72 '00 C.691 B.A. L.273 J.D. (adm. in MD; not adm. in IL) [Ⓐ Wildman,H.A.&D.]
Hale, Lola Miranda, (AV) .... '44 '69 C.19 B.A. L.262 J.D. [Epstein B.&G.]
Hale, Thomas A., (AV) .... '57 '82 C.597 B.A. L.228 J.D. [Skadden,A.S.M.&F.]
Hales, Bryan S. .... '— '96 C.701 B.S. L.477 J.D. [Kirkland&E.]
Hales, Daniel B., (AV) '41 '66 C.477 B.A. L.597 J.D. 200 East Randolph Drive, Suite 7300
Halevy, Beth M., (AV) .... '— '85 C.347 B.A. L.209 J.D. Asst. Atty.
Haley, Robert E., (AV) .... '46 '72 C.424 B.A. L.597 J.D. [Swanson,M.&B.]
Haley, Timothy F. .... '51 '78 C.902 B.A. L.893 J.D. [Seyfarth S.]
Halferty, Jean M. .... '64 '89 C&L.966 B.A., J.D. Mead Data Central
Halfman, Peggy A. .... '67 '92 C.436 B.S. L.477 J.D. [McDermott W.&E.]
Halfpenny, Harold T., (AV) .... '05 '30 C&L.339 B.S., J.D. 20 N. Wacker Dr.‡
Hall, Angela Renee .... '— '94 C.597 B.A. L.339 J.D. 20 N. Clark St.
Hall, Calvin H. .... '24 '53 C.1016 B.S. L.146 LL.B. Assoc. Cir. Ct. J.
Hall, Carrie A. .... '74 '99 C.339 B.A. L.209 J.D. [Ⓐ Hill G.&B.]
Hall, David C., (AV) .... '58 '83 C.475 B.A. L.477 J.D. [Hall,P.&S.]
Hall, David V., (BV) .... '66 '91 C&L.800 J.D. [DLPiper R.G.C.U.]
Hall, Douglas M. .... '72 '99 C.228 B.A. L.229 J.D. [Ⓐ Niro,S.H.&N.]
Hall, J. Robert .... '69 '97 C.659 B.A. L.146 J.D. [Meckler B.&T.]
Hall, Jeffrey A., (AV) .... '60 '89 C.659 B.S. L.477 J.D. [Bartlit B.H.P.&S.]
Hall, Larry G., (AV) .... '54 '79 C.252 B.S. L.477 J.D. [Matkov,S.M.&G.]
Hall, Mary M. .... '11 '45 C.852 A.B. L.365 LL.B. 8 S. Michigan Ave.‡
Hall, Michael R. .... '72 '02 C.911 B.A. L.145 J.D. [Ⓐ Barack F.K.P.&N.]
Hall, Robin Ann .... '50 '89 C.927 B.A. L.424 J.D. Sr. Atty., Akzo Nobel Inc.
Hall, Shelvin Louise Marie, (Ms.) .... '48 '75 C.302 B.A. L.94 J.D. Cir. Ct. J.
Hall, Sophia H. .... '43 '67 C.966 B.S. L.597 J.D. J
Hall, Stephen E. .... '— '94 C.597 B.A. L.339 J.D. [Jones D.]
Hall, Steven S. .... '— '04 C.375 B.S. L.1556 J.D. [Ⓐ Kirkland&E.]
Hall Prangle & Schoonveld, LLC, (AV) .... 225 West Washington Street, Suite 2700
Hallab, Charles Salem .... '— '98 C.273 B.A. L.276 J.D. [Ⓐ Baker&M.]
Hallagan, James, (AV) .... '54 '80 C.339 B.A. L.209 J.D. [Minsky,M.&H.]
Hallberg, Krista S. .... '— '98 C.473 B.A. L.424 J.D. [Ⓐ DLPiper R.G.C.U.]
Haller, Rebecca R. .... '60 '89 C.339 B.A. L.209 J.D. [Meckler B.&T.]
Haller, Timothy J., (AV) '46 '75 C.158 B.S.M.E. L.276 J.D. [Niro,S.H.&N.] (See Pat. Sect.)
Halleron, L. Timothy .... '72 '99 C.321 B.A. L.1019 J.D. [Ⓐ Winston&S.]
Hallerud, John C. .... '60 '86 C.145 B.A. L.352 J.D. Fed. Trade Comm.
Halliday, Patrick E. .... '78 '04 C.589 B.A. L.209 J.D. [Ⓐ Cassiday,S.&G.]
Halligan, R. Mark, (AV) .... '53 '78 C.150 B.A. L.597 J.D. [Welsh&K.]
Hallihan, William J. (Hal) .... '— '96 C.339 B.S. L.365 J.D. [Hallihan L.] (Pat.)

Hallihan Intellectual Property Law, Ltd.
125 South Wacker Drive, Suite 2080, 60606
Telephone: 312-223-0010 Fax: 312-873-4383 URL: http://www.hiplaw.net
Email: questions@hallihan.com URL: http://www.hallihan.com
William J. (Hal) Hallihan.
Litigation, Intellectual Property Law, Patents, Trademarks, Copyrights, Trade Secrets and Entertainment Law.
See Professional Biographies, CHICAGO, ILLINOIS

Halliman, Colleen Leonie .... '70 '97 C.589 B.A. L.352 J.D. 1340 S. Michigan, 3rd Fl.
Halloran, Claudia .... '56 '85 C.339 B.S. L.146 J.D. [Ⓐ S.G.Thomas]
Hallsten, Donald R., Jr. .... '70 '97 C.338 B.S. L.424 J.D. Ctr. for Disability & Elder Law
Halper, Edward J., (AV) .... '46 '73 C.999 A.B. L.209 J.D. [Shefsky&F.]
Halper, Joel D. .... '48 '73 C&L.339 B.S., J.D. [Ⓒ K.B.Moll&Assoc.]

Halperin, Errol R., (AV) '41 '68 C&L.209 B.S., J.D. [DLPiper R.G.C.U.]
Halperin, Julie R. '— '00 C.339 B.A. L.424 J.D. [Swanson,M.&B.]
Halperin, Karl L. '41 '67 C.28 L.94 LL.B. [Rosenfield,K.&H.]
Halpern, Guy '65 '90 C.589 B.A. L.209 J.D. [Laser,P.S.F.&E.]
Halpern, Julia L. '— '04 C.339 B.A. L.146 J.D. [Pircher,N.&M.]
Halpern, Marcelo '— '92 C.918 B.A. L.178 J.D. [Latham&W.]
Halpern, Sheryl Jaffee '69 '93 C.339 B.A. L.146 J.D. [Patzik,F.&S.]
Halpin, Marie A., (BV) '— '92 C&L.424 B.B.A., J.D. [McDermott W.&E.]
Halprin, Judith A., (AV) '42 '77 C.1016 B.A. L.209 J.D. [Feldman&H.]
Halprin, Rick A., (AV) '40 '70
C.1016 B.A. L.1389 J.D. 542 South Dearborn Street, Suite 750
Halsted, Kellie S. '— '93 C.476 B.A. L.209 J.D. [Scott,H.&B.]
Halverson, Eric P. '— '01 C.399 B.A. L.966 J.D. [Katten M.R.]
Halverson-Cross, Karen '— '91 C.966 B.A. L.309 J.D.
(adm. in NY; not adm. in IL) John Marshall Law Sch.
Ham, Eldon L. '52 '76 20 N. Clark St.
Hamann, Ardath A. '55 '77 C.679 B.S. L.945 J.D.
Assoc. Prof., John Marshall Law Sch.
Hamann, Malinda C. '66 '91 C.790 B.A. L.273 J.D.
(adm. in GA; not adm. in IL) U.S. Dept. of Health & Human Servs.
Hamann, Steven L., (BV) '52 '87 C.475 B.A. L.215 J.D. [Vedder,P.K.&K.]
Hamblet, Michael J., (AV) '40 '65 C.339 B.A. L.477 J.D. [Hamblet,O.&L.]
Hamblet, Oremus & Little, (AV) 1 E. Wacker Dr.
Hambleton, Douglas M. '55 '81 C.893 B.A. L.276 J.D. [Vedder,P.K.&K.]
Hamblin, Janice K. '61 '87 C.350 B.B.A. L.339 J.D. [McGuirewoods]
Hamblin, William H. '38 '74 C.112 B.A. L.800 J.D.
(adm. in CA; not adm. in IL) Consultant & Project Dir., Amer. Bar Assn.
Hambourger, David R., (AV) '55 '80 C.339 B.S. L.424 J.D. [Winston&S.]
Hamburg, Jaimy Levine '69 '95 C.910 B.A. L.659 J.D. [Mayer,B.R.&M.]
Hamburg, Jeffrey A. '69 '95
C.228 B.A. L.910 J.D. Assoc. Coun., Interstate Insurance Group
Hameder, Brian W. '75 '00 C.701 B.S.M.E. L.365 J.D. [Ladas&P.]
Hamera, Jeffrey L. '64 '94 C.339 B.S.C.E. L.597 J.D. [Jenkens&G.]
Hamill, Cheryl Urbanski '59 '85 C&L.352 B.S., J.D. Sr. Atty., AT&T Corp.
Hamill, James J., (AV) '33 '61
C.277 B.M.E. L.273 LL.B. [Fitch,E.T.&F.] (See Pat. Sect.)
Hamill, John J., (AV) '68 '93 C.602 B.A. L.309 J.D. [Jenner&B.]
Hamill, Mark S. '— '01 C.901 B.A. L.597 J.D. [Kirkland&E.]
Hamilton, Deborah F. '— '88 C.339 B.A. L.245 J.D. [Neal&L.]
Hamilton, Lawrence R. '57 '96 C.309 A.B. L.145 J.D. [Mayer,B.R.&M.]
Hamilton, Marc M. '71 '99 C.511 B.A. L.209 J.D. 10244 S. Beverly Ave.
Hamilton, Maria L. '76 '02 C.585 B.A. L.309 J.D. [Katten M.R.]
Hamilton, R. Dickey, (AV) '35 '60 C.604 B.A. L.145 J.D. [Miller S.&H.]
Hamilton, Robert L. '43 '70 C&L.339 B.A., J.D. Contl. Ill. Nat. Bk. & Tr. Co. of Chic.
Hamilton, Thomas M., Jr., (AV) '44 '69 C.347 B.A. L.1119 J.D. [Hinshaw&C.]
Hamm, Kimberly M. '68 '96 C.339 B.A. L.602 J.D. [Lord,B.&B.]
Hamm, Leisa J., (AV) '53 '84 C.352 B.A. L.209 J.D. [Lord,B.&B.]
Hamman, George W., (AV) '33 '61 C.347 A.B. L.1119 LL.B. [George W.H.]
Hamman, James S., Jr. '69 '94 C.602 B.B.A. L.597 J.D.
V.P. & Assoc. Coun., Zurich Kemper Investments, Inc.

Hamman & Benn
(See Much Shelist Freed Denenberg Ament & Rubenstein, P.C.)

Hammar, John C. '52 '78 C.477 B.S. L.911 J.D.
(adm. in WA; not adm. in IL; Pat.) Coun., The Boeing Co.
Hammatt, Matthew '70 '96 C.72 B.A. L.966 J.D.
Assoc. Gen. Coun., True North Communications, Inc. (Legal Department)
Hammer, Aaron L. '— '97 C.477 A.B. L.597 J.D. [Freeborn&P.]
Hammer, Alan '— '75 C&L.477 B.A., J.D. V.P., Harris Trust and Savings Bank
Hammer, Allison G. '73 '98 C.477 B.A. L.597 J.D. [Goldberg,K.B.B.R.&M.]
Hammer, Scott, (AV) '57 '82 C.276 B.S.F.S. L.365 J.D. [Fraterrigo,B.F.&K.]
Hammerle, John C. '— '05 C.108 B.S. L.209 J.D. [Freeborn&P.]

Hammerman, Alan H., (AV) '33 '59 C.309 A.B. L.597 J.D.
640 North La Salle Street Suite 670, 60610
Telephone: 312-642-1322 Fax: 312-642-9401
Email: LAWOFF@AMERITECH.NET
Of Counsel: Stephen L. Seftenberg.
Federal Tax, Estate Planning and Probate Law.

See Professional Biographies, CHICAGO, ILLINOIS

Hammerman, Joel M. '72 '97 C.846 B.A. L.309 J.D. [Sidley A.B.&W.]
Hammersmith, Timothy J. '— '93 C.1111 B.S. L.365 J.D. [Masuda,F.E.&M.]
Hammes, Jeffrey C., (P.C.) '— '85
C.966 B.B.A. L.597 J.D. [Kirkland&E.] (©San Fran., CA)
Hammesfahr, Robert W., (AV) '54 '78 C.165 B.A. L.597 J.D. [Cozen O.]
Hammond, Caroline E. '77 '02 C&L.477 B.A., J.D. [Goldberg,K.B.B.R.&M.]
Hammond, Celeste M. '45 '69 C.424 B.S. L.145 J.D. Prof., John Marshall Law Sch.
Hammond, Craig B., (BV) '42 '79 C.572 A.B. L.146 J.D. [C.B.Hammond]
Hammond, John P. '— '02 C.273 B.S.B.A. L.477 J.D. [McDermott W.&E.]
Hammond, Julie S. B. '— '99 C&L.101 B.A., J.D. [Latham&W.]
Hammond, Rick L. '51 '88 C.801 B.A. L.365 J.D. [Johnson&B.]

Hammond, Craig B., Ltd., (BV)
77 West Washington, Suite 1805, 60602
Telephone: 312-236-5006 Fax: 312-236-2103
Email: chammon2@ix.netcom.com URL: http://www.lawyers.com/craigbhammondlaw
Craig B. Hammond.
Child Custody, Visitation Rights, Family Law, Matrimonial Law, Divorce, Child Support, Domestic Violence, Premarital Agreements, Spousal Support, Mediation and Tax Law and Retirement Benefit Plans.

See Professional Biographies, CHICAGO, ILLINOIS

Hamper, Sidney C. '31 '58 C.98 B.S. L.365 J.D. 9956 S. Damen Ave.‡
Hampton, Carl Bernard '72 '99 C.813 A.B. L.966 J.D.
(adm. in WI; not adm. in IL) 8920 S. Euclid Ave.
Hampton, Steven J., (AV) '51 '86
C.339 B.S. L.146 J.D. [McAndrews,H.&M.] (See Pat. Sect.)
Hanaford, Robert H. '57 '82 C.927 B.A. L.221 J.D. 205 W. Randolph St., Ste. 1700
Hanahan, Michael J., (BV) '— '91 C.602 B.A. L.424 J.D. [Schiff H.]
Hanauer, Benjamin '78 '03 C.228 A.B. L.145 J.D. [McDermott W.&E.]
Hanbury, Marshall E., (AV) '44 '69 C.500 A.B. L.356 LL.B.
(adm. in MS; not adm. in IL) [Mayer,B.R.&M.]
Hanchett, Paul E. '16 '79 L.146 J.D. 5510 N. Sheridan Rd.‡
Hancuch, Thomas G. '60 '88 C.602 B.A. L.966 J.D. [Vedder,P.K.&K.]
Handa, Jennifer A. '72 '97 C.326 B.A. L.339 J.D. Arthur Andersen, LLP
Handelman, Arthur Z., (BV) '62 '89 C.183 B.A. L.245 J.D. [Giordano&N.]
Handelman, Jeffery A. '59 '84 C.339 B.A. L.276 J.D. [Brinks H.G.&L.]
Handelman, Joel L. '40 '65 C.477 A.B. L.145 J.D. Pres., Metrocenter Corp.
Handelman, Stuart B. '62 '87 C.589 B.A. L.365 J.D. [S.B.Handelman]
Handelman, Stuart B. Law Offices of, P.C. 332 S. Michigan Ave.
Handelsman, Norman A., (AV) '18 '56 C.339 B.S. L.146 J.D. 20 N. Clark St.‡
Handler, David A., (AV) '— '92 C.339 B.S. L.597 J.D. [Kirkland&E.]

Handler, Joel F., (AV) '51 '75 C.339 B.A. L.209 J.D.
55 West Wacker Drive, Suite 950, 60601
Telephone: 312-621-0008 FAX: 312-629-2916
Email: jhandler@cogan-mcnabola.com
General Trial and Appellate Practice in State and Federal Courts. Administrative Law, General Business and Commercial Law, Personal Injury, Matrimonial Law, Chancery and Employment Law including State and Federal Discrimination Actions. Termination, Retaliatory Discharge and Breach of Employment Contracts, Torts, Wills, Premises Liability, Products Liability, Defamation and Trade Secrets.

See Professional Biographies, CHICAGO, ILLINOIS

Handler, Robert P. '55 '80 C.293 B.A. L.352 J.D. 203 N. Lasalle St., Ste. 2100
Handler, Steven P., (AV) '46 '71 C.477 A.B. L.145 J.D. [McDermott W.&E.]
Handler, Thomas J. '56 '83 C.339 B.S. L.209 J.D. [Handler,T.&D.]
Handler Ackerman, Lisa '74 '99 C.341 B.A. L.146 J.D. [Wilson E.M.E.&D.]

Handler, Thayer & Duggan, LLC
191 N. Wacker Drive 23rd Floor, 60606
Telephone: 312-641-2100 Fax: 312-641-6866
URL: http://www.htdlaw.com
Partners: Thomas J. Handler; Steven J. Thayer; James M. Duggan; Douglas S. Robson; Gregory J. Bertsch. Associates: Steven M. Bonneau; Sharon A. Hannaford; Susan F. Lifvendahl; Heather A. Nichols; Giselle C. Piraro; Catherine A. Battin; Andrew M. Stroth; Eric E. Kalnins; Jeffrey J. Budzik. Of Counsel: Richard D. Hart; Barry N. Morrell.
Transactional Practice, Business, Finance, Estate Planning, Tax, Real Estate, Sports and Entertainment.

See Professional Biographies, CHICAGO, ILLINOIS

Handmacher, Leonard E. '14 '38 C&L.209 LL.B. 161 N. Clark St.
Handwerker, Barry A. '61 '86 C.94 B.S.B.A. L.209 J.D. V.P., Midwest Canvas Corp.
Hanebutt, Pamela R., (AV) '59 '84 C.339 B.A. L.861 J.D. [Eimer S.K.&S.]
Hanekamp, Thomas K., (AV) '61 '86 C.347 B.A. L.209 J.D. [Tressler,S.M.&P.]
Haney, Marian C., (AV) '40 '74 C&L.424 B.S., J.D. [Mayer,B.R.&M.]
Haney, Paul Richard '59 '00 C.1458 B.S. L.146 J.D. 125 S. Franklin St.
Haney, Robert E. '59 '85 C.597 B.A. L.767 J.D. [Marks,M.&K.]
Haney, Thomas M. '38 '63 C.424 B.S. L.145 J.D.
Assoc. Dean, Loyola Univ. Chicago Sch. of Law
Hanfling, Norman, & Associates, (AV) '34 '59 C&L.145 B.A., J.D. 208 S. LaSalle St.
Hanfling, Scott A. '73 '98 C.597 B.A. L.146 J.D. [Kerns,P.F.&P.]
Hangebrauck, Wendi J. '57 '88 C.678 B.S. L.424 J.D. Sr. Tax Atty., BP America Inc.
Hanigan, Brian '74 '04 C.339 B.S. L.597 J.D. [Skadden,A.S.M.&F.]
Hankin, Robert L. '31 '56 C.339 B.S. L.209 J.D. Asst. Corp. Coun.
Hanley, Edward T., Jr. '56 '84 C.123 B.A. L.146 J.D. 29 S. LaSalle St.
Hanley, Mark G. '65 '01 C.436 B.S.E.E. L.209 J.D. [Grossman&F.] (Pat.)
Hanlon, James E., Jr. '59 '84 C&L.209 B.A., J.D. [Howrey]
Hanlon, Kay M. '60 '85 C.339 B.S. L.209 J.D. Asst. State's Atty.
Hanna, Adam Keith '70 '96 C.477 B.A. L.347 J.D. [Taylor,M.S.H.&M.]
Hanna, Albert C. '30 '55 C&L.966 B.B.A., LL.B.
(adm. in WI; not adm. in IL) Pres. & CEO, Mid North Financial Servs., Inc.
Hanna, Alfred E. '— '04 C.388 B.A. L.365 J.D. [Sachnoff&W.]
Hanna, Brad '— '01 C.801 B.A. L.966 J.D. [Kirkland&E.]
Hanna, Dolores K., (AV) '— '52 C.610 A.B. L.146 J.D. [Bell,B.&L.]
Hanna, Jennifer M. '— '02 C.424 B.S. L.339 J.D. [Hinshaw&C.]
Hanna, Joshua P. '75 '99 C.608 B.A. L.597 J.D. [Mayer,B.R.&M.]
Hannafan, Blake T. '73 '98 C.880 B.A. L.910 J.D. [M.T.Hannafan&Assoc.]
Hannafan, Michael T., (AV) '42 '70 C.502 B.J. L.910 J.D. [M.T.Hannafan&Assoc.]

Hannafan, Michael T., & Associates, Ltd., (AV)
One East Wacker Drive, Suite 1208, 60601
Telephone: (312) 527-0055 Fax: (312) 527-0220 URL: http://www.lawyers.com/hannafan
Email: mth@hannafanlaw.com URL: http://www.hannafanlaw.com
Michael T. Hannafan;—Nicholas A. Pavich; Blake T. Hannafan.
General Trial and Appellate Practice in State and Federal Courts Including General Business, Commercial, Patent Infringement, Antitrust, Securities, Legal and Medical Malpractice, Employment Termination and Discrimination, Products Liability, Class Action, Estate and Probate Litigation, Personal Injury, Contract, White Collar Criminal Defense and Bankruptcy Trial Law.
Reference: The Northern Trust Co.

See Professional Biographies, CHICAGO, ILLINOIS

Hannaford, Sharon A. '48 '93 [Handler,T.&D.]
Hannah, Judith '54 '79 C.604 B.A. L.178 J.D. 980 North Michigan Avenue, Suite 1400
Hannah, Wayne R., Jr., (AV) '31 '57 C.337 A.B. L.569 J.D. [Sonnenschein N.&R.]
Hannay, William M., (AV) '— '73 C.976 B.A. L.276 J.D. [Schiff H.]
Hannigan, Keith C. '65 '91 C.145 A.B. L.813 J.D. [Jenkens&G.]
Hannigan, Susan Marzec '— '83 C.424 B.A. L.209 J.D. [Anderson,R.]
Hannon, Edward J. '— '91 C.734 B.S. L.424 J.D. [Freeborn&P.]
Hanover, Mark L. '68 '93 C.659 B.A. L.494 J.D. [Sonnenschein N.&R.]
Hanrahan, Thomas P. '42 '72 L.209 J.D. 208 S. La Salle St., Rm. 1273
Hansche, Heather L. '— '80 C.477 A.B. L.215 J.D. [Chapman&C.]
Hanscom, Weston W. '53 '78 C&L.188 B.A., J.D. 30 N. LaSalle St.
Hanselman, David L., Jr. '71 '98 C.309 A.B. L.145 J.D. [McDermott W.&E.]
Hansen, Brian D. '75 '00 C&L.352 B.A., J.D. [Jenner&B.]
Hansen, Christina Tomaras '75 '00 C.602 B.A. L.910 J.D. [Jenner&B.]
Hansen, Clinton P. '72 '01 C&L.879 B.S., J.D. [FagelHaber]
Hansen, Gene H., (AV) '44 '75 C&L.477 B.A., J.D. 19 S. La Salle St., Ste. 1300
Hansen, Jeffrey M. '— '99 C.221 B.A. L.597 J.D. [Freeborn&P.]
Hansen, Jennifer L. '71 '97 C.201 B.A. L.861 J.D. [Goodsmith G.&U.]
Hansen, Kristin N. '69 '02 C.57 B.A. L.365 J.D. Law Clerk
Hansen, Laurence A. '50 '75 C.746 B.A. L.966 J.D. [Lord,B.&B.]
Hansen, Leland G. '65 '95 C.101 B.S. L.145 J.D. [McAndrews,H.&M.]
Hansen, Mark D., (BV) '56 '87 C.339 B.A. L.365 J.D. [Graefe&H.]
Hansen, William M. '42 '68 C.424 B.S. L.365 J.D. 3310 West Peterson Avenue
Hanses, Eugene Joseph, Jr. '65 '90 C.597 B.A L.910 J.D. 1990 [Robbins,S.N.L.&T.]
Hansfield, Paul '30 '82 C&L.209 B.Sc., J.D. [Fuchs&R.]
Hansher, Beth L. '75 '00 C&L.966 B.A., J.D. [FagelHaber]
Hanson, David L., (AV) '37 '62 C.309 A.B. L.976 LL.B. 191 N. Wacker Dr.
Hanson, David P. '74 '01 C.1119 B.S. L.209 J.D. [Garofalo,S.H.&S.]
Hanson, Donald S. '36 '67 C.339 B.A. L.365 LL.B.
Asst. Coun., Ill. Dept. of Employ. Sec.
Hanson, Douglas A., (AV) '61 '87 C.339 B.S. L.146 J.D. [Schuyler,R.&Z.]
Hanson, Marion H. '75 '02 C.143 B.A. L.209 J.D.
Staff Atty., National Assn. of Realtors
Hanson, Mark C. '59 '90 C.234 B.A. L.365 J.D. [Williams&Ma.]
Hanson, Richard A. '46 '72 C.976 B.A. L.145 J.D. [McDermott W.&E.]
Hanson, Ronald W., (AV) '— '75 C.747 B.A. L.145 J.D. [Latham&W.]
Hantzos, Elizabeth G. '62 '88 C.339 A.B. L.365 J.D. Asst. States Atty.
Hanus, George D. '48 '71 C.1016 B.A. L.597 J.D. 333 W. Wacker Dr.

Hanus, Richard, Law Offices of '63 '88 C.597 B.S. L.339 J.D.
Suite 2500, 161 North Clark Street, 60601
Telephone: 312-357-0033 Fax: 312-357-0286 URL: http://www.lawyers.com/usavisacounsel
Email: rhanus@usavisacounsel.com URL: http://www.usavisacounsel.com
Immigration and Naturalization, Business Immigration, Citizenship, Consular Law, Deportation, Employment Authorizations, Employment Immigration, Employment Visas, Family Immigration Law, Immigration Law, Investor Vistas, Labor Certifications, Permanent Visas, Political Asylum, Refugee Law, Religious Visas, Visas.
See Professional Biographies, CHICAGO, ILLINOIS

Hanusa, Julie M. ... '64 '89 C.352 B.A. L.597 J.D. [Much S.F.D.A.&R.]
Hanzlik, Blair B. ... '76 '03 C.918 B.A. L.339 J.D. [Ⓐ McGuirewoods]
Hanzlik, Jodie Distler ... '77 '03 C&L.339 B.S., J.D. [Ⓐ McDermott W.&E.]
Hanzlik, Paul F., (AV) ... '— '71 C.918 B.A. L.178 LL.B. [Foley&L.]
Hara, Colin ... '— '78 C.424 A.B. L.209 J.D. [Masuda,F.E.&M.]
Haracz, David '61 '89 C.321 A.B. L.1065 J.D.
Supervisory Atty., Legal Asisstance Found. of Chicago
Haraguchi, Bruce K. ... '70 '98 C.101 B.A. L.893 J.D. [Ⓐ Seyfarth S.]
Harakas, Dean ... '63 '89 C&L.734 B.S.B.A., J.D. 30 S. Wacker Dr., Suite 2900
Harbaugh, Richard A. ... '47 '72 C.937 B.A. L.597 J.D. [Fuchs&R.]
Harbecke, Fred R., (BV) ... '56 '81 C.339 B.S. L.209 J.D. [F.R.Harbecke]
Harbecke, Fred R., Inc., (BV) ... 134 N. La Salle St., Ste. 2222
Harbert, James ... '54 '79 C.945 A.B. L.893 J.D. [Hinshaw&C.]
Harchuck, Kara E. ... '78 '03 C.25 B.A. L.597 J.D. [Ⓐ Mayer,B.R.&M.]
Hardgrove, James A., (AV) ... '45 '70 C&L.602 B.A., J.D. [Sidley A.B.&W.]
Hardgrove-Koleno, Sarah ... '71 '96 C&L.339 B.S., J.D. [Ⓐ Jenner&B.]
Hardiman, A. J., (Ltd.), (AV) ... '32 '60 C.188 B.S. L.209 J.D. 39 S. LaSalle St.
Hardiman, Eugene C., (AV) ... '52 '79 C.454 B.A. L.365 J.D. [P.A.Hardiman]
Hardiman, Megan ... '68 '93 C&L.339 B.S., J.D. [Katten M.R.]
Hardiman, Patricia A., (BV) ... '54 '81 C.93 B.S. L.365 J.D. [P.A.Hardiman]
Hardiman, Patrick M. ... '61 '87 C&L.339 B.S., J.D. [Winston&S.]

Hardiman, Patricia A., Ltd, Law Offices of, (AV)
77 W. Washington Street, Suite 600, 60602
Telephone: 312-782-3090 Facsimile: 312-782-0993
Email: PAHardiman@aol.com URL: http://www.hardimanlawoffices.com
Members of Firm: Patricia A. Hardiman; Eugene C. Hardiman.
Worker's Compensation, Personal Injury, Negligence, Construction Defects, Medical Malpractice.
See Professional Biographies, CHICAGO, ILLINOIS

Harding, David G., (AV) '54 '81 C.801 B.A. L.365 J.D.
100 North LaSalle Street, Suite 1610, 60602
Telephone: 312-782-3039 Fax: 312-236-0678
Email: hardlaw@netzero.com URL: http://www.lawyers.com/harding
Bankruptcy, Lawsuits, Business Litigation, Contracts, Corporate Law, Limited Liability Company Law, Environmental Law, Estate Planning, Wills, Probate, Real Estate, Residential Real Estate.
See Professional Biographies, CHICAGO, ILLINOIS

Harding, Joseph F. '69 '00
C.679 B.S.M.E. L.477 J.D. [McAndrews,H.&M.] (See Pat. Sect.)
Harding, Ryan K. ... '— '01 C.533 B.B.A. L.329 J.D. [Ⓐ Neal&L.]
Harding, Ryan M. ... '77 '02 C.602 B.B.A. L.477 J.D. 227 West Monroe Street
Harding, Thomas N. ... '47 '73 C.339 B.A. L.145 J.D. [Ⓒ Pugh,J.J.&Q.]
Harding, Virginia M., (AV) ... '47 '72 C.339 B.A. L.145 J.D. [Ⓒ Gould&R.]
Hardman-Burt, Trina ... '70 '99 C.589 B.S. L.146 J.D. Dept. of Law
Hardt, James R. ... '43 '70 C&L.424 B.S., J.D. [Hardt&S.]
Hardt, Renee M. ... '70 '97 C.477 A.B. L.94 J.D. [Vedder,P.K.&K.]
Hardt & Stern, P.C., (AV) ... 311 S. Wacker Dr.
Hardwicke, Tim ... '— '89 C.880 B.A. L.145 J.D. [Latham&W.]
Hardy, Gabriel P. ... '— '95 C.97 L.124 J.D. [Ⓐ Hickey,M.&Assoc.]
Hardy, James B. ... '66 '04 C.597 B.A. L.879 J.D. [Ⓐ Anesi,O.R.N.&K.]
Hardy, Sean J., (BV) ... '63 '91 C.145 B.A. L.424 J.D. [Ⓐ Johnson&B.]
Hardy, Whitnie D. ... '78 '04 C.302 B.A. L.228 J.D. [Ⓐ Franczek S.]
Hare, Jamie ... '74 '99 C.428 B.A. L.146 J.D. [Ⓐ Robbins,S.&P.]
Hare, Verlanteree, (Ms.) ... '— '78 C.234 B.A. L.879 J.D. 200 N. LaSalle
Harenza, Katherine L. ... '— '98 C.339 B.S. L.209 J.D. [Ⓐ Winston&S.]
Hargadon, D. Scott, (AV) ... '— '83 C.893 B.A. L.659 J.D. [Bryan C.]
Harig, Robert E. ... '64 '92 C.602 B.B.A. L.209 J.D. [Ⓐ Holland&K.]
Harjani, Sunil R. ... '74 '00 C&L.597 B.A., J.D. Sr. Atty., Chicago, M.R.O., S.E.C.
Harkins, Christopher A. '65 '91
C.338 B.S. L.339 J.D. [Ⓒ Brinks H.G.&L.] (See Pat. Sect.)
Harkless, Angela ... '— '95 C.424 B.A. L.1119 J.D. 734 N. LaSalle Street
Harlan, Heather A. '— '97 C.145 B.A. L.602 J.D.
(adm. in NY; not adm. in IL) [Ⓐ Mayer,B.R.&M.]
Harley, Keith Ian ... '60 '88 Environ. Law Prog. Dir., Chicago Legal Clinic
Harlin, Michael B. '68 '96 C.976 B.S. L.146 J.D.
[McAndrews,H.&M.] (See Pat. Sect.)
Harman, James C. ... '58 '87 C.801 B.S. L.365 J.D. [Cirignani H.H.&L.]
Harman, Pamela K., (AV) ... '50 '78 C.339 B.A. L.209 J.D. [Ⓒ Dowd&D.]
Harman, Theodore E. ... '— '89 C.98 B.S. L.339 J.D. [Ungaretti&H.]
Harmelin, Edward I. ... '38 '64 C.339 B.S. L.209 J.D. Sr. Spec. Coun.
Harmon, Julie M. ... '54 '79 C.436 B.A. L.146 J.D. Asst. Pub. Def.
Harmon, Meighan A. ... '71 '96 C.339 B.S. L.602 J.D. [Schiller,D.&F.]
Harmon, Robert J. ... '30 '55 C.602 B.S.C. L.209 J.D. 180 N. LaSalle St.
Harmon, Teresa Wilton ... '68 '94 C.16 B.S. L.145 J.D. [Ⓐ Sidley A.B.&W.]
Harmon, William J. ... '— '79 C.98 B.A. L.339 J.D. [Ⓒ Jones D.]
Harned, Nicholas S. ... '72 '98 C&L.966 B.S., J.D. [Ⓐ Vedder,P.K.&K.]
Harner, Michelle Morgan ... '— '95 C.93 B.A. L.608 J.D. [Jones D.]
Harner, Nicole ... '73 '99 C.932 B.B.A. L.966 J.D. 10 South Dearborn
Harner, Paul E. ... '— '90 C&L.228 B.A., J.D. [Jones D.]
Harp, Jason G. ... '— '98 C.597 B.A. L.494 J.D. [Ⓐ Schiff H.] (Pat.)
Harp, R. Kymn, (AV) ... '— '78 C.894 B.A. L.365 J.D. [Arnstein&L.]
Harp, Robert Kymn ... '53 '78 C.894 B.A. L.1000 J.D. 111 W. washington St.
Harper, Charles E., Jr. ... '— '99 C.597 B.A. L.339 J.D. [Ⓐ Quarles&B.]
Harper, David S. ... '61 '98 C.589 B.A. L.146 J.D. [McDonnell B.H.&B.] (See Pat. Sect.)
Harper, Douglas B. ... '59 '85 C.976 B.A. L.569 J.D. 70 West Madison Street, Suite 1400
Harper, Steven J., (P.C.), (AV) ... '— '79 C.597 B.A. L.309 J.D. [Kirkland&E.]
Harper, Tyson K. ... '76 '01 C.477 B.A. L.309 J.D. [Ⓐ Cotsirilos,T.&S.]
Harpest, David ... '78 '04 C.209 B.M. L.339 J.D. [Ⓐ Schwartz C.]
Harrell, Jacob W. ... '76 '04 C.597 B.A. L.477 J.D. [Ⓐ Grippo&E.]
Harrigan, Donna R. ... '40 '67 C&L.352 B.A., J.D. [Harrigan&Assoc.]
Harrigan, Marie G. ... '66 '92 Chicago Legal Clinic, Inc.
Harrigan & Associates ... 122 South Michigan Avenue, Suite 1220
Harrington, Alison M. ... '— '97 C.352 B.S. L.436 J.D. [Best,V.&H.] ⊙
Harrington, Carol A., (AV) ... '53 '77 C&L.339 B.S., J.D. [McDermott W.&E.]
Harrington, Cornelius J., III, (AV) ... '55 '80 C.602 B.B.A. L.851 J.D. [Bullaro&C.]
Harrington, James T., (AV) ... '42 '67 C&L.602 B.A., J.D. [McGuirewoods]
Harrington, John R. ... '68 '95 C.597 B.A. L.347 J.D. [Jenner&B.]
Harrington, Patrick J., (AV) ... '60 '85 C.363 B.A. L.424 J.D. [Harrington,T.A.&H.]
Harrington, Robert E., III ... '77 '02 C.363 B.A. L.424 J.D. [Ⓐ Harrington,T.A.&H.]
Harrington, Robert E., Jr., (AV) ... '50 '76 C.363 B.A. L.146 J.D. [Harrington,T.A.&H.]
Harrington, Ryan J. ... '66 '92 C.755 B.A. L.146 J.D. [Ⓐ Yelton&K.]
Harrington, Vernon D. '14 '42 L.180 LL.B.
(adm. in DC; not adm. in IL) Amer. Airlines Inc.
Harrington, William J. ... '65 '92 C.347 B.A. L.1187 J.D. [Ⓐ Rusin M.&F.]

Harrington, Thompson, Acker & Harrington, Ltd., (AV) BB
310 South Michigan Avenue, Suite 2000, 60604
Telephone: 312-922-8833 Fax: 312-922-3044
URL: http://www.harringtonlaw.com
Robert E. Harrington, Jr.; Robert B. Thompson; Laurence C. Acker; Patrick J. Harrington; Kenneth J. Sophie, Jr.;—Vincent B. Browne; Robert E. Harrington, III; Daniel W. Pisani.
Civil Trial and Appellate Practice in all Courts. Plaintiff Personal Injury, Wrongful Death, Federal Employers Liability Act (FELA), Medical Malpractice, Products Liability, Civil Rights and Construction Related Torts.
Reference: American National Bank and Trust Co., Chicago, Illinois.
See Professional Biographies, CHICAGO, ILLINOIS

Harris, Allan M. ... '34 '60 C.1016 B.S. L.209 LL.B. 1501 N. State‡
Harris, Alton B., (AV) ... '— '67 C&L.309 B.A., LL.B. [Ungaretti&H.]
Harris, Andrew B. ... '71 '97 C.347 B.A. L.209 J.D. Soc. Sec. Admn.
Harris, Beth A., (AV) '53 '80 C.145 B.A. L.597 J.D.
V.P & Gen. Coun., The University of Chicago
Harris, C. Murray ... '76 '03 C.478 B.A. L.94 J.D. [Ⓐ Hunt]
Harris, Charles, (AV) ... '61 '89 C.209 B.S. L.146 J.D. [Katten M.R.]
Harris, Charles E., II ... '— '03 C.575 B.S. L.989 J.D. [Ⓐ Mayer,B.R.&M.] (Pat.)
Harris, Cheryl I. '52 '79 C.914 B.A. L.597 J.D.
Asst. Prof. of Law, Chicago-Kent College of Law
Harris, Daniel M. ... '51 '78 C.367 B.A. L.309 J.D. [D.Harris]
Harris, David G. ... '52 '77 C.339 A.B. L.801 J.D. Coopers & Lybrand
Harris, Donald R., (Ltd.), (AV) ... '38 '63 C&L.352 B.A., J.D. [Jenner&B.]
Harris, Duncan G. ... '54 '80 C.24 B.A. L.365 J.D. Chicago Transit Auth.
Harris, Erick Steven ... '75 '02 C.966 B.A. L.309 J.D. [Ⓐ Mayer,B.R.&M.]
Harris, Harold A. ... '12 '36 C.999 A.A. L.209 LL.B. 29 S. LaSalle St.‡
Harris, James L. ... '22 '50 C.852 L.365 J.D. 6326 S. Cottage Grove Ave.
Harris, Jeff D., (AV) ... '53 '78 C.473 B.A. L.902 J.D. [Figliulo&S.]
Harris, Jeremy B. ... '74 '01 C.37 B.A. L.209 J.D. [Ⓐ Gunty&M.]
Harris, Jonathan A. ... '72 '98 C.228 B.S. L.184 J.D. [Wildman,H.A.&D.] (Pat.)
Harris, Karen K. ... '69 '94 C.674 B.A. L.309 J.D. [Ⓒ Seyfarth S.]
Harris, Kenneth L. ... '60 '85 C.299 A.B. L.145 J.D. [Neal,G.&E.]
Harris, Lee ... '47 '73 C.339 B.S. L.608 J.D. 141 W. Jackson
Harris, Linda Chaplik ... '49 '74 C.477 B.A. L.128 J.D. [Sonnenschein N.&R.]
Harris, Mark A. ... '57 '82 C.734 A.B. L.597 J.D. [McDermott W.&E.]
Harris, Martin ... '63 '87 C.674 A.B. L.477 J.D. [Connelly S.H.]
Harris, Michael J. ... '— '03 C.879 B.S.E.E. L.339 J.D. [Ⓐ Banner&W.]
Harris, Natalie A. ... '— '00 C.477 B.A. L.966 J.D. [Ⓐ Mandell M.]
Harris, Philip L. ... '58 '83 C.597 B.A. L.145 J.D. [Jenner&B.]
Harris, Phillip H. '48 '73 C.347 B.S. L.276 J.D.
Gen. Coun., Evangelical Lutheran Church in Amer.
Harris, Richard D., (AV) ... '48 '75 C.339 B.S. L.209 J.D. [Greenberg T.] (Pat.)
Harris, Richard M. ... '44 '74 C.339 B.A. L.146 J.D. 2029 N. Cleveland‡
Harris, Robert J., (AV) ... '60 '85 C.299 A.B. L.976 J.D. [Stein,R.&H.]
Harris, Robert M. ... '63 '88 C.339 B.A. L.1000 J.D. [Ⓐ Knell&P.]
Harris, Roger B., (AV) ... '38 '62 C&L.477 B.A., LL.B. [Fox,H.S.L.&C.]
Harris, Ryan ... '— '02 C.1365 B.A. L.597 J.D. [Ⓐ McDermott W.&E.]
Harris, Sarah L. ... '74 '01 C.773 B.A. L.597 J.D. [Ⓐ Mayer,B.R.&M.]
Harris, Sharon A. ... '67 '98 C.475 B.S. L.209 J.D. [Ⓐ Barnow&Assoc.]
Harris, Stephanie J. ... '76 '04 C.185 B.A. L.280 J.D. [Ⓐ Novack&M.]
Harris, Steven M., (AV) ... '56 '81 C.589 B.S. L.46 J.D. [Harris K.&G.]
Harris, Susan V. ... '61 '92 C.694 B.A. L.145 J.D. [Ⓐ Sidley A.B.&W.]
Harris, Thomas M., Jr., (BV) ... '63 '88 C.339 B.A. L.174 J.D. [Ⓐ J.Mirza&Assoc.] ⊙
Harris, Timothy S. ... '60 '88 C.851 B.A. L.608 J.D. [DLPiper R.G.C.U.]
Harris, Wendell W. ... '— '01 C.679 B.S.C.E. L.309 J.D. [Ⓐ Banner&W.]
Harris, Zelda B. ... '66 '91 C.823 B.S. L.910 J.D. Northwestern Univ. Sch. of Law

Harris, Daniel, The Law Offices of
150 North Wacker Drive Suite 3000, 60606
Telephone: 312-960-1802 Fax: 312-960-1936
Email: lawofficedh@yahoo.com URL: http://www.lawyers.com/danielharris
Daniel M. Harris.
Class Actions, Consumer Protection.
See Professional Biographies, CHICAGO, ILLINOIS

Harris Kessler & Goldstein LLC, (AV)
A Limited Liability Company
640 North La Salle Street Suite 590, 60610-3731 ⊙
Telephone: 312-280-0111 Fax: 312-280-8232
URL: http://www.hkgold.com
Steven M. Harris; Richard N. Kessler; John A. Goldstein; Rick L. Hindmand; Ryann Whalen; James W. Marks; Jayme R. Matchinski;—Pamela Mitchell Belyn; Jasmine de la Torre; Todd L. Erdman; Alan D. Leib; Beatriz M. Olivera.
General Business Practice including Litigation, Secured Lending, Real Estate, Health Care and Estate Planning.
Waukegan, Illinois Office: 404 Water Street, 60085. Telephone: 847-263-1919. Fax: 847-244-8891.
See Professional Biographies, CHICAGO, ILLINOIS

Harrison, Arnold, (AV) ... '45 '70 C.339 B.S. L.597 J.D. [Jenner&B.]
Harrison, Benjamin E. '59 '96
C.201 B.A. L.365 J.D. 55 East Washington Street, Suite 1722
Harrison, Bernard P. ... '22 '51 C.339 B.S. L.209 J.D. Amer. Medical Assn.
Harrison, Charles J. '57 '88 C.1320 B.A. L.146 J.D.
VP Real Estate & Gen. Coun., CMC Heartland Partners
Harrison, Edward S. ... '71 '01 C.301 B.A. L.329 J.D. [Ⓐ Baker&M.]
Harrison, Holly A. ... '58 '84 C.208 B.A. L.94 J.D. [Sidley A.B.&W.]
Harrison, Joseph H., Jr. ... '50 '79 C.674 A.B. L.597 J.D. [Sidley A.B.&W.]
Harrison, Louis S., (AV) ... '59 '84 C.165 B.A. L.228 J.D. [Harrison&H.]
Harrison, Sean C. ... '66 '94 C.846 B.A. L.861 J.D. 222 N. La Salle St., Ste. 200

Harrison & Held, LLP, (AV) BB
333 W. Wacker Drive, Suite 950, 60606
Telephone: 312-332-1111 Fax: 312-332-1150
URL: http://www.harrisonheld.com
Louis S. Harrison; Robert S. Held; Edward O. Pacer; Charles F. Newlin; Emily J. Kuo; Michael J. Durkin; Gregory A. Frezados.
Trust Litigation, Estate Planning, Probate, Employment Discrimination, Commercial Dispute Litigation, General Litigation, Nonprofit Corporations, Guardianship, Premarital Agreements, Elder Law, Trusts and Estates.
See Professional Biographies, CHICAGO, ILLINOIS

Harrold, Bernard, (AV) ... '25 '51 C.347 A.B. L.1119 LL.B. [Ⓒ Wildman,H.A.&D.]
Harsch, Roy M., (AV) ... '46 '72 C.350 B.S. L.352 J.D. [Gardner C.&D.]
Harsha, H. Vincent ... '20 '53 C&L.352 B.S.E.E., J.D. [Ⓒ Rockey,M.&K.] (Pat.)

Harstad, Clifford A. '47 '73 C.475 B.A. L.339 J.D. [Gozdecki&D.]
Hart, Alexis B. '76 '03 C.209 B.S. L.1398 J.D. 1700 W. Huron St., Ste. 2
Hart, Bennett F., (BV) '54 '79 C&L.352 B.B.A., J.D. [Garofalo,S.H.&S.]
Hart, Brett J. '69 '94 C.477 B.S. L.145 J.D. Dep. Gen. Coun., Sara Lee Corp.
Hart, Brian S. '62 '87 C.339 B.S. L.1068 J.D. [Winston&S.]
Hart, Herbert D., III, (AV) '52 '77
C.347 B.A. L.1119 J.D. [McAndrews,H.&M.] (See Pat. Sect.)
Hart, Jeffrey C., (BV) '69 '95 C.475 B.A. L.424 J.D. [Garofalo,S.H.&S.]
Hart, Richard D. '53 '78 C.221 B.S. L.209 J.D. [Handler,T.&D.]
Hart, Steven A. '67 '92 C.966 B.A. L.365 J.D. [Segal M.S.&M.]
Hart, Trisha M. '77 '01 C.999 B.A. L.365 J.D. [Cassiday,S.&G.]
Hart, William T. '29 '51 C&L.424 J.D. U.S. Sr. Dist. J.
Harte, Meghan Kathleen '68 '99
C.880 B.S. L.424 J.D. City of Chicago, Office of the Mayor
Harte, Michael F. '— '00 C&L.602 B.S., J.D. [Latham&W.]
Harte, William J., (AV) '31 '59 C.1082 B.A. L.602 J.D. [W.J.Harte]

Harte, William J., Ltd., (AV)
Suite 1100, 111 West Washington Street, 60602
Telephone: 312-726-5015 Fax: 312-641-2455
William J. Harte;—Erik D. Gruber; Dana M. Pesha. Of Counsel: David J. Walker.
Negligence, Tort, Chancery, Antitrust and Securities Law. Trials and Appeals. State and Local Taxation.
See Professional Biographies, CHICAGO, ILLINOIS

Hartford, Richard S. '46 '72 C.424 B.B.A. L.209 J.D. [Abramson&F.]
Hartgering, William E., (AV) '49 '75 C.154 B.A. L.597 J.D. Jams
Harth, Danita Y. '54 '81 C&L.209 B.A., J.D. 10051 S. May St.‡
Hartigan, David M., (AV) '40 '66 C.276 A.B. L.424 J.D. [Carroll,H.&C.]
Hartigan, John M., (AV) '32 '58 C.602 B.S. L.597 J.D. [Carroll,H.&C.]
Hartigan, Mary K. '62 '91 C.276 B.S.F.S. L.602 J.D. [Carroll,H.&C.]
Hartigan, Russell W., (AV) '46 '76 C.209 B.S.C. L.365 J.D. 222 N. LaSalle St.
Hartl, Donna F. '58 '83 C.578 B.A. L.424 J.D. [Field&G.]
Hartlaub, Lawrence P. '13 '39 C.597 L.365 LL.B. Salerno-Megowen Biscuit Co.
Hartley, Katherine L. '75 '04 C.213 B.A. L.424 J.D. [Bollinger,R.&G.]
Hartley, Kirk T., (AV) '— '83 C.339 B.S. L.365 J.D. [Butler R.S.&B.]
Hartman, Allen '27 '59 C&L.597 B.S.L., LL.B. Appl. Ct. Jus.
Hartman, Kendra Kekelis '73 '98 C.1036 B.A. L.976 J.D. [Sonnenschein N.&R.]
Hartman, Marshall J. '34 '58 C&L.145 A.B., J.D. Chief Pub. Def., Lake Co.
Hartman, Stacie R. '— '96 C&L.597 B.A., J.D. [Schiff H.]
Hartmann, Albert E. '72 '98 C.339 B.A. L.477 J.D. [DLPiper R.G.C.U.]
Hartmann, Frederick L., Jr., (AV) '— '69 C.674 A.B. L.145 J.D. [Schiff H.]
Hartmann, H. Michael, (AV) '48 '76
C.171 B.S. L.209 J.D. [Leydig,V.&M.] (See Pat. Sect.)
Hartmann, Jennifer Lynn '67 '95 C.339 B.S. L.365 J.D. 222 N. La Salle St.
Hartmann, John F., P.C. '— '87 C&L.494 B.S., J.D. [Kirkland&E.]
Hartmann, Steven M. '— '83 C.597 B.A. L.339 J.D. [Freeborn&P.]
Hartnett, Daniel, (AV) '57 '86 C&L.597 B.A., J.D. [Kaye S.]
Hartnett, Daniel T., (AV) '52 '77 C.602 B.A. L.424 J.D. [Martin,B.&S.]
Hartnett, Patrick I. '52 '77 C.755 B.S. L.365 J.D. 79 W. Monroe
Hartnett, Thomas P. '64 '90 C.966 B.A. L.209 J.D. Zurich-American Insurance Group
Hartsell, David L. '55 '83 C&L.477 B.A., J.D. [McGuirewoods]
Hartstein, Barry A., (AV) '51 '76 C.188 B.S. L.597 J.D. [Morgan,L.&B.]
Hartunian, Aram A., (AV) '32 '55 C.339 L.209 LL.B. [A.A.Hartunian] (⊙Chicago)
Hartunian, Aram A., (AV) '32 '55 C.339 L.209 LL.B. [Levin,R.] (⊙Chicago)
Hartunian, Aram A., A Professional Corporation, (AV) 1124 West George Street
Hartwell, David C. '65 '98 C.393 B.A. L.209 J.D. One N. LaSalle St., Ste. 1515
Harty, Daniel J. '— '02 C.339 B.S. L.209 J.D. 140 S. Dearborn, Suite 1610
Hartz, Michael O., (AV) '53 '80 C.373 B.A. L.215 J.D. [Katten M.R.]
Hartzell, Julianne '— '01 C.228 B.S. L.477 J.D. [Marshall,G.&B.] (See Pat. Sect.)
Harvey, Bennet B., Jr., Law Offices of, (AV) '34 '60 C.674 A.B. L.309 LL.B.
39 South LaSalle St., Suite 200 (⊙Lake Forest)
Harvey, Debra A. '— '88 C.597 B.S. L.365 J.D. Asst. Gen. Coun.
Harvey, Elizabeth '70 '02 C.741 B.A. L.597 J.D. [Shefsky&F.]
Harvey, Elizabeth Schroer, (AV) '— '86 C.352 B.A. L.801 J.D. [Swanson,M.&B.]
Harvey, Stuart C., Jr. '61 '86 C.723 B.A. L.273 J.D. Options Clearing Corp.
Harvey, Waddell, Monahan & Layton, (AV)
345 N. LaSalle Boulevard, Suite 3105 (⊙Lake Worth, FL)
Harvick, Thomas M., (AV) '45 '71 C.742 B.A. L.602 J.D. [Bresler&H.]
Hasan, Salim A. '67 '93 C&L.347 B.A., J.D. [Leydig,V.&M.] (See Pat. Sect.)
Hasch, Jennifer A. '74 '00 C.880 B.A. L.1066 J.D. [Jenner&B.]
Hasday, Jill Elaine '72 '98 C&L.976 B.A., J.D.
(adm. in NY; not adm. in IL) Univ. of Chicago Law School
Hasenbalg, Stacee A., (AV) '65 '90
C.679 B.A. L.112 J.D. V.P. & Tr. Coun., Harris Tr. & Svgs. Bk.
Hasenmiller, John D. '46 '73 C.352 B.B.A. L.209 J.D. [Blatt,H.L.&M.]
Haskell, Donald M., (AV) '32 '57 C.970 B.A. L.477 J.D. [Haskell&P.]
Haskell, Laurel A. '— '97 C.1369 B.S. L.494 J.D. [Michael B.&F.]
Haskell & Perrin, (AV) P.O. Box 2672
Haskin, Warren C., (AV) '33 '58 C&L.597 B.A., J.D. [Bell,B.&L.] ‡
Haskins, Charles, Jr. '51 '76 C.339 B.A. L.1000 J.D. 35 E. Wacker Dr., Ste. 1760
Haskins, Gail Ferbend, (AV) '58 '83 C.597 B.S. L.424 J.D. [Ferbend&F.]
Hasman, Joseph J., (AV) '41 '66 C&L.339 A.B., J.D. [Chittenden,M.&N.]
Hassan, Michael R., (AV) '48 '74 C.674 B.A. L.145 J.D. [Lord,B.&B.]
Hassan, Susan S. '70 '96 C&L.477 B.A., J.D. [Skadden,A.S.M.&F.]
Hasse, Mary '— '00 C.128 B.S.N. L.146 J.D. [Alholm,M.K.H.&O.]
Hassen, S. R. '10 '34 C&L.145 Ph.B., J.D. 33 N. LaSalle St.
Hasson, Joseph K. '— '87 C.228 B.A. L.339 J.D. [Ungaretti&H.]
Hastings, John M., (P.C.), (AV) '32 '59 C&L.424 B.S., J.D. 35 E. Wacker Dr.
Hastings, Steven G., (AV) '— '87 C&L.339 B.S., J.D. [Chapman&C.]
Haszto, Stephen J., Law Offices of, (AV) '60 '85
C.1024 B.A. L.365 J.D. 225 W. Washington St., Ste 1400
Hatcher, Merrick D. '68 '96 C&L.477 B.A., J.D. [Bell,B.&L.]
Hatchett, Bonita L. '70 '96 C.477 B.A. L.705 J.D. [Bell,B.&L.]
Hathaway, Katherine A. '— '04 C.910 B.A. L.424 J.D. [Schad,D.&S.]
Hatlestad, Douglas J. '72 '00 C.339 B.S. L.424 J.D. [Bell,B.&L.]
Hatseras, Angela M. '63 '99 C.879 B.S. L.424 J.D. Staff Coun., YMCA of the USA
Hatzenbuehler, Mari Rose '61 '86 C.966 B.A. L.424 J.D. State's Atty's. Off.
Haugh, Michael A. '53 '78 C&L.424 B.A., J.D. [Veverka,R.&H.]
Haugh, Todd J. '76 '02 C.103 B.A. L.339 J.D. [Stetler&D.]
Haugh, Valerie A. '59 '88 C.424 B.A. L.365 J.D. [Gardner C.&D.]
Haughey, Joseph C. '43 '77 C.1016 B.S. L.365 J.D. 6252 N. Harlem Ave.
Haule, Anne M., (BV) '— '81 C.424 B.A. L.365 J.D. [Ungaretti&H.]
Hauselman, Martin F., (AV) '36 '60 C.1016 B.A. L.146 J.D. [Hauselman&R.]
Hauselman & Rappin, (AV) 39 S. La Salle St.
Hauseman, Stanley Robt. '10 '35 C&L.597 Contl. Cas. Co.
Hauser, Crane C., (AV) '23 '50 C.264 A.B. L.597 J.D. 1515 Astor Ct., #14C‡
Hauser, Henry A., (AV) '45 '70 C.755 B.A. L.424 J.D. [Schoenberg,F.N.&R.]
Hauser, James C., (AV) '50 '77 [Tressler,S.M.&P.]
Hauser, Marc D. '73 '98 C&L.597 B.A., J.D.
Assoc. Gen. Coun., Equity Group Investments
Hauser, Robert M. '58 '82 C.339 B.A. L.801 J.D. 8019 S. California
Hausken, Philip D. '58 '82 C.339 B.A. L.209 J.D.
1st V.P., Dir. of Compliance, Zurich Kemper Investments, Inc.
Hausler, Charla L. '— '00 C.339 B.S. L.879 J.D. [Barnes&T.]
Hauslinger, Morton J. '07 '32 L.145 LL.B. 33 N. La Salle St.
Hausman, Madelynn J. '55 '81 C.659 B.A. L.494 J.D. 77 W. Washington St., Ste. 1119
Hausman, Susan L. '75 '00 C.339 B.S. L.146 J.D. Law Clerk, Cir. Ct. of Cook Co.
Haussmann, Brian C. '79 '04 C.347 B.A. L.1556 J.D. [Jenner&B.]
Hausten, Lisa A. '56 '83 C.162 B.A. L.145 J.D. [Sidley A.B.&W.]
Havey, Brian R. '64 '89 C.436 B.S. L.424 J.D. Asst. U.S. Atty., U.S. Atty.'s Off.
Haw, Jeanny '— '01 C.197 B.A. L.597 J.D. [Mayer,B.R.&M.] (Pat.)
Hawekotte, Thomas J., (P.C.) '34 '60
C.602 A.B. L.209 J.D. Leg. Advisor, Ill. Secy. of State
Hawilo, Cristina T. '— '04 C&L.477 B.A., J.D. [Jenkens&G.]
Hawker, Alexis A. '75 '00 C.210 B.A. L.477 J.D. [Lovells]
Hawkins, Brent A. '71 '97 C.477 B.S.E. L.339 J.D.
[Wallenstein W.&R.] (See Pat. Sect.)
Hawkins, Maureseta T. '54 '97 C.999 B.A.B.A. L.365 J.D. [Gomberg,S.G.&O.]
Hawkins, William J. '— '85 C.339 B.S. L.365 J.D. [Hennessy&R.]
Hawksley, Alan J. '55 '82 C.338 B.A. L.339 J.D. [McDermott W.&E.]
Hawley, Alicia M. '— '02 C.473 B.A. L.597 J.D. [Jones D.]
Hay, Linda J., (BV) '— '86 C.339 B.A. L.365 J.D. [Alholm,M.K.H.&O.]
Hayden, Mark '60 '89 C.589 B.S. L.966 J.D. Dir. & Sr. Coun., CNA
Hayden, Thomas P. '37 '66 C.177 B.A. L.365 LL.B. 9334 Muskegon Ave.
Hayes, Dale C. '48 '77 C.72 B.A. L.150 J.D. Staff Atty., U.S. Dist. Ct.
Hayes, Daniel J. '72 '97 C.93 B.A. L.602 J.D. [Bell,B.&L.]
Hayes, David J. A., Jr. '29 '61 C.309 A.B. L.146 J.D. Amer. Bar Assn.
Hayes, Dina Pascarelli '73 '99 C.945 B.S. L.209 J.D. [Niro,S.H.&N.]
Hayes, Gregory W. '70 '96 C.591 B.S. L.477 J.D. [DLPiper R.G.C.U.]
Hayes, James H. '57 '83 C.602 A.B. L.597 J.D. 140 S. Dearborn Street
Hayes, John J. '58 '83 C.98 B.S. L.209 J.D. [Pedersen&H.]
Hayes, John L. '— '01 C.339 B.A. L.145 J.D. [Sachnoff&W.]
Hayes, Maryann C., (AV) '55 '81 C.602 B.A. L.424 J.D. [Bates&C.]
Hayes, Michael '59 '89 C.339 B.S. L.424 J.D. 3260 North Clark Street, Apt. 502
Hayes, Michael D. '59 '84 C.67 B.A. L.209 J.D. [Varga B.L.H.&C.]
Hayes, Michael J., Jr. '— '96 C.339 B.A. L.209 J.D. [Ungaretti&H.]
Hayes, Michael J., Sr., (AV) '46 '74 C.424 B.A. L.209 J.D. [Bell,B.&L.]
Hayes, Neil B. '71 '97 C.813 A.B. L.477 J.D.
V.P. & Chf. Legal Offr., Classified Ventures, LLC, Apartments.com, Cars.com, Homescape Div.
Hayes, Thomas J. '76 '03 C.436 B.S. L.209 J.D. [Johnson&B.]
Hayes, Thomas W., (BV) '51 '76 C.755 B.A. L.602 J.D. [Fuchs&R.]
Hayes, Thomas W. '— '86 C.870 B.S. L.209 J.D. [McKenna S.]
Haynes, Alton C., (AV) '55 '80 C.477 B.G.S. L.188 J.D. [Haynes,S.K.O.&M.]
Haynes, Helen '56 '82 C.93 B.S. L.184 J.D. Asst. State's Atty.
Haynes, Jacquelyn C. '52 '80 C.629 B.A. L.597 J.D. [Borovsky&E.]
Haynes, Leslie D. '72 '00 C.339 B.A. L.146 J.D. IL Commerce Commission
Haynes, Linda J. '65 '94 C.679 B.S. L.424 J.D. [Seyfarth S.]
Haynes, Thomas B. '56 '83 C.197 B.A. L.145 J.D. Pres., Enzo Provolone Productions
Haynes, Todd James '59 '86 C.198 B.A. L.801 J.D. Sr. Atty., Legal Div., F.D.I.C.
Haynes, Studnicka, Kahan, O'Neill and Miller, LLC, (AV)
208 South LaSalle Street, Suite 1154
Haynie, Howard E., (AV) '28 '59 C.597 B.S.B.A. L.424 J.D. One 1st. National Plz.‡
Haynie, Laurie A. '58 '85 C.878 B.A. L.101 J.D. [Welsh&K.]
Hays, Antonia '74 '01 C&L.424 B.S., J.D. [Asperger&Assoc.]
Hays, Brian I. '70 '98 C.311 B.A. L.597 J.D. [Lord,B.&B.]
Hays, Keith J. '72 '98 C.967 B.A. L.345 J.D.
(adm. in IN; not adm. in IL) [Segal M.S.&M.]
Hays, Mary Vidal '70 '95 C.339 B.S. L.208 J.D. [Aronberg G.D.&G.]
Hayward, Robert M. '— '97 C&L.597 B.S., J.D. [Kirkland&E.]
Hayward, Thomas Z., Jr., (AV) '40 '66 C&L.597 B.A., J.D. [Bell,B.&L.]
Haywood, Amy C. '— '03 C.502 B.A. L.276 J.D.
(adm. in VA; not adm. in IL) [Kirkland&E.]
Hazel, Kristen E. '62 '88 C.912 B.A. L.424 J.D. [McDermott W.&E.]
Hazelwood, Laura A. '65 '02 C.347 B.S. L.145 J.D. [Skadden,A.S.M.&F.]
Hazlitt, Walter C., Jr. '69 '96 C.216 B.A. L.273 J.D. [Sonnenschein N.&R.]
Head, Brendan P. '66 '93 C&L.276 B.A., J.D. [Winston&S.]
Head, Donna L. '57 '83 C.685 B.A. L.424 J.D. 222 N. La Salle St.‡
Head, Martin P. '67 '92 C.276 A.B. L.597 J.D. [Bollinger,R.&G.]
Head, Tracy R. Cassens '70 '95 C.339 B.A. L.879 J.D. 150 S. Wacker Drive
Head, Wallace L. '50 '76 C.934 B.A. L.502 J.D.,MBA 69 W. Washington‡
Headrick, David D. '66 '93
C.436 B.S.E.E. L.494 J.D. [McAndrews,H.&M.] (See Pat. Sect.)
Healey, Brendan J. '— '97 C.813 A.B. L.569 J.D. [Mandell M.]
Healy, George R. '42 '71 C.339 B.A. L.146 J.D. 25 E. Wash.
Healy, James P., Jr. '76 '02 C.1176 B.A. L.209 J.D. [Winston&S.]
Healy, John C., (AV) '24 '50 C.932 A.B. L.597 J.D. [Heineke,B.&B.]
Healy, John Patrick, (AV) '47 '72 C.602 B.A. L.477 J.D. 29 South La Salle - Suite 640
Healy, Martin J., Jr., (AV) '44 '68 C.602 B.A. L.424 J.D. [Healy]
Healy, Patrick F., III, (AV) '61 '86 C.177 B.A. L.365 J.D. [Pretzel&S.]
Healy, Sheryl E. '50 '85 C.352 B.A. L.424 J.D. [Gunty&M.]
Healy, Stephen J. '65 '92 C.338 B.S. L.365 J.D. [Pappas,J.&M.]
Healy, Thomas P., Jr., (AV) '52 '79 C.893 B.A. L.902 J.D.
V.P. & Assoc. Gen. Coun., American Medical Association
Healy, William J. '64 '92 C.602 B.A. L.276 J.D. Animation Technologies

Healy Law Firm, The, (AV)
111 West Washington Street, Suite 1425, 60602
Telephone: 312-977-0100; 1-800-922-4500 Fax: 312-977-0795
URL: http://www.healylawfirm.com
Martin J. Healy, Jr.; Daniel B. Malone; J.T. Terence Geoghegan; John P. Scanlon. Associates: David P. Huber; Kevin T. Veugeler; Diana M. Jacob; Jack Cannon. Of Counsel: Terry Sullivan.
Personal Injury, Wrongful Death, Products Liability, Bus Accidents, SUV Rollover, Crashworthiness, Automotive Defects, Defective Tires, Defective Airbags, Defective Seatbelts, Defective Restraints, Roof Crush, Quadriplegia, Paraplegia, Brain Injury, Brain Trauma, Spinal Injury, Traumatic Brain Injury, Medical Malpractice, Airplane Crashes, Automobile Accidents, Railroad, Trucking and Construction Injuries, Workers Compensation.
See Professional Biographies, CHICAGO, ILLINOIS

Heap, Frank K., (AV) '41 '66 C.597 B.S. L.145 J.D. [Bell,B.&L.]
Heaphy, John M. '55 '81 C&L.477 B.S.E., J.D. [Vurdelja&H.]
Heard, H. Roderic, (AV) '46 '73 C.597 B.S. L.945 J.D. [Wildman,H.A.&D.]

Heard, James H. '40 '75 C.1149 B.S. L.209 J.D. Kennedy-King Coll.
Hearn, Edward W., (CVⓉ) '69 '95 C.679 B.S. L.879 J.D.
(adm. in IN; not adm. in IL) [Johnson&B.] (⊙Highland, IN)
Heaston, Curtis '31 '58 C&L.424 J.D. Cir. Ct. J.
Heath, Timothy W. '56 '84 C.339 B.A. L.424 J.D. 3 First National Plz., Ste. 2070
Heaton, David L. '71 '98 C.589 B.A. L.209 J.D. [Ⓐ Fisher K.]
Heaton, J. Michael, (AV) '46 '71 C&L.602 A.B., J.D. [O'Keefe,L.&H.]
Heaton, James B., III '69 '99 C.339 A.B. L.145 J.D. [Bartlit B.H.P.&S.]
Heatwole, Mark M., (AV) '48 '72 C&L.902 B.A., J.D. [Winston&S.]
Heavrin, Thomas C. '48 '74 C.1150 B.A. L.421 J.D.
(adm. in KY; not adm. in IL) Merit Systems Protec. Bd.
Hebbeln, Mark F. '70 '97 C.896 B.A. L.245 J.D. [Gardner C.&D.]
Hebeisen, Keith A., (AV) '53 '83 C.339 B.A. L.209 J.D. [Clifford]
Hebenstreit, Sandra L. '50 '81 C.347 B.A. L.209 J.D. [Righeimer M.&C.]
Heber, Albert H. '53 '79 C.959 B.A. L.365 J.D. 8430 W. Bryn Mawr Ave.
Hechinger, John F. '28 '57 C.424 B.S. L.146 J.D. [Ⓒ Rock F.]
Hecht, Edward M. '38 '65 C.210 A.B. L.146 J.D. Treas., The Hecht Co., Inc.
Hecht, F. Thomas, (AV) '— '75 C.813 A.B. L.145 J.D. [Ungaretti&H.]
Hechtman, Jeffrey A. '64 '89 C.659 B.S.E. L.145 J.D. [Horwood M.&B.]
Heck, Judith Rea, (AV) '— '77 C.319 B.A. L.982 J.D. Northern Trust Corporation
Heck, R. Chris '— '01 C.31 B.A. L.145 J.D. [Ⓐ Kirkland&E.]
Heckathorne, Holly E. '61 '87 C.105 B.S.B.A. L.665 J.D. 430 N. Michigan Ave.
Heckelman, David R. '47 '76 C.234 B.A. L.339 J.D.
Chicago Law Bulletin Publishing Co.
Hector, Brian D. '61 '89 C.339 B.A. L.146 J.D. [Morgan,L.&B.]
Hedberg, Victor, (AV) '05 '28 C&L.597 M.A., J.D. 3 1st Nat. Pl.
Hedberg, Tobin, Flaherty & Whalen, A Professional Corporation, (AV)
Three First Natl. Plz., Ste. 2150
Hedblom, John M. '53 '83 C.339 B.S. L.146 J.D. United Airlines Inc.
Hedeen, Herbert V., Jr. '42 '69 C.388 B.A. L.339 J.D. 1117 W. Belmont Ave.
Hedeen, Karen L. '67 '99 C.339 B.S. L.424 J.D. [Ⓐ Tressler,S.M.&P.]
Hedges, John A. '58 '89 C.309 A.B. L.273 J.D. 421 W. Melrose
Hedges, Leslie Lackey '70 '01 C.990 B.A. L.879 J.D. 180 N. Lasalle St., Ste. 2901
Hedges, Ryan S. '71 '01 C.597 B.S. L.800 J.D.
(adm. in CA; not adm. in IL) [Ⓐ Eimer S.K.&S.]
Hedin, Eliott M. '74 '00 C.339 B.S. L.910 J.D. [Ⓐ Hinshaw&C.]
Hedlund, Reuben L., (AV) '36 '59 C.207 B.A. L.976 LL.B. [Hedlund&H.]
Hedlund & Hanley, LLC, (AV) 77 West Wacker Drive, Suite 4800
Hedman, Jared E. '— '02 C.589 B.S. L.424 J.D. [Ⓐ Kirkland&E.]
Hedrich, John F. '66 '92 C.350 B.A. L.424 J.D. [Ⓐ R.B.Patterson]
Hedrick, Michael S. '69 '01 C.34 B.S. L.365 J.D. [Ⓐ Reibman,H.B.H.&O.]
Heeren, Geoffrey James '74 '00
C.145 B.A. L.569 J.D. Sr. Atty., National Center on Poverty Law
Heffernan, Kim M. '67 '92 C.174 B.S. L.742 J.D. [Ⓐ Pretzel&S.]
Heffernan, Robert T. '71 '02 C.861 B.S. L.339 J.D. [Ⓐ DLPiper R.G.C.U.]
Heffernan, William P. '— '92 C.846 B.S.S. L.744 J.D. [Ⓐ O'Hagan,S.&A.]
Heffner, Anastasia '69 '00 C.339 B.S. L.209 J.D. [Ⓐ Brinks H.G.&L.] (See Pat. Sect.)
Heffner, Matthew T. '71 '97 C.347 B.A. L.846 J.D. [Ⓐ Susman,W.&W.]
Hefler, Marcie L. '68 '93 C.966 B.A. L.365 J.D. [Ⓐ Pretzel&S.]
Hefner, M. Daniel '67 '96 C.340 B.A. L.339 J.D. [Leydig,V.&M.] (See Pat. Sect.)
Hefter, Daniel S., (AV) '56 '80 C.339 B.A. L.477 J.D. [Fox,H.S.L.&C.]
Heftman, Jeffery M. '74 '02 C&L.339 B.A., J.D. [Ⓐ Vedder,P.K.&K.]
Heftman, Lawrence H. '— '04 C.1365 B.A. L.1565 J.D. [Ⓢ Schiff H.]
Heftman, Mark A. '75 '03 C.549 B.A. L.365 J.D. 212 N Canal St Ste 300
Heftman, Ronald N., (AV) '45 '71 C.910 B.S.B.A. L.597 J.D. [R.N.Heftman]
Heftman, Ronald N., PC, (AV) 30 N. LaSalle St., Ste. 2024
Hefty, Thomas L., (AV) '55 '80 C&L.339 A.B., J.D. [McDermott W.&E.]
Hegarty, James J. '71 '99 C.228 A.B. L.145 J.D. [Ⓐ Wildman,H.A.&D.]
Hegarty, Terrence K., (AV) '44 '69 C&L.424 B.S., J.D. [T.K.Hegarty&Assoc.]
Hegarty, Terrence K., & Associates, Ltd., (AV) 3 1st Nat. Plza., Ste. 27D
Hegedus, Lisa M. '70 '95 C.426 B.A. L.276 J.D. [Quinlan&C.]
Heggie, Corinne Cantwell '76 '02 C.339 B.A. L.209 J.D. [Ⓐ Hinshaw&C.]
Heglar, Ronald O. '51 '81 C.339 B.S. L.209 J.D. 10040 S. Eberhart
Hegy, Sheila Ann '41 '80 C.388 B.A. L.339 J.D. Asst. Reg. Coun., Dept. of HHS
Heidelberger, Brian L. '69 '94 C.347 B.S. L.146 J.D. [Winston&S.]
Heiden, Thomas J., (AVⓉ) '— '71 C.602 B.A. L.1556 J.D. [Latham&W.]
Heidenreich, Sarah E. '76 '01 C.339 B.A. L.221 J.D. [Bollinger,R.&G.]
Heidenry, Eve M. '71 '96 C.276 B.S.F.S. L.597 J.D.
Asst. VP & Sr. Atty., LaSalle Bank Corporation
Heifetz, Elmer M. '12 '37 C.477 A.B. L.145 J.D. Rollins, Burdick, Hunter of Ill.
Heil, Stephen W., (AV) '65 '90 C.1151 B.A. L.339 J.D. [Iwan C.H.H.&V.]
Heil, Summer E. '69 '94 C.347 B.A. L.209 J.D. [Williams M.&J.]
Heilizer, Glenn E. '59 '87 C.347 B.A. L.273 J.D. [G.Heilizer]
Heilizer, Glenn, Law Offices of 5 N. Wabash Ave., Apt. 1304
Heilman, Shannon M. '64 '90 C.597 B.A. L.94 J.D. 150 N. Wacker Dr.
Heilmann, David M., (BV) '62 '87 C.339 B.S. L.209 J.D. [Clausen M.]
Heiman, Adam M. '76 '01 C.347 B.A. L.146 J.D. [Ⓐ T.S.Eisner]
Hein, Ronald J., Jr., (AV) '50 '75 C&L.602 B.A., J.D. [Franczek S.]
Heineke, Burke & Bodach, (AV) 2 N. La Salle St., Ste. 1110
Heineman, Ben W., (AV) '14 '36 C.477 L.597 LL.B. 9400 Sears Twr.‡
Heinig, Randy J. '71 '02 C.937 B.A. L.976 J.D. [Ⓐ Barack F.K.P.&N.]
Heinke, Matthew Darren '78 '03 C&L.339 B.S., J.D. [Ⓐ Holland&K.]
Heinle, Mark R. F. '78 '04 C.436 B.A. L.94 J.D. [Ⓐ Ancel,G.D.B.D.&R.]
Heinle, Michael J. '— '02 C.424 B.A. L.146 J.D. [Ⓐ Litchfield C.]
Heinrich, Brett D., (BV) '59 '86 C.339 B.S. L.209 J.D. [Meckler B.&T.]
Heintskill, Christopher M. '74 '00 C.424 B.A. L.46 J.D. [Ⓐ Levenfeld P.]
Heintz, George W., (BVⓉ) '46 '72
C.894 B.A. L.339 J.D. [Bowman,H.B.&V.] (⊙Merrillville, IN)
Heintzelman, Yvette, (AV) '— '89 C&L.190 B.A., J.D. [Ⓒ Seyfarth S.]
Heinz, Ann B. '65 '90 C.339 B.A. L.477 J.D. Dearborn Fin. Publishing, Inc.
Heinz, John P. '36 '62 C.910 A.B. L.976 LL.B.
Prof. of Law, Northwestern Univ. School of Law
Heinz, Kurt J. '— '80 C.602 B.A. L.245 J.D. [Arnstein&L.]
Heinz, William D., (AV) '47 '73 C.357 B.S. L.339 J.D. [Jenner&B.]
Heinz Huston, Rebecca '76 '03 C.966 B.A. L.339 J.D. [Ⓐ Burke,W.M.&S.]
Heinze, Stephen Lawrence '58 '83 C.424 B.B.A. L.309 J.D. Asst. U.S. Atty.
Heiser, James '— '03 C.223 B.A. L.602 J.D. [Ⓐ Chapman&C.]
Heisler, David M. '56 '80 C.339 B.A. L.146 J.D. Mng. Atty., Heller Fin. Inc.
Heisler, Quentin G., Jr., (AV) '43 '68 C&L.309 A.B., J.D. [McDermott W.&E.]
Heiss, Cheryl L. '75 '00 C.210 B.A. L.146 J.D. [Ⓐ Fisher K.]
Heiss, David E. '70 '97 C.210 B.A. L.365 J.D. [Fisher K.]
Heiss, Frederick P. '40 '65 C.801 B.S. L.365 LL.B. 188 W. Randolph St.
Heiss, Robin, (AV) '— '69 C.145 B.A. L.569 J.D. [Sachnoff&W.]
Heist, Robert C. '64 '90 C.339 B.A. L.365 J.D. 120 South Riverside Plaza
Heitz, Philip G., (AV) '49 '74 C.597 B.S.J. L.424 J.D. [Garretson&S.]
Hejna, David T. '53 '78 C&L.477 A.B., J.D. [Ⓒ DLPiper R.G.C.U.]
Helbraun, Fred '40 '66 C.1016 B.A. L.209 LL.B. 120 W. Madison St.
Held, John J., (AV) '38 '65
C.679 B.S.M.E. L.276 J.D. [McAndrews,H.&M.] (See Pat. Sect.)
Held, Robert S. '57 '96 C.107 B.A. L.209 J.D. [Harrison&H.]
Heldt, Bruce A. '50 '74 C.145 B.A. L.339 J.D. Coopers & Lybrand
Helenhouse, Colleen E. '69 '98 C.339 B.A. L.146 J.D. [Ⓐ McGuirewoods]
Helfand, Mark J. '46 '71 C.339 B.S. L.365 J.D. 180 N. LaSalle St.
Helfand, Marvin S., (AV) '36 '60 C&L.597 B.S., J.D. [Ⓒ Defrees&F.]
Helfer, Erica Tina '56 '80 C.910 A.B. L.733 J.D. [Ⓢ Katten M.R.]
Helfgot, Alvin J., (AV) '46 '74 C.339 B.A. L.424 J.D. [Deutsch,L.&E.]

Helfgot, Ira N., Law Offices of, (AV) '56 '82 C.589 B.A. L.209 J.D.
Three First National Plaza, 70 West Madison Street, Suite 3700, 60602
Telephone: 312-558-3013 Fax: 312-263-9104
Email: iralaw@aol.com
Commercial Litigation, Business Law, Contracts, Creditor's Rights, Civil Trial and Plaintiff's Professional Liability, Legal Malpractice, Commodities, Securities, Investments.
See Professional Biographies, CHICAGO, ILLINOIS

Helis, Steven '— '80 C.339 B.A. L.209 J.D. [Querrey&H.]
Heller, Bennett R. '59 '84 C.339 B.A. L.424 J.D. [Wilson E.M.E.&D.]
Heller, David S., (AV) '— '78 C.597 B.A. L.276 J.D. [Latham&W.]
Heller, John A., (AV) '52 '82 C.98 B.S. L.146 J.D. [Ⓒ Sidley A.B.&W.]
Heller, Paul M., (AV) '43 '68 C.20 L.146 LL.B. [Heller&F.]
Heller, Stanley J. '41 '88 C.367 A.B. L.597 J.D. [Cirignani H.H.&L.]
Heller, Stephen B., (AV) '55 '80
C.350 B.S.Aero E. L.339 J.D. [Cook,A.M.M.C.&M.] (See Pat. Sect.)
Heller, Todd A. '53 '78
C.367 B.A. L.209 J.D. 25 East Washington, Suite 925 (⊙Deerfield)

Heller and Frisone, Ltd., (AV)
33 North LaSalle Street, Suite 1200, 60602
Telephone: 312-236-3644 Fax: 312-236-3595 Email: nick@hellerfrisone.com
Email: paul@hellerfrisone.com URL: http://www.hellerandfrisone.com
Paul M. Heller; Nicholas J. Frisone;—Jason R. Ziemann.
Commercial and Consumer Collection Litigation.
Representative Clients: Avondale Federal Savings; Banc One Financial; City of Chicago; Eagle Finance Co.; Great American Finance Co.; Jewel Food Stores, Inc.; Old Kent Bank; The Peoples Gas Light & Coke Co.; State Farm Insurance Co.
See Professional Biographies, CHICAGO, ILLINOIS

Hellerman, Richard K. '— '87 C.910 B.A. L.245 J.D. [Arnstein&L.]
Hellige, James R., (AV) '— '76 C.742 B.A. L.602 J.D. [Foley&L.]
Hellman, Jean A. '51 '79 C.424 B.A. L.209 J.D. Loyola University
Hellman, Joel M. '50 '78 C&L.145 B.A., J.D. 122 S. Michigan Ave., Ste. 1850
Hellman, Michael P. '72 '99 C.1016 B.A. L.365 J.D. [Ⓐ Anesi,O.R.N.&K.]
Helman, Robert A., (AV) '34 '56 C&L.597 B.S.L., LL.B. [Mayer,B.R.&M.]
Helmer, Colleen M. '69 '96 C.879 B.A. L.365 J.D. [Ⓐ Sidley A.B.&W.]
Helmholz, Richard '40 '65 C.674 A.B. L.309 LL.B.
(adm. in MO; not adm. in IL) Univ. of Chicago
Helmink, Meri-jo '54 '83 C.323 B.A. L.1187 J.D. Ticor Title Ins. Co.
Helms, Brenda Porter, (AV) '53 '84 C.965 B.A. L.424 J.D.
Gen. Coun., Albany Bank & Trust Company, N.A.
Helms, F. James '— '73 C.679 B.S. L.347 J.D. [Tenney&B.]
Helms, Judith Fournie, (AV) '52 '78 C&L.209 B.A., J.D. [Tressler,S.M.&P.]
Helms, Lawrence, (AV) '51 '78 C.945 B.A. L.893 J.D. [Swanson,M.&B.]
Helou, Elie '— '73 C.1016 B.S. L.146 J.D. Asst. Gen. Coun., Peoples Energy Corp.
Helsinger, Howard M., (AV) '40 '78 C.311 B.A. L.145 J.D. [Sugar,F.&F.]
Helt, Christopher '69 '94 C&L.424 B.A., J.D. 325 W. Huron St., Ste. 515A
Helton, Jonathan R. '75 '01 C&L.383 B.A., J.D. [Ⓐ DLPiper R.G.C.U.]
Helton, Tonita M. '— '01 C.221 B.A. L.352 J.D. [Ⓐ Freeborn&P.]
Heltzer, Michael '60 '87 C.174 B.A. L.597 J.D. 4853 N. Ravenwood Ave.
Helwig, Ted S., (AV) '54 '80 C.1106 B.A. L.424 J.D. [Katten M.R.]
Hemeryck, Sondra A. '— '91 C.976 B.A. L.309 J.D. [Schiff H.]
Hemmer, James P. '42 '67 C.436 A.B. L.309 LL.B. [Ⓒ Bell,B.&L.]
Hemmesch, Donald F., Jr., (AV) '53 '78 C.177 B.A. L.365 J.D. [Smith,H.B.&B.]
Hemming, Seth M., (BV) '— '85 C.339 B.S. L.424 J.D. [Sachnoff&W.]
Hemmingsen, Amy Jo '62 '92 C.352 B.A. L.190 J.D. [Ⓐ Garretson&S.]
Hender, George S. '42 '69 C.901 B.A. L.904 J.D.
(adm. in PA; not adm. in IL) Sr. Exec. V.P., The Options Clearing Corp.
Hendershot, Michael K. '75 '01 C.608 B.S. L.893 J.D. [Ⓐ Brinks H.G.&L.]
Henderson, Henry L., (AV) '52 '82 C.385 A.B. L.910 J.D. Comr., Dept. of Envir.
Henderson, James A., (AV) '41 '67
C.477 A.B. L.966 J.D. V.P. & Corp. Coun., Amer. Hospital Assn.
Henderson, Janet E., (AV) '56 '82 C.623 B.A. L.178 J.D. [Sidley A.B.&W.]
Henderson, Jeffry M. '58 '85 C.746 B.A. L.365 J.D. [Henderson&L.]
Henderson, John R. '50 '80 C.150 L.365 J.D. Dept. of Planning & Development
Henderson, Kyle W., (AV) '— '86 C.385 A.B. L.477 J.D. [Chapman&C.]
Henderson, Matthew R., (AV) '66 '92 C.602 B.A. L.494 J.D. [Hinshaw&C.]
Henderson, Ryan M. '71 '97 C.347 B.S. L.424 J.D. [Ⓐ Lord,B.&B.]
Henderson, Victor P., (BV) '61 '88 C.659 B.S.E. L.276 J.D. [Holland&K.]

Henderson & Lyman, (AV)
175 West Jackson Boulevard Suite 240, 60604 ⊙
Telephone: 312-986-6960 Fax: 312-986-6961
Email: administrator@Henderson-Lyman.com URL: http://www.henderson-lyman.com
Members of Firm: Jeffry M. Henderson; Mark M. Lyman; Joseph A. Girardi; Douglas E. Arend; Robert Christie. Associates: Anthony A. Cavallo; Ryan Fox; Brian E. Lewis; Kurt Newsom; Michael D. Sefton; Scott P. Slykas; Andrea Stulgies-Clauss.
Practice concentrated in Commodities, Securities, Corporate Transactions, Commercial and Residential Real Estate Development, Commercial Litigation and Transaction, Environmental Law and Estate Planning.
New York, N.Y. Office: 152 West 57th Street, 18th Floor, 10019. Telephone: 212-957-4600.
See Professional Biographies, CHICAGO, ILLINOIS

Hendricks, James F., Jr., (AV) '44 '73 C.347 B.S. L.424 J.D. [Fisher&P.]
Hendrickson, Cara Ann '— '01 C.597 B.A. L.309 J.D. [Ⓐ Hughes S.P.R.&D.]
Hendrickson, James J., II '73 '04 C.723 B.A. L.477 J.D. [Ⓐ McGuirewoods]
Hendrickson, John C. '43 '68 C.145 B.A. L.178 LL.B. Reg. Atty., EEOC
Hendrickson, John P. '55 '80 C.791 B.S. L.602 J.D. [McDermott W.&E.]
Hendrickson, Michele F. '66 '92 C.801 B.S. L.365 J.D. Asst. Pub. Def.
Hendrickson, Nancy L., (AV) '61 '91 C.597 B.S.G.S. L.209 J.D. [Gardner C.&D.]
Henegan, James K., (AV) '56 '81 C.602 B.S. L.339 J.D. [Ⓐ Schain,B.R.&C.]
Heneghan, Patrick J. '57 '83 C.801 B.S. L.128 J.D. [Schopf&W.]
Henehan, Thomas J. '— '97 C.339 B.S. L.309 J.D. [Schiff H.]
Henehan, Donovan & Isaacson, Ltd., (AV) 150 S. Wacker Dr.
Henely, John J., (AV) '44 '71 C.339 B.A. L.209 J.D. [J.J.Henely]
Henely, John J., Ltd., (AV) 60 E. Chestnut St.

Hengesbaugh, Brian '69 '95 C.910 B.A. L.494 J.D.
(adm. in IN; not adm. in IL) [Ⓐ Baker&M.]
Hengsbach, Bethany L. .... '72 '97 C.339 B.A. L.209 J.D. [Ⓐ Wildman,H.A.&D.]
Henmueller, Paul A. .... '67 '92 C.339 B.A. L.365 J.D. Litig. Coun., Aon Corporation
Henn, Julie L. .... '70 '03 C.317 B.A. L.94 J.D. [Ⓐ McCullough,C.&L.]
Henn, Kathleen T. .... '72 '98 C.602 B.A. L.424 J.D. [Ⓐ Klein,T.&J.]
Hennecke, Curt F. .... '69 '95 C.339 B.A. L.365 J.D. [Ⓐ Roddy,L.&Z.]
Hennelly, Thomas .... '50 '80 C.750 B.A. L.209 J.D. Supvr., Off. of State's Atty.
Henneman, Margaret M. '64 '91
C.720 B.A. L.1187 J.D. Staff Atty., Amer. Fam. Ins. Grp.
Hennessey, Gilbert H., Jr., (Ltd.), (AV) .... '16 '40 C&L.339 B.S., J.D. 1 IBM Plaza
Hennessy, Bernard J., (AV) .... '31 '56 C&L.424 B.S., J.D. 111 W. Wash. St.
Hennessy, Christopher S. .... '67 '96 C.589 B.S. L.365 J.D. [Meckler B.&T.]
Hennessy, Colleen M. .... '61 '86 C.602 B.A. L.309 J.D. [Lord,B.&B.]
Hennessy, Edward L., (BV) .... '— '94 C.589 B.A. L.1187 J.D. [Hennessy&R.]
Hennessy, J. Kevin, (AV) .... '51 '76 C.339 B.A. L.424 J.D. [Vedder,P.K.&K.]
Hennessy, Mary Ellen, (AV) .... '50 '79 C.706 B.A. L.276 J.D. [Katten M.R.]
Hennessy, Robert A., (AV) .... '21 '53 C&L.209 LL.B. 3501 W. Higgins Rd.
Hennessy, Robert J. .... '48 '73 C.339 B.S. L.209 J.D. 8501 W. Higgins
Hennessy, Thomas G., (BV) .... '— '88 C.338 B.S. L.365 J.D. [Hennessy&R.]
Hennessy, William J. .... '44 '79 C.339 B.A. L.1151 J.D. 111 W. Wash. St.

Hennessy & Roach, P.C., (AV)
Marquett Building, 140 S. Dearborn Street, Suite 520, 60603 ⊙
Telephone: 312-346-5310 Fax: 312-346-5330
Email: hennroach@hennessyroach.com URL: http://www.hennessyroach.com
Managing Partners: Thomas G. Hennessy; James P. Roach, II; Guy N. Maras. Partners: Joseph J. Higgins; Edward L. Hennessy; Michael P. Geary; Joseph A. Zwick; Mary Anne H. Capron; Sheryl R. Lapka; William J. Hawkins; James L. Clarke;—John C. Wilson; Natalie J. Romo; Thomas C. Flaherty; Jason D. Kolecke; Laura D. Hrubec; Christopher S. Crawford; Lisa R. Rozen; Maria L. Cappiello; James W. Lowry; Heather L. Boyer. Of Counsel: John J. Murphy, Jr.; P. Neill Petronella.
Languages: English, Spanish.
Workers Compensation Defense, including litigation, mediation and arbitration; Liability Defense, including insurance defense, construction accidents, post-structured work act; Employer Liability, retaliatory discharge; Premises Liability, industrial machinery, auto and truck, consumer products; Insurance Coverage, Transportation, Property Damage, Fire Loss, Motor Vehicle Accidents, Industrial Accidents; Civil, State and Federal Appeals, Industrial Commission Appeals.
St. Louis, Missouri Office: 720 Olive Street, Suite 2222, 63101. Telephone: 314-231-0770. Fax: 314-231-0990.
Springfield, Illinois Office: 2501 Chatham Road, Suite 220, 62704. Telephone: 217-726-0037. Fax 217-726-0137.

See Professional Biographies, CHICAGO, ILLINOIS

Hennig, Bernard A. .... '40 '64 C.723 A.B. L.365 LL.B. 77 W. Wash. St.
Hennig, Bernard A., Sr. .... '17 '39 C.723 L.365 LL.B. 77 W. Wash. St.
Hennig, Michael J., (AV) .... '56 '81 C.723 B.S. L.365 J.D. [Cassiday,S.&G.]
Henning, Beth A. '64 '89 C.339 A.B. L.879 J.D.
(adm. in IN; not adm. in IL) U.S. Envir. Protec. Agcy.
Henning, Grace W. .... '39 '65 C.477 A.B. L.309 J.D. 5723 S. Blackstone Ave.
Henning, Mark G., (AV) .... '53 '78 C.339 B.A. L.424 J.D. [Winston&S.]
Henninger, Jodi L., (AV) .... '69 '95 C.339 B.A. L.209 J.D. [Dykema G.P.]
Henrichs, Canella E., (BV) '46 '73 C.530 B.A. L.365 J.D.
Asst. U.S. Atty., Dept. of Just.
Henrikson, Mark Allen .... '62 '97 C.357 B.M. L.801 J.D. LaSalle Bank N.A./ABN Amro
Henry, Brian T., (AV) .... '54 '80 C.424 B.A. L.339 J.D. [Pretzel&S.]
Henry, Frederick E. .... '47 '72 C&L.228 A.B., J.D. [Baker&M.]
Henry, Gregory T. .... '73 '00 C.37 B.A. L.209 J.D. [Ⓐ Fraterrigo,B.F.&K.]
Henry, James F. .... '51 '77 C.746 B.A. L.209 J.D. Cir. J.

Henry, Kenneth A., (AV) '51 '76 C.966 B.S. L.146 J.D.
120 West Madison Street, Suite 600, 60602-4106
Telephone: 312-857-0100 Fax: 312-857-1157 URL: http://www.kahlaw.com
Email: khenry@kahlaw.com URL: http://www.lawyers.com/kahlaw
Labor and Employment Law, OSHA, Wage and Hour Matters, Sexual Harassment, Employment Discrimination, Wrongful Termination, Union Management Relations, Real Estate, Commercial Real Estate, Residential Real Estate, Buying and Selling a House or Business, Bankruptcy, Chapter 7, Chapter 11, Corporate and Commercial Law, Litigation, Alternative Dispute Resolution, Mediation.

See Professional Biographies, CHICAGO, ILLINOIS

Henry, Robert J. .... '50 '75 C&L.424 B.A., J.D. [Scopelitis,G.L.&H.]
Henry, Scott W. .... '75 '00 C.880 B.A. L.124 J.D. [Ⓐ Segal M.S.&M.]
Henry-Turner, Kelly M. .... '72 '03 C.546 B.A. L.424 J.D. [Ⓐ Richardson,S.B.&M.]
Hensel, Paul H. .... '48 '72 C.339 B.S. L.477 J.D. [Winston&S.]
Henson, Emily J. .... '74 '02 C.201 B.A. L.209 J.D. [Ⓐ Katten M.R.]
Hepburn, Laura A. .... '— '95 C.339 B.S. L.597 J.D. [Kirkland&E.]
Hepburn, Michael T. .... '68 '95 C.184 B.S. L.209 J.D. [Gordon&G.L.]
Heppermann, Roger A. '— '92 C.502 B.S. L.597 J.D.
[Marshall,G.&B.] (See Pat. Sect.)
Hepplewhite, David W. .... '51 '81 C.170 B.A. L.221 J.D. [Ⓐ P.D.Kasdin]
Herald, J. Patrick, (AV) .... '47 '72 C.363 A.B. L.602 J.D. [Baker&M.]
Heraty, Peter E. .... '43 '77 C.436 B.A. L.424 J.D. Chicago Tribune Co.
Herber, Linda J. .... '56 '81 C.741 B.A. L.209 J.D. [Jaros,T.&O.]
Herbert, Antonia Rago, (Mrs.) .... '18 '38 C&L.209 B.S., LL.B. 1150 N. Lake Shore Dr.‡
Herbert, Barry S. .... '52 '81 C.597 B.S. L.209 J.D. Library of the U.S. Cts.
Herbert, Margaret L. .... '47 '77 C.383 B.A. L.424 J.D. Admin. Law J., E.E.O.C.
Herbert, T. Ronald .... '38 '64 C&L.209 A.B., J.D. 5944 N. Milwaukee Ave.‡
Herbert, Wm. Carlisle, (AV) .... '— '76 C.674 A.B. L.597 J.D. [Foley&L.]
Herbst, David I., (AV) .... '40 '64 C.339 B.A. L.145 J.D. [Butler R.S.&B.]
Hercule, Gail M. .... '— '01 C.209 B.S. L.365 J.D. 206 South Jefferson
Herendrother, Thos. E. .... '31 '58 C&L.597 B.S., J.D. 4827 W. Belmoral Ave.
Hergott, Bradley D. .... '78 '03 C.801 B.A. L.477 J.D. [Ⓐ Lord,B.&B.]
Heriaud, Neal, (AV) .... '54 '81 C.228 A.B. L.145 J.D. 150 N. Michigan Ave., Ste. 2700
Hering, Glenn Z. .... '52 '77 C.30 B.A. L.365 J.D. [Dykema G.P.]
Herkal, Craig J. .... '74 '00 C.197 B.A. L.862 J.D. Off. of the Gen. Coun., Dept. of HHS
Hermalyn, Lawrence L. '50 '75
C.563 B.A. L.1119 J.D. Asst. Gen. Coun., Fleet Bus. Credit Corp.
Herman, Harvey R., (BV) .... '55 '82 C&L.477 B.A., J.D. [Clausen M.]
Herman, Jack J., P.C. .... '26 '51 C.347 L.145 J.D. 180 N. Wacker Dr.
Herman, Nancy .... '— '79 C.393 B.A. L.146 J.D. Asst. Dean, Chicago-Kent Coll. of Law
Herman, Sidney N., (AV) .... '53 '78 C.311 B.A. L.597 J.D. [Bartlit B.H.P.&S.]
Hermanek, Kevin J., (BV) .... '54 '81 C.339 B.S. L.209 J.D. 417 S. Dearborn
Hermann, Donald H. J., III '43 '68 C.813 A.B. L.178 J.D.
Prof. of Law & Dir. of Health Law Institute, DePaul Univ.
Hermann, Susan M. .... '62 '87 C.66 A.B. L.597 J.D. [Pedersen&H.]
Hermann, William C. .... '— '90 C.602 B.A. L.347 J.D. [Chapman&C.]
Hermansen, Barbara E., (AV) .... '— '82 C.187 B.A. L.597 J.D. [Ⓒ Schiff H.]
Hermanson, Christopher S. .... '69 '01 C.339 B.S. L.146 J.D. [Ⓐ Seyfarth S.]
Hermes, Robert N., (AV) .... '54 '79 C.347 B.A. L.209 J.D. [Butler R.S.&B.]
Hermsen, Michael L. .... '57 '86 C.436 B.S. L.966 J.D. [Mayer,B.R.&M.]
Hernandez, Angelita E. .... '— '04 C.350 B.A. L.209 J.D. [Ⓐ Katten M.R.]
Hernandez, Louis R. .... '— '96 C.339 B.S. L.813 J.D. [Kirkland&E.]
Hernandez, Marisel A. .... '56 '82 C.262 B.A. L.569 J.D. [Jacobs,B.O.S.&H.]
Hernandez, Michael J. .... '58 '86 C.424 B.A. L.477 J.D. [Franczek S.]
Hernandez, Nora M. .... '72 '98 C.597 B.S. L.352 J.D. [Ⓐ Evans,L.S.&M.]
Heroux, Francis A., (AV) .... '34 '59 C.742 B.S. L.597 J.D. [Ⓒ Clausen M.]
Heroy, David F., (AV) .... '51 '76 C&L.477 A.B., J.D. [Bell,B.&L.]
Heroy, Donna Tuke .... '50 '80 C.347 B.A. L.209 J.D. Alert Publications, Inc.
Herpe, David A., (AV) .... '53 '78 C.339 B.A. L.145 J.D. [McDermott W.&E.]
Herrington, Elizabeth B. .... '71 '97 C.473 B.A. L.339 J.D. [Ⓐ McDermott W.&E.]
Herriott, Allison Verderber .... '75 '04 C.951 B.A. L.597 J.D. [Ⓐ Skadden,A.S.M.&F.]
Herrmann, John R., (AV) '55 '80
C.880 B.A. L.145 J.D. V.P. & Sr. Coun., Bank of America
Herrmann, Kathleen H. .... '56 '83 C.339 M.U.P. L.146 J.D. City Transit Auth.
Herrmann, Kristina K. .... '— '04 C.1150 B.A. L.1119 J.D. [Ⓐ Mayer,B.R.&M.]
Herron, Russell J. '68 '95 C&L.477 B.A., J.D.
Assoc. Gen. Coun., The Univ. of Chicago
Herseth, Stephen S., (AV) .... '47 '82 C.976 B.A. L.146 J.D. [Schwartz C.]
Hersh, Mark S. .... '— '83 C.339 B.A. L.813 J.D. [Sachnoff&W.]
Hershman, Don S. .... '57 '82 C.339 B.S. L.424 J.D. [Much S.F.D.A.&R.]
Hershman, Ellyn A. .... '42 '72 C.966 B.B.A. L.1066 J.D. 10754 S. Wood
Hershman, Stuart, (AV) .... '59 '84 C&L.477 B.A., J.D. [DLPiper R.G.C.U.]
Herst, Lawrence A. .... '53 '83 C.454 B.A. L.424 J.D. Pres., Lawrence Financial Assoc.
Hertel, Robert G. .... '— '85 C.475 B.S. L.910 J.D. [Ⓒ DLPiper R.G.C.U.]
Hertz, Jack A., (AV) .... '49 '75 C.665 B.A. L.365 J.D. 205 W. Randolph St., Ste. 1630
Hertzberg, William A. .... '33 '57 C.339 L.209 LL.B. 33 N. Dearborn, 24th Fl.
Herzel, Leo, (AV) .... '23 '52 C.352 A.B. L.145 J.D. [Ⓒ Mayer,B.R.&M.]
Herzog, Adam .... '— '04 C.659 B.S. L.145 J.D. [Ⓐ Latham&W.]
Herzog, Jordan .... '61 '93 C.339 B.S.C.S. L.209 J.D. [Ⓐ Greenberg T.] (Pat.)
Herzog, Peter F., (AV) .... '59 '85 C.966 B.S. L.146 J.D. [Michael B.&F.]
Hess, Elizabeth S. .... '— '04 C&L.145 A.B., J.D. [Ⓐ Kirkland&E.]
Hess, Glen E., (AV) '— '67 C.188 B.A. L.309 LL.B.
[Kirkland&E.] (⊙New York, NY)
Hess, Henry H. .... '72 '02 C.608 B.A. L.999 J.D. [Ⓐ Tabet D.&R.]
Hess, Mary J., (BV) .... '59 '91 C.700 B.A. L.209 J.D. [Hinshaw&C.]
Hess, Patrick C. .... '64 '91 C.494 B.A. L.339 J.D. [Ⓐ Ellison,N.Z.&A.]
Hess, Richard Jay '43 '69 C.645 B.S. L.146 J.D.
Supervisory Atty., Legal Assistance Found. of Chicago
Hess, Sidney J., Jr., (AV) .... '10 '32 C&L.145 Ph.B., J.D. [Ⓒ Seyfarth S.]
Hesse, Carolyn S., (AV) .... '— '83 C.339 B.S. L.209 J.D. [Barnes&T.]
Hesse, Channing Blair .... '68 '94 C.589 B.A. L.146 J.D. [Ⓒ Shefsky&F.]
Hessell, Scott F. .... '75 '01 C.477 B.A. L.145 J.D. [Ⓐ Kirkland&E.]
Hesser, Jeffrey A. .... '72 '98 C.502 B.A. L.209 J.D. [Ⓐ Cassiday,S.&G.]
Hession, Christopher D. .... '71 '97 C.347 B.S. L.209 J.D. [Cummins&H.]
Hesterberg, Brett A., (AV) '59 '84
C&L.339 B.S.E.E., J.D. [Leydig,V.&M.] (See Pat. Sect.)
Heston, Kristopher S. .... '56 '90 C.234 B.A. L.339 J.D. Sr. Atty., Chicago M.R.O., S.E.C.
Hetherington, W. Joseph, (AV) .... '47 '77 C.397 B.A. L.309 J.D. [Lewis,D.&H.]
Hetler, Dennis W. .... '40 '66 C.597 B.S. L.424 J.D. [McCracken,W.d.&H.]
Hetman, Joseph E. .... '45 '75 C.339 B.S. L.365 J.D. 7657 W. Ardmore Ave.
Hettinger, Lee T., (BV) .... '41 '66 C.436 B.A. L.477 J.D. [Dykema G.P.]
Hetz, Joseph F. .... '72 '96 C.597 B.S.E.E. L.477 J.D. [Brinks H.G.&L.] (See Pat. Sect.)
Hetzel, Daniel A. .... '— '04 C.597 B.A. L.145 J.D. [Ⓐ Morgan,L.&B.]
Hetzler, Mark W., (AV) '66 '93
C.597 B.S.M.E L.424 J.D. [Fitch,E.T.&F.] (See Pat. Sect.)
Heuberger, John H., (AV) .... '48 '74 C.589 B.S. L.472 J.D. [DLPiper R.G.C.U.]
Heuberger Yura, Julie .... '73 '98 C.352 B.A. L.209 J.D. [Ⓐ Franczek S.]
Heverin, Allison S. .... '72 '97 C.478 B.A. L.602 J.D. 333 West Wacker Drive, Suite 500
Heverin, Timothy J. .... '— '97 C&L.602 B.S., J.D. [Ⓐ Jones D.]
Hewitt, Carrie E. .... '56 '80 C.597 B.S.J. L.424 J.D. 225 N. Michigan Ave., 11th Fl.
Hewitt, Douglass G., (AV) .... '55 '82 C.966 B.S. L.424 J.D. [Schuyler,R.&Z.]
Hewitt, Sarah J. .... '59 '86 C.339 B.S.W. L.145 J.D. Atty., Chicago M.R.O., S.E.C.
Hextell, Julie Marie .... '66 '93 C.424 B.A. L.209 J.D. 550 W. Washington Blvd., Ste. 300
Heyda, Clifton J. .... '74 '02 C.339 B.A. L.846 J.D. [Ⓐ Jenner&B.]
Heyda, James J. .... '37 '66 C.560 B.A. L.365 J.D. Cir. J.
Heyde, Christina R. .... '66 '92 C.309 A.B. L.597 J.D. Northwestern Univ. Sch. of Law
Heyde, John M. .... '65 '95 C.309 A.B. L.145 J.D. [Ⓐ Sidley A.B.&W.]
Heydemann, Helaine Wachs, (AV) '— '73 C.112 A.B. L.813 J.D.
[Wildman,H.A.&D.]
Heyer, David J., Jr. .... '63 '89 C.209 B.S. L.146 J.D. 212 W. Washington St., Apt. 908
Heyke, J. Ericson, III .... '43 '93 C.976 B.S. L.145 J.D. [Ⓒ Winston&S.]
Heyman, Glenn R., (AV) .... '30 '53 C.339 L.146 LL.B. [Crane,H.S.W.&C.]
Heyman, Michael G. .... '45 '72 C.831 B.A. L.273 J.D. Prof., John Marshall Law Sch.
Heyman, Rachel C. .... '63 '90 C.659 B.A. L.145 J.D. [Ⓐ Nadler,P.&M.]
Heyman, Scott J., (AV) .... '62 '87 C.659 B.S. L.145 J.D. [Sidley A.B.&W.]
Heyman, Steven J. '59 '86 C&L.309 A.B., J.D.
(adm. in PA; not adm. in IL) Assoc. Prof. of Law, Chicago-Kent Coll. of Law
Heymann, Idrienne L. .... '23 '45 C.680 L.575 LL.B. 105 W. Madison (⊙Highland Park)
Heyne, Robert J., (AV) .... '53 '79 C.927 B.B. L.365 J.D. [Tressler,S.M.&P.]
Heyrman, Mark J. .... '49 '77 C.339 B.A. L.145 J.D. Univ. of Chgo. Law Sch.
Heytow, Richard D., (AV) .... '47 '77 C.339 B.A. L.146 J.D. [Crystal,H.&W.]
Hianik, Mark W., (AV) '60 '87 C.339 B.S. L.424 J.D.
V.P./Asst. Gen. Coun. & Asst. Secy., Tribune Co.
Hibbard, Tamara K., (AV) .... '68 '93 C.473 B.S. L.209 J.D. [Schain,B.R.&C.]
Hibben, David A. .... '60 '87 C.208 B.A. L.339 J.D. 1130 N Dearborn, Ste. 1405
Hickel, Susan S. '— '92 C.338 B.A. L.209 J.D.
Sr. Corp. Coun., SSA Global Technologies, Inc.
Hickey, James J. .... '62 '88 C.226 B.A. L.146 J.D. [Meckler B.&T.]
Hickey, John T., Jr. (P.C.), (AV) .... '— '77 C.276 A.B. L.145 J.D. [Kirkland&E.]
Hickey, Peter J., III, (AV) .... '45 '76 C.415 B.A. L.365 J.D. [Hickey&N.]
Hickey, Richard J., III, (AV) .... '— '80 C&L.339 B.A., J.D. [Hickey,M.&Assoc.]
Hickey, Timothy A. .... '64 '90 C.210 B.A. L.260 J.D. [Hinshaw&C.]

Hickey, Melia & Associates, Chartered, (AV) BR
77 West Washington Street, Suite 800, 60602
Telephone: 312-422-9400 Fax: 312-422-9410
Email: Firm@hmklawfirm.com URL: http://www.hmalawfirm.com
Richard J. Hickey, III; Edward J. Melia;—Christopher R. Zink; Gabriel P. Hardy; Kelly Maureen O'Malley; Kristin A. Ahmadian. Counsel: Daniel C. Hofert.
General, Civil Trial and Appellate Practice. Medical Malpractice, Commercial Litigation, Criminal, Casualty Litigation, Health Care and Hospital, Employment, Products Liability, Toxic Tort Law, Corporate Law and Estate Planning and Administration.

See Professional Biographies, CHICAGO, ILLINOIS

Hickey and Nemzin, (AV) .... 2536 S. California Ave.
Hickman, Kristin E. .... '69 '99 C.859 B.S. L.597 J.D. 333 West Wacker Drive
Hickman, Susan M., (BV) .... '51 '79 C.597 B.S. L.801 J.D. [Hinshaw&C.]
Hickok, Arthur F. .... '68 '94 C.674 A.B. L.145 J.D. [Ⓐ Sidley A.B.&W.]

Hicks, Stephen L. ... '69 '95 C.475 B.A. L.209 J.D. 79 W. Monroe St.
Hickstein-Foley, Donna ... '54 '80 C.694 A.B. L.209 J.D. [Foley&F.]
Hierl, Michael A., (AV) ... '53 '80 C.801 B.S. L.365 J.D. [Olson&H.] (See Pat. Sect.)
Higer, David W. '— '04 C.911 B.S. L.285 J.D.
(adm. in ID; not adm. in IL) [[A] Kirkland&E.]
Higgens, Cathy L. ... '73 '99 C.209 B.A. L.146 J.D. [[A] Hughes S.P.R.&D.]
Higginbotham, James M. '39 '64
C.473 B.S. L.365 J.D. Dept. Chair, Northwestern Business College‡
Higgins, Bart F. ... '65 '90 C.893 B.S. L.1356 J.D. [Arnett G.]
Higgins, Cathy Ann Buge' ... '49 '78 C.972 B.A. L.209 J.D. Asst. Atty. Gen.
Higgins, Denise M. '57 '84 C.742 B.A. L.589 J.D.
Sr. Coun., Bank One Corp. (Law Dept.)
Higgins, Francis J., (AV) ... '36 '61 C.321 A.B. L.309 LL.B. [Bell,B.&L.]
Higgins, Joseph J., (BV) ... '— '89 C.260 B.A. L.365 J.D. [Hennessy&R.]
Higgins, Lauretta J. ... '58 '89 C.388 B.A. L.146 J.D. 155 N. Harbor Dr.
Higgins, Peter F., (AV) ... '60 '86 C.352 B.A. L.209 J.D. [Lipkin&H.]
Higgins, Roger J. ... '— '97 C.763 B.A. L.1049 J.D. [Kirkland&E.]
Highland, Ashlee Bamber ... '72 '00 C.1119 B.S. L.146 J.D. 3333 W. Arlington
Hightman, Carrie Jankauer ... '57 '82 C.339 B.A. L.259 J.D. 225 W. Randolph St.
Hiken Lapens, Cynthia E. ... '58 '84 C&L.966 B.A., J.D. Amoco Corp.
Hilbert, Bethany A. ... '78 '03 C.967 B.A. L.209 J.D. [[A] Barlow,K.&D.]
Hilbert, Robert N., (AV) ... '47 '81 C.424 B.A. L.365 J.D. [Hilbert,L.&P.]
Hilbert, Lawler & Power, (AV) ... 36 South Wabash, Suite 1300
Hilborn, Harold B. ... '70 '95 C.477 B.A. L.597 J.D. [[A] Varga B.L.H.&C.]
Hilborn, Michael G., (AV) '43 '68 C.339 B.S. L.209 J.D.
Sr. V.P. & Gen. Coun., Urban Retail Properties Co.
Hild, Jeffrey ... '— '00 55 Monroe Street, Suite 4100
Hildebrand, Daniel G. ... '66 '93 C.103 A.B. L.976 J.D. [[C] Mayer,B.R.&M.]
Hildy, John T. ... '71 '96 C.339 A.B. L.597 J.D. [Mayer,B.R.&M.]
Hilfman, Louis, (AV) ... '43 '69 C.475 B.S. L.365 J.D. [Hilfman,M.&B.]

Hilfman, Martin & Barr, P.C., (AV)
Suite 1700, 33 North Dearborn Street, 60602
Telephone: 312-236-5207 Facsimile: 312-236-2321 URL: http://www.hfmblaw.com
URL: http://www.hfmb.com
Louis Hilfman; William F. Martin; William L. Barr, Jr.; Patrick J. Sullivan;—James P. Tutaj. Of Counsel: Philip E. Lane; Jerry L. Lambert.
Medical Malpractice, Legal Malpractice, Professional Negligence, Personal Injury, Airplane Crash Litigation, Automobile Accidents, Hospital Negligence, Automotive Products Liability, Wrongful Death, Railroad Accidents, Product Liability, Drug and Medical Device Litigation, Construction Injuries, General Negligence, Personal Injury, Workers Compensation and Commercial Litigation.
See Professional Biographies, CHICAGO, ILLINOIS

Hilicki, Michael S. ... '69 '94 C&L.352 B.A., J.D. [[A] Schad,D.&S.]
Hilke, Karen M. ... '77 '03 C.602 B.A. L.597 J.D. [[A] Mayer,B.R.&M.]
Hill, Arthur F., Jr., (AV) ... '53 '78 C.932 B.S. L.597 J.D. Chf. Dep. States Atty.
Hill, Celeste A., (AV) ... '60 '86 C.339 A.B. L.597 J.D. [Clausen M.]
Hill, Christopher R. '64 '92 C.145 B.A. L.569 J.D.
Atty. II, Chicago Board Options Exchange, Incorporated
Hill, Dana ... '74 '99 C.221 B.A. L.597 J.D. [[A] Seyfarth S.]
Hill, David R. ... '57 '84 C.174 B.A. L.966 J.D. [[C] Sidley A.B.&W.]
Hill, Deborah Fish, (AV) ... '56 '81 C&L.339 B.S., J.D. [Hill]
Hill, Everette M., Jr., (AV) ... '45 '75 C.937 A.B. L.365 J.D. [Klein,T.&J.]
Hill, Frank, (AV Ⓣ) ... '40 '66 C.1142 B.A. L.802 LL.B. [Hill G.&B.] ⊙
Hill, Hamilton H. ... '75 '01 C.378 B.G.S. L.145 J.D. [[A] Bartlit B.H.P.&S.]
Hill, James J., (AV) ... '37 '65 C.436 B.E.E. L.209 J.D. [Emrich&D.] (See Pat. Sect.)
Hill, Janile S. ... '73 '98 C.705 B.A. L.976 J.D. [[A] Mayer,B.R.&M.]
Hill, Joal M. '56 '87 C.836 B.A. L.838 J.D.
(adm. in NY; not adm. in IL)
The Park Rdge. Ctr. for the Study of Health, Faith & Ethics
Hill, John R. ... '13 '41 C&L.273 LL.B. 6314 S. Central Ave.
Hill, Jonathan ... '72 '98 C.886 B.S.M.E. L.945 J.D. [[A] Jenner&B.]
Hill, Lawrence N. ... '67 '00 C.1016 B.S.B.A. L.146 J.D. [[A] Gardner C.&D.]
Hill, Reginald J. ... '62 '94 C.864 B.S.E.E. L.365 J.D. [Jenner&B.] (Pat.)
Hill, Ronald Michael, (AV) '57 '82 C&L.424 B.S., J.D.
Sr. Asst. Atty., Metro. Water Reclamation Dist. of Greater Chicago
Hill, Stanley L., (AV) ... '49 '74 C.597 B.S. L.477 J.D. [S.L.Hill&Assoc.]
Hill, Thomas E., (AV) ... '44 '78 C.927 B.S. L.273 J.D. [Emrich&D.] (See Pat. Sect.)
Hill, Thomas R., (AV) ... '60 '85 C.339 B.A. L.424 J.D. [Dykema G.P.]
Hill, Warren P. ... '24 '49 C.112 B.S. L.597 J.D. 205 N. Mich. Ave.
Hill Gilstrap & Balson, A Professional Corporation, (AV Ⓣ)
303 West Madison, Suite 1050 (⊙Arlington, Fort Worth, TX)

Hill Law Offices, (AV)
211 East Ontario Suite 1225, 60611
Telephone: 312-640-6331 Fax: 312-640-6333
Email: deborahhill@msn.com
Deborah Fish Hill. Of Counsel: George Vernon.
Commercial Real Estate Leasing and Transactions.
See Professional Biographies, CHICAGO, ILLINOIS

Hill, Stanley L., P.C., & Associates, (AV)
10 South La Salle Street, Suite 1301, 60603
Telephone: 312-917-8888 Fax: 312-781-9401
Email: stanhill@megsinet.net URL: http://www.stanleyhilllaw.com
Stanley L. Hill.
Criminal Law, Felonies, Misdemeanors, Driving While Intoxicated, DUI, Assaults, Traffic Violations, Civil Litigation, Plaintiffs Personal Injury, Automobile Accidents, Truck Accidents, Wrongful Death, Municipal Law, School Law, Employment Law, Wrongful Termination, Harassment.
See Professional Biographies, CHICAGO, ILLINOIS

Hiller, David D. ... '53 '80 C&L.309 A.B., J.D. Tribune Corp.
Hiller, James B. ... '74 '02 C.1154 B.A. L.209 J.D. [[A] Cassiday,S.&G.]
Hiller, R. Matthew ... '75 '02 C.502 A.B. L.339 J.D. [[A] DLPiper R.G.C.U.]
Hilliard, David Craig, (AV) ... '37 '62 C.860 B.S. L.145 J.D. [Pattishall,M.N.H.&G.]
Hilliard, James P., (AV) ... '37 '64 C.602 A.B. L.424 J.D. 29 S. LaSalle St.
Hilliard, James W. ... '58 '83 C.597 B.A. L.339 J.D. Jud. Clk.
Hilliard-Smith, Emlee '— '88 C.788 B.A. L.588 J.D.
(adm. in WI; not adm. in IL) Sr. Coun., U.S. Secs. & Exchange Comm.
Hillier, Patricia B. ... '79 '03 C.1557 B.A. L.145 J.D. [[A] Seyfarth S.]
Hilliker, Donald B., (AV) ... '44 '69 C.424 B.S. L.597 J.D. [McDermott W.&E.]
Hillman, Barbara J., (AV) ... '42 '67 C&L.145 A.B., J.D. [Cornfield&F.]
Hillman, Lisa M. W. ... '— '99 L.260 J.D. [McDonnell B.H.&B.] (See Pat. Sect.)
Hillstrom, Bruce G. ... '39 '63 C.210 B.A. L.339 LL.B. [Hillstrom&H.]
Hillstrom, Scott L. ... '43 '68 C.210 B.A. L.339 J.D. [Hillstrom&H.]
Hillstrom & Hillstrom ... 11212 S. Western Ave.
Hillyard, Clare ... '31 '61 C.530 A.B. L.862 LL.B. Asst. Pub. Def.
Hilmert, James M. ... '77 '02 C.323 B.A. L.74 J.D. [[A] Winston&S.]
Himelfarb, Allison J. ... '72 '97 C.188 B.A. L.659 J.D. [[A] Sidley A.B.&W.]
Himelhoch, Richard C. '63 '90 C&L.966 B.S., J.D.
[Wallenstein W.&R.] (See Pat. Sect.)
Himley-Grandi, Dawn A. ... '54 '84 C.274 B.S. L.146 J.D. Liberty Mutual Ins. Co.
Hinchliff, James, (AV) '39 '72 C.221 B.Mus. L.145 J.D.
Sr. V.P. & Gen. Coun., Peoples Gas Light & Coke Co., The
Hinchman, Timothy K. ... '67 '94 C.339 B.S. L.365 J.D. [[A] Charity&Assoc.]
Hind, Anthony S. ... '— '99 C.1059 B.A. L.424 J.D. [[A] Marshall,G.&B.] (See Pat. Sect.)
Hinderman, Matthew M. ... '— '04 C.602 B.B.A. L.424 J.D. [[A] Katten M.R.]
Hindmand, Rick L., (BV) ... '59 '86 C.597 B.A. L.477 J.D. [Harris K.&G.]
Hinds, Melissa M. '78 '03 C.97 B.S. L.477 J.D.
(adm. in IN; not adm. in IL) [[A] Jenner&B.]
Hines, Erin B. ... '69 '98 C.966 B.A. L.424 J.D. [[A] Kane,C.&M.]
Hines, John L., Jr. ... '— '81 C.674 A.B. L.597 J.D. [Sachnoff&W.]
Hines, Justin M. ... '69 '99 C.1030 B.A. L.245 J.D. [[A] Katten M.R.]
Hinkemeyer, Jonathan E. ... '— '98 C.597 B.A. L.146 J.D. [Kirkland&E.]
Hinkhouse, Joseph A., (AV) ... '63 '88 C.238 B.A. L.46 J.D. [Lord,B.&B.]
Hinkle, Daniel M. ... '75 '04 C.103 A.B. L.1565 J.D. [[A] Funkhouser V.L.&D.]
Hinman, Cynthia McKee '47 '82
C.393 B.A. L.146 J.D. Asst. Prof., The John Marshall Law School

Hinshaw & Culbertson LLP, (AV) [BR]
Hinshaw & Culbertson LLP is an Illinois registered limited liability partnership that has elected to be governed by the Illinois Uniform Partnership Act (1997)
222 North La Salle Street, Suite 300, 60601-1081 ⊙
Telephone: 312-704-3000 Facsimile: 312-704-3001 Telex: 880248
Email: kfox@hinshawlaw.com URL: http://www.hinshawlaw.com
Partners: Leo J. Athas (Also at Lisle, Illinois Office); Dan L. Boho; Steven R. Bonanno; Roy M. Bossen; Thomas L. Browne; Kevin Joseph Burke; Lisa M. Burman; Peter H. Carlson; Paul J. Cherner; Paul J. Clementi; Shawn P. Clifford; William J. Connelly; Clare Connor Ranalli; David R. Creagh; Andrew B. Cripe; James G. Culbertson (1934-1969); Kent J. Cummings; Michael J. Cunningham; Stanley J. Davidson; Aimee E. Delaney; John W. Dubbs, III; Carlton D. Fisher; Lyndon M. Flosi; Stephanie R. Gaines; Thomas F. Ging; Alan I. Greene; Edmund Gronkiewicz; Thomas M. Hamilton, Jr.; James Harbert; Matthew R. Henderson; Mary J. Hess; Timothy A. Hickey; Susan M. Hickman; Joseph H. Hinshaw (1934-1973); James M. Hofert; William J. Holloway; Cecilia A. Horan; Linda K. Horras; Kurt L. Hudson; Fritz K. Huszagh; Anthony J. Jacob; Robert M. Konop (Not admitted in IL); Kristy M. Kelly; Philip Reed Kujawa; John Y. Lee; Michael J. Leech; Samuel G. Levin; David H. Levitt; Craig T. Liljestrand; Alan R. Lipton; Nancy G. Lischer; Tom H. Luetkemeyer; Stephen H. Malato; Thomas Y. Mandler; Paul M. Markese; Newton C. Marshall, II; Terrence P. McAvoy; Thomas P. McGarry; Daniel W. McGrath; Christine Olson McTigue; Gary E. Medler; Gregg I. Minkow; Lawrence R. Moelmann; Caroline A. Mondschean; Renee J. Mortimer; Donald L. Mrozek; Thomas R. Mulroy, III; Brendan A. O'Brien; Donald A. O'Brien; Yvonne C. Ocrant; Renee P. O'Neill; Dean E. Parker; Richard B. Polony; Carol Proctor; Steven M. Puiszis; Daniel M. Purdom; Bernard E. Jude Quinn; Laurie S. Randolph; Marcos Reilly; David J. Richards; J. William Roberts (Also at Springfield, Illinois Office); Daniel K. Ryan; Adam L. Saper; David M. Schultz; John E. Sebastian; Jennifer M. Sender; Robert T. Shannon; Harvey M. Sheldon; Timothy G. Shelton; Kevin R. Sido; David A. Sorensen; Elizabeth F. Staruck; Thomas P. Sukowicz (Also at Fort Lauderdale, Florida Office); Peter D. Sullivan; Timothy M. Sullivan; Robert H. Summers, Jr.; Stephen R. Swofford; Jerome R. Vainisi; Kathryn S. Vander Broek; James C. Vlahakis; Joshua G. Vincent; Matthew P. Walsh, II; Peter A. Walsh; Jennifer W. Weller; Todd M. Young; Clifford E. Yuknis. Associates: David J. Alfini; Anthony E. Antognoli; V. Brette Bensinger; Jason S. Bentley; Matthew J. Canna; Clint B. Charnes; Renee C. Choy; April M. Dahl; Karen M. Eiche; Sharon M. Figliulo; Robert J. Finley; Katherine Foley; Barbara A. Gallant; Jennifer K. Gust; Jennifer L. Guthrie; Jennifer M. Hanna; Eliott M. Hedin; Corinne Cantwell Heggie; Melina T. Hipskind; Betty Y. Jang; Kimberly A. Jansen; Valerie L. Kahn; Max J. Kanter; Chadwel D. Kasdin; Angela S. Kelver; Peter M. King; Steven M. Klaczynski; Danielle R. LeBlang; Abel Leon; James M. Lydon; Barry F. MacEntee; Christopher G. Markey; Frank J. Marsico; Kourtney A. Mulcahy; Conrad C. Nowak; Timothy S. O'Brien; Thomas L. O'Carroll; Peter E. Pederson; Justin M. Penn; Jennifer R. Riccolo; Joseph E. Rubas; Linnea L. Schramm; Michael P. Smith; Todd P. Stelter; Shannon K. Stevens; Daniel A. Trevino; Clay M. Ullrick; Richard Velázquez; Terry Wand; Diane E. Webster; William Yu; Javier E. Zamora. Of Counsel: Robert E. Ellis; James L. Fletcher; William P. Grogan; Michael J. Kasper; Courtney C. Nottage; Timothy J. O'Brien; William O. Shank (Also at Crystal Lake, Illinois Office); Clive M. Topol.
Appellate, Banking & Financing, Bankruptcy & Creditors' Rights, Class Action Litigation, Civil Rights Defense, Commercial Litigation, Corporate, Construction Law, Director & Officer Liability, Employee Benefits, Environmental, Fidelity & Surety, General Liability Litigation, Government, Health Care, Insurance Coverage, Insurance and Reinsurance, Labor & Employment, Legal Malpractice, Medical Malpractice, Mergers & Acquisitions, Municipal Liability, Personal Injury Defense, Public Law, Products Liability Litigation, Professional Liability, Regulatory, Real Estate, School Law, Securities, Taxation, Transportation, White Collar Crime and Workers' Compensation Defense.
Representative Clients: Aetna Life & Casualty Co.; Allstate Insurance Co.; Continental Insurance; Farmers Insurance Group; Fireman's Fund American; Hartford Insurance Group; Maryland Casualty Co.; Unigard Security; U.S. Fidelity & Guaranty Co.
Other Office Locations: Appleton, Wisconsin; Belleville, Illinois; Boston, Massachusetts; Champaign, Illinois; Crystal Lake, Illinois; Edwardsville, Illinois; Fort Lauderdale, Florida; Jacksonville, Florida; Joliet, Illinois; Lisle, Illinois; Los Angeles, California; Miami, Florida; Milwaukee, Wisconsin; Minneapolis, Minnesota; New York, New York; Peoria, Illinois; Phoenix, Arizona; Portland, Oregon; Providence, Rhode Island; Rockford, Illinois; St. Louis, Missouri; San Francisco, California; Schererville, Indiana; Springfield, Illinois; Tampa, Florida; Waukegan, Illinois.
See Professional Biographies, CHICAGO, ILLINOIS

Hipp, Brian J. ... '74 '99 C.966 B.A. L.477 J.D. [[S] Seyfarth S.]
Hipskind, Melina T. ... '79 '04 C.339 B.A. L.209 J.D. [[A] Hinshaw&C.]
Hira, Archana ... '69 '94 C.705 B.A. L.93 J.D. Mgr., Price Waterhouse Coopers LLP
Hirsch, Adam N. ... '76 '01 C.846 B.A. L.1565 J.D. [[A] Robinson C.&C.]
Hirsch, Austin L., (AV) ... '— '73 C.339 B.S. L.597 J.D. [Sachnoff&W.]
Hirsch, Barbara B., (AV) ... '38 '66 C.339 L.209 LL.B. 20 E. Cedar St.
Hirsch, Cory M. ... '70 '99 C.188 B.S. L.910 J.D. [[A] Seyfarth S.]
Hirsch, Davi L. ... '57 '82 C.339 B.S.W. L.209 J.D. [[C] Klein D.&H.]
Hirsch, Donald J. '40 '68 C.687 B.A. L.966 J.D.
(adm. in WI; not adm. in IL) Editor in Chf., Defense Rsch. Ins.
Hirsch, Gordon S. ... '59 '82 C.339 B.A. L.589 J.D. 5901 N. Cicero Ave., Ste. 405
Hirsch, Jocelyn A. ... '— '95 C&L.966 B.A., J.D. [Kirkland&E.]
Hirsch, John B., (AV) ... '33 '57 C.309 A.B. L.976 LL.B. 2305 N. Commonwealth Ave.
Hirsch, Laurence B. ... '74 '99 C.352 B.A. L.146 J.D. [[A] Berger S.]
Hirsch, Martin J. ... '— '85 C&L.339 B.S., J.D. [Marshall,G.&B.] (See Pat. Sect.)
Hirsch, Nancy L., (BV) ... '57 '83 C.352 B.A. L.365 J.D. [Reibman,H.B.H.&O.]
Hirsch, Norman M., (AV) ... '55 '81 C.145 B.A. L.813 J.D. [Jenner&B.]
Hirsch, Richard M. ... '37 '61 C.966 B.B.A. L.597 J.D. Pres., Gold Eagle Co.
Hirsch, Robert H. ... '38 '62 C.221 B.S. L.209 J.D. 180 N. LaSalle St.
Hirsch, Steven A. ... '51 '78 C&L.209 B.A., J.D. 2914 W. Gregory St.
Hirschey, David B., (AV) '50 '75
C.597 B.A. L.477 J.D. Sr. Atty., Northern Trust Corporation
Hirschhaut, Suanne P., (AV) ... '56 '81 C.347 B.A. L.146 J.D. [Fisher K.]
Hirschtick, Michael J. ... '42 '67 C.339 B.S. L.209 J.D. 6321 N. Avondale
Hirschtritt, Richard, (AV) ... '34 '58 C&L.597 B.S., J.D. [[C] Abramson&F.]
Hirschtritt, Shelly Matthew ... '— '98 C.477 A.B. L.309 J.D. [Kirkland&E.]
Hirsh, Bobbe, (AV) ... '53 '81 C.103 B.A. L.309 J.D. [Lord,B.&B.]
Hirsh, Jason B. ... '— '04 C.473 B.S. L.146 J.D. [[A] Arnstein&L.]
Hirsh, Steven J. ... '53 '84 C.339 B.S. L.146 J.D. Hyatt Legal Servs
Hirshman, Harold C., (AV) ... '45 '69 C.187 B.S. L.145 J.D. [Sonnenschein N.&R.]
Hirshman, Linda R., (AV) '44 '69
C.188 B.A. L.145 J.D. Prof. of Law, Chicago-Kent College of Law
Hirshman, Neil S., (AV) ... '— '90 C.339 B.S.E.E. L.309 J.D. [Kirkland&E.] (Pat.)
Hirst, Morgan R. ... '— '01 C.347 B.A. L.339 J.D. [[A] Jones D.]

Hirst, Ronald Vance '47 '73
C.338 B.S. L.424 J.D. Assoc. Gen. Coun., National Futures Assn.
Hisaw, J. Richard, & Associates, (CV) '48 '74
C.801 B.A. L.146 J.D. 222 North LaSalle, Ste. 2100
Hiss, Ryan A. ....'70 '95 C.576 B.A. L.575 J.D. [Stein,R.&H.]
Hitselberger, Carol A. ....'64 '89 C.104 B.A. L.659 J.D. [Mayer,B.R.&M.]
Hitt, John C., Jr. ....'— '90 C.976 B.A. L.893 J.D. [Chapman&C.]
Hitt, Mark Donald ....'70 '97 C.238 B.A. L.209 J.D. Off. of State Atty.
Hittle, Byron D. ....'74 '02 C.210 B.A. L.1119 J.D. [Vedder,P.K.&K.]
Hittle, Richard M. ....'50 '75 C.339 B.A. L.365 J.D. Liberty Mutual Ins. Co.
Hitzeman, James W., (AV) ....'62 '87 C&L.339 B.A., J.D. [Sidley A.B.&W.]
Hiza, Paula E. ....'43 '78 C.145 B.A. L.209 J.D. [Carl&H.]
Hlavin, Brian C. ....'67 '92 C.209 B.S. L.365 J.D. [Baum S.A.&N.]
Hlustik, Jack R., (AV) ....'35 '64 C.597 L.880 LL.B. [Hlustik,H.W.&V.]
Hlustik, Huizenga, Williams & Vander Woude, Ltd., (AV)
20 North Wacker Drive, Suite 2800
Ho, Cynthia Ming-Wai '69 '94 C.94 B.A. L.228 J.D.
(adm. in XX; not adm. in IL) Loyola University School of Law
Ho, Frankie ....'74 '99 C.37 B.S.E.E. L.36 J.D. [Grossman&F.] (Pat.)
Ho, Li-Chung Daniel ....'65 '97 C.477 B.S.M.E. L.930 J.D. [Jenner&B.] (Pat.)
Hoard, Michael ....'74 '99 C.999 B.A. L.801 J.D. State Atty. Gen. Off.
Hoban, George S., (AV) ....'14 '38 C.694 A.B. L.597 J.D. 222 N. La Salle St.‡
Hoban, Robert G., (AV) ....'47 '75 C.976 B.A. L.597 J.D. [McDermott W.&E.]
Hoban, Robert P., III ....'69 '94 C.589 B.A. L.436 J.D. [Condon&C.]
Hobbins, Kathleen L. ....'56 '95 C.918 B.A. L.146 J.D. [Freeborn&P.]
Hobbs, Jeremy W. ....'60 '87 C.668 B.A. L.145 J.D. Exec. V.P., Draupnir, LLC
Hobbs, Melvin G. ....'— '99 C.838 M.S.N. L.209 J.D. [Alholm,M.K.H.&O.]
Hoberman, Robin ....'68 '94 C.860 B.A. L.146 J.D. 100 North LaSalle Street
Hobgood, William P. '39 '72 C.259 B.S. L.421 J.D.
(adm. in DC; not adm. in IL) 1313 N. Ritcie Ct.‡
Hoch, Guy A. ....'45 '77 C.1191 B.A. L.365 J.D. Asst. Pub. Def.
Hoch, Kenneth H., (AV) ....'47 '71 C.116 A.B. L.602 J.D. [Sonnenschein N.&R.]
Hoch, Ramon R. '59 '91 C.378 B.S.Ch.E. L.1209 J.D.
(adm. in VA; not adm. in IL; See Pat. Sect.) [Fitch,E.T.&F.] (Wash., DC)
Hochberg, Burton S., (AV) ....'49 '74 C.966 B.B.A. L.209 J.D. [Schiller,D.&F.]
Hochberg, Kevin J. ....'54 '84 C.446 B.A. L.145 J.D. [Sidley A.B.&W.]
Hochhausen, Jaime L. ....'78 '04 C.961 B.A. L.365 J.D. [McGuirewoods]
Hochler, Don L. '57 '82 C.994 B.A. L.724 J.D.
(adm. in NY; not adm. in IL) [McBreen&K.]
Hochman, David J., (AV) ....'46 '73 C.502 B.A. L.339 J.D. [Kamensky,R.H.&D.]
Hochstetler, Douglas C. ....'— '77 C.674 A.B. L.276 J.D. [Schiff H.] (Pat.)
Hodes, Michael G. ....'52 '76 C.339 B.A. L.424 J.D. [Hodes,K.&P.]
Hodes, Scott, (AV) ....'— '59 C.145 A.B. L.477 J.D. [Bryan C.]
Hodes, Scott D., (AV) ....'51 '76 C.1029 B.A. L.209 J.D. 180 N. LaSalle St.
Hodes, Sheldon ....'24 '51 C&L.221 B.A., LL.B. 205 W. Randolph St.

Hodes, Keating & Pilon, (AV)
39 South LaSalle Street, Suite 1020, 60603-1731
Telephone: 312-553-1440 Fax: 312-553-1470
Email: hkp@hkp-customs.com URL: http://www.hkp-customs.com
Michael G. Hodes; Thomas M. Keating; Lawrence R. Pilon;—Jessica T. DePinto; Michelle Welsh.
Customs Law, International Trade Regulation, Administrative Law, Commercial Litigation, International Transportation Law.
See Professional Biographies, CHICAGO, ILLINOIS

Hodge, Karen E. ....'— '92 C&L.347 B.A., J.D. Asst. State's Atty.
Hodges, Charisse K. ....'64 '92 C.966 B.S. L.589 J.D. 3348 South Giles Avenue
Hodges, George A., (Ltd.) ....'35 '63 C&L.597 B.A., J.D. 155 N. Michigan Ave.
Hodgman, David R., (AV) ....'— '74 C.293 B.A. L.976 J.D. [Schiff H.]
Hodyl, Richard A., Jr., (AV) ....'64 '89 C.927 B.S. L.209 J.D. [Meckler B.&T.]
Hoeflich, Adam L., (AV) ....'64 '92 C.165 B.A. L.339 J.D. [Bartlit B.H.P.&S.]
Hoeft, Steven H., (AV) ....'51 '76 C.578 B.A. L.597 J.D. [McDermott W.&E.]
Hoeg, Andrew D. ....'— '03 C.352 B.B.A. L.339 J.D. [Katten M.R.]
Hoeksema, Kristin E. ....'— '92 C&L.879 B.A., J.D. 122 S. Michigan Ave.
Hoellen, John J. ....'14 '38 C&L.597 B.A., J.D. [Hoellen&L.] ‡
Hoellen, Robert B. ....'57 '83 C.1106 B.A. L.365 J.D. 1940 W. Irving Pk. Rd.
Hoellen & Lukes ....1940 W. Irving Park Rd.
Hoellwarth, Larry A. ....'— '83 C.20 B.A. L.597 J.D. [Karbal,C.E.S.&D.]
Hoerman, Timothy E. ....'64 '98 C.424 B.S. L.801 J.D. [Cremer,K.S.&S.]
Hoevel, John J. ....'60 '85 C&L.339 B.A., J.D. [Hoevel&Assoc.]
Hoevel, Talbot C. ....'60 '86 C&L.801 B.S., J.D. [Hoevel&Assoc.]
Hoevel & Associates, P.C. ....3725 N. Western Avenue
Hoey, James M., (AV) ....'52 '77 C.679 B.S.M.E. L.424 J.D. [Clausen M.] (Pat.)

Hoey & Farina, P.C., (AV)
542 South Dearborn, Suite 200, 60605
Telephone: 312-939-1212 Toll Free: 888-425-1212 Fax: 312-939-7842
Email: info@hoeyfarina.com URL: http://www.hoeyfarina.com
James L. Farina.
Federal Employers' Liability Act, Personal Injury.
See Professional Biographies, CHICAGO, ILLINOIS

Hofeld, Albert F., (Ltd.), (AV) ....'36 '64 C.309 B.A. L.145 J.D. [Hofeld&S.]
Hofeld, Albert Francis, III '66 '01 C.685 B.A. L.597 J.D.
Legal Assistance Foundation of Metropolitan Chicago

Hofeld and Schaffner, (AV)
A Partnership including A Professional Corporation
Suite 3120, 30 North La Salle Street, 60602-2506
Telephone: 312-372-4250 Telecopier: 312-372-1766
Email: bmurphy@hofeldandschaffner.com URL: http://www.hofeldandschaffner.com
Albert F. Hofeld (Ltd.); Howard Schaffner; Brian Murphy;—John J. MacInerney; Lynne Plum Duffey.
Plaintiffs Personal Injury and Wrongful Death, Aviation, Medical Negligence, Professional Negligence, Product Liability, Premises Liability, Construction Accidents FELA and Automobile Accidents. Litigation Practice.
See Professional Biographies, CHICAGO, ILLINOIS

Hofer, Roy E., (AV) '35 '61 C.679 B.Ch.E. L.276 J.D.
[Brinks H.G.&L.] (See Pat. Sect.)
Hofert, Daniel C., (BV) ....'— '85 C.238 B.A. L.146 J.D. [Hickey,M.&Assoc.]
Hofert, Edward C. ....'26 '51 C.145 Ph.B. L.146 J.D. Cir. Ct. J.
Hofert, James M., (AV) ....'54 '79 C.293 B.A. L.146 J.D. [Hinshaw&C.]
Hoff, John Scott, (AV) ....'46 '76 C.221 B.S.B.A. L.809 J.D. [J.S.Hoff]
Hoff, Robert T. '48 '73 C&L.221 B.S.B.A., J.D.
(adm. in IA; not adm. in IL) [J.S.Hoff]
Hoff, John Scott, P.C., (AV) .... 20 N. Clark Street, Suite 3000
Hoffa, Thomas E. ....'35 '72 C.350 B.S. L.365 J.D. 30 W. Chicago Ave.‡
Hoffenberg, Alan D. ....'42 '67 C.98 B.A. L.365 LL.B. 180 N. LaSalle St.
Hoffman, Aaron E., (AV) '47 '72 C.910 A.B. L.145 J.D.
Sr. V.P., Loss Prevention, Attorneys' Liability Assurance Society, Inc.

Hoffman, Alan C. ....'44 '73 C.123 B.A. L.365 J.D. [A.C.Hoffman&Assoc.]
Hoffman, Burton L., (AV) ....'32 '55 C&L.209 LL.B. [Reibman,H.B.H.&O.]
Hoffman, Dean V. ....'— '03 C.112 B.A. L.893 J.D. [Katten M.R.]
Hoffman, Debra B., (AV) ....'55 '86 C.694 B.A. L.209 J.D [Mayer,B.R.&M.]
Hoffman, Douglas R. ....'— '82 C.750 B.S. L.146 J.D. [Chapman&C.]
Hoffman, George M., (AV) ....'48 '81 C.1042 B.A. L.209 J.D. [Stamos&T.]
Hoffman, James F., (AV) '62 '87 C.339 B.S. L.309 J.D.
Exec. V.P., Gen. Coun. & Secy., Prime Grp. Realty Tr.
Hoffman, James Garland, Jr. '64 '91 C.802 B.B.A. L.862 J.D.
(adm. in TX; not adm. in IL) Asst., V.P., Salomon Smith Barney
Hoffman, Janet Goelz, (AV) ....'49 '79 C.393 B.A. L.597 J.D. [Katten M.R.]
Hoffman, Jay R. ....'62 '86 C.597 B.A. L.276 J.D. [Hoffman]
Hoffman, Kenneth A. ....'66 '91 C.347 B.A. L.910 J.D. [Mitchell H.&W.]
Hoffman, Maya ....'74 '01 C.339 B.A. L.365 J.D. [Cozen O.]
Hoffman, Nancy M. ....'— '90 C.385 B.A. L.424 J.D. [Querrey&H.]
Hoffman, Nathan E. ....'75 '00 C.243 B.A. L.597 J.D. [Winston&S.]
Hoffman, Paul R. ....'62 '88 C.436 B.S. L.209 J.D. [Vedder,P.K.&K.]
Hoffman, Richard B., (AV) '— '73
C.339 B.S.G.E. L.209 J.D. [Marshall,G.&B.] (See Pat. Sect.)
Hoffman, Richard H., (AV) '35 '62
C.340 B.S. L.209 J.D. 175 West Jackson Boulevard, Suite 1600‡
Hoffman, Richard M., (AV) ....'63 '90 C&L.494 B.S., J.D. [Wildman,H.A.&D.]
Hoffman, Robert A., (BV) ....'52 '77 C.339 B.A. L.365 J.D. [Brady,C.&M.]
Hoffman, Robert B., (AV) '38 '65 C.966 B.S. L.597 J.D.
Harris Trust and Savings Bank
Hoffman, Stephanie A. M. ....'56 '81 C.19 B.A. L.597 J.D. Def. Resch. Institute
Hoffman, Stephen D. '66 '91 C.999 B.S. L.1049 J.D.
(adm. in AZ; not adm. in IL) [Worker,S.&H.]
Hoffman, Thomas E. ....'47 '71 C.424 B.B.A. L.365 J.D. Appl. J.
Hoffman, Thomas G., (AV) ..... '49 '74 C.424 B.S. L.276 J.D. 11 E. Adams St., Ste. 1600
Hoffman, Timothy V., (BV) ....'58 '84 C.347 B.S. L.424 J.D. [Sanchez&D.]
Hoffman, Valerie J., (AV) ....'53 '78 C.867 B.A. L.94 J.D. [Seyfarth S.]
Hoffman, Alan C., & Associates .... 180 N. LaSalle St.
Hoffman Legal .... 19 S. La Salle St., Ste. 802
Hoffmann, Eric C. '63 '97 C.145 B.A. L.365 J.D.
Dept. of Jus. Antitrust Div. Midwest Field Off.
Hoffmann, Howard M., (AV) ....'41 '68 C.424 B.S. L.146 J.D. [Duane M.]
Hoffmann, Jeanne M. ....'65 '89 C.339 B.A. L.209 J.D. [BryceDowney]
Hoffmeyer, Kevin T. ....'— '98 C&L.477 B.A., J.D. [Sidley A.B.&W.]
Hoffnagle, James J., (AV) ....'27 '52 C.339 B.A. L.976 LL.B. [Taylor,M.S.H.&M.]
Hofmann, William E., (BV) ....'49 '74 C.118 B.A. L.910 J.D. [Shaheen,N.S.F.&E.]
Hofmeister, Dan J., Jr. ....'64 '90 C.546 B.J. L.424 J.D. [Neal,G.&E.]
Hofstra, Patricia S., (AV) ....'52 '78 C.645 B.S. L.607 J.D. [Bell,B.&L.]
Hoft, Janine L. ....'59 '84 C.429 B.S. L.146 J.D. 180 N. Milwaukee
Hogan, Albert L., III ....'66 '97 C.608 B.S. L.145 J.D. [Skadden,A.S.M.&F.]
Hogan, Brian D., (BV) ....'— '69 C.679 B.S. L.309 J.D. 200 East Randolph St., Fl. 54
Hogan, Carol A., (AV) ....'— '89 C.339 B.A. L.424 J.D. [Jones D.]
Hogan, Carol C., (AV) ....'— '86 C.741 B.A. L.424 J.D. [Hogan M.]
Hogan, Deborah Rzasnicki ..... '70 '95 C.579 B.A. L.597 J.D. [Goldberg,K.B.B.R.&M.]
Hogan, Edward M., (AV) ....'— '77 C.602 A.B. L.146 J.D. [Hogan M.]
Hogan, Frederic G., (AV) ....'47 '73 C.966 B.S.C.E. L.602 J.D. [O'Rourke,H.F.&D.]
Hogan, Kenneth J. ....'70 '95 C&L.339 B.A., J.D. [Meckler B.&T.]
Hogan, Margaret Parnell ....'71 '99 C.966 B.A. L.146 J.D. [Littler M.]
Hogan, Michael J. ....'46 '72 C&L.424 B.A., J.D. Cir. Ct. J., Cook Co.
Hogan, Patricia J., (AV) ....'59 '90 C.338 B.S. L.339 J.D. [Cassiday,S.&G.]
Hogan, Patricia K., Law Office of '— '75 C.473 B.A. L.146 J.D.
39 South LaSalle Street
Hogan, Thomas L. ....'54 '80 C.602 A.B. L.146 J.D. Cir. Ct. J.
Hogan, Thomas M. .... '39 '65 C&L.209 B.S.C., J.D. Asst. Coun., Dept. of Law

Hogan Marren, Ltd., (AV)
180 North Wacker Drive Suite 600, 60606
Telephone: 312-946-1800 FAX: 312-946-9818
Email: hmadm@aol.com URL: http://www.hmltd.com
Edward M. Hogan; John P. Marren; Carol C. Hogan; Patrick E. Deady; Kelly McCloskey Cherf; Limo T. Cherian; Laura C. Liu; Cheryl L. Segal; Jeffrey M. Teske;—Timothy B Caprez; Matthew J. Cleveland; John Michael Tecson.
Health Care, Labor, Corporate, Venture Capital and Business Litigation Law.
See Professional Biographies, CHICAGO, ILLINOIS

Hogg, Kevin D., (AV) '— '84 C&L.150 B.S.M.E., J.D.
[Marshall,G.&B.] (See Pat. Sect.)
Hogg, Michael J. ....'45 '74 L.999 LL.B. Business Council
Hogren, Charles V. '36 '61
C.937 A.B. L.597 J.D. Exec. Dir., Cabrini Green Legal Aid Clinic
Hogstrom, Erik A. ....'78 '04 C.429 B.A. L.477 J.D. [Skadden,A.S.M.&F.]
Hohmann, Joseph G. '58 '83
C.339 B.S. L.209 J.D.,MBA Sr. Mng. Dir., The Chicago Corporation
Hohner, Hallie G. ..... '69 '94 C.188 B.S. L.477 J.D. Human Resource Coun., Tribune Co.
Hoke, Stephen ....'— '85 C.347 B.S. L.276 J.D. [Ungaretti&H.]
Holahan, Kathryn J. ....'74 '02 C.280 B.B.A. L.597 J.D. [Mayer,B.R.&M.]
Holbrook, Jeremy R. ....'— '04 C.221 B.A. L.146 J.D. [Anderson,R.]
Holcomb, Barbara Levine, (AV) '38 '84 C.1044 B.S. L.209 J.D.
4147 N. Keeler Avenue
Holden, John K. ....'58 '91 C.1191 B.A. L.365 J.D. 11418 S. Forrestville Ave.
Holden, Virginia H., (AV) ....'53 '80 C.822 B.A. L.209 J.D. [McDermott W.&E.]
Holderman, James F. ....'46 '71 C&L.339 B.S., J.D. U.S. Dist. J.
Holderman, Paula Hudson, (AV) ....'52 '79 C.339 B.A. L.365 J.D. [Winston&S.]
Holdvogt, Jeffrey ....'78 '03 C.723 B.A. L.477 J.D. [McDermott W.&E.]
Hole, Nathan J. ....'79 '04 C.861 B.A. L.477 J.D. [Loeb&L.]
Holen, Andrew J. ....'74 '99 C.679 B.S. L.326 J.D. [Pretzel&S.]
Holihan, Gary M. ..... '— '93 C.602 B.B.A. L.146 J.D. [Kirkland&E.] (San Fran., CA)
Holingue, David R., Ltd. ....'52 '85 C.424 B.S. L.365 J.D. 2420 N. Geneva Terr.
Holisky, Jerald ....'56 '89 C.494 B.A. L.365 J.D. [Holland&K.]
Holkeboer, Van E. ....'— '83 C.114 B.A. L.477 J.D. [Chapman&C.]
Holland, Dennis K. ....'52 '79 C.98 B.S. L.365 J.D. 500 West Monroe
Holland, J. William, (AV) ....'37 '63 C.1029 B.S. L.477 J.D. [Holland&H.]
Holland, Patricia A. '66 '94 C.732 B.A. L.365 J.D.
Assoc. Gen. Coun., Chicago Mercantile Exchange Inc.
Holland, Patricia C. ....'— '83 C.339 B.A. L.145 J.D. [Albert,W.]
Holland, Steven B. ....'63 '88 C&L.339 B.A., J.D. 205 W. Wacker Drive
Holland & Holland, (Associated), (AV) .... 135 South La Salle Street Suite 2435

Holland & Knight LLP, (AV)
131 South Dearborn Street, 30th Floor, 60603
Telephone: 312-263-3600 Fax: 312-578-6666
URL: http://www.hklaw.com

(This Listing Continued)

Holland & Knight LLP (Continued)

Chicago Members: Barbara A. Adams; Henry S. Allen, Jr.; Thomas P. Arden; Michael J. Boland; Malcolm H. Brooks; Mark E. Burkland; Scott F. Burns; Martin J. Campanella; James R. Carr; Martin G. Durkin, Jr.; Steven M. Elrod; Victor P. Filippini, Jr.; Shayle P. Fox; Peter M. Friedman; Anthony L. Frink; Steffanie N. Garrett; Andrew R. Gelman; Robert H. Gerstein; Steven L. Gillman; Victor P. Henderson; Kenneth A. Jenero; Charles E. Joern, Jr.; Michael J. Kanute; Naomi F. Katz; Thomas J. Kinasz; Charles D. Knight; Jerry Kokolis; Frances H. Krasnow; Robert J. Labate; David M. Lefkow; Bruce D. Loring; David S. Mann; Elias N. Matsakis; James T. Mayer; C. Grant McCorkhill; Craig McCrohon; Gregory R. Meeder; Robert M. Mintz; James A. Moehling; Donald G. Mulack; Christopher J. Murdoch; Martin P. Murphy; John R. Mussman; Carl A. Neumann (Also at Oakbrook Terrace Office); Matthew E. Norton; John R. Nyweide; Jennifer S. Oosterbaan; Morgan J. Ordman; Todd S. Parkhurst; George M. Pearce; Scott W. Petersen; Charles L. Philbrick; S. Richard Pincus; Frances E. Prell; Michael J. Ranallo; Michael D. Rechtin; Richard A. Redmond; Edward F. Ryan; Anne Hamblin Schiave; Todd J. Schneider; Robert C. Schnitz; Phillip M. Schreiber; Mark L. Shapiro; Michele E. Sibley Gonzales; Colin Smith; Mark A. Spognardi; Lewis T. Steadman, Jr.; Todd D. Steenson; Mark J. Steger; William M. Stevens; Maureen Strauts; Jonathan E. Strouse; Julie A. Tappendorf; Robert E. Tonn; Steven B. Varick; Robert W. Vyverberg, Jr.; Richard R. Winter; Thomas R. Woodrow; David E. Zajicek; Larry M. Zanger. Senior Counsel: Daniel Acosta; Lawrence A. Coles, Jr.; James G. Haft; Iain Johnston; Mark Kingsley; Mark J. Nora; Sarah E. Pace; Carole Laude Pechi; John D. Ryan; Peter J. Strand. Associates: Naser Baseer; Steven C. Bauer; Terri L. Brieske; Marissa Cashy Brinkley; Timothy A. Brinkley; Andrea L. Briski; Maureen Elizabeth Browne; Christopher W. Carmichael; James P. Chivilo (Also at Oakbrook Terrace Office); Laura A. Derouin; Kelly D. DeWitt; Eric Dorkin; Lisa A. Ellis; Kristen E. Fligel Cochrane; Laura Christine Garofalo; Barbara A. Gimbel; Karen E. Gossman; Robert E. Harig; Matthew Darren Heinke; Jerald Holisky; Troy D. Hoyt; Lisa Johnson; Staci L. Ketay; Amy E. McShane; Jennifer E. Miller; James T. Mueller; Sean Nash; Eric Robben; Suzanne E. Rollier; Matthew Singer; Leah Wardak; David Scott Warner. Of Counsel: Robert O. Case; David L. Fargo; Donald A. Gillies; Robert C. Newman; David G. O'Leary; G. Gale Roberson, Jr.; David Shayne; Jack M. Siegel; Michael L. Weissman.
Litigation, Government Law, Business Law, Real Estate Law and Private Wealth Services.
Annapolis, Maryland Office: State Circle Building, 47 State Circle, Suite 400, 21401. Telephone: 410-263-7800. Fax: 410-263-3768.
Atlanta, Georgia Office: One Atlantic Center, 1201 West Peachtree Street, N.E., Suite 2000, 30309. Telephone: 404-817-8500. Fax: 404-881-0470.
Beijing, China Office: No. 33, 14th Floor, IBM Tower, Pacific Century Place, 2 A Workers Stadium Road North, Chaoyang District, 100027. Telephone: 86-10-653-91232. Fax: 86-10-653-91060.
Bethesda, Maryland Office: 3 Bethesda Metro Center, Suite 800, 20814. Telephone: 301-654-7800. Fax: 301-656-3978.
Boston, Massachusetts Office: 10 St. James Avenue, 11th Floor, 02116. Telephone: 617-523-2700. Fax: 617-523-6850.
Bradenton, Florida Office: Bradenton Financial Center, 1401 West Manatee Avenue, Suite 1200, 34205. Telephone: 941-748-7076. Fax: 941-747-9774.
Fort Lauderdale, Florida Office: One East Broward Boulevard, Suite 1300, 33301. Telephone: 954-525-1000. Fax: 954-463-2030.
Jacksonville, Florida Office: 50 North Laura Street, Suite 3900, 32202. Telephone: 904-353-2000. Fax: 904-358-1872.
Lakeland, Florida Office: 92 Lake Wire Drive, 33815. Telephone: 863-682-1161. Fax: 863-688-1186.
Los Angeles, California Office: 633 West Fifth Street, 21st Floor, 90071. Telephone: 213-896-2400. Fax: 213-896-2450.
Mexico City, Mexico Office: Holland & Knight - Gallastegui y Lozano, S.C., Edificio Arcos Bosques Corporativo, Paseo de los Tamarindos 400-B, Piso 2, Delegación Cuajimalpa, Bosques de las Lomas, 05120. Telephone: 525-55-261-1866. Fax: 525-55-261-1867.
Miami, Florida Office: 701 Brickell Avenue, Suite 3000, 33131. Telephone: 305-374-8500. Fax: 305-789-7799.
New York, New York Office: 195 Broadway, 24th Floor, 10007. Telephone: 212-513-3200. Fax: 212-385-9010.
Northern Virginia: 1600 Tysons Boulevard, Suite 700, McLean, Virginia, 22102. Telephone: 703-720-8600. Fax: 703-720-8610.
Oakbrook Terrace, Illinois Office: One Mid America Plaza, Suite 1000, 60181. Telephone: 630-954-2100. Fax: 630-954-2112.
Orlando, Florida Office: SunTrust Building, Suite 2600, 200 South Orange Avenue, 32801. Telephone: 407-425-8500. Fax: 407-244-5288.
Portland, Oregon Office: 2300 U.S. Bancorp Tower, 111 Southwest Fifth Avenue, 97204. Telephone: 503-243-2300. Fax: 503-241-8014.
Providence, Rhode Island Office: One Financial Plaza, Suite 1800, 02903. Telephone: 401-751-8500. Fax: 401-553-6850.
Rancho Santa Fe, California Office: 6050 El Tordo, 92067. Telephone: 858-756-4410. Fax: 858-756-4386.
Sacramento, California Office: 1215 K Street, 17th Floor, 95814. Telephone: 916-503-1695. Fax: 916-503-2401.
San Antonio, Texas Office: 112 East Pecan Street, Suite 2700, 78205. Telephone: 210-229-3000. Fax: 210-229-1194.
San Francisco, California Office: 50 California Street, Suite 2800, 94111. Telephone: 415-743-6900. Fax: 415-743-6910.
Seattle, Washington Office: 2600 Pike Tower, 520 Pike Street, 98101. Telephone: 206-340-1825. Fax: 206-623-4363.
St. Petersburg, Florida Office: 200 Central Avenue, Suite 1600, 33701. Telephone: 727-896-7171. Fax: 727-822-8048.
Tallahassee, Florida Office: 315 South Calhoun Street, Suite 600, 32301. Telephone: 850-224-7000. Fax: 850-224-8832.
Tampa, Florida Office: 100 North Tampa Street, Suite 4100, 33602. Telephone: 813-227-8500. Fax: 813-229-0134.
Tokyo, Japan Office: Akasaka Tokyu Building, 7th Floor, 2-14-3 Nagatacho, Chiyoda-Ku, Tokyo, 100-0014. Telephone: 03-3539-5881. Fax: 03-3503-1033.
Washington, D.C. Office: 2099 Pennsylvania Avenue, N.W., Suite 100, 20006. Telephone: 202-955-3000. Fax: 202-955-5564.
West Palm Beach, Florida Office: 222 Lakeview Avenue, Suite 1000, 33401. Telephone: 561-833-2000. Fax: 561-650-8399.
Representative Offices:
Caracas, Venezuela Office: Tinoco, Travieso, Planchart & Núñez, Avenida Francisco De Miranda, Torre Country Club, Pisos 1 y 2, Chacaito, 1050. Telephone: 582-12-952-9033 (Master). Fax: 582-12-953-1053/8365/7583.
Helsinki, Finland Office: Holland & Knight Oy, Pohjoisesplanadi 33, FIN-00100. Telephone: 358-9-684-1520. Fax: 358-9-6841-5252.
Tel Aviv, Israel Office: Haim Samet, Steinmetz, Haring & Co. Advocates, 23 Begin Road, 66814. Telephone: 972-3-567-0100. Fax: 972-3-567-01010.

See Professional Biographies, CHICAGO, ILLINOIS

Hollander, Adam K. .... '67 '92 C.347 B.A. L.209 J.D. [Ⓖ Mayer,B.R.&M.]
Hollander, Eugene K. .... '61 '86 C.339 B.A. L.146 J.D. [Ⓖ Lane&L.] (ⓒChicago)
Hollander, Eugene K., The Law Offices of, (AV) '61 '86
C.339 B.A. L.146 J.D. 33 North Dearborn Suite 2300 (ⓒChicago)
Hollander, George M. .... '34 '58 C&L.597 B.S., J.D. 11 S. LaSalle St.
Holleb, Joshua D., (AV) .... '57 '83 C.478 B.A. L.146 J.D. [Klein D.&H.] ⓒ
Holleb, Marshall M., (AV) .... '16 '47 C.966 B.A. L.309 J.D. [Ⓖ Wildman,H.A.&D.]
Holleb Hotaling, Keri L. .... '73 '00 C.25 B.A. L.893 J.D. [Ⓐ Jenner&B.]
Hollenbeck, Andrew D. .... '79 '04 C.74 B.S. L.1119 J.D. [Ⓐ Mayer,B.R.&M.]
Holley, Charles J. .... '65 '91 C&L.966 B.A., J.D. [Ⓐ Sales,G.G.&B.]
Holliday, Laura E. .... '72 '99 C&L.597 .B.S., J.D. [Ⓐ Sidley A.B.&W.]
Hollis, Amanda J. .... '— '03 C.339 B.S. L.577 J.D. [Ⓐ Latham&W.]
Hollis, Bobby J., II .... '74 '00 C.260 B.A. L.352 J.D. [Ⓐ Jenner&B.]
Hollis, Everett L. .... '14 '40 C.339 B.S. L.309 LL.B. 190 S. LaSalle St.
Holloway, Philip S. .... '71 '00 C.339 B.S. L.150 J.D. [Ⓐ Gonzalez,S.&H.]

Holloway, Sheryl Y. '51 '93 C.339 B.A. L.329 J.D.
70 W. Madison, Suite 1400, 60602
Telephone: 312-214-3144 Fax: 773-660-8686
Email: sherylholloway507@yahoo.com URL: http://www.sherylholloway.com
Language: English.
Real Estate Closings, Evictions, Divorces, Wills, Personal Injury, Guardianships, Expungements.

See Professional Biographies, CHICAGO, ILLINOIS

Holloway, William J., (AV) .... '35 '65 C.350 B.S. L.597 J.D. [Hinshaw&C.]
Holm, Clifford R. '61 '91 C.820 B.A. L.1019 J.D.
V.P. & Tr. Coun., Harris Trust and Savings Bank
Holman, Brian R. .... '67 '92 C.221 B.S. L.146 J.D. [K.B.Moll&Assoc.]
Holman, David W. .... '40 '65 C.207 B.A. L.608 J.D. Northern Tr. Co.
Holmen, Neil E., (AV) .... '50 '76 C.339 B.S. L.209 J.D. [Winston&S.]
Holmen, Ralph W. '52 '78
C.339 B.S. L.424 J.D. Assoc. Gen. Coun., Natl. Assn. of Realtors
Holmes, David M. .... '62 '88 C&L.339 B.S., J.D. [Wilson E.M.E.&D.]
Holmes, Laurie A. '62 '93 C.706 B.A. L.276 J.D.
(adm. in NY; not adm. in IL) [Gardner C.&D.]
Holmes, Patricia Brown .... '— '87 C.342 B.S. L.339 J.D. [Schiff H.]
Holmes, Paul B., (BV) .... '— '81 C.98 B.S. L.339 J.D. [Ungaretti&H.]
Holmes, Scott M. .... '— '00 C.608 B.M. L.846 J.D. [Ⓐ Gardner C.&D.]
Holmes, William C., (AV) .... '— '73 C.813 B.A. L.309 J.D. [Ⓖ Freeborn&P.]
Holohan, G. Courtney .... '— '98 C.597 B.S. L.228 J.D. [Kirkland&E.]
Holsapple, Dennis L., (AVⓣ) .... '53 '78 C.352 B.A. L.477 J.D. [Kutak R.]
Holstein, Robert A., (AV) ...'36 '62 C.385 A.B. L.477 J.D. 100 W. Randolph St.Ste 7-900
Holt, Colette, & Associates ....'58 '85 C.976 B.A. L.145 J.D. 541 W. Arlington Place
Holt, Geraldine .... '— '95 C.1016 M.A. L.589 J.D. [Grant H.&S.]
Holt, Nancy H. .... '48 '76 C.340 B.F.A. L.209 J.D. Ticor Title Ins. Co.
Holt, Thomas L. .... '71 '97 C.502 B.S. L.424 J.D. [Brinks H.G.&L.] (See Pat. Sect.)
Holtaway, John A. .... '52 '82 C.339 B.A. L.209 J.D. Coun., Amer. Bar Assn.
Holte, Yvonne M. .... '60 '87 C.424 B.A. L.146 J.D. Co. Guardian Ad Litem
Holtz, Charlene L., (AV) .... '48 '76 C.705 A.B. L.209 J.D. [Friedman&H.]
Holtzman, Arthur M., (AV) .... '49 '76 C.597 B.A. L.910 J.D. [Pedersen&H.]
Holtzman, David Stuart ....'59 '93 C.1507 B.S. L.1048 J.D. 100 W Monroe St., 4th Fl.
Holubar, Lisa M. .... '— '99 C.473 B.S. L.209 J.D. [Kirkland&E.]
Holy, Michael C., (AV) .... '69 '94 C.589 B.S. L.436 J.D. [Ⓐ Johnson&B.]
Holzhall, Marianne Craigmile .... '— '90 C.597 B.S.J. L.424 J.D. [Foley&L.]
Holzhauer, James D., (AV) .... '48 '80 C.569 B.A. L.477 J.D. [Mayer,B.R.&M.]
Holzman, William M., (BV) .... '49 '75 C.966 B.A. L.1049 J.D. [Schwartz C.]
Holzwarth, Elsie G. .... '42 '66 C.118 A.B. L.339 J.D. 134 N. La Salle St.
Homan, Cynthia A., (BV) .... '54 '81 C.339 B.A. L.209 J.D. [Brinks H.G.&L.]
Homburger, Thomas C., (AV) .... '41 '66 C&L.178 B.A., LL.B. [Bell,B.&L.]
Homer, Jennifer D. .... '65 '95 C.910 B.A. L.221 J.D. [DLPiper R.G.C.U.]
Homer, Paul, (P.C.), (AV) .... '23 '51 C.145 B.A. L.597 J.D. [DLPiper R.G.C.U.]
Homer, Richard S., (AV) .... '34 '58 C.145 B.A. L.597 J.D. [Ⓖ DLPiper R.G.C.U.]
Homola, Harry F. '30 '56 C.188 B.A. L.309 J.D.
(adm. in NY; not adm. in IL) U.S. Postal Serv.
Homsy, Joseph G., (BV) .... '45 '78 C.659 B.A. L.1202 J.D. [Guibord H.]
Hong, Grace .... '73 '98 C.597 B.S. L.146 J.D. Asst. State Atty.
Hong, Jane C. .... '— '01 C.93 A.B. L.966 J.D. [Ⓐ Chapman&C.]
Hood, Gary A. ....'69 '94 C.338 B.S. L.339 J.D. Gen. Cou. & Corp. Sec., Transora
Hood, Gary E. .... '— '96 C.800 B.S.E.E. L.285 J.D. [Ⓖ Baniak P.&G.] (See Pat. Sect.)
Hood, Mary Stark '50 '77
C.1154 B.A. L.1187 J.D. Mng. Sr. Coun., Natl. Assn. of REALTORS
Hood, Vicki Vallen, (AV) .... '— '77 C&L.597 B.A., J.D. [Kirkland&E.]
Hood Ackerman, Julie M. .... '70 '96 C.228 A.B. L.966 J.D. 227 W. Monroe
Hoogendoorn, Case, (AV) .... '43 '69 C.114 A.B. L.145 J.D. [Hoogendoorn&T.]

Hoogendoorn & Talbot, (AV)
122 South Michigan Avenue Suite 1220, 60603-6107
Telephone: 312-786-2250 FAX: 312-786-0708
URL: http://www.hoogendoorntalbot.com
Members of Firm: Case Hoogendoorn; Earl A. Talbot; Thomas J. Godfrey, Jr.; Kathryn E. Skelton; Bruce J. Van Heukelem; Brian L. Dobben; Richard D. Boonstra; Richard M. Sawdey; David G. Strom; Kevin J. Todd; Todd M. Van Baren; Laurence J. Kline. Associates: Melissa Hoogendoorn De Vries; Joseph Wright; Sally R. Wagenmaker; Brian D. Yeley; Robert A. Janoski; Sharon M. Buccino.
Estate Tax and Financial Planning, Business and Corporate Law, Commercial, Personal Injury, Insurance Disputes, Litigation, Real Estate Law and Charitable Tax Planning.

See Professional Biographies, CHICAGO, ILLINOIS

Hooker, Darrick J. .... '74 '01 C.339 B.S.B.A. L.1119 J.D. [Ⓐ Jenner&B.]
Hooks, William H., (AV) .... '53 '81 C.209 B.A. L.146 J.D. [Hooks]

Hooks Law Offices, P.C., (AV)
29 S. LaSalle Street, Suite 333, 60603
Telephone: 312-553-5252 Telefax: 312-553-1510 International Cable Address: Chgolawyer
Email: chgolawyer@sbcglobal.net URL: http://www.hookslaw.com
William H. Hooks.
Federal and State Criminal Defense Trial and Appellate Practice (all Felony Crimes including: White Collar, Fraud, Sexual, Weapons, Homicide, Bribery, Conspiracy and Drug Offenses; all Misdemeanor Crimes, including D.U.I., D.W.I. and D.W.B., involving: professionals, doctors, lawyers, business owners/executives, clergy and law enforcement officials). Commercial Litigation, Contract Litigation, Corporate Internal Investigations, Major Incident Management, Civil Fraud, Class Action, Defamation, Election Law and Sexual Harassment Defense. Premises Liability Defense, serious Personal Injury, Wrongful Death, selective Police Misconduct Litigation (Plaintiff and Defense), selective Professional Liability and Governmental Liability. Representation before Military Criminal Courts Martial and Administrative Boards, Disciplinary Labor Arbitrations, Professional Disciplinary License Boards, Academic/Disciplinary hearing/appeals panels (undergraduate, graduate and professional schools); Liquor Licensing Boards and Zoning and Permit Boards.

See Professional Biographies, CHICAGO, ILLINOIS

Hoopingarner, Kirk A., (AV) .... '58 '84 C.323 B.A. L.477 J.D. [Gardner C.&D.]
Hoornstra, Dennis W., Attorney
(See Wheaton)
Hooven, Julie Osswald '68 '93 C.339 B.S. L.424 J.D.
30 North La Salle Street, Suite 4300
Hoover, Allen E., (AV) .... '— '93 C&L.339 B.S., J.D. [Banner&W.] (See Pat. Sect.)
Hoover, Allen J., (AV) '40 '65
C.436 B.M.E. L.209 J.D. [Wood,P.K.C.&M.] (See Pat. Sect.)
Hoover, Marsha K., (AV) .... '55 '80 C&L.597 B.S., J.D. [Davis M.]
Hoover, Mike J. '48 '78 C.321 B.A. L.930 J.D.
V.P., Gen. Coun. & Secy., Pechiney Plastic Packaging, Inc.
Hoover, R. Sam .... '31 '94 C.602 B.S. L.424 J.D. [R.S.Hoover&Assoc.]
Hoover, Robert S. .... '66 '93 C.174 B.A. L.365 J.D. [R.S.Hoover&Assoc.]
Hoover, Russell J., (AV) .... '40 '65 C.602 A.B. L.276 J.D. [Jenner&B.]
Hoover, R. S., & Associates .... 20 North Clark Street, Suite 3600
Hopf, Rachel A. .... '78 '04 C.602 B.A. L.145 J.D. [Ⓐ Mayer,B.R.&M.]
Hopkins, Alexander G. .... '69 '96 C.188 B.A. L.597 J.D. [Ⓐ Lord,B.&B.]
Hopkins, Catherine E. .... '59 '85 C.350 B.S. L.221 J.D. 222 N. La Salle St.
Hopkins, David H., (AV) .... '44 '69 C.228 A.B. L.178 J.D. [Schiller,D.&F.]
Hopkins, Nkrumah Lumumba ... '70 '98 C.339 B.S. L.910 J.D. 1525 E. 53rd St., Ste. 1103
Hopkinson, James R., (AV) .... '59 '85 C.363 B.S.B.A. L.424 J.D. [Ⓐ Cooney&C.]
Hopp, Anthony G., (AV) .... '62 '88 C&L.339 B.A., J.D. [Wildman,H.A.&D.]
Hopp, Gregory D. .... '59 '84 C.339 B.A. L.477 J.D. [Cozen O.]
Hopp, Jason L. .... '73 '98 C.339 B.A. L.365 J.D. [Ⓐ Dykema G.P.]
Hoppe, John C. '47 '75 C.378 B.A. L.309 J.D.
(adm. in MA; not adm. in IL) President, General Counsel Corporation

Hoppe, Wayne G. '50 '75 C&L.352 B.A., J.D.
Sr. Div. Coun., American Medical Association
Hopper, Penelope S. .... '68 '96 C.910 B.A. L.1439 J.D. [Wilson E.M.E.&D.]
Horan, Cecilia A. .... '66 '97 C.999 B.A. L.365 J.D. [Hinshaw&C.]
Horan, David W. ....'52 '83 C.893 B.A. L.910 J.D. [R.P.Etherton&Assoc.]
Horan, Janet K. .... '39 '79 C.351 B.A. L.146 J.D. Sr. Legis. Coun., AMA
Horan, Kevin W. .... '54 '79 C.436 B.S. L.209 J.D. [Rock F.]
Horbenko, Rachell M., The Law Office of '75 '01
C.742 B.A. L.146 J.D. 7527 North Seeley Avenue
Horenkamp, Thomas H. .... '— '04 C.602 B.A. L.472 J.D. [McGuirewoods]
Horie, Tadashi ...... '— '98 C.688 M.B.A. L.424 J.D. [Brinks H.G.&L.] (See Pat. Sect.)
Horiszny, Laurene H. ....'55 '80 C.475 B.A. L.608 J.D. Gen. Coun., BorgWarner Inc.
Hormeku, Lebene Abena '74 '00 C&L.94 B.A., J.D.
(adm. in MA; not adm. in IL) 30 S. Wacker Dr., Ste. 3900
Horn, James T. .... '49 '81 C&L.597 B.S., J.D. Aechdiosie of Chicago
Horn, Lizabeth F., (AV) .... '47 '74 C.210 B.A. L.424 J.D. [Katten M.R.]
Horn, Stanley J. .... '38 '63 C.339 B.A. L.597 J.D. [Azulay,H.&S.] (⊙New York, NY)
Hornbrook, Michael J., (BV) '55 '80
C.424 B.A. L.1292 J.D. 77 West Wacker Drive, Suite 4500
Horne, Mark J., (AV) ....'46 '73 C.801 B.S. L.209 J.D. [Quarles&B.]
Hornewer, Charles A., (AV) ...... '56 '81 C&L.209 B.A., J.D. 161 N. Clark St., Ste. 4925
Hornish, Michele Lynn ....'75 '01 C&L.502 B.A., J.D. [Lovells]
Hornsby, William E., Jr., (AV) ....'51 '80 C.339 B.A. L.209 J.D. 541 N. Fairbanks Ct.
Hornstein, Charlotte, (Miss), (AV) ..... '12 '35 C.145 Ph.B. L.365 LL.B. Asst. States Atty.
Horowitz, Paul, (Ltd.) .... '51 '76 C.823 B.A. L.365 J.D. [Horowitz&W.]
Horowitz and Weinstein, A Professional Corporation
311 West Superior Street Suite 525
Horras, Linda K. ....'61 '89 C.424 B.S. L.365 J.D. [Hinshaw&C.]
Horrigan, Molly A. ... '— '93 C.373 B.A. L.424 J.D. 208 South La Salle Street, Suite 950
Horsch, Christopher J. .... '41 '69 C.797 B.A. L.228 LL.B. Gen. Coun., Shorebank Corp.
Horsnail, Joanna K. .... '71 '96 C.174 B.S. L.146 J.D. [Mayer,B.R.&M.]
Horstman, James K., (AV) ....'53 '80 C.210 B.A. L.910 J.D. [Iwan C.H.H.&V.]
Horton, Keith E. .... '— '04 C.976 B.A. L.339 J.D. [Cozen O.]
Horton, Margaret Glunz .... '— '02 C&L.602 B.A., J.D. [Winston&S.]
Horton, Timothy E. ....'— '02 C.321 B.A. L.602 J.D. [Ungaretti&H.]
Horvat, Stephen P., Jr. '46 '74 C.918 B.A. L.597 J.D.
Senior Vice President - Legal & Secretary, North America Co. for Life & Health Ins.
Horvath, Donald S., (AV) ....'58 '84 C.339 B.S. L.46 J.D. [Jenner&B.]
Horvath, John F., (AV) .... '46 '74 C.209 B.S.C. L.365 J.D. [Horvath&L.]

Horvath & Lieber, P.C., (AV)
10 South La Salle, Suite 1400, 60603
Telephone: 312-419-6600 Fax: 312-419-6666
URL: http://www.hlpc-law.com
Rosemarie J. Guadnolo; John F. Horvath; Howard L. Lieber; David L. Poindexter; Joel S. Siegel; Duane C. Weaver. Of Counsel: John J. Enright.
Insurance Coverage Defense and Subrogation. Professional Liability Defense, Inland Marine, Warehouse Legal Liability and Cargo Legal Liability, Product Liability, Commercial Litigation, Environmental and Directors and Officers Liability. Appellate Practice.
See Professional Biographies, CHICAGO, ILLINOIS

Horvay, Christopher J., (AV) ....'51 '76 C.823 A.B. L.597 J.D. [Gould&R.]
Horwich, Allan, (AV) ....'— '69 C.674 A.B. L.145 J.D. [Schiff H.]
Horwich, Terri Finesmith, (AV) ....'58 '85 C.966 B.A. L.597 J.D. [Ballard,D.B.&H.]
Horwitch, David S. ....'— '97 C&L.339 B.A., J.D. [Arnstein&L.]
Horwitch, Mark H. ....'— '00 C&L.339 B.A., J.D. [Tabet D.&R.]
Horwitch, Robert M., (AV) .... '31 '55 C.477 B.B.A. L.309 J.D. [Schuyler,R.&Z.] ‡
Horwitz, Clifford W. .... '59 '84 C.260 B.A. L.146 J.D. [Horwitz,H.&Assoc.]
Horwitz, Donald L. '47 '72 C.477 B.A. L.912 J.D.
(adm. in MI; not adm. in IL) Dir. & Gen. Coun. Global Futures, ABN Amro Inc.
Horwitz, Donald P., (AV) ....'36 '60 C.597 B.S. L.976 LL.B. [Sonnenschein N.&R.]
Horwitz, Marc A. .... '69 '94 C.477 B.A. L.347 J.D. [Baker&M.]
Horwitz, Mitchell W. .... '54 '79 C.589 B.A. L.365 J.D. [Horwitz,H.&Assoc.]
Horwitz, Robert A., Law Offices of '62 '95 C.429 B.A. L.146 J.D.
407 S. Dearborn Street
Horwitz, Samantha H. .... '74 '99 C&L.893 B.A., J.D. [BryceDowney]
Horwitz, Stephen B., (AV) .... '45 '70 C.221 B.A. L.597 J.D. [Sugarman&H.]

Horwitz, Horwitz & Associates, (BV)
25 E. Washington Street, Suite 900, 60602
Telephone: 312-372-8822 Fax: 312-372-1673
Email: office@horwitzlaw.com URL: http://www.horwitzlaw.com
Clifford W. Horwitz; Mitchell W. Horwitz; Marc A. Perper; O. Randolph Bragg; Jay R. Luchsinger; Wayne L. Newman. Associates: Valerie C. Barich; Michael D. Carter, Jr.; Richard J. Doherty; Daniel E. McKenzie; Ray Podobnik; Craig M. Shapiro; James M. Smith; Mark Weissburg.
Languages: Spanish and Polish.
Work-Related Injuries, Auto Accidents, Personal Injury, Negligence, Railroad Injuries, Riverboat Injuries, Consumer Fraud, Defective Products, Malpractice.
See Professional Biographies, CHICAGO, ILLINOIS

Horwood, Daniel L. .... '— '99 C.183 B.A. L.659 J.D. [Mayer,B.R.&M.]
Horwood, Richard M., (AV) ....'40 '65 C.165 A.B. L.659 LL.B. [Horwood M.&B.]

Horwood Marcus & Berk, Chartered, (AV)
180 North LaSalle Street, Suite 3700, 60601
Telephone: 312-606-3200 Telecopier: 312-606-3232
URL: http://www.hmblaw.com
Keith H. Berk; Kenneth W. Bosworth; Brian L. Browdy; Lawrence J. Feller; Joel M. Friedman; Kenneth A. Goldstein; Jordan M. Goodman; Jeffrey A. Hechtman; Richard M. Horwood; David A. Hughes; James L. Jerue; Howard D. Lerman; Fred O. Marcus; David S. Ruskin; Marilyn A. Wethekam; Hal J. Wood; Jeffrey A. Zaluda;—Brenda M. Allison; J. David Ballinger; C. Eric Fader; Benjamin N. Feder; Stavros S. Giannoulias; Chadwick A. Hoyt; Jennifer A. Jors; Scott A. Josephson; Kate Kanabay; Peter J. Kenny; Kenneth Klassman; Shelley H. Koren; Aaron D. Rachelson; Angela L. Vitale; Kristin L. Vucinovich; Lauren J. Wolven. Of Counsel: James H. Ryan.
Corporate, Federal and State Taxation, Real Estate, Trust and Estate Planning and Probate Law. Commercial and Tax Litigation.
See Professional Biographies, CHICAGO, ILLINOIS

Hoseman, Daniel, (AV) .... '35 '59 C&L.339 B.A., J.D. Trustee in Bkrptcy.
Hoseman, Linda Lemel ....'— '89 C.880 B.A. L.861 J.D. [Winston&S.]
Hoskins, Richard J., (AV) .... '— '71 C.378 B.A. L.597 J.D. [Schiff H.] (Pat.)
Hosko, Ronald T. '58 '84 C.649 B.A. L.831 J.D.
(adm. in PA; not adm. in IL) F.B.I.
Hoste, Peter D. ....'72 '97 C.475 B.A. L.424 J.D. [Leahy&H.]
Hosteny, Joseph N., III, (AV) '45 '76
C.436 B.S.M.E. L.209 J.D. [Niro,S.H.&N.] (See Pat. Sect.)
Hosty, Gretchen M. .... '— '03 C.339 B.S. L.146 J.D. [Michael B.&F.] (See Pat. Sect.)
Hosty, Patrick J., (AV) ....'47 '74 C.602 A.B. L.365 J.D. 910 W. Jackson Blvd.
Hotaling, Christopher Paul .... '73 '00 C.228 B.A. L.893 J.D. Law Clk., Dist. Ct.
Houchens, Matthew C. ....'71 '97 C.339 B.S.E. L.365 J.D. [Mayer,B.R.&M.]
Houck, Cara M. .... '65 '97 C.597 B.S. L.1187 J.D. [McGuirewoods]
Hough, John W., (AV) .... '27 '52 C.976 L.424 LL.B. 181 West Madison St.
Houlihan, Daniel L., (AV) .... '36 '62 C&L.424 B.S., J.D. 111 W. Wash. St.
Houlihan, Sean M. .... '68 '02 C.339 B.A. L.209 J.D. [Power R.&S.]
Houpt, Richard V., (AV) '— '52
C.145 A.B. L.339 LL.B. [Pedersen&H.] (⊙Oak Brook)‡
Hourihan, Paul F. .... '51 '79 C.745 B.A. L.602 J.D. 1877 North Leavitt Street‡
Hourihane, John N., Jr. ....'— '98 C.424 B.B.A. L.146 J.D. [Murphy&H.]
House, Emmitt C. .... '49 '78 C.118 B.A. L.597 J.D. [Gonzalez,S.&H.]
Houser, Ann .... '43 '72 C.1016 B.S.B.A. L.209 J.D. Assoc. J.
Hovis, Kevin S. ....'— '99 C.347 B.A. L.339 J.D. [Schiff H.]
Howard, Bradley D. .... '— '98 C.145 A.B. L.813 J.D. [Sidley A.B.&W.]
Howard, Bruce C., (BV) '56 '81 C.162 B.A. L.902 J.D.
122 S. Michigan Ave., Ste. 1850
Howard, David A. ....'— '96 C.352 B.A. L.209 J.D. [Schiff H.]
Howard, Deborah Anne ....'68 '94 C.339 B.A. L.209 J.D. Asst. Dean
Howard, Frank M. ....'54 '80 C.742 B.A. L.589 J.D. 5801 N. Northwest Hwy.
Howard, Jason A. '77 '04 C.378 B.A. L.424 J.D.
Atty., Div. of Enforce., U.S. Secs. & Exch. Comm.
Howard, Jeffrey M. .... '55 '80 C&L.597 B.A., J.D. Capitol Case Coord.
Howard, Joseph G. ....'62 '87 C.339 B.S. L.896 J.D. [J.G.Howard]
Howard, Karen Wilson '61 '86 C.339 B.S. L.424 J.D.
333 S. Wabash Avenue, 25th Floor
Howard, Kathleen M. ....'— '91 C.1183 B.S. L.424 J.D. [Perkins C.]
Howard, Lee M. ....'33 '60 C.207 B.A. L.597 J.D. 2 N. LaSalle St.
Howard, Marjorie C., (AV) .... '63 '92 C.991 B.A. L.597 J.D. [Weinberg R.]
Howard, Mark D. ....'56 '81 C.597 B.S. L.339 J.D. [McDonald&M.]
Howard, Melissa M. '73 '04 C.340 B.A. L.893 J.D.
(adm. in NY; not adm. in IL) [McDermott W.&E.]
Howard, Peter M. .... '58 '85 C.33 B.S. L.976 J.D. [Wildman,H.A.&D.]
Howard, Robert C. .... '42 '67 C.475 B.A. L.309 J.D. [Futterman&H.]
Howard, Rodney C. ....'47 '76 C.542 B.A. L.146 J.D. 8541 S. Cottage Grove
Howard, Thomas F. ....'— '99 C.393 B.A. L.339 J.D. [Chapman&C.]
Howard, William N. ....'— '85 C.339 B.S. L.146 J.D. [Freeborn&P.]
Howard, Joseph G., P.C., Law Offices of .... 217 N. Jefferson St., Ste. 602

Howard & Nemoy, (AV)
111 W. Washington Street, Suite 1023, 60602
Telephone: 312-782-7120 Fax: 312-782-7126 URL: http://www.howardandnemoylaw.com
Email: pnemoy@howardandnemoy.com URL: http://www.howardandnemoy.com
Members of Firm: Paul I. Nemoy; Joseph Pierotti.
Personal Injury, Wrongful Death, Automobile Accidents, Trucking Accidents, Professional Negligence, Nursing Home Abuse, Sexual Abuse, Dog Bites, Railroad Accidents, Slip and Fall, Automotive Products Liability, Aviation Accidents, Airplane Crashes, Boating Accidents, Workers' Compensation.
See Professional Biographies, CHICAGO, ILLINOIS

Howe, Arthur J., (AV) .... '60 '85 C.894 B.A. L.228 J.D. [Schopf&W.]
Howe, Jonathan T., (AV) ......'40 '66 C.597 B.A. L.228 J.D. [Howe&H.] (⊙Wash., DC)

Howe & Hutton, Ltd., (AV)
20 North Wacker Drive, Suite 4200, 60606-9833 ⊙
Telephone: 312-263-3001 Fax: 312-372-6685
Email: hh@howehutton.com URL: http://www.howehutton.com
Jonathan T. Howe; Terrence Hutton; John M. Peterson; Barbara Dunn; Samuel J. Erkonen; C. Michael Deese;—Leland J. Badger (Resident, Washington, D.C. Office); David Walter Norris; Nathan J. Breen; Naomi R. Angel. Of Counsel: Layton E. Olson; Gerard P. Panaro.
General Representation of Not for Profit Organizations, Associations and Related Entities, Antitrust, Corporate, Employment, Contract, Administrative, Tax, Travel, Transportation, Meetings, Expositions and Hospitality Industry, Intellectual Property Law, Arbitration, Alternative Dispute Resolution, Trial and Appellate Practice.
Washington, D.C. Office: 1901 Pennsylvania Avenue, N.W., Suite 1007, 20006. Telephone: 202-466-7252. Fax: 202-466-5829.
Ballwin (St. Louis), Missouri Office: 1421 Buckhurst Court, 63021. Telephone: 636-256-3351. Fax: 636-256-3727.
See Professional Biographies, CHICAGO, ILLINOIS

Howell, Gary W., (AV) .... '50 '77 C&L.352 B.A., J.D. [Gardner C.&D.]
Howell, R. Thomas, Jr. .... '42 '68 C.951 B.A. L.966 J.D. [Seyfarth S.]
Howie, Julie N. ....'69 '94 C.910 B.A. L.146 J.D. [Stamos&T.]
Howie, Scott Langford .... '66 '94 C.597 B.A. L.146 J.D. [Pretzel&S.]
Howlett, Kathleen F. ....'49 '85 C.436 B.S. L.424 J.D. [Shefsky&F.]

Howrey LLP, (AV)
321 North Clark Street, Suite 3400, 60610 ⊙
Telephone: 312-595-1239 Fax: 312-595-2250
URL: http://www.howrey.com
Resident Partners: Joel G. Chefitz; David W. Clough; Christine A. Dudzik; James E. Hanlon, Jr.; Kenneth M. Kliebard; Stephen D. Libowsky; Todd L. McLawhorn; Edward M. O'Toole; Michael P. Padden; Ernest Summers III. Resident Associates: Daniel A. Dorfman; Michael K. Obernesser; Salmaan Quader; Thomas L. Ruffner; Joseph J. Siprut; Lisa C. Sullivan. Resident Senior Associates: Thomas W. Jenkins, Jr.; Teddy C. Scott.
General and Trial Practice including Antitrust, Commercial Litigation, Complex Tort, Corporate Responsibility, Corporate and Transactional, Environmental, Government Contracts, Insurance Coverage, Intellectual Property, International Trade, Products Liability, Securities Litigation, Supreme Court and Appellate and White Collar Criminal Defense.
Washington, D.C. Office: 1299 Pennsylvania Avenue, N.W., 20004-2402. Telephone: 202-783-0800. Fax: 202-383-6610.
Los Angeles, California Office: 550 South Hope Street, Suite 1100, 90071-2604. Telephone: 213-892-1800. Fax: 213-892-2300.
Menlo Park, California Office: 301 Ravenswood Avenue, 94025. Telephone: 650-463-8100. Fax: 650-463-8400.
Houston, Texas Office: 1111 Louisiana, 25th Floor, 77002. Telephone: 713-787-1400. Fax: 713-787-1440.
Other Houston, Texas Office: Wells Fargo Plaza, 1000 Louisiana Street, Suite 1800, 77002. Telephone: 713-654-7600. Fax: 713-654-7690.
Irvine, California Office: 2020 Main Street, Suite 1000. Telephone: 949-721-6900.
London Office: City Point, One Ropemaker Street, EC2Y 9HS. Telephone: 011 44 207 6283303. Fax: 011 44 207 065 6650.
San Francisco, California Office: 525 Market Street, Suite 3600. Telephone: 415-848-4900. Fax: 415-848-4999.
Brussels, Belgium Office: Avenue des Nerviens 9-31, 1040. Telephone: 011 322-741-1011. Fax: 011 322-741-1012.
Amsterdam, The Netherlands Office: The Rembrandt Tower, 31st Floor, One Amstelplein, 1096 HA. Telephone: +31 (0) 20 592 4411. Fax: +31 (0) 20 463 7296.
See Professional Biographies, CHICAGO, ILLINOIS

Howse, Natalie Lynn '73 '01
C.424 B.A. L.329 J.D. Asst. State Atty., Cook Co. State Atty. Off.
Howser, Richard G., (AV) ....'51 '77 C.339 B.A. L.424 J.D. [Clausen M.]
Hoying, Kathryn R. ....'74 '01 C.150 B.B.A. L.209 J.D. [Johnson&B.]
Hoyle, Patricia M. '— '00 C.054 Ph.D. L.966 J.D.
(adm. in WI; not adm. in IL; See Pat. Sect.) [Ladas&P.]
Hoyne, Scott W., (AV) .... '50 '75 C&L.597 B.A., J.D. [Johnson&B.]
Hoyt, Chadwick A. .... '71 '96 C.352 B.S. L.145 J.D. [Horwood M.&B.]
Hoyt, Merrill C., (AV) ....'42 '68 C.339 B.S. L.146 J.D. [Hoyt&W.]
Hoyt, Troy D. .... '— '02 C.36 B.S. L.145 J.D. [Holland&K.]
Hoyt & Waller, P.C., (AV) .... 20 N. Clark Street (⊙Wheaton)

Hrajnoha, James A. ....'52 '77 C.686 B.S. L.365 J.D. 1754 W. Walnut St.
Hrebec, John E., (AV) ....'61 '88 C.602 B.A. L.145 J.D. [Lord,B.&B.]
Hrubec, Laura D. ....'— '02 C.578 B.S. L.209 J.D. [[A] Hennessy&R.]
Hsu, Diana Juliet ....'64 '93 C.477 B.B.A. L.209 J.D. [Winston&S.]
Hsu, Jack C. ....'68 '93 C.145 A.B. L.347 J.D. [Christensen&E.] ⊙
Hsu, Yuan-Ying ....'76 '02 C.976 B.A. L.569 J.D. [[A] Skadden,A.S.M.&F.]
Hu, Shoufen ....'73 '97 L.999 J.D. [[A] Mayer,B.R.&M.]
Hua, Jennifer H. ......'71 '98 C&L.339 B.A., J.D. Sr. Coun., Bank One Corp. (Law Dept.)
Huang, Joe Lee ....'75 '00 C.1375 B.A. L.1529 J.D. 180 N. LaSalle St., Ste. 2901
Huang, John Z., & Associates ....'53 '91 C&L.999 B.A., LL.B. 20 N. Clark
Huang, Roy '58 '83 C.112 A.B. L.276 J.D.
(adm. in CA; not adm. in IL) Arthur Andersen (Legal Department)
Hubachek, F. B., Jr., (AV) ....'— '50 C.976 L.145 J.D. [[C] Chapman&C.]
Hubalik, Timothy M. ....'50 '79 C.424 A.B. L.209 J.D. 3805 N. Oconto
Hubbard, Elizabeth Louise, (AV) .... '49 '74 C.383 B.A. L.146 J.D. [Hubbard&O.]
Hubbard, G. William, II ....'51 '78 C.870 B.S. L.146 J.D. [Hubbard B.]
Hubbard, Meghan M. ....'— '01 C.932 B.A. L.146 J.D. [[A] Wildman,H.A.&D.]

Hubbard, Michael V. '— '00 C.339 B.A. L.209 J.D.
200 West Madison Street, Suite 710, 60606
Telephone: 312-345-9290 Fax: 312-372-8456
Email: advice@idolaw2.com URL: http://www.idolaw2.com
Elder Law, Bankruptcy, Real Estate, Wills and Trusts, Probate, Chapter 7 and 11 Bankruptcy.
See Professional Biographies, CHICAGO, ILLINOIS

Hubbard, Patricia L. ....'57 '92 C.339 B.S. L.424 J.D. [[C] Seyfarth S.]
Hubbard, William H. J. ....'76 '02 L.145 J.D. [[A] Mayer,B.R.&M.]

Hubbard Business Counsel
222 N. LaSalle Street, Suite 300, 60601-1013
Telephone: 312-704-3624 Fax: 312-704-3001
Email: b.h@hbcounsel.com URL: http://www.hbcounsel.com
Member of Firm: G. William Hubbard, II.
Closely Held Businesses, Mergers and Acquisitions.
See Professional Biographies, CHICAGO, ILLINOIS

Hubbard & O'Connor, Ltd., (AV)
900 West Jackson Boulevard, Suite 6W, 60607
Telephone: 312-421-5960 Fax: 312-421-5310
Email: ehubbard@hubbardoconnor.com URL: http://www.lawyers.com/hubbardoconnorlaw
Elizabeth Louise Hubbard; John Campbell O'Connor;—Brian D. Ekstrom.
General Civil Trial Practice. Employment Related Litigation and Counsel. Domestic Relations and Family Law. Probate. Labor and Employment, Americans with Disabilities Act, Employment Discrimination, Family and Medical Leave Act, Sexual Harassment, Wrongful Termination, Executive Compensation.
See Professional Biographies, CHICAGO, ILLINOIS

Hubbarth, Michael P. ... '53 '79 C.477 B.B.A. L.215 J.D. Sr. Atty., General Growth Prop.
Hubbell, Angela Marie '69 '95 C.477 B.S. L.607 J.D.
(adm. in MI; not adm. in IL) [[A] Matkov,S.M.&G.]
Hubbuch, John A. ....'49 '74 C.880 B.A. L.145 J.D. [McCullough,C.&L.]
Huber, Anne Marrs ....'— '92 C.436 B.A. L.494 J.D. [Kirkland&E.]
Huber, David P. ....'68 '93 C.339 B.A. L.424 J.D. [[A] Healy]
Huber, Helga E. ....'48 '73 C.94 B.A. L.597 J.D. 9535 S. Damen Ave.‡
Huber, Michael D., (AV) ....'60 '85 C.894 A.B. L.345 J.D. [Iwan C.H.H.&V.]
Hubert, Donald, (AV) .... '48 '73 C.424 B.A. L.477 J.D. [Hubert&F.]

Hubert & Fowler, P.C., (AV)
188 West Randolph Street Suite 801, 60601
Telephone: 312-368-0213 Fax: 312-782-4811 URL: http://www.hubert-fowler.com URL: http://www.hfqlaw.com
Email: info@Hubert-Fowler.com URL: http://www.hubert-fowlerlaw.com
Members of Firm: Donald Hubert; Philip ⊙ Fowler. Associates: Myron F. Mackoff; Stephanie L. Stewart-Page; Ted S. Li; Gabriel A. Caravello; Ethan P. Mandziara; Sherry J. Daun.
Administrative Law, Appellate Practice, Chancery and Equity, Civil Rights, Commercial Law, Complex Litigation, Constitutional Law, Construction Law, Contracts, Corporate Law, Criminal Defense, Employment Discrimination, Environmental Law, Government Law, Health Care, Insurance Defense, Libel and Slander, Defamation, Litigation, Products Liability, Professional Liability, Torts, Toxic Torts, Civil Litigation.
See Professional Biographies, CHICAGO, ILLINOIS

Huberty, James J. ....'69 '98 C&L.352 B.S., J.D. [Walker W.M.]
Hubertz, Elizabeth J. ....'65 '93 C.937 B.A. L.893 J.D. [Robinson C.&C.]
Hubka, Ronald J. ....'32 '55 C.999 L.209 LL.B. Asst. States Atty.

Hucek, Jeffrey M.
(See Oak Brook)

Huck, John B., (AV) ....'32 '56 C.197 B.A. L.477 J.D. 500 W. Madison, 40th Fl.‡
Hucker, Brian S., (AV) ....'48 '73 C&L.424 B.A., J.D. [McDermott W.&E.]
Huckman, Andrew G. ....'67 '92 C.674 A.B. L.597 J.D. Illinois Commerce Commission
Huddle, Mark A. ....'59 '92 C.388 B.A. L.339 J.D. [[A] Wildman,H.A.&D.]
Hudgins, Margaret Lee ....'— '04 C.145 A.B. L.146 J.D. [[A] Kirkland&E.]
Hudson, Judith M. ....'67 '92 C.966 B.A. L.145 J.D. Mng. Dir., Major, Lindsey & Africa
Hudson, Kristen E. ....'— '03 C.575 A.B. L.365 J.D. [[A] Sachnoff&W.]
Hudson, Kurt L. ....'49 '77 C.589 B.S. L.209 J.D. [Hinshaw&C.]
Hudson, Maaike S. ....'— '99 C.966 B.A. L.477 J.D. [[A] Latham&W.]
Hudson, Rockney W. ....'58 '83 [Hackbarth&H.]
Hudson, Sally A. ......'57 '83 C.207 B.A. L.209 J.D. Natl. Off. Machine Dealers Assn.
Hudson, Timothy A. ....'74 '00 C.966 B.A. L.477 J.D. [[A] Jenner&B.]
Hudson-Winfield, Gilda, Attorney at Law '55 '85
C.966 B.A. L.424 J.D. 203 N. Wabash Ave., Ste. 1012
Huebsch, Robert P., (AV) ....'— '75 C.201 B.S. L.146 J.D. [Querrey&H.]
Huettel, Richard C., (AV) ....'60 '85 C.477 B.A. L.209 J.D. [Cassiday,S.&G.]
Huff, Andrea L. '73 '99 C.347 B.A. L.365 J.D.
General Adjuster, Fireman's Fund/Interstate Insurance Group‡
Huff, Carol Anne ....'— '96 C.446 B.A. L.228 J.D. [Kirkland&E.]
Huff, Carrie Kiger, (AV) ....'49 '85 C.645 B.A. L.145 J.D. [Mayer,B.R.&M.]
Huff, Diane M. ....'59 '84 C.57 B.A. L.339 J.D. [[C] Mayer,B.R.&M.]
Huff, John Chafer ....'57 '84 C&L.477 B.S., J.D. [[C] Mayer,B.R.&M.]
Huff, John L., (AV) ....'48 '73 C.1030 B.A. L.276 J.D. [Huff&G.]
Huff, Roger M., Law Offices of, (AV) '47 '76
C.33 B.A. L.145 J.D. 1525 E. 53rd Street, Suite 502
Huff, William A. ....'46 '70 C.347 B.S. L.339 J.D. [Huff&K.]
Huff & Gaines Ltd., (AV) ....10 S. La Salle St., Ste. 3500
Huff & Kennedy ....10450 S. Western Ave.
Huffman-Gottschling, David ....'69 '99 C.747 B.A. L.477 J.D. [[A] Jacobs,B.O.S.&H.]
Hufford, Catherine A. ....'64 '91 C.719 B.B.A. L.1187 J.D. Asst. State's Atty.
Huft, Michael J. ....'— '97 C.602 B.S. L.477 J.D. [[C] Schiff H.]
Huggins, Rollin C., Jr., (AV) ....'31 '58 C.388 A.B. L.309 LL.B. [[C] Bell,B.&L.]
Hughes, A. Blair ....'58 '91 C.701 B.S. L.209 J.D. [McDonnell B.H.&B.] (See Pat. Sect.)
Hughes, Carolyn Cozad ....'50 '75 C.813 B.A. L.597 J.D. Dept. of Health & Human Servs.
Hughes, Charles S. ....'— '76 C.57 B.A. L.597 J.D. [Chapman&C.]
Hughes, David A. ....'66 '91 C.602 B.A. L.178 J.D. [Horwood M.&B.]
Hughes, Jane E. ....'78 '04 C&L.347 B.S., J.D. [[A] Dowd&D.]
Hughes, John A. ....'— '01 C.475 B.A. L.273 J.D. [[A] DLPiper R.G.C.U.]
Hughes, John K., (AV) ....'48 '74 C.321 A.B. L.145 J.D. [Hughes S.P.R.&D.]
Hughes, John M. ....'51 '86 C.339 B.S. L.46 J.D. [Vedder,P.K.&K.]
Hughes, Julie K. ....'— '78 C.221 B.A. L.190 J.D. Gen. Coun., State Educ. Labor Rel Bd.
Hughes, Matthew J. ....'68 '93 C&L.339 B.A., J.D. Gen. Coun., Natl. Wrecking Co.
Hughes, Michael F. ....'— '03 C.46 B.S. L.146 J.D. Two North LaSalle Street, Suite 2200
Hughes, Michael J. ....'64 '89 C.145 B.A. L.910 J.D. [Neal,G.&E.]
Hughes, Miles W. ....'68 '97 C.260 B.A. L.259 J.D. [[A] McDermott W.&E.]
Hughes, Susan M. ....'68 '94 C.339 B.A. L.209 J.D. [Sonnenschein N.&R.]
Hughes, Timothy M. ....'62 '92 C&L.209 M.B.A., J.D. 208 S. LaSalle

Hughes Socol Piers Resnick & Dym, Ltd., (AV)
70 West Madison, Suite 4000, 60602
Telephone: 312-580-0100 Telecopy: 312-580-1994
URL: http://www.ghsltd.com
Robert R. Anderson; José J. Behar; Mark S. Dym; John K. Hughes; Bernice Jacobs; Richard F. Johnson; Joshua Karsh; Peter M. Katsaros; Barry Locke; Kimberley Marsh; Terence J. Moran; Donald G. Peterson; Matthew J. Piers; Kalman D. Resnick; Frederick S. Rhine; Mary M. Rowland; Donna Kaner Socol; J. Eric Vander Arend; Mark B. Weiner;—Natalie A. Bautista; Juliet V. Berger-White; Samir Zia Chowhan; Cara Ann Hendrickson; Cathy L. Higgens; Allison G. Margolies; Peter C. McLeod; Alex R. Montgomery; Fazila Vaid. Of Counsel: Gary Chodorow.
General Civil and Litigation Practice in all Courts. Insurance and Reinsurance. Personal Injury, Immigration, Civil Rights, Class Actions, Labor and Employment, Commercial, Professional Liability, Litigation.
See Professional Biographies, CHICAGO, ILLINOIS

Hugi, Robert F., (AV) ....'58 '86 C.597 B.S. L.145 J.D. [Mayer,B.R.&M.]
Huizenga, Timothy '54 '79
C.114 B.A. L.145 J.D. Atty., Legal Assistance Found. of Chicago
Hulbert, Bradley J., (AV) '52 '77
C&L.494 B.E.E., J.D. [McDonnell B.H.&B.] (See Pat. Sect.)
Hulbert, James W. ....'56 '82 C.575 B.A. L.93 J.D. [Schiff&H.]
Hulbert-Batiste, Lesia M. ....'61 '89 C.801 B.A. L.803 J.D. Asst. Pub. Def.
Hull, David M. '55 '84 C.900 B.B.A. L.378 J.D.
Contl. Ill. Natl. Bk. & Tr. Co. of Chicago
Hull, Edwin J., III, (BV) ....'53 '79 C.893 B.A. L.880 J.D. [McGowan&H.] ⊙
Hull, Jamie L. ....'75 '01 C.473 B.A. L.1000 J.D. [[A] Cassiday,S.&G.]
Hull, Paul Gerald, Jr. ....'70 '96 C.966 B.A. L.989 J.D. [Stahl&B.]
Hullihan, James A. ....'49 '76 C.602 B.A. L.146 J.D. 33 N. Dearborn Street
Hulse, Benjamin W. ....'— '02 C.309 A.B. L.145 J.D. [[A] Kirkland&E.]
Hulse, Minard E., Jr., (AV) ....'38 '64 C.293 B.A. L.309 J.D. 195 N. Harbon Dr.
Hulshizer, Robin M. ....'— '92 C.597 B.S. L.352 J.D. [Latham&W.]
Hult, Keith C., (AV) ....'50 '76 C.339 A.B. L.608 J.D. [Littler M.]
Hultquist, James T. ....'— '90 C.340 B.S. L.424 J.D. [Sachnoff&W.]
Hultquist, Michael D. '61 '86 C.436 B.S. L.424 J.D. [Sonnenschein N.&R.]
Hummel, Brandon G. ....'— '04 C.367 B.A. L.597 J.D. [[A] Wildman,H.A.&D.]
Hummel, Gregory W., (AV) ....'49 '74 C.430 B.A. L.597 J.D. [Bell,B.&L.]
Humphrey, J. Scott ....'71 '97 C.967 B.A. L.365 J.D. [[A] Seyfarth S.]
Hundley, David M., II ....'71 '98 C.150 B.A. L.209 J.D. Asst. Corp. Coun.
Hunken, Alan J. ....'37 '62 C.966 B.A. L.174 LL.B. Hunken
Hunnewell, Todd W. ....'75 '00 C.589 B.A. L.209 J.D. [[A] Busse&B.]
Hunt, Brian J. ....'64 '91 C.477 B.B.A. L.339 J.D. [Hunt]
Hunt, Ellen M. ....'62 '90 C.323 B.A. L.365 J.D. 203 N. La Salle St.
Hunt, Keith L. ....'60 '85 C.1044 B.A. L.365 J.D. [Hunt&Assoc.] (Pat.)
Hunt, Lawrence H., Jr., (AV) ....'43 '70 C.197 A.B. L.145 J.D. [Sidley A.B.&W.]

Hunt, Thaddeus, Law Offices of '74 '02 C.679 B.A. L.1000 J.D.
53 West Jackson Boulevard, Suite 1620, 60604
Telephone: 312-834-0609 Fax: 312-834-0610
Email: huntlaw@innoport.com URL: http://www.thaddeusjhunt.com
Bankruptcy, Consumer Bankruptcy, Commercial Bankruptcy, Foreclosures, Libel, Slander and Defamation, Consumer Fraud, Automobile Accidents, Dog Bites, Slip and Fall, Condominium Law, Homeowners Association Law, Landlord and Tenant Law, Residential Real Estate, Buying and Selling a Home, Business Law, Mechanics Liens, Breach of Contract, Identity Theft, Commercial Transactions, Civil Litigation, Federal Litigation, Trial Practice.
See Professional Biographies, CHICAGO, ILLINOIS

Hunt & Associates, P.C. ....70 W. Madison St. (Pat.)

Hunt Law Group, The, L.L.C.
101 North Wacker Drive Suite 612, 60606
Telephone: 312-780-7481 Fax: 312-780-7587
Email: bhunt@hunt-lawgroup.com
Brian J. Hunt;—W. Scott Trench; C. Murray Harris. Of Counsel: Mark R. Mayer.
Commercial Litigation, Professional Liability, Construction Litigation, Products Liability, Transportation Litigation, Premises Liability, Insurance Coverage, Appellate Practice.
See Professional Biographies, CHICAGO, ILLINOIS

Hunter, Darren J. ....'— '88 C.339 B.A. L.146 J.D. [[C] LeBoeuf,L.G.&M.]
Hunter, James G., Jr., (AV) ....'— '67 C.124 B.S. L.145 J.D. [Latham&W.] (Pat.)
Hunter, John C. ....'74 '00 C&L.352 B.A., J.D. [[A] Wilson E.M.E.&D.]
Hunter, Karen A. '54 '81 C.260 B.S. L.424 J.D.
Coun., Quaker Foods & Beverages (Pat.)
Hunter, Luke ....'45 '77 C.339 B.S. L.209 J.D. 1507 E. 53rd St.
Hunter, Nancy Scheurwater ....'— '83 C.914 B.A. L.309 J.D. [[C] Latham&W.]
Hunter, R. William ....'— '91 C.802 B.B.A. L.339 J.D. [Chapman&C.]

Hunter, Steven R. '62 '87 C&L.477 A.B., J.D.
820 West Jackson Boulevard, Suite 310, 60607
Telephone: 312-466-9466 Fax: 312-993-1554
Email: srhunterlaw@sbcglobal.net URL: http://www.lawyers.com/srhlaw
Criminal Trial and Appellate Practice. Drug Cases, Drugs and Narcotics, Drug Crimes, Cocaine, Heroin, Conspiracy, Fraud, Bank Fraud, Theft, Murder, Homicide, Guns, Weapons, Juvenile Criminal Law, Forgery, White Collar Crime, Felonies, Misdemeanors.
See Professional Biographies, CHICAGO, ILLINOIS

Hunter, Steven V. ....'77 '02 C.103 A.B. L.276 J.D. [[A] DLPiper R.G.C.U.]
Hunter, William H. ....'45 '72 C.46 B.S. L.146 J.D. 29 S. La Salle St., Ste 950
Huntington, Howard L. ....'72 '98 C.339 B.A. L.146 J.D. [[A] Williams M.&J.]
Huntley, John S. ....'49 '79 C.477 B.A. L.365 J.D. [Sanchez&D.]
Huntzicker, Joseph C. ....'73 '00 C&L.477 B.A., J.D. [Fox,H.S.L.&C.]
Huon, Meanith ....'70 '96 C.293 B.A. L.424 J.D. [[A] Johnson&B.]
Hupp, John W., (AV) ....'27 '53 C.597 B.S. L.477 J.D. [[C] Defrees&F.]
Hurd, Matthew A., (BV) ....'57 '85 C.338 B.S. L.602 J.D. 415 N. LaSalle St.
Hurd, Robert J. ....'34 '72 C.602 B.S. L.597 J.D. Bank of America Ill.
Hurka, Thomas F. ....'71 '99 C.696 B.A. L.665 J.D. [[A] Baker&M.]
Hurlbut, John F. '59 '84 C&L.879 B.A., J.D.
Asst. Dist. Coun., Immigration & Naturalization Serv.
Hurley, Annette Brands ....'— '95 C.424 B.A. L.602 J.D. [Sachnoff&W.]
Hurley, Brian E., & Associates '59 '84 C.93 B.A. L.365 J.D.
39 S. LaSalle Street, Ste. 707

Hurley, Christopher T., (AV) .... '59 '84 C.165 B.A. L.424 J.D. [Hurley,M.&M.]
Hurley, David J. .... '68 '99 C.886 B.S. L.365 J.D. [© Thiedmann&E.] (Pat.)
Hurley, Edward C., III .... '54 '80 C.436 B.S. L.365 J.D. Ill. Com. Comm.
Hurley, Joanne F. .... '50 '78 C.475 B.A.B.S. L.209 J.D. [Hurley S.]
Hurley, Robert E. .... '55 '82 C.602 B.A. L.178 J.D. 22 W. Monroe St.
Hurley, Thomas J. .... '30 '69 C.597 B.B.A. L.1340 J.D. 777 N. Michigan Ave.
Hurley, William J., III .... '56 '82 C.388 B.A. L.365 J.D. [Ⓐ Crowley&L.]

Hurley, McKenna & Mertz, (AV)
33 N. Dearborn Street Suite 1430, 60602
Telephone: 312-553-4900 Fax: 312-553-0964 URL: http://www.hurley-lawfirm.com
Email: cthurley@hurley-law.com URL: http://www.hurley-law.com
Christopher T. Hurley; Mark R. McKenna; Michael T. Mertz. Associates: Lara M. Palles; Michael S. Keating.
Personal Injury, Plaintiff, Medical Negligence, Nursing Home Abuse.
See Professional Biographies, CHICAGO, ILLINOIS

Hurley Stanners, Limited
30 South Wacker Drive, Suite 2300, 60606-7410
Telephone: 312-236-6700 Fax: 312-236-6706 URL: http://www.lawyers.com/hurleystanners
Email: jhurley@komdr.com URL: http://www.hurleystanners.com
Joanne F. Hurley.
International and Domestic Business, Commercial Transactions and Real Estate Practice, with Concentrations in the Marketing, Creative Arts and Entertainment Fields.
See Professional Biographies, CHICAGO, ILLINOIS

Hurowitz, Merle .... '32 '56 C.597 B.S. L.209 J.D. Swan Cleaners, Inc.
Hurse, Lonathan .... '48 '80 C.475 B.S. L.765 J.D. Sears Roebuck & Co.
Hurst, Brian .... '70 '95 C.234 B.A. L.146 J.D. [Taxman&H.]
Hurst, James F., (AV) .... '64 '89 C.205 B.S. L.659 J.D. [Winston&S.]
Hurst, Matthew T. .... '73 '99 C.787 B.A. L.597 J.D. [Ⓐ Susman,W.&W.]
Hurt, Blanche O. '46 '80 C.57 B.A. L.146 J.D.
V.P. & Gen. Coun., Harris Bankcorp, Inc.
Hurtado, Daniel J. .... '49 '93 C.477 B.A. L.597 J.D. [Jenner&B.]
Hurwitz, Joel M., (AV) .... '— '76 C.665 B.A. L.145 J.D. [Arnstein&L.]
Hurwitz, Robert S. '47 '73
C.339 B.S. L.597 J.D. Assoc. Gen. Coun., Employ. Law, Aon Corp.
Huseby, Laura S. .... '71 '97 C&L.884 B.A.B.S., J.D. [Ⓐ Stamos&T.]
Husman, David L. .... '34 '57 C.339 L.209 LL.B. 1200 N. Ashland Ave.
Husmann, John A. .... '69 '00 C.190 B.A. L.424 J.D. [Ⓐ Tressler,S.M.&P.]
Husnick, Chad J. .... '— '04 C.966 B.S. L.145 J.D. [Ⓐ Kirkland&E.]
Hussain, Khurram .... '69 '95 C.035 B.A. L.801 J.D. [Hussain E.B.&F.]
Hussain, M. Faiyaz .... '71 '01 C&L.339 B.S., J.D. [Ⓐ Winston&S.]
Hussain Egan Bendersky and Franczyk LLC .... 430 West Erie Street, Suite 500
Hussein, Ferris J. .... '77 '03 C.477 B.A. L.893 J.D. [Ⓐ Katten M.R.]
Hussey, James E. .... '48 '73 C.339 B.A. L.424 J.D. 200 W. Madison, Ste. 3660
Hussey, Sean P. .... '72 '99 C.719 B.A. L.424 J.D. [Ⓐ Johnson&B.]
Huston, John H., (AV) .... '41 '76 C.976 B.S. L.424 J.D. [Tressler,S.M.&P.]
Huszagh, Fritz K., (AV) .... '53 '81 C.747 B.A. L.146 J.D. [Hinshaw&C.]
Hutchins, Harley, (AV) .... '42 '73 C.951 B.A. L.597 J.D. 190 South La Salle Street‡
Hutchinson, Alan D., (BV) .... '62 '87 C.210 B.A. L.345 J.D. 664 West Aldine Avenue
Hutchinson, Leland E., (AV) .... '48 '73 C.675 B.A. L.145 J.D. [Winston&S.]
Hutchinson, Leland W., Jr., (AV) .... '— '75 C&L.339 A.B., J.D. [© Freeborn&P.]
Hutchison, Andrew M. .... '78 '04 C.309 B.A. L.352 J.D. [Ⓐ Meckler B.&T.]
Hutchison, James Wellington .... '69 '95 C.597 B.A. L.569 J.D. [Katten M.R.]
Hutchison, Roger S. .... '67 '92 C.339 B.A. L.146 J.D. [Dobbs&H.]
Huttenhower, James A. .... '59 '87 C.197 A.B. L.976 J.D. Chicago-Kent College of Law
Hutton, Doressia L. .... '75 '01 C.852 B.A. L.589 J.D. [Ⓐ Mayer,B.R.&M.]
Hutton, Terrence, (AV) .... '39 '72 C.602 B.B.A. L.597 J.D. [Howe&H.]
Hutul, Pamela J., (AV) .... '— '75 C.393 B.A. L.365 J.D. [Beermann S.W.B.B.G.&L.]
Huyck, William Thomas, (AV) '38 '63
C.197 B.A. L.145 J.D. 122 South Michigan Avenue, Suite 1850
Hwang, Christina .... '— '03 C&L.846 B.A., J.D. [Ⓐ DLPiper R.G.C.U.]
Hwang, David S. ..... '— '98 C.339 B.A. L.910 J.D. [Ⓐ Masuda,F.E.&M.] (⊙Schaumburg)
Hwang, Sharon A. .... '68 '93 C.339 B.S. L.93 J.D. [McAndrews,H.&M.] (See Pat. Sect.)
Hwu, Jackson .... '74 '97 L.597 J.D. [Ⓐ Barack F.K.P.&N.]
Hybel, Paul A. .... '— '88 C.197 B.A. L.569 J.D. [© Freeborn&P.]
Hyde, Henry J., (AV) .... '24 '50 C.276 B.S. L.424 J.D. [Redding&H.]
Hyer, Kathryn Burrer '55 '82 C.1121 B.A. L.1003 J.D.
(adm. in OH; not adm. in IL)
Investment Banker & Mng. Dir., Health Care Grp., Everen Secs.‡
Hylton, Maria O'Brien '60 '87 C.309 A.B. L.976 J.D.
(adm. in MA; not adm. in IL) Assoc. Prof., DePaul Coll. of Law
Hyman, Barry S., (AV) .... '— '84 C.183 B.A. L.930 J.D. [Schiff H.]
Hyman, Douglas W. .... '70 '95 C&L.347 B.A., J.D. [Ⓐ DLPiper R.G.C.U.]
Hyman, Joshua S. .... '63 '89 C.966 B.A. L.910 J.D. [Chuhak&T.]
Hyman, Lawrence H., (AV) ... '51 '76 C.597 B.A. L.209 J.D. 111 W. Wash. St., Ste. 1625
Hyman, Michael B., (AV) .... '52 '77 C&L.597 B.S.J., J.D. [Much S.F.D.A.&R.]
Hymen, Robert A. .... '54 '78 C.37 B.A. L.146 J.D. 55 W. Wacker Dr., Ste. 400
Hyndman, Cynthia H. .... '56 '82 C.1100 A.B. L.966 J.D. [Robinson C.&C.]
Hynes, Brian F. .... '70 '96 C.339 B.A. L.424 J.D. [Shefsky&F.]
Hynes, Carol Pelton '74 '00
C.352 B.A. L.146 J.D. Pilsen Imm. Atty., Chicago Legal Clinic
Hynes, Daniel W., (AV) .... '68 '93 C.602 B.A. L.424 J.D. 100 W. Randolph Street
Hynes, James P., (BV) .... '54 '81 C.388 B.A. L.365 J.D. [S.G.Thomas]
Hynes, John M., (AV) .... '54 '79 C.597 B.A. L.424 J.D. [Clausen M.]
Hynes, Karen K. .... '— '02 C.339 B.A. L.424 J.D. [Ⓐ Franczek S.]
Hynes, Kathryn A. '50 '84 C.531 B.A. L.1340 J.D.
(adm. in FL; not adm. in IL) Managing Director, Law Registry, Inc.
Hynes, Kevin B., (BV) .... '66 '91 C.723 B.S. L.424 J.D. [O'Keefe,L.&H.]
Hynes, Matthew J. .... '71 '97 C.602 B.A. L.424 J.D. [Quinlan&C.]
Hynes, Michael E. ..... '73 '98 C.602 B.B.A. L.424 J.D. Credit Analyst, LaSalle Natl. Bk.
Hynes, Robert E., (AV) .... '44 '69 C&L.424 B.B.A., J.D. [O'Keefe,L.&H.]
Hynes, Thomas C., (AV) .... '38 '62 C&L.424 B.S., J.D. [Quinlan&C.]
Hynes, Thomas F. .... '66 '97 C.602 B.A. L.145 J.D. V.P., Mesirow Financial
Hyun, Jonathan E. .... '73 '98 C&L.94 B.A., J.D. [Ⓐ Gardner C.&D.]
Iadevaia, Lisa A. .... '79 '05 C.690 B.A. L.209 J.D. [Ⓐ Adler,M.&M.]
Ialongo, A. Mark, (AV) ..... '49 '74 C.209 B.A. L.602 J.D. 33 N. Dearborn St., Ste. 1300
Iannazzo, Anthony C. '76 '03 C.723 B.A. L.1565 J.D.
(adm. in NY; not adm. in IL) [Ⓐ Skadden,A.S.M.&F.]
Ibach, Darcy Lynn .... '60 '86 C.339 B.S. L.209 J.D. [Bollinger,R.&G.]

Ice Miller, (AV)
200 West Madison Suite 3500, 60606-3417 ⊙
Telephone: 312-726-1567 Fax: 312-726-7102
Email: info@icemiller.com URL: http://www.icemiller.com
Partners: John D. Burke; Anthony Nimmo; Robert J. Schillerstrom; Richard A. Schnurr; James A. Shanahan; Thomas C. Smith. Of Counsel: Patra S. Geroulis; Brian J. Lum. Associate: Joan G. Ritchey.

(This Listing Continued)

Ice Miller (Continued)
Administrative Law, Antitrust, Appellate Practice, Architectural Malpractice Law, Banking, Bankruptcy, Broadcasting and Communications, Cable TV Franchising, Civil and Criminal Litigation, Civil Rights, Coal Law, College and University Law, Commercial and Business Litigation, Complex Litigation, Computer Law, Contracting and Litigation, Construction Law, Corporate Law, Corporate Finance, Creditors Rights Law, Drug and Medical Device Litigation, Economic Development and Incentives, Education Law, Employee Benefits Law, Entrepreneurial Services, Environmental Law, Estate Development and Finance, Franchise Law, Gaming Law, Gift and Estate Tax, Governmental Affairs, Governmental Relations, Governmental Services and Lobbying, Government Law, Government (Public) Contract Law, Government Procurement, Guardianship, Health Care Law, Immigration Law, Insurance Law, Intellectual Property and Licensing, International Law, Labor and Employment Law (including Equal Employment Litigation, ERISA Practice and Occupational Safety and Health Matters), Liability Risk Management, Licensing, Management Labor Relations Law, Mergers and Acquisitions, Minerals and Mining, Municipal Finance (Bond) Law, Municipal Finance (Bond), Dispute Resolution and Litigation, Municipal Litigation, Municipal Solid Waste Resource Recovery, Municipal Utility Regulation, Occupational Hazards Law (Black Lung, Asbestosis, etc.), Patent, Trademark and Copyright, Plaintiff's Trial Practice, Probate Law, Product Liability Law, Public Agency, Public Authority Financing Law, Public Contract Law, Public Employment Relations, Public Entity Law, Public Finance, Public Health Law, Public Housing Law, Public Schools, Public Sector Collective Bargaining, Public Utility Law, Public Works, Professional Malpractice Law, Real Estate Law (including Sales, Development and Financing, Mortgage Banking, Secured Transactions, Sale/Leasebacks, Condominiums and Zoning), Regulation, Risk and Claims Management, Securities Regulation Law, Sports Law, Taxation (Federal, State and Local), Tax Exempt Organizations, Tort Law, Toxic Torts, Transportation Law, Utility Law, Venture Capital, Venture Finance Services, Workers' Compensation.
Indianapolis, Indiana Office: One American Square, Box 82001. Telephone: 317-236-2100. Fax: 317-236-2219. Internet Email: info@icemiller.com. Web Site Address: http://www.icemiller.com.
Washington, D.C. Office: 1090 Vermont Avenue, N.W., Suite 920. Telephone: 202-824-8600. Fax: 202-824-8601. Email: info@icemiller.com. Web Site Address: http://www.icemiller.com
Reviser of the Indiana Law Digest for this Directory.
See Professional Biographies, CHICAGO, ILLINOIS

Idrizi, Shefik .... '66 '94 134 N. La Salle St., Ste. 2116
Igasaki, Paul M. .... '55 '80 C.597 B.A. L.1067 J.D. Comm. on Asian Amer. Affairs
Ignoffo, Gregory R. .... '79 '04 C.999 B.A. L.365 J.D. [Ⓐ J.G.Kelly]
Igoe, Michael L., Jr., (AV) .... '30 '56 C.276 B.S.S. L.145 J.D. [Vedder,P.K.&K.]

Igoe, Philip A., The Law Offices of '— '77 C.339 B.A. L.146 J.D.
221 N. La Salle Street, Suite 655, 60601
Telephone: 312-372-4298 Fax: 312-372-5147
Bankruptcy Law, Criminal Law, DUI/DWI, Traffic Violations, Transportation Law, White Collar Crimes.
See Professional Biographies, CHICAGO, ILLINOIS

Ihrke, James H., (AV) .... '43 '68 C.597 B.A. L.477 J.D. [Dykema G.P.]
Ilhardt, Lora S. .... '57 '82 C.478 B.A. L.309 J.D. Sara Lee Corp.
Illinois Defense Group, The, PC .... 605 W. Madison St., Ste. 331

Immigration Law Center, P.C.
53 West Jackson Boulevard, Suite 860, 60604
Telephone: 312-461-1005 Fax: 312-461-1012
Email: immigrationlawcenter@att.net URL: http://www.guycroteaulaw.com
Guy V. Croteau.
Immigration Law, Visas, Work Permits, Employment Immigration, Citizenship, Business Law, Small Business Law, Family Businesses, Contracts, Civil Litigation, Consumer Bankruptcy.
See Professional Biographies, CHICAGO, ILLINOIS

Imoukhuede, Areto A. .... '77 '02 C.597 B.A. L.276 J.D. [Ⓐ Sonnenschein N.&R.]
Imparl, Steven D. .... '63 '92 C&L.209 B.S., J.D. 12 S. Michigan Ave.
Impey, W. Richard .... '29 '58 C.221 B.A. L.146 LL.B. 8 S. Michigan Ave., 35th Fl.
Inbau, Fred E. '09 '34 C&L.861 B.S., LL.B.
Prof. of Law, Emeritus, Northwestern Univ.
Indomenico, Sal, (AV) .... '58 '87 C.597 B.A. L.365 J.D. 161 N. Clark St.
Inendino, James V., (BV) .... '60 '85 C.123 B.A. L.209 J.D. [© McDermott W.&E.]
Ingraham, Lesa M. .... '63 '93 C.475 B.A. L.146 J.D. [Ⓐ Sonnenschein N.&R.]
Ingraham, Nancy A. .... '58 '94 C.571 B.S. L.424 J.D. [REFCO]
Ingram, Cheryl D. .... '53 '79 C.966 B.A. L.365 J.D. Asst. Pub. Def.
Ingram, Forrest L., (BV) .... '38 '81 C.812 A.B. L.146 J.D. [F.L.Ingram]
Ingram, John D. .... '29 '66 C.309 A.B. L.365 J.D. Prof., John Marshall Law Sch.
Ingram, Richard L. .... '56 '81 C.234 B.A. L.838 J.D. [Shefsky&F.]
Ingram, Sherrin Ross .... '68 '92 C.940 B.A. L.352 J.D. [© Tressler,S.M.&P.]
Ingram, Forrest L., P.C., (BV) .... 79 West Monroe, Suite 1210
Ingrim, Kathryn Rohde ...... '62 '87 C.424 B.B.A. L.190 J.D. Tax Atty., BP America Inc.
Inlander, David W., (AV) .... '51 '75 C.339 B.A. L.424 J.D. [Fischel&K.]
Inlow, Micah R. .... '74 '02 C.339 B.S. L.424 J.D. [Ⓐ Segal M.S.&M.]
Inman, Lynne C. '64 '91 C.518 B.A. L.128 J.D.
(adm. in MD; not adm. in IL) Principal Consultant, Pricewaterhouse Coopers LLP
Inman, Michael, (AV) .... '51 '79 C.932 B.A. L.365 J.D. 33 N. Dearborn St., Ste. 1825
Innes, Mary Genevieve .... '74 '01 C.475 B.A. L.209 J.D. State Atty. Off. Juv. Div.
Innis, E. Eugene '27 '55 C.378 B.S.Ch.E. L.982 J.D.
(adm. in KS; not adm. in IL; Pat.) 200 South Michigan Avenue, Suite 1000
Innis, Mary E. .... '62 '87 C.57 B.A. L.94 J.D. [Loeb&L.]
Inocelda, Camille D. .... '— '03 C.966 B.A. L.494 J.D. [Ⓐ Sachnoff&W.]
Insalata, S. John .... '33 '58 C.339 L.424 J.D. 426 W. Briar Place
Inskeep, Leroy G., (AV) .... '48 '73 C&L.339 B.S., J.D. [DLPiper R.G.C.U.]
Integris Law, Professional Corporation .... 79 W. Monroe Street (Pat.)
Interlandi, Jessica Bank .... '72 '01 C.276 B.A. L.146 J.D. [Ⓐ Schiller,D.&F.]
Ioppolo, Donna Krier .... '53 '85 C&L.424 A.B., J.D. DePaul Univ.
Iorio-Power, Sandra G. .... '— '94 C&L.436 B.A., J.D. [Ⓐ Anderson,R.]
Irle, Judith L. .... '45 '77 C.1183 B.A. L.209 J.D. Dist. Coun., Small Business Admn.
Irons, Ernest W., (AV) .... '49 '76 C.894 B.A. L.910 J.D. [Schuyler,R.&Z.]
Irukera, Babatunde A. '— '89 L.999 LL.B.
(adm. in WA; not adm. in IL) [DAC]
Irvin, Scott E. .... '— '98 C.910 B.A. L.209 J.D. [Ⓐ Anderson,R.]
Irvine, Katie A. .... '— '97 C.473 B.A. L.365 J.D. [Ⓐ O'Hagan,S.&A.]
Irvine, Robert J., III '62 '94
C.339 B.S. L.597 J.D. [McDonnell B.H.&B.] (See Pat. Sect.)
Irwin, Barbara Jane .... '55 '80 C.475 B.A. L.477 J.D. Hewitt Assoc.
Irwin, Barry F., (AV) .... '— '92 C&L.602 B.S.A.E., J.D. [Kirkland&E.] (Pat.)
Irwin, Jonathan E. .... '— '89 C.324 B.A. L.879 J.D. [Querrey&H.]
Irwin, Shirley A. .... '66 '96 C.806 B.A. L.1015 J.D. [Ⓐ Schueler,D.&C.]
Isaac, Gary A., (AV) .... '60 '85 C.178 B.A. L.976 J.D. [© Mayer,B.R.&M.]
Isaacs, Dean Alan, (AV) .... '61 '86 C&L.339 B.A., J.D. [© Mayer,B.R.&M.]
Isaacs, Elissa L., (AV) .... '66 '91 C.597 B.S. L.273 J.D. [Gardner C.&D.]
Isaacs, Lori D. .... '64 '89 C.475 B.A. L.339 J.D. Brokers Risk Placement Service, Inc.
Isaacs, Steve E. .... '— '95 C.39 B.A. L.569 J.D. [Schiff H.]
Isaacson, Annette '— '99 C.860 B.A. L.178 J.D.
Sr. Coun., Bank One Corp. (Law Dept.)
Isaacson, Barry W. .... '52 '77 C.221 B.A. L.339 J.D. IL Dept. of Employ. Sec.
Isaacson, Nicholas O. .... '— '98 C.309 A.B. L.178 J.D. [Ⓐ Latham&W.]
Isaacson, Samuel B., (AV) .... '57 '82 C.216 B.A. L.1017 J.D. [DLPiper R.G.C.U.]

Isaacson, Sandy N., Law Offices of '41 '67 C.1016 B.S.B.A. L.209 J.D.
1000 North Halsted, Suite 203, 60622
Telephone: 312-255-0007 Fax: 312-255-0009
Email: snilaw@comcast.net URL: http://www.sandynisaacson.com
Family, Divorce, Child Custody, Child Support, Personal Injury, Medical Malpractice, Automobile Accidents, Workers Compensation, Wrongful Death, Probate, Real Estate, Corporate, Business, Contracts, Trusts and Estates, Business Litigation, General Practice.
See Professional Biographies, CHICAGO, ILLINOIS

Isaacson, Steven B., (BV) '56 '81 C.339 B.A. L.188 J.D. [(A) Shaw G.F.G.W.&T.]
Isaly, William Britt '70 '96 C.477 B.A. L.146 J.D. [(A) Ancel,G.D.B.D.&R.]
Isasi, José A., II '— '92 C.228 A.B. L.276 J.D. [Sachnoff&W.]
Isbell, Gregory D. '66 '95 C&L.597 B.A., J.D.
Sr. Coun., Bank One Corporation (Law Dept.)
Isenbergh, Joseph '45 '76 C.178 B.A. L.976 J.D.
(adm. in DC; not adm. in IL) Prof., Univ. of Chicago Law Sch.
Ishbia, Justin R. '— '04 C.475 B.A. L.880 J.D. [(A) Kirkland&E.]
Iskalis, Thomas C. '56 '82 C.602 B.A. L.851 J.D.
(adm. in WI; not adm. in IL) Northern Trust Co., The
Iskowich, David Harris '71 '97 C.659 B.A. L.1119 J.D. Asst. Atty. Gen.
Ismail, Tarek '69 '94 C.118 B.A. L.339 J.D. [Bartlit B.H.P.&S.]
Israel, Deborah J. '70 '97 C.145 A.B. L.339 J.D. State Appl. Def.
Israel, Elliott B. '44 '65 C.339 B.S. L.146 J.D. Contl. Nat. Bk. & Tr. Co. of Chic.
Israel, Harold D., (AV) '— '93 C.477 B.B.A. L.339 J.D. [(C) Kaye S.]
Israel, Ivy D. '74 '99 C.966 B.A. L.146 J.D. [(A) Marks,M.&K.]
Israel, Michael H. '71 '99 C&L.597 B.A., J.D. [(A) Johnson&B.]
Isselhard, Terrell J., (AV) '42 '67 C.1024 B.S. L.339 J.D. [Chuhak&T.]
Itoga, Tomoko '— '00 C.103 B.S. L.597 J.D. [(A) Kirkland&E.] (Pat.)
Ivansek, Donald F., (AV) '61 '90 C.742 B.A. L.365 J.D. [(C) Cassiday,S.&G.]
Iveljic, Mario M. '77 '03 C.976 B.A. L.146 J.D. [(A) Cremer,K.S.&S.]
Iversen, Christine J. '71 '98 C.350 B.S. L.365 J.D. [(A) Pretzel&S.]
Iverson, Matthew J., (AV) '— '64 C&L.966 B.B.A., LL.B. [Litchfield C.]
Ivester, J. Eric '60 '85 C&L.623 B.A., J.D. [Skadden,A.S.M.&F.]
Ivory, Danita V. '76 '00 C&L.209 B.A., J.D. [(A) Edelman,C.&L.]
Iwan, Lori E., (AV) '58 '83 C&L.339 B.S., J.D. [Iwan C.H.H.&V.]

Iwan Cray Huber Horstman & VanAusdal LLC, (AV) [BB]
303 West Madison Street, Suite 2200, 60606 ⊙
Telephone: 312-332-8450 Fax: 312-332-8451
Email: attorneys@iwancray.com URL: http://www.iwancray.com
Lori E. Iwan; Daniel K. Cray; Michael D. Huber; James K. Horstman; Rodney E. VanAusdal; Stephen W. Heil;—Benjamin B. Belcher; LaDonna L. Boeckman; Bryan T. Butcher; Adam C. Carter; Douglas M. DeWitt; David J. Farina; David E. Kravitz; Timothy C. Samuelson; Jennifer L. Tweeton; Christopher D. Wehrman; Ronald L. Wisniewski.
Litigation Practice. Product Liability, Insurance Coverage, E-Commerce, Commercial, Professional Liability, Medical Malpractice, Transportation Liability, Premises Liability, Hospital Liability, Toxic Tort, Environmental Litigation and Civil Appeals in State and Federal Courts.
Clarendon Hills, Illinois Office: 115 W. 55th Street, Suite 400, 60514. Telephone: 630-789-8200.
See Professional Biographies, CHICAGO, ILLINOIS

Iwerebon, Felix E. '63 '89 C.1016 B.S. L.365 J.D. Asst. Corp. Coun.
Izadpanah, Shermin '77 '02 C.025 B.S. L.477 J.D. [(A) Barack F.K.P.&N.]
Izenman, Jeffrey D., (AV) '57 '82 C.339 B.S. L.477 J.D. 525 W. Monroe St., Ste. 1600
Izraelewicz, Jennifer R. '— '00 C.910 B.A. L.846 J.D. [(A) Schiff H.]
Izraelewicz, Mark H. '— '01 C.107 B.S. L.145 J.D.
[(A) Marshall,G.&B.] (See Pat. Sect.)
Izzo, David A. '58 '83 C.209 B.A. L.365 J.D. Mng. Trial Atty.
Jablonski, Carrie A. '— '03 C&L.309 A.B., J.D. [(A) Bartlit B.H.P.&S.]
Jaburek, Donald W., Jr. '55 '81 C.339 B.A. L.365 J.D. 1 N. La Salle St., Ste. 1940
Jachimiak, Tany L. '70 '98 C.339 B.S. L.209 J.D. [(A) Fisher&P.]
Jachimowski, Phyllis A. '13 '38 C.597 L.209 LL.B. 535 N. Michigan Ave.‡
Jaci, Elizabeth Emilia '— '01 C.597 B.A. L.339 J.D. [(A) Anderson,R.]
Jacks, Ronald A., (AV) '35 '59 C&L.494 B.S.L., J.D. 190 S. LaSalle St.‡
Jackson, Bruce B. '— '91 C.1023 B.A. L.365 J.D. [(C) A.J.Madonia&Assoc.]
Jackson, Charles C., (AV) '52 '77 C.1144 B.A. L.597 J.D. [Morgan,L.&B.]
Jackson, Denise R. '59 '92 C.184 B.A. L.209 J.D. Atty., Natl. Labor Rel. Bd.
Jackson, Douglas H. '66 '92 C.103 A.B. L.228 J.D. BancAmerica Robertson Stephens
Jackson, Durman Zolly '60 '87 C.46 B.S. L.339 J.D. Asst. State's Atty.
Jackson, Edward S. '17 '52 C.209 L.365 J.D. 180 N. LaSalle St.
Jackson, Heather A. '71 '97 C.477 B.A. L.597 J.D. [(A) Shefsky&F.]
Jackson, John H. '40 '65 C.910 B.S. L.502 J.D. [Morgan,L.D.&J.]
Jackson, Joshua M. '80 '05 C.966 B.A. L.209 J.D. [(A) Schiller,D.&F.]
Jackson, Kathleen P. '76 '02 C.602 B.A. L.276 J.D.
(adm. in PA; not adm. in IL) [(A) McDermott W.&E.]
Jackson, Linda M. '62 '93 C.424 B.S. L.602 J.D. MWH Energy & Infrastructure, Inc.
Jackson, Nicola '— '96 C.188 B.A. L.309 J.D. [(C) Mayer,B.R.&M.]
Jackson, Nicole A. '71 '97 C.103 A.B. L.145 J.D. 322 S. Green St., Ste. 400
Jackson, Robert F. '21 '49 C&L.597 B.S., J.D. [Henehan,D.&I.]
Jackson, William D. '64 '91 C.339 B.A. L.209 J.D. [(A) Brinks H.G.&L.]
Jackson, Yusef D. '70 '96 C&L.893 B.A., J.D. River North Sales & Service
Jackson, Zachary C. '79 '03 C.880 B.A. L.910 J.D. [(A) Connelly S.H.]

Jackson Lewis LLP, (AV)
320 West Ohio Street, Suite 500, 60610 ⊙
Telephone: 312-787-4949 Facsimile: 312-787-4995
URL: http://www.jacksonlewis.com
Partners: Cathryn E. Albrecht; Robert E. Arroyo; James F. Botana; Peter R. Bulmer; Michael R. Flaherty.
Employment, Labor, Benefits, Immigration Law, and Other Related Litigation, On Behalf of Management Exclusively.
Other offices located in: Atlanta, GA; Boston, MA; Cary, NC; Dallas, TX; Greenville, SC; Hartford, CT; Long Island, NY; Los Angeles, CA; Miami, FL; Minneapolis, MN; Morristown, NJ; New York, NY; Orlando, FL; Pittsburgh, PA; Sacramento, CA; San Francisco, CA; Seattle, WA; Stamford, CT; Vienna, VA; White Plains, NY.
Satellite Offices: 127 Dorrance Street, Providence, Rhode Island 02903. Phone: 401-490-3444. Fax: 401-454-8855.
1225 Market Street, Wheeling, West Virginia 26003. Phone: 304-230-1461. Fax: 304-230-1462.
11 Federal Plaza, Suite 300, Youngstown, OH 44503. Phone: 330-746-2324. Fax: 330-746-7023.
See Professional Biographies, CHICAGO, ILLINOIS

Jacob, Anthony J. '72 '98 C.589 B.A. L.365 J.D. [Hinshaw&C.]
Jacob, Ayad Paul '— '03 C&L.339 B.A., J.D. [(A) Schiff H.]
Jacob, Diana M. '70 '97 C.424 B.S. L.146 J.D. [(A) Healy]
Jacobi, Joseph J. '— '97 C.107 B.A. L.1565 J.D. [Kirkland&E.]
Jacobi, Paula K., (AV) '50 '77 C.477 B.Ed. L.597 J.D. [Sugar,F.&F.]
Jacobs, Alan, (BV) '38 '66 C.209 B.S.C. L.365 LL.B. 33 N. LaSalle St.
Jacobs, Ashley A. '76 '02 C.347 B.S. L.339 J.D. 10 South Lasalle, Ste. 2102
Jacobs, Bernice '46 '83 C.347 B.A. L.146 J.D. [Hughes S.P.R.&D.]
Jacobs, Caryn L. '58 '84 C.813 A.B. L.309 J.D. [Mayer,B.R.&M.]
Jacobs, Darryl P., (AV) '63 '88 C.339 B.S. L.309 J.D. [Levenfeld P.]
Jacobs, Eugene, (AV) '47 '73 C.966 B.A. L.569 J.D. [Seyfarth S.]
Jacobs, Harry S. '06 '29 C.597 L.209 LL.B. 746 N. LaSalle St.‡
Jacobs, James S. '62 '89 C.945 B.A. L.464 J.D. Asst. Pub. Def.
Jacobs, Jeffrey D., (AV) '50 '74 C.98 B.A. L.424 J.D. [Jacobs&Assoc.]
Jacobs, Jennifer L. '76 '01 C.36 B.A. L.209 J.D. [(A) Tribler O.&M.]
Jacobs, John F. '— '93 C.339 B.A. L.209 J.D. [(S) Freeborn&P.]
Jacobs, John G., (AV) '47 '72 C.623 B.A. L.145 J.D. [Jacobs]
Jacobs, Karen L. '52 '87 C.1031 B.S. L.215 J.D. Jud. Clk., Appellate Ct.
Jacobs, Marc M., (AV) '60 '85 C&L.477 A.B., J.D. [Barack F.K.P.&N.]
Jacobs, Marc R., (AV) '60 '85 C.966 B.A. L.94 J.D. [Seyfarth S.]
Jacobs, Mark J. '52 '77 C&L.436 B.S., J.D. [Dale,J.&G.]
Jacobs, Michael David '61 '86 C.966 B.B.A. L.910 J.D. Asst. State's Atty.
Jacobs, Michael J. '57 '82 C.686 B.S.B.A. L.190 J.D.
(adm. in WI; not adm. in IL) U.S. Treas. Dept.
Jacobs, Paul L. '71 '96 C.234 B.A. L.190 J.D. [(A) J.J.Corbett&Assoc.]
Jacobs, Robert S., (AV) '31 '54 C.145 Ph.B. L.309 J.D. 150 N. Michigan Ave.
Jacobs, Todd C. '63 '89 C.352 B.A. L.893 J.D. [Grippo&E.]
Jacobs, Walter D., (AV) '30 '58 C&L.966 B.S., J.D. 33 N. Dearborn St.
Jacobs & Associates, Ltd., (AV) 110 N. Carpenter St.
Jacobs, Burns, Orlove, Stanton & Hernandez, (AV) 122 S. Michigan Avenue
Jacobs Law Firm, The, Chtd., (AV) 122 S. Michigan Ave., Ste. 1850
Jacobsen, John J., Jr., (AV) '44 '75 C.999 B.A. L.145 J.D. [Vedder,P.K.&K.]
Jacobsen, Joni S. '67 '97 C.878 B.A. L.145 J.D. [(A) Katten M.R.]
Jacobsen, Thomas P. '53 '79 C.882 B.A. L.209 J.D. Legal Aid Bur.
Jacobsen, Vanessa G. '72 '97 C.879 B.A. L.209 J.D. [Eimer S.K.&S.]
Jacobsen, William V., Jr. '72 '97 C.475 B.A. L.209 J.D. [(A) Mayer,B.R.&M.]
Jacobson, Alan P., Law Offices of '53 '89 C.801 B.S. L.365 J.D.
10917 S. Campbell Ave.
Jacobson, Andrew A. '64 '92 C.424 B.A. L.339 J.D. [Jenner&B.]
Jacobson, Arent J., (AV) '25 '49 C.999 L.209 LL.B. 247 E. Chestnut St.‡
Jacobson, Catherine A. '57 '82 C.813 A.B. L.309 J.D. [Applegate&T.]
Jacobson, Craig A. '76 '02 C.477 B.A. L.209 J.D. [(A) Swanson,M.&B.]
Jacobson, David C., (AV) '51 '76 C.367 B.A. L.276 J.D. [Sonnenschein N.&R.]
Jacobson, Eric L. '75 '01 C.966 B.S. L.94 J.D. [(A) Winston&S.]
Jacobson, Fruman, (AV) '48 '73 C.339 B.A. L.597 J.D. [Sonnenschein N.&R.]
Jacobson, Jacqueline S. '65 '90 C&L.966 B.A., J.D. [Monico,P.&S.]
Jacobson, James D., (BV) '56 '81 C.347 B.S. L.209 J.D. [Griffith&J.]
Jacobson, Jessica R. '77 '02 C.293 B.A. L.209 J.D. IL State Bd. of Ed.
Jacobson, Keith D. '71 '01 C.999 B.S. L.209 J.D. [(A) K.B.Moll&Assoc.]
Jacobson, Kenneth M., (AV) '54 '79 C.339 B.A. L.813 J.D. [Katten M.R.]
Jacobson, Larry, (AV) '— '81 C.910 B.A. L.276 J.D. [Schiff H.]
Jacobson, Marian S., (AV) '45 '72 C.611 B.A. L.145 J.D. [Sonnenschein N.&R.]
Jacobson, Michael A. '69 '94 C.352 B.B.A. L.209 J.D. [Katten M.R.]
Jacobson, Milton C. '36 '60 C.339 L.209 LL.B. [Jacobson&S.]
Jacobson, Nancy S. '— '85 C.174 B.A. L.276 J.D. [(A) Mayer,B.R.&M.]
Jacobson, P. Michelle '76 '01 C.597 B.A. L.94 J.D. [(A) Vedder,P.K.&K.]
Jacobson, Richard A., (BV) '48 '76 C.992 B.A. L.362 J.D. [(A) Ruff,W.&R.]
Jacobson, Richard J. '43 '77 C.309 A.B. L.893 J.D. [Flaherty&J.]
Jacobson, Richard M. '54 '79 C.339 B.A. L.209 J.D. [S.G.Thomas]
Jacobson, Ronald H., (AV) '63 '88 C.339 B.A. L.424 J.D. [Winston&S.]
Jacobson, Ryan B. '— '99 C.347 B.A. L.146 J.D. [(A) O'Hagan,S.&A.]
Jacobson, Scott B. '56 '81 C.339 B.S. L.46 J.D. V.P., LaSalle Natl. Tr., N.A.
Jacobson, Seth E., (AV) '63 '88 C&L.477 B.A., J.D. [Skadden,A.S.M.&F.]
Jacobson, Steven W. '62 '89 C.352 B.A. L.1000 J.D. [Jacobson&S.]
Jacobson, Thomas A. '73 '03 C&L.209 B.A., J.D. [(A) Dowd&D.]
Jacobson, Brandvik & Anderson, Ltd., (AV) Suite 3800, 20 North Wacker Drive

Jacobson & Sorkin, LTD.
77 West Washington Street, Suite 1500, 60602
Telephone: 312-236-8628 Fax: 312-236-6905
URL: http://www.JacobsonSorkin.com
Members of Firm: Milton C. Jacobson; Steven W. Jacobson; Lynne F. Shapiro.
Personal Injury, Construction Accidents, Workers Compensation, Nursing Home Litigation, Medical Malpractice, Automobile Accidents, Truck Accidents, Dog Bites, Railroad Accidents, Bus Accidents, Sexual Abuse, Slip and Fall, Pedestrian Injuries, Wrongful Death, Products Liability.
See Professional Biographies, CHICAGO, ILLINOIS

Jacobus, Alan P. '68 '93 C&L.861 B.A., J.D. [(A) Karbal,C.E.S.&D.]
Jacoby, John, (BV) '41 '65 C&L.339 B.S., LL.B. [Vedder,P.K.&K.]
Jacoby, John P., (AV) '57 '87 C.593 B.S. L.910 J.D. [Pappas,J.&M.]
Jaconetty, Thomas A. '53 '78
C.424 A.B. L.597 J.D. Chief Dep. Comm., Co. Bd. of Review
Jacover, Aric S. '74 '02 C.477 B.Mus. L.276 J.D. [(A) Mayer,B.R.&M.]
Jacover, Jerold A., (AV) '45 '72
C.966 B.S.E.E. L.276 J.D. [Brinks H.G.&L.] (See Pat. Sect.)
Jadwin, Ted R., (AV) '48 '74 C.659 B.A. L.145 J.D.
Sr. V.P., Gen. Coun & Corp Secy, Trizec Properties, Inc.
Jafari, Sam '74 '04 C.424 B.A. L.209 J.D. [(A) Madsen,F.&P.]
Jaffe, Aaron '30 '53 C.339 B.A. L.209 J.D. Cir. J.
Jaffe, Alvin N. '46 '74 C.836 B.B.A. L.339 J.D. Off. of Gen. Coun., Dept. of HHS
Jaffe, Frank W. '60 '87 C&L.597 B.A., J.D. 111 W. Washington St., Ste. 1401
Jaffe, Jennifer R. '— '02 C.910 B.A. L.597 J.D. [(A) Latham&W.]
Jaffe, Laurie D., (BV) '54 '85 C.604 B.A. L.424 J.D. [Albert,W.]

Jaffe, Maria J. '— '02 C.424 B.S. L.365 J.D.
8 South Michigan Avenue, Suite 3200, 60603 ⊙
Telephone: 312-641-1050 Fax: 312-641-1052
URL: http://www.mariajaffelawfirm.com
Adoption, Child Support, Criminal Law, Custody and Visitation, Debtor/Creditor, Divorce, Family Law, Immigration Law, Landlord/Tenant, Mediation, Medical Malpractice, Motor Vehicle Accidents, Plaintiff Personal Injury, Real Estate.
Northfield, Illinois Office: 1 Northfield Plaza, Suite 300, 60093. Telephone: 847-441-1814.
See Professional Biographies, CHICAGO, ILLINOIS

Jaffe, Martin S. '48 '74 C&L.912 B.A., J.D. Assoc. Prof., Univ. of Ill., Chicago

Jaffe, Richard, (AV) '51 '76 C.966 B.A. L.146 J.D.
100 West Monroe Street, Suite 714, 60603
Telephone: 312-372-1245 Fax: 312-372-1247
Email: RICKYJAFFE@AOL.COM URL: http://www.lawyers.com/jaffelaw
Business Law, Family Law, Commercial Litigation, Debtor and Creditor, Collections, Commercial Real Estate, Residential Real Estate, Personal Injury, Probate.
See Professional Biographies, CHICAGO, ILLINOIS

Jaffe, Stephen L., Law Offices of '52 '88
C.597 B.S. L.209 J.D. 30 North Michigan Avenue
Jaffee, Heidi M. '65 '92 C.860 B.S. L.588 J.D.
Assoc. Gen. Coun., Oil-Dri Corporation of America
Jafri, Rafi K. '76 '03 C.145 B.A. L.209 J.D. [(A) Dykema G.P.]
Jagadich, Adam '78 '03 C.679 B.A. L.966 J.D. [(A) Segal M.S.&M.]
Jager, Melvin F., (AV) '37 '62 C&L.339 B.S., J.D. Ocean Tomo LLC (Pat.)
Jagielski, Raymond L. '53 '81 C.894 B.A. L.365 J.D. Richard J. Daley Ctr.
Jaglowski, David R. '72 '02 C.475 B.S.E. L.477 J.D. 120 S. LaSalle Street, Suite 1600

Jagodzinski, Christine M. ....'76 '02 C&L.424 B.S., J.D. [Ⓐ Wiedner&M.]
Jahn, Stephen Michael ....'59 '86 C.190 B.A. L.352 J.D. Legal Assist. Found.
Jahns, Jeffrey, (AV) ....'46 '71 C.884 A.B. L.145 J.D. [Seyfarth S.]
Jahrling, John C. ....'43 '68 C.363 B.A. L.597 J.D. 2301 W. Chicago Ave.
Jain, Ashok K. '59 '84 C.645 B.A. L.831 J.D.
(adm. in PA; not adm. in IL) Mgr., Price Waterhouse
Jain, Tamara G. ....'— '02 C.188 B.A. L.477 J.D. [Ⓐ Kirkland&E.]
Jain, Veena K. ....'68 '94 C.597 B.A. L.477 J.D. [Ⓐ Bell,B.&L.]
Jakobe, Neill P. ....'— '02 C.602 B.A. L.477 J.D. [Ⓐ Mayer,B.R.&M.]
Jakobe, Stacy S. ....'— '03 C&L.477 B.A., J.D. [Ⓐ Goldberg,K.B.B.R.&M.]
Jakofsky, Wm. ....'24 '52 L.365 LL.B. 188 W. Randolph
Jakola, Adrianne K. ....'— '01 C.597 B.A. L.145 J.D. [Ⓐ Kirkland&E.]
Jakubco, Nicholas Jerome ....'74 '02 C.473 B.A. L.365 J.D. 2224 W. Irving Park Rd.
Jakubco, P. Jerome ....'41 '69 C.424 B.B.A. L.365 J.D. 2224 W. Irving Pk. Rd.
Jakubiak, Paul C. ....'70 '97 C.477 B.A. L.424 J.D. [Ⓐ Patton&R.]
Jakubik, Jerome W. ....'45 '72 C.276 A.B. L.339 J.D. [Baker&M.]
Jakubowski, Steven R. '57 '85 C.867 B.S. L.145 J.D.
Suite 4800 77 West Wacker Drive (ⓒChicago)
Jakubowski, Steven R. '57 '85
C.867 B.S. L.145 J.D. [Ⓟ R.F.Coleman&Assoc.] (ⓒChicago)
Jalovec, Richard S., (AV) ....'40 '65 C.602 B.A. L.597 J.D. [R.S.Jalovec&Assoc.]
Jalovec, Richard S., & Associates, Ltd., (AV) ....1021 W. Adams St.
Jambois, Steven K., (AV) ....'57 '82 C.347 B.S. L.146 J.D. [Kralovec,J.&S.]
Jambor, Robert V., (AV) ....'36 '63 C.1229 B.M.E. L.365 J.D. [Ⓒ Jenner&B.] (Pat.)
James, Gregory R., Jr. ....'59 '88 C.705 B.A. L.365 J.D. [Laner,M.D.B.L.&T.]
James, Hilary A. ....'50 '78 C.597 B.A. L.365 J.D. Asst. Pub. Def.
James, Kristin R. ....'— '96 L.145 J.D. 6732 North Glenwood Ave.
James, Mary Galloway '20 '44 C.449 B.A. L.966 J.D.
(adm. in WI; not adm. in IL) Bus. & Prof. People for the Pub. Interest
James, Michael E. ....'52 '77 C.98 B.A. L.424 J.D. 19 S. La Salle St.
James, Sally Ann ....'49 '86 C.999 B.A. L.145 J.D. The First Ntl. Bk.
James, Thomas Michael '56 '80 C.728 B.A. L.831 J.D.
(adm. in PA; not adm. in IL) The Northern Trust Company
James, Thomas P. ....'53 '82 C.999 B.A. L.1066 J.D. Dir., Reg. Ofc. of the Atty. Gen.
James, Thomas W. ....'25 '52 C.309 A.B. L.477 LL.B. Ret. U.S. Bkrptcy. J.‡
James-Moore, Beatrice L. ....'58 '90 C.420 B.S. L.145 J.D. SBC Corp.
Jamil, Deyar M. ....'— '97 C.477 B.A. L.912 J.D. Spec. Agent
Jamison, Theodore R., III '61 '92 C.966 B.A. L.879 J.D.
Dep. Gen. Coun., Chicago Transit Auth. Law Dept., Enforce & Investigations
Janatka, Joseph J. ....'62 '87 C.388 B.A. L.910 J.D. [Ⓐ McGuirewoods]
Jancasz, Richard J. ....'— '02 C.477 B.A. L.209 J.D. [Ⓐ Wildman,H.A.&D.]
Janci, David F., (BV) '49 '81 C.401 B.S. L.273 J.D.
(adm. in NY; not adm. in IL; Pat.) Sr. Pat. Atty., USG Corp.
Janci, Richard M., (AV) ....'54 '80 C.339 B.S. L.365 J.D. 105 W. Madison, Ste. 1300
Jancovich, Karen L. ....'72 '99 C.597 B.A. L.146 J.D. 515 N. State Street
Janda, Michael L. ....'54 '82 C.424 B.B.A. L.209 J.D. 500 W. Monroe Street, 29th floor
Jandacek, Christopher J. ....'68 '01 C.691 B.S.E.E. L.477 J.D. [Ⓐ Mayer,B.R.&M.]
Janello, Frank ....'74 '99 C.340 B.S. L.801 J.D. [Ⓐ Blatt,H.L.&M.]
Janes, Jean K. ....'54 '93 C.694 B.A. L.494 J.D. [Much S.F.D.A.&R.]
Jang, Betty Y. ....'— '94 C.339 B.A. L.146 J.D. [Ⓐ Hinshaw&C.]
Janger, Richard K., (AV) ....'36 '61 C&L.597 B.S., J.D. [Eisenberg&J.]
Jani, Maitreya P. ....'74 '99 C.339 B.S.G.E. L.273 J.D. [Ⓐ Welsh&K.] (See Pat. Sect.)
Janich, Daniel N. ....'52 '78 C.1216 B.A. L.365 J.D. [Janich]

Janich Law Group
222 North LaSalle Street, Suite 2500, 60601
Telephone: 312-609-4528 Fax: 312-609-5005
Email: djanich@janichlawgroup.com URL: http://www.janichlawgroup.com
Daniel N. Janich.
Employee Benefits, Executive Compensation, Employee Benefits Litigation, Estate Litigation, Estate Planning and Administration, Business Successorship Planning.
See Professional Biographies, CHICAGO, ILLINOIS

Janicik, John A., (AV) ....'57 '86 C.388 B.A. L.424 J.D. [Mayer,B.R.&M.]
Janik, Anthony P. ....'55 '79 C.719 B.A. L.424 J.D. [Abramson&F.]
Janik, Laurene K. ....'53 '78 C.589 B.A. L.424 J.D. Gen. Coun., Natl. Assn. of Realtors
Janka, John C., (BV) ....'50 '87 C.46 B.S. L.145 J.D. [Niro,S.H.&N.] (See Pat. Sect.)
Jann, Norma Finley ....'54 '79 C.339 B.A. L.209 J.D. Sr. Contract Admr., Metra
Janney, Rana H. ....'74 '00 C.597 B.A. L.146 J.D. [Ⓒ Schopf&W.]
Janney, Richard A. ....'72 '00 C.108 B.S. L.146 J.D. [Ⓐ Krasnow S.C.]
Jannisch, James W. ....'73 '99 C.578 B.A. L.209 J.D. [Ⓐ Wiedner&M.]
Jannusch, Matthew W. ....'75 '01 C.578 B.A. L.589 J.D. Asst. State Atty.
Janoski, Robert A., (AV) ....'37 '62 C.602 A.B. L.145 J.D. [Ⓐ Hoogendoorn&T.]
Janovich, Karen L. ....'72 '99 C.597 B.A. L.146 J.D. 515 North State Street
Janovsky, Rebecca ....'62 '88 C.473 B.A. L.345 J.D. [Ⓢ Katten M.R.]
Janowicz, Alene M. ....'68 '00 C.208 B.S. L.809 J.D. 50 S. LaSalle St.
Jansen, Brad L. ....'54 '83 C.339 B.A. L.146 J.D. Chicago Transit Auth.
Jansen, Gary T. ....'59 '84 C.589 B.S. L.209 J.D. [Cremer,K.S.&S.]
Jansen, Greg E. ....'74 '99 C.340 B.A. L.494 J.D. [Ⓐ Katten M.R.]
Jansen, Kimberly A. ....'73 '99 C.388 B.A. L.339 J.D. [Ⓐ Hinshaw&C.]
Janser, Marc D., (AV) ....'52 '78 C.188 B.A. L.339 J.D. [Pedersen&H.]
Janus, Mark James ....'57 '86 C.589 B.S. L.365 J.D. U.S. Dept. of Labor
Janusonis, Joseph Kenneth ....'73 '01 C.1024 B.A. L.734 J.D. 318 West Adams Street
Januszyk, Ximen J. ....'74 '99 C.597 B.A. L.347 J.D. [Ⓐ Magnani&B.]
Japlon, Mary Gilhooly ....'54 '79 C&L.339 B.A., J.D. Admin. Law J., Ill. Dept. of Rev.
Jarcho, Jane E. ....'60 '86 C.478 B.A. L.966 J.D. U.S. Sec. & Exch. Comm.
Jardine, Matthew C. ....'— '01 C.966 B.A. L.146 J.D. [Ⓐ Schiff H.]
Jarecki, Michael R. ....'79 '04 C.424 B.A. L.339 J.D. [Ⓐ M.C.R.Madrid-Crost]
Jared, Cynthia, (AV) ....'— '80 C.108 B.A. L.209 J.D. [Sachnoff&W.]
Jarema, Kathleen A. ....'46 '87 C.801 B.A. L.213 J.D. [Ⓒ Katten M.R.]
Jarik, Charles L. ....'— '78 C.228 B.A. L.880 J.D. [Chapman&C.]
Jarol, Shelbee ....'78 '03 C.339 B.S. L.209 J.D. [Ⓐ Winston&S.]
Jaros, Joseph J., Jr., (AV) ....'37 '62 C.276 A.B. L.597 J.D. [Jaros,T.&O.]
Jaros, Thomas G. ....'67 '92 C.388 B.A. L.146 J.D. [Levenfeld P.]

Jaros, Tittle & O'Toole, Limited, (AV)
20 North Clark Street, Suite 510, 60602
Telephone: 312-750-1000 Fax: 312-332-6136
Email: info@jtolaw.com URL: http://www.jtolaw.com
Joseph J. Jaros (1899-1975); Vernon Tittle (1906-1981); Joseph J. Jaros, Jr.; William G. O'Toole; James E. Trausch; Linda J. Herber; Monique N. O'Toole.
Real Estate, Foreclosure, Probate, Corporate, Savings and Loan Law, Banking and Mortgage Banking. Litigation in State and Federal Courts. Estate Planning, Bankruptcy. Designated Counsel, Federal Home Loan Mortgage Corporation (Freddie Mac).
See Professional Biographies, CHICAGO, ILLINOIS

Jarosch, Jami A. ....'— '01 C.1365 B.A. L.477 J.D. [Ⓐ Kirkland&E.]
Jarosik, Gary R. ....'— '91 C.105 B.S.E.E. L.446 J.D. [Greenberg T.] (Pat.)

Jarrett, Valerie Bowman, (AV) '56 '81
C.813 A.B. L.477 J.D. Comr., Dept. of Planning & Development
Jartz, John G. '53 '78 C.966 B.A. L.610 J.D.
V.P., Gen. Coun. Bus. Develop. & Corp. Sec., Quaker Oats Co.
Jarvis, James S., (AV) ....'38 '62 C.742 B.A. L.597 J.D. [Aronberg G.D.&G.]
Jarvis, Kristina L. ....'72 '00 C.790 B.A. L.146 J.D. [Ⓐ Berger S.]
Jarvis, Lawrence M., (AV) '50 '77
C.339 B.S.E.E. L.128 J.D. [McAndrews,H.&M.] (See Pat. Sect.)
Jasionowski, James S. '59 '85
C.589 B.S. L.146 J.D. Sr. V.P. & Dir. of Tax, Heller Financial, Inc.
Jaskoviak, Dennis H., Jr. ......'64 '02 C.589 B.S.M.E. L.145 J.D. [Ⓐ McAndrews,H.&M.]
Jaskula, Michael ....'58 '97 C.339 B.A. L.146 J.D. 155 North Michigan Avenue, Suite 556
Jason, Mark N. ....'55 '81 C.260 B.A. L.589 J.D. Attorney, A.T. Kearney, Inc.
Jasper, Joseph T. ....'77 '02 C.436 B.S. L.446 J.D. [Ⓐ Grossman&F.] (Pat.)
Jast, Raymond J. ....'47 '72 C.430 A.B. L.477 J.D. [Wilson E.M.E.&D.]
Jaszczuk, Mark A. ....'44 '80 L.365 J.D. 2956 N. Milwaukee Ave.
Jaszczuk, Martin W. ....'76 '00 C&L.011 LL.B. [Ⓐ Lord,B.&B.]
Jaunal, Garry W. ....'— '99 C.679 M.S. L.597 J.D. [Kirkland&E.]
Jawad, Nahlah ....'65 '91 C&L.424 B.S., J.D. 836 W. Wellington Avenue
Jawgiel, Michael B., Law Office of, (CV) '65 '91
C.339 B.S.B.A. L.910 J.D. 5487 N. Milwaukee Ave.
Jayaram, Vivek ....'78 '04 C.966 B.A. L.1398 J.D. [Ⓐ Youkhana&S.]
Jeddeloh, Norman P., (AV) ....'— '71 C.602 B.A. L.597 J.D. [Arnstein&L.]
Jefferson, Carl S., III ....'45 '76 C.339 B.A. L.146 J.D. 535 N. Michigan Ave.‡
Jeffery, Heidi H. ....'— '96 C.597 B.A. L.352 J.D. [Foley&L.]
Jeffery, Joseph R. ....'70 '97 C.352 B.A. L.734 J.D. [Ⓐ Chittenden,M.&N.]
Jeffords, Julie K. ....'72 '98 C.352 B.A. L.801 J.D. [Ⓐ Horowitz&W.]
Jeffrey, Craig D. ....'— '00 C.1138 B.A. L.352 J.D. [Ⓐ Bryan C.]
Jeffrey, Terry D., (AV) ....'49 '75 C.339 B.S. L.209 J.D. [Burke,W.M.&S.]
Jeffries, John A., (AV) ....'— '61 C.347 B.S. L.1119 J.D. [Lord,B.&B.]
Jendryk, Chester F. J. ....'28 '53 C.1024 L.209 LL.B. 5556 S. Kedze St.
Jenero, Kenneth A., (AV) ....'— '80 C&L.209 B.A., J.D. [Holland&K.]

Jenkens & Gilchrist, A Professional Corporation, (AV)
225 West Washington, Suite 2600, 60606-3418 ⓒ
Telephone: 312-425-3900 Facsimile: 312-425-3909
Email: jenkens@jenkens.com URL: http://www.jenkens.com
Shareholders: Daniel J. Burnham; Janet M. Garetto; John C. Gatz; Donna Zak Guerin; Keith C. Hannigan; Paul R. Kitch; Charles B. Lewis; Edward F. McCormack; Margo Wolf O'Donnell; Stephen G. Rudisill; Jodi Rosen Wine. Of Counsel: Paul M. Daugerdas; Erwin Mayer; Harold N. Wells (Not admitted in IL). Counsel: John P. Luther (Not admitted in IL). Associates: Mark Anderson; Sorinel Cimpoes; Russell J. Genet; Jeffrey L. Hamera; Cristina T. Hawilo; Nick Kahlon; Jeremie D. Moll; William D. Pegg; Amy L. Sierocki; Justin D. Swindells; Cynthia Thompson; Elizabeth Wiszowaty.
General Practice including Corporate and Securities Law, Estates and Trusts, Bankruptcy. Administrative Law, Antitrust, Aviation, Commercial Lending, Communications, Computer Law, Construction Law, Employee Benefits (ERISA); Energy, Environmental Law, Federal Practice, Financial Institutions, Finance, Franchise and Distribution Law, Governmental Affairs, Health Law, Hospitality (REIT), Immigration, Intellectual Property (Prosecution, Litigation and Transactional), International Law, Internet Law, Labor and Employment Law, Land Use, Litigation (Commercial, Tax and Fiduciary), Mergers and Acquisitions, Product Liability, Real Estate Services, Securities, Tax, Toxic Tort, Trade Regulation, Transportation, Venture Capital.
Austin, Texas Office: 401 Congress, Suite 2500. Telephone: 512-499-3800. Facsimile: 512-499-3810.
Dallas, Texas, Office: 1445 Ross Avenue, Suite 3700. Telephone: 214-855-4500. TWX: 910-861-4047. Telex: 73-2595. Facsimile: 214-855-4300. International Facsimile: 214-855-4300.
Los Angeles, California Office: Jenkens & Gilchrist, LLP, 12100 Wilshire Boulevard, 15th Floor. Telephone: 310-820-8800. Facsimile: 310-820-8859.
Houston, Texas Office: 1401 McKinney, Suite 2700. Telephone: 713-951-3300. Facsimile: 713-951-3314.
Washington, D.C. Office: 901 15th Street N.W. Telephone: 202-326-1500. Facsimile: 202-326-1555.
San Antonio, Texas Office: 112 East Pecan Street, Suite 900. Telephone: 210-246-5000. Facsimile: 210-246-5999.
Pasadena, California Office: Jenkins & Gilchrist, 55 South Lake Avenue, Suite 650. Telephone: 626-578-7400. Fax: 626-304-9711.
See Professional Biographies, CHICAGO, ILLINOIS

Jenkins, Ellen D. ....'63 '93 C&L.945 B.A., J.D. [Boundas S.W.&B.]
Jenkins, Gerald L., (AV) ....'48 '75 C.234 B.A. L.309 J.D. [Goldberg,K.B.B.R.&M.]
Jenkins, James R. ....'61 '91 C&L.597 B.A., J.D. 8410 W. Bryn Mawr
Jenkins, Kenneth D. ....'62 '02 C.339 B.A. L.209 J.D. Asst. State Atty.
Jenkins, Kimberly '71 '96 C.859 B.S. L.276 J.D.
(adm. in MO; not adm. in IL) 111 N. Canal St.
Jenkins, Kirk C., (AVⓉ) ....'61 '86 C.309 B.A. L.1565 J.D. [Sedgwick,D.M.&A.]
Jenkins, Robert J. ....'46 '79 C.339 B.A. L.209 J.D. [Krohn&J.]
Jenkins, Thomas M. ....'48 '77 C&L.209 B.S., J.D. V.P., Heller Financial, Inc.
Jenkins, Thomas M. '58 '84 C.297 B.A. L.1018 J.D.
(adm. in MN; not adm. in IL) Assoc. Gen. Coun., Fannie Mae
Jenkins, Thomas W. ....'50 '77 C.927 B.A. L.146 J.D. [Lord,B.&B.]
Jenkins, Thomas W., Jr. ....'74 '00 C.475 B.S. L.477 J.D. [Ⓐ Howrey]
Jenner, Richard E. '47 '79 C.46 B.S.E.E. L.589 J.D.
Metro. Water Reclamation Dist. of Greater Chicago

Jenner & Block LLP, (AV) BB
A Partnership including Professional Corporations
One IBM Plaza, 60611 ⓒ
Telephone: 312-222-9350 FAX: 312-527-0484 Telex: 270469 TWX: 9102215409 Cable Address: "Jenblock"
URL: http://www.jenner.com
Chairman of the Firm: Jerold S. Solovy. Partners: Catherine Abbott (Resident, Washington, D.C. Office); Aaron A. Barlow; Timothy J. Barron; Matt D. Basil; Donald E. Batterson; David R. Bennett; Debbie L. Berman; Joseph G. Bisceglia; Samuel W. Block (1911-1970); Brian R. Boch; George S. Bosy; Gregory M. Boyle; David J. Bradford; Traci M. Braun; Peter J. Brennan; Michael T. Brody; Patricia A. Bronte; Jerry J. Burgdoerfer; Jennifer A. Burke; John J. Buttita; Robert L. Byman; Julia M. Carpenter (Resident, Washington, D.C. Office); Donald R. Cassling; Theresa Chmara (Resident, Washington, D.C. Office); Timothy J. Chorvat; David A. Churchill (Resident, Washington, D.C. Office); Elizabeth Abbene Coleman; Jeffrey D. Colman; Deirdre E. Connell; Jacob I. Corré; Joseph P. Covington (Resident, Washington, D.C. Office); John F. Cox; Elizabeth A. Davidson; Geoffrey M. Davis; David W. DeBruin (Resident, Washington, D.C. Office); Michael B. DeSanctis (Resident, Washington, D.C. Office); Christopher C. Dickinson; Michael A. Doornweerd; Kevin B. Duckworth; Kevin C. Dwyer (Resident, Washington, D.C. Office); Larry P. Ellsworth (Resident, Washington, D.C. Office); Jerome L. Epstein (Resident, Washington, D.C. Office); Steven B. Fabrizio (Resident, Washington, D.C. Office); Jill Sugar Factor; Katherine A. Fallow (Resident, Washington, D.C. Office); James H. Feldman; James P. Fieweger; Bill S. Forcade; Richard T. Franch; Chris C. Gair; Gregory S. Gallopoulos; Ian Heath Gershengorn (Resident, Washington, D.C. Office); Elaine J. Goldenberg (Not admitted in IL; Resident, Washington, D.C. Office); Marc A. Goldman (Resident, Washington, D.C. Office); Robert L. Graham; Richard J. Gray; E. Lynn Grayson; David M. Greenwald; Joseph P. Gromacki; David K. Haase; John J. Hamill; David A. Handzo (Resident, Washington, D.C. Office); John R. Harrington; Donald R. Harris (Ltd.); Philip L. Harris; Arnold Harrison; Mark R. Heilbrun (Resident, Washington, D.C. Office); William D. Heinz; Reginald J. Hill; Norman M. Hirsch; Sam Hirsch (Resident, Washington, D.C. Office); William A. Hohengarten (Resident, Washington, D.C. Office); Russell J. Hoover; Donald S. Horvath; Daniel J. Hurtado; Andrew A. Jacobson; Albert E. Jenner, Jr. (1907-1988); David Jiménez-Ekman; Paul F. Jock II (Resident, New York, N.Y. Office); Elmer W. Johnson; Chester T. Kamin; Kathleen E. Karelis (Resident, Washington, D.C. Office); Brent E. Kidwell; Christian E. Kimball; Carter H. Klein; Tobias L. Knapp (Resident, New York, N.Y. Office); C. John Koch; Jeffrey A. Koppy; David M. Kroeger; Kenneth A. Kroot; David C. Layden; Vincent E. Lazar; Leslie H. Lepow (Resident, Washington, D.C. Office); Barry Levenstam; Richard F. Levy; Susan C. Levy; Christopher D. Liguori; Teri A. Lindquist; S. Tony Ling; Linda L. Listrom;

(This Listing Continued)

Jenner & Block LLP (Continued)

Eric L. Lohrenz; Daniel Mach (Resident, Washington, D.C. Office); Thaddeus J. Malik; Edward F. Malone; Julie Montz Mandanas; Robert T. Markowski; Ronald L. Marmer; Sarah R. Marmor; Arthur Mead Martin; Craig C. Martin; Jeff J. Marwil; Terri L. Mascherin; Lorelie S. Masters (Resident, Washington, D.C. Office); John H. Mathias, Jr.; J. Kevin McCall; Thomas J. McCarthy; James A. McKenna; Thomas A. Monson; Scott J. Moore; Gail H. Morse; Daniel R. Murray; Matthew M. Neumeier; Edward J. Neveril; John W. Newlin, III; Raymond N. Nimrod; Catherine R. Nolan (Resident, Washington, D.C. Office); Matthew J. Oppenheim (Resident, Washington, D.C. Office); Robert S. Osborne; Dean N. Panos; Patrick L. Patras; Joel T. Pelz; Thomas J. Perrelli (Resident, Washington, D.C. Office); Ronald R. Peterson; Adam V. Petravicius; Megan B. Poetzel; Anthony C. Porcelli; Robert M. Portman (Resident, Washington, D.C. Office); Paul V. Possinger; Suzanne J. Prysak; R. Douglas Rees; Ronald Ian Reicin; Matthew J. Renaud; Donald I. Resnick; Harry J. Roper; Carla J. Rozycki; Michael C. Rupe; Roibin J. Ryan; Eric A. Sacks; David P. Sanders; Lawrence S. Schaner; Stephanie A. Scharf; Stanley A. Schlitter; Marshall John Schmitt; Mark D. Schneider (Resident, Washington, D.C. Office); Scott T. Schutte; Daniel J. Schwartz; William L. Scogland; Jeffrey T. Shaw; Gabrielle Sigel; John B. Simon; Steven M. Siros; Charles B. Sklarsky; Robert Z. Slaughter; Daniel W. Smith; Paul M. Smith (Resident, Washington, D.C. Office); Shelley Smith; Lise T. Spacapan; Tanya J. Stanish; Robert R. Stauffer; Catherine L. Steege; Barbara S. Steiner; Richard P. Steinken; Avidan J. Stern; William R. Stoughton (Resident, Dallas, Texas Office); Barry Sullivan; Thomas P. Sullivan (Ltd.); Howard S. Suskin; Brian I. Swett; Jerry L. Switzer, Jr.; Jeremy M. Taylor; Michael S. Terrien; Mark K. Thomas; Matthew J. Thomas; James L. Thompson; John E. Titus; William L. Tolbert, Jr. (Resident, Washington, D.C. Office); C. Steven Tomashefsky; Seth A. Travis; Terrence J. Truax; Steven R. Trybus; Anton R. Valukas; Marc Van Allen; Donald B. Verrilli, Jr. (Resident, Washington, D.C. Office); Mark P. Vrla; James A. Vroman; Charlotte L. Wager; Michael S. Walsh; Ronald L. Wanke; J. Alex Ward (Resident, Washington, D.C. Office); John F. Ward, Jr.; Kathy Coleman Weinberg (Resident, Dallas, Texas Office); John E. Welch (Resident, Washington, D.C. Office); Daniel J. Winters. Associates: Jonathan F. Allen; Amanda S. Amert; Ginger D. Anders (Resident, Washington, D.C. Office); Joseph F. Arias; Richard W. Arnholt (Resident, Washington, D.C. Office); David W. Austin; Marek H. Badyna; Terence G. Banich, II; Angela M. Barry; Shannon P. Bartlett; Courtney M. Beemer; Iris Bennett (Resident, Washington, D.C. Office); Eric Berger (Resident, Washington, D.C. Office); Bethany Kaye Biesenthal; Robert J. Blazejowski; Gregory D. Bonifield; Denise Kirkowski Bowler; Donald S. Boyce, Jr.; Patricia Boye-Williams; Kali N. Bracey (Resident, Washington, D.C. Office); Aaron Bruhl (Resident, Washington, D.C. Office); Evan Jay Budin; Ana R. Bugan; Christine L. Childers; Marilyn J. Chimes; Martez M. Clark; Robert H. Clarke; John F. Costello, Jr.; Suzanne M. Courtheoux; Craig A. Cowie (Resident, Washington, D.C. Office); Robert J. Dart; Damien P. Delaney; Matthew R. Devine; Alison A. Dieterichs; Matthew R. DiPentima; Nada Djordjevic; Irina Y. Dmitrieva; Chris-Tia Donaldson; Daniel S. Dooley; Debra M. Doyle; David S. Drachler; John Wesley Drury; Jeffrey S. Eberhard; Lisa M. Eddington; Frank J. Eichenlaub IV; Elizabeth L. Fine; Emily M. Frank; Jared O. Freedman (Resident, Washington, D.C. Office); Wendy L. Fritz; Anthony S. Gabrielson; Ami J. Galani; Claudia Gallo; Stephen M. Geissler; Rick Y. Gelboim; Jason J. Green; Anthony J. Grzyb; Michael S. Gulland; John Haarlow, Jr.; Adam A. Hachikian; Brian D. Hansen; Christina Tomaras Hansen; Sarah Hardgrove-Koleno; Kathleen Hartnett (Resident, Washington, D.C. Office); Jennifer A. Hasch; Brian Hauck (Resident, Washington, D.C. Office); Brian C. Haussmann; Matthew Hersh (Resident, Washington, D.C. Office); Clifton J. Heyda; Jonathan Hill; Melissa M. Hinds (Not admitted in IL); Li-Chung Daniel Ho; Keri L. Holleb Hotaling; Bobby J. Hollis II; Darrick J. Hooker; Timothy A. Hudson; Rachel A. Jeris; Kathy A. Karcher; David M. Kavanaugh; Benjamin J. Keith; Fazal R. Khan; Kristopher R. Kiel; Bryan D. King; Rebecca J. Krasaeath; Jayne Laiprasert; Oliver Larson; Lisa S. Lauer; William R. Lee; Jorge M. Leon; Jennifer S. Levin; Darren H. Lubetzky (Resident, Washington, D.C. Office); Paul D. Margolis; Joseph F. Marinelli; Galen R. Mason; Michelle M. McAtee; Edward P. McKenna; Daniel P. McLaughlin; Daniel C. McMurtrie; Steven R. Meier; Brian H. Meldrum; Robin M. Meriweather (Resident, Washington, D.C. Office); Zachary V. Moen; Thomas P. Monroe; Molly J. Moran; Meghan C. Morrissey; Darren M. Mungerson; Thalia L. Myrianthopoulos; Maya D. Nath (Not admitted in IL); Phillip W. Nelson; Kathryn C. Newman; Andrew S. Nicoll; Erin M. O'Connell; Christopher M. O'Connor; Brian P. O'Donnell; Andrew J. Olejnik; Vera Ovadia; Vito M. Pacione; Emily S. Palmer; Christopher V. Parente; Christine A. Parker; Iordan A. Peev; Laura E. Pelanek; Damon D. Perry; Elayna T. Pham; Monica R. Pinciak; Luke C. Platzer (Resident, Washington, D.C. Office); Elizabeth G. Porter (Resident, Washington, D.C. Office); Duane Pozza (Not admitted in IL); Edward G. Quinlisk; Katherine Rahill (Not admitted in IL); Gayle A. Rana; Jay S. Readey; Matthew H. Rice; David B. Robbins (Resident, Washington, D.C. Office); Cynthia J. Robertson (Resident, Washington, D.C. Office); Ross M. Rosenberg; Alexander Rozenblat; Laura A. Sakulich; Joseph A. Saltiel; Brian S. Scarbrough; John R. Schleppenbach; Darren J. Schmidt; Ruth A. Schoenmeyer; Joseph A. Schouten; Erin R. Schrantz; Kristen Garvey Schulz (Resident, Dallas, Texas Office); Lisa T. Scruggs; Sally K. Sears Coder; Jill R. Sheiman; Shana A. Shifrin; Jeffrey R. Shuman; Peter A. Siddiqui; Margaret J. Simpson; Raymond D. Sinnappan; Marc D. Sokol; Douglas A. Sondgeroth; Michelle Speller-Thurman; Scott A. Spencer; Courtney A. Stevens; Clay Stiffler; Jeremy T. Stillings; John R. Storino; Emma J. Sullivan; Joanne H. Sweeney; Shehla F. Syed; Mary C. Talarico; Amy L. Tenney (Resident, Washington, D.C. Office); Angela M. Terry; Wade A. Thomson; Jessica Tillipman (Resident, Washington, D.C. Office); Sandi J. Toll; Christopher Tompkins; Heather M. Trew (Resident, Washington, D.C. Office); Amy K. Trueblood; Andrew W. Vail; Martina E. Vandenberg (Resident, Washington, D.C. Office); Shyni R. Varghese; Hillary A. Victor; David E. Walters; Erinn L. Wehrman; Daniel J. Weiss; Anders C. Wick; Scott Wilkens (Resident, Washington, D.C. Office); John P. Wolfsmith; Caroline Lewis Wolverton (Resident, Washington, D.C. Office); Gregory M. Wu; Jason E. Yearout; Peter J. Young; Bradley M. Yusim; Blair R. Zanzig; Steven McMahon Zeller. Of Counsel: Ronald DeKoven; Edward Jackson (Resident, Washington, D.C. Office); Robert V. Jambor; Charles J. McCarthy (Ltd.); Benjamin K. Miller; Henry M. Schaffer.

Administrative Law; Advertising and Marketing; Agency and Distributorships; Alternative Dispute Resolution; Antitrust and Trade Regulation; Appellate Practice; Aviation and Aerospace; Bankruptcy; Banks and Banking; Biotechnology; Business Law; Chancery and Equity; Civil Practice; Class Action; Commercial Law; Commercial Real Estate; Commodities; Communications and Media; Complex and Multi District Litigation; Computers and Software; Constitutional Law; Construction Law; Consumer Law; Contracts; Copyrights; Corporate Law; Debtor and Creditor; Disabilities; Employee Benefits; Energy; Environmental Law; Family Law; Finance; Franchises and Franchising; Government; Government Contracts; Health Care; Hospital Law; Intellectual Property; International Law; Labor and Employment; Libel, Slander and Defamation; Litigation; Mergers, Acquisitions and Divestitures; Occupational Safety and Health; Partnership Law; Patents; Privacy Law; Probate; Products Liability; Professional Liability; Real Estate; Regulatory Law; RICO; Securities; Taxation; Technology and Science; Torts; Toxic Torts; Trade and Professional Associations; Trade Secrets; Trademarks; Trusts and Estates; Unfair Competition; Utility Law; Wills.

Washington, D.C. Office: 601 Thirteenth Street, N.W., Twelfth Floor. Telephone: 202-639-6000. FAX: 202-639-6066. Cable Address: "Jenblock."

Dallas, Texas Office: 1717 Main Street, Suite 3150. Telephone: 214-746-5700. FAX: 214-746-5757.

New York, N.Y. Office: 919 Third Avenue.

See Professional Biographies, CHICAGO, ILLINOIS

Jennings, Diane I. ... '— '82 C.597 B.S. L.365 J.D. [Anderson,R.]
Jennings, James J. ... '32 '57 C&L.209 LL.B. 6117 W. Addison St.
Jennings, John M. ... '— '97 C.893 B.A. L.597 J.D. [Kirkland&E.]
Jennings, Jonathan S. ... '64 '90 C.1365 B.A. L.597 J.D. [Pattishall,M.N.H.&G.]
Jennings, Lee T., (BV) ... '54 '81 C.339 B.A. L.365 J.D. 309 W. Washington St.
Jennings, Mark J. ... '18 '42 L.209 LL.B. 3906 N. Hoyne Ave.‡
Jensen, David A. ... '— '00 C.473 B.S./B.A. L.966 J.D. [[A] Mayer,B.R.&M.]
Jensen, David B. '38 '66 C.339 L.209 LL.B.
V.P. & Assoc. Gen. Coun., Claims, Chicago Title Ins. Co.
Jensen, *Elizabeth D.* ... '— '01 C&L.209 B.A., J.D. [Field&G.]
Jensen, Helen M. ... '47 '87 C&L.209 B.A., J.D. [Nisen&E.]
Jensen, J. Aaron ... '69 '99 C.877 B.A. L.424 J.D. [[A] Meckler B.&T.]
Jensen, Kenneth E. ... '56 '81 C.57 B.A. L.209 J.D. 20 N. Clark St.
Jensen, Ryan L. ... '— '01 C.877 B.A. L.101 J.D. [[A] Kirkland&E.]
Jenson, Paul T. ... '71 '96 C.436 B.S. L.424 J.D. [Shefsky&F.]
Jentry-Green, Anne ... '46 '76 C&L.424 J.D. [[C] McCullough,C.&L.]
Jepsen, Tori M. ... '55 '82 C.339 B.A. L.210 J.D. Sr. Staff Atty., Amer. Fam. Ins. Grp.
Jepson, Edward C., Jr., (AV) ... '55 '80 C.388 B.A. L.309 J.D. [Vedder,P.K.&K.]
Jerdee, Chad T. '67 '94 C.747 B.A. L.494 J.D.
(adm. in MN; not adm. in IL) Corp. Coun., Accenture
Jeris, Rachel A. ... '78 '03 C.880 B.A. L.339 J.D. [[A] Jenner&B.]
Jernberg, Donald V., (AV) ... '47 '72 C.880 B.A. L.597 J.D. [Jernberg]
Jernberg Law Group, (AV) ... 10 South LaSalle, Suite 3300

Jerrick, Ronald M., (AV) '— '70 C.602 A.B. L.209 J.D.
[Querrey&H.] (⊙Crystal Lake)
Jersey, Russell J. ... '52 '78 C.1183 B.A. L.209 J.D. 415 N. LaSalle St.
Jersild, Thomas N., (AV) ... '36 '62 C&L.145 B.A., J.D. [[C] Mayer,B.R.&M.]
Jeruchimowitz, Howard K. ... '72 '97 C.1036 B.A. L.188 J.D. [[A] Greenberg T.]
Jerue, James L., (AV) ... '56 '82 C.597 B.A. L.1068 J.D. [Horwood M.&B.]
Jerzy, Jennifer L. ... '71 '01 C.1369 B.A. L.424 J.D. [[A] Askounis&B.]
Jesani, Priya K. ... '74 '99 C.473 B.S. L.623 J.D. [Pretzel&S.]
Jeske, Dean M. ... '— '89 C&L.339 B.A., J.D. [Foley&L.]
Jessee, Bret C. ... '71 '03 C.838 B.S. L.146 J.D. [[A] Baker&E.]
Jester, Andrew T. ... '69 '95 C.97 B.A. L.1000 J.D. [Jester,K.&E.]

Jester, Kenworthy & Eagle LLC
53 W. Jackson Boulevard, Suite 1324, 60604
Telephone: 312-435-9901 Fax: 312-435-9903
URL: http://www.jkelaw.com
Members of Firm: Andrew T. Jester; Diana L. Kenworthy; Ross M. Eagle.
Criminal Law, Federal Criminal Law, Drug Crimes, DUI, Traffic Violations, Juvenile Law, Criminal Appeals.

See Professional Biographies, CHICAGO, ILLINOIS

Jeter, Sheldon Leigh ... '69 '96 C&L.790 B.S.B.A., J.D. [Seyfarth S.]
Jett, Daci L. ... '74 '01 C.338 B.A. L.846 J.D. [D.Jett]
Jett, Rick L. ... '56 '86 C&L.339 B.A., J.D. [Sidley A.B.&W.]
Jett, Daci, Law Offices of ... 731 W. Bittersweet Place, Suite 1S
Jewkes, Joshua D. ... '— '02 C&L.101 B.A., J.D. [[A] Kirkland&E.]
Jha, Pran ... '66 '91 C&L.477 A.B., J.D. [Sidley A.B.&W.]
Jiganti, John J., (AV) ... '41 '64 C&L.602 A.B., LL.B. [Madden,J.M.&S.]
Jiganti, Mel R. ... '32 '56 C.602 B.S. L.209 LL.B. 190 S. La Salle St.
Jiganti, Mia P. ... '67 '94 C.388 B.A. L.365 J.D. [DLPiper R.G.C.U.]
Jiménez-Ekman, David ... '67 '92 C.145 A.B. L.1066 J.D. [Jenner&B.]
Jin, Laural S. ... '70 '97 C&L.145 A.B., J.D. [McLachlan,R.&D.]
Jindal, Unmaish ... '— '03 C.477 B.A. L.213 J.D. [[A] DLPiper R.G.C.U.]
Jiongco, E. Charles ... '70 '97 C.436 B.A. L.365 J.D. [[A] Veverka,R.&H.]
Jirut, Panasarn Aim '78 '04
C.880 B.E. L.209 J.D. [[A] Cook,A.M.M.C.&M.] (See Pat. Sect.)
Jischke, Mary A. ... '50 '78 C.589 B.S. L.146 J.D. State Attys. Off.
Joaquin, Arcadio A., Jr. ... '39 '76 C&L.999 LL.B. 300 N. State St.
Joens, Thomas H. ... '55 '82 C.339 B.A. L.209 J.D. Ste 1000, 11 S Lasalle St
Joern, Charles E., Jr., (BV) ... '51 '80 C.388 B.A. L.209 J.D. [Holland&K.]
Joffe, Jo Curie ... '— '78 C.145 B.A. L.146 J.D. 656 W. Buena, Ste. 2
Johansen, Kyle B. ... '76 '02 C.589 B.A. L.146 J.D. [[A] Franczek S.]
Johlie, Christopher A., (BV) ... '61 '88 C.347 B.S. L.209 J.D. [Matkov,S.M.&G.]
John, Peter C., (AV) ... '41 '66 C.188 B.A. L.884 J.D. [Williams M.&J.]
John Rokacz & Associates, PC ... 55 East Monroe St
Johns, LaVon M. ... '68 '96 C.190 B.A. L.597 J.D. [Pugh,J.J.&Q.]
Johnson, Adam ... '— '01 C.339 B.A. L.1119 J.D. [[A] Katten M.R.]
Johnson, Andrea L. ... '— '04 C.898 B.A. L.861 J.D. [[A] Kirkland&E.]
Johnson, Anita Senese, (AV) ... '— '76 C.597 B.A. L.209 J.D. [O'Hagan,S.&A.]
Johnson, Barbara ... '54 '80 C.1082 B.A. L.424 J.D. [O'Keefe,L.&H.]
Johnson, Brad ... '71 '02 C.597 B.A. L.424 J.D. [[C] Roth]
Johnson, Brett R. ... '61 '04 C.494 B.A. L.477 J.D. [[A] McDermott W.&E.]
Johnson, Brian A. ... '60 '85 C.813 B.S. L.309 J.D. McKinsey & Co.
Johnson, Bruce ... '35 '63 C.937 A.B. L.597 J.D. [B.E.Johnson]
Johnson, C. Richard, (AV) ... '— '65 C.694 A.B. L.145 J.D. [Foley&L.]
Johnson, Carol Cozzi ... '52 '94 C.424 B.S. L.146 J.D. 203 N. La Salle St., Suite 1800
Johnson, Carol L. ... '57 '84 C&L.339 B.A., J.D. [Bollinger,R.&G.]
Johnson, Christian A. ... '61 '91 C.878 B.A. L.178 J.D. Loyola Univ. Chicago Sch. of Law
Johnson, Christine M. ... '51 '94 C.339 B.A. L.945 J.D. [[A] Eimer S.K.&S.]
Johnson, Cindy M. ... '63 '88 C.145 B.A. L.146 J.D. [Johnson&N.]
Johnson, Daniel L. ... '— '75 C.187 B.A. L.339 J.D. [Chapman&C.]
Johnson, Daniel R. ... '— '04 C.31 B.A. L.597 J.D. [[A] Cozen O.]
Johnson, David B. ... '56 '83 C.436 B.A. L.424 J.D. [Sidley A.B.&W.]
Johnson, Dawn L. ... '74 '01 C&L.339 B.A., J.D. [[A] Bell,B.&L.]
Johnson, Dawn L. ... '— '97 C.800 B.A. L.365 J.D. [[A] A.J.Madonia&Assoc.]
Johnson, Dennis P. W., (AV) ... '54 '80 C.21 A.B. L.145 J.D. [Pugh,J.J.&Q.]
Johnson, Dexter ... '58 '84 C.472 B.B.A. L.276 J.D. [Mallon&J.]

Johnson, Donald L., (AV) '37 '62 C.427 B.A. L.352 J.D. [BR]
Suite 1401, 33 North Dearborn Street, 60602
Telephone: 312-263-7000 Fax: 312-263-3051
Civil and Trial Practice, Business, Real Estate and Partnership Litigation, Professional Malpractice.

See Professional Biographies, CHICAGO, ILLINOIS

Johnson, Dorothy Bertram, (AV) ... '47 '73 C.473 B.A. L.146 J.D. [Johnson&Assoc.]
Johnson, Douglas R. ... '67 '93 C.339 B.S. L.597 J.D. 77 West Wacker Drive Suite 4800
Johnson, Eddie C. ... '20 '52 C.1016 L.365 LL.B. Ret. Cir. J.
Johnson, Edward A. ... '53 '77 C.388 B.A. L.880 J.D. Hartmarx Corp.
Johnson, Elmer W., (AV) ... '32 '57 C.976 B.A. L.145 J.D. [Jenner&B.]
Johnson, Eugene E., Jr. ... '51 '77 C.339 B.S. L.146 J.D. The Northern Tr.Co.
Johnson, Eugenie R. ... '38 '80 C.597 Ph.B. L.146 J.D. 2250 W. Ohio St.
Johnson, Garrett B., (AV) ... '— '73 C.674 A.B. L.477 J.D. [Kirkland&E.]
Johnson, Geoffrey G., (AV) ... '47 '74 C.911 B.A. L.365 J.D. [[A] J.M.Goldberg]
Johnson, Glenn T. ... '17 '50 C.943 B.S. L.365 LL.B. 5050 S. Lake Shore Drive
Johnson, Harold V., (AV) '56 '84
C.474 B.S.E.E. L.982 J.D. [Brinks H.G.&L.] (See Pat. Sect.)
Johnson, James C., Sr. '52 '78 C&L.659 B.A., J.D.
(adm. in PA; not adm. in IL) V.P., Corp. Secy. & Asst. Gen. Coun., The Boeing Co.
Johnson, James M. ... '57 '82 C.338 B.S. L.46 J.D. Internal Rev. Agent
Johnson, Janet M., (AV) ... '— '80 C&L.352 B.B.A., J.D. [Schiff H.]
Johnson, Jay ... '65 '98 C.383 B.A. L.365 J.D. [[A] C.Woodruff&Assoc.] ⊙
Johnson, Jennifer Jerit, (AV) ... '60 '85 C.339 B.A. L.424 J.D. [Tressler,S.M.&P.]
Johnson, Jenny L. ... '— '98 C.797 B.A. L.309 J.D. [[A] Katten M.R.]
Johnson, Karen Litscher ... '61 '88 C.966 B.A. L.188 J.D. [[C] DLPiper R.G.C.U.]
Johnson, Kathleen A., (AV) ... '— '87 C.238 B.A. L.365 J.D. [[A] Clausen M.]
Johnson, Kathryn L. '62 '90
C.373 B.A. L.477 J.D. Dir. Advocacy Res. Ctr., Amer. Med. Assn.
Johnson, Lael F., (AV) ... '— '63 C.937 A.B. L.597 J.D. [[C] Schiff H.]
Johnson, Larry L. ... '51 '77 C.338 B.S. L.365 J.D. Sr. Atty., U.S. EPA
Johnson, Lars S. ... '56 '88 C.339 B.S. L.146 J.D. Coun., Quaker Foods & Beverages
Johnson, Leslie, (BV) ... '— '86 C.339 B.A. L.910 J.D. [[A] O'Hagan,S.&A.]
Johnson, Linda Urbanik ... '58 '93 C.679 B.A. L.424 J.D. [DLPiper R.G.C.U.]
Johnson, Lisa ... '76 '03 C.145 B.A. L.309 J.D. [[A] Holland&K.]
Johnson, Marie C. Bellamy '11 '48 C.943 L.365 LL.B.
Ret. Admin. Law J., Ill. Dept. of Employ. Sec.‡
Johnson, Marilyn F. ... '54 '80 C.145 B.A. L.339 J.D. Chicago Bd of Ed
Johnson, Mark D., (AV) ... '65 '93 C.436 B.A. L.365 J.D. [Johnson&B.]
Johnson, Mark L. ... '65 '90 C&L.339 B.A., J.D. [Seyfarth S.]

Johnson, Matthew E. ... '64 '89 C&L.352 B.B.A., J.D. [Sidley A.B.&W.]
Johnson, Matthew L. ... '70 '96 C.967 B.A. L.365 J.D. [Johnson&B.]
Johnson, Matthew M. ... '— '95 C.602 B.A. L.221 J.D. [Sachnoff&W.]
Johnson, Michael A. ... '57 '82 C.339 B.A. L.365 J.D. 415 N. LaSalle
Johnson, Michael G. ... '48 '90 C.767 B.A. L.1068 J.D. Asst. Pub. Def.
Johnson, Michael L. ... '58 '86 C.1293 B.A. L.477 J.D. 203 North La Salle Street
Johnson, Michael L. ... '75 '03 C.436 B.A. L.190 J.D. [Keating,K.P.&B.]
Johnson, Parker H. ... '50 '96 C.491 B.S. L.209 J.D. [Ancel,G.D.B.D.&R.]
Johnson, Paul K. ... '51 '76 C&L.597 B.A., J.D. Sr. Coun., Bank One Corp.
Johnson, Phillip J., (AV) ... '43 '69 C.424 B.S. L.146 J.D. [Scopelitis,G.L.&H.]
Johnson, Prentis Llewellyn ... '51 '99 C.629 B.S. L.589 J.D. Asst. States Atty.
Johnson, Richard F., (AV) ... '44 '69 C.473 B.S. L.597 J.D. [Hughes S.P.R.&D.]
Johnson, Richard K., (AV) ... '55 '82 C.597 B.S. L.209 J.D. [Katz,F.E.E.&J.]
Johnson, Richard M., Jr., (AV) '46 '72
C.597 B.A. L.208 J.D. 30 North La Salle Street, Suite 4300
Johnson, Robert Bradley ... '71 '02 C.597 B.A. L.424 J.D. [Kelly,O.M.D.&R.]
Johnson, Robert C., (AV) ... '48 '73 C.187 B.A. L.569 J.D. [Sonnenschein N.&R.]
Johnson, Robert Earl ... '47 '94 Chicago Legal Clinic, Inc.
Johnson, Robert V. ... '39 '65 C.373 B.A. L.145 J.D. 5648 S. Dorchester Ave.‡
Johnson, Robt. N. ... '28 '54 C.973 B.S. L.209 J.D. Small Bus. Admn.
Johnson, Russell N. ... '62 '87 C.880 B.A. L.477 J.D. 3145 N. Cambridge Ave.
Johnson, Ryan T. ... '77 '03 C.352 B.A. L.221 J.D. [McKay,N.T.D.&K.]
Johnson, Sara E. ... '52 '77 C&L.597 B.A., J.D. Legal Assist. Found.
Johnson, Shelley A. ... '53 '78 C.509 B.A. L.1338 J.D. 29 S. LaSalle St., Suite 620
Johnson, Shelly Ann '75 '02 C.1082 B.A. L.209 J.D.
Staff Atty., Merchandise Mart Properties, Inc.
Johnson, Sonja R. ... '56 '81 C.999 B.A. L.209 J.D. [Weinberg R.]
Johnson, Stacy L. ... '61 '86 C.347 B.A. L.597 J.D. 2 N. Riverside Plaza
Johnson, Steven R. ... '63 '92 C.597 B.S. L.365 J.D. [Falk J.]
Johnson, Suzanne H. ... '74 '00 C.259 B.S. L.502 J.D. [Vedder,P.K.&K.]
Johnson, Thomas E., (AV) ... '50 '75 C.30 B.A. L.309 J.D. [Johnson,J.S.G.&D.]
Johnson, Thomas E., (AV) ... '48 '75 C.878 B.S. L.597 J.D. [Sandler,T.&R.]
Johnson, Tige C. ... '70 '98 C.560 B.A. L.880 J.D. [Clark&J.]
Johnson, William V., (AV) ... '40 '66 C.436 B.A. L.146 J.D. [Johnson&B.]

Johnson & Associates, P.C., (AV)
887 North La Salle Street, 60610-3219
Telephone: 312-236-1616 Facsimile: 312-642-3609
Email: japc@ix.netcom.com URL: http://www.lawyers.com/johnson&assoc
Dorothy Bertram Johnson;—Coleen A. Blake.
Family Law, Probate and Estate Planning, Criminal, Appellate, Real Estate Transactions and Commercial Litigation.
See Professional Biographies, CHICAGO, ILLINOIS

Johnson & Bell, Ltd., (AV) BR
55 East Monroe Street Suite 4100, 60603-5896 ⊙
Telephone: 312-372-0770 Facsimile: 312-372-9818
Email: info@johnsonandbell.com URL: http://www.johnsonandbell.com
Shareholders: William V. Johnson; John W. Bell; Jack T. Riley, Jr.; Brian C. Fetzer; Thomas J. Andrews; William G. Beatty; John A. Childers; Margaret A. Unger; H. Patrick Morris; Scott W. Hoyne; Frederick S. Mueller; Joseph R. Marconi; Robert M. Burke; Glenn F. Fencl; David J. Loughnane; Joseph F. Spitzzeri; Dennis C. Cusack; Steven B. Novy; Joseph B. Carini, III; Rick L. Hammond; James K. Toohey; Michael P. Siavelis; William A. Geiser; Kevin G. Owens; Charles P. Rantis; Robert J. Comfort; Daniel C. Murray; William K. McVisk; Kathryn K. Loft; Gregory D. Conforti; Frank P. Nowicki; Gregory E. Schiller; Howard W. Foster; Robert R. McNamara; Marilyn McCabe Reidy; David M. Macksey; Terry A. Takash; Patrick T. Garvey; Mark D. Johnson; Andrew J. Kovarik; Lynn M. Reid; Robert Spitkovsky, Jr.; Steve C. Canty; Matthew L. Johnson; Julie M. Kennedy; Charlene S. Mitchell; Edward W. Hearn (Not admitted in IL); Keith L. Gibson; Michael A. LaTona. Associates: Julie E. Benes; Garrett L. Boehm, Jr.; Paul E. Brady; Christopher J. Carlos; Steven G. Carlson; Jeffery G. Chrones; Tracie V. Coleman; Timothy R. Couture; Mary K. Cryar; David A. Cyr; David F. Fanning; Cecilio L. Franco, IV; Matthew A. Galin; Eydie R. Glassman; Jonathon W. Goken; Richard R. Gordon; Katie E. Gorrie; Sean J. Hardy; Thomas J. Hayes; Michael C. Holy; Kathryn R. Hoying; Meanith Huon; Sean P. Hussey; Michael H. Israel; Kurt E. Keagle (Not admitted in IL); Angela M. Kotsalieff; Michael J. Laux; William J. Leeder, III; Christopher W. Loweth; Nicholas R. Lykins; Paige C. Manley; Rory L. Margulis; Eric W. Moch; Cristina Mungai; Meiko L. Ogura; Jason Orleans; Henry A. Parkhurst; Michael A. Pauletto; James E. Phelan; Victor Pioli; Deborah G. Relihan; Justin A. Relihan; Sammi L. Renken; Jennifer Tomsak Rose; Peter R. Ryndak; Justin D. Scheid; Carl M. Schultz; Jared M. Scott; Ronald E. Scott; Joshua S. Singewald; Martha C. Szatkowski; Lauren Ann Wieland; Matthew K. Wollin; William T. Young; Daniel J. Zlatic.
Trial practice in state and federal courts, including national coordinating counsel. Appellate Law, Asbestos Litigation, Automotive Product Liability Litigation, Aviation Litigation, Benefits, Business Litigation and Practice, Complex Plaintiff Litigation, Construction Litigation, Corporate Health Care, Criminal Litigation, Employment Law, ERISA, Environmental Law, Financial Crimes, Financial Institution Representation, General Negligence and Premises Liability, Gun Litigation, Hospital Law and Medical Liability, Insurance Coverage, Intellectual Property, Long Term Care/Nursing Home Liability, Mass Tort, Medical Device Liability, Mold Litigation, Municipal Liability, National Coordinating Counsel, Probate, Product Liability, Professional Liability, Railroad Litigation, Toxic Tort and Trucking and Transportation.
References available upon request.
Waukegan, Illinois Office: 325 Washington Street, Suite 200, 60085. Telephone: 847-662-7458. Facsimile: 847-662-7366.
Highland, Indiana Office: 9000 Indianapolis Boulevard, Suite A, 46322. Telephone: 219-923-5250. Facsimile: 219-923-6170.
See Professional Biographies, CHICAGO, ILLINOIS

Johnson, Bruce Earl ... 500 N. Michigan Ave., Ste. 300

Johnson and Colmar, (AV)
300 South Wacker Drive Suite 1000, 60606
Telephone: 312-922-1980 Fax: 312-922-9283
URL: http://www.jocolaw.com
Russell E. Q. Johnson (1938-1980); Craig P. Colmar; Michael Bonn; Mark V. Chester; Joan S. Cherry; Robin C. Friedman; Joan M. Meyers; Peter J. Daane; Murray J. Lewison. Of Counsel: John L. Colmar (1916-2004).
Business Planning, Acquisitions, Securities, Business and Governmental Litigation, Employee Benefits, State and Local Government Law, Real Estate and Estate Planning and Probate.
See Professional Biographies, CHICAGO, ILLINOIS

Johnson, Jones, Snelling, Gilbert & Davis, P.C., (AV) ... 36 S. Wabash Ave.

Johnson & Newby, LLC, (AV)
39 S. LaSalle Street Suite 820, 60603
Telephone: 312-345-1306 Fax: 312-345-1308
URL: http://www.lawyers.com/johnsonnewby
Members of Firm: Cindy M. Johnson; David A. Newby. Associates: Beth Anne Alcantar; Rebecca M. Shanaman.
Bankruptcy, Business Litigation and Commercial Collections.
See Professional Biographies, CHICAGO, ILLINOIS

Johnson, Theresa V., Law Office of
(See Westmont)

Johnson-Weinberger, Daniel E. ... '74 '00 C.339 B.A. L.145 J.D. Nat'l Field Dir.
Johnston, Alan R., (AV) ... '14 '41 C.674 B.S. L.477 J.D. 1 IBM Plaza
Johnston, Benjamin A. '61 '88 C&L.339 B.A., J.D.
Gen. Coun., V.P. & Secy., James McHugh Const. Co.
Johnston, Christopher R., (AV) ... '— '82 C.695 B.B.A. L.209 J.D. [Querrey&H.]
Johnston, Daniel P. ... '— '97 C.339 B.A. L.221 J.D. [Litchfield C.]
Johnston, Iain, (AV) ... '65 '90 C.697 B.S.G.S. L.365 J.D. [Holland&K.]
Johnston, James P. ... '61 '87 C.209 B.S. L.146 J.D. [Donohue B.M.&S.]
Johnston, Jennifer A. ... '73 '01 C&L.124 B.S.N., J.D. [Wildman,H.A.&D.]
Johnston, Julie N. ... '— '97 C.339 B.S. L.365 J.D. [Lord,B.&B.]
Johnston, Randolph M. ... '48 '80 C.475 B.S. L.146 J.D. Asst. States Atty.
Johnston, Richard Blake '63 '97 C.608 B.S.M.E. L.424 J.D.
[DLPiper R.G.C.U.] (Pat.)
Johnston, Robert G. '31 '60 C&L.145 J.D.
Prof. & Assoc. Dean, The John Marshall Law Sch.
Johnston-Ahlen, Julie A. ... '71 '02 C.915 B.A. L.494 J.D. [Novack&M.]
Johnstone, Andrew M. ... '73 '98 C.339 B.A. L.477 J.D. [Winston&S.]
Joike, Trevor B. ... '— '70 C.339 B.S.E.E. L.904 J.D. [Schiff H.] (Pat.)
Jolivette, David J., (AV) ... '42 '70 C&L.966 B.S., J.D. [Jolivette&T.]

Jolivette & Templer, P.C., (AV)
10 South La Salle Street Suite 1017, 60603
Telephone: 312-419-8800 Facsimile: 312-419-0705
Email: jolidave@juno.com
David J. Jolivette; Lawrence M. Templer.
General Civil Trial and Commercial Law. Corporate, Real Property, Mortgage Law, Appellate Practice, Professional Conduct of Attorneys.
See Professional Biographies, CHICAGO, ILLINOIS

Jona, Ildiko ... '— '98 [Latham&W.]
Jones, Adam E. ... '74 '02 C&L.352 B.A., J.D. [Ross,D.&B.]
Jones, Amanda ... '— '05 C.623 B.A. L.880 J.D. [DLPiper R.G.C.U.]
Jones, Amy B. Gendleman '71 '96
C.477 B.A. L.145 J.D. Human Resource Coun., Tribune Co.
Jones, Christian T. ... '— '68 C.605 B.A. L.597 J.D. [Chapman&C.]
Jones, Eric D. ... '73 '98 C.424 B.A. L.146 J.D. [Bullaro&C.]
Jones, Gregory C., (AV) ... '42 '67 C.188 B.A. L.477 J.D. [Grippo&E.]
Jones, Helen Hart ... '21 '45 C.473 B.A. L.930 LL.B. 140 S. Dearborn St.
Jones, Jacqueline ... '— '85 C&L.597 B.S., J.D. 4469 S. Lake Park
Jones, Jerry D., (AV) ... '42 '67 C.999 A.B. L.339 J.D. [Bell J.&Q.]
Jones, Jetta N. ... '— '55 L.976 LL.B. 4907 S. Kimbark St.
Jones, Katherine A. ... '72 '98 C.399 B.A. L.902 J.D. [Christensen&E.]
Jones, Kenneth L. ... '46 '70 C.339 L.146 J.D. Asst. State Appl. Def.
Jones, Kevin M. ... '76 '01 C.116 B.A. L.209 J.D. [Freeman,F.&S.]
Jones, Leslie Ann ... '52 '83 C.976 B.A. L.309 LL.B. [Johnson,J.S.G.&D.]
Jones, Linzey D. ... '22 '62 C.339 L.365 J.D. Comm., Industrial Commission of Ill.
Jones, Linzey D., Jr., (AV) ... '— '82 C.145 B.A. L.339 J.D. [Pugh,J.J.&Q.]
Jones, Loren D. '57 '82 C.579 B.A. L.585 J.D.
(adm. in ND; not adm. in IL) TechLaw Automation Partners, Inc.
Jones, Margaret B. '60 '88 C.276 B.A. L.477 J.D.
VP & Sr. Coun., Global Hyatt Corp.
Jones, Mark E., Jr., (AV) ... '20 '50 C.1016 A.B. L.424 J.D. 111 W. Washington St.
Jones, Miranda B. ... '70 '96 C.104 A.B. L.477 J.D. Atty., Dept. of HHS, Gen. Coun. Off.
Jones, Mitchell E., (BV) ... '52 '80 C.415 B.A. L.365 J.D. [Jones]
Jones, Nathaniel M. ... '45 '97 C.1183 B.A. L.589 J.D. [Baumgert,J.&Assoc.]
Jones, Pamela P. ... '— '02 C.1040 B.A. L.146 J.D. [Franczek S.]
Jones, Philip A. ... '66 '93 C.674 A.B. L.94 J.D. [Brinks H.G.&L.]
Jones, Richard C. ... '28 '63 C&L.209 Ph.B., J.D. 30 S. Wacker Dr., 29th Fl.
Jones, Rickey ... '55 '86 C.801 M.S. L.325 J.D. Cir. J.
Jones, Robert B., (AV) ... '32 '60 C.350 B.S. L.477 J.D. [Fitch,E.T.&F.] (See Pat. Sect.)
Jones, Robert L., Jr. '58 '84 C.602 B.A. L.309 J.D.
Bus. and Professional People for the Pub. Interest
Jones, Roger J. ... '— '87 C.1044 B.A. L.107 J.D. [Latham&W.]
Jones, Ronald R. ... '50 '79 C.112 A.B. L.1151 J.D. 6332 1/2 S. Archer Ave.
Jones, Sandra Y. ... '52 '78 C.339 B.S. L.879 J.D. Admin. Law J., Dept. of Human Rights
Jones, Shawn K. ... '— '97 C.101 B.A. L.46 J.D. [Clausen M.]
Jones, Sidney A., III ... '43 '73 C.339 B.S. L.597 J.D. Cir. J.
Jones, Stephanie D. ... '69 '94 C.951 B.A. L.477 J.D. [Figliulo&S.]
Jones, T. Monique ... '77 '02 C.475 B.A. L.273 J.D. [Dahm&E.]
Jones, Thomas M., (AV) ... '47 '75 C.339 B.A. L.188 J.D. [McDermott W.&E.]
Jones, Walter, Jr., (AV) ... '46 '72 C&L.339 B.A., J.D. [Pugh,J.J.&Q.]
Jones, William H., (AV) ... '63 '89 C.352 B.B.A. L.365 J.D. [Canel,D.&K.]
Jones, William P. ... '49 '78 C.339 B.A. L.424 J.D. 3 1st. National Plaza, Ste 2200

Jones Day, (AV)
77 West Wacker, 60601-1692 ⊙
Telephone: 312-782-3939 Telecopier: 312-782-8585
Email: counsel@jonesday.com URL: http://www.jonesday.com
Members of Firm in Chicago: Joni L. Andrioff; Robert Dean Avery; Eric P. Berlin; John F. Bibby, Jr.; Scott W. Burt; Steven T. Catlett; Richard A. Chesley; Peter D. Clarke; Lynn Leland Coe; James R. Daly; Lawrence C. DiNardo; Michael F. Dolan; Brian W. Easley; Susan Elliott; Brad B. Erens; Irene S. Fiorentinos; Christopher W. Flynn; Thomas F. Gardner; June K. Ghezzi; Robert J. Graves; Michael J. Gray; James C. Hagy; Stephen E. Hall; Michelle Morgan Harner; Paul E. Harner; Carol A. Hogan; Robert J. Joseph; David J. Kates; Elizabeth Clough Kitslaar; Robert C. Lee; John A. Marlott; Thomas P. McNulty; Timothy J. Melton; Michael J. Mitchell; Edward A. Purnell; Daniel E. Reidy; William P. Ritchie; Mark P. Rotatori; Lee Ann Russo; Paul T. Ruxin; Ronald A. Sandler; Debra J. Schnebel; Paul W. Schroeder; Brian L. Sedlak; Tina M. Tabacchi; Richard K. Tomei; Charles T. Wehland; James A. White; Edward B. Winslow; David L. Witcoff. Of Counsel: Daniel J. Bacastow; Joseph H. Golant; William J. Harmon; William S. McKay, Jr.; Dan B. Miller; James B. Raden; Ronald S. Rizzo; Boyd J. Springer; Robert A. Yolles. Counsel: John B. Carothers III; James C. Dunlop; Susan I. Matejcak; Jane K. Murphy; Sandra Byster Weiss; Daniel E. White. Associates: Stacy A. Baim; Carrie E. Bassi; Melissa R. Beiting; Charles N. Bensinger, III; Marc S. Blackman; Jon-Thomas Bloch; Cassandra L. Boyle; Bradley C. Brasser; Amy L. Cobb; Mark A. Cody; Emily A. Colantino; Lindsey D. Dates; Rachael E. Dehner (Not admitted in IL); Catherine M. Dietz; Patrick M. D'Onofrio; Laura M. Earl; Michael P. Earley; Sarah H. Eberhard; Kevin P. Ferguson; Michael S. Ferrell; Yelena Fertman; Mindy A. Finnigan; James A. Francque; Tara A. Fumerton; Gregory J. Gallagher; Carol P. Geisler; Kelly P. Glauberman; Ilana Glazier; Rebecca L. Graines; Robert C. Griffith; Alicia M. Hawley; Timothy J. Heverin; Morgan R. Hirst; Charles E. Juister; Matthew D. Kellam; Mary M. Kimura; Brent D. Knight; Robert E. Krebs; Kristan Q. Laden; Phuong T. Lam; Joel T. May; Elizabeth B. McRee; Amanda E. Meyers; Nenad M. Milenkovich; Michelle L. Miller; John K. Min; J. Ryan Mitchell; Thomas N. Molins; Kendra L. Morrill; Trisha L. Mowbray; Brian S. Mulcahy; Brian J. Murray; Kelly M. Neff; John D. Neumann; Beth A. O'Connor; Heather M. O'Shea (Not admitted in IL); Gregory S. Otsuka; Nikki J. Palmer; Kristin L. Parker; Jennifer Pelic; Giselle M. Pérez; John T. Perugini; Michelle S. Quintos; Paula S. Quist; Michael J. Rausch; Sheila Saegh; Ericka K. Scarpace (Not admitted in IL); Leslie E. Schafer; Efrat R. Schulman; Krista S. Schwartz; Margaret M. Seurynck; Joseph P. Shereda; Karey V. Skiermont; Tatjana Stoljarova; Michael G. Strohmeier; Albert D. Sturtevant, III; Tamara Irwin Travis; Heather A. Varon; Jill S. Vorobiev; Adam W. Wiers (Not admitted in IL); Jason G. Winchester; Megan M. Wolfinger; John M. Wright; Michelle Yokoyama; Kate L. Zarczynski; Grazia M. Zorub (Not admitted in IL). Staff Attorneys: Wendy A. Aeschlimann; Laura A. Dahl.
Languages: French, German, Hebrew, Hindi, Korean, Marathi, Russian, Serbo-Croatian, Spanish, and Ukrainian.
Full-Service Civil Practice, Antitrust and Competition Law, Business Restructuring and Reorganization, Capital Markets, Complex Commercial and Multrijurisdictional Litigation, Corporate Criminal Investigations, Employee Benefits and Executive Compensation, Energy Delivery and Power, Government Regulation, Health Care, Intellectual Property and Technology, International Litigation and Arbitration, Issues and Appeals, Labor and Employment, Lending/Structured Finance and

(This Listing Continued)

Jones Day (Continued)

Derivatives, Life Sciences, Mergers and Acquisitions, Oil and Gas, Private Equity, Products Liability, Personal Injury Torts and Health Litigation, Real Estate and Environment, Securities and Shareholder Litigation, Tax.
In Atlanta, Georgia: 1420 Peachtree Street, N.E., Suite 800. Telephone: 404-521-3939. Telecopier: 404-581-8330.
In Beijing, China: 3201 China World Tower 1, No. 1 Jianguomenwai Avenue. Telephone: 86-10-5866-1111. Telecopier: 86-10-5866-1122.
In Brussels, Belgium: Boulevard Brand Whitlocklaan 165, 1200 Brussels. Telephone: 32-2-645-14-11. Telecopier: 32-2-645-14-45.
In Cleveland, Ohio: North Point, 901 Lakeside Avenue. Telephone: 216-586-3939. Telecopier: 216-579-0212.
In Columbus, Ohio: 325 John H. McConnell Boulevard, Suite 600. Telephone: 614-469-3939. Telecopier: 614-461-4198.
In Dallas, Texas: 2727 North Harwood Street. Telephone: 214-220-3939. Telecopier: 214-969-5100.
In Frankfurt, Germany: Hochhaus am Park, Grüneburgweg 102, 60323 Frankfurt am Main. Telephone: 49-69-9726-3939. Telecopier: 49-69-9726-3993.
In Hong Kong, China: 31st Floor, Edinburgh Tower, The Landmark, 15 Queen's Road, Central. Telephone: 852-2526-6895. Telecopier: 852-2868-5871.
In Houston, Texas: 717 Texas, Suite 3300. Telephone: 832-239-3939. Telecopier: 832-239-3600.
In Irvine, California: 3 Park Plaza, Suite 1100. Telephone: 949-851-3939. Telecopier: 949-553-7539.
In London, England: 21 Tudor Street. Telephone: 44-20-7039-5959. Telecopier: 44-20-7039-5999.
In Los Angeles, California: 555 South Flower Street, Fiftieth Floor. Telephone: 213-489-3939. Telecopier: 213-243-2539.
In Madrid, Spain: Velázquez 51, 4th Floor. Telephone: 34-91-520-39-39. Telecopier: 34-91-520-39-38.
In Menlo Park, California: 2882 Sand Hill Road, Suite 240. Telephone: 650-739-3939. Telecopier: 650-739-3900.
In Milan, Italy: Via Turati, 16/18. Telephone: 39-02-7645-4001. Telecopier: 39-02-7645-4400.
In Moscow, Russia: Smolenskaya Square 3, 9th Floor, 121099 Moscow. Telephone: 7-095-980-6769. Telecopier: 7-095-980-6765.
In Munich, Germany: Prinzregentenstr. 11, 80538 Munich. Telephone: 089-20 60 42-200. Telecopier: 089-20 60 42-293.
In New York, New York: 222 East 41st Street. Telephone: 212-326-3939. Telecopier: 212-755-7306.
In Paris, France: 120, rue du Faubourg Saint-Honoré. Telephone: 33-1-56-59-39-39. Telecopier: 33-1-56-59-39-38.
In Pittsburgh, Pennsylvania: 500 Grant Street, One Mellon Bank Center, 31st Floor. Telephone: 412-391-3939. Telecopier: 412-394-7959.
In San Diego, California: 12750 High Bluff Drive, Suite 300. Telephone: 858-314-1200. Telecopier: 858-314-1150.
In San Francisco, California: 555 California Street, 26th Floor. Telephone: 415-626-3939. Telecopier: 415-875-5700.
In Shanghai, China: 30th Floor, Shanghai Kerry Centre, 1515 Nanjing Road West. Telephone: 86-21-2201-8000. Telecopier: 86-21-5298-6569.
In Singapore, Singapore: 30 Cecil Street, #29-01 Prudential Tower. Telephone: 65 6 538 3939. Telecopier: 65 6 536 3939.
In Sydney, Australia: Australia Square, Level 38, 264-278 George Street. Telephone: 61-2-8272-0500. Telecopier: 61-2-8272-0599.
In Taipei, Taiwan: 6th Floor, 2 Tun Hwa South Road, Section 2. Telephone: (886-2) 2704-6808 or (886-2) 7712-3399. Telecopier: (886-2) 2704-6791.
In Tokyo, Japan: Shiroyama MT Building, 6th Floor, 1-17 Toranomon 4-chome, Minato-ku, Tokyo 105-0001. Telephone: 81-3-3433-3939. Telecopier: 81-3-5401-2725.
In Washington, D.C.: 51 Louisiana Avenue, N.W. Telephone: 202-879-3939. Telecopier: 202-626-1700.

See Professional Biographies, CHICAGO, ILLINOIS

Jones Klopfer, Gail . . . . . '68 '94 [Ⓐ Rosenthal,M.C.]

Jones Law Offices, (BV)
25 East Washington Street, Suite 906, 60602
Telephone: 312-236-2112 Facsimile: 312-236-2634
Email: mej@joneslaw.org URL: http://www.lawyers.com/joneslaw
Mitchell E. Jones.
All Aspects of General Business, Corporate, Partnership and Limited Liability Law with emphasis on Business, Financial and Legal Consulting, Commercial Mediation, Dispute Resolution, Business and Commercial Litigation, Public and Private Bond Finance, Mergers, Acquisitions, and Divestitures, Business Turnaround, Financial Restructuring and Workouts, Commercial Bankruptcy and Reorganizations, Creditors Rights, Contracts, Secured Transactions, Commercial Real Estate including Construction and Mortgage Foreclosure Litigation, Business Succession and Estate Planning, Elder Law.

See Professional Biographies, CHICAGO, ILLINOIS

Jones-Beatty, Leslye E. . . . . '— '85 C.210 B.A. L.150 J.D. [Ⓐ Robbins,S.N.L.&T.]
Jonusaitis, Andy V. . . . . . '— '86 C&L.597 B.A., J.D. [Ⓒ Freeborn&P.]
Joranko, David B. '60 '85 C.228 B.A. L.608 J.D.
(adm. in OH; not adm. in IL) Price Waterhouse
Jordan, Daniel C. . . . . '60 '91 C.339 A.B. L.146 J.D. Off. of the Comptr. of the Currency
Jordan, Daniel G. . . . . '59 '86 C.424 A.B. L.339 J.D. [Caron,C.&W.]
Jordan, Edward R. . . . . '36 '73 C.1016 B.A. L.365 J.D. Cir. J.
Jordan, Gregory J., (AV) . . . . '58 '84 C.602 B.B.A. L.1119 J.D. [Dykema G.P.]
Jordan, Horace W., (AV) . . . . '16 '40 C.31 A.B. L.597 J.D. 180 N. LaSalle St., Ste. 1801
Jordan, Jeffrey S. . . . . . '79 '04 C&L.424 B.A., J.D. [Ⓐ Anesi,O.R.N.&K.]
Jordan, Marie I. . . . '61 '91 C.589 B.A. L.339 J.D. Sr. Coun., Bank One Corp. (Law Dept.)
Jordan, Michael F. . . . . '55 '83 C.966 B.B.A. L.365 J.D. 4609 N. Westfra
Jordan, Michelle W. . . . . '— '02 C.608 B.S.M.E. L.597 J.D. [Ⓐ Kirkland&E.]
Jordan, Scott E. . . . . '64 '92 C.608 B.S.B.A. L.930 J.D. CEO & Pres., ScotteVest LLC
Jordan, Susan P. . . . . '— '85 C.597 B.A. L.276 J.D. [Lord,B.&B.]
Jordan, Tracey A. . . . . '67 '92 C.473 B.A. L.930 J.D. [Clausen M.]
Jorgensen, Kelly A. . . . . '— '02 C.352 B.B.A. L.209 J.D. [Ⓐ Clausen M.]
Jors, Jennifer A. . . . . '73 '98 C.958 B.A. L.209 J.D. [Ⓐ Horwood M.&B.]
Jorzak, Richard H. . . . . '31 '54 6049 W. Belmont St.
Joseph, Burton, (AV) . . . . '30 '52 C.339 L.209 LL.B. Spec. Coun., Playboy Magazine
Joseph, Georgann . . . . '58 '85 C.494 B.A. L.597 J.D. 16 N. May St., Ste. 544
Joseph, George A., (AV) . . . . '— '76 C.477 B.A. L.94 J.D. [Kirkland&E.]
Joseph, Howard . . . . '25 '51 C.966 L.597 LL.B. 3200 Broadway

Joseph, Jack, (AV) '27 '52 C&L.145 B.A., J.D.
77 West Wacker Drive, Suite 4800, 60601
Telephone: 312-346-9887 Fax: 312-346-3468
(Also, Of Counsel to Hedlund & Hanley, LLC).
General Civil and Trial Practice in State and Federal Courts.

Joseph, Marc S., (BV) . . . . '56 '81 C&L.339 B.S., J.D. [Levenfeld P.]
Joseph, Maria Sewell . . . . '51 '85 Appellate Cts.
Joseph, Robert J., (AV) . . . . '— '88 C.347 B.A. L.309 J.D. [Jones D.]
Joseph, Robert T., (AV) . . . . '46 '71 C.973 A.B. L.477 J.D. [Sonnenschein N.&R.]
Josephson, Edwin I. . . . . '44 '68 C.1016 B.S. L.209 J.D. [Chuhak&T.]
Josephson, Eliott . . . . '42 '69 C.597 B.S.B.A. L.209 J.D. 1 S. Wacker Dr.
Josephson, Kathy P. . . . . '— '02 C&L.597 B.A., J.D. [Ⓐ Katten M.R.]
Josephson, Mark Lee . . . . '67 '97 C.145 B.A. L.597 J.D. U.S. Ct. App.
Josephson, Scott A. . . . . '71 '98 C.37 B.A. L.1202 J.D. [Ⓐ Horwood M.&B.]
Josephson Bernat, Laura A. . . . . '— '93 C.347 B.S. L.424 J.D. [Ⓒ Chuhak&T.]
Joshi, Ronak T. . . . . '77 '04 C.025 B.A. L.365 J.D. [Ⓐ Garofalo,S.H.&S.]
Joshua, Fred A. . . . . '78 '03 C.339 B.S. L.146 J.D. 220 S. State St., Ste. 2026
Joslin, James C. . . . . '— '96 C.340 B.A. L.608 J.D. [Kirkland&E.]
Joslyn, David L. . . . . '48 '75 C&L.597 B.A., J.D. [Ⓒ McCullough,C.&L.]
Jostock, Eric H. . . . . '65 '90 C.352 B.B.A. L.339 J.D. [Jostock&J.]
Jostock, Henry J., (AV) . . . . '29 '55 C.339 B.S. L.146 J.D. [Jostock&J.]
Jostock & Jostock, P.C., (AV) . . . . 20 North Wacker Drive
Joung, J. Kenneth . . . . '69 '94 C.197 A.B. L.597 J.D. [DLPiper R.G.C.U.] (Pat.)
Jovan, William J. . . . . '35 '61 C&L.597 B.S., J.D. [Ⓐ Nolan]
Joy, Mark, (AV) . . . . '65 '90 C.339 B.S. L.477 J.D. [Leydig,V.&M.] (See Pat. Sect.)
Joyce, Catherine Wozniak . . . . '62 '88 C&L.424 B.B.A., J.D. [Winston&S.]
Joyce, Christopher P. . . . . '49 '75 C.339 B.A. L.365 J.D. Drovers Nat. Bk. of Chic.
Joyce, Edward T., (AV) . . . . '42 '67 C.145 B.B.A. L.424 J.D. [E.T.Joyce&Assoc.]
Joyce, Georgia L. . . . . '55 '94 C.339 B.S. L.446 J.D. [Ⓐ Chittenden,M.&N.]
Joyce, Jennifer A. . . . . '73 '00 C.960 B.A. L.436 J.D. [Ⓐ Masuda,F.E.&M.]
Joyce, Mary Patricia '70 '95 C.209 B.A. L.146 J.D.
Claims Coun., Chicago Title Ins. Co.
Joyce, Molly M. . . . . '77 '02 C.209 B.A. L.146 J.D. [Ⓐ Seyfarth S.]
Joyce, Robert H., (AV) . . . . '28 '56 C.177 B.A. L.209 J.D. [Seyfarth S.] ‡
Joyce, Sean G. . . . . '69 '03 C.209 B.S. L.424 J.D. [Ⓐ Williams M.&J.]
Joyce, Thomas F., (AV) . . . . '52 '81 C.145 B.S. L.309 J.D. [Bell,B.&L.]
Joyce, Thomas J., (AV) . . . . '21 '49 C.1024 B.A. L.209 J.D. 1 N. Franklin St., Ste. 900
Joyce, Thomas M. . . . . '29 '74 C.339 B.A. L.209 J.D. 333 N. Michigan Ave.
Joyce, Thomas P. . . . . '15 '48 C.424 L.146 LL.B. 6203 N. Keeler Ave.
Joyce, Edward T., & Associates, P.C., (AV) . . . . Eleven South La Salle Street, Suite 1600
Joyce-Romani, Sheila D. '71 '96
C.338 B.S. L.146 J.D. Assoc. Gen. Coun., Braun Consulting, Inc.
Jozefiak, Stanley W. . . . . '57 '83 C.145 B.A. L.597 J.D. 33 W. Monroe St.‡
Jozefowicz, James J. . . . . '61 '89 C.145 B.A. L.589 J.D. [Ⓐ Patton&R.]
Jozwiak, John R. . . . . '27 '55 C&L.424 A.B., J.D. Prof. of Law, Loyola Univ.
Juarez, Richard J. . . . . '66 '92 C.339 B.S. L.209 J.D. [Schuyler,R.&Z.]
Judd, Zachary A. . . . . '— '02 C.894 B.A. L.339 J.D. [Ⓐ Latham&W.]
Judge, James E. . . . . '63 '97 C.339 B.F.A. L.146 J.D. [Ⓐ Vanasco,G.&M.]
Judge, Jonathan M. . . . . '— '01 C.399 B.A. L.966 J.D. [Ⓐ Schiff H.]
Judge, McRay, II . . . . '69 '94 C.352 B.S. L.45 J.D. [Ⓐ Swanson,M.&B.]
Juenger, Jon M. . . . . '66 '02 C.339 B.A. L.494 J.D. [Ⓐ Mayer,B.R.&M.]
Juergensmeyer, John E., (AV) . . . . '34 '63 C&L.339 A.B., J.D. [Juergensmeyer&Assoc.] ⊙
Juergensmeyer and Associates, (AV) . . . . 39 South La Salle Street, Suite 915 (⊙Elgin)
Juettner, Paul G., (AV) . . . . '54 '81 C.339 B.S.C.E. L.146 J.D. [Greer,B.&C.] (Pat.)
Juettner, Thomas R., (AVⓉ) '24 '50 C.436 B.M.E. L.424 J.D.
[Ⓒ Greer,B.&C.] (Pat.) ⊙
Juffernbruch, Thomas K. . . . . '— '95 C.339 B.S. L.1119 J.D. [Schiff H.]
Juhl, Loren E., (AV) . . . . '18 '49 C.339 B.S. L.309 LL.B. 1 1st Nat. Plaza
Juhnke, Laura E. . . . . '75 '02 C.945 B.A. L.477 J.D. 10 South Dearborn
Juister, Charles E. . . . . '— '01 C.339 B.S.M.E. L.597 J.D. [Ⓐ Jones D.]
Julian, David C., Attorney at law '48 '74
C.339 B.A. L.146 J.D. 2800 N. Lake Shore Dr., Ste. 1202
Julian, Paul T. . . . . '47 '77 C.1046 B.S. L.146 J.D. 1038 N. LaSalle
Julius, Norman B. . . . . '56 '81 C.339 B.S. L.145 J.D. [Vedder,P.K.&K.]
Jump, R. Howard, (AV) . . . . '53 '79 C&L.469 B.A., J.D. 11 S. Lasalle St., Ste. 2000
Juneau, William Jerome . . . . '33 '83 C.742 B.S. L.209 J.D. 218 North Jefferson Street
Junewicz, James J. . . . . '50 '77 C.276 B.S. L.229 J.D. [Mayer,B.R.&M.]
Jung, Bryan T. D. . . . . '— '90 C.340 B.F.A. L.145 J.D. [Foley&L.]
Jung, Jeffrey A. . . . . '64 '90 C.976 B.A. L.477 J.D. [McDermott W.&E.]
Jungels, Gary A. . . . . '— '97 C.602 B.B.A. L.339 J.D. [Kirkland&E.]
Jurasek, Michael C. . . . . '73 '98 C.475 B.A. L.424 J.D. [Latimer L.J.]
Jurek, Kenneth J., (AV) . . . . '48 '73 C&L.339 B.S., J.D. [McDermott W.&E.]
Jurgeleit, Peter B. . . . . '68 '98 C.197 A.B. L.347 J.D. [Ⓐ Barack F.K.P.&N.]
Jurgens, Larry C. . . . . '49 '81 C.339 B.S. L.862 J.D. [Sanchez&D.]
Jurgovan, Richard J. . . . . '43 '69 C.339 B.A. L.209 J.D. Contl. Ill. Nat. Bk. & Tr. Co.
Juric, Catherine '54 '87 C.700 B.A. L.424 J.D.
Courts Dept. Mgr., Law Bulletin Pub. Co.
Jurish, Kenneth M., (BV) . . . . '65 '90 C.856 B.A. L.902 J.D. Envir. Res. Mgmt.
Jurkacek, Elizabeth . . . . '59 '91 C.30 B.S. L.146 J.D. 180 N. Michigan Avenue, Suite 340
Jurusik, Michael T. . . . . '66 '93 C.299 B.A. L.424 J.D. [Klein,T.&J.]
Jurva, Jon K. . . . . '— '99 C&L.477 B.A., J.D. [Ⓐ Schiff H.]
Justak, Mel M. . . . . '74 '01 C.602 B.A. L.74 J.D. [Ⓐ Sachnoff&W.]
Juster, Mark L., (AV) . . . . '50 '76 C.473 B.A. L.910 J.D. [Laner,M.D.B.L.&T.]
Jutila, Gerald D., (AV) . . . . '43 '75 C.494 B.A. L.365 J.D. Arbitrator
Kaatz, Ryan M. '75 '04 C.494 B.A. L.300 J.D.
(adm. in MN; not adm. in IL) [Ⓐ Ladas&P.]
Kaba, Richard A. '47 '89 C.160 B.S. L.477 J.D.
(adm. in MI; not adm. in IL; See Pat. Sect.) [Fitch,E.T.&F.]
Kabaker, William L., (AV) . . . . '46 '72 C.339 B.A. L.209 J.D. [W.L.Kabaker&Assoc.]
Kabaker, William L., P.C., & Associates, (AV) . . . . 55 E. Monroe St., Ste. 3420
Kabat, David L., (AV) . . . . '46 '72 C&L.602 B.A., J.D. [Tressler,S.M.&P.]
Kabumoto, Cary K., (Mr.) . . . . '48 '81 C.1016 B.A. L.146 J.D. 5204 N. Christiana Ave.
Kachelhoffer, Scott S. . . . . '58 '91 C.388 B.A. L.46 J.D. Dept. of Employ. Sec. (⊙Aurora)
Kaczmarek, Mary L. . . . . '— '01 C.668 B.A. L.145 J.D. [Ⓐ Kirkland&E.]
Kaczynski, Christopher . . . . '68 '93 C.339 B.A. L.209 J.D. [Ⓐ Smith,H.B.&B.]
Kaden, Jonathan . . . . '74 '99 C.228 A.B. L.597 J.D. [Ⓐ Sonnenschein N.&R.]
Kaderabek, Lisa M., (AV) . . . . '60 '85 C.475 B.A. L.145 J.D. [McDermott W.&E.]
Kadish, Marc R. . . . . '43 '68 C&L.705 B.A., J.D. Clinical Prof., Chicago-Kent Coll. of Law
Kadison, Steven J., (AV) . . . . '44 '69 C.103 B.S. L.365 J.D. [Kamenear K.S.&C.]
Kadjan, Daniel N., (AV) . . . . '34 '60 C&L.209 B.A., J.D. [Arnold&K.]
Kadlec, Randall J. '45 '72 C.966 B.A. L.146 J.D.
V.P. & Sr. Underwriting Coun., Chicago Title Ins. Co.

Kagan, Linda S., (AV) '52 '80 C&L.424 B.A., J.D.
Monadnock Building, 53 West Jackson Boulevard, Suite 1108, 60604
Telephone: 312-362-1500 Fax: 312-362-0052
Email: lskagan@speakeasy.net URL: http://www.lawyers.com/lindaskaganlaw
Appellate and Civil Practice, Family, Domestic Relations and Real Estate Law. Immigration and Naturalization Law.

See Professional Biographies, CHICAGO, ILLINOIS

Kagan, Rosalyn H. . . . . '51 '76 C.339 B.S. L.146 J.D. Asst. States Atty.
Kagay, Sara J. '74 '00 C.221 B.A. L.352 J.D.
(adm. in MO; not adm. in IL) [Ⓐ Vedder,P.K.&K.]
Kahan, Dan M. '63 '90 C.478 B.A. L.309 J.D.
(adm. in MD; not adm. in IL) Asst. Prof., Univ. of Chicago Law School
Kahan, Ilana S. '67 '92 C.339 B.S. L.209 J.D.
ABN-AMRO North America, Inc. (Legal Department)
Kahan, Penny Nathan, (AV) . . . . '44 '79 C.1016 B.A. L.1066 J.D. [P.N.Kahan&Assoc.]
Kahan, Shimon B., (BV) . . . . '66 '91 C.339 B.A. L.209 J.D. [Haynes,S.K.O.&M.]

Kahan, Penny Nathan, & Associates, Ltd., (AV)
208 South LaSalle Street Suite 1660, 60604
Telephone: 312-855-1660 Fax: 312-855-1431 URL: http://www.lawyers.com/pennykahanlaw
Email: pnkahan@pnkahan.com URL: http://www.pnkahan.com
Penny Nathan Kahan;—Kristin M. Case.
Employment Contracts, Employment Litigation, Severance Agreements, Executive Employment Agreements, Alternative Dispute Resolution, Expatriate Employment Issues, Counseling on Employ-

(This Listing Continued)

Kahan, Penny Nathan, & Associates, Ltd. (Continued)

ment-Related Problems, Disability Accommodation, Discrimination, Sexual Harassment and Wrongful Termination, Family and Medical Leave Act, Americans with Disabilities Act.

See Professional Biographies, CHICAGO, ILLINOIS

Kahley, Jennifer Roling ... '74 '00 C.339 B.A. L.1000 J.D. Judicial Clerk
Kahlon, Nick ... '75 '00 C.205 B.Sc. L.1271 J.D. [🄰 Jenkens&G.]
Kahn, Alan M. ... '31 '60 C.1016 B.A. L.209 J.D. 4801 W. Peterson
Kahn, Bennett A. ... '43 '70 C.1016 B.A. L.209 J.D. 14 E Jackson Blvd
Kahn, Claude B. ... '36 '60 C&L.30 B.A., LL.B. [Kipnis&K.]
Kahn, Edward J., (AV) ... '— '55 C.174 B.S. L.477 J.D. [🄲 Tenney&B.]
Kahn, Eileen Susan ... '69 '94 C.339 B.A. L.365 J.D. 180 N. Lasalle, Ste. 2025
Kahn, Glenn J. ... '65 '91 C.393 B.A. L.146 J.D. [Kipnis&K.] (⊙Joliet)
Kahn, Harlan D., (AV) ... '61 '86 C&L.477 A.B., J.D. [Bronson&K.]
Kahn, Ira ... '56 '83 C.339 B.S. L.365 J.D. 53 West Jackson Boulevard, Suite 725
Kahn, Sanford, (AV) ... '51 '76 C.339 B.A. L.209 J.D. [S.Kahn]
Kahn, Valerie L. ... '75 '01 C.94 B.A. L.124 J.D. [🄰 Hinshaw&C.]
Kahn, Sanford, Ltd., (AV) ... 180 N. LaSalle St.
Kahng, David B. ... '67 '97 C&L.477 B.A., J.D. [🄰 Seyfarth S.]
Kailus, Sheila Considine ... '— '97 C.674 A.B. L.339 J.D. 2 N. Riverside #2100
Kain, Cole S. ... '63 '90 C.352 B.A. L.365 J.D. [Clausen M.]
Kairis, David G. ... '— '03 C.597 B.A. L.365 J.D. [🄰 Schiff H.]
Kais, Michael G. ... '— '89 C.588 B.S. L.365 J.D. 1 N. Lasalle, Ste. 1525
Kaiser, Anne-Marie W. ... '68 '93 C&L.602 B.A., J.D. Atty., National Futures Assn.
Kaiser, Charlotte E. ... '73 '01 C.145 B.A. L.597 J.D. [🄰 Skadden,A.S.M.&F.]
Kaitis, Frank S. ... '54 '79 C.436 B.A. L.209 J.D. Hearings Ref., Dept. of Employ. Sec.
Kajfes, Larry S. ... '44 '69 C.424 B.S. L.365 J.D. [L.S.Kajfes]
Kajfes, Larry S., Ltd. ... 30 N. La Salle Street, Suite 2140
Kakacek, John J., (AV) ... '58 '84 C&L.339 B.S., J.D. [🄰 Stamos&T.]
Kakoma, Diana K. ... '72 '01 C.339 B.A. L.589 J.D. 69 W. Washington
Kakuda, Eldon H. ... '— '86 C&L.276 B.S.F.S., J.D. [Masuda,F.E.&M.] (⊙Schaumburg)
Kalas, Becky L. ... '— '03 C.352 B.A. L.146 J.D. [🄰 Matkov,S.M.&G.]
Kalcheim, Elliott ... '15 '39 C&L.339 B.A., LL.B. 79 W. Monroe St.‡
Kalcheim, Michael W., (AV) ... '43 '67 C.966 B.S. L.209 J.D. [Kalcheim H.&K.]

Kalcheim Haber & Kuzniar, (AV)
134 N. La Salle, 21st Floor, 60601
Telephone: 312-236-9445; 773-782-3456 Fax: 312-236-7932
URL: http://www.khk-law.com
Members of Firm: Michael W. Kalcheim; Michael A. Haber; Pamela J. Kuzniar.
Family Law, Divorce, Child Custody, Child Support, Modifications.

See Professional Biographies, CHICAGO, ILLINOIS

Kale, Scott A. ... '47 '99 C.910 B.A. L.365 J.D. 30 S. Michigan Ave.
Kaleba, John J. '73 '99 C.1372 B.A. L.861 J.D.
Enforce. Div., U.S. Secs. & Exch. Comm.
Kales, Ronald S. ... '— '76 C.37 B.A. L.146 J.D. Apt 19-C, 1100 N Lake Shore Dr
Kalich, John W., (AV) ... '51 '86 C.378 B.A. L.309 J.D. [Karaganis,W.&M.]
Kalika, Michael ... '25 '51 C.1016 B.A. L.597 LL.B. Ill. Dept. of Employ. Sec.
Kalina, Ira M. ... '69 '94 C.477 B.A. L.145 J.D. [Gardner C.&D.]
Kalinich, Gail Chaney, (AV) ... '62 '87 C&L.339 A.B., J.D. [McGuirewoods]
Kalinsky, Robert H. ... '62 '88 C.610 B.S. L.117 J.D. Sr. Atty., General Growth Prop.
Kalish, Ronald, (AV) ... '67 '92 C.473 B.S. L.365 J.D. [🄰 Steinberg,P.&G.]
Kalish, Sheila Beth ... '36 '88 C.597 B.S. L.146 J.D. 79 W. Monroe
Kalishman, Amy S. ... '70 '95 C.861 B.A. L.472 J.D. State Medical Soc.
Kalita, Shelley J. ... '— '00 C.339 M.S. L.209 J.D. 800 S. Oakley
Kallas, Edward N., Jr. ... '51 '78 C.339 B.S. L.209 J.D. 601 W. Randolph St., 2nd Fl.
Kallas, Jay A. ... '75 '00 C.339 B.S. L.597 J.D. [🄰 Lord,B.&B.]
Kallianis, James H., Jr. ... '65 '90 C.339 B.A. L.209 J.D. [Meckler B.&T.]
Kallick, David A., (AV) ... '45 '71 C.674 A.B. L.597 J.D. [Tishler&W.]
Kallish, Marc H. ... '— '96 C.339 B.A. L.1000 J.D. [🄰 Freeborn&P.]
Kallman, John K., (AV) ... '45 '70 C&L.494 B.A., J.D. 221 N. La Salle St.
Kallos, Chris P. ... '— '94 C.893 B.S. L.309 J.D. [Kirkland&E.]
Kallow, Arthur S. ... '48 '73 C&L.597 B.A., J.D. [Kallow&M.]
Kallow & Muchunas ... 79 W. Monroe St.
Kallus, Mindy L. ... '58 '85 C.102 B.A. L.276 J.D. [🄰 Karmel&G.]
Kalmewicki, Jessica M. '75 '00 C.1121 B.A. L.477 J.D.
Atty., Legal Asst. Found. of Metropolitan Chicago
Kalnins, Eric E. ... '73 '99 C.57 B.A. L.1187 J.D. [🄰 Handler,T.&D.]
Kalnitz, Arnold B. ... '28 '51 C.339 L.146 LL.B. [A.B.Kalnitz]
Kalnitz, Arnold B., P.C. ... 10 S. LaSalle Street
Kalousdian, Raffi ... '56 '81 C&L.477 B.B.A., J.D. 115 S. La Salle St.‡
Kalra, Amit ... '72 '97 C.910 B.S.B.A. L.145 J.D. [🄰 Winston&S.]
Kalra, Mohit ... '77 '02 C.477 B.A. L.309 J.D. [🄰 Mayer,B.R.&M.]
Kalscheur, Katherine M. '77 '02 C.597 B.A. L.477 J.D.
(adm. in CO; not adm. in IL) One IBM Plaza
Kalt, Owen D. ... '60 '88 C.569 B.A. L.262 J.D. State's Atty. Off.
Kaltenbach, Barry P. ... '72 '99 C.589 B.S. L.365 J.D. [🄰 Kubasiak,F.R.&R.]
Kalyna, Adrianne, (BVⓉ) ... '58 '83 C.37 B.A. L.36 J.D. 224 S. Michigan Ave.‡
Kaman, C. Noel ... '— '01 C.383 B.S. L.273 J.D. [🄰 Brinks H.G.&L.]
Kamberos, Peter G. ... '46 '75 C.339 B.A. L.365 J.D. 50 E. Bellevue
Kambic, Karla L. ... '64 '89 C.589 B.A. L.339 J.D. V.P & Assoc. Gen. Coun., CNA

Kamenear Kadison Shapiro & Craig, (AV)
20 North Clark Street, Suite 2200, 60602
Telephone: 312-332-0490 FAX: 312-332-6163
Members of Firm: Maurice Kamenear (1904-1975); Joseph L. Kadison (1907-2003); Steven J. Kadison; Joel H. Shapiro; Thomas M. Craig.
General Civil and Criminal Trial Practice. Bankruptcy and Reorganization, Commercial and Creditors Rights, Probate, Estate Planning, Real Estate, Mechanics Lien, Corporation Law and Federal Practice.
Representative Clients: Graybar Electric Co.; Revere Electric Supply Co.

See Professional Biographies, CHICAGO, ILLINOIS

Kamensky, Marvin, (Ltd.), (AV) '39 '66 C.339 B.S. L.209 J.D.
[Kamensky,R.H.&D.] ⊙
Kamensky, Robert N. ... '69 '98 C.352 B.A. L.209 J.D. [🄰 FagelHaber]

Kamensky, Rubinstein, Hochman & Delott, LLP, (AV)
An LLP Including Professional Corporations
Suite 4300, 30 North LaSalle Street, 60602 ⊙
Telephone: 312-368-1776; 312-807-3960 Telecopier: 312-807-3652 By Appointment only
URL: http://www.kr-law.com
Members of Firm: Marvin Kamensky (Ltd.); Sherwin R. Rubinstein; Michael G. Erens; Ben M. Roth; Michael B. Brohman; David J. Hochman; Avery Delott; Roger B. Mandel; Stuart M. Gimbel; Miles J. Zaremski; Dorothy Voss Ward; James K. Shaw; Lee J. Levin; John B. Waters; Ericka L. Adler. Associates: Alon Stein; Adrienne Butler. Of Counsel: Howard W. Carroll (Also with Carroll & Sain); Kenneth W. Sain (Also with Carroll & Sain); Samuel H. Young; Joseph L. Matz; Michael D. Batler. Health Care, Taxation, Corporate Real Estate, Pension and Employee Benefits, Estate Planning and Probate, Bankruptcy, and Commercial Litigation.

(This Listing Continued)

Kamensky, Rubinstein, Hochman & Delott, LLP (Continued)

Lincolnwood, Illinois Office: Suite 200, 7250 North Cicero Avenue, 60712-1693. Telephone: 847-982-1776. Telecopier: 847-982-1676.

Kamerlink, Lydia Gross, (BV) ... '53 '80 C.347 B.A. L.365 J.D. [Kamerlink,S.&M.] ⊙
Kamerlink, Stark & McCormack, (AV) ... 221 N. LaSalle St., Ste. 1800 (⊙Deerfield)
Kamin, Chester T., (AV) ... '40 '65 C.309 A.B. L.145 J.D. [Jenner&B.]
Kamin, Kay H. ... '40 '81 C.881 B.A. L.597 J.D. Pres., Sutton Pl. Financial Inc.
Kamin, Kim A. ... '— '97 C.813 B.A. L.145 J.D. [🄰 Schiff H.]
Kamin, Malcolm S., (AV) ... '39 '64 C.976 B.A. L.145 J.D. [🄲 Abramson&F.]

Kamin, Scott T., Law Offices of '66 '95 C.605 B.A. L.221 J.D.
20 East Jackson Boulevard, Suite 600, 60604
Telephone: 312-322-0077 Cell Phone: 312-307-8848 Fax: 312-322-1041
Email: ScottTKamin@aol.com URL: http://www.chicagodefenseattorney.net
Criminal Defense, Felonies, Homicide, Misdemeanors, Sexual Assault and Wrongful Convictions.

See Professional Biographies, CHICAGO, ILLINOIS

Kamins, Clive D., (AV) ... '36 '60 C.339 B.S. L.209 J.D. [🄰 Laser,P.S.F.&E.]
Kaminski, David P. ... '71 '97 C.339 B.A. L.209 J.D. [🄰 Vedder,P.K.&K.]
Kaminski, Helen N. '63 '91 C&L.477 B.B.A., J.D.
Asst. Gen. Coun., Corp. & Secs., Sara Lee Corp.
Kaminski, Julie Lynn ... '66 '91 C.424 B.A. L.989 J.D. [Wolin&R.]
Kaminski, Mark G. '70 '99 C.589 B.A. L.146 J.D.
Asst. Atty. Gen., IL Atty. Gen.'s Off.
Kaminski, Stanley R., (AV) ... '55 '80 C&L.209 B.S.C., J.D. [Duane M.]
Kaminski, Yvonne M. ... '55 '86 C.339 B.A. L.146 J.D. 120 N. LaSalle St.,19th Fl.
Kaminsky, Peter ... '64 '91 C.597 B.A. L.209 J.D. Accenture
Kaminsky, Richard A., (AV) '51 '76
C.367 B.A. L.477 J.D. V.P. & Assoc. Gen. Coun., CNA
Kamm, Robert M., (AV) ... '38 '61 C&L.966 B.B.A., LL.B. 318 W. Adams
Kamman, Susan E. ... '63 '97 C.597 B.S. L.378 J.D. 180 N. LaSalle St., Ste. 2101
Kammula, Zubin S. ... '70 '97 C.1494 B.S. L.61 J.D. [🄰 Siegel M.&S.]
Kamowski, Richard M. ... '51 '76 C.339 B.A. L.477 J.D. 541 W. Oakdale
Kamp, Allen R. ... '42 '69 C.112 A.B. L.145 J.D. Prof., The John Marshall Law Sch.
Kamphuis, Wanda G. ... '48 '74 C&L.966 B.A., J.D. Ill. Com. Comm.
Kampsen, Patricia J., (BV) ... '52 '85 C.741 B.A. L.734 J.D. [S.G.Thomas]
Kamraczewski, Kevin P. ... '56 '82 C.145 A.B. L.339 J.D. [Sonnenschein N.&R.]
Kamradt, Tara Goff ... '67 '92 C.645 B.S. L.564 J.D. [Katten M.R.]
Kanabay, Kate ... '71 '96 C&L.436 B.A., J.D. [🄰 Horwood M.&B.]
Kanaris, Peter E. ... '59 '85 C.228 B.A. L.910 J.D. [Fisher K.]
Kanarish, Shelby H., (AV) '41 '71
C.339 B.S. L.209 J.D. [S.H.Kanarish] & [H.L.Walner&Assoc.]

Kanarish, Shelby H., P.C., (AV)
123 N. Wacker Drive, Suite 880, 60606
Telephone: 312-782-8550 Fax: 312-782-2646
Email: Shelby@Walnerlaw.com
Shelby H. Kanarish.
Personal Injury, Medical Malpractice, Automobile Accidents, Construction Accidents, Wrongful Death, Slip and Fall, Dog Bites, Products Liability, Drug and Medical Device Litigation and Insurance Bad Faith Law.

Kandalepas, Jamie C. ... '77 '02 C.597 B.A. L.436 J.D. [🄰 Tressler,S.M.&P.]
Kandaras, Kenneth ... '47 '73 C.801 B.S. L.209 J.D. John Marshall Law Sch.
Kandelman, Steven ... '71 '98 C.597 B.A. L.146 J.D. [🄰 Sarnoff&B.]
Kandyba, Mary L. ... '56 '81 C.339 B.S. L.209 J.D. [Daley&M.]
Kane, Amy Hoagland ... '— '91 C.966 B.A. L.209 J.D. [Anderson,R.]
Kane, Arthur O., (AV) ... '18 '39 C&L.145 A.B., J.D. [Kane,D.&H.]
Kane, David L. ... '— '02 C.966 B.A. L.124 J.D. [🄰 Freeborn&P.]
Kane, David W. ... '67 '93 C.339 B.A. L.209 J.D. [🄲 Bollinger,R.&G.]
Kane, Gregory ... '— '02 C.293 B.A. L.145 J.D. [🄰 Krasnow S.C.]
Kane, Howard E., (AV) ... '27 '52 C.477 B.B.A. L.597 J.D. [DLPiper R.G.C.U.]
Kane, Ivan P., (AV) ... '56 '81 C&L.145 B.A., J.D. [Mayer,B.R.&M.]
Kane, J. Christopher ... '53 '81 C.602 B.A. L.1049 J.D. 5844 W. Irving Park Rd.‡
Kane, James M., (AV) ... '— '79 C&L.209 B.A., J.D. [Schiff H.]
Kane, James M., (AV) ... '52 '77 C.424 B.A. L.146 J.D. [Vedder,P.K.&K.]
Kane, James P., Jr ... '43 '72 C.424 B.B.A. L.365 J.D. 2038 N. Mohawk St.
Kane, Larry R., (P.C.), (AV) ... '40 '65 C.339 B.S. L.209 J.D. [Davis F.Z.K.M.M.&R.]
Kane, Laura A. ... '64 '91 C.339 B.A. L.597 J.D. [🄲 Lord,B.&B.]
Kane, Maritoni D. ... '64 '93 C.597 B.A. L.209 J.D. [🄲 Mayer,B.R.&M.]
Kane, Michelle D. ... '69 '95 C.914 B.A. L.145 J.D. [DLPiper R.G.C.U.]
Kane, Ronald P., (AV) ... '47 '72 C.589 B.S. L.424 J.D. [Kane&F.]
Kane, Stephen J. ... '73 '00 C.858 B.A. L.276 J.D. [🄰 Mayer,B.R.&M.]
Kane, Susan H. ... '70 '99 C.966 B.A. L.659 J.D. [🄰 Goldberg,K.B.B.R.&M.]
Kane, William K. ... '60 '86 C.473 B.S. L.365 J.D. [Kane,C.&M.]

Kane, Carbonara & Mendoza, Ltd., (AV)
One North Franklin, Suite 2700, 60606
Telephone: 312-726-2322 Telecopier: 312-726-2425
Email: info@kcmfirm.com URL: http://www.kcmfirm.com
William K. Kane; Richard M. Carbonara; Adrian Mendoza; Marina Popovic;—Ben Capraro; Allison Seger Noback; Brian M. Wishnow; Erin B. Hines. Of Counsel: Don H. Reuben; Charles A. Brizzolara.
Commercial Litigation and Business Advice, Government Controversy and Investigations, Administrative Law, Employment Law, Constitutional Law and Civil Rights, Government Contracting, Negligence and Insurance Coverage Litigation.

See Professional Biographies, CHICAGO, ILLINOIS

Kane, Doy & Harrington, Ltd., (AV) BR
One North La Salle Street, Suite 1825, 60602
Telephone: 312-236-7788 FAX: 312-236-5721
Email: kd&h@insnet.com URL: http://www.illinoisworkerscompdefenselaw.com
Arthur O. Kane; Gregory E. Ahern; Michael J. Brennan; Frank I. Gaughan; Nancy J. Doyle; Richard A. Kimnach; Michael S. Rolenc; Samuel J. Doy (Retired); Henry L. Kane (1886-1963); Robert E. Harrington (1935-1991).
Workers Compensation Defense including all Levels of Appeal. Trials in all Courts.
Representative Clients: Berkley Risk Administrators; ESIS; One Beacon Insurance Company; Crawford & Company; Gallagher Bassett Services, Inc.; Travelers / St. Paul Insurance Group; United Heartland; AON Group (Martin Boyer Company; Virginia Surety; ASIC; Cambridge Integrated Services.

Kane & Fischer, Ltd., (AV) BR
208 South La Salle Street, Suite 1800, 60604
Telephone: 312-422-7200 Fax: 312-422-7217
Ronald P. Kane; Diane C. Fischer;—Thomas A. Volz; Robert C. Scremin; Jennifer L. Klebes.
Securities, Securities Litigation, Securities Arbitration, Business Litigation, Banking Litigation, Broker Dealer Arbitration, SEC Enforcement.

See Professional Biographies, CHICAGO, ILLINOIS

Kang, Carolyn '— '04 C.475 B.A. L.1119 J.D.
(adm. in IN; not adm. in IL) [🄰 O'Hagan,S.&A.]
Kannensohn, Kimberly J. ... '65 '90 C.477 B.A. L.309 J.D. [McGuirewoods]
Kanner, Steven A., (AV) ... '54 '79 C.21 B.A. L.209 J.D. [Much S.F.D.A.&R.]
Kano, Kazumune V. ... '54 '86 C.46 B.A. L.146 J.D. [Barnes,R.&C.]

Kanofsky, Martin A., (AV) '49 '81 C.1183 B.A. L.589 J.D. [Merlo K.B.&G.]
Kansa, Kenneth Paul '72 '99 C.273 B.A. L.893 J.D. [[A] Sidley A.B.&W.]
Kant, Dean A., (AV) '50 '80 C.569 B.A. L.884 J.D. [McDermott W.&E.]
Kanter, Craig A. '56 '81 C.339 B.S. L.46 J.D. V.P. & Corp. Coun., Alper Servs., Inc.
Kanter, Edward J. '39 '68 C.1016 B.A. L.146 J.D. 222 N. LaSalle Street
Kanter, Herbert, (AV) '39 '65 C.339 B.S. L.365 J.D. [Rieff S.&K.]
Kanter, Joshua S. '62 '87 C.1365 B.A. L.145 J.D. [[C] Barack F.K.P.&N.]
Kanter, Martha D., (BV) '64 '91 C.321 B.A. L.424 J.D. [Wildman,H.A.&D.]
Kanter, Max J. '76 '05 C.339 B.S. L.146 J.D. [[A] Hinshaw&C.]
Kanter, Suzanne Rubens '66 '91 C.197 B.A. L.597 J.D. De Paul Univ. Coll. of Law
Kantor, Jonathan D. '55 '81 C.103 A.B. L.178 J.D.
(adm. in NY; not adm. in IL) Exec. V.P., Gen. Coun. & Secy., CNA
Kantor, Michelle F., Law Offices of '59 '87 C.98 B.A. L.424 J.D. 2539 N. Kedzie Blvd.
Kantrow, Josh M., (AV) '65 '91 C&L.420 B.S., J.D. [Cozen O.]
Kantz, Erik L. '— '00 C.340 B.A. L.209 J.D. [[A] Arnstein&L.]
Kanute, Michael J. '65 '90 C.602 B.A. L.425 J.D. [Holland&K.]
Kanwit, Glen H., (AV) '— '68 C.821 B.A. L.178 LL.B. [Foley&L.]
Kao, Frances P.H. '63 '92 C.187 B.S.S. L.146 J.D. [Skadden,A.S.M.&F.]
Kapernekas, Dina M. '73 '00 C.339 B.A. L.146 J.D. [[A] Seyfarth S.]
Kaplan, Alan M., (AV) '— '80
C.597 B.S.E. L.209 J.D. [Masuda,F.E.&M.] (⊙Schaumburg)
Kaplan, Allen L. '43 '69 C.1016 B.S.B.A. L.146 J.D. 120 N. LaSalle St.
Kaplan, Alvin L. '24 '51 C&L.339 B.S., J.D. [[C] Kelly,O.M.D.&R.]
Kaplan, Arnold G., & Associates '59 '85
C.966 B.B.A. L.146 J.D. Suite 3315, 221 North LaSalle Street
Kaplan, Aubrey F. '26 '60 C.800 B.S. L.597 J.D. Cir. J.
Kaplan, Bennett E. '65 '90 C.477 B.B.A. L.597 J.D. [Kaplan]
Kaplan, Brian J. '63 '89 C.347 B.A. L.1049 J.D. 20 S. Clark, Ste. 510
Kaplan, Daniel S. '58 '90 C.36 B.S. L.424 J.D. [Kaplan&G.] ⊙
Kaplan, Diane S. '49 '76 C.112 B.A. L.976 J.D. 315 S. Plymouth Ct.
Kaplan, Eric D. '66 '92 C.388 B.A. L.910 J.D. [Kaplan P.&G.]
Kaplan, Ethel R. '43 '84 C.605 A.B. L.597 J.D. 860 N. Lake Shore Drive
Kaplan, Frederick M., (AV) '54 '80 C.273 B .A. L.146 J.D. [Krasnow S.C.]
Kaplan, Gary S., (BV) '56 '84 C.165 B.A. L.597 J.D. [Seyfarth S.]
Kaplan, Harold L., (AV) '— '76 C.966 B.A. L.145 J.D. [Gardner C.&D.]
Kaplan, Harold Z. '25 '50 C.339 L.209 LL.B. 5455 N. Sheridan Rd.
Kaplan, Howard Gordon, (AV) '41 '67 C.339 B.S. L.365 J.D. [Kaplan]
Kaplan, James Lewis, (AV) '44 '71 C.37 B.A. L.146 J.D. [Kaplan&S.]
Kaplan, Jared, (AV) '38 '63 C.112 A.B. L.309 LL.B. [McDermott W.&E.]
Kaplan, Jason N. '70 '95 C.846 B.B.A. L.146 J.D. [DLPiper R.G.C.U.]
Kaplan, Jeffrey B. '77 '02 C.966 B.B.A. L.309 J.D. [[A] Kirkland&E.]
Kaplan, Joel H., (AV) '46 '69 C.188 B.S. L.145 J.D. [Seyfarth S.]
Kaplan, Joel M. '47 '73 C.339 B.A. L.209 J.D. [[A] Karlin&F.]
Kaplan, Josh S. '76 '02 C.966 B.A. L.146 J.D. [[A] Levin G.]
Kaplan, Lane A. '51 '76 C.339 B.A. L.146 J.D. 205 W. Randolph St.
Kaplan, Larry S., (AV) '50 '75 C.800 B.A. L.145 J.D. [Kaplan,v.&M.]
Kaplan, Lawrence M. '63 '89 C&L.339 B.S., J.D. NAVTEQ Corporation (Pat.)
Kaplan, Marshall, (AV) '31 '56 C&L.209 B.S., J.D. 111 W. Wash. St.
Kaplan, Melvin J. '31 '58 C.1016 B.A. L.146 LL.B. 14 E. Jackson Blvd., Rm. 1200
Kaplan, Morton C. '36 '61 C.477 B.A. L.597 J.D. 20 N. Wacker Dr.
Kaplan, Myriam Benhamou '57 '84 C.659 LL.M. L.46 J.D. [[A] Barack F.K.P.&N.]
Kaplan, Richard A., (AV) '57 '82
C.674 B.S.E. L.982 J.D. [Brinks H.G.&L.] (See Pat. Sect.)
Kaplan, Richard M., (AV) '50 '75 C.367 B.A. L.597 J.D. [Clausen M.]
Kaplan, Richard N. '43 '67 C.339 B.S. L.209 J.D. [Rosenfield,K.&H.]
Kaplan, Ronald '49 '76 C.679 B.S.E.E. L.365 J.D. 134 N. La Salle St., Ste. 1108
Kaplan, Ronald B., Ltd. '35 '59 C.339 B.A. L.209 LL.B. 188 w. Randolph St.
Kaplan, Rosalyn B. '47 '81 C.339 B.A. L.365 J.D. Solr. Gen.
Kaplan, Stanley F., (AV) '37 '62 C.966 B.S. L.597 J.D. [S.F.Kaplan]
Kaplan, Wayne S., (AV) '46 '89 C.659 B.S. L.309 J.D. [[C] Mayer,B.R.&M.]
Kaplan Fox & Kilsheimer, LLP
203 North LaSalle Street (⊙L.A., San Fran., CA; Wash., DC; Morristown, NJ; New York, NY; Richmond, VA)
Kaplan & Greenswag LLC 600 W. Jackson Boulevard, Suite 200 (⊙Northfield)

Kaplan Group, The, Ltd., (AV) [BR]
180 North La Salle Street, 60601
Telephone: 312-641-2555 Facsimile: 312-641-6265
URL: http://www.lawyers.com/kaplangroup
Howard Gordon Kaplan; Rhonda D. Kaplan-Katz; Bennett E. Kaplan. Associate: Mercy T. Tang-Tellez. Of Counsel: Karnig Kerkonian.
General Civil and Corporate Law, Real Estate and Real Estate Taxes, Federal and State Tax Matters, Construction and Mechanics Liens, Merger and Acquisitions, Banking, Non-Profit Organizations, Immigration, Insurance Law, Probate, Personal Planning, Estate Planning, Estate and Trust Administration, Mediation, Estate and Gift Taxes, Employment Law, Employee Benefits, Pension Plans, Profit Sharing Plans, 401(K) Plans, Litigation, International Corporate, Transactional Law. Internal Investigations, White Collar Criminal Process, Securities Litigation, Tax Controversies.
See Professional Biographies, CHICAGO, ILLINOIS

Kaplan Papadakis & Gournis, LLP
180 North La Salle Street, Suite 2108, 60601
Telephone: 312-726-0531 Fax: 312-726-4928
Email: dpapadakis@kpglaw.com URL: http://www.lawyers.com/kaplanpapadakisandgournis
Eric D. Kaplan; Dean J. Papadakis; Dean Gournis;—Spiro G. Zarkos. Of Counsel: Michael H. Berman.
Professional Liability Defense; Errors and Omissions, Insurance Defense; Civil Litigation; Construction Law; Employment Law; Real Estate Transactions; Business Law.
See Professional Biographies, CHICAGO, ILLINOIS

Kaplan & Sorosky, Ltd., (AV) 158 West Erie Street
Kaplan, Stanley F., P.C., (AV) 39 S. LaSalle St.

Kaplan, von Ohlen & Massamillo, LLC, (AV) [BR]
120 North La Salle Street 24th Floor, 60602-2421 ⊙
Telephone: 312-345-3000 Fax: 312-345-3119
URL: http://www.kvolaw.com
***Members of Firm:* Larry S. Kaplan; Robert C. von Ohlen, Jr.; Eugene Massamillo (Not admitted in IL; Resident, New York, NY Office); Richard A. Walker; James S. Stickles, Jr.; Keith S. Yamaguchi; Thomas C. Sokol; Telly Andrews; Nicholas E. Pantelopoulos (Not admitted in IL; Resident, New York, NY Office); Lawrence Mentz (Not admitted in IL; Resident, New York, NY Office). Of Counsel: Anthony W. Eckert, III (Not admitted in IL; Resident, New York, NY Office). Associates: Walter L. Buzanowski; Christopher T. Conrad; Paul H. Kuznetsky; Luke C. McHenry; Daniel V. Santiago; Todd M. Saranecki; Catherine N. Tetzlaff; John R. Zillmer.**
Civil Litigation, Trial and Appellate Practice in all Courts. Aviation, Employment and Labor, Environmental, Commercial, Construction, Insurance and Reinsurance, Mass Disaster, Outer Space, Products Liability, Professional Liability, Toxic Torts and Transportation.
New York, New York Office: 90 Park Avenue, 18th Floor, 10016.
See Professional Biographies, CHICAGO, ILLINOIS

Kaplan-Katz, Rhonda D. '63 '89 C.966 B.S. L.365 J.D. [Kaplan]
Kaplansky, David '64 '93 C.178 B.S. L.209 J.D. 3500 Three 1st Nat. Plz.
Kapnick, Richard B. '55 '82 C.813 B.A. L.145 J.D. [Sidley A.B.&W.]

Kapp, James W., III '— '94 C.597 B.S. L.494 J.D. [Kirkland&E.]
Kapp, Scott H. '— '98 C.966 B.A. L.575 J.D. [Arnstein&L.]
Kappeler, Amy J. '— '98 C&L.597 B.A., J.D. [[A] Latham&W.]
Kapplin, Shira J. '— '03 C.277 B.S. L.145 J.D. [[A] Kirkland&E.]
Kapshandy, Timothy E. '56 '81 C&L.602 A.B., J.D. [Sidley A.B.&W.]
Kapur, Reema '78 '04 C.145 B.A. L.424 J.D. [[A] Tabet D.&R.]
Karaba, Thomas F. '55 '80 C&L.597 B.S., J.D. [Crowley B.&K.]
Karabatsos, Peter T. '40 '66 C.339 L.209 LL.B. Bank of America Illinois
Karacic, Thomas J., (AV) '29 '54 C.339 A.B. L.146 LL.B. 55 West Monroe St
Karafiol, Emile '— '79 C.674 A.B. L.145 J.D. [[C] Kirkland&E.]
Karafotias, George N. '26 '51
C&L.597 B.S.L., J.D. Dist. Coun., U.S. Army Corps of Engrs.
Karaganis, Joseph V., (AV) '42 '66 C.475 B.A. L.145 J.D. [Karaganis,W.&M.]
Karaganis, White & Magel, Ltd., (AV) 414 North Orleans
Karahalios, James N., The Law Offices, (AV) '45 '70
C.339 L.209 J.D. 77 W. Washington St., Ste. 1100
Karalekas, Sylvia '— '93 C.424 B.B.A. L.365 J.D. [Querrey&H.]
Karamanis, James A. '56 '87 C.966 B.S. L.564 J.D. [J.A.Karamanis]
Karamanis, James A., P.C. 20 North Clark Street, Suite 2450
Karamchandani, Sangeeta '71 '96
C.339 B.S. L.424 J.D. Atty., Americas, Wm. Wrigley Jr. Co.
Karamuzis, Anthony G. '— '91 C.424 B.A. L.209 J.D. [O'Hagan,S.&A.]
Karan, Alexander L. '— '00 C.145 A.B. L.893 J.D. [[A] Kirkland&E.]
Karasik, Mark L., (AV) '56 '81 C&L.800 B.A., J.D. [Baker&M.]
Karasik, Paul, Law Office of, (AV) '58 '84
C.477 B.A. L.209 J.D. 188 West Randolph, Suite 1119
Karasik, Victoria P. '49 '83 C.1099 B.S. L.209 J.D. [[A] Kiesler&B.]
Karavidas, Theodore G., (AV) '54 '79 C.436 B.A. L.365 J.D. [Karavidas]
Karavidas Law Offices, (AV) 2 North La Salle Street, Suite 1776
Karbal, Wayne S., (BV) '— '91 C.477 B.A. L.209 J.D. [Karbal,C.E.S.&D.]

Karbal, Cohen, Economou, Silk & Dunne, LLC, (AV)
200 South Michigan, 20th Floor, 60604
Telephone: 312-431-3700 Fax: 312-431-3670
URL: http://www.karballaw.com
Steven R. Apel; Edward A. Cohen; Roderick T. Dunne; Dena Economou; Stacy S. Freel; Samuel M. Greenberg; Larry A. Hoellwarth; Wayne S. Karbal; Michele T. Oshman; John K. Silk. Associates: Adam R. Bunge; Patricia M.B. Caracci; Linda J. Carwile; Dennis B. Condon; Cathleen G. Crowley; Alan P. Jacobus; Charles F. Morrissey; Paul Parker; Suverna Patel; Gerald E. Ziebell.
Insurance, Reinsurance, Civil Litigation, Commercial Litigation, Insurance Coverage, Environmental Law, Environmental Coverage, Toxic Torts, Products Liability, Directors and Officers Liability Insurance, Fidelity and Surety Bonds, Employment Practices Liability, Labor and Employment, Professional Liability, Legal Malpractice, Accountant Malpractice, Agents and Brokers Errors and Omissions, Design Professional Liability, Architect's Liability, Engineers' Liability, Casualty Insurance, Bankers' Bond, Insurance Defense, Excess Liability Coverage, Bad Faith, Property Insurance.
See Professional Biographies, CHICAGO, ILLINOIS

Karcazes, Dimitri G. '74 '99 C&L.145 B.A., J.D. [[A] Goldberg,K.B.B.R.&M.]
Karcazes, George D., (AV) '38 '60 C&L.145 B.A., J.D. [Martin&K.]
Karch, Gary C., (AV) '54 '80 C&L.959 B.B.A., J.D. [McDermott W.&E.]
Karcher, Kathy A. '— '01 C&L.339 B.A., J.D. [[A] Jenner&B.]
Karchmar, Larry, (AV) '48 '73 C.98 B.A. L.209 J.D. [Karchmar&S.]
Karchmar & Stone, (AV) 111 W. Washington
Karczewski, Joseph P. '57 '83 C.424 B.B.A. L.209 J.D. 33 W. Monroe‡
Karey, Jennie C. '18 '51 C&L.209 LL.B. Legal Aid Bur.
Karg, Karl A., IV '— '94 C.37 B.S. L.1194 J.D. [[A] Latham&W.]
Karimi, Afshin, M.D. '66 '00 C.112 Ph.D. L.801 J.D. [Karimi]
Karimi Law Offices 4950 N. Marine Dr., Ste. 207
Karinattu, Jeffrey J. '69 '94 C.339 B.S. L.146 J.D. State Dept. Human Rights
Karis, Hariklia '— '95 C.424 B.B.A. L.209 J.D. [Kirkland&E.]
Kariya, Jean M. '60 '85 C&L.209 B.S., J.D. Price Waterhouse
Karkula, Elizabeth A. '62 '87 C.602 B.A. L.209 J.D. 3310 N. Clifton Ave.
Karlen, Douglas M., (AV) '49 '75 C&L.339 B.A., J.D.
Reg. Coun., Chicago Title Ins. Co.
Karlin, Edward J., (AV) '52 '77 C.347 B.A. L.597 J.D. [Seyfarth S.]
Karlin, Lawrence M. '54 '79 C.339 B.A. L.146 J.D. [Weinberg R.]

Karlin & Fleisher, L.L.C., (AV)
Suite 1505, 111 West Washington Street, 60602-2703
Telephone: 312-346-8620 Fax: 312-346-8743
Leo S. Karlin (1908-1974); Richard S. Fleisher;—Charles V. Falkenberg, III; Jonathan B. Fleisher; Ronald G. Fleisher; Joel M. Kaplan; Charles E. Tannen.
General Negligence, Trials and Appeals, Medical Malpractice and other Professional Liability, Products Liability, Railroad, Maritime and Aviation Negligence Law and Workers Compensation Law.
Reference: The La Salle National Bank, Chicago, Illinois.
See Professional Biographies, CHICAGO, ILLINOIS

Karlyn, Matthew A. '— '97 C.867 B.A. L.831 J.D.
Two North LaSalle Street, Suite 2200
Karmel, Jonathan D., (AV) '55 '82 C.966 B.A. L.365 J.D. [Karmel&G.]
Karmel, Joshua N. '60 '91 C.966 B.A. L.365 J.D. [[A] Karmel&G.]
Karmel & Gilden, (AV) 221 N. LaSalle
Karmgard, Robert T. '49 '74 C&L.209 B.A., J.D. Chief Asst. Corp. Coun.
Karnegis, Theodora A. '— '76 C.424 B.A. L.365 J.D. [[S] Schiff H.]
Karnes, Evan B., II, (AV) '54 '78 C.424 A.B. L.209 J.D. 20 S. Clark St., Ste. 2000
Karnezis, John T., (AV) '66 '91 C.339 B.S. L.424 J.D. [Clifford]

Karno, Mark L., & Associates, (BV) '57 '82 C.339 B.S. L.146 J.D.
33 North La Salle Street, Suite 3200, 60602
Telephone: 312-701-0090 Fax: 312-701-0600
Email: mlkarno@sbcglobal.net URL: http://www.karnolaw.com
Associate: Scott David DeSalvo.
Language: Spanish.
Wrongful Death, Personal Injury, Premises Liability, Products Liability, Medical Malpractice, Automobile Accidents, Real Estate Transactions, Insurance and Worker's Compensation, Spinal Injury, Head Injury, Pedestrian Injuries.
See Professional Biographies, CHICAGO, ILLINOIS

Karnuth, Michael R. '65 '99 C.424 B.B.A. L.146 J.D. [[A] Krislov&Assoc.]
Karol, Martin B. '75 '00 C&L.347 B.A., J.D.
Sr. V.P. & Corp. Coun., JP Morgan Property Exchange, Inc.
Karolewski, Arnold E., (BV) '52 '76 C.589 B.S.Ed. L.146 J.D. [Chuhak&T.]
Karoll, Paul, (Prof. Corp.) '48 '84 C.597 B.S. L.146 J.D. 5136 N. Bernard St.
Karon, Sheldon, (AV) '— '55 C.597 B.S. L.309 J.D. [[C] Foley&L.]
Karottki, Salvador K. '74 '00 C.347 B.S. L.228 J.D. [[A] Goldberg,K.B.B.R.&M.] (Pat.)
Karp, Harold E. '32 '63 C.1016 B.S. L.209 J.D. 77 W. Washington St.
Karpel, Alan P., (BV) '61 '87 C.339 B.A. L.146 J.D. [[A] Lewis,D.&H.]
Karpeles, Michael D., (AV) '58 '85 C.937 B.A. L.309 J.D. [Goldberg,K.B.B.R.&M.]
Karpuk, Brian P. '74 '00 C.190 B.A. L.276 J.D. [[A] Skadden,A.S.M.&F.]
Karr, Richard M. '52 '80 C.659 B.A. L.146 J.D. 150 N. Wacker Dr., Ste. 1650
Karr, Robert W., Jr. '69 '99 C.352 B.A. L.209 J.D. [Freeborn&P.]
Karras, Angela Rose '75 '00 C.597 B.S.J. L.1119 J.D. [[A] Swanson,M.&B.]

Karris, Nicholas A., (Ltd.) ... '37 '61 C.72 A.B. L.209 J.D. 415 N. La Salle St
Karsh, Joshua ... '63 '90 C.976 B.A. L.145 J.D. [Hughes S.P.R.&D.]
Karson, Michael J. '50 '78 C.927 B.A. L.365 J.D.
V.P. & Gen. Coun., Ameritech Info. Ind. Serv., Inc.
Karsten, Christopher R. ... '67 '94 C.424 B.A. L.879 J.D. [🄰 Daley&M.]
Kart, Eugene, (AV) ... '11 '36 C&L.597 B.S., J.D. [🄲 Fisk K.K.&R.]
Kart, Gilbert, (AV) ... '21 '51 C.1106 L.365 J.D. [🄲 Fisk K.K.&R.]
Kartha, Sunith V. ... '75 '02 C.597 B.A. L.146 J.D. [🄰 Wildman,H.A.&D.]
Kartheiser, Erin A. ... '— '02 C.589 B.S. L.339 J.D. [🄰 Winston&S.]
Kartholl, Robert J., Jr. ... '48 '73 C.1182 B.A. L.209 J.D. [🄲 Knell&P.]
Karton, Robert M., (AV) ... '41 '65 C.339 B.S. L.209 LL.B. [R.M.Karton]
Karton, Robert M., Ltd., (AV) ... 77 W. Washington St.
Kasanov, Joel S. ... '49 '74 C.339 B.A. L.209 J.D. HSA Commercial Inc.
Kasbohm, Francis P., (AV) ... '55 '81 C.589 B.S. L.424 J.D. [Fraterrigo,B.F.&K.]
Kasdin, Chadwel D. ... '75 '00 C.787 B.A. L.910 J.D. [🄰 Hinshaw&C.]
Kasdin, Michael ... '— '04 C.188 B.A. L.146 J.D. [🄰 DLPiper R.G.C.U.]
Kasdin, Peter D., (AV) ... '42 '67 C.705 A.B. L.880 J.D. [P.D.Kasdin]

Kasdin, Peter D., Ltd., (AV)
120 North La Salle Street, Suite 1000, 60602
Telephone: 312-630-1990 Facsimile: 312-630-1103
Email: pdkltd@kasdinlaw.com URL: http://www.lawyers.com/peterdkasdin
Peter D. Kasdin;—David W. Hepplewhite.
General Civil Trial and Appellate Practice. Personal Injury, Negligence, Medical Negligence, Professional Negligence, Product Liability, Premises Liability, Construction Injury, Wrongful Death Law, Vehicular Injury Law, Railroad Litigation and Injury, and General Commercial Litigation.

See Professional Biographies, CHICAGO, ILLINOIS

Kase, Aaron S. ... '68 '95 C.966 B.A. L.145 J.D. [Levenfeld P.]
Kash, Bernard B. ... '24 '52 C&L.209 A.B., J.D. 4192 Archer Ave.
Kash, James J. ... '59 '84 C&L.424 B.A., J.D. 6545 W. Archer Ave.
Kasher, John M. '— '95 C.378 B.S. L.273 J.D.
V.P. & Gen. Coun., Beltone Electronics Corporation
Kasko, Nancy L., (BV) ... '— '78 C.339 B.A. L.597 J.D. [Schiff H.]
Kaspar, Scott R. ... '75 '03 C.339 B.S.M.E. L.221 J.D. [🄰 Kelley D.&W.] (Pat.)
Kasper, James P. ... '76 '04 C.177 B.A. L.365 J.D. [🄰 Gunty&M.]
Kasper, Michael J. ... '64 '89 C.602 B.A. L.597 J.D. [🄲 Hinshaw&C.]
Kass, Andrew L. ... '66 '91 C.823 B.A. L.365 J.D. [Kass&M.]
Kass, Geoffrey R. ... '64 '89 C.951 B.A. L.597 J.D. [Vedder,P.K.&K.]
Kass, Terry Horwitz ... '66 '91 C.1365 B.B.A. L.597 J.D. 525 W. Monroe St., Suite 1600
Kass & Moses, P.C. ... 79 W. Monroe, Ste. 914
Kassak, Christine M. ... '46 '91 C.454 B.A. L.424 J.D. U.S. Dept. of Labor, Off. of Solr.
Kassen, Patrick J. '75 '02 C.674 A.B. L.1565 J.D.
(adm. in NY; not adm. in IL) [🄰 Mayer,B.R.&M.]
Kasserman, Shawn S., (AV) ... '65 '90 C.927 B.A. L.209 J.D. [Corboy&D.]
Kassis, Ellen ... '— '01 C.323 B.A. L.879 J.D. [🄰 Azulay,H.&S.]
Kassof, Andrew A. ... '— '98 C.893 B.A. L.273 J.D. [Kirkland&E.]
Kasson, Constantine D., (AV) ... '29 '55 C.209 B.A. L.477 J.D. [Bullwinkel]
Kastel, Howard L., (AV) ... '32 '60 C.309 A.B. L.424 J.D. [Fox,H.S.L.&C.]
Kasten, Daniel D. ... '61 '87 C.72 B.A. L.145 J.D. Sr. Litig. Coun., Aon Corp.
Katalinic, Marc F. ... '65 '90 C.209 B.S. L.365 J.D. [Fisher K.]
Katauskas, Anthony P., (AV) ... '38 '73 C.177 B.A. L.365 J.D. [🄲 Williams M.&J.]
Kates, David J. ... '— '95 C.1036 B.A. L.910 J.D. [Jones D.]
Kates, Richard M. ... '40 '64 C&L.145 A.B., J.D. 155 N. Michigan Ave.
Katilius, Catherine ... '— '04 C.475 B.A. L.424 J.D. [🄰 Epstein B.&G.]
Kato, Yvonne M. ... '73 '99 C.145 A.B. L.146 J.D. [🄰 BryceDowney]
Katris, Basileios ... '71 '97 C.424 B.A. L.146 J.D. [🄰 Tressler,S.M.&P.]
Katsaros, Peter M., (AV) ... '50 '78 C.347 B.A. L.339 J.D. [Hughes S.P.R.&D.]
Katsoudas, George K. ... '70 '95 C&L.424 B.A., J.D. [🄰 Meckler B.&T.]
Katsuyama, Michael '51 '81
C.72 B.A. L.209 J.D. Div. Coun., American Medical Association
Katten, Betsy L. ... '69 '94 C.910 B.A. L.597 J.D. [🅂 Winston&S.]
Katten, Melvin L., (P.C.), (AV) ... '36 '63 C.339 B.S. L.365 J.D. [🄲 Katten M.R.]
Katten, Mitchell B. ... '62 '88 C.399 B.A. L.910 J.D. [O'Rourke M.&M.]

Katten Muchin Rosenman LLP, (AV) BR
A Partnership including Professional Corporations
525 West Monroe Street, Suite 1600, 60661-3693 ⊙
Telephone: 312-902-5200 Fax: 312-902-1061
URL: http://www.kattenlaw.com
Partners: Kristin J. Achterhof; James Craig Anderson; Brian D. Annulis; Nicole Nehama Auerbach; Steven F. Banghart; Sheldon I. Banoff (P.C.); Steven L. Bashwiner (P.C.); Jonathan K. Baum; Alan M. Berry (P.C.); Victor H. Bezman (P.C.); Craig C. Bradley; Matthew S. Brown; David J. Bryant; Denise S. Burn; James A. Burns, Jr.; Michael R. Callahan; Dawn M. Canty; Stuart J. Chanen; Charles Chejfec; Eric C. Cohen; Tanya L. Curtis; Theresa L. Davis; W. Kenneth Davis, Jr.; Denise M. Devine; David R. Dlugie; Leah J. Domitrovic; David M. Dunbar; Jeffrey L. Elegant; Jonathan S. Feld; Leonard A. Ferber; Kurt W. Florian, Jr.; Gary J. Fox; Renée M. Friedman; James M. Gecker; Scott M. Gettleson; René Ghadimi; Susan L. Goldenberg; Julie L. Gottshall; Stuart E. Grass; Bryan J. Green; Lewis Greenbaum; Russell E. Greenblatt (P.C.); Arthur W. Hahn; Megan Hardiman; Charles Harris; Michael O. Hartz; Ted S. Helwig; Mary Ellen Hennessy; Janet Goelz Hoffman; James Wellington Hutchison; Kenneth M. Jacobson; Michael A. Jacobson; Tara Goff Kamradt; Christian T. Kemnitz; David H. Kistenbroker; Adam R. Klein; Charles R. Krikorian; Stewart T. Kusper; Howard S. Lanznar; Mark E. Laughman; Lawrence D. Levin; Kevin S. MacKinnon; Seth R. Madorsky; Reid A. Mandel; Floyd A. Mandell (P.C.); Jonathan L. Marks; Laura Keidan Martin; Nina B. Matis (P.C.); William E. Mattingly (P.C.); Thomas J. McFadden; Adam M. Meek; Kenneth W. Miller; Leslie Dawn Minier; Warren Y. Nakatani; Terry E. Newman (P.C.); Douglas L. Noren; J. Phillip O'Brien; Steven R. Olson; Kenneth J. Ottaviano; John S. Paniaguas; Keith D. Pascus; Timothy J. Patenode; Jeffrey R. Patt; Daniel J. Perlman; Michael M. Philipp; Gregory P. L. Pierce; Debra S. Rade; Nancy J. Rich; Howard M. Richard (P.C.); Brian F. Richards; Saul E. Rudo; Russell B. Selman; Vincent A. F. Sergi (P.C.); Steven A. Shapiro (P.C.); David R. Shevitz (P.C.); Stuart P. Shulruff; John Sieger; Harvey M. Silets; Ross O. Silverman; Mark C. Simon; Ann Marie Sink; Nina Momtazee Sitzer; Andrew D. Small; Pamela G. Smith; Ziemowit T. Smulkowski; Gil M. Soffer; Bonita L. Stone; Marcia W. Sullivan (P.C.); Ira J. Swidler; Martin T. Tully; James D. Van De Graaff; Alexander S. Vesselinovitch; Timothy J. Vezeau; Carl E. Volz; Zachary D. Wagman; Milton S. Wakschlag; Herbert S. Wander (P.C.); Maryann A. Waryjas; Elizabeth Fleming Weber; Neil H. Weinberg; Walter S. Weinberg; John Robert Weiss; Peter R. Wilson; Janet H. Winningham; Mark D. Wood; Sheldon T. Zenner; Mark S. Zolno. Retired Founding Partner: Michael Wm. Zavis (P.C.). Associates: Seth M. Aigner; Geoff AuYeung; William F. Baarsma; Karl R. Barnickol; David F. Benson; Fritz E. Berckmueller; Bethany N. Bonner; Cathleen A. Booth; Kellye Bowers (Not admitted in IL); Rachel S. Brown; David J. Calicchia; Jeffrey A. Chadwick; Sonja K. Clayton-Pedersen; David P. Cohen; Genevieve M. Daniels; Kristen M. Danyluk; Sampreeti De; Angela J. Delph; Laura M. Dreznes; Chad A. Diehl; Joseph B. DiRago; Michael J. Diver; Adam M. Docks; Steve J. Dollear; Kimberly F. Dombrow; Michael A. Dorfman; William J. Dorsey; Daniel M. Entsminger; Phillip M. Estaver; Valentina Famparska; Megan A. Flaherty; Michael T. Foley; Barrie M. Friend; Amy Moor Gaylord; Lauren Geoffrey; Brooks Giles; Jonathan Graber; Adam M. Grant; Gregory S. Grossman; Mark Richard Grossmann; Mark D. Guidubaldi; Allen B. Gutterman; Eric P. Halverson; Maria L. Hamilton; Emily J. Henson; Angelita E. Hernandez; Matthew M. Hinderman; Justin M. Hines; Andrew D. Hoeg; Dean V. Hoffman; Ferris J. Hussein; Joni S. Jacobsen; Greg E. Jansen; Adam Johnson; Jenny L. Johnson; Kathy P. Josephson; Tye J. Klooster; John Krol; David M. Kushnir; Derek F. Ladgenski; Sharron C. Lamoreaux; Christian J. Lane; Daniel B. Lange; Melissa F. Langsdorf; Jeannie Lee (Not admitted in IL); Ryan J. Liebl; Alex Liker; Michael J. Lohnes; Stephen J. Lombardo, III; Amy E. Lum; Scott E. Lyons; Katherine A. Majewski; Jason M. Marks; Belinda I. Mathie; Michelle McGuiness; Megan P. McKnight; Carolyn E. Miller; James E. Mitchell; Monica J. Mosby; Matthew A. Olins; Heather Kuhn O'Toole; Ram Padmanabhan; Alyx S. Pattison; Kyle A. Petersen; Carolynn

(This Listing Continued)

Katten Muchin Rosenman LLP (Continued)

Pfaff; Daniel J. Polatsek; Angela C. Ramey; Bradley S. Rochlen; Eric R. Rock; Kirk Ross; Jeffrey L. Rudd; Jennifer C. Ryan; Blake Evan Schulman; Steven A. Schwab; Julie P. Setren; Jason P. Shaffer; Brian T. Sheedy (Not admitted in IL); Victoria Shusterman; David S. Slovick; Eric Anthony Smith; Kimberly Thompson Smith; Jennifer A. Smulin; David J. Stagman; Christopher J. Stetler; Joanna R. Stevanson; Bryan F. Stroh; Michael J. Summerhill; Philip Tortorich; David J. Valeck; Aaron J. VanGetson; Joseph A. Venzon; Ritu Vig (Not admitted in IL); Rachel M. Vorbeck; Michael S. Weisman; Becky A. Williams; Jennifer I. Wolfe; Todd D. Yaross; Lance A. Zinman; John E. Zummo. Staff Attorneys: Erica Tina Helfer; Rebecca Janovsky; Kelli Chase Plotz. Of Counsel: Lizabeth F. Horn; Kathleen A. Jarema; Melvin L. Katten (P.C.); Allan B. Muchin (P.C.); Stephen M. Neumer; Melvin E. Pearl (P.C.). Special Counsel: Margaret P. Griffiths; Stacey Komon; Patricia Levy; Lisa K. Shebar; Linda K. Shore (Not admitted in IL); Thomas E. Sweeney; Melissa L. Westbrook (Not admitted in IL).

Advertising, Anti-Fraud Counseling and Litigation, Antitrust, Apparel and Fashion, Aviation, Bankruptcy, Reorganization and Creditors' Rights, Corporate and Securities, Corporate Governance, Customs and International Trade, Employee Benefits and Executive Compensation, Entertainment and Media, Entertainment and Media Finance, Entertainment and Media Litigation, Environmental, FCC and Telecommunications, Finance and Structured Finance, Financial Institutions, Financial Markets and Products, Financial Services, Health Care, Health Care Compliance, Health Care Insolvency, Health Information and HIPAA Compliance, Hotel and Hospitality, Intellectual Property, Intellectual Property Litigation, Investment Management, Labor and Employment, Licensing and Distribution, Life Sciences, Litigation and Dispute Resolution, Matrimonial and Family Law, Mergers and Acquisitions, Music Law, Private Client Services, Private Equity, Public Finance, Publishing, Real Estate, Real Estate Development, Real Estate Finance, Real Estate Litigation, Real Estate Taxation, Securities, Securities Litigation, Shopping Center and Retail Law, Sports Law and Sports Facilities, Tax Planning and Litigation, Taxation of Financial Products, Technology, Trusts and Estates, White Collar Criminal and Civil Litigation.

Charlotte, North Carolina Office: 401 South Tryon Street, Suite 2600, 28202-1935. Telephone: 704-444-2000. Fax: 704-444-2050.

Los Angeles, California Office: 2029 Century Park East, Suite 2600, 90067-3012. Telephone: 310-788-4400. Fax: 310-788-4471.

New York, New York Office: 575 Madison Avenue, 10022-2585. Telephone: 212-940-8800. Fax: 212-940-8776.

Palo Alto, California Office: 260 Sheridan Avenue, Suite 450, 94306-2047. Telephone: 650-330-3652. Fax: 650-321-4746.

Washington, D.C. Office: 1025 Thomas Jefferson Street, N.W., East Lobby, Suite 700, 20007-5201. Telephone: 202-625-3500. Fax: 202-298-7570.

Irving, Texas Office: 5215 N. O'Connor Boulevard, Suite 200, 75039-3732. Telephone: 972-868-9058. Fax: 972-868-9068.

See Professional Biographies, CHICAGO, ILLINOIS

Katubig, Belle L. ... '66 '97 C.339 B.S. L.365 J.D. [🄰 Pretzel&S.]
Katz, A. Sidney, (AV) ... '39 '66 C.46 B.S.E.E. L.273 J.D. [Welsh&K.] (See Pat. Sect.) ⊙
Katz, Alan D., (AV) ... '27 '51 C.339 L.146 J.D. 33 N. Dearborn St.
Katz, Alvin Charles, (AV) ... '52 '77 C.477 B.A. L.813 J.D. [Mayer,B.R.&M.]
Katz, Barry R., (AV) ... '— '78 C.477 B.A. L.597 J.D. [Arnstein&L.]
Katz, Bruce M., (AV) ... '42 '68 C.1016 B.S.B.A. L.209 J.D. 330 S. Wells Street
Katz, Charles D. '59 '85 C.982 B.A. L.262 J.D.
(adm. in NY; not adm. in IL) [Duane M.]
Katz, Charles I., (AV) ... '50 '75 C.563 B.A. L.209 J.D. [🄰 B.L.Gordon&Assoc.]
Katz, Diane ... '67 '97 C.918 B.A. L.597 J.D. [🄰 Sidley A.B.&W.]
Katz, Erwin I. ... '35 '62 C.978 B.A. L.146 J.D. 2839 W. Morse Ave.
Katz, Gail ... '62 '87 C.1044 B.A. L.982 J.D. Expedited Child Support Div., Co. Cir. Ct.
Katz, Harold A., (AV) ... '21 '48 C.880 B.A. L.145 J.D. [Katz,F.E.E.&J.]
Katz, Heidi H. ... '52 '79 C.966 B.A. L.424 J.D. [Robbins,S.N.L.&T.]
Katz, James L. ... '68 '98 C.477 B.S.C.E. L.347 J.D. [Brinks H.G.&L.] (See Pat. Sect.)
Katz, Jason H. ... '64 '89 C&L.597 B.A., J.D. V.P., Bus. Affairs, KBA Mktg.
Katz, Jerome M. ... '29 '56 C&L.597 B.S., J.D. 33 N. Dearborn St.
Katz, Julie A., (CV) ... '65 '90 C.347 B.A. L.339 J.D. [Welsh&K.]
Katz, Martin L. '42 '68 C.690 B.S. L.276 J.D.
[Wood,P.K.C.&M.] (See Pat. Sect.) (⊙Arlington, VA)
Katz, Michele S. ... '75 '01 C.347 B.A. L.146 J.D. [🄰 Welsh&K.] ⊙
Katz, Nancy J. ... '55 '83 C.1183 B.A. L.146 J.D. Legal Asst. Found. of Chgo.
Katz, Naomi F. ... '70 '96 C.910 B.A. L.477 J.D. [Holland&K.]
Katz, P. André, (AV) ... '64 '89 C.966 B.A. L.424 J.D. [Berger S.]
Katz, Rhonda D. Kaplan ... '63 '89 C.966 B.S. L.365 J.D. 180 N. LaSalle
Katz, Steven F., (BV) ... '64 '91 C.880 B.A. L.339 J.D. [🄰 Sidley A.B.&W.]
Katz, Steven L. ... '— '92 C.477 B.A. L.589 J.D. [Masuda,F.E.&M.]
Katz, Stuart C., (AV) '37 '64
C.1016 B.A. L.365 J.D. Exec. V.P. & Gen. Coun., Heitman LLC
Katz, Tracy E. ... '76 '00 C.276 B.S.F.S. L.145 J.D. [Fox,H.S.L.&C.]
Katz, Friedman, Eagle, Eisenstein & Johnson, Chartered, (AV)
77 W. Washington St., 20th Fl.
Katznelson, Cary L. ... '44 '70 C.339 B.S. L.209 J.D. Sr. Atty., U.S. Postal Serv.
Kauffman, Jeffrey C. ... '— '83 C.20 B.A. L.477 J.D. [Seyfarth S.]
Kauffman, Nicholas J. ... '69 '96 C.208 B.S.B.A. L.982 J.D. [🄰 Wilson E.M.E.&D.]
Kauffman, Peter H. '46 '72 C&L.339 A.B., J.D.
Asst. Gen. Coun. & Secy., Peoples Energy Corp.
Kaufman, Andrew M., (AVⓉ) ... '— '74 C.976 B.A. L.880 J.D. [Kirkland&E.]
Kaufman, Daniel A., (AV) ... '61 '87 C.31 B.A. L.145 J.D. [Michael B.&F.]
Kaufman, David J., (AV) ... '63 '90 C&L.477 B.A., J.D. [Duane M.]
Kaufman, Jacob J. ... '65 '92 C.976 B.A. L.659 J.D. [Ruttenberg&R.]
Kaufman, Lisa G. ... '— '01 C.347 B.A. L.1009 J.D. [🄰 O'Hagan,S.&A.]
Kaufman, Robert W., (AV) ... '51 '77 C.477 B.B.A. L.446 J.D. [Fischel&K.]
Kaufmann, Fred R., Jr., (AV) ... '30 '54 C&L.209 B.S., J.D. 525 W. Monroe St.‡
Kaufmann, Mark L. ... '64 '89 C&L.339 B.S., J.D. [Sidley A.B.&W.]
Kaufmann, Thomas C. ... '— '84 C&L.339 B.S., J.D. [Querrey&H.]
Kaul, Ramji B. ... '— '05 C&L.477 B.A., J.D. [🄰 Sonnenschein N.&R.]
Kaulas, Paul V., (BV) ... '40 '66 C.210 B.A. L.209 J.D. [Purcell&W.]
Kavanagh, John B. ... '62 '88 C.393 B.A. L.424 J.D. Coun., Quaker Foods & Beverages
Kavanaugh, Brian P. ... '— '99 C.597 B.A. L.339 J.D. [Kirkland&E.]
Kavanaugh, David M. ... '78 '04 C.546 B.S.B.A. L.846 J.D. [🄰 Jenner&B.]
Kavanaugh, James R., (AV) '41 '68
C.215 B.S. L.365 J.D. Prof. of Law, City Coll. of Chicago
Kavathas, Saml. A. ... '21 '48 C&L.209 LL.B. 33 N. Dearborn St.‡
Kavathas, Samuel ... '53 '79 [Kavathas&C.]
Kavathas & Castanes ... 33 N. Dearborn St.
Kaveny, Elizabeth A., (AV) ... '65 '92 C.401 B.A. L.930 J.D. [Propes&K.]
Kawala, David E., (BV) ... '60 '85 C.597 B.A. L.339 J.D. [Swanson,M.&B.]
Kawamoto, Lynne ... '50 '81 C.1106 B.A. L.209 J.D. Assoc. Cir. J.
Kawashima, Neil T. ... '71 '96 C.145 A.B. L.188 J.D. [McDermott W.&E.]
Kawitt, Alan ... '37 '66 C.679 L.146 J.D. 226 S. Wabash Ave., Ste. 905
Kawula, Walter J., Jr. ... '63 '94 C.339 B.S.E.E. L.146 J.D. [Welsh&K.] (See Pat. Sect.)
Kay, David N. ... '55 '90 C.999 B.A. L.46 J.D. [Gardner C.&D.]
Kay, Edward M., (AV) ... '52 '79 C.424 B.A. L.589 J.D. [Clausen M.]
Kay, Jennifer H. ... '66 '93 C.846 B.J. L.802 J.D. [🄰 Tribler O.&M.]

Kerr, Michael H., (P.C.), (AV) .... '— '72 C.228 B.A. L.178 J.D. [Kirkland&E.]
Kerr, Michael R. '70 '97 C.813 A.B. L.800 J.D.
(adm. in CA; not adm. in IL)
Lgl Cnsl & Dir., National Conf. of Comm. on Uniform State Laws
Kerr, William D. .... '58 '84 C.976 B.A. L.309 J.D. [Sidley A.B.&W.]
Kerschner, Stephen L. .... '48 '78 C.797 B.A. L.339 J.D. 1 N. LaSalle St., Ste. 3900
Kersten, Steven A. .... '55 '80 C.309 B.A. L.145 J.D. Pres., Water Saver Faucet Co.
Kerstetter, Wayne A. .... '39 '68 C&L.145 B.A., J.D. Sr. Resch. Fellow, Amer. Bar Found.
Kertez, Jay M. .... '57 '85 C.146 B.S. L.597 J.D. Asst. Corp. Coun., City Law Dept.
Kerwin, Brian P. .... '64 '89 C.477 B.A. L.273 J.D. [Duane M.]
Kerwin, Kristina M. .... '68 '93 C.839 B.S. L.846 J.D. [[A] Seyfarth S.]
Kerwin, Richard A. .... '38 '64 C.424 L.146 LL.B. 36 S. Wabash Ave.
Keryczynskyj, Leo '48 '81 C.209 B.A.B.S. L.1151 J.D.
Dep. Treas. & Gen. Coun., Co. Treasurer's Off.
Keske, Roland Scott .... '74 '00 C.210 B.A. L.365 J.D. [[A] Leahy,E.&F.]
Kessel, Herbert A., (AV) .....'— '68 C.339 A.B. L.597 J.D. [Beermann S.W.B.B.G.&L.]
Kessel, Renee F. ....'— '73 C&L.339 B.S., J.D. [[A] Neal&L.]
Kessel, Roy D., Law Offices of '65 '91
C.966 B.B.A. L.597 J.D. 223 West Jackson Boulevard, Suite 850
Kesselring, Amy M. ....'76 '04 C.373 B.A. L.209 J.D. [[A] Colky&K.]
Kessinger, Jennifer F. .... '68 '94 C.112 B.A. L.1065 J.D. 525 W. Monroe St.
Kessler, Barry C., (AV) .... '53 '78 C.209 B.A. L.602 J.D. [Kessler,K.&C.]
Kessler, Hal "Corky", (BV) ... '49 '74 C.608 B.S.B.A. L.365 J.D. [Funkhouser V.L.&D.]
Kessler, Richard N., (AV) .... '57 '82 C.339 B.A. L.146 J.D. [Harris K.&G.] ⊙
Kessler, Stanton A., (AV) ....'34 '58 C.31 B.A. L.309 LL.B. [[C] Mayer,B.R.&M.]
Kessler, Krantz & Christensen, (AV) ....318 West Randolph Street, 5th Floor
Keta, Mishel ....'— '98 C.999 B.S. L.597 J.D. [[A] Latham&W.]
Ketay, Staci L. ....'— '97 C.339 B.A. L.146 J.D. [[A] Holland&K.]
Ketcham, Christina D. .... '71 '98 C&L.339 B.S., J.D. [[A] Williams M.&J.]
Ketcham, Paula M. ....'— '94 C.597 B.A. L.145 J.D. [Schiff H.]
Ketchens, Jason P. ....'75 '00 C.276 B.A. L.145 J.D. [[A] Skadden,A.S.M.&F.]
Ketter, Barry A. ...... '51 '83 C.960 B.S. L.365 J.D. Commissioner, Industrial Commission
Ketterman, Travis J. .... '71 '96 C.436 B.A. L.424 J.D. 2 N. LaSalle St., Ste. 1601
Ketzback, Thor W. ....'70 '95 C&L.209 B.A., J.D. [Bell,B.&L.]
Kevenides, Brendan H. ....'69 '96 C.665 B.A. L.209 J.D. [[A] P.J.Kenneally]

Kevin Edward White & Associates
77 West Wacker Drive, Suite 4800, 60601
Telephone: 312-606-8602 Fax: 312-606-8603
Email: kwhite@kevinedwardwhiteassociates.com URL: http://www.kevinedwardwhiteassociates.com
Kevin E. White.
Complex Litigation, Civil Litigation, Commercial Law, Corporate Law, Franchises.
See Professional Biographies, CHICAGO, ILLINOIS

Keys, Arlander .... '43 '75 C&L.209 B.A., J.D. U.S. Dist. Ct. J.
Keysor, Deanna L. ....'73 '99 C.473 B.A. L.976 J.D. [[A] Bell,B.&L.]
Keysor, Glen T., (AV) ....'51 '76 C.339 B.S. L.365 J.D. [FagelHaber]
Keyt, Bryan E. ....'66 '93 C.165 B.A. L.209 J.D. [Bell,B.&L.]
Keywell, Synde B., (AV) ....'50 '78 C&L.477 B.A., J.D. [Neal,G.&E.]
Kezelis, Algimantas, (AV) ....'— '55 C.339 L.209 LL.B. [Prusik S.D.&K.]
Kezelis, Robert A., (AV) ....'57 '86 C.597 B.A. L.365 J.D. (⊙Palos Heights)
Khalaf, Vivian R. ....'66 '92 C.339 B.A. L.46 J.D. [Azulay,H.&S.] (⊙Palos Hills)
Khambati, Mohsin N. ....'73 '98 C&L.37 B.A., J.D. [[A] McDermott W.&E.]
Khambatta, Daisy ....'— '01 C.846 B.A. L.796 J.D. [[A] O'Hagan,S.&A.]
Khan, Fazal R. ....'— '01 C.145 B.A. L.339 J.D. [[A] Jenner&B.]
Khan, Safia ....'— '95 C.145 B.A. L.339 J.D. [[A] Sachnoff&W.]
Khan, Zubair A. ....'76 '01 C.597 B.A. L.477 J.D. [[A] Grippo&E.]
Khanna, Jai S. ....'68 '99 C.597 B.S. L.910 J.D. [[A] Winston&S.]
Khodadad, Camille N., (AV) ....'65 '91 C.597 B.A. L.424 J.D. [[C] Lord,B.&B.]
Khodosh, Vladimir ....'— '02 C&L.339 B.A., J.D. [[A] Barnes&T.] (See Pat. Sect.)
Khosla, Reena B. ....'70 '95 C.424 B.A. L.339 J.D. Mgr., Price Waterhouse Coopers
Kibble-Smith, Brian G. ....'57 '86 C.477 B.G.S. L.146 J.D. V.P., Citicorp Servs. Inc.
Kiburz, Robert ....'— '04 C.210 B.A. L.477 J.D. [[A] Kirkland&E.]
Kickhaefer, Kyle D. '71 '99 C.378 B.G.S. L.1066 J.D.
(adm. in CA; not adm. in IL) [[A] Connelly S.H.]
Kidd, Janet Engel ....'54 '79 C.555 B.A. L.904 J.D. I.R.S.
Kidder, Jacquelyn F. ....'57 '81 C.184 B.A. L.365 J.D. [McGuirewoods]
Kidder, Rex E. '53 '79 C.184 B.A. L.365 J.D.
Asst. Gen. Coun., Ins. Law, Western U.S., Aon Corp.
Kidwell, Brent E. ....'67 '93 C&L.347 B.A., J.D. [Jenner&B.]
Kiel, Kristopher R. ....'— '02 C.597 B.S.I.E. L.477 J.D. [[A] Jenner&B.] (Pat.)
Kielian, Robert C. .... '51 '80 C.339 B.A. L.221 J.D. [Kielian&W.]
Kielian & Walther .... 33 W. Jackson Blvd.
Kiely, John C. .... '22 '49 C&L.209 B.S., J.D. 20 N. Wacker Dr., Ste. 2000
Kiely, John J. .... '54 '83 C.742 B.A. L.209 J.D. 401 S. LaSalle St.
Kienzle, James W., Jr. ....'78 '04 C&L.339 B.A., J.D. [[A] Walker W.M.]
Kiepura, Thomas A., (AV) ....'45 '71 C&L.339 B.A., J.D. [[A] Stellato&S.]
Kierpiec, Charles ....'79 '04 C.477 B.A. L.178 J.D. [[A] Winston&S.]
Kiersch, Lawrence .... '14 '40 C.137 A.A. L.209 LL.B. 8120 W. Catherine Ave.‡
Kierscht, Charles M. '39 '62 C&L.352 B.A., J.D.
Pres. & CEO, Kemper Financial Services, Inc.
Kies, Sheila M. ....'— '99 C.424 B.S. L.209 J.D. State Atty. Off.
Kieselstein, Marc, (P.C.), (AV) ....'— '88 C.994 B.A. L.145 J.D. [Kirkland&E.]
Kiesler, David J., (BV) .... '60 '86 C.339 B.A.S. L.424 J.D. [Kiesler&M.]
Kiesler, Robert L., (AV) .... '32 '56 C&L.339 B.S., J.D. [Kiesler&B.]

Kiesler & Berman, (AV) [BB]
70 West Madison, Suite 4200, 60602 ⊙
Telephone: 312-332-2840 FAX: 312-332-4547
Email: info@thekillerbees.com URL: http://www.kieslerberman.com
Founders: Marvin D. Berman; Robert L. Kiesler. Partners: Stephen B. Frew (Managing Partner); Clinton J. Feil; Alan P. Miller; John R. Garofalo; Dale L. Schlafer; Patti Olson Deuel; William P. McElligott. Senior Trial Counsel: Edward L. Cooper. Associates: Bryan W. Luce; Donna D. Ciancio; Victoria P. Karasik; Alan E. Neumann; Jeanne M. Zeiger; Richard L. Elsliger; Thomas E. Gonzales; Lingzhi Zhao. Senior Counsel: William M. Stroud; Frank N. Rago.
General Civil Trial and Appellate Practice. Insurance, Workers Compensation, Trucking Law, Construction Litigation, Corporation, Real Estate and Probate Law. Asbestos Litigation, Civil Rights Law, Estate Planning, Insurance Coverage, Insurance Defense Law, Medical Malpractice Law, Police Misconduct, RICO, Surety and Fidelity Bond Law, Tort Law, Toxic Substances Law and Toxic Torts, Lanham Act Litigation, Condemnation Litigation, Arbitrations.
Joliet Office: 57 North Ottawa Street, Suite 210. Telephone: 815-723-2755. Fax: 815-723-2763.
See Professional Biographies, CHICAGO, ILLINOIS

Kiesler & McQuillan, LLC, (AV) ....33 N. Dearborn St., Ste. 1621
Kieszkowski, Laura A. ....'77 '02 C.352 B.A. L.146 J.D. Coun., Friedman Properties
Kight, Douglas P., (AVⓉ) '56 '81 C.939 B.S. L.1065 J.D.
(adm. in CA; not adm. in IL)
VP & Asst. Gen. Coun., Labor, Employ. & Benefits, The Boeing Co.
Kight, Jaclyn A. ....'77 '02 C.423 B.A. L.424 J.D. [[A] Perkins C.]

Kijowski, Lori Ann .... '66 '91 C.339 B.S. L.424 J.D. United Automobile Ins. Group
Kikoler, Stephen P., (AV) ....'45 '69 C&L.477 B.A., J.D. [Much S.F.D.A.&R.]
Kilduff, James K. .... '36 '68 C.424 B.S. L.365 J.D. 222 Merchandise Mart Plz.
Kileen, Kevin M. ....'— '04 C.602 B.B.A. L.339 J.D. [[A] Kirkland&E.]
Kilens, Kearney W., (AV) ....'— '85 C.207 B.A. L.209 J.D. [Litchfield C.]
Kiley, Rachel ....'78 '04 C.823 B.A. L.424 J.D. [Bollinger,R.&G.]
Kiley, Roger J., Jr., (AV) '37 '66
C.602 B.A. L.424 J.D. Sr. VP, Gen. Coun. and Secretary, SBC
Kilgallon, Michael B., (AV) ....'55 '83 C.339 B.S. L.146 J.D. 218 N. Jefferson Street
Kilkenney, Ryan ....'— '03 C.124 B.A. L.608 J.D. [[A] Kirkland&E.]
Kill, Annemarie E. ....'70 '95 C.338 B.S. L.209 J.D. [Avery C.K.]
Killacky, John P. ....'71 '01 C.871 B.S. L.339 J.D. [[A] McDermott W.&E.]
Kilyk, John, Jr., (AV) '59 '83
C.385 B.A.Chem. L.276 J.D. [Leydig,V.&M.] (See Pat. Sect.)
Kim, Amy S.M. '69 '95
C.104 B.A. L.1119 J.D. Asst. Gen. Coun., The University of Chicago
Kim, Andrew W. ....'70 '97 C.976 B.A. L.188 J.D. [Schwartz C.]
Kim, Ann M. ....'71 '01 C.589 B.S. L.146 J.D. [[A] Gardner C.&D.]
Kim, Ben H. ....'32 '69 C.502 M.A. L.365 J.D. 3403 W. Lawrence
Kim, Charles C. ....'68 '95 C.228 B.A. L.597 J.D. [Wildman,H.A.&D.]
Kim, David ....'77 '03 C&L.477 B.A., J.D [[A] Bell,B.&L.]
Kim, Grace M. ....'64 '90 C.477 B.A. L.424 J.D. Asst. Reg. Coun., S.S.A.
Kim, Helen J. .... '70 '97 C&L.424 B.S.W., J.D. Off. of Co. Pub. Def.
Kim, Hyun-Jung A. '73 '04 C.604 B.A. L.1556 J.D.
(adm. in NY; not adm. in IL) [[A] Mayer,B.R.&M.]
Kim, Jae Choi ....'61 '02 C.145 B.A. L.209 J.D. [[A] Boodell D.&S.]
Kim, Jason C. .... '70 '99 C.597 B.A. L.339 J.D. Two North LaSalle Street, Suite 2200
Kim, Jenny S. .... '— '02 C.477 B.A. L.339 J.D. Two North LaSalle Street, Suite 2200
Kim, Jonathon J.H. .... '73 '00 C.976 B.A. L.910 J.D. [[A] Goldberg,K.B.B.R.&M.]
Kim, Joo Hyang ....'— '00 C.347 B.A. L.494 J.D. [[A] Mayer,B.R.&M.]
Kim, June Y. ....'78 '03 C.118 B.A. L.597 J.D. [[A] McDermott W.&E.]
Kim, Kate E. ....'— '03 C.112 B.A. L.145 J.D. [[A] Stein,R.&H.]
Kim, Mimi Y. ....'75 '00 C.473 B.S. L.608 J.D. [[A] Christensen&E.]
Kim, Peter C. ....'— '03 C.339 B.S. L.424 J.D. [[A] Adler,M.&M.]
Kim, Soo Jin ....'— '98 C.571 B.A. L.879 J.D. [[A] O'Hagan,S.&A.]
Kim, Stephanie J. ....'— '96 C.597 B.A. L.365 J.D. [Arnstein&L.]
Kim, Tony ....'76 '03 C.679 B.A. L.365 J.D. [[A] Schad,D.&S.]
Kimball, Anne Giddings, (AV) ......'— '76 C.788 B.A. L.145 J.D. [Wildman,H.A.&D.]
Kimball, Christian E. ....'55 '83 C.309 B.A. L.145 J.D. [Jenner&B.]
Kimball, Robert R. '64 '90 C&L.477 B.A., J.D.
Staff Atty., IBM North America-Chicago
Kimbarovsky, Ross E. ....'— '95 C.597 B.A. L.339 J.D. [Ungaretti&H.]
Kimbrel, Douglas Ethan .... '70 '00 C.145 B.A. L.273 J.D. Law Clk., App. Ct.
Kimmelman, Susan ....'48 '80 C.145 A.B. L.597 J.D. 5319 N. Lakewood St.‡
Kimmeth, Robert C., Jr. ....'— '96 C.188 B.A. L.477 J.D. [[A] Kubasiak,F.R.&R.]
Kimnach, Richard A., (AV) ....'53 '80 C.339 B.A. L.424 J.D. [Kane,D.&H.]
Kimrey, Blaine C. ....'69 '98 C.378 B.S. L.846 J.D. [[A] Winston&S.]
Kimura, Mary M. ....'— '00 C.276 B.S.F.S. L.145 J.D. [[A] Jones D.]
Kinasz, Thomas J. ....'— '82 C.424 B.S. L.597 J.D. [Holland&K.]
Kincaid, Joseph P., (BV) ....'61 '90 C.340 B.A. L.424 J.D. [Swanson,M.&B.]
Kinchen, Robert E., (AVⓉ) '55 '81
C&L.309 B.A., J.D. Special Asst. to President, Legal Affairs
Kinczewski, Greg A. '49 '78
C.597 B.S.J. L.209 J.D. V.P. & Gen. Coun., Marco Consulting Group
Kindelin, Mark Thomas ....'57 '82 C.97 B.S. L.930 J.D. [Bell,B.&L.]
Kindorf, William A., III, (AV) '52 '77
C.339 B.S. L.477 J.D. [Tressler,S.M.&P.] (⊙Wheaton)
Kindschy, Eileen F. ....'51 '81 Asst. Secy. & Coun., Constitution Life Ins. Co.
Kindstrand, Rachel ....'— '03 C.475 B.A. L.957 J.D. [[A] Seyfarth S.]
King, Alan S., (BV) ....'63 '88 C.57 B.A. L.339 J.D. [Gardner C.&D.]
King, Amy C. '73 '99 C&L.339 B.A., J.D.
Corp. Coun., CNA Member Insurance Cos., Law Dept.
King, Brian E. ....'70 '96 C.475 B.S. L.209 J.D. [[A] Drunken D.D.o.I.] (⊙Chicago)
King, Brian E. ....'70 '96 C.475 B.S. L.209 J.D. [[A] Komie&Assoc.] (⊙Chicago)
King, Bryan D. ....'73 '98 C.813 B.A. L.178 J.D. [[A] Jenner&B.]
King, Catherine A. '67 '93 C&L.734 B.A., J.D.
Compliance & Ethics Liaison, Blue Cross/Blue Shield Assn.
King, Celeste M., (AV) ....'58 '83 C.679 B.A. L.424 J.D. [Walker W.M.]
King, Christopher Q., (AV) ....'58 '83 C.597 B.A. L.880 J.D. [Sonnenschein N.&R.]
King, Clarence C. .... '43 '80 C.112 B.S. L.61 J.D. 8541 S. Cottage Grove Ave.
King, Deborah Lynn ....'61 '86 C.597 B.A. L.339 J.D. Admin. Law J.
King, Irving M., (AV) ....'31 '59 C.302 B.S. L.976 LL.B. P.O. Box 497262
King, Jennifer Durham ....'67 '98 C.473 B.A. L.146 J.D. [[A] Vedder,P.K.&K.]
King, Jonathan D., (AV) ....'64 '89 C.145 A.B. L.597 J.D. [DLPiper R.G.C.U.]
King, Maria L. ....'76 '02 C.585 B.A. L.1565 J.D. [[A] Fox,H.S.L.&C.]
King, Melissa A. ....'78 '04 C.393 B.A. L.424 J.D. [[A] Meckler B.&T.]
King, Michael H., P.C., (AV) ....'43 '70 C&L.910 B.S., J.D. [LeBoeuf,L.G.&M.]

King, Patricia D., Law Practice of, (AV) '52 '77 C&L.966 B.A., J.D.
211 East Ontario Street, Suite 1800, 60611
Telephone: 312-283-5350 Fax: 312-283-5005
Email: patking@patkinglaw.com URL: http://www.patkinglaw.com
Health Care Law, Hospital Law, Computers and Software Law.
See Professional Biographies, CHICAGO, ILLINOIS

King, Patrick G. ....'67 '93 C.750 B.A. L.365 J.D. [Neal,G.&E.]
King, Peter M., (AV) ....'56 '82 C.339 B.S. L.146 J.D. [Canel,D.&K.]
King, Peter M. ....'74 '03 C.234 B.A. L.365 J.D. [[A] Hinshaw&C.]
King, Philip R. ....'59 '84 C.294 B.A. L.930 J.D. [Meckler B.&T.]
King, Robert H., Jr. ....'53 '78 C.197 B.A. L.477 J.D. [Sonnenschein N.&R.]
King, Robert L., (BV) ....'63 '89 C.447 A.B. L.910 J.D. [Swedlow&Assoc.]
King, Robin S. ....'58 '83 C.893 B.A. L.597 J.D. [[C] Goldberg,K.B.B.R.&M.]
King, Sally Doubet ....'51 '89 C.388 B.A. L.209 J.D. [McGuirewoods]
King, Sharon L., (AV) ....'32 '57 C.518 A.B. L.879 J.D. [[C] Sidley A.B.&W.]
King, Sheila M. ....'53 '79 C.424 B.S.Ed. L.146 J.D. Asst. States Atty.
King, Therese C. ....'75 '00 C.750 B.S. L.146 J.D. [[A] Mayer,B.R.&M.]
King, Thomas G. ....'34 '63 C&L.209 A.B., LL.B. 200 W. Adams St., Ste. 1005
King, Thomas L. '48 '83 C.475 B.S. L.1187 J.D.
(adm. in MI; not adm. in IL) V.P. & Dep. Gen. Coun., Fannie Mae
King, Yolanda M. ....'76 '02 C.347 B.A.J. L.309 J.D. [[A] Brinks H.G.&L.]
Kingery, Heather ....'— '01 C.1064 B.A. L.260 J.D. [[A] O'Hagan,S.&A.]
Kingsbury, Colby Anne ....'— '00 C.631 B.F.A. L.209 J.D. [[A] Kirkland&E.]
Kingsbury, John F., Jr. ....'52 '79 C.424 B.A. L.339 J.D. 111 W. Jackson Blvd.
Kingsley, Adam ....'65 '91 C.188 B.S L.228 J.D. [[C] Holland&K.]
Kinn, Michael J. ....'54 '79 C.339 B.S.B.A. L.597 J.D. [Sidley A.B.&W.]
Kinnaman, Jackie A. ....'54 '79 C&L.966 B.A., J.D. State Industrial Comm.

Kinne, Charles C., (AV) '58 '84 C.696 B.S. L.846 J.D. [Baniak P.&G.] (See Pat. Sect.)
Kinnerk, Patrick J. .... '32 '64 C&L.209 B.Sc., LL.B. Cook Co. States Atty's Off.
Kinney, Elizabeth '43 '68 C.914 A.B. L.477 J.D. (adm. in OH; not adm. in IL) Reg. Dir., NLRB
Kinney, John F. .... '48 '73 C&L.276 A.B., J.D. [Freeman,F.&S.]
Kinney, Terry M. ....'56 '84 C.1200 B.A. L.602 J.D. Dep. Sr. Staff Atty., U.S. Ct. of App.
Kinoy, Joanne, (AV) .... '49 '77 [Kinoy,T.&G.]
Kinoy, Taren & Geraghty, P.C., (AV) .... 224 South Michigan Avenue, Suite 300
Kinra, Sonia S. .... '— '00 C.1365 B.A. L.796 J.D. [🄰 Scott&K.]
Kins, Juris, (AV) .... '42 '69 C&L.966 B.S.Ch.E., J.D. [🄲 Abramson&F.]
Kinsella, Daniel V., (AV) .... '51 '77 C.1154 B.A. L.339 J.D. [Schuyler,R.&Z.]
Kinsella, John J. .... '28 '65 C.424 A.B. L.276 J.D. Loyola Law School
Kinton, Christina .... '62 '87 C.502 B.J. L.597 J.D. [Hlustik,H.W.&V.]
Kinzie, Harry E. .... '47 '78 C.399 B.A. L.424 J.D. [Nyhan,P.B.K.&L.]
Kinzie, Raymond W. '30 '56 C.118 B.A. L.976 J.D. Sr. V.P. & Asst. Secy., LaSalle Natl. Tr., N.A.
Kinzy, Kyle M. .... '70 '96 C.69 B.A. L.796 J.D. [Kinzy&Assoc.]

Kinzy & Associates, P.C.
3053 West Armitage, Suite 1F, 60647
Telephone: 773-486-9529 Fax: 773-486-9344
Email: kapconline@ameritech.net URL: http://www.kinzyandassociates.com
Kyle M. Kinzy.
Immigration, Deportation, Real Estate, Business Law, Asset Protection, Estate Planning.

See Professional Biographies, CHICAGO, ILLINOIS

Kipnis, Ira A., (AV) .... '21 '55 C.597 B.A. L.145 J.D. 919 N. Michigan
Kipnis, Irwin .... '26 '50 C&L.209 LL.B. 205 W. Randolph
Kipnis, Mark S., (AV) .... '47 '74 C.339 B.S. L.597 J.D. 401 N. Wabash, Ste. 740
Kipnis, Robert S., (BV) .... '65 '90 C.966 B.A. L.209 J.D. [Grund&L.]

Kipnis & Kahn, Ltd.
30 North La Salle Street, Suite 2024, 60602 ⊙
Telephone: 312-726-3700 Fax: 312-726-4644
Email: kipniskahnlaw@aol.com URL: http://www.kipniskahnlaw.com
Claude B. Kahn; Glenn J. Kahn.
Civil Litigation, Family Law, Corporate Litigation, Church Law, Personal Injury, Worker's Compensation, Auto Accidents, Medical Malpractice, Slip and Fall, Airplane Crashes, Train Crashes, Wrongful Death.
Joliet, Illinois Office: 54 N. Ottawa, Suite 305, 60432. Telephone: 815-726-7370.

See Professional Biographies, CHICAGO, ILLINOIS

Kipp, Matthew R., (AV) .... '63 '89 C.976 B.A. L.178 J.D. [Skadden,A.S.M.&F.]
Kipperman, Lawrence I., (AV) .... '41 '66 C&L.339 B.A., J.D. [Sidley A.B.&W.]
Kirchhoefer, Gregg, (AV) .... '— '82 C&L.734 B.S.C., J.D. [Kirkland&E.]
Kirchner, John R. '28 '64 C&L.569 B.S., LL.B. (adm. in NY; not adm. in IL) V.P., CT Corp. Sys.
Kiriakos, Thomas S., (AV) .... '56 '81 C.293 B.A. L.352 J.D. [Mayer,B.R.&M.]
Kirk, Daniel A. .... '— '96 C.234 B.A. L.146 J.D. [Querrey&H.]
Kirk, Shannon Capone .... '— '98 C.724 B.A. L.818 J.D. [Ungaretti&H.]

Kirkland & Ellis LLP, (AV) BR
And Affiliated Partnerships
200 East Randolph Drive, 60601 ⊙
Telephone: 312-861-2000 Facsimile: 312-861-2200
URL: http://www.kirkland.com
Partners of Firm: Weymouth Kirkland (1877-1965); Howard Ellis (1892-1968); Ellen Therese Ahern; Cindy S. Ahn; Imron T. Aly; John J. Amberg; Amy Curtner Andrews; Gary E. Axelrod; Janet S. Baer; Gabor Balassa; Jon A. Ballis; Michael D. Belsley; David M. Bernick (P.C.); Jack N. Bernstein; Wendy L. Bloom; Andrew B. Bloomer; James J. Boland; Nader R. Boulos; Michael P. Bregenzer; Michelle H. Browdy; Robert T. Buday; Jonathan Bunge; Christopher Butler; David K. Callahan; Richard J. Campbell, Jr.; Thomas L. Campbell; Carole A. Cheney; Frank Cicero, Jr., (P.C.); Kevin J. Coenen; Paul David Collier; James B. Coughlan; Keith S. Crow (P.C.); Luke L. Dauchot; Brian E. Davis; Robert C. Davis III; Terrence J. Dee; William E. Devitt; Nick DiCrescenzo; Martin A. DiLoreto, Jr.; Alex Dimitrief; John Donley; Timothy A. Duffy; Deborah Dunn; David L. Eaton; Barack S. Echols; Robert B. Ellis (P.C.); Carter W. Emerson; David T. Erie; Lisa G. Esayian; Bruce I. Ettelson; Kevin R. Evanich; James P. Faley, Jr.; R. Scott Falk, P.C.; Michael G. Fatall; Catherine E. Fazio; Mark A. Fennell; Barry E. Fields; Jeffrey A. Fine; Karen M. Fine; Catherine L. Fitzpatrick; Michael P. Foradas; Michael D. Foster; Scott W. Fowkes; Ariel A. Fox; Michelle A.H. Francis; Willard G. Fraumann (P.C.); Jonathan P. Friedland; Angela Bonfield Frye; Jody S. Gale; Todd A. Gale; Gregory W. Gallagher; Paul R. Garcia; C. Graham Gerst; Douglas C. Gessner; Margaret A. Gibson, P.C.; Richard C. Godfrey; Robert B. Goldberg; Christopher J. Greeno; Stephen C. Hackney; John F. Hagan Jr.; Bryan S. Hales (Also at San Francisco, California Office); Jeffrey C. Hammes (P.C.); David A. Handler; Steven J. Harper (P.C.); John F. Hartmann, P.C.; Robert M. Hayward; Laura A. Hepburn; Louis R. Hernandez; Glen E. Hess; John T. Hickey, Jr. (P.C.); Roger J. Higgins; Jonathan E. Hinkemeyer; Jocelyn A. Hirsch; Shelly Matthew Hirschtritt; Neil S. Hirshman; Gary M. Holihan; G. Courtney Holohan; Lisa M. Holubar; Vicki Vallen Hood; Anne Marrs Huber; Carol Anne Huff; Barry F. Irwin; Joseph J. Jacobi; Garry W. Jaunal; John M. Jennings; Garrett B. Johnson; George A. Joseph; James C. Joslin; Gary A. Jungels; Chris P. Kallos; James W. Kapp, III; Hariklia Karis; Andrew A. Kassof; Andrew M. Kaufman; Brian P. Kavanaugh; Natalie Hoyer Keller; Stacey Tobin Kern; Michael H. Kerr (P.C.); Marc Kieselstein (P.C.); Gregg Kirchhoefer; Sarah E. Kirson; Matthew N. Kleiman; Norbert B. Knapke, II; Robert J. Kopecky; Howard G. Krane (P.C.); Robert G. Krupka (P.C.); Thomas Otman Kuhns; Douglas J. Kurtenbach (P.C.); Walter R. Lancaster; James Andrew Langan; Daniel Edward Laytin; Garret Leach; Craig D. Leavell; Elli Leibenstein; Jack S. Levin (P.C.); Adam J. Levine; Russell E. Levine, P.C.; Mark S. Lillie; Jeremy Seth Liss; Olga A. Loy; Nathaniel M. Marrs; Daryll V. Marshall; Mariano Elí Martínez; Todd F. Maynes, P.C.; Steven D. McCormick, P.C.; Jamie H. McDole; Andrew R. McGaan (P.C.); Janette A. McMahan; Scott McMillin; Toni B. Merrick; Gregory R. Metz; Roberto S. Miceli; Alexandra Mihalas; Todd A. Miller; J. Chad Mitchell; Scott A. Moehrke (Not admitted in IL); Gabriela I. Monahan; Kenneth P. Morrison, P.C.; James C. Munson; James H. Mutchnik; Dennis M. Myers, P.C.; Linda K. Myers, P.C.; Michael Newman; Emily Nicklin; Mark Nomellini; Jeffery S. Norman; James N. Nowacki (P.C.); Gerald T. Nowak; Maureen O'Brien; Jeffrey S. O'Connor; John R. O'Neil; Reed S. Oslan; Stacey Garbis Pagonis; Michael D. Paley; Mark A. Pals, Ph.D. (Also at San Francisco, California Office); Jane S. Park; Thomas G. Pasternak; Stephen R. Patton, P.C.; Adam Paul; Drew G. A. Peel; Francesco Penati; Sanford E. Perl, P.C.; Richard W. Porter (P.C.); Jeffrey S. Quinn; Robin A. Rademacher; James W. Rankin; Matthew T. Regan; Tracy L. Reilly; Linda S. Resh; Geoffrey A. Richards; Jeffrey W. Richards; Stephen L. Ritchie, P.C.; Bradley V. Ritter; Maria Pellegrino Rivera; J. Robert Robertson (P.C.); Donald E. Rocap; James S. Rowe; David S. Royal; Andrew R. Running; Anup Sathy; James H. Schink (P.C.); John A. Schoenfeld (P.C.); Ray C. Schrock; Steven C. Seeger; Jeffrey Seifman (P.C.); David R. Seligman; Marcus E. Sernel; Jeffrey T. Sheffield (P.C.); James A. Shimota; Anne M. Sidrys; Brian D. Sieve, P.C.; Michael Slade; Douglas G. Smith; Leslie M. Smith (P.C.); Renee D. Smith; Tefft W. Smith; Sallie G. Smylie (P.C.); Karen G. Sodke; Gregory E. Spitzer; James H. M. Sprayregen; John H. Stassen (P.C.); Paul R. Steadman; Matthew E. Steinmetz; James A. Stempel; William A. Streff, Jr., P.C.; Edward T. Swan; Maureen E. Sweeney; Christian Chadd Taylor; Andrew J. Terry; Angelo F. Tiesi; Douglas D. Timmer; Michael G. Timmers, P.C.; Stephen G. Tomlinson, P.C.; Thomas A. Tozer; Seth Traxler; Christopher M.R. Turner; William E. Tymm; Brian C. Van Klompenberg; Kevin T. Van Wart (P.C.); Keith E. Villmow; Gregory Vogelsperger; H. Kurt von Moltke; Michael H. Weed; Ross M. Weisman; John A. Weissenbach; Donna M. Welch; William R. Welke; Raymond P. Wexler (P.C.); Jeffrey L. Willian (P.C.); Robert A. Wilson; Helen E. Witt; W. Allen Woolley; Michael D. Wright; Mary E. Zaug; Robert R. Zitko; Ted H. Zook; David J. Zott. Associates: David A. Agay; Ameer I. Ahmad; George P. Alexander; Suzanne Milne Alexander; James Allen (Not admitted in IL); Kristen J. Allen; John A. Amash; Matthew Antinossi; James J. Antonopoulos; Shuaib A. Atique (Not admitted in IL); Alison R. Aubry (Not admitted in IL); Dean C. Bachus; Justin A. Barker; James P. Bartley; Benjamin Will Bates; Andrew Bautista; Heather Bawden; Eric Bennett; Ryan Blaine Bennett; Salvatore Bianca; Jessica L. Bina; Thomas N. Blanchard; Samuel Blatnick; Tanya Brady; Stephanie A. Brennan; Paul S. Brown (Not admitted in IL); Matthew S. Bryant; William R. Burke; Jason W. Callen; Rachel Cantor (Not admitted in IL); Marc J. Carmel; Susan Campbell Caudell (Not admitted in IL); Erik W. Chalut; Tarun J. Chandran; Aaron D. Charfoos; Brandi L. Chudoba; Scott

(This Listing Continued)

Kirkland & Ellis LLP (Continued)

Clair; Khara Coleman; Lisa H. Cox; Katherine M. Cunningham; Tiffany P. Cunningham; Gianni L. Cutri; Michael B. Daniel (Not admitted in IL); Dawn H. Dawson; David H. DeCelles; Jason P. Desai; Michael T. Dierkes; Edward A. Donovan; Michael A. Duffy; Andrew Dustin; Stephanie R. Dykeman; Scott M. Edenfield; Jamal M. Edwards; Katheleen A. Ehrhart; Israel J. Encinosa; Wendy Netter Epstein; Christopher J. Esbrook; Leonid Feller; Wendy A. Fleske; Paul S. Fondahn; Corey D. Fox; Ted M. Frankel; John C. Gekas; Jeffrey W. Gettleman; Adam Gill; John A. Glassgow; Serena Jean Gondek; Warren R. Goodworth (Not admitted in IL); Uday Gorrepati; David Grassmick; Steven S. Hall; Mark S. Hamill; Brad Hanna; Amy C. Haywood (Not admitted in IL); R. Chris Heck; Jared E. Hedman; Elizabeth S. Hess; Scott F. Hessell; David W. Higer (Not admitted in IL); Margaret Lee Hudgins; Benjamin W. Hulse; Chad J. Husnick; Justin R. Ishbia; Tomoko Itoga; Tamara G. Jain; Adrianne K. Jakola; Jami A. Jarosch; Ryan L. Jensen; Joshua D. Jewkes; Andrea L. Johnson; Michelle W. Jordan; Mary L. Kaczmarek; Jeffrey B. Kaplan; Shira J. Kapplin; Alexander L. Karan; Robert Kiburz; Kevin M. Kileen; Ryan Kilkenney; Colby Anne Kingsbury; S. Raja Krishnamoorthi; Ross Kwasteniet; Elizabeth A. Larsen; Deneese Walia Levin; Alex C. Levine; Chuan Li; Stephanie S. Liang; Russell S. Light; Christopher R. Liro; Eva Lo; Jeffrey M. Loeb; Matthew S. Lovell; Samantha M. Mann; Micah E. Marcus; Elisabeth M. Martin; Rachel Masory; Bryce A. Mautner; James J. Mazza, Jr.; Jamenda A. McCoy; Ryan J. McCrate; James T. McLaughlin, Jr.; Andrew H. McWhirter; Maria A. Meginnes; Jamie L. Mignon; Jeffrey Richard Miller; Christina D. Mitakis; Tom Monagan; Daniel C. Moore; Jonathan Moore; Thomas J. Morel; Kevin L. Morris; John M. Muno; Marisa Murillo; Karen Nelson; Alexander T. Nguyen; Howard S. Norber (Not admitted in IL); Krista L. Nunemaker; Sven Nylen; Larry J. Obhof; Sean P. O'Brien; Jason Osborn; Erick S. Ottoson; Lucy K. Park; Rachel L. Pernic; Rachel Perrier; Amy R. Peters; Theodore A. Peto; D. Joseph Piech; Clare M. Pinkert; Eleftheria Terry Platis; Karin Wray Preusse; Travis Quick; Joshua Z. Rabinovitz; Richard S. Radnay; Sara K. Rankin; Ramya Ravindran; John W. Reale; Neal J. Reenan; Jennifer M. Rhodes; Jillian Rice; Matthew Richards; Ann Marie T. Rizzo; Sara A. Robinson; David Rokach; C.W. Ross; Edward K. Runyan; Joseph Michael Russell; Bryan C. Rutsch; Colleen Ryan; Peter J. Ryan; Tana M. Ryan; Nabil Sabki; Kathryn B. Sanderson; Amanda Cochran Sarafa; George D. Sax; Renee M. Schreiber; Justin K. Schwartz; Nicholas Joseph Secco; Kyle P. Seelbach; Kal K. Shah; Palak V. Shah; Christopher T. Shannon; Jesse Sheley; Jessica Helena Sicsu (not admitted in the United States); Robert D. Snow, Jr.; John Soave, III; Aaron D. Spira; Linnea C. Stack; Benjamin D. Stanley; Nyika O. Strickland; David E. Suchar; Scott D. Sugino; Michael E. Sullivan; Arek Sycz; Wendy L. Tamblyn; John E. Tangren; Bernard Taylor; Kathryn F. Taylor; John C. Thurmond; Daniel M. Trevino; Kevin S. Ueland; Mark Varboncouer; Rebecca D. Walker; Noah F. Webster; Susan L. Welsh; Charla Ann Willian; Guohua Wu (Not admitted in IL); Qi (Alexander) Yang (Not admitted in IL); Seth R. Yohalem; Thomas H. Young; Jeffrey J. Zeiger; Scott R. Zemnick; Christopher A. Ziebarth; Meredith Zinanni; Erica B. Zolner. Of Counsel: James M. Amend (P.C.); Kristine L. Anderson; Debra Beinstein; Holden Bixler; Erica Beutler; Lauren Hennessey Breit; Holly W. Bull; Jennifer Clarke-Smith; Rebecca O'Neal Fruchtman; Francis J. Gerlits (P.C.); Emile Karafiol; John E. Kirkpatrick (P.C.); Lori A. Lenard; Kevin M. McKenna; Cheryl L. Meier; Kelly A. Schell; Joseph U. Schorer; Rachel Reagler Schulman; William S. Singer; Stephanie Stern; Jeffrey W. Stevenson; Kristal S. Stippich; Roger L. Taylor; P. Renée Wicklund. Visiting Attorneys: Christiane Albrecht (Not admitted in the United States); Oscar Stephens C. (Not admitted in the United States).
Advertising, Advertising and Marketing, Alternative Dispute Resolution, Antitrust Litigation, Antitrust and Trade Regulation, Appellate, Arbitration, Asset-Backed Securities, Asset-Backed Finance, Banking, Bankruptcy and Workouts, Bankruptcy Reorganization, Biotechnology, Business Law, Civil Litigation, Class Action, Commercial Litigation, Competition and Antitrust Law, Computer Law, Computer and Technology, Computers and Software, Contested Tax Matters, Contract, Copyrights, Corporate, Counseling, Creditor's Rights, Debtor-Creditor Law, Digital Commerce, Distribution Litigation, Divestitures, Employee Benefits, Employment Litigation, Employment Law, Environmental Litigation, ERISA, Estate Planning, Executive Compensation, Finance, Financial Services, Foreign Tax Planning, Franchise Law, Franchise and Distribution, Fund Formation, Futures Law, Health Care, Institutional Investment, Insurance Coverage, Intellectual Property, Intercompany Transfer-Pricing, International Law, Joint Ventures, Labor and Employment, Legislative, Leveraged Acquisitions, Leveraged Buyouts, Licensing, Litigation, Marketing, Mass Torts, Mergers and Acquisitions, Patent Litigation, Planning and Administration, Private Equity, Product Liability, Real Estate, Restructuring, Secured Lending, Securities, Strategic Alliances, Tax, Taxation, Technology and Science, Technology Licensing, Technology Transactions, Telecommunications, Torts, Trade Secrets and intellectual Property, Trademarks, Trusts and Estates, Unfair Competition, Venture Capital, White Collar Crime, Workout and Bankruptcy, Workouts, Reorganizations and Bankruptcy, Worldwide Litigation and Arbitration.
Los Angeles, California Office: 777 South Figueroa Street. Telephone: 213-680-8400. Facsimile: 213-680-8500.
San Francisco, California Office: 555 California Street. Telephone: 415-439-1400. Facsimile: 415-439-1500.
Washington, D.C. Office: 655 Fifteenth Street, N.W. Telephone: 202-879-5000. Facsimile: 202-879-5200.
New York, New York Office: Citigroup Center, 153 East 53rd Street. Telephone: 212-446-4800. Facsimile: 212-446-4900.
London, England Office: Kirkland & Ellis International LLP, Tower 42, 25 Old Broad Street. Telephone: 011-44-20-7816-8700. Facsimile: 011-44-20-7816-8800.
Munich, Germany Office: Kirkland & Ellis International LLP, Maximilianstrasse 11. Telephone: +49 89 2030 6000. Facsimile: +49 89 2030 6100.

See Professional Biographies, CHICAGO, ILLINOIS

Kirkpatrick, Bruce .... '48 '75 C.473 B.A. L.597 J.D. Ste. 1411, 115 N. Harbor Dr.
Kirkpatrick, John E., (P.C.), (AV) .... '— '55 C.31 A.B. L.309 J.D. [🄲 Kirkland&E.]
Kirkpatrick, Sharon Roos .... '53 '81 C.339 B.A. L.146 J.D. Mgr., Law Title Insurance
Kirkpatrick, Thomas B., Jr. '42 '66 C&L.339 B.A., J.D. Exec. Dir., Ill. Dangerous Drugs Comm.
Kirkton, John L. '53 '79 C.339 B.S. L.146 J.D. Editor, Cook County Jury Verdict Rptr., Law Bulletin Pub. Co.
Kirsch, Bryan J. .... '— '02 C.165 B.A. L.339 J.D. [🄰 Donohue B.M.&S.]
Kirschbaum, Howard J., (AV) .... '55 '79 C.597 B.A. L.477 J.D. [Barack F.K.P.&N.]
Kirschner, Daniel S. .... '71 '98 C.966 B.A. L.146 J.D. [🄰 Corboy&D.]
Kirsh, Allen S. .... '64 '89 C.339 B.A. L.209 J.D. 550 W. Washington St.
Kirsh, Matthew A., (AV) .... '64 '89 C&L.339 B.A., J.D. [Colky&K.]
Kirsh, Sanford, (AV) .... '31 '52 C.999 L.146 [Kirsh&B.]
Kirsh & Berman, Ltd., (AV) .... 10 S. LaSalle St.
Kirshenbaum, David L. .... '61 '86 C.1365 B.A. L.597 J.D. V.P., LR Develop. Co.
Kirshner, Sheldon G., (CV) .... '41 '78 C.959 Ph.D. L.597 LL.M. 221 N. La Salle St.
Kirsner, Bernard M. .... '39 '66 C.339 B.A. L.209 J.D. 400 E. Randolph St.
Kirson, Sarah E. .... '— '94 C.339 B.S. L.309 J.D. [Kirkland&E.]
Kirsons, Mark R. .... '72 '97 C&L.597 B.A., J.D. [🄰 Sidley A.B.&W.]
Kiser, Charles R. .... '62 '00 C.1016 B.A. L.146 J.D. [🄰 Baum S.A.&N.]
Kiser, Livia M. .... '— '01 C.339 B.A. L.597 J.D. [🄰 Latham&W.]
Kish, Joseph L. .... '58 '88 C.477 B.G.S. L.209 J.D. [Kish]
Kish Law Firm .... P.O. Box 2914
Kisicki, Nancy Grauer .... '59 '85 C.860 B.A. L.1066 J.D. State Atty.'s Off.
Kissel, James W., (AV) .... '15 '42 C.966 B.A. L.365 J.D. 1 1st Nat. Plaza
Kissel, Richard J., (AV) .... '36 '62 C&L.597 B.A., J.D. [🄲 Gardner C.&D.]
Kisser, Cynthia S. .... '49 '00 L.146 J.D. 111 W. Washington St., Ste. 1625
Kistenbroker, David H., (AV) .... '— '80 C.965 B.S. L.436 J.D. [Katten M.R.]
Kita, George .... '20 '45 C.763 B.A. L.221 J.D. 3248 N. Clark St.‡
Kitch, Paul R., (AV) .... '66 '93 C&L.477 B.S.E.E, J.D. [Jenkens&G.] (Pat.)
Kite, M. Leslie, (BV) .... '36 '61 C&L.145 A.B., J.D. [M.L.Kite&Assoc.]
Kite, Steven B., (AV) .... '49 '74 C.339 B.A. L.1565 J.D. [Sonnenschein N.&R.]
Kite, M. Leslie, & Associates, P.C., (BV) .... 1 N. Franklin St.
Kitslaar, Elizabeth Clough .... '— '88 C.518 A.B. L.930 J.D. [Jones D.]
Kitterlin, Neal D. .... '— '05 C.418 B.S. L.146 J.D. [🄰 Ashman]
Kittle-Kamp, Thomas L. .... '60 '88 C.98 B.A. L.597 J.D. [Mayer,B.R.&M.]
Kittling, Nesheba M. .... '79 '04 C&L.597 B.A., J.D. [🄰 Fisher&P.]
Kitzinger, Paige A. '68 '94 C.436 B.S. L.209 J.D. [Trexler,B.G.B.&M.] (See Pat. Sect.)
Kitzinger, Stanley A. .... '67 '94 C.867 B.S. L.982 J.D. [🄰 Condon&C.]

Kiwala, Terrence E., (AV) ....'45 '70 C.602 B.A. L.597 J.D. [Dykema G.P.]
Klabacha, Barbara C. ....'— '87 C.741 B.S. L.597 J.D. [🄲 Chapman&C.]
Klaczek, Kristin A. ....'77 '04 C.597 B.A. L.146 J.D. [🄰 Shefsky&F.]
Klaczynski, Steven M., (AV) ....'65 '90 C.477 B.A. L.215 J.D. [🄰 Hinshaw&C.]
Kladis, Patricia Anastasia ....'73 '02 C.424 B.S. L.365 J.D. 210 West Illinois
Klages, Gary W., (BV) ....'— '82 C.546 B.S. L.365 J.D. [Matushek,N.&S.]
Klages, John A., (AV) ....'62 '87 C.339 B.S. L.904 J.D. [Quarles&B.]
Klamrzynski, Gregory A. ....'— '95 C.209 B.S. L.339 J.D. [Chapman&C.]
Klapman, Daniel S. ....'72 '97 C.339 B.S. L.146 J.D. [🄰 Schoenberg,F.N.&R.]
Klassman, Debra Ann '58 '85
C.399 B.A. L.424 J.D. Assoc. Reg. Coun., U.S. Envir. Prot. Agcy.
Klassman, Kenneth ....'78 '03 C.966 B.A. L.146 J.D. [🄰 Horwood M.&B.]
Klauke, George F., Jr., (BV) ....'— '85 C.347 B.S. L.209 J.D. [Alholm,M.K.H.&O.]
Klawans, Steven L. '70 '95 C.347 B.A. L.209 J.D.
Branch Chief, U.S. Secs. and Exchange Comm.
Klawiter, Richard F. ....'63 '90 C.747 B.A. L.813 J.D. [DLPiper R.G.C.U.]
Kleban, Debra Ann ....'70 '95 C.477 A.B. L.273 J.D. [Applegate&T.]
Klebba, John F., (AV) ....'56 '81 C.602 B.A. L.424 J.D. 158 W. Erie St.
Klebes, Jennifer L. ....'73 '99 C.1116 B.A. L.665 J.D. [🄰 Kane&F.]
Klee, Albert H. ....'17 '40 C.209 L.146 LL.B. Bear, Stearns & Co.
Kleehamer, Melinda M. ....'62 '86 C.1044 B.A. L.145 J.D. 227 W Monroe St
Kleiman, Matthew N., (AV) ....'— '92 C.659 B.A. L.597 J.D. [Kirkland&E.]
Kleiman, S. Leslie, (BV) .....'52 '77 C.966 B.A. L.424 J.D. 940 W. Adams St., Suite 300
Klein, Adam R. ....'71 '95 C.188 B.S. L.309 J.D. [Katten M.R.]
Klein, Andrew F. ....'41 '70 C.145 B.A. L.209 J.D. State Dept. of Pub. Aid
Klein, Arthur L., (AV) ....'— '62 C&L.597 B.S.L., LL.B. [Arnstein&L.]
Klein, Barbara D. ....'54 '78 C.339 B.A. L.146 J.D. 23 E. Division St.
Klein, Beverley J., (AV) ....'49 '75 C.339 B.A. L.424 J.D. [🄲 Mayer,B.R.&M.]
Klein, Carter H., (AV) ....'47 '72 C&L.339 B.A., J.D. [Jenner&B.]
Klein, Daniel, (AV) ....'— '90 C&L.608 B.A., J.D. [Kurasch&K.]
Klein, Deborah J. ....'70 '94 C.339 B.A. L.209 J.D. [🄰 LaBarge,C.&L.]
Klein, Eugene '63 '94 L.1018 J.D.
(adm. in NB; not adm. in IL) Britannica.com Inc.
Klein, Frederic R., (AV) ....'50 '80 C.860 B.A. L.477 J.D. [Goldberg,K.B.B.R.&M.]
Klein, Gregory A. ....'50 '75 C&L.802 B.A., J.D. A.T. Kearney, Inc.
Klein, J. Douglas '62 '87 C&L.945 A.B., J.D.
Off. of Legal Coun., Illinois Masonic Medical Center
Klein, Jewel N., (AV) ....'41 '66 C.1036 B.A. L.145 J.D. 20 N. Clark St.
Klein, Jill Swerdloff '64 '91 C&L.893 B.A., J.D.
(adm. in VA; not adm. in IL) BlueCross BlueShield Association
Klein, Jordan A., (AV) ....'64 '89 C.659 B.S. L.145 J.D. [Sidley A.B.&W.]
Klein, Joseph J. ....'57 '83 C.339 B.S. L.146 J.D. [Stitt,K.D.A.&G.] ⊙
Klein, Joshua A. ....'72 '97 C.860 B.A. L.659 J.D. [Neal,G.&E.]
Klein, Leslie A., (AV) ....'55 '80 C.339 B.S. L.46 J.D. [Sonnenschein N.&R.]
Klein, Michael A. ....'57 '83 C.978 B.A. L.597 J.D. 2715 W. Birchwood
Klein, Randall L., (AV) ....'65 '90 C.339 B.A. L.597 J.D. [Goldberg,K.B.B.R.&M.]
Klein, Richard F. ....'— '81 C.339 B.S. L.602 J.D. [Chapman&C.]
Klein, Robert M., (AV) ....'57 '82 C&L.966 B.B.A., J.D. [Klein D.&H.] ⊙
Klein, Steven H., (AV) ....'65 '90 C.477 B.A. L.309 J.D. [Wildman,H.A.&D.]
Klein, Steven N., Law Offices of '42 '67 C&L.569 B.A., J.D.
300 W. Adams St., Ste. 517
Klein, Todd P. ....'76 '01 C.338 B.S. L.365 J.D. [🄰 Conway&C.]
Klein, Wendy S. ....'— '80 C.145 A.B. L.146 J.D. Resch. Atty., Appl. Ct.
Klein, William J. ....'— '95 C.645 B.S. L.1292 J.D. [🄰 Banner&W.] (See Pat. Sect.)
Klein, William R. ....'58 '83 C&L.339 B.A., J.D. [Young,R.F.&S.]

Klein Dub & Holleb, Ltd., (AV)
303 West Madison Street, 23rd Floor, 60606-3308 ⊙
Telephone: 312-464-9400
Email: info@labor-law.com URL: http://www.labor-law.com
Robert M. Klein; Allen W. Dub; Joshua D. Holleb; Michael Paull. Of Counsel: Lawrence A. Reich; Davi L. Hirsch.
Private and Public Sector Labor Law, Employment Law, Employment Discrimination and Affirmative Action. Litigation in State and Federal Courts and before Administrative Agencies in all listed practice areas.
Lake County Office: 660 La Salle Place, Suite 100, Highland Park, Illinois, 60035. Telephone: 847-681-9100. Fax: 847-681-1600.
See Professional Biographies, CHICAGO, ILLINOIS

Klein, Thorpe and Jenkins, Ltd., (AV) ....20 North Wacker Drive, Suite 1660
Kleindorfer, J. William '28 '55 C.347 B.S. L.1119 J.D.
(adm. in IN; not adm. in IL) Dir., Atty. Search, The Registry, Inc.
Kleinman, Anne Kenny ....'58 '85 C.665 B.A. L.146 J.D. Soc. Sec. Admn.
Kleinman, Jeremy C. ....'74 '99 C.1494 B.A. L.477 J.D. [🄰 Quarles&B.]
Kleinman, Robert W., (AV) ....'46 '71 C.659 B.S. L.94 J.D. [DLPiper R.G.C.U.]

Kleinman, Sidney C., (AV) '32 '57 C&L.447 B.A., J.D. 🄱🄱
14 North Peoria Street - 5H, 60607
Telephone: 312-850-8050 FAX: 312-850-8053
Email: sidc@kleinmansnet.com URL: http://www.lawyers.com/sckleinman
Business Law, Corporate Law, Estate Planning, Financial Law and Real Estate.
See Professional Biographies, CHICAGO, ILLINOIS

Klem, Stanley M. ....'56 '81 C.57 B.A. L.477 J.D. Gen. Coun., Managcare, Inc.
Klem, Steven A. ....'46 '73 C.801 B.A. L.146 J.D. 134 N. LaSalle St.
Klempay, Laura G. ....'78 '04 C&L.477 B.S., J.D. [🄰 Winston&S.]
Klemt, LeRoy C. ....'45 '71 C.747 B.A. L.339 J.D. 53 W. Jackson Blvd.
Klenck, Paul R. '58 '85
C.597 B.A. L.209 J.D. Dep. Gen. Coun., Illinois Educ. Assn. - NEA
Klenk, James A., (AV) ....'49 '74 C.72 B.A. L.966 J.D. [Sonnenschein N.&R.]
Klenk, Timothy C., (AV) ....'— '67 C.937 B.A. L.597 J.D. [🄲 Bryan C.]
Klepak, Ralla ....'36 '64 C.597 B.S. L.365 J.D. 5158 N. Ashland Ave.
Kleper, Ann-Louise, (AVⓉ) ....'49 '73 C.1036 A.B. L.94 J.D. [Lewis,D.&H.]
Klepper, Matthew S. ....'71 '96 C.578 B.A. L.945 J.D. [Lord,B.&B.]
Kleppetsch, Paul T. ....'78 '03 C.201 B.A. L.365 J.D. [🄰 Cassiday,S.&G.]
Klevatt, David S. ....'61 '88 C.174 B.S. L.209 J.D. 33 North LaSalle St
Klevorn, Andrew G., (AV) ....'61 '87 C.145 B.A. L.477 J.D. [Eimer S.K.&S.]
Klicka, William J. ....'16 '43 L.365 J.D. 680 S. Federal St.‡
Kliebard, Kenneth M. ....'63 '89 C.966 B.A. L.1066 J.D. [Howrey]
Klimas, Robert J. ....'— '87 C.339 B.S. L.146 J.D. Spec. Agent, F.B.I.
Klimek, John M. ....'59 '84 C&L.339 B.S., J.D. [Merrick&K.]
Klimesh, Mary Kay ....'54 '86 C.859 B.A. L.352 J.D. [Seyfarth S.]
Kline, Gary H. ....'39 '66 C.477 B.A. L.309 J.D. [Quarles&B.]
Kline, Laurence J., (AV) ....'46 '72 C.597 B.S.B.A. L.477 J.D. [Hoogendoorn&T.]

Kline, Mitchell A., Law Office of '53 '78 C.309 B.A. L.1119 J.D.
203 N. LaSalle Street Suite 2100, 60601
Telephone: 312-558-1454 Fax: 312-346-9603 URL: http://www.klinelawfirm.com
Email: mitchellakline@aol.com URL: http://www.mitchellkline.com
(This Listing Continued)

Kline, Mitchell A., Law Office of (Continued)
Sexual Harassment, Discrimination, Age Discrimination, Sex Discrimination, Disability Discrimination, Race Discrimination, Religious Discrimination, Workers' Compensation.
See Professional Biographies, CHICAGO, ILLINOIS

Kling, Andrew A. ....'— '84 C.966 B.A. L.893 J.D. [Schiff H.]
Kling, Richard S., (AV) ... '45 '71 C.339 B.A. L.597 J.D. 565 W. Adams Street, 6th Floor
Kling, Tamara ....'65 '90 C.424 B.A. L.146 J.D. CT Corp. Sys.
Kling, William C. ....'61 '88 C.174 B.A. L.146 J.D. [Ancel,G.D.B.D.&R.]
Klinghoffer, Jon Eric ....'70 '99 C.679 B.S. L.339 J.D. [🄰 Goldberg,K.B.B.R.&M.]
Klinowski, Jason R. ....'78 '04 C.152 B.A. L.365 J.D. [Illinois,D.]
Klintworth, Sheri K. ....'75 '02 C.339 B.A. L.276 J.D. Coun. to the Gov.
Klintworth, Timothy K. ....'70 '96 C.339 B.S. L.502 J.D. [Wildman,H.A.&D.] (Pat.)
Klise, John D. ....'67 '97 C.477 B.A. L.365 J.D. [Klise&B.]

Klise & Biel, Ltd.
1478 West Webster Avenue, 60614
Telephone: 773-871-6446 Fax: 773-871-6902 URL: http://www.kliseandbiel.com
Email: zoe@kliseandbiel.com URL: http://www.lawyers.com/kliseandbiel
John D. Klise; Zoe G. Biel.
Business Formation, Limited Liability Company Law, Chancery Practice, Commercial Real Estate Acquisitions, Commercial Real Estate Contracts, Commercial Real Estate Sales, Construction Contracts, Breach of Contract, Commercial Contracts, Contract Litigation, Corporate Formation, Nonprofit Corporations, Small Business Corporations, Commercial Landlord and Tenant Law, Commercial Leasing, Evictions, Landlord and Tenant Law, Lease Terminations, Leasing, Office Leasing, Civil Litigation, Limited Partnerships, Partnership Dissolution, Partnership Formation, Partnership Organization, Condominium Association Law, Condominium Conversions, Condominium Development, Condominium Law, Real Estate Acquisitions, Real Estate Brokers and Agents Liability, Real Estate Contracts, Real Estate Development, Real Estate Leasing, Real Estate Litigation, Residential Real Estate, Residential Real Estate Development, Residential Real Estate Sales.
See Professional Biographies, CHICAGO, ILLINOIS

Klobuchar, Peter M. '72 '96
C.679 B.S.MetE L.146 J.D. [Wallenstein W.&R.] (See Pat. Sect.)
Klockars, Karl N., (AV) '45 '74 C.1106 B.A. L.146 J.D.
V.P., Legal Affs., Covenant Ministries of Benevolence
Kloecker, John F. ....'66 '95 C.309 B.A. L.597 J.D. [Lord,B.&B.]
Klomann, Karl, (AV) ....'19 '51 C.207 A.B. L.209 J.D. 676 N. La Salle St.‡
Klooster, Tye J. ....'— '03 C.352 B.B.A. L.221 J.D. [🄰 Katten M.R.]
Klopfenstein, Keith A., Law Office of, (AV) '49 '74
C.602 A.B. L.145 J.D. 161 W. Harrison St., Ste. 102
Klotnia, Diane F. ....'61 '88 C.339 B.S. L.145 J.D. [Miller S.&H.]
Klotz, Michael R. ....'76 '04 C&L.347 B.A., J.D. [🄰 Swanson,M.&B.]
Kluchenek, Matthew F. '— '91 C.424 B.A. L.146 J.D.
Assoc. Gen. Coun., Chicago Mercantile Exchange Inc.
Kluever, Brian D. ....'— '89 C.210 B.A. L.597 J.D. [Schiff H.]
Klumpe, Kerry J. '49 '75 C.150 B.A. L.1161 J.D.
(adm. in OH; not adm. in IL) Mng. Editor, ABA Journal
Klunder, Patrick F. ....'46 '72 C&L.424 B.S., J.D. [🄲 Haynes,S.K.O.&M.]
Klupchak, Michael ....'51 '82 C.197 A.B. L.597 J.D. [Laner,M.D.B.L.&T.]
Klyber, Troy B. ....'75 '01 C.339 B.S. L.276 J.D. [🄰 Mayer,B.R.&M.]
Klyman, Marc L. ....'63 '88 C.477 B.A. L.309 J.D. [Mayer,B.R.&M.]
Klytta, Anthony Michael ....'60 '89 C.339 B.A. L.365 J.D. [Klytta&K.]
Klytta, John R. ....'60 '89 C.339 B.A. L.365 J.D. [Klytta&K.]
Klytta and Klytta .... 5680 N. Elston Ave.
Knabe, Robert M. ....'53 '78 C.597 B.S. L.209 J.D. [McNish,K.&K.]
Knape, Frederic T. ....'71 '98 C.477 B.A. L.146 J.D. [🄰 Vedder,P.K.&K.]
Knapke, Norbert B., II ....'— '92 C.602 B.A. L.228 J.D. [Kirkland&E.]
Knapp, Dolores M. ....'28 '68 C.530 B.S. L.365 J.D. 3016 S Lowe Ave.
Knapp, Moyenda Mutharika ....'69 '94 C.197 A.B. L.94 J.D. [🄰 Deutsch,L.&E.]
Kneafsey, John K., (AV) ....'39 '65 C.363 B.S. L.424 J.D. [Nisen&E.]
Knecht, Kristen S. ....'80 '04 C&L.477 A.B., J.D. [🄰 Pattishall,M.N.H.&G.]
Knechtel, Robert L. '59 '89 C.589 B.S. L.1187 J.D.
(adm. in MI; not adm. in IL; Pat.) [M.E.Wiemelt]
Kneedy, Mark J. ....'— '72 C&L.339 A.B., J.D. [Chapman&C.]
Knell, Bradley C., (BV) ....'62 '88 C.234 B.A. L.607 J.D. [Knell&P.] ⊙

Knell & Poulos, A Professional Corporation, (AV)
555 West Jackson Boulevard Suite 700, 60661-5700 ⊙
Telephone: 312-277-3000 Fax: 312-277-3008
Email: home@knellpoulos.com URL: http://www.knellpoulos.com
Bradley C. Knell; David T. Poulos; John J. O'Connor;—Tina R. Swanson; Paul-Eric Seal; Robert M. Harris; Ryan M. Mahoney. Of Counsel: Robert J. Kartholl, Jr.
Workers Compensation Defense, Insurance Defense, Employment Defense.
Wheaton, Illinois Office: 511 West Wesley, 60187. Telephone: 630-681-1512.
See Professional Biographies, CHICAGO, ILLINOIS

Knepper, Thomas M., (AV) ....'45 '72 C.602 B.A. L.146 J.D. [Knepper&G.]

Knepper & Gladney, (AV)
150 North Wacker Drive, Suite 3050, 60606
Telephone: 312-957-1300 Fax: 312-957-1070 URL: http://www.kg-legal.com
URL: http://www.lawyers.com/knepper&gladney
Members of Firm: Thomas M. Knepper; Jill J. Gladney.
Commercial Litigation and Appellate Practice, Securities and Commodities Law, Labor and Employment Law.
See Professional Biographies, CHICAGO, ILLINOIS

Kneubuhler, Kenneth K. ....'— '75 C.63 B.A. L.597 J.D. [Freeborn&P.]
Knight, Brent D. ....'— '98 C&L.477 B.A., J.D. [🄰 Jones D.]
Knight, Charles D., (AV) ....'53 '78 C&L.339 A.B., J.D. [Holland&K.]
Knight, Christopher N., (AV) ....'— '71 C.976 B.A. L.228 J.D. [Foley&L.]
Knight, John A. .. '60 '89 C.813 B.A. L.145 J.D. Ste. 3900, Xerox Ctr., 55 W. Monroe St.
Knight, Peter P. ....'— '99 C.373 B.A. L.569 J.D. [🄰 Latham&W.]
Knight, Sarah R. '73 '01 C.951 B.A. L.569 J.D.
(adm. in WA; not adm. in IL) [🄰 Perkins C.]
Knight, Timothy P. ....'65 '90 C.436 B.S. L.209 J.D. 435 N. Michigan Ave.
Knipmeyer, Jeffrey J., (CVⓉ) ....'71 '96 C.502 B.A. L.209 J.D. [🄰 Nottage&W.]
Knippen, Michael S., (AV) ....'55 '83 C.746 B.A. L.209 J.D. [Bollinger,R.&G.]
Knipstein, Julie E. ....'65 '90 C.347 B.A. L.339 J.D. Legal Coun., Barton Inc.
Knobloch, Jennifer ....'73 '01 C.340 B.A. L.209 J.D. [🄰 Baal&O.]
Knohl, Kevin C. ....'— '99 C.896 B.A. L.477 J.D. [🄰 Schiff H.]
Knopf, Alvin N. ....'48 '76 C.705 B.S. L.146 J.D. 3525 W. Peterson Ave., Ste. 510
Knopp, Anne-Marie K. ....Chicago Legal Clinic
Knowles, Jessica C. ....'— '02 C&L.494 B.A., J.D. 10 S. Dearborn Street
Knowles, Lawrence M. ....'56 '83 C.494 B.A. L.145 J.D. [🄲 Mayer,B.R.&M.]
Knowles, Robert S. ......'56 '83 C.339 A.B. L.209 J.D. Dir. of Claims, Coregis Grp., Inc.
Knox, James A., Jr., (AV) ....'57 '84 C.802 B.A. L.846 J.D. [Tressler,S.M.&P.]
Knox, James M. ......'44 '79 C.339 B.A. L.209 J.D. 121 West Chestnut Street, Apt. 3202

Knox, William R. '— '02 C.219 B.A. L.209 J.D.
3376 North Central, 60634
Telephone: 773-383-7748 Fax: 312-873-4699
(This Listing Continued)

Knox, William R. (Continued)
Civil Litigation, Criminal Law, Drug Crimes, Driving While Intoxicated, Traffic Violations, Evictions, Family Law, Divorce, Child Custody, Child Support, Domestic Relations, Personal Injury, Automobile Accidents, Trucking Accidents, Slip and Fall, Wrongful Death.
See Professional Biographies, CHICAGO, ILLINOIS

Knuepfer, Robert C., Jr. .... '52 '78 C.207 B.A. L.597 J.D. [Baker&M.]
Knuti, Robert A., (AV) .... '42 '69 C.207 B.A. L.339 J.D. [🄱 Lord,B.&B.]
Kobayashi, George H. ....'— '01 C.190 B.S.B.A. L.365 J.D. [🄰 Masuda,F.E.&M.]
Kobayashi, Jennifer L. ....'75 '01 C.966 B.A. L.1375 J.D. [🄰 Winston&S.]
Kobialka, Karen ....'57 '82 C.339 B.S. L.209 J.D. [🄰 Horowitz&W.]
Koch, Brian J. ....'70 '98 C.339 B.S. L.209 J.D. [🄰 Wiedner&M.]
Koch, C. John ....'56 '81 C.910 A.B. L.145 J.D. [Jenner&B.]
Koch, Elissa Boysen ....'— '04 C.597 B.S. L.424 J.D. [🄰 McGuirewoods]
Koch, James A. ....'51 '79 C.338 B.S. L.365 J.D. Asst. Atty. Gen.
Koch, James B. ....'52 '79 C.424 B.A. L.146 J.D. [Gardiner K.&W.]
Koch, John P. ....'39 '64 C.276 B.S.F.S. L.597 J.D. 100 W. North Ave.
Koch, Kristina S. .....'70 '97 C.234 B.A. L.801 J.D. Sr. Coun., Ill. Develop. Finance Auth.
Koch, Thomas J., (BV) ....'55 '84 C.177 B.A. L.146 J.D. [🄱 Swanson,M.&B.]
Kocheny, Brigitte T. ....'— '93 C&L.957 B.A., J.D. [Gardner C.&D.]
Kochis, Stephen T. '46 '73 C.436 A.B. L.477 J.D.
Contl. Ill. Nat. Bk. & Tr. Co. of Chic.
Koci, Susan Kurzydlo ....'— '88 C&L.424 B.A., J.D. [🄰 Schiff H.]
Kocol, Mark S., (CV) ....'67 '94 C.589 B.S. L.365 J.D. 79 West Monroe
Kocoras, Charles P. ....'38 '69 C&L.209 B.S.C., J.D. Chf. U.S. Dist. J.
Kocoras, Peter J. ....'69 '93 C.347 B.S. L.209 J.D. [Winston&S.]
Kocour, Patricia S. ....'66 '91 C.339 B.S. L.146 J.D. [Swanson,M.&B.]
Koczwara, Christopher S. ....'65 '94 [C.Koczwara]
Koczwara, Christopher, Law Office of ....6808 W. Archer Ave.
Kodjayan, Nicole J. ....'72 '98 C.424 B.S. L.146 J.D. Off. of States Atty.
Koehler, A. Jay, III ....'66 '91 C.510 B.A. L.365 J.D. [Swanson,M.&B.]
Koehler, Douglas T. ....'38 '67 C.959 B.S. L.966 J.D. V.P., The Northern Trust Co.
Koehler, Ernest K., (BV) ....'33 '56 C&L.145 A.B., J.D. 111W. Washington
Koehler, Julie Ann ....'69 '96 C.98 B.S. L.209 J.D. Off. of Pub. Def.
Koenders, Matthew T. ....'— '03 C.912 B.S. L.309 J.D. [🄰 Mayer,B.R.&M.]
Koenig, Amy Listick ....'62 '87 C.339 B.A. L.597 J.D. [Barack F.K.P.&N.]
Koenig, Ray J., III ....'73 '99 C.475 B.A. L.209 J.D. [🄰 Peck,B.A.&M.] ⊙
Koenigsberg, Ilene C. ....'66 '91 C.1365 B.B.A. L.273 J.D. 360 N. Michigan Ave.
Koenigsberger, Michael, (AV) ....'70 '95 C.339 B.A. L.209 J.D. [Grund&L.]
Koenigsknecht, John J. '68 '96
C.309 A.B. L.273 J.D. Two North LaSalle Street, Suite 2200
Koeppl, Kelly L. ....'— '03 C.746 B.A. L.597 J.D. [🄰 Foley&L.]
Koering, Jacob D. ....'— '01 C.966 B.S. L.424 J.D. [🄰 Freeborn&P.]
Koerth, Jenny Friedman ....'76 '02 C.494 B.A. L.597 J.D. [🄰 Vedder,P.K.&K.]
Koerth, Theodore J. ....'— '02 C.893 B.A. L.273 J.D. [🄰 Freeborn&P.]
Koessl, Thomas C. ....'71 '96 C.1172 B.A. L.146 J.D. [Williams M.&J.]
Koester, Ted A. ....'72 '98 C.234 B.S. L.997 J.D. [🄰 Bischoff]
Koff, Jonathan A. ....'— '85 C.339 B.A. L.209 J.D. [Chapman&C.]
Kofkin, Leonard R. ....'33 '58 C&L.597 B.S., J.D. [Scopelitis,G.L.&H.]
Koga, Steven A., (AV) ....'50 '77 C.209 B.A. L.365 J.D. [Kelly,O.M.D.&R.]
Kogan, Randye A. ....'49 '78 C.966 B.A. L.209 J.D. Assoc. Cir. Ct. J.
Kogut, James Kenneth ....'56 '83 [🄱 Wolf&W.]
Kohen, Bruce M., (AV) ....'53 '79 C.339 B.S. L.146 J.D. [Anesi,O.R.N.&K.]
Kohen, Stefanie W. ....'67 '94 C.705 B.A. L.365 J.D. [Littler M.]
Kohl, Leonard F. ....'31 '63 C.363 B.S. L.209 2474 West Estes‡
Kohler, Edward G. ....'51 '78 C.339 B.A. L.424 J.D. S.E.C.
Kohn, Andrew J. ....'57 '85 C.720 B.A. L.146 J.D. Chf. Dep. Clk., The U.S. Fed. Ct.
Kohn, Carole J. ....'43 '77 C.289 A.B. L.424 J.D. U.S. Dept. of H.H.S.
Kohn, Daniel, (AV) ....'62 '87 C.1036 B.A. L.309 J.D. [Duane M.]
Kohn, Daniel R. '52 '77 C.579 B.A. L.585 J.D.
Dir. & Sr. Coun., CNA Property & Casualty Oper.
Kohn, Henry, III ... '63 '90 C.228 A.B. L.597 J.D. Sr. Coun., Bank One Corp. (Law Dept.)
Kohn, Jerrold H. ....'57 '84 C.589 B.S. L.146 J.D. Secs. & Exch. Com.
Kohn, Richard M., (AV) ....'44 '69 C&L.477 B.A., J.D. [Goldberg,K.B.B.R.&M.]
Kohn, Shalom L., (AV) ....'49 '75 C.102 B.S. L.309 J.D. [Sidley A.B.&W.]
Kohn, Stuart J., (AV) ....'— '87 C.477 B.B.A. L.424 J.D. [Levin&S.]
Kohn, William B. ....'60 '87 C.477 A.B. L.1119 J.D. 150 N. Wacker Dr., Ste. 1400
Kohn, William I., (AVⓣ) ....'— '76 C.150 B.A. L.608 J.D. [Schiff H.]
Kohnen, Daniel J. '49 '82 C.339 B.A. L.424 J.D.
Dir. Bur. of Archit., Chic. Pub. Schools
Kohnke, John J. ....'59 '84 C&L.221 B.A., J.D. [Segal M.S.&M.]
Kohut, Michelle M. ....'74 '02 C&L.424 B.S., J.D. [🄰 Corboy&D.]
Kokolis, Aphrodite, (AV) ....'— '87 C.339 B.A. L.597 J.D. [Schiff H.]
Kokolis, Jerry ....'65 '90 C.145 B.A. L.597 J.D. [Holland&K.]
Kokoski, Jo-Anne ....'— '99 C.453 S.B. L.910 J.D. [🄰 Schiff H.] (Pat.)
Kokoszka, Frank J. ....'64 '89 C.424 B.A. L.228 J.D. 140 South Dearborn, Suite 1610
Kolak, Raymond P., (AV) ....'52 '78 C.145 B.A. L.273 J.D. [Eckhart K.]
Kolar, Deanna L. ....'69 '99 C.477 B.A. L.209 J.D. Richard J Daley Ctr.

Kolar, Kurt J., Law Office of '68 '96 C.436 B.A. L.990 J.D.
123 West Madison, Suite 1800, 60602
Telephone: 312-641-3230 Fax: 312-641-3225
Email: kjkolar@kjkolarlaw.com URL: http://www.kjkolarlaw.com
Business Organization/Advising; Contract Law, Contract Drafting/Revision/Negotiation; Breach of Contract Litigation, Economic Torts, Interference with Prospective Economic Advantage, Defamation, Patent/Trademark/Copyright Infringement, Deceptive Business Practices, Fraud; Commercial Bankruptcy/Reorganization; Entertainment Law, Civil Litigation; Condominium Law; Recording Artist, Independent Record Label Representation, Real Estate Transactions, Litigation, and Consumer and Creditors Rights.
See Professional Biographies, CHICAGO, ILLINOIS

Kolar, Robert D., (AV) ....'38 '67 C.1016 B.S. L.365 J.D. [Tressler,S.M.&P.]
Kolasa, Natalia A. ....'79 '04 C.587 B.A. L.1556 J.D. [🄰 Reardon G.&R.]
Kolb, William A. ....'54 '98 C.145 B.A. L.1209 J.D. 53 W. Jackson Boulevard
Kole, James D., (AVⓣ) ....'60 '87 C.477 B.A. L.145 J.D. [🄱 Sidley A.B.&W.]
Kolecke, Jason D. ....'— '01 C.436 B.S. L.365 J.D. [🄰 Hennessy&R.]
Kolek, Robert E., (AV) ....'— '68 C&L.424 B.B.A., J.D. [Schiff H.]
Kolin, Charles J. ....'— '99 C.363 B.S.B.A. L.365 J.D. [🄰 Chapman&C.]
Kolin, David F. ....'55 '87 C.475 B.A. L.477 J.D. [🄱 Skadden,A.S.M.&F.]
Kolin, Renata A. ....'66 '98 C.801 B.S. L.1000 J.D. [🄰 Fraterrigo,B.F.&K.]
Kolkmeier, Kiplund R. ....'62 '88 C.813 B.A. L.424 J.D. [🄱 Wildman,H.A.&D.]
Kolliniatis, Christina ....'79 '04 C.339 B.S. L.61 J.D. [🄰 Amin L.]
Kolloway, Michael R. '60 '85
C.746 B.A. L.339 J.D. Consoer Townsend Envirodyne Engineers
Kollross, Melinda S. ....'67 '92 C.209 B.A. L.146 J.D. [Clausen M.]
Kolman, Judith N. ....'51 '84 C.273 B.A. L.209 J.D. [Rosenthal,M.C.]
Kolman, Ludwig E., (AV) ....'48 '75 C.339 B.S. L.597 J.D. [Vedder,P.K.&K.] (Pat.)

Kolmin, Kenneth G., (AV) ....'51 '76 C.1044 B.S. L.823 J.D. [Sonnenschein N.&R.]
Kolodziej, Stephen A. ....'68 '93 C&L.339 B.A., J.D. [Brenner,F.M.&S.]
Kolomayets, Andrew G., (BV) '61 '88
C.424 B.A. L.339 J.D. [Cook,A.M.M.C.&M.] (See Pat. Sect.)
Kolton, Bryan G. ....'74 '99 [🄰 Jacobs]
Kolton, Kevin L. ....'— '90 C.339 B.S.E. L.796 J.D. [Schiff H.]
Kolz, Aimee Boss ....'— '99 C.277 B.S. L.365 J.D. [Banner&W.] (See Pat. Sect.)
Koman, Christine M. ....'64 '93 C.210 B.A. L.209 J.D. [Hall,P.&S.]
Komie, James L., (AV) ....'62 '87 C&L.477 B.A., J.D. [Schuyler,R.&Z.]
Komie, Lowell B., (AV) ....'27 '55 C.477 B.A. L.597 J.D. 155 N. Michigan
Komie, Stephen M., (AV) '49 '76
C.37 B.A. L.209 J.D. [Komie&Assoc.] & [Drunken D.D.L.I.]

Komie and Associates, Law Offices of, (AV)
One North La Salle Street Suite 4200, 60602-4005
Telephone: 312-263-2800 Fax: 312-263-2803 URL: http://www.komie-and-associates.com
URL: http://www.lawyers.com/komielaw
Stephen M. Komie. Associates: Darius R. Dirmantas; Elisabeth A. Ritter; Brian E. King; Sarah E. Toney. Of Counsel: Marc D. Wolfe.
Civil and Criminal Litigation. Federal, State, International, Trial and Appellate Practice. Complex Litigation, Criminal Defense, Divorce, Family Law, Probate, Taxation, Immigration Law, International Criminal Law, Real Estate Law.
See Professional Biographies, CHICAGO, ILLINOIS

Kommers, Theodore F. ....'65 '92 C&L.602 B.A., J.D. [Gould&R.]
Komoll, Michael S. ....'66 '90 C&L.209 B.A., J.D. Suite 1040, 20 North Wacker Drive
Komon, Stacey ....'— '94 C.339 B.S. L.424 J.D. [🄱 Katten M.R.]
Komosa, Edward J., (AV) ....'27 '58 C.734 A.B. L.424 J.D. 4013 W. Wellington‡
Koncius, Brian E. ....'78 '03 C.228 A.B. L.477 J.D. [🄰 Butler R.S.&B.]
Konetzki, Jennifer A. ....'63 '89 C.966 B.A. L.436 J.D. U.S. Bank
Konieczny, Daniel I. ....'76 '01 C.674 A.B. L.309 J.D. [🄰 Tabet D.&R.] (Pat.)
Kono, Dayne ....'— '82 C.477 A.B. L.262 J.D. [Masuda,F.E.&M.]
Konop, Robert M., (AV) '46 '73 C&L.966 B.S., J.D.
(adm. in WI; not adm. in IL) [Hinshaw&C.]
Konopack, Anne Marie ....'69 '94 C&L.424 B.B.A., J.D. [Mayer,B.R.&M.]
Konstantopoulos, Dimitrios '73 '01
C.145 B.A. L.209 J.D. Coun., United Investors, Inc. (Realty Co.)
Kooy, Ralph J. ....'67 '92 C&L.339 B.A., J.D. [Tressler,S.M.&P.]
Kopec, William F. ....'46 '76 C.209 B.S.C. L.365 J.D. Asst. States Atty.
Kopecky, James L. ....'68 '94 C.339 B.A. L.424 J.D. [J.L.Kopecky]
Kopecky, Robert J., (AV) ....'— '79 C.373 B.A. L.145 J.D. [Kirkland&E.]

Kopecky, James L., P.C.
321 N. Clark Street, Suite 2200, 60610
Telephone: 312-527-3966 Fax: 312-527-3968 URL: http://www.jlkopecky.com
Email: info@jlkopecky.com URL: http://www.jlkopeckylaaw.com
James L. Kopecky.
Securities, Securities Fraud, Securities Arbitration and Litigation, Shareholder Disputes, Business and Contract Litigation, General Civil Litigation and Personal Injury.
See Professional Biographies, CHICAGO, ILLINOIS

Kopelman, Ian S., (AV) ....'49 '74 C.388 B.A. L.352 J.D. [DLPiper R.G.C.U.]
Kopiwoda, Jeffrey E. ....'69 '95 C.475 B.A. L.146 J.D. 70 W. Madison
Kopka, Pinkus, Dolin & Eads, (AV)
200 N. LaSalle Street, Suite 2850 (⊙Buffalo Grove, IL; Crown Point, Indpls., South Bend, IN; Farmington Hills, MI)
Kopko, Frederick H., Jr. ....'55 '80 C.184 B.A. L.602 J.D. [McBreen&K.]
Kopko, Mary Elizabeth ....'58 '83 C.741 B.A. L.424 J.D. [McBreen&K.]
Koplin, Caroline ....'61 '86 C.602 B.A. L.424 J.D. Asst. State's Atty.
Kopon, Andrew, Jr., (AV) ....'54 '80 C.676 B.A. L.365 J.D. [Cremer,K.S.&S.]
Kopoulos, Peter C. ....'60 '85 C.209 B.S. L.146 J.D. 55 W. Wacker Dr.
Kopp, Daniel J. ....'62 '87 C.602 B.A. L.1119 J.D. [Schwartz C.]
Koppelman, Andrew ....'57 '90 C.145 A.B. L.976 J.D. 357 E. Chicago Avenue
Koppelman, David ....'63 '89 C.588 B.S. L.424 J.D. 200 N. LaSalle St., Ste. 2000
Koppy, Jeffrey A. ....'69 '94 C&L.477 B.A., J.D. [Jenner&B.]
Kopriva, James W., (AV) ....'51 '79 C.339 B.A. L.589 J.D. [Cassiday,S.&G.]
Kopriva, Teresa C. '58 '87 C&L.190 B.A., J.D.
Assoc. Gen. Coun., Westport Ins. Corp., GE ERC Comm. Ins.
Koptik, Michael T. ....'66 '01 C.339 B.A. L.365 J.D. [🄰 Hall,P.&S.]
Koran, Janet M., (AV) '49 '78
C.388 B.A. L.597 J.D. General Counsel, YMCA of the USA
Kordish, Eric J. ....'74 '05 C.597 B.A. L.424 J.D. [🄰 Pedersen&H.]
Kordys, Richard A. '54 '82 C.347 B.A. L.607 J.D.
(adm. in IN; not adm. in IL) U.S. Dept. of Labor, Off. of the Solr.

Korein Tillery
(See St. Louis, Missouri)

Koren, Shelley H. ....'74 '93 C&L.910 A.B., J.D. [🄰 Horwood M.&B.]
Korengold, Howard ....'33 '57 C&L.597 B.S.L., LL.B. 208 S. LaSalle St.
Korey, Carter Andrew ....'72 '98 C.36 B.S. L.365 J.D. [🄰 Stone,P.&K.]
Korey, Ilene M., (AV) ....'57 '83 C.174 B.A. L.209 J.D. [Clausen M.]
Korey, Martin S. ....'45 '70 C.339 B.S. L.209 J.D. [Stone,P.&K.]
Koritz, Matthew H. '69 '94 C.339 B.S. L.597 J.D.
Litig. & Govt. Affs. Coun., Equity Off. Properties Tr.
Korman, Thomas A., (AV) ....'48 '74 C.339 B.S. L.209 J.D. [Gould&R.]
Kormendy, Charlotte ....'73 '98 C.454 B.A. L.146 J.D. [🄰 Meckler B.&T.]
Korn, Kathryn E., (AV) ....'51 '76 C.475 B.A. L.339 J.D. 8501 W. Higgins, Ste. 440
Kornak, Michael P. ....'— '96 C.347 B.S. L.339 J.D. [Freeborn&P.]
Kornfeld, Jerome J. ....'18 '58 C.145 A.B. L.365 LL.B. 105 W. Madison St.
Kornfeld, N. David, The Law Offices of '56 '81
C.339 B.A. L.94 J.D. 203 North LaSalle Street (⊙Evanston)
Korniczky, Paul J., (AV) '61 '86 C.186 B.E. L.107 J.D.
[Leydig,V.&M.] (See Pat. Sect.)
Koropp, David E. ....'64 '89 C&L.339 B.A., J.D. [Winston&S.]
Kors, Geoffrey R. '61 '87 C.867 B.A. L.813 J.D.
(adm. in CA; not adm. in IL) ACLU
Korshak, Kracoff, Kong & Sugano, LLP
70 West Madison Street (⊙L.A., Oakl., Sacra., CA)
Korte, Amy S. ....'71 '99 C.945 B.A. L.910 J.D. [🄰 Mayer,B.R.&M.]
Kosc, Jeffrey ....'71 '96 C.164 B.A. L.209 J.D. [🄰 Wildman,H.A.&D.]
Kosciolek, James F. ....'63 '92 C.813 B.A. L.145 J.D. 311 West Superior St.
Kosiak, Mary Ann ....'53 '78 C.720 B.A. L.365 J.D. 2020 N. Lincoln Park W.
Kosiarek, Renee K. ....'73 '98 C.339 B.A. L.424 J.D. Consult., Broadview, Inc.
Kosin, Paul C. ....'— '68 C&L.597 B.S., J.D. [Chapman&C.]
Kosin, Robert S., (Ltd.), (BV) ....'34 '56 L.365 LL.B. 134 N. LaSalle St.
Kosinski, Maria L. ....'58 '92 C.339 B.S.I.E. L.146 J.D. V.P. Mktg., By-Lo Mfg.
Koski, John C. ....'67 '92 C.880 B.A. L.472 J.D. [Sonnenschein N.&R.]
Kosky, John E. ....'— '98 C.436 B.S. L.365 J.D. [🄰 Augustine,K.&L.]
Koslow, Stephen D. ....'69 '94 C.339 B.S. L.209 J.D. [🄰 McCullough,C.&L.]

Kosman, Joseph J. ... '57 '89 C.963 B.S. L.365 J.D. Asst. State's Atty.
Kosmond, James N., (AV) ... '— '59 C.98 B.S. L.597 J.D. [Querrey&H.]
Kosowski, Lisa Anne ... '66 '00 C.801 B.S. L.424 J.D. Off. of the Pub. Guardian
Kossek, Regina M. ... '51 '75 C.645 B.A. L.659 J.D. Reg. Jud. Offr., U.S.E.P.A.
Kossoff, Sinclair ... '32 '59 C&L.145 M.A., J.D. 2901 W. Birchwood Ave.
Kossow, Todd M. ... '62 '87 C.967 B.A. L.597 J.D. Law Clk., App. Ct. J.
Kost, Kelly K., (AV) ... '— '86 C.504 B.A. L.880 J.D. [Chapman&C.]
Kostecki, Gabriel A. ... '40 '66 C.424 B.S. L.146 J.D. 5850 N. Milwaukee Ave.
Kostopulos, Margaret ... '58 '84 C.424 B.A. L.1000 J.D. [Ⓒ Ancel,G.D.B.D.&R.]
Kostro, Victor S. ... '59 '93 C.339 B.S. L.1187 J.D. [Ⓐ Martin,B.&S.]
Kosuri, Praveen ... '69 '94 C.228 A.B. L.910 J.D. Asst. Dir., Univ. Chicago Law School
Kosztya, Ryan S. ... '74 '02 C.912 B.A. L.365 J.D. 200 West Adams Street
Kotelman, Laura Mary ... '72 '97 C.393 B.A. L.339 J.D. 10 South Dearborn Street
Kotin, Daniel M., (AV) ... '65 '91 C.93 B.A. L.424 J.D. [Corboy&D.]
Kotler, Bradley E. ... '— '95 C.1365 B.B.A. L.276 J.D. [Latham&W.]
Kotler, Jennifer P. ... '71 '97 C.31 B.A. L.145 J.D. Atty., Northern Trust Corp.
Kotsalieff, Angela M. ... '— '00 C.339 B.S. L.146 J.D. [Ⓐ Johnson&B.] (⊙Waukegan)
Kott, Andrea H., (BV) ... '64 '90 C.910 B.A. L.930 J.D. [McKay,N.T.D.&K.]
Kott, Marcelle R. ... '67 '92 C.347 B.A. L.365 J.D. [Ⓐ Berger S.]
Kottaras, Demetrios G. ... '57 '84 C.597 B.S. L.146 J.D. Supvr., Fin. Crimes Unit
Kotte, John D. ... '63 '88 C&L.339 A.B., J.D. Consultant, CNA‡
Kotze, Sarah B. ... '71 '99 C.98 B.A. L.339 J.D. Coun., Urban Retail Properties Co.
Koucky, Joseph P. ... '37 '62 C.197 B.A. L.477 J.D. 134 La Salle St.
Kouimelis, Eleni Skoulikas, (AV) ... '60 '85 C.339 B.S. L.424 J.D. [Winston&S.]
Kourasis, Tina D. ... '71 '97 C.339 B.A. L.145 J.D. [Gardner C.&D.]
Kouris, John R. '46 '71 C.999 B.A. L.424 J.D.
(adm. in IN; not adm. in IL) Exec. Dir., Defense Rsch. Inst.
Kourvetaris, Nicholas G. ... '— '00 C.597 B.S. L.146 J.D. [Ⓐ O'Hagan,S.&A.]
Koury, David L. ... '67 '93 C&L.352 B.B.A., J.D. [Walker W.M.]
Koutsky, Kenneth F., (AV) ... '26 '51 L.365 LL.B. 33 N. Dearborn St.
Kovach, Karl D. ... '63 '96 C.608 B.S.M.E. L.365 J.D. Stratos International, Inc. (Pat.)
Kovacs, James A. ... '75 '00 C.477 B.A. L.309 J.D. [Ⓐ Gordon&G.L.]
Kovar, Andrea K. ... '— '99 C.145 B.A. L.365 J.D. [Ⓐ Baker&M.]
Kovar-Hersh, Marlene ... '47 '78 C.112 B.A. L.809 J.D. The Northern Trust Co.
Kovarik, Andrew J., (BV) ... '60 '92 C.424 B.A. L.365 J.D. [Johnson&B.]
Koven, Edward L. ... '40 '65 C&L.597 B.A., J.D. Asst. Reg. Coun., Social Sec. Admn.
Kovitz, Alan D., (AV) ... '34 '58 C&L.597 B.S.L., J.D. [Kovitz S.N.] ⊙
Kovitz, Samuel H. ... '63 '88 C.339 B.S. L.597 J.D. 2 N. La Salle St., Ste. 725
Kovitz Shifrin Nesbit, A Professional Corporation, (AV)
134 North LaSalle Street, Suite 1600 (⊙Buffalo Grove)
Kowal, Steven M., (AV) ... '49 '74 C.750 B.A. L.597 J.D. [Bell,B.&L.]
Kowalczyk, Larry S., (AV) ... '— '94 C&L.424 B.A., J.D. [Querrey&H.]
Kowalczyk, Ronald B. ... '71 '01 C.362 B.A. L.209 J.D. [Kowalczyk&B.] ⊙
Kowalczyk & Bell, P.C. ... 203 North LaSalle Street, Suite 2100 (⊙Geneva)
Kowalik, John J. ... '18 '40 C&L.209 LL.B. 53 W. Jackson (Pat.)
Kowalski, Karen M. ... '75 '00 C.339 B.A. L.209 J.D. [Ⓐ Winston&S.]
Kowalski, Walter J. ... '18 '39 C.597 B.S. L.146 J.D. Cir. J.
Koya, Devi S. ... '69 '94 C.340 B.A. L.209 J.D. [Ⓐ McDermott W.&E.]
Koyn, Jonathan R. ... '69 '98 C.589 B.A. L.209 J.D. [Ⓐ Nasharr&S.]
Koyner, Robyn ... '74 '00 C.367 B.A. L.477 J.D. [Ⓐ DLPiper R.G.C.U.]
Kozacky, Paul J., (AV) ... '59 '84 C.339 A.B. L.276 J.D. [Kozacky&W.]

Kozacky & Weitzel, P.C., (AV)
One North LaSalle, Suite 3150, 60602
Telephone: 312-696-0900 Fax: 312-696-0905
Email: pkozacky@kozacky.com URL: http://www.kozacky.com
Paul J. Kozacky; Jerome R. Weitzel;—Jeffrey S. Becker.
Admiralty and Maritime Law, Commercial Law, Business Litigation, Construction, Contract Litigation, Litigation, Real Estate Litigation, Business Fraud, Business Arbitration, Chancery Practice, Federal Civil Practice, Contracts, Insurance Coverage, Commercial Landlord and Tenant Law, Long-Arm Litigation, Transportation Law.
See Professional Biographies, CHICAGO, ILLINOIS

Kozak, Barry ... '65 '00 C.1044 B.S. L.365 J.D. Dir.
Kozak, John W., (AV) '43 '68
C.602 B.S.E.E. L.276 J.D. [Leydig,V.&M.] (See Pat. Sect.)
Kozel, Edward J., Jr. ... '— '92 C.589 B.S. L.365 J.D. [Querrey&H.]
Koziboski, Edward J. '67 '92 C.436 B.A. L.966 J.D.
(adm. in WI; not adm. in IL) 1024 N Oakley Blvd.‡
Koziol, Christopher S. ... '59 '84 C.339 B.A. L.365 J.D. 6060 N. Milwaukee Avenue
Kozlowski, Amy K. ... '61 '91 C.339 B.S. L.424 J.D. [Weinberg R.]
Kozlowski, Brian J. ... '69 '95 C.339 B.A. L.424 J.D. [Winston&S.]
Kozlowski, Robert ... '58 '89 C.1320 B.A. L.365 J.D. 2610 W. Montrose Ave.
Kozlowski, Susan M. ... '59 '85 C&L.424 B.A., J.D. Assoc. Gen. Coun., Fannie Mae
Kozminski, Brian K. ... '70 '95 C.339 B.A. L.209 J.D. [Levenfeld P.]
Kozubek, S. Michael ... '47 '74 C.453 B.S. L.982 J.D. 2845 N Wolcott Ave. Unit A
Kracik, Deborah Kashul ... '65 '91 C.597 B.A. L.602 J.D. 360° Communications Co.
Kraemer, Elizabeth Opper ... '— '98 C.597 B.S.J. L.1068 J.D. [Ⓐ Latham&W.]
Kraetsch, Neil A. ... '73 '99 C.339 B.A. L.910 J.D. [Ⓐ Leo&W.]
Krafsur, Jay V., (AV) ... '56 '84 C.174 B.A. L.146 J.D. [Krafsur]

Krafsur Law Group, The, LLC, (AV)
30 North LaSalle Street, Suite 4300, 60602
Telephone: 312-899-0911 Fax: 312-899-0220
URL: http://www.krafsurlaw.com
Jay V. Krafsur; Eric L. Routman.
Captive Insurance Formation and Management, Insurance Coverage Counseling, Enterprise Risk Management and Alternative Risk Financing Advice, Alternative Dispute Resolution, Emergency Services and Emergency Products Counseling, All Litigation Relating to These Specialties.
See Professional Biographies, CHICAGO, ILLINOIS

Kraft, Jeffrey G., (AV) ... '49 '77 C.563 B.A. L.930 J.D. [Neal,G.&E.]
Kraft, Jennifer A. ... '— '96 C.477 B.A. L.494 J.D. [Ⓐ Seyfarth S.]
Kraft, Jennifer L. '71 '96 C.576 B.A. L.276 J.D.
Assoc. Gen. Coun., Securities Law, Aon Corp.
Kraft, Kelly A. ... '74 '99 C.57 B.A. L.879 J.D. [Ⓐ Wilson E.M.E.&D.]
Kraft, Sumner ... '23 '48 C.588 L.94 LL.B. 3712 N. Bwy. St.
Kraft, Vicki M. ... '54 '84 C.589 M.A. L.107 J.D. 121 N. LaSalle St.
Krafthefer, Keri-Lyn J., (BV) ... '63 '88 C.339 B.A. L.365 J.D. [Ancel,G.D.B.D.&R.]
Krahl, William F. ... '46 '72 C.197 B.A. L.477 J.D. Legal Aid Bur.
Krajewski, Henry L. ... '15 '37 C&L.209 LL.B. 8812 S. Coml. Ave.
Krakauer, Bryan, (AV) ... '56 '81 C.228 A.B. L.145 J.D. [Sidley A.B.&W.]
Krakowski, Richard J. ... '46 '84 C.209 B.A. L.365 J.D. 1550 N. Lake Shore Dr., Apt. 16E
Krakus, Beata K. ... '73 '03 C.067 LL.M. L.424 J.D. [Ⓐ Sonnenschein N.&R.]
Kral, Franklin I. ... '32 '55 C.999 L.146 LL.B. Ret. Cir. J., Jud. Panelist‡
Kralovec, Celeste Ebers ... '56 '81 C.339 B.A. L.365 J.D. [Ⓒ Davis M.]
Kralovec, John B., (AV) ... '56 '81 C.339 B.S. L.424 J.D. [Kralovec,J.&S.]
Kralovec, Michael J., (AV) ... '51 '77 C.602 B.A. L.424 J.D. 30 N La Salle St Ste 1526

Kralovec, Jambois & Schwartz, (AV)
Goodman Theatre Building, 60 West Randolph Street, 4th Floor, 60601
Telephone: 312-782-2525 Fax: 312-855-0068
URL: http://www.kjs-law.com
Members of Firm: John B. Kralovec; Steven K. Jambois; Allen N. Schwartz; David E. Schwartz. Associates: Robert J. Kelleher; Craig P. Mannarino; Nathan J. Mirocha; Alexander Sukhman; Ryan E. Yagoda; Michael S. Shinsky.
Representing Plaintiff's Medical Malpractice, Personal Injury and Products Liability Law.
See Professional Biographies, CHICAGO, ILLINOIS

Kralovec & Marquard, Chartered, (AV) ... 55 West Monroe Street Suite 1000
Kramer, Andrea S., (AV) ... '55 '78 C.339 B.A. L.597 J.D. [McDermott W.&E.]
Kramer, Bernard S., (AV) ... '54 '81 C.910 A.B. L.145 J.D. [McDermott W.&E.]
Kramer, Cheryl ... '59 '86 C.959 B.B.A. L.966 J.D. Off. of Corp. Coun.
Kramer, Heather L. ... '74 '00 C.352 B.A. L.846 J.D. [Ⓐ Schwartz C.]
Kramer, Jack L. ... '56 '81 C.339 B.A. L.46 J.D. [Mackey&K.]
Kramer, John M. '63 '89 C.164 B.A. L.597 J.D.
Dep. Gen. Coun., Bank One Corp. (Law Dept.)
Kramer, Jon J. ... '— '00 C&L.597 B.A., J.D. [Ⓐ Winston&S.]
Kramer, Ronald J. ... '66 '92 C.475 B.A. L.146 J.D. [Seyfarth S.]
Kramer, Samuel G. ... '64 '91 C.604 B.A. L.597 J.D. [Baker&M.]
Kramer, Terry L. '43 '68 C.375 B.S. L.900 J.D.
Assoc. Exec. Dir., Professional Servs. Grp., Amer. Bar Assn.
Kramer, William J., (AV) '— '92
C.339 B.S. L.597 J.D. [Marshall,G.&B.] (See Pat. Sect.)
Krammer, Reinhold F. ... '— '93 C.339 B.S. L.209 J.D. [Masuda,F.E.&M.]
Kramzyk, Henry S. ... '47 '85 C.031 B.A. L.213 J.D. Asst. Reg. Coun., S.S.A.
Krane, Howard G., (P.C.), (AV) ... '— '57 C.293 A.B. L.145 J.D. [Kirkland&E.]
Krane, Marie Campbell ... '62 '86 C&L.597 B.A., J.D. 4943 S. Woodlawn St.‡
Krantz, Brian ... '76 '04 [Benes S.&K.]
Krantz, Hillary P. ... '71 '01 C&L.597 B.A., J.D. [Ⓐ Freeborn&P.]
Krantz, Kevin R., (AV) ... '59 '91 C.597 B.A. L.424 J.D. [Kessler,K.&C.]
Krasaeath, Rebecca J. ... '77 '04 C.1365 B.S. L.597 J.D. [Ⓐ Jenner&B.]
Krasnove, Jason D. ... '77 '03 C.260 B.A. L.365 J.D. [Ⓐ Garretson&S.]
Krasnow, Frances H., (AV) ... '53 '78 C.477 B.A. L.597 J.D. [Holland&K.]
Krasnow, Henry C., (AV) ... '42 '67 C.477 A.B. L.145 J.D. [Krasnow S.C.]
Krasnow, Melissa J. ... '— '93 C.914 A.B. L.597 J.D. [Schiff H.]

Krasnow Saunders Cornblath, LLP, (AV)
The Boyce Building, 500 North Dearborn Street, Second Floor, 60610
Telephone: 312-755-5700 Fax: 312-755-5720
Email: bizlaw@ksc-law.com URL: http://www.ksc-law.com
Francis A. Beninati; Dina A. Bradford; Glen R. Cornblath; Sue Ann Fishbein; Frederick M. Kaplan; Henry C. Krasnow; Lora K. Sanberg; David A. Saunders; Charles A. Valente; Richard Demarest Yant. Senior Counsel: Robert M. Berger;—Richard A. Janney; Gregory Kane; Margaret A. Lavanish; Stanley F. Wruble, III.
Business Law, Real Estate Development, Leasing and Lending, Land Use, Corporate, Commercial and Municipal Finance, Mergers and Acquisitions, Municipal Law, State and Federal Civil Litigation, Intellectual Property, Intellectual Property Infringement and Trademark Litigation, Wills, Trusts and Estates, Estate Planning for Unmarried Couples, Disability Law.
See Professional Biographies, CHICAGO, ILLINOIS

Krasny, Paula Jill, (BV) ... '63 '88 C.881 A.B. L.597 J.D. [Baker&M.]
Krasny, Philip ... '47 '73 C.339 B.A. L.209 J.D. 150 N. Wacker Dr.
Krasovec, Joseph J., III ... '— '89 C.208 B.S. L.597 J.D. [Schiff H.]
Kratz, Rudy I. ... '67 '93 C&L.339 B.S./B.A., J.D. [Fitch,E.T.&F.]
Kraus, Daniel J. ... '57 '83 C.339 B.S. L.209 J.D. 200 E. Randolph Dr.
Kraus, Daniel L., (AV) ... '58 '84 C&L.494 B.S., J.D. [Greenberg T.]
Kraus, Eugene S. ... '64 '89 C.393 B.A. L.209 J.D. [Scott&K.]
Kraus, Jeffrey T., (AV) '56 '83 C.363 B.A. L.145 J.D.
Loss Prevention Coun., Attorneys' Liability Assurance Society, Inc.
Kraus, Kenneth E., (AV) ... '56 '86 C.608 B.A. L.966 J.D. [Schopf&W.]
Krause, Avrum ... '41 '69 C.1016 B.S. L.365 J.D. 3450 N. Lake Shore Dr.
Krause, Joseph P. ... '55 '83 C.46 B.S.E.E. L.365 J.D. [Ⓐ Ladas&P.] (See Pat. Sect.)
Krause, Michael J. '72 '00 C&L.851 J.D.
(adm. in FL; not adm. in IL) Tax Atty., Abbott Laboratories
Krause, Michele L. ... '69 '94 C.338 B.S. L.146 J.D. [Ⓐ Levenfeld P.]
Krause, Paul ... '— '04 C.221 B.S. L.436 J.D. [Ⓐ Littler M.]
Krauskopf, Mark D., (AV) '61 '86
C.205 B.S. L.365 J.D. Sr. Coun., Bank One Corp. (Law Dept.)

Krauskopf, Stuart P., The Law Offices of, (AV) '59 '85 C.339 B.A. L.146 J.D.
2 North LaSalle Street, Suite 1200, 60602
Telephone: 312-377-9592 Fax: 312-264-5618
Email: stu@stuklaw.com
Litigation, Business Litigation, Business Law, Insurance.
See Professional Biographies, CHICAGO, ILLINOIS

Krauskopf, Tammie G. ... '— '87 C.645 B.A. L.665 J.D. [Ⓒ Bryan C.]
Krauter, Paul A., (BV) ... '70 '95 C.339 B.A. L.365 J.D. [Ⓐ Roddy,L.&Z.]
Krauze, Raymond M. ... '— '03 C.94 B.A. L.276 J.D [Ⓐ Michael B.&F.]
Kravets, Alan R., (AV) '40 '66
C&L.477 B.B.A., J.D. Pres. & Gen. Coun., Sheldon Good & Co.
Kravitz, David E. ... '68 '94 C.966 B.A. L.146 J.D. [Ⓐ Iwan C.H.H.&V.]
Kravitz, Tamar Gela '60 '84 C.1044 B.A. L.1003 J.D.
Mktg. Dir., The Raterman Grp. Ltd.
Krawczak, Dennis M. '51 '79
C.424 B.A. L.365 J.D. Asst. Dir., Prof. Educ., Amer. Bar Assn.
Krawczyk, Jolanda B. ... '78 '03 C.209 B.S. L.365 J.D. [Ⓐ Hill G.&B.]
Krawiec, Kimberly Dawn '65 '93 C.576 B.A. L.276 J.D.
(adm. in NY; not adm. in IL) Northwestern Univ. Sch. of Law
Krawiec, Martin P. ... '50 '79 C.424 B.A. L.365 J.D. 5357 W. Devon Ave.
Krawitz, Michael J. ... '64 '89 C&L.339 B.A., J.D. 2 N. LaSalle Street
Krawzak, Helen M., (BV) ... '51 '77 C&L.424 A.B., J.D. CNA Ins. Cos.
Krebs, Peter ... '73 '03 C.602 B.A. L.608 J.D. [Ⓐ Skadden,A.S.M.&F.]
Krebs, Robert E. ... '— '02 C.858 B.A. L.112 J.D. [Ⓐ Jones D.]
Krebs, Thomas P. ... '— '95 C.602 B.A. L.608 J.D. [Foley&L.]
Kreger, Donald J., (AV) ... '— '63 C&L.209 B.S., J.D. [Schiff H.]
Kreger, Mark A. ... '55 '80 C.1365 B.A. L.245 J.D. [Lord,B.&B.]
Krehbiel, Karen Rose ... '76 '02 C.197 B.A. L.477 J.D. [Ⓐ Berger S.]
Kreid, Christopher A. "Kit" ... '61 '86 C.339 B.S. L.910 J.D. [Metge,S.&K.]
Kreisberg, Howard L. ... '58 '83 C.339 B.S. L.146 J.D. Price Waterhouse
Kreisler, Barry B. ... '45 '70 C.597 B.S. L.145 J.D. [B.B.Kreisler]
Kreisler, Barry B., P.C, Law Offices of ... 3001 W. Armitage Ave.
Kreisman, Bruce S. ... '57 '82 C.339 B.S. L.477 J.D. [Goldstein&F.]
Kreisman, Robert D., (AV) ... '50 '76 C.502 B.A. L.365 J.D. [Kreisman]

Kreisman Law Offices, (AV)
A Professional Corporation
55 West Monroe Street Suite 3720, 60603-5011
Telephone: 312-346-0045 Fax: 312-346-2380
Email: bob@robertkreisman.com URL: http://www.robertkreisman.com

(This Listing Continued)

Kreisman Law Offices (Continued)

Robert D. Kreisman.
Language: Spanish.
Practice in all State and Federal Courts. Plaintiff's Personal Injury Litigation, Medical Negligence, Health Care, Wrongful Death Litigation, Premises Liability, Vehicular Accidents, Construction Accidents, Employment Litigation, Product Liability, Commercial Litigation.
See Professional Biographies, CHICAGO, ILLINOIS

Kreissl, J. F., Jr. ....'15 '39 L.209 LL.B. 4921 N. Keeler Ave.
Kreiter, Mitchell D. .... '48 '78 C.966 B.A. L.365 J.D. 70 W. Hubbard St.
Kreiter, Byck and Associates, LLC ....180 W. Washington
Kreitzer, Joshua S. ....'72 '97 C.309 B.A. L.597 J.D. [M.J.Lane]
Krejci, Erin .... '79 '04 C.339 B.S,. L.276 J.D. [DLPiper R.G.C.U.]
Kreliner, Jason .... '74 '00 C.1349 B.A. L.494 J.D. [DLPiper R.G.C.U.]
Kreloff, Michael A., (AV) ....'46 '71 C&L.339 B.S., J.D. Dir. of Policy
Kremin, David K. '55 '83 C.339 B.S. L.146 J.D.
[D.K.Kremin&Assoc.] & [1800AskALawyer] (⊙Chicago)
Kremin, David K. '55 '83
C.339 B.S. L.146 J.D. [1-800-Ask-A-Lawyer&Assoc.] (⊙Chicago)

Kremin, David K., & Associates, P.C.
221 N. LaSalle Street, Suite 1900, 60601
Telephone: 312-456-9000 Toll Free: 1-800-ASK-A-LAWYER (1-800-275-2529) Fax: 312-456-9900
Email: ASKALAWYER@aol.com URL: http://www.1800askalawyer.com
David K. Kremin.
Personal Injury, Litigation, Automobile Accidents, Work Accidents, Premises Liability, Product Liability, Fire and Casualty Cases, Medical Malpractice, Birth Defects, Dram Shop, Workers Compensation, Catastrophic Injuries, Spinal Cord, Airplane Crash and Slip and Fall, Wrongful Death.
See Professional Biographies, CHICAGO, ILLINOIS

Krent, Harold J. '56 '83 C.674 A.B. L.569 J.D.
(adm. in DC; not adm. in IL) Assoc. Prof., Chicago-Kent School of Law
Kress, Michael J. ....'44 '69 C.801 B.A. L.365 J.D. Asst. State Atty.
Kresse, William J. ....'58 '85 C.602 B.B.A. L.339 J.D. 10221 S. California Ave.
Kretchman, John E. .... '20 '54 C.8 B.S. L.7 B.L. United Ins. Co. of Amer.

Kretchmar, S. Randolph
(See Wilmette)

Krichiver, Bernard M. .... '16 '57 C.339 B.S. L.146 LL.B. Ill. Dept. of Public Aid
Krichiver, David M., Law Offices of ....'10 '33 C&L.145 Ph.B., J.D. 1 N. LaSalle St.
Krider, Scott B. ....'— '85 C.966 B.S. L.365 J.D. [Querrey&H.]
Kriegel, Jeremy R. '— '95 C.696 B.S.M.E. L.910 J.D.
[Marshall,G.&B.] (See Pat. Sect.)
Krieger, Cameron R. .... '74 '01 C.293 B.A. L.145 J.D. [Goodsmith G.&U.]
Kriezelman, Jeffrey, (BV) .... '47 '73 C.589 B.S.Ed. L.146 J.D. 20 N. Clark St., Ste. 725
Kriha, Darcy L. .... '68 '92 C.530 B.A. L.365 J.D. [Franczek S.]
Krikorian, Charles R. ....'61 '95 C.339 B.S. L.209 J.D. [Katten M.R.] (Pat.)
Krimbel, Rosemary, (BV) '53 '90 C.238 B.S. L.145 J.D.
Asst. Corp. Coun., Contracts & Aviation Div.
Krinsky, Steven P. .... '56 '83 C.339 B.S. L.365 J.D. Ronald A. Landsman & Co.
Krippner, Timothy L., (BV) ....'65 '90 C.339 B.A. L.209 J.D. [Segal M.S.&M.]
Krishnamoorthi, S. Raja ....'— '00 C.674 B.S.E. L.309 J.D. [Kirkland&E.]
Krisik, Dennis J. .... '50 '80 C.339 B.A. L.589 J.D. 208 S. LaSalle St.
Krislov, Clinton A., (AV) ....'49 '74 C.597 B.A. L.188 J.D. [Krislov&Assoc.]

Krislov & Associates, Ltd., (AV)
20 North Wacker Drive, Suite 1350, 60606
Telephone: 312-606-0500 Telecopier: 312-606-0207
Email: mail@krislovlaw.com URL: http://www.krislovlaw.com
Clinton A. Krislov;—Kenneth T. Goldstein; Michael R. Karnuth; Jessica J. Mead; Jason P. Stiehl; W. Joel Vander Vliet; Elizabeth Neugent-Dixon.
Trials and Appeals. Class and Derivative Actions in Pension, Municipal, Securities Law, Tax Litigation and Consumer Law, Public Interest and Whistleblower Cases.
See Professional Biographies, CHICAGO, ILLINOIS

Kriss, Robert J., (AV) .... '53 '78 C.188 B.A. L.309 J.D. [Mayer,B.R.&M.]
Krit, Jonathan J., (BV) ....'64 '89 C&L.597 B.S., J.D. [Emrich&D.] (See Pat. Sect.)
Kritt, Lisa Helene ....'63 '89 C.927 B.S. L.861 J.D. Stathies Construction
Krivicich, John A., (AV) .... '55 '80 C.597 B.S. L.339 J.D. [Donohue B.M.&S.]
Krizman, Tracy Hensler .... '67 '94 C.473 B.A. L.146 J.D. 205 W. Randolph
Krkljes, Stevan .... '61 '88 C.339 B.S. L.146 J.D. 1 E. Wacker Dr., Ste. 35
Krob, Brian E. ....'— '97 C.378 B.A. L.339 J.D. [Ungaretti&H.]
Kroeger, David M. .... '65 '92 C.602 B.A. L.339 J.D. [Jenner&B.]
Kroft, Brandon J. ....'72 '99 C.879 B.A. L.209 J.D. [Cassiday,S.&G.]
Krohn, Adam J. ....'68 '94 C.37 B.A. L.112 J.D. [Krohn&M.]
Krohn, Micah R. .... '59 '93 C.1036 B.A. L.1398 J.D. [Frank/ G.]
Krohn, William O., (AV) ....'16 '48 C.690 B.S. L.146 J.D. [Krohn&J.]
Krohn & Jenkins, (AV) ....175 W. Jackson Blvd.
Krohn & Moss, Ltd. ....120 West Madison, 10th Floor
Krol, John ....'72 '97 C.339 B.A. L.209 J.D. [Katten M.R.]
Krol, Katarzyna A. .... '77 '02 C.340 B.A. L.146 J.D. 550 W. Washington Blvd., Ste. 1600
Krol, Kenneth A. .... '55 '85 C.72 B.A. L.146 J.D. Martin E. Segal Co.
Krol, Michael A. ....'65 '04 C&L.477 B.Sc., J.D. [Welsh&K.] (See Pat. Sect.)
Krolick, Jordan E. .... '68 '93 C.339 B.S. L.477 J.D. Dir., Corp. Strag., McDonald's Corp.
Krolick, Marshall D., (AV) ....'38 '62 C.221 B.A. L.597 J.D. [Deutsch,L.&E.]
Kroll, Barry L., (AV) ....'34 '58 C&L.477 A.B., J.D. [Williams M.&J.]
Kroll, Jeffrey J., (AV) .... '64 '90 C&L.209 B.S., J.D. [Clifford]
Kroll, Robert A. .... '37 '62 C&L.597 B.S., J.D. [Kroll&R.]
Kroll, Steven L., (AV) .... '59 '84 C.197 B.A. L.477 J.D. [Wolin&R.] (⊙Schaumburg)
Kroll & Rubin, Ltd. ....415 N. LaSalle St.
Kromelow, Marc R., (AV) '35 '59
C.477 B.A. L.976 J.D. Suite 3800, One East Wacker Drive
Kromkowski, Mark A. ....'70 '98 C&L.602 B.A., J.D. [Wildman,H.A.&D.]
Kromm, Matthew Carl ....'76 '01 C.339 B.S. L.146 J.D. 77 W. Walker, 50th Fl.
Kron, Jonathan D. ....'60 '85 C&L.339 B.S., J.D. [Mayer,B.R.&M.]
Kronenberg, David ....'56 '02 C.1375 B.S. L.146 J.D. [Baker&M.]
Kronenwetter, Patrick J., (AV) .... '54 '78 C.602 B.A. L.665 J.D. [G.E.W.Kelter,Jr.]
Kroning, Linda J. ....'49 '75 C.914 B.A. L.276 J.D. [McNish,K.&K.]
Kronsnoble, Joseph M. ....'— '91 C.966 B.B.A. L.145 J.D. [Latham&W.]
Kroot, Jason M. .... '72 '99 C.846 B.S. L.146 J.D. 1 E Wacker Dr Ste 2920
Kroot, Kenneth A., (AV) .... '56 '81 C.373 B.A. L.477 J.D. [Jenner&B.]
Kropik, Chas. T. .... '10 '37 C&L.597 B.S., J.D. 120 S. LaSalle St.
Krucks, William N., (AV) .... '— '76 C.861 B.A. L.500 J.D. [Freeborn&P.] (⊙Skokie)
Krueger, Herbert W. .... '48 '74 C.959 B.A. L.145 J.D. [Mayer,B.R.&M.]
Krueger, James P. .... '58 '93 C.999 B.A. L.46 J.D. [Fitch,E.T.&F.] (See Pat. Sect.)
Krueger, Ryan Gray .... '71 '96 C&L.339 B.A., J.D. 120 N. LaSalle Street
Krueger, Steven Philip .... '62 '87 C.927 B.S. L.365 J.D. Asst. State's Atty.
Krueger, Thomas J. .... '59 '84 C.602 B.A. L.893 J.D. Asst. Reg. Coun., U.S. EPA
Krug, Leonard A. ....'32 '61 C.502 A.B. L.145 J.D. 5467 Ridgewood Ct.
Krug, Robert F., Jr., (AV) .... '48 '73 C.589 B.S. L.339 J.D. [Carponelli&K.]
Krug, Robert W. ....'70 '99 C.339 B.A. L.209 J.D. [Fragomen,D.B.&L.]
Kruger, Marvin J. .... '40 '66 C.477 B.B.A. L.424 J.D. Continental Bk.
Krugly, Ruth E. ....'— '83 C.1036 A.B. L.145 J.D. [Schiff H.]
Krugman, Kimberly A. .... '65 '95 C.36 B.S. L.809 J.D. [Much S.F.D.A.&R.]
Kruizenga, Lori J., (CV) .... '57 '90 C&L.589 B.S., J.D. 208 S. La Salle St., Ste. 1650
Kruley, Harold ....'10 '34 C&L.145 Ph.B., J.D. 1 IBM Plaza
Kruley, Michael F. '47 '73 C.145 B.A. L.1066 J.D.
Spec. Asst., U.S. Dept. of Health & Human Servs.
Krull, Angel M. .... '76 '01 C.98 B.A. L.146 J.D. [Robinson C.&C.]
Krull, Frederick John ....'61 '86 C.123 B.A. L.801 J.D. Ernst & Young
Krull, Robert J., Law Offices of, (AV) '44 '69
C.347 B.S. L.1119 J.D. 200 North Dearborn Avenue, Suite 1202
Krumdick, Eric A., (BV) ....'59 '85 C.879 B.A. L.146 J.D. [Fraterrigo,B.F.&K.]
Krupin O'Brien LLC
203 North La Salle Street Suite 2100 (⊙Phoenix, AZ; Wash., DC; Boston, MA; New York, NY)
Krupka, Robert G., (P.C.), (AV) '— '74 C.276 B.S. L.145 J.D.
[Kirkland&E.] (Pat.) (⊙L.A., CA; Wash., DC)
Krupoff, Jana .... '— '00 C.1119 B.S. L.146 J.D. [Sonnenschein N.&R.]
Krupp, Peter C. .... '61 '86 C.20 B.A. L.477 J.D. [Skadden,A.S.M.&F.]
Kruse, Alvin L., (AV) .... '43 '69 C&L.597 B.A., J.D. [Seyfarth S.]
Kruse, Corinne R. .... '66 '92 C.98 B.A. L.365 J.D. V.P. of Claims, ISBA Mutual Ins. Co.
Kruss, Richard S. .... '65 '98 C.339 B.S.E. L.365 J.D. Asst. Co. Pub. Def.
Kruszynski, Julie A. ....'— '04 C.339 B.S. L.209 J.D. [Anderson,R.]
Kryder, Andrew S., Law Office .... '72 '98 C.608 L.209 134 N. LaSalle St., Ste. 1515
Krzak, Michael S. ....'70 '97 C.1183 B.A. L.209 J.D. [Clifford]
Kuban, Anne Scrivner ....'— '88 C.207 B.A. L.910 J.D. [Anderson,R.]
Kubasiak, Daniel J., (AV) .... '49 '81 C.973 B.A. L.424 J.D. [Kubasiak,F.R.&R.]
Kubasiak, Gerald E., (AV) .... '40 '68 C.932 B.B.A. L.424 J.D. [Kubasiak,F.R.&R.]

Kubasiak, Fylstra, Reizen & Rotunno, Professional Corporation, (AV) BR
Two First National Plaza, 20 South Clark Street, Suite 2900, 60603
Telephone: 312-630-9600 Fax: 312-630-7939
URL: http://www.kfrrlaw.com
Gerald E. Kubasiak; Raymond A. Fylstra; Daniel J. Kubasiak; Richard S. Reizen; Steven J. Rotunno; Gregory A. Thorpe; John A. Dienner, III; Daniel C. McCabe;—John C. Anderson; Clarke M. Gillespie, III; Noël P. Goudreau; Barry P. Kaltenbach; Robert C. Kimmeth, Jr.; Manuel J. Placencia, Jr.; Jeannie M. Ridings; Eric P. Sparks. Of Counsel: Ellen Chapelle.
General Practice including representation of Business Entities (Formation, Operation, Acquisition and Merger), Commercial Litigation (Ownership Disputes, Contract, Trust and Estate, Construction, Securities and Financial Litigation), Taxation (Federal, State, Local and International), and Commercial Real Estate (Finance, Construction, Defaults and Workouts and Environmental Matters), Municipal Law (Development Agreements, Land Use Planning and Governmental Relations).
See Professional Biographies, CHICAGO, ILLINOIS

Kubes, Jeffrey T., (AV) ....'56 '81 C.234 B.S. L.589 J.D. [Crisham&K.]
Kubes, Kenneth G. ....'— '02 C.597 B.A. L.1119 J.D. [Sachnoff&W.]
Kubiatowski, Steve A. .... '35 '63 C.597 B.S. L.209 LL.B. 5339 N. Milwaukee Ave.
Kubik, James J. ....'45 '70 C&L.424 B.S., J.D. Asst. U.S. Atty.
Kuby, Raymond ....'31 '61 C.33 B.A. L.145 J.D. 5842 S. Stony Island Ave.‡
Kucera, William R. .... '72 '97 C.165 B.A. L.597 J.D. [Mayer,B.R.&M.]
Kuchii, Craig M. ....'72 '04 C.861 B.S. L.597 J.D. [Welsh&K.]
Kuchler, Mark A., (AV) ....'64 '91 C.436 B.S. L.424 J.D. [Ronaldson&K.]
Kuczma, Linda A. '56 '81
C.742 B.A.Biol. L.424 J.D. [Wallenstein W.&R.] (See Pat. Sect.)
Kuczwara, Thomas P. ....'51 '76 C.424 A.B. L.790 J.D. Postal Inspec. Atty.
Kuehl, Robert Thomas .... '72 '00 C.747 B.A. L.879 J.D. [Regas,F.&D.]
Kuehn, Robert O. .... '43 '69 C.1106 B.A. L.424 J.D. [Karavidas] (⊙Barrington)
Kuehn, William R. .... '70 '95 C.197 B.A. L.146 J.D. [Karavidas] (⊙Barrington)
Kuehnel, Kathi A. '57 '82 C.597 B.A. L.188 J.D.
(adm. in MI; not adm. in IL) Dir., State Govt. Rel., Ford Motor Co.
Kuelper, Jean Dudek, (AV) '54 '80
C.602 B.S.E.E. L.424 J.D. [McAndrews,H.&M.] (See Pat. Sect.)
Kuenn, Neil J. .... '46 '73 C.755 B.A. L.209 J.D. [Keeley,K.&R.]
Kuenstler, John F., (CV) ....'66 '93 C.339 B.A. L.910 J.D. [Wildman,H.A.&D.]
Kuffer, Dorene A. .... '58 '85 C.338 B.S. L.339 J.D. Atty. Supervisor
Kugel, Robert W. ....'42 '85 C.589 B.S. L.365 J.D. CFO, Ill Housing Develop. Auth.
Kugler, Isabel A. '71 '04 C.112 B.A. L.1117 J.D.
(adm. in CA; not adm. in IL) [Fragomen,D.B.&L.]
Kugler, Jerry A. .... '52 '78 C.339 B.A. L.365 J.D. 3376 N. Central Avenue
Kuh, Steven H., (AV) .... '59 '84 C.860 A.B. L.276 J.D. [S.H.Kuh]

Kuh, Steven H., P.C., (AV)
One North Franklin Street, Suite 650, 60606-3420
Telephone: 312-236-5500 Facsimile: 312-236-3462
Email: stevenkuh@hotmail.com
Steven H. Kuh.
Commercial Litigation. Employment Litigation. General Practice.
See Professional Biographies, CHICAGO, ILLINOIS

Kuhlman, George A. '47 '79 C.755 A.B. L.1003 J.D.
(adm. in OH; not adm. in IL) Ethics Coun., Amer. Bar Assn.
Kuhlman, Richard S., (AV) ....'43 '69 C.339 B.A. L.597 J.D. [Wolin&R.]
Kuhn, Deborah L. ....'69 '94 C&L.228 M.A., J.D. MCI Worldcom
Kuhn, James Michael .... '57 '87 C.927 B.S. L.146 J.D. U.S. Dept. of Justice
Kuhn, John D., (BV) ....'36 '84 C&L.424 B.S., J.D. [Fedota C.]
Kuhn, Kevin J. .... '62 '92 C.589 B.S. L.365 J.D. [Vedder,P.K.&K.]
Kuhn, William L. .... '75 '99 C.37 B.A. L.309 J.D. [McGuirewoods]
Kuhns, Thomas Otman, (AV) .... '— '80 C.390 B.A. L.597 J.D. [Kirkland&E.]
Kuhr, Marilyn T. '48 '75 C&L.424 B.A., J.D.
Admin. Law J., State Human Rights Comm.
Kuhs, Muriel, (AV) .... '41 '78 C.188 A.B. L.365 J.D. [Davis F.Z.K.M.M.&R.]
Kujawa, Jerome ....'— '87 C.293 B.A. L.424 J.D. Assoc. Reg. Coun.
Kujawa, Philip Reed, (AV) ....'63 '91 C.424 B.S. L.146 J.D. [Hinshaw&C.]
Kujundjic, Vildana ....'74 '00 C.339 B.S. L.146 J.D. [DLPiper R.G.C.U.]
Kukac, Jennifer J. ....'70 '99 C.172 B.A. L.146 J.D. Natl. Treasury Employees Union
Kukankos, John A. ....'46 '74 C.602 B.A. L.597 J.D. [Coghlan K.C.]
Kuker, Robert J. ....'63 '89 C.742 B.A. L.365 J.D. Urban Street Properties, LLC
Kula, Keith M., (BV) .... '56 '81 C.72 B.A. L.209 J.D. 20 N. Clark St., Ste. 820
Kulas, James A. .... '49 '84 C.679 B.S. L.146 J.D. Sr. Labor Coun., Tribune Co.
Kulas, Julian E. .... '33 '59 C&L.209 B.S., J.D. 2329 W. Chicago Ave.
Kulas, Paul J. ....'60 '91 C.927 B.A. L.365 J.D. 2329 W. Chicago Ave.
Kulek, Gershon S., Attorney at Law '— '82
C.802 B.A. L.982 J.D. 432 N. Clark St., Ste. 305
Kulevich, Frederick J. .... '65 '93 C.920 B.S. L.365 J.D. Dep. Compl. Offr., Aon Corp.
Kulis, Gregory E. .... '56 '81 C.602 B.B.A. L.209 J.D. 30 N. LaSalle St., Ste. 2140
Kull, Geary W. ....'46 '75 C.37 B.S.B.A. L.365 J.D. 910 W. Jackson Blvd.
Kulpa, Lorraine A. '39 '75 C&L.107 B.A., LL.B.
(adm. in MI; not adm. in IL) 130 E. Randolph St.‡

Kulwiec, Alexia M. ... ’70 ’96 C.602 B.A. L.146 J.D. [🄰 Baum S.A.&N.]
Kulwin, Jeffrey R. ... ’70 ’96 C.424 B.A. L.221 J.D. [🄰 Kulwin&Assoc.]
Kulwin, Shelly B., (AV) ... ’54 ’79 C.339 A.B. L.424 J.D. [Kulwin&Assoc.]
Kulwin & Associates, (AV) ... 161 North Clark Street, Suite 2500
Kumar, Sapna ... ’— ’03 C.846 B.S. L.145 J.D. [🄰 Pattishall,M.N.H.&G.]
Kumer, Kathleen ... ’71 ’98 C.597 B.A. L.665 J.D. Coun., Aon Corp.
Kumlin, Richard L. ... ’40 ’65 C.339 L.209 J.D. 205 W. Randolph
Kummer, Scott W. ... ’71 ’00 C.959 B.A L.209 J.D. 20 South Clark Street, Suite 500
Kummerer, William A., (AV) ... ’63 ’88 C.352 B.A. L.276 J.D. [Vedder,P.K.&K.]
Kumor, John ... ’75 ’00 C.145 A.B. L.910 J.D. [Kumor&H.]
Kumor & Hipple, P.C. ... 8711 West Bryn Mawr Avenue, Ste. 708
Kundmueller, Michelle M. ... ’— ’04 C.1418 B.A. L.602 J.D. [🄰 Wildman,H.A.&D.]
Kunetka, Julie A. ’62 ’89
C.339 B.S. L.477 J.D. Associate General Counsel, Bank of America
Kunkel, Paul J., (AV) ... ’56 ’92 C.674 B.A. L.597 J.D. [🄲 Mayer,B.R.&M.]
Kunkel, William R., (AV) ... ’56 ’81 C.190 B.S. L.309 J.D. [Skadden,A.S.M.&F.]
Kunkle, William J. ... ’41 ’69 C&L.597 B.A., J.D. Cir.J.
Kunshek, Rudy ... ’45 ’82 C.357 B.A. L.365 J.D. Commonwealth Edison Co.
Kuntz, Richard M., (BV) ... ’50 ’84 C.923 B.A. L.273 J.D. [Bollinger,R.&G.]
Kuo, Emily J. ... ’73 ’97 C.575 B.S. L.145 J.D. [Harrison&H.]
Kuo, Joseph M. ... ’68 ’93 C.597 B.S. L.861 J.D. [Olson&H.] (See Pat. Sect.)
Kuo, Winnie J. ... ’72 ’99 C.976 B.A. L.910 J.D. Two North LaSalle Street, Suite 2200
Kupelian, Sandra E. ... ’65 ’90 C.589 B.A. L.339 J.D. [🄲 Cassiday,S.&G.]
Kupets, David J., (AV) ... ’52 ’90 C.999 B.A. L.365 J.D. [Kupets&D.]
Kupets & DeCaro, P.C., Law Offices of, (AV) ... 30 North LaSalle Street Suite 4020
Kupferberg, Lloyd S., (AV) ... ’31 ’56 C.966 B.S. L.309 J.D. [🄲 Schwartz C.]

Kupiec, Mark J., (AV) ’— ’75 C.597 B.A. L.365 J.D.
77 West Washington, Suite 519, 60602
Telephone: 312-541-1878 Fax: 312-641-1745
URL: http://www.chicago-zoning.com
Zoning, Planning and Land Use, Eminent Domain, Condemnation, Real Estate, Building Code Compliance, Business Licensing.
See Professional Biographies, CHICAGO, ILLINOIS

Kupka, James J. ... ’52 ’76 C.504 B.A. L.146 J.D. [🄰 Conklin&C.]
Kuppersmith, Michael P., (AV) ... ’59 ’84 C.280 B.A. L.846 J.D. [DLPiper R.G.C.U.]
Kuprys, Saulius V. ... ’52 ’79 C.424 B.A. L.146 J.D. [Henehan,D.&I.]
Kurasch, Donald A., (AV) ... ’45 ’72 C.293 B.A. L.339 J.D. [Kurasch&K.]
Kurasch, Teri J. ’56 ’79 C.339 B.S. L.146 J.D.
V.P./Assoc. Gen. Coun., Fed. Reserve Bk. of Chgo.

Kurasch & Klein, (AV)
188 West Randolph Street, Suite 1201, 60601 ⊙
Telephone: 312-372-7250 Fax: 312-372-7254
Email: dkurasch@chicagopilaw.com URL: http://www.chicagopilaw.com
Members of Firm: Donald A. Kurasch; Daniel Klein. Associate: Elissa A. Tisdahl.
Personal Injury; Accidents, Automobile Accidents and Injuries; Wrongful Death, Workers Compensation, Medical Malpractice, Nursing Home Accidents, Catastrophic Injury, Trusts Accidents, Motorcycle Accidents, Boating Accidents.
Milwaukee, Wisconsin Office: 1640 North Jackson Street, 53202. Telephone: 414-313-5677. Fax: 414-277-0907.
See Professional Biographies, CHICAGO, ILLINOIS

Kurcz, Jennifer M. ... ’— ’03 C&L.546 B.S., J.D. [🄰 McDonnell B.H.&B.]
Kurfirst, Leonard S., (AV) ... ’59 ’84 C.813 B.A. L.1119 J.D. [Wildman,H.A.&D.]
Kurilla, Marlene A., (AV) ... ’55 ’88 C.381 B.B.A. L.365 J.D. [🄰 Mora,B.W.&U.]
Kurland, Amy L. ... ’— ’85 C.339 B.S. L.966 J.D. [DLPiper R.G.C.U.]
Kurland, Joseph G. ... ’44 ’69 C.1024 B.A. L.146 J.D. Asst. States Atty.
Kurlander, Michele S., (AV) ... ’44 ’69 C.477 B.A. L.597 J.D. [Kurlander&G.]

Kurlander & Grippo, LLP, (AV)
155 North Michigan Avenue, Suite 620, 60601
Telephone: 312-616-4246 Facsimile: 312-239-9343
URL: http://www.kurlanderandgrippo.com
Michele S. Kurlander; Theodore W. Grippo, Jr. Of Counsel: William F. Coale (1921-1989); Amos J. Coffman, Jr.; Leon E. Lindenbaum.
General Civil Practice, Antitrust and Trade Regulation, Civil Litigation, Commercial Litigation, Corporate Law, Business Law, Bankruptcy, Employee Benefits, Family Law, Divorce, Taxation, Insurance, Labor Law, Mergers and Acquisitions, Product Liability, Real Estate, Commercial Real Estate, Trusts and Estates, Trademarks, Copyrights.
See Professional Biographies, CHICAGO, ILLINOIS

Kurpis, Sue Roberts ... ’48 ’92 C.112 B.A. L.146 J.D. [S.R.Kurpis]
Kurpis, Sue Roberts, P.C. ... 3845 W. 58th Place
Kurson, Amy C. ... ’68 ’95 C.92 B.S. L.146 J.D. [🄲 Greenberg T.]
Kurtenbach, Douglas J., (P.C.) ... ’— ’86 C.698 B.A. L.178 J.D. [Kirkland&E.]
Kurtenbach, Jerome P. ... ’53 ’86 C.174 B.S. L.276 J.D. [Kurtenbach&Assoc.]
Kurtenbach & Associates ... 321 S. Plymouth Court
Kurth, Dale R. ... ’52 ’84 C&L.339 B.S., J.D. [🄰 Tressler,S.M.&P.]
Kurtis, William H. ’40 ’66 C.378 B.S. L.900 J.D.
(adm. in KS; not adm. in IL) WBBM-TV
Kurtos, Linda P. ... ’66 ’91 C.475 B.S. L.597 J.D. [🄰 Eimer S.K.&S.]
Kurtz, Brian J. ... ’72 ’97 C.910 B.A. L.273 J.D. [🄰 Matkov,S.M.&G.]
Kurtz, William A. ... ’27 ’59 C.597 B.S. L.365 J.D. CNA Plaza
Kurtzon, Michael S., (AV) ... ’47 ’73 C.188 A.B. L.145 J.D. [Schwartz C.]
Kurzeja, Michael L. ’70 ’97 C&L.589 B.A., J.D.
Sr. Coun., Bank One Corp. (Law Dept.)
Kus, Edward J., (AV) ... ’53 ’78 C.209 B.A. L.589 J.D. [Shefsky&F.]
Kushen, Amy R. ... ’— ’92 C.477 B.A. L.424 J.D. [🄲 Wilkow&W.]
Kushner, Colleen A. ... ’— ’92 C.339 B.S. L.884 J.D. [🄰 Chapman&C.]
Kushnir, David M. ... ’72 ’97 C.477 B.A. L.424 J.D. [🄰 Katten M.R.]
Kushnir, Melanie Leigh ... ’73 ’00 C.473 B.A. L.608 J.D. ABA Ctr. for Pro Bono
Kuska, Tina ... ’— ’02 C.209 B.S. L.146 J.D. [🄰 Gardner C.&D.]
Kusman, George D. ... ’34 ’67 C&L.209 LL.B. 5032 S. Archer Ave.
Kusper, Stanley T., Jr. ... ’35 ’60 C.602 B.A. L.597 J.D. [Kusper&R.]
Kusper, Stewart T., (AV) ... ’64 ’91 C.602 B.A. L.146 J.D. [Katten M.R.]
Kusper & Raucci, Chartered, (AV) ... Ste. 3400, 30 N. La Salle St.
Kuta, Alexander E., Jr. ... ’34 ’58 C.742 B.A. L.209 J.D. 6116 N. Naples Ave.‡
Kuta, Ann Marie ... ’55 ’79 C.707 B.A. L.352 J.D. Assoc. Dir., Chgo NOW
Kuta, Jeffrey, (AV) ... ’— ’72 C&L.145 B.A., J.D. [Schiff H.]

Kutak Rock LLP, (AV)
One South Wacker Drive, 60606-4614 ⊙
Telephone: 312-602-4100 Facsimile: 312-602-4101
URL: http://www.kutakrock.com
Partners: Jerry B. Wallack; Robert M. Star; Dennis L. Holsapple; Jay Gilbert; Kevin L. Barney.
Civil Litigation and Bankruptcy, Public Finance, Corporate and Structured Finance, Banking and Commercial Lending, Real Estate Law, Taxation Law, Health Care and Hospital Law.
Atlanta, Georgia Office: Suite 2100, 225 Peachtree Street, NE, 30303-1731. Telephone: 404-222-4600. Facsimile: 404-222-4654.
Denver, Colorado Office: Suite 3100, 1801 California Street, 80202-2658. Telephone: 303-297-2400. Facsimile: 303-292-7799.

(This Listing Continued)

Kutak Rock LLP (Continued)
Des Moines, Iowa Office: Suite 124, Highland Building, 4201 Westown Parkway, Des Moines, 50266-6720. Telephone: 515-224-1266. Facsimile: 515-457-7669.
Fayetteville, Arkansas Office: The Three Sisters Building, 214 West Dickson Street, 72701-5221. Telephone: 501-973-4200. Facsimile: 501-973-0007.
Kansas City, Missouri Office: Valencia Place, Suite 200, 444 West 47th Street, 64112-1914. Telephone: 816-960-0090. Telefax: 816-960-0041.
Little Rock, Arkansas Office: Suite 1100, 425 West Capitol Avenue, 72201-3409. Telephone: 501-975-3000. Facsimile: 501-975-3001.
Los Angeles, California Office: Suite 3000, 555 West Fifth Street, 90013-1010. Telephone: 213-996-8478. Facsimile: 213-996-8479.
Oklahoma City, Oklahoma Office: Suite 475, 6305 Waterford Boulevard, 73118-1116. Telephone: 405-848-2475. Facsimile: 405-842-5748.
Omaha, Nebraska Office: The Omaha Building, 1650 Farnam Street, 68102-2186. Telephone: 402-346-6000. Facsimile: 402-346-1148.
Scottsdale, Arizona Office: Suite 300, 8601 N. Scottsdale Road, 85253-2742. Telephone: 480-429-5000. Facsimile: 480-429-5001.
Washington, D.C. Office: Suite 1000, 1101 Connecticut Avenue, NW, 20036-4374. Telephone: 202-828-2400. Facsimile: 202-828-2488.
Irvine, California Office: Suite 1100, 18201 Von Karman Avenue, 92612-1077. Telephone: 949-417-0999. Facsimile: 949-417-5394.
Pasadena, California Office: Suite 308, 201 South Lake Avenue, 91101-3004. Telephone: 626-432-1630. Facsimile: 626-432-1614.
Richmond, Virginia Office: Bank of America Center, Suite 800, 1111 East Main Street, 23219-3103. Telephone: 804-644-0313. Facsimile: 804-783-6192.
Wichita, Kansas Office: Suite 370, 8301 East 21st Street North, 67206-2935. Telephone: 316-609-7900. Facsimile: 316-630-8021.
See Professional Biographies, CHICAGO, ILLINOIS

Kutnick, Joshua Bateman ... ’72 ’99 C.966 B.A. L.146 J.D. [J.B.Kutnick]
Kutnick, Joshua B., The Law Office of ... 820 W. Jackson Blvd., Ste. 300
Kutty, Thoufiq A. ... ’76 ’03 C.597 B.A. L.145 J.D. [🄰 Skadden,A.S.M.&F.]
Kutyla, Elizabeth Y. ’62 ’87 C&L.145 A.B., J.D.
Gen. Coun., Sr. V.P. & Sec., Barton Inc.
Kutylo, Janine E. ... ’72 ’00 C.30 B.A. L.424 J.D. [🄰 Clausen M.]
Kuzas, Robert D., (BV) ... ’61 ’89 C.1191 B.A. L.365 J.D. [Wise&K.]
Kuznetsky, Paul H. ... ’56 ’81 C.339 B.A. L.209 J.D. [🄰 Kaplan,v.&M.]
Kuzniar, Jason M. ... ’73 ’99 C.424 B.A. L.146 J.D. [🄰 Wilson E.M.E.&D.]
Kuzniar, Pamela J., (BV) ... ’57 ’91 C&L.424 B.S., J.D. [Kalcheim H.&K.]
Kwall, Roberta ... ’55 ’80 C.103 A.B. L.659 J.D. Prof., DePaul Univ. Coll. Of Law
Kwan, Angela L. ... ’69 ’01 C.339 B.A. L.146 J.D. 4001 West Devon Avenue
Kwasniewski, Charles V. ... ’57 ’96 C.801 B.S. L.209 J.D. [🄰 Pyes&C.]
Kwasteniet, Ross ... ’— ’02 C.114 B.A. L.477 J.D. [🄰 Kirkland&E.]
Kwon, Jae K. ... ’78 ’03 C.187 B.A. L.209 J.D. 608 W. Briar Place
Kye, J. Katelyn ... ’72 ’99 C&L.145 B.A., J.D. Major, Lindsey & Africa
Kye, Joseph H. ... ’70 ’97 C.597 B.A. L.145 J.D. [🄰 Vedder,P.K.&K.]
Kyte, Janet M. ... ’53 ’91 C&L.793 B.A., J.D. 320 West Ohio Street, Suite 500
Laabs, Karyn A. ... ’76 ’02 C.339 B.A. L.494 J.D. Cook Co. Pub. Guard. Off.
Laatsch, Gary K., (AV) ... ’54 ’79 C.57 B.A. L.424 J.D. [Pavalon,G.L.&M.]
LaBant, Terrence M. ... ’66 ’92 C.363 B.A. L.597 J.D. [Fuchs&R.]
LaBarbera, John D. ... ’— ’01 C.339 B.A. L.146 J.D. [🄰 O’Hagan,S.&A.]
LaBarbera, Salvatore J. ... ’58 ’85 C&L.424 B.S., J.D. 205 W. Randolph
LaBarge, James A., (AV) ... ’62 ’90 C.475 B.A. L.589 J.D. [Pretzel&S.]
LaBarge, Michael R., (AV) ... ’56 ’82 C.602 B.A. L.339 J.D. [LaBarge,C.&L.]
LaBarge, Richard M., (AV) ’— ’85
C.339 B.S.C.E. L.896 J.D. [Marshall,G.&B.] (See Pat. Sect.)

LaBarge, Campbell & Lyon, L.L.C., (AV)
200 West Jackson Boulevard Suite 2050, 60606
Telephone: 312-580-9010 Fax: 312-580-9011
Email: kcampbell@lcllaw.com URL: http://www.lcllaw.com
Michael R. LaBarge; Kevin Campbell; Bruce W. Lyon;—Deborah J. Klein; Melanie A. Strubbe; Angie M. Grove; Brooke H. Matteucci; Lisa L. Lantero; Diana D. McCall; Katherine M. Benson; Cindy Dobbins; Michael J. MacFarlane.
General Civil and Trial Practice in all Courts, with Emphasis in Transportation Liability Law, Building Construction Liability Law, Products Liability Law, Medical Malpractice Law, Asbestos Litigation, Commercial Litigation, Insurance Coverage and Appellate Practice.
See Professional Biographies, CHICAGO, ILLINOIS

Labate, Robert J. ... ’53 ’83 C.976 B.A. L.930 J.D. [Holland&K.]
Labbe, John ... ’— ’02 C&L.597 B.A., J.D. [🄰 Sonnenschein N.&R.] (Pat.)
LaBella, Jason L. ... ’69 ’97 C.645 B.A. L.146 J.D. [🄰 Much S.F.D.A.&R.]
Laben, Nancy Jill ... ’61 ’87 C.788 A.B. L.178 J.D. Accenture LLP
Labeots, Laura A. ... ’— ’03 C.347 B.A. L.1000 J.D. [🄲 Welsh&K.]
Labinsky, H. Carl ... ’73 ’99 C.339 B.S. L.966 J.D. Arthur Andersen, LLP
Labinsky, Todd A. ... ’— ’00 C&L.339 B.A., J.D. [🄰 Freeborn&P.]
Labkon, Jordan R. ... ’70 ’95 C.659 B.A. L.146 J.D. [🄰 Vedder,P.K.&K.]
Labuda, Thomas A., Jr. ... ’69 ’94 C.357 B.A. L.424 J.D. [Sonnenschein N.&R.]
Lach, Kathleen M. ... ’— ’97 C.1288 B.A. L.107 J.D. [Arnstein&L.]
LaCien, Brian ... ’76 ’02 C.352 B.A. L.209 J.D. [🄰 Power R.&S.]
Lacroix, Jennifer E. ’— ’00 C.971 B.S. L.597 J.D.
[McAndrews,H.&M.] (See Pat. Sect.)
Lacy, Albert S. ... ’57 ’83 C.477 B.A. L.1119 J.D. Sr. Tax Mgr., KGN
Lacy, Maricarol, (BV) ... ’60 ’86 C.424 B.S. L.602 J.D. [Rinella&R.]

Ladas & Parry LLP, (AV)
224 South Michigan Avenue, 60604 ⊙
Telephone: 312-427-1300 Telecopy: 312-427-6663; 312-427-6668
Email: chmail@ladasparry.com URL: http://www.ladas.com
Members of Firm: Richard J. Streit; Frederick W. Meyers; John E. McKie (Not admitted in IL). Associates: Edward J. Chalfie; W. Dennis Drehkoff; Burton S. Ehrlich; Brian W. Hameder; Patricia M. Hoyle (Not admitted in IL); Ryan M. Kaatz (Not admitted in IL); Joseph P. Krause; Valerie R. Neymeyer-Tynkov; W. William Park (Not admitted in IL). Of Counsel: Donald P. Reynolds.
Patent, Trademark, Copyright, Unfair Competition, Licensing, Entertainment and Litigation.
New York, N.Y. Office: 26 West 61st Street. Telephone: 212-708-1800. Telecopy: 212-246-8959; 212-246-8925.
Los Angeles, California Office: 5670 Wilshire Boulevard. Telephone: 323-934-2300. Telecopier: 323-934-0202.
London, England Office: High Holborn House, 52-54 High Holborn, WC1V 6RR. Telephone: 44-71-242-5566. Telex: 262433 MONREF G. Telecopy: 44-207-405-1908.
Munich, Germany Office: Dachauerstrasse 37, 80335 Munich, Germany. Telephone: (089) 269077. Fax: 49-89-269040.
See Professional Biographies, CHICAGO, ILLINOIS

Ladd, Jeffrey R., (AV) ... ’41 ’73 C.177 B.A. L.146 J.D. [Bell,B.&L.]
Ladden, Ronald S. ... ’31 ’56 C.221 B.A. L.209 J.D. [Ladden&A.]

Ladden & Allen, Chartered, (AV) 🄱🄱
55 West Monroe Street, Suite 3950, 60603
Telephone: 312-853-3000 Fax: 312-201-1436
URL: http://www.lawyers.com/l&alaw
Ronald S. Ladden; Gemma B. Allen.
Family Law, Complex Matrimonial Litigation, Premarital Agreements, Postnuptial Agreements, Child Custody, Paternity, Divorce and the interrelationship of Corporate Law and Estate Planning.
See Professional Biographies, CHICAGO, ILLINOIS

Laden, Kristan Q. ... ’— ’96 C.93 B.A. L.146 J.D. [🄰 Jones D.]

Ladenson, Robert F. .... '43 '80 C.966 B.A. L.209 J.D. Ill. Institute Of Tech.
Ladgenski, Derek F. ....'74 '99 C&L.339 B.A. and B.S., J.D. [🄰 Katten M.R.]
Ladner, Tracey R., (AV) '60 '85 C&L.339 B.S., J.D.
Chief Asst. Corp. Coun., City Of Chicago Dept. of Law
Ladon, Richard J. ....'35 '61 C&L.597 B.S., LL.B. 640 N. LaSalle St.
Laduzinsky, Steven M. .... '61 '86 C.209 B.A. L.365 J.D. 20 S. Clark St., Ste. 2000
Lafakis, Gregory J. ....'45 '82 C.801 M.A. L.146 J.D. 33 N La Salle # 27
Laff, Charles A., (AV) '34 '59
C.679 B.S.Ch.E. L.309 J.D. [Michael B.&F.] (See Pat. Sect.)
LaFratta, Brian K. ....'73 '01 C.94 B.A. L.339 J.D. [🄰 Fisher&P.]
Lagerquist, Jerry C. ....'43 '68 C.1106 B.A. L.146 J.D. 1476 W. Berwyn
LaGory, Dennis G. ....'— '89 C.912 B.A. L.1340 J.D. [Schiff H.]
La Grone, Yvonne Spradley .... '63 '87 C.597 B.A. L.339 J.D. Asst. Corp. Coun.
Lahey, Matthew D. ....'— '99 C.602 B.B.A. L.893 J.D. [🄰 Schiff H.]
Lahiff, Lisa Kay '65 '92 C.81 B.A. L.734 J.D.
Asst. to the Pres. & Risk Mgr. & Gov. Rel., St. Marys of Nazareth Hospital Ctr.
Laidlaw, Andrew R., (AV) ....'46 '72 C.597 B.A. L.575 J.D. [Seyfarth S.]
Laing, Susan K. ....'— '92 C.602 B.A. L.209 J.D. [Anderson,R.]
Laiprasert, Jayne .... '80 '04 C.145 B.A. L.178 J.D. [🄰 Jenner&B.]
Laird, Evalyn Walsh, (Mrs.) ....'02 '26 L.209 J.D. 4319 W. Devon Ave.‡
Laird, Michael J. ....'49 '75 C.973 L.602 J.D. Asst. Atty. Gen.
Lake, Catherine A. '63 '89 C.347 B.A. L.879 J.D.
(adm. in IN; not adm. in IL) [🄰 S.P.Polick&Assoc.]
Lake, Micheal D., (BV) '54 '88
C.5 B.S.Chem. L.365 J.D. 311 S. Wacker Dr., 53rd Fl. (Pat.)
Lake, Steven R., (BV) ....'48 '74 C.339 B.A. L.174 J.D. [Lake,T.&D.]

Lake, Toback & D'Arco, (AV) 🄱🄱
A Partnership including a Professional Corporation
33 North Dearborn, Suite 900, 60602
Telephone: 312-726-7111 Fax: 312-726-2385 URL: http://www.ltddivorce.com
URL: http://www.lawyers.com/ltddivorce
Members of Firm: Steven R. Lake; Alan J. Toback; John M. D'Arco. Associates: Laura N. Ashmore; Holly Ann Bencivenga; Michael G. Di Domenico; Erin J. Bognar; Andrew M. Engle; Bernadette I. Rossmoore. Of Counsel: Rebecca B. Feinberg.
Family Law including Complex Matrimonial Litigation, Domestic Relations, Financial Discovery and Analysis, Tax Considerations and Retirement Benefits, Divorce Mediation and Negotiation, Custody, Visitation Rights, Adoptions and Appeals, Parentage and Paternity Proceedings.
See Professional Biographies, CHICAGO, ILLINOIS

Lakerdas, James G. .... '53 '84 C.229 B.A. L.365 J.D. [Chadwick&L.]
Lakernick, Harriette G., (BV) '45 '78 C.831 B.A. L.365 J.D.
111 W. Washington, Ste. 737
Laks, Perry M., (AV) ....'43 '72 C.339 B.S. L.365 LL.B. 200 N. LaSalle St.
Lally, John, (AV) ....'40 '69 C&L.424 B.A., J.D. 2224 W. Irving Park Rd.
Lam, Edward W. '66 '95 C.801 B.A. L.823 J.D.
V.P. & Dep. Gen. Coun., Natl. Equity Fund, Inc.
Lam, Phuong T. ....'— '98 C.339 B.S. L.602 J.D. [🄰 Jones D.]
Lamar, Marilyn ....'55 '79 C.339 B.S. L.145 J.D. [McDermott W.&E.]
Lamb, Michael T. .... '58 '84 C.436 B.A. L.724 J.D. Natl. Treas. Employees Union
Lamb, Patrick D., (BV) ....'54 '80 C.201 B.S. L.365 J.D. [Crowley&L.]
Lamb, Patrick J., (AV) ....'57 '82 C.597 B.S. L.477 J.D. [Butler R.S.&B.]
Lambe, James P. ....'74 '00 C.602 B.B.A. L.209 J.D. [🄰 Vedder,P.K.&K.]
Lambe, Malcolm D. ....'55 '84 C.966 B.B.A. L.209 J.D. Price Waterhouse
Lamberson, Linda A.O. ....'— '02 C.347 B.A. L.145 J.D. [🄰 McDermott W.&E.]
Lambert, Jerry L. ....'39 '72 C.234 B.S. L.146 J.D. [🄲 Hilfman,M.&B.]
Lambert, Joseph D. ....'74 '00 C.475 B.A. L.309 J.D. [🄰 Barack F.K.P.&N.]
Lambert, Stanford L., (AV) ....'39 '66 C.1016 B.S.B.A. L.146 J.D. [Cohn,L.R.S.&G.]
Lambrechts, Carla K. .... '44 '82 C.424 B.S. L.209 J.D. Sr. Writer/ Analyst, CCH, Inc.
Lambur, Laura M. ....'59 '86 C.174 B.Arch. L.365 J.D. State Attys. Off.
Lamden, Seth D. ....'— '99 C.1036 B.A. L.365 J.D. [🄰 Schiff H.]
Lamendella, Joseph A., (AV) ....'37 '64 C.424 B.Sc. L.365 J.D. [Lamendella&D.]
Lamendella & Daniel, P.C., (AV) ....36th Floor Twenty North Clark Street
Lamerato, Amanda Marie .... '— '01 C.477 B.A. L.879 J.D. Pub. Guardian Off.
Lamere, Donna L. '49 '79 C&L.879 B.A., J.D.
(adm. in IN; not adm. in IL)
National Loss Prevention Coordinator, Chicago Title Ins. Co.
Lamet, Jerome S., & Associates, (AV) '30 '55
C&L.597 B.S., J.D. 542 South Dearborn Street Suite 1260
Lamfalusi, Melissa E. ....'72 '97 C.597 B.A. L.813 J.D. [🄰 Sidley A.B.&W.]
Lamm, Richard H. ....'53 '78 C.867 B.A. L.597 J.D. 30 S. Wacker Dr.‡
Lammiman, Forrest B., (AV) ....'44 '83 C.678 B.A. L.352 J.D. [Lord,B.&B.]
Lamoreaux, Sharron C. ....'63 '93 C.101 B.A. L.902 J.D. [🄰 Katten M.R.]
Lamperis, Eleni S. ....'73 '98 C&L.209 B.S.A., J.D. [🄰 Freeborn&P.]
Lampert, Andrew F. ....'71 '96 C.860 B.A. L.273 J.D. [Seyfarth S.]
Lampert, Steven A., (AV) ....'44 '69 C.339 B.S. L.597 J.D. [Neal,G.&E.]
Lampinen, Timothy J., Law Offices of '60 '94
C.477 B.A. L.424 J.D. 330 North Wabash, 26th Floor
Lampkin, Bertina E. ....'48 '74 C.1016 B.A. L.209 J.D. Cir. J.
Lamsens, Catherine E. ....'66 '96 C.278 B.A. L.597 J.D. [Butler R.S.&B.]
Lancaster, Walter R., (AV) ....'— '87 C.339 B.A. L.309 J.D. [Kirkland&E.]
Lancaster, William J. ....'— '78 C.424 B.S. L.365 J.D. 1440 N. Lake Shore Dr.‡
Lancheros, James M. ....'— '01 C.651 B.A. L.209 J.D. [Weaver]
Lanciloti, Daniel F. ....'67 '94 C.388 B.A. L.879 J.D. [Seyfarth S.]
Lanctot, Thomas E., (AV) ....'54 '79 C.597 B.A. L.145 J.D. William Blair & Co.
Land, Penny A. ....'65 '92 C.424 B.S. L.692 J.D. 65 E. Wacker Pl., Ste. 1700
Land, Peter G. ....'68 '95 C.210 B.A. L.597 J.D. [Babbitt&M.]
Landau, Melvin M. ....'23 '47 L.597 LL.B. [Albin&L.] ‡
Lande, Charles A. ....'69 '95 C.966 B.A. L.597 J.D. [Baker&M.]
Landeck, Katherine A. '59 '85
C.424 B.S. L.209 J.D. Sr. Atty., American Medical Association
Landenberger, James T. '60 '86 C.475 B.A. L.602 J.D.
Exec. V.P. & Gen. Coun., Amalgamated Bank of Chicago
Landes, Stephen J., (AV) ....'45 '70 C&L.597 B.A., J.D. [Wildman,H.A.&D.]
Landesman, Judith L., (AV) ....'— '77 C.339 B.A. L.46 J.D. [🄲 Neal,G.&E.]
Landgraff, Christopher D. ....'68 '94 C.575 B.A. L.1068 J.D. [Bartlit B.H.P.&S.]
Landis, Arnold H. ....'50 '74 C.339 B.A. L.209 J.D. 77 W. Wash. St.
Landis, John R. ....'— '88 C.399 B.A. L.494 J.D. [Foley&L.]
Landis, Kenneth R., Jr. '64 '92 C.665 B.A. L.273 J.D.
Loss Prevention Coun., Attorneys' Liability Assurance Society, Inc.
Landon, J. Herbert, (AV) ....'31 '60 C.339 B.S. L.910 J.D. [Landon&W.]

Landon & Wickersty, Ltd., (AV)
Suite 1119, 77 West Washington Street, 60602
Telephone: 312-782-4780 Fax: 312-372-9399
Email: lwltd@ameritech.net
J. Herbert Landon; William J. Wickersty;—Jennifer A. Atkin.
(This Listing Continued)

Landon & Wickersty, Ltd. (Continued)
Wills and Probate, Trusts and Estate Planning Law. Corporate Law, Business Law, Real Estate and Drainage Law, General Civil and Trial Practice.
See Professional Biographies, CHICAGO, ILLINOIS

Landow-Esser, Janine M., (AV) ....'51 '76 C.966 B.A. L.273 J.D. [Quarles&B.]
Landsberg, Erica M. ... '62 '87 C.976 B.A. L.145 J.D. Asst. Gen. Coun., Univ. of Chicago
Landsman, Laurence M. ....'64 '89 C.823 B.A. L.146 J.D. [Block&L.]
Landsman, Stephan A., (AV©) '46 '73 C.385 A.B. L.309 J.D.
(adm. in NY; not adm. in IL) Prof. of Law, DePaul Univ. Coll. of Law
Landsman, Stephen A., (AV) ....'42 '67 C.659 B.S. L.477 J.D. [DLPiper R.G.C.U.]
Landt, Judith G. ....'47 '77 C.145 B.A. L.146 J.D. 1330 N. La Salle St.
Lane, Bradley G. .... '63 '88 C.339 B.S. L.477 J.D. [Brinks H.G.&L.] (See Pat. Sect.)
Lane, Christian J. ....'— '98 C.813 A.B. L.494 J.D. [🄰 Katten M.R.]
Lane, Cristina ....'79 '04 C.477 B.A. L.597 J.D. [🄰 Mayer,B.R.&M.]
Lane, Fred ....'25 '50 L.424 J.D. [Lane&L.]
Lane, Frederic S., (AV) ....'35 '60 C.659 B.A. L.145 J.D. [🄲 Robbins,S.N.L.&T.]
Lane, Kevin C. ....'68 '96 C.602 B.A. L.209 J.D. [Sonnenschein N.&R.]
Lane, Marc J., (AV) ....'46 '71 C.339 B.A. L.597 J.D. [M.J.Lane]
Lane, Michael M., (AV) ....'41 '66 C.602 A.B. L.1066 LL.B. [McCullough,C.&L.]
Lane, Philip E. ....'48 '97 C.339 B.S. L.146 J.D. [🄲 Hilfman,M.&B.]
Lane, Robert G., (AV) ....'38 '63 C.228 B.A. L.477 J.D. [Winston&S.]
Lane, Scott D., (AV) ....'62 '88 C.802 B.A. L.424 J.D. [Lane&L.]
Lane, Stephen I., (AV) ....'53 '78 C.339 B.A. L.46 J.D. [Lane&L.]

Lane & Lane, (AV) 🄱🄱
33 North Dearborn Street, Suite 2300, 60602-3199
Telephone: 312-332-1400 Fax: 312-899-8003
Email: lanelaw@lane-lane.com URL: http://www.lane-lane.com
Members of Firm: Fred Lane; Stephen I. Lane; Scott D. Lane. Associate: Mark A. Brown. Of Counsel: John F. Sandner; Daniel M. Cullan (Not admitted in IL); Eugene K. Hollander (Also practicing individually).
Trial Practice in all areas involving Serious Personal Injury and Wrongful Death. Emphasis in Medical and Professional Negligence, Products Liability, Premises Liability and Vehicular Negligence, Medical Malpractice, Automobile Accidents, Slip and Fall, Animal Bites, Railroad Accidents, Toxic Torts, Class Actions, Jones Act, OSHA.
See Professional Biographies, CHICAGO, ILLINOIS

Lane, Marc J., A Prof. Corp., The Law Offices of, (AV) 🄱🄱
Suite 2100 180 North La Salle Street, 60601-2701
Telephone: 312-372-1040 800-372-1040 Fax: 312-346-1040 URL: http://www.marcjlane.com
Email: success@marcjlane.com URL: http://www.lawyers.com/marcjlane
Marc J. Lane. Of Counsel: Rosalyn S. Watson;—Joshua S. Kreitzer; John J. Lapinski.
Federal and International Taxation, Trust and Estate Planning, Probate, Elder Law, Real Estate, Nonprofit, Internet Law, Corporation, Securities and Banking Law.
See Professional Biographies, CHICAGO, ILLINOIS

Laner, Richard W., (AV) ....'33 '56 C&L.597 B.S.L., LL.B. [🄲 Laner,M.D.B.L.&T.]

Laner, Muchin, Dombrow, Becker, Levin and Tominberg, Ltd., (AV) 🄱🄱
515 North State Street, Suite 2800, 60610
Telephone: 312-467-9800 Fax: 312-467-9479
URL: http://www.lmdblt.com
Lawrence F. Doppelt (1935-1979); Arthur B. Muchin; Anthony E. Dombrow; Alan M. Levin; Carl S. Tominberg; Mark L. Juster; Gary Alan Wincek; Michael Klupchak; Joseph H. Yastrow; Joseph M. Gagliardo; Robert H. Brown; James J. Convery; Robert S. Letchinger; Violet M. Clark; James F. Vanek; Jeffrey P. Carren; Jill P. O'Brien; Neil P. Stern; Thomas Bradley; Scott A. Gore; Jeffrey S. Fowler; Clifford R. Perry III; Gregory R. James, Jr.; Jennifer A. Naber; Janice M. Rauen; Andrew S. Goldberg; Mark W. Bennett; Robert T. Bernstein;—Joshua A. Dombrow; Debrai G. Haile; Monica B. Lasky; Allison M. Lynn; Margaret C. McGrath; Laura R. Meehan; Devlin J. Schoop; Sonya Olds Som; Mark L. Stolzenburg; William P. Sweeney. Of Counsel: Isaiah S. Dorfman; Daniel J. Ashley; Herman J. De Koven; Seymour Cohen; Richard W. Laner; Lawrence Jay Weiner; William L. Becker.
Labor and Employment Relations Law, Employee Benefits Law and Related Litigation.
References: NBD Bank Chicago; Illinois; La Salle National Bank & Trust Co.
See Professional Biographies, CHICAGO, ILLINOIS

Laney, Frederick C. ....'72 '01 C.420 B.S.M.E. L.425 J.D. [🄰 Niro,S.H.&N.]
Lang, Angela R. ....'71 '95 C&L.347 B.S., J.D. [Mayer,B.R.&M.]
Lang, C. Kyle ....'— '03 C.207 B.A. L.365 J.D. [🄰 Clausen M.]
Lang, George K. ....'64 '92 C&L.221 B.A., J.D. [🄰 Childress D.G.]
Lang, Gina L., Attorney at Law '61 '87 C.861 B.A. L.803 J.D.
(adm. in LA; not adm. in IL) 1416 W. Lunt Ave., Ste. 109
Lang, Gordon, Jr., (AV) ....'33 '60 C.976 B.A. L.309 LL.B. [🄲 Gardner C.&D.]
Lang, Joseph W. ....'39 '67 C&L.424 B.S.C., J.D. Sr. V.P., LaSalle Natl. Tr., N.A.
Lang, Louis I. ....'49 '74 C.339 B.A. L.209 J.D. State Rep.
Lang, Richard A., (AV) ....'50 '75 C.309 A.B. L.365 J.D. [McDermott W.&E.]
Lang, Richard J., (AV) ....'45 '70 C.424 B.S. L.597 J.D. [Schain,B.R.&C.]
Lang, Robert H. ....'69 '94 C.339 B.A. L.896 J.D. [FagelHaber]
Lang, Scott H. .... '46 '72 C&L.309 B.A., J.D. Rodman & Renshaw, Inc.
Lang, Thomas A., II ....'75 '00 C.339 B.A. L.209 J.D. [🄰 Pretzel&S.]
Langan, James Andrew, (AV) ....'— '82 C.339 A.B. L.309 J.D. [Kirkland&E.]
Lange, Daniel B. ....'— '01 C.999 B.A. L.911 J.D. [🄰 Katten M.R.]
Lange, Douglas A. ....'66 '93 C.959 B.A. L.424 J.D. [Ellison,N.Z.&A.]
Lange, Justin T. ....'78 '03 C&L.352 B.B.A., J.D. [🄰 Dykema G.P.]
Langendorf, Robert A. ....'55 '80 C&L.339 B.S., J.D. [R.A.Langendorf]
Langendorf, Robert A., P.C. ....134 N. La Salle Street
Langer, Ned ....'21 '50 L.209 LL.B. 6221 N. Niagara
Langer, Paul L. ....'59 '85 C.339 B.S. L.424 J.D. [Mayer,B.R.&M.]
Langer, Sharon M. ....'60 '89 C.1183 B.A. L.424 J.D. 2851 W. Greenleaf
Langford, Anna R. ....'17 '56 C.1016 L.365 LL.B. 1249 W. 63rd St.‡
Langford, Brady J. ....'52 '77 C.589 B.S. L.209 J.D. Coopers & Lybrand
Langhenry, John G., III, (AV) ......'58 '85 C.602 A.B. L.424 J.D. [Mangan,L.G.&L.] ⊙
Langie, Jean M., (AV) ....'60 '85 C.350 B.S. L.352 J.D. [Vedder,P.K.&K.]
Langlotz, Susan M. ....'60 '86 C.98 B.S. L.365 J.D. [🄰 Hedberg,T.F.&W.]
Langone, Christopher V., (BV) ....'67 '92 C.188 B.A. L.597 J.D. [Langone]
Langone Law Firm, The, (BV) ....25 East Washington - Suite 1805
Langsdorf, Melissa F. ....'76 '03 C.188 B.A. L.597 J.D. [🄰 Katten M.R.]
Langston-Cox, Pamela D. '57 '85 C&L.8 B.A., J.D.
Coun., Office of the Chief Coun., Dept. of Treas.
Lanigan, Joanne L. ....'34 '58 C.339 L.209 LL.B. Cir.J.
Lanigan, Michael F. ....'46 '77 C&L.424 B.A., J.D. [S.G.Thomas]
Lannan, Robert W. ....'69 '97 C&L.276 A.B., J.D. [🄰 Greenberg T.]
Lannert, Pamela Schick '71 '00
C.347 B.A. L.146 J.D. U.S. Customs and Border Protection
Lanning, James C., Jr. '48 '74 C&L.546 B.A., J.D.
(adm. in NE; not adm. in IL) Asst. Reg. Coun., I.R.S.
Lannon, Lannon & Barr, Ltd., (AV) ....221 N. LaSalle St.
Lannon-Kus, Patricia C., (AV) ....'53 '78 C.363 B.S. L.146 J.D. [Lannon,L.&B.]
Lanser, Joseph R. ....'73 '00 C.801 B.S. L.146 J.D. [🄰 Seyfarth S.] (Pat.)
Lansing, David S. ....'52 '77 C.966 B.A. L.910 J.D. Dean of Admin., Roosevelt Univ.
Lansky, Marvin S. ....'39 '64 C.1016 B.A. L.365 LL.B. [🄰 H.L.Walner&Assoc.]
Lansu, Brian F. ....'72 '99 C.210 B.A. L.589 J.D. [🄰 Cassiday,S.&G.]

Lanter, James E. .... '46 '73 C&L.339 B.A., J.D. Admin. Law J., SSA
Lantero, Lisa L. .... '58 '83 C.174 B.A. L.209 J.D. [🄰 LaBarge,C.&L.]
Lanznar, Howard S., (AV) .... '55 '83 C.31 B.A. L.145 J.D. [Katten M.R.]
Lapacek, James V., (AV) '44 '74
C.46 B.S.E.E. L.424 J.D. Gen. Coun., S & C Elec. Co. (Pat.)
Lape, Rachael R. .... '73 '00 C.502 B.A. L.893 J.D. [🄰 Goldberg,K.B.B.R.&M.]
Lapidus, Allan E., (AV) .... '43 '67 C.966 B.S. L.477 J.D. [🄲 Vedder,P.K.&K.]
Lapin, Andrew W. .... '53 '78 C.347 B.A. L.365 J.D. [Much S.F.D.A.&R.]
Lapins, David A., (AV) .... '58 '83 C.339 B.A. L.597 J.D. [Drane F.&L.]
Lapins, Scott M., (AV) .... '55 '80 C.339 B.S. L.597 J.D. [Schwartz C.]
Lapinski, John J. .... '61 '88 C.238 B.S. L.146 J.D. [🄰 M.J.Lane]
Lapka, Sheryl R. .... '— '97 C.339 B.A. L.146 J.D. [Hennessy&R.]
Lapka, Theodore A. .... '20 '48 C.707 B.A. L.209 J.D. Fed. Trade Comm.
LaPointe, Martin K. .... '52 '87 C.1208 B.A. L.146 J.D. [Burke,W.M.&S.]
LaPorte, Damon .... '63 '95 C.604 B.A. L.146 J.D [Worker,S.&H.]
LaPorte, David L. .... '— '96 C.475 B.A. L.209 J.D. [Querrey&H.]
LaPorte, Michael R. .... '69 '96 C.951 B.A. L.146 J.D. [🄰 Wildman,H.A.&D.]
LaPorte, Robert D. .... '— '04 C.932 B.S. L.1370 J.D. [🄰 Cantwell&C.]
Lapp, Richard B., (BV) .... '58 '85 C.476 B.A. L.966 J.D. [Morgan,L.&B.]
Lapping, Norman E., (AV) .... '32 '56 C&L.597 B.S.L., LL.B. 345 N. Canal St.
Lapres, Marie T. .... '— '94 C.477 B.S.N. L.209 J.D. [🄰 Lowery&Assoc.]
Lara, Constance H. .... '— '88 C.424 B.A. L.602 J.D. [C.H.Lara]
Lara, Eduardo X. .... '45 '76 C.339 B.S. L.800 J.D. 2553 South Ridgeway
Lara, Roland C. ..... '75 '00 C.597 B.A. L.339 J.D. 180 North La Salle Street, Suite 3400
Lara, Wendy Z. .... '71 '01 C.339 B.A. L.378 J.D. Supm. Ct.
Lara, Constance H., P.C. .... 3749 West 26th Street
La Raus, David William .... '66 '97 C.118 B.A. L.339 J.D. Assoc. Corp. Coun.
Larcher, Carol .... '61 '94 C.531 B.S. L.424 J.D. [🄲 Gardner C.&D.] (Pat.)
Larkin, James M. .... '45 '73 C.424 B.B.A. L.365 J.D. 1415 N. Dayton St.
Larkin, Jerome '51 '78 C&L.424 B.S., J.D.
Atty. Regr. & Disciplinary Comm. of the State Supm. Ct.
Larkin, Richard W., (AV) .... '29 '56 C.321 A.B. L.309 J.D. 1 N. La Salle St.
Larkin, Rosemary Filter .... '41 '80 C.719 B.S. L.146 J.D. 2621 W. 102nd Pl.
Larned, Carla P. .... '75 '02 C.477 B.A. L.209 J.D. [🄰 Bollinger,R.&G.]
LaRocco, Joseph J. .... '20 '48 C.339 A.B. L.597 J.D. 79 W. Monroe St.
LaRocque, James E. .... '28 '56 C.436 L.424 J.D. 2222 S. Indiana Street‡
Larsen, Anne Edelman .... '58 '83 C.339 B.S. L.597 J.D. 77 W. Washington St.
Larsen, Bryan C. .... '77 '04 C.846 B.A. L.146 J.D. [🄰 Lloyd&C.]
Larsen, Darrell R., Jr., (AVⓉ) .... '— '76 C&L.878 B.A., J.D. [Chapman&C.]
Larsen, Diane J. .... '58 '83 C.209 B.A. L.424 J.D. J. Cir. Ct. of Cook Co.
Larsen, Elizabeth A. .... '— '02 C.674 A.B. L.145 J.D. [🄰 Kirkland&E.]
Larsen, Mark A. .... '63 '92 C.801 B.S. L.365 J.D. Atty's Liability Assur. Soc.
Larsen, Scott .... '70 '95 C.98 B.S. L.209 J.D. [🄰 W.J.Sneckenberg&Assoc.]
Larson, Anne E. .... '— '89 C.339 A.B. L.477 J.D. [Much S.F.D.A.&R.]
Larson, David A. .... '69 '94 C.597 B.A. L.61 J.D. [🄰 Bollinger,R.&G.]
Larson, James A. .... '59 '87 C.350 B.A. L.352 J.D. 11 S. LaSalle
Larson, Julie A. .... '64 '93 C.752 B.A. L.146 J.D. [🄱 Sidley A.B.&W.]

Larson, Keil M. '60 '85 C.339 B.A. L.365 J.D.
800 N. Clark Street, Suite 222, 60610
Telephone: 312-664-9300 Fax: 312-664-5363
Email: keil@keillarson.com URL: http://www.keillarson.com
Real Estate Litigation, Condominium Disputes, Real Estate Transactions, Probate Litigation, Partition Suits, Foreclosures, Lien Litigation, Specific Performance, Contract Litigation, Appraisal Litigation, Builder Litigation, Construction Defects, Landlord Tenant Law, Fraud Litigation, Immigration.
See Professional Biographies, CHICAGO, ILLINOIS

Larson, Oliver .... '75 '99 C&L.477 B.A., J.D. [🄰 Jenner&B.]
Larson, Richard A. .... '57 '92 C.750 B.A. L.1000 J.D. [🄰 G.B.Mullin]
Larson, Steven L., (AV) '52 '77 C.339 B.A. L.910 J.D.
[Swanson,M.&B.] (⊙Libertyville, Waukegan)
Lartz, John A. '57 '83 C.679 B.A. L.209 J.D.
Chf. Bus. Prosecutor, Ill. Dept. of Prof. Regulation
Larvick, Matthew P. .... '69 '94 C&L.339 B.S., J.D. [McDermott W.&E.]
Lascari, Elizabeth R. '48 '83 C&L.966 B.A., J.D.
(adm. in WI; not adm. in IL) 140 S. Dearborn St.‡
Lascari, Scott C. .... '72 '97 C&L.436 B.S., J.D. [🄰 Gardner C.&D.]
LasCola, James Gregory .... '65 '98 C.999 B.A. L.209 J.D. 227 W. Monroe, Ste. 2000
Laser, Adam M. .... '69 '97 C&L.597 B.A., J.D. [Goldberg,K.B.B.R.&M.]
Laser, Gary S. .... '37 '65 C&L.472 B.B.A., J.D. Chicago-Kent Coll. of Law
Laser, Jules M., (AV) .... '36 '62 C.339 B.A. L.209 J.D. [Laser,P.S.F.&E.]
Laser, Megan E. .... '74 '04 C.972 B.S. L.146 J.D. [🄰 J.M.Goldberg]
Laser, Pokorny, Schwartz, Friedman & Economos, P.C., (AV)
6 West Hubbard Street 8th Floor
Laski, James E. .... '50 '75 C.424 B.A. L.339 J.D. 9204 S. Commercial Ave.
Lasko, Bennett W., (AV) .... '61 '87 C.293 A.B. L.309 J.D. [Mayer,B.R.&M.]
Lasko, Norman .... '37 '67 C.472 B.B.A. L.365 J.D. Dept. of Prof. Reg. (Prosecute)
Lasko, William E., II, P.C. .... '45 '71 C&L.597 A.B., J.D. 79 W. Monroe
Lasko, William E., Sr. .... '15 '46 C.339 L.365 J.D. 79 W. Monroe St.‡
Lasky, Allan N. .... '30 '58 C.339 B.A. L.1000 J.D. 250 S. Wacker Dr.
Lasky, Jerald H. .... '55 '79 C.611 B.A. L.339 J.D. 414 N. Orleans Street, Suite 610
Lasky, Monica B. .... '66 '92 C.31 B.A. L.309 J.D. [🄰 Laner,M.D.B.L.&T.]
Lasky, Robert J., (AV) .... '— '62 C.597 L.209 J.D. [Arnstein&L.]

Lasky & Rifkind, Ltd., (AV)
351 W. Hubbard Street, 60610 ⊙
Telephone: 312-634-0057 Fax: 312-634-0059
Email: Lasky@Laskyrifkind.com URL: http://www.laskyrifkind.com
Leigh R. Lasky (Resident, New York, N.Y. Office); Norman Rifkind.
Litigation Practice including Securities, Business, Commercial, Class Actions, Professional Malpractice and Appellate Practice.
New York, New York Office: 100 Park Avenue, 10017. Telephone: 212-907-0800.
See Professional Biographies, CHICAGO, ILLINOIS

LaSota, David J. .... '— '98 C.339 B.A. L.602 J.D. [🄰 Chapman&C.]
Lassar, Scott R., (AV) .... '50 '75 C.604 B.A. L.597 J.D. First Asst. U.S. Atty.
Lassers, Willard J. .... '19 '42 C&L.145 A.B., J.D. Cir. J.
Lastimosa, C. Kinnier .... '76 '02 C.597 B.A. L.910 J.D. [🄰 Sedgwick,D.M.&A.]
Latchana, David .... '77 '02 C.373 B.A. L.602 J.D. [🄰 Winston&S.]
Laterza, B. Franco .... '62 '87 C.801 B.A. L.339 J.D. [Keegan,L.L.&G.]
Latham, Mark A., (AV) .... '57 '89 C.340 B.S. L.1066 J.D. [Gardner C.&D.]

Latham & Watkins LLP, (AV)
Sears Tower, Suite 5800, 60606 ⊙
Telephone: 312-876-7700 Telecopier: 312-993-9767
URL: http://www.lw.com
Partners: Mary Rose Alexander; Josef S. Athanas; J. Douglas Bacon; Stephen S. Bowen; James A. Cherney; David G. Crumbaugh; James W. Doran; Diana Slyfield Doyle; David S. Foster; Douglas A. Freedman; Mark D. Gerstein; William J. Gibbons; Robert G. Goldman; Marcelo Halpern; Ronald W.

(This Listing Continued)

Latham & Watkins LLP (Continued)

Hanson; Tim Hardwicke; Thomas J. Heiden; David S. Heller; Robin M. Hulshizer; James G. Hunter, Jr.; Roger J. Jones; Thomas E. Keim, Jr.; Bradley E. Kotler; Joseph M. Kronsnoble; Michael D. Levin; Laurence H. Levine; Richard A. Levy; Janet Malloy Link; Christopher D. Lueking; John P. Lynch; Ellen L. Marks; Juli Wilson Marshall; Richard S. Meller; Mark S. Mester; Jeffrey G. Moran; Kevin M. Murphy; David A. Nelson; Cary R. Perlman; Philip J. Perzek; Michael A. Pucker; Vik Puri; David K. Rathgeber; Kevin A. Russell; Nancy L. Schimmel; Kenneth G. Schuler; Donald L. Schwartz; Robin L. Struve; Robert W. Tarun; Matthew W. Walch. Of Counsel: Sandhya C. Budinger; Nancy Scheurwater Hunter. Associates: Kristine A. Ackerman; ManChit AuYeung; Julie D. Bailey; Jenny C. Baker; Stephanie Barker; Brendan S. Beasley; Christopher P. Bennett; Cathy A. Birkeland; Carrie Bordewick; Roderick O. Branch (Not admitted in IL); David M. Buchanan; B. John Casey; Yael M. Citro; Lisa Plunkett Conlon; Alice E. Decker; Joshua P. Dehnke; Mia Grace DiBella; Robert A. Drobnak; Jacob B. Drouillard; Kerry Ducey; Bradley C. Faris; Michael J. Faris; Fred C. Fisher; Timothy P. FitzSimons; Arthur F. Foerster; André M. Geverola; Tasneem K. Goodman; Nicholas B. Gorga; Scott W. Hairston; Julie S. B. Hammond; Michael F. Harte; Adam Herzog; Amanda J. Hollis; Maaike S. Hudson; Nicholas O. Isaacson; Jennifer R. Jaffe; Ildiko Jona; Zachary A. Judd; Amy J. Kappeler; Karl A. Karg, IV; Danielle Susan Kemp; Mishel Keta; Livia M. Kiser; Peter P. Knight; Elizabeth Opper Kraemer; Erik A. Lopez, Sr.; John J. Marhoefer; Julie M. Marion; Kevin C. May; Sasha Mayergoyz; David McKone; Matthew B. Mock; Peter Moore; Joann P. Murphy; Joel Steven Neckers; Allison O'Neill; Paige S. Ormond; Lopa Patel; Mark Paul Ramsey; Caroline A. Reckler; Andrew R. Roberson; Leslie N. Rosen; Scott Schoettes; Erin S. Shaw; Veronica A. Silva-Minin; Keith A. Simon; Adam R. Skilken; Amanda J. Smith; Cindy Sobel; Deborah L. Steiner; Daniel B. Stolarsky; R. Brian Tanner; Stephen R. Tetro, II; Kaitlin Reidy Verber; Peter N. Witty; Fan Zhang.
Complex Commercial Litigation, Distributor Termination, Franchise Arbitration and Litigation, Antitrust, General Corporate, Corporate Governance, Public Corporations, Corporate Workouts, Securitization, Corporate Reorganization, Corporate Finance, Corporate Contracts, Takeovers, Tender Offers, Securities, Mergers, Acquisitions and Divestitures, Corporate Tax Controversies, Federal and State Tax Controversies, Federal Taxation, Illinois Taxation, Corporate Control Contests, Employee Benefits, Environmental Law, Environmental Insurance Coverage, Toxic Tort Defense, Commercial Finance, Debt and Equity Finance, Structured Finance, Financial Restructuring, Secured Finance, Unsecured Finance Insolvency, Fraudulent Conveyance, Pre-Bankruptcy Workouts, Information Technology Contracts, Information Technology Licensing, Intellectual Property Infringement, Intellectual Property Litigation, Intellectual Property Licensing, Information and Privacy, Trademarks, Real Estate Development, Real Estate Finance.
Brussels, Belgium; Costa Mesa, California; Frankfurt, Germany; Hamburg, Germany; Hong Kong, China; London, England; Los Angeles, California; Menlo Park, California; Milan, Italy; Moscow, Russia; Newark, New Jersey; New York, N.Y.; Paris, France; Reston, Virginia; San Diego, California; San Francisco, California; Shanghai, China; Singapore; Tokyo, Japan; Washington, D.C.
See Professional Biographies, CHICAGO, ILLINOIS

Latherow, Jerry A., (AV) .... '51 '76 C.338 B.S. L.424 J.D. [Latherow&P.]
Latherow & Porretta Law Office, (AV) .... 321 North Clark, Suite 2222
Latimer, Cary R. .... '— '97 C.477 B.A. L.424 J.D. [Latimer L.J.]
Latimer, Kenneth A., (AV) .... '43 '69 C.966 B.S. L.273 J.D. [Duane M.]

Latimer LeVay Jurasek LLC, (AV)
55 West Monroe Street, Suite 1100, 60603
Telephone: 312-422-8000 Fax: 312-422-8001
Email: info@lljlaw.com URL: http://www.lljlaw.com
Cary R. Latimer; Brian D. LeVay; Michael C. Jurasek; Sheryl A. Fyock; Donald B. Levine;—Vanessa E. Seiler.
Corporate Law, Mergers and Acquisitions, Commercial Finance, Securities, Real Estate, Estate Planning, Commercial Litigation, Business Law, Tax.
See Professional Biographies, CHICAGO, ILLINOIS

LaTona, Michael A. .... '56 '81 C.209 B.A. L.424 J.D. [Johnson&B.]
Latreille, Daniel M. .... '64 '93 C.477 B.A. L.215 J.D. [🄰 Norton,M.W.&D.]
Latta, James R., Law Offices of, (AV) '46 '81
C.388 B.A. L.209 J.D. 140 S. Dearborn St., Ste. 1610
Latturner, James O. .... '38 '63 C.473 B.S. L.145 J.D. [Edelman,C.&L.]
Latz, Michael P. .... '63 '89 C&L.602 B.A., J.D. [Bollinger,R.&G.]
Lau, Laura L. .... '— '03 C.493 B.S. L.957 J.D. [🄰 Arnstein&L.]
Laub, Joseph M. .... '60 '85 C.831 B.B.A. L.365 J.D. [Gould&R.]
Laubhan, Daniel B. '62 '96 C.209 B.A. L.146 J.D.
Assist. Gen. Counsel, Chicago Mercantile Exchange Inc.
Lauderbach, Elizabeth M. .... '80 '05 C.174 B.A. L.424 J.D. [🄰 Smith O.&W.]
Lauer, Lisa S. .... '77 '04 C.912 B.S. L.477 J.D. [🄰 Jenner&B.]
Lauer, Rebecca J. '57 '82
C.879 B.A. L.597 J.D. Vice President & General Counsel, Com Ed
Lauerman, Marc S. .... '58 '87 C.1168 B.A. L.966 J.D. [Grippo&E.]
Laughlin, John F. .... '28 '54 C.209 B.A. L.602 LL.B. 221 N. LaSalle St.
Laughlin, Paul J. .... '53 '78 C&L.602 B.B.A., J.D. 33 W. Monroe St.‡
Laughman, Mark E. .... '67 '94 C.766 B.A. L.602 J.D. [Katten M.R.]
Laughton, Deborah A. .... '73 '02 C.339 B.S. L.146 J.D. [🄰 McAndrews,H.&M.]
Laurens, Claudia M. .... '74 '99 C&L.339 B.A., J.D. [🄰 Grippo&E.]
Laurent, Bernard '62 '90 C&L.999
(adm. in Belgium; not adm. in IL) [🄲 Susman&Assoc.]
Laurent, Katherine Harvie .... '73 '98 C.597 B.A. L.910 J.D. Atty. Gen.'s Off.
Laureto, Nancy K. .... '47 '85 C.700 B.A. L.209 J.D. Bd. of Educ.
Laurie, John G. .... '45 '70 C.742 B.A. L.209 J.D. Cir. J.
Laurie, Ty D., (AV) .... '61 '86 C.597 B.A. L.477 J.D. [DLPiper R.G.C.U.]
Lausen, Carrie J. .... '63 '92 C.347 B.S. L.365 J.D. Rm 460, 430 S Michigan Ave
Lauter, Leonard H. .... '27 '54 C.339 B.S. L.209 J.D. 5717 N. Elston Ave.
Lauter, Richard S., (BV) .... '— '82 C.378 B.A. L.589 J.D. [Seyfarth S.]
Laux, Michael J. .... '73 '02 C&L.966 B.A., J.D. [🄰 Johnson&B.]
Lavanish, Margaret A. .... '69 '01 C.228 A.B. L.145 J.D. [🄰 Krasnow S.C.]
Lavelle, Michael E., (AV) .... '38 '70 C.424 L.365 J.D. 218 N. Jefferson St.
Lavender, Timothy R. .... '60 '87 C.602 B.B.A. L.421 J.D. [Kelley D.&W.]
Laverty, David A. .... '58 '84 C&L.477 B.A., J.D. 200 S. Wacker Dr.
Lavery, Mark T. .... '72 '00 C.209 B.A. L.146 J.D. [🄰 Langone]
Lavey, Warren G. .... '53 '79 C&L.309 B.A., J.D. [Skadden,A.S.M.&F.]
Lavieri, Vincent A., (BV) '52 '80
C.494 B.S.B.A. L.146 J.D. 53 W. Jackson Boulevard, Suite 950
Lavin, Allen S. .... '31 '55 C.339 L.365 LL.B. 222 North La Salle Street, Suite 1910
Lavin, David M. .... '59 '84 C.338 B.S. L.209 J.D. [🄲 Neal,G.&E.]
Lavin, Dawn Projansky .... '63 '88 C.339 B.A. L.1065 J.D. 134 N. LaSalle, 13th Fl.
Lavin, Jerold R. .... '60 '86 C.339 B.A. L.309 J.D. [Lavin&W.]
Lavin, Steven H. .... '55 '80 C.339 B.S. L.424 J.D. [Lavin&W.]

Lavin & Waldon, P.C., (AV) 🄱🄱
444 North Michigan Avenue Suite 2600, 60611
Telephone: 312-670-4260 Fax: 312-670-4275
Steven H. Lavin; Dennis C. Waldon; Jerold R. Lavin; Jennifer J. Gedville.
Corporate, Finance, Real Estate Transactions, and Commercial Litigation.
See Professional Biographies, CHICAGO, ILLINOIS

LaVoie, Anne E. .... '60 '85 C&L.339 B.A., J.D. [McCullough,C.&L.]
Lawler, Christopher E. .... '62 '88 C.190 BA L.146 JD [Hilbert,L.&P.]
Lawler, Daniel J., (AV) .... '55 '81 C.679 B.S.Mech.E. L.801 J.D. [Bell,B.&L.]
Lawler, Thomas James, (AV) '62 '87 C.145 B.A. L.966 J.D.
Asst.Corp.Coun.,City of Chicago, Dept.of Law
Lawler, W. Gale '49 '75 C&L.846 B.B.A., J.D.
(adm. in TX; not adm. in IL) Mgr., R.R. Donnelley & Sons Co.
Lawless, Michelle A. .... '73 '99 C.347 B.A. L.734 J.D. [🄰 Schiller,D.&F.]

Lawlor, James H., III, (BV) .... '60 '87 C.1183 B.A. L.365 J.D. [🄰 Nolan]
Lawlor, John F. .... '63 '88 C.276 A.B. L.602 J.D. [Mayer,B.R.&M.]
Lawlor, John J., (AV) .... '51 '76 C&L.597 B.A., J.D. [Sonnenschein N.&R.]
Lawrence, Andrea C. .... '72 '97 C.589 B.A. L.209 J.D. [🄰 Anderson&Assoc.] ⊙
Lawrence, Andrew M. '— '99 C.602 B.S. L.174 J.D.
[🄰 Marshall,G.&B.] (See Pat. Sect.)
Lawrence, Kent, (AV) ....'44 '69 C.1036 B.A. L.597 J.D. [Lawrence,K.S.&U.]
Lawrence, Peter Gibbons .... '72 '97 C.602 B.A. L.339 J.D. [🄰 DLPiper R.G.C.U.]
Lawrence, Robert J., (AV) ...... '44 '69 C.477 B.S.E. L.597 J.D. [🄲 Lawrence,K.S.&U.]

Lawrence, Kamin, Saunders & Uhlenhop, L.L.C., (AV) 🄱🄱
208 South La Salle Street, Suite 1750, 60604-1188
Telephone: 312-372-1947 Telecopier: 312-372-2389
Email: LKSU@LKSU.com
Members of Firm: Raymond E. Saunders; Paul B. Uhlenhop; Kent Lawrence; Robert L. Schlossberg; Charles J. Risch; Michael Wise; Peter E. Cooper; David L. Reich; John S. Monical; John D. Ruark. Associates: Paul M. Weltlich; Mitchell B. Goldberg; Rhonda V. Turner. Members: A. Charles Lawrence (1907-1990); James J. Lawrence (1910-1992); Max Frederick Goldberg (1899-1996); Howard P. Kamin (1929-1997). Of Counsel: Robert J. Lawrence.
General Civil Practice. Securities, Commodities, Futures and Securities Regulation. Corporate, Business and Closely Held Businesses. Acquisitions, Divestitures and Mergers, Products Liability, Construction, Commercial and General Litigation, Arbitration and Mediation. Federal Taxation, Estate Planning, Probate, Trust, Real Estate and Employment Law.
See Professional Biographies, CHICAGO, ILLINOIS

Lawrie, Henry deVos, Jr., (AV) .... '42 '67 C.95 A.B. L.597 J.D. [McGuirewoods]
Lawson, Fred C. '62 '97 C.339 B.A. L.209 J.D.
Asst. Gen. Coun., Federal Home Loan Bank of Chicago
Lawson, Gary S. '58 '83 C.999 B.A. L.976 J.D.
(adm. in WA; not adm. in IL) Dir. of Research; Prof., Northwestern Univ. Sch. of Law
Lawyer, Catherine A. '60 '88
C.477 B.M.A. L.365 J.D. Law Libr., John Marshall Law School
Layden, David C. .... '67 '93 C.910 B.A. L.477 J.D. [Jenner&B.]
Layden, Michael T. .... '70 '95 C.966 B.A. L.146 J.D. [🄰 R.J.Prendergast]
Layfer, Seymour J., (AV) .... '19 '48 C.405 L.146 J.D. Spec. State Asst. Atty. Gen.
Layng, Karen P., (AV) .... '62 '87 C&L.339 B.A., J.D. [Vedder,P.K.&K.]
Laytin, Daniel Edward ....'— '98 C&L.477 A.B., J.D. [Kirkland&E.]
Laytin, Kerrie Elizabeth Maloney .... '71 '98 C.569 B.A. L.178 J.D. Asst. Corp. Coun.
Laytin, William M. .... '47 '72 C&L.623 B.A., J.D. [🄲 Flamm&T.]
Layton, Chad J. ....'72 '97 C.339 B.A. L.365 J.D. [🄰 Segal M.S.&M.]
Lazar, Bart A., (AV) ....'61 '87 C.145 B.A. L.146 J.D. [Seyfarth S.]
Lazar, Denise A. ....'— '98 C.937 B.A. L.188 J.D. [🄰 Wildman,H.A.&D.]
Lazar, Vincent E., (AV) ....'65 '90 C.597 B.A. L.339 J.D. [Jenner&B.]
La Zara, Joseph A. ....'58 '83 C&L.209 B.S.C., J.D. 7246 W. Touhy Ave.
Lazarczyk, Laura J. ...... '66 '98 C.800 B.A. L.209 J.D. Sr. Coun., Rewards Network Inc.
Lazaro, Rafael E. ....'— '00 C&L.188 B.A., J.D. [🄰 Seyfarth S.]
Lazzara, Elizabeth Olen, (BV) ....'64 '90 C.363 B.A. L.425 J.D. [Aronberg G.D.&G.]
Le, Tan H. ....'70 '96 C.597 B.A. L.966 J.D. [🄰 Patzik,F.&S.]
Lea, Christopher G. ....'59 '84 C.880 B.A. L.802 J.D. [C.Lea]
Lea, Christopher .... 101 W. Grand Ave., Ste. 200
Leach, Chris A. .... '64 '91 C.347 B.S. L.365 J.D. [🄰 Daley&G.]
Leach, Garret .... '— '96 C.339 B.S. L.424 J.D. [Kirkland&E.] (Pat.)
Leach, Jonathan D. ....'— '04 C.339 B.S. L.146 J.D. [🄰 Neal&L.]
Leacock, Stephen J. '43 '72 C&L.999 B.A., LL.M.
(adm. in NY; not adm. in IL) Prof. of Law, De Paul Univ. Coll. of Law
Leaf, Marc J., (AV) ....'61 '86 C.339 B.S. L.146 J.D. One North LaSalle St.
Leahy, Daniel J., (AV) .... '33 '59 C.884 B.S. L.209 LL.B. [🄲 Leahy,E.&F.]
Leahy, Edward J. .... '55 '87 C.927 B.A. L.209 J.D. [Leahy,E.&F.]
Leahy, Steven A., The Law Office of '62 '00
C.424 B.A. L.365 J.D. 150 North Michigan Avenue, Suite 1100
Leahy, Tom, (AV) ....'51 '77 C.602 B.A. L.424 LL.B. [Leahy&H.]
Leahy, W. Daniel, (AV) ....'45 '71 C.424 B.S. L.209 J.D. [Roddy,L.&Z.]
Leahy, Eisenberg & Fraenkel, Ltd., (AV) .... 161 N. Clark St., Ste. 1325
Leahy & Hoste, (AV) .... 321 N. Clark Street. Suite 2222
Leamy, Richard J., Jr. .... '52 '78 C.932 B.A. L.209 J.D. [Wiedner&M.]
Learner, Howard A., (AV) ..... '55 '80 C.477 A.B. L.309 J.D. Envir. Law & Policy Center
Leary, Shandra L. ....'69 '99 C.957 B.A. L.209 J.D. State's Atty. Off.
Leathem, William W. ....'56 '89 C.339 B.A. L.365 J.D. [🄰 Jacobs,B.O.S.&H.]
Leathers, Wade S., (AV) ....'— '86 C&L.352 B.B.A., J.D. [Sachnoff&W.]
Leatherwood, Nicole Marie Briski .... '71 '01 C&L.424 B.B.A., J.D. 10 S. Dearborn Street
Leavell, Craig D. ....'— '98 C&L.339 B.S., J.D. [Kirkland&E.]
Leavens, Thomas R., (AV) ... '48 '75 C.477 A.B. L.912 J.D. Gen. Coun., MusicNow LLC
Leavitt, Jamie .... '77 '02 C.338 B.S. L.1187 J.D. [🄰 Baker&E.]
Leavitt, Josh M., (AV) .... '60 '85 C.976 B.A. L.569 J.D. [Bell,B.&L.]
Leavitt, Marvin J. ....'49 '76 C.589 B.A. L.146 J.D. [Grund&L.]
Leavitt, Robert D. ....'54 '80 C.165 B.A. L.209 J.D. [🄲 Lowis&G.]
LeBlang, Danielle R. .... '78 '05 C.338 B.S. L.365 J.D. [🄰 Hinshaw&C.]

LeBoeuf, Lamb, Greene & MacRae, L.L.P., (AV)
A Limited Liability Partnership including Professional Corporations
Two Prudential Plaza, 180 North Stetson Avenue, Suite 1175, 60601 ⊙
Telephone: 312-794-8000 Fax: 312-794-8100
URL: http://www.llgm.com
Partners: Elizabeth M. Bradshaw; James R. Dwyer; Michael H. King, P.C.; Keith P. Schoeneberger; Neal L. Wolf. Counsel: Timothy A. Barnes; Darren J. Hunter; Spencer R. Wood.
General Practice including Banking, Bankruptcy, Copyrights, Corporate, Corporate Finance, Energy, Health Care, Insurance, Intellectual Property, Interactive Media, Internet and Telecommunications, International (Corporate, M&A, Energy), Life Insurance, Litigation, Mergers and Acquisitions, Municipal Bonds, Patents, Project Finance, Public Finance, Privatization, Real Estate, Taxation, Trademarks, Trusts and Estates, Utilities and Venture Capital.
Eastern United States:
New York, N.Y. Office: 125 West 55th Street. Telephone: 212-424-8000. Facsimile: 212-424-8500. Telex: 423416 or 1561363.
Washington, D.C. Office: 1875 Connecticut Avenue, N.W. Telephone: 202-986-8000. Facsimile: 202-986-8102. Telex: 440274.
Albany, New York Office: One Commerce Plaza, 99 Washington Avenue, Suite 2020. Telephone: 518-626-9000. Facsimile: 518-626-9010.
Boston, Massachusetts Office: 260 Franklin Street. Telephone: 617-439-9500. Facsimile: 617-439-0341; 439-0342.
Harrisburg, Pennsylvania Office: 200 North Third Street, Suite 300, P.O. Box 12105. Telephone: 717-232-8199. Facsimile: 717-232-8720.
Hartford, Connecticut Office: Goodwin Square, 225 Asylum Street, 13th Floor. Telephone: 860-293-3500. Facsimile: 860-293-3555.
Pittsburgh, Pennsylvania Office: One Gateway Center, Fort Duquesne Boulevard, Suite 1600. Telephone: 412-594-2300. Facsimile: 412-594-5237.
Western United States:
Los Angeles, California Office: 725 South Figueroa Street, Suite 3100. Telephone: 213-955-7300. Facsimile: 213-955-7399. Telex: 679982.
San Francisco, California Office: One Embarcadero Center, Suite 400. Telephone: 415-951-1100. Facsimile: 415-951-1180; 951-1181. Telex: 470167.
Southern United States:
Houston, Texas Office: 1000 Main Street, Suite 2550. Telephone: 713-287-2000. Facsimile: 713-287-2100.

(This Listing Continued)

LeBoeuf, Lamb, Greene & MacRae, L.L.P. (Continued)
Jacksonville, Florida Office: 50 North Laura Street, Suite 2800. Telephone: 904-354-8000. Facsimile: 904-353-1673.
European Offices:
Brussels, Belgium Office: Rue de Luxemburgstr 14A, B-1000 Brussels, Belgium. Telephone: 011-32-2-227-0900. Facsimile: 011-32-2-227-0909.
London, England Office: LeBoeuf, Lamb, Greene & MacRae (A London Based Multinational Partnership); One Minster Court, Mincing Lane, 6th Floor, London EC3R 7AA England. Telephone: 011-44-20-7-459-5000. Facsimile: 011-44-20-7-459-5099.
Moscow, Russian Federation Office: Nikitsky Pereulok, 5 (formerly Ulitsa Belinskogo) 103473 Moscow, Russian Federation. Telephone: 011-7-095-737-5000. Facsimile: 011-7-095-737-5050.
Paris, France Office: 130 rue du Faubourg Saint-Honoré 75008 Paris, France. Telephone: 011-33-1-53-93-77-00. Facsimile: 011-33-1-42-56-08-06.
Asian Offices:
Almaty, Kazakhstan Office: Prospect Seyfullin, 531, 5th Floor, 480083, Almaty, Republic of Kazakhstan. Telephone: 011-7-3272-50-7575. Facsimile: 011-7-3272-50-7576.
Beijing, China Office: Room B8, 21st Floor, Hanwei Plaza, No. 7 Guanghau Road, Chaoyang District, Beijing 10004, China. Telephone: 011-8610-6561-0422. Facsimile: 011-8610-6561-0425.
Bishkek, Kyrgyz Office: Ulitsa Panfilova, 205 Bishkek, Kyrgyz Republic. Telephone: 011-996-3312-22-2994. Facsimile: 011-996-3312-66-2233.
Tashkent, Uzbekistan Office: Ulitsa Turab Tula, 1 700003 Tashkent, Republic of Uzbekistan. Telephone: 011-7-3712-40-6050. Facsimile: 011-7-3712-40-6052.
African Office:
Johannesburg, South Africa Office: 11 Alice Lane, 2nd Floor, West Wing, Standard Bank Building, Sandton 2196, Johannesburg, South Africa. Telephone: 27-011-784-0233. Fax: 27-11-784-2855.
See Professional Biographies, CHICAGO, ILLINOIS

Leckie, David John '72 '97 C.879 B.S. L.602 J.D.
Arthur Andersen (Legal Department)‡
Lederer, Caren A. ....'67 '98 C.846 B.A. L.365 J.D. [🄰 Field&G.]
Lederman, Scott J. '56 '82
C.659 B.S.E. L.145 J.D. Ptnr., Grosvenor Capital Management, L.P.
Ledesma, Hector ....'64 '94 C.188 — L.589 J.D. 333 West Wacker Drive, Suite 500
Ledsky, Jonathan N. .... '59 '86 C.264 B.A. L.880 J.D. [Varga B.L.H.&C.]
LeDuc, John André, (AV) ....'54 '78 C.674 A.B. L.309 J.D. [Skadden,A.S.M.&F.]
LeDuc, Robert J. ....'67 '97 C.957 B.B.A. L.569 J.D. [🄰 DLPiper R.G.C.U.]
Le Duc, Timothy J. ... '69 '03 C.966 B.S. L.494 J.D. [🄰 Brinks H.G.&L.] (See Pat. Sect.)
Lee, Aleen .... '79 '04 C.228 B.S. L.477 J.D. [🄰 Schwartz C.]
Lee, Alexandra .... '74 '00 C.145 B.A. L.477 J.D. [🄰 Baker&M.]
Lee, Christine S. .... '72 '00 C.339 B.A. L.424 J.D. [🄰 Lewis,O.&F.]
Lee, Christopher J., (AV) '64 '93 C.339 B.S. L.146 J.D.
[Niro,S.H.&N.] (See Pat. Sect.)

Lee, David L., Law Offices of, (AV) '52 '77 C&L.597 B.A., J.D. 🄱🄱
Suite 660, 53 West Jackson Boulevard, 60604
Telephone: 312-347-4400 Facsimile: 312-347-3272
Email: d-lee@davidleelaw.com URL: http://www.davidleelaw.com
Civil Rights, Employment Law, Employment Discrimination, Employment Contracts, Employee Benefits, Retaliation, Unpaid Wages, Unpaid Overtime, Unpaid Commissions, Executive Employment Contracts and Executive Severance Negotiations.
See Professional Biographies, CHICAGO, ILLINOIS

Lee, David S. .... '77 '04 C.339 B.S. L.145 J.D. [🄰 McDermott W.&E.]
Lee, George I. '64 '94 C.966 B.S.E.E. L.339 J.D.
[McDonnell B.H.&B.] (See Pat. Sect.)
Lee, Grace Hwang .... '76 '01 C.597 B.A. L.273 J.D. [🄰 Krupin O.] (⊙Wash., DC)
Lee, Grace Soyon .... '74 '03 C.951 B.A. L.597 J.D. [🄰 Mayer,B.R.&M.]
Lee, Harold S. ....'32 '55 C.145 B.A. L.209 J.D. P.O. Box 59302
Lee, Hyun Ah .... '68 '93 C.339 B.A. L.117 J.D. [Baumann,S.&L.]
Lee, Inhak ....'— '99 C.145 B.A. L.352 J.D. [🄰 O'Hagan,S.&A.]
Lee, Jeannie '72 '04 C.788 B.A. L.904 J.D.
(adm. in NY; not adm. in IL) [🄰 Katten M.R.]
Lee, Joanne .... '— '04 C.339 B.A. L.145 J.D. [🄰 Foley&L.]
Lee, John A. ....'59 '98 C.966 B.S. L.209 J.D. [🄰 Michaels&M.]
Lee, John W. ....'72 '00 C&L.145 B.A., J.D. [🄰 Skadden,A.S.M.&F.]
Lee, John Y. .... '60 '86 C.197 B.A. L.597 J.D. [Hinshaw&C.]
Lee, John Z. ....'— '92 C&L.309 B.A., J.D. [Freeborn&P.]
Lee, Joshua ....'— '03 C.879 B.A. L.477 J.D. [🄰 Schiff H.]
Lee, Karen M. ....'69 '96 C.911 B.A. L.145 J.D. [🄲 Skadden,A.S.M.&F.]
Lee, Kevin T. .... '58 '83 C.597 B.S. L.146 J.D. [Wilson&L.]
Lee, Kim Barker .... '67 '93 C.976 B.A. L.569 J.D. [Pugh,J.J.&Q.]
Lee, Kyong ... '70 '00 C.597 B.A. L.146 J.D. City of Chicago, Dept. of Consumer Servs.
Lee, Marcus M. .... '73 '99 C.589 B.S. L.910 J.D. [🄰 Bell,B.&L.]
Lee, Michael D. .... '68 '94 C.339 B.S. L.146 J.D. [🄰 Schuyler,R.&Z.]
Lee, Michael P. ....'— '98 C.911 B.S. L.145 J.D. [Sachnoff&W.]
Lee, Michael S. .... '64 '94 C&L.861 B.S., J.D. Wealth Advsr., William Blair & Co.
Lee, Nicholas S. .... '— '04 C.679 B.S. L.209 J.D. 1327 W. Washington, Ste. 5G/H
Lee, Robert C. ....'— '85 C.893 B.Plan. L.477 J.D. [Jones D.]
Lee, Sang-yul .... '68 '96 C.597 B.A. L.339 J.D. [🄰 DLPiper R.G.C.U.]
Lee, Shawn P. .... '75 '01 C.597 B.A. L.910 J.D. [🄰 Wilson E.M.E.&D.]
Lee, Soojung '73 '03 L.1522 J.D.
(adm. in CA; not adm. in IL) [🄰 Sonnenschein N.&R.] (⊙L.A., CA)
Lee, Thomas C. ....'— '89 C.178 B.A. L.659 J.D. [Chapman&C.]
Lee, Thomas J., (AV) .... '37 '63 C.742 B.A. L.209 J.D. [T.J.Lee]
Lee, William M., Jr., (AV) ... '— '75 C.188 B.S. L.273 J.D. [Barnes&T.] (See Pat. Sect.)
Lee, William R. .... '79 '03 C.597 B.S.J. L.145 J.D. [🄰 Jenner&B.]

Lee, Mann, Smith, McWilliams, Sweeney & Ohlson
(See Barnes & Thornburg)

Lee, Thomas J., Ltd., (AV) ....134 N. La Salle St.
Leech, Michael J., (AV) ....'51 '76 C&L.893 B.A., J.D. [Hinshaw&C.]
Leeder, William J., III ....'— '05 C.896 B.A. L.209 J.D. [🄰 Johnson&B.]
Leeders, Terrance S. .... '71 '98 C.339 B.S. L.1187 J.D. [Leeders&D.]
Leeders & Doyle, Ltd. ....20 East Jackson Boulevard, Suite 850
Leeds, Paul L., (AV) ....'40 '64 C&L.477 B.A., J.D. 100 W. Monroe St.
LeeLun, Laura A. ....'77 '03 C&L.477 B.A., J.D. [🄰 Lord,B.&B.]
LeFever, John C. '29 '60 C.911 B.S. L.724 LL.B.
(adm. in NY; not adm. in IL; Pat.) One IBM Plaza‡
LeFevour, Mark L. ....'58 '83 C.687 B.A. L.424 J.D. [Kelley,K.&K.] ⊙
LeFevour, Terrence P. ....'54 '79 C.273 B.S.F.S. L.597 J.D. 221 N. LaSalle St.
Leff, Sherwin H., (AV) .... '41 '67 C.966 B.B.A. L.365 J.D. [Leff,C.&W.]

Leff, Cohen & Winkler, Ltd., (AV) 🄱🄱
303 West Madison Street, Suite 1700, 60606
Telephone: 312-782-2700 Fax: 312-782-9300
Email: lcw@lcwchicago.com URL: http://www.lcwchicago.com
Sherwin H. Leff; Aaron Cohen; Thomas W. Winkler;—Ronald G. Glosniak; Robert S. McCarty; Richard M. Cohen; Robert C. Ansani.
General Commercial, Federal and State Taxation, Property Tax and Assessment Law, Estate Planning, Probate and Real Estate Law.
See Professional Biographies, CHICAGO, ILLINOIS

Leffert, Kim A., (AV) .... '61 '86 C.188 A.B. L.145 J.D. [🄲 Mayer,B.R.&M.]

Lefkow, David M., (AV) .... '50 '78 C.339 B.A. L.117 J.D. [Holland&K.]
Lefkow, Joan H. .... '44 '71 C.937 A.B. L.597 J.D. U.S. Dist. Ct. J.
Lefkow, Michael F. .... '40 '66 C.578 B.A. L.597 J.D. 53 W. Jackson Blvd.
Lefkow, Michael R. '42 '67
C.1036 B.A. L.309 J.D. Gen. Atty., R. R. Donnelley & Sons Co.
Leftwich, Harold A. .... '26 '50 C.46 L.209 LL.B. 10 S. Riverside Pl.
Legal Helpers .... 444 North Wells Street, Suite 301
Legamaro, Michael J., (AV) .... '61 '86 C.910 A.B. L.597 J.D. [Schwartz C.]
Legator, Sheldon P. .... '29 '54 C.1016 B.S. L.209 J.D. 171 N. Clark St.
Legatos, Nick S. .... '73 '98 C.597 B.A. L.339 J.D. [Ⓐ Levenfeld P.]
Legatzke, Stephen J. .... '67 '92 C.602 B.A. L.893 J.D. [Winston&S.]
Legenza, Sharon K. .... '65 '91 C.145 B.A. L.597 J.D. [Ⓒ Miner,B.&G.]
Legg, Kari A. .... '— '00 C.339 B.A. L.209 J.D. Two North LaSalle Street, Suite 2200
Legittino, Tricia L. .... '71 '96 C.999 B.A. L.365 J.D. 209 South LaSalle Street, Suite 800
Legner, James J. .... '70 '95 C.201 B.A. L.365 J.D. [Levin,M.P.&M.]
LeHew, Steven J. '68 '99 C.339 B.A.T. L.424 J.D.
200 East Randolph Drive, Suite 7300
Lehman, Beth A. .... '44 '75 C.145 M.A. L.365 J.D. [Lehman&F.]
Lehman, David O. .... '— '73 C.309 A.B. L.659 J.D. [D.Lehman]
Lehman, Julie S. .... '62 '91 C.178 B.A. L.94 J.D. [Ravitz&P.]

Lehman, David, Law Offices
Suite 520, 55 West Van Buren Street, 60605-1110
Telephone: 312-360-0050 Fax: 312-360-0725
Email: davidlehmanlaw@davidlehmanlaw.com URL: http://www.davidlehmanlaw.com
David O. Lehman.
Immigration Law, Investor, Entertainer and International Business Personnel Transfers. All Immigrant, Non-Immigrant and Business Visas, Immigration Court Proceedings. Sarbanes-Oxley, Employment, State and Federal Civil Litigation.
See Professional Biographies, CHICAGO, ILLINOIS

Lehman & Fox, (AV) .... 6 East Monroe Street
Lehner, Paul E., (AV) .... '48 '75 C.178 B.A. L.276 J.D. [Adducci,D.L.M.&B.]
Lehner, Randall D. .... '— '96 C.477 B.A. L.228 J.D. [Sachnoff&W.]
Lehr, L. Anthony, (AV) .... '59 '84 C.436 B.S. L.339 J.D. [Lord,B.&B.]
Lehr, Louis A., Jr., (AV) .... '— '51 C&L.424 J.D. [Arnstein&L.]
Lehrer, Julius M. .... '21 '49 C&L.145 A.B., J.D. 20 N. Clark St.‡

Lehrer, Robert E., Law Offices, (AV) '45 '71 C.976 A.B. L.309 J.D.
36 South Wabash Street, Suite 1310, 60603
Telephone: 312-332-2121 Fax: 312-422-0708 Email: relehrer@aol.com
Email: lehrerlawoffice@aol.com URL: http://www.lawyers.com/relehrer
Civil Litigation, Civil Rights, Constitutional Law, Family Law, Children.
See Professional Biographies, CHICAGO, ILLINOIS

Leib, Alan D. .... '62 '87 C&L.339 B.S., J.D. [Ⓐ Harris K.&G.]
Leib, Lisa C. .... '64 '90 C.339 B.S. L.569 J.D. Asst. V.P. - Legal, Equity Residential
Leib, Michael S. .... '— '96 C.228 B.A. L.309 J.D. [Sachnoff&W.]
Leib, Sandra Miller '66 '91 C.347 B.S. L.966 J.D.
V.P. & Assoc. Gen. Coun., True North Communications, Inc. (Legal Department)
Leibenstein, Elli, (AV) .... '— '92 C.1183 B.A. L.145 J.D. [Kirkland&E.]
Leibovitz, Jay Byron .... '— '96 C&L.477 A.B., J.D. [Ⓐ Pircher,N.&M.]
Leibsker, Donald M., (BV) .... '42 '67 C.339 B.S. L.209 J.D. 29 S. LaSalle St.
Leibsker, Ira F. .... '50 '76 C.801 B.S. L.209 J.D. [Blatt,H.L.&M.]
Leichtman, Julie L. .... '77 '04 C.145 B.A. L.424 J.D. [Ⓐ Brinks H.G.&L.]
Leifel, Elizabeth A. .... '78 '03 C.339 B.A. L.477 J.D. [Ⓐ Sonnenschein N.&R.]
Leigh, Mari Henry .... '58 '83 C.679 B.A. L.930 J.D. [Meckler B.&T.]
Leighton, George N. .... '— '46 C.329 A.B. L.309 LL.B. [Ⓒ Neal&L.]
Leikin, Mitchell .... '21 '49 C.339 B.S. L.209 J.D. Assoc. Cir. J.
Leinberger, Karl G. .... '69 '96 C.352 B.A. L.209 J.D. [Crowley B.&K.]
Leinenweber, Harry D. .... '37 '62 C.602 A.B. L.145 J.D. Sr. U.S. Dist. J.
Leinheiser, Stacey L. .... '76 '02 C.340 B.A. L.209 J.D. [Ⓐ D.A.Axelrod&Assoc.]
Leipold, Mark E., (AV) .... '60 '86 C.597 B.S. L.209 J.D. [Gould&R.]
Leist, M. Shawn .... '— '03 C.502 B.A. L.910 J.D. [Ⓐ Schiff H.]
Leisten, Arthur G., (AV) '41 '66
C.424 A.B. L.309 J.D. Sr. V.P. & Gen. Coun., USG Corp.
Leiter, Manning K. .... '30 '51 C&L.145 B.A., J.D. 200 N. La Salle St.
Leitson, Mark '52 '89 C.477 B.A. L.145 J.D.
V.P. & Dep. Gen. Coun., National Equity Fund, Inc.
Leja, John A. .... '69 '98 C.679 B.S. L.188 J.D. [Ⓐ McGuirewoods]
Leka, Jill, (BV) .... '— '85 C&L.801 B.S., J.D. [Seyfarth S.]
Lele, Sal A. .... '71 '98 C.339 B.A. L.577 J.D. [Ⓐ DLPiper R.G.C.U.]
Lello, Victor W. .... '14 '50 C&L.339 B.S., LL.B. 6440 S. St. Louis Ave.‡
Lemack, Danielle B. .... '72 '98 C.1375 B.A. L.477 J.D. [Ⓐ Pattishall,M.N.H.&G.]
LeMar, Bruce R. '46 '71 C.347 B.S. L.477 J.D.
(adm. in CO; not adm. in IL) [Early C.&O.]
Lemberis, Theodore T., (AV) '48 '82 C.679 B.A. L.365 J.D.
Sr. VP & Assist. Gen Coun., Diners Club Intl. Ltd.
Lemein, Gregg D. .... '50 '76 C.339 B.S. L.597 J.D. [Baker&M.]
Lemker, John F., Jr. .... '38 '71 C&L.597 B.A., J.D. [Bell,B.&L.]
Lemley, Brandon K. .... '— '01 C.1119 B.A. L.1000 J.D. [Ⓐ Querrey&H.]
Lemmens, Alison A. .... '74 '01 C.436 B.S. L.209 J.D. [Ⓐ O'Keefe,L.&H.]
Lemming, Raymond M. .... '52 '97 C.201 B.S. L.146 J.D. CNA Plz., 13 South
Lemmon, Kristin J. .... '76 '01 C.57 B.A. L.424 J.D. [Ⓐ Burke,W.M.&S.]
LeMoine, Charles A., (AV) .... '57 '87 C.339 B.A. L.365 J.D. [Dykema G.P.]
Lemon, Donald J. .... '53 '83 C.937 B.A. L.365 J.D. Fred S. James & Co.
Lemon, Katherine Amy .... '75 '02 C.347 B.A. L.345 J.D. [Ⓐ Brenner,F.M.&S.]
Lempia, Bryan J. ... '— '93 C.645 B.S.M.E. L.215 J.D. [Marshall,G.&B.] (See Pat. Sect.)
Lempke, George J. .... '37 '63 C.424 B.S. L.209 LL.B. 1930 W. 21st Pl.‡
Lenahan, James J. '52 '77 C.339 B.S. L.424 J.D.
Assoc. Gen. Tax Coun., BP America Inc.
Lenahan, John T. '51 '77 C.339 B.S. L.209 J.D.
Asst. Gen. Coun., Fed. Regulatory, Ameritech Corp.
Lenane, Pamela A. '45 '71 C.700 B.A. L.597 J.D.
Acting Dir., Ill. Housing Develop. Auth.
Lenard, Cheryl Marie .... '76 '01 C.27 B.A. L.879 J.D. State's Atty. Off.
Lenard, Lori A. .... '— '92 C.927 B.A. L.46 J.D. [Ⓒ Kirkland&E.]
Lenczowski, Mark '63 '90 C.309 B.A. L.339 J.D.
Sr. Coun., Bank One Corp. (Law Dept.)
Lending, Randall Marc .... '64 '88 C.477 B.A. L.880 J.D. [Vedder,P.K.&K.]
Lengiewicz, Katherine .... '— '99 C.338 B.S. L.589 J.D. [Ⓐ O'Hagan,S.&A.]
Lenhart, Douglas W. '52 '79 C.746 B.A. L.1137 J.D.
(adm. in CA; not adm. in IL) FBI Spec. Agent
Lenkov, Richard W. .... '70 '96 C.012 B.A. L.589 J.D. [BryceDowney]
Lennard, Jeffrey, (AV) .... '48 '75 C.273 A.B. L.145 J.D. [Sonnenschein N.&R.]
Lennon, Robert F. .... '28 '52 C.340 B.A. L.365 J.D. 30 N. LaSalle St.‡
Lentz, James E., (AV) .... '— '75 C.177 B.A. L.352 J.D. [Ungaretti&H.]
Lentz, Robert J. .... '64 '89 C.927 B.A. L.365 J.D. [Ⓐ Fisher K.]
Lenz, Mark .... '56 '86 C.477 B.A. L.846 J.D. [Ⓒ Dykema G.P.]
Lenz, William J. '68 '99
C.339 B.S.M.E. L.365 J.D. 1327 W. Washington Blvd., Ste. 5G/H (Pat.)
Leo, T. Scott .... '54 '80 C.339 B.A. L.910 J.D. [Leo&W.]

Leo & Weber, P.C., (AV)
One N. LaSalle Street Suite 3600, 60602
Telephone: 312-857-0910 Fax: 312-857-1240
URL: http://www.leoweber.com
T. Scott Leo; Michael J. Weber; Grace Winkler Cranley. Associates: Neil A. Kraetsch; Jennifer Susnjara; Bryan M. Seifert. Of Counsel: Joel R. Page, Jr.
Bankruptcy, Fidelity and Surety Bonds, Commercial Litigation, Construction Law and General Litigation.
See Professional Biographies, CHICAGO, ILLINOIS

Leon, Abel .... '— '03 C.118 B.A. L.209 J.D. [Ⓐ Hinshaw&C.]
Leon, Jeffrey A., (AV) .... '65 '91 C.684 B.A. L.347 J.D. [Winston&S.]
Leon, Jorge M. .... '72 '98 C&L.339 B.S., J.D. [Ⓐ Jenner&B.]
Leon, Norman M. .... '66 '93 C.94 B.A. L.1009 J.D. [DLPiper R.G.C.U.]
Leonard, Donna Mullen .... '56 '85 C.209 B.S. L.365 J.D. Asst. Atty. Gen.
Leonard, John J., Jr. .... '50 '81 C.46 B.S. L.146 J.D. 300 N. State St.
Leonard, John L. .... '46 '71 C.424 B.S. L.597 J.D. [Teeple&L.]
Leonard, John M., Jr. .... '17 '47 C.209 L.365 J.D. 140 S. Dearborn
Leonard, Laura L., (AV) .... '56 '83 C.112 A.B. L.424 J.D. [Sidley A.B.&W.]
Leonard, Melanie C. .... '— '02 C.339 B.A. L.146 J.D. [Ⓐ Defrees&F.]
Leonard, Michael I. .... '65 '91 C.352 B.A. L.424 J.D. [Meckler B.&T.]
Leonas, Amy E. .... '76 '02 C.879 B.S. L.910 J.D. Co. State Atty.
Leonas, Theodore S., Jr. .... '51 '90 C.1016 B.S. L.879 J.D. [Leonas]
Leonas Law Office .... 30 N. LaSalle, Ste. 3400
Leone, Eugene J. M. .... '— '83 C.188 B.A. L.273 J.D. [Pircher,N.&M.]
Leonhard, Chunlin .... '64 '95 C.999 B.A. L.94 J.D. [Ⓒ Sonnenschein N.&R.]
Leopold, Valerie A., (AV) .... '53 '77 C.350 B.A. L.309 J.D. [Leopold&Assoc.]

Leopold & Associates, L.L.C., (AV)
150 North Michigan Avenue Suite 2700, 60601
Telephone: 312-781-6212 Fax: 312-781-6213
Email: leopoldlaw@sbcglobal.net URL: http://www.valerieleopold.com
Valerie A. Leopold.
Languages: English and Spanish.
Medical Malpractice, Birth Injury, Hospital Negligence, Obstetric Malpractice, Orthopedic Malpractice, Emergency Room Errors, Pregnancy Problems, Brain Damage, Cerebral Palsy, Surgical Mistakes, Nursing Errors, Cancer Misdiagnosis, Wrongful Death, Amputations, Nursing Home Negligence, Paralysis Cases, Motorcycle, Truck, Car and Pedestrian Accidents, Burn Injury, Drug and Medical Device Litigation, Sports Injury, Railroad Accidents and Injuries, Torts, Defective Products Liability, Toxic Torts and Class Action Litigation.
See Professional Biographies, CHICAGO, ILLINOIS

LePar, Lori J. .... '— '98 C.473 B.A. L.424 J.D. [Ⓐ Sidley A.B.&W.]
Lepinskas, Ronald M. .... '67 '93 C.197 B.A. L.145 J.D. [Lord,B.&B.]
Lepman, Carol S. .... '61 '83 C.477 L.347 LL.B. [Ⓒ DLPiper R.G.C.U.]
Lepp, Alan W. .... '63 '92 C.188 B.A. L.477 J.D. Staff Atty., U.S. Ct. of App.
Lepri, Julie A., (AV) '57 '81 C&L.424 A.B., J.D.
Sr. Assoc. Gen. Coun., Bank One Corp. (Law Dept.)
Lerman, Alice C. '54 '78 C.959 B.A. L.436 J.D.
(adm. in WI; not adm. in IL) 6531 N. Saint Louis Ave.‡
Lerman, Bradley E., (AV) .... '56 '81 C.976 B.A. L.309 J.D. [Winston&S.]
Lerman, Howard D., (AV) .... '40 '65 C.339 B.S. L.597 J.D. [Horwood M.&B.]
Lerman, Julie Chatz .... '57 '82 C.477 B.A. L.597 J.D. 3500 Three 1st Natl. Plz.
Lerman, Nancy .... '54 '85 C.72 B.A. L.145 J.D. 1813B N. Mohawk‡
Lerner, Barbara A. .... '35 '77 C&L.145 Ph.D, J.D. 1642 E. 65th St.‡
Lerner, Frederick M. .... '62 '87 C.352 B.S. L.339 J.D. 19 S. La Salle St., Ste. 802
Leroy, Michael D. .... '— '68 C.339 A.B. L.477 J.D. [Neal&L.]
LeRoy, Spencer, III '46 '74 C&L.477 A.B., J.D.
Sr. V.P., Gen. Coun. & Secy., Old Republic International Corp.
Lerum, Norman J., (AV) .... '49 '75 C&L.602 B.A., J.D. [N.J.Lerum]

Lerum, Norman J., P.C., (AV)
Suite 2100, 100 West Monroe Street, 60603
Telephone: 312-782-1087 Facsimile: 312-782-3773
Email: njlerum@msn.com URL: http://www.normanjlerum.com
Norman J. Lerum. Of Counsel: Michael J. Samis.
Trial and Appellate Practice in all State and Federal Courts concentrating in the following areas: Business Litigation, Contract Litigation, Chancery Practice, Plaintiff's Personal Injury (with emphasis on brain and spinal cord injuries), Construction Litigation, Aviation Law, Wrongful Death Law, Professional Negligence, Railroad Accidents and Injuries, Employment Litigation, Arbitration and Mediation.
See Professional Biographies, CHICAGO, ILLINOIS

Lervick, Jeana R. .... '77 '02 C.506 B.S. L.209 J.D. [Ⓐ Bell,B.&L.]
Lesavich, Stephen .... '59 '96 C&L.966 B.S., J.D. [Lesavich H.] (Pat.)

Lesavich High-Tech Law Group, PC
39 S. LaSalle Street, 60603
Telephone: 312-332-3751 Fax: 312-332-3752 URL: http://www.hightech-iplaw.com
Email: stephen.lesavich@lhtlg.com URL: http://www.lhtlg.com
Stephen Lesavich.
Software Patents, High-Tech Patents, Patent, Trademark Copyright Law, Licensing, Litigation, Internet Law, E-Commerce Law, Business Method Patents.
See Professional Biographies, CHICAGO, ILLINOIS

Lesch, Ian S. .... '70 '00 C.209 B.A. L.424 J.D. [Ⓐ Schuyler,R.&Z.]
Lesch, John Foster, (AV) .... '40 '66 C.597 B.S. L.146 J.D. [Nisen&E.]
Lescher, H. W. .... '20 '43 C&L.209 Ph.B., LL.B. 1 E. Superior St.
Lesht, David, (AV) '51 '81 C.339 B.S. L.46 J.D.
[Cook,A.M.M.C.&M.] (See Pat. Sect.)
Leslie, William D. .... '59 '85 C.339 B.A. L.209 J.D. IL Atty. Gen. Off.
Lesniak, Edward J., (AV) .... '49 '74 C.209 B.S.C. L.228 J.D. [Burke,W.M.&S.]
Less, Peter .... '20 '56 C.999 L.365 LL.B. 105 W. Madison
Lesser, Barbara A. .... '48 '79 C.339 B.A. L.1355 J.D. Brokers' Risk Placement Serv., Inc.
Lesser, Daniel J. .... '57 '84 C.674 A.B. L.597 J.D. Legal Assistance Found. of Chicago
Lessman, Timothy R. .... '78 '05 C.339 B.A. L.209 J.D. [Ⓐ Tressler,S.M.&P.]
Lessmeister, James J. .... '67 '94 C.338 B.S. L.1243 J.D. [Ⓐ Collins&B.]
Lester, Bruce W. .... '53 '78 C.424 B.A. L.597 J.D. Cir. J.
Letchinger, John S. .... '66 '91 C.597 B.S. L.339 J.D. [Wildman,H.A.&D.]
Letchinger, Robert S., (AV) .... '55 '82 C.118 B.A. L.597 J.D. [Laner,M.D.B.L.&T.]
Letchinger, Sharon Zaban .... '68 '93 C&L.339 A.B., J.D. [Schwartz C.]
Letkewicz, Lawrence C. .... '52 '77 C.602 A.B. L.339 J.D. Spec. Trial Atty.
Letsche, Keith E., (BV) .... '48 '81 C.121 B.A. L.209 J.D. Asst. Atty. Gen.
Letts, Eileen M., (AV) .... '54 '79 C.608 B.A. L.146 J.D. [Greene&L.]
Letvin, David J., (AV) .... '48 '73 C.1154 B.A. L.910 J.D. [Letvin&S.]
Letvin & Stein, (AV) .... 541 N. Fairbanks Ct.
Leuin, Charles B. .... '68 '94 C.228 A.B. L.339 J.D. [Greenberg T.]
Leung, Gary Y., Jr. .... '76 '02 C&L.597 B.A., J.D. [Ⓐ McGuirewoods]

Lev, Arnold M. '35 '60 C.146 B.S. L.589 J.D. 105 W. Madison St., Ste. 804
Lev, Ronald A. '46 '71 C.339 B.S. L.597 J.D. 40 E. Cedar St.
Levaccare, Lucien D. '12 '46 C&L.597 B.S.L., J.D. 953 W. 34th Pl.‡
Leval, Alain '49 '75 C.339 B.A. L.209 J.D. [Anesi,O.R.N.&K.]
Levatino, Jerome '19 '54 C.894 A.B. L.365 LL.B. 134 N. La Salle St.
LeVay, Brian D., (AV) '— '88 C.860 B.A. L.910 J.D. [Latimer L.J.]
LeVee, Janet Smerling, (AV) '62 '88 C.477 B.A. L.597 J.D. [Gordon&G.L.]
Levenberg, Richard S. '37 '63
C.188 B.A. L.813 J.D. Corp. Coun., Columbia Pipe & Supply Co.
Levenberg, Thomas O. '70 '96 C.813 B.A. L.597 J.D. [Gordon&G.L.]
Levenfeld, Andrew W. '48 '73 C.475 B.S. L.1292 J.D. [A.W.Levenfeld&Assoc.]
Levenfeld, Milton A., (AV) '27 '50 C&L.145 Ph.B., J.D. [Levenfeld P.]

Levenfeld, Andrew W., & Associates, Ltd.
221 N. LaSalle Street, Suite 2800, 60601-1206
Telephone: 312-782-5858 Fax: 312-419-9876
Email: levenfeld@yahoo.com URL: http://www.levenfeldlaw.com
Andrew W. Levenfeld. Associate: Jeffrey Scott Sell.
Civil Litigation, Trial Practice, Commercial and Residential Real Estate, Buying and Selling a Home, Condominium Law, Cooperative Housing Law, Homeowners Association Law, Land Acquisitions, Sales, Trusts, Real Estate Arbitration, Real Estate Development, Real Estate Development, Real Estate Leasing, Real Estate Mediation, Real Estate Tax Liens, Construction Law, Trusts and Estates, Elder Law, Estate Administration, Estate Planning, Estate Litigation, Family Trust, Powers of Attorney, Trust Litigation, Wealth Preservation, Probate Litigation, Asset Protection, Guardianship, Tax Litigation, Wills, Probate, Employment Discrimination, Sex Discrimination, Age Discrimination, Conservatorship, Corporate Law, Nonprofit Organization Law, Corporate Litigation, S Corporations, Small Business Corporations, Litigation, Consumer Fraud.
See Professional Biographies, CHICAGO, ILLINOIS

Levenfeld Pearlstein, LLC, (AV)
2 North LaSalle Street, Suite 1300, 60602 ⊙
Telephone: 312-346-8380 Facsimile: 312-346-8434
Email: lplegal@lplegal.com URL: http://www.lplegal.com
Members of Firm: David B. Berzon; Gary I. Blackman; Steven Bright; Mitchell Bryan; Jordan M. Cramer; Howard S. Dakoff; Katherine Smith Dedrick; Peter F. Donati; Leon I. Edelson; Steven "Sonny" F. Ginsberg; Donald A. Glassberg; Steven P. Gomberg; Beau T. Greiman; Darryl P. Jacobs; Thomas G. Jaros; Marc S. Joseph; Aaron S. Kase; Brian K. Kozminski; Scott A. Meyers; Mark D. Pearlstein; Scott H. Reynolds; Robert Alan Romanoff; Keith A. Ross; Philip E. Ruben; Bryan I. Schwartz; William S. Schwartz; Russell I. Shapiro; Abraham Trieger; Michael J. Tuchman; Mary K. Wasik. Associates: Mark A. Biesiada; Rebecca Edwards (Not admitted in IL); Jeffrey C. Friedman; Linda A. Gallagher; Eric J. Genin; Charles J. Goetz; Christopher S. Griesmeyer; Valli V. Gupta; Christopher M. Heintskill; Michele L. Krause; Nick S. Legatos; Jamie E. LeVine; Amy W. Mahone; James G. Martignon; Heather L. Moore; Jason P. Neumark; Patricia A. O'Connor; Neha A. Parikh; Natalie M. Perry; Brian J. Pleviak; Keara M. Roethke; Adam B. Rome; Jason M. Romick; Steven M. Weiss; Matthew R. Zakaras. Of Counsel: James D. Brusslan; William Case Clarke; Joseph S. Farrell; Milton A. Levenfeld. Counsel: G. John Blumberg.
Business Law, Corporate Law, Technology Law, Mergers, Acquisitions and Divestitures, Litigation, Real Estate, Banks and Banking, Financial Institutions Law, Finance, Secured Lending, Federal Taxation, State Taxation, Securities, Bankruptcy, Workouts, Homeowners Association Law, Condominium Law, Intellectual Property, Employee Benefits, Wealth Preservation, Estate Planning, Trust Law, Probate, International Asset Protection, Commercial Law, Franchise Law, Employment Law, Executive Employment Law, Environmental Litigation.
Northfield Office: 211 Waukegan Road, Suite 300, 60093. Telephone: 847-441-7676. Facsimile: 847-441-9976.
See Professional Biographies, CHICAGO, ILLINOIS

Levens, Jeffrey B. '— '75 C.339 B.A. L.424 J.D. [Augustine,K.&L.]
Levenstam, Barry, (AV) '53 '78 C&L.339 B.S., J.D. [Jenner&B.]
Levenstein, Gary I., (AV) '— '76 C.339 B.A. L.597 J.D. [Ungaretti&H.]
Leventhal, Donald B. '60 '86 C.475 B.A. L.608 J.D. [Chittenden,M.&N.]
Leventhal, Michael L., Jr. '38 '65 C.197 B.A. L.976 J.D. 120 S. LaSalle St.
Levey, Ross S., (BV) '68 '93 C.339 B.S. L.209 J.D. [Yavitz&L.]
Levi, Edward H. '11 '36 C&L.145 Ph.B., J.D.
Prof. of Law, Emeritus, Univ. of Chicago Law Sch.
Levi, John G., (AV) '48 '73 C.696 B.A. L.309 J.D. [Sidley A.B.&W.]
Levin, Alan M., (AV) '47 '74 C.976 B.A. L.145 J.D. [Laner,M.D.B.L.&T.]
Levin, Alisa M. '75 '04 C.36 B.S. L.424 J.D. [Fuchs&R.]
Levin, Allan Earl '25 '59 C&L.1035 B.S.L., LL.B. 221 N. LaSalle St.
Levin, Brad A. '58 '83 C.597 B.A. L.209 J.D. [Laser,P.S.F.&E.]
Levin, Brian T., (BV) '64 '92 C.339 B.A. L.365 J.D. [Lowis&G.]
Levin, Charles E., (AV) '46 '71 C.209 B.A. L.597 J.D. [McDermott W.&E.]
Levin, David B. '67 '92 C.851 B.A. L.608 J.D. 120 W. Madison, 10th Fl.
Levin, David M. '46 '74 C.608 B.A. L.161 J.D. 19 S. La Salle St., Ste. 1300
Levin, Deneese Walia '— '03 C.597 B.A. L.145 J.D. [Kirkland&E.]
Levin, H. Debra, (AV) '50 '75 C.188 B.A. L.309 J.D. [Seyfarth S.]
Levin, Herbert M. '36 '63 C.1016 B.S. L.209 J.D. 180 N. LaSalle St.
Levin, Ian H. '39 '66 C&L.209 B.S., J.D. U.S. Mag. J.
Levin, Ira M., (AV) '60 '86 C.472 B.B.A. L.46 J.D. [Burke,W.M.&S.]
Levin, Jack R. '50 '81 C.339 B.A. L.1000 J.D. [Borovsky&E.]
Levin, Jack S., (P.C.), (AV) '— '61 C.597 B.S. L.309 LL.B. [Kirkland&E.]
Levin, James R., (AV) '46 '71 C.188 B.S.M.E. L.976 J.D. 1001-C S. Plymouth Ct.‡
Levin, Jason W., (AV) '— '83 C.347 B.S. L.1119 J.D. [DLPiper R.G.C.U.]
Levin, Jennifer S. '77 '02 C.1365 B.A. L.597 J.D. [Jenner&B.]
Levin, Joel C., (AV) '49 '74 C.339 B.A. L.910 J.D. [Aronberg G.D.&G.]
Levin, Joel J. '48 '73 C.801 B.S. L.146 J.D. 130 E. Randolph Dr., Ste. 1200
Levin, Judith A. '55 '80 C.910 A.B. L.178 J.D. 4542 N. Paulina St.
Levin, Laurie A. '56 '85 C.999 B.M. L.262 J.D. [Fox,H.S.L.&C.]
Levin, Lawrence D. '59 '85 C&L.339 B.S., J.D. [Katten M.R.]
Levin, Lawrence R., (AV) '39 '65 C.37 B.A. L.976 LL.B. [Funkhouser V.L.&D.]
Levin, Lee A. '35 '59 C.221 B.A. L.209 J.D. 77 W. Wash. St.
Levin, Lee J. '61 '86 C&L.339 B.A., J.D. [Kamensky,R.H.&D.] ⊙
Levin, Leonard L. '23 '48 C&L.209 J.D. Cir. J.
Levin, Leslie Broder, (AV) '61 '86 C.339 B.A. L.146 J.D. 20 N. Wacker Dr.
Levin, Michael A. '53 '78 C.339 B.A. L.46 J.D. Harris Trust & Savings Bank
Levin, Michael D., (AV) '— '67 C&L.477 A.B., J.D. [Latham&W.]
Levin, Neal H. '62 '90 C.208 B.A. L.209 J.D. [Freeborn&P.] (⊙Chicago)
Levin, Neal H. '62 '90 C.208 B.A. L.209 J.D. [N.H.Levin&Assoc.] (⊙Chicago)
Levin, Ralph L. '30 '53 C.339 A.B. L.209 J.D. [Levin,R.]
Levin, Richard I., (AV) '60 '86 C.966 B.B.A. L.146 J.D. [Levin,R.]
Levin, Robert E., (AV) '12 '36 C&L.145 B.A., J.D. [McCarthy&L.] ‡
Levin, Robert M., (AV) '— '67 C.453 B.S. L.145 J.D. [Levin&S.]
Levin, Robert S., (AV) '— '66 C.339 L.209 J.D. [Levin G.]
Levin, Roger '41 '66 C.178 B.A. L.145 J.D. Ill. Com. Comm.
Levin, Samuel G. '60 '85 C.399 B.A. L.209 J.D. [Hinshaw&C.]
Levin, Sander D., (AV) '48 '74 C.1016 B.S.B.A. L.424 J.D. [Levin&B.]
Levin, Scott M., (AV) '54 '83 C.339 B.S. L.146 J.D. [Defrees&F.]
Levin, Steven M., (AV) '51 '76 C.966 B.A. L.424 J.D. [Levin&P.]
Levin, Steven R., (AV) '57 '81 C&L.861 B.A., J.D. [Levin,R.]
Levin, Thomas J. '23 '51 C.209 L.365 221 N. LaSalle St.‡

Levin, William E., & Associates, (AV) '40 '66 C.597 Ph.B. L.209 J.D.
200 West Madison Street, Suite 710, 60606-3412
Telephone: 312-372-6544 Facsimile: 312-372-8456 URL: http://www.lawyers.com/levin&associates
Email: WmELevinChgo@cs.com URL: http://www.williamelevinlawoffice.com
Federal Taxation, Corporate, Partnerships, Real Estate, Estate Planning, Trusts and Estates, Trials and Appeals.
Representative Clients: Bar-Ilan University in Israel; Compus System, S.A.; Miami Free Zone Corp.; North Suburban Cardiology Group, Ltd.; ORIX Real Estate Equities, Inc.; Quantum Cable, Inc.; Reese Development Company; TMK Development Ltd.
References: Harris Trust and Savings Bank; The Northern Trust Company.
See Professional Biographies, CHICAGO, ILLINOIS

Levin & Brend, P.C., (AV) BB
20 N. Wacker Drive, Suite 2920, 60606
Telephone: 312-726-4440 Fax: 312-726-0029
URL: http://www.levinbrend.com
Sander D. Levin; Jeffrey W. Brend; Gregory A. Papiernik;—Jennifer M. Fletchall; J. Denise Niemczyk.
Family Law, Complex Domestic Relations Issues, Divorce/Dissolution of Marriage, Financial Discovery, Forensic Accounting and Analysis related to Divorce, Business Valuation as related to Divorce, Tax Considerations related to Divorce, Property Rights, Prenuptial Agreements/Premarital Agreements, Postnuptial Agreements, Administration, Child Custody and Visitation, Spousal Support/Alimony/Maintenance, Matrimonial Law and Litigation, Marital Settlement Agreements, Separation Agreements, Appeals; Commodities, Real Estate Ventures, Corporate Law.
See Professional Biographies, CHICAGO, ILLINOIS

Levin & Funkhouser, Ltd.
(See Funkhouser Vegosen Liebman & Dunn Ltd.)

Levin Ginsburg, (AV)
180 North LaSalle Street, Suite 3200, 60601-2800
Telephone: 312-368-0100 Fax: 312-368-0111
Email: lg@lgattorneys.com URL: http://www.lgattorneys.com
Joseph A. Ginsburg; Anne C. Keays; Robert S. Levin; Lisa Arlyn Lowe; Morris R. Saunders; Jonathan M. Weis;—Keith Shaylan Baldwin; Saskia Nora Bryan; Josh S. Kaplan; Robert S. Strauss.
Mergers and Acquisitions, Business Litigation, Commercial Litigation, Employment Litigation, Real Estate Litigation, Corporate, Closely Held Business Estate Planning, Closely Held Business Law, Closely Held Corporations, Commercial Real Estate, Construction Contracts, Divestitures, Employment Law, Entrepreneurial Business Law, Estate Planning, Family Business Law, Family Corporations, International Business Law, Landlord and Tenant Law, Probate, Taxation, Transportation, Trusts and Estates and Wills, Tobacco Master Settlement Agreement Expertise, Internet Law, Trademarks, Ownership and Management Succession Planning.
See Professional Biographies, CHICAGO, ILLINOIS

Levin, McParland, Phillips & Minetz 221 N. La Salle St., Ste. 463
Levin, Neal H., & Associates, P.C. 954 W. Washington Boulevard Suite 2 SW

Levin & Perconti, (AV) BB
325 North LaSalle Street Suite 450, 60610
Telephone: 312-332-2872 Fax: 312-332-3112
URL: http://www.levinperconti.com
Members of Firm: Steven M. Levin; John J. Perconti; Susan Levin Novosad; Mary Ellen Cagney. Associates: Jeffrey E. Martin; Lawrence B. Finn; Anna Polyak; Stephen J. Coukos.
Catastrophic personal injury, wrongful death, personal injury, medical malpractice including birth injuries, cancer, AIDS, failure to diagnose or misdiagnosis, obstetric, surgical, cardiac, orthopedic and nursing malpractice. Nursing home abuse and neglect including bedsores, malnutrition, dehydration, wandering, falls, fractures, physical, verbal and sexual abuse and assault, restraints, medication errors and burns. Aviation, defective products, defective drugs, attorney malpractice, airplane crashes, automobile, construction, workplace, commercial litigation, Federal Tort Claims Act and insurance.
See Professional Biographies, CHICAGO, ILLINOIS

Levin, Riback Law Group P.C., (AV) BB
(Formerly Pekin & Levin & Associates)
200 North LaSalle Street, Suite 2300, 60601
Telephone: 312-782-6717 Fax: 312-782-5128 URL: http://www.levinriback.com
Email: info@levinriback.com URL: http://www.personalinjurylawyer1.com
Richard I. Levin; Steven R. Levin; Adam Riback; Amy R. Perlman;—Robert J. Adelman; Robert J. Domol. Of Counsel: Aram A. Hartunian; Ralph L. Levin.
Personal Injury, Catastrophic Injuries, Construction Accidents, Brain Injury, Spinal Cord Injury, Mild Head Injury, Premises Liability, Product Liability, Lasik Surgery, Medical Malpractice, Obstetric Malpractice, Reflex Sympathetic Dystrophy, Neurological Injuries, Automobile Accidents, Truck Accidents, Wrongful Death, Construction Site Safety, OSHA, Unsafe Job Conditions, Workers Compensation, Disability, Dog Bites, FELA, Railroad Accidents, Psychological Injury, Sever Burns and Birth Trauma.
See Professional Biographies, CHICAGO, ILLINOIS

Levin & Schreder, Ltd, (AV)
120 North La Salle Street, Suite 3800, 60602 ⊙
Telephone: 312-332-6300 Fax: 312-332-6393
Email: taxes@levinschreder.com URL: http://www.levinschreder.com
Robert M. Levin; Carleen L. Schreder; James R. Carey; Stuart J. Kohn; Margot Gordon; Theodore E. Froum; Julie J. Olenn. Of Counsel: Daniel G. Cedarbaum (Resident, Evanston Office).
Federal and International Income Tax Matters, Estate Planning, Family Wealth Counseling, Probate, Trust Administration, Probate and Trust Litigation and Contested Tax Matters.
Evanston, Illinois Office: 500 Davis Street, Suite 812, 60612-4269. Telephone: 847-492-5200. Fax: 847-492-9650.
See Professional Biographies, CHICAGO, ILLINOIS

Levine, Adam J. '— '95 C.659 B.S. L.145 J.D. [Kirkland&E.]
Levine, Alex C. '— '02 C.604 B.A. L.813 J.D. [Kirkland&E.]
Levine, Andrew N. '67 '92 C.339 B.S. L.209 J.D. [O'Rourke M.&M.]
Levine, Beth M. '62 '87 C.477 B.A. L.597 J.D. Legal Dept., Fed. Reserve Bk. of Chgo.
Levine, Catherine Mafee, (BV) '64 '91 C.475 B.S. L.215 J.D. [Wiedner&M.]
Levine, Donald B., (AV) '45 '69 C.966 B.A. L.209 J.D. [Latimer L.J.]
Le Vine, Edw. '10 '35 C&L.209 LL.B. 111 W. Wash. St.
Levine, Herzl E. '29 '52 C.999 B.Com L.365 J.D. 309 W. Washington
Levine, Howard J., (AV) '51 '79 C.378 B.A. L.472 J.D. [Gardner C.&D.]
Levine, Jamie E. '70 '03 C.367 B.A. L.597 J.D. [Levenfeld P.]
Levine, Jay D., (AV) '39 '63
C.264 B.S. L.178 LL.B. V.P. & Gen. Coun., Hawthorn Realty Grp.
Levine, Karen L., (AV) '52 '86 C.293 B.A. L.597 J.D. [Novack&M.]
Levine, Kenneth L. '47 '73 C.46 B.S. L.365 J.D. 1324 W. Touhy
Levine, Laurence H., (AV) '— '71 C.930 B.A. L.597 J.D. [Latham&W.]
Levine, Mark E. '71 '96 C&L.790 B.A., J.D. 55 E. Monroe St.
Levine, Mark L., (AV) '64 '90 C.674 A.B. L.976 J.D. [Bartlit B.H.P.&S.]
Levine, Robert S. '50 '77 C.930 B.S. L.1003 J.D.
(adm. in OH; not adm. in IL) Ernst & Young
Levine, Russell E., P.C., (AV) '60 '86 C.477 B.S. L.145 J.D. [Kirkland&E.] (Pat.)
Levine, Samuel H., (AV) '— '81 C.910 B.A. L.146 J.D. [Arnstein&L.]
Levine, Scott David '63 '89 C.659 B.A. L.597 J.D. Asst. U.S. Atty.
Levine, Sidney M., (AV) '52 '76 C&L.339 B.S., J.D. [Cohen,G.&R.]
Leving, Jeffery M. '51 '79 C.801 B.S. L.46 J.D. [J.M.Leving]

Leving, Jeffery M., Ltd., A Professional Corporation, Law Offices of
19 South La Salle Street, Suite 450, 60603
Telephone: 312-807-3990 Fax: 312-807-4782 URL: http://www.dadsrights.com
Email: pr@dadsrights.com URL: http://www.lawyers.com/Jeffery_Leving
Jeffery M. Leving.

(This Listing Continued)

Leving, Jeffery M., Ltd., A Professional Corporation, Law Offices of (Continued)
Family Law, Matrimonial Litigation, Sophisticated Financial Discovery and Analysis, Tax Considerations and Retirement Benefits, Negotiation and Mediation, Father's Custody and Visitation Trials and Appeals. Interstate and Intrastate Litigation, International Child Abduction Cases.
See Professional Biographies, CHICAGO, ILLINOIS

Levin-Muriel, Jayme . . . '69 '93 C.861 B.A. L.424 J.D. [A Spain,S.&V.]
Levins, Debra Homer . . . '58 '83 C&L.597 B.A., J.D. Stone Container Corp.
Levinsohn, Michael J. . . . '68 '94 C.94 B.S. L.861 J.D. 200 W. Superior St., Ste. 210
Levinson, Arthur H. . . . '56 '81 C.339 B.S. L.365 J.D. J.
Levinson, Irving B., (AV) . . . '47 '74 C.910 B.A. L.424 J.D. [Bell,B.&L.]
Levinson, Michael Gregg . . . '60 '86 C.339 B.S. L.365 J.D. Ann Anovitz Assocs.
Levinson, Michael R., (AV) . . . '54 '79 C.154 B.A. L.309 J.D. [Seyfarth S.]
Levinson, Michele . . . '58 '84 C.339 B.S. L.209 J.D. Asst. Atty. Gen.
Levinson, Myron N. . . . '12 '36 C.597 L.146 LL.B. 3600 Lake Shore Dr.‡
Levinson, Patti S. . . . '— '96 C.1349 B.A. L.146 J.D. [Arnstein&L.]
Levinson, Roberta A. . . . '51 '75 C&L.339 B.A., J.D. [Abrahamson V.&L.]
Levinson, Samantha A. . . . '— '01 C.276 B.S. L.365 J.D. [A Litchfield C.]
Levinson, William, (AV) . . . '25 '52 C&L.597 B.S.L., LL.B. 312 W. Randolph St.
Levit, Steven B. . . . '55 '80 C.339 B.S. L.46 J.D. [Levit&L.]
Levit & Lipshutz . . . 1120 W. Belmont Ave.
Levitt, Adam J., (AV) '69 '93
C.178 A.B. L.597 J.D. [Wolf H.A.F.&H.] (⊙New York, NY)
Levitt, David . . . '— '03 C.424 B.A. L.145 J.D. [A Ungaretti&H.]
Levitt, David H., (AV) . . . '54 '79 C.339 B.A. L.424 J.D. [Hinshaw&C.]
Levitt, Judith E. . . . '60 '86 C.771 B.A. L.209 J.D. Off. for Civil Rights
Levitt, Mark L. . . . '64 '90 C&L.339 B.A., J.D. Asst. Pub. Def.
Levitt, Renee S. . . . '— '86 C.339 B.A. L.146 J.D. [C Sedgwick,D.M.&A.]
Levstik, Betsy J. . . . '78 '04 C.945 B.S. L.209 J.D. [A Cook,A.M.M.C.&M.]
Levstik, Timothy E., (AV) '45 '70 C.124 B.S. L.494 J.D.
[Fitch,E.T.&F.] (See Pat. Sect.)
Levun, Charles R., Ltd., (AV) . . . '44 '70 C.339 B.S. L.145 J.D. [Levun,G.&C.] ⊙

Levun, Goodman & Cohen, LLP, (AV)
Comprised of Professional Corporations
One North La Salle Street Suite 1920, 60602 ⊙
Telephone: 312-263-4661
Email: lgc@lgclaw.com URL: http://www.lgclaw.com
Charles R. Levun, Ltd.; Lawrence S. Goodman, Ltd.; Michael J. Cohen, Ltd.
General Business and Tax Practice including Federal and State Taxation, Corporate Law, Partnership Law, Employee Benefits and Executive Compensation, Real Estate, Estate Planning, Trust Administration, and Commercial Litigation.
Northbrook, Illinois Office: 500 Skokie Boulevard, Suite 650. Telephone: 847-509-7700. Fax: 847-509-7709.
See Professional Biographies, CHICAGO, ILLINOIS

Levy, Andrew B. . . . '— '01 C.107 B.A. L.188 J.D. [A Ungaretti&H.]
Levy, Brooke A. . . . '79 '04 C.846 B.A. L.597 J.D. [A Skadden,A.S.M.&F.]
Levy, Charles, (AV) . . . '39 '65 C.1016 B.S.B.A. L.365 J.D. 1 N. La Salle St.
Levy, Charles G., (BV) . . . '35 '59 C.339 B.S.L. L.597 LL.B. One N. La Salle St.
Levy, David H., (P.C.), (AV) . . . '51 '76 C.610 B.G.S. L.146 J.D. [Berger S.]
Levy, George . . . '30 '56 C&L.145 A.B., J.D. 155 N. Michigan St.
Levy, Harry M., (AV) '40 '65 C.679 B.S.Ch.E. L.597 J.D.
[Emrich&D.] (See Pat. Sect.)
Levy, Jay K. . . . '49 '74 C.589 B.S. L.146 J.D. [Weltman,W.&R.]
Levy, Jon L. . . . '38 '63 C&L.861 B.A., LL.B. CNA Plaza‡
Levy, Jonathan D., (BV) . . . '— '91 C&L.477 B.A., J.D. [Pircher,N.&M.]
Levy, Joy E. . . . '— '01 C.800 B.S. L.809 J.D. [A Arnstein&L.]
Levy, Monica M. '77 '02 C.97 B.S.B.A L.596 J.D.
Two North LaSalle Street, Suite 2200
Levy, Morris A., (AV) . . . '36 '61 C.339 B.S. L.597 LL.B. 134 N. La Salle St.
Levy, Patricia . . . '59 '85 C.473 B.Phil. L.893 J.D. [C Katten M.R.]
Levy, Paul A. . . . '42 '68 C.477 M.B.A. L.276 J.D. [Levy&A.]
Levy, Paul M., (AV) . . . '35 '60 C.97 B.S. L.209 J.D. [Deutsch,L.&E.]
Levy, Peter A., (AV) . . . '49 '74 C&L.339 B.A., J.D. [DLPiper R.G.C.U.]
Levy, Richard A., (AV) . . . '— '83 C.31 B.A. L.976 J.D. [Latham&W.]
Levy, Richard B. . . . '— '81 C.210 B.A. L.146 J.D. [Freeborn&P.]
Levy, Richard F., (AV) . . . '30 '54 C.659 B.S. L.178 LL.B. [Jenner&B.]
Levy, Richard H., (AV) . . . '43 '76 C.801 B.S. L.209 J.D. [Schain,B.R.&C.]
Levy, S. Jerome, (AV) . . . '30 '54 C.597 B.S.L. L.497 LL.B. [S.J.Levy&Assoc.]
Levy, Scott J. . . . '66 '94 C.910 B.A. L.221 J.D. 1525 East 53rd Street, Suite 524
Levy, Stephen, (AV) . . . '29 '55 C.339 L.365 J.D. 33 N. LaSalle
Levy, Steven A. . . . '63 '88 C.473 B.S. L.339 J.D. [Goldberg,K.B.B.R.&M.]
Levy, Steven M., (AV) . . . '58 '82 C.597 B.A. L.309 J.D. [Sonnenschein N.&R.]
Levy, Susan C., (AV) . . . '57 '82 C.188 A.B. L.309 J.D. [Jenner&B.]
Levy, William A. . . . '63 '88 C.659 B.A. L.145 J.D. [Mayer,B.R.&M.]
Levy & Augustine . . . 333 N. Michigan Ave., Ste. 1600

Levy, S. Jerome, & Associates, P.C., (AV)
One East Wacker Drive, Suite 2500, 60601
Telephone: 312-832-1616 FAX: 312-832-0270
URL: http://www.jeromelevylaw.com
S. Jerome Levy; Karin A. Olson. Of Counsel: Leslie A. Stulberg.
Practice limited to Litigation including Plaintiff's Personal Injury, Wrongful Death, Medical and Dental Malpractice, Products Liability, Premises Liability, Commercial and Private Aviation Litigation, Chemical Exposure, Torts, Injuries, Insurance, Income Tax, Tax Planning.
See Professional Biographies, CHICAGO, ILLINOIS

Lew, Michael I. . . . '39 '65 C&L.597 B.S., J.D. Coopers & Lybrand
Lewandowski, Rita L., (BV) . . . '54 '81 C.424 B.A. L.209 J.D. 121 N. LaSalle St.
Lewey, Virginia S. . . . '53 '80 C.893 B.A. L.128 J.D. 2446 N. Albany
Lewin, David M. . . . '65 '92 C.424 B.A. L.209 J.D. [A Tribler O.&M.]
Lewin, Herbert M. . . . '11 '39 C.999 A.A. L.365 J.D. 29 S. LaSalle St.‡
Lewin, Jeremy B. . . . '— '99 C.209 B.A. L.424 J.D. [A Barnes&T.]
Lewin, Matthew R. . . . '— '81 C.1044 B.S. L.1119 J.D. [Chapman&C.]
Lewinbuk, Ekaterina Parton . . . '72 '00 C.999 B.A. L.1000 J.D. 25 E Jackson
Lewis, Adam F. . . . '58 '84 400 E. Randolph
Lewis, Adam S. . . . '73 '98 C.339 B.S. L.424 J.D. [A Vedder,P.K.&K.]
Lewis, Amy Elizabeth . . . '76 '03 C&L.339 A.B., J.D. [A Vedder,P.K.&K.]
Lewis, Andrew '63 '90 C&L.999
(adm. in England; not adm. in IL) Sr. Atty., Northern Trust Corporation

Lewis, Barry Michael '50 '75 C.597 B.A. L.365 J.D.
211 East Ontario Street Suite 1800, 60611
Telephone: 312-372-2221 Fax: 312-377-1771
Email: blewislaw@aol.com URL: http://www.barrylewislaw.com
Personal Injury, Medical Malpractice, Product Liability, Criminal, DUI, DWI, Traffic Violations, Felonies, Serious Misdemeanors, Drug Cases.
See Professional Biographies, CHICAGO, ILLINOIS

Lewis, Brian E. . . . '70 '98 C.347 B.A. L.879 J.D. [A Henderson&L.]
Lewis, Brian W. . . . '59 '85 C.339 B.A. L.424 J.D. [Wildman,H.A.&D.]
Lewis, Charles B., (AV) . . . '50 '76 C.477 B.A. L.767 J.D. [Jenkens&G.]
Lewis, Douglas I. . . . '66 '93 C.339 B.S. L.145 J.D. [A Sidley A.B.&W.] (Pat.)
Lewis, Garth F. . . . '67 '98 C.209 B.A. L.339 J.D. [A Spain,S.&V.]
Lewis, Gregory L. . . . '48 '76 C.347 A.B. L.678 J.D. Mgr., Housing Develop. Auth.
Lewis, Hilary E. . . . '— '78 C.597 B.A. L.381 J.D. Dir. & Sr. Coun., CNA Healthpro
Lewis, Irving . . . '15 '39 C&L.352 B.A., J.D. [Galvin,L.W.G.&S.] ‡
Lewis, Jay D. . . . '78 '04 C.861 L.146 J.D. 221 N. LaSalle St., Ste. 1763
Lewis, Jeannette L. . . . '63 '88 C.339 B.A. L.424 J.D. Assoc. Reg. Dir., M.R.O., S.E.C.
Lewis, Jill B. . . . '64 '97 C.1111 B.A. L.209 J.D. 1 E Wacker Drive
Lewis, John A. '45 '85 C.660 B.S. L.424 J.D.
Staff Atty., SAFECO Prop. & Cas. Ins. Co.
Lewis, Jonathan L. . . . '70 '99 C.446 B.A. L.477 J.D. [A Mayer,B.R.&M.]
Lewis, Julius, (AV) . . . '31 '57 C.145 B.A. L.976 LL.B. [Sonnenschein N.&R.]
Lewis, Kenneth S., (AV) . . . '32 '57 C&L.597 B.S., J.D. [Lewis,D.&H.]
Lewis, Philip S. . . . '39 '64 C.477 B.B.A. L.309 LL.B. [Gass&L.] ⊙
Lewis, Renee P. . . . '— '97 C&L.209 B.S., J.D. [A Morgan,L.&B.]
Lewis, Richard A. . . . '54 '80 C.352 B.A. L.339 J.D. Asst. Corp. Coun.
Lewis, Robert J. . . . '66 '95 C.674 A.B. L.494 J.D. [A Sidley A.B.&W.]
Lewis, Robert V., (AV) . . . '— '64 C.674 B.a. L.477 J.D. [C Chapman&C.]
Lewis, Roger A. . . . '70 '95 C.813 B.A. L.309 J.D. [Goldberg,K.B.B.R.&M.]
Lewis, Roger F. . . . '36 '60 C.339 B.S. L.597 J.D. [C Sidley A.B.&W.]
Lewis, Stephen B. . . . '52 '78 C.210 B.A. L.347 J.D. 500 West Monroe
Lewis, Tod A. . . . '66 '98 C.932 B.B.A. L.146 J.D. [Freed&W.]
Lewis, William J. . . . '— '95 C.436 B.S. L.285 J.D. [Ungaretti&H.]
Lewis, Willie F., Jr. . . . '— '99 C&L.209 B.A., J.D. [A Chapman&C.]
Lewis, Davidson & Hetherington, Ltd., (AV) . . . 1 N. Franklin St.

Lewis, Overbeck & Furman, LLP, (AV)
135 South La Salle Street, Suite 2300, 60603-4274
Telephone: 312-580-1200 Fax: 312-580-1201
Email: Firm@LEWISOVERBECK.COM URL: http://www.lewisoverbeck.com
Members of Firm: David J. Creagan, Jr.; Tim J. Emmitt; James R. Gannon; Robert A. Subkowsky; Douglas A. Lindsay; John W. Loseman; F. Richard Skweres. Associates: Christine S. Lee; Sage Fattahian; Lisa M. Simioni. Of Counsel: Perry H. Lewis (1908-1995); John H. Overbeck, Jr. (1918-2003); Victor E. Furman (1906-1992); John M. Teevan (1918-2000); O. Keith Stoutner (1913-1995); Paul L. Freter; George W. Phillips; Thomas H. Varner.
ERISA, Employee Benefits, Pension and Profit Sharing Plans, Apprenticeship Programs, Labor, State and Federal Courts Trials and Appeals, ERISA Litigation, Corporate, Federal and State Taxation, Business, Estate Planning, Real Estate, Trusts, Probate.
See Professional Biographies, CHICAGO, ILLINOIS

Lewison, Edward . . . '11 '32 C&L.145 Ph.B., J.D. 505 N. Lake Shore Dr.‡
Lewison, Murray J. . . . '52 '77 C.347 B.S. L.221 J.D. [Johnson&C.]
Lewitas, Bruce . . . '65 '91 C.475 B.A. L.46 J.D. 55 E. Monroe St., Ste. 3910
Leydig, C. Frederick, (AV) '25 '50
C.46 B.S.Ch.E. L.209 J.D. [C Leydig,V.&M.] (See Pat. Sect.)
Leydig, Gary W., (AV) . . . '55 '80 C.339 B.A. L.945 J.D. [C Worker,S.&H.]

Leydig, Voit & Mayer, Ltd., (AV) BB
Two Prudential Plaza, 180 North Stetson Avenue, Suite 4900, 60601-6780 ⊙
Telephone: 312-616-5600 Telecopier: 312-616-5700
Email: mail@leydig.com URL: http://www.leydig.com
James B. Muskal; Dennis R. Schlemmer; Gordon R. Coons; John W. Kozak; Mark E. Phelps; H. Michael Hartmann; Bruce M. Gagala; Charles H. Mottier; John Kilyk, Jr.; Robert F. Green; John B. Conklin; James D. Zalewa; Mark J. Liss; John M. Belz (Resident, Washington, D.C. Office); Brett A. Hesterberg; Jeffrey A. Wyand (Resident, Washington, D.C. Office); Paul J. Korniczky; Pamela J. Ruschau; Steven P. Petersen; John M. Augustyn; Christopher T. Griffith; Wesley O. Mueller; Jeremy M. Jay (Resident, Washington, D.C. Office); Lynn A. Sullivan; Jeffrey B. Burgan; Eley O. Thompson; Mark Joy; David M. Airan; Xavier Pillai; Y. Kurt Chang; Gregory C. Bays; Steven H. Sklar; Tamara A. Miller; M. Daniel Hefner; Salim A. Hasan; Roger D. Wylie (Resident, Seattle, Washington Office); Kenneth P. Spina;—Phillip M. Pippenger; Anne E. Naffziger (Resident, Seattle, Washington Office); Vladan M. Vasiljevic; Claudia W. Stangle; Paul J. Filbin; John L. Gase; Jeremy C. Lowe; John T. Bretscher; Robert T. Wittmann; J. Karl Gross; Seth A. Rose; Saumil S. Mehta; Jason T. Murata; Scott H. Schulhof; Aaron R. Feigelson; L. Scott Beall; Lisa K. Kelly; Stephen R. Auten; Mark A. Nieds; Caroline L. Stevens; Douglas A. Robinson; Nancy J. Gettel; Peter H. Domer; Jeffrey N. Turner; Susan L. Steele; Stephanie M. Lawley (Resident, Washington, D.C. Office); Kurt T. Buechle; Thomas K. McBride, Jr.; Jennifer M. Duk; Marcos P. Rivas (Not admitted in IL); Christine M. Cochran; Kevin C. Parks. Of Counsel: C. Frederick Leydig; Theodore W. Anderson; John P. Bundock, Jr. (Resident, Washington, D.C. Office); Berton Scott Sheppard; John E. Rosenquist; Charles S. Oslakovic (Resident, Rockford, Illinois Office); John D. Foster (Resident, Washington, D.C. Office).
Patent, Trademark, Copyright, Unfair Competition, Licensing and Related Antitrust and International Trade Law. Trials and Appeals.
Rockford, Illinois Office: 6815 Weaver Road, Suite 300. Telephone: 815-963-7661. Telecopier: 815-963-7664.
Washington, D.C. Office: Leydig, Voit & Mayer, 700 Thirteenth Street, N.W., Suite 300. Telephone: 202-737-6770. Telecopier: 202-737-6776.
Seattle, Washington Office: 1420 Fifth Avenue, Suite 2200. Telephone: 206-521-5985. Telecopier: 206-224-3557.
See Professional Biographies, CHICAGO, ILLINOIS

Leyhane, Francis J. (Jack), III, (AV) . . . '57 '80 C&L.424 A.B., J.D. [Leyhane&Assoc.]

Leyhane & Associates, Ltd., (AV)
11 East Adams Street, Suite 1600, 60603
Telephone: 312-922-2996 Fax: 312-922-0323
Email: Leyhane329@aol.com URL: http://www.lawyers.com/leyhanelaw
Francis J. (Jack) Leyhane, III. Of Counsel: Eugene P. Sullivan.
Insurance Litigation, Insurance Coverage, Appellate Practice, General Practice, Commodities.
Other Chicago Office: 9924 S. Walden Parkway, 60643. Telephone: 773-238-5881. Fax: 312-922-0323.
See Professional Biographies, CHICAGO, ILLINOIS

Li, Chuan . . . '— '99 L.352 J.D. [A Kirkland&E.]
Li, Julie Y. . . . '— '95 L.910 J.D. [C Susman&Assoc.]
Li, Ted S. . . . '78 '03 C.1349 B.A. L.145 J.D. [A Hubert&F.]
Liang, Stephanie S. . . . '76 '02 C.276 B.S.F.S. L.145 J.D. [A Kirkland&E.]
Liapis, Telly J. . . . '72 '97 C.424 B.A. L.146 J.D. [A Tressler,S.M.&P.]
Libbey, Heather A., (AV) '59 '87
C.518 A.B. L.880 J.D. Asst. V.P. & Asst. Gen. Coun., CNA
Libby, Eileen B., (CV) '46 '90
C.339 B.A. L.424 J.D. Assoc. Ethics. Council, Amer. Bar Assn.
Libert, Marshall C. . . . '52 '82 C.339 B.A. L.589 J.D. Asst. States Atty.
Liberti, Daniel J. '51 '84 C.184 B.A. L.365 J.D.
V.P. & Chf. Enforc. Coun., Chicago Stock Exchange, Incorporated
Libit, William M. . . . '— '85 C.1365 B.A. L.597 J.D. [Chapman&C.]
Libman, Robert H. . . . '44 '83 C.339 M.D. L.209 J.D. 901 S. Ashland
Libman, Robert S. . . . '63 '88 C&L.813 B.A., J.D. [Miner,B.&G.]
Libman, Stephen M. . . . '59 '86 C.589 B.A. L.1187 J.D. 2 N. LaSalle St.
Libowsky, Stephen D., (AV) . . . '57 '82 C.880 B.A. L.280 J.D. [Howrey]
Licari, Mary F. . . . '— '86 C.338 B.S. L.339 J.D. [Bates&C.]
Licari, Ralph J. . . . '65 '91 C.927 B.S. L.365 J.D. 20 S. Clark St.
Licata, Anthony R., (AV) . . . '54 '79 C.430 B.S. L.309 J.D. [Shefsky&F.]
Licata, James J. . . . '53 '87 C.602 B.A. L.146 J.D. Draper & Kramer, Inc.
Lichtsein, Bruce M. . . . '64 '90 C.597 B.A. L.930 J.D. [Cozen O.]
Lichten, Thomas R., (AV) . . . '46 '73 C.309 B.A. L.477 J.D. [T.R.Lichten]

Lichten, Thomas R., Ltd., (AV) .... 53 W. Jackson Blvd.
Lichtenberger, Vincent M. ... '64 '91 C.178 B.A. L.93 J.D. Corp. Coun., Borg-Warner Inc.
Lichtenfeld, Samuel A. .... '76 '02 C.597 B.A. L.94 J.D. [Ⓐ Shaw G.F.G.W.&T.]
Lichtenfeld, Susan Grob, (AV) ...... '52 '77 C.273 B.A. L.910 J.D. [DLPiper R.G.C.U.]
Lichtenstein, Daniel H. ...... '70 '96 C.477 B.B.A. L.339 J.D. Atty., Grant Thornton Intl.
Lichtenstein, David G. .... '45 '74 C&L.910 A.B., J.D. Cir. J.
Lichtenstein, Larry B., & Associates, (AV) '42 '67
C&L.339 B.S., J.D. 20 North Clark Street, Suite 801
Lichtenstein, Nathan H., (AV) ....'53 '77 C.597 B.A. L.209 J.D. [Aronberg G.D.&G.]
Lichtenstein, Susan R., (AV) '57 '81
C.494 B.A. L.597 J.D. 225 West Randolph Street, 27th Floor
Lichterman, Jonathan D. .... '69 '96 C.477 B.A. L.276 J.D. [Ⓐ Meckler B.&T.]
Lichtman, Marc S. .... '50 '85 C.347 B.S. L.209 J.D. 123 North Wacker Drive
Lickerman, Michael A. ....'70 '95 C.597 B.A. L.659 J.D. [M.A.Lickerman]
Lickerman, Michael A., P.C. .... 120 W. Madison Street, Suite 225
Lidbury, James T. ....'65 '90 C&L.597 B.A., J.D. [Mayer,B.R.&M.]
Lidbury, Thomas A., (AV) .... '67 '92 C.145 B.A. L.910 J.D. [Ⓒ Mayer,B.R.&M.]
Lidd, Dorothea J. .... '60 '87 C.145 A.B. L.424 J.D. [Ⓐ Schwartz C.]
Lieb, Philip S. ....'36 '61 C.339 B.S. L.209 J.D. Assoc. Cir. J.
Lieb, Roslyn C. ....'42 '76 C.705 A.B. L.209 J.D. Pub. Interest Law Initiative
Liebentritt, Donald J. '50 '76
C.424 A.B. L.145 J.D. Pres., Equity Group Investments, LLC
Lieber, Howard L., (BV) .... '57 '83 C&L.424 B.A., J.D. [Horvath&L.]
Lieber, Michael R. ....'— '96 C.67 B.A. L.347 J.D. [Sachnoff&W.]
Lieberman, David E. ....'— '92 C.103 Sc.B. L.145 J.D. [Sachnoff&W.]
Lieberman, Karen M. .... '68 '94 C.1375 B.A. L.477 J.D. Coun., Heller Fin., Inc.
Lieberman, Mark C. ......'49 '75 C.339 B.S. L.146 J.D. 111 W. Washington St., Ste. 1030
Lieberman, Mitchell A., (AV) .... '61 '86 C.347 B.A. L.209 J.D. [Noonan&L.]
Lieberman, Myron, (AV) ....'31 '54 C.813 B.S. L.597 LL.B. [Ⓒ Greenberg T.]
Lieberman, Peter H. .... '62 '89 C.477 A.B. L.309 J.D. [Greenberg T.]
Lieberman, Richard E., (AV) .... '46 '71 C.473 B.A. L.150 J.D. [McGuirewoods]
Liebl, Ryan J. ....'75 '04 C.602 B.A. L.146 J.D. [Ⓐ Katten M.R.]
Liebling, Jeffrey H. .... '70 '98 C.338 B.S. L.365 J.D. [Ⓐ Seyfarth S.]
Liebman, Joshua E. ....'76 '04 C.861 B.A. L.424 J.D. [Ⓐ Swanson,M.&B.]
Liebman, Richard D. ....'49 '75 C.46 B.S. L.597 J.D. Ernst & Young
Liebman, Vance L., (AV) ....'52 '77 C.293 B.A. L.597 J.D. [Funkhouser V.L.&D.]
Liebow, Deborah A. ....'57 '83 C.339 L.146 J.D. Asst. Dir., Amer. Library Assn.
Lien, John D., (AV) ....'— '68 C.966 B.A. L.309 J.D. [Foley&L.]
Lies, Mark A., II, (AV) ....'46 '74 C.602 B.A. L.209 J.D. [Seyfarth S.]
Lifshitz, Richard A., (AV) .... '51 '76 C&L.910 B.A., J.D. [Mandel,L.&S.]
Lifson, Steven R. .... '60 '87 C.94 B.A. L.339 J.D. [Seyfarth S.]
Lifton, Fred B. ....'28 '52 C&L.912 A.B., J.D. [Robbins,S.N.L.&T.]
Lifvendahl, Eric R., (AV) ....'66 '92 C.93 B.A. L.424 J.D. [Williams M.&J.]
Lifvendahl, Susan F. ....'67 '93 C.95 B.S. L.424 J.D. [Ⓐ Handler,T.&D.]
Ligas, Andrew, Law Office of ...... '67 '92 C.424 B.A. L.365 J.D. 5097 S. Archer, Ste. Z
Ligda, Matthew J. ....'68 '95 C.1365 B.B.A. L.209 J.D. [Ⓐ Pretzel&S.]
Liggio, Carl D., Sr., (AVⓉ) .....'43 '67 C.276 A.B. L.569 J.D. [Ⓒ McCullough,C.&L.] ‡
Light, Corey E. .... '56 '82 C.339 B.S. L.209 J.D. [Greenberg T.]
Light, Russell S. ....'— '01 C.453 B.S. L.145 J.D. [Ⓐ Kirkland&E.]
Lightfoot, Lori E. ....'62 '89 C.477 B.A. L.145 J.D. 10 W. 35th Street, 12th Floor
Liguori, Christopher D., (AV) .... '62 '87 C.477 B.A. L.904 J.D. [Jenner&B.]
Liker, Alex ....'— '01 C.424 B.S. L.146 J.D. [Ⓐ Katten M.R.]
Liljequist, Jon L. '36 '64 C.339 B.S.M.E. L.424 J.D.
Pat. Consultant & Lic. Offr., Univ. of Ill. (Pat.)
Liljestrand, Craig T., (AV) .... '65 '90 C.234 B.A. L.365 J.D. [Hinshaw&C.]
Lillie, Mark S., (AV) ....'— '84 C.597 B.S. L.208 J.D. [Kirkland&E.]
Lillios, Paul C. '57 '82 C.352 B.A. L.190 J.D.
(adm. in IA; not adm. in IL) Reg. Chf. Admin. Law J.
Lilly, Lisa M. ....'65 '00 C.999 B.A. L.209 J.D. [Ⓐ Sonnenschein N.&R.]
Lillya, Erik J. ......'63 '91 C.604 B.A. L.597 J.D. Atty. Adviser, Chicago, M.R.O., S.E.C.
Lim, Arlene ....'73 '98 C&L.597 B.S., J.D. [Ⓐ Winston&S.]
Limperis, Chris E., (BV) '54 '78 C.597 B.A. L.477 J.D.
Assoc. Gen. Coun., Rush Presbyterian St. Luke's Med. Ctr.
Lin, Christopher K. ....'76 '02 C.910 A.B. L.477 J.D. [Ⓐ McDermott W.&E.]
Lin, Jennifer Lee ....'74 '00 C.846 B.A. L.146 J.D. State's Atty. Off.
Lin, Laura '62 '88 C&L.800 B.S., J.D.
(adm. in CA; not adm. in IL) Assoc. Prof., Northwestern Univ. Sch. of Law
Linares, Juan Carlos '76 '02 C.339 B.A. L.209 J.D.
Asst. Corp. Coun., City of Chicago Law Dept., Fin. Div.
Lind, Carol M. .... '67 '94 C.951 B.A. L.145 J.D. [Ⓐ Sidley A.B.&W.]
Lind, Chris ....'68 '94 C.477 B.A. L.597 J.D. [Bartlit B.H.P.&S.]
Lind, Jon R., (AV) .... '35 '61 C&L.309 A.B., LL.B. 227 W. Monroe St.‡
Lindahl, Katherine L. ....'79 '04 C.861 B.A. L.145 J.D. [Ⓐ Skadden,A.S.M.&F.]
Lindau, Peter D. .... '63 '96 C.882 B.A. L.93 J.D. [Ⓐ Ross,D.&B.]
Lindauer, April J. .... '74 '03 C.145 A.B. L.209 J.D. [Ⓐ Shaheen,N.S.F.&E.]
Lindberg, Elizabeth A. ... '61 '88 C.597 B.S. L.424 J.D. Dr. Ins. Litig. Dept., Boeing Co.
Lindberg, George W. .... '32 '58 C&L.597 B.S., J.D. U.S. Sr. Dist J.
Linde, Derek P. ....'75 '00 C.502 B.A. L.880 J.D. [Ⓐ Winston&S.]
Lindeman, Janet A., (AV) .... '63 '87 C.282 B.A. L.724 J.D. [DLPiper R.G.C.U.]
Lindemann, John S. .... '66 '92 C.879 B.A. L.347 J.D. [Lord,B.&B.]
Linden, Richard F. .... '60 '89 C.352 B.S. L.424 J.D. [Ⓐ O'Rourke M.&M.]
Lindenbaum, Leon E., (AV) .... '37 '61 C&L.966 B.B.A., J.D. [Ⓒ Kurlander&G.]
Lindenmuth, Noel C., (AV) .... '40 '70 L.424 J.D. 161 North Clark Street, 21st Floor‡
Linder, David C. '64 '90 C&L.494 B.A., J.D.
(adm. in MO; not adm. in IL) [Lovells]
Lindgren, James T. ......'52 '77 C.976 B.A. L.145 J.D. Prof., Northwestern Univ. Law Sch.
Lindgren, William D. .... '32 '56 C&L.597 B.S.L., J.D. 6919 N. Oriole Ave.‡
Lindland, Kurt N., (BV) ....'63 '91 C.475 B.S. L.146 J.D. Asst. U.S. Atty.
Lindner, Burton R., (Ltd.) ....'43 '70 C.339 B.S. L.209 J.D. 150 S. Wacker Dr.
Lindner, David P. ....'— '04 C.339 B.S. L.209 J.D. [Ⓐ Brinks H.G.&L.]
Lindo, Lorelle L. ....'— '04 C&L.352 [Ⓐ Chapman&C.]
Lindquist, Alan V. ....'54 '83 C&L.339 B.S., J.D. [Ⓐ Winston&S.]
Lindquist, Scott A., (AV) ....'57 '82 C&L.477 B.A., J.D. [Sonnenschein N.&R.]
Lindquist, Teri A., (AV) ....'59 '86 C.1044 B.A. L.597 J.D. [Jenner&B.]
Lindsay, Douglas A., (AV) ....'51 '76 C.373 B.A. L.365 J.D. [Lewis,O.&F.]
Lindsay, Nancy J. '52 '77 C.477 B.A. L.597 J.D.
Sr. Assoc. Gen. Coun., Bank One Corp. (Law Dept.)
Lindt, Marketa ....'68 '94 C&L.665 B.A., J.D. 10 S. Dearborn
Linebarger Goggan Blair & Sampson, LLP, (BVⓉ)
233 S. Wacker Dr., Suite 4030 (60606) (⊙Phoenix, AZ; L.A., CA; Denver, CO; Jacksnvl., Miami, FL; Dublin, OH; Harrisburg, Phila., PA; Memphis, TN; Austin, Beaumont, Brownsville, Conroe, Corpus Christi, Corsicana, Dallas, Edinburg, El Paso, Fort Worth, Greenville, Hous., Jacksboro, Longview, Lufkin, Odessa, Orange, Pampa, Rich-

(This Listing Continued)

Linebarger Goggan Blair & Sampson, LLP, (Continued)
mond, San Angelo, San Antonio, Sherman, Texas City, The Woodlands, Tyler, Victoria, Waco, TX; Richmond, VA)
Lines, John K. ....'— '84 C.679 B.S. L.1119 J.D. [Ⓒ Schiff H.]
Ling, S. Tony ....'70 '96 C.597 B.A. L.1119 J.D. [Jenner&B.]
Lingertat, Jessica G. ....'72 '97 C.339 B.A. L.436 J.D. [Gould&R.]
Lingren, Kristin L. ....'— '96 C&L.966 B.A., J.D. [Ⓐ Mandell M.]
Linguanti, Thomas V. M. ....'63 '91 C.136 B.S. L.262 J.D. [Baker&M.]
Link, Amanda L. ....'78 '04 C.339 B.A. L.209 J.D. 150 S. Wacker, Ste. 2400
Link, Janet Malloy ....'— '95 C.976 B.A. L.178 J.D. [Latham&W.]
Link, Matthew R. ....'79 '04 C.424 B.A. L.209 J.D. [Ⓐ Dowd&D.]
Linker, Meredith J. '73 '98
C.846 B.A. L.146 J.D. Legal Placement Consultant, Co-Counsel
Linklater, William J., (AV) .... '42 '68 C.602 B.A. L.424 J.D. [Baker&M.]
Linn, Debra J. .... '56 '85 C.999 B.A. L.659 J.D. Quaker Oats Co.
Linn, Estelle ....'— '59 C.597 B.S. L.209 J.D. 200 E. Delaware Place
Linn, Herbert J., (AV) ....'44 '69 C.477 A.B. L.339 J.D. [Pedersen&H.]
Linn, James B., (AV) .... '49 '77 C.98 B.S. L.365 J.D. Asst. States Atty.
Linn, Scott J. '52 '79 C.339 B.A. L.734 J.D.
Corp. Cnsl, General Growth Properties, Inc.
Linneman, Michael Joseph .....'75 '01 C.436 B.A. L.365 J.D. 218 N. Jefferson, Suite 300
Linnemeyer, Kara L. .... '72 '98 C.999 B.A. L.209 J.D. [Ⓐ E.T.Joyce&Assoc.]
Linsley, Sarah M., (AV) .... '56 '84 C.309 A.B. L.597 J.D. [Quarles&B.]
Linton, Robert C. .... '64 '89 C.477 B.A. L.276 J.D. [Schwartz C.]
Lione, Richard G., (AV) '31 '60 C.966 B.S. L.273 J.D.
[Brinks H.G.&L.] (See Pat. Sect.) (⊙Arlington, VA)
Liou, Timothy K. ....'66 '95 C.589 B.S. L.146 J.D. 575 W. Madison Street, Suite 361
Lipe, Jay A., (AV) ....'30 '53 C.145 A.B. L.893 LL.B. [Ⓒ Dykema G.P.]
Lipe, Jeffrey H., (AV) .... '58 '83 C.861 B.A. L.339 J.D. [Williams M.&J.]
Lipezker, Enrique A. .... '66 '99 C.424 B.S. L.146 J.D. 221 N. LaSalle St., Ste. 2040
Lipinski, Laura Ann, (AV) .... '63 '87 C.424 B.S. L.339 J.D. [Schwartz C.]
Lipinski, Marc S., (AV) ....'54 '79 C.145 A.B. L.813 J.D. [Riordan,D.L.&M.]
Lipinski, Ronald L., (AV) ....'50 '76 C.373 B.A. L.365 J.D. [Seyfarth S.]
Lipke, Douglas J., (AV) .... '53 '79 C.436 B.S. L.424 J.D. [Vedder,P.K.&K.]
Lipkin, Marcia S., (AV) ....'49 '76 C.339 B.A. L.209 J.D. [M.S.Lipkin]
Lipkin, Mitchell S., (AV) .... '51 '85 C.339 B.A. L.209 J.D. [Lipkin&H.]
Lipkin & Higgins, (AV) .... 222 North LaSalle Street Suite 2100
Lipkin, Marcia S., PC, (AV) .... 120 N. LaSalle St., Ste. 1160
Lipman, Joel L. ....'67 '95 C.112 B.A. L.426 J.D. [Ⓐ O'Rourke M.&M.]
Lipman, Nancy G. ....'45 '83 C.339 B.A. L.597 J.D. Asst. Pub. Def.
Lipnick, Stanley M., (AV) ....'— '60 C.178 B.A. L.273 J.D. [Ⓒ Arnstein&L.]
Lippert, Kevin M. .... '70 '03 C.473 B.A. L.276 J.D. [Ⓐ Shefsky&F.]
Lippold, Sara S. '72 '97 C.339 B.S. L.910 J.D.
(adm. in MO; not adm. in IL)
Sr. V.P., Legal & Compliance, Terra Nova Trading, L.L.C.
Lipschultz, Brent S. ....'66 '91 C.347 B.S. L.146 J.D. KPMG Peat Marwick
Lipschultz, Jerry R. ....'47 '74 C.436 B.A. L.209 J.D. [Lipschultz]
Lipschultz, Noah G. ....'— '01 C.966 B.A. L.145 J.D. [Ⓐ Seyfarth S.]
Lipschultz Law Firm .... 205 W. Randolph St., Ste. 1000
Lipshutz, Hal A. ....'56 '80 C.339 B.A. L.146 J.D. [Levit&L.]
Lipsitz, Michael '64 '89 C.597 B.A. L.424 J.D.
Sr. Assoc. Gen. Coun., Bank One Corp. (Law Dept.)
Lipson, Wayne David .... '58 '83 C.339 B.S. L.209 J.D. Asst. Pub. Def.
Lipton, Alan R. .... '50 '80 C.339 B.A. L.464 J.D. [Hinshaw&C.]
Lipton, Alfred R., (AV) ....'42 '66 C.966 B.S. L.145 J.D. [Mandel,L.&S.]
Lipton, Clara E. ....'76 '03 C.30 B.S. L.145 J.D. [Ⓐ Baker&M.]
Lipton, Lois J. ....'46 '74 C.477 B.A. L.209 J.D. [Ⓒ Robinson C.&C.]
Lipton, Richard M., (AV) ....'52 '77 C.31 B.A. L.145 J.D. [Baker&M.]
Liro, Christopher R. ....'— '01 C.453 S.B. L.477 J.D. [Ⓐ Kirkland&E.]
Lis, Shabsa A. .... '58 '86 C.976 B.A. L.569 J.D. [S.A.Lis]
Lis, Shabsa A., P.C. ....33 N. Dearborn St.
Lischer, Nancy G., (AV) .... '52 '81 C.879 B.A. L.209 J.D. [Hinshaw&C.]
Lisco, Robert F., (AV) ....'28 '51 C.339 L.209 J.D. 20 N. Clark St.
Lisiecki, Lucy ....'— '98 C&L.145 B.A., J.D. [Ⓐ Wildman,H.A.&D.]
Liskar, Jeffrey E. ....'59 '84 C.477 B.A. L.339 J.D. V.P., The Appraisal Institute
Lisnek, Paul M. ....'58 '83 C&L.339 B.A., J.D. V.P., Natl. Instit.for Legal Educ.
Liss, Debra A. ....'78 '02 C.477 B.A. L.146 J.D. 20 N. Clark St., Ste. 2300
Liss, Jeffrey G., (AV) ....'43 '68 C.103 A.B. L.309 J.D. [J.G.Liss]
Liss, Jeremy Seth ....'— '99 C&L.477 B.B.A., J.D. [Kirkland&E.]
Liss, Laura Shroyer .... '— '96 C.477 B.A. L.146 J.D. [Michael B.&F.]
Liss, Mark J., (AV) ....'56 '81 C.339 B.A. L.146 J.D. [Leydig,V.&M.]

Liss, Jeffrey G., P.C., (AV)
130 South Jefferson Street, Suite 501, 60661
Telephone: 312-876-0600 Fax: 312-782-7789
Email: JGLJGL@aol.com
Jeffrey G. Liss.
Business and Real Estate Law, Estate Planning, Wills and Trusts.
See Professional Biographies, CHICAGO, ILLINOIS

Lissner, Talia Anna .... '72 '01 C.339 B.S. L.146 J.D. [Ⓐ Sonnenschein N.&R.]
List, David P., (AV) ....'20 '48 C.197 A.B. L.309 LL.B. One 1st. National Plz.‡
List, Steven S. .... '61 '86 C.966 B.A. L.209 J.D. Accenture
Listecki, Jerome E. '49 '76
C.424 B.A. L.209 J.D. Gen. Coun., Catholic Bishop of Chicago
Listokin, Stephanie P. '75 '02 C.309 A.B. L.659 J.D.
(adm. in NY; not adm. in IL) [Ⓐ Sugar,F.&F.]
Liston, Brian P., (AV) ....'61 '91 C.679 B.S. L.989 J.D. 33 North La Salle Street
Listrom, Linda L., (AV) .... '52 '77 C.326 B.A. L.309 J.D. [Jenner&B.]
Liszewski, Paul R. '56 '91
C.999 B.A. L.365 J.D. Underwriting Coun., Chicago Title Ins. Co.
Liszka, Walter J. .... '45 '70 C.597 B.A. L.424 J.D. [Wessels&P.]
Litak, Michael J. ....'— '83 C.679 B.A. L.209 J.D. 1335 N. Vermont St.★
Litchfield, Daniel G., (AV) .... '— '83 C.221 B.A. L.145 J.D. [Litchfield C.]

Litchfield Cavo LLP, (AV)
Suite 300 303 West Madison Street, 60606-3300 ⊙
Telephone: 312-781-6677 Fax: 312-781-6630
Email: firm@litchfieldcavo.com URL: http://www.litchfieldcavo.com
Partners: Kenneth J. Barrish; Jonathan E. Barrish; Alan I. Becker; Tracy C. Beggs; John R. Catizone (Resident, Tampa, Florida Office); Richard C. Cavo (Resident, Avon, Connecticut Office); Elizabeth M. Christofaro (Resident, Avon, Connecticut Office); Robert L. Ciociola (Not admitted in IL; Resident, Lynnfield, Massachusetts Office); Thomas C. Clark (Not admitted in IL; Resident, Avon, Connecticut Office); Bradford Cooke (Resident, New York, N.Y. Office); Thomas M. Crawford; Mark A. Darling (Resident, Lynnfield, Massachusetts Office); Michael J. Dugan (Resident, Cherry Hill, New Jersey Office/Avon, Connecticut Office); Carrie A. Durkin; Marc S. Edrich (Not admitted in IL; Resident, Avon, Connecticut Office); Edward M. Fogarty, Jr. (Resident, New York, N.Y. Office); Mitchell H. Frazen; Dawn M. Gonzalez; Daniel T. Hughes (Resident, New York, N.Y. Office);

(This Listing Continued)

Litchfield Cavo LLP (Continued)

Matthew J. Iverson; John J. Jarosak (Not admitted in IL; Resident, Lynnfield, Massachusetts Office); Eileen P. Kavanagh (Not admitted in IL; Resident, Lynnfield, Massachusetts Office); Kearney W. Kilens; Peter C. Kober (Resident, Lynnfield, Massachusetts Office); Daniel G. Litchfield; Lynne M. Mueller (Resident, Brookfield, Wisconsin Office); Mark W. Murphy (Resident, Lynnfield, Massachusetts Office); Hope G. Nightingale; Lisa A. Oonk (Resident, Tampa, Florida Office); Nicholas J. Parolisi, Jr.; Peter J. Ponziani (Not admitted in IL; Resident, Avon, Connecticut Office); Mark W. Rattan (Resident, Brookfield, Wisconsin Office); Paul G. Roche (Resident, Avon, Connecticut Office); Joseph B. Royster; J. Rodney Runyons (Resident, Tampa, Florida Office); George P. Smyrniotis; Scott D. Stephenson; Patrick J. Sullivan; Charles E. Vermette, Jr. (Not admitted in IL; Resident, Avon, Connecticut Office). Associates: Alan M. Bernover; James M. Bonalsky (Resident, New York, N.Y. Office); Kathleen J. Collins (Resident, Cherry Hill, New Jersey Office); David A. Corbett (Not admitted in IL; Resident, Avon, Connecticut Office); Peter Cusick (Resident, New York, N.Y. Office); Luana DiSarra (Resident, Lynnfield, Massachusetts Office); Dennis Dolan; Stephanie L. Dykeman (Resident, Brookfield, Wisconsin Office); Jodi Zils Gagne (Resident, Avon, Connecticut Office); Kathleen M. Hansberry (Resident, Cherry Hill, New Jersey Office); Michael J. Heinle; Timothy S. Jajliardo (Not admitted in IL; Resident, Avon, Connecticut Office); Daniel P. Johnston; Samantha A. Levinson; Richard A. Lord, Jr. (Resident, Avon, Connecticut Office); Mark S. Nazarof; James P. Odda (Resident, Brookfield, Wisconsin Office); Daniel S. Orenstein; Jacob W. Osher (Resident, Cherry Hill, New Jersey Office); Ohn Park; William J. Perry; Brian M. Reid; Deborah E. Roser (Not admitted in IL; Resident, Avon, Connecticut Office); James W. Sexton (Resident, Lynnfield, Massachusetts Office); Christopher J. Sochacki (Resident, Avon, Connecticut Office); Kevin J. Spagnoli (Resident, New York, N.Y. Office); Melicent B. Thompson (Not admitted in IL; Resident, Avon, Connecticut Office); Stephanie Wing Tipton; Matthew D. Walker; Renee H. Wiszowaty.

General Liability, Business Litigation, Bad Faith/Extra Contractual Liability, Environmental/Toxic Tort Defense, Product Liability, Insurance Coverage Litigation, Construction, Executive Liability, Reinsurance, Professional Liability-Non Medical, Professional Liability - Medical, Truckers' Liability, Appellate Practice, Employment Liability, Intellectual Property, Workers' Compensation, First Party Property.

Avon: 40 Tower Lane, Suite 200, Avon CT 06001-4222. Telephone: (860) 255-5577. Fax: (860) 255-5566.

Boston: 6 Kimball Lane, Suite 100, Lynnfield, MA 01940-2682. Telephone: (781) 309-1500. Fax: (781) 245-0167.

New Jersey: Commerce Center, 1800 Chapel Avenue West, Suite 140, Cherry Hill, NJ 08002. Telephone: (856) 854-3636. Fax: (856) 751-1230.

New York: 420 Lexington Avenue, Suite 1750, New York, NY 10170. Telephone: (212) 434-0100. Fax: (212) 434-0105.

Tampa: 5201 West Kennedy Boulevard, Suite 450, Tampa, FL 33609. Telephone: (813) 289-0690. Fax: (813) 289-0692.

Wisconsin: 13555 Bishop's Court, Suite 230, Brookfield, WI 53005-6224. Telephone: (262) 784-8800. Fax: (262) 784-8812.

See Professional Biographies, CHICAGO, ILLINOIS

Lithgow, Bruce E. . . . '67 '94 C.877 B.A. L.145 J.D. [Bell,B.&L.]
Litner, Mark S., (AV) . . . '59 '85 C.860 B.A. L.597 J.D. [Much S.F.D.A.&R.]
Litt, Paula E., (AV) . . . '52 '84 C.608 B.S. L.309 J.D. [Schopf&W.]
Little, J. Joseph, (AV) . . . '51 '79 C.608 B.S.B.A. L.424 J.D. [Hamblet,O.&L.]
Littlejohn, William L., (AV) . . . '31 '56 C&L.893 B.A., LL.B. 2258 N. Lincoln Pk. W.‡

Littler Mendelson, A Professional Corporation, (AV)
200 North LaSalle Street, Suite 2900, 60601-1014 ⊙
Telephone: 312-372-5520 Facsimile: 312-372-7880
Email: info@littler.com URL: http://www.littler.com
Jody A. Ballmer; Paul E. Bateman; Dana S. Connell; Shanthi V. Gaur; Keith C. Hult; Stefanie W. Kohen; Robert C. Long (Also at Columbus, Ohio); James J. Oh; David J. Parsons; Garrison L. Phillips; Frederick L. Schwartz; Adam C. Wit; John A. Ybarra;—D. Chad Anderton; Asilia S. Backus; Rachel F. Barner; David L. Christlieb; Terese Connolly; Melodie K. Craft; John Dijohn; Erin Dougherty Foley; Puamuh T. Ghogomu, II; Margaret Parnell Hogan; Stephanie Seay Kelly; Paul Krause; Mary C. O'Neil; Marissa Ross; Alan Satyr; Amy R. Schaefer; Amy Toepper; Amanda Helm Wright.
Employment and Labor Law; Affirmative Action; Age Discrimination in Employment Civil Service; Collective Bargaining; Confidentiality Agreements; Covenants Not To Compete; Employee Drug Testing; Employee Privacy; Employer Liability; Employment Arbitration; Employment Breach of Contract; Employment Civil Rights; Employment Class Actions; Employment Discrimination; Employment Litigation; Equal Employment Opportunity Law; Fair Labor Standards; Family and Medical Leave Act; Harassment; Labor Relations; Labor Strikes; National Labor Relations Act; Noncompete Litigation; Noncompetition and Non-Solicitation Agreements; Personnel Policies; Prevailing Wage Litigation; Reductions in Force; Restrictive Covenants; Sexual Harassment; Title VII Discrimination; Unfair Labor Practices; Union Contract Negotiations; Union Elections; Union Organization; Wage and Hour Law; WARN Act; Whistleblower Litigation; Workplace Violence; Wrongful Termination; Wrongful Termination Defense.
Offices located in: Phoenix, Arizona; California — Fresno, Los Angeles, Sacramento, San Diego, San Francisco, San Jose, Santa Maria, Stockton and Walnut Creek; Denver, Colorado; Washington, D.C.; Miami, Florida; Atlanta, Georgia; Boston, Massachusetts; Minneapolis, Minnesota; Reno and Las Vegas, Nevada; Newark, New Jersey; New York, New York; Charlotte, North Carolina; Columbus, Ohio; Philadelphia and Pittsburgh, Pennsylvania; Dallas and Houston, Texas; Seattle, Washington.

See Professional Biographies, CHICAGO, ILLINOIS

Littles, Lorenzo S. . . . '51 '83 C.188 B.A. L.309 J.D. COO for U.S. Senator
Littman, Roger, (AV) . . . '— '79 C&L.339 B.A., J.D. [Querrey&H.]
Litvak, Matthew M. . . . '61 '91 C.339 B.S. L.365 J.D. 155 N. Harbor Dr.
Litwin, Burton H., (AV) . . . '44 '70 C.1016 B.S.B.A. L.597 J.D. [Neal,G.&E.]

Litwin, Leonard D., (BV) '57 '82 C.339 A.B. L.209 J.D.
205 West Randolph Street Suite 1410, 60606-1894
Telephone: 312-346-9733 Fax: 312-704-4323
Email: leonardlitwin@sbcglobal.net URL: http://www.lawyers.com/ldlitwinlaw
Personal Injury, Workers Compensation, Family Law, Divorce, Real Estate, Landlord and Tenant Law, Medical Malpractice, Wrongful Death, Social Security Disability, Trusts and Estates, Guardianship and Conservatorship, Consumer Bankruptcy, Adoption Law, Child Custody, Child Support, Premarital Agreements, Spousal Support, Automobile Accidents and Injuries, Dog Bites, Slip and Fall.

See Professional Biographies, CHICAGO, ILLINOIS

Litwin, Stuart M., (AV) . . . '59 '85 C.339 B.S. L.145 J.D. [Mayer,B.R.&M.]
Liu, Eileen M. . . . '72 '97 C&L.597 B.A., J.D. [Sidley A.B.&W.]
Liu, Grace I. . . . '— '04 C.309 A.B. L.145 J.D. [Beem]
Liu, Laura C. . . . '— '91 C.980 B.S. L.150 J.D. [Hogan M.]
Liutikas, L. Daniel . . . '71 '00 L.146 J.D. [Much S.F.D.A.&R.]
Lively, Jonathan Mark . . . '— '99 C.373 B.A. L.904 J.D. [Schiff H.]
Lively, Paul T., (AV) . . . '48 '73 C.339 A.B. L.597 J.D. [Foran G.P.&P.]

Livensparger, John C., Law Office of, (AV) '45 '76 C.37 B.A. L.365 J.D.
4753 North Broadway Suite 620, 60640
Telephone: 773-784-2102 Fax: 773-784-2281
Email: livensparger@ameritech.net
Estate Administration, Probate, Real Estate, Corporate, Federal Taxation and Banking Law.

See Professional Biographies, CHICAGO, ILLINOIS

Livergood, Julie Lynn . . . '— '02 C.98 B.S.N. L.209 J.D. [Lord,B.&B.]
Livermore, Brian M., (CV) . . . '61 '92 C.424 B.A. L.425 J.D. 9019 S. Damen Ave.
Livingston, Bradford L., (AV) . . . '54 '79 C&L.477 B.A., J.D. [Seyfarth S.]
Livingston, John, Attorney at Law '67 '93 C&L.502 B.S., B.S. 1616 W. Montrose, Ste. 3A
Livingston, Nancy R. . . . '53 '83 C.914 B.A. L.209 J.D. [Schwartz C.]
Livingston, Terrance K. '56 '81 C.602 B.A. L.477 J.D. Assoc. Gen. Coun., Chicago Board of Trade
Livingston, Theodore A., Jr. . . . '46 '73 C.467 B.A. L.378 J.D. [Mayer,B.R.&M.]
Llerena, Elaine A. . . . '75 '03 C.259 B.S. L.365 J.D. [Beaulieu]
LL.M. Law Group . . . 12 S. Michigan Ave., Ste. 5

Lloyd, David J. . . . '48 '73 C.477 B.A. L.966 J.D. [Rohlfing&O.]
Lloyd, Kathryn A. . . . '74 '00 C.608 B.S. L.597 J.D. [Seyfarth S.]
Lloyd, Kurt D., (AV) . . . '59 '85 C.209 B.A. L.146 J.D. [Lloyd&C.]
Lloyd, Neil . . . '— '94 C.668 B.A. L.145 J.D. [Schiff H.]
Lloyd, Robert A., (AV) . . . '41 '69 C.339 B.S.E.E. L.424 J.D. [Greer,B.&C.] (Pat.)
Lloyd, William M. . . . '43 '68 C.388 B.A. L.339 J.D. Federal reserve Bank of Chicago

Lloyd & Cavanagh, (AV)
Suite 2050, 200 West Madison Street, 60606
Telephone: 312-425-1900 Facsimile: 312-425-1904
Email: law@lloydcavanagh.com URL: http://www.lloydcavanagh.com
Members of Firm: Kurt D. Lloyd; Timothy J. Cavanagh. Associates: Matthew M. Rundio; Bryan C. Larsen.
Plaintiff's Personal Injury, Motor Vehicle Accidents and Injuries, Catastrophic Injury, Birth Trauma, Automotive Products Liability, Product Defects, Medical Negligence, Drug and Medical Device Litigation, Railroad Accidents and Injuries, Aviation Liability, Construction Accidents, Government Tort Liability, Health Care Liability, Nursing Home Negligence, Managed Care Liability, Wrongful Death.

See Professional Biographies, CHICAGO, ILLINOIS

Lo, Benjamin T. . . . '— '94 C.477 B.A. L.1119 J.D. [Ungaretti&H.]
Lo, Eva . . . '— '98 C.659 B.A. L.724 J.D. [Kirkland&E.]
Lo, Tracy W. . . . '76 '99 C.910 B.A. L.339 J.D. Sr. Atty., Chicago, M.R.O., S.E.C.
Locallo, Daniel M. . . . '52 '77 C.339 B.S. L.365 J.D. Cir. J.
Locallo, John G., (AV) . . . '59 '86 C.339 B.S. L.146 J.D. [Amari&L.]
Locallo, Joseph F., Jr., (AV) . . . '48 '76 C.209 B.A. L.365 J.D. [Amari&L.]
Lochbihler, Frederick V., (AV) . . . '— '76 C.602 A.B. L.145 J.D. [Chapman&C.]
Locher, Stephen . . . '78 '04 C.602 B.A. L.1565 J.D. [Goldberg,K.B.B.R.&M.]

Lock, Robert K., Jr. '58 '89 C.112 B.A. L.365 J.D.
7144 North Harlem Avenue, Suite 323, 60631
Telephone: 773-631-0064 Fax: 206-338-6036
Email: debtlawyer@sbcglobal.net URL: http://www.rklockandassociates.com
Complex Corporate Litigation and Negotiation, Credit Collection, Complex Class Action Litigation.

See Professional Biographies, CHICAGO, ILLINOIS

Locke, Barry . . . '47 '91 C.831 M.B.A. L.365 J.D. [B.Locke&Assoc.]
Locke, Jane Hoffman '— '75 C.477 B.A. L.188 J.D. Assoc. Prof., Loyola Univ. Sch. of Law
Locke, Leslie D. . . . '47 '75 C.902 B.A. L.188 J.D. [McGuirewoods]

Locke, Barry, & Associates, LTD.
205 West Wacker Drive, Suite 2333, 60606
Telephone: 312-553-1911 Fax: 312-251-0021
Email: blocke@205wacker.com URL: http://www.barrylockechicagolaw.com
Barry Locke.
Family Law, Divorce, Child Custody, Child Support, Paternity, Parentage, Visitation Rights.

See Professional Biographies, CHICAGO, ILLINOIS

Lockhart, Jamie '— '02 C.93 B.A. L.966 J.D. (adm. in MN; not adm. in IL) [DLPiper R.G.C.U.]
Lockner, Robert E. . . . '— '79 C.494 B.A. L.1565 J.D. [Chapman&C.]

Locks, David H., Law Offices of '45 '71 C.339 B.A. L.597 J.D.
5901 North Cicero, Suite 406, 60646-5711
Telephone: 773-736-5700 Fax: 773-736-5444
Email: lockslaw@aol.com URL: http://www.lockslawfirm.com
Contested Wills, Trusts and Estates, Real Estate Transactions and Litigation, Mechanics Liens, Encroachments, Business and Commercial Transactions and Litigation and Insurance Coverage.

See Professional Biographies, CHICAGO, ILLINOIS

Lockwood, Fred S., (P.C.), (AV) '16 '42 C.823 B.Ch.E. L.365 J.D. [Cook,A.M.M.C.&M.] (See Pat. Sect.)
Lockwood, Gary L., (AV) . . . '46 '76 C.353 B.A. L.597 J.D. [Walker W.M.]
Lodato, Phillip . . . '— '03 C.347 B.A. L.1119 J.D. [Chapman&C.]
Lodermeier, Michael L. . . . '74 '99 C.957 B.S. L.365 J.D. [Muller]
Lodge, Kenneth M., (AV) . . . '49 '74 C.276 B.S. L.776 J.D. [Lord,B.&B.]
Loeb, Jeffrey M. . . . '— '04 C.197 A.B. L.1565 J.D. [Kirkland&E.]

Loeb, Robert A. '51 '76 C.95 B.A. L.209 J.D.
221 N. LaSalle Street, 60601
Telephone: 312-368-0611 Fax: 312-606-9133 URL: http://www.robertloeblaw.com
Email: robertloeb@att.net URL: http://www.lawyers.com/robertaloeblaw
State and Federal Criminal Defense, Felonies, Misdemeanors, Criminal Law, DUI, Traffic Violations, Drug Crimes, White Collar Crime, Murder, Fraud, Wire Fraud, Mail Fraud, Mortgage Fraud, Social Security Fraud, Forfeiture, Gambling Law.

See Professional Biographies, CHICAGO, ILLINOIS

Loeb, Susan H. . . . '54 '81 C.966 B.A. L.146 J.D. 5660 S. Blackstone‡

Loeb & Loeb LLP, (AV)
A Limited Liability Partnership including Professional Corporations
Suite 2300, 321 North Clark Street, 60610-4714 ⊙
Telephone: 312-464-3100 Facsimile: 312-464-3111
URL: http://www.loeb.com
Members of Firm: Daniel D. Frohling; Mary E. Innis; Douglas N. Masters; Edward G. Wierzbicki. Associates: Nathan J. Hole; Nerissa Coyle McGinn.
Advertising Law; Antitrust Law; Appellate Practice; Banking Law; Bankruptcy Law; Civil Litigation; Corporate Securities Law; Entertainment Law; Entertainment Finance; Environmental Law; General Corporate Law; Healthcare Law; Intellectual Property Law; International Law; Labor and Employment Law; Real Estate Law; Tax Law; Tax Exempt Organizations Law; Patent, Trademark, Copyright and Unfair Competition; Trusts and Estates, Wills and Probates; White Collar Criminal Investigation.
Los Angeles, California Office: Suite 2200, 10100 Santa Monica Boulevard, Los Angeles, 90067-4164. Telephone: 310-282-2000. Facsimile: 310-282-2200.
New York, New York Office: 345 Park Avenue, 10154-0037. Telephone: 212-407-4000. Facsimile: 212-407-4990.
Nashville, Tennessee Office: 1906 Acklen Avenue, 37212-3700. Telephone: 615-749-8300. Facsimile: 615-749-8308.

See Professional Biographies, CHICAGO, ILLINOIS

Loeffler, Michael S. . . . '59 '85 C.339 B.S. L.1068 J.D. [Meckler B.&T.]
Loesch, William R. . . . '65 '92 C.674 A.B. L.597 J.D. [Goldberg,K.B.B.R.&M.]
Loew, Jonathan L., (AV) . . . '56 '82 C.694 B.A. L.209 J.D. [Weinberg R.]
Loewenstein, Daniel M. . . . '54 '80 C&L.910 A.B., J.D. [Evans,L.S.&M.]
Lofgren, Richard J. . . . '61 '85 C.801 B.S. L.365 J.D. [Keegan,L.L.&G.]
Loft, Kathryn K., (AV) . . . '52 '87 C.1171 B.S. L.146 J.D. [Johnson&B.]
Loftus, Anna M. . . . '69 '98 C.477 B.A. L.424 J.D. [Hall,P.&S.]
Loftus, Bianca M. . . . '70 '95 C.339 B.S. L.365 J.D. [Bates&C.]
Loftus, Mark P. . . . '60 '85 C.388 B.A. L.209 J.D. 100 W. Monroe Street, 19th Floor
Loftus, P. Michael . . . '52 '78 C.363 B.S. L.209 J.D. 53 W. Jackson Blvd.
Loftus, Patrick B., (AV) '58 '83 C.136 B.S. L.365 J.D. V.P., Law & Govt. Affs., TTX Company (Law Department)
Logan, Bruce T., (AV) . . . '43 '70 C&L.209 B.S.C., J.D. [Ash,A.F.&L.]
Logan, David S. . . . '18 '41 C&L.145 A.B., J.D. 919 N. Michigan
Loggans, Susan E., (AV) . . . '49 '74 C.339 A.B. L.209 J.D. [S.E.Loggans&Assoc.]

Loggans, Susan E., & Associates, P.C., (AV)
33 North LaSalle Street, Suite 1910, 60602-2604
Telephone: 312-201-8600 Telecopier: 312-201-1180
URL: http://www.loggans law.com
Susan E. Loggans;—Matthew R. Basinger.
Plaintiffs Personal Injury Litigation, General Civil Trial Practice, Negligence Aviation, Product Liability, Wrongful Death, Medical Negligence and Tort Law, Commercial Litigation.
See Professional Biographies, CHICAGO, ILLINOIS

Logue, Patricia M., (AV) '60 '86 C.103 A.B. L.597 J.D. Mng. Atty., Lambda Legal Def. & Educ. Fund, Inc.
Lohmar, Douglas W., Jr. '53 '87 C.494 B.A. L.46 J.D. 111 West Washington Street - Suite 823
Lohnes, Michael J. '77 '04 C.800 B.A. L.273 J.D. [[A] Katten M.R.]
Lohrenz, Eric L., (AV) '62 '87 C.339 B.S. L.813 J.D. [Jenner&B.] (Pat.)
Loiacono, Mark Thomas '62 '96 C.262 B.A. L.146 J.D. Trust Ofc., LaSalle Bank National Association
Loies, Kimberly V. '71 '00 C.339 B.A. L.280 J.D. Archipelago Holdings, Inc.
Loizzi, Nicholas V., (BV) '63 '92 C.209 B.S. L.365 J.D. [N.V.Loizzi]
Loizzi, Nicholas V., LLC, Law Offices of, (BV) 320 West Ohio Street, Suite 501
Lollino, Laurie A. '63 '88 C.209 B.S. L.365 J.D. Asst. Atty. Gen.
Lombaer, Forest R., Jr. '49 '78 C.880 B.A. L.472 J.D. Asst. Corp. Coun., City Dept. of Law
Lombardi, George C., (AV) '58 '84 C.197 A.B. L.477 J.D. [Winston&S.]
Lombardo, Joseph P. '— '99 C.201 B.S. L.228 J.D. [[A] Chapman&C.]
Lombardo, Kim '— '00 C.550 B.A. L.276 J.D. [[A] Skadden,A.S.M.&F.]
Lombardo, Pasquale G. '54 '81 C.860 B.A. L.588 J.D. (adm. in MA; not adm. in IL) Sr. Atty., Ill. Migrant Legal Assistance Project
Lombardo, Stephen J., III '74 '99 C&L.276 B.S.B.A., J.D. [[A] Katten M.R.]
Lombardo, Thomas M. '77 '03 C.209 B.A. L.424 J.D. [[A] Cassiday,S.&G.]
Lona, Marie A. '66 '91 C.597 B.A. L.813 J.D. [Winston&S.]
Londe, Carl L. '52 '77 C&L.910 A.B., J.D. (adm. in MO; not adm. in IL) Acct. Mgr., Watson Wyatt Worldwide
London, Alfred L., (AV) '31 '58 C.597 B.S. L.178 LL.D. 1220 N. State Pkwy.
London, Howard A., (AV) '— '78 C.597 B.A. L.273 J.D. [Beermann S.W.B.B.G.&L.]
London, Jeffrey L., (AV) '— '84 C.311 B.A. L.228 J.D. [Sachnoff&W.]
London, William A. '42 '67 C.473 A.B. L.145 J.D. Asst. State Atty.
London, William H., (AV) '62 '87 C.823 B.A. L.146 J.D. [Much S.F.D.A.&R.]
Long, J. Craig, (AV) '— '78 C.165 B.A. L.209 J.D. [Foley&L.]
Long, Jennifer L. '— '96 C&L.879 B.A., J.D. [[A] Baker&M.]
Long, Joan L. '56 '92 C.338 B.S. L.424 J.D. [[G] Mayer,B.R.&M.]
Long, John D. '58 '88 C.93 B.S. L.424 J.D. 222 N. La Salle St.
Long, John W. '36 '66 C.1032 B.A. L.365 LL.B. 20 N. Clark St.
Long, Martin P. '51 '84 C.209 B.A. L.146 J.D. Sr. Negotiator, Fed. Natl., Mtge. Assn.
Long, Nicholas A. '— '99 C&L.966 B.A., J.D. [[A] Sachnoff&W.]
Long, Rebecca R. '76 '01 C.477 B.A. L.424 J.D. [[A] Wildman,H.A.&D.]
Long, Robert A., Jr. '47 '73 C.691 B.A. L.145 J.D. Sr. Coun., Bank One Corp. (Law Dept.)
Long, Robert C., (AV) '53 '79 C.388 B.A. L.309 J.D. [Littler M.] (⊙Columbus, OH)
Long, Thomas J. '58 '83 C.602 B.A. L.424 J.D. [Norton,M.W.&D.] ⊙
Long, William Michael '— '86 C.98 B.S. L.365 J.D. [McGuirewoods]
Longman, Scott T. '— '93 C.597 B.A. L.339 J.D. [Barnes&T.]
Longo, Anthony J. '79 '05 C.424 B.A. L.365 J.D. [[A] Cassiday,S.&G.]
Longo, Elizabeth A. '65 '91 C.424 B.B.A. L.209 J.D. [Coghlan K.C.]
Longstreet, Cheryl Maria '— '96 C.339 B.A. L.209 J.D. Sr. Staff Coun., Merchandise Mart Properties, Inc.
Longtin, Roger L., (P.C.), (AV) '45 '73 C.602 B.A. L.339 J.D. [DLPiper R.G.C.U.]
Longwell, Marilyn F., (AV) '43 '73 C.608 B.A. L.209 J.D. [Longwell] ⊙

Longwell Associates, Chartered, (AV) [BB]
111 West Washington Street, Suite 1625, 60602-2703 ⊙
Telephone: 312-263-4730 Fax: 312-263-2055
Email: longwell@interaccess.com URL: http://www.longwell-law.com
Marilyn F. Longwell;—Deanna R. Blair; Diana T. Epstein.
Family Law including Divorce/Dissolution of Marriage, Child Custody, Child Support, Visitation Rights, Spousal Support/Maintenance/Alimony, Pre-Marital/Post-Marital Agreements, Separation Agreements, QDROS, Marital Property Distribution, Guardianship, School Law including Special Education and Teacher, Dismissal.
Oak Brook, Illinois Office: 1301 West 22nd Street, Suite 914, 60523. Telephone: 630-954-1480.
See Professional Biographies, CHICAGO, ILLINOIS

Lonoff, Alice S., (AV) '50 '77 C.604 B.A. L.93 J.D. [[G] Bell,B.&L.]
Lonstein, Carmen H. '— '88 C.331 B.A. L.569 J.D. [Bell,B.&L.]
Looker, Maureen C. '— '02 C.190 B.A. L.424 J.D. Legal Assistance Found. of Chicago
Looman, James R., (AV) '52 '78 C.879 B.A. L.145 J.D. [Sidley A.B.&W.]
Loomis, Walter P., (AV) '27 '52 C&L.597 B.S., LL.B. [Seyfarth S.] ‡
Loop, Sheila A. '— '03 C.494 B.A. L.424 J.D. [[A] Quinlan&C.]
Loos, Dietrich A. '73 '98 C.990 B.A. L.145 J.D. [[A] Duane M.]
Lopatka, Kenneth T., (AV) '47 '71 C.750 B.A. L.1565 J.D. [Perkins C.]
Lopez, Abad '76 '01 C&L.339 B.A., J.D. [[A] Pedersen&H.]
Lopez, Denise '— '04 C.846 B.B.A. L.1556 J.D. [[A] Mayer,B.R.&M.]
Lopez, Erik A., Sr. '— '00 C.1513 B.A. L.569 J.D. [[A] Latham&W.]
Lopez, Honoratus '30 '56 1718 S. Ashland
Lopez, Jose A., (AV) '70 '95 C.209 B.A. L.597 J.D. [Schopf&W.]
Lopez, Joseph R., (P.C.) '55 '84 C.339 B.A. L.146 J.D. 53 W. Jackson
Lopez, M. Susan '53 '85 C.339 B.A. L.209 J.D. Asst. Corp. Coun.
Lopez, Mark J. '57 '84 C.339 B.S. L.589 J.D. Asst. States Atty.
Lopez, Mary E., (BV) '67 '92 C&L.602 B.A., J.D. [[A] Lowis&G.]
Lopez, Sarah E. '68 '00 C.1400 B.A. L.146 J.D. [[A] Bollinger,R.&G.]
LoPrete, Robert D., (AV) '— '89 C.210 B.A. L.477 J.D. [Sachnoff&W.]
Lopuszynski, George '51 '76 C.339 B.A. L.365 J.D. Dir.- Law Dept., CNA Financial Corp., Environ. & Mass Tort
Lorber, Sara E. '67 '95 C.1349 B.A. L.930 J.D. [[A] Seyfarth S.]
Lord, Cristofer E. '52 '82 C.893 B.A. L.910 J.D. 10 S. La Salle St., Ste. 3500
Lord, Erica E. '— '02 C.475 B.A. L.273 J.D. [[A] Sachnoff&W.]
Lord, Bissell & Brook LLP, (AV) 115 South LaSalle Street (Pat.) (⊙L.A., CA; Wash., DC; Atlanta, GA; New York, NY)
Lore, John Corson, III. '73 '99 C.1214 B.A. L.597 J.D. Northwestern Legal Clinic
Lorenc, Susan M. '76 '02 C.477 B.A. L.966 J.D. [[A] FagelHaber]
Lorentzen, John C. '55 '80 C.221 B.S.B.A. L.145 J.D. [Winston&S.]
Lorenz, Hugo A. '26 '54 C.597 B.S. L.309 LL.B. 123 N. Wacker Dr.
Lorenz, Peter J., (BV) '63 '89 C.424 B.A. L.190 J.D. [Braun S.L.B.&M.]
Lorenzen, Donald R., (AV) '— '91 C.424 B.S. L.477 J.D. Asst. U.S. Atty., Northern Dist. of Ill.
Lorenzen, John M., (AV) '41 '70 C.610 B.S.M.E. L.851 J.D. (adm. in OH; not adm. in IL; Pat.) Pat. Coun., USG Corp.
Lorenzini, Agostino '63 '98 C&L.424 B.A., J.D. [[A] Mayer,B.R.&M.]
Lorge, Michael M. '53 '78 C.339 B.A. L.150 J.D. [Laser,P.S.F.&E.]

Loring, Bruce D., (AV) '48 '73 C&L.966 B.B.A., J.D. [Holland&K.]
Loring, John C. '44 '71 C&L.966 B.S., J.D. 700 W. Irving Pk. Rd.
Loseman, John W. '64 '89 C&L.339 B.A., J.D. [Lewis,O.&F.]
Lotsoff, Jonathan D. '69 '94 C.188 A.B. L.309 J.D. [[A] Sidley A.B.&W.]
Lott, Gay-Lloyd '37 '65 C.1016 B.A. L.365 J.D. Cir. J.‡
Lotus, Joseph J. '— '01 C&L.352 B.A., J.D. [[A] Foley&L.]
Lotus, Michael J., (AV) '63 '93 C.145 B.A. L.347 J.D. [Winston&S.]
Loucks, Thomas J. '58 '83 C.340 B.S. L.365 J.D. [Childress D.G.]
Loudermilk, Alan R. '58 '85 C.679 B.S.E.E. L.1119 J.D. 1550 N. Lake Shore Dr.
Lough, Mark H. '59 '86 C.197 B.A. L.178 J.D. Chf. Coun., The Boeing Co.
Loughlin, Kevin J. '54 '80 C.339 B.S. L.861 J.D. Chief Asst. Corp. Coun.

Loughman, Peter B. '48 '73 C.385 A.B. L.597 J.D.
155 North Michigan Avenue Suite 600, 60601
Telephone: 312-616-4250 Fax: 312-616-4252
Real Estate Transaction Law.
See Professional Biographies, CHICAGO, ILLINOIS

Loughnane, David J., (AV) '47 '72 C.966 B.A. L.424 J.D. [Johnson&B.]
Loukas, Pat '74 '01 C.339 B.S. L.209 J.D. [Lucas L.]
Loukas, Tom '76 '03 C.424 B.A. L.146 J.D. [Loukas L.]
Loukas Law, LLC 4061 North Milwaukee Avenue
Loumbas, Angelo J. '66 '93 C.210 B.A. L.347 J.D. [Eckhart K.]
Loundy, Christina King '68 '93 C.118 B.A. L.352 J.D. [[G] DLPiper R.G.C.U.]
Loundy, Richard A. '35 '60 C.966 B.B.A. L.597 J.D. Chmn. of the Bd. & CEO, Devon Bk.‡
Lounsbury, Lincoln J. '70 '01 C.801 B.A. L.597 J.D. [[A] McGuirewoods]
Lourie, Alexander, (AV) '57 '83 C.228 B.S. L.145 J.D. [Barack F.K.P.&N.]
Lourie, Marvin H. '32 '59 C.831 B.S. L.94 LL.B. (adm. in MA; not adm. in IL) 1212 Lake Shore Dr.‡
Lousin, Ann M. '43 '70 C.293 B.A. L.145 J.D. Prof. of Law, The John Marshall Law Sch.
Loutfi, Tarick '60 '87 C.477 B.A. L.209 J.D. 221 N. La Salle Street, Suite 2970
LoVallo, Michael A., (AV) '— '80 C.276 A.B. L.178 J.D. [Sachnoff&W.]
Lovato, Peter F., III '50 '76 C.674 A.B. L.976 J.D. [Boundas S.W.&B.]
Love, David B., (AV) '56 '80 C.597 B.A. L.477 J.D. [Winston&S.]
Love, Janet Otsuka, (AV) '53 '81 C.927 B.S. L.597 J.D. [Lord,B.&B.]
Love, Simon L. '50 '76 C.659 B.A. L.597 J.D. Sr. Coun., Chicago Park District

Love, Emily, P.C., Law Office of
(See Evanston)

Lovell, Matthew S. '76 '02 C.938 B.A. L.309 J.D. [[A] Kirkland&E.]
Lovell, Richard D. '46 '87 C.720 B.A. L.146 J.D. Asst. State's Atty.

Lovells
One IBM Plaza, 330 North Wabash Avenue, Suite 1900, 60611 ⊙
Telephone: 312-832-4400 Fax: 312-832-4444
Email: information@lovells.com URL: http://www.lovells.com
Partners: Thomas F. Bush, Jr.; Gail M. Goering; Eric A. Haab; David C. Linder (Not admitted in IL); Joseph T. McCullough IV; Neal J. Moglin; Kay E. Wilde. Of Counsel: Adam B. Goodman; John M. O'Bryan; Brad Ockene; Frank B. Slepicka; MaryBeth Wilkinson. Associates: Darrow Abrahams; Jodi L. Ahlman (Not admitted in IL); Rachael Blackburn; Ed Diffin; Robin C. Dusek; Jonathan R. Glusman; Alexis A. Hawker; Michele Lynn Hornish; Kris L. McCoy; R. Chad McCracken; Richard Alexander Nelson; Erin O'Brien; Peter B. Steffen; Mitchell B. Weiss.
Alternative Risk Transfer, Arbitration, Aviation, Banking, Banking Litigation, Capital Markets, Commercial and Trading Law, Commodities, Competition Trade and European Law, Computers Communications and Media, Construction, Consumer Financial Services, Corporate, Employees' Share Incentives, Employment, Energy, Environmental Law, Financial Service and Investment Funds, Fraud and Asset Recovery, Insolvency and Business Restructuring, Insurance and Reinsurance, International Arbitration, Intellectual Property, Litigation, Pensions, Private Equity, Product Liability, Project Finance, Property and Planning, Public Policy, Retail Finance, Tax.
Other Offices:
Alicante, Spain
Amsterdam, Netherlands
Beijing, Republic of China
Berlin, Germany
Brussels, Belgium
Budapest, Hungary Associated Office
Dusseldorf, Germany
Frankfurt, Germany
Hamburg, Germany
Ho Chi Minh City, Vietnam
Hong Kong
London, England
Madrid, Spain
Milan, Italy
Moscow, Russia
Munich, Germany
New York, N.Y.
Paris, France
Prague, Czech Republic
Rome, Italy
Shanghai, China
Singapore
Tokyo, Japan
Vienna, Austria Associated Office
Warsaw, Poland
Zagreb, Croatia Associated Office
Reviser of the Germany Law Digest for this Directory.
See Professional Biographies, CHICAGO, ILLINOIS

Lovely, Victoria B. '67 '93 C.299 B.A. L.861 J.D. [[G] Wolf&W.]
Lovestrand, Sandra P. '66 '91 C.597 B.A. L.424 J.D. Asst. Atty. Gen.
Lovett, Tammara M. '— '95 C.966 B.A. L.146 J.D. [[A] Morgan,L.&B.]
Low, Theodore J., (AV) '52 '77 C.1208 B.A. L.477 J.D. [Williams M.&J.]
Lowder, Charles Lynn '45 '80 C.339 B.A. L.209 J.D. [[G] DLPiper R.G.C.U.]
Lowdon, Jane E. '63 '89 C.424 B.A. L.146 J.D. 107 W. Van Buren St.
Lowe, Barry N. '51 '76 C.823 B.A. L.146 J.D. 432 N. Clark St.
Lowe, Carlton '48 '77 C.340 B.A. L.597 J.D. Fed. Trade Comm.
Lowe, Jeremy C. '74 '00 C.502 B.S.Ch.E. L.910 J.D. [[A] Leydig,V.&M.]
Lowe, John E., (AV) '55 '80 C.339 A.B. L.1565 J.D. [Schuyler,R.&Z.]
Lowe, Lisa Arlyn, (AV) '— '79 C.260 B.A. L.208 J.D. [Levin G.]
Lowery, Ann W. '55 '88 C&L.424 B.S.N., J.D. Dept. of Prof. Regulation
Lowery, D. Sanders '74 '99 C.880 B.S. L.424 J.D. [[A] Franczek S.]
Lowery, Martin B. '26 '52 L.209 J.D. [[G] Lowery&Assoc.]
Lowery, Timothy J., (AV) '59 '86 C.339 B.A. L.146 J.D. [Lowery&Assoc.]

Lowery & Associates, LLC, (AV) [BB]
333 West Wacker Drive Suite 420, 60606-1225
Telephone: 312-460-8788 Facsimile: 312-460-8790
Email: loweryllc@loweryllc.com URL: http://www.loweryandassociatesllc.com
Timothy J. Lowery. Of Counsel: Martin B. Lowery; Kathleen A. Smith-Haszto. Associates: John R. Withall; Marie T. Lapres.

(This Listing Continued)

Lowery & Associates, LLC (Continued)

Insurance Defense, Transportation Law, Truck Accidents, Motor Carrier Defense, Motor Vehicle/ Automobile Accidents, Subrogation, Cargo Claims, Commercial Litigation, Wrongful Death, Automobile Accidents and Injuries, Collections, General Business.

See Professional Biographies, CHICAGO, ILLINOIS

Loweth, Christopher W. '— '99 C.966 B.S. L.477 J.D. [Ⓐ Johnson&B.]
Lowinger, Alexander I., (AV) '17 '41
C&L.145 A.B., J.D. 111 West Washington St., Ste. 1900‡
Lowinger, Frederick C., (AV) '55 '82 C.659 B.S. L.145 J.D. [Sidley A.B.&W.]
Lowis, Jennifer A., (AV) '49 '78 C.502 B.A. L.146 J.D. [Lowis&G.]
Lowis & Gellen, (AV) 200 West Adams Street
Lowrey, John J., (AV) '39 '69 C.424 B.S. L.208 J.D. [Ⓒ Nolan]
Lowry, James W. '— '04 C.840 L.801 J.D. [Ⓐ Hennessy&R.]
Lowry, William A. '62 '88 C.393 B.A. L.424 J.D. [Nyhan,P.B.K.&L.]
Loy, Olga A. '— '98 C.338 B.A. L.339 J.D. [Kirkland&E.]
Loye, Linda '61 '92 Asst. Corp. Coun., Chicago Sun-Times, Inc.
Lu, Dianne M. '— '99 C.976 B.A. L.588 J.D. [Ⓐ Pircher,N.&M.]
Lu, Linda Enn '69 '94 C.145 A.B. L.276 J.D. [Ⓐ Lowis&G.]
Lubeck, Michael J. '— '94 C.588 B.A. L.424 J.D. [Ⓐ Cooney&C.]
Lubelchek, Douglas J., (AV) '63 '87 C.339 B.S. L.145 J.D. [Neal,G.&E.]
Luber, Zachary A. '75 '00 C.276 B.S.F.S. L.597 J.D. [Ⓐ Mayer,B.R.&M.]
Lubet, Steven '49 '73 C.597 B.A. L.1066 J.D. Prof., Northwestern Univ. Sch. of Law
Lubezny, Steven M. '75 '01 C.339 B.S.E.E. L.146 J.D. [Ⓐ Sonnenschein N.&R.]
Lubin, Donald G., (AV) '34 '57 C.659 B.S.E. L.309 LL.B. [Sonnenschein N.&R.]
Lubin, Edmond L. '62 '00 C.339 B.A. L.146 J.D. P.O. Box 1677
Lubin, Peter S., (AV) '57 '83 C.197 A.B. L.145 J.D.
737 West Washington Street Suite 3304 (⊙Oakbrook Terrace)
Lubinski, Kenneth M. '74 '01 C.347 B.A. L.424 J.D. [Ⓐ Busse&B.]
Luburic, John A. '75 '00 C.209 B.S. L.424 J.D. [Ⓐ Wildman,H.A.&D.]
Lucaccioni, Kent M., (AV) '62 '88 C.473 B.S. L.209 J.D. 33 N. Dearborn
Lucaccioni, Ronald J., (AV) '34 '59 C&L.209 J.D. 33 N. Dearborn, Ste. 2400
Lucansky, Patrick A., (AV) '36 '64 C.209 B.S.C. L.146 J.D. [Klein,T.&J.]
Lucas, David H., (AV) '36 '65 C.321 L.146 LL.B. [D.H.Lucas]
Lucas, Edward J. '27 '50 L.209 LL.B. V.P., LaSalle Natl. Bk.
Lucas, Jo Desha '21 '52 C.823 A.B. L.893 LL.B.
(adm. in VA; not adm. in IL) Prof. of Law, Univ. of Chicago Law Sch.
Lucas, John K., (AV) '46 '72 C.46 B.S. L.209 J.D. [Brinks H.G.&L.] (See Pat. Sect.)
Lucas, Martin J., (BV) '63 '91 C.363 B.A. L.46 J.D. [Ⓐ Anesi,O.R.N.&K.]
Lucas, Roger S. '66 '93 C&L.477 B.B.A., J.D. [Winston&S.]
Lucas, Thomas F. '— '78 C.339 B.A. L.424 J.D. [McKenna S.]
Lucas, Vanessa Melendez '70 '97 C.976 B.A. L.262 J.D.
Northwestern Univ. Sch. of Law
Lucas, David H., Ltd., (AV) 77 W. Washington St., Ste. 10
Lucas Law, LLC 4061 N. Milwaukee
Lucchese-Soto, Lynn '54 '79 C.424 B.A. L.209 J.D. [Berger,N.&F.]
Lucchesi, Adela C. '74 '00 C.1097 B.A. L.424 J.D. [Ⓐ Crowley&L.]
Luce, Bryan W. '61 '86 C&L.339 B.A., J.D. [Ⓐ Kiesler&B.]
Lucenti, Robert C. '51 '76 C.424 A.B. L.365 J.D. 6832 W. North Ave.
Lucey, Lawrence H. '47 '82 C.679 B.S. L.424 J.D. Alpha Advisors, Inc.
Luchsinger, Jay R. '50 '89 C.927 B.A. L.365 J.D. [Horwitz,H.&Assoc.]
Lucier, Timothy P. '71 '98
C.1229 B.S.M.E. L.424 J.D. [Ⓐ Brinks H.G.&L.] (See Pat. Sect.)
Luck, Dawn K. '71 '03 C.589 B.A. L.146 J.D. [Ⓐ Daspin&A.]
Luck, Max M. '40 '65 C&L.966 B.S., LL.B. S.E.C.
Lucy, Cecil B., Law Offices of '— '95 C&L.339 B.S., J.D. 1507 E. 53rd St.
Lucy, Richard H., (AV) '32 '59 C&L.597 B.S., J.D. [Ⓒ Dowd&D.]
Luczak, Gregory S. '52 '78 C.436 B.S. L.339 J.D. Touche Ross & Co.
Ludwig, Marek W. '55 '81
C.221 B.A. L.589 J.D. Sr. Portfolio Coun., General Growth Prop.
Ludwig, Samera S. '— '00 C.918 B.A. L.178 J.D. [Ungaretti&H.]
Luebchow, James E., (AV) '— '73 C.589 B.S. L.228 J.D. [Chapman&C.]
Luedde, Shawn F. '77 '04 C.1208 B.A. L.365 J.D. [Ⓐ Garofalo,S.H.&S.]
Lueking, Christopher D. '— '84 C.747 B.A. L.477 J.D. [Latham&W.]
Luenz, Jeffrey W. '73 '00 C.347 B.A. L.1119 J.D. [Ⓐ Grippo&E.]
Luepke, Ellen L. '— '97 C.879 B.A. L.352 J.D. [Ⓐ Barnes&T.]
Luepker, Wayne R. '49 '79 C.293 B.A. L.145 J.D. [Mayer,B.R.&M.]
Luetkemeyer, Tom H., (AV) '56 '82 C&L.424 B.A., J.D. [Hinshaw&C.]
Lufrano, Michael R. '65 '92 C.339 B.A. L.309 J.D. Sr. Coun., Tribune Co.
Lugardo, David D. '71 '98 C&L.589 B.A., J.D. 70 West Madison, Suite 1400
Lugo, Ricardo, (CVⓉ) '62 '91 C.750 B.A. L.966 J.D. [Lugo]
Lugo Law Office, (CVⓉ) 4244 West North Avenue
Lujan, John-Paul '69 '97 C.339 B.S.A.S. L.209 J.D. [Ⓐ Stein,R.&H.]
Lukanich, J. Mark '55 '80 C.602 B.A. L.209 J.D. 221 N. LaSalle St.
Lukas, James J., Jr. '74 '99 C.340 B.A. L.209 J.D. [Ⓐ Williams M.&J.]
Lukas, Joseph P. '70 '95 C.93 B.S. L.966 J.D. [Winston&S.]
Luken, Martin G., Jr. '12 '40 C.276 B.A. L.597 LL.B. 1448 North Lake Shore Drive
Lukes, Paul M. '44 '69 C.209 B.S.C. L.365 J.D. [Hoellen&L.]
Lukowski, Gina M. '78 '03 C.209 B.A. L.365 J.D. [Ⓐ Cassiday,S.&G.]
Lulich, Ingrid, (BV) '67 '92 C.446 B.A. L.209 J.D. [Ⓐ Wiedner&M.]
Lullo, David A. '— '87 C.339 B.A. L.477 J.D. [Chapman&C.]
Lum, Amy E. '— '96 C.475 B.A. L.424 J.D. [Ⓐ Katten M.R.]
Lum, Brian J. '60 '98 C.145 B.A. L.424 J.D. [Ⓒ Ice M.] (Pat.)
Lumb, Kenneth T., (AV) '66 '91 C.602 B.A. L.209 J.D. [Ⓐ Corboy&D.]
Lunardini, Claire L. '75 '00 C&L.209 B.A., J.D. [Ⓐ Williams M.&J.]
Lund, Mary M. '47 '92 C.530 B.A. L.424 J.D. 1030 N. State St.
Lund, Sara D. '72 '98 C.339 B.A. L.989 J.D. [Ⓐ Connelly R.&M.]
Lund, Toria L. '80 '05 C.436 B.A. L.1000 J.D. [Ⓐ Tressler,S.M.&P.]
Lundahl, Margaret Ann '48 '80 C.145 L.146 J.D. 10128 Ave. J‡
Lundeen, David M. '76 '04 C.477 B.A. L.1119 J.D. [Ⓐ Mayer,B.R.&M.]
Lundeen, Ronald Edward, Jr. '73 '04 C.878 B.S. L.145 J.D. [Ⓐ McGuirewoods]
Lundgren, Colleen D. '64 '97 C.476 B.S. L.912 J.D. [Ⓐ Bell,B.&L.]
Lundgren, Erik B. '70 '98 C.502 B.A. L.352 J.D. [Ⓐ Winston&S.]
Lundquist, Troy A. '67 '92 C.339 B.A. L.365 J.D. [Mangan,L.G.&L.] ⊙
Lundy, James G. '70 '96 C.339 B.A. L.209 J.D.
Branch Chf., Div. of Enforce., U.S. Secs. & Exch. Comm.
Lungmus, John B., (AV) '— '54 C&L.597 B.S., J.D.
[Ⓒ Marshall,G.&B.] (See Pat. Sect.)
Luning, Thomas P., (AV) '— '68 C.973 H.A.B. L.276 J.D. [Schiff H.]
Lunn, Robin R., (AV) '50 '75 C&L.665 B.A., J.D. [Mayer,B.R.&M.]
Lunt, Aaron E. '78 '04 C.999 B.A. L.365 J.D. [Ⓐ Fisher K.]
Lupa, Edward M. '31 '57 C&L.209 B.S.C., J.D. 5796 S. Archer
Lupa, Gary C. '51 '78 C.1024 B.A. L.365 J.D. U.S. Dept. of Agric.
Lupel, Warren, (AV) '42 '68 C.1016 A.B. L.365 J.D. [Weinberg R.]
Lupo, James A., Jr. '64 '89 C.597 B.A. L.424 J.D. [Ⓒ Bollinger,R.&G.]
Lupo, Thomas D., (AV) '59 '85 C&L.602 B.A., J.D. [Seyfarth S.]
Luque-Rosales, Mercedes '62 '89 C.424 B.A. L.190 J.D. Asst. State's Atty.
Lura, Mark J., (BV) '— '86 C.999 B.A. L.365 J.D. [Anderson,R.]
Lurie, Gerald B., (AV) '44 '69 C.477 B.A. L.209 J.D. [DLPiper R.G.C.U.]
Lurie, Michael D., (AV) '68 '93
C.813 B.A. L.1049 J.D. V.P. & Sr. Assoc. Gen. Coun., Barton Inc.
Lurie, Michael H., (AV) '43 '68 C.339 B.S. L.209 J.D. 30 N. LaSalle St.
Lurie, Paul M., (AV) '— '65 C&L.477 A.B., J.D. [Schiff H.]
Lusak, John E. '39 '65 C.1016 A.B. L.339 LL.B. 221 N. LaSalle St., Suite 1700
Luscombe, George A., II '44 '69 C&L.339 B.S., J.D. [Mayer,B.R.&M.]
Lusk, Kimberly R. '70 '03 C.36 B.A. L.424 J.D. [Ⓐ Mandel,L.&S.]
Lusk, Michael P. '64 '95 C&L.421 B.S.B.A., J.D. [Wildman,H.A.&D.]
Luskin, Joshua Dante '72 '97 C.429 B.A. L.477 J.D. [Ⓐ Nyhan,P.B.K.&L.]
Lusky, Barbara E.
(See Skokie)
Lussem, James J., Law Offices of '— '80 C.424 B.S. L.589 J.D. 6864 N. Tonty Ave.
Lustgarten, Marvin '22 '52 2850 W. Fitch St.
Lustgarten, Ralph W. F., (AV) '37 '63 C&L.597 B.A., J.D. [Taylor,M.S.H.&M.]
Lustig, Jacqueline Stanley '49 '79
C.563 B.A. L.209 J.D. Chf. Legal Coun. Dept. of Human Rights
Lustig, Patrick Foran, (AV) '56 '82 C.209 B.S.C. L.146 J.D.
50 W. Washington, Ste. 1403
Luther, Daniel W., (AV) '61 '86 C&L.276 A.B., J.D. [Mayer,B.R.&M.]
Luther, John P. '53 '85 C.454 B.S. L.623 J.D.
(adm. in OK; not adm. in IL; Pat.) [Ⓒ Jenkens&G.]
Luthringshausen, Jacqueline R. '66 '91
C.602 B.A. L.209 J.D. Staff Coun., The Options Clearing Corp.
Lutner, Rebecca Leah '69 '96 C.172 B.S. L.146 J.D. [Ⓐ Fraterrigo,B.F.&K.]
Lutter, Paul A. '— '71 C.118 B.A. L.976 J.D. [Ⓒ Bryan C.]
Lutterbeck, Ann G. '— '49 C&L.209 A.B., J.D. 5000 East End Ave., #21B‡
Luzadder, Matthew C. '— '04 C.347 B.A. L.74 J.D. [Ⓐ Kelley D.&W.]
Luzzie, Edward L. '09 '35 C&L.976 B.A., LL.B. Examiner of Titles Torrens System
Lydiksen, Mary Jo Montgomery '60 '86 C.991 B.A. L.365 J.D. Asst. States Atty.
Lydon, James M. '66 '92 C.477 B.A. L.146 J.D. [Ⓐ Hinshaw&C.]
Lydon, John J. '63 '89 C.424 B.A. L.209 J.D. [Ⓐ Gomberg,S.G.&O.]
Lydon, Matthias A., (AV) '42 '69 C&L.209 B.A., J.D. [Winston&S.]
Lydon, Maureen H. '54 '87 C&L.276 B.A., J.D. Dep. Exec. Dir.
Lyerla, Bradford P., (AV) '— '80 C&L.339 A.B., J.D.
[Marshall,G.&B.] (See Pat. Sect.)
Lyhus, John E. '57 '84 C.966 B.B.A. L.564 J.D. [Fitch,E.T.&F.]
Lyke, John Fitzgerald, Jr. '— '94 C.1191 B.S. L.146 J.D.
1505 East 53rd Street, Suite 200
Lyke, Sarah R. '68 '94 C.918 B.A. L.597 J.D. [Ⓐ Sidley A.B.&W.]
Lykins, Nicholas R. '74 '03 C.339 B.S. L.209 J.D. [Ⓐ Johnson&B.]
Lyman, Mark M., (AV) '59 '85 C.676 B.A. L.365 J.D. [Henderson&L.]
Lyman, Thomas J., III, (AV) '— '87 C.321 B.A. L.365 J.D. [O'Hagan,S.&A.]
Lynam, David J. '51 '78 C&L.424 B.A., J.D. [Lynam&Assoc.]
Lynam, Gregory S. '73 '01 C.350 B.S. L.352 J.D. [Ⓐ Baker&M.]
Lynam & Associates 1 North LaSalle, Suite 3100
Lynch, Barbara J. '58 '83 C.602 B.B.A. L.339 J.D. S.E.C.
Lynch, Bryan P. '71 '96 C.339 B.A. L.365 J.D. [Ⓐ Nasharr&S.]
Lynch, Daniel, (AV) '59 '88 C.174 B.A. L.597 J.D. [Cirignani H.H.&L.]
Lynch, David G., (AV) '47 '74 C.589 B.A. L.339 J.D. [DLPiper R.G.C.U.]
Lynch, Eric E. '67 '92 C.823 B.A. L.365 J.D. [Meckler B.&T.]
Lynch, Francine D. '— '90 C.238 B.A. L.365 J.D. [Ⓐ Neal&L.]
Lynch, George J., (AV) '48 '73 C.201 B.A. L.602 J.D. [Burke,W.M.&S.]
Lynch, James M., (AV) '51 '77 C.973 B.S.B.A. L.365 J.D. [Winston&S.]
Lynch, Jamison '70 '98 C&L.966 B.S.M.E., J.D. [Ⓐ Mayer,B.R.&M.] (Pat.)
Lynch, John J., (AV) '45 '73 C.999 B.A. L.209 J.D. [Figliulo&S.]
Lynch, John P. '74 '01 C.234 B.S. L.1000 J.D. [Ⓐ Crisham&K.]
Lynch, John P., (AV) '— '67 C.436 B.A. L.597 J.D. [Latham&W.] (⊙Paris, France)
Lynch, John P., Jr., (AV) '63 '88 C.746 B.B.A. L.209 J.D. [Cremer,K.S.&S.]
Lynch, Julia Kelleher '68 '95 C.339 B.S. L.424 J.D. [Ⓐ Donohue B.M.&S.]
Lynch, Michael T. '78 '04 C.188 B.A. L.93 J.D. [Ⓐ Cassiday,S.&G.]
Lynch, Robert M. '50 '75 C&L.734 A.B., J.D.
(adm. in MO; not adm. in IL) Sr. V.P. & Assoc. Gen. Coun., SBC Ameritech
Lynch, Thomas M., (AV) '54 '84 C.201 B.A. L.597 J.D. [Wildman,H.A.&D.]
Lynch, Thomas W., P.C.
(See Oak Lawn)
Lyndon, T. Edward '57 '92 C.475 Ch.E. L.146 J.D. [Robbins&R.]
Lynk, M. Jane '51 '78 C.339 B.S. L.146 J.D. Assoc. Gen. Coun., Bus. Law, Aon Corp.
Lynn, Allison M. '73 '03 C.623 B.A. L.966 J.D. [Ⓐ Laner,M.D.B.L.&T.]
Lynn, Nicholas J., (BV) '52 '80 C.221 B.S. L.365 J.D. [Duane M.]
Lynott, Genevieve M. '74 '01 C&L.209 B.A., J.D. [Ⓐ Riordan,D.L.&M.]
Lynott, Melissa A. '79 '04 C.338 B.S. L.879 J.D. [Ⓐ Brenner,F.M.&S.]
Lyon, Andrea D. '52 '76 C.705 B.A. L.1162 J.D. 25 E. Jackson Boulevard
Lyon, Bruce W., (AV) '59 '84 C.747 B.A. L.209 J.D. [LaBarge,C.&L.]
Lyon, Damon '75 '00 C.475 B.A. L.477 J.D. [Ⓐ McDermott W.&E.]
Lyon, Nancy Anne '56 '81 C.123 B.S. L.424 J.D. Northern Tr. Co.
Lyon, Richard M., (AV) '26 '54 C.188 Ph.D. L.1009 LL.B. [Seyfarth S.] ‡
Lyons, Christine G. '74 '99 C.597 B.S. L.276 J.D. Assoc., Gunther Group LLC;
Lyons, Christopher P. '65 '90 C&L.339 B.S., J.D. [Peters&L.]
Lyons, Francis X. '62 '88 C.494 B.A. L.424 J.D. [Bell,B.&L.]
Lyons, John K., (AV) '64 '89 C.276 B.S.F.S. L.884 J.D. [Skadden,A.S.M.&F.]
Lyons, Joseph G., (BV) '62 '87 C.323 B.A. L.215 J.D. [Cozen O.]
Lyons, Kathleen A., (AV) '54 '84
C.424 B.S. L.209 J.D. [Wallenstein W.&R.] (See Pat. Sect.)
Lyons, Kathleen Liu '— '94 C.477 B.B.A. L.424 J.D. IL Educ. Labor Rel. Bd.
Lyons, Michael J. '54 '78 C.734 B.A. L.178 J.D.
Illinois Dept. of Professional Regulation
Lyons, Raymond, Jr., (AV) '51 '80 C.424 B.S. L.209 J.D. [Williams M.&J.]
Lyons, Robert P. '54 '82 C.424 B.A. L.365 J.D. Assoc. Gen. Coun.
Lyons, Scott E. '70 '96 C&L.339 B.S., J.D. [Ⓐ Katten M.R.]
Lyons, Thomas G., (AV) '31 '57 C&L.424 B.S., J.D. [O'Keefe,L.&H.]
Lysik, David A. '56 '96 C.1258 B.A. L.146 J.D.
Staff Atty., Liturgy Training Publications
Lythcott, Stephen X. '50 '78
C.33 B.A. L.966 J.D. Asst. Gen. Atty., Law Dept., Chgo. Pk. Dist.
Ma, Dennis H. '76 '01 C.597 B.A. L.1556 J.D./LL.M. [Ⓐ Olson&H.] (See Pat. Sect.)
Ma, Yufeng '74 '02 C.999 B.Sc. L.880 J.D. [Ⓐ McAndrews,H.&M.] (See Pat. Sect.)
Maatman, Gerald L., Jr., (AV) '56 '81 C.902 B.A. L.597 J.D. [Seyfarth S.]
Mabery, Leah L. '74 '04 C.155 B.A. L.879 J.D. [Ⓐ Rusin M.&F.]
MacAloon, Martha A. '52 '84 C.93 B.A. L.209 J.D. [Monico,P.&S.]
Macaluso, Joseph A. '46 '73 C&L.424 B.A., J.D. [J.A.Macaluso]

Macaluso, J. A., Law Offices of ....100 W. Monroe St., Ste. 1310
MacArthur, Diane, (AV) .... '57 '82 C.339 B.A. L.424 J.D. Asst. U.S. Atty.
Macaulay, Joan M. '69 '96 C.112 B.A. L.276 J.D.
(adm. in CA; not adm. in IL) [🄰 Sidley A.B.&W.]
Macaulay, Susan J. ....'52 '84 C.604 B.M. L.424 J.D. [Gardner C.&D.]
MacAyeal, Linda S. .... '57 '83 C.103 B.A. L.659 J.D. Northern Trust Corp.
MacBride, Owen E. ....'— '75 C.477 B.A. L.976 J.D. [Schiff H.]
MacCabe, Edward H., (AV) ....'48 '78 C.339 B.S. L.589 J.D. [MacCabe&M.]

MacCabe & McGuire, (AV)
Suite 3333, 77 West Wacker Drive, 60601
Telephone: 312-357-2600 Fax: 312-357-0317
Email: thefirm@maccabe-mcguire.com
Members of Firm: Edward H. MacCabe; Maureen A. McGuire; Anthony R. Rutkowski. Associates: Timothy J. Murphy; Michael O. Vates; Timothy J. Deffet. Of Counsel: Brian J. Mulhern.
Civil Litigation, Transportation, Railroad, Trucking, Premises Liability, Security, Hospitality, Products Liability, Asbestos Defense, Commercial Transactions and Litigation, Employment Law and General Practice.

See Professional Biographies, CHICAGO, ILLINOIS

MacCarthy, John L. ....'59 '85 C.951 B.A. L.813 J.D. [Winston&S.]
MacCarthy, Sean Patrick .... '63 '88 C.339 B.A. L.424 J.D. [Chittenden,M.&N.]
MacCarthy, Terence F. .... '34 '60 C.1024 A.B. L.209 J.D. Exec. Dir., Fed. Def. Prog.
MacDonald, Brittany Cathleen .... '73 '99 C.911 B.S. L.37 J.D. [🄰 Greer,B.&C.] (Pat.)
MacDonald, Diane A. .... '— '90 C.105 B.A. L.146 J.D. [🄰 Barnes,R.&C.]
MacDonald, Lenore L. ....'56 '81 C.860 B.A. L.436 J.D. Asst. State's Atty.
MacDonald, Lynn C. ....'72 '97 C.339 B.S. L.597 J.D. [🄰 Winston&S.]
MacDonald, Robert W., (AV) .... '12 '39 C.385 B.S. L.145 J.D. 208 S. LaSalle St.
MacDowall, Alexis ....'64 '89 C&L.352 B.A., J.D. [Winston&S.]
MacEntee, Barry F. ....'76 '01 C.363 B.A. L.424 J.D. [🄰 Hinshaw&C.]
Macey, Eric N., (AV) ....'51 '78 C.674 A.B. L.276 J.D. [Novack&M.]
MacFarlane, Michael J. ....'75 '01 C.234 B.A. L.209 J.D. [🄰 LaBarge,C.&L.]
Machalinski, Donald G. ....'— '89 C.338 B.S. L.424 J.D. [Merlo K.B.&G.]
Machen, Monika J. ....'— '00 C.659 B.A. L.477 J.D. [🄰 Sonnenschein N.&R.]
Machlin, Barry N. ....'59 '85 C.1036 B.A. L.309 J.D. [Mayer,B.R.&M.]
Machnik, Thaddeus S. ....'56 '82 C.209 B.S. L.424 J.D. Circuit Crt of Cook Cty
Machonkin, Richard A. '68 '96
C.477 B.S. L.309 J.D. [McDonnell B.H.&B.] (See Pat. Sect.)
Maciariello, Domenic C. ....'75 '02 C.1024 L.209 J.D. 134 N. LaSalle Street
Maciasz, Mark ....'— '92 C.339 B.S. L.209 J.D. [FagelHaber]
MacInerney, John J. ....'60 '96 C.1374 B.A./B.S. L.424 J.D. [🄰 Hofeld&S.]
MacIntyre, Shona M. ....'— '98 C.945 B.A. L.597 J.D. [🄰 Sidley A.B.&W.]
Maciorowski, John A., (AV) ....'55 '80 C.750 B.A. L.209 J.D. [Rusin M.&F.]
Maciorowski, Robert E., (AV) ...... '49 '74 C.750 B.A. L.209 J.D. [Maciorowski,S.&U.]

Maciorowski, Sackmann & Ulrich, (AV)
221 North LaSalle Street, Suite 3600, 60601
Telephone: 312-236-4600 Fax: 312-236-8459
URL: http://www.msulaw.com
Members of Firm: Robert E. Maciorowski; Jeremy P. Sackmann; Robert B. Ulrich. Associates: Geraldine M. Balow; Tina L. DePaul; Gary K. Gale; Julie A. Garrison; Eric S. Grodsky; Robert T. Newman.
Worker's Compensation Defense Law, including Hospital, Corporations and Business Defense and Labor and Employment Law.

See Professional Biographies, CHICAGO, ILLINOIS

MacIver, Anne Keyes .... '69 '96 C.674 A.B. L.477 J.D. Arthur Andersen, LLP
Mack, Brian P. ....'63 '88 C.477 B.A. L.201 J.D. [Richardson,S.B.&M.]
Mack, Charles J. ....'59 '85 C.477 B.A. L.608 J.D. [Wolin&R.]
Mack, Karen Kavanagh ....'73 '98 C&L.424 B.A., J.D. [🄰 Deutsch,L.&E.]
Mack, William D. '68 '99
C.1268 B.A. L.424 J.D. Metropolitan Dier & Exposition Authority
MacKay, Karen K., (AV) .... '44 '71 C.788 B.A. L.477 J.D. [Burke,W.M.&S.]
MacKelvie, Charles F., (BV) .... '44 '74 C.966 B.S. L.365 J.D. 120W.Madisonst.
Mackey, Montgomery William ....'47 '85 C.477 B.A. L.424 J.D. [Mackey&K.]

Mackey & Kramer, P.C., Law Offices of
77 W. Washington Street, Suite 1300, 60602
Telephone: 312-263-2000 Fax: 312-263-3484
Email: info@mackey-kramer.com URL: http://www.mklawoffices.com
Montgomery William Mackey; Jack L. Kramer.
Personal Injury, Medical Malpractice, Workers Compensation, Auto Accidents, Wrongful Death, Trucking Accidents, Boating Accidents, Bicycle Accidents, Tractor Accidents, Lawnmower Accidents, Products Liability, Railroad Accidents.

See Professional Biographies, CHICAGO, ILLINOIS

Mackie, Katie .... '79 '04 C.577 B.S. L.597 J.D. [🄰 Winston&S.]
Mackin, Daniel E. J. ....'58 '84 C.347 B.A. L.1119 J.D. Mgr., Bk. of America
MacKinnon, Kevin S. ....'58 '83 C.112 B.A. L.770 J.D. [Katten M.R.]
Macklin, Heather J. .... '74 '99 C.578 B.A. L.145 J.D. [🄰 Barack F.K.P.&N.]
Macknin, Mitchell H., (AV) ....'53 '78 C&L.597 B.A., J.D. [Sperling&S.]
Mackoff, Benjamin S. ....'33 '58 C.145 A.B. L.597 J.D. [Schiller,D.&F.]
Mackoff, Myron F. ....'— '94 C.477 B.A. L.597 J.D. [🄰 Hubert&F.]
Macksey, David M., (BV) ....'63 '90 C&L.352 B.A., J.D. [Johnson&B.]
Maclaren, Anne L. .... '60 '93 C.477 B.A. L.912 J.D. 1040 W. Rosemont, Suite 3
Maclean, Susan M., (AV) ....'63 '94 C.604 B.A. L.61 J.D. [Zulkie]
MacLellan, Allison A. ....'74 '02 C.273 B.A. L.209 J.D. Asst. State. Atty.
Macmanus, Sheila ....'46 '88 C.700 B.A. L.146 J.D. Admin. Law J.
MacMaster, Sarah R. .... '74 '99 C.473 B.A. L.608 J.D. [Gleason&M.]
MacNeil, Donald L. '43 '68 C.504 A.B. L.597 J.D.
Pres. & CEO, Heritage Bancorp., Inc.
MacNeil, Ian R. '29 '56 C.882 B.A. L.309 LL.B.
(adm. in NH; not adm. in IL) Prof. of Law, Northwestern Univ. Law Sch.
MacQueen, Aaron ....'72 '02 C.550 B.A. L.124 J.D. [🄰 McDermott W.&E.]
MacRae, Roderick E., (AV) .....'45 '71 C.276 B.S. L.880 J.D. [🄲 Davis F.Z.K.M.M.&R.]
Madaan, Ram Tirath '63 '96 C.999 B.A. L.309 LL.M.
(adm. in NY; not adm. in IL) [Madaan]
Madaan & Co. .... 6033 N. Sheridan Rd.
Madans, Alan S., (AV) .... '57 '82 C.597 B.A. L.228 J.D. [Rothschild,B.&M.]
Madauss, Alison C. .... '78 '03 C.880 B.A. L.145 J.D. [🄰 McLachlan,R.&D.]
Madda, Eileen E. ....'— '03 C.676 B.A. L.1000 J.D. [🄰 Querrey&H.]
Madden, Daniel P. ....'48 '80 C.454 B.A. L.597 J.D. 20 N. Clark St.
Madden, David M. ....'— '03 C.475 B.A. L.209 J.D. [🄰 Freeborn&P.]
Madden, J. Christopher ....'71 '97 C.770 B.A. L.146 J.D. [🄰 Quinlan&C.]
Madden, John K. .... '43 '68 C&L.436 B.A., J.D. Cir. J.
Madden, Mary M. ....'68 '98 C.103 B.A. L.1478 J.D. [🄰 E.K.Hollander]
Madden, Terrence J., (AV) ....'48 '73 C.734 B.A. L.339 J.D. [BryceDowney]

Madden, Jiganti, Moore & Sinars LLP, (AV)
Suite 1700, 190 South La Salle Street, 60603
Telephone: 312-346-4101 Fax: 312-346-4885
Email: mjms@mjms.com URL: http://www.mjms.com

(This Listing Continued)

Madden, Jiganti, Moore & Sinars LLP (Continued)
Members of Firm: John J. Jiganti; John G. Moore; Theodore A. Sinars; Paul M. Sheridan, III; Joseph S. Capitani;—Leila T. Francis; Holly A. Bailey.
William F. Madden (1945-1992).
Tax and General Business.

See Professional Biographies, CHICAGO, ILLINOIS

Maddox, Devin C. .... '78 '04 C.339 B.A. L.1000 J.D. [🄰 Tressler,S.M.&P.]
Maddux, William D. ....'35 '59 C.602 B.A. L.276 J.D. Cir. J.
Madea, Frank P. ....'53 '79 C.424 A.B. L.365 J.D. Cook Co. Pub. Def.
Madiar, Eric M. .... '— '00 C.587 B.A. L.146 J.D. [🄰 Freeborn&P.]
Madigan, Carol M. ....'34 '81 C.449 B.S. L.589 J.D. 1120 N. Lake Shore Dr.
Madigan, Daniel T., (AV) ....'68 '93 C&L.339 B.A., J.D. [🄰 Motherway&N.]
Madigan, James P. ....'74 '02 C.124 B.A. L.145 J.D. [🄰 Goldberg,K.B.B.R.&M.]
Madigan, Michael J., (AV) ....'42 '67 C.602 B.A. L.424 J.D. [Madigan&G.]
Madigan & Getzendanner, (AV) .... 30 N. LaSalle St.
Madler, James R. ....'37 '64 C.1082 B.S. L.597 J.D. 350 N. LaSalle St., 8th Fl.
Madlock, Ashanti L. ....'— '04 C.597 B.S. L.273 J.D. [🄰 Wildman,H.A.&D.]
Madock, Daniel R. ....'58 '86 C.339 B.A. L.365 J.D. [Barlow,K.&D.]
Madoff, Jeffrey L., (AV) ....'45 '74 C.912 A.B. L.145 J.D. [Matkov,S.M.&G.]
Madonia, Anthony J., (AV) ....'— '90 C.339 B.S. L.365 J.D. [A.J.Madonia&Assoc.]
Madonia, Joseph F., (AV) ....'59 '85 C.602 B.A. L.802 J.D. [Wildman,H.A.&D.]

Madonia, Joseph J., & Associates '62 '90 C.339 B.S. L.424 J.D.
5757 North Sheridan, Suite 10A, 60660
Telephone: 773-654-5065 Fax: 773-654-5066
Email: joemadonia@aol.com
Entertainment and Sports Law, including Multimedia, Intellectual Property, Copyright and Trademark Law, Music Law, Motion Pictures, Television, Publishing, Radio Stations and Labeling, Commercial and Contract Litigation.

See Professional Biographies, CHICAGO, ILLINOIS

Madonia, Anthony J., & Associates, Ltd., (AV) .... 150 North Wacker, Suite 2600
Madormo, Anthony J. ....'— '86 C.339 B.A. L.365 J.D. [Querrey&H.]
Madorsky, Seth R., (AV) ....'61 '86 C.477 B.A. L.188 J.D. [Katten M.R.]

Madrid-Crost, Mary Carmen R., Law Offices of '57 '94 C&L.662 A.B., LL.B.
10 S. LaSalle Street Suite 3320, 60603
Telephone: 312-857-0857 Fax: 312-857-0858
URL: http://www.madridcrostlaw.com
(Not admitted in IL).
Associate: Michael R. Jarecki.
Immigration.

See Professional Biographies, CHICAGO, ILLINOIS

Madsen, Brandt R., (AV) .... '63 '89 C.473 B.S. L.365 J.D. [Madsen,F.&P.]
Madsen, Craig A. '45 '75 C.966 B.A. L.365 J.D.
Contl. Ill. Nat. Bk. & Tr. Co. of Chicago
Madsen, Gillian D. ....'72 '97 C.674 B.S.E. L.597 J.D. [🄰 DLPiper R.G.C.U.]
Madsen, Farkas & Powen, L.L.C., (AV) ....111 W. Washington St., Ste. 1550
Maduff, Aaron B. ....'70 '95 C.187 B.S.S. L.352 J.D. [Maduff M.&M.]
Maduff, Michael L. ....'41 '88 C.352 B.A. L.1348 J.D. [Maduff M.&M.]
Maduff Medina & Maduff, LLC .... One East Wacker Drive, Suite 2122
Maganuco, Robert J., (AV) ....'50 '75 C.93 A.B. L.339 J.D. [Sidley A.B.&W.]
Maganzini, Teresa A. ....'51 '76 C.602 B.A. L.884 J.D. Asst. States Atty.
Magdaleno, Leticia '63 '89 C.424 B.A. L.597 J.D.
Clinical Staff Atty., Loyola University Community Law Center
Magel, Barbara A., (AV) ....'54 '79 C.918 B.A. L.575 J.D. [Karaganis,W.&M.]
Mages, Lawrence M. ....'43 '68 C.197 B.A. L.309 J.D. [Bell,B.&L.]
Maggio, Andrew P., Jr. ....'56 '80 C&L.209 B.S.C., J.D. [A.P.Maggio,Jr.&Assoc.]
Maggio, Nicole M. '76 '02 C.338 B.S. L.146 J.D.
Mgr. Copyrights & Licensing, American Bar Association (Legal Department)
Maggio, Paula C. '68 '94 C&L.339 B.A., J.D.
Vice President & Associate General Counsel, Strategic Hotel Capital, L.L.C.
Maggio, Timothy M. ....'60 '85 C&L.602 B.A., J.D. [Lord,B.&B.]
Maggio, Andrew P., Jr. and Associates ....7824 West Belmont Ave.
Magidson, Sherman C., (AV) '32 '59
C.976 B.A. L.597 J.D. 321 S. Plymouth Ct., Suite 950
Magidson, William H. '31 '56
C&L.597 B.S., J.D. [🄲 Cook,A.M.M.C.&M.] (See Pat. Sect.)
Magiera, John S., (BV) ....'52 '79 C.597 B.A. L.1151 J.D. [🄲 Scopelitis,G.L.&H.]
Magill, Michael K. ....'50 '78 C.339 B.S. L.209 J.D. Harris Trust & Svgs. Bk.
Magill, R. Hugh ....'57 '85 C.747 B.A. L.494 J.D. Sr. V.P., Northern Tr. Co., The
Magill, Thomas J., (AV) ....'48 '77 C.339 B.S. L.365 J.D. [Quarles&B.]
Maglione, Daniel F., (BV) ....'60 '87 C.1172 B.S. L.365 J.D. [Wittenberg,D.&M.]
Magnani, Peter J., (AV) ....'46 '74 C&L.347 B.E., J.D. [Magnani&B.]

Magnani & Buck Ltd., (AV)
321 South Plymouth Court Suite 1700, 60604
Telephone: 312-294-4800 Facsimile: 312-294-4815
Email: law@magnanibuck.com
Peter J. Magnani; Thomas L. Buck;—Ximen J. Januszyk; Allison A. Batt; Matthew T. Volk; Jennifer K. Rawe.
Civil Trial and Appellate Practice in State and Federal Courts. Civil Rights Defense, Construction Liability, Insurance Coverage, Insurance Defense, Medical Malpractice, Professional Liability, Municipal Liability, Premises Liability, Products Liability and Transportation Liability.

See Professional Biographies, CHICAGO, ILLINOIS

Magner, Michele G., (AV) .... '51 '77 C.388 B.A. L.910 J.D. [🄲 DLPiper R.G.C.U.]
Magnone, Richard ....'70 '96 C.436 B.S. L.602 J.D. 8501 W. Higgins, Ste. 440
Magnusson, Laura Lee ....'66 '91 C.475 B.A. L.910 J.D. Lexis Nexis
Mago, Louis M. ....'54 '83 C.589 B.S. L.365 J.D. Dep. Atty. & Pros.
Maguire, Paula K. ....'45 '91 C.589 B.A. L.989 J.D. [Friedman&H.]
Magyar-Africk, Julie A. '65 '91 C.424 B.A. L.365 J.D.
Admin. Law J., State & Local Labor Rel. Bd.
Mahajan, Vaishali .... '69 '97 C.846 B.A. L.46 J.D. Midwest Acct. Mgr., Real Legal
Mahalek, David J. ....'70 '03 C.546 B.A. L.209 J.D. [🄰 Niro,S.H.&N.]
Mahaney-Turley, Nora, Law Offices of '54 '79
C.98 B.A. L.802 J.D. 205 W. Randolph St., Ste. 1310
Mahdi Ali, Sajida ....'77 '02 C&L.597 B.A., J.D. [🄰 Mayer,B.R.&M.]
Maher, Brian S. ....'57 '85 C.589 B.S. L.146 J.D. [🄰 Weis&D.]
Maher, Crystal S. ......'65 '91 C.338 B.S. L.209 J.D. Atty., State Comr., Bks. & Trust Cos.
Maher, David W., (AV) ......'34 '60 C&L.309 A.B., LL.B. [Sonnenschein N.&R.] (Pat.)
Maher, David W., Ph.D. '61 '99 C.602 B.S. L.770 J.D.
(adm. in CA; not adm. in IL; See Pat. Sect.) [Fitch,E.T.&F.]
Maher, Jerome A. ....'34 '58 C&L.424 A.B., J.D. Sr. V.P., Hanover Capital
Maher, John N. ....'70 '96 C.98 B.S. L.589 J.D. [🄰 Mayer,B.R.&M.]
Maher, Joy E. ....'65 '90 C.352 B.A. L.424 J.D. [Condon&C.]
Maher, Karen Wojtowicz ....'71 '97 C.680 B.A. L.209 J.D. 2245 W. Ogden
Maher, Michael J., (AV) ....'57 '85 C&L.589 B.A., J.D. [Swanson,M.&B.]
Maher, Robin Drey ....'79 '04 C.784 B.A. L.352 J.D. [🄰 Winston&S.]

Maher, Teresa R., (BV) ....'55 '90 C.602 B.S. L.46 J.D. [Brenner,F.M.&S.]
Maher, William K. ....'64 '94 C.589 B.S. L.146 J.D. V.P., First Options of Chicago, Inc.
Maheras, Theodore G. .... '20 '49 C.103 A.B. L.309 LL.B. 53 W. Jackson
Mahin, Charles B., (AV) '08 '36
C.942 A.B. L.145 J.D. 77 West Wacker Drive, Suite 4400‡
Mahler, Alex ....'69 '00 C.36 B.S. L.345 J.D. [Ⓐ Ross,D.&B.]
Mahlo, James D. .... '76 '01 C.57 B.A. L.424 J.D. [Ⓐ Schuyler,R.&Z.]
Mahone, Amy W. .... '74 '99 C.999 B.A. L.838 J.D. [Ⓐ Levenfeld P.]
Mahoney, Eugene L., (AV) '48 '74
C&L.424 B.B.A., J.D. [E.L.Mahoney&Assoc.] (⊙Tel Aviv, Israel)
Mahoney, James E. ....'52 '78 C.145 B.A. L.1119 J.D. [Griffith&J.]
Mahoney, James P. ....'38 '64 C.174 B.S. L.597 J.D. 1648 N. Burling St.
Mahoney, Jason McClain ....'73 '01 C.350 B.A. L.365 J.D. [Ⓢ Wildman,H.A.&D.]
Mahoney, John F. ... '62 '89 C.475 B.A. L.477 J.D. 208 South La Salle Street, Suite 1750
Mahoney, John H. ...... '43 '68 C&L.966 B.S., J.D. U.S. Dept. of Housing & Urban Dev.
Mahoney, Joseph A. ....'63 '93 C.546 Phar.D. L.734 J.D. [Mayer,B.R.&M.]
Mahoney, Matthew Locke ....'— '88 C.37 B.A. L.597 J.D. 820 West Jackson
Mahoney, Michael G., (AV) ....'60 '89 C.602 B.B.A. L.424 J.D. [Burke,M.&W.]
Mahoney, Patrick E., (AV) ....'37 '61 C.339 B.S. L.209 J.D. [Mahoney,C.&G.]
Mahoney, Ryan A. ....'— '01 C.201 B.A. L.602 J.D. [Ⓐ O'Hagan,S.&A.]
Mahoney, Ryan M. ....'71 '00 C.827 B.S. L.365 J.D. [Ⓐ Knell&P.]
Mahoney, Steven Michael, (AV) ....'55 '80 C.597 B.S. L.339 J.D. [Ⓐ Heineke,B.&B.]
Mahoney, Terence J., (AV) ....'45 '71 C.602 B.A. L.209 J.D. 221 N. LaSalle St.
Mahoney, Timothy P. ....'66 '93 C.424 B.A. L.146 J.D. [Ⓒ Neal,G.&E.]
Mahoney, William F., (AV) ....'53 '78 C.424 B.A. L.339 J.D. [Segal M.S.&M.]
Mahoney, Crowe & Goldrick, P.C., (AV) ....36 S. Wabash Avenue
Mahoney, Eugene L., & Associates, P.C., (AV) ....100 N. La Salle St.
Mahony, Rhona '57 '84 C.103 B.A. L.309 J.D.
Legal Assistance Found. of Chicago, Inc.
Maillis, Eric F. ....'67 '92 C.846 B.A. L.273 J.D. [Ⓐ Rohlfing&O.]
Main, Arthur W., Jr., (Ltd.) .....'24 '50 C.145 A.B. L.365 LL.B. 2139 N. Cleveland Ave.‡
Main, Chad W. '70 '97 C.1165 B.A. L.879 J.D.
(adm. in CA; not adm. in IL) [Ⓐ Meckler B.&T.]
Maina, Arthur A., Jr. ....'23 '50 C.999 L.146 LL.B. 4861 W. Hutchinson St.
Mainzer, James M. ....'51 '78 C.339 B.S. L.146 J.D. [Ⓒ Regas,F.&D.]
Mairone, Gavriel ....'52 '82 C.999 B.A. L.146 J.D. [Mann&M.] (⊙Tel Aviv, Israel)
Maiter, Iris M. ....'— '80 C&L.424 B.S., J.D. 201 E. Chestnut
Majers, Elizabeth L., (AV) ....'58 '82 C.339 B.S. L.1119 J.D. [McDermott W.&E.]
Majewski, Katherine A. ....'— '03 C.154 B.A. L.477 J.D. [Ⓐ Katten M.R.]
Majid, Ameena Y. ....'— '98 C.352 B.A. L.424 J.D. [Ⓐ Seyfarth S.]
Majka, Erin L. ....'76 '02 C.210 B.A. L.209 J.D. [Ⓐ Tressler,S.M.&P.]
Major, Justin James ....'69 '01 C.793 B.S. L.146 J.D. State Appellate Def. Off.
Major, Karrick L. ....'— '77 C.691 B.A. L.424 J.D. 640 N. LaSalle St.
Major, Ruth I. ....'— '90 C.339 B.S. L.352 J.D. [Gardner C.&D.]
Makarski, David S. ....'71 '96 C&L.597 B.A., J.D. [Ⓐ Schoenberg,F.N.&R.]
Makarski, Richard A., (AV) ....'38 '63 C&L.339 A.B., LL.B. 11 W. Monroe St.‡
Makauskas, Andrew R., (BV) ....'— '91 C.477 B.A. L.339 J.D. [Brady,C.&M.]
Maki, Alison J. ....'— '00 C.589 B.Mus. L.477 J.D. [Ⓐ Vedder,P.K.&K.]
Maki-Rusk, Emily M. ....'76 '02 C.373 B.A. L.910 J.D. [Ⓐ Seyfarth S.]
Maksym, Walter P., (BV) .... '46 '72 C.339 B.S. L.365 J.D. [W.P.Maksym&Assoc.]
Maksym, Walter P., & Assoc., Ltd., (BV) ....2056 N. Lincoln Ave.
Malahowski, Andrew A. ....'77 '02 C&L.602 B.A., J.D. [Ⓐ Franczek S.]
Malak, Jeffrey A. ....'40 '64 C&L.879 B.A., J.D. Assoc. Cir. J.
Malamis, Kathy Karaboyas .... '76 '01 C.424 B.A. L.209 J.D. [Ⓐ Tressler,S.M.&P.]
Malarkey, John D. ....'49 '83 C.93 B.A. L.597 J.D. [Schain,B.R.&C.]
Malatesta, Michael J. ....'75 '02 C.352 B.A. L.209 J.D. [Ⓐ Ellison,N.Z.&A.]
Malato, Stephen H., (AV) ....'53 '78 C.927 B.A. L.146 J.D. [Hinshaw&C.]
Malavia, Roger A. ....'67 '93 C&L.424 B.A., J.D. [Odim&M.]
Maldonado, Nancy L. ....'— '01 C.309 B.A. L.178 J.D. [Ⓐ Miner,B.&G.]
Malek, Joseph A. .... '35 '60 C&L.424 B.S.S.S., J.D. 77 W. Jackson Blvd. S.E.
Malfar, David E. ....'22 '48 C&L.339 B.A., LL.B. 77 W. Wash. St.
Malik, Terry John, (AV) ....'51 '80 C.602 B.A. L.424 J.D. [Winston&S.]
Malik, Thaddeus J., (AV) ....'66 '91 C.597 B.A. L.309 J.D. [Jenner&B.]
Malin, Martin H. ....'53 '76 C.475 B.A. L.273 J.D. Chicago-Kent College of Law
Malina, Lance C. ....'60 '89 C.1016 B.A. L.209 J.D. [Ⓐ Klein,T.&J.]
Malina, Steven M. ....'62 '87 C.477 B.A. L.339 J.D. [Morgan,L.&B.]
Malinger, David N. ....'73 '98 C.339 B.S. L.221 J.D. [Ⓐ Mayer,B.R.&M.]
Malinowski, Arthur A. ....'29 '60 C&L.209 B.S.C., LL.B. 5409 W. Hutchinson St.
Malinowski, Sybil C. '49 '77 C.530 B.A. L.146 J.D.
V.P. & Assoc. Gen. Coun., Federal Home Loan Bk. of Chicago
Malis, Michele K. ....'70 '96 C.800 B.A. L.1117 J.D. [Ⓐ DLPiper R.G.C.U.]
Malitz, Steven N. ....'— '95 C.347 B.A. L.982 J.D. [Arnstein&L.]
Malk, Charles R. ....'52 '77 C.339 B.S. L.209 J.D. CRM Properties Group, Ltd.
Malkan, Jeffrey D. '54 '89 C.178 A.B. L.563 J.D.
(adm. in NY; not adm. in IL) Chicago-Kent College of Law
Malki, Roger S. ....'— '03 C.014 B.A. L.213 J.D. [Ⓐ Freeborn&P.]
Malkin, Cary J., (AV) ....'49 '74 C.273 B.A. L.597 J.D. [Mayer,B.R.&M.]
Malkin, Earle A. ....'31 '56 C.339 B.A. L.365 J.D. 30 N. La Salle St.
Malkin, Howard I. ....'35 '60 C.339 B.A. L.597 LL.B. NLRB, Region 13
Malkin, Leonard M., (AV) ....'41 '65 C.966 B.B.A. L.339 LL.B. [Mandel,L.&S.]
Malkin, Rachael G. .... '— '02 C.473 B.A. L.424 J.D. [Ⓐ Bates&C.]
Malkin, Sherwin J. ....'32 '56 C.597 B.S. L.477 J.D. [S.J.Malkin]
Malkin, Sherwin J., Ltd. ....155 N. Michigan
Mallen, Richard F. ....'52 '79 C.339 B.S. L.146 J.D. [R.F.Mallen&Assoc.]
Mallen, Richard F., & Associates, Ltd. ....188 West Randolph Street Suite 1750
Mallers, Thomas J., (BV) ....'56 '81 C.57 B.A. L.209 J.D. [Nyhan,P.B.K.&L.]
Malliband, David J. ....'72 '91 C&L.1382 B.Comm., LL.B. [Baker&M.]
Mallin, Robert S. .... '63 '90 C.339 B.S. L.424 J.D. [Brinks H.G.&L.] (See Pat. Sect.)
Mallon, Barbara A., (AV) ....'58 '86 C.597 B.A. L.365 J.D. [Mallon&J.]
Mallon, Clifford P. '35 '59 C&L.209 LL.B.
Managing Attorney, Allstate Insurance Company

Mallon & Johnson, P.C., (AV)
19 South La Salle Street, Suite 1202, 60603
Telephone: 312-346-8890 Fax: 312-346-8896 Email: bmallon@mallonandjohnson.com
Email: djohnson@mallonandjohnson.com URL: http://www.mallonandjohnson.com
Barbara A. Mallon; Dexter Johnson.
Securities Regulation and Compliance.
See Professional Biographies, CHICAGO, ILLINOIS

Mallory, Ramsey L. ....'70 '99 C.234 B.S. L.879 J.D. [Ⓐ Williams M.&J.]
Malloy, James W. ....'31 '62 C.276 B.S. L.597 J.D. 53 W. Jackson Blvd.
Malloy, Kevin R. ....'71 '97 C.602 B.A. L.904 J.D. [Ⓐ K.M.Forde]
Malloy, Timothy J., (AV) '44 '69
C&L.602 B.S.E.E., J.D. [McAndrews,H.&M.] (See Pat. Sect.)

Malman, Steven J., & Associates, Law Offices of '66 '91
C.352 B.A. L.424 J.D. 205 W. Randolph Street, Suite 1040
Malone, Daniel B., (AV) ....'57 '86 C.339 B.A. L.209 J.D. [Healy]
Malone, Edward F. ....'64 '91 C.145 A.B. L.1068 J.D. [Jenner&B.]
Malone, Patrick R. ....'77 '02 C.602 B.A. L.597 J.D. [Ⓐ Grippo&E.]
Malone, W. Bruck, (AV) ....'33 '63 C.424 B.S. L.339 J.D. 3550 N. Lake Shore Dr.‡
Maloney, C. Vincent, (AV) '59 '87 C.436 B.A. L.339 J.D.
Suite 4000, 10 South Wacker Drive (⊙Chicago)
Maloney, C. Vincent (Vince), (AV) '59 '87
C.436 B.A. L.339 J.D. [Perkins C.] (⊙Chicago)
Maloney, Douglas P., (AV) ....'31 '59 C.367 A.B. L.597 J.D. 1 E.Wacker Dr.
Maloney, Joan E. ....'55 '94 C.238 B.S. L.365 J.D. [Ⓒ Field&G.]
Maloney, Kathryn Ann ....'70 '98 C.116 B.A. L.424 J.D. Asst. Pub. Def.
Maloney, Marylove '46 '72 C.436 B.A. L.494 J.D.
(adm. in CA; not adm. in IL) 680 N. Lake Shore Drive
Maloney, Michael F., (AV) ....'43 '70 C.742 B.A. L.146 J.D. [Fishman,F.&S.]
Maloney, Patrick E., (AV) ....'45 '70 C&L.602 A.B., J.D. [Tressler,S.M.&P.]
Maloney, Patrick J. ....'57 '84 C&L.145 B.A., J.D. [Bell,B.&L.]
Maloney, Sean T. ....'— '87 C.602 B.A. L.1119 J.D. [Schiff H.]
Maloney, Sheila M. '76 '03 C.339 B.A. L.597 J.D.
Prof., Northwestern Univ. Law School
Maloney, Timothy P., (BV) '66 '93
C&L.339 B.S.Ch.E., J.D. [Fitch,E.T.&F.] (See Pat. Sect.)
Malovance, Gregory J. ....'54 '78 C.1365 B.A. L.145 J.D. [Winston&S.]
Malovany, Howard '50 '77 C.608 B.A. L.851 J.D.
V.P., Secy. & Gen. Coun., Wm. Wrigley Jr. Co.
Malstrom, Edward W., (AV) '51 '75
C.1183 B.A. L.339 J.D. Asst. Gen. Coun., Exelon Bus. Servs. Co.
Malstrom, Robert A., (AV) .... '46 '73 C.339 B.S. L.477 J.D. [Sidley A.B.&W.]
Maltby, Kimberly A. ....'62 '91 L.339 J.D. [Ⓐ Dowd&D.]
Malter, David J., & Associates, Law Offices of '59 '85
C.339 B.A. L.146 J.D. 19 South La Salle Street, Suite 1300
Malysiak, James T. .... '46 '76 C.197 B.A. L.976 J.D. [Freeman,F.&S.]
Mamet, Bernard M. ....'23 '46 L.597 LL.B. 327 S. La Salle St.
Mammel, Christopher N., (AVⓉ) ....'54 '81 C&L.208 B.A., J.D. [Childress D.G.]
Man, Thomas Y. ....'61 '97 C.999 B.A. L.347 J.D. [Ⓐ Baker&M.]
Manalli, J. Christian ....'70 '97 C.679 L.424 J.D. 130 S. Jefferson St., Ste. 500
Manaster, Ira B. ....'37 '61 C.597 B.S.B.A. L.145 J.D. David Berg & Co.
Manchik, Craig ....'66 '94 C.378 BS L.213 JD 29 S. LaSalle St., Ste. 945
Mancini, Lorenzo A., (AV) .... '46 '77 C.742 B.A. L.209 J.D. [Norton,M.W.&D.] ⊙
Mancoff, Neal A., (AV) ....'— '65 C.966 B.B.A. L.597 J.D. [Schiff H.]
Manczak, Mary Rose C. ....'59 '86 C.209 B.A. L.424 J.D. [Nisen&E.]
Mandanas, Julie Montz ....'69 '97 C.597 B.A. L.339 J.D. [Jenner&B.]
Mandel, Alan J. ....'58 '84 C.339 B.A. L.276 J.D. [A.J.Mandel&Assoc.]
Mandel, Jed R., (AV) ....'52 '77 C.477 B.A. L.597 J.D. [Neal,G.&E.]
Mandel, Laura G., (AV) '62 '87
C&L.424 B.A., J.D. Sr. Atty., Northern Trust Corporation
Mandel, Martha Pink ....'26 '58 C&L.597 B.S., J.D. 860 Lake Shore Dr.‡
Mandel, Miranda Kiser, (AV) ....'56 '81 C&L.347 B.A., J.D. [Neal,G.&E.]
Mandel, Reid A. ....'54 '81 C.976 B.A. L.569 J.D. [Katten M.R.]
Mandel, Richard L., (AV) ...... '27 '50 L.145 J.D. Suite 2210, 203 North La Salle Street‡
Mandel, Robert J., (BV) ....'56 '82 C&L.1019 B.B.A., J.D. 10 S. Wacker Drive
Mandel, Roger B., (AV) ....'39 '66 C.339 B.S. L.146 J.D. [Kamensky,R.H.&D.] ⊙
Mandel, Alan J., & Associates Ltd. ....77 W. Wacker Drive, #2500

Mandel, Lipton and Stevenson Limited, (AV)
Suite 2210, 203 North La Salle Street, 60601
Telephone: 312-236-7080 Facsimile: 312-236-0781
URL: http://www.mandellipton.com
Alfred R. Lipton; Leonard M. Malkin; R. Peter Carey; Henry A. Waller; Kathleen Roseborough; Richard A. Lifshitz; Terry Yale Feiertag; Carolyn E. Winter; Andrés J. Gallegos; Reuben A. Bernick; Joan E. Comiskey;—Tracey A. Salinski; Amanda Petersen (Not admitted in IL); Kimberly R. Lusk.
General Civil Practice. Corporation, Retirement Plans, Banking, Labor and Employment Relations, Family, Adoption and Child Custody, Mental Health and Developmental Disabilities, Probate, Estate and Tax Planning, Real Estate, Personal Injury, Bankruptcy, State and Federal Civil Trials and Appeals, Intellectual Property, Immigration and Nationality Law, College and University, International Trade.
References: Northern Trust Co.; Bank One; La Salle Bank FSB.
See Professional Biographies, CHICAGO, ILLINOIS

Mandell, Floyd A., (P.C.), (AV) ....'48 '73 C.589 B.A. L.339 J.D. [Katten M.R.]
Mandell, Gregg, Law Offices of, (AV) '52 '81
C.1080 B.A. L.209 J.D. 33 N. LaSalle St., Ste. 1925
Mandell, Keith W. ....'72 '99 C.597 B.A. L.273 J.D. [Ⓐ Reardon G.&R.]
Mandell, Philip L. ....'35 '62 C.339 B.S. L.365 LL.B. [Pitler&M.]
Mandell, Steven P., (AV) ....'57 '82 C.966 B.B.A. L.276 J.D. [Mandell M.]

Mandell Menkes LLC, (AV) BR
333 West Wacker Drive, Suite 300, 60606
Telephone: 312-251-1000 Fax: 312-251-1010
URL: http://www.mandellmenkes.com
Steven L. Baron; Joan S. Callan; Bruce E. de'Medici; J. David Duffy; Steven P. Mandell; Bruce N. Menkes; Daniel V. O'Leary, Jr.; Ned S. Othman; Stephen J. Rosenfeld. Associates: Keith E. Allen; Ryan T. Brown; Natalie A. Harris; Brendan J. Healey; Kristin L. Lingren; Alexis E. Payne; Elizabeth N. Pendleton; Michael A. Rakov; Suzanne M. Scheuing; Patrick G. Somers; Joshua J. Wallar. Of Counsel: Susan S. O'Byrne; Jennifer A. Widmer.
General Civil Practice, Class Action Defense, Consumer Finance and Banking, Corporate, Commercial Litigation, Employment, Media, Entertainment and Intellectual Property Law including Copyright and Trademark Law, Computer and Technology Law, Health Care, Captive Insurance and Purchasing and Risk Retention Groups and Insurance Coverage, Directors and Officers Liability, Professional Liability, Casualty, Life, Health and Disability.
See Professional Biographies, CHICAGO, ILLINOIS

Mandler, Thomas Y., (AV) ....'46 '72 C.966 B.A. L.339 J.D. [Hinshaw&C.]
Mandrell, D. Matthew '69 '96 C.338 B.S. L.61 J.D.
A.V.P./Coun., Harris Tr. & Svgs. Bk.
Mandziara, Ethan P. ....'71 '03 C.339 B.A. L.424 J.D. [Ⓐ Hubert&F.]
Manelis, Epaminondas Eddie ....'63 '87 C.145 B.A. L.208 J.D. 29 S. LaSalle
Mangan, Jerald M. ....'57 '82 C.378 B.A. L.209 J.D. [Mangan,L.G.&L.] ⊙
Mangan, John J., (AV) .... '51 '76 C.378 B.A. L.365 J.D. [Dykema G.P.] (⊙Lisle)
Mangan, Thomas P., (AV) ....'49 '78 C.602 B.A. L.1151 J.D. [Schoen&S.]

Mangan, Langhenry, Gillen & Lundquist, (AV)
29 South La Salle Street, Suite 720, 60603 ⊙
Telephone: 312-704-6700 Fax: 312-704-6777
Email: mlgl@mlglaw.com
Members: Jerald M. Mangan; John G. Langhenry III; Suzanne Favia Gillen; Troy A. Lundquist. Associates: Melissa J. Gordon; John P. Palumbo; Adam M. Berger; Pedro Cervantes.
General Liability Defense, Medical Malpractice Defense, Insurance Coverage, Class Action Defense and Insurance Defense.
Joliet, Illinois Office: 18 West Cass Street, Suite 200, 60432. Telephone: 815-726-3600. Fax: 815-726-3676.

(This Listing Continued)

Mangan, Langhenry, Gillen & Lundquist (Continued)
Rockford, Illinois Office: 6785 Weaver Road, Suite 2E, 61114. Telephone: 815-636-1800. Fax: 815-636-2860.
Wheaton, Illinois Office: 311 South County Farm Road, Suite K, 60187. Telephone: 630-653-5775. Fax: 630-653-5980.
See Professional Biographies, CHICAGO, ILLINOIS

Mangiaforte, Cynthia S. '64 '90 C.801 B.A. L.602 J.D. [Ⓐ Bell,B.&L.]
Mangoni, August M., (Ltd.) '23 '52 L.365 J.D. 221 N. LaSalle St.
Mangum, Charles D. '71 '98 C.477 B.A. L.930 J.D. [Ⓐ Schain,B.R.&C.]
Manhart, Maria T. '62 '88 C.190 B.A. L.436 J.D. [Neal,G.&E.]
Maniatis, John P., (AV) '56 '82 C.146 B.S. L.365 J.D. [Tressler,S.M.&P.]
Manikas, Donald J. '62 '87 C.339 B.A. L.145 J.D. [Lord,B.&B.]
Manilow, Floyd B. '29 '56 C.339 A.B. L.597 J.D. Ste 200, 4725 N Western Ave
Manilow, Lewis, (AV) '27 '51 C.145 Ph.B. L.309 LL.B. 30 S. Wacker Dr., Suite 2900
Manis, Peter E. '57 '83 C&L.477 A.B., J.D. [Ⓒ Varga B.L.H.&C.]
Manley, Paige C. '74 '01 C.473 B.A. L.365 J.D. [Ⓐ Johnson&B.]
Manly, Anne E. '59 '91 C.801 B.S. L.339 J.D. [Robbins&R.]
Manly, Michael P. '71 '96 C&L.546 B.A., J.D. [Neal,G.&E.]
Mann, David S., (AV) '— '62 C.602 A.B. L.597 J.D. [Holland&K.]
Mann, Eric N. '71 '96 C.339 B.S. L.46 J.D. Two North LaSalle Street, Suite 2200
Mann, Gregory B. '68 '93 C.966 B.A. L.146 J.D. [Much S.F.D.A.&R.]
Mann, Monte L. '70 '95 C.659 B.A. L.597 J.D. [Novack&M.]
Mann, Neil R. '— '75 C&L.477 B.A., J.D. [Chapman&C.]
Mann, Nicole K. '74 '99 C.970 B.A. L.146 J.D. [Ⓐ McDermott W.&E.]
Mann, Philip J. '57 '82 C.339 B.A. L.209 J.D. F.B.I.
Mann, Robert E., (Ltd.), (AV) '29 '56 C.339 B.S. L.145 LL.B. 5539 S. Harper St.
Mann, Robert M. '48 '77 C&L.424 A.B., J.D.
Sr. V.P. & Assoc. Dep. Gen. Coun., CNA Insurance Companies
Mann, Samantha M. '— '00 C&L.339 B.A., J.D. [Ⓐ Kirkland&E.]
Mann, Scott '54 '79 C.473 B.A. L.365 J.D. [Mann&M.] (ⓞTel Aviv, Israel)
Mann, Vicki L. '43 '81 C.473 A.B. L.365 J.D. 644 Webster
Mann, Vijai Singh '34 '82 C&L.999 B.A., LL.B. Ck. Co. Law Library
Mann & Mairone 100 N. LaSalle St.
Mannarino, Craig P. '69 '96 C.918 B.A. L.209 J.D. [Ⓐ Kralovec,J.&S.]
Manning, Amy B., (AV) '67 '92 C.1108 B.A. L.145 J.D. [McGuirewoods]
Manning, Blanche M. '34 '67 C.1191 L.365 J.D. U.S. Dist. J.
Manning, Christopher R., (AV) '49 '74 C.276 A.B. L.145 J.D. [Burke,W.M.&S.]
Manning, Frederick J. '47 '73 C.659 B.S. L.309 J.D. Pres., Celtic Group, Inc.
Manning, Heather H. '76 '02 C.477 B.S. L.276 J.D.
(adm. in NY; not adm. in IL) [Ⓐ Gould&R.]
Manning, James E. '24 '52 C.209 L.424 J.D. 10827 S. Western Ave.
Manning, Mack P. '17 '47 C.999 L.146 1624 W. Bryn Mawr Ave.
Manning, Richard L., (AV) '43 '68 C&L.602 B.A., J.D. [Burman&M.]
Mannis, Michael D. '58 '84 C&L.861 B.A., J.D. [Skaletsky&M.]
Mannix, Gerald J., (AV) '30 '59 C&L.209 B.A., J.D. [Ⓒ Davis M.]
Manno, Vincent P. '18 '45 C.999 L.365 J.D. 6273 N. Lemont Ave.‡
Mannon, Joseph M. '76 '01 C.475 B.A. L.424 J.D. [Ⓐ Vedder,P.K.&K.]
Mano, Julia '— '04 C.958 B.S. L.597 J.D. [Ⓐ Winston&S.]
Manocheo, D. Nicholas '40 '65 C&L.352 B.A., J.D.
Contl. Ill. Nat. Bk. & Tr. Co. of Chic.
Manos, Bruce J. '53 '88 C.1027 B.S. L.365 J.D. [Ⓐ Morris&S.]
Manos, George J., (BV) '61 '86 C&L.209 B.A., J.D. [Bollinger,R.&G.]
Manos, Nicholas G., (AV) '22 '43 L.209 J.D. 53 W. Jackson Blvd.
Mansell, Eric Reed '73 '01 C.911 B.A. L.424 J.D. [Ⓐ Sonnenschein N.&R.]
Mansfield, Bruce R., (AV) '48 '75
C.46 B.S.E.E. L.365 J.D. [Ⓐ Olson&H.] (See Pat. Sect.)
Manson, Julie N., (BV) '50 '77 C.339 B.A. L.146 J.D.
Assoc. Gen. Coun., Rush Presbyterian St. Luke's Med. Ctr.
Manson, Patricia A. '56 '83 C&L.378 B.S., J.D.
(adm. in KS; not adm. in IL) Rept., Law Bulletin Pub. Co.

Manson, Lawrence A.
(See Highland Park)

Mansour, Constance A. '64 '89 C.597 B.S. L.424 J.D. Comm. of Banks & Trust Co.
Mantas, John '73 '99 C.209 B.S. L.365 J.D. 6601 N. Avondale
Mantel, Helen '72 '00 C.019 B.A. L.145 J.D. [Ⓐ Baker&M.]
Manter, Gregory A. '78 '04 C.893 B.A. L.228 J.D.
(adm. in NY; not adm. in IL) [Ⓐ Mayer,B.R.&M.]
Manter, Jennifer S. '— '03 C.597 B.A. L.228 J.D. [Ⓐ Pircher,N.&M.]
Mantynband, Ralph A., (AV) '29 '53 C.339 B.S. L.145 J.D. [Shefsky&F.]
Mantz, Rachel Williams '72 '97 C.910 B.A. L.966 J.D. [Ⓐ McGuirewoods]
Manuel, Chad M. '79 '04 C.504 B.A. L.1187 J.D. [Manuel&Assoc.]
Manuel, Donna '63 '91 C.378 B.S. L.424 J.D. Two N. LaSalle St.
Manuel, Michael B. '60 '88 C.477 B.S. L.597 J.D. [Goldberg,K.B.B.R.&M.]
Manuel & Associates 2446 N. Clark
Manus, Neil '24 '51 C&L.597 B.S.L., LL.B. 330 S. Wells St.
Manzo, Edward D., (AV) '50 '76
C.667 B.S. L.107 J.D. [Cook,A.M.M.C.&M.] (See Pat. Sect.)
Mapes-Riordan, Lynne D. '63 '89 C.477 B.A. L.1059 J.D. [Barack F.K.P.&N.]
Maragos, Samuel C. '22 '48 C.145 A.B. L.365 J.D. Cir. J.

Maramba & Associates, LLC
(See Arlington Heights)

Maras, Guy N., (BV) '— '95 C.436 B.A. L.365 J.D. [Hennessy&R.]
Maras, Marcia '56 '82 C.338 B.S. L.209 J.D. Cir. Ct. J.
Marasa, Francis James, (AV) '50 '76 C.300 B.A. L.365 J.D. [F.J.Marasa]
Marasa, Francis J., Ltd., (AV) One East Wacker Drive 35th Floor
Marasco, Joelle T. '66 '91 C.107 B.A. L.851 J.D. Atty. Gen. Off.
Marback, William '— '88 C.424 B.A. L.209 J.D. P.O. Box 2996
Marcaurelle, Myra A. '— '02 C.30 B.A. L.424 J.D. [Ⓐ Sachnoff&W.]
Marcheschi, Elena '50 '91 C.999 B.A. L.365 J.D.
Chicago Federation of Labor Wkrs. Assistance Committee
Marchese, John C. '68 '95 C.276 B.A. L.145 J.D. Arthur Andersen, LLP
Marchetti, Frances F. '16 '40 L.146 J.D. 151 N. Michigan Ave.‡
Marchion, Philip '77 '04 C.473 B.S. L.424 J.D. [Ⓐ Rusin M.&F.]
Marciniak, Joseph A. '63 '90 C.338 B.S. L.146 J.D. [Ⓐ Rusin M.&F.]
Marcisz, Sharon M. '59 '01 C.209 B.S. L.424 J.D. PricewaterhouseCoopers LLP
Marco, David M. '70 '00 C.999 B.S. L.146 J.D. [Ⓐ Swanson,M.&B.]
Marconi, Jerome F., Jr., (AV) '60 '86 C.927 B.A. L.209 J.D. 218 N. Jefferson, Ste. 300
Marconi, Joseph R., (AV) '49 '76 C.350 B.S. L.365 J.D. [Johnson&B.]
Marcotte, Paul A. '54 '85 C.966 B.A. L.146 J.D. Amer. Bar Assn.
Marcovitch, Paul B. '58 '84 C.178 B.A. L.597 J.D. 2729 W. Fullerton Ave.
Marcus, Alan R. '51 '77 [Chapekis,M.&C.]
Marcus, Debra Kramer '— '81 C.339 B.A. L.146 J.D. [Pappas,J.&M.]
Marcus, Dorene, (AV) '40 '78 C.1016 B.A. L.424 J.D. [Davis F.Z.K.M.M.&R.]
Marcus, Fred O. '48 '74 C.339 B.S. L.209 J.D. [Horwood M.&B.]
Marcus, Ira J., (AV) '45 '71 C&L.861 B.A., J.D. [Marcus,P.&C.]
Marcus, James I. '45 '70 C.339 B.A. L.424 J.D. [Williams&Ma.]
Marcus, Joseph R., (AV) '36 '65
C.119 B.S.Ch.E. L.146 J.D. [Welsh&K.] (See Pat. Sect.)
Marcus, Lenard S. '48 '75 C.339 B.A. L.209 J.D. [Linebarger G.B.&S.]
Marcus, Micah E. '— '99 C.37 B.A. L.209 J.D. [Ⓐ Kirkland&E.]
Marcus, Neal D. '63 '90 C.339 B.S.E.E. L.425 J.D. 333 W. Hubbard St., Ste. 3D
Marcus, Richard L., (AV) '38 '62 C&L.145 A.B., J.D. [Sonnenschein N.&R.]
Marcus, Stephen A., (AV) '— '68 C.339 B.S. L.597 J.D. [Ⓒ Schiff H.]
Marcus, Stephen D., (AV) '41 '67 C&L.309 B.A., J.D.
[Clausen M.] (ⓞLondon, England; Paris, France; Rome, Italy)
Marcus, Perres & Campanale, (AV) 19 South La Salle Street Suite 1500
Marczak, Susan B. '51 '77 C.339 B.A. L.424 J.D. Asst. Corp. Coun.
Mardell, Fred R. '34 '58 C.209 B.S. L.145 J.D. 401 N. Michigan Ave.‡
Mardell, Howard '31 '63 C.1016 B.S.C. L.209 J.D. [H.Mardell]
Mardell, Howard, Ltd. 221 N. LaSalle St.
Marderosian, Steven A. '69 '96 C.339 B.A. L.209 J.D. [Ⓐ Field&G.]
Marek, Richard J. '46 '76 C.1265 B.A. L.912 J.D.
(adm. in MI; not adm. in IL) Harris Tr. & Svgs. Bk.
Marek, Sherman P., Law Office of '62 '89
C.723 B.A. L.494 J.D. 1120 N. LaSalle Dr., Ste. 19 F
Maremont, James K. '36 '61 C.221 B.S. L.209 LL.B. 134 W. LaSalle St.
Marengo, Paul C., (AV) '— '74 C.674 A.B. L.145 J.D. [Schiff H.]
Margolies, Allison G. '71 '00 C.659 B.A. L.273 J.D. [Ⓐ Hughes S.P.R.&D.]
Margolies, Marjorie M. '62 '88 C.103 B.A. L.477 J.D. [Ⓒ Mayer,B.R.&M.]
Margolin, Stephen M., (AV) '35 '63 C.339 B.S. L.365 J.D. [Chuhak&T.]
Margolis, Edward S., (AV) '43 '68 C&L.339 B.A., J.D. [Teller,L.&S.]
Margolis, Jeremy, (AV) '47 '73 C.339 B.A. L.597 J.D. [Sonnenschein N.&R.]
Margolis, Jordan L., (BV) '54 '79 C.339 B.A. L.597 J.D. [Margolis]
Margolis, Marvin '27 '62 C.1016 B.S. L.365 LL.B. 221 N. LaSalle, Ste. 1320
Margolis, Paul D. '76 '01 C&L.339 B.S., J.D. [Ⓐ Jenner&B.]
Margolis, Robert L. '63 '89 C.228 B.A. L.145 J.D. [Ⓐ Robinson C.&C.]

Margolis, Sidney, (AV) '46 '80 L.597 J.D.
123 West Madison Street Suite 606, 60602
Telephone: 312-578-9382 Facsimile: 312-578-9384
Email: sidsume@sbcglobal.net
Litigation and Environmental Law.
See Professional Biographies, CHICAGO, ILLINOIS

Margolis, Sidney B., (AV) '40 '65 C&L.339 B.S., J.D. [S.B.Margolis]
Margolis Firm, The, PC, (BV) 77 West Wacker Drive, Suite 3200
Margolis, Sidney B., Ltd., (AV) 20 N. Clark St.
Margulis, Rory L. '73 '00 C.352 B.A. L.365 J.D. [Ⓐ Johnson&B.]
Margulis, Ryan Adam '75 '01 C.347 B.S.B. L.910 J.D. [Seidman]
Marhoefer, John J. '— '03 C.63 B.S. L.146 J.D. [Ⓐ Latham&W.]
Mariano, Michael A. '49 '74 C.1151 L.365 J.D.
Asst. Gen. Coun. & Asst. Corp. Secy., Unisys Corp.
Marick, Michael M., (AV) '57 '82 C.207 B.A. L.146 J.D. [Meckler B.&T.]
Marinakis, Dean C., Attorney at Law '68 '93
C.339 B.S. L.424 J.D. 20 N. Clark St., Ste. 2450
Marinakis, George G. '30 '64 C.339 B.S. L.365 LL.B. 77 W. Washington St.
Marinelli, Joseph F. '72 '99 C.679 B.S.M.E. L.966 J.D. [Ⓐ Jenner&B.]
Marinello, Mitchell L., (AV) '54 '81 C.918 B.A. L.569 J.D. [Novack&M.]
Marino, Frank A. '50 '75 C.742 B.A. L.209 J.D. [Ⓐ Tobin P.&M.]
Marino, Frank C., (AV) '48 '83 C.399 B.A. L.146 J.D. [Pavalon,G.L.&M.]
Marino, Herman J. '51 '76 C.424 B.S. L.597 J.D.
53 West Jackson Boulevard, Suite 1442
Marino, Jack F., (BV) '40 '65 C.424 B.S. L.209 J.D. 123 W. Madison St.
Marino, Nahrin S. '74 '03 C.338 B.S. L.365 J.D. [Ⓐ Dykema G.P.]
Marion, James M., (AV) '60 '89
C.375 B.A. L.378 J.D. Trust Coun., LaSalle Natl. Tr., N.A.
Marion, Julie M. '— '01 C.339 B.S. L.577 J.D. [Ⓐ Latham&W.]
Maris, George P. '68 '94 C.821 B.A. L.339 J.D. 3500 Three First Nat. Plz.
Maritote, R. Mark '56 '81 C.812 B.S. L.209 J.D. [M.Maritote]
Maritote, Mark 188 West Randolph Street
Mark, Warren W., (P.C.) '41 '66 C.1016 L.209 LL.B. 205 W. Randolph St.
Markese, Paul M. '71 '99 C.424 B.A. L.365 J.D. [Hinshaw&C.]
Markey, Christopher G. '50 '96 C.424 B.A. L.365 J.D. [Ⓐ Hinshaw&C.]
Markey, Patrick B. '75 '02 C.494 B.A. L.146 J.D. [Ⓐ Nottage&W.]
Markham, Bradford M. '49 '74
C.72 B.A. L.966 J.D. Sr. Coun., Bank One Corp. (Law Dept.)
Markham, Harold '32 '77 C&L.209 B.A., J.D. James McHugh Construstion Co.
Markin, Robert S., (AV) '59 '84 C.103 B.A. L.276 J.D. [DLPiper R.G.C.U.]
Markley, G. Roger '48 '73 C.276 B.S. L.831 J.D. Sr. Atty., I.R.S.
Marko, Daniel '73 '00 C.477 B.S.E. L.146 J.D. [Ⓐ Daley&M.]
Markoff, Paul F., IV '70 '96 C.477 A.B. L.209 J.D. [Crowley B.&K.]
Markoutsis, Nina '64 '95 C.339 B.S. L.365 J.D. [Ⓐ Bates&C.]
Markovic, Milos '— '99 C.339 B.A. L.209 J.D. [Ⓐ Mayer,B.R.&M.]
Markovitz, Rhoda Elvove '51 '77 C.823 B.S. L.146 J.D. [Ⓐ Hauselman&R.]
Markowski, Robert T., (AV) '53 '78 C.209 B.A. L.339 J.D. [Jenner&B.]
Marks, Dennis A., (AV) '— '74 C.424 B.B.A. L.365 J.D. [Querrey&H.]
Marks, Ellen L. '— '91 C.597 B.A. L.477 J.D. [Latham&W.]
Marks, Howard, (AVⓉ) '52 '77 C&L.861 B.S., J.D. [Berger,N.&F.]
Marks, James W. '56 '84 C.145 B.A. L.861 J.D. [Harris K.&G.]
Marks, Jason M. '76 '01 C.145 A.B. L.273 J.D. [Ⓐ Katten M.R.]
Marks, Jeffrey M., Law Offices of '53 '79
C.339 B.S. L.365 J.D. 33 N. Dearborn St., Ste. 700
Marks, Jerome, (AV) '31 '55 C&L.597 B.S., J.D. 203 N. La Salle St., Suite 1800
Marks, Jonathan L. '— '89 C.976 B.A. L.477 J.D. [Katten M.R.]
Marks, Lisa R. '67 '97 C.216 B.A. L.597 J.D. 53 W. Jackson Blvd., Ste. 1550
Marks, Roger H. '51 '76 C.659 B.S. & B.A. L.188 J.D.
Sr. V.P., Gen. Coun. & Secy., H20 Plus, Inc., Pres., Int'l Div.
Marks, Spencer J., (AV) '47 '74 C.591 B.A. L.365 J.D. [Marks,M.&K.]

Marks, Marks and Kaplan, Ltd., (AV)
55 West Monroe Street, Suite 3300, 60603
Telephone: 312-332-5200 Fax: 312-332-2952 URL: http://www.mmklawoffice.com
URL: http://www.mmk-ltd.com
Arnee J. Eisenberg; Gilbert W. Gordon; Spencer J. Marks; Richard W. Rappold; Gerald M. Tenner;—Stephen A. Cohen; Susan L. Dawson; Robert E. Haney; Ivy D. Israel. Of Counsel: Howard D. Galper; Ronald R. Rassin.
General Civil, Corporate and Partnership. Business, Real Estate, Trial and Appellate Practice, Zoning, Environmental, Estate Planning, Trust, Probate and Negligence Law, Medical Malpractice, Professional Sports Injuries, Employment Law, Corporate Law, Business Law, Litigation.
See Professional Biographies, CHICAGO, ILLINOIS

Markus, Terry A. '61 '86 C.339 B.S. L.597 J.D. Exec. V.P., Prism Mortgage Co.

Marler, Eric J. '76 '02 C&L.352 B.S., J.D. [Ⓐ Reardon G.&R.]
Marlott, John A. '— '95 C.339 B.S. L.273 J.D. [Jones D.] (See Pat. Sect.)
Marlow, Christopher K. '74 '04
C.502 B.S.E.E. L.597 J.D. [Ⓐ Welsh&K.] (See Pat. Sect.)
Marmer, Ronald L., (AV) '52 '77 C.597 B.S. L.893 J.D. [Jenner&B.]
Marmor, Randall I., (AV) '53 '78 C.234 B.A. L.365 J.D. [Clausen M.]
Marmor, Sarah R. '65 '93 C.674 B.A. L.597 J.D. [Jenner&B.]
Marotta, Gina T. '76 '02 C.999 B.A. L.146 J.D. 53 West Jackson Boulevard, Suite 1460
Marovich, George M. '31 '55 C&L.339 B.S., J.D. Sr. U.S. Dist. J.
Marovitz, Abraham Lincoln '05 '27 L.146 LL.B. U.S. Sr. Dist. J.‡
Marovitz, Andrew S., (AV) '64 '89 C.31 B.A. L.976 J.D. [Mayer,B.R.&M.]
Marquard, Henry J., (AV) '21 '49 L.209 J.D. 122 S. Michigan Ave., Ste. 1720‡
Marquette, I. Edward, (AVⓉ) '50 '76 C.502 B.A. L.309 J.D.
(adm. in MO; not adm. in IL) [Sonnenschein N.&R.] (⊙Kansas City, MO)
Marr, Bruce B., (AV) '— '81 C.893 B.A. L.209 J.D. [McKenna S.]
Marr, David J. '58 '87 C.339 B.S. L.146 J.D. [Trexler,B.G.B.&M.] (See Pat. Sect.)
Marre, Daniel G.M. '67 '92 C.145 A.B. L.597 J.D. [Perkins C.]
Marren, Daniel F., (AV) '61 '88 C.436 B.A. L.424 J.D. [Ⓐ Chuhak&T.]
Marren, John P., (AV) '— '83 C.999 B.A. L.424 J.D. [Hogan M.]
Marrinson, Thomas A. '64 '89 C.178 A.B. L.1068 J.D. [Morgan,L.&B.]
Marroquin, Terri Lynn '67 '95 C.1273 B.A. L.846 J.D. Off. of the State Appl. Def.
Marrs, Judith L. '59 '90 C.597 B.S. L.910 J.D. Application Consultant, Lexis Nexis
Marrs, Michael A. '66 '94 C.1119 B.S. L.209 J.D. 20 N. Wacker Drive, Suite 1660
Marrs, Nathaniel M. '— '96 C&L.477 A.B., J.D. [Kirkland&E.]
Marsalek, Diann K., (AV) '61 '90 C.209 B.A. L.589 J.D. Asst. Atty. Gen.
Marsalli, Daniel V. '61 '87 C.734 B.A. L.339 J.D. [Ⓒ Reardon G.&R.]
Marschel, Karl L. '78 '03 C.502 B.A. L.910 J.D. [Ⓐ Bell,B.&L.]
Marsh, Aberdeen W. '70 '94 C.477 A.B. L.339 J.D. 3440 N. Lake Shore Dr., Ste. 6A
Marsh, Daniel A., Jr., (AV) '41 '71 C.424 B.B.A. L.365 J.D. 135 S. LaSalle St.
Marsh, Evelyn L. '43 '98 C.145 B.A. L.209 J.D. 5433 S.E. View Park
Marsh, Georganne E. '46 '81 C.339 B.A. L.146 J.D. 2821 W. Estes
Marsh, Kevin B. '70 '94 C.309 A.B. L.276 J.D. [Plotkin,J.&O.]
Marsh, Kimberley, (AV) '57 '86 C.914 B.A. L.146 J.D. [Hughes S.P.R.&D.]
Marsh, Michael V. '66 '92 C.97 B.S.B.A. L.161 J.D. [Ⓐ Sarles&O.]
Marsh, Weston W., (AV) '— '76 C.976 B.A. L.339 J.D. [Freeborn&P.]
Marshall, Abike '46 '85 C.112 B.A. L.1065 J.D. 105 W. Madison St.‡
Marshall, Christine S. '47 '81 C.352 B.A. L.221 J.D. 33 West Delaware
Marshall, Daryll V. '— '99 C.831 B.B.A. L.94 J.D. [Kirkland&E.]
Marshall, Elmer Paul "Al" '51 '85 C.209 B.A. L.365 J.D. 7026 W. North Ave., Ste. 207
Marshall, Eric C. '58 '84 C.976 B.A. L.477 J.D. [Ⓒ Sonnenschein N.&R.]
Marshall, James H. '— '97 C&L.597 B.A., J.D. [Daspin&A.]
Marshall, John D., (AV) '40 '65 C.339 B.A. L.146 J.D. [Mayer,B.R.&M.]
Marshall, Joseph '12 '34 C.999 L.144 7141 N. Kedzie Ave.
Marshall, Juli Wilson, (AV) '— '84 C.475 B.A. L.477 J.D. [Latham&W.]
Marshall, Kenneth N., (AV) '48 '78 C.589 B.S.E. L.339 J.D. [Rusin M.&F.]
Marshall, Lawrence C. '59 '87 C.999 B.S. L.597 J.D. Prof. of Law, Northwestern Univ.
Marshall, Marilyn O. '54 '80 C.1080 L.803
(adm. in LA; not adm. in IL) Chapter 13 Trustee Off.
Marshall, Newton C., II '64 '92 C.207 B.A. L.930 J.D. [Hinshaw&C.]
Marshall, Prentice H., Jr., (AV) '52 '77 C.339 B.A. L.352 J.D. [Sidley A.B.&W.]
Marshall, Robert S. '63 '94 C.207 B.A. L.150 J.D. [Bates&C.]
Marshall, Tamika D. '77 '03 C.1128 B.A. L.1187 J.D. [Ⓐ Gunty&M.]
Marshall, Thomas A., Jr. '45 '75 C.273 B.A. L.280 J.D. Spec. Asst. Atty. Gen.
Marshall, Zofia Kessler '49 '83 C.477 B.A. L.424 J.D. Dept. of Pub. Guardian

Marshall, Gerstein & Borun LLP, (AV) BB
Sears Tower 6300, 233 South Wacker Drive, 60606-6357
Telephone: 312-474-6300 Fax: 312-474-0448
Email: info@marshallip.com URL: http://www.marshallip.com
Partners: Richard H. Anderson; Scott E. Baxendale; Michael F. Borun; Paul C. Craane; Jeffrey H. Dean; Thomas L. Duston; Patrick D. Ertel; Kevin M. Flowers; David A. Gass; Robert M. Gerstein; Michael R. Graham; Roger A. Heppermann; Martin J. Hirsch; Richard B. Hoffman; Kevin D. Hogg; William J. Kramer; Jeremy R. Kriegel; Richard M. LaBarge; Bryan J. Lempia; Bradford P. Lyerla; Gregory C. Mayer; William K. Merkel; Carl E. Moore, Jr.; Michael Muczynski; James J. Napoli; Sandip H. Patel; David C. Read; Li-Hsein (Lily) Rin-Laures, M.D.; Thomas I. Ross; Jeffrey S. Sharp; Anthony G. Sitko; Paul B. Stephens; Thomas K. Stine; Michael R. Weiner; Joseph A. Williams, Jr.; James P. Zeller. Of Counsel: Allen H. Gerstein. Special Counsel: Meggan F. Duffy; John B. Lungmus. Associates: Matthias Abrell; Jill Anderfuren; George Christopher Braidwood; Gregory J. Chinlund; Pamela L. Cox; Rashmi V. Gupta; Julianne Hartzell; Anthony S. Hind; Mark H. Izraelewicz; Adam G. Kelly; Andrew M. Lawrence; Nabeela R. McMillian; Matthew C. Nielsen; Oliver T. Ong; Chirag B. Patel; Cullen N. Pendleton; Aaron M. Peters; Russell C. Petersen; Andrew D. Raymond; Randall G. Rueth; Alisa C. Simmons; Sharon M. Sintich; Gregory E. Stanton.
Patent, Trademark, Copyright Litigation and Prosecution; Intellectual Property, Antitrust Law and Related Litigation.
See Professional Biographies, CHICAGO, ILLINOIS

Marsico, Frank J. '69 '95 C.436 B.A. L.209 J.D. [Ⓐ Hinshaw&C.]
Marsico, Nick '66 '91 C&L.209 B.S., J.D. [Dykema G.P.]
Marszal, Lisa A. '68 '93 C.608 B.S./B.A. L.150 J.D. Pres., Legal Edge, Inc.
Marszalek, James J., (AV) '47 '76 C.339 B.S. L.365 J.D. 29 S. Lasalle St., Ste. 830

Marszalek, John E., (AV) '51 '76 C.699 B.A. L.365 J.D.
29 South La Salle Street, Suite 830, 60603
Telephone: 312-263-4570 Fax: 312-263-5939
Email: jmarszalek@aol.com URL: http://www.johnmarszaleklaw.com
Plaintiff Personal Injury including Automobile Accidents, Trucking Accidents, Motorcycle Accidents, Catastrophic Accidents, Wrongful Death, Medical Malpractice, Workers Compensation, Workplace Injuries.
See Professional Biographies, CHICAGO, ILLINOIS

Marszewski, Thomas C. '66 '92 C.589 B.A. L.146 J.D. [J.D.Montgomery&Assoc.]
Marta, Martin P., (AV) '42 '72 C.1016 B.S. L.228 J.D. [Seyfarth S.]
Marta, Peter M. '75 '04 C.945 B.B.A. L.1565 J.D.
(adm. in NY; not adm. in IL) [Ⓐ McDermott W.&E.]
Martay, David W. '71 '97 C.210 B.A. L.365 J.D. 134 N. LaSalle, 13th Fl.
Martell, Matthew T., Law Offices of '72 '99
C.145 B.A. L.959 J.D. 53 W. Jackson, Suite 1556 (⊙Summit)
Marten, John S. '77 '04 C&L.424 B.A., J.D. [Ⓐ Vedder,P.K.&K.]
Martens, Richard A. '45 '73 C.207 B.A. L.477 J.D. 20 N. Wacker Dr., Ste. 1660
Marti, Vanessa C. '— '04 C.1365 B.A. L.276 J.D. [Ⓐ Sachnoff&W.]
Martier, Robert L., (AV) '49 '77 C.597 B.A. L.146 J.D. 100 W. Monroe St., Ste. 2200
Martignon, James G. '68 '02 C.276 B.S.F.S. L.910 J.D. [Ⓐ Levenfeld P.]
Martin, Alan J. '59 '85 C.339 B.A. L.893 J.D. [Mayer,B.R.&M.]
Martin, Alice O., (AV) '— '90 C.1150 B.S. L.424 J.D. [Barnes&T.] (See Pat. Sect.)
Martin, Arlene E. '47 '85 C.597 Ph.B. L.365 J.D. Asst. Corp. Coun.
Martin, Arthur Mead, (AV) '42 '66 C.674 A.B. L.309 LL.B. [Jenner&B.]
Martin, Brian E., (AV) '56 '82 C.184 B.A. L.209 J.D. [Bell,B.&L.]
Martin, Charles Blake '48 '79
C.293 A.B. L.597 J.D. Gen. Atty., R. R. Donnelley & Sons Co.
Martin, Charles T., (AV) '15 '41 C.894 A.B. L.597 J.D. [Ⓒ Bell,B.&L.]

Martin, Craig C., (AV) '63 '88 C.602 B.A. L.309 J.D. [Jenner&B.]
Martin, D. Eric '71 '01 C&L.424 B.B.A., J.D. [Ⓐ Nisen&E.]
Martin, Daniel G. '— '85 C.209 B.A. L.146 J.D. Staff Atty., Fed Def. Program
Martin, David A., (AV) '51 '76 C.674 A.B. L.1119 J.D. [Righeimer M.&C.]
Martin, David S., (AV) '53 '82 C.373 B.A. L.365 J.D. [Neal,G.&E.]
Martin, Donald '37 '61 C&L.145 B.A., J.D. [Martin&K.]
Martin, Elisabeth M. '— '02 C.309 A.B. L.178 J.D. [Ⓐ Kirkland&E.]
Martin, Ellen S. '56 '89 C.145 B.A. L.146 J.D. [Ⓒ Schopf&W.]
Martin, Eric P. '76 '01 C.966 B.S. L.602 J.D. [Ⓐ Bell,B.&L.] (Pat.)
Martin, Erin F. '— '01 C.602 B.A. L.597 J.D. [Ⓐ Bryan C.]
Martin, Frank R., (AV) '46 '72 C.72 B.A. L.309 J.D. [Righeimer M.&C.]
Martin, Gerard C. '71 '98 C.976 B.A. L.145 J.D. [Ⓐ Skadden,A.S.M.&F.]
Martin, Jeffrey E., (AV) '56 '82 C.1106 B.A. L.424 J.D. [Ⓐ Levin&P.]
Martin, Jil L. '— '01 C.966 B.B.A. L.424 J.D. [Ⓐ Chapman&C.]
Martin, Joanne '49 '81 C.610 B.A. L.424 J.D. Asst. Dir., Amer. Bar Foundation
Martin, John C. '— '94 C.976 B.A. L.145 J.D. [Schiff H.]
Martin, John J. '— '00 C.201 B.S. L.209 J.D. [Ⓐ Chapman&C.]
Martin, Joseph M. '66 '91 C.234 B.A. L.339 J.D. [Ⓒ Goldberg,K.B.B.R.&M.]
Martin, Julie A. '70 '96 C.477 A.B. L.309 J.D.
Assoc. V.P. & Corp. Coun., NovaMed Eyecare
Martin, Kelly Lynn '73 '98 C.30 B.A. L.128 J.D. Asst. State Atty.
Martin, Kevin T., (AV) '40 '67 C.424 B.S. L.146 J.D. [Swanson,M.&B.]
Martin, Larry W., (AV) '51 '80 C.231 B.A. L.597 J.D.
V.P. & Asst. Gen. Coun., John Nuveen & Co., Inc.
Martin, Laura Keidan, (AV) '64 '89 C.477 B.A. L.309 J.D. [Katten M.R.]
Martin, Lisa A. '70 '97 C.188 B.S. L.477 J.D. Assoc. Coun., MCI, Inc.
Martin, Marc W., (AV) '61 '87 C&L.424 B.S., J.D. 53 W. Jackson Blvd., Ste. 1420
Martin, Marilyn J. '45 '77 C.112 B.A. L.426 J.D. [Ⓐ Ambrose&C.]
Martin, Matthew E. '— '03 C.679 B.S. L.1000 J.D. [Ⓐ Foley&L.] (Pat.)
Martin, Michael J. '60 '85 C.602 B.A. L.424 J.D. [Burke,W.M.&S.]
Martin, Michael J. '58 '85 C&L.209 B.S., J.D. [M.J.Martin&Assoc.]

Martin, Patrick W. '57 '83 C.25 B.A. L.146 J.D.
203 North LaSalle Street, Suite 2100, 60601
Telephone: 312-332-3343 Fax: 312-346-9603
Workers Compensation, Third Party Liability, Insurance Defense.
See Professional Biographies, CHICAGO, ILLINOIS

Martin, R. Eden, (AV) '40 '67 C.339 B.A. L.309 LL.B. [Sidley A.B.&W.]
Martin, Renee M. '55 '82 C&L.966 B.A., J.D. 200 N. LaSalle St.
Martin, Robyn '74 '00 C.597 B.S. L.477 J.D. [Ⓐ Winston&S.]
Martin, Royal B., (AV) '45 '70 C.767 B.A. L.911 J.D. [Martin,B.&S.]
Martin, S. Marshall '67 '97
C.1222 B.B.A. L.339 J.D. Reg. Consultant, KPMG Peat Marwick, LLP
Martin, Siva '25 '53 C.597 M.A. L.209 J.D. 5860 W. Higgins‡
Martin, Steven G. '64 '91 C.477 B.B.A. L.597 J.D. 525 W. Monroe St.
Martin, Steven John, (BV) '66 '92 C.477 B.A. L.339 J.D. [Price T.R.]
Martin, William F., (BV) '58 '83 C.436 B.A. L.424 J.D. [Hilfman,M.&B.]

Martin, Brown & Sullivan, Ltd., (AV)
321 South Plymouth Court 10th Floor, 60604
Telephone: 312-360-5000 Fax: 312-360-5026
Email: FIRM@MBSLAW.COM URL: http://WWW.MBSLAW.COM
Royal B. Martin; Steven S. Brown; William G. Sullivan; Leigh D. Roadman; Daniel T. Hartnett; Robert S. Grabemann;—Victor S. Kostro; Mason N. Floyd. Of Counsel: Denis J. Conlon.
Federal and State Trial and Appellate Practice, both Criminal and Civil. Federal and State Taxation.
See Professional Biographies, CHICAGO, ILLINOIS

Martin, Craig, Chester & Sonnenschein
(See Oak Brook)

Martin & Karcazes, Ltd., (AV) 161 N. Clark, Ste. 550
Martin, Michael J., & Associates, PC 401 South LaSalle Street
Martinez, Bonnie A. '49 '77 C.1191 B.S. L.209 J.D. 6230 N. Leona Ave.
Martinez, Christine H. '— '03 C&L.424 B.A., J.D. [Ⓐ Barnes,R.&C.]
Martinez, Guillermo F., (CV) '45 '83 C.120 B.A. L.365 J.D. [G.F.Martinez&Assoc.]
Martinez, Marcie M. '68 '97 C&L.424 B.S., J.D.
Sr. Coun., Bank One Corp. (Law Dept.)
Martínez, Mariano Elí '— '99 C.93 B.S. L.145 J.D. [Kirkland&E.]
Martínez, Michael E. '72 '97 C.679 B.A. L.966 J.D. [Bell,B.&L.]
Martinez, Guillermo F., & Assocs., A Prof. Corp., (CV) 2651 N. Milwaukee Ave.
Martini, Christina L. '— '94 C.339 B.S. L.597 J.D. [DLPiper R.G.C.U.]
Martire, Mary Kay McCalla, (AV) '— '85 C.475 B.A. L.477 J.D. [Foley&L.]
Martwick, Cathleen R. '64 '91 C.1149 B.S. L.424 J.D. Asst. Reg. Coun., U.S. E.P.A.
Martwick, Robert F., (AV) '37 '62 C.424 L.209 LL.B. [Firm of Finkel,M.&C.]
Marutzky, Eileen M., (AV) '— '80 C.209 B.S.C. L.146 J.D. Asst. U.S. Atty.
Marvel, Janet A. '61 '89 C.347 B.A. L.477 J.D. [Pattishall,M.N.H.&G.]
Marvet, Jodi R. '62 '88 C&L.260 B.A., J.D. [Ⓐ Kerns,P.F.&P.]
Marvin, James L. '61 '86 C&L.339 B.A., J.D.
Asst. Gen. Coun. & Asst. Secy., FMC Technologies, Inc.
Marwedel, Warren J., (AV) '— '72 C.1027 B.S. L.424 J.D. [Marwedel,M.&R.]

Marwedel, Minichello & Reeb, P.C., (AV)
10 South Riverside Plaza, Suite 720, 60606
Telephone: 312-902-1600 Fax: 312-902-9900
URL: http://www.mmr-law.com
Shareholders: Warren J. Marwedel; Dennis Minichello; Robert L. Reeb. Limited Shareholders: Shari L. Friedman; William P. Ryan.
General Civil Trial and Appellate Practice including Complex Litigation, Administrative Hearings, Alternate Dispute Resolution, Transportation Law, Admiralty and Maritime Law, Commercial Law, Technology Law, Personal Injury, Professional Liability and Insurance.
See Professional Biographies, CHICAGO, ILLINOIS

Marwil, Jeff J., (AV) '61 '86 C.477 B.A. L.209 J.D. [Jenner&B.]
Marx, David, Jr., (AV) '50 '76 C.31 B.A. L.823 J.D. [McDermott W.&E.]
Marx, Jeffrey A. '78 '05 C.94 B.S. L.966 J.D. [Ⓐ Brinks H.G.&L.] (See Pat. Sect.)
Marx, Theresa M.H. '— '03 C.201 B.S. L.424 J.D. [Ⓐ Schiff H.]
Marzal, V. Andrew '50 '79 C.339 B.F.A. L.1151 J.D. [Baum,R.&M.]
Marzec, Megan S. '79 '04 C.339 B.A. L.146 J.D. [Ⓐ Matushek,N.&S.]
Marziani, Gini S., (AV) '55 '80 C.575 B.A. L.146 J.D. [Davis M.]
Marzo, Katherine F. '76 '04 C&L.597 B.A., J.D. [Ⓐ DLPiper R.G.C.U.]
Marzullo, Bradley W. '78 '04 C.910 B.A. L.477 J.D. [Ⓐ Barack F.K.P.&N.]
Marzullo, Sara F. '75 '00 C.112 B.A. L.424 J.D. [Ⓐ Cassiday,S.&G.]
Mas, Edward A., II '65 '92
C.597 B.S.M.E. L.659 J.D. [McAndrews,H.&M.] (See Pat. Sect.)
Masarachia, Sarah R. '72 '97 C.771 B.A. L.245 J.D. Lit. Coun.
Maschek, Linda J. '55 '80 C&L.339 B.A., J.D. Admin. J., Dept. of Pub. Health
Mascherin, Terri L., (AV) '59 '84 C.228 A.B. L.597 J.D. [Jenner&B.]
Masciopinto, Anthony J. '66 '91 C&L.209 B.S., J.D. [Ⓐ P.B.Episcope]
Masciopinto, Vito M. '63 '89 C.190 B.A. L.365 J.D. [Lowis&G.]
Masia, Adam H. '65 '90 C.1349 B.S. L.146 J.D. [Bell,B.&L.] (Pat.)

Masini, Jon B. '60 '89 C.602 B.A. L.424 J.D. [Fisher K.]
Maslanka, Michael J. '59 '84 C.720 B.A. L.801 J.D. 100 W. Monroe St., Ste. 804
Masliansky, Tzivia A. '76 '01
C.339 B.A. L.146 J.D. Two North LaSalle Street, Suite 2200
Maslowsky, Len '45 '79 C.339 B.A. L.589 J.D. 2317 N. Cambridge
Mason, David M. '59 '84 C.339 B.S. L.813 J.D. [Goldberg,K.B.B.R.&M.]
Mason, Edwin D. '— '80 C.339 B.S. L.477 J.D. [Foley&L.]
Mason, Galen R. '76 '02 C.747 B.A. L.502 J.D. [Jenner&B.]
Mason, Lawrence D., (AV) '64 '89 C&L.339 B.A., J.D. [Fisher K.]
Mason, Lloyd W., (AV) '22 '51 C.388 A.B. L.813 LL.B. 500 W. Madison St.‡
Mason, Mary Anne '52 '77 C.93 B.A. L.424 J.D. Cir.J.
Mason, Michael T. '42 '77 C.37 B.A. L.365 J.D. Mag.
Mason, Molly C., (AV) '56 '85 C.309 B.A. L.424 J.D. [Corti,F.&A.]
Mason, Peter I. '— '76 C.65 A.B. L.94 J.D. [Freeborn&P.]
Mason, Richard J., P.C., (AV) '51 '77 C.339 B.A. L.602 J.D. [McGuirewoods]
Mason, Steven C. '— '88 C.602 B.A. L.339 J.D. [Chapman&C.]
Masory, Rachel '— '03 C.597 B.S.J. L.309 J.D. [Kirkland&E.]
Masover, Jos. '12 '35 C.209 L.146 LL.B. 1313 Ritchie Ct.‡
Massa, Heidi, (AV) '57 '83 C&L.145 B.A., J.D. 55 West Monroe Street, Suite 3200
Massari, Jeffrey T. '57 '86 C.999 B.A. L.424 J.D.
Asst. Gen. Coun., Akzo America Inc.
Massel, Suzanne J. '65 '92 C.860 B.S. L.910 J.D. [Madsen,F.&P.]
Massengill, Brian J. '62 '95 C.347 B.S. L.145 J.D. [Mayer,B.R.&M.]
Massin, Kimberlee '68 '93 C.338 B.S. L.810 J.D. [DiVincenzo S.S.]
Mastandrea, Linda L. '64 '95 C.339 B.A. L.146 J.D. [L.Mastandrea]
Mastandrea, Linda, Law Offices of 1327G W. Greenleaf Ave.
Masterly, John G. '49 '75 C.705 B.A. L.365 J.D. 2301 S. Western Ave.
Masters, Anndra L. '77 '02 C.339 B.A. L.209 J.D. [Williams M.&J.]
Masters, Catherine M. '— '83 C&L.145 B.A., J.D. [Schiff H.]
Masters, Charles J., (AV) '49 '74 C.339 B.A. L.146 J.D. [C.J.Masters]
Masters, Douglas N. '63 '88 C.188 B.A. L.309 J.D. [Loeb&L.]
Masters, Erin E. '80 '04 C.112 B.A. L.424 J.D. [Nadler,P.&M.]
Masters, Charles J., Ltd., (AV) 340 W. Diversey Pkwy.
Masuda, Beverly N., (AV) '— '81 C.312 B.A. L.46 J.D. [Brady,C.&M.]

Masuda, Funai, Eifert & Mitchell, Ltd., (AV)
Suite 2500, 203 North LaSalle Street, 60601-1262 ⊙
Telephone: 312-245-7500 Fax: 312-245-7467
Email: lawfirm@masudafunai.com URL: http://www.masudafunai.com
Principals: Anthony J. Bruozas; James M. Coonan; Laura Tallroth Edmonds; Helmut Eifert (1929-1995); Jerrold E. Fink; Bryan Y. Funai; Masaru Funai; Kathleen M. Gaber; Keith Walter Groebe; Timothy J. Hammersmith; Colin Hara; Eldon H. Kakuda; Alan M. Kaplan; Steven L. Katz; Dayne Kono; Reinhold F. Krammer; Thomas Masuda (1905-1986); Thomas P. McMenamin; Gerald L. Morel; Joseph S. Parisi; Stephen M. Proctor; Gary D. Santella; Nancy E. Sasamoto; Mary W. Shellenberg; John B. Stanis; Edward J. Underhill; Robert S. White. Associates: Laurence P. Becker; David S. Hwang; Jennifer A. Joyce; George H. Kobayashi; Jason M. Metnick; Shinobu Nishida; Reynard L. Tanig; Gary Vist; Jennifer R.M.C. Watson; Shinya Yamamoto. Of Counsel: Jeremy A. Gibson; Jeffrey M. Hucek; James C. Shanley (P.C.).
International Business, Corporations, Corporate Financing and Reorganizations, Mergers and Acquisitions, Joint Ventures, Real Estate, Environmental Law, Banking, Finance and Lending, Antitrust and Trade Regulations, Unfair Competition, Commercial Transactions, Employment and Labor Relations, Immigration, Technology Licensing, Intellectual Property, Multistate and Local Taxation, Probate, Insurance Defense, Product and Professional Liability, Arbitration, Corporate and Commercial Litigation and Trials in all Courts, and General Civil Practice.
Schaumburg, Illinois Office: Suite 800, 1475 East Woodfield Road, 60173-5485. Telephone: 847-734-8811. Fax: 847-734-1089.
Torrance, California Office: Suite 420, 19191 South Vermont Avenue, 90502-1051. Telephone: 310-630-5900. Fax: 310-630-5909.
See Professional Biographies, CHICAGO, ILLINOIS

Matanky, James E. '60 '85 C&L.339 B.S., J.D. 1332 N. Halsted St.
Matasar, Richard A. '52 '77 C&L.659 B.A., J.D.
(adm. in PA; not adm. in IL) Dean & Prof., Chicago-Kent College of Law/IIT
Matchinski, Jayme R. '66 '92 C.591 B.S. L.879 J.D. [Harris K.&G.]
Mateiu, Ramona '— '03 C.339 B.S. L.1066 J.D. [Schiff H.]
Matejcak, Gary J. '60 '85 Sr. Staff Atty., American Family Insurance Group
Matejcak, Susan I. '— '86 C.589 B.A. L.424 J.D. [Jones D.]
Matek, Michael S. '57 '83 C.1036 B.A. L.146 J.D. [Matek]

Matek Law Offices, P.C.
77 West Washington Street Suite 1313, 60602-3236
Telephone: 312-372-5800 Fax: 312-372-1276 URL: http://www.mateklaw.com
Email: mmatek@mateklaw.com URL: http://www.michaelmateklawoffices.com
Michael S. Matek.
Subrogation, Collections, Commercial Litigation, Bankruptcy, Commercial Law.
See Professional Biographies, CHICAGO, ILLINOIS

Matela, Eva Alexandra '75 '01
C.1176 B.S. L.1000 J.D. 111 W. Washington Street, Suite 1150
Matern, Christopher W. '59 '88 C.46 B.S.Ch.E. L.209 J.D. 205 W. Wacker Drive
Mates, Christopher I. '56 '98 C.473 B.S.B.A. L.146 J.D. 440 S. LaSalle
Matevich, William J. '57 '83 C&L.472 B.B.A., J.D. 6453 S. Bell Ave.
Mathai, Tom V. '40 '80 C.347 B.A. L.589 J.D. [Mathai&T.]
Mathai & Thorson, P.C. 3601 N. Ashland Ave.
Mathelier, Val D. '75 '03 C.966 B.A. L.597 J.D. [DLPiper R.G.C.U.]
Matheny, Jennifer Beth '68 '99 C.1182 B.A. L.209 J.D. 180 N. LaSalle Street
Mathew, Michael J. '76 '03 C.424 B.A. L.209 J.D. [Corboy&D.]
Mathews, Andrew L. '— '03 C.477 B.A. L.597 J.D. [Sachnoff&W.]
Mathews, David J. '49 '74 C.645 B.A. L.884 J.D. 225 W. Washington St.
Mathews, Elizabeth Drahold '71 '01 C.36 B.S. L.1358 J.D.
Collateral Admr., ABN-AMRO North America, Inc. (Asset-Backed Sec. Tr. Serv. Dept.)
Mathews, Gregory S., Law Offices of, (AV) '55 '80
C.976 B.A. L.1119 J.D. 30 La Salle St., Ste. 3440
Mathews, Katherine A. '— '03 C.229 B.A. L.597 J.D. [Sachnoff&W.]
Mathews Graf, Catherine '70 '95 C.475 B.A. L.209 J.D. [Wildman,H.A.&D.]
Mathewson, J. Kent, (AV) '57 '82 C.197 A.B. L.145 J.D. [Donohue B.M.&S.]
Mathewson, Kathleen D. '— '85 C.209 B.S. L.424 J.D. [Schiff H.]
Mathias, John H., Jr., (AV) '47 '72 C.197 A.B. L.309 J.D. [Jenner&B.]
Mathias, Megan M. '77 '03 C.475 B.A. L.146 J.D. [Hardt&S.]
Mathie, Belinda I. '— '02 C.477 B.A. L.145 J.D. [Katten M.R.]
Mathura, Karen B. '— '00 C.276 B.S.N. L.64 J.D. [Anderson,R.]
Matis, Nina B., (P.C.), (AV) '47 '73 C.788 A.B. L.569 J.D. [Katten M.R.]
Matkov, George J., Jr., (AV) '42 '66 C.388 L.352 LL.B. [Matkov,S.M.&G.]

Matkov, Salzman, Madoff & Gunn, (AV)
Suite 2900, 55 East Monroe Street, 60603-5709
Telephone: 312-332-0777 Telecopier: 312-332-6130
URL: http://www.matkovsalzman.com
Members of Firm: George J. Matkov, Jr.; James John Salzman; Jeffrey L. Madoff; Larry G. Hall; Michael W. Duffee; Steven L. Brenneman; Christopher A. Johlie; Craig R. Thorstenson; Thomas M. Dugard; Melissa Crawford Mazzeo. Associates: Brian J. Kurtz; Angela Marie Hubbell (Not admitted in IL); Karin Anderson; Elizabeth A. Ward; Becky L. Kalas. Of Counsel: Allan Gunn; Jay G. Swardenski; Deborah Lee Smith; Teri Firmiss Thompson.

(This Listing Continued)

Matkov, Salzman, Madoff & Gunn (Continued)
Representing Management in Labor Relations, Employment Discrimination, Employee Benefits, Administrative Law and Civil and Administrative Litigation.
See Professional Biographies, CHICAGO, ILLINOIS

Matlack, Joan '56 '88 C.118 B.A. L.1178 J.D. [Futterman&H.]
Matlaw, Leslie V. '61 '92 C.209 B.A. L.46 J.D. [L.V.Matlaw]

Matlaw, Leslie V., P.C.
P.O. Box 4426, 60680-4426
Telephone: 312-804-3527 Fax: 312-896-9412
Email: send_2_leslie@hotmail.com
Leslie V. Matlaw.
Housing Discrimination, Fair Housing Law.
See Professional Biographies, CHICAGO, ILLINOIS

Matlin, Susanne Summer '49 '82
C.801 B.S. L.424 J.D. Field Atty., Fed. Labor Relations Auth.
Matousek, Joanne J., (AV) '62 '87 C.823 B.S. L.602 J.D. [Duane M.]
Matousek, Paul F. '62 '87 C.62 B.A. L.602 J.D. [Walker W.M.]
Matranga, Mark P., (BV) '47 '76 C.339 B.A. L.146 J.D. [Wiedner&M.]
Matsakis, Elias N., (AV) '51 '74 C.145 B.A. L.309 J.D. [Holland&K.]
Matsas, Constantine Dean '61 '86 C&L.424 B.B.A., J.D. 5069 N. Bway. Ave.
Matschke, Kristin Weaver '71 '01 C.385 B.A. L.146 J.D. The Northern Trust Co.
Matsis, Demetra K. '67 '92 C.94 B.A. L.436 J.D.
Asst. V.P. & Sr. Atty., Federal Home Loan Bk. of Chicago
Matsunaga Conrad, Kim '72 '98
C.424 B.B.A. L.209 J.D. Assoc. Gen. Coun., Levy Restaurants
Mattes, Barry A. '53 '81 C.696 B.A. L.146 J.D. 3320 N. Central Ave.
Matteson, David M. '— '77 C.605 B.A. L.424 J.D. [Gardner C.&D.]
Matteucci, Brooke H. '— '02 C.352 B.A. L.209 J.D. [LaBarge,C.&L.]
Matteucci, Michael A. '75 '03 C.210 B.A. L.424 J.D. [Chico&N.]
Matthews, Albert L. '50 '78 C.339 B.S. L.597 J.D. P.O. Box 277964 (Pat.)
Matthews, Dorothy Gibson '62 '87 C.339 B.A. L.329 J.D. Atty., Metra
Matthews, Richard J. '55 '84 C.966 B.A. L.1019 J.D.
(adm. in NY; not adm. in IL) 33 West Monroe Street, Suite 21
Mattingly, William E., (P.C.), (BV) '48 '75 C.679 B.S.I.E. L.345 J.D. [Katten M.R.]
Mattos Neto, Sebastiao de Souza '51 '80 C&L.146 J.D. [Baker&M.]
Mattson, Brian M., (BV) '64 '92 C.350 B.S.E.E. L.1209 J.D. [Patents&T.] (Pat.)
Mattson, Eric S. '65 '94 C.477 B.A. L.597 J.D. [Sidley A.B.&W.]
Mattson, Jeffrey M., (AV) '— '90 C.339 B.S. L.145 J.D. [Freeborn&P.]
Matusak, John J. '63 '90
C.927 B.S. L.209 J.D. Admin. Law J., State Dept. of Employ. Sec.
Matushek, Edward J., III, (AV) '54 '82 C.340 B.A. L.365 J.D. [Matushek,N.&S.]

Matushek, Nilles & Sinars, L.L.C., (AV) BR
One North LaSalle Street, Suite 2100, 60602
Telephone: 312-750-1215 Fax: 312-750-1273
Email: ejmatushek@matushek.com URL: http://www.matushek.com
Edward J. Matushek III; David A. Nilles; Douglas M. Sinars; Gary W. Klages. Associates: Kristen M. Streepey; Melissa M. Fallah; Megan S. Marzec; Jenny M. Norenberg.
Complex Litigation including Asbestos, Toxic Torts, Benzene, Mold, Construction Law, Transportation Law, Aviation, Insurance Coverage, Products Liability Defense and Professional Malpractice, Civil Trials and Appeals.
See Professional Biographies, CHICAGO, ILLINOIS

Matusinec, Colette A. '74 '02 C.959 B.A. L.146 J.D. 53 W. Jackson Blvd., Ste. 950
Matuszewich, Lewis F., (AV) '41 '66 C.210 B.A. L.597 J.D. [Matuszewich,K.&M.] ⊙
Matuszewich, Kelly & Mckeever, LLP, (AV)
2121 N. Fremont, Suite 400 (⊙Crystal Lake)
Matyas, Harlene G., (BV) '49 '73 C.339 B.S. L.564 J.D. [Tribler O.&M.]
Matyas, Jordan D. '78 '04 C.273 B.A. L.365 J.D. City of Chicago
Matyas, Lisa J. '— '99 C&L.597 B.S., J.D. [Schiff H.]
Matyas, Thomas I., (AV) '47 '73 C.1016 B.A. L.564 J.D. [Wildman,H.A.&D.]
Matz, Joseph L., (AV) '29 '54 C&L.339 B.A., J.D. [Kamensky,R.H.&D.] ⊙
Mauck, Fred A., (AV) '37 '63
C.855 B.A. L.145 J.D. Chmn. of the Bd. & CEO, FNP Corp.
Mauck, John W. '47 '72 C.976 B.A. L.145 J.D. [Mauck&B.]
Mauck & Baker, Attorneys at Law, (AV) 1 North La Salle Street
Maupin, Shonda K. '— '01 C.1321 B.A. L.602 J.D.
(adm. in MO; not adm. in IL) [Bryan C.]
Maurer, Christopher J. '72 '97 C.339 B.S. L.424 J.D. [Anderson&Assoc.] ⊙
Maurer, Erik S. '— '01 C.339 B.S. L.597 J.D. [Banner&W.] (See Pat. Sect.)
Maurides, George D., (AV) '50 '79 C.339 B.S. L.209 J.D. [Maurides&F.]
Maurides & Foley, L.L.C., (AV) Two North LaSalle Street Suite 1900
Maus, Erin McCloskey '74 '99 C.188 B.S. L.424 J.D. [Baker&M.]
Mauser, Robert E., (AV) '53 '79
C&L.665 B.A., J.D. V.P. & Sen. Coun., Harris Tr. & Svgs. Bk.
Mautner, Bryce A. '— '05 C.477 B.S.E. L.339 J.D. [Kirkland&E.]
Mavrothalasitis, Spiridoula '— '03 C.597 B.A. L.477 J.D. [DLPiper R.G.C.U.]
Maxcy, Patrick C. '70 '99 C&L.431 B.A., J.D.
(adm. in ME; not adm. in IL) [Sonnenschein N.&R.]
Maxson, Finley P. ... '— '97 C.385 B.A. L.910 J.D. Assoc. Coun., Natl. Assn. of Realtors
Maxson, M. Finley, (AV) '34 '62 C.228 A.B. L.309 LL.B. [Winston&S.]
Maxwell, Dawn M., (BV) '58 '88 C.338 B.S. L.365 J.D. 39 S. LaSalle, Ste. 610
May, Brian T. '74 '98 C.549 B.S. L.477 J.D. [Mayer,B.R.&M.] (Pat.)
May, Chas. M. '27 '58 C.254 A.B. L.209 LL.B. 641 W. Lake St.
May, Christopher J., (BV) '70 '95 C.339 B.S. L.146 J.D. [Hall,P.&S.]
May, Jane Wells, (AV) '58 '86 C.967 B.A. L.880 J.D. [McDermott W.&E.]
May, Joel T. '— '00 C.879 B.A. L.74 J.D. [Jones D.]
May, Kevin C. '— '96 C.352 B.A. L.659 J.D. [Latham&W.]
May, Ronald D. '58 '86 C.347 B.S. L.880 J.D. U.S. Atty's. Off.
May, Theodore J., (AV) '61 '87 C&L.494 B.A., J.D. [Michaels&M.]
Mayer, Charles H. '65 '91 C&L.802 B.B.A., J.D.
(adm. in TX; not adm. in IL) 233 S. Wacker Drive
Mayer, Deborah H., (AV) '48 '81 C.118 B.A. L.424 J.D. Spec. Asst. Atty. Gen.
Mayer, Elizabeth A. '73 '97 C.340 B.A. L.477 J.D. [Novack&M.]
Mayer, Erwin '63 '87 C.339 B.S. L.424 J.D. [Jenkens&G.]
Mayer, Frank D., Jr., (AV) '33 '59 C.31 B.A. L.339 J.D. [Mayer,B.R.&M.] ‡
Mayer, Gregory C. '— '93
C.339 B.S.A.A.E. L.145 J.D. [Marshall,G.&B.] (See Pat. Sect.)
Mayer, Irving B. '07 '30 C&L.339 LL.B. 77 W. Washington St. K
Mayer, James T., (AV) '58 '84 C.1365 B.A. L.245 J.D. [Holland&K.]
Mayer, Jeffrey J., (AV) '— '86 C.228 B.A. L.910 J.D. [Freeborn&P.]
Mayer, Mark R. '54 '83 C.424 B.A. L.146 J.D. [Hunt]
Mayer, Michael P. '75 '00 C.932 B.S. L.966 J.D. [Winston&S.]
Mayer, Phillip H., (AV) '28 '55 C.350 B.S.M.E. L.30 J.D. 180 N. Stetson Ave. (Pat.)
Mayer, Ronald A. '39 '67 C.1016 B.S.B.A. L.365 J.D. 19 S. LaSalle St.

Mayer, Brown, Rowe & Maw LLP, (AV) BR

71 S. Wacker, 60606-4637 ⊙

Telephone: 312-782-0600 Facsimile: 312-701-7711 Telex: 190404 Cable: LEMAY

URL: http://www.mayerbrownrowe.com

Retired Partner: Frank D. Mayer, Jr. Partners: David F. Abbott (New York, N.Y. Office); Karen Heather Holland Abbott (London, England Office); Lee N. Abrams; Fiona Adams (London, England Office); Rodney E. Alexander (Charlotte, North Carolina Office); Robert Allan (London, England Office); David Martin Allen (London, England Office); J. Trent Anderson; Bradley J. Andreozzi; Brian Aronson (Los Angeles, California Office); Jean-Marie L. Atamian (New York, N.Y. Office); Laura E. Bader; Mary Bagnall (London, England Office); Robert C. Baptista, Jr.; Robert N. Barnard (New York, N.Y. Office); Jonathan A. Barrett (Charlotte, North Carolina Office); James R. Barry; Mary R. Barry; Gregory L. Barton; Stephanie Bates (London, England Office); Scott Baugh (Los Angeles, California Office); Brandon D. Baum (Palo Alto, California Office); Teresa A. Beaudet (Los Angeles, California Office); Kenneth D. Bell (Charlotte, North Carolina Office); Richard Ben-Veniste (Washington, D.C. Office); John C. Berghoff, Jr.; Joel D. Bertocchi; Edward S. Best; Bruce M. Bettigole (Washington, D.C. Office); Michael E. Bieniek; Dr. Ulrike Binder (Frankfurt/Main, Germany Office); Christian F. Binnig; Gillian Mary Birkby (London, England Office); Timothy S. Bishop; James Arthur Black (London, England Office); Michael T. Blair; Francis J. Blanchfield, Jr. (Charlotte, North Carolina Office); Robert E. Bloch (Washington, D.C. Office); David I. Bloom (Washington, D.C. Office); Bruce C. Bloomingdale (London, England Office); David C. Bolstad (Los Angeles, California Office); Fern C. Bomchill; Thomas W. Bottomlee; Stephen John Bottomley (London, England Office); David N. Bowen (Board Certified Tax Lawyer, Florida Bar Board of Legal Specialization) (Washington, D.C. Office); Gary Bownes (London, England Office); Francis R. Bradley, III (Houston, Texas Office); Christopher J. Brady (Charlotte, North Carolina Office); Addison D. Braendel; Philip O. Brandes (New York, N.Y. Office); Richard S. Brennan; Robert I. Bressman (New York, N.Y. Office); Susan Brice; Andrew Briggs (London, England Office); Ronald S. Brody (New York, N.Y. Office); Hayden D. Brown (Charlotte, North Carolina Office); Michael Brown (London, England Office); Rachel Brown (London, England Office); Stephen Barnett Brown (London, England Office); Ulrich Brückmann (Frankfurt/Main, Germany Office); Richard F. Bulger; Amy Marlyse Burgert (Houston, Texas Office); J. Keith Burt (Washington, D.C. Office); Michael R. Butowsky (New York, N.Y. Office); Sarah Byrt (Partner, Intellectual Property and Information Technology Group, London) (London, England Office); Timothy P. Callahan; Richard A. Campbell; William Candelaria (New York, N.Y. Office); Jeffrey P. Cantrell (Charlotte, North Carolina Office); James B. Carlson (New York, N.Y. Office); David A. Carpenter; Andrew James Carruthers (London, England Office); James A. Casey; David Chadwick (London, England Office); Tony Child (London, England Office); Jean S. Chin (New York, N.Y. Office); C. Cabell Chinnis, Jr. (Palo Alto, California Office); Ian Christie (London, England Office); David A. Ciancuillo; Katherine M. Clark; Jeremy Clay (London, England Office); Paul B. Clemenceau (Houston, Texas Office); Ian R. Coles (Partner in Charge, London, England Office); Joseph P. Collins; Gary S. Colton, Jr.,; John M. Conlon (New York, N.Y. Office); Vincent J. Connelly; Sean Michael Connolly (London, England Office); Pat S. Conti (Washington, D.C. Office); Gary Cooper (London, England Office); Andrew Copley (London, England Office); Robert B. Cordle (Charlotte, North Carolina Office); J. Tyson Covey; George W. Craven; Paul M. Crimmins; Robert E. Curley; David S. Curry; Peter V. Darrow (New York, N.Y. Office); Raniero D'Aversa, Jr. (New York, N.Y. Office); Sally Alexandra Davies (London, England Office); Robert P. Davis (Washington, D.C. Office); Scott J. Davis; Debora de Hoyos; Daniel J. Delaney; Kiran Simon Desai (London, England Office); Joseph DeSimone (New York, N.Y. Office); Julian C. D'Esposito, Jr.; Julie Mellinda Dickins (London, England Office); Peter J.G. Dickinson (London, England Office); Thomas W. Dimond; Douglas A. Doetsch; Robert M. Dow, Jr.; David F. Dowd (Washington, D.C. Office); Joseph E. Doyle; Ralph P. Dudziak; David K. Duffee (New York, N.Y. Office); Robert T. Duffy (Charlotte, North Carolina Office); Daniel Dumezich; Thomas C. Durham; Thomas M. Durkin; Louis P. Eatman (Los Angeles, California Office); Dr. Christofer Eggers (Frankfurt/Main, Germany Office); Russell R. Eggert; Rebecca S. Eisner; Timothy B. Ellwood (Houston, Texas Office); Allen Erenbaum (Los Angeles, California Office); Grant J. Esposito (New York, N.Y. Office); Richard Marshall Evans (London, England Office); Tyrone C. Fahner; Donald M. Falk (Palo Alto, California Office); Richard J. Favretto (Washington, D.C. Office); John A. Faylor (Frankfurt/Main, Germany Office); Michael R. Feagley; Ronald M. Feiman (New York, N.Y. Office); Ian N. Feinberg (Palo Alto, California Office); James R. Ferguson; Robert F. Finke; Sheila M. Finnegan; Christopher Fisher (London, England Office); Robert V. Fitzsimmons; Delilah B. Flaum; Ian Flowers (London, England Office); Mary C. Fontaine; Michael K. Forde; Anna Forge (London, England Office); J. Paul Forrester; Douglas B. Frank (Los Angeles, California Office); Ron D. Franklin (Charlotte, North Carolina Office); Andrew L. Frey; Michele-Anne Mary Freyne (London, England Office); Dennis G. Friedman; Gary D. Friedman (New York, N.Y. Office); Claudia W. Frost (Houston, Texas Office); Alfred-Carl Gaedertz (Frankfurt/Main, Germany Office); Dr. Johann-Christoph Gaedertz (Frankfurt/Main, Germany Office); Stephen David Gare (London, England Office); Barry Gassman (Not admitted in IL; New York, New York Office); Christof Gaudig (Cologne, Germany Office); John J. Gearen; Dr. Markus Geisler (Cologne, Germany Office); Kenneth S. Geller (Washington, D.C. Office); Bruce L. Gelman; Bettina Getz; Randall R. Gibeau (New York, N.Y. Office); Steven R. Gilford; Michael J. Gill; Julie A. Gillespie; Mark H. Gitenstein (Washington, D.C. Office); Ronald B. Given; Robert E. Glennon, Jr. (Washington, D.C. Office); David M. Goldman (New York, N.Y. Office); Robert D. Goldschein (Los Angeles, California Office); Joseph I. Goldstein (Washington, D.C. Office); Hector Gonzalez (New York, N.Y. Office); Marcia E. Goodman; Jeffrey I. Gordon (London, England Office); Robert E. Gordon; Maureen J. Gorman (Palo Alto, California Office); David M. Gossett (Washington, D.C. Office); Robert F. Gray, Jr. (Houston, Texas Office); Diane Green-Kelly; Richard Gregorian (London, England Office); Terri Truitt Griffiths (Houston, Texas Office); Ulf H. Grundmann (Frankfurt/Main, Germany Office); Salvatore Guerrera (New York, N.Y. Office); Paul R. Gupta (Not admitted in IL; New York, N.Y. Office); Frederic L. Hahn; C. Wells Hall III (Charlotte, North Carolina Office); Robert Hamill (London, England Office); Lawrence R. Hamilton; Samantha Hampshire (London, England Office); Cameron Street Hamrick (Washington, D.C., Office); Marshall E. Hanbury (Not admitted in IL); Kevin P. Hawken (London, England Office); Dr. Manfred Heemann (Frankfurt/Main, Germany Office); Werner J. Hein (Washington, D.C. Office); Robert A. Helman; Nicholas Henchie (London, England Office); Frank H. Henneburg (Washington, D.C. Office); Michael L. Hermsen; Dr. Rüdiger Herrmann (Frankfurt/Main, Germany Office); Robert M. Hertzberg (Los Angeles, California Office); Dr. Ralf Hesdahl (Frankfurt/Main, Germany Office); John T. Hildy; Andreas Hilfrich (Frankfurt/Main, Germany Office); Dr. Mark C. Hilgard (Frankfurt/Main, Germany Office); Carol A. Hitselberger; Ingrid Hobbs (London, England Office); Louise Hobbs (London, England Office); Debra B. Hoffman; Dr. Hans Hofmann (Frankfurt/Main, Germany Office); Fiona Holland (London, England Office); James D. Holzhauer; Thomas R. Hood (New York, N.Y. Office); Diana L. Hoover (Houston, Texas Office); Charles M. Horn (Washington, D.C. Office); Joanna K. Horsnail; Jonathan Hosie (London, England Office); Nigel L. Howard (New York, N.Y. Office); David M. Hudanish (New York, N.Y. Office); Carrie Kiger Huff; Robert F. Hugi; Charles P. Hurley (Washington, D.C. Office); Michael Hutchinson (London, England Office); Frederick D. Hyman (New York, N.Y. Office); Sharon A. Israel (Houston, Texas Office); David Ive (London, England Office); Rebecca L. Jackson (Washington, D.C. Office); Caryn L. Jacobs; Philippa Susan James (London, England Office); John A. Janicik; Robert M. Jenkins, III (Washington, D.C. Office); William Edward Jewitt (London, England Office); James J. Jochum (Washington, D.C. Office); Trefor Morgan John (London, England Office); Edward D. Johnson (Palo Alto, California Office); Anita Jones (London, England Office); Erika Z. Jones (Washington, D.C. Office); Paul A. Jorissen; James J. Junewicz; Dr. Hans-Georg Kamann (Frankfurt/Main, Germany Office); Ivan P. Kane; Michael ("Mickey") Kantor (Washington, D.C. Office); Alvin Charles Katz; J. Bradley Keck; Charles S. Kelley (Houston, Texas Office); Christopher J. Kelly (Washington, D.C. Office); Robert A. Kelman; Terry D. Kernell (Houston, Texas Office); Michael F. Kerr (Los Angeles, California Office); William H. Kiekhofer, III (Los Angeles, California Office); Roger J. Kiley, Jr.; Jin K. Kim (New York, N.Y. Office); Thomas S. Kiriakos; Thomas L. Kittle-Kamp; Dr. Ingo Kleutgens (Frankfurt/Main, Germany Office); Marc L. Klyman; Elizabeth M. Knoblock (Washington, D.C. Office); William H. Knull, III (Houston, Texas Office); Kenneth E. Kohler (Los Angeles, California Office); Anne Marie Konopack; David S. Krakoff (Washington, D.C. Office); Jason H. P. Kravitt (New York, N.Y. Office); Simeon M. Kriesberg (Washington, D.C. Office); Robert J. Kriss; Jonathan D. Kron; Herbert W. Krueger; William R. Kucera; Kathryn A. Kusske (Washington, D.C. Office); Michael E. Lackey, Jr. (Washington, D.C. Office); Douglas J. Landy (New York, N.Y. Office); Angela R. Lang; Dr. Jörg Michael Lang (Frankfurt/Main, Germany Office); Larry R. Langdon (Palo Alto, California Office); Reinhart Lange (Frankfurt/Main, Germany Office); Paul L. Langer; Christopher Peter Langford (London, England Office); Bennett W. Lasko; John F. Lawlor; Lorie Soares Lazarus (Los Angeles, California Office); Charles J.E. Leach (London, England Office); Andrew R. Legg (London, England Office); Wolfgang Leip (Frankfurt/Main, Germany Office); Mary B. Lemuth (Houston, Texas Office); Fredrick S. Levin (Los Angeles, California Office); William A. Levy; Peter S. Liaskos (New York, N.Y. Office); James T. Lidbury; Richard Duncan Linsell (London, England Office); Stuart M. Litwin; Theodore A. Livingston, Jr.; Alvin J. Lorman (Washington, D.C. Office); Warren R. Loui (Los Angeles, California Office); Wayne R. Luepker; Robin R. Lunn; George A. Luscombe, II; Daniel W. Luther; Keith Lyon (London, England Office); Barry N. Machlin; Marcia G. Madsen (Washington, D.C. Office); Paul Joseph Maher (London, England Office); Joseph A. Mahoney; Cary J. Malkin; A. John P. Mancini (New York, N.Y. Office); Mary K. Mandeville (Charlotte, North Carolina Office); Mark D. Manela (Houston, Texas Office); Kristin Pernoll Manzano (Charlotte, North Carolina

(This Listing Continued)

Mayer, Brown, Rowe & Maw LLP (Continued)

Office); Andrew S. Marovitz; Daniel R. Marschollek (Frankfurt/Main, Germany Office); John D. Marshall; Alan J. Martin; Brian J. Massengill; Geoffrey L. Master (Washington, D.C. Office); Daniel A. Masur (Washington, D.C. Office); Andrew Mattei (New York, N.Y. Office); Wayne C. Matus (New York, N.Y. Office); Terri A. Mazur (New York, N.Y. Office); Gregory R. McClintock (Los Angeles, California Office); Hugh R. McCombs; Howard M. McCue, III; Ian James McDonald (London, England Office); Kathleen A. McGill (Charlotte, North Carolina Office); Kathryn B. McGrath (Washington, D.C. Office); David Martin McIntosh, II (Washington, D.C. Office); Ian McKenna (London, England Office); T. Mark McLaughlin; Patrick J. McNerney; Jonathan C. Medow; David R. Melton; Robert L. Mendenhall (Charlotte, North Carolina Office); Demetrios G. Metropoulos; Paul Meyer; James R. Mogle (Washington, D.C. Office); Michael A. Molano (Palo Alto, California Office); Stephanie M. Monaco (Washington, D.C. Office); Jay Parry Monge (Charlotte, North Carolina Office); Jonathan Moody (London, England Office); Donna Evensen Morgan; Louis P. Moritz; Andrew J. Morris (Washington, D.C. Office); Neil Morrison (London, England Office); Richard J. Morvillo (Washington, D.C. Office); Beverley Moss (London, England Office); William S. Moss III (Houston, Texas Office); Dr. Klaus J. Müeller (Frankfurt/Main, Germany Office); Thomas M. Mueller (New York, N.Y. Office); John E. Muench; J. Thomas Mullen; D. Michael Murray; John Nadolenco (Los Angeles, California Office); Peter Nägele (Frankfurt/Main, Germany Office); Lucia Nale; David Narefsky; Miriam R. Nemetz (Washington, D.C. Office); Brian E. Newhouse (Los Angeles, California Office); Andrew A. Nicely (Washington, D.C. Office); Trevor Anthony Nicholls (London, England Office); C. Mark Nicolaides (London, England Office); Michael E. Niebruegge (Houston, Texas Office); Philip J. Niehoff; Kenneth E. Noble (New York, N.Y. Office); John W. Noell; Tim Nosworthy (London, England Office); Jonathan Edward Nugent (London, England Office); Keith F. Oberkfell (Charlotte, North Carolina Office); Lennine Occhino; Ger P. O'Donnell; Michele L. Odorizzi; Michael A. Olsen; Anna M. O'Meara; Joseph B. Organ; Dennis P. Orr (New York, N.Y. Office); Carolyn P. Osolinik (Washington, D.C. Office); Jonathan Michael Oulton (London, England Office); Michael Pabst (London, England Office); Richard Page (London, England Office); Danuta Bembenista Panich; Dean Constantine Pappas (Los Angeles, California Office); Stanley J. Parzen; James P. Patti; Mark G. Paulson (Washington, D.C. Office); George A. Pecoulas; Eileen Penner (Washington, D.C. Office); Bruce F. Perce; Stuart P. Pergament (Washington, D.C. Office); Scott P. Perlman (Washington, D.C. Office); Robert (Bob) Peters (London, England Office); Brad L. Peterson; Antony Douglas Phillips (London, England Office); Jeffrey S. Piell; Scott N. Pierpont (New York, N.Y. Office); Andrew J. Pincus (Washington, D.C. Office); Matthew A. Posthuma; Ashish S. Prasad; Mark Adam Prinsley (London, England Office); Kevin A. Rang; George A. Ranney, Jr.; Mitchell D. Raup (Washington, D.C. Office); Elizabeth A. Raymond; Philip R. Recht (Los Angeles, California Office); Phillip S. Reed; Christopher F. Regan; Michael Regan (London, England Office); N. Neville Reid; Peter W. Richards-Carpenter (London, England Office); Mary B. Richardson-Lowry; Laura D. Richman; Michael P. Richman (New York, N.Y. Office); Robert S. Rigg; Daniel L. Ring; Michael P. Rissman; Jeffrey F. Robertson (Washington, D.C. Office); Nicholas Robertson (London, England Office); Melville Rodrigues (London, England Office); Anna Rogers (London, England Office); Howard J. Roin; David L. Ronn (Houston, Texas Office); Matthew A. Rooney; Leonard X Rosenberg; Andrew S. Rosenman; Martin G. Rosenstein; Marc E. Rosenthal; Julian Wentworth Roskill (London, England Office); Philip R. Rotner; Paul Rowell (London, England Office); Paul J.N. Roy; Stuart M. Rozen; Lee H. Rubin (Palo Alto, California Office); Javier H. Rubinstein; Deborah Schavey Ruff; George Ruhlen; Donald W. Rupert; John Rushton (London, England Office); Mark W. Ryan (Washington, D.C. Office); John R. Sagan; Alan N. Salpeter; Drew Dana Salvest (London, England Office); Gail C. Saracco; Jeffrey W. Sarles; John M. Satalic; Edmund Mark Sautter (London, England Office); Andrew H. Schapiro (New York, N.Y. Office); Peter L. Scher (Washington, D.C. Office); William A. Schmalzl; John R. Schmidt; John P. Schmitz; Edward J. Schneidman; James C. Schroeder; David A. Schuette; Andrea J. Schwartzman (New York, N.Y. Office); Ami G. Scott; Zaldwaynaka L. Scott; Steven R. Selsberg (Houston, Texas Office); Devi Shah (London, England Office); Stephen M. Shapiro; Paul L. Sharer (Not admitted in IL); Cate Sharp (London, England Office); Andrew Sharples (London, England Office); Kevin L. Shaw (Houston, Texas Office); Richard W. Shepro; Timothy C. Sherck; Ronald M. Shoss (Houston, Texas Office); Jodi Ann Simala; Michael N. Sloyer (New York, N.Y. Office); Richard Smith (London, England Office); Neil M. Soltman (Los Angeles, California Office); Richard A. Spehr (New York, N.Y. Office); Dominic Paul Spenser Underhill (London, England Office); Marc F. Sperber; Gillian Sproul (London, England Office); Andrew Stanger (Not admitted in IL; London, England Office; not admitted in the U.S.); James S. Stanhaus; Adrian L. Steel, Jr. (Washington, D.C. Office); Peter Alan Steiner (London, England Office); Richard M. Steuer (New York, N.Y. Office); Andrew Kenneth Stewart (London, England Office); Scott M. Stewart; Marshall C. Stoddard, Jr. (Los Angeles, California Office); J. Robert Stoll; Jeffrey M. Strauss; Markus Strelow (Frankfurt/Main, Germany Office); Evan M. Tager (Washington, D.C. Office); James E. Tancula (Houston, Texas Office); John D. Taylor; Mark R. Taylor; Christoph M. Tegel (Frankfurt/Main, Germany Office); Joel S. Telpner (New York, N.Y. Office); Mark R. Ter Molen; Bernd Thalmann (Frankfurt/Main, Germany Office); John J. Tharp, Jr.; Paul W. Theiss; Frederick B. Thomas; Iain Victor Thomas (London, England Office); William C. Tompsett; John M. Touhy; Charles S. Triplett (Washington, D.C. Office); Brian Trust (New York, N.Y. Office); George J. Tzanetopoulos; Mark R. Uhrynuk (London, England Office); Angela M. Ulum; Robert W. Unikel; Jeffrey A. Usow; Lane W. Vanderslice; Barry Alan Van Dyke; Jon D. Van Gorp; Terry Otero Vilardo (Houston, Texas Office); John S. Vishneski III; Thomas M. Vitale (New York, N.Y. Office); Pierre Vogelenzang (Los Angeles, California Office); Hoang Quan Vu (Houston, Texas Office); Arthur C. Walker, Jr. (Washington, D.C. Office); Richard Mark Walker (London, England and Frankfurt/Main, Germany Offices); Michael A. Wallin (London, England Office); Kathleen Anne Walsh (New York, N.Y. Office); Stephen Joseph Walsh (London, England Office); James R. Walther (Los Angeles, California Office); Robert J. Ward (New York, N.Y. Office); Michael O. Warnecke; Steven L. Washington; Neil A. Wasserstrom (Houston, Texas Office); Don L. Weaver (Los Angeles, California Office); Seth J. Weinberger; Harry "Hap" Weitzel (Houston, Texas Office); Andrew George White (London, England Office); Nigel Julian White (London, England Office); Peter H. White (Washington, D.C. Office); Jeffrey R. Whyte (New York, N.Y. Office); Robert J. Wild; Edward H. Williams; Spencer Howard Kerven Williams (London, England Office); Joel V. Williamson; Richard S. Williamson; Keith J. Willner (Washington, D.C. Office); Gary A. Winters (Washington, D.C. Office); Douglas L. Wisner (New York, N.Y. Office); Mark S. Wojciechowski (New York, N.Y. Office); Steven Wolowitz (New York, N.Y. Office); Ian Charles Wood (London, England Office); Craig A. Woods; Stephen Woodward (London, England Office); Nigel A. Wright (London, England Office); Dr. Jörg Wulfken (Frankfurt/Main, Germany Office); Russell R. Young; Patricia Anne Yurchak; Herbert L. Zarov; Dr. Guido Zeppenfeld (Frankfurt/Main, Germany Office); Nazim Zilkha (New York, N.Y. Office). Senior Counsel: Thomas Young Allman (Not admitted in IL); Roger W. Barrett; Stuart Bernstein; Jerome F. Donohoe; David B. Finnegan (Washington, D.C. Office); James W. Gladden, Jr.; Leo Herzel; Thomas N. Jersild; Wayne S. Kaplan; M. Marvin Katz (Houston, Texas Office) (Board Certified, Commercial Real Estate Law, Texas Board of Legal Specialization); Kenneth Klein (Washington, D.C. Office); Philip Allen Lacovara (New York, N.Y. Office); Harvey Nixon; Patrick W. O'Brien. Special Counsel: Stanton A. Kessler; Charles A. Rothfeld (Washington, D.C. Office). Counsel: Frank E. Arado; Debra Rae Bernard; Carol J. Bilzi (Washington, D.C. Office); Alexander B. Blades (New York, N.Y. Office); Robert A. Bloom; Susan J. Booth (Los Angeles, California Office); Daniel T. Brown (Washington, D.C. Office); Susan T. Brown (Washington, D.C. Office); Dr. Günter Burghardt (Not admitted in IL; Brussels, Belgium Office); Paul Chandler; Timothy J. Choppin (Washington, D.C. Office); Victoria R. Collado; Leslie S. Cruz (Washington, D.C. Office); Richard C. Cummings, Jr.; Kevin G. Desharnais; Sharon L. De Vault; Ronald R. Dietrich; Boise A. Ding (Los Angeles, California Office); Lisa A. Dunsky; Linda H. Earle (Houston, Texas Office); Jack Edelbrock; Julian P. Gehman (Washington, D.C. Office); Patricia V. Gentry; Kara K. Gibney; Jeffrey A. Goldman; Karen F. R. Grotberg; Marian C. Haney; William J. Healey (Washington, D.C. Office); John R. Hewitt (New York, N.Y. Office); Daniel G. Hildebrand; Adam K. Hollander; Diane M. Huff; John Chafer Huff; Gary A. Isaac; Dean Alan Isaacs; Nicola Jackson; Christine Jagde (New York, N.Y. Office); Sultana Kaldis (Houston, Texas Office); Maritoni D. Kane; Beverley J. Klein; Lawrence M. Knowles; Andrew M. Kofsky (New York, N.Y. Office); Paul J. Kunkel; Laurence Dumure Lambert (Paris, France Office); Benjamin W. Lau (New York, N.Y. Office); Kim A. Leffert; Thomas A. Lidbury; Serge A. Lomako (Houston, Texas Office); Joan L. Long; William M. Mann (Washington, D.C. Office); Marjorie M. Margolies; Kevin C. McDonald; Virginia A. Melvin (New York, N.Y. Office); Clifford R. Michel (New York, N.Y. Office); Dr. Joachim J. Modlich (Cologne, Germany Office); Judith A. Mondello; Deborah Alfred Monson; Robert L. Morgan (Houston, Texas Office); Donald C. Morris; Adriaen M. Morse, Jr. (Washington, D.C. Office); Christopher P. Murphy (Los Angeles, California Office); Stanley C. Nardoni; Daniel B. Nelson (New York, N.Y. Office); Richard M. Newman; Lisa O'Keefe; Rosaria Vivo Owen; Dena Palermo (Not admitted in IL); Rex A. Palmer; James A. Parker; Roger W. Patrick (Washington, D.C. Office); Ross Pazzol; Kathleen H. Pender; George N. Polydoros, Jr. (Houston, Texas Office); Karen L. Prena; Susan R. Proffitt; Dennis M. Quinn; Charles F. Regan, Jr.; Lauri Blum Regan (New York, N.Y. Office); Craig E. Reimer; Linda L. Rhodes (Washington, D.C. Office); Cecilia A. Roth; Abigail L. Rudoff; Pamela J. Sackmann (New York, N.Y. Office); Patricia F. Sharkey; Mark T. Shipley (Los Angeles, California Office); Shira A. Silver (New York, N.Y. Office); Adam C. Sloane (Washington, D.C. Office); Richard A. Speer (Not admitted in IL); Richard A. Steinberg (Washington, D.C. Office); Catherine Ann Stevens (Washington, D.C. Office); Doreen A. Sullivan (New York, N.Y. Office); Michael T. Sullivan; Ilana Z. Sultan (Washington, D.C. Office); Wayne L. Tang; David M. Thimmig; Richard J. Timmel; Jeffrey G. Tougas (New York, N.Y. Office); Marguerite E. Trossevin

(This Listing Continued)

Mayer, Brown, Rowe & Maw LLP (Continued)

(Washington, D.C. Office); Timothy J. Tyler (Houston, Texas Office); Stephen Van Dolsen (New York, N.Y. Office); Robert C. Varnell (Washington, D.C. Office); John J. Voorhees, Jr.; Kenneth N. Weinstein (Washington, D.C. Office); Kimberly S. Winick (Los Angeles, California Office); Richard G. Ziegler. Senior Associate: Jason K. Schmitz. Associates: K. Robin Abraham; Priti Seksaria Agrawal (Resident, Washington D.C. Office); Andres E. Aguila (New York, N.Y. Office); Thais M. Alexander (Charlotte, North Carolina Office); Suzanne V. Alwan (Charlotte, North Carolina Office); Lisa M. An; Courtney L. Anderson; Mack D. Anderson (Los Angeles, California Office); Jeffrey B. Andrews (New York, N.Y. Office); Michelle J. Annunziata (New York, N.Y. Office); Monica A. Aquino (Washington, D.C. Office); Michael Robert Arbogast (Not admitted in IL); Richard M. Assmus; Grace K. Avedissian (New York, N.Y. Office); Gianluca G. Bacchiocchi; Andrew C. Baek (Resident, Washington D.C. Office); Joseph R. Baker (Washington, D.C. Office); Violeta I. Balan; Sonia Baldia (Washington, D.C. Office); Marcella J. Barganz (New York, N.Y. Office); Zachary K. Barnett; Rafic H. Barrage (New York, N.Y Office); Amanda T. Barry; Jason S. Bazar (New York, N.Y. Office); Emilie M. Beavers; Patricia H. Becker (Washington, D.C. Office); Nina Behring (Frankfurt/Main, Germany Office); Wendy Watkins Bera (Houston, Texas Office); William T. Bergin (Not admitted in IL; New York, N.Y. Office); Ellen Bergmann (Frankfurt/Main, Germany Office); Catherine A. Bernard; Christy-Anne V. Betler (Charlotte, North Carolina Office); Andrew J. Bettwy (New York, N.Y. Office); Thorsten Beyerlein (Not admitted in IL; Frankfurt/Main, Germany Office); Vivek G. Bhatt; Mark S. Biskamp (Houston, Texas Office); Barry R. Blankfield; Michael P. Bodosky (Washington, D.C. Office); John P. Boelter; Dr. Marius A. Boewe (Cologne, Germany Office); Debra L. Bogo-Ernst; Ryan W. Borho (New York, N.Y. Office); Todd E. Bowen (New York, N.Y. Office); Patrick Brady; Dr. Martin Braun (Frankfurt/Main, Germany Office); Jeannine Braune (Frankfurt/Main, Germany Office); Sarah Elizabeth Breslin (New York, N.Y. Office); Maria A. Bries; Patricia Ann Brito (Houston, Texas Office); Michael E. Brogan; Robert L. Bronston (Washington, D.C. Office); Mark D. Brookstein; Caroline E. Brown (Washington, D.C. Office); Gabriela Rivero Brown (Houston, Texas Office); Gerald F. Brown; Jay S. Brown (Washington, D.C. Office); Jessica E. Brown; Jeffrey M. Bruns; Henninger S. Bullock (New York, N.Y. Office); Matthew B. Burke; J. Brett Busby (Houston, Texas Office); Alison M. Butler; John T. Bycraft; Nicole R. Byrd; Christine D. Cagnina (Charlotte, North Carolina Office); Eileen M. Candia; Craig W. Canetti (Washington, D.C. Office); Lourdes M. Cano; Nathaniel Carden; Stephen A. Chan (Houston, Texas Office); Susan Charles; Leslie Chebli (New York, N.Y. Office); David K. Cheng (Palo Alto, California Office); Scott A. Chesin (New York, N.Y. Office); Lana Chiariello (Los Angeles, California Office); Rena S. Chng (Palo Alto, California Office); Elizabeth Choi (Los Angeles, California Office); Casarine H. Chong; Michael W. Christopherson (Los Angeles, California Office); Sujata Barai Chugh; Allison D. Citron (New York, N.Y. Office); Angela L. Clark (New York, N.Y. Office); Berwin Cohen (Palo Alto, California Office); Daniel A. Cook; Michael D. Coppin; Dennis S. Corgill (Palo Alto, California Office); Eric H. Cottrell (Charlotte, North Carolina Office); Susan E. Cowell; Therese Craparo (New York, N.Y. Office); Mariel Creo (New York, N.Y. Office); Evan A. Creutz (New York, N.Y. Office); Brian S. Cromwell (Charlotte, North Carolina Office); Theresa M. Cummings (Los Angeles, California Office); Sheri Drucker Davis; Sean P. Dailey; Rebecca C. Davenport; Edward A. Davis (New York, N.Y. Office); John P. Davis (New York, N.Y. Office); Margaret N. Davis (Houston, Texas Office); Shane D. Deaton (New York, N.Y. Office); Katherine Deibert; J. Gregory Deis; Lauren A. DeKoven (New York, N.Y. Office); Franco Destro (New York, N.Y. Office); Richard D. Deutsch (Houston, Texas Office); Kimberly E. Diamond (New York, N.Y. Office); Anthony J. Diana (New York, N.Y. Office); Gina M. Diomedi; Paul A. DiSangro (Palo Alto, California Office); Michelle V. Dohra; Dana S. Douglas; Paul M. Drucker; John R. Duff (New York, N.Y. Office); Brian J. Dunn; Jean-Jacques B. Dupré (Los Angeles, California Office); Ariel M. Dybner (New York, N.Y. Office); J. Benjamin Earthman (Charlotte, North Carolina Office); Dirk Ehle (Cologne, Germany Office); Jochen Eimer (Frankfurt/Main, Germany Office); Frank David Endebrock (Frankfurt/Main, Germany Office); Stefan W. Engelhardt (New York, N.Y. Office); Mauricio A. Espana (New York, N.Y. Office); Eric B. Evans (Palo Alto, California Office); Douglas M. Eveleigh; Christopher L. Exberger (Los Angeles, California Office); Christian W. Fabian; M. C. Georgina Fabian (Not admitted in IL); Claire A. L. Fallone (New York, N.Y. Office); Mariam A. Farah; Ryan P. Farley (New York, N.Y. Office); Gregory S. Feder (Washington, D.C. Office); Petra Fendt (Frankfurt/Main, Germany Office); Lisa J. Fine; Ryan J. Fitts; Jason B. Fliegel; Dirk-Peter Flor (Frankfurt/Main, Germany Office); Monica C. Flores (Houston, Texas Office); David B. Fournier; Gregory A. Frantz (Resident, New York Office); Shauna L. Fulbright; David W. Fuller; Paul A. Galante (Not admitted in IL); Michelle A. Gale; Wendy Dodson Gallegos; William Gardner (New York, N.Y. Office); Jeremy J. Gaston (Houston, Texas Office); Christopher Michael Gavin; Carolyn R. Georgiade (Charlotte, North Carolina Office); Thomas Geraghty; Hans J. Germann; Peter Gey (Frankfurt/Main, Germany Office); Michele Lew Gibbons (New York, N.Y. Office); Claire K. Gibson; James P. Gignac; Reginald R. Goeke (Washington, D.C. Office); Jason J. Goitia; Lauren Rosenblum Goldman (New York, N.Y. Office); Antonia Golianopoulos (New York, N.Y. Office); Erika Gosker; Michael Gottschalk (Frankfurt/Main, Germany Office); Jonathan M. Grandon; Barbara Grayson; Brian F. Gredder (New York, N.Y. Office); Simon G. Grieser (Frankfurt/Main, Germany Office); David A. Grossman; Mascha Julia Grundmann (Frankfurt/Main, Germany Office); Peter T. Gruszka; Loic Erick Guerin (Not admitted in United States); Britton B. Guerrina; Shirish Gupta (Palo Alto, California Office); Jennifer T. Ha (Charlotte, North Carolina Office); A. David Hakim (Not admitted in the United States) (New York, N.Y. Office); Jaimy Levine Hamburg; Judy Song Han (New York, N.Y. Office); Emily R. Hanks (Washington, D.C. Office); Joshua P. Hanna; Stacey J. Hanna (New York, N.Y. Office); Gayle C. Hanz (Houston, Texas Office); Kara E. Harchuck; Heather A. Harlan (Not admitted in IL); Charles E. Harris, II; Erick Steven Harris; Sarah L. Harris; Dara M. Hartman (New York, N.Y. Office); Fred W. Hartman (Charlotte, North Carolina Office); Stephanie G. Hartung (Frankfurt/Main, Germany Office); Jeanny Haw; W.C. Turner Herbert (Charlotte, North Carolina Office); Dr. Caroline Herkströter (Frankfurt/Main, Germany Office); Kristina K. Herrmann; Thomas J. Hershenson (Washington, D.C. Office); Michael-Bryant Hicks (Houston, Texas Office); Gesine K. Hild (Frankfurt/Main, Germany Office); Karen M. Hilke; Janile S. Hill; Natalie M. Hiott-Levine (New York, N.Y. Office); Kathryn J. Holahan; Michelle R. Holl (New York, N.Y. Office); Andrew D. Hollenbeck; Houdin Honarvar (New York, N.Y. Office); Rachel A. Hopf; Christopher B. Horn (New York, N.Y. Office); Daniel L. Horwood; Matthew C. Houchens; Shoufen Hu; William H. J. Hubbard; David G. Hume (New York, N.Y. Office); Doressia L. Hutton; Matthew D. Ingber (New York, N.Y. Office); Nancy S. Jacobson; William V. Jacobsen, Jr.; Aric S. Jacover; Neill P. Jakobe; Christopher J. Jandacek; John W. Jarrell, Jr. (Washington, D.C. Office); Jerome M.J.F. Jauffret (Los Angeles, California Office); Tiloma Jayasinghe (New York, N.Y. Office); Bradford Jealous, III (New York, N.Y. Office); David A. Jensen; Jay C. Johnson (Washington, D.C. Office); Leeta Jordan (New York, N.Y. Office); Sarah E. Josephson (Washington, D.C. Office); Jon M. Juenger; Mohit Kalra; Stephen J. Kane; Flore Kanmacher (Los Angeles, California Office); Jason Kanner (New York, N.Y. Office); Loan Anh Tran Kao (Houston, Texas Office); Patrick J. Kassen (Not admitted in IL); Jennifer Keating; Jennifer L. Keegan; Asieh Kehyari (Washington, D.C. Office); Hyun-Jung A. Kim (Not admitted in IL); Joo Hyang Kim; Suzy Kim (New York, N.Y. Office); Yale K. Kim (Los Angeles, California Office); Therese C. King; Dr. Gabriele Kirchhoff (Cologne, Germany Office); John C. Kloosterman (Palo Alto, California Office); Troy B. Klyber; Jack M. Knight, Jr. (Charlotte, North Carolina Office); Annette Knoth (Frankfurt/Main, Germany Office); Mollie S. Knox (New York, N.Y. Office); Matthew T. Koenders; Amy S. Korte; Dr. Dr. Adem Koyuncu (Cologne, Germany Office); Jan Kraayvanger (Frankfurt/Main, Germany Office); Andrew T. Kugler (Los Angeles, California Office); James M. Kunick (Frankfurt/Main, Germany Office); Germain D. Labat, III (Los Angeles, California Office); Richard A. Lafont (New York, N.Y. Office); Timothy C. Lambert (Washington, D.C. Office); Cristina Lane; Dr. Andreas Lange (Frankfurt/Main, Germany Office); Deann Kay Lanz (Houston, Texas Office); Saul R. Laureles (Houston, Texas Office); Nicholas A. Laveris (New York, N.Y. Office); Jennifer D. Lawrence (Charlotte, North Carolina Office); Grace Soyon Lee; Ian B. Leong (Los Angeles, California Office); Nickolai G. Levin (Washington, D.C. Office); Jeffrey H. Lewis (Washington, D.C. Office); Jonathan L. Lewis; Kai Liebrich (Frankfurt/Main, Germany Office); David A.K. Linley (Resident, New York Office); Denise Lopez; Simon Lopez (Houston, Texas Office); Agostino Lorenzini; Zachary A. Luber; Susanne Lührmann (Frankfurt/Main, Germany Office); David M. Lundeen; Todd E. Lundell (New York, N.Y. Office); Jamison Lynch; Sajida Mahdi Ali; John N. Maher; Mark J. Maier (Washington, D.C. Office); Eldad Z. Malamuth (Washington, D.C. Office); David N. Malinger; Jennifer C. Maloney (Washington, D.C. Office); William Malpica (New York, N.Y. Office); Gregory A. Manter (Not admitted in IL); Michael K. Marion (Washington, D.C. Office); Milos Markovic; Heather H. Martin (Washington, D.C. Office); Michael C. Mascia (Charlotte, North Carolina Office); Joshua M. Masur; John E. Mauk (Washington, D.C. Office); Brian T. May; Douglas E. McCormack (New York, N.Y. Office); Jill K. McDowell (Resident, Washington D.C. Office); Mark A. Mears (Los Angeles, California Office); Matthias J. Meckert (Frankfurt/Main, Germany Office); Steven J. Meiner (New York, N.Y. Office); Mirja Mertin, LLM, Maîtrise en Droit (Cologne, Germany Office); Tobias Messer (Frankfurt/Main, Germany Office); Tiffany L. Metz (Not admitted in IL); Laura Dawn Metzger (New York, N.Y. Office); Vazantha Meyers; Adam B. Miller (Resident, Washington D.C. Office); Britt M. Miller; Charles A. (Van) Miller (Washington, D.C. Office); Anshuman Mishra; Christopher A. Monsour; Isela Morales; Michael V. Morelli (New York, N.Y. Office); Lee Morlock; Carol A. Morrison (New York, N.Y. Office); Matthew Mozian (New York, N.Y. Office); Monique J. Mulcare (New York, N.Y. Office); Melissa Mulrooney (New York, N.Y. Office); Trent M. Murch; Christopher Charles Murray; Dr. Ariane Musil (Frankfurt/Main, Germany Office); Vera A. Nackovic; Anthony J. Napolitano (Los Angeles, California Office); Michael T. Neidigh; Peter T. Nelson (Houston, Texas Office); Jade Earl

(This Listing Continued)

Mayer, Brown, Rowe & Maw LLP (Continued)

Newburn; Cara L. Newman (New York, N.Y. Office); Mark A. Nicholson (Not admitted in IL); Nancy V. Nieto (Not admitted in IL); Lauren F. Noll; Angela D. O'Brien; Margaret A. O'Connor; Thomas O'Donnell (New York, N.Y. Office); Cristin Obsitnik; Francisco Ochoa (Los Angeles, California Office); Jason M. Osborn (Washington, D.C. Office); Archis A. Parasharami (Washington, D.C. Office); Diane Park (Los Angeles, California Offiice); James T. Parkinson (Washington, D.C. Office); Melissa Pastrana; Heike Paul (Frankfurt/Main, Germany Office); William Paxton (Washington, D.C. Office); Dennis F. Penepacker; Heiko Penndorf (Frankfurt/Main, Germany Office); Erin C. Perkins; Amy Ward Pershkow (Washington, D.C. Office); Emily S. Petrovic; Mark A. Petry (Washington, D.C. Office); Anthony R. Pflum (Houston, Texas Office); Lori Philipson (Not admitted in IL; New York, N.Y. Office); Mackenzie K. Phillips; Marcus Pickel (Frankfurt/Main, Germany Office); Edward A. Pionke; Kirsten Pirzkall (Frankfurt/Main, Germany Office); Bronwyn F. Pollock (Los Angeles, California Office); David D. Pope; Christine Poulon (Washington, D.C. Office); Matthew R. Powers (Houston, Texas Office); Jason L. Portnoy (New York, N.Y. Office); Pearl H. Prokosh (Los Angeles, California Office); Tristan E. Propst (Houston, Texas Office); Sharon N. Purcell (New York, N.Y. Office); David H. Pyun (Los Angeles, California Office); Maria M. Rabassa (Los Angeles, California Office); Jennifer L. Rakstad; Daniel R. Read (New York, N.Y. Office); Constantin Rehaag (Frankfurt/Main, Germany Office); Laura A. Reilly (Washington, D.C. Office); Lianne S. Reilly (Washington, D.C. Office); Steven E. Rich (Los Angeles, California Office); Christopher Jene Richart (Houston, Texas Office); Luke S. Richbourg (New York, N.Y. Office); Thomas D. Ricks (Charlotte, North Carolina Office); Curtis Dean Ripley; Sandra Rodriguez (New York, N.Y. Office); Jamie L. Romick; Brad P. Rosenberg (Washington, D.C. Office); Jordan H. Rosenfeld (New York, N.Y. Office); Eve B. Ross; Araceli Ruano Pineda (Los Angeles, California Office); Gregory D. Ruback (New York, N.Y. Office); Dr. Isabella V. Rudes (Frankfurt/Main, Germany Office); Jordan M. Rudnick; Richard T. Ruzich; Allan C. ("Kelly") Ryan, IV; Diane Renae Sabol; Jonathan A. Sambur (Washington, D.C. Office); Marcela D. Sanchez; Douglas Lawrence Sawyer; Andrew John Schaefer; Eva Schalast (Frankfurt/Main, Germany Office); Terry Schiff (New York, N.Y. Office); Vincent Paul (Trace) Schmeltz III; Dr. Jens Peter Schmidt (Brussels, Belgium Office); Dr. Burkhard Schmitt (Not admitted in IL; Frankfurt/Main, Germany Office); Maggie J. Schneider; Steven E. Schraibman (New York, N.Y. Office); Gero F. Schreiber (Cologne, Germany Office); Beth Ann Schultz (New York, N.Y. Office); Evan P. Schultz (Washington, D.C. Office); Peter Schultz; Dietmer Schulz (Frankfurt/Main, Germany Office); Sean T. Scott; Ruby G. Sekhon (New York, N.Y. Office); Joseph Seliga; Michael A. Serafini; Sumana Setty (New York, N.Y. Office); Nathan H. Sevilla (New York, N.Y. Office); Matthew A. Shabat; Andrew D. Shaffer (New York, N.Y. Office); Shari A. Shepard (New York, N.Y. Office); Jonathan A. Shiffman (New York, N.Y. Office); David T. Shin; Daniel H. Shulman; Scott Jacob Siegler (New York, N.Y. Office); Dr. Patrick Sinewe (Frankfurt/Main, Germany Office); Parita Singla; John A. Sloat; Gilda M. Smart (New York, N.Y. Office); Hutson Smelley (Houston, Texas Office); Claudius O. Sokenu (New York, N.Y. Office); Jonathan Sokotch (New York, N.Y. Office); Matthew C. Sostrin; Todd Robert Southwell; Veronica L. Spicer; William R. Springer (New York, N.Y. Office); Shannon L. Steege (Houston, Texas Office); Heidi L. Steiber (Washington, D.C. Office); Andrew W. Steigleder; Jeffrey T. Steiner (New York, N.Y. Office); Michael Steingo (Not admitted in IL); Adrian R. Stewart (New York, N.Y. Office); Rebecca K. Stewart (Houston, Texas Office); Daniel K. Storino; Mary M. Streett; Sarah E. Streicker; Ms. Reiko E. Suber; Kenneth Suh (New York, N.Y. Office); Carl J. Summers (Washington, D.C. Office); Joseph Ronald Suster; Mo Taherzadeh (Houston, Texas Office); Sagi Tamir (New York, N.Y. Office); James Alexander Tanaka (New York, N.Y. Office); Karen H. Tang (Los Angeles, California Office); Ashley E. Tatman (Not admitted in IL); Andrew E. Tauber (Washington, D.C. Office); Daniel L. Tedrick (Charlotte, North Carolina Office); Amy G. Thompson (New York, N.Y. Office); Margaret J. Thompson Anderson (Charlotte, North Carolina Office); Tara E. Thompson; Heather O'Farrell Townsend; Brian Kelly Trachtenberg (Houston, Texas Office); Brian P. Trauman (New York, N.Y. Office); Christopher N. Travers (New York, N.Y. Office); Amit K. Trehan (Not admitted in IL); Benjamin C. Tschann (Los Angeles, California Office); Lorraine M. Tyson; Isabelle van Sambeck (Cologne, Germany Office); Carlos A. Vazquez; Elefteris Velesiotis (Houston, Texas Office); Neeraj Verma (Houston, Texas Office); Dani L. Vogt (Los Angeles, California Office); Heinrich von Bünau (Frankfurt/Main, Germany Office); Gary K. Wachtel; Jonathan C. Wagner; Lisa A. Walgenbach (Not admitted in IL; Los Angeles, California Office); Ingo Wallenborn (Frankfurt/Main, Germany Office); Michael O. Ware (New York, N.Y. Office); Bonnie Sarah Weinstein (Palo Alto, California Office); Lyman C. Welch; Reb D. Wheeler (New York, N.Y. Office); Samantha B. Whitehouse; Daniel P. Whitmore; Dr. Marco Wilhelm (Frankfurt/Main, Germany Office); Brent E. Williams; Nick S. Williams (New York, N.Y. Office); Maya Y. Wilson (Washington, D.C. Office); Tamela M. Woods; Catherine F. Wong (New York, N.Y. Office); Mitchell M. Wong (New York, N.Y. Office); Jamie E. Wrage (Los Angeles, California Office); Charles Qiong Wu; Tim Wybitul (Frankfurt/Main, Germany Office); Yasmin Yavar (Houston, Texas Office); Daniel I. Yeh (New York, N.Y. Office); Chae Uk Yi; Joshua D. Yount; Kimberly M. Zielinski. Consultant: Arantzazu Golderos (Brussels, Belgium Office).

Antitrust, Appellate, Asia, Bankruptcy, Biotech, Pharma & Life Science, Chemicals, Collateralized Debt Obligation, Company Secretarial, Construction & Engineering, Corporate & Securities, Corporate Governance, Derivatives, E-commerce, Emerging Companies, Employee Benefits & Executive Compensation, Employee Share Incentives, Employment & Labour, Energy, Environment, Finance, Financial Services, Global Trade, Government, Government Contracts, Health Care, Information Technology, Insurance & Reinsurance, Intellectual Property, International Arbitration, Investment Management, Latin America, Legislative, Litigation & Dispute Resolution, Natural Resources, Outsourcing, Pensions, PPP/PFI & Infrastructure, Private Equity, Private Investment Fund, Pro Bono, Professional Practices, Project Finance, Property Rights, Public Law, Rail, Real Estate, Regulated Industries, Restructuring & Insolvency, Securitisation, Tax Controversy & Transfer Pricing, Tax Transactions & Consulting, Telecommunications & Media, Venture & Technology, Wealth Management.

Brussels, Belgium Office: Square de Meeûs 35, B-1000. Telephone: +011-32 2 502 55 17. Facsimile: + 011-32 2 502 54 21.

Charlotte, North Carolina Office: 214 N. Tryon Street, Suite 3800. Telephone: (704) 444-3500. Fax: (704) 377-2033.

Cologne, Germany Office: Kaiser-Wilhelm-Ring 27-29, 50672. Telephone: +49-221-5771-100. Facsimile: +49-221-5771-199.

Frankfurt am Main, Germany Office: Bockenheimer Landstraße 98-100, D-60323. Telephone: 011-49-69 79 41-0. Facsimile: 011-49-69 79 41-100.

Houston, Texas Office: 700 Louisiana Street, Suite 3600, 77002-2730. Telephone: (713) 221-1651. Facsimile: (713) 224-6410. Telex: 775809. Cable: LEMAYHOU.

London, England Office: 11 Pilgrim Street, London EC4V 6RW. Telephone: 011-44-207-248-4282. Facsimile: 011-44-207-248-2009.

Los Angeles, California Office: 350 South Grand Avenue, 25th Floor, 90071-1503. Telephone: (213) 229-9500. Facsimile: (213) 625-0248. Telex: 188089. Cable: LEMAYLA.

New York, New York Office: 1675 Broadway, 10019-5820. Telephone: (212) 506-2500. Facsimile: (212) 262-1910. Telex: 701842. Cable: LEMAYEN.

Palo Alto, California Office: Two Palo Alto Square, Suite 300, 94306. Telephone: (650) 331-2000. Facsimile: (650) 331-2060.

Paris, France Office: 41 Avenue Hoche, 75008. Telephone: 011-33-1-53-53-43-43. Facsimile: 011-33-1-53-96-03-83.

Washington, D.C. Office: 1909 K Street, N.W., 20006-1101. Telephone: (202) 263-3000. Facsimile: (202) 263-3300. Telex: 892603. Cable: LEMAYDC.

Representative Offices:

Beijing, People's Republic of China: 7-1-31, Qijayuanr, 9 Jianguomen Wai Avenue, Chaoyang District, 100600. Telephone: 011-86-10-85322221. Facsimile: 011-86-10-85322156.

Shanghai, People's Republic of China: 2805 Plaza 66, 1266 Nanjing Road West. Telephone: 011-86-21-6288-1250. Facsimile: 011-86-21-6288-1255.

Mexico City, Mexico, D.F., Independent Mexico Correspondent: Jáuregui, Navarrete, Nader y Rojas, S.C., Abogados Torre Arcos, Paseo de los Tamarindos No. 400-B. Col. Bosques de las Lomas, 05120. Telephone: 011-5255-5-267-45-00. Facsimile: 011-5255-5-267-45-98.

See Professional Biographies, CHICAGO, ILLINOIS

Mayer, Friedlich, Spiess, Tierney, Brown & Platt
(See Mayer, Brown, Rowe & Maw)

Mayergoyz, Sasha .... '— '00 C.188 B.S.E.E. L.597 J.D. [🄰 Latham&W.]

Maynard, Jerome I., (AV) .... '47 '89 C.474 B.S. L.966 J.D. [Dykema G.P.]

Maynard, Kent, Jr. .... '55 '90 C.145 A.B. L.365 J.D. [Meckler B.&T.]

Maynes, Todd F., P.C. ....'— '88 C&L.101 B.A., J.D. [Kirkland&E.]

Mays, John H., (AV) .... '46 '74 C&L.209 B.S., J.D. [Gould&R.]

Mayster, Courtney E. .... '76 '01 C.276 B.A. L.424 J.D. [🄰 Schain,B.R.&C.]

Mayster, Jerrold H. .... '46 '72 C.679 B.S. L.209 J.D. [J.H.Mayster]

Mayster, Jerrold H., Ltd. ....Ste. 1404, 221 N. La Salle St.

Mazar, Adrian E. .... '58 '84 C.388 B.A. L.46 J.D. [A.Mazar]

Mazar, Adrian, Law Office of .... 20 South Clark St., Ste. 2000

Mazur, Todd A. ....'75 '00 C.347 B.A. L.1119 J.D. [Ⓐ Greenberg T.]
Mazura, Adrianne C., (AV) ....'51 '78 C.477 B.A. L.912 J.D. [DLPiper R.G.C.U.]
Mazurek, Janet L. ....'65 '91 C.801 B.S. L.365 J.D. [Ⓐ Pasulka&W.]
Mazurk, Mary A. ....'— '84 C.238 B.A. L.365 J.D. 77 W. Washington # 505
Mazza, James J., Jr. ....'— '01 C.880 B.A. L.339 J.D. [Ⓐ Kirkland&E.]
Mazzeo, Melissa Crawford ....'67 '95 C.477 B.A. L.1194 J.D. [Matkov,S.M.&G.]
Mazzochi, Deanne M. ....'— '97 C.94 B.A. L.273 J.D. [Rakoczy M.M.S.] (Pat.)
Mazzone, John Anthony ....'26 '58 C&L.209 B.S., J.D. Kelvyn Pk. High School
McAdams, Richard H. '60 '87 C.575 B.A. L.893 J.D.
(adm. in PA; not adm. in IL) Assoc. Prof. of Law, Chicago-Kent College of Law
McAleenan, A. Frank, (AV) ....'43 '69 C.1151 B.A. L.209 J.D. [Garretson&S.]
McAleenan, Brian A. ....'— '98 C&L.339 B.A., J.D. [Ⓐ Sidley A.B.&W.]
McAllister, Kent W. '62 '89 C.1119 B.A. L.575 J.D.
(adm. in VA; not adm. in IL) Branch Chf., U.S. Secs. & Exch. Comm.
McAnally, Daniel P. ....'65 '90 C&L.424 B.S., J.D. 2 N. LaSalle St., Ste. 1650
McAnany, Patrick D. ....'30 '60 C.698 A.B. L.309 LL.B. Dept. of Crim. Jus.
McAndrew, Mark J., (AV) ....'— '80 C.339 B.S. L.365 J.D. [Ⓒ Barnes&T.]
McAndrew, Mark T. ....'69 '01 C.352 B.B.A. L.365 J.D. [Ⓐ Schueler,D.&C.]
McAndrew, Michelle Kaplan ....'62 '90 C.93 B.A. L.276 J.D. 812 North Dearborn
McAndrews, George P., (AV) '35 '62
C&L.602 B.S.M.E., J.D. [McAndrews,H.&M.] (See Pat. Sect.)
McAndrews, John M., (BV) ....'64 '89 C.436 B.S. L.365 J.D. [Gurber,M.&N.]
McAndrews, Matthew G. '66 '95 C.602 B.A. L.365 J.D.
[Niro,S.H.&N.] (See Pat. Sect.)
McAndrews, Peter J. '68 '95
C.436 B.S.E.E. L.365 J.D. [McAndrews,H.&M.] (See Pat. Sect.)

McAndrews, Held & Malloy, Ltd., (AV)
34th Floor, 500 West Madison Street, 60661
Telephone: 312-775-8000 Fax: 312-775-8100
URL: http://www.mhmlaw.com
George P. McAndrews; John J. Held; Timothy J. Malloy; William M. Wesley; Lawrence M. Jarvis; Gregory J. Vogler; Jean Dudek Kuelper; Herbert D. Hart III; Robert W. Fieseler; Thomas J. Wimbiscus; Steven J. Hampton; Priscilla F. Gallagher; Stephen F. Sherry; Patrick J. Arnold, Jr.; George F. Wheeler; Janet M. McNicholas; Christopher C. Winslade; Edward A. Mas, II; Gregory C. Schodde; Edward W. Remus; Donald J. Pochopien; Sharon A. Hwang; David D. Headrick; Alejandro Menchaca; Kirk A. VanderLeest; Richard T. McCaulley, Jr.; Peter J. McAndrews; Leland G. Hansen; James M. Hafertepe; Jonathan R. Sick; Eligio C. Pimentel; James P. Murphy; Dean A. Pelletier; Michael B. Harlin; James R. Nuttall; Robert A. Surrette; Joseph M. Barich; Scott P. McBride; Patricia J. McGrath; Troy A. Groetken; Gerald C. Willis, Jr.; John A. Wiberg; Wilhelm L. Rao; Sandra A. Frantzen; Ronald Spuhler; Christopher V. Carani; Mirut P. Dalal; Ronald A. DiCerbo; Jennifer E. Lacroix; Joseph F. Harding; Joseph M. Butscher;—Sara Bartos; John L. Abramic; Michael J. Fitzpatrick; David Z. Petty; Michael T. Cruz (Not admitted in IL); Christopher N. George; Matthew A. Anderson; Yufeng Ma; Dennis H. Jaskoviak, Jr.; Deborah A. Laughton; William B. Gont; Dennis P. Hackett; Hopeton Walker; Shawn L. Peterson; Ognyan (Oggie) Beremski; Philip H. Sheridan; Christopher R. Carroll; Christopher M. Scharff; Consuelo G. Erwin; Peter J. Prommer; Merle Elliott; Brian C. Bianco; Laura M. Personick; Jonathan M. Rushman; Jeremy N. Gayed; Christopher J. Buchko; Leonard D. Conapinski. Of Counsel: S. Jack Sauer.
Federal and State Trial, Appellate and Agency Practice, Dispute Resolution and Licensing Involving Patents, Trademarks and Copyrights, Environmental Law, Trade Association, Warranty, Complex Technology and Antitrust Matters.
See Professional Biographies, CHICAGO, ILLINOIS

McArdle, James M., (BV) ....'— '90 C.339 A.B. L.209 J.D. [Ⓐ Scott&K.]
McArdle, Michael J., (AV) ....'36 '61 C.679 L.209 J.D. 20 N. Clark St.
McArdle, Richard P. ....'65 '93 C.161 B.B.A. L.930 J.D. [Seyfarth S.]
McArdle, Timothy I. ....'61 '87 C.339 B.A. L.365 J.D. 20 North Clark, 36th Floor
McAtee, Jane A., (BV) ......'51 '78 C.608 B.S.Ed. L.477 J.D. Univ. of Chicago Hospitals
McAtee, Michelle M. ....'73 '99 C.436 B.S. L.352 J.D. [Ⓐ Jenner&B.]
McAuley, John G. ....'52 '88 C.665 B.S. L.365 J.D. [Ⓐ Adler,M.&M.]
McAuley, Michael J. '54 '81 C.276 A.B. L.982 J.D.
Natl. Coun., Natl. Treasury Employees Union
McAuliff, James L., Jr. ....'46 '75 C.597 B.S. L.424 J.D. Asst. Atty. Gen.
McAuliffe, Jeremiah D., (AV) ....'21 '49 C&L.597 B.S., J.D. [Pattishall,M.N.H.&G.]
McAuliffe, John P., (AV) ....'21 '56 C.424 Ph.B. L.365 [Wiedner&M.] ‡
McAuliffe, Lester E. '34 '63 C.755 B.A. L.494 J.D.
(adm. in MN; not adm. in IL) U.S. Postal Service
McAvoy, Katherine A. ....'71 '98 C.339 B.A. L.602 J.D. [Ⓐ Winston&S.]
McAvoy, Terrence P., (AV) ....'61 '87 C.339 B.S. L.365 J.D. [Hinshaw&C.]
McBreen, Hugh G., (AV) ....'55 '80 C.197 A.B. L.602 J.D. [McBreen&K.]
McBreen, Maura Ann, (AV) ....'53 '78 C.788 A.B. L.309 J.D. [Baker&M.]
McBreen, Michele Tate ....'54 '81 C&L.602 B.A., J.D. [McBreen&K.]
McBreen, Paul J. ....'60 '86 C.208 B.A. L.209 J.D. [McBreen&K.]

McBreen & Kopko, (AV)
Suite 2520, 20 North Wacker Drive, 60606 ⊙
Telephone: 312-332-6405 Fax: 312-332-2657
Email: counsel@mmklaw.com
Members of Firm: Frederick H. Kopko, Jr.; Hugh G. McBreen; Brian J. Hogan (Resident, Irvine, California Office); James Russell Stern; Thomas J. Bradley (Resident, Philadelphia, Pennsylvania Office); Leonard D. Kirsch (Resident, Jericho, N.Y. Office); Richard A. Auerbach (Resident, Jericho, N.Y. Office); Mary Elizabeth Kopko; Robert S. Moran, Jr. (Resident, Montvale, New Jersey Office); Paul J. McBreen; Anjali Dayal; Helene Gorman Bradley (Resident, Philadelphia, Pennsylvania Office); Michele Tate McBreen; Annie K. Strobl; Don L. Hochler (Not admitted in IL); Norman N. Bluth (Resident, Jericho, N.Y. Office). Associates: Regina Movsesyan (Resident, Jericho, N.Y. Office); T. Brent Costello (Not admitted in IL); Nancy J. Leddy (Resident, Philadelphia, Pennsylvania Office); Christopher J. Boyle (Resident, Philadelphia, Pennsylvania Office); Andrea Maier (Resident, Philadelphia, Pennsylvania Office). Of Counsel: Ralph T. Verrill (Not admitted in IL); Gerard Terry (Not admitted in IL).
General Practice, Corporate, Mergers and Acquisitions, Securities, Commodities, Real Estate, Aviation, General and Commercial Litigation, Appellate Practice, Toxic Torts, Products Liability, Medical Malpractice and Environmental Law.
Irvine, California Office: 2 Venture Avenue, Suite 240. Telephone: 949-453-8900. Fax: 949-453-8989.
Philadelphia, Pennsylvania Office: Eight Penn Center, 1628 John F. Kennedy Boulevard, Suite 1400. Telephone: 215-864-2600. Fax: 215-864-2610.
Montvale, New Jersey Office: 110 Summit Avenue. Telephone: 201-476-5400. Fax: 201-573-0574.
Jericho, New York Office: 500 North Broadway. Telephone: 516-364-1095. Fax: 516-364-0612.
See Professional Biographies, CHICAGO, ILLINOIS

McBride, Danny R. ....'23 '51 C.8 B.A. L.597 J.D. 134 N. La Salle St.
McBride, David N., (AV) ....'31 '55 C&L.602 B.A., J.D. [Ⓒ McGuirewoods]
McBride, J. Scott ....'70 '02 C.197 A.B. L.145 J.D. [Ⓐ Bartlit B.H.P.&S.]
McBride, Katarinna '— '00 C.1028 B.A. L.200 J.D.
[Ⓐ Beermann S.W.B.B.G.&L.] (Pat.)
McBride, Laurie J. ....'52 '80 C.339 B.A. L.424 J.D. Asst. State's Atty.
McBride, Margaret Stanton ....'51 '76 C.999 B.A. L.209 J.D. App. Ct. J.
McBride, Michael P. ....'— '04 L.477 J.D. [Ⓐ Ungaretti&H.]
McBride, Scott P. .....'73 '98 C.966 B.S. L.201 J.D. [McAndrews,H.&M.] (See Pat. Sect.)
McBride, Thomas K., Jr. '67 '04
C.339 B.S. L.424 J.D. [Ⓐ Leydig,V.&M.] (See Pat. Sect.)

McBride Baker & Coles
(See Holland & Knight LLC)

McCabe, Daniel C. ....'68 '94 C.597 B.A. L.146 J.D. [Kubasiak,F.R.&R.]
McCabe, John B., (AV) ....'45 '71 C.436 B.C.E. L.365 J.D. [McDonald&M.]
McCabe, John M. '39 '68 C.813 A.B. L.508 J.D.
Legal Coun. & Dir., National Conf. of Comm. on Uniform State Laws
McCabe, Kathleen M., (BV) ....'64 '90 C.339 B.S. L.1000 J.D. [Cassiday,S.&G.]
McCabe, Peter C., III, (AV) ....'60 '85 C.309 B.A. L.1119 J.D. [Winston&S.]
McCabe, Regina K. ....'56 '81 C.339 B.A. L.597 J.D. [Ⓒ Boundas S.W.&B.]
McCabe, Terrence D. ....'59 '87 C.337 B.S. L.365 J.D. [Ⓐ Ryan&R.]

McCaffery, Joseph P., Attorney at Law
(See Aurora)

McCaffrey, John W., (BV) ....'— '74 C.801 B.A. L.146 J.D. [Foley&L.]
McCaffrey, Timothy J. ....'70 '95 C&L.347 B.S., J.D. [Winston&S.]
McCahill, Jane K., (AV) ....'53 '78 C.98 B.S. L.910 J.D. [Bell,B.&L.]
McCain, Taryn Marie, (BVⓉ) '59 '84 C.788 A.B. L.846 J.D.
(adm. in TX; not adm. in IL) Boeing Company, The
McCain, Trent A. ....'74 '02 C.257 B.S.B.A. L.879 J.D. [Ⓐ J.D.Montgomery&Assoc.]
McCaleb, Malcolm, Jr., (AV) ....'— '71 C.165 B.A. L.597 J.D. [Barack F.K.P.&N.]
McCall, Diana D. ....'— '02 C.801 B.S. L.339 J.D. [Ⓐ LaBarge,C.&L.]
McCall, J. Kevin, (AV) ....'53 '79 C&L.424 A.B., J.D. [Jenner&B.]
McCall, Kara Lynn ....'76 '00 C.108 B.A. L.145 J.D. 10 South Dearborn
McCallister, Gary D., (AV) '50 '75
C.375 B.S. L.900 J.D. [G.D.McCallister&Assoc.] (⊙Topeka, KS)
McCallister, Marc E. ....'79 '05 C.645 B.A. L.146 J.D. [Ⓐ Bollinger,R.&G.]

McCallister, Gary D., & Associates, Ltd., (AV)
120 North La Salle Street, 60602
Telephone: 312-345-0611 Fax: 312-345-0612
Email: gdm@gdmlawfirm.com URL: http://www.lawyers.com/gdmlawfirm
Gary D. McCallister; Eric I. Unrein; Thomas A. Kelliher.
Plaintiff's Personal Injury, Products Liability, Medical, Legal Malpractice, Wrongful Death, Insurance, Pharmaceutical, Antitrust, Business, Commercial, Complex and Multi-District Litigation and Class Actions in all State and Federal Trial and Appellate Courts.
See Professional Biographies, CHICAGO, ILLINOIS

McCallum, Lisa A. '67 '92 C&L.347 B.A., J.D.
(adm. in IN; not adm. in IL) 616 W. Berry #1E
McCallum, Stephanie ....'— '02 C&L.966 B.A., J.D. [Ⓐ Winston&S.]
McCambridge, Edward J., (AV) ....'49 '75 C.755 B.A. L.365 J.D. [Segal M.S.&M.]
McCambridge, John R., (AV) ....'52 '77 C&L.309 A.B., J.D. [Grippo&E.]
McCambridge, Michael J. ......'52 '86 C.339 B.S. L.365 J.D. State Pollution Control Bd.
McCann, Bradley S. ....'71 '98 C.589 B.S. L.1252 J.D. [Nisen&E.]
Mc Cann, Dennise L. ....'63 '88 C.965 B.S. L.365 J.D. Law Clk. to U.S. Bkrptcy. J.
McCann, Patrick J., II ....'75 '01 C.36 B.S. L.365 J.D. [Ⓐ Noonan&L.]
McCann, R. Michael ....'68 '01 C.425 B.B.A. L.424 J.D. [Ⓐ Wildman,H.A.&D.]
McCareins, R. Mark, (AV) ....'56 '81 C.597 B.A. L.910 J.D. [Winston&S.]
McCarter, James V. ....'50 '76 C.1034 B.A. L.146 J.D. Asst. States Atty.
McCarthy, Brian D. ......'— '96 C.1109 B.S. L.365 J.D. 320 West Ohio Street, Suite 500
McCarthy, Charles J., (Ltd.), (AV) ....'37 '62 C.686 B.S. L.276 J.D. [Ⓒ Jenner&B.]
McCarthy, David S. ....'— '88 C.976 B.A. L.145 J.D. [Schiff H.]
McCarthy, Edward Quentin .....'50 '77 C.276 A.B. L.365 J.D. Fin. Advsr., Paine Webber
McCarthy, Emmett R. ....'73 '99 C.339 B.S. L.209 J.D. [Ⓐ Flamm&T.]
McCarthy, Hugh J., (AV) ....'09 '35 C&L.209 LL.B. [H.J.McCarthy&Assoc.]
McCarthy, James G. ....'66 '95 C.276 A.B. L.209 J.D. [Ⓐ Dwyer,M.&Assoc.]
McCarthy, James M. '69 '94
C.602 B.S.E.E. L.201 J.D. [McDonnell B.H.&B.] (See Pat. Sect.)
McCarthy, James P., (AV) ....'59 '84 C.602 B.B.A. L.365 J.D. [Gunty&M.]
McCarthy, James Patrick ....'48 '78 C.1157 B.S. L.589 J.D. Asst. Corp. Coun.
McCarthy, John T., (AV) ....'41 '66 C.1024 B.S. L.597 J.D. [Bell,B.&L.]
McCarthy, Kevin J. ....'66 '91 C.602 B.B.A. L.339 J.D. [Bell,B.&L.]
McCarthy, Mary Margaret ....'58 '89 L.424 J.D. Dir., Midwest Immigrant Law Center
McCarthy, Maurice J., (AV) ....'38 '63 C&L.424 A.B., J.D. 30 N. LaSalle St.
McCarthy, Paul ....'40 '72 C.188 A.B. L.477 J.D. [Ⓒ Baker&M.]
McCarthy, Paul B. ....'66 '94 C.31 B.A. L.602 J.D. 203 N. La Salle St., Suite 1800
McCarthy, Thomas A. ....'74 '00 C&L.966 B.S., J.D. [Ⓐ Quarles&B.]
McCarthy, Thomas J., (AV) ....'55 '81 C.188 A.B. L.276 J.D. [Jenner&B.]
McCarthy, Thomas J., (AV) ....'47 '74 C.602 A.B. L.365 J.D. [McCarthy&Assoc.]
McCarthy, Timothy M., (AV) '54 '81
C.339 B.S. L.326 J.D. [Trexler,B.G.B.&M.] (See Pat. Sect.)

McCarthy & Associates, (AV)
20 N. Wacker Drive, Suite 1701, 60606
Telephone: 312-634-5200 Telecopier: 312-634-5220
Member of Firm: Thomas J. McCarthy. Associate: Rachel L. Oesch. Of Counsel: Jeffrey W. Finke; Edward R. Rabe, Jr.
Government and Legislative Relations, State and Local Taxation, General Corporate Law, Health Care and Aviation Law.
Representative Clients: Ameritech Information Systems, Inc.; CPC International, Inc.; Inland Steel Industries, Inc.; Lutheran General Health Care System; Shearson Lehman Brothers, Inc.
Reference: Amalgamated Bank, Chicago, Illinois.
See Professional Biographies, CHICAGO, ILLINOIS

McCarthy Duffy, (AV)
180 North LaSalle Street Suite 1400, 60601 ⊙
Telephone: 312-726-0355 Fax: 312-726-6383; 312-726-6609 URL: http://www.mccarthyduffylaw.com
URL: http://www.mccarthyduffy.com
Members of Firm: John M. Duffy; Forest J. Miles; Thomas J. Montgomery; Terrence Leigh Schaul; Stephen A. Snakard; Timothy E. Weilandt; Richard J. Witry; Steven N. Zaris. Associate: Julie M. Realmuto.
Commercial Litigation. Banking, Real Estate, Probate, Trusts & Estates, Corporate, Employment, Appellate, Municipal and Bankruptcy Law.
Skokie, Illinois Office: 8022 Lincoln Avenue. Telephone: 847-673-0355. Fax: 847-673-2354.
Palos Park, Illinois Office: 8102 West 119th Street, Suite 800, 60464. Telephone: 708-923-7345. Fax: 708-923-0963.
See Professional Biographies, CHICAGO, ILLINOIS

McCarthy, Hugh J., & Associates, Ltd., (AV) ....35 E. Wacker Dr.
McCarthy and Levin, (AV) ....100 West Monroe
McCarty, Jon P. ....'70 '98 C.338 B.A. L.339 J.D. [Ⓐ Vedder,P.K.&K.]
McCarty, Matthew G. '69 '96 C.201 B.A. L.365 J.D.
V.P. & Gen. Coun., Globalcom, Inc.
McCarty, Robert S. ....'62 '89 C.339 B.S. L.424 J.D. [Ⓐ Leff,C.&W.]
McCarty, Tonya M. ....'66 '97 C.629 B.A. L.146 J.D. [Ⓐ Condon&C.]
McCauley, James Brent ....'— '93 C.63 B.S. L.345 J.D. [Ungaretti&H.]
McCauley, Thomas V., (AV) ....'50 '75 C.276 A.B. L.424 J.D. [Nisen&E.]
McCaulley, Richard T., Jr. '65 '94
C.855 B.S. L.602 J.D. [McAndrews,H.&M.] (See Pat. Sect.)
McClain, Barat S., (BV) ....'51 '90 C.530 B.A. L.146 J.D. [Much S.F.D.A.&R.]
McClary, Michael J. ....'57 '86 U.S. EPA
McClear, Kevin R. '61 '87 C.207 B.A. L.597 J.D.
V.P, Spec. Coun., Board of Trade Clearing Corp.
McClellan, Holly Klus ....'71 '97 C.1372 B.A. L.823 J.D. [Ⓐ Baker&M.]

McClelland, Marion G., (Ms.) ... '13 '38 L.365 LL.B. 909 W. Foster Ave.‡
McClintic, Kelly Jeanne ... '73 '98 C.589 B.A. L.146 J.D. [Ⓐ Keating&S.]
McClinton, Vanessa D. ... '73 '98 C.477 B.A. L.597 J.D. [Ⓐ Eimer S.K.&S.]
McCloskey, Kelly A. ... '64 '90 C.602 B.A. L.273 J.D. [O'Rourke M.&M.]
McCloy, Elizabeth K., (AV) ... '59 '84 C.197 B.A. L.597 J.D. [Sidley A.B.&W.]
McCluggage, Michael L., (AV) ... '47 '72 C.611 B.A. L.145 J.D. [Wildman,H.A.&D.]
McClung, Megan Healy ... '73 '98 C.339 B.A. L.589 J.D. Dept. of Law
McClure, James J., Jr., (AV) ... '20 '50 C&L.145 B.A., J.D. [Ⓒ Gardner C.&D.]
McClure, John F., (AV) ... '23 '51 C.210 A.B. L.597 LL.B. Hearing Off., Labor Rel. Bd.
McClure, Lorie A. ... '59 '89 C.470 B.A. L.209 J.D. 2712 N. Mildred Ave.‡
McColgan, Arthur J., II, (AV) ... '64 '89 C&L.602 B.A., J.D. [Lord,B.&B.]
McColl, Michael H. ... '70 '94 C.207 B.A. L.597 J.D. [Foran G.P.&P.]
McCollam, Brian J. ... '51 '76 C.597 B.A. L.145 J.D. [Barnard&M.]
McCombs, Hugh R., (AV) ... '46 '75 C.976 B.A. L.94 J.D. [Mayer,B.R.&M.]
McCombs, Mark J., (AV) ... '59 '84 C.30 B.S. L.597 J.D. [Greenberg T.]
McConkey, James W. ... '63 '89 C.198 A.B. L.988 J.D. [Dykema G.P.]
McConnell, Gregory A. ... '64 '90 C.339 B.A. L.273 J.D. [Ⓢ Winston&S.]
McConnell, James G. ... '— '73 C.350 B.S. L.597 J.D. [Ⓐ Neal&L.]
McConville, Terrence James ... '55 '83 C.602 B.A. L.365 J.D. Asst. Gen. Coun.
McCorkhill, C. Grant ... '61 '88 C.970 B.A. L.930 J.D. [Holland&K.]
McCormack, Beth Fawver, (AV) ... '64 '92 C.338 B.A. L.365 J.D. [Kamerlink,S.&M.] ⊙
McCormack, Edward F., (AV) ... '62 '89 C.477 B.A. L.893 J.D. [Jenkens&G.]
McCormack, John L. ... '42 '68 C.959 B.S. L.966 J.D. Prof., Loyola Univ. Sch. of Law
McCormick, Carl ... '35 '63 C.1016 B.S.B.A. L.365 LL.B. 9415 S. State St.
McCormick, Chas. B., Jr. ... '28 '52 C.602 L.365 LL.B. U.S. Bkrptcy. J.
McCormick, Gregory A. ... '65 '89 C.209 B.A. L.146 J.D. [Ⓐ Garfield&M.]
McCormick, Linda Claire '50 '76 C.881 B.A. L.421 J.D.
(adm. in KY; not adm. in IL) NLRB
McCormick, Margaret H., (AV) ... '51 '78 C.530 B.A. L.209 J.D. [Minsky,M.&H.]
McCormick, Michael T. ... '62 '88 C.473 B.S. L.879 J.D. [McCormick]
McCormick, Steven D., P.C., (AV) ... '— '72 C.602 A.B. L.597 J.D. [Kirkland&E.]
McCormick Law Group, LLC ... 217 N. Jefferson St., Ste. 500
McCown, Harrison J. '56 '81 C.802 B.B.A. L.339 J.D.
Sr. Counsel, LaSalle Bank National Association
McCoy, Jamenda A. ... '— '03 C.502 B.A. L.597 J.D. [Ⓐ Kirkland&E.]
McCoy, Joseph Q. ... '72 '98 C.145 B.A./M.A. L.597 J.D. [Schwartz C.]
McCoy, Kris L. ... '73 '99 C&L.339 B.A., J.D. [Ⓐ Lovells]
McCoy, Megan L. ... '75 '05 C.473 B.A. L.365 J.D. [Ⓐ Shefsky&F.]
McCoy, Ruth Goldwater, (CV) ... '64 '89 C.339 B.A. L.146 J.D. [Bollinger,R.&G.]
McCoy, Tene LaVi ... '72 '98 C&L.329 B.A., J.D. Asst. State's Atty., Cook Co.
McCracken, Amy E. ... '59 '91 C.912 B.S.N. L.477 J.D. [Ⓐ Duane M.]
McCracken, David E., III, (AV) ... '38 '63 C&L.339 B.S., LL.B. [McCracken&M.]
McCracken, R. Chad ... '67 '99 C.976 B.A. L.846 J.D. [Ⓐ Lovells]
McCracken, Thomas J. ... '25 '54 C.145 L.424 J.D. [McCracken,W.d.&H.]
McCracken, Thomas J., Jr., (AV) ... '52 '77 C.436 B.A. L.424 J.D. [McCracken,W.d.&H.]
McCracken, William E., (AV) '55 '80 C.339 B.S.E.E. L.424 J.D.
[McCracken&F.] (Pat.)

McCracken & Frank LLP, (AV)
200 West Adams, Suite 2150, 60606
Telephone: 312-263-4700 Fax: 312-263-3990
URL: http://www.pattm.com
Members of the Firm: William E. McCracken; J. William Frank, III. Associates: Nicholas P. Schmidbauer; Thomas P. Riley. Of Counsel: Thomas R. Stiebel, Jr.
Intellectual Property.

See Professional Biographies, CHICAGO, ILLINOIS

McCracken & McCracken, P.C., (AV) ... 134 N. LaSalle St.
McCracken, Walsh, de LaVan & Hetler, (AV) ... 134 North La Salle Street
McCrate, Ryan J. ... '— '03 C.124 B.S. L.976 J.D. [Ⓐ Kirkland&E.]
McCraw, Johnny, Jr. ... '— '03 C.837 B.A. L.477 J.D. [Ⓐ Sonnenschein N.&R.]
McCray, Jacque ... '79 '04 C.309 B.A. L.276 J.D. [Ⓐ Sonnenschein N.&R.]
McCready, Michael P., The Law Offices of '68 '92
C.692 B.A. L.1509 J.D. 10008 S. Western Ave.
McCreery, Mary Kathryn ... '74 '99 C.436 B.A. L.602 J.D. [Ⓐ Greenberg T.]
McCrohon, Craig ... '— '89 C.309 B.A. L.659 J.D. [Holland&K.]
McCue, Howard M., III, (AV) ... '46 '71 C.674 A.B. L.309 J.D. [Mayer,B.R.&M.]
McCue, Judith W., (AV) ... '48 '72 C.659 B.A. L.309 J.D. [McDermott W.&E.]
McCulloh, John R. '54 '81 C.309 A.B. L.893 J.D.
Sr. Coun., Bank One Corp. (Law Dept.)
McCullough, Edwin R. ... '41 '73 C.339 B.S.E.E. L.424 J.D. 19 S. LaSalle Street
McCullough, Jane B., (AV) ... '45 '81 C.238 B.A. L.209 J.D. [Greenberg T.]
McCullough, John W. ... '40 '66 C.597 B.A. L.477 J.D. [McCullough,C.&L.]
McCullough, Joseph T., IV ... '56 '85 C.276 B.A. L.597 J.D. [Lovells]
McCullough, Michael D. ... '67 '95 C.347 B.S. L.424 J.D. [Ⓐ DLPiper R.G.C.U.]

McCullough, Campbell & Lane, (AV)
205 North Michigan Avenue, Suite 4100, 60601
Telephone: 312-923-4000 Facsimile: 312-923-4329
Email: firm@mcandl.com
Partners: John W. McCullough; John G. Campbell; Michael M. Lane; Dennis L. Frostic; John A. Hubbuch; F. Dennis Nelson; Paul S. Turner; Patrick M. Graber; Ann P. Goodman; Anne E. LaVoie; Mark D. Siebert; Debra A. Emry; Bart Rinn; Myra J. Brown. Associates: Stephen D. Koslow; Veronica Nulman; Brian J. Dusek; Julie L. Henn. Of Counsel: Marvin Green; Anne Jentry-Green; David L. Joslyn; Carl D. Liggio, Sr.
General Civil Trial and Appellate Practice in all State and Federal Courts. Aviation, Banking, Commercial, Corporation and Corporation Financing, Directors and Officers Liability, Employee Benefits, Employment Discrimination, Environmental, Insurance, Reinsurance and Insurance Defense, International Business, Medical Malpractice, Products Liability, Professional Liability, Real Estate, Securities and Taxation.

See Professional Biographies, CHICAGO, ILLINOIS

McCune, Andrew W. ... '63 '89 C.910 A.B. L.145 J.D. [DLPiper R.G.C.U.]
McCurdy, Kay W., (AV) ... '50 '75 C.98 A.B. L.145 J.D. [Lord,B.&B.]
McCurry, Kenneth T. ... '42 '75 C.1121 B.A. L.365 J.D. Asst. States Atty.
McCutchen, Peter B. '64 '90 C.927 B.A. L.597 J.D.
Bigelow Teaching Fellow and Lecturer, U. of Chicago Law School
McCutcheon, Michael C. ... '75 '01 C.339 B.S. L.424 J.D. [Ⓐ Baker&M.]
McDermott, Andrew P.R. ... '76 '03 C.494 B.A. L.597 J.D. [Ⓐ Bell,B.&L.]
McDermott, John H., (AV) ... '31 '56 C.951 B.A. L.477 J.D. 227 West Monroe Street
McDermott, Mark A. ... '66 '91 C.350 B.S. L.597 J.D. [Ⓢ Skadden,A.S.M.&F.]
McDermott, Michael L., (AV) ... '38 '63 C.812 B.S. L.597 J.D. [O'Keefe,L.&H.]
McDermott, Richard O., (AV) ... '66 '93 C.860 B.A. L.602 J.D. [Ⓐ Lord,B.&B.]
McDermott, Ronald J. ... '64 '91 C.339 B.A. L.424 J.D. [Ⓐ Shefsky&F.]
McDermott, William F. ... '52 '78 C.433 B.E. L.146 J.D. [Ⓐ Morris&S.] (Pat.)
McDermott Will & Emery, (AV)
227 W. Monroe St. (Pat.) (⊙Irvine, L.A., Palo Alto, San Diego, CA; Wash., DC; Miami, FL; Boston, MA; New York, NY; Dusseldorf, Munich, Germany)
McDevitt, Daniel D. ... '60 '92 C.604 A.B. L.665 J.D. 30 N. LaSalle St., Ste. 3900
McDevitt, Donna L. ... '54 '88 C.882 B.A. L.145 J.D. [Ⓢ Skadden,A.S.M.&F.]

McDole, Jamie H. ... '— '99 C.352 B.S.E. L.146 J.D. [Kirkland&E.]
McDonagh, Mary ... '73 '01 C.999 B.A. L.365 J.D. 5366 North Elston Ave. Ste. 201
McDonald, Heather R. ... '— '03 C.475 B.A. L.209 J.D. [Ⓐ Schiff H.]
McDonald, James F., (AV) ... '54 '79 C.976 B.A. L.145 J.D. Asst. Corp. Coun.
McDonald, John A., (AV) ... '40 '64 C&L.477 A.B., J.D. [Quarles&B.]
McDonald, John D. ... '71 '96 C.436 B.S. L.597 J.D. [Baker&M.]
McDonald, Kathleen '67 '95 C.597 B.S. L.365 J.D.
One South Wacker Drive, Suite 2500
McDonald, Kevin C. ... '55 '80 C.145 A.B. L.309 J.D. [Ⓒ Mayer,B.R.&M.]
McDonald, Sally J. ... '64 '90 C.347 B.S. L.228 J.D. [DLPiper R.G.C.U.]
McDonald, Thomas A., (AV) ... '42 '69 C.276 A.B. L.424 J.D. [McDonald&M.]

McDonald & McCabe, LLC, (AV) BR
300 S. Wacker Drive, Suite 1600, 60606
Telephone: 312-845-5190 Fax: 312-845-5825
Email: tmcdonald@mcdonaldmccabe.com URL: http://www.mcdonaldmccabe.com
Thomas A. McDonald; John B. McCabe;—David R. Edsey; Jeremy F. Goldstein; Mark D. Howard; James K. Schultz; Thomas A. Smith.
Complex Litigation, Technical Litigation, Fires, Explosions, Construction Failures; Construction Liability, Product Liability, Property Insurance Coverage and Litigation; Liability Insurance Coverage; Subrogation; Insurance Bad Faith, Civil RICO, Employment Law.

See Professional Biographies, CHICAGO, ILLINOIS

McDonnell, E. F., Jr. ... '24 '53 C.602 B.S. L.209 J.D. 200 S. Wacker Dr.‡
McDonnell, John J., (AV) '39 '74
C.589 B.S. L.146 J.D. [McDonnell B.H.&B.] (See Pat. Sect.)
McDonnell, Thomas J., (AV) ... '32 '60 C.424 B.S. L.597 J.D. 203 N. La Salle St.‡

McDonnell Boehnen Hulbert & Berghoff LLP, (AV) BR
300 South Wacker Drive, 60606-6709
Telephone: 312-913-0001 Fax: 312-913-0002
Email: info@mbhb.com URL: http://www.mbhb.com
John J. McDonnell; Daniel A. Boehnen; Bradley J. Hulbert; Paul H. Berghoff; Grantland G. Drutchas; James C. Gumina; David M. Frischkorn; Leif R. Sigmond, Jr.; A. Blair Hughes; Lawrence H. Aaronson; Thomas A. Fairhall; Matthew J. Sampson; Curt J. Whitenack; Michael S. Greenfield; Steven J. Sarussi; Christopher M. Cavan; Kevin E. Noonan; George I. Lee; Joshua R. Rich; James M. McCarthy; Robert J. Irvine, III; Thomas E. Wettermann; Sean M. Sullivan; Richard A. Machonkin; Emily Miao; Patrick G. Gattari; David S. Harper; Marcus J. Thymian; Stephen H. Docter; Lisa M. W. Hillman; Anita J. Terpstra; S. Richard Carden; Jeremy Edward Noe; Paul S. Tully; Anthoula Pomrening; Alison Jameen Baldwin; Nicole F. Keenan; Jeffrey A. Steck; Paul W. Churilla (Not admitted in IL). Of Counsel: Denis A. Berntsen. Associates: Eric R. Moran; Andrew W. Williams; Daniel P. Williams; Aaron F. Barkoff; Mark L. Chael; Donald L. Zuhn; Bradley W. Crawford; Lisa Schoedel; Dennis D. Crouch; David L. Ciesielski; Victoria Friedman; Paula S. Fritsch; Jennifer M. Kurcz; Raef Shaltout.
Intellectual Property Law, Federal Trial and Appellate Practice in Patent, Trademark, Trade Dress, Trade Secrets, International Trade, Unfair Competition, Copyright and Antitrust Causes before Federal and State Courts and Administrative Agencies; All phases of Prosecution before the United States and Foreign Patent and Trademark Offices.

See Professional Biographies, CHICAGO, ILLINOIS

McDonough, Andrew J. ... '60 '86 C&L.608 B.A., J.D. [Winston&S.]
McDonough, Courtney Anne ... '79 '04 C&L.602 B.A., J.D. [Ⓐ Vedder,P.K.&K.]
McDonough, John D. ... '59 '85 C&L.339 B.F.A., J.D. Asst. Corp. Coun.
McDonough, John M., (AV) ... '44 '69 C.674 A.B. L.976 LL.B. [Sidley A.B.&W.]
McDonough, Kathleen ... '69 '94 C.741 B.A. L.146 J.D. [Segal M.S.&M.]
McDonough, Lucille K. ... '34 '59 C.530 B.A. L.424 J.D. 10951 S. Hermosa St.
McDonough, Michael J. ... '63 '95 [Ⓐ A.S.Gomberg]
McDonough, Thomas C. ... '63 '88 C.339 B.S. L.966 J.D. [Neal,G.&E.] (Pat.)
McDougall, Donald T. ... '45 '73 C.694 A.B. L.145 J.D. Dept. of Health & Human Servs.
McDowell, Allen W. ... '40 '75 C.531 B.S. L.146 J.D. [McDowell&D.]
McDowell, Steven Frederick ... '55 '77 C&L.352 B.A., J.D. [Arnold&K.]
McDowell, William S., Jr. ... '41 '66 C&L.477 B.B.A., J.D. [Ⓒ Baker&M.]
McDowell & Drew Ltd. ... 35 E. Wacker Drive, Suite 1212
McDuffie, Elizabeth A. '63 '90 C.121 B.S. L.436 J.D.
(adm. in WI; not adm. in IL) [Gonzalez,S.&H.] (⊙Milw., WI)
McEachran, Daniel C., (AV) '32 '59
C.350 B.S.E.E. L.424 J.D. [Ⓒ Cook,A.M.M.C.&M.] (See Pat. Sect.)
McElligott, John A. ... '13 '39 C&L.597 B.A., J.D. Cir. J.
McElligott, Thos. J., (BV) ... '24 '51 C.424 B.S.C. L.276 J.D. 77 W. Washington
McElligott, William P. ... '63 '89 C.339 B.A. L.146 J.D. [Kiesler&B.]
McElroy, Christopher J., (AV) '50 '76
C.674 A.B. L.477 J.D. Sr. Corp. Coun., USG Corp.
Mcelwee, Terence Patrick ... '48 '78 C.959 B.S L.802 J.D. 1737 W. Polk St., Ste. 405
McEnery, Matthew T. ... '71 '99 C.742 B.A. L.365 J.D. [Gurber,M.&N.]
McEnroe, John T., (AV) ... '52 '77 C.339 B.S. L.976 J.D. [Vedder,P.K.&K.]
McErlean, William M., (AV) ... '— '78 C.602 B.A. L.276 J.D. [Barnes&T.]
McEvoy, Arthur ... '52 '89 C&L.813 A.B., J.D. Resch. Fellow, Amer. Bar Found.
McFadden, Christopher R. ... '75 '00 C.309 A.B. L.597 J.D. [Ⓐ Sidley A.B.&W.]
McFadden, Jennifer J. ... '76 '01 C.93 B.A. L.424 J.D. [Ⓐ Schueler,D.&C.]
McFadden, Patrick M. '55 '81 C.375 B.A. L.276 J.D.
(adm. in TX; not adm. in IL) Prof., Loyola Univ. Chicago Sch. of Law
McFadden, Roger J., (AV) ... '45 '71 C.602 A.B. L.339 J.D. [McFadden&D.]
McFadden, Sharon A. ... '50 '80 C&L.424 B.A., J.D. Arthur Andersen, LLP
McFadden, Thomas J., (BV) ... '54 '79 C&L.602 B.A., J.D. [Katten M.R.]
McFadden, Timothy S. ... '74 '01 C&L.602 B.A., J.D. [Ⓐ Lord,B.&B.]

McFadden & Dillon, A Professional Corporation, (AV)
120 South La Salle, Suite 1530, 60603
Telephone: 312-201-8300 Facsimile: 312-201-0535
Email: mcfaddendillonlaw@ameritech.net
Roger J. McFadden; Thomas J. Dillon;—Wendy Kaleta Skrobin; Timothy J. Somen.
General Civil Trial and Appellate Practice. Corporation, Securities, Estate Planning, Probate, Banking, Real Estate and Employment Law.

See Professional Biographies, CHICAGO, ILLINOIS

McFarland, Thomas F., (AV) ... '39 '65 C.636 B.S. L.424 J.D. [T.F.McFarland]
McFarland, Thomas F., PC, (AV) ... 208 South LaSalle Street, Suite 1890
McFarron, Gary W., (AV) '48 '74
C.679 B.S.M.E. L.597 J.D. [Cook,A.M.M.C.&M.] (See Pat. Sect.)
McFetridge, Jane M., (AV) ... '58 '89 C.339 B.S. L.597 J.D. [Fisher&P.]
McGaan, Andrew R., (P.C.), (AV) ... '— '86 C&L.188 A.B., J.D. [Kirkland&E.]
McGann, Patrick E., (AV) '47 '72 C.201 B.A. L.209 J.D.
Cir. Ct. of Cook Co., Chan. Div.
McGann, Terrance B. ... '61 '89 C.339 L.365 J.D. 2 N. LaSalle St., Ste. 1650
McGann-Ryan, Maureen J., (AV) '51 '76
C.338 B.S.Ed. L.209 J.D. 29 S. La Salle St., Ste. 640
McGarrah, Donald R., (AV) ... '53 '78 C.812 B.A. L.734 J.D. [Salvi,S.&P.]
McGarrity, Lisa A., (AV) ... '62 '88 C.966 B.B.A. L.597 J.D. [Franczek S.]
McGarry, John M., (AV) ... '58 '83 C.385 B.A. L.902 J.D. [Dykema G.P.]
McGarry, John T. ... '39 '65 C.1021 B.A. L.365 J.D. 1609 E. 53rd St.
McGarry, Thomas P., (AV) ... '51 '80 C.436 B.A. L.209 J.D. [Hinshaw&C.]
McGaugh, Raymond S. ... '54 '84 C&L.190 B.A., J.D. [Ⓒ Greenberg T.]
McGavic, Erin Ryan ... '— '94 C.321 B.A. L.424 J.D. 2018 N. Wolcott (Pat.)

McGee, Michael G., (AV) ....'— '77 C.1016 B.S.B.A. L.477 J.D. [Chapman&C.]
McGee, Michael J. '70 '97
C.259 B.S.E.E. L.365 J.D. [Cook,A.M.M.C.&M.] (See Pat. Sect.)
McGeehan, Christopher J. .....'70 '03 C.197 A.B. L.365 J.D. 300 S. Wacker Dr., Ste. 2500
Mcgeehan, Kelly Lynn ....'74 '01 C.1049 B.A. L.602 J.D. State Atty. Off.
McGill, Sandra Parker ....'67 '90 C.378 B.A. L.477 J.D. [McDermott W.&E.]
McGillen, Edward J. ....'57 '82 C.436 B.A. L.424 J.D. [Fuchs&R.]
McGing, James M. ....'61 '86 C&L.209 B.A., J.D. 6723 N. Northwest Highway
McGinn, Nerissa Coyle ....'72 '97 C.339 B.S. L.309 J.D. [Ⓐ Loeb&L.] (Pat.)
McGinness, Jeffrey K. ....'75 '01 C&L.352 B.A., J.D. [Ⓐ Wildman,H.A.&D.]
McGinnis, F. John ....'— '74 [Ⓑ Huff&G.]
McGinnis, Sheila M. ....'61 '89 C.436 B.A. L.365 J.D. Asst. State's Atty.
Mcginty, Kathleen A. ....'63 '97 C.339 B.S.N. L.424 J.D. [Ⓐ Salvi,S.&P.]
McGivern, Arthur J., (AV) ....'47 '74 C.973 B.S.B.A. L.597 J.D. 77 West Wacker Drive‡
McGivern, Arthur T. ....'09 '34 C&L.209 J.D. 1737 Howard St.‡
McGivern, Michael J., (BVⓉ) '52 '85
C.339 B.S. L.1119 J.D. Asst. Atty Gen., Off. of IL Atty. Gen.
McGivney, Catherine ....'60 '86 C.339 B.A. L.569 J.D. [Connelly R.&M.]
McGlothlen, Condon A., (AV) ....'61 '87 C.383 B.A. L.966 J.D. [Seyfarth S.]
McGonegle, Timothy J., (AV) ....'52 '77 C.352 B.A. L.424 J.D. [Schain,B.R.&C.]
McGonigal, Leo T., (BV) ....'52 '77 C.339 L.209 J.D. 53 W. Jackson Blvd., Ste. 1430
McGonigle, Tracy ....'— '93 C.424 B.A. L.209 J.D. [Ⓐ McKenna S.]
McGough, James J. '31 '61 C.103 A.B. L.705 J.D.
(adm. in AZ; not adm. in IL) 901 S. Plymouth‡
McGovern, John E., Jr., (AV) ... '31 '59 C.674 B.S.E. L.309 J.D. [Ⓑ Wildman,H.A.&D.]
McGovern, Linda A. '49 '80 C.150 B.S. L.1003 J.D.
(adm. in OH; not adm. in IL) Reg. Dir., U.S. Dept. of Educ.
McGovern, Lynn M. ....'61 '86 C.339 B.S. L.477 J.D. [Skadden,A.S.M.&F.]
McGovern, Patrick F. '72 '97 C.339 B.S. L.424 J.D.
Asst. U.S. Atty., Criminal Div., North. Dist. of IL.
McGovern, Peter J. '38 '64
C.602 A.B. L.262 J.D. Prof. of Law, John Marshall Law School
McGovern, Timothy S. ....'75 '01 C.339 B.A. L.365 J.D. [Snyder&M.]
McGowan, J. Geoffrey ....'55 '86 C.378 B.A. L.365 J.D. [McGowan&H.] ⊙
McGowan, Mark L. .....'51 '80 C.602 B.A. L.339 J.D. Coun., Quaker Foods & Beverages
McGowan, Michael J., (AV) ....'— '88 C.602 B.A. L.424 J.D. [O'Hagan,S.&A.]
McGowan and Hull, (BV) ....3 1st National Plaza, 70 West Madison (⊙Geneva)
McGrady, Paul D., Jr. ....'71 '96 C.130 B.A. L.209 J.D. [Greenberg T.]
McGrane, Michael P. ....'73 '01 C.339 B.S. L.146 J.D. [Ⓐ Skadden,A.S.M.&F.]
McGrath, Alastar S. ....'74 '99 C.339 B.S. L.424 J.D. 227 W. Monroe, Ste. 2000
Mcgrath, Bonnie C. ....'50 '93 C.339 B.S. L.365 J.D. 221 N Lasalle Street
McGrath, Brigid M. ....'59 '84 C.190 B.A. L.494 J.D. Assoc. Cir. J.
McGrath, Daniel W., (AV) ....'57 '82 C&L.424 B.A., J.D. [Hinshaw&C.]
Mcgrath, Katherine M. ....'— '94 C.347 B.S. L.146 J.D. P.O. Box 410533
McGrath, Margaret C. ....'58 '04 C.424 B.A. L.365 J.D. [Ⓐ Laner,M.D.B.L.&T.]
McGrath, Mary Ellen '— '90
C.436 B.A. L.424 J.D. V.P., Atty., Leo Burnett Worldwide, Inc.
McGrath, Patricia J. '— '98 C.720 B.S. L.146 J.D.
[McAndrews,H.&M.] (See Pat. Sect.)
McGrath, Richard A., (AV) ....'31 '56 C&L.424 B.S., J.D. 111 W. Wash. St.
McGrath, Robt. A. ....'16 '41 C.602 B.A. L.128 LL.B. Chi. Metal Mfg. Co.
McGrath, William J., (AV) .... '43 '70 C.363 A.B.cl. L.309 J.D. [McDermott W.&E.]
McGrath, William T., (AV) ....'51 '76 C.602 B.A. L.910 J.D. [Davis M.]
McGrath, William V. ....'51 '77 C.436 B.A. L.365 J.D. 303 W. Madison St.
McGree, Timothy V., (AV) ....'— '73 C&L.145 A.B., J.D. [Chapman&C.]
McGreevey, Robert M. ....'48 '76 C&L.608 B.A., J.D. 200 East Randolph Drive‡
McGrew, Theresa M. ....'— '77 C.720 B.A. L.209 J.D. Fed. Trade Comm.
McGrory, Timothy P. ....'70 '97 C.597 B.A. L.94 J.D. [Ⓐ Franczek S.]
McGuane, Melissa ....'77 '02 C.473 B.S. L.904 J.D. [Ⓐ Ross,D.&B.]
McGuffage, William M. ....'39 '94 C.801 B.S. L.365 J.D. 111 W. Washington St.
McGuigan, Philip P., (AVⓉ) ....'44 '69 C.103 A.B. L.494 J.D. [Gordon&G.L.]
McGuiness, Michelle ....'70 '01 C.339 B.A. L.145 J.D. [Ⓐ Katten M.R.]
McGuinn, William F. ....'68 '93 C.589 B.S. L.339 J.D. [Sugar,F.&F.]
McGuire, Bernadette C. '74 '03 C.174 B.A. L.1035 J.D.
(adm. in CO; not adm. in IL) [Ⓐ M.Cianciolo]
McGuire, Daniel J. ....'70 '96 C.884 B.A. L.145 J.D. [Winston&S.]
McGuire, David A., (AV) ....'46 '74 C.1016 B.S.B.A. L.209 J.D. [Stone,M.&S.] ⊙
McGuire, John A. ....'28 '60 C.589 B.E. L.365 B.L. 77 W. Washington St.
McGuire, Katriina S. ....'68 '96 C.911 B.A. L.424 J.D. [Ⓐ Schain,B.R.&C.]
McGuire, Mark ....'59 '97 C.767 B.A. L.209 J.D. Law Clk., Off. of Chf. J.
McGuire, Mark J., (AVⓉ) ....'53 '81 C.1102 B.A. L.734 J.D. [McGuirewoods]
McGuire, Maureen A., (AV) ....'56 '81 C.424 B.A.B.S. L.209 J.D. [MacCabe&M.]
McGuire, Patrick M. ....'64 '89 C&L.424 B.A., J.D. Asst. State Atty.
McGuire, Philip J., (AV) ..... '34 '62 C&L.424 A.B., J.D. 203 N. La Salle St., Suite 2100
Mcguire, Thomas F. ....'56 '00 C&L.209 Co. Ct. Crim. Div.
McGuire, Thomas F. ....'— '85 C&L.339 B.S., J.D. [Arnstein&L.]
McGuire-Martino, Paige '60 '85 C.347 B.S. L.365 J.D.
Staff Atty., National Ofc. Machine Dealers Assn.

McGuireWoods LLP, (AV)
77 West Wacker Drive Suite 4100, 60601-1815 ⊙
Telephone: 312-849-8100 Fax: 312-849-3690
Email: info@mcguirewoods.com URL: http://www.mcguirewoods.com
Partners: Richelle L. Aschenbrenner; Scott Becker; Lonni E. Berkley; Patrick E. Brady; Frederick H. Branding; Michael A. Chabraja; Leland H. Chait; Jeffrey C. Clark; Craig R. Culbertson; Darryl R. Davidson; Keith A. Dorman; Scott P. Downing; Linda B. Dubnow; Paul D. Durbin; Paul E. Fisher; Kara M. Friedman; Donald J. Gibson, Jr.; Larry R. Goldstein; Arnold E. Grant; Richard T. Greenberg; W. Kirk Grimm; David S. Guin; Janice K. Hamblin; James T. Harrington; David L. Hartsell; Gail Chaney Kalinich; Kimberly J. Kannensohn; Michael E. Kernan; Jacquelyn F. Kidder; Sally Doubet King; Henry deVos Lawrie, Jr.; Richard E. Lieberman; Leslie D. Locke; William Michael Long; Amy B. Manning; Richard J. Mason, P.C.; Mark J. McGuire; Richard L. Menson; John J. Michels, Jr.; Thomas R. Mulroy; Donald C. Pasulka; Russell M. Pelton; Michael R. Phillips; John F. Pollick; Robert J. Pristave, P.C.; Richard J. Rappaport; David L. Rieser; James B. Riley, Jr.; Jeffrey E. Rogers; Lawrence R. Samuels; Edward W. Schwartz; John L. Senica; William D. Serritella; Patricia K. Smoots; Joel H. Spitz; Gary L. Starkman; Marta A. Stein; Robert E. Wangard; Jay A. Yalowitz; Kevin J. Young; Paul C. Ziebert; Robert T. Zielinski. Retired Partners: Bruce J. McWhirter; David F. Sterling. Of Counsel: Joann Tansey Angarola; David N. McBride; James C. Williams. Associates: Tammy L. Adkins; Deborah Beerman; Melissa M. Bien; Philip S. Brewster (Not admitted in IL); Daniel Philip Bubar; Robert L. Carter; Carla M. Casas; Charles A. Cavallo, III; Bernard Cherkasov; Lisa L. Clay; Dawn M. Cutlan; Paul W. Doerscheln; Donald A. Ensing; Steven M. Evans; Thomas B. FitzGibbon; John Charles Gardner; Samantha C. Gordon; Blair B. Hanzlik; Colleen E. Helenhouse; James J. Hendrickson II; Jaime L. Hochhausen; Thomas H. Horenkamp; Cara M. Houck; Joseph J. Janatka; Rachel Goldstein Kempler; Elissa Boysen Koch; William L. Kuhn; John A. Leja; Gary Y. Leung, Jr.; Lincoln J. Lounsbury; Ronald Edward Lundeen, Jr.; Rachel Williams Mantz; David T. Meehan; Carlin R. Metzger; Alison Vratil Mikula; Peter A. Milianti; Pamela M. Miller; David A. P. Neboyskey; Brian P. O'Meara; Anne M. Peterson; Katie M. Rak; Nancy Mary Riley; Angelo M. Russo; Andrew S. Ryerson; Scott A. Schlautman; Michael M. Schmahl; Karen

(This Listing Continued)

McGuireWoods LLP (Continued)

Sewell; Jennifer A. Stojak; Melissa Szabad; Elizabeth S. Tenney; Jeffrey C. Torres; Carolyn M. Trenda; Christopher J. Verstrate; Barton C. Walker; Amber McGraw Walsh; Jacob A. Warden; Undray Wilks; Brianna J. Zielke.
Accountants Liability, Administrative Law, Advertising Law, Affordable Housing, Alternative Dispute Resolution, Americans with Disabilities Act, Antitrust, Appellate Practice, Asbestos Litigation, Asset Based Finance, Automotive Products Liability, Bankruptcy, Banks and Banking, Business Acquisitions, Business Divestitures, Business Law, Business Litigation, Buying and Selling of Businesses, Capital Markets, Charitable Giving, Class Actions, Coal Mining, Cogeneration; College and University Law, Commercial Litigation, Commercial Real Estate, Communications and Media, Complex Commercial Litigation, Computer Contracts, Confidentiality Agreements, Construction Equipment Liability, Construction Litigation, Consumer Finance, Content Licensing, Contracts, Copyright Licensing, Corporate Control Contests, Corporate Finance, Corporate Governance, Corporate Investigations, Corporate Law, Corporate Reorganization, Covenants Not to Compete, Creditors Rights, Criminal Taxation, Digital Signatures, Domain Name Infringement, Domain Names, Drug and Medical Device Defense, Drug and Medical Device Litigation, E-Commerce, Education Law, Electric Utilities, Emerging Growth Companies, Employee Benefits, Employee Benefits Litigation, Employment Breach of Contract, Employment Contracts, Employment Discrimination, Energy, Energy Acquisitions, Energy Project Development, Energy Regulation, Entertainment Law, Environmental Administrative Law, Environmental Compliance, Environmental Land Use, Environmental Law, Environmental Litigation, Environmental Real Estate, ERISA, Executive Compensation, False Advertising, Family Business Law, Fiduciary Litigation, Finance, First Amendment Law, Franchises and Franchising, Gas Utilities, Government Investigations, Government Relations, Health Care, High Technology Contracts, Hospital Administration, Hospital Law, Hostile Takeovers, Immigration Law, Independent Power, Insurance Litigation, Intellectual Property, Intellectual Property Licensing, Intellectual Property Litigation, Intellectual Property Portfolio Management, Intellectual Property Procurement, Intellectual Property Rights, International Arbitration, International Mergers and Acquisitions, International Taxation, International Trade, Internet Licensing, Joint Venture Litigation, Joint Ventures, Labor and Employment, Labor Relations, Land Use, Latex Allergy Litigation, Lead Poisoning, Leasing, Legal Ethics and Professional Responsibility, Leveraged Buyouts, Litigation, Litigation Management, Lobbying, Local Taxation, Marketing Law, Media Law, Merger Reorganization, Mergers and Acquisitions Finance, Mergers, Acquisitions and Divestitures, Motorcycle Products Liability, Municipal Law, Music Law, Natural Gas, North American Energy Trade, Oil and Gas Law, Partnership Law, Partnership Litigation, Partnership Taxation, Patent Litigation, Patent Prosecution, Patents, Petroleum Trading, Products Liability, Products Liability Insurance Coverage, Project Finance, Promotion Law, Proprietary Rights, Proxy Contests, Public Finance, Public Utility Law, Railroad Law, Real Estate, Real Estate Acquisitions, Real Estate Development, Real Estate Investment Trusts, Real Estate Leasing, Regulatory Law, Resorts and Leisure, Securities, Securities Litigation, Securities Regulation, Securitization, Software Copyright, Software Licensing, Software Protection, Spin-Offs, Sponsorship Law, Sports Law, Sports Licensing, Sports Marketing Law, State Taxation, Structured Finance, Sweepstakes, Takeovers, Tax Audits, Tax Credits, Tax Exempt Organizations, Tax Litigation, Taxation, Technology Licensing, Telephone Utility Regulation, Toxic Tort Class Actions, Toxic Torts, Trade Regulation, Trade Secrets, Trademark Registration, Trademarks, Transportation, Trusts and Estates, Trusts and Estates Taxation, Union Labor Law, Utility Law, Utility Regulation, Vaccine Injury, Web Site Development, White Collar Crime, Wrongful Termination.
Atlanta, Georgia Office: The Proscenium, 1170 Peachtree Street, N.E., Suite 2100, 30309-7649. Telephone: 404-443-5500. Fax: 404-443-5599.
Baltimore, Maryland Office: 7 Saint Paul Street, Suite 1000, 21202-1671. Telephone: 410-659-4400. Fax: 410-659-4599.
Charlotte, North Carolina Office: Bank of America Corporate Center, Suite 2900, 100 North Tryon Street, 28202-4011. Telephone: 704-373-8999. Fax: 704-373-8935.
Charlottesville, Virginia Office: Court Square Building, 310 Fourth Street N.E., Suite 300, P.O. Box 1288, 22902-1288. Telephone: 434-977-2500. Fax: 434-980-2222.
Jacksonville, Florida Office: Bank of America Tower, 50 North Laura Street, Suite 3300, 32202-3661. Telephone: 904-798-3200. Fax: 904-798-3207.
Los Angeles, California Office: 11601 Wilshire Boulevard, 90025. Telephone: 310-575-1848.
McLean, (Tysons Corner) Virginia Office: 1750 Tysons Boulevard, Suite 1800, 22102-4215. Telephone: 703-712-5000. Fax: 703-712-5050.
New York, New York Offices: 1345 Avenue of the Americas, 10105-0106. Telephone: 212-548-2100. Fax: 212-548-2150.
Norfolk, Virginia Office: World Trade Center, 101 West Main Street, Suite 9000, 23510-1655. Telephone: 757-640-3700. Fax: 757-640-3701.
Pittsburgh, Pennsylvania Office: Dominion Tower, 23rd Floor, 625 Liberty Avenue, 15222-3142. Telephone: 412-667-6000. Fax: 412-667-6050.
Richmond, Virginia Office: One James Center, 901 East Cary Street, 23219-4030. Telephone: 804-775-1000. Fax: 804-775-1061.
Washington, D.C. Office: Washington Square, 1050 Connecticut Avenue, N.W., Suite 1200, 20036-5317. Telephone: 202-857-1700. Fax: 202-857-1737.
Almaty, Republic of Kazakhstan Office: McGuireWoods Kazakhstan LLP, 41B, Kazibek Bi Street, 5th Floor, 480100. Telephone: +7-3272-596-100. Fax: +7-3272-596-116.
Brussels, Belgium Office: Avenue Louise 250, bte 64, 1050. Telephone: +32-(0)2-629-42-11. Fax: +32 (0)2 629 42 22.
Reviser of the Virginia Law Digest for this Directory.
See Professional Biographies, CHICAGO, ILLINOIS

McGunn, Lori R. ....'— '94 C.347 B.S. L.345 J.D. [Ungaretti&H.]
McGurk, James A., (AV) ....'48 '73 C&L.339 B.A., J.D. [Ⓑ Stack&F.]
McGury, Kathleen M. ....'52 '77 C.741 B.A. L.146 J.D. Asst. States Atty.
Mchale, Michael ....'63 '91 C.912 B.S. L.209 J.D. Asst. States Atty.
McHenry, Luke C. ....'76 '03 C.910 B.A. L.597 J.D. [Ⓐ Kaplan,v.&M.]
McHugh, David P. ....'— '97 C.882 B.A. L.823 J.D. [Schiff H.]
McHugh, John J., (AV) ....'34 '61 C&L.424 B.S., J.D. [Michael B.&F.]
McHugh, Robert D., (AV) ....'32 '59 C.276 B.S. L.424 J.D. 20 N. Wacker Dr.
McIlroy, Terry A., (AV) ....'— '70 C.911 B.A. L.145 J.D. [Chapman&C.]
McInerney, Donald B. ....'34 '68 C.966 B.S. L.146 J.D. 50 S. La Salle St.
McInerney, John J., Jr., (AV) ....'54 '80 C.602 A.B. L.209 J.D. [Leahy,E.&F.]
McInerney, Mary M. .....'— '79 C&L.424 B.A., J.D. Assoc. Exec. Dir., Health Fac. Auth.
McInnis, Gerard A., (BV) '64 '90 C.801 B.A. L.339 J.D.
320 West Ohio Street, Suite 500
McIntosh, Joseph Thomas ....'— '97 C.352 B.B.A. L.597 J.D. Invest. Bkg., Merrill Lynch
McIntyre, J. Bates ....'— '00 C.293 B.A. L.339 J.D. [Ⓐ Perkins C.]
McKann, George C., (AV) ....'42 '66 C.399 B.A. L.597 J.D. [Gardner C.&D.]
McKay, Daniel C., II, (AV) ....'58 '84 C.602 B.A. L.424 J.D. [Vedder,P.K.&K.]
McKay, James P., Jr. ....'58 '84 C.209 B.A. L.146 J.D. Asst. States Atty.
McKay, John J. ....'62 '91 C.700 B.A. L.424 J.D. Asst. State's Atty.
McKay, Laura S. ....'66 '91 C.550 B.S. L.94 J.D. [Lord,B.&B.]
McKay, Neil, (AV) ....'17 '46 C&L.477 A.B., J.D. 1 First National Plaza‡
McKay, Timothy J. ....'54 '79 C.602 B.A. L.424 J.D. [McKay,N.T.D.&K.]
McKay, William S., Jr. ....'— '72 C.25 B.A. L.597 J.D. [Ⓑ Jones D.]

McKay, Nora, Tanzillo, Daddino & Kott, LLP, (AV)
10 South LaSalle Street, Suite 2700, 60603
Telephone: 312-650-7900 Fax: 312-650-7910
Members of Firm: Timothy J. McKay; Robert L. Nora; Paul A. Tanzillo; Christopher M. Daddino; Andrea H. Kott; Lynne M. Reardon Damsma. Associates: Vincent Michael Auricchio; Stuart L. Berman; Kevin M. Bugos; Caroline E. Carlson; Ryan T. Johnson; Brad Schulman.
Insurance Defense, Medical Malpractice, Pharmacist Liability, Premises Liability, Insurance Fraud and Coverage Issues.
See Professional Biographies, CHICAGO, ILLINOIS

McKee, Dovette ....'— '80 4939 S. Saint Lawrence Ave
McKee, H. Anne ....'60 '85 C.132 B.A. L.209 J.D. 222 N. La Salle St.
McKee, Harold E. ....'60 '87 C.734 B.S.B.A. L.365 J.D. [Riordan,D.L.&M.]
McKee, Howard A., (AV) ....'15 '41 C.132 A.B. L.597 J.D. 2 First Natl. Plaza
McKee, Kathleen J. ....'59 '84 C.734 B.S. L.744 J.D. Asst. States Atty., Cook Cty.
McKeever, Michael ....'— '90 C.813 B.A. L.597 J.D. [Pircher,N.&M.]
McKeever, Roberta Sessa ....'64 '90 C.93 B.A. L.597 J.D. 2844 N. Cambridge‡

McKeever, Susan L. .... '63 '97 C.31 B.A. L.597 J.D. [🄰 Sidley A.B.&W.]
McKenna, Edward P. .... '75 '04 C.846 B.A. L.597 J.D. [🄰 Jenner&B.]
McKenna, Gregory James .... '74 '01 C.602 B.A. L.424 J.D. [🄰 Cremer,K.S.&S.]
McKenna, James A., (AV) .... '52 '77 C.201 B.A. L.597 J.D. [Jenner&B.]
McKenna, Kevin M. .... '— '90 C.602 B.A. L.477 J.D. [🄲 Kirkland&E.]
McKenna, Mark R., (BV) .... '68 '94 C.597 B.A. L.339 J.D. [Hurley,M.&M.]
McKenna, Michael R., (AV) '48 '76 C.339 B.S. L.146 J.D.
[Firm of M.R.McKenna] (Pat.) (⊙Kailua-Kona, HI; Northbrook, IL)
McKenna, Shannon D. .... '69 '97 C.612 B.A. L.209 J.D. 321 S. Plymouth Court
McKenna, William J., Jr., (AV) .... '— '79 C.478 B.A. L.145 J.D. [Foley&L.]

McKenna, Michael R., P.C., The Law Firm of, (AV)
500 West Madison Street, Suite 3800, 60661
Telephone: 312-321-0123 Fax: 312-876-2020 URL: http://www.ChicagoPatent.com
Email: info@ChicagoPatent.com URL: http://www.lawyers.com/mckennalawfirm
Michael R. McKenna.
Patent, Trademark and Copyright Law, including prosecution, licensing and dispute resolution.
See Professional Biographies, CHICAGO, ILLINOIS

McKenna Storer, (AV)
33 N. La Salle Street 14th Floor, 60602-2610 ⊙
Telephone: 312-558-3900 Fax: 312-558-8348
Email: postmaster-@mckenna-law.com URL: http://www.mckenna-law.com
William J. McKenna (1923-1975); John F. White (1929-2002). Attorneys: Richard M. Clark (Resident, Waukegan Office) (For complete biographical data, see Waukegan Office); Gregory L. Cochran; Sara E. Cook (Resident, Woodstock Office) (For complete biographical data, see Woodstock Office); John A. Culver; James P. DeNardo; John W. Egan; Dawn E. Ehrenberg; Tina L. Fink; Margaret Marie Foster; Terry A. Fox; Thomas W. Hayes; Patricia C. Kraft (Resident, Woodstock Office) (For complete biographical data, see Woodstock Office); Thomas F. Lucas; Bruce B. Marr; Tracy McGonigle; Timothy J. Murtaugh, III; Paige Moray Neel; William S. Piper; Robert P. Pisani; Samuel A. Purves; Julie A. Ramson; Thomas A. Reed; Richard J. Rettberg; Kristin Dvorsky Tauras; Justin L. Terry.
Administrative Hearings, Appellate, Banking and Lending, Bankruptcy, Civil Rights, Commercial, Construction, Employment, Estate Planning, Fidelity, Insurance Coverage, Legal Malpractice, Mediation Services, Medical Malpractice, National Coordination, Personal Injury, Products Liability, Professional Liability, Surety, Tax and Toxic Tort.
Waukegan, Illinois Office: 33 North County Street, 6th Floor, 60085-4343. Telephone: 847-249-1620. Fax: 847-249-8457.
Woodstock, Illinois Office: 666 Russel Court, Suite 303, 60098-2672. Telephone: 815-334-9690. Fax: 815-334-9697.
See Professional Biographies, CHICAGO, ILLINOIS

McKenzie, Ann C. .... '62 '90 C.597 B.S. L.209 J.D. Dev. Mgr., The Habitat Co.
McKenzie, Claire R. .... '60 '91 C.589 B.A. L.424 J.D. [🄰 Schiller,D.&F.]
McKenzie, Daniel E. .... '— '03 C.477 B.A. L.597 J.D. [🄰 Horwitz,H.&Assoc.]
McKenzie, Diana J.P., (AV) .... '59 '86 C.385 B.A. L.245 J.D. [Neal,G.&E.]
McKenzie, Martin J. '61 '96
C.338 B.A. L.424 J.D. Client Development, Applied Discovery, Inc.
McKenzie, Robert E., (AV) .... '— '79 C.475 B.A. L.146 J.D. [Arnstein&L.]
McKenzie, Steven Q. .... '66 '97 C.475 B.A. L.146 J.D. App. Def. Off.
Mckenzie, Theresa Wolf .... '— '77 C.339 L.365 120 S. Riverside Plaza
McKeon, Megan M., Attorney at Law '79 '05 C.741 B.B.A L.365 J.D.
320 W. Illinois St.
McKevitt, Martin O., Jr. '29 '57
C.602 B.S. L.477 J.D. Secy. & Coun., Energy Cooperative, Inc.
McKey, S. Patrick .... '60 '89 C&L.966 B.S., J.D. [Bell,B.&L.]
McKie, John E. '56 '82 C.602 B.A. L.273 J.D.
(adm. in DC; not adm. in IL) [Ladas&P.]
McKinley, Anne Catherine '74 '99
C.597 B.A. L.339 J.D. Sr. Atty., U.S. Secs. & Exchange & Comm.
McKinley, Richard B. .... '53 '84 C.966 B.A. L.209 J.D. 77 W. Washington St.
McKinney, Jason .... '76 '02 C.502 B.A. L.910 J.D. [🄰 Patterson]
McKinney, Laura L. .... '— '00 C.806 B.A. L.37 J.D. [🄰 Chapman&C.]
McKinney, Luther C., (AV) .... '31 '59 C.350 B.S. L.339 LL.B. Sr. V.P., Quaker Oats Co.
Mckinzie, L. Rachel '— '91 C.339 B.S. L.146 J.D.
Legal Coun., State Dept. of Corrections
McKnight, Cornelius E. .... '64 '92 C.436 B.A. L.861 J.D. [🄰 Condon&C.]
McKnight, James L. .... '66 '91 C.273 B.A. L.94 J.D. [S.G.Thomas]
McKnight, Megan P. .... '— '03 C.373 B.A. L.477 J.D. [🄰 Katten M.R.]
McKone, David .... '— '02 C.475 B.S. L.477 J.D. [🄰 Latham&W.]

McLachlan, Rissman & Doll
676 North Michigan Avenue, Suite 2800, 60611
Telephone: 312-266-2444 Telecopier: 312-266-3330
Members of Firm: Donald J. McLachlan (1937-1992); Thomas W. Rissman; John H. Doll; Laural S. Jin. Associate: Alison C. Madauss. Counsel: Anthony E. Rothschild.
Acquisition and Financing Transactions; General Corporate; Railroads; Rail Equipment Finance; Commercial Transactions.
See Professional Biographies, CHICAGO, ILLINOIS

McLaren, Richard W., Jr., (AVⓉ) .... '45 '73 C.976 B.A. L.597 J.D. [Welsh&K.]
McLauchlan, David C., (AV) .... '46 '72 C.98 B.A. L.339 J.D. [Lord,B.&B.]
McLaughlin, Daniel P. .... '77 '04 C.436 B.A. L.339 J.D. [🄰 Jenner&B.]
McLaughlin, Ellen E., (AV) .... '56 '81 C&L.602 B.A., J.D. [Seyfarth S.]
McLaughlin, F. William, (AV) '56 '85
C.602 B.S.E.E. L.209 J.D. [Wood,P.K.C.&M.] (See Pat. Sect.)
McLaughlin, James T., Jr. .... '— '05 C.260 B.A. L.597 J.D. [🄰 Kirkland&E.]
McLaughlin, Kenneth S., Jr. '68 '95
C.597 B.A. L.365 J.D. 290 S. County Farm Rd., Ste. M
McLaughlin, Robert Hugh '72 '98 C.178 B.A. L.145 J.D.
(adm. in NY; not adm. in IL) Anthropolgy Dept., Univ. of Chicago
McLaughlin, Robert John .... '75 '00 C.234 B.S. L.1000 J.D. [🄰 Segal M.S.&M.]
McLaughlin, T. Mark, (AV) .... '53 '78 C&L.602 B.A., J.D. [Mayer,B.R.&M.]
McLawhorn, Todd L. .... '67 '92 C.232 B.A. L.575 J.D. [Howrey]
McLean, Lisa J. '77 '02 C.347 B.S. L.309 J.D.
Asst. Gen. Coun., Deerfield Capital Mgmt. LLC
McLean, Michael .... '48 '79 C.234 B.A. L.990 J.D. IL Dept. of Employ. Sec.
McLees, John A., (AV) .... '48 '74 C&L.145 B.A., J.D. [Baker&M.]
McLeese, Richard H., (AV) '52 '81
C.72 B.A. L.145 J.D. 900 West Jackson Boulevard, Suite 6W
McLellan, Ann .... '— '02 C.477 B.A. L.597 J.D. [🄰 O'Hagan,S.&A.]
McLennan, Ryan H. .... '— '02 C.880 B.A. L.597 J.D. [🄰 Greenberg T.]
McLennon, Paul A., Jr., (AV) ...... '50 '76 C.602 B.B.A. L.209 J.D. [McLennon&Assoc.]
McLennon & Associates, (AV) .... 100 North La Salle Street
McLeod, Peter C. .... '70 '02 C.679 B.A. L.146 J.D. [🄰 Hughes S.P.R.&D.]
McMahan, Carol Sharpe .... '51 '85 C&L.878 J.D. [Carroll,H.&C.]
McMahan, Charles .... '52 '89 C.1183 B.S. L.365 J.D. 5345 W. Ardmore
McMahan, Janette A. .... '— '98 C.197 B.A. L.597 J.D. [Kirkland&E.]
McMahan, Parker F., Jr., (BV) .... '38 '68 C.72 B.A. L.146 J.D. [McMahan&C.]
McMahan & Cavenagh, Ltd., (BV) .... 216 W. Jackson Blvd.
McMahon, Anthony J. '68 '02
C.424 B.A. L.365 J.D. Claims Consultant, CNA Insurance Cos.

McMahon, Brendan T. .... '71 '02 C.473 B.A. L.146 J.D. [🄰 Schuyler,R.&Z.]
McMahon, Charles M. '74 '99
C.602 B.S.E.E. L.273 J.D. [🄰 Brinks H.G.&L.] (See Pat. Sect.)
McMahon, Daniel J., (AV) .... '63 '89 C&L.602 B.A., J.D. [Wilson E.M.E.&D.]
McMahon, Eugene F., (AV) .... '30 '62 C&L.424 B.S., J.D. 120 W. Madison St., Ste. 725
McMahon, Gregory M. .... '73 '02 C.800 B.S. L.209 J.D. [🄰 Segal M.S.&M.]
McMahon, Jennifer .... '66 '94 C.339 B.S. L.276 J.D. Asst. Gen. Coun., Exelon Corp.
McMahon, Kristin Dodge .... '65 '90 C.1030 B.S. L.94 J.D. [🄲 Kerns,P.F.&P.]
McMahon, Marshal I., Jr., (AV) '34 '63 C.174 A.B. L.424 J.D.
180 N. Stetson, Ste. 4525
McMahon, Thomas E. '45 '74 C.602 B.A. L.424 J.D.
(adm. in VA; not adm. in IL)
V.P., Wash. Rel. & Eastern Coun., National Automatic Merchandising Assn.
McMahon, Timothy D., (AV) .... '52 '77 C.363 B.A. L.209 J.D. [Wiedner&M.]
McMannon, Steven R. .... '57 '83 C.1193 B.B.A. L.336 J.D. [Tressler,S.M.&P.]
McManus, Brian J., (AV) .... '46 '73 C.602 B.A. L.209 J.D. [B.J.McManus&Assoc.]
McManus, Colleen E. .... '72 '97 C.347 B.A. L.209 J.D. [🄰 DLPiper R.G.C.U.]
McManus, James J. .... '40 '66 C&L.209 B.A., J.D. [Henehan,D.&I.]
McManus, Brian J., & Associates, Ltd., (AV) .... 30 N. La Salle St.
McMaster, William G., Jr., (AV) .... '— '73 C.473 B.A. L.597 J.D. [Foley&L.]
McMasters, James W. .... '62 '90 C&L.597 B.S., J.D. Northwestern Univ. Sch. of Law
McMenamin, J. Robert, (AV) .... '46 '71 C&L.602 B.A., J.D. [McDermott W.&E.]
McMenamin, Paula Hunt .... '67 '93 C.800 B.S. L.910 J.D. [McDermott W.&E.]
McMenamin, Thomas P. .... '— '80 C.602 B.A. L.276 J.D. [Masuda,F.E.&M.]
McMillan, Bart M. .... '70 '99 C.1131 B.A. L.569 J.D. [🄰 Baker&M.]
McMillan, D. Mark, (BV) .... '63 '89 C.938 B.A. L.424 J.D. [Bell,B.&L.]
McMillian, Nabeela R. .... '— '03 [🄰 Marshall,G.&B.] (See Pat. Sect.)
McMillin, Scott .... '— '96 C.951 B.A. L.309 J.D. [Kirkland&E.]
McMorrow, Doris Schumacher, (BV) '51 '77
C.881 B.A. L.818 J.D. [Davis F.Z.K.M.M.&R.]
McMorrow, Michael J. .... '— '00 C.976 B.A. L.339 J.D. [🄰 Foley&L.]
McMullan, Sandra J. .... '67 '02 C.1375 B.A. L.472 J.D. [🄰 Meckler B.&T.]
McMurry, Gayle M. .... '52 '89 C.477 B.S.N. L.209 J.D. 1210 Astor St.
McMurtrie, Amanda H. .... '77 '03 C.477 B.A. L.966 J.D. [🄰 Grippo&E.]
McMurtrie, Daniel C. .... '77 '03 C.477 B.A. L.966 J.D. [🄰 Jenner&B.]
McNab, Kay .... '62 '88 C&L.339 B.A., J.D. [Winston&S.]
McNabola, Edward W., (AV) .... '66 '92 C.473 B.A. L.426 J.D. [Cogan&M.]
McNabola, Mark E., (AV) .... '59 '85 C&L.209 B.A., J.D. [Cogan&M.]
McNair, Andrew D. .... '78 '03 C.260 B.S. L.1565 J.D. [🄰 Gardner C.&D.]
McNally, Carrie C. .... '69 '95 C.228 B.A. L.276 J.D. [Bell,B.&L.]
McNally, Laura K. .... '69 '95 C.597 B.A. L.861 J.D. [Grippo&E.]
McNamara, Ana M. .... '68 '98 C.209 B.S. L.365 J.D. 910 W. Van Buren, Suite 119
McNamara, Jill M. .... '70 '95 C.597 B.S. L.436 J.D. [🄰 Gould&R.]
McNamara, John L. .... '70 '95 C.339 B.A. L.146 J.D. [McNamara&A.]
McNamara, Kevin J. .... '69 '95 C.347 B.A. L.365 J.D. [McNamara&A.]
McNamara, Paddy Harris .... '43 '73 C.112 B.A. L.209 J.D. Cir. J.
McNamara, Robert R., (AV) .... '62 '87 C.602 B.A. L.424 J.D. [Johnson&B.]
McNamara, Thomas W., (AV) .... '31 '56 C.602 B.A. L.597 LL.B. 1 IBM Plaza

McNamara & Austin, P.C.
25 East Washington - Suite 1501, 60602
Telephone: 312-201-8850 Fax: 312-201-8853
Email: austin@mafirm.com URL: http://www.mafirm.com
Edward J. Austin; John L. McNamara; Kevin J. McNamara.
Civil Trial Practice, Criminal Defense, Driving While Intoxicated, Drug Crimes, Felonies, Homicide, Misdemeanors, Parole and Probation, Sexual Assault, Traffic Violations, Suspended License Offenses, Personal Injury, Automobile Accidents, Medical Malpractice and Real Estate Law.
See Professional Biographies, CHICAGO, ILLINOIS

McNamer, Amy M. '68 '96 C.309 B.A. L.276 J.D.
(adm. in CA; not adm. in IL) Staff Atty., Midwest Reg. Off., Secs. & Exch. Comm.
McNaughton, Michael .... '72 '00 C.145 B.A. L.146 J.D. [🄰 Michaels&M.]
McNeil, Donald J., (AV) .... '— '86 C.276 B.S. L.424 J.D. [Barnes&T.]
McNerney, Patrick J., (AV) .... '57 '82 C.424 B.S. L.365 J.D. [Mayer,B.R.&M.]
McNicholas, Janet M., (AV) '51 '86
C.700 B.A. L.145 J.D. [McAndrews,H.&M.] (See Pat. Sect.)
McNish, Robert J., Jr., (AV) .... '43 '69 C&L.494 B.A., J.D. [McNish,K.&K.]
McNish, Knabe and Kroning, (AV) .... 20 S. Clark St.
McNown, Lynne E. .... '44 '69 C&L.339 A.B., J.D. Coun., Ameritech Corp.
McNulty, Jill .... '35 '60 C&L.597 B.A., J.D. 160 N. Lasalle St., Ste. 1608
McNulty, John W., (AV) .... '27 '55 C.309 A.B. L.597 J.D. Asst. State Atty.
McNulty, Peter J., (AV) .... '51 '76 C&L.276 B.S.B.A., J.D. [🄲 Huff&G.]
McNulty, Shannon M. .... '71 '04 C.424 B.S. L.209 J.D. [🄰 Clifford]
McNulty, Thomas J., (AV) .... '51 '76 C.602 B.S. L.1292 J.D. [Neal,G.&E.]
McNulty, Thomas P., (AV) .... '— '89 C&L.347 B.A., J.D. [Jones D.]
McParland, James E., (AV) .... '46 '72 C.750 B.A. L.365 J.D. [McParland&P.]

McParland & Phillips, LLC, (AV)
221 N. La Salle Street, Suite 463, 60601
Telephone: 312-634-1100 Fax: 312-634-1101
Email: jmcpar8174@aol.com
James E. McParland; William B. Phillips.
Corporate, Commercial, Real Estate, Employment and Health Care Law.
See Professional Biographies, CHICAGO, ILLINOIS

McPherson, Marena L. .... '49 '83 C.97 B.A. L.365 J.D. The Committee of 200
McPike, Timothy K. '49 '76 C&L.37 B.S., J.D.
(adm. in AZ; not adm. in IL) Asst. Atty. Gen.
McQueen, Thomas K., (AV) .... '— '74 C.172 B.A. L.209 J.D. [Sonnenschein N.&R.]
McQueeney, Neal B. '74 '99 C.94 B.A. L.1202 J.D.
(adm. in MA; not adm. in IL) 333 West Wacker Drive, Suite 500
McQuillan, Kevin K., (AV) .... '51 '77 C&L.966 B.S.M.E., J.D. [Kiesler&M.]
McQuillen, Michael G., (AV) .... '— '84 C.338 B.S. L.365 J.D. [Adler,M.&M.]
McRee, Elizabeth B. .... '— '01 C.198 B.A. L.1191 J.D. [🄰 Jones D.]
McShane, Amy E. .... '72 '97 C.712 B.A. L.94 J.D. [🄰 Holland&K.]
McShane, Antony J. .... '60 '85 C.339 B.A. L.209 J.D. [Neal,G.&E.]
McSherry, Jerome G. '52 '79 C.927 B.A. L.801 J.D.
Insurance Staff Counsel, American International Companies
McSweeney, Helen J., (AV) .... '59 '84 C.976 B.A. L.597 J.D. [Gardner C.&D.]
McSweeney, W. Donald, (AV) .... '20 '48 C&L.309 A.B., LL.B. [🄲 Schiff H.]
McSweeny, Thomas A. .... '40 '65 C.734 B.S. L.145 J.D. Price Waterhouse
McTigue, Christine Olson .... '60 '84 C.494 B.A. L.424 J.D. [Hinshaw&C.]
McTurnan, Sarah D. .... '73 '02 C.597 B.A. L.145 J.D. [🄰 Grippo&E.]
McVane, Jim '— '79 C.93 B.A. L.589 J.D.
Asst. Cable Admin., City of Chicago Off. of Cable Comm.
McVety, Christopher A. .... '— '01 C&L.477 B.A., J.D. [🄰 Sachnoff&W.]
McVicker, Tricia E. .... '71 '02 C.999 B.S.N. L.365 J.D. [🄰 Dykema G.P.]
McVisk, William K., (AV) '53 '77 C.339 B.A. L.597 J.D.
[Johnson&B.] (⊙Highland, IN)

McWhirter, Andrew H. ... '— '00 C.659 B.A. L.477 J.D. [Ⓐ Kirkland&E.]
McWhirter, Bruce J., (AV) ... '31 '55 C.597 B.S. L.309 LL.B. [McGuirewoods] ‡
McWilliams, Dennis M., (AV) '— '68
C.602 B.A. L.424 J.D. [Barnes&T.] (See Pat. Sect.)
McWilliams, Janet Lynn '70 '00
C.427 B.A. L.146 J.D. Sr. Atty., Driehaus Capital Management, Inc.
McWilliams, Mary Kruit ... '67 '95 C.999 B.A. L.424 J.D. [Ⓐ McDermott W.&E.]
McWilliams, Robert A. ... '— '83 C.347 B.S. L.339 J.D. [Freeborn&P.]
Meacham, Clifford L. ... '45 '77 C.238 B.A. L.365 J.D. Assoc. Cir. J.
Meacham, Owen Thomas '71 '98 C.676 B.S. L.818 J.D.
V.P. & Prod. Analyst, ABN AMRO Asset Management, Prod. Strategy & Develop.
Meachum, Lauren K. ... '55 '80 C.927 B.A. L.339 J.D. Liberty Mutual Ins. Grp.
Mead, Jessica J. ... '77 '03 C.162 B.A. L.221 J.D. [Ⓐ Krislov&Assoc.]
Mead, Stephen B. ... '69 '95 C.494 B.A. L.966 J.D. Sr. Coun., SBC Communications Inc.
Meador, Mark D. '64 '89 C&L.245 B.A., J.D.
(adm. in GA; not adm. in IL) Reg. Gen. Coun., Aetna U.S. Healthcare Inc.
Meadors, Gayle M. ... '46 '77 C.339 A.B. L.209 J.D. [G.M.Meadors]

Meadors, Gayle M., P.C.
20 South Clark Street, 25th Floor, 60603
Telephone: 312-558-1255
Email: gmm@erisalaw-chicago.com URL: http://www.erisalaw-chicago.com
Gayle M. Meadors.
Employee Benefits, ERISA.
See Professional Biographies, CHICAGO, ILLINOIS

Meadows, Stanley H., (AV) ... '45 '70 C.339 B.A. L.145 J.D. [McDermott W.&E.]
Meany, John Stewart, Jr. ... '45 '70 C&L.602 B.A., J.D. 9200 S. Winchester Ave.
Mears, John S. '23 '51 C&L.273 A.B., J.D.
(adm. in DC; not adm. in IL) Asst. Dist. Coun., Vet. Admn.
Mebane, Adrienne D. ... '59 '84 C&L.209 B.A., J.D. Asst. State's Atty.
Mech, Raymond R. ... '30 '53 C&L.146 B.L., J.D. 39 S. LaSalle St.
Meckler, Bruce R., (AV) ... '55 '81 C.98 B.A. L.365 J.D. [Meckler B.&T.]

Meckler Bulger & Tilson, (AV) BR
123 North Wacker Drive, Suite 1800, 60606
Telephone: 312-474-7900 Facsimile: 312-474-7898
URL: http://www.mbtlaw.com
Members of Firm: Jeffrey A. Berman; Anne L. Blume; Brian W. Bulger; Jack J. Carriglio; Janet R. Davis; John E. DeLascio; Karen M. Dixon; J. Stuart Garbutt; Paul R. Garry; Brent J. Graber; J. Robert Hall; Rebecca R. Haller; Brett D. Heinrich; Christopher S. Hennessy; James J. Hickey; Richard A. Hodyl, Jr.; James H. Kallianis, Jr.; Christopher E. Kentra; Philip R. King; Mari Henry Leigh; Michael I. Leonard; Michael S. Loeffler; Eric E. Lynch; Michael M. Marick; Kent Maynard, Jr.; Bruce R. Meckler; Ziyad I. Naccasha; Steven D. Pearson; Pamela G. Perrone; Alan M. Posner; Don R. Sampen; Jason R. Schulze; Scott M. Seaman; Mark J. Seplak; Jerome C. Studer, Jr.; Joseph E. Tilson; Julie L. Trester; Peter J. Valeta; Matthew R. Wildermuth; Brian J. Williams; Timothy A. Wolfe. Associates: Robert J. Ambrose; James G. Argionis; Eileen E. Baker; Phillip Beth; Lauren W. Blatt; David D. Brown; Robert E. Browne, Jr.; Yukyong Choi; Matthew C. Cohn; Seth E. Darmstadter; Blair L. Dawson; Victoria Dizik; Mitchell J. Edlund; Lynn Geerdes-Lugo; Jeremy J. Glenn; Carrie L. Graziani; Jeffrey Greenspan; Kenneth J. Hogan; Andrew M. Hutchison; J. Aaron Jensen; George K. Katsoudas; Melissa A. King; Charlotte Kormendy; Jonathan D. Lichterman; Chad W. Main (Not admitted in IL); Sandra J. McMullan; Eric E. Newman; Omar S. Odland; Jacob Rubinstein; Meaghan L. Schneider; E. Lynette Stafford; Elizabeth J. M. Strobel; Sara G. Uffelman; Timothy J. Walsh; Kristen A. Weisse; Anneliese Wermuth. Of Counsel: Lisa C. Breen; John K. Daly; Thomas J. O'Brien; Peter Petrakis; Georgene M. Wilson.
Practice concentrated in all areas of general commercial litigation, insurance, reinsurance, excess and professional liability coverage, labor and employment, product liability and white collar criminal litigation and counseling.
See Professional Biographies, CHICAGO, ILLINOIS

Medansky, Keith W., (AV) ... '61 '87 C.597 B.A. L.339 J.D. [DLPiper R.G.C.U.]
Medenwald, Jennifer L. ... '— '01 C.347 B.A L.1119 J.D. [Ⓐ Querrey&H.]
Medina, Deanne S. ... '— '00 L.209 J.D. [Maduff M.&M.]
Medler, Gary E., (AV) ... '52 '80 C.475 B.A. L.209 J.D. [Hinshaw&C.]
Medley, Mindy M. ... '76 '01 C&L.910 B.A., J.D. [Ⓐ Clausen M.]
Medow, Arthur ... '16 '49 C.597 B.S. L.309 LL.B. 680 N. Lake Shore Dr.
Medow, Jonathan C., (AV) ... '57 '81 C.813 B.A. L.309 J.D. [Mayer,B.R.&M.]
Medvin, Steven M. ... '68 '96 C.339 B.S. L.589 J.D. Aon Re, Inc.
Meece, Timothy C., (AV) '— '95
C.339 B.S.E.E. L.365 J.D. [Banner&W.] (See Pat. Sect.)
Meeder, Gregory R. ... '56 '83 C.339 B.A. L.146 J.D. [Holland&K.]
Meegan, Cathleen E. ... '50 '83 C.707 B.A. L.424 J.D. 11 S. LaSalle St.
Meehan, David T. ... '70 '98 C.347 B.A. L.209 J.D. [Ⓐ McGuirewoods]
Meehan, Frances, (AV) ... '— '78 C.589 B.A. L.146 J.D. [Ⓒ Sachnoff&W.]
Meehan, John J. ... '66 '90 C&L.427 B.S., J.D. 33 North Dearborn Street, Suite 300
Meehan, Karen Osiecki ... '49 '81 C.597 B.S.G.Ed. L.424 J.D. [Ⓐ Gould&R.]
Meehan, Laura R. ... '74 '99 C.473 B.A. L.146 J.D. [Ⓐ Laner,M.D.B.L.&T.]
Meehan, Lori L. ... '64 '89 C.339 B.A. L.597 J.D. 525 W. Monroe St., Ste. 1600
Meehan, Mary C. ... '70 '01 C.201 B.S. L.365 J.D. Atty. Gen. Off.
Meek, Adam M. ... '65 '91 C.477 A.B. L.597 J.D. [Katten M.R.]
Meek, David T. ... '69 '98 C.918 B.A. L.146 J.D. [Ⓐ Quarles&B.]
Meenan, Daniel C., Jr., (AV) ... '48 '74 C.770 B.S.C. L.424 J.D. 10 S. La Salle St.
Megaro, Kim M. ... '56 '79 C&L.209 B.A., J.D. 1st Dep. Purchasing Agent
Meginnes, Maria A. ... '— '04 C.145 A.B. L.1565 J.D. [Ⓐ Kirkland&E.]
Megley, Richard Burns, Jr. ... '67 '95 C.966 B.S.I.E. L.209 J.D. [Niro,S.H.&N.]
Megna, Ronald J. '49 '77 C.855 B.A. L.1209 J.D.
(adm. in VA; not adm. in IL)
Asst. Gen. Coun. & Asst. Secy., Smurfit-Stone Container Corp.
Mehl, James B. ... '43 '68 C&L.424 B.B.A., J.D. 161 N. Clark Street
Mehler, Raymond M., (AV) '44 '74
C.46 B.S. L.145 J.D. [Cook,A.M.M.C.&M.] (See Pat. Sect.)
Mehlman, Mark F., (AV) ... '47 '73 C.339 B.A. L.477 LL.B. [Sonnenschein N.&R.]
Mehrberg, Randall E., (AV) '55 '80
C.659 B.S. L.477 J.D. Exec. V.P. & Gen. Coun., Exelon Corp.
Mehta, Amit ... '— '00 C.734 B.S.B.A. L.276 J.D. [Ⓐ Greenberg T.]
Mehta, Mina ... '77 '01 C.339 B.A. L.597 J.D. [Ⓐ Gardner C.&D.]
Mehta, Saumil S. ... '67 '02 C.966 B.S. L.494 J.D. [Ⓐ Leydig,V.&M.]
Meidan, Lanelle K. ... '70 '00 C.659 B.A. L.910 J.D. [Ⓐ Skadden,A.S.M.&F.]
Meier, Cheryl L. ... '— '96 C&L.339 B.S., J.D. [Ⓒ Kirkland&E.]
Meier, Roger A. ... '39 '64 C.589 B.A. L.477 LL.B. V.P., Chicago Title & Tr. Co.
Meier, Steven R. ... '— '98 C.966 B.A. L.178 J.D. [Ⓐ Jenner&B.]
Meier, Thomas J. '69 '94 C.133 B.A. L.597 J.D.
Branch Chf., Div. of Enforce., U.S. Secs. & Exch. Comm.
Meier, W. Kurt ... '48 '77 C.800 B.S. L.339 J.D. Alexander Grant & Co.
Meinertzhagen, Nicole D. ... '72 '97 C.1169 B.A. L.339 J.D. Staff Atty., U.S. SEC
Meinertzhagen, Stephen R. ... '68 '94 C.918 B.A. L.339 J.D. [Burke,W.M.&S.]
Meisler, Liat R. ... '72 '98 C&L.477 B.A., J.D. [Ⓐ Field&G.]
Meisler, Ron E. ... '72 '99 C&L.477 B.A., J.D. [Ⓐ Skadden,A.S.M.&F.]
Meister, Jacob J., (AV) ... '65 '90 C.30 B.A. L.966 J.D. 65 E. Wacker Place, Suite 1700
Meister, Paul A. '62 '87 C.339 B.S. L.597 J.D.
Partner, Grosvenor Capital Management, L.P.

Meites, Jerome B. ... '55 '79 C.674 A.B. L.145 J.D. Off. Of Gen. Coun., Dept. of HHS
Meites, Thomas R., (AV) ... '43 '69 C&L.309 B.A., J.D. [Meites,M.B.&M.]

Meites, Mulder, Burger & Mollica, (AV)
208 S. LaSalle Street, Suite 1410, 60604-1003
Telephone: 312-263-0272 Fax: 312-263-2942
URL: http://www.mmbmlaw.com
Thomas R. Meites; Michael M. Mulder; Paul W. Mollica; Joan H. Burger (Retired); Shona B. Glink. Associates: Josie Raimond; Jamie S. Franklin.
Class Actions, Federal Practice, Employment Rights, Employment Law, Government Contracts, Toxic Torts, Employment Discrimination, Appellate Practice, ERISA, Consumer Law, Civil Rights, Environmental Litigation, Securities Litigation, Complex Litigation.
See Professional Biographies, CHICAGO, ILLINOIS

Melamed, Earl N. ... '57 '82 C&L.597 B.S., J.D. [Neal,G.&E.]
Melamed, Leo ... '32 '55 C.339 L.365 LL.B. 10 South Wacker Drive‡
Melamed, Mitchell J., (AV) ... '43 '68 C&L.339 B.S., J.D. [Aronberg G.D.&G.] ⊙
Meland, Creighton R., Jr. ... '56 '89 C.659 B.S. L.477 J.D. [Baker&M.]
Melbinger, Michael S., (AV) ... '58 '83 C.602 B.A. L.339 J.D. [Winston&S.]
Melby, Charles B. ... '20 '49 C.966 A.B. L.309 LL.B. Gen. Coun., Boulevard Bk. N.A.
Melchert, Karen ... '71 '96 Dir. Gov't Rel., CNA
Meldrum, Brian H. ... '74 '00 C&L.477 A.B., J.D. [Ⓐ Jenner&B.]
Melia, Edward J., (AV) ... '— '81 C.597 B.S.J. L.424 J.D. [Hickey,M.&Assoc.]
Melichar, William J. ... '— '93 C.339 B.A. L.424 J.D. [Ⓐ A.Barinholtz]
Melickian, Mark S. ... '59 '95 C.172 B.A. L.597 J.D. [Ⓒ Gardner C.&D.]
Melidis, Ceasar J. ... '72 '01 C.424 B.S. L.365 J.D. [Ⓐ Tucker B.R.&M.]
Meliker, Matthew S., Law Office of '74 '02
C.37 B.A. L.589 J.D. 1360 North Lakeshore Drive Suite 1802
Meller, Richard S. ... '— '82 C.103 A.B. L.477 J.D. [Latham&W.]
Mellican, Robert M. ... '75 '05 C.339 B.A. L.146 J.D. [Ⓐ Schwartz C.]
Mellinger, Michelle K. ... '72 '97 C.339 B.A. L.209 J.D. [Ⓐ Seyfarth S.]
Mellow, Karen R. '50 '76
C.339 B.S. L.424 J.D. Admin. Law J., Dept. of Employment Sec.
Melnick, Irving H. ... '28 '75 C.46 B.S. L.424 J.D. 4528 N. Wolcott Ave.‡
Melnick, Jeffry A., (AVⓉ) ... '46 '72 C.118 B.A. L.976 J.D. [Shefsky&F.]
Melnick, Sam S. ... '49 '83 C.1183 B.A. L.365 J.D. 155 N. Michigan Ave., Ste. 600
Melnyk, Yaro M. ... '73 '00 C.424 B.S. L.146 J.D. [Ⓐ Cassiday,S.&G.]
Melody, Thomas M. ... '66 '94 C&L.424 B.A., J.D. [Ⓐ Klein,T.&J.]
Melsher, Melissa Glass ... '— '99 C.30 B.A. L.146 J.D. [Ⓐ Ungaretti&H.]
Meltesen, Lon D. ... '69 '94 C.340 B.A. L.209 J.D. Illinois Dept. of Human Rights
Melton, Bruce W. ... '60 '86 C.187 B.Ph. L.145 J.D. [Babbitt&M.]
Melton, David R., (AV) ... '52 '77 C.966 B.A. L.145 J.D. [Mayer,B.R.&M.]
Melton, Timothy J. ... '— '89 C.999 B.A. L.912 J.D. [Jones D.]
Meltzer, Bernard D., (AV) '14 '38 C&L.145 A.B., J.D.
Prof. of Law, Emeritus, Univ. of Chic. Law Sch.
Meltzer, Renee F. ... '63 '88 C.477 B.B.A. L.910 J.D. [Ⓐ Fisher&F.]
Meltzer, Susan Joan '54 '80 C.881 B.A. L.1009 J.D.
(adm. in NY; not adm. in IL) NASD
Melvin, Daniel H., II ... '56 '95 C.1232 B.A. L.209 J.D. [McDermott W.&E.]
Melvoin, Hugo, (P.C.), (AV) ... '29 '53 C.339 B.S. L.309 LL.B. 115 S. LaSalle St.
Memon, Kamran ... '69 '97 C.273 B.A. L.145 J.D. 200 S. Michigan Ave.
Mena, Carlos R. ... '68 '94 C.31 B.A. L.146 J.D. Gen. Coun. and Partner, MCI WorldCom
Menaker, Pamela S., (CV) ... '— '84 C.597 B.S. L.424 J.D. [Clifford]
Menaker, Ronald D., (AV) ... '— '70 C.801 B.A. L.146 J.D. [Arnstein&L.]
Menchaca, Alejandro, (AV) '63 '89
C.453 B.S.Ch.E. L.424 J.D. [McAndrews,H.&M.] (See Pat. Sect.)
Mendel, Scott M., (AV) ... '52 '76 C&L.597 B.A., J.D. [Bell,B.&L.]
Mendeloff, Scott, (AV) ... '57 '83 C.966 B.A. L.276 J.D. [Sidley A.B.&W.]
Mendelsohn, David E., (BV) ... '64 '91 C.065 LL.B. L.146 J.D. [DLPiper R.G.C.U.]
Mendelsohn, Frederic A. ... '60 '86 C.1036 B.A. L.436 J.D. [Burke,W.M.&S.]
Mendelson, Alan C., (BV) ... '42 '66 C&L.339 B.A., J.D. 77 West Washington Street
Mendenhall, Samuel, (AV) ... '64 '91 C&L.339 B.A., J.D. [Winston&S.]
Mendoza, Adrian ... '68 '94 C.209 B.S. L.365 J.D. [Kane,C.&M.]
Mendoza, Maria A. ... '78 '04 C.623 B.A. L.602 J.D. [Ⓐ Bell,B.&L.]
Mendoza, Patricia ... '60 '84 C&L.209 B.A., J.D. M.A.L.D.E.F.
Mendoza Adleman, Maria Lourdes C. '67 '94
C.597 B.S. L.1194 J.D. Off. of the Gen. Coun., US Dept. of HHS
Menge, Jerry S., (AV) ... '59 '86 C.209 B.A. L.146 J.D. [Ⓐ R.F.Coleman&Assoc.]
Menges, Charles P., (AV) ... '36 '61 C&L.477 A.B., LL.B. [Ⓒ Menges&M.]
Menges & Molzahn, LLC, (AV) ... 20 North Clark Street Suite 2300
Menkes, Bruce N. ... '59 '84 C.945 B.A. L.145 J.D. [Mandell M.]
Menna, Ronald D., Jr. ... '62 '88 C.797 A.B. L.339 J.D. [Ⓐ Fischel&K.]
Menon, Pia ... '50 '89 C.999 B.Sc. L.46 J.D. Staff Atty., Ofc. of the Pub. Guardian
Menotti, Maria ... '71 '95 C.679 B.A. L.146 J.D. [Ⓐ Segal M.S.&M.]
Mensch, Linda Susan, (AV) ... '51 '77 C.299 B.A. L.569 J.D. [L.S.Mensch]
Mensch, Linda Susan, P.C., (AV) ... 200 S. Michigan Ave.
Mensheha, Paul N. ... '— '03 Atty., Chicago, M.R.O., S.E.C.
Mensik, Michael S. ... '53 '80 C.813 B.A. L.1066 J.D. [Baker&M.]
Menson, Richard L., (AV) ... '43 '68 C.694 A.B. L.597 J.D. [McGuirewoods]
Mentel, Kathleen Lori '67 '95 C.338 B.S. L.365 J.D.
Corp. Claims Analyst, TIG Specialty Insurance Solutions
Mercado, Kristen L. ... '— '04 C.145 A.B. L.1191 J.D. [Ⓐ Schiff H.]
Mercado, Silvia Liliana ... '74 '00 C.385 B.A. L.424 J.D. [Ⓐ Rock F.]
Mercherson, Denise M. ... '— '79 C.429 B.A. L.878 J.D. 25 E. Washington St., Ste. 1320
Meredith, Donna K. '56 '81
C.421 B.A. L.209 J.D. Dep. Reg. Coun., Fed. Deposit Ins. Corp.
Merel, Jonathan B. ... '77 '02 C.966 B.A. L.146 J.D. [Ⓐ Kamerlink,S.&M.]
Merel, Richard A., (AV) ... '50 '75 C.339 B.S. L.209 J.D. [Garfield&M.]
Merens, Henry B., (AV) ... '56 '81 C.855 B.A. L.910 J.D. [Adelman&G.]
Meriwether, Porter L. ... '40 '82 C.832 B.S. L.329 J.D. 8137 St. Lawrence
Merkel, William K. ... '— '94 C.388 Ph.D. L.569 J.D. [Marshall,G.&B.] (See Pat. Sect.)
Merker, Timothy G., (BV) ... '59 '84 C.201 B.A. L.602 J.D. [Tucker B.R.&M.]
Merlin, Peter H., (AV) ... '28 '54 C.999 LL.B. L.477 J.D. [Ⓒ Gardner C.&D.]
Merlo, Michael J., (AV) ... '42 '67 C.363 B.A. L.597 J.D. [Merlo K.B.&G.]

Merlo Kanofsky Brinkmeier & Gregg Ltd., (AV) BR
208 South La Salle Street, Suite 950, 60604
Telephone: 312-553-5500 Facsimile: 312-553-1586
URL: http://www.merlolaw.com
Michael J. Merlo; Martin A. Kanofsky; Alan J. Brinkmeier; Michael R. Gregg; Linda J. Schneider; Donald G. Machalinski; John D. Dalton; Ross D. Roloff; Mark H. Shanberg;—Michelle B. Balfour; Anthony N. Balice; Amelia Christensen; Mary C. Clifford; C. Edward Craft; Thomas D. Donofrio; Jason R. Donovan; Michael G. Patrizio; Christopher J. Raistrick; Todd M. Rowe (Not admitted in IL); Thomas Edward Sarikas.
Civil Trials and Appeals in State and Federal Courts. Aviation, Civil Rights, Excess Insurance, Insurance Coverage, Municipal Liability, Product Liability, Professional Liability, Reinsurance and General Civil Litigation.
See Professional Biographies, CHICAGO, ILLINOIS

Mermall, Michael E. ... '— '86 C.473 B.A. L.910 J.D. [Gardner C.&D.]

Merouse, Steven L. '64 '97 C.57 B.A. L.569 J.D. [Sonnenschein N.&R.]
Merrick, Michael J. '66 '92 C.546 B.A. L.190 J.D. [Merrick]
Merrick, Robert A., Jr., (AV) '51 '77 C.674 A.B. L.597 J.D. [R.A.Merrick,Jr.]
Merrick, Stephen M., (AV) '41 '67 C&L.597 B.A., J.D. [Merrick&K.]
Merrick, Toni B., (BV) '— '75 C.914 B.A. L.616 J.D. [Kirkland&E.]
Merrick & Klimek, P.C., (AV) 33 North LaSalle Street, Suite 2200
Merrick Law Firm, LLC 150 N. Michigan Ave., Ste. 2700

Merrick, Robert A., Jr., Ltd., (AV)
53 West Jackson Boulevard Suite 1235, 60604
Telephone: 312-922-0772 Fax: 312-922-0851
Email: ramerrick@sbcglobal.net
Robert A. Merrick, Jr.
Attorney Discipline Defense, Professional Responsibility, Legal Ethics.
See Professional Biographies, CHICAGO, ILLINOIS

Merrill, Adam P. '68 '95 C&L.101 B.S., J.D. [Sperling&S.]
Merrill, Thomas W., (AV) '49 '80 C.293 B.A. L.145 J.D. [Sidley A.B.&W.]
Merriman, James J. '66 '91 C.597 B.A. L.930 J.D. Asst. V.P., CNA Insurance Cos.
Merrinette, Jenifer '63 '91 C.578 B.S. L.589 J.D. Ill. Industrial Comm.
Merten, William W., (AV) '55 '80 C.475 B.A. L.912 J.D. [McDermott W.&E.]
Mertes, Tyler '79 '04 C&L.339 B.A., J.D. [Ross,D.&B.]
Mertz, Michael T. '72 '97 C.297 B.A. L.209 J.D. [Hurley,M.&M.]
Mervine, Sarah Naomi '72 '00 C.228 B.A. L.597 J.D. 111 W. Jackson
Merwise, Stephen D. '67 '94 C.860 B.A. L.569 J.D. Sr. Coun., Bank One Corp.
Meserow, Nancy J. '49 '82 C.174 B.A. L.596 J.D. [Tucker B.R.&M.]
Mesic, Robert E. '23 '55 C&L.145 B.A., J.D. 171 N. Clark St.
Mesires, George R. '69 '95 C.165 B.A. L.823 J.D. [Barack F.K.P.&N.]
Messer, Joseph S. '62 '88 C.393 B.A. L.146 J.D. [Messer&S.]
Messer, Michael C. '52 '84 C.339 B.A. L.209 J.D. Asst. Reg. Coun., Social Sec. Admn.
Messer & Stilp, Ltd. 160 West Washington Street
Messerly, Robert F. '62 '87 C.973 A.B. L.597 J.D. [Sonnenschein N.&R.]
Messersmith, Michael D. '— '99 C.611 B.A. L.209 J.D. [Kaye S.]
Messersmith, Peter '76 '02 C.846 B.A. L.365 J.D. 55 E. Washington
Messina, Cherisse M. '73 '98 C.339 B.A. L.365 J.D. [Haynes,S.K.O.&M.]
Messutta, Stephen S. '50 '76 C.165 A.B. L.365 J.D. 325 N. La Salle Dr.
Mester, Mark S. '— '87 C&L.976 B.A., J.D. [Latham&W.]
Metcalfe, Imogene L. '42 '99 C.347 B.S. L.209 J.D. 14 E. Jackson Blvd. #1500
Metge, Marvin F., (AV) '29 '53 C&L.597 B.S.L., J.D. [Metge,S.&K.]

Metge, Spitzer & Kreid, (AV)
30 West Monroe Street, Suite 630, 60603
Telephone: 312-580-1710 Fax: 312-580-1711
Members of Firm: Marvin F. Metge; Bruce C. Spitzer; Christopher A. "Kit" Kreid.
Transportation, Freight Loss and Damage, Personal Injury, Property Damage, Contract and Regulatory Claims Disputes, Commercial Litigation, Construction Litigation, Commercial, Employment, ERISA, Health Care, Insurance, Banking, Environmental, Construction, Real Estate, Transactions and Corporate Law. Mediation, Arbitration and Litigation Practice.
See Professional Biographies, CHICAGO, ILLINOIS

Metnick, Jason M. '— '03 C.477 B.A. L.209 J.D. [Masuda,F.E.&M.]
Metoyer, Michael A., (BV) '60 '90 C.209 B.A. L.339 J.D. 3937 West Fullerton Avenue
Metropoulos, Demetrios G. '63 '93 C.477 B.B.A. L.813 J.D. [Mayer,B.R.&M.]
Metskas, Thomas S., (AV) '31 '58 C&L.339 B.S., J.D. 35 W. Wacker Dr.
Metts, Amanda J. '73 '99 C.610 B.S. L.94 J.D.
(adm. in MA; not adm. in IL) [McDermott W.&E.]
Metz, Carl E., II '68 '94 C.145 B.A. L.596 J.D. [Falk J.]
Metz, Gregory R. '— '99 C.910 B.A. L.597 J.D. [Kirkland&E.]
Metz, Howard A. '67 '93 C.352 B.S. L.146 J.D. [Robbins,S.N.L.&T.]
Metz, Jill '52 '78 C.929 B.S. L.424 J.D. 2000 N. Racine
Metz, Tiffany L. '69 '98 C.1021 B.A. L.477 J.D.
(adm. in MI; not adm. in IL) [Mayer,B.R.&M.]
Metzcus, Leanne M. '69 '95 C.347 B.A. L.879 J.D. 500 N. Michigan Ave., Ste. 1050
Metzger, Carlin R. '76 '01 C.210 B.A. L.146 J.D. [McGuirewoods]
Metzger, David R., (AV) '59 '87 C.679 B.S.E.E. L.930 J.D.
[Sonnenschein N.&R.] (Pat.)
Metzger, Donald L. F., (AV) '45 '70 C.976 B.A. L.597 J.D. [Metzger&Assoc.]
Metzger, Paul T., (AV) '50 '76 C&L.309 A.B., J.D. [Bell,B.&L.]
Metzger, Timothy M. '68 '93 C.339 B.S. L.597 J.D. [Sonnenschein N.&R.]
Metzger & Associates, Ltd., (AV) 39 South La Salle Street Suite 808
Metzler, Donna K. '37 '92 C.436 B.S. L.339 J.D. 1739 W. Barry Ave.
Metzner, Richard J. '47 '73 C&L.966 B.A., J.D. Sr. V.P., Davis St. Land Co.
Meyer, Allen H., (BV) '25 '51 C.309 A.B. L.597 J.D. 111 W. Wash. St.‡
Meyer, Corey E. '60 '85 C.184 B.A. L.209 J.D. [Meyer&B.]
Meyer, Daniel B. '— '96 C.679 B.A. L.209 J.D. [O'Hagan,S.&A.]
Meyer, Derek J. '66 '91 C&L.347 B.S., J.D. [McDermott W.&E.]
Meyer, Eileen M. '60 '85 C.363 B.S.B.A. L.365 J.D.
Sr. Coun. & V.P., Merrill Lynch Bus. Financial Servs., Inc.
Meyer, Elizabeth Leah '76 '02 C.475 B.A. L.209 J.D. 10 S. LaSalle, Ste. 2800
Meyer, J. Theodore '36 '62 C.363 B.S. L.209 J.D. State Pollution Control Bd.
Meyer, John A., (AV) '46 '72 C.350 B.S. L.352 J.D. 20 S. Clark St., Ste. 2210
Meyer, Joyce L., (AV) '53 '90 C.347 B.S. L.209 J.D. [Gardner C.&D.]
Meyer, Kendall R., (AV) '43 '68 C.187 B.A. L.352 J.D. [Quarles&B.]
Meyer, Larry J. '52 '78 C.339 B.A. L.365 J.D. 205 W. Randolph, Ste. 820
Meyer, Leon S., (BV) '15 '39 C&L.209 LL.B. 100 E. Bellevue Pl.
Meyer, Lisa S. '66 '94 C.893 B.A. L.879 J.D. [Eimer S.K.&S.]
Meyer, Max E., (AV) '18 '42 C&L.546 A.B., J.D. 115 S. La Salle St.
Meyer, Michael J., (BV) '61 '86 C.338 B.S. L.424 J.D. [Tribler O.&M.]
Meyer, Michael L., (AV) '— '65 C.674 A.B. L.309 LL.B. [Schiff H.]
Meyer, Paul '62 '87 C.190 B.A. L.602 J.D. [Mayer,B.R.&M.]
Meyer, Peter J. '56 '84 C.502 B.J. L.146 J.D. [Gardner C.&D.]
Meyer, Raymond J. '34 '62 C.862 B.S. L.209 LL.B. 120 W. Madison
Meyer, Robert J., (AV) '52 '87 C&L.209 B.A., J.D. [Swanson,M.&B.]
Meyer, Susan '— '94 C.1350 B.A. L.146 J.D. [Schwartz C.]
Meyer, Thomas A., (BV) '— '84 C.746 B.B.A. L.209 J.D. [O'Hagan,S.&A.]
Meyer, Wayne A. '38 '75 C.597 B.A. L.209 J.D. Ret. Cir. J.‡
Meyer, William E., Jr. '— '91 C.309 A.B. L.424 J.D. [Schiff H.]
Meyer & Blumenshine, (BV) 221 N. La Salle St.
Meyer & Njus, P.A. 25 E. Washington, Suite 500 (⊙Southfield, MI; Mpls., MN)
Meyers, Alaya B. '74 '98 C.1375 B.A. L.597 J.D. [Seyfarth S.]
Meyers, Amanda E. '— '99 C&L.276 B.A., J.D. [Jones D.]
Meyers, Evan M. '77 '02 C.477 B.A. L.339 J.D. [Gardner C.&D.]
Meyers, Frederick W., (BV) '55 '81 C.45 B.A. L.930 J.D. [Ladas&P.] (See Pat. Sect.)
Meyers, Irving '07 '30 L.365 LL.B. [Meyers&M.]
Meyers, Joan M. '62 '90 C.25 B.S. L.564 J.D. [Johnson&C.]
Meyers, Megan E. '74 '99 C.602 B.B.A. L.345 J.D. [Vedder,P.K.&K.]
Meyers, Peter R., (AV) '47 '74 C.477 B.A. L.597 J.D. [Meyers&M.]
Meyers, Scott A. '66 '92 C.659 B.S. L.276 J.D. [Levenfeld P.]
Meyers, Vazantha '71 '04 C.679 B.A. L.879 J.D. [Mayer,B.R.&M.]
Meyers, William Buddy, (BV) '42 '70
C.339 B.S. L.146 J.D. 640 N. LaSalle Street, Suite 556
Meyers, William C. '62 '87 C.475 B.A. L.477 J.D. [Goldberg,K.B.B.R.&M.]
Meyers & Meyers, (AV) 360 E. Randolph St.
Meza, Ricardo '64 '90 C.338 B.A. L.365 J.D.
Mexician Amer. Legal Def. & Educ. Fund
Meza Utreras, Celia '69 '94 C.339 B.A. L.352 J.D. Asst. Gen. Coun., Exelon Corp.
Miao, Emily '60 '97 C.569 Ph.D. L.146 J.D. [McDonnell B.H.&B.] (See Pat. Sect.)
Miarecki, Greg J. '73 '97 C&L.145 B.A., J.D. [Winston&S.]
Miceli, Roberto S. '— '96 C.966 B.B.A. L.494 J.D. [Kirkland&E.]
Miceli, William A. '58 '84 C&L.424 B.A., J.D. [Miner,B.&G.]
Michael, David N. '— '93 C.347 B.S. L.424 J.D. [Gould&R.]
Michael, Howard S. '70 '98 C.477 B.A. L.94 J.D. [Brinks H.G.&L.]
Michael, Jeffrey E. '72 '97 C&L.339 B.S., J.D. Horizon Realty Group
Michael, Jonathan W. '68 '94 C.473 B.S. L.472 J.D. [Burke,W.M.&S.]
Michael, Richard A. '33 '58 C&L.424 B.S., J.D. Prof. of Law, Loyola Univ.
Michael, Tracy H. '— '02 C.1365 B.A. L.597 J.D. [Freeborn&P.]

Michael Best & Friedrich LLP, (AV)
401 North Michigan Avenue Suite 1900, 60611 ⊙
Telephone: 312-222-0800 Facsimile: 312-222-0818
Email: info@michaelbest.com URL: http://www.michaelbest.com
Partners: Regina W. Calabro; Lisa C. Childs; Ronald S. Cope; G. A. Finch; Judith L. Grubner; Kerryann M. Haase; Laurel A. Haskell; Peter F. Herzog; Daniel A. Kaufman; Charles A. Laff; Laura Shroyer Liss; John J. McHugh; Bridget M. O'Keefe; Larry L. Saret; Joseph F. Schmidt; Martin L. Stern; Michael A. Stiegel; Sarah E. Swartzmeyer; Steven J. Teplinsky. Of Counsel: Louis Altman; Julian L. Berman; Kenneth H. Denberg; S. Richard Fine; Julian J. Frazin; Richard L. Freeman; Steven B. Randall; William L. Sharp. Associates: Gretchen M. Hosty; Raymond M. Krauze; Christopher R. Parker; Brian P. Paul; Susan D. Reinecke; Jamie A. Robinson; Stephen C. Smith.
Litigation, Corporate and Commercial Law, Management Labor and Employment, Employee Benefits, Patents, Trademarks, Internet Law, Computer Technology, Intellectual Property, Financial Institutions, Securities and Mergers and Acquisitions, Real Property and Commercial, Industrial and Residential Land Development, Federal and State Taxation, Associations, Antitrust and Unfair Trade Practices, Public and Corporate Finance, Creditors' Rights, Bankruptcy and Insolvency, International Business, Estate and Trust Planning, Business Succession Planning, Health Care, Immigration, Environmental, Government Relations and Administrative, Retail Distribution, Communications, Sports and Entertainment, Trade and Professional, Alternative Dispute Resolution, Venture Capital, Insurance Defense, Law Firm Disputes, Divorce and Family Law, Construction Law.
Milwaukee, Wisconsin Office: 100 East Wisconsin Avenue, 53202-4108. Telephone: 414-271-6560. Telecopier: 414-277-0656.
Madison, Wisconsin Office: One South Pinckney Street, Firstar Plaza, P.O. Box 1806, 53701-1806. Telephone: 608-257-3501. Telecopier: 608-283-2275.
Manitowoc, Wisconsin Office: 1000 Maritime Drive, 54220. Telephone: 920-686-2800. Telecopier: 920-686-2810.
Waukesha, Wisconsin Office: Two Riverwood Place, Suite 200, N19 W24133 Riverwood Drive, 53188-1174. Telephone: 262-956-6560. Telecopier: 262-956-6565.
Center Valley, Pennsylvania Office: Stabler Corporate Center, 3773 Corporate Parkway, 18034. Telephone: 610-798-2170. Telecopier: 610-798-2180.
See Professional Biographies, CHICAGO, ILLINOIS

Michaelides, Barbara I. '61 '96 C.1044 B.A. L.424 J.D. [Clausen M.]
Michaels, Brian S. '— '92 C.351 B.A. L.1018 J.D. V.P., ATG Trust Company
Michaels, Jan M., (AV) '63 '89 C.1044 B.A. L.602 J.D. [Michaels&M.]
Michaels, Kenneth A., Jr. '58 '83 C.424 A.B. L.365 J.D. [Bauch&M.]
Michaels, Kristin Edell '66 '91 C.436 B.A. L.597 J.D. [Seyfarth S.]
Michaels, Richard B. '39 '64 C.472 B.B.A. L.597 J.D. 309 W. Washington St.
Michaels, Richard E., (AV) '52 '77 C.209 B.S.C. L.597 J.D. [Schuyler,R.&Z.]
Michaels, Robert S. '63 '91 C.477 B.A. L.228 J.D. [Robinson C.&C.]
Michaels, Thomas P. '38 '67 C.209 B.S. L.144 J.D. Amer. Nat. Bk. & Tr. Co.

Michaels & May, P.C., (AV)
Sears Tower, Suite 5620, 233 South Wacker Drive, 60606
Telephone: 312-428-4720 Facsimile: 312-575-8679
URL: http://www.michaelsmay.com
Members: Jan M. Michaels; Theodore J. May; Alfred L. Buchanan; Steven Schulwolf. Associates: Scott M. Salerno; John M. Duczynski; Kathryn A'Hearn; Stephen A. Skardon; Neal F. Thompson; John A. Lee; Michael McNaughton; William D. Ellison.
Insurance Coverage, Commercial Litigation, Excess and Reinsurance, Environmental, Professional Liability Insurance Coverage, Directors and Officers Liability, Complex and General Civil Litigation, Insurance Bad Faith, Appellate Practice, International Dispute Resolution, Alternative Dispute Resolution, Class Action Defense, Intellectual Property Litigation, Product Liability.
See Professional Biographies, CHICAGO, ILLINOIS

Michaelson, Shirley M. '50 '74 C&L.477 B.A., J.D.
Off. of the Gen. Coun., Dept. of HHS
Michal, Jon A. '53 '92 L.365 J.D. 5576 N. Elston Ave.
Michalak, Edward F., (AV) '37 '62 C.597 B.S. L.309 LL.B. [McDermott W.&E.]
Michalak, Robert A., (AV) '45 '70 C.602 B.B.A. L.424 J.D. [Schuyler,R.&Z.]
Michalik, Michelle A. '69 '97 C.188 B.A. L.424 J.D. Appellate Law Clerk
Michalik, Paul A., (AV) '58 '88 C.424 B.S. L.146 J.D. [Dykema G.P.]
Michas, Christopher J. '39 '63 C&L.145 A.B., J.D. 30 North LaSalle Street, Suite 3400
Michaud, Douglas W. '67 '94 C.860 B.Sc. L.209 J.D. [Guibord H.]
Michel, James E. '— '04 C.679 B.A. L.424 J.D. [Barnes&T.]
Michelotti, Carla R., (AV) '50 '75 C&L.209 B.A., J.D.
Exec. V.P. & Gen. Coun., Global Opers., Leo Burnett Worldwide, Inc.
Michels, Deborah N. '50 '75 C.914 B.A. L.930 J.D. U.S. Dept. of Labor
Michels, John J., Jr. '55 '85 C.1070 B.S. L.228 J.D. [McGuirewoods]
Michels, Robert L. '63 '88 C.602 B.B.A. L.209 J.D. [Winston&S.]
Michmerhuizen, Susan '49 '86 C&L.209 J.D.
Mng. Editor, Amer. Bar Assn., Ctr. for Prof. Responsibility
Michod, Charles L., (AV) '17 '42 C.339 A.B. L.309 J.D. [Kelly,O.M.D.&R.]
Michod, Charles L., Jr. '43 '68 C.674 A.B. L.477 J.D. [Kelly,O.M.D.&R.]
Michon, Dennis M. '54 '80 C.209 B.S.C. L.365 J.D. V.P. & Gen. Coun., JPS Interests
Mick, Mitchel A. '65 '93 C&L.347 B.S., J.D. [Sidley A.B.&W.]
Mick, Pamela '70 '96 C.210 B.A. L.1119 J.D. [Zulkie]
Mickelson, Carole A. '— '00 C.119 B.S. L.146 J.D. [Greer,B.&C.] (Pat.)
Mickelson, Ralph R., (AV) '27 '55 C&L.209 B.S., J.D. 10 E. Ontario Street‡
Mickey, Douglas J. '— '84
C&L.972 B.S., J.D. Sr. Staff Atty., American Family Insurance
Mickus, Christopher D. '74 '99 C.999 L.365 J.D. Two North LaSalle Street, Suite 2200
Middendorf, Brett A. '77 '05 C.424 B.B.A. L.352 J.D. [Wildman,H.A.&D.]
Middleton, Robert O. '53 '80 C.436 B.A. L.285 J.D. [Nisen&E.]
Midgley, David B. '40 '65 C.893 B.A. L.145 J.D. 1550 N. Lake Shore Drive
Mierzwa, Peter V. '65 '92 C.399 B.A. L.209 J.D. Law Bulletin Publishing Company
Migala, Steven A. '71 '96 C.98 B.S. L.339 J.D. [Tishler&W.]
Migdal, Bradley '— '02 C.966 B.A. L.365 J.D. 120 W. Madison, 10th Fl.
Migdal, Sheldon P., (AV) '36 '61 C.339 B.S. L.597 J.D. [Wildman,H.A.&D.]
Mignin, Robert J., (AV) '48 '73 C.388 B.A. L.339 J.D. [Seyfarth S.]
Mignon, Jamie L. '— '01 C.591 B.S. L.209 J.D. [Kirkland&E.]
Mihael, Nicholas H. '68 '93 C&L.339 B.A., J.D. [Rosenfeld H.S.&F.]
Mihalache, Marin I. '52 '96 C.999 LL.B. L.1000 LL.M.
(adm. in MI; not adm. in IL) 3617 W Foster
Mihalas, Alexandra '— '91 C.311 B.S. L.309 J.D. [Kirkland&E.]

Mihalopoulos, Jorge T. . . . . . '79 '04 C.209 B.S. L.146 J.D. [🄰 Reott]
Mihm, Jacob M. . . . . . '— '00 C.177 B.A. L.801 J.D. [🄰 Ungaretti&H.]
Miksa, Gregory A. '49 '77 C.276 B.S. L.912 J.D.
Admin. Law J., U.S. Merit Systems Protection Bd.
Mikula, Alison Vratil . . . . . '— '04 C.478 B.A. L.477 J.D. [🄰 McGuirewoods]
Mikula, Jeffrey T.E. . . . . . '49 '77 C.1151 B.A. L.424 J.D. I.R.S.
Mikulich, Kara Kellaher '63 '93 C.321 B.A. L.813 J.D.
Prog. Offr., The Joyce Found.‡
Mikulina, Jennifer . . . . . '76 '01 C&L.966 B.S., J.D. [🄰 McDermott W.&E.]
Mikuzis, Steven P. . . . . . '75 '03 C.339 B.Arch. L.146 J.D. [🄰 Swanson,M.&B.]
Mikva, Abner J. . . . . . '26 '51 C.966 L.145 J.D. 5020 S. Lake Shore Dr.
Milam-Perez, Lisa A. '64 '98 C&L.209 B.A., J.D.
Legal Assistance Foundation of Chicago
Milano, John A. . . . . '64 '89 C.597 B.A. L.602 J.D. Asst. Chief Coun., Ill. Dept. of Transp.
Milberg, David A. . . . . . '— '79 C.477 A.B. L.365 J.D. [Schiff H.]
Milenkovich, Nenad M. . . . . . '— '00 C.608 B.S. L.365 J.D. [🄰 Jones D.]
Miles, Forest J., (BV) . . . . . '48 '77 C.1262 B.A. L.365 J.D. [McCarthy D.]
Milew, Rosemary G. . . . . . '66 '91 C.112 B.S. L.424 J.D. Lexis Nexis
Miley, David A. . . . . . '68 '04 C.999 B.A. L.862 J.D. 1133 W. Fulton Market
Milia, Martha K. . . . . . '— '00 C.477 B.A. L.209 J.D. [🄰 Arnstein&L.]
Milianti, Peter A. . . . . . '72 '97 C.352 B.A. L.146 J.D. [🄰 McGuirewoods]
Milissis, Nicholas G. . . . . . '74 '02 C.339 B.A. L.146 J.D. 6601 N. Avondale, Ste. 203
Millar, Sarah Bassler . . . . . '75 '01 C&L.602 B.A., J.D. [🄰 Gardner C.&D.]
Millard, Dianne H. . . . . . '51 '76 C.112 B.A. L.365 J.D. Cameron General Corp.
Millen, Douglas A. . . . . . '69 '94 C.477 B.G.S. L.339 J.D. [Much S.F.D.A.&R.]
Miller, Alan P., (AV) . . . . . '38 '65 C.103 A.B. L.477 J.D. [Kiesler&B.]
Miller, Amanda M. . . . '77 '02 C.117 B.A. L.608 J.D. [🄰 Brinks H.G.&L.] (See Pat. Sect.)
Miller, Barbara . . . . '— '92 L.209 J.D. Dir. & Sr. Coun., CNA Property & Casualty Oper.
Miller, Barry A., (AV) . . . . . '54 '78 C.976 B.A. L.309 J.D. Asst. U.S. Atty.
Miller, Benjamin K. . . . . . '36 '61 C.801 B.A. L.880 J.D. [🄲 Jenner&B.]
Miller, Beth A. . . . . . '64 '90 C.352 B.A. L.365 J.D. [🄰 Pontikes&Assoc.]
Miller, Brian T. . . . . . '76 '02 C.705 B.A. L.945 J.D. [🄰 Riordan,D.L.&M.]
Miller, Britt M. . . . . . '73 '98 C.10 B.A. L.597 J.D. [🄰 Mayer,B.R.&M.]
Miller, Carolyn E. . . . . . '79 '04 C.473 L.209 J.D. [🄰 Katten M.R.]
Miller, Catherine A. . . . . . '— '99 C&L.339 B.A., J.D. [🄰 Freeborn&P.]
Miller, Charles . . . . . '— '99 C.801 B.A. L.1209 J.D. [Banner&W.] (See Pat. Sect.)
Miller, Claudette P., (AV) . . . . . '— '88 C.788 A.B. L.145 J.D. [Ungaretti&H.]
Miller, Dale T., (AV) . . . . . '57 '86 C.20 B.A. L.880 J.D. [Lord,B.&B.]
Miller, Dan B., (AV🅃) . . . . . '— '94 C.378 B.S. L.846 LL.B. [🄲 Jones D.]
Miller, David '25 '76 C.262 B.S. L.7 J.D.
(adm. in OH; not adm. in IL) Exec. Dir., Jewish Children's Bur. of Chicago
Miller, David L., (BV) . . . . . '62 '87 C.31 B.A. L.912 J.D. [Dykema G.P.]
Miller, David S., (AV) . . . . . '50 '75 C.352 B.A. L.146 J.D. 11 S. La Salle St.
Miller, Douglas A. . . . . . '59 '86 C.93 B.S. L.146 J.D. [Haynes,S.K.O.&M.]
Miller, Elissa . . . . . '70 '00 C.589 B.A. L.1187 J.D. Chicago Public Schools
Miller, Florence E. . . . . . '13 '42 L.365 J.D. 850 Dewitt Pl.‡
Miller, Gary M. . . . . . '69 '95 C.339 B.A. L.575 J.D. [Grippo&E.]
Miller, Geoffrey P. '50 '80 C.674 A.B. L.178 J.D.
(adm. in DC; not adm. in IL) 1111 E. 60th St.
Miller, Gerald M. . . . . . '50 '75 C.209 B.S. L.597 J.D. [Vanasco,G.&M.]
Miller, Gregory V. . . . . . '58 '83 C.511 B.A. L.209 J.D. [Miller&F.]
Miller, Gretchen N. . . . . . '71 '96 C.37 B.A. L.273 J.D. [Greenberg T.]
Miller, Harry S., (AV) . . . . . '32 '58 C&L.145 B.A., J.D. 135 S. La Salle St.
Miller, Jason H. . . . . . '— '97 C.101 B.A. L.178 J.D. [🄰 Sidley A.B.&W.]
Miller, Jeffrey Richard . . . . . '— '02 C.477 B.A. L.145 J.D. [🄰 Kirkland&E.]
Miller, Jennifer E. . . . . . '76 '01 C.473 B.A. L.8 J.D. [🄰 Holland&K.]
Miller, Jennifer G. . . . . . '59 '88 C.66 B.A. L.146 J.D. 3100 N. Sheridan Rd., Apt 6C
Miller, Joel L., (AV) . . . . . '35 '61 C.339 B.S. L.597 J.D. [🄲 Kaye S.]
Miller, Kenneth C., (AV) . . . . . '43 '72 C.734 B.S.A.E. L.150 J.D. [K.C.Miller]
Miller, Kenneth W. . . . . . '60 '85 C.339 B.S. L.597 J.D. [Katten M.R.]
Miller, Kerri L. . . . . . '72 '00 C.1236 B.S. L.910 J.D. 2 N Lasalle St, Ste 1300
Miller, Kerry A. . . . . . '64 '94 C.597 B.A. L.145 J.D. Arthur Andersen, LLP
Miller, Kimberly . . . . . '66 '91 C.914 B.A. L.597 J.D. Sr. Coun., Huron Corp.
Miller, Laura A. . . . . . '— '92 C&L.209 B.S., J.D. [🄰 Crystal,H.&W.]
Miller, Laura Beth, (AV) '60 '85
C.893 B.A. L.945 J.D. [Brinks H.G.&L.] (See Pat. Sect.)

Miller, Lawrence T. '42 '69 C.436 B.A. L.339 J.D.
230 West Monroe Street, Suite 250, 60606
Telephone: 312-236-2431 Fax: 312-641-6174
Email: ltmjd@aol.com
Language: English.
Civil Trial and Appellate Practice, Litigation, Business Law, Commercial Litigation, Creditors' Rights, Corporate Law, Real Estate Law, Elder Law, Trusts and Estates, Wills and Probate, Administrative Law, Medical Malpractice, Personal Injury, Premises Liability, Professional Liability, Libel, Slander, Insurance, Labor and Employment Law, Election, Campaign and Political.
See Professional Biographies, CHICAGO, ILLINOIS

Miller, Lee I., (AV) . . . . . '47 '73 C&L.276 B.S.B.A., J.D. [DLPiper R.G.C.U.]
Miller, Leslie J. '44 '75 C.508 B.A. L.352 J.D.
Div. Coun., American Medical Association
Miller, Mark F., (AV) . . . . . '— '79 C&L.597 B.A., J.D. [Arnstein&L.]
Miller, Mark P., (AV) . . . . . '60 '85 C&L.339 A.B., J.D. [Wildman,H.A.&D.]
Miller, Marvin A., (AV) . . . . . '44 '70 C.1019 B.B.A. L.46 J.D. [Miller F.&C.]
Miller, Matthew S. . . . . . '71 '96 C.966 B.A. L.424 J.D. [Miller&S.]
Miller, Matthew W. . . . . . '77 '03 C.347 B.S. L.146 J.D. [🄰 Cremer,K.S.&S.]
Miller, Maureen A., (AV) . . . . . '60 '86 C&L.436 B.A., J.D. [Vedder,P.K.&K.]
Miller, Maurice J., (AV) . . . . . '26 '55 C&L.966 B.B.A., J.D. 1 1st Nat. Plaza
Miller, Maxwell M. . . . . . '58 '88 C.221 B.A. L.976 J.D. [Skadden,A.S.M.&F.]
Miller, Michael G. . . . . . '61 '86 C.597 B.A. L.209 J.D. [🄲 D.R.Fichera&Assoc.]
Miller, Michael I., (AV) . . . . . '37 '60 C&L.597 B.A., J.D. [🄲 Eimer S.K.&S.]
Miller, Michele Danine . . . . . '— '00 L.589 J.D. 233 S. Wacker Drive, 27th Floor
Miller, Michelle L. . . . . . '— '02 C&L.966 B.S., J.D. [🄰 Jones D.]
Miller, Nancy Chase . . . . . '46 '80 C.145 B.A. L.208 J.D. Sr. Atty., F.D.I.C
Miller, Noah B. '78 '03 C&L.477 B.A., J.D.
(adm. in PA; not adm. in IL) [🄰 Butler R.S.&B.]
Miller, Pamela M. . . . . . '77 '02 C.260 B.S.B.A. L.339 J.D. [🄰 McGuirewoods]
Miller, Paul A. '75 '00 C.339 B.S. L.146 J.D.
Asst. Gen. Coun., Govt. Off. of Mgmt. & Budg.
Miller, Paul J., (AV) . . . . . '29 '53 C.976 B.A. L.309 LL.B. [Sonnenschein N.&R.]
Miller, Peter C. . . . . . '65 '90 C.436 B.A. L.292 J.D. [Seyfarth S.]
Miller, Peter J., (AV) . . . . . '44 '70 C.1016 B.S. L.209 J.D. [Sinar K.M.&F.]
Miller, Phillip N. . . . . . '36 '83 C.475 B.S. L.146 J.D. Admin. J.
Miller, Richard L., II . . . . . '70 '97 C&L.339 B.S., J.D. [🄰 Novack&M.]
Miller, Richard T. . . . . . '— '98 C.597 B.S. L.424 J.D. [Schiff H.]
Miller, Robert F. . . . . . '56 '81 C.293 B.A. L.861 J.D. [🄲 Birndorf&B.]
Miller, Robert Joel . . . . . '57 '85 C.473 B.A. L.597 J.D. [R.J.Miller]

Miller, Rochelle C., Law Offices of '51 '86 C.477 B.S. L.146 J.D.
155 North Michigan Avenue, Suite 500, 60601-7511
Telephone: 312-565-4800 Fax: 312-565-4810
Email: rochmiller@aol.com URL: http://www.lawyers.com/rcmillerlaw
Estate Planning, Trusts and Estates, Wills and Probate, Estate and Gift Taxation, Fiduciary Income Tax, Generation-Skipping Tax, Charitable Giving.
See Professional Biographies, CHICAGO, ILLINOIS

Miller, Ronald S., (AV) . . . . . '31 '55 C&L.339 B.S., LL.B. [Miller S.&H.]
Miller, S. Ira . . . . . '37 '62 C.339 A.B. L.209 J.D. 111 W Washington St Ste 1900
Miller, Sam L. . . . . . '26 '51 C.424 L.146 J.D. [🄲 Dowd&D.]
Miller, Sheldon P. . . . . . '29 '52 C&L.597 B.S., J.D. 505 N. Lake Shore Dr.
Miller, Stanton, (AV) . . . . . '44 '69 C.473 A.B. L.339 J.D. [Schwartz C.] (Pat.)
Miller, Stephanie Kathryn . . . . . '72 '99 C.597 B.A. L.424 J.D. Pub. Def. Off.
Miller, Stephen R., (AV) . . . . . '50 '75 C.976 B.A. L.188 J.D. [McDermott W.&E.]
Miller, Stephen R., (AV) . . . . . '— '90 C.339 B.S. L.1565 J.D. [Sachnoff&W.]
Miller, Steve A. . . . . . '70 '97 C.351 B.A. L.477 J.D. [🄲 Fisher&P.]
Miller, Steven A., (AV) . . . . . '— '79 C&L.910 B.A., J.D. [Sachnoff&W.]
Miller, Tamara A. . . . . . '70 '96 C.347 B.A. L.424 J.D. [Leydig,V.&M.]
Miller, Terry . . . . . '— '98 C.339 B.S. L.209 J.D. [🄰 Greene&L.]
Miller, Timothy J., (AV) . . . . . '60 '85 C.27 B.A. L.228 J.D. [Novack&M.]
Miller, Todd A. . . . . . '— '97 C.339 B.A. L.602 J.D. [Kirkland&E.]
Miller, Willie J., Jr. '53 '79 C.339 B.S. L.424 J.D.
Assoc. Gen. Coun., Chicago Div., ABN-AMRO North America, Inc. (Legal Department)

Miller, Alan Benjamin
(See Highland Park)

Miller Faucher and Cafferty LLP, (AV)
30 North La Salle Street, Suite 3200, 60602 ⊙
Telephone: 312-782-4880 Telecopier: 312-782-4485
URL: http://www.millerfaucher.com
Members of Firm: Marvin A. Miller; Patrick E. Cafferty (Resident, Ann Arbor, Michigan Office); Ellen Meriwether (Resident, Philadelphia, Pennsylvania Office); Bryan L. Clobes (Resident, Philadelphia, Pennsylvania Office); Jennifer Winter Sprengel; William R. Kane (Resident, Philadelphia, Pennsylvania Office); Michael J. Willner (Resident, Philadelphia, Pennsylvania Office). Associates: Lori A. Fanning; Melody Forrester (Resident, Philadelphia, Pennsylvania Office); Christopher B. Sanchez; Michael S. Tarringer (Resident, Philadelphia, Pennsylvania Office); Anthony F. Fata; Nyran Rose Pearson. Of Counsel: J. Dennis Faucher (Resident, Philadelphia, Pennsylvania Office); Dom J. Rizzi; Matthew E. Van Tine.
Arbitration, Antitrust Class Actions, Deceptive Trade Practices, Appellate Practice, Federal Civil Practice, Commercial Fraud and Commercial Liability, Complex Commercial Litigation, Commodities Fraud, Complex and Multi-District Litigation, Consumer Fraud, Consumer Class Actions, ERISA Litigation, ERISA Class Actions, Civil Litigation, Federal Civil Litigation, Trial Practice.
Philadelphia, Pennsylvania Office: One Logan Square, Suite 1700, 18th and Cherry Streets, 19103. Telephone: 215-864-2800. Telecopier: 215-864-2810.
Ann Arbor, Michigan Office: 101 North Main Street, 48104. Telephone: 734-769-2144. Telecopier: 734-769-1207.
See Professional Biographies, CHICAGO, ILLINOIS

Miller & Ferguson . . . . . 9415 S. State St.
Miller, Kenneth C., Ltd., (AV) . . . . . 33 N. Dearborn St., Suite 1505
Miller, Robert J., Law Office . . . . . 219 S. Dearborn St., Ste. 2378

Miller Shakman & Hamilton LLP, (AV)
Suite 3600, 180 North La Salle Street, 60601
Telephone: 312-263-3700 FAX: 312-263-3270
URL: http://www.millershakman.com
Members of Firm: Marc O. Beem; Stephen J. Bisgeier; Daniel M. Feeney; Edward W. Feldman; Arthur W. Friedman; R. Dickey Hamilton; Diane F. Klotnia; Ronald S. Miller; Michael L. Shakman; Thomas M. Staunton; Stuart M. Widman. Associates: Julie H. Friedman; Roberta G. Evans; Jennifer E. Smiley; Fredrick E. Vars; Roger J. Perlstadt; Zachary J. Freeman.
Civil Trial and Appellate Practice in state and federal courts, as well as Arbitration and Mediation practice, in an array of commercial matters: Business Litigation; Corporate Litigation; Legal Malpractice and Legal Ethics; Representation of Lawyers and Law Firms; Bankruptcy Litigation and Creditors' Rights; Securities Litigation; Constitutional Litigation; Employment Litigation and Counseling; Environmental Litigation; Governmental and Regulatory Litigation; Intellectual Property and Media Litigation; Closely-Held Business and Partnership Disputes; Professional Malpractice and Directors and Officers Liability; Real Estate and Construction Litigation; Specialized Corporate Representations; Estate Planning; Counseling and Transactional Practice.
See Professional Biographies, CHICAGO, ILLINOIS

Miller & Sweeney
111 West Washington Street, Suite 1160, 60602
Telephone: 312-384-0500 Fax: 312-384-0600
Members of Firm: Matthew S. Miller; Robert D. Sweeney.
Litigation, Commercial Litigation, Civil Practice, Appellate Practice.
See Professional Biographies, CHICAGO, ILLINOIS

Millichap, Paul A. . . . . . '52 '78 C.893 B.A. L.209 J.D. [Franczek S.]
Millman, Craig, (BV) . . . . . '50 '75 C.724 B.A. L.365 J.D. [Braun S.L.B.&M.]
Millner, Gordon H. . . . . . '34 '58 C.339 B.A. L.597 J.D. [🄲 FagelHaber]
Millner, Robert B., (AV) . . . . . '50 '75 C.918 B.A. L.145 J.D. [Sonnenschein N.&R.]
Mills, Alan . . . . . '56 '81 C.103 A.B. L.597 J.D. Uptown People's Law Ctr.
Mills, Bryan L. '72 '98 C.299 B.A. L.208 J.D.
(adm. in VT; not adm. in IL) 1411 W. Berteau Ave.
Mills, Daniel B. . . . . . '63 '89 C.234 B.S. L.589 J.D. [Pretzel&S.]
Mills, Elizabeth M., (AV) . . . . . '52 '84 C.378 B.A. L.597 J.D. [McDermott W.&E.]
Mills, Jonathan L., (AV) . . . . . '47 '77 C.966 B.A. L.145 J.D. [Sugar,F.&F.]
Mills, Linda . . . . . '50 '79 C&L.629 B.S., J.D. 353 W. Chicago Ave.
Mills, Martha A., (AV) . . . . . '41 '66 C.429 B.A. L.494 J.D. 118 N. Clark
Mills, Mary L. . . . . . '61 '91 C.910 B.A. L.46 J.D. [🄰 Sonnenschein N.&R.]
Mills, Pamela J., (BV) . . . . . '58 '82 C.597 B.A. L.602 J.D. [Duane M.]
Milnamow, Alison . . . . . '80 '04 C.436 B.A. L.339 J.D. [🄰 Bollinger,R.&G.]
Milnamow, John P., (AV) '36 '64 C.436 B.S.M.E. L.365 LL.B.
[Rockey,M.&K.] (Pat.) ⊙
Milner, Morgan J. . . . . . '— '04 C.164 B.A. L.128 J.D. [🄰 Chittenden,M.&N.]
Milnikel, Robert S., (AV) '26 '53
C&L.145 A.B., J.D. 200 East Randolph Drive, Suite 7300
Milos, Nicole D. . . . . . '76 '01 C.741 B.S. L.365 J.D. [🄰 Cremer,K.S.&S.]
Milos, Vivian L. . . . . . '— '79 C&L.209 B.S., J.D. [V.L.Milos]
Milos, V. L., Ltd., Law Office of . . . . . 6617 W. Archer Ave.
Milosevic, Vladan . . . . . '73 '02 C.424 B.A. L.365 J.D. IL Com. Comm.
Milott, Stephen K. . . . . . '50 '77 C.1183 B.A. L.365 J.D. [🄰 Gunty&M.]
Milstein, Albert, (AV) . . . . . '46 '72 C.978 B.A. L.145 J.D. [Winston&S.]
Miltonberger, Paul C. . . . . . '58 '83 C&L.339 B.A., J.D. [Epstein B.&G.]
Milz, Michael E. . . . . . '60 '90 C.339 B.S. L.146 J.D. [Brinks H.G.&L.] (See Pat. Sect.)
Mims, Trasha D. '— '93 C.597 B.A. L.893 J.D.
Sr. Coun., Bank One Corp. (Law Dept.)
Min, John K. . . . . . '— '04 C&L.145 B.A., J.D. [🄰 Jones D.]
Minarik, Ann E. '57 '82 C.58 B.A. L.146 J.D.
Comm. Underwriter, Chicago Title Ins. Co.
Minc, Gabriel J., (AV) '— '83
C.350 B.A. L.209 J.D. 1700 West Irving Park Road, Suite 205A

Mindell, Gerald D., (AV) .... '43 '68 C.597 B.S. L.659 J.D. 70 W. Burton Pl.
Mine, Andrew S. .... '61 '85 C.145 B.A. L.477 J.D. Asst. Corp. Coun.
Minear, Nicholas R. .... '56 '81 C.352 B.B.A. L.813 J.D. [DLPiper R.G.C.U.]
Miner, Alison L. .... '— '96 C&L.352 B.B.A., J.D. [Bollinger,R.&G.]
Miner, Amy L. .... '64 '90 C&L.352 B.B.A., J.D. [Bollinger,R.&G.]
Miner, Judson H., (AV) .... '41 '67 C.597 B.A. L.145 J.D. [Miner,B.&G.]
Miner, Thomas H. .... '27 '54 C.388 B.A. L.339 J.D. [T.H.Miner&Assoc.]

Miner, Barnhill & Galland, P.C., (AV)
14 West Erie Street, 60610 ⊙
Telephone: 312-751-1170 Facsimile: 312-751-0438
URL: http://www.lawmbg.com
Charles Barnhill, Jr. (Resident, Madison, WI Office); Jeffrey I. Cummings; William P. Dixon (Resident, Madison, WI Office); George F. Galland, Jr.; Robert S. Libman; William A. Miceli; Judson H. Miner; Sarah E. Siskind (Resident, Madison, WI Office); Paul L. Strauss; Laura E. Tilly;—Lisa T. Alexander; Elizabeth J. Eberle (Not admitted in IL; Resident, Madison, WI Office); Nancy L. Maldonado; Rebecca Onie. Of Counsel: Sharon K. Legenza; Bradley Scott Weiss.
General Practice, Trial and Appellate Litigation, Commercial, Employment, Employee Benefits, Civil Rights and Securities Litigation, Banking Law, Single and Multi-Family Housing Finance and Development, Non-Profit Corporations.
Madison, Wisconsin Office: Suite 803, 44 East Mifflin Street. Telephone: 608-255-5200. Facsimile: 608-255-5380.

See Professional Biographies, CHICAGO, ILLINOIS

Miner, Thomas H., & Associates, Inc. .... 150 N. Michigan Ave.
Mines, Kimberly A. .... '75 '01 C&L.424 B.A., J.D. Asst. Pub. Def., Cook Co. Pub. Def.
Ming, Marian S. K. .... '40 '73 C.700 M.A. L.209 J.D. 1 N. La Salle Street
Minichello, Dennis, (AV) .... '— '78 C.610 B.A. L.597 J.D. [Marwedel,M.&R.]
Minier, Leslie Dawn .... '65 '94 C.864 B.S.E.E. L.597 J.D. [Katten M.R.]
Minkin, Jason P. .... '71 '98 C.494 B.A. L.209 J.D. [Ⓐ Kerns,P.F.&P.]
Minkow, Gregg I. .... '57 '81 C.393 B.A. L.339 J.D. [Hinshaw&C.]
Minkus, Robert J., (AV) .... '— '80 C.976 B.A. L.145 J.D. [Schiff H.]
Minnaert, Trev M. .... '— '93 C.339 B.A. L.424 J.D. [Arnstein&L.]
Minor, Denise '57 '88 C.170 B.A. L.1051 J.D.
(adm. in OK; not adm. in IL) F.B.I.
Minor, Lance R. .... '68 '98 C.1147 B.S. L.146 J.D. [Ⓐ Belofsky&B.]
Minor, Maria J. .... '69 '98 C.145 B.S. L.597 J.D. Two North LaSalle Street, Suite 2200
Minow, Newton N., (AV) .... '26 '50 C&L.597 B.S., J.D. [Ⓒ Sidley A.B.&W.]
Minsky, McCormick & Hallagan, P.C., (AV) ...... 122 South Michigan Avenue, Suite 1800
Mintz, Joshua J., (AV) '55 '81 C.174 B.A. L.472 J.D.
Gen. Coun., John D. & Catherine T. MacArthur Found.
Mintz, Robert M. .... '60 '87 C.347 B.S. L.146 J.D. [Holland&K.]
Mintzer, Ari D. .... '74 '03 C.477 B.A. L.597 J.D. [Ⓐ Winston&S.]
Minwalla, Sherizaan .... '70 '02 C.150 B.A. L.146 J.D. Staff Atty.
Miossi, William G., (AV) .... '59 '85 C&L.276 B.S., J.D. [Winston&S.] (⊙Wash., DC)
Mirabella, Laurel A. .... '47 '87 C.145 B.A. L.365 J.D. I.R.S.
Mirabelli, Enrico J., (BV) .... '56 '81 C.742 B.A. L.365 J.D. [Nadler,P.&M.]
Miraglia, John M. .... '68 '01 C.1122 B.A. L.1000 J.D. [Ⓐ R.L.Prusak]
Miranda, Daniel F. .... '53 '79 C.112 A.B. L.178 J.D. General Electric Capital Corp.
Miriani, Steven P. .... '63 '87 C.209 L.861 J.D. [Ⓒ Skadden,A.S.M.&F.]
Mirman, Rita .... '69 '95 C.1390 B.E. L.1019 J.D. Coun., Intell. Prop., Tribune Co.
Miroballi, Joseph J., (AV) .... '53 '79 C.589 B.A. L.365 J.D. [Miroballi,D.&R.]

Miroballi, Durkin & Rudin, (AV)
6 W. Hubbard, Suite 300, 60610
Telephone: 312-229-5555 Fax: 312-229-5556
URL: http://www.mdr-law.com
Members of Firm: Joseph J. Miroballi; Albert E. Durkin, Jr.; Scott H. Rudin.
Personal Injury, Civil Torts.

See Professional Biographies, CHICAGO, ILLINOIS

Mirocha, Nathan J. .... '74 '99 C.339 B.A. L.209 J.D. [Ⓐ Kralovec,J.&S.]
Miron, Joseph A. .... '68 '99 C.475 B.A. L.146 J.D. [Ⓒ Skadden,A.S.M.&F.]
Mirza, Fawzia .... '— '03 C.347 B.A. L.146 J.D. [Ⓐ Patton&R.]
Mirza, Jerome, (AV) .... '37 '63 C.340 B.S. L.339 LL.B. [J.Mirza&Assoc.] ⊙

Mirza, Jerome, and Associates, Ltd., (AV)
Three First National Plaza, 60602 ⊙
Telephone: 312-368-1903 Facsimile: 312-368-0528
URL: http://www.mirzalaw.com
Jerome Mirza;—Thomas M. Harris, Jr.
Trial and Appellate Practice. Products Liability, Malpractice and Railroad Law.
Bloomington, Illinois Office: 705 East Washington Street. Telephone: 309-827-8011. Facsimile: 309-829-8638.

See Professional Biographies, CHICAGO, ILLINOIS

Miscimarra, Philip A., (AV) .... '56 '82 C.229 B.A. L.659 J.D. [Morgan,L.&B.]
Miselman, Michael D., (AV) .... '42 '67 C.477 A.B. L.309 J.D. [Seyfarth S.]
Misetic, Luka S., Law Offices of ..... '70 '96 C.597 B.A. L.602 J.D. 207 E. Ohio, Ste. 217
Misheff, Alexander P. .... '34 '60 C&L.309 A.B., LL.B. 19 S. LaSalle St.
Mishkin, Melvin I., (AV) .... '31 '57 C&L.597 J.D. [Rothschild,B.&M.]
Mishra, Anshuman .... '74 '02 C&L.999 B.A., LL.B. [Ⓐ Mayer,B.R.&M.]
Missner, David N., (AV) .... '— '67 C.473 A.B. L.597 J.D. [DLPiper R.G.C.U.]
Mitakis, Christina D. .... '— '04 C.597 B.A. L.880 J.D. [Ⓐ Kirkland&E.]
Mitchel, Maureen A. .... '— '78 C.347 B.A. L.424 J.D. [Ⓐ A.L.Gaynor&Assoc.]
Mitchel, Michael M. .... '29 '53 C&L.597 B.S.L., LL.B. Economy Folding Box Corp.
Mitchell, Alison M., (AV) .... '65 '90 C.477 B.A. L.597 J.D. [DLPiper R.G.C.U.]
Mitchell, Anne W. .... '74 '02 C.6 B.A. L.597 J.D. [Ⓐ Sonnenschein N.&R.]
Mitchell, Charlene S. .... '68 '95 C.602 B.A. L.365 J.D. [Johnson&B.]
Mitchell, D. Rebecca .... '53 '80 C.823 B.A. L.107 J.D. [Peck,B.A.&M.] ⊙
Mitchell, Dianna L. .... '— '81 C.339 B.A. L.276 J.D. 247 E. Chestnut
Mitchell, Gregory A. .... '51 '76 C&L.229 B.S., J.D. 188 W. Randolph Street
Mitchell, J. Chad .... '— '98 C.1104 B.S. L.101 J.D. [Kirkland&E.]
Mitchell, J. Ryan .... '— '99 C.878 B.S. L.546 .D. [Ⓐ Jones D.]
Mitchell, J. Wesley .... '60 '90 C.347 B.S. L.146 J.D. [Mitchell H.&W.]
Mitchell, James E. .... '66 '97 C.210 B.A. L.209 J.D. [Ⓐ Katten M.R.]
Mitchell, John Eric .... '— '89 C&L.597 B.S., J.D. 1341 W. Fullerton Ave., Ste. 222
Mitchell, Joseph R. .... '44 '77 C.679 B.S. L.365 J.D. 3501 E. 106th St., Ste. 205
Mitchell, Karla .... '— '01 C.812 B.S. L.910 J.D. [Ⓐ DLPiper R.G.C.U.]
Mitchell, Lee M., (AV) '43 '68
C.918 A.B. L.145 J.D. Thoma Cressey Equity Partners, Inc.
Mitchell, Michael J. .... '— '80 C&L.339 B.S., J.D. [Jones D.]
Mitchell, Nancy A. .... '62 '88 C.347 B.A. L.477 J.D. [Greenberg T.]
Mitchell, Patricia M. .... '68 '97 C.339 B.A. L.209 J.D. 100 N. LaSalle
Mitchell, Philip H. .... '49 '76 C.424 B.B.A. L.365 J.D. Asst. States Atty.
Mitchell, Randall L., (AV) .... '42 '67 C.477 B.A. L.339 J.D. [Adducci,D.L.M.&B.]
Mitchell, Raymond W. .... '69 '93 C.423 A.B. L.424 J.D. [Winston&S.]
Mitchell, Robert D. .... '18 '42 C&L.477 A.B., J.D. 312 W. Randolph

Mitchell Hoffman & Wolf LLC
221 North LaSalle, Suite 1148, 60601
Telephone: 312-726-6722 Fax: 312-726-3220
URL: http://www.mitchellhoffmanwolf.com

(This Listing Continued)

Mitchell Hoffman & Wolf LLC (Continued)
J. Wesley Mitchell; Kenneth A. Hoffman; Paul P. Wolf.
Plaintiffs Personal Injury, Automobile Accidents, Wrongful Death, Medical Malpractice, Construction Accidents, Premises Liability.

See Professional Biographies, CHICAGO, ILLINOIS

Mitchem, Russell L. .... '24 '50 C.210 A.B. L.1119 J.D. Harris Tr. & Svgs. Bk.
Mitka, Gloria R. .... '56 '88 C.182 B.A. L.494 J.D. Sr. Coun., Bank One Corp. (Law Dept.)
Mitrius, Janice V. .... '— '97 C.46 B.S.M.E. L.36 J.D. [Banner&W.] (See Pat. Sect.)
Mitzenmacher, Allen, (AV) .... '35 '58 C&L.339 A.B., LL.B. [Ⓒ J.A.Schechter]
Mix, B. John, Jr., (AV) .... '28 '56 C&L.597 B.S., J.D. 203 N. La Salle St.
Mix, Katherine S. .... '57 '85 C.597 B.A. L.424 J.D. [Morrison&M.]
Mizen, Gregory T. .... '67 '94 C&L.339 B.S., J.D. 730 W. Randolph, 6th Floor
Mizerk, Don Joseph, (AV) .... '63 '88 C.340 B.A. L.880 J.D. [Winston&S.]
Mizock, Phillip P. .... '11 '34 C.405 B.S. L.146 LL.B. 655 W. Irving Pk. Rd.
Mobley, Sharon Steinberg .... '70 '00 C.477 B.A. L.1494 J.D. [Ⓐ Berger S.]
Mocerf, Howard L., (AV) .... '46 '71 C.902 B.A. L.421 J.D. [Duane M.]
Moch, Eric W. .... '72 '97 C.201 B.A. L.365 J.D. [Ⓐ Johnson&B.]
Mock, Donald J. .... '58 '83 C.894 B.A. L.365 J.D. [Ⓐ Borovsky&E.]
Mock, Karen E. .... '64 '90 C.608 B.A. L.966 J.D. U.S. Dept. of Labor
Mock, Matthew B. .... '— '00 C.1349 B.A. L.477 J.D. [Ⓐ Latham&W.]
Mock, Matthew S. .... '75 '03 C.623 B.A. L.477 J.D. [Ⓐ McDermott W.&E.]
Mock, William B.T., Jr. '52 '79 C.311 B.A. L.276 J.D.
Prof. & Dir., John Marshall Law Sch., Intl. Law Ctr.
Mockaitis, Vitas J., (BV) .... '56 '85 C.339 B.A. L.365 J.D. [Ⓐ Corti,F.&A.]
Modestas, Saulius V. .... '70 '02 C.339 B.S. L.146 J.D. [Ⓐ Langone]
Moehling, James A., (AV) .... '— '65 C&L.597 B.A., J.D. [Holland&K.]
Moehrke, Scott A. '— '89 C.436 B.A. L.228 J.D.
(adm. in WI; not adm. in IL) [Kirkland&E.]
Moeller, Chad W. .... '71 '97 C.966 B.A. L.209 J.D. [Neal,G.&E.]
Moelmann, Lawrence R., (AV) .... '47 '73 C.674 A.B. L.477 J.D. [Hinshaw&C.]
Moen, Zachary V. .... '78 '03 C.938 B.A. L.424 J.D. [Ⓐ Jenner&B.]
Moenning, Richard C., (AV) .... '37 '62 C&L.597 B.S., J.D. 135 S. La Salle St.
Moffic-Silver, Joanne, (AV) '52 '77 C.966 B.A. L.597 J.D.
Gen. Coun. & Corp. Secy., Chicago Board Options Exchange, Incorporated
Moffitt, Thomas G., (AV) .... '55 '81 C.602 B.A. L.209 J.D. [Ⓐ McCracken,W.d.&H.]
Moglin, Neal J. .... '63 '88 C&L.880 B.A., J.D. [Lovells]
Mogul, Alyssa .... '70 '98 C.1365 B.A. L.146 J.D. [Ⓐ Grund&L.]
Mogul, Edward .... '45 '70 C.976 B.A. L.999 J.D. 5250 N. Broadway St.
Mohan, Daniel J., (AV) .... '59 '84 C.602 B.A. L.424 J.D. [Daley&M.]
Mohan, Timothy P. .... '— '85 C.475 B.A. L.209 J.D. [Chapman&C.]
Mohapatra, Seema .... '74 '00 C.367 B.A. L.597 J.D. 10 S. Dearborn
Mohip, Ranjeev S. .... '76 '02 C.999 B.A. L.1187 J.D. [R.Mohip]
Mohip, Ranj, Law Office of .... 1738 W. Wallen Ave.
Mohyuddin, Fatima G. '— '03 C.734 B.A. L.30 J.D.
(adm. in MO; not adm. in IL) [Ⓐ S.D.Pollock&Assoc.]
Moirano, Michael H., (AV) .... '52 '79 C.339 B.A. L.424 J.D. [Nisen&E.]

Mojarad, Azita M. '65 '00 C.1461 B.S. L.424 J.D.
Three First National Plaza, 70 W. Madison Street, Suite 3700, 60602
Telephone: 312-641-0771 Fax: 312-641-0480
Email: amojarad@aol.com URL: http://www.azitalaw.com
Collections, Contracts, Family Law, Immigration and Naturalization and Real Estate.

See Professional Biographies, CHICAGO, ILLINOIS

Mokshagundam, Smita .... '75 '01 C.477 B.A. L.339 J.D. [Ⓐ Wilson E.M.E.&D.]
Molano, Anita T., (AV) .... '51 '80 C.273 B.A. L.150 J.D. [DLPiper R.G.C.U.]
Moles, Charles F. .... '53 '79 C.475 B.A. L.209 J.D. [Ashcraft&A.]
Molina, Teresa .... '— '01 C.49 B.S. L.608 J.D. Asst. State Atty.
Molinaro, Michael L., (AV) .... '57 '82 C.1024 B.S. L.209 J.D. [Neal,G.&E.]
Molino, Paul J. .... '— '91 C.221 B.S. L.209 J.D. [Rakoczy M.M.S.] (Pat.)
Molins, Marcel J. .... '36 '67 C.999 B.A. L.597 J.D. [Baker&M.]
Molins, Thomas N. .... '— '93 C.276 B.A. L.1049 J.D. [Ⓐ Jones D.]
Molk, Elliot I. .... '64 '89 C.477 B.B.A. L.145 J.D. [Barack F.K.P.&N.]
Molk, Laura D. .... '64 '89 C.477 B.A. L.597 J.D. LR Develop. Co.
Moll, Jeremie D. .... '78 '03 C.340 B.A. L.365 J.D. [Ⓐ Jenkens&G.]
Moll, Kenneth B. .... '61 '89 C.966 B.A. L.146 J.D. [K.B.Moll&Assoc.]
Moll, Kenneth B., & Associates, Ltd. .... Three First National Plaza, 50th Floor
Mollet, Chris J. '54 '79 C&L.966 B.A., J.D.
Assoc. Univ. Coun., Univ. of Illinois at Chicago
Mollica, Paul W., (AV) .... '61 '86 C.145 B.A. L.209 J.D. [Meites,M.B.&M.]
Molony, Winifred D. .... '12 '38 C.700 L.424 J.D. 3550 N. Lake Shores Dr.‡
Moltz, Marshall J., (AV) .... '30 '54 C&L.597 B.S., J.D. [M.J.Moltz]
Moltz, Marshall J., P.C., (AV) .... 77 West Washington Street, Suite 1620
Moltzen, Edward W., (AV) ..... '44 '68 C.1106 B.A. L.365 J.D. [Momkus M.M.M.M.&S.]
Moltzen, Karl E. .... '71 '00 C.966 B.A. L.365 J.D. [Ⓐ S.F.Ginsberg]
Molzahn, Lyndon C., (AV) .... '47 '72 C.228 B.A. L.477 J.D. [Menges&M.]
Molzon, Justina A. .... '50 '85 C.690 B.S. L.146 J.D. Supr. St. & Fairbanks Ct.‡
Momblanco, Eileen M. .... '73 '98 C.477 B.A. L.424 J.D. [Ⓐ Minsky,M.&H.]
Momkus McCluskey Moltzen Monroe Marsh & Spyratos, LLC, (AV)
33 North LaSalle Street, 34th Floor (⊙Downers Grove)
Monaco, Anthony J. .... '75 '03 C.436 B.S. L.209 J.D. [Ⓐ Swanson,M.&B.]
Monaco, Meredith A. .... '71 '97 C.473 B.A. L.597 J.D. [Ⓐ Sonnenschein N.&R.]
Monagan, Tom .... '— '02 C.597 B.S.J. L.608 J.D. [Ⓐ Kirkland&E.]
Monaghan, Robert F. .... '22 '49 C.145 L.424 J.D. 20 N. Clark St.
Monahan, Amy B. .... '75 '99 C.367 B.A. L.228 J.D. [Ⓐ Sidley A.B.&W.]
Monahan, Brian P. .... '— '03 C.339 B.A. L.424 J.D. [Ⓐ Shefsky&F.]
Monahan, Daniel L., (AV⊙) .... '42 '72 C.742 B.A. L.365 J.D. [Harvey,W.M.&L.] ⊙
Monahan, Gabriela I. .... '— '93 C.69 B.A. L.424 J.D. [Kirkland&E.]
Monahan, John T. .... '28 '51 C&L.209 B.Sc., LL.B. Sears, Roebuck & Co.
Monahan, Joseph T. '55 '85 C.339 B.S.W. L.209 J.D.
225 W. Washington St., Ste. 2300
Monahan, Peter A., (AV) .... '— '81 C.388 B.A. L.209 J.D. [Alholm,M.K.H.&O.]
Monarch, Joel R., (AV) .... '50 '80 C.339 B.A. L.597 J.D. Dep. Dir. of Rev.
Monat, William M. '62 '89
C&L.352 B.B.A., J.D. V.P., Financial & Prof. Risk Solutions, Inc.
Monco, Dean A., (AV) '50 '79 C.424 B.S. L.209 J.D.
[Wood,P.K.C.&M.] (See Pat. Sect.)
Monco, Walter J., (AV) .... '42 '69 C&L.424 B.B.A., J.D. 1 N. La Salle St., Ste. 3400
Mondello, Judith A. .... '— '85 C.966 B.A. L.146 J.D. [Ⓒ Mayer,B.R.&M.]
Mondero, Dennis J. .... '68 '93 C.339 B.A. L.347 J.D. [Mondero D.&G.]
Mondero D'Souza & Gosrisirikul, Ltd. .... 2303 W. North Avenue
Mondrowski, Laura A. .... '65 '90 C.209 B.A. L.424 J.D. Chart House Enterprises Inc.
Mondschean, Caroline A. .... '63 '89 C.1024 B.S. L.221 J.D. [Hinshaw&C.]
Mone, Peter J., (AV) .... '40 '65 C.95 A.B. L.145 J.D. [Baker&M.]
Monfils, Julie Edwards '54 '83 C.477 B.M. L.213 J.D.
(adm. in MI; not adm. in IL) V.P. & Gen. Mgr., Marketing Resources, Inc.

Mongolis, Gregory P. '46 '73
C.424 B.A. L.365 J.D. Asst. Gen. Coun., Chicago Title Ins. Co.
Monical, John S. ... '68 '94 C.339 B.S. L.589 J.D. [Lawrence,K.S.&U.]
Monico, Michael D., (AV) ... '47 '73 C.276 A.B. L.597 J.D. [Monico,P.&S.]

Monico, Pavich & Spevack, (AV) BB
20 South Clark Street, Suite 700, 60603-1894
Telephone: 312-782-8500 Fax: 312-759-2000
Members of Firm: Michael D. Monico; Robert J. Pavich; Barry A. Spevack; Martha A. MacAloon; Melanie K. Fairman; Jacqueline S. Jacobson;—Anastasia Pavich; Theodore Eppel. Of Counsel: Steven J. Seidman.
Federal Criminal and Civil Litigation. Products Liability and Medical Malpractice Law. Appellate Practice.
See Professional Biographies, CHICAGO, ILLINOIS

Monroe, Lee A. ... '32 '60 C.951 B.A. L.597 J.D. 455 North Cityfront Plaza Drive
Monroe, Mark A. '48 '75 C.589 B.A. L.146 J.D.
Coun., Corp. Governance & Securities, & Asst. Secy, Wm. Wrigley Jr. Co.
Monroe, Randall C. ... '59 '84 C.879 B.A. L.339 J.D. [Brenner,F.M.&S.]
Monroe, Thomas P. ... '73 '01 C.504 B.A. L.424 J.D. [Ⓐ Jenner&B.]
Monroe-Sampson, Lara ... '— '02 C.597 B.S. L.273 J.D. [Ⓐ Rakoczy M.M.S.]
Monson, Deborah Alfred, (AV) ... '59 '85 C.674 A.B. L.477 J.D. [Ⓒ Mayer,B.R.&M.]
Monson, Paul D. ... '57 '82 C&L.339 B.S., J.D. [Sidley A.B.&W.]
Monson, Thomas A. ... '60 '85 C.339 B.S.M.E. L.309 J.D. [Jenner&B.]
Monsour, Christopher A. ... '79 '05 C.259 B.A. L.1565 J.D. [Ⓐ Mayer,B.R.&M.]
Montague, Valerie Breslin ... '— '03 C.436 B.A. L.276 J.D. [Ⓐ Ungaretti&H.]
Montana, James S., Jr., (AV) ... '43 '69 C.276 A.B. L.597 J.D. [Vedder,P.K.&K.]
Montes, Jorge Luis ... '63 '88 C&L.424 B.A., J.D. [Montes&Assoc.]
Montes & Associates ... 831 N. Ashland Ave.
Montgomery, Alex R. ... '73 '02 C.951 B.A. L.145 J.D. [Ⓐ Hughes S.P.R.&D.]
Montgomery, Brian M. '63 '89 C.477 B.G.S. L.209 J.D.
Asst. Gen. Coun., Exelon Corp.
Montgomery, Bruce Gartner '59 '91 C.339 B.A. L.146 J.D.
Corp. Purchasing Agent, Wm. Wrigley Jr. Co.
Montgomery, C. Barry, (AV) ... '37 '62 C.532 B.A. L.477 J.D. [Williams M.&J.]
Montgomery, Fred H. ... '46 '76 C.821 B.A. L.209 J.D. Sr. Tax Atty., Sara Lee Corp.
Montgomery, James D., (AV) ... '32 '56 C&L.339 B.A., J.D. [J.D.Montgomery&Assoc.]
Montgomery, James D., Jr. ... '57 '82 C.813 B.A. L.339 J.D. [J.D.Montgomery&Assoc.]
Montgomery, Jane Ellen, (AV) ... '— '90 C.339 B.S. L.597 J.D. [Schiff H.]
Montgomery, Sari W. '69 '94 C.145 B.A. L.424 .D.
Sr. Coun., Attorney Registration and Disciplinary Commission
Montgomery, Thomas J. ... '47 '73 C.339 A.B. L.424 J.D. [McCarthy D.]
Montgomery, Virgil R., Jr. ... '— '92 C.1165 B.A. L.309 J.D. [Schiff H.]
Montgomery, William A., (P.C.), (AV) ... '— '58 C.951 A.B. L.309 LL.B. [Schiff H.]

Montgomery, James D., & Associates, Ltd., (AV)
One North LaSalle Street Suite 2450, 60602
Telephone: 312-977-0200 Fax: 312-977-0209
Email: missp@jdmlaw.com URL: http://www.lawyers.com/jamesdmontgomery
James D. Montgomery; James D. Montgomery, Jr.; Thomas C. Marszewski; Melvin Brooks. Associates: Mark Parts; James M. Sanford; Beverly P. Spearman; Trent A. McCain.
Complex Litigation, including Personal Injury, Wrongful Death, Aviation, Medical Malpractice and Products Liability.
See Professional Biographies, CHICAGO, ILLINOIS

Monto, Richard L. '64 '90 C.477 B.A. L.94 J.D.
Assoicate Counsel, MCI Telecommunications Corporation
Montoya, Paul A. '66 '94 C.840 B.B.A. L.424 J.D.
Asst. Reg. Dir., Div. of Enforce., U.S. Secs. & Exch. Comm.
Montpas, Scott M. ... '72 '97 C.477 B.A. L.201 J.D. [Ⓐ Sidley A.B.&W.]
Montplaisir, Laurie Martin ... '— '96 C.679 B.S. L.424 J.D. [Ⓐ Schuyler,R.&Z.]
Montroy, Nancy J. '60 '86 C.741 B.A. L.602 J.D.
VP & Dir. Underwriting Svces., Attorneys' Liability Assurance Society, Inc.
Moody, Alexander J., Jr. ... '41 '66 C.436 B.S. L.597 J.D. 2912 N. Lincoln Ave.
Moody, Michael C. ... '63 '90 C.338 B.S. L.365 J.D. [O'Rourke M.&M.]
Moon, Jessika J. ... '74 '00 C.276 B.S. L.94 J.D. [Ⓐ Ross,D.&B.]
Mooney, Cynthia C., (BV) ... '48 '88 C.441 B.A. L.424 J.D. [Ⓒ Seyfarth S.]
Mooney, John E. ... '66 '95 C.884 B.A. L.209 J.D. [Winston&S.]
Mooney, Sara Marie ... '76 '01 C.1400 B.A. L.112 J.D. Atty.
Moor, Edward R., (AV) ... '59 '90 C&L.347 B.A., J.D. [Williams M.&J.]
Moore, Abram I. ... '74 '02 C.508 B.A. L.602 J.D. [Ⓐ Bell,B.&L.]
Moore, Ayrie ... '41 '76 C.183 B.A. L.209 J.D. U.S. Dept. of H.H.S.
Moore, Carl E., Jr., (AV) '— '69 C&L.424 B.S., J.D.
[Marshall,G.&B.] (See Pat. Sect.)
Moore, Christopher S. ... '60 '98 C.145 B.A. L.339 J.D. [Ⓐ Novack&M.]
Moore, Daniel C. ... '— '05 C.674 B.A. L.494 J.D. [Ⓐ Kirkland&E.]
Moore, David A. ... '— '04 C.346 B.S. L.1119 J.D. [Ⓐ Foley&L.]
Moore, Donna L. ... '65 '04 C.1016 B.G.S. L.365 J.D. [Ⓐ Cassiday,S.&G.]
Moore, Gary K., (AV) ... '46 '74 C.339 B.A. L.424 J.D. [Moore,S.&W.]
Moore, Heather L. ... '70 '01 C&L.209 B.A., J.D. [Ⓐ Levenfeld P.]
Moore, Hugh L., (AV) ... '40 '65 C&L.347 A.B., J.D. [Lord,B.&B.]
Moore, Jane A. ... '59 '86 C.477 B.A. L.569 J.D. Mgr./Atty., Protection & Advocacy, Inc.
Moore, John G. ... '53 '79 C.602 B.B.A. L.209 J.D. [Madden,J.M.&S.]
Moore, Jonathan ... '— '02 C.938 B.A. L.893 J.D. [Ⓐ Kirkland&E.]
Moore, Keith L. ... '51 '77 C.347 B.A. L.276 J.D. [Ⓒ Stamos&T.]
Moore, Kevin A. ... '52 '76 C&L.339 B.S., J.D. Asst. States Atty.
Moore, Kevin J. ... '58 '84 C.436 B.A. L.209 J.D. [Rothschild,B.&M.]
Moore, Leon W., (BV) ... '50 '81 C.624 B.S. L.365 J.D. [Blatt,H.L.&M.]
Moore, Lisa M. ... '78 '03 C.339 B.S. L.966 J.D. [Ⓐ Pretzel&S.]
Moore, M. Read, (AV) ... '65 '90 C.691 B.A. L.893 J.D. [McDermott W.&E.]
Moore, Mary Katherine ... '53 '86 C.145 B.A. L.365 J.D. Asst. State's Atty.
Moore, Mary Margaret ... '— '91 C.993 B.A. L.597 J.D. [Bryan C.]
Moore, Mary Szews, (AV) '62 '88 C.436 B.S.E.E. L.813 J.D.
[Ⓒ Bartlit B.H.P.&S.] (Pat.)
Moore, Michael Allen ... '60 '94 C.145 B.A. L.424 J.D. [Ⓐ J.J.Roche&Assoc.]
Moore, Michelle L. ... '— '97 C.112 B.A. L.477 J.D. [Sachnoff&W.]
Moore, Peter ... '— '03 C&L.597 B.S., J.D. [Ⓐ Latham&W.]
Moore, Peter W. ... '53 '85 C.602 B.A. Law Clk. to U.S. Mag.
Moore, Raven ... '— '03 C.201 B.A. L.861 J.D. [Ⓐ Sachnoff&W.]
Moore, Robert Charles ... '52 '77 C.363 B.S.B.A. L.424 J.D. [Stone&M.]
Moore, Scott J. ... '60 '88 C&L.339 B.S., J.D. [Jenner&B.]
Moore, Thomas N., III ... '49 '75 C.597 B.A. L.146 J.D. Asst. Pub. Def.
Moore, William F. ... '— '04 C.591 B.S. L.1000 J.D. [Ⓐ Adler,M.&M.]

Moore, Strickland & Whitson-Owen, (AV)
One East Wacker Drive, Suite 3510, 60601
Telephone: 312-464-1890 Fax: 312-464-1627
Email: attorneys@moore-strickland.com
Members: Gary K. Moore; Darlene Strickland; Eugena A. Whitson-Owen. Associates: Thomas J. Branit (1958-1993); Robert P. Kile (1955-2005); Christine M. Quintos; Rhett Strom; Brett A. Skean.

(This Listing Continued)

Moore, Strickland & Whitson-Owen (Continued)
Automobile Insurance Defense, Commercial Insurance Defense, General Liability Defense, Insurance Defense, Local Government Defense, Municipal Defense, Premises Liability Defense, Products Liability Defense, Property Insurance Defense, School District Liability, Self Insured Defense.
See Professional Biographies, CHICAGO, ILLINOIS

Moorehead, Lisa L. ... '64 '91 C.388 B.A. L.145 J.D. 233 S. Wacker Dr.
Moorhead, David J. ... '76 '03 C.93 A.B. L.477 J.D. [Ⓐ Gardner C.&D.]
Moorhead, James P. ... '72 '99 C.276 B.A. L.424 J.D. [Ⓐ FagelHaber]
Mora, Ronald N., (AV) ... '33 '58 C.347 B.S. L.597 J.D. [Gould&R.]
Mora, Steven H., (AV) ... '44 '68 C.1036 B.A. L.309 J.D. [Mora,B.W.&U.] ⊙
Mora, Baugh, Waitzman & Unger, (AV)
55 West Monroe Street, Suite 600 (⊙Lincolnshire)
Morales, Isela ... '76 '02 C.681 A.B. L.477 J.D. [Ⓐ Mayer,B.R.&M.]
Morales, Melinda J. ... '67 '94 C.118 B.A. L.494 J.D. [Much S.F.D.A.&R.]
Moran, Alfred C. ... '48 '76 C.226 B.A. L.597 J.D. 1227 E. Madison Park‡
Moran, Donald J., (AV) ... '51 '77 C.597 B.A. L.823 J.D. [Pedersen&H.]

Moran, Edmund B., Jr., (AV) '47 '73 C.602 B.B.A. L.424 J.D.
53 West Jackson Boulevard, Suite 857, 60604
Telephone: 312-408-1544 Fax: 312-408-1539
Email: moran_law@earthlink.net
General Civil Litigation. Trials and Appeals. Environmental, Commercial, Civil Rights and Torts, Criminal, Constitutional and Defamation.
See Professional Biographies, CHICAGO, ILLINOIS

Moran, Eric R. ... '71 '01 C.602 B.S. L.146 J.D. [Ⓐ McDonnell B.H.&B.] (See Pat. Sect.)
Moran, Erin E. ... '73 '98 C.999 B.A. L.365 J.D. [Clausen M.]
Moran, James A. ... '67 '96 C.338 B.S. L.209 J.D. [Nyhan,P.B.K.&L.]
Moran, James B. ... '30 '58 C.477 B.A. L.309 LL.B. Sr. U.S. Dist. J.
Moran, Jeffrey G. ... '— '88 C.98 B.S. L.477 J.D. [Latham&W.]
Moran, Jeffrey R., Jr. ... '79 '04 C&L.93 B.A., J.D. [Ⓐ Daar&V.]
Moran, Jody Wilner, (AV) '58 '83
C.1044 B.A. L.424 J.D. 320 West Ohio Street, Suite 500
Moran, John J., Jr. ... '51 '78 C.589 B.S.Ed. L.424 J.D. State Attys. Off.
Moran, John Thomas, Jr., (AV) ... '— '69 C.602 A.B. L.276 J.D. [J.T.Moran&Assoc.]
Moran, José A. ... '70 '94 L.999 J.D. [Baker&M.]
Moran, Karen Andersen ... '66 '92 C&L.339 B.A., J.D. [Ⓐ N.R.Novak]
Moran, Kathryn Montgomery, (AV) ... '59 '84 C&L.477 B.B.A., J.D. [Lord,B.&B.]
Moran, Lauretta J., (AV) ... '47 '83 L.145 J.D. [Ⓒ Kaye S.]
Moran, Mariah E. ... '71 '00 C.473 B.A. L.1119 J.D. [Ⓐ Durkin&R.]
Moran, Matthew T. ... '54 '79 C&L.339 A.B., J.D. Chicago Mercantile Exch.
Moran, Molly J. ... '68 '98 C.347 B.A. L.1119 J.D. [Ⓐ Jenner&B.]
Moran, Patrick G., (AV) ... '50 '76 C.309 B.A. L.276 J.D. [Sonnenschein N.&R.]
Moran, Robert J., (AV) ... '45 '70 C.602 A.B. L.209 J.D. [Vedder,P.K.&K.]
Moran, Terence J., (AV) ... '54 '83 C.339 B.A. L.424 J.D. [Hughes S.P.R.&D.]
Moran, Thomas E., (AV) ... '15 '39 C&L.145 A.B., J.D. 30 S. Wacker Dr.‡

Moran, John T., & Associates, (AV)
Suite 900, 309 West Washington, 60606
Telephone: 312-630-0200 Telefax: 312-630-0203
Email: j.moran@comcast.net URL: http://www.lawyers.com/jmoran
John Thomas Moran, Jr.
Civil and Criminal Appeals, Labor and Employment, Discrimination Law, Wrongful Termination, State and Federal Criminal Law, Business Litigation.
See Professional Biographies, CHICAGO, ILLINOIS

Morano, Donald V. ... '34 '78 C.597 Ph.D. L.1068 J.D. 1231 Jarvis Ave.
Morask, Dean C. ... '56 '80 C&L.424 B.A., J.D. Asst. State's Atty.
Morawicz, Marion A., (BV) ... '57 '83 C.966 B.S. L.365 J.D. [M.A.Morawicz]
Morawicz, Marion A., Ltd., (BV) ... 20 S. Clark St., Ste. 410
Mordini, Mark A. ... '64 '89 C.123 B.A. L.365 J.D. [Mordini&S.]
Mordini & Schwartz ... 188 W. Randolph
More, Donna B., (AV) ... '— '83 C.860 B.A. L.276 J.D. [Greenberg T.]
More, Joshua R. ... '— '00 C.339 B.S. L.146 J.D. [Ⓐ Schiff H.]
Morel, Gerald L., (AV) ... '— '72 C.589 B.S. L.424 J.D. [Masuda,F.E.&M.]
Morel, Thomas J. ... '— '00 C.976 B.A L.145 J.D. [Ⓐ Kirkland&E.]
Moreland, Adam Robert ... '73 '98 C.339 B.S. L.209 J.D. [Ⓐ Rock F.]
Morella, Timothy M. '72 '97
C.602 B.S.E.E. L.851 J.D. Two North LaSalle Street, Suite 2200 (Pat.)
Morency, Paula J., (AV) ... '— '80 C.674 A.B. L.893 J.D. [Schiff H.]
Moreno, Joseph Mario, (Ltd.) ... '52 '79 C&L.209 B.A., J.D. Commissioner
Morey, Richard J. ... '71 '96 C.339 B.A. L.659 J.D. [DLPiper R.G.C.U.]
Morgan, Alan J. ... '46 '75 C.597 B.S. L.209 J.D. 227 W. Monroe St., Ste. 2000
Morgan, Belinda S. ... '— '00 C.679 B.A. L.339 J.D. [Ⓐ Foley&L.]
Morgan, Betsy Stelle ... '63 '89 C.210 B.A. L.365 J.D. [Baker&M.]
Morgan, Deborah L. ... '— '04 C&L.339 B.A., J.D. [Ⓐ Wildman,H.A.&D.]
Morgan, Donna Evensen, (AV) ... '57 '85 C.165 B.A. L.477 J.D. [Mayer,B.R.&M.]
Morgan, Ellen J. '53 '79 C.597 B.S. L.976 J.D.
Assoc. Dean, Northwestern Univ. School of Law
Morgan, James E. ... '68 '93 C&L.347 B.S., J.D. [Much S.F.D.A.&R.]
Morgan, Karen A. ... '66 '92 C.93 B.A. L.424 J.D. [Ⓐ Ruff,W.&R.]
Morgan, Keevan D., (BV) ... '50 '76 C.966 B.A. L.904 J.D. 900 W. Jackson Blvd., Ste. 4E
Morgan, Timothy B. ... '55 '80 C.742 B.A. L.365 J.D. Vets. Adm.
Morgan, Wendy R. '55 '81
C.424 B.A. L.146 J.D. 333 W. Wacker Dr. (⊙Arlington Heights)
Morgan, William A. ... '56 '82 C.340 B.A. L.339 J.D. Bd. of Educ.
Morgan, Lanoff, Denniston & Jackson, Ltd., (AV) ... 33 North LaSalle Street

Morgan, Lewis & Bockius LLP, (AV)
77 West Wacker Drive, 60601 ⊙
Telephone: 312-324-1000 eFax: 877-432-9652; Fax: 312-324-1001
Email: postmaster@morganlewis.com URL: http://www.morganlewis.com
Members of Firm in Chicago: David Ackerman; Sari M. Alamuddin; Miriam G. Bahcall; Theodore M. Becker; Barry A. Hartstein; Brian D. Hector; Charles C. Jackson; Richard B. Lapp; Steven M. Malina; Thomas A. Marrinson; Philip A. Miscimarra; Grady B. Murdock Jr.; Elizabeth S. Perdue; John D. Shugrue; Nina G. Stillman. Of Counsel in Chicago: Andy R. Anderson; Mary A. Smigielski. Associates in Chicago: Gregory P. Abrams; James E. Bayles, Jr.; Beth A. Black; Shannon Callahan; Deborah S. Davidson; Todd E. Domjan; Kevin Dreher; Ross H. Friedman; Laura M. Geiger; Daniel A. Hetzel; Renee P. Lewis; Tammara M. Lovett; M. Emily Osborne; Michael H. Peipert; Christopher Rizzo; Charis A. Runnels; Daniel J. Struck; Heather Ann Wright; Ethan G. Zelizer.
Acquisitions and Mergers, Antitrust, Banking, Bankruptcy, Civil Litigation, Construction, Corporate, Elections and Campaign Financing, Employee Benefits and Pensions, Environmental, Estate Planning, Government Regulation, Health and Biotechnology, Immigration, Intellectual Property, Insurance, Insurance Recovery, International Law, Investment Management and Financial Services, Labor and Employment, Legislative, Litigation, Municipal Finance, Natural Resources, Non-Profit Organizations, Partnerships, Patent Litigation, Patent Prosecution, Personal Injury, Personal Law and Probate, Product Liability, Public Utilities, Real Estate, Savings and Loan, Securities Offerings, Trademarks and Copyrights, Taxation and White Collar Defense. Unless otherwise indicated, lawyers listed are not certified by the Texas Board of Legal Specialization.
Philadelphia, Pennsylvania Office: 1701 Market Street, 19103-2921. Telephone: 215-963-5000. eFax: 877-432-9652; Fax: 215-963-5001.

(This Listing Continued)

Morgan, Lewis & Bockius LLP (Continued)

Washington, DC Office: 1111 Pennsylvania Avenue, NW, 20004. Telephone: 202-739-3000. eFax: 877-432-9652; Fax: 202-739-3001.
New York, New York Office: 101 Park Avenue, 10178-0060. Telephone: 212-309-6000. eFax: 877-432-9652; Fax: 212-309-6001.
Los Angeles, California Office: 300 South Grand Avenue, Twenty-Second Floor, 90071-3132. Telephone: 213-612-2500. eFax: 877-432-9652; Fax: 213-612-2501.
San Francisco, California Office: One Market, Spear Street Tower, 94105. Telephone: 415-442-1000. eFax: 877-432-9652; Fax: 415-442-1001.
Miami, Florida Office: 5300 Wachovia Financial Center, 200 South Biscayne Boulevard, 33131-2339. Telephone: 305-415-3000. eFax: 877-432-9652; Fax: 305-415-3001.
Pittsburgh, Pennsylvania Office: One Oxford Centre, Thirty-Second Floor, 15219-6401. Telephone: 412-560-3300. eFax: 877-432-9652; Fax: 412-560-7001.
Princeton, New Jersey Office: 502 Carnegie Center, 08540-6241. Telephone: 609-919-6600. eFax: 877-432-9652; Fax: 609-919-6701.
Palo Alto, California Office: 2 Palo Alto Square, 3000 El Camino Real, Suite 700, 94306. Telephone: 650-843-4000. eFax: 877-432-9652; Fax: 650-843-4001.
Dallas, Texas Office: 1717 Main Street, Suite 3200, 75201-7347. Telephone: 214-466-4000. eFax: 877-432-9652; Fax: 214-466-4001.
Harrisburg, Pennsylvania Office: One Commerce Square, 417 Walnut Street, 17101-1904. Telephone: 717-237-4000. eFax: 877-432-9652; Fax: 717-237-4001.
Irvine, California Office: 5 Park Plaza, Suite 1750, 92614. Telephone: 949-399-7000. eFax: 877-432-9652; Fax: 949-399-7001.
Boston, Massachusetts Office: 225 Franklin Street, Suite 1705, 02110. Telephone: 617-451-9700. eFax: 877-432-9652; Fax: 617-451-9710.
London, England Office: Morgan, Lewis & Bockius, 2 Gresham Street, London EC2V 7PE. Telephone: 44-20-7710-5500. Fax: 44-20-7710-5600.
Paris, France Office: Morgan, Lewis & Bockius, 68, rue du Faubourg Saint-Honoré, 75008 Paris. Telephone: +33 (0) 1-53-30-43-00. Fax: +33 (0) 1-53-30-43-01.
Brussels, Belgium Office: Morgan, Lewis & Bockius, 7 Rue Guimard, B-1040. Telephone: 32-2-507-75-00. Fax: 32-2-507-75-55.
Frankfurt, Germany Office: Guiollettstraße 54, D-60325 Frankfurt am Main. Telephone: 49-69-714-007-0. Fax: 49-69-714-007-10.
Tokyo, Japan Office: Shin-Tokyo Building, 9th Floor, 3-1, Marunouchi 3-chome, Chiyoda-ku, Tokyo 100-0005. Telephone: 81-3-5219-2500. Fax: 81-3-5219-2501.

See Professional Biographies, CHICAGO, ILLINOIS

Morgan, Wendy R., The Law Firm of
(See Arlington Heights)

Morgenthaler, Diane M., (BV) .... '61 '87 C.104 A.B. L.94 J.D. [McDermott W.&E.]
Moriarty, Daniel J. .... '67 '92 C.436 B.S. L.209 J.D. 140 South Dearborn, Suite 520
Moriarty, Kathleen Ann .... '73 '00 C.966 B.A. L.146 J.D. Pub. Def. Off.
Morissette, Sherri .... '70 '98 C.927 B.A. L.597 J.D. [🄰 Greenberg T.]
Moritz, Jeremy C. .... '71 '97 C.967 B.A. L.1119 J.D. [Franczek S.]
Moritz, Louis P. .... '64 '90 C&L.145 A.B., J.D. [Mayer,B.R.&M.]
Moritz, Michelle K. .... '72 '97 C.114 B.A. L.347 J.D. [🄰 Eimer S.K.&S.]
Moritz, Terry F., (AV) .... '42 '70 C&L.424 B.S., J.D. [Goldberg,K.B.B.R.&M.]
Morkin, Michael L. .... '65 '90 C.57 A.B. L.339 J.D. [Baker&M.]
Morlas, Toni M. .... '71 '99 C.339 B.A. L.365 J.D. State Atty.
Morlock, Lee .... '— '04 C.012 B.Com. L.1565 J.D. [🄰 Mayer,B.R.&M.]
Morneault, Monique A. '62 '94
C.339 B.S. L.146 J.D. [Wallenstein W.&R.] (See Pat. Sect.)
Morof, Jeffrey W. '— '79 C.477 A.B. L.910 J.D.
(adm. in MO; not adm. in IL) [Bryan C.]
Moroney, John J., IV, (AV) .... '64 '91 C.436 B.A. L.365 J.D. [Bollinger,R.&G.]
Morowitz, Donald H., (Ltd.) .... '33 '57 C.339 L.209 LL.B. 208 S. La Salle St.

Morreale, John F., & Associates, P.C.
(See Glen Ellyn)

Morrell, Barry N. .... '43 '75 C.659 A.B. L.904 J.D. [🄲 Handler,T.&D.]
Morrill, Kendra L. .... '— '94 C.602 B.A. L.146 J.D. [🄰 Jones D.]
Morrill, Stephen S. .... '59 '86 C&L.597 B.A., J.D. 203 N. LaSalle Street, 15th Floor
Morrin, James R., (AV) .... '49 '76 C.46 B.S.M.E. L.146 J.D. [Morrin]
The Morrin Group, (AV) .... 3034 N. Kenmore Ave.
Morris, Arthur I. .... '14 '37 L.209 LL.B. 4132 W. Peterson Ave.
Morris, Brian W. .... '75 '02 C.27 B.A. L.339 J.D. [🄰 Conway&M.]
Morris, David J. .... '66 '91 C.339 B.S. L.1068 J.D. [Fox,H.S.L.&C.]
Morris, Donald C., (AV) .... '49 '78 C.339 A.B. L.209 J.D. [🄲 Mayer,B.R.&M.]
Morris, Gael .... '57 '82 C.339 B.S. L.800 J.D. 2835 N. Sheffield
Morris, Gareth G.R. .... '49 '74 C.1100 B.A. L.36 J.D. 1704 N. Dayton St., Ste. 100
Morris, H. Patrick, (AV) .... '56 '84 C.339 B.A. L.46 J.D. [Johnson&B.]
Morris, Hal R., (BV) .... '— '85 C.145 B.A. L.146 J.D. [Arnstein&L.]
Morris, Henry M., (AV) .... '39 '62 C&L.597 B.S.L., J.D. [Aronberg G.D.&G.]
Morris, James J. '46 '76 C.1100 B.A. L.339 J.D.
V.P. & Assoc. Gen. Coun., CNA Insurance Companies
Morris, Joseph A. .... '51 '76 C&L.145 B.A., J.D. [Morris,R.&D.]
Morris, Kathy .... '50 '75 C.477 B.A. L.588 J.D. 541 N. Fairbanks Ct.
Morris, Kevin L. .... '— '02 C.108 B.S. L.145 J.D. [🄰 Kirkland&E.]
Morris, Lee Ann '65 '95
C.575 B.A. L.945 J.D. Assoc. Coun., BlueCross BlueShield Assoc.
Morris, Louis A. '41 '73 C.912 B.S. L.424 J.D.
Sr. Intell. Prop. Coun., Akzo Nobel Inc. (Pat.)
Morris, R. Cabell, Jr. .... '60 '87 C.475 B.A. L.209 J.D. [Winston&S.]
Morris, Ralph A., (AV) .... '— '70 C.879 B.A. L.477 J.D. [Schiff H.]
Morris, Sandy L. .... '74 '99 C.823 B.A. L.145 J.D. [🄰 Dahm&E.] ⊙
Morris, Steven W. .... '39 '75 C.563 B.S. L.309 J.D. Chicago Tribune
Morris, Vivian P. ... '69 '97 C.813 B.A. L.1066 J.D. Two North LaSalle Street, Suite 2200
Morris, Wendy E. .... '75 '03 C.339 B.S. L.365 J.D. Staff Atty.
Morris, William J., (AV) .... '30 '65 C.339 B.S.M.E. L.365 J.D. [Morris&S.] (Pat.)
Morris, Rathnau & De La Rosa
100 West Monroe Street 21st Floor (⊙London, England)

Morris & Stella, (AV) BR
Suite 1200, 200 West Adams Street, 60606
Telephone: 312-782-2345 Telecopier: 312-750-0924
Email: morrisandstella@ameritech.net
Members of Firm: William J. Morris; Joseph N. Stella; Jeffrey W. Gunn. Associates: Bruce J. Manos; William F. McDermott; Ronald Eric Bentsen.
Products Liability Litigation. General Civil and Commercial Litigation.

See Professional Biographies, CHICAGO, ILLINOIS

Morrison, Claire R. .... '46 '78 C.697 B.A. L.209 J.D. Dept. of Vet. Affs.
Morrison, Daniel .... '— '99 L.477 J.D. [🄰 Sachnoff&W.]
Morrison, David E. .... '68 '93 C.347 B.A. L.477 J.D. [Goldberg,K.B.B.R.&M.]
Morrison, Douglas K. .... '47 '76 C.383 B.A. L.365 J.D. [Morrison&M.]
Morrison, Ian H. .... '70 '95 C.145 B.A. L.910 J.D. [Seyfarth S.]
Morrison, John J., (AV) .... '49 '78 C.339 B.S. L.209 J.D. [J.J.Morrison]
Morrison, John P. (Pete), (AV) .... '56 '82 C.976 B.A. L.276 J.D. [Bell,B.&L.]
Morrison, Kathleen Hogan, (AV) .... '49 '76 C.734 B.A. L.365 J.D. [K.H.Morrison]
Morrison, Kenneth P., P.C., (AV) .... '— '83 C.976 B.A. L.94 J.D. [Kirkland&E.]
Morrison, Michael P., (AV) .... '— '72 C.475 B.A. L.846 J.D. [🄲 Gardner C.&D.]
Morrison, Michael W. .... '53 '79 C.339 B.A. L.424 J.D. [Tressler,S.M.&P.]
Morrison, Portia Owen, (AV) .... '44 '78 C.6 B.A. L.145 J.D. [DLPiper R.G.C.U.]
Morrison, Sidney E., (AV) .... '34 '57 C&L.597 B.S., LL.B. [🄲 Berger,N.&F.]
Morrison, Thomas J. .... '47 '76 C.801 B.S. L.146 J.D. 77 W. Wacker Dr., 6th Fl.
Morrison, William L., (AV) .... '31 '58 C&L.309 A.B., LL.B. [🄲 Gardner C.&D.]
Morrison, John J., Ltd., Law Offices of, (AV) .... 134 N. La Salle

Morrison, Kathleen Hogan, P.C., (AV)
Three First National Plaza, Suite 2100, 70 West Madison Street, 60602
Telephone: 312-977-4477 Fax: 312-977-0872
Email: kmorrison@adoptionattorneys.org URL: http://www.chicagoadoptionattorney.com
Kathleen Hogan Morrison.
Adoption and Child Welfare.

See Professional Biographies, CHICAGO, ILLINOIS

Morrison & Mix .... 120 N. LaSalle Street, Suite 2750
Morrisroe, Richard F. '38 '78 C.424 M.A. L.597 J.D.
Assoc. Atty., Chicago Transit Auth.
Morrissey, Charles F. .... '— '97 C.707 L.1000 J.D. [🄰 Karbal,C.E.S.&D.]
Morrissey, Corinne Seither ..... '37 '85 C.821 B.A. L.424 J.D. John Marshall Law School
Morrissey, Francis D., (AV) '30 '58
C.993 A.B. L.424 J.D. Of Counsel, Archdiocese of Chicago
Morrissey, Francis P., (BV) .... '— '93 C.321 B.A. L.424 J.D. [Schiff H.]
Morrissey, James W. .... '71 '00 C.93 B.A. L.209 J.D. [🄰 Vedder,P.K.&K.]
Morrissey, Lawrence E., (AV) '36 '64
C.339 B.S. L.365 LL.B. 135 S. La Salle St. (⊙Joliet)
Morrissey, Mary Kay .... '62 '87 C.436 B.S. L.862 J.D. [🄰 Mora,B.W.&U.]
Morrissey, Mary M. .... '70 '95 C.741 B.A. L.734 J.D. 1103 Paulina St. Suite 3
Morrissey, Matthew J., (AV) ...... '55 '81 C.436 B.A. L.734 J.D. [M.J.Morrissey&Assoc.]
Morrissey, Meghan C. .... '78 '04 C.339 B.A. L.145 J.D. [🄰 Jenner&B.]
Morrissey, Michael J., (AV) .... '48 '74 C.424 B.A. L.209 J.D. [Cassiday,S.&G.]
Morrissey, Raymond A. .... '64 '89 C.339 B.A. L.381 J.D. Asst. Pub. Def.
Morrissey, Thomas G. .... '55 '79 C&L.276 B.S.B.A., J.D. [T.G.Morrissey]
Morrissey, Matthew J., & Associates, Ltd., (AV) .... 33 N. Dearborn
Morrissey, Thomas G., Ltd. .... 10249 S. Western
Morrone, Ann M. .... '66 '91 C&L.339 B.A., J.D. Dep. Gen. Coun., Arthur Andersen
Morrone, Anthony J. .... '32 '57 C&L.209 B.S.C., LL.B. Contl. Ill. Nat. Bk. & Tr. Co.
Morrone, Anthony J. .... '74 '99 C.339 B.A. L.365 J.D. [Cozen O.]
Morrow, John E., (AV) .... '43 '69 C.800 B.S. L.145 J.D. [Baker&M.]
Morsch, James A. .... '65 '92 C.602 B.A. L.597 J.D. [Butler R.S.&B.]
Morsch, Thomas H., (AV) '31 '55
C&L.597 B.S.L., J.D. Northwestern University School of Law
Morse, Gail H. .... '57 '82 C&L.1049 B.B.A., J.D. [Jenner&B.]
Morse, Hartwell P., III .... '57 '82 C.207 B.A. L.201 J.D. [Welsh&K.]
Morse, John W. .... '— '98 C.210 B.A. L.597 J.D. [🄲 Barnes&T.]
Morse, Leslie .... '66 '94 C.424 B.A. L.209 J.D. [Hill G.&B.]
Morse, Miriam G. .... '60 '85 C.1036 B.A. L.597 J.D. 233 S. Wacker Dr., Ste. 8000
Mortimer, John J., (AV) .... '07 '34 C.339 L.146 LL.B. 9200 S. Winchester‡
Mortimer, John S., (AV) '54 '80
C.602 B.S.M.E. L.209 J.D. [Wood,P.K.C.&M.] (See Pat. Sect.)
Mortimer, Renee J., (CV) '67 '91
C.347 B.A. L.424 J.D. [Hinshaw&C.] (⊙Schererville, IN)
Morton, Paul K., (BV) .... '62 '87 C.477 B.A. L.597 J.D. [Greenberg T.]
Morton, Robert B. .... '57 '82 C.477 B.A. L.309 J.D. 70 W. Madison St., Ste. 1400
Morton, Robert C. .... '29 '53 C&L.145 Ph.B., J.D. 105 W. Madison
Morton, Steven J., (BV) .... '57 '83 C.861 B.A. L.426 J.D. [S.J.Morton&Assoc.]
Morton, Steven J., & Associates, (BV) .... 10 S. LaSalle St., Ste. 3310
Morzy, Anna .... '74 '01 C.209 B.A. L.424 J.D. [🄰 Fragomen,D.B.&L.]
Mosbacher, Bruce E., (AV) .... '54 '81 C.910 A.B. L.1019 J.D. Asst. Pub. Def.
Mosby, Lori Lanciani .... '60 '85 C.454 B.A. L.910 J.D. Asst. App. Def.
Mosby, Monica J. .... '73 '04 C&L.209 B.S., J.D. [🄰 Katten M.R.]
Moscardini, Frank A., Jr., (AV) .... '63 '88 C.209 B.A. L.424 J.D. [Evans,L.S.&M.]
Mosconi, William .... '63 '91 C.424 B.S. L.365 J.D. [Childress D.G.]
Moscovitch, Ruth M. .... '47 '74 C.681 B.A. L.597 J.D. City Colleges of Chicago
Moser, Patricia M., (BV) .... '50 '83 C.1291 B.A. L.209 J.D. Asst. Corp. Coun.
Moses, Herman H. .... '19 '42 L.145 LL.B. 2613 W. Lunt Ave.
Moses, Joel D. .... '62 '92 C.475 B.A. L.365 J.D. [Kass&M.]
Moses, Margaret L., (AVⓉ) '42 '76
C.6 B.A. L.178 J.D. Loyola Univ., Chicago Sch. of Law
Moses, Max G. '49 '73 C&L.900 B.A., J.D.
(adm. in KS; not adm. in IL) Comm. Law League of America
Moses, Michael A., (AV) .... '50 '75 C.477 B.G.S. L.215 J.D. [Siegel M.&S.]
Mosh, Maureen A., (AV) '50 '83 C.553 B.A. L.145 J.D.
Asst. Gen. Coun., Northern Trust Corporation
Mosher, Michael P. .... '47 '76 C.475 B.A. L.209 J.D. 19 S. La Salle St., Ste. 1400
Moshman, Diane K. .... '— '02 C.597 B.S. L.146 J.D. Cir. Ct. Law Clk.

Moskovic & Associates
(See Arlington Heights)

Moskovitz, Michael .... '70 '96 C.347 B.A. L.569 J.D. [Much S.F.D.A.&R.]
Moskowitz, Harold L., (BV) .... '53 '77 C.423 B.A. L.446 J.D. [H.Moskowitz]
Moskowitz, M. Keith .... '71 '98 C.477 B.A. L.306 J.D. [Sonnenschein N.&R.]

Moskowitz, Harold, L.L.C., Law Offices of, (BV)
55 West Monroe Street, Suite 1100, 60603
Telephone: 312-977-0223 Fax: 312-422-8001
Email: hlmatty@aol.com
Harold L. Moskowitz.
Civil Litigation in Federal and State Courts, Secured Lending, Real Estate, Banking, Bankruptcy, Breach of Contract, Business, Partnerships, Debtor and Creditor, Asset Protection, Estate Planning.

See Professional Biographies, CHICAGO, ILLINOIS

Moss, Andrew .... '— '99 C.860 B.A. L.210 J.D. [🄰 Sachnoff&W.]
Moss, Debra Cassens .... '56 '83 C.339 B.A. L.209 J.D. News Editor, ABA Journal
Moss, Gregory H. .... '70 '95 C.966 B.A. L.365 J.D. [Krohn&M.]
Moss, John W. .... '64 '95 C.597 B.A. L.209 J.D. [Winston&S.]
Moss, Joseph .... '27 '62 C.1016 L.365 LL.B. Pres., Joseph Moss Realty Corp.
Moss, Lawrence J., (AV) .... '55 '82 C.178 B.A. L.145 J.D. [Seyfarth S.]
Moss, Robert G. .... '41 '73 C.597 Ph.B. L.146 J.D. 3238 N. Seminary Ave., Apt. 3
Moss, Saul J. .... '08 '30 L.365 LL.B. 5901 N. Sheridan Rd.‡

Moss and Bloomberg, Ltd.
(See Tressler, Soderstrom, Maloney & Priess)

Mossina, Elena .... '72 '95 C.999 B.A. L.597 J.D. [🄰 Baker&M.]
Mossing, Adria East, (BV) .... '61 '88 C.597 B.A. L.209 J.D. [🄰 Cogan&M.]
Moster, James T., Jr. .... '45 '75 C.707 L.146 J.D. [Grotta&M.]
Mosterd, Edward H. '53 '79 C.578 B.A. L.209 J.D.
Assoc. Coun., Allstate Insurance Co.
Mostow, Gary S. .... '— '80 C.966 B.A. L.365 J.D. [🄲 Pedersen&H.]
Mostow, Michael S., (AV) .... '65 '91 C.339 B.A. L.597 J.D. [Quarles&B.]

Mote, Jeffrey G. .... '64 '97 C&L.339 B.S.I.E., J.D. [Ⓐ Greenberg T.]
Motherway, Nicholas J., (AV) .... '40 '65 C.424 B.S.C. L.209 J.D. [Motherway&N.]
Motherway, Nicholas T. .... '71 '98 C.347 B.A. L.209 J.D. [Ⓐ Motherway&N.]

Motherway & Napleton, (AV) BB
100 West Monroe Street Suite 200, 60603
Telephone: 312-726-2699 Fax: 312-726-6851
Email: mn@mnlawoffice.com URL: http://www.mnlawoffice.com
Members of Firm: Nicholas J. Motherway; Robert J. Napleton. Associates: John M. Saletta; Daniel T. Madigan; Kevin J. Golden; Nicholas T. Motherway.
General Civil Practice. Commercial, Negligence, Trial, Malpractice, Products Liability and Aviation Litigation.

See Professional Biographies, CHICAGO, ILLINOIS

Motta, Robert M. .... '45 '72 C.209 L.146 J.D. 218 N. Jefferson St.
Mottier, Charles H., (AV) '55 '81
C&L.339 B.S.G.E., J.D. [Leydig,V.&M.] (See Pat. Sect.)
Motto, Joseph D. .... '13 '35 C&L.209 LL.B. 53 W. Jackson
Motto, Patricia, (AV) .... '47 '79 C.339 B.A. L.209 J.D. 770 N. Halsted St.
Motto, William P. .... '57 '84 C.973 B.A. L.365 J.D. Asst. States Atty.
Mottweiler, Richard R. .... '52 '79 C.339 B.A. L.146 J.D. Off. of the State's Atty.
Motz, Linda B. '54 '79
C.145 B.A. L.477 J.D. Assoc. Gen. Coun., Bally Total Fitness Corp.
Mousin, Craig B. '51 '78
C.367 B.A. L.339 J.D. DePaul Univ. Ctr. for Church/State Studies
Moutoussamy, Penelope .... '45 '86 C.393 B.A. L.424 J.D. Asst. State's Atty.
Mowatt, Cecillia A. ....'60 '87 C.813 A.B. L.112 J.D. Illinois Bell
Mowbray, Brian J. .... '78 '03 C.575 B.S. L.477 J.D. [Ⓐ Grippo&E.]
Mowbray, Trisha L. .... '— '04 C.577 B.A. L.477 J.D. [Ⓐ Jones D.]
Mowder, Gary L., (P.C.), (AV) .... '— '65 C&L.339 B.S., LL.B. [Schiff H.]
Mowery, Philip L., (BV) .... '63 '88 C&L.145 A.B., J.D. [Vedder,P.K.&K.]
Moy, Wallace K. .... '55 '80 C.927 B.S. L.365 J.D. 53 W. Jackson Blvd.
Moya, Jose .... '— '04 C.436 B.S. L.339 J.D. [Ⓐ Flamm&T.]
Moye, Robert M. .... '67 '94 C.101 B.A. L.597 J.D. [Bell,B.&L.]
Moyer, Lane R. .... '63 '88 C.589 B.S. L.597 J.D. [Vedder,P.K.&K.]
Moynihan, John W. .... '— '93 C.339 B.S. L.477 J.D. [Sachnoff&W.]
Moynihan, Michael A., (AV) .... '— '92 C.602 B.S. L.424 J.D. [Freeborn&P.]
Mozdzierz, Kimberly A. .... '64 '89 C.347 B.A. L.46 J.D. Asst. State's Atty.
Mozer, Stefan I., (AV) .... '51 '77 C.393 B.A. L.209 J.D. 39 S. LaSalle St.
Mraz, Frank A. .... '54 '84 C.424 B.S. L.1066 J.D. 5520 S. Mason Ave.
Mrksich, K. Shannon ... '66 '97 C.324 B.S. L.276 J.D. [Brinks H.G.&L.] (See Pat. Sect.)
Mrowiec, John S., (AV) .... '54 '83 C.589 B.A. L.209 J.D. [Conway&M.]
Mrozek, Donald L., (AV) .... '47 '73 C.597 B.S.E. L.209 J.D. [Hinshaw&C.]
Mrozowski, Gail E. .... '55 '81 C.589 B.S. L.146 J.D. [Ⓐ Cornfield&F.]
Mruk, Kevin G. ... '70 '96 C.107 B.A. L.659 J.D. Sr. Coun., Bank One Corp. (Law Dept.)
Msall, Anita M. '52 '83 C.339 B.A. L.209 J.D.
Assoc. Gen. Coun., Off. of Spec. Dep. Receiver
Muceus, Emily K. .... '— '02 C.198 B.S. L.1119 J.D. [Ⓐ Stein,R.&H.]
Much, Morrie, (AV) .... '38 '62 C.339 B.S. L.145 J.D. [Much S.F.D.A.&R.]

Much Shelist Freed Denenberg Ament & Rubenstein, P.C., (AV)
191 North Wacker Drive Suite 1800, 60606-1615 ⊙
Telephone: 312-521-2000 Fax: 312-521-2100
URL: http://www.muchshelist.com
David Alan Alman; Joseph D. Ament; William N. Anspach, Jr.; Marvin N. Benn; Steven P. Blonder; Steven H. Blumenthal; Lawrence H. Brenman; David T. Brown; Penny Brown; Stephen J. Cassin; Leslee Moss Cohen; James M. Dash; Scott L. David; Howard M. Denenberg; Rachel E. Feldstein; Michael J. Freed; Irving M. Geslewitz; Carol V. Gilden; Neal T. Goldstein; David Goodman; Julie M. Hanusa; Don S. Hershman; Michael B. Hyman; Jean K. Janes; Steven A. Kanner; Stephen P. Kikoler; Andrew W. Lapin; Anne E. Larson; Mark S. Litner; William H. London; Gregory B. Mann; Barat S. McClain; Douglas A. Millen; Melinda J. Morales; James E. Morgan; Michael Moskovitz; Morrie Much; Norman B. Newman; Michael L. O'Shaughnessy; Joel S. Polisky; Mitchell S. Roth; Jeffrey C. Rubenstein; Michael B. Sadoff; Joanne A. Sarasin; Scott N. Schreiber; Steven Schwartz; Thomas B. Shapira; Edward D. Shapiro; Michael R. Shelist; Norman A. Shubert; Gregg M. Simon; Steven A. Stender; Christopher J. Stuart; Glenn D. Taxman; Anthony C. Valiulis; Michael B. Viner; John H. Ward; Oran F. Whiting; Philip Wong;—Lisa H. Ben-Isvy; Michael D. Burstein; Soo Choi; Joseph L. Cohen; Jonna Daleiden Eimer; William Silas Hackney, III; Kimberly A. Krugman; Jason L. LaBella; L. Daniel Liutikas; Donal M. O'Brien; Tina Paries; David Matthew Pilotto; Adam K. Sacharoff; Lorne T. Saeks; Michael B. Shaw; Lisa Marie Spelhaug; Robert J. Wozniak (Not admitted in IL). Of Counsel: Jack Shore.
Corporate, Secured Lending, Real Estate, Federal Taxation, Estate Planning and Probate Law, Business, Antitrust, Commodities and Securities Law, Litigation, Trade Regulations Law, Bankruptcy, Environmental Law.
References: American National Bank; NBD Chicago Bank; Harris Trust and Savings Bank and Bank Hapoalim.
Irvine, California Office: 2030 Main Street, Suite 1200, 92614. Telephone: 949-851-7475. Fax: 949-250-1714.

See Professional Biographies, CHICAGO, ILLINOIS

Mucha, Jeff .... '50 '82 C.597 B.A. L.209 J.D. 420 West Belmont Avenue, Apt. 5C
Muchin, Allan B., (P.C.), (AV) .... '36 '61 C&L.966 B.B.A., LL.B. [Ⓒ Katten M.R.]
Muchin, Andrea K., (BV) .... '62 '87 C.475 B.A. L.94 J.D. [Schiller,D.&F.]
Muchin, Arthur B., (AV) .... '43 '67 C&L.966 B.S., J.D. [Laner,M.D.B.L.&T.]
Muchin, Marc L. .... '53 '82 C.966 B.S. L.861 J.D. Ill. Dept. of Rev.
Muchoney, Andrew A. .... '64 '93 C.589 B.A. L.209 J.D. [Ⓐ Coston&R.]
Muchunas, Peter J. .... '64 '89 C.886 B.S. L.146 J.D. [Kallow&M.]
Muczynski, Michael .... '— '98 C.475 B.S. L.477 J.D. [Marshall,G.&B.] (See Pat. Sect.)

Mudd, Charles Lee, Law Offices of '68 '97 C.679 B.A. L.1252 J.D.
3344 North Albany Avenue, 60618
Telephone: 773-588-5410 Fax: 773-588-5440 URL: http://www.muddfirm.com
Email: cmudd@muddlawoffices.com URL: http://www.muddlawoffices.com
Language: English.
Civil and Commercial Litigation, Internet Law, Intellectual Property, Technology Law, Privacy Law, Real Estate, Elder Law.

See Professional Biographies, CHICAGO, ILLINOIS

Mudd, Susan R. '56 '83 C&L.966 B.A., J.D.
(adm. in WI; not adm. in IL) 6707 N. Newgard Ave.
Mudd Leutheuser, Shannon .... '76 '03 C.502 B.S. L.911 J.D. [Ⓐ Winston&S.]
Muehlstein, John H. .... '55 '80 C.1111 B.A. L.201 J.D. [Pedersen&H.]
Muehlstein, Mary C., (AV) .... '55 '85 C.339 B.S. L.146 J.D. [Pedersen&H.]
Muelhausen, James A. .... '50 '75 C.472 B.B.A. L.146 J.D. [Serkland&M.]
Mueller, Bradley A. .... '60 '86 C.957 B.A. L.365 J.D. [Righeimer M.&C.]
Mueller, Edward B., (AV) .... '47 '73 C.424 B.S. L.597 J.D. [Nisen&E.]
Mueller, Frederick S. .... '51 '76 C.347 B.S. L.345 J.D. [Johnson&B.]
Mueller, James T. .... '68 '95 C&L.339 B.A., J.D. [Ⓐ Holland&K.]
Mueller, Kevin J. .... '79 '05 C.473 B.S. L.597 J.D. [Ⓐ Butler R.S.&B.]
Mueller, Kristine A. .... '77 '04 C.338 B.S. L.209 J.D. [Ⓐ Coghlan K.C.]
Mueller, Kurt J. H. .... '— '91 C.966 B.B.A. L.94 J.D. [Cinnamon M.]
Mueller, Leslye A. .... '50 '75 C&L.69 B.A., J.D. Amer. Natl. Bk.
Mueller, Lisa von Bargen '67 '92
C.879 B.S. L.897 J.D. [Wood,P.K.C.&M.] (See Pat. Sect.)

Mueller, Michael J. .... '— '86 C.339 B.A. L.209 J.D. [Ⓒ Barnes&T.]
Mueller, Patricia B. .... '71 '04 C.347 B.S. L.365 J.D. [Ⓐ Pretzel&S.]
Mueller, Richard E., (AV) .... '27 '51 C&L.597 B.S., LL.B. 115 S. La Salle St.
Mueller, Wesley O., (AV) '61 '88
C.150 B.S.E.E. L.608 J.D. [Leydig,V.&M.] (See Pat. Sect.)
Muench, John E., (AV) .... '48 '76 C.321 A.B. L.597 J.D. [Mayer,B.R.&M.]
Muensterman, Peggy A., (AV) '54 '92
C.238 B.S. L.209 J.D. Corp. Coun., Borg-Warner Inc.
Muentzer, Ralph .... '40 '66 C.347 B.A. L.365 LL.B. Harris Tr. & Svgs. Bk.
Mug, John W. .... '46 '77 C&L.424 A.B., J.D. [Ⓐ Carpenter&C.]
Muhl, Charles J. .... '70 '00 C.910 B.A. L.276 J.D. 200 W. Adams St., Suite 800
Muhlenbeck, Sandra A. .... '70 '95 C.896 B.A. L.178 J.D. [McDermott W.&E.]
Muhr, Robert A. .... '49 '74 C.424 B.A. L.365 J.D. [Stellato&S.]
Muir, Arthur B., (AV) .... '46 '77 C.659 A.B. L.597 J.D. [Neal,G.&E.]
Muir, John S. .... '65 '93 C.840 B.S. L.365 J.D. [Ⓐ Salvi,S.&P.]
Mulack, Donald G., (AV) .... '— '66 C.589 B.S. L.146 J.D. [Holland&K.]
Mulaney, Charles W., Jr., (AV) .... '49 '75 C.276 A.B. L.976 J.D. [Skadden,A.S.M.&F.]
Mulaney, Ellen Stanton .... '50 '75 C.276 B.S.F.S. L.976 J.D. 2525 N. Burling St.
Mulcahy, Brian J. .... '— '94 C.1100 B.A. L.117 J.D. Gen. Coun., Greater Ill. Title Co.
Mulcahy, Brian S. .... '— '02 C&L.477 B.B.A., J.D. [Ⓐ Jones D.]
Mulcahy, Daniel J. .... '47 '72 C.742 B.A. L.424 J.D. Sr. Coun., Aon Corp.
Mulcahy, Kourtney A. .... '75 '02 C.339 B.A. L.1000 J.D. [Ⓐ Hinshaw&C.]
Mulcahy, Michael R. .... '64 '93 C.338 B.S. L.365 J.D. [Ⓐ Vedder,P.K.&K.]
Mulcahy, Thomas W. .... '74 '00 C.347 B.A. L.365 J.D. [Ⓐ Crisham&K.]
Mulder, Emily L. .... '76 '01 C.477 B.A. L.597 J.D. Two North LaSalle Street, Suite 2200
Mulder, Michael M. .... '49 '75 C.932 B.A. L.879 J.D. [Meites,M.B.&M.]
Muldoon, John J. .... '30 '56 C.602 A.B. L.146 LL.B. 105 W. Madison St.
Muldoon, John J., III, (AV) .... '58 '83 C.602 B.A. L.146 J.D. 10 S. La Salle St.
Muldowney, Patrick T. .... '65 '91 C.339 B.A. L.46 J.D. 642 N. Dearborn St.
Muldrow, Wayne S. .... '64 '90 C.188 B.S. L.659 J.D. Northern Trust Corporation
Mulherin, Joseph Kevin .... '74 '02 C.436 B.S. L.1117 J.D. [Ⓐ Vedder,P.K.&K.]
Mulhern, Brian J. .... '56 '81 C.602 B.A. L.597 J.D. [Ⓒ MacCabe&M.]
Mulhern, Joseph P., (AV) .... '21 '51 C.1191 B.E. L.209 J.D. 227 W. Monroe St.
Mulhern, Joseph P., (AV) .... '49 '75 C.602 B.A. L.597 J.D. [Ⓒ Gozdecki&D.]
Mulhern, Michael L. .... '61 '86 C&L.602 B.A., J.D. [Winston&S.]
Mulholland, Kristin A. '57 '88 C&L.347 B.A., J.D.
(adm. in IN; not adm. in IL) [Ⓐ S.P.Polick&Assoc.]
Mulholland, Toby Patrick .... '74 '00 C.352 B.A. L.209 J.D. One East Walker Dr.
Mullen, Christopher, (P.C.), (AV) .... '45 '80 C.424 B.S. L.209 J.D. [Mullen&K.]
Mullen, Edward B., III .... '67 '98 C.659 B.A. L.273 J.D. [Ⓐ Ross,D.&B.]
Mullen, J. Thomas, (AV) .... '40 '67 C.674 B.S.E. L.477 J.D. [Mayer,B.R.&M.]
Mullen, John C., (Ltd.), (AV) .... '22 '49 C.424 A.B. L.209 LL.B. [Ⓒ Mullen&K.]
Mullen, Michael J., (AV) .... '54 '82 C.424 B.S. L.365 J.D. [Kralovec&M.]
Mullen, Michael T., (AV) .... '56 '81 C.436 B.A. L.424 J.D. [P.B.Episcope]

Mullen & Kelliher, (AV) BB
A Partnership including Professional Corporations
Three First National Plaza, Suite 2060, 60602
Telephone: 312-346-2998 Fax: 312-346-6024
Members of Firm: Christopher Mullen (P.C.); Suzanne Dvorak Kelliher. Of Counsel: John C. Mullen (Ltd.); Jon G. Carlson.
Personal Injury, Wrongful Death, Product Liability, Malpractice and Railroad F.E.L.A. Cases, Civil and Trial Practice in all State and Federal Courts.

See Professional Biographies, CHICAGO, ILLINOIS

Mullenix, Philip A. .... '53 '83 C.597 B.S. L.365 J.D. 55 W. Wacher Dr.
Muller, Kurt A., (BV) .... '55 '86 C.966 B.S. L.365 J.D. [Muller]
Muller, Susan Garrity '70 '97 C.674 A.B. L.477 J.D.
U.S. Enviro. Protection Agency, Reg. Coun. Off.

Muller Firm, The, Ltd., (BV)
The Muller Building, 110 West Grand Avenue, 60610-4269
Telephone: 312-467-6700 Facsimile: 312-467-0252 URL: http://www.mullaw.com
Email: kmuller@mullaw.com URL: http://www.lawyers.com/mullerlaw
Kurt A. Muller;—Todd A. Walters; Michael L. Lodermeier.
Practice concentrated in Trial/Settlement of High-Profile Domestic Relations Cases concerning Property Division, Child Custody, Child Support, Domestic Violence, Paternity, Alternative Living Arrangements, Adoption, Ante-and Post-Nuptial Agreements, Probate Matters including Guardianships, Wills and Trusts, Contract Preparation, Negotiation and Litigation, Criminal charge Trial and Settlement, analysis of Stock, Option, Commodity, Real Estate and Insurance Offerings and Holdings, Business Valuations, Hidden-Asset Discovery and Appellate Advocacy.

See Professional Biographies, CHICAGO, ILLINOIS

Mullin, George L. .... '66 '91 C.276 B.S.F.S. L.145 J.D. [Sidley A.B.&W.]
Mullin, Gerald B., (AV) .... '32 '57 C.145 A.B. L.365 J.D. [G.B.Mullin]
Mullin, Joseph C. .... '70 '95 C.276 B.A. L.145 J.D. [Ⓐ Sidley A.B.&W.]
Mullin, Mary Anne .... '— '89 C.399 B.A. L.966 J.D. [Ⓒ Schiff H.]
Mullin, Patricia E. '— '60 C.157 B.A. L.209 J.D.
V.P. & Corp. Secy., Bankers Life & Cas. Co.
Mullin, Gerald B., P.C., (AV) .... 55 East Monroe Street, Suite 3420
Mullins, Laura J. .... '— '95 C.823 B.S. L.365 J.D. [Ⓐ W.G.Pintas&Assoc.]
Mullins, Michael T. .... '72 '97 C.436 B.S. L.209 J.D. [Ⓐ Winston&S.]
Mulroe, John G. .... '59 '88 C&L.424 B.B.A., J.D. [J.G.Mulroe]
Mulroe, John G., P.C. .... 6687 N. Northwest Hwy.
Mulroy, Thomas R., (AV) .... '46 '73 C.770 B.A. L.424 J.D. [McGuirewoods]
Mulroy, Thomas R., III .... '73 '98 C.339 B.A. L.424 J.D. [Hinshaw&C.]
Mulvaney, James N. '34 '62 C&L.209 A.B., J.D.
Sr. Atty., ABN-AMRO North America, Inc. (Legal Department)
Mulvanny, Barbara J. .... '52 '84 C.959 B.S. L.424 J.D. [Ⓐ Davis M.]
Mulvihill, Michael D., (AV) .... '63 '88 C.436 B.A. L.209 J.D. [Ⓐ Cooney&C.]
Muncy, Judith K. .... '55 '80 C.713 B.A. L.602 J.D. [Ⓒ Barack F.K.P.&N.]
Munday, John J., (AV) .... '43 '68 C.801 B.A. L.146 J.D. [Munday&N.]
Munday, M. Madeleine .... '49 '78 C.450 B.A. L.734 J.D. Sisters of Good Shepherd

Munday & Nathan, The Law Offices of, (AV) BB
33 North Dearborn Street, Suite 2220, 60602
Telephone: 312-346-5678 Fax: 312-346-8394
John J. Munday; Thomas J. Nathan; Edward G. Proctor, Jr.;—Jeffrey A. Schulkin; Andrew Eisenberg.
Plaintiff's Personal Injury Litigation, Negligence, Medical and Professional Negligence, Products Liability, Premises Liability, Construction Accidents, Railroad and Aviation Law and Police Pursuit Litigation.

See Professional Biographies, CHICAGO, ILLINOIS

Mundo, John P. .... '66 '91 C&L.602 B.A., J.D. [Duffy&M.]
Mundt, David Michael '70 '97
C.352 B.S.B.M.E. L.365 J.D. [Cook,A.M.M.C.&M.] (See Pat. Sect.)
Mungai, Cristina .... '68 '96 C.424 B.A. L.146 J.D. [Ⓐ Johnson&B.]
Mungerson, Darren M. .... '72 '98 C.339 B.S. L.365 J.D. [Ⓐ Jenner&B.]
Mungy, Virgil W. .... '35 '74 C.1016 B.A. L.365 J.D. 5453 W. Diversey Ave.
Munitz, Gerald F., (AV) .... '33 '60 C.477 B.A. L.145 J.D. [Goldberg,K.B.B.R.&M.]

Munitz, Gillian E. '74 '02 C.477 B.A. L.1494 J.D.
(adm. in NY; not adm. in IL) Ⓐ Barack F.K.P.&N.]
Muniz, Lizabeth A. '76 '01 C.878 B.S. L.477 J.D. [Ⓐ Stein,R.&H.]
Muno, John M. '— '04 C.339 B.S. L.597 J.D. [Ⓐ Kirkland&E.]
Muñoz, Eric J. '69 '99 C.813 B.A. L.352 J.D. [Ⓐ Scandaglia&R.]
Muñoz, George, (AV) '51 '81 C.846 B.B.A. L.309 J.D. [Tobin P.&M.] ⊙
Munoz, Gustavo '58 '84 C&L.339 B.A., J.D. Off. of State's Atty.
Munoz, Ricardo J. '69 '96 C.960 B.S. L.589 J.D. 6321 N. Avondale Ave., Ste. 211
Munro, Ellen Kane, (AV) '43 '72 C.424 B.B.A. L.597 J.D.
V.P. & Gen. Coun., Loyola University of Chicago
Munson, James C., (AV) '— '70 C.976 B.A. L.966 J.D. [Kirkland&E.]
Munzer, Cynde Hirschtick '— '83 C.339 B.S. L.146 J.D. [Arnstein&L.]
Muraff, James P. '67 '94 C.339 B.S. [Wallenstein W.&R.] (See Pat. Sect.)
Murata, Jason T. '78 '03 C.013 B.S. L.910 J.D. [Ⓐ Leydig,V.&M.]
Murawski, Steven J. '— '97 C.209 B.S. L.146 J.D. [Ⓐ Gardner C.&D.]
Murch, Jill L. '— '98 C.145 A.B. L.339 J.D. [Ⓑ Foley&L.]
Murch, Trent M. '71 '98 C.98 B.S. L.339 J.D. [Ⓐ Mayer,B.R.&M.]
Murday, Donald A. '60 '85 C.602 B.B.A. L.128 J.D. [Chittenden,M.&N.]
Murdoch, Christopher J., (AV) '62 '87 C.276 B.A. L.477 J.D. [Holland&K.]
Murdock, Charles W., (AV) '35 '63 C.46 B.S.Ch.E. L.424 J.D. School of Law
Murdock, Grady B., Jr., (AV) '48 '74 C.293 B.A. L.597 J.D. [Morgan,L.&B.]
Murer, Matthew J. '69 '94 C&L.339 B.A., J.D. 321 North Clark, Suite 2800
Murges, George J., (AV) '27 '51 C&L.209 LL.B. 33 N. Dearborn
Muriel, Robert H. '— '93 C.339 B.S. L.424 J.D. [Muriel R.]
Muriel Renner LLC 566 W. Lake St., Ste. 200 (⊙Chicago)
Murillo, Marisa '03 C.976 B.A. L.800 J.D. [Ⓐ Kirkland&E.]
Murnane, Mark, (AV) '67 '92 C.321 B.A. L.424 J.D. [Ⓐ Anesi,O.R.N.&K.]
Murnighan, F. Kevin '50 '76 C.103 A.B. L.365 J.D. [Carey,F.W.&B.]
Murnighan, John B., (AV) '20 '48 C.424 Ph.B. L.597 J.D. 235 South Wacker Drive
Murnighan, Thomas J., (AV) '55 '81 C.209 B.A. L.597 J.D. [Lord,B.&B.]
Murov, Jacob C. '78 '04 C.347 B.S. L.209 J.D. [Ⓑ Cremer,K.S.&S.]
Murov, Lauren Jill '— '04 C.347 B.A. L.209 J.D. [Ⓐ DLPiper R.G.C.U.]
Murphey, John B. '51 '76 C.177 B.A. L.424 J.D. [Rosenthal,M.C.]
Murphy, Aileen T. '— '02 C.104 B.A. L.477 J.D. [Ⓐ DLPiper R.G.C.U.]
Murphy, Anne M. '61 '86 C.95 A.B. L.94 J.D. Il. Dept. of Pub. Health
Murphy, Arthur J. '50 '78 C.128 B.A. L.365 J.D. [Murphy&S.]
Murphy, Brenda J. '60 '89 C.967 B.A. L.424 J.D. Providus
Murphy, Brian, (AV) '64 '89 C.742 B.A. L.424 J.D. [Hofeld&S.]
Murphy, Byran F. '56 '84 C.229 B.S. L.262 J.D. The Hartford
Murphy, Charles E., (AV) '42 '67 C.861 B.S. L.145 J.D. [Ogletree,D.N.S.&S.]
Murphy, Charles G. '46 '74 C.436 B.A. L.146 J.D. 542 S. Dearborn St., Ste. 750
Murphy, Christopher H. '74 '99 C.477 B.A. L.93 J.D. [Ⓑ Cozen O.]
Murphy, Christopher M. '64 '90 C.276 B.S. L.145 J.D. [McDermott W.&E.]
Murphy, Claire P., (BV) '60 '89 C.602 B.A. L.424 J.D. [Sperling&S.]
Murphy, Clyde E. '48 '76 C.976 B.A. L.178 J.D. Exec. Dir., Chicago Lawyers Comm.
Murphy, Cornelius M. '— '97 C.602 B.A. L.276 J.D. [Ⓐ Winston&S.]
Murphy, Daniel E. '60 '85 C.966 B.B.A. L.436 J.D. 300 W Washington St # 1120
Murphy, David H. '20 '43 C.363 L.209 LL.B. 111 W. Wash. St.‡
Murphy, Donald X. '32 '58 L.209 J.D. 651 S. Wells
Murphy, Edward J., (AV) '47 '80 C.46 B.S. L.209 J.D. [Williams M.&J.]
Murphy, Elizabeth O. '58 '89 C.201 B.Tech. L.966 J.D.
(adm. in WI; not adm. in IL) U.S. EPA
Murphy, Eugene E., Jr. '— '87 C.177 B.A. L.146 J.D. [Murphy&H.]
Murphy, Francis Patrick, (AV) '48 '75 C.597 B.S.B.A. L.146 J.D. [Corboy&D.]
Murphy, James D. '30 '54 C&L.597 B.S.L., LL.B. 180 N. LaSalle St.
Murphy, James F., (AV) '— '81 C.589 B.S. L.209 J.D. [Adler,M.&M.]
Murphy, James P. '65 '92 C.475 B.S. L.209 J.D. [McAndrews,H.&M.] (See Pat. Sect.)
Murphy, Jane K. '— '90 C.602 B.A. L.273 J.D. [Ⓑ Jones D.]
Murphy, Joann P. '— '03 C.347 B.S. L.597 J.D. [Ⓐ Latham&W.]
Murphy, John G. '58 '84 C.597 B.S. L.209 J.D. Asst. States Atty.
Murphy, John J., Jr., (AV) '— '81 C.424 B.A. L.146 J.D. [Ⓑ Hennessy&R.]
Murphy, John M. '62 '88 C.602 B.A. L.339 J.D. [Baker&M.]
Murphy, Kathleen M. '— '85 C.720 B.A. L.424 J.D. [Gardner C.&D.]
Murphy, Kevin M., (AV) '— '81 C.937 B.A. L.145 J.D. [Latham&W.]
Murphy, Kevin W. '— '89 C.339 B.S. L.280 J.D. [Adler,M.&M.]
Murphy, Kris R. '— '96 C.602 B.A. L.180 J.D. [Ⓑ Freeborn&P.]
Murphy, Madeleine Sullivan '60 '85 C.93 B.A. L.602 J.D. Asst. U.S. Atty.
Murphy, Mark J. '64 '89 C.602 B.S. L.436 J.D.
[Cook,A.M.M.C.&M.] (See Pat. Sect.)
Murphy, Martin P. '63 '90 C.602 B.B.A. L.597 J.D. [Holland&K.]
Murphy, Matthew M. '56 '82 C.339 B.A. L.146 J.D. [Bates&C.]
Murphy, Matthew M. '73 '99 C&L.477 B.A., J.D. [Ⓐ Skadden,A.S.M.&F.]
Murphy, Maureen A., (AV) '59 '84
C.424 B.B.A. L.188 J.D. Sr. Coun., Archdiocese of Chicago
Murphy, Michael F. '51 '78 C.912 B.A. L.215 J.D. [S.G.Thomas]
Murphy, Michael J. '41 '70 C.424 B.S. L.365 J.D. Cir. J.
Murphy, Morgan F., III '60 '86 C.597 B.A. L.146 J.D. 221 N. La Salle St., Ste 2500
Murphy, Nicole Ciszak '71 '00 C&L.93 B.A., J.D. [Ⓐ DLPiper R.G.C.U.]
Murphy, Patrick J. '63 '86 C&L.128 B.A., J.D. F.B.I.
Murphy, Richard D., Jr., (AV) '60 '85
C.602 B.B.A. L.107 J.D. First V.P. - Legal, Equity Residential
Murphy, Richard Joseph '71 '98 C.1372 B.A. L.602 J.D. [Ⓐ Dahl&B.]
Murphy, Richard L., (AV) '51 '76 C.602 B.A. L.93 J.D. [Clausen M.]
Murphy, Robert '23 '49 C&L.602 LL.B. [R.Murphy]
Murphy, Rose M. '57 '82 C.339 B.A. L.221 J.D.
Sr. Coun., Bldg. Materials Grp., International Paper Co.
Murphy, Sandra R., (AV) '49 '76 C.597 B.A. L.424 J.D. [McDermott W.&E.]
Murphy, Sheila M. '37 '70 C.436 B.S. L.209 J.D. [Ⓑ Rothschild,B.&M.]
Murphy, Siobhan M. '65 '92
C.999 B.A. L.146 J.D. 53 West Jackson Boulevard, Suite 1150
Murphy, Thaddeus '66 '91 C.339 B.S. L.424 J.D. Sr. Cnsl, Merrill Lynch & Co.
Murphy, Thomas J., (AV) '56 '81 C.340 B.A. L.309 J.D. [McDermott W.&E.]
Murphy, Thomas J. '43 '67 C.602 B.A. L.597 J.D. [T.J.Murphy]
Murphy, Thomas P. '53 '85 C&L.209 B.A., J.D. 6247 W. 63rd St.
Murphy, Thomas W., (AV) '54 '77 C.276 B.A.B.S. L.365 J.D. [Burke,W.M.&S.]
Murphy, Timothy J., (AV) '54 '79 C.597 B.S.S. L.209 J.D. [Ⓐ MacCabe&M.]
Murphy, Todd M. '— '03 C.602 B.A. L.365 J.D. [Ⓐ Clausen M.]
Murphy, William J. '70 '95 C.724 B.A. L.300 J.D. [Ⓐ Barnes,R.&C.]
Murphy, William P., (AV) '43 '68 C.436 B.S. L.146 J.D. 542 S. Dearborn St.

Murphy & Hourihane, L.L.C.
77 West Wacker Drive, Suite 4800, 60601
Telephone: 312-606-9300 Fax: 312-606-8765
Email: info@mhlitigation.com URL: http://www.mhlitigation.com
Eugene E. Murphy Jr.; John N. Hourihane, Jr.

(This Listing Continued)

Murphy & Hourihane, L.L.C. (Continued)
Litigation Practice including Commercial Litigation, Government Relations, Contracts, Employment Agreements, Construction Disputes, Real Estate, White Collar Crime and Professional Malpractice.
See Professional Biographies, CHICAGO, ILLINOIS

Murphy, Robert, Ltd. 77 W. Washington St., Ste. 10
Murphy & Smith, Ltd. 53 W. Jackson Blvd.
Murphy, Thomas J., P.C. 111 W. Washington St.
Murphy-Petros, Melissa A. '65 '95 C.347 B.A. L.424 J.D. [Clausen M.]
Murray, A. John, Ph.D. '53 '99 C.1481 B.S.C. L.146 J.D. [Ⓐ Brinks H.G.&L.]
Murray, Bernard J. '57 '83 C.339 B.S.C. L.209 J.D. Asst. State's Atty.
Murray, Brian J. '— '00 C&L.602 B.S., J.D. [Ⓐ Jones D.] (See Pat. Sect.)
Murray, Catherine A. '63 '88 C.741 B.A. L.1000 J.D. [Linebarger G.B.&S.]
Murray, Christopher Charles '71 '02 C.124 B.A. L.659 J.D. [Ⓐ Mayer,B.R.&M.]
Murray, D. Michael '71 '97 C.589 B.S. L.209 J.D. [Mayer,B.R.&M.]
Murray, Daniel C., (AV) '— '76 C.436 B.A. L.424 J.D. [Johnson&B.]
Murray, Daniel R., (AV) '46 '70 C.602 A.B. L.309 J.D. [Jenner&B.]
Murray, Donald X. '22 '50 C&L.424 A.B., J.D. 10320 S. Seeley Ave.‡
Murray, Douglas C. '— '05 C.597 B.A. L.424 J.D. [Ⓐ Gardner C.&D.]
Murray, Gregory S., (AV) '49 '74 C.602 A.B. L.893 J.D. [Winston&S.]
Murray, Jacqueline B. '47 '74 C.339 B.A. L.209 J.D. 175 E. Delaware
Murray, James B. '43 '70 C.436 A.B. L.209 J.D. 100 E. Erie St.‡
Murray, James C. '17 '40 C&L.209 LL.B. 9432 S. Leavitt St.
Murray, James E., (BV) '58 '84 C.602 B.A. L.365 J.D. [J.E.Murray]
Murray, James R., (AV) '60 '86 C.339 B.S. L.365 J.D. [Tressler,S.M.&P.]
Murray, Joel '40 '64 C.966 B.S. L.597 LL.M. 29 E. Scott St.
Murray, John C. '45 '70 C&L.477 B.B.A., J.D. Sr. Coun., Bank of America Illinois
Murray, John M., (AV) '30 '54 C&L.424 B.S., J.D. 30 N. La Salle St.
Murray, John P. '28 '52 C.424 L.365 LL.B. 123 W. Madison St.
Murray, Leonard '46 '74 C.717 B.S. L.597 J.D. J.D. Touche Ross & Co.
Murray, Lynn Hagman '60 '85 C&L.339 B.S., J.D. [Grippo&E.]
Murray, Mary Ann '62 '91 C.999 B.A. L.734 J.D. [Ⓐ Burke B.&P.]
Murray, Michael A. '40 '79 C.339 B.A. L.597 J.D. Prof. of Law, DePaul Univ.
Murray, Michael J., (BV) '56 '82 C&L.424 B.B.A., J.D. [Carey,F.W.&B.]
Murray, Nicole '— '02 C.679 B.S.Ch.E. L.893 J.D. [Ⓐ Gardner C.&D.]
Murray, Sean P. '76 '01 C.927 B.A. L.424 J.D. [Ⓐ Anesi,O.R.N.&K.]
Murray, Siobhan C. '72 '97 C.424 B.A. L.209 J.D. Off. of the Pub. Guard.
Murray, Stephen M., (AV) '47 '72 C.210 B.A. L.597 J.D. [Lord,B.&B.]
Murray, Thomas '57 '84 C.966 B.A. L.424 J.D. [Wilson E.M.E.&D.]
Murray, James E., Ltd., (BV) 53 W. Jackson, Ste. 1540
Murtagh, Thomas B. '72 '98 C.424 B.B.A. L.339 J.D. KPMG Peat Marwick, LLP
Murtaugh, Christopher D., (AV) '45 '70 C&L.339 A.B., J.D. [Winston&S.]
Murtaugh, Timothy J., III, (AV) '— '62 C.602 A.B. L.477 LL.B. [McKenna S.]
Murthy, Sanjay K. '75 '00 C.425 B.S. L.61 J.D. [Ⓐ Bell,B.&L.] (Pat.)

Murzyn, Brenda L., Law Office of '54 '83 C.347 B.S. L.589 J.D.
1255 North State Parkway, 60610 ⊙
Telephone: 312-330-3458 Fax: 312-266-5967
Email: brendamurzynlaw@ameritech.net URL: http://www.lawyers.com/murzyn
Real Estate Closings, For Sale By Owner Investment Property, Foreclosure, Probate, Wills, Residential Real Estate, Commercial Real Estate, Real Estate Investment, Land Trusts, Land Sales, Real Estate Acquisitions, Real Estate Contracts.
See Professional Biographies, CHICAGO, ILLINOIS

Musburger, Todd W., (AV) '44 '73 C.208 B.A. L.209 J.D. [T.W.Musburger]
Musburger, Todd W., Ltd., (AV) 142 E. Ontario
Musca, Albert M. '63 '02 C.424 L.365 J.D. 401 East Ontario, Suite 902
Muschler, David E., (AV) '46 '73 C.210 B.A. L.597 J.D. [D.Muschler]

Muschler, David, Law Office of, (AV)
135 South LaSalle Street, Suite 3950, 60603
Telephone: 312-759-0102 Fax: 312-629-0174
Email: cubmusch@aol.com URL: http://www.lawyers.com/muschlerlaw
David E. Muschler.
Construction, Real Estate, Litigation, Arbitration.
See Professional Biographies, CHICAGO, ILLINOIS

Muskal, James B., (AV) '38 '63
C.339 B.S.M.E. L.209 J.D. [Leydig,V.&M.] (See Pat. Sect.)
Mussar, Martin M. '54 '79 C.597 B.A. L.424 J.D. [Pierce,D.B.O.&M.]
Musschoot, Arthur R., (AV) '17 '54 C.103 A.B. L.94 J.D. 300 W. Washington St.
Mussman, John R. '52 '83 C.373 B.A. L.477 J.D. [Holland&K.]
Mutchnik, James H., (AV) '— '89 C.659 B.S. L.597 J.D. [Kirkland&E.]
Muther, Paul S. '44 '74 C.309 B.A. L.813 J.D. 1st Natl. Bk. of Chicago
Mutz, Gregory T. '45 '73 C.210 B.A. L.477 J.D.
Chmn. of the Bd., Amli Residential Props. Tr.
Myalls, Kathleen M. '62 '87 C.477 A.B. L.339 J.D.
Associate Counsel, MCI Worldcom Communications, Inc.
Myers, Benjamin '62 '85 C.1183 B.S. L.365 J.D. 6525 N. Clark St.
Myers, Dennis M., P.C. '— '90 C.930 B.A. L.309 J.D. [Kirkland&E.]
Myers, Holly I. '— '80 C.174 B.A. L.365 J.D. Exec. V.P., Myers-Baker & Co., Inc.
Myers, Leah C. '77 '02 C.228 B.A. L.339 J.D. Asst. Atty. Gen.
Myers, Lewis, Jr. '47 '72 C.329 B.A. L.500 J.D. 25 E Washington St
Myers, Linda K., P.C., (AV) '— '90 C.966 B.A. L.276 J.D. [Kirkland&E.]
Myers, Lonn W. '46 '76 C.475 B.A. L.309 J.D. [McDermott W.&E.]
Myers, Lowell J. '30 '56 C.1016 B.S.C. L.365 J.D. 1060 W. North Shore‡
Myers, Samuel D. '34 '59 C.339 B.A. L.145 J.D. 5875 N. Lincoln Ave.
Myers, Solomon M. '63 '88 C.966 B.A. L.339 J.D. 5875 N. Lincoln Ave., Ste. 244
Myers, Therese M. '58 '97 C.937 B.A. L.276 J.D. Atty., Natl. Assn. of Realtors
Myers, William G., (P.C.), (AV) '30 '53 C&L.597 B.S., J.D. [Rothschild,B.&M.]

Myking, Stephen T., (AV) '47 '72 C.903 B.A. L.893 J.D.
300 South Wacker Drive Suite 3400, 60606-6785
Telephone: 312-786-6176 Fax: 312-986-9192
Email: smyking@cs.com
Immigration Law, Employment Relations Law (U.S. and International) confined to Management.
See Professional Biographies, CHICAGO, ILLINOIS

Myrianthopoulos, Thalia L. '73 '01 C.311 B.A. L.309 J.D. [Ⓐ Jenner&B.]
Myrick, James J., (AV) '43 '69 C.339 B.S. L.477 J.D. [Ⓑ Welsh&K.] (See Pat. Sect.)
N. Velazquez, Mona, Law Office of 8505 S. Pulaski Rd.
Naar, Sonya D. '70 '94 C.788 A.B. L.795 J.D. [DLPiper R.G.C.U.]
Naber, Jennifer A. '62 '88 C.209 B.A. L.424 J.D. [Laner,M.D.B.L.&T.]
Nabor, Joseph T. '57 '89 C.1183 B.A. L.46 J.D. [Fitch,E.T.&F.]
Naborowski, Clarence T. '33 '55 C&L.209 J.D. 303 W. Madison St.
Nacca, Joseph S. '— '03 C.893 B.A. L.178 J.D. [Ⓐ Novack&M.]
Naccasha, Ziyad I. '65 '90 C.1074 B.S. L.602 J.D. [Meckler B.&T.]
Nace, Jill Joyce '74 '00 C.345 B.A. L.813 J.D. [Ⓐ Lord,B.&B.]
Nachman, James L., (AV) '42 '66 C.188 B.A. L.145 J.D. 28 E. Scott St.
Nachman, Robert D., (AV) '50 '83 C.477 B.A. L.309 J.D. [Schwartz C.]

Nachsin, Jonathan . . . . '51 '85 C.930 B.A. L.146 J.D. [J.Nachsin]

Nachsin, Jonathan, P.C.
105 West Adams Street, Suite 3000, 60603-6209
Telephone: 312-327-1777 Fax: 312-431-1456
Email: nachsin@att.net URL: http://www.jonathannachsin.com
Jonathan Nachsin.
Class Actions, Consumer Litigation, Contract Litigation, Warranty Law.
See Professional Biographies, CHICAGO, ILLINOIS

Nachtwey, Steven J. . . . . '75 '00 C.966 B.S. L.494 J.D. [Ⓐ Bartlit B.H.P.&S.]
Nacker, Wayne E. . . . . '47 '78 C.238 B.A. L.209 J.D. Morton International, Inc. (Pat.)
Nackovic, Vera A. . . . . '— '03 C.741 B.S. L.879 J.D. [Ⓐ Mayer,B.R.&M.]
Nadelhoffer, Sarah . . . . '59 '85 C.95 B.A. L.910 J.D. [Bailey B.N.]
Nader, G. Terence . . . . '59 '87 C&L.424 A.B./B.S., J.D. [Ⓐ Young,R.F.&S.]
Nadler, Floyd N. . . . . '34 '59 C.339 A.B. L.365 LL.B. [Nadler,P.&M.]
Nadler, James A., (AV) . . . . '63 '89 C.339 B.A. L.192 J.D. [Nadler,P.&M.]
Nadler, Janice . . . . '63 '90 C.188 B.A. L.1066 J.D. American Bar Found.
Nadler, Lisa Reilly . . . . '63 '88 C.197 A.B. L.276 J.D. THF Realty, Inc.

Nadler, Pritikin & Mirabelli, L.L.C., (AV)
One Prudential Plaza, 130 East Randolph Drive, Suite 1200, 60601
Telephone: 312-861-4600 Fax: 312-861-4666
Email: r.dorus@npmfamlaw.com URL: http://www.npmfamlaw.com
Floyd N. Nadler; James B. Pritikin; Enrico J. Mirabelli; Ilene E. Shapiro; James A. Nadler; Francis A. Gembala; Jacalyn Birnbaum; Matthew C. Arnoux; Sam F. Cannizzaro; Steven D. Gerage; Michael Ian Bender; Amy L. Gertler;—Shalom D. Bersson; Cynthia J. Vocat; Tania K. Gray; Erin E. Masters; Rachel C. Heyman.
Family Law and Domestic Relations Law including Dissolution of Marriage, Division and Valuation of Marital and Non-Marital Property, Maintenance and Support, Custody and Visitation, Domestic Violence, Establishment of Paternity, Prenuptial and Postnuptial Agreements and, When Necessary, Litigation of Cases and the Prosecution and Defense of Appeals. Mediation and Arbitration.
See Professional Biographies, CHICAGO, ILLINOIS

Nadoff, David H. . . . . '54 '82 C.424 A.B. L.597 J.D. [Barack F.K.P.&N.]
Naffziger, Jeffrey David . . . . '74 '01 C.352 B.A. L.424 J.D. 36 S. Wabash, Ste. 1310
Nagel, Marc . . . . '49 '77 C.339 B.S. L.146 J.D. 221 E. Walton St.‡
Nagel, Mary T., (BV) . . . . '63 '88 C.339 B.A. L.365 J.D. Asst. Atty. Gen.
Nagela, Margaret A. . . . . '— '98 C.999 B.A. L.365 J.D. [Ⓢ Schiff H.]
Nagelberg, Howard A., (AV) . . . . '47 '73 C.477 B.A. L.145 J.D. [Barack F.K.P.&N.]
Nagelberg, Sheldon B., Law Offices of, (BV) '46 '75
C.659 B.A. L.209 J.D. 53 W. Jackson Blvd., Ste. 1657
Nagle, Jane E. . . . . '— '93 C.397 B.S. L.602 J.D. [Ⓐ Chapman&C.]
Nagle, Kimberly A. . . . '73 '01 C.30 B.A. L.124 J.D. Two North LaSalle Street, Suite 2200
Nagle, Richard L. '59 '88 C.645 B.S. L.477 J.D.
Asst. Reg. Coun., U.S. Environ. Protection Agcy.
Nagler, Arnold . . . . '16 '39 C&L.209 LL.B. 5519 N. Lincoln Ave.
Nagorka, Frank W. . . . . '55 '79 C.597 B.A. L.608 J.D. [Ⓐ Mora,B.W.&U.]
Nagorsky, Marsha Ferziger '71 '96 C.1349 B.S. L.145 J.D.
(adm. in NY; not adm. in IL) [M.F.Nagorsky]
Nagorsky, Marsha F. . . . . 3733 N. Pine Grove Ave.
Nagy, Robert J., (BV) '61 '88 C.645 B.S. L.228 J.D.
(adm. in PA; not adm. in IL) Asst. Gen. Coun., Bk. of America
Nahmod, Sheldon . . . . '40 '65 C.145 B.A. L.309 J.D. Chicago-Kent College of Law
Nahnsen, Mark J. . . . . . '— '00 C.679 B.S.C.E. L.365 J.D. [Ⓐ Barnes&T.] (See Pat. Sect.)
Nahrstadt, Bradley C. . . . . '67 '92 C.504 B.A. L.333 J.D. [Williams M.&J.]
Naidu, Sree '67 '92 C.477 B.A. L.861 J.D.
(adm. in OH; not adm. in IL) Coun., Accenture Ltd
Naiman, Robert M., (Ltd.), (BV) . . . . '37 '67 C.339 B.S. L.209 J.D. 180 N. LaSalle
Nakatani, Warren Y. . . . . '70 '95 C.910 B.A. L.665 J.D. [Katten M.R.]
Nakos, Telly C., (AV) . . . . '65 '90 C.894 B.A. L.930 J.D. [Anesi,O.R.N.&K.]
Nale, Lucia . . . . '64 '89 C&L.424 B.A., J.D. [Mayer,B.R.&M.]
Nalley, Denise M., Law Office of '65 '93
C.504 B.A. L.424 J.D. 203 N. La Salle, Ste. 2100
Nally, James P. . . . . '59 '84 C.209 B.A. L.365 J.D. [J.P.Nally]
Nally, James P., PC . . . . 8 S. Michigan, Ste. 3500
Namovice, John A. '55 '82 C.347 M.B.A. L.1119 J.D.
(adm. in TX; not adm. in IL) 1520 W. Byron St.‡
Nance, Dale A. '52 '77 C.691 B.A. L.813 J.D.
(adm. in CA; not adm. in IL) Chicago-Kent College of Law
Nani, David T., (AV) . . . . '56 '85 C.602 B.A. L.365 J.D. [Kralovec&M.]
Naper, Christine M. . . . . '50 '77 C.856 A.B. L.209 J.D. [C.Naper]
Naper, Christine, Law Office of . . . . 2701 N. Marshfield Ave.
Napier, Elizabeth '59 '90 C.705 B.A. L.976 J.D.
(adm. in NY; not adm. in IL) Area Mktg. Coun., IBM North America-Chicago
Napier, Robert T., (AV) . . . . '61 '87 C.436 B.S. L.209 J.D. [R.T.Napier&Assoc.]
Napier, Robert T., & Associates, P.C., (AV) . . . . 208 South LaSalle Street, Suite 2070
Napleton, Robert J., (AV) . . . . '63 '88 C&L.424 B.B.A., J.D. [Motherway&N.]
Napoli, James J., (AV) '— '91 C.608 B.S. L.209 J.D.
[Marshall,G.&B.] (See Pat. Sect.)
Napoli, Richard G. . . . . . . '41 '67 C.602 A.B. L.209 J.D. Chief Dep. Clk., U.S. Bkrptcy. Ct.
Napolski, Paul M. . . . . '74 '00 C.686 B.S. L.365 J.D. [Tamari&B.]
Narayan, Harsha S. . . . . '68 '00 C.424 B.A. L.365 J.D. [Ⓐ P.J.Kenneally]
Nardi, Catherine D., (BV) . . . . '60 '85 C.518 B.A. L.597 J.D. 233 S. Wacker St.
Nardomarino, Christine N. . . . . '73 '99 C.352 B.A. L.146 J.D. 28 N. Clark St.
Nardoni, Stanley C., (BV) . . . . '56 '81 C&L.209 B.A., J.D. [Ⓒ Mayer,B.R.&M.]
Narea, Amy Weiss . . . . . '52 '83 C.104 B.A. L.146 J.D. Princ., LaSalle Language Academy
Narefsky, David, (AV) . . . . '55 '79 C.1044 B.A. L.477 J.D. [Mayer,B.R.&M.]
Narey, Sally Brewster, (AVⓉ) '52 '77 C.352 B.A. L.494 J.D.
Sr. V.P. & Dep. Gen. Coun., CNA Property & Casualty Oper.
Narko, Kathleen Dillon '63 '89 C.976 B.A. L.188 J.D.
Clinical Asst. Prof. of Law, Northwestern University School of Law
Narko, Kevin J. . . . . '64 '89 C.339 A.B. L.597 J.D. [Winston&S.]
Naron, Gregory R. . . . . '66 '91 C.378 B.A. L.178 J.D. [Ⓒ Sonnenschein N.&R.]
Naser-Velazquez, Mona . . . . '74 '02 C.339 B.A. L.209 J.D. [M.N.Velazquez]
Nash, Ann O'Boyle '52 '78 C.741 B.A. L.424 J.D.
V.P., Develop., Children's Memorial Med. Ctr.
Nash, Brian Thomas . . . . '71 '99 C.339 B.S. L.209 J.D. [Ⓐ Clifford]
Nash, Caroline A. . . . . '70 '96 C.477 B.A. L.209 J.D. [Ⓐ Schain,B.R.&C.]
Nash, Gordon B., (AV) . . . . '06 '28 L.424 LL.B. Ret. Cir. Ct. J.‡
Nash, Gordon B., Jr., (AV) . . . . '44 '69 C.602 B.A. L.424 J.D. [Gardner C.&D.]
Nash, Mary Ellen, (BV) . . . . '47 '76 C.991 B.A. L.146 J.D. [Dillon&N.]
Nash, Patrick J., Jr. '71 '96
C.602 B.A. L.339 J.D. [Ⓐ Skadden,A.S.M.&F.] (⊙New York, NY)
Nash, Patrick T., (AV) . . . . '66 '91 C.8 B.A. L.597 J.D. [Grippo&E.]
Nash, Robert C., (AV) . . . . '— '69 C.197 A.B. L.1565 J.D. [Chapman&C.]
Nash, Sean . . . . '71 '98 C.813 B.A. L.597 J.D. [Ⓐ Holland&K.]
Nash, Susan M. . . . . '64 '91 C.276 B.A. L.597 J.D. [McDermott W.&E.]
Nash, Thomas D., Jr., (AV) . . . . '21 '48 C.602 A.B. L.209 J.D. 30 N. La Salle St.
Nash, Thomas R., (AV) . . . . '52 '77 C.602 B.A. L.424 J.D. [T.R.Nash]
Nash, Thomas R., P.C., (AV) . . . . 8 S. Michigan Ave., Ste. 1616
Nasharr, Anthony J., III . . . . '58 '83 C.473 B.S. L.365 J.D. [Nasharr&S.]

Nasharr & Shea LLC, (AV)
Two Prudential Plaza, 180 N. Stetson Avenue, Suite 4525, 60601
Telephone: 312-819-1900 Fax: 312-819-1910
Email: attorneys@nashea-law.com URL: http://www.nasharr-law.com
Anthony J. Nasharr, III; Brian C. Shea; John J. Curry, Jr.;—Bryan P. Lynch; Jonathan R. Koyn.
Banking Law, Finance Law, Loans, Business Law, Corporate Law, Real Estate, Commercial Real Estate, Leasing, Commercial Landlord and Tenant Law, Civil Litigation, Eminent Domain, Employment Law, Wills, Trusts and Estates, Probate.
See Professional Biographies, CHICAGO, ILLINOIS

Nassau, Richard J. . . . . '44 '69 C.645 B.S. L.665 J.D. V.P., CC Industries
Nasser, Catherine . . . . '78 '04 C.477 B.A. L.597 J.D. [Ⓐ Sonnenschein N.&R.]
Nassopoulos, Evdoxia C. . . . . '— '02 C&L.424 B.S., J.D. [Ⓐ Querrey&H.]
Nassos, Ernest J. . . . . '30 '55 C.597 B.S. L.339 LL.B. Sears, Roebuck & Co.
Nassos, John G. . . . . '— '90 C.347 B.S. L.597 J.D. [Ungaretti&H.]
Natarus, Burton F., (AV) . . . . '33 '60 C&L.966 B.S., J.D. 30 N. La Salle St., Ste. 2900
Nath, Maya D. '79 '05 C.178 B.A. L.569 J.D.
(adm. in MA; not adm. in IL) [Ⓐ Jenner&B.]
Nathan, Bernard B. . . . . '33 '59 C.1016 B.A. L.209 J.D. 19 S. La Salle St.
Nathan, Gilbert . . . . '31 '55 C.679 B.S. L.597 J.D. 20 N. Clark St.
Nathan, Harvey A. . . . . '42 '67 C.823 A.B. L.597 J.D. 1350 E. 49th St.
Nathan, Joel R. . . . . '48 '76 C.347 B.A. L.209 J.D. Spec. Asst. Atty. Gen.
Nathan, Kimberley Alice . . . . '73 '00 C.927 L.801 Asst. State's Atty.
Nathan, Robert S. . . . . '61 '90 C.208 B.A. L.365 J.D. 53 W. Jackson Blvd., Ste. 1556
Nathan, Thomas J., (AV) . . . . '50 '78 C.399 B.A. L.365 J.D. [Munday&N.]
Nathanson, Natalie . . . . '71 '00 C.861 B.S. L.228 J.D. [Ⓐ McDermott W.&E.]
Nathenson, Wm. Allen, (AV) . . . . '12 '35 C&L.966 B.A., LL.B. 200 E. Chestnut St.‡
Nations, Marlene D., (AV) . . . . '54 '82 C.339 B.S. L.597 J.D. [Sonnenschein N.&R.]
Natkin, Bruce G. . . . . '47 '80 C.347 B.A. L.589 J.D. 2727 N. Milwaukee Ave.
Naughton, James P., (AV) '57 '81
C&L.339 B.S.E.E., J.D. [Brinks H.G.&L.] (See Pat. Sect.)
Naughton, Stephen M., (AV) '60 '85
C.436 B.A. L.602 J.D. Coun., Quaker Foods & Beverages
Naumann, Steven T. . . . . . '50 '88 C.688 B.S. L.46 J.D. Commonwealth Edison Co. (Pat.)
Naurich, William P. . . . . '50 '79 C.801 B.S. L.365 J.D. Admin. Law J.
Navarre, James P. . . . . '— '93 C.339 B.S. L.424 J.D. [Ⓐ Cogan&M.]
Navarre, Stephen J. . . . . '60 '97 C.602 B.A. L.146 J.D. [Minsky,M.&H.]
Naveja, Christopher S. . . . . '— '95 C.347 B.S. L.339 J.D. [Arnstein&L.]
Naviaux, Wesley . . . . '70 '96 C.108 B.S. L.347 J.D. 53 W. Jackson Blvd., Ste. 1610
Navid, Barry B. . . . . '14 '37 C.999 L.365 LL.B. 7619F N. Eastlake Ter.‡
Navigato, John E., (AV) . . . . '42 '66 C.1024 B.A. L.209 J.D. [Serpico,N.&N.]
Navin, William H., (AV) '45 '69 C.602 A.B. L.976 LL.B.
Exec. V.P. of Gen. Council, The Options Clearing Corp.
Nawracaj, Richard E. . . . . '68 '93 C.339 B.S. L.424 J.D. [Entwistle&C.]
Naylor, Emory S., Jr., (AV) . . . . '17 '46 C&L.597 B.S., J.D. 227 W. Monroe St.
Nazarof, Mark S. . . . . '— '03 C.338 B.S. L.146 J.D. [Ⓐ Litchfield C.]
Neal, Andrew G., (AV) . . . . . '59 '85 C.813 B.A. L.94 J.D. 2438 North Marshfield Avenue
Neal, Earl L., (AV) . . . . '— '53 C.339 A.B. L.477 J.D. [Neal&L.]
Neal, Gerald J., (AV) . . . . '— '68 C.309 B.A. L.976 LL.B. [Foley&L.]
Neal, Langdon D., (AV) . . . . '— '81 C.188 A.B. L.339 J.D. [Neal&L.]
Neal, Linda Thoren, (AV) . . . . '43 '67 C&L.145 B.A., J.D. [L.T.Neal]
Neal, Michelle Giawaya . . . . '63 '90 C.289 B.A. L.705 J.D. 20 East Jackson Boulevard
Neal, Phil C., (AV) . . . . '19 '43 C&L.309 B.A., LL.B. [Neal,G.&E.]
Neal, Phillip G. . . . . '51 '78 C.339 B.S. L.801 J.D. 440 S. LaSalle St.
Neal, Sharon M. . . . . '62 '89 C&L.424 B.A., J.D. Asst. Gen. Coun., Exelon Corp.

Neal, Gerber & Eisenberg LLP, (AV)
Two North LaSalle Street Suite 2200, 60602
Telephone: 312-269-8000 FAX: 312-269-1747
URL: http://www.ngelaw.com
Partners of Firm: Harvey M. Adelstein; Claudia Harri Allen; Diane M. Anderson; Scott J. Bakal; Jeffrey J. Bakker; Peter H. Barrow; Robert A. Bedore; Wendy L. Bendersky; Lawrence M. Benjamin; H. Nicholas Berberian; Paula Kaplan Berger; Stephen L. Berger; Stephen S. Berkeley; Howard L. Bernstein; Jerry H. Biederman; Eugene A. Boyle; Karen A. Broucek; Scott A. Browdy; Alan C. Brown; Robert E. Browne; Christopher M. Burky; Timothy W. Burns; Patricia S. Cain; Susan Feingold Carlson; Michael A. Carrillo; Jill Ann Coleman; Andrea M. Despotes; Jennifer Desser; Victoria L. Donati; Marshall E. Eisenberg; Douglas M. Ellis; Ross D. Emmerman; Lee J. Eulgen; Stephen Fedo; Avram I. Feldman; Bruce A. Fox; Timothy A. French; Ellen B. Friedler; Jeffrey M. Galkin; Norman J. Gantz; James K. Gardner; Charles E. Gerber (1941-1998); Robert G. Gerber; Gerald A. Golden; David V. Goodsir; John W. Guarisco; Irwin I. Gzesh; Kenneth L. Harris; Dan J. Hofmeister, Jr.; Michael J. Hughes; Philip M. Kayman; Michael G. Kelber; Synde B. Keywell; Patrick G. King; Joshua A. Klein; Jeffrey G. Kraft; Steven A. Lampert; Douglas J. Lubelchek; Jed R. Mandel; Miranda Kiser Mandel; Maria T. Manhart; Michael P. Manly; David S. Martin; Thomas C. McDonough; Diana J.P. McKenzie; Thomas J. McNulty; Antony J. McShane; Earl N. Melamed; Chad W. Moeller; Michael L. Molinaro; Arthur B. Muir; Phil C. Neal; Marlene Mathes Nelson; Peter B. Newton; Kimberly A. Pendo; Mark A. Rabinowitz; Robert Radasevich; Timothy Ray; Stephen M. Reiches; Rawn Howard Reinhard; Meg M. Reynolds; Lawrence I. Richman; David B. Ritter; Kathryn A. Roe; Jack A. Rovner; Ralph T. Russell, Jr.; John S. Santa Lucia; Jerry M. Santangelo; Cheryl Kehoe Schaul; Leah A. Schleicher; Harry J. Secaras; Audrey E. Selin; Michael D. Sher; Lisa A. Stegink; David S. Stone; William J. Tarnow; Elaine M. Taussig; Kevin D. Tessier; Winfield S. Thom; Martin H. Tish; Elizabeth Matich Todorovic; Jonathan D. Wasserman; Robert M. Weiss; Terry D. Weissman; Tina L. Winer; Thomas C. Wolford; Elizabeth D. Wright; Amy J. Zdravecky; Lisa S. Zebovitz; Robert D. Zimelis. Senior Counsel: Sarah C. Bender; Thomas D. Bixby; Angela Elbert; Christine C. Franklin; Judith L. Landesman; David M. Lavin; Burton H. Litwin; Timothy P. Mahoney; Milton L. Petersen; Beth J. Rosner; Francis J. Wirtz. Of Counsel: Sheri E. Warsh.
General Civil Practice. Corporate Law, Commodities, Securities, Governance, Bankruptcy, Real Estate, Labor and Employment, Employee Benefits, Estate Planning, Environmental Law, Federal, State and International Tax, Finance, Health Law, Information Technology, Intellectual Property, State and Local Property Law, Wealth Preservation, Insurance Coverage and Litigation including Antitrust, Commercial Litigation, White Collar Crime, Products Liability Defense, Exempt Organizations and Association Law.
See Professional Biographies, CHICAGO, ILLINOIS

Neal & Leroy, LLC, (AV)
203 North LaSalle, Suite 2300, 60601
Telephone: 312-641-7144 Fax: 312-641-5137
Email: lneal@nealandleroy.com URL: http://www.nealandleroy.com
Earl L. Neal; Langdon D. Neal; Michael D. Leroy; Anne L. Fredd; Richard F. Friedman. Attorneys: Lenny D. Asaro; Paul E. Bennett, II; Nicole L. Castillo; Terrance L. Diamond; Thomas W. Goedert; Deborah F. Hamilton; Ryan K. Harding; Renee F. Kessel; Jonathan D. Leach; Francine D. Lynch; James G. McConnell; Tobin M. Richter; Lawrence K. Sezer; Jerome A. Siegan; Bradley A. Smith; Carol D. Stubblefield; Jeanette Sublett. Of Counsel: Benjamin Ghess; George N. Leighton.
Eminent Domain, Condemnation, Labor and Employment, Litigation, Public Finance and Project Finance, Real Estate and Real Estate Finance, Zoning, Development and Land Use, Business Reorganization and Bankruptcy and Construction Law.
See Professional Biographies, CHICAGO, ILLINOIS

Neal, Linda Thoren, Ltd., (AV) . . . . 5629 Blackstone Avenue

Neal & McDevitt
(See Evanston)

Nealon, Marian C. .... '— '82 L.146 J.D. Off. of the Gen. Coun., Dept. of HHS
Neary, Eileen F. '62 '92 C.589 B.A. L.365 J.D. Vice Pres. & Exchange Coun., Exchange Services Group
Nebel, Theodore H., (AV) ....'46 '71 C.602 B.A. L.145 J.D. 10 S. La Salle St.
Neboyskey, David A. P. ....'69 '00 C.477 B.A. L.1119 J.D. [Ⓐ McGuirewoods]
Nechin, Herbert B., (AV) '35 '60 C.597 B.A. L.309 J.D. 120 North La Salle Street, Suite 3800‡
Neckers, Joel Steven ....'— '04 C.323 B.A. L.477 J.D. [Ⓐ Latham&W.]
Needham, Joseph ....'72 '99 C.424 B.S. L.365 J.D. [Ⓐ Keefe&Assoc.]
Needham, Patricia A. '53 '82 C.363 B.A. L.424 J.D. Senior Vice President & General Counsel, Strategic Hotels
Needles, James L. '48 '76 C.352 B.A. L.365 J.D. Coun., Atty. Regis. & Disiplinary Comm.
Needles, Nancy K., (AV) ....'49 '76 C.350 B.S. L.365 J.D. 1147 W. Ohio St., #505
Neel, Paige Moray ....'— '01 C&L.347 B.A., J.D. [Ⓐ McKenna S.]
Neely, Ellen J. '64 '89 C.846 B.A. L.145 J.D. Sr. V.P. & Gen. Coun., Chicago Stock Exchange, Inc.
Neff, Alan H., (AV) ....'49 '73 C&L.477 B.A., J.D. Asst. Corp. Coun., Dept. of Law
Neff, David M., (AV) ....'60 '85 C.597 B.S.J. L.209 J.D. [DLPiper R.G.C.U.]
Neff, Kelly M. ....'— '03 C.209 B.A. L.146 J.D. [Ⓐ Jones D.]
Neff, Mary V., P.C., (AV) ....'13 '43 C.999 A.B. L.365 J.D. 2013 Prairie
Neff, Nathan I. ....'72 '00 C.800 B.A. L.424 J.D. [Ⓐ Cassiday,S.&G.]
Nega, Marya '55 '80 C.209 B.S.C. L.424 J.D. Metro. Water Reclamation Dist. of Greater Chicago
Neiberg, Maurine J. ....'64 '96 C.914 B.A. L.145 J.D. [Ⓐ Tressler,S.M.&P.]
Neidigh, Michael T. ....'— '98 C.597 B.S. L.424 J.D. [Ⓐ Mayer,B.R.&M.]
Neil, Mark T., (AV) ....'49 '75 C.1100 B.A. L.597 J.D. [Ⓒ J.S.Rothman&Assoc.]
Neilan, Paul G. ....'58 '83 C.178 B.A. L.145 J.D. [Giordano&N.]
Neiman, Ira S. ....'60 '83 C.424 B.B.A. L.209 J.D. [Shefsky&F.]
Neiman, Robert E., (AV) ....'41 '66 C.347 B.S. L.1119 J.D. [Greenberg T.]
Neiman, Robert K., (AV) ....'— '82 C.339 B.S.J. L.910 J.D. [Sachnoff&W.]
Neiman, William J. ....'37 '63 C.659 B.S. L.597 LL.B. Pres., Neiman Bros. Co., Inc.
Neis, James M. ....'46 '73 C&L.209 B.A., J.D. [Winston&S.]
Neish, Clive Woodsworth ....'61 '00 C.801 B.S. L.424 J.D. 11720 S. Throop St.
Neistein, Bernard S. ....'16 '37 C&L.209 LL.B., D.J. 33 N. La Salle St.
Nekritz, Barry B., (AV) ....'38 '62 C&L.339 B.A., LL.B. [Sonnenschein N.&R.]
Nelligan, Brendan J. ....'71 '96 C.602 B.A. L.276 J.D. [Ⓐ Pretzel&S.]
Nelsen, Timothy A., (AV) ....'47 '73 C.118 B.A. L.477 J.D. [Skadden,A.S.M.&F.]
Nelson, Adam ....'— '92 C.37 B.A. L.146 J.D. IBM Corp.
Nelson, Andrew B. ....'70 '02 C.339 B.A. L.146 J.D. 55 E. Monroe St., Ste. 3400
Nelson, Anne Stalder ....'67 '92 C.597 B.A. L.276 J.D. 206 West Division
Nelson, Bradley P., (AV) ....'60 '86 C.960 B.S. L.966 J.D. [Schopf&W.]
Nelson, Bruce C. ....'61 '91 C.597 B.A. L.94 J.D. [Vedder,P.K.&K.]
Nelson, Cameron M. ....'76 '01 C.339 B.S.M.E. L.146 J.D. [Ⓐ Greenberg T.]
Nelson, Catherine A.T., (BV) ....'61 '86 C.339 B.S. L.365 J.D. [Cozen O.]
Nelson, Catherine B. ....'— '96 C.339 B.S. L.597 J.D. [Ⓒ Foley&L.]
Nelson, Craig E. ....'— '91 C.602 B.B.A. L.846 J.D. [Entwistle&C.]
Nelson, David A. ....'— '92 C.813 B.S.E.E. L.597 J.D. [Latham&W.]
Nelson, David C. ....'67 '94 C.966 B.S. L.221 J.D. [Ⓢ Nelson]
Nelson, F. Dennis ....'52 '78 C&L.477 A.B., J.D. [McCullough,C.&L.]
Nelson, Heather L. ....'69 '93 C.589 B.A. L.209 J.D. 20 North Clark St., Ste. 2725,
Nelson, Heather M., Law Office of '— '96 C.966 B.B.A. L.146 J.D. 1727 South Indiana Ave, Suite G02
Nelson, Herbert O. ....'31 '60 C&L.145 A.B., J.D. 6215 W. Touhy Ave.
Nelson, Jack D. ....'44 '72 C.238 B.A. L.365 J.D. Allstate Ins. Co.
Nelson, James R. ....'— '91 C.162 B.A. L.352 J.D. [Chapman&C.]
Nelson, James R., II ....'64 '89 C.589 B.S. L.365 J.D. Asst. State Atty.

Nelson, Jay Scott, (AV) '41 '75 C.641 B.A. L.365 J.D.
5757 North Lincoln Avenue, Suite 20, 60659-4720
Telephone: 773-907-9010 Fax: 773-907-9013
General Civil Practice in all State and Federal Courts, Business Transactions.
See Professional Biographies, CHICAGO, ILLINOIS

Nelson, Jerold T. ....'42 '75 C.474 B.S. L.146 J.D. St. Anthony Hospital
Nelson, Jon O., (AV) ....'— '66 C.679 B.S. L.339 J.D. [Banner&W.] (See Pat. Sect.)
Nelson, Karen ....'— '00 C.188 B.S. L.597 J.D. [Ⓐ Kirkland&E.]
Nelson, Kathryn Zeledon ....'50 '84 C.339 B.S. L.209 J.D. Asst. Corp. Coun.
Nelson, Kenneth B. .....'43 '69 C.912 B.A. L.273 J.D. Admin. Law J., State Com. Comm.
Nelson, Kevin M. ....'76 '01 C.347 B.A. L.209 J.D. [Ⓐ Lord,B.&B.]
Nelson, Leonard A., (AV) '48 '74 C.197 A.B. L.309 J.D. Div. Coun., American Medical Association
Nelson, Lisa E. ....'71 '96 C.1106 B.A. L.209 J.D. 3514 Hawthorne Street
Nelson, Margaret Grembala '70 '99 C&L.339 B.S., J.D. Sr. Atty., Chicago, M.R.O., S.E.C.
Nelson, Mark D., (AV) ....'57 '82 C&L.339 B.A., J.D. [Gardner C.&D.]
Nelson, Marlene Mathes ....'46 '95 C.209 B.A. L.146 J.D. [Neal,G.&E.]
Nelson, Paul C. '27 '58 C.028 B.A. L.472 J.D. Litigation Counsel, Equipment Manufacturers Institute‡
Nelson, Paul S. ......'54 '89 C.1106 B.A. L.145 J.D. Sr. Atty., Northern Trust Corporation
Nelson, Phillip W. ....'78 '04 C.894 A.B. L.228 J.D. [Ⓐ Jenner&B.]
Nelson, Richard Alexander ....'— '03 C.228 B.A. L.597 J.D. [Ⓐ Lovells]
Nelson, Robert D. ....'56 '83 C.608 B.S.B.A. L.209 J.D. Sr. Atty., MCI Worldcom, Inc.
Nelson, Scott, (AV) ....'56 '81 C.1106 B.A. L.424 J.D. [Ⓐ Ruff,W.&R.]
Nelson, Sharon C. ....'— '01 C.424 B.A. L.339 J.D. [Ⓐ Foley&L.]
Nelson, Stephen T. ....'— '99 C&L.597 B.A., J.D. [Ⓐ Baker&M.]
Nelson, T. Leverett '59 '85 C.118 B.A. L.174 J.D. (adm. in CO; not adm. in IL) U.S.E.P.A.
Nelson, Thomas R., (AV) ....'36 '64 C&L.623 B.A., LL.B. 130 E. Randolph Dr.‡
Nelson Law Office .... P.O. Box 803595
Nemec, Michelle Victoria ....'72 '02 C.741 B.A. L.146 J.D. Law Clk.
Nemeroff, David ....'61 '95 C.446 B.S. L.1529 J.D. [Nemeroff]
Nemeroff, Michael A., (BV) ....'63 '88 C.1044 B.A. L.273 J.D. [Vedder,P.K.&K.]
Nemeroff Law Offices .... 161 N. Clark Street, Suite 3575
Nemerovski, Steven H. ....'51 '77 C.659 B.S. L.339 J.D. [Ⓒ Aronberg G.D.&G.]
Nemeth, Chris ....'76 '01 C.597 B.A. L.477 J.D. [Ⓐ McDermott W.&E.]
Nemeth, Elizabeth Anne ....'73 '97 C.339 B.S. L.597 J.D. [Ⓐ Winston&S.]
Nemoy, Paul I., (AV) ....'53 '78 C.339 B.A. L.146 J.D. [Howard&N.]
Nemvalts, Janet K. ......'48 '80 C.477 B.A. L.588 J.D. Legal Assistance Found. of Chicago
Nemzin, Robert F., (AV) ....'51 '77 C.608 B.S.Ed. L.365 J.D. [Hickey&N.]
Nemzura, Marjorie '50 '76 C.741 B.A. L.597 J.D. Asst. Gen. Coun., Chicago Title Ins. Co.
Nentwig, Christine E. ....'71 '00 C.1326 B.A. L.446 J.D. [Ⓐ Smith O.&W.]
Nereim, Mardell '48 '82 C.339 A.B. L.597 J.D. Chf. Asst. Corp. Coun., City of Chicago Dept. of Law
Nerney, Susan C. ....'67 '94 C.602 B.B.A. L.424 J.D. 77 W. Wacker, 50th Fl.
Nero, Mark J., (AV) '54 '81 C.959 B.A. L.966 J.D. Sr. Atty., Northern Trust Corporation
Nery, Joseph F. ....'73 '98 C.597 B.A. L.1019 J.D. [Nery&M.]
Nery & Muriel LLC ....4124 W. 63rd St. (⊙Chicago)
Nesbit, Charles L., Law Offices '46 '80 L.150 J.D. (adm. in PA; not adm. in IL) 105 W. Madison St., Ste. 700
Nesbitt, Amber M. ....'78 '04 C.477 B.A. L.424 J.D. [Ⓐ Wexler]
Nesburg, Alan D., (AV) ....'47 '72 C.373 B.A. L.597 J.D. [McDermott W.&E.]
Neschis, Samuel E. ....'68 '00 C.966 B.A. L.262 J.D. [Ⓐ Horowitz&W.]
Nestor, Daniel C. ....'47 '72 C&L.339 B.S., J.D. Sr. Atty. Supvr., City Law Dept.
Nethery, John F. ....'68 '97 C.350 B.S. L.339 J.D. [Ⓐ Brinks H.G.&L.] (See Pat. Sect.)
Netsch, Dawn Clark '26 '52 C&L.597 B.A., J.D. Prof. Emeritus, Northwestern Law Sch.‡
Netzel, Tracy L. ....'74 '00 C&L.966 B.A., J.D. [Netzel&Assoc.]

Netzel & Associates, P.C.
211 E. Ontario Street, Suite 1800, 60611
Telephone: 312-283-5200 Fax: 312-283-5005
Email: tnetzel@whistlelaw.com URL: http://www.whistlelaw.com
Tracy L. Netzel.
Whistle Blower, Qui Tam Litigation/Whistleblower Litigation, Health Care Fraud, Employment Retaliation, Class Action Litigation, Commercial Litigation.
See Professional Biographies, CHICAGO, ILLINOIS

Neuckranz, Thomas H., (AV) ....'47 '74 C.674 B.S.E. L.597 J.D. [Williams M.&J.]
Neudel, Marian Henriquez '41 '77 C.309 A.B. L.209 J.D. Lawyers Commitee for Better Housing
Neue, Nadine ....'76 '01 C.299 B.A. L.209 J.D. [Ⓐ Rusin M.&F.]
Neuffer, Brian E. ....'63 '90 C.597 B.A. L.101 J.D. [Winston&S.]
Neugent-Dixon, Elizabeth ....'77 '03 C.436 B.A. L.221 J.D. [Ⓐ Krislov&Assoc.]
Neuman, James M. ....'60 '85 C.339 B.S. L.424 J.D. [Baum S.A.&N.]
Neumann, Alan E., (BV) ....'43 '77 C.475 B.A. L.146 J.D. [Ⓐ Kiesler&B.]
Neumann, Carl A., (AV) '— '68 C.959 B.A. L.966 J.D. [Holland&K.] (⊙Oakbrook Terrace)
Neumann, John D. ....'— '99 C.902 B.A. L.957 J.D. [Ⓐ Jones D.]
Neumann, Kenneth K. ....'— '93 C.597 B.A. L.209 J.D. [Copeland,F.&F.]
Neumann, Otto C. '08 '34 C.918 A.B. L.472 J.D. (adm. in FL; not adm. in IL) Barbara Oil Co.
Neumann, Robert R. '64 '90 C.966 B.A. L.146 J.D. Gen. Coun. & Mng. Dir., Burwood Group
Neumann, Sylvia J., (BV) ....'45 '81 C.338 B.S. L.146 J.D. [Pierce&Assoc.]
Neumark, Jason P. ....'70 '95 C.674 A.B. L.597 J.D. [Ⓐ Levenfeld P.]
Neumark, Neil T., (AV) ....'47 '73 C.679 B.S.I.E. L.345 J.D. [Schwartz C.]
Neumeier, Matthew M., (AV) ....'54 '87 C.477 B.G.S. L.309 J.D. [Jenner&B.]
Neumeister, David E. ....'— '91 C.352 B.A. L.209 J.D. [Querrey&H.]
Neumer, Stephen M., (AV) ....'40 '66 C.477 B.B.A. L.813 J.D. [Ⓒ Katten M.R.]
Nevel, Ira T. ....'55 '83 C.424 B.A. L.365 J.D. 175 N. Franklin St., Ste. 201
Neveril, Edward J. ....'68 '96 C.870 B.S. L.597 J.D. [Jenner&B.]
Neville, Arthur J., (AV) ....'52 '78 C.339 B.A. L.209 J.D. V.P., Community Svgs. Bk.
Neville, Richard E. ....'42 '66 C&L.209 A.B., J.D. Cir. J. (Crim.)
Neville, Ronald F., (AV) ....'46 '71 C&L.209 B.A., J.D. 221 N. LaSalle St.
Nevoral, Bernard R., (AV) ....'43 '71 C&L.209 B.A., J.D. [B.R.Nevoral&Assoc.]

Nevoral, Bernard R., and Associates Ltd., (AV) BR
One East Wacker Drive, Suite 3610, 60601
Telephone: 312-263-7058 Fax: 312-263-4566
Email: brnltd@nevoral.com
Bernard R. Nevoral;—David F. Szczecin; Andrew A. Galich; Robert J. Drummond.
General Civil Practice in all State and Federal Courts. Appellate Practice, Products Liability, Workers Compensation and Negligence Law. Federal Employers Liability Act.
See Professional Biographies, CHICAGO, ILLINOIS

New, Jason G. ....'69 '94 C.25 B.A. L.228 J.D. [Ⓐ Sidley A.B.&W.]
Newburn, Jade Earl ....'74 '05 C.103 A.B. L.1565 J.D. [Ⓐ Mayer,B.R.&M.]
Newbury, Robert M., (AV) ......'31 '59 C.118 B.A. L.976 LL.B. [Pattishall,M.N.H.&G.]
Newby, David A., (AV) ....'59 '85 C.894 A.B. L.178 J.D. [Johnson&N.]
Newcomb, Christopher W. ....'62 '95 C.145 B.A. L.146 J.D. [Ⓐ Karaganis,W.&M.]
Newell, John F., (BV) ....'47 '78 C&L.221 B.A., J.D. [Ⓐ K.J.Wysoglad&Assoc.]
Newey, Paul D. ....'14 '46 C.214 B.A. L.365 LL.B. 1034 W. Altgeld St.
Newhouse, Richard H., Jr., (AV) ....'24 '61 C.94 B.S. L.145 LL.B. State Sen.
Newitt, George B., (AV) ....'18 '48 C.912 B.S. L.602 J.D. 10 S. Wacker Dr. (Pat.)‡
Newkirk, Douglas R. ....'— '82 C.118 B.A. L.976 J.D. [Sachnoff&W.]
Newlin, Charles F., (AV) ....'53 '78 C.340 B.A. L.309 J.D. [Harrison&H.]
Newlin, John W., III ....'69 '94 C.645 B.A. L.339 J.D. [Jenner&B.]
Newman, A. Marcy, (AV) '48 '73 C.966 B.B.A. L.930 J.D. 205 W. Randolph St., Ste. 2000
Newman, C. Brooks ....'76 '03 C.473 B.A. L.424 J.D. [Ⓐ Gardner C.&D.]
Newman, Charlotte ....'51 '85 C&L.966 B.A., J.D. Hearing Offr.
Newman, David L. ....'— '92 C.608 B.S. L.209 J.D. [Seyfarth S.] (Pat.)
Newman, Dennis Nathan, (AV) ...'46 '72 C.1036 B.A. L.477 J.D. [Sonnenschein N.&R.]
Newman, Eric E. ....'70 '97 C.473 B.A. L.477 J.D. [Ⓐ Meckler B.&T.]
Newman, Eric S. ....'66 '91 C.477 B.B.A. L.597 J.D. [Ⓒ Rachlis D.D.&A.]
Newman, Gerald M., (AV) '39 '64 C.339 B.S.M.E. L.597 J.D. [Schoenberg,F.N.&R.] (Pat.)
Newman, Glenn D., (AV) '60 '86 C&L.966 B.B.A., J.D. V.P. & Dep. Gen. Coun., Labor & Empl., Exelon Bus. Servs. Co. (⊙Phila., PA)
Newman, James P. ....'64 '94 C.260 B.A. L.365 J.D. [Newman&P.]
Newman, James T., (AV) ....'50 '78 C&L.424 B.A., J.D. [Ⓐ Cooney&C.]
Newman, John H. '46 '73 C&L.347 A.B., J.D. (adm. in IN; not adm. in IL) Asst. U.S. Atty.
Newman, Justin M. ....'77 '02 C.339 B.A. L.910 J.D. [Field&G.]
Newman, Kathryn C. ....'73 '99 C&L.276 B.A., J.D. [Ⓐ Jenner&B.]
Newman, Lauren, (AV) ....'57 '82 C.910 A.B. L.734 J.D. [Ⓐ FagelHaber]
Newman, Leonard E. ....'32 '56 C&L.339 A.B., LL.B. 134 N. LaSalle St.
Newman, Linda F. ....'— '02 C.339 B.A. L.209 J.D. [Ⓐ O'Hagan,S.&A.]
Newman, Marc Laurence ....'67 '92 C.29 B.S. L.146 J.D. 33 N. LaSalle St.
Newman, Margery, (AV) ....'— '83 C.102 B.A. L.365 J.D. [Ogletree,D.N.S.&S.]
Newman, Margo R. ....'51 '76 C.477 B.A. L.273 J.D. 1124 W. Lill St.
Newman, Meagan Noel '76 '03 C.477 B.A. L.446 J.D. (adm. in MD; not adm. in IL) [Ⓐ Seyfarth S.]
Newman, Melvin S., (AV) ....'36 '60 C.339 B.S. L.145 J.D. [Schoenberg,F.N.&R.]
Newman, Michael ....'— '98 C.352 B.S.I.E. L.146 J.D. [Kirkland&E.] (Pat.)
Newman, Norman B., (AV) ....'51 '75 C.339 B.A. L.365 J.D. [Much S.F.D.A.&R.]
Newman, Richard M., (AV) ....'43 '68 C&L.178 A.B., J.D. [Ⓒ Mayer,B.R.&M.]
Newman, Robert C., (AV) ....'43 '72 C&L.339 B.S., J.D. [Ⓒ Holland&K.]
Newman, Robert T., (BV) ....'51 '76 C.367 B.A. L.446 J.D. [Ⓐ Maciorowski,S.&U.]

Newman, Robert W., (AV) .... '33 '57 C.339 L.209 LL.B. [Wildman,H.A.&D.]
Newman, Sandra K. .... '64 '92 C.587 B.A. L.823 J.D. [Bell,B.&L.]
Newman, Terry E., (P.C.), (AV) .... '47 '77 C.424 B.A. L.209 J.D. [Katten M.R.]
Newman, Wayne L., (BV) .... '61 '86 C&L.339 B.S., J.D. [Horwitz,H.&Assoc.]
Newman, William S., Sr. '40 '67
C.1106 B.S. L.146 J.D. Reinsurance Coun., Chicago Title Ins. Co.
Newman & Pelafas .... 120 W. Madison, Suite 200
Newmark, Jodi Ann .... '59 '85 C.942 B.A. L.597 J.D. 333 W. Wacker Dr.
Newquist, Elaine T. .... '61 '86 C.700 B.A. L.209 J.D. 210 W. Illinois
Newsham, Katie '54 '78
C.424 B.A. L.365 J.D. Admin. Law J., State Dept. of Mental Health
Newsom, Kurt .... '78 '04 C.477 B.A. L.472 J.D. [[A] Henderson&L.]
Newton, Grace A., (AV) .... '41 '82 C.477 B.A. L.146 J.D. 300 S. Wacker Dr.
Newton, John E. .... '71 '01 C.597 B.S. L.146 J.D. [[A] Crisham&K.]
Newton, Natalie M. .... '76 '03 C.861 A.B. L.228 J.D. [[A] McDermott W.&E.]
Newton, Peter B., (AV) .... '52 '83 C.1301 B.S. L.146 J.D. [Neal,G.&E.]
Neymeyer-Tynkov, Valerie R. .... '69 '01 C.352 B.A. L.146 J.D. [[A] Ladas&P.]
Nguyen, Alexander T. .... '— '03 C.309 A.B. L.976 J.D. [[A] Kirkland&E.]
Nguyen, Rachel T. .... '73 '99 C.477 B.A. L.424 J.D. [[A] Schuyler,R.&Z.]
Nicastro, Tracey A. .... '69 '94 C.339 B.A. L.879 J.D. [[A] Sidley A.B.&W.]
Nicgorski, Alan W. .... '71 '97 C.602 B.A. L.597 J.D. [[A] Scandaglia&R.]
Nichele, John B. .... '35 '60 C&L.424 B.Sc., J.D. 6043 W. Irving Pk. Rd.
Nicholas, Frank C., (AV) .... '61 '89 C.436 B.S.M.E. L.966 J.D. [Cardinal] (Pat.) ⊙
Nichols, Christine K. .... '71 '96 C.679 B.A. L.347 J.D. [Barack F.K.P.&N.]
Nichols, Dale K. '56 '81 C&L.477 A.B., J.D.
Asst. Gen. Coun., Northern Trust Corporation
Nichols, G. Peter, (AV) '58 '89
C.494 B.S.Ch.E. L.209 J.D. [Brinks H.G.&L.] (See Pat. Sect.)
Nichols, Heather A. .... '71 '99 C&L.209 B.S., J.D. [[A] Handler,T.&D.]
Nichols, Jeffry M. ..... '75 '00 C.587 B.S. L.306 J.D. [[A] Brinks H.G.&L.] (See Pat. Sect.)
Nichols, Julie M. .... '68 '94 C.228 A.B. L.146 J.D. [[A] Wildman,H.A.&D.]
Nichols, Kristin A. .... '69 '94 C&L.477 B.A., J.D. [[A] Sidley A.B.&W.]
Nichols, William H., (AV) .... '— '79 C.31 B.A. L.188 J.D. [Ungaretti&H.]
Nicholson, Emily Jo .... '74 '00 C.589 B.A. L.146 J.D. 2724 N. Jansen Ave.
Nicholson, Janetta Fowler '38 '71
C.597 L.209 J.D. V.P., Bank One Tr. Co., N.A. Chicago‡
Nicholson, Julia M. .... '43 '78 C.362 B.A. L.209 J.D. 1522 West Elmdale‡
Nicholson, Mark A. '75 '02 C.602 B.A. L.893 J.D.
(adm. in CA; not adm. in IL) [[A] Mayer,B.R.&M.]
Nicholson, Marlene A. '39 '69 C.112 B.A. L.1068
(adm. in CA; not adm. in IL) Prof., De Paul Univ. Sch. of Law
Nicholson, Patrick B., (BV) '54 '79 C.602 B.B.A. L.424 J.D.
35 E. Wacker Dr., Ste. 1760
Nicholson, Peter A., (BV) .... '59 '85 C.339 B.A. L.146 J.D. [Goldberg&G.]
Nickel, Daniel J. .... '70 '02 C.1314 B.A. L.146 J.D. 19 W. Jackson
Nickele, Gary A. .... '52 '77 C.602 B.B.A. L.477 J.D. 900 North Michigan Avenue
Nickels, Timothy G., (AV) .... '57 '82 C&L.602 B.A., J.D. [Swanson,M.&B.]
Nickl, Fred A. .... '73 '98 C.339 B.A. L.209 J.D. [[A] Brenner,F.M.&S.]
Nicklin, Emily, (AV) .... '— '77 C&L.145 B.A., J.D. [Kirkland&E.]
Nicolaides, Mary .... '27 '82 C.563 B.C.E. L.209 J.D. 233 E. Erie St. (Pat.)
Nicolaides, Richard H., Jr., (AV) .... '63 '91 C.228 B.A. L.46 J.D. [Bates&C.]
Nicolas, Michael A. .... '73 '98 C.589 B.S. L.146 J.D. [[A] Gardner C.&D.]
Nicoll, Andrew S. .... '77 '04 C&L.101 B.S., J.D. [[A] Jenner&B.]
Niederman, Allan N., (AV) .... '29 '58 C.472 B.B.A. L.597 LL.B. 2558 W. Fitch Ave.‡
Nieds, Mark A. .... '65 '94 C.473 B.A. L.146 J.D. [[A] Leydig,V.&M.]
Niehaus, Mary C. .... '61 '88 C.293 B.A. L.597 J.D. [Sidley A.B.&W.]
Niehoff, Philip J. .... '59 '85 C&L.966 B.B.A., J.D. [Mayer,B.R.&M.]
Nieland, Robert G., (AV) '54 '81
C.589 B.A. L.597 J.D. Gen. Atty., R. R. Donnelley & Sons Co.
Nield, Eric J. .... '67 '99 C.339 B.A. L.146 J.D. Coun., Caylon Financial Inc.
Nielsen, Edward H., (AV) .... '46 '73 C.589 B.A. L.879 J.D. [Pretzel&S.]
Nielsen, Erik W. .... '67 '92 C.999 B.A. L.879 J.D. [Ellison,N.Z.&A.]
Nielsen, Marjie M. .... '78 '02 C&L.597 B.A., J.D. Chicago Legal Clinic
Nielsen, Mary N. .... '69 '94 C.339 B.A. L.801 J.D. [Hall,P.&S.]
Nielsen, Matthew C. ..... '— '99 C&L.602 B.S., J.D. [[A] Marshall,G.&B.] (See Pat. Sect.)
Nielsen, Paul C. .... '56 '81 C.679 B.S. L.893 J.D. JNB Realty Corp.
Niemczyk, J. Denise .... '76 '02 C.98 L.365 J.D. [[A] Levin&B.]
Niemira, Edwin R. .... '51 '81 C.209 L.365 J.D. 1110 N. Ashland Ave.
Nierling, Donald Wayne .... '56 '90 C&L.352 B.A., J.D. 11 S. LaSalle, Ste. 2500
Niersbach, C. .... '— '93 C.424 B.S.N. L.365 J.D. 30 N. La Salle
Niersbach, Clifford D. .... '50 '85 C.597 B.S. L.365 J.D. V.P., Natl. Assn. of Realtors
Niersbach, Donald C. '28 '51 C.424 L.209 LL.B.
Ret., Adm. Law J., Social Sec. Admn.‡
Nieto, Nancy V. '50 '95 C.763 B.S. L.1049 J.D.
(adm. in CA; not adm. in IL) [[A] Mayer,B.R.&M.]
Nieves, Ivan .... '74 '00 C.976 B.A. L.339 J.D. [[A] Rusin M.&F.]
Niewiara, James A. .... '68 '93 C.339 B.A. L.309 J.D. [Quinlan&C.]
Niewoehner, Christopher S. .... '70 '97 C&L.309 A.B., J.D. [[A] Sidley A.B.&W.]
Nightingale, Hope G., (AV) .... '— '81 C.293 B.A. L.145 J.D. [Litchfield C.]
Nihill, Burke J. .... '78 '03 C.340 B.A. L.146 J.D. [[A] Tressler,S.M.&P.] (⊙Wheaton)
Nijm, Michelle .... '— '04 C.424 B.A. L.145 J.D. [[A] Wildman,H.A.&D.]
Nijman, Jennifer T., (AV) .... '62 '87 C.339 B.A. L.145 J.D. [Winston&S.]
Nikas, Nikolas T. '57 '86 C.599 B.A. L.36 J.D.
(adm. in AZ; not adm. in IL) Gen. Coun., Americans United for Life
Nikchevich, Richard S. .... '62 '87 C.123 B.A. L.145 J.D. [Barack F.K.P.&N.]
Niles, Martha A. .... '54 '92 C.446 B.A. L.46 J.D. [[A] BryceDowney]
Nilles, David A., (AV) .... '62 '89 C.339 B.S. L.365 J.D. [Matushek,N.&S.]
Nilsen, Svenerik .... '71 '00 C.299 B.A. L.880 J.D. [[A] Scott&K.]
Nilson, Richard P., (BV) .... '55 '81 C.589 B.S. L.209 J.D. [Nilson,S.G.&C.]

Nilson, Stookal, Gleason & Caputo, (AV)
205 West Randolph Street, Suite 440, 60606
Telephone: 312-443-1331 Fax: 312-443-0746
Email: NSGCLaw@aol.com
Richard P. Nilson; Marc B. Stookal; Steven M. Gleason; William P. Caputo.
Personal Injury, Workers Compensation, Medical Malpractice, Airplane Crash Litigation, Automobile Accidents and Injuries, Wrongful Death, Federal Employers Liability Act (FELA), Construction Accidents, Employment Law and Divorce Law.
See Professional Biographies, CHICAGO, ILLINOIS

Nimerala, Natalie P. .... '— '03 C.797 B.A. L.424 J.D. [[A] Flamm&T.]
Nimmo, Anthony, (AV) .... '54 '83 C.679 B.S. L.347 J.D. [Ice M.] (Pat.)
Nimrod, Raymond N., (AV) .... '59 '84 C.602 B.S.Ch.E. L.424 J.D. [Jenner&B.] (Pat.)
Nimz, Jack D., (AV) '61 '90 C.339 B.S.M.E. L.365 J.D.
Sr. Coun.-Intell. Prop., Wm. Wrigley Jr. Co. (Pat.)
Nimz, Jeffrey E. .... '65 '91 C.881 B.A. L.477 J.D. Infinity Management Co., Inc.
Niro, Cheryl I., (AV) .... '50 '81 C.339 B.S. L.589 J.D. [Quinlan&C.]
Niro, Dean D., (BV) .... '65 '91 C.174 B.S. L.209 J.D. [Niro,S.H.&N.] (See Pat. Sect.)
Niro, Raymond P., (AV) '42 '70
C.665 B.S.Ch.E. L.273 J.D. [Niro,S.H.&N.] (See Pat. Sect.)
Niro, Raymond P., Jr., (AV) .... '66 '91 C.347 B.S. L.209 J.D. [Niro,S.H.&N.]
Niro, William L. ..... '45 '74 C.665 B.S.Ch.E. L.209 J.D. [Niro,S.H.&N.] (See Pat. Sect.)

Niro, Scavone, Haller & Niro, (AV) [BR]
181 West Madison, Suite 4600, 60602-4515
Telephone: 312-236-0733 Facsimile: 312-236-3137
URL: http://www.niroscavone.com
Members and Associates: Raymond P. Niro; Thomas G. Scavone; Timothy J. Haller; William L. Niro; Joseph N. Hosteny, III; Robert A. Vitale, Jr.; John C. Janka; Paul K. Vickrey; Dean D. Niro; Raymond P. Niro, Jr.; Patrick F. Solon; Arthur A. Gasey; Christopher J. Lee; David J. Sheikh; Vasilios (Bill) D. Dossas; Robert P. Greenspoon; Sally Wiggins; Richard Burns Megley, Jr.; Matthew G. McAndrews; Paul C. Gibbons; William W. Flachsbart; Brady J. Fulton; Gregory P. Casimer; Dina Pascarelli Hayes; Douglas M. Hall; Frederick C. Laney; David J. Mahalek; Kara L. Szpondowski; Robert A. Conley.
Intellectual Property and Technology-Related Law including Patent, Trademark, Trade Secret, Copyright, Licensing, Unfair Competition, Related Antitrust Matters.
See Professional Biographies, CHICAGO, ILLINOIS

Nisen & Elliott, LLC, (AV)
200 West Adams Street, Suite 2500, 60606
Telephone: 312-346-7800 Facsimile: 312-346-9316
URL: http://www.nisen.com
Members of Firm: Paul F. Gerbosi; Edward B. Mueller; Anthony Packard; Mark F. Zaenger; Michael J. Daley; John Foster Lesch; John K. Kneafsey; Michael H. Moirano; Robert O. Middleton; William G. Daluga, Jr.; Kenneth J. Rojc; Thomas V. McCauley; Helen M. Jensen; William A. Walker; Daniel P. Dawson; William J. Raleigh; Mary Rose C. Manczak; Bradley S. McCann;—Donald F. Froehlke; Patrick Vining; D. Eric Martin; Elena Gallo; David E. Gemperle; Jessica R. Falk; Claire E. Gorman; Sara B. Robertson; Matthew Sollitto. Of Counsel: Donald C. Shine.
Corporate Law, Commercial Litigation in all Federal and State Courts, Insurance Coverage, Financial Services, Employee Benefits, Estate Planning and Administration, Health Care Law, Taxation, Transportation Law, Employment Law, Commodities Law, Real Estate, Mergers and Acquisitions, Exempt Organizations, Antitrust, International Litigation, Aviation Law, Bankruptcy Reorganizations and Family-Owned-Business Law.
See Professional Biographies, CHICAGO, ILLINOIS

Nishida, Shinobu .... '— '03 C.347 B.A. L.1119 J.D. [[A] Masuda,F.E.&M.]
Nishigai, Makoto .... '73 '02 C.118 B.A. L.999 LL.B. [[A] Baker&M.]
Nissen, William J., (AV) .... '47 '76 C.597 B.A. L.309 J.D. [Sidley A.B.&W.]
Nissim-Sabat, Charles, Ph.D. '38 '95
C.178 B.S. L.146 J.D. [[C] Cherskov&F.] (See Pat. Sect.)
Nitikman, Franklin W., (AV) .... '40 '66 C.597 B.A. L.976 LL.B. [McDermott W.&E.]
Nix, James N. .... '67 '00 C&L.209 B.S., J.D. Enforcement Atty., IL Securities Dept.
Nix-Hodes, Patricia .... '64 '93 C.190 L.209 J.D. Legal Assistance Found. of Chicago
Nixon, Charles W. .... '36 '68 C.210 A.B. L.365 J.D. 29 S. La Salle St.
Nixon, David L. .... '56 '82 C.597 B.A. L.339 J.D. Ill. Com. Comm.
Nixon, Harvey, (AV) .... '31 '60 C.293 B.A. L.309 LL.B. [[C] Mayer,B.R.&M.]
Nixon, Lewis M. ..... '49 '75 C.723 B.A. L.209 J.D. Asst. Gen. Coun., U.S. Dept. of HUD
Noback, Allison Seger .... '77 '03 C.339 B.A. L.424 J.D. [[A] Kane,C.&M.]
Noble, Patricia E. .... '24 '55 C.352 B.A. L.209 J.D. Admin. Law J., Dept. of Employ. Sec.
Nocera, Nicole .... '71 '98 C.610 B.A. L.424 J.D. [[A] Wildman,H.A.&D.]
Nochowitz, Matthew M. .... '71 '98 C.347 B.S. L.1119 J.D. [[A] Baker&M.]
Noe, Jeremy Edward '63 '00
C.339 B.S. L.146 J.D. [McDonnell B.H.&B.] (See Pat. Sect.)
Noel, Jena M. .... '56 '87 C.209 B.A. L.146 J.D. [Dillard&N.]
Noell, John W., (AV) .... '56 '85 C.602 B.B.A. L.424 J.D. [Mayer,B.R.&M.]
Nolan, Brett .... '73 '98 C.478 B.A. L.910 J.D. [Shefsky&F.]
Nolan, Cristina C. .... '72 '97 C.209 B.A. L.734 J.D. [[A] Rusin M.&F.]
Nolan, Daniel J. .... '— '97 C.732 B.A. L.146 J.D. [[A] O'Hagan,S.&A.]
Nolan, Donald J., (AV) .... '52 '77 C.238 B.A. L.209 J.D. [Nolan]
Nolan, Heather E. .... '— '03 C.966 B.S. L.424 J.D. [[A] Wildman,H.A.&D.]
Nolan, James O., (AV) .... '39 '66 C&L.209 B.A., LL.B. [[C] Clausen M.]
Nolan, Michael J. .... '51 '82 C.177 B.A. L.424 J.D. [Nolan&N.]
Nolan, Nan R. .... '43 '76 C.424 B.S. L.209 J.D. U.S. Mag.
Nolan, Robert Emmett, (AV) .... '48 '75 C.177 B.A. L.424 J.D. [Nolan&N.]
Nolan, Timothy M. .... '61 '86 C.145 B.A. L.597 J.D. [Nolan]

Nolan Law Group, (AV) [BR]
20 North Clark Street, 30th Floor, 60602
Telephone: 312-630-4000 Toll Free: 888-630-9340 Facsimile: 312-630-4011 URL: http://www.nolanlawgroup.net
Email: contact@nolan-law.com URL: http://www.lawyers.com/nolan-law
Donald J. Nolan;—William J. Jovan; Floyd A. Wisner; Jerome L. Skinner (Not admitted in IL); James H. Lawlor, III; Orla M. Brady. Of Counsel: John J. Lowrey; Charles Rayburn Barnett, III.
Plaintiff's Personal Injury, Aviation, Traumatic Brain Injury, Wrongful Death, Medical Malpractice, Product Liability, FELA, Construction Accidents, Transportation Law, Automobile Accidents, Civil Trial and Appellate Practice.
See Professional Biographies, CHICAGO, ILLINOIS

Nolan Law Office .... 53 W. Jackson Blvd., Ste. 1137
Nolan and Nolan, P.C., (AV) .... 33 N. Dearborn St.
Noland, Daniel M. .... '68 '96 C.602 B.A. L.365 J.D. [Dykema G.P.]
Noland, Jennifer L. .... '— '03 C.210 B.A. L.209 J.D. [[A] Chittenden,M.&N.]
Noland, Michael .... '60 '89 C.602 B.A. L.365 J.D. Gen. Coun., Metra
Nolen, William D., (AV) .... '— '89 C.309 A.B. L.276 J.D. [Anderson,R.]
Noll, Lauren F. .... '— '00 C.473 B.A. L.339 J.D. [[A] Mayer,B.R.&M.]
Noll, Steven H., (AV) .... '— '78 C.475 B.S. L.608 J.D. [Schiff H.] (Pat.)
Nomellini, Mark .... '— '97 C.309 A.B. L.976 J.D. [Kirkland&E.]
Noonan, Gerald P. '36 '72 C.478 B.A. L.262 J.D.
(adm. in NE; not adm. in IL) Paramount Pictures
Noonan, James V., (AV) .... '63 '89 C.436 B.A. L.209 J.D. [Noonan&L.]
Noonan, Joseph P., III .... '70 '02 C.128 B.A. L.597 J.D. [[A] Butler R.S.&B.]
Noonan, Kevin E. '54 '93 C.1350 B.S. L.989 J.D.
[McDonnell B.H.&B.] (See Pat. Sect.)
Noonan, Kevin M. .... '— '97 C.150 B.B.A. L.424 J.D. [Sachnoff&W.]
Noonan, Patricia M. .... '— '88 L.339 J.D. [[C] Alholm,M.K.H.&O.]

Noonan & Lieberman, Ltd., (AV)
105 West Adams Street, Suite 3000, 60603-6209
Telephone: 312-431-1455 Fax: 312-431-1456
Email: JNoonan@noonandlieberman.com
James V. Noonan; Mitchell A. Lieberman;—Patrick J. McCann, II; Craig C. Smith; Jonathan D. Nusgart; Ralph T. Wutscher. Of Counsel: Michael J. Weik.
Real Estate Litigation, Lenders Rights and Lenders Litigation, Foreclosure, Commercial Litigation, and Civil Rights and Appellate Practice.
See Professional Biographies, CHICAGO, ILLINOIS

Nora, Gerald E. .... '51 '78 C&L.276 B.A., J.D. State's Atty.
Nora, Mark J., (AV) .... '52 '81 C.838 B.A. L.365 J.D. [[C] Holland&K.]
Nora, Robert L., (AV) .... '55 '80 C.597 B.A. L.209 J.D. [McKay,N.T.D.&K.]
Norber, Howard S. '— '01 C.475 B.A. L.145 J.D.
(adm. in NY; not adm. in IL) [[A] Kirkland&E.]

Norcross, John D., (AV) ....'36 '61 C.813 A.B. L.597 J.D. [Crane&N.]
Nord, Donald C., (AV) ....'43 '69 C.691 B.A. L.597 J.D. [Stahl C.C.]
Nord, Henry J. ....'17 '50 C.597 L.209 J.D. 55 W. Monroe St.‡
Nordahl, Andrew C. ....'— '95 C.424 B.A. L.365 J.D. [[A] Freeborn&P.]
Nordberg, John A. ....'26 '50 C.118 L.477 J.D. U.S. Sr. Dist. J.
Nordenberg, Arthur D. ....'30 '58 C.339 B.S. L.309 J.D. 6430 North Richmond‡
Nordgren, Gerald P. ....'54 '79 C.339 B.A. L.597 J.D. Supv. Atty., Chicago Legal Clinic
Nordwall, David R. ....'68 '93 C.10 B.A. L.597 J.D. [[A] Propes&K.]
Norek, Joan I., Law Office of, (AV) '45 '75
C.339 B.A. L.209 J.D. 180 N. La Salle, Ste. 1800 (Pat.)
Noren, Douglas L. ....'67 '92 C.910 B.A. L.597 J.D. [Katten M.R.]
Norenberg, Jenny M. ....'79 '04 C.966 B.A. L.494 J.D. [[A] Matushek,N.&S.]

Norgaard, Steven K., P.C.
(See Glen Ellyn)

Norgle, Charles R., Sr. ....'37 '69 C.597 B.B.A. L.365 J.D. U.S. Dist. J.
Norgle, Christine R. ....'67 '94 C.436 B.S. L.365 J.D. [[C] Bevilacqua&R.]
Norgle, Denise A. .....'61 '86 C.694 B.A. L.339 J.D. Asst. Gen. Coun., Trans Union LLC
Norgle, Gregory M. ....'70 '97 C.238 B.S. L.365 J.D. [Gurber,M.&N.]
Norgle, Gwendolyn M. ....'— '01 C.602 B.A. L.146 J.D. [[A] Bevilacqua&R.]
Norgle, Renee C. ....'— '98 C.57 B.A. L.365 J.D. [[A] Bevilacqua&R.]
Norkett, Brian W., (AV) ....'61 '87 C.276 A.B. L.597 J.D. [[C] Bullaro&C.]
Norkus, Jennifer L. ....'77 '04 C.575 B.A. L.339 J.D. [[A] Schuyler,R.&Z.]
Norman, Andy, (BV) ....'52 '79 C.589 B.A. L.796 J.D. [Mauck&B.]
Norman, Donald L., Jr. ....'61 '86 C.339 B.A. L.378 J.D. [Barack F.K.P.&N.]
Norman, Irving R. ....'14 '36 L.209 LL.B. 3150 N. Lake Shore Dr.‡
Norman, Jeffery S. ....'— '92 C&L.910 A.B., J.D. [Kirkland&E.]
Norman, Lynn E. ....'55 '86 C.276 B.S.F.S. L.94 J.D. Cash Station, Inc.
Norris, Craig W. ....'61 '86 C.861 B.S.M. L.744 J.D. Chicago Mercantile Exch.
Norris, David Walter ....'50 '87 C&L.46 B.S., J.D. [[A] Howe&H.]
Norris, John K., Jr., (AV) ....'54 '83 C.1111 B.A. L.146 J.D. [Rubin&N.] ⊙
Norris, Samantha C. ....'— '01 C.352 B.A. L.597 J.D. [[A] Schiff H.]
Norris, Scott ....'60 '85 C.589 B.A. L.209 J.D. 2 N. La Salle
Norris, Tanya L. ....'74 '02 C.174 B.A. L.424 J.D. Off. of the Pub. Guard.
Norrod, Gregory S. ....'— '88 C&L.347 B.A., J.D. [Foley&L.]
Norton, Brian P., (AV) ....'— '84 C&L.424 B.A., J.D. [Freeborn&P.]
Norton, Dennis H. '51 '80
C.746 B.A. L.365 J.D. Asst. V.P., CNA Property & Casualty Oper.
Norton, Jerry E. ....'37 '62 C.379 A.B. L.900 J.D. Prof. of Law, Loyola Univ.
Norton, John E., (AV) ....'49 '75 C.602 A.B. L.209 J.D. [Norton,M.W.&D.] ⊙
Norton, Joseph A., (AV) '35 '64
C.602 B.A. L.209 J.D. 175 West Jackson Boulevard, Suite 1600‡
Norton, Matthew E. ....'64 '89 C.707 B.A. L.339 J.D. [Holland&K.]
Norton, Terrance A. ....'45 '70 C.602 B.A. L.209 J.D. [Sonnenschein N.&R.]

Norton, Mancini, Weiler & DeAno, (AV)
Suite 835, 111 West Washington Street, 60602 ⊙
Telephone: 312-807-4999 Fax: 312-807-4998
Email: firm@nortonmancini.com
John E. Norton; Lorenzo A. Mancini; Thomas R. Weiler; James L. DeAno; Thomas J. Long; W. Anthony Andrews;—Daniel M. Latreille; David H. Capizzi; Mark W. Conrad.
Trial Practice. Personal Injury, Malpractice, Products Liability, Corporate Litigation, Municipal Litigation, Insurance, Corporate, Probate and Environmental Law, Medical Malpractice.
Wheaton, Illinois Office: 109 North Hale Street. Telephone: 630-668-9440. Fax: 630-668-9489.
See Professional Biographies, CHICAGO, ILLINOIS

Norum, David P. ....'31 '64 C.340 B.S. L.365 J.D. Sears, Roebuck & Co.
Norvell, Joseph V. ....'68 '94 C.339 B.S. L.276 J.D. [Brinks H.G.&L.]
Norwell, Gregory E., (AV) ....'43 '67 C.145 B.A. L.597 J.D. [Defrees&F.]
Nosek, Lisa ....'— '99 C.1016 B.A. L.589 J.D. [[A] S.M.Beller&Assoc.]
Nosek, William G. ....'— '71 C.424 A.B. L.145 J.D. [Arnstein&L.]
Notkin, Nathan T. ....'17 '38 C.339 L.365 LL.M. 105 W. Madison St.
Nottage, Courtney C. ....'60 '90 C.346 B.S. L.347 J.D. [[C] Hinshaw&C.]
Nottage, Rosaire M., (AV) ....'48 '76 C.475 B.A. L.424 J.D. [Nottage&W.]

Nottage and Ward, (AV)
Ten North Dearborn Street, Penthouse, 60602
Telephone: 312-332-2915 Fax: 312-332-3075
Members of Firm: Rosaire M. Nottage; Eunice Ward. Associates: Jeffrey J. Knipmeyer; Patrick B. Markey; Isa-Lee Wolf; Annemarie Tarara.
Family, Divorce, Child Custody, Premarital and Postnuptial Agreements, Visitation and Matrimonial Litigation, Appeals.
See Professional Biographies, CHICAGO, ILLINOIS

Notz, Jane Elinor ......'67 '99 C.659 B.A L.145 J.D. Appeals Div., Chicago Dept. of Law
Notz, John K., Jr., (AV) ....'— '56 C.951 B.A. L.597 J.D. [Gardner C.&D.]
Novack, Stephen, (AV) ....'46 '72 C.1347 B.A. L.597 J.D. [Novack&M.]

Novack and Macey LLP, (AV) BB
100 North Riverside Plaza, 60606
Telephone: 312-419-6900 Fax: 312-419-6928
Email: nminfo@novackandmacey.com URL: http://www.novackandmacey.com
Members of Firm: P. Andrew Fleming; Karen L. Levine; Eric N. Macey; Monte L. Mann; Mitchell L. Marinello; Timothy J. Miller; Stephen Novack; Stephen J. Siegel; Donald A. Tarkington; Michael A. Weinberg. Associates: Kenneth M. Abell; Allan V. Abinoja; Andrew D. Campbell; Steven J. Ciszewski; Kristen Werries Collier; Richard G. Douglass; Shelby L. Drury; Brian M. Dunn; Stephanie J. Harris; Julie A. Johnston-Ahlen; Elizabeth A. Mayer; Richard L. Miller II; Christopher S. Moore; Joseph S. Nacca; Vincent M. Roche; Alison Talbert Schwartz; John F. Shonkwiler; Louis C. Szura; Courtney Douglass Tedrowe.
General Trial and Appellate Practice in State and Federal Courts and in Arbitration, including Civil Appeals, Bankruptcy Litigation, Banks and Banking, Business Torts, Class Actions, Complex Commercial Litigation, Commercial Real Estate, Creditors' Rights, Energy, Environmental Litigation, Financial Institutions Litigation, Fraud and Deceit, including Art Fraud, Insurance Litigation, Lender Liability, Partnership Law, Professional Liability, Securities Litigation, Trademark Litigation, Trust Litigation, Unfair Competition.
See Professional Biographies, CHICAGO, ILLINOIS

Novak, David M., (AV) ....'48 '82 C&L.145 B.A., J.D. [Bell,B.&L.]
Novak, Mark, (AV) ....'52 '77 C.696 B.A. L.424 J.D. [Anesi,O.R.N.&K.]
Novak, Neal R., (AV) ....'51 '77 C&L.150 B.A., J.D. [N.R.Novak]
Novak, Rita M. ....'49 '78 C.20 B.A. L.209 J.D. Cir. Ct. J.
Novak, Theodore J., (P.C.), (AV) .....'40 '67 C.339 B.S. L.146 J.D. [DLPiper R.G.C.U.]

Novak, Neal R., Ltd., Law Offices of, (AV)
33 North LaSalle Street, Suite 1900, 60602
Telephone: 312-425-2500 Fax: 312-425-2525
Email: novak@novakjuris.com URL: http://www.lawyers.com/nealnovak
Neal R. Novak;—Karen Andersen Moran; Reid J. Rozen; Julia M. Core; Laura E. Pryst.
Insurance Coverage and Defense, Reinsurance and Fidelity/Crime Coverage Matters.
See Professional Biographies, CHICAGO, ILLINOIS

Novay, Christian ....'68 '98 C.258 B.S. L.1187 J.D. [[A] Wilson E.M.E.&D.]
Novelle, Robert A., (AV) ....'41 '66 C&L.209 B.S., J.D. [Serpico,N.&N.]

Novelli, Geoffrey M., (AV) '47 '74
C.846 B.S.Ch.E. L.209 J.D. 105 W. Adams St., 36th Fl. (Pat.)
Novello, William J. '50 '80
C.424 B.B.A. L.365 J.D. Treas. & Sr. Dir., The NutraSweet Co.
Novick, Michelle G., (BV) ....'67 '91 C&L.339 B.S., J.D. [[A] FagelHaber]
Novit, Kent E., (Ltd.) ....'55 '84 C.597 L.365 J.D. 100 N. LaSalle Street
Novit, Nancy Ann, (BV) ....'51 '81 C.388 B.A. L.365 J.D. 100 N. LaSalle
Novit, Sidney ....'27 '52 C.475 B.S. L.209 LL.B. 100 N. LaSalle St.
Novosad, Steven N., (BV) ....'53 '84 C.801 B.S. L.365 J.D. [Clausen M.]
Novosad, Susan Levin, (AV) ....'56 '86 C.339 B.S. L.365 J.D. [Levin&P.]
Novoselsky, Benj. E. ....'15 '38 C.137 B.A. L.209 J.D. Presiding J., Cir. Ct. (Probate)
Novoselsky, David A., (AV) ....'47 '73 C&L.424 A.B., J.D. [Novoselsky]
Novoselsky, Henry N., (AV) ....'42 '66 C.1016 B.A. L.209 J.D. [Shaheen,N.S.F.&E.]

Novoselsky Law Offices, (AV) BB
120 North La Salle Street, Suite 1400, 60602-2401
Telephone: 312-346-8930 Fax: 312-346-9453
Email: mail@novoselsky.com URL: http://www.novoselsky.com
Member of Firm: David A. Novoselsky. Associates: Leslie J. Rosen; Jeffrey M. Brown. Of Counsel: Linda A. Bryceland; James J. Ayres (Also practicing individually).
General Civil Trial and Appellate Practice. Probate, Class Actions and Civil Rights Litigation.
See Professional Biographies, CHICAGO, ILLINOIS

Novota, Miluska L. '— '99 C.57 B.A. L.597 J.D.
Asst. Corp. Coun., City of Chicago Law Dept.
Novotny, David J., (AV) ....'53 '78 C&L.209 B.S.C., J.D. [Chittenden,M.&N.]
Novotny, Kimberly D. ....'72 '98 C.210 L.209 J.D. [Bell,B.&L.]
Novy, Christopher M. ....'69 '96 C.424 B.S. L.589 J.D. [[A] Rock F.]
Novy, Fredric G., (AV) ....'39 '64 C.742 B.A. L.424 J.D. 350 N. La Sallle Dr.
Novy, Michael D. ....'45 '78 C.602 B.B.A. L.365 J.D. Appls. Div., IRS
Novy, Steven B., (AV) ....'47 '73 C.339 B.A. L.602 J.D. [Johnson&B.] (⊙Waukegan)
Nowacki, James N., (P.C.), (AV) ....'— '73 C.674 A.B. L.976 J.D. [Kirkland&E.]
Nowaczewski, Jeanne L. '56 '84 C&L.145 B.A., J.D.
Coun., Bus. & Professional People for the Pub. Interest
Nowak, Conrad C. ....'73 '03 C.209 B.A. L.424 J.D. [[A] Hinshaw&C.]
Nowak, Gerald T. ....'— '93 C.475 B.A. L.477 J.D. [Kirkland&E.]
Nowak, Jeffrey S. ....'72 '99 C&L.347 B.A., J.D. [[A] Franczek S.]
Nowak, John E. ....'72 '97 C.340 B.A. L.494 J.D. Asst. State's Atty.
Nowak, Patricia Cari, (AV) ....'56 '86 C&L.424 B.S.N., J.D. [Dykema G.P.]
Nowakowski, Annette '54 '85 C.700 B.A. L.339 J.D.
Asst. Atty., Mayor's Off. for People with Disabil.
Nowicki, Frank P., (AV) ....'54 '79 C.209 B.A. L.424 J.D. [Johnson&B.]
Nowicki, Julia M. ....'48 '75 C.966 B.A. L.424 J.D. Cir. J.
Nowicki, Mark E. '57 '84 C.209 B.A. L.365 J.D.
Sr. Atty., NASD Dispute Resolution, Inc.
Nowotarski, Christopher T., (P.C.) ....'58 '83 C&L.209 B.S., J.D. [Stone,P.&K.]
Noyes, Eric B. ....'62 '92 C.659 B.A. L.94 J.D. 335 S. Wabash, 25th Fl.
Nozette, Mark D., (AV) '50 '74 C.165 B.A. L.188 J.D.
Pres., Attorneys' Liability Assurance Society, Inc.
Nudelman, Paul A. ....'67 '92 C.352 B.S. L.209 J.D. 440 W. Randolph St.
Nudelman, Stuart A. ....'46 '72 C.339 B.S. L.146 J.D. Assoc. Cir. J.
Nugent, Lori S., (BV) ....'62 '87 C.388 B.A. L.597 J.D. [Cozen O.]
Nulman, Veronica ....'73 '98 C.597 B.A. L.94 J.D. [[A] McCullough,C.&L.]
Nunemaker, Krista L. ....'— '00 C&L.477 B.B.A., J.D. [[A] Kirkland&E.]
Nunes, Marcus J. ....'60 '84 C&L.597 B.A., J.D. [Chico&N.]
Nurnberg, D. Tyler ....'— '94 C.339 B.S. L.597 J.D. [[A] Kaye S.]
Nusgart, Jonathan D. ....'66 '92 C.260 B.A. L.61 J.D. [[A] Noonan&L.]
Nussbaum, Bernard J., (AV) ......'31 '56 C.388 A.B. L.145 J.D. [Sonnenschein N.&R.]
Nussbaum, Gerald S. ....'31 '58 C.966 B.B.A. L.209 LL.B. 134 N. LaSalle St.
Nutley, Deborah ....'59 '86 C.36 B.S. L.146 J.D. CNA Plz.
Nuttall, James R. '72 '97 C.339 B.S.I.E. L.424 J.D.
[McAndrews,H.&M.] (See Pat. Sect.)
Nutter, Michael K. ....'69 '97 C.339 B.S.Ch.E. L.146 J.D. [[A] Winston&S.] (Pat.)
Nwaomah, Amanu M. ....'77 '05 C.597 B.A. L.146 J.D. [[A] Bollinger,R.&G.]
Nyberg, David W., (AV) ....'55 '80 C&L.209 B.S.C., J.D. [[C] Shefsky&F.]
Nybo, Christopher L. ....'— '02 C.197 B.A. L.145 J.D. [[A] Vedder,P.K.&K.]
Nye, Jonathan D., (CV) ....'62 '92 C.991 B.A. L.365 J.D. [Nye&Assoc.]
Nye, Robert J., (AV) '31 '54 C.145 B.A. L.569 J.D.
Prof., The John Marshall Sch. of Law
Nye, Ronald J. ....'64 '89 C.602 B.B.A. L.893 J.D. [Winston&S.]
Nye, Sandra G., (BV) ....'35 '63 C.145 B.A. L.569 J.D. [Nye&Assoc.]
Nye & Associates, Ltd., Law Offices of, (BV) ..... 151 North Michigan Avenue, Suite 804
Nyhan, Lawrence J., (AV) ....'55 '80 C.145 B.A. L.424 J.D. [Sidley A.B.&W.]
Nyhan, Thomas D., (AV) ....'29 '58 C&L.424 B.S.C., J.D. [[A] Nyhan,P.B.K.&L.]
Nyhan, Pfister, Bambrick, Kinzie & Lowry, P.C., (BV) ..... 20 N. Clark Street, Suite 1000
Nykaza, Paul J. ....'66 '93 C.146 B.S.M.E. L.424 J.D. [Wallenstein W.&R.]
Nylen, Sven ....'— '05 C.597 B.A. L.339 J.D. [[A] Kirkland&E.]
Nyweide, John R., (AV) ....'47 '73 C.473 B.A. L.880 J.D. [Holland&K.]
Oak, Anita S. ....'78 '03 C.608 B.A. L.365 J.D. [[A] Garofalo,S.H.&S.]
Oakley, James L. ....'78 '03 C.659 B.A. L.960 J.D. [[A] FagelHaber]
Oates, Mark A. ....'60 '85 C.347 B.S. L.477 J.D. [Baker&M.]
O'Banion, Dana K. ...... '64 '93 C.254 B.A. L.145 J.D. Chicago Housing Auth., Sr. Coun.
Oberhardt, William P., (AV) '52 '78 C.602 B.S.M.E. L.209 J.D.
[W.P.Oberhardt] (Pat.)

Oberhardt, William P., LLC, (AV)
2100 Three First National Plaza, 70 West Madison, Suite 2100, 60602
Telephone: 312-251-1100 Fax: 312-251-1175
Email: wpoberhardt@aol.com URL: http://www.wpoberhardt.com
William P. Oberhardt.
Intellectual Property including Patents, Trademarks, Copyrights, Trade Secrets, and Unfair Competition, Litigation, Prosecution, Appeals, Licensing, Technology Transfer, Opinions, and Counseling.
See Professional Biographies, CHICAGO, ILLINOIS

Oberholtzer, James B., (AV) ....'53 '79 C.231 B.A. L.902 J.D. [Rohlfing&O.]
Oberlies, Robert M. ....'74 '02 C.321 B.A. L.597 J.D. [[A] Goldberg,K.B.B.R.&M.]
Oberman, Alicia S. ... '— '03 C.31 B.A. L.597 J.D. Two North LaSalle Street, Suite 2200
Oberman, Martin J., (AV) ....'45 '69 C.976 B.A. L.966 J.D. [M.Oberman]
Oberman, Mattathias H. ....'78 '04 C&L.893 B.A., J.D. [[A] DLPiper R.G.C.U.]
Oberman, Martin, (AV) ....36 S. Wabash, Ste. 1310
Obernesser, Michael K. ....'74 '01 C.973 B.A. L.597 J.D. [[A] Howrey]
Obhof, Larry J. ....'— '04 C.608 B.A. L.976 J.D. [[A] Kirkland&E.]
Obiala, John R., (AV) ....'54 '79 C.602 B.A. L.424 J.D. [Vedder,P.K.&K.]
O'Brien, Anastasia M. '64 '88 C.1016 B.A. L.365 J.D.
Assoc. Gen. Coun., Exelon Corp.
O'Brien, Angela D. ....'— '98 C.326 B.A. L.345 J.D. [[A] Mayer,B.R.&M.]
O'Brien, Barbara Jean '59 '89 C.150 B.A. L.1029 J.D.
Supervising Atty., Cabrini Green Legal Aid Clinic
O'Brien, Barton J. ....'75 '02 C.436 B.A. L.365 J.D. [[A] Shefsky&F.]

O'Brien, Brendan A. '69 '96 C.338 B.S. L.365 J.D. [Hinshaw&C.]
O'Brien, Carrie E. '— '00 C.602 B.A. L.339 J.D. [Ⓐ Gardner C.&D.]
O'Brien, Daniel E. '65 '92 C.339 B.A. L.365 J.D. [Stowick&S.]
O'Brien, Deborah M. '65 '91 C.260 B.S. L.46 J.D. [Ⓐ Lowis&G.]
O'Brien, Dennis M., (AV) '32 '60 C&L.424 B.S.C., J.D. 20 North Clark St., 36th Fl.
O'Brien, Donal M. '73 '98 C.999 B.A. L.424 J.D. [Ⓐ Much S.F.D.A.&R.]
O'Brien, Donald A., (AV) '48 '77 C.424 B.A. L.365 J.D. [Hinshaw&C.]
O'Brien, Donald J., (AV) '13 '36 C&L.209 J.D. 111 W. Wash. St.‡
O'Brien, Donald J., Jr. '38 '63 C.973 B.S.B.A. L.597 J.D. Cir. J.
O'Brien, Erin '75 '00 C&L.339 B.A., J.D. [Ⓐ Lovells]
O'Brien, Grace Law '70 '00 C.1169 B.A. L.146 J.D. [Ⓐ Fitch,E.T.&F.] (See Pat. Sect.)
O'Brien, Gregory M. '51 '77 C&L.209 B.A., J.D. 39 S. LaSalle St.
O'Brien, J. Phillip, (AV) '49 '74 C.927 B.A. L.339 J.D. [Katten M.R.]
O'Brien, James B., (AV) '40 '64 C&L.339 B.A., J.D. [Schiller,D.&F.]
O'Brien, James M., (AV) '56 '81 C.602 B.A. L.309 J.D. [Baker&M.]
O'Brien, James P., (AV) '58 '83 C.602 B.S. L.966 J.D. [Baker&M.]
O'Brien, Janet A. '42 '81 C.689 Ed.B. L.107 J.D. 1448 N. Lake Shore Dr. Apt. 7-8A‡
O'Brien, Jill P., (AV) '64 '89 C.927 B.S. L.365 J.D. [Laner,M.D.B.L.&T.]
O'Brien, John J. '19 '53 C.145 B.E. L.209 J.D. 6230 N. Lundy‡
O'Brien, John R. '53 '78 C.973 B.A. L.209 J.D. [J.R.O'Brien]
O'Brien, Kevin J., (AV) '61 '86 C.602 B.A. L.145 J.D. [Butler R.S.&B.]
O'Brien, Kevin M., (BV) '54 '80 C.201 B.A. L.200 J.D. [K.O'Brien]
O'Brien, Marc W. '51 '84 C.323 B.A. L.365 J.D. [Bronson&K.]
O'Brien, Margaret R., (BV) '62 '87 C.436 B.S. L.365 J.D. [G.K.Stern]
O'Brien, Maureen '— '98 C.1494 B.A. L.146 J.D. [Kirkland&E.]
O'Brien, Michael J. '57 '85 C.927 B.S. L.365 J.D. State's Atty.
O'Brien, Michael P. '60 '85 C.424 B.B.A. L.597 J.D. [Winston&S.]
O'Brien, Monica C. '65 '93 C.424 B.S. L.146 J.D. [G.K.Stern]
O'Brien, Neal J. '56 '91 C.1191 B.A. L.365 J.D. Off. of State Comr. of Bks. & Tr. Cos.
O'Brien, Patrick W., (AV) '27 '51 C&L.597 B.S., J.D. [Ⓒ Mayer,B.R.&M.]
O'Brien, Richard J., Jr., (AV) '54 '79 C.734 B.A. L.276 J.D. [Sidley A.B.&W.]
O'Brien, Sean P. '— '98 C.602 B.A. L.345 J.D. [Ⓐ Kirkland&E.]
O'Brien, Sheila M. '55 '80 C&L.602 B.A., J.D. App. Ct. Jus.
O'Brien, Susan M. '73 '98 C.602 B.A. L.424 J.D. [Ⓐ Hall,P.&S.]
O'Brien, Terence P. '— '99 C.339 B.S.M.E. L.146 J.D. Wilson Sporting Goods Co.
O'Brien, Thomas C. '41 '66 C&L.910 B.S.Ch.E., J.D. 151 N. Michigan Ave.
O'Brien, Thomas J. '32 '60 C&L.209 B.A., J.D. [Ⓒ Meckler B.&T.]
O'Brien, Timothy J., (AV) '48 '81 C.339 B.A. L.365 J.D. [Ⓒ Hinshaw&C.]
O'Brien, Timothy S. '74 '05 C.436 B.S. L.365 J.D. [Ⓐ Hinshaw&C.]
O'Brien, William T., (AV) '59 '84 C.363 B.S.B.A. L.146 J.D. Asst. States Atty.

O'Brien, Hanrahan & Fay, (AV)
53 West Jackson Boulevard, 60604 ⊙
Telephone: 312-427-4540 Fax: 312-427-9048
Member of Firm: E. Garnet Fay. Of Counsel: Thomas J. Keevers.
General Civil Practice. Casualty Insurance, Probate Administration and Litigation. Trials in all Courts.
Woodstock, Illinois Office: O'Brien, Hanrahan & Fay. 722 East Calhoun Street, P.O. Box 668, 60098. Telephone: 815-338-7780. Fax: 815-338-1003.

O'Brien, John R., P.C. 33 N. Dearborn St.
O'Brien, Kevin, Law Office of, (BV) 407 Dearborn St., Ste. 1125
O'Bryan, John M. '68 '97 C.188 A.B. L.597 J.D. [Ⓒ Lovells]
Obsitnik, Cristin '— '97 C.31 B.A. L.424 J.D. [Ⓐ Mayer,B.R.&M.]
Obucina, Lillian '62 '02 C.597 L.365 J.D. 104 S. Michigan Avenue, Ste. 727
O'Byrne, Francis J., Jr., (AV) '61 '89 C.339 B.A. L.365 J.D. 162 W. Grand Ave.
O'Byrne, Francis J., Sr. '28 '52 C.339 L.209 J.D.
Chf. Admin. Law J., Soc. Sec. Admin.
O'Byrne, Stephen F. '49 '77 C&L.145 B.A., J.D. Price Waterhouse
O'Byrne, Susan S. '— '00 C.399 B.A. L.209 J.D. [Ⓒ Mandell M.]
O'Callaghan, Joseph M. '43 '67 C&L.424 B.S., J.D. [O'Callaghan&C.]
O'Callaghan, Mary Aileen '45 '77 C.530 B.F.A. L.424 J.D. [Smith O.&W.]
O'Callaghan and Colleagues, P.C. 208 W. Washington Street
O'Carroll, Thomas L. '72 '97 C.861 B.A. L.209 J.D. [Ⓐ Hinshaw&C.]
Ocasek, James E., (AV) '52 '81 C.597 B.A. L.209 J.D. [Ⓐ Cooney&C.]
Ocasek, Timothy R., (AV) '54 '79 C.339 B.A. L.209 J.D. [Ⓐ Cooney&C.]
Ocasio, Eve Troczynski '74 '02 L.146 J.D. [Ⓐ Azulay,H.&S.]
Occhino, Lennine '56 '82 C.966 B.A. L.209 J.D. [Mayer,B.R.&M.]
Ochal, Frank J. '57 '84 C.339 B.S. L.209 J.D. [F.Ochal]
Ochal, Frank, Law Office of 5433 N. Ashland Ave.
Ockene, Brad '— '89 C.976 B.A. L.1365 J.D. [Ⓒ Lovells]
O'Connell, David J. '62 '88 C.436 B.S.M.E. L.910 J.D. [Wiedner&M.]
O'Connell, Donald P. '43 '68 C.72 B.A. L.597 J.D. Spec. Coun.
O'Connell, Erin M. '78 '04 C.188 B.A. L.813 J.D. [Ⓐ Jenner&B.]
O'Connell, Karin T., (AV) '60 '86 C.477 B.A. L.602 J.D. [Gould&R.]
O'Connell, Katherine N. '64 '93 C.339 B.A. L.30 J.D. [Ⓒ Gardner C.&D.]
O'Connell, Michael S. '53 '79 C.172 B.S. L.146 J.D. [O'Connell&R.]
O'Connell & Ryan, (AV) 53 W. Jackson Blvd., Suite 1350
O'Connell-Diaz, Erin M. '— '83
C.741 B.A. L.424 J.D. Comm., Illinois Commerce Comm.
O'Connor, Allyn M. '61 '94 C.856 B.A. L.190 J.D. 3270 N. Lake Shore Drive
O'Connor, Beth A. '— '98 C&L.477 A.B., J.D. [Ⓐ Jones D.]
O'Connor, Brendan '74 '02 C&L.424 B.A., J.D. [Ⓐ Quarles&B.]
O'Connor, Brian T. '45 '70 C&L.436 B.A., J.D. [B.O'Connor]
O'Connor, Bryan J., III, (AV) '52 '77 C.589 B.A. L.597 J.D. [Baal&O.]
O'Connor, Caitlin '78 '03 C.347 B.A. L.424 J.D. [Ⓐ Pretzel&S.]
O'Connor, Charles J., (AV) '31 '58 C&L.424 B.S., J.D. 6079 N. Sauganash Ave.
O'Connor, Christopher M. '75 '00 C.20 B.A. L.124 J.D. [Ⓐ Jenner&B.]
O'Connor, Daniel J., (AV) '47 '74 C.424 B.S. L.276 J.D. [Baker&M.]
O'Connor, Daniel V., (AV) '67 '92 C&L.424 B.S., J.D. [Anesi,O.R.N.&K.]
O'Connor, David J. '— '87 Cook Co. State's Attorney's Off.
O'Connor, James J. '37 '64 C.321 B.S. L.276 J.D.
Chmn. of the Bd. & Pres., Commonwealth Edison Co.
O'Connor, James W., (AV) '46 '85 C.960 B.S. L.365 J.D. [K.C.Miller]
O'Connor, Jeffrey S. '— '91 C.436 B.S. L.800 J.D. [Kirkland&E.]
O'Connor, John Campbell, (AV) '65 '90 C.339 B.A. L.347 J.D. [Hubbard&O.]
O'Connor, John J. '— '86 C.338 B.A. L.365 J.D. [Knell&P.] ⊙
O'Connor, Joseph F. '46 '79 C.966 B.A. L.424 J.D. 9531 S. Longwood Dr.‡
O'Connor, Margaret A. '73 '01 C.602 B.S. L.424 J.D. [Ⓐ Mayer,B.R.&M.]
O'Connor, Mary Ann '55 '80
C.321 A.B. L.602 J.D. Sr. Coun., Bank One Corp. (Law Dept.)
O'Connor, Mary C., (AV) '51 '76 C.339 B.A. L.597 J.D. [Foran G.P.&P.]
O'Connor, Matthew T. '65 '94 C.347 B.S. L.146 J.D. [Ⓐ Vedder,P.K.&K.]
O'Connor, Michael '68 '97 C.602 B.B.A. L.145 J.D. McKinsey & Co.
O'Connor, Michael T. '62 '88 C.347 B.S. L.424 J.D. [Fuchs&R.]
O'Connor, Neil D., (AV) '49 '74 C.602 A.B. L.597 J.D. 20 S. Clark St., Ste. 2000
O'Connor, Patricia A. '59 '85 C.339 B.A. L.365 J.D. [Ⓐ Levenfeld P.]
O'Connor, Patricia W. '51 '82 C.801 B.S. L.209 J.D. 20 S. Clark, 20th Fl.
O'Connor, Thomas F. '33 '58 C&L.424 J.D. 77 W. Wash. St.
O'Connor, Timothy P. '64 '89 C.339 B.A. L.477 J.D. [Winston&S.]
O'Connor, William J. '37 '64 C.350 B.S. L.352 J.D.
(adm. in IA; not adm. in IL) 53 W. Jackson Blvd.‡
O'Connor, Brian 1507 N. Cleveland, Ste. 3S
Ocrant, Yvonne C. '73 '99 C.589 B.S. L.209 J.D. [Hinshaw&C.]
O'Danovich, A. Mark '73 '98 C.347 B.S. L.365 J.D. [Ⓐ Bullaro&C.]
Odarczenko, Sonia V., (BV) '64 '88 C.98 B.A. L.424 J.D. [Clausen M.]
Odeh, Reem H. '— '03 C.720 B.A. L.365 J.D. [Brodsky&O.]
Odell, Diane Danzy '52 '94 C.999 B.S. L.146 J.D. [D.D.Odell]
Odell, Paul M., (AV) '45 '73
C.966 B.S.N.E. L.209 J.D. [Wood,P.K.C.&M.] (See Pat. Sect.)

Odell, Diane Danzy, Attorney At Law, P.C.
70 West Madison Street, Suite 1400, 60602
Telephone: 773-624-9828 Fax: 773-624-0790
Email: odelldia@ameritech.net URL: http://www.dianeodelllaw.com
Diane Danzy Odell.
Residential and Commercial Real Estate, Buying and Selling, Leasing, Real Estate Transactions, Housing Code Violations, Landlord/Tenant, Evictions, Disabled Estates, Guardianship.
See Professional Biographies, CHICAGO, ILLINOIS

Odem, Nathan H.B. '— '03 C&L.352 B.A., J.D. [Ⓐ Chapman&C.]
Oden, Sharon D. '70 '96 C.98 B.S. L.329 J.D. [S.D.Oden]
Oden, S.D., Law Offices of 1525 E. 53rd St., Ste. 819
Odendahl, Sean R. '72 '01 C&L.339 B.A., J.D. [Ⓐ Bell,B.&L.]
Odim & Malavia, P.C. 19 S. LaSalle Street, Suite 1402
Odland, Omar S. '61 '96 C.589 B.A. L.1000 J.D. [Ⓐ Meckler B.&T.]
Odom, Raymond C. '55 '80 C.879 B.A. L.608 J.D. 122 S. Michigan Ave., Ste. 1220
O'Donnell, Arthur J. '24 '50 C&L.209 J.D. 122 S. Michigan Ave.‡
O'Donnell, Brian P. '71 '01 C.339 B.A. L.424 J.D. [Ⓐ Jenner&B.]
O'Donnell, Ger P. '67 '92 C.339 B.S. L.477 J.D. [Mayer,B.R.&M.]
O'Donnell, Hugh C. '63 '89 C.145 A.B. L.339 J.D. [Sanchez&D.]
O'Donnell, John A., (AV) '56 '81 C.723 B.A. L.424 J.D. [Belgrade&O.]
O'Donnell, John R. '75 '01 C.436 B.A. L.365 J.D.
Cir. Ct. of Cook Co., Off. of the Chf. J.
O'Donnell, Kelley A. '65 '00 C.1183 B.A. L.209 J.D. State Farm Insurance Co.
O'Donnell, Margaret C. '62 '88 C.201 B.S. L.365 J.D.
V.P., Aon Corp., Professional Servs. Grp., Inc.
O'Donnell, Margo Wolf '68 '94 C.976 B.A. L.477 J.D. [Jenkens&G.]
O'Donnell, Stephen '60 '86 C.910 B.A. L.339 J.D. [Gardner C.&D.]
O'Donnell, Thomas J., (AV) '46 '73 C.1086 B.S. L.424 J.D.
[Rodriguez O.R.F.G.W.&E.]
O'Donnell, Timothy W. '61 '89 C.352 B.B.A. L.209 J.D. [Vedder,P.K.&K.]
O'Donovan, Jill A. '70 '95 C.1356 B.S. L.352 J.D. [Walker W.M.]
Odorizzi, Michele L. '52 '76 C.597 B.A. L.145 J.D. [Mayer,B.R.&M.]
O'Driscoll, John M. '71 '96 C.339 B.A. L.347 J.D. [Ⓐ Tressler,S.M.&P.]
Odunsi, Abosede O. '74 '01 C.339 B.A. L.966 J.D. [Ⓐ Swanson,M.&B.]
Oduye, Adewale A. '79 '05 C.178 B.A. L.597 J.D. [Ⓐ Bollinger,R.&G.]
Oehring, Thomas S. '28 '56 C.597 B.S. L.339 LL.B. V.P. & Secy., Miami Corporation
Oertle, Heidi '— '01 C.118 B.A. L.145 J.D. [Ⓐ Schiff H.]
Oesch, Rachel L. '— '01 C.107 B.A. L.146 J.D. [Ⓐ McCarthy&Assoc.]
Oest, John N., (AV) '52 '77 C.207 B.A. L.966 J.D. [Lord,B.&B.]
Oesterle, Eric A., (AV) '48 '73 C&L.477 B.S., J.D. [Sonnenschein N.&R.]
Offenbach, Daniel J., (BV) '56 '82 C.1365 B.A. L.209 J.D. [Leahy,E.&F.]
Offenbach, Sigi M. '50 '80 C.293 B.A. L.424 J.D. [Pitler&M.]
Offutt, Gerald M., (AV) '50 '76 C&L.309 A.B., J.D. [McDermott W.&E.]
O'Flaherty, Paul B., (AV) '— '49 C&L.424 J.D. [Schiff H.] ‡
O'Flaherty, Paul B., Jr., (AV) '55 '80 C.197 A.B. L.424 J.D. [Cheely,O.&A.]
O'Flaherty, Tracy A. '69 '94 C.94 B.A. L.884 J.D. [Winston&S.]
Ofsthun, D. Glenn, (AV) '— '50 C&L.309 A.B., LL.B. [Dykema G.P.] ‡
O'Gallagher, Brian A. '67 '92 C.339 B.S. L.602 J.D. [Cremer,K.S.&S.]
O'Gara, Lawrence D. '42 '69 C.424 B.S. L.209 J.D. Chief Asst. States Atty.
Ogden, Bryan C. '43 '69 C.1074 B.S. L.1065 J.D.
(adm. in NY; not adm. in IL; Pat.) Boeing Company, The
Ogden, Seymour '19 '56 C.597 B.S. L.365 134 N. La Salle St.

Ogletree, Deakins, Nash, Smoak & Stewart, P.C., (AV) (BV)
Twenty-Fifth Floor, Two First National Plaza 20 South Clark Street, 60603-1891 ⊙
Telephone: 312-558-1220 Telecopier: 312-807-3619
Email: clientservices@ogletreedeakins.com URL: http://www.ogletreedeakins.com
Charles E. Murphy; Arthur B. Smith Jr.; Robert P. Casey; Richard L. Samson; Carol A. Poplawski; Tracey L. Truesdale; Randolph E. Ruff; Thomas Vasiljevich; Margery Newman; Michael H. Cramer;—Michael D. Ray. Of Counsel: Gayle M. Meadors; Matthew J. Straub; Julia A. Donnelly; Nancy Ann Case; Karen N. Brandon; Michael R. Cannon.
Labor Relations, Employment Litigation, Workers' Compensation. Civil Litigation in all State and Federal Courts and Administrative Agencies.
Atlanta, Georgia Office: 600 Peachtree Street, N.E., Suite 2100. Telephone: 404-881-1300.
Austin, Texas Office: 301 Congress Avenue, Suite 1250. Telephone: 512-344-4700.
Birmingham, Alabama Office: One Federal Place, Suite 1000, 1819 Fifth Avenue North. Telephone: 205-328-1900.
Charleston, South Carolina Office: 134 Meeting Street, Suite 160, P.O. Box 1808. Telephone: 843-853-1300.
Charlotte, North Carolina Office: 400 West Trade Street. Telephone: 704-342-2588.
Columbia, South Carolina Office: 1320 Main Street, Suite 600. Telephone: 803-252-1300.
Dallas, Texas Office: 700 Preston Commons, 8117 Preston Road. Telephone: 214-987-3800.
Greensboro, North Carolina Office: 2725 Horse Pen Creek Road, Suite 101. Telephone: 336-375-9737.
Greenville, South Carolina Office: The Ogletree Building, 300 North Main Street, P.O. Box 2757. Telephone: 864-271-1300.
Houston, Texas Office: One Allen Center, 500 Dallas Street, Suite 3000. Telephone: 713-655-0855.
Kansas City, Missouri Office: 4717 Grand Avenue, Suite 300. Telephone: 816-471-1301.
Los Angeles, California Office: 633 West Fifth Street, Suite 5300. Telephone: 213-239-9800.
Indianapolis, Indiana Office: Suite 4600, 111 Monument Circle. Telephone: 317-916-1300.
Miami, Florida Office: 80 S.W. 8th Street, Suite 1830. Telephone: 305-374-0506.
Morristown, New Jersey Office: 10 Madison Avenue, Suite 402. Telephone: 973-656-1600.
Nashville, Tennessee Office: SunTrust Center, Suite 800, 424 Church Street. Telephone: 615-254-1900.
Phoenix, Arizona Office: 2415 East Camelback Road, Suite 800. Telephone: 602-778-3700.
Raleigh, North Carolina Office: 2301 Sugar Bush Road, Suite 600, P.O. Box 31608. Telephone: 919-787-9700.
San Antonio, Texas Office: 2600 Weston Centre, 112 East Pecan Street. Telephone: 210-354-1300.
St. Thomas, U.S. Virgin Islands Office: The Tunick Building, 1336 Beltjen Road, Suite 202. Telephone: 340-714-1235.
Tampa, Florida Office: 100 North Tampa Street, Suite 3600. Telephone: 813-289-1247.
Washington, D.C. Office: Fifth Floor, 2400 N Street, N.W. Telephone: 202-887-0855.
See Professional Biographies, CHICAGO, ILLINOIS

O'Grady, John '— '90 C.339 B.A. L.46 J.D. [Ⓐ Foran G.P.&P.]
Ogron, Bruce D. '61 '88 C.589 B.A. L.146 J.D. [Ⓐ Nyhan,P.B.K.&L.]
Ogura, Meiko L. '70 '95 C.339 B.A. L.801 J.D. [Ⓐ Johnson&B.]
Ogus, Lonny B. '49 '78 C.563 B.B.A. L.1151 J.D. 39 S. LaSalle St.
Oguss, Douglas A. '77 '05 C.880 B.E. L.770 J.D. [Ⓐ Brinks H.G.&L.]
Oh, James J., (AV) '63 '87 C&L.597 B.A., J.D. [Littler M.]

O'Hagan, James J., (AV) .... '— '63 C&L.209 B.S.C., J.D. [O'Hagan,S.&A.]
O'Hagan, Kevin M. ....'67 '92 C.321 B.A. L.209 J.D. [O'Hagan,S.&A.]

O'Hagan, Smith & Amundsen, (AV)
150 North Michigan Avenue, Suite 3300, 60601 ⊙
Telephone: 312-894-3200 Fax: 312-894-3210
Email: choffice@osalaw.com URL: http://www.osalaw.com
Members of Firm: Glen E. Amundsen; James P. Balog; Benjamin A. Blume; Lew R.C. Bricker; Patrick B. Cage; Craig A. Cappas; Gerald V. Cleary, III; Carmel M. Cosgrave; Dennis J. Cotter; Ronald L. Drozdzik; Jerome J. Duchowicz; Timothy J. Fagan; Thomas F. Falkenberg; James W. Fessler; Rita M. Filiaggi; Rosalyn M. Golden; Anita Senese Johnson; Anthony G. Karamuzis; Patrick Keating; Thomas J. Lyman, III; Michael J. McGowan; Thomas A. Meyer; James J. O'Hagan; Kevin M. O'Hagan; Victor J. Piekarski; Jill A. Pignotti; Michael Resis; Julie P. Rubin; Eric L. Samore; Larry A. Schechtman; James S. Smith, III; Lawrence R. Smith; Marcie Thorp; Richard T. Valentino; Aleen R. Tiffany. Associates: Christine V. Anto; Cynthia L. Besecker; Molly A. Caprez; James Caronis; Daniel P. Derechin; Elizabeth Dillon; Joseph M. Eichberger; Timothy Liam Epstein; Kristine S. Estacio; Brian T. Flood; Steven Fuoco; Frederic C. Goodwill, II; William P. Heffernan; Katie A. Irvine; Ryan B. Jacobson; Leslie Johnson; Carolyn Kang (Not admitted in IL); Lisa G. Kaufman; Daisy Khambatta; Soo Jin Kim; Heather Kingery; Nicholas G. Kourvetaris; John D. LaBarbera; Inhak Lee; Katherine Lengiewicz; Ryan A. Mahoney; Ann McLellan; Daniel B. Meyer; Linda F. Newman; Daniel J. Nolan; Lisa M. Pagel; Kenneth Perry; Tanya Petermann; Troy S. Radunsky; Brian A. Rosenblatt; Andrew C. Seiber; Elana K. Seifert; Luke P. Sheridan; Carrie A. Von Hoff; Ginger Rae Wiley; Gary Zhao.
Commercial; Commercial Transportation; Appellate; Complex Litigation; Construction; Corporate Transactions; Employment; Extra-Contractual/Insurance Litigation; Healthcare; Insurance Coverage; Personal Lines; Product Liability; Professional Liability; Property Litigation.
Rockford, Illinois Office: Stewart Square, 308 West State Street, Suite 320, 61101-1140. Telephone: 815-987-0441. Fax: 815-987-9891.
St. Charles, Illinois Office: 3815 E. Main Street, Suite A-1, 60174-2488. Telephone: 630-587-7910. Fax: 630-587-7960.
Waukegan, Illinois Office: 415 West Washington Street, Suite 204, 60079-0410. Telephone: 847-599-9503. Fax: 847-599-9525.
Woodstock, Illinois Office: 666 Russell Court, 60098. Telephone: 815-337-4900. Fax: 815-337-4910.
Milwaukee, Wisconsin Office: 4811 South 76th Street, Suite 305, 53220. Telephone: 414-282-7103. Fax: 414-282-1830.

See Professional Biographies, CHICAGO, ILLINOIS

O'Hair, Dee Ann ...... '64 '94 C.375 B.S. L.1003 J.D. Sr. Atty., Chicago, M.R.O., S.E.C.
O'Halleran, Katherine .... '— '01 C.276 B.A. L.597 J.D. [🄰 Winston&S.]
O'Halloran, James E., III ....'66 '92 C.861 B.A. L.436 J.D. [Deutsch,L.&E.]
O'Halloran, John M., (AV) .... '48 '74 C.436 B.A. L.339 J.D. [Coleman&O.]
O'Halloran, Joseph P. ....'54 '79 C&L.424 A.B., J.D. 222 S. Riverside Plz.
O'Halloran, Loari M. .....'76 '02 C.219 B.A. L.436 J.D. 111 W. Washington St., Ste. 802

O'Halloran, Kosoff, Geitner & Cook, P.C.
(See Northbrook)

O'Hara, Brian J. ....'55 '80 C.424 B.A. L.597 J.D. 19 W. Jackson Blvd.
O'Hara, Joseph J., Jr., (AV) .... '— '81 C.436 B.S. L.597 J.D. [Schiff H.]
O'Hara, Kevin J. P. .... '61 '88 C.145 B.A. L.276 J.D. Gen. Coun., Archipelago, LLC
O'Hara, Margaret L. '— '86 C.473 B.A. L.930 J.D.
(adm. in OH; not adm. in IL) Dir. & Sr. Coun., CNA Property & Casualty Oper.
O'Hara, Martin J. ....'68 '95 C.338 B.A. L.365 J.D. [Quinlan&C.]
O'Hara, Matthew J. .... '— '96 C.597 B.A. L.146 J.D. [Sachnoff&W.]
O'Hara, Timothy D. ....'32 '57 C&L.602 B.A., LL.B. Asst. Corp. Coun.
O'Hare, John M. ....'46 '71 C.339 A.B. L.309 J.D. [Sidley A.B.&W.]
Ohlms, Todd J. ....'— '95 C.502 B.S. L.910 J.D. [Freeborn&P.]
Ohlson, Glenn W., (AV) '— '76 C.339 B.S.C.E. L.365 J.D.
[Barnes&T.] (See Pat. Sect.)
Ohm, Michael K., (BV) ....'60 '85 C.339 B.S.W. L.209 J.D. [Bell,B.&L.]
Ohren, Ronald L. .... '60 '86 C.150 B.A. L.365 J.D. [Baker&M.]
O'Kane, Brian Patrick .... '72 '97 C&L.339 B.A., J.D. [Weldon-Linne&V.]
O'Keefe, Bridget M., (AV) .... '59 '87 C.741 B.A. L.276 J.D. [Michael B.&F.]
O'Keefe, David J., (AV) ....'56 '81 C.602 B.A. L.424 J.D. [Schain,B.R.&C.]
O'Keefe, Kevin M., (AV) .... '46 '73 C.339 B.S. L.146 J.D. [O'Keefe,L.&H.]
O'Keefe, Lisa .... '59 '91 C.338 B.A. L.424 J.D. [🄲 Mayer,B.R.&M.]
O'Keefe, Nicholas J. '64 '95
C.812 B.S. L.365 J.D. Corp. Coun., Anteros Capital Markets LLC
O'Keefe, Paul F., (BV) .... '65 '90 C.321 B.A. L.339 J.D. [P.F.O'Keefe] ⊙
O'Keefe, William P., Jr., (AV) .... '38 '63 C.321 A.B. L.145 J.D. [W.P.O'Keefe,Jr.]

O'Keefe, Lyons & Hynes, LLC, (AV)
30 North La Salle Street, Suite 4100, 60602
Telephone: 312-621-0400 Facsimile: 312-621-0297
Email: info@okeefe-law.com URL: http://www.okeefe-law.com
Christine M. Biebel; James E. Carroll; Daniel W. Coyne; Mark R. Davis; Patricia Quinn Ford; Brian P. Forde; Elizabeth L. Gracie; J. Michael Heaton; Kevin B. Hynes; Robert E. Hynes; Barbara Johnson; Alison A. Lemmens; Thomas G. Lyons; Michael L. McDermott; Kevin M. O'Keefe; Marguerite Quinn; Jason T. Shilson; John F. Ward, Jr., (P.C.).
Taxation (State and Local) Law, Ad Valorem Law, Finance Law, Finance: Mergers and Acquisitions, Health and Hospital Law, Litigation, International, Matrimonial Law, Estate Planning, Probate Law, Real Estate Law, Environmental Law.
Reference: The First National Bank of Chicago.

See Professional Biographies, CHICAGO, ILLINOIS

O'Keefe, Paul F., P.C., (BV)
20 North Clark Street, Suite 2550, 60602 ⊙
Telephone: 312-263-9200 Fax: 312-263-6245
Email: okeefelaw@msn.com URL: http://www.okeefelawoffice.com
Paul F. O'Keefe.
Languages: Spanish.
Arbitration, Business Law, Business Litigation, Complex Business Litigation, Federal Civil Practice, Commercial Law, Complex Commercial Litigation, Contracts, Breach of Contracts, Contract Litigation, Corporate Law, Corporate Litigation, Criminal law, Criminal Defense, Governmental Law, Labor and Employment, Employment Breach of Contract, Litigation, Civil Litigation, Complex Litigation, Defense Litigation, Federal Litigation, Trial Practice, Medical Malpractice, Personal Injury, Probate, Ancillary Probate, Probate Administration, Probate Litigation, Criminal Taxation, Trusts and Estates, Contested Trusts and Estates, Decedents Estates, Estate Litigation, Estate Settlements, White Collar Crimes, White Collar Criminal Defense, Wills, Contested Wills, Inheritance, Decedents Estates, Estate Administration, Estate Litigation, Estate Planning, Internet Crimes, Felonies.
Waukegan, Illinois Office: 32 N. West Street. Second Floor. 60085. Telephone: 847-263-9262.

See Professional Biographies, CHICAGO, ILLINOIS

O'Keefe, William P., Jr., P.C., (AV) .... 150 North Wacker Drive Suite 1500
O'Kelly, Cathy G., (AV) .... '53 '78 C.945 B.A. L.893 J.D. [Vedder,P.K.&K.]
O'Kelly, Paul B. '49 '74 C&L.424 B.A., J.D.
Chief Operating Officer, Chicago Stock Exchange, Incorporated
Okey, David W. ......'46 '00 C.174 B.A. L.365 J.D. [🄰 Brinks H.G.&L.] (See Pat. Sect.)
Okitipi, Bernard I. ....'59 '89 C.1016 B.S. L.472 J.D. Asst. Pub. Def.
Okizaki, Carrie Lynn H. '— '00 C.276 B.S. L.174 J.D.
(adm. in CO; not adm. in IL) [🄰 Schiff H.]
Okmin, Mara .... '72 '97 C.966 B.A. L.146 J.D. Amer. Natl. Bk. & Tr. Co.
Okun, Andrea Caplan, (BV) .... '— '95 C&L.477 B.A., J.D. [Seyfarth S.]
Olatunji, Kenny .... '— '03 L.365 J.D. [K.Olatunji]
Olatunji, Kenny, P.C. .... 166 W. Washington St., Ste. 640
O'Laughlin, Charles J., (AV) .... '18 '42 C.424 B.S.C. L.477 J.D. 1 IBM Plaza
O'Laughlin, Ellen ....'63 '91 C.399 B.A. L.424 J.D. [🄰 Kerns,P.F.&P.]
Olbrysh, Ronald .... '41 '67 C.381 B.S. L.930 J.D. [🄲 George W.H.]
Old, Philip E. ....'64 '93 C.436 B.S. L.424 J.D. [Carroll,H.&C.]
Oldenburg, Anne Marie, (BV) ......'— '87 C.694 B.A. L.365 J.D. [Alholm,M.K.H.&O.]
Olderman, Neil S. .... '— '90 C.347 B.A. L.128 J.D. [Gardner C.&D.]
Oldford, William G., Jr. ....'65 '91 C.477 B.A. L.61 J.D. [🄲 Christensen&E.]
Oldham, Douglas M. .... '— '04 C&L.597 B.A., J.D. [🄰 Barnes&T.]
Oldham, Marie C., (AV) ....'61 '86 C.801 B.S. L.339 J.D. [Winston&S.]
O'Leary, Daniel V., Jr., (AV) ....'42 '67 C.276 A.B. L.976 LL.B. [Mandell M.]
O'Leary, David G. ....'48 '78 C.339 B.S. L.424 J.D. [🄲 Holland&K.]
O'Leary, Frank J. ....'53 '78 C.165 B.A. L.309 J.D. 916 Armitage
O'Leary, John J. ....'62 '89 C.339 B.A. L.365 J.D. 203 South Sangamon Street
O'Leary, John J. '— '80 C.743 B.A. L.597 J.D.
20 N. Clark Street, Suite 1725, 60602
Telephone: 312-782-8807 Fax: 312-372-6067
Email: joleary@olearylawfirm.com URL: http://www.olearylawfirm.com
Construction Law and Commercial and Residential Real Estate Law, Lending Law.

See Professional Biographies, CHICAGO, ILLINOIS

O'Leary, Mary Margaret .... '69 '99 C.27 B.A. L.209 J.D. 1 N. LaSalle St., Ste. 2400
O'Leary, Maureen P. '66 '02 C.720 B.S.N. L.365 J.D.
33 North LaSalle Street, Suite 1910
O'Leary, Susan Wood, (AV) '49 '85 C.436 B.S. L.146 J.D.
Assoc. Gen. Coun., Asst. V.P., & Risk Mgr., Rush Presbyterian St. Luke's Med. Ctr.
Olejnik, Andrew J. ....'79 '04 C.602 B.A. L.813 J.D. [🄰 Jenner&B.]
Oleksa, Laurence ....'75 '01 C.378 B.S. L.966 J.D. [🄰 Perkins C.]
Olenn, Julie J. ....'— '02 C.722 B.A. L.1529 J.D. [Levin&S.]
Olenski, Maribeth, (AV) ...'— '86 C.424 B.A. L.365 J.D. [🄰 Beermann S.W.B.B.G.&L.]
Oles, Frank J., (AV) .... '48 '73 C.589 B.A. L.424 J.D. 120 N. La Salle St.
Oleszkiewicz, Robert T., (BV) ....'60 '85 C.597 B.A. L.209 J.D. [🄰 Daley&G.]
Oleszkiewicz, Stephen M. ....'33 '58 C.1024 B.A. L.209 J.D. 4012 S. Archer Ave.
Oleszkiewicz, Vincent S., (AV) ....'57 '82 C.475 B.A. L.209 J.D. [Duane M.]
Olian, Robert M., (AV) ....'53 '77 C&L.309 A.B., J.D. [Sidley A.B.&W.]
Olins, Matthew A. ....'74 '01 C.385 B.A. L.910 J.D. [🄰 Katten M.R.]
Oliver, Darlene M. ....'70 '94 C.98 B.S. L.276 J.D. [🄰 Robinson C.&C.]
Oliver, Lawrence, II ....'61 '91 C.679 B.S.I.E. L.213 J.D. Chf. Coun., Boeing Co. .
Oliver, Roseann, (AV) ....'47 '72 C.597 B.A. L.424 J.D. [Perkins C.]
Oliver, Wallace L., (AV) ...'44 '74 C.111 B.S. L.597 J.D. [🄲 Welsh&K.] (See Pat. Sect.)
Olivera, Beatriz M. ....'56 '80 C.597 B.A. L.477 J.D. [🄰 Harris K.&G.]
Olivi, Ralph L., Jr., (AV⊙) '27 '55 C.112 A.B. L.1065 J.D.
(adm. in CA; not adm. in IL) 900 N. Michigan Ave.
Ollis, Robert W., Jr. ....'— '74 C.502 B.A. L.477 J.D. [Chapman&C.]
Olmstead, David J. ....'68 '95 C.477 B.A. L.128 J.D. [🄰 Tressler,S.M.&P.]
Olofsson, Thomas J. ....'57 '92 C.339 B.A. L.365 J.D. 10001 S. Western Ave.
O'Loughlin, William P. ....'50 '77 C.338 B.S. L.46 J.D. 10143 S. Prospect Ave.‡
Olsen, Kurt E. ....'58 '84 C.927 B.S. L.365 J.D. [Fitzgerald&C.]
Olsen, Lisa A. ....'— '89 C&L.477 B.A., J.D. [Chapman&C.]
Olsen, Michael A. ....'71 '96 C.477 B.A. L.209 J.D. [Mayer,B.R.&M.]
Olshansky, Amy L. ....'— '98 C.188 B.A. L.602 J.D. [🄰 Chapman&C.]
Olshansky, David S. ....'73 '00 L.146 J.D. [Giovannini&O.]
Olson, Arne M., (AV) .... '55 '80 C.145 A.B. L.209 J.D. [Olson&H.] (See Pat. Sect.)
Olson, B. Tucker ....'53 '79 C.339 B.S. L.146 J.D. [Early C.&O.]
Olson, Camille A., (AV) .... '58 '83 C&L.477 B.A., J.D. [Seyfarth S.]
Olson, Diana C. ... '48 '81 C.783 B.A. L.966 J.D. Asst. Dean, De Paul Univ. Coll. of Law
Olson, Glen R. '56 '83 C.112 B.A. L.1065 J.D.
(adm. in CA; not adm. in IL) V.P., CNA Insurance
Olson, Jeryl, (AV) .... '57 '85 C.879 B.S. L.209 J.D. [Seyfarth S.]
Olson, Karin A., (AV) ....'60 '90 C&L.209 B.A., J.D. [S.J.Levy&Assoc.]
Olson, Layton E. ....'42 '68 C.668 B.A. L.1066 J.D. [🄲 Howe&H.]
Olson, Nancy M. ....'— '94 C.597 B.A. L.424 J.D. [🄲 Skadden,A.S.M.&F.]
Olson, Peter M. ...... '59 '91 C.385 A.B. L.339 J.D. Gen. Coun. & Sec., Morningstar, Inc.
Olson, Ronald W. ....'31 '56 C&L.597 B.S.L., J.D. Cir. J.
Olson, Sarah L., (AV) ....'53 '86 C.112 B.A. L.146 J.D. [Wildman,H.A.&D.]
Olson, Scott H. ....'— '00 C.813 L.602 [🄰 Chapman&C.]
Olson, Steven J. ....'65 '90 C.966 B.S. L.477 J.D. 18th Floor, 33 West Monroe Street
Olson, Steven R., (AV) .... '55 '82 C.243 B.S. L.365 J.D. [Katten M.R.]

Olson & Hierl, Ltd., (AV)
20 North Wacker Drive 36th Floor, 60606-3181
Telephone: 312-580-1180 Telecopier: 312-580-1189
Email: firm@olsonhierl.com URL: http://www.olsonandhierl.com
Michael A. Hierl; Arne M. Olson; Dolores T. Kenney; Talivaldis Cepuritis; Kathryn E. Garipay; Joseph M. Kuo;—Dennis H. Ma; Bruce R. Mansfield; Mark R. Bagley. Of Counsel: Seymour Rothstein.
Intellectual Property and Technology-Related Law including Patents, Trademarks, Trade Secrets, Copyrights and Unfair Competition, Related Licensing and Litigation.

See Professional Biographies, CHICAGO, ILLINOIS

Olswang, Daniel H. .... '70 '96 C.966 B.A. L.146 J.D. [🄰 Weltman,W.&R.] (⊙Deerfield)
Olthoff, Linda M. ....'70 '98 C.1348 B.A. L.339 J.D. Appl. Def.
Oltman, Gregory ....'59 '86 C.347 B.S. L.365 J.D. [Cosby,O.&B.]
Oltmanns, Julia K. ....'75 '00 C.339 B.S. L.424 J.D. [🄰 Franczek S.]
Omahana, Robin J., (AV) ...... '50 '75 C.293 B.A. L.910 J.D. 230 W. Monroe Street
O'Malley, Denise ....'40 '81 C.530 B.A. L.365 J.D. Cir. J.
O'Malley, Francis W. ....'65 '90 C.602 B.B.A. L.209 J.D. [🄰 Worsek&V.]
O'Malley, James A. '74 '99
C.436 B.S.M.E. L.1000 J.D. [Trexler,B.G.B.&M.] (See Pat. Sect.)
O'Malley, James D. ....'33 '70 C.742 B.A. L.365 J.D. V.P., Great Amer. Fed. Svgs.
O'Malley, John C. ....'49 '75 C&L.424 B.A., J.D. Archdiocese of Chicago
O'Malley, John D. ....'26 '53 C&L.424 B.S., J.D. Professor, Loyola University‡
O'Malley, John J., (AV) ....'13 '40 L.209 LL.B. 30 N. La Salle St., Ste. 1740
O'Malley, John J., (AV) ....'48 '74 C.321 B.A. L.209 J.D. [Seyfarth S.]
O'Malley, John M., (AV) ....'51 '81 C.424 B.S. L.145 J.D. States Atty.
O'Malley, John P. ....'65 '91 C.436 B.S. L.209 J.D. [Crisham&K.]
O'Malley, Kelly Maureen ....'— '00 C.477 B.A. L.424 J.D. [🄰 Hickey,M.&Assoc.]
O'Malley, Lisa '68 '94 C.602 B.A. L.477 J.D.
Asst. Dir. Underwriting Servs., Atty.'s Liability Assurance Soc. Inc.
O' Malley, Michael A., (BV) ......'— '91 C&L.209 B.S.C., J.D. Coun., GE Capital Corp.
O'Malley, Richard F., Jr. ....'58 '83 C.602 A.B. L.339 J.D. [Sidley A.B.&W.]
O'Malley, Robert E., (AV) '35 '60 C.602 A.B. L.597 J.D.
(adm. in DC; not adm. in IL) 311 S. Wacker Dr.
O'Malley, Robert E., (AV) ....'60 '86 C.436 B.A. L.146 J.D. [Segal M.S.&M.]
Oman, Darrel F. ....'74 '99 C.424 B.A. L.146 J.D. Asst. Appellate Def.
O'Mara Frossard, Margaret ....'51 '76 C.597 B.A. L.405 J.D. Appellate Ct. J.
O'Meara, Anna M. ....'47 '84 C&L.424 B.S., J.D. [Mayer,B.R.&M.]
O'Meara, Brian P. ....'75 '01 C.93 B.A. L.424 J.D. [🄰 McGuirewoods]
O'Meara, Daniel C., (AV) '45 '77
C.436 B.S.B.A. L.339 J.D. Asst. Atty. Gen., Chief, Public Info. Div.

O'Meara, Donald J., Jr., (AV) .... '66 '91 C.1030 B.A. L.365 J.D. [Pretzel&S.]
O'Meara, John F., (AV) ....'36 '60 C.424 B.S. L.597 J.D. 1737 N. Wolcott Ave.
O'Meara, Mark R. ....'— '96 C.610 B.A. L.146 J.D. [Ⓐ Chapman&C.]
O'Meara, Matthew D. .... '69 '96 C&L.424 B.A., J.D. [Winston&S.]
O'Meara, Robert S. ....'— '97 C.475 B.A. L.339 J.D. [Sachnoff&W.]
O'Meara, Terence T. ....'— '73 C.965 B.S. L.424 J.D. [Chapman&C.]
O'Melia, Corinne S. .... '76 '01 C.339 B.A. L.597 J.D. [Ⓐ Franczek S.]

1-800-Ask-A-Lawyer & Associates
aka David K. Kremin & Associates, A.P.C.
221 N. La Salle Street, Suite 1900, 60601
Telephone: 800-275-2529 Fax: 312-456-9900 Toll Free: 1-800-ASK A LAWYER (1-800-275-2529)
URL: http://www.askdavidkremin.com URL: http://www.lawyers.com/davidkremin
Email: ASKALAWYER@aol.com URL: http://www.1800askalawyer.com
David K. Kremin.
Personal Injury, Litigation, Automobile Accidents, Work Accidents, Premises Liability, Product Liability, Fire and Casualty Cases, Medical Malpractice, Birth Defects, Dram Shop, Workers Compensation, Catastrophic Injuries, Spinal Cord, Airplane Crash and Slip and Fall, Wrongful Death.
See Professional Biographies, CHICAGO, ILLINOIS

O'Neil, Daniel E., III ....'35 '60 C.475 B.A. L.893 LL.B. 10 S. Wacker Dr.‡
O'Neil, John R. .... '— '98 C.966 B.B.A. L.597 J.D. [Kirkland&E.]
O'Neil, Mary C. .... '— '93 C&L.602 B.A., J.D. [Ⓐ Littler M.]
O'Neil, Michael C. .... '61 '89 C.102 B.A. L.209 J.D. [DLPiper R.G.C.U.]
O'Neil, Stephen J., (AV) .... '55 '80 C.602 B.A. L.273 J.D. [Bell,B.&L.]
O'Neil, William ....'78 '03 C.207 B.A. L.910 J.D. [Ⓐ Winston&S.]
O'Neill, Allison ....'— '04 C.319 B.A. L.1556 J.D. [Ⓐ Latham&W.]
O'Neill, Brian P. .... '55 '90 C.1183 B.A. L.146 J.D. [Haynes,S.K.O.&M.]
O'Neill, Bridget R. ....'63 '88 C.276 B.S.B.A. L.966 J.D. [Sidley A.B.&W.]
O'Neill, Constance R., (AV) ....'61 '86 C.339 B.S. L.146 J.D. [Ⓒ Cassiday,S.&G.]
O'Neill, Francis P. ....'10 '35 C.339 L.209 LL.B. 6430 S. Pulaski Rd.
O'Neill, James T. ....'58 '85 C.98 B.S. L.597 J.D. 411 W. Ontario Street
O'Neill, John P. .... '26 '52 C.999 L.209 LL.B. Director, INTERIM Legal Professionals
O'Neill, Renee P. ....'70 '95 C.1030 B.A. L.209 J.D. [Hinshaw&C.]
O'Neill, Timothy P. ....'50 '75 C.309 A.B. L.477 J.D. Prof., John Marshall Law Sch.
O'Neill Macro, Stephanie M. ..... '70 '95 C.94 B.A. L.424 J.D. [Ⓐ Sonnenschein N.&R.]
Onesto, Anthony J., (AV) .... '42 '67 C.215 B.A. L.597 J.D. 6832 W. North Avenue
Oney, Claudia, P.C., & Associates .... '47 '78 C.1142 B.A. L.209 J.D. [C.Oney&Assoc.]

Oney, Claudia, & Associates
134 North La Salle Street, Suite 300, 60602
Telephone: 312-782-1900 Fax: 312-782-1965
Email: claudiaoney@mac.com URL: http://www.claudiaoney.com
Claudia Oney & Associates, P.C.
Employment Law, Age, Race and Sex Discrimination, Family Law and Divorce.
See Professional Biographies, CHICAGO, ILLINOIS

Ong, Oliver T. ......'— '03 C.339 B.S.E.E. L.597 J.D. [Ⓐ Marshall,G.&B.] (See Pat. Sect.)
Onie, Rebecca ....'77 '03 C.309 B.A. L.1565 J.D. [Ⓐ Miner,B.&G.]
Onixt, Micah R. ....'72 '98 C.477 B.A. L.424 J.D. [Ⓐ DLPiper R.G.C.U.] (Pat.)
Onorato, Nicole M. ....'75 '04 C.966 B.A. L.209 J.D. [Ⓐ Rinella&R.]
Oommen, Sanju D. ....'75 '00 C&L.424 B.A., J.D. Cook Co. State's Atty. Off.
Oosterbaan, Jennifer S. ....'66 '95 C&L.339 B.S., J.D. [Holland&K.]
Opdycke, Stuart W., (AV) .... '42 '74 C.473 B.A. L.365 J.D. [S.Opdycke]
Opdycke, Stuart, (AV) .... 53 W. Jackson Blvd., Ste. 224
Opferman, Thomas G., (AV) ...... '56 '80 C.610 A.B. L.608 J.D. [Sonnenschein N.&R.]
Opp, Christine A. ....'50 '75 C.597 B.A. L.575 J.D. Off. of State Atty.
Oppenheim, David M. ....'— '02 C.976 B.A. L.309 J.D. [Ⓐ Wildman,H.A.&D.]
Oppenheim, Judy B. .... '— '88 C.429 B.A. L.424 J.D. 525 W. Monroe St., Ste. 1600
Oppenheim, Mary G. ....'12 '34 C&L.209 B.S., J.D. 400 E Randolph St Apt 2103
Opryszek, Sharon D. ....'57 '92 C.339 B.S.N. L.209 J.D. Asst. States Atty.
Orbon, Margaret J., (AV) ....'51 '76 C.741 B.A. L.424 J.D. [Clausen M.]
Ordman, Morgan J. .... '42 '67 C.210 B.A. L.145 J.D. [Holland&K.]
Ordonez, Edward M., (BV) ....'62 '88 C.339 B.S. L.1119 J.D. [Sanchez&D.]
Ordower, Benj. .... '13 '34 C&L.145 Ph.B., J.D. 20 N. Clark
Ordower, Lawrence B., (AV) '45 '72 C.188 A.B. L.1066 J.D.
1 N. LaSalle St., Ste. 1300
Ordower, Peter, (AV) ....'— '80 C.339 A.B. L.145 J.D. [Ⓒ Huff&G.]
O'Reilly, Gerald J. ....'31 '56 C.475 B.A. L.215 J.D. Sears, Roebuck & Co.
O'Reilly, Lawrence X. ....'— '91 C.98 B.S. L.117 J.D. Asst. State's Atty.
O'Reilly, Mary Ann ....'54 '82 C.339 B.S.N. L.209 J.D. [Ⓐ Gunty&M.]
Orel-Padjen, Kimberly A. .... '61 '87 C.741 B.A. L.424 J.D. [Ⓐ Gomberg,S.G.&O.]
Oremus, Dorothy A. ....'45 '75 C.999 B.A. L.424 J.D. [Hamblet,O.&L.]
Orenstein, Daniel S. ....'— '00 C.352 B.A. L.146 J.D. [Ⓐ Litchfield C.]
Organ, Joseph B., (AV) .... '51 '77 C.699 B.A. L.597 J.D. [Mayer,B.R.&M.]
Orlando, Frank, (AV) ....'28 '53 C.1016 B.A. L.597 LL.B. 2405 Richad J. Daley Ctr.
Orlando, Louis R. ....'50 '87 C.424 B.S. L.365 J.D. 161 N Clark Street, Suite 2210
Orlando, Thomas B. .... '65 '88 C.473 B.S. L.339 J.D. [Foran G.P.&P.]
Orleans, Jason .... '73 '99 C.339 B.A. L.146 J.D. [Ⓐ Johnson&B.] (⊙Waukegan)
Orlikoff, Richard, (AV) ....'23 '50 C.477 B.A. L.145 J.D. [Ⓒ Flamm&T.]
Orloff, Ronald L. ....'32 '58 C.901 B.A. L.976 LL.B. 1030 North State Street, #32-E
Orlofsky, Jonah, (AV) ....'55 '80 C.1044 B.A. L.597 J.D. [Plotkin,J.&O.]
Orlove, Charles, (AV) ....'37 '60 C&L.209 LL.B. [Jacobs,B.O.S.&H.]
Ormond, Paige S. ....'— '02 C.823 B.F.A. L.818 J.D. [Ⓐ Latham&W.]
Ormsby, John F. ....'53 '85 C.589 B.A. L.424 J.D. Tax Atty., Sara Lee Corp.
Ornduff, Jason S. ....'71 '96 C&L.339 B.A., J.D. [Eckhart K.]
Orner, Ronald A. ....'35 '60 C&L.597 B.S., J.D. 200 N. La Salle St.
O'Rourke, Daniel, (AV) ....'47 '72 C.321 A.B. L.276 J.D. [Vedder,P.K.&K.]
O'Rourke, Ellen Joan .....'65 '93 C.339 B.S. L.209 J.D. 120 North La Salle St., Ste. 1900
O'Rourke, James M., (AV) '53 '81 C.339 B.A. L.365 J.D.
Supervisor, 1st Munic. Div., Ofc. of the Pub. Def.
O'Rourke, John C., Jr., (AV) ....'47 '73 C.602 B.A. L.209 J.D. [O'Rourke,H.F.&D.]
O'Rourke, John W. ....'42 '99 C.339 B.A. L.365 J.D. 4239 W. 63rd S.
O'Rourke, Kathleen ....'43 '78 C.1191 M.Ed. L.146 J.D. 4239 W. 63rd St.
O'Rourke, Kevin B. ....'63 '95 C.339 B.A. L.365 JD 205 W. Randolph, Suite 1240
O'Rourke, Michael J. ....'51 '77 C.309 B.A. L.893 J.D. [O'Rourke M.&M.]

O'Rourke, Hogan, Fowler & Dwyer, (AV)
10 South La Salle Street, Suite 2900, 60603
Telephone: 312-739-3500 Fax: 312-739-3535
Members of Firm: William T. Dwyer, Jr.; W. Craig Fowler; Michael A. Gilman; Frederic G. Hogan; John C. O'Rourke, Jr. (Resident); Howard I. Goldblatt.
General Trial and Appellate Practice in all Courts, State and Federal Arbitrations and Dispute Resolution Board Proceedings. Our practice includes Construction Related (Public and Private) Contracts, Litigation, Claims, Bonds, Surety Law and Construction Liens. We also practice in the areas of Management Labor Relations Law, Employment Relations Law and Commercial Litigation.
See Professional Biographies, CHICAGO, ILLINOIS

O'Rourke McCloskey & Moody .... 161 North Clark Street, Suite 2230
Orpett, Mitchell A., (AV) ....'54 '78 C&L.339 B.A., J.D. [Tribler O.&M.]
Orr, Dana ....'— '04 C.197 B.A. L.276 J.D. [Ⓐ Sonnenschein N.&R.]
Orrico, Jennifer ....'— '00 C.436 B.A. L.209 J.D. [Ⓐ Ungaretti&H.]
Orschel, Alan Rauh, (AV) ....'39 '66 C.197 B.A. L.145 J.D. [Crowley B.&K.]
Orseno, Jay Christopher ....'76 '01 C.57 B.A. L.146 J.D. 205 West Wacker Drive
Orsic, Eric ....'71 '96 C.145 B.A. L.309 J.D. [Ⓐ McDermott W.&E.]
Orszula, Stanley F. .... '72 '98 C.93 B.A. L.424 J.D. [Ⓐ Adelman&G.]
Ortega-Piron, D. Jean '56 '81 C.700 B.A. L.146 J.D.
Off. of Gov. of Spec. Coun. for Child Welf. Servs.
Ortiz, Angela ....'71 '96 C.477 B.A. L.966 J.D. Atty., Northern Trust Corporation
Ortiz, Henry ....'73 '01 C.679 B.A. L.879 J.D. [Ⓐ Cassiday,S.&G.]
Ortiz, Susana Lynn ....'67 '01 C.999 B.A. L.146 J.D. 565 W. Adams, Ste. 600
Ortlieb, Mark R. ....'57 '82 C&L.477 B.A., J.D. Coun., Ameritech Corp.
Orton, Michelle D. ....'72 '97 C.339 B.F.A. L.209 J.D. [Raimondi&O.]
Orum, Keith H. ....'58 '89 C.339 B.S. L.365 J.D. [Orum&R.]
Orum & Roth, (AV) .... 53 West Jackson Boulevard (Pat.)
Ory, Samuel S. ....'— '94 C.375 B.A. L.986 J.D. [Ⓐ Skadden,A.S.M.&F.]
Osacky, Arika J. ....'— '01 C.473 B.A. L.146 J.D. [Ⓐ Schwartz C.]
Osanloo, O. Michael ...... '66 '91 C.477 A.B. L.339 J.D. 1313 N. Ritchie Ct., Apt. 1404‡
Osborn, Jason ....'— '03 C.569 B.A. L.477 J.D. [Ⓐ Kirkland&E.]
Osborne, David S. ....'68 '96 C.910 A.B. L.597 J.D. [Ⓐ Pretzel&S.]
Osborne, M. Emily ....'— '00 C.112 B.A. L.1355 J.D. [Ⓐ Morgan,L.&B.]
Osborne, Robert S. ....'— '79 C&L.309 A.B., J.D. [Jenner&B.]
Osenga, Matthew R. '75 '00 C.477 B.S.E. L.339 J.D.
(adm. in VA; not adm. in IL; Pat.) [Ⓐ Winston&S.]
Osgood, Karen M. ....'— '00 C.174 B.A. L.424 J.D. [Ⓐ Seyfarth S.]
O'Shaughnessy, Michael L. .... '49 '87 C.1034 B.A. L.150 J.D. [Much S.F.D.A.&R.]
O'Shea, Edward J. ....'73 '00 C&L.589 B.A., J.D. [Ⓐ Davis&C.]
O'Shea, Heather M. '— '95 C.840 B.S. L.425 J.D.
(adm. in TX; not adm. in IL) [Ⓐ Jones D.]
O'Shea, Kevin J. ....'59 '84 C.339 B.S. L.424 J.D. 61 W. Superior St.
O'Shea, Kevin J. ....'66 '99 C.339 B.S. L.424 J.D. [Ⓐ Winston&S.] (Pat.)
Osheff, Alan ....'42 '68 C.339 B.A.S. L.365 J.D. Admin. Law J., Dept. of Rev.
Oshman, Michele T. ....'58 '86 C.445 B.A. L.64 J.D. [Karbal,C.E.S.&D.]
Osick, James P. '55 '80 C.645 B.A. L.902 J.D.
Dir./ Sr. Coun., Labor & Employee Rel., Tibune Co.
Osimitz, Dennis V. ....'51 '76 C&L.966 B.A., J.D. [Sidley A.B.&W.]
Oskorep, John J. '68 '98
C.339 B.S.E.E. L.146 J.D. 980 N. Michigan Ave., Ste. 1400 (Pat.)
Oslan, Reed S., (AV) ....'— '87 C.174 B.A. L.345 J.D. [Kirkland&E.]
Osoba, Wayne F., (BV) ....'— '85 C&L.339 B.S., J.D. [Foley&L.]
Osowski, Edward L. ....'40 '66 C&L.602 B.A., LL.B. 345 N. Canal St.
Ossyra, James D. ....'— '83 C.309 A.B. L.94 J.D. [Foley&L.]
Osterhoff, Michael R. ....'72 '98 C.339 B.S. L.502 J.D. [Bell,B.&L.] (Pat.)
Osterkamp, Jeffrey M. ....'69 '98 C&L.597 B.S.J., J.D. [Ⓐ Stein,R.&H.]
Osterman, Peggy Joyce ....'— '02 C.190 L.276 [Ⓐ Chapman&C.]
Ostfeld, Gregory E. ....'73 '98 C.273 B.A. L.145 J.D. [Ⓐ Greenberg T.]
Ostler, James P., Jr., (AV) ....'49 '79 C.927 B.A. L.209 J.D. 208 S. LaSalle St.
Ostler, Raymond J., (AV) ....'50 '76 C.339 B.A. L.209 J.D. [Gomberg,S.G.&O.]
Ostojic, John R., (AV) ....'61 '85 C.339 B.A. L.365 J.D. 161 North Clark Street
Ostojic, Radusa ...... '60 '86 C.339 B.A. L.365 J.D. Sr. Staff Atty., Amer. Fam. Ins. Grp.
Ostrow, Richard D., (AV) ....'31 '56 C.477 A.B. L.209 J.D. [Seyfarth S.] ‡
Ostrowski, Sharon L. '57 '82 C.339 B.A. L.209 J.D.
Sr. Div. Coun., American Medical Association
Osty, Michael J. ....'68 '94 C.679 B.A. L.365 J.D. [Ⓐ Field&G.]
O'Sullivan, John J. ....'64 '94 C.339 B.A. L.420 J.D. [Ⓒ Swanson,M.&B.]
Otaka, Sandra Reiko ....'52 '87 C.112 B.A. L.1068 J.D. E.P.A.
Othman, Ned S., (AV) ....'— '77 C&L.477 B.A., J.D. [Mandell M.]
Otis, James T., (AV) '23 '53 C.309 A.B. L.597 J.D.
77 West Wacker Drive, Suite 4400‡
O'Toole, Amy G. ....'68 '95 C.347 B.A. L.365 J.D. [Bell,B.&L.]
O'Toole, Barbara P. '38 '69
C.741 B.A. L.424 J.D. Roger Baldwin Foundation of ACLU, Inc.
O'Toole, Edward M., (AV) ....'35 '62 C&L.602 B.S., J.D. [Howrey] (Pat.)
O'Toole, Heather Kuhn ....'— '02 C.339 B.S. L.424 J.D. [Ⓐ Katten M.R.]
O'Toole, Mark T. ....'60 '85 C.473 B.S. L.424 J.D. [Foran,O.&B.]
O'Toole, Monique N. ....'67 '92 C.174 L.365 J.D. [Jaros,T.&O.]
O'Toole, Paul G. ....'63 '90 C.436 B.A. L.365 J.D. [Reibman,H.B.H.&O.]
O'Toole, William G., (AV) ....'34 '61 C.215 B.S. L.209 J.D. [Jaros,T.&O.]
Otsuka, Gregory S. ....'— '99 C.339 B.S. L.597 J.D. [Ⓐ Jones D.]
Otsuka, Lara C. ....'71 '99 C.147 B.A. L.597 J.D. [Ⓐ Drinker B.&R.]
Ottaviano, Kenneth J. ....'70 '96 C.393 B.A. L.1187 J.D. [Katten M.R.]
Ottenfeld, Heather A. ....'76 '02 C.339 B.A. L.424 J.D. CMS Services, LLC
Ottley, Bruce L. ....'47 '72 C.986 B.A. L.352 J.D. 25 E. Jackson Blvd.
Ottley, Younghee J. ....'51 '82 C.999 B.A. L.209 J.D. [Winston&S.]
Ottmer, Nicole J. ....'73 '98 C.347 B.S. L.910 J.D. [Ⓐ Winston&S.]
Ottoson, Erick S. ....'— '99 C.575 B.S. L.494 J.D. [Ⓐ Kirkland&E.]
Ourth, Joe ....'— '88 C.1281 B.A. L.339 J.D. [Arnstein&L.]
Ouska, John A. ....'55 '80 C.201 B.S. L.365 J.D. Supvr., Indus. Claims Sect.
Ouweleen, Mark S. ....'64 '96 C.276 A.B. L.976 J.D. [Bartlit B.H.P.&S.]
Ouzounov, Nikolay A. ....'75 '04 C.587 B.A. L.365 J.D. [Ⓐ Barnes,R.&C.]
Ovadia, Vera ....'64 '91 C&L.893 B.A., J.D. [Ⓐ Jenner&B.]
Overgaard, Cordell J., (P.C.), (AV) .... '34 '60 C.339 B.S. L.309 LL.B. 70 W. Madison St.
Owen, Brian '45 '89 C.352 M.A. L.146 J.D.
Appl. Report Editor, Law Bulletin Pub. Co,
Owen, Carla Rendina .... '62 '90 C.339 B.S. L.424 J.D. 239 Berry Pkwy.
Owen, Jeffrey N., (AV) ....'54 '79 C.373 B.A. L.365 J.D. [DLPiper R.G.C.U.]
Owen, Michael L., (AV) ....'63 '88 C.597 B.A. L.347 J.D. [Bell,B.&L.]
Owen, Nathan P. ....'36 '60 C.472 B.B.A L.145 J.D. Fed. Trade Comm.‡
Owen, Rosaria Vivo ....'63 '91 C.339 B.S. L.424 J.D. [Ⓒ Mayer,B.R.&M.]
Owens, Kevin G., (AV) ....'58 '83 C.436 B.A. L.209 J.D. [Johnson&B.]
Owens, Marcia Klenk ....'73 '98 C&L.352 B.B.A., J.D. [Ⓐ Wildman,H.A.&D.]
Owens, Michelle C. .... '68 '92 C.589 B.A. L.209 J.D. Ticor Title Insurance Company
Owens, Richard J. ....'46 '71 C&L.209 A.B., J.D. Dep. Gen. Coun.

Owens, Owens & Rinn, Ltd.
(See Park Ridge)

Owings, Alice G. .... '66 '92 C.228 B.A. L.477 J.D. [Goldberg,K.B.B.R.&M.]
Oxley, Timothy J., (BV) ....'53 '80 C.937 B.A. L.365 J.D. [Winston&S.]
Oyebanji, Adam ....'63 '01 C.1469 LL.B. L.309 J.D. [Ⓐ Eimer S.K.&S.]
Oyler, Randall L., (AV) ....'— '92 C.937 B.A. L.145 J.D. [Barack F.K.P.&N.]
Ozmon, Nat P., (AV) ....'25 '54 C.569 L.597 J.D. [Anesi,O.R.N.&K.]
Ozog, Brian M. ....'73 '99 C.339 B.A. L.146 J.D. [Ⓐ Carponelli&K.]
Ozog, Edward J., (AV) '48 '73 C&L.209 B.A., J.D.
[Clausen M.] (⊙London, England; Paris, France; Rome, Italy)
Ozog, James W., (AV) ....'52 '77 C.597 B.S. L.910 J.D. [Wiedner&M.]
Pabarue, Andre C. ....'74 '01 C.476 B.S. L.607 J.D. Wilson Sporting Goods Co.

Pabian, Michael S. ....'49 '76 C.309 B.A. L.477 J.D. Asst. Gen. Coun., Exelon Corp.
Pabst, Jody L., (AV) ....'65 '93 C.881 A.B. L.966 J.D. [Swanson,M.&B.]
Pace, Michael R. ....'64 '89 C.339 B.S. L.597 J.D. Reg. Coun., Kroll Associates, Inc.
Pace, Sarah E. ....'62 '93 C.72 B.A. L.597 J.D. [Ⓒ Holland&K.]
Pacer, Edward O., (AV) ....'62 '88 C.339 B.A. L.424 J.D. [Harrison&H.]
Pachciarek, Anne M. ....'57 '82 C.339 B.A. L.597 J.D. [DLPiper R.G.C.U.]
Pacher, Nancy A. '50 '75 C.276 B.A. L.597 J.D.
Pres. & COO, U.S. Equities Realty, Inc.

Pachter, Gregory & Finocchiaro, P.C.
(See Deerfield)

Pacini, James J. ....'66 '92 C.145 B.A. L.146 J.D. [J.Pacini]
Pacini, James ....4784 N. Elston
Pacione, Vito M. ....'78 '03 C&L.339 B.A., J.D. [Ⓐ Jenner&B.]
Pacioni, Mark R. ....'65 '91 C&L.276 B.A., J.D. Assit. Corp. Sec., Boeing Co., The
Pacis, Cecilia F. '37 '84 C&L.662 LL.B.
(adm. in NY; not adm. in IL) 5011 N. Monticello Ave.
Pacis, Felipe H. '33 '82 C&L.662 A.B., LL.B.
(adm. in NY; not adm. in IL) 5011 N. Monticello Ave.
Packard, Anthony, (AV) ....'42 '69 C.31 A.B. L.597 J.D. [Nisen&E.]
Packer, Andrew E. ....'70 '95 C&L.339 B.A., J.D. Ge Capital
Packowitz, Ronald S. ....'67 '94 C.339 B.S. L.209 J.D. Asst. Def.
Pacocha, John F., (AV) ....'46 '73 C.424 B.B.A. L.146 J.D. 221 N. LaSalle
Padden, Michael P. ....'56 '82 C.602 B.A. L.813 J.D. [Howrey]
Padegimas, Julius V. ....'45 '69 C&L.424 B.S., J.D. 111 W. Wash. St.
Padgham, Kenneth A., Jr. ....'43 '68 C&L.352 B.A., J.D. MorganStanleyDeanWitter
Padgitt, Sarah M. ....'— '96 C.165 A.B. L.597 J.D. Litig. Coun., Aon Corp.
Padilla, Diane T. '— '97 C.424 B.A. L.209 J.D.
Sr. Coun., Bank One Corporation (Law Dept.)
Padilla, José D. '58 '83 C.851 B.Ed. L.477 J.D.
Assoc. Gen. Coun., Illinois Institute of Technology
Padmanabhan, Ram ....'68 '93 C.012 B.A. L.597 J.D. [Ⓐ Katten M.R.]
Padron, Paul Arthur ....'74 '02 C.339 B.A. L.146 J.D. 70 W. Madison, Suite 650
Paetsch, Christopher E. ....'70 '95 C.228 B.A. L.477 J.D. [Seyfarth S.]
Paflas, Allyson W. ....'— '04 C.916 B.A. L.228 J.D. [Ⓐ Wildman,H.A.&D.]
Pagano, Richard C. '53 '78 C.746 B.A. L.597 J.D.
Sr.V.P., Gen. Coun. & Secy., USFreightways Corp.
Pagano, Vincent J., Law Offices of '70 '99
C.623 B.S. L.734 J.D. 1829 N. Milwaukee Avenue
Page, Jeremy R. ....'61 '86 C.339 B.A. L.146 J.D. [Sandler,T.&R.]
Page, Joel R., Jr. ....'58 '83 C.894 A.B. L.347 J.D. [Ⓒ Leo&W.]
Page, Mark W. '64 '92
C.790 B.A./B.S. L.494 J.D. Sr. Coun., Bank One Corp. (Law Dept.)
Page, Steven C., (AV) '43 '68
C.188 A.B. L.477 J.D. 150 North Michigan Avenue, Suite 2500
Page, Thomas H., (AV) ....'52 '78 C&L.477 B.A., J.D. [Barack F.K.P.&N.]
Pagel, Lisa M. ....'— '02 C.378 B.G.S. L.365 J.D. [Ⓐ O'Hagan,S.&A.]
Pagniucci, Arnold A., (AV) ....'— '74 C.209 B.A. L.597 J.D. [Sachnoff&W.]
Pagonis, Stacey Garbis ....'— '99 C.966 b.a. L.597 J.D. [Kirkland&E.]
Paik, Nam H. ....'62 '88 C&L.597 B.A., J.D. [Baker&M.]
Paine, Andrew S. ....'73 '98 C.477 B.A. L.347 J.D. [Ⓐ Burke,W.M.&S.]
Paine, Marianne D., (P.C.), (AV) ... '48 '73 C.103 B.A. L.813 J.D. [Fitzsimmons,R.P.&C.]
Paison, Curt A. ....'73 '00 C.210 B.A. L.424 J.D. [Ⓐ Bell,B.&L.]
Pak, Kevin Y. ....'67 '95 C.339 B.A. L.880 J.D. [Ⓐ Bell,B.&L.]
Pakkala, Nicole S. ....'75 '00 C&L.477 B.A., J.D. [Ⓐ Sonnenschein N.&R.]
Palal, Binu George ....'— '04 C.1494 B.A. L.957 J.D. [Ⓐ Schiff H.]
Palanca, Christopher L. ....'63 '90 C.339 B.S. L.209 J.D. 410 S. Michigan Ave.
Palandech, Douglas J., (AV) ....'51 '77 C.846 B.A. L.146 J.D. [Foran G.P.&P.]
Paler, Scott '80 '05 C&L.966 B.A., J.D.
(adm. in WI; not adm. in IL) [Ⓐ Seyfarth S.]
Paler-Amaya, Catherine ....'67 '04 C.477 B.A. L.46 J.D. [Ⓢ Sidley A.B.&W.]
Palermo, Dena, (AVⓉ) '— '84 C.1349 B.S. L.94 J.D.
(adm. in NY; not adm. in IL) [Ⓒ Mayer,B.R.&M.]
Palermo, Mario C. ....'71 '96 C.93 B.A. L.146 J.D. [Ⓐ C.Woodruff&Assoc.] ⊙
Palermo, Michael A., Jr. ....'65 '92 C.98 B.A. L.1000 J.D. [Ⓐ Riordan,D.L.&M.]
Palese, Luke Allan, (BVⓉ) ....'66 '91 C&L.436 B.S., J.D. [Winston&S.]
Paley, Michael D. ....'— '95 C.174 B.A. L.910 J.D. [Kirkland&E.]
Paley, Robert J. ....'33 '60 C&L.477 B.B.A., J.D. [Seyfarth S.]
Pallardy, Janet D., (BV) ....'65 '90 C.339 B.S. L.966 J.D. [Wiedner&M.]
Pallasch, A. Maxim ....'28 '55 C.209 B.A. L.365 LL.B. 5487 Milwaukee Ave.
Pallasch, B. Michael ....'33 '57 C.276 B.S. L.309 LL.B. 35 W. Wacker Dr.‡
Palles, Eric S. ....'51 '77 C&L.910 A.B., J.D. [Ravitz&P.]
Palles, Lara M. ....'75 '02 C.1301 B.A. L.209 J.D. [Ⓐ Hurley,M.&M.]
Pallis, Peter E. ....'21 '50 C.145 L.365 J.D. [Constantine,Z.&P.]
Pallmeyer, Rebecca R. ....'54 '80 C.879 B.A. L.145 J.D. Dist. J.
Palm, Gary H. ....'42 '67 C.967 A.B. L.145 J.D. Prof., Univ. of Chicago Law Sch.
Palmatier, Francois N., (AV) ....'23 '49 C&L.966 B.S., LL.B. [Palmatier&Z.] (Pat.)
Palmatier & Zummer, (AV) ....Suite 1222, 39 South La Salle Street (Pat.)
Palmer, Alan G. ....'60 '85 C&L.339 B.S., J.D. 116 S. Mich. Ave.
Palmer, Angelique ....'— '04 C.025 B.A. L.213 J.D. [Ⓐ Querrey&H.]
Palmer, Ann T. ....'51 '78 C.602 B.A. L.424 J.D. Lincoln Legal Foundation
Palmer, Dwight B. ....'49 '78 C.174 B.A. L.146 J.D. [Ⓒ Frank/ G.]
Palmer, Emily S. ....'77 '04 C.951 B.A. L.477 J.D. [Ⓐ Jenner&B.]
Palmer, Gregory G., (AV) ....'57 '83 C.201 B.S. L.145 J.D. [McDermott W.&E.]
Palmer, John B., III, (AV) ....'— '77 C.475 B.A. L.477 J.D. [Foley&L.]
Palmer, Margaret M.H. ....'44 '80 C.881 B.A. L.365 J.D. 536 W. Deming Pl.
Palmer, Nikki J. ....'— '00 C.861 B.A. L.597 J.D. [Ⓐ Jones D.]
Palmer, Rex A., (AV) ....'52 '81 C&L.813 A.B., J.D. [Ⓒ Mayer,B.R.&M.]
Palmer, Richard C., (AV) ....'57 '83 C.58 B.A. L.209 J.D. [Wildman,H.A.&D.]
Palmerlee, Amy C. ....'74 '01 C.893 B.A. L.174 J.D. [Ⓐ Baker&M.]
Palmersheim, Robert J. ....'68 '96 C.966 B.A. L.209 J.D. [Schopf&W.]
Palmisano, Joseph D., (P.C.) ....'49 '75 C.597 B.A. L.424 J.D. 79 W. Monroe St.
Palmore, Roderick A., (AV) '52 '77 C.976 B.A. L.145 J.D.
Sr. V.P., Gen. Coun. & Sec.y., Sara Lee Corp.
Paloian, Gus A., (AV) ....'58 '84 C.597 B.A. L.209 J.D. [Seyfarth S.]
Palomar, Linda L. '68 '94
C.679 B.S.A.A.E. L.424 J.D. [Trexler,B.G.B.&M.] (See Pat. Sect.)
Palomo, Ernesto Rafael ....'— '02 C&L.339 B.A., J.D. [Ⓐ Lord,B.&B.]
Pals, Mark A., Ph.D. .... '— '89 C.197 A.B. L.597 J.D. [Kirkland&E.] (⊙San Fran., CA)
Paluch, Edw. J. ....'17 '49 C.145 L.424 LL.B. 4444 N. Richmond
Palumbo, John P. ....'67 '94 C.321 B.A. L.209 J.D. [Ⓐ Mangan,L.G.&L.]
Palumbo, Timothy M., (BV) '— '85
C.98 B.A. L.734 J.D. 200 N. LaSalle Street, Suite 2850
Pamel, Nicholas C. ....'32 '62 C.339 A.B. L.966 J.D. 300 W. Washington St.
Pamenter, Kathryn A. ....'70 '95 C&L.602 B.B.A., J.D. [Ⓐ Goldberg,K.B.B.R.&M.]

Pampel, Jaclyn J. ....'77 '02 C.879 B.S. L.245 J.D. [Ⓐ McDermott W.&E.]
Panagakis, George N., (AV) ....'65 '90 C&L.597 B.A., J.D. [Skadden,A.S.M.&F.]
Panarese, Joseph D. ....'63 '88 6808 W. Archer Ave.
Panchal, Nita Marie '71 '97 C.643 B.A. L.1252 J.D.
(adm. in CT; not adm. in IL) Assoc. Atty., Enforcement & Investigation
Pancratz, James E., (AV) ....'52 '83 C.966 B.S. L.365 J.D. [Pancratz,R.&S.] ⊙
Pancratz, Riffner & Scott, LLP, (AV)
33 North Dearborn Street, Suite 1430 (⊙Schaumburg)
Pando, Mark ....'— '04 C.424 B.A. L.146 J.D. [Ⓐ Asonye&Assoc.]
Pandya, Sameer Bakul ....'73 '00 C.930 B.A. L.424 J.D. Atty. Gen.
Panek, Kendra J. ....'— '95 C.339 B.A. L.146 J.D. [Ⓒ Schiff H.]
Paniaguas, John S., (AV) ....'51 '82 C.679 B.S.E. L.209 J.D. [Katten M.R.] (Pat.)
Paniak, Meryl Daskal ....'62 '91 C.910 B.A. L.146 J.D. Off. of the Pub. Guardian
Panich, Danuta Bembenista ....'54 '78 C.347 A.B. L.1119 J.D. [Mayer,B.R.&M.]
Panici, John ....'30 '56 C.999 L.209 LL.B. 6036 W. Montrose
Pannkoke, Theodore W. ....'71 '00 C&L.339 B.A., J.D. [Ⓐ Cozen O.]
Panos, Dean N., (AV) ....'65 '90 C.473 B.S. L.879 J.D. [Jenner&B.]
Panos, Nicholas C., (AV) ....'35 '67 C.388 B.A. L.365 J.D. [Ⓐ Stride,C.&S.]
Panter, Irwin, (AV) ....'14 '37 C&L.145 A.B., J.D. 225 W. Washington St.
Panter, Michael R., & Associates, (BV) '52 '78
C.966 B.A. L.209 J.D. 30 North La Salle Street (⊙Waukegan)
Panter, Ronald L. ....'44 '69 C.966 B.A. L.209 J.D. 70 W. Madison, Ste. 610
Pantoga, Ann Addis ....'— '97 C.741 B.M. L.209 J.D. [Ⓐ Tenney&B.]
Panzica, Anthony N. ....'55 '80 C.209 B.A. L.365 J.D. 3604 W. Irving Pk. Rd.
Paolucci, Dean D. ....'75 '01 C.970 B.A. L.365 J.D. [Select]
Paolucci, Joseph M., Jr. '63 '89 C.145 A.B. L.188 J.D.
V.P., Gen. Coun., Equity Group Investments, LLC
Papadakis, Dean J. ....'69 '94 C.339 B.A. L.146 J.D. [Kaplan P.&G.]
Papadopoulos, Athanasios (Tom) '76 '02
C.339 B.S. L.146 J.D. Two North LaSalle Street, Suite 2200
Papadopoulos, Elaine Cindy ....'75 '00 C.339 B.A. L.209 J.D. 11 S. La Salle Street
Papahronis, Jennifer ....'72 '98 C.860 B.A. L.209 J.D. [Ⓐ Aronberg G.D.&G.]
Papaj, William E. '43 '71 C.215 B.S.M.E. L.276 J.D.
Sr. V.P. & Gen. Coun., National Equity Fund, Inc.

Pape Law Firm, The
(See Wheaton)

Papiernik, Gregory A. ....'58 '83 C.602 B.B.A. L.146 J.D. [Levin&B.]
Papin, Jon C., (AV) ....'56 '84 C.101 B.S. L.383 J.D. [Rapoport]
Pappas, John J., Jr. ....'71 '97 C.475 B.A. L.365 J.D. [Ⓐ Pappas,J.&M.]
Pappas, John J., Sr., (AV) ....'45 '70 C.477 B.A. L.602 J.D. [Pappas,J.&M.]
Pappas, Nickolas ....'— '95 C&L.424 B.B.A., J.D. [Ⓐ Querrey&H.]
Pappas, Phoebe M. '65 '98
C.705 B.A. L.1194 J.D. Coun., CNA Property & Casualty Oper.
Pappas, Thomas R. ....'72 '98 C.339 B.A. L.146 J.D. [Ⓐ Shefsky&F.]

Pappas, Jacoby & Marcus, (AV)
30 West Monroe Street Suite 800, 60603
Telephone: 312-782-5363 Telecopier: 312-782-9590
URL: http://www.pjmlaw.net
Members of Firm: John J. Pappas, Sr.; John P. Jacoby; Debra Kramer Marcus. Associates: Stephen J. Healy; John J. Pappas, Jr.
Trial Practice in all State, Federal and Appellate Courts. Products Liability, Crashworthiness, Product Defects, Recreational Vehicle, Negligence, Personal Injury, Wrongful Death, Automobile Accidents, Pedestrian Injuries, Railroad Accidents, Medical Malpractice, Birth Trauma, Warranty Law, Insurance and Corporate Litigation.
See Professional Biographies, CHICAGO, ILLINOIS

Paprocki, Thomas J. ....'52 '81 C.424 B.A. L.209 J.D. Archdiocese of Chicago
Papuga, Charanne M. ....'— '00 C.472 B.A. L.365 J.D. 120 S. Lasalle, Ste. 1327
Papuga, Stanley W., (AV) '44 '74 C.472 B.B.A. L.146 J.D.
120 S. LaSalle St., Ste. 1327
Papushkewych, Darka, (AV) ....'53 '80 C.339 B.S. L.801 J.D. Dep. Corp. Coun.
Paquin, Joseph H., Jr. ....'60 '87 C.608 B.S.E.E. L.276 J.D. [McDermott W.&E.] (Pat.)
Para, Bruno G. ....'59 '86 C.209 B.S. L.589 J.D. 225 W. Washington St., Ste 1400
Para, Marina C. ....'76 '01 C.769 B.A. L.879 J.D. Asst. State Atty.
Paravola, Thomas J. ....'— '81 C.238 B.A. L.339 J.D. [Ⓒ Schuyler,R.&Z.]
Pardo, Maria Elena ....'75 '01 C.1494 B.A. L.339 J.D. 55 W. Monroe
Pardys, David F., (BV) '57 '82 C.339 B.A. L.146 J.D.
[Swanson,M.&B.] (⊙Libertyville, Waukegan)
Pardys, Michael ....'50 '75 C.339 B.A. L.365 J.D. [Pardys&V.]
Pardys and Vargas ....1300 W. Belmont
Parekh, Milind ....'68 '95 C.477 A.B. L.262 J.D. [Ⓐ Ross,D.&B.]
Parente, Christopher V. ....'79 '04 C.754 B.S. L.602 J.D. [Ⓐ Jenner&B.]
Parham, Michael M. ...'63 '90 C.475 B.A. L.477 J.D. Atty., IBM North America-Chicago
Paridy, Nancy E., (AV) '60 '83
C.927 B.A. L.146 J.D. Gen. Coun., Rehab. Inst. of Chicago
Paries, Tina ....'69 '01 C.589 B.A. L.146 J.D. [Ⓐ Much S.F.D.A.&R.]
Parikh, Amol A. ....'79 '05 C.679 B.S.E.E. L.209 J.D. [Ⓐ Wallenstein W.&R.]
Parikh, Neha A. ....'75 '00 C&L.260 B.S., J.D. [Ⓐ Levenfeld P.]
Paris, James J. '70 '97 C.347 B.S. L.309 J.D.
(adm. in NY; not adm. in IL) Global Inv. Banking Dept., Deutsche Bank Securities Inc.
Parisi, Joseph S. ...... '— '75 C.339 B.S. L.424 J.D. [Masuda,F.E.&M.] (⊙Schaumburg)
Parisi, Michael ....'29 '59 C.056 L.209 LL.B. 6049 W. Belmont Ave.
Park, Faith .... '— '04 C&L.145 B.A., J.D. Two North LaSalle Street, Suite 2200
Park, Jane S. ....'— '98 C&L.309 B.A., J.D. [Kirkland&E.]
Park, Jeanah ....'76 '02 C.597 B.A. L.339 J.D. [Ⓐ Quinlan&C.]
Park, Lucy K. ....'— '00 C.788 B.A. L.146 J.D. [Ⓐ Kirkland&E.]
Park, Ohn ....'— '96 C.197 B.A. L.339 J.D. [Ⓐ Litchfield C.]
Park, Sally L. ....'38 '88 C.477 B.A. L.597 J.D. 161 Chicago Ave., E.
Park, Samuel S. ....'73 '01 C.145 B.A. L.424 J.D. [Ⓐ Winston&S.]
Park, Stephanie S. ....'— '96 C.339 B.S. L.146 J.D. [Ⓒ Rieff S.&K.]
Park, Tanya ....'67 '98 C.477 B.A. L.879 J.D. [Ⓐ Cassiday,S.&G.]
Park, W. William '67 '01 C.339 B.S.E.E L.209 J.D.
(adm. in CO; not adm. in IL) [Ⓐ Ladas&P.]
Parker, Christine A. ....'74 '02 C.999 B.S. L.945 J.D. [Ⓐ Jenner&B.]
Parker, Christopher R. ....'— '99 C.966 B.A. L.339 J.D. [Ⓐ Michael B.&F.]
Parker, Dean E., (AV) ....'54 '79 C&L.966 B.B.A., J.D. [Hinshaw&C.]
Parker, Druella A. ....'73 '98 C.123 L.879 J.D. 130 S. Jefferson St., Suite 500
Parker, James A. ....'46 '77 C.1050 B.A. L.46 J.D. [Ⓒ Mayer,B.R.&M.]
Parker, Janice M. ....'65 '89 C.589 B.A. L.879 J.D. Asst. Atty. Gen.
Parker, Kristin L. ....'— '99 C.608 B.A. L.597 J.D. [Ⓐ Jones D.]
Parker, Paul ....'— '81 C.801 B.S. L.365 J.D. [Ⓐ Karbal,C.E.S.&D.]
Parker Gates, Lisa ....'62 '99 C.473 B.A. L.424 J.D. [Ⓐ Baker&M.]
Parkerson, Frank J. ....'46 '73 C.123 B.A. L.146 J.D. Asst. State's Atty.
Parkhurst, Beverly Susler, (AV) ....'— '69 C&L.339 B.A., J.D. [Ⓒ Hedlund&H.]
Parkhurst, Henry A. ....'74 '02 C.910 B.A. L.352 J.D. [Ⓐ Johnson&B.]
Parkhurst, Todd S., (AV) ....'41 '68 C.339 B.S. L.659 LL.B. [Holland&K.] (Pat.)

Parks, Kevin C. '59 '85 C&L.352 B.A., J.D. [A Leydig,V.&M.]
Parks, Michael A., (AV) '64 '93
C.597 B.S.E.E. L.209 J.D. Sr. Coun., Intell. Prop., Tribune Co.
Parks, Reginald L. '71 '02 C.339 B.A. L.209 J.D. [A Sonnenschein N.&R.]
Parks, Suzanne Montague '63 '88 C.339 B.S. L.424 J.D. 1 S. Wacker Dr.
Parma, Rowena T. '67 '92 C.339 B.S. L.424 J.D. [A E.T.Joyce&Assoc.]
Parmelee, Steven G. '53 '78 C.701 B.S.E.E. L.190 J.D.
(adm. in MN; not adm. in IL; See Pat. Sect.) [Fitch,E.T.&F.]
Parolisi, Nicholas J., Jr. '— '89 C.454 B.A. L.209 J.D. [Litchfield C.]
Parr, Keith D., (AV) '57 '81 C&L.339 B.S., J.D. [Lord,B.&B.]
Parrillo, Marianne J. '— '70 C.339 B.S. L.424 J.D. 3002 South Emerald Ave.
Parrino, Jack L. '74 '00 C.597 B.S. L.209 J.D. [A FagelHaber]
Parson, Jason A., (AV) '— '89 C.347 B.A. L.910 J.D. [Anderson,R.]
Parsons, Brian T. '72 '00 C.338 B.S. L.424 J.D. [A Foran G.P.&P.]
Parsons, David J., (AV) '46 '72 C.207 B.A. L.339 J.D. [Littler M.]
Parsons, Lisa B. '62 '88 C.112 B.S. L.1065 J.D.
Mandel Legal Aid Clinic, Univ. of Chicago Law School
Partee, Jennifer S. '70 '99 C.210 B.A. L.146 J.D. [A Baker&M.]
Partee, Michael C. '69 '00 C.477 B.S. L.146 J.D. Asst. Atty. Gen.
Partelow, John E. '59 '84 C.597 B.A. L.424 J.D. 820 W. Jackson Blvd., Ste. 300
Partilla, Shelly A. '72 '98
C.338 B.A. L.365 J.D. Staff Atty., U.S. Court of Appeals, 7th Cir.
Partin, Mark A. '— '02 C.347 L.209 [A Chapman&C.]
Partridge, Ellen L., (AV) '48 '77 C.473 B.A. L.276 J.D.
Dep. Gen. Coun., Chicago Transit Auth., Law Dept.
Partridge, Mark V. B., (AV) '54 '81 C.546 B.A. L.309 J.D. [Pattishall,M.N.H.&G.]
Parts, Mark '61 '90 C.108 B.A. L.145 J.D. [A J.D.Montgomery&Assoc.]
Parzen, Stanley J., (AV) '52 '78 C.231 B.A. L.309 LL.B. [Mayer,B.R.&M.]
Pascal, Erica '50 '76 C.94 B.A. L.597 J.D. 1217 W. Oakdale St.
Pascal, Roger, (AV) '— '65 C.477 A.B. L.309 J.D. [Schiff H.]
Pasche, Paul W., (BV) '66 '91 C&L.879 B.S., J.D. [A Brady,C.&M.]
Paschke, Joel C. '— '98 C.492 B.A. L.300 J.D. [A Wildman,H.A.&D.]
Pascus, Keith D., (AV) '56 '82 C&L.339 B.A., J.D. [Katten M.R.]
Pasin, Mario A. '30 '55 C&L.602 B.Ph.C., LL.B. 6515 W. Grand Ave.
Paskar, Mark A. '— '99 C.228 A.B. L.273 J.D. [A Bryan C.]
Paskin, Deborah Corthier '52 '83 C.347 B.A. L.597 J.D.
Brookdale Living Communities
Pasko, Cristina '63 '89 C.424 B.S.N. L.339 J.D. Asst. State Atty.
Pasowicz, Ronald J. '56 '02 C.46 B.S.M.E. L.365 J.D. [R.J.Pasowicz]
Pasowicz, Ronald J., P.E. 231 W. 25th Place
Pasqual, Morris, (CV) '56 '81 C.776 B.A. L.190 J.D. 219 S Dearborn, Rm. 1200
Pasquesi, Frank E. '— '90 C.597 B.A. L.94 J.D. [Ungaretti&H.]
Passen, Stephen M., (AV) '48 '73 C.112 B.A. L.966 J.D. [S.M.Passen]

Passen, Stephen M., Ltd., (AV) BB
One East Wacker, Suite 2406, 60601
Telephone: 312-527-4500 Facsimile: 312-527-4435 URL: http://www.passenlaw.com
Email: spassen@passenlaw.com URL: http://www.stephenmpassen.com
Stephen M. Passen;—John J. Driscoll.
Practice Limited to Major Personal Injury Cases, Catastrophic Accidents and Injuries, Head Injuries, Spinal Cord Injuries, Paralysis, Surgical and Physician Malpractice, Automobile, Construction Accidents, Medical Malpractice, Work-Related Accidents, Products Liability Accidents.
See Professional Biographies, CHICAGO, ILLINOIS

Pasternak, Thomas G., (AV) '— '91 C.871 B.S.M.E. L.477 J.D. [Kirkland&E.] (Pat.)
Pastin, Max '26 '56 C.1016 B.A. L.209 J.D. 1 N. LaSalle St.‡
Pastors, Charles R., II '46 '80 C.453 S.B. L.424 J.D.
Prof. & Chair, Northeastern Ill. Univ.
Pastrana, Melissa '— '01 C.309 A.B. L.145 J.D. [A Mayer,B.R.&M.]
Pastroff, Sanford M., (AV) '63 '88 C.477 B.B.A. L.597 J.D. [Sonnenschein N.&R.]
Pasulka, David P., (AV) '59 '84 C.145 A.B. L.1049 J.D. [Pasulka&W.]
Pasulka, Donald C., (AV) '61 '86 C.145 A.B. L.309 J.D. [McGuirewoods]

Pasulka & White, LLC, (AV) BB
Three First National Plaza, 70 West Madison Street, Suite 650, 60602
Telephone: 312-236-9150 Fax: 312-236-9157
Email: pasulkalaw@pasulkalaw.com URL: http://www.pasulkalaw.com
Members of Firm: David P. Pasulka; William P. White III. Associates: William K. Bass; Janet L. Mazurek; Mitchell B. Gordon.
Family Law including all phases of Matrimonial and Paternity Litigation, Custody, Visitation and Appeals.
See Professional Biographies, CHICAGO, ILLINOIS

Pasulka-Brown, Kathleen R. '— '86 C.112 B.A. L.309 J.D. [Foley&L.]
Pate, Jerome L. '71 '00 Coun., Standard Parking Corp.
Pate, Kristen N. '76 '01 C&L.420 B.A., J.D. [C Schopf&W.]
Patek, James M. '15 '39 C&L.209 LL.B. [C Heineke,B.&B.]
Patel, Ahmed A., (BV) '30 '76 L.999 LL.B. 25 E. Washington St.
Patel, Avani A. '— '03 C.424 B.A. L.597 J.D. [A Schiff H.]
Patel, Avani C. '77 '03 C.576 B.S. L.209 J.D. [A Wallenstein W.&R.]
Patel, Binal J. '— '96 C.339 B.S.E.E. L.597 J.D. [Banner&W.] (See Pat. Sect.)
Patel, Chirag B. '— '02 C.999 B.E. L.276 J.D. [A Marshall,G.&B.] (See Pat. Sect.)
Patel, Kavita Mukund '— '02 C.273 B.A. L.245 J.D. [A Schiff H.]
Patel, Lopa '— '04 C.228 B.A. L.597 J.D. [A Latham&W.]
Patel, Parin N. '— '01 C.477 B.B.A. L.608 J.D. [A Anderson,R.]
Patel, S. Charles '79 '05 C.597 B.A. L.424 J.D. [S Winston&S.]
Patel, Sailesh K. '— '99 C.597 B.S.Ch.E. L.93 J.D. [A Schiff H.] (Pat.)
Patel, Sandip H. '— '96 C.475 B.S. L.1119 J.D. [Marshall,G.&B.] (See Pat. Sect.)
Patel, Sanjay H. '74 '00 C.025 B.A. L.475 J.D. State's Atty. Off.
Patel, Suverna '— '01 C.424 B.B.A. L.209 J.D. [A Karbal,C.E.S.&D.]
Patenode, Timothy J., (BV) '56 '81 C&L.597 B.A., J.D. [Katten M.R.]

Patents & TMS, P.C., (BV)
1914 North Milwaukee Avenue Third Floor, 60647
Telephone: 773-772-6009 Fax: 773-772-3210 URL: http://www.patents-tms.com
URL: http://www.lawyers.com/patentstmspc
Brian M. Mattson.
Patent, Trademark and Copyright Law.
See Professional Biographies, CHICAGO, ILLINOIS

Patinkin, Hugh M. '50 '75 C.860 B.A. L.145 J.D.
Pres. & CEO, Whitehall Jewellers, Inc.
Patner, Marshall, (AV) '31 '56 C.966 B.S. L.145 J.D. [M.Patner&Assoc.]
Patner, Marshall, & Associates, P.C., (AV) 135 South La Salle Street, 27th Floor
Patras, Patrick L. '67 '92 C&L.339 B.S., J.D. [Jenner&B.] (Pat.)
Patrick, Thomas M. '45 '73
C.906 B.A. L.145 J.D. V.P., Peoples Gas Light & Coke Co., The
Patricoski, Matthew T. '63 '94 C.602 B.B.A. L.209 J.D.
Mgr., Gen. Investigations, Chicago Merc. Exchange
Patrizio, Michael G. '52 '84 C.923 A.B. L.209 J.D. [A Merlo K.B.&G.]

Patsavos, Evelyn C. '55 '80 C.914 B.A. L.309 J.D.
(adm. in FL; not adm. in IL) U.S. Dept. of Health & Human Servs.
Patt, Aldon W. '59 '85 C.999 B.A. L.365 J.D. 120 W. Madison
Patt, Eric G. '65 '90 C.347 B.S. L.146 J.D. [Robbins,S.&P.]
Patt, Jeffrey R. '62 '87 C.339 B.S. L.146 J.D. [Katten M.R.]
Patt, Stephen P. '39 '64 C.209 B.S.C. L.365 J.D. [Robbins,S.&P.] ⊙
Pattee, Jeffrey C., (AV) '45 '75 C.156 B.A. L.209 J.D. 33 N. LaSalle St., Ste. 2100
Patten, Jefferson D. '72 '01 C.339 B.S. L.365 J.D. [A Fisher K.]
Patten, Paul A. '65 '90 C.145 A.B. L.309 J.D. 320 West Ohio Street, Suite 500
Patterson, Alisa L. '64 '89 C.347 B.A. L.46 J.D. [A Cohn,L.R.S.&G.]
Patterson, Ann Crowley '59 '85 C.228 B.A. L.597 J.D.
(adm. in NY; not adm. in IL) Asst. V.P., Secy. & Gen. Coun., Globe Builders, Inc
Patterson, Benjamin E., (AV) '65 '93 C.608 B.S.,B.A. L.146 J.D. [Hall,P.&S.]
Patterson, Robert B., (AV) '46 '71 C.645 B.A. L.597 J.D. [R.B.Patterson]
Patterson, Stephen R. '68 '03 C&L.209 B.A., J.D. [A Gardner C.&D.]
Patterson, Thomas E., (AV) '53 '79 C.340 B.A. L.209 J.D. [Patterson]
Patterson Law Firm, The, (AV) 33 N. LaSalle Street, Suite 3350

Patterson, Robert B., Ltd., Law Offices of, (AV)
221 North La Salle Street, Suite 1050, 60601
Telephone: 312-236-0995 FAX: 312-984-5791
Email: rbpltd@sbcglobal.net URL: http://www.lawyers.com/pattersonfirm
Robert B. Patterson;—John F. Hedrich.
Civil Trial Practice. Personal Injury, Medical Malpractice, Products Liability, Wrongful Death, Transportation, Railroad and Aviation Law. Appellate Practice.
See Professional Biographies, CHICAGO, ILLINOIS

Patti, James P. '67 '94 C.276 B.S.B.A. L.145 J.D. [Mayer,B.R.&M.]
Patti, John C. '56 '89 C.424 B.A. L.365 J.D.
V.P. & Chf. Underwriter, Greater Ill. Title Co.
Patti, Sebastian '53 '79 C.228 B.A.B.S. L.378 J.D. Chambers 1111

Pattishall, McAuliffe, Newbury, Hilliard & Geraldson LLP, (AV) BB
311 South Wacker Drive Suite 5000, 60606 ⊙
Telephone: 312-554-8000 Facsimile: 312-554-8015
URL: http://www.pattishall.com
Members of Firm: Brett A. August; Diana Lee Bixler; Thad Chaloemtiarana; Bradley L. Cohn; Raymond I. Geraldson, Jr.; David Craig Hilliard; Jonathan S. Jennings; Janet A. Marvel; Jeremiah D. McAuliffe; Robert M. Newbury; Mark V. B. Partridge; Beverly W. Pattishall (1916-2002); Robert W. Sacoff; Sanjiv D. Sarwate; Belinda Jayne Scrimenti (Not admitted in IL; Resident, Alexandria, Virginia Office); Benjamin S. Warren III (Resident Partner, Alexandria, Virginia Office); Joseph N. Welch II; Uli Widmaier. Of Counsel: Melvyn A. Silver;—Annie L. Albertson; Phillip Barengolts; Chad J. Doellinger; Andrew N. Downer; Matthew A. Griffin; Kristen S. Knecht; Sapna Kumar; Danielle B. Lemack; Jared D. Solovay; Angela K. Steele; Teresa D. Tambolas.
Litigation and Counseling in the Areas of Domestic and International Trademark, Unfair Competition, Copyright, Internet, e-Commerce, Technology and Computer Law, Licensing, Advertising and Promotions, Right of Publicity, Counterfeiting and Trade Secrets.
Alexandria, Virginia Office: 225 Reinekers Lane, Alexandria, VA 22314. Telephone: 703-684-7550. Fax: 703-684-7888.
See Professional Biographies, CHICAGO, ILLINOIS

Pattison, Alyx S. '74 '03 C.878 B.A. L.597 J.D. [A Katten M.R.]
Patton, J. Jeffrey '66 '94 C.473 B.Phil L.309 J.D. [Tabet D.&R.]
Patton, John W., Jr., (AV) '58 '83 C.473 B.A. L.209 J.D. [Patton&R.]
Patton, Mary B. '21 '59 C.681 A.B. L.365 J.D. 122 S. Michigan Ave.‡
Patton, Scott C. '71 '01 C.1154 B.S. L.146 J.D. [A Cirignani H.H.&L.]
Patton, Stephen R., P.C., (AV) '— '78 C.347 A.B. L.276 J.D. [Kirkland&E.]

Patton & Ryan LLC, (AV) BB
One IBM Plaza, Suite 2900, 60611
Telephone: 312-261-5160 Fax: 312-261-5161
Email: jpatton@pattonryan.com URL: http://www.pattonryan.com
Partners of Firm: John W. Patton, Jr.; David F. Ryan; W. Mark Sickles. Associates: David S. Atlas; Fernando M. Bustamante; Andrew N. Coleman; Paul C. Jakubiak; James J. Jozefowicz; Sarah A. Kennedy; Fawzia Mirza; Mark R. Penney (Not admitted in IL); Kathryn A. Starck; Paul S. Steinhofer; Brian J. Weig.
Languages: Spanish, French, German, Vietnamese and Urdu.
Tort Litigation, Commercial Litigation, Product Liability Law, Environmental Law, Construction Law, Insurance Coverage, Civil Litigation, Insurance Defense, Professional Liability, Medical Malpractice.
See Professional Biographies, CHICAGO, ILLINOIS

Patton-Gentert, Nancy A. '60 '91
C.546 B.S.B.A. L.1048 J.D. Atty., SAFECO Prop. & Cas. Ins. Co.
Pattullo, Robert L., Jr. '56 '82 C.424 B.A. L.146 J.D. [A Rock F.]
Patula, Timothy T., (AV) '58 '83 C.679 B.S.E.E. L.879 J.D. [Patula&Assoc.] (Pat.)
Patula & Associates, (AV) 116 South Michigan Avenue 14th Floor (Pat.)
Patzik, Alan B., (AV) '59 '84 C.339 B.S. L.597 J.D. [Patzik,F.&S.]

Patzik, Frank & Samotny Ltd., (AV)
Suite 900, 150 South Wacker Drive, 60606
Telephone: 312-551-8300 Facsimile: 312-551-1101
Email: lawyers@pfs-law.com URL: http://www.pfs-law.com
Alan B. Patzik; Steven M. Prebish; Marc Z. Samotny; Max Shaftal; Joel G. Shapiro; James M. Teper; Thomas J. Verticchio; Gary Irwin Walt; Allan L. Yusim; Chadwick I. Buttell; Sheryl Jaffee Halpern;—Patrick G. Cooke; Scott M. Curran; Tan H. Le; David J. Schwartz; Scott W. Smilie; Sean S. Swidler; Joseph C. Vitek. Of Counsel: Jeffrey H. Frank.
Corporate, Federal and State Securities, Federal Taxation, Estate Planning, Real Estate, Patent, Copyright and Trademark, Commercial and Business Law and Litigation.
See Professional Biographies, CHICAGO, ILLINOIS

Patzke, Michelle '56 '88 C.1016 B.G.S. L.145 J.D. 4541 S. Whipple St.
Pauel, Linda J. '65 '91 C.187 B.A. L.146 J.D. Sr. Supvring. Atty.
Pauka, Andre M. '66 '96 C.870 B.S. L.597 J.D. [Bartlit B.H.P.&S.]
Pauker, David H., (AV) '31 '54 C.339 B.S. L.597 J.D. [Pauker&R.]
Pauker & Rubin, Ltd., (AV) 180 N. LaSalle
Paul, Adam '— '97 C.1369 B.A. L.180 J.D. [Kirkland&E.]
Paul, Brian P. '— '03 C.1365 B.A. L.880 J.D. [A Michael B.&F.]
Paul, Michelle E. '70 '96 C.339 B.S. L.734 J.D. The Jacobson Group‡
Paul, Robert J. '51 '77 C.339 B.A. L.146 J.D. 155 N. Michigan, Ste. 600
Paul Wright, L.L.C. 1748 West Diversey Pkwy.
Pauletto, Michael A. '69 '96 C.347 B.A. L.365 J.D. [A Johnson&B.]
Pauling, Gerald L., II '67 '92 C.339 B.S. L.1068 J.D. [Seyfarth S.]
Paull, Michael, (AV) '61 '86 C.339 B.S. L.597 J.D. [Klein D.&H.] ⊙
Paulson, Lele E. '60 '92 C.273 B.A. L.209 J.D. Univ. of Chicago
Paulson, Mark D. '— '92 C.801 B.A. L.365 J.D. [Clausen M.]
Paulus, Amy Rich, (AV) '63 '89 C.597 B.A. L.587 J.D. [Clausen M.]
Pause, Frank J., (AV) '12 '46 C.339 L.146 LL.B. 30 N. La Salle St.
Paustian, Jeffrey Lee '68 '00 C.352 B.B.A. L.424 J.D. 55 W. Monroe Street
Pavalon, Eugene I., (AV) '33 '56 C&L.597 B.S.L., J.D. [Pavalon,G.L.&M.]

Pavalon, Gifford, Laatsch & Marino, (AV) BB
Two North La Salle Street, Suite 1600, 60602
Telephone: 312-419-7400 Fax: 312-419-7408
Email: info@pglmlaw.com URL: http://www.pglmlaw.com
Members of Firm: Eugene I. Pavalon; Geoffrey L. Gifford; Gary K. Laatsch; Frank C. Marino. Associate: John J. Simonetti. Of Counsel: Martin Whittaker.

(This Listing Continued)

Pavalon, Gifford, Laatsch & Marino (Continued)

Language: Spanish.
Civil Trial and Appellate Practice in all Courts. Personal Injury, Wrongful Death, Railroad Injuries, (F.E.L.A.), Medical Malpractice, Products Liability, Aviation Law, Complex Commercial Litigation and Class Actions.

See Professional Biographies, CHICAGO, ILLINOIS

Pavela, Jean '38 '81 C.480 B.A. L.365 J.D.
Dir., The Chicago Bar Assoc. Lawyer Referral Service
Pavich, Anastasia .... '79 '04 C.746 B.A. L.424 J.D. [🄰 Monico,P.&S.]
Pavich, Nicholas A. .... '72 '99 C.705 B.A. L.910 J.D. [🄰 M.T.Hannafan&Assoc.]
Pavich, Robert J., (AV) .... '47 '75 C.309 B.A. L.209 LL.B. [Monico,P.&S.]
Pavlatos, Angela C. .... '75 '00 C.357 B.A. L.424 J.D. [🄰 Vedder,P.K.&K.]
Pavlicek, Joan M. .... '57 '82 C.741 B.A. L.209 J.D. Univ. of Chicago
Pavlidis, Nicholas '72 '98
C.311 B.A. L.145 J.D. V.P., Invest. Bkg.; Robert W. Baird & Co.
Pavlik, George S. .... '74 '04 C.378 B.S. L.1000 J.D. [🄰 Welsh&K.]
Pavlow, Susan M. '73 '98 C.339 B.A. L.734 J.D.
53 West Jackson Boulevard, Suite 1460
Pawlak, Frank M., (AV) .... '53 '81 C&L.424 B.A., J.D. 333 N. Michigan Ave., Ste. 912
Pawlykowycz, Leon, (BV) .... '50 '78 C.339 B.A. L.365 J.D. Coun., Chicago Park District
Payne, Alexis E. .... '— '99 C.477 B.A. L.608 J.D. [🄰 Mandell M.]
Payne, Jason H., (BV) .... '66 '92 C.339 B.A. L.146 J.D. [Nyhan,P.B.K.&L.]
Payne, Jennifer J. .... '64 '90 C.602 B.A. L.347 J.D. Legal Assistance Found. of Chicago
Payne, Rosary '50 '85 C.974 B.S. L.1000 J.D.
Div. Coun., American Medical Association
Payne, Sue .... '53 '85 C.207 B.A. L.597 J.D. Information Resources, Inc.
Payne, Timothy G. .... '66 '93 C.339 B.A. L.146 J.D. [🄰 Sidley A.B.&W.]

Paynter, Bruce D., The Law Offices of
(See Arlington Heights)

Pazen, Thea M. .... '52 '77 C.597 B.A. L.209 J.D. 3839 North Kenneth Avenue, Suite 300
Pazzol, Ross .... '59 '87 C.339 B.A. L.424 J.D. [🄲 Mayer,B.R.&M.]
Peaceman, Karen L. '55 '80 C.910 A.B. L.94 J.D.
(adm. in MA; not adm. in IL) U.S. EPA
Pearce, George M., (AV) .... '54 '79 C.388 B.A. L.209 J.D. [Holland&K.]
Pearce, Mary Sinclair '52 '79
C.72 B.A. L.209 J.D. U.S. Dept. of Agric., Off. of Gen. Coun.
Pearl, Edward M. .... '38 '67 C.1016 L.209 LL.B. 222 E. Pearson
Pearl, Howard M., (AV) .... '54 '80 C.103 A.B. L.309 J.D. [Winston&S.]
Pearl, Kenneth B. .... '42 '68 C.966 B.S. L.209 J.D. 62 W. Huron St.
Pearl, Melvin E., (P.C.), (AV) .... '36 '60 C.966 B.B.A. L.597 J.D. [🄲 Katten M.R.]
Pearl, Richard J. .... '— '01 C.589 B.S. L.424 J.D. [🄰 Wildman,H.A.&D.]
Pearlman, Jason Randall .... '71 '00 C.347 B.A. L.365 J.D. 200 N. LaSalle, Ste. 2750
Pearlman, Kimberlie .... '73 '01 C.339 B.A. L.365 J.D. [🄰 DLPiper R.G.C.U.]
Pearlman, Marc J. .... '65 '91 C.188 B.A. L.477 J.D. [Kerns,P.F.&P.]
Pearlman, Steven J. .... '72 '98 C.339 B.S. L.1068 J.D. [🄰 Franczek S.]
Pearlstein, Mark D., (AV) .... '48 '75 C.339 B.A. L.209 J.D. [Levenfeld P.]
Pearse, Richard W. .... '52 '84 C.94 B.A. L.597 J.D. [Vedder,P.K.&K.]
Pearson, Frederic C. .... '45 '79 C.546 B.A. L.209 J.D. Law Libr., Cook Co. Law Libr.
Pearson, Marilyn A. '51 '76 C&L.494 B.A., J.D.
(adm. in MN; not adm. in IL) [DLPiper R.G.C.U.]
Pearson, Nyran Rose .... '74 '99 C.340 B.A. L.629 J.D. [🄰 Miller F.&C.]
Pearson, Steven D., (AV) .... '61 '85 C.494 B.A. L.209 J.D. [Meckler B.&T.]
Peart, Sharon M. .... '65 '90 C.357 B.S. L.1017 J.D. 150 S. Wacker Dr.
Pechette, Michael A. .... '56 '81 C.347 B.S. L.1119 J.D. Pres., Founders Capital Corp.
Pechi, Carole Laude .... '62 '90 C.339 A.B. L.146 J.D. [🄲 Holland&K.]
Pechter, Barry S. .... '54 '79 C.1016 B.A. L.365 J.D. Asst. State's Atty.
Pechter, Marvin .... '23 '50 C&L.339 A.B., J.D. 105W Madison St.‡
Peck, Joseph .... '25 '56 C&L.209 B.S.C., J.D. [J.Peck&Assoc.]
Peck, Kerry R., (AV) .... '52 '78 C.589 B.S.Ed. L.146 J.D. [Peck,B.A.&M.] ⊙
Peck, S. Michael, (AV) .... '— '73 C.145 B.A. L.477 J.D. [Schiff H.]

Peck, Bloom, Austriaco & Mitchell, LLC, (AV)
105 West Adams, 31st Floor, 60603 ⊙
Telephone: 312-201-0900 Facsimile: 312-201-0803
URL: http://www.peckbloom.com
Kerry R. Peck; Kenneth M. Bloom; D. Rebecca Mitchell;—Ray J. Koenig III; Jeanine M. Cunningham; Alexander Drapatsky; Marisa T. Cipolla. Of Counsel: Aurora Austriaco.
Probate, Estate Planning, Guardianship, Elder Law, Probate Litigation, Estate Administration, Asset Protection Planning, Real Estate, Real Estate Litigation, Corporate, Business Transactions, Public Aid Law, Medicaid Law.
Northbrook, Illinois Office: 601 Skokie Boulevard, 60062. Telephone: 847-509-1099.

See Professional Biographies, CHICAGO, ILLINOIS

Peck, Joseph, & Associates .... 105 W. Adams St., 34th Flr.

Peck, Shaffer & Williams LLP
11 South LaSalle Street, Suite 2100, 60603 ⊙
Telephone: 312-372-6060; 877-372-6060 Fax: 312-372-6085
Email: lawinfo@peck-shaffer.com URL: http://www.peck-shaffer.com
Members of Firm: Bruce D. Agin; George D. Buzard III.
Public Finance, Municipal Bonds, Municipal Bond Taxation, Municipal Securities. Tax Exempt Bonds, Housing and Urban Development, Health Care Finance, Tax Increment Finance, Municipal Leasing, Public Finance Taxation, Securities Finance, Blue Sky Law, Low Income Housing, Industrial Development Bonds, Municipal Bankruptcy, Public Construction Law.
Atlanta, Georgia Office: Peck, Shaffer & Williams LLP, Atlanta Financial Center, Suite M20, 3353 Peachtree Road, N.E. Telephone: 404-995-3850. Fax: 404-995-3851.
Cincinnati, Ohio Office: Peck, Shaffer & Williams LLP, 201 E. 5th Street, Suite 900. Telephones: 513-621-3394; 800-927-2663. Telecopier: 513-621-3813.
Columbus, Ohio Office: Peck, Shaffer & Williams LLP, 175 South Third Street, Suite 600, 43215. Telephone: 614-224-5205; 888-900-5205. Telecopier: 614-224-0069.
Covington, Kentucky Office: Peck, Shaffer & Williams LLP, 118 West 5th Street, 41011. Telephones: 859-431-7000; 888-431-7511. Telecopier: 859-431-0673.
Denver, Colorado Office: Peck, Shaffer & Williams LLP, 555 17th Street, Suite 845 South, 80202. Telephone: 303-296-3996; 877-296-0333. Fax: 303-296-0344.
Louisville, Kentucky Office: Peck, Shaffer & Williams LLP, 239 S. Fifth Street, Suite 1603, 40202. Telephone: 502-561-0054. Telecopier: 502-561-0058.

See Professional Biographies, CHICAGO, ILLINOIS

Peckham, Thomas H. .... '62 '87 C&L.597 B.A., J.D. [Seyfarth S.]
Pecoulas, George A. .... '49 '87 C.801 B.A. L.365 J.D. [Mayer,B.R.&M.]
Pecquet, William J. .... '44 '77 C&L.424 A.B., J.D. 77 W. Wacker Dr.
Pecyna, Daniel W. .... '24 '52 C.424 B.S.C. L.209 J.D. 100 W. Monroe St.
Pedersen, Erik J. .... '66 '95 C.94 B.A. L.1035 J.D. [🄰 Pedersen&H.]
Pedersen, Erika E. .... '70 '95 C.589 B.A. L.209 J.D. [Pedersen&W.]
Pedersen, Peer, (AV) .... '25 '49 C&L.339 B.S., J.D. [Pedersen&H.]
Pedersen, Sandra S. .... '72 '00 C.473 B.S. L.884 J.D. [🄰 Wildman,H.A.&D.]
Pedersen, Susan M. .... '— '87 C.741 B.B.A. L.146 J.D. [🄰 DLPiper R.G.C.U.]

Pedersen & Houpt, A Professional Corporation, (AV)
161 North Clark Suite 3100, 60601-3242 ⊙
Telephone: 312-641-6888 Telecopier: 312-641-6895
URL: http://www.pedersenhoupt.com

(This Listing Continued)

Pedersen & Houpt, A Professional Corporation (Continued)

Peer Pedersen; John H. Muehlstein; Paul S. Altman; Joseph Benedict Brocato; Lawrence W. Byrne; Stacy P. Chronopoulos; Kimberly J. Cornell; Stephen A. Frost; John J. Hayes; Susan M. Hermann; Arthur M. Holtzman; Marc D. Janser; Thomas J. Kelly; Herbert J. Linn; Donald J. Moran; Mary C. Muehlstein; David B. Solomon;—Christine Decke Alt; Lauren Blair; Brian P. Collins; Richard L. DiNardo; Eric J. Kordish; Abad Lopez; Erik J. Pedersen; Kelee J. Schwenn; Michael P. Sullivan. Of Counsel: Sheldon Davidson; Richard V. Houpt (Retired); Gary S. Mostow; Gregory J. Perry; Thomas F. Sax; James B. Sloan (Resident, Lake Forest Office); Stanley C. Sneeringer; Steven M. Stone.
Mergers and Acquisitions, Employee Benefits and Executive Compensation, Banking and Financing, Municipal Law and Land Use, Real Estate, Trusts and Estates, Taxation and Organizational Planning, Private Equity and Venture Capital, Public Securities, Litigation and Dispute Resolution, Family Law, Employment Law, Antitrust, Technology and Intellectual Property.
Lake Forest, Illinois Office: One Westminister Place. Telephone: 708-295-4317.

See Professional Biographies, CHICAGO, ILLINOIS

Pedersen & Weinstein LLP
309 West Washington Suite 1200, 60606
Telephone: 312-855-1200 Fax: 312-855-1207
Email: info@pwllp.com URL: http://www.pwllp.com
Members of Firm: Erika E. Pedersen; Jill S. Weinstein.
Employment Discrimination, Employment Litigation and Counseling, Mediation and Arbitration, Sexual Harassment, Employment Contracts, Executive Severance Contracts, Civil Rights.

See Professional Biographies, CHICAGO, ILLINOIS

Pederson, David M. .... '— '02 C&L.494 [🄰 Chapman&C.]
Pederson, Peter E. .... '74 '99 C.339 B.A. L.94 J.D. [🄰 Hinshaw&C.]
Pedicone, Michael A., (CV) .... '60 '79 C.205 B.A. L.1338 J.D. [M.A.Pedicone]
Pedicone, Michael A., Ltd., (CV) .... 30 N. Michigan Ave., Ste. 1201
Pedwell, Edward B. .... '68 '00 C.034 B.A. L.1325 J.D. Mgr., Jus. Web Collaboratory
Peel, Drew G. A., (AV) .... '— '92 C.198 A.B. L.145 J.D. [Kirkland&E.]
Peev, Iordan A. .... '65 '00 C&L.801 B.S, J.D. [🄰 Jenner&B.]
Pegg, William D. .... '67 '98 C.705 B.S.M.E. L.146 J.D. [🄰 Jenkens&G.] (Pat.)
Peipert, Michael H. .... '— '98 C.339 B.S. L.146 J.D. [🄰 Morgan,L.&B.]
Pekala, Beverly A., Law Offices of, (BV) .... '57 '82 C.209 B.A. L.146 J.D. 432 N. Clark
Pekay, Michael, (P.C.), (AV) .... '43 '68 C.477 B.A. L.209 J.D. 77 W. Wash. St.
Pekin, Marshall J. .... '31 '53 C.339 L.209 LL.B. 200 North LaSalle Street, Suite 2300

Pekin Levin & Associates
(See Levin, Riback Lawgroup P.C.)

Pekkala, Lisa M. .... '71 '97 C.957 B.A. L.966 J.D. [🄰 Sonnenschein N.&R.]
Pekow, Eugene .... '30 '55 C.103 A.B. L.597 J.D. Pres., Midland Bldg. Corp.
Pelafas, James P. .... '62 '88 C.801 B.A. L.365 J.D. [Newman&P.]
Pelanek, Laura E. .... '79 '04 C.893 B.A. L.846 J.D. [🄰 Jenner&B.]
Peldyak, Paul E. .... '48 '73 C.742 B.A. L.602 J.D. 12 S. Michigan Ave.
Pelic, Jennifer .... '— '04 C.741 B.B.A. L.597 J.D. [🄰 Jones D.]
Pelican, Edward J. .... '— '93 C.602 B.B.A. L.597 J.D. [Chapman&C.]
Pelka, Joann C. .... '45 '81 C.530 B.A. L.146 J.D. Dep. Gen. Coun., Litig., Metra
Pellegrino, Mark A. .... '— '92 C.399 B.A. L.436 J.D. [🄰 Anderson,R.]
Pellegrino, Salvatore A. .... '— '02 C.589 B.A. L.365 J.D. [🄰 Clausen M.]
Pelletier, Dean A. .... '69 '95 C.597 B.S. L.910 J.D. [McAndrews,H.&M.] (See Pat. Sect.)
Pelletier, Michael J. .... '50 '76 C.589 B.A. L.365 J.D. Dep. Def.
Pellett, Clark D. '54 '81 C.309 B.A. L.190 J.D.
Associate Counsel, MCI Telecommunications Corporation
Pellish, Stuart, (BV) .... '56 '85 C.339 B.A. L.209 J.D. [Rusin M.&F.]
Peltin, William J., (AV) .... '62 '87 C.339 B.S. L.966 J.D. [Fox,H.S.L.&C.]
Pelton, Russell M., (AV) .... '38 '63 C.210 B.A. L.145 J.D. [McGuirewoods]
Peltz, Jason L. .... '67 '92 C.477 A.B. L.145 J.D. [Bartlit B.H.P.&S.]
Pelz, Joel T., (AV) .... '55 '80 C.879 B.A. L.309 J.D. [Jenner&B.]
Pemberton, Heidi '61 '87 C.104 A.B. L.659 J.D.
(adm. in MA; not adm. in IL) [🄰 Baker&M.]
Penati, Francesco .... '— '93 C.276 B.S. L.602 J.D. [Kirkland&E.]
Pender, Kathleen H. .... '66 '92 C&L.339 B.A., J.D. [🄲 Mayer,B.R.&M.]
Pender, Thomas R. .... '62 '88 C.473 B.A. L.902 J.D. [Cremer,K.S.&S.]
Pendergast, Francis J., III, (BV) .... '56 '80 C&L.424 B.S., J.D. [🄰 Crowley&L.]
Pendleton, Cullen N. .... '68 '04 C.326 B.S. L.145 J.D. [🄰 Marshall,G.&B.]
Pendleton, Elizabeth N. .... '— '01 C.385 B.A. L.93 J.D. [🄰 Mandell M.]
Pendo, Kimberly A. .... '— '98 C.339 B.A. L.597 J.D. [Neal,G.&E.]
Pendola, Michael H., Law Offices of '61 '89 C.424 B.S. L.209 J.D.
105 W. Madison Street
Penepacker, Dennis F. .... '69 '99 C.870 B.S. L.597 J.D. [🄰 Mayer,B.R.&M.]
Pengra, Brian L. .... '62 '91 C.972 B.S. L.494 J.D. Atty., IBM North America-Chicago
Pengra, R. René .... '67 '95 C.972 B.A. L.569 J.D. [🄰 Sidley A.B.&W.]
Penick, Elena B. .... '76 '02 C.477 B.A. L.339 J.D. Asst. Defender
Penland, Kathleen A. .... '45 '88 C.209 B.A. L.424 J.D. 1 N. LaSalle St., Ste. 1515
Penn, Amir N. .... '67 '94 C.150 B.S.E.E. L.597 J.D. [🄲 Brinks H.G.&L.] (See Pat. Sect.)
Penn, Dortricia Kenyatta .... '76 '01 C.329 B.A. L.1000 J.D. Asst. State Atty.
Penn, Justin M. .... '76 '04 C.602 B.A. L.1000 J.D. [🄰 Hinshaw&C.]
Penner, Gerald M., (AV) '40 '64
C.477 A.B. L.145 J.D. 525 West Monroe Street, Suite 1300
Penney, Mark R. '74 '00 C.674 B.A. L.1565 J.D.
(adm. in IN; not adm. in IL) [🄰 Patton&R.]
Pennington, Joan, (BV) .... '51 '80 C.923 B.S.E.E. L.365 J.D. 535 N. Michigan Ave. (Pat.)
Pennington, Rachel S. .... '52 '00 C.437 B.S. L.424 J.D. 343 S. Dearborn St., Ste. 503
Penovich, Gerald George .... '43 '80 C.597 B.A. L.365 J.D. 100 W. Monroe St.
Penrose, Craig Gordon .... '62 '96 C.025 B.M. L.1358 J.D. [🄰 Tressler,S.M.&P.]
Pensyl, Claire E., (AV) .... '— '78 C&L.145 B.A., J.D. [Bell&P.]
Pentecost, Todd E. .... '72 '99 C.436 B.A. L.145 J.D. [🄰 Bell,B.&L.]
People's Law Office .... 1180 N. Milwaukee Avenue
Pepper, Joyce M. .... '46 '79 C.597 B.S. L.209 J.D. 2728 N. Hampden Ct., Ste. 1405
Pepple, Bronwyn H. .... '73 '04 C.174 B.A. L.365 J.D. 320 West Ohio Street, Suite 500
Peracke, Nicole K. .... '— '04 C.589 B.S. L.424 J.D. [🄰 Seyfarth S.]
Perce, Bruce F. .... '64 '90 C.165 A.B. L.966 J.D. [Mayer,B.R.&M.]
Perconti, John J., (AV) .... '57 '82 C.339 B.A. L.365 J.D. [Levin&P.]
Perdew, P. Russell .... '74 '99 C.98 B.A. L.597 J.D. [🄰 Lord,B.&B.]
Perdue, Elizabeth S. .... '54 '82 C.668 B.A. L.145 J.D. [Morgan,L.&B.]
Peregrine, Michael W., (AV) .... '55 '80 C.840 B.A. L.597 J.D. [McDermott W.&E.]
Pereiro, Francisco J. .... '58 '81 C.145 A.B. L.209 J.D. First Nat. Bk. of Chicago
Perellis, Andrew H., (AV) .... '55 '81 C.477 B.A. L.273 J.D. [Seyfarth S.]
Perera, Ruwan C. .... '76 '04 C.608 B.S. L.365 J.D. [Fedota C.]
Perera, Valerie C. '— '94 C.371 B.A. L.209 J.D.
V.P., Cambridge Human Resource Group
Peretz, Elan .... '— '03 C.911 B.S. L.145 J.D. [🄰 Goldberg,K.B.B.R.&M.]
Perez, Christina B. .... '78 '03 C.339 B.S. L.146 J.D. [🄰 Aronberg G.D.&G.]
Perez, Enrique .... '— '95 C.597 B.S.E.E. L.146 J.D. [🄲 Sonnenschein N.&R.] (Pat.)
Pérez, Giselle M. .... '— '04 C.94 B.A. L.597 J.D. [🄰 Jones D.]
Perez, Jessica M. '75 '03 C.602 B.B.A. L.339 J.D.
(adm. in MN; not adm. in IL) [🄰 Barack F.K.P.&N.]

Perez, Michael A., Law Office of, (BV) '61 '86
C.209 B.A. L.365 J.D. 1608 North Milwaukee Avenue
Pérez-Serrano, Alejandro .... '71 '94 L.424 J.D. [Ⓐ Baker&M.]
Pergericht, Frances L. .... '52 '79 C.930 B.A. L.910 J.D. U.S. Dept. of HHS
Perille, Christine Ciabotti .... '58 '87 C.321 B.A. L.424 J.D. Special Asst. State's Atty.
Periolat, Mary K., (AV) .... '58 '83 C&L.347 B.A., J.D. [Pugh,J.J.&Q.]
Perisin, Mary C. .... '— '42 C.137 L.365 J.D. 233 S. Wacker Dr.
Peritz, Revelle G. .... '32 '80 C.339 B.A. L.146 J.D. Asst. State's Atty.
Perivolidis, Arthur C. .... '41 '67 C.393 B.A. L.597 J.D. Cir. J.
Perkins, Erin C. .... '69 '98 C.976 B.A. L.597 J.D. [Ⓐ Mayer,B.R.&M.]
Perkins, Floyd D. .... '— '77 C.339 B.S. L.365 J.D. [Ungaretti&H.]
Perkins, James L. .... '31 '54 C&L.221 A.B., J.D. 35 W. Wacker Dr.
Perkins, Jefferson, (AV) .... '55 '83 C.339 B.S.E.E. L.365 J.D. [Daspin&A.] (Pat.) ⊙
Perkins, Joan .... '46 '73 C.418 B.A. L.209 J.D. Chicago Title & Tr. co.
Perkins, Raymond .... '68 '94 C&L.339 B.A., J.D. [Winston&S.]

Perkins Coie LLC, (AV)
131 S. Dearborn Street, Suite 1700, 60603-5559 ⊙
Telephone: 312-324-8400 Facsimile: 312-324-9400
Email: perkins@perkinscoie.com URL: http://www.perkinscoie.com
Partners: Craig Boggs; Bruce A. Bonjour; Eric D. Brandfonbrener; William T. Cahill; Robert L. Capizzi; John M. Christian; Alexandra R. Cole; William E. Corbin; Ken Crane; James R. Cruger; Susan Daley; Jan Feldman; Matthew J. Gehringer; Phillip Gordon; Scott B. Greene; Mary Kathryn Kelly; Kenneth T. Lopatka; C. Vincent (Vince) Maloney; Daniel G.M. Marre; Roseann Oliver; Richard E. Peterson; Robert Stephan; Hugh Totten; Edward E. Wicks; Christopher B. Wilson; Daniel A. Zazove. Of Counsel: Darrell J. Graham; Kathleen M. Howard. Associates: Amina Abrahams; Bevin M. Brennan; Jonathan Buck (Not admitted in IL); Jason Burlingame; Jeanne M. Cullen; Scott H. Gingold; Jaclyn A. Kight; Sarah R. Knight (Not admitted in IL); J. Bates McIntyre; Laurence Oleksa; Chad D. Striker; Theodore Wern; Ryan Whitacre.
General Civil Trial and Appellate Practice in Federal and State Courts and before various Federal and State Administrative Tribunals. Administrative; Antitrust and Trade Regulation; Aviation and Aerospace; Banks and Banking; Bankruptcy; Biotechnology; Business Law; Commercial Law; Construction Law; Corporate Law; Employee Benefits; Energy; Environmental; Estate Planning; Federal Indian Law; Franchising; General Litigation; Government Contracts; Government Relations; Immigration; Intellectual Property; International Trade; International Law; Internet and Electronic Commerce; Labor and Employment; Land Use; Life Sciences; Mergers, Acquisitions and Divestitures; Municipal/Public Finance; Natural Resources; Nonprofit and Charitable Organizations; Probate; Patents; Products Liability; Project Finance; Political Law; Public Utility; Real Estate; School Law; Securities Law and Litigation; Taxation; Technology; Telecommunications; Toxic Torts; Trademarks and Copyrights; Venture Capital and Investment Funds; Water Rights; White-Collar Criminal Representation; Workers' Compensation.
Other Offices: Anchorage, Alaska; Bellevue, Washington; Boise, Idaho; Denver, Colorado; Los Angeles, California; Menlo Park, California; Olympia, Washington; Phoenix, Arizona; Portland, Oregon; San Francisco, California; Seattle, Washington; Washington, D.C.
Reviser of the Washington Law Digest for this Directory.
See Professional Biographies, CHICAGO, ILLINOIS

Perkins, Leonard F., & Associates
(See Arlington Heights)

Perkins, Y. Jacqueline
(See Arlington Heights)

Perkoski, Joseph J. .... '63 '93 C&L.608 B.A., J.D. [Ⓐ Robbins,S.N.L.&T.]
Perkovich, Robert '51 '81
C.1016 B.A. L.365 J.D. Exec. Dir., Ill. Educ. Labor Relations Bd.
Perl, Michael W. .... '78 '04 C.978 B.S. L.597 J.D. [Ⓐ Skadden,A.S.M.&F.]
Perl, Sanford E., P.C., (AV) .... '— '90 C.339 B.S. L.477 J.D. [Kirkland&E.]
Perla, Alicia A. .... '70 '99 C.178 B.A. L.477 J.D. [Ⓐ Bell,B.&L.]
Perla, Saul N. '46 '73 C.161 B.M.E. L.276 J.D.
(adm. in DC; not adm. in IL) Assoc. Chf. Coun., U.S. Customs Serv.
Perlberg, Michael T. '72 '97 C.228 A.B. L.477 J.D.
V.P./Gen. Coun., Levy Restaurants
Perlin, Alice S. .... '50 '75 C.597 B.A. L.209 J.D. Loyola Univ.
Perlman, Amy R., (AV) .... '58 '83 C.347 B.A. L.209 J.D. [Levin,R.]
Perlman, Cary R., (AV) .... '— '88 C.477 A.B. L.309 J.D. [Latham&W.]
Perlman, Charles H., (AV) .... '45 '71 C.966 B.B.A. L.597 J.D. [Barack F.K.P.&N.]
Perlman, Daniel J., (AV) .... '60 '85 C.477 B.A. L.597 J.D. [Katten M.R.]
Perlman, Felicia Gerber .... '64 '92 C.659 B.A./B.S.E. L.597 J.D. [Skadden,A.S.M.&F.]
Perlman, Gary S. .... '60 '85 C.589 B.S. L.209 J.D. 30 N. Lasalle St., Ste. 3922
Perlman, Kenneth S., (AV) .... '47 '72 C.339 A.B. L.309 J.D. [Bailey B.N.]
Perlman, Richard R., (AV) .... '52 '76 C.597 B.A. L.309 J.D. [Schoenberg,F.N.&R.]
Perlman, Stuart D., (AV) '34 '59
C.178 A.B. L.976 LL.B. Suite 2040, 30 North La Salle Street
Perlstadt, Roger J. .... '75 '02 C.118 B.A. L.145 J.D. [Ⓐ Miller S.&H.]
Perna, Richard C., (BV) .... '61 '86 C.742 B.A. L.300 J.D. [Fuchs&R.]
Pernic, Rachel L. .... '— '01 C.347 B.S. L.597 J.D. [Ⓐ Kirkland&E.]
Perona, Alison Ryan .... '59 '86 C.338 B.S. L.209 J.D. Asst. State's Atty.
Perper, Marc A. .... '53 '84 C.339 B.A. L.146 J.D. [Horwitz,H.&Assoc.]
Perres, Lee Scott .... '56 '81 C.107 B.A. L.365 J.D. [Marcus,P.&C.]
Perri, Brad C. .... '72 '02 C.742 B.A. L.221 J.D. [Ⓐ Ancel,G.D.B.D.&R.]
Perri, Dennis D. .... '50 '75 C.338 B.A. L.221 J.D. U.S. Dept. of Agric.
Perrier, Rachel .... '— '00 C.182 B.A. L.145 J.D. [Ⓐ Kirkland&E.]
Perrin, James Kirk, (AV) .... '40 '65 C.611 B.A. L.477 LL.B. [Haskell&P.]
Perrone, Alicia Brumbach .... '— '99 C.1059 B.A. L.146 J.D. [Ⓐ Anderson,R.]
Perrone, Pamela G. .... '57 '81 C.1044 B.A. L.273 J.D. [Meckler B.&T.]
Perrotta, Augustine R. '72 '01 C.959 B.S. L.209 J.D.
Assoc. Gen. Coun., Quadriga Asset Management, Inc.
Perry, Ann Killian .... '67 '93 C&L.339 B.A., J.D. 547 S. Clark St., Suite 1003
Perry, Cheryl A. .... '79 '04 C&L.436 B.A., J.D. [Ⓐ Cohon R.&R.]
Perry, Christopher S. .... '78 '03 C.321 B.A. L.228 J.D. [Ⓐ Winston&S.]
Perry, Clifford R., III .... '65 '90 C.597 B.S.I.E. L.910 J.D. [Laner,M.D.B.L.&T.]
Perry, Damon D. .... '78 '03 C&L.477 B.A., J.D. [Ⓐ Jenner&B.]
Perry, Denise A. '58 '87
C.338 B.S. L.365 J.D. Asst. Coun., Exelon Business Services Co.
Perry, Elizabeth M. .... '— '01 C.475 B.A. L.424 J.D. [Ⓐ Arnstein&L.]
Perry, Eydie R. .... '76 '01 C.477 B.A. L.424 J.D. [Ⓐ Brenner,F.M.&S.]
Perry, Gregory J., (BV) '— '65
C.966 B.S. L.276 LL.B. [Ⓒ Pedersen&H.] (⊙San Jose, Costa Rica)
Perry, Julie K. .... '70 '01 C&L.339 B.A., J.D. Attorney, Integrated E. Solutions
Perry, Kenneth .... '— '04 C.340 B.A. L.602 J.D. [Ⓐ O'Hagan,S.&A.]
Perry, Michael J. '45 '74 C.276 A.B. L.178 J.D.
(adm. in NY; not adm. in IL) Prof. of Law, Northwestern Univ. Sch. of Law
Perry, Natalie M. .... '67 '95 C.345 B.S. L.209 J.D. [Ⓐ Levenfeld P.]
Perry, Rodney .... '— '98 C.832 B.A. L.910 J.D. [Ⓐ Bryan C.]
Perry, William J. .... '— '95 C.966 B.A. L.339 J.D. [Ⓐ Litchfield C.]

Perry & Associates
(See Spring Grove)

Persin, Raymond C., (BV) .... '54 '79 C.999 B.A. L.365 J.D. [Ⓐ Brady,C.&M.]
Persky, Jonathan Edward .... '63 '02 C.145 A.B. L.597 J.D. Parliament Enterprises
Persky, Seymour H. .... '22 '52 C.1016 A.B. L.209 J.D. 123 W. Madison St., 20th Fl.‡

Person, Roland E. .... '50 '75 C&L.597 B.A., J.D. 8549 S. Rhodes Ave.
Personick, Laura M. .... '— '04 C.893 B.S. L.145 J.D. [Ⓐ McAndrews,H.&M.]
Perugini, John T. .... '— '96 C&L.602 B.A., J.D. [Ⓐ Jones D.]
Perzek, Philip J., (BV) .... '86 C.589 B.S. L.597 J.D. [Latham&W.]
Pesavento, Raymond R., (AV) '48 '86
C.339 B.A. L.209 J.D. 30 North La Salle Street, Suite 4300
Pesch, Christopher A. .... '— '95 C.393 B.A. L.988 J.D. [Ⓐ Chapman&C.]
Peschke, John E. .... '— '02 C.602 B.A. L.145 J.D. [Ⓐ Goldberg,K.B.B.R.&M.]
Pesha, Dana M. .... '78 '03 C.98 B.S. L.365 J.D. [Ⓐ W.J.Harte]
Peskin, Bernard M. .... '22 '50 L.365 J.D. 900 N. Michigan Ave.
Petacque, Gerald M., (AV) .... '30 '55 C&L.339 LL.B. 19 W. Jackson
Petchenik, Larry A. .... '58 '87 C.966 B.S.,M.S.I.R. L.424 J.D. Educ. Labor Relations Bd.
Peter, Bernard G., Jr. .... '44 '69 C.321 A.B. L.446 J.D. The Wyatt Co.
Peterman, Nancy A., (BV) .... '66 '91 C&L.477 B.A., J.D. [Greenberg T.]
Petermann, Tanya .... '— '04 C.201 B.A. L.1000 J.D. [Ⓐ O'Hagan,S.&A.]
Petermann, Thomas J. '50 '75 C.424 B.S. L.146 J.D.
Asst. Gen. Coun., Litig., Amsted Industries (Legal Department)
Peters, Aaron M. '— '00 C.477 B.S.E.E. L.1218 J.D.
[Ⓐ Marshall,G.&B.] (See Pat. Sect.)
Peters, Amy R. .... '— '02 C.880 B.A. L.276 J.D. [Ⓐ Kirkland&E.]
Peters, Charles H.R. .... '— '86 C.473 B.S. L.597 J.D. [Schiff H.]
Peters, David A. .... '72 '99 C.880 B.A. L.352 J.D. Global Hyatt Corporation
Peters, Donald F., (AV) .... '45 '71 C.602 B.A. L.339 J.D. [Peters&L.]
Peters, Edmund A. .... '38 '72 C.209 B.S. L.146 J.D. 6247 S. Kedzie Ave.‡
Peters, Grant H. .... '— '91 C.352 B.S. L.424 J.D. [Barnes&T.] (See Pat. Sect.)
Peters, Jordan H., (AV) .... '— '72 C.103 A.B. L.365 J.D. [Freeborn&P.]
Peters, Kenneth D., (BV) .... '57 '83 C.478 B.A. L.339 J.D. [Ⓐ Askounis&B.]
Peters, Kenneth D., (AV) .... '48 '74 C.679 B.S. L.365 J.D. [Cronin,P.&C.]

Peters, Kevin R., (AV) '52 '83 C.357 B.A. L.365 J.D.
407 South Dearborn Street, Suite 1675, 60605
Telephone: 312-697-0022; Cell: 312-543-6365 Fax: 312-697-0812
Email: kp6970022@aol.com URL: http://www.kevinpeterslaw.com
Driving While Intoxicated, Drug Crimes, Felonies, Homicide, Misdemeanors, Sexual Assault, Traffic Violations, Police Misconduct, Civil Rights.
See Professional Biographies, CHICAGO, ILLINOIS

Peters, Lynda A. .... '61 '86 C.477 A.B. L.209 J.D. Asst. State's Atty.
Peters, Nicholas T. ...... '76 '03 C.880 B.S. L.424 J.D. [Ⓐ Fitch,E.T.&F.] (See Pat. Sect.)
Peters, Pamela Lee .... '67 '92 C&L.477 B.A., J.D. Sr. Atty., Northern Trust Corporation
Peters, R. Delacy, Jr. .... '— '89 C&L.64 B.S., J.D. [Arnstein&L.]
Peters, Randall F., (AV) .... '52 '81 C.188 A.B. L.209 J.D. 53 W. Jackson Blvd., Ste. 1009
Peters, Scott N. '56 '87 C.197 A.B. L.145 J.D.
Asst. Secy., SEC & PUHCA Coun., Exelon Corp.
Peters, Thomas M. .... '48 '75 C.430 B.A. L.365 J.D. 542 S. Dearborn St., Ste. 750
Peters, Troy R. .... '76 '02 C.966 B.S. L.276 J.D. [Ⓐ Skadden,A.S.M.&F.]
Peters, Victoria J., (AV) .... '48 '74 C.208 B.A. L.424 J.D. Asst. U.S. Atty.
Peters, Wayne .... '33 '58 C.339 B.S. L.145 J.D. 1204 W. Chase, Suite 1N

Peters & Lyons, Ltd., (AV)
25 East Washington Street, Suite 1000, 60602
Telephone: 312-346-7300 Fax: 312-782-6690 URL: http://www.peterslyons.com
Email: Laborlaw@peterslyons.com URL: http://www.lawyers.com/laborlaw
Donald F. Peters; Christopher P. Lyons.
Management Labor Law, Employment Litigation, Opposition to Union Organization, Unfair Labor Practice Charges, Union Contract Negotiations, Employment Discrimination, Employment Contracts and Wage and Hour Law.
See Professional Biographies, CHICAGO, ILLINOIS

Petersen, Amanda '67 '93 C.02 B.A. L.05 J.D.
(adm. in ME; not adm. in IL) [Ⓐ Mandel,L.&S.]
Petersen, Ann C., (AV) '50 '76 C.352 B.A. L.477 J.D.
180 East Pearson Street, Suite 5103
Petersen, Beth A. .... '— '96 C&L.597 B.A., J.D. [Sachnoff&W.]
Petersen, Carol M., (AV) .... '40 '67 C.339 B.S. L.813 J.D. Bank One‡
Petersen, Dale R. .... '51 '77 C.589 B.A. L.365 J.D. [Weil,F.&P.]
Petersen, Donald S., (AV) .... '29 '57 C.57 A.B. L.597 J.D. One 1st. National Plz.‡
Petersen, Jeffrey T. .... '71 '01 C.966 B.B.A. L.276 J.D. [Ⓐ Bell,B.&L.]
Petersen, Kyle A. .... '73 '01 C.347 B.A. L.146 J.D. [Ⓐ Katten M.R.]
Petersen, Laurette .... '62 '96 C.475 B.A. L.145 J.D. [Winston&S.]
Petersen, Matthew J. .... '— '94 C.339 B.A. L.146 J.D. [Sachnoff&W.]
Petersen, Milton L. .... '58 '00 C.350 B.S. L.477 J.D. [Ⓒ Neal,G.&E.]
Petersen, Russell C. .... '— '01 C.966 B.S. L.273 J.D. [Ⓐ Marshall,G.&B.] (See Pat. Sect.)
Petersen, Scott W. .... '47 '73 C.57 B.A. L.46 J.D. [Holland&K.]
Petersen, Steven P., (AV) '62 '87
C.597 B.S.E.E. L.477 J.D. [Leydig,V.&M.] (See Pat. Sect.)
Petersen, Warren G., (AV) .... '24 '51 C.145 B.A. L.597 J.D. 180 N. LaSalle St., Ste. 1801
Petersen, William O., (AV) .... '26 '52 C&L.309 A.B., LL.B. [Ⓒ Vedder,P.K.&K.]
Petersmarck, Stephanie .... '— '02 C&L.477 B.A., J.D. [Ⓐ McDermott W.&E.]
Peterson, Amy Fitzsimmons .... '58 '84 C.966 B.A. L.209 J.D. Equip for Equality
Peterson, Anne M. .... '— '02 C&L.602 B.A., J.D. [Ⓐ McGuirewoods]
Peterson, Brad L. .... '59 '88 C.145 M.B.A. L.309 J.D. [Mayer,B.R.&M.]
Peterson, Craig A. .... '41 '66 C.188 B.A. L.309 J.D. The John Marshall Law Sch.
Peterson, David R. .... '— '96 C.350 B.S. L.589 J.D. [Querrey&H.]
Peterson, Dennis A. .... '71 '98 C&L.494 B.S., J.D. [Ⓐ Baker&M.]
Peterson, Dixie L., (AV) .... '47 '75 C.174 B.A. L.365 J.D. Dep. Gen. Coun.
Peterson, Donald G., (AV) .... '40 '66 C.473 B.A. L.597 J.D. [Hughes S.P.R.&D.]
Peterson, Edward C. .... '41 '71 C.999 B.A. L.209 J.D. Bd. of Education
Peterson, Gerald C. .... '48 '77 C&L.424 B.A., J.D. [Winston&S.]
Peterson, Henry A. .... '10 '42 C.337 B.A. L.365 J.D. 6101 N. Nassau Avenue
Peterson, James A. .... '35 '61 C&L.966 B.B.A., LL.B. 2455 N. Racine
Peterson, James H. '52 '78 C.1082 B.S. L.339 J.D.
Tax Mgr., R.R. Donnelley & Sons Co.
Peterson, James R. ...... '45 '73 C&L.976 B.A., J.D. Arthur Andersen (Legal Department)
Peterson, Jan Marc .... '52 '76 C&L.923 B.S.Ec., J.D. V.P., MB Financial Bank
Peterson, John M., (AV) .... '47 '74 C.589 B.S. L.365 J.D. [Howe&H.]
Peterson, Kenneth A., Jr., (BV) .... '66 '91 C.679 B.A. L.1119 J.D. [Bell,B.&L.]
Peterson, Krista S. .... '76 '02 C.63 B.A. L.209 J.D. Cook Co. State Atty. Off.
Peterson, Paul L., (AV) '49 '75 C.339 B.A. L.146 J.D.
Asst. Gen. Coun., Underwriting, Chicago Title Ins. Co.
Peterson, Paul R. '41 '66 C.679 B.S. L.608 J.D.
(adm. in OH; not adm. in IL) Sr. V.P., Gen. Coun. & Sec., Technology Solutions Corp.
Peterson, Rebecca S. .... '74 '00 C.30 B.A. L.276 J.D. Pub. Def.
Peterson, Richard E., (AV) .... '64 '89 C.209 B.S. L.178 J.D. [Perkins C.]
Peterson, Ronald R., (AV) .... '48 '74 C.694 A.B. L.145 J.D. [Jenner&B.]
Peterson, Shawn L. .... '— '02 C.966 B.S.E.E. L.36 J.D. [Ⓐ McAndrews,H.&M.]
Petkus, Tomas .... '52 '80 C.339 B.A. L.146 J.D. [Tobin P.&M.]
Peto, Theodore A. .... '— '02 C&L.339 B.S., J.D. [Ⓐ Kirkland&E.]
Petrakis, Peter, (AV) .... '51 '76 C&L.424 B.A., J.D. [Ⓒ Meckler B.&T.]

Petravicius, Adam V. '70 '95 C.477 B.S.E.E. L.309 J.D. [Jenner&B.]
Petrek, Francis R., Jr., (AV) '49 '77 C.339 B.S. L.209 J.D. [Bollinger,R.&G.]
Petrich, David S. '61 '86 C.424 B.B.A. L.146 J.D. 134 N. LaSalle St.
Petrich, Matthew J. '65 '92 C.338 B.S. L.209 J.D. Deloitte & Touche
Petrie, James S., (AV) '36 '61 C.184 A.B. L.144 J.D. [Vedder,P.K.&K.]
Petrie, Paul E. '26 '55 C.578 L.365 LL.B. 5605 S. Dorchester St.‡
Petro, F. Daniel '59 '86 C.802 B.A. L.365 J.D. 310 S. Michigan Ave., Ste. 1310
Petro, Frank W. '35 '65 C.363 B.A. L.424 J.D. 310 S. Michigan Ave.
Petro, Michael J. '— '89 C&L.347 B.S., J.D. 53 West Jackson Boulevard Suite 1264
Petrone, Angela M. '56 '85 C.339 L.365 J.D. Asst. State's Atty.
Petrone, Anthony M., (BV) '55 '79 C.339 B.A. L.365 J.D. [A.M.Petrone]
Petrone, Anthony M., A Professional Corporation, (BV)
150 North Wacker Drive Suite 2460
Petronella, P. Neill '— '64 C.347 B.S. L.472 LL.B. [C Hennessy&R.]
Petrovic, Douglas '69 '95 C.597 B.A. L.1119 J.D. [A Corboy&D.]
Petrovic, Emily S. '77 '03 C.383 B.S. L.309 J.D. [A Mayer,B.R.&M.]
Petrozzi, Pablo L. '— '99 C.602 B.A. L.494 J.D. [A Pircher,N.&M.]
Petruso, Tracy E. '66 '97 C.188 B.S. L.146 J.D. 50 W. Washington, Suite 2108
Petsche, Janet N. '32 '90 C.999 L.365 J.D. [Klein,T.&J.]
Petti, Philip T., (AV) '58 '85 C.118 B.S. L.221 J.D. [Fitch,E.T.&F.] (See Pat. Sect.)
Pettinger, Sara L. '65 '90 C.145 B.A. L.209 J.D. [C Scopelitis,G.L.&H.]
Pettit, Karin Virginai '73 '00 C.436 B.A. L.818 J.D. State's Atty. Off.
Petty, David Z. '76 '01 C.350 B.S. L.546 J.D. [A McAndrews,H.&M.]
Peven, Jerrold M., (AV) '55 '80 C.910 B.A. L.597 J.D. [Schwartz C.]
Peyton, Theresa M. '63 '95 C.893 B.A. L.146 J.D. [Vedder,P.K.&K.]
Pezanoski, Diane M. '57 '85 C.959 B.A. L.597 J.D. Chief Asst. Corp. Coun.
Pezza, David J., Sr. '60 '85 C&L.209 B.S., J.D. [C Seyfarth S.]
Pfaff, Bruce R., (AV) '54 '79 C.197 A.B. L.1065 J.D. [Pfaff&G.]
Pfaff, Carolynn '68 '99 C.473 B.S. L.74 J.D. [A Katten M.R.]

Pfaff & Gill, Ltd., (AV)
One East Wacker Drive, Suite 3310, 60601
Telephone: 312-828-9666 Fax: 312-828-0880
Email: info@pfaffgill.com URL: http://www.pfaffgill.com
Bruce R. Pfaff; Michael Thomas Gill;—Matthew Douglas Ports; Mark Szaflarski.
Medical Malpractice including physician and surgical malpractice, birth defects, cerebral palsy, anesthesia negligence, failure to diagnose. Automotive Defects and Products Liability, Plaintiff Personal Injury including automobile accidents, catastrophic accidents, trucking accidents, head and spinal cord injuries, wrongful death.
See Professional Biographies, CHICAGO, ILLINOIS

Pfannkuche, Christopher E. K. '55 '80 C&L.424 B.A., J.D. Asst. State's Atty.
Pfau, Andrew T. '70 '02 C.399 B.A. L.145 J.D. [A Sidley A.B.&W.]
Pfeifer, Jeremy Todd '73 '99 C.966 B.A. L.146 J.D. Pub. Def., Cook Co.
Pfeiffer, J. Matthew '74 '00 C.679 B.S. L.589 J.D. [A Fuchs&R.]
Pfeiffer, John G. '61 '87 C.1532 B.A. L.1066 J.D. [Pfeiffer&A.]
Pfeiffer, Scott D. '73 '00 C.801 B.A. L.1000 J.D. [A Gunty&M.]
Pfeiffer & Adams, (AV) 300 West Adams, Suite 601
Pfeiler, Thomas A. '29 '57 C&L.966 B.S., LL.B. Pres., SCBA Ins. Servs., Inc.
Pfister, Edward M. '50 '80 C.259 B.S. L.209 J.D. [Nyhan,P.B.K.&L.]
Pfister, Todd B. '— '86 C.393 B.A. L.976 J.D. [Foley&L.]
Pflaum, Steven F., (AV) '55 '79 C.339 B.A. L.477 J.D. [McDermott W.&E.]
Pflaumer, John S. '51 '79 C.424 B.B.A. L.365 J.D. Northwest Indus. Inc.
Pfleger, Erika L. '72 '00 C.610 B.A. L.976 J.D. [A Sidley A.B.&W.]
Pfrang, Pamela '45 '84 C.747 B.S. L.146 J.D. Asst. Pub. Def.
Phalen, Stephen S., (AV) '60 '85 C.473 B.A. L.851 J.D. [S.S.Phalen]

Phalen, Stephen S., LLC, Law Offices of, (AV)
77 W. Wacker, Suite 4800, 60601
Telephone: 312-606-8718
Email: steve@phalenlaw.com URL: http://www.stephenphalen.com
Member of Firm: Stephen S. Phalen.
Personal Injury, Wrongful Death, Automobile Accidents, Boating Accidents, Motorcycle Accidents, Trucking Accidents, Bus Accidents, Train Accidents, Construction Accidents, Medical Malpractice, Head Trauma, Spinal Injuries.
See Professional Biographies, CHICAGO, ILLINOIS

Pham, Elayna T. '— '99 C.30 B.A. L.146 J.D. [A Jenner&B.]
Phanthavong, Christy E. '— '99 C.938 B.A. L.339 J.D. [A Bryan C.]
Phelan, Francis J. '33 '59 C&L.262 B.S., LL.B. 2 N. LaSalle St.
Phelan, James E. '71 '97 C.424 B.S. L.209 J.D. [A Johnson&B.]
Phelan, Joseph F. '36 '70 C.812 B.S.C. L.365 J.D. 100 W. Monroe St.
Phelan, Richard J., (AV) '— '61 C.602 Ph.B. L.276 J.D. [Foley&L.]
Phelps, Joseph G., (AV) '52 '82 C&L.424 B.A., J.D. [Rinella&R.]
Phelps, Mark E., (AV) '48 '75
C.453 B.S.M.E. L.597 J.D. [Leydig,V.&M.] (See Pat. Sect.)
Phelps, P. Michael '33 '58 C.918 B.A. L.309 LL.B. 100 N. Riverside Plz.
Pherson, Steven P., (AV) '59 '94 C.882 B.A. L.365 J.D. [Schuyler,R.&Z.]
Philbrick, Charles L., (BV) '— '88 C.859 B.A. L.1202 J.D. [Holland&K.]
Philbrick, James '72 '98 C.182 B.A. L.209 J.D. [A J.A.Schechter]
Philipp, Guenther M., (P.C.), (AV) '— '56 C.999 A.B. L.424 J.D. [Schiff H.]
Philipp, Michael M. '59 '92 C.145 B.A. L.209 J.D. [Katten M.R.]
Philippi, Michael J., (AV) '— '84 C.340 B.A. L.879 J.D. [Ungaretti&H.]
Phillips, Arthur A., (Ltd.) '30 '54 C&L.221 B.A., J.D. 200 N. LaSalle St.
Phillips, Charles '79 '04 C.473 B.S.A. L.1365 J.D. [A Beermann S.W.B.B.G.&L.]
Phillips, Clay H., (AV) '51 '76 C.502 A.B. L.276 J.D. [Bollinger,R.&G.]
Phillips, Edward H. '46 '75 C.1016 B.G.S. L.209 J.D. Asst. States Atty.
Phillips, Garrison L. '71 '96 C.477 B.A. L.339 J.D. [Littler M.]
Phillips, George W., (AV) '34 '59 C.210 B.A. L.597 J.D. [C Lewis,O.&F.]
Phillips, John G., (AV) '19 '43 C&L.209 Ph.B., J.D. [J.G.Phillips&Assoc.]
Phillips, Karen K. '51 '76 C.597 B.A. L.276 J.D.
Loss Prevention Coun., Attorney's Liability Assurance Society, Inc.
Phillips, Kevin Michael '71 '97 C.273 B.B.A. L.365 J.D. [A Fisher K.]
Phillips, Louis J. '74 '03 C.339 B.A. L.1000 J.D. [A Swanson,M.&B.]
Phillips, Mackenzie K. '— '04 C.188 A.B. L.477 J.D. [A Mayer,B.R.&M.]
Phillips, Matthew A. '68 '93 C.674 B.A. L.597 J.D.
Assistant General Counsel, Unilever Home & Personal Care
Phillips, Michael G. '68 '96 C.197 B.A. L.945 J.D.
(adm. in DE; not adm. in IL) Atty., Northern Trust Corp.
Phillips, Michael R. '69 '94 C.112 A.B. L.477 J.D. [McGuirewoods]
Phillips, Phoebe K. '— '02 C.893 B.S.S.E. L.339 J.D. [A Banner&W.] (See Pat. Sect.)
Phillips, Regina, & Associates '59 '85 C.339 B.S. L.146 J.D. 3530 W. Peterson Ave.
Phillips, Richard S., (AV) '26 '51
C&L.339 B.S., LL.B. [C Wood,P.K.C.&M.] (See Pat. Sect.)
Phillips, Robert S., (BV) '48 '76 C.347 B.A. L.209 J.D. [S.G.Thomas]
Phillips, Thomas R. '40 '65 C&L.597 B.S., J.D. 227 W. Monroe St., 13th Fl.‡
Phillips, William B. '46 '73 C.597 B.S. L.339 J.D. [McParland&P.]
Phillips, William E., (AV) '28 '53 C.388 B.A. L.597 J.D. 134 N. LaSalle St.
Phillips, William L. '49 '75 C.145 A.B. L.659 J.D. 6224 N. Livermore Ave.
Phillips, John G., & Associates, (AV) 200 N. La Salle St.
Phipps, Garrett '73 '04 C.767 B.A. L.477 J.D. [A Baker&M.]
Phipps, James M. '52 '77 C.813 B.S. L.910 J.D. [DLPiper R.G.C.U.]
Pialis, Stefania '69 '96 C.025 B.A. L.213 J.D. [A Beermann S.W.B.B.G.&L.]
Pick, Kay L., (AV) '44 '80 C.696 A.B. L.209 J.D. [C Rachlis D.D.&A.]
Pickens, Scott E., (AV) '— '78 C.339 B.S. L.424 J.D. [Schiff H.]
Picker, Randal C., (AV) '59 '86 C&L.145 B.A., J.D. [C Sidley A.B.&W.]
Pickus, Miriam I. '62 '87 C&L.477 B.A., J.D. City Human Rel. Comm.
Pico, Steven A. '56 '84 C.347 B.S. L.365 J.D. Univ. of Chicago Medical Ctr.
Picone, Christopher L. '56 '81 C.424 B.B.A. L.365 J.D. [Sinar K.M.&F.]
Picton, Charles E., III '72 '02 C&L.339 B.A., J.D. [A Barack F.K.P.&N.]
Piech, D. Joseph '— '04 C.477 B.S.E. L.1565 J.D. [A Kirkland&E.]
Piech, Hanna T. '57 '82 C.339 B.A. L.770 J.D. 2716 W Logan Blvd‡
Pieczonka, James P. '56 '83 C.1183 B.S. L.365 J.D. Admin. Law J., Dept. of Rev.
Piegore, John J., (BV) '55 '81 C.424 B.S. L.46 J.D. [Sanchez&D.]
Piekarski, Victor J., (AV) '— '74 C.93 B.A. L.597 J.D. [O'Hagan,S.&A.]
Piekut, Kenneth E. '47 '72 C.339 B.A. L.209 J.D. Harris Tr. & Svgs. Bk.
Piell, Hilda Harris '67 '92 C&L.477 B.A., J.D.
Assis. Gen. Coun., Chicago Mercantile Exchange Inc.
Piell, Jeffrey S. '66 '91 C.477 B.A. L.309 J.D. [Mayer,B.R.&M.]
Pieper, Gabrielle P., (BV) '34 '69 C.530 B.A. L.365 J.D. 188 W. Randolph St.
Pieper, Joseph W. '54 '88 C.297 B.A. L.209 J.D. 188 W. Randolph St., Ste. 2424
Pierce, Allen S., (AV) '18 '46 C.209 L.365 LL.B. 9024 S. Bennett Ave.‡
Pierce, Arthur R. '45 '72 C.209 B.A. L.146 J.D. [Pierce&R.]
Pierce, Daniel J., (AV) '— '72 C&L.209 B.S., J.D. [C Ungaretti&H.]
Pierce, Daniel M., (AV) '28 '52 C&L.309 A.B., J.D. [A Rubin&N.]
Pierce, Denis B. '44 '69 C.385 A.B. L.424 J.D. [Pierce&Assoc.]
Pierce, Gregory P. L., (AV) '57 '84 C&L.339 B.A., J.D. [Katten M.R.]
Pierce, Louis D. '44 '69 C.339 A.B. L.477 J.D.
V.P. & Ass. Gen. Coun., Reinsurance, Chicago Title Ins. Co.
Pierce & Associates, (AV) 1 North Dearborn, Suite 1300

Pierce, Daley, Baffes, O'Sullivan & Mussar, (AV)
La Salle Plaza, 180 N. La Salle Street, Suite 2320, 60601
Telephone: 312-236-7492 FAX: 312-236-2032
Members of Firm: Robert C. Pierce (1935-1971); Donal D. O'Sullivan (1928-1995); Thomas G. Baffes (1923-1998); Richard J. Dafey; Martin M. Mussar.
General Practice. Litigation. Medical Legal Law.
See Professional Biographies, CHICAGO, ILLINOIS

Pierce & Rogul 4246 W. 63rd St.
Pierotti, Joseph '68 '94 C.209 B.S. L.146 J.D. [Howard&N.]
Pierro, Pamela L. '77 '04 C.679 B.A. L.424 J.D. [A Momkus M.M.M.M.&S.]
Piers, Matthew J., (AV) '51 '74 C.188 L.145 J.D. [Hughes S.P.R.&D.]
Pierson, Craig D. '69 '95 C.385 B.A. L.861 J.D. [Kennedy&P.]
Pierson, Diayara Chanice '76 '01 C.477 B.S. L.209 J.D. Cook Co. State's Atty. Off.
Pierson, Michael D. '54 '89
C.1375 B.A. L.767 J.D. V.P., Gen. Coun., TD Equity Options, Inc.
Pierson, Stanley W. '— '02 C.112 B.A. L.424 J.D. [A Schad,D.&S.]
Pietrkowski, Henry '— '95 C.597 B.A. L.146 J.D. [Sachnoff&W.]
Pietrucha, Edward N. '51 '76 C&L.209 B.A., J.D. Cir. J.
Pietrzyk, Joseph W. '72 '97 C.37 B.A. L.145 J.D. [A Sidley A.B.&W.]
Pignotti, Jill A. '— '96 C.339 B.A. L.602 J.D. [O'Hagan,S.&A.]
Pigott, Jane DiRenzo, (AV) '57 '81 C.893 B.A. L.575 J.D. [R3]
Pikarski, Maureen C. '69 '96 C.104 B.A. L.128 J.D. 25 E. Washington St.
Pike, Connie S. '77 '04 C.1182 B.A. L.986 J.D. [A Bellows&B.]
Pike, Paulita A. '71 '96 C&L.602 B.A., J.D. [Bell,B.&L.]
Pike, Richard J. '71 '98 L.209 J.D. Asst. Coun., Allstate Insurance Co.
Pike, Stacy K. '— '87 C.15 B.A. L.966 J.D. [Chapman&C.]
Pikel, Howard J., (AV) '53 '81 C.339 B.A. L.365 J.D. [A Pretzel&S.]
Pikowsky, Harry '11 '36 L.146 LL.B. 1737 W. Howard St.
Pilati, August A., (AV) '53 '79 C.597 B.A. L.209 J.D. [Gesas,P.&G.]
Pildes, Michael E. '42 '66 C.339 B.A. L.209 J.D. [Wolin&R.]
Pileggi, William G., (AV) '50 '76 C.1151 B.A. L.146 J.D. 120 N. LaSalle
Pilgrim, Jeffrey D. '70 '99 C.352 B.B.A. L.146 J.D. [Arnstein&L.]
Piliponis, John A. '53 '77 C.424 B.A. L.597 J.D. Sr. Atty., Northern Trust Corporation
Pilja, George Daniel '71 '96 C.578 B.A. L.339 J.D [A Foran G.P.&P.]
Pilkington, Cathy Ann '54 '80 C.259 B.A. L.365 J.D. 20 North Clark Street
Pillai, Xavier '52 '94 C.930 Ph.D. L.146 J.D. [Leydig,V.&M.] (See Pat. Sect.)
Pille, Ann '78 '04 C.597 B.S. L.477 J.D. [A DLPiper R.G.C.U.]
Piller, Michael C. '54 '79 C.339 B.A. L.365 J.D. Coun., SAFECO Prop. & Cas. Ins. Co.
Pillsbury, Andrew P. '— '96 C&L.477 B.B.A., J.D. [A Kelley D.&W.]
Pilon, Lawrence R. '52 '84 C.338 B.M.E. L.146 J.D. [Hodes,K.&P.]
Pilotto, David Matthew '70 '00 C.927 B.B. L.424 J.D. [A Much S.F.D.A.&R.]
Pimentel, Eligio C. '66 '95 C.813 B.S. L.494 J.D.
[McAndrews,H.&M.] (See Pat. Sect.)
Pimentel, Julio G. '61 '92 C.209 B.S.C. L.365 J.D. P.O. Box A3761
Pincham, R. Eugene, (AV) '25 '51 C.832 A.B. L.597 J.D. 9316 S. Michigan Ave.
Pinchot, Dov J. '67 '94 C.978 B.A. L.145 J.D. [DLPiper R.G.C.U.]
Pinciak, Monica R. '74 '99 C.209 B.S. L.146 J.D. [A Jenner&B.]
Pincus, Elkin '25 '53 C.1016 B.S. L.209 J.D. 25 E. Wash.
Pincus, Laura B. '63 '88 C.860 B.S. L.145 J.D. 1 E. Jackson Blvd., Ste. 70331465
Pincus, S. Richard, (AV) '36 '61 C.273 B.A. L.145 J.D. [Holland&K.]
Pinderski, James A., (AV) '64 '89 C&L.339 B.A., J.D. [Tressler,S.M.&P.]

Pinderski & Pinderski, Ltd.
(See Palatine)

Pine, Francine Jaffe '66 '91 C.347 B.A. L.424 J.D. 1810 N. Fremont, Unit 11‡
Pine, Jeffrey A. '62 '91 C.339 B.S.E.E. L.424 J.D. [Baniak P.&G.] (See Pat. Sect.)
Pinelli, Anthony, Law Offices of, (AV) '48 '73
C.424 B.A. L.146 J.D. 53 W. Jackson Blvd., Ste. 1460
Pinelli, Vincent D., (AV) '53 '78 C.424 B.A. L.209 J.D. [Burke B.&P.]
Pinhasik, Annette E., (AV) '54 '78 C.339 B.A. L.365 J.D. 230 W. Monroe St.
Pinkert, Clare M. '— '04 C.197 A.B. L.145 J.D. [A Kirkland&E.]
Pinkert-Lieb, Karen, (AV) '66 '93 C.846 B.A. L.46 J.D. [Schiller,D.&F.]
Pinkstaff, James M. '77 '02 C&L.339 A.B., J.D. [A Sedgwick,D.M.&A.]
Pinkston, J. Murray, III, (BV) '59 '85
C.861 B.A. L.500 J.D. 30 North La Salle Street, Suite 4300
Pinkus, D. C. '15 '38 C.597 L.365 LL.B. 3500 N. Lake Shore Dr.
Pinski, Ronald L. '36 '60 C.339 B.S. L.597 LL.B. [Zalutsky&P.]
Pinsky, Michael S., (AV) '45 '71 C.339 B.S. L.209 J.D. [Schain,B.R.&C.]
Pintar, Janice M. '67 '02 C.959 B.S. L.966 J.D. [A Maduff M.&M.]
Pintas, William G. '60 '85 C.472 B.A. L.1187 J.D. [W.G.Pintas&Assoc.]

Pintas, William G., & Associates, Ltd.
368 West Huron Street, Suite 100, 60610
Telephone: 312-664-4411 Fax: 312-664-8833 URL: http://www.ineedanattorney.com
Email: pintas@msn.com URL: http://www.mylawyerteam.com
(This Listing Continued)

Pintas, William G., & Associates, Ltd. (Continued)

William G. Pintas. Associates: Laura J. Mullins; Linda Keck.
Personal Injury, Workers Compensation, Accidents, Automobile Accidents and Injuries, Automobile Negligence, Bodily Injury, Brain Injury, Plaintiffs Personal Injury, Motorcycle Accidents, Head Injury, Electrical Injury, Slip and Fall, Spinal Injury, Medical Malpractice, Birth Trauma, Gynecology Malpractice, Medical Negligence, Physicians Professional Liability, Psychiatric Malpractice, Surgeons Liability.

See Professional Biographies, CHICAGO, ILLINOIS

Pinto, Anthony M., (AV) .... '70 '95 C&L.424 B.B.A., J.D. [Ⓐ Donohue B.M.&S.]
Pinzur, Neil S. .... '52 '77 C&L.339 B.S., J.D. LaSalle Natl. Tr., N.A.

Pinzur, Cohen & Kerr, Ltd.
(See Long Grove)

Pioli, Janet A., (AV) '59 '84 C.338 B.S. L.589 J.D.
[Ⓒ Brinks H.G.&L.] (See Pat. Sect.)
Pioli, Victor .... '73 '98 C.569 B.A. L.276 J.D. [Ⓐ Johnson&B.]
Pionke, Edward A. ....'— '99 C.339 B.S. L.209 J.D. [Ⓐ Mayer,B.R.&M.]
Piontek, Michael, (AV) .... '42 '69 C.339 B.S.M.E. L.365 J.D. [Pyle&P.] (Pat.)
Pipal, Faustin A., Jr., (AV) .... '55 '80 C&L.597 B.S., J.D. [Keating,K.P.&B.]
Pipal, Frank F. ....'27 '51 C&L.209 A.B., J.D. 5935 S. Pulaski Rd.‡
Pipal, Susan A. ....'67 '93 C.602 B.A. L.597 J.D. [Winston&S.]
Piper, William S. ....'— '78 C&L.424 A.B., J.D. [McKenna S.]
Pippenger, Phillip M. '69 '98
C.111 B.S.E.E. L.188 J.D. [Ⓐ Leydig,V.&M.] (See Pat. Sect.)
Piraro, Giselle C. .... '74 '00 C.209 B.A. L.365 J.D. [Ⓐ Handler,T.&D.]

Pircher, Nichols & Meeks, (BV)
900 North Michigan Avenue, 60611-1575 ⊙
Telephone: 310-201-8900 FAX: 310-201-8922
URL: http://www.pircher.com
Resident Members: Marc A. Benjamin; Eugene J. M. Leone; Jonathan D. Levy; Michael McKeever; Miryam Rosie Rees. Resident Associates: Elchanan Finestone; Julia L. Halpern; Jay Byron Leibovitz; Dianne M. Lu; Jennifer S. Manter; Pablo L. Petrozzi; Aaron M. Potter; John M. Valentine.
Real Estate Law including Representation of Partnerships, Limited Liability Companies and Tax-Exempt Organizations in Acquisition, Development and Financing. Corporation, Federal and State Securities, Federal and State Taxation, Partnership, Environmental Law, Litigation, Bankruptcy and Limited Liability Company.
Los Angeles, California Office: 1925 Century Park East, Suite 1700. Telephone: 310-201-8900. FAX: 310-201-8922.

See Professional Biographies, CHICAGO, ILLINOIS

Pirogovsky, Alex ....'— '98 C.597 B.A. L.910 J.D. [Ungaretti&H.]
Pirpiris, Irene V. .... '65 '90 C.1278 B.A. L.1206 J.D. Atty., U.S. Dept. of Labor
Pirruccello, Frank W., Jr. .... '50 '76 C.623 B.A. L.209 J.D. 155 N. Michigan Ave.
Pisani, Daniel W. ....'67 '92 C.436 B.A. L.146 J.D. [Ⓐ Harrington,T.A.&H.]
Pisani, Robert P., (AV) ....'— '86 C.966 B.A. L.209 J.D. [McKenna S.]
Pisano, Anne Marie ....'— '99 C.884 B.A.H. L.145 J.D. [Ⓐ Goldberg,K.B.B.R.&M.]
Piskorski, Thomas J., (AV) .... '55 '81 C.436 B.S. L.602 J.D. [Seyfarth S.]
Pissetzky, Gal ....'72 '00 C.339 B.A. L.365 J.D. 111 W. Washington, Ste. 1625
Pistorius, William P., (AV) ....'62 '87 C.339 B.A. L.209 J.D. [Clausen M.]
Pitler, Barry A. ....'31 '53 L.146 J.D. [Pitler&M.]
Pitler, Lisa R. '63 '01 C.249 B.S.N. L.209 J.D.
Asst. Dir., Research Compl., Rush University Medical Center
Pitler & Mandell ....39 S. LaSalle St.
Pitrack, Howard B., Law Offices of ......'48 '73 C&L.209 B.A., J.D. 205 West Randolph
Pitrof, Elizabeth A. ....'46 '85 C.209 B.A. L.424 J.D. [Kerns,P.F.&P.]
Pitt, George, (AVⓉ) ....'38 '63 C&L.597 B.A., J.D. Mng. Dir., UBS Painewebber Inc.
Pittman, Anna C. ....'75 '01 C.201 B.S. L.365 J.D. [Ⓐ A.J.Madonia&Assoc.]
Pittman, Elizabeth L. ....'71 '98 C.886 B.S.C.E. L.209 J.D. GE Ins. Solutions
Pitts, Adrienne Banks .... '68 '95 C.659 B.S. L.94 J.D. [Winston&S.]
Pitts, Henry L., (AV) ....'— '39 C.339 B.S. L.477 J.D. [Dykema G.P.] ‡
Pitulla, Joanne Pelton '— '84
C.339 B.S. L.146 J.D. Asst. Ethics Counsel, Amer. Bar Assn.
Pivar, Ruth A. ....'48 '91 C.959 B.B.A. L.436 J.D. [DLPiper R.G.C.U.]
Pizer, Edwin, (BV) ....'12 '35 C&L.209 LL.B. 135 S. LaSalle St.
Pizer, Howard C., (AV) '41 '66 C.966 B.B.A. L.597 J.D.
Exec. V.P., Chicago White Sox
Placek, Marijane, (AV) ....'48 '73 C.700 B.A. L.209 J.D. Asst. Pub. Def.
Placencia, Manuel J., Jr. .... '72 '98 C.197 B.A. L.339 J.D. [Ⓐ Kubasiak,F.R.&R.]
Plain, Kass A. ....'63 '88 C.339 B.A. L.597 J.D. Cook Co. Pub. Guard.
Planek, Charles W., (AV) ....'— '81 C&L.209 B.A., J.D. [Ⓒ Wilson E.M.E.&D.]
Plante, John R., (AV) '45 '77
C.801 B.A. L.365 J.D. Mng. Atty., Claims, Chicago Transit Auth.
Plasz, Andrew Nicholas ....'74 '99 C&L.910 A.B., J.D. [Crowley B.&K.]
Plater, Caroline C. ....'71 '98 C.436 B.A. L.209 J.D. [Ⓐ Kelley D.&W.]
Platis, Eleftheria Terry .... '— '03 C.597 B.A. L.569 J.D. [Ⓐ Kirkland&E.]
Platt, Andrew L. ....'61 '86 C.339 B.A. L.146 J.D. 55 West Monroe Street
Platt, L. Steven, (AV) ....'53 '78 C.597 B.A. L.424 J.D. [Arnold&K.]
Platt, Michael ....'38 '62 C.221 B.S. L.597 J.D. Platt Luggage, Inc.
Platt, Steven Keith '57 '83 C&L.94 B.S. B.A., J.D.
(adm. in MA; not adm. in IL) AM&G Financial Servs., Inc.
Platt, Thomas Joseph ....'54 '81 C.98 B.A. L.365 J.D. 30 N. Lasalle St.
Plaza, Wayne F., (AV) .....'45 '70 C.388 B.A. L.146 J.D. [Dykema G.P.] (⊙Detroit, MI)
Plazibat, Stephen E., (BV) ....'57 '82 C.209 B.A. L.365 J.D. Asst. Atty. Gen.
Plesha, Gregory G. '61 '86
C.190 B.A. L.365 J.D. 10540 South Western Avenue, Suite 103
Pleshivoy, Julie Sirlin '— '03 C.145 A.B. L.146 J.D.
Two North LaSalle Street, Suite 2200
Pleviak, Brian J. ....'75 '00 C.966 B.A. L.146 J.D. [Ⓐ Levenfeld P.]
Plewes, Stanley Frank '46 '81 C.659 A.B. L.813 J.D.
(adm. in CT; not adm. in IL) Coun., The Boeing Co.
Plochinski, Kenneth E. ....'55 '03 C&L.477 B.S.E., J.D. [Ⓐ Fitch,E.T.&F.]
Plonka, Alicja G., Law Offices of ....'58 '88 C.734 B.A. L.424 J.D. 4111 W. 47th St.
Plotkin, Robert, (AV) ....'28 '54 C&L.339 LL.B. [Plotkin,J.&O.]
Plotkin, Steven J. ....'49 '78 C.339 A.B. L.209 J.D. [Ⓒ Plotkin,J.&O.]
Plotkin, Jacobs & Orlofsky, Ltd., (AV) .... 122 S. Michigan Ave., Ste. 1850
Plotner, Todd R. ....'— '98 C.339 B.A. L.477 J.D. [Ⓐ Sidley A.B.&W.]
Plotnick, Gary L., (AV) ....'62 '87 C.339 B.A. L.209 J.D. [Schain,B.R.&C.]
Plotnick, Harry D. ....'12 '35 C&L.209 Ph.B., LL.B. 29 S. LaSalle St.
Plotz, Kelli Chase ....'61 '86 C.339 B.S. L.209 J.D. [Ⓢ Katten M.R.]
Plumb, George T., (AV) ....'50 '77 C&L.209 A.B., J.D. [DLPiper R.G.C.U.]
Plumlee, Melissa L. '76 '01 C.846 B.A. L.602 J.D.
(adm. in TX; not adm. in IL) [Ⓐ Skadden,A.S.M.&F.]
Plunkett, Andrew M., (AV) ....'63 '92 C.347 B.A. L.424 J.D. [Ⓐ Childress D.G.]
Plunkett, Paul E. ....'35 '60 C&L.309 B.S., J.D. U.S. Sr. Dist. J.
Pluta, Robert G. ....'— '02 C.436 B.S. L.209 J.D. [Ⓐ Brinks H.G.&L.] (See Pat. Sect.)
Pluth, Robert R., Jr., (AV) ....'— '80 C.1151 B.A. L.597 J.D. [Schiff H.]
Plzak, Louis Anthony ....'67 '93 C.339 B.A. L.1000 J.D. [Ⓐ Meyer&B.]

Pochis, David S., (AV) ....'28 '51 C.339 L.146 J.D. 33 N. Dearborn St.
Pochopien, Donald J., (BV) '46 '88
C.424 B.S. L.365 J.D. [McAndrews,H.&M.] (See Pat. Sect.)
Podbelsek, Glenn ....'59 '85 C&L.339 B.A., J.D. [Treumann&P.]
Podgers, James .... '50 '84 C.966 B.A. L.146 J.D. Asst. Editor, Amer. Bar Assn.
Podkowa, Daniel ....'65 '91 C.339 B.A. L.365 J.D. 6620 W. Diversey Ave.
Podlasek, Robert M. ....'55 '85 C.424 B.S. L.146 J.D. Asst. State Atty.
Podlewski, Joseph R., Jr., (AV) ....'53 '78 C.589 B.A. L.146 J.D. [Ⓒ Schwartz C.]
Podliska, John F., (AV) ......'47 '72 C&L.597 B.S., J.D. Asst. U.S. Atty., U.S. Atty. Off.
Podobnik, Ray .... '43 '79 C.589 B.S. L.1151 J.D. [Ⓐ Horwitz,H.&Assoc.]
Podulka, Holly A. ....'— '02 C.1049 B.A. L.145 J.D. [Ⓐ Schiff H.]
Poduska, Joseph J. .... '41 '67 C.363 B.S. L.146 J.D. 6059 W. Irving Park Rd.
Poe, Grace Y. ....'72 '97 C&L.597 B.S., J.D. [Ⓐ DLPiper R.G.C.U.]
Poe, Steven F. ....'68 '95 C.108 B.S. L.146 J.D. Sr. Coun., Grant Thornton, LLP
Poedtke, Carl H., III .... '69 '96 C.362 B.A. L.365 J.D. [Ⓐ DLPiper R.G.C.U.]
Poetzel, Megan B. ....'73 '97 C.477 B.S. L.146 J.D. [Jenner&B.]
Pogorzelski, Agnes, & Associates, Law Offices of '75 '03
C.424 B.A. L.209 J.D. 5934 W. Montrose Ave.
Pogrund, David B. ....'59 '83 C&L.861 B.A., J.D. [Stone,P.&K.]
Pogrund, Sherwin I., (P.C.), (AV) ....'34 '57 C.1016 B.A. L.597 J.D. [Stone,P.&K.]
Pogue, Peter A. ....'67 '94 C.679 B.S. L.284 J.D. [Ⓐ Swanson,M.&B.]
Pogwizd, James L. ....'48 '86 C.424 B.A. L.209 J.D. 2301 S. Western Ave.
Poh, Linda S. ....'51 '84 C.123 B.A. L.209 J.D. 505 N. lakeshore Dr.
Pohl, Timothy R., (AV) ....'66 '91 C.31 B.A. L.145 J.D. [Skadden,A.S.M.&F.]
Pohlenz, Jennifer J. Sackett ....'— '94 C.174 B.A. L.879 J.D. [Querrey&H.]
Poindexter, David L., (CV) .... '57 '82 C&L.339 B.A., J.D. [Horvath&L.]
Pokorny, Stephen J., (AV) .... '44 '70 C.1016 B.A. L.424 J.D. [Laser,P.S.F.&E.]
Pokorny, William R. ....'— '01 C.57 B.A. L.145 J.D. [Ⓐ Wildman,H.A.&D.]
Polacheck, Joan F., (AV) ....'55 '81 C.976 B.A. L.309 J.D. [McDermott W.&E.]
Polachek, Michael J., (AV) '50 '76
C.339 B.A. L.146 J.D. [Tressler,S.M.&P.] (⊙Wheaton)
Polachek, Thomas A., (AV) .... '42 '68 C.475 B.A. L.339 J.D. [Quarles&B.]
Polales, Dean J., (AV) ....'— '79 C&L.145 B.A., J.D. [Ungaretti&H.]
Polales, John C., (P.C.) ....'24 '51 C.209 L.365 LL.B. 111 W. Wash. St.
Polance, Michael E. ....'43 '77 C.209 B.A. L.365 J.D. Asst. Pub. Def.
Poland, Christian M. ....'— '92 C.937 B.A. L.602 J.D. [Bryan C.]
Polansky, Marc A. ....'66 '94 C.446 B.A. L.146 J.D. [Cozen O.]
Polaski, Anne Spencer '52 '79
C.25 B.A. L.273 J.D. Asst. Gen. Coun., Chicago Board of Trade
Polatsek, Daniel J. ....'70 '97 C.861 B.A. L.365 J.D. [Ⓐ Katten M.R.]
Polega, Gary R. ....'— '88 C.98 B.S. L.209 J.D. [Chapman&C.]
Polelle, Michael J. ....'38 '65 C.424 A.B. L.309 LL.B. Prof., John Marshall Sch. of Law
Poli, Carl E. ....'52 '78 C.424 A.B. L.209 J.D. [Stone,M.&S.] ⊙
Polich, Melissa K. ....'71 '96 C.352 B.A. L.597 J.D. [Ⓐ Sidley A.B.&W.]
Polichak, James W. ....'— '03 C.867 B.A. L.477 J.D. [Ⓐ Wildman,H.A.&D.]
Polick, Steven P. ....'54 '81 C.173 B.A. L.365 J.D. [S.P.Polick&Assoc.] ⊙
Polick, Steven P., & Associates, P.C. ...... 218 North Jefferson, 3rd Floor (⊙Highland, IN)
Polikoff, Bernard A. .... '12 '40 C&L.209 J.D. 3180 N. Lake Shore Dr., Apt. 21-F‡
Polinski, Thomas John .... '58 '86 C.934 B.A. L.365 J.D. 5844 W. Irving Park Rd.
Polish, Jonathan S. ....'— '96 C&L.477 A.B., J.D. [Sachnoff&W.]
Polisky, Joel S. ....'52 '79 C.339 B.S. L.365 J.D. [Much S.F.D.A.&R.]
Polisky, Philip Scott '50 '79 C.597 B.A. L.569 J.D.
30 East Huron Street, Suite 3509 (⊙New York, NY)
Polisner, Jori L. ....'73 '00 C.966 B.A. L.146 J.D. [Ⓐ Cassiday,S.&G.]
Polit, Robert B., (BV) '62 '91
C.339 B.S.E.E. L.365 J.D. [Ⓒ Brinks H.G.&L.] (See Pat. Sect.)
Polites, Gregory E. .... '64 '89 C&L.30 B.A., J.D. 6157 N. Sheridan Rd.
Polizzi, Stuart D. .....'63 '02 C.209 B.S. L.339 J.D. Two North LaSalle Street, Suite 2200
Polk, Christine M. ....'75 '02 C.910 B.A. L.424 J.D. Clk.
Polk, Lee T., (AV) ....'— '70 C.162 A.B. L.145 J.D. [Barnes&T.]
Polk, Michael R. ....'56 '82 C.209 B.Sc. L.146 J.D. [Walinski&T.]
Pollack, Frank S. ....'35 '60 C&L.477 B.A., LL.B. 33 North LaSalle Street, Suite 2900
Pollack, Mark D., (AV) ...'59 '85 C&L.477 B.A., J.D. Gen. Coun., Arthur Andersen, LLP
Pollack, Wendy ....'51 '89 C.339 A.B. L.309 J.D. Legal Assistance Found. of Chicago
Pollard, Hugh E. ....'52 '83 C.424 B.A. L.46 J.D. ATG Trust Company
Pollard, Michael A., (AV) ....'54 '83 C.602 A.B. L.339 J.D. [Baker&M.]
Polley, Theodore Zane, III ....'— '03 C.477 B.A. L.1565 J.D. [Ⓐ Winston&S.]
Pollick, John F., (AV) ....'52 '80 C.976 B.A. L.477 J.D. [McGuirewoods]
Pollock, Ann H. ....'56 '82 C.976 B.A. L.309 J.D. [Skadden,A.S.M.&F.]
Pollock, Earl E., (AV) ....'28 '55 C.494 B.A. L.597 J.D. 233 S. Wacker Dr.‡
Pollock, Scott D., (AV) .... '58 '86 C.33 B.A. L.1009 J.D. [S.D.Pollock&Assoc.]

Pollock, Scott D., & Associates, P.C., (AV) ⊞
105 West Madison, Suite 2200, 60602
Telephone: 312-444-1940 Fax: 312-444-1950 URL: http://www.lawfirm1.com
Email: info@lawfirm1.com URL: http://www.lawyers.com/scottdpollock&assoc
Scott D. Pollock;—Marta Delgado; Maria T. Baldini-Potermin; Kathryn Weber; Fatima G. Mohyuddin (Not admitted in IL); Anne G. Relias.
Languages: Spanish, French, Urdu/Hindi, German, Serbo-Croatian, Russian, Czech.
Immigration and Nationality, Citizenship, Visas, Asylum, Deportation, Family and Litigation Practice.

See Professional Biographies, CHICAGO, ILLINOIS

Pollyea, Sarah D. .... '75 '00 C.347 B.A. L.930 J.D. 150 North Wacker Dr., Ste. 2600
Polony, Richard B. ....'64 '95 C.424 B.B.A. L.146 J.D. [Hinshaw&C.]
Polovin, Andrew K. ....'73 '01 C.165 B.A. L.597 J.D. [Ⓐ Bartlit B.H.P.&S.]
Polovin, Robert K. .... '42 '68 C.339 B.S. L.209 J.D. [Wolfe&P.]
Polsby, Daniel D. '45 '71 C.1154 B.A. L.494 J.D.
Prof. of Law, Northwestern Univ. Sch. of Law
Polsby, Daniel L. ....'72 '99 C.999 B.A. L.597 J.D. [Ⓐ Dowd&D.]
Polsky, Samuel J., (AV) ....'50 '74 C.1016 B.A. L.597 J.D. [Polsky&Assoc.]

Polsky & Associates, Ltd., (AV)
205 North Michigan Avenue 41st Floor, 60601-5925
Telephone: 312-540-0200 Fax: 312-540-0207
Email: postmaster@polskylaw.com URL: http://www.polskylaw.com
Samuel J. Polsky; Deborah A. Faktor. Associate: Lauren E. Brady.
Tax Increment Finance, Commercial Real Estate Development, Commercial Real Estate Finance, Industrial Real Estate Law, Shopping Center Development, Municipal Finance, Redevelopment Law, Real Estate Development, Property Tax Abatement, Sales and Use Tax, Land Development, Land Entitlement.

See Professional Biographies, CHICAGO, ILLINOIS

Polster, David ....'69 '94 C.978 B.A. L.309 J.D. [Skadden,A.S.M.&F.]
Poltrock, Jennifer K. ....'69 '92 C.965 B.A. L.365 J.D. [Poltrock&P.]
Poltrock, Lawrence A. ....'41 '66 C.576 B.A. L.146 J.D. [Poltrock&P.]
Poltrock & Poltrock .... 123 W. Madison, 18th Floor
Polyak, Anna ....'75 '04 C&L.424 B.S., J.D. [Ⓐ Levin&P.]

Polyakov, Mark V. '— '05 C&L.930 B.A., J.D.
(adm. in NY; not adm. in IL) [A] Wood,P.K.C.&M.]
Polycarpe, Yanick E. '70 '96 C.339 B.S. L.146 J.D. [A] S.B.Handelman]
Pomerance, Philip L., (AV) '— '81 C&L.597 B.A., J.D. [Arnstein&L.]
Pomerantz, Harold B., (AV) '53 '79 C&L.910 B.A., J.D. [DLPiper R.G.C.U.]
Pomerantz, William A. '41 '66 C.399 B.A. L.145 J.D. 55 E. Monroe St.

Pomerantz Haudek Block Grossman & Gross LLP
One North LaSalle Street, Suite 2225, 60602-3908 ⊙
Telephone: 312-377-1181 Fax: 312-377-1184
Email: pomerantz@pomlaw.com URL: http://www.pomlaw.com
Patrick V. Dahlstrom.
Corporate, Securities, Antitrust and Insurance Litigation.
New York, New York Office: 100 Park Avenue, 10017. Telephone: 212-661-1100. Fax: 212-661-8665.
Washington, D.C. Office: 1025 Connecticut Avenue, N.W., Suite 1000. Telephone: 202-327-5420. Fax: 202-327-5422.
See Professional Biographies, CHICAGO, ILLINOIS

Pomeranz, Jacob '46 '73 C.966 B.S. L.976 J.D. [Cornfield&F.]
Pomierski, William R., (AV) '58 '83 C.475 B.B.A. L.339 J.D. [McDermott W.&E.]
Pomper, Howard '34 '57 C&L.145 B.A., J.D. 22 W. Monroe St.
Pomper, Mitchell H. '58 '84 C.597 B.S. L.146 J.D.
Ins. Consul./Agent, American Family Insurance
Pomrening, Anthoula '67 '99
C.46 B.S.M.E. L.365 J.D. [McDonnell B.H.&B.] (See Pat. Sect.)
Pomrenze, Nathaniel J. '54 '84 C.112 B.A. L.273 J.D. 123 N. Wacker Dr.
Ponce de Leon, Edmund '53 '84 C.1183 B.A. L.365 J.D. Cir. J.
Pond, Jacob C. '74 '01 C.910 B.S.B.A. L.347 J.D. [A] Vedder,P.K.&K.]

Pond, Robert A., (AV) '47 '72 C.477 A.B. L.309 J.D.
10 South La Salle Street, Suite 1017, 60603
Telephone: 312-609-1600 Fax: 312-609-1720; 312-419-0705
Email: rpond@ameritech.net
Commercial Law & Litigation, Employment Law & Litigation, Bankruptcy, Probate, Banks and Banking.

Ponder, Anita J. '— '85 C.254 B.A. L.260 J.D. [Gardner C.&D.]
Ponsetto, Joseph L., (BV) '56 '82 C&L.209 B.A., J.D. Asst. Atty. Gen.
Pontikes, George C., & Associates, (AV) '36 '61
C&L.309 A.B., LL.B. 11 South LaSalle Street
Pontikes, Rachael G. '74 '01 C.918 B.A. L.145 J.D. [A] Duane M.]
Pontikes, Steven M., (AV) '57 '82 C.145 B.A. L.597 J.D. [Pontikes&Assoc.]
Pontikes & Associates, (AV) 111 W. Washington, Suite 1221
Pontikis, Thomas J., (AV) '61 '86 C&L.209 B.A., J.D. [Williams M.&J.]
Ponzi, Matthew S. '63 '88 C.210 B.A. L.273 J.D. [Foran G.P.&P.]
Ponzio, Anthony V., (BV) '48 '74 C.716 B.S. L.602 J.D. 205 W. Randolph St.
Pool, Gregory R., (AV) '50 '76 C.347 B.A. L.146 J.D.
Assoc. Gen. Coun., Claims, Chicago Title Ins. Co.
Poole, Jay J. '30 '57 L.209 LL.B. 9753 Hoyne St.
Poole, Leslie P. '54 '81 C&L.424 B.B.A., J.D. [A] Bellows&B.]
Poor, E. King, (AV) '54 '80 C.197 A.B. L.245 J.D. [Winston&S.]
Poor, J. Stephen '55 '80 C.347 B.A. L.893 J.D. [Seyfarth S.]
Poorman, John Kevin, (AV) '51 '77
C&L.623 B.S., J.D. Exec. V.P. & Gen. Coun., Penguin Group
Pope, David D. '75 '01 C.170 B.A. L.145 J.D. [A] Mayer,B.R.&M.]
Pope, Harold N. '34 '58 C&L.597 B.S.L., LL.B. 1 N. La Salle St.
Pope, Jerome W., (AV) '51 '76 C.98 B.S. L.209 J.D. [Winston&S.]
Pope, LeAnn Pedersen, (AV) '57 '83 C.123 B.A. L.365 J.D. [Burke,W.M.&S.]
Pope, Michael A., (AV) '44 '69 C.424 B.S. L.597 J.D. [McDermott W.&E.]
Popel, Orest J. '29 '56 C&L.339 B.A., LL.B. 2300 W. Chicago Ave.‡
Popelka, John M., (AV) '61 '87 C.436 B.A. L.365 J.D. [Anesi,O.R.N.&K.]
Popham, David M. '71 '97 C.187 B.A. L.365 J.D. 203 N. La Salle St., Suite 1800
Popko, Jerome G., (AV) '38 '65 C.98 B.A. L.597 J.D. [Tinkoff,P.&D.]
Poplawski, Carol A., (BV) '60 '86 C.339 B.S. L.209 J.D. [Ogletree,D.N.S.&S.]
Poplett, Ray E., (AV) '23 '51 C&L.145 A.B., J.D. [R.E.Poplett]
Poplett, Ray E., P.C., (AV) 221 N. La Salle St.
Popovic, Marina '71 '96 C.209 B.A. L.424 J.D. [Kane,C.&M.]
Popovits, Renée M., (AV) '64 '89 C.720 B.A. L.209 J.D. [Popovits&Assoc.]
Popovits & Associates, P.C., (AV) 3600 3 1st Nat. Plaza
Popovsky, Carl L. '64 '91 C&L.339 B.S., J.D. [Stein,R.&H.]
Popp, James P. '68 '93 C.424 B.A. L.365 J.D. Sr. Claims Analyst, CNA
Popp, Noah Nathaniel '73 '99 C&L.966 B.S., J.D. 10 S. Dearborn Street
Porcelli, Anthony C., (AV) '69 '94 C.602 B.B.A. L.597 J.D. [Jenner&B.]
Porcelli, William P. '24 '55 C.46 B.S.M.E. L.424 J.D. 9920 S. Seeley Avenue (Pat.)‡
Poremba, Carol A. '49 '82 C.94 B.S. L.589 J.D. Asst. Corp. Coun.
Porretta, Charles A., (AV) '65 '91 C.436 B.S. L.365 J.D. [Latherow&P.]
Port, M. L. '15 '39 C.137 A.A. L.146 LL.B. 7141 N. Kedzie
Portela, Maria Elena, (BV) '58 '84 C.597 B.A. L.221 J.D. [B] Scopelitis,G.L.&H.]
Porteous, David W. '68 '98 C.966 B.A. L.861 J.D. [A] Gardner C.&D.]
Porter, David '60 '86 C.477 B.A. L.1019 J.D. 11 South LaSalle Street, Suite 1020
Porter, David William, (BV) '55 '82 C.339 B.S. L.146 J.D. 150 S. Wacker Dr.
Porter, Karen J., (BV) '57 '83 C.553 B.A. L.477 J.D. [K.J.Porter]
Porter, Marc S. '54 '79 C.190 B.S.B.A. L.589 J.D. [Figliulo&S.]
Porter, Richard W., (P.C.), (AV) '— '87 C.478 B.A. L.145 J.D. [Kirkland&E.]
Porter, Simon S. '24 '52 C.350 L.472 LL.B. Asso. Cir. J.
Porter, Todd M., (AV) '60 '90 C.339 B.A. L.365 J.D. [A] Ruff,W.&R.]
Porter, Tracie R. '69 '94 C.187 B.A. L.221 J.D. [T.R.Porter]
Porter, Karen J., Ltd., The Law Offices of, (BV) 11 East Adams Street, Suite 1100
Porter, Tracie R., LLC, Law Offices of 1507 E. 53rd St.
Porterfield, W. Scott, (AV) '54 '79 C&L.597 B.A., J.D. [Barack F.K.P.&N.]
Portes, Herbert, (AV) '13 '36 C&L.145 B.A., J.D. 333 W. Wacker Dr.
Ports, Matthew Douglas '72 '00 C.174 B.A. L.209 J.D. [A] Pfaff&G.]
Posen, Kevin E. '61 '90 C.424 B.A. L.365 J.D. [Teller,L.&S.]
Posey, Thomas J. '71 '03 C.338 B.S. L.146 J.D. [A] Franczek S.]
Poskanzer, Steven G. '58 '83 C.674 A.B. L.309 J.D.
(adm. in DC; not adm. in IL) Univ. of Chicago
Posner, Alan M., (AV) '53 '77 C.309 A.B. L.145 J.D. [Meckler B.&T.]
Posner, Neil B. '— '96 C.569 B.A. L.436 J.D. [Sachnoff&W.]
Posner, Richard '39 '63 C.976 A.B. L.309 LL.B. U.S. Ct. App. J.
Possinger, Paul V., (AV) '68 '93 C.981 B.A. L.945 J.D. [Jenner&B.]
Postel, Joseph P. '56 '82 C&L.950 B.A., J.D.
(adm. in OR; not adm. in IL) 2960 N. Lake Shore Dr.‡
Postel, Theodore R. '25 '51 C.209 L.365 LL.B. 2960 N. Lake Shore Dr.
Posthuma, Matthew A. '69 '94 C.477 A.B. L.309 J.D. [Mayer,B.R.&M.]
Postilion, Laura G., (BV) '66 '94 C.424 B.A. L.365 J.D. [Hall,P.&S.]
Postlewaite, Philip F. '45 '70
C.840 B.B.A. L.112 J.D. Prof., Northwestern Univ. Sch. of Law
Potapova, Linda '— '01 C.999 B.S. L.880 J.D. [A] Schiff H.]
Potasiak, Joseph T. '56 '87 C.339 B.A. L.1187 J.D. Asst. Corp. Coun.

Potenza, Robert J. V. '50 '82 C.1044 B.A. L.107 J.D. 1535 W. Lunt Ave.
Poth, Tanya '73 '01 C.502 B.S. L.208 J.D. [A] Bollinger,R.&G.]
Potter, Aaron M. '— '03 C.1259 B.M. L.602 J.D. [A] Pircher,N.&M.]
Potter, Donald C. '31 '59 C&L.339 A.B., LL.B. 5338 S. Normandy‡
Potter, John W., (AV) '68 '93 C.861 B.A. L.146 J.D. [A] S.J.Haszto]
Potter, Julie K. '77 '02 C.976 B.A. L.1565 J.D. [A] Sidley A.B.&W.]
Potter, Robin B., (AV) '54 '78 C.563 B.A. L.352 J.D. [R.Potter&Assoc.]
Potter, Tracy L. '— '87 C.860 B.A. L.145 J.D. 10 S. Wacker Dr.
Potter, Robin, & Associates, P.C., (AV) 208 S. LaSalle Street, Suite 1615
Pottratz, Ruth Chodur '75 '01 C.351 B.A. L.221 J.D. Exelon Business Serv. Co.
Potts, J. Ryan '77 '02 C.339 B.S. L.209 J.D. [A] Clifford]
Potucek, Charlotte S. '— '97 C.597 B.A. L.339 J.D. [A] Sachnoff&W.]
Potym, Igor, (AV) '54 '80 C.959 B.A. L.436 J.D. [Vedder,P.K.&K.]
Pouk, Robert J. '55 '91 C.145 B.A. L.339 J.D. 5828 Archer Ave.
Poulakidas, Alexander G., (AV) '25 '50 C&L.209 J.D. 161 N. Clark St.
Poulakidas, Angelos G., (AV) '27 '50 C&L.209 J.D. 111 W. Washington St.
Poulakidas, Mark G. '68 '95 C.347 B.S. L.209 J.D. [Haynes,S.K.O.&M.]
Poullaos, Ivan M. '— '02 C.143 B.S. L.910 J.D. [A] Winston&S.]
Poulos, David T., (AV) '67 '92 C.339 B.A. L.46 J.D. [Knell&P.] ⊙
Poulos, Michael S., (AV) '61 '86 C.293 B.S. L.930 J.D. [DLPiper R.G.C.U.]
Poulos, Peter W. '68 '95 C.339 B.S. L.1066 J.D. [Winston&S.]
Poulos, Theodore T., (AV) '61 '87 C.679 B.A. L.424 J.D. [Cotsirilos,T.&S.]
Poust, Brian '65 '93 C.1101 B.A. L.339 J.D. 3419 N. Marshfield, #G‡
Poust, John G., (AV) '— '46 C&L.597 B.S.L., LL.B. [Dykema G.P.] ‡
Powalisz, Michael Stephan '74 '00 C.221 B.A. L.879 J.D. 162 W. Grand Ave.
Powell, Barry L. '51 '80 C.846 B.A. L.146 J.D.
Sr. V.P., Gen. Coun. & Secy., Starcom Mediavest Group, Inc.
Powell, Byron M. '34 '59 C.72 A.B. L.339 LL.B. V.P., Chicago Trust Co., The
Powell, Charles A. '42 '71 C.596 B.A. L.674 J.D. [Powell&R.]
Powell, Connie Davis '75 '00 C.575 B.A. L.1119 J.D. Global Hyatt Corporation
Powell, Ernest N., Jr. '30 '57 L.365 LL.B. 8110 S. Cottage Ave.
Powell, Harlan C. '69 '98 C.597 B.A. L.464 J.D. [A] Webster W.C.]
Powell, Joan E. '48 '92 C.446 B.A. L.365 J.D. 1509 W. Jackson Blvd.
Powell, Lewis W., III, Law Office of '57 '90
C.589 B.A. L.365 J.D. 53 W. Jackson Blvd., Ste. 1519
Powell, Victoria A. '51 '82 C.589 B.A. L.339 J.D. 3930 North Pine Grove Avenue
Powell, William H. '19 '47 C.340 B.S. L.209 J.D. 5479 N. Milwaukee Ave.‡
Powell & Reilly, P.C. 111 West Washington Street Suite 955
Powen, John T. '63 '88 C.339 B.S. L.365 J.D. [B] Smith O.&W.]
Power, Berve M. '75 '98 C.511 B.A. L.209 J.D. [Power&D.]
Power, Elizabeth Anne '72 '99 C.475 B.A. L.879 J.D.
Asst. Dir., New Member Programs, American Bar Assoc.
Power, John M., (AV) '62 '88 C&L.424 B.B.A., J.D. [A] Cogan&M.]
Power, Joseph A., Jr., (AV) '52 '77 C.602 B.A. L.424 J.D. [Power R.&S.]
Power, Justin J., (BV) '— '85 C.973 H.A.B. L.365 J.D. [Hilbert,L.&P.]
Power, Margaret M., (AV) '43 '86 C.262 B.A. L.424 J.D. [A] Corboy&D.]
Power, Melinda L. '53 '80 C.276 B.A. L.284 J.D. West Town Community Law Office
Power, Thomas M., (AV) '57 '85 C.757 B.A. L.364 J.D. [A] Power R.&S.]
Power, William R., (AV) '55 '81 C.339 B.S. L.209 J.D. 4211 S. Lowe‡
Power & Dixon 123 West Madison, Suite 900

Power Rogers & Smith, P.C., (AV) BB
70 West Madison Street, 55th Floor, 60602
Telephone: 312-236-9381 Fax: 312-236-0920
Email: law@prslaw.com URL: http://www.prslaw.com
Joseph A. Power, Jr.; Larry R. Rogers; Todd A. Smith;—Thomas G. Siracusa; Thomas M. Power; Larry R. Rogers, Jr.; Devon C. Bruce; Joseph W. Balesteri; Sean M. Houlihan; Brian LaCien.
Plaintiffs Personal Injury and Wrongful Death, Litigation, Including Aviation, Medical and Professional Negligence, FELA, Products Liability, Premises Liability, Construction Accidents and Vehicular Accidents.
See Professional Biographies, CHICAGO, ILLINOIS

Powers, Brian P. '66 '92 C.446 B.S. L.365 J.D. Legal Svc., U.S. Navy
Powers, Dennis J., (AV) '58 '83 C.927 B.S. L.209 J.D. [DLPiper R.G.C.U.]
Powers, Erika K. '— '94 C.27 B.A. L.477 J.D. [B] Barnes&T.]
Powers, Francis J. '13 '37 C.707 A.B. L.588 LL.B.
(adm. in MA; not adm. in IL) Loyola Univ.
Powers, Howard J., II '68 '97 C.37 B.S. L.809 J.D. [Weitzman&P.]
Powers, James J. '70 '98 C.597 B.A. L.146 J.D. [A] Seyfarth S.]
Powers, John E. '38 '63 C&L.424 A.B., J.D. Chi. Transit Auth.
Powers, John W., (AV) '49 '76 C.309 A.B. L.94 J.D. [Seyfarth S.]
Powers, Michael J. '57 '84 C.927 B.B.A. L.339 J.D. [Defrees&F.]
Powers, Philip T. '47 '73 C.823 B.A. L.477 J.D. 657 W. Wellington
Powers, Richard A. '47 '72 C.121 B.S. L.597 J.D. Contl. Ill. Nat. Bk. & Tr. Co.
Powers, Rita Alliss '64 '90 C.210 B.A. L.880 J.D. [Greenberg T.]
Powers, Robin K. '67 '92 C.659 B.A. L.597 J.D. [Rothschild,B.&M.]
Powers, Theodore J., (BV) '55 '93 C.339 B.A. L.46 J.D. [Rusin M.&F.]
Powis, Kelly '— '02 C.475 B.A. L.1119 J.D. [A] Gardner C.&D.]
Powles, Peter B. '36 '58 C&L.050 B.A., LL.B. 130 E. Randolph Dr.
Poynter, Pamela F. Sorensen '52 '85 C.339 B.S. L.146 J.D.
Legal Aid Bureau of United Charities of Chicago
Pozdol, Richard J. '40 '66 C&L.424 B.A., J.D.
V.P. & Sr. Underwriting Coun., Chicago Title Ins. Co.
Pozen, Joseph P. '57 '93 C.597 B.A. L.209 J.D. [Bates&C.]
Prager, Mark L., (AV) '— '76 C.339 B.A. L.910 J.D. [Foley&L.]
Pramuk, Daniel A., (AV⑦) '46 '72 C.347 A.B. L.1119 J.D.
(adm. in OH; not adm. in IL) 1515 N. Astor Street
Pranger, James R., (AV) '60 '85 C.424 B.A. L.339 J.D. [Chuhak&T.]
Prangle, Michael E., (AV) '64 '90 C.378 B.S. L.339 J.D. [Hall,P.&S.]
Prasad, Ashish S. '67 '94 C.477 A.B. L.145 J.D. [Mayer,B.R.&M.]
Pratt, Andrew F. '70 '98 C.911 B.S. L.831 J.D. [A] Baniak P.&G.] (See Pat. Sect.)
Pratt, Robert W., (AV) '50 '75 C.967 A.B. L.976 J.D. Asst. Atty. Gen.
Pratt, Thomas K., (AV) '— '92 C&L.378 B.S.E.E., J.D. [Banner&W.] (See Pat. Sect.)
Pravecek, Jody B. '70 '95 C.401 B.A. L.365 J.D. [A] Cogan&M.]
Prayor, Sharon E. '59 '91 C.338 B.S. L.46 J.D. Chicago Park District
Prebil, Richard L., (AV) '— '79 C.339 B.A. L.734 J.D. [B] Foley&L.]
Prebish, Steven M. '65 '90 C&L.339 B.A., J.D. [Patzik,F.&S.]
Preece, Lynn S. '— '81 L.424 J.D. [Baker&M.]
Preece, Nora A. '70 '02 C.339 B.A. L.146 J.D. [B] Alter&W.]
Preiner, Barbara Ann '50 '75 C.339 B.A. L.424 J.D. Solr. Gen.
Prell, Frances E. '49 '78 C.234 B.A. L.339 J.D. [Holland&K.]
Prena, Karen L. '60 '89 C.602 B.A. L.569 J.D. [B] Mayer,B.R.&M.]
Prendergast, James, (AV) '53 '80 C.1082 B.A. L.589 J.D. [A] R.J.Prendergast]
Prendergast, Jean M. '— '94 C&L.424 B.A., J.D. [Crisham&K.]
Prendergast, Richard F. '25 '55 C&L.209 B.S.C., J.D. 175 W. Jackson Blvd.‡
Prendergast, Richard J., (AV) '45 '69 C&L.424 B.B.A., J.D. [R.J.Prendergast]
Prendergast, Robert J. '54 '81 C.339 B.S. L.146 J.D. [A] K.J.Wysoglad&Assoc.]

Prendergast, William F., (AV) '65 '90
C.424 B.S. L.339 J.D. [Brinks H.G.&L.] (See Pat. Sect.)

Prendergast, Richard J., Ltd., (AV)
111 West Washington-Suite 1100, 60602-2768
Telephone: 312-641-0881 Fax: 312-641-3562
Email: lawfirm@rjpltd.com URL: http://www.rjpltd.com
Richard J. Prendergast;—James Prendergast; Michael T. Layden; Deirdre Ann Close; Jennifer M. Ryder.
General Trial and Appellate Practice. Personal Injury, Antitrust, Securities and Commercial Litigation.
See Professional Biographies, CHICAGO, ILLINOIS

Prendiville, John R. .... '62 '88 C.234 B.A. L.209 J.D. Sr. Coun., The Bank of NY
Prero, Elisha M., (AV) .... '54 '81 C.424 B.A. L.477 J.D. [Schuyler,R.&Z.]
Presser, Jay E. .... '70 '96 C.107 B.A. L.117 J.D. [Ⓐ Fuchs&R.]
Presser, Stephen B. '46 '71 C&L.309 A.B., J.D.
(adm. in MA; not adm. in IL) Prof., N. western Univ. Sch. of Law
Pressman, Charles, (P.C.), (AV) .... '22 '51 C&L.145 A.B., J.D. 120 S. Riverside Plz
Preston, Henry A., (AV) .... '19 '49 C.976 A.B. L.309 J.D. Bank One Plz.‡
Preston, Lee S. .... '44 '72 C.339 B.S. L.209 J.D. Cir. J.
Preston, Peter J. .... '70 '95 C&L.472 B.B.A., J.D. [Ⓐ Sedgwick,D.M.&A.]
Preston, Stanley W., III '66 '97 C.608 B.S. L.146 J.D.
Corp. Coun., Alaron Trading Corp.
Pretekin, Louis .... '57 '82 C.477 A.B. L.880 J.D. Imperial Real Co.

Pretzel & Stouffer, Chartered, (AV) [BB]
One South Wacker Drive Suite 2500, 60606-4673
Telephone: 312-346-1973 FAX: 312-346-8242; 346-8060
URL: http://www.pretzel-stouffer.com
Cynthia H. Alkhouja; Scott L. Anderson; Darryl L. Awick; Rena A. Ballard; David M. Bennett; Brendan M. Burns; Christopher C. Cassidy; Robert Marc Chemers; Michael A. Clarke; Brendan S. Crowley; Suzanne Marie Crowley; Mary H. Cusack; Melissa Giovanini Deptula; Matthew J. Egan; William W. Elinski; Michael A. Faccenda; Patrick F. Healy, III; Kim M. Heffernan; Marcie L. Hefler; Brian T. Henry; Andrew J. Holen; Scott Langford Howie; Christine J. Iversen; Priya K. Jesani; Belle L. Katubig; Richard P. Kenyon; James A. LaBarge; Thomas A. Lang, II; Matthew J. Ligda; Daniel B. Mills; Lisa M. Moore; Patricia B. Mueller; Brendan J. Nelligan; Edward H. Nielsen; Caitlin O'Connor; Donald J. O'Meara, Jr.; David S. Osborne; Howard J. Pikel; Neil K. Quinn; Mark S. Ratner; Charles F. Redden; D. Scott Rendleman; Brian C. Rocca; Edward B. Ruff, III; Miguel A. Ruiz; Steven W. Ryan; Lewis M. Schneider; Alan J. Schumacher; Robert E. Sidkey; Richard J. Siebert; James J. Sipchen, Jr.; Kathryn A. Smetana; John V. Smith, II; Jane Solmor-Mordini; Brian C. Sundheim; Amy J. Thompson; Michael P. Turiello; Stephen C. Veltman; Anne E. Wall; John J. Walsh, III; Richard M. Waris; Timothy A. Weaver; Daniel G. Wills; Alan S. Zelkowitz. Of Counsel: Paula Meyer Besler; Paul W. Pretzel (1906-1987); Ralph E. Stouffer, Jr.
General Civil Litigation, Dispute Resolution, Trial and Appellate Practice. Insurance, Environmental, Corporate, Commercial, Probate, Tax, Real Estate, Employee Benefits, Construction and Admiralty Law.
See Professional Biographies, CHICAGO, ILLINOIS

Preusse, Karin Wray .... '— '04 C.339 B.S. L.145 J.D. [Ⓐ Kirkland&E.]
Prewitt, Matthew .... '73 '96 C.206 B.A. L.145 J.D. [Ⓐ Greenberg T.]
Prezant, Eric S. .... '70 '97 C.259 B.S. L.365 J.D. [Vedder,P.K.&K.]
Price, Charles T., (AVⓉ) .... '44 '69 C.611 B.A. L.309 J.D. [Ⓖ Bell,B.&L.]
Price, Derke J. .... '63 '88 C.937 B.A. L.309 J.D. [Ancel,G.D.B.D.&R.]
Price, Paul L., (AV) .... '45 '71 C.424 B.B.A. L.146 J.D. [Price T.R.]
Price, Ralph M. .... '60 '92 C&L.424 B.S., J.D. 6255 N. Newark Ave.
Price, Roger L., (AV) .... '44 '68 C.477 B.A. L.145 J.D. [Seyfarth S.]
Price, Sarah E. .... '73 '99 C.477 B.A. L.1375 J.D. 20 N. Clark St.
Price, William S., (AV) .... '42 '68 C.208 B.S.B.A. L.597 J.D. [Bell,B.&L.]

Price Tunney Reiter, A Professional Corporation, (AV)
123 N. Wacker Drive, Suite 2220, 60606
Telephone: 312-230-9100 Fax: 312-230-9201
URL: http://www.ptrlaw.com
Paul L. Price; Anthony J. Tunney; Catherine Coyne Reiter; Steven John Martin;—Dina L. Torrisi; Daniel J. Deleo; Robert E. Elworth; Christopher Richard Reinkall; Jeffrey Tabares.
Trial and Appellate Practice in State and Federal Courts. Alternative Dispute Resolution, Litigation Prevention, Health Care Professionals Liability, Legal Malpractice, Accountant's Malpractice, Hospital Litigation, Products Liability, Premises Liability, Commercial Litigation, Fraud, Real Estate Broker and Insurance Agent Errors and Omissions, Nursing Home Litigation, Insurance Coverage Disputes, Breach of Lease, Toxic Tort Litigation, Contract Disputes, Environmental Litigation.
See Professional Biographies, CHICAGO, ILLINOIS

Priess, Howard K., II, (AV) .... '44 '71 C.597 B.S. L.146 J.D. [Tressler,S.M.&P.]
Prihoda, Virginia D. .... '50 '92 C.597 B.S. L.146 J.D. [V.Prihoda]

Prihoda, Virginia, Law Offices of
7551 North Oakley Avenue, 60645
Telephone: 773-262-1712 Fax: 847-589-8072 URL: http://www.prihodalaw.com
Email: virginiaprihoda@hotmail.com URL: http://www.virginiaprihoda.com
Virginia D. Prihoda.
Taxation, Tax Consulting, Tax Audits, Collection Matters, Wills, Trusts, Living Trusts, Insurance Trusts, Guardianships, Powers of Attorney, Living Wills, Gifts to Minors, Probate, Tax Planning, Estate Planning, Tax and Estate Planning for Senior Citizens, Income Tax Return Preparation, Business Entity Planning, Business Succession Planning, Business Tax Planning, Representation before the Internal Revenue Service, IRS Liens, IRS Offers in Compromise.
See Professional Biographies, CHICAGO, ILLINOIS

Primack, Marc A., (AV) .... '52 '77 C.145 B.A. L.813 J.D. [Dykema G.P.]
Prince, James E. .... '71 '99 C.385 B.A. L.1066 J.D. 180 N. La Salle St., Ste. 3850
Prince, Matthew Browning .... '74 '01 C.855 B.A. L.145 J.D. [Unspain]
Prince, Venus McGhee .... '— '98 C.309 B.A. L.1375 J.D. [Ⓐ Sachnoff&W.]
Prindable, Thomas K., (AV) .... '43 '73 C.999 B.A. L.146 J.D. [Clifford]
Prins, Richard H., (AV) .... '23 '50 C.118 B.A. L.145 J.D. 33 N. Dearborn St.‡
Priola, Victoria C. .... '69 '96 C.679 B.A. L.209 J.D. [Ⓐ Madsen,F.&P.]
Prioleau, Jennifer A. .... '— '02 C.860 B.A. L.597 J.D. [Ⓐ Brinks H.G.&L.]
Prior, Gary L., (AV) .... '43 '68 C.861 B.S. L.145 J.D. [Tabet D.&R.]
Pristave, Robert J., P.C. .... '42 '67 C.145 B.A. L.597 J.D. [McGuirewoods]
Pristelski, James S., (AV) '43 '73
C.966 B.S.E.E. L.352 J.D. [Cook,A.M.M.C.&M.] (See Pat. Sect.)
Pristo, Christine M. .... '67 '92 50 S. La Salle St.
Pritchard, David J., (AV) .... '52 '77 C.424 B.B.A. L.209 J.D. [Salvi,S.&P.]
Pritchard, J. Brett .... '62 '90 C.67 B.A. L.188 J.D. [Lord,B.&B.]
Pritikin, David T., (AV) .... '49 '74 C.188 A.B. L.309 J.D. [Sidley A.B.&W.]
Pritikin, James B., (AV) .... '39 '65 C.339 B.S. L.209 J.D. [Nadler,P.&M.]
Pritikin, Renee Zarbin .... '— '59 C&L.597 B.S., J.D. Admin. Hearing Offr.‡
Prittis, Nickolas Kosmas .... '73 '00 C.424 B.S. L.146 J.D. Legal Advocates Group
Pritzker, Daniel F. .... '59 '88 C.860 B.A. L.597 J.D. [Pritzker&P.]
Pritzker, J. B. .... '65 '94 C.228 B.A. L.589 J.D. New World Equities
Pritzker, Jay A., (AV) .... '22 '47 C&L.597 B.S., J.D. [Pritzker&P.]
Pritzker, Penny Sue, (AV) .... '59 '85 C.309 B.A. L.813 J.D. [Pritzker&P.]
Pritzker, Thomas J., (AV) .... '50 '76 C&L.145 M.B.A., J.D. [Pritzker&P.]
Pritzker & Pritzker, (AV) .... 200 W. Madison
Prochnow, Douglas L., (AV) .... '52 '77 C.546 B.A. L.597 J.D. [Wildman,H.A.&D.]
Prochnow, Herbert V., Jr., (AV) .... '31 '57 C&L.309 A.B., J.D. 155 N. Michigan Ave.

Proctor, Carol, (AV) .... '51 '85 C.58 B.A. L.209 J.D. [Hinshaw&C.]
Proctor, Darcy L. .... '63 '88 C&L.424 B.A., J.D. [Ancel,G.D.B.D.&R.]
Proctor, Edward G., Jr., (AV) .... '62 '89 C.339 B.S. L.424 J.D. [Munday&N.]
Proctor, Stephen M. '— '82 C.347 B.A. L.1119 J.D.
[Masuda,F.E.&M.] (ⓒSchaumburg)
Procyk, Kalyna A. .... '76 '04 C.918 B.A. L.146 J.D. [Ⓐ DLPiper R.G.C.U.]
Proczko, Taras R. '54 '80 C.750 B.A. L.365 J.D.
Sr. V.P., Gen. Coun., & Secy., Hartmarx Corp.
Proffitt, Susan R. .... '60 '93 C.347 B.S. L.424 J.D. [Ⓖ Mayer,B.R.&M.]
Progar, Michael J., (BV) .... '53 '81 C.602 B.A. L.209 J.D. [Doherty&P.] ⓒ
Prohofsky, David S. .... '— '99 C.475 B.A. L.276 J.D. [Ⓐ Skadden,A.S.M.&F.]
Prohov, Fredric B. .... '54 '79 C.339 B.A. L.209 J.D. 30 North La Salle Street
Proietti, Ralph Anthony .... '61 '86 C.339 B.A. L.209 J.D. Asst. State's Atty.
Projansky, Sidney H. .... '35 '61 L.209 LL.B. 6043 N. Central Park Ave.
Prommer, Peter J. '— '03
C&L.339 B.S.C.E., J.D. [Ⓐ McAndrews,H.&M.] (See Pat. Sect.)
Propes, Lorna E., (AV) .... '— '75 C.347 B.S. L.424 J.D. [Propes&K.]

Propes & Kaveny, L.L.C., (AV)
833 West Jackson, Suite 200, 60607
Telephone: 312-334-3111 Fax: 312-829-3367 URL: http://www.pktrialaw.com
Email: propes@pktriallaw.com URL: http://www.lawyers.com/propeskaveny
Lorna E. Propes; Elizabeth A. Kaveny;—David R. Nordwall. Of Counsel: Patricia C. Bobb.
Medical Malpractice, including Failure to Diagnose, Birth Trauma, Obstetrics, Surgical, Oncological, Cardiac, Urological, Neurosurgical and Psychiatric Malpractice; Products Liability, Personal Injury.
See Professional Biographies, CHICAGO, ILLINOIS

Propp, Eugene, (AV) .... '21 '47 C&L.209 J.D. [Propp&S.]
Propp & Schultz, (AV) .... 19 S. La Salle St.
Prosperi, Mark S., (AV) .... '46 '73 C&L.424 B.S., J.D. Asst. U.S. Atty.
Prosser, Raymond J., (AV) .... '47 '74 C.597 B.A. L.365 J.D. [R.J.Prosser]
Prosser, Raymond J., Ltd., (AV) .... 105 W. Madison St.
Prossnitz, Howard B. .... '— '76 C.311 B.A. L.813 J.D. [Ⓖ Birndorf&B.]
Prousis, Danae K., (AV) '49 '75 C.597 B.A. L.228 J.D.
V.P., Legal Servs. & Gen. Coun., Northwestern Med. Found., Inc.
Prout, Susan W. .... '58 '85 C.399 B.A. L.424 J.D. Assoc. Reg. Coun., U.S. EPA
Provencher, Jennifer M.K. .... '77 '04 C.999 B.S. L.209 J.D. [Ⓐ Vedder,P.K.&K.]
Provenzano, Ronald C. .... '66 '91 C&L.339 B.S., J.D. Gen. Coun., Huron Corp.
Provis, Peggy .... '74 '99 C&L.424 B.A., J.D. Fireman's Fund Ins Co
Provost, Christine A. .... '65 '91 C.659 B.A. L.597 J.D. 660 W. Wrightwood
Pruchnicki, Raymond H. .... '— '99 C.350 B.S. L.209 J.D. [Ⓐ Freeborn&P.]
Prudden, Gerard William .... '56 '85 C.927 B.A. L.796 J.D. 77 W Washington St.
Pruhs, Nicholas C. .... '73 '01 C.215 B.S. L.966 J.D. [Ⓐ Wallenstein W.&R.]
Prusak, Raymond L., Law Office of '55 '80
C.424 B.A. L.365 J.D. 1021 W. Adams, Suite 102
Prusiecki, John F., Law Offices of, (AV) '48 '75
C.477 B.A. L.597 J.D. 30 S. Wacker Dr., Ste. 2200
Prusik, John P., (AV) .... '45 '75 C.999 B.A. L.424 J.D. [Prusik S.D.&K.]

Prusik Selby Daley & Kezelis, P.C., (AV)
209 West Jackson Boulevard, Suite 900, 60606
Telephone: 312-427-4700 Fax: 312-427-8090
Email: advocates@psdlegal.com
John P. Prusik; Terence R. Selby; John J. Daley III; Algimantas Kezelis;—Louise L. Daley; Daniel J. Connell.
Insurance Defense, Product Liability, Class Actions, Medical Negligence, Toxic Torts, Construction, Environmental, FELA, Asbestos, Contract Coverage, Consumer Products and Workers' Compensation, plus ADR and Arbitration, First Response Claim Investigation.
See Professional Biographies, CHICAGO, ILLINOIS

Pruzan, Gloria E. .... '54 '78 C.107 B.A. L.597 J.D. Legal Assist. Found. of Chicago
Prygrosky, Carol R. .... '— '87 C.347 B.A. L.966 J.D. [Schiff H.]
Pryor, Kevin R. .... '70 '97 C.101 B.A. L.145 J.D. [Ⓐ Sidley A.B.&W.]
Prypchan, Andre Bohdan '54 '80 C.424 B.A. L.209 J.D.
Asst. Dist. Coun., U.S. Army Corps of Engrs.
Prysak, Suzanne J. .... '71 '97 C&L.477 B.A., J.D. [Jenner&B.]
Pryst, Laura E. .... '74 '01 C&L.352 B.A., J.D. [Ⓐ N.R.Novak]
Przybylo, Chester M. .... '— '65 C.276 A.B. L.146 J.D. 5339 N. Milwaukee Ave.
Ptacek, Edward A., (AV) .... '41 '70 C.966 B.S. L.424 J.D. Asst. Pub. Def. (Pat.)
Ptak, Edwin A. .... '51 '77 C&L.602 B.A., J.D. Corp. Coun., Pepes Inc.
Ptasinski, Martin .... '76 '02 C.477 B.A. L.912 J.D. [M.Ptasinski]
Ptasinski, Martin, P.C., Law Offices of .... 5725 S. Archer Ave.
Puchalski, Connie Lou '58 '81
C.209 B.S. L.146 J.D. U.S. Environmental Protection Agency
Puchalski, Donald, (AV) .... '54 '79 C.209 B.A. L.365 J.D. [D.E.Puchalski]
Puchalski, Richard J., (AV) .... '46 '70 L.365 J.D. 111 W. Washington St.
Puchalski, Donald E., Law Offices of, (AV) .... 111 W. Washington St., Ste. 1000
Pucin, John S. .... '66 '92 C.973 B.A. L.117 J.D. [Weltman,W.&R.] (ⓒDeerfield)
Puckelwartz, Christopher M. .... '72 '97 C.339 B.A. L.424 J.D. [Ⓐ BryceDowney]
Pucker, Michael A. .... '— '89 C&L.178 B.A., J.D. [Latham&W.]
Pugh, Donna J., (AV) .... '58 '83 C.260 B.A. L.424 J.D. [Vedder,P.K.&K.]
Pugh, Stephen H., Jr., (AV) .... '42 '73 C&L.424 A.B., J.D. [Pugh,J.J.&Q.]
Pugh, Todd S. .... '67 '97 C.1086 B.A. L.209 J.D. 53 W. Jackson Blvd., Ste. 1460

Pugh, Jones, Johnson & Quandt, P.C., (AV)
180 North La Salle Street, Suite 3400, 60601
Telephone: 312-768-7800 Fax: 312-768-7801
URL: http://www.PJJQ.com
Stephen H. Pugh, Jr.; Walter Jones Jr.; Dennis P. W. Johnson; Eric F. Quandt; Jorge V. Cazares; Scott A. Bremer; Linzey D. Jones, Jr.; Mary K. Periolat; Carole A. Corns; Kim Barker Lee; Daniel A. Rowin; LaVon M. Johns; Mark D. Andrews; Eduardo M. Cotillas;—Paul C. Do; Gil R. Cubia. Of Counsel: Thomas N. Harding.
Complex Civil and White Collar Criminal Litigation, Employment Discrimination, Management and Labor Law, Drug and Medical Device Litigation, Pharmaceutical Litigation, Medical Malpractice, Trade Secrets, Contract and Commercial Litigation, Mediation and Arbitration, Products Liability, Patent Litigation, Antitrust, RICO, Securities, Banking Litigation, Business Fraud and Tort Litigation, Local Government Defense, Real Estate, Corporate Transactions and Public Finance.
See Professional Biographies, CHICAGO, ILLINOIS

Puglia, Nina .... '58 '88 C.881 B.A. L.597 J.D. Asst. Corp. Coun., Appeals Div.
Pugliese, Kevin M. .... '69 '94 C.436 B.A. L.209 J.D. [Ⓐ Fisher K.]
Pugliese, Maria S. .... '71 '98 C.602 B.A. L.597 J.D. [Ⓐ Baker&M.]
Pugliese, Robert J., (AV) .... '53 '78 C.221 B.A. L.339 J.D. [Lord,B.&B.]
Puiszis, Steven M., (AV) .... '54 '79 C.209 B.S. L.424 J.D. [Hinshaw&C.]
Pulcanio, Stephanie J. .... '— '02 C.207 B.A. L.146 J.D. [Ⓐ Seyfarth S.]
Puljic, Ivan .... '72 '98 C.424 B.A. L.146 J.D. [Huff&G.]
Pullano, Richard L., Law Offices of, (AV) '57 '82
C.602 B.B.A. L.209 J.D. 100 W. Monroe St., 19th Fl.
Pullappally, Ligy J. ..... '69 '95 C.339 B.A. L.424 J.D. Lifespan Center for Legal Services
Pulmanova, Barbora '77 '04 C&L.209 B.A., J.D.
(adm. in CA; not adm. in IL) [Ⓐ Tressler,S.M.&P.] (ⓒCosta Mesa, CA)
Puma, Scott A., (BV) .... '68 '93 C.602 B.A. L.424 J.D. [Ⓐ Ancel,G.D.B.D.&R.]

Puplis, A. Ryan ....'74 '00 C.339 B.A. L.146 J.D. Trans. Atty., Accenture LLP
Purcell, Amy P. ....'— '03 C&L.477 B.A., J.D. [Ⓐ Foley&L.]
Purcell, Andrew J. .... '74 '99 C.234 B.A. L.365 J.D. [Ⓐ Tressler,S.M.&P.]
Purcell, Charles R. .... '31 '56 C&L.424 B.S., J.D. Prof. of Law, Loyola Univ.
Purcell, Christopher H. ....'71 '98 L.209 J.D. 407 S. Dearborn
Purcell, Edward C., (AV) .... '32 '63 C.424 L.365 LL.B. [Purcell&W.]
Purcell, Kenneth P. .... '54 '89 C&L.352 B.A., J.D. [Ⓐ Winston&S.]
Purcell, William L. ....'22 '51 C.209 L.365 LL.B. 300 S. Wacker Dr.‡
Purcell & Wardrope, Chtd., (AV) ....10 S. LaSalle St., Ste. 1200
Purdom, Daniel M. ....'52 '78 C.338 B.S. L.801 J.D. [Hinshaw&C.] (⊙Lisle)
Purevich-Cardenas, Katherine A. '70 '96
C.347 B.S. L.424 J.D. 77 W. Washington St., Ste. 900
Puri, Vik ....'— '93 C.339 B.A. L.94 J.D. [Latham&W.]
Purmal, Marthe C., (AV) ....'42 '66 C.597 B.A. L.146 J.D. [Ⓐ J.P.Greene&Assoc.]
Purnell, Edward A. .... '— '90 C.674 B.A. L.309 J.D. [Jones D.]
Purves, Samuel A., (AV) ....'— '66 C.813 A.B. L.477 J.D. [Ⓒ McKenna S.]
Puryear Jonas, Valerie R. ......'76 '04 C.436 B.A. L.424 J.D. [Ⓐ Momkus M.M.M.M.&S.]
Pusemp, Christina A. ....'75 '03 C.209 B.A. L.629 J.D. [Ⓐ Giordano&N.]
Putlak, Kenneth J. .... '39 '65 C&L.339 A.B., LL.B. 4340 S. Spaulding Ave.
Putnick, Joseph J. ....'44 '73 221 N. LaSalle St.
Putta, Barbara J., (AV) .... '46 '75 C.339 B.A. L.597 J.D. [Ⓒ Butler R.S.&B.]
Pyes, Harvey, (AV) ....'30 '54 C.221 B.A. L.209 J.D. [Pyes&C.]

Pyes & Cherin, LLP, (AV)
29 South La Salle Street Suite 1100, 60603
Telephone: 312-236-5888 Fax: 312-236-1288
Email: pyescherin@usa.net
Harvey Pyes; Steven Cherin;—Charles V. Kwasniewski; Marietta L. Kerr.
General, Civil Practice including Banking, Commercial, Collection, Personal Injury, Corporate, Family and Real Estate.

See Professional Biographies, CHICAGO, ILLINOIS

Pykosz, Carolyn A. ....'80 '05 C.345 B.A. L.424 J.D. [Gozdecki&D.]
Pyle, Russell W., (AV) .... '41 '66 C.694 B.A.Chem. L.966 J.D. [Pyle&P.] (Pat.)
Pyle & Piontek, (AV) .... 221 North La Salle Street, Suite 850 (Pat.)
Pyszka, Kathryn A. '64 '89
C.966 B.A. L.339 J.D. Sr. Trial Coun., Chicago, M.R.O., S.E.C.
Qasim, Imad I. ....'57 '83 C.299 A.B. L.276 J.D. [Sidley A.B.&W.]

Qiu, Peter Y., Law Offices of '61 '98 C.999 B.A. L.146 J.D.
736 W. 35th Street, 60616
Telephone: 773-843-9808 Fax: 773-843-9812
Email: pyqlawfirm@sbcglobal.net URL: http://www.lawyers.com/pqiulaw
Languages: Chinese and Spanish.
Business Litigation, Commercial Litigation, Collection of Judgments, Bankruptcy, Immigration, Civil Litigation, Personal Injury, Workers Compensation, Real Estate, Family Law, Wills and Probate, Trusts and Estates, Estate Planning, Criminal Defense, Copyrights.

See Professional Biographies, CHICAGO, ILLINOIS

Quader, Salmaan ....'— '04 C.475 B.A. L.213 J.D. [Ⓐ Howrey]
Quaid, Dennis E., (AV) ....'— '70 C.339 B.A. L.209 J.D. [FagelHaber]
Quaini, Duane C., (AV) .... '45 '70 C.145 B.A. L.813 J.D. [Sonnenschein N.&R.]
Quam, Lester ....'58 '83 C.472 B.S. L.365 J.D. Spec. Asst. Atty. Gen.
Quanbeck, Maridee A., (AV) .... '46 '76 C.906 B.A. L.309 J.D. 105 W. Delaware, Unit G
Quandt, Eric F., (AV) ....'51 '76 C&L.966 B.S., J.D. [Pugh,J.J.&Q.]

Quarles & Brady LLP, (AV) BR
Citicorp Center, 500 West Madison Street, Suite 3700, 60661-2511 ⊙
Telephone: 312-715-5000 Fax: 312-715-5155
URL: http://www.quarles.com
Partners: Patrick J. Bitterman; Thomas E. Chomicz; Gary R. Clark; Melanie Rovner Cohen; Christopher Combest; Faye B. Feinstein; Robert F. Forrer; H. James Fox; Eric J. Fuglsang; Robert L. Gamrath III; James J. Gatziolis; Mark J. Horne; John A. Klages; Gary H. Kline; Janine M. Landow-Esser; Sarah M. Linsley; Thomas J. Magill; John A. McDonald; Kendall R. Meyer; Michael S. Mostow; Thomas A. Polachek; Janice E. Rodgers; Peter A. Sarasek (Managing Partner, Chicago Office); Leonard S. Shifflett; John P. Vail; D. Scott Watson. Associates: Sowmya Bharathi; Joel A. Brodsky; Meridith G. Cannon; Christopher T. De Ment; Jennifer Dorn; Ellen Marie Girard; Charles E. Harper, Jr.; Jeremy C. Kleinman; Thomas A. McCarthy; David T. Meek; Brendan O'Connor; Benjamin L. Schneider; Monica Maria Tynan.
General Corporate Practice, including Administrative, Antitrust, Trade Regulation and Franchising, Creditors' Rights and Bankruptcy, Business Planning, Commercial, Community Associations and Country Clubs, Construction, Corporate Finance and Securities, E-Commerce, Employee Benefits, Energy and Telecommunications, Environmental, Estate Planning, Exempt Organizations, Family, Financial Institutions, Government Relations, Hospital and Health, Immigration, Insurance, Intellectual Property, International, Labor and Employment (Management), Litigation (Civil, Products Liability, Toxic Tort and Environmental Defense), Mergers and Acquisitions, Municipal, Privately Held Businesses, Public Finance, Real Estate and Land Use, School, Taxation and White Collar Crime.
Milwaukee, Wisconsin Office: Quarles & Brady LLP, 411 East Wisconsin Avenue, Suite 2040, 53202-4497. Telephone: 414-277-5000. Fax: 414-271-3552.
Madison, Wisconsin Office: One South Pinckney Street, Suite 600, P.O. Box 2113, 53701-2113. Telephone: 608-251-5000. Fax: 608-251-9166.
Naples, Florida Office: 1395 Panther Lane, 34109-7874. Telephone: 239-262-5959. Fax: 239-434-4999.
Boca Raton, Florida Office: One Lincoln Place, 1900 Glades Road, Suite 355, 33431. Telephone: 561-368-5400. Fax: 561-368-1996.
Phoenix, Arizona Office: Quarles & Brady Streich Lang, LLP, One Renaissance Square, Two North Central Avenue, 85004-2391. Telephone: 602-229-5200. Fax: 602-229-5690.
Tucson, Arizona Office: Quarles & Brady Streich Lang, LLP, One South Church Avenue, Suite 1700, 85701-1621. Telephone: 520-770-8700. Fax: 520-623-2418.
Reviser of the Wisconsin Law Digest for this Directory.

See Professional Biographies, CHICAGO, ILLINOIS

Queen, Craig D., (BV) '65 '91 C.210 B.A. L.46 J.D.
550 W. Washington Blvd., Ste. 1600
Quentel, Debra L. ....'57 '88 C&L.966 B.M., J.D. 565 W. Adams St.

Querrey & Harrow, Ltd., (AV)
175 West Jackson Boulevard, Suite 1600, 60604-2827 ⊙
Telephone: 312-540-7000 Fax: 312-540-0578
URL: http://www.querrey.com
Paul A. Rettberg; Ronald M. Jerrick; Kevin J. Caplis; Dennis A. Marks; Robert P. Huebsch; James S. Jendryk (Resident, Wheaton Office); James N. Kosmond; Daniel F. Gallagher; Thomas P. Burke (Resident, Waukegan Office); Roger Littman; Charles E. Blackman, Jr.; Thomas C. Kaufmann; James M. Bream; Janet M. Farmans (Resident, Joliet Office); Anthony J. Madormo; David J. Flynn; Charles E. Whalen; Christopher R. Johnston; John M. Green; David E. Neumeister; Larry S. Kowalczyk; Michael B. Stillman (Resident, Joliet Office); Bruce H. Schoumacher; Thomas E. Stahr; Scott B. Krider; Jerome M. Sonnefeldt; George J. Vogrin, Jr. (Resident, New York, N.Y. Office); Kevin T. Salter (Resident, New York, N.Y. Office); Steven Helis; Jonathan E. Irwin; Karen M. Vivian; Sylvia Karalekas; Edward J. Kozel, Jr.; Jeffrey W. Clymer (Resident, Merrillville, Indiana Office); Lissa L. Hamer (Resident, Wheaton Office); R. John Anderson; Thomas J. Bracken (Resident, New York, N.Y. Office); David L. LaPorte; Mia M. Lucas (Resident, Crystal Lake Office); Jennifer J. Sackett Pohlenz; Timothy R. Rabel; Ellen E. Gibson (Resident, Waukegan Office); Anne M. Belanger; April R. Walkup; Terrence F. Guolee; Christine McAsey (Resident, Joliet Office); Gary C. Sachs (Resident, New York, N.Y., Office); David R. Peterson; Robert Eric Traul; Galen A. Bradley (Also at Merrilville, Indiana Office); Daniel A. Kirk;—Emily J. Bardelas; Barry C. Brotine; Mason L. Budelier; Ernie Burden; Megan A. Byrnes; Kevin M. Casey; Thomas Comstock; Omar J. Fayez; Paul L. Friman (Resident, New York, N.Y. Office); Michael J. Frimet (Resident, New York, N.Y. Office); Cynthia E. Garcia; Jennifer J. Gross; John H. Halstead (Resident, Merrillville, Indiana Office); Nicholas Johnson (Resident, Waukegan Office); Konstantinos Katsaros (Resident, New York, N.Y.

(This Listing Continued)

Querrey & Harrow, Ltd. (Continued)

Office); Brandon K. Lemley; Eileen E. Madda; Meghan P. McCarthy (Resident, New York, N.Y., Office); Lauren McSweeney (Resident, New York, N.Y., Office); Jennifer L. Medenwald; Jeanne M. Miller (Resident, Crystal Lake Office); Crystal D. Monahan (Resident, New York, NY Office); Evdoxia C. Nassopoulos; Angelique Palmer; Nickolas Pappas; Ryan J. Rodman; Jennifer M. Scarlett; Lawrence A. Steingold (Resident, Waukegan Office); Joan R. Stohl; Fuad R. Sulayman; Marie J. Taraska; Cynthia D. Traynor; Richard J. Turiello (Resident, Joliet Office); Joseph V. Vito. Of Counsel: Thomas P. Carney, Jr.; Donald C. Gancer; Nancy M. Hoffman; Robert F. Sharp; Lawrence S. Speyer.
General Civil and Trial Practice. Appellate, Banking, Commercial Litigation, Construction, Corporate, Dental, Employment, Environmental, Healthcare Liability, Insurance Coverage, Intellectual Property, Information Technology, Governmental Affairs/Government Procurement, Municipal Law, Personal Injury Defense, Product Liability, Professional Liability, Real Estate, Reinsurance, Tax, Transportation, Trusts, Estate Planning, Wills and Probate Law.
Crystal Lake, Illinois Office: 651 West Terra Cotta Avenue, Suite 221. Telephone: 815-479-1929. Fax: 815-479-1978.
Wheaton, Illinois Office: 310 South County Farm Road, Third Floor. Telephone: 630-653-2600. Fax: 630-653-0178.
Waukegan, Illinois Office: 415 West Washington Street, Suite 205. Telephone: 847-249-4440. Fax: 847-249-4932.
Joliet, Illinois Office: 2 Rialto Square, Suite 401, 116 North Chicago Street. Telephone: 815-726-1600. Fax: 815-726-1674.
Merrillville, Indiana Office: 8585 Broadway, Suite 510. Telephone: 219-738-1820. Fax: 219-738-1821.
New York, N.Y. Office: 120 Broadway, Suite 2800. Telephone: 212-233-0130. Fax: 212-233-0172.
London, England Office: 141-142 Fenchurch Street, Fifth Floor. Telephone: 207-929-6670. Fax: 207-929-6671.

See Professional Biographies, CHICAGO, ILLINOIS

Questal, Nina H. '52 '76 C&L.966 B.A., J.D.
(adm. in WI; not adm. in IL) 2735 N. Dayton St.‡
Quiceno, William A. ....'70 '97 C.209 B.A. L.879 J.D. 332 S. Michigan Ave.
Quick, Travis .... '— '03 C.338 B.A. L.339 J.D. [Ⓐ Kirkland&E.]
Quigg, Mary E. ....'62 '93 C.277 B.E. L.365 J.D. [Quigg&Assoc.]
Quigg & Associates, P.C. ....3336 N. Clifton Ave.
Quigley, James M. '66 '92 C.966 B.A. L.209 J.D.
[Beermann S.W.B.B.G.&L.] (⊙Bannockburn, Chicago)
Quigley, James M. '66 '92
C.966 B.A. L.209 J.D. [Quigley&Assoc.] (⊙Bannockburn, Chicago)
Quigley & Associates, P.C., Law Offices of
30 N. LaSalle Street, Suite 2340 (⊙Bannockburn)
Quijano, Alfred ....'74 '02 C.339 B.A. L.209 J.D. [Linebarger G.B.&S.]
Quilici, Peter A. .... '48 '81 C.1151 B.S. L.365 J.D. 300 W. Wash. St., 17th Fl.‡
Quinlan, William J. ....'— '95 C.339 B.A. L.275 J.D. [Quinlan&C.]
Quinlan, William J., Jr., (AV) ....'39 '66 C&L.424 A.B., J.D. [McDermott W.&E.]
Quinlan, William R., (AV) ....'39 '64 C&L.424 B.Sc., J.D. [Quinlan&C.]

Quinlan & Carroll, Ltd., (AV) BR
30 North La Salle Street, Suite 2900, 60602
Telephone: 312-263-0900 Telecopier: 312-263-5013
URL: http://www.qclaw.com
William R. Quinlan; James R. Carroll; Thomas C. Hynes; Cheryl I. Niro; Brian J. Alesia; Michael T. Beirne; Richard C. Bollow; Nicholas G. Grapsas; Lisa M. Hegedus; Matthew J. Hynes; James A. Niewiara; Martin J. O'Hara; William J. Quinlan; John H. Scheid, Jr.; Michael A. Steigmann;—Amy E. Bullock; Sheila A. Loop; J. Christopher Madden; Jeanah Park; Jessica A. Sohl.

See Professional Biographies, CHICAGO, ILLINOIS

Quinlisk, Edward G. .... '72 '00 C.1016 B.A. L.209 J.D. [Ⓐ Jenner&B.]
Quinlisk, John J., (BV) ....'43 '70 C&L.424 B.B.A., J.D. [Bell J.&Q.]
Quinn, Bernard E. Jude, (BVⓉ) ....'60 '86 C.602 B.A. L.884 J.D. [Hinshaw&C.]
Quinn, Dennis M. ....'— '79 C.602 B.A. L.378 J.D. [Ⓒ Mayer,B.R.&M.]
Quinn, E. Paul ....'— '91 C.352 B.B.A. L.893 J.D. [Greenberg T.]
Quinn, James R. ....'41 '66 C&L.209 B.S.C., J.D. [Ruff,W.&R.]
Quinn, Jeffrey S. .... '— '98 C.476 B.A. L.209 J.D. [Kirkland&E.]
Quinn, Jennifer R. ....'— '99 C.560 B.B.A. L.365 J.D. [Ⓐ Ungaretti&H.]
Quinn, Jonathan S., (AV) ....'— '86 C.311 B.A. L.597 J.D. [Sachnoff&W.]
Quinn, Marguerite, (BV) ....'59 '86 C.352 B.A. L.424 J.D. [Ⓐ O'Keefe,L.&H.]
Quinn, Michael J., (AV) ....'52 '82 C.436 B.A. L.966 J.D. [Seyfarth S.]
Quinn, Neil K., (AV) ....'29 '57 C.339 B.A. L.209 J.D. [Pretzel&S.]
Quinn, Owen P. ....'75 '01 C&L.339 B.A., J.D. [Ⓐ Field&G.]
Quinn, Patrick J., (AV) ....'53 '80 C.339 B.A. L.365 J.D. Illinois Appellate Ct.
Quinn, Patrick J. ....'48 '80 C.276 B.S.B.F. L.597 J.D. 1852 N. Nashville Ave.
Quinn, Sheila Beary ....'64 '89 C.741 B.A. L.339 J.D. DARC Corp.
Quinn, Thomas B. ....'— '78 C&L.813 A.B., J.D. [Schiff H.]

Quinn, John M., & Associates, Ltd.
(See Bloomingdale)

Quintos, Christine M. ....'76 '02 C.602 B.S. L.209 J.D. [Ⓐ Moore,S.&W.]
Quintos, Michelle S. ....'— '02 C&L.339 B.S., J.D. [Ⓐ Jones D.]
Quirk, Catherine Ann ....'60 '86 C.966 B.B.A. L.365 J.D. Asst. States Atty.
Quirk, Karen Caraher ....'68 '95 C.741 B.A. L.602 J.D. [Winston&S.]
Quirke, Barry J. ....'60 '85 C.436 B.S. L.339 J.D. [McDermott W.&E.]
Quist, Paula S. ....'— '02 C.547 B.A. L.546 J.D. [Ⓐ Jones D.]
R3 Group LLC, (AV) ....1 N. LaSalle St., Ste. 1904
Raam, Jani S. ....'77 '04 C.602 B.B.A. L.276 J.D. [Ⓐ McDermott W.&E.]
Rabe, Edward R., Jr. .... '48 '74 C.1106 B.A. L.146 J.D. [Ⓒ McCarthy&Assoc.]
Rabe, Lee Ann ....'— '03 C&L.608 B.A., J.D. [Ⓐ Schiff H.]
Rabel, Timothy R. ....'— '91 C.339 B.A. L.365 J.D. [Querrey&H.]
Rabens, Geo. C., (AV) ....'08 '31 C&L.339 B.S., LL.B. 33 N. La Salle St.
Rabin, Robert F. ....'65 '90 C.861 B.A. L.209 J.D. [Ⓐ Robbins,S.&P.]
Rabinovitz, Joshua Z. ....'— '00 C.597 B.A. L.145 J.D. [Ⓐ Kirkland&E.]
Rabinowitz, Fred ....'49 '76 C.1373 B.S. L.365 J.D. [Schaffner,R.&F.]
Rabinowitz, Mark A., (AV) ....'54 '78 C.339 B.A. L.309 J.D. [Neal,G.&E.]
Rabinsky, Alex P. ....'— '01 C.861 B.A. L.94 J.D. [Ⓐ Schiff H.]
Racette, Thomas C. '49 '79
C.494 B.A. L.1035 J.D. V.P., Ins & Risk Mgt., General Growth Prop.
Rachelson, Aaron D. ....'73 '98 C&L.477 B.A., J.D. [Ⓐ Horwood M.&B.]
Rachlis, Michael ....'66 '90 C.339 B.A. L.966 J.D. [Rachlis D.D.&A.]

Rachlis Durham Duff & Adler, (AV)
542 South Dearborn Street, Suite 1310, 60605
Telephone: 312-733-3950 Fax: 312-733-3952
URL: http://www.rddlaw.net
Partners: Michael Rachlis; Edwin L. Durham; Kevin B. Duff; Marion B. Adler. Of Counsel: Eric S. Newman; Kay L. Pick.
Commercial Litigation, Corporate Litigation, Contract Litigation, Civil Appeals, Construction Litigation, Insurance Coverage, Securities, Employment, Consumer Fraud and Class Defense, Mass Torts, Accountants Liability.

See Professional Biographies, CHICAGO, ILLINOIS

Rachoy, Trisha M. .... '77 '04 C.209 B.S. L.146 J.D. [Ⓐ Seyfarth S.]
Rachwalski, Karla ....'— '04 C.118 B.A. L.146 J.D. [Ⓐ Sachnoff&W.]
Rackauskas, Tracy Noelle '70 '99 C.352 B.A. L.589 J.D.
Law Clerk, U.S. Bankruptcy Ct.

Radak, Michael '— '03 C.339 B.A. L.209 J.D. [Ⓐ Busse&B.]
Radakovich, Daniel E., (AV) '49 '74 C.197 A.B. L.880 J.D. 900 W. Jackson Blvd.
Radasevich, Robert, (AV) '56 '81 C.801 B.A. L.209 J.D. [Neal,G.&E.]
Radde, Susan M. '64 '92 C.494 B.S. L.1035 J.D.
(adm. in MN; not adm. in IL) Assoc. Gen. Coun., TruServ Corp.
Rade, Debra S. '53 '80 C.339 B.A. L.209 J.D. [Katten M.R.]
Radelet, David P., (AV) '55 '81 C.475 B.A. L.477 J.D. [Franczek S.]
Rademacher, Patricia E. '61 '90 C.475 B.A. L.365 J.D. [Coston&R.]
Rademacher, Robin A. '— '98 C.477 B.A. L.209 J.D. [Kirkland&E.]
Rademaker, Bradley F. '63 '91 C.357 B.S. L.146 J.D. [Wallenstein W.&R.]
Rademaker, Julie K. '61 '86 C.388 B.A. L.597 J.D. [Barack F.K.P.&N.]
Rademaker, Randall J. '56 '82 C.388 B.A. L.145 J.D. [Skadden,A.S.M.&F.]
Raden, James B. '— '66 C.339 B.S. L.145 J.D. [Ⓒ Jones D.] (See Pat. Sect.)
Radick, Alicia J. '55 '89 C.339 B.A. L.146 J.D. E.E.O.C.
Radke, Arthur F., (AV) '52 '79 C.436 B.A. L.1068 J.D. [Dykema G.P.]
Radke, Bruce A. '68 '96 C&L.339 B.A., J.D. [Ⓐ Vedder,P.K.&K.]
Radnay, Richard S. '— '00 C.188 B.S. L.597 J.D. [Ⓐ Kirkland&E.]
Radner, Keith G. '68 '96 C.477 B.A. L.339 J.D. [Goldberg,K.B.B.R.&M.]
Rados, James L., (AV) '52 '77 C.363 A.B. L.201 J.D. 30 N. La Salle St., Ste. 1740
Radovich, Joan '62 '97 C.597 B.S. L.145 J.D. [Ⓐ Sidley A.B.&W.]
Radtke, Mark L. '75 '01 C.352 B.B.A. L.146 J.D. [Ⓐ Shaw G.F.G.W.&T.]
Radtke, Michael J., (AV) '51 '76 C.589 B.A. L.146 J.D. 39 S. La Salle St., Ste. 408
Radtke, Steven R., (AV) '54 '79 C.339 B.A. L.146 J.D. [Chill,C.&R.]
Radunsky, Troy S. '— '99 C.36 B.A. L.365 J.D. [Ⓐ O'Hagan,S.&A.]
Radziłowsky, Michael, Law Offices of '50 '76 C.238 B.A. L.209 J.D.
234 S. Wabash Ave.
Radzin, Bruce E. '48 '76 C.339 B.A. L.146 J.D. 415 N. LaSalle
Rafanelli, Cara Moore '62 '88 C.560 B.A. L.862 J.D. 680 N. Lake Shore Dr.
Raffals, Reeghan '67 '00 C.145 A.B. L.309 J.D.
(adm. in MA; not adm. in IL) [Ⓐ Bartlit B.H.P.&S.]
Rafferty, John R. '29 '56 C.177 L.365 LL.B. 111 W. Wash. St.
Rafkin, John M. '62 '89 C.309 A.B. L.597 J.D. [Sidley A.B.&W.]
Rafter, Thomas D. '42 '71
C.705 B.A. L.424 J.D. Gen. Coun., Grant Thornton International
Raghavan, Tara M. '— '03 C&L.339 B.S., J.D. [Ⓐ Rakoczy M.M.S.] (Pat.)
Rago, Brad E. '76 '01 C.679 B.A. L.339 J.D. [Ⓐ Barnes&T.]
Rago, Frank N. '19 '48 L.209 LL.B. [Ⓒ Kiesler&B.]
Rago, Gail Buoscio '52 '81 C.339 B.S. L.209 J.D. Gen. Coun., Seven World Wide, Inc.
Ragus, Lori A. '— '88 C.339 B.A. L.146 J.D.
Atty.-Advsr., Midwest Reg. Off., U.S. Secs. & Exch. Comm.
Raguse, Rick A. '— '98 C.339 B.S. L.597 J.D. [Ⓐ Sidley A.B.&W.]
Rahe, Paul A. '— '96 C.347 B.A. L.893 J.D. [Schiff H.]
Rahill, Katherine '77 '02 C.597 B.A. L.477 J.D.
(adm. in CO; not adm. in IL) [Ⓐ Jenner&B.]
Rahilly, Sean G. '73 '99 C&L.209 B.S., J.D. [Ⓐ]
Rahman, Tanvir A. '78 '03 C&L.813 B.A., J.D. [Ⓐ Gardner C.&D.]
Raimi, Zachary M. '75 '00 C.477 B.A. L.424 J.D. [Ⓐ Bollinger,R.&G.]
Raimond, Josie '68 '95 C.299 B.A. L.880 J.D. [Ⓐ Meites,M.B.&M.]
Raimondi, Lisa M. '71 '96 C.339 B.A. L.365 J.D. [Raimondi&O.]
Raimondi, Marianne '— '99 C.424 B.B.A. L.365 J.D. [Ⓐ DLPiper R.G.C.U.]
Raimondi & Orton, Ltd. 19 S. La Salle, Suite 1500
Raines, Lana J. '— '02 C&L.477 B.A., J.D. [Ⓐ Sachnoff&W.]
Rainey, Samuel B. '76 '02 C.473 B.A. L.665 J.D. [Ⓐ Sedgwick,D.M.&A.]
Raistrick, Christopher J. '71 '96 C.340 B.A. L.424 J.D. [Ⓐ Merlo K.B.&G.]
Raitt, Sandra '67 '92 C.477 B.A. L.145 J.D. Assoc., Gunther Group LLC
Raizes, Maurice P., (AV) '29 '53 C&L.339 B.S.L., J.D. [Cohon R.&R.]
Rajfer, Sol '48 '73 C.339 B.A. L.146 J.D. Asst. State's Atty.
Rak, Katie M. '78 '04 C&L.602 B.A., J.D. [Ⓐ McGuirewoods]
Rakers, Kevin C. '63 '88 C.339 B.A. L.910 J.D. [Falasz&R.]
Rakley, Barbara J. '54 '89 C.378 B.A. L.339 J.D. Loyola Univ.
Rakoczy, Mark E., (AV) '52 '76 C.385 B.A. L.365 J.D. [Ⓒ Skadden,A.S.M.&F.]
Rakoczy, William A. '— '95 C.894 A.B. L.880 J.D. [Rakoczy M.M.S.]

Rakoczy Molino Mazzochi Siwik LLP
6 West Hubbard Street, Suite 500, 60610
Telephone: 312-527-2157 Fax: 312-527-4205
URL: http://www.rmmslegal.com
Partners: William A. Rakoczy; Paul J. Molino; Deanne M. Mazzochi; Christine J. Siwik. Associates: Amy D. Brody; Lara Monroe-Sampson; Tara M. Raghavan; Alice L. Riechers.
Litigation, Intellectual Property, Antitrust and Complex Commercial. Patent and Regulatory Counseling, Licensing, Patent Prosecution.
See Professional Biographies, CHICAGO, ILLINOIS

Rakov, Michael A. '— '95 C.309 B.A. L.910 J.D. [Ⓐ Mandell M.]
Rakowski, Thomas R. '43 '70 C.209 B.S.C. L.365 J.D. [Connelly R.&M.]
Rakstad, Jennifer L. '— '98 C.57 B.A. L.569 J.D. [Ⓐ Mayer,B.R.&M.]
Raleigh, Philip M. '48 '82 C.339 B.A. L.851 J.D. Sr. Atty., National Futures Assn.
Raleigh, William J., (AV) '53 '80 C&L.424 B.S., J.D. [Nisen&E.]
Rallo, David T., (BV) '— '75 C.30 B.A. L.365 J.D. [Ⓒ Arnstein&L.]
Ralph, Michael L., Jr. '74 '99 C.347 B.A. L.146 J.D. [Ⓐ Richards,R.&S.] ⊙
Ralph, Michael L., Sr., (AV) '47 '72 C.123 B.A. L.436 J.D. [Richards,R.&S.] ⊙
Ramel, Gregory J., Sr. '48 '77 C&L.209 B.A., J.D. Dep. Coun., Dept. Of Employ. Sec.
Ramelow, Geo. E. '20 '42 C.999 L.209 LL.B. 20 N. Michigan St.
Ramey, Angela C. '— '04 C.339 B.A. L.144 J.D. [Ⓐ Katten M.R.]
Ramey, Judith A. '38 '79 C.546 B.S. L.424 J.D. Fed. Labor Rel. Auth.
Rammelt, David A., (AV) '— '90 C.299 B.A. L.347 J.D. [Kelley D.&W.]
Ramos, Sandra G., (BV) '60 '86 C&L.209 B.A., J.D. [Ramos]
Ramos Ltd., (BV) 2538 S. California, 1st Fl.
Rampson, Edward J., (BV) '53 '78 C.602 B.A. L.365 J.D.
SAFECO Prop. & Cas. Ins. Co.
Ramsden, Lisa M. '62 '90 C.932 B.B.A. L.1187 J.D. Law Clk., U.S. Bkrptcy. Ct.
Ramsey, Douglas M. '72 '98 C.802 B.A. L.209 J.D. [Shefsky&F.]
Ramsey, J. Timothy, (AV) '— '78 C.674 A.B. L.910 J.D. [Weinberg R.]
Ramsey, Jeffrey F. '67 '97 C.340 B.A. L.146 J.D. John Nuveen & Co.
Ramsey, Laura C. '62 '88 C.855 B.A. L.94 J.D.
V.P. & Compliance Coun., Everen Securities, Inc.
Ramsey, Mark Paul '— '98 C&L.347 B.A., J.D. [Ⓐ Latham&W.]
Ramson, Julie A., (AV) '— '82 C.966 B.S.N. L.424 J.D. [McKenna S.]
Rana, Gayle A. '77 '02 C.597 B.A. L.309 J.D. [Ⓐ Jenner&B.]
Ranallo, Michael J., (AVⓉ) '54 '80 C.381 B.A. L.608 J.D. [Holland&K.]
Ranard, William W., (BV) '66 '92 C.597 B.A. L.502 J.D.
[Cassiday,S.&G.] (⊙Rockford)
Rand, Justin B. '75 '00 C.347 B.S. L.94 J.D. [Ⓐ Brinks H.G.&L.] (See Pat. Sect.)
Randall, Benjamin J., (AV) '48 '72 C.608 B.A. L.930 J.D. [Randall&K.]
Randall, Jeffrey M. '42 '69 C.1016 B.S.B.A. L.365 J.D. [Robbins,S.&P.] ⊙
Randall, Paula Vincich, (BV) '65 '90 C.424 B.S. L.365 J.D. [Ⓐ Ancel,G.D.B.D.&R.]
Randall, R. Nathan '58 '88 C&L.597 B.A., J.D. [Boundas S.W.&B.]
Randall, Steven B., (AV) '36 '62 C.340 B.S. L.966 J.D. [Ⓒ Michael B.&F.]

Randall & Kenig LLP, (AV)
NBC Tower, Suite 3160, 455 North CityFront Plaza Drive, 60611
Telephone: 312-822-0800 Fax: 312-822-0215
Benjamin J. Randall; Scott H. Kenig.
Commercial Real Estate, Commercial Law, Business Law, Banking Law, Construction Law, Zoning, Planning and Land Use, Real Estate.
See Professional Biographies, CHICAGO, ILLINOIS

Randell, David F. '64 '90 C.674 B.A. L.309 J.D. 5800 Sears Twr.
Randell, Howard B. '65 '90 C.477 B.S. L.209 J.D. [Leahy,E.&F.]
Randolph, Carole '61 '85 C.145 B.A. L.976 J.D. Sears Tower
Randolph, Laurie S., (AV) '54 '79 C.589 B.S. L.209 J.D. [Hinshaw&C.]
Randolph, Robert D., Jr. '61 '86 C.27 B.S. L.213 J.D. 2501 North Bosworth
Rane, Andrew L. '67 '94 C.339 B.A. L.589 J.D. [Garofalo,S.H.&S.]
Rang, Kevin A. '68 '95 C.475 B.A. L.477 J.D. [Mayer,B.R.&M.]
Rangel, Diego R. '33 '78 C.1183 M.Ed. L.1151 J.D. 2314 N. Milwaukee Ave.
Rangel-Campos, Linda '74 '00 C.339 B.A. L.209 J.D. 10602 S. Ewing Ave.
Rankin, James W., (AV) '— '68 C.604 A.B. L.145 J.D. [Kirkland&E.]
Rankin, Sara K. '— '00 C.629 B.A. L.569 J.D. [Ⓐ Kirkland&E.]
Ranney, George A., Jr., (AV) '40 '66 C.309 B.A. L.145 J.D. [Mayer,B.R.&M.]
Ransel, C. Zachary '75 '01 C.473 B.S. L.1119 J.D. [Ⓐ Foran G.P.&P.]
Ransford, Kathleen, (AV) '51 '78 C&L.424 B.A., J.D. Chief Asst. Corp. Coun.

Ransom, William H. '60 '94 C.424 B.A. L.365 J.D.
415 North La Salle Street, Suite 203, 60610
Telephone: 312-222-9120 Fax: 312-222-1656
Email: WRansom@aol.com URL: http://www.williamhransom.com
Personal Injury, Automobile Accidents and Injuries, Wrongful Death, Collections, Workers' Compensation, Commercial Law, Business Law, Breach of Contract, Discrimination, Wrongful Termination, Family Law, Divorce, Adoption Law, General Practice, Appellate Practice, Criminal Practice, Driving While Intoxicated, Felonies, Traffic Violations, Homicide, Drug Crimes, Parole and Probation.
See Professional Biographies, CHICAGO, ILLINOIS

Ranson, Arik B. '71 '96 C&L.923 B.S.I.E., J.D. [Ⓐ Greer,B.&C.] (Pat.)
Rantis, Charles P., (AV) '60 '85 C.209 B.S. L.146 J.D. [Johnson&B.]
Rantisi, Naheel M. '68 '93 C.238 B.A. L.879 J.D. 5435 W. Diversey
Rao, Wilhelm L. '— '99 C.910 B.S.C.E. L.146 J.D. [McAndrews,H.&M.]
Raphael, Alan '45 '79 C.311 B.A. L.345 J.D. Assoc. Prof. of Law, Loyola Univ.
Raphael, Arthur, (AV) '40 '65 C.339 L.209 J.D. [Teller,L.&S.]
Raphael, Max '09 '32 L.209 LL.B. 77 W. Wash. St.
Rapoport, David E., (AV) '56 '81 C.589 B.S. L.146 J.D. [Rapoport]

Rapoport Law Offices, P.C., (AV)
20 North Clark Street, Suite 3500, 60602
Telephone: 312-327-9880 1-800-545-6437 Fax: 312-327-9881 URL: http://www.rapoportlaw.com
Email: reception@rapoportlaw.com URL: http://www.rapoportlaw.com
David E. Rapoport; Jon C. Papin; Paul David Richter; Steven M. Sandler. Of Counsel: Ira J. Furman (Not admitted in IL).
Plaintiffs' Personal Injury Litigation; Wrongful Death Litigation; Commercial Aviation Litigation; Medical Malpractice; General Aviation Litigation; Product Liability; Vehicular Accidents; Boating Accidents; Personal Watercraft Accidents; Construction Accidents; Premises Liability; Head and Spinal Injuries; Slip and Fall; Trucking Accidents; Drug and Medical Devices.
See Professional Biographies, CHICAGO, ILLINOIS

Rapp, Geoffrey C. '— '03 C.309 A.B. L.976 j.D. 14 W. Erie
Rapp, Ronald J. '60 '85 C.879 B.A. L.494 J.D. [Ⓒ Vedder,P.K.&K.]
Rappaport, Bret A. '61 '86 C.347 B.S. L.365 J.D. [Schwartz C.]
Rappaport, Earle S., (AV) '35 '58 C&L.597 B.S.L., J.D. 180 N. La Salle St.
Rappaport, Richard J., (AV) '43 '67 C&L.424 B.S., J.D. [McGuirewoods]
Rappin, Jeffrey C., (AV) '43 '66 C.679 B.A. L.145 J.D. 350 W. Hubbard St.
Rappin, Steven R., (AV) '61 '86 C.347 B.A. L.209 J.D. [Hauselman&R.]
Rappold, Richard W., (AV) '53 '78 C.98 B.A. L.424 J.D. [Marks,M.&K.]
Rascia, Louis A. '61 '87 C.209 B.S. L.424 J.D. [Griffith&J.]
Rashid, George Jacob '62 '87 C.190 B.S.B.A. L.734 J.D. 79 W. Monroe, Ste. 914
Raskin, Kenneth A. '47 '73 C.1036 B.A. L.569 J.D. Sanwa Business Credit Corp.
Raskin, Richard D., (AV) '57 '85 C.103 A.B. L.150 J.D. [Sidley A.B.&W.]
Rasmussen, Mark D. '— '92 C&L.477 B.B.A., J.D. [Chapman&C.]
Rasor, Robert D., (AV) '— '73 C.210 B.A. L.597 J.D. [Anderson,R.]
Rassin, Ronald R. '43 '67 C&L.209 B.S., J.D. [Ⓒ Marks,M.&K.]
Ratana, Alvin S. '67 '97 C.1163 B.A. L.365 J.D. Asst. St. Atty.
Ratcliffe, James M. '25 '50 C&L.145 A.B., J.D. V.P., R.R. Donnelley & Sons Co.‡
Rathgeber, David K. '— '85 C.602 B.A. L.597 J.D. [Latham&W.]
Rathje, Theron L., (AV) '18 '49 C.188 B.C. L.597 J.D. 20 N. Clark St.
Rathnau, Joseph N. '35 '77 C.1191 B.A. L.146 J.D. [Ⓒ Morris,R.&D.]
Rathsack, Michael W., (AV) '47 '72 C.966 B.S. L.339 J.D. 111 W. Washington St.
Ratnaswamy, John P. '— '85 C&L.597 B.S., J.D. [Foley&L.]
Ratner, Gerald, (AV) '13 '37 C&L.145 Ph.B., J.D. [Gould&R.]
Ratner, Joshua D. '76 '02 C.1036 B.A. L.145 J.D.
(adm. in MI; not adm. in IL) [Ⓐ Skadden,A.S.M.&F.]
Ratner, Mark S. '68 '94 C.475 B.A. L.213 J.D. [Ⓐ Pretzel&S.]
Rattner, William E., (AV) '36 '62 C.659 B.S. L.309 J.D. 213 W. Institute Place
Ratts, Andrew W. '62 '87 C.339 B.S. L.309 J.D. [Winston&S.]
Ratzburg, Courtney '77 '03 C.880 B.S. L.911 J.D. [Ⓐ Bell,B.&L.]
Raucci, Andrew M., (AV) '45 '68 C.209 B.A. L.365 J.D. [Kusper&R.]
Rauch, Christopher P. '69 '01 C.46 B.S. L.365 J.D. [Ⓐ Sonnenschein N.&R.] (Pat.)
Rauch, George W., (AV) '19 '48 C.347 B.S. L.893 LL.B. 111 W. Monroe St.
Rauch, John G. '61 '92 C.679 B.S.E.E. L.46 J.D. [Brinks H.G.&L.] (See Pat. Sect.)
Rauch, Lisa F. '63 '89 C.424 B.S. L.589 J.D.
V.P. & Sr. Cnsl, Merrill Lynch Bus. Financial Servs., Inc.
Rauch, Paul E., Ph.D. '65 '98 C.604 B.A. L.273 J.D. [Evan] (Pat.)
Rauchwerger, Dean S., (AV) '59 '84 C&L.910 B.A., J.D. [Clausen M.]
Rauen, Janice M. '64 '90 C.339 B.A. L.146 J.D. [Laner,M.D.B.L.&T.]
Rauner, Vincent J. '27 '53 C&L.477 B.S.E., J.D. 620 Fullerton Pkwy.‡
Rausch, Michael J. '— '04 C.966 B.S. L.597 J.D. [Ⓐ Jones D.]
Rauschert, Donald R. '47 '73 L.146 [Rauschert&R.]
Rauschert, Robert P. '71 '98 C.209 B.S. L.146 J.D. [Rauschert&R.]
Rauschert & Rauschert 1025 Webster Ave.
Ravago, Joseph Shun Mendoza '72 '98 C.347 B.S. L.424 J.D. 5757 N. Lincoln Ave.
Raval, Rupal '77 '03 C.63 B.A. L.602 J.D. [Ⓐ Gardner C.&D.]
Raven, Marc E., (AV) '59 '84 C.309 B.A. L.477 J.D. [Sidley A.B.&W.]
Ravid, Steven M. '46 '73 C.966 B.B.A. L.424 J.D. IL Appl. Ct.
Ravindran, Ramya '— '04 C.691 B.S. L.1565 J.D. [Ⓐ Kirkland&E.]
Ravitz, Gary '51 '76 C.589 B.A. L.365 J.D. [Ravitz&P.]
Ravitz & Palles, P.C. 203 North La Salle Street, Suite 2100
Rawe, Jennifer K. '78 '03 C.351 B.A. L.352 J.D. [Ⓐ Magnani&B.]
Rawson, William L., (AV) '52 '79 C.221 B.A. L.861 J.D. [DLPiper R.G.C.U.]
Ray, John J., III '59 '83 C.454 B.A. L.221 J.D.
Chief Adm. Off., Gen. Coun. & Secy., Fruit of the Loom, Ltd.

Ray, Jordan Herschel '72 '00 C.367 B.A. L.146 J.D. 3601 W. Devon Ave., Ste. 9
Ray, Michael D. '79 '04 C.970 B.A. L.1119 J.D. [🄰 Ogletree,D.N.S.&S.]
Ray, Stephen E., (AV) '56 '81 C.165 B.A. L.188 J.D. [Stein,R.&H.]
Ray, Timothy '— '95 C.974 B.A. L.352 J.D. [Neal,G.&E.]
Raya, Paul '72 '04 C.388 B.C. L.365 J.D. [🄰 Cook,A.M.M.C.&M.]
Rayford, Konrad J. '41 '86
C.1191 B.S.Ed. L.209 J.D. U.S. Dept. of Housing & Urban Develop.
Rayis, John D. '54 '81 C.475 B.A. L.912 J.D. [Skadden,A.S.M.&F.]
Raymer, Debra L., (AV) '56 '81
C.958 B.A. L.1565 J.D. Asst. Gen. Coun., Bk. of America
Raymond, Andrew D. '— '03 C.124 B.S. L.1565 J.D. [🄰 Marshall,G.&B.]
Raymond, Cari Jay '73 '99 C.589 B.S. L.1338 J.D. [🄰 Tressler,S.M.&P.]
Raymond, Elizabeth A., (AV) '57 '84 C.674 A.B. L.569 J.D. [Mayer,B.R.&M.]
Raymond, Spencer H., (AV) '26 '53 C.674 B.S.E. L.309 J.D. 1 IBM Plaza
Raynal, Lazar Pol, (AV) '63 '88 C.966 B.S. L.602 J.D. [McDermott W.&E.]
Rea, Anne E., (AV) '59 '84 C.103 A.B. L.145 J.D. [Sidley A.B.&W.]
Read, David C., (AV) '— '92
C.679 B.S.C.E. L.879 J.D. [Marshall,G.&B.] (See Pat. Sect.)
Read, Sarah J., (AV) '56 '81 C.976 B.A. L.966 J.D. [🄲 Sidley A.B.&W.]
Readey, Jay S. '72 '04 C&L.976 B.A., J.D. [🄰 Jenner&B.]
Reagan, Paul V., (AVⓉ) '47 '74 C.705 B.A. L.602 J.D.
(adm. in NY; not adm. in IL) Sr. V.P. & U.S. Gen. Coun., Harris Tr. & Svgs. Bk.
Reale, John W. '— '02 C.708 B.A. L.345 J.D. [🄰 Kirkland&E.]
Reali, Janet L., (AV) '51 '77 C.347 B.A. L.424 J.D.
Sr. Exec. V.P., Gen. Coun. & Corp. Secy., Everen Securities, Inc.
Realmuto, Julie M. '67 '00 C.209 B.A. L.146 J.D. [🄰 McCarthy D.]
Ream, Davidson '37 '72 C.976 B.A. L.893 J.D.
(adm. in DC; not adm. in IL) Editor for the Defense, Defense Resch. Institute
Reames, Jane E. '56 '87 C.424 B.B.A. L.46 J.D. 33 North Dearborn Street, Suite 300
Reardon, Karen A., (AV) '59 '86 C.659 B.A. L.880 J.D. [Reardon G.&R.]
Reardon, Mark W., (BVⓉ) '56 '80 C.388 B.A. L.776 J.D. Coun., The Boeing Co.
Reardon, Patrick G., (AV) '40 '75 C.999 B.A. L.365 J.D. 221 N. La Salle St., Rm. 1938

Reardon Golinkin & Reed, (AV)
208 South La Salle Street, Suite 1290, 60604-1102
Telephone: 312-855-3700 Fax: 312-855-1089
Email: info@rgrlaw.com URL: http://www.rgrlaw.com
Karen A. Reardon; Scott G. Golinkin; Scott O. Reed. Associates: Keith W. Mandell; Eric J. Marler; Natalia A. Kolasa. Of Counsel: Daniel V. Marsalli.
Insurance Coverage, Litigation, Directors and Officers Liability, Professional Liability, Labor and Employment, Reinsurance, Alternative Dispute Resolution.
See Professional Biographies, CHICAGO, ILLINOIS

Reategui, Lisa J. '66 '96 C.674 B.A. L.597 J.D. [🄰 Sidley A.B.&W.]
Rebey, Paul J. '58 '82 C.339 B.A. L.209 J.D. 200 N. LaSalle
Recht, Leslie, (Ms.), (AV) '49 '74 C.145 A.B. L.146 J.D. [Defrees&F.]
Rechtin, Michael D., (AV) '— '82 C.339 B.S. L.146 J.D. [Foley&L.] (Pat.)
Rechtin, Michael D. '67 '92 C.453 B.S. L.602 J.D. [Holland&K.]
Rechtoris, Kenneth E. '61 '85 C&L.352 B.B.A., J.D. [Bell,B.&L.]
Reckamp, Christopher J. '61 '91 C.436 B.S.E.E. L.209 J.D. [Vedder,P.K.&K.]
Reckler, Caroline A. '— '01 C.228 B.A. L.477 J.D. [🄰 Latham&W.]
Recktenwald, William E. '23 '52 C.679 B.Mech.E. L.273 J.D. 500 W. Madison‡

Rector, Laurel Black, (BV) '53 '78 C.696 B.A. L.910 J.D.
53 W. Jackson, Suite 1118, 60604
Telephone: 312-322-7900 Fax: 312-922-8027
Email: laurelrector@lawyer.com URL: http://www.laurelblackrector.com
Family Law, Divorce, Child Custody, Child Support, Visitation Rights, Domestic Violence, Spousal Support.
See Professional Biographies, CHICAGO, ILLINOIS

Reda, Ltd., (AV) 8 South Michigan Avenue, Suite 3400
Reda, Edward E. '23 '51 C&L.209 A.B., LL.B. 8501 W. Higgins Rd.
Reda, Edward E., Jr., (AV) '51 '76 C&L.209 B.S., J.D. [Reda]
Reda, Robert S. '— '89 C.221 B.A. L.365 J.D. 8 South Michigan Avenue, Suite 3400
Redden, Charles F., (AV) '58 '84 C.94 B.A. L.424 J.D. [Pretzel&S.]
Reddick, Erica L. '65 '91 C.597 B.A. L.150 J.D. Asst. Pub. Def.
Redding, Brian J., (AV) '45 '70 C.602 B.B.A. L.424 J.D.
V.P. & Loss Prevention Coun., Attorneys' Liability Assurance Society, Inc.
Redding, James M., (AV) '23 '49 C.477 A.B. L.209 J.D. [Redding&H.]
Redding & Hyde, (AV) 111 W. Wash. St.
Reddington, G. Joseph '41 '66 C&L.352 B.A., J.D.
(adm. in IA; not adm. in IL) Sears, Roebuck & Co.
Reddy, Ajitha L. '72 '99 C.309 B.A. L.477 J.D. 29 S. La Salle, Ste. 960
Redfield, Susan T. '46 '80
C.509 B.A. L.46 J.D. Dir., Estate Planning, Ill. Institute of Tech.
Reding, Nancy A. '66 '92 C.597 B.A. L.910 J.D. 3500 Three 1st Nat. Plz.
Redman, Clarence Owen, (AV) '42 '66 C&L.339 B.S., J.D. [🄲 Lord,B.&B.]
Redman, Scott D.H. '64 '89 C&L.339 A.B., J.D. [Crowley B.&K.]
Redmond, Lawrence C., Jr. '43 '86 C.339 B.A. L.365 J.D. 7544 S. Phillips Ave.
Redmond, Richard A., (AV) '— '72 C.602 A.B. L.188 J.D. [Holland&K.]
Reeb, Robert L., (BV) '62 '88 C.1105 B.A. L.424 J.D. [Marwedel,M.&R.]
Reed, Bryan V. '67 '92 C.421 B.S. L.1161 J.D. [Reed,C.&Z.]
Reed, David R., (AV) '54 '79 C.178 A.B. L.339 J.D. [Lord,B.&B.]
Reed, Irene M. '74 '98 C&L.309 B.A., J.D. [🄰 Schwartz C.]
Reed, Keith A., (AV) '39 '63 C&L.352 B.B.A., J.D. [🄲 Seyfarth S.]
Reed, Kimberly '77 '02 C.597 B.A. L.339 J.D. [🄰 Winston&S.]
Reed, Mary Hutchings, (AV) '51 '76 C.103 B.A. L.976 J.D. [🄲 Winston&S.]
Reed, Michael E., (AV) '42 '68 C.385 B.A. L.597 J.D. [Vedder,P.K.&K.]
Reed, Phillip S. '56 '84 C.150 B.A. L.597 J.D. [Mayer,B.R.&M.]
Reed, Scott O., (AV) '57 '80 C&L.339 B.A., J.D. [Reardon G.&R.]
Reed, Thomas A., (AV) '— '75 C.339 B.S. L.846 J.D. [McKenna S.]
Reed, Thomas J., Law Offices of, (AV) '47 '73
C.276 A.B. L.209 J.D. 208 South La Salle Street, Suite 1600
Reed, Timothy J., (AV) '59 '85 C.338 B.S. L.365 J.D. [Menges&M.]

Reed, Centracchio & Zac, LLC, Law Offices of
75 East Wacker Drive 4th Floor, 60601
Telephone: 312-551-1552 Fax: 312-551-1559
Email: bvreed@bryanvreed.net URL: http://www.rczlaw.com
Bryan V. Reed; Nicole Centracchio; Anthony Zac.
Languages: French, Spanish, Arabic and Polish.
Contract Litigation, Commercial Litigation, Creditor Rights, Debtor Rights, Divorce, Child Support, Child Custody, Visitation Rights, Personal Injury, International Advisement.
See Professional Biographies, CHICAGO, ILLINOIS

Reedy, Daniel P. '58 '87 C.145 B.A. L.146 J.D. Asst. State's Atty.
Reedy, Tara M. '78 '04 C.37 B.A. L.209 J.D. [🄰 Fitch,E.T.&F.]
Reenan, Neal J. '— '03 C.309 A.B. L.477 J.D. [🄰 Kirkland&E.]
Rees, Miryam Rosie '— '81 C.1183 B.A. L.424 J.D. [Pircher,N.&M.]
Rees, R. Douglas '62 '89 C.101 B.A. L.597 J.D. [Jenner&B.]

Reese, Judith R. '42 '77 C.339 B.S. L.424 J.D. 1200 N. Lake Shore Dr.
Reese, Lucius E. '60 '88 C.210 B.A. L.477 J.D. Sears Tower
Reese-Gordon, Edith '56 '80 C.801 B.S. L.273 J.D. Claims Specialist, CNA HealthPro‡
Reetz, Margaret A. '60 '87 C.339 B.A. L.209 J.D. [Cozen O.]
Reeves, Eric '72 '98 C.477 B.A. L.608 J.D. [🄰 McDermott W.&E.]
Reeves, Kathryn E. '75 '01 C.473 B.A. L.209 J.D. [🄰 Azulay,H.&S.]
Reeves, Rodney F. '46 '74 C.339 B.A. L.365 J.D. 19 S. Lasalle Street, Suite 1500
REFCO, LLC 550 W. Jackson
Regal, Seymour I., (AV) '29 '53 C&L.339 B.S., J.D. 208 S. La Salle St., Ste. 1860‡
Regan, Ann W., (AV) '48 '73 C.260 B.A. L.813 J.D. Harris Assoc. L.P.
Regan, Charles F., Jr. '59 '88 C.145 A.B. L.597 J.D. [🄲 Mayer,B.R.&M.]
Regan, Deborah Mitchell '56 '85 C.813 B.A. L.597 J.D. R. R. Donnelley & Sons Co.
Regan, James P., (AV) '34 '79 C.999 B.A. L.724 J.D. [Fisk K.K.&R.]
Regan, Margaret M. '56 '86 C.1183 B.A. L.365 J.D. Asst. States Atty.
Regan, Matthew T. '— '95 C.276 B.S. L.309 J.D. [Kirkland&E.]
Regan, Michael J. '55 '80 C.597 B.A. L.209 J.D.
Vice President & Senior Counsel, Citibank, FSB
Regan, Robert John '— '82 C.165 B.A. L.188 J.D. [Schiff H.]
Regan, Thomas J., (AV) '32 '59 C&L.209 B.A., J.D. 20 North Clark Street, Suite 510‡
Regas, James A., (AV) '30 '53 C.339 B.S.C. L.209 J.D. [🄲 Regas,F.&D.]
Regas, Peter L., (AV) '45 '74 C.589 B.S. L.365 J.D. [Regas,F.&D.]
Regas, Suzanne '58 '84 C.201 B.S. L.365 J.D. Asst. State's Atty.
Regas, Frezados & Dallas LLP, (AV) 111 W. Washington St., Ste. 1525
Regenbogen, Laurie B. '45 '75 C.659 B.S. L.588 J.D. 2350 N. Lincoln Park W
Regnier, Mari Yamamoto '— '93 C.999 B.A. L.1119 J.D. [Barnes&T.]
Regunathan, Ravi '66 '92 C&L.339 B.S., J.D. 211 East Ontario, Suite 1800
Rehling, William R. '44 '77 C&L.209 B.A., J.D. Asst. State's Atty.
Rehm, Joan L. '49 '86 C.209 B.A. L.365 J.D. Hearing Offr.
Reibman, Richard T., (AV) '— '78 C.999 B.A. L.146 J.D. [Schwartz C.]
Reibman, Sheldon N., (BV) '29 '51 C.145 A.B. L.597 J.D. 69 W. Wash. St.

Reibman, Hoffman, Baum, Hirsch & O'Toole, (AV)
20 North Clark Street, Suite 1700, 60602
Telephone: 312-372-6367 Fax: 312-372-0531
Email: mailrhb@aol.com URL: http://www.rhblawfirm.com
Burton L. Hoffman; David M. Baum; Nancy L. Hirsch; Paul G. O'Toole. Associate: Michael S. Hedrick.
Construction Law, Construction Accidents and Defects, Legal Malpractice, Medical Malpractice, Personal Injury, Airplane Crash Litigation, Automobile Accidents, Truck Accidents, Dog Bites, Railroad Accidents, Sexual Abuse, Slip and Fall, Wrongful Death, Products Liability, Drug and Medical Device Litigation, Toxic Torts, Workers Compensation.
See Professional Biographies, CHICAGO, ILLINOIS

Reich, Allan J., (AV) '48 '73 C.188 A.B. L.477 J.D. [Seyfarth S.]
Reich, David L. '63 '91 C.347 B.S. L.597 J.D. [Lawrence,K.S.&U.]
Reich, Elaine '59 '84 C&L.424 B.B.A., J.D. 1350 N. Lake Shore Dr.‡
Reich, Kim Slotky '— '91 C.339 B.S. L.597 J.D. Coun., GE Capital
Reich, Lawrence A., (AV) '37 '74 C.813 A.B. L.365 J.D. [🄲 Klein D.&H.] ⊙
Reich, Michael S. '51 '78 C.597 B.S. L.365 J.D. Asst. Corp. Coun.
Reichelderfer, Frank A., (AV) '19 '43 C&L.339 B.S., J.D. 500 W. Madison
Reiches, Stephen M., (AV) '61 '87 C.597 B.A. L.145 J.D. [Neal,G.&E.]
Reichstein, Richard P. '50 '91 C.597 M.M. L.146 J.D. [R.P.Reichstein]
Reichstein, Richard P., Ltd., Law Offices of 1327 N. Greenview Ave., 1st Fl.
Reicin, Ronald Ian, (AV) '42 '67 C&L.477 B.B.A., J.D. [Jenner&B.]
Reid, Beverly A. '55 '83 C.610 B.A. L.608 J.D. 1316 W. Lexington St.
Reid, Brian M. '— '93 C.692 B.S. L.146 J.D. [🄰 Litchfield C.]
Reid, Ellis E. '34 '59 C.339 A.B. L.145 J.D. Jus., App. Ct.
Reid, Kevin James '68 '96 C.94 B.A./B.A. L.209 J.D. [Garofalo,S.H.&S.]
Reid, Lynn M., (AV) '61 '90 C.879 B.S. L.209 J.D. [Johnson&B.]
Reid, Michael T. '49 '74 C.966 B.A. L.209 J.D. [Keeley,K.&R.]
Reid, N. Neville, (AV) '61 '87 C&L.309 B.A., J.D. [Mayer,B.R.&M.]
Reidy, Daniel E., (AV) '— '74 C.424 B.A. L.477 J.D. [Jones D.]
Reidy, John J., (AV) '41 '66 C&L.209 B.S., J.D. [Ruff,W.&R.]
Reidy, John J., III '61 '91 C.602 B.A. L.365 J.D. Sr. Atty., AT&T Corp.
Reidy, Marilyn McCabe '52 '91 C.589 B.S. L.46 J.D. [Johnson&B.]
Reidy, Paul N. '69 '94 C.352 B.A. L.365 J.D. [🄰 Ruff,W.&R.]
Reif, Burton, (AV) '31 '56 C.597 B.S. L.309 J.D. 1333 W. Greenleaf Ave.
Reifenberg, Robert L., (AV) '56 '81 C.742 B.S. L.589 J.D. [Clausen M.]
Reifer, Avrum '— '84 3016 W. Sherwin Ave.
Reiff, Erin E. '77 '02 C&L.602 B.B.A., J.D. Deloitte
Reifman, Arkady A. '74 '02 C.589 B.A. L.365 J.D. [Reifman]
Reifman, David L., (AV) '59 '88 C.339 B.A. L.597 J.D. [DLPiper R.G.C.U.]
Reifman Law Offices 1221 N. Dearborn St., Apt. 1003N
Reifsteck, Reneé M. '71 '96 C&L.339 B.A., J.D.
Asst. Univ. Coun., Univ. of Ill.- Chicago
Reiland, James M. '76 '03 C.910 B.A. L.597 J.D. [🄰 Kelley D.&W.]
Reilly, James M. '55 '80 C&L.424 B.A., J.D. Dept. of Admin. Hearings
Reilly, James R., Jr. '45 '72 C.337 A.B. L.145 J.D.
Chf. Exec. Offr., Metroplitan Pier & Expo. Auth.
Reilly, Lori A. '67 '92 C.190 B.S. L.424 J.D. [🄰 E.T.Joyce&Assoc.]
Reilly, Marcos, (BV) '62 '86 C.597 B.A. L.477 J.D. [Hinshaw&C.]
Reilly, Paul J. '54 '79 C.1082 B.S. L.424 J.D. [Powell&R.]
Reilly, Tracy L. '— '96 C.589 B.A. L.879 J.D. [Kirkland&E.]
Reilly-Bates, Gabriel '75 '03 C.145 A.B. L.597 J.D. [🄰 Shefsky&F.]
Reimer, Craig E. '67 '92 C.860 B.A. L.424 J.D. [🄲 Mayer,B.R.&M.]
Reimers, Charles H. '23 '49 C&L.597 B.S., J.D. 880 N. Lake Shore Dr.‡
Rein, Eric S., (AV) '56 '81 C.910 B.A. L.473 J.D. [Schwartz C.]
Rein, Thomas D., (AV) '58 '84 C.165 B.A. L.309 J.D. [Sidley A.B.&W.]
Reinberg, Daniel S. '— '91 C.473 B.S. L.597 J.D. [Foley&L.]
Reinbold, Gary W. '68 '93 C.474 B.S. L.477 J.D. Asst. Reg. Coun.
Reinecke, Susan D. '— '99 C.831 B.S. L.107 J.D. [🄰 Michael B.&F.] (See Pat. Sect.)
Reiners, Jennifer '66 '93 C.966 B.A. L.276 J.D. Gen Atty., R. R. Donnelley & Sons Co.
Reinhard, Constance W. '51 '77
C.930 B.A. L.608 J.D. Asst. Gen. Coun., Exelon Bus. Servs. Co.
Reinhard, Rawn Howard '63 '89 C.1064 B.A. L.228 J.D. [Neal,G.&E.]
Reinish, Richard L., (P.C.), (AV) '41 '66 C.477 B.B.A. L.597 J.D. [Seyfarth S.]
Reinkall, Christopher Richard '75 '02 C&L.424 B.A., J.D. [🄰 Price T.R.]
Reinke, Mark W. '58 '85 C&L.966 B.S., J.D. 161 N. Clark, Ste. 2900
Reinsdorf, Jonathan M. '69 '95 C.37 B.A. L.597 J.D. 560 W. Fulton St., Apt. 601
Reinshagen, Kendra, (BV) '50 '80 C.1183 B.A. L.209 J.D.
(adm. in FL; not adm. in IL)
Supervising Atty., Fam. Law Proj./Proj. SAFE, Legal Assistance Found. of Chicago
Reinstein, Arthur '66 '91 C.659 B.S. L.145 J.D.
Dep. Gen. Coun., Chicago Board Options Exchange, Incorporated
Reisberg, Darren Ross '74 '99 C.228 A.B. L.976 J.D. 10 South Dearborn Street
Reisman, Andrew L. '— '93 C.338 B.S. L.339 J.D. [Enterprise]

Reisner, Ralph '31 '59 C.911 B.A. L.273 LL.B.
Prof. of Law (Acting), Northwestern Univ. School of Law
Reiter, Catherine Coyne, (AV) .... '50 '81 C.477 B.S.N. L.209 J.D. [Price T.R.]
Reiter, Gregory M. .... '67 '95 C.107 B.A. L.1187 J.D. 19 S. La Salle St.
Reiter, Michael A., (AV) .... '41 '67 C&L.966 B.S., J.D. [Duane M.]
Reiter, Susan K., (AV) .... '42 '68 C.938 A.B. L.569 J.D. 415 W. Aldine‡
Reizen, Richard S., (BV) .... '54 '80 C.156 B.A. L.424 J.D. [Kubasiak,F.R.&R.]
Rejowski, Joseph A. .... '51 '78 C.927 B.A. L.365 J.D. [J.A.Rejowski]
Rejowski, Joseph A., P.C. .... 5746 W. 63rd St.
Relf, Burton .... '31 '56 C.597 B.S. in B.A. L.309 J.D. 190 S. Lasalle Street
Relias, Anne G. .... '— '01 C.477 B.A. L.209 J.D. [[A] S.D.Pollock&Assoc.]
Relias, George J. .... '64 '95 C.436 B.S. L.365 J.D. [Fisk K.K.&R.]
Relias, John A., (AV) .... '46 '72 C&L.597 B.A., J.D. [Franczek S.]
Reliford, Arthur J., Jr. .... '74 '99 C.299 B.A. L.209 J.D. [[A] Swanson,M.&B.]
Relihan, Deborah G. .... '79 '04 C.339 B.S. L.209 J.D. [[A] Johnson&B.]
Relihan, Justin A. .... '74 '00 C.321 B.A. L.365 J.D. [[A] Johnson&B.]
Relosky, Patricia M. .... '53 '81 C.901 B.A. L.145 J.D. [[C] DLPiper R.G.C.U.]
Remien, Natalie A. .... '74 '99 C.174 B.S.B.A. L.209 J.D. [[A] Welsh&K.]
Remijas, Jonathan P., Law Offices of '68 '94
C.339 B.S. L.209 J.D. 30 West Monroe, Suite 710
Remus, Edward W., (AV) '42 '70
C.494 B.Ch.E. L.209 J.D. [McAndrews,H.&M.] (See Pat. Sect.)
Remus, Mark H. .... '72 '97 C&L.339 B.S., J.D. [Brinks H.G.&L.]
Renaud, Matthew J. .... '64 '92 C&L.477 B.S.E., J.D. [Jenner&B.]
Rendell, Bradley E. '61 '87
C.280 B.B.A. L.365 J.D. V.P., Sales & Mktg., Rendell Sales Co.
Render, Paula Wilson .... '62 '96 C.30 B.A. L.145 J.D. [Bell,B.&L.]
Rendleman, D. Scott, (AV) .... '68 '93 C.338 B.S. L.339 J.D. [Pretzel&S.]
Rendler-Kaplan, Donald .... '47 '80 C.209 B.A. L.365 J.D. [D.Rendler-Kaplan]
Rendler-Kaplan, Donald, & Associates .... 1541 W. Chicago Ave.
Reneau, Andrae P. .... '78 '03 C.309 B.A. L.966 J.D. [[A] Wexler]
Reneau, Peter J. '57 '84 C.959 B.A. L.966 J.D.
(adm. in WI; not adm. in IL) U.S. Dept. of Jus.
Renetzky, Michael K. .... '72 '96 C.734 B.S.B.A. L.309 J.D. [Lord,B.&B.]
Renfroe, James Scott '57 '85 C&L.339 B.S., J.D.
Sr. Coun., Atty. Registration & Disciplinary Comm.
Renier, Elaine C. .... '49 '74 C.424 B.A. L.146 J.D. 6457 N. Hiawatha Ave.
Renk, Christopher J., (AV) '— '88 C.350 B.S. L.494 J.D.
[Banner&W.] (See Pat. Sect.)
Renken, Sammi L. .... '74 '00 C&L.846 B.A., J.D. [[A] Johnson&B.]
Renner, Edward G. .... '70 '00 C.57 A.B. L.365 J.D. [Muriel R.]
Reno, Scott G. .... '60 '90 C.679 B.S. L.879 J.D. [Menges&M.]

Rentschler, Susan M., Law Offices of, (AV) '59 '90 C.679 B.S. L.365 J.D.
203 North LaSalle Street, Suite 2100, 60601
Telephone: 312-558-1457 Fax: 312-346-9603
Email: rentschlerlaw@aol.com
Estate Planning, Estate Administration, Wills and Probate, Trusts and Estates, Guardianship.
See Professional Biographies, CHICAGO, ILLINOIS

Reott, Raymond T., (AV) .... '55 '80 C.276 B.A. L.145 J.D. [Reott]

Reott Law Offices, LLC, (AV)
35 East Wacker Drive, Suite 650, 60601
Telephone: 312-332-7544 Fax: 312-782-4519
Email: rreott@reottlaw.com URL: http://www.reottlaw.com
Raymond T. Reott;—Jorge T. Mihalopoulos.
Environmental, Toxic Tort Defense, Environmental Bankruptcy, Environmental Insurance Coverage.
See Professional Biographies, CHICAGO, ILLINOIS

Repel, Robert J., (AV) '48 '77
C.209 A.B. L.365 J.D. Off. of Mayor, Intergovernmental Affairs
Repo, Geoffrey J. .... '70 '99 C.112 B.A. L.94 J.D. [[A] Sonnenschein N.&R.]
Reppas, Agelo L. .... '73 '00 C.352 B.S. L.910 J.D. [[A] Clausen M.]
Reschke, Michael W. '55 '80 C.589 B.S. L.339 J.D.
Pres. & Chmn. of the Bd., Prime Grp., Inc., The
Resh, Linda S., (AV) .... '— '89 C.959 B.S. L.424 J.D. [Kirkland&E.] (Pat.)
Resis, Michael, (AV) .... '— '81 C&L.339 B.A., J.D. [O'Hagan,S.&A.]
Resis, Robert H., (AV) '— '86 C.339 B.S.Ch.E. L.597 J.D.
[Banner&W.] (See Pat. Sect.)
Resnick, David P. .... '— '00 C.477 L.597 J.D. [[A] Foley&L.]
Resnick, Donald I., (AV) .... '50 '75 C.339 B.S. L.309 J.D. [Jenner&B.]
Resnick, Elise .... '67 '91 C.966 B.A. L.477 J.D. Asst. Corp. Coun., City of Chicago
Resnick, Kalman D., (AV) .... '48 '73 C.604 B.A. L.477 J.D. [Hughes S.P.R.&D.]
Resnick, Michael '66 '92 C.976 B.A. L.309 J.D.
(adm. in NY; not adm. in IL) William Harris Investors
Resnicoff, Steven H. '52 '80 C.674 A.B. L.976 J.D.
(adm. in NJ; not adm. in IL) De Paul Univ. Coll. of Law
Resnik, Mark E., (AV) .... '55 '80 C.339 B.S. L.424 J.D. 10 S. Wacker Dr., Ste. 2150
Restall, Jennie L. .... '77 '02 C.585 B.A. L.629 J.D. Off. of State App. Def.
Retke, Robert R. .... '41 '71 C&L.145 A.B., J.D. Dep. Corp. Coun.
Retsky, Jonathan E., (AV) '62 '89
C.98 B.S.E.E. L.846 J.D. [Brinks H.G.&L.] (See Pat. Sect.)
Rettberg, Kyle D. .... '— '98 C.894 A.B. L.145 J.D. [[A] Sidley A.B.&W.]
Rettberg, Paul A., (AV) .... '— '70 C&L.209 B.A., J.D. [Querrey&H.]
Rettberg, Richard J., (AV) .... '— '76 C.339 B.A. L.146 J.D. [McKenna S.]
Reuben, Don H., (AV) '28 '52 C&L.597 B.S., J.D.
[[C] Kane,C.&M.] (⊙Indian Wells, CA)
Reum, James M. .... '46 '73 C&L.309 B.A., J.D. [Winston&S.]
Reum, Walter J., (AV) .... '14 '38 L.146 LL.B. [Reum&C.]
Reum & Casello, (AV) .... 2960 N. Lake Shore Dr., Apt. 2401
Reutebuch, Wendy M. .... '74 '99 C.339 B.A. L.209 J.D. [Berger,N.&F.]

Reveliotis, George N., Law Office of '74 '99 C.339 B.S. L.1000 J.D.
30 N. Michigan Avenue, Suite 1619, 60602
Telephone: 312-230-0160 Fax: 312-230-0161
Email: greveliotis@reveliotislaw.com URL: http://www.reveliotislaw.com
(Of Counsel, Peter G. Karahalios).
Property Tax and Ad Valorem Tax.
See Professional Biographies, CHICAGO, ILLINOIS

Revis, Courtney A. .... '68 '99 C.473 B.A. L.150 J.D. [Revis&W.]

Revis & Ward, LLC
123 West Madison Street Suite 950, 60602
Telephone: 312-701-0380 Fax: 312-701-1161
URL: http://www.revisandward.com
Courtney A. Revis; Jennifer R. Ward.
Family Law, Divorce, Child Custody, Child Support, Paternity, Premarital Agreements, Postnuptial Agreements.
See Professional Biographies, CHICAGO, ILLINOIS

Revord, Lisa Maria Carrizales .... '63 '88 C.602 B.A. L.802 J.D. 1248G W. Fletcher‡
Rexer, Christian .... '46 '82 C.46 B.S. L.146 J.D. Contl. Bk.
Rexroat, Christopher L. .... '— '93 C&L.966 B.A., J.D. [Ungaretti&H.]
Reyes, Manuel .... '18 '57 C&L.597 B.S., J.D. 1624 W. 18th St.
Reyes, Marcos D. .... '70 '00 C&L.424 B.S., J.D. Off of the Cook Co. Pub. Def.
Reyes-Villanueva, Adriana I. '71 '96 C.188 B.S. L.309 J.D.
Quaker Foods & Beverages
Reynolds, Donald P. .... '29 '61 C&L.188 B.E.E., J.D. [[C] Ladas&P.] (See Pat. Sect.)
Reynolds, Frances P. .... '75 '04 C&L.966 B.A., J.D. [[A] Bell,B.&L.]
Reynolds, Frank R., Jr., (AV) .... '37 '62 C.602 B.A. L.424 J.D. [Reynolds&R.]
Reynolds, Jeanne M. .... '61 '86 C.741 B.A. L.424 J.D. [Reynolds&R.]
Reynolds, Meg M. .... '— '94 C.597 B.A. L.339 J.D. [Neal,G.&E.]
Reynolds, Michael T. .... '53 '81 C&L.424 B.A., J.D. [Rieff S.&K.]
Reynolds, N. Elizabeth .... '69 '97 C.976 B.A. L.846 J.D. [[A] Allison,S.&K.]
Reynolds, Scott H., (AV) .... '51 '76 C.339 B.A. L.597 J.D. [Levenfeld P.]
Reynolds, Thomas A., III, (AV) .... '52 '77 C.276 B.S.B.A. L.245 J.D. [Winston&S.]
Reynolds, Thomas A., Jr., (AV) .... '28 '51 C.276 A.B. L.477 J.D. [Winston&S.]
Reynolds & Reynolds, Law Offices of, Ltd., (AV) .... 111 W. Washington St.
Reynolds-Quillin, Michika R. '67 '98 C.811 B.A. L.1338 J.D.
(adm. in GA; not adm. in IL) Assoc. Gen. Coun., American Bar Association
Rezabek, James L. .... '32 '67 C.597 B.S. L.146 J.D. 4640 N. Olcott Ave.
Rezner, Ray G., (AV) .... '51 '77 C&L.352 B.G.S., J.D. [Barack F.K.P.&N.]
Rhee, David Y. .... '71 '01 C.477 B.A. L.284 J.D. 2 N. Lasalle Street
Rheingans, Karen .... '72 '99 C.966 B.A. L.365 J.D. [[A] Segal M.S.&M.]
Rheintgen, Kathleen A. .... '63 '88 C.339 B.S. L.424 J.D. [Welsh&K.] (See Pat. Sect.)
Rhiew, Margaret J. .... '— '05 C.477 B.A. L.146 J.D. [[S] Dykema G.P.]
Rhind, David S. '63 '90 C.299 B.A. L.347 J.D.
Gen. Coun., North America Hudson Highland Group, Inc.
Rhind, James T., (AV) .... '22 '50 C.608 A.B. L.309 LL.B. [[C] Bell,B.&L.]
Rhine, Alan, Law Offices of '51 '75 C.339 L.424 J.D.
111 W. Washington St., Ste. 1025
Rhine, Frederick S., (AV) .... '60 '86 C.46 B.S. L.178 J.D. [Hughes S.P.R.&D.]
Rhine, Wayne .... '41 '65 C.339 L.209 LL.B. Assoc. Cir. J.
Rhiner, Joel J., (AV) .... '64 '90 C.352 B.A. L.1068 J.D. [Stein,R.&H.]
Rhoades, Jennifer T. .... '75 '01 C.347 B.A. L.424 J.D. [[A] Cassiday,S.&G.]
Rhode, Christine M., (AV) .... '48 '73 C.597 B.A. L.477 J.D. [Vedder,P.K.&K.]
Rhodes, Anne-Marie, (AV) .... '51 '76 C.19 B.A. L.309 J.D. 30 S. Wacker Dr., 29th Fl.
Rhodes, Jennifer M. .... '— '04 C.339 B.S. L.145 J.D. [[A] Kirkland&E.]
Rhodes, Rhonda Alicia '— '76 C.597 B.A. L.209 J.D.
Assoc. Gen. Coun. & V.P., Amer. Hospital Assn.‡
Rhodes, Richard S., (AV) '31 '53 C.347 B.S. L.1119 LL.B.
125 S. Wacker Dr., Ste. 1700
Rhoten, Alison M. .... '77 '02 C.339 B.A. L.228 J.D. [[A] Skadden,A.S.M.&F.]
Riahei, Melissa M. .... '73 '98 C.1356 B.A. L.692 J.D. [[A] Wildman,H.A.&D.]
Riback, Adam .... '— '94 C.339 B.A. L.999 J.D. [Levin,R.]
Ribaudo, Anthony J. .... '71 '96 C.309 B.A. L.145 J.D. [[A] Sidley A.B.&W.]
Riccione, John M. .... '64 '89 C.116 B.A. L.823 J.D. [Aronberg G.D.&G.]
Riccolo, Jennifer R. .... '78 '04 C.352 B.A. L.424 J.D. [[A] Hinshaw&C.]
Rice, Aaron N. .... '77 '03 C.1365 B.A. L.339 J.D. [[A] Schwartz C.]
Rice, Andrea D. .... '— '97 C.801 L.424 330 S. Wells St., Suite 1100
Rice, Andrew .... '71 '97 C.475 B.A. L.209 J.D. 333 West Wacker Drive, Suite 500
Rice, Craig C. .... '51 '77 C.976 B.A. L.606 J.D. Contl. Ill. Nat. Bk. & Trust Co.
Rice, David J., (BV) '53 '80 C.293 B.A. L.424 J.D.
Assoc. Gen. Coun., Rush Presbyterian St. Luke's Med. Ctr.
Rice, Edward H. .... '61 '88 C&L.477 A.B., J.D. [Sonnenschein N.&R.]
Rice, Glenn A. .... '59 '85 C.589 B.S. L.146 J.D. [Funkhouser V.L.&D.]
Rice, Jillian .... '— '03 C.339 B.A. L.597 J.D. [[A] Kirkland&E.]
Rice, Joel W., (BV) .... '57 '83 C.894 B.A. L.145 J.D. [[C] Fisher&P.]
Rice, Julia A. .... '33 '79 C.999 A.B. L.589 J.D. Univ. of Ill. at Chicago
Rice, Matthew H. .... '75 '03 C.477 B.A. L.813 J.D. [[A] Jenner&B.]
Rice, Saundra L. .... '71 '96 C.867 B.A. L.597 J.D. [[A] McDermott W.&E.]
Rice, Sharon .... '58 '83 C.575 B.A. L.145 J.D. [[A] Bollinger,R.&G.]
Rich, Joshua R. '69 '94 C.446 B.S.B.A. L.893 J.D.
[McDonnell B.H.&B.] (See Pat. Sect.)
Rich, Nancy J., (BV) .... '59 '84 C&L.424 A.B., J.D. [Katten M.R.]
Richard, Edward C. .... '49 '74 C.861 B.A. L.910 J.D. [Chuhak&T.]
Richard, Howard M., (P.C.), (AV) .... '44 '68 C.188 B.A. L.309 LL.B. [Katten M.R.]
Richards, Alan E., (AV) .... '49 '76 C.123 B.A. L.436 J.D. [Richards,R.&S.] ⊙
Richards, Brian F. .... '67 '92 C.339 B.S. L.893 J.D. [Katten M.R.]
Richards, David J. .... '70 '95 C.424 B.A. L.879 J.D. [Hinshaw&C.]
Richards, Geoffrey A. .... '— '95 C.966 B.A. L.1009 J.D. [Kirkland&E.]
Richards, Jeffrey W. .... '— '95 C.98 B.S. L.145 J.D. [Kirkland&E.]
Richards, Marc V. '60 '93 C.910 B.S.Ch.E. L.424 J.D.
[Brinks H.G.&L.] (See Pat. Sect.)
Richards, Matthew .... '— '00 C.367 B.A. L.145 J.D. [[A] Kirkland&E.]
Richards, Patrick D. .... '75 '00 C.339 B.S. L.893 J.D. [[A] McDermott W.&E.]
Richards, Robert E., (AV) .... '63 '88 C.367 B.A. L.477 J.D. [Sonnenschein N.&R.]
Richards, Stanley H. .... '22 '49 C&L.309 B.S., LL.B. 25 E. Washington

Richards, Ralph & Schwab, Chartered, (AV)
39 South LaSalle Street, Suite 905, 60603 ⊙
Telephone: 312-641-6696 Fax: 847-367-9621
Email: attorney@rrs-chtd.com URL: http://www.lawyers.com/richardandschwab
Michael L. Ralph, Sr.; Alan E. Richards; David J. Schwab;—Michael L. Ralph, Jr.; Lauren B. Schreeder.
Corporate and Business. Banking and Finance. Bankruptcy and Creditors' Rights. Real Estate. Commercial Litigation.
Vernon Hills, Illinois Office: One Hawthorn Place, 175 East Hawthorn Parkway, Suite 345, 60061. Telephone: 847-367-9699. Fax: 847-367-9621. Email: attorney@rrs-chtd.com.
See Professional Biographies, CHICAGO, ILLINOIS

Richardson, David M. .... '71 '98 C.478 B.A. L.597 J.D. [Nery&M.]
Richardson, Elliot .... '72 '98 C.98 B.A. L.201 J.D. [Richardson,S.B.&M.]
Richardson, James R., (AV) .... '— '69 C.210 B.A. L.145 J.D. [Chapman&C.]
Richardson, John L. .... '47 '82 C.161 B.B.A. L.1003 J.D. 5800 N. Sheridan Rd.
Richardson, Julieanna L. '54 '80 C.1036 B.A. L.309 J.D.
Showcase Chicago Channel 25 Teleproductions
Richardson, Michael I., (AV) .... '58 '87 C&L.602 B.A., J.D. [Franczek S.]
Richardson, Michele Baker '63 '90 C.103 B.A. L.976 J.D.
(adm. in GA; not adm. in IL) Asst. Prof. of Law, Chicago-Kent College of Law
Richardson, Travis .... '67 '97 C.659 B.A. L.477 J.D. 5 E. Superior St.

Richardson, Patrick, Westbrook & Brickman, LLC
218 N. Jefferson Street, Suite 400, 60661 ⊙
Telephone: 312-466-1669 Fax:312-466-1513
URL: http://www.rpwb.com
Nicholas J. Vogelzang.

(This Listing Continued)

Richardson, Patrick, Westbrook & Brickman, LLC (Continued)

Antitrust and Trade Regulation, Business Torts, Class Actions, Commercial Litigation, Complex and Multi-District Litigation, Consumer Law, Drug and Medical Device Litigation, Environmental Law, Healthcare, Mass Torts, Medical Malpractice, Occupational Disease, Plaintiffs Personal Injury, Premises Liability, Products Liability, Securities, Railroad Accidents and Injuries, Tax Litigation, Toxic Torts, White Collar Criminal Defense.
Barnwell, South Carolina Office: 1730 Jackson Street, P.O. Box 1368, 29812. Telephone: 803-541-7850. Fax: 803-541-9625.
Mt. Pleasant, South Carolina Office: 1037 Chuck Dawley Boulevard, Building A, P.O. Box 1007, 29464. Telephone: 843-727-6500. Fax: 843-216-6509.
Charleston, South Carolina Office: 174 East Bay Street, P.O. Box 879, 29401. Telephone: 843-727-6541. Fax: 843-727-3103.

See Professional Biographies, CHICAGO, ILLINOIS

Richardson, Stasko, Boyd & Mack, LLC .... 20 South Clark Street, Suite 500
Richardson-Lowry, Mary B. .... '57 '86 C.766 B.A. L.325 J.D. [Mayer,B.R.&M.]
Richek, Stephen D. .... '48 '73 C.910 A.B. L.424 J.D. 20 N. Clark St., Ste. 2550
Richert, Elizabeth E. .... '76 '01 C.938 B.A. L.228 J.D. [A R.F.Coleman&Assoc.]
Richman, Arlene B. .... '57 '82 C.188 B.S. L.930 J.D. 203 N. La Salle St., Suite 1800
Richman, Daniel A. .... '53 '79 C.910 A.B. L.209 J.D. Modern Healthcare
Richman, Edward S. .... '32 '57 C.1016 L.209 LL.B. 33 N. La Salle St.
Richman, Jerald F. .... '40 '67 100 N La Salle St Ste 910
Richman, Jerome R. .... '65 '90 C.339 B.S. L.597 J.D. [Weinberg R.]
Richman, Joan M. .... '65 '92 C.012 B.Com. L.276 J.D. [Baker&M.]
Richman, Kenneth H. .... '47 '73 C.98 B.S. L.966 J.D. [Burke,W.M.&S.]
Richman, Laura D. .... '56 '81 C.976 B.A. L.145 J.D. [Mayer,B.R.&M.]
Richman, Lawrence I., (AV) .... '54 '77 C.178 B.A. L.145 J.D. [Neal,G.&E.]
Richman, Michael D., (AV) .... '— '79 C.347 B.A. L.930 J.D. [Sachnoff&W.]
Richmond, James G., (AVⓉ) .... '44 '69 C.347 B.S. L.1119 J.D. [Greenberg T.]
Richmond, Janet A. .... '56 '81 C.20 B.A. L.424 J.D. Admr., Dept. of Corrections
Richmond, Mark S., (AV) .... '51 '76 C.339 B.S. L.365 J.D. [Weinberg R.]
Richter, Alison Marie .... '75 '00 C.339 B.A. L.597 J.D. [B Sidley A.B.&W.]
Richter, Brian K. '67 '92 C.188 B.A. L.145 J.D.
V. P. & Assoc. Gen. Coun., Equity Group Investments, LLC
Richter, David J. .... '40 '70 C.966 B.S.M.E. L.339 J.D. [B DLPiper R.G.C.U.] (Pat.)
Richter, Mindi .... '79 '04 C.347 B.S. L.424 J.D. [A Sonnenschein N.&R.]
Richter, Paul David .... '69 '96 C.339 B.A. L.209 J.D. [Rapoport]
Richter, Paul J., (AV) .... '46 '71 C.1016 L.365 J.D. [Kelly,O.M.D.&R.]
Richter, Tobin M., (AV) .... '— '73 C&L.893 B.C.P., J.D. [A Neal&L.]
Ricordati, Raymond R., III .... '77 '02 C.602 B.S. L.365 J.D. [A Brinks H.G.&L.]
Riddick, Catherine Lynn .... '56 '83 C.1083 B.S. L.902 J.D. KPMG Peat Marwick
Riddle, Benjamin L. .... '77 '03 C.347 B.A. L.345 J.D. [A Wiedner&M.]
Rider, Susan H. .... '65 '90 C.547 B.S. L.188 J.D. Assoc. Gen. Coun., Excelon Corp.
Ridge, Anita S., (AV) .... '66 '91 C.504 B.A. L.145 J.D. [B J.S.Rothman&Assoc.]
Ridings, Jeannie M. .... '— '05 C.519 B.A, L.597 J.D. [A Kubasiak,F.R.&R.]
Ridley, Kevin L. .... '58 '87 C.1090 B.S. L.329 J.D. Asst. Gen. Coun., Exelon Corp.
Ridsdale, Matthew T. .... '71 '02 C.477 B.S.M.E. L.146 J.D. [A Bell,B.&L.] (Pat.)
Riebman, Hyman I. '53 '78
C.209 B.A. L.589 J.D. Assoc. J., 1st Munic. Dist. Ct. of Cook Co.
Riechers, Alice L. .... '— '00 C.957 B.A. L.966 J.D. [A Rakoczy M.M.S.]
Rieck, Thomas W., (AV) .... '45 '71 C.602 B.B.A. L.597 J.D. [Rieck&C.]
Rieck and Crotty, A Professional Corporation, (AV) ... 55 West Monroe Street Suite 3390
Riecke, Charles Sanford .... '— '97 C.629 B.A. L.861 J.D. [A Seyfarth S.]
Rieff, Melvyn A., (AV) .... '44 '69 C&L.339 B.A., J.D. [Rieff S.&K.]

Rieff Schramm & Kanter, (AV)
100 North LaSalle Street, Suite 2300, 60602-2402
Telephone: 312-372-2500 Fax: 312-372-2550
Email: mel@realproptax.com URL: http://www.rieffschrammkanter.com
Members of Firm: Melvyn A. Rieff; Donald L. Schramm; Herbert Kanter; Lawrence B. Brodsky; Glenn S. Guttman; Margaret E. Graham; Michael T. Reynolds. Of Counsel: Stephanie S. Park.
Real Estate Taxation, Property Tax Appeals, Property Tax Assessments, Tax Incentives, Tax Abatement, Exemption, Eminent Domain, Condemnation, Assessments.

See Professional Biographies, CHICAGO, ILLINOIS

Rieger, Mitchell S., (AV) .... '— '50 C.597 A.B. L.309 J.D. [Schiff H.] ‡
Riekes, Suzanne S. .... '67 '93 C.861 B.A. L.569 J.D. 1615 N. Oakley E.‡
Ries-Buntain, Jennifer .... '72 '97 C.477 B.A. L.209 J.D. [A Hall,P.&S.]
Rieser, David L., (AV) .... '56 '80 C.145 A.B. L.910 J.D. [McGuirewoods]
Riess, Daniel M., (AV) '36 '68
C.597 B.S.Ch.E. L.276 J.D. [Cook,A.M.M.C.&M.] (See Pat. Sect.)
Rietz, Eric J. .... '67 '92 C.966 B.A. L.597 J.D. [A Vedder,P.K.&K.]
Riewer, John J. .... '64 '99 C.424 B.A. L.365 J.D. [Bollinger,R.&G.]
Riewer, Nicholas A., (AV) .... '55 '84 C.424 B.A. L.365 J.D. [Bollinger,R.&G.]
Rifkind, Norman, (AV) .... '60 '85 C.347 B.S. L.424 J.D. [Lasky&R.]
Rigg, Robert S., (AV) .... '64 '90 C.679 B.S.I.D.E. L.879 J.D. [Mayer,B.R.&M.] (Pat.)
Riggle, David A., (AV) .... '46 '78 C.1044 B.A. L.215 J.D. [Riggle&C.]

Riggle and Craven, (AV)
Suite 525 8430 West Bryn Mawr, 60631
Telephone: 312-368-8787 Telefax: 312-368-0939
Email: RandC@tradelaw.com URL: http://www.tradelaw.com
Members of Firm: David A. Riggle; David J. Craven. Of Counsel: Jack D. Mlawski (Not admitted in IL); John J. Galvin (Not admitted in IL); John P. Craven (Not admitted in IL).
Customs Law, International Trade, Export Regulation, Import and Export Law, Antidumping, International Law of the Sea. Federal, Administrative and Legislative Practice.

See Professional Biographies, CHICAGO, ILLINOIS

Riggs, Charles T., Jr. .... '68 '94 C.339 B.S. [A Patula&Assoc.] (Pat.)

Righeimer Martin & Cinquino, P.C., (AV)
20 North Clark, Suite 1900, 60602
Telephone: 312-726-5646 Telecopier: 312-609-2277
Frank R. Martin; Leo N. Cinquino; David A. Martin; Sandra L. Hebenstreit; Bradley A. Mueller; Celeste P. Cinquino; Frank S. Righeimer (1882-1980); Alvah T. Martin (1908-1993); Frank S. Righeimer, Jr. (1909-1998).
General Civil and Trial Practice. Eminent Domain, Banking, Probate, Health Care and Hospital Law, Corporate.

See Professional Biographies, CHICAGO, ILLINOIS

Riley, Barbara A. .... '— '85 C.339 B.A. L.365 J.D. Ofc. Of State's Atty.
Riley, Charles E., III '48 '74 C.754 B.S. L.229 J.D.
(adm. in PA; not adm. in IL) FBI
Riley, Colleen M. .... '72 '97 C.597 B.S. L.424 J.D. 20 N. Wacker Dr.
Riley, Jack T., Jr., (AV) .... '46 '73 C.207 B.A. L.276 J.D. [Johnson&B.]
Riley, James B., Jr., (AV) .... '54 '79 C.339 B.S. L.273 J.D. [McGuirewoods]
Riley, Joan R., (AV) '52 '85 C.597 B.A. L.424 J.D.
Gen. Coun., V.P. & Secy., Quixote Corporation
Riley, Nancy Mary .... '78 '04 C.597 B.A. L.800 J.D. [A McGuirewoods]
Riley, Reed F. .... '29 '71 C.339 B.S. L.178 J.D. Amoco Corp.
Riley, Robert E. .... '55 '80 C.927 B.A. L.209 J.D. [Robbins,S.N.L.&T.]
Riley, Robert H., (AV) ..... '— '78 C.207 B.A. L.145 J.D. [Schiff H.] (ⓞNew York, NY)
Riley, Shellé E. .... '72 '99 C.393 B.A. L.900 J.D. [A Borovsky&E.]
Riley, Thomas H., Jr. .... '60 '88 C.966 B.S.J. L.425 J.D. 1737 W. Polk St., Ste. 405
Riley, Thomas P. .... '73 '02 C.679 B.S.C.E. L.879 J.D. [A McCracken&F.] (Pat.)
Rimland, Jack P., (AV) .... '42 '66 C.339 B.A. L.209 J.D. 820 W. Jackson Blvd.
Rinder, Lawrence J. .... '52 '79 C.339 B.A. L.146 J.D. 6305 N. Hamlin Ave.‡
Rinella, Bernard B., (AV) .... '36 '61 C.477 B.A. L.209 J.D. [Rinella&R.]

Rinella and Rinella, Ltd., (AV) BB
One North La Salle Street Suite 3400, 60602-4094
Telephone: 312-236-5454 Fax: 312-236-6975 URL: http://www.rinellaandrinella.com
Email: donnaw@rinellaandrinella.com URL: http://www.lawyers.com/rinellaandrinella
Samuel A. Rinella (1906-1982); Kathryn B. Rinella (1906-1991); Bernard B. Rinella; Joseph G. Phelps; Maricarol Lacy; Karen J. Bowes; Michael J. Chiero. Associate: Nicole M. Onorato.
Practice Limited to Family Law and Divorce including the areas of Legal Separation, Negotiating and Drafting Premarital and Postnuptial Agreements, Judgment Enforcement, Child Custody and Child Support Actions, Domestic Violence, Spousal Support, Appeals, Adoption, Parentage Actions and Interstate Support Enforcement.

See Professional Biographies, CHICAGO, ILLINOIS

Ring, Daniel L. .... '67 '93 C.597 B.A. L.424 J.D. [Mayer,B.R.&M.]
Ring, Gerard D., (AV) .... '57 '86 C.339 B.A. L.365 J.D. [Burke,W.M.&S.]
Ring, Jack Samuel, (AV) .... '— '57 C&L.472 B.B.A., J.D. [J.S.Ring&Assoc.]
Ring, Kathleen A., (BV) '57 '86
C.209 B.S. L.365 J.D. V.P., Sr. Atty., Leo Burnett Worldwide, Inc.
Ring, Thomas J., (AV) ... '52 '78 C.966 B.S.C.E.E. L.365 J.D. [Wildman,H.A.&D.] (Pat.)
Ring, Jack Samuel, & Associates, Ltd., (AV) .... 1 East Wacker Drive, Suite 2406
Ringhofer, Robert B. .... '78 '02 C.37 B.S. L.424 J.D. 200 W. Adams, Ste. 1900
Ringler, Meredith J. .... '73 '99 C.210 B.A. L.424 J.D. Supr. Ct., Jud. Clk.
Ringo, Wesley L. '50 '92 C.734 B.A. L.957 J.D.
(adm. in WI; not adm. in IL) 50 South LaSalle St.
Rink, Paul W. .... '46 '70 C.424 B.S. L.597 J.D. Asso. Coun., Indus. Comm. of Ill.
Rinkov, Jeffrey S. .... '78 '04 C.966 B.S. L.145 J.D. [A Barack F.K.P.&N.]
Rin-Laures, Li-Hsein (Lily), M.D. '— '93
C.367 B.A. L.309 J.D. [Marshall,G.&B.] (See Pat. Sect.)
Rinn, Bart .... '63 '88 C.589 B.S. L.339 J.D. [McCullough,C.&L.]
Rioja, Amalia S. ...... '68 '93 C&L.597 B.S., J.D. Dep. Gen. Coun. Off. of the Comptroller
Riordan, Anne M. '55 '81 C.822 A.B. L.285 J.D.
(adm. in WI; not adm. in IL) Law Clk. to U.S. Bkrptcy. Ct. J.
Riordan, Brian J. .... '71 '96 C.234 B.A. L.424 J.D. [Clausen M.]
Riordan, Brian K. .... '43 '69 C.755 B.A. L.602 J.D. 2629 N. Hampden Ct.
Riordan, Cornelius F., (AV) .... '51 '76 C.602 B.A. L.365 J.D. [Riordan,D.L.&M.]
Riordan, Joan Marie .... '38 '63 C&L.209 A.B., J.D. [Riordan&R.]
Riordan, Mary J., (BV) .... '54 '87 C.719 B.A. L.424 J.D. [M.J.Riordan]
Riordan, Michael J. .... '60 '90 C.475 B.A. L.215 J.D. U.S. Securities & Exch. Comm.
Riordan, Molly Bridget .... '69 '97 C.339 B.S. L.209 J.D. 2629 N. Hampden Ct.
Riordan, Timothy J., (AV) .... '41 '65 C.177 B.A. L.597 J.D. [Defrees&F.]

Riordan, Donnelly, Lipinski & McKee, Ltd., (AV)
(Formerly McNeela & Griffin, Ltd.)
10 North Dearborn 4th Floor, 60602
Telephone: 312-663-9400 Fax: 312-663-1028
Email: webbaddress@rdlmlaw.com URL: http://www.rdlmlaw.com
Cornelius F. Riordan; Patrick G. Donnelly; Marc S. Lipinski; Harold E. McKee;—Michael A. Palermo, Jr.; Jamie L. Schwartz; Genevieve M. Lynott; Brian T. Miller. Of Counsel: Gary L. Griffin.
Commercial and Tort Litigation, Construction, Mechanics Liens, Employment Practice, Surety and Fidelity Law, Insurance, Real Estate Law, Corporate Law; Estate Planning and Probate.

See Professional Biographies, CHICAGO, ILLINOIS

Riordan, Mary J., Ltd., (BV) ....980 N. Michigan
Riordan & Robbins .... 134 N. LaSalle St.
Ripani, Michael N. ...... '61 '90 C.339 B.S. L.146 J.D. 30 South Wacker Drive, 26th Floor
Ripley, Curtis Dean .... '75 '01 C.492 B.A. L.494 J.D. [A Mayer,B.R.&M.]
Ripley, Regina .... '71 '01 C&L.339 B.S., J.D. [A Ross,D.&B.]
Ripp, Amanda J. '69 '97 C.966 B.A. L.146 J.D.
Three First National Plaza, 7000 Madison Avenue
Ripp, Paul J. .... '67 '03 C.339 B.A. L.145 J.D. [A Williams M.&J.]
Rippie, E. Glenn, (AV) .... '— '85 C.597 B.A. L.976 J.D. [Foley&L.]
Ripple, Stephanie Ann ...... '75 '02 C.573 B.A. L.146 J.D. 205 W. Randolph St., Ste. 925
Risch, Charles J. .... '49 '82 C&L.966 B.A., J.D. [Lawrence,K.S.&U.]
Rising, Julie Claire .... '— '02 C.966 B.A. L.145 J.D. [A Schiff H.]
Rissman, Burton R., (P.C.), (AV) .... '— '51 C&L.339 B.S., J.D. [Schiff H.]
Rissman, Francine G. .... '— '77 C.705 B.A. L.597 J.D. 180 E. Pearson St.‡
Rissman, Michael P., (AV) .... '60 '86 C.329 A.B. L.145 J.D. [Mayer,B.R.&M.]
Rissman, Steven E. .... '49 '77 Asst. States Atty.
Rissman, Thomas W. .... '57 '82 C.188 A.B. L.145 J.D. [McLachlan,R.&D.]
Rist, Dianne E. .... '— '92 C.185 B.A. L.352 J.D. [Chapman&C.]
Ristanovic, Zorka .... '70 '95 C.339 B.A. L.209 J.D. [A Davis F.Z.K.M.M.&R.]
Ritchey, Joan G. .... '72 '01 C.94 B.A. L.910 J.D. [A Ice M.]
Ritchie, Paul Scott, (AV) .... '60 '89 C.679 B.S. L.209 J.D. [Clausen M.]
Ritchie, Stephen L., P.C., (AV) .... '— '89 C.893 B.A. L.145 J.D. [Kirkland&E.]
Ritchie, William P., (AV) .... '— '71 C.608 B.S. L.893 J.D. [Jones D.]
Ritenour, Megan E. .... '77 '03 C.339 B.A. L.209 J.D. [A Grotefeld&D.]
Ritsos, Geo. T. .... '14 '38 L.365 LL.B. 29 S. LaSalle St.
Ritsos, Peter C., (BV) .... '42 '66 C.1016 B.A. L.209 J.D. 29 S. La Salle St.
Rittenberg, Ivan M., (AV) .... '45 '72 C.339 B.A. L.209 J.D. [Rittenberg,B.&G.]
Rittenberg, Buffen & Gulbrandsen, Ltd., (AV) ..... 309 West Washington Street, Suite 900
Ritter, Bradley V., (BV) .... '— '91 C.597 B.A. L.339 J.D. [Kirkland&E.]
Ritter, David B., (AV) .... '58 '85 C.188 B.S. L.930 J.D. [Neal,G.&E.]
Ritter, Elisabeth A., (BV) .... '69 '94 C.597 B.A. L.910 J.D. [A Komie&Assoc.]
Ritter, Gerald L., (BV) .... '48 '73 C.393 B.A. L.209 J.D. 445 N. La Salle St.
Ritter, S. Michael .... '53 '79 C.477 B.B.A. L.424 J.D. [Ritter&C.]
Ritter & Cassano, (BV) .... 1 N. La Salle St. Suite 3950
Rivas, Marcos P. '69 '03 C.145 B.A. L.659 J.D.
(adm. in MA; not adm. in IL; See Pat. Sect.) [A Leydig,V.&M.]
Rivelli, Timothy J., (BV) .... '54 '79 C.597 B.A. L.424 J.D. [Winston&S.]
River, Regina M. ..... '72 '99 C.352 B.B.A. L.209 J.D. Claims Analyst, CNA Surety Corp.
Rivera, Christian R. .... '69 '94 C.597 B.A. L.273 J.D. [Haynes,S.K.O.&M.]
Rivera, Gilberto R. '54 '89 C.178 B.A. L.677 J.D.
(adm. in NY; not adm. in IL) 6160 N. Cicero Avenue, Suite 305
Rivera, Jesus Ricardo .... '71 '02 C.339 B.A. L.879 J.D. 2030 W. Armitage
Rivera, Maria Pellegrino .... '— '95 C.597 B.A. L.145 J.D. [Kirkland&E.]
Rivers, D. Adolphus .... '28 '51 C.999 L.365 J.D. Ret. Cir. J.
Rives Band, Kathryn .... '65 '04 C.339 B.A. L.1000 J.D. [A Belgrade&O.]
Rivkin, Bernard L., (AV) .... '47 '74 C.1016 B.A. L.365 J.D. 33 N. Dearborn St.
Rivkin, Robert S., (AV) '60 '87
C.309 A.B. L.813 J.D. V.P. & Dep. Gen. Coun., Aon Corp.
Rizzi, Dom J. .... '32 '61 C&L.209 B.S.C., J.D. [B Miller F.&C.]
Rizzo, Ann Marie T. .... '— '01 C&L.209 B.S., J.D. [A Kirkland&E.]
Rizzo, Christopher .... '— '03 C.597 B.A. L.339 J.D. [A Morgan,L.&B.]

Rizzo, Ronald S., (AVⓉ) . . . '— '65 C.746 B.S. L.276 LL.B. [Ⓒ Jones D.]
Rizzo, Tracy M. . . . '71 '96 C.700 B.A. L.365 J.D. [T.M.Rizzo]
Rizzo, Tracy M., P.C., Law Office of . . . 30 N. La Salle St., Ste. 1530
Roach, David M. . . . '75 '01 C.1458 B.A. L.209 J.D. [Ⓐ Fisher K.]
Roach, Derek A. . . . '74 '99 C.340 B.A. L.145 J.D. [Ⓐ Gordon&G.L.] (Pat.)
Roach, James P., II, (AV) . . . '— '90 C&L.339 B.A., J.D. [Hennessy&R.]
Roach, John L., (AV) . . . '24 '50 C.644 L.146 J.D. 77 W. Wash. St.
Roach, Kathleen L., (AV) . . . '62 '85 C.1375 A.B. L.145 J.D. [Sidley A.B.&W.]
Roach, William H., Jr., (AV) . . . '44 '75 C.178 A.B. L.880 J.D. [McDermott W.&E.]
Roache, John T. . . . '68 '93 C.602 B.B.A. L.339 J.D. [Bell,B.&L.]
Roadman, Leigh D., (AV) . . . '59 '86 C.339 B.S. L.209 J.D. [Martin,B.&S.]
Robben, Eric . . . '— '02 C.602 B.A. L.910 J.D. [Ⓐ Holland&K.]
Robbins, Ellen S. . . . '67 '91 C.339 B.S. L.309 J.D. [Sidley A.B.&W.]
Robbins, Elliott H. . . . '61 '86 C.145 B.A. L.424 J.D. [Robbins&R.]
Robbins, Gregory J. . . . '69 '97 C&L.966 B.A., J.D. [Ⓐ Sidley A.B.&W.]
Robbins, Harold J. . . . '37 '81 C.201 B.A. L.209 J.D. [Riordan&R.]
Robbins, Jenifer M. . . . '73 '98 C.339 B.A. L.309 J.D. Gen. Coun., FPL Advsry. Grp.
Robbins, Laurence S. . . . '30 '56 C.339 L.365 LL.B. [Robbins&R.]
Robbins, Leslie . . . '54 '78 C.339 B.A. L.424 J.D. Cook Co. Pub. Guardian
Robbins, Manuel J., (AV) . . . '17 '41 C.1016 L.209 J.D. [Ⓒ Robbins,S.&P.]
Robbins, Richard A. . . . '33 '58 C&L.966 B.S.E., LL.B. 4503 N. Oakley St.
Robbins, Richard E. . . . '62 '91 C.453 B.S. L.145 J.D. [Sidley A.B.&W.]
Robbins, Ronnie Orzoff, (Mrs.) . . . '33 '57 C.1016 B.A. L.209 J.D. [Robbins&R.]
Robbins Atwood, Reagen C. . . . '— '97 C.309 A.B. L.477 J.D. [Ⓐ Foley&L.]
Robbins & Robbins, Ltd. . . . 70 W. Madison Street
Robbins, Salomon & Patt, Ltd., (AV) . . . 10th Floor (⊙Glenview)
Robbins, Schwartz, Nicholas, Lifton & Taylor, Ltd., (AV)
20 North Clark Street Suite 900 (⊙Collinsville, Decatur, Macomb)
Roberson, Andrew R. . . . '— '00 C.911 B.A. L.1117 J.D. [Ⓐ Latham&W.]
Roberson, Eric M. . . . '— '91 C.98 B.S. L.339 J.D. [Chapman&C.]
Roberson, G. Gale, Jr., (AV) . . . '— '60 C.197 A.B. L.309 LL.B. [Ⓒ Holland&K.]
Robert, Linda A. . . . '77 '02 C&L.424 B.A., J.D. [Ⓐ Wiedner&M.]
Roberts, Albert J., III '72 '02 C.589 B.S. L.365 J.D.
Asst. V.P., General Star Management Company
Roberts, David J. . . . '51 '82 C.589 B.S. L.209 J.D. DePaul Univ.
Roberts, Dorothy . . . '10 '31 L.209 LL.B. 655 W. 80th‡
Roberts, Dorothy E. '56 '81 C.976 B.A. L.309 S.J.D.
(adm. in NY; not adm. in IL) Northwestern Univ. School of Law
Roberts, J. William, (AV) '— '68 C.340 B.A. L.910 J.D.
[Hinshaw&C.] (⊙Springfield)
Roberts, James D. . . . '59 '89 C.937 B.A. L.365 J.D. [DLPiper R.G.C.U.]
Roberts, Janis D. . . . '48 '80 C.338 B.S. L.436 J.D. [Durkin&R.]
Roberts, Jerome J., (P.C.), (AV) . . . '43 '68 C&L.477 B.B.A., J.D. [Fitzsimmons,R.P.&C.]
Roberts, John A. . . . '68 '94 C.477 B.A. L.352 J.D. [Wildman,H.A.&D.]
Roberts, John C. . . . '40 '69 C.597 B.S. L.976 LL.B. Dean, DePaul Univ.
Roberts, John W., (AV) . . . '57 '82 C.393 B.A. L.309 J.D. [Barack F.K.P.&N.]
Roberts, Kenneth M., (AV) . . . '— '85 C&L.352 B.G.S., J.D. [Schiff H.]
Roberts, Kimberly Marie . . . '75 '00 C&L.801 B.S., J.D. City of Chicago, Dept. of Law
Roberts, Lindsay E. . . . '56 '86 C.914 B.A. L.145 J.D. 837 Oakdale Ave.‡
Roberts, Mary Colleen . . . '59 '89 C.750 B.A. L.209 J.D. Asst. State Atty.
Roberts, Michael G. . . . '57 '84 C.339 B.A. L.365 J.D. [Roberts]
Roberts, Michael S. . . . '61 '87 C.589 B.S. L.209 J.D. [Connelly R.&M.]
Roberts, Paul G. . . . '64 '90 C&L.352 B.A., J.D. ITT Hartford
Roberts, Peter J., (AV) . . . '66 '91 C.93 A.B. L.228 J.D. [Shaw G.F.G.W.&T.]
Roberts, Randall E., (AV) . . . '56 '81 C&L.424 B.A., J.D. Exec. Asst. States Atty.
Roberts, Sheri . . . '66 '95 C.912 B.A. L.477 J.D. [Ⓐ Sidley A.B.&W.]
Roberts Law Office . . . 535 North Michigan Avenue Suite 2302
Roberts-Kurpis, Sue . . . '48 '92 C.112 A.B. L.146 J.D. 3845 W. 58th Pl.
Robertson, David H., Jr., (BVⓉ) . . . '52 '81 C.197 B.A. L.146 J.D. [D.H.Robertson]
Robertson, Francesca J. '58 '83 C.339 B.S. L.424 J.D.
V.P. & Sr. Coun., United Ins. Co. of America
Robertson, J. Robert, (P.C.), (AV) . . . '— '90 C.885 B.A. L.145 J.D. [Kirkland&E.]
Robertson, Ned S., (AV) . . . '45 '71 C.319 B.A. L.146 J.D. [Aronberg G.D.&G.]
Robertson, Sara B. . . . '76 '02 C.20 B.A. L.424 J.D. [Ⓐ Nisen&E.]
Robertson and Wall, P.C., (BVⓉ) . . . 670 N. Clark St., Ste. 300
Robin, Barry A. . . . '57 '83 C.339 B.S. L.365 J.D. [Tucker B.R.&M.]
Robin, Neil A., (BV) . . . '50 '76 C.339 B.A. L.146 J.D. 30 N. La Salle St.
Robin, Richard C., (AV) . . . '45 '70 C.861 B.A. L.209 J.D. [Vedder,P.K.&K.]
Robin, Robert S., (P.C.), (AV) . . . '35 '59 C.966 B.S. L.309 LL.B. 200 S. Wacker Dr.
Robin, Shawn M. . . . '75 '02 C.347 B.A. L.209 J.D. [Ⓐ J.S.Ring&Assoc.]
Robin, Sidney, (AV) . . . '35 '60 C.339 B.A. L.597 J.D. 155 N. Michigan Ave.
Robins, Lawrence A., (P.C.), (AV) . . . '49 '73 C.339 B.A. L.273 J.D. [DLPiper R.G.C.U.]
Robinson, Aron D., (BV) . . . '56 '87 C.475 B.A. L.365 J.D. 19 S. La Salle St.
Robinson, Clarke C., (AV) . . . '29 '55 C&L.309 A.B., LL.B. 3500 Three 1st Nat. Plz.‡
Robinson, Douglas A. . . . '78 '04 C.502 B.S. L.910 J.D. [Ⓐ Leydig,V.&M.]
Robinson, Ellen G. . . . '75 '01 C.339 B.A. L.146 J.D. [Ⓐ Clausen M.]
Robinson, Ellen G., (AV) . . . '44 '77 C.659 B.A. L.209 J.D. [Ⓒ Robinson C.&C.]
Robinson, Howard M. . . . '46 '72 C.966 B.A. L.209 J.D. 405 N. Wabash Ave.
Robinson, Jamie A. . . . '— '99 C&L.966 B.A., J.D. [Ⓐ Michael B.&F.]
Robinson, Janice Holman . . . '56 '83 C.313 B.A. L.7 J.D. Hyatt Legal Servs.
Robinson, Kevin M. . . . '59 '85 C.162 B.A. L.352 J.D. 100 S. Wacker Dr., 20th Fl.
Robinson, Kimberly J. . . . '60 '86 C.350 B.S. L.352 J.D. [Barack F.K.P.&N.]
Robinson, Kimberly L. . . . '64 '89 C&L.589 B.S., J.D. [Cassiday,S.&G.]
Robinson, Maria Theresa . . . '54 '80 C.771 B.A. L.477 J.D. U.S. Postal Serv.
Robinson, Mary Beth S., (AV) '62 '90 C.475 B.A. L.424 J.D.
VP & Sr. Claims Coun., Attorney's Liability Assurance Society, Inc.
Robinson, Melvin A. . . . '— '84 C.801 B.S.E. L.734 J.D. [Schiff H.] (Pat.)
Robinson, Michael G., (AV) . . . '57 '82 C&L.339 B.S., J.D. [Winston&S.]
Robinson, Paul H. '48 '74 C.688 B.S. L.1068 J.D.
(adm. in MA; not adm. in IL) Prof. of Law, Northwestern University
Robinson, Robert H. . . . '34 '62 C.401 B.S. L.273 LL.B. 125 South Franklin (Pat.)
Robinson, Sara A. . . . '— '00 C.602 B.A. L.145 J.D. [Ⓐ Kirkland&E.]
Robinson, Stacey L. . . . '64 '97 C.277 B.C.E. L.1059 J.D. [Ⓐ Seyfarth S.]

Robinson Curley & Clayton, P.C., (AV)
300 South Wacker Drive Suite 1700, 60606
Telephone: 312-663-3100 Telecopier: 312-663-0303
URL: http://www.robinsoncurley.com
C. Philip Curley; Fay Clayton; Alan F. Curley; Cynthia H. Hyndman; Susan Valentine; John H. Wickert; Alan R. Dolinko; Robert S. Michaels; Elizabeth J. Hubertz;—Carl T. Bergetz; Adam N. Hirsch; Angel M. Krull; Robert L. Margolis; Darlene M. Oliver. Of Counsel: Ellen G. Robinson; Lois J. Lipton.
General Commercial Litigation, Litigation arising from Insurance Company and other Financial Institution Insolvencies, Reinsurance Recovery Disputes, RICO, Securities, Professional Liability, Intellectual Property, Class Actions, Civil Rights and Employment Litigation, Insurance Regulatory

(This Listing Continued)

Robinson Curley & Clayton, P.C. (Continued)

and Receivership Matters, Civil and Criminal Trial and Appellate Practice and Alternative Dispute Resolution in all State and Federal Courts and Tribunals.

See Professional Biographies, CHICAGO, ILLINOIS

Robison, Charles B., (AV) . . . '13 '37 C.388 A.B. L.597 J.D. 1 Bank One Plaza‡
Robison, William P. . . . '— '98 C.228 A.B. L.659 J.D. [Ⓐ Sachnoff&W.]
Robles, Edward N. . . . '60 '88 C.424 B.A. L.966 J.D. [Sanchez&D.]
Robot, George S. . . . '60 '96 C.339 B.S. L.146 J.D. [Ⓐ Stowell&F.]
Robovsky, Nicolette L. . . . '73 '02 C.162 B.A. L.209 J.D. Admin. Hearings Dept.
Robson, Douglas S. . . . '67 '92 C.347 B.A. L.209 J.D. [Handler,T.&D.]
Robson, Michael D. . . . '— '99 C&L.602 B.A., J.D. [Ⓐ Chapman&C.]
Rocap, Donald E., (AV) . . . '— '80 C.228 B.A. L.893 J.D. [Kirkland&E.]
Rocawich, Michele M. . . . '47 '94 C.523 B.A. L.146 J.D. [Ⓒ Susman&Assoc.]
Rocca, Brian C., (AV) . . . '53 '82 C.351 B.A. L.352 J.D. [Pretzel&S.]
Roccanova, Bernard, (AV) . . . '46 '72 C.1046 B.A. L.339 J.D. [Daley&M.]
Rocco, Perry C., (AV) . . . '57 '83 C.679 B.S. L.879 J.D. [Menges&M.]
Roche, Brian D., (AV) . . . '— '82 C.145 A.B. L.276 J.D. [Sachnoff&W.]
Roche, Brian P. . . . '— '99 C.436 B.S. L.146 J.D. [Ⓒ Seyfarth S.]
Roche, David I., (AV) . . . '51 '84 C.339 B.S. L.146 J.D. [Baker&M.] (Pat.)
Roche, James J., & Associates, (AV) '48 '75
C&L.424 B.A., J.D. 642 North Dearborn Street
Roche, James M., (AV) . . . '34 '59 C.321 A.B. L.309 LL.B. 227 W. Monroe St.‡
Roche, Michael B., (AV) . . . '41 '66 C&L.602 A.B., J.D. [Schuyler,R.&Z.]
Roche, Michael P. . . . '67 '93 C&L.339 B.S., J.D. [Winston&S.]
Roche, Michael T. . . . '75 '02 C.436 B.S. L.424 J.D. [Ⓐ Schuyler,R.&Z.]
Roche, Thomas F., (AV) . . . '27 '55 C&L.424 LL.B. [Ⓒ Keeley,K.&R.]
Roche, Vincent M. . . . '77 '03 C.57 B.A. L.893 J.D. [Ⓐ Novack&M.]
Rochelle, L. Raquel . . . '64 '89 C.388 B.A. L.910 J.D. Trans Union LLC
Rochlen, Bradley S. . . . '73 '98 C&L.477 B.A., J.D. [Ⓐ Katten M.R.]
Rochman, Jeffrey E. . . . '47 '73 C.339 B.A. L.209 J.D. 55 W. Monroe St.
Rock, Eric R. . . . '— '04 C&L.424 B.A., J.D. [Ⓐ Katten M.R.]
Rock, John J. . . . '69 '96 C.473 B.S. L.424 J.D. [Rock F.]
Rock, Philip J., (AV) . . . '37 '64 C.999 A.B. L.424 J.D. [Rock F.]
Rock Fusco, LLC, (AV) . . . 321 N. Clark Street, Suite 2200
Rockey, Keith V., (AV) '41 '67
C.679 B.S.Ch.E. L.273 J.D. [Wallenstein W.&R.] (See Pat. Sect.)
Rockey, Milnamow & Katz, Ltd., (AV)
500 W. Madison St. (Pat.) (⊙Moline, IL; Arlington, VA)
Rockman, Howard B., (AV) '— '63
C.223 B.S.M.E. L.273 J.D. [Barnes&T.] (See Pat. Sect.)
Rocks, Patrick J., Jr., (AV) . . . '57 '85 C.424 B.A. L.365 J.D. Gen. Coun.
Roddy, John P., (AV) . . . '20 '48 C.339 B.A. L.209 J.D. [Roddy,L.&Z.]
Roddy, Joseph P. . . . '— '90 C.321 B.A. L.146 J.D. [Freeborn&P.]
Roddy, Joseph V., (AV) . . . '38 '62 C.339 B.S. L.146 J.D. 77 W. Washington St.
Roddy, Leahy & Zima, Ltd., (AV) . . . 162 W. Grand Avenue
Rode, Arne R., (AV) . . . '40 '65 C.976 B.A. L.309 LL.B. 1147 West Ohio Street Suite 505
Rode, Gregory A., (BV) . . . '60 '88 C.578 B.A. L.589 J.D. [Rusin M.&F.]
Rode, Janice I. . . . '— '77 C.187 B.A. L.365 J.D. Admin. Law J.
Rodelli, Richard Nicholas . . . '72 '99 C.1128 B.A. L.575 J.D. Atty.
Rodenberg, Peter H. . . . '63 '98 C.339 B.A.S. L.424 J.D. [Ⓐ Conklin&C.]
Rodenburg, Margaret T. . . . '— '97 C.339 B.A. L.146 J.D. [Ⓐ Williams M.&J.]
Rodenkirch, Julia Suzanne . . . '75 '00 C.339 B.A. L.146 J.D. State Atty. Off.
Rodewald, April J. '53 '83 C.1212 B.A. L.1067 J.D.
(adm. in CA; not adm. in IL) General Atty., Asst. Gen. Coun., SBC
Rodewald, Jeffrey P. '54 '87 C.63 B.S. L.365 J.D.
Dir. Employ. Rel., Chief Labor Coun., USG Corp.
Rodewald, John E., (AV) . . . '65 '90 C&L.424 B.A., J.D. [Bates&C.]
Rodey, Laura . . . '76 '04 C.587 B.A. L.339 J.D. [Ⓐ Baker&M.]
Rodgers, Janice E., (AV) . . . '52 '76 C.339 B.S. L.309 J.D. [Quarles&B.]
Rodgers, Lance R., (AV) . . . '— '75 C&L.309 A.B., J.D. [Sachnoff&W.]
Rodin, Curt N., (AV) . . . '50 '75 C.339 B.A. L.424 J.D. [Anesi,O.R.N.&K.]
Rodman, Ryan J. . . . '— '04 C.352 B.A. L.146 J.D. [Ⓐ Querrey&H.]
Rodosky, Katherine Ann . . . '67 '92 C.174 B.A. L.645 J.D. [Ⓐ Schueler,D.&C.]
Rodriguez, Beth Clark, (AV) '59 '87
C.136 B.S. L.424 J.D. V.P. Wealth Strategy, J. P. Morgan FSB‡
Rodriguez, David Anthony . . . '72 '00 L.477 J.D. 10 S. Dearborn St.
Rodriguez, David Sergio '57 '84 C.1111 B.A. L.339 J.D.
IL Off. of Banks & Real Estate
Rodriguez, Gabriel M., (AV) . . . '— '84 C.597 B.A. L.587 J.D. [Schiff H.]
Rodriguez, Theresa . . . '66 '91 C.339 B.S. L.209 J.D. Asst. States Atty.

Rodriguez O'Donnell Ross Fuerst Gonzalez Williams & England, P.C., (AV)
8430 W. Bryn Mawr Avenue, Suite 525, 60631 ⊙
Telephone: 312-372-7000 Fax: 312-372-1719
Email: rodriguez@rorfgw.com URL: http://www.rorfgw.com
Thomas J. O'Donnell; R. Kevin Williams.
International Transportation, Trade, Customs, Maritime, Commercial Transactions Law, Government Relations, Tax and Tax Litigation.
Washington, D.C. Office: 1211 Connecticut Avenue, N.W., Suite 800, 20036-3007. Telephone: 202-293-3300. Fax: 202-293-3307.
Miami, Florida Office: 1001 Brickell Bay Drive, Suite 2002, 33131. Telephone: 305-350-5690. Fax: 305-371-8989.
New York, New York Office: 45 Rockefeller Plaza, 10111. Telephone: 212-332-8136. Fax: 212-332-3401.
Los Angeles, California Office: 5777 W. Century Boulevard, Suite 1500, 90045-5659. Telephone: 310-410-4414. Fax: 310-410-1017.

See Professional Biographies, CHICAGO, ILLINOIS

Rodriguez-Del Moral, Juan A. . . . '70 '04 C.209 B.A. L.146 J.D. [Ⓐ Garofalo,S.H.&S.]
Roe, David J. . . . '63 '93 C.352 B.A. L.213 J.D. [Ⓐ Clausen M.]
Roe, John R. . . . '48 '74 C.973 B.A. L.602 J.D. 100 W. Monroe St., 21st Fl.
Roe, Kathryn A. . . . '66 '91 C.602 B.A. L.597 J.D. [Neal,G.&E.]
Roeder, Craig A. . . . '60 '85 C.208 B.S. L.94 J.D. [Baker&M.]
Roeder, Steven J. . . . '58 '84 C.145 B.A. L.339 J.D. [Williams M.&J.]
Roehl, Rex A. . . . '50 '84 C&L.146 B.S.M.E., J.D. Bus. Mgr., Midwest Generation
Roesel, James L. . . . '51 '89 C.801 B.S.E.M.M. L.146 J.D. Commonwealth Edison Co.
Roeser, Lori LePar '73 '98 C.473 B.A. L.424 J.D.
Sr. Coun., Attorneys' Liability Assurance Society, Inc.
Roeser, Peter S. . . . '70 '98 C.966 B.A. L.424 J.D. [Ⓐ Grippo&E.]
Roethke, Keara M. . . . '78 '03 C.436 B.A. L.1000 J.D. [Ⓐ Levenfeld P.]
Rogal, Helen R. . . . '— '78 C.19 B.A. L.365 J.D. 29 S. La Salle
Rogers, Alfred M., Jr. . . . '27 '53 C&L.966 B.B.A., LL.B. 190 S. La Salle St.‡
Rogers, Jeffrey E., (AV) . . . '49 '76 C.424 B.A. L.365 J.D. [McGuirewoods]
Rogers, Joanne M. . . . '63 '89 C.608 B.S. L.989 J.D. [Ⓐ Ellison,N.Z.&A.]
Rogers, Joanne S. . . . '62 '87 C&L.339 B.S., J.D. Sr. Coun., Bank One Corp. (Law Dept.)
Rogers, John E. . . . '— '67 C.602 A.B. L.309 LL.B. [Seyfarth S.]
Rogers, John L., III, (AV) . . . '— '74 C.893 B.A. L.309 J.D. [Foley&L.]

Rogers, John W. ...'18 '48 C.1191 B.Ed. L.145 J.D. Cir. J.
Rogers, Kevin B. ...'— '86 C.1183 B.A. L.365 J.D. 20 S. Clark St., Ste. 2000
Rogers, Larry R., (AV) ...'47 '83 C.720 B.A. L.209 J.D. [Power R.&S.]
Rogers, Larry R., Jr., (AV) ...'68 '94 C.1067 B.S. L.146 J.D. [Ⓐ Power R.&S.]
Rogers, Melinda C. ...'68 '95 C.810 B.A. L.209 J.D. [Ⓐ Berger S.]
Rogers, Michael G. ...'63 '89 C.686 B.A. L.46 J.D. Asst. State Atty.
Rogers, Michael G. '60 '87 C.347 B.A. L.1119 J.D.
Assoc. Gen. Coun., National Equity Fund, Inc.
Rogers, Scott E. ...'56 '90 C.339 B.A. L.259 J.D. [Ⓒ Scandaglia&R.]
Rogers, William J., (AV) ...'50 '75 C.1030 B.A. L.597 J.D. [Bollinger,R.&G.]
Rogers, Yolande B. ...'52 '78 C&L.734 A.B., J.D. Asst. States Atty.
Rogina, Erica N. ...'58 '88 C.966 B.A. L.424 J.D. [Ⓐ Wiedner&M.]
Roginski-Kord, Jaime S. ...'76 '01 C.927 B.A. L.597 J.D. [Ⓐ Varga B.L.H.&C.]
Rogoff, Richard A., (AVⓉ) '52 '77 C.378 B.A. L.802 J.D.
(adm. in OK; not adm. in IL) Sr. Assoc. Gen. Coun., Bank One Corporation (Law Dept.)
Rogul, Joseph W. ...'52 '77 C.339 B.A. L.365 J.D. [Pierce&R.]
Rogus, Gregory E. ...'55 '80 C.424 B.A. L.339 J.D. [Segal M.S.&M.]
Rohan, Michael Patrick ...'70 '99 C.339 B.A. L.424 J.D. [Ⓐ Winston&S.]
Rohde, Harry Q. ...'32 '59 C.31 A.B. L.146 J.D. 300 N. State St.
Rohlfing, James T., (BV) ...'57 '82 C.436 B.S. L.209 J.D. [Rohlfing&O.]
Rohlfing & Oberholtzer, (AV) ...One East Wacker Drive Suite 2420
Rohlfsen, Ryan J. ...'74 '99 C&L.221 B.A., J.D. [Ⓐ Skadden,A.S.M.&F.]
Rohn, Walter A. ...'46 '72 C.46 B.S. L.424 J.D. 6300 N. Milwaukee Ave.
Rohner, William M. ...'74 '02 C.118 B.A. L.597 J.D. [Ⓐ Skadden,A.S.M.&F.]
Rohrbacher, Christopher ...'71 '01 C.118 B.A. L.145 J.D. [Ⓐ Skadden,A.S.M.&F.]
Rohrer, Gerald T., Jr. ...'68 '97 C.201 B.A. L.365 J.D. [Ⓐ Schuyler,R.&Z.]
Rohrman, Douglass F., (AV) ...'41 '66 C.228 A.B. L.597 J.D. [Lord,B.&B.]
Roin, Howard J., (AV) ...'53 '78 C.31 B.A. L.145 J.D. [Mayer,B.R.&M.]
Rojas, Olga R. ...'70 '96 C.339 B.A. L.209 J.D. [Ⓐ Minsky,M.&H.]
Rojc, Kenneth J. ...'55 '80 C.339 B.A. L.345 J.D. [Nisen&E.]
Rokach, David ...'— '03 C.999 B.H.L. L.145 J.D. [Ⓐ Kirkland&E.]
Rokacz, John ...'46 '71 C.645 B.A. L.1000 J.D. [John R.&Assoc.]
Rokos, Rebecca P. ...'— '96 C&L.477 B.S.Ch.E., J.D. [Banner&W.] (See Pat. Sect.)
Rokosz, Ronald E., (AV) ...'— '69 C.424 B.S. L.597 J.D. [Chapman&C.]
Rolek, Robert W. ...'51 '87 C.94 A.B. L.365 J.D. [Ancel,G.D.B.D.&R.]
Rolenc, Michael S., (AV) ...'53 '79 C.209 B.S. L.1151 J.D. [Kane,D.&H.]
Rolewicz, Peter C. ...'37 '63 C.103 A.B. L.146 J.D. 9226 S. Commercial Ave.
Rolfes, James A. ...'— '88 C.477 B.B.A. L.339 J.D. [Sachnoff&W.]
Rolla, Lawrence Thomas ...'54 '78 C.262 B.A. L.339 J.D. [Rolla,L.&Assoc.]
Rolla, Lawrence & Associates ...407 S. Dearborn St., Ste. 1735
Rollier, Suzanne E. ...'70 '04 C.597 B.A. L.36 J.D. [Ⓐ Holland&K.]
Rollin, Arthur S., (AV) ...'32 '58 C.475 B.A. L.597 J.D. [Ⓒ Skadden,A.S.M.&F.]
Rollins, J. Andrew ...'49 '72 C.839 L.69 J.D. F.D.I.C.
Rollins, Susan E., (AV) ...'— '77 C.597 B.A. L.1556 J.D. [Ⓒ Chapman&C.]
Rollman, Dina G. ...'— '00 C.604 B.A. L.597 J.D. [Ⓐ Sperling&S.]
Rollman, Eli M. ...'70 '99 C.604 B.A. L.597 J.D. 1429 N. Paulino St.
Rollo, Sherry L. ...'77 '04 C.846 B.S. L.365 J.D. [Ⓐ Welsh&K.]
Roloff, Ross D., (AV) ...'68 '93 C.898 B.A. L.879 J.D. [Merlo K.B.&G.]
Roma-Kutz, Diane J. ...'— '82 C.927 B.S. L.589 J.D. [Epstein B.&G.]
Roman, Ronald B. ...'52 '83 C.339 B.A. L.146 J.D. 180 N. LaSalle St.
Romanchek, Robert A. ...'60 '85 C.238 B.S. L.209 J.D. Price Waterhouse
Romani, Michael E. ...'63 '02 C.589 B.S. L.365 J.D. [Ⓢ Seyfarth S.] (Pat.)
Romaniuk, William G. ...'49 '75 C.436 B.S. L.209 J.D. Clybourn Metal Finishing Co.
Romanoff, Melvyn L. ...'45 '69 C.339 B.A. L.209 J.D. 1 N. LaSalle St., Ste. 2600
Romanoff, Robert Alan, (AV) ...'63 '89 C.352 B.A. L.477 J.D. [Levenfeld P.]
Romanoff, William A., (BV) ...'35 '59 L.209 J.D. [Ⓒ Regas,F.&D.]
Romanucci, Antonio M., (AV) ...'60 '85 C.966 B.A. L.365 J.D. [Romanucci&B.]
Romanucci & Blandin, (AV) ...33 N. La Salle St., Ste. 20
Rome, Adam B. ...'76 '02 C.347 B.A. L.146 J.D. [Ⓐ Levenfeld P.]
Romei, Randall C. ...'54 '81 C.339 B.A. L.209 J.D. [Ashcraft&A.]
Romero, Jessica ...'— '04 C.259 B.A. L.145 J.D. [Ⓐ Schiff H.]
Romick, Jamie L. ...'78 '04 C.228 B.A. L.276 J.D. [Ⓐ Mayer,B.R.&M.]
Romick, Jason M. ...'71 '97 C.910 B.S.B.A. L.339 J.D. [Ⓐ Levenfeld P.]
Romick, Jonathan ...'— '02 C&L.339 B.S., J.D. Two North LaSalle Street, Suite 2200
Romo, Natalie J. ...'— '00 C&L.339 B.A., J.D. [Ⓐ Hennessy&R.]
Rompon, John P. ...'63 '88 C.597 B.A. L.347 J.D. Booz-Allen & Hamilton, Inc.
Ronaldson, Glenn C., (AV) ...'59 '84 C.927 B.S. L.365 J.D. [Ronaldson&K.]
Ronaldson and Kuchler, L.L.C., (AV) ...205 W. Wacker Dr., Ste. 1015
Ronin, Michael D. ...'51 '76 C.801 B.A. L.365 J.D. Asst. States Atty.
Ronson, Alan B., (BV) ...'67 '92 C.367 B.A. L.910 J.D. [Chuhak&T.]
Roodman, Sheldon H. '41 '66 C.477 B.A. L.910 J.D.
Exec. Dir., Legal Assistance Found. of Chicago

Rooks Pitts
(See Dykema Gossett PLLC)

Rooney, James A., Attorney at Law, (AV) '44 '69
C&L.597 B.S., J.D. 77 W. Washington St., Ste. 1414
Rooney, James C., Jr. '34 '58 C&L.436 A.B., LL.B.
(adm. in WI; not adm. in IL) Commerce Clearing House
Rooney, John E., (AV) ...'63 '88 C.424 B.B.A. L.365 J.D. [Sonnenschein N.&R.]
Rooney, Matthew A., (AV) ...'49 '75 C.276 A.B. L.145 J.D. [Mayer,B.R.&M.]
Rooney, Patricia A. ...'57 '85 C.276 B.S. L.273 J.D. [Ⓒ Ungaretti&H.]
Rooney, Robert W., Jr., (AV) ...'45 '69 C&L.209 B.A., J.D. [R.W.Rooney,Jr.]
Rooney, Robert W., Sr., (AV) ...'17 '42 L.209 LL.B. One N. La Salle St.
Rooney, Ronald J., Jr. ...'69 '98 C.1147 B.B.A. L.623 J.D. 415 N. LaSalle St., Ste. 500
Rooney, Robert W., Jr., Chartered, (AV) ...1 N. LaSalle
Roos, Robert T. ...'— '01 C.597 B.S. L.880 J.D. [Ⓐ Winston&S.]
Roosevelt, Kermit ...'71 '97 C.309 A.B. L.976 J.D. Mayer, Brown & Platt
Root, Jeremy A. ...'75 '03 C.67 B.A. L.569 J.D. [Ⓐ McDermott W.&E.]
Roper, Harry J., (AV) ...'40 '66 C.688 B.E.E. L.569 LL.B. [Jenner&B.] (Pat.)
Roper, Steven C. ...'57 '88 C.1074 B.S. L.309 J.D. [Lord,B.&B.]

Roper & Quigg
(See Jenner & Block LLP)

Ropiequet, John L., (AV) ...'— '72 C.367 B.A. L.597 J.D. [Arnstein&L.]
Ropski, Gary M., (AV) '52 '76 C.119 B.S. L.597 J.D.
[Brinks H.G.&L.] (See Pat. Sect.)
Rosas, James D., (BV) '46 '75 C&L.209 B.A., J.D.
33 North Dearborn Street Suite 1850
Rose, Alexandra D. ...'— '01 C.477 B.A. L.273 J.D. [Ⓐ DLPiper R.G.C.U.]
Rose, Charles P., (AV) ...'57 '82 C.884 B.A. L.209 J.D. [Franczek S.]
Rose, Henry G. ...'49 '75 C.597 B.A. L.46 J.D. Asst. Prof., Loyola Univ. Sch. of Law
Rose, Jeffrey B., (BV) ...'52 '83 C.339 B.A. L.209 J.D. [Tishler&W.]
Rose, Jennifer Tomsak ...'72 '00 C.30 B.A. L.146 J.D. [Ⓐ Johnson&B.]
Rose, Judith L. ...'41 '82 C.94 B.A. L.145 J.D. Art Institute of Chicago
Rose, Kirk A. ...'60 '85 C.228 A.B. L.1119 J.D. V.P., Fin., Hyatt Corporation

Rose, Mark J., Law Offices of, (AV) '52 '77 C.339 B.A. L.597 J.D. BB
200 West Adams Street, Suite 2850, 60606-5206
Telephone: 312-704-1446 Fax: 312-704-8233
Email: MJRoseEsq@aol.com URL: http://www.markjrose.com
Litigation Practice, including Bankruptcy, Creditor Rights, Mechanic's Lien Foreclosure, Mortgage Foreclosure and Commercial Law; Real Estate, Commercial Leasing, Buying and Selling of Businesses and Commercial Transactions.

See Professional Biographies, CHICAGO, ILLINOIS

Rose, Marya J. ...'72 '97 C.475 B.A. L.93 J.D. Jud. Clk.
Rose, Michael Paul ...'66 '92 C.339 B.A. L.893 J.D. 401 N. Michigan
Rose, Mitchell D. ...'65 '90 C.477 B.G.S. L.966 J.D. [Bollinger,R.&G.]
Rose, Seth A. ...'77 '02 C.893 B.A. L.608 J.D. [Ⓐ Leydig,V.&M.]
Roseborough, Kathleen, (AV) ...'44 '77 C.276 B.S.F.S. L.209 LL.B. [Mandel,L.&S.]
Roselle, James E. '46 '73 C.597 B.A. L.893 J.D.
Assoc. Gen. Coun., Northern Trust Corp.
Roselli, John T., (AV) ...'49 '75 C.602 B.A. L.365 J.D. [Fuchs&R.]

Rosemarin, Carey S., P.C., Law Offices of
(See Northbrook)

Rosen, Alan, (AV) ...'46 '74 C.339 B.S. L.424 J.D. [Young,R.F.&S.]
Rosen, Allan P. ...'52 '81 C.1036 B.A. L.209 J.D. 850 W. Jackson Blvd., Ste. 405
Rosen, Arnold A. ...'14 '36 L.209 LL.B. 180 N. LaSalle St.
Rosen, Barry S., (AV) ...'— '77 C.339 B.S. L.309 J.D. [Sachnoff&W.]
Rosen, Claire I. ...'12 '33 C.145 L.209 LL.B. 180 N. LaSalle St.
Rosen, Courtney A. ...'74 '98 C.234 B.A. L.146 J.D. [Ⓐ Sidley A.B.&W.]
Rosen, Harold, (AV) ...'49 '75 C.473 B.A. L.365 J.D. [Wolin&R.]
Rosen, Jack W. ...'30 '55 C.339 B.S. L.209 J.D. 55 W. Monroe St., 3rd Fl., E.
Rosen, Leslie J., (AV) ...'53 '81 C.339 B.A. L.588 J.D. [Ⓐ Novoselsky]
Rosen, Leslie N. ...'— '02 C.188 B.A. L.145 J.D. [Ⓐ Latham&W.]
Rosen, Lester, (AV) ...'30 '55 C.659 B.S. L.309 LL.B. [Ⓒ DLPiper R.G.C.U.]
Rosen, Louis E., (AV) ...'37 '62 C.339 B.S. L.145 J.D. [Ⓒ Lord,B.&B.]
Rosen, Michael J. ...'61 '86 C.1168 B.A. L.910 J.D. [Boundas S.W.&B.]
Rosen, Richard S. ...'44 '69 C.339 B.A. L.146 J.D. [Veverka,R.&H.]
Rosen, Robert B. ...'42 '67 C.1016 B.S. L.146 J.D. 77 W. Wash. St.
Rosen, Sue-Ann ...'— '81 C.472 B.B.A. L.146 J.D. Sr. Atty., Metra
Rosen, William H. ...'50 '77 C.966 B.A. L.365 J.D. 19 S. LaSalle St., Ste. 1300
Rosenbaum, Jody B. ...'54 '84 C.208 B.A. L.146 J.D. Three First National Plaza
Rosenbaum, Judith Ann ...'51 '76 C.696 B.A. L.477 J.D. Northwestern Univ. Sch. of Law
Rosenbaum, Mark R. ...'51 '76 C.477 A.B. L.145 J.D. [Fischel&K.]
Rosenbaum, Michael D. ...'62 '87 C.475 B.A. L.966 J.D. [Gardner C.&D.]
Rosenbaum, Murray S. ...'44 '73 C.477 B.A. L.94 J.D. 542 S. Dearborn
Rosenbaum, N. Rosie ...'54 '79 C.339 B.A. L.477 J.D. [McDermott W.&E.]
Rosenbaum, Neil M. ...'79 '04 C.477 B.A. L.146 J.D. [Ⓐ Funkhouser V.L.&D.]
Rosenberg, Betsy R. ...'— '01 C.966 B.A. L.910 J.D. [Ⓐ Clausen M.]
Rosenberg, Burton X., (AV) ...'41 '66 C.659 B.A. L.597 J.D. [Seyfarth S.]
Rosenberg, Carolyn Hope, (AV) ...'— '82 C&L.477 B.A., J.D. [Sachnoff&W.]
Rosenberg, Daniel G. ...'75 '01 C.473 B.S. L.424 J.D. [Ⓐ Bell,B.&L.]
Rosenberg, Gerald N. '54 '84 C.197 B.A. L.477 J.D.
(adm. in DC; not adm. in IL) Univ. of Chicago, Poli. Sci. Dept.
Rosenberg, Harry B., (AV) ...'— '52 C.604 B.A. L.309 LL.B. [Sachnoff&W.]
Rosenberg, Herbert B. ...'41 '67 C&L.209 B.S.C., J.D. [Schoenberg,F.N.&R.]
Rosenberg, Jeffrey R. ...'64 '97 C.1016 B.A. L.424 J.D. [Ⓐ Schuyler,R.&Z.]
Rosenberg, Jonah ...'40 '66 C.1191 L.144 J.D. 39 S. LaSalle St.
Rosenberg, Leonard L., (AVⓉ) '46 '71 C.994 B.A. L.273 J.D.
(adm. in MD; not adm. in IL) [Sandler,T.&R.]
(⊙L.A., San Fran., CA; Wash., DC; Miami, FL; New York, NY)
Rosenberg, Leonard X. (AV) ...'67 '92 C.1036 B.A. L.597 J.D. [Mayer,B.R.&M.]
Rosenberg, Merwin S., (AV) ...'12 '34 C&L.145 Ph.B., J.D. 203 N. La Salle St.
Rosenberg, Richard M., (AV) '34 '60
C&L.309 B.A., LL.B. Visiting Prof., Loyola Univ. Sch. of Law
Rosenberg, Ross M. ...'70 '02 C.659 B.A. L.597 J.D. [Ⓐ Jenner&B.]
Rosenberg, Scott D. ...'61 '86 C&L.339 B.S., J.D. Baker Robbins & Co.
Rosenberg, Seth Mann ...'— '03 C.339 B.A. L.146 J.D. [Ⓐ Schwartz C.]
Rosenberg, Steven J. ...'47 '72 C.339 B.A. L.575 J.D. [S.J.Rosenberg]
Rosenberg, Susan H. ...'61 '90 C&L.145 B.A, J.D. 5416 S. University
Rosenberg, Steven J., P.C. ...53 W. Jackson Blvd.
Rosenblat, Stephen ...'59 '90 C.339 B.A. L.209 J.D. [Baum S.A.&N.]

Rosenblat, Michael C., P.C.
(See Glenview)

Rosenblatt, Brian A. ...'— '97 C.910 B.A. L.146 J.D. [Ⓐ O'Hagan,S.&A.]
Rosenbloom, David S., (AV) ...'59 '85 C.170 B.A. L.309 J.D. [McDermott W.&E.]
Rosenbloom, James B., (AV) ...'47 '72 C.976 B.A. L.145 J.D. [Goldberg,K.B.B.R.&M.]
Rosenbloom, Lewis S., (AV) ...'53 '77 C.393 B.A. L.209 J.D. [McDermott W.&E.]
Rosenblum, Arthur ...'16 '40 C.339 L.209 LL.B. Assoc. Cir. J.
Rosenblum, Daniel W. ...'50 '76 C.910 A.B. L.597 J.D. Legal Assist. Found. of Chic.
Rosenblum, Ronald, & Associates, (AV) '58 '83
C.339 B.A. L.424 J.D. 111 W. Washington St., Ste. 823
Rosenblum, Sarah Carlin '66 '91 C.966 B.A. L.146 J.D.
Liason, Chicago Pub. Sch., Civil Rights Off.‡
Rosenblum, Victor G. ...'25 '49 C&L.178 A.B., LL.B. Prof., Northwestern Univ.
Rosenburg, Howard J. ...'73 '98 C.339 B.S. L.146 J.D. [Ⓐ Gardner C.&D.]
Rosencranz, Linda ...'48 '73 C&L.339 A.B., J.D. Ticor Title Ins. Co
Rosenfeld, Deena Newlander '65 '89
C.477 B.A. L.339 J.D. Asst. Gen. Coun., Deerfield Capital Mgmt.
Rosenfeld, Howard H., (AV) ...'38 '62 C.339 L.209 LL.B. [Rosenfeld H.S.&F.]
Rosenfeld, Jonathan A. '74 '00 C.401 B.A. L.146 J.D.
345 North Canal Street, Suite 507
Rosenfeld, Neal D., (AV) ...'34 '58 C.597 B.S. L.145 J.D. 1130 N. Dearborn St.
Rosenfeld, Stephen J., (AV) ...'68 '93 C.477 B.A. L.339 J.D. [Mandell M.]
Rosenfeld Hafron Shapiro & Farmer, (AV)
221 North La Salle Street, Suite 1763 (⊙Schaumburg)
Rosenfield, Andrew M. ...'51 '78 C.385 B.A. L.145 J.D. Pres., Lexecon Inc.
Rosenfield, Harry N., (AVⓉ) '11 '34 C.563 B.A. L.178 LL.B.
(adm. in DC; not adm. in IL) 1755 E. 55th St., Apt. 803
Rosenfield, Neal G. ...'44 '67 C.339 L.209 LL.B. [Rosenfield,K.&H.]
Rosenfield, Kaplan & Halperin ...6160 N. Cicero Ave.
Rosenheim, Margaret K. '26 '49 C.914 L.145 J.D.
Univ. of Chicago, Sch. of Soc. Servs. Admin.
Rosenman, Andrew S. ...'69 '95 C.477 B.A. L.146 J.D. [Mayer,B.R.&M.]
Rosenoff, Eric B. ...'72 '00 C.36 B.S. L.37 J.D. [Ⓐ Skadden,A.S.M.&F.]
Rosenquist, John E., (AV) '40 '68
C.742 B.A.Chem. L.365 J.D. [Ⓒ Leydig,V.&M.] (See Pat. Sect.)
Rosenson, Arthur E. ...'62 '86 C.659 B.A. L.597 J.D. [Cohen,G.&R.]
Rosenstein, Martin G. ...'53 '79 C.339 B.S. L.424 J.D. [Mayer,B.R.&M.]
Rosenstrock, Philip ...'15 '57 C.597 B.S. L.365 J.D. 801 N. Clark St.

Rosenthal, Arla G. . . . .'63 '89 C.966 B.B.A. L.424 J.D. [Ⓐ Tribler O.&M.]
Rosenthal, Jason M. . . . .'72 '97 C.347 B.S. L.146 J.D. [Schopf&W.]
Rosenthal, Lauren S. . . . .'57 '82 C.597 B.A. L.339 J.D. 1407 W. Hood Ave.
Rosenthal, Lawrence . . . .'58 '81 C.339 B.A. L.309 J.D. City of Chicago, Dept. of Law
Rosenthal, Marc E. . . . .'63 '90 C.385 B.A. L.365 J.D. [Mayer,B.R.&M.]
Rosenthal, Matthew B. . . . .'75 '02 C.473 B.A. L.228 J.D. [Ⓐ Williams M.&J.]
Rosenthal, Michael D. . . . .'64 '89 C.910 A.B. L.477 J.D. [Sonnenschein N.&R.]
Rosenthal, Norbert N. . . . .'32 '59 C.1016 B.A. L.209 J.D. [N.N.Rosenthal&Assoc.]
Rosenthal, Peter M., (AV) . . . .'50 '75 C.659 B.A. L.477 J.D. [Rosenthal,M.C.]
Rosenthal, Murphey, Coblentz, (AV) . . . . .30 N. La Salle Street, Suite 1624
Rosenthal, Norbert N., & Associates, Ltd. . . . . .400 E. Randolph Dr.
Rosenwein, Thomas D., (Ltd.), (AV) . . .'43 '78 C.145 A.B. L.209 J.D. [Gordon,G.F.&R.]
Rosenzweig, Darryl B. . . . .'60 '88 C.589 B.S. L.365 J.D. 33 N. LaSalle St.
Rosenzweig, Ellis B., (AV) . . . .'— '65 L.365 LL.B. [Sachnoff&W.]
Roseth, H. David . . . .'60 '01 C.477 B.A L.569 J.D. [Ⓐ D.A.Axelrod&Assoc.]
Roshanali, Dabeer M. '71 '97
C.597 B.A. L.146 J.D. Sr. Coun., Bank One Corp. (Law Dept.)
Rosiello, Thomas A. '47 '77 C.397 B.A. L.424 J.D.
Sr. Coun., Chicago Div., ABN-AMRO North America, Inc. (Legal Department)
Rosin, Robert A., (BV) . . . .'53 '79 C.659 B.S. L.910 J.D. 70 W. Madison Street
Rosing, Sheldon . . . .'31 '64 C&L.209 B.S., J.D. 120 W. Madison St.
Rosmarin, Shurl . . . .'11 '33 C&L.597 B.S.L., J.D. 111 W. Wash. St.
Rosner, Beth J. . . . .'53 '78 C.393 B.A. L.597 J.D. [Ⓒ Neal,G.&E.]

Ross, Curtis Bennett, The Law Office of, (BV) '55 '80 C&L.339 B.S., J.D.
19 South La Salle Street, 13th Floor, 60603
Telephone: 312-984-1514 Fax: 312-984-1504
Email: RossatLaw@aol.com URL: http://www.divorce-chicago.com
Family Law, Divorce, Child Custody, Child Support, Paternity, Visitation.
See Professional Biographies, CHICAGO, ILLINOIS

Ross, C.W. . . . .'— '04 C.101 B.A. L.1565 J.D. [Ⓐ Kirkland&E.]
Ross, Dina B. . . . .'63 '94 C.1036 B.A. L.424 J.D. [Schwartz C.]
Ross, Eve B. . . . .'— '95 C.822 A.B. L.209 J.D. [Ⓐ Mayer,B.R.&M.]
Ross, Gilbert J., (AV) . . . .'46 '80 C.176 B.A. L.146 J.D. [Sussman,S.&R.]
Ross, Heather . . .'68 '93 C.347 B.A. L.339 J.D. Atty., Legal Assistance Found. of Chicago
Ross, Jamie L. . . . .'74 '99 C.388 B.A. L.801 J.D. [Ⓐ Crisham&K.]
Ross, Jay B., (AV) . . . .'42 '68 C.966 B.S. L.339 J.D. [J.B.Ross&Assoc.]
Ross, Jeffrey K., (AV) . . . .'51 '76 C&L.188 B.S., J.D. [Seyfarth S.]
Ross, Keith A., (AV) . . . .'67 '92 C.339 B.S. L.146 J.D. [Levenfeld P.]
Ross, Kenneth P., (AV) . . . . '51 '77 C.966 B.A. L.588 J.D. [Ⓐ R.F.Coleman&Assoc.]
Ross, Kimberly A. . . . .'70 '96 C.477 B.A. L.209 J.D. [Cremer,K.S.&S.]
Ross, Kirk . . . .'74 '04 C.78 B.S.B.A. L.597 J.D. [Ⓐ Katten M.R.]
Ross, Marissa . . . .'77 '02 C.732 B.A. L.823 J.D. [Ⓐ Littler M.]
Ross, Michael E., (AV) . . . .'51 '76 C.339 B.A. L.146 J.D. [Schain,B.R.&C.]
Ross, Nancy G., (AV) . . . .'56 '85 C.174 B.A. L.424 J.D. [McDermott W.&E.]
Ross, Nathan L. . . . .'73 '99 C.346 B.A. L.365 J.D. Secy., Sigma Mortgage Corp.
Ross, Peter B. . . . .'61 '86 C.976 B.A. L.597 J.D. [DLPiper R.G.C.U.]
Ross, Rakhael . . . .'47 '79 C.966 B.A. L.146 J.D. [Ⓒ Sussman,S.&R.]
Ross, Rebecca L., (AVⓉ) . . . .'51 '76 C.164 B.A. L.546 J.D. [Ross,D.&B.]
Ross, Stephanie L. . . . . . .'— '97 C.801 B.A. L.424 J.D. Atty., Leo Burnett Worldwide, Inc.
Ross, Steven J. . . . .'63 '95 C.339 B.S. L.365 J.D. [Ⓐ Kroll&R.]
Ross, Steven O. . . . . '53 '85 C.477 A.B. L.146 J.D. 1749 N. Wells St.
Ross, Terry Ann . . . . '48 '81 C.597 B.S.B.A. L.209 J.D. 5711 S. Dorchester Ave.
Ross, Thomas I., (AV) '— '79
C.679 B.S.M.E. L.276 J.D. [Marshall,G.&B.] (See Pat. Sect.)

Ross, Dixon & Bell, LLP, (AV) BB
55 West Monroe Street Suite 3000, 60603-5758 ⊙
Telephone: 312-759-1920 Fax: 312-759-1939
Email: info@rdblaw.com URL: http://www.rdblaw.com
Partners: Eileen King Bower; Michael G. Bruton; Clinton E. Cameron; Hallie Miller Fahey; Rebecca L. Ross; Michael P. Tone; Daniel J. Zollner. Of Counsel: Scott E. Turner. Associates: Kimberly E. Blair; Julie L. Burgener; David I. Curkovic; David F. Cutter; Eóin M. Dempsey; Patrick Frye; Timothy Furrow; Stephanie Haas; Adam E. Jones; Peter D. Lindau; Alex Mahler; Melissa McGuane; Tyler Mertes; Jessika J. Moon; Edward B. Mullen, III; Milind Parekh; Regina Ripley; Carol Threlkeld; Christopher White.
Commercial Litigation and Appellate Practice, Insurance Coverage Litigation and Counseling, Directors and Officers Liability, Professional Liability, Environmental/Mass Tort Coverage, General Liability.
Washington, D.C. Office: 2001 K Street, N.W., 20006-1040. Telephone: 202-662-2000. Fax: 202-662-2190.
Irvine, California Office: 5 Park Plaza, Suite 1200, 92614-8592. Telephone: 949-622-2700. Fax: 949-622-2739.
San Diego, California Office: 550 West B Street, Suite 400, 92101-3538. Telephone: 619-235-4040. Fax: 619-231-8796.
See Professional Biographies, CHICAGO, ILLINOIS

Ross & Hardies
(See McGuireWoods LLP)

Ross, Jay B., & Associates, P.C., (AV) . . . . 838 W. Grand Ave., 2nd Fl.
Rossa, Joseph W. . . . .'41 '87 C.424 D.D.S. L.209 J.D. 5400 N. Milwaukee
Rossiter, John W. . . . . '64 '03 C.20 B.A. L.365 J.D. [Ⓐ Gomberg,S.G.&O.]
Rossiter, Peter L., (AV) . . . .'— '73 C.674 A.B. L.976 J.D. [Schiff H.]
Rossman, Jeffrey A. . . . .'70 '97 C&L.477 A.B., J.D. [McDermott W.&E.]
Rossmoore, Bernadette I. . . . .'74 '99 C.477 B.A. L.904 J.D. [Ⓐ Lake,T.&D.]
Rosso, Anthony R. . . . .'— '85 C.966 B.A. L.477 J.D. [Chapman&C.]
Rosso, Christine Hehmeyer, (AV) . . . .'47 '72 C.1168 B.A. L.597 J.D. 77 w. wacker Dr.
Rotatori, Mark P. . . . .'— '94 C.602 B.A. L.930 J.D. [Jones D.]
Rotenberg, David M. . . . .'— '04 C.881 B.A. L.145 J.D. [Ⓐ Wildman,H.A.&D.]
Rotenberry, William J. '54 '83 C.98 B.S. L.209 J.D.
Dir. Corp. Development, R. R. Donnelley & Sons Company

Rotert, Mark L., The Law Office of, (AV) '52 '77 C.723 B.A. L.424 J.D.
11 South LaSalle Street, Suite 1200, 60603
Telephone: 312-236-8115 Fax: 312-236-8116
Email: mlr@markrotertlaw.com URL: http://www.markrotertlaw.com
Associate: Matthew J. Gulde.
White Collar Criminal Defense, Commercial Litigation, Appellate Practice.
See Professional Biographies, CHICAGO, ILLINOIS

Roth, Alan B., (AV) . . . .'57 '84 C.228 B.A. L.910 J.D. [Wildman,H.A.&D.]
Roth, Ben M., (AV) . . . .'50 '75 C.339 B.S. L.146 J.D. [Kamensky,R.H.&D.]
Roth, Bradford D., (AV) . . . .'52 '79 C.352 B.B.A. L.146 J.D. [Cassiday,S.&G.]
Roth, Cecilia A. . . . .'54 '84 C.145 A.B. L.477 J.D. [Ⓒ Mayer,B.R.&M.]
Roth, Daniel J., (AV) '49 '80 C.602 B.A. L.424 J.D.
V.P., Gen. Coun. & Secy., National Futures Assn.
Roth, Harvey A. . . . .'43 '70 C.102 B.S. L.339 J.D. Reg. Atty., NLRB
Roth, James A., Attorney at Law '52 '85 C.801 B.A. L.365 J.D.
171 N. Clark St., 8th Fl.
Roth, Karl W. . . . .'65 '01 C.234 B.S. L.424 J.D. [Roth]
Roth, Mark D., (AV) . . . .'60 '87 C.589 B.A. L.365 J.D. [Orum&R.]
Roth, Michael J., Jr. . . . .'76 '04 C.587 B.A. L.910 J.D. [Ⓐ Bell,B.&L.]
Roth, Mitchell S. . . . .'67 '92 C&L.339 B.S., J.D. [Much S.F.D.A.&R.]
Roth, Robert A. . . . .'— '89 C.339 B.S. L.365 J.D. [Sachnoff&W.]
Roth, Shira . . . .'— '01 C.1375 B.A. L.1068 J.D. [Ⓐ Goldberg,K.B.B.R.&M.]
Roth, Steven . . . .'62 '88 C.309 B.A. L.477 J.D. Coun., GE Capital Corp.
Roth, Walter, (AV) . . . .'29 '52 C.339 L.145 J.D. [Ⓒ Seyfarth S.]

Roth Law Group, The, LLC
111 West Washington Street, Suite 1440, 60602
Telephone: 312-419-9599 Fax: 312-419-9559
Email: kwr@rothlawgroup.com URL: http://www.rothlawgroup.com
Member of Firm: Karl W. Roth. Of Counsel: Brad Johnson.
Corporate Law: Business Litigation and Counseling, Prosecution and Defense of Contractual, Statutory and Common Law Claims, Equipment Leasing Contracts, Construction Contracts, Insurance Defense: Premises Liability, Coverage Analysis, Aviation: Prosecution and Defense of Mishap Claims, Real Estate: Buy-Sell Contracts, Closings, Condominium Conversions, Personal Injury: Accidents, Drug Injury.
See Professional Biographies, CHICAGO, ILLINOIS

Rothaar, Lucas M. . . . .'79 '04 C.879 B.A. L.424 J.D. [Ⓐ Rusin M.&F.]
Rothbart, Herbert I., Law Offices of, (AV) '29 '53
C.221 B.S. L.597 J.D. 200 W. Madison St., Ste. 2430
Rothe, Edward W., (AV) . . . .'27 '50 C.674 A.B. L.477 J.D. 839 N. Dearborn St.‡
Rothe, Mary B. '37 '84 C.121 B.S. L.285 J.D.
(adm. in WI; not adm. in IL) Artists, Events & Entertainment, Inc.
Rothenberg, Ian N. . . . .'72 '97 C.339 B.S. L.424 J.D. [Ⓐ Sedgwick,D.M.&A.]
Rothenberg, Sheribel F., (AV) . . . . '44 '67 C&L.597 B.A., J.D. 36 S. Wabash
Rothman, Joel S., (AV) '55 '80 C&L.597 B.A., J.D.
[J.S.Rothman&Assoc.] & [Ⓒ Otis]
Rothman, Richard B. . . . .'33 '63 C.597 B.S. L.146 LL.B. 205 W. Randolph St.

Rothman, Joel S., & Associates, Ltd., (AV)
55 West Monroe Street, Suite 3330, 60603
Telephone: 312-578-0900 Fax: 312-578-0905
Email: joel@rothmanlaw.com
Joel S. Rothman;—Thomas D. Sterling; Christopher R. Fleck. Of Counsel: Stuart A. Cohn; Mark T. Neil; Anita S. Ridge; Robert E. Stigger; Michel Winkelstein.
Estate Planning, Estate and Trust Administration. Business Planning, Probate, Tax Planning, Corporate and Charitable Contribution Law.
See Professional Biographies, CHICAGO, ILLINOIS

Rothmann, Rebecca . . . .'71 '96 C.966 B.A. L.146 J.D. [Wilson E.M.E.&D.]
Rothschild, Anthony E. . . . .'57 '83 C.309 A.B. L.597 J.D. [Ⓒ McLachlan,R.&D.]
Rothschild, Edward I., (P.C.), (AV) . . . '21 '49 C&L.309 A.B., LL.B. [Rothschild,B.&M.]
Rothschild, George W. . . . .'17 '42 C.309 A.B. L.145 J.D. Assoc. Cir. J.
Rothschild, Jonathan E., (AV) . . . . '54 '80 C.385 B.A. L.597 J.D. [Rothschild,B.&M.]

Rothschild, Barry & Myers, (AV)
A Partnership including Professional Corporations
Suite 3900, 55 West Monroe Street, 60603-5012
Telephone: 312-372-2345 FAX: 312-372-2350
Email: firm@rbmchicago.com URL: http://www.rbmchicago.com
Members of Firm: Norman J. Barry (P.C.) (1921-1998); Edward I. Rothschild (P.C.); William G. Myers (P.C.); Melvin I. Mishkin; John J. Coffey, III; Joseph P. Della Maria, Jr.; Michael J. Wall; Daniel Cummings; Kenneth P. Taube; Jonathan E. Rothschild; Alan S. Madans; Kevin J. Moore; Robin K. Powers; John D. Silk. Of Counsel: Sheila M. Murphy.
General Civil, Trial and Appellate Practice in Federal and State Courts. General, Corporate and Business Law, Real Estate, Estate Planning, Trusts and Probate, Antitrust, Aviation, Creditor, Bankruptcy, Class Actions, Constitutional Law, Construction Law, Employment Discrimination, Environmental, Franchising, Insurance, Intellectual Property, Pensions, Secured Transactions and Taxation.
See Professional Biographies, CHICAGO, ILLINOIS

Rothstein, Jeffrey S., (AV) . . . . '56 '82 C.309 A.B. L.145 J.D. [Sidley A.B.&W.]
Rothstein, Lisa A. . . . .'64 '93 C.477 A.B. L.608 J.D. [Chuhak&T.]
Rothstein, Michael D. . . . .'71 '97 C.260 B.S.B.A. L.339 J.D. [Schwartz C.]
Rothstein, Michael I, (AV) . . . .'60 '87 C.347 B.S. L.94 J.D. [Tabet D.&R.]
Rothstein, Ronald Y. . . . .'69 '95 C.011 B.A. L.879 J.D. [Winston&S.]
Rothstein, Seymour, (AV) '31 '58
C.124 B.S.M.E. L.273 LL.B. [Ⓒ Olson&H.] (See Pat. Sect.)
Rotman, Michael H. '36 '62 C.1016 B.S.C. L.209 J.D. [Rotman&E.]
Rotman, Orin S., (AV) . . . .'53 '78 C.597 B.A. L.209 J.D. [Stein&R.]
Rotman, Robert D. . . . .'60 '90 C.338 B.A. L.1000 J.D. [Rotman&E.]
Rotman & Elovitz, Ltd. . . . . .180 N. La Salle St.
Rotner, Philip R., (AVⓉ) . . . .'— '72 C.112 A.B. L.1565 J.D. [Mayer,B.R.&M.]
Rotstein, Harold B. . . . .'12 '35 C.145 L.209 Hearings Ref., Dept. of Employ. Sec.
Rottner, Jack H., (BV) . . . . '57 '82 C.339 B.A. L.146 J.D. 105 W. Madison St.
Rotunno, Donna A. . . . .'75 '00 C.700 B.A. L.146 J.D. State's Atty.
Rotunno, John W., (AV) . . . .'51 '76 C.339 B.A. L.145 J.D. [Bell,B.&L.]
Rotunno, Melissa '71 '97 C.1111 L.339 J.D.
Brand Coun., Blue Cross Blue Shield Assoc.
Rotunno, Steven J., (AV) . . . . '53 '78 C.339 B.A. L.424 J.D. [Kubasiak,F.R.&R.]
Rougeau, Vincent D. '63 '89 C.103 A.B. L.309 J.D.
(adm. in MD; not adm. in IL) Asst. Prof., Loyola University-Chicago School of Law
Roumell, Michael T., (AV) . . . .'54 '81 C.477 B.A. L.215 J.D. [Epstein B.&G.]
Rouse, Steven P., (AV) . . . .'57 '85 C.98 B.A. L.365 J.D. [Menges&M.]
Routman, Eric L., (AV) . . . . '— '80 C.273 B.B.A. L.365 J.D. [Krafsur]
Rovell, Michael J., Law Offices of, (AV) . . . . .'49 '72 C&L.339 B.A., J.D. 20 N. Clark St.
Rovner, Gary S. . . . .'— '95 C.197 B.A. L.273 J.D. [Ⓒ Foley&L.]
Rovner, Ilana Diamond . . . .'38 '72 C.104 A.B. L.146 J.D. U.S. Cir. J.
Rovner, Jack A., (AV) . . . . '46 '76 C.1036 B.A. L.94 J.D. [Neal,G.&E.]
Rovner, Suzanne Karbarz . . . . '70 '95 C.339 B.A. L.273 J.D. [Ⓐ DLPiper R.G.C.U.]
Rowan, Karen A. . . . .'56 '89 C.536 B.A. L.424 J.D. Legal Officer, Police Dept.
Rowe, Anita M., Arbitrator and Mediator '59 '84 C.241 B.S. L.276 J.D.
P.O. Box 14525
Rowe, Heidi Hennig . . . .'— '01 C.879 B.A. L.146 J.D. [Ⓐ Schiff H.]
Rowe, James S., (AV) . . . . '— '91 C.339 B.A. L.228 J.D. [Kirkland&E.]
Rowe, Todd M. '74 '00 C.476 B.S. L.436 J.D.
(adm. in MI; not adm. in IL) [Ⓐ Merlo K.B.&G.]
Rowells, Timothy L. . . . .'51 '79 C.339 B.A. L.146 J.D. [Starr,Y.&R.]
Rowels, L. Victoria . . . .'58 '83 C.477 A.B. L.569 J.D. P.O. Box 1095
Rowen, Lyle D. . . . .'70 '97 C.436 B.A. L.957 J.D. [Ⓐ Dowd,B.&B.]
Rowin, Daniel A. . . . .'61 '89 C.1494 B.A. L.597 J.D. [Pugh,J.J.&Q.]
Rowland, David J. . . . .'62 '88 C&L.477 A.B., J.D. [Seyfarth S.]
Rowland, Frank C., (AV) . . . .'54 '76 C.436 B.A. L.365 J.D. [Ⓐ BryceDowney]
Rowland, Mary M., (BV) . . . .'61 '89 C.477 B.A. L.145 J.D. [Hughes S.P.R.&D.]
Rowley, Richard C. . . . .'46 '76 C.187 B.A. L.365 J.D. F.D.I.C.
Rownd, David M. . . . .'65 '91 C.597 B.A. L.910 J.D. [Ⓐ FagelHaber]
Roy, Paul J.N. . . . . '55 '85 C.164 B.A. L.424 J.D. [Mayer,B.R.&M.]
Roy, Shima S. . . . .'74 '99 C.104 A.B. L.477 J.D. [Ⓐ Baker&M.]
Royal, Carl A. . . . .'— '74 C.894 B.A. L.976 J.D. [Ⓒ Schiff H.]

Royal, David S. .... '— '97 C&L.976 B.A., J.D. [Kirkland&E.]
Royce, Merle L., II, (AV) '42 '67
C&L.352 B.A., J.D. 111 West Washington Street Suite 1710
Roy-Singh, Pradeep, Law Office of '48 '84
C.999 B.A. L.146 J.D. 2335 West Devon, Suite 204
Royster, Joseph B., (BV) .... '— '90 C.940 B.A. L.245 J.D. [Litchfield C.]
Roytberg, Nan .... '49 '95 C.846 B.A. L.146 J.D. Assoc. Coun., Nat'l Assn of Realtors
Rozak, James M. .... '64 '91 C.436 B.S. L.365 J.D. [🄰 Wiedner&M.]
Rozen, Lisa R. .... '— '02 C.966 B.A. L.260 J.D. [🄰 Hennessy&R.]
Rozen, Reid J. .... '60 '88 C.340 B.A. L.477 J.D. [🄰 N.R.Novak]
Rozen, Stuart M., (AV) .... '56 '81 C&L.339 B.A., J.D. [Mayer,B.R.&M.]
Rozenblat, Alexander .... '78 '03 C.597 B.A. L.209 J.D. [🄰 Jenner&B.] (Pat.)
Rozenblat, David .... '73 '98 C.339 B.S.M.E. L.146 J.D. [🄰 Sonnenschein N.&R.] (Pat.)
Rozman, Alexander Gregory .... '74 '99 C.339 B.A. L.146 J.D. [RozmanPractice]
Rozman Law Practice .... 2615 North Sheffield
Rozran, Jack L. .... '39 '63 C.597 B.A. L.309 LL.B. 875 W. Huron‡
Rozycki, Carla J. .... '52 '77 C.339 B.S. L.597 J.D. [Jenner&B.]
Ruark, John D., (BV) .... '64 '92 C.976 B.A. L.365 J.D. [Lawrence,K.S.&U.]
Rubas, Joseph E. .... '73 '98 C.339 B.A. L.424 J.D. [🄰 Hinshaw&C.]
Rubel, Kimberly K. .... '68 '95 C.339 B.S. L.145 J.D. [Gardner C.&D.]
Ruben, Gary N., (AV) .... '57 '81 C.339 B.S. L.309 J.D. [Goldberg,K.B.B.R.&M.]
Ruben, Philip E. .... '58 '83 C.339 B.S. L.146 J.D. [Levenfeld P.] ⊙
Rubens, Barrett E. .... '75 '02 C.966 B.A. L.146 J.D. Asst. Corp. Coun.
Rubens, James L., (AV) .... '54 '79 C.339 B.A. L.209 J.D. [Davis F.Z.K.M.M.&R.]
Rubenstein, Alan J. .... '64 '90 C.966 B.A. L.209 J.D. Chicago Legal Search, Ltd.
Rubenstein, Amy M. .... '— '02 C.1365 B.A. L.145 J.D. [🄰 Schiff H.]
Rubenstein, Corey B. .... '70 '95 C.477 A.B. L.309 J.D. [Stetler&D.]
Rubenstein, David A. .... '58 '83 C.339 B.A. L.477 J.D. [Gardner C.&D.]
Rubenstein, I. H. .... '08 '32 C.999 L.209 LL.B. 1611 Chicago Ave.
Rubenstein, Jeffrey C., (AV) .... '42 '66 C&L.477 A.B., J.D. [Much S.F.D.A.&R.]
Ruber, Norman, (BV) .... '52 '78 C.1183 B.A. L.365 J.D. [Berger S.]
Ruberry, Edward F., (AV) .... '47 '73 C.162 B.A. L.424 J.D. [Bollinger,R.&G.]
Ruberry, Patrick J. .... '59 '84 C&L.339 B.A., J.D. [Dowd&D.]
Rubesh, Karl G., II .... '51 '78 C.415 B.A. L.146 J.D. [Carper&R.]
Rubin, Arnold G., (AV) .... '54 '78 C.597 B.A. L.46 J.D. [A.G.Rubin]
Rubin, Beth S. .... '— '87 C&L.477 A.B.Ed., J.D. [🄲 Barack F.K.P.&N.]
Rubin, David M., (AV) .... '45 '71 C.1016 B.S. L.209 J.D. [Gould&R.]
Rubin, Donald T., (AV) .... '50 '80 C.339 B.A. L.365 J.D. [Rubin&N.] ⊙
Rubin, E. Leonard, (AV) .... '— '60 C&L.472 A.B., J.D. [🄲 Sachnoff&W.]
Rubin, Erwin .... '37 '64 C.1016 B.S.B.A. L.365 LL.B. [Kroll&R.]
Rubin, Howard M. '45 '71 C.339 B.S. L.209 J.D.
Assoc. Dean, DePaul Univ. Col. of Law
Rubin, Ira E. .... '32 '55 L.209 LL.B. [Pauker&R.]
Rubin, James I., (AV) .... '46 '71 C.339 A.B. L.424 J.D. [Butler R.S.&B.]
Rubin, Jamie .... '— '00 C.352 B.A. L.365 J.D. [🄰 Wildman,H.A.&D.]
Rubin, Jason L. .... '73 '98 C.188 B.A. L.145 J.D. [🄰 Sonnenschein N.&R.]
Rubin, J.D. .... '76 '03 C.966 B.A. L.597 J.D. [🄰 Barack F.K.P.&N.]
Rubin, Joel D., (AV) .... '44 '68 C.659 B.S. L.597 J.D. [Seyfarth S.]
Rubin, Julie P. .... '— '92 C.165 B.A. L.930 J.D. [O'Hagan,S.&A.]
Rubin, Lawrence C., (AV) .... '48 '72 C.339 B.S. L.597 J.D. [Shefsky&F.]
Rubin, M. H. .... '10 '34 C&L.209 LL.B. 3200 N. Lake Shore Dr.‡
Rubin, Mark S. .... '57 '81 C.475 B.A. L.597 J.D. American Dental Assn.
Rubin, Martin J., Law Offices of '39 '62 C.339 L.365 J.D.
155 N. Michigan Ave., Ste. 620
Rubin, Robert C., (BV) .... '55 '83 C.221 B.A. L.861 J.D. [🄲 Scopelitis,G.L.&H.]
Rubin, Roger A., (BV) .... '— '71 C.347 B.A. L.339 J.D. [Beermann S.W.B.B.G.&L.]
Rubin, Ross N. .... '48 '73 C.475 B.A. L.339 J.D. V.P., Legis Affs., Amer. Med. Assn.
Rubin, Arnold G., Ltd., (AV) .... 100 W. Monroe St., Ste. 1710

Rubin & Norris, LLC, The Law Offices of, (AV)
205 West Wacker Drive, Suite 705, 60606-1212 ⊙
Telephone: 312-263-1360 Fax: 312-263-1368 URL: http://www.propertytaxattorneys.com
Email: johnknorrisattorney@msn.com URL: http://www.lawyers.com/johnknorris
John K. Norris, Jr.; Donald T. Rubin;—Daniel M. Pierce. Of Counsel: Marshall A. Fleischman.
Real Estate Taxation, Ad Valorem Property Taxation, Property Tax Assessments and Property Tax Appeals.
Wood Dale Office: 189 North Cedar Avenue, 60191-2084. Telephone: 630-787-1234. Fax: 630-787-1236.

See Professional Biographies, CHICAGO, ILLINOIS

Rubinelli, Joseph O., (AV) .... '16 '40 C&L.209 B.S., J.D. [🄲 Chuhak&T.]
Rubinelli, Joseph O., Jr., (AV) .... '54 '78 C.813 A.B. L.597 J.D. [McDermott W.&E.]
Rubinoff, N. Arthur, (AV) .... '18 '40 L.209 LL.B. 5519 N. Lincoln Ave.
Rubinowitz, Leonard S. '43 '68 C.966 B.A. L.976 LL.B.
(adm. in CT; not adm. in IL) Prof., Northwestern Univ. Sch. of Law
Rubinson, Adolph A., (AV) .... '10 '34 C&L.145 Ph.B., J.D. 221 N. LaSalle St.
Rubinstein, Jacob .... '27 '58 C.339 B.A. L.146 J.D. [🄰 Meckler B.&T.]
Rubinstein, Javier H. .... '63 '89 C.477 B.A. L.276 J.D. [Mayer,B.R.&M.]
Rubinstein, Sherwin R., (AV) .... '47 '73 C.339 B.A. L.209 J.D. [Kamensky,R.H.&D.] ⊙
Ruble, Lisa A. '58 '84 C.788 B.A. L.146 J.D.
Dep. Chief Admin. Officer, City Finance Comm.
Ruby, Lauren S. .... '63 '89 C.477 A.B. L.309 J.D. Asst. Reg. Coun., Dept. of HHS
Rucker, William R. .... '— '00 C.16 B.S. L.365 J.D. [🄰 Gardner C.&D.]
Ruda, Mark B., (AV) .... '58 '83 C.424 B.A. L.146 J.D. [Condon&C.]
Rudd, Anne Ciser .... '62 '98 C.339 B.S. L.879 J.D. [🄰 K.B.Moll&Assoc.]
Rudd, Jeffrey L. .... '75 '00 C.339 B.A. L.276 J.D. [🄰 Katten M.R.]
Ruddy, John R. .... '28 '78 C.424 B.S.C. L.1151 J.D. 29 S. LaSalle St.
Ruder, David S., (AV) '29 '57 C.951 B.A. L.966 J.D.
William W. Gurley Memorial Prof. of Law, Northwestern Univ. School of Law
Rudin, Scott H., (AV) .... '64 '89 C.338 B.S. L.146 J.D. [Miroballi,D.&R.]
Rudin, Sheila H. .... '59 '84 C.339 B.S. L.146 J.D. Off. of State's Atty.
Rudinsky, Jason .... '79 '04 C.309 A.B. L.602 J.D. [🄰 Skadden,A.S.M.&F.]
Rudis, Mark A. .... '53 '80 C.338 L.424 J.D. Creditors Benefit Corp.
Rudisill, Stephen G., (AV) .... '— '64 C.228 B.S.E.E. L.569 J.D. [Jenkens&G.] (Pat.)
Rudman, Jerry I. .... '42 '68 C.339 B.S. L.209 J.D. [Deutsch,L.&E.]
Rudnick, Jordan M. .... '67 '95 C.145 B.A. L.365 J.D. [🄰 Mayer,B.R.&M.]
Rudnick, Lewis G., (AV) .... '35 '64 C.339 A.B. L.597 J.D. [DLPiper R.G.C.U.]
Rudnick, Paul D., (AV) .... '40 '65 C.861 B.S. L.597 J.D. [🄲 DLPiper R.G.C.U.]
Rudnick, Raymond M. .... '73 '00 C.927 B.S. L.365 J.D. [🄰 Carponelli&K.]
Rudnick, William A., (AV) .... '64 '89 C.860 B.A. L.597 J.D. [DLPiper R.G.C.U.]
Rudo, Saul E., (BV) .... '58 '83 C.339 B.S. L.309 J.D. [Katten M.R.]
Rudoff, Abigail L. .... '57 '94 C.589 B.S. L.145 J.D. [🄲 Mayer,B.R.&M.]
Rudolph, David L. .... '70 '95 C.94 B.A. L.608 J.D. 111 W. Washington Street Suite 823
Rudoy, Herbert L., Ltd. .... '42 '67 C.228 B.A. L.597 J.D. 230 W. Superior St.
Rudstein, David S. '46 '71
C.339 B.S. L.597 J.D. Prof. of Law, Chicago-Kent Coll. of Law
Ruebner, Ralph .... '44 '69 C.339 B.A. L.30 J.D. Chicago Law Sch.

Rueth, Randall G. .... '— '98 C.927 B.S. L.209 J.D. [🄰 Marshall,G.&B.] (See Pat. Sect.)
Ruff, Deborah Schavey, (AV) .... '59 '86 C.679 B.S. L.879 J.D. [Mayer,B.R.&M.] (Pat.)
Ruff, Edward B., III, (AV) .... '54 '81 C.966 B.S.M.E. L.209 J.D. [Pretzel&S.]
Ruff, Randolph E., (AV) .... '58 '86 C.174 B.A. L.879 J.D. [Ogletree,D.N.S.&S.]
Ruff, Stephen L., Jr., (AV) .... '46 '71 C.1024 B.A. L.209 J.D. [Ruff,W.&R.]
Ruff, Weidenaar & Reidy, Ltd., (AV) .... 222 N. La Salle St.
Ruffalo, Steven M., (AV) .... '62 '89 C.339 B.S. L.365 J.D. [Fuchs&R.]
Ruffner, Thomas L. .... '78 '03 C.896 B.S. L.209 J.D. [🄰 Howrey]
Ruffolo, Samuel J., (AV) .... '44 '75 C.932 B.S. L.209 J.D. [Baum,R.&M.]
Rugg, Nathan Q. .... '75 '00 C.197 B.A. L.339 J.D. [🄰 Adelman&G.]
Ruggiero, Richard, (BV) '63 '92
C.209 B.A. L.365 J.D. Atty., SAFECO Prop. & Cas. Ins. Co.
Ruggio, Mary A. .... '56 '99 C.1016 B.A. L.365 J.D. 741 North Dearborn
Ruhlen, George, (AVⓉ) .... '50 '75 C.691 B.A. L.846 J.D. [Mayer,B.R.&M.]
Ruiz, Jean-Pierre .... '58 '90 C.012 B.E. L.146 J.D. 10 S. La Salle St.‡
Ruiz, Jesse H. .... '65 '95 C.339 B.A. L.145 J.D. [Gardner C.&D.]
Ruiz, Michele I. .... '69 '94 C.188 B.S. L.145 J.D. [🄰 Sidley A.B.&W.]
Ruiz, Miguel A., (AV) .... '63 '92 C.339 B.A. L.966 J.D. [Pretzel&S.]
Ruiz, Robert J. .... '49 '78 C.339 B.A. L.209 J.D. Solr. Gen.
Ruksakiati, Scott A. .... '68 '93 C.347 B.A. L.209 J.D. [Fisher K.]
Rummel, George T. .... '45 '70 C.597 B.A. L.339 J.D. 538 W. Hawthorne Pl.
Rummel, Philip P. .... '34 '68 C.604 A.B. L.209 J.D. 8912 S. Constance St.‡
Rumsey, Richard L., (AV) .... '50 '78 C.234 B.S. L.424 J.D. 111 W. Washington St.
Runcie, Diana T. .... '62 '87 C&L.309 A.B., J.D. 525 W. Monroe St., Suite 1600
Rundell, Ralph .... '13 '35 L.209 LL.B. 222 E. Pearson St.‡
Rundin, Nancy M. .... '54 '80 C.339 B.A. L.365 J.D. [S.G.Thomas]
Rundio, Louis M., Jr., (AV) .... '43 '72 C&L.424 B.S., J.D. [McDermott W.&E.]
Rundio, Matthew M. .... '75 '00 C.339 B.S. L.424 J.D. [🄰 Lloyd&C.]
Runnels, Charis A. .... '72 '99 C.436 B.A. L.146 J.D. [🄰 Morgan,L.&B.]
Running, Andrew R., (AV) .... '— '82 C.145 A.B. L.976 J.D. [Kirkland&E.]
Runyan, Edward K. .... '— '00 C.679 B.S. L.209 J.D. [🄰 Kirkland&E.] (Pat.)
Rupe, Michael C. .... '— '98 C.608 B.A. L.150 J.D. [Jenner&B.]
Rupert, Donald W., (AV) .... '46 '77 C.473 B.S. L.900 J.D. [Mayer,B.R.&M.] (Pat.)
Rupert, Douglas S. .... '70 '97 C.475 B.S.E.E. L.424 J.D. [🄰 Seyfarth S.] (Pat.)
Rupp, Brian C. .... '62 '90 C&L.209 B.S., J.D. [Gardner C.&D.]
Ruschau, Pamela J. '59 '87 C.1229 B.M.E. L.608 J.D.
[Leydig,V.&M.] (See Pat. Sect.)
Rusche, Laura S. .... '— '01 C.550 B.A. L.424 J.D. Two North LaSalle Street, Suite 2200
Rush, Peter G., (AV) .... '59 '85 C.602 B.A. L.228 J.D. [Bell,B.&L.]
Rush, Robert H. .... '— '01 C.67 B.A. L.569 J.D. [🄰 Sachnoff&W.]
Rush, Sharon E. '51 '80 C&L.188 B.A., J.D.
(adm. in DC; not adm. in IL) Assoc. Prof., DePaul Coll. of Law
Rusher, Robert H. .... '28 '53 C&L.209 LL.B. Pres., COO, North Fed. Svgs. Bk.
Rushman, Jonathan M. '77 '04
C.477 B.S.E. L.209 J.D. [🄰 McAndrews,H.&M.] (See Pat. Sect.)
Rusin, Mark P., (AV) .... '63 '90 C.339 B.A. L.146 J.D. [Rusin M.&F.]
Rusin, Michael E., (AV) .... '55 '78 C&L.597 B.A., J.D. [Rusin M.&F.]

Rusin Maciorowski & Friedman, Ltd., (AV) 🄱🅁
Suite 1530 10 South Riverside Plaza, 60606 ⊙
Telephone: 312-454-5110 Fax: 312-454-6166
URL: http://www.rusinlaw.com
Michael E. Rusin; Stephen J. Friedman; John A. Maciorowski; Kenneth N. Marshall; Gregory G. Vacala; Daniel W. Arkin; Randall R. Stark; Mark P. Rusin; Daniel R. Egan; Theodore J. Powers; Gregory A. Rode; R. Mark Cosimini (Resident, Champaign Office); Joseph N. Casciato; Stuart Pellish; Thomas E. Margolis (Resident, Carbondale Office);—Farrah L. Anderson (Resident, Carbondale Office); Joseph P. Basile; Amber M. Clark; Timothy D. Denny (Resident, Carbondale Office); Steven R. Dyki; Brent W. Halbleib; William J. Harrington; Leah L. Mabery; Philip Marchion; Joseph A. Marciniak; Nadine Neue; Ivan Nieves; Cristina C. Nolan; Lucas M. Rothaar; Robert P. Sabetto; Terry E. Schroeder (Resident, Champaign Office); Douglas J. Sullivan; Edward R. Tomkowiak.
Workers Compensation Law. Insurance Defense, Personal Injury, Products Liability, Auto and Trucking Liability, Structural Work Act, Commercial Litigation, Subrogation, Contract Insurance, Employment Discrimination. Wrongful Discharge.
Champaign, Illinois Office: 2506 Galen Drive, Suite 104, 61821-7047. Telephone: 217-351-1700. Fax: 217-351-1732.
Carbondale, Illinois Office: 239 South Lewis Lane, Suite A, 62901-3443. Telephone: 618-351-8100. Fax: 618-351-8109.

See Professional Biographies, CHICAGO, ILLINOIS

Ruskin, David S. .... '66 '91 C.966 B.A. L.424 J.D. [Horwood M.&B.]
Ruskusky, John T. .... '— '98 C.602 B.A. L.273 J.D. [🄰 Ungaretti&H.]
Russ, Donald J., Jr., (AV) .... '52 '77 C.927 B.B.A. L.326 J.D. [Chuhak&T.]
Russ, Michael M. .... '57 '82 C.339 B.S. L.273 J.D. U.S. Envir. Protec. Agcy.
Russell, James H., (AV) .... '43 '70 C.611 B.A. L.608 J.D. [Winston&S.]
Russell, Jan .... '55 '97 C.1016 B.G.S. L.146 J.D. 4044 S. Archer Ave.
Russell, Jennifer W. '71 '96
C.475 B.A. L.424 J.D. Litig. & Claims Managt., The Boeing Co.
Russell, Joseph M. '47 '77 C.339 B.S. L.146 J.D.
Sr. Coun., Bank One Corp. (Law Dept.)
Russell, Joseph Michael .... '— '03 C.276 B.A. L.597 J.D. [🄰 Kirkland&E.]
Russell, Kevin A. .... '— '80 C.20 A.B. L.477 J.D. [Latham&W.]
Russell, Maynard B. .... '26 '58 C.339 B.S. L.209 J.D. [🄲 FagelHaber]
Russell, Paul F., (BV) .... '48 '73 C.597 B.A. L.477 J.D. [Vedder,P.K.&K.]
Russell, Ralph T., Jr., (AV) .... '48 '74 C.694 A.B. L.145 J.D. [Neal,G.&E.]
Russell, Scott David '62 '88 C.27 B.A. L.215 J.D.
Asst. Gen. Coun. & Asst. Sec., R. R. Donnelley & Sons Co.
Russell, Suzanne M. .... '— '90 C.321 B.A. L.602 J.D. [Chapman&C.]
Russell, Thomas J., (AV) .... '21 '49 C&L.209 A.B., J.D. 6509 W. 63rd St.
Russell, Thomas J., (BV) '52 '78 C.502 B.A. L.94 J.D.
Asst. Gen. Coun., Exelon Corp.
Russell, Victor W. '40 '70
C.957 B.S. L.966 J.D. Adm J., U.S. Merit Systems Protection Bd.
Russell, William E., (AV) .... '— '84 C.228 B.A. L.910 J.D. [Freeborn&P.]
Russo, Allyson B. .... '75 '01 C.93 B.A. L.477 J.D. [🄰 Vedder,P.K.&K.]
Russo, Andrea Renee .... '74 '00 C.225 B.S. L.502 J.D. West Group
Russo, Angelo M. .... '75 '00 C.339 B.S. L.209 J.D. [🄰 McGuirewoods]
Russo, Carl L., (AV) .... '46 '71 C.436 B.S. L.597 J.D. [Seyfarth S.]
Russo, Lee Ann, (AV) .... '— '82 C.602 B.A. L.893 J.D. [Jones D.]
Russo, Steven S., (BV) .... '52 '82 C.589 B.A. L.209 J.D. 210 W. Illinois St.
Rust, Mark E., (AV) .... '— '89 C.602 B.A. L.424 J.D. [Barnes&T.]
Rustik, James A. .... '65 '92 C.209 B.A. L.365 J.D. Asst. Atty. Gen.
Rutkoff, Alan S., (AV) .... '52 '76 C.477 B.A. L.597 J.D. [McDermott W.&E.]
Rutkowski, Anthony R. .... '66 '91 C.276 B.S. L.424 J.D. [MacCabe&M.]
Rutkowski, Jamie A. .... '76 '02 C.347 B.S. L.424 J.D. Staff Atty.
Rutsch, Bryan C. .... '— '05 C&L.966 B.S., J.D. [🄰 Kirkland&E.] (Pat.)
Rutstein, Leonard David, (AV) .... '33 '55 C&L.145 A.B., J.D. [Williams,G.M.K.&R.]
Rutstein, Neal D. .... '62 '91 C.118 B.A. L.145 J.D. 5553 Glenwood‡
Ruttenberg, Barnett P., (AV) .... '45 '72 C.339 B.A. L.597 J.D. [Gardner C.&D.]

Ruttenberg, David C., (AV) ... '09 '33 C.966 B.S. L.597 J.D. [Ruttenberg&R.]
Ruttenberg, David W., (AV) ... '41 '66 C.188 B.A. L.597 J.D. [Ruttenberg&R.]
Ruttenberg, Daymon L. ... '— '01 C.363 B.S. L.365 J.D. [Ⓐ Brinks H.G.&L.]
Ruttenberg & Ruttenberg, (AV) ... 833 N. Orleans Street
Ruxin, Paul T., (AVⓉ) ... '— '68 C.31 B.A. L.893 LL.B. [Jones D.]
Ruzich, Richard T. ... '69 '96 C.98 B.S.E.E.T. L.801 J.D. [Ⓐ Mayer,B.R.&M.]
Ryan, Aaron P. ... '— '03 C&L.209 B.S., J.D. [Ⓐ Anderson,R.]
Ryan, Agnes C. ... '28 '50 C.329 A.B. L.262 LL.B. Legal Aid Bureau
Ryan, Allan C. ("Kelly"), IV ... '73 '98 C.321 B.A. L.597 J.D. [Ⓐ Mayer,B.R.&M.]
Ryan, Charles J., Jr., (AV) ... '49 '82 C.602 B.A. L.146 J.D. [O'Connell&R.]
Ryan, Colleen ... '— '03 C.957 B.A. L.597 J.D. [Ⓐ Kirkland&E.]
Ryan, Daniel K. ... '59 '85 C.602 B.A. L.424 J.D. [Hinshaw&C.]
Ryan, David F. ... '53 '85 C.602 B.B.A. L.1252 J.D. [Patton&R.]

Ryan, David J., (AV) '53 '77 C.597 B.A. L.276 J.D.
111 West Washington Street Suite 1900, 60602
Telephone: 312-782-7099 Facsimile: 312-807-4858
Civil Litigation, Health Care Law, Insurance Law, Arbitration, Mediation.
See Professional Biographies, CHICAGO, ILLINOIS

Ryan, Edward F., (AV) ... '43 '68 C.1268 B.A. L.276 J.D. [Holland&K.]
Ryan, Heather Heath ... '— '04 C.880 B.A. L.910 J.D. [Ⓐ Gardner C.&D.]
Ryan, J. Hayes ... '74 '01 C.385 B.A. L.365 J.D. [Ⓐ Cassiday,S.&G.]
Ryan, James H., (AV) ... '40 '66 C.874 A.B. L.309 LL.B. [Ⓒ Horwood M.&B.]
Ryan, James J. ... '56 '84 C.339 B.A. L.1000 J.D. [Ⓐ Ambrose&C.]
Ryan, Jennifer C. ... '75 '01 C.589 B.A. L.339 J.D. [Ⓐ Katten M.R.]
Ryan, John Clemens ... '59 '85 C.197 A.B. L.309 J.D. V.P., Goldman, Sachs & Co.
Ryan, John D. ... '— '73 L.262 J.D. [Ⓒ Holland&K.]
Ryan, Joseph Gerald ... '75 '01 C&L.424 B.A., J.D. 180 N. La Salle St., Ste. 2310
Ryan, Kevin J. ... '56 '87 C.602 B.S. L.146 J.D. [Burke,W.M.&S.]
Ryan, Kevin M. ... '73 '98 C.93 B.A. L.424 J.D. [Ⓐ Winston&S.]
Ryan, Kristyna C., Law Office of '71 '00
C.608 B.S. L.146 J.D. 1530 South State Street, Suite 605
Ryan, Laura D. '61 '88 C.145 B.A. L.966 J.D.
V.P. & Coun., Harris Trust and Savings Bank
Ryan, Lauren E. ... '77 '02 C.884 B.S. L.209 J.D. [Ⓐ Ryan&R.]
Ryan, Martin P. ... '67 '92 C.339 B.A. L.424 J.D. [Burke,W.M.&S.]
Ryan, Martin Q. ... '69 '95 C.597 B.A. L.365 J.D. [Ⓐ Mora,B.W.&U.]
Ryan, Michael W. ... '75 '02 C.473 B.A. L.597 J.D. [Ⓐ Ryan&R.]
Ryan, Michaela ... '63 '91 C.276 B.A. L.146 J.D. [Ⓐ Kerns,P.F.&P.]
Ryan, Patricia A. ... '69 '94 C.339 B.A. L.424 J.D. [Cassiday,S.&G.]
Ryan, Patrick J., (AV) ... '48 '74 C&L.209 B.A., J.D. [Cohn,L.R.S.&G.]
Ryan, Patrick Thomas ... '80 '05 C.339 B.A. L.209 J.D. [Ⓐ Schiller,D.&F.]
Ryan, Peter J. ... '— '04 C.602 B.A. L.910 J.D. [Ⓐ Kirkland&E.]
Ryan, Priscilla E., (BV) ... '47 '82 C.436 B.A. L.424 J.D. [Sidley A.B.&W.]
Ryan, Richard L. ... '47 '72 C.339 B.A. L.146 J.D. Chief Admin. Law J., Dept. of Rev.
Ryan, Richard T., (AV) ... '34 '62 C.424 B.S. L.365 J.D. [Ⓐ J.L.Flynn]
Ryan, Roibin J. ... '61 '88 C.339 B.S. L.276 J.D. [Jenner&B.]
Ryan, Seamus M. ... '75 '04 C.93 B.A. L.597 J.D. [Ⓐ Marcus,P.&C.]
Ryan, Steven W. ... '68 '93 C&L.424 B.A., J.D. [Pretzel&S.]
Ryan, Tana M. ... '— '03 C.112 B.A. L.145 J.D. [Ⓐ Kirkland&E.]
Ryan, Terry I. ... '— '03 C.188 B.A. L.597 J.D. [Ⓐ DLPiper R.G.C.U.]
Ryan, Thomas F., (AV) ... '43 '72 C.252 B.S. L.912 J.D. [Sidley A.B.&W.]
Ryan, Thomas M. ... '64 '89 C.347 B.A. L.146 J.D. 500 W. Madison St.
Ryan, Thomas W. ... '69 '97 C.966 B.S. L.201 J.D. [Ⓐ DLPiper R.G.C.U.] (Pat.)
Ryan, Timothy J. ... '51 '78 C.973 A.B. L.365 J.D. [Ryan&R.]
Ryan, W. Michael, (AV) ... '65 '92 C.976 B.A. L.339 J.D. [Sonnenschein N.&R.]
Ryan, William E., (AV) ... '49 '75 C.973 B.A. L.209 J.D. [Ryan&R.]
Ryan, William J., (AV) ... '63 '91 C.1044 B.A. L.309 J.D. [Scandaglia&R.] (Pat.)
Ryan, William P. ... '— '82 C.801 B.A. L.209 J.D. [Marwedel,M.&R.]

Ryan and Ryan, (AV) BB
33 North Dearborn Street, Suite 1530, 60602
Telephone: 312-236-1386 Fax: 312-236-2556
URL: http://www.ryanandryanchicago.com
William E. Ryan; Timothy J. Ryan. Associates: Terrence D. McCabe; Michael W. Ryan; Lauren E. Ryan.
Eminent Domain, Condemnation.
See Professional Biographies, CHICAGO, ILLINOIS

Rybicki, Michael J. ... '46 '70 C.750 B.A. L.339 J.D. [Seyfarth S.]
Ryder, David R. ... '46 '71 C.210 B.A. L.477 J.D. [McDermott W.&E.]
Ryder, Jennifer M. ... '— '04 C.966 B.A. L.424 J.D. [Ⓐ R.J.Prendergast]
Ryerson, Andrew S. ... '69 '95 C.473 B.A. L.209 J.D. [Ⓢ McGuirewoods]
Ryken, Robert L. ... '50 '75 C.793 B.A. L.309 J.D. 1426 S. Federal St.‡
Rymer, Terrie A., (AV) '46 '81 C.477 B.A. L.597 J.D.
Legal Advocate, Advocacy Servs., Jewish Federation of Metro. Chicago
Ryndak, James D., (AV) '52 '77
C.679 B.S.Ch.E. L.146 J.D. [Ryndak&S.] (See Pat. Sect.)
Ryndak, Peter R. ... '70 '96 C.597 B.A. L.424 J.D. [Ⓐ Johnson&B.]

Ryndak & Suri, (AV) BB
200 West Madison Street, Suite 2100, 60606
Telephone: 312-214-7770 Fax: 312-214-7715
URL: http://www.ryndaksuri.com
James D. Ryndak; Mark K. Suri; Eric H. Weimers.
Intellectual Property, Patents, Trademarks, Copyrights, Unfair Competition, Litigation, Computer Software.
See Professional Biographies, CHICAGO, ILLINOIS

Ryther, James P., (AV) ... '34 '61 C.602 B.S. L.276 J.D. [DLPiper R.G.C.U.] (Pat.)
Rywak, Walter Z., Law Office of ... '48 '74 C&L.424 B.A., J.D. 1016 N. Western
Rywalski, Eric Alan ... '74 '01 C.473 B.S. L.851 J.D. [Ⓐ Brenner,F.M.&S.]
Rzepczynski, Gregg M. ... '61 '89 C&L.424 B.B.A., J.D. [Bevilacqua&R.]
Rzepka, Natalia K. ... '77 '02 C.424 B.S. L.146 J.D. [Tishler&W.]
Sabath, Michael S., (BV) ... '66 '92 C.174 B.A. L.146 J.D. [Berger S.]
Sabatini, David P. ... '51 '75 C.424 B.S. L.879 J.D. State Attys. Off.
Sabesin, Marcia L. ... '— '80 C.703 B.S. L.836 J.D. 561 W. Diversey Pkwy., Ste. 200
Sabetto, Robert P. ... '70 '03 C.381 B.A. L.209 J.D. [Ⓐ Rusin M.&F.]
Sabin, Arthur J. ... '30 '59 C.1016 A.B. L.365 J.D. [Ⓒ Deutsch,L.&E.]
Sabin, Nettie F., (BV) ... '51 '81 C.339 B.S. L.424 J.D. [Ⓐ B.L.Gordon&Assoc.]
Sabin, Paul ... '49 '86 C.872 B.A. L.365 J.D. Asst. State's Atty.
Sabki, Nabil ... '— '99 C.477 B.A. L.494 J.D. [Ⓐ Kirkland&E.]
Sablich, Christopher G. ... '56 '94 C.357 B.S. L.146 J.D. Comptr. Off.
Sabo, Werner A., (AV) ... '46 '81 C.597 B.A. L.146 J.D. [Sabo&Z.]

Sabo & Zahn, (AV) BB
401 N. Michigan Avenue, Suite 2050, 60611
Telephone: 312-655-8620 Fax: 312-655-8622
Email: wsabo@sabozahn.com URL: http://www.sabozahn.com
Werner A. Sabo; James K. Zahn; Shawn E. Goodman.

(This Listing Continued)

Sabo & Zahn (Continued)
Construction Law, Construction Litigation, Construction Contracts, Construction Claims, Construction Defects, Construction Intellectual Property, Copyright Infringement, Architects and Engineers Liability, Mechanics Liens, Structural Work Act, Mediation, Arbitration.
See Professional Biographies, CHICAGO, ILLINOIS

Sabol, Diane Renae ... '77 '02 C.602 B.A. L.880 J.D. [Ⓐ Mayer,B.R.&M.]
Sabol, Martha A. ... '60 '99 C.550 B.S. L.424 J.D. 200 W. Madison
Saccone, Joseph A., Jr. ... '23 '49 C.209 L.146 J.D. 6310 N. Cicero Ave.‡
Sacha, Alfred N. ... '55 '88 C.339 B.S. L.209 J.D. [Sidley A.B.&W.]
Sacharoff, Adam K. ... '72 '98 C.679 B.S.A.E. L.1218 J.D. [Ⓐ Much S.F.D.A.&R.] (Pat.)
Sachat, Marilyn R. ... '— '77 C.1183 B.A. L.146 J.D. 612 S. Laflin St.
Sachnoff, Lowell E., (AV) ... '— '57 C&L.309 A.B., LL.B. [Sachnoff&W.]
Sachnoff, Scott D. ... '54 '79 C.1275 B.A. L.1065 J.D. Sr. Sup. Asst. Corp. Coun.

Sachnoff & Weaver, Ltd., (AV) BB
10 South Wacker Drive, 60606-7507
Telephone: 312-207-1000 Telecopier: 312-207-6400
URL: http://www.sachnoff.com
Evelyn C. Arkebauer; J. Todd Arkebauer; Frank D. Ballantine; Carey L. Bartell; Greg L. Berenstein; Jeffrey H. Bergman; Peter T. Berk; Jack L. Block; Stephen T. Bobo; David C. Bohan; Mark A. Brand; Gary S. Caplan; H. Brian Centeno; Kit Chaskin; Christopher R. Clark; Loletta L. Darden; Charles E. Dobrusin; Stewart Dolin; William E. Doran; Marilyn P. Dunn; David C. Fuechtman; Roselyn L. Friedman; Arlene N. Gelman; Jeffrey T. Gilbert; Neil Greenbaum; James J. Greenberger; Lewis B. Greenblatt; Robin Heiss; Seth M. Hemming; Mark S. Hersh; John L. Hines, Jr.; Austin L. Hirsch; James T. Hultquist; Annette Brands Hurley; José A. Isasi, II; Cynthia Jared; Wade S. Leathers; Michael P. Lee; Randall D. Lehner; Michael S. Leib; Michael R. Lieber; David E. Lieberman; Jeffrey L. London; Robert D. LoPrete; Michael A. LoVallo; Stephen R. Miller; Steven A. Miller; Michelle L. Moore; John W. Moynihan; Robert K. Neiman; Douglas R. Newkirk; Kevin M. Noonan; Matthew J. O'Hara; Robert S. O'Meara; Arnold A. Pagniucci; Beth A. Petersen; Matthew J. Petersen; Henry Pietrkowski; Jonathan S. Polish; Neil B. Posner; Jonathan S. Quinn; Michael D. Richman; Brian D. Roche; Lance R. Rodgers; James A. Rolfes; Barry S. Rosen; Carolyn Hope Rosenberg; Harry B. Rosenberg; Ellis B. Rosenzweig; Robert A. Roth; Lowell E. Sachnoff; Bina Sanghavi; Joel R. Schaider; Bradley S. Schmarak; Charles P. Schulman; Jeffrey A. Schumacher; Marshall Seeder; Clifford J. Shapiro; Duane F. Sigelko; Daniel J. Slattery; Abraham J. Stern; J. Samuel Tenenbaum; George A. Vinyard; Edward V. Walsh, III; Angela M. Washelesky; William N. Weaver, Jr.; Jeffrey B. Whitt; Sarah R. Wolff; Richard K. Wray; Mary Lou Zwick. Associates: Katie R. Aune; Mary Ann Becker; Bradley James Bolerjack; Benjamin L. Brimeyer; Erich S. Buck; Briggitte Marie Carlson; Hsing-Hua Pam Chen; Adam R. Chiss; Jennifer Yule DePriest; Patrick J. Elder; Robin J. Elowe; Tracy Gregar Ferak; Alexandra Grigoras; Alfred E. Hanna; John L. Hayes; Kristen E. Hudson; Camille D. Inocelda; Matthew M. Johnson; Mel M. Justak; Danail Kazachki; Lisa Kellmeyer; Safia Khan; Kenneth G. Kubes; Nicholas A. Long; Erica E. Lord; Myra A. Marcaurelle; Vanessa C. Marti; Andrew L. Mathews; Katherine A. Mathews; Christopher A. McVety; Raven Moore; Daniel Morrison; Andrew Moss; Charlotte S. Potucek; Venus McGhee Prince; Karla Rachwalski; Lana J. Raines; William P. Robison; Robert H. Rush; David Z. Smith; Max A. Stein; Emily Wolf Torre; Michele L. Walton; Hillary A. Weis; Casey L. Westover; Maryanne C. Woo. Of Counsel: Jules G. Cogan; Frances Meehan; E. Leonard Rubin; Ernest D. Simon.
Antitrust Law, Appellate Practice, Arbitration, Bankruptcy/Creditors Rights, Business Planning Law, Class Actions, Commercial Litigation, Complex Litigation, Construction Litigation, Corporate Finance, Corporate Law, Electronic Commerce, Emerging Growth Companies, Employee Benefits, Environmental Law, ERISA, Executive Compensation, Family Business Law, Finance, Government Investigations, Health Care Regulation, Immigration, Information Technology, Insurance Coverage, International, Intellectual Property, Labor and Employment, Lending, Litigation, Mergers and Acquisitions, Patents, Probate Administration, Products Liability, Professional Liability, Real Estate, Securities Law, Tax, Technology, Transportation, Trusts and Estates, Venture Capital, White Collar Crime Defense, Workouts.
See Professional Biographies, CHICAGO, ILLINOIS

Sachs, Andrew M. ... '62 '87 C.339 B.A. L.146 J.D. [Robbins,S.&P.]
Sachs, David H. ... '63 '88 C.339 B.A. L.146 J.D. [Aronberg G.D.&G.]
Sachs, Gerald M. ... '35 '58 C.209 B.S. L.597 J.D. One N. LaSalle St.
Sachs, Joshua ... '49 '74 C.293 B.A. L.339 J.D. 600 W. Jackson Blvd., Ste. 600
Sack, Nathaniel, (AV) ... '41 '65 C.477 B.A. L.309 J.D. [Seyfarth S.]
Sackmann, Jeremy P., (AV) ... '51 '77 C.475 B.S. L.339 J.D. [Maciorowski,S.&U.]
Sackrider, Gregg R. ... '48 '75 C.378 B.A. L.502 J.D. Mng. Coun., U.S. Postal Serv.
Sacks, Eric A. ... '67 '92 C.118 B.A. L.309 J.D. [Jenner&B.]
Sacks, Marvin, (Ltd.) ... '30 '56 C.339 B.S. L.145 J.D. 100 W. Monroe St.
Sacks, Michael J. '62 '88 C.861 B.A. L.597 J.D.
Mng. Partner, Grosvenor Capital Management, L.P.
Sacks, Robert N., (BVⓉ) '53 '79 C.597 B.A. L.818 J.D.
(adm. in MA; not adm. in IL)
Exec. V.P., Gen. Coun. & Secy., APCOA/Standard Parking, Inc.
Sacoff, Robert W., (AV) ... '47 '73 C.602 A.B. L.597 J.D. [Pattishall,M.N.H.&G.]
Sadewater, Brent E. ... '57 '82 C.697 B.A. L.209 J.D. 221 N. LaSalle St.
Sadler, Joe ... '76 '02 C.347 B.A. L.339 J.D. [Ⓐ Tressler,S.M.&P.]
Sadler, Thomas W. '47 '72
C.436 B.A. L.339 J.D. Asst. Gen. Coun., U.S. R.R. Retirement Bd.
Sadoff, Michael B., (AV) ... '49 '75 C.352 B.B.A. L.209 J.D. [Much S.F.D.A.&R.]
Saef, Scott E. ... '64 '92 C.309 B.A. L.597 J.D. [Ⓐ Sidley A.B.&W.]
Saegh, Sheila ... '— '98 C.930 B.S. L.659 J.D. [Ⓐ Jones D.]
Saeks, Lorne T. ... '66 '91 C.339 B.A. L.347 J.D. [Ⓐ Much S.F.D.A.&R.]
Saez, Maria T. ... '— '04 C.477 B.S. L.339 J.D. Two North LaSalle Street, Suite 2200
Safapour, Shayda A. ... '74 '01 C.932 B.A. L.818 J.D. [Ⓐ Fragomen,D.B.&L.]
Safer, Ronald S., (AV) ... '— '83 C.659 B.A.B.S. L.276 J.D. [Schiff H.]
Safranek, Stephen J. ... '60 '88 C.767 B.A. L.602 J.D. Sears Twr., Ste. 5800
Sagan, John R. ... '50 '83 C.399 B.A. L.966 J.D. [Mayer,B.R.&M.]
Saharack, Paul T. ... '43 '69 C&L.339 B.S., J.D. [Robbins,S.&P.]
Sahebjami, Dara ... '73 '98 C.597 B.A. L.276 J.D. [Ⓐ Funkhouser V.L.&D.]
Saibert, Frank J., (AV) ... '— '83 C.339 B.A. L.477 J.D. [Ungaretti&H.]
Sain, Kenneth W., (AV) ... '37 '66 C.424 B.S. L.880 J.D. [Ⓒ Kamensky,R.H.&D.] ⊙
Saindon, Kelly A. ... '71 '98 C.477 B.A. L.221 J.D. [Ⓐ Asperger&Assoc.]
Saines, Richard M. ... '69 '96 C.473 B.S. L.146 J.D. [Ⓐ Baker&M.]
St. Eve, Amy J. '65 '91 C&L.188 B.A., J.D.
(adm. in NY; not adm. in IL) U.S. Dist. J.
St. John, Gregory J. ... '50 '80 C.339 B.A. L.209 J.D. 1932 N. Newland
St. Lawrence, Franklin R. ... '36 '62 C.424 A.B. L.276 J.D. Apps. Officer, IRS
St. Vicina, Valeria C. '— '93 C.802 B.A. L.861 J.D.
Atty., ABN-AMRO North America, Inc. (Legal Department)
Saipe, Gary Scott, (AV) ... '48 '74 C.339 B.S. L.597 J.D. [Boodell D.&S.]
Saitlin, Sheldon I., (AV) ... '41 '70 C.966 B.S. L.30 J.D. 875 N. Michigan Ave.‡
Saito, Marina N. ... '— '95 C.339 B.S. L.146 J.D. [Sonnenschein N.&R.] (Pat.)
Sakaguchi, Daniel '— '02 C&L.1375 B.A., J.D.
(adm. in CA; not adm. in IL) [Ⓐ Sonnenschein N.&R.] (⊙St. Louis, MO)
Sakas, Laura N. ... '61 '86 C.720 B.A. L.365 J.D. Mng. Atty.
Sakol, Jeffrey N. ... '59 '90 C.608 B.S. L.1187 J.D. 500 North Dearborn Street, Suite 302
Sakulich, Laura A. ... '76 '04 C.932 B.M. L.101 J.D. [Ⓐ Jenner&B.]
Sakurada, Lance R. ... '— '81 C.339 L.209 J.D. 219 S. Dearborn St.
Salajanu, Ioana ... '74 '00 C.477 B.A. L.424 J.D. [Ⓐ BryceDowney]
Saldaña, Maria N., (AV) '55 '81 C.813 B.A. L.1066 J.D.
120N. LaSalle Street, Ste. 1420
Saldinger, Richard A. ... '66 '92 C&L.339 B.S., J.D. [Shaw G.F.G.W.&T.]
Salemi, Michael G. ... '73 '03 C.966 B.A. L.424 J.D. [Ⓐ Lord,B.&B.]

Salerno, Anthony J. '72 '97 C.424 B.A. L.365 J.D.
Asst. Atty. Gen. [Ⓐ Weldon-Linne&V.]
Salerno, Scott M. ... '72 '98 C.801 B.S. L.209 J.D. [Ⓐ Michaels&M.]
Sales, Goodloe, Golden & Blakemore ... 222 N. La Salle Street, Suite 300 (⊙Atlanta, GA)
Saletta, John M., (AV) ... '61 '88 C.602 B.A. L.424 J.D. [Ⓐ Motherway&N.]
Saletta, John S. ... '62 '88 C.347 B.S. 218 N. Jefferson St.
Salgado, David L. ... '57 '85 C.720 B.A. L.365 J.D. [D.L.Salgado]
Salgado, Enrique, Jr. ... '70 '95 C.339 B.A. L.146 J.D. Sr. Coun., Aon Corporation
Salgado, David L., P.C. ... 205 W. Randolph Street Suite 920
Salinas, Sharon A. ... '61 '89 C.999 B.S. L.89 J.D. [Ⓐ Dykema G.P.]
Salinger, Debra R. ... '60 '84 C&L.424 B.A., J.D. Asst. Appl. Def.
Salins, Stuart M. ... '50 '78 C.280 B.B.A. L.30 J.D. VMS Realty, Inc.
Salinski, Tracey A. ... '66 '92 C.477 A.B. L.213 J.D. [Ⓐ Mandel,L.&S.]
Salisbury, Linda ... '56 '91 C.788 B.A. L.424 J.D. 1540 N. Lake Shore Dr.
Salita, Matthew L. ... '10 '36 C.597 L.365 LL.B. 200 N. LaSalle St.
Salk, Steven B. ... '48 '74 C.98 B.S. L.365 J.D. [S.B.Salk&Assoc.]
Salk, Steven B., & Associates, Ltd. ... 150 N. Wacker Drive, Suite 2570
Sallerson, Samuel I. '50 '75 C&L.494 B.A., J.D.
(adm. in MN; not adm. in IL) 442 W. Wellington Ave.‡
Salmon, Bradley A. ... '73 '00 C&L.608 B.A., J.D. [Ⓐ Gordon&G.L.]
Salmon, Jeffrey W. ... '66 '93 C.597 B.S. L.347 J.D. [Welsh&K.] (See Pat. Sect.)
Salomon, Edward S., (AV) ... '42 '66 C&L.339 B.A., J.D. [Robbins,S.&P.]
Salovaara, Kaarina, (AV) ... '55 '81 C.788 A.B. L.893 J.D. Asst. U.S. Atty.
Salpeter, Alan N., (AV) ... '47 '72 C.30 B.A. L.884 J.D. [Mayer,B.R.&M.]
Saltarelli, Gerald G., (AV) ... '47 '73 C.674 A.B. L.145 J.D. [Butler R.S.&B.]
Salter, Cody ... '75 '04 C.339 B.S. L.1494 J.D. [Ⓐ Daspin&A.]
Salti, Rana H. ... '76 '01 C.424 B.S. L.966 J.D. [Ⓐ Winston&S.]
Saltiel, David M., (AV) ... '54 '80 C.477 B.B.A. L.339 J.D. [Bell,B.&L.]
Saltiel, Joseph A. ... '— '01 C&L.339 B.S., J.D. [Ⓐ Jenner&B.] (Pat.)
Saltoun, Diane L., (AV) ... '— '88 C.31 B.A. L.93 J.D. Asst. U.S. Atty., Dep. Chf.
Saltz, Jeffrey T. ... '51 '76 C.208 B.A. L.46 J.D. [Ⓒ Berger,N.&F.]
Saltz, Sidney G., (AV) ... '— '63 C.597 B.A. L.976 LL.B. [Barnes&T.]
Saltzberg, Gerald B., (AV) ... '28 '55 C.1016 B.S. L.146 LL.B. [Fishman,F.&S.]
Saltzberg, Sally H. ... '54 '82 C.339 B.A. L.209 J.D. 53 N. Jackson Boulevard
Saltzman, Steven I. ... '48 '74 C.910 B.A. L.145 J.D. 122 S. Michigan Ave., Ste. 1850
Saltzman-Jones, Tiffany S. ... '67 '04 C.267 B.F.A. L.145 J.D. [Ⓐ Walker W.M.]
Saltzstein, Robert S. ... '63 '89 C.347 B.S. L.146 J.D. 1473 W. Irving Park
Salvi, Patrick A., (AV) ... '53 '78 C.742 B.A. L.602 J.D. [Salvi,S.&P.] ⊙

Salvi, Schostok & Pritchard P.C., (AV)
181 West Madison, Suite 3800, 60602 ⊙
Telephone: 312-372-1227 Facsimile: 312-372-3720
Email: psalvi@salvilaw.com URL: http://www.salvilaw.com
Patrick A. Salvi; David J. Pritchard (Resident); Mark N. Senak; Donald R. McGarrah;—Kathleen A. Mcginty (Resident); John S. Muir. Of Counsel: James H. Canel.
Concentration in representing Plaintiffs in personal injury, medical malpractice, wrongful death, transportation liability, aviation, product liability and commercial litigation.
Waukegan, Illinois Office: 218 North Martin Luther King Jr. Avenue, 60085. Telephone: 847-249-1227. Telefax: 847-249-0138.
See Professional Biographies, CHICAGO, ILLINOIS

Salyers, Nancy Sidote ... '49 '78 C.700 B.A. L.209 J.D. Presiding J., Child Protec. Div.
Salzberg, Jerry M. ... '51 '77 C.184 B.A. L.365 J.D. [J.Salzberg]
Salzberg, Jerry, Law Offices of ... 205 W. Randolph St., Ste. 1020
Salzeider, John A., (AV) ... '63 '88 C.338 B.S. L.589 J.D. [Ⓐ Anesi,O.R.N.&K.]
Salzer, Kathleen A. ... '54 '79 C.602 B.A. L.659 J.D. 2 N. LaSalle St.
Salzman, James John, (AV) ... '43 '73 C.276 B.S.F.S. L.209 J.D. [Matkov,S.M.&G.]
Salzman, Jerrold E., (AV) ... '40 '65 C.477 A.B. L.309 LL.B. [Freeman,F.&S.]
Salzman, Martin J., (Ltd.) ... '45 '69 C.339 L.209 J.D. 5807 N. Kolmar Avenue
Salzman, Martin W., (AV) ... '45 '71 C.339 B.A. L.276 J.D. [Schwartz C.]
Salzman, Steven A., (AV) '53 '78
C.339 B.A. L.1194 J.D. 222 North La Salle Street, Suite 1910
Samardzija, Tanja ... '74 '00 C.339 B.S. L.424 J.D. [Ⓐ Epstein B.&G.]
Samis, Michael J. ... '48 '73 C.973 B.A. L.424 J.D. [Ⓒ N.J.Lerum]
Samko, Robert C. ... '46 '71 C&L.209 B.S.C., J.D. [R.C.Samko]
Samko, Robert C., PC ... 100 W. Monroe St., 19th Fl.
Samlan, Alan B., (AV) ... '48 '76 C.339 B.S.M.E. L.365 J.D. [Ⓒ Thiedmann&E.] (Pat.)
Samore, Eric L., (BV) ... '— '81 C&L.966 B.S., J.D. [O'Hagan,S.&A.]
Samotny, Marc Z., (AV) ... '49 '75 C.801 B.S. L.365 J.D. [Patzik,F.&S.]
Sampen, Don R., (AV) ... '50 '75 C&L.597 B.A., J.D. [Meckler B.&T.]
Samples, Kenneth H., (AV) '46 '73
C.546 B.S.E.E. L.365 J.D. [Fitch,E.T.&F.] (See Pat. Sect.)
Sampson, Matthew J., (AV) '63 '91
C.339 B.S.E.E. L.209 J.D. [McDonnell B.H.&B.] (See Pat. Sect.)
Samsa, Mary K. ... '— '96 C.339 B.S. L.209 J.D. [Ⓐ Gardner C.&D.]
Samson, Richard L., (BV) ... '60 '85 C.339 B.A. L.146 J.D. [Ogletree,D.N.S.&S.]
Samuels, Craig E. '66 '91 C.311 B.A. L.477 J.D.
Asst. Dir., Bus. Dev., National Patient Safety Foundation
Samuels, Lawrence R. ... '46 '72 C.145 B.A. L.309 J.D. [McGuirewoods]
Samuels, Ronald S. ... '41 '69 C.1191 B.A. L.365 J.D. 29 South LaSalle, Suite 434
Samuels, Simonetti, (BV) ... '57 '89 C.66 B.A. L.966 J.D. 525 W. Monroe St.
Samuels, Steven G. ... '60 '86 C.339 B.A. L.146 J.D. Bear Kaufman Realty
Samuelson, Kathryn L. ... '50 '77 C.801 B.A. L.339 J.D. Cook Cty. Dev. Planning Board
Samuelson, Timothy C. ... '72 '98 C.879 B.A. L.347 J.D. [Ⓐ Iwan C.H.H.&V.]
Sanberg, Lora K., (AV) ... '43 '80 C.999 B.S. L.597 J.D. [Krasnow S.C.]
Sanchez, Christopher B. ... '74 '00 C.560 B.A. L.209 J.D. [Ⓐ Miller F.&C.]
Sanchez, Jeffrey ... '53 '79 C.321 B.A. L.209 J.D. 55 W. Monroe St.
Sanchez, Jorge ... '67 '98 C.103 B.A. L.1066 J.D. [Ⓐ Despres,S.&G.]
Sanchez, Manuel "Manny", (AV) ... '47 '74 C.589 B.A. L.659 J.D. [Sanchez&D.] ⊙
Sanchez, Marcela D. ... '— '01 C.556 B.A. L.477 J.D. [Ⓐ Mayer,B.R.&M.]
Sanchez, Vincent A. ... '68 '94 C&L.602 B.A., J.D. [DLPiper R.G.C.U.]

Sanchez & Daniels, (AV)
333 West Wacker Drive, Suite 500, 60606 ⊙
Telephone: 312-641-1555 Fax: 312-641-3004
Email: sd@sanchezdaniels.com URL: http://www.sanchezdaniels.com
Members of Firm: Manuel "Manny" Sanchez; John D. Daniels; Timothy V. Hoffman; Edward M. Ordonez; Franklin U. Valderrama; Edward N. Robles; Hugh C. O'Donnell; John S. Huntley; John J. Piegore; Mark S. Vilimek; Gerald M. Dombrowski; Susan K. Chae; Paige Donaldson; Mark E. Winters; Hugo Chaviano; Nilgun Aykent Zahour; Larry C. Jurgens.
Defense Litigation, including Insurance Defense; Products Liability, including automobile, construction, pharmaceutical, medical devices, machines and mechanical devices; Transportation Liability, including automobiles, trucks, aircraft and watercraft; Construction Liability, including contractors, architects and owners; Warranty Liability, including the Magnuson-Moss Warranty Act and Lemon Law; Premises Liability, including landlord-tenant and hotel; Professional Liability, including attorneys, engineers, accountants, insurance agents and brokers, physicians and hospitals; Employer Liability, including wrongful termination; Commercial Liability, including breach of contract; Real Estate Liability; Environmental Liability, including pollution and toxic torts; Public Finance, including bond issues.

(This Listing Continued)

Sanchez & Daniels (Continued)
Wheaton, Illinois Office: 2100 Manchester Road, Suite 201. Telephone: 630-752-9880. Fax: 630-752-9881.
See Professional Biographies, CHICAGO, ILLINOIS

Sandberg, Craig M. ... '71 '99 C.475 B.A. L.365 J.D. Asst. State's Atty.
Sandberg, Susan E. '66 '91
C.339 B.A. L.209 J.D. Staff Atty., State Dept. of Mental Health
Sandberg, Verona M. ... '— '03 C.339 B.S. L.597 J.D. [Ⓐ Freeborn&P.]
Sandel, Wantland L., Jr. '27 '54 C&L.208 B.S.L., J.D.
(adm. in CO; not adm. in IL) Dir., Div. for Judicial Servs., Amer. Bar Assn.
Sander, Richard G., Jr. ... '37 '61 C.238 L.339 LL.B. P.O. Box 7600‡
Sanders, Catherine D., (BV) ... '— '84 C.720 B.A. L.146 J.D. Asst. States Atty.
Sanders, David P., (AV) ... '49 '74 C.966 B.A. L.276 J.D. [Jenner&B.]
Sanders, Douglas B. ... '72 '98 C.276 B.S.F.S. L.597 J.D. [Ⓐ Baker&M.]
Sanders, Elizabeth A. '62 '87
C.339 B.A. L.145 J.D. Asst. V.P. & Asst. Gen. Coun., CNA
Sanders, George M., (BV) ... '64 '90 C.724 B.A. L.145 J.D. [Ⓐ A.L.Gaynor&Assoc.]
Sanders, Jon P. ... '— '00 C.138 B.A. L.1194 J.D. [Ⓐ Ungaretti&H.]
Sanders, Jos. H. ... '21 '50 C.137 L.365 LL.B. 11 S. La Salle St.
Sanders, Madge O'Brien ... '44 '91 C.72 B.A. L.879 J.D. Asst. Pub. Def.
Sanders, Richard H., (AV) ... '44 '69 C.424 B.S. L.597 J.D. [Vedder,P.K.&K.]
Sanders, Yvette S. ... '— '00 C.855 B.A. L.146 J.D. 200 W. Adams, 30th Fl.
Sanderson, Kathryn B. ... '— '04 C.597 B.A. L.893 J.D. [Ⓐ Kirkland&E.]
Sandler, Gilbert Lee, (AVⓉ) '44 '69 C.197 A.B. L.569 J.D.
(adm. in FL; not adm. in IL) [Sandler,T.&R.]
(⊙L.A., San Fran., CA; Wash., DC; Miami, FL; New York, NY)
Sandler, Jeffrey R. ... '68 '93 C.339 B.A. L.365 J.D. [Cassiday,S.&G.]
Sandler, Mitchell H. '53 '82
C.339 B.A. L.209 J.D. Off. of Hearings & Apps., Soc. Sec. Admn.
Sandler, Philip W. ... '51 '76 C.339 B.S. L.146 J.D. [Sandler&Assoc.]
Sandler, Richard L., (AV) ... '55 '80 C.910 A.B. L.352 J.D. [Fox,H.S.L.&C.]
Sandler, Ronald A., (AV) ... '— '66 C.339 B.S.I.E. L.273 J.D. [Jones D.] (See Pat. Sect.)
Sandler, Stephen P., (AV) ... '39 '67 C.910 B.S. L.597 J.D. [Gould&R.]
Sandler, Steven M. ... '53 '78 C.339 B.A. L.146 J.D. [Rapoport]
Sandler & Associates ... 10 S. La Salle St., Ste. 1301

Sandler, Travis & Rosenberg, P.A., (AV)
225 West Washington Street, Suite 1550, 60606 ⊙
Telephone: 312-641-0000 Telecopier: 312-641-0005
Email: info@strtrade.com URL: http://www.strtrade.com
Gilbert Lee Sandler (Not admitted in IL; See Miami, Florida Listing); Thomas G. Travis (Not admitted in IL; See Miami, Florida Listing); Leonard L. Rosenberg (Not admitted in IL; See Miami, Florida Listing); Jeremy R. Page; Thomas E. Johnson; Shannon E. Fura. Associate: Donna L. Bade.
Customs Law, International Trade and Transportation Law. International Corporate, Copyright and Trademark Law. Trial, Appellate, Federal and Administrative Practice. Immigration and Nationality Law. International Labor Law, NAFTA, Government Relations, Trade Negotiations, International Trade Policy, Intellectual Property, Import and Export Law, Foreign Trade Sanctions, Shipping Law, Surety.
Miami, Florida Office: 5200 Blue Lagoon Drive, Suite 600, 33126-2022. Telephone: 305-267-9200. Telecopier: 305-267-5155.
Washington, D.C. Office: 1300 Pennsylvania Avenue, Suite 400, 20004. Telephone: 202-216-9307. Fax: 202-842-2247.
New York, New York Office: 551 Fifth Avenue, Suite 614, 10176. Telephone: 212-883-1300. Fax: 212-883-0068.
Baltimore, Maryland Office: 111 South Calvert Street, Suite 2700, 21202. Telephone: 410-385-5208. Fax: 410-837-2441.
San Francisco, California Office: Sandler, Travis & Rosenberg and Glad & Ferguson, P.C., 1 Sutter Street, 10th Floor, 94014. Telephone: 415-986-1088. Fax: 415-986-2271.
Los Angeles, California Office: Sandler, Travis & Rosenberg and Glad & Ferguson, P.C., 801 South Flower Street, Fifth Floor, 90017. Telephone: 213-327-0155. Telecopier: 213-327-0157.
See Professional Biographies, CHICAGO, ILLINOIS

Sandman, Sheldon J., (BV) ... '36 '62 C.339 A.B. L.365 J.D. 134 N. La Salle St.
Sandner, John F. ... '41 '68 C.801 B.A. L.602 J.D. [Ⓒ Lane&L.]
Sandon, Mara ... '78 '04 C.569 B.A. L.94 J.D. Asst. Corp. Coun.
Sandri, Mark R. ... '— '05 C.477 B.A. L.209 J.D. [Ⓐ Scott,H.&B.]
Sands, John C., (AV) ... '29 '59 C.339 B.A. L.365 LL.B. 33 N. Dearborn St.
Sands, Paul T., Jr. '43 '68
C.177 B.A. L.623 J.D. V.P. & Gen. Coun., Chicago Title Ins. Co.
Sanford, James M. ... '61 '87 C.475 B.A. L.179 J.D. [Ⓐ J.D.Montgomery&Assoc.]
Sang, George E. ... '49 '73 C.705 B.A. L.145 J.D. [Ⓒ Young,R.F.&S.]
Sangerman, Harry M., (AV) ... '41 '65 C.339 B.S. L.597 J.D. 1854 N. Burling Street
Sanghavi, Bina ... '— '94 C.46 B.S. L.424 J.D. [Sachnoff&W.]
Sanguinetti, Raymond J. ... '71 '98 C.1073 B.A. L.365 J.D. 2 N. LaSalle St., Ste. 1650
Sannes, Andrew J. ... '— '04 C.966 B.A. L.1000 J.D. [Ⓐ DLPiper R.G.C.U.]
Sansonetti, Mark P. ... '77 '02 C.436 B.S. L.365 J.D. [M.P.Sansonetti]
Sansonetti, Vincent ... '45 '71 C.424 B.S.B.A. L.365 J.D. 5521 N. Cumberland Ave.
Sansonetti, Mark P., P.C. ... 5521 N. Cumberland, Ste. 1109
Santa Lucia, John S., (AV) ... '63 '88 C&L.597 B.A., J.D. [Neal,G.&E.]
Santangelo, Jerry M., (AV) ... '59 '84 C.473 B.S. L.209 J.D. [Neal,G.&E.]
Santella, Gary D. ... '— '79 C&L.424 B.A., J.D. [Masuda,F.E.&M.]
Santiago, Beatriz ... '70 '96 C.339 B.A. L.365 J.D. 2 N. LaSalle
Santiago, Daniel V. ... '70 '96 C.597 B.A. L.477 J.D. [Ⓐ Kaplan,v.&M.]
Santibanez-Bania, Giselle ... '74 '00 C.910 B.A. L.424 J.D. 161 N. Clark St.
Santilli, Frank A. ... '58 '89 C.339 B.A. L.365 J.D. 100 N. LaSalle St.
Santis, Elizabeth D. ... '65 '92 C.659 B.A. L.597 J.D. 510 West Erie Street, Suite 1306
Santoni, Dennis J., II ... '71 '99 C.823 B.S. L.424 J.D. 27 N. Wacker Dr., Ste. 248
Santora, Thomas M., (AV) ... '32 '60 C&L.209 B.S., LL.B. [Garretson&S.]
Santori, David J., (AV) ... '47 '72 C.209 B.A. L.339 J.D. 105 W. Madison St., Ste. 1300
Santoro, Michael Vito ... '72 '97 C.98 B.S. L.589 J.D. Sr. Tax. Assoc, Arthur Anderen
Santucci, James A. ... '64 '91 C.339 B.A. L.209 J.D. 150 S. Wacker Dr., Ste. 2400
Saper, Adam L. ... '— '98 C.209 B.A. L.365 J.D. [Hinshaw&C.]
Saper, Daliah ... '80 '04 C&L.339 B.S., J.D. 845 West Oakdale
Saper, Jaclyn D. ... '— '90 V.P. & Coun., Harris Tr. & Svgs. Bk.
Saper, Michael S., (AV) ... '41 '65 C.103 A.B. L.309 J.D. [M.S.Saper&Assoc.]
Saper, Michael S., & Associates, P.C., (AV) ... 222 S. Riverside Plz.
Saperstein, Gerald W. ... '33 '72 C.1016 B.S.C. L.365 J.D. 4801 W. Peterson Ave.
Saphire-Bernstein, Leonard D. ... '54 '80 C&L.309 A.B., J.D. 2 N. LaSalle St., Ste. 1601
Saporito, Frank '53 '80 C.424 B.A. L.589 J.D.
Asst. V.P. & Tr. Offr., Drovers Bk. of Chicago
Saposnik, Gary H., Law Offices of '57 '84
C.339 B.A. L.426 J.D. 105 W. Madison St., Ste. 700
Sarabia, Antonio R., (AV) ... '13 '50 C.999 B.S.Ch.E. L.145 J.D. 79 W. Monroe St.‡
Saracco, Gail C., (AV) ... '66 '91 C.976 B.A. L.477 J.D. [Mayer,B.R.&M.]
Sarafa, Amanda Cochran ... '— '02 C.477 B.B.A. L.597 J.D. [Ⓐ Kirkland&E.]
Sarafa, Derek J. ... '72 '97 C.475 B.A. L.477 J.D. [Ⓐ Winston&S.]
Saranecki, Todd M. ... '70 '96 C.352 B.A. L.146 J.D. [Ⓐ Kaplan,v.&M.]
Saranow, Mitchell H. ... '45 '71 C.597 B.S.B.A. L.309 J.D. [Ⓒ George W.H.]

Saranteas, James .... '69 '99 C.388 B.A. L.424 J.D. [Ⓐ Belgrade&O.]
Sarasek, Peter A., (AV) .... '45 '74 C.128 B.A. L.966 J.D. [Quarles&B.]
Sarasin, Joanne A. .... '60 '85 C&L.339 B.A., J.D. [Much S.F.D.A.&R.]
Saret, Larry L., (AV) .... '50 '75 C.188 B.A. L.424 J.D. [Michael B.&F.] (See Pat. Sect.)
Sargent, Sally Larson '50 '75 C.187 B.A. L.339 J.D.
V.P., Harris Trust and Savings Bank
Sargis, Mark R., (AV) .... '59 '86 C.976 B.A. L.209 J.D. [Bellande&S.]
Sarikas, Thomas Edward .... '58 '94 C.602 B.S.C.E. L.209 J.D. [Ⓐ Merlo K.B.&G.]
Sarles, Gary D. '62 '87 C.347 B.A. L.597 J.D.
(adm. in TX; not adm. in IL) [Sarles&O.]
Sarles, Jeffrey W. .... '48 '94 C.918 B.A. L.597 J.D. [Mayer,B.R.&M.]
Sarles & Ouimet, L.L.P. .... 820 West Jackson Boulevard, Suite 300 (©Dallas, TX)
Sarley, Bernard J. .... '54 '81 C.742 B.A. L.365 J.D. Asst. Pub. Def.
Sarnoff, James B. .... '— '03 C.823 B.S. L.146 J.D. [Ⓐ Sarnoff&B.]
Sarnoff, Kenneth R. .... '72 '98 C.823 B.S. L.146 J.D. [Ⓐ Sarnoff&B.]
Sarnoff, Robert M., (AV) .... '43 '68 C.339 B.S. L.146 J.D. [Sarnoff&B.]

Sarnoff & Baccash, (AV)
One North La Salle Street Suite 1920, 60602-3907
Telephone: 312-782-8310 Fax: 312-782-8635
URL: http://www.sarnoffbaccash.com
Members of Firm: Michael F. Baccash; Robert M. Sarnoff. Associates: Kenneth R. Sarnoff; Steven Kandelman; Curtis L. Durik; Allon D. Skidelsky; James B. Sarnoff.
Practice Limited to Real and Personal Property Taxation.
See Professional Biographies, CHICAGO, ILLINOIS

Sarron, Julia R. .... '57 '81 C.976 B.A. L.178 J.D. [Greenberg T.]
Sarsany, Dennis M., (P.C.) ..... '45 '70 C&L.339 B.S., J.D. 3857 North Hamilton Avenue
Sarto, Charlene M. .... '61 '99 C.209 B.A. L.365 J.D. Atty, General Growth Prop.
Sartorio, Dion J., (AV) .... '56 '81 C&L.339 B.S., J.D. [Tressler,S.M.&P.]
Sarussi, Steven J. '60 '92 C.424 A.B. L.365 J.D.
[McDonnell B.H.&B.] (See Pat. Sect.)
Sarwate, Sanjiv D. .... '72 '97 C&L.339 B.A., J.D. [Pattishall,M.N.H.&G.]
Sasamoto, Nancy E. .... '— '80 C.339 B.S. L.910 J.D. [Masuda,F.E.&M.]
Saslow, Judy A. .... '— '82 C.861 B.A. L.424 J.D. 300 West Superior
Sass, Nancy S. .... '49 '75 C.427 B.A. L.146 J.D. Asst. States Atty.
Sassan, Anthony J., The Law Offices of '66 '93
C.742 B.A. L.365 J.D. 221 N. LaSalle St., Ste. 2100
Satalic, John M. .... '59 '86 C&L.309 B.A., J.D. [Mayer,B.R.&M.]
Sathy, Anup .... '— '95 C.339 B.S. L.588 J.D. [Kirkland&E.]
Satin, Max J. .... '07 '30 C&L.339 A.B., LL.B. 320 W. Oakdale Ave.‡
Sato, Shorge K. .... '— '02 C.597 B.A. L.569 J.D. [Ⓐ Stein,R.&H.]
Sattar, Uzma .... '76 '01 C.597 B.A. L.145 J.D. [Integris L.] (Pat.)
Satter, Susan L. .... '55 '83 C.966 B.A. L.146 J.D. Asst. Atty. Gen.
Satyr, Alan .... '71 '96 C.339 B.S. L.910 J.D. [Ⓐ Littler M.]
Satyr, Allison J. .... '72 '97 C.188 B.A. L.659 J.D. [Ⓐ Sidley A.B.&W.]
Satz, Michael B. .... '53 '82 C.597 B.A. L.365 J.D. [Ⓒ Sedgwick,D.M.&A.]
Sauer, Lisa S. .... '71 '97 C.121 B.S. L.365 J.D. [Ⓐ Sinar K.M.&F.]
Sauer, S. Jack .... '34 '63 C&L.597 B.A., J.D. [Ⓒ McAndrews,H.M.M.]
Saunders, David A. .... '39 '64 C.604 A.B. L.145 J.D. [Krasnow S.C.]
Saunders, LaVerne Rolle .... '45 '87 C.188 B.S. L.365 J.D. Asst. State's Atty.
Saunders, Morris R., (BV) .... '— '79 C.893 B.A. L.365 J.D. [Levin G.]
Saunders, Raymond E., (AV) .... '32 '56 C&L.597 B.S., J.D. [Lawrence,K.S.&U.]
Saunders, Rebecca L. '51 '84 C.788 A.B. L.424 J.D.
Legal Assistance Found. of Chicago
Saunders, Terry Rose, (AV) .... '42 '73 C.66 B.A. L.569 J.D. [Saunders&D.]
Saunders, Tyanika L. .... '73 '00 C.339 B.A. L.179 J.D. [Ⓐ BryceDowney]

Saunders & Doyle, (AV)
20 South Clark Street Suite 1720, 60603
Telephone: 312-551-0051 Fax: 312-551-4467
Terry Rose Saunders; Thomas A. Doyle.
Securities, Trade Regulation, Class Actions and Business Litigation.
See Professional Biographies, CHICAGO, ILLINOIS

Sauser, Michael Paul .... '69 '96 C.209 B.A. L.146 J.D. [Sauser]
Sauser Law Office LLC .... 332 S. Michigan Ave.
Sauter, Stephanie Ann .... '65 '98 C.66 B.A. L.424 J.D. Co. Pub. Def.
Savage, Colette M. .... '— '01 C.477 B.A. L.1119 J.D. [Ⓐ Seyfarth S.]
Savage, Janelle M. .... '74 '00 C.473 B.S. L.597 J.D. [Ⓐ Barack F.K.P.&N.]
Savage, Timothy G. .... '— '03 C&L.424 B.A., J.D. [Ⓐ Anderson,R.]
Savaiano, Dominick W., (AV) .... '56 '81 C.339 B.A. L.424 J.D. [Clausen M.]
Savard, Elizabeth A. .... '— '01 C.424 B.A. L.477 J.D. [Ⓐ McDermott W.&E.]
Savini, Gina M. .... '65 '91 C.1121 B.A. L.128 J.D. Asst. States Atty.
Savitz, Stuart M., (AV) .... '60 '85 C.1369 B.A. L.910 J.D. [S.M.Savitz]
Savitz, Stuart M., Law Offices of, LLC, (AV) .... 444 North Wells Street, Suite 430
Sawdey, Richard M. .... '43 '68 C.475 B.S. L.477 J.D. [Hoogendoorn&T.]
Sawin, John S. .... '68 '94 C.352 B.S. L.30 J.D. [Ⓐ Childress D.G.]
Sawislak, Richard S. ... '31 '55 C&L.339 B.A., LL.B. 55 West Wacker Drive, 10th Floor‡
Sawkar, Ashish Laxmidas .... '73 '00 C.94 B.A. L.37 J.D. State's Atty. Off.
Sawko, Victor J. .... '32 '59 C&L.424 B.S., J.D. Heitman Mortgage Co.
Sawula, Andrew N. .... '— '02 C.339 B.M.E. L.597 J.D. [Ⓐ Schiff H.]
Sawyer, Allison Marie '— '03 C.912 B.A. L.424 J.D.
Staff Atty., Chicago, M.R.O., S.E.C.
Sawyer, Douglas Lawrence .... '73 '01 C.339 B.S. L.209 J.D. [Ⓐ Mayer,B.R.&M.]
Sawyer, Harold Z. .... '32 '56 C.339 L.146 LL.B. 221 N. LaSalle St.
Sawyer, James L. .... '— '94 C.867 B.A. L.146 J.D. [Gardner C.&D.]
Sawyer, Roderick T. .... '63 '90 C.209 B.S. L.46 J.D. 609 E. 75th St.
Sawyer, V. Mishaune .... '67 '96 C.1365 B.A. L.209 J.D. 222 N. La Salle St.
Sawyer, Wendy J. .... '74 '01 C.347 B.A. L.209 J.D. [Ⓐ Bell,B.&L.]
Sawyier, David R., (AV) .... '51 '77 C&L.309 B.A., J.D. [Sidley A.B.&W.]

Sawyier, Michael T., Law Offices of, (AV) '48 '72 C.309 A.B. L.145 J.D. BR
150 North Michigan Avenue, Suite 2700, 60601 ⊙
Telephone: 312-856-9741 Fax: 312-856-9743
Email: mtsawyier@mtsatlaw.com URL: http://www.mtsatlaw.com
Trusts and Estates, Asset Protection, Wills and Probate, Elder Law, Real Estate, Business Law.
Highland, Indiana Office: 2646 Highway Avenue, Suite 201, 46322. Telephone: 219-923-8846. Fax: 219-838-0554.
See Professional Biographies, CHICAGO, ILLINOIS

Sax, George D. .... '— '03 C.597 B.S.J. L.813 J.D. [Ⓐ Kirkland&E.]
Sax, Jerome M. .... '12 '39 C.405 L.146 LL.B. 220 S. State St.‡
Sax, Thomas F. .... '59 '85 C.477 A.B. L.145 J.D. [Ⓒ Pedersen&H.]
Saxman, Suzanne L., (AV) .... '56 '81 C.477 B.A. L.339 J.D. [Seyfarth S.]
Saxner, Morris .... '14 '38 L.365 J.D. 5415 N. Sheridan Rd.‡
Sayre, Stephen D. .... '62 '92 C.174 B.S. L.209 J.D. [Dykema G.P.]
Sazdanoff, Michael L. .... '54 '79 C&L.602 B.A., J.D. [Ⓐ K.J.Wysoglad&Assoc.]
Scalambrino, Bruce C. .... '55 '82 C.62 B.A. L.930 J.D. 33 N. La Salle
Scalise, Amy C. .... '63 '91 C.886 B.S. L.424 J.D. Sr. Coun., Bank One Corp. (Law Dept.)

Scallan, Stephen .... '69 '95 C.597 B.A. L.602 J.D. [Staes&S.]
Scandaglia, Gregory J., (AV) .... '61 '87 C.1044 B.A. L.904 J.D. [Scandaglia&R.]

Scandaglia & Ryan, (AV)
55 East Monroe Street, Suite 3930, 60603
Telephone: 312-580-2020 Fax: 312-782-3806
Email: contact@scandagliaryan.com URL: http://www.scandagliaryan.com
Gregory J. Scandaglia; William J. Ryan. Associates: James R. Ahler; Amy C. Crawford; Eric J. Muñoz; Alan W. Nicgorski; Matthew B. Steffens; Therese L. Tully. Counsel: Scott E. Rogers.
ADA Counseling/Litigation, Administrative Law, Admiralty Law, Antitrust, Commercial Litigation, Contracts, Copyright Law, Education Law, Employment Law, Environmental Law, Fiduciary Law, Government Contracts, Hospitality Law, Insurance Coverage, Intellectual Property Litigation, Not-for-Profit Corporate Law, Partnership Law, Product Liability, Real Estate Litigation, Securities Litigation, Technology Law, Trade Association Law, Trademark Law, UCC Sales, and White Collar Defense.
See Professional Biographies, CHICAGO, ILLINOIS

Scanlan, Edmund J., (AV) .... '49 '76 C.602 A.B. L.209 J.D. [E.J.Scanlan]
Scanlan, Edmund J., Ltd., Law Offices of, (AV) .... 8 S. Michigan Avenue, Fl. 2700
Scanlon, James E. .... '40 '65 C.973 B.S.B.A. L.477 J.D. 332 S. Michigan Ave.
Scanlon, John P. .... '62 '90 C.750 B.A. L.209 J.D. [Healy]
Scanlon, Lawrence R. .... '69 '97 C.602 B.A. L.424 J.D. [Ⓐ Tribler O.&M.]
Scannicchio, Regina A., (AV) .... '63 '89 C.209 B.S. L.365 J.D. [Scannicchio&Assoc.]

Scannicchio & Associates, Chtd., (AV)
Suite 1210 33 North LaSalle Street, 60602
Telephone: 312-782-8274 Fax: 312-782-1595
Email: rscannicchio@aol.com
Regina A. Scannicchio.
Family Law, Residential and Commercial Real Estate, Estate Planning, Appellate Practice, Probate.
See Professional Biographies, CHICAGO, ILLINOIS

Scarborough, Theodore R. .... '— '93 C.352 B.A. L.145 J.D. [Ⓐ Sidley A.B.&W.]
Scarbrough, Brian S. .... '79 '04 C.228 B.A. L.1565 J.D. [Ⓐ Jenner&B.]
Scarlati, Steven R., Jr. .... '63 '90 C.234 B.A. L.146 J.D. [Garofalo,S.H.&S.]
Scarlett, Jennifer M. .... '— '03 C.679 B.A. L.365 J.D. [Ⓐ Querrey&H.]
Scarnavack, Alan M. .... '37 '73 C.339 B.S. L.146 J.D. Asst. Pub. Def.
Scarpace, Ericka K. '— '04 C&L.966 B.S., J.D.
(adm. in WI; not adm. in IL) [Ⓐ Jones D.]
Scarpelli, Craig M. .... '70 '96 C.966 B.S. L.209 J.D. [Garofalo,S.H.&S.]
Scarpelli, Nicholas J. .... '64 '88 C.123 B.A. L.365 J.D. [Ⓐ Stellato&S.]
Scavone, Thomas G., (AV) '46 '73
C.215 B.S.Ch.E. L.912 J.D. [Niro,S.H.&N.] (See Pat. Sect.)
Schaab, Shannon M. .... '73 '98 C.339 B.S. L.209 J.D. [Ⓐ Ungaretti&H.]
Schaal, John Eric, (AV) '43 '68 C.973 M.A.B. L.477 J.D.
Asst. Gen. Coun., USG Corp.
Schaar, Marvin B. .... '48 '73 C.339 A.B. L.145 J.D. 33 W. Monroe St.‡
Schachman, David .... '52 '78 C.112 B.A. L.1119 J.D. 122 South Michigan Avenue
Schachner, Jason R. .... '77 '03 C.475 B.S. L.1187 J.D. [Ⓐ Wiedner&M.]
Schad, Lawrence W., (AV) .... '45 '70 C.207 B.A. L.477 J.D. [Schad,D.&S.]

Schad, Diamond & Shedden, P.C., (AV)
332 South Michigan Avenue Suite 1000, 60604-4398
Telephone: 312-939-6280 Facsimile: 312-939-4661
URL: http://www.bsdlaw.com
Lawrence W. Schad; Stephen B. Diamond; James Shedden;—Steven J. Tomiello; Michael S. Hilicki; Stanley W. Pierson; Tony Kim; Katherine A. Hathaway.
Class Action Litigation (Securities, Insurance, Consumer Protection and Fair Debt Collection Practices), False Claims-Qui Tam Litigation, Whistleblower Litigation, Consumer Protection and Consumer Fraud Litigation, Business Transactions and Litigation, Environmental Law and Appellate Practice.
See Professional Biographies, CHICAGO, ILLINOIS

Schade, Rudolf G., Jr., (AV) .... '41 '68 C.313 B.A. L.365 J.D. [Cassiday,S.&G.]
Schaefer, Amy R. .... '72 '99 C.36 B.A. L.209 J.D. [Ⓐ Littler M.]
Schaefer, Andrew John .... '70 '97 C.145 A.B. L.276 J.D. [Ⓐ Mayer,B.R.&M.]
Schaefer, Sarah E. .... '68 '99 L.597 J.D. [Ⓐ Bell,B.&L.]
Schaefer, Susan Peters, (BV) .... '65 '89 C.293 B.A. L.339 J.D. [McDermott W.&E.]
Schaefers, Scott A. .... '77 '02 C.602 B.A. L.339 J.D. [Ⓐ Seyfarth S.]
Schaeffer, Adam R. .... '78 '03 C.1372 B.A. L.145 J.D. [Ⓐ Bell,B.&L.]
Schaeffner, Sean Patrick .... '39 '72 C.602 B.B.A. L.215 J.D. Fleet Capital Corp.
Schafer, Brian M. .... '68 '96 C.276 B.A. L.309 J.D. [Winston&S.]
Schafer, Christopher J. .... '76 '02 C.623 B.S. L.1066 J.D. [Ⓐ Burke,W.M.&S.]
Schafer, Heather N. .... '— '05 C.352 B.S. L.1059 J.D. [Ⓐ Brinks H.G.&L.]
Schafer, Leslie E. .... '— '00 C.734 B.A. L.74 J.D. [Ⓐ Jones D.]
Schaffer, David S. .... '61 '89 C.145 B.A. L.309 J.D. [Gardner C.&D.]
Schaffer, Henry M. .... '43 '73 C.178 A.B. L.1066 J.D. [Ⓒ Jenner&B.]
Schaffner, Ariel .... '63 '89 C.273 B.A. L.146 J.D. Towers Productions, Inc.
Schaffner, Howard, (AV) .... '43 '70 C.1016 B.A. L.365 J.D. [Hofeld&S.]
Schaffner, Michael .... '19 '43 C.339 L.209 LL.B. [Schaffner,R.&F.] ‡
Schaffner, Rabinowitz & Feinartz, P.C., (BV) .... 118 N. Clinton Street, Penthouse 425
Schaider, Joel R. .... '— '82 C.339 B.S. L.146 J.D. [Sachnoff&W.]
Schain, Jerome S., (AV) .... '41 '66 C.339 B.S. L.209 J.D. [Schain,B.R.&C.]
Schain, Linda .... '46 '74 C.966 B.S. L.424 J.D. 222 N. La Salle St., Ste. 1910

Schain, Burney, Ross & Citron, Ltd., (AV)
222 North La Salle Street, Suite 1910, 60601-1102
Telephone: 312-332-0200 Fax: 312-332-4514
Joan T. Berg; Patrick T. Brankin; Thomas R. Burney; Bernard I. Citron; Richard G. Golab; James R. Griffin; Tamara K. Hibbard; Robert C. Kenny; Richard J. Lang; Richard H. Levy; John D. Malarkey; Timothy J. McGonegle; David J. O'Keefe; Michael S. Pinsky; Gary L. Plotnick; Michael E. Ross; Jerome S. Schain; Glenn C. Sechen; Jerome Wiener;—Jennifer Morrison Bloom; Jessica Marie Boudreau; Linsey N. Cohen; James K. Henegan; Charles D. Mangum; Courtney E. Mayster; Katriina S. McGuire; Caroline A. Nash; Daniel C. Shapiro; Donald C. Wennlund; Maribeth Hope Whitfield; Kevin J. Wolfberg.
Real Estate practice including Contracts, Leases, Liens, Loans for Lenders, Borrower Financing, Lender Financing, Mezzanine and Conduit Financing, Residential, Industrial and Commercial Developments, Condominium Conversions and Tax Increment Financing.
Land Use Regulation practice including Annexations, Annexation Agreements, Zoning Relief including Planned Developments, Map Amendments, Subdivision Approvals, Variances, Licenses and Permits.
Environmental Law practice including Enforcement Defense, Permits and Transactions.
Commercial Litigation practice including Business, Bankruptcy and Creditor Litigation, Unfair Competition, Construction and Zoning Disputes and Property Rights Law.
Business and Corporate Law practice including Acquisitions, General Representation, LLC and Partnerships.
Municipal Law practice including Civil Rights, Condemnation, Contract, Annexation, Zoning, Negotiation and Enforcement of Intergovernmental Agreements and Special Financing Techniques including Special Service Areas and Tax Increment Financing districts.
Income and Estate Tax Law practice including Wealth Preservation, Estate Planning, Business Tax Planning and Contested Matters.
See Professional Biographies, CHICAGO, ILLINOIS

Schall, Hope D. ... '73 '98 C.218 B.A. L.209 J.D. Atty., Federal Reserve Bank of Chicago
Schaller, Michael J., (AV) .... '50 '75 C&L.339 B.S., J.D. [Shefsky&F.]
Schaller, William Lynch, (AV) .... '56 '81 C.339 B.S. L.209 J.D. [Baker&M.]

Schamis, Jeffrey B., (AV) '47 '76 C.696 A.B. L.145 J.D. [Seyfarth S.]
Schaner, Lawrence S. '60 '87 C.228 A.B. L.813 J.D. [Jenner&B.]
Schank, Timothy M. '76 '01 C&L.602 B.A., J.D. [Vedder,P.K.&K.]
Schanks, Scott A. '60 '90 C.932 B.S. L.365 J.D. 5329 N. St. Louis
Schar, Stephen L., (AV) '45 '70 C.145 B.A. L.209 J.D. [Seyfarth S.]
Scharf, Stephanie A., (AV) '— '85 L.145 J.D. [Jenner&B.]
Scharff, Christopher M. '78 '03
C.597 B.S. L.188 J.D. [McAndrews,H.&M.] (See Pat. Sect.)
Scharkey, John J. '72 '99 C.910 B.A. L.424 J.D. [Gould&R.]
Schatz, Barry A., (P.C.), (AV) '46 '74 C.645 B.A. L.365 J.D. [Berger S.]
Schauer, John S., (AV) '40 '65 C.475 B.A. L.597 J.D. [Seyfarth S.]
Schauerte, Mark '— '05 C.976 B.A. L.602 J.D. [Gardner C.&D.]
Schaul, Cheryl Kehoe, (AV) '59 '85 C.589 B.A. L.424 J.D. [Neal,G.&E.]
Schaul, Terrence Leigh '63 '88 C.339 B.A. L.209 J.D. [McCarthy D.]
Schechter, Erika Schafer '69 '97 C.473 B.S. L.339 J.D. [Baker&M.]
Schechter, Joel A., (AV) '53 '78 C.910 B.A. L.146 J.D. [J.A.Schechter]
Schechter, Mark J. '52 '78 C.339 B.A. L.146 J.D. Sr. Asst. Corp. Coun.‡
Schechter, Joel A., Law Offices of, (AV) 53 W. Jackson Blvd.
Schechtman, Ellen Rae '53 '83
C.597 B.S. L.424 J.D. Roosevelt Univ. Lawyers' Ass't. Program
Schechtman, Florence B., (BV) '52 '77 C.260 B.A. L.209 J.D. 116 S. Michigan Ave.
Schechtman, Larry A., (AV) '— '83 C.338 B.S. L.146 J.D. [O'Hagan,S.&A.]
Schecter, Bradley I. '76 '01 C.473 B.A. L.339 J.D. [Burke,W.M.&S.]
Schecter, Carole, (CV) '53 '84
C.112 B.A. L.424 J.D. Sr. Coun., Commonwealth Edison Co.
Scheer, James A., (AV) '47 '78 C.602 B.S. L.589 J.D. [Welsh&K.] (See Pat. Sect.)
Scheffres, Alan J. '36 '60 3241 W. Victoria St.
Scheid, John H., (AV) '35 '62
C&L.424 A.B., J.D. Prof. of Law, John Marshall Law School
Scheid, John H., Jr. '— '94 C.339 B.A. L.989 J.D. [Quinlan&C.]
Scheid, Justin D. '79 '04 C.339 B.S. L.146 J.D. [Johnson&B.]
Scheidt, Kathleen Sheil '72 '98 C.602 B.A. L.352 J.D. [Gardner C.&D.]
Scheiner, Eric C. '69 '97 C.383 B.A. L.365 J.D. [Sedgwick,D.M.&A.]
Schell, Kelly A. '— '95 C.209 B.S. L.365 J.D. [Kirkland&E.]
Scheller, Arthur M., III '— '93 C.602 B.A. L.365 J.D. [Gardner C.&D.]
Schellinger, Laurie L. '63 '89 C.961 B.S. L.365 J.D. Asst. Dep. Chf., Legal Coun.
Schelly, Ralph M. '18 '53 C.339 B.S. L.146 J.D. 220 S. State St.
Schemm, John M., Jr. '44 '77 C.64 B.A. L.365 J.D. Amer. Natl. Can Co.
Schenk, David R. '— '68 C.477 B.B.A. L.365 J.D. [Barnes&T.]
Schenk, Gerald L., (AV) '43 '68 C&L.339 B.A., J.D. [Schenk,A.B.&T.]
Schenk, Marion H. '23 '48 C.209 L.597 LL.B. 1931 Bradley Pl.
Schenk, Stefanie I. '— '95 C.188 B.A. L.477 J.D. [Sidley A.B.&W.]
Schenk, Todd S., (BV) '70 '95 C&L.347 B.A., J.D. [Tressler,S.M.&P.]

Schenk, Annes, Brookman & Tepper, Ltd., (AV)
311 South Wacker Drive, Suite 5125, 60606-6657
Telephone: 312-554-3100 Fax: 312-554-3115 URL: http://www.sabt.com
Email: sabt@sabt.com URL: http://www.sabtlaw.net
Gerald L. Schenk; Andrew J. Annes; Robert K. Brookman; Robert D. Tepper;—John W. Campbell, Jr.; Charles G. Blair.
Business and Commercial Litigation, Commercial Real Estate, including Representation of Management/Ownership, Estate Planning and Administration, Probate, Corporate Law, Corporate Planning, Financial Planning, Tax, Commercial Transactions, General Civil Trial/Litigation, Creditors Rights and Bankruptcy, Business Immigration, Insurance Law, including Insurance Coverage, Insurance Defense and Professional Liability and Employment Law.
See Professional Biographies, CHICAGO, ILLINOIS

Schenkier, Sidney I. '55 '79 C&L.597 B.J.S., J.D. Mag.
Scherer, Maria '— '01 C.602 B.A. L.893 J.D. [DLPiper R.G.C.U.]
Scherrer, Stephen T. '72 '98 C.750 B.S. L.1119 J.D. [McDermott W.&E.] (Pat.)
Schetz, John P. '— '01 C&L.477 A.B., J.D. [McDermott W.&E.]
Scheu, Ralph G., (AV) '28 '55 C.210 B.A. L.597 J.D. 20 N. Clark St.‡
Scheuerlein, Paul H., (AV) '52 '84 C&L.823 B.S., J.D. [Cantwell&C.]
Scheuing, Suzanne M. '— '99 C.228 B.A. L.846 J.D. [Mandell M.]
Scheurich, Rita W. '17 '42 C.856 B.A. L.424 J.D. 2318 W. 109th St.‡
Schey, Robert, (AV) '32 '56 C.1016 L.46 J.D. [R.Schey&Assoc.]
Schey, Robert, & Associates, P.C., (AV) 188 West Randolph Street, Suite 1000
Schiave, Anne Hamblin, (AV) '— '73 C&L.145 A.B., J.D. [Holland&K.]
Schiavone, Nancy E., (AV) '58 '83 C.339 B.A. L.209 J.D. 2511 N. Campbell Ave
Schichtel, Kay L., (AV) '49 '74 C.373 B.A. L.145 J.D. [Swanson,M.&B.]
Schick, Paul E. '65 '95 C&L.378 B.S., J.D. [Baker&M.]
Schieber, Judith A., (BV) '57 '81 C.531 B.A. L.339 J.D. 125 S. Franklin St.
Schiefelbein, Chad A. '70 '96 C&L.879 B.S., J.D. [Vedder,P.K.&K.]
Schienberg, Marvin B. '31 '86 C.679 B.S. L.365 J.D. 400 McClurg Ct., Ste. 1416
Schiff, Mark H., (AV) '53 '77 C.339 B.S. L.365 J.D. [Fuchs&R.]
Schiff, Matthew B., (AV) '57 '82 C.188 B.A. L.94 J.D. [Schiff&H.]

Schiff Hardin LLP, (AV)
A Limited Liability Partnership Including Professional Corporations
Founded in 1864
6600 Sears Tower, 60606-6473
Telephone: 312-258-5500 Facsimile: 312-258-5600
Email: attorneys@schiffhardin.com URL: http://www.schiffhardin.com
Partners: Thomas W. Abendroth; John F. Adams; Barry S. Alberts; Kristy L. Allen; David H. Anderson; Dirk W. Andringa; Darren C. Baker; John A. Bannon; Svetlana V. Bekman; Lauralyn G. Bengel; Robert I. Berger; Jill B. Berkeley; Scott Bieber; David C. Blickenstaff; Chris L. Bollinger; Stephen J. Bonebrake; Felice Bressler Rose; Max G. Brittain, Jr.; Harmon A. Brown; James E. Brown; Lisa A. Brown; Antony S. Burt; Kevin J. Byrne; Joseph A. Cancila, Jr.; Jennifer M. Cerven; Everett J. Cygal; Heidi Dalenberg; Paul E. Dengel; Sharon A. Doherty; Patricia Dondanville; Stephen J. Dragich; Michael W. Drumke; Marci A. Eisenstein; James F. X. Fahy (Resident at Dublin, Ireland Office); Peter V. Fazio, Jr.; Robert C. Feldmeier; Matthew J. Fischer; J. Mark Fisher; Steven D. Friedland; Mark C. Friedlander; Julie J. Furer; Matthew G. Galo; James P. Gaughan; Eugene J. Geekie, Jr.; Lawrence M. Gill; Walter C. Greenough; Paul Edwin Greenwalt, III; David A. Grossberg; Michael J. Hanahan; William M. Hannay; Stacie R. Hartman; Frederick L. Hartmann, Jr.; Sondra A. Hemeryck; Thomas J. Henehan; Douglas C. Hochstetler; David R. Hodgman; Patricia Brown Holmes; Allan Horwich; Richard J. Hoskins; David A. Howard; Barry S. Hyman; Steve E. Isaacs; Larry Jacobson; Janet M. Johnson; Trevor B. Joike; Thomas K. Juffernbruch; James M. Kane; Nancy L. Kasko; Paula M. Ketcham; Andrew A. Kling; Brian D. Kluever; William I. Kohn; Aphrodite Kokolis; Robert E. Kolek; Kevin L. Kolton; Melissa J. Krasnow; Joseph J. Krasovec, III; Ruth E. Krugly; Jeffrey Kuta; Dennis G. LaGory; Neil Lloyd; Thomas P. Luning; Paul M. Lurie; Owen E. MacBride; Sean T. Maloney; Paul C. Marengo; John C. Martin; Catherine M. Masters; David S. McCarthy; David P. McHugh; Michael L. Meyer; William E. Meyer, Jr.; Richard T. Miller; Robert J. Minkus; Jane Ellen Montgomery; Virgil R. Montgomery, Jr.; Paula J. Morency; Ralph A. Morris; Francis P. Morrissey; Gary L. Mowder (P.C.); Steven H. Noll; Joseph J. O'Hara, Jr.; Roger Pascal; S. Michael Peck; Randolph M. Perkins (Resident at Lake Forest, Illinois Office); Charles H.R. Peters; Scott E. Pickens; Robert R. Pluth, Jr.; Carol R. Prygrosky; Thomas B. Quinn; Paul A. Rahe; Robert John Regan; Robert H. Riley; Kenneth M. Roberts; Melvin A. Robinson; Gabriel M. Rodriguez; Peter L. Rossiter; Ronald S. Safer; John N. Scholnick; Henry W. Sledz, Jr.; Patricia Costello Slovak; Jeffery N. Smith; Edward Spacapan, Jr.; David M. Spector; Robin M. Spencer; Frederick J. Sperling; Mark A. Sternberg; Debra L. Stetter; Linda K. Stevens; Ross D. Taylor; Patricia J. Thompson; Clay A. Tillack; Michael F. Tomasek; Scott C. Tomassi; Patricia S. Ullman; Brett A. Valiquet; Darren M. R. Van Puymbrouck; Everett S. Ward; Thomas R. Wechter; Bruce P. Weisenthal; Adam S. Weiss; Thomas P. White; Robert B. Wilcox, Jr.; Roger R. Wilen; Jay Williams; Helen T. Wilson; Brenna B.

(This Listing Continued)

Schiff Hardin LLP (Continued)

Woodley; Mark C. Zaander; Sheldon A. Zabel; Kathryn D. Zalewski; Christopher J. Zinski. Special Partners: Lawrence Block (P.C.); Stuart L. Goodman; Donald J. Kreger; Neal A. Mancoff; William A. Montgomery (P.C.); Guenther M. Philipp (P.C.); James M. Van Vliet, Jr.; John J. Voortman; Ronald Wilder. Retired Partners: Paul B. O'Flaherty; Mitchell S. Rieger; Burton R. Rissman (P.C.); James B. Wilson (P.C.). Senior Counsel: W. Donald McSweeney; Keith Shay. Of Counsel: Howard R. Barron; Kathleen C. Bassi; Susan M. Carlson (Resident at Lake Forest, Illinois Office); James A. Clark; Nicole Finitzo (Resident at Lake Forest, Illinois Office); Barbara E. Hermansen; Lael F. Johnson; Katherine J. Levy (Resident at Lake Forest, Illinois Office); Stephen A. Marcus; Kathleen D. Mathewson; Kendra J. Panek; Carl A. Royal; John D. Simpson; Richard L. Verkler (Resident at Lake Forest, Illinois Office). Counsel: Todd D. Freer; Daniel J. Deeb; Michael J. Huft; John K. Lines; Mary Anne Mullin; Michael Yetnikoff. Associates: Andrew M. Alul; Mark A. Bergner; Elizabeth Anne Blackwood; Michael J. Boffa; Matthew Brett; Fiona A. Burke; Benjamin C. Butler; Tracy A. Campbell; John Capone; Edward M. Casmere; Jeffrey Colvin; Alexis Andrews Cooper; Erika Csicsila, L.; John C. deMoulpied; Nathan A. Engel (Resident at Lake Forest, Illinois Office); Michelle J. Fisk; Patricia J. Fokuo; Aaron M. Forester; Laura B. Friedel; David C. Giles; Jason G. Harp; Lawrence H. Heftman; Kevin S. Hovis; Jennifer R. Izraelewicz; Ayad Paul Jacob; Matthew C. Jardine; Jonathan M. Judge; Jon K. Jurva; David G. Kairis; Charlene Q. Kalebic (Resident at Lake Forest, Illinois Office); Kim A. Kamin; Brendan J. Kelly; Charlene M. Kelly; Ian T. Kelly; Kevin C. Knohl; Susan Kurzydlo Koci; Jo-Anne Kokoski; Matthew D. Lahey; Seth D. Lamden; Joshua Lee; M. Shawn Leist; Jonathan Mark Lively; Theresa M.H. Marx; Ramona Mateiu; Lisa J. Matyas; Heather R. McDonald; Kristen L. Mercado; Joshua R. More; Samantha C. Norris; Heidi Oertle; Carrie Lynn H. Okizaki (Not admitted in IL); Binu George Palal; Avani A. Patel; Kavita Mukund Patel; Sailesh K. Patel; Holly A. Podulka; Linda Potapova; Lee Ann Rabe; Alex P. Rabinsky; Julie Claire Rising; Jessica Romero; Heidi Hennig Rowe; Amy M. Rubenstein; Andrew N. Sawula; Reid A. Schultz; David C. Scott; Marla R. Shade; Peter C. Spier; Sonia Macias Steele; Heidi Anne Steiner; Margaret Strothkamp; Jason M. Torf; Jon Carlo Vigano; Doug J. Wagenbach; Nora A. Kersten Walsh; Kelly M. Warner; Dorothy A. Weber (Not admitted in IL); Alexander B. Young; Andrew P. Young; Jason L. Zgliniec; Jeanette Sanniola Zimmer; Gladys C. Zolna. Staff Attorneys: Andrew Finko; Theodora A. Karnegis; Margaret A. Nagela; Steven D. Welhouse. Director of Marketing and Communications: David A. Milberg.
General Practice.
Washington, D.C. Office: 1101 Connecticut Avenue, N.W. Telephone: 202-778-6400. Facsimile: 202-778-6460.
New York, New York Office: 623 Fifth Avenue, 28th Floor, 10022. Telephone: 212-753-5000. Facsimile: 212-753-5044.
Dublin, Ireland Office: 3 Burlington Road, Dublin 4 Ireland. Telephone: +011-353-1-202-6555. Facsimile: +011-353-1-668-1212.
Lake Forest, Illinois Office: One Westminster Place, 60045. Telephone: 847-295-9200. Facsimile: 847-295-7810.
Atlanta, Georgia Office: 1230 Peachtree Street, 18th Floor. Telephone: 404-806-3800. Facsimile: 404-806-3801.
See Professional Biographies, CHICAGO, ILLINOIS

Schiff & Hulbert, (AV)
150 N. Wacker Drive, Suite 1300, 60606
Telephone: 312-726-2800 Fax: 312-726-2100
Email: mschiff@schiffandhulbert.com URL: http://www.schiffandhulbert.com
Members of Firm: Matthew B. Schiff; James W. Hulbert.
Labor and Employment Law, Workers Compensation.
See Professional Biographies, CHICAGO, ILLINOIS

Schiffman, David M., (AV) '53 '77 C&L.309 A.B., J.D. [Sidley A.B.&W.]
Schigelone, Jason W. '— '05 C.477 B.S. L.912 J.D. [Brinks H.G.&L.]
Schiller, Donald C., (AV) '42 '66 C.393 L.209 J.D. [Schiller,D.&F.]
Schiller, Eric M., (AV) '46 '71 C.347 A.B. L.597 J.D. [Sonnenschein N.&R.]
Schiller, Gregory E., (BV) '60 '85 C.477 B.A. L.1119 J.D. [Johnson&B.]
Schiller, Jay A., Jr., (BV) '29 '52 C.103 L.209 LL.B. 1 N. LaSalle St.
Schiller, Jeffrey E., (AV) '54 '79 C.477 B.A. L.597 J.D. [Schuyler,R.&Z.]
Schiller, Philip J., & Assoc., P.C., (AV) '36 '58
C.145 B.A. L.597 LL.B. 33 N. Dearborn St.
Schiller, Scott Y. '64 '90 C.861 B.A. L.339 J.D. Chmn., S & S Home Builders, Inc.
Schiller, Stephen A. '37 '61 C.1016 B.S.C. L.145 J.D. Cir. J.

Schiller, DuCanto and Fleck, (AV)
200 North La Salle Street, 30th Floor, 60601
Telephone: 312-641-5560 Fax: 312-641-6361
Email: schillerducantoandfleck@sdflaw.com URL: http://www.sdflaw.com
Partners: Joseph N. DuCanto; Donald C. Schiller; Charles J. Fleck (Resident, Lake Forest Office); David H. Hopkins; Arnold B. Stein; Burton S. Hochberg; Carlton R. Marcyan (Resident, Lake Forest Office); Timothy M. Daw (Resident, Wheaton Office); Benjamin S. Mackoff; James B. O'Brien; Michael R. Galasso (Resident, Wheaton Office); Sarane Crowther Siewerth; Anita M. Ventrelli; Andrea K. Muchin; David A. King (Resident, Wheaton Office); Karen Pinkert-Lieb; Daniel R. Stefani; Celia G. Gamrath (Resident, Lake Forest Office); Eric L. Schulman (Resident, Lake Forest Office); Mario R. Ventrelli (Resident, Lake Forest Office); Meighan A. Harmon. Associates: Jason N. Sposeep; Neal A. Simon (Resident, Lake Forest Office); Jennifer L. Dillon Kotz; Deborah A. Carder (Resident, Wheaton Office); Claire R. McKenzie; Patrick Thomas Ryan; Jessica Bank Interlandi; Joshua M. Jackson; Stewart J. Auslander; Elizabeth A. Theyssen; Mary A. Zambreno (Resident, Lake Forest Office); Michelle A. Lawless; Abigail M. Chiesa (Resident, Wheaton Office); Jay P. Dahlin. Of Counsel: Harold G. Field (Resident, Wheaton Office).
Family Law, Complex Domestic Relations Issues, Divorce/Dissolution of Marriage, Prenuptial Agreements/Premarital Agreements, Child Custody and Visitation, Spousal Support/Alimony/Maintenance, Matrimonial Law and Litigation, Appeals, Mediation-Family/ Divorce, Marital Settlement Agreements, Separation Agreements, Property Rights, Financial Discovery and Analysis Related to Divorce, and Tax Considerations Related to Divorce.
Lake Forest, Illinois Office: Suite 300, 207 East Westminster Avenue. Telephone: 847-615-8300. Fax: 847-615-8284.
Wheaton, Illinois Office: 311 South County Farm Road, Suite G. Telephone: 630-665-5800. Fax: 630-665-6082.
See Professional Biographies, CHICAGO, ILLINOIS

Schillerstrom, Robert J., (AV) '52 '80 C.337 B.A. L.146 J.D. [Ice M.]
Schilling, Jennifer L. '73 '98 C.966 B.A. L.424 J.D. [DLPiper R.G.C.U.]
Schiltz, Eugene J. '56 '81 C.338 B.S. L.145 J.D. [R.F.Coleman&Assoc.]
Schimberg, A. Bruce, (AV) '27 '52 C&L.145 Ph.B., J.D. 55 W. Monroe St.‡
Schimmel, Jacqueline M. '64 '93 C.691 B.A. L.966 J.D. [Gardner C.&D.]
Schimmel, Nancy L. '— '81 C.951 B.A. L.276 J.D. [Latham&W.]
Schindel, Donald M., (AV) '32 '56 C.339 B.S. L.145 J.D. [Sonnenschein N.&R.] ‡
Schink, David F. '— '98 C.299 B.A. L.94 J.D.
Gen. Coun., Contego Capital Partners, LLC
Schink, James H., (P.C.), (AV) '— '68 C&L.976 B.A., J.D. [Kirkland&E.]
Schippers, David P., (AV) '29 '59 C&L.424 J.D. 20 N. Clark St.
Schirle, K. Clark '63 '88 C.339 B.A. L.1068 J.D. [Clausen M.]
Schlack, David A., (AV) '44 '74 C.1016 B.S.B.A. L.209 J.D. 155 N. Michigan Ave.
Schlack, Jonathan Becket '71 '01 C.57 B.A. L.966 J.D.
(adm. in WI; not adm. in IL) [Anesi,O.R.N.&K.]
Schlade, Daniel I. '— '00 C.339 B.S. L.146 J.D. [Arnstein&L.]
Schlade, Terry M., (AV) '42 '66 C.339 B.S. L.309 LL.B. [Connelly R.&M.]
Schlafer, Dale L., (AV) '38 '62 C.31 A.B. L.145 J.D. [Kiesler&B.]
Schlanger, David A. '55 '80 C.339 B.S. L.365 J.D. Asst. States Atty.
Schlautman, Scott A. '— '03 C.861 B.S.M. L.602 J.D. [McGuirewoods]
Schleder, John G. '54 '78 C&L.209 B.A., J.D. Airline Employees Assn.
Schlegel, Stephen J., (AV) '45 '69 C.597 B.A. L.146 J.D. [S.J.Schlegel]
Schlegel, Stephen J., Ltd., (AV) 111 W. Washington St., Ste. 1020
Schleicher, Leah A. '71 '97 C.475 B.A. L.262 J.D. [Neal,G.&E.]
Schleifer, Andrea M., (AV) '— '79 C.347 B.A. L.424 J.D. [A.M.Schleifer&Assoc.]

Schleifer, Andrea M., & Associates, P.C., (AV)
20 North Clark Street, Suite 2200, 60602
Telephone: 312-673-7373 Fax: 312-236-7660
Email: ams1esq@aol.com
Andrea M. Schleifer.
Family Law, Divorce, Parentage, Child Custody, Visitation, Child Support, Contested Paternity, Contested Adoptions, Guardianship, Mediation, Alternative Dispute Resolution, Post Divorce Issues, Buying and Selling a Home, Buying and Selling a Business, Landlord Tenant Agreements and Residential Real Estate.
See Professional Biographies, CHICAGO, ILLINOIS

Schleiter, John R. ... '71 '96 C.339 B.A. L.365 J.D. [Fisher K.]
Schlemmer, Dennis R., (AV) '39 '64 C&L.339 B.S., J.D. [Leydig,V.&M.] (See Pat. Sect.)
Schlemmer, Robert N. ... '72 '98 C.108 L.421 [Ⓐ Cohn,L.R.S.&G.]
Schlenz, Gregory G. ... '77 '02 C&L.339 B.S., J.D. [Ⓐ Wallenstein W.&R.]
Schleppenbach, John R. ... '78 '03 C.357 B.A.B.S. L.339 J.D. [Ⓐ Jenner&B.]
Schlesinger, Michael D., (AV) ... '45 '70 C.216 B.A. L.365 J.D. [Robbins,S.&P.]
Schlessinger, Daniel I., (AV) ... '54 '78 C.1036 B.A. L.339 J.D. [Lord,B.&B.]
Schlickman, J. Andrew, (AV) ... '52 '78 C.276 A.B. L.145 J.D. [Sidley A.B.&W.]
Schlickman, Stephen E. ... '53 '79 C.276 A.B. L.209 J.D. Chicago Transit Auth.
Schlifke, Bernard A., (AV) ... '40 '66 C.597 B.S. L.145 J.D. [Aronberg G.D.&G.]
Schlifke, James S. '48 '73 C&L.339 B.S., J.D. Pres. & Gen. Coun., GNP Securities Inc. (Pat.)
Schlifkin, Lewis W. ... '07 '30 C.209 B.A. L.144 B.L. 2 N. LaSalle St.
Schlitter, Stanley A., (AV) ... '50 '77 C.350 B.S.E.E. L.352 J.D. [Jenner&B.] (Pat.)
Schloerb, John M. ... '62 '92 C.477 B.A. L.659 J.D. [Winston&S.]
Schloerb, Robert G., (AV) '24 '51 C.604 A.B. L.145 J.D. 200 East Randolph Drive, Suite 7300
Schlom, Curt J. ... '63 '90 C.966 B.A. L.209 J.D. [Wilson E.M.E.&D.]
Schlossberg, Robert L., (AV) ... '40 '64 C.209 B.S.C. L.597 J.D. [Lawrence,K.S.&U.]
Schlossberg, Ruth Alderman '62 '87 C.477 B.A. L.976 J.D. Northwestern Univ. School of Law
Schlueter, Tobias ... '74 '02 C.1391 B.A. L.365 J.D. [Ⓐ Sonnenschein N.&R.]
Schmahl, Michael M. ... '— '01 C.95 A.B. L.966 J.D. [Ⓐ McGuirewoods]
Schmall, Steven Todd ... '60 '87 C&L.910 A.B., J.D. [Schmall&Assoc.]
Schmall & Associates ... 134 N. La Salle St., Ste. 1924
Schmalzl, William A., (AV) ... '53 '77 C.665 B.A. L.309 J.D. [Mayer,B.R.&M.]
Schmanski, Matthew B. ... '— '04 C.472 B.A. L.602 J.D. [Ⓐ Chapman&C.]
Schmarak, Bradley S. ... '— '87 C.339 B.S. L.597 J.D. [Sachnoff&W.]
Schmedlen, Daniel G., Jr. '70 '96 C.976 B.A. L.902 J.D. (adm. in NC; not adm. in IL) [Ⓒ Lord,B.&B.] (⊙New York, NY)
Schmeiderman, Maria S. '62 '87 C&L.966 B.A., J.D. (adm. in WI; not adm. in IL) U.S. Dept. of Labor
Schmeltz, Vincent Paul (Trace), III '69 '97 C.675 B.A. L.378 J.D. [Ⓐ Mayer,B.R.&M.]
Schmetterer, Jack B. ... '31 '55 C&L.976 B.A., LL.B. U.S. Bkrptcy J.
Schmetterer, Kenneth L., (AV) ... '63 '89 C.966 B.A. L.309 J.D. [DLPiper R.G.C.U.]
Schmidbauer, Nicholas P. ... '77 '03 C.477 B.S. L.339 J.D. [Ⓐ McCracken&F.] (Pat.)
Schmidt, Alan W. ... '47 '72 C.388 A.B. L.424 J.D. 2663 N. Lincoln
Schmidt, Darren J. ... '74 '01 C.347 B.A. L.178 J.D. [Ⓐ Jenner&B.]
Schmidt, David F. ... '58 '90 C.162 B.A. L.424 J.D. [Chittenden,M.&N.]
Schmidt, David R., (AV) ... '49 '79 C.602 A.B. L.884 J.D. [Fedota C.]
Schmidt, Jason ... '74 '99 C&L.477 B.A., J.D. [Ⓐ Epstein B.&G.]
Schmidt, Jennifer Ann .. '66 '91 C&L.436 B.A., J.D. Claims Atty., American Inter. Group
Schmidt, John J. ... '28 '55 C.209 B.S. L.424 J.D. 35 E. Wacker Dr.‡
Schmidt, John M. ... '71 '98 C.57 B.A. L.365 J.D. [Ⓐ Fisher K.]
Schmidt, John R., (AV) ... '43 '67 C&L.309 B.A., J.D. [Mayer,B.R.&M.]
Schmidt, Joseph F., (AV) '48 '73 C.424 B.A. L.146 J.D. [Michael B.&F.] (See Pat. Sect.)
Schmidt, Joseph K. ... '14 '36 C&L.145 Ph.B., J.D. 1525 E. 53rd St.
Schmidt, Patricia Kane ... '64 '95 C.884 B.S.E.E. L.201 J.D. [Bell,B.&L.] (Pat.)
Schmidt, Peter J. ... '71 '98 C.339 B.S. L.209 J.D. [Ⓐ Dykema G.P.]
Schmidt, Philip J. ... '45 '71 C.973 B.S. L.602 J.D. 11 South LaSalle Street, Suite 1020
Schmidt, Randall D. ... '54 '79 C.339 B.A. L.145 J.D. Mandel Legal Aid Clinic
Schmiedel, Peter J. ... '48 '74 C.776 B.A. L.365 J.D. [Ⓐ Fischel&K.]
Schmiege, Colleen M. ... '76 '02 C.93 B.S. L.424 J.D. [Ⓐ Figliulo&S.]
Schmiege, Robert ... '41 '66 C&L.602 B.A., J.D. 150 N.Wacker Dr., Ste., 1550
Schmitt, David K., (AV) ... '55 '80 C.174 B.A. L.424 J.D. [Field&G.]
Schmitt, Marshall John ... '59 '83 C.145 B.S. L.309 J.D. [Jenner&B.]
Schmitt, Ruth Ann ... '49 '75 C.879 B.A. L.209 J.D. Exec. Dir., Lawyers Tr. Fund of Ill.
Schmitz, Dieter A. ... '58 '84 C.602 B.A. L.597 J.D. [Baker&M.]
Schmitz, Jason K. ... '74 '99 C.475 B.A. L.209 J.D. [Ⓐ Mayer,B.R.&M.]
Schmookler, Scott L. ... '71 '96 C.98 B.A. L.146 J.D. [Clausen M.]
Schmucker, Christina ... '79 '04 C.880 B.A. L.472 J.D. 203 N. LaSalle St., Ste. 2100
Schnack, Steven O. ... '72 '97 C.597 B.A. L.352 J.D. Dir. & Sr. Coun., CNA
Schnadig, Richard H., (AV) ... '39 '65 C.855 B.A. L.309 LL.B. [Vedder,P.K.&K.]
Schnayer, Jerold B., (AV) '50 '77 C.339 B.S.E.E. L.146 J.D. [Welsh&K.] (See Pat. Sect.)
Schnebel, Debra J., (AV) ... '— '75 C.25 B.A. L.597 J.D. [Jones D.]
Schneck, Steven Paul ... '62 '88 C.188 B.S. L.569 J.D. [Ⓐ R.D.Allison&Assoc.]
Schneider, Arnold C. ... '22 '52 C.966 Ph.B. L.912 J.D. Bankers Life & Cas. Co.
Schneider, Benjamin L. ... '— '03 C.966 B.S. L.494 J.D. [Ⓐ Quarles&B.]
Schneider, Dan W. ... '47 '74 C.747 B.A. L.950 J.D. [Baker&M.]
Schneider, David Alan ... '69 '94 C.966 B.S. L.146 J.D. [Ⓒ Smith O.&W.]
Schneider, Earl G. ... '33 '55 L.146 J.D. 1633 N. North Park Ave.
Schneider, Frank L., (AV) ... '37 '62 C.210 A.B. L.145 J.D. 10 S. LaSalle St.
Schneider, Gregg D., (BV) .. '52 '77 C.339 A.B. L.910 J.D. 33 N. LaSalle St., Ste. 1700A
Schneider, Harris J. ... '63 '88 C.575 B.A. L.910 J.D. 2464 W. estes St.‡
Schneider, Harvey Jay ... '34 '58 C&L.597 B.S., J.D. Chicago Transit Auth.
Schneider, Jaime Erin ... '76 '01 C.477 B.A. L.146 J.D. [Ⓐ Seyfarth S.]
Schneider, Jerold H. ... '49 '74 C.597 B.A. L.424 J.D. 8410 W. Bryn Mawr Ave., Ste. 400
Schneider, John C. ... '58 '83 C.927 B.S. L.424 J.D. 2 N. Riverside Plaza
Schneider, Joseph ... '22 '56 C.910 B.S. L.365 J.D. Cir. J.
Schneider, Lee S., (Ltd.) ... '56 '82 C.597 B.S. L.424 J.D. 77 W. Wacker Dr.
Schneider, Lewis M., (AV) ... '44 '73 C.238 B.A. L.365 J.D. [Pretzel&S.]
Schneider, Linda J., (AV) ... '60 '89 C.801 B.A. L.209 J.D. [Merlo K.B.&G.]
Schneider, Lisa A. ... '— '94 C.494 B.S. L.597 J.D. [Ⓐ Sidley A.B.&W.]
Schneider, Maggie J. ... '76 '01 C.339 B.A. L.477 J.D. [Ⓐ Mayer,B.R.&M.]
Schneider, Meaghan L. ... '75 '01 C.602 B.A. L.424 J.D. [Ⓐ Meckler B.&T.]
Schneider, Michael R., (AV) ... '49 '76 C&L.339 B.S., J.D. [Cohn,L.R.S.&G.]
Schneider, Miriam M. ... '31 '70 C.480 B.S. L.546 J.D. 171 N. Clark St.
Schneider, Robert J., (AV) ... '— '73 C&L.150 B.S.M.E., J.D. [Chapman&C.] (Pat.)
Schneider, Robert R. ... '57 '83 C.339 B.S. L.597 J.D. Tax Counsel, BP America Inc.
Schneider, Todd J. ... '— '95 C.597 B.A. L.436 J.D. [Holland&K.]

Schneider, Linda K., and Associates
(See Palatine)
Schneidman, Edward J., (AV) ... '55 '80 C.659 B.S. L.228 J.D. [Mayer,B.R.&M.]
Schnitz, Robert C. ... '— '75 C&L.309 B.A., J.D. [Holland&K.]
Schnitz, Robert V. '62 '88 C.597 B.A. L.424 J.D. (adm. in GA; not adm. in IL) V.P. & Assoc. Gen. Coun., Hyatt Hotels Corp.
Schnitzer, Michael ... '72 '97 C.608 B.A.S. L.365 J.D. [Ⓐ Worker,S.&H.]
Schnur, Thomas E., (BV) ... '61 '86 C.339 B.S. L.209 J.D. [Vedder,P.K.&K.]
Schnurr, Mary Jankousky, (AV) '55 '82 C.339 B.S. L.94 J.D. Intell. Prop. Coun., Rexam Beverage Can Company (Pat.)
Schnurr, Richard A., (AV) ... '55 '81 C.347 B.S. L.339 J.D. [Ice M.] (Pat.)
Schodde, Gregory C. '64 '92 C.659 B.S.E.E. L.221 J.D. [McAndrews,H.&M.] (See Pat. Sect.)
Schoedel, Lisa ... '— '03 C.910 B.S. L.209 J.D. [Ⓐ McDonnell B.H.&B.]
Schoen, Dennis T., (AV) ... '44 '74 C.742 B.A. L.424 J.D. [D.T.Schoen]
Schoen, Lee J., (AV) ... '48 '73 C.963 B.S. L.602 J.D. [Schoen&S.]
Schoen, Dennis T., P.C., Law Offices, (AV) ... Ste. 663, 221 N. La Salle St.
Schoen & Smith, Ltd., (AV) ... 200 W Adams Street
Schoenberg, David W., (AV) ... '42 '66 C.347 A.B. L.339 J.D. [Ⓒ Greenberg T.]
Schoenberg, Renee M., (AV) ... '52 '76 C.597 B.A. L.477 J.D. [DLPiper R.G.C.U.]

Schoenberg, Fisher, Newman & Rosenberg, Ltd., (AV)
222 South Riverside Plaza, Suite 2100, 60606-6101
Telephone: 312-648-2300 Fax: 312-648-1212
URL: http://www.sfnr.com
Kenneth C. Prince (1912-2005); Samuel Schoenberg (1913-1989); David L. Fisher (1929-1993); Melvin S. Newman; Gerald M. Newman; Daniel E. Beederman; Robert C. Goldberg; Richard R. Perlman; Bruce E. Bell; Herbert B. Rosenberg; Leonard J. Gambino; Henry A. Hauser; Adam J. Glazer;— Eileen B. Cozzi; Daniel S. Klapman; David S. Makarski. Of Counsel: Paul W. Gabler.
General Business Practice, including Corporate, Litigation, Trade Associations, Independent Manufacturers Representatives, Labor Law, Employee Benefits, Federal, State and Real Estate Taxation, Estate Planning, Probate, Real Estate, Environmental Law, Mergers and Acquisitions, Securities, Banking, Intellectual Property, Bankruptcy, Family Law, Unfair Trade Practices, Legal Ethics and Professional Responsibility.
See Professional Biographies, CHICAGO, ILLINOIS

Schoeneberger, Carl A. ... '08 '31 C&L.597 B.S.L., J.D. 6733 N. Lightfoot Ave.‡
Schoeneberger, Keith P. ... '48 '74 C.276 B.A. L.597 J.D. [LeBoeuf,L.G.&M.]
Schoenfeld, David E., (AV) ... '59 '85 C.118 B.A. L.910 J.D. [Grippo&E.]
Schoenfeld, John A., (P.C.) ... '— '91 C.399 B.A. L.309 J.D. [Kirkland&E.]
Schoenfield, Rick M., (BV) ... '51 '76 C&L.597 B.A., J.D. [DiVincenzo S.S.]
Schoenmeyer, Ruth A. ... '70 '95 C&L.477 A.B., J.D. [Ⓐ Jenner&B.]
Schoenstadt, Richard G., (AV) ... '53 '78 C.339 A.B. L.424 J.D. [Siegel M.&S.]
Schoettes, Scott ... '— '04 C.800 B.F.A. L.276 J.D. [Ⓐ Latham&W.]
Schofield, Paul F., (P.C.), (AV) ... '48 '73 C.686 A.B. L.424 J.D. [Schofield&V.]
Schofield & Varde, LLP, (AV) ... 30 West Monroe Street
Scholes, Steven S., (AV) ... '60 '85 C.234 B.A. L.339 J.D. [McDermott W.&E.]
Scholl, Steven M. ... '60 '85 C.339 B.S. L.424 J.D. [Chuhak&T.]
Scholnick, John N., (AV) ... '— '79 C.311 B.A. L.597 J.D. [Schiff H.]
Schols, Bethany ... '74 '01 C.339 B.S. L.146 J.D. [Ⓐ Schwartz C.]
Scholz, David A. ... '41 '69 C.546 B.S. L.178 LL.B. Secy., Commonwealth Edison Co.
Schooley, Virginia G. '46 '80 C.339 B.A. L.146 J.D. V.P. & Secy., Rollins Burdick Hunter Co.
Schoon, Eugene A., (AV) ... '52 '80 C.114 B.A. L.879 J.D. [Sidley A.B.&W.]
Schoonhoven, Ray J., (AV) ... '21 '49 C.602 B.S.C. L.597 J.D. [Seyfarth S.] ‡
Schoonmaker, Peter W., (BV) ... '56 '80 C.966 B.S.Ed. L.146 J.D. [Condon&C.]
Schoonveld, Eric P., (AV) ... '66 '91 C.999 B.A. L.597 J.D. [Hall,P.&S.]
Schoop, Devlin J. ... '71 '97 C&L.339 B.A., J.D. [Ⓐ Laner,M.D.B.L.&T.]
Schopf, William G., (AV) ... '48 '73 C.674 A.B. L.188 J.D. [Schopf&W.]

Schopf & Weiss LLP, (AV)
312 West Randolph Street, Suite 300, 60606-1721
Telephone: 312-701-9300 Fax: 312-701-9335
URL: http://www.sw.com
Members of Firm: Peter V. Baugher; Ian H. Fisher; Todd H. Flaming; Verónica Gómez; Patrick J. Heneghan; Arthur J. Howe; Kenneth E. Kraus; Paula E. Litt; Jose A. Lopez; Bradley P. Nelson; Robert J. Palmersheim; Jason M. Rosenthal; William G. Schopf; Steven A. Weiss. Associates: William B. Berndt; Marcus D. Fruchter; Anna Eisner Seder; Autumn L. Sharp (Not admitted in IL); Jennifer A. Waters. Counsel: Ellen S. Martin; Rana H. Janney; Kristen N. Pate.
Business Litigation.
See Professional Biographies, CHICAGO, ILLINOIS

Schorer, Joseph U., (AV) ... '— '78 C.597 B.A. L.309 J.D. [Ⓒ Kirkland&E.]
Schottler, Mark R. ... '70 '96 C.723 B.A. L.436 J.D. [Schottler&Z.]
Schottler & Zukosky, LLC ... 10 S. Lasalle, Suite 3410
Schoumacher, Bruce H., (AV) ... '— '66 C.597 B.S. L.145 J.D. [Querrey&H.]
Schouten, Joseph A. ... '78 '04 C.201 B.A. L.945 J.D. [Ⓐ Jenner&B.]
Schraidt, James A. ... '51 '78 C.339 B.S. L.801 J.D. [Seyfarth S.]
Schramm, Cynthia L. ... '52 '79 C.424 B.A. L.146 J.D. Dept. of Labor, Admin. Law J.
Schramm, Donald L. ... '49 '78 C.347 B.A. L.365 J.D. [Rieff S.&K.]
Schramm, Linnea L. ... '58 '96 C&L.260 B.S., J.D. [Ⓐ Hinshaw&C.]
Schramm, Mark A. ... '56 '82 C.602 B.A. L.424 J.D. [Esposito&S.]
Schrank, Charles E., (AV) ... '60 '86 C&L.966 B.B.A., J.D. [Sidley A.B.&W.]
Schrantz, Erin R. ... '75 '00 C.339 B.A. L.1119 J.D. [Ⓐ Jenner&B.]
Schreck, Robert A., Jr. ... '52 '78 C.276 B.S.B.A. L.597 J.D. [McDermott W.&E.]
Schreder, Carleen L., (AV) ... '— '82 C.393 B.A. L.145 J.D. [Levin&S.]
Schreeder, Lauren B. ... '70 '95 C.1365 B.A. L.861 J.D. [Ⓐ Richards,R.&S.] ⊙
Schreiber, Gay R. ... '61 '87 C.1365 B.A. L.94 J.D. 150 N. Wacker Dr., Ste. 2950
Schreiber, Glenn E. ... '47 '75 C.210 B.A. L.145 30 N. La Salle St., Ste. 3906
Schreiber, Jayne C. '— '82 C.813 B.A. L.597 J.D. Dir., Client Develop., Broadview, Inc.
Schreiber, Joseph P. ... '59 '84 C.436 B.A. L.424 J.D. 30 North LaSalle Street, Suite 2800
Schreiber, Julian D. ... '33 '60 C&L.477 A.B., LL.B. [Borovsky&E.]
Schreiber, Myron N. ... '55 '81 C.424 B.S.W. L.146 J.D. Dep. Dir., Policy & Planning
Schreiber, Phillip M. ... '— '92 C.339 B.A. L.597 J.D. [Holland&K.]
Schreiber, Renee M. ... '— '02 C.424 L.597 [Ⓐ Kirkland&E.]
Schreiber, Rodd M., (AV) ... '61 '87 C&L.477 B.A., J.D. [Skadden,A.S.M.&F.]
Schreiber, Ronald, (AV) ... '53 '77 C.994 B.A. L.145 J.D. [Seyfarth S.]
Schreiber, Scott N., (BV) ... '56 '85 C.475 B.A. L.146 J.D. [Much S.F.D.A.&R.]
Schreiber, Scott T., (BV) ... '56 '81 C&L.879 B.A., J.D. [Garofalo,S.H.&S.]
Schreiber, Susan, (AV) ... '54 '80 C.33 B.A. L.107 J.D. DePaul Univ.
Schreiber-Murray, Beth V. '60 '87 C.597 B.A. L.945 J.D. Asst. Coun., Chicago Title Ins. Co.
Schreier, James M. ... '40 '65 C.276 A.B. L.209 J.D. Assoc. Cir. J.
Schrepfer, Katherine Hilton '65 '90 C.339 B.A. L.424 J.D. Sr. Atty., Federal Reserve Bank of Chicago
Schriar, Seymour ... '20 '47 C&L.145 A.B., J.D. 29 S. La Salle St.
Schriver, John T., III, (AV) ... '45 '71 C.321 A.B. L.276 J.D. [Duane M.]
Schrock, Ray C. ... '— '98 C.932 B.B.A. L.146 J.D. [Kirkland&E.]
Schrodt, David I. ... '— '90 C.339 B.S. L.893 J.D. [Chapman&C.]

Schroeder, Brian A. ....'67 '92 C.339 B.A. L.589 J.D. [Cassiday,S.&G.]
Schroeder, David E. ....'59 '84 C.578 B.A. L.145 J.D. CNA Ins. Co.
Schroeder, Dolores K. ....'59 '87 C.741 B.A. L.424 J.D. 77 W. Washington Suite 1510
Schroeder, Gilbert J. ....'45 '70 C&L.209 A.B., J.D. [Clausen M.]
Schroeder, James C., (BV) ....'56 '81 C.72 B.A. L.966 J.D. [Mayer,B.R.&M.]
Schroeder, Louis R., (AV) '48 '76
C.97 B.A. L.851 J.D. Claims Coun., Chicago Title Ins. Co.
Schroeder, Paul W., (AV) ....'— '72 C&L.339 B.A., J.D. [Jones D.]
Schroeder, Thomas M., & Associates, Counselors at Law, (AV) '47 '72
C.393 B.A. L.597 J.D. 980 N. Michigan Ave., Ste. 1120
Schroedter, Gregory J., (AV) ....'46 '72 C&L.966 B.A., J.D. [Bell,B.&L.]
Schroer, Steven C., (AVⓉ) '48 '76
C.747 B.A. L.178 J.D. [Fitch,E.T.&F.] (⊙Boulder, CO)
Schub, Moshe ....'53 '79 C.589 B.A. L.1151 LL.M. Lawyers, Inc., P.C.
Schuber, Chas. L. ....'20 '50 C&L.597 B.B.A., J.D. 4615 W. Huron St.
Schubert, Elizabeth M. '67 '00 C.104 A.B. L.273 J.D.
(adm. in NY; not adm. in IL) [Ⓐ McDermott W.&E.]
Schubert, Margareth '59 '84 C.339 B.A. L.424 J.D.
Asst. Gen. Coun., Loyola University of Chicago
Schuch, Judith L. ....'68 '00 C.339 B.A. L.365 J.D. [Ⓐ DLPiper R.G.C.U.]
Schueler, Matthew J., (AV) ....'60 '89 C.927 B.S. L.424 J.D. [Schueler,D.&C.]

Schueler, Dallavo & Casieri, (AV)
233 South Wacker Drive, Suite 6150, 60606
Telephone: 312-831-1099 Facsimile: 312-831-4144
Matthew J. Schueler; Christopher J. Dallavo; Vincent M. Casieri;—Katherine Ann Rodosky; Mark T. McAndrew; Shirley A. Irwin; Jennifer J. McFadden.
Medical Malpractice, Products Liability, Directors and Officers Liability, Employment Law and Errors and Omissions.
See Professional Biographies, CHICAGO, ILLINOIS

Schueller, James R. ....'74 '00 C&L.602 B.B.A., J.D. [Ⓐ Bell,B.&L.]
Schuette, David A. ....'60 '85 C.276 A.B. L.477 J.D. [Mayer,B.R.&M.]
Schuitmaker, Helen J. '47 '72 C.881 B.A. L.575 J.D.
(adm. in NC; not adm. in IL) Solr. Off., U.S. Dept of Law
Schuler, Gregory G. '52 '90 C.339 B.A. L.424 J.D.
Sr. Coun., Real Estate, Commonwealth Edison Co.
Schuler, Kenneth G. ....'— '94 C.351 B.A. L.477 J.D. [Latham&W.]
Schuler, Nicholas J., Jr. ....'67 '04 C.128 B.A. L.339 J.D. [Ⓐ Winston&S.]
Schulhof, Scott H. ......'71 '03 C.597 B.A. L.146 J.D. [Ⓐ Leydig,V.&M.] (See Pat. Sect.)
Schulkin, Jeffrey A. ....'70 '95 C.339 B.A. L.146 J.D. [Ⓐ Munday&N.]
Schuller, Edward L., (AV) ....'41 '76 C.209 L.424 J.D. 415 N. LaSalle St.
Schulman, Blake Evan ....'77 '02 C&L.477 B.B.A., J.D. [Ⓐ Katten M.R.]
Schulman, Brad ....'79 '05 C.401 B.A. L.1000 J.D. [Ⓐ McKay,N.T.D.&K.]
Schulman, Charles P., (AV) ....'— '87 C.94 B.A. L.904 J.D. [Sachnoff&W.]
Schulman, Efrat R. ....'— '03 C&L.477 B.B.A., J.D. [Ⓐ Jones D.]
Schulman, Jeffrey, (BV) ....'44 '68 C.966 B.S. L.209 J.D. [Wolin&R.]
Schulman, Marc S. .....'55 '79 C.208 B.S.B.A. L.597 J.D. Pres., The Eli's Cheesecake Co.
Schulman, Rachel Reagler ....'— '89 C.347 B.S. L.339 J.D. [▣ Kirkland&E.]
Schulson, Susan Buckman '44 '80
C.339 B.A. L.365 J.D. Off. of the Cook Co. Pub. Guard.
Schulte, Mark J. '53 '79 C&L.734 B.A., J.D.
(adm. in NY; not adm. in IL) Exec. V.P., Prime Grp. Realty Tr.
Schulte, Stephen C., (AV) ....'52 '76 C&L.734 B.A., J.D. [Winston&S.]
Schultz, Carl M. ....'70 '00 C.966 B.A. L.146 J.D. [Ⓐ Johnson&B.]
Schultz, Charles J. ....'— '85 C.597 B.A. L.146 J.D. [Barnes&T.]
Schultz, David M. ....'61 '88 C.339 B.S. L.365 J.D. [Hinshaw&C.]
Schultz, David V. ....'45 '69 C&L.339 B.S., J.D. [Propp&S.]
Schultz, Donald ....'32 '57 C.1016 B.S. L.146 LL.B.,J.D 70 W. Madison
Schultz, James K. ....'71 '97 C.436 B.A. L.209 J.D. [Ⓐ McDonald&M.]
Schultz, James W. ....'53 '86 C.276 B.S.F.S. L.146 J.D. 6054 W. Touhy, Ste. 108
Schultz, Kurt L., (AV) ....'46 '72 C.659 B.S. L.608 J.D. [Winston&S.]
Schultz, Marc L. ....'69 '97 C.475 B.A. L.146 J.D. [Ⓐ Sonnenschein N.&R.]
Schultz, Martin A., & Associates '52 '82
C.861 B.A. L.365 J.D. 10 South La Salle Street Suite 3500
Schultz, Peter ....'66 '94 C.339 B.A. L.309 J.D. [Ⓐ Mayer,B.R.&M.]
Schultz, Reid A. ....'— '04 C.502 B.A. L.424 [Ⓐ Schiff H.]
Schultz, Richard G., (AV) ....'38 '64 C.339 L.209 J.D. [Schwartz C.]
Schultz, Ryan T. '— '03 C.679 B.S. L.145 J.D.
(adm. in NV; not adm. in IL) [Ⓐ Chapman&C.]
Schultz, Susan M. '55 '80
C.363 B.A. L.365 J.D. Assoc. Gen. Coun., Caylon Financial Inc.
Schulwolf, Steven ....'69 '94 C.339 B.A. L.477 J.D. [Michaels&M.]
Schulz, Carl W., Jr. ....'37 '67 C.197 A.B. L.146 J.D. Amer. Intl. Cos.
Schulz, Fred E., (AV) ....'43 '70 C.679 B.S. L.597 J.D. [Wildman,H.A.&D.]
Schulz, Mary K., (BV) ....'49 '81 C.960 B.S. L.966 J.D. [▣ Sinar K.M.&F.]
Schulze, Jason R. ....'70 '96 C.352 B.A. L.209 J.D. [Meckler B.&T.]
Schulze, Richard L. '45 '75 C.546 B.S.M.E. L.309 J.D.
(adm. in NE; not adm. in IL) 200 W. Madison St.
Schumacher, Alan J., (AV) ....'59 '84 C.602 B.B.A. L.339 J.D. [Pretzel&S.]
Schumacher, Daryl M. ....'72 '98 C.746 B.B.A. L.365 J.D. [Ⓐ Gardner C.&D.]
Schumacher, Florence Hackman ....'65 '89 C&L.383 B.A., J.D. [Sudekum,C.&S.]
Schumacher, Jeffrey A., (AV) ....'— '80 C.597 B.A. L.309 J.D. [Sachnoff&W.]
Schumacher, Paul W., (AV) ....'58 '84 C.339 B.A. L.365 J.D. [Roddy,L.&Z.]
Schuman, Joseph, (AV) ....'46 '76 C.118 B.A. L.145 J.D. 5000 N. Marine Drive, Suite 6E
Schuman, Susan J. '52 '79 C.475 B.A. L.945 J.D.
V.P., Gen. Coun. & Secy., AMA Insurance Agency, Inc.
Schuman, William P., (AV) ....'54 '79 C.477 B.B.A. L.309 J.D. [McDermott W.&E.]
Schumann, Anthony L., (AV) ....'59 '85 C.57 B.A. L.803 J.D. [Grant H.&S.]
Schumann, Bryan G. ....'58 '85 C.589 B.S. L.146 J.D. [Bollinger,R.&G.]
Schupp, Anastasia Luka ....'44 '82 C&L.424 B.S., J.D. 5425 S. Richmond
Schupp, August "Jamie" H. '— '99
C.597 B.A. L.339 J.D. Two North LaSalle Street, Suite 2200
Schur, Gerald S., (AV) ....'35 '63 C.679 B.Ch.E. L.365 J.D. [Welsh&K.] (See Pat. Sect.)
Schur, Jerome, (AV) ....'27 '51 C.966 B.A. L.976 J.D. [Katz,F.E.E.&J.]
Schur, William G., (AV) '50 '75 C.197 A.B. L.188 J.D. ▣
111 West Washington Street - Suite 737, 60602
Telephone: 312-853-0156 FAX: 312-853-0158
Email: wgs1972@aol.com URL: http://www.lawyers.com/schur
Commercial and Civil Litigation. Commercial Collection. Enforcement of Foreign Judgments. Real Estate.
Representative Clients: Clear Channel Broadcasting; Woman's Clinic; Three Star Adjustment Co.
See Professional Biographies, CHICAGO, ILLINOIS

Schurgin, William P., (AV) ....'56 '80 C.477 A.B. L.94 J.D. [Seyfarth S.]
Schurman, Linda S., (AV) ....'60 '85 C.478 B.A. L.145 J.D. [Goodsmith G.&U.]
Schurr, Steven C. ....'57 '94 C.210 B.A. L.424 J.D. 203 N. La Salle Street, Suite 2100
Schusteff, Howard ....'60 '85 C.339 B.A. L.146 J.D. 200 N. LaSalle, Ste. 2650

Schutt, Thomas R., (BV) ....'53 '82 C.679 B.S.C.E. L.209 J.D. [Ⓐ Menges&M.]
Schutte, Scott T. ....'66 '95 C.338 B.S. L.146 J.D. [Jenner&B.]
Schutzel, Peter M. ....'79 '04 C.1365 B.A. L.477 J.D. [Ⓐ McDermott W.&E.]
Schuyler, Daniel M., (AV) ....'12 '37 C.197 A.B. L.597 J.D. 130 E. Randolph St

Schuyler, Roche & Zwirner, a professional corporation, (AV)
One Prudential Plaza, Suite 3800, 130 East Randolph Street, 60601 ⊙
Telephone: 312-565-2400 Facsimile: 312-565-8300
URL: http://www.srzlaw.com
Shareholders: Michael B. Roche; Richard T. Zwirner; Ralph E. Brown; Edward J. Copeland; Harry C. Benford III; Joseph J. Stevens; Robert A. Michalak; David M. Allen; Ernest W. Irons; Alison Barkley; Charles H. Cole; Daniel V. Kinsella; Richard E. Michaels; L. Andrew Brehm; David M. Giangrossi; Jeffrey E. Schiller; Thomas G. Draths; John E. Lowe; Michael F. Braun; Eric M. Fogel; Douglas A. Hanson; James L. Komie; David I. Addis; Camille B. Conway; Justin L. Weisberg; Ronald F. Geimer; Lauren E. DeJong. Partners: Catherine C. Gryczan; Douglass G. Hewitt; Richard J. Juarez; Steven P. Pherson; Elisha M. Prero; Robert J. Trizna; Mary K. Walter. Associates: Dolores Ayala; Jin-Ho Chung; Andrew M. Geier; Michael D. Lee; Ian S. Lesch; James D. Mahlo; Brendan T. McMahon; Laurie Martin Montplaisir; Rachel T. Nguyen; Jennifer L. Norkus; Michael T. Roche; Gerald T. Rohrer, Jr.; Jeffrey R. Rosenberg. Counsel: Walter L. Adams; Robert M. Horwitch; Thomas J. Paravola; Richard J. Walsh; Richard S. Weinberg; David E. Zarski.
Business Enterprise: Closely Held Businesses, International Business Transactions, Structured Finance and Asset Securitization, Corporate and Personal Taxation, Employment and Benefits, Technology Startups and E-Commerce, Real Estate. Business Litigation: Securities and Commodities Litigation, Commercial and Employment Litigation, Labor Arbitration and Litigation, Professional Liability Litigation, Intellectual Property Litigation, Construction Contracts and Litigation. Estate Management: Estate Planning and Administration, Trusts, Probate and Trust Litigation, Estate and Transfer Taxation, Wealth and Health Planning.
Evanston, Illinois Office: Suite 2050, 1603 Orrington Avenue. Telephone: 312-565-2400.
See Professional Biographies, CHICAGO, ILLINOIS

Schwab, Carl E. '46 '73 C.475 B.A. L.213 J.D.
(adm. in MI; not adm. in IL) Price-Waterhouse
Schwab, David J., (BV) ....'63 '90 C.347 B.S. L.209 J.D. [Richards,R.&S.] ⊙
Schwab, John H., Jr. '53 '78 C.339 B.A. L.424 J.D.
Corp. Coun., Fed. Deposit Ins. Corp.
Schwab, Stephen W., (AV) ....'— '82 C.597 B.A. L.1017 J.D. [DLPiper R.G.C.U.]
Schwab, Steven A. ....'77 '02 C.473 B.A. L.424 J.D. [Ⓐ Katten M.R.]
Schwalb, David D. '70 '96 C.94 B.A. L.339 J.D.
V.P. & Gen. Coun., EJD Properties LLC
Schwanbeck, Wm. J. ....'13 '46 C.597 L.365 LL.B. Touche Ross & Co.
Schwartz, Alison Pollock '72 '97
C.339 B.S.E.E. L.145 J.D. [Ⓐ Sonnenschein N.&R.] (Pat.)
Schwartz, Alison Talbert ....'74 '99 C&L.339 B.A., J.D. [Ⓐ Novack&M.]
Schwartz, Allen D., (AV) ....'28 '52 C&L.597 B.S.L., LL.B. [Robbins,S.N.L.&T.] ‡
Schwartz, Allen N., (AV) ....'59 '84 C.339 B.A. L.146 J.D. [Kralovec,J.&S.]
Schwartz, Andrew R., (AV) ....'63 '88 C.477 A.B. L.424 J.D. [Sugar,F.&F.]
Schwartz, Arnold M. ....'38 '63 C.477 A.B. L.597 J.D. 111 N. Canal St.
Schwartz, Brian S. ....'— '00 C.608 B.A. L.851 J.D. [Ⓐ B.A.Gomberg&Assoc.]
Schwartz, Bryan I., (AV) ....'60 '86 C.260 B.S.B.A. L.365 J.D. [Levenfeld P.]
Schwartz, Chas. P., Jr. ....'27 '50 C.145 A.B. L.309 LL.B. 1501 N. State Pkwy.
Schwartz, Daniel J. ....'70 '95 C&L.597 B.S., J.D. [Jenner&B.]
Schwartz, David A. ....'69 '94 C&L.477 B.A., J.D. U.S. Dept. of Education
Schwartz, David E., (AV) ....'58 '83 C.340 B.A. L.209 J.D. [Kralovec,J.&S.]
Schwartz, David J. ....'72 '98 C.999 B.S. L.201 J.D. [Ⓐ Patzik,F.&S.]
Schwartz, David L. '70 '95 C.339 B.S. L.477 J.D.
[Wallenstein W.&R.] (See Pat. Sect.)
Schwartz, Donald ....'54 '79 C.880 B.S. L.910 J.D. [Arnold&K.]
Schwartz, Donald L., (AV) ....'— '74 C.429 B.A. L.145 J.D. [Latham&W.]
Schwartz, Edward W., (AV) ....'63 '90 C.597 B.S. L.339 J.D. [McGuirewoods]
Schwartz, Esther Joy, (AV) ....'56 '81 C.145 B.A. L.146 J.D. [Stellato&S.]
Schwartz, Francine J. '52 '77
C.118 B.A. L.904 J.D. 135 S. LaSalle St. (⊙Daytona Beach, FL)‡
Schwartz, Frederick L. ....'63 '90 C.188 B.S. L.494 J.D. [Littler M.]
Schwartz, Gary H. ....'51 '84 C.339 B.A. L.146 J.D. Asst. Atty. Gen.
Schwartz, Glenn A. '29 '55
C.597 A.B. L.174 J.D. Asst. Prof. of Law, John Marshall Law Sch.
Schwartz, Glenn P. ....'40 '64 C.999 B.A. L.597 J.D. The John Marshall Law Sch.
Schwartz, Harvey ....'29 '56 321 N. LaSalle St.
Schwartz, Jamie Brooke ....'72 '97 C.966 B.A. L.146 J.D. [Ⓐ FagelHaber]
Schwartz, Jamie L. ....'72 '97 C.999 B.A. L.209 J.D. [Ⓐ Riordan,D.L.&M.]
Schwartz, Jeffrey M., (AV) ....'67 '92 C&L.339 B.S., J.D. [Gardner C.&D.]
Schwartz, John B., (AV) ....'39 '66 C.597 B.A. L.209 J.D. [J.B.Schwartz&Assoc.]
Schwartz, John D. ....'25 '50 C&L.145 Ph.B., J.D. U.S. Bkrptcy. J.
Schwartz, Justin K. ....'— '99 C.674 A.B. L.608 J.D. [Ⓐ Kirkland&E.]
Schwartz, Krista S. ....'— '96 C.339 B.S. L.146 J.D. [Ⓐ Jones D.] (See Pat. Sect.)
Schwartz, L. Bradley ....'66 '92 C.378 B.S. L.365 J.D. [Mordini&S.]
Schwartz, Marc H. ....'53 '79 C.339 B.A. L.146 J.D. [Laser,P.S.F.&E.]
Schwartz, Mark A. ....'72 '99 C.112 B.A. L.477 J.D. [Ⓐ Butler R.S.&B.]
Schwartz, Marty J., (AV) ....'54 '79 C.976 B.A. L.904 J.D. [M.J.Schwartz]
Schwartz, Michael L. '58 '83
C.37 B.S.B.A. L.597 J.D. V.P., Schwartz Insurance Servs. Inc.
Schwartz, Michael N. ....'64 '90 C.174 B.A. L.767 J.D. S & S Home Builders, Inc.
Schwartz, Robert S. ....'65 '91 C&L.339 B.A., J.D. [Shapiro&S.]
Schwartz, Ronald B. ....'55 '80 C.339 B.A. L.146 J.D. [Katz,F.E.E.&J.]
Schwartz, Stanley D. ....'48 '79 C.912 B.S. L.1187 J.D. 10 S. La Salle St., Ste. 3300
Schwartz, Steven ....'52 '77 C.339 B.S. L.597 J.D. [Much S.F.D.A.&R.]
Schwartz, Stuart R., (AV) ....'49 '73 C.659 B.A. L.597 J.D. Fleet Business Credit Corp.‡
Schwartz, Susan J., (AV) ....'56 '80 C.276 B.S.F.S. L.424 J.D. [Corboy&D.]
Schwartz, William S. ....'65 '90 C.339 B.A. L.146 J.D. [Levenfeld P.] ⊙

Schwartz Cooper Chartered, (AV)
180 North La Salle Street Suite 2700, 60601
Telephone: 312-346-1300 Telecopier: 312-782-8416
Email: postmaster@schwartzcooper.com URL: http://www.schwartzcooper.com
Dennis R. Ainger; Charles M. Baum; Richard M. Bendix, Jr.; Jay S. Berlinsky; Mark B. Butterman; Carmen D. Caruso; John L. Conlon; Andrew H. Connor; Edward A. Cooper (1897-1977); Derek L. Cottier; C. Elizabeth Darke (Not admitted in IL); Robert G. Davidson; Joan M. Eagle; Richard J. Firfer; Steven H. Gistenson; Robert Dunn Glick; Ronald B. Grais (Administrative Managing Partner); Michael B. Gray; Ernest Greenberger (1923-2001); Stephen S. Herseth; William M. Holzman; Andrew W. Kim; Ira S. Kolb (1908-1988); Daniel J. Kopp; Hyman J. Krauss (1922-1977); Michael S. Kurtzon; Scott M. Lapins; Michael J. Legamaro; Sharon Zaban Letchinger; Robert C. Linton; Laura Ann Lipinski; Nancy R. Livingston; Joseph Q. McCoy; Stanton Miller; Robert D. Nachman; Neil T. Neumark; Jerrold M. Peven; Bret A. Rappaport; Richard T. Reibman; Eric S. Rein; Dina B. Ross; Michael D. Rothstein; Martin W. Salzman; Richard G. Schultz; Joseph H. Schwartz (1895-1971); Franklin S. Schwerin; Gary P. Segal; Robert A. Smoller; Patrick T. Stanton; Bryan R. Sup; Steven W. Swibel; Edward S. Weil; Thomas M. White;—Heather Aeschleman; Roberto Anguizola; David E. Beker; Magda Boyles; Christopher Cahill; B. Wayne Creel; Peter O. Farah; Jeremy Gottschalk; Robert Groholski; David Harpest; Heather L. Kramer; Aleen Lee; Dorothea J. Lidd; Robert M. Mellican; Arika J. Osacky; Irene M. Reed; Aaron N. Rice; Seth Mann Rosenberg; Bethany Schols; David Seidman; Diana Tsai; Shane T. Young. Of Counsel: Anne Kathryn Berg; Harry G. Comerford; Malcolm M. Gaynor; Mary Louise Haddad; Lloyd S. Kupferberg; Susan Meyer; Joseph R. Podlewski, Jr.

(This Listing Continued)

Schwartz Cooper Chartered (Continued)

Administrative and Regulatory, Banking, Corporate Finance, Corporate Law, Mergers and Acquisitions, Leveraged Buy-Outs, Private Equity and Venture Capital, Not-for-Profit Corporations, Bankruptcy, Creditors' Rights, Reorganizations, Workouts, Commodities, Employment Law, Estate Planning and Administration, Probate, Elder Law, Employee Benefits and Executive Compensation, Wealth Managment, Federal and State Tax, Commercial Litigation, White Collar Defense, Professional Liability, Appellate Law, Alternative Dispute Resolution, Asset Recovery, Franchise Law, Environmental Law, Real Estate, Condominiums, Leasing, Affordable Housing, Secured Transactions, Securities, Technology and Intellectual Property, Trademarks, Copyrights, Trade Secrets.

See Professional Biographies, CHICAGO, ILLINOIS

Schwartz, Cooper, Kolb & Gaynor
(See Schwartz Cooper Chartered)

Schwartz, John B., & Associates, (AV) BB
Suite 408, Thirty-Nine South La Salle Street, 60603
Telephone: 312-332-1586 Fax: 312-332-7009
Email: JBSLAWOFF@aol.com
John B. Schwartz. Associate: David J. Spira.
Civil Litigation Practice including Plaintiffs Personal Injury Litigation, Negligence, Medical and Professional Malpractice, Premises Liability, Wrongful Death Law, Vehicular Accident Law and Civil Appeals.

See Professional Biographies, CHICAGO, ILLINOIS

Schwartz, Marty J., P.C., (AV)
Three First National Plaza, Suite 3700, 60602
Telephone: 312-558-4293 Fax: 312-558-7750
Email: sosueme@savaho.com URL: http://www.savaho.com
Marty J. Schwartz.
Business Litigation, Commercial Litigation, Construction Litigation, Employment Litigation, Real Estate Litigation.

See Professional Biographies, CHICAGO, ILLINOIS

Schwartzberg, Hugh J., (AV) .... '33 '56 C.309 A.B. L.976 J.D. [Schwartzberg,B.&C.]
Schwartzberg, Barnett & Cohen, (AV) .... 111 West Washington Street, Suite 820
Schwarz, Jeffrey C. ....'64 '92 C.350 B.B.A. L.930 J.D. [McDermott W.&E.]
Schwarz, Mark L. ....'48 '73 C.209 B.S. L.146 J.D. 5097 N. Elston Avenue, Suite 304
Schwarz, Robert J. ....'31 '57 C.46 B.S. L.209 J.D. 3 1st National Plz. (Pat.)
Schwarzbach, Marshall J., (BV) ....'26 '52 C.339 L.365 J.D. 25 E. Wash. St.
Schwechter, Arnold ....'10 '36 L.209 LL.B. 1110 Lake Shore Dr., 28th Fl.‡
Schweikart, Scott J. ....'77 '04 C.910 B.A. L.930 J.D. Hispanic Legal Ctr.
Schwenn, Kelee J. .... '67 '95 C.597 B.S. L.146 J.D. [Ⓐ Pedersen&H.]
Schwerin, Franklin S., (AV) ....'39 '64 C.347 A.B. L.309 LL.B. [Schwartz C.]
Schwertfeger, Timothy R. '49 '74
C.597 B.A. L.276 J.D. Chmn. & CEO, John Nuveen & Co.
Schwimmer, Robert I. .... '48 '74 C.30 B.S. L.209 J.D. [Greenberg T.]
Schwob, Amanda A. ....'— '01 C.1061 B.S. L.339 J.D. [Fox,H.S.L.&C.]
Schy, David A. ....'51 '78 C.339 B.A. L.146 J.D. Hyatt Legal Servs.
Sciaccotta, John C., (AV) .... '62 '87 C.190 B.S.B.A. L.209 J.D. [Shefsky&F.]
Scimeca, Colleen M. '— '92 C.388 B.A. L.209 J.D.
Atty/Legal Consultant, Huron Consulting Group
Scinto, Shelly A. ....'— '93 C.234 B.A. L.146 J.D. [Ⓐ Chapman&C.]
Sciortino, Richard J. ....'57 '83 C.184 B.S. L.861 J.D. The Habitat Co.‡
Scofield, Douglas W. ....'52 '77 C.801 B.S. L.339 J.D. 6650 N. Northwest Hwy., Ste. 207
Scogland, William L., (AV) ....'49 '75 C.57 B.A. L.309 J.D. [Jenner&B.]
Scolaro, Cindy Anne .... '70 '00 C.1172 B.A. L.146 J.D. [Ⓐ Karchmar&S.]

Scopelitis, Garvin, Light & Hanson, P.C., (AV)
30 West Monroe Street, Suite 600, 60603-2427 ⊙
Telephone: 312-422-1200 FAX: 312-422-1224
Email: chicago@scopelitis.com URL: http://www.scopelitis.com
Gerald F. Cooper, Jr.; William D. Brejcha; Victor P. Shane; Leonard R. Kofkin; Donald J. Vogel; Robert J. Henry. Of Counsel: Robert C. Rubin; Maria Elena Portela; Donald W. Devitt; Sara L. Pettinger; John S. Magiera; James D. Ellman; Adam C. Smedstad; Phillip J. Johnson.
General Civil Practice. Litigation in all State and Federal Courts, including Appellate Practice, Transportation, Motor Carrier, Corporate, Administrative, Antitrust and Trade Regulation, Business, Insurance Defense, Negligence, Labor and Employment, Environmental, Workers Compensation, Probate and Estate Planning and Public Utility Law.
Indianapolis, Indiana Office: 10 West Market Street, Suite 1500, 46204-2968. Telephone: 312-637-1777. Fax: 317-687-2414.
Washington, D.C. Office: 1850 M Street, N.W., Suite 280, 20036-5804. Telephone: 202-783-9222. Fax: 202-783-9230.
Kansas City, Missouri Office: Two Pershing Square, 2300 Main Street, Suite 900, 64108. Telephone: 816-279-9835. Fax: 816-279-1973.
Pasadena, California Office: 790 East Colorado Boulevard, 9th Floor, 91101. Telephone: 626-795-4700. Fax: 626-795-4790.

See Professional Biographies, CHICAGO, ILLINOIS

Scordino, Lawrence A., (BV) '49 '75
C.1044 B.A. L.365 J.D. 111 E. Wacker Dr., Ste. 2622
Scordino, Michael A. ....'58 '88 C.93 B.S. L.818 J.D. V.P. & Gen. Coun., One-USA, Inc.
Scot, Risa Renee ....'74 '99 C.338 B.A. L.705 J.D. State's Atty. Off.
Scotellaro, John P. ....'43 '68 C.436 B.A. L.569 J.D. [Bell,B.&L.]
Scotillo, Anthony J. ....'30 '57 C&L.209 B.S., J.D. Cir. J.
Scott, Allison ....'79 '04 C.339 B.S. L.347 J.D. [Ⓐ Segal M.S.&M.]
Scott, Ami G. ....'— '99 C.608 B.S.B.A. L.477 J.D. [Mayer,B.R.&M.]
Scott, Andrew P. ....'66 '96 C.860 B.A. L.146 J.D. [DLPiper R.G.C.U.]
Scott, Anne O'Laughlin ....'48 '74 C.174 B.A. L.365 J.D. Ret. Assoc. Cir. J.
Scott, Cynthia L. ....'47 '82 C.611 B.A. L.46 J.D. [Ⓐ Kegan&K.]
Scott, David C. ....'— '03 C.473 B.A. L.145 J.D. [Ⓐ Schiff H.]
Scott, Drew J. ....'60 '86 C&L.339 B.S. in B.A., J.D. [Scott&K.]
Scott, Jared M. ....'76 '01 C.339 B.A. L.365 J.D. [Ⓐ Johnson&B.]
Scott, Lisa, Law Offices of, (AV) ....'59 '86 C.881 A.B. L.930 J.D. P.O. Box 2286
Scott, Mary Kay, (AV) ....'59 '84 C&L.339 B.A., J.D. [Brenner,F.M.&S.]
Scott, Robert K. ....'— '82 C.801 B.A. L.209 J.D. [Scott,H.&B.]
Scott, Ronald E. ....'73 '01 C.339 B.S. L.365 J.D. [Ⓐ Johnson&B.]
Scott, Sally J. ....'64 '90 C.114 B.A. L.477 J.D. [Franczek S.]
Scott, Sean T. ....'— '00 C.910 B.A. L.602 J.D. [Ⓐ Mayer,B.R.&M.]
Scott, Steven J. ....'74 '99 C.114 B.A. L.879 J.D. [Ⓐ Connelly R.&M.]
Scott, Teddy C. ....'66 '00 C.845 B.S. L.597 J.D. [Ⓐ Howrey] (Pat.)
Scott, Theodore R., (AV) ....'24 '50 C&L.339 A.B., J.D. [Ⓒ Rockey,M.&K.] (Pat.)‡
Scott, Timothy A. ....'70 '97 C.388 B.A. L.146 J.D. [Hagens B.S.S.]
Scott, Zaldwaynaka L., (AV) ....'58 '83 C.339 B.S. L.1119 J.D. [Mayer,B.R.&M.]

Scott, Halsted & Babetch, P.C.
117 N. Jefferson Street, Suite 205, 60661
Telephone: 312-463-1045 Fax: 312-463-1046
Email: info@shblaw.net URL: http://www.shblaw.net
Robert K. Scott; Kellie S. Halsted; Daniel I. Babetch;—Mark R. Sandri.
Civil Litigation, Trials, Defense Litigation, Appeals, Personal Injury, Automobile, Premises Liability, Uninsured, Underinsured Motorists, Negligence, Strict Liability Law, Construction, Commercial and Insurance Law.

See Professional Biographies, CHICAGO, ILLINOIS

Scott & Kraus, LLC, (BV)
150 South Wacker Drive, Suite 2900, 60606
Telephone: 312-327-1050 Fax: 312-327-1051
URL: http://www.lawyers.com/skcounsel
Drew J. Scott; Eugene S. Kraus; Thomas P. Egan;—Miles V. Cohen; Sonia S. Kinra; Jason R. Sleezer; Svenerik Nilsen; James M. McArdle.
Litigation, Corporate, Public Finance, Municipal Bonds, Commercial Litigation, Secured Lending, Real Estate and Health Care Law, General Business Practice.

See Professional Biographies, CHICAGO, ILLINOIS

Scotti, Michael J., III, (BV) .... '— '91 C.317 B.A. L.862 J.D. [Freeborn&P.]
Scoville, Joseph .... '09 '34 L.209 LL.B. 39 S. LaSalle St.
Scranton, Kenneth E., Ltd., (AV) .... '15 '41 C&L.597 B.A., J.D. 134 N. La Salle St.
Scremin, Robert C., (CVⓉ) ....'64 '98 C.1111 B.A. L.793 J.D. [Ⓐ Kane&F.]
Scriven-Young, David J. ....'78 '03 C.436 B.A. L.209 J.D. [Ⓐ McDermott W.&E.]
Scrivner, Anne C. ....'63 '88 C.207 B.A. L.910 J.D. Asst. States Atty.
Scruggs, Lisa T. .... '71 '98 C.276 B.A. L.145 J.D. [Ⓐ Jenner&B.]
Scruton, Michele P. '58 '84 C.976 B.A. L.273 J.D.
(adm. in NY; not adm. in IL) V.P. & Sr. Coun., Diners Club Intl. Ltd.
Scullen, Anne M. .... '72 '97 C.477 B.A. L.209 J.D. Law Clk., Appl. Ct.
Scully, J. Page ....'76 '03 C.797 B.A. L.469 J.D. [Ⓐ McDermott W.&E.]
Scully, Michael J. .... '75 '02 C.209 B.S. L.365 J.D. 200 N. LaSalle St., Ste. 2850
Scully, Patrice ....'49 '77 C.801 B.A. L.209 J.D. Asst. Reg. Coun., U.S. Customs Serv.
Scully, Thomas J., III, (BVⓉ) '45 '73 C.831 B.A. L.1292 J.D.
[T.J.Scully,III&Assoc.] ⊙

Scully, Thomas J., III, & Associates, Law Offices of, (BVⓉ)
53 West Jackson, Suite 523, 60604 ⊙
Telephone: 800-628-1934 Fax: 219-836-5514
Email: tscully506@aol.com URL: http://www.scullydisabilitylaw.com
Thomas J. Scully, III;—Veda Praveen Dasari.
Practice limited to the area of Social Security Disability.
Munster, Indiana Office: 506 Ridge Road, 46321. Telephone: 219-836-1380. Fax: 219-836-5514.
Chesterton, Indiana Office: 372 Indian Boundary Road, 46304. Telephone: 800-628-1934. Fax: 219-836-5514.

See Professional Biographies, CHICAGO, ILLINOIS

Seaberry, James J., Jr., (AV) .... '53 '78 C.339 B.A. L.569 J.D. [Ⓐ D.T.Schoen]
Seabright, David W. ....'65 '93 C.429 B.S. L.424 J.D. 221 N. LaSalle, Ste. 2500
Seagle, Catherine A. '62 '88 C&L.424 B.A., J.D.
Asst. Reg. Coun., U.S. Soc. Sec. Admn.
Seal, Paul-Eric, (BV) ....'62 '88 C&L.424 A.B., J.D. [Ⓐ Knell&P.]
Seaman, Scott M., (AV) ....'62 '87 C.991 B.A. L.424 J.D. [Meckler B.&T.]
Sears, Roy W., (AV) ....'33 '61 C&L.597 B.S., J.D. [Ⓒ Eckhart K.]
Sears Coder, Sally K. ....'74 '99 C.475 B.A. L.477 J.D. [Ⓐ Jenner&B.]
Sebastian, John E. ....'68 '95 C.679 B.S. L.589 J.D. [Hinshaw&C.]
Seberger, Donald P. ....'52 '80 C&L.879 B.A., J.D. Pechiney Servs. America
Secaras, Harry J., (AV) ....'63 '89 C&L.339 B.A., J.D. [Neal,G.&E.]
Secco, Nicholas Joseph ....'— '01 C.420 B.A. L.597 J.D. [Ⓐ Kirkland&E.]
Sechen, Glenn C., (AV) ...... '47 '74 C.679 B.S.E.E. L.365 J.D. [Schain,B.R.&C.] (Pat.)
Seder, Anna Eisner .... '74 '01 C.339 B.A. L.276 J.D. [Ⓐ Schopf&W.]

Sedgwick, Detert, Moran & Arnold LLP, (AV)
One North Wacker Drive Suite 4200, 60606-2841 ⊙
Telephone: 312-641-9050 Fax: 312-641-9530
Email: E-Mail@SDMA.com URL: http://www.sdma.com
Partners: Anthony J. Anscombe; Erica Lewis Battaglia; Thomas A. Brusstar; Richard J. Geddes; Kirk C. Jenkins (Certified Specialist, Appellate Law, The State Bar of California Board of Legal Specialization); Eric C. Scheiner; Evan T. Smith; Fred A. Smith III; James D. Wangelin. Special Counsel: Carol J. Gerner; Renee S. Levitt; Michael B. Satz; David K. Subramanian. Associates: Scott D. Braun; Jennifer Quinn Broda; Melanie M. Brown; Jenna L. Buda; Nicholas D. Butovich; Elizabeth J. Cotter; Gary L. Gassman; David M. Goldhaber; C. Kinnier Lastimosa; James M. Pinkstaff; Peter J. Preston; Samuel B. Rainey; Ian N. Rothenberg; M. Miles Sukovic; Kristine Tejano; Frank E. Valenti.
Advertising and Marketing, Agency and Distributorships, Agricultural Law, Alternative Dispute Resolution, Antitrust and Trade Regulation, Appellate Practice, Aviation and Aerospace, Bankruptcy, Banks and Banking, Business Law, Class Actions, Collections, Commercial Law, Commercial Real Estate, Communications and Media, Complex and Multi-District Litigation, Computers and Software, Construction Law, Consumer Law, Contracts, Copyrights, Corporate Law, Debtor and Creditor, Disabilities, Education Law, Employee Benefits, Entertainment and the Arts, Environmental Law, Equipment Finance and Leasing, Fidelity and Surety, Franchises and Franchising, Fraud and Deceit, Health Care, Hospital Law, Insurance, Insurance Defense, Intellectual Property, International Law, Labor and Employment, Leases and Leasing, Legal Ethics and Professional Responsibility, Libel, Slander and Defamation, Litigation, Media Law, Medical Practice, Natural Resources, Negligence, Patents, Personal Injury, Premises Liability, Privacy Law, Products Liability, Professional Liability, Real Estate, Regulatory Law, RICO, Securities, Technology and Science, Torts, Toxic Torts, Trade Secrets, Trademarks, Transportation, Unfair Competition, Zoning, Planning and Land Use.
Dallas, Texas Office: 1717 Main Street, Suite 5400. Telephone: 469-227-8200. Fax: 469-227-8004.
Irvine, California Office: 3 Park Plaza, 17th Floor. Telephone: 949-852-8200. Fax: 949-852-8282.
London, England Office: Candlewick House, 120 Cannon Street, EC4N 6LR. Telephone: +011-44-20-7929-1829. Fax: +011-44-20-7929-1808. Telex: 927037.
Los Angeles, California Office: 801 South Figueroa Street, 18th Floor. Telephone: 213-426-6900. Fax: 213-426-6921.
Newark, New Jersey Office: Three Gateway Center, 12th Floor. Telephone: 973-242-0002. Fax: 973-242-8099.
New York, New York Office: 125 Broad Street, 39th Floor. Telephone: 212-422-0202. Fax: 212-422-0925.
Paris, France Office: 104 Avenue Kléber, 75116. Telephone/Fax: 011-33-1-4704-5502.
San Francisco, California Office: One Market Plaza, Steuart Tower, 8th Floor. Telephone: 415-781-7900. Cabel Address: "Sedma". Fax: 415-781-2635.
Zurich, Switzerland Office: Spluegenstrasse 3, CH-8002. Telephone: +011-411-201-1730. Fax: +011-411-201-4404.

See Professional Biographies, CHICAGO, ILLINOIS

Sedlak, Brian L. ....'— '93 C.1183 B.A. L.146 J.D. [Jones D.]
Seeder, Marshall, (AV) ....'— '80 C.145 A.B. L.146 J.D. [Sachnoff&W.]
Seeger, Kristen R. ....'— '02 C.937 B.A. L.145 J.D. [Ⓐ Sidley A.B.&W.]
Seeger, Steven C. ....'— '97 C.937 B.A. L.477 J.D. [Kirkland&E.]
Seelbach, Kyle P. ....'— '04 C&L.339 B.A., J.D. [Ⓐ Kirkland&E.]
Seely, John J. '55 '80 C&L.424 B.A., J.D.
Sr. V.P., Gen. Coun. & Secy., Newly Weds Foods, Inc.
Seery, David ....'60 '85 C&L.597 B.S., B.A., J.D. Corp. Coun.
Seftenberg, Stephen L. '35 '59 C&L.309 A.B., LL.B.
[Ⓒ A.H.Hammerman] (⊙West Palm Beach, FL)
Sefton, Beau C. ....'74 '99 C.473 B.A. L.309 J.D. [Ⓐ Wildman,H.A.&D.]
Sefton, Michael D. ....'73 '99 C.112 B.A. L.209 J.D. [Ⓐ Henderson&L.]

Segal, Alan F. '45 '70 C.276 B.S.B.A. L.145 J.D.
29 S. La Salle Street, Suite 334, 60603
Telephone: 312-444-1700 Fax: 312-444-1766
Email: asegal@megsinet.net URL: http://www.asegal.com
Taxation, Individual Taxation, Business Taxation, Tax Audits, Employment Tax, Appellate Practice, Tax Law.

See Professional Biographies, CHICAGO, ILLINOIS

Segal, Bryan ....'67 '94 C.339 A.B. L.597 J.D. [Barack F.K.P.&N.]
Segal, Cheryl L. ....'— '88 C&L.597 B.A., J.D. [Hogan M.]

Segal, Diana R. '39 '69 C.112 B.A. L.966 J.D.
(adm. in WI; not adm. in IL) 2142 N. Sedgwick‡
Segal, Donald, (AV) ... '38 '63 C.966 B.S. L.145 J.D. [Segal M.S.&M.]
Segal, Donald W. ... '27 '52 C.339 B.S. L.597 J.D. [Segal&S.]
Segal, Elmer R. ... '21 '49 C.260 L.146 LL.B.,J.D 55 W. Monroe St.
Segal, Gary P. ... '69 '95 C&L.339 B.A., J.D. [Schwartz C.]
Segal, Marshall B., Law Office ... '40 '66 C.112 B.A. L.1066 J.D. 2142 N. Sedgwick
Segal, Marshall D. ... '22 '52 C.339 B.S. L.597 LL.B. [Segal&S.]
Segal, Robert D., (BV) ... '61 '86 C.659 B.A. L.831 J.D. [Davis F.Z.K.M.M.&R.]

Segal McCambridge Singer & Mahoney, Ltd., (AV)
One IBM Plaza, Suite 200 330 North Wabash, 60611 ⊙
Telephone: 312-645-7800 Facsimile: 312-645-7711
URL: http://www.smsm.com
Partners: Donald Segal; Edward J. McCambridge; William F. Mahoney; Gregory E. Rogus; Phillip Mark Crane; Robert E. O'Malley; Paul E. Wojcicki; Timothy L. Krippner; Steven A. Hart; Kathleen McDonough; John J. Kohnke; Jason L. Kennedy. Senior Counsel: Jeffrey Singer. Associates: Christy J. Benton; Nicholas A. Caputo; Amina S. Choudhry; John L. Dillenbeck; Brian H. Eldridge; Bernard Gawne, III; Catherine E. Boyd Goldhaber; Keith J. Hays (Not admitted in IL); Scott W. Henry; Micah R. Inlow; Adam Jagadich; Kimberly Alina Kayiwa; Scott L. Kellogg; Tara K. Kennedy; Chad J. Layton; Robert John McLaughlin; Gregory M. McMahon; Maria Menotti; Karen Rheingans; Allison Scott; Katherine L. Sleeker; Holly R. Stevens; Ben M. Swallow; J. Yasmin Tayyab; Cameron D. Turner; Scott J. Vold; Alexis K. Weed.
Product Liability, Toxic Torts, General Insurance Defense, General Liability, Medical Malpractice, Professional Liability, Commercial Litigiation, Coverage Issues, Municipal Liability, Law Enforcement Liability, Construction Litigation, Premises Liability, Employment Discrimination, Civil Rights, Automobile.
Brighton, Michigan Office: 7960 Grand River Ave., Suite 260, 48114. Telephone: 810-225-4227. Facsimile: 810-225-4201.
Austin, Texas Office: 100 Congress Avenue, Suite 700, 78701. Telephone: 512-476-7834. Facsimile: 512-476-7832.
Philadelphia, Pennsylvania Office: United Plaza 30 S. 17th Street, Suite #1700, 19103. Telephone: 215-972-8015. Fascimile: 215-972-8016.
Princeton, New Jersey Office: 103 Carnegie Center, Suite 103, 08540. Telephone: 609-452-1558. Facsimile: 609-452-1559.
Baltimore, Maryland Office: 217 Redwood Street, 21st Floor, 21202. Telephone: 410-779-3960. Fax: 410-779-3967.
New York, New York Office: 830 Third Avenue, Suite 400, 10022. Telephone: 212-651-7500. Fax: 212-651-7499.
See Professional Biographies, CHICAGO, ILLINOIS

Segal & Segal ... 77 W. Wash. St.
Segall, Michael B. ... '— '01 C.1365 B.A. L.569 J.D. 10 S. Dearborn St.
Segel, Donald H. ... '47 '73 C.339 B.A. L.365 J.D. 200 North LaSalle Street, Suite 2675
Segler, Judith M. ... '58 '83 C.338 B.S. L.1119 J.D. [A Keating&S.]
Segrest, Philip D., Jr. '67 '92 C&L.16 B.S., J.D.
[© Welsh&K.] (See Pat. Sect.) (⊙Tallassee, AL)
Seham Seham Meltz & Petersen, LLP, (AV)
33 North LaSalle, Suite 2222 (⊙Bloomington, MN; New York, White Plains, NY; Hous., TX; Mercer Island, WA)
Sehr, Michael J., (AV) '50 '77 C.424 B.A. L.339 J.D.
Sr. V.P. & Dep. Gen. Coun., CNA
Seibel, John N., (AV) ... '52 '78 C.475 B.S. L.215 J.D. [Cassiday,S.&G.]
Seiber, Andrew C. ... '— '97 C.339 B.A. L.365 J.D. [A O'Hagan,S.&A.]
Seidel, W. Michael ... '53 '78 C.602 B.A. L.339 J.D. [Defrees&F.]
Seiden, Glenn ... '47 '74 C.1016 B.S.B.A. L.365 J.D. [Azulay,H.&S.]
Seidenfeld, Glenn K., (AV) ... '14 '38 C.393 B.A. L.477 J.D. 1 IBM Plaza
Seidler, Marc, (AV) ... '— '73 C&L.145 B.A., J.D. [© DLPiper R.G.C.U.]
Seidler, Sharon Y. '44 '73 C&L.209 B.A., J.D.
(adm. in FL; not adm. in IL) V.P., Creative Research Assocs.
Seidman, A. Jeffrey, (AV) ... '46 '74 C.679 B.S. L.146 J.D. [Cassiday,S.&G.]
Seidman, David ... '72 '97 C.659 B.A. L.910 J.D. [A Schwartz C.]
Seidman, Rachel E. ... '58 '87 C.339 B.S. L.588 J.D. Ct. Facilitator
Seidman, Steven J., (BV) ... '56 '81 C.339 B.S. L.209 J.D. [Seidman]

Seidman Law Offices, (BV)
20 S. Clark Street, Suite 700, 60602
Telephone: 312-781-1977 Fax: 312-853-2187
URL: http://www.seidmanlawoffices.com
Members of Firm: Steven J. Seidman; Sean M. Baker; Ryan A. Margulis.
Insurance Defense; Corporate Litigation; Workers Compensation.
See Professional Biographies, CHICAGO, ILLINOIS

Seieroe, Warren C. ... '22 '50 L.508 LL.B. 227 W. Monroe St.
Seifert, Bryan M. ... '75 '03 C.46 B.Arch. L.146 J.D. [A Leo&W.]
Seifert, Elana K. ... '— '98 C.705 B.A. L.424 J.D. [A O'Hagan,S.&A.]
Seifman, Jeffrey, (P.C.) ... '— '92 C&L.477 B.A., J.D. [Kirkland&E.] (Pat.)
Seifman, Michelle G. '69 '95 C.477 B.A. L.146 J.D.
Dir., Annual Giving, Chicago-Kent Coll. of Law, Illinois Institute of Tech.
Seiler, Vanessa E. ... '74 '99 C.221 B.A. L.146 J.D. [A Latimer L.J.]
Seilheimer, Lisa K. ... '74 '99 C.339 B.A. L.273 J.D. [A Winston&S.]
Seimetz, Karen G. ... '53 '85 C&L.339 B.S., J.D. Chf. Asst. Corp. Coun.
Seitz, William J. ... '61 '86 C.339 B.S. L.424 J.D. [Fisk K.K.&R.]
Seiwert, Lawrence P., (BV) ... '48 '73 C&L.209 B.A., J.D. [L.Seiwert]
Seiwert, Lawrence, Law Office of, (BV) ... 33 N. La Salle St., Ste. 2600
Selan, Steven M., Law Office, (BV) '47 '73 C&L.209 B.A., J.D.
11 S. LaSalle, Ste. 2301
Selander, Larry, (AV) ... '46 '72 C.602 B.S.Ch.Eng. L.339 J.D. [Duane M.]
Selby, Terence R., (AV) ... '— '86 C.999 M.E. L.209 J.D. [Prusik S.D.&K.]
Selden, Lynde, III ... '72 '00 C.112 B.A. L.1049 J.D. [A Cassiday,S.&G.]
Select Legal, P.C. ... 53 West Jackson Boulevard, Suite 1520
Selig, David B., (AV) ... '41 '66 C.339 B.S. L.597 J.D. [Sussman,S.&S.]
Selig, Michelle L. ... '73 '99 C.188 B.S. L.273 J.D. [A Gould&R.]
Selig, Randal J. ... '56 '81 C.347 B.A. L.273 J.D. [DLPiper R.G.C.U.]
Seliga, Joseph ... '72 '00 C.276 A.B. L.597 J.D. [A Mayer,B.R.&M.]
Seliger, Stephen G., (AV) ... '44 '69 C.659 B.A. L.597 J.D. [Seliger&E.]
Seliger & Elkin, Ltd., (AV) ... 155 North Michigan Avenue, Suite 500
Seligman, David R. ... '— '96 C.197 A.B. L.472 J.D. [Kirkland&E.]
Selin, Audrey E., (AV) ... '52 '77 C.339 B.S. L.424 J.D. [Neal,G.&E.]
Sell, Jeffrey Scott ... '69 '95 C.98 B.A. L.339 J.D. [A A.W.Levenfeld&Assoc.]
Sell, Robert J. ... '65 '90 C.337 B.A. L.597 J.D. [Seyfarth S.]
Sellstrom, Dawn E. ... '66 '93 C.597 B.A. L.424 J.D. [© Seyfarth S.]
Sellstrom, Joy ... '58 '84 C.260 B.S. L.424 J.D. [© Seyfarth S.]
Selman, Russell B., (AV) ... '54 '80 C.1275 B.A. L.910 J.D. [Katten M.R.]
Selmer, David R., (AV) ... '53 '78 C.932 B.A. L.477 J.D. [Barack F.K.P.&N.]
Seltzer, Robert A. ... '53 '92 C.966 B.A. L.477 J.D. [Cornfield&F.]
Seltzer, Wendy L. ... *'— '01 C.882 B.A. L.665 J.D. [A Gardner C.&D.]*
Semenek, Scott A., (AV) ... '67 '92 C.966 B.B.A. L.597 J.D. [© Wildman,H.A.&D.]
Semer, Barry E., Law Office of, (AV) '39 '64
C.339 B.S. L.365 J.D. 30 North LaSalle Street, Suite 2040
Semerling, Joseph A. ... '48 '80 C.339 B.A. L.365 J.D. 3805 N. Lincoln Ave.
Semmelhack, Charles A. ... '60 '85 C.597 B.A. L.966 J.D. [Defrees&F.]
Semple, John M. ... '36 '63 C&L.424 B.S., J.D. 3200 N. Lake Shore Dr.‡
Semrad, Robert James, Jr. ... '68 '94 C.493 B.A. L.209 J.D. 53 W. Jackson Blvd.
Senak, Mark N. ... '61 '87 C.347 B.A. L.209 J.D. [Salvi,S.&P.]
Sender, Jennifer M., (BV) ... '66 '91 C.589 B.A. L.424 J.D. [Hinshaw&C.]
Senderowitz, Stephen J., (AV) ... '49 '74 C&L.597 B.A., J.D. [Winston&S.]
Sendziak, Steven J., Jr. ... '28 '57 C.339 B.S. L.365 LL.B. 6108 S. Archer Ave.
Sener, Martin C. ... '59 '84 C.597 B.S. L.365 J.D. [Clausen M.]
Seng, Michael P. ... '42 '67 C&L.602 B.A., LL.B. Prof., John Marshall Law Sch.
Senica, John L. ... '60 '85 C.602 B.A. L.597 J.D. [McGuirewoods]
Senner, Gary, (AV) ... '42 '68 C.966 B.A. L.597 J.D. [Sonnenschein N.&R.]
Sennet, Charles J. '52 '79 C.188 A.B. L.273 J.D.
Sr. Coun./Broadcasting & Entertainment, Tribune Co.
Sennett, Michael, (AV) ... '51 '77 C.1082 A.B. L.424 J.D. [Bell,B.&L.]
Seno, John J., & Associates ... '51 '85 C.750 B.A. L.146 J.D. 5901 N. Cicero Avenue
Seplak, Mark J., (AV) ... '59 '85 C.209 B.S. L.589 J.D. [Meckler B.&T.]
Sepulveda, Cheryl L. ... '69 '95 C&L.339 B.A., J.D. Asst. Atty., City Bd. of Educ.
Serafini, Michael A. ... '— '01 C.201 B.S. L.477 J.D. [A Mayer,B.R.&M.]
Sered, Lynne O. ... '61 '87 C.347 B.A. L.209 J.D. Educ. Labor Rel. Bd.
Sergi, Vincent A. F., (P.C.), (AV) ... '46 '74 C.72 B.A. L.597 J.D. [Katten M.R.]
Sergienko, Gregory S. '58 '86 C&L.309 A.B., J.D.
(adm. in WA; not adm. in IL) Univ. of Chicago
Serkland, James C. ... '39 '66 C.182 B.A. L.146 J.D. [Serkland&M.]
Serkland, John C., & Associates, Law Offices of '71 '02
C.742 B.S. L.1000 J.D. 3245 W. Fullerton Avenue
Serkland & Muelhausen ... 55 W. Wacker Dr.
Sernel, Marcus E. ... '— '97 C.339 B.S.Ch.E. L.424 J.D. [Kirkland&E.]
Serota, Barry ... '48 '78 C.178 B.A. L.209 J.D. 3012 Jarvis
Serota, Sidney ... '24 '49 C.63 L.209 LL.B. 105 W. Madison St.
Serpe, Roger A. ... '50 '75 C.339 B.S. L.146 J.D. Indiana Harbor Belt Railroad Co.
Serpico, William D., (AV) ... '41 '66 C.966 B.S. L.209 LL.B. [Serpico,N.&N.]
Serpico, Novelle and Navigato, (AV) ... 61 West Superior
Serritella, James A., (AV) ... '42 '71 C.1044 B.A. L.145 J.D. [Burke,W.M.&S.]
Serritella, William D., (AV) ... '46 '71 C&L.339 B.A., J.D. [McGuirewoods]
Serritella, William J., Jr. ... '67 '92 C.750 B.A. L.209 J.D. [Aronberg G.D.&G.]
Server, Randall E., (AV) ... '51 '76 C.674 A.B. L.597 J.D. [© Tucker B.R.&M.]
Serwer, Alan M., (AV) ... '44 '69 C.477 B.A. L.597 J.D. [Bell,B.&L.]
Serwer, David M. ... '70 '96 C.477 B.A. L.146 J.D. [A Baker&M.]
Sessions, Barbara C. ... '— '86 C.477 B.A. L.209 J.D. [Winston&S.]
Sessions, Rex L. ... '59 '84 C.597 B.A. L.477 J.D. [Winston&S.]
Setren, Julie P. ... '78 '03 C.273 B.A. L.597 J.D. [A Katten M.R.]
Seurynck, Margaret M. ... '— '01 C.602 B.B.A. L.597 J.D. [A Jones D.]
Sevcik, Richard L., (AV) ... '60 '85 C.352 B.A. L.145 J.D. [Bell,B.&L.]
Severs, Emily S. ... '75 '01 C.966 B.S. L.597 J.D. 1530 S. State St., Ste. 717
Severson, Donald S. '27 '53 C.297 B.A. L.966 LL.B.
(adm. in WI; not adm. in IL) Borg-Warner Corp.
Severson, Sarah Kerr ... '72 '98 C.352 B.A. L.597 J.D. [McDermott W.&E.]
Sewell, Karen ... '79 '04 C.597 B.S. L.339 J.D. [A McGuirewoods]
Sexton, John Patrick '64 '90 C&L.602 B.A., J.D.
Asst. Gen. Coun., Chicago Board Options Exchange, Incorporated
Sexton, Michael F. ... '58 '83 C.357 B.A. L.339 J.D. [Dykema G.P.]
Sexton, Thomas W., III '63 '88
C&L.602 B.A., J.D. Asst. Gen. Coun., National Futures Assn.

Seyfarth Shaw LLP, (AV) BR
55 E. Monroe Street, Suite 4200, 60603-5803 ⊙
Telephone: 312-346-8000 Fax: 312-269-8869
Email: seyfarthshaw@seyfarth.com
Partners: John H. Anderson; David S. Baffa; James Baird; Edward W. Bergmann; Daniel M. Blouin; Michael E. Blount; Eric E. Boyd; Jerome F. Buch; J. Kelly Bufton; Scott A. Carlson; Philip V. Carter (Retired); Mark Casciari; Brent I. Clark; R. Theodore Clark, Jr.; Philip L. Comella; Theodore E. Cornell III; James L. Curtis; Douglas A. Darch; Gregory M. Davis; Christopher J. DeGroff; Thomas G. Dent; Joshua L. Ditelberg; Kenneth R. Dolin; Arthur Don; Gregg M. Dorman; William F. Dugan; Diane V. Dygert; Hillary A. Ebach; William J. Factor; William J. Fairbanks; Owen Fairweather (1913-1987); Jennifer Kelly Fardy; Brenda Hofman Feis; Michel J. Feldman; Ira Fierstein; Noah A. Finkel; Fredric H. Fischer; Robert P. Flanagan; Elizabeth Pfeiler Foley; James R. FortCamp; Elaine S. Fox; Paul E. Freehling; Jeffrey D. Friedman; Joan E. Gale; Christopher A. Garcia; Durward J. (James) Gehring; Raymond I. Geraldson (Retired); George H. Gerstman; Jay A. Gitles; William I. Goldberg; Beth T. Golub; Deborah C. Gordon; Adam Greetis; Geoffrey F. Grossman; Timothy F. Haley; Linda J. Haynes; Valerie J. Hoffman; Eugene Jacobs; Marc R. Jacobs; Jeffrey Jahns; Sheldon Leigh Jeter; Mark L. Johnson; Robert H. Joyce (Retired); Gary S. Kaplan; Joel H. Kaplan; Edward J. Karlin; Jeffrey C. Kauffman; Timothy J. Keefer; Raymond J. Kelly, Jr.; Mary Kay Klimesh; Ronald J. Kramer; Alvin L. Kruse; Andrew R. Laidlaw; Andrew F. Lampert; Daniel F. Lanciloti; Richard S. Lauter; Bart A. Lazar; Jill Leka; H. Debra Levin; Michael R. Levinson; Mark A. Lies, II; Steven R. Lifson; Ronald L. Lipinski; Bradford L. Livingston; Walter P. Loomis (Retired); Thomas D. Lupo; Richard M. Lyon (Retired); Gerald L. Maatman, Jr.; Martin P. Marta; Richard P. McArdle; Condon A. McGlothlen; Ellen E. McLaughlin; Kristin Edell Michaels; Robert J. Mignin; Peter C. Miller; Michael D. Miselman; Ian H. Morrison; Lawrence J. Moss; David L. Newman; Andrea Caplan Okun; Camille A. Olson; Jeryl Olson; John J. O'Malley; Richard D. Ostrow (Retired); Christopher E. Paetsch; Robert J. Paley; Gus A. Paloian; Gerald L. Pauling, II; Thomas H. Peckham; Andrew H. Perellis; Thomas J. Piskorski; J. Stephen Poor; John W. Powers; Roger L. Price; Michael J. Quinn; Allan J. Reich; Richard L. Reinish (P.C.); John E. Rogers; Burton X. Rosenberg; Jeffrey K. Ross; David J. Rowland; Joel D. Rubin; Carl L. Russo; Michael J. Rybicki; Nathaniel Sack; Suzanne L. Saxman; Jeffrey B. Schamis; Stephen L. Schar; John S. Schauer; Ray J. Schoonhoven (Retired); James A. Schraidt; Ronald Schreiber; William P. Schurgin; Robert J. Sell; Henry E. Seyfarth (1908-1991); Jeremy P. Sherman; Robert J. Smith, Jr.; Harold V. Stotland; Joseph S. Turner; Alan L. Unikel; Michael A. Warner; Robert F. Weber; David M. Weiner; John T. Weise (Retired); Michael D. Wexler; Hannah B. Widlus; Phillip Shawn Wood; Peter C. Woodford; Joseph E. Wyse (Retired); Sandra P. Zemm. Of Counsel: Glenn I. Becker; Paul S. Drizner; Ann E. Dustman (Not admitted in IL); Garrettson Ellis; Merrill A. Freed (Retired); Patricia L. Gillman; Cheryl L. Haack; Karen K. Harris; Yvette Heintzelman; Sidney J. Hess, Jr.; R. Thomas Howell, Jr.; Patricia L. Hubbard; Andi S. Kenney; Cynthia C. Mooney; David J. Pezza, Sr.; Keith A. Reed; Brian P. Roche; Walter Roth; Dawn E. Sellstrom; Joy Sellstrom; Gerald D. Skoning; Sheldon R. Stein; Joseph L. Stone; Paul H. Vishny. Associates: Stephan W. Addison; Alysa M. Barancik; Brian William Barrett; Frank A. Bear; Justin K. Beyer; Tracy M. Billows; Rebecca Pratt Bromet; Anne E. C. Brynn; Alyssa C. Burghardt; Scott T. Buser; Jessica E. Chmiel; James R. Cho; Sarah Norem Chomiak; Louis S. Chronowski Jr.; Michael A. Cox; Richard Cutshall; Joshua N. Dalley; Pamela Quigley Devata; Robert W. Diehl; Ada W. Dolph; W. Andrew Douglass; Anne Duprey; Molly Eastman; Kathleen M. Eggers; Sarah J. Golden; John A. Graham; Jason Greis; Amy L. Grider; Janessa M. Griffin; Bruce K. Haraguchi; Christopher S. Hermanson; Dana Hill; Patricia B. Hillier; Cory M. Hirsch; J. Scott Humphrey; Molly M. Joyce; David B. Kahng; Dina M. Kapernekas; Kristina M. Kerwin; Rachel Kindstrand; Jennifer A. Kraft; Joseph R. Lanser; Rafael E. Lazaro; Jeffrey H. Liebling; Noah G. Lipschultz; Kathryn A. Lloyd; Sara E. Lorber; Ameena Y. Majid; Emily M. Maki-Rusk; Michelle K. Mellinger; Alaya B. Meyers; Meagan Noel Newman (Not admitted in IL); Karen M. Osgood; Scott Paler (Not admitted in IL); Nicole K. Peracke; James J. Powers; Stephanie J. Pulcanio; Trisha M. Rachoy; Charles Sanford Riecke; Stacey L. Robinson; Douglas S. Rupert; Colette M. Savage; Scott A. Schaefers; Jaime Erin Schneider; Scott J. Smith; Amanda A. Sonneborn; Brian M. Stolzenbach; David L. Streck; Daniel W. Tarpey; Michael D. Thompson; Jason M. Torres; Annette Tyman; John M. Vande Walle; Tyler A. VanLonkhuyzen; Judith L. Wethall; Alison B. Willard; Lindsay Wolter; Winnie Wong; Jason K. Zachary; Patrick Zeller. Staff Attorneys: Melanie H. Berkowitz; James L. Flatley; Brian J. Hipp; Michael E. Romani.
Labor and Employment Law, Employee Benefits, Employment Discrimination, Employment-at-Will, Health Care, Occupational, Safety and Health, Worker's Compensation. Government Contracts. White-Collar Criminal. Litigation, Administrative Law, Business Contract Disputes, Construction, Corporations and Partnerships, General Tort, Insurance, Intellectual Property, Product Liability,

(This Listing Continued)

Seyfarth Shaw LLP (Continued)

Professional Liability, Securities and Commodities. Corporate, Acquisitions, Antitrust, Bankruptcy and Creditors' Rights, Commercial and Financial Transactions, Contracts, Divestitures, Joint Ventures, Mergers, Real Estate, Tax Law, Trust and Probate. Environmental, Safety and Toxic Torts.
Washington, D.C. Office: 815 Connecticut Avenue, N.W. Telephone: 202-463-2400. Facsimile: 202-828-5393.
Los Angeles, California Office: 2029 Century Park East. Telephone: 310-277-7200. Facsimile: 310-201-5219.
New York, N.Y. Office: 1270 Avenue of the Americas, Suite 2500. Telephone: 212-218-5500. Facsimile: 212-218-5526.
San Francisco, California Office: 560 Mission Street, Suite 3100. Telephone: 415-397-2823. Facsimile: 415-397-8549.
Sacramento, California Office: 400 Capitol Mall, Suite 2350. Telephone: 916-448-0159. Facsimile: 916-558-4839.
Houston, Texas Office: 700 Louisiana Street, Suite 3700. Telephone: 713-225-2300. Facsimile: 713-225-2340.
Atlanta, Georgia Office: 1545 Peachtree Street, N.E., One Peachtree Pointe, Suite 700. Telephone: 404-885-1500. Facsimile: 404-892-7056.
Boston, Massachusetts Office: Two Seaport Lane, Suite 300. Telephone: 617-946-4800. Facsimile: 617-946-4801.
Brussels, Belgium Office: Avenue Louise 500, Box 8. Telephone: (32) (2) 647. 60. 25. Fax: (32) (2) 640. 70. 71.

See Professional Biographies, CHICAGO, ILLINOIS

Seyferth, Horst R. .... '37 '66 C.339 B.A. L.209 LL.B. [H.R.Seyferth]
Seyferth, Horst R., Ltd .... 4001 N. Elston
Seymour, Julie K. ....'— '90 C.697 B.A. L.339 J.D. [Ungaretti&H.]
Seymour, Linda C. .... '51 '97 C.679 B.A. L.424 J.D. Resch. Atty., Cir. Ct.
Seyring, Gary W. .... '50 '78 C.589 B.S. L.1000 J.D. [Galvin,L.W.G.&S.]
Sezer, Lawrence K. ....'— '77 C.388 B.A. L.910 J.D. [Ⓐ Neal&L.]
Sfikas, Ellen M. .... '68 '94 C.597 B.A. L.424 J.D. 70 W. Madison St.
Sfikas, Peter M., (AV) .... '37 '62 C.347 B.S. L.597 J.D. [Bell,B.&L.]
Sha, Jie .... '54 '97 C.999 B.S.E.E. L.1000 J.D. [Sha&Assoc.]
Sha & Associates .... 195 N. Harbor Drive
Shabat, Matthew A. .... '75 '00 C.813 B.A. L.659 J.D. [Ⓐ Mayer,B.R.&M.]
Shade, Marla R. ....'— '00 C&L.339 B.A., J.D. [Ⓐ Schiff H.]
Shadle, Paul W. .... '64 '96 C.118 B.A. L.145 J.D. [DLPiper R.G.C.U.]
Shadur, Milton I. ....'24 '49 C&L.145 B.S., J.D. U.S. Sr. Dist. J.
Shaff, Grace L. ....'66 '91 C.597 B.A. L.352 J.D. [Winston&S.]
Shaffer, Daniel R. ....'70 '95 C.473 B.A. L.146 J.D. [Ⓐ Stamos&T.]
Shaffer, Jason P. ....'75 '00 C.130 B.A. L.146 J.D. [Ⓐ Katten M.R.]
Shafis, Robert M. '55 '80 C.679 B.A. L.879 J.D.
Dir., Museum of Sci. & Indus.,Maj. Gift Plan.
Shaftal, Max, (AV) .... '56 '82 C.339 B.S.C.E. L.209 J.D. [Patzik,F.&S.] (Pat.)
Shah, Bansari M. .... '66 '92 C&L.966 B.B.A., J.D. Corp. Coun., Trizec Properties, Inc.
Shah, Charulata (Charu) Jain '75 '02
C.124 B.S. L.477 J.D. [Ⓐ Sonnenschein N.&R.] (Pat.)
Shah, Huma P. .... '71 '98 C.378 B.S. L.146 J.D. [Ⓐ Tressler,S.M.&P.]
Shah, Kal K. ....'— '01 C.339 B.S. L.424 J.D. [Ⓐ Kirkland&E.] (Pat.)
Shah, Nirav N., Attorney at Law '76 '04
C.477 B.S. L.276 J.D. 6116 S. University, Ste. 300
Shah, Palak V. ....'— '02 C.188 B.S. L.145 J.D. [Ⓐ Kirkland&E.]
Shah, Raj N. .... '73 '98 C&L.477 B.B.A., J.D. [Ⓐ DLPiper R.G.C.U.]
Shah, Sulin B. ....'77 '04 C.339 B.S. L.597 J.D. [Ⓐ McDermott W.&E.]
Shaheen, Raymond, (AV) .... '18 '49 C&L.209 [Shaheen,N.S.F.&E.]

Shaheen, Novoselsky, Staat, Filipowski & Eccleston, P.C., (AV)
20 North Wacker Drive, Suite 2900, 60606-3192
Telephone: 312-621-4400 Fax: 312-621-0268
Email: info@snsfe-law.com URL: http://www.snsfe-law.com
Shareholders: Raymond Shaheen; Henry N. Novoselsky; Lawrence G. Staat; Steven C. Filipowski; James J. Eccleston. Partners: William E. Hofmann; Scott E. Galbreath; Michael D. Weis; Jack L. Haan;—Sharyn Beth Alpert; Jeffrey M. Gershon; Ronald M. Amato; April J. Lindauer; Scott Sissel.
Banking, Debtor and Creditor, Corporate Law, Commercial Law, Employee Benefits, Estate Planning, Estate Administration, Estate and Trust Litigation, Employment Relations Law, Litigation, Minority Business Law, Real Estate, Arbitration, Securities, Securities Industry Disputes, Taxation, Tax Exempt Organizations.

See Professional Biographies, CHICAGO, ILLINOIS

Shaker, Omar H. ....'75 '00 C.424 B.S. L.146 J.D. Atty. Gen. Off.
Shakman, Michael L., (AV) .... '42 '66 C&L.145 A.B., J.D. [Miller S.&H.]
Shakula, Peter J. ....'— '90 C.679 B.S. L.347 J.D. [Barnes&T.]
Shallcross, Brian ....'72 '05 C&L.209 B.A., J.D. [Ⓐ Clifford]
Shallenberger, Susan ....'— '86 C.201 B.A. L.339 J.D. [Chapman&C.]
Shaltout, Raef .... '69 '04 C.804 B.S. L.146 J.D. [Ⓐ McDonnell B.H.&B.] (See Pat. Sect.)
Shaman, Jeffrey M. '41 '68
C.645 B.A. L.800 J.D. Prof. of Law, DePaul Univ. Coll. of Law
Shamberg, Jeffrey S. ....'67 '95 C.339 B.S. L.597 J.D. [Barack F.K.P.&N.]
Shan, Xiaokui Katie .... '67 '93 L.602 J.D. [Ⓐ Baker&M.]
Shanahan, James A., (AVⓉ) '51 '77 C.602 B.B.A. L.1119 J.D.
[Ice M.] (⊙Indpls., IN)
Shanahan, Margaret A. .... '58 '84 C.197 A.B. L.659 J.D. V.P., Northern Trust Co.
Shanaman, Rebecca M. ....'76 '04 C.397 B.A. L.424 J.D. [Ⓐ Johnson&N.]
Shanberg, Edwin H. ....'31 '55 C&L.145 A.B., J.D. 30 N. LaSalle St.
Shanberg, Mark H. ....'67 '92 C.347 B.A. L.365 J.D. [Merlo K.B.&G.]
Shancer, Jeffrey M., Law Offices of '61 '86
C.339 B.A. L.209 J.D. 10 S. LaSalle St., Ste. 3500
Shane, Victor P., (AV) .... '57 '84 C.209 B.S. L.770 J.D. [Scopelitis,G.L.&H.]
Shanes, Abraham .... '09 '30 C.339 L.365 LL.B. 134 N. La Salle St., Ste. 1606
Shanfield, Jason Gabriel ....'— '01 C.145 B.A. L.209 J.D. [Ⓐ Edelman,C.&L.]
Shani, Vishal Raj ....'79 '04 C.228 B.S.E. L.1375 J.D. [Ⓐ Winston&S.]
Shanin, Steven R. .... '— '73 C.339 B.S. L.424 J.D. 53 W. Jackson Blvd., Ste. 920
Shank, William O., (AV) '24 '51
C.473 A.B. L.976 J.D. [Ⓑ Hinshaw&C.] (⊙Crystal Lake)
Shankman, Jack L. .... '49 '79 C.339 B.A. L.146 J.D. 1120 W. Montana St.
Shanley, James C., (P.C.) ....'— '74 C&L.209 B.S.C., J.D. [Ⓑ Masuda,F.E.&M.]
Shannon, Christopher T. ....'— '01 C.999 B.S. L.145 J.D. [Ⓐ Kirkland&E.]
Shannon, David R. ....'— '90 C.877 B.S. L.365 J.D. [Tenney&B.]
Shannon, Joseph P. ....'63 '88 C.670 B.A. L.602 J.D. [Dolan&S.]
Shannon, Lori L. .... '72 '97 C.238 B.S. L.209 J.D. [Ⓐ Gardner C.&D.]
Shannon, Robert T. ....'69 '95 C.347 B.A. L.424 J.D. [Hinshaw&C.]
Shannon, Robert V., (AV) ....'51 '78 C.238 B.A. L.339 J.D. [Bell,B.&L.]
Shannon, Thomas J., (AV) ....'— '73 C&L.424 B.A., J.D. [Shannon&Assoc.]

Shannon & Associates, Ltd., (AV)
8 South Michigan, 26th Floor, 60603
Telephone: 312-332-2804 Fax: 312-332-0600
Email: tshannon@shannonlawoffice.com URL: http://www.shannonlawoffice.com
Thomas J. Shannon.

(This Listing Continued)

Shannon & Associates, Ltd. (Continued)

Business Law, Construction Law, Labor and Employment, Real Estate, Construction Defects, Mechanics Liens, Contracts, Franchises and Franchising, Employment Contracts, Personnel Policies, Mergers and Acquisitions.

See Professional Biographies, CHICAGO, ILLINOIS

Shapira, John S., (AV) ....'36 '61 C.103 B.A. L.976 LL.B. [Ⓑ Lord,B.&B.]
Shapira, Thomas B. .... '67 '92 C.103 A.B. L.659 J.D. [Much S.F.D.A.&R.]
Shapiro, Andrew D. ....'75 '00 C.473 B.S. L.339 J.D. [Ⓐ Winston&S.]
Shapiro, Benjamin P., (AV) ....'— '68 C.339 B.S. L.597 J.D. [Wolin&R.]
Shapiro, Clifford J., (AV) ....'— '82 C.910 B.A. L.273 J.D. [Sachnoff&W.]
Shapiro, Craig M. ....'— '05 [Ⓐ Horwitz,H.&Assoc.]
Shapiro, Daniel C. ....'61 '87 C.477 B.A. L.29 J.D. [Ⓐ Schain,B.R.&C.]
Shapiro, Daniel P., (AV) .... '57 '82 C.339 B.A. L.145 J.D. [Goldberg,K.B.B.R.&M.]
Shapiro, David A., (AV) ....'54 '80 C.597 B.S. L.209 J.D. [Laser,P.S.F.&E.]
Shapiro, Edward D. .... '62 '91 C.1349 B.A. L.94 J.D. [Much S.F.D.A.&R.]
Shapiro, Harold D., (AV) ....'27 '52 C&L.597 B.S., J.D. [Sonnenschein N.&R.]
Shapiro, Howard '47 '73 C.339 B.A. L.209 J.D.
Gen. Coun. & Exec. V.P., Law & Admin., Playboy Magazine (Law Department)
Shapiro, Ilene E., (AV) .... '53 '78 C.597 B.A. L.424 J.D. [Nadler,P.&M.]
Shapiro, Jack E. .... '28 '51 C&L.209 LL.B. 188 W. Randolph St.
Shapiro, James A., (AV) ....'59 '85 C.855 B.A. L.945 J.D. [Shapiro&S.]
Shapiro, Jay M., (AV) ....'42 '66 C.966 L.209 LL.B. [Ganan&S.]
Shapiro, Jeffrey Stewart '59 '85
C.339 B.A. L.146 J.D. 180 North LaSalle Street, Suite 2010
Shapiro, Jennifer R. ....'70 '96 C.145 B.A. L.209 J.D. [Ⓐ Minsky,M.&H.]
Shapiro, Jerrold M. .... '43 '69 C&L.597 B.A., J.D. 1000 N. State St., Apt. 15
Shapiro, Joel ....'72 '98 C.477 B.S. L.597 J.D. 401 N. Mich. Ave.
Shapiro, Joel G. ....'61 '85 C.473 B.S. L.339 J.D. [Patzik,F.&S.]
Shapiro, Joel H., (AV) .... '49 '75 C.339 B.A. L.209 J.D. [Kamenear K.S.&C.]
Shapiro, John T. ....'— '91 C.118 B.A. L.494 J.D. [Freeborn&P.]
Shapiro, Judith Hope '44 '88 C.477 B.A. L.146 J.D.
U.S. Dept. of Labor, Off. of the Solr.
Shapiro, Julius H., (AV) ....'34 '59 C.339 B.S. L.597 J.D. [Berger,N.&F.] ⊙
Shapiro, Keith J., (AV) .... '58 '83 C.339 B.S. L.245 J.D. [Greenberg T.]
Shapiro, Lewis R. ....'44 '69 C.966 B.S. L.209 J.D. 29 S. LaSalle St.
Shapiro, Lynne F. ....'— '91 C.347 B.A. L.424 J.D. [Jacobson&S.]
Shapiro, Mark L., (AV) ....'49 '74 C.918 B.A. L.145 J.D. [Holland&K.]
Shapiro, Michael S. ....'— '03 C.339 B.S. L.146 J.D. [Ⓐ Foley&L.]
Shapiro, Rebecca .... '75 '01 C.881 B.A. L.597 J.D. [Ⓐ Azulay,H.&S.]
Shapiro, Richard A. ....'50 '80 C&L.339 B.A., J.D. 676 N. La Salle St.
Shapiro, Richard Harry ....'46 '72 C.339 B.A. L.146 J.D. Asst. States Atty.
Shapiro, Robert E. ....'50 '79 C.309 A.B. L.145 J.D. [Barack F.K.P.&N.]
Shapiro, Robert Lee ....'10 '33 C&L.145 Ph.B., J.D. 100 W. Monroe
Shapiro, Russell I. ....'64 '89 C.339 B.S. L.659 J.D. [Levenfeld P.]
Shapiro, Stephen M., (AV) ....'46 '71 C&L.976 B.A., J.D. [Mayer,B.R.&M.]
Shapiro, Steven A., (P.C.) ....'50 '75 C.339 B.S. L.146 J.D. [Katten M.R.]
Shapiro, Stuart M. .... '41 '65 C.1016 B.A. L.209 LL.B. 180 N. La Salle St.
Shapiro, Wayne S. ....'49 '78 C.339 B.S. L.424 J.D. [W.S.Shapiro]
Shapiro & Schwartz, (AV) ....222 N. La Salle St., Ste. 200

Shapiro, Wayne S., P.C.
111 West Washington Street Suite 1028, 60602
Telephone: 312-704-8400 Fax: 312-704-0366 URL: http://www.honstlawyr.com
Email: honstlawyr@aol.com URL: http://www.lawyers.com/wayneshapiro
Wayne S. Shapiro.
Family, Divorce, Dissolution of Marriage, Paternity, Child Custody, Prenuptial Agreements, Postnuptial Agreements, Visitation, Real Estate, Landlord and Tenant, Commercial Real Estate, Residential Real Estate, Probate, Estate Planning, Guardianship, Wills and Litigation, Personal Injury, Medical Malpractice, Business, Bankruptcy, Felonies and Misdemeanors.

See Professional Biographies, CHICAGO, ILLINOIS

Shapo, Helene S. '38 '76 C.788 B.A. L.893 J.D.
Prof., Northwestern Univ. School of Law
Shapo, Nathaniel S. ....'67 '98 C&L.145 B.A., J.D. Dir., State Dept. Ins.
Shaps, Adrienne Zipperman ....'— '73 C.339 B.S. L.146 J.D. 4268 S. Archer Ave.
Shaps, Morris C. ....'07 '34 C.339 L.365 LL.B. 134 N. LaSalle St.
Sharer, Jeffrey C. ....'69 '97 C.477 A.B. L.145 J.D. [Ⓐ Sidley A.B.&W.]
Sharer, Paul L. '61 '91 C.223 B.S. L.1338 J.D.
(adm. in PA; not adm. in IL; Pat.) [Mayer,B.R.&M.] (⊙Wash., DC)
Sharfman, Robert J., (AV) ....'36 '60 C.339 B.S. L.209 J.D. [Ⓑ Gomberg,S.G.&O.]
Sharkey, Patricia F., (AV) ....'52 '80 C.145 B.A. L.629 J.D. [Ⓑ Mayer,B.R.&M.]
Sharp, Autumn L. '76 '03 C.610 B.A. L.893 J.D.
(adm. in OH; not adm. in IL) [Ⓐ Schopf&W.]
Sharp, Jeffrey S., (AV) '— '84 C.674 B.S.E. L.280 J.D.
[Marshall,G.&B.] (See Pat. Sect.)
Sharp, Marjorie C. ....'— '46 L.365 LL.B. 34 E. 112th Pl.
Sharp, Robert F., (AV) ....'— '62 C.339 B.S. L.209 J.D. [Ⓑ Querrey&H.]
Sharp, Stephen D., (AV) .... '52 '78 C.210 B.A. L.352 J.D. [Ⓑ Flaherty&J.]
Sharp, William L., (AV) .... '39 '64 C.976 B.A. L.145 J.D. [Ⓑ Michael B.&F.]
Sharpe, Eleanor F. Dein '55 '84
C.183 B.A. L.365 J.D. Coun., Stewart Title Guaranty Company
Sharuzi, Jacqueline B. .... '72 '98 C.589 B.A. L.365 J.D. [Ⓐ Hall,P.&S.]
Shatz, Susan, Law Office of '54 '89 C.597 B.S. L.365 J.D.
542 S. Dearborn St., Ste. 750
Shaughnessy, Brian P. ....'52 '79 C.436 B.S. L.146 J.D. [Cremer,K.S.&S.]
Shaughnessy, Colleen T. .... '66 '91 C.339 B.S. L.209 J.D. [Winston&S.]
Shaw, Andrew H., (AV) ....'54 '79 C.197 A.B. L.188 J.D. [Sidley A.B.&W.]
Shaw, Brian L., (AV) ....'67 '93 C.860 B.A. L.339 J.D. [Shaw G.F.G.W.&T.]
Shaw, David L., (AV) .... '43 '66 C&L.477 A.B., J.D. [Shaw G.F.G.W.&T.]
Shaw, Erin S. ....'— '98 C.602 B.A. L.477 J.D. [Ⓐ Latham&W.]
Shaw, James K. ....'54 '82 C.339 B.S. L.424 J.D. [Kamensky,R.H.&D.] ⊙
Shaw, Jeffrey T., (AV) ....'60 '86 C.597 B.A. L.352 J.D. [Jenner&B.]
Shaw, Kyan E. .... '76 '02 C.999 B.A. L.425 J.D. Staff Atty., Compsych
Shaw, Leonora L. '65 '90 C.339 B.S. L.365 J.D.
Sr. Coun., Bank One Corp. (Law Dept.)
Shaw, Michael B. ....'73 '98 C&L.597 B.A., J.D. [Ⓐ Much S.F.D.A.&R.]

Shaw Gussis Fishman Glantz Wolfson & Towbin LLC, (AV) BR
321 N. Clark Street Suite 800, 60610
Telephone: 312-541-0151 Fax: 312-980-3888
Email: info@shawgussis.com URL: http://www.shawgussis.com
Members of Firm: Robert M. Fishman; Samuel Gussis; Robert W. Glantz; Randy S. Gussis; Peter J. Roberts; Richard A. Saldinger; Brian L. Shaw; David L. Shaw; George J. Spathis; Steven B. Towbin; Jeffrey L. Widman. Associates: John M. Sheldon; Allen J. Guon; Janice A. Alwin; Mark L. Radtke; Brian M. Graham; Ann Stockman; Patrick A. Clisham; Samuel A. Lichtenfeld; Matthew A. Swanson; Kristina M. Summers; Thomas C. Wendt; Steven B. Isaacson; Gordon E. Gouveia. Of Counsel: Richard M. Fogel; Jay S. Geller.

(This Listing Continued)

Shaw Gussis Fishman Glantz Wolfson & Towbin LLC (Continued)

Bankruptcy and Insolvency Law, Creditors Rights, Real Estate and related services, Land Use and Zoning, Commercial Litigation, and Secured Lending.

See Professional Biographies, CHICAGO, ILLINOIS

Shawver, Elizbeth A. ... '— '02 C.145 A.B. L.188 J.D. 10 S. Dearborn
Shay, Keith, (AV) ... '— '49 C.31 B.A. L.976 LL.B. [Schiff H.]
Shayne, David, (AV) ... '— '60 C.976 B.A. L.309 LL.B. [Holland&K.]
Shayne, Lara ... '69 '96 C.477 B.S. L.146 J.D. Chicago Board of Education
Shea, Brian C., (AV) ... '— '86 C.597 B.S. L.424 J.D. [Nasharr&S.]
Shea, Kevin P. ... '— '97 C&L.339 B.A., J.D. [Ungaretti&H.]
Shea, Pamela A. '52 '79 C&L.838 B.A., J.D.
(adm. in TN; not adm. in IL) Reg. Coun., F.D.I.C.
Sheahan, Patricia '69 '96
C.347 B.A. L.146 J.D. Assoc. Gen. Coun., Rehab. Inst. of Chicago
Sheahan, Terrence J. ... '— '99 C.347 B.A. L.209 J.D. [Freeborn&P.]
Sheahin, Matthew J. ... '71 '97 C.339 B.S. L.424 J.D. 208 S. LaSalle St.
Shear, Steven M. ... '74 '01 C.475 B.A. L.209 J.D. [Cassiday,S.&G.]
Shearer, Merle ... '55 '90 C.1106 B.A. L.146 J.D. 2953 W. Howard
Shearer, Robert D., Jr. ... '47 '73 C.393 A.B. L.209 J.D. 1400 W. Sherwin
Shearn, Cynthia L. ... '69 '96 C.94 B.A. L.904 J.D. [Fragomen,D.B.&L.]
Sheats, Letitia Spunar ... '— '72 105 W. Madison St., Ste., 1300
Shebar, Lisa K. ... '93 C.937 B.A. L.339 J.D. [Katten M.R.]
Shebesta, Jeffrey J. ... '77 '02 C.966 B.S. L.339 J.D. 35 West Wacker Dr.
Shebuski, Matthew A. ... '71 '97 C&L.477 B.B.A., J.D. [Skadden,A.S.M.&F.]
Shedd, David A. ... '74 '00 C.45 B.A. L.910 J.D. [Boundas S.W.&B.]
Shedden, James ... '— '82 C&L.339 A.B., J.D. [Schad,D.&S.]
Sheean, Christopher T., (AV) ... '— '92 C&L.37 B.A., J.D. [Wildman,H.A.&D.]
Sheedy, Brian T. '— '01 C.602 B.A. L.228 J.D.
(adm. in GA; not adm. in IL) [Katten M.R.]
Sheehan, Jamie M. ... '66 '99 C.519 B.A. L.209 J.D. State Atty.
Sheehan, Kevin M. ... '56 '83 C.424 B.A. L.146 J.D. Chf., Protec. Div. Juv. Bur.
Sheehan, Michael J., (BV) ... '59 '84 C.317 B.A. L.896 J.D. [Connelly S.H.]
Sheehan, Michael P. ... '71 '96 C.339 B.A. L.209 J.D. [Shefsky&F.]
Sheehan, Nancy Drew '42 '83
C.741 B.A. L.365 J.D. Comm., Water Reclamation Dist. Metro.
Sheehan, Robert R. '28 '66
C&L.424 B.S., J.D. Gen. Claims Coun., Bankers Life & Cas. Co.

Sheehan & Lower
(See Cary)

Sheen, Dennis M. ... '56 '83 C.959 M.A. L.146 J.D. Contl. Ill. Natl. Bk. & Tr. Co.
Sheets, Charles P., (BV) ... '— '83 C.339 B.A. L.365 J.D. [Foley&L.]
Sheetz, Martha G. ... '62 '87 C.20 B.A. L.597 J.D. Ofc. of the Corp. Coun.
Sheffert, David G. '63 '93
C.347 B.S. L.424 J.D. Vice Pres. & Gen. Coun., NeuroSource, Inc.
Sheffield, Jeffrey T., (P.C.), (AV) ... '— '80 C.145 B.A. L.309 J.D. [Kirkland&E.]
Sheffield, Thomas M. ... '71 '99 C.336 B.S. L.209 J.D. [Boundas S.W.&B.]
Shefsky, Lloyd E., (AV) ... '41 '65 C.209 B.S.C. L.145 J.D. [Shefsky&F.]

Shefsky & Froelich Ltd., (AV)
111 East Wacker Drive, Suite 2800, 60601
Telephone: 312-527-4000 Fax: 312-527-4011
Email: sfltd@shefskylaw.com URL: http://www.shefskylaw.com
Richard E. Aderman; James D. Anderson; Kathryn Kovitz Arnold; James R. Asmussen; Michael J. Choate; Erhard R. Chorlé; Kimberly M. Copp; Michael A. Cramarosso; Brian L. Crowe; Howard A. Davis; Cary E. Donham; Lynn A. Ellenberger; David M. Franek; Cezar M. Froelich; Theodore G. Gertz; Mitchell D. Goldsmith; Karen R. Goodman; Jack Guthman; Jack J. Hagerty; Edward J. Halper; Brian F. Hynes; Richard L. Ingram; Paul T. Jenson; Paul L. Kelley; John F. Kennedy; Lawrence M. Kern; Edward J. Kus; Anthony R. Licata; Ralph A. Mantynband; Jeffry A. Melnick; Ira S. Neiman; Brett Nolan; Douglas M. Ramsey; Lawrence C. Rubin; Michael J. Schaller; John C. Sciaccotta; Michael P. Sheehan; Judith S. Sherwin; Allan T. Slagel; Patricia S. Spratt; Joel J. Sprayregen; Jeremy Stonehill; Lawrence J. Suffredin, Jr.; Stuart K. Taussig; Susan W. Wiles; James D. Wilson;—Ellen M. Avery; Susanna M. Brown; Christopher M. Gibbs; Elizabeth Harvey; Heather A. Jackson; Kristin A. Klaczek; Kevin M. Lippert; Megan L. McCoy; Ronald J. McDermott; Brian P. Monahan; Barton J. O'Brien; Thomas R. Pappas; Gabriel Reilly-Bates; Suzanne L. Sias; Nicolette L. Sonntag; Kim R. Walberg; Brent R. Walters. Of Counsel: Paul D. Fischer; Channing Blair Hesse; Lloyd E. Shefsky. Senior Counsel: Elizabeth J. Boddy; Joseph P. Gattuso; Kathleen F. Howlett; David W. Nyberg.
Acquisitions, Divestitures and Mergers, Banking and Financial Institutions, Gaming, Food Industry, Construction, Corporate, Securities, Securitization and Financing, Venture Capital, Real Estate and Land Use, Employment, Employee Benefits and ESOPs, Franchise, Government, Health Care and Hospital, Insurance and Insurance Regulatory, State and Federal Litigation and Appellate Practice, Bankruptcy, Debtors'/Creditors' Rights, Partnerships, Estate Planning and Probate, Taxation, Technology.

See Professional Biographies, CHICAGO, ILLINOIS

Shehadeh, Samuel E. '— '02 C.966 B.S. L.273 J.D.
[Brinks H.G.&L.] (See Pat. Sect.)
Shehigian, Ruben B., Jr. ... '56 '84 C.347 B.S. L.365 J.D. [Bullaro&C.]
Sheikh, David J. ... '65 '92 C.339 B.S. L.209 J.D. [Niro,S.H.&N.]
Sheiman, Jill R. ... '75 '00 C.477 B.A. L.597 J.D. [Jenner&B.]
Shein, James B. ... '42 '97 C.679 B.S.I.E. L.424 J.D. [McDermott W.&E.]
Sheinfeld, Kari B. ... '71 '96 C.339 B.S. L.145 J.D. [Sidley A.B.&W.]
Shekleton, Gerald T., (AV) '47 '73
C.973 B.S.Chem. L.1003 J.D. [Welsh&K.] (See Pat. Sect.)
Sheldon, Ann P. ... '— '71 C.788 B.A. L.597 J.D. Gen. Coun., State Dept. of Labor
Sheldon, Harvey M., (AV) ... '42 '68 C.31 B.A. L.309 J.D. [Hinshaw&C.]
Sheldon, John M. ... '69 '98 C.823 B.S. L.424 J.D. [Shaw G.F.G.W.&T.]
Sheldon, Paul A. ... '67 '92 C.750 B.A. L.424 J.D. [Grippo&E.]
Shelest, Irina ... '— '01 C.597 B.A. L.424 J.D. [Arnstein&L.]
Sheley, Jesse ... '— '03 C.347 B.A. L.1119 J.D. [Kirkland&E.]
Shelist, Michael R., (AV) ... '36 '61 C&L.597 B.S., J.D. [Much S.F.D.A.&R.]
Shelist, Robert J. ... '61 '88 C.339 B.S. L.597 J.D. 1061 W. Monroe St.
Shellenback, Stephanie B., (AV) ... '— '82 C.966 B.A. L.245 J.D. [Gardner C.&D.]
Shellenberg, Mary W. ... '— '74 C.530 B.A. L.424 J.D. [Masuda,F.E.&M.]
Shelley, David N. '57 '90 C.870 B.S. L.861 J.D.
(adm. in TN; not adm. in IL) U.S. Postal Inspector
Shelly, Jennifer O'Reilly ... '71 '00 C.1119 B.G.S. L.365 J.D. [Dolan&S.]
Shelly, Joseph D., III ... '61 '91 C.473 B.S. L.365 J.D. Nuveen Institutional Advisory Grp.
Shelton, David A. ... '67 '97 C.339 B.A. L.424 J.D. New World Solutions
Shelton, Julie P. ... '55 '82 C.1307 B.S. L.209 J.D. [Butler R.S.&B.]
Shelton, Timothy G. ... '47 '92 C.668 B.A. L.276 J.D. [Hinshaw&C.]
Shenoo, Edward G., (CV) ... '55 '80 C.209 B.A. L.365 J.D. 9618 S. Commercial Ave.
Shepard, Debra ... '— '89 C.477 B.G.S. L.424 J.D. 17 N. State Street, Suite 1850
Shepard, Elizabeth A. ... '71 '96 C.339 B.A. L.602 J.D. [Sugar,F.&F.]
Shepherd, Stewart R., (AV) ... '48 '73 C.697 B.A. L.145 J.D. [Sidley A.B.&W.]
Sheppard, Barry D., (BV) ... '51 '76 C.801 B.S. L.209 J.D. 180 N. LaSalle St.
Sheppard, Berton Scott, (AV) '36 '62
C.475 B.S.Engr. L.597 J.D. [Leydig,V.&M.] (See Pat. Sect.)

Sheppard, Fred A. ... '74 '99 C.200 B.S. L.146 J.D. State's Atty. Off.
Sheppard, Hille R. ... '69 '95 C&L.145 A.B., J.D. [Sidley A.B.&W.]
Shepro, Richard W. ... '53 '79 C&L.309 A.B., J.D. [Mayer,B.R.&M.]
Sher, Brian A., (BV) ... '— '87 C.477 B.A. L.228 J.D. [Bryan C.]
Sher, Harry D. ... '15 '39 C.405 L.209 LL.B. 875 N. Mich. Ave.
Sher, Michael D., (AV) ... '50 '74 C.477 B.A. L.966 J.D. [Neal,G.&E.]
Sher, Stephen N. ... '67 '92 C.347 B.S. L.146 J.D. [Winston&S.]
Sher, Susan S. ... '48 '74 C.273 B.A. L.424 J.D. Corp. Coun., City of Chicago
Sherck, Timothy C. ... '49 '75 C.597 B.A. L.309 J.D. [Mayer,B.R.&M.]
Shereda, Joseph P. ... '— '98 C.477 B.A. L.273 J.D. [Jones D.]
Sheridan, Daniel James '64 '89 C&L.477 A.B., J.D.
V.P., Asst. Gen. Cnsl, General Growth Properties, Inc.
Sheridan, Deborah M. ... '68 '94 C&L.1019 B.B.A., J.D. [Cassiday,S.&G.]
Sheridan, Luke P. ... '— '92 C.602 B.A. L.424 J.D. [O'Hagan,S.&A.]
Sheridan, Mark G., (AV) ... '65 '91 C.602 B.A. L.424 J.D. [Bates&C.]
Sheridan, Paul M., III, (AV) ... '63 '88 C.602 B.B.A. L.424 J.D. [Madden,J.M.&S.]
Sheridan, Philip H. ... '78 '03 C.352 B.S.E.E. L.365 J.D. [McAndrews,H.&M.]
Sheridan, Robert C. ... '55 '82 C.339 B.S.A.S. L.146 J.D. [B.A.Pekala]
Sheridan, Robert P. ... '46 '75 C.352 L.209 J.D. [Clifford]
Sheriff, Matthew P. ... '68 '93 C.352 B.A. L.910 J.D. [Brady,C.&M.]
Sherlock, Daniel T. ... '56 '81 C.424 B.A. L.602 J.D. [Vedder,P.K.&K.]
Sherlock, Patrick J., Law Office of '65 '90
C.1082 B.S. L.339 J.D. 11 S. La Salle St., Ste. 1600
Sherman, Amy E. ... '— '90 C&L.597 B.A., J.D. Northwestern Unv. Sch. of Law
Sherman, Anthony B. ... '67 '92 C&L.966 B.B.A., J.D. [Lord,B.&B.]
Sherman, Eugene T. ... '28 '58 C.339 B.S. L.209 J.D. 70 W. Madison St.
Sherman, Gerald J., (AV) ... '38 '63 C.339 A.B. L.145 J.D. [Sonnenschein N.&R.]
Sherman, Ian M., (AV) ... '53 '78 C.339 B.A. L.94 J.D. [Dykema G.P.]
Sherman, Jeffrey G. '46 '72 C&L.309 A.B., J.D.
(adm. in MN; not adm. in IL) Chicago-Kent Coll. of Law
Sherman, Jeremy P., (AV) ... '51 '76 C.30 B.A. L.273 J.D. [Seyfarth S.]
Sherman, Jonathan D., (BV) ... '58 '83 C.477 B.A. L.597 J.D. [Weinberg R.]
Sherman, Laurence A. ... '35 '94 C.145 B.A. L.424 J.D. 20 N. Clark St.
Sherman, Max E. ... '27 '52 C&L.339 A.B., J.D. 135 S. La Salle St., Ste. 1940
Sherman, Mindy Wolin ... '59 '84 C.339 B.S. L.597 J.D. 900 N. Michigan Avenue
Sherman, Seymour I. ... '27 '52 C.966 L.569 LL.B. 2 N. LaSalle St.
Sherman, Sidney ... '27 '53 C.477 A.B. L.145 J.D. 105 W. Madison St.
Sherman, Susan Kaye ... '70 '00 C.477 B.A. L.365 J.D. 77 W. Wacker
Sherpy, Della L. Anderson ... '53 '79 C.299 B.A. L.966 J.D. Asst. Pub. Def.
Sherrer, Emily ... '78 '04 C.388 B.A. L.424 J.D. [Richardson,S.B.&M.]
Sherrill, Benjamin Michael ... '74 '01 C.101 B.A. L.145 J.D. 10 South Dearborn St.
Sherrod, Theodore R., Jr. '46 '73 C.103 B.A. L.309 J.D.
Admin. Law J., Off. of Admin. Hearings, IL Dept. of Rev.
Sherry, Anne M. ... '— '02 C.502 B.A. L.145 J.D. [Goldberg,K.B.B.R.&M.]
Sherry, Stephen F., (AV) '56 '82
C.886 B.S. L.209 J.D. [McAndrews,H.&M.] (See Pat. Sect.)
Sherwin, Judith S., (AV) ... '45 '78 C.196 B.A. L.365 J.D. [Shefsky&F.]
Sherwin, Robert A., (AV) ... '42 '67 C.966 B.A. L.339 J.D. [R.A.Sherwin]
Sherwin, Theodore R., (AV) ... '13 '37 C.999 B.A. L.146 LL.B. 39 S. LaSalle St.‡
Sherwin, Robert A., Ltd., (AV) ... 350 W. Hubbard St., 3rd Fl.
Sherwood, Marc E. ... '48 '74 C.352 B.B.A. L.146 J.D. 309 W. Washington St., Ste. 550
Shevitz, David R., (AV) ... '41 '66 C.385 B.A. L.477 J.D. [Katten M.R.]
Sheyka, Joseph W., (AV) ... '46 '74 C.339 B.A. L.597 J.D. [DLPiper R.G.C.U.]
Sheynes, Matthew ... '69 '00 C&L.861 B.A., J.D. Cir. Ct. of Cook Cty.
Shidenko, Yuri M. '76 '98
(adm. in NY; not adm. in IL) [Fox,H.S.L.&C.]
Shiel, Colleen Reppen ... '61 '86 C.424 B.B.A. L.339 J.D. Prudential Ins. Co.
Shields, Brian Stuart ... '65 '91 C.339 B.S. L.209 J.D. [B.S.Shields]
Shields, Geoffrey B., (AV) ... '— '73 C.309 L.976 J.D. [Gardner C.&D.]
Shields, Heather J. ... '67 '93 C.966 B.A. L.424 J.D. Sr. Coun., Risk Mgmt., Aon Corp.
Shields, Karen G. ... '52 '80 C.339 B.A. L.209 J.D. 2805 Daley Center
Shields, Mary E. ... '59 '84 C.339 B.A. L.209 J.D. Asst. State Atty.
Shields, Thomas C., (AV) ... '41 '66 C.276 A.B. L.597 J.D. [Bell,B.&L.]
Shields, Brian S. ... 410 S. Michigan Ave., Ste. 622
Shier, Suzanne L., (AV) ... '— '85 C.477 B.A. L.424 J.D. [Chapman&C.]
Shifflett, Leonard S. ... '49 '74 C.339 A.B. L.145 J.D. [Quarles&B.]
Shiffrin, Daniel '58 '84 C.118 B.A. L.1119 J.D.
(adm. in CA; not adm. in IL) 111 E. Wacker Dr.
Shifley, Charles W., (AV) '— '76 C&L.608 B.S.M.E., J.D.
[Banner&W.] (See Pat. Sect.)
Shifrin, Chad ... '— '04 C.339 B.A. L.146 J.D. [DLPiper R.G.C.U.]
Shifrin, Dmitry ... '— '02 C&L.502 B.A., J.D. [Bryan C.]
Shifrin, Shana A. ... '78 '03 C.659 B.A. L.597 J.D. [Jenner&B.]
Shilov, Anna, Law Offices of '— '03
C.339 B.S. L.424 J.D. 321 S. Plymouth Ct., Ste. 1525
Shilson, Jason T. ... '68 '93 C.477 B.A. L.209 J.D. [O'Keefe,L.&H.]
Shimanovsky, David L. ... '63 '88 C.338 B.S. L.365 J.D. [Evans,L.S.&M.]
Shimota, James A. ... '— '99 C&L.477 B.S.E., J.D. [Kirkland&E.]
Shin, David T. ... '— '03 C.605 B.A. L.880 J.D. [Mayer,B.R.&M.]
Shin, Edward M. ... '73 '01 C.477 B.A. L.910 J.D. [Greenberg T.]
Shin, Miyoung ... '71 '03 C.999 B.S. L.597 J.D. [Brinks H.G.&L.] (See Pat. Sect.)
Shinall, Greg, (AV) ... '65 '90 C.145 B.A. L.879 J.D. [Sperling&S.]
Shindler, Donald A., (AV) ... '46 '71 C.910 B.S.B.A. L.861 J.D. [DLPiper R.G.C.U.]
Shine, Donald C., (AV) ... '40 '70 C.363 B.S. L.424 J.D. [Nisen&E.]
Shine, Gerald J. ... '26 '52 C.1024 B.A. L.209 LL.B. 20 N. Wacker Dr.
Shine, Patrick M. ... '60 '88 C.1183 B.A. L.365 J.D. [Caron,C.&W.]
Shiner, David B. ... '69 '96 C.94 B.S.B.A. L.365 J.D. [Chuhak&T.]
Shines, Gayle B. ... '48 '76 C.393 B.A. L.329 J.D. Asst. States Atty.
Shinglman, Gregory J. ... '48 '74 C.46 B.S. L.146 J.D. 150 E. Huron St.
Shinitzky, Edwin J. ... '32 '55 C.999 A.D. L.146 J.D. Admin. Law J., Soc. Sec. Admn.
Shinsky, Michael S. ... '76 '01 C.339 B.S. L.146 J.D. [Kralovec,J.&S.]
Shipley, Joseph E., (AV) '56 '82
C.597 B.S.M.E. L.339 J.D. [Fitch,E.T.&F.] (See Pat. Sect.)
Shipley, Robert A., (AV) ... '53 '79 C.339 B.A. L.589 J.D. [Shipley]
Shipley Law Group, Ltd., (AV) ... 100 West Monroe Street, Suite 1510
Shipps, Riana N. ... '— '03 C.910 B.A. L.477 J.D. [Greene&L.]
Shishem, Edward M. ... '60 '85 C.209 B.A. L.365 J.D. 53 W. Jackson Blvd.
Shishem, Karen L. ... '59 '85 C.424 B.A. L.365 J.D. 53 W. Jackson Blvd., Ste. 1650
Shivakumar, Dhananjai '72 '98 C.309 A.B. L.976 J.D.
(adm. in NY; not adm. in IL) [Skadden,A.S.M.&F.]
Shkolnik, Barry J., (AV) ... '55 '80 C.339 B.A. L.813 J.D. [Ungaretti&H.]
Shmikler, Daniel A. ... '69 '96 C.145 B.A. L.597 J.D. [Sperling&S.]
Shoenberger, Allen E. ... '44 '73 C.821 B.A. L.178 J.D. [Hablutzel&Assoc.]
Shoenberger, Elisabeth E. ... '71 '97 C.231 B.A. L.588 J.D. 770 N. Halsted St., Ste. 205

Shoffner, Robin D. ... '60 '90 C.502 B.J. L.190 J.D. Litig. Coun., Aon Corporation
Sholder, Iris E. ... '48 '73 C.145 B.A. L.477 J.D. Gen. Coun., Co. Assessor
Shollenberger, Richard C., Jr. ... '64 '89 C.94 B.A. L.659 J.D. [Ⓐ Lewis,D.&H.]
Shonder, Steven S. ... '61 '96 C.1016 B.M. L.209 J.D. [Ⓐ Gardner C.&D.]
Shonkwiler, John F. ... '70 '98 C.477 B.A. L.339 J.D. [Ⓐ Novack&M.]
Shopiro, Richard S. ... '52 '78 [Sulzer&S.]
Shore, Jack ... '26 '52 C.46 B.S. L.273 LL.B. [Ⓒ Much S.F.D.A.&R.] (Pat.)
Shore, Linda K. '59 '84 C.94 B.A. L.477 J.D.
(adm. in FL; not adm. in IL) [Ⓒ Katten M.R.]
Shorris, Perry M. ... '68 '93 C.477 A.B. L.339 J.D. [Bollinger,R.&G.]
Short, John J. ... '47 '80 C.597 B.A. L.424 J.D. 3500 S. Union Ave.★
Short, M. David ... '— '95 C.602 B.A. L.339 J.D. [Kelley D.&W.]
Shortridge, Deborah Green, (AVⓉ) '52 '82 C&L.64 B.A., J.D.
Loss Prevent. Coun., Attorneys' Liab. Assur. Soc., Inc.
Shorts, Kenneth R. ... '26 '50 C.504 B.A. L.339 J.D. 820 W. Belmont Ave.
Shoto, Lorraine Clarice ... '73 '98 C.97 B.A. L.608 J.D. Asst. States Atty.
Shoub, David E. ... '41 '67 C.475 B.A. L.209 J.D. [Ⓒ A.J.Madonia&Assoc.]
Shragal, Otto J. ... '78 '05 C.854 B.A. L.365 J.D. [Ⓐ Cassiday,S.&G.]
Shrallow, Dale Phillip '53 '78 C.473 B.A. L.608 J.D.
Assoc. Gen. Tax Coun., Planning & Litig., BP America Inc.
Shreder, Elaine A. ... '77 '02 C.339 B.A. L.424 J.D. Asst. Pub. Guard.
Shroba, Jane, (AV) ... '57 '86 C.504 B.A. L.365 J.D. J.P. Morgan Chase Bk.
Shu, Tony T., (BV) ... '55 '80 C.679 B.S.M.E. L.146 J.D. 208 S. LaSalle St., Suite 1400
Shubert, Norman A., (AV) ... '35 '60 C.477 A.B. L.597 J.D. [Much S.F.D.A.&R.]
Shudnow, Ronald A. ... '40 '69 C&L.209 B.S.C., J.D. [R.A.Shudnow]
Shudnow, Scott Michael ... '77 '02 C&L.339 J.D. [R.A.Shudnow]
Shudnow, Ronald A., LTD ... 77 W. Washington St., Ste. 1620
Shuftan, Robert L., (AV) ... '54 '79 C.339 B.A. L.309 J.D. [Wildman,H.A.&D.]
Shuger, Marc S. ... '52 '84 C.347 B.A. L.365 J.D. P.O. Box 963
Shugrue, John D., (AV) ... '62 '87 C.208 B.A. L.575 J.D. [Morgan,L.&B.]
Shuldiner, Paul R., (BV) '53 '80 C.454 B.A. L.851 J.D.
[Baumann,S.&L.] (⊙Des Plaines)
Shuler, Aaron J. ... '78 '04 C.966 B.A. L.494 J.D. [Bollinger,R.&G.]
Shull, Jason ... '— '00 C.475 B.S. L.146 J.D. [Banner&W.] (See Pat. Sect.)
Shulman, Bennett H., (AV) ... '27 '51 C&L.597 B.S.L., LL.B. 208 S. LaSalle St.
Shulman, Daniel H. ... '74 '99 C.597 B.A. L.424 J.D. [Ⓐ Mayer,B.R.&M.] (Pat.)
Shulruff, Henry L. ... '63 '88 C.352 B.A. L.209 J.D. Attorney's Title Guaranty Fund Inc.
Shulruff, Lawrence, (AV) ... '59 '88 C.339 B.A. L.597 J.D. [Sudekum,C.&S.]
Shulruff, Stuart P. ... '59 '84 C.339 B.S. L.424 J.D. [Katten M.R.]
Shuman, Jeffrey R. ... '78 '03 C.339 B.A.B.S. L.309 J.D. [Ⓐ Jenner&B.]
Shuman, Marc Jeffrey ... '61 '86 C.339 L.146 [M.J.Shuman&Assoc.]
Shuman, Stanley J. '42 '70 C.1303 B.S. L.1202 J.D.
(adm. in MA; not adm. in IL) Gen. Atty., U.S. RR Retire. Bd.
Shuman, Marc J., & Associates, Ltd. ... 2 N. LaSalle Street
Shuman-Moore, Elizabeth '56 '82
C.339 B.S.W. L.1119 J.D. Chicago Lawyers' Comm. for Civil Rights
Shumpert, Shanon ... '70 '97 C.209 B.A. L.329 J.D. [Ⓐ Cremer,K.S.&S.]
Shure, Leon R. ... '47 '75 U.S. of Amer. R.R. Retirement Bd.
Shure, Mark E., (AV) ... '58 '84 C.589 B.S. L.424 J.D. [Keating&S.]
Shurr, Barbara K. ... '47 '85 C.338 B.S. L.589 J.D. F.D.I.C.
Shurtz, Steven P., (BV) '56 '83
C&L.878 B.S.Ch.E., J.D. [Brinks H.G.&L.] (See Pat. Sect.)
Shusterman, Victoria ... '73 '98 C.597 B.A. L.910 J.D. [Ⓐ Katten M.R.]
Sias, Suzanne L. ... '73 '03 C.475 B.A. L.146 J.D. [Ⓐ Shefsky&F.]
Siatis, Perry C. ... '74 '00 C.1356 B.A. L.101 J.D. 203 North La Salle Street, Suite 1900
Siavelis, Michael P., (AV) ... '— '67 C&L.209 B.S., J.D. [Johnson&B.]
Siavelis, Peter M. ... '71 '00 C.475 B.S.M.E. L.146 J.D. [Ⓐ Wallenstein W.&R.]
Sibley Gonzales, Michele E. ... '— '94 C.145 B.A. L.146 J.D. [Holland&K.]
Sibrava, John C., (AV) ... '49 '74 C.210 B.A. L.424 J.D. [Hardt&S.]
Sick, Jonathan R. '69 '95 C.339 Ch.E. L.146 J.D.
[McAndrews,H.&M.] (See Pat. Sect.)
Sickle, David B., (AV) ... '59 '86 C.659 B.S. L.477 J.D. [DLPiper R.G.C.U.]
Sickles, W. Mark ... '— '91 C.999 B.S. L.365 J.D. [Patton&R.]
Sickman, Jordan M. ... '— '01 C.1494 B.A. L.880 J.D. [Ⓐ Chapman&C.]
Sicsu, Jessica Helena ... '— '96 L.339 LL.M. [Ⓐ Kirkland&E.]
Siddall, James L. '38 '68 C.930 B.B.A. L.1003 J.D.
(adm. in OH; not adm. in IL) Mgr., State Income Tax Planning, BP America Inc.
Siddique, Saadia ... '75 '01 C.339 B.A. L.209 J.D. [Ⓐ Azulay,H.&S.]
Siddiqui, Peter A. ... '76 '02 C.210 B.A. L.345 J.D. [Ⓐ Jenner&B.]
Siddon O'Brien, Katherine Ann ... '— '98 C.174 B.A. L.1017 J.D. [Ⓐ Foley&L.]
Sider, Norman L. ... '12 '36 C.405 L.209 LL.B. 4200 Marine Drive
Sidkey, Robert E. ... '74 '99 C.879 B.A. L.146 J.D. [Ⓐ Pretzel&S.]
Sidley Austin Brown & Wood, (AV)
10 S. Dearborn Street, 48th Floor (Pat.) (⊙L.A., San Fran., CA; Wash., DC; New York, NY; Dallas, TX; Seattle, WA)
Sido, Kevin R., (AV) ... '51 '75 C&L.339 B.A., J.D. [Hinshaw&C.]
Sidor, Matthew A. ... '76 '02 C.172 B.S. L.146 J.D. [Ⓐ Gardiner K.&W.]
Sidrys, Anne M. ... '— '92 C.352 B.B.A. L.276 J.D. [Kirkland&E.]
Siebel, Richard A., (P.C.) ... '39 '64 C.103 A.B. L.597 J.D. Cir. J.
Siebert, Mark D. ... '60 '86 C&L.339 A.B., J.D. [McCullough,C.&L.]
Siebert, Richard J. ... '66 '91 C.209 B.S. L.597 J.D. [Ⓐ Pretzel&S.]

Siebert, William Newell '43 '69 C.475 B.A. L.215 J.D.
307 North Michigan Avenue, Suite 924, 60601
Telephone: 312-329-0646 Fax: 312-553-4419
Email: wsiebert@siebert-immigrationlaw.com URL: http://www.williamsiebert.com
Naturalization, Working Visas, Consular Practice, Family and Employment Based Permanent Residency Cases, PERM Labor Certification, Kennedy McCain.
See Professional Biographies, CHICAGO, ILLINOIS

Sieburg, Jeffrey J. ... '53 '78 C&L.339 B.A., J.D. Asst. Reg. Coun., IRS
Siedlecki, Charles T. ... '55 '97 C.1191 B.A. L.146 J.D. [C.Siedlecki&Assoc.]
Siedlecki, Charles, & Associates, P.C. ... 10540 S. Western Ave.
Siegan, Jerold N., (AV) ... '— '72 C.339 B.A. L.209 J.D. [Arnstein&L.]
Siegan, Jerome A. ... '— '73 C.209 B.S. L.339 J.D. [Ⓐ Neal&L.]
Siegan, Kenneth R., (AV) ... '43 '69 C.339 B.S. L.209 J.D. 1 North Franklin
Siegel, Albert ... '18 '43 C.145 A.B. L.209 5850 N. Whipple St.‡
Siegel, Andrew J. ... '63 '88 C.475 B.S. L.365 J.D. Staff Atty., Chan. Div.

Siegel, Arnold G., (AV) '47 '76 C.424 B.A. L.209 J.D.
20 North Clark Street, Suite 2200, 60602
Telephone: 312-629-0222 FAX: 312-236-7660
Email: arnsiegel@aol.com URL: http://www.lawyers.com/siegellaw
Real Estate Tax Assessment Law.
See Professional Biographies, CHICAGO, ILLINOIS

Siegel, Charles W., Law Offices of '57 '83
C.1024 B.A. L.365 J.D. 10345 South Western Avenue
Siegel, David J. ... '69 '94 C.477 A.B. L.309 J.D. [Ⓐ Sidley A.B.&W.]
Siegel, Elaine K. B. ... '49 '82 C.112 A.B. L.1119 J.D. [E.K.B.Siegel&Assoc.] ⊙
Siegel, Evan ... '66 '92 C.103 A.B. L.245 J.D. Sr. Atty., WorldCom, Inc.
Siegel, Howard Bruce ... '66 '91 C.473 B.S. L.146 J.D. Pub. Def.
Siegel, Jack M., (AV) ... '26 '51 C&L.145 J.D. [Ⓒ Holland&K.]
Siegel, Joel E., (AV) '43 '69
C.679 B.S.I.E. L.904 J.D. [Wood,P.K.C.&M.] (See Pat. Sect.)
Siegel, Joel S., (AV) ... '36 '60 C.477 B.A. L.309 J.D. [Horvath&L.]
Siegel, Marc J. ... '71 '96 C.228 A.B. L.339 J.D. [Caffarelli&S.]
Siegel, Michael L., (AV) ... '50 '75 C.293 B.A. L.339 J.D. [Stone,M.&S.] ⊙
Siegel, Morton, (AV) ... '34 '60 C.477 B.Econ. L.209 J.D. [Siegel M.&S.]
Siegel, Ronald E., (BV) '48 '75
C.339 B.A. L.209 J.D. Assoc. Gen. Coun., Bally Total Fitness Corp.
Siegel, Stephen J. ... '62 '92 C.478 B.A. L.477 J.D. [Novack&M.]

Siegel, Elaine K. B., & Associates, P.C.
39 South La Salle Street, Suite 617, 60603 ⊙
Telephone: 312-236-8088 Facsimile: 312-236-3451 URL: http://www.siegeledlaw.com
Email: siegeledlaw@aol.com URL: http://www.siegel-law.com
Elaine K. B. Siegel;—Katherine J. Eder.
Education, School Law, Discrimination.
Skokie, Illinois Office: 5005 Touhy Avenue, 60076. Telephone: 847-329-7500. Facsimile: 847-675-1884.
See Professional Biographies, CHICAGO, ILLINOIS

Siegel Moses & Schoenstadt PC, (AV)
444 North Michigan Avenue Suite 2600, 60611
Telephone: 312-658-2000 Fax: 312-658-2022
Email: sms@smslaw.com URL: http://www.smslaw.com
Morton Siegel; Michael A. Moses; Richard G. Schoenstadt;—Jennifer G. Gallery; Zubin S. Kammula.
Civil Trial and Appellate Practice in state and federal courts throughout the U.S. Alcoholic Beverages, Antitrust, Constitutional, Commercial, Administrative, Arbitration, Corporate, Licensing and Real Estate Law.
See Professional Biographies, CHICAGO, ILLINOIS

Sieger, John ... '69 '94 C.339 B.S. L.477 J.D. [Katten M.R.]
Siegert, Edmund J. ... '60 '86 C.177 B.S. L.209 J.D. [Cremer,K.S.&S.]
Sieland, Robert P. ... '76 '03 C.602 B.A. L.339 J.D. [Ⓐ McDermott W.&E.]
Siemsen, John P. ... '70 '00 C.475 B.S. L.146 J.D. [Ⓐ DLPiper R.G.C.U.]
Sienko, David C. ... '68 '94 C.604 B.A. L.436 J.D. [Bell,B.&L.]
Siepker, Frank G. ... '39 '68 C.679 B.S. L.339 J.D. [Kelly,O.M.D.&R.]
Sierig, Miriam ... '71 '02 L.339 J.D. Asst. App. Def.
Sierocki, Amy L. ... '— '03 C.477 B.S. L.424 J.D. [Ⓐ Jenkens&G.] (Pat.)
Sieve, Brian D., P.C., (AV) ... '— '88 C.967 B.A. L.145 J.D. [Kirkland&E.]
Sievers, Eric W. ... '70 '01 C.821 B.A. L.976 J.D. [Ⓐ Baker&M.]
Sievert, Anthony J. ... '76 '00 C&L.966 B.A., J.D. [Ⓐ Wexler]
Siewerth, Sarane Crowther, (AV) ... '40 '81 C.597 B.S. L.365 J.D. [Schiller,D.&F.]
Sigal, Howard, (AV) '58 '84 C&L.494 B.A., J.D.
V.P. & Asst. Gen. Coun., General Growth Prop.
Sigal, Michael S., (AV) ... '42 '67 C.966 B.S. L.145 J.D. [Sidley A.B.&W.]
Sigale, Jordan A. ... '67 '92 C&L.339 B.S., J.D. [Sonnenschein N.&R.] (Pat.)
Sigale, Keith A. ... '73 '97 C.339 B.S. L.309 J.D. [Goldberg,K.B.B.R.&M.]
Sigel, Gabrielle, (AV) ... '57 '83 C.604 B.A. L.94 J.D. [Jenner&B.]
Sigelko, Duane F., (AV) ... '— '86 C.215 A.B. L.597 J.D. [Sachnoff&W.]
Sigman, Louis E., (AV) ... '44 '69 C.966 B.A. L.597 J.D. [Baum S.A.&N.]
Sigmond, Leif R., Jr., (AV) '65 '90
C.390 B.S. L.1338 J.D. [McDonnell B.H.&B.] (See Pat. Sect.)
Sigmond, Steven A. ... '60 '85 C&L.339 B.S., J.D. 150 North Wacker Drive
Sikes, Richard T. ... '28 '57 C&L.424 A.B., J.D. 11 S. La Salle St.
Sikes, Richard T., Jr., (AV) ... '— '80 C.436 B.S.B.A. L.209 J.D. [Freeborn&P.]
Sikora, John J., Jr. '66 '91 C.859 B.A. L.597 J.D.
Assist. Regional Dir., Chicago, M.R.O., S.E.C.
Silberman, Alan H., (AV) ... '40 '64 C.597 B.A. L.976 LL.B. [Sonnenschein N.&R.]
Silbert, Ronald G. ... '46 '72 C.339 B.A. L.209 J.D. [Young,R.F.&S.]
Siler, Edith E. '55 '79 C.881 B.A. L.145 J.D.
Prog. Admr., Div. of Professional Educ., Amer. Bar Assn.
Silets, Harvey M., (AV) ... '31 '55 C.209 B.S.C. L.477 J.D. [Katten M.R.]
Silfen, Stuart A. ... '29 '54 C&L.597 B.S., J.D. 260 E. Chestnut St.
Silk, John D. ... '70 '95 C.602 B.A. L.93 J.D. [Rothschild,B.&M.]
Silk, John K. ... '— '79 C.976 B.A. L.1119 J.D. [Karbal,C.E.S.&D.]
Sill, Andrea L. ... '71 '96 C.105 B.A. L.904 J.D. [Ⓐ Barack F.K.P.&N.]
Siller, Gustavo, Jr., (AV) '56 '83
C.597 B.S.M.E. L.209 J.D. [Brinks H.G.&L.] (See Pat. Sect.)
Sillins, Herbert J. ... '45 '78 C.1106 B.A. L.146 J.D. Asst. Pub. Def.
Silton, Herbert ... '11 '38 C.339 L.146 LL.B. 77 W. Wash. St.
Silva-Minin, Veronica A. ... '— '03 C.999 L.659 LL.M. [Ⓐ Latham&W.]
Silver, Candice Alison '73 '99 C.012 B.Com. L.424 J.D.
Sr. Coun., Bank One Corporation (Law Dept.)
Silver, Marc S. ... '— '96 C.696 B.A. L.339 J.D. [Barnes&T.]
Silver, Melvyn A. ... '40 '65 C&L.597 B.A., J.D. [Ⓒ Pattishall,M.N.H.&G.]
Silver, Stacey Rubin ... '65 '96 C.339 B.S. L.146 J.D. 1700 W. Irving Park Rd., Ste. 102
Silver, Warren E., Law Office of '57 '82
C.597 B.A. L.339 J.D. 1700 West Irving Park Rd.
Silverberg, Janet Lynn '61 '86 C.477 B.A. L.309 J.D.
Coun., Quaker Foods & Beverages
Silverman, Adam P. ... '70 '98 C.339 B.A. L.146 J.D. [Adelman&G.]
Silverman, Clifford A., (AV) '44 '69
C.339 L.209 LL.B. 180 N. LaSalle St. (⊙Homewood)
Silverman, Gary R., (AV) ... '61 '86 C.1036 B.A. L.597 J.D. [Kaye S.]
Silverman, Gregory J. ... '70 '95 C.339 B.S. L.146 J.D. [Ⓐ S.B.Salk&Assoc.]
Silverman, Howard E., (AV) ... '58 '84 C.679 B.S.E.E. L.910 J.D. [Greenberg T.] (Pat.)
Silverman, Howard S. ... '49 '74 C.339 B.A. L.365 J.D. 114 W. Illinois St.‡
Silverman, Martin L., (AV) ... '28 '51 C.339 L.365 J.D. 100 W. Monroe St.
Silverman, Michael Evan '68 '93 C.339 B.A. L.365 J.D.
Gen Coun., Smith, Bucklin & Associates, Inc.
Silverman, Michael J. ... '63 '90 C.339 B.S. L.597 J.D. [Duane M.]
Silverman, Norman R. ... '10 '34 C&L.209 LL.B. 79 W. Monroe #1020
Silverman, Peter A. ... '61 '87 C.597 B.A. L.94 J.D. [Figliulo&S.]
Silverman, Ross O., (AV) ... '60 '86 C.608 B.A. L.851 J.D. [Katten M.R.]
Silverman, S Jonathan ... '61 '92 C.976 B.A. L.145 J.D. [Gardner C.&D.]
Silverman, Cass & Singer, Ltd., (AV) ... 105 West Adams Street (Pat.)
Silverstein, Abraham ... '— '78 L.146 J.D. 3025 W. Granville
Silverstein, Burton ... '34 '62 C&L.569 B.S., LL.B. 30 S. Wacker Dr., Suite 2900‡
Silverstein, Ira Isaac ... '60 '85 C.424 B.A. L.365 J.D. 111 W. Washington St.
Silverstein, Leo A. ... '— '38 C.145 L.597 LL.B. 860 Dewitt Pl.
Silverstein, Steven '62 '87 C.477 B.B.A. L.280 J.D.
(adm. in GA; not adm. in IL) Equity Property & Develop. Co.
Silverstein, Zachary B. ... '68 '99 C.977 B.A. L.597 J.D. [Ⓐ Babbitt&M.]
Silvert, Donald J. ... '53 '92 C.674 A.B. L.569 J.D. [Ⓒ Brinks H.G.&L.] (See Pat. Sect.)

Silvestri, Arnold A., (AV) '— '50 L.145 J.D. [🄲 Dykema G.P.]
Silvestri, Laurie A. '60 '86 C.145 B.A. L.146 J.D. 70 W. Madison Street
Silvestri, Peter N. '57 '82 C&L.209 B.A., J.D. Co. Comr.
Silvey, Steve C. '57 '88 C.238 B.S. L.209 J.D. [Grotefeld&D.]
Simala, Jodi Ann '68 '93 C.94 B.A. L.309 J.D. [Mayer,B.R.&M.]
Simard, Raymond M., Law Offices of, (BV) '50 '77
C.1107 B.A. L.365 J.D. 221 N. LaSalle St.
Simioni, Lisa M. '71 '03 L.365 [🄰 Lewis,O.&F.]
Simmons, Alisa C. '— '99 C.345 B.A. L.597 J.D. [🄰 Marshall,G.&B.] (See Pat. Sect.)

Simmons, Geraldine C. '— '81 C.1016 B.A. L.365 J.D.
7316 South Cottage Grove, 60619
Telephone: 773-994-2600 Fax: 773-994-2606
Email: geresimmon@aol.com
Elder, Probate, Real Estate law, Elder, Probate.

Simmons, Henry R., Jr. '55 '80 C.679 B.S. L.209 J.D. 2650 S. California
Simmons, Jade G. '74 '99 C.145 B.A. L.339 J.D. Assoc. Atty., Chicago Transit Auth.
Simmons, Jerome G. '76 '02 C.1133 B.S. L.879 J.D. [🄰 Grant H.&S.]
Simmons, Lisa S. '61 '86 C&L.966 B.A., J.D. [Wildman,H.A.&D.]
Simmons-Gill, Catherine '49 '75 C.339 A.B. L.597 J.D. [C.Simmons-Gill]

Simmons-Gill, Catherine, LLC, Offices of
221 North LaSalle Street Suite 850, 60601
Telephone: 312-609-6611 Fax: 312-609-6610 URL: http://www.simmonsgill.com
Email: csimmonsgil@netscape.net URL: http://www.lawyers.com/simmons-gill
Catherine Simmons-Gill.
Intellectual Property, Trademark, Copyright, Internet, Trade Secret, Commercial Litigation, Corporate, Employment.
See Professional Biographies, CHICAGO, ILLINOIS

Simon, Adam B. '72 '97 C.910 B.S. L.276 J.D. [🄰 Ancel,G.D.B.D.&R.]
Simon, Arthur Gary, (AV) '54 '79 C.339 B.S. L.424 J.D. [Crane,H.S.W.&C.]
Simon, Arthur J., (AV) '54 '79 C.880 B.S. L.597 J.D. Gen. Coun., William Blair & Co.
Simon, Bradley F. '69 '94 C.339 B.S. L.597 J.D. Bond Cos.
Simon, Charles S. '42 '67 C.339 B.S. L.209 J.D. [C.S.Simon]
Simon, David M., (AV) '64 '89 C.367 B.A. L.966 J.D. [Wildman,H.A.&D.]
Simon, Donald R. '72 '03 C.1310 B.A. L.365 J.D./LL.M. [EntertainmentChicago]
Simon, Elliott M. '31 '53 C.1016 L.209 J.D. One E. Wacker Dr.
Simon, Ernest D., (AV) '— '60 C.339 B.A. L.597 J.D. [🄲 Sachnoff&W.]
Simon, George T., (AV) '— '73 C.855 B.A. L.309 J.D. [Foley&L.]
Simon, Gregg M., (AV) '62 '87 C.339 B.S. L.424 J.D. [Much S.F.D.A.&R.]
Simon, Gregory B. '77 '02 19 S. LaSalle, Ste. 700
Simon, Gregory J. '63 '88 C.309 A.B. L.477 J.D. [Kerns,P.F.&P.]
Simon, John A., (AV) '60 '85 C.770 B.S. L.424 J.D. [Gardner C.&D.]
Simon, John B., (AV) '42 '67 C.966 B.S. L.209 J.D. [Jenner&B.]
Simon, John P., (AV) '53 '76 C.112 A.B. L.1068 J.D. [Sidley A.B.&W.]
Simon, Keith A. '— '99 C.339 B.S. L.597 J.D. [🄰 Latham&W.]
Simon, Kevin S. '— '92 C.321 B.A. L.1065 J.D. [Fisher&P.]
Simon, Lauren Beth '52 '82 C.801 B.S. L.209 J.D. Legal Assistance
Simon, Linda J. '67 '95 C&L.145 B.A., J.D. [🄰 Lord,B.&B.]
Simon, Mark C., (AV) '54 '79 C.118 B.A. L.477 J.D. [Katten M.R.]
Simon, Mark S., Law Office of, (AV) '56 '83
C.339 B.S. L.209 J.D. 70 W. Madison St., Suite 1400
Simon, Raymond F., (AV) '32 '56 C&L.424 B.S., J.D. [Simon&S.]
Simon, Robert F. '53 '82 C.473 B.A. L.209 J.D. [Vedder,P.K.&K.]
Simon, Seymour F., (AV) '15 '38 C&L.597 B.S., J.D. [DLPiper R.G.C.U.]
Simon, Charles S., Ltd. 10 South La Salle St.

Simon, Lapidos & Simon, LLC
(See Skokie)

Simon & Spitalli, (AV) 55 W. Wacker Dr.
Simonetti, John A. '54 '81 C.93 B.A. L.365 J.D. [🄲 Cohen,G.&R.]
Simonetti, John J., (AV) '68 '94 C.93 B.A. L.424 J.D. [🄰 Pavalon,G.L.&M.]
Simoni, Christopher '46 '80 C.477 B.A. L.596 J.D.
(adm. in OR; not adm. in IL) Assoc. Dean, Northwestern Univ.‡
Simons, Broudy '25 '52 C.477 B.S. L.597 J.D. [🄲 Cornfield&F.]
Simons, Douglas A. '60 '85 C.477 B.B.A. L.209 J.D. 680 N. Peoria St.
Simons, Paul R. '64 '89 C.350 B.B.A. L.352 J.D. [Sinar K.M.&F.]
Simonsen, Karen A. '— '88 C.172 B.A. L.597 J.D. [McDermott W.&E.]
Simpson, David W. '47 '80
C.879 B.A. L.424 J.D. Asst. Exec. Dir., Dept. of Youth Guidance
Simpson, John D., (AV) '— '61 C.350 B.S. L.209 J.D. [🄲 Schiff H.] (Pat.)
Simpson, John H. '57 '84
C.951 A.B. L.309 J.D. Mng. Dir., Wasserstein Perella & Co., Inc.
Simpson, Laura E. '75 '03 C.31 B.A. L.880 J.D. [🄰 Bell,B.&L.]
Simpson, Manliff M. '42 '72 C.339 B.A.B.S. L.209 J.D. [Simpson&C.]
Simpson, Margaret J. '61 '97 C.747 B.A. L.145 J.D. [🄰 Jenner&B.]
Simpson, Roger M., Jr. '36 '62 C.813 B.A. L.597 J.D. Rollins Burdick Hunter Co.
Simpson & Cybak 33 N. LaSalle St., 34th Fl.
Sims, Steven K., Sr. '64 '89 C.234 B.A. L.910 J.D. [Enterprise]
Simutis, Jennifer L. '72 '02 C.339 B.A. L.209 J.D. [🄰 Zulkie]
Sinar, Scott A. '62 '87 C.339 B.S. L.146 J.D. [Sinar K.M.&F.]
Sinar Keldermans Miller & Friedman, LLC, (AV) 303 W. Madison St.
Sinars, Douglas M., (AV) '68 '93 C.602 B.A. L.209 J.D. [Matushek,N.&S.]
Sinars, Laura Manzi '68 '93 C&L.602 B.A., J.D. [Robbins,S.N.L.&T.]
Sinars, Theodore A., (AV) '43 '67 C&L.602 B.B.A., J.D. [Madden,J.M.&S.]
Siner, Jonathan P. '44 '69 C&L.966 B.A., J.D. Lyric Opera of Chicago
Singer, Cecile '39 '72 122 S. Michigan
Singer, David B. '77 '03 C&L.477 B.A., J.D. [🄰 Fox,H.S.L.&C.]
Singer, David E. '69 '96 C.674 A.B. L.446 J.D. [🄰 DLPiper R.G.C.U.]
Singer, Henry M. '52 '76 C.1016 B.S.B.A. L.146 J.D. 6323 N. Monticello
Singer, Herbert J., (AV) '41 '67 C.339 B.S. L.424 J.D. [Silverman,C.&S.] (Pat.)
Singer, Jeffrey, (AV) '50 '75 C&L.221 B.A., J.D. [🄲 Segal M.S.&M.]
Singer, Matthew '79 '04 L.1119 J.D. [🄰 Holland&K.]
Singer, Paul H. '36 '63 C.674 A.B. L.309 J.D. 500 North Dearborn St., Ste. 726
Singer, Simone Alysa '67 '99 C.608 B.A. L.365 J.D. Singer Properties
Singer, Stacy E. '68 '93 C&L.477 B.A., J.D.
VP, Estate Admin., Harris Trust & Savings Bank
Singer, William S., (AV) '— '65 C.1036 B.A. L.178 LL.B. [🄲 Kirkland&E.]
Singewald, Joshua S. '72 '99 C.93 B.A. L.365 J.D. [🄰 Johnson&B.]
Singh, A. Paul '60 '86 C.188 A.B. L.569 J.D. 6645 N. Rockwell‡
Singh, Amy K. '62 '87 C.477 B.A. L.597 J.D.
The Entertainment & Intellectual Property Grp., LLC
Singh, Annapurna '— '05 C.188 B.A. L.424 J.D. [🄰 Gardner C.&D.]
Singh, Julia J. '— '04 C.1138 L.494 [🄰 Chapman&C.]
Singla, Parita '71 '98 C&L.999 [🄰 Mayer,B.R.&M.]
Sink, Ann Marie '53 '82 C.424 B.A. L.209 J.D. [Katten M.R.]
Sinnappan, Raymond D. '72 '97 C.339 B.S. L.597 J.D. [🄰 Jenner&B.]

Sinnott, Edmund W., (AV) '18 '42 C&L.424 A.B., J.D. 55 W. Monroe St., Ste. 800
Sinson, Junie L., (Mr.), (AV) '30 '57 C.72 B.A. L.597 J.D. 111 W. Washington St.
Sinson, Kent D. '61 '87 C.299 B.A. L.209 J.D. 111 W. Washington, Ste. 737
Sinson, Scott R. '70 '97 C.674 B.A. L.221 J.D. [🄰 Bullaro&C.]
Sintich, Sharon M. '— '04 [🄰 Marshall,G.&B.] (See Pat. Sect.)
Sipari, Orazio (Ross) '17 '48 C&L.608 B.S., J.D.
(adm. in OH; not adm. in IL) S.E.C.
Sipchen, James J., Jr. '68 '94 C.347 B.A. L.365 J.D. [Pretzel&S.]
Sipe, Stephen Todd '— '91 C.276 L.477 [🄰 Chapman&C.]
Siprut, Joseph J. '77 '03 C.436 B.A. L.597 J.D. [🄰 Howrey]
Sir, Brian T. '61 '86 C.1082 B.S. L.339 J.D. Guggenheim Capital, LLC
Siracusa, Thomas G., (AV) '61 '86 C.424 B.A. L.146 J.D. [🄰 Power R.&S.]
Siragusa, Charles W., (AV) '49 '74 C&L.597 B.A., J.D. [Crowley B.&K.]
Sircus, Gary M., (BV) '61 '85 C.861 B.S.E. L.597 J.D. 928 W. Montana St.
Siros, Steven M., (AV) '69 '94 C.338 B.A. L.589 J.D. [Jenner&B.]
Sirota, Michael L. '49 '75
C.1044 B.A. L.339 J.D. V.P., Sr. Atty., Leo Burnett Worldwide, Inc.
Sirus, Richard A., (BV) '58 '83 C&L.424 B.B.A., J.D. [Greenberg T.]
Siske, Roger C., (AV) '44 '69 C.608 B.S. L.477 J.D. [Sonnenschein N.&R.]
Sissel, Scott '79 '04 C&L.352 B.B.A., J.D. [🄰 Shaheen,N.S.F.&E.]
Sisul, J. Jerome '45 '73 C.339 B.A. L.209 J.D. Asst. Atty. Gen.
Sitko, Anthony G., (AV) '— '93
C.477 B.S.M.E. L.912 J.D. [Marshall,G.&B.] (See Pat. Sect.)
Sitko, Mary F. '— '91 L.213 J.D. [Worker,S.&H.]
Sitkoff, Erica S. '79 '04 C.597 B.A. L.276 J.D. [🄰 DLPiper R.G.C.U.]
Sitkoff, Robert Henry '74 '01 C.893 B.A. L.145 J.D.
Asst. Prof. of Law, Northwestern Univ. Sch. of Law
Sitkowski, Robert J. '61 '96 C.339 B.Arch. L.665 J.D.
(adm. in PA; not adm. in IL) [Freeborn&P.]
Sitrick, Gregory P. '76 '03 C.37 B.S.E.E. L.597 J.D. [🄰 Bell,B.&L.]
Sitzer, Matthew O. '66 '92 C.602 B.A. L.597 J.D. [Grippo&E.]
Sitzer, Nina Momtazee '67 '92 C.1365 B.A. L.597 J.D. [Katten M.R.]
Siu, Woon-Wah, (AV) '51 '93 C.999 M.A. L.339 J.D. [Bell,B.&L.]
Siwik, Christine J. '— '95 C.475 B.A. L.424 J.D. [Rakoczy M.M.S.]

Skadden, Arps, Slate, Meagher & Flom LLP, (AV)
333 West Wacker Drive, 60606 ⊙
Telephone: 312-407-0700 Fax: 312-407-0411
URL: http://www.skadden.com
Partners: Wayne W. Whalen; Charles W. Mulaney, Jr.; Timothy A. Nelsen; Marian P. Wexler; Warren G. Lavey; Andrew S. Kenoe; William R. Kunkel; John D. Rayis; David E. Springer; John Wm. Butler, Jr.; Edward M. Crane; Thomas A. Hale; Randall J. Rademaker; Christina M. Tchen; Gary P. Cullen; John André LeDuc; Ann H. Pollock; Peter C. Krupp; Brian W. Duwe; J. Eric Ivester; Charles F. Smith; Seth E. Jacobson; Maxwell M. Miller; Rodd M. Schreiber; Louis S. Freeman; Matthew R. Kipp; Lynn M. McGovern; George N. Panagakis; R. Ryan Stoll; Timothy R. Pohl; L. Byron Vance III; John K. Lyons; Felicia Gerber Perlman; Frances P.H. Kao; Charles B. Taylor; Susan S. Hassan; Kimberly A. deBeers; David Polster; Albert L. Hogan, III. Of Counsel: Arthur S. Rollin. Counsel: Elizabeth A. Devine; Steven H. Forbes; Lee P. Garner; Eric J. Gorman; Shilpi Gupta; David F. Kolin; Karen M. Lee; Mark A. McDermott; Donna L. McDevitt; Steven P. Miriani; Nancy M. Olson; Mark E. Rakoczy; Dhananjai Shivakumar (Not admitted in IL); Deborah G. Solmor. Associates: Carolyn G. Aberman; Christopher Athas; Gregory S. Bailey; Carmin D. Ballou; Nick Campanario (Not admitted in IL); Jennifer J. Carlson; Christopher P. Connors; Laura D. Cullison; Eugene A. DeAngelis; Christine M. DeMott; Chris L. Dickerson; Hugo Dubovoy, Jr.; Brian M. Fern; Benjamin R. Foster; Robert P. Gal; Amy M. Gardner; Randell J. Gartin (Not admitted in IL); Rebecca M. Girsch; Jeffrey A. Greenblatt; John Guzzardo; Brian Hanigan; Laura A. Hazelwood; Allison Verderber Herriott; Erik A. Hogstrom; Yuan-Ying Hsu; Anthony C. Iannazzo (Not admitted in IL); Charlotte E. Kaiser; Brian P. Karpuk; Jason P. Ketchens; Peter Krebs; Thoufiq A. Kutty; John W. Lee; Brooke A. Levy; Katherine L. Lindahl; Kim Lombardo; Gerard C. Martin; Michael P. McGrane; Lanelle K. Meidan; Ron E. Meisler; Joseph A. Miron; Matthew M. Murphy; Patrick J. Nash, Jr.; Samuel S. Ory; Michael W. Perl; Troy R. Peters; Melissa L. Plumlee (Not admitted in IL); David S. Prohofsky; Joshua D. Ratner (Not admitted in IL); Alison M. Rhoten; Ryan J. Rohlfsen; William M. Rohner; Christopher Rohrbacher; Eric B. Rosenoff; Jason Rudinsky; Matthew A. Shebuski; Susan J. Smith; Kelly Smith-Haley; Nathan Stuart; Grey Alexandra Tanzi; Jakub Teply; Janet Byrne Thabit; Jenelle M. Todryk; Amy Van Gelder; Courtney E. VanLonkhuyzen; Xiaojie Wang; Joseph N. Wharton; Jon-Micheal A. Wheat; Amanda S. Williamson; Stephen D. Williamson; Lindsay E. Wilson-Gowin; Richard C. Witzel, Jr.; Gretchen M. Wolf.
General Practice.
Offices of Affiliates:
New York, New York: Four Times Square, 10036. Telephone: 212-735-3000. Fax: 212-735-2000.
Boston, Massachusetts: One Beacon Street, 02108. Telephone: 617-573-4800. Fax: 617-573-4822.
Washington, D.C.: 1440 New York Avenue, N.W., 20005. Telephone: 202-371-7000. Fax: 202-393-5760.
Wilmington, Delaware: One Rodney Square, 19801. Telephone: 302-651-3000. Fax: 302-651-3001.
Los Angeles, California: 300 South Grand Avenue, Suite 3400, 90071. Telephone: 213-687-5000. Fax: 213-687-5600.
San Francisco, California: Four Embarcadero Center, Suite 3800, 94111. Telephone: 415-984-6400. Fax: 415-984-2698.
Houston, Texas: 1600 Smith Street, Suite 4400, 77002. Telephone: 713-655-5100. Fax: 713-655-5200.
Palo Alto, California: 525 University Avenue, Suite 1100, 94301. Telephone: 650-470-4500. Fax: 650-470-4570.
Tokyo, Japan: Izumi Garden Tower, 21st Floor, 1-6-1 Roppongi, Minato-ku, 106-6021. Telephone: 011-813-3568-2600. Fax: 011-813-3568-2626.
London, England: Skadden, Arps, Slate, Meagher & Flom (UK) LLP, 40 Bank Street, Canary Wharf, E14 5DS. Telephone: 011-44-20-7519-7000. Fax: 011-44-20-7519-7070.
Hong Kong, China: 30/F Tower Two, Lippo Centre, 89 Queensway, Central. Telephone: 011-852-2820-0700. Fax: 011-852-2820-0727.
Sydney, New South Wales 2000, Australia: Skadden, Arps, Slate, Meagher & Flom (International), Level 13, 131 Macquarie Street. Telephone: 011-61-2-9253-6000. Fax: 011-61-2-9253-6044.
Toronto, Ontario, Canada: 222 Bay Street, Suite 1750, P.O. Box 258, M5K 1J5. Telephone: 416-777-4700. Fax: 416-777-4747.
Brussels, Belgium: 523 avenue Louise, Box 30, 1050. Telephone: 011-32-2-639-0300. Fax: 011-32-2-639-0339.
Frankfurt am Main, Germany: An der Welle 5, 60322. Telephone: 011-49-69-742200. Fax: 011-49-69-74220300.
Munich, Germany: Karl-Scharnagl-Ring 7, 80539. Telephone: +011-49-89-244-495-0. Fax: +011-49-89-244-495-300.
Paris, France: 68, rue du Faubourg Saint-Honoré, 75008. Telephone: 011-331-55-27-11-00. Fax: 011-331-55-27-11-99.
Beijing, China: East Wing Office, Level 4, China World Trade Center, No 1 Jian Guo Men Wai Avenue, 100004. Telephone: 011-86-10-6505-5511. Fax: 011-86-10-6505-5522.
Moscow, Russia: Degtyarniy Pereulok 4, Building 1, 125009. Telephone: 011-7-501-797-4600. Fax: 011-7-501-797-4601.
Singapore, Singapore: Skadden, Arps, Slate, Meagher & Flom (International), 9 Temasek Boulevard, Suite 29-01, Suntec Tower Two, 038989. Telephone: 011-65-6434-2900. Fax: 011-65-6434-2988.
Vienna, Austria: Schwarzenbergplatz 6, A-1030. Telephone: 011-43-1-710-77-300. Fax: 011-43-1-710-77-303.
See Professional Biographies, CHICAGO, ILLINOIS

Skafish, Bradley A., Law Offices of '— '02
C&L.347 B.S., J.D. 180 N. LaSalle Street, Suite 1925
Skaletsky, Scott, (AV) '56 '81 C.339 B.A. L.734 J.D. [Skaletsky&M.]
Skaletsky and Mannis, P.C., (AV) 180 N. Wacker Dr., Suite 201
Skalitzky, William G. '65 '91 C&L.597 B.A., J.D. 322 S. Green Street
Skallas, A. Thomas '— '98 C.339 B.S. L.209 J.D. [Arnstein&L.]
Skardon, Stephen A. '72 '03 C.608 B.A. L.339 J.D. [🄰 Michaels&M.]
Skean, Brett A. '73 '03 C.352 B.A. L.589 J.D. [🄰 Moore,S.&W.]

Skeffington, John F., (AV) '30 '57
C&L.424 B.S., J.D. 175 West Jackson Boulevard, Suite 1600‡
Skelton, Kathryn E. ..... '49 '76 C.475 B.A. L.339 J.D. [Hoogendoorn&T.]
Skey, Christopher N. ..... '69 '97 C&L.597 B.A., J.D. [🄰 DLPiper R.G.C.U.]
Skidelsky, Allon D. ..... '— '98 C.339 B.S. L.146 J.D. [🄰 Sarnoff&B.]
Skidmore, David ..... '65 '98 C.1564 B.A. L.665 J.D. Asst. Regional Coun.,
Skiermont, Karey V. ..... '— '02 C&L.546 B.A., J.D. [🄰 Jones D.]
Skiermont, Paul J. ..... '73 '02 C.383 B.A. L.145 J.D. [🄰 Bartlit B.H.P.&S.]
Skiko, Peter G., (BV) ..... '67 '92 C&L.602 B.A., J.D. [Swanson,M.&B.]
Skilken, Adam R. ..... '— '01 C.197 B.A. L.597 J.D. [🄰 Latham&W.]
Skilken, Melissa Suzanne ..... '72 '98 C.385 A.B. L.150 J.D. [🄰 Wildman,H.A.&D.]
Skinner, Jerome L., (AVⓉ) '51 '79 C.1044 B.A. L.607 J.D.
(adm. in OH; not adm. in IL) [🄰 Nolan]
Skinner, Joel R. ..... '55 '84 C.339 B.A. L.146 J.D. Blue Cross and Blue Shield Assn.
Skinner, Mary Jacobs, (AV) ..... '57 '81 C.309 B.A. L.597 J.D. [Sidley A.B.&W.]
Skinner, Samuel K., (AV) ..... '38 '66 C.339 B.S. L.209 J.D. [🄲 Greenberg T.]
Skinner, Steven E., II ..... '72 '01 C.801 B.A. L.424 J.D. Asst. D. A.
Skinner-Lewis, Frances J., (AV) ..... '— '80 C.37 B.A. L.146 J.D. [F.J.Skinner-Lewis]

Skinner-Lewis, F. J., Law Offices of, (AV)
1 North La Salle Street, Suite 1375, 60602
Telephone: 312-346-0336 Fax: 312-346-0192
Email: fjsl.law@attglobal.net URL: http://www.lawyers.com/franceskinnerlewis
Frances J. Skinner-Lewis.
General Practice.
See Professional Biographies, CHICAGO, ILLINOIS

Skittone, John R. ..... '10 '34 C&L.597 B.S.L. 5070 W. Pensacola
Sklar, Michael L., (AV) ..... '38 '63 C.477 B.A. L.309 J.D. [DLPiper R.G.C.U.]
Sklar, Ruth L. ..... '40 '78 C.477 B.A. L.209 J.D. 2041 North Cleveland
Sklar, Stanley P., (AV) ..... '38 '64 C.339 B.S. L.597 J.D. [Bell,B.&L.]
Sklar, Steven H. ..... '69 '96 C.910 B.S.Ch.E. L.597 J.D. [Leydig,V.&M.] (See Pat. Sect.)
Sklarsky, Charles B., (AV) ..... '46 '73 C.309 B.A. L.966 J.D. [Jenner&B.]
Sklaver, Julie Ann ..... '69 '95 C.659 B.A. L.146 J.D. 2729 N. Janssen
Sklodowski, Robert L. ..... '35 '59 C.1016 B.A. L.146 J.D. 111 W. Washington
Skoning, Gerald D., (AV) ..... '42 '67 C.674 A.B. L.477 J.D. [🄲 Seyfarth S.]
Skontos, George J. ..... '36 '62 C&L.209 B.S.C., J.D. 20 South Clark St., 29th Fl.
Skony, Gregory J. ..... '79 '05 C.602 B.S. L.209 J.D. [🄰 Welsh&K.]
Skrel, Vicki Heltman ..... '54 '80 C.150 B.A. L.201 J.D. Corp. Coun., City of Chicago
Skrobin, Wendy Kaleta ..... '69 '94 C.597 B.A. L.424 J.D. [🄰 McFadden&D.]
Skweres, F. Richard ..... '70 '95 C&L.424 B.A., J.D. [Lewis,O.&F.]
Slade, Michael ..... '— '99 C.1365 B.A. L.309 J.D. [Kirkland&E.]
Sladnick, Clifford M., (AV) '56 '81 C&L.339 B.S., J.D.
Sr. V.P. & Corp. Coun., St. Paul Fed. Bank for Sugs
Slagel, Allan T. ..... '60 '88 C&L.347 B.S., J.D. [Shefsky&F.]
Slajchert, Michael C. ..... '48 '82 C&L.424 B.A., J.D. Guardian Ad Litem
Slamar, Paul T. ..... '49 '75 C.477 B.A. L.365 J.D. Fl 18, 200 E Randolph St
Slate, Peter J. ..... '67 '94 C.477 B.A. L.273 J.D. 525 W. Monroe St., Suite 1600
Slater, Bernard J., Jr. ..... '62 '94 C.352 B.B.A. L.424 J.D. 120 W. Madison
Slater, John, III ..... '64 '91 C.352 B.B.A. L.502 J.D. Off. of the Pub. Guardian
Slater, Paul E., (AV) ..... '45 '70 C.178 B.A. L.597 J.D. [Sperling&S.]
Slater, Peggy H. ..... '44 '75 C.112 B.A. L.597 J.D. Northwestern Univ. Legal Clinic
Slattery, Christine Kentopp, (AV) '61 '88
C.518 A.B. L.575 J.D. Dep. Comr., Dept. of Planning
Slattery, Daniel J., (AV) ..... '— '85 C.72 B.A. L.910 J.D. [Sachnoff&W.]
Slattery, Kerrin Brennan ..... '69 '96 C.1049 B.B.A. L.424 J.D. [🄰 McDermott W.&E.]
Slaughter, Christopher S. ..... '73 '98 C.155 B.A. L.589 J.D. [C.Slaughter&Assoc.]
Slaughter, Kevin E. ..... '70 '95 C.302 B.A. L.597 J.D. [Burris,W.S.&T.]
Slaughter, Robert Z. ..... '54 '82 C.674 A.B. L.145 J.D. [Jenner&B.]
Slaughter, Chris, & Associates, Law Offices of ..... 2011 East 75th Street, Suite 114
Slavick, Scott J. ..... '73 '98 C.597 B.A. L.276 J.D. [🄰 Brinks H.G.&L.]
Slavin, Mark F., (AV) ..... '61 '87 C.339 B.A. L.146 J.D. [Kusper&R.]
Slavin, Stephen M., (AV) ..... '— '64 C.165 A.B. L.145 J.D. [Foley&L.] ‡
Slavis, Harry, (Ltd.) ..... '24 '47 C.209 L.37 LL.B. 79 W. Monroe St.
Slawkowski, David J., (AV) ..... '— '75 C.602 A.B. L.309 J.D. [Anderson,R.]
Sledz, Henry W., Jr., (AV) ..... '— '74 C.339 B.S. L.424 J.D. [Schiff H.]
Sleeker, Katherine L. ..... '75 '02 C.945 B.A. L.260 J.D. [🄰 Segal M.S.&M.]
Sleezer, Jason R. ..... '79 '05 C.578 B.A. L.209 J.D. [🄰 Scott&K.]
Slepicka, Frank B. ..... '67 '92 C.597 B.A. L.339 J.D. [🄲 Lovells]
Slewitzke, Ronald T. ..... '47 '75 C.966 B.A. L.365 J.D. [Morgan,L.D.&J.]
Slezak, Walter T., (AV) ..... '50 '75 C.750 B.A. L.597 J.D. [Lord,B.&B.]
Slick, G. Christopher ..... '71 '97 C.69 B.A. L.602 J.D. [🄰 Swanson,M.&B.]
Sliwa, Barbara ..... '75 '01 C.958 B.S. L.365 J.D. Atty.
Sloan, James D. ..... '— '98 C.339 B.A. L.146 J.D. [🄰 Donohue B.M.&S.]
Sloan, Maol Murray, (AV) ..... '39 '69 C&L.424 A.B., LL.B. [Sloan&Assoc.]

Sloan and Associates, Inc., (AV)
111 West Washington Street Suite 1020, 60602
Telephone: 312-332-3771 Fax: 312-332-1319
URL: http://www.lawyers.com/sloanandassoc
Member of Firm: Maol Murray Sloan.
Family Law Practice including Child Custody, Divorce, Domestic Violence, Premarital Agreements, Paternity.
See Professional Biographies, CHICAGO, ILLINOIS

Sloane, Wendi E., (AV) ..... '57 '82 C.103 B.A. L.145 J.D. [Barack F.K.P.&N.]
Sloat, John A. ..... '70 '02 C.604 B.A. L.477 J.D. [🄰 Mayer,B.R.&M.]
Slobig, Robert J., (AV) ..... '57 '82 C.436 A.B. L.597 J.D. [Torshen,S.G.D.&A.]
Slobodien, Andrew M. ..... '— '94 C.311 B.A. L.146 J.D. [Wildman,H.A.&D.]
Slocum, Robert Bruce ..... '64 '95 C.589 B.S. L.365 J.D. Litig. Coun., Aon Corporation
Slodki, Alan H. ..... '47 '72 C.339 B.A. L.365 J.D. [A.H.Slodki&Assoc.]
Slodki, Alan H., & Associates, Ltd. ..... 111 West Washington Street, Suite 1023
Slominski, Gabriel S. ..... '77 '02 C.475 B.A. L.209 J.D. Claims Atty., Argonaut Ins. Co.
Slonim, Nancy Cowger '46 '79 C.502 B.J. L.146 J.D.
Dep. News Secy. & Dir., Media Servs., Amer. Bar Assn.
Slota, Thomas J. ..... '55 '80 C.367 B.A. L.365 J.D. 1640 W. Van Buren Street
Slotky, Solomon ..... '11 '34 C.999 L.209 LL.B. Asst. States Atty.
Slovak, Patricia Costello, (AV) ..... '— '77 C.734 B.A. L.145 J.D. [Schiff H.]
Slovick, David S. ..... '72 '98 C.966 B.A. L.146 J.D. [🄰 Katten M.R.]
Slutsky, Michael H., (AV) ..... '51 '76 C.860 A.B. L.145 J.D. [Allison,S.&K.]
Slutzky, Lorence H., (AV) ..... '46 '72 C.801 B.S. L.365 J.D. [Robbins,S.N.L.&T.]
Slutzky, Rodney C., (AV) ..... '48 '74 C.475 B.A. L.339 J.D. 33 N. Dearborn St., Ste. 800
Slykas, Scott P. ..... '68 '98 C.1049 B.A. L.365 J.D. [🄰 Henderson&L.]
Small, Andrew D. ..... '64 '89 C.477 B.B.A. L.145 J.D. [Katten M.R.]
Small, Michael H. ..... '59 '85 C.339 B.S. L.365 J.D. Ernst & Young
Small, Michael J., (AV) ..... '— '91 C.103 A.B. L.145 J.D. [Foley&L.]
Small, Norman H. ..... '26 '52 C.339 B.A. L.209 LL.B. 77 W. Wash. St.
Smalling, Cheryl Lee ..... '52 '79 C.209 B.A. L.365 J.D. Allstate Ins. Co.‡
Smalling, Stephen J. ..... '58 '84 C.352 B.A. L.365 J.D. 30 N. LaSalle St.
Smart, Allen R., (AV) ..... '34 '61 C.674 A.B. L.309 LL.B. [🄲 Bell,B.&L.]
Smart, Patricia S. ..... '— '78 C&L.339 B.A., J.D. [Smart&B.]

Smart & Bostjancich
19 South La Salle Street, Suite 1300, 60603
Telephone: 312-857-2424 Facsimile: 312-201-0737
John Bostjancich; Patricia S. Smart.
Litigation and Counseling. Domestic and International Trademark, Copyright, Unfair Competition and Computer Law, Licensing, Franchising, False Advertising, Right of Publicity, Counterfeiting and Trade Secrets.
See Professional Biographies, CHICAGO, ILLINOIS

Smeda, Reid J. '67 '92 C.114 B.A. L.1209 J.D.
Vice President & Dir., Fifth Third Bank, Chicago
Smedinghoff, Thomas J., (AV) ..... '51 '78 C.388 B.A. L.477 J.D. [🄲 Baker&M.]
Smedstad, Adam C. ..... '67 '92 C.145 B.A. L.273 J.D. [🄲 Scopelitis,G.L.&H.]
Smeltzer, Robert H. ..... '65 '91 C.473 B.S. L.150 J.D. 200 W. Adams St., Ste. 1900
Smerling, David W. ..... '33 '58 C.477 A.B. L.597 J.D. Chmn., L.C. Industries
Smetana, Gerard C., (AV) ..... '32 '58 C.563 B.A. L.477 J.D. [Smetana&A.]
Smetana, Kathryn A. ..... '73 '02 C.339 B.S. L.424 J.D. [🄰 Pretzel&S.]
Smetana & Avakian, (AV) ..... 39 South La Salle Street, Suite 1218
Smiejek, Steven D. ..... '70 '97 C.589 B.S. L.365 J.D. [🄰 Wilson E.M.E.&D.]
Smierciak, Robert M. ..... '46 '71 C.424 B.A. L.597 J.D. Assoc. Cir. J.
Smigelskis, Marianne R. ..... '43 '68 C.788 A.B. L.976 LL.B. Legal Assist. Found. of Chic.
Smigiel, Chester W. ..... '17 '52 C.137 L.146 LL.B. 2392 N Milwaukee Ave
Smigielski, Mary A. ..... '68 '93 C&L.1049 B.A., J.D. [🄲 Morgan,L.&B.]
Smiley, Jennifer E. ..... '72 '01 C.881 B.A. L.597 J.D. [🄰 Miller S.&H.]
Smilie, Scott W. ..... '71 '97 C.339 B.S.G.E. L.146 J.D. [🄰 Patzik,F.&S.] (Pat.)
Smiricky, Stacey Lynn ..... '76 '02 C.352 B.A. L.589 J.D. [🄰 Wilson E.M.E.&D.]
Smirl, Richard W. '67 '92 C.1?2 B.A. L.426 J.D.
(adm. in CA; not adm. in IL) Sr. Coun., William Blair & Co.
Smith, Aaron C. ..... '73 '99 C&L.352 B.A., J.D. [🄰 Lord,B.&B.]
Smith, Alys C. ..... '72 '99 C.475 B.A. L.352 J.D. Suite 1310, 10 South Lasalle Street
Smith, Amanda J. ..... '— '03 C.339 B.S. L.577 J.D. [🄰 Latham&W.]
Smith, Amy E. ..... '64 '89 C.802 B.B.A. L.424 J.D. 525 W. Monroe St., Suite 1600
Smith, Arthur B., Jr., (AV) ..... '44 '69 C.188 B.S. L.145 J.D. [Ogletree,D.N.S.&S.]
Smith, Ashley Lynn ..... '73 '98 C&L.802 B.B.A., J.D. Off. of Pub. Guardian
Smith, Barbara Lee ..... '67 '91 C&L.145 A.B., J.D. [🄰 Sonnenschein N.&R.]
Smith, Bradley A. ..... '— '04 C.350 B.S. L.146 J.D. [🄰 Neal&L.]
Smith, Brett D. ..... '74 '99 C.339 B.S. L.424 J.D. [🄰 Burke,W.M.&S.]
Smith, Brian A. ..... '— '98 C&L.347 B.S., J.D. [🄰 Freeborn&P.]
Smith, Charles F. ..... '62 '87 C.388 B.A. L.145 J.D. [Skadden,A.S.M.&F.]
Smith, Christine E., Law Office of, (AV) '40 '65
C.424 A.B. L.209 J.D. 120 W. Madison St.
Smith, Colin ..... '55 '80 C.210 B.A. L.910 J.D. [Holland&K.]
Smith, Coree ..... '— '01 C.351 B.A. L.352 J.D. [🄰 DLPiper R.G.C.U.]
Smith, Craig C. ..... '66 '96 C.339 B.A. L.365 J.D. [🄰 Noonan&L.]
Smith, Daniel W. ..... '65 '92 C.602 B.A. L.339 J.D. [Jenner&B.]
Smith, David E.B. ..... '58 '94 C.597 B.A. L.146 J.D. Asst. Corp. Coun.
Smith, David Z. ..... '— '98 C.1036 B.A. L.309 J.D. [🄰 Sachnoff&W.]
Smith, Deborah Lee ..... '55 '88 C.477 B.A. L.597 J.D. [🄲 Matkov,S.M.&G.]
Smith, Debra K. '— '91 C&L.352 B.A., J.D.
Asst. Reg. Coun., U.S. Environ. Protec. Agcy.
Smith, Derek C. ..... '72 '98 C.851 B.B.A. L.150 J.D. [Wildman,H.A.&D.]
Smith, Donald P. ..... '44 '72 C&L.209 B.A., J.D. 100 N. La Salle St., 23rd Fl.
Smith, Douglas G. ..... '— '96 C.107 B.S./B.A. L.597 J.D. [Kirkland&E.] (Pat.)
Smith, Douglas W. ..... '49 '80 C.424 B.B.A. L.365 J.D. 3407 N. Pulaski Rd.
Smith, Edward J. ..... '47 '71 C.339 A.B. L.597 J.D. 2100 N. Lincoln Pk. W.
Smith, Eric Anthony ..... '74 '99 C&L.339 B.S., J.D. [🄰 Katten M.R.]
Smith, Eugene M. '57 '83 C.98 B.S. L.329 J.D.
(adm. in MI; not adm. in IL) P.O. Box 5321‡
Smith, Evan T. ..... '61 '87 C.309 A.B. L.608 J.D. [Sedgwick,D.M.&A.]
Smith, Frank J., III ..... '49 '82 C.177 B.A. L.209 J.D. [Murphy&S.]
Smith, Fred A., III, (AV) ..... '50 '82 C.339 B.S. L.146 J.D. [Sedgwick,D.M.&A.]
Smith, Gary H. ..... '53 '80 C.575 B.A. L.910 J.D. [G.H.Smith]
Smith, Gordon H., (AV) ..... '15 '39 C.674 A.B. L.976 LL.B. [🄲 Gardner C.&D.] ‡
Smith, Gregory J. ..... '62 '89 C.1229 B.S.E.E. L.273 J.D. [Competition L.] (Pat.)
Smith, Gregory M. ..... '68 '98 C.174 B.S. L.365 J.D. [🄰 Wildman,H.A.&D.] (Pat.)
Smith, Henry E. '65 '97 C.309 A.B. L.976 J.D.
Asst. Prof. of Law, Northwestern Univ. Sch. of Law
Smith, Herman, (AV) ..... '09 '32 L.209 J.D. 440 W. Randolph St., Suite 500
Smith, James A. ..... '48 '80 C.339 B.A. L.146 J.D. 4746 N. Milwaukee Ave.
Smith, James A., Law Offices of '52 '76
C.903 B.A. L.339 J.D. 300 W. Adams St., Ste. 330
Smith, James B., (AV) ..... '— '74 C.165 B.A. L.94 J.D. [Ungaretti&H.]
Smith, James F. ..... '60 '89 C.893 B.S. L.602 J.D. [Clausen M.]
Smith, James G. F. ..... '43 '75 C.436 A.B.B.S. L.365 J.D. Cir. J.
Smith, James M. ..... '— '05 [🄰 Horwitz,H.&Assoc.]
Smith, James S., III, (BV) ..... '— '90 C.436 B.A. L.365 J.D. [O'Hagan,S.&A.]
Smith, Jeffery N. ..... '— '85 C.477 B.B.A. L.597 J.D. [Schiff H.]
Smith, John V., II, (AV) ..... '57 '82 C&L.602 A.B., J.D. [Pretzel&S.]
Smith, Joshua L. ..... '71 '96 C.205 B.S. L.347 J.D. [🄰 Wildman,H.A.&D.]
Smith, Judy A. ..... '70 '95 C.475 B.A. L.477 J.D. [🄰 Grippo&E.]
Smith, Karen P. ..... '48 '74 C.293 A.B. L.145 J.D. 7259 S. Rhodes Ave.
Smith, Kathleen K. ..... '69 '95 C.339 B.A. L.879 J.D. [🄰 Rieck&C.]
Smith, Kimberly A. ..... '77 '02 C&L.347 B.A., J.D. [🄰 Burke,W.M.&S.]
Smith, Kimberly Thompson ..... '72 '98 C.339 B.A. L.276 J.D. [🄰 Katten M.R.]
Smith, Laura E. ..... '76 '02 C.228 A.B. L.597 J.D. [🄰 Gould&R.]
Smith, Lawrence E., Jr. ..... '21 '51 C.137 L.365 LL.B. 7801 S. Cottage Grove Ave.‡
Smith, Lawrence R., (AV) ..... '— '73 C.321 A.B. L.477 J.D. [O'Hagan,S.&A.]
Smith, Lenora ..... '64 '95 C.161 B.A. L.597 J.D. Atty., Northern Trust Corporation
Smith, Leslie M., (P.C.) ..... '— '87 C&L.276 B.A., J.D. [Kirkland&E.]
Smith, Lute ..... '25 '62 C.1016 B.S. L.365 J.D. 5125 Ellis Ave.
Smith, Martin A. ..... '34 '57 C&L.597 B.S.L., LL.B. 180 N. Wacker Dr.
Smith, Mary Anne '44 '77 C.530 B.A. L.146 J.D.
V.P. & Gen. Coun., Illinois Institute of Technology
Smith, Matthew M. ..... '— '03 C.502 B.S.B.A. L.61 J.D. [🄰 Weldon-Linne&V.]
Smith, Michael A. ..... '— '72 C.112 A.B. L.1067 J.D. [🄲 Freeborn&P.]
Smith, Michael J., & Associates '44 '69
C.602 B.B.A. L.597 J.D. 39 South LaSalle Street, Suite 305
Smith, Michael P. ..... '74 '03 C.357 B.A. L.339 J.D. [🄰 Hinshaw&C.]
Smith, Michael Sawyer, (AV) ..... '67 '93 C.93 B.A. L.880 J.D. [Baker&M.]
Smith, Pamela G. ..... '62 '90 C.597 B.S. L.424 J.D. [Katten M.R.]
Smith, Paul M., Jr. ..... '18 '48 C.365 LL.B. 77 W. Washington St.
Smith, Randall ..... '60 '85 C.436 B.S. L.424 J.D. [Schoen&S.]

Smith, Renato L. .....'72 '97 C&L.339 B.S., J.D. [Bell,B.&L.]
Smith, Renee D. .....'— '95 C.473 B.A. L.309 J.D. [Kirkland&E.]
Smith, Richard E. .....'55 '81 C.734 B.A. L.339 J.D. Sr. Coun., Quaker Foods Corp.
Smith, Robert H., (AV) .....'55 '82 C.589 B.S. L.46 J.D. [Lowis&G.]
Smith, Robert Harold ....'71 '97 C&L.107 B.A., J.D. U.S. Envir. Protection Agcy., Reg. 5
Smith, Robert J., Jr. .....'56 '81 C&L.209 B.A., J.D. [Seyfarth S.]
Smith, Robert L., (AV) .....'64 '89 C.72 B.A. L.589 J.D. [Wiedner&M.]
Smith, Ronald C. .....'33 '65 C&L.424 B.S., J.D. John Marshall Law Sch.
Smith, Sarah E. .....'— '00 C.597 B.A. L.145 J.D. Two North LaSalle Street, Suite 2200
Smith, Scott J. .....'— '96 C.477 B.S. L.146 J.D. [Seyfarth S.]
Smith, Shelley .....'61 '88 C.1044 B.A. L.178 J.D. [Jenner&B.]
Smith, Shelley R., (AV) .....'49 '78 C.228 A.B. L.424 J.D. [Engelberg&S.]
Smith, Shevonn K. .....'78 '04 C.339 B.A. L.46 [Tressler,S.M.&P.]
Smith, Stephen C. .....'50 '03 C&L.339 B.S., J.D. [Michael B.&F.] (See Pat. Sect.)
Smith, Stephen Conrad .....'— '04 C.679 B.S. L.276 J.D. [Brinks H.G.&L.]
Smith, Stephen E., Law Offices of, (AV) '50 '76
C.94 A.B. L.910 J.D. 55 W. Monroe St., Suite 2410
Smith, Steven R., (BV) .....'— '80 C.145 B.A. L.770 J.D. [Bryan C.]
Smith, Stuart, (AV) .....'46 '72 C&L.546 B.S.Ch.E., J.D. [Gordon&G.L.]
Smith, Susan J. .....'72 '01 C.893 B.A. L.477 J.D. [Skadden,A.S.M.&F.]
Smith, Susan T., (BVⓉ) .....'50 '82 C.352 B.S.N. L.208 J.D. Global Hyatt Corporation
Smith, Ted A. .....'67 '00 C.801 B.A. L.365 J.D. [Smith O.]
Smith, Tefft W., (AVⓉ) .....'— '71 C.103 B.A. L.145 J.D. [Kirkland&E.] (Wash., DC)
Smith, Terence B., (BVⓉ) .....'34 '71 C.1060 A.B. L.169 J.D. Cir. Ct. of Cook Co.
Smith, Terence P. .....'68 '00 C.754 B.A. L.146 J.D. [Connelly S.H.]
Smith, Terry J. .....'58 '84 C.399 B.A. L.188 J.D. [Smith O.&W.]
Smith, Theresa Marie .....'72 '99 C&L.339 A.B., J.D. State's Atty.
Smith, Thomas A. .....'63 '94 C.871 B.S. L.424 J.D. [McDonald&M.]
Smith, Thomas C., (AV) .....'61 '88 C.347 B.A. L.1119 J.D. [Ice M.] (Indpls., IN)
Smith, Tiffini D. .....'77 '04 C.803 B.S. L.597 J.D. [McDermott W.&E.]
Smith, Timothy W. .....'70 '95 C.679 B.S. L.178 J.D. [Winston&S.]
Smith, Todd A., (AV) .....'49 '76 C.378 B.S.B. L.424 J.D. [Power R.&S.]
Smith, Virginia A. .....'— '85 C.930 B.A. L.365 J.D. Atty., A.T. Kearney, Inc.
Smith, William L., Jr. .....'46 '71 C&L.352 B.A., J.D. [Smith,H.B.&B.]
Smith, William P., (AV) .....'52 '77 C.188 B.A. L.150 J.D. [McDermott W.&E.]
Smith, Wm. B. .....'29 '55 C&L.424 B.S., J.D. 515 N. State St.
Smith, Zane D. .....'57 '83 C.801 B.A. L.365 J.D. [Z.D.Smith&Assoc.]

Smith, Gary H., P.C., Law Offices of
180 North La Salle Street, Suite 2001, 60601
Telephone: 312-236-7447 Fax: 312-236-7961
Email: gary@garyhsmith.com URL: http://www.garyhsmith.com
Gary H. Smith;—Jennifer Allen-Goldstein.
Property Tax, Property Tax Appeals and Real Estate Law.
See Professional Biographies, CHICAGO, ILLINOIS

Smith, Hemmesch, Burke & Brannigan, (AV)
11 East Adams Street, Suite 1400, 60603
Telephone: 312-939-0100 Fax: 312-939-7765 URL: http://www.propertytaxlawfirm.com
Email: shb-law.com URL: http://www.shbb-law.com
Members of Firm: William L. Smith, Jr.; Donald F. Hemmesch, Jr.; Kevin P. Burke; Thomas E. Brannigan, Sr. Associate: Christopher Kaczynski.
Real Property Taxation, General Civil Practice in State and Federal Courts, Real Estate and Personal Injury Law.
References: Oldkent Bank - Trust Dept.; American National Bank of Chicago.
See Professional Biographies, CHICAGO, ILLINOIS

Smith O'Callaghan & White
33 North La Salle Street Suite 3800, 60602
Telephone: 312-419-1000 Facsimile: 312-419-1007
Email: socw@socw.com
Terry J. Smith; Mary Aileen O'Callaghan; Laura A. White. Of Counsel: John T. Powen; David Alan Schneider. Associates: Robert R. Duda Jr.; Rebecca A. Figler; Christine E. Nentwig; Elizabeth M. Lauderbach.
Labor and Employment. Trial and Appellate Litigation: Federal and State Courts. Employment Litigation. Management Labor Law. Unfair Competition, Trade Secrets and Non-Compete Agreements. Administrative Agency: Federal, State and Local. Employment Mediation and Arbitration.
See Professional Biographies, CHICAGO, ILLINOIS

Smith Ortiz, LLP ..... 4309 West Fullerton
Smith, Zane D., & Associates, Ltd. .....415 N. LaSalle St., Ste. 300
Smith-Haley, Kelly .....'77 '04 C.602 B.A. L.424 J.D. [Skadden,A.S.M.&F.]
Smith-Haszto, Kathleen A. .....'— '84 C.209 B.S. L.46 J.D. [Lowery&Assoc.]
Smolen, Lee M., (AV) .....'60 '85 C.339 B.S. L.145 J.D. [Sidley A.B.&W.]
Smolens, Mark F. .....'57 '85 C.597 B.A. L.365 J.D. Asst. Co. State Atty.
Smoler, Robert J., (BV) .....'— '83 C&L.339 B.S., J.D. [R.J.Smoler&Assoc.]
Smoler, Robert J., & Associates, Ltd., (BV) ..... 188 W. Randolph Street, Suite 1518
Smolin, David Michael .....'53 '94 C.188 B.S. L.94 J.D. 20 S. Clark St., Ste. 410
Smoller, Robert A., (AV) .....'46 '71 C.339 B.S. L.597 J.D. [Schwartz C.]
Smoots, Patricia K. .....'54 '86 C.339 B.S. L.209 J.D. [McGuirewoods]
Smuckler, Lisa .....'71 '02 C.966 B.A. L.146 J.D. [Bollinger,R.&G.]
Smuda, Joan E. .....'53 '78 C&L.209 B.A., J.D. Atty. Gen. Off.
Smuda, Marie Elayne .....'60 '85 C&L.209 B.S.C., J.D. Asst. State's Atty.
Smulin, Jennifer A. .....'— '03 C.339 B.S. L.209 J.D. [Katten M.R.]
Smulkowski, Ziemowit T. .....'70 '96 C.424 B.A. L.597 J.D. [Katten M.R.]
Smyk, Rostyslaw J. .....'71 '98 C.339 B.A. L.1292 J.D. [Bollinger,R.&G.]
Smylie, Sallie G., (P.C.) .....'— '89 C.758 B.A. L.209 J.D. [Kirkland&E.]
Smyrniotis, George P. .....'— '89 C.1183 B.A. L.146 J.D. [Litchfield C.]
Smyth, Patrick H., & Associates ...'39 '68 C.602 B.B.A. L.30 J.D. 105 W. Madison Street
Smyth, Robert W., Jr., (AV) .....'57 '82 C.477 B.A. L.209 J.D. [Donohue B.M.&S.]
Snakard, Stephen A. .....'45 '70 C.37 B.S. L.365 J.D. [McCarthy D.]
Snapp, Erik W. .....'68 '95 C.723 B.S. L.494 J.D. [Winston&S.]
Sneckenberg, William J., (AV) '46 '72
C.627 B.S.B.A. L.190 J.D. [W.J.Sneckenberg&Assoc.]
Sneckenberg, W. J., & Associates, (AV) ..... 161 N. Clark St.
Sneed, Sekret T. '75 '01 C.813 B.A. L.276 J.D.
(adm. in CA; not adm. in IL) [Sonnenschein N.&R.]
Sneed, William M., (AV) .....'62 '87 C.813 A.B. L.597 J.D. [Sidley A.B.&W.]
Sneeringer, Stanley C. .....'72 '99 C.309 A.B. L.276 J.D. [Pedersen&H.]
Snell, Robert H. .....'35 '60 C.668 A.B. L.424 J.D. 200 W. Madison St.
Snelling, Phillip H. .....'50 '75 C&L.879 B.A., J.D. [Johnson,J.S.G.&D.]
Snider, Debra H. '54 '79 C.477 A.B. L.145 J.D.
Exe. V.P., Gen. Coun. & Chief Admin. Officer, Heller Financial, Inc.
Snider, Josh C. .....'— '99 C.966 B.S.E.E. L.424 J.D. [Greer,B.&C.] (Pat.)
Snider, Rowe W., (AV) .....'54 '79 C.133 B.A. L.145 J.D. [Lord,B.&B.]
Snider, Teresa, (AV) .....'67 '92 C.339 B.A. L.477 J.D. [Butler R.S.&B.]
Snieg, Ann H. .....'48 '79 C.424 B.S. L.209 J.D. 4750 N. Milwaukee Ave.
Snively, Gregory Scott .....'76 '01 C&L.209 B.A., J.D. 150 N. Wacker Drive, Ste. 1400
Snorf, Lowell D., III .....'54 '82 C.94 B.A. L.1338 J.D. 77 W. Washington Street
Snow, Edward C. .....'54 '79 C.93 A.B. L.424 J.D. Asst. States Atty.
Snow, Martin B. .....'48 '72 C.221 B.S.B.A. L.424 J.D. [Snow&S.]
Snow, Richard A. .....'32 '57 C&L.597 B.S., J.D. 100 N. LaSalle St.
Snow, Robert D., Jr. .....'— '01 C.927 B.A. L.365 J.D. [Kirkland&E.]

Snow & Snow, Ltd.
33 N. La Salle Street, Suite 2000, 60602
Telephone: 312-263-4858 Facsimile: 312-263-4860
Email: martin.snow@snowandsnow.com URL: http://www.snowandsnow.com
Robert H. Snow (1916-2003); Martin B. Snow.
Estate Planning, Asset Protection, Wills and Probate, Trusts and Estates, Guardianships, Elder Law, Trust, Taxation, Small Closely Held Business Law, Business Succession Planning, Estate Planning, General Practice, Real Estate, Buying and Selling a Home, Buying and Selling a Business and IRS Audits.
See Professional Biographies, CHICAGO, ILLINOIS

Snyder, Edward A. .....'— '80 C.942 B.B.A. L.893 J.D. [Arnstein&L.]
Snyder, Guy E., (AV) .....'54 '79 C.436 B.S. L.424 J.D. [Vedder,P.K.&K.]
Snyder, James A. .....'76 '02 C.339 B.A. L.273 J.D. Two North LaSalle Street, Suite 2200
Snyder, Jean Maclean, (BV) .....'42 '79 C&L.145 B.A., J.D. Univ. of Chicago Law Sch.
Snyder, Martin D. .....'70 '96 C.174 B.A. L.424 J.D. [Wildman,H.A.&D.]
Snyder, Michael A., (AV) .....'38 '68 C.1027 B.S. L.365 J.D. [Snyder&M.]
Snyder, Richard D. '58 '82 C&L.477 B.G.S., J.D.
(adm. in MI; not adm. in IL) Coopers & Lybrand
Snyder, Susan D., (AV) '— '90
C.942 B.A. L.597 J.D. Sr. Atty., Northern Trust Corporation
Snyder, Thomas H., (AV) .....'43 '68 C.276 A.B. L.477 J.D. [Wildman,H.A.&D.]
Snyder, William E., (AV) .....'44 '69 C&L.597 B.S., J.D. [Connelly R.&M.]

Snyder & McGovern, LLC, (AV)
343 South Dearborn Street Suite 2015, 60604
Telephone: 312-447-0260 Fax: 312-447-0261
Email: shiplaw@juno.com URL: http://www.snydermcgovern.com
Michael A. Snyder; Timothy S. McGovern.
Admiralty and Maritime Law, Civil Practice, Litigation, Commercial Litigation, Transportation, Torts.
See Professional Biographies, CHICAGO, ILLINOIS

Snyderman, Perry J., (AV) .....'32 '60 C.98 B.S. L.209 J.D. [DLPiper R.G.C.U.]
Soave, John, III .....'— '01 C&L.477 B.S.E., J.D. [Kirkland&E.]
Sobel, Cindy .....'— '04 C.910 B.A. L.597 J.D. [Latham&W.]
Sobel, Jeffrey G. .....'58 '83 C.477 B.A. L.846 J.D. 30 N. Michigan Ave., Ste. 900
Sobieraj, James R., (AV) '57 '82
C&L.477 B.S.E.E., J.D. [Brinks H.G.&L.] (See Pat. Sect.)
Soble, Jeffrey A., (AV) .....'— '96 C.112 B.A. L.424 J.D. [Foley&L.]
Socha, Daniel P. .....'30 '55 C&L.597 B.S., J.D. 10 S. Wacker Dr.
Socol, Donna Kaner, (AV) .....'52 '76 C.597 B.A. L.209 J.D. [Hughes S.P.R.&D.]
Soderstrom, Edward H., II .....'45 '73 C.674 A.B. L.597 J.D. 2204 W. Greenleaf
Soderstrom, Robert S., (AV) .....'44 '69 C.385 A.B. L.424 J.D. [Tressler,S.M.&P.]
Sodikoff, Brian J. .....'77 '03 C.880 B.S. L.209 J.D. [Welsh&K.] (See Pat. Sect.)
Sodikoff, Robert N., (AV) .....'48 '73 C.339 B.A. L.597 J.D. [Aronberg G.D.&G.]
Sodini, Ronald P. .....'64 '96 C.209 B.A. L.424 J.D. Chicago Police Department
Sodke, Karen G. .....'— '98 C&L.597 B.S., J.D. [Kirkland&E.]
Soehlig, Deborah Jo, (AV) .....'63 '87 C.560 B.A. L.910 J.D. [Fischel&K.]
Soffer, Gil M. .....'64 '89 C.103 A.B. L.309 J.D. [Katten M.R.]
Sohl, Jessica A. .....'77 '04 C.999 B.A. L.424 J.D. [Quinlan&C.]

Sohn, Alan E., Law Offices of, (AV) '44 '68 C&L.339 B.A., J.D.
30 North La Salle Street, Suite 2040, 60602
Telephone: 312-236-7005 Fax: 312-236-6906
Email: aeslaw@ameritech.net URL: http://www.alansohnlaw.com
Closely Held Business Law, Estate Planning and Probate, Business Organizations, Real Estate, Litigation, Business Litigation, Representation of Child Day Care Centers.
See Professional Biographies, CHICAGO, ILLINOIS

Sohn, Herbert .....'27 '82 C.893 B.A. L.365 J.D. 4640 N. Marine
Sohn, Nancy .....'56 '81 C.228 B.A. L.339 J.D. Staff Coun., ACLU
Sokal, Joseph F., (AV) .....'08 '36 C.145 L.146 LL.B. 79 W. Monroe
Sokol, Deborah J. '66 '92 C.477 A.B. L.188 J.D.
Sr. Corp. Coun., AT&T Wireless Servs.
Sokol, Marc D. .....'70 '01 C.597 B.A. L.347 J.D. [Jenner&B.]
Sokol, Mary Sue F. .....'63 '88 C.121 B.A. L.966 J.D. Asst. Atty. Gen.
Sokol, Thomas C. .....'44 '95 C.734 B.S. L.347 J.D. [Kaplan,v.&M.]
Sokolnicki, Zygmunt K. .....'32 '95 C.339 B.S. L.1000 J.D. 2331 West 22nd Place
Solari, Alfred J. .....'51 '75 C.602 B.A. L.424 J.D. SCT Productions
Solberg, Scott C., (AV) .....'63 '90 C.57 B.A. L.880 J.D. [Eimer S.K.&S.]
Solberg, Wallace C. .....'60 '86 C.339 B.A. L.146 J.D. [Bell,B.&L.]
Soldat, Kenneth M. .....'57 '83 C.1024 B.S. L.365 J.D. [B.F.Dorn&Assoc.]
Soler, Nilda M. .....'45 '76 C.298 B.A. L.209 J.D. Chief Asst. Corp. Coun.
Solganick, Irwin J. .....'48 '72 C.339 B.A. L.146 J.D. 850 N. State St.
Solinski, Paulette .....'57 '83 C.719 B.A. L.209 J.D. Assoc. Gen. Coun., Aon Corp.
Solis, Tina B. .....'71 '97 C&L.352 B.A., J.D. [Ungaretti&H.]
Solis-Szukala, Maile H. .....'73 '98 C.352 B.A. L.145 J.D. [Grippo&E.]
Sollinger, Rachel Levitt .....'70 '96 C.608 B.A. L.146 J.D. 515 North State St. Ste 2800
Sollitto, Matthew .....'— '04 C.276 B.A. L.602 J.D. [Nisen&E.]
Solmor, Deborah G. .....'— '91 [Skadden,A.S.M.&F.]
Solmor-Mordini, Jane .....'61 '90 C.339 B.A. L.46 J.D. [Pretzel&S.]
Solock, Mark W. .....'49 '78 C.339 B.A. L.209 J.D. 221 N. LaSalle St.
Solomon, Aaron L. .....'— '02 C.918 B.A. L.145 J.D. [Wildman,H.A.&D.]
Solomon, Alfred B. .....'16 '40 C.597 L.146 J.D. 2906 W. Peterson
Solomon, Benna Ruth, (AV) .....'53 '80 C&L.280 B.A., J.D. Chf. Asst. Corp. Coun.
Solomon, David B. .....'— '94 C.477 B.B.A. L.209 J.D. [Pedersen&H.]
Solomon, Harold N. .....'08 '31 C.339 A.B. L.145 J.D. 25 E. Wash. St.
Solomon, Jack, Jr., (AV) '28 '51 C&L.546 B.S., LL.B.
Solomon & Solomon Fine Art, Ltd.
Solomon, Joan G. .....'67 '93 C&L.910 B.A., J.D. Law Clk., U.S. Dist. Ct.
Solomon, Leonard V. .....'18 '42 C.145 L.209 LL.B. 2726 N. Dayton St.
Solomon, Rayman L. '47 '76 C.918 B.A. L.145 J.D.
Assoc. Dean, Northwestern Univ. Sch. of Law
Solomon, Robert S., (AV) .....'29 '52 C.339 L.145 J.D. 225 W. Wacker Dr., 30th Fl.
Solomon, Todd A. .....'73 '98 C.477 B.B.A. L.145 J.D. [McDermott W.&E.]
Solon, Patrick F. .....'64 '89 C&L.477 B.B.A., J.D. [Niro,S.H.&N.]
Solotke, Manuel, (AV) .....'26 '54 C.339 L.365 J.D. 30 N. LaSalle St.
Solotorovsky, Julian, (AV) .....'51 '78 C.893 B.A. L.365 J.D. [Kelley D.&W.]
Solov, Tanya .....'63 '89 C.46 B.B.A. L.146 J.D. Dir., IL Security Dept.
Solovay, Jared D. .....'74 '99 C.178 B.A. L.1066 J.D. [Pattishall,M.N.H.&G.]
Solovy, Jerold S., (AV) .....'30 '55 C.477 B.A. L.309 LL.B. [Jenner&B.]
Solovy, Joel S. .....'37 '62 C&L.339 B.S., LL.B. 5445 N. Sheridan Rd.
Solow, Alan P., (AV) .....'54 '79 C.339 A.B. L.309 J.D. [Goldberg,K.B.R.&M.]
Solow, Michael B., (AV) .....'59 '84 C.339 A.B. L.309 J.D. [Kaye S.]
Solow, Sheldon L., (AV) .....'50 '75 C.339 B.A. L.309 J.D. [Kaye S.]
Soloway, Julie L. .....'67 '92 C.477 A.B. L.339 J.D. [Winston&S.]

Soltman, Nelson A. ....'43 '71 C.976 B.A. L.145 J.D. Legal Assist. Found.
Soltysinski, Henry M., Jr. ....'58 '83 C.679 B.A. L.365 J.D. [H.M.Soltysinski,Jr.]
Soltysinski, Henry M., Jr., Ltd. ....9618 S. Commercial
Som, Sonya Olds ....'72 '97 C.373 B.A. L.188 J.D. [Ⓐ Laner,M.D.B.L.&T.]
Somen, Timothy J. ....'76 '03 C.746 B.B.A. L.1000 J.D. [Ⓐ McFadden&D.]
Somerlot, Douglas K. '43 '68 C.97 B.A. L.608 J.D.
(adm. in OH; not adm. in IL) Dir., Family Jus. Leadership Institute
Somers, Patrick G. ....'— '05 C.999 B.A. L.209 J.D. [Ⓐ Mandell M.]
Somerville, John ....'62 '89 C.999 B.A. L.365 J.D. Ofc. of the State's Atty.
Sommario, Frank Anthony ....'75 '00 C&L.209 B.S., J.D. 200 N. LaSalle, Ste. 700
Sommer, Edward V., (AV) ....'— '82 C.299 A.B. L.602 J.D. [Chapman&C.]
Sommer, Lisa Marré ....'— '92 C.339 B.A. L.602 J.D. [Spellmire&S.]
Sonalla, Majd Ed Deen Isam ....'61 '00 C.608 B.S. L.424 J.D. 79 West Monroe
Sondej, Denise ....'— '87 C.339 B.F.A. L.365 J.D. Sr. Atty., ABN AMRO N. Amer., Inc.
Sonderby, Peter R., (AV) .... '41 '67 C&L.339 B.A., J.D. [P.R.Sonderby] (⊙Chicago)
Sonderby, Peter R., (AV) '41 '67 C&L.339 B.A., J.D.
[Ⓒ Ulmer&B.] & [P.R.Sonderby] (⊙Chicago)
Sonderby, Susan Pierson ....'47 '73 C.339 B.S. L.365 J.D. Chf. U.S. Bkrptcy. J.
Sonderby, Peter R., P.C., (AV) ....29 South LaSalle Street, Suite 620
Sondgeroth, Douglas A. ....'76 '02 C.57 B.A. L.93 J.D. [Ⓐ Jenner&B.]
Sone, Maurice A. ....'65 '94 C.145 B.A. L.966 J.D. 2030 W. Armitage Ave.
Sonenthal, Lloyd M. ....'42 '70 70 W. Madison St.
Soni, Leena ....'66 '92 C.502 B.J. L.352 J.D. [Cozen O.]
Sonkin, Andrea Laurel ....'71 '96 C.105 B.A. L.30 J.D. Off. of Banks & Real Estate
Sonneborn, Amanda A. ....'78 '03 C&L.339 B.A., J.D. [Ⓐ Seyfarth S.]
Sonnefeldt, Jerome M. ....'— '87 C.424 B.A. L.209 J.D. [Querrey&H.]
Sonnenberg, Steven P., (AV) ....'48 '74 C.238 B.A. L.146 J.D. [Sonnenberg&A.]
Sonnenberg & Anderson, (AV) .... 300 South Wacker Drive, Suite 1220

Sonnenschein Nath & Rosenthal LLP, (AV) BB
Sears Tower, Suite 8000, 233 South Wacker Drive, 60606 ⊙
Telephone: 312-876-8000 Cable Address: "Sonberk" Telex: 25-3526 Telecopier: 312-876-7934
URL: http://www.sonnenschein.com

Edward Sonnenschein (1881-1935); Hugo Sonnenschein (1883-1956). Partners: Roy M. Adams (Resident, New York, N.Y. Office); Neal Aizenstein; David Albenda (Not admitted in IL; Resident, New York, N.Y. Office); Mitchell Edward Albert (Not admitted in IL; Resident, Kansas City, Missouri Office); Christine Comer Alfaro (Resident, St. Louis, Missouri Office); Jean Allard; Mina Amir-Mokri; Robert M. Andalman; Thomas A. Andreoli; Joseph J. Andrew (Not admitted in IL; Resident, Washington, D.C. Office); Reid L. Ashinoff (Not admitted in IL; Resident, New York, N.Y. Office); Gayle M. Athanacio (Not admitted in IL; Resident, San Francisco, California Office); Katharina E. Babich (Not admitted in IL; Resident, Kansas City, Missouri Office); John R. F. Baer; Pamela Baker; Michael A. Bamberger (Not admitted in IL; Resident, New York, N.Y. Office); William T. Barker; Michael A. Barnes (Not admitted in IL; Resident, San Francisco, California Office); Daniel D. Barnowski (Not admitted in IL; Resident, Washington, D.C. Office); Michael H. Barr (Not admitted in IL; Resident, New York, N.Y. Office); Kara S. Baysinger (Resident, San Francisco, California Office); Carol Anne Been; Rudolf H. Beese; Cheryl Dyer Berg (Not admitted in IL; Resident, San Francisco, California Office); Joshua G. Berman (Resident, Washington, D.C. Office); Amy L. Bess (Resident, Washington, D.C. Office); Jana Cohen Blackman; Allison C. Blakley; G. Harley Blosser (Not admitted in IL; Resident, St. Louis, Missouri Office); Joel N. Bock (Not admitted in IL; Resident, Short Hills, New Jersey Office); Valarie Tatem Bomar; Douglas G. Bonner (Not admitted in IL; Resident, Washington, D.C. Office); Alan B. Bornstein (Not admitted in IL; Resident, St. Louis, Missouri Office); Victor H. Boyajian (Not admitted in IL; Resident, New York, N.Y. and Short Hills, New Jersey Offices); Roger T. Brice; Jeffrey Brill (Not admitted in IL; Resident, San Francisco, California Office); Lynda L. Brothers (Not admitted in IL; Resident, San Francisco, California Office); Richard M. Brown; Mark S. Bryant (Not admitted in IL; Resident, Kansas City, Missouri Office); Jeffry Butler (Not admitted in IL; Resident, San Francisco, California Office); John J. Calkins (Not admitted in IL; Resident, Washington, D.C. Office); Donald M. Carley (Not admitted in IL; Resident, San Francisco, California Office); Leo J. Carlin (Deceased, 1988); Phillip A. Casey; Martin R. Castro; Gina M. Cavalier (Resident, Washington, D.C. Office); Caryn L. Chalmers; Devereux Chatillon (Resident, New York, N.Y. Office); Kevin P. Chavous (Resident, Washington, D.C. Office); William W. Choe (Not admitted in IL; Resident, San Francisco, California Office); John Franklin Clark (Resident, Washington, D.C. Office); Kimani Clark (Resident, Washington, D.C. Office); John L. Cleary (Not admitted in IL; Resident, Short Hills, New Jersey Office); Denise M. Clolery (Not admitted in IL; Resident, New York, N.Y. Office); Robert W. Cockren (Not admitted in IL; Resident, Short Hills, New Jersey Office); David E. Crawford, Jr. (Resident, St. Louis, Missouri Office); Shirley E. Curfman (Not admitted in IL; Resident, Los Angeles, California Office); Steven R. Davidson; Leslie D. Davis; Bruce C. Davison (Not admitted in IL; Resident, Kansas City, Missouri Office); Eric R. Decator; Dennis S. Diaz (Not admitted in IL; Resident, Los Angeles, California Office); J. Ross Docksey; Mark L. Dosier; Arlene G. Dubin (Not admitted in IL; Resident, New York, N.Y. Office); Robin M. Edwards (Not admitted in IL; Resident, San Francisco, California Office); Michael J. Emont (Not admitted in IL; Resident, New York, N.Y. Office); Ralph M. Engel (Not admitted in IL; Resident, New York, N.Y. Office); Todd R. Eskelsen (Not admitted in IL; Resident, Washington, D.C. Office); Phyllis A. Ewer; Holly S. Falkowitz Wallman (Not admitted in IL; Resident, New York, N.Y. Office); Cynthia A. Faur; Richard L. Fenton; Elizabeth A. Ferrell (Not admitted in IL; Resident, Washington, D.C. Office); Brian W. Fields (Resident, Kansas City, Missouri Office); Samuel Fifer; Sheldon I. Fink; John F. Finston (Resident, San Francisco, California Office); Christine Bay Fisher; G. Robert Fisher (Not admitted in IL; Resident, Kansas City, Missouri Office); Mark A. Flessner; Michael R. Flynn (Resident, New York, N.Y. Office); Martin J. Foley (Not admitted in IL; Resident, Los Angeles, California Office); Jeffrey C. Fort; Gerald E. Fradin; Steven H. Frankel (Resident, San Francisco, California Office); Bruce Merlin Fried (Not admitted in IL; Resident, Washington, D.C. Office); Michael M. Froy; Paul A. Gajer (Not admitted in IL; Resident, New York, N.Y. Office); Sarah N. Galioto; Philip S. Gallas (Resident, Kansas City, Missouri Office); Catherine B. Gardner (Not admitted in IL; Resident, Washington, D.C. Office); Brit L. Geiger (Not admitted in IL; Resident, New York, N.Y. Office); Christian S. Genetski (Not admitted in IL; Resident, Washington, D.C. Office); Brent Matthew Giddens (Not admitted in IL; Resident, Los Angeles, California Office); Alan S. Gilbert; John T. Gilbertson (Not admitted in IL; Resident, Los Angeles, California Office); Robert D. Girard (Not admitted in IL; Resident, Los Angeles, California Office); Paul E. B. Glad (Not admitted in IL; Resident, San Francisco, California Office); Michael M. Godsy (Resident, St. Louis, Missouri Office); Martin R. Gold (Not admitted in IL; Resident, New York, N.Y. Office); Alvin J. Goldman (Not admitted in IL; Resident, New York, N.Y. Office); Jeffrey S. Goldman; James A. Goniea (Not admitted in IL; Resident, San Francisco, California Office); Gary A. Goodman (Not admitted in IL; Resident, New York, N.Y. Office); Robert N. Grant; Steven J. Gray; Ronald Greenberg (Not admitted in IL; Resident, New York, N.Y. Office); Andrew R. Greene; Kevin P. Groarke (Not admitted in IL; Resident, New York, N.Y. Office); John I. Grossbart; Michael Guerra; Rosemary L.L. Gullikson; Kevin W. Guynn; Frank H. Hackmann (Resident, St. Louis, Missouri Office); Wayne R. Hannah, Jr.; Mark L. Hanover; Mark T. Hansen (Not admitted in IL; Resident, Los Angeles, California Office); Kevin T. Haroff (Resident, San Francisco, California Office); Linda Chaplik Harris; Kendra Kekelis Hartman; Harumi Hata (Not admitted in IL; Resident, Los Angeles, California Office); Sandra D. Hauser (Not admitted in IL; Resident, New York, N.Y. Office); James A. Heeter (Not admitted in IL; Resident, Kansas City, Missouri Office); Roger K. Heidenreich (Resident, St. Louis, Missouri Office); J. Dean Heller (Resident, Los Angeles, California Office); Frances J. Henderson (Not admitted in IL; Resident, Washington, D.C. Office); Gary A. Hernandez (Not admitted in IL; Resident, San Francisco, California Office); Raymond J. Heslin (Not admitted in IL; Resident, New York, N.Y. Office); Ellen P. Hession (Resident, New York, N.Y. Office); William Reece Hirsch (Not admitted in IL; Resident, San Francisco, California Office); Harold C. Hirshman; Kenneth H. Hoch; Donald R. Holland (Resident, St. Louis, Missouri Office); Donald P. Horwitz; Paul J. Housey (Not admitted in IL; Resident, New York, New York Office); James L. Hsu (Not admitted in IL; Resident, Los Angeles, California Office); Susan M. Hughes; Michael D. Hultquist; David C. Jacobson; Fruman Jacobson; Marian S. Jacobson; Robert J. Jakubeck (Not admitted in IL; Resident, St. Louis, Missouri Office); Christopher G. Janney (Resident, Washington, D.C. Office); Thomas C. Jensen (Resident, Washington, D.C. Office); John Grayson Johnson (Resident, San Francisco, California Office); Mark P. Johnson (Not admitted in IL; Resident, Kansas City, Missouri Office); Robert C. Johnson; Robert M. Johnson (Resident, Los Angeles, California Office); Robert T. Joseph; Kevin P. Kamraczewski; Arthur S. Katz (Not admitted in IL; Resident, New York, N.Y. Office); Michelle Stark Kaufman (Not admitted in IL; Resident, Kansas City, Missouri Office); Ronald D. Kent (Not admitted in IL; Resident, Los Angeles, California Office); Michael L. Kiklis (Not admitted in IL; Resident, Washington, D.C. Office); Christopher Q. King; Robert H. King, Jr.; Sanford Kingsley (Resident, San Francisco, California Office); James M. Kirkland (Not admitted in IL; Resident, Kansas City,

(This Listing Continued)

Sonnenschein Nath & Rosenthal LLP (Continued)

Missouri Office); Matt A. Kirmayer (Not admitted in IL; Resident, San Francisco, California Office); Steven B. Kite; Leslie A. Klein; Shaun M. Klein (Not admitted in IL; Resident, Kansas City, Missouri Office); H. Frances Kleiner (Resident, New York, N.Y. Office); James A. Klenk; Edward Klimerman (Not admitted in IL; Resident, New York, N.Y. Office); Elaine D. Kolish (Resident, Washington, D.C. Office); Kenneth G. Kolmin; John C. Koski; Thomas A. Labuda, Jr.; Mary Kay Lacey (Not admitted in IL; Resident, San Francisco, California Office); David S. Ladwig (Not admitted in IL; Resident, Kansas City, Missouri Office); Kevin C. Lane; Robert J. Lanza (Resident, New York, N.Y. Office); John J. Lawlor; Mark R. Lehrer (Not admitted in IL; Resident, New York, N.Y. Office); J. Bradley Leitch (Not admitted in IL; Resident, Kansas City, Missouri Office); Jeffrey Lennard; Christine Lepera (Not admitted in IL; Resident, New York, N.Y. Office); Trina R. LeRiche (Not admitted in IL; Resident, Kansas City, Missouri Office); Robert O. Lesley (Resident, Kansas City, Missouri Office); Jack B. Levitt (Not admitted in IL; Resident, New York, N.Y. Office); Fred L. Levy (Not admitted in IL; Resident, Washington, D.C. Office); Steven M. Levy; Julius Lewis; Paul V. LiCalsi (Not admitted in IL; Resident, New York, N.Y. Office); Yabo Lin (Resident, Kansas City, Missouri Office); Mark J. Linderman (Not admitted in IL; Resident, San Francisco, California Office); Scott A. Lindquist; Karen Litsinger (Resident, Washington, D.C. Office); Lloyd C. Loomis (Resident, Los Angeles, California Office); Michael B. Lubic (Resident, Los Angeles and San Francisco CA, Offices); Donald G. Lubin; Holley T. Lutz (Resident, Washington, D.C. Office); Lisa A. MacVittie (Not admitted in IL; Resident, Washington, D.C. Office); David W. Maher; Richard L. Marcus; Jeremy Margolis; I. Edward Marquette (Not admitted in IL; Resident, Kansas City, Missouri Office); Drew W. Marrocco (Not admitted in IL; Resident, Washington, D.C. Office); Stephen A. Marshall (Not admitted in IL; Resident, New York, N.Y. Office); Sonia Renee Martin (Not admitted in IL; Resident, San Francisco, California Office); John F. Marvin (Not admitted in IL; Resident, Kansas City, Missouri Office); Michael R. Maryn (Not admitted in IL; Resident, Washington, D.C. Office); Sandra R. McCandless (Not admitted in IL; Resident, San Francisco, California Office); Frederick D. McClure (Resident, Washington, D.C. Office); Douglas McCormack (Resident, Washington, D.C. Office); Thomas E. McDonald (Resident, San Francisco, California Office); Sean McEneaney (Not admitted in IL; Resident, San Francisco, California Office); Brian R. McGinley (Resident, Kansas City, Missouri Office); Michael T. McNamara (Not admitted in IL; Resident, Washington, D.C. Office); Thomas K. McQueen; Mark F. Mehlman; Donna D. Melby (Resident, Los Angeles, CA Office); Cynthia L. Mellema (Not admitted in IL; Resident, San Francisco, California Office); Shepard W. Melzer (Resident, New York, N.Y. Office); Scott A. Memmott (Not admitted in IL; Resident, Washington, D.C. Office); Robert F. Messerly; David R. Metzger; Timothy M. Metzger; Gary Meyerhoff (Not admitted in IL; Resident, New York, N.Y. Office); Martin P. Michael (Not admitted in IL; Resident, New York, N.Y. Office); Paul J. Miller; Robert B. Millner; Martin J. Moderson (Not admitted in IL; Resident, Kansas City, Missouri Office); James L. Moeller (Not admitted in IL; Resident, Kansas City, Missouri Office); Patrick G. Moran; M. Keith Moskowitz; Stacey L. Murphy (Resident, St. Louis, Missouri Office); Bernard Nath (1899-1996); Marlene D. Nations; Barry B. Nekritz; Carole Neville (Not admitted in IL; Resident, New York, N.Y. Office); David B. Newman (Not admitted in IL; Resident, New York, N.Y. Office); Dennis Nathan Newman; Terrance A. Norton; Bernard J. Nussbaum; Stephen J. O'Brien (Not admitted in IL; Resident, St. Louis, Missouri Office); Philip A. O'Connell, Jr. (Resident, San Francisco, California Office); Eric A. Oesterle; Thomas G. Opferman; David J. Papier (Not admitted in IL; Resident, Short Hills, New Jersey Office); Michael E. Pappas (Not admitted in IL; Resident, Los Angeles, California Office); Sanford M. Pastroff; Demian L. Pay (Not admitted in IL; Resident, San Francisco, California Office); Barbara Lynn Pedersen (Not admitted in IL; Resident, New York, N.Y. Office); Kenneth J. Pfaehler (Not admitted in IL; Resident, Washington, D.C. Office); Timothy Pfister (Resident, New York, N.Y. Office); Elliott I. Portnoy (Resident, Washington, D.C. Office); Caryl A. Potter, III (Resident, Washington, D.C. Office); Pamela K. Prickett (Not admitted in IL; Resident, Los Angeles, California Office); Christopher E. Prince (Resident, Los Angeles, CA Office); Duane C. Quaini; Edward J. Radlo (Resident, San Francisco, California Office); Charles A. Redd (Resident, St. Louis, Missouri Office); Edwin B. Reeser, III (Not admitted in IL; Resident, Los Angeles, California Office); Edward J. Reich (Not admitted in IL; Resident, New York, N.Y. Office); Peter S. Reichertz (Resident, Washington, D.C. Office); Allen G. Reiter (Not admitted in IL; Resident, New York, N.Y. Office); Edward H. Rice; Robert E. Richards; Steven L. Rist (Not admitted in IL; Resident, Kansas City, Missouri Office); Gary M. Roberts (Resident, Los Angeles, California Office); John E. Rooney; Martin Rosen (Not admitted in IL; Resident, New York, N.Y. Office); Allan M. Rosenbloom (Not admitted in IL; Resident, New York, N.Y. Office); Kenneth A. Rosenblum (Not admitted in IL; Resident, New York, N.Y. Office); Douglas E. Rosenthal (Not admitted in IL; Resident, Washington, D.C. Office); Michael D. Rosenthal; Samuel R. Rosenthal (1899-1994); Stephen H. Rovak (Resident, St. Louis, Missouri Office); Ira I. Roxland (Not admitted in IL; Resident, New York, N.Y. Office); Howard R. Rubin (Resident, Washington, D.C. Office); Arthur H. Ruegger (Not admitted in IL; Resident, New York, N.Y. Office); Kirk R. Ruthenberg (Resident, Washington, D.C. Office); W. Michael Ryan; Marina N. Saito; Marc A. Salle (Resident, Kansas City, Missouri Office); Ivor E. Samson (Not admitted in IL; Resident, San Francisco, California Office); Charles D. Satinover (1906-1998); Mitchell D. Schepps (Not admitted in IL; Resident, West Palm Beach, Florida Office); Eric M. Schiller; Donald M. Schindel; Michael A. Schlanger (Not admitted in IL; Resident, Washington, D.C. Office); Kenneth B. Schnoll (Resident, San Francisco, California Office); Ira A. Schreger (Not admitted in IL; Resident, New York, N.Y. Office); Robert L. Schuchard (Not admitted in IL; Resident, Los Angeles, California Office); Arnold P. Schuster (Not admitted in IL; Resident, San Francisco, California Office); Jordana Schwartz (Resident, New York, N.Y. Office); Lewis M. Schwartz (Not admitted in IL; Resident, New York, N.Y. Office); Robert F. Scoular (Not admitted in IL; Resident, Los Angeles, California Office); Gary Senner; J. A. Shafran (Not admitted in IL; Resident, Los Angeles, California Office); Harold D. Shapiro; Albert W. Shay (Not admitted in IL; Resident, Washington, D.C. Office); Gerald J. Sherman; Jordan A. Sigale; Alan H. Silberman; Roger C. Siske; Janu Sivanesan (Resident, New York, N.Y. Office); Susan B. Slater-Jansen (Not admitted in IL; Resident, New York, N.Y. Office); Christopher Smith (Not admitted in IL; Resident, Washington, D.C. Office); John L. Snyder (Resident, Kansas City, Missouri Office); Stephen L. Solomon (Not admitted in IL; Resident, New York, N.Y. Office); Margo C. Soulé (Not admitted in IL; Resident, Kansas City, Missouri Office); Rochelle Buchsbaum Spandorf (Not admitted in IL; Resident, Los Angeles, California Office); Natalie J. Spears; Darry Sragow (Not admitted in IL; Resident, Los Angeles, California Office); Ronald E. Stauffer (Not admitted in IL; Resident, Washington, D.C. Office); T. Reed Stephens (Resident, Washington, D.C. Office); Thomas M. Stephens; David H. Stern (Not admitted in IL; Resident, Los Angeles, California Office); Jane G. Stevens (Not admitted in IL; Resident, New York, N.Y. Office); David P. Stoeberl (Resident, St. Louis, Missouri Office); Errol L. Stone; Sarah Toevs Sullivan (Resident, Kansas City, Missouri Office); Kevin R. Sweeney (Not admitted in IL; Resident, Kansas City, Missouri Office); Daniel R. Swett; Louis L.S. Tao (Not admitted in IL; Resident, Washington, D.C. Office); Marc D. Teitelbaum (Not admitted in IL; Resident, New York, N.Y. Office); Rhonda C. Thomas; Elizabeth Thompson (Not admitted in IL; Resident, San Francisco, California Office); D. McCarty Thornton (Not admitted in IL; Resident, Washington, D.C. Office); Denise M. Tormey (Not admitted in IL; Resident, New York, N.Y. Office); Eileen Bannon Trost; Scott Turow; Frank P. VanderPloeg; Thomas K. Vandiver (Resident, St. Louis, Missouri Office); Jacqueline M. Vidmar; Donna J. Vobornik; David L. Volk (Not admitted in IL; Resident, Los Angeles, California Office); John E. Walker (Not admitted in IL; Resident, Los Angeles, California Office); Susan M. Walker (Not admitted in IL; Resident, Los Angeles, California Office); Thomas M. Walsh (Not admitted in IL; Resident, St. Louis, Missouri Office); Lori Anne Ward; Paige D. Waters; Andrew L. Weil; Michael J. Weinberger (Not admitted in IL; Resident, New York, N.Y. Office); Gadi Weinreich (Resident, Washington, D.C. Office); Margo Weinstein; Jerome P. Weiss (1934-1996); Barry Leigh Weissman (Resident, Los Angeles, California Office); Linda D. White; G. Marc Whitehead; James G. Wiehl (Not admitted in IL; Resident, St. Louis, Missouri Office); C. Hunter Wiggins; John Leland Williams (Not admitted in IL; Resident, San Francisco, California Office); Mary G. Wilson; Robert L. Winikoff (Not admitted in IL; Resident, New York, N.Y. Office); Bradley A. Winters (Resident, St. Louis, Missouri Office); Jerome T. Wolf (Not admitted in IL; Resident, Kansas City, Missouri Office); Benjamin E. Wolff III (Resident, New York, N.Y. Office); Peter D. Wolfson (Not admitted in IL; Resident, New York, N.Y. Office); Clement B. Wood (Not admitted in IL; Resident, New York, N.Y. Office); Curtis E. Woods (Resident, Kansas City, Missouri Office); Melvin M. Wright, Jr.; Michael J. Wynne; Laura Ann Wytsma (Not admitted in IL; Resident, Los Angeles, California Office); D. Farrington Yates (Resident, New York, N.Y. Office); Alan T. Yoshitake (Not admitted in IL; Resident, Los Angeles, California Office); Nicholas C. Yost (Not admitted in IL; Resident, San Francisco, California Office); Paula M. Yost (Not admitted in IL; Resident, San Francisco, California Office); Howard J. Young (Resident, Washington, D.C.); Henry S. Zangwill (Not admitted in IL; Resident, Los Angeles, California Office); Marjorie J. Zessar; Janice H. Ziegler (Resident, Washington, D.C. Office); Robert B. Zimmerman (Not admitted in IL; Resident, New York, N.Y. Office); Karl Zobrist (Resident, Kansas City, Missouri Office); Richard M. Zuckerman (Not admitted in IL; Resident, New York, N.Y. Office); Marc Zwillinger (Resident, Washington, D.C. Office). Of Counsel: Yong J. An (Resident, Kansas City, Missouri Office); Jennifer A. Barrett; Thomas G. Barrett (Not admitted in IL; Resident, New York, N.Y. Office); Brian C. Behrens (Resident, St. Louis, Missouri Office); Camille E. Bennett; Belinda A. Boyer (Resident, St. Louis, Missouri Office); Amadeo F. Cantu, Jr. (Resident, Los Angeles, California Office); Clarissa Cerda; Debra S. Clark; Juliet A. Cox (Resident, Kansas City, Missouri Office); Karen Davis (Resident, St. Louis, Missouri Office); Zack Z. Dong; Marco P. Ferreira (Not admitted in IL; Resident, Los Angeles, California Office); Theresa M. Fitzgerald (Not admitted in IL; Resident, San Francisco,

(This Listing Continued)

Sonnenschein Nath & Rosenthal LLP (Continued)

California Office); Julie R. Formwalt (Not admitted in IL; Resident, Kansas City, Missouri Office); Alexander H Fukui (Resident, Los Angeles, CA Office); Andrew I. Gavil (Resident, Washington, D.C. Office); Stephen L. Gibson (Not admitted in IL; Resident, Washington, D.C. Office); Allison T. Godfrey (Resident, Kansas City, Missouri Office); Debra Goldberg (Not admitted in IL; Resident, New York, N.Y. Office); Helise Harrington (Not admitted in IL; Resident, New York, N.Y. Office); Jacob Inwald (Not admitted in IL; Resident, New York, N.Y. Office); Lars E. Johansson (Not admitted in IL; Resident, San Francisco, California Office); Dee Joyce-Hayes (Not admitted in IL; Resident, St. Louis, Missouri Office); Ralph B. Kelley (Not admitted in IL; Resident, New York, N.Y. Office); Andrew P. Lederman (Not admitted in IL; Resident, New York, N.Y. Office); Chunlin Leonhard; Arthur S. Levine (Not admitted in IL; Resident, Los Angeles, California Office); Marci Rose Levine (Not admitted in IL; Resident, Washington, D.C. Office); Matthew L. Lifflander (Resident, New York, N.Y. Office); Harold I. Loring (Not admitted in IL; Resident, Washington, D.C. Office); Jennifer A. Marler (Resident, St. Louis, Missouri Office); Eric C. Marshall; Wendy Byers Marvin (Not admitted in IL; Resident, Kansas City, Missouri Office); Edward J. McCaffery (Resident, Los Angeles, California Office); John Gary McDavid (Resident, Washington, D.C. Office); Jane A. Meyer (Not admitted in IL; Resident, New York, N.Y. Office); Eric T. Mikkelson (Resident, Kansas City, Missouri Office); Grace E. Mueller (Not admitted in IL; Resident, Los Angeles, California Office); Robert P. Mulvey (Not admitted in IL; Resident, New York, N.Y. Office); Gregory R. Naron; Enrique Perez; Abraham D. Piontnica (Resident, New York, N.Y. Office); David C. Reintjes (Not admitted in IL; Resident, Kansas City, Missouri Office); Burton R. Rubin (P.C.) (Not admitted in IL; Resident, New York, N.Y. Office); Richard L. Sadowsky (Resident, New York, N.Y. Office); Joseph H. Schmitt (Not admitted in IL; Resident, New York, N.Y. Office); Martin J. Schwartz (Not admitted in IL; Resident, New York, N.Y. Office); Victor H. Sim (Resident, Los Angeles, California Office); Daniel A. Spirn (Resident, St. Louis, Missouri Office); Todd M. Stennes; Letitia Rei Todd (Not admitted in IL; Resident, San Francisco, California Office); Elizabeth A. Tosaris (Not admitted in IL; Resident, San Francisco, California Office); Wendy S. Weingart (Not admitted in IL; Resident, New York, N.Y. Office); Howard H. Weller (Not admitted in IL; Resident, New York, N.Y. Office); Donna M. Wilson (Resident, Kansas City, Missouri Office); Morris K. Withers (Not admitted in IL; Resident, Kansas City, Missouri Office); Charles M. Yablon (Not admitted in IL; Resident, New York, N.Y. Office); Debra B. Yale. Special Counsel: Daniel R. Brown (Resident, San Francisco, California Office). Associates: Jill L. Abitbol (Not admitted in IL; Resident, New York, N.Y. Office); Kirill Y. Abramov (Resident, St. Louis, Missouri Office); Philip F. Ackerman; Joshua Akbar (Resident, New York, N.Y. Office); David S. Alverson (Not admitted in IL; Resident, Los Angeles, California Office); Leanna M. Anderson (Resident, Los Angeles, California Office); Shannon Skinner Anglin; Kathryn B. Ashton; Eric M. Baim (Resident, Washington, D.C. Office); Rachel G. Balaban (Not admitted in IL; Resident, New York, N.Y. Office); Carole Bass (Resident, New York, N.Y. Office); David R. Baum (Not admitted in IL; Resident, New York, N.Y. Office); Laura Becker (Resident, Los Angeles, California Office); Jason Beckerman (Resident, Los Angeles, California Office); Imanta M. Bergmanis (Not admitted in IL; Resident, Washington, D.C. Office); Wenyu Ho Blanchard; Kathleen Boergers (Not admitted in IL; Resident, San Francisco, California Office); Howard S. Bonfield (Resident, New York, N.Y. Office); Richard J. Brightman (Not admitted in IL; Resident, Short Hills, New Jersey Office); Christopher A. Brown (Not admitted in IL); Leah R. Bruno; Kevin W. Buckley (Not admitted in IL; Resident, St. Louis, MO Office); Jennifer A. Bunshoft (Not admitted in IL; Resident, San Francisco, California Office); Thomas J. Burton; Kwame N. Cain (Not admitted in IL; Resident, New York, N.Y. Office); Julie Calhoun (Resident, St. Louis, Missouri Office); Letissa Carver Reid; Patricia N. Chock (Not admitted in IL; Resident, Los Angeles, California Office); Zenas J. Choi (Resident, Washington, D.C. Office); Michael W. Chou (Resident, Los Angeles, California Office); Kevin M. Christensen (Not admitted in IL; Resident, San Francisco, California Office); Kevin J. Clancy; William E. Copley, III (Not admitted in IL; Resident, Washington, D.C. Office); Mona E. Dajani; Andrew Dalin (Not admitted in IL; Resident, New York, N.Y. Office); Keith A. Davidson (Not admitted in IL; Resident, Los Angeles, California Office); Jeffery S. Davis; David Aloysius Diepenbrock (Resident, San Francisco, California Office); Katherine Hale Donnelly (Not admitted in IL); Michael G. Donohue (Resident, Kansas City, Missouri Office); Staci E. Dresher (Resident, San Francisco, California Office); Deborah Druley (Resident, St. Louis, Missouri Office); Stephanie A. Duchene (Resident, San Francisco, California Office); Charles A. Duffield; Katherine Jean Eddy (Resident, San Francisco, California Office); Anthony T. Eliseuson; Benjamin S. Ellenbogen (Not admitted in IL; Resident, New York, N.Y. Office); Cynthia J. Emry (Resident, Los Angeles, California Office); Wendy N. Enerson; Ramy Fayed (Resident, Washington, D.C. Office); Daniel Feinberg; Robert L. Fernandez; A. Wesley Ferrebee (Not admitted in IL; Resident, Washington, D.C. Office); Scott T. Filmore (Resident, St. Louis, MO Office); Elizabeth S. Finberg (Resident, Washington, D.C. Office); Mark A. Fink (Resident, New York, N.Y. Office); Jacqueline H. Finnegan (Resident, New York, N.Y. Office); Debra L. Fogelman (Resident, Los Angeles, California Office); Stephen E. Fox (Not admitted in IL; Resident, New York, N.Y. Office); Saundra N. Fried; Katherine I. Funk (Not admitted in IL; Resident, Washington, D.C. Office); Todd A. Gangel (Not admitted in IL; Resident, Kansas City, Missouri Office); R. Matt Garms (Not admitted in IL; Resident, Kansas City, Missouri Office); Patricia K. Garringer (Not admitted in IL; Resident, Kansas City, Missouri Office); Susan J. Germer (Not admitted in IL; Resident, San Francisco, California Office); Terance A. Gonsalves; Dina Gorodess; Amanda R. Grainger (Resident, Washington, D.C. Office); Thomas E. Greiff (Resident, Los Angeles, CA Office); Walter C. Hazlitt, Jr.; Chris S. Heller (Resident, Kansas City, Missouri Office); Robert W. Hoffman (Not admitted in IL; Resident, San Francisco, California Office); Hillary Hera Hughes (Not admitted in IL; Resident, New York, N.Y. Office); Areto A. Imoukhuede; Lesa M. Ingraham; James E. Jasaitis (Not admitted in IL; Resident, Short Hills, New Jersey Office); Sanchitha Jayaram (Not admitted in IL; Resident, Washington, D.C. Office); Joma R. Jones (Not admitted in IL; Resident, San Francisco, California Office); Karen M. Jordan (Resident, St. Louis, Missouri Office); Jonathan Kaden; Gaurav Kalra (Resident, San Francisco, California Office); Christopher N. Kanagawa (Resident, St. Louis, Missouri Office); Lee Kaster (Not admitted in IL; Resident, San Francisco, California Office); Justin N. Kattan (Resident, New York, N.Y. Office); Ramji B. Kaul; Nadim Kazi; Derrick Kedziora; Lilly Kim (Resident, Los Angeles, California Office); Leslie E. Klein (Not admitted in IL; Resident, Washington, D.C. Office); Jennifer B. Kleiner (Not admitted in IL; Resident, New York, N.Y. Office); Beata K. Krakus; Jana Krupoff; Azniv Ksachikyan (Not admitted in IL; Resident, Los Angeles, CA Office); Merrillyn Erskine Kulis (Resident, Los Angeles, California Office); John Labbe; Meleana E. Leaverton (Not admitted in IL; Resident, San Francisco, California Office); Soojung Lee (Not admitted in IL; Resident, Los Angeles, California Office); Elizabeth A. Leifel; Kevin D. Lesh (Resident, San Francisco, California Office); Cliona A. Levy (Not admitted in IL; Resident, New York, N.Y. Office); Lisa M. Lilly; Talia Anna Lissner; Steven M. Lubezny; Mark R. Ludwikowski (Resident, Washington, D.C. Office); Monika J. Machen; Kashmira M. Makwana (Not admitted in IL; Resident, Washington, D.C. Office); Eric Reed Mansell; Patrick C. Maxcy (Not admitted in IL); Kevin C. May (Resident, St. Louis, Missouri Office); Johnny McCraw, Jr.; Jacque McCray; Elizabeth J. McCubrey (Resident, Washington, D.C. Office); Shane M. McGee (Not admitted in IL; Resident, Washington, D.C. Office); Steven L. Merouse; Mary L. Mills; Sarah M. Minchener (Not admitted in IL; Resident, Washington, D.C. Office); Anne W. Mitchell; Meredith A. Monaco; Kim Morimoto (Not admitted in IL; Resident, San Francisco, California Office); M. Quinn Murphy (Resident, St. Louis, Missouri Office); Mickki D. Murray (Resident, St. Louis, Missouri Office); Catherine Nasser; Tara A. Nealey (Resident, St. Louis, Missouri Office); James C. Neeld (Resident, Kansas City, Missouri Office); Jessica M. Norris (Resident, Kansas City, Missouri Office); Emily S. Nozick (Resident, San Francisco, California Office); Stephanie M. O'Neill Macro; Dana Orr; Eric I. Orseck (Not admitted in IL; Resident, Short Hills, New Jersey Office); Ashley H. Osbourne (Not admitted in IL; Resident, San Francisco, California Office); Monica Pa (Resident, New York, N.Y. Office); Reid A. Page (Not admitted in IL; Resident, Washington, D.C. Office); Nader Pakfar (Resident, Los Angeles, California Office); Nicole S. Pakkala; Jake A. Palumbo (Resident, St. Louis, Missouri Office); Reginald L. Parks; Lisa M. Pekkala; Shahrzad Poormosleh (Resident, Washington, D.C. Office); Justin D. Pulikkan (Resident, Kansas City, Missouri Office); Sarah J. Ratcliffe (Not admitted in IL; Resident, San Francisco, California Office); Christopher P. Rauch; Jo Christine Reed (Resident, New York, N.Y. Office); Kerry E. Reichs (Not admitted in IL; Resident, Washington, D.C. Office); Deborah Renner (Not admitted in IL; Resident, New York, N.Y. Office); Geoffrey J. Repo; Mindi Richter; Traci Rittenberg (Resident, Washington, D.C. Office); David Rozenblat; Andrew L. Ruben (Not admitted in IL; Resident, St. Louis, Missouri Office); Jason L. Rubin; Daniel Sakaguchi (Not admitted in IL; Resident, St. Louis, Missouri Office); Timothy J. Santoli (Not admitted in IL; Resident, New York, N.Y. Office); Tobias Schlueter; James M. Schoenecker (Not admitted in IL; Resident, New York, N.Y. Office); Marc L. Schultz; Alison Pollock Schwartz; Richard Adam Senzer (Not admitted in IL; Resident, New York, N.Y. Office); Joseph D. Serrano (Not admitted in IL; Resident, Kansas City, Missouri Office); Aaron Shafer (Not admitted in IL; Resident, New York, N.Y. Office); Charulata (Charu) Jain Shah; Andrea Sharetta (Resident, New York, N.Y. Office); James A. Silver (Not admitted in IL; Resident, Washington, D.C. Office); David R. Simonton (Not admitted in IL; Resident, San Francisco, California Office); Ron B. Sitton (Not admitted in IL); Heather L. Skidmore (Resident, Los Angeles, California Office); Barbara Lee Smith; Dianne M. Smith-Misemer (Resident, Kansas City, Missouri Office); Sekret T. Sneed (Not admitted in IL); Peter Soares (Resident, San Francisco, California Office); Milena J. Spencer; Bryan P. Stanley (Resident, Kansas City, Missouri Office); William A. Stetson (Resident, West Palm Beach, Florida Office); Daniele B. Strain (Resident, New York, N.Y. Office); Rebecca S. Stroder (Resident, Kansas City, Missouri Office); Kelly S. Sullivan Deady (Resident, Kansas City, Missouri Office); Daphnee Surpris (Not admitted in IL; Resident, New

(This Listing Continued)

Sonnenschein Nath & Rosenthal LLP (Continued)

York, N.Y. Office); Jadene M.W. Tamura (Resident, Los Angeles, CA Office); Timothy P. Terry (Not admitted in IL; Resident, Los Angeles, California Office); Pia N. Thompson; Emilio Torres-Lumsden (Resident, New York, N.Y. Office); Rheanna Towner; Mei Tsang (Resident, Los Angeles, California Office); Michael Ritchie Y. Ty (Not admitted in IL; Resident, Los Angeles, California Office); Noel B. Vales (Not admitted in IL; Resident, New York, N.Y. Office); Carey P. Wagner (Resident, New York, N.Y. Office); Elizabeth L. Warren-Mikes; Anne Nicholson Weber; Grace Catherine Wen (Not admitted in IL; Resident, Los Angeles, California Office); Jonathan R. Whitehead (Resident, Kansas City, Missouri Office); Roderic M. Williams; Linda Yassky (Not admitted in IL; Resident, New York, N.Y. Office); Paula M. Yost (Not admitted in IL; Resident, San Francisco, California Office); Virginia K. Young (Not admitted in IL; Resident, San Francisco, California Office); Jennifer S. Yu (Not admitted in IL; Resident, Los Angeles, California Office); Saul L. Zackson (Resident, St. Louis, Missouri Office); Stephanie L. Zeppa (Not admitted in IL; Resident, San Francisco, California Office); Ellen Prince Zivitz; Michael Zolandz (Not admitted in IL; Resident, Washington, D.C. Office).

Antitrust, Aviation Litigation, Banking, Bankruptcy, Commercial Financing, Corporate, Employee Benefits, Environmental, Estate Planning, Executive Compensation, First Amendment, Franchising, Government Contracts, Health Care, Insurance, Intellectual Property, International Trade, Labor and Employment, Land Use, Litigation, Media, Municipal Bonds, Outsourcing, Probate, Product Liability, Professional Liability, Real Estate, Securities, Taxation, Trade Regulation, Venture Capital, Workouts, Zoning.

New York, N.Y. Office: 1221 Avenue of the Americas. Telephone: 212-768-6700. Facsimile: 212-768-6800.

Washington, D.C. Office: 1301 K Street, N.W., Suite 600 East Tower. Telephone: 202-408-6400. Facsimile: 202-408-6399.

San Francisco, California Office: 685 Market Street, 6th Floor. Telephone: 415-882-5000. Facsimile: 415-543-5472.

Los Angeles, California Office: 601 South Figueroa Street, Suite 1500. Telephone: 213-623-9300. Facsimile: 213-623-9924.

St. Louis, Missouri Office: One Metropolitan Square, Suite 3000. Telephone: 314-241-1800. Facsimile: 314-259-5959.

Kansas City, Missouri Office: Suite 1100, 4520 Main Street, 64111. Telephone: 816-460-2400. Facsimile: 816-531-7545.

West Palm Beach, Florida Office: Phillips Point, West Tower, 777 South Flagler Drive, Suite 1102. Telephone: 561-833-2410. Facsimile: 561-833-8387.

Short Hills, New Jersey Office: 101 JFK Parkway. Telephone: 973-912-7100. Fax: 973-912-7199.

See Professional Biographies, CHICAGO, ILLINOIS

Sonntag, Nicolette L. ....'66 '97 C&L.209 B.A., J.D. [🄰 Shefsky&F.]
Soodek, Caroline S. ....'— '97 C.494 B.A. L.597 J.D. [🄰 Bryan C.]
Sophie, Kenneth J., Jr., (AV) ....'50 '77 C.363 B.A. L.365 J.D. [Harrington,T.A.&H.]
Sorce, Joseph P., (AV) ....'48 '87 C.209 B.A. L.365 J.D. 1 E. Wacker
Sorensen, David A., (BVⓉ) ....'65 '93 C.477 B.A. L.347 J.D. [Hinshaw&C.]
Sorensen, Sharp ....'57 '86 C.878 B.S. L.597 J.D. [Sidley A.B.&W.]
Sorenson, Kristine M. ....'63 '95 C.966 B.A. L.209 J.D. [Walker W.M.]
Sori-Marin, Mariano L. ....'63 '89 C.347 B.S. L.146 J.D. KPMG Peat Marwick
Sorkin, David E. '64 '89
C.347 B.A.,B.S. L.309 J.D. Asst. Prof. of Law, John Marshall Law Sch.
Sorman, Richard J. ....'49 '76 C.966 B.A. L.146 J.D. 203 N. La Salle St., Ste. 2350
Soroka, Walter ....'29 '53 C.477 A.B. L.339 J.D. 39 S. La Salle St.
Sorosky, Sheldon M., (AV) ....'41 '67 C.424 B.S. L.209 J.D. [Kaplan&S.]
Sorrow, Susan, (CVⓉ) '58 '88 C.843 B.B.A. L.280 J.D.
(adm. in GA; not adm. in IL) 100 South Wacker Drive, 9th Floor
Sorvino, Krista C. ....'72 '01 C.880 B.A. L.209 J.D. [🄰 Bates&C.]
Soseman, Thomas W. ....'66 '91 C.187 B.S.S. L.352 J.D. [🄰 Thiedmann&E.]
Soso, Daniel P. ....'52 '79 C.801 B.A. L.365 J.D. 39 S. LaSalle St.
Sostrin, Ellis M., (AV) ....'49 '72 C.339 L.209 J.D. Spec. Asst. Atty. Gen.
Sostrin, Matthew C. ....'78 '03 C&L.339 B.A., J.D. [🄰 Mayer,B.R.&M.]
Sostrin, Rachel N. ....'77 '02 C.1365 B.A. L.1355 J.D. 2 N. La Salle St., Ste. 1606
Soule, Jennifer K. ....'63 '88 C.234 B.A. L.46 J.D. 155 N. Michigan, 5th Fl.
Soule, Kevin M. '56 '81 C&L.352 B.A., J.D.
(adm. in IA; not adm. in IL) V. P. & Asst. Gen. Coun., General Growth Prop.
Souris, Theodore, (AVⓉ) '25 '49 C&L.477 A.B., J.D.
(adm. in MI; not adm. in IL) 737 N. Michigan Avenue‡
South, Galen R. ....'43 '68 C.478 A.B. L.145 J.D. Sr. Coun., Aon Corp.
Southerland, Lisa G. '65 '02
C.78 B.A. L.424 J.D. Legal Assistance Found. of Metro. Chicago

Southern, Robert A.
(See Grayslake)

Southward, Eric S. ....'69 '99 C.106 B.A. L.345 J.D. 20 W Kinzie, Suite 1300
Southwell, Todd Robert ....'71 '97 C.201 B.S.B.A. L.1000 J.D. [🄰 Mayer,B.R.&M.]
Sowers, Don M., Jr., (AV) ....'59 '86 C.840 B.B.A. L.365 J.D. [🄰 J.M.Goldberg]
Sowle, Mary E. ....'50 '95 C.959 B.A. L.146 J.D. 39 South LaSalle Street, Suite 1020‡
Sowle, Stephen D. '60 '91 C.951 B.A. L.976 J.D.
(adm. in MA; not adm. in IL) Asst. Prof. of Law, Chicago-Kent Coll. of Law
Spacapan, Edward, Jr., (AV) ....'— '79 C.880 B.S. L.597 J.D. [Schiff H.]
Spacapan, Lise T., (AV) ....'57 '84 C.880 B.S. L.209 J.D. [Jenner&B.]
Spadoni, Robert S. '64 '89 C.424 B.A. L.209 LL.M.
Assoc. Gen. Coun., Rush Presbyterian St. Luke's Med. Ctr.
Spadoni, Robin E., Law Offices of '64 '99
C.424 B.A. L.365 J.D. 200 W. Madison, Ste. 710
Spadoro, Mark A. ....'50 '76 C.705 B.A. L.209 J.D. 29 S. LaSalle St., Ste. 425
Spagat, Martin, (P.C.), (AV) ....'40 '64 C&L.339 B.S., J.D. 221 N. LaSalle St. 32nd Fl.
Spagnuolo, Marta ....'76 '01 C.339 B.S. L.146 J.D. 33 N. Dearborn St., Ste. 1910
Spain, Nancy M., (AV) ....'51 '76 C.183 B.A. L.930 J.D. [Spain,S.&V.]
Spain, Richard C., (AV) '50 '75 C.399 B.A. L.930 J.D.
[Spain,S.&V.] (⊙Rolling Meadows, Schaumburg, IL; Northborough, MA)

Spain, Spain & Varnet, P.C., (AV)
33 North Dearborn, Suite 2220, 60602-4302 ⊙
Telephone: 312-220-9112 Facsimile: 312-220-9261
Email: nspain@spainspainvarnet.com URL: http://www.spainspainvarnet.com
Richard C. Spain; Nancy M. Spain; Theresa M. Varnet (Resident, Northborough, Massachusetts);— Sheri L. Willard; Jayme Levin-Muriel; M. Catherine Taylor; Garth F. Lewis.
Estate Planning, Probate, Guardianship, Disability, Elder, Real Estate and Corporate Law.
Northborough, Massachusetts Office: 2 Brigham Street. Telephone: 508-393-4380. Fax: 508-393-4381.
Rolling Meadows, Illinois Office: 1600 Golf Road, Suite 450, 60008. Telephone: 847-434-1162. Fax: 312-220-9261.

Spak, Bernard R. ....'27 '54 C.1016 B.S.C. L.146 LL.B. 20 N. Clark St.

Spak, Donald F., (AV) '48 '74 C.910 A.B. L.209 J.D.
180 N. LaSalle Street, Suite 2510, 60601
Telephone: 312-214-1818 Fax: 312-609-0578
Email: don@spaklaw.com
Commercial Litigation, Real Estate Title Litigation, White Collar Crimes, Real Estate Tax Deed Litigation, Advertising and Copyright Law, Debtor and Creditor Law.

See Professional Biographies, CHICAGO, ILLINOIS

Spak, Marsha C. ....'42 '79 C.307 B.A.Ed. L.146 J.D. 680 N. Lake Shore Dr.‡
Spak, Michael I. '36 '61 C&L.209 B.S., J.D.
Prof. of Law, Chicago-Kent College of Law
Spak, Theodore ....'32 '56 C&L.597 B.S.B.A., LL.B. 30 N. La Salle St.
Spalding, Angela R. ....'— '01 C.339 L.209 J.D. 20 W. Kenzie, Ste. 1300

Spalding, Robert M. .... '— '98 C.605 B.A. L.597 J.D. [Ⓐ Baker&M.]
Spang, Brian Edward .... '72 '97 C.945 A.B. L.339 J.D. [Ⓐ Connelly S.H.]
Spangler, Andrew M. .... '62 '92 C.150 B.F.A. L.93 J.D. [Ⓒ Dahm&E.]
Spangler, Cardelle B. .... '69 '97 C&L.910 B.A., J.D. [Ⓐ Winston&S.]
Spangler, James C., (AV) .... '24 '49 C&L.436 Ph.B., J.D. 20 South Clark St., #2210‡
Spann, Chante D. .... '77 '01 C.1365 B.A. L.569 J.D. [Ⓐ Goldberg,K.B.B.R.&M.]
Sparacio, Steven J. .... '52 '77 C.339 B.S. L.146 J.D. 205 W. Randolph Street
Sparks, Eric P. .... '70 '03 C.339 B.S. L.145 J.D. [Ⓐ Kubasiak,F.R.&R.]
Sparks, Jerry D. .... '42 '67 C.347 B.S. L.1119 J.D. 333 W. Wacker Dr.
Sparks, Karol K., (AVⓉ) '51 '79 C.108 B.A. L.345 J.D.
(adm. in IN; not adm. in IL) [Barack F.K.P.&N.]
Sparks, Kenneth F. .... '63 '92 C.453 B.S. L.477 J.D. [Vedder,P.K.&K.]
Sparks, Lyle Wayne, (AV) .... '44 '77 C.894 A.B. L.309 J.D. [Lord,B.&B.]
Spataro, George S. .... '53 '80 C.820 B.A. L.365 J.D. 120 S. State St., 4th Fl.
Spathis, George J., (BV) .... '65 '90 C.339 B.A. L.146 J.D. [Shaw G.F.G.W.&T.]
Spatuzza, John G., (AV) .... '25 '51 C.209 B.A. L.597 J.D. [Spatuzza&S.]
Spatuzza and Spatuzza, (AV) .... Suite 2000, 221 North La Salle Street
Spatz, George R. .... '72 '02 C.597 B.S.E.D. L.145 J.D. [Ⓐ Gordon&G.L.]
Spatzek, James F., Jr. '71 '97 C.436 B.A. L.209 J.D.
Sr. Coun., Bank One Corporation (Law Dept.)
Spatzek, Jay F. .... '71 '97 C.436 B.A. L.209 J.D. Asst. V.P.
Spearman, Beverly P. ..... '64 '01 C.734 B.S.N. L.560 J.D. [Ⓐ J.D.Montgomery&Assoc.]
Spears, Natalie J. .... '70 '95 C.352 B.B.A. L.477 J.D. [Sonnenschein N.&R.]
Spears, Scott Douglas .... '73 '01 C.589 B.S. L.209 J.D. [Ⓐ Ancel,G.D.B.D.&R.]
Specht, Frederick L., (AV) .... '39 '68 C.424 B.B.A. L.365 J.D. 207 East Ohio Street
Specks, Gary L., (AV) .... '51 '75 C.597 B.A. L.209 J.D. [Ⓒ Kaplan F.&K.]
Specks, Granvil I., (AV) ..... '26 '50 C.802 B.B.A. L.597 J.D. 10 S. Wacker Dr., Ste. 3600
Spector, David M., (AV) .... '— '71 C.597 B.A. L.477 J.D. [Schiff H.]
Spector, Kenneth L. .... '50 '75 C.976 B.A. L.145 J.D. 19 South LaSalle St.
Spector, Richard S. .... '26 '55 C.597 B.S. L.146 LL.B. [R.S.Spector]
Spector, Steven .... '57 '81 C.339 B.S. L.352 J.D. [S.S.Llc]
Spector, Richard S., Ltd. .... 3740 N. Lake Shore Dr., Apt. 12B

Spector, Steven, LLC
150 South Wacker Drive, Suite 1200, 60606-4201
Telephone: 312-357-9408 Fax: 312-357-9404
Email: sspector@spectorllc.com URL: http://www.spectorllc.com
Steven Spector.
Tax, Business Planning, Estate Planning, Tax Return Preparation, Probate, Wealth Management, Trust Administration, Corporate Formation, Limited Liability Companies.
See Professional Biographies, CHICAGO, ILLINOIS

Speer, Richard A. '28 '56 C.608 B.M.E. L.273 LL.B.
(adm. in VA; not adm. in IL; Pat.) [Ⓒ Mayer,B.R.&M.]
Speidel, Elizabeth West .... '48 '80 C.612 B.S. L.597 J.D. [Ⓒ Daley&M.]
Speidel, Richard E. '33 '57 C.207 B.A. L.150 J.D.
(adm. in OH; not adm. in IL) Prof. of Law, Northwestern Univ.
Spelhaug, Lisa Marie .... '69 '97 C.494 B.A. L.300 J.D. [Ⓐ Much S.F.D.A.&R.]
Speller-Thurman, Michelle .... '68 '99 C.339 B.S. L.597 J.D. [Ⓐ Jenner&B.]
Spellmire, George W., Jr., (AV) .... '— '74 C.608 B.A. L.209 J.D. [Spellmire&S.]

Spellmire & Sommer, (AV)
77 West Wacker Drive, Suite 4800, 60601
Telephone: 312-606-8721 Fax: 312-606-8731
Email: gws@spellmiresommer.com URL: http://www.spellmireandsommer.com
George W. Spellmire, Jr.; Lisa Marré Sommer; John M. Foley.
Legal Malpractice, Accounting Malpractice, Insurance Coverage, Medical Hospital Malpractice, Professional Ethics and Attorney Discipline, Directors and Officers, Errors and Omissions, Insurance Law, General Litigation.
See Professional Biographies, CHICAGO, ILLINOIS

Spence, William A., (AV) .... '— '71 C.597 B.A. L.424 J.D. [Ⓒ Freeborn&P.]
Spencer, Harold E., (AV) '12 '38
C.546 A.B. L.145 J.D. 860 N. Lake Shore Drive, Ste. 25 K
Spencer, Lewis D. .... '17 '42 C.210 A.B. L.178 J.D. 5555 N. Sheridan Rd.‡
Spencer, Milena J. .... '78 '04 C.424 B.S. L.1066 J.D. [Ⓐ Sonnenschein N.&R.]
Spencer, Robin M. .... '— '94 C.878 B.A. L.893 J.D. [Schiff H.]
Spencer, Scott A. .... '72 '03 C.845 B.S. L.339 J.D. [Ⓐ Jenner&B.]
Sperber, Marc F. .... '64 '92 C.696 B.A. L.276 J.D. [Mayer,B.R.&M.]
Sperling, Bruce S., (AV) .... '45 '70 C&L.597 B.S.M.E., J.D. [Sperling&S.]
Sperling, Frederick J., (AV) .... '— '80 C.31 B.A. L.145 J.D. [Schiff H.]
Sperling, Jeffrey C. .... '69 '94 C.347 B.A. L.365 J.D. 53 W. Jackson
Sperling, Robert Y., (AV) .... '47 '72 C.339 A.B. L.209 J.D. [Winston&S.]

Sperling & Slater, A Professional Corporation, (AV)
55 West Monroe Street Suite 3200, 60603
Telephone: 312-641-3200 Fax: 312-641-6492
URL: http://www.sperling-law.com
Bruce S. Sperling; Paul E. Slater; Eugene J. Frett; Mitchell H. Macknin; Gregg R. Hague; Greg Shinall; Steven C. Florsheim; Claire P. Murphy; Robert D. Cheifetz; Thomas D. Brooks; Adam P. Merrill;—Celiza P. Bragança; Daniel A. Shmikler; Michael G. Dickler; Matthew Weisman; Dina G. Rollman; Monazza Arain. Of Counsel: Harvey J. Barnett; Stephen J. Spitz; Angie A. Chen. Commercial and Business Litigation, Antitrust, Intellectual Property, Appellate Practice.
See Professional Biographies, CHICAGO, ILLINOIS

Spevacek, Lucia Ann .... '66 '95 C.260 B.A. L.1206 J.D. Pricewaterhouse Coopers, L.L.P.
Spevack, Barry A., (AV) .... '50 '78 C.30 B.A. L.424 J.D. [Monico,P.&S.]
Speyer, Lawrence S., (AV) .... '— '64 C.1016 B.S.B.A. L.365 J.D. [Ⓒ Querrey&H.]
Sphar, Troy M. .... '— '02 C.473 B.S. L.910 J.D. [Ⓐ Griffin]
Spicer, Veronica L. .... '74 '01 C.986 B.A. L.145 J.D. [Ⓐ Mayer,B.R.&M.]
Spiegel, Joelle Hillory .... '64 '89 C.1119 B.A. L.365 J.D. 2218 N. Seminary

Spiegel, Mark L. '53 '78 C.1183 B.A. L.146 J.D.
25 East Washington, Suite 1501, 60602
Telephone: 312-782-2860 Fax: 312-782-2870
Email: mark.spiegel@markspiegel.com URL: http://www.markspiegel.com
Real Estate, including Residential, Commercial and Industrial, Condominium Development and Conversion, Leases and Leasing, Contract Negotiation and Disputes; Family Law, including Divorce, Child Custody, Child Support, Spousal Support/Alimony, Separation Agreements, Distribution/Separation of Property, Visitation Rights; Commercial Litigation, including Commercial Collections.
See Professional Biographies, CHICAGO, ILLINOIS

Spiegel, Robert I., P.C. .... '40 '65 C.477 A.B. L.597 J.D. [R.I.Spiegel]
Spiegel, Scott Lee .... '76 '01 C.966 B.A. L.146 J.D. Asst. State's Atty.
Spiegel, Stuart .... '47 '71 C.339 B.A. L.424 J.D. [Spiegel&D.]
Spiegel & DeMars, (BV) .... 100 W. Monroe St.
Spiegel, Robert I., P.C. .... 1150 N. Lake Shore Dr.
Spiegler, Joseph A. .... '68 '94 C.569 B.A. L.602 J.D. [Winston&S.]
Spiegler, Lisa M. .... '72 '97 C.378 B.A. L.910 J.D. [Ⓐ Franczek S.]
Spier, Peter C. .... '— '98 C.659 B.A. L.597 J.D. [Ⓐ Schiff H.]
Spiliopoulos, Elaine M. .... '71 '97 C.477 B.A. L.209 J.D. Off. of the Appl. Def.
Spina, Francis A., (AV) .... '55 '80 C.602 B.A. L.209 J.D. [Cremer,K.S.&S.]
Spina, Kenneth P. .... '62 '96 C.424 M.S. L.209 J.D. [Leydig,V.&M.] (See Pat. Sect.)

Spinak, Michael D. .... '47 '72 C.641 B.A. L.352 J.D. 134 N. La Salle St., Ste. 1020
Spingola, Joseph J., Ltd. .... '42 '70 C.679 B.S. L.146 J.D. 47 W. Polk St., 3rd Fl.
Spingola, Peter M. .... '71 '97 C.197 B.A. L.146 J.D. [Chapman&S.]
Spinka, Dorothy W., (Mrs.) .... '18 '47 C.597 L.146 LL.B. 10412 S. Whipple St.‡
Spiotto, James E., (AV) .... '— '72 C.999 A.B. L.145 J.D. [Chapman&C.]
Spira, Aaron D. .... '— '04 C.231 B.A. L.597 J.D. [Ⓐ Kirkland&E.]
Spira, David J. .... '46 '93 C.959 B.A. L.365 J.D. [Ⓐ J.B.Schwartz&Assoc.]
Spitalli, Joseph A., (AV) .... '39 '63 C&L.209 B.A., J.D. [Simon&S.]
Spitkovsky, Robert, Jr. .... '62 '88 C&L.221 B.A., J.D. [Johnson&B.]
Spitz, Alan .... '52 '77 C.339 B.A. L.146 J.D. 111 W. Washington St., Ste. 1401
Spitz, Edward .... '45 '70 L.146 J.D. Vitell & Spitz
Spitz, Joel H. .... '65 '90 C.966 B.A. L.436 J.D. [McGuirewoods]
Spitz, Stephen J., (AV) .... '44 '71 C.347 B.A. L.597 J.D. [Ⓒ Sperling&S.]
Spitzer, Bruce C. .... '47 '72 C&L.339 A.B., J.D. [Metge,S.&K.]
Spitzer, Gregory E. .... '— '89 C.339 B.S. L.597 J.D. [Kirkland&E.]
Spitzer, Addis, Susman & Enders, (AV) .... 100 West Monroe Street, Suite 1500
Spitzzeri, Joseph F., (AV) .... '57 '83 C.339 B.S. L.365 J.D. [Johnson&B.]
Spivack, Aaron, Law Offices of, (AV) '46 '75 C.208 B.A. L.365 J.D.
811 W. Superior St.
Spivak, Marc E. .... '50 '75 C.589 B.A. L.365 J.D. 19 S. LaSalle St.
Spivey, Dawn M. .... '71 '98 C.375 B.A. L.339 J.D. [Ⓐ Franczek S.]
Spivey, Donna R. .... '48 '80 C&L.209 B.S., J.D. Northern Trust Co.‡
Spivey, Jonathan R. .... '— '97 C.671 B.S. L.1463 J.D. [Ⓐ Foley&L.] (Pat.)
Spiwak, Andrew D. '60 '86 C.966 B.A. L.365 J.D.
Dir. Legal Div. & Chf. Atty., Chicago Board Options Exchange, Incorporated
Spizzirri, William E., (AV) .... '41 '75 C.999 B.A. L.365 J.D. [Kralovec&M.]
Spizzo, James A., (BV) .... '52 '79 C.337 A.B. L.352 J.D. [Vedder,P.K.&K.]
Spognardi, Mark A., (AV) .... '— '84 C.352 B.A. L.209 J.D. [Holland&K.]
Sposeep, Jason N. .... '77 '03 C.347 B.S. L.146 J.D. [Ⓐ Schiller,D.&F.]
Spotts, Richard C. .... '58 '85 C.589 B.S. L.221 J.D. 2628 N. Orchard St.
Spracker, Marilyn S. .... '55 '81 C.881 B.A. L.966 J.D. Sr. Atty., SBC Corp.
Sprague, Kara Dailey .... '71 '97 C.1150 B.A. L.421 J.D. Pub. Def.
Spratt, Patricia S., (AV) .... '49 '91 L.424 J.D. [Shefsky&F.]
Sprayregen, James H. M., (AV) .... '— '85 C.477 B.A. L.339 J.D. [Kirkland&E.]
Sprayregen, Joel J., (AV) .... '34 '58 C.597 B.S. L.976 LL.B. [Shefsky&F.]
Sprengel, Jennifer Winter, (AV) .... '65 '90 C.679 B.A. L.209 J.D. [Miller F.&C.]
Sprenger, Katherine S. .... '68 '94 C.999 B.A. L.597 J.D. [Barack F.K.P.&N.]
Spring, Linda E., (BV) '45 '83 C.494 B.S. L.424 J.D.
[Swanson,M.&B.] (⊙Libertyville, Waukegan)
Springer, Boyd J., (AV) .... '— '78 C&L.339 A.B., J.D. [Ⓒ Jones D.]
Springer, David E., (AV) .... '52 '77 C&L.976 A.B., J.D. [Skadden,A.S.M.&F.]
Springer, Edward M., (AV) .... '42 '67 C.339 A.B. L.209 J.D. [Springer,C.&D.] ⊙
Springer, Olga M. .... '25 '50 C.597 L.146 J.D. Immigration J., Dept. of Jus.
Springer, William R. '— '03
C.477 B.A. L.597 J.D. [Ⓐ Mayer,B.R.&M.] (⊙New York, NY)

Springer, Casey & Dienstag, P.C., (AV)
100 West Monroe Street, 60603 ⊙
Telephone: 312-372-0800 Fax: 312-372-0842
Email: SCDCHGO@global.net
Wyatt Jacobs (1906-1994); Joseph E. Springer (1937-1983); Donald E. Casey; Gary E. Dienstag; Edward M. Springer.
General Practice. Civil Trial and Appellate Litigation in State and Federal Courts. Insurance Law, Regulatory Defense and Coverage Litigation. Administrative Agencies. Corporation, Estate Planning and Probate, Federal Taxation, Matrimonial, Municipal and Real Estate Law.
Barrington, Illinois Office: 509 West Old Northwest Highway 60010. Telephone: 847-382-9797.
See Professional Biographies, CHICAGO, ILLINOIS

Springman, Sean P. .... '75 '01 C.701 B.S.M.E. L.1119 J.D. [Ⓐ Brinks H.G.&L.]
Sproger, Charles E., (AV) '33 '58 C&L.597 B.S. in B.A., J.D.
2800 W. Birchwood Ave.
Sproule, Dianne M. '— '87 C.700 B.A. L.209 J.D.
Dept. of Admin. Hearings, Secy. of St., Legal Advsr.
Sprowl, Charles R., (AV) .... '10 '35 C&L.477 A.B., J.D. [Ⓒ Taylor,M.S.H.&M.]
Spry, Jennifer .... '79 '04 C.201 B.S.B.A. L.602 J.D. [Ⓐ Winston&S.]
Spuhler, Beata K. .... '74 '99 C.209 B.A. L.146 J.D. [Ⓒ Gardner C.&D.]
Spuhler, Ronald .... '73 '99 C.679 B.S. L.146 J.D. [McAndrews,H.&M.]
Spychalski, Derek M. .... '71 '03 C.367 B.A. L.146 J.D. [Ⓐ Vedder,P.K.&K.]
Spytek, Eryk J. .... '68 '94 C.276 B.A. L.424 J.D. [Winston&S.]
Squillace, Craig J. .... '73 '02 C.338 B.S. L.365 J.D. [Ⓐ Clifford]
Squires, John H. .... '46 '71 C&L.339 A.B., J.D. U.S. Bkrptcy. J.
Squyres, Mary M. .... '50 '82 C.706 A.B. L.879 J.D. [Ⓒ Brinks H.G.&L.]
Sreenan, Michael J. .... '61 '86 C.589 B.S. L.339 J.D. [M.J.Sreenan,Sr.]
Sreenan, Michael J., P.C. .... 2540 N. Seminary
Srodulski, Marc L. .... '71 '97 C.174 B.A. L.146 J.D. 30 N. LaSalle St.
Staas, Laurie .... '70 '95 C.97 B.S.B.A. L.608 J.D. Coopers & Lybrand
Staat, Lawrence G. .... '49 '74 C.339 B.S. L.209 J.D. [Shaheen,N.S.F.&E.]
Stabrawa, David J. .... '63 '88 C&L.602 B.B.A., J.D. Off. of States Atty.
Stacey, Christ S., Law Office of, (BV) '57 '82
C.966 B.A. L.365 J.D. 19 S. LaSalle, Suite 1400
Stach, Victoria F. .... '66 '92 C.597 B.A. L.245 J.D. [Winston&S.]
Stachnik, Raymond E. .... '49 '75 C.508 B.A. L.365 J.D. [Connelly R.&M.]
Stachyra, Frank E. .... '46 '73 C.1049 B.A. L.597 J.D. 3319 West Belden Avenue
Stack, James F., (AV) .... '31 '59 C&L.209 B.A., LL.B. 2 N. LaSalle St.
Stack, John W., (AV) .... '37 '63 C.966 B.S. L.1066 J.D. 35 W. Wacker Dr.‡
Stack, Lawrence R. .... '41 '85 C.209 B.A. L.424 J.D. 20 N. Wacker Dr.
Stack, Linnea C. .... '— '03 C.477 B.A. L.146 J.D. [Ⓐ Kirkland&E.]
Stack, Paul F., (AV) .... '46 '71 C.37 B.S. L.276 J.D. [Stack&F.]

Stack & Filpi, Chartered, (AV)
Suite 411, 140 South Dearborn Street, 60603-5298
Telephone: 312-782-0690 Facsimile: 312-782-0936
URL: http://www.stackfilpi.com
Paul F. Stack; Robert A. Filpi. Associate: Cori A. Szczucki. Of Counsel: James A. McGurk.
Federal and state commercial litigation with extensive experience in contract and intellectual property matters.
See Professional Biographies, CHICAGO, ILLINOIS

Stadheim, Rolf O., (AV) .... '40 '67 C.966 B.S. L.145 J.D. [Stadheim&G.]

Stadheim & Grear, (AV)
Wrigley Tower - 22nd Floor, 400 North Michigan Avenue, 60611-4102
Telephone: 312-755-4400 Fax: 312-755-4408
Rolf O. Stadheim; Joseph A. Grear; George C. Summerfield, Jr. (Not admitted in IL); Keith A. Vogt. Patent Licensing and Litigation.
See Professional Biographies, CHICAGO, ILLINOIS

Staes, Andrew T., (AV) .... '58 '83 C.339 B.S.B.A. L.146 J.D. [Staes&S.]

Staes & Scallan, P.C., (AV)
111 W. Washington Street Suite 1310, 60602
Telephone: 312-201-8969 Fax: 312-201-9233
Email: staesandscallan@earthlink.net
Andrew T. Staes; Stephen Scallan.
Business, Commercial and Federal White Collar Criminal Litigation. Appellate Practice in the Federal and State Courts of Appeals.
See Professional Biographies, CHICAGO, ILLINOIS

Stafford, E. Lynette ... '72 '00 C.254 B.A. L.1051 J.D. [Ⓐ Meckler B.&T.]
Stafford, Mary F., (AV) ... '51 '76 C.339 B.A. L.365 J.D. [Clausen M.]
Stagman, David J., (AV) ... '— '93 C.647 B.A. L.597 J.D. [Ⓐ Katten M.R.]
Stahl, David M., (AV) ... '46 '72 C.339 B.A. L.477 J.D. [Eimer S.K.&S.]
Stahl, Jeffrey J., (AV) ... '58 '83 C.602 B.B.A. L.802 J.D. [Stahl&B.]
Stahl, Philip C., (AV) ... '48 '74 C.446 B.A. L.273 J.D. [Grippo&E.]
Stahl & Brashler LLC, (AV) ... 55 W. Monroe Street
Stahl Cowen Crowley LLC, (AV) ... 55 West Monroe Street
Stahr, Scott M. '56 '82 C.893 B.A. L.846 J.D.
(adm. in CA; not adm. in IL) 200 E. Randolph St.
Stahr, Thomas E., (AV) ... '— '79 C.234 B.A. L.209 J.D. [Querrey&H.]
Stainthorp, John L. ... '50 '80 L.107 J.D. People's Law Office
Staley, Charles R., (AV) '38 '63
C.309 A.B. L.145 J.D. 29 South La Salle Street, Suite 950
Stallworth, Stanley B. ... '63 '90 C.1010 B.S. L.966 J.D. [Sidley A.B.&W.]
Stalmack, John M., (AV) ... '47 '74 C.162 B.A. L.424 J.D. [Bollinger,R.&G.]
Stalmack, Todd J. ... '76 '01 C.393 B.A. L.1410 J.D. [Ⓐ Donohue B.M.&S.]

Stalmack, Joseph, & Associates, P.C.
(See Hammond, Indiana)

Stamas, Arthur ... '51 '78 C.424 B.A. L.365 J.D. 330 N. Wabash Ave., Ste. 3208
Stamatakos, Philip S. ... '63 '93 C&L.477 A.B., J.D. [Baker&M.]
Stamatis, Peter S., Law Offices of '68 '93
C.339 B.A. L.146 J.D. 77 W. Wacker Dr., Ste. 4800
Stamato, Anthony G. ... '— '91 C.813 A.B. L.145 J.D. [Kaye S.]
Stamos, James A., (AV) ... '39 '65 C.388 B.A. L.597 J.D. [J.A.Stamos]
Stamos, James J., (AV) ... '56 '80 C.879 B.A. L.339 J.D. [Stamos&T.]
Stamos, John J. ... '24 '49 C&L.209 LL.B. [Ⓒ Stamos&T.]
Stamos, James A., Ltd., (AV) ... 61 W. Superior St.

Stamos & Trucco, (AV)
30 W. Monroe, Suite 1600, 60603
Telephone: 312-630-7979 Telecopier: 312-630-1183
James J. Stamos; Michael T. Trucco; George M. Hoffman; Gus J. Athas; Raymond Gupta. Associates: John J. Kakacek; Julie N. Howie; Laura S. Huseby; Daniel R. Shaffer; Jenni L. Young; Julie Bruce Zogbaum. Of Counsel: John J. Stamos; Keith L. Moore.
Commercial Litigation and Health Care Litigation.
See Professional Biographies, CHICAGO, ILLINOIS

Stanczak, William R. ... '71 '98 C.475 B.A. L.210 J.D. [Ⓐ Garofalo,S.H.&S.]
Standlee, Russell P., (AV) ... '49 '75 C.347 B.S. L.362 J.D. [Wiedner&M.]
Stanek, Debra J., (AV) ... '59 '86 C.424 B.A. L.145 J.D. [Sidley A.B.&W.]
Stanger, Andrew '— '97
(adm. in England; not adm. in IL) [Mayer,B.R.&M.] (⊙London, England)
Stangle, Claudia W. ... '70 '97 C.477 B.A. L.209 J.D. [Ⓐ Leydig,V.&M.]
Stanhaus, James S. ... '45 '70 C.276 A.B. L.309 J.D. [Mayer,B.R.&M.]
Staniec, Denise Y., Law Offices of, (AV) '56 '84
C.446 B.A. L.146 J.D. 900 N. Franklin St., Ste. 406
Staniec, Marjan P. ... '14 '41 C.999 L.180 LL.B. Ret. Assoc. Cir. J.‡
Stanis, John B. ... '— '88 C.338 B.S. L.339 J.D. [Masuda,F.E.&M.] (⊙Schaumburg)
Stanish, Tanya J., (BV) ... '69 '95 C.210 B.A. L.209 J.D. [Jenner&B.]
Stanisha, Therese J. ... '62 '92 C.477 A.B. L.589 J.D. 333 W. Wacker Dr.
Stankevicius, Vladas ... '71 '03 L.424 J.D. 443 W. Wrightwood, Suite 1405
Stanko, John W., Jr. ... '62 '88 C.723 B.A. L.365 J.D. [Flamm&T.]
Stankovic, Bratislav '— '04 C.999 B.S. L.966 J.D.
(adm. in WI; not adm. in IL) [Ⓐ Brinks H.G.&L.]
Stanley, Benjamin D. ... '— '03 C&L.101 B.S., J.D. [Ⓐ Kirkland&E.]
Stanley, Frank C., Jr., (AV) ... '28 '55 C.221 B.C.S. L.597 J.D. 7929 Wellington Ave.
Stanley, James R. ... '33 '59 C.645 A.B. L.1017 LL.B. 100 N. Riverside Plz.‡
Stanley, Justin A., (AV) ... '11 '37 C.197 A.B. L.178 LL.B. 190 S. LaSalle St.
Stanley, Richard E., Jr. '67 '99
C.792 B.S.M.E. L.69 J.D. [Ⓐ Brinks H.G.&L.] (See Pat. Sect.)
Stanner, Daniel L., (AV) ... '67 '92 C.93 B.A. L.424 J.D. [Crisham&K.]
Stansbury, Thomas A. ... '25 '49 C&L.597 B.S., J.D. 180 N. LaSalle St. (Pat.)
Stanton, Daniel T. ... '55 '80 C.424 B.A. L.365 J.D. [Ⓐ Cooney&C.]
Stanton, Gregory E. '— '99
C.339 B.S.E.E. L.597 J.D. [Ⓐ Marshall,G.&B.] (See Pat. Sect.)
Stanton, John R., (AV) ... '19 '48 C&L.209 A.B., J.D. 135 S. LaSalle St.
Stanton, Karen M. ... '69 '94 C.893 B.S. L.352 J.D. [Ⓐ Sidley A.B.&W.]
Stanton, Michael F. ... '50 '85 C.339 B.S. L.365 J.D. Soc. Sec. Admn.
Stanton, Patrick T. ... '66 '93 C.602 B.A. L.424 J.D. [Schwartz C.]
Stanton, Richard M. ... '41 '68 C&L.339 B.S., J.D. [Jacobs,B.O.S.&H.]
Stanton, Robert L. ... '46 '79 C.424 B.A. L.209 J.D. Univ. of Chgo./NORC
Stanton, Timothy J. ... '65 '94 C.966 B.A. L.424 J.D. [Gardner C.&D.]
Staples, James G., (AV) '31 '56 C.679 B.S.M.E. L.477 LL.B.
130 E. Randolph Dr. (Pat.)
Stapleton, Margaret ... '45 '71 C.700 B.A. L.145 J.D. Legal Asst. Found. of Chicago
Star, James A. ... '61 '87 C.309 A.B. L.976 J.D. 222 N. LaSalle St.
Star, Leon P. ... '10 '35 L.339 LL.B. 3750 Lake Shore Dr.
Star, Robert M. ... '45 '73 C.112 A.B. L.145 J.D. [Kutak R.]
Star, Sara Crown ... '60 '87 C.575 B.A. L.276 J.D. 222 North La Salle Street, 8th Floor
Starcevich, Lisa M. ... '70 '94 C.679 B.A. L.209 J.D. [Weinberg R.]
Starck, Kathryn A. ... '— '02 C.209 L.146 J.D. [Ⓐ Patton&R.]
Starck, Walter J., (AV) ... '— '76 C.309 B.A. L.861 J.D. [Arnstein&L.]
Stark, Blooma, (AV) ... '47 '81 C.589 B.S. L.597 J.D. [Aronberg G.D.&G.]
Stark, Jarmila ... '21 '60 C.597 Ph.B. L.365 LL.B. 5647 W. Irving Pk. Rd.
Stark, Lawrence J., (AV) ... '60 '85 C.1036 B.A. L.146 J.D. [Stone,P.&K.]
Stark, Randall R., (BV) ... '61 '87 C.436 B.A. L.209 J.D. [Rusin M.&F.]
Stark, Vincent J., (BV) ... '62 '88 C.338 B.S. L.365 J.D. [Kamerlink,S.&M.] ⊙
Stark-Hood, Mary C. ... '50 '77 C.1154 B.A. L.1187 J.D. 430 N. Michigan State
Starkman, Gary L., (AV) ... '46 '71 C.339 A.B. L.597 J.D. [McGuirewoods]
Starkman, Leah Jo ... '73 '02 C.209 B.A. L.365 J.D. 6150 N. Lincoln Ave.
Starkman, Paul E. ... '— '84 C.966 B.A. L.209 J.D. [Arnstein&L.]
Starkopf, Lawrence S., (BV) ... '49 '75 C.37 B.A. L.64 J.D. [Grund&L.]
Starks, Benjamin E., Sr. ... '43 '77 C.1191 B.S. L.46 J.D. 11528 S. Halsted Street
Starr, Daniel M. ... '53 '78 C.1111 B.A. L.424 J.D. [Starr,Y.&R.]
Starr, Kelly A. ... '66 '95 C.188 B.S. L.339 J.D. [Vedder,P.K.&K.]
Starr, Yanoff & Rowells ... 35 E. Wacker Dr.
Starshak, Kathryn ... '76 '02 C&L.209 B.A., J.D. [Ⓐ Bell,B.&L.]
Starshak, William A. ... '72 '00 C.893 B.A L.597 J.D. [Ⓐ Goldberg,K.B.B.R.&M.]
Staruck, Elizabeth F. ... '70 '95 C.352 B.A. L.146 J.D. [Hinshaw&C.]
Stascia, Lawrence R. ... '— '81 C.339 A.B. L.424 J.D. Asst. States Atty.
Stasiulis, Stanley P., (BV) ... '48 '75 C.597 B.A. L.861 J.D. 6639 S. Kilbourn Ave.
Stasko, Christopher J. ... '71 '98 C.98 B.A. L.146 J.D. [Richardson,S.B.&M.]
Stassen, John H., (P.C.), (AV) ... '— '68 C.597 B.S. L.309 J.D. [Kirkland&E.]
Stathopoulos, Chris ... '77 '01 C.276 B.A. L.477 J.D. [Ⓐ Winston&S.]
Statland, Donald A., (AV) '38 '63
C.102 B.S. L.569 LL.B. Suite 1600, 175 West Jackson Blvd.
Statland, Jay L., (AV) ... '49 '74 C.589 B.A. L.209 J.D. [Statland&V.]
Statland & Valley, (AV) ... 10 S. LaSalle Street

Statman, Harris, Siegel & Eyrich, LLC, (AV)
333 West Wacker Drive, Suite 1710, 60606 ⊙
Telephone: 312-263-1070 Fax: 312-263-1201
Members of Firm: Alan I. Ehrenberg; Scott C. Frost. Associates: Joshua Bernstein; Denise D. Keliuotis; Julie Davis Egan.
General Civil Trial and Appellate Practice in Federal and State Courts. Commercial Litigation, Bankruptcy, Banking, Personal Injury and Family Law. Corporate Acquisitions, Dispositions, Spin-Offs, Corporate Formation, Financings, Real Estate, Banking and Commercial Law, Reorganizations, Restructurings, Bankruptcy, Civil Litigation, General Business, Intellectual Property, Taxation, Estate Planning.
References: Bank One, Cincinnati, N.A.; Fifth Third Bank.
Dayton, Ohio Office: Fifth Third Center, 110 North Main Street, Suite 1520, 45402. Telephone: 937-222-1090. Fax: 937-222-1046.
Cincinnati, Ohio Office: 2900 Chemed Center, 255 East Fifth Street, 45202-2912. Telephone: 513-621-2666. Telecopier: 513-621-4896.
See Professional Biographies, CHICAGO, ILLINOIS

Statz, Kathryn Marie '66 '00 C.530 B.A. L.436 J.D.
(adm. in WI; not adm. in IL) DePaul Athletic Dept.
Statza, Gerald R. ... '50 '79 C.966 B.A. L.365 J.D. 53 W. Jackson Blvd.
Staub, David K., (AV) ... '53 '77 C.339 B.S. L.309 J.D. [Stahl C.C.]
Staubus, Bradley K. ... '70 '95 C.608 B.S. L.209 J.D. [Esposito&S.]
Staudacher, Edward ... '72 '04 [Benes S.&K.]
Staudt, Ronald W. '46 '70
C.1024 B.A. L.145 J.D. Prof. of Law, Chicago-Kent Coll. of Law
Stauff, Lisa M., Law Offices of '70 '01
C.145 A.B. L.146 J.D. 1658 N. Milwaukee Avenue
Stauffer, Robert R., (AV) ... '61 '86 C.502 B.A. L.309 J.D. [Jenner&B.]
Staulcup, James M., Jr. ... '— '68 C.894 A.B. L.209 J.D. [Ⓒ Bryan C.]
Staunton, Thomas M. ... '63 '93 C.339 B.A. L.569 J.D. [Miller S.&H.]
Stavins, Richard Lee, (AV) ... '43 '68 C&L.597 B.S.J., J.D. [Robbins,S.&P.]
Stavropoulos, Peter J. ... '69 '96 C.1183 B.A. L.365 J.D. [Ⓐ Brady,C.&M.]
Stavropoulos, Sandra M., (BV) ... '54 '80 C.597 B.S. L.209 J.D. Asst. States Atty.
Stavrou, Tina G. ... '— '01 L.146 J.D. Enforcement Atty., Illinois Securities Department
Steadman, Lewis T., Jr., (AV) ... '56 '82 C.597 B.A. L.365 J.D. [Holland&K.]
Steadman, Lewis T., Sr., (AV) '26 '52
C.823 B.M.E. L.273 J.D. [Trexler,B.G.B.&M.] (See Pat. Sect.)
Steadman, Paul R. ... '— '96 C.691 B.S. L.145 J.D. [Kirkland&E.] (Pat.) (⊙Wash., DC)
Stearn, Robert Alan '59 '89 C.339 B.S. L.966 J.D.
Coun., State Off. of Bks. & Real Estate
Stears, George T. '47 '74 C.477 B.A. L.424 J.D.
Chief Atty., Ofc. of the Pub. Guardian (Divorce Div.)
Stec, Natalie Marie ... '75 '00 C.339 B.S. L.564 J.D. 105 W. Madison St., Ste. 2000
Stec, Sean C. ... '71 '97 C.205 B.A. L.851 J.D. Two N. LaSalle St., Ste. 1650
Steck, Jeffrey A. '72 '01 C.145 B.A. L.1375 J.D.
[McDonnell B.H.&B.] (See Pat. Sect.)
Steed, John M. ... '55 '80 C.436 B.S.B.A. L.209 J.D. [Dykema G.P.]
Steege, Catherine L., (AV) ... '56 '82 C.597 B.S.J. L.209 J.D. [Jenner&B.]
Steele, Angela K. ... '76 '02 C.575 B.S. L.145 J.D. [Ⓐ Pattishall,M.N.H.&G.]
Steele, Geoffrey Paul ... '58 '00 C&L.424 B.A., J.D. [Steele]
Steele, Heidi J. ... '— '92 C.914 B.A. L.477 J.D. [McDermott W.&E.]
Steele, Sonia Macias ... '— '03 C.276 B.A. L.228 J.D. [Ⓐ Schiff H.]
Steele, Susan L. ... '70 '04 C.323 B.S. L.477 J.D. [Ⓐ Leydig,V.&M.]
Steele & Co. ... 510 W. Belmont Ave., Ste. 2403
Steen, Jeffrey C., (AV) ... '59 '84 C.197 B.A. L.145 J.D. [Sidley A.B.&W.]
Steenson, Todd D. ... '66 '93 C.55 B.A. L.494 J.D. [Holland&K.]
Stefan, Barbara S. '53 '00 C.1032 B.B.A. L.988 J.D.
(adm. in WA; not adm. in IL) Region Coun., Aetna Inc.
Stefaneas, Telly ... '72 '97 C&L.209 B.A., J.D. [Ⓐ Cantwell&C.]
Stefani, Daniel R., (AV) ... '66 '94 C.339 B.A. L.365 J.D. [Schiller,D.&F.]
Stefanich, Matthew W., Jr. ... '46 '72 C.597 A.B. L.209 J.D. Homart Devel. Co.
Stefanowicz, Dennis H., Jr. ... '67 '92 C&L.209 B.A., J.D. 30 S. Wacker Dr., Ste. 2425
Stefans, Arthur ... '47 '72 C.339 B.A. L.209 J.D. 134 N. LaSalle St.
Stefans, Donald J. ... '36 '63 C.145 B.A. L.365 LL.B. [Stefans&S.]
Stefans, Laurance A. ... '41 '65 C.1016 B.S.B.A. L.365 J.D. [Stefans&S.]
Stefans & Stefans ... 134 N. La Salle St.
Steffen, Peter B. ... '77 '01 C.910 A.B. L.145 J.D. [Ⓐ Lovells]
Steffens, Matthew B. ... '71 '03 C.602 B.A. L.145 J.D. [Ⓐ Scandaglia&R.]
Steffenson, Douglas S. ... '65 '91 C.350 B.A. L.209 J.D. [Nyhan,P.B.K.&L.]
Steffes, Katherine M. ... '66 '93 C&L.339 B.A., J.D. 2476 W. Estes, Ste. 2
Steger, Mark J., (AV) ... '— '85 C.339 B.S. L.1358 J.D. [Holland&K.]
Stegink, Lisa A., (AV) ... '62 '91 C.114 B.A. L.145 J.D. [Neal,G.&E.]
Stegmaier, Jennifer S. ... '70 '98 C.339 B.S. L.146 J.D. [Ⓐ Chittenden,M.&N.]
Stegman, Clement A., Jr. '38 '68
C&L.424 B.S.C., J.D. Contl. Ill. Nat. Bk. & Tr. Co. of Chi.
Steigleder, Andrew W. ... '73 '02 C.425 B.B.A. L.190 J.D. [Ⓐ Mayer,B.R.&M.]
Steigmann, Michael A. ... '69 '94 C.339 B.A. L.309 J.D. [Quinlan&C.]
Stein, Allison Zousmer ... '65 '90 C&L.477 B.A., J.D. [Connelly S.H.]
Stein, Alon ... '— '02 C.339 B.A. L.966 J.D. [Ⓐ Kamensky,R.H.&D.] ⊙
Stein, Arnold B., (AV) ... '48 '75 C.339 B.S. L.597 J.D. [Schiller,D.&F.]
Stein, Carey M. ... '47 '74 C.801 B.S. L.209 J.D. 150 N. Wacker Dr., Ste. 3000
Stein, Charles D., (AV) ... '22 '47 C&L.145 A.B., J.D. Two N. La Salle St.
Stein, David M., (AV) ... '49 '73 C.339 B.S. L.209 J.D. [Letvin&S.]
Stein, Edward T., Law Offices of, (AV) '42 '68
C.569 B.S. L.1009 LL.B. 202 S. Michigan Avenue
Stein, Giel ... '72 '01 C.145 B.A. L.597 J.D. [Ⓐ Winston&S.]
Stein, Jay D., (AV) ... '57 '81 C.597 B.S. L.424 J.D. 55 E Monroe Ste.3910
Stein, Jeffrey M. ... '77 '02 C.589 B.S. L.209 J.D. Asst. State's Atty
Stein, Joel A., (AV) ... '49 '78 C.1044 B.A. L.145 J.D. [Deutsch,L.&E.]
Stein, Joseph, (AV) ... '18 '42 C&L.145 A.B., J.D. 30 S. Wacker Dr., 29th Fl.
Stein, Marta A., (AV) ... '— '88 C.477 B.A. L.608 J.D. [McGuirewoods]
Stein, Max A. ... '— '01 C.118 B.A. L.146 J.D. [Ⓐ Sachnoff&W.]
Stein, Michael L. ... '40 '67 C.103 B.A. L.145 J.D. 20 N. Wacker Dr.
Stein, Michele Grimaldi '56 '80
C.602 B.A. L.424 J.D. Asst. States Atty., Cook Co. State Atty. Off.
Stein, Miriam R. ... '— '96 C.597 B.A. L.146 J.D. [Arnstein&L.]

Stein, Robert J., III .... '67 '95 C.1044 B.A. L.146 J.D. [Stein]
Stein, Roger H., (AV) '58 '84
C&L.339 B.S.G.E., J.D. [Wallenstein W.&R.] (See Pat. Sect.)
Stein, Sanford M., (AV) .... '49 '75 C.339 B.S. L.273 J.D. [Gardner C.&D.]
Stein, Scott D. .... '— '98 C.597 B.A. L.145 J.D. [Ⓐ Sidley A.B.&W.]
Stein, Sheldon R., (AV) .... '28 '51 C&L.145 B.A., J.D. [Ⓒ Seyfarth S.]
Stein, Steven A., (AV) .... '55 '81 C.589 B.S. L.365 J.D. [Stein&C.] ⊙
Stein, Steven G. M., (AV) .... '51 '76 C.966 B.A. L.145 J.D. [Stein,R.&H.]
Stein, Stuart J. .... '48 '73 C.927 B.A. L.209 J.D. [Stein&R.]
Stein, Terrence W. .... '— '86 C.966 B.B.A. L.309 J.D. [Burke,W.M.&S.]
Stein & Cherney, Ltd., (AV) .... 205 West Randolph Street, Suite 1250 (⊙Wheeling)
Stein Law Firm .... 401 E. Ontario St., Ste. 2302

Stein, Ray & Harris LLP, (AV)
222 West Adams Street, Suite 1800, 60606
Telephone: 312-641-3700 Telecopier: 312-641-3701
URL: http://www.steinrayharris.com
Members of Firm: Steven G. M. Stein; Stephen E. Ray; Robert J. Harris; Jeffrey H. Winick; Joel J. Rhiner; Carl L. Popovsky; Jeffrey B. Charkow; John N. Walker; Scott R. Fradin; Ryan A. Hiss. Associates: John-Paul Lujan; Jeffrey M. Osterkamp; Carrie L. Berger; Charles Henry Wahtola, III; Michael J. Kelly; Peter J. Bedard; Kate E. Kim; Lizabeth A. Muniz; Shorge K. Sato; Emily K. Muceus. Construction and Design Law, Mechanics Liens, Government Contracts, Insurance, Complex Litigation and Construction Related Insurance Bankruptcy.
See Professional Biographies, CHICAGO, ILLINOIS

Stein & Rotman, (AV) .... 105 W. Madison St.
Steinback, Steven C. .... '— '95 C.597 B.S. L.146 J.D. [Ⓐ Anderson,R.]
Steinberg, Allan R., (AV) .... '31 '55 C.339 B.A. L.597 J.D. [Steinberg,B.&G.]
Steinberg, Bradley D., (AV) .... '33 '58 C.118 B.A. L.597 J.D. [Steinberg,P.&G.]
Steinberg, Charles M. ... '43 '68 C.823 A.B. L.597 J.D. 111 W. Washington St., Ste. 1421
Steinberg, Frances S. ... '44 '85 C.966 A.B. L.146 J.D. 111 W. Washington St., Ste. 1421
Steinberg, Jay A., (AV) .... '— '71 C.1016 B.S. L.209 J.D. [Ⓒ Foley&L.]
Steinberg, Maynerd I., (AV) .... '52 '79 C.339 B.Arch. L.424 J.D. [Lord,B.&B.]
Steinberg, Morton M., (AV) .... '45 '71 C.339 A.B. L.597 J.D. [DLPiper R.G.C.U.]
Steinberg, Burtker & Grossman, Ltd., (AV) .... 55 E. Monroe St.

Steinberg, Polacek & Goodman, (AV) BB
309 West Washington Street, Suite 500, 60606
Telephone: 312-782-1386 FAX: 312-782-6739 URL: http://www.spglawyers.com
URL: http://www.lawyers.com/spg
Members of Firm: Bradley D. Steinberg; Bruce D. Goodman. Associate: Ronald Kalish. Personal Injury, Automobile Accidents, Products Liability and Medical Malpractice Law.
See Professional Biographies, CHICAGO, ILLINOIS

Steinbrecher, William P., (AV) .... '17 '43 C&L.145 A.B., J.D. [Ⓒ Defrees&F.]
Steiner, Barbara S., (AV) .... '49 '74 C&L.477 B.A., J.D. [Jenner&B.]
Steiner, Benjamin D., (AV) .... '40 '65 C&L.477 A.B., LL.B. [Weinberg R.]
Steiner, Carl L., (AV) .... '15 '38 C.597 B.S. L.365 LL.B. 39 S. La Salle St.
Steiner, Deborah L. .... '— '98 C.432 B.A. L.188 J.D. [Ⓐ Latham&W.]
Steiner, Heidi Anne .... '— '00 C.30 B.A. L.597 J.D. [Ⓐ Schiff H.]
Steiner, Joel H., (AV) .... '46 '71 C&L.966 B.A., J.D. [Axelrod,G.S.&B.]
Steiner, Rachel C. .... '— '04 L.957 J.D. [Ⓐ Ungaretti&H.]
Steiner, Samantha H. .... '69 '01 C.339 B.A. L.46 J.D. [Ⓐ Goldstein&L.]
Steingo, Michael '72 '99 C.659 B.A. L.178 J.D.
(adm. in NY; not adm. in IL) [Ⓐ Mayer,B.R.&M.]
Steingold, Eugene, (AV) '47 '73
C.477 B.S. L.339 J.D. 111 W. Washington Street, Suite 1437
Steinhaus, Elizabeth T. .... '59 '99 C.476 B.B.A. L.424 J.D. Access Financial, Inc.
Steinhofer, Paul S. .... '65 '93 C&L.347 B.S., J.D. [Ⓐ Patton&R.]
Steinken, Richard P., (AV) .... '54 '80 C.597 B.S.J. L.339 J.D. [Jenner&B.]
Steinman, Joan E. '47 '73 C.696 A.B. L.309 J.D.
Prof. of Law, Chicago-Kent Coll. of Law, Ill. Inst. of Tech.
Steinmetz, Matthew E. .... '— '88 C.27 B.A. L.602 J.D. [Kirkland&E.]
Steinmeyer, Heather C., (AV) '62 '91
C.388 B.A. L.424 J.D. Brand Coun., Blue Cross Blue Shield Assn.
Steinmeyer, Peter A., (AV) .... '65 '90 C.893 B.A. L.144 J.D. [Epstein B.&G.]
Stejkowski, David G. .... '65 '93 C.388 B.A. L.800 J.D. [Stejkowski&Z.]

Stejkowski & Zaffere LLC, (AV) BB
77 West Wacker Drive, Suite 4800, 60601-1604
Telephone: 312-606-8611 Fax: 312-606-8608
URL: http://www.sandzlaw.com
Members of Firm: David G. Stejkowski; Frank D. Zaffere, III. Business Law, Commercial Real Estate, Mergers and Acquisitions.
See Professional Biographies, CHICAGO, ILLINOIS

Steketee, John Powers .... '64 '89 C.477 B.A. L.347 J.D. Assoc. Reg. Coun., U.S.E.P.A.
Stella, Joseph N., (AV) .... '47 '74 C.724 B.A. L.146 J.D. [Morris&S.]
Stellato, Donald E., (AV) .... '45 '73 C&L.339 B.A., J.D. [Stellato&S.]
Stellato & Schwartz, Ltd., (AV) .... 120 North La Salle Street, 34th Floor
Stelnicki, Phillip J. .... '54 '84 C.1183 B.A. L.424 J.D. Chicago Fire Dept.
Stelter, Todd P. .... '76 '02 C.339 B.A. L.424 J.D. [Ⓐ Hinshaw&C.]
Stelzer, Gregory L. .... '73 '98 C.597 B.S. L.494 J.D. [Ⓐ Figliulo&S.]
Stempel, James A. .... '— '89 C.477 B.G.S. L.146 J.D. [Kirkland&E.]
Stempel, Samuel B., (AV) .... '67 '92 C.477 B.A. L.597 J.D. [DLPiper R.G.C.U.]
Stenander, Katherine .... '71 '96 C.339 B.S. L.146 J.D. [Ⓐ McDermott W.&E.]
Stencel, Deborah A. .... '70 '01 C.576 B.A. L.575 J.D. 20 W. Kinzie St., Ste. 1300
Stendahl, Kathleen E. .... '75 '02 C.597 B.A. L.494 J.D. [Ⓐ DLPiper R.G.C.U.]
Stender, Steven A., (AV) .... '55 '80 C.339 B.A. L.146 J.D. [Much S.F.D.A.&R.]
Stenhouse, Wallace J., Jr. .... '27 '55 C.976 B.A. L.145 J.D. 440 S. LaSalle St.
Stenn, Irving, Jr., Law Offices of '31 '55
C&L.477 B.A., J.D. 20 North Clark St., Ste. 3100
Stennes, Todd M. .... '66 '92 C.339 B.S. L.145 J.D. [Ⓒ Sonnenschein N.&R.]
Stephan, Edmund A., III .... '66 '95 C&L.602 B.A., J.D. [Ⓒ Dowd&D.]
Stephan, Robert, (AV) .... '66 '91 C.597 B.A. L.345 J.D. [Perkins C.]
Stephen, Joel .... '64 '92 C.1105 B.A. L.1187 J.D. 30 N. Lasalle St., Ste. 1740
Stephens, John P. .... '56 '83 C&L.602 B.A., J.D. [Burke,W.M.&S.]
Stephens, Mark K. '57 '82 C.651 B.A. L.607 J.D.
(adm. in PA; not adm. in IL) V.P. & Staff Coun., CNA Insurance Co.
Stephens, Matthew B. ... '68 '98 C.112 B.A. L.146 J.D. 30 North LaSalle Street, Ste. 4300
Stephens, Paul B. .... '— '98 C&L.477 B.S.E., J.D. [Marshall,G.&B.] (See Pat. Sect.)
Stephens, Robert C. .... '45 '74 C.966 B.S. L.146 J.D. Asst. Reg. Coun., Dept. of HHS
Stephens, Thomas M. .... '56 '82 C.184 B.A. L.128 J.D. [Sonnenschein N.&R.]
Stephenson, Brian J. .... '61 '88 C.1044 B.A. L.365 J.D. [Ferolie&S.]
Stephenson, Robert M., (AV) .... '— '73 C&L.339 B.A., J.D. [Foley&L.]
Stephenson, Scott D. .... '— '87 C.502 B.A. L.365 J.D. [Litchfield C.]

Stephenson, R.M., LLC
(See Oak Park)

Stephenson-Cohn, Jan Meyer '74 '01 C.352 B.A. L.365 J.D.
Underwriting Atty., Near North Natl. Title Corp.

Stepnowski, Francis E. .... '59 '84 C.1105 B.A. L.597 J.D. [Coghlan K.C.]
Sterling, David F., (AV) .... '36 '61 C&L.597 B.S., J.D. [McGuirewoods]
Sterling, Hillard M. .... '64 '89 C.589 B.A. L.276 J.D. [Freeborn&P.]
Sterling, Kevin A. ... '65 '93 C.597 B.A. L.146 J.D. General Counsel, Friedman Properties
Sterling, Thomas D. .... '— '97 C&L.597 B.A., J.D. [Ⓐ J.S.Rothman&Assoc.]
Stern, Abraham J., (AV) .... '— '79 C.1016 B.S.B.A. L.146 J.D. [Sachnoff&W.]
Stern, Avidan J., (AV) .... '64 '89 C.659 B.A. L.145 J.D. [Jenner&B.]
Stern, Charles A., (AV) .... '30 '58 C.597 B.S. L.309 J.D. [Wildman,H.A.&D.]
Stern, Gary B., (AV) .... '57 '82 C.477 B.A. L.597 J.D. [Sidley A.B.&W.]
Stern, Gary J. .... '59 '83 C.188 B.A. L.145 J.D. [Chuhak&T.]
Stern, Gregory K., (BV) .... '52 '82 C.37 B.A. L.365 J.D. [G.K.Stern]
Stern, James Russell .... '56 '81 C.477 B.A. L.1066 J.D. [McBreen&K.]
Stern, John C. .... '52 '78 C.103 A.B. L.1119 J.D. [Hardt&S.]
Stern, Mark O., (BV) .... '72 '96 C.339 B.A. L.145 J.D. [Burke,W.M.&S.]
Stern, Martin L., (AV) ... '52 '77 C.146 B.S. L.597 J.D. [Michael B.&F.] (See Pat. Sect.)
Stern, Nancy L. .... '70 '94 C&L.477 A.B., J.D. [Gardner C.&D.]
Stern, Neil P., (AV) .... '58 '84 C.604 B.A. L.608 J.D. [Laner,M.D.B.L.&T.]
Stern, Phillip L. .... '49 '75 C&L.209 B.S.C., J.D. [Freeman,F.&S.]
Stern, Rhonda Liebman '58 '82 C.339 B.A. L.597 J.D.
Adjunct Prof. of Law, Chicago-Kent Coll. of Law
Stern, Stephanie .... '— '01 C.103 B.A. L.976 J.D. [Ⓒ Kirkland&E.]
Stern, Stephen ..... '49 '77 C.339 B.A. L.910 J.D. Legal Assistance Foundation of Chicago
Stern, Gregory K., P.C., (BV) .... 53 West Jackson Boulevard
Sternberg, Arthur B. .... '— '80 C.927 B.A. L.339 J.D. [FagelHaber]

Sternberg, David M. '56 '83 C.1036 B.A. L.904 J.D.
1 N. LaSalle Avenue, Suite 1525, 60602
Telephone: 312-372-6271 Fax: 312-333-6290
URL: http://www.davidsternberglaw.com
Automobile Accidents and Injuries, Slip and Fall, Wrongful Death, Personal Injury and Workers Compensation Law.
See Professional Biographies, CHICAGO, ILLINOIS

Sternberg, Mark A. .... '— '88 C&L.339 B.S., J.D. [Schiff H.]
Sternic, Ivan M. .... '— '02 C.999 L.424 J.D. [Sternic]
Sternic Law Offices .... 1130 N. Dearborn St., Apt. 1311
Sternstein, Allan J., (AV) .... '48 '77 C.339 B.S. L.424 J.D. [Dykema G.P.] (Pat.)
Sterrett, James R. '40 '73 C.560 B.S. L.502 J.D.
(adm. in MO; not adm. in IL) Dept. of Jus.
Stetler, Christopher J. .... '— '04 C.911 B.A. L.339 J.D. [Ⓐ Katten M.R.]
Stetler, David J., (AV) .... '49 '74 C&L.884 B.A., J.D. [Stetler&D.]

Stetler & Duffy, Ltd., (AV)
11 S. LaSalle Street, Suite 1200, 60603
Telephone: 312-338-0200 Fax: 312-338-0070
URL: http://www.stetlerandduffy.com
David J. Stetler; Joseph J. Duffy; Jonathan M. Cyrluk; William P. Ziegelmueller; Corey B. Rubenstein;—Joni M. Green; Todd J. Haugh.
White Collar Criminal Defense; Commercial Litigation.
See Professional Biographies, CHICAGO, ILLINOIS

Stetson, Everett C. .... '16 '43 C.597 A.B. L.424 J.D. 5555 N. Sheridan Rd.‡
Stetson, James Lee .... '57 '82 C.957 B.A. L.966 J.D. [Baker&M.]
Stetson, Roger H. .... '78 '03 C.800 B.A. L.477 J.D. [Ⓐ Barack F.K.P.&N.]
Stetter, Debra L., (AV) .... '— '92 C.104 A.B. L.597 J.D. [Schiff H.]
Stevanson, Joanna R. .... '— '04 C.951 B.A. L.893 J.D. [Ⓐ Katten M.R.]
Stevens, Caroline L. .... '74 '01 C.188 B.F.A. L.477 J.D. [Ⓐ Leydig,V.&M.]
Stevens, Courtney A. .... '79 '04 C.798 B.S. L.339 J.D. [Ⓐ Jenner&B.]
Stevens, Cynthia Bushnell, (CV) ... '56 '81 C.347 B.S. L.146 J.D. [Ⓒ Wildman,H.A.&D.]
Stevens, Douglas R., (AV) '55 '82
C.347 B.A. L.846 J.D. Assoc. Gen. Coun., Litigation, Aon Corp.
Stevens, Emily Leigh .... '74 '01 C.232 B.A. L.1187 J.D. Cook Co. State's Atty's Off.
Stevens, Eva B. .... '— '78 C.145 B.A. L.146 J.D. Sr. Coun., United Airlines, Inc.
Stevens, Frank C. .... '54 '80 C.597 B.A. L.209 J.D. [Taylor,M.S.H.&M.]
Stevens, Holly R. .... '72 '00 C.477 B.A. L.1000 J.D. [Ⓐ Segal M.S.&M.]
Stevens, James C., Jr. .... '59 '85 C.477 B.A. L.209 J.D. Spec. Asst. Atty. Gen.
Stevens, Jane A. .... '77 '02 C.108 B.A. L.345 J.D. [Ⓐ Hall,P.&S.]
Stevens, Jeanine L., (AV) .... '59 '85 C.210 B.A. L.209 J.D. [Clancy&S.]
Stevens, John E. .... '— '78 C.177 B.A. L.589 J.D. [Freeborn&P.]
Stevens, John Spencer .... '63 '89 C.966 B.A. L.146 J.D. Sr., Reg. Atty., FDIC
Stevens, Joseph J., (AV) .... '35 '64 C&L.209 B.A., J.D. [Schuyler,R.&Z.]
Stevens, Kathryn L. .... '75 '99 C.966 B.A. L.209 J.D. [Ⓐ Vedder,P.K.&K.]
Stevens, LeRoy E. .... '22 '48 C.339 L.209 LL.B. 4800 Milwaukee Ave.
Stevens, Linda K., (AV) .... '— '87 C.373 B.A. L.477 J.D. [Schiff H.]
Stevens, Mark .... '47 '73 C&L.923 B.A., J.D. Cont. Ill. Nat. Bk. & Tr. Co. of Chicago
Stevens, Peter L. .... '25 '51 C.145 L.365 LL.B. 4659 S. Springfield Ave.‡
Stevens, Richard A. .... '57 '82 C.602 B.B.A. L.229 J.D. Asst. States Atty.
Stevens, Richard James, (AV) .... '15 '38 C&L.145 A.B., J.D. 135 S. LaSalle St.
Stevens, Shannon K. .... '70 '99 C.959 B.A. L.209 J.D. [Ⓐ Hinshaw&C.]
Stevens, Shannon L. .... '75 '01 C.339 B.A. L.608 J.D. [Ⓐ Winston&S.]
Stevens, Stanley M. '48 '73 C.502 B.A. L.145 J.D.
Exec. V.P., Chf. Legal Coun. & Secy., Equity Office Properties Trust
Stevens, William M., (AV) .... '43 '68 C.473 B.A. L.597 J.D. [Holland&K.]
Stevenson, Adlai E. .... '30 '57 C&L.309 B.A., LL.B. 225 W. Wacker Dr.
Stevenson, David E. .... '52 '78 C.475 B.A. L.861 J.D. [Williams M.&J.]
Stevenson, Ian R. .... '65 '91 C.399 B.A. L.966 J.D. [Tressler,S.M.&P.]
Stevenson, James W., Jr., (AV) .... '60 '87 C.210 B.A. L.365 J.D. [Wiedner&M.]
Stevenson, Jeffrey W. .... '— '89 C.221 B.S. L.146 J.D. [Ⓒ Kirkland&E.]
Stevenson, Nicholas '21 '55
C.156 B.B.A. L.597 J.D. Suite 2900, 120 North La Salle Street‡
Stevenson, Tracy E. .... '66 '91 C.679 B.A. L.215 J.D. [Chuhak&T.]
Stevenson, Wm. J. .... '10 '35 C&L.209 Ph.B., J.D. Asst. Corp. Coun.
Stewart, Ian A. .... '71 '96 C.910 B.A. L.734 J.D. [Wilson E.M.E.&D.]
Stewart, Joseph A. .... '59 '89 C.339 B.A. L.146 J.D. Asst. Corp. Coun. City of Chicago
Stewart, Judith A. .... '45 '70 C&L.339 B.A., J.D. Asst. Pub. Def.
Stewart, Margaret G. '47 '72 C.373 B.A. L.597 J.D.
(adm. in NY; not adm. in IL) Prof., ITT Chicago-Kent Coll. of Law
Stewart, Roland M. .... '24 '57 C.339 B.S. L.365 LL.B. 30 N. LaSalle St.
Stewart, Roma Jones ... '36 '73 C.254 B.A. L.276 J.D. 39 South LaSalle Street, Suite 1425
Stewart, Scott M. .... '61 '89 C.190 B.S. L.309 J.D. [Mayer,B.R.&M.]
Stewart, William A. '45 '70 C.36 B.S. L.802 J.D.
(adm. in TX; not adm. in IL) Pres., Stewarts Private Blend Foods
Stewart-Page, Stephanie L. .... '— '94 C.350 B.A. L.597 J.D. [Ⓐ Hubert&F.]
Stick, Michael A., (AV) .... '54 '81 C.198 B.A. L.575 J.D. [Butler R.S.&B.]
Stickler, K. Bruce, (AV) .... '46 '70 C&L.802 B.A., J.D. [Gardner C.&D.]
Stickles, James S., Jr., (AV) .... '51 '79 C.430 B.S. L.365 J.D. [Kaplan,v.&M.]
Stiebel, Thomas R., Jr. .... '62 '99 C.801 B.S. L.597 J.D. [Ⓒ McCracken&F.] (Pat.)
Stiefel, John C. .... '— '65 C.145 B.A. L.597 J.D. [Freeborn&P.]

Stiegel, Michael A., (AV) ....'46 '71 C.37 B.A. L.424 J.D. [Michael B.&F.]
Stiehl, Jason P. ....'76 '01 C.859 B.S.B.A. L.146 J.D. [Ⓐ Krislov&Assoc.]
Stiehl, Jason Patrick '76 '01
C.859 B.S.B.A. L.146 J.D. 20 North Wacker Drive, Suite 1350
Stiffler, Clay ....'71 '99 C.475 B.A. L.424 J.D. [Ⓐ Jenner&B.]
Stigger, Robert E. ....'49 '76 C.429 B.A. L.145 J.D. [Ⓑ J.S.Rothman&Assoc.]
Still, Ashley M. '73 '98 C.475 B.A. L.851 J.D.
Investigator, U.S. Dept. of Labor-PWBA
Stillings, Jeremy T. ....'77 '03 C.861 B.S.M. L.846 J.D. [Ⓐ Jenner&B.]
Stillman, Nina G., (AV) ....'48 '73 C.788 A.B. L.597 J.D. [Morgan,L.&B.]
Stillman, Thomas P. ....'44 '68 C.823 A.B. L.145 J.D. Sr. V.P. & Dep. Gen. Coun., CNA
Stine, Molly McGinnis, (AV) ....'65 '90 C.429 B.A. L.477 J.D. [Lord,B.&B.]
Stine, Thomas K., (AV) '— '84
C.679 B.S.E.E. L.209 J.D. [Marshall,G.&B.] (See Pat. Sect.)
Stinespring, Donald C. '49 '73 C.747 B.A. L.365 J.D.
20 N. Clarke St. (⊙Spring Grove)
Stinneford, Anne T. ....'55 '83 C.025 B.A. L.904 J.D. [Ⓐ Cheely,O.&A.]
Stinson, James R., (AV) '52 '77 C.347 A.B. L.339 J.D.
10 S. Dearborn Street, 50th Floor
Stinson-Marti, Angela L. ....'71 '03 C&L.339 B.A., J.D. [Ⓐ Lord,B.&B.]
Stippich, Kristal S. ....'— '98 C.938 B.A. L.145 J.D. [Ⓑ Kirkland&E.]
Stiscak, Michael J. ....'69 '01 C.63 B.S. L.365 J.D. 4240 N. Clarendon, Ste. 407-S
Stitcher, Kurt, (AVⓉ) ....'63 '90 C.276 B.S. L.813 J.D. [Winston&S.]
Stitt, Klein, Daday, Aretos & Giampietro, LLC, (AV)
300 W. Adams Street (⊙Arlington Heights)
Stiven, Janet A. ....'60 '85 C.339 B.A. L.209 J.D. [Dykema G.P.]
Stock, Richard M. ....'52 '77 C.339 B.S. L.424 J.D. [Gardner C.&D.]
Stockman, Ann ....'— '00 C.221 B.A. L.494 J.D. [Ⓐ Shaw G.F.G.W.&T.]
Stockton, Richard ....'— '00 C&L.339 B.S., J.D. [Banner&W.] (See Pat. Sect.)
Stoesser, Fred J. ....'32 '55 C&L.209 LL.B. 20 N. Clark St.
Stoesser, Paulette E. ....'49 '78 C.1106 B.A. L.424 J.D. Asst. Atty. Gen.
Stohl, Joan R. ....'65 '91 C.578 B.A. L.209 J.D. [Ⓐ Querrey&H.]
Stojak, Jennifer A. ....'75 '01 C.1030 B.A. L.276 J.D. [Ⓐ McGuirewoods]
Stokas, Robert M. ....'77 '02 C&L.424 B.S., J.D. Asst. State's Atty.
Stoker, Patrick R. ....'34 '69 C.597 B.S. L.424 J.D. 200 N. LaSalle St.
Stokes, Gary W. ....'71 '02 C.801 B.A. L.146 J.D. Fed. Labor Rel. Auth.
Stokes, Tracey J., (AV) '60 '85
C.787 B.A. L.365 J.D. Sr. Staff. Atty., James M. Hoffman & Co.
Stoklas, Patrick J. ....'76 '04 C.385 B.A. L.424 J.D. [Ⓐ Vedder,P.K.&K.]
Stolar, Donna ....'53 '91 C.597 B.A. L.209 J.D. Staff Atty., Dom. Rel. Div.
Stolarsky, Daniel B. ....'— '00 C.1494 B.A. L.477 J.D. [Ⓐ Latham&W.]
Stolberg, Lawrence R., (BV) .....'63 '88 C.339 B.A. L.146 J.D. [Ⓐ Alholm,M.K.H.&O.]
Stoljarova, Tatjana ....'— '03 C.1456 B.A. L.880 J.D. [Ⓐ Jones D.]
Stoll, J. Robert, (AV) ....'50 '75 C.311 B.A. L.178 J.D. [Mayer,B.R.&M.]
Stoll, R. Ryan, (AV) ....'64 '90 C.813 B.A. L.309 J.D. [Skadden,A.S.M.&F.]
Stolte, Keith M. ....'64 '98 C.145 B.A. L.365 J.D. [McDermott W.&E.]
Stoltmann, Andrew J. ....'71 '99 C.966 B.B.A. L.209 J.D. [Stoltmann]

Stoltmann Law Offices, P.C.
10 South LaSalle Street, Suite 3300, 60603-1002
Telephone: 312-332-4200 Fax: 312-332-4201
Email: stoltmann1234@hotmail.com
Andrew J. Stoltmann.
Securities Arbitration.
See Professional Biographies, CHICAGO, ILLINOIS

Stoltz, Kelly Link ....'79 '04 C.424 B.A. L.734 J.D. [Ⓐ Bollinger,R.&G.]
Stoltz, Richard B., Jr. ....'30 '64 C.57 A.B. L.146 LL.B. 1st Natl. Bk. of Chi.
Stoltz, Richard G. '74 '04 C&L.734 B.A., J.D.
(adm. in MO; not adm. in IL) Atty., Div. of Enforce., U.S. Secs. & Exch., Comm.
Stolz, Paul C. '53 '81 C.895 B.A. L.776 J.D.
(adm. in FL; not adm. in IL) 1100 E. 55th St.‡
Stolzenbach, Brian M. ....'— '00 C.502 A.B. L.477 J.D. [Ⓐ Seyfarth S.]
Stolzenburg, Mark L. ....'78 '03 C.188 B.S. L.910 J.D. [Ⓐ Laner,M.D.B.L.&T.]
Stomberg, Stephanie R. ....'70 '92 C.679 B.A. L.424 J.D. [Cassiday,S.&G.]
Stone, Bonita L., (AV) ....'55 '79 C.339 B.A. L.597 J.D. [Katten M.R.]
Stone, Charles D. ....'66 '92 C.966 B.A. L.424 J.D. [Stahl C.C.]
Stone, Charles F., Law Office ....'56 '84 C&L.339 B.S., J.D. 79 W. Monroe, Ste. 1300
Stone, David S. ....'60 '85 C&L.477 B.A., J.D. [Neal,G.&E.]
Stone, Earl ....'54 '80 C.339 B.S. L.146 J.D. [Sulzer&S.]
Stone, Erin Glezen ....'79 '04 C.339 B.A. L.880 J.D. [Ⓐ Winston&S.]
Stone, Errol L., (AV) ....'39 '64 C.659 A.B. L.309 LL.B. [Sonnenschein N.&R.]
Stone, Gary P., (AV) ....'61 '86 C.339 B.S. L.146 J.D. [Karchmar&S.]
Stone, Geoffrey R. '46 '72 C.659 B.S. L.145 J.D.
(adm. in NY; not adm. in IL) Provost, Univ. of Chicago
Stone, Howard L., (AV) ....'41 '72 C.1016 B.S.B.A. L.209 J.D. [Stone,M.&S.] ⊙
Stone, Ileana C. ....'69 '97 C.846 B.A. L.146 J.D. Bank of America
Stone, J. Andrew P. ....'72 '00 C.910 B.A. L.188 J.D. [Ⓐ Winston&S.]
Stone, Jan E. ....'52 '91 C.659 B.A. L.569 J.D. The Chicago Trust Co.
Stone, Jeffrey E., (AV) ....'56 '85 C.813 A.B. L.309 J.D. [McDermott W.&E.]
Stone, Joel A. ....'44 '70 C&L.209 B.S.C., J.D. VMS Realty, Inc.
Stone, Joseph L., (AV) ....'33 '59 C.966 B.S. L.597 J.D. [Ⓑ Seyfarth S.]
Stone, Mona M. ....'73 '98 C.98 B.A. L.861 J.D. [Ⓐ Lord,B.&B.]
Stone, Robert D. ....'46 '71 C.473 B.A. L.477 J.D. Chmn. & CEO, Richstone, Ltd.
Stone, Robert L. ....'46 '82 C.813 B.A. L.145 J.D. [R.L.Stone&Assoc.]
Stone, Robin R. ....'— '00 C.788 B.A. L.1556 J.D. [Ⓑ Sidley A.B.&W.]
Stone, Steven M. ....'— '80 C.802 B.A.S. L.209 J.D. [Ⓑ Pedersen&H.] (⊙Chicago)
Stone, Steven M. ....'— '80 C.802 B.A.S. L.209 J.D. [S.M.Stone] (⊙Chicago)
Stone, Susan A., (AV) ....'61 '87 C.976 B.A. L.309 J.D. [Sidley A.B.&W.]
Stone, William G., (AV) ....'49 '80 C.1111 B.A. L.45 J.D. [Stone&M.]

Stone & Associates L.L.C.
(See Waukegan)

Stone, McGuire & Siegel, (AV) .... Suite 3230, 55 East Monroe Street (⊙Northbrook)

Stone & Moore, Chartered, (AV)
30 North La Salle Street, Suite 4300, 60602
Telephone: 312-332-5656 Fax: 312-332-5858
URL: http://www.stonemoore.com
William G. Stone; Robert Charles Moore.
Products Liability, Mass Injury Litigation, Professional Malpractice Defense and Prosecution, Construction Litigation, Insurance Coverage Opinions and Litigation, Bad Faith, Reinsurance Arbitration, Personal Injury Defense, Appellate Practice, Workmans Compensation.
See Professional Biographies, CHICAGO, ILLINOIS

Stone, Pogrund & Korey, (AV)
A Partnership including Professional Corporations
221 North La Salle Street, 32nd Floor, 60601
Telephone: 312-782-3636 Fax: 312-782-1482
Email: attorney@spklaw.com URL: http://www.spklaw.com
(This Listing Continued)

Stone, Pogrund & Korey (Continued)
Members of Firm: Bertram A. Stone (1915-1994); Sherwin I. Pogrund (P.C.); Martin S. Korey; James P. Ziegler; David B. Pogrund; Christopher T. Nowotarski (P.C.); Lawrence J. Stark. Associate: Carter Andrew Korey.
General Practice. Corporate, Commercial, Banking, Real Estate, Litigation, Environmental, Construction, Employment Law, Commercial and Residential Real Estate, Business, Contract Law, Health Care Law, OSHA, Mechanic Liens, Government Liens, Employment Discrimination, Workers Compensation.
See Professional Biographies, CHICAGO, ILLINOIS

Stone, Robert L., and Associates, P.C. .... 1518 E. 59th St.
Stone, Steven M., Attorney-at-Law, LLC .... 399 W. Fullerton Pkwy.
Stonebraker, Kelly L., (AV) ....'55 '81 C.293 B.A. L.569 J.D. [DLPiper R.G.C.U.]
Stonebraker, Robert D. ....'75 '02 C.976 B.A. L.597 J.D. [Ⓐ Grippo&E.]
Stonehill, Jeremy ....'70 '97 C.477 B.B.A. L.424 J.D. [Shefsky&F.]
Stookal, Marc B., (BV) ....'56 '81 C.339 B.A. L.209 J.D. [Nilson,S.G.&C.]
Storcel, Susan M. ....'55 '91 C.578 B.A. L.209 J.D. Asst. Pub. Guard., Juv. Ct.
Storino, Daniel K. ....'— '04 C&L.602 B.A., J.D. [Ⓐ Mayer,B.R.&M.]
Storino, John R. ....'74 '00 C&L.602 B.A., J.D. [Ⓐ Jenner&B.]
Storm, Derek A., (AV) ....'59 '84 C.234 B.A. L.209 J.D. [Garofalo,S.H.&S.]
Storm, Philip N. ....'62 '92 C.57 B.A. L.365 J.D. Labor & Employ. Coun., Accenture
Storm, Timothy J. ....'65 '92 C.145 B.A. L.365 J.D. [T.J.Storm]
Storm, Timothy J., P.C. ....11 S. LaSalle St., Ste. 1000
Storning, F. Allan ....'66 '98 C.886 B.S. L.1162 J.D. 1344 N. Dearborn St., Apt. 13D
Storto, David E. ....'54 '86 C.477 B.A. L.424 J.D. Exec. V.P., Rehab. Inst. of Chicago
Stortz, Alvin A. ....'25 '51 C&L.966 B.S., LL.B. 1555 N. Sandburg Ter.‡
Stotland, Hanna L. ....'75 '02 C.309 A.B. L.1565 J.D. Law Clk.
Stotland, Harold, (AV) ....'40 '64 C.145 B.A. L.365 J.D. [Teller,L.&S.]
Stotland, Harold V., (AV) ....'41 '66 C.46 B.S. L.209 J.D. [Seyfarth S.] (Pat.)
Stotts, Retha R. ....'74 '00 C&L.339 B.A., J.D. Staff Law Clk.
Stouffer, Ralph E., Jr., (AV) ....'17 '41 C&L.597 B.S., J.D. [Ⓑ Pretzel&S.]

Stovall, Howard L., Law Office of '52 '81 C.20 B.A. L.846 J.D.
2131 North Racine Avenue, 60614
Telephone: 773-248-8896 Fax: 773-248-8897
Email: howard@stovall-law.com URL: http://www.stovall-law.com
Languages: Arabic.
International Arbitration, International Commercial Law, International Business Law, International Distribution, particularly Commercial Law of the Arabic-Speaking countries of the Middle East.
See Professional Biographies, CHICAGO, ILLINOIS

Stover, Andrew D. '65 '94 C.910 B.S.M.E. L.597 J.D.
[Brinks H.G.&L.] (See Pat. Sect.)
Stowell, Mary, (AV) ....'46 '74 C.502 B.A. L.597 J.D. [Stowell&F.]
Stowell, Richard P., (AV) ....'53 '82 C.339 B.A. L.365 J.D. [Ⓐ Lord,B.&B.]
Stowell & Friedman, Ltd., (AV) ....321 S. Plymouth Ct., Ste. 1400
Stowick, Paul C. ....'16 '39 L.209 LL.B. [Stowick&S.]
Stowick, Paul J. ....'45 '85 C.209 B.A. L.365 J.D. [Stowick&S.]
Stowick & Stowick ....1614 N. Pulaski Rd.
Strader, Kent David ....'67 '94 C.475 B.A. L.150 J.D. Ernst & Young LLP‡
Strain, Derek W. ....'66 '97 C.378 B.A. L.209 J.D. [Ⓐ Minsky,M.&H.]
Stralka, Daniel C. '58 '83 C.436 B.A. L.365 J.D.
Assoc. Clk., Human Res. Off.of the Clk., Cir. Ct.
Stralka, Paul ....'50 '76 C.424 A.B. L.365 J.D. Asst. Pub. Def.
Strand, Peter J. ....'— '87 C&L.966 B.A., J.D. [Ⓑ Holland&K.]
Strang, Eileen, (AV) ....'— '54 C.33 B.A. L.477 J.D. [Ⓑ Chapman&C.]
Strasser, Adam C. '68 '96 C.589 B.A. L.209 J.D.
Tax Consultant, Arthur Andersen LLP‡
Stratton, Maureen M. ....'57 '84 C.93 A.B. L.597 J.D. Legal Assistance Found.
Stratton, Timothy A. ....'— '99 C.63 B.S. L.1187 J.D. [Ⓐ Chapman&C.]
Straub, Matthew J. ....'74 '00 C.602 B.A. L.124 J.D. [Ⓑ Ogletree,D.N.S.&S.]
Straus, Karen '60 '86 C.309 B.A. L.569 J.D.
(adm. in NY; not adm. in IL) Asst. Prof. of Law, Chicago-Kent Coll. of Law
Strauss, David A. '52 '80 C&L.309 A.B., J.D.
(adm. in DC; not adm. in IL) Prof., Univ. of Chicago Law Sch.
Strauss, Jeffrey M. ....'55 '81 C&L.145 A.B., J.D. [Mayer,B.R.&M.]
Strauss, Jonathan, (AV) '54 '79
C.659 B.A. L.910 J.D. V.P. & Gen. Coun., Century America Corp.
Strauss, Paul L., (AV) ....'56 '81 C.951 B.A. L.976 J.D. [Miner,B.&G.]
Strauss, Robert S. ....'72 '00 C.339 B.S. L.146 J.D. [Ⓐ Levin G.]

Strauss & Malk LLP
(See Northbrook)

Strauts, Maureen ....'50 '76 C.340 B.A. L.597 J.D. [Holland&K.]
Straw, Gerald K. '43 '79 C&L.851 B.B.A., J.D.
(adm. in OH; not adm. in IL) Assoc. Aviation Underwriters
Straw, Kathleen A. ....'75 '02 C.321 B.A. L.424 J.D. [Ⓐ Weldon-Linne&V.]
Strawbridge, Richard Wm. ....'47 '78 C.165 B.A. L.365 J.D. [Clausen M.]
Strayhorn, Earl E. ....'18 '48 C.339 B.A. L.209 J.D. 53 W. Jackson Blvd.‡
Streber, Danielle M. ....'71 '97 C.694 A.B. L.966 J.D. [Ⓐ Sidley A.B.&W.]
Streck, David L. ....'70 '95 C.597 B.A. L.424 J.D. [Ⓐ Seyfarth S.]
Streckert, Herbert P. ....'13 '50 C.57 A.B. L.146 LL.B. 41165 N. Lincoln Ave.‡
Streckert, Kenneth E. ....'35 '61 C.238 B.A. L.597 J.D. 200 N. Lasalle, Ste. 700
Streepey, Kristen M. ....'73 '00 C.827 B.A. L.347 J.D. [Ⓐ Matushek,N.&S.]
Street, R. John, (AV) ....'60 '86 C.610 B.S. L.930 J.D. [Wildman,H.A.&D.]
Streets, Nabil D. ......'— '01 C.118 B.A. L.347 J.D. Two North LaSalle Street, Suite 2200
Streett, Mary M. ....'68 '98 C.862 B.S.B.A. L.45 J.D. [Ⓐ Mayer,B.R.&M.]
Streff, Denise A. ....'58 '83 C.742 B.A. L.424 J.D. Asst Pub. Def.
Streff, William A., Jr., P.C., (AV) '— '74 C&L.597 B.S.M.E., J.D.
[Kirkland&E.] (Pat.)
Streicher, Paul D., (AV) ....'52 '80 C.966 B.A. L.861 J.D. [Fedota C.]
Streicker, James R., (AV) ....'44 '69 C.473 A.B. L.339 J.D. [Cotsirilos,T.&S.]
Streicker, Sarah E. ....'— '04 C.477 B.A. L.1565 J.D. [Ⓐ Mayer,B.R.&M.]
Streit, Elizabeth M. ....'59 '84 C.339 B.S. L.145 J.D. Fed. Agcy.
Streit, Richard J., (AV) '35 '65 C.602 B.S.M.E. L.365 LL.B.
[Ladas&P.] (See Pat. Sect.)
Strelecky, Robert A., (AV) ....'53 '80 C.339 B.S. L.209 J.D. [Clifford]
Strellis, Gregg E. ....'72 '98 C.339 B.S. L.347 J.D. [Strellis&F.]
Strellis, Jack A., (AV) ....'44 '71 C.339 B.A. L.424 J.D. [Strellis&F.] (⊙Waterloo)
Strellis & Field, Chartered, (AV) ....444 North Wells Street, Suite 202 (⊙Waterloo)
Stremsterfer, Mary Achsah ....'75 '00 C.339 B.A. L.910 J.D. 121 N. LaSalle St.
Stretch, Charlotte K. ....'50 '76 C.312 B.A. L.1065 J.D. Spec. Coun., American Bar Assoc.
Strickland, Darlene ....'53 '92 C.589 B.A. L.424 J.D. [Moore,S.&W.]
Strickland, Nyika O. ....'— '01 C.453 B.S. L.597 J.D. [Ⓐ Kirkland&E.]
Stride, Herbert F., (AV) ....'33 '57 C&L.879 B.A., J.D. [Stride,C.&S.]
Stride, Herbert L., (AV) ....'60 '86 C&L.879 B.A., J.D. [Stride,C.&S.]

Stride, Craddock & Stride, (AV) BB
111 West Washington Street, Suite 1837, 60602-2773
Telephone: 312-346-5800 Fax: 312-346-3870
Herbert F. Stride; J. Patrick Craddock; Herbert L. Stride;—Nicholas C. Panos; Deborah A. Stride-Saran; Michael J. Craddock; Joseph P. Giamanco.
General Civil and Trial Practice. Medical, Legal Malpractice and Negligence Law.
See Professional Biographies, CHICAGO, ILLINOIS

Stride-Saran, Deborah A. .... '59 '85 C.879 B.S. L.424 J.D. [Ⓐ Stride,C.&S.]
Striker, Chad D. .... '71 '97 C&L.477 B.B.A, J.D. [Ⓐ Perkins C.]
Strimaitis, Andrius K. ....'— '96 C&L.424 B.B.A., J.D. [Ⓐ Baker&M.]
Stringer, David N. .... '62 '87 C.20 B.A. L.213 J.D. Amer. Nat. Bk. & Tr.
Strizak, Ellen Maureen ....'74 '02 C.352 B.A. L.365 J.D. Brd. Atty., Educ. Lab. Rels. Brd.
Strizak, Ira R., (BV) ....'40 '66 C.339 B.S. L.209 LL.B. 11 S. LaSalle St.
Strobel, Elizabeth J. M. .... '72 '00 C.860 B.A. L.424 J.D. [Ⓐ Meckler B.&T.]
Strobel, John A., (AV) ....'41 '67 C.477 B.A. L.424 J.D. [Braun S.L.B.&M.]
Strobel, Pamela B., (AV) '52 '77 C&L.339 B.S., J.D.
Sen. V.P. & Gen. Coun., Commonwealth Edison Co.
Strobl, Annie K. .... '60 '86 C.424 B.S. L.146 J.D. [McBreen&K.]
Stroh, Bryan F. ....'— '02 C.674 A.B. L.893 J.D. [Ⓐ Katten M.R.]
Stroh, Timothy J. '46 '75 C&L.546 B.S., J.D.
(adm. in NE; not adm. in IL) FBI
Strohm, Bruce C., (AV) '55 '80
C.339 B.S. L.597 J.D. Exec. V.P. & Gen. Coun., Equity Residential
Strohm, Ronald A. .... '54 '79 C.339 B.A. L.273 J.D. [Leahy,E.&F.]
Strohmeier, Michael G. ....'— '99 L.339 J.D. [Ⓐ Jones D.]
Strom, David G. .... '47 '74 C&L.477 A.B., J.D. [Hoogendoorn&T.]
Strom, Michael A., (AV) ....'52 '77 C.339 B.A. L.94 J.D. 333 S. Wabash, 25th Fl.
Strom, Neal B., (AV) .... '51 '77 C.98 B.A. L.209 J.D. [Strom&Assoc.]
Strom, Rhett .... '71 '04 C.967 B.A. L.209 J.D. [Ⓐ Moore,S.&W.]
Strom and Associates Ltd., (AV) .... 180 N. LaSalle St., Ste. 2510
Strong, Stacie I. '65 '95 C.112 B.A. L.228 J.D.
(adm. in NY; not adm. in IL) [Ⓐ Baker&M.]
Strosnider, David C. .... '73 '99 L.1017 J.D. [Ⓐ Chuhak&T.]
Stroth, Andrew M. .... '67 '01 C.339 B.A. L.597 J.D. [Ⓐ Handler,T.&D.]
Strothkamp, Margaret ....'— '01 C.339 B.A. L.209 J.D. [Ⓐ Schiff H.]
Strothkamp, Mark A. .... '71 '02 C.424 L.209 J.D. 101 N. Wacker Dr., Ste. 200
Stroud, William M. .... '35 '83 C.1016 B.S.C. L.146 J.D. [Ⓒ Kiesler&B.]
Stroup, Beth A. ....'71 '98 C.136 B.S. L.209 J.D. [Ⓐ Cozen O.]
Strouse, Harry D., (AV) ....'23 '50 C.473 L.477 J.D. 150 N. Michigan Ave.
Strouse, Jonathan E. ....'— '86 C&L.966 B.B.A., J.D. [Holland&K.]
Strubbe, Joseph A., (BV) ....'59 '85 C.927 B.A. L.146 J.D. [Vedder,P.K.&K.]
Strubbe, Mary Rose .... '48 '81 C.530 B.A. L.146 J.D. Chicago-Kent College of Law
Strubbe, Matt D. ....'68 '93 C.597 B.A. L.1119 J.D. [Fisher&P.]
Strubbe, Melanie A. .... '70 '95 C.597 B.A. L.326 J.D. [Ⓐ LaBarge,C.&L.]
Strubbe, Thomas F. .... '37 '65 C&L.424 B.S., J.D. Clk., U.S. Ct. of App.
Struck, Daniel J. ....'65 '94 C.1105 B.A. L.569 J.D. [Ⓐ Morgan,L.&B.]
Strup, Nathaniel L. ....'— '02 C.608 B.A. L.209 J.D. [Ⓐ Foley&L.]
Strusz, Mary Jo .... '57 '82 C&L.424 B.A., J.D. 4113 N. Paulina St.
Strutzenberg, Beth Eileen .... '72 '00 C.674 A.B. L.145 J.D. [Ⓐ Sidley A.B.&W.]
Struve, Robin L., (AV) ....'— '87 C.174 B.A. L.309 J.D. [Latham&W.]
Strybel, Robert C. ....'67 '92 C.436 B.A. L.146 J.D. Coun., Chicago Title Ins. Co.
Strye, John A. .... '66 '92 C.966 B.B.A. L.365 J.D. [Bronson&K.]
Strzalka, Daniel P. ....'— '03 C.352 B.A. L.209 J.D. [Ⓐ Ungaretti&H.]
Strzalka, Mary Alice C. '57 '90 C&L.209 B.S., J.D.
5440 N. Cumberland Ave., Ste. 140
Strzalka, Philip R. .... '71 '98 C.339 B.S. L.146 J.D. [Ⓐ Wildman,H.A.&D.]
Stuart, Cheri A. ....'— '04 C.719 B.S. L.146 J.D. [Ⓐ Anderson,R.]
Stuart, Christopher J. ....'60 '85 C&L.339 B.A., J.D. [Much S.F.D.A.&R.]
Stuart, Ellen D. '— '03 C.208 B.A. L.61 J.D.
(adm. in CA; not adm. in IL) [Ⓐ Connelly S.H.]
Stuart, Michael G. ....'51 '81 C&L.1040 B.B.A., J.D. [Ⓒ A.J.Madonia&Assoc.]
Stuart, Nathan ....'77 '02 C&L.477 A.B., J.D. [Ⓐ Skadden,A.S.M.&F.]
Stuart, William W. .... '43 '70 C.813 A.B. L.902 J.D. Prof. of Law, DePaul Univ.
Stubbee, Kirk A. '— '82
C.747 B.A. L.352 J.D. Claims Coun., American International Group
Stubblefield, Carol D. .... '— '96 C.1121 B.S. L.215 J.D. [Ⓐ Neal&L.]
Stubenvoll, Eric D. .... '66 '92 C&L.339 B.A., J.D. [Christensen&E.]
Stucker, Robert J., (AV) ....'45 '70 C.276 A.B. L.145 J.D. [Vedder,P.K.&K.]
Stucki, Hans U. ....'48 '74 C.608 B.A. L.602 J.D. [Epstein B.&G.]
Studer, Jerome C., Jr. .... '64 '95 C.145 B.A. L.146 J.D. [Meckler B.&T.]
Studnicka, James R., (BV) .... '62 '88 C.188 B.A. L.209 J.D. [Haynes,S.K.O.&M.]
Studzinski, Edward P. .... '60 '86 C&L.339 B.A., J.D. 200 W. Adams St. 30th Fl.
Stulberg, Leslie A. .... '— '78 C.477 B.A. L.145 J.D. [Ⓒ S.J.Levy&Assoc.]
Stulgies-Clauss, Andrea ....'— '89 C.209 B.A. L.597 J.D. [Ⓐ Henderson&L.]
Sturges, Emily A. '— '00 C.138 B.A. L.838 J.D.
(adm. in TN; not adm. in IL) [Ⓐ McDermott W.&E.]
Sturino, Denean K. .... '— '96 C.1172 B.A. L.365 J.D. [FagelHaber]
Sturm, Barry .... '60 '85 C&L.339 B.A., J.D. Mgmt. Asst. II, Co. Housing Auth.
Sturms, David A., (AV) .... '60 '85 C.608 B.S. L.424 J.D. [Vedder,P.K.&K.]
Sturtevant, Albert D., III ....'— '02 C.813 B.A. L.569 J.D. [Ⓐ Jones D.]
Sturtevant, Charles L., (AVⓉ) '08 '34 C.976 L.537 LL.B.
(adm. in DC; not adm. in IL; Pat.) 105 West Adams St.
Stutland, Donielle Tigay .... '77 '02 C.477 B.A. L.597 J.D. [Ⓐ Lord,B.&B.]
Stutland, Gary ....'40 '66 C.1016 B.S.B.A. L.146 J.D. Admin. Law J., Dept. of Rev.
Stutz, Robert B. '64 '90 C.98 B.S. L.339 J.D.
Asst. Gen. Coun., Exelon Bus. Servs. Co.
Stuyvesant, Cindy S. ....'— '03 C.475 B.A. L.146 J.D. [Ⓐ Vedder,P.K.&K.]
Styka, Sylvia A. .... '59 '90 C.424 B.S. L.365 J.D. 230 W. Monroe
Suarez, Jeanette A. ....'79 '04 C.597 B.A. L.280 J.D. [Ⓐ McDermott W.&E.]
Suber, Daniel G. ....'51 '79 C.494 B.A. L.950 J.D. 77 W. Washington Street
Suber, Reiko E. ....'— '03 C.302 B.A. L.329 J.D. [Ⓐ Mayer,B.R.&M.]
Subkowsky, Robert A. .... '49 '74 C.184 B.A. L.597 J.D. [Lewis,O.&F.]
Sublett, Jeanette ....'— '82 C.927 B.A. L.339 J.D. [Ⓐ Neal&L.]
Subramanian, David K. ....'— '93 C.57 B.A. L.209 J.D. [Ⓒ Sedgwick,D.M.&A.]
Such, Domingo P., III ....'— '96 C.910 B.A. L.424 J.D. [McDermott W.&E.]
Suchar, David E. ....'— '02 C.209 B.A. L.276 J.D. [Ⓐ Kirkland&E.]
Sucher, Jennifer L., (BV) ....'63 '89 C&L.424 B.A., J.D. Coun., GE Capital
Sudak, Fred, (AV) ....'30 '54 C&L.209 J.D. 230 W. Monroe St.‡
Sudekum, Frederick J., III, (AV) .... '54 '80 C.502 B.A. L.734 J.D. [Sudekum,C.&S.]
Sudekum, Cassidy & Shulruff, Chartered, (AV) .... 20 N. Clark St., Ste. 1400
Sudel, Saren K. ....'74 '03 C.494 B.A. L.145 J.D. [Ⓐ Bell,B.&L.]
Sudzus, David B. ....'64 '90 C.750 B.A. L.597 J.D. [Drinker B.&R.]
Sufalko, Kira E. .... '67 '92 C.800 B.S. L.228 J.D. Coun., Accenture LLP
Suffredin, Lawrence J., Jr. .... '47 '73 C.424 B.A. L.276 J.D. [Shefsky&F.]

Sufrin, Barry W., (AV) .... '48 '74 C&L.339 B.S., J.D. [Gardner C.&D.] (Pat.)
Sugar, Bryan Paul .... '74 '01 C.966 B.A. L.146 J.D. [Ⓐ Wildman,H.A.&D.]
Sugar, David, (AV) ....'— '76 C.339 B.A. L.597 J.D. [Arnstein&L.]
Sugar, Paul .... '28 '56 C.1016 B.S.C. L.365 J.D. [P.Sugar]
Sugar, Richard A., (AV) .... '47 '72 C.347 B.S. L.145 J.D. [Sugar,F.&F.]

Sugar, Friedberg & Felsenthal LLP, (AV)
30 North La Salle Street, Suite 3000, 60602
Telephone: 312-704-9400 Facsimile: 312-372-7951
URL: http://www.sff-law.com
Members of Firm: Richard A. Sugar; Michael R. Friedberg; Steven A. Felsenthal; Andrew B. David; Leslie J. Weiss; Paula K. Jacobi; Jonathan L. Mills; Howard M. Helsinger; Martin M. Weinstein; Etahn M. Cohen; Kathryn A. Erickson; William F. McGuinn; Andrew R. Schwartz; Adam J. Grais. Associates: Andrew J. Abrams; Brett N. Cagan; Pamela S. DiCarlantonio; Stephanie P. Listokin (Not admitted in IL); Elizabeth A. Shepard; Megan I. Witzel.
Business and Transactional Practice, including Corporate, Partnership and Securities Law, Mergers and Acquisitions, Securities and Futures Regulation, Real Estate, and Subsidized Housing, Federal Income Tax Planning and Litigation, Estate Planning and Administration, Commercial Litigation, Securities Litigation, Insolvency, Bankruptcy and Reorganization, Insurance Law, Franchise Law, Intellectual Property.
See Professional Biographies, CHICAGO, ILLINOIS

Sugar, Paul, Ltd. .... 1 E. Wacker Dr., Ste. 3430
Sugarman, Renan I., (AV) '59 '85 C.112 B.A. L.978 J.D.
Sr. V.P. & Asst. Gen. Coun., Everen Securities, Inc.
Sugarman, Robert S., (AV) .... '31 '58 C.608 B.S.B.A. L.477 J.D. [Sugarman&H.]
Sugarman & Horwitz, (AV) ....221 North LaSalle Street, Suite 626
Sugayan, Catalina J. .... '60 '85 C.477 A.B. L.94 J.D. [Lord,B.&B.]
Sugino, Scott D. ....'— '03 C.309 A.B. L.145 J.D. [Ⓐ Kirkland&E.]
Sujack, Gregory P. ....'59 '84 C.93 B.S. L.424 J.D. [Garofalo,S.H.&S.]
Sukhman, Alexander .... '73 '99 C.339 B.A. L.146 J.D. [Ⓐ Kralovec,J.&S.]
Sukovic, M. Miles ....'71 '00 C.339 B.A. L.347 J.D. [Ⓐ Sedgwick,D.M.&A.]
Sukowicz, Thomas P. .....'55 '85 C.424 B.A. L.209 J.D. [Hinshaw&C.] (⊙Ft Laud., FL)
Sulayman, Fuad R. ....'— '99 C.94 B.S.B.A. L.146 J.D. [Ⓐ Querrey&H.]
Sulkin, Ryan T. ....'— '04 C.597 B.S.J. L.1565 J.D. [Ⓐ Wildman,H.A.&D.]
Sullivan, Allison Z. .... '76 '02 C.477 B.A. L.146 J.D. [Ⓐ Swanson,M.&B.]
Sullivan, Arthur A. ....'39 '64 C.31 A.B. L.597 J.D. Cir. Ct. J.
Sullivan, Barbara J., (AV) ....'47 '85 C.209 B.A. L.365 J.D. [B.Sullivan&Assoc.]
Sullivan, Barry, (AV) .... '49 '75 C.478 A.B. L.145 J.D. [Jenner&B.]
Sullivan, Brian T. '59 '89 C.869 B.S. L.309 J.D.
(adm. in CT; not adm. in IL) Pres. & Gen. Coun., Sullivan Companies, Inc. The
Sullivan, Bryan R. .... '47 '75 C.951 B.A. L.629 J.D. 180 N. Stetson Ave.
Sullivan, C. David .... '32 '69 C.712 B.B.A. L.818 J.D. [Ⓒ Tressler,S.M.&P.]
Sullivan, Christopher B. ....'67 '95 C.188 A.B. L.597 J.D. [Duane M.]
Sullivan, Colleen H. ....'61 '96 C.813 B.A. L.145 J.D. [Ⓐ Sidley A.B.&W.]
Sullivan, David J. ....'71 '96 C.602 B.B.A. L.424 J.D [Ⓐ Crisham&K.]
Sullivan, Douglas J. ....'64 '92 C.723 B.A. L.221 J.D [Ⓐ Rusin M.&F.]
Sullivan, Emma J. ....'75 '99 C&L.339 B.S., J.D. [Ⓐ Jenner&B.]
Sullivan, Eugene P. ....'58 '91 C.238 B.S. L.589 J.D. [Ⓒ Leyhane&Assoc.]
Sullivan, Heather C. ....'73 '98 C.339 B.A. L.424 J.D. [Ⓐ Tressler,S.M.&P.]
Sullivan, James F. ......'55 '81 C&L.424 B.A., J.D. 33 North Dearborn Street, Suite 1630
Sullivan, James Michael ....'59 '87 C.750 B.A. L.365 J.D. State's Atty's. Off.
Sullivan, James P. ....'— '98 C.339 B.A. L.209 J.D. [Ⓐ Chapman&C.]
Sullivan, John J. ....'14 '36 C&L.209 B.S., LL.B. Appl. Ct. J.
Sullivan, John P. ....'63 '89 C.608 B.S. L.117 J.D. [Bollinger,R.&G.]
Sullivan, John T. ....'43 '68 C.1024 B.S. L.424 J.D. Asst. States Atty.
Sullivan, Kelly ....'75 '00 C.424 B.S. L.146 J.D. [Ⓐ Swanson,M.&B.]
Sullivan, Lisa C. ....'72 '97 C.340 B.A. L.309 J.D. [Ⓐ Howrey]
Sullivan, Lisa M. '62 '88 C.264 B.A. L.902 J.D.
(adm. in NY; not adm. in IL) 400 E. Ohio St.‡
Sullivan, Lynn A. ....'50 '90 C.312 B.A. L.209 J.D. [Leydig,V.&M.]
Sullivan, Marcia W., (P.C.), (AV) ....'50 '75 C.210 B.A. L.1119 J.D. [Katten M.R.]
Sullivan, Marita C. ....'58 '84 C.1049 B.A. L.424 J.D. Asst. Atty. Gen.
Sullivan, Matthew J. ....'77 '02 C&L.339 B.A., J.D. [Ⓐ Winston&S.]
Sullivan, Michael E. ....'— '99 C.966 B.A. L.597 J.D. [Ⓐ Kirkland&E.]
Sullivan, Michael L., (AV) ....'— '91 C&L.339 B.S., J.D. [Goldberg,K.B.B.R.&M.]
Sullivan, Michael P. ....'67 '95 C.473 B.S. L.424 J.D. [Ⓐ Pedersen&H.]
Sullivan, Michael T. ....'68 '93 C.228 A.B. L.309 J.D. [Ⓒ Mayer,B.R.&M.]
Sullivan, Michelle ....'66 '91 C.339 B.A. L.365 J.D. Asst. Pub. Guardian
Sullivan, Monica T., (AV) ....'68 '93 C.339 B.S. L.209 J.D. [Bates&C.]
Sullivan, Patrick J. ....'37 '83 C.321 A.B. L.424 J.D. 150 E. Huron‡
Sullivan, Patrick J., (AV) ....'43 '69 C.884 B.A. L.209 J.D. [Hilfman,M.&S.]
Sullivan, Patrick J. ....'— '90 C.589 B.A. L.352 J.D. [Litchfield C.]
Sullivan, Peter D., (AV) ....'58 '83 C.602 B.A. L.424 J.D. [Hinshaw&C.]
Sullivan, Robert K. ....'45 '70 C.424 B.B.A. L.209 J.D. Oak Tr. & Svgs. Bk.
Sullivan, Sean M. ....'60 '85 C.234 B.A. L.339 J.D. [Daley&M.]
Sullivan, Sean M. '70 '95
C.339 B.S.M.E. L.424 J.D. [McDonnell B.H.&B.] (See Pat. Sect.)
Sullivan, Thomas F. '39 '64 C.973 B.S. L.209 J.D.
Pres. & CEO, Virginia Surety Co., Inc.
Sullivan, Thomas P., (Ltd.), (AV) ....'30 '52 C.177 L.424 LL.B. [Jenner&B.]
Sullivan, Timothy M. ....'49 '75 C&L.424 B.S., J.D. [Hinshaw&C.]
Sullivan, William G. .... '49 '78 C.589 B.S. L.146 J.D. [Martin,B.&S.]
Sullivan, William R., Jr., (AV) ....'43 '71 C.321 A.B. L.145 J.D. [Franczek S.]
Sullivan, BJ, & Associates, (AV) .... 79 West Monroe Street, Suite 900

Sullivan Firm, The, Ltd.
(See Rolling Meadows)

Sullivan Hincks & Conway, Law Offices of
(See Oak Brook)

Sulzer, James M. .... '53 '77 C&L.339 B.S., J.D. [Sulzer&S.]
Sulzer & Shapiro, Ltd. .... 20 S. La Salle St.
Summerfield, Craig A. '— '93
C.378 B.S.E.E. L.146 J.D. [Brinks H.G.&L.] (See Pat. Sect.)
Summerfield, George C., Jr. '58 '87 C.1113 B.A. L.912 J.D.
(adm. in MI; not adm. in IL) [Stadheim&G.]
Summerhill, Michael J. ....'71 '98 C.608 B.A. L.365 J.D. [Ⓐ Katten M.R.]
Summers, Ernest, III ....'53 '80 C.347 A.B. L.1119 J.D. [Howrey]
Summers, Kristina M. ....'75 '02 C.339 B.A. L.861 J.D. [Ⓐ Shaw G.F.G.W.&T.]
Summers, Lawrence L., (AV) ....'48 '73 C.347 A.B. L.1119 J.D. [Vedder,P.K.&K.]
Summers, Robert H., Jr., (AV) ....'65 '91 C.339 B.A. L.365 J.D. [Hinshaw&C.]
Sumner, Thomas R. .... '49 '77 C.339 B.A. L.365 J.D. Assoc. Cir. J.
Sun, Gregory R., Law Office of, (AV) '49 '83
C.46 B.S. L.146 J.D. 431 S. Dearborn St., Ste. 1102
Sunderland, Louise A. ....'48 '73 C.881 A.B. L.813 J.D. Coun., Ameritech Corp.
Sundheim, Brian C., (AV) ....'57 '86 C.424 B.A. L.365 J.D. [Pretzel&S.]

Sundheim, George M., (AV) '26 '53
C.597 B.A. L.365 J.D. 111 W. Washington St. (⊙Oak Brook)
Sundvall, Sheila A. '63 '88 C&L.477 B.A., J.D. [Sidley A.B.&W.]
Sunstein, Cass R. '— '80 C&L.309 A.B., J.D.
(adm. in DC; not adm. in IL) Prof., Univ. of Chicago Law Sch.
Sunu, H. Wesley, (AV) '60 '85 C.966 B.A. L.424 J.D. [Tribler O.&M.]
Suomala, Robert L. '55 '81 C.964 B.A. L.477 J.D.
200 East Randolph Drive, Suite 7300
Sup, Bryan R. '70 '96 C.477 B.A. L.209 J.D. [Schwartz C.]
Surges, Edward N. '29 '74 C.999 M.A. L.424 J.D. Catholic Charities of Chicago
Suri, Mark K., (AV) '60 '88 C.427 B.A. L.352 J.D. [Ryndak&S.] (See Pat. Sect.)
Suria, Fred G., Jr. '27 '53 C.339 L.424 LL.B. Cir. J.
Suriano, Donald J. '56 '83 C.339 B.A. L.365 J.D. Richard J. Daley Ctr., Ste. 1306
Surie, Irving '14 '39 C&L.339 B.A., LL.B. 3600 N. Lake Shore Dr.‡
Surowiec, Kathleen E. '78 '03 C.20 B.A. L.602 J.D. [🄰 Dykema G.P.]
Surrette, Robert A. '66 '97 C.454 B.S.M.E. L.146 J.D. [McAndrews,H.&M.]
Sus, Geo. M., (AV) '17 '42 C.976 B.A. L.477 J.D. Cont. Ill. Nat. Bk. & Tr. Co.
Suse, Philip F. '54 '81 C.321 B.A. L.659 J.D. [Baker&M.]
Susina, Mark S. '— '89 C.436 B.A. L.424 J.D. [Adler,M.&M.]
Suskin, Howard S., (AV) '59 '83 C.597 B.A. L.477 J.D. [Jenner&B.]
Susler, Janis M. '49 '75 C&L.339 B.A., J.D. Peoples Law Off.
Susman, Arthur T., (AV) '34 '58 C.339 B.S. L.597 J.D. [Susman,W.&W.]
Susman, Barbara A., (AV) '58 '83 C.339 A.B. L.146 J.D. [Susman&Assoc.]
Susman, David I. '67 '97 C.966 B.A. L.436 J.D. [Spitzer,A.S.&E.]
Susman, Michael B., (AV) '38 '62 C.339 B.S. L.597 J.D. [Spitzer,A.S.&E.]

Susman & Associates, P.C., (AV)
203 North Wabash Avenue 14th Floor, 60601
Telephone: 312-444-9600 Facsimile: 312-444-9612
Email: SusmanUSA@aol.com URL: http://www.susmanlaw.com
Barbara A. Susman. Of Counsel: David G. Duggan; Michele M. Rocawich; Alejandro de Eguren Santisteban (Not Admitted in the United States); José Antonio Rodríguez Marquez (Not Admitted in the United States) (Resident, Mexico Office); Bernard Laurent (Not admitted in IL; Not admitted in the United States); James Godwill Issa (Not admitted in the United States); Julie Y. Li; Julian Torres (Not admitted in IL; Not admitted in United States).
Languages: English, Spanish, Portuguese, French, German, Polish.
Customs, International Trade, International Transactions, Commercial and Foreign Trade Laws, Immigration Law, Visas, Work Permits, Employment Immigration, Related Administrative Law and Litigation, Commercial Transactions, Import and Export Law.
Mexico Office: Lago Alberto 442-27, Col. Anahuac, 11320 Mexico, D.F.
Spain Office: Alejandro de Eguren Santisteban Abogado, Marqués del Puerto n° 9, 1° izda. Bilbao.
Belgian Office: Rue Faider 18, B 1060 Bruxelles, Belgium.
Peru Office: Calle 6, No. 193, Las Lilas, Santiago de Surco, Lima, Peru.
See Professional Biographies, CHICAGO, ILLINOIS

Susman, Watkins & Wylie, LLP, (AV)
Two First National Plaza, 20 South Clark Street, Suite 600, 60603
Telephone: 312-346-3466 FAX: 312-346-2829
Email: chuckwatkins@ameritech.net
Arthur T. Susman; Charles R. Watkins; John R. Wylie. Associates: Matthew T. Heffner; Matthew T. Hurst. Of Counsel: William T. Gotfryd.
Securities, Corporate, Antitrust, Pension, Commodities, Antitrust and Class Action Litigation. General Civil and Trial Practice. Business and Corporation Law.
See Professional Biographies, CHICAGO, ILLINOIS

Susnjara, Jennifer '77 '03 C.347 B.S. L.146 J.D. [🄰 Leo&W.]
Susoreny, John '71 '04 C.679 B.S. L.446 J.D. [🄰 Bell,B.&L.]
Sussman, Arthur M., (AV) '42 '66 C.188 B.S. L.309 LL.B. 140 S. Dearborn St.
Sussman, Carl B. '13 '37 L.146 LL.B. U.S. Mag.
Sussman, Jeffrey B., (AV) '47 '75 C.472 B.A. L.146 J.D.
[Sussman,S.&R.] (⊙Bronx, NY)
Sussman, Paul J. '48 '73 C.339 B.S. L.597 J.D. 200 West Jackson Boulevard
Sussman, Selig & Ross, (AV) 1 East Wacker Drive, Suite 2920
Suster, Dewey D. '42 '67 C.210 B.A. L.597 J.D. 856 W. Buena‡
Suster, Joseph Ronald '76 '01 C.363 B.S.B.A. L.608 J.D. [🄰 Mayer,B.R.&M.]
Suszynski, Kristina '62 '88
C.216 B.A. L.424 J.D. Community Econ. Develop. Law Project
Suter, Ronald E. '47 '75 C.339 B.S. L.273 J.D.
(adm. in VA; not adm. in IL) Chf. Coun., The Boeing Co.
Suth, Brian T. '64 '89 C.354 B.A. L.209 J.D. [Ellison,N.Z.&A.]
Suth, Phillip R. '33 '56 L.365 LL.B. 20 N. Clark
Sutherland, Joe A., (AV) '34 '59 C.840 B.A. L.145 J.D. 321 N. Clark St.‡
Sutherland, Steven '59 '84 C.424 B.S. L.339 J.D. [Sidley A.B.&W.]
Sutton, James E. '— '77 C.357 B.S. L.733 J.D. 420 E. Ohio St., Apt. 39D
Sutton, Peter A. '53 '79 C.321 B.A. L.1202 J.D.
(adm. in MA; not adm. in IL) Fed. Labor Rel. Auth.
Svanascini, Michael '66 '91 C.424 B.B.A. L.365 J.D. 39 S. LaSalle St.
Svoboda, Paul A., (AV) '60 '86 C.747 B.A. L.178 J.D. [Sidley A.B.&W.]
Swain, John W., Jr. '65 '92
C.602 B.B.A. L.597 J.D. 203 North Wabash Avenue, Suite 711
Swain, Theodore M., (AV) '— '54 C.339 A.B. L.309 LL.B. [🄲 Gould&R.]
Swallow, Ben M. '— '03 C.347 L.146 J.D. [🄰 Segal M.S.&M.]
Swan, Edward T., (AV) '— '77 C.197 A.B. L.597 J.D. [Kirkland&E.]
Swan, Kathleen J. '— '85 C.880 B.A. L.472 J.D. [🄲 Dykema G.P.]
Swaney, Thomas E., (AV) '42 '68 C&L.477 B.A., J.D. [Sidley A.B.&W.]
Swanson, Alfred M., Jr. '46 '82 C.339 B.S. L.146 J.D. [🄰 Greene&L.]
Swanson, Brian C. '71 '01 C.31 B.A. L.597 J.D. [🄰 Bartlit B.H.P.&S.]
Swanson, Lenard C., (AV) '37 '67 C&L.339 B.S., J.D. [🄲 Swanson,M.&B.] (⊙Lisle)
Swanson, Mary Ellen Rosen, (AV) '39 '81 C.734 B.S. L.146 J.D. [🄲 Tucker B.R.&M.]
Swanson, Matthew A. '75 '00 C.477 B.A. L.800 J.D. [🄰 Shaw G.F.G.W.&T.]
Swanson, Peter C. '69 '98 C.352 B.A. L.588 J.D. [🄰 Cornfield&F.]
Swanson, Sheila Hegy '41 '80 C.388 B.A. L.339 J.D. Asst. Reg. Coun., Dept. of H.H.S.
Swanson, Stephen C. '— '98 C.339 B.A. L.607 J.D. [🄰 Anderson,R.]
Swanson, Steven C. '69 '00 C.339 B.S. L.966 J.D. [🄰 Fisher K.]
Swanson, Tina R. '70 '98 C.424 B.A. L.146 J.D. [🄰 Knell&P.]

Swanson, Martin & Bell, (AV)
330 North Wabash, Suite 3300, 60611 ⊙
Telephone: 312-321-9100 Fax: 312-321-0990
URL: http://www.smbtrials.com
Partners: Brian W. Bell; Stanley V. Boychuck; Kevin V. Boyle; Margaret O. Byrne; David J. Cahill (Resident, Lisle Office); Steven E. Danekas; P. Stephen Fardy; George F. Fitzpatrick, Jr.; Robert E. Haley; Elizabeth Schroer Harvey; Lawrence Helms; Matthew D. Jacobson (Resident, Lisle Office); David E. Kawala; Joseph P. Kincaid; Patricia S. Kocour; A. Jay Koehler, III; Steven L. Larson; ***Michael J. Maher; Kevin T. Martin; Robert J. Meyer; Timothy G. Nickels; Jody L. Pabst;*** **David F. Pardys; Kay L. Schichtel; Peter G. Skiko; Linda E. Spring; Joseph P. Switzer; Bruce S. Terlep (Resident, Lisle Office); John A. Terselic (Waukegan Office); William B. Weiler; Dale G. Wills. Associates: James Adamson; John P. Arranz; Ross W. Bartolotta; Nicole L. Bjork; Elizabeth A. Bruer; Patricia E. Charles; Leanne W. Conn; Lindsy A. Elkins; Suzanne M. Fitch (Resident, Lisle Office); Misti H. Floyd; Meredith A. Gaffke; David S. Goles; John A. Gollwitzer; Richard L. Haas; Julie R. Halperin; Craig A. Jacobson; McRay Judge, II; Angela Rose Karras; Richard J. Keating, Jr.; Michael R. Klotz; Michone J. Kuhlman (Resident, Libertyville and Waukegan Offices); Joshua E. Liebman;**

(This Listing Continued)

Swanson, Martin & Bell (Continued)
David M. Marco; Steven P. Mikuzis; Amy R. Miller (Resident, Lisle Office); Anthony J. Monaco; Abosede O. Odunsi; Joy I. Padnos (Resident, Waukegan and Libertyville Offices); Louis J. Phillips; Peter A. Pogue; Arthur J. Reliford, Jr.; David J. Riski (Resident, Lisle Office); G. Christopher Slick; Allison Z. Sullivan; Christian A. Sullivan (Resident, Lisle Office); Kelly Sullivan; Aiju C. Thevatheril; Alain Villeneuve; Catherine Basque Weiler; Andrew M. Weisberg. Of Counsel: Lenard C. Swanson; Edward T. Butt, Jr.; John J. O'Sullivan; John C. Church; Thomas J. Koch.
Asbestos Litigation, Class Action Lawsuits, Commercial Litigation, Construction Litigation/Disputes, Consumer and Warranty Law, Creditor's Rights, Drugs & Medical Devices, Employment Litigation, Environmental Law, Equipment Leasing, General Tort Liability, Healthcare, Insurance Coverage, Intellectual Property, Medical Negligence, Municipal Law, Product Liability, Professional Negligence, Real Estate Development/Zoning, Real Estate Litigation, Toxic and Mass Tort Litigation and White Collar Criminal Defense.
DuPage County, Illinois Office: 2525 Cabot Drive, Lisle, Illinois, 60532. Telephone: 630-799-6900. Fax: 630-799-6901.
Lake County, Illinois Office: 1860 West Winchester Road, Suite 201, Libertyville, Illinois, 60048. Telephone: 847-949-0025. Fax: 847-247-0555.
Waukegan, Illinois, Satellite Office: 415 Washington Street, Suite 1B, Waukegan, Illinois, 60085. Telephone: 847-949-0025. Fax: 847-247-0555.
See Professional Biographies, CHICAGO, ILLINOIS

Swardenski, Jay G. '39 '64 C.966 B.A. L.309 LL.B. [🄲 Matkov,S.M.&G.]
Swartz, Marla '77 '03 C.597 B.A. L.477 J.D. [🄰 Goldberg,K.B.B.R.&M.]
Swartzman, Daniel, (BV) '51 '75 C.911 B.A. L.597 J.D. [DiVincenzo S.S.]
Swartzmeyer, Sarah E. '69 '95 C.1350 B.A. L.107 J.D. [Michael B.&F.]
Swedberg, Richard L. '39 '68 C.1106 A.B. L.424 J.D. 111 W. Wash.
Swedlow, Stephen A. '— '95 C.473 B.A. L.608 J.D. [Swedlow&Assoc.]
Swedlow & Associates, (BV) 70 West Madison Street, Suite 660
Sweeney, George E., (AV) '25 '52
C.602 A.B. L.597 J.D. Gen. Coun. & Secy., J.M. Sweeney Co.
Sweeney, Gerald O., Jr., (AV) '52 '79 C.210 B.A. L.365 J.D. [Lord,B.&B.]
Sweeney, Jalyn '— '02 C.910 B.A. L.477 J.D. [🄰 McDermott W.&E.]
Sweeney, Joanne H. '73 '99 C.473 B.S. L.424 J.D. [🄰 Jenner&B.]
Sweeney, Kevin '45 '69 C.855 B.A. L.145 J.D. Asst. States Atty.
Sweeney, Kevin R., (AVⓋ) '57 '82 C.602 B.B.A. L.1439 J.D.
(adm. in MO; not adm. in IL) [Sonnenschein N.&R.] (⊙Kansas City, MO)
Sweeney, Lisa '68 '97 C.339 B.A. L.365 J.D. Project Staff Atty., Greater Ill. Title Co.
Sweeney, Margaret B. '57 '85 C.893 B.A. L.209 J.D. 556 W. Roscoe St.
Sweeney, Maureen E. '— '96 C&L.477 B.S., J.D. [Kirkland&E.]
Sweeney, Michael J. '53 '76 C.339 B.A. L.145 J.D. [Sidley A.B.&W.]
Sweeney, Rhoda Davis '39 '81 C.597 B.S. L.146 J.D. Cir. J.
Sweeney, Robert D. '71 '96 C.602 B.A. L.424 J.D. [Miller&S.]
Sweeney, Robert E., Jr., (AV) '55 '80 C.184 B.S. L.276 J.D. [Lord,B.&B.]
Sweeney, Thomas E. '57 '88 C.801 B.S. L.424 J.D. [🄲 Katten M.R.]
Sweeney, William P. '76 '02 C.357 B.S. L.365 J.D. [🄰 Laner,M.D.B.L.&T.]
Sweet, Allan J., (AV) '47 '73 C&L.477 B.B.A., J.D. Pres., Amli Residential Props. Tr.
Sweetnam, William M. '— '94 C.477 A.B. L.209 J.D. [Freed&W.]
Sweigard, Edward C. '32 '60 C&L.190 B.S., LL.B.
(adm. in NE; not adm. in IL) Ford Co. Bk. & Tr. Co.
Sweitzer, Kathleen Ann '68 '94 C.339 B.S. L.61 J.D. [🄰 Tressler,S.M.&P.]
Sweitzer, Stephanie L. '78 '03 C.477 B.A. L.1556 J.D. [🄰 Baker&M.]
Swenson, Irving G., (AV) '21 '50 C&L.145 A.B., LL.B. 200 E. Delaware Pl.‡
Swerdlove, Nathan B., (AV) '— '58 C.339 L.209 LL.B. [🄲 Beermann S.W.B.B.G.&L.]
Swerdlow, Marc '63 '88 C.352 B.B.A. L.209 J.D. V.P., Heitman Advisory Corporation
Swett, Brian I. '70 '96 C.367 B.A. L.569 J.D. [Jenner&B.]
Swett, Daniel R., (AV) '36 '62 C&L.309 A.B., LL.B. [Sonnenschein N.&R.]
Swiatek, Michael G., (BV) '47 '80 C.602 B.S.C.E. L.365 J.D. [Kelly,O.M.&D.]
Swibel, Howard J., (AV) '— '75 C&L.309 A.B., J.D. [Arnstein&L.]
Swibel, Lawrence B., (AV) '54 '78 C.696 B.A. L.880 J.D. [Fox,H.S.L.&C.]
Swibel, Steven W., (AV) '46 '71 C.453 B.S. L.309 J.D. [Schwartz C.]
Swick, Gerard A. '40 '65 C&L.424 B.B.A., J.D. Walton, Joplin, Langer & Co.
Swidler, Ira J., (AV) '54 '79 C&L.339 B.S., J.D. [Katten M.R.]
Swidler, Sean S. '73 '99 C.352 B.S.E. L.146 J.D. [🄰 Patzik,F.&S.] (Pat.)
Święcicki, Peter '54 '82 C.276 B.S.F.S. L.477 J.D.
(adm. in MI; not adm. in IL) [🄲 Baker&M.]
Swien, Kathleen Ann '— '89 C.477 A.B. L.215 J.D. [Winston&S.]
Swietnicki, Mary L. '— '02 C.103 A.B. L.145 J.D. [🄰 Grippo&E.]
Swift, Thomas Nye '49 '86 C.94 B.A. L.146 J.D. 650 N. Dearborn St., Ste. 750
Swiger, Elinor P. '27 '51 C&L.608 B.A., J.D. [🄲 Robbins,S.N.L.&T.]
Swill, Douglas B. '64 '89 C.529 B.A. L.910 J.D. [Gardner C.&D.]
Swindells, Justin D. '73 '98 C.688 B.S.E.E. L.146 J.D. [🄰 Jenkens&G.]
Swinehart, James R. '57 '82 C.602 B.A. L.851 J.D. [Clausen M.]
Swinnea, Natalie R. '76 '02 C.623 B.A. L.424 J.D. Off. of the Pub. Guard.
Swiss, Sally A. '56 '80 C&L.339 B.A., J.D. State Asst. Appl. Def.
Swistak, Michael P. '79 '04 C.213 B.A. L.209 J.D. [🄰 Grotefeld&D.]
Switzer, Jerry L., Jr., (AV) '65 '92 C.388 B.A. L.352 J.D. [Jenner&B.]
Switzer, Joseph P., (AV) '55 '80 C&L.339 B.S., J.D. [Swanson,M.&B.]
Swofford, Stephen R., (AV) '47 '75 C.597 B.S. L.365 J.D. [Hinshaw&C.]
Swords, Mark C. '60 '92 C&L.339 B.A., J.D. [Baker&M.]
Sycz, Arek '— '03 C.999 B.A. L.597 J.D. [🄰 Kirkland&E.]
Syed, Shehla F. '77 '01 C.367 B.A. L.645 J.D. [🄰 Jenner&B.] (Pat.)
Sykes, Alan O. '54 '84 C.945 B.A. L.976 J.D.
(adm. in MA; not adm. in IL) Prof. of Law, Univ. of Chicago
Sykes, James E. '34 '64 C.597 Ph.B. L.339 LL.B. 1130 S. Michigan St.‡
Sykes, Thomas D. '54 '79 C.957 B.A. L.608 J.D. [McDermott W.&E.]
Synchef, James S. '52 '79 C.801 B.A. L.209 J.D. 19 S. LaSalle St.
Synol, Stephanie J. '66 '03 C.209 B.A. L.597 J.D. [🄰 Drinker B.&R.]
Syracuse, Russell D. '57 '82 C&L.209 B.A., J.D. Chief Hearing Officer, Dept. of Labor
Syregelas, Christopher S. '64 '94 C.339 B.S. L.146 J.D. [🄰 D.S.Dussias]
Syregelas, Nicholas C. '44 '78 C.801 B.A L.589 J.D. [Syregelas]

Syregelas Law Offices
Suite 1800, 180 N. La Salle Street, 60601-2604
Telephone: 312-855-0400 Fax: 312-855-0535
Email: ns@syregelaslaw.com URL: http://www.syregelaslawoffices.com
Member of Firm: Nicholas C. Syregelas.
Medical Malpractice, Personal Injury, Premises Liability, Automobile Accidents, Commercial Litigation, White Collar Criminal Law.
See Professional Biographies, CHICAGO, ILLINOIS

Szabad, Melissa '73 '00 C.385 B.A. L.209 J.D. [🄰 McGuirewoods]
Szaflarski, Mark, (AV) '57 '85 C.602 B.A. L.209 J.D. [🄰 Pfaff&G.]
Szala, Scott J., (AV) '53 '78 C.388 B.A. L.597 J.D. [Winston&S.]
Szarmack, Stephen M. '62 '87 C.339 B.A. L.146 J.D.
Assoc. Gen. Coun., Chicago Mercantile Exchange Inc.
Szatkowski, Martha C. '78 '04 C.347 B.S. L.365 J.D. [🄰 Johnson&B.]
Szczecin, David F. '70 '98 C.339 B.A. L.365 J.D. [🄰 B.R.Nevoral&Assoc.]
Szczepanski, Slawomir (Steve) Z., (AV) '48 '76
C.688 B.S.Ch.E. L.982 J.D. [Kelley D.&W.] (Pat.)

Szczucki, Cori A. ....'77 '02 C.339 B.A.S. L.209 J.D. [[A] Stack&F.]
Szego, Stephen Donald Oliver ....'49 '74 C.1338 B.A. L.500 J.D. P.O. Box 10032‡
Szesny, Henry C. ....'48 '74 C.339 B.S. L.209 J.D. 150 N. Michigan Ave.
Szeszel, Steven E. ....'57 '83 C.339 B.A. L.365 J.D. 39 S. La Salle St., Ste. 200
Szilagyi, Gregg E., (AV) ....'— '88 C&L.339 B.A., J.D. [Ungaretti&H.]
Szot, Andrew ....'74 '01 C&L.477 B.A., J.D. [[A] Grippo&E.]
Szpondowski, Kara L. '74 '04
C.679 B.S.I.E. L.146 J.D. [[A] Niro,S.H.&N.] (See Pat. Sect.)
Szukala, Danielle J. ....'74 '99 C&L.352 B.A., J.D. [[A] Burke,W.M.&S.]
Szura, Louis C. ....'76 '03 C.477 B.A. L.1556 J.D. [[A] Novack&M.]
Szybist, Kathleen A. '74 '00 C.645 B.A. L.665 J.D.
(adm. in PA; not adm. in IL) Atty./Advsr., US Dept. of Housing & Urban Development
Tabacchi, Tina M. ....'— '92 C.473 A.B. L.608 J.D. [Jones D.]
Tabangay, Adrian ....'69 '95 C.477 B.A. L.209 J.D. [[A] Maurides&F.]
Tabares, Jeffrey ....'70 '02 C.999 B.A. L.209 J.D. [[A] Price T.R.]
Tabata, Marie A. ....'68 '93 C.420 B.S. L.146 J.D. Off. of the Clk., Cir. Ct.
Taber, Steven M., Law Office of, (BV) '59 '86 C.475 B.A. L.477 J.D.
1220 North Harvey
Tabet, Caesar A., (AV) ....'60 '87 C.723 B.A. L.494 J.D. [Tabet D.&R.]

Tabet DiVito & Rothstein LLC, (AV)
The Rookery Building, 209 South La Salle Street, Seventh Floor, 60604
Telephone: 312-762-9450 Fax: 312-795-9801 URL: http://www.tdrlawfirm.com
URL: http://www.lawyers.com/tabetdivito&rothsteinllc
Caesar A. Tabet; Gino L. DiVito; Michael I Rothstein; Gary L. Prior; J. Jeffrey Patton; Deborah E. Decker; Karina H. DeHayes;—Stephen J. Keeley; Mark H. Horwitch; Michael J. Grant; Daniel I. Konieczny; Henry H. Hess; Mary Beth Wynn; Reema Kapur; Rachel N. Cruz (Not admitted in IL).
General Civil Trial Practice. Commercial Litigation, Corporate Litigation, Appellate Practice, Arbitration and Mediation, Class Actions, Antitrust and Unfair Competition, Commercial Real Estate Litigation, Intellectual Property Litigation, Professional Liability, Product Liability, Insurance/Reinsurance Coverage, Trade Secret Misappropriation, Executive Compensation and Employment Litigation, Civil RICO, Construction Litigation, Constitutional Law, Governmental Litigation, Banking Litigation, Corporate Investigation, False Claims Act and Qui Tam Litigation, Securities Litigation, Sports Law.
See Professional Biographies, CHICAGO, ILLINOIS

Tabin, Julius, (AV) '19 '49 C.145 B.S. L.309 LL.B.
[Fitch,E.T.&F.] (See Pat. Sect.) (⊙San Diego, CA)
Tabis, Bruno W., Jr., (AV) ....'46 '73 C.339 B.S. L.146 J.D. [Crowley B.&K.]
Tabor, Katherine L. ....'65 '90 C.800 B.S. L.879 J.D. [⊡ Kelley D.&W.] (Pat.)
Tabrizi, Maryam ....'75 '03 C.769 B.S. L.602 J.D. [[A] Vedder,P.K.&K.]
Taffe, Paula M. '50 '88 C.999 B.M. L.146 J.D.
Chf. Brand Coun., Assoc. Gen. Coun., Blue Cross Blue Shield Assn. (⊙New York, NY)
Tafilaw, Amy Renee ....'— '99 C.339 B.S. L.209 J.D. [[A] Rosenfeld H.S.&F.]
Tagler, George J. ....'50 '77 C.339 B.S. L.365 J.D. 100 N. La Salle St.
Tagli, Hugo, Jr. ......'42 '70 C.424 B.B.A. L.365 J.D. Asst. Coun., Health Care Serv. Corp.
Taglia, Anthony R. ....'69 '94 C.589 B.S. L.209 J.D. [Field&G.]
Taglia, Daniel Paul '62 '89 C.602 B.S. L.477 J.D.
(adm. in MI; not adm. in IL) Univ. of Ill.
Tague, Philip N. '49 '77 C.597 B.A. L.608 J.D.
Co-C.E.O., Amli Residential Props. Tr.‡
Takada, Joji ....'— '04 C.939 B.A. L.146 J.D. [[A] Freeborn&P.]
Takash, Terry A., (AV) ....'60 '86 C.927 B.S. L.365 J.D. [Johnson&B.]
Talaga, Bruce J. ....'50 '74 C.742 B.A. L.209 J.D. Chicago Transit Auth.
Talan, Randall G., (AV) ....'47 '72 C.145 B.A. L.339 J.D. [Menges&M.]
Talanki, Venu V. '76 '01 C.477 B.A. L.339 J.D.
(adm. in MI; not adm. in IL) [[A] Vedder,P.K.&K.]
Talarico, Mary C. ....'65 '95 C.20 B.A. L.365 J.D. [[A] Jenner&B.]
Talbert, Bernard M. '42 '74 C.1016 B.S.B.A. L.365 J.D.
Assoc. Gen. Coun., BlueCross BlueShield Assoc.
Talbot, Earl A., (AV) ....'39 '64 C.894 A.B. L.339 J.D. [Hoogendoorn&T.]
Talbot, John J. '56 '83 C.602 B.S.C.E. L.365 J.D.
Exec. V.P., A. Epstein & Sons Intl., Inc.
Tallant, David, Jr., (AV) ....'31 '56 C.154 B.A. L.228 LL.B. 111 W. Monroe St.
Tallis, Jeffrey J., (AV) ....'55 '81 C.21 B.A. L.365 J.D. 221 N. LaSalle St., Ste. 2800
Tallon, Patrick A., (AV) ....'47 '78 C.1151 B.A. L.365 J.D. [Corti,F.&A.]
Talty, Karen M., (BV) ....'63 '89 C.207 B.S. L.904 J.D. [[A] Yelton&K.]
Tama Oblander, Cheryl ....'— '88 C.801 B.A. L.424 J.D. [Winston&S.]
Tamari, Walid Joseph ....'72 '99 C.94 B.S.B.A. L.365 J.D. [Tamari&B.]

Tamari & Blumenthal, LLC
980 N. Michigan Avenue, 14th Floor, 60611
Telephone: 312-922-8900
Members of Firm: Walid Joseph Tamari; Grant Blumenthal;—Paul M. Napolski. Of Counsel: Christopher T. Considine.
Commercial Litigation, Consumer Litigation, Corporate Law, Personal Injury Litigation, Business Litigation, Landlord Tenant Litigation.
See Professional Biographies, CHICAGO, ILLINOIS

Tamblyn, Wendy L. ....'— '99 C.187 B.A. L.424 J.D. [[A] Kirkland&E.]
Tambolas, Teresa D. ....'74 '99 C.178 B.A. L.209 J.D. [[A] Pattishall,M.N.H.&G.] (Pat.)
Tamisiea, John P. ....'64 '90 C.352 B.B.A. L.659 J.D. [McDermott W.&E.]
Tamkin, Samuel J., (BV) ....'61 '86 C.659 B.A. L.339 J.D. [S.Tamkin]
Tamkin, Samuel, (BV) ....165 N. Canal, Ste. 1425
Tammaro, Katherine E. ....'67 '92 C.602 B.A. L.276 J.D. [Tressler,S.M.&P.]
Tan, Mox '53 '85 C.453 B.Sc. L.309 J.D.
(adm. in NY; not adm. in IL) Invest. Bkr., Banc America Robertson Stephens
Tanaka, Vanessa G. ....'69 '00 C.94 B.A. L.966 J.D. [McDermott W.&E.]
Tanasijevich, Rudolph Chris '64 '92 C.477 B.A. L.1119 J.D.
(adm. in PA; not adm. in IL) Off. of Reg. Coun., U.S. Environ. Protect. Agcy.
Tanay, Anita ....'55 '80 C&L.477 B.A., J.D. [[A] Jacobs,B.O.S.&H.]
Tanchum, Letty W. '49 '73 C&L.228 B.A., J.D.
(adm. in NY; not adm. in IL) VP& Gen. Coun., Harpo Productions, Inc.
Tanck, Nancy A. ....'63 '88 C&L.966 B.A., J.D. 4626 N. Kenmore, #1N‡
Tandy, Scott B. ....'69 '94 Sr. Atty., U.S. Sec. and Exchange Comm.
Tang, Wayne L., (BV) ....'66 '91 C&L.477 B.A., J.D. [⊡ Mayer,B.R.&M.]
Tangren, John E. ....'— '03 C&L.145 B.A., J.D. [[A] Kirkland&E.]
Tang-Tellez, Mercy T. ....'— '96 C.1183 B.S. L.1187 J.D. [[A] Kaplan]
Tanig, Reynard L. ....'68 '93 C.339 B.A. L.209 J.D. [[A] Masuda,F.E.&M.]
Tanis, Cornelius J., (AV) ....'58 '83 C.114 B.A. L.1292 J.D. [Bell,B.&L.]
Tannen, Catherine V. ....'70 '97 C.299 B.A. L.94 J.D. Asst. Pub. Guard.
Tannen, Charles E., (AV) ....'33 '60 L.209 LL.B. [[A] Karlin&F.]
Tannen, Michael Murphy, Law Offices of, (BV) '62 '90
C.424 A.B. L.209 J.D. 39 S. Lasalle St., Ste. 905
Tannenbaum, Fredric D. ....'56 '81 C.611 B.A. L.966 J.D. [Gould&R.]
Tanner, David Neal ....'74 '01 C.502 A.B. L.734 J.D. [[A] Gardner C.&D.]
Tanner, Matthew D. ....'59 '90 C&L.339 B.S., J.D. 53 W. Jackson Boulevard
Tanner, R. Brian ....'— '03 C.277 B.S. L.245 J.D. [[A] Latham&W.]
Tansey, James G. ....'41 '78 C.999 A.B. L.589 J.D. Asst. States Atty.
Tantillo, Steven J. ....'60 '87 C.602 A.B. L.145 J.D. City of Chicago Law Dept.

Tantleff, Aaron K. ....'77 '04 C.597 B.A. L.146 J.D. [[A] Bell,B.&L.]
Tanz, Jill S. ....'50 '77 L.145 J.D. [Chicago M.]
Tanzar, Philip A. ....'50 '92 C.801 B.A. L.46 J.D. Asst. Gen. Coun., Man Financial Inc.
Tanzi, Grey Alexandra ....'79 '04 C.910 B.A. L.477 J.D. [[A] Skadden,A.S.M.&F.]
Tanzillo, Paul A. ....'60 '86 C.750 B.A. L.146 J.D. [McKay,N.T.D.&K.]
Tapia-Ruano, Carlina, (AV) ....'55 '80 C.340 B.A. L.209 J.D. [Minsky,M.&H.]
Tappendorf, Julie A. ....'64 '97 C.338 B.A. L.312 J.D. [Holland&K.]
Taradash, Dean W. ....'72 '99 C.209 B.A. L.146 J.D. 33 N. Dearborn St., Ste. 1910
Taradji, Nima B. ....'— '98 C.845 B.A. L.365 J.D. [Taradji]

Taradji Law Offices
Suite 1310, 205 West Randolph, 60606
Telephone: 312-252-5252; 782-3400 Fax: 312-252-5253 Email: ntpc@taradji.com
Email: nbt@taradji.com URL: http://www.taradji.com
Nima B. Taradji.
Languages: French, Farsi and English.
Personal Injury, Workers Compensation, Premises Liability, Automobile Accidents, Negligence, Products Liability, Construction Accidents, Dog Bites, Slip and Fall, Wrongful Death, Medical Malpractice, Tort Law and Civil, Commercial and Business Litigation. Libel and Slander, Contracts and Small Business Law.
See Professional Biographies, CHICAGO, ILLINOIS

Tarara, Annemarie ....'— '03 C.209 B.S. L.146 J.D. [[A] Nottage&W.]
Taraska, Marie J. ....'— '97 C.339 B.A. L.209 J.D. [[A] Querrey&H.]
Tardiff, Daniel M. '— '02 C.602 B.A. L.424 J.D.
U.S. Atty.'s Off., Dist. for N. Dist. of IL
Taren, Jeffrey L., (AV) ....'52 '77 C.705 B.A. L.93 J.D. [Kinoy,T.&G.]
Tarkington, Donald A. ....'56 '83 C.347 B.S. L.597 J.D. [Novack&M.]
Tarlock, A. Dan '40 '65 C&L.813 A.B., LL.B.
(adm. in CA; not adm. in IL) Prof. of Law, Chicago-Kent College of Law
Tarman, James I., Jr. ....'60 '87 C.645 B.S. L.1017 J.D. [Cozen O.]
Tarnoff, Stephen ....'50 '81 C.589 B.A. L.365 J.D. [[A] Minsky,M.&H.]
Tarnow, Georgette H. ....'48 '80 C.1183 B.A. L.365 J.D. 6123 N. Karlov Ave.
Tarnow, William J. ....'73 '97 C&L.339 B.A., J.D. [Neal,G.&E.]
Tarpey, Daniel W. ....'72 '97 C.339 B.A. L.602 J.D. [[A] Seyfarth S.]
Tarpey, L. Michael, (AV) ....'63 '89 C.339 B.A. L.884 J.D. [Donohue B.M.&S.]
Tarpey, Leo M., Jr., (AV) ....'34 '58 C&L.424 B.S., J.D. Ste 700, 140 S Dearborn St
Tarpey, Peter D., (BV) ....'65 '90 C.477 B.G.S. L.770 J.D. [[A] P.B.Episcope]
Tarshis, Jay P. ....'— '80 C.597 B.A. L.339 J.D. [Arnstein&L.]
Tarsney, Peter J. '69 '95 C&L.602 B.A., J.D.
Sr. Atty., Div. of Enforce., Secs. & Exch. Comm.
Tarun, Robert W., (AV) ....'— '74 C.813 A.B. L.209 J.D. [Latham&W.]
Tarver, Vivian T. ....'— '03 C.999 B.A. L.365 J.D. [[A] Clifford]
Tassone, Bruno J. ....'40 '70 C.209 B.S.C. L.146 J.D. 33 N. La Salle Street
Tassone, Caterina P. ....'— '97 C.424 B.A. L.146 J.D. [[A] Fragomen,D.B.&L.]
Tate, Emory A. ....'18 '51 C.339 L.365 LL.B. 9606 S. Yale Ave.
Tate, June B. '31 '79 C.424 B.S. L.597 J.D.
Hearing Examiner, State Commerce Comm.
Tate, Ricardo L. ....'— '80 C.309 A.B. L.145 J.D. Legal Assist. Found. of Chic.
Tatman, Ashley E. '— '05 C.651 B.A. L.345 J.D.
(adm. in IN; not adm. in IL) [[A] Mayer,B.R.&M.]
Tatooles, Dean J. ....'73 '99 C.475 B.A. L.365 J.D. [[A] Tressler,S.M.&P.]
Tatum, Kenyatta L. ....'64 '92 C.811 B.A. L.209 J.D. Asst. Fed. Def.
Taube, Kenneth P. ....'49 '79 C.309 B.A. L.339 J.D. [Rothschild,B.&M.]
Taubert, Nicholas D. ....'43 '69 C.910 A.B. L.209 J.D. Asst. States Atty.
Tauke, Dale B. ....'52 '77 C.352 B.B.A. L.145 J.D. [Fox,H.S.L.&C.]
Tauras, Kristin Dvorsky ....'— '93 C.352 B.A. L.209 J.D. [[A] McKenna S.]
Tauras, Richard P. ....'67 '95 C.352 B.S. L.597 J.D. [[A] Bollinger,R.&G.]
Tausche, Charles A. ....'38 '63 C.602 A.B. L.309 LL.B. 1360 N. Sandburg Ter.
Taussig, Elaine M. ....'65 '95 C.66 B.A. L.597 J.D. [Neal,G.&E.]
Taussig, Stuart K., (AV) ....'37 '60 C&L.966 B.B.A., J.D. [Shefsky&F.]
Taxman, Glenn D. ....'70 '96 C.112 B.A. L.365 J.D. [Much S.F.D.A.&R.] ⊙
Taxman, Marc A., (AV) ....'62 '88 C.339 B.S. L.146 J.D. [Anesi,O.R.N.&K.]
Taxman, Phillip ....'36 '85 C.339 B.S. L.424 J.D. [Taxman&H.]

Taxman & Hurst
100 West Monroe Street Suite 1605, 60603
Telephone: 312-263-3040 Fax: 312-263-7944
Email: info@taxmanlaw.com URL: http://www.taxmanlaw.com
Phillip Taxman; Brian Hurst. Of Counsel: Ernest W. Beutel, M.D.
Tort Litigation Practice, Medical Malpractice, Negligence, Trials, Professional Malpractice and Products Liability Law.
See Professional Biographies, CHICAGO, ILLINOIS

Taylor, Ann Caroline ....'62 '92 C.473 A.B. L.150 J.D. [Lord,B.&B.]
Taylor, Anne E. ....'54 '81 C.050 B.A. L.145 J.D. [[A] R.T.Napier&Assoc.]
Taylor, Bernard ....'— '02 C.309 B.A. L.477 J.D. [[A] Kirkland&E.]
Taylor, Byron F. ....'64 '90 C.976 B.A. L.145 J.D. [Sidley A.B.&W.]
Taylor, Charles B. ....'63 '92 C.339 B.S. L.145 J.D. [Skadden,A.S.M.&F.]
Taylor, Christian Chadd ....'— '94 C.701 B.S.E.E. L.347 J.D. [Kirkland&E.]
Taylor, Darrell W. ....'64 '03 C.1337 B.S.M.T. L.602 J.D. [[A] DLPiper R.G.C.U.]
Taylor, Don F. ....'61 '98 C.477 B.S.M.E. L.213 J.D. [[A] Carponelli&K.]
Taylor, Jacqueline M. '58 '99 C.597 B.S. L.424 J.D.
Gen. Coun., Holsten Real Estate Development Corp.
Taylor, Jean L. ....'73 '00 C.597 B.A. L.477 J.D. Consult., Broadview, Inc.
Taylor, Jeremy M. ....'70 '97 C.893 B.A. L.500 J.D. [Jenner&B.]
Taylor, John D. ....'66 '94 C.276 B.S.F.S. L.893 J.D. [Mayer,B.R.&M.]
Taylor, Karen E. ....'— '82 C.597 B.A. L.245 J.D. [⊡ Harrigan&Assoc.]
Taylor, Kathryn F. ....'— '01 C.934 B.A. L.910 J.D. [[A] Kirkland&E.]
Taylor, Lance D., (BV) ....'49 '81 C.339 B.A. L.209 J.D. 900 N. Mich. Ave., Ste. 130
Taylor, Laura Yates ....'— '05 C&L.910 B.A., J.D. [[A] Gardner C.&D.]
Taylor, Lawrence M., Jr. ....'45 '73 C.103 A.B. L.94 J.D. Walter E. Heller Intl. Corp.
Taylor, Lillian O. ....'42 '84 C.1183 B.A. L.352 J.D. Asst. States Atty.
Taylor, M. Catherine ....'48 '93 C.339 B.A. L.209 J.D. [[A] Spain,S.&V.]
Taylor, Mark R. ....'57 '90 C.338 B.S. L.424 J.D. [Mayer,B.R.&M.]
Taylor, Mary P. ....'54 '80 C&L.339 B.A., J.D. [[A] M.Black&Assoc.]
Taylor, Pamela L. ....'65 '90 C.914 B.A. L.94 J.D. [Bell,B.&L.]
Taylor, R. Vincent ....'59 '92 C.1031 B.S. L.228 J.D. Accenture
Taylor, Rick ....'58 '97 C.432 B.S. L.424 J.D. Asst. Corp. Coun.
Taylor, Robert J. ....'— '96 C.339 B.S. L.146 J.D. [Arnstein&L.]
Taylor, Rodney J. ....'46 '80 C.446 B.S. L.101 J.D. Fred S. James & Co.
Taylor, Roger L., (AV) ....'— '71 C.388 B.A. L.597 J.D. [⊡ Kirkland&E.]
Taylor, Ross D. ....'— '88 C.589 B.S. L.893 J.D. [Schiff H.]
Taylor, Ryan ....'80 '05 C.339 B.S. L.209 J.D. [[A] Tressler,S.M.&P.]
Taylor, Sean F. ....'65 '93 C.347 B.S. L.365 J.D. Sr. Coun., Chicago Park District
Taylor, Ursula ....'80 '05 C.477 B.A. L.597 J.D. [[A] Vedder,P.K.&K.]
Taylor, William H., II '54 '80 C.188 B.A. L.597 J.D.
Gen. Coun., Co. Recorder of Deeds
Taylor, William M. ....'37 '62 C.352 B.A. L.597 J.D. Cir. J.

Taylor, Miller, Sprowl, Hoffnagle & Merletti, (AV) .... Suite 2222
Taylor Poppe, Emily S. ....'77 '04 C.228 B.A. L.597 J.D. [McDermott W.&E.]
Tayyab, J. Yasmin ....'73 '98 C.880 B.A. L.93 J.D. [Segal M.S.&M.]
Tchen, Christina M., (AV) ....'56 '84 C.681 A.B. L.597 J.D. [Skadden,A.S.M.&F.]
Teaney, Douglas B. ....'60 '87 C.146 B.S.M.A.E. L.589 J.D. [Greenberg T.] (Pat.)
Tecson, Andrew P., (AV) ....'55 '80 C.597 B.A. L.145 J.D. [Chuhak&T.]
Tecson, David J. ....'61 '88 C.429 B.A. L.339 J.D. [Chuhak&T.]
Tecson, John Michael ....'75 '01 C.339 B.A. L.1018 J.D. [Hogan M.]
Tecson, Joseph A., (AV) ....'28 '55 C.694 B.A. L.966 J.D. [Chuhak&T.]
Tecu, Amy Elizabeth Obrist '75 '01 C.378 B.S.W. L.1000 J.D.
Mgr., The Boeing Co., Ins. Litig. & Risk Mgmt.
Tedeschi, Donald A. '50 '81
C.339 B.A. L.365 J.D. Mng. Claim Atty., Amer. Fam. Ins. Grp.

Tedesso, Frank A. '68 '93 C.597 B.A. L.209 J.D.
39 South La Salle, Suite 808, 60603-1603
Telephone: 312-578-9770 Fax: 312-899-0048
Email: ftedesso@ameritech.net URL: http://www.frankatedesso.com
Criminal Law, Traffic Violations, Domestic Violence, Driving While Intoxicated, Drug Crimes Sexual Assaults, Felonies, Misdemeanors, Armed Robbery, Robbery, Weapons Offense, Murder and Attempted Murder.
See Professional Biographies, CHICAGO, ILLINOIS

Tedrowe, Courtney Douglas ....'70 '01 C.881 B.A. L.188 J.D. [Novack&M.]
Teeple, Ronald W., (AV) ....'42 '67 C.145 B.A. L.659 LL.B. [Teeple&L.]

Teeple & Leonard, (AV)
175 W. Jackson Boulevard, Suite 240, 60604
Telephone: 312-986-3228 Fax: 312-986-3981
Ronald W. Teeple; John L. Leonard;—Michael H. Erdman.
Commercial and Civil Litigation, Antitrust Law, Environmental Law, Intellectual Property Law.
See Professional Biographies, CHICAGO, ILLINOIS

Teggelaar, Michelle R. ....'71 '97 C.339 B.A. L.146 J.D. [Edelman,C.&L.]
Teibloom, Joel D. ....'54 '80 C.1036 A.B. L.94 J.D. [Flamm&T.]
Teich, Michael L. ....'68 '94 C.188 B.S. L.1065 J.D. [Lewis,D.&H.]
Teichgraeber, Thomas G. '45 '72 C.375 B.A. L.900 J.D.
(adm. in KS; not adm. in IL) Exec. V.P. & Gen. Coun., Diners Club Intl. Ltd.
Teichner, Leon J., & Associates, (BV) '49 '74
C.339 B.S. L.209 J.D. 180 North LaSalle Street Suite 1601
Teixeira, Maurice E. ....'71 '99 C.679 B.S.C.E. L.339 J.D. [Wallenstein W.&R.]
Tejano, Kristine ....'71 '00 C.659 B.A. L.209 J.D. [Sedgwick,D.M.&A.]
Tellefsen, Charmaine ....'51 '76 C.238 B.A. L.365 J.D. Law Clk., Appl. Ct. J.

Teller, Levit & Silvertrust, P.C., (AV)
11 East Adams, Suite 800, 60603
Telephone: 312-922-3030 Toll-Free: 800-922-0342 Fax: 312-922-3048; 312-922-4105 URL: http://www.lawyers.com/tellerlevit&silvertrust
Email: TLS@TellerLevit.com URL: http://www.TellerLevit.com
Arthur Raphael; Harold Stotland; Edward S. Margolis; Kevin E. Posen.
Creditors Rights, Collections, Civil Practice, Commercial Arbitration, Commercial Litigation, Preference Defense, Sale of Goods, Secured Transactions, Uniform Commercial Code, Breach of Contract, Commercial Contracts, Insurance Premium Collection, Mortgage Foreclosures, Construction Litigation, Mechanics Liens, Commercial Evictions, Post Judgment Collections, Appeals.
See Professional Biographies, CHICAGO, ILLINOIS

Telman, Deborah H. '64 '93
C.659 B.A. L.94 J.D. Asst. Corp. Secy. & Coun, The Boeing Co.
Temple, Kurt T., Law Office of '65 '92
C.350 B.B.A. L.209 J.D. 5343 South Drexel Avenue
Templer, Lawrence M., (AV) ....'46 '71 C.339 B.S. L.597 J.D. [Jolivette&T.]
Ten Brink, Charles J. ....'54 '79 C.475 B.S. L.477 J.D. Libr., Univ. of Chicago
TenBroeck, James C. ....'42 '69 C.602 B.B.A. L.424 J.D. 1652 N. Humboldt Blvd.
Tenenbaum, J. Samuel, (AV) ....'— '73 C.608 B.A. L.597 J.D. [Sachnoff&W.]
Tenenbaum, Marvin A., (AV) ....'51 '76 C&L.597 B.S., J.D. LECG
Tennant, Francis K., (AV) ....'54 '79 C.602 A.B. L.424 J.D. [Wolf&T.]
Tenner, David S. ....'51 '75 C.597 B.A. L.145 J.D. 2803 W. Summerdale Ave.
Tenner, Gerald M., (AV) ....'45 '69 C&L.339 B.S., J.D. [Marks,M.&K.]
Tenney, Elizabeth S. ....'75 '01 C&L.475 B.A., J.D. [McGuirewoods]

Tenney & Bentley, LLC, (AV)
Founded 1847
111 West Washington Street Suite 1900, 60602
Telephone: 312-407-7800 Telefax: 312-807-4858
Email: TENBEN@interaccess.com
Henry F. Tenney (1915-1971); Richard Bentley (1922-1970). Members of Firm: Arthur H. Anderson, Jr.; Richard J. Cochran; Edwin H. Conger; John S. Eskilson; Solomon Gutstein; F. James Helms; David R. Shannon; Timothy K. Travers. Of Counsel: Irwin J. Askow; Albert L. Finston; Edward J. Kahn. Associates: Ann Addis Pantoga; David J. Wolf.
General Civil Practice, including Business and Personal Litigation, Corporate, Probate, Real Estate, Tax and Estate Planning.
See Professional Biographies, CHICAGO, ILLINOIS

Tenyak, Carol L., (BV) '56 '82 C.97 B.A.C. L.608 J.D.
Sr. Assoc. Gen. Coun., Chicago Div., ABN-AMRO North America, Inc. (Legal Department)
Tenzer, Steven J., (BV) ....'53 '79 C.966 B.A. L.1151 J.D. [S.J.Tenzer]
Tenzer, Steven J., Ltd., The Law Offices of, (BV) ....20 S. Clark St., Ste. 2900
Teper, James M. ....'62 '87 C&L.966 B.B.A., J.D. [Patzik,F.&S.]
Teplinsky, Steven J., (AV) ....'53 '78 C.589 B.A. L.46 J.D. [Michael B.&F.]
Teply, Jakub ....'77 '04 C.339 B.S. L.477 J.D. [Skadden,A.S.M.&F.]
Tepper, Robert D., (AV) ....'49 '82 C.801 B.A. L.365 J.D. [Schenk,A.B.&T.]
Tepper, Robert R., (AV) ....'45 '69 C&L.477 B.A., J.D. 111 W. Washington
Tepper, Sharyn A., (BV) '58 '83
C.473 B.S. L.930 J.D. Mng. Dir., Zurich Scudder Investments, Inc.
Terman, James L. ....'48 '74 C.208 B.S.B.A. L.146 J.D. 730 N. Franklin
Ter Molen, David ....'68 '99 C.197 A.B. L.597 J.D. [Freeborn&P.]
Ter Molen, Mark R., (BV) ....'62 '88 C.188 A.B. L.145 J.D. [Mayer,B.R.&M.]
Termondt, M. Jas. ....'28 '52 C&L.602 B.A., LL.B. 30 N. La Salle St.‡
Terney, Risë J. '44 '99 C.991 B.A. L.424 J.D.
Legal Assistance Found. of Metro. Chicago
Terpstra, Anita J. ...'61 '98 C.67 B.A. L.734 J.D. [McDonnell B.H.&B.] (See Pat. Sect.)
Terras, Alexander ....'52 '77 C.145 B.A. L.209 J.D. [DLPiper R.G.C.U.]
Terrazino, Imelda R. '29 '75 C.700 B.A. L.365 J.D.
10 South La Salle Street, Suite 1600‡
Terrien, Michael S. ....'64 '92 C.494 B.S. L.597 J.D. [Jenner&B.]
Terry, Andrew J. ....'— '98 C.347 B.A. L.345 J.D. [Kirkland&E.]
Terry, Angela M. ....'71 '04 C.746 B.A. L.424 J.D. [Jenner&B.]
Terry, Gerard '54 '86 C.994 B.A. L.724 J.D.
(adm. in NY; not adm. in IL) [McBreen&K.]
Terry, Jeffrey L. ....'— '00 C.339 B.S. L.424 J.D. [Greenberg T.]
Terry, Justin L. ....'— '00 C.597 B.S. L.602 J.D. [McKenna S.]

Terselic, John A. '67 '92 C.801 B.A. L.209 J.D.
[Swanson,M.&B.] (⊙Libertyville, Waukegan)
Tesija, Miki V. ....'— '97 C.339 B.A. L.273 J.D. [Foley&L.]
Teske, Jeffrey M. ....'55 '82 C.347 B.A. L.1119 J.D. [Hogan M.]
Tesmer, Trisha K. ....'76 '01 C.347 B.S. L.209 J.D. [Cassiday,S.&G.]
Tessier, Kevin D. ....'— '96 C.684 B.A. L.1119 J.D. [Neal,G.&E.]
Teton, Alfred B. ....'14 '36 C&L.145 A.B., J.D. Cir. Ct. J.
Tetro, Stephen R., II ....'— '95 C.188 B.S. L.145 J.D. [Latham&W.]
Tetzlaff, Catherine N. ....'74 '02 C.436 B.A. L.209 J.D. [Kaplan,v.&M.]
Tetzlaff, Janna D., (AV) ....'55 '80 C.587 B.S.E. L.502 J.D. 1432 N. State Pkwy.
Tetzlaff, Theodore R., (AV) ....'— '69 C.674 A.B. L.976 LL.B. [Ungaretti&H.]
Teuscher, Julie A., (AV) ....'60 '85 C.339 B.A. L.209 J.D. [Cassiday,S.&G.]
Teven, Brian D. ....'77 '02 C.966 B.B.A. L.910 J.D. 77 W. Wacker, Ste. 4025
Tews, Herbert R., (AV) ....'06 '27 L.146 J.D. [Tews,T.&T.]
Tews, Theisen & Theisen, (AV) ....One N. La Salle St. (⊙Glenview)
Thabit, Janet Byrne ....'67 '95 C.210 B.A. L.424 J.D. [Skadden,A.S.M.&F.]
Thacker, Stephen M. ....'53 '83 C.927 B.A. L.209 J.D. 1 E. Wacker Dr.
Thakkar, Mona ....'— '04 C.339 B.S. L.209 J.D. [Foley&L.]
Thakrar, Anooj M. ....'77 '04 C.1372 B.A. L.1000 J.D. [Grotefeld&D.]
Thar, Anne E., (AV) ....'57 '83 C.518 B.A. L.597 J.D. [Winston&S.]
Tharp, John J., Jr., (AV) ....'60 '90 C.228 B.A. L.597 J.D. [Mayer,B.R.&M.]
Tharpe, Lisa L. ....'— '98 C.112 B.A. L.245 J.D. [Foley&L.]
Thaviu, Lisa ....'56 '88 C.119 B.F.A. L.424 J.D. [Bollinger,R.&G.]
Thayer, Scott D. '59 '86 C&L.190 B.A., J.D.
(adm. in NE; not adm. in IL) Sr. Coun., Americas/Pacific, Wm.Wrigley Jr. Co.
Thayer, Stephen C. ....'39 '67 C.951 A.B. L.802 J.D. Principal Fin.
Thayer, Steven J. ....'66 '91 C.339 B.A. L.209 M.B.A./J.D. [Handler,T.&D.]
Theis, John T., (AV) ....'47 '73 C.424 B.A. L.1355 J.D. 29 S. LaSalle, Ste. 220
Theis, Mary Jane W. ....'49 '74 C.424 B.A. L.765 J.D. Appl. Ct. J. 1st Dist. of IL
Theisen, Herbert J., (AV) ....'40 '65 C.424 B.S. L.597 J.D. [Tews,T.&T.]
Theisen, Kenneth F., (AV) ....'46 '77 C.1016 B.A. L.1187 J.D. [Tews,T.&T.] ⊙
Theiss, James R., Jr. ....'— '79 C.602 B.A. L.209 J.D. [Chapman&C.]
Theiss, Paul W., (AV) ....'60 '85 C.31 B.A. L.145 J.D. [Mayer,B.R.&M.]
Thelen, Betsy ......'— '01 C.477 A.B. L.1565 J.D. Two North LaSalle Street, Suite 2200
Therieau, Anne ....'— '04 C.602 B.A. L.424 J.D. [Vedder,P.K.&K.]
Thevatheril, Aiju C. ....'73 '99 C.339 B.S. L.209 J.D. [Swanson,M.&B.]
Theyssen, David L. ....'73 '99 C&L.347 B.A., J.D. 525 West Monroe Street, Suite 1600
Theyssen, Elizabeth A. ....'75 '02 C.345 B.A. L.424 J.D. [Schiller,D.&F.]
Thiedmann, Klaus U., (AV) ....'54 '83 L.597 J.D. [Thiedmann&E.]

Thiedmann & Edler, (AV)
222 South Riverside Plaza, Suite 1410, 60606
Telephone: 312-831-4440 Fax: 312-831-4447
Email: thiedmann@thiedmannedler.com URL: http://www.thiedmannedler.com
Members of Firm: Klaus U. Thiedmann; Robert W. Edler; Sarah A. A. Ames; Thomas W. Soseman. Of Counsel: Annette E. Gustafsson Guenther; Alan B. Samlan; Jamie S. Freveletti; David J. Hurley.
Corporate Law, Business Law, Mergers, Acquisitions and Divestitures, Finance, Securities, Business Immigration, Labor and Employment, Foreign Investment in the United States, Intellectual Property, International Commercial Arbitration.
See Professional Biographies, CHICAGO, ILLINOIS

Thiel, Michael F. '52 '88
C.339 B.S. L.424 J.D. Assoc. Coun., Natl. Assn. of Realtors (Pat.)
Thiel, Sandra L. '— '77 C.966 B.A. L.146 J.D.
(adm. in FL; not adm. in IL) [S.L.Thiel]
Thiel, Sandra Lynn .... 432 N. Clark St., Ste. 305
Thiersch, Alex R. ....'75 '01 C.352 B.A. L.209 J.D. [Williams M.&J.]
Thill, Timothy J. ....'46 '72 C&L.424 B.A., J.D. [T.J.Thill]
Thill, Timothy J., P.C. ....6415 W. 63rd Street
Thillens, Stephanie M. ....'— '99 C.741 B.A. L.405 J.D. [Gunty&M.]
Thimmig, David M., (AV) '62 '91 C.1229 B.S.M.E. L.477 J.D.
[Mayer,B.R.&M.] (Pat.)
Thom, Winfield S. ....'64 '97 C.813 B.A.S. L.966 J.D. [Neal,G.&E.]
Thomas, Angela C. '57 '85 C.228 B.A. L.128 J.D.
Dep. Corp. Coun., Labor Div., City of Chicago Law Dept.
Thomas, Barbara A. ....'46 '78 C.339 B.A. L.209 J.D. 145 W. Schiller St.
Thomas, Carolyn, (Ms.) '52 '96 C.502 B.A. L.46 J.D.
Cook Co. Off. of the Pub. Guardian
Thomas, Dale E., (AV) ....'47 '75 C.674 A.B. L.976 J.D. [Sidley A.B.&W.]
Thomas, David C. ....'54 '79 C.385 A.B. L.477 J.D. 180 N. Wacker Drive
Thomas, Edwin C., III, (AV) ....'40 '66 C.629 B.S. L.1066 LL.B. [Lord,B.&B.]
Thomas, Frederick B. ....'49 '74 C.197 A.B. L.145 J.D. [Mayer,B.R.&M.]
Thomas, Howard C., Jr. ....'23 '49 C&L.329 A.B., LL.B. 720 E. 89th St.
Thomas, James A. ....'42 '76 C.1016 B.S. L.209 J.D. 53 W. Jackson Blvd.
Thomas, James M. '53 '81 C.339 B.A. L.365 J.D.
Dir. of Legal Services, Dept. of Water
Thomas, Jas. J. ....'27 '52 C&L.209 LL.B. 2256 W. Cermak Rd.
Thomas, Jessica K. ....'— '99 C.477 B.F.A. L.209 J.D. [Ungaretti&H.]
Thomas, Kathryn C. ....'— '93 C.340 B.A. L.365 J.D. [Freeborn&P.]
Thomas, Liisa M. ....'71 '96 C.311 B.A. L.145 J.D. [Gardner C.&D.]
Thomas, Mark K., (AV) ....'55 '81 C.597 B.A. L.1049 J.D. [Jenner&B.]
Thomas, Matthew J. ....'72 '97 C&L.477 B.B.A., J.D. [Jenner&B.]
Thomas, Rhonda C., (AVⓉ) ....'47 '73 C.225 A.B. L.502 J.D. [Sonnenschein N.&R.]
Thomas, Scott G., (AVⓉ) '56 '82
C.957 B.A. L.436 J.D. [S.G.Thomas] (⊙New Berlin, WI)
Thomas, Vernon B., Jr. ....'34 '60 C.309 B.A. L.597 J.D. 53 W. Jackson Blvd.

Thomas, Scott G., Law Offices of, (AVⓉ)
500 West Madison Street, Suite 2790, 60661-2511
Telephone: 312-930-5500 Fax: 312-993-9896
Staff Counsel American International Companies: Managing Attorney: Scott G. Thomas. Supervising Attorney: James L. McKnight. Senior Trial Attorneys: James P. Hynes; Richard M. Jacobson; Patricia J. Kampsen; Michael F. Lanigan; Robert S. Phillips; Nancy M. Rundin. Trial Attorneys: Michael F. Murphy; Andrew Touloupakis. Associate Attorney: Claudia Halloran.
Products Liability, Professional Liability, Securities Arbitration, Premises Liability, Automobile Accident Liability, Employment Law, General Liability, and Workers' Compensation.
See Professional Biographies, CHICAGO, ILLINOIS

Thompson, Amy J. ....'72 '97 C.347 B.S.Ph. L.879 J.D. [Pretzel&S.]
Thompson, Brian J. '70 '00 C.339 B.S. L.575 J.D.
(adm. in NC; not adm. in IL) 333 West Wacker Drive
Thompson, Carol K. ....'— '89 C&L.352 B.A., J.D. [Chapman&C.]
Thompson, Cherie E. ....'67 '92 C.589 B.A. L.365 J.D. [Thompson&T.]
Thompson, Cynthia ....'74 '00 C.879 B.S. L.597 J.D. [Jenkens&G.]
Thompson, David A. '52 '78 C.338 B.S. L.339 J.D.
Sr. Assoc. Gen. Coun., Bank One Corp. (Law Dept.)
Thompson, Donald M. ....'41 '66 C.597 B.A. L.145 J.D. [D.Thompson]
Thompson, Eley O., (AV) '64 '90
C.886 B.S.E.E. L.1189 J.D. [Leydig,V.&M.] (See Pat. Sect.)

Thompson, Elizabeth L. '57 '89 C&L.347 B.A., J.D. [Bartlit B.H.P.&S.]
Thompson, Erica '61 '91 L.209 J.D. People's Law Off.
Thompson, Erik J. '67 '92 C.352 B.B.A. L.365 J.D. [Thompson&T.]
Thompson, Howard S. '— '88 C.477 B.B.A. L.228 J.D. [Daspin&A.]
Thompson, Hubert O., (AV) '55 '79 C.484 B.A. L.569 J.D. [Brothers&T.]
Thompson, James L. '63 '88 C.118 B.A. L.477 J.D. [Jenner&B.]
Thompson, James R., Jr., (AV) '36 '59 C.339 L.597 J.D. [Winston&S.]
Thompson, Kevin A. '71 '98 C.966 B.A. L.209 J.D. [Ⓐ Davis M.]
Thompson, Lily '— '80 C.1138 B.B.A. L.262 J.D.
Gen. Coun., Johnson Products Co., Inc.
Thompson, Matthew '79 '04 C.966 B.B.A. L.424 J.D. [Ⓐ Chuhak&T.]

Thompson, Michael '51 '76 C.351 B.A. L.352 J.D.
401 North Michigan Avenue, Suite 1200, 60611
Telephone: 312-840-8556 Fax: 847-733-1807
Email: michaelthompsonlaw@earthlink.net URL: http://www.michaelthompsonlaw.com
International Trade and Investment, Acquisition of Fine Art and Cultural Property, Transactions involving Literary and Artistic Property.
See Professional Biographies, CHICAGO, ILLINOIS

Thompson, Michael D. '75 '01 C&L.352 B.B.A., J.D. [Ⓐ Seyfarth S.]
Thompson, Michelle Farrar '64 '91 C.93 B.A. L.273 J.D. 821 W. Van Buren
Thompson, Monica L., (P.C.), (AV) '53 '81 C.421 B.A. L.910 J.D.
[DLPiper R.G.C.U.]
Thompson, Nancy J. '58 '87 C&L.273 B.A., J.D.
(adm. in VA; not adm. in IL) John Marshall Law Sch.
Thompson, Neal F. '52 '81 C.339 B.A. L.597 J.D. [Ⓐ Michaels&M.]
Thompson, Patricia J. '— '88 C.112 B.S. L.424 J.D. [Schiff H.]
Thompson, Patrick Daley '— '99 C.741 B.A. L.365 J.D. [Ⓐ DLPiper R.G.C.U.]
Thompson, Pia N. '69 '94 C.914 B.A. L.477 J.D. [Ⓐ Sonnenschein N.&R.]
Thompson, Robert B. '50 '75 C.357 B.S. L.146 J.D. [Harrington,T.A.&H.]
Thompson, Steven J., (AV) '— '87 C&L.966 B.A., J.D. [Ungaretti&H.]
Thompson, Steven M. '53 '93 C.502 B.S.B.A. L.365 J.D. [Ⓐ W.J.Sneckenberg&Assoc.]
Thompson, Tara E. '— '03 C.878 B.A. L.145 J.D. [Ⓐ Mayer,B.R.&M.]
Thompson, Teri Firmiss '63 '92 C.966 B.A. L.659 J.D. [Ⓒ Matkov,S.M.&G.]
Thompson, Timothy H. '62 '88 C.602 B.B.A. L.477 J.D.
Chicago Bd. Options Exch., Inc. (Market Regul.)
Thompson, Tomas M. '74 '01 C.894 A.B. L.508 J.D. [Ⓐ Lord,B.&B.]
Thompson, Donald 55 W. Monroe, Ste. 3950
Thompson & Thompson 19 S. LaSalle St.
Thomson, Catherine M. '68 '96 C.477 B.A. L.146 J.D. [Ⓐ Barack F.K.P.&N.]
Thomson, Paige J. '— '02 C.37 B.S. L.146 J.D. [Ⓐ Patula&Assoc.] (Pat.)
Thomson, Wade A. '76 '04 C.373 B.A. L.339 J.D. [Ⓐ Jenner&B.]
Thorkelson, Mary M. '46 '71 C.771 B.A. L.145 J.D. 5220 S. Blackstone Ave.
Thorn, Dennis W., (AV) '49 '75 C.823 B.A. L.365 J.D. [D.W.Thorn&Assoc.]
Thorn, Paul J., Jr. '24 '52 C&L.209 B.S., J.D. Int. Rev. Dept.
Thorn, Dennis W., & Associates, (AV) 180 N. Michigan Avenue, Suite 2105
Thornber, Judy P. '41 '69 C.145 B.A. L.309 J.D. 5555 N. Sheridan Rd.
Thorne, Deborah L., (AV) '— '83 C.429 B.A. L.146 J.D. [Barnes&T.]
Thorne-Thomsen, Thomas, (AV) '49 '76 C.880 B.A. L.174 J.D. [Applegate&T.]
Thornton, John B. '59 '02 C.602 B.A. L.597 J.D. [Ⓐ Vedder,P.K.&K.]
Thornton, Peter '44 '78 C.93 A.B. L.339 J.D. Assoc. Gen. Coun., Exelon Corp.
Thorp, Marcie '— '94 C.339 B.S. L.146 J.D. [O'Hagan,S.&A.]
Thorpe, Barry K. '41 '69 221 N. LaSalle St., Ste. 2800
Thorpe, Gregory A., (AV) '50 '78 C.339 B.A. L.146 J.D. [Kubasiak,F.R.&R.]
Thorpe, Lynn Urkov '— '79 C.910 B.A. L.146 J.D. [Mora,B.W.&U.]
Thorsen, Robert, (AV) '12 '35 C.597 B.S. L.145 J.D. 200 W. Adams St.
Thorson, Sondra J. '41 '95 C.966 B.S. L.365 J.D.
V.P., Corp. & Intl. Trans. Coun., Leo Burnett Worldwide, Inc.
Thorson, Thomas J. '55 '81 C.339 A.B. L.477 J.D. [Mathai&T.]
Thorstenson, Craig R., (AV) '61 '88 C.1165 B.S. L.339 J.D. [Matkov,S.M.&G.]
Thraya, Tom '— '01 C.037 B.A. L.477 J.D. [Ⓐ Baker&M.]
Threlkeld, Carol '70 '02 C.801 B.A. L.339 J.D. [Ⓐ Ross,D.&B.]
Threlkeld, Sheila '— '85 C.123 B.A. L.803 J.D. Asst. State Atty.
Thrower, Susan E. '62 '87 C.893 B.A. L.896 J.D. De Paul Univ.
Thuma, Raymond Paul '64 '96 C&L.589 B.S., J.D. Appl. Courthouse
Thuma, William A., Jr. '37 '64
C.72 B.A. L.339 LL.B. Sr. V.P. & Tr. Offr., Mid-City Natl. Bk.‡
Thurmond, John C. '— '02 C&L.602 B.A., J.D. [Ⓐ Kirkland&E.]
Thurston, James K. '62 '89 C.659 B.A. L.436 J.D. [Wilson E.M.E.&D.]
Thurston, Robert C. '62 '87 C.477 A.B. L.608 J.D. [Ⓒ Kerns,P.F.&P.]
Thymian, Marcus J. '72 '98
C&L.494 B.S.E.E., J.D. [McDonnell B.H.&B.] (See Pat. Sect.)
Tibble, Matthew '77 '04 C&L.209 B.A., J.D. [Ⓐ Cremer,K.S.&S.]
Tierney, Theodore J., (AV) '40 '64 C&L.190 B.A., J.D. [Vedder,P.K.&K.]
Tiersky, Martin '35 '63 C.339 B.S. L.149 J.D. 2640 Touhy Ave.
Tiersky, Terri S. '59 '91 C.339 B.A. L.365 J.D. 4200 W. Peterson Ave.‡
Tiesi, Angelo F., (AV) '— '87 C.339 B.S. L.424 J.D. [Kirkland&E.]
Tiffany, Aleen R., (BV) '— '93 C.339 B.S. L.365 J.D. [O'Hagan,S.&A.]
Tighe, Ann C., (AV) '40 '73 C.813 B.A. L.597 J.D. [Cotsirilos,T.&S.]

Tighe, Frank P., III, (AV) '60 '86 C.602 B.A. L.424 J.D.
8700 West Bryn Mawr Avenue, Suite 800 South, 60631
Telephone: 630-574-5015 Fax: 630-574-1501
Trials and Appeals in Federal and State Courts.
See Professional Biographies, CHICAGO, ILLINOIS

Tighe, Joseph E., (AV) '57 '81 C&L.597 B.A., J.D. [Tighe,J.E.]
Tighe, Joseph E., P.C., (AV) 111 West Washington Street, Suite 1100
Tigue, Mary E. '58 '84 C.145 A.B. L.569 J.D. Sr. Coun., JMB Realty Corp.
Tilbury, Tara Wagner '— '01 C.399 B.A. L.494 J.D. [Ⓐ Chapman&C.]
Tiliks, Tina Y. '75 '00 C.339 B.A. L.209 J.D. City of Chicago Law Dept.
Tillack, Clay A., (AV) '— '82 C.197 A.B. L.846 J.D. [Schiff H.]
Tiller, Sharon L. '56 '87 C.1191 B.S.Ed. L.352 J.D. Sr. Asst. Atty., Bd. of Educ.
Tilles, Gayle Podell, P.C. '47 '77 C.703 B.A. L.823 J.D. 61 W. Schiller Street
Tillman, Paula S. '49 '79 C.424 B.A. L.209 J.D. Public Def.
Tilly, Laura E., (AV) '59 '84 C.118 B.A. L.477 J.D. [Miner,B.&G.]
Tilson, Joseph E., (AV) '56 '81 C&L.477 B.A., J.D. [Meckler B.&T.]
Tilton, Timothy L., (AV) '23 '50
C.679 B.S.C. L.597 J.D. 100 S. Wacker Dr., Ste. 960 (Pat.)
Timble, Suzanne M., (AV) '45 '82 C.696 B.A. L.597 J.D. V.P., LaSalle Bank
Timm, Kari A. '71 '98 C.589 B.A. L.209 J.D. [Ⓐ Walker W.M.]
Timmel, Richard J. '55 '90 C.959 B.S.N. L.309 J.D. [Ⓒ Mayer,B.R.&M.]
Timmer, Douglas D. '— '95 C.187 B.A. L.893 J.D. [Kirkland&E.]
Timmerman, Scott A. '79 '04 C&L.352 B.S., J.D. [Ⓐ Brinks H.G.&L.]
Timmers, Michael G., P.C., (AV) '— '82 C.145 B.A. L.597 J.D. [Kirkland&E.]

Tinaglia, Michael Lee, (BV) '52 '77 C.597 B.A. L.209 J.D. 161 N. Clark St., Ste. 2550
Tingler, Robert A. '42 '69 C.801 B.S. L.146 J.D. Asst. Atty. Gen./ Franchise Bur. Chf.
Tinglin, Karen Elaine, Law Offices of '68 '97
C.597 B.A. L.209 J.D. 500 North Michigan Ave., Suite 300
Tinker, Catherine E. '55 '80 C.399 B.A. L.910 J.D.
Columbian Model and Exhibit Work
Tinkoff, Bruce N. '57 '82 C.427 B.S. L.146 D.L. 4326 N. Lincoln Ave.
Tinkoff, Paysoff, Jr., (AV) '29 '50 [Tinkoff,P.&D.]
Tinkoff, Popko & DuVal, (AV) 4326 N. Lincoln Ave.
Tipescu, Mircea A. '— '01 C.674 B.S.E. L.273 J.D. [Ⓐ Brinks H.G.&L.]
Tippins, Bedell A., (AV) '48 '78 C.705 B.A. L.365 J.D. [DLPiper R.G.C.U.]
Tipton, Stephanie Wing '— '99 C.1248 B.A. L.146 J.D. [Ⓐ Litchfield C.]
Tisdahl, Elissa A. '— '04 C.67 B.S. L.146 J.D. [Ⓐ Kurasch&K.] (Pat.)
Tish, Martin H., (AV) '57 '81 C&L.597 B.A., J.D. [Neal,G.&E.]
Tishler, Louis B., Jr., (AV) '33 '59 C.477 A.B. L.597 J.D. [Tishler&W.]

Tishler & Wald, Ltd., (AV)
Suite 3000, 200 South Wacker Drive, 60606
Telephone: 312-876-3800 Telecopier: 312-876-3816
Email: tishlerandwald@tishlerandwald.com URL: http://www.tishlerandwald.com
Kurt M. Carlson; Lawrence R. Drumm; David A. Kallick; Alexander D. Kerr, Jr.; Steven A. Migala; Jeffrey B. Rose; Natalia K. Rzepka; Louis B. Tishler, Jr.; Inez K. Tremain; Bruce L. Wald.
General Civil Practice. Bankruptcy and Reorganization, Corporate, Taxation, Estate Planning, Franchise, Probate, Real Estate, Banking, State and Federal Litigation.
Reference: Bank One, Chicago, Chicago, Illinois.
See Professional Biographies, CHICAGO, ILLINOIS

Titus, John E. '66 '94 C.576 B.S.E.E. L.575 J.D. [Jenner&B.]
Titus, Kevin A. '66 '93 C.659 B.S. L.477 J.D. [Ⓐ Tribler O.&M.]
Toal, Helen L. '— '73 C.477 B.A. L.813 J.D. [Ⓒ Foley&L.]
Toback, Alan J., (AV) '58 '82 C.1044 B.A. L.365 J.D. [Lake,T.&D.]
Tober, Stephen J. '64 '91 C.31 B.A. L.893 J.D. 5800 Sears Tower
Tobey, Paul A. '10 '79 L.146 J.D. 1959 W. Hood Ave.‡
Tobin, Craig Daniel, (AV) '54 '80 C.339 B.A. L.146 J.D. [Tobin P.&M.]
Tobin, Edmund M., (AV) '31 '55 C&L.424 B.S.C., J.D. [Hedberg,T.F.&W.]
Tobin, James B., (AV) '— '87 C.473 B.A. L.424 J.D. [Worker,S.&H.]
Tobin, Jeanine F. '39 '81 C.589 B.S.Ed. L.146 J.D. Hyatt Legal Servs.
Tobin, Paul X. '61 '87 C.385 B.A. L.564 J.D.
(adm. in NJ; not adm. in IL) Cheif Leg. Off., Computershare Grp. of Cos.
Tobin, Paula Fuller, (AV) '— '87 C.502 B.S. L.146 J.D. [Ⓐ Tobin P.&M.]

Tobin Petkus & Muñoz, (AV) BB
Three First National Plaza, Suite 1950, 60602-4298 ⊙
Telephone: 312-641-1321 Fax: 312-641-5220
Email: TomasPetkus@barristers.com URL: http://www.barristers.com
Hon. Robert J. Collins (1911-1997); Craig Daniel Tobin; Tomas Petkus; George Muñoz; Paula Fuller Tobin; Frank A. Marino.
Languages: Spanish and Lithuanian.
Trial Practice, International Business Law, International Tax Law, Corporate Law, Commercial Law, Latin American Transactions, Civil Litigation.
Washington, DC Office: 1300 Pennsylvania Avenue, N.W., Suite 700, 20004-3024. Telephone: 202-204-2530. Fax: 202-347-2312.
See Professional Biographies, CHICAGO, ILLINOIS

Todd, Kevin J. '63 '88 C.130 B.A. L.494 J.D. [Hoogendoorn&T.]
Todd, Thomas N. '38 '63 C&L.803 B.A., LL.B. 1 N. LaSalle St.
Todhunter, L. Judson, (AV) '50 '76 C.174 B.A. L.365 J.D. [Defrees&F.]
Todorovic, Elizabeth Matich '62 '87 C.597 B.A. L.94 J.D. [Neal,G.&E.]
Todryk, Jenelle M. '72 '01 C.884 B.S. L.209 J.D. [Ⓐ Skadden,A.S.M.&F.]
Toepper, Amy '— '01 C&L.424 B.A., J.D. [Ⓐ Littler M.]
Toerber, Charlotte C. '49 '77 C.339 B.S. L.209 J.D. Suite 213, 55 W. Delaware
Toffenetti, William L. '50 '85 C.339 B.A. L.209 J.D. States Atty.'s Ofc.
Toft, Jeanne G. '— '92 C.597 B.S.J. L.1000 J.D. Sr. Coun., Chicago Park District
Tokarz, Kenneth James '56 '82 C.1151 B.A. L.365 J.D. 900 W. Jackson Blvd., Ste. 6E
Tolbert, James E., III '59 '87 C.162 B.A. L.352 J.D. Continental Bk.
Toliopoulos, Maria '— '01 C.424 B.A. L.365 J.D. [Ⓐ Daspin&A.]
Toliopoulos, Vasilios '— '01 C.424 B.A. L.209 J.D. [Ⓐ DLPiper R.G.C.U.]
Tolitano, Tami A. '69 '97 C.424 B.B.A. L.365 J.D. [Ⓐ Horowitz&W.]
Toll, Sandi J. '75 '02 C.188 B.S. L.424 J.D. [Ⓐ Jenner&B.]
Tolone, James J. '45 '75 C.46 B.S. L.365 J.D. Hearing Ref., Dept. of Employ. Sec.
Tolpin, Brett M. '71 '96 C.352 B.A. L.285 J.D. [Ⓐ Welsh&K.]
Tolpin, Thomas W., (AV) '45 '70 C.339 B.S. L.30 J.D. [Welsh&K.] (See Pat. Sect.) ⊙
Tolva, Elizabeth Catherine '74 '99 C.880 B.S. L.424 J.D. 311 S. Wacker, Ste. 3000
Tolve, Vincent J., (AV) '49 '74 C.145 A.B. L.477 J.D.
V.P. & Gen. Coun., Lakeside Bank
Tom, Darryl '70 '96 C.188 A.B. L.597 J.D. [Burris,W.S.&T.]
Tomaras, Peter A., (AV) '52 '81 C.238 B.A. L.365 J.D. [Wildman,H.A.&D.]
Tomas, Jennifer A. '75 '02
C.347 B.S. L.1194 J.D.M.S.E.L. Asst. Atty. Gen., Envir. Bur. N.
Tomas, Jerome Peter '73 '01 C.475 B.A. L.424 J.D.
Sr. Atty., Div. of Enforce., U.S. Secs. and Exch. Comm.
Tomasek, Michael F. '— '94 C&L.424 B.S., J.D. [Schiff H.]
Tomashefsky, C. Steven, (AV) '50 '85 C.309 A.B. L.145 J.D. [Jenner&B.]
Tomasik, Timothy S., (AV) '64 '89 C.174 M.S. L.208 J.D. [Clifford]
Tomaso, Alphonse R. '46 '77 C.424 B.A. L.146 J.D. Dep. State's Atty.
Tomassi, Scott C., (AV) '— '88 C&L.424 B.B.A., J.D. [Schiff H.]
Tomczak, Peter '77 '02 C.339 B.S. L.477 J.D. [Ⓐ Baker&M.]
Tomeczko, Michael G. '43 '77 C.707 B.A. L.146 J.D. 7446 N Harlem
Tomei, Richard K., (AV) '— '87 C&L.339 B.S., J.D. [Jones D.]
Tomic, Ivan '71 '00 C&L.46 M.B.A., LL.M. [Avila,T.]
Tomiello, Steven J. '— '93 C&L.209 B.A., J.D. [Ⓐ Schad,D.&S.]
Tominberg, Carl S., (AV) '49 '74 C.1016 B.S.B.A. L.209 J.D. [Laner,M.D.B.L.&T.]
Tomino, Carla A. '51 '80 C.363 A.B. L.424 J.D. 1146 W. Farwell Ave.
Tomkiewicz, Vincent P. '61 '86 C&L.966 B.A., J.D. [Bollinger,R.&G.]
Tomkowiak, Edward R. '55 '80 C.746 B.A. L.339 J.D. [Ⓐ Rusin M.&F.]
Tomlinson, Michael P. '— '03 C.339 B.S. L.46 J.D. [Ⓐ Foley&L.]
Tomlinson, Stephen G., P.C. '— '84
C&L.477 A.B., J.D. [Kirkland&E.] (⊙New York, NY)
Tompkins, Christopher '75 '00 C.128 B.A. L.424 J.D. [Ⓐ Jenner&B.]
Tompsett, William C. '48 '74 C.311 B.A. L.188 J.D. [Mayer,B.R.&M.]
Tomse, Deanne M. '65 '90 C.750 B.A. L.602 J.D.
Associate Counsel, MCI Telecommunications Corporation
Tone, Jeffrey R., (AV) '53 '78 C.674 A.B. L.339 J.D. [Sidley A.B.&W.]
Tone, Michael P., (AV) '49 '74 C.207 B.A. L.790 J.D. [Ross,D.&B.]
Tone, Philip W., (AV) '23 '48 C&L.352 B.A., J.D. 1 IBM Plaza
Toney, Sarah E. '78 '04 C.473 B.S. L.424 J.D. [Ⓐ Drunken D.D.o.I.] (⊙Chicago)
Toney, Sarah E. '78 '04 C.473 B.S. L.424 J.D. [Ⓐ Komie&Assoc.] (⊙Chicago)
Tonn, Robert E. '68 '96 C.112 B.A. L.767 J.D. [Holland&K.]
Tonos, Robert J., (AV) '42 '72 C&L.145 A.B., J.D. [Fisk K.K.&R.]

Toohey, James B. '70 '00 C.1062 B.A. L.424 J.D. [🄰 Fuchs&R.]
Toohey, James K., (AV) '44 '69 C.602 B.B.A. L.597 J.D. [Johnson&B.]
Toole, Arnold E. '65 '93 C.1036 B.A. L.477 J.D. [Toole]
Toole, Cornelius E. '33 '62 C.221 A.B. L.574 LL.B. Cir. J.

Toole Law Offices, LLC
1525 East 53rd Street, 60615
Telephone: 773-684-5730 Fax: 773-684-5740
Email: info@toolelaw.com URL: http://www.toolelaw.com
Arnold E. Toole.
Corporate Law, Contracts, Commercial Transactions, Mergers and Acquisitions, Joint Ventures, Licensing, International Business Transactions, Foreign Investment, Trademarks, Copyrights, Entertainment Law, Employment Law, Civil Rights, Litigation.
See Professional Biographies, CHICAGO, ILLINOIS

Toolis, Shannon A. '71 '97 C.276 B.S.F.S. L.309 J.D. [🄰 Sidley A.B.&W.]
Toomey, James P. '78 '03 C.340 B.A. L.494 J.D.
(adm. in NM; not adm. in IL) 741 N. Dearborn St.
Toomey, John J. '52 '78 C.339 B.S. L.365 J.D. [Arnold&K.]
Toomin, Michael P. '38 '67 C.597 B.A. L.209 J.D. Cir. J.
Toon, Jason M. '— '99 C.734 B.A. L.190 J.D. [🄰 Greenberg T.]
Toosley, Adam C. '74 '02 C&L.339 B.A., J.D. [🄰 FagelHaber]
Tootooian, Michael W. '51 '77 C.424 B.A. L.365 J.D. [🄰 Ancel,G.D.B.D.&R.]
Top, Franklin H., III '— '88 C.385 B.A. L.608 J.D. [Chapman&C.]
Topacio, Charmagne '77 '02 C.424 B.S. L.146 J.D. [🄰 Tressler,S.M.&P.]
Topalis, Panos T., (AV) '63 '89 C.589 B.S. L.146 J.D. [Tribler O.&M.]
Topol, Clive M., (AV) '49 '75 C&L.339 B.S., J.D. [🄲 Hinshaw&C.]
Topoluk, R. Elizabeth '59 '85 C.713 B.A. L.1035 J.D. [🄲 Varga B.L.H.&C.]
Topper, Gary '42 '67 C.339 B.S. L.209 J.D. 19 S. LaSalle
Toppins, Roger K. '56 '80 C&L.502 B.J., J.D.
(adm. in MO; not adm. in IL) Gen. Atty. & Asst. Gen. Coun., SBC
Torain, Ernest W., Jr. '65 '91 C.197 A.B. L.477 J.D. [Vedder,P.K.&K.]
Torbert, Preston M. '43 '74 C.674 A.B. L.309 J.D. [Baker&M.]
Torem, Christopher C. H. '50 '80
C.31 B.A. L.276 J.D. First Dep. Coun., Chicago Park District
Torf, Jason M. '— '98 C&L.339 B.S., J.D. [🄰 Schiff H.]
Tornheim, Milton A., (Ltd.) '29 '62 C.339 B.S. L.365 LL.B. 221 N. LaSalle St.
Toronyi, Kelli A. '— '96 C.238 B.S. L.365 J.D. [🄰 DLPiper R.G.C.U.]
Torosian, Jeffrey S. '68 '93 C.145 B.A. L.990 J.D. [Greenberg T.]
Torrado, René A., Jr., (AV) '47 '73 C.602 B.A. L.276 J.D. [Corboy&D.]
Torre, Andrew '— '04 C.276 B.A. L.145 J.D. [🄰 Goldberg,K.B.B.R.&M.]
Torre, Emily Wolf '— '04 C.276 A.B. L.1565 J.D. [🄰 Sachnoff&W.]
Torres, Jaime L. '55 '81 C.102 B.S. L.339 J.D. 980 N Michigan Ave.
Torres, Jason M. '— '02 C.347 B.S. L.345 J.D. [🄰 Seyfarth S.]
Torres, Jeffrey C. '67 '97 C.602 B.B.A. L.477 J.D. [🄰 McGuirewoods]
Torres, Joseph James '63 '90 C.145 B.A. L.339 J.D. [Winston&S.]
Torres, Julian '41 '66 L.999 J.D.
(adm. in Peru; not adm. in IL) [🄲 Susman&Assoc.]
Torres, Katherine C. '60 '94
C.597 B.A. L.879 J.D. Claims Atty., Fireman's Fund, Interstate Ins.
Torrey, N. Morrison '50 '78
C.914 A.B. L.221 J.D. Assoc. Prof., DePaul Univ. Coll. of Law
Torrey, Suzanne K. '48 '75 C.429 B.A. L.597 J.D. Sr. Corp. Coun., USG Corp.
Torrisi, Dina L. '69 '94 C.339 B.A. L.365 J.D. [🄰 Price T.R.]
Torshen, Jacqueline J. '— '98 C.659 B.A. L.146 J.D. [🄰 Beermann S.W.B.B.G.&L.]

Torshen, Slobig, Genden, Dragutinovich & Axel, Ltd., (AV) 🄱🄱
105 West Adams Street, Suite 3200, 60603
Telephone: 312-372-9282 Fax: 312-372-7914
Email: law@torshen.com URL: http://www.torshen.com
Jerome H. Torshen (1929-2002); Robert J. Slobig; James K. Genden; Zoran Dragutinovich; Bradley J. Axel.
Trial and Appellate Practice in State and Federal Courts. Corporate and Insurance, Zoning and Land Use, Eminent Domain, Real Estate Litigation, Commercial Real Estate Litigation.
See Professional Biographies, CHICAGO, ILLINOIS

Tortorich, Philip '74 '99 C&L.424 B.A., J.D. [🄰 Katten M.R.]
Toth, Bruce A., (AV) '53 '81 C.277 B.S. L.813 J.D. [Winston&S.]
Toth, Richard A. '65 '94 C.339 B.S. L.146 J.D. [🄰 Daley&G.]
Totten, Hugh, (AV) '— '85 C.679 B.A. L.597 J.D. [Perkins C.]

Tottis, Kevin, Law Offices of, (AV) '61 '86 C&L.477 A.B., J.D.
One East Wacker Drive, Suite 2420, 60601
Telephone: 312-923-9620 Fax: 312-923-9626
Email: ktottis@tottislaw.com
Commercial Litigation and Intellectual Property Litigation.
See Professional Biographies, CHICAGO, ILLINOIS

Touchi, Karen Grace '68 '98 C.1060 B.A. L.146 J.D. 745 N. Dearborn St.
Touhy, John M., (AV) '55 '80 C.145 B.A. L.569 J.D. [Mayer,B.R.&M.]
Touloupakis, Andrew '— '00 C.339 B.A. L.365 J.D. [S.G.Thomas]
Touras, George C. '61 '88 C.1106 B.A. L.365 J.D.
Exec. V. P. & Gen. Coun, Equity Group Investments, LLC
Tourek, James M. '32 '57 C.750 B.A. L.209 LL.B.
300 W. Washington St. (⊙Riverside)
Tovrov, Jessica '— '90 C.145 B.A. L.146 J.D. [Arnstein&L.]
Towbin, Steven B., (AV) '49 '75 C.339 B.A. L.209 J.D. [Shaw G.F.G.W.&T.]
Towers, John G. '15 '40 C.339 L.146 LL.B. 3831 W. 109 Pl.
Towne, Carole K., (AV) '51 '77 C.477 B.G.S. L.597 J.D. [Goldberg,K.B.B.R.&M.]
Towne, Michael J. '70 '96 C.339 L.424 J.D. [🄰 Winston&S.]
Towner, Rheanna '77 '04 C&L.597 B.A., J.D. [🄰 Sonnenschein N.&R.]
Towner, Stephanie '— '01 C&L.209 B.F.A., J.D. [🄰 Freeborn&P.]
Townsend, Christopher J., (BV) '66 '91 C.56 B.A. L.352 J.D. [DLPiper R.G.C.U.]
Townsend, Heather O'Farrell '71 '98 C.178 A.B. L.145 J.D. [🄰 Mayer,B.R.&M.]
Townsend, John '70 '98 C.276 B.S.F.S. L.145 J.D. [McDermott W.&E.]
Townsend, Luke '56 '81 C.72 B.A. L.188 J.D. City Finance Council
Townsley, Darrell Shannon '62 '88 C.801 B.S. L.128 J.D. Coun., MCI
Tozer, Elizabeth C. '49 '80 C.475 B.S. L.144 J.D.
Dir., Editorial Servs. & Issues Develop., Amer. Bar Assn.
Tozer, Thomas A. '— '91 C.145 B.A. L.347 J.D. [Kirkland&E.]
Trabaris, Douglas W. '59 '85 C.339 B.A. L.146 J.D. Sr. Atty., AT&T Corp.
Trachtman, Steven B. '48 '73 C.339 B.S. L.146 J.D. Ste. 2215, 100 N. La Salle St.‡
Tracy, Janet L. '51 '81 C.339 B.A. L.209 J.D. [🄲 DLPiper R.G.C.U.]
Tracy, Johanna L. '77 '02 C.597 B.S. L.209 J.D. Asst. State Atty.
Tracy, Robert E. '62 '87 C.750 B.A. L.209 J.D. [🄰 Kroll&R.]
Tracy, Tiffany J. '— '02 C.339 B.A. L.424 J.D. [🄰 Clausen M.]
Trafelet, Janet J. '42 '79 C.597 B.A. L.589 J.D. 120 S. Riverside Plaza
Trafelet, Raymond E. '07 '35 C.339 B.A. L.597 J.D. 11159 Regency Dr.‡
Trafman, Howard T. '68 '96 C.589 B.S. L.209 J.D. 1 S. Wacker, Ste. 3400
Trager, Mark A. '— '94 C&L.339 B.S., J.D. Vice Pres., Equity Residential
Tragesser, Olivia Kate '76 '01 C.973 B.S.B.A. L.209 J.D. City Corp. Coun.
Trainor, David E. '49 '79 C.338 B.S. L.365 J.D. [Tressler,S.M.&P.]
Trainor, Richard D., Law Offices of '49 '76 L.365 J.D. 33 N. Dearborn St., Ste. 1700
Tranen, Daniel E. '70 '97 C.659 B.A. L.339 J.D. [🄰 Wilson E.M.E.&D.]
Trapani, Michelle C. '67 '92 C&L.339 B.A., J.D.
(adm. in CA; not adm. in IL) Sr. Corp. Coun., Oracle USA, Inc.

Trapp, Jamie M., & Associates, (AV) '56 '81 C.927 B.A. L.209 J.D.
221 North La Salle Street, Suite 2910, 60601
Telephone: 312-368-1444 Fax: 312-263-1108 URL: http://www.lawyers.com/jamietrapp
Email: trapplaw@yahoo.com URL: http://www.trapplaw.com
Associates: Douglas C. Dorn; Jeremy L. Geller.
Personal Injury, Catastrophic Accidents and Injuries, Head Trauma, Spinal Cord Injuries, Motorcycle Accidents, Tort Litigation, Medical Malpractice, Birth Defects, Physician and Obstetric Malpractice, Surgical Malpractice, Airplane Crash Litigation, Automobile Accidents, Dog Bites, Railroad Accidents, Sexual Abuse, Wrongful Death, Construction Negligence.
See Professional Biographies, CHICAGO, ILLINOIS

Traub, Richard J., (AV) '— '87 C&L.602 B.A., J.D. [Freeborn&P.]
Traul, Robert Eric '— '93 C.259 B.A. L.146 J.D. [Querrey&H.]
Trausch, James E., (AV) '57 '82 C.602 B.A. L.146 J.D. [Jaros,T.&O.]
Traver, Jerry M. '41 '68 C.477 B.B.A. L.802 J.D.
(adm. in TX; not adm. in IL) 400 E. Randolph‡
Travers, Timothy K., (AV) '— '83 C.424 B.B.A. L.146 J.D. [Tenney&B.]
Traversa, Halyna M. '— '84 C.424 B.S. L.126 J.D.
V.P. & Gen. Coun., Rexam Beverage Can Co.
Travis, Seth A. '72 '96 C.1138 B.B.A. L.597 J.D. [Jenner&B.]
Travis, Sherrie, (AV) '— '76 C.339 B.A. L.146 J.D. [Wildman,H.A.&D.]
Travis, Tamara Irwin '— '98 C.347 B.A. L.813 J.D. [🄰 Jones D.]
Travis, Thomas G., (AVⓉ) '47 '72 C.674 A.B. L.178 J.D.
(adm. in NJ; not adm. in IL) [Sandler,T.&R.]
(⊙L.A., San Fran., CA; Wash., DC; Miami, FL; New York, NY)
Traxler, Seth '— '97 C.378 B.A. L.597 J.D. [Kirkland&E.]
Traynor, Cynthia D. '— '88 C.694 A.B. L.365 J.D. [🄰 Querrey&H.] (⊙Wheaton)
Treacy-Maloney, Sheila '59 '86 C.209 B.A. L.365 J.D. Off. of The Public Guardian
Treadway, Anne E. '53 '77 C.518 A.B. L.215 J.D.
(adm. in MI; not adm. in IL) Gen. Atty., TTX Co.
Treat, Jonathon '71 '03 C.338 B.S. L.365 J.D. [🅂 Winston&S.]
Treece, John W., (AV) '52 '78 C.309 B.A. L.178 J.D. [Sidley A.B.&W.]
Trees, George S., Jr. '43 '68 C.31 A.B. L.339 J.D. Harris Trust & Savings Bk.
Treger, Tracy L. '— '93 C.659 B.A. L.146 J.D. [Gardner C.&D.]
Trehan, Amit K. '— '04 C.103 A.B. L.477 J.D.
(adm. in NY; not adm. in IL) [🄰 Mayer,B.R.&M.] (⊙New York, NY)
Treimer, Ann L. '59 '85 C.221 B.S. L.352 J.D. McDermott Will & Emery
Trela, Constantine L., Jr., (AV) '55 '79 C&L.597 B.A., J.D. [Sidley A.B.&W.]
Tremain, Inez K. '40 '80 C.823 B.A. L.424 J.D. [Tishler&W.]
Tremblay, E. Jason '00 C.264 B.A. L.146 J.D. [🄰 Arnstein&L.]
Tremko, Norbert J. '23 '51 C.602 L.365 LL.B. 5770 N. Rogers Ave.
Trench, W. Scott '73 '99 C.36 B.S. L.209 J.D. [🄰 Hunt]
Trenda, Carolyn M. '77 '02 C&L.602 B.A., J.D. [🄰 McGuirewoods]
Trenda, Regis J. '45 '69 C.177 A.B. L.602 J.D. Asst. Gen. Coun., Borg-Warner Inc.
Trepel, John E. '— '79 C.966 B.S. L.365 J.D. 5844 W. Irving Park Rd.
Tresnowski, Bernard Richard '32 '00 C.477 B.S. L.146 J.D. Staff Atty.
Tressler, Jay H., (AV) '42 '67 C.210 A.B. L.339 J.D. [Tressler,S.M.&P.]

Tressler, Soderstrom, Maloney & Priess, (AV)
233 South Wacker Drive, Sears Tower 22nd Floor, 60606 ⊙
Telephone: 312-627-4000 FAX: 312-627-1717
Email: tsmp@tsmp.com URL: http://www.tsmp.com
Members of Firm: Jay H. Tressler; Robert S. Soderstrom; Patrick E. Maloney; Howard K. Priess II; Daniel R. Formeller; William A. Kindorf, III; Judith Fournie Helms; David E. Trainor; Shaun McParland Baldwin; Jacqueline A. Criswell; Stephen T. Grossmark; Michael W. Morrison; John P. Maniatis; Jennifer Jerit Johnson; Thomas K. Hanekamp; Mary E. McPherson (Resident Member, Los Angeles, California Office); John H. Huston; Dion J. Sartorio; James R. Murray; Michael J. Duffy; Maureen A. Coleman; James K. Borcia; James A. Pinderski; Durga M. Bharam; David L. Kabat; Daniel J. Cunningham; Catherine Connelly-Warren; Robert D. Kolar; Robert J. Heyne; James A. Knox, Jr.; Katherine E. Tammaro; Mark T. Banovetz; Michael J. Polachek (Resident Member, Wheaton Office); Bruce M. Engel; Todd S. Schenk; Paul S. White (Resident Member, Los Angeles, California Office); Mark R. Vespole (Resident Member, Newark, New Jersey Office); Andrew S. Boris; Ralph J. Kooy; John W. Carver; David Simantob (Resident Member, Los Angeles, California Office); Wen-Shin Cheng; Carrie E. Cope; Linda Tai Hoshide (Resident Associate, Los Angeles, California Office); Linda Bondi Morrison (Resident Member, Costa Mesa, California Office); Joanna L. Crosby (Resident Member, Newark, New Jersey Office); Theresa E. Mullen (Certified by the Supreme Court of New Jersey as a Civil Trial Attorney) (Resident Member, Newark, New Jersey Office); Katherine Klima Liner (Resident Member, Costa Mesa, California Office); Donald W. McCormick (Resident Member, Los Angeles, California Office); Robert J. Fettweis (Resident Member, Newark, New Jersey Office); Ian R. Stevenson; Steven R. McMannon; Harry E. Bartosiak (Resident Member, Wheaton Office); Janelle K. Christensen; Michaela L. Sozio (Resident Member, Los Angeles, California Office); Barry L. Moss (Resident Member, Bolingbrook Office); Steven P. Bloomberg (Resident Member, Bolingbrook Office); George A. Marchetti (Resident Member, Bolingbrook Office); David J. Freeman (Resident Member, Bolingbrook Office); James Boan (Resident Member, Bolingbrook Office). Of Counsel: Katherine Streicher Arnold; Sherrin Ross Ingram; Bernard E. Drew, Jr.; C. David Sullivan; C. Jackson Darnall (Resident Of Counsel, Wheaton Office). Associates: Pete V. Albanis; Jeffrey Mark Alperin; Lara A. Anderson (Resident Associate, Bolingbrook Office); James P. Arrigo (Resident Associate, Bolingbrook Office); Jeffrey D. Barclay; Daneen Fitzpatrick Berres; Heather M. Brown-Smith (Resident Associate, Costa Mesa, California Office); Kristen S. Burns; Marcos G. Cancio; Rina Carmel (Resident Associate, Los Angeles, California Office); Jason M. Craft; Matthew J. Devereux; Thomas G. Drennan; Jill Jennings Drzewiecki; Donald E. Elder; Bonny Garcha; Stephen M. Green (Resident Associate, Los Angeles, California Office); Adam C. Hackett (Resident Associate, Costa Mesa, California Office); Katherine L. Haennicke; James C. Hauser; Karen L. Hedeen; John A. Husmann; Jamie C. Kandalepas; Basileios Katris; Meghan M. Kelly; Dale R. Kurth; Maureen LePochat (Resident Associate, Newark, New Jersey Office); Timothy R. Lessman; Cari-ann R. Levine (Resident Associate, Newark, New Jersey Office); Telly J. Liapis; Toria L. Lund; Devin C. Maddox; Erin L. Majka; Kathy Karaboyas Malamis; Katherine E. Mast (Resident Associate, Los Angeles, California Office); Christian D. Molloy (Resident Associate, Los Angeles, California Office); Maurine J. Neiberg; Burke J. Nihill; John M. O'Driscoll; David J. Olmstead; Craig Gordon Penrose; Barbora Pulmanova (Not admitted in IL; Resident Associate, Costa Mesa, California Office); Andrew J. Purcell; Cari Jay Raymond; Joe Sadler; Huma P. Shah; Connie J. Sheng (Resident Associate, Los Angeles, California Office); Shevonn K. Smith; Evan B. Sorensen (Resident Associate, Los Angeles, California Office); Heather C. Sullivan; Kathleen Ann Sweitzer; Dean J. Tatooles; Ryan Taylor; Charmagne Topacio; Brian E. Turnauer (Resident Associate, Los Angeles, California Office); Dana M. Ugolini; Kelly D. Waller; David O. Yuen.
General Civil Litigation and Trial Practice, Insurance, Reinsurance, Litigation, Insurance Bad Faith, Appellate Practice, Business Litigation, Business Transactions, Class Action Defense, Commercial Litigation, Complex Litigation, Directors and Officers Liability, Construction Law, Architects and Engineers, Fidelity and Surety, Real Estate Litigation and Transactions, Alternative Dispute Resolution, Product Liability, Intellectual Property, Internet Law, Electronic Commerce, Environmental Law, Asbestos Litigation, Health Care, ERISA, Labor and Employment, Technology Law, Securities Litigation, Health Care, Bankruptcy, Advertising Law, Personal Injury, Trusts and Estates, Contracts, Professional Liability, Regulatory, White Collar Crime, Corporate Law, Mergers and Acquisitions, Commodities, Condominium and Common Interest Community Law, Municipal Law.
Wheaton, Illinois Office: 2100 Manchester Road, Suite 950, 60187. Telephone: 630-668-2800. FAX: 630-668-3003.
Bolingbrook, Illinois Office: 305 West Briarcliff Road, Suite 201, 60440-0858. Telephone: 630-759-0800. FAX: 630-759-8504.

(This Listing Continued)

Tressler, Soderstrom, Maloney & Priess (Continued)

Newark, New Jersey Office: 744 Broad Street, Suite 1510, 07102. Telephone: 973-848-2900. Fax: 973-623-0405.
Los Angeles, California Office: 1901 Avenue of the Stars, Suite 450, 90067. Telephone: 310-203-4800. Fax: 310-203-4850.
Costa Mesa, California Office: 3070 Bristol Street, Suite 450, 92626. Telephone: 714-429-2900. Fax: 714-429-2901.

See Professional Biographies, CHICAGO, ILLINOIS

Trester, Julie L. ... '64 '91 C&L.339 B.A., J.D. [Meckler B.&T.]
Treston, Sherry S. ... '50 '83 C.679 B.A. L.209 J.D. [Sidley A.B.&W.]
Tretter, Frances "Alexis" ... '— '04 C.383 B.A. L.880 J.D. [🄰 Foley&L.]
Treumann, Julie E. ... '— '01 C.747 B.A. L.424 J.D. [🄰 Ungaretti&H.]
Treumann & Podbelsek, P.C. ... 33 N. La Salle St.
Trevino, Daniel A. ... '75 '99 C.339 B.A. L.209 J.D. [🄰 Hinshaw&C.]
Trevino, Daniel M. ... '— '02 C.589 B.S. L.339 J.D. [🄰 Kirkland&E.]

Trevino, Fern N., Law Offices of, (AV) '45 '83 C&L.424 B.A., J.D.
120 North LaSalle Street, Suite 1050, 60602
Telephone: 312-630-4491 Fax: 312-630-9281 URL: http://www.chicagoemploymentlawyer.net
Email: ferntrevino@chicagoemploymentlawyer.net URL: http://www.ferntrevinolaw.com
Associates: Alenna K. Bolin; Antoinette Choate.
Employment Law, Employment Discrimination, Sexual Harassment, Retaliatory Discharge, Family and Medical Leave Act, Severance Agreements, Fair Labor Standards Act, Qui Tam, Whistleblower Law, Wrongful Termination and Civil Rights.

See Professional Biographies, CHICAGO, ILLINOIS

Trew, Mary S. ... '55 '81 C.932 B.S. L.475 J.D. Exec. Dir., Pro Bono Advocates

Trexler, Bushnell, Giangiorgi, Blackstone & Marr, Ltd., (AV)
The Clark Adams Building, 105 West Adams Street Suite 3600, 60603-6299
Telephone: 312-704-1890 Fax: 312-704-8023
Email: info@trexlaw.com URL: http://www.trexlaw.com
Richard R. Trexler (1906-1995); Richard A. Giangiorgi; Raiford A. Blackstone, Jr.; David J. Marr; Linda L. Palomar; James R. Foley; James A. O'Malley; Timothy M. McCarthy; Paige A. Kitzinger; Robert J. Depke; Lewis T. Steadman, Sr.
Intellectual Property Law including Patent, Trademark, Trade Secrets, Copyright, Unfair Competition Law, all phases including Prosecution, Licensing and Litigation.

See Professional Biographies, CHICAGO, ILLINOIS

Tribbett, Charles A., III '55 '81
C.436 B.A. L.893 J.D. Mng. Dir., Russell Reynolds Assoc., Inc.
Tribler, Willis R., (AV) ... '34 '60 C.98 B.S. L.339 J.D. [Tribler O.&M.]

Tribler Orpett & Meyer, P.C., (AV) BR
30 North La Salle Street Suite 2200, 60602
Telephone: 312-201-6400 Fax: 312-201-6401
Email: admin@tribler.com URL: http://www.tribler.com
Daniel D. Drew; Harlene G. Matyas; Michael J. Meyer; Mitchell A. Orpett; H. Wesley Sunu; Panos T. Topalis; Willis R. Tribler; Douglas C. Crone;—Daniel J. Arnett; Paul R. Gamperl; Jennifer L. Jacobs; Jennifer H. Kay; David M. Lewin; Arla G. Rosenthal; Lawrence R. Scanlon; Kevin A. Titus; Stephen S. Weiss.
General Civil Trial and Appellate Practice, including Professional Liability, Insurance Coverage, Reinsurance, Environmental, Municipal, School Board, Construction, Product Liability, Premises Liability, Petroleum Industry Practice, Labor and Employment, General Tort Defense, Unfair Competition, Corporate, Commercial and Business Law, Real Estate, and Administration.

See Professional Biographies, CHICAGO, ILLINOIS

Trieger, Abraham, (AV) ... '51 '75 C.597 B.A. L.424 J.D. [Levenfeld P.]
Trienens, Howard J., (AV) ... '23 '49 C&L.597 B.S., J.D. [Sidley A.B.&W.]
Trier, Michael P. ... '49 '86 C.966 B.A. L.145 J.D. [Lord,B.&B.]
Triffler, Fay L. ... '50 '79 C.966 B.A. L.424 J.D. Sr. Coun., Bank One Corp. (Law Dept.)
Trimarco, Christine L. ... '72 '97 C.209 B.A. L.365 J.D. [🄰 Cassiday,S.&G.]
Trio, Edward A. ... '52 '77 C.602 B.B.A. L.300 J.D. [Gould&R.]
Triplett, Rosemary A. ... '— '93 C.1016 B.S.B.M. L.325 J.D. P.O. Box 23501
Triptow, Janice Lynn ... '61 '87 C.550 B.A. L.209 J.D. [🄰 Menges&M.]
Tristan, Gerardo, Jr. ... '70 '02 C.103 A.B. L.209 J.D. Asst. State Atty.
Trittipo, Walter E., (AV) ... '36 '61 C&L.477 B.B.A., J.D. [W.E.Trittipo]
Trittipo, Walter E., P.C., (AV) ... 33 N. La Salle St., Ste. 2020
Trizna, Robert J. ... '52 '79 C.602 A.B. L.365 J.D. [Schuyler,R.&Z.]
Trkla, Kathryn M., (AV) ... '— '83 C.145 B.A. L.597 J.D. [Foley&L.]
Troesken-Koczur, Lora ... '69 '97 C.338 B.S. L.146 J.D. 205 W. Randolph
Trofa, Gretchen Anne ... '63 '88 C.228 A.B. L.597 J.D. [Barack F.K.P.&N.]
Trofa, M. John ... '— '81 C.93 B.A. L.339 J.D. [Chapman&C.]
Troglia, Brian W. ... '67 '92 C&L.339 B.A., J.D. [Stahl C.C.]
Troiani, John ... '52 '84 C.338 B.S. L.365 J.D. 1 N. Franklin St.
Trop, Harriet ... '48 '78 C.597 B.S. L.209 J.D. 2130 N. Racine Ave.‡
Trost, Eileen Bannon, (AV) ... '51 '76 C.1100 B.A. L.494 J.D. [Sonnenschein N.&R.]

Trott Nelson, P.C.
(See Oak Brook)

Trovato, Nicholas F. ... '— '59 C&L.209 B.S., J.D. Dep. Corp. Coun.
Trowbridge, Penelope C. ... '60 '87 C.788 A.B. L.228 J.D. 3517 N. Marshfield Ave.
Troxclair, Jeffrey L. ... '— '04 C.576 B.A. L.602 J.D. [🄰 Chapman&C.]
Troy, Terry ... '49 '75 C.477 B.A. L.209 J.D. Asst. Atty. Gen.
Truax, James C. ... '57 '83 C.589 B.S. L.146 J.D. 100 W. Monroe St., Ste. 2001
Truax, Terrence J. ... '61 '88 C.259 B.A. L.575 J.D. [Jenner&B.]
Trubitt, Ari M. ... '62 '87 C.339 B.A. L.365 J.D. [🄰 Borovsky&E.]
Trubow, George B. ... '33 '58 C&L.477 A.B., J.D. Prof. of Law, John Marshall Law Sch.
Trucco, Michael T., (AV) ... '57 '82 C.98 B.S. L.209 J.D. [Stamos&T.]
Trudell, Jeanette K. '78 '04 C.477 A.B. L.145 J.D.
(adm. in NY; not adm. in IL) [🄰 Goldberg,K.B.R.&M.]
True, John C. ... '36 '70 C.339 B.S. L.209 J.D. Sears, Roebuck & Co.
Trueblood, Amy K. ... '78 '02 C.309 A.B. L.893 J.D. [🄰 Jenner&B.]
Truesdale, Tracey L. ... '67 '91 C.530 B.A. L.146 J.D. [Ogletree,D.N.S.&S.]
Truglio, Fred ... '57 '84 C.4 B.B.A. L.365 J.D. 1 N Franklin St.
Truitt, Craig C. ... '61 '92 C.473 B.A. L.146 J.D. [Truitt&T.]
Truitt, David M., (AV) ... '33 '62 C.473 B.S. L.146 J.D. [Truitt&T.]
Truitt, Richard B. ... '05 '31 L.146 LL.B. 1642 E. 56th St.‡
Truitt & Truitt, (AV) ... 1642 E. 56th St.
Trujillo, Luisa F., (BV) ... '68 '93 C.188 B.A. L.910 J.D. [Bollinger,R.&G.]
Trull, Lisa A. ... '— '94 C.104 A.B. L.146 J.D. [🄰 Alholm,M.K.H.&O.]
Trumbull-Harris, Jill R. ... '75 '01 C.37 B.A. L.597 J.D. [🄰 Bartlit B.H.P.&S.]
Trummel, Rachael M. ... '71 '98 C.145 B.A. L.880 J.D. [McDermott W.&E.]
Trunk, Wm. L. ... '29 '55 C&L.209 B.S., LL.B. 5151 N. Harlem
Trunkett, Kerry S., (AV) ... '59 '84 C.93 B.A. L.365 J.D. [Walinski&T.]
Truskowski, John B., (AV) ... '45 '70 C.339 B.S. L.145 J.D. [🄲 Lord,B.&B.]
Trutenko, Nicholas N. ... '55 '80 C.424 B.S. L.589 J.D. Asst. States Atty.
Truty, John E. "Jay" ... '74 '99 C.340 B.A. L.502 J.D. [🄰 Bell,B.&L.]
Tryban, Esther Elizabeth, (BV) ... '58 '89 C.1016 B.S. L.145 J.D. Senior Counsel
Tryboski, Thomas K. ... '61 '86 C.339 B.S. L.209 J.D. [Robbins,S.&P.]
Trybus, Steven R., (AV) ... '60 '86 C.46 B.S.Ch.E. L.146 J.D. [Jenner&B.] (Pat.)
Tryzna, Jennifer M. ... '67 '02 C.339 B.A. L.146 J.D. Asst. Corp. Coun.

Tsai, Diana ... '74 '00 C.145 B.A. L.339 J.D. [🄰 Schwartz C.]
Tsantilis, Peter ... '78 '03 C&L.424 B.B.A., J.D. 33 N. LaSalle St., Ste. 2500
Tsoris, Stephen A., (AV) ... '57 '82 C.436 B.A. L.188 J.D. [Gardner C.&D.]
Tsoumas, Theodore Joseph, (AV) '30 '53
C&L.597 B.S.L., J.D. 200 East Randolph Drive, Suite 7300
Tsoutsias, John A. ... '74 '99 C.473 B.A. L.424 J.D. [🄰 Fuchs&R.]
Tsu, Brian P. ... '78 '04 C.93 B.S. L.201 J.D. PricewaterhouseCoopers
Tsukuno, Paul A., (BV) ... '51 '78 C.339 B.S. L.365 J.D. Asst. States Atty.
Tu, Amy '67 '96 C.914 B.A. L.45 J.D.
(adm. in AR; not adm. in IL) Asst. Corp Secy & Coun., The Boeing Co.
Tuber, Harold F. ... '16 '41 C&L.209 LL.B. 200 N. La Salle St.
Tuchman, Michael J., (AV) ... '58 '84 C.589 B.S. L.339 J.D. [Levenfeld P.]
Tucker, Creed T., (AV) ... '56 '85 C.339 A.B. L.589 J.D. [Tucker B.R.&M.]
Tucker, Debra J. ... '68 '95 C.339 B.S. L.145 J.D. [Tucker]
Tucker, Harve D. ... '46 '70 C.597 B.S. L.424 J.D. Tax Specialist
Tucker, Jessica B. ... '59 '85 C.477 B.B.A. L.1187 J.D. [🄲 Tucker B.R.&M.]
Tucker, M. Jeffrey ... '65 '90 C.365 B.A. L.624 J.D. 3500 Three 1st Nat. Plz.
Tucker, Martin B. ... '— '01 C.1161 B.A. L.209 J.D. [🄰 F.L.Ingram]
Tucker, Robert G. ... '— '92 C.1365 B.A. L.966 J.D. [Chapman&C.]
Tucker, Tiffanie B. ... '75 '00 C.999 B.S. L.1439 J.D. [🄰 Cassiday,S.&G.]

Tucker Bower Robin & Merker, LLC, (AV) BR
200 West Madison Suite 1900, 60606
Telephone: 312-346-4700 Fax: 312-346-4711
Email: firm@tbrmlaw.com URL: http://www.tbrmlaw.com
Creed T. Tucker; Robert A. Bower; Barry A. Robin; Timothy G. Merker;—Rebecca A. Weber; Ceasar J. Melidis; Nancy J. Meserow. Of Counsel: Randall E. Server; Mary Ellen Rosen Swanson; Jessica B. Tucker.
Insurance Coverage and Defense, Products Liability, Medical Malpractice, Labor and Employment, Civil Trial Practice, Construction Law, Liquor Liability, Toxic Torts, Medical Device Liability, Directors and Officers, Errors and Omissions.

See Professional Biographies, CHICAGO, ILLINOIS

Tucker Firm, The, LLC ... 1723 N. Halsted St.
Tuerk, Edward B. ... '73 '02 C.339 B.S. L.209 [🄰 McDermott W.&E.]
Tueting, William F., (AV) ... '— '69 C&L.178 B.S., LL.B. [Chapman&C.]
Tuhey, John Matthew '68 '00
C.174 B.A. L.146 J.D. Dep. Gen. Coun., Click Commerce, Inc.
Tuite, Patrick A., (AV) ... '— '61 C&L.339 B.A., LL.B. [🄲 Arnstein&L.]
Tullio, Christine C.A. '52 '81 C.156 B.A. L.128 J.D.
(adm. in PA; not adm. in IL) F.D.I.C.
Tullman, Howard A., (AV) ... '45 '70 C&L.597 B.A., J.D. Eager Enterprises, Inc.
Tully, John J., Jr. ... '69 '94 C.976 B.A. L.597 J.D. [Winston&S.]
Tully, John P. ... '36 '70 C.46 B.Ed. L.209 J.D. Presiding Jus., Appl. Ct.
Tully, Martin T. ... '— '90 C.339 B.A. L.209 J.D. [Katten M.R.]
Tully, Paul S. ... '67 '00 C.234 B.S. L.365 J.D. [McDonnell B.H.&B.] (See Pat. Sect.)
Tully, Therese L. ... '67 '96 C.1154 B.S. L.424 J.D. [🄰 Scandaglia&R.]
Tully, Thomas M., (AV) ... '37 '63 C.363 B.Sc. L.209 J.D. 33 N. Dearborn, Ste. 2450
Tulupan, L. Zoe ... '— '82 C.339 B.A. L.365 J.D. 6323 N. Minnehaha Ave.
Tumialan, Rosa ... '70 '94 C.502 B.A. L.424 J.D. [🄰 Dykema G.P.]
Tun, Marla ... '76 '01 C&L.339 B.S., J.D. [🄰 Sidley A.B.&W.]
Tunney, Anthony J., (AV) ... '47 '77 C.1268 B.A. L.365 J.D. [Price T.R.]
Tuohy, Joseph P. ... '33 '63 C&L.424 B.S., J.D. Hearing Offr., Ill. Commerce Comm.
Tuohy, Thomas W., (AV) ... '— '82 C&L.209 B.A., J.D. [Tuohy]
Tuohy Law Offices, (AV) ... 218 N. Jefferson Street, Suite 300
Tupper, Richard J. ... '57 '86 C.114 B.A. L.309 J.D. [Cornfield&F.]
Turano, Guerino J. ... '29 '54 C&L.209 B.S.C., LL.B. 2960 North Lake Shore Drive
Turansick, Michael F. '57 '83 C&L.262 B.A., J.D.
(adm. in NY; not adm. in IL) [Fragomen,D.B.&L.]
Turcy, Philip E. ... '56 '82 C.184 B.A. L.209 J.D. [🄰 Goldberg,W.&C.]
Turgeon, Michael J. ... '68 '94 C.436 B.S. L.365 J.D. [Vedder,P.K.&K.] (Pat.)
Turiello, Michael P. ... '70 '96 C.98 B.S. L.884 J.D. [🄰 Pretzel&S.]
Turk, Julia A. ... '68 '97 C.477 B.A. L.424 J.D. [🄰 DLPiper R.G.C.U.]
Turk, Mary Lee, (AV) ... '55 '80 C.347 B.A. L.145 J.D. [McDermott W.&E.]
Turley, Elizabeth ... '52 '80 C.477 B.A. L.902 J.D. Bank of America
Turnbaugh, Amy Lynn ... '73 '00 C.697 B.A. L.705 J.D. 210 W. Illinois St.
Turner, A. Kelly ... '66 '93 C.103 A.B. L.94 J.D. [Lord,B.&B.]
Turner, Allen M., (AV) ... '37 '61 C.966 B.B.A. L.145 J.D. 200 W. Madison, 38th Fl.
Turner, Cameron D. ... '72 '97 C.602 B.A. L.209 J.D. [🄰 Segal M.S.&M.]
Turner, Christopher M.R. ... '— '96 C.918 B.A. L.813 J.D. [Kirkland&E.]
Turner, Dale R., (AV) ... '46 '72 C&L.339 B.S., J.D. Acting Gen. Coun. to Comr. of Bks.
Turner, Howard M., (AV) ... '36 '60 C&L.145 A.B., J.D. [🄲 Gould&R.]
Turner, Jeffrey N. ... '78 '04 C.339 B.S.G.E. L.326 J.D. [🄰 Leydig,V.&M.]
Turner, John J. ... '30 '55 C&L.209 B.S., J.D. 527 S. Wells St.
Turner, Joseph S. ... '61 '87 C&L.575 B.A., J.D. [Seyfarth S.]
Turner, Patrick C. ... '64 '90 C.589 B.S. L.365 J.D. 527 S. Wells St.
Turner, Patrick J. ... '57 '83 C.347 B.S. L.1119 J.D. Dynaprop Investment, Ltd.
Turner, Paul S. ... '53 '78 C&L.309 B.A., J.D. [McCullough,C.&L.]

Turner, Phillip A., Law Offices of '54 '78 C.436 B.A. L.966 J.D.
100 West Monroe Street, Suite 2204, 60603-1925
Telephone: 312-899-0009 Fax: 312-899-8087
Email: pturner98@sbcglobal.net
Language: Spanish.
Civil Practice, Criminal Law, Trial Practice, Medical Malpractice, Administrative Law.

See Professional Biographies, CHICAGO, ILLINOIS

Turner, Rhonda V. ... '— '04 C.14 B.A. L.1565 J.D. [🄰 Lawrence,K.S.&U.]
Turner, Scott E. ... '68 '95 C.37 B.A. L.597 J.D. [🄲 Ross,D.&B.]
Turner, Thomas P., IV '60 '85 C.674 A.B. L.966 J.D.
(adm. in WI; not adm. in IL) Staff Atty.
Turner, William E., II ... '70 '95 C.149 B.A. L.597 J.D. [Barack F.K.P.&N.]
Turoff, Alison G. ... '76 '02 C.1119 B.A. L.597 J.D. [🄰 Colky&K.]
Turoff, Michael R., (AV) ... '— '64 C.477 B.B.A. L.145 J.D. [Arnstein&L.]
Turotsy, Barbara ... '62 '87 C.31 B.A. L.945 J.D. [🄲 Sudekum,C.&S.]
Turow, Scott, (AV) ... '49 '78 C.31 B.A. L.309 J.D. [Sonnenschein N.&R.]
Turpin, Carl K. ... '50 '88 C.329 B.A. L.209 J.D. [🄰 Greene&L.]
Tutaj, James P., (BV) ... '64 '93 C.436 B.A. L.365 J.D. [🄰 Hilfman,M.&B.]
Tuttle, Patti L. ... '49 '93 C.597 B.A. L.424 J.D. [🄰 Cogan&M.]
Tweeton, Jennifer L. ... '— '05 C.494 B.A. L.1018 J.D. [🄰 Iwan C.H.H.&V.]
Tyksinski, Peter R. '68 '03 C.967 B.A. L.209 J.D.
Mng. Director, Legal Recruiting, Spherion Professional Services Grp.
Tyksinski, Terence J., (AV) ... '33 '62 C.475 A.B. L.597 J.D. [T.Tyksinski]
Tyksinski, Terence, Law Offices of, (AV) ... 77 W. Washington St., Ste. 408

Tyler, Katharine Barr '56 '81 C.339 B.A. L.365 J.D.
Suite 725 - 53 West Jackson Boulevard, 60604
Telephone: 312-663-1311 Fax: 312-663-1312
Email: KBTylerlaw@aol.com URL: http://www.lawyers.com/katharinebarrtyler

(This Listing Continued)

Tyler, Katharine Barr (Continued)

Residential Real Estate, Commercial Real Estate, Estate Planning, Real Estate Tax Rate Objections.
See Professional Biographies, CHICAGO, ILLINOIS

Tyma, Stephen L. .... '50 '84 C.475 B.A. L.477 J.D. [S.L.Tyma]

Tyma, Stephen L., P.C.
105 West Madison Street, Suite 2200, 60602-4648
Telephone: 312-372-3920 Fax: 312-372-3780 URL: http://www.tymalaw.com
Email: STYMA@TYMALAW.COM URL: http://www.lawyers.com/tymalaw
Stephen L. Tyma.
Federal and State Litigation, Trial and Appellate Practice, Business Law, Commercial Law, Construction Law, Contracts, Corporate Law, Environmental Law, Family Law, Divorce, Partnership Law, Probate, Professional Liability, Real Estate, RICO, General Practice.
See Professional Biographies, CHICAGO, ILLINOIS

Tyman, Annette .... '69 '05 C.347 B.S. L.424 J.D. [Ⓐ Seyfarth S.]
Tymm, William E., (AV) .... '— '70 C&L.209 B.S., J.D. [Kirkland&E.]
Tynan, Monica Maria .... '— '92 C.339 B.S. L.146 J.D. [Ⓐ Quarles&B.]
Tyner, Randall Louis .... '57 '01 C&L.424 B.A., J.D. Asst. State's Atty.
Tyree, Colleen T. .... '61 '86 C&L.424 B.B.A., J.D. 111 W. Washington St.
Tyrrell, Michael A., (AV) '46 '73
C.602 B.A. L.477 J.D. 3150 N. Lake Shore Drive, Unit 24 A
Tyrrell, Ross, (Ltd.), (AV) .... '41 '67 C.742 B.A. L.146 J.D. 111 W. Wash. St.
Tyson, Alma Learetta '51 '91 C.339 B.A. L.329 J.D.
10540 South Western Avenue, #310
Tyson, Lorraine M. .... '— '99 C.597 B.A. L.339 J.D. [Ⓐ Mayer,B.R.&M.]
Tzanetopoulos, George J., (AV) .... '60 '85 C.145 B.A. L.477 J.D. [Mayer,B.R.&M.]
Tzinberg, Scott William .... '68 '96 C.966 B.A. L.365 J.D. 11 S. Lasalle, Ste. 2600
Uber, Edw. J. .... '15 '55 C.597 B.S. L.209 J.D. 5509 W. Windsor Ave. #2‡
Udoni, Joseph O., (AV) .... '23 '51 C&L.424 Ph.B., J.D. 221 N. LaSalle St.
Ueland, Kevin S. .... '— '02 C.473 B.A. L.209 J.D. [Ⓐ Kirkland&E.]
Uffelman, Sara G. .... '76 '04 C.578 B.A. L.209 J.D. [Ⓐ Meckler B.&T.]
Ugaste, Daniel J., (BV) .... '63 '88 C.393 B.A. L.209 J.D. [Nyhan,P.B.K.&L.]
Ugolini, Dana M. .... '70 '03 C.339 B.A. L.424 J.D. [Ⓐ Tressler,S.M.&P.]
Uhlarik, Stephanie L. .... '59 '84 C.436 B.A. L.309 J.D. Chf. Asst. Corp. Coun.
Uhlenhop, Paul B., (AV) .... '36 '61 C&L.339 B.A., J.D. [Lawrence,K.S.&U.]
Uhler, Scott F. .... '56 '86 C.339 M.S.W. L.209 J.D. [Klein,T.&J.]
Uhlig, Christine Greener '67 '93 C.352 B.B.A. L.339 J.D.
Sr. Atty., Northern Trust Corp.
Ukman, Laren A. .... '60 '85 C.429 B.A. L.146 J.D. IE6, Inc.
Ullman, Patricia S. .... '— '00 C.945 B.A. L.597 J.D. [Schiff H.]
Ullrich, David A. '48 '73 C.197 B.A. L.966 J.D.
(adm. in WI; not adm. in IL) Dep. Reg. Adm., U.S. EPA
Ullrich, David A. .... '52 '76 C&L.339 B.A., J.D. Assoc. Gen. Coun.
Ullrick, Clay M. .... '— '99 C.589 B.A. L.365 J.D. [Ⓐ Hinshaw&C.]
Ulm, Anthony P. .... '71 '97 C.339 B.A. L.801 J.D. [Ⓐ Clausen M.]

Ulmer & Berne LLP, (AV)
One N. Franklin Street, Suite 1825, 60606-3401 ⊙
Telephone: 312-324-8000 FAX: 312-324-8001
Email: infochicago@ulmer.com URL: http://www.ulmer.com
Partner: Kenneth F. Berg. Of Counsel: Peter R. Sonderby. Associate: Sean M. Downey.
Antitrust; Banking and Commercial Lending; Broker/Dealer and Securities Litigation; Business Law; Business Litigation; Business Restructuring; Class Action Defense; Construction Law; Corporate Finance; Corporate Restructuring and Creditors' Rights; Corporate Succession Planning; Emerging Businesses; Employee Benefits; Employment and Labor; Environmental; Fair Housing; Financial Institution Compliance; General Counsel Services; Health Care; Income Tax; Insurance Coverage; Intellectual Property and Technology; Joint Ventures; Liability Defense; Mass Torts; Mergers, Acquisitions and Divestitures; Nonprofit; OSHA; Pharmaceutical; Product Liability; Public Law; Real Estate; Securities; Securities Regulatory Compliance; Subrogation; Tax; Technology Transactions; Toxic Tort Defense; Trade Secrets/Unfair Competition; Trusts and Estates; Venture Capital; Workers' Compensation; Trial and Appellate Practice in All Courts.
Cleveland, Ohio Office: Skylight Office Tower, 1660 West 2nd Street, Suite 1100. Telephone: 216-583-7000. FAX: 216-583-7001.
Columbus, Ohio Office: 88 East Broad Street, Suite 1600. Telephone: 614-229-0000. FAX: 614-229-0001.
Cincinnati, Ohio Office: 600 Vine Street, Suite 2800. Telephone: 513-698-5000. FAX: 513-698-5001.
See Professional Biographies, CHICAGO, ILLINOIS

Ulrich, Kenneth S. .... '63 '87 C&L.597 B.A., J.D. [Goldberg,K.B.B.R.&M.]
Ulrich, Robert B., (AV) .... '51 '80 C&L.209 B.S., J.D. [Maciorowski,S.&U.]
Ulrich, Thomas W. '63 '92 C.546 B.A. L.190 J.D.
Gen. Coun., Geneva Investment Management of Chicago, LLC
Ulum, Angela M. .... '73 '97 C&L.477 B.A., J.D. [Mayer,B.R.&M.]
Umansky, Boris .... '75 '00 C&L.347 B.A., J.D. [Ⓐ Davis M.]
Underhill, Edward J. .... '— '84 C&L.589 B.A., J.D. [Masuda,F.E.&M.]
Underwood, Henry J., (AV) .... '44 '69 C.575 B.A. L.339 J.D. [Defrees&F.]
Underwood, T. Bryan, Jr. '32 '57 C.970 B.A. L.608 J.D.
(adm. in OH; not adm. in IL) 50 S. La Salle St.
Underwood, Thomas B., (AV) .... '52 '78 C&L.339 B.A., J.D. 10 S. LaSalle, Ste. 1200
Ungaretti, Richard A., (AV) .... '— '70 C&L.209 B.S.C., J.D. [Ungaretti&H.]

Ungaretti & Harris, (AV)
3500 Three First National Plaza, 60602 ⊙
Telephone: 312-977-4400 Fax: 312-977-4405
Email: info@uhlaw.com URL: http://www.uhlaw.com
Partners: R. Scott Alsterda; Nicholas Anaclerio; Vincent M. Aquilino; Stephen H. Armstrong; Charles R. Bernardini; Michael W. Black; Dennis G. Bouxsein; Thomas F. Brett, II; David A. Bronner; John P. Buckley; Stacey Cavanagh; Kathleen Holper Champagne; Edward Clancy; Kris E. Curran; Leslie M. Darling; Carol M. Douglas; John J. Durso; James T. Easterling; J. Timothy Eaton; Theodore T. Eidukas; Francis J. Emmons; John D. English; Thomas M. Fahey; Susan G. Feibus; Michael A. Ficaro; Raymond C. Fricke; Robert H. Griffith; Theodore E. Harman; Alton B. Harris; Joseph K. Hasson; Anne M. Haule; F. Thomas Hecht; Paul B. Holmes; Ross E. Kimbarovsky; Shannon Capone Kirk; Brian E. Krob; James E. Lentz; Gary I. Levenstein; William J. Lewis; Benjamin T. Lo; Samera S. Ludwig; James Brent McCauley; Lori R. McGunn; Claudette P. Miller; John G. Nassos; William H. Nichols; Frank E. Pasquesi; Floyd D. Perkins; Michael J. Philippi; Alex Pirogovsky; Dean J. Polales; Christopher L. Rexroat; Frank J. Saibert; Julie K. Seymour; Kevin P. Shea; Barry J. Shkolnik; James B. Smith; Tina B. Solis; Gregg E. Szilagyi; Theodore R. Tetzlaff; Steven J. Thompson; Richard A. Ungaretti; Sam Vinson; Robert S. Winner; Jennifer Zordani. Of Counsel: Kevin M. Foley; Eric F. Greenberg; Stephen Hoke; Daniel J. Pierce; Patricia A. Rooney; Degee D. Wilhelm. Associates: Brian V. Alcala; Anna L. Benjamin; Joel A. Blanchet; Brenda N. Broderick; James M. Carlson; Jolynn C. Caroline; Kamau A. Coar; Brecken Joy Cutler; Elizabeth A. Davis; Hallie A. Diethelm; Keith E. Edeus, Jr.; Catherine T. Gonzalez; Michael J. Hayes, Jr.; Timothy E. Horton; David Levitt; Andrew B. Levy; Michael P. McBride; Melissa Glass Melsher; Jacob M. Mihm; Valerie Breslin Montague; Jennifer Orrico; Jennifer R. Quinn; John T. Ruskusky; Jon P. Sanders; Shannon M. Schaab; Rachel C. Steiner; Daniel P. Strzalka; Jessica K. Thomas; Julie E. Treumann; Angela Williams-Walker; Jeffrey D. Woods.
General Practice, including Business and Corporate, Financial Services and Securities, Litigation and Appeals, Real Estate, Health Care, Information Technology, Public Finance, Legislative and Regulatory Affairs, Labor and Employment, Employee Benefits, Taxation, Affordable Housing, Bankruptcy and Creditors' Rights, Estates and Trusts, Gaming Law, Intellectual Property and Patent Litigation, Class Actions and Securities Arbitration.
Washington, D.C. Office: 1500 K Street, N.W., Suite 250, 20005-1714. Telephone: 202-639-7500. Fax: 202-639-7505.
See Professional Biographies, CHICAGO, ILLINOIS

Unger, Daniel P. .... '28 '53 C.1016 L.209 LL.B. 35 E. Wacker Dr.
Unger, Donald J., (AVⓉ) .... '50 '76 C.339 B.A. L.365 J.D. [Barnes,R.&C.]
Unger, Linda E., (AV) .... '54 '79 C.339 B.A. L.146 J.D. [Mora,B.W.&U.] ⊙
Unger, Margaret A., (AV) .... '53 '79 C.424 B.A. L.365 J.D. [Johnson&B.]
Unger, Michael A. .... '37 '64 C.260 B.A. L.30 LL.B. 2802 W. 26th St.
Unger, Stuart C., (AV) '41 '66
C.473 B.S. L.477 J.D. Asst. Gen. Coun., Chicago Brd. of Ed.
Unger, Theresa H., Attorney at Law .... '72 '00 C.966 B.S. L.365 J.D. 6133 S. Ellis
Ungerleider, Robert N. .... '40 '65 C&L.705 B.A., LL.B. 850 N. State St., Ste. 14F‡
Unikel, Alan L., (AV) .... '43 '68 C.46 B.S. L.276 J.D. [Seyfarth S.] (Pat.)
Unikel, Robert W., (BV) .... '69 '93 C.197 B.A. L.597 J.D. [Mayer,B.R.&M.]
Unkrich, Micki A. .... '— '01 C.352 B.S. L.597 J.D. Two North LaSalle Street, Suite 2200
Unrein, Eric I., (BVⓉ) '68 '93
C.378 B.A. L.846 J.D. [G.D.McCallister&Assoc.] (⊙Topeka, KS)
Unruh, Marilee C. .... '57 '81 C.813 B.A. L.1068 J.D. [Goodsmith G.&U.]
Unspain, LLC .... 850 W. Adams, Ste. 4E
Upshaw, David A. .... '59 '86 C.72 B.A. L.146 J.D. Reg. Coun.
Urban, Ronald F. .... '37 '76 C.46 B.S. L.365 J.D. Christian-Roge & Assocs., Inc.
Urban, Tod M., (AV) .... '58 '84 C.1016 B.S.B.A. L.146 J.D. [T.M.Urban]

Urban, Tod M., Ltd., Law Offices of, (AV) BB
820 West Jackson Boulevard Suite 310, 60607
Telephone: 312-474-1144 Fax: 312-993-1554
Email: Urbanlaw@ameritech.net URL: http://www.lawyers.com/urbantod
Tod M. Urban.
Complex Criminal Law Practice including Capital Offenses, Murder, Drugs, Serious Felonies, Federal Criminal and Criminal Appeals.
See Professional Biographies, CHICAGO, ILLINOIS

Urgell, Maria E. .... '62 '87 C.1036 B.A. L.309 J.D. Asst. Corp. Coun.
Urso, Frank W. .... '45 '85 C.589 B.A. L.365 J.D. State Dept. of Pub. Health
Urtis, James M. .... '65 '91 C.696 B.A. L.879 J.D. [J.Urtis]
Urtis, James, Law Office of .... 20 N. Clark St., Ste. 2550
Ury, Robert I., (AV) .... '— '64 C.209 B.S. L.597 J.D. [Arnstein&L.]
Usman, Azhar M. .... '75 '02 C.339 B.A. L.494 J.D. [Integris L.]
Usow, Jeffrey A., (AV) .... '52 '77 C.960 B.A. L.309 J.D. [Mayer,B.R.&M.]
Utreras, Mario E. .... '69 '95 C.339 B.A. L.352 J.D. [Utreras]
Utreras Law Offices LLC .... 4937 W. Foster Avenue
Uvena, Frank J., (AV) .... '34 '63 C.610 A.B. L.608 LL.B. 33 W. Huron St.
Uzzell, James G., (BV) .... '49 '75 C.575 B.A. L.477 J.D. 39 S. La Salle St.
Vaca, Monica E. .... '70 '97 C.893 B.A. L.597 J.D. Law Clk., U.S. Dist. Ct.
Vacala, Gregory G., (BV) .... '58 '83 C&L.209 B.S., J.D. [Rusin M.&F.]
Vaid, Fazila .... '75 '00 C.339 B.A. L.146 J.D. [Ⓐ Hughes S.P.R.&D.]
Vail, Andrew W. .... '76 '03 C.577 B.A. L.339 J.D. [Ⓐ Jenner&B.]
Vail, Anne Findlay .... '64 '90 C.597 B.A. L.477 J.D. Asst. Dir., Amer. Med. Assn.
Vail, James N., (AV) .... '32 '60 C&L.424 B.S., J.D. 33 N. Dearborn
Vail, John P. .... '55 '80 C&L.424 B.A., J.D. [Quarles&B.]
Vainikos, Jim M. .... '63 '90 C.597 B.A. L.130 J.D. [Cornfield&F.]
Vainisi, Jerome R., (AV) .... '41 '69 C.276 B.S.B.A. L.146 J.D. [Hinshaw&C.]
Vainisi, Mark E. '72 '97
C&L.477 B.A., J.D. Coun., Mergers & Acquisitions, Tribune Co.
Vaisvilas, Terrance A., M.D. .... '53 '78 C.679 B.S. L.838 J.D. [⊚ Karavidas] ‡
Valaik, Michael J. .... '65 '97 C.871 B.S. L.276 J.D. [Bartlit B.H.P.&S.]
Valauskas, Charles C., (AV) '52 '81
C.339 B.S. L.209 J.D. [Baniak P.&G.] (See Pat. Sect.)
Valderrama, Franklin U. .... '62 '88 C.339 B.A. L.209 J.D. [Sanchez&D.]
Valderrama, Pamela Griffith '63 '88
C.893 B.A. L.659 J.D. Gen.Atty., R.R. Donnelley & Sons Co.
Valdes, Ariel Omar '66 '91
C.339 B.A. L.589 J.D. Pilsen Mng. Atty., Chicago Legal Clinic
Valdes-Cruz, Jose Manuel .... '55 '84 C.259 B.A. L.144 J.D. Pragmaton
Valdez, James J. '48 '74 C&L.546 B.A., J.D.
(adm. in NE; not adm. in IL) V.P. & Assoc. Gen. Coun., Bankers Life & Cas. Co.
Valdez, Maria G. .... '62 '88 C.112 B.A. L.1065 J.D. U.S. Mag.
Valeck, David J. .... '72 '99 C.475 B.A. L.477 J.D. [Ⓐ Katten M.R.]
Valek, Richard A. .... '61 '87 C&L.209 B.S., J.D. 30 North La Salle Street, Suite 4300
Valencic, Michelle R. .... '70 '96 C.97 A.B. L.930 J.D. [Clausen M.]
Valenta, Marcel .... '72 '03 L.597 J.D. [Ⓐ Baker&M.]
Valente, Charles A., (AV) .... '62 '88 C.1044 B.A. L.910 J.D. [Krasnow S.C.]
Valenti, Alfred T. .... '17 '49 L.209 LL.B. 2825 N. Campell
Valenti, David A. .... '57 '83 C.597 B.A. L.602 J.D. Sr. V.P., La Salle Bank, N.A.
Valenti, Frank E. .... '— '02 C.589 B.A. L.339 J.D. [Ⓐ Sedgwick,D.M.&A.]
Valenti, Thomas P., (AV) .... '52 '77 C.93 B.A. L.209 J.D. [T.P.Valenti]
Valenti, Thomas P., P.C., (AV) .... 350 North LaSalle St.
Valentine, John M. .... '— '01 C.477 B.A. L.424 J.D. [Ⓐ Pircher,N.&M.]
Valentine, Susan .... '62 '87 C.20 B.A. L.146 J.D. [Robinson C.&C.]
Valentini, Fabio .... '66 '91 C.724 B.S. L.1009 J.D. Asst. State's Atty.
Valentino, Karie J. .... '71 '96 C.352 B.A. L.365 J.D. [Bollinger,R.&G.]
Valentino, Richard T., (AV) .... '— '84 C.209 B.A. L.365 J.D. [O'Hagan,S.&A.]
Valenzona, Elisa M. .... '68 '98 C.339 B.A. L.146 J.D. [Ⓐ Brinks H.G.&L.]
Valenzuela, Sandra .... '63 '96 C.741 B.B.A. L.209 J.D. [Ⓐ Minsky,M.&H.]
Valerious, Randi L. .... '— '90 C.477 B.A. L.309 J.D. [Greenberg T.]
Valeta, Peter J., (AV) .... '53 '80 C.665 B.A. L.472 J.D. [Meckler B.&T.]
Valiquet, Brett A., (AV) .... '— '75 C.46 B.S.E.E. L.146 J.D. [Schiff H.] (Pat.)
Valiulis, Anthony C., (AV) .... '47 '74 C.436 B.A. L.424 J.D. [Much S.F.D.A.&R.]
Valladarez-Ortiz, Raquel .... '75 '00 C.339 B.A. L.1000 J.D. [Smith O.]
Vallar, James M. .... '52 '87 C&L.424 B.A., J.D. 5421 S. New England Ave.
Vallas, David P. .... '73 '00 C.951 B.A. L.1119 J.D. [Ⓐ Wildman,H.A.&D.]
Valley, Mark R. .... '52 '78 C.966 B.A. L.146 J.D. [Statland&V.]
Vallone, Melissa A. .... '— '96 C.679 B.S. L.879 J.D. [Barnes&T.]
Vallort, Joseph R. .... '67 '92 C.436 B.A. L.365 J.D. 150 S. Wacker Dr., Ste. 2400
Valukas, Anton J. .... '20 '43 C.999 L.209 LL.B. Superv. J., Cir. Ct.
Valukas, Anton R., (AV) .... '43 '68 C.399 B.A. L.597 J.D. [Jenner&B.]
Vamos, Teresa M. .... '65 '91 C.927 B.S. L.734 J.D. 2302 W. North Ave.
Van Alkemade, Sara A. '53 '84
C.612 B.A. L.623 J.D. Asst. Gen. Coun., Jesus People USA
Van Allen, Marc .... '66 '92 C.145 B.A. L.477 J.D. [Jenner&B.]
Vanasco, Gina G. .... '64 '98 C.597 B.A. L.146 J.D. Cir. Ct.
Vanasco, Robert A., (AV) .... '41 '67 C.812 B.A. L.262 J.D. [Vanasco,G.&M.]
Vanasco, Genelly & Miller, (AV) .... 33 N. La Salle St., Ste. 2200
VanAusdal, Rodney E., (AV) .... '58 '83 C.347 B.S. L.1119 J.D. [Iwan C.H.H.&V.]
Van Baren, Todd M. .... '67 '93 C.114 B.A. L.145 J.D. [Hoogendoorn&T.]
Van Blargan, Jennifer .... '77 '03 C.201 B.S. L.424 J.D. [Ⓐ BryceDowney]
Van Bree, Frank E. .... '39 '63 C&L.424 LL.B. 542 S. Dearborn
Vance, Geoffrey A. .... '70 '96 C.475 B.A. L.365 J.D. [Ⓐ McDermott W.&E.]
Vance, L. Byron, III .... '68 '92 C&L.69 B.B.A., J.D. [Skadden,A.S.M.&F.]

Vance, Lawrence N. ... '49 '77 C.1016 B.S. L.146 J.D. [L.N.Vance&Assoc.]
Vance, L.N., & Associates ... 60 W. Randolph St., Ste. 200
Van Cleave, Roy M., (P.C.), (AV) '47 '73
C.210 A.B. L.477 J.D. 65 W. Jackson Boulevard
VanDaele, Lanny ... '74 '03 C.352 B.A. L.879 J.D. [Ⓐ Brenner,F.M.&S.]
Vande Walle, John M. ... '60 '98 C.1275 B.A. L.146 J.D. [Ⓐ Seyfarth S.]
Van de Burgt, David W. ... '64 '91 C.121 B.S. L.801 J.D. Atty. Gen. Off.
Van De Graaff, James D., (BV) ... '60 '87 C.101 B.A. L.276 J.D. [Katten M.R.]
VanDemark, Ruth E., Law Offices of, (AV) '44 '76
C.881 A.B. L.184 J.D. 2046 West Pierce Avenue
Vander Arend, J. Eric ... '58 '91 C.1316 B.F.A. L.597 J.D. [Hughes S.P.R.&D.]
Vander Broek, Kathryn S. ... '63 '94 C.475 B.A. L.424 J.D. [Hinshaw&C.]
Vander Ploeg, David J., Jr. ... '75 '04 C.399 B.A. L.190 J.D. 368 W. Huron St., Ste. 100
Vander Pol, Brian ... '78 '03 C&L.352 B.A., J.D. [Ⓐ McDermott W.&E.]
Vander Vliet, W. Joel ... '77 '05 C.323 B.A. L.477 J.D. [Ⓐ Krislov&Assoc.]
Vander Woude, Paul S., (AV) ... '51 '76 C.114 B.A. L.146 J.D. [Hlustik,H.W.&V.]
Vanderlaan, Lori A. ... '68 '95 C.569 L.365 J.D. [Best,V.&H.] ⊙
VanderLeest, Kirk A. '64 '94
C.350 B.S.I.E. L.146 J.D. [McAndrews,H.&M.] (See Pat. Sect.)
VanderPloeg, Frank P., (AV) ... '44 '73 C.597 B.A. L.477 J.D. [Sonnenschein N.&R.]
Vanderslice, Lane W. ... '65 '93 C&L.178 B.A., J.D. [Mayer,B.R.&M.]
Van Derveer, Sarah ... '74 '03 C.210 B.A. L.273 J.D. [Ⓐ Vedder,P.K.&K.]
Vandeveld, Dirk J. ... '58 '84 C.174 B.S. L.221 J.D. Jefferies Grp., Inc.
VanDeWeert, John K. ... '73 '98 C.674 A.B. L.145 J.D. [Ⓐ Sidley A.B.&W.]
Vandewerken, Walter '49 '74 C&L.209 B.A., J.D.
Courts Info. Dir., Law Bulletin Pub. Co.
Van Dorf, Steven, (Ltd.) ... '35 '59 C.1016 A.B. L.209 J.D. 25 E. Washington St.
Van Duerm, James '51 '76 C.424 B.A. L.209 J.D.
Sr. Coun., Bank One Corp. (Law Dept.)
Van Duzer, Jane '60 '86 C.477 B.A. L.597 J.D.
Sr. Coun., Focal Communications Corporation
Van Duzer, John B., (AV) ... '17 '40 C.894 B.A. L.597 J.D. 180 N. LaSalle St., Ste. 1801
Van Dyke, Barry Alan ... '54 '84 C.1304 B.A. L.145 J.D. [Mayer,B.R.&M.]
Van Dyke, David C., (BV) ... '57 '90 C.352 B.S. L.221 J.D. [Cassiday,S.&G.] (Pat.)
Vanecko, Mari-Rose McManus ... '66 '97 C.321 B.A. L.209 J.D. Asst. State Atty.
Vanek, James F., (AV) ... '59 '85 C.734 B.S. L.365 J.D. [Laner,M.D.B.L.&T.]
Vanek, Joseph M., (AV) ... '61 '87 C.190 B.A. L.93 J.D. [Daar&V.]
Van Emden, Geo. J., (AV) ... '32 '56 C&L.339 A.B., LL.B. 105 W. Madison St.
van Es, J. Pieter ... '— '92 C&L.339 B.A.Ec., J.D. [Banner&W.] (See Pat. Sect.)
Van Gelder, Amy ... '77 '03 C.597 B.S. L.273 J.D. [Ⓐ Skadden,A.S.M.&F.]
VanGetson, Aaron J. ... '— '03 C&L.339 B.S., J.D. [Ⓐ Katten M.R.]
Van Gorp, Jon D. ... '69 '94 C.114 B.A. L.802 J.D. [Mayer,B.R.&M.]
Van Hecke, Jeremiah C. ... '74 '99 C.597 B.A. L.861 J.D. [Ⓐ Kelly,O.M.D.&R.]
Van Heukelem, Bruce J. ... '53 '79 C.114 B.A. L.879 J.D. [Hoogendoorn&T.]
Van Hook, Robert W. '50 '76 C&L.893 B.A., J.D.
(adm. in OH; not adm. in IL) Sr. Tax Atty., BP America Inc.
Van Hoose, Judith A. ... '75 '94 C.597 B.A. L.477 J.D. [Ⓐ Barack F.K.P.&N.]
Vanker, Frank B. ... '59 '85 C.475 B.A. L.477 J.D. [Sidley A.B.&W.]
Van Klompenberg, Brian C. ... '— '98 C.475 B.A. L.145 J.D. [Kirkland&E.]
VanLonkhuyzen, Courtney E. ... '74 '04 C.323 B.A. L.597 J.D. [Ⓐ Skadden,A.S.M.&F.]
VanLonkhuyzen, Tyler A. ... '74 '00 C.323 B.A. L.209 J.D. [Ⓐ Seyfarth S.]
Van Lysebettens, Paul D. ... '61 '94 C.999 B.Mus. L.146 J.D. [Gunty&M.]
Van Meter, Karen, (AV) ... '63 '91 C.893 B.A. L.976 J.D. [McDermott W.&E.]
Vano, Alfred S., (AV) ... '52 '77 C.424 B.A. L.365 J.D. [Leahy,E.&F.]
VanPopering, Melissa P. ... '68 '93 C&L.209 B.A., J.D. [Women's R.]
VanPopering, Randy E., & Associates, Law Offices of '65 '90
C.477 B.A. L.213 J.D. 205 W. Wacker Dr.
Van Puymbrouck, Darren M. R., (AV) ... '— '86 C.911 B.A. L.424 J.D. [Schiff H.]
Van Roeyen, Eileen W. '57 '82 C.597 B.A. L.146 J.D.
V.P. & Regulatory Coun., Chicago Title Ins. Co.
Van Santen, James, (AV) ... '22 '50 C.46 B.S. L.145 h.D. 233 South Wacker Drive (Pat.)
Van Santen, William A., (AV) '39 '65
C.46 B.S.C. L.273 J.D. [Ⓒ Wood,P.K.C.&M.] (See Pat. Sect.)‡
Van Timmeren, Kevin ... '— '05 C.323 B.A. L.910 J.D. [Ⓐ Gardner C.&D.]
Van Tine, Matthew E. ... '58 '83 C.309 A.B. L.94 J.D. [Ⓒ Miller F.&C.]
Van Tine, Rena M. ... '61 '86 C.1154 B.A. L.564 J.D. Asst. States Atty.
VanVlierbergen, Brian '37 '65 C.424 B.S. L.365 LL.B.
Senior Vice President, Law & Audit & Secretary, Blue Cross & Blue Shield of Illinois
Van Vliet, James M., Jr., (AV) ... '— '57 C&L.352 B.A., J.D. [Schiff H.]
Van Vranken, John W., (AV) ... '47 '75 C.177 B.A. L.339 J.D. Exelon Corp.
Van Vuren, Theresa G. ... '— '03 C.477 B.A. L.146 J.D. [Ⓐ Wildman,H.A.&D.]
Van Wart, Kevin T., (P.C.) ... '— '82 C.611 B.A. L.94 J.D. [Kirkland&E.]
Van Zandt, David E. '53 '85 C.674 A.B. L.976 J.D.
(adm. in NY; not adm. in IL) Dean & Prof., Northwestern Univ. Sch. of Law
Varboncouer, Mark ... '— '00 C&L.339 B.S., J.D. [Ⓐ Kirkland&E.]
Varde, John M., (P.C.) ... '49 '81 C.679 B.S.Ch.E. L.209 J.D. [Schofield&V.]
Varga, Craig A., (AV) ... '54 '80 C.901 B.A. L.597 J.D. [Varga B.L.H.&C.]
Varga, James M. ... '53 '78 C.801 B.A. L.602 J.D. 2808 R.J. Daley Center

Varga Berger Ledsky Hayes & Casey, A Professional Corporation, (AV)
Santa Fe Building, 224 South Michigan Avenue, Suite 350, 60604-2507
Telephone: 312-341-9400 Fax: 312-341-2900
Craig A. Varga; Norman B. Berger; Jonathan N. Ledsky; Michael D. Hayes; Michael V. Casey; Anne E. Viner; Joshua D. Davidson;—Harold B. Hilborn; Jaime S. Roginski-Kord; Julie F. Grosch. Of Counsel: R. Elizabeth Topoluk; Peter E. Manis.
General Civil Practice in State and Federal Courts. Trials and Appeals in all Courts. General Commercial Litigation, Class Action Defense, Consumer Financial Services Litigation, Regulatory and Compliance, Environmental Safety and Health Law and Litigation, Real Estate, Insurance Coverage, Banking and Financial Institution Regulation, RICO, Civil Rights and Employment Litigation. Alternative Dispute Resolution.

See Professional Biographies, CHICAGO, ILLINOIS

Vargas, Teresa M. '72 '98 C.339 B.S.W. L.209 J.D.
Off. of the Gen. Coun., Dept. of HHS
Vargas, Vanessa L. '69 '94 C&L.339 B.A., J.D.
Ethics & Compl. Offr., Abbott Laboratories, Intl. Div., Dept. EC05
Vargas, Yvonne ... '— '88 [Pardys&V.]
Varghese, Shyni R. ... '74 '02 C.145 A.B. L.339 J.D. [Ⓐ Jenner&B.]
Vargo, Paul M., (AV) ... '41 '77 C.124 B.S.E.E. L.146 J.D. [Welsh&K.] (See Pat. Sect.)
Vargo, Stephen E., (BV) ... '55 '81 C.475 B.A. L.365 J.D. 77 W. Wash. St.
Varhola, Steven Michael ... '70 '01 C.686 B.A. L.209 J.D. [Ⓐ A.J.Madonia&Assoc.]
Varick, Steven B., (AV) ... '— '79 C.388 B.A. L.145 J.D. [Holland&K.]
Varner, Thomas H. ... '34 '61 C.339 B.S. L.597 J.D. [Ⓒ Lewis,O.&F.]
Varon, Heather A. ... '— '03 C.228 B.S. L.309 J.D. [Ⓐ Jones D.]
Vars, Fredrick E. ... '73 '99 C.674 A.B. L.976 J.D. [Ⓐ Miller S.&H.]
Vasaturo, Gaylene '— '83 C.1111 B.A. L.1049 J.D.
(adm. in CA; not adm. in IL) Assoc. Reg. Coun., U.S. E.P.A.

Vasic, Ivan ... '64 '97 L.365 J.D. 10020 South Western
Vasilatos, Christina S. ... '75 '01 C.36 B.A. L.1000 J.D. [Fedota C.]
Vasiljevic, Vladan M. '74 '98 C&L.339 B.S.E.E., J.D.
[Ⓐ Leydig,V.&M.] (See Pat. Sect.)
Vasiljevich, Thomas, (AV) ... '57 '82 C.966 B.A. L.209 J.D. [Ogletree,D.N.S.&S.]
Vasys, Dalius F. ... '55 '80 C.309 B.A. L.597 J.D. [Vedder,P.K.&K.]
Vates, Michael O. ... '75 '00 C.597 B.A. L.209 J.D. [Ⓐ MacCabe&M.]
Vathis, Maria Z. ... '— '02 C.339 B.A. L.209 J.D. [Ⓐ Clausen M.]
Vaughan, Kenneth J. ... '— '61 C&L.276 B.S., J.D. [Ⓒ Chapman&C.]
Vaughn, Sherry L. ... '— '95 C.1111 B.A. L.209 J.D. 161 N. Clark St., Ste. 4950
Vaughn, Thomas E. ... '52 '78 C.39 B.S. L.378 J.D. [T.Vaughn]
Vaughn, Tom ... P.O. Box 2937
Vazquez, Carlos A. ... '52 '86 C.424 B.B.A. L.146 J.D. 3129 W. Logan Blvd.
Vazquez, Carlos A. ... '79 '04 C.339 B.A. L.813 J.D. [Ⓐ Mayer,B.R.&M.]
Vazquez, Gregory P. ... '51 '77 C&L.209 B.A., J.D. 53 W. Jackson Blvd.
Vazquez, Respicio F. ... '60 '86 C&L.209 B.S.C., J.D. [Ⓒ Franczek S.]
Veal, Beverly E. ... '— '84 C.339 B.A. L.365 J.D. [B.Veal]
Veal, Edward Thomas ... '46 '77 C.976 B.A. L.339 J.D. Dir., Deloitte & Touche
Veal, Beverly ... 10540 S. Western Ave., Ste. 312
Vechiola, Robert J. ... '— '92 C.338 B.S. L.209 J.D. [Foley&L.]

Vedder, Price, Kaufman & Kammholz, P.C., (AV) BR
222 North La Salle Street, 60601-1003 ⊙
Telephone: 312-609-7500 Fax: 312-609-5005 Email: See addresses for individual attorneys
URL: http://www.vedderprice.com
Members of Firm: Thomas G. Abram; Bruce R. Alper; Dana Simaitis Armagno; James A. Arpaia; Anthony J. Ashley; Thomas A. Baker; Robert S. Beiser; David E. Bennett; William J. Bettman; George P. Blake; John T. Blatchford (Not admitted in IL); Stanley B. Block; Jonathan H. Bogaard; Mark I. Bogart; Gabrielle M. Buckley; Angelo J. Bufalino; Mitchell A. Carrel; Lawrence J. Casazza; Thomas P. Cimino, Jr.; Michael G. Cleveland; Mark A. Dalla Valle; Jeffrey C. Davis; Thomas R. Dee; Thomas P. Desmond; David L. Doyle; Terence M. Dunleavy; Deborah Bielicke Eades (Not admitted in IL); Michael M. Eidelman; Karin Jagel Flynn; Andrew M. Gardner; James V. Garvey; Joshua D. Gentner; Dean N. Gerber; Lynne A. Gochanour; Steven L. Hamann; Douglas M. Hambleton; Thomas G. Hancuch; Renee M. Hardt; J. Kevin Hennessy; Paul R. Hoffman; John M. Hughes; Michael L. Igoe, Jr.; John J. Jacobsen, Jr.; John Jacoby; Edward C. Jepson, Jr.; Norman B. Julius; Theophil C. Kammholz (1909-1992); James M. Kane; Geoffrey R. Kass; Charles R. Kaufman (1908-1990); Diane M. Kehl; Peter J. Kelly; Ludwig E. Kolman; Kevin J. Kuhn; William A. Kummerer; Jean M. Langie; Karen P. Layng; Randall Marc Lending; Douglas J. Lipke; John T. McEnroe; Daniel C. McKay, II; Maureen A. Miller; James S. Montana, Jr.; Robert J. Moran; Philip L. Mowery; Lane R. Moyer; Bruce C. Nelson; Michael A. Nemeroff; John R. Obiala; Timothy W. O'Donnell; Cathy G. O'Kelly; Daniel O'Rourke; Richard W. Pearse; James S. Petrie; Theresa M. Peyton; Igor Potym; Eric S. Prezant; William F. Price (1909-1973); Donna J. Pugh; Christopher J. Reckamp; Michael E. Reed; Christine M. Rhode; Richard C. Robin; Paul F. Russell; Richard H. Sanders; Chad A. Schiefelbein; Richard H. Schnadig; Thomas E. Schnur; Daniel T. Sherlock; Robert F. Simon; Guy E. Snyder; Kenneth F. Sparks; James A. Spizzo; Kelly A. Starr; Joseph A. Strubbe; Robert J. Stucker; David A. Sturms; Lawrence L. Summers; Theodore J. Tierney; Ernest W. Torain, Jr.; Michael J. Turgeon; Dalius F. Vasys; Beverly B. Vedder (1887-1955); William F. Walsh; Charles H. Wiggins, Jr.; Thomas M. Wilde; Richard L. Williams III; Charles B. Wolf; Gregory G. Wrobel; Richard A. Zachar; Pearl A. Zager. Associates: Leslie Allen Bayles; David C. Blum; David J. Borkon (Not admitted in IL); Sarah M. Brown; Mark A. Camero; Timothy J. Carroll; Christopher T. Collins; D. Kathryn Colvin; Laura Carroll DeBolt; Michael R. Demnicki; Robert W. Dixon; Scot J. Foley (Not admitted in IL); Nicole A. Frankel; David W. French; Allen J. Gable; Aaron R. Gelb; Jennifer M. Goodman; Nicholas S. Harned; Jeffery M. Heftman; Byron D. Hittle; P. Michelle Jacobson; Suzanne H. Johnson; Sara J. Kagay (Not admitted in IL); David P. Kaminski; Jennifer Durham King; Frederic T. Knape; Jenny Friedman Koerth; Joseph H. Kye; Jordan R. Labkon; James P. Lambe; Adam S. Lewis; Amy Elizabeth Lewis; Alison J. Maki; Joseph M. Mannon; John S. Marten; Jon P. McCarty; Courtney Anne McDonough; Megan E. Meyers; James W. Morrissey; Michael R. Mulcahy; Joseph Kevin Mulherin; Christopher L. Nybo; Matthew T. O'Connor; Angela C. Pavlatos; Jacob C. Pond; Jennifer M.K. Provencher; Bruce A. Radke; Eric J. Rietz; Allyson B. Russo; Timothy M. Schank; Derek M. Spychalski; Kathryn L. Stevens; Patrick J. Stoklas; Cindy S. Stuyvesant; Maryam Tabrizi; Venu V. Talanki (Not admitted in IL); Ursula Taylor; Anne Therieau; John B. Thornton; Sarah Van Derveer; Mark L. Winget; Peter T. Wynacht; Amy L. Young; Jin W. Yun; Michael Derek Zolner. Of Counsel: Margaret A. Arnold; Michael G. Beemer; Bernard J. Echlin; James T. FitzGibbon; Philip L. Kennedy; Allan E. Lapidus; William O. Petersen. Counsel: Ronald J. Rapp.
General Practice. Complex Litigation, Civil Litigation, Class Actions, Alternate Dispute Resolution, Corporate Law, Commercial Law, Equipment Finance and Leasing, Project Finance, Municipal Finance, Banking Law, International Trade, Labor and Employment, Employee Benefits, Occupational Safety and Health, Municipal Law, School Law, Securities, Investment Company Law, Professional Liability Defense, Insurance Coverage, Insurance Litigation, Tax Planning, Tax Litigation, Intellectual Property, Mergers and Acquisitions, Bankruptcy, Real Estate, Health Care, Trade and Professional Associations, Estate Planning, Trust Administration.
New York, New York Office: 805 Third Avenue. Telephone: 212-407-7700. Facsimile: 212-407-7799. Roseland, New Jersey Office: Five Becker Farm Road. Telephone: 973-579-1100. Facsimile: 973-579-9607.

See Professional Biographies, CHICAGO, ILLINOIS

Vedova, Stephen R. ... '71 '98 C.013 B.A. L.209 J.D. 20 N. Clark, Ste. 2300
Veed, Mary Cannon, (AV) ... '— '77 C.546 B.A. L.190 J.D. [Arnstein&L.]
Veerhusen, Katrina, (AV) ... '49 '78 C.94 B.A. L.424 J.D. 1433 North State Parkway
Vega, Katherine Davis '73 '98
C.228 A.B. L.597 J.D. Two North LaSalle Street, Suite 2200
Vega, Librado Arreola ... '63 '90 C.339 B.A. L.588 J.D. [Ⓐ Asher,G.G.&D.]
Vega-Byrnes, Thomas J. ... '58 '90 C.424 B.A. L.145 J.D. [T.Vega-Byrnes]

Vega-Byrnes, Thomas, LLC
The Monadnock Building, 53 West Jackson Boulevard Suite 1057, 60604
Telephone: 312-360-1562 Mobile: 773-230-0228 Fax: 312-360-1607
Email: tvb@vegabyrnes.com URL: http://www.vegabyrnes.com
Thomas J. Vega-Byrnes.
Languages: Spanish, Portuguese, French and Italian.
International Construction Law, Electric Power, International Loans, International Investments, International Mergers and Acquisitions, International Joint Ventures, International Corporate Law, International Licensing.

See Professional Biographies, CHICAGO, ILLINOIS

Vegosen, Jonathan, (AV) ... '49 '76 C&L.597 B.A., J.D. [Funkhouser V.L.&D.]
Veith, Paul E. ... '65 '90 C.339 B.S. L.309 J.D. [Sidley A.B.&W.]
Velarde, Cesar A. ... '46 '72 C.424 B.S. L.209 J.D. 1624 W. 18th St.
Velazquez, Orlando ... '67 '92 C&L.424 B.B.A., J.D. P.O. Box 410533
Velázquez, Richard ... '76 '03 C.424 B.A. L.209 J.D. [Ⓐ Hinshaw&C.]
Velchek, Laurence A. ... '51 '76 C.602 B.A. L.365 J.D. 9130 S. Houston Ave.
Velcich, George M. ... '55 '80 C.602 B.A. L.424 J.D. [Belgrade&O.]
Veldman, Jane H., (AV) ... '54 '79 C.114 B.A. L.912 J.D. [Lord,B.&B.]
Velez, Lisa ... '72 '98 C.339 B.A. L.1068 J.D. [Ⓐ Cassiday,S.&G.]
Velk, Seymour ... '22 '48 C.339 B.S. L.209 LL.B. 221 N. LaSalle St.
Velky, Joanne M. ... '63 '89 C.608 B.S. L.1003 J.D. Asst. Pub. Def.
Veltman, Stephen C. ... '54 '79 C&L.424 A.B., J.D. [Pretzel&S.]
Veniaminova, Maria ... '75 '01 C.999 B.S. L.209 J.D. [Ⓐ Fragomen,D.B.&L.]
Ventrelli, Anita M., (BV) ... '64 '90 C.477 A.B. L.209 J.D. [Schiller,D.&F.]
Ventress, Michelle B. '58 '83
C.116 B.A. L.597 J.D. 1st V.P. & Sr. Coun., La Salle Bank Corp.
Ventura, Dennis N. ... '79 '04 C.339 B.S. L.1000 J.D. [Ⓐ Cremer,K.S.&S.]
Venverloh, Sally L. ... '70 '96 C&L.734 B.A., J.D. [Ⓐ Gardner C.&D.]
Venzon, Joseph A. ... '— '97 C.309 A.B. L.597 J.D. [Ⓐ Katten M.R.]

Veon, Leslie L., Law Offices of, (AV) '53 '78 C.473 A.B. L.150 J.D.
303 West Madison Street, Suite 1150, 60606
Telephone: 312-578-1721 Facsimile: 312-578-1743
URL: http://www.lawyers.com/veonlaw
Associates: Christina M. Dardick; Deborah L. Dencer; Kate Curler.
Practice limited to Matrimonial Law, Family Law, Domestic Relations Law, Trial and Appellate Practice.
See Professional Biographies, CHICAGO, ILLINOIS

Verber, Kaitlin Reidy .....'— '04 C.197 B.A. L.597 J.D. [Latham&W.]
Vergara, Vanessa B.M. .....'— '00 C.300 B.A. L.597 J.D. [Goldberg,K.B.B.R.&M.]
Verhey, John .....'— '89 C.114 B.A. L.1565 J.D. [DLPiper R.G.C.U.]
Verhey, Scott D. .....'65 '91 C.436 B.A. L.365 J.D. 734 N. Wells St.
Vermiglio, Ivan Antonio .....'67 '95 C.688 B.S. L.597 J.D. General Electric Corp.
Vernon, George, (AV) .....'45 '75 C.309 B.A. L.145 J.D. [Hill] (Monroe, WI)
Verr, Steven R. .....'57 '86 C.309 A.B. L.339 J.D. 455 N. Cityfront Plz., Suite 1800
Verrill, Ralph T. '37 '65 C.178 A.B. L.569 LL.B.
(adm. in NY; not adm. in IL) [McBreen&K.]
Verschoor, Katherine Anne .....'55 '86 C.339 B.S. L.209 J.D. D. J. Lessin & Assocs., Inc.
Verstrate, Christopher J. .....'74 '99 C.999 B.A. L.597 J.D. [McGuirewoods]
Verticchio, Thomas J., (AV) .....'60 '85 C.337 B.S. L.801 J.D. [Patzik,F.&S.]
Vertuno, Maria L. .....'68 '93 C.424 B.A. L.602 J.D. [Cassiday,S.&G.]
Vesole, Martin K. .....'47 '79 C.910 B.A. L.209 J.D. 2708 W. Birchwood
Vesselinovitch, Alexander S., (AV) .....'— '78 C.145 B.A. L.178 J.D. [Katten M.R.]
Veugeler, Kevin T. .....'71 '96 C.589 B.A. L.339 J.D. [Healy]
Veverka, Donald J., (AV) .....'35 '63 C.424 B.S. L.209 J.D. [Veverka,R.&H.]
Veverka, Rosen & Haugh, (AV) .....180 N. Michigan Avenue
Veys, Richard S. .....'54 '81 C.546 B.A. L.339 J.D. Sr. Coun., A.T. Kearney, Inc.
Vezeau, Timothy J., (AV) .....'44 '72 C.734 B.S.E.E. L.276 J.D. [Katten M.R.] (Pat.)
Vezino, Patrick J. .....'70 '95 C.37 B.A. L.209 J.D. [Baker&E.]
Vickers, Thomas A. .....'63 '94 C.234 B.S. L.146 J.D. [Daar&V.]
Vickery, Randall G. .....'— '88 C.1365 B.A. L.309 J.D. [Freeborn&P.]
Vickrey, Paul K., (AV) .....'55 '80 C.339 B.A. L.424 J.D. [Niro,S.H.&N.]
Victor, David A. .....'63 '89 C.339 B.A. L.209 J.D. 20 N. Clark St., Ste. 1000
Victor, Dean M. .....'— '92 C.966 B.A. L.365 J.D. [Foley&L.]
Victor, Hillary A. .....'76 '01 C.578 B.A. L.365 J.D. [Jenner&B.]
Victor, Marvin M. .....'25 '50 C.597 L.209 LL.B. 300 N. LaSalle St.
Videtto, Keli M. .....'— '01 C.853 B.A. L.966 J.D. [Arnstein&L.]
Vidis, Jennifer D. .....'61 '89 C.788 A.B. L.276 J.D. Exec. Dir., Human Rights Comm.
Vidmar, Jacqueline M., (AV) .....'63 '88 C.659 B.A. L.597 J.D. [Sonnenschein N.&R.]
Vidovic, Christopher M. .....'63 '88 C.339 B.S. L.145 J.D. 200 E. Randolph Dr., Ste. 4322
Vieth, Perry J. .....'56 '82 C.436 B.S. L.602 J.D. Chicago Research & Trading
Vig, Ritu '— '02 C&L.339 B.S., J.D.
(adm. in MI; not adm. in IL) [Katten M.R.]
Vigano, Jon Carlo .....'— '99 C.426 B.A. L.424 J.D. [Schiff H.]
Vigil, Angela C. .....'— '95 C.575 B.A. L.597 J.D. [Baker&M.]
Vigil, Thomas R., (AV) '38 '66 C.46 B.S.E.E. L.209 J.D.
[Welsh&K.] (See Pat. Sect.)
Vihon, Robert S., (AV) .....'52 '77 C.339 B.S. L.146 J.D. [Worsek&V.]
Viktora, Philip R. .....'52 '80 C.801 B.S. L.589 J.D. State Atty.
Vilimek, Mark S. .....'56 '83 C.1151 B.A. L.146 J.D. [Sanchez&D.]
Vilkelis, Peter J., (BV) .....'55 '80 C.339 B.A. L.365 J.D. 53 W. Jackson Blvd.
Villa, Robert K. .....'70 '95 C.339 B.S. L.209 J.D. [Dykema G.P.]
Villalobos, Melissa M. .....'76 '04 C.910 A.B. L.597 J.D. [Barack F.K.P.&N.]
Villar, Ronnie Lebita .....'75 '03 C.999 B.A. L.209 J.D. 227 W. Monroe, Ste. 2000
Villarreal, Irma .....'58 '83 C.339 B.A. L.209 J.D. Playboy Enterprises, Inc.
Villarreal, Judith A. .....'52 '90 C.476 L.146 J.D. Man Financial Inc.
Villeneuve, Alain .....'67 '03 C.999 B.E L.339 J.D. [Swanson,M.&B.]
Villmow, Keith E. .....'— '93 C.821 B.A. L.813 J.D. [Kirkland&E.]
Vincent, Brent W. .....'72 '99 C.902 B.A. L.597 J.D. [Bell,B.&L.]
Vincent, Joshua G. .....'58 '83 C.477 A.B. L.209 J.D. [Hinshaw&C.]
Vine, Eli B. .....'78 '04 C.608 B.A. L.1000 J.D. 188 W. Randolph, Ste. 300
Viner, Anne E. .....'68 '93 C.207 B.A. L.597 J.D. [Varga B.L.H.&C.]
Viner, Jonathan T. .....'68 '93 C.339 B.S. L.597 J.D. [Bates&C.]
Viner, Michael B., (AV) .....'63 '88 C&L.339 B.S., J.D. [Much S.F.D.A.&R.]
Viner, Monte .....'34 '57 C.339 B.S. L.209 J.D. Suite 4620, 55 East Monroe Street
Vinikoor, Robert D. .....'49 '76 C.205 B.S. L.64 J.D. U.S. Immigration J.
Vining, Patrick .....'— '00 C.321 A.B. L.1119 J.D. [Nisen&E.]
Vink Venegas, Krista '— '01 L.1522 J.D.
(adm. in CA; not adm. in IL) [McDermott W.&E.]
Vinson, B. Todd .....'72 '98 C.260 B.S. L.880 J.D. [Drinker B.&R.]
Vinson, Sam, (AV) .....'— '79 C.197 B.A. L.276 J.D. [Ungaretti&H.] (Springfield)
Vinyard, George A., (AV) .....'— '77 C.340 B.A. L.477 J.D. [Sachnoff&W.]
Virgil, Michael S. .....'42 '67 C&L.879 B.A., J.D. [Burke,W.M.&S.]
Virgilio, John V. .....'38 '66 C.801 L.209 J.D. Ret. Cir. J.‡
Virmani, Aalok .....'74 '99 C&L.339 B.S., J.D. Mng., K.P.M.G. L.P.P.
Vishneski, John S., III, (AV) .....'63 '88 C&L.893 B.A., J.D. [Mayer,B.R.&M.]
Vishny, Paul H., (AV) .....'31 '53 C.339 L.209 J.D. [Seyfarth S.]
Visk, F. Kilburn .....'25 '50 C.597 L.209 LL.B. Bkrs. Life & Cas. Co.
Vist, Gary .....'— '99 C.424 B.S. L.597 J.D. [Masuda,F.E.&M.]
Vitacco, Elene F. .....'72 '97 C.477 B.A. L.424 J.D. 30 N. LaSalle St.
Vital, Leroy P. .....'23 '52 C.262 B.S. L.145 J.D. 9415 S. State St.
Vitale, Angela L. .....'77 '02 C.273 B.B.A. L.880 J.D. [Horwood M.&B.]
Vitale, Robert A., Jr. '60 '85 C.105 B.S.C.E. L.229 J.D.
[Niro,S.H.&N.] (See Pat. Sect.)

Vitale, Michael J., The Law Offices of
(See Berwyn)

Vitek, Joseph C., (CV) .....'64 '89 C&L.546 B.A., J.D. [Patzik,F.&S.]
Vitek, Michael G. .....'58 '87 C.612 B.S. L.862 J.D. Coun., The Options Clearing Corp.
Vitek, Shana L. .....'79 '03 C.927 B.S. L.365 J.D. [Beermann S.W.B.B.G.&L.]
Vitell, Joseph A., (AV) .....'40 '69 C.98 B.S. L.879 J.D. 200 N. LaSalle St.‡
Vitellaro, Lizabeth K. '75 '00
C.385 A.B. L.1000 J.D. [Brinks H.G.&L.] (See Pat. Sect.)
Vito, Joseph V. .....'— '04 C.339 B.A. L.146 J.D. [Querrey&H.]
Vitu, Joseph F., Jr. .....'71 '97 C.339 B.A. L.190 J.D. [Ambrose&C.]
Vitullo, Louis P., (AV) .....'44 '69 C.363 B.A. L.424 J.D. [Wildman,H.A.&D.]
Vitullo, Vincent F., (AV) .....'30 '55 C&L.424 A.B., J.D. Prof., DePaul Univ. Coll. of Law
Vivek, Mali V. .....'— '04 C.373 B.A. L.365 J.D. 1142 W. Drummond PL.
Viverito, John B. .....'71 '00 C.428 B.A. L.1000 J.D. Asst. Corp. Coun.
Vivian, Karen M. .....'— '89 C.1154 B.S.N. L.930 J.D. [Querrey&H.]
Viz, Stephen A. .....'67 '92 C.602 B.A. L.146 J.D. [Figliulo&S.]
Vizer, Nancy M. .....'56 '99 C.1041 B.A. L.1209 J.D. [N.M.Vizer]
Vizer, Nancy M., P.C. .....105 W. Madison, Suite 2200
Vizza, Mark, (BV) .....'56 '81 C&L.209 B.S.C., J.D. [Brady,C.&M.]
Vlahakis, James C. .....'70 '95 C.475 B.A. L.424 J.D. [Hinshaw&C.]

Vlaming, Julie M. '72 '99 C.602 B.A. L.424 J.D.
(adm. in NY; not adm. in IL) 333 West Wacker Drive, Suite 500
Vobornik, Donna J., (AV) .....'62 '87 C.597 B.A. L.966 J.D. [Sonnenschein N.&R.]
Vocat, Cynthia J. .....'70 '02 C.338 B.S.Ed. L.209 J.D. [Nadler,P.&M.]
Voelker, Daniel J., (AV) .....'— '85 C.339 B.S. L.146 J.D. [Freeborn&P.]
Vogel, Donald J., (AV) .....'59 '85 C.347 B.S. L.1119 J.D. [Scopelitis,G.L.&H.]
Vogel, Mark Joseph .....'47 '73 C.742 B.A. L.588 J.D. Off. of U.S. Atty.
Vogel, Raymond F. .....'12 '38 L.146 LL.B. 7003 W. Higgins Ave.
Vogelsang, Donald A., (AV) .....'49 '79 C.347 B.A. L.365 J.D. [Grippo&E.]
Vogelsperger, Gregory .....'— '00 C.321 B.A. L.145 J.D. [Kirkland&E.]
Vogelzang, Nicholas J. .....'74 '99 C.114 B.A. L.734 J.D. [Richardson,P.W.&B.]
Voges, Mickie A. '50 '79 C&L.846 B.A., J.D.
(adm. in TX; not adm. in IL) Assoc. Prof. of Law, Chicago-Kent Legal Info. Ctr.
Vogler, Gregory J., (AV) '54 '84
C.679 B.S. L.209 J.D. [McAndrews,H.&M.] (See Pat. Sect.)
Vogler, James R., (AV) .....'— '77 C.309 B.A. L.801 J.D. [Barack F.K.P.&N.]
Vogt, Keith A. .....'61 '91 C.339 B.S. L.46 J.D. [Stadheim&G.] (Pat.)
Vogt, Robert P. .....'60 '85 C.177 B.A. L.146 J.D. [Weldon-Linne&V.]
Vogts, James B., (AV) .....'58 '84 C.473 A.B. L.209 J.D. [Wildman,H.A.&D.]
Voit, Richard L., (AV) .....'17 '44 C.966 B.S.E.E. L.273 J.D. 2 Prudential Plaza (Pat.)
Vojcanin, Sava Alexander, (BV) .....'64 '88 C.210 B.A. L.910 J.D. [Clausen M.]
Vold, Scott J. .....'— '03 C.339 B.A. L.910 J.D. [Segal M.S.&M.]
Volk, Eugene J. .....'31 '56 C.723 B.A. L.602 LL.B. V.P., Bankers Life & Cas. Co.
Volk, Lesley Milbury .....'72 '97 C.339 B.A.U.P. L.589 J.D. 77 W. Wacker Dr., Ste. 4025
Volk, Matthew T. .....'72 '02 C.475 B.A. L.352 J.D. [Magnani&B.]
Volk, Phyllis L. .....'52 '78 C.339 B.S. L.146 J.D. 2 N. Riverside Plaza
Volpe, Jason Alex .....'74 '99 C&L.846 B.A., J.D. 500 W. Madison St., Ste.2300
Volz, Carl E. .....'70 '95 C.610 B.A. L.146 J.D. [Katten M.R.]
Volz, Thomas A. .....'69 '96 C.945 B.A. L.910 J.D. [Kane&F.]
Vonder Heide, Susan M. .....'52 '86 C.694 A.B. L.424 J.D. 405 N. Wabash, Ste. 612
Vonder Heide, William C. .....'28 '53 C&L.424 B.S.C., J.D. 2621 W. 103rd Pl.
Vonderheide, Gregory Paul .....'50 '78 C.1183 B.A. L.146 J.D. F.B.I.
Von Drathen, Karl W. .....'— '00 C.800 B.S. L.339 J.D. [Foley&L.]
Von Hoene, William A., Jr., (AV) '54 '81 C.976 B.A. L.145 J.D.
Sr. V.P., Acting Gen. Coun., & Dep. Gen. Coun., Exelon Corp.
Vonhof, Jeanne M. .....'52 '83 C.72 B.A. L.339 J.D. 4031 N. Hermitage Ave.
Von Hoff, Carrie A. .....'— '03 C.597 L.880 J.D. [O'Hagan,S.&A.]
von Kluck, Kenneth A. .....'44 '68 C.694 A.B. L.966 J.D. [Defrees&F.]
von Mandel, Mary D., (AV) .....'52 '88 C.665 B.A. L.209 J.D. [von Mandel&v.]
von Mandel, Michael J., (AV) .....'41 '69 C.276 A.B. L.128 J.D. [von Mandel&v.]

von Mandel & von Mandel, (AV)
79 West Monroe Street, Suite 1000, 60603
Telephone: 312-726-2145 Telecopier: 312-726-2261
Email: mvmtax@aol.com URL: http://www.lawyers.com/mvmtax
Michael J. von Mandel; Mary D. von Mandel.
Tax Controversies, Tax Litigation, Federal Taxation, Estate and Gift Taxation, State Tax Controversies, Employment Tax, Criminal Tax Audits.
See Professional Biographies, CHICAGO, ILLINOIS

von Meier, Joseph E. .....'72 '02 C.477 B.B.A. L.966 J.D. [Burke,W.M.&S.]
von Moltke, H. Kurt .....'— '86 C.597 B.A. L.477 J.D. [Kirkland&E.]
von Ohlen, Robert C., Jr., (AV) .....'59 '84 C&L.602 B.A., J.D. [Kaplan,v.&M.]
Voorhees, John J., Jr., (AV) .....'66 '92 C.228 B.A. L.910 J.D. [Mayer,B.R.&M.]
Voortman, John J., (AV) .....'— '60 C.475 B.A. L.145 J.D. [Schiff H.]
Vorachek, Darlene A., (AV) .....'56 '82 C.477 B.A. L.273 J.D. [Abrahamson V.&L.]
Vorbeck, Rachel M. .....'71 '96 C.502 B.A. L.597 J.D. [Katten M.R.]
Vorberg, Elaine S. .....'71 '95 C.679 B.S. L.339 J.D. [Childress D.G.]
Voris, Stephen C., (AV) .....'54 '79 C.93 A.B. L.209 J.D. [Burke,W.M.&S.]
Vorobiev, Jill S. .....'— '96 C.31 B.A. L.602 J.D. [Jones D.]
Vos, Amy Kuemmel '72 '99 C.436 B.A. L.145 J.D.
(adm. in WI; not adm. in IL) Prudential Capital Grp.
Vosicky, Joseph F., Jr., (BV) .....'49 '81 C.210 B.A. L.365 J.D. 53 W. Jackson Blvd.
Voss, Paul J. .....'67 '94 C.339 B.S. L.424 J.D. [T.J.Reed]

Vournazos, George J., The Law Offices of, (AV) '62 '87 C&L.424 B.B.A., J.D.
2334 West Lawrence Avenue, Suite 100, 60625
Telephone: 708-636-5900; 773-784-5006 Fax: 773-784-5068
Email: LawFind@flash.net URL: http://www.georgejvournazos.com
Personal Injury, Medical Malpractice, Legal Malpractice, Slip and Fall, Product Liability, Automobile Accidents, Workers Compensation, Assault and Battery, Consumer Bankruptcy, Business, Corporate, Contract Litigation, Chancery, Real Estate, Collections and Administrative Hearings.
See Professional Biographies, CHICAGO, ILLINOIS

Voyles, Sherrie E. .....'65 '90 C.97 B.S. L.851 J.D. [Jacobs,B.O.S.&H.]
Voytovich, Anna M. '60 '83 C.338 B.S. L.339 J.D.
Vice. Pres. & Asst. Gen. Coun., Federal Reserve Bank of Chicago
Vranicar, John E. .....'49 '84 C.589 B.A. L.424 J.D. [Field&G.]
Vrdolyak, Catherine .....'49 '82 C.209 B.A. L.365 J.D. 9618 S. Coml. Ave.
Vrdolyak, Edward R., Ltd. .....'37 '63 C.1024 B.A. L.145 J.D. 741 N. Dearborn St.
Vree, Roger A. .....'43 '69 C.937 B.A. L.813 J.D. [Sidley A.B.&W.]
Vrla, Mark P. .....'59 '97 C&L.339 B.S.E., J.D. [Jenner&B.] (Pat.)
Vroman, James A., (AV) .....'48 '77 C&L.339 B.S., J.D. [Jenner&B.]
Vroustouris, Alexander, (BV) .....'54 '80 C.424 B.S. L.365 J.D. Inspector Gen. Off.
Vucinovich, Kristin L. .....'75 '00 C.1268 B.A. L.424 J.D. [Horwood M.&B.]
Vuckovic, Sladjana .....'68 '95 C.339 B.A. L.589 J.D. 2 North LaSalle
Vuckovich, Adrian M. .....'65 '91 C.966 B.A. L.424 J.D. [Collins&B.]
Vurdelja, George N., Jr., (AV) .....'56 '81 C.475 B.A. L.145 J.D. [Vurdelja&H.]

Vurdelja & Heaphy, (AV)
120 North La Salle Street, Suite 1150, 60602
Telephone: 312-345-2000 Fax: 312-345-2005
John M. Heaphy; George N. Vurdelja, Jr.; Griswold L. Ware.
Civil Litigation including Insurance Coverage Litigation, Reinsurance Litigation and Arbitration, Bankruptcy Litigation, Breach of Contract, Construction Litigation, Commercial Torts, Employment Litigation, Collection, Personal Injury, Product Liability, Fraud, Probate Litigation.
See Professional Biographies, CHICAGO, ILLINOIS

Vyas, Ujjval K. .....'60 '03 C.581 B.A. L.146 J.D. [Foran G.P.&P.]
Vyverberg, Kerry A. .....'69 '94 C.347 B.A. L.339 J.D. [Lord,B.&B.]
Vyverberg, Robert W., Jr. .....'68 '93 C&L.339 B.S., J.D. [Holland&K.]
Waack, Kirsten Radler .....'69 '94 C.229 B.A. L.896 J.D. [Christensen&E.]
Wabich, James A. .....'49 '74 C.424 B.B.A. L.472 J.D. Dir., Tax Planning, Sara Lee Corp.
Wacaser, Carol Hines .....'— '93 C.882 B.S. L.209 J.D. [Gardner C.&D.]
Wachspress, Eric S. .....'54 '80 C.529 B.A. L.128 J.D. 1727 N. Natoma Ave.
Wachtel, Eugene H., (AV) .....'38 '62 C&L.145 B.A., J.D. [Lord,B.&B.]
Wachtel, Gary K. .....'73 '03 C.529 B.A. L.365 J.D. [Mayer,B.R.&M.]
Wacks, Peter J. '40 '66 C.116 B.S. L.823 LL.B.
(adm. in NY; not adm. in IL) 10334 S. Leavitt St.
Wade, Jacqueline J. .....'71 '96 C.309 A.B. L.347 J.D. [Connelly S.H.]

Wadhwa, Anuj K. ...... '75 '00 C.999 B.S. L.124 J.D. [Ⓐ Baniak P.&G.] (See Pat. Sect.)
Wadington, Robert N., & Associates, (AV) '57 '86
C.347 B.S. L.365 J.D. 111 W. Washington St., Ste., 1460
Wadley, Christopher A. ....'78 '02 C.339 B.A. L.424 J.D. [Ⓐ Walker W.M.]
Wagenbach, Doug J. ....'— '04 C.350 B.S. L.352 J.D. [Ⓐ Schiff H.]
Wagener, Jason B. ....'69 '95 C.112 B.A. L.146 J.D. 10 S. La Salle
Wagener, John T., (AV) ....'— '83 C.812 B.A. L.339 J.D. [Arnstein&L.]
Wagener, Susan Ann ....'59 '87 C.966 B.S. L.436 J.D. [Ⓐ Alholm,M.K.H.&O.]
Wagenmaker, Sally R. ....'66 '90 C.500 B.A. L.245 J.D. [Ⓐ Hoogendoorn&T.]
Wager, Charlotte L. ....'64 '92 L.051 LL.B. [Jenner&B.]
Wagman, Heidi A. .... '64 '91 C.861 B.S. L.569 J.D. 2669D N. Greenview Ave.‡
Wagman, Sandra Dee '54 '79
C.347 B.A. L.424 J.D. Asst. V.P. & Asst. Gen. Coun., CNA
Wagman, Zachary D. ....'64 '89 C.966 B.A. L.339 J.D. [Katten M.R.]
Wagner, David L. '64 '91 C.951 B.A. L.94 J.D.
(adm. in NY; not adm. in IL) 5447 S. Hyde Park Blvd.‡
Wagner, Irvin J. ....'56 '81 C.339 B.A. L.146 J.D. [Cin&W.]
Wagner, Janet ....'61 '00 C.530 B.A. L.424 J.D. [Ⓐ Sinar K.M.&F.]
Wagner, Jeffrey C. ....'68 '93 C.602 B.B.A. L.424 J.D. [McDermott W.&E.]
Wagner, Jeffrey M., (AV) ....'62 '88 C.684 B.A. L.145 J.D. [Winston&S.]
Wagner, Michael J., (AV) ....'57 '81 C.597 B.S.J. L.966 J.D. [Baker&M.]
Wagner, Richard R. .....'47 '74 C.1024 B.A. L.1119 J.D. Sr. Atty., U.S. Envir. Pro. Agcy.
Wagner, Robert ....'— '01 C.1167 B.S. L.124 J.D. [Ⓐ Wildman,H.A.&D.]
Wagner, Robert E., (AV) '30 '61
C.350 B.S.E. L.30 J.D. [Ⓒ Wallenstein W.&R.] (See Pat. Sect.)
Wagner, Robert J. ....'36 '64 C.502 B.S. L.862 LL.B. Amoco Corp.‡
Wagner, Steven M. ....'— '79 C.234 B.A. L.365 J.D. [Ⓒ Gardner C.&D.]
Wagreich, Ian D. ....'66 '95 C.966 B.S. L.424 J.D. [Wagreich&C.]
Wagreich & Choi ....75 East Wacker Drive
Wah, Angela C. .... '72 '97 C.339 B.A. L.436 J.D. Atty., Equity Off. Properties Tr.
Wahlen, Edwin A., (AV) ....'19 '48 C&L.145 A.B., J.D. [Ⓒ Wildman,H.A.&D.]
Wahlers, John L., (AV) ....'51 '77 C.31 B.A. L.880 J.D. [Ⓒ Dolgin&F.]
Wahtola, Charles Henry, III ....'71 '98 C.966 B.A. L.424 J.D. [Ⓐ Stein,R.&H.]

Wai, Minh C., Law Offices of
(See Merrillville, Indiana)

Waintroob, Andrea R., (AV) ....'52 '78 C.103 A.B. L.145 J.D. [Franczek S.]
Waite, Norman, Jr., (AV) ....'36 '63 C.976 B.A. L.309 LL.B. 35 W. Wacker Dr.‡
Waitzman, Gary R. ....'52 '80 C.339 B.S. L.365 J.D. [Mora,B.W.&U.] ⊙
Wake, Kenneth R. ....'69 '95 C.234 B.A. L.801 J.D. [Ⓐ Blatt,H.L.&M.]
Wakeen, Linda M. ....'58 '83 C&L.477 B.S., J.D. Assoc. Gen. Coun., Amer. Dental Assn.
Wakely, James M. ....'75 '00 C.98 B.S.E.E. L.597 J.D. [Ⓐ Fitch,E.T.&F.] (See Pat. Sect.)
Wakschlag, Milton S. ....'55 '80 L.145 J.D. [Katten M.R.]
Walberg, Kim R. ....'74 '99 C.309 B.A. L.424 J.D. [Ⓐ Shefsky&F.]
Walch, Matthew W. ....'— '94 C.473 B.A. L.276 J.D. [Latham&W.]
Walchirk, Victor L. '32 '56 C.347 A.B. L.145 J.D.
Exec. Dir., Housing Auth. of Cook Co.
Wald, Barbara Anderson '51 '84
C.696 B.A. L.145 J.D. Coun., Bank One Corporation (Law Dept.)
Wald, Bruce L., (AV) ....'46 '72 C.966 B.A. L.597 LL.B. [Tishler&W.]
Wald, David S. ....'16 '39 C&L.597 B.A., J.D. 4980 Marine Dr.‡
Walden, David V. .....'47 '78 C.339 B.A. L.146 J.D. Hearings Ref., Dept. of Employ. Sec.
Walden, Kenneth M. ....'63 '90 C.705 B.A. L.446 J.D. 614 W. Roosevelt Road
Waldier, Sandra L. ....'73 '97 C&L.339 B.A., J.D. [Bell,B.&L.]
Waldman, Bruce J., (BV) ....'52 '77 C.352 B.S. L.339 J.D. [Cohon R.&R.]
Waldman, Carol A. ....'54 '85 C.478 B.A. L.597 J.D. Legal Assistance Found. of Chicago
Waldman, Joey B. ....'74 '99 C.352 B.A. L.209 J.D. [Ⓐ Robbins,S.&P.]
Waldon, Dennis C., (AV) ....'46 '73 C.145 B.A. L.309 J.D. [Lavin&W.]
Waldron, Austin J., (AV) ....'26 '53 C.209 B.S. L.365 LL.B. 10526 S. Talman‡
Waldron, John J., Jr. '34 '60 C&L.424 B.S., J.D.
Sr. Atty., Northern Trust Corporation
Wales, Samuel W. ....'74 '00 C&L.276 B.A., J.D. [Ⓐ McDermott W.&E.]
Walgenbach, Lisa A. '— '04 C.679 B.S. L.1522 J.D.
(adm. in CA; not adm. in IL) [Ⓐ Mayer,B.R.&M.] (⊙L.A., CA)
Walinski, Robert J., (AV) ....'49 '76 C.597 B.A. L.424 J.D. [Walinski&T.]
Walinski & Trunkett, P.C., (AV) ....25 E. Washington St., Suite 1927
Walker, Allen P. ....'61 '87 C&L.209 B.S., J.D. [Greene&L.]
Walker, Barton C. ....'79 '04 C.575 B.A. L.602 J.D. [Ⓐ McGuirewoods]
Walker, Carl Anthony, Law Offices of '63 '92
C.339 B.S. L.352 J.D. 120 W. Madison, Ste. 910
Walker, Carlon B. ....'52 '77 C.411 B.A. L.329 J.D. 2743 N. Greenview Ave.
Walker, David E. ....'64 '89 C.174 B.A. L.339 J.D. [Walker W.M.]
Walker, David J., (AV) ....'39 '80 C.999 M.A. L.424 LL.D. [Ⓒ W.J.Harte]
Walker, Debra B., (AV) ....'60 '87 C&L.339 B.S., J.D. [Clausen M.]
Walker, Douglas W. ....'68 '94 C.210 B.A. L.339 J.D. [Ⓐ Walker W.M.]
Walker, Gregory Ronald ....'74 '00 C.130 B.A. L.477 J.D. [Ⓐ McDermott W.&E.]
Walker, Hopeton ....'— '02 C.570 B.S. L.552 J.D. [Ⓐ McAndrews,H.&M.]
Walker, Howard, (AV) '39 '63 C&L.339 B.S., J.D.
Pres., & CEO, Manufactured Home Communities, Inc.
Walker, John Craig ....'57 '83 C.813 A.B. L.477 J.D. [Bell,B.&L.]
Walker, John N. ....'64 '92 C.145 B.A. L.309 J.D. [Stein,R.&H.]
Walker, Matthew D. ....'— '97 C&L.339 B.A., J.D. [Ⓐ Litchfield C.]
Walker, Megan G. ....'75 '00 C.475 B.S. L.477 J.D. [Ⓐ Goldberg,K.B.B.R.&M.]
Walker, Rebecca D. ....'— '03 C.339 B.S. L.1117 J.D. [Ⓐ Kirkland&E.] (Pat.)
Walker, Richard A. ....'55 '87 C&L.623 B.A., J.D. [Kaplan,v.&M.]
Walker, Richard G. ....'35 '66 C.165 A.B. L.365 LL.B. Lake View Tr. & Svgs. Bk.
Walker, William A. ....'59 '87 C.337 B.S. L.424 J.D. [Nisen&E.]

Walker Wilcox Matousek LLP, (AV) BR
225 W. Washington Street, Suite 2400, 60606-3418
Telephone: 312-244-6700 Fax: 312-244-6800
URL: http://www.wwmlawyers.com
Partners of Firm: William P. Bila; Joseph J. Borders; Joyce F. Clough; Robert P. Conlon; Edward P. Gibbons; James J. Huberty; Celeste M. King; David L. Koury; Gary L. Lockwood; Paul F. Matousek; Jill A. O'Donovan; Kristine M. Sorenson; David E. Walker; Mark D. Wilcox. Associates: Eric D. Blanchard; Marnie N. Bozic; Peter G. Daniels; Jannis E. Goodnow; James W. Kienzle, Jr.; Tiffany S. Saltzman-Jones; Kari A. Timm; Christopher A. Wadley; Douglas W. Walker.
Insurance Law, Coverage, Counseling, Alternative Dispute Resolution, Litigation, Civil Trial Practice, Aviation Coverage and Defense, Casualty Insurance Coverage and Defense, Class Action Defense, Commercial Litigation, Construction Defense, Contract Litigation, Directors and Officers Liability Coverage, Employment Practices Liability Insurance Coverage and Defense, Environmental Insurance Coverage and Defense, Financial Institutions Liability Insurance Coverage and Defense, First and Third Party Insurance Coverage and Defense, Life, Accident and Health, and Disability Insurance Coverage and Defense, Media and Defamation Coverage and Defense, Medical Liability Insurance Coverage, Premises Liability Defense, Products Liability Defense, Professional Liability Insurance Coverage, Professional Liability Counseling and Defense, Property Insurance Coverage and Defense, Reinsurance Coverage and Arbitrations, Tort Defense, Accountants Liability, Insurance Agents and

(This Listing Continued)

Walker Wilcox Matousek LLP (Continued)
Brokers Liability, Attorneys, Data Processors, Tech and eBusiness, Directors and Officers Liability, Fiduciaries, Public Officials, School Boards, Real Estate Agents and Brokers, Registered Representatives, Third Party Administrators, Trustees.
See Professional Biographies, CHICAGO, ILLINOIS

Walker-Bright, Paul R. ....'— '94 C.145 B.A. L.146 J.D. [Anderson K.&O.]
Walkington, Sarah M. ....'76 '02 C.352 B.S. L.365 J.D. [Ⓐ Fitch,E.T.&F.]
Walkowicz, Victoria A. ....'50 '84 C.339 B.A. L.146 J.D. Asst. V. P., Aon Re Inc.
Walkup, April R. ....'— '96 C.679 B.A. L.365 J.D. [Querrey&H.]
Wall, Anne E. ....'76 '02 C.473 B.A. L.209 J.D. [Ⓐ Pretzel&S.]
Wall, Bernard T., P.C., (AV) ....'38 '62 C&L.339 A.B., LL.B. 70 W. Madison St.
Wall, Bruce M., (AV) ....'51 '76 C.209 B.S.C. L.146 J.D. [Cassiday,S.&G.]
Wall, Donald J. ....'52 '77 C.118 B.A. L.436 J.D. Coun., to the Cir. Exec.
Wall, Jeanine M. ....'46 '81 C.966 B.A. L.146 J.D. [D.H.Robertson]
Wall, Julie Freund ....'74 '99 C.201 B.S. L.339 J.D. [Ⓐ Chittenden,M.&N.]
Wall, Michael J. ....'46 '75 C.339 B.A. L.146 J.D. [Rothschild,B.&M.]
Wall, Robert F., (AV) ....'52 '77 C.597 B.A. L.770 J.D. [Winston&S.]
Wallace, Donna B. ....'49 '89 C.652 B.A. L.365 J.D. [Ⓐ J.A.Baldi&Assoc.]
Wallace, Edward A. ....'69 '95 C.234 B.A. L.209 J.D. [Wexler]
Wallace, Elizabeth A., (BV) ....'54 '89 C.339 B.A. L.365 J.D. Asst. Atty. Gen.
Wallace, Frances .....'59 '95 C.999 B.S. L.424 J.D. 1130 S. Michigan Avenue, Suite 613
Wallace, Gary J. ....'57 '83 C.352 B.A. L.146 J.D. [Nyhan,P.B.K.&L.]
Wallace, Karen C. ....'60 '86 C.339 B.A. L.801 J.D. HIPAA Chf. Compl. Offr.
Wallace, Michael J. ....'39 '65 C&L.597 B.A., J.D. 924 S. Bishop
Wallace, Peggy C., (BV) ....'50 '79 C.801 B.A. L.365 J.D. 4201 N. Sheridan Road.
Wallack, Jerry B. ....'52 '78 C.604 B.A. L.145 J.D. [Kutak R.]
Wallar, Joshua J. ....'— '02 C.957 B.A. L.966 J.D. [Ⓐ Mandell M.]
Wallenfelsz, Rebecca ....'— '97 C.602 B.A. L.424 J.D. [Ⓐ Chapman&C.]

Wallenstein Wagner & Rockey, Ltd., (AV) BR
Suite 5300 311 South Wacker Drive, 60606-6630
Telephone: 312-554-3300 Facsimile: 312-554-3301
Email: iplaw@wwrfirm.com URL: http://www.wwrfirm.com
Daniel N. Christus; Thomas C. Elliott, Jr.; Jeffrey R. Gargano; Matthew J. Gryzlo; Brent A. Hawkins; Richard C. Himelhoch; Peter M. Klobuchar; Linda A. Kuczma; Kathleen A. Lyons; Monique A. Morneault; James P. Muraff; Paul J. Nykaza; Bradley F. Rademaker; Keith V. Rockey; David L. Schwartz; Roger H. Stein; Sidney Wallenstein (1907-1999). Of Counsel: Robert E. Wagner;—Joseph T. Bernstein; Amy M. Crout Ziegler; Amol A. Parikh; Avani C. Patel; Nicholas C. Pruhs; Gregory G. Schlenz; Peter M. Siavelis; Maurice E. Teixeira.
Intellectual Property and Technology Related Law including Protection and Licensing of United States and International Patent, Trademark, Copyright Trade Secret and Unfair Competition Matters and Related Litigation in the Courts and United States International Trade Commission.
See Professional Biographies, CHICAGO, ILLINOIS

Waller, Amy Suzanne ....'75 '01 C.352 B.A. L.424 J.D. Off. of State Appl. Def.
Waller, Harvey Jack .....'48 '74 C.1016 B.S.B.A. L.209 J.D. 30 N. La Salle St., Ste. 2040
Waller, Henry A., (AV) ....'40 '66 C.966 B.S. L.145 J.D. [Mandel,L.&S.]
Waller, Kelly D. ....'78 '03 C&L.339 B.A., J.D. [Ⓐ Tressler,S.M.&P.]
Waller, Richard W., (P.C.), (AV) ....'35 '59 C&L.597 B.A., J.D. 525 W. Monroe St.
Waller, Wayne M. ....'49 '75 C.589 B.S. L.365 J.D. [Wilk&W.]
Wallin, Harold L. ....'66 '94 C.145 B.A. L.910 J.D. 33 North Dearborn, Suite 1850
Wallin, Paul K. ....'65 '93 C.339 B.S. L.146 J.D. Gen. Coun.
Wallin, William R. ....'42 '69 C&L.145 A.B., J.D. Coun., State Dept. Human. Servs.
Wallman, Suzanne M. ....'69 '96 C.245 L.597 J.D. [Ⓐ McDermott W.&E.]
Walls, Linda Ann ....'74 '99 C.679 B.A. L.365 J.D. [Linebarger G.B.&S.]
Walls, Virginia A. ....'— '05 C.575 B.A. L.276 J.D. [Ⓐ Gardner C.&D.]
Walner, Harvey L. ....'36 '62 C.1016 B.A. L.209 LL.B. [H.L.Walner&Assoc.] ‡
Walner, Jonathan E. ....'— '88 C.477 B.B.A. L.146 J.D. [H.L.Walner&Assoc.]
Walner, Lawrence, (BV) ....'32 '56 C&L.209 B.A., J.D. [L.Walner&Assoc.]

Walner, Harvey L., & Associates, Ltd., (AV)
123 N. Wacker Drive, Suite 880, 60606
Telephone: 312-782-8550 Fax: 312-782-2646
Email: jon.walner@walnerlaw.com URL: http://www.walnerlaw.com
Harvey L. Walner (Retired); Jonathan E. Walner; Shelby H. Kanarish; Debra I. Crystal;—Marvin S. Lansky.
Construction Accidents, Heath Insurance, Long Term Care, Nursing Home Litigation, Medical Malpractice, Personal Injury, Airplane Crash Litigation, Automobile Accidents, Dog Bites, Railroad Accidents, Sexual Abuse, Slip and Fall, Wrongful Death, Products Liability, Workers Compensation.
See Professional Biographies, CHICAGO, ILLINOIS

Walner, Lawrence, & Associates, Ltd., (BV) ....150 N. Wacker Dr., Ste. 2150
Walrath, Christopher F. ....'— '91 C.589 B.A. L.209 J.D. [Chapman&C.]
Walschlager, Raymond J. '38 '81 C.209 B.A. L.365 J.D.
Sr. V.P. & Coun., GMAC Comm. Mtge. Corp.‡
Walsen, Paul J. ....'66 '94 C&L.339 B.A., J.D. [Bell,B.&L.]
Walsh, Amber McGraw ....'76 '02 C.378 B.A. L.910 J.D. [Ⓐ McGuirewoods]
Walsh, Ann Marie, (AV) ....'55 '80 C.339 B.A. L.209 J.D. [Lord,B.&B.]
Walsh, Brian F. ....'60 '85 C.475 B.A. L.424 J.D. [Barnes,R.&C.]
Walsh, Brian J. ....'— '90 C.602 B.S. L.589 J.D. Asst. Pub. Def.
Walsh, Carl M., (AV) '41 '65 C.602 B.S. L.209 J.D.
39 South La Salle Street, Suite 1400
Walsh, Carl P., Law Offices of '62 '02
C.896 B.A. L.339 J.D. 5550 S. Dorchester Ave., Apt. 602

Walsh, Christopher G., Jr., (AV) '48 '76 C.424 A.B. L.569 J.D.
111 West Washington Street, Suite 1150, 60602 ⊙
Telephone: 312-372-1155 Fax: 312-372-1974
Email: cgw@chriswalshlaw.com URL: http://www.chriswalshlaw.com
Property Tax Appeals and Civil Litigation.
Oak Park Office: 1111 South Boulevard, 60302. Telephone: 708-386-4571. Fax: 708-386-8413.
See Professional Biographies, CHICAGO, ILLINOIS

Walsh, Daniel J. ....'47 '74 C.363 B.S. L.424 J.D. Walsh Construction Co.
Walsh, Dennis G. ....'58 '86 C.1044 B.P.S. L.365 J.D. [Klein,T.&J.]
Walsh, Diane N. ....'55 '86 C.424 B.S. L.589 J.D. Asst. States Atty.
Walsh, Edward V., III, (AV) ....'— '83 C.801 B.S. L.597 J.D. [Sachnoff&W.]
Walsh, Elizabeth A. '71 '04 C.973 B.A. L.365 J.D.
Atty., NASD Dispute Resolution, Inc.
Walsh, James P. .....'69 '96 C.309 A.B. L.228 J.D. Off. of the Gen. Coun., Dept. of HHS
Walsh, John J., III, (AV) ....'46 '82 C.602 B.A. L.424 J.D. [Pretzel&S.]
Walsh, John O. ....'50 '89 C.720 B.A. L.146 J.D. [Ⓐ Borovsky&E.]
Walsh, Joseph A., Jr., (AV) ....'49 '74 C.347 B.A. L.345 J.D. [Winston&S.]
Walsh, Louise T. ....'59 '95 C.602 B.S. L.209 J.D. [Welsh&K.] (See Pat. Sect.)
Walsh, Matthew, Jr. ....'46 '72 C.602 B.A. L.424 J.D. Walsh Constr. Co.
Walsh, Matthew P., II ....'67 '92 C.98 B.S. L.146 J.D. [Hinshaw&C.]
Walsh, Matthew T. ....'63 '90 C.339 B.S. L.1049 J.D. [Cozen O.]
Walsh, Michael S., (AV) ....'51 '78 C.165 A.B. L.802 J.D. [Jenner&B.] (Pat.)
Walsh, Michael T., (AV) ....'62 '91 C.723 B.S. L.365 J.D. [Bollinger,R.&G.]
Walsh, Natalie A., (AV) ....'59 '86 C.966 B.A. L.146 J.D. [Walsh]
Walsh, Nora A. Kersten ....'— '02 C.321 B.A. L.966 J.D. [Ⓐ Schiff H.]

Walsh, Patrick T. '64 '89 C&L.424 B.S., J.D. [Lord,B.&B.]
Walsh, Peter A. '58 '83 C&L.602 B.A., J.D. [Hinshaw&C.]
Walsh, Richard A., (AV) '30 '54 C&L.424 B.S., J.D. [McCracken,W.d.&H.]
Walsh, Richard J., (AV) '26 '52 C.209 L.477 LL.B. [Ⓒ Schuyler,R.&Z.]
Walsh, Robert P., Jr., (AV) '59 '86 C.723 B.A. L.424 J.D. [Clifford]
Walsh, Susan E. '— '98 C.339 B.S. L.146 J.D. [Ⓐ Freeborn&P.]
Walsh, Thomas C. '54 '79 C.477 B.A. L.309 J.D. [Lord,B.&B.]
Walsh, Thomas M., (AVⓉ) '52 '76 C.894 A.B. L.910 J.D.
(adm. in MO; not adm. in IL) [Sonnenschein N.&R.] (⊙St. Louis, MO)
Walsh, Thomas P. '50 '78 C.339 B.S. L.209 J.D. Asst. U.S. Atty.
Walsh, Timothy J. '77 '02 C.502 B.S. L.910 J.D. [Ⓐ Meckler B.&T.]
Walsh, William F. '47 '73 C.477 B.A. L.309 J.D. [Vedder,P.K.&K.]
Walsh, Wm. J. '17 '47 C.973 Ph.B. L.209 J.D. 10310 S. Seeley Ave.
Walsh Law Office, (AV) 4434 N. Tripp Ave.
Walt, Bonnie G. '40 '67 C.518 A.B. L.276 J.D. Exec. Dir., Ill Racing Bd.
Walt, Gary Irwin, (AV) '57 '82 C.477 B.A. L.188 J.D. [Patzik,F.&S.]
Walter, Jennifer K., (AV) '64 '90 C.966 B.A. L.209 J.D. 70 W. Madison St.
Walter, Mary K. '— '90 C.352 B.B.A. L.602 J.D. [Schuyler,R.&Z.]
Walter, Priscilla A. (Pam), (AV) '43 '78 C.914 B.A. L.597 J.D. [Gardner C.&D.]
Walters, Brent R. '73 '03 C.546 B.A. L.352 J.D. [Ⓐ Shefsky&F.]
Walters, David E. '72 '98 C&L.602 B.S., J.D. [Ⓐ Jenner&B.]
Walters, Jon '66 '91 C&L.597 B.A., J.D. Asst. States Atty.
Walters, Roger C. '54 '80 C.173 B.A. L.365 J.D.
(adm. in CO; not adm. in IL) 625 W. Madison‡
Walters, Sandra J. '50 '92 C.1191 B.S. L.365 J.D. 203 E. 113th St.
Walters, Todd A. '69 '95 C.354 B.A. L.1187 J.D. [Ⓐ Muller]
Walther, Karen E. '75 '01 C.475 B.A. L.424 J.D. [Ⓐ Bell,B.&L.]
Walther, M. Jacqueline '55 '79 C&L.424 A.B., J.D. [Kielian&W.]
Walton, Edward A. '74 '00 C.475 B.A. L.365 J.D. 2 N. LaSalle St.
Walton, Gordon K. '68 '94 C.145 B.A. L.365 J.D. [Clausen M.]
Walton, Michele L. '— '99 C.475 B.A. L.209 J.D. [Ⓐ Sachnoff&W.]
Walton, Robert S. '71 '96 C.339 B.S. L.309 J.D. [Baker&M.]
Walton, Scott '— '03 C.187 B.A. L.352 J.D. [Ⓐ Winston&S.]
Walton, Wesley S., (AV) '38 '64 C&L.309 A.B., LL.B. [Ⓒ Lord,B.&B.]
Walts, C. Alan '68 '96 C.918 B.A. L.477 J.D.
(adm. in MI; not adm. in IL) Asst. Reg. Coun., U.S. E.P.A.
Wambach, Douglas E., (AV) '56 '81 C&L.276 B.S., J.D. [Burke,W.M.&S.]
Wanamaker, Brian '— '03 C.378 B.A. L.910 J.D. [Ⓐ Winston&S.]
Wand, Terry '— '04 C.974 B.S. L.1119 J.D. [Ⓐ Hinshaw&C.]
Wander, Herbert S., (P.C.), (AV) '35 '60 C.477 A.B. L.976 LL.B. [Katten M.R.]
Wanek, Laura R. '77 '02 C.966 B.S. L.209 J.D. 300 S. Walker, Ste. 2500
Wang, Andrew D. '69 '94 C.477 B.A. L.597 J.D. [Ⓐ Winston&S.]
Wang, Kathy '— '03 C.1133 B.S. L.365 J.D. Leg. Recr., Spherion Corp.
Wang, Xiaojie '71 '02 C.999 B.A. L.352 J.D. [Ⓐ Skadden,A.S.M.&F.]
Wangard, Robert E. '41 '69 C.966 B.S. L.339 J.D. [McGuirewoods]
Wangelin, James D., (AV) '47 '74 C&L.477 A.B., J.D. [Sedgwick,D.M.&A.]
Wanger, Eric David '62 '99 C.339 B.S. L.813 J.D. 161 N. Clare Street, Suite 2950
Wangerin, Paul T. '47 '79 C.986 A.B. L.365 J.D. Assoc. Prof., John Marshall Law Sch.
Wang-Grimm, Jessie '68 '93 C.145 B.A. L.424 J.D. Asst. Reg. Coun., Soc. Sec. Adm.
Wangler, Daniel J. '62 '92 C.477 B.A. L.912 J.D.
(adm. in MI; not adm. in IL) [D.J.Wangler]
Wangler, Daniel J., Law Office of 3933 N. Hermitage Ave.
Wanke, Ronald L., (AV) '41 '68 C.597 B.S.E.E. L.209 J.D. [Jenner&B.] (Pat.)
Wanless, Marion '— '96 C.910 B.A. L.339 J.D. Dept. of HHS
Wanninger, Albert M. '38 '70 C.339 B.S.E.E. L.365 J.D. 205 W. Randolph St
Wappel, John P. '— '04 C.339 B.S.M.E. L.146 J.D. [Ⓐ Barnes&T.] (See Pat. Sect.)
Warchol, Louis C. '30 '54 C.339 L.365 LL.B. 134 N. LaSalle
Ward, Brooke B. '73 '99 C.477 B.A. L.1065 J.D. [Ⓐ Winston&S.]
Ward, Dennis P. '47 '73 C.436 B.S.M.E. L.966 J.D. Sargent & Lundy
Ward, Dorothy Voss, (BV) '49 '81 C.239 B.A. L.146 J.D. [Kamensky,R.H.&D.] ⊙
Ward, Elizabeth A. '68 '94 C.353 B.A. L.365 J.D. [Ⓐ Matkov,S.M.&G.]
Ward, Eunice '46 '80 C.608 B.S. L.146 J.D. [Nottage&W.]
Ward, Everett S., (AV) '— '86 C.674 A.B. L.309 J.D. [Schiff H.]
Ward, Guy G. '62 '93 C.145 B.A. L.339 J.D. Fed. Trade Comm.
Ward, Jennifer R. '77 '02 C.502 B.A. L.365 J.D. [Revis&W.]
Ward, John A., (AV) '40 '65 C.31 A.B. L.145 J.D. 11 W. Monroe St.‡
Ward, John Andrew '54 '79 C.436 B.S. L.597 J.D. Asst. Atty. Gen.
Ward, John F., (AV) '58 '83 C.338 B.S. L.146 J.D. 225 W. Washington
Ward, John F., Jr. '65 '91 C&L.477 B.A., J.D. [Jenner&B.]
Ward, John F., Jr., (P.C.), (AV) '41 '66 C.602 A.B. L.209 J.D. [O'Keefe,L.&H.]
Ward, John H., (AV) '42 '78 C.870 B.S. L.209 J.D. [Much S.F.D.A.&R.]
Ward, Kathleen R. '49 '89 C.530 B.A. L.46 J.D. State Dept. of Mental Health
Ward, Lori Anne '66 '92 C&L.37 B.A., J.D. [Sonnenschein N.&R.]
Ward, Molly A. '— '02 C.339 B.A. L.209 J.D. [Ⓐ Chuhak&T.]
Ward, Thomas P., (AV) '31 '58
C&L.966 B.S.M.E., J.D. 500 West Madison Street, 40th Floor‡
Ward, Thomas P. '71 '96 C.602 B.B.A. L.477 J.D. [Ⓐ McDermott W.&E.]
Ward, Torrick Alan '72 '98 C.589 B.S. L.209 J.D. Sr. Coun.
Ward, William F., III '76 '02
C.436 B.S.C.E. L.365 J.D. [Ⓐ Baniak P.&G.] (See Pat. Sect.)
Ward, William L. '40 '70 C.424 B.S. L.209 J.D. Bankers Life & Cas. Co.
Ward, William Parker, (AV) '17 '40 C&L.209 J.D. 111 W. Wash. St.‡
Wardak, Leah '77 '05 L.424 J.D. [Ⓐ Holland&K.]
Ward-Brown, Gwyndolette '63 '89 C&L.436 B.A., J.D. Asst. Pub. Def.
Warden, Jacob A. '— '04 C.659 B.A. L.597 J.D. [Ⓐ McGuirewoods]
Wardlaw, Byron M. '73 '04 C.338 B.A. L.365 J.D. [Ⓐ Greene&L.]
Wardrope, John T., (AV) '28 '56 C.145 B.A. L.209 J.D. [Purcell&W.]
Wardzala, Pamela M. '77 '02 C.597 B.S. L.424 J.D. State Appl. Def.
Ware, Bobby L. '62 '93 C.475 B.S. L.1338 J.D. [B.L.Ware&Assoc.]
Ware, Griswold L. '63 '92 C.207 B.A. L.365 J.D. [Vurdelja&H.]
Ware, Bobby L., and Associates, L.L.C. 8333 S. Perry Ave.
Wargula, David A. '67 '95 C.37 B.S. L.209 J.D. Corp. Coun., MarCap Corp.
Waris, Richard M., (AV) '54 '80 C&L.602 B.A., J.D. [Pretzel&S.]
Warman, Thomas D. '78 '03 C.123 B.A. L.339 J.D. [Ⓐ Figliulo&S.]
Warnecke, Andrew C. '— '96 C.679 B.S.C. L.273 J.D. [Ⓐ Winston&S.] (Pat.)
Warnecke, Michael O., (AV) '41 '67 C.679 B.S.M.E. L.273 J.D.
[Mayer,B.R.&M.] (Pat.)
Warner, David Scott '66 '95 C.597 B.A. L.1068 J.D. [Ⓐ Holland&K.]
Warner, Dina '67 '92 C.178 B.A. L.976 J.D. [Ⓐ Berger S.]
Warner, G. Ray '55 '80 C.1365 B.A. L.597 J.D. [Ⓒ Greenberg T.]
Warner, Jared M. '77 '03 C.303 B.A. L.477 J.D. [Ⓐ DLPiper R.G.C.U.]
Warner, Kelly M. '— '00 C.475 B.A. L.424 J.D. [Ⓐ Schiff H.]
Warner, Michael A., (AV) '41 '65 C.966 B.S. L.477 LL.B. [Seyfarth S.]
Warner, Michael A., Jr., (AV) '66 '91 C.228 A.B. L.597 J.D. [Franczek S.]

Warnick, Jeffrey L., (AV) '53 '78 C.339 B.S. L.146 J.D. [Crystal,H.&W.]
Warning, Brett L. '62 '88 C.57 B.A. L.879 J.D. [Ⓐ Bollinger,R.&G.]
Warren, Jeffrey D., (AV) '46 '72 C.597 A.B. L.145 J.D. [Burke,W.M.&S.]
Warren, Morrison C. '— '91 C.605 A.B. L.602 J.D. [Chapman&C.]
Warren, Myriam Pierre '70 '99 C.197 B.A. L.597 J.D. [Ⓐ McDermott W.&E.]
Warren, Renne Annette '75 '99 C.927 B.S. L.893 J.D. Ct. of Appeals
Warren, Timothy L. '59 '85 C.813 B.A. L.424 J.D. U.S. Securities & Exchange Comm.
Warren-Mikes, Elizabeth L. '69 '99 C.575 B.S.B.A. L.597 J.D.
[Ⓐ Sonnenschein N.&R.]
Warsawsky, Samuel N. '27 '76 C.339 B.A. L.146 J.D. 53 W. Jackson Blvd.
Warsh, Sheri E. '64 '89 C.477 B.B.A. L.339 J.D. [Ⓒ Neal,G.&E.]
Warshauer, Marshall A. '30 '54 C.339 L.209 LL.B. Levanthol & Horwath
Wartman, Bradley J. '60 '87 C.1191 B.S.B.A. L.989 J.D. [Ⓐ P.Andjelkovich]
Waryjas, Maryann A. '— '83 C.424 B.S. L.597 J.D. [Katten M.R.]
Warzala, Stanley W. '22 '53 C&L.209 Ph.B., LL.B. 3543 N. Harlem Ave.
Warzynski, Cheryl A. '72 '97 C.339 B.A. L.869 J.D. [Dykema G.P.]
Wascher, James D. '53 '78 C.813 B.A. L.597 J.D. [Friedman&H.]
Washburn, Elisabeth '64 '93 C.352 B.A. L.209 J.D.
Coun./Broadcasting & Entertainment, Tribune Co.
Washburn, John A. '51 '76 C.813 B.A. L.145 J.D. [Gould&R.]
Washburn, Melville W. '44 '87 C.894 B.A. L.966 J.D. [Sidley A.B.&W.]
Washelesky, Angela M. '— '92 C&L.209 B.A., J.D. [Sachnoff&W.]
Washington, Ernestine B. '19 '46 C.999 L.365 LL.B. 6326 S. Cottage Grove Ave.
Washington, Kara M. '— '94
C.329 B.S. L.597 J.D. Sr. Atty., U.S. Secs. and Exchange Comm.
Washington, Steven L. '71 '99 C.339 B.A. L.597 J.D. [Mayer,B.R.&M.]
Wasik, Mary K. '56 '81 C.424 B.B.A. L.339 J.D. [Levenfeld P.]
Wasik, Richard J. '58 '85 C&L.424 B.A., J.D. Asst. State's Atty.
Wasilewski, John A. '52 '78 C.209 B.A. L.1151 J.D. Asst. States Atty.
Wasserman, Bronna L. '46 '73 C.597 B.A. L.184 J.D.
Assoc. Gen. Coun., GATX Corp.
Wasserman, Jonathan D., (AV) '63 '88 C.112 B.A. L.145 J.D. [Neal,G.&E.]
Wasserman, Michael H. '61 '85 C.1365 B.A. L.424 J.D. 221 N. LaSalle Street
Wasserman, Norton, (AV) '36 '59 C.145 A.B. L.976 LL.B. 200 N. La Salle St.
Wasserman, Rachel L. '66 '95
C.347 B.S.B.A. L.209 J.D. Sr. Corp. Coun., Oracle, USA, Inc.

Wasserman, Laurie J., Law Offices of
(See Skokie)

Wasylik, Katheryn M. '71 '02 C.494 B.A. L.209 J.D. The Chicago Legal Clinic, Inc.
Waters, Jennifer A. '76 '02 C.674 A.B. L.597 J.D. [Ⓐ Schopf&W.]
Waters, John B. '63 '91 C.350 B.S. L.336 J.D. [Kamensky,R.H.&D.] ⊙
Waters, Paige D., (BV) '64 '89 C.473 B.A. L.146 J.D. [Sonnenschein N.&R.]
Waters, Stephen M. '43 '69 C.1100 B.A. L.623 J.D. 180 North Wacker Drive, Suite 201
Watkins, Barbara Bidell '53 '81 C.475 B.A. L.477 J.D.
V.P. & Assoc. Gen. Coun., Federal Home Loan Bk. of Chicago
Watkins, Charles R., (AV) '53 '79 C.475 B.A. L.477 J.D. [Susman,W.&W.]
Watkins, Richard D. '75 '00 C.511 B.S. L.276 J.D.
(adm. in PA; not adm. in IL; See Pat. Sect.) [Ⓐ Brinks H.G.&L.]
Watkins, Steven G. '64 '91 C.329 B.S. L.209 J.D. [S.G.Watkins&Assoc.]
Watkins, Steven G., & Associates, P.C. 609 E. 75th Street
Watkins-Asiyanbi, Joycelynn '— '04 C.966 B.A. L.597 J.D. [Ⓐ DLPiper R.G.C.U.]
Watroba, Amy Margaret '76 '01 C.477 B.A. L.424 J.D. Asst. State Atty.
Watson, Adrienne Redding '68 '93 C.94 B.S. L.910 J.D.
Dir. of Admin., AIDSCARE, Inc.
Watson, Barbara K. '43 '77 C.424 B.S. L.365 J.D. [Galvin,L.W.G.&S.]
Watson, Caroline '65 '01 C.338 B.S. L.161 J.D. [Ⓐ BryceDowney]
Watson, Charles E., II '64 '90 C.378 B.A. L.276 J.D. [Freeborn&P.]
Watson, D. Scott '63 '95 C.346 B.S. L.339 J.D. [Quarles&B.]
Watson, David R. '62 '92 C.385 B.A. L.930 J.D.
(adm. in OH; not adm. in IL) Dep. Exec. Dir., Defense Research Inst.
Watson, Jennifer R.M.C. '— '01 C.578 B.A. L.597 J.D. [Ⓐ Masuda,F.E.&M.]
Watson, John W., III, (AV) '63 '88 C.747 B.A. L.146 J.D. [Gardner C.&D.]
Watson, Krista L. '75 '01 C.477 B.A. L.494 J.D. [Ⓐ Gardner C.&D.]
Watson, Robert R., (AV) '44 '72 C.937 B.A. L.145 J.D. [Sidley A.B.&W.]
Watson, Rosalyn S. '65 '98 C&L.477 B.A., J.D. [Ⓒ M.J.Lane]
Watson, S. Ana '— '90 C.597 B.A. L.188 J.D. [Fedota C.]

Watson-Wesley Coleman, L.C.
(See St. Louis)

Watt, Garland W., (AV) '32 '61 C.574 A.B. L.209 J.D. [G.W.Watt&Assoc.]
Watt, Marsha '65 '91 C.103 A.B. L.597 J.D. [Ⓐ G.W.Watt&Assoc.]
Watt, Richard F., (AV) '17 '42 C.911 A.B. L.145 LL.B. 5000 S. East End Ave.
Watt, Garland W., & Associates, LLC, (AV) 53 W. Jackson Blvd., Ste. 504
Watterson, Heather '73 '01 C.967 B.A. L.209 J.D. [Ⓐ Cremer,K.S.&S.]
Watts, Charles M., Jr. '— '01 C.476 B.S. L.424 J.D. [Ⓐ Anderson,R.]
Watts, Daniel Gerard '59 '84 C.597 B.A. L.424 J.D. Cosmopolitan Bk. & Tr.
Waud, Morrison, (AV) '10 '35 C.674 A.B. L.597 J.D. 321 N. Clark St.‡
Wawrzyn, Matthew M. '74 '01 L.209 J.D. [Ⓐ Winston&S.]
Wawzenski, Linda A. '47 '78 C&L.424 A.B., J.D. Asst. U.S. Atty.
Wax, Jeffrey S. '64 '90 C.679 B.S.E.E. L.61 J.D. [Wax] (⊙Santa Monica, CA)
Wax, Michael A. '77 '02 C.210 B.A. L.424 J.D. [Ⓐ Fisher K.]
Wax Law Group 30 N. Michigan Ave.
Waxman, David S., (AV) '— '85 C.347 B.S. L.659 J.D. [Arnstein&L.]
Waxman, Herbert S., (AV) '34 '59 C&L.597 B.A., J.D. 180 N. La Salle St.
Way, Karen S. '68 '98 C.645 P.S.B.S. L.146 J.D. [Ⓐ DLPiper R.G.C.U.]
Wayne, David S. '— '96 C.597 B.A. L.424 J.D. [Arnstein&L.]
Weatherhead, Paul D. '50 '75 C&L.339 B.S., J.D. [Fernholz&E.]
Weaver, A. Denison, (AV) '29 '54 C.894 A.B. L.146 LL.B. [A.D.Weaver]
Weaver, Alexander '56 '83 C.602 B.A. L.146 J.D. 12 S. Michigan Ave., Ste. 1209
Weaver, Duane C., (BV) '52 '87 C&L.424 B.A., J.D. [Horvath&L.]
Weaver, George E., Law Office of, (AV) '45 '72
C.597 B.S. L.150 J.D. 221 North La Salle Street, Suite 850
Weaver, Karen A. '58 '94 C.851 B.S. L.209 J.D. [Weaver]
Weaver, Lionel W. '75 '01 C&L.352 B.A., J.D. [Ⓐ Gardner C.&D.]
Weaver, Lynn K. '65 '90 C.339 B.A. L.209 J.D. [Grotefeld&D.]
Weaver, Timothy A., (AV) '48 '74 C.103 A.B. L.339 J.D. [Pretzel&S.]
Weaver, William N., Jr., (AV) '— '64 C.604 A.B. L.365 J.D. [Sachnoff&W.]
Weaver, William T., (AV) '43 '68 C.813 A.B. L.1065 J.D. [Ⓒ Lord,B.&B.]
Weaver, A. Denison, Ltd., (AV) 180 N. Michigan Ave.

Weaver Law Group, LLC
549 West Randolph Street, Suite 400, 60661
Telephone: 312-876-3686 Fax: 312-876-3680
Email: lramirez@weaverlawgroup.com URL: http://www.weaverlawgroup.com
Members of the Firm: Karen A. Weaver; James M. Lancheros.
Language: Spanish.

(This Listing Continued)

Weaver Law Group, LLC (Continued)

Regulatory and Administrative Practice to the Food, Drug, Cosmetic, Device and Dietary Supplement Industry. Trademark and Copyright Practice, Direct Sales, Telemarketing, Network Marketing, US Customs, Federal Trade Commission, Civil Litigation and Business Transactions.

See Professional Biographies, CHICAGO, ILLINOIS

Webb, Dan K., (AV) .... '45 '70 C.927 L.424 J.D. [Winston&S.]
Webb, Jerome J. .... '47 '73 C.589 B.S. L.146 J.D. Chief, Unemp. Ins. Div., Atty. Gen.
Webb, Marland O. '48 '74 C.210 A.B. L.145 J.D.
(adm. in NY; not adm. in IL) GATX Corp.
Webb, Nichole C. .... '72 '97 C.14 B.A. L.365 J.D. Asst. States Atty.
Webb, Ralanda, (AV) .... '55 '80 C.339 B.A. L.1066 J.D. [Webb&Assoc.]
Webb, Robert W., (AV) '39 '70 C.339 B.S. L.46 J.D.
Sr. V.P. & Gen. Coun., The Marmon Group, Inc.
Webb, Stephen Wilson, JR. '69 '02
C.1378 B.S. L.1509 J.D. Claims Atty., Argonaut Ins. Co.
Webb & Associates, (AV) .... 25 East Washington Street, Suite 1908
Webber, Andrea M. .... '76 '02 C.347 B.A. L.209 J.D. Pub. Def.
Webber, William G. .... '21 '48 C&L.424 J.D. 20 S. Clark St.
Weber, Adam J.C. ..... '73 '00 C.352 B.A. L.146 J.D. 222 North La Salle Street, 8th Floor
Weber, Anne Nicholson .... '57 '85 C&L.976 B.A., J.D. [Ⓐ Sonnenschein N.&R.]
Weber, Dorothy A. '— '05 C.746 B.A. L.966 J.D.
(adm. in WI; not adm. in IL) [Ⓐ Schiff H.]
Weber, Elizabeth A. .... '76 '01 C.602 B.A. L.209 J.D. 333 West Wacker Drive, Suite 500
Weber, Elizabeth Fleming, (AV) .... '49 '74 C.339 B.A. L.94 J.D. [Katten M.R.]
Weber, Frederic W. .... '39 '72 C&L.602 A.B., J.D. [Ⓒ Lord,B.&B.]
Weber, Gerald A., (AV) .... '39 '63 C&L.477 B.B.A., J.D. [Gould&R.]
Weber, Jonathan S. .... '72 '98 C.37 B.A. L.209 J.D. [Ⓐ Fisher K.]
Weber, Kathryn .... '— '04 C.436 B.A. L.494 J.D. [Ⓐ S.D.Pollock&Assoc.]
Weber, Kathy A. '47 '80 C.898 B.A. L.1035 J.D.
(adm. in MN; not adm. in IL) I.R.S.
Weber, Louis J., III .... '57 '85 C&L.602 B.S.E.E., J.D. [Winston&S.]
Weber, Mark C. .... '53 '78 C.178 B.A. L.976 J.D. Prof. of Law, DePaul Univ.
Weber, Michael J., (AV) .... '58 '83 C.347 B.S. L.1119 J.D. [Leo&W.]
Weber, Rebecca A. .... '69 '96 C.932 B.S. L.209 J.D. [Ⓐ Tucker B.R.&M.]
Weber, Richard E., II ... '69 '94 C.475 B.A. L.880 J.D. Gen.Coun., Pax Technologies, Inc.
Weber, Robert .... '28 '61 C.339 B.S. L.209 J.D. Barristers, Inc.
Weber, Robert F., (AV) .... '50 '76 C.276 A.B. L.145 J.D. [Seyfarth S.]
Weber, Robert J. ..... '39 '64 C.602 A.B. L.597 J.D. Suite 3000, 30 North La Salle Street
Weber, Susan A. .... '58 '90 C.221 B.A. L.567 J.D. [Sidley A.B.&W.]
Weber, Thomas W. .... '56 '84 C.589 B.A. L.365 J.D. [Ⓐ Wiedner&M.]
Webster, Bryan M. .... '78 '03 C.502 B.A. L.477 J.D. [Ⓐ McDermott W.&E.]
Webster, Charles W., (AV) .... '— '79 C.973 A.B. L.1119 J.D. [Freeborn&P.]
Webster, Diane E. .... '79 '04 C.36 B.A. L.1202 J.D. [Ⓐ Hinshaw&C.]
Webster, James L. .... '53 '82 C.966 B.A. L.209 J.D. [Webster W.C.]
Webster, Megan .... '— '01 C.383 B.B.A. L.209 J.D. [Ⓐ DLPiper R.G.C.U.]
Webster, Noah F. .... '— '04 C.870 B.S. L.339 J.D. [Ⓐ Kirkland&E.]

Webster Wilcox Christopoulos P.C.
320 West Ohio, Suite 501, 60610
Telephone: 312-587-8800 Fax: 312-587-8808
Email: jwebster@wwclaw.com URL: http://www.wwclaw.com
James L. Webster; Mark Wilcox; Dimitrios G. Christopoulos;—Harlan C. Powell.
Beverage, Alcohol and Hospitality Industry Practice, including, Federal and State Alcoholic Beverage Regulation and Trade Practice, Administrative Hearings and Appeals, Excise and Sales Tax Litigation, Commercial Litigation, Commercial Transactions, Mergers and Acquisitions and Licensure.

See Professional Biographies, CHICAGO, ILLINOIS

Wechter, Thomas R., (AV) .... '— '66 C.477 B.A. L.145 J.D. [Schiff H.]
Weclew, Robt. G. .... '11 '34 C&L.597 B.S.L., J.D. 5766 N. Kercheval Ave.‡
Weed, Alexis K. .... '— '03 C.475 B.A. L.424 J.D. [Ⓐ Segal M.S.&M.]
Weed, Michael H. .... '— '96 C.352 B.S. L.178 J.D. [Kirkland&E.]
Weed, Monica M. '60 '85 C&L.597 B.A., J.D.
Exec. V.P., Gen. Coun. & Asst. Corp. Secy., Information Res., Inc.
Weersing, Sarah A. .... '71 '99 C.597 B.S. L.93 J.D. [Ⓐ DLPiper R.G.C.U.]
Wegerzyn, Norbert J., (AV) .... '39 '64 C.477 A.B. L.597 J.D. [Ⓒ Boundas S.W.&B.]
Weging, James E. .... '50 '77 C&L.209 B.S., J.D. Spec. Asst. Atty. Gen.
Wegman, Paula LoMonaco .... '— '96 C.36 B.A. L.146 J.D. [Adler,M.&M.]
Wegman, Todd E. .... '69 '96 C.338 B.S. L.46 J.D. [Garofalo,S.H.&S.]
Wegner, Janice A. .... '50 '89 C.209 B.A. L.46 J.D. 120 S. La Salle St.
Wegner, Julie Kristin .... '73 '01 C.338 B.S. L.365 J.D. 745 North Dearborn
Wehland, Charles T. .... '— '86 C.893 B.A. L.569 J.D. [Jones D.]
Wehrman, Christopher D. .... '76 '02 C.475 B.A. L.213 J.D. [Ⓐ Iwan C.H.H.&V.]
Wehrman, Erinn L. .... '78 '03 C.475 B.A. L.424 J.D. [Ⓐ Jenner&B.]
Weicher, Mary Ann MacLaughlan .... '77 '02 C.321 B.A. L.818 J.D. Asst. App. Def.
Weicher, Richard T. .... '76 '01 C.321 B.A. L.602 J.D. [Ⓐ Sidley A.B.&W.]
Weidenaar, William B. .... '37 '62 C.114 A.B. L.145 J.D. [Ruff,W.&R.]
Weidner, Brant C. '60 '87 C.945 B.A. L.209 J.D.
Sr. Claims Coun., Attorneys' Liability Assurance Society, Inc.
Weier, Lisa M. .... '— '00 C.339 B.S. L.146 J.D. [Ⓐ Chapman&C.]
Weig, Brian J., (CVⓉ) .... '64 '95 C&L.585 B.S., J.D. [Ⓐ Patton&R.]
Weigand, Dale F., (BV) .... '51 '78 C.1151 B.A. L.589 J.D. [Ellison,N.Z.&A.]
Weigel, Robert K., Jr. .... '65 '99 C.966 B.A. L.436 J.D. [Ⓒ Madsen,F.&P.]
Weik, Michael J. .... '53 '78 C&L.339 B.S., J.D. [Ⓒ Noonan&L.]
Weil, Andrew L., (AV) .... '60 '86 C&L.597 B.A., J.D. [Sonnenschein N.&R.]
Weil, Daniel W., (AV) .... '— '65 C.966 B.S. L.597 J.D. [Ⓒ Chapman&C.]
Weil, Edward S. .... '60 '86 C.918 B.A. L.597 J.D. [Schwartz C.]
Weil, Loren A. .... '61 '85 C&L.228 A.B., J.D. [Winston&S.]
Weil, Richard B., (AV) .... '45 '69 C&L.597 B.S.B.A., J.D. [Weil,F.&P.]
Weil, Freiburg & Petersen, P.C., (AV) .... 20 S. Clark St.
Weiland, Lisa A. .... '52 '76 C.679 B.A. L.893 J.D. 999 N. Lake Shore Dr.
Weiland, Michael A. .... '70 '96 C.339 B.A. L.146 J.D. Bank One Trust Co., N.A.
Weilandt, Timothy E. .... '61 '87 C.966 B.B.A. L.209 J.D. [McCarthy D.]
Weiler, Catherine Basque .... '74 '00 C.602 B.A. L.424 J.D. [Ⓐ Swanson,M.&B.]
Weiler, Claire A., (AV) '58 '83 C.788 A.B. L.145 J.D.
Employee Benefits Coun., BlueCross BlueShield Assoc.
Weiler, Thomas R., (BV) .... '58 '83 C.602 B.B.A. L.424 J.D. [Norton,M.W.&D.] ⊙
Weiler, William B. .... '63 '89 C.602 B.A. L.365 J.D. [Swanson,M.&B.]
Weimers, Eric H., (AV) .... '58 '85 C&L.861 B.S., J.D. [Ryndak&S.] (See Pat. Sect.)
Weinberg, Arnold, (AV) .... '42 '67 C.339 B.S. L.597 J.D. [Weinberg R.]
Weinberg, Idele L. .... '53 '84 C.339 B.A. L.424 J.D. Asst. Corp. Coun.
Weinberg, Marshall R. .... '42 '67 C.339 B.A. L.209 J.D. 1021 W. Adams St.
Weinberg, Michael A. .... '52 '76 C.881 A.B. L.477 J.D. [Novack&M.]
Weinberg, Neil H., (AV) .... '64 '91 C.339 B.S. L.910 J.D. [Katten M.R.]
Weinberg, Richard S., (AV) .... '36 '61 C&L.309 B.A., J.D. [Ⓒ Schuyler,R.&Z.]
Weinberg, Sara A. .... '74 '99 C.861 B.A. L.146 J.D. 320 West Ohio Street, Suite 500
Weinberg, Shelley Rice .... '59 '83 C.477 B.A. L.309 J.D. Univ. of Chicago
Weinberg, Steven J. .... '63 '89 C.339 B.S. L.146 J.D. 53 W. Jackson, Ste. 1460
Weinberg, Walter S. .... '56 '81 C.145 B.A. L.597 J.D. [Katten M.R.]
Weinberg Richmond LLP, (AV) .... 333 West Wacker Drive
Weinberger, Benjamin David .... '— '93 C.477 B.A. L.966 J.D. Baker Robbin & Co.
Weinberger, Seth J., (AV) .... '55 '80 C&L.477 A.B., J.D. [Mayer,B.R.&M.]
Weinberger, Stanley R., (AV) .... '30 '54 C&L.477 A.B., J.D. [Ⓒ Dykema G.P.]
Weiner, D. A. .... '14 '38 C.137 L.209 LL.B. 3950 N. Lake Shore Dr.
Weiner, David M., (AV) .... '54 '80 C.339 B.S. L.424 J.D. [Seyfarth S.]
Weiner, Debra F. '54 '83 C.339 B.S. L.424 J.D.
Off. of Legal Affs., St. Lukes Med. Ctr.
Weiner, Janice M. .... '— '91 C.1183 B.A. L.365 J.D. Acct. Exec., Lexis Nexis
Weiner, Kenneth I. .... '— '00 C.591 B.S. L.424 J.D. [Ⓐ DLPiper R.G.C.U.]
Weiner, Lawrence Jay, (AV) '41 '64 C.472 B.B.A. L.1565 LL.B.
[Ⓒ Laner,M.D.B.L.&T.]
Weiner, Mark B. .... '63 '89 C.339 B.A. L.208 J.D. [Hughes S.P.R.&D.]
Weiner, Michael R. .... '— '93 C&L.339 B.S., J.D. [Marshall,G.&B.] (See Pat. Sect.)
Weinfield, Neal H., (AV) .... '61 '87 C.188 B.A. L.880 J.D. [Bell,B.&L.]
Weingarten, J. Douglas .... '48 '73 C.546 B.A. L.339 J.D. 8 S. Michigan Ave.
Weinger, Kerry R. .... '— '79 C.339 B.S. L.424 J.D. [Baker&M.]
Weininger, David A., (AV) ..... '48 '73 C&L.339 B.A., J.D. 222 N. La Salle St., Ste. 1525
Weininger, Michael, (AV) .... '41 '65 C.339 B.A. L.597 J.D. [Weinberg R.]
Weinkopf, Friedrich J., (AV) .... '30 '67 C.999 L.146 J.D. [Ⓒ Baker&M.]
Weinsheimer, William C., (AV) .... '— '65 C.602 B.B.A. L.597 J.D. [Foley&L.]
Weinshel, Norman E. '17 '40 C&L.966 Ph.B., LL.B.
(adm. in WI; not adm. in IL) 5555 N. Sheridan Rd.‡
Weinstein, Brooke P. .... '77 '03 C.966 B.A. L.145 J.D. [Ⓐ Bell,B.&L.]
Weinstein, Burton I., (AV) .... '40 '65 C.339 L.209 LL.B. [Baskin,S.B.&W.]
Weinstein, David L., (AV) .... '51 '79 C.801 B.A. L.597 J.D. [Wildman,H.A.&D.]
Weinstein, Donna Morros '46 '72
C.339 A.B. L.309 J.D. Off. of the Gen. Coun., Dept. of HHS
Weinstein, Glenn E. .... '— '91 C.103 A.B. L.597 J.D. [Ⓐ Chapman&C.]
Weinstein, Jeffrey D. .... '72 '98 C.860 B.A. L.910 J.D. 77 West Wacker
Weinstein, Jill S. .... '72 '97 C.346 B.S. L.345 J.D. [Pedersen&W.]
Weinstein, Lisa .... '— '82 L.209 J.D. 1909 W. Belmont Ave. #101
Weinstein, Marc S. '52 '78 C.347 B.A. L.345 J.D.
(adm. in IN; not adm. in IL)
Natl. Mgr., State Income Tax & Franchise Taxes, Sears, Roebuck & Co.
Weinstein, Margo .... '60 '88 C.976 B.A. L.597 J.D. [Sonnenschein N.&R.]
Weinstein, Martin M. .... '43 '74 C.446 B.S. L.128 J.D. [Sugar,F.&F.]
Weinstein, Melvin A. .... '29 '51 C&L.209 LL.B. 134 N. LaSalle St.
Weinstein, Mitchell D. .... '68 '92 C.339 B.S. L.597 J.D. [Chuhak&T.]
Weinstein, Mitchell J. '58 '93 C.1044 B.S.Ch.E. L.365 J.D.
[Welsh&K.] (See Pat. Sect.)
Weinstein, Scott A. .... '68 '00 C.446 B.A. L.831 J.D. [Ⓐ Bischoff]
Weinstein, Seymour B. .... '16 '50 C.966 B.A. L.309 J.D. 1525 E. 53rd St.
Weintraub, Greg J. .... '75 '01 C.94 B.S.B.A. L.145 J.D. [Ⓐ Eimer S.K.&S.]
Weinum, Christopher A., Law Office of '65 '00
C.302 B.S. L.424 J.D. 407 South Dearborn, Suite 515
Weis, Anastasia G. .... '67 '96 C.602 B.A. L.209 J.D. [Ⓐ Winston&S.]
Weis, Byron H. .... '35 '60 C.174 B.A. L.477 J.D. [Weis&D.]
Weis, Hillary A. .... '— '02 C.477 B.A. L.813 J.D. [Ⓐ Sachnoff&W.]
Weis, Jonathan M. .... '— '96 C.188 B.A. L.339 J.D. [Levin G.]
Weis, Marsha F. .... '— '62 C.477 B.A. L.597 J.D. 221 N. LaSalle St.
Weis, Michael D. .... '63 '88 C&L.339 B.S., J.D. [Shaheen,N.S.F.&E.]
Weis & DuBrock .... 1 N La Salle St., Ste. 1300
Weisbard, Mark W., (AV) .... '54 '79 C.197 B.A. L.597 J.D. [Dykema G.P.]
Weisberg, Andrew M. .... '70 '96 C.339 B.A. L.502 J.D. [Ⓐ Swanson,M.&B.]
Weisberg, Justin L., (BV) .... '62 '92 C.339 B.S. L.146 J.D. [Schuyler,R.&Z.]
Weisberg, Lynn N. .... '63 '93 C.966 B.A. L.597 J.D. [Gardiner K.&W.]
Weisberg, Mark S. .... '63 '88 C&L.659 B.S., J.D. [Winston&S.]
Weise, John T., (AV) .... '32 '59 C.210 B.A. L.597 J.D. [Seyfarth S.] ‡
Weisenthal, Bruce P., (AV) .... '— '83 C.966 B.A. L.659 J.D. [Schiff H.]
Weiser, Andrea M. .... '77 '02 C.339 B.A. L.146 J.D. [Ⓐ Adamski&C.]
Weisman, Howard Dean .... '64 '89 C.861 B.A. L.365 J.D. Asst. State's Atty.
Weisman, James T. .... '46 '77 C.966 B.B.A. L.145 J.D. Touche Ross & Co.
Weisman, Jay .... '34 '60 C.118 B.A. L.597 J.D. [Weisman&W.]
Weisman, Larry E., (AV) .... '49 '74 C.339 B.A. L.209 J.D. [Goldberg,W.&C.]
Weisman, M. David .... '63 '89 C.893 B.S. L.846 J.D. Asst. Corp. Coun.
Weisman, Mark D., Law Offices of .... '50 '75 C.388 B.A. L.365 J.D. 100 W. Monroe
Weisman, Matthew .... '72 '00 C.659 B.A. L.145 J.D. [Ⓐ Sperling&S.]
Weisman, Michael S. .... '58 '99 C.339 B.A. L.146 J.D. [Ⓐ Katten M.R.]
Weisman, Robert A., (BV) .... '48 '74 C&L.339 B.S., J.D. 33 North La Salle Street
Weisman, Ross .... '63 '88 C.477 L.365 J.D. [Weisman&W.]
Weisman, Ross M. .... '— '93 C.597 B.A. L.94 J.D. [Kirkland&E.]
Weisman & Weisman .... 188 W. Randolph St.
Weiss, Adam S. .... '— '98 C.339 B.S. L.146 J.D. [Schiff H.]
Weiss, Adeena J. .... '— '02 C.783 B.A. L.365 J.D. 333 West Wacker Drive, Suite 500
Weiss, Barry .... '43 '68 C.339 B.S. L.146 J.D. 19 S. LaSalle St.
Weiss, Bradley Scott .... '54 '88 C.424 B.A. L.46 J.D. [Ⓒ Miner,B.&G.]
Weiss, Daniel J. .... '73 '98 C.30 B.A. L.145 J.D. [Ⓐ Jenner&B.]
Weiss, Deborah E., (BV) ... '59 '84 C.966 B.A. L.910 J.D. 77 W. Washington St., 20th Fl.
Weiss, Donald S. .... '44 '71 C.103 A.B. L.273 J.D. [Bell,B.&L.]
Weiss, Elaine '— '85 C.597 B.S.J. L.273 J.D.
Dir., Comm. on Women in the Profession, Amer. Bar Assn.
Weiss, Howard A., (AV) .... '24 '52 C.871 B.S. L.309 LL.B. 180 E. Pearson St.‡
Weiss, James D., (AV) .... '64 '93 C.385 B.A. L.494 J.D. [Ⓐ Sidley A.B.&W.]
Weiss, Jamie E. Saltzman .... '70 '95 C.347 B.A. L.146 J.D. [Freed&W.]
Weiss, Jennifer S. .... '71 '96 C.66 B.A. L.146 J.D. Off. of States Atty.
Weiss, John Robert, (AV) .... '61 '85 C&L.597 B.A., J.D. [Katten M.R.]
Weiss, Keren L. .... '76 '02 C.367 B.A. L.273 J.D. [Ⓐ Goodsmith G.&U.]
Weiss, Lawrence '49 '74 C.893 B.A. L.280 J.D.
(adm. in PA; not adm. in IL) [Ⓒ Giordano&N.]
Weiss, Lee A. .... '60 '85 C&L.597 B.A., J.D. West Servs., Inc.‡
Weiss, Leslie J. .... '57 '82 C.788 A.B. L.597 J.D. [Sugar,F.&F.]
Weiss, Marilyn J. .... '62 '94 C.597 B.A. L.178 J.D. 910 W. Gunnison St., 3rd Fl.
Weiss, Mary '48 '94 C.856 A.B. L.273 J.D.
Sr. V.P., Secretary & General Counsel, Driehaus Capital Management, Inc.
Weiss, Mitchell B. .... '69 '00 C.801 B.S. L.145 J.D. [Ⓐ Lovells]
Weiss, Paul M. .... '67 '93 C.347 B.S. L.1119 J.D. [Freed&W.]
Weiss, Phillip A., (AV) .... '27 '60 C.46 B.S.E.E. L.146 J.D. [Ⓒ Alter&W.] (Pat.)‡
Weiss, Richard L. .... '45 '71 C&L.209 B.S., J.D. [Weiss&B.]
Weiss, Robert M. .... '65 '90 C.197 A.B. L.813 J.D. [Neal,G.&E.]
Weiss, Sandra Byster, (AV) '— '84 C.339 B.S. L.209 J.D.
[Ⓒ Jones D.] (See Pat. Sect.)

Weiss, Stephen S. ... '68 '94 C.494 B.S. L.209 J.D. [Ⓐ Tribler O.&M.]
Weiss, Steven A., (AV) ... '55 '80 C.188 B.A. L.477 J.D. [Schopf&W.]
Weiss, Steven M. ... '73 '02 C.846 B.A. L.146 J.D. [Ⓐ Levenfeld P.] ⊙
Weiss, Susan B. ... '— '91 C.188 B.A. L.477 J.D. Asst. Gen. Coun., Exelon Bus. Servs.
Weiss & Block, Chtd. ... 1 E. Wacker Dr.

Weiss, Steven C., Law Offices of
(See Northbrook)

Weissbeck, William W. ... '57 '83 C.378 B.S.J. L.339 J.D. 25 E. Washington St.
Weissberg, Ariel ... '54 '79 C.910 A.B. L.734 J.D. [Weissberg&Assoc.]
Weissberg and Associates, Ltd. ... 401 S. La Salle St., Ste. 403
Weissbluth, Samantha E. ... '— '97 C&L.597 B.A., J.D. [Ⓒ Foley&L.]
Weissbourd, Bernard B. ... '22 '48 C&L.145 B.S., J.D. Met. Structures, Inc.
Weissburg, Mark ... '— '95 C.966 B.S. L.1000 J.D. [Ⓐ Horwitz,H.&Assoc.]
Weissburg, Robyn Meyer '65 '91
C.966 B.A. L.424 J.D. Dir., Mktg., Duray Fluorescent Mfg. Co.
Weisse, Kristen A. ... '— '02 C&L.424 B.A., J.D. [Ⓐ Meckler B.&T.]
Weissenbach, John A. ... '— '80 C.674 B.A. L.309 J.D. [Kirkland&E.]
Weissman, Andrew E. ... '74 '00 C&L.339 B.A., J.D. [Ⓐ Gardner C.&D.]
Weissman, Michael L., (AV) ... '— '58 C.597 B.S. L.309 J.D. [Ⓒ Holland&K.]
Weissman, Terry D. ... '57 '82 C.188 B.A. L.1019 J.D. [Neal,G.&E.]
Weisz, Ellen S. ... '53 '82 C.589 B.A. L.145 J.D. 3305 N. Nagle Ave.
Weisz, Lee M., Law Office of '49 '73 C.966 B.A. L.276 J.D.
33 N. Dearborn St., Ste. 500
Weithers, Mariola K. ... '61 '86 C.388 B.A. L.209 J.D. Fireman's Fund Ins. Co.
Weitzel, Jerome R., (BV) ... '69 '93 C.424 B.A. L.209 J.D. [Kozacky&W.]
Weitzel, Naomi Braude '58 '87
C.966 B.A. L.999 J.D. Atty., LaSalle Bank National Association
Weitzenfeld, Burton Y., (AV) ... '15 '42 L.209 J.D. Dep. Comm. Bd. of Appeals
Weitzman, Arden S. ... '69 '02 C.37 B.A. L.209 J.D. [Weitzman&P.]
Weitzman, Robert H. ... '37 '62 C.293 B.A. L.209 J.D. Group One Investments
Weitzman & Powers ... P.O. Box 87655
Wejnert, Jason M. ... '— '04 C.1556 B.S. L.36 J.D. [Ⓐ Brinks H.G.&L.]
Welch, David K., (BV) ... '56 '82 C.339 B.A. L.365 J.D. [Crane,H.S.W.&C.]
Welch, Donna M. ... '— '94 C.145 B.A. L.209 J.D. [Kirkland&E.]
Welch, Emanuel Christopher ... '71 '97 C.597 B.S. L.365 J.D. [Ⓐ J.J.Roche&Assoc.]
Welch, James M. ... '23 '53 L.365 LL.B. 4931 Cuyler St.
Welch, Joseph N., II, (AV) ... '54 '84 C.309 B.A. L.597 J.D. [Pattishall,M.N.H.&G.]
Welch, Lyman C. ... '— '93 C.165 A.B. L.597 J.D. [Ⓐ Mayer,B.R.&M.]
Welch, Lyman W., (AV) ... '43 '68 C.388 B.A. L.309 J.D. [Sidley A.B.&W.]
Welch, Meghan A. ... '74 '02 C.197 A.B. L.861 J.D. [Ⓐ Kerns,P.F.&P.]
Welch, Michael T., (AV) '50 '75
C&L.339 B.A., J.D. V.P. Legal Srvcs., Quaker Oats Corp.
Welch, Shea D. ... '73 '98 C.502 B.S. L.1439 J.D. [Ⓐ Gould&R.]
Welch, Terry L., Jr. ... '76 '01 C.880 B.A. L.861 J.D. 10 S. Riverside Plaza
Welch, William R. ... '52 '77 C.801 B.A. L.339 J.D. Claims Coun., Chicago Title Ins. Co.
Weldon-Linne, Madeleine, (AV) ... '54 '81 C.597 B.A. L.209 J.D. [Weldon-Linne&V.]
Weldon-Linne & Vogt, (AV) ... 105 West Madison Street, Suite 1400
Welhouse, Steven D. ... '— '97 C.966 B.A. L.146 J.D. [Ⓢ Schiff H.]
Welke, William R. ... '— '83 C.453 S.B. L.477 J.D. [Kirkland&E.]
Well, Brett E. ... '69 '96 C.823 B.S. L.339 J.D. Quaker Foods & Beverages
Weller, Christopher A. ... '— '02 C.337 B.A. L.339 J.D. [Ⓐ Winston&S.]
Weller, Jennifer W. ... '74 '99 C.339 B.A. L.424 J.D. [Hinshaw&C.]
Weller, Matthew H. ... '75 '02 C.238 B.A. L.146 J.D. [Ⓐ Cassiday,S.&G.]
Welling, Christopher M. ... '75 '00 C&L.734 B.A., J.D. [Ⓐ Cassiday,S.&G.]
Wellisch, Fred A. ... '47 '84 C.145 B.A. L.365 J.D. 1021 W. Adams
Wells, Chevez M. '66 '93 C.597 B.A. L.352 J.D.
Assoc. Gen. Coun., American Bar Association
Wells, David A., Jr. ... '64 '91 C.999 B.A. L.469 J.D. [David W.]
Wells, Elizabeth M., Law Offices of '54 '96
C.300 B.A. L.146 J.D. 980 N. Michigan Avenue, Suite 1400
Wells, Harold N. '30 '74 C.401 B.S.Ch.E. L.776 J.D.
(adm. in NJ; not adm. in IL; Pat.) [Ⓒ Jenkens&G.]
Wells, Michele L. ... '70 '97 C.36 B.S. L.209 J.D. [Ⓐ Robbins,S.N.L.&T.]
Wells, Patrick J., Law Office of '— '99 C.436 B.S. L.30 J.D.
(adm. in NY; not adm. in IL) 1039 W. Altgeld St.
Wells, Sharon B. '43 '81
C.209 B.A. L.365 J.D. Admin. Law J., Ill. & State Labor Rel. Bd.
Wells, Valerie C. ... '60 '88 C&L.966 B.A., J.D. Corp. Coun., City of Chic. Off.
Wells Law Firm, LLC ... 609B W. Addison St.
Welnhofer, William G. ... '54 '80 C&L.597 B.A., J.D. 55 W. Monroe St.
Welsch, Barbara J. ... '47 '77 C.98 B.S. L.209 J.D. Reg. Coun., Interstate Com. Comm.
Welsh, Julie T. ... '70 '95 C.934 B.A. L.424 J.D. 2150 W. North Ave.
Welsh, Kelly R., (AV) '52 '79 C&L.309 A.B., J.D.
Exec. V.P. & Gen. Coun., Northern Trust Corporation
Welsh, Michelle ... '79 '04 C.477 B.A. L.424 J.D. [Ⓐ Hodes,K.&P.]
Welsh, Susan L. ... '— '01 C.477 B.A. L.339 J.D. [Ⓐ Kirkland&E.]

Welsh & Katz, Ltd., (AV) BR
120 South Riverside Plaza 22nd Floor, 60606-3912 ⊙
Telephone: 312-655-1500 Fax: 312-655-1501
URL: http://www.welshkatz.com
A. Sidney Katz; Richard L. Wood; Jerold B. Schnayer; Joseph R. Marcus; Gerald S. Schur; Gerald T. Shekleton; James A. Scheer; Daniel R. Cherry; Robert B. Breisblatt; James P. White; R. Mark Halligan; Hartwell P. Morse, III; Edward P. Gamson; Kara Eve Foster Cenar; Kathleen A. Rheintgen; Thomas W. Tolpin; Richard W. McLaren, Jr.; Elliott C. Bankendorf; Mitchell J. Weinstein; Eric D. Cohen; John L. Ambrogi; Julie A. Katz; Jon P. Christensen; Walter J. Kawula, Jr.; Leonard Friedman; Steven E. Feldman; Jeffrey W. Salmon; Thomas L. Gemmell; Louise T. Walsh; Paul M. Vargo; Joseph E. Cwik; J. Aron Carnahan; Erik B. Flom;—Richard J. Gurak; Daniel M. Gurfinkel; Michele S. Katz; Natalie A. Remien; Brian J. Sodikoff; Brett M. Tolpin; George S. Pavlik; Michael A. Krol; Sherry L. Rollo; Christopher K. Marlow; Maitreya P. Jani; Craig M. Kuchii; Stephen P. Benson; Gregory J. Skony. Of Counsel: Laurie A. Haynie; James J. Myrick; Thomas R. Vigil; Philip D. Segrest, Jr.; Wallace L. Oliver; Laura A. Labeots.
Technology and Intellectual Property Law including Patent, Trademark, Copyright, Trade Secret, Unfair Competition and Related Antitrust Law, and Trials and Appeals.
Arlington, Virginia Office: Crystal Plaza One, Suite 311, 2001 Jefferson Davis Highway, 22202-3603. Telephone: 703-415-4777.

See Professional Biographies, CHICAGO, ILLINOIS

Welter, James E. ... '38 '63 C.602 A.B. L.424 J.D. 100 W. Monroe St.
Weltlich, Paul M. ... '64 '95 C.339 B.A. L.365 J.D. [Ⓐ Lawrence,K.S.&U.]
Weltman, Stewart M., (AV) ... '52 '78 C.1016 B.A. L.365 J.D. [S.M.Weltman]
Weltman, Stewart M., P.C., (AV) ... 39 South La Salle Street

Weltman, Weinberg & Reis Co., L.P.A.
10 S. La Salle Street Suite 900, 60603 ⊙
Telephone: 312-782-9676 Fax: 312-782-4201
Email: wwr@weltman.com URL: http://www.weltman.com
Jeffrey M. Feingold; John S. Pucin; Jay K. Levy;—John J. Grieger, Jr.; Daniel H. Olswang; John R. Booker.

(This Listing Continued)

Weltman, Weinberg & Reis Co., L.P.A. (Continued)
Creditors Rights, Collections, Creditor Bankruptcy, Foreclosure/Eviction, Title Insurance Law, Fair Debt Collections Practices Act, Probate/Deceased Collections, Subrogation, Credit Union Law, Banks and Banking, Creditor Defense, Complex Consumer and Commercial Litigation, Real Estate Title & Closing Services.
Burlington, New Jersey Office: Telephone: 609-914-0437.
Deerfield, Illinois Office: Telephone: 847-940-9812.
Cincinnati, Ohio Office: Telephone: 513-723-2200.
Cleveland, Ohio Office: Telephone: 216-685-1000.
Columbus, Ohio Office: Telephone: 614-228-7272.
Philadelphia, Pennsylvania Office: Telephone: 215-599-1500.
Pittsburgh, Pennsylvania Office: Telephone: 412-434-7955.
Troy, Michigan Office: Telephone: 248-362-6100.

See Professional Biographies, CHICAGO, ILLINOIS

Wendlinger, David M. '76 '02 C.999 B.A. L.879 J.D.
Trust Admr., LaSalle Bank National Association
Wendt, Debra ... '54 '81 C.475 B.A. L.365 J.D. Mng. Atty., Heller Financial, Inc.
Wendt, Thomas C. ... '65 '02 C.424 B.A. L.146 J.D. [Ⓐ Shaw G.F.G.W.&T.]
Wendte, Dennis R. ... '57 '82 C.339 B.S. L.477 J.D. [Barack F.K.P.&N.]
Wendy, Richard A., (AV) ... '— '83 C.273 B.A. L.910 J.D. [DLPiper R.G.C.U.]
Wenig, Donald R. ... '66 '91 C.209 B.A. L.365 J.D. Princ., Blackacre Advisors, LLC
Wenig, Leonard N. ... '28 '57 C.339 B.S. L.597 J.D. 2640 W. Touhy Avenue, Suite 12
Wennlund, Donald C. ... '66 '91 C.965 B.A. L.365 J.D. [Ⓐ Schain,B.R.&C.]
Wentzel, David F. ... '65 '90 C.339 B.A. L.678 J.D. [McDermott W.&E.]
Wenzloff, Warren P. ... '63 '88 C.475 B.S. L.879 J.D. [Applegate&T.]
Wermuth, Anneliese ... '69 '99 C.209 B.A. L.424 J.D. [Ⓐ Meckler B.&T.]
Wern, Theodore ... '— '00 C.473 B.A. L.608 J.D. [Ⓐ Perkins C.]
Werner, Brian D. ... '75 '00 C.98 B.A. L.477 J.D. [Ⓐ Winston&S.]
Werner, Christopher J. ... '— '02 C.347 B.A. L.273 J.D. [Ⓐ Foley&L.]
Werner, Herman S. ... '30 '53 C.339 L.209 LL.B. 20 N. Clark
Werner, Mark D. ... '76 '02 C.339 B.S. L.893 J.d. 10 S. Dearborn Street
Werner, Raymond J., (AV) ... '— '71 C.209 B.S.C. L.146 J.D. [Arnstein&L.]
Wernick, Alan S., (AV) ... '— '78 C.608 B.S. L.117 J.D. [Chuhak&T.]
Wernikoff, Steven M. ... '69 '94 C.645 B.A. L.597 J.D. Federal Trade Commission
Werth, Meera ... '— '84 C.999 B.A. L.146 J.D. 565 W. Adams St.‡
Wertheimer, Douglas ... '48 '73 C.966 B.A. L.209 J.D. 1228 W. Monroe St.
Wertman, Tracey A. ... '66 '91 C.226 B.A. L.7 J.D. [Berger S.]
Wesley, William M., (AV) '43 '71
C.436 B.E.E. L.424 J.D. [McAndrews,H.&M.] (See Pat. Sect.)
Wesolowski, Allen C., (BV) ... '54 '79 C.597 B.A. L.245 J.D. [Martin&K.]
Wesolowski, James J. ... '50 '77 C.339 B.S. L.424 J.D. 333 W. Wacker Dr.

Wessels & Pautsch, P.C., (AV)
Chicago Bar Association Building, 321 South Plymouth Court, Suite 900, 60604 ⊙
Telephone: 312-461-0500 Fax: 312-461-0595
Email: wessels@stch.w-p.com URL: http://www.w-p.com
Walter J. Liszka;—Michael H. Berendt; Sean F. Darke.
Representing Employers in Labor and Employment Law Matters. NLRA, RLA, all Federal and State Employment Discrimination Laws, Federal and State Disability Laws, Wrongful Discharge, Employment Contracts, Collective Bargaining Negotiations and Arbitrations, Employee Substance Abuse, Safety and Health, Unemployment Insurance, Benefits Law, Wage and Hour, and Employment-Based Immigration Matters. Litigation before all Federal and State Courts and Agencies, Trial and Appellate Practice.
St. Charles, Illinois Office: Dunham Center, 2035 Foxfield Drive. Telephone: 630-377-1554. Fax: 630-377-1653.
Milwaukee, Wisconsin Office: Two Plaza East, 330 East Kilbourn Avenue, Suite 1475. Telephone: 414-291-0600. Fax: 414-291-0200.
Davenport, Iowa Office: Northwest Bank Building, 101 W. Second Street, Suite 307. Telephone: 563-333-9102. Fax: 563-333-9105.
Minneapolis, Minnesota Office: MoneyGram Tower, 1550 Utica Avenue South, Suite 450. Telephone: 952-746-1700. Fax: 952-746-1704.
Indianapolis, Indiana Office: Market Tower, 10 West Market Street, Suite 1770. Telephone: 317-656-8800. Fax: 317-656-8855.

See Professional Biographies, CHICAGO, ILLINOIS

Wessman, Emily Elaine ... '76 '01 C.597 B.A. L.1365 J.D. City Dept. of Law
Wesson, Felisia A. ... '61 '87 C.976 B.A. L.477 J.D. Field Museum of Nat. History
West, A. Reneé '56 '89 C.801 B.S. L.809 J.D.
(adm. in CA; not adm. in IL) 934 W. 123 St.
West, Paul C. ... '47 '75 C.339 B.A. L.879 J.D. 1936 W. Waveland Ave.
Westbrook, Melissa L. '69 '94 C.502 B.A. L.569 J.D.
(adm. in NY; not adm. in IL) [Ⓒ Katten M.R.]
Wester, Barbara Leibhardt '63 '92 C.597 B.A. L.1066 J.D.
Assoc. Reg. Coun., U.S.E.P.A.
Westerberg, Gary W. ... '45 '71 C.187 B.A. L.802 J.D. [Lord,B.&B.]
Westerfield, Evan B. ... '64 '93 C.976 B.A. L.145 J.D. [Ⓐ Sidley A.B.&W.]
Westhoff, Mark R. ... '59 '84 C.221 B.S. L.424 J.D. 33 W. Monroe‡
Weston, Jeffrey M., (AV) ... '46 '73 C&L.339 B.S., J.D. 20 N. Clark St.
Westover, Casey L. ... '— '01 C.339 B.S. L.309 J.D. [Ⓐ Sachnoff&W.]
Wethall, Judith L. ... '— '97 C.966 B.A. L.362 J.D. [Ⓐ Seyfarth S.]
Wethekam, Marilyn A. ... '51 '77 C.424 B.A. L.146 J.D. [Horwood M.&B.]
Wetherell, Weston B. '56 '85
C.291 B.A. L.146 J.D. V.P. & Dep. Gen. Coun., PPM America, Inc.
Wettermann, Thomas E. '64 '95
C.436 B.S.E.E. L.209 J.D. [McDonnell B.H.&B.] (See Pat. Sect.)
Wetzler, Donna S., (BV) '50 '75
C.976 B.A. L.309 J.D. Gen. Coun., Children's Memorial Med. Ctr.
Wexler, A. Colin ... '72 '99 C.976 B.A. L.477 J.D. [Ⓐ Goldberg,K.B.R.&M.]
Wexler, James R. ... '72 '99 C.976 B.A. L.475 J.D. [Ⓢ Sidley A.B.&W.]
Wexler, Jerome E., (AV) ... '40 '64 C&L.597 B.A., J.D. Pres., JDS Advisors
Wexler, Kenneth A., (AV) ... '55 '80 C.910 B.A. L.276 J.D. [Wexler]
Wexler, Leon C. ... '35 '61 C&L.339 B.S., J.D. 77 W. Washington
Wexler, Marian P., (AV) ... '51 '77 C.393 B.A. L.209 J.D. [Skadden,A.S.M.&F.]
Wexler, Michael D. ... '— '91 C.339 B.A. L.146 J.D. [Seyfarth S.]
Wexler, Mitchell H. ... '64 '91 C.352 B.B.A. L.146 J.D. 500 W. Madison St., Ste. 2910
Wexler, Norman P., (AV) '42 '68 C.209 B.A.S. L.146 J.D.
500 W. Madison St., Ste. 2910
Wexler, Raymond P., (P.C.), (AV) ... '— '67 C&L.910 B.A., J.D. [Kirkland&E.]
Wexler, Richard L., (AV) ... '41 '65 C.477 L.365 J.D. [Lord,B.&B.]
Wexler, Saul R., (AV) ... '43 '68 C.966 B.S. L.209 J.D. [Ⓒ K.B.Moll&Assoc.]
Wexler, Warren M. ... '32 '56 C.339 B.S. L.597 LL.B. 55 W. Wacker Dr., 9th Fl.

Wexler Firm, The, LLP, (AV)
One North LaSalle Street, Suite 2000, 60602
Telephone: 312-346-2222 Fax: 312-346-0022
Email: info@wexlerfirm.com URL: http://www.wexlerfirm.com
Founding Partner: Kenneth A. Wexler. Partner: Edward A. Wallace. Associates: Jennifer Fountain Connolly; Anthony J. Sievert; Andrae P. Reneau; Amber M. Nesbitt.

(This Listing Continued)

Wexler Firm, The, LLP (Continued)

Complex Multi-District Commercial Litigation, Class Actions, Consumer Litigation, Accountants' Liability, Defamation, Antitrust, Securities Fraud, Commodities, Fraud, RICO Litigation, Civil Rights, Legal Malpractice and Municipal Litigation.

See Professional Biographies, CHICAGO, ILLINOIS

Weyeneth, Jamie A. '76 '00 C.597 B.A. L.145 J.D. [Ⓐ McDermott W.&E.]
Weyls, Brigitte C. '76 '02 C.207 B.A. L.209 J.D. [Ⓐ Williams M.&J.]
Whalen, Charles E. '— '64 C&L.339 B.A., J.D. [Querrey&H.]
Whalen, Charles T. '46 '91 C.734 B.A. L.365 J.D. App. Offr., I.R.S.
Whalen, Edward J., Jr. '44 '73 C.597 B.A. L.146 J.D. [Hedberg,T.F.&W.]
Whalen, Ryann '69 '93 C.966 B.A. L.436 J.D. [Harris K.&G.]
Whalen, Wayne W., (AV) '39 '67 C.1070 B.S. L.597 J.D. [Skadden,A.S.M.&F.]
Wharton, Joseph N. '70 '98 C.800 B.A. L.146 J.D. [Ⓐ Skadden,A.S.M.&F.]
Wharton, Kathleen J. '40 '84 C&L.424 A.B., J.D. Coun., Consumer Credit Ins. Assn.
Wheat, Jon-Micheal A. '78 '04 C.602 B.A. L.477 J.D. [Ⓐ Skadden,A.S.M.&F.]
Wheatley, Charles N., Jr. '50 '82 C.150 B.B.A. L.424 J.D. Sahara Enterprises Inc.
Wheeland, David R. '65 '98 C.589 B.S.A. L.146 J.D. Sr. Fin. Analyst, S & C Elec. Co.
Wheeler, David A. '63 '99 C.446 B.S. L.424 J.D. [Ⓐ Dykema G.P.]
Wheeler, Ellen M. '— '97 C.293 B.A. L.477 J.D. [Ⓒ Foley&L.]
Wheeler, George F., (AV) '53 '77
C&L.966 B.S., J.D. [McAndrews,H.&M.] (See Pat. Sect.)
Wheeler, Harold C., (AV) '45 '74 C.309 A.B. L.893 J.D. [Butler R.S.&B.]
Wheeler, Mark S. '65 '91 C.1121 B.A. L.1187 J.D. [Ⓐ T.Vaughn]
Wheeler, Mary Elizabeth '44 '80 C.526 B.A. L.365 J.D. [M.B.Wheeler]
Wheeler, Paula Becker '56 '80 C.339 B.A. L.424 J.D.
Dep. Comr., Chicago Dept. of Consumer Servs.
Wheeler, Trayne S. '73 '00 C.145 A.B. L.94 J.D. [Ⓐ Bell,B.&L.]
Wheeler, Mary Beth 29 N. LaSalle, Ste. 430
Wheelock, Richard M. '54 '82 C.478 B.A. L.966 J.D.
Housing Supervising Atty., Legal Assistance Found. of Chicago
Whelan, John M. '39 '67 C.178 B.A. L.145 J.D. Amer. Nat. Bk. & Tr. Co.
Whelan, Stephen A. '67 '92 C.93 B.A. L.424 J.D. [Fisher K.]
Whelan-Kapanowski, Maureen K. '56 '80 C.339 B.A. L.209 J.D.
Metro. Water Reclamation Dist. of Greater Chicago
Whicher, Jane M. '49 '76 C.350 B.S. L.352 J.D. Staff Coun., ACLU
Whipple, Benjamin M. '— '04 C.477 B.A. L.602 J.D. [Ⓐ Wilson E.M.E.&D.]
Whitacre, Ryan '75 '00 C.475 B.A. L.1556 J.D. [Ⓐ Perkins C.]
Whitcup, Leonard S. '31 '56 C&L.597 B.S., J.D. 155 N. Michigan St., 7th Fl.
White, A. Bruce, (AV) '52 '78 C.339 A.B. L.145 J.D. [Karaganis,W.&M.]
White, Alexander P. '32 '64 C.589 B.S. L.146 J.D. Cir. J.
White, Andrew T. '78 '03 C.1030 B.S. L.424 J.D. [Ⓐ Greenberg T.]
White, Barry A. '48 '73 C.966 B.A. L.597 J.D. 190 South La Salle Street‡
White, Brian A. '77 '02 C&L.352 B.A., J.D. [Ⓐ Boundas S.W.&B.]
White, Christopher '77 '04 C.674 A.B. L.597 J.D. [Ⓐ Ross,D.&B.]
White, Craig M., (AV) '52 '77 C.197 B.A. L.1119 J.D. [Wildman,H.A.&D.]
White, Daniel E. '— '95 C.475 B.S. L.7 J.D. [Ⓒ Jones D.]
White, Diana Churchill, (AV) '44 '81 C.788 B.A. L.145 J.D.
Dep. Dir., Legal Assistance Found. of Chicago
White, Dierdre K. '71 '97 C.911 B.A. L.146 J.D. United Airlines
White, Edward M., (AV) '28 '51 C&L.424 J.D. [Carey,F.W.&B.]
White, Frederick L., (AV) '44 '70 C.188 A.B. L.477 J.D.
Gen. Coun. & Mng. Dir., Deerfield Capital Mgmt. LLC
White, Gerald K. '38 '72 C.645 B.S. L.128 J.D. 205 West Randolph St. (Pat.)
White, Gregory M., (AV) '49 '75 C&L.209 B.A., J.D. [Crowley B.&K.]
White, H. Blair, (AV) '27 '51 C&L.352 B.A., J.D. 1 1st Nat. Plaza
White, James A. '— '85 C.145 A.B. L.966 J.D. [Jones D.]
White, James P. '46 '73 C.475 B.S. L.818 J.D. [Welsh&K.]
White, Jason C. '70 '96 C.436 B.S.E.E. L.201 J.D. [Brinks H.G.&L.]
White, John E. '57 '91 C.801 B.S. L.365 J.D. Admin. J., State Dept. of Rev.
White, Kevin E. '54 '81 C.388 B.A. L.966 J.D. [Kevin E.W.&Assoc.]
White, Laura A. '69 '96 C&L.201 B.A., J.D. [Smith O.&W.]
White, Lawrence E. '— '90 C.846 B.B.A. L.659 J.D. [Chapman&C.]
White, Linda D., (AV) '52 '76 C.659 A.B. L.597 J.D. [Sonnenschein N.&R.]
White, Michael E. '54 '79 C.602 B.B.A. L.365 J.D. [Carey,F.W.&B.]
White, Neal J., (AV) '51 '77 C.976 B.A. L.309 J.D. [McDermott W.&E.]
White, Pamela K. '54 '83 C.966 B.S. L.597 J.D. 515 W. Belden Ave.‡
White, R. Quincy, (AV) '33 '60 C.976 B.A. L.309 J.D. 1 1st Nat. Plaza
White, Rick A. '48 '74 C.339 B.A. L.209 J.D. 77 W. Washington St.
White, Robert G. '45 '85 C.999 B.S. L.146 J.D. [R.White]
White, Robert S., (AV) '— '93
C.602 B.A. L.146 J.D. [Masuda,F.E.&M.] (⊙Schaumburg)
White, Tess A. '70 '95 C.210 B.A. L.879 J.D. 150 S. Wacker Dr.
White, Thomas M. '49 '75 C.1230 B.A. L.597 J.D. [Schwartz C.]
White, Thomas P. '— '84 C.231 B.A. L.145 J.D. [Schiff H.]
White, William P., III, (AV) '47 '74 C.602 B.B.A. L.209 J.D. [Pasulka&W.]
White, Robert, Law Office of 6832 W. North Ave., Ste. 3A
Whitefield, Edward '37 '60 C.1016 B.L.S. L.209 LL.B. 4603 N. Sheridan Rd.
Whitehead, G. Marc, (AVⓉ) '40 '64 C.674 B.A. L.976 J.D. [Sonnenschein N.&R.]
Whitehead, Gregory C., (AV) '60 '85 C&L.893 B.A., J.D. [Albert,W.]
Whitehead, James S., (AV) '48 '74 C.976 B.A. L.145 J.D. [Sidley A.B.&W.]
Whitehouse, Joel A. '58 '83 C.589 B.S. L.146 J.D. 61 W. Superior
Whitehouse, Samantha B. '72 '98 C.477 B.A. L.276 J.D. [Ⓐ Mayer,B.R.&M.]
Whiteman, Adam B. '64 '91 C&L.966 B.A., J.D. [Whiteman]
Whiteman Law Offices 221 N. LaSalle St., Ste. 1938
Whitenack, Curt J. '61 '91 C&L.966 B.S., J.D. [McDonnell B.H.&B.] (See Pat. Sect.)
Whiteside, Joshua J. '76 '02 C.339 B.A. L.910 J.D. [Ⓐ Purcell&W.]
Whitfield, Collins P. '49 '76 C.966 B.A. L.365 J.D. 2 N. La Salle St., Ste. 1650
Whitfield, Maribeth Hope '77 '04 C.339 B.A. L.146 J.D. [Ⓐ Schain,B.R.&C.]
Whiting, Oran F. '61 '87 C.659 B.A. L.276 J.D. [Much S.F.D.A.&R.]
Whiting, Timothy M., (AV) '68 '94 C.1172 B.S. L.966 J.D. [Whiting] ⊙
Whiting, Willie M. '26 '51 C.254 L.365 LL.B. Cir. J.

Whiting Law Group, Ltd., (AV)
One East Wacker Drive Suite 2300, 60601 ⊙
Telephone: 312-372-1655 Toll Free: 877-936-7200 Fax: 312-279-1111
Email: twhiting@wlglaw.net URL: http://www.wlglaw.net
Timothy M. Whiting; Michael J. Goldberg.
Personal Injury, wrongful death, automobile accidents, trucking accidents, slip and fall injuries, construction accidents, products liability and farming injuries; Medical Malpractice, including nursing home negligence, birth injuries, labor and delivery injuries, brain and spinal cord injuries, obstetric malpractice and hospital negligence.
Delavan, Wisconsin Office: 125 North Second Street, 53115. Telephone: 877-936-7200.

See Professional Biographies, CHICAGO, ILLINOIS

Whitlock, Brian T. '54 '79 C.597 B.A. L.46 J.D.
Ptnr., Wealth Transfer Servs., Blackman Kallick Bartelstein LLP
Whitmer, James L. '51 '84 C.1151 B.A. L.146 J.D. F.B.I.
Whitmer, Steven T. '71 '97 C.937 B.A. L.145 J.D. [Lord,B.&B.]
Whitmore, Daniel P. '55 '96 C.684 B.A. L.209 J.D. [Ⓐ Mayer,B.R.&M.]
Whitney, Douglas E. '68 '99 C.976 B.A. L.569 J.D. [McDermott W.&E.]
Whitson-Owen, Eugena A. '70 '96 C.234 B.S. L.365 J.D. [Moore,S.&W.]
Whitt, Jeffrey B. '— '81 C.338 B.S. L.424 J.D. [Sachnoff&W.]
Whittaker, Martin, (AV) '62 '91
C.602 B.A. L.146 J.D. Two North LaSalle Street, Suite 1600
Whitted, John B., Jr. '24 '50 C.388 B.A. L.597 J.D. Pres., Whitso Inc.
Whitten, Patricia J., (AV) '50 '74 C.420 B.S. L.146 J.D. [Franczek S.]
Whitty, Michael D., (AV) '62 '89 C&L.846 B.B.A., J.D. [Winston&S.]
Whitty, Raynarldo K. '74 '01 C.259 B.S. L.472 J.D.
(adm. in FL; not adm. in IL) [Ⓐ Brinks H.G.&L.]
Wiacek, Robt. A. '22 '51 C.209 L.597 LL.B. 2108 N. Sheffield Ave.
Wiberg, John A. '68 '98 C.959 B.S.E.E. L.146 J.D.
[McAndrews,H.&M.] (See Pat. Sect.)
Wichern, Nadine Jean '75 '00 C.347 B.A. L.209 J.D. Asst. Atty. Gen.
Wick, Anders C. '74 '01 C.145 A.B. L.477 J.D. [Ⓐ Jenner&B.]
Wickersty, William J. '65 '90 C.894 B.A. L.378 J.D. [Landon&W.]
Wickert, John H. '60 '84 C.436 A.B. L.597 J.D. [Robinson C.&C.]
Wickham, Lizabeth J. '63 '89 C.436 B.A. L.424 J.D. Asst. Corp. Coun.
Wicklund, P. Renée '— '98 C.823 B.A. L.976 J.D. [Ⓒ Kirkland&E.]
Wicks, Edward E., (AV) '50 '75 C.339 A.B. L.145 J.D. [Perkins C.]
Widen, Melissa S. '66 '91 C.228 A.B. L.466 J.D. Arthur Andersen, LLP
Widerborg, Sandra M. '59 '84 C.209 B.S. L.424 J.D. United Airlines
Widlus, Hannah B. '55 '79 C.473 B.S.B.A. L.273 J.D. [Seyfarth S.]
Widmaier, Uli '62 '94 C.103 B.A. L.976 J.D. [Pattishall,M.N.H.&G.]
Widman, Jeffrey L. '67 '94 C.477 B.A. L.424 J.D. [Shaw G.F.G.W.&T.]
Widman, Stuart M., (AV) '48 '77 C.659 B.S. L.597 J.D. [Miller S.&H.]
Widmer, Jennifer A. '65 '90 C.504 B.A. L.276 J.D. [Ⓒ Mandell M.]
Wieczorek, Dennis E., (AV) '52 '77 C.910 A.B. L.228 J.D. [DLPiper R.G.C.U.]
Wiedner, Frank J., (AV) '23 '49 C&L.209 J.D. [Wiedner&M.]
Wiedner, Mark C., (AV) '55 '80 C.210 B.A. L.209 J.D. [Wiedner&M.]
Wiedner, Paul W., (AV) '51 '77 C.172 B.S. L.209 J.D. [Wiedner&M.]

Wiedner & McAuliffe, Ltd., (AV)
One North Franklin Suite 1900, 60606
Telephone: 312-855-1105 Fax: 312-855-1792
URL: http://www.wmlaw.com
Frank J. Wiedner; John P. McAuliffe (Retired); Russell P. Standlee; Paul W. Wiedner; Richard J. Leamy, Jr.; Mark C. Wiedner; Timothy D. McMahon; Mark D. Wilkening; Michael F. Doerries; James W. Stevenson Jr.; Janet D. Pallardy; Catherine Mafee Levine; Mark P. Matranga; Robert L. Smith; James W. Ozog; David J. O'Connell;—Thomas W. Weber; James Jason Coggins; Brian J. Koch; Ingrid Lulich; Christine M. Jagodzinski; Brian H. Driscoll; Emily E. Borg; James M. Rozak; James W. Jannisch; Karen E. Coon; Jason R. Schachner; Robert H. Fredian; Linda A. Robert; Daniel M. Anders; Tricia L. Anderson; Benjamin L. Riddle; Erica N. Rogina.
Workers' Compensation, Wrongful Discharge, ADA, Sexual Harassment and Human Rights Claims, Product Liability and Personal Injury Law. General Civil, Trial and Appellate Practice in both State and Federal Courts.

See Professional Biographies, CHICAGO, ILLINOIS

Wiegand, Thomas J., (AV) '62 '87 C.976 B.A. L.309 J.D. [Winston&S.]
Wieland, Lauren Ann '72 '99 C.473 B.S. L.209 J.D. [Ⓐ Johnson&B.]
Wiemelt, Mark E. '65 '91 C.98 B.S.M.E. L.801 J.D. [M.E.Wiemelt] (Pat.)

Wiemelt, Mark E., P.C., Law Offices of
10 South La Salle Street, Suite 3300, 60603
Telephone: 312-372-7664 Fax: 312-372-6568 URL: http://www.wiemeltlawoffices.com
Email: mark@wiemeltlaw.com URL: http://www.wiemeltlaw.com
Mark E. Wiemelt; Robert L. Knechtel (Not admitted in IL).

See Professional Biographies, CHICAGO, ILLINOIS

Wiener, Jerome, (AV) '43 '68 C.401 B.S. L.276 J.D. [Schain,B.R.&C.]
Wiener, Todd R., (AV) '61 '86 C.150 B.A. L.309 J.D. [McDermott W.&E.]
Wier, Jonathan M. '74 '99 C.659 B.S. L.966 J.D. [Ⓐ Eimer S.K.&S.]
Wiers, Adam W. '— '02 C.114 B.A. L.477 J.D.
(adm. in PA; not adm. in IL) [Ⓐ Jones D.]
Wierzbicki, Edward G., (AV) '49 '75 C.98 B.A. L.145 J.D. [Loeb&L.]
Wierzbicki, Michael T. '74 '99 C.20 B.A. L.209 J.D. 25 E. Washington, Ste. 900
Wiese, David M. '70 '01 C.339 B.S. L.352 J.D. [Ⓐ Barack F.K.P.&N.]
Wiesen, Tracy Bauer '48 '86 C&L.424 B.A., J.D. Off. of Thrift Super.
Wiesenthal, Robert L., (AV) '39 '64 C.937 B.A. L.597 J.D. [Bell,B.&L.]
Wietecha, Ronald O. '71 '02 C.813 A.B. L.597 J.D. Atty. Advsr.
Wiggins, A. Leo, Jr. '51 '80 C&L.803 B.S., J.D. [L.A.Wiggins]
Wiggins, C. Hunter '67 '95 C.352 B.A. L.477 J.D. [Sonnenschein N.&R.]
Wiggins, Charles H., Jr., (AV) '39 '65 C&L.339 B.S., J.D. [Vedder,P.K.&K.]
Wiggins, Sally '63 '94 C.536 B.A. L.365 J.D. [Niro,S.H.&N.]
Wiggins, Leo A., The Law Office of 188 W. Randolph St., Ste. 926
Wiggs, Sara T. '63 '88 C&L.801 B.A., J.D. 122 S. Michigan Ave., Ste. 1720‡
Wigoda, Gary I., (AV) '52 '80 C.273 B.A. L.365 J.D. [Ⓐ Wigoda&W.]
Wigoda, Paul T., (BV) '22 '50 C.1016 B.A. L.209 J.D. [Wigoda&W.]
Wigoda, Robert M., (BV) '55 '79 C.339 B.A. L.365 J.D. [Wigoda&W.]
Wigoda, Susan Seligman '47 '85 C.1036 B.A. L.146 J.D. Cook Co. Pub. Guard.
Wigoda, William S., (AV) '46 '74 C.1016 B.S.B.A. L.365 J.D. 150 N. Wackerd Avenue
Wigoda & Wigoda, (BV) 444 N. Michigan Ave., 26th Fl.
Wiktor, John R. '— '00 C.477 B.A. L.424 J.D. [Ⓐ Gardner C.&D.]
Wilcox, Allyson L. '77 '03 C.112 B.A. L.990 J.D. [Ⓐ Bell,B.&L.]
Wilcox, Angela C. '74 '99 C.339 B.S. L.209 J.D. [Daar&V.]
Wilcox, Barbara L. '47 '78 C.339 A.B. L.597 J.D. [Wilcox&G.]
Wilcox, Gary E. '52 '77 C.103 A.B. L.1017 J.D. [Hardt&S.]
Wilcox, L. Kent '43 '70 C&L.945 A.B., J.D.
(adm. in IN; not adm. in IL) U.S. Dept. of Health & Human Servs.
Wilcox, Mark '56 '82 C.339 B.S. L.209 J.D. [Webster W.C.]
Wilcox, Mark D., (AV) '52 '76 C.602 B.B.A. L.597 J.D. [Walker W.M.]
Wilcox, Robert B., Jr., (AV) '— '84 C.309 B.A. L.1066 J.D. [Schiff H.]
Wilcox & Grimbau 205 W. Randolph St.
Wilczek, Robert J. '44 '68 C.201 B.A. L.602 LL.B. [Gardner C.&D.]
Wild, Robert J. '61 '89 C&L.424 B.B.A., J.D. [Mayer,B.R.&M.]
Wilda, Susan '73 '98 C.352 B.A. L.365 J.D. [Ⓐ Hall,P.&S.]
Wilde, Kay E. '64 '89 C.957 B.A. L.477 J.D. [Lovells]
Wilde, Thomas M. '67 '93 C.589 B.A. L.209 J.D. [Vedder,P.K.&K.]
Wilder, John R. '24 '52 C&L.215 J.D.
(adm. in MI; not adm. in IL) Admin. Law J., Off. of Hearings & App.
Wilder, Robert '68 '98 C.1182 B.S. L.365 J.D. [Ⓐ Busse&B.]
Wilder, Ronald, (AV) '— '62 C&L.339 LL.B. [Schiff H.]
Wildermuth, Matthew R. '64 '89 C&L.347 B.A., J.D. [Meckler B.&T.]
Wildman, Max, (AV) '19 '48 C.108 B.S. L.477 J.D. [Ⓒ Wildman,H.A.&D.]
Wildman, Sally, Law Offices of '— '74 C.910 B.A. L.209 J.D. 180 N. LaSalle St.
Wildman, Wesley A. '31 '54 C&L.145 A.B., J.D. [Ⓒ Franczek S.]

Wildman, Harrold, Allen & Dixon LLP, (AV) [BB]
225 West Wacker Drive Suite 3000, 60606-1229 ⊙
Telephone: 312-201-2000 Fax: 312-201-2555
Email: info@wildmanharrold.com URL: http://www.wildmanharrold.com
Partners: Anthony L. Abboud; Fred M. Ackerson; Stephen A. Allison; Aimee B. Anderson; John J. Arado; Brent R. Austin; Joseph E. Bender; Michael P. Bennett; Todd A. Bickel; Michael R. Blankshain; Scott R. Borstein; Bruce L. Boruszak; John T. Brown; Cal R. Burnton; Adam Scott Calisoff; Douglas R. Carlson; James A. Christman; Geoffrey C. Cockrell; William J. Cook; John W. Costello; Paul R. Diamond; Stewart S. Dixon; Michael Dockterman; Leo P. Dombrowski; James P. Dorr; Vilia M. Drazdys; Thomas P. Duffy; Mark L. Durbin; James B. Durkin (Lisle Office); John L. Eisel; Diane G. Elder; Jerald P. Esrick; Lawrence W. Falbe; Beth L. Fancsali; David J. Fischer; Donald Flayton; Craig Steven Fochler; Lisa M. Fontoura; Kathy Pinkstaff Fox; John E. Frey; Howard N. Gilbert; Gary R. Gillen; Kathleen M. Gilligan; Kenneth M. Gorenberg; Jeffrey P. Gray; Jonathan A. Harris; H. Roderic Heard; Helaine Wachs Heydemann; David H. Hight (Lisle Office); Richard M. Hoffman; Anthony G. Hopp; Peter M. Howard; Richard C. Johnson (Lisle Office); Martha D. Kanter; Charles C. Kim; Anne Giddings Kimball; Steven H. Klein; Timothy K. Klintworth; John F. Kuenstler; Leonard S. Kurfirst; Stephen J. Landes; Dean J. Leffelman (Lisle Office); John S. Letchinger; Brian W. Lewis; Michael P. Lusk; Thomas M. Lynch; Joseph F. Madonia; Thomas I. Matyas; Michael L. McCluggage; Mark P. Miller; Bart T. Murphy (Lisle Office); Robert W. Newman; Sarah L. Olson; Richard C. Palmer; Douglas L. Prochnow; Thomas J. Ring; John A. Roberts; Alan B. Roth; Michael M. Roth (Lisle Office); Fred E. Schulz; Christopher T. Sheean; Robert L. Shuftan; Lisa S. Simmons; David M. Simon; Eric L. Singer (Lisle Office); Andrew M. Slobodien; Derek C. Smith; James M. Snyder (Lisle Office); Charles A. Stern; R. John Street; Peter A. Tomaras; Sherrie Travis; James B. Vogts; David L. Weinstein; Craig M. White; Neil G. Wolf; Allan A. Wulfstat; Jonathan W. Young; Justine Young Gottshall. Associates: Ana L. Acena (Not admitted in IL); Rebecca Alfert; William M. Barnes, Jr.; Jennifer L. Baugh; Jonathan A. Bohlen; Albert M. Bower; Matthew J. Caccamo; Brian R. Carnie; Michael J. Castellino; Gina M. Chang; David J. Chroust (Lisle Office); Chad E. Clark; Alison C. Conlon; David A. Copland; Mohammed A. Diwan; Christopher J. Douglass; Nathan E. Ferguson; Paul K. Freeborn; Jeffrey L. Gansberg; Matthew M. Garrett; Christy S. Gerst; Jeremy S. Goldkind; Jonathan S. Goodman; Velisha L. Haddox; David R. Hale (Not admitted in IL); James J. Hegarty; Bethany L. Hengsbach; Meghan M. Hubbard; Mark A. Huddle; Brandon G. Hummel; Richard J. Jancasz; Jennifer A. Johnston; Sunith V. Kartha; Jeffrey Kosc; Mark A. Kromkowski; Michelle M. Kundmueller; Michael R. LaPorte; Denise A. Lazar; Lucy Lisiecki; Rebecca R. Long; John A. Luburic; Ashanti L. Madlock; Jason McClain Mahoney; R. Michael McCann; Jeffrey K. McGinness; Elizabeth A. McKillip (Lisle Office); Brett A. Middendorf; Laurie M. Miller (Lisle Office); Deborah L. Morgan; Julie M. Nichols; Michelle Nijm; Nicole Nocera; Heather E. Nolan; David M. Oppenheim; Marcia Klenk Owens; Allyson W. Paflas; Joel C. Paschke; Richard J. Pearl; Sandra S. Pedersen; William R. Pokorny; James W. Polichak; Melissa M. Riahei; David M. Rotenberg; Jamie Rubin; Beau C. Sefton; Melissa Suzanne Skilken; Gregory M. Smith; Joshua L. Smith; Martin D. Snyder; Aaron L. Solomon; Jenee M. Straub (Lisle Office); Philip R. Strzalka; Bryan Paul Sugar; Ryan T. Sulkin; David P. Vallas; Corrie E. Valrose (Lisle Office); Theresa G. Van Vuren; Robert Wagner; Pedro J. Windsor, Jr.; Wayne Yao; John W. Young; Edward P. Zaengle. Of Counsel: Thomas D. Allen; Howard Arvey; Marshall L. Burman; Thomas R. Field; Lori A. Goldstein; Robert M. Gunn; Duane P. Hagerty; Bernard Harrold; Marshall M. Holleb; Elizabeth Keiley; Kiplund R. Kolkmeier; Catherine Mathews Graf; John E. McGovern, Jr.; Sheldon P. Migdal; Scott A. Semenek; Thomas H. Snyder; Cynthia Bushnell Stevens; Louis P. Vitullo; Edwin A. Wahlen; Max Wildman.
General Practice. Accreditation, Alternative Dispute Resolution, Antitrust, Appellate, Asbestos, Automotive, Aviation, Banking, Bankruptcy, Business Organizations, Closely-Held Corporations, Commercial Litigation, Consumer, Corporate, Creditors' Rights, Criminal, Drug and Medical Device, E-Commerce, EMF, Employee Benefits, Environmental, Estate Planning, Family Law, Financial Services, Governmental Affairs, Health Care, Industrial Machinery, Insurance Industry, Intellectual Property, Labor and Employment, Land Use Regulation, Mergers and Acquisitions, Municipal Bonds, Patents, Probate, Probate Administration, Procurement and Contracting, Product Liability, Real Estate, Recreational Products, SBIC, Securities, Superfund, Tax, Toxic Torts, Trial, Venture Capital and Workouts.
Lisle, Illinois Office: 2300 Cabot Drive, Suite 455. Telephone: 630-955-0555. Fax: 630-955-0662.
See Professional Biographies, CHICAGO, ILLINOIS

Wile, Cindy F. '49 '79 C.861 B.A. L.424 J.D.
Admin. Atty., Clerk's Off., State Appl. Ct.
Wile, Kenneth Edward, (AV) '— '82
C.178 B.A. L.145 J.D. 10 S. Dearborn Street, 48th Floor
Wilen, Roger R., (AV) .... '— '88 C&L.477 A.B., J.D. [Schiff H.]
Wilen, William P. .... '46 '73 C.352 B.A. L.597 J.D. Legal Assist. Found. of Chicago
Wilens, Gene .... '23 '51 C.1016 L.365 LL.B. Asso. Cir. J.
Wilens, Robert E. .... '65 '90 C.477 B.G.S. L.910 J.D. [Clausen M.]
Wiles, Susan W. .... '64 '91 C.62 B.A. L.597 J.D. [Shefsky&F.]
Wiley, Ginger Rae .... '— '97 C.437 B.A. L.424 J.D. [[A] O'Hagan,S.&A.]
Wilhelm, Degee D. .... '— '02 C.69 B.B.A. L.146 J.D. [[C] Ungaretti&H.]
Wilhelm, John H., (BV) .... '44 '77 C.589 B.A. L.801 J.D. 11 S. La Salle St., Ste. 1800
Wilhoite, Edward .... '58 '87 C.276 A.B. L.339 J.D. 19 S. La Salle St., Ste. 802
Wilk, Jack .... '60 '90 C.340 B.A. L.365 J.D. Cook Co. State's Attorney's Off.
Wilk, Lawrence A. .... '46 '70 C.978 B.A. L.365 J.D. [Wilk&W.]
Wilk, Michele L. .... '67 '92 C.339 B.A. L.146 J.D. [[A] Laser,P.S.F.&E.]
Wilk & Waller .... 77 W. Wash.
Wilkening, Mark D., (AV) .... '53 '80 C.338 B.S. L.209 J.D. [Wiedner&M.]
Wilkes, Tonya N. .... '70 '02 L.966 J.D. [[A] McDermott W.&E.]
Wilkins, Arthur D. '34 '67 C.317 B.A. L.213 LL.B.
Attorney's Title Guaranty Fund Inc.
Wilkins, Norma G. .... '30 '89 C.530 B.A. L.146 J.D. Leslie Lewis Sch.
Wilkins, Thaddeus .... '67 '96 C.1191 B.A. L.615 J.D. Sr. Admin. Law Officer
Wilkinson, MaryBeth .... '72 '97 C.741 B.A. L.597 J.D. [[C] Lovells]
Wilkinson, William J. .... '41 '76 C.1191 B.S.E. L.146 J.D. Chic. Fire Dept.
Wilkow, Marc R., (AV) .... '50 '74 C.112 B.A. L.145 J.D. [Wilkow&W.]
Wilkow & Wilkow, P.C., (AV) .... 180 N. Michigan Ave., 2nd Fl.
Wilks, Undray .... '62 '87 C.597 B.A. L.477 J.D. [[A] McGuirewoods]
Willard, Alison B. .... '76 '01 C.347 B.A. L.477 J.D. [[A] Seyfarth S.]
Willard, Sheri L. .... '57 '91 C.508 B.A. L.209 J.D. [[A] Spain,S.&V.]
Willenborg, Susan J. .... '58 '83 C.118 B.A. L.145 J.D. Asst. Bd. Coun.
Willens, Matthew L. .... '69 '95 C.589 B.S. L.424 J.D. [[A] Clifford]
Willer, Edward G., (AV) .... '48 '73 C&L.209 B.A., J.D. [[A] Corboy&D.]
Williams, Andrew S., (AV) .... '45 '73 C.894 B.A. L.477 J.D. [Aronberg G.D.&G.]
Williams, Andrew W. '66 '01
C.352 B.S. L.273 J.D. [[A] McDonnell B.H.&B.] (See Pat. Sect.)
Williams, Ann Claire .... '49 '76 C.212 B.S. L.602 J.D. Dist. J.
Williams, Becky A. .... '73 '00 C.436 B.A. L.209 J.D. [[A] Katten M.R.]
Williams, Beth L. '51 '78 C.608 B.A. L.659 J.D.
(adm. in PA; not adm. in IL) I.R.S.
Williams, Brent E. .... '— '03 C.201 B.S. L.608 J.D. [[A] Mayer,B.R.&M.]
Williams, Brian J. .... '59 '86 C.927 B.S. L.146 J.D. [Meckler B.&T.]
Williams, Brian S. '64 '89 C.388 B.A. L.347 J.D.
Instructor, Northwestern University Sch. of Law‡
Williams, Carol A., (AV) '46 '80 C.629 B.S. L.424 J.D.
V.P. & Asst. Gen. Coun., General Growth Prop.
Williams, Collin B. .... '76 '03 C.478 B.A. L.861 J.D. [[A] Greenberg T.]
Williams, Daniel P. .... '76 '01 C.477 C.S.E. L.309 J.D. [[A] McDonnell B.H.&B.]
Williams, David G., (AV) .... '— '64 C.226 B.A. L.477 J.D. 111 West Monroe Street‡
Williams, Donna M. .... '65 '90 C&L.597 B.A., J.D. [[A] Baker&M.]
Williams, Dorian R. .... '60 '87 C.679 B.S. L.145 J.D. 203 N. La Salle St., Suite 1800
Williams, Douglas H., (AV) .... '48 '77 C.477 B.A. L.145 J.D. [Sidley A.B.&W.]
Williams, Edward A. ... '— '67 C&L.209 B.S., J.D. 655 West Irving Park Road, Suite 702
Williams, Edward H. .... '67 '93 C.293 B.A. L.477 J.D. [Mayer,B.R.&M.]
Williams, Elaine L. .... '58 '83 C.31 B.A. L.145 J.D. 525 W. Monroe St., Suite 1600
Williams, Elizabeth Anne .... '68 '96 C.01 B.A. L.597 J.D. [Gardner C.&D.]
Williams, George H. '18 '46 C.1019 A.B. L.569 LL.B.
(adm. in NY; not adm. in IL) Exec. Dir., Amer. Jud. Soc.
Williams, H. Randolph, (AV) .... '42 '67 C.378 A.B. L.802 J.D. [Williams&B.]
Williams, Hanson L. .... '68 '94 C.165 B.A. L.208 J.D. [Williams M.&J.]
Williams, J. Michael .... '— '86 C.36 B.A. L.145 J.D. [Cohon R.&R.]
Williams, James C. .... '55 '80 C.276 B.S. L.184 J.D. [[C] McGuirewoods]
Williams, Jason R. .... '73 '03 C.209 B.A. L.146 J.D. [[A] Foran G.P.&P.]
Williams, Jay .... '— '87 C.597 B.A. L.339 J.D. [Schiff H.]
Williams, Jeffrey P., Office .... '51 '81 C.339 B.A. L.209 J.D. 134 N. LaSalle St., Ste. 450
Williams, John T. .... '62 '88 C.297 B.A. L.494 J.D. [Lord,B.&B.]
Williams, John T. '46 '75 C.602 B.A. L.910 J.D.
Coun., Wolters Kluwer U.S. Corporation
Williams, Joseph A., Jr. '— '00 C.576 B.S. L.209 J.D.
[Marshall,G.&B.] (See Pat. Sect.)
Williams, Karl T. .... '— '86 C.976 B.A. L.477 J.D. [Chapman&C.]
Williams, La Vetta D. ...... '54 '90 C.339 B.A. L.365 J.D. 25 E. Washington St., Ste. 820
Williams, Lisa G. .... '68 '96 C.477 B.A. L.339 J.D. 120 North La Salle Street
Williams, Lloyd E., Jr., (AV) .... '34 '61 C.976 B.A. L.477 J.D. [Williams M.&J.]
Williams, Mark R. .... '66 '93 C.339 B.A. L.178 J.D. [DLPiper R.G.C.U.]
Williams, Nancy A., (AV[T]) '54 '78 C.608 B.S. L.117 J.D.
10 S. Riverside Plz., Ste. 1600
Williams, Neil G. '56 '82 C.228 B.A. L.145 J.D.
Assoc. Prof. of Law, Loyola Univ. of Chic. School of Law
Williams, Paul L. .... '53 '84 C.1191 B.A. L.209 J.D. 9415 S. State St.
Williams, R. Kevin .... '54 '87 C&L.339 B.S., J.D. [Rodriguez O.R.F.G.W.&E.]
Williams, Richard John, (AV) .... '40 '66 C.187 A.B. L.276 J.D. [Hlustik,H.W.&V.]
Williams, Richard L., III, (AV) ...... '40 '65 C.674 B.A. L.893 LL.B. [Vedder,P.K.&K.]
Williams, Robert B. .... '42 '67 C.145 B.A. L.209 J.D. [Williams&Ma.]
Williams, Robert E. .... '44 '72 C.403 B.S. L.424 J.D. Chief, Industrial Comm.
Williams, Robert L. .... '15 '37 L.209 LL.B. 135 S. La Salle St.‡
Williams, Roderic M. .... '76 '02 C.597 B.S.E.D. L.665 J.D. [[A] Sonnenschein N.&R.]
Williams, Roger H. .... '41 '73 C.1016 B.A. L.424 J.D. 205 W. Randolph St.
Williams, Scott M. .... '63 '88 C&L.966 B.A., J.D. [McDermott W.&E.]
Williams, Sharon S. '53 '78 C.329 B.A. L.597 J.D.
Admin. Law J., Dept. of Employ. Sec.
Williams, Shelli D. .... '— '84 C.881 B.A. L.1119 J.D. Asst. Chf. Atty.
Williams, Steven A. .... '62 '87 C.210 B.A. L.146 J.D. [[A] Pontikes&Assoc.]
Williams, Thomas E. .... '65 '03 C.679 B.S.A.A.E. L.209 J.D. 2 N. LaSalle St. (Pat.)
Williams, Thomas L. '58 '82 C.347 B.S. L.502 J.D.
(adm. in IN; not adm. in IL) Sr. Coun., Bank One Corp. (Law Dept.)
Williams, Thomas M. .... '— '96 C.966 B.A. L.339 J.D. [Brinks H.G.&L.]
Williams, Tracy D. .... '— '94 C.339 B.A. L.309 J.D. [Foley&L.]
Williams, Zeophus Joy .... '58 '86 C.209 B.S.C. L.1000 J.D. Dep. Supvr.

Williams & Baerson, LLC, (AV)
One North LaSalle Street, Suite 1350, 60602
Telephone: 312-629-9003 Fax: 312-629-9020
H. Randolph Williams; Steven L. Baerson. Of Counsel: Irene Sheridan Brewick.
Trusts and Estates, Estate Planning and Administration, Taxation, International Taxation; Closely Held Businesses.
See Professional Biographies, CHICAGO, ILLINOIS

Williams, Goldfarb, Midura, Kayne & Rutstein, Ltd., (AV) .... 140 S. Dearborn St.
Williams & Marcus, Ltd. .... 33 N. LaSalle St.

Williams Montgomery & John Ltd., (AV)
20 North Wacker Drive Suite 2100, 60606 ⊙
Telephone: 312-443-3200 Facsimile: 312-630-8500
Email: WMJINFO@WILLMONT.COM URL: http://www.willmont.com
Lloyd E. Williams, Jr.; C. Barry Montgomery; Peter C. John; Thomas H. Neuckranz; Edward J. Murphy; David E. Stevenson; Jeffrey H. Lipe; Deborah H. Bornstein; Steven J. Roeder; Gregory J. Bird; Thomas J. Pontikis; Raymond Lyons, Jr.; Brigid E. Kennedy; Bradley C. Nahrstadt; Alyssa M. Campbell; Edward R. Moor; Summer E. Heil; David L. Applegate; Theodore J. Low; Eric R. Lifvendahl; Hanson L. Williams; Thomas C. Koessl;—Christina D. Ketcham; Claire L. Lunardini; Brian Y. Boyd; Beth B. Woods; Alex R. Thiersch; Brigitte C. Weyls; Rodney C. Bashford; Sean G. Joyce; Christina M. Alderfer; Anndra L. Masters; Matthew B. Rosenthal; Margaret T. Rodenburg; James J. Lukas, Jr.; Paul J. Ripp; Ramsey L. Mallory; Howard L. Huntington. Of Counsel: Anthony P. Katauskas; Barry L. Kroll.
Commercial Litigation, Professional Liability (Accountants, Agents and Brokers, Architects and Engineers, Directors and Officers, and Lawyers), Antitrust, Securities Litigation, Class Actions, Mass Torts, Toxic Torts, Products Liability, Construction Liability, Employer Liability, Employment Discrimination, Environmental Insurance Coverage, Environmental Defense, Insurance Coverage, Automobile Liability Defense, General Liability, Insurance Bad Faith, Government Tort Liability, Police Liability, Railroad Accidents and Injuries, Trucking Liability, Maritime Negligence, Farm Equipment Liability, Premises Liability Defense, and Civil Appeals.
Representative Clients: Alpha Therapeutics; Bell Helicopter; Best Buy; Blockbuster; Fisher-Price; Fortune Brands; IBM; PepsiAmerica; Quest Diagnostics.
Miami, Florida Office: Clarke, Silverglate, Campbell, Williams & Montgomery, 799 Brickell Plaza, Suite 900. Telephone: 305-377-0700. Facsimile: 305-377-3001.
See Professional Biographies, CHICAGO, ILLINOIS

Williamson, Amanda S. .... '76 '03 C&L.597 B.A., J.D. [[A] Skadden,A.S.M.&F.]
Williamson, Joel V., (AV) .... '45 '70 C.198 B.A. L.383 J.D. [Mayer,B.R.&M.]
Williamson, Richard S., (AV) .... '49 '74 C.674 A.B. L.893 J.D. [Mayer,B.R.&M.]
Williamson, Stephen D. .... '69 '97 C.352 B.A. L.597 J.D. [[A] Skadden,A.S.M.&F.]
Williams-Walker, Angela .... '— '00 C.197 B.A. L.966 J.D. [[A] Ungaretti&H.]
Willian, Charla Ann .... '— '04 C.473 B.S. L.1119 J.D. [[A] Kirkland&E.]
Willian, Jeffrey L., (P.C.), (AV) .... '— '86 C.473 B.S. L.30 J.D. [Kirkland&E.]
Willis, Gerald C., Jr. '68 '96 C.338 B.S. L.365 J.D.
[McAndrews,H.&M.] (See Pat. Sect.)
Willis, Joleen S. '47 '94 C.966 B.A. L.146 J.D.
Sr. Assoc. Gen. Coun., Bank One Corp. (Law Dept.)
Willis, Ronald M. '46 '72 C.659 B.S. L.597 J.D.
Coun., Chicago & Central States Joint Bd., ACTWU
Willrich, Wendy Jayne '65 '90 C.918 B.A. L.569 J.D.
(adm. in MA; not adm. in IL) City Dept. of Cultural Affs.
Wills, Dale G., (AV) .... '55 '82 C.357 B.S. L.339 J.D. [Swanson,M.&B.]
Wills, Daniel G., (AV) .... '— '90 C&L.209 B.S.Econ., J.D. [Pretzel&S.]
Wills, Garry L. .... '— '03 C.976 B.A. L.597 J.D. [[A] Freeborn&P.]
Wilneff, Robert .... '45 '73 C&L.209 B.S.C., J.D. Philip Rootberg & Co.
Wilner, Noel S. .... '54 '80 C.339 B.S. L.146 J.D. Philip Rootberg & Co.
Wilner, Susan J. .... '46 '81 C.1016 B.A. L.209 J.D. Chicago Housing Auth.
Wilsey, Allen G. .... '29 '50 C&L.209 B.A., LL.B. 221 N. La Salle St.
Wilson, Bruce G., (AV) '49 '77 C.350 B.S. L.352 J.D.
Assoc. Gen. Coun. & Asst. Secy., Exelon Corp.
Wilson, Christopher B., (AV) .... '62 '89 C.577 B.A. L.597 J.D. [Perkins C.]
Wilson, Dennis M., (AV) .... '44 '69 C.602 B.A. L.597 J.D. [DLPiper R.G.C.U.]
Wilson, Donald N. .... '65 '91 C.339 B.S. L.378 J.D. 101 N. Wacker Dr., Ste. 1800
Wilson, Doris K. .... '61 '86 C.813 B.A. L.477 J.D. 1st Natl. Bk. of Chicago

Wilson, Elizabeth A. '— '86 C.217 B.A. L.608 J.D.
V.P. & Assoc. Gen. Coun., CNA Property & Casualty Oper.
Wilson, Felicia H. '58 '95 C.697 B.A. L.1206 J.D.
Chicago Housing Auth., Off. of the Gen. Coun.
Wilson, Georgene M., (AV) .... '52 '81 C.347 B.A. L.209 J.D. [Ⓒ Meckler B.&T.]
Wilson, Gloria E. ....'17 '45 C.597 B.S. L.365 J.D. 4850 Lake Park Ave.
Wilson, Harry L., (AV) ....'42 '75 C.475 B.A. L.477 J.D. [Ⓒ Clausen M.]
Wilson, Helen T. ....'— '88 C.999 B.A. L.209 J.D. [Schiff H.]
Wilson, James B., (P.C.), (AV) ....'— '53 C.276 A.B. L.477 J.D. [Schiff H.] ‡
Wilson, James D., (AV) ....'50 '78 C.628 B.S. L.146 J.D. [Shefsky&F.]
Wilson, John C. ....'— '78 C.879 B.A. L.365 J.D. [Ⓐ Hennessy&R.]
Wilson, Johner T., III ....'77 '02 C.339 B.A. L.209 J.D. [Albert,W.]
Wilson, Joseph L. ....'55 '82 C.338 B.S. L.734 J.D. [Wilson&L.]
Wilson, Mark E. ....'63 '89 C.373 B.A. L.494 J.D. [Kerns,P.F.&P.]
Wilson, Martin J. ....'36 '79 C.1191 B.S. L.209 J.D. 7847 S. Crandon Ave.
Wilson, Mary Ann S. .... '— '84 C.588 B.A. L.365 J.D. Asst. State's Atty., Cook Co.
Wilson, Mary G., (AV) ....'67 '92 C.976 B.A. L.145 J.D. [Sonnenschein N.&R.]
Wilson, Patricia Shea ....'52 '85 C&L.424 B.A., J.D. Asst. States Atty.
Wilson, Peter R. ....'68 '95 C.165 B.A. L.339 J.D. [Katten M.R.]
Wilson, Richard Allen, (BV) ....'59 '92 C&L.424 B.A., J.D. [R.A.Wilson]
Wilson, Robert A. ....'— '99 C.966 B.A. L.597 J.D. [Kirkland&E.]
Wilson, Roger G. '50 '75 C.197 A.B. L.309 J.D.
Sr. V.P., Gen. Coun. & Corp. Secy., BlueCross BlueShield Assoc.
Wilson, Thaddeus L. ....'66 '94 C.602 B.B.A. L.589 J.D. 11 E. Adams St., Ste. 902

Wilson Elser Moskowitz Edelman & Dicker LLP, (AV)
120 N. La Salle Street 26th Floor, 60602 ⊙
Telephone: 312-704-0550 Facsimile: 312-704-1522
URL: http://www.wemed.com
Resident Partners: Anjali C. Das; Bennett R. Heller; David M. Holmes; Raymond J. Jast; Daniel J. McMahon; Thomas Murray; Rebecca Rothmann; Curt J. Schlom; Ian A. Stewart; James K. Thurston. Resident Associates: Edna S. Bailey; Stefan R. Dandelles; James R. Dougherty; Jacinta Epting; Benjamin Falloon; Jamie L. Filipovic; Anthony M. Goldner; Cinthia Granados Motley; Lisa Handler Ackerman; Penelope S. Hopper; John C. Hunter; Nicholas J. Kauffman; Kelly A. Kraft; Jason M. Kuzniar; Shawn P. Lee; Smita Mokshagundam; Christian Novay; Steven D. Smiejek; Stacey Lynn Smiricky; Daniel E. Tranen; Benjamin M. Whipple; Daniel A. Wolberg. Resident Of Counsel: Loren S. Cohen; Charles W. Planek.
Accounting Liability, Admiralty Law, Agents and Brokers Liability, Alternative Dispute Resolution, Appellate Practice, Architects and Engineers Liability, Asbestos Defense, Aviation Law, Commercial Law, Construction Law, D&O Liability, Employment Law, Environmental Law, General Liability, Health Care, Insurance Bad Faith, Insurance Coverage, Intellectual Property, Lawyers' Malpractice, Medical Malpractice, Municipal Law, Product Liability, Professional Liability, Toxic Torts, Trucking Law, Transportation Liability.
Los Angeles, CA; San Diego, CA; San Francisco, CA; Washington, D.C.; McLean, VA; Newark, NJ; Philadelphia, PA; Baltimore, MD; Miami, FL; White Plains, NY; Dallas, TX; Houston, TX; Albany, NY; Garden City, NY; New York, NY; Boston, MA; Stamford, CT; Las Vegas, NV; London, England. Affiliates: HPMBC/Clyde & Co.: Paris, France; Bach, Langheid Dallmayr: Cologne, Germany; Frankfurt/Main, Germany; Berlin, Germany; Munich, Germany.
See Professional Biographies, CHICAGO, ILLINOIS

Wilson & Lee ....111 W. Washington St.

Wilson & McIlvaine
(See Quarles & Brady LLC)

Wilson, Richard A., P.C., The Law Offices of, (BV)
35 East Wacker Drive, Suite 650, 60601
Telephone: 312-987-0191 Fax: 312-546-5140 URL: http://www.rwlex.com
Email: rwilson@rwlex.com URL: http://www.richardwilsonlawoffice.com
Richard Allen Wilson.
Litigation and Appellate Practice concentrating in Domestic Relations Law, Same-Sex Law, including Marriage, Domestic Partnerships, Parentage, Custody and Visitation, Divorce, Custody and Visitation, and Related Matters, Pre- and Post-Decree, Pre- and Post-Nuptial Agreements, Cohabitation Agreements.
See Professional Biographies, CHICAGO, ILLINOIS

Wilson-Gowin, Lindsay E. ....'79 '04 C.339 B.A. L.178 J.D. [Ⓐ Skadden,A.S.M.&F.]
Wilson-Lokken, Anne E. ....'72 '97 C.221 B.A. L.209 J.D. [Ⓐ Franczek S.]
Wimbiscus, Thomas J., (AV) '60 '85
C&L.339 B.S., J.D. [McAndrews,H.&M.] (See Pat. Sect.)
Wimmer, Richard T. ....'49 '74 C.932 B.B.A. L.209 J.D. [Klein,T.&J.]
Wincek, Gary Alan ....'57 '82 C.424 B.S. L.146 J.D. [Laner,M.D.B.L.&T.]
Wincek, Todd M. ....'69 '99 C.347 B.A. L.831 J.D. 53 W. Jackson, Ste. 560
Winchester, Jason G. .... '— '96 C&L.339 B.A., J.D. [Ⓐ Jones D.]
Windham, Danny ....'61 '89 [Childers,W.&W.]
Windsor, Pedro J., Jr. ....'— '04 C.1139 B.A. L.352 J.D. [Ⓐ Wildman,H.A.&D.]
Wine, Jodi Rosen ....'60 '92 C.174 B.S. L.145 J.D. [Jenkens&G.]
Wine-Banks, Jill, (AV) '43 '69 C.339 B.S. L.178 J.D.
Maytag Corp., V.P., Alliance Mgmt.
Winer, Barbara S. ....'47 '79 C.98 B.A. L.209 J.D. 205 W. Randolph, Ste. 1530
Winer, Sherwin M. ....'35 '60 C.118 B.A. L.597 J.D. 205 W. Randolph
Winer, Tina L. ....'70 '94 C&L.339 B.A., J.D. [Neal,G.&E.]
Winfield, Prentice H., Jr. ....'21 '49 C.597 B.S. L.209 LL.B. Asst. Corp. Coun.
Wing, John A. ....'35 '63 C.867 B.A. L.273 LL.B. 208 South LaSalle Street
Winger, Harold R. ....'13 '50 C&L.966 A.B., LL.B. Contl. Assurance Co.
Winger, Steven J. ....'67 '00 C.951 B.A. L.597 J.D. [Ⓐ Babbitt&M.]
Winget, Mark L. ....'68 '95 C.367 B.A. L.309 J.D. [Ⓐ Vedder,P.K.&K.]
Winick, Jeffrey H., (AV) ....'63 '88 C.352 B.A. L.477 J.D. [Stein,R.&H.]
Winiecki, Kurt A. ....'66 '97 C.339 B.S. L.424 J.D. [Ⓐ DLPiper R.G.C.U.]
Winkelstein, Michel ....'51 '87 C.1044 B.A. L.365 J.D. [Ⓒ J.S.Rothman&Assoc.]
Winkler, Charles H., (AV) '54 '79
C.1365 B.B.A. L.597 J.D. Circuit Court of Cook County
Winkler, Thomas W. ....'56 '82 C&L.339 B.S., J.D. [Leff,C.&W.]
Winn, Wm. S. ....'19 '48 C.597 L.365 LL.B. 6338 N. Artesian Ave.
Winner, Robert S. ....'— '97 C.910 B.A. L.209 J.D. [Ungaretti&H.]
Winner, Sarie E. ....'77 '02 C.165 B.A. L.424 J.D. [Ⓐ Kusper&R.]
Winningham, Janet H. ....'— '82 C.210 B.A. L.424 J.D. [Katten M.R.]
Winslade, Christopher C. '65 '92
C.602 B.A. L.608 J.D. [McAndrews,H.&M.] (See Pat. Sect.)
Winslow, Edward B. ....'— '95 C.93 B.A. L.893 J.D. [Jones D.]
Winston, Harold J. ....'45 '86 C.563 B.A. L.424 J.D. Asst. Pub. Def.
Winston, Ina S. '— '71 C.145 B.A. L.209 J.D.
Metro. Water Reclamation Dist. of Greater Chicago
Winston, Sarah H. .... '73 '98 C.477 B.A. L.213 J.D. [Ⓐ Baker&M.]

Winston & Strawn LLP, (AV) BB
35 West Wacker Drive, 60601 ⊙
Telephone: 312-558-5600 Facsimile: 312-558-5700
Email: postmaster@winston.com URL: http://www.winston.com
Frederick H. Winston (1853-1886); Frederick S. Winston (1878-1909); Silas Hardy Strawn (1891-1946). Partners: George B. Christensen (1905-1997); Calvin P. Sawyier (1921-2003); Thomas A. Reynolds, Jr.; Edward L. Foote; Bruce L. Bower (Retired); M. Finley Maxson; Robert G. Lane (Retired); Stephen C. Bruner (Retired); Terry M. Grimm; Duane M. Kelley; Albert Milstein; Kurt L.

(This Listing Continued)

Winston & Strawn LLP (Continued)

Schultz; Paul H. Hensel; Columbus R. Gangemi, Jr.; Christopher D. Murtaugh; Robert F. Denvir; Hurd Baruch (Retired); Gregory S. Murray; James M. Neis; Michael V. Hasten (1946-1997); Susan E. Cremin; Robert W. Ericson (New York, N.Y. Office); Neil E. Holmen; Gerald C. Peterson; Kimball R. Anderson; Jerome W. Pope; Thomas A. Reynolds, III; Robert F. Wall; Dan K. Webb; Wayne D. Boberg; Mark G. Henning; Gregory J. Malovance; Scott J. Szala; Charles E. Stahl (1944-1998); James H. Russell; Thomas P. Fitzgerald; Timothy J. Rivelli; Stephen C. Schulte; Edward F. Gerwin, Jr. (Washington, D.C. Office); F. Ellen Duff; Terry John Malik; Bruce A. Toth; Arnold G. Gough, Jr.; Dennis J. Kelly; R. Mark McCareins; Stephen P. Durchslag; Richard B. Teiman (New York, N.Y. Office); Anthony J. D'Auria (New York, N.Y. Office); Jonathan Goldstein (New York, N.Y. Office); Joseph A. DiBenedetto (New York, N.Y. Office); Jeffrey H. Elkin (New York, N.Y. Office); Susan Berkwitt-Malefakis (New York, N.Y. Office); Joseph A. Walsh, Jr.; Michael G. Robinson; Mark M. Heatwole; Leonard W. Belter (Washington, D.C. Office); Thomas M. Buchanan (Washington, D.C. Office); Donald K. Dankner (Washington, D.C. Office); Peter N. Hiebert (Washington, D.C. Office); Eric L. Hirschhorn (Washington, D.C. Office); John C. Kirtland (Washington, D.C. Office); William J. Madden, Jr. (Washington, D.C. Office); J. Michael McGarry, III (Washington, D.C. Office); Nicholas S. Reynolds (Washington, D.C. Office); Mark J. Wetterhahn (Washington, D.C. Office); Howard M. Pearl; Lawrence R. Desideri; Thomas J. Quigley (New York, N.Y. Office); David A. Repka (Washington, D.C. Office); Norman Newman (1952-1998); Anthony F. LoFrisco (New York, N.Y. Office); James R. Thompson, Jr.; Thomas F. Blakemore; Thomas J. Frederick; George C. Lombardi; Rex L. Sessions; John A. Waits, II (Washington, D.C. Office); Christine L. Albright; Marc S. Palay (Geneva, Switzerland Office); Benjamin P. Fishburne, III (Washington, D.C. Office); Barry J. Hart (Washington, D.C. Office); Charles L. Kinney (Washington, D.C. Office); James R. Curtiss (Washington, D.C. Office); Nicolas C. Ulmer (Geneva, Switzerland Office); Julie A. Bauer; Charles B. Boehrer; Deborah K. Boling; Terrence R. Brady; Steven J. Gavin; John L. MacCarthy; Peter C. McCabe, III; William G. Miossi; Louis J. Weber III; John C. Lorentzen; James M. Reum; William D. Brewer (New York, N.Y. Office); Christina Karcher Corsiglia; W. Gordon Dobie; Patrick O. Doyle; Andrew J. McDonough; Michael L. Mulhern; Lori J. Van Auken (New York, N.Y. Office); John Albert Whittaker, IV (Washington, D.C. Office); Gordon Alan Coffee (Washington, D.C. Office); Patrick F. Murray (Paris, France Office); Timothy M. Broas (Washington, D.C. Office); Leland E. Hutchinson; M. David Galainena; William A. Carmell (New York, N.Y. Office); Matthias A. Lydon; Christopher C. McIsaac (Washington, D.C. Office); Eric W. Bloom (Washington, D.C. Office); Oscar A. David; Anthony DiSarro (New York, N.Y. Office); Brian S. Hart; Eleni Skoulikas Kouimelis; R. Cabell Morris, Jr.; Jennifer T. Nijman; Andrew W. Ratts; Michael L. Sibarium (Washington, D.C. Office); Thomas J. Wiegand; Daniel C. Bird, Jr.; Vincent Sol (Paris, France Office); Thomas L. Mills (Washington, D.C. Office); Constantine G. Papavizas (Washington, D.C. Office); Jeffrey G. Berman (Washington, D.C. Office); John Fehrenbach (Washington, D.C. Office); William N. Hall (Washington, D.C. Office); Younghee J. Ottley; Robert Everett Bostrom (New York, N.Y. Office); William A. Anderson, II (Washington, D.C. Office); Daniel R. Murdock (New York, N.Y. Office); Joan B. Tucker Fife (San Francisco, California Office); William A. Kapell (New York, N.Y. Office); Catherine Wozniak Joyce; W. Paul Bishop (Paris, France Office); Carol A. Joffe (Washington, D.C. Office); Charles B. Molster, III (Washington, D.C. Office); Stanford J. Goldblatt; Michael S. Melbinger; Bruce R. Braun; Ronald H. Jacobson; Robert L. Michels; Timothy P. O'Connor; Ronald J. Nye; Patrick M. Hardiman; Brian T. Black; James F. Hurst; David E. Koropp; Kathleen Ann Swien; Eric J. Marcotte (Washington, D.C. Office); Vincent D. Salvatore, Jr. (Washington, D.C. Office); Bradley E. Lerman; Christoph C. Heisenberg (New York, N.Y. Office); David B. Love; Mary E. Wall (Washington, D.C. Office); Jack Crowe; Susan W. Drewke; Bradley C. Graveline; Alexis MacDowall; Don Joseph Mizerk; Kevin J. Narko; Cheryl Tama Oblander; Joseph James Torres; Louise Rembar Radin (New York, N.Y. Office); Loren A. Weil; Matthew J. Botica; Michael L. Brody; Susan F. Klein (New York, N.Y. Office); Joël Alquezar (Paris, France Office); James A. Beha II (New York, N.Y. Office); Edward G. H. Chin (Not admitted in IL; New York, N.Y. Office); Steven M. Schwartz (New York, N.Y. Office); David C. Romm (Washington, D.C. Office); Garry R. Boehlert (Washington, D.C. Office); Manes M. Merrit (New York, N.Y. Office); Stuart Altschuler; Mary Patricia Benz; Timothy J. Oxley; E. King Poor; Marie A. Lona; Samuel Mendenhall; Grace L. Shaff; Colleen T. Shaughnessy; Jeffrey M. Wagner; Joseph J. Zaknoen; Raymond B. Wuslich (Washington, D.C. Office); Joëlle Herschtel (Paris, France Office); Lee T. Paterson (Los Angeles, California Office); Laura R. Petroff (Los Angeles, California Office); Susan M. Benton-Powers; Debra J. Albin-Riley (Los Angeles, California Office); Richard F. Williamson (Washington, D.C. Office); Susan Cannon Longstreet (Washington, D.C. Office); Neal R. Marder (Los Angeles, California Office); Kay McNab; Marie C. Oldham; David W. Wirt; Virginia R. Richard (New York, N.Y. Office); Vincent A. Sama (New York, N.Y. Office); William C. Seligman (Not admitted in IL; Los Angeles, California and New York, New York Offices); Corey A. Tessler (New York, N.Y. Office); Jay Gladis (New York, N.Y. Office); Alan S. Hoffman (New York, N.Y. Office); H. Sidney Holmes III (New York, N.Y. Office); David F. Kroenlein (New York, N.Y. Office); Eric M. Nelson (New York, N.Y. Office); James S. Normile (New York, N.Y. Office); Stephen L. Sheinfeld (New York, N.Y. Office); John H. Denne (New York, N.Y. Office); William F. Dudine, III (New York, N.Y. Office); Patricia Van B. Madsen (New York, N.Y. Office); John E. Tardera (New York, N.Y. Office); Eric P. Taylor (Not admitted in IL; New York, N.Y. Office); Loran T. Thompson (New York, N.Y. Office); Alexander T. Deland (New York, N.Y. Office); Richard F. Lawler (New York, N.Y. Office); C. MacNeil Mitchell (New York, N.Y. Office); Brian L. Sullivan (New York, N.Y. Office); Neil Underberg (New York, N.Y. Office); Lina M. Viviano (New York, N.Y. Office); William A. Horin (Washington, D.C. Office); Gerald P. Farano (Washington, D.C. Office); Andreas H. Leskovsek (Washington, D.C. Office); Jay L. Levine (Washington, D.C. Office); Michael P. O'Brien; Anne E. Thar; Gregory J. Bynan; John M. Dickman; Joseph P. Franklin; Jeffrey A. Leon; David R. Hambourger; James M. Lynch; Allan A. Fanucci (New York, N.Y. and Washington D.C. Offices); David M. Traitel; Peter M. D'Ambrosio (Washington, D.C. Office); Alexandre Brue (Paris, France Office); John W. Christopher; Todd J. Ehlman; Paul S. Pilecki (Washington, D.C. Office); Stephen J. Senderowitz; Timothy J. Dable; Dane Drobny; John R. Grier; Brendan P. Head; Lawrence I. Kiern (Washington, D.C. Office); Peter J. Kocoras; Stephen J. Legatzke; Roger S. Lucas; Brian E. Neuffer; Susan A. Pipal; J. David Reich (New York, N.Y. Office); Michael P. Roche; Julie L. Soloway; Michael E. Emrich (New York, N.Y. Office); Lana C. Marina (New York, N.Y. Office); Nikolai Krylov (New York, N.Y. Office); Eric M. Robinson (New York, N.Y. Office); Howard R. Majev (Washington, D.C. Office); Jeanne M. Dennis (Washington, D.C. Office); Anna Segobia Masters (Los Angeles, California Office); Ronald S. Betman; Robert Y. Sperling; Andrew P. Bridges (San Francisco, California Office); John D. Fredericks (San Francisco, California Office); Amanda Groves (San Francisco, California Office); Demetra V. Georgelos (Los Angeles, California Office); David A. Honig (San Francisco, California Office); Robert A. Julian (San Francisco, California Office); Michael Kip Maly (San Francisco, California Office); Patrick A. Murphy (San Francisco, California Office); John C. Nishi (San Francisco, California Office); Mark A. Olson (San Francisco, California Office); Randy Rogers (San Francisco, California Office); Paul P. Sagan (Los Angeles, California Office); Eric E. Sagerman (Los Angeles, California Office); Margaret Sheneman (San Francisco, California Office); Rolf S. Woolner (Los Angeles, California Office); Derek G. Barella; Matthew F. Bergmann; Stephen V. D'Amore; Damon DiCastri; Patricia M. Dineen (New York, N.Y. Office); David J. Doyle; M. Christine Graff; Brian L. Heidelberger; Luke Allan Palese; Raymond Perkins; Tracy A. O'Flaherty; Ronald Y. Rothstein; John M. Schloerb; Joseph A. Spiegler; John J. Tully, Jr.; Ricardo E. Ugarte (Geneva, Switzerland Office); Michael D. Whitty; Francisco J. Pavia (Washington, D.C. Office); Christine A. Edwards; Raul R. Herrera (Washington, D.C. Office); John L. Carr, Jr. (Not admitted in IL); Norman K. Beck; Jon Michael Brown, Jr.; Taras A. Gracey; Diana Juliet Hsu; Brian J. Kozlowski; Michael J. Lotus; Joseph P. Lukas; Timothy J. McCaffrey; Daniel J. McGuire; Raymond W. Mitchell; John E. Mooney; John W. Moss; Adrienne Banks Pitts; Peter W. Poulos; Timothy W. Smith; Erik W. Snapp; Eryk J. Spytek; Victoria F. Stach; Mark A. de Bernardo (Washington, D.C. Office); H. Allen Black III (Washington, D.C. Office); M. Carter DeLorme (Washington, D.C. Office); Catherine DiFiglia (New York, N.Y. Office); Michael T. Dyson (Washington, D.C. Office); Marion Kristal Goldberg (Washington, D.C. Office); Charles B. Klein (Washington, D.C. Office); Jessie A. Kohler (Los Angeles, California Office); James S. Richter (New York, N.Y. Office); Jeffrey A. Wolfson (Washington, D.C. Office); Stacy Yakaboski (New York, N.Y. Office); Charles S. Birenbaum (San Francisco, California Office); Stephen I. Berkman (San Francisco, California Office); Jeffrey S. Bosley (San Francisco, California Office); Tyler M. Paetkau (San Francisco, California Office); William M. Doyle, Jr.; Linda Lemel Hoseman; William M. Sullivan, Jr. (Washington, D.C. Office); David E. Mollón (New York, N.Y. Office); Mark S. Weisberg; James L. Malone III (New York, N.Y. Office); Zoe J. Ashcroft (London, England Office); Peggy M. Balesteri; Kevin A. Banasik; Lori A. Bean (London, England Office); Thomas J. Benz (London, England Office); Christine M. Cahill (New York, N.Y. Office); Jared R. Cloud; Luke A. Connelly (New York, N.Y. Office); Jerome O. Herbet (Paris, France Office); Louis C. Katsoris (New York, N.Y. Office); David Neier (New York, N.Y. Office); Antoine Martin (Paris, France Office); John McMickle (Washington, D.C. Office); Matthew D. O'Meara; Laurette Petersen; Karen Caraher Quirk; Brian M. Schafer; Scott A. Schipma (Washington, D.C. Office); Amanda C. Sommerfeld (Los Angeles, California Office); Gail J. Standish (Los Angeles, California Office); Stephen R. Smerek (Los Angeles, California Office); Barry S. Vitou (London, England Office); Paul J. Coady (Los Angeles, California Office); Gregory S. Shatan (New York, N.Y. Office); G. Thomas Stromberg, Jr. (Los Angeles, California Office); Randa A. Jaafar (New York, N.Y. Office); Michael A. Moser (New York, N.Y. Office); Adam J. Schlatner (New York, N.Y. Office); Linda T. Coberly; Ross A. Honig (New York, N.Y. Office); David M. Hickey (Los Angeles, California Office); Paolo Di Rosa (Washington, D.C. Office); Scott H. Blackman (Washington, D.C.

(This Listing Continued)

Winston & Strawn LLP (Continued)

Office); (Mr.) Thomas C. Mavrakakis (San Francisco, California Office); Edmund S. Cohen (New York, N.Y. Office); Milton K. Buckingham; Kurt Stitcher; Barbara C. Sessions. Of Counsel: Mary Hutchings Reed; J. Ericson Heyke, III; John M. Hadlock (New York, N.Y. Office); Judith A. Gelb (Not admitted in IL; New York, N.Y. Office); John P. Proctor (Washington, D.C. Office); Hill Blackett, III (San Francisco, California Office); S. Shane Sagheb (Not admitted in IL); Gaela K. Gehring Flores (Washington, D.C. Office). Senior Counsel: Peter Whitridge Williams (New York, N.Y. Office). Senior Attorneys: Barry L. Salkin (New York, N.Y. Office); Alan V. Lindquist; Deborah S. K. Jagoda (New York, N.Y. Office); William M. Sunkel (New York, N.Y. Office); Marcia R. Gelman (Not admitted in IL); N. Dwight Cary (San Francisco, California Office). Associates: Maureen Aidasani; Lana Alamat; Laura J. Alexander; Tracy J. Allen; Brian N. Anderson; Stacey Austin; Courtney Engelbrecht Barr; Michael D. Bess; Matthew A. Bills; Monika M. Blacha; Kellie Blattner; Todd M. Bloomquist; Jason L. Booth; Katherine Borden; Lester G. Bovia, Jr.; Eric L. Broxterman (Not admitted in IL); Dean M. Burau; Alfonso Canela; Romy Elisabeth Carr; Hortensia S. Carreira; Tracy S. Cassidy; Christine R. Chase; Pei Yuan Chung; Kevin M. Cloutier; Kendric M. Cobb; Danielle A. R. Coffman; Mindy D. Cohn; J. Erik Connolly; Larissa Cooper; Matthew D. Costigan; Kristen Cowan; Catherine L. Crisham; Christopher J. Cullen; Bryna Dahlin; David Dahlquist; Kareem A. Dale; Kyle DeJong; Joseph L. Devaney, III; Michael P. DiGiannantonio; Justin Endres; Elizabeth Epstein; Elizabeth Erickson; Christopher Blair Essig; Michael G. Falk; Jared R. Feehan; Brian D. Fergemann; Amy L. Flaherty; Stacy J. Flanigan; Michael A. Flomenhoft; Brian L. Franklin; Melissa Gadowski; Jennifer Gallinson; Rodger Lee Gardy, Jr.; Megan E. Gervase (Not admitted in IL); Gwenn E. Girard; Scott P. Glauberman; Anne Graber Blazek; Maria Guiao; Ankur Gupta; Adam K. Gusman; J. Eric Guth; L. Timothy Halleron; Katherine L. Harenza; James P. Healy, Jr.; James M. Hilmert; Nathan E. Hoffman; Margaret Glunz Horton; M. Faiyaz Hussain; Eric L. Jacobson; Shelbee Jarol; Andrew M. Johnstone; Amit Kalra; Erin A. Kartheiser; Jai S. Khanna; Charles Kierpiec; Blaine C. Kimrey; Laura G. Klempay; Jennifer L. Kobayashi; Karen M. Kowalski; Jon J. Kramer; David Latchana; Arlene Lim; Derek P. Linde; Erik B. Lundgren; Lynn C. MacDonald; Katie Mackie; Robin Drey Maher; Julia Mano; Robyn Martin; Michael P. Mayer; Katherine A. McAvoy; Stephanie McCallum; Greg J. Miarecki; Ari D. Mintzer; Shannon Mudd Leutheuser; Michael T. Mullins; Cornelius M. Murphy; Elizabeth Anne Nemeth; Michael K. Nutter; Katherine O'Halleran; William O'Neil; Mat thew R. Osenga (Not admitted in IL); Kevin J. O'Shea; Nicole J. Ottmer; Samuel S. Park; Christopher S. Perry; Theodore Zane Polley, III; Ivan M. Poullaos; Kenneth P. Purcell; Kimberly Reed; Michael Patrick Rohan; Robert T. Roos; Kevin M. Ryan; Rana H. Salti; Derek J. Sarafa; Nicholas J. Schuler, Jr.; Lisa K. Seilheimer; Vishal Raj Shani; Andrew D. Shapiro; Cardelle B. Spangler; Jennifer Spry; Chris Stathopoulos; Giel Stein; Shannon L. Stevens; Erin Glezen Stone; J. Andrew P. Stone; Matthew J. Sullivan; Michael J. Towne; Scott Walton; Brian Wanamaker; Andrew D. Wang; Brooke B. Ward; Andrew C. Warnecke; Matthew M. Wawrzyn; Anastasia G. Weis; Christopher A. Weller; Brian D. Werner; Nicole E. Wrigley; Ethan R. York. Staff Attorneys: Edward M. Coffman; Kelly Cordes; Jennifer L. Cuculich; Patrick Sean Ginty; Betsy L. Katten; Gregory A. McConnell; S. Charles Patel; Stephen N. Sher; Jonathon Treat; Paula Hudson Holderman.

Alternative Dispute Resolution, Antitrust, Asset Securitization, Banking, Bankruptcy, Workouts and Financial Restructurings, Commercial Lending, Contracts, Corporate, Corporate Finance, E-Commerce, Employee Benefits and Executive Compensation, Energy, Environmental Law, Healthcare, Immigration, Intellectual Property, International, Labor and Employment Relations, Lease Finance, Litigation, Maritime, Mergers and Acquisitions, Product Liability, Project Finance, Public Finance, Real Estate, Securities, State and Federal Governmental Relations and Regulatory Affairs, Tax, Technology, Transportation, Trusts and Estates and White Collar Criminal Defense.

Washington, D.C. Office: 1700 K Street, N.W., 20006-3817. Telephone: 202-282-5000. Telecopier: 202-282-5100.

New York, N.Y. Office: 200 Park Avenue, 10166-4193. Telephone: 212-294-6700. Telecopier: 212-294-4700.

Los Angeles, California Office: 333 South Grand Avenue, 38th Floor, 90071-1543. Telephone: 213-615-1700. Fax: 213-615-1750.

Geneva, Switzerland Office: 43 Rue du Rhone, CH 1204. Telephone: +41-22 317 75 75. Fax: +41-22 317 75 00.

Paris, France Office: 21 Avenue Victor Hugo. 75116. Telephone: 331-5364-8282. Fax: 331-5364-8220.

San Francisco, California Office: 101 California Street, 94111. Telephone: 415-591-1000. Fax: 415-591-1400.

London, England Office: Bucklersbury House, 3 Queen Victoria Street, EC4N 8NH. Telephone: 011-44-20-7429-0000. Fax: 011-44-20-7429-0100.

See Professional Biographies, CHICAGO, ILLINOIS

Winter, Carolyn E., (AV) ... '44 '85 C.1016 B.S. L.424 J.D. [Mandel,L.&S.]
Winter, Daniel J., (CV) '66 '91
C.966 B.A. L.910 J.D. 53 W. Jackson Boulevard, Suite 725
Winter, Frank L., (AV) ... '28 '54 C&L.597 B.S., J.D. 527 S. Wells St.
Winter, Patricia J. ... '49 '75 C&L.546 B.A., J.D. Sr. Atty., Northern Trust Corporation
Winter, Richard R. ... '— '87 C.339 B.S. L.146 J.D. [Holland&K.]
Winter, Robert Mc Kenna ... '53 '78 C&L.209 B.A., J.D. [Robbins,S.&P.]
Winters, Daniel J. ... '— '92 C.276 B.A. L.339 J.D. [Jenner&B.]
Winters, David P. ... '55 '92 C.659 A.B. L.209 J.D. Sr. Staff Atty.
Winters, Gregory M. ... '69 '94 C.339 B.S. L.424 J.D. [Burke,W.M.&S.]
Winters, John David ... '68 '02 C.1111 B.A. L.597 J.D. [Ⓐ Butler R.S.&B.]
Winters, John F., Jr. ... '53 '91 C.338 B.A. L.364 J.D. 111 West Washington Street
Winters, Mark E. ... '66 '91 C.597 B.A. L.424 J.D. [Sanchez&D.]
Wintroub, Cary J. ... '53 '78 C.910 B.A. L.209 J.D. 30 N. LaSalle St.
Wintroub, Shana B. ... '— '01 C.823 B.A. L.339 J.D. [Ⓐ McDermott W.&E.]
Wippold, William M., (BV) ... '43 '72 C&L.339 A.B., J.D. [Ⓐ Dwyer,M.&Assoc.]
Wirt, David W., (BV) ... '65 '91 C.1375 A.B. L.597 J.D. [Winston&S.]
Wirth, Jennifer ... '— '02 C.339 B.A. L.365 J.D. 53 West Jackson Street, Suite 1002
Wirth, Karen C. ... '39 '83 C.399 B.Mus.Ed. L.365 J.D. Asst. States Atty.
Wirtz, Francis J. ... '54 '80 C.339 B.S. L.477 J.D. [Ⓒ Neal,G.&E.]
Wise, David C., (AV) ... '67 '93 C.339 B.A. L.365 J.D. [Burke,M.&W.]
Wise, Howard J. ... '68 '97 C.37 B.F.A. L.1187 J.D. [Ⓐ W.H.Wise&Assoc.] ⊙
Wise, Jolene M. ... '59 '89 C.338 B.S. L.365 J.D. Securities and Exchange Comm.
Wise, Michael, (AV) ... '54 '79 C.178 B.A. L.910 J.D. [Lawrence,K.S.&U.]

Wise, William H., & Associates, Law Offices of, (AV) '40 '65 C.1016 A.B. L.365 J.D.
134 North LaSalle Street Suite 1515, 60602 ⊙
Telephone: 312-346-4555 Fax: 847-272-4255
Email: william@wiseattorneys.net URL: http://www.wiseattorneys.net
Associate: Howard J. Wise.
Criminal Law, Driving While Intoxicated, Traffic Violations, Juvenile Law, Expungements, Parole and Probation, Drug Crimes, Felonies, Homicide, Misdemeanors, Secretary of State Drivers License Revocation, White Collar Crime, Personal Injury, Automobile Accidents, Constitutional Law and Workers Compensation.
Schaumburg, Illinois Office: 1821 Walden Office Square, 4th Floor, 60173. Telephone: 847-397-1112. Fax: 847-272-4255.

See Professional Biographies, CHICAGO, ILLINOIS

Wise & Kuzas, Ltd., (BV) ... 150 N. Wacker Dr.
Wiser, Steven ... '69 '98 C&L.424 B.A., J.D. [Ⓐ Defrees&F.]
Wishnick, Susan ... '63 '88 C.477 A.B. L.309 J.D. Staff Coun, ACLU
Wishnoff, Jory I. ... '52 '79 C.966 B.S. L.146 J.D. Sr. Supervising Atty.
Wishnow, Brian M. ... '78 '03 C.367 B.A. L.880 J.D. [Ⓐ Kane,C.&M.] (Pat.)
Wisner, Floyd A. ... '— '77 C&L.209 B.A., J.D. [Ⓐ Nolan]
Wisniewski, David L. ... '71 '00 C.209 B.A. L.365 J.D. 20 N. Wacker Dr., Ste. 1900
Wisniewski, Ronald L. ... '66 '92 C.602 B.A. L.879 J.D. [Ⓐ Iwan C.H.H.&V.]
Wissman, Angela B. '70 '97 C.118 B.A. L.1119 J.D.
(adm. in IN; not adm. in IL) Ill. Legal Times
Wiszowaty, Elizabeth ... '— '04 C.602 B.S. L.424 J.D. [Ⓐ Jenkens&G.]
Wiszowaty, Renee H. ... '— '02 C.340 B.A. L.221 J.D. [Ⓐ Litchfield C.]
Wit, Adam C. ... '70 '95 C.273 B.A. L.93 J.D. [Littler M.]
Witcoff, David L., (AV) ... '— '82 C.813 B.S.E.E. L.1066 J.D. [Jones D.] (See Pat. Sect.)
Witcoff, Sheldon W., (AV) '— '53
C.446 B.S.E.E. L.273 J.D. [Ⓒ Banner&W.] (See Pat. Sect.)

Withall, John R. ... '47 '76 C.58 B.A. L.146 J.D. [Ⓐ Lowery&Assoc.]
Witney, Morris D. ... '34 '61 C.339 B.A. L.145 J.D. 33 N. LaSalle St.
Witous, John J., (AV) ... '21 '51 C&L.602 B.S., LL.B. 10 S. La Salle St.‡
Witry, Richard J., (AV) ... '50 '76 C.321 B.A. L.365 J.D. [McCarthy D.]
Witt, Alan M. ... '52 '77 C&L.339 B.S., J.D. Touche Ross & Co.
Witt, Amy L. ... '— '02 C.475 B.A. L.209 J.D. [Ⓐ Clausen M.]
Witt, Burton T., & Associates, (BV) ... '32 '60 C.1016 B.A. L.209 LL.B. 1 N. La Salle St.
Witt, Helen E., (AV) ... '— '82 C.976 B.A. L.145 J.D. [Kirkland&E.]
Witt, Kathryn L. '59 '84
C.927 B.A. L.209 J.D. V.P. & Corp. Coun., Information Res., Inc.
Witt, Melanie L. ... '63 '92 C.477 B.A. L.602 J.D. [Burke,W.M.&S.]
Witt, Michael A. ... '69 '95 C.339 B.A. L.424 J.D. [Duane M.]
Witt, Richard M. ... '59 '85 C.597 B.A. L.424 J.D. Sr. Staff Atty., Amer. Fam. Ins. Grp.
Witt, Robert J. ... '64 '92 C&L.424 B.A., J.D. 1 N. La Salle St.
Witt, Stephen A. ... '61 '89 C.118 B.A. L.1066 1 N. La Salle St., Ste. 3900
Wittebort, Robert J., Jr. ... '47 '74 C.976 B.A. L.602 J.D. [Smetana&A.]
Witten, Earl A. '47 '73 C.112 B.A. L.1067 J.D.
(adm. in CA; not adm. in IL) Chief Admin. Law J., U.S. Merit Systems Protec. Bd.
Wittenberg, David M. ... '36 '62 C.608 B.S. L.145 J.D. [Wittenberg,D.&M.]
Wittenberg, Elissa G. ... '72 '98 C.339 B.S. L.597 J.D. [Ⓐ Sidley A.B.&W.]
Wittenberg, Howard I. ... '30 '55 C&L.966 B.A., LL.B. 50 S. La Salle St.‡
Wittenberg, Dougherty & Maglione, Ltd., (AV) ... 100 W. Monroe St.
Wittenstein, Edwin M. ... '62 '87 C.477 B.A. L.209 J.D. [Ⓐ Worsek&V.]
Wittmann, Robert T. '67 '00
C.436 B.S.E.E. L.209 J.D. [Ⓐ Leydig,V.&M.] (See Pat. Sect.)
Witty, Peter N. ... '— '97 C&L.602 B.S., J.D. [Ⓐ Latham&W.]

Witwer & Waldron, LLC
(See Evanston)

Witz, Charles J., (AV) ... '35 '60 C.976 B.A. L.597 J.D. 1230 N. State Pkwy.
Witz, James M. ... '— '92 C.918 B.A. L.1068 J.D. [Freeborn&P.]
Witz, Susan J. '58 '86 C&L.966 B.A., J.D.
(adm. in WI; not adm. in IL) U.S. Dept of Labor
Witzel, Megan I. ... '72 '97 C.741 B.A. L.910 J.D. [Ⓐ Sugar,F.&F.]
Witzel, Richard C., Jr. ... '71 '97 C.276 B.S.F.S. L.910 J.D. [Ⓐ Skadden,A.S.M.&F.]
Wix, David G. ... '67 '94 C.674 A.B. L.146 J.D. [Baker&M.]
Wiznitzer, Michelle ... '59 '85 C.597 B.A. L.146 J.D. 1310 Ritchie Ct.
Wnuczek, Robert J. ... '41 '79 C.436 B.A. L.146 J.D. 5455 W. Sheridan Rd.
Woelkers, William G. ... '60 '98 C.477 B.G.S. L.209 J.D. Asst. Pub. Def.
Woerthwein, Theodore A. ... '41 '71 C.694 A.B. L.477 J.D. 155 North Michigan Avenue
Wohl, Steven N., (AV) ... '— '70 C.473 B.A. L.597 J.D. [Chapman&C.]
Wohlleber, Richard A. ... '— '79 C.339 B.A. L.145 J.D. [Chapman&C.]
Wojcicki, Paul E., (AV) ... '64 '89 C.178 A.B. L.209 J.D. [Segal M.S.&M.]
Wojciechowksi, Paul ... '78 '03 C.145 A.B. L.424 J.D. [Ⓐ C.C.Kendall]
Wojcik, Lawrence A., (AV) ... '51 '77 C.209 B.S. L.597 J.D. [DLPiper R.G.C.U.]
Wojcik, Mark E. '61 '86 C.98 B.A. L.365 J.D.
Prof. of Law, The John Marshall Law Sch.

Wojteczko, John C. '46 '75 C.755 B.A. L.930 J.D.
77 West Washington Street, 60602
Telephone: 312-782-4780 Fax: 312-372-9399
Email: jcwrefax@ameritech.net
Residential and Commercial Real Estate, Condominium, Real Estate Taxation, Income Tax, Business, Corporate, Estate Planning, Probate, Pension and Profit Sharing Law. Litigation.

See Professional Biographies, CHICAGO, ILLINOIS

Wolanyk, Katharine A. '63 '96 C.475 B.S. L.145 J.D.
President & Chief Legal Officer, Soverain Software
Wolberg, Charles L., (AV) ... '38 '64 C&L.597 B.A., J.D. 5348 N. Paulina St.
Wolberg, Daniel A. ... '71 '02 C.966 B.A. L.424 J.D. [Ⓐ Wilson E.M.E.&D.]
Woldenberg, James R. ... '64 '90 C.228 A.B. L.145 J.D. Sears Tower
Wolf, Alan J., (AV) ... '50 '74 C.107 B.A. L.597 J.D. [Robbins,S.&P.]
Wolf, Benjamin S. ... '53 '79 C.910 B.A. L.93 J.D. Roger Baldwin Found. of ACLU Inc.
Wolf, Charles B., (AV) ... '50 '75 C.103 A.B. L.145 J.D. [Vedder,P.K.&K.]
Wolf, Daniel A. '52 '77 C.930 B.S. L.339 J.D.
Friedman, Eisenstein, Raemer & Schwartz
Wolf, David J. ... '64 '94 C.597 B.S. L.209 J.D. [Ⓐ Tenney&B.]
Wolf, Gretchen M. ... '76 '02 C.221 B.A. L.352 J.D. [Ⓐ Skadden,A.S.M.&F.]
Wolf, Isa-Lee ... '— '99 C.347 B.A. L.124 J.D. [Ⓐ Nottage&W.]
Wolf, J. Henry ... '25 '50 L.209 LL.B. 120 W. Madison St.
Wolf, James H., (AV) ... '41 '67 C.177 B.A. L.146 J.D. [Wolf&T.]
Wolf, James M. ... '70 '95 C.884 B.A. L.146 J.D. [Ⓐ Wolf&T.]
Wolf, John G. ... '50 '78 C.46 B.S. L.365 J.D. 3901 N. Lincoln Ave.
Wolf, Michael K., (AV) '49 '74 C.659 B.A. L.910 J.D.
Exec. VP & Assoc. Gen. Coun., APCOA/Standard Parking, Inc.
Wolf, Neal L., (AV) ... '49 '74 C.674 B.A. L.145 J.D. [LeBoeuf,L.G.&M.]
Wolf, Neil G. ... '52 '91 C.347 B.A. L.209 J.D. [Wildman,H.A.&D.]
Wolf, Paul P. ... '59 '85 C.347 B.A. L.365 J.D. [Mitchell H.&W.]
Wolf, Robert A. ... '56 '80 C.339 B.A. L.424 J.D. 155 N. Michigan Ave.
Wolf, Steven B. ... '56 '82 C.589 B.S. L.365 J.D. [S.B.Wolf&Assoc.]
Wolf, Steven C. ... '56 '88 C.650 B.A. L.365 J.D. [Wolf&W.]

Wolf Haldenstein Adler Freeman & Herz LLC, (AV)
55 West Monroe Street, Suite 1111, 60603 ⊙
Telephone: 312-984-0000 Fax: 312-984-0001
URL: http://www.whafh.com
Mary Jane Edelstein Fait; Adam J. Levitt.
Corporate and Securities, Estate and Trust, Real Estate, Licensing and Intellectual Property, Tax, Not-For-Profit, Employee Benefits, Labor, Commercial Collections, Elder Law and Litigation including Commercial, Securities and Class Actions.
New York, New York Office: 270 Madison Avenue, 10016. Telephone: 212-545-4600. Fax: 212-686-0114; 212-545-4653; 212-545-4677.
San Diego, California Office: Symphony Towers, Suite 2770, 750 B Street, 92101. Telephone: 619-239-4599. Fax: 619-234-4599.
West Palm Beach, Florida Office: 625 North Flagler Drive, 9th Floor, 33401. Telephone: 561-833-1776.

See Professional Biographies, CHICAGO, ILLINOIS

Wolf, Steven B., and Associates, Ltd. ... 205 W. Wacker Dr., Ste 1600
Wolf & Tennant, (AV) ... 33 N. Dearborn St.
Wolf & Wolfe, LTD, The Law Offices of, (BV) ... 25 East Washington St.
Wolfberg, Kevin J. ... '72 '99 C.347 B.A. L.365 J.D. [Ⓐ Schain,B.R.&C.]
Wolfe, Bernard B. ... '14 '37 L.146 LL.B. Ret. Cir. J.‡
Wolfe, David H., (BV) ... '69 '94 C.339 B.S. L.910 J.D. [Wolf&W.]
Wolfe, David L., (AV) ... '51 '76 C.339 B.S. L.477 J.D. [Gardner C.&D.]
Wolfe, Francis Dunnan, Jr. ... '32 '98 C.966 M.S. L.424 J.D. 327 W. Belden Avenue
Wolfe, Howard O. ... '23 '49 C.339 L.424 J.D. Suite 3550, 20 North Wacker Dr.
Wolfe, Janice E. '39 '64 C.610 A.B. L.608 J.D.
(adm. in OH; not adm. in IL) Dep. Dist. Dir., Small Business Admn.
Wolfe, Jennifer I. ... '74 '00 C.347 B.S. L.209 J.D. [Ⓐ Katten M.R.]
Wolfe, Kenneth B., Jr., (AV) ... '50 '75 C.188 B.A. L.365 J.D. [Wolfe&E.]

Wolfe, Kerry B. '53 '79 C.339 B.S. L.424 J.D. 20 N. Wacker Dr., Ste. 3550
Wolfe, Marc D. '51 '76 C.208 B.A. L.365 J.D.
[C Komie&Assoc.] & [C Drunken D.D.L.I.] (⊙Woodridge)
Wolfe, Mark F., (AV) '58 '83 C.966 B.S. L.436 J.D. [Bollinger,R.&G.]
Wolfe, Richard A. '47 '72 C.339 B.A. L.209 J.D. [Wolfe&P.]
Wolfe, Timothy A. '63 '88 C&L.339 B.A., J.D. [Meckler B.&T.]
Wolfe, Tracey L. '72 '98 C.338 B.A. L.339 J.D. [A L.DeGrand&Assoc.]
Wolfe and Elfenbaum, P.C., (AV) 940 W. Adams St.
Wolfe & Polovin 180 N. Lasalle St.
Wolfersberger, Karissa '70 '95 C&L.339 B.A., J.D. [A Menges&M.]
Wolff, Aaron S., (AV) '30 '55 C&L.597 B.S., J.D. 33 N. Dearborn St.
Wolff, John B. '24 '51 C&L.145 Ph.B., J.D. 77 W. Wash. St.
Wolff, Randall A. '59 '84 C.339 B.A. L.146 J.D. 39 S. LaSalle
Wolff, Sarah R., (AV) '— '79 C&L.597 B.S., J.D. [Sachnoff&W.]
Wolfinger, Megan M. '— '00 C.1372 B.A. L.107 J.D. [A Jones D.]
Wolfinger, Travis B. '74 '00 C.383 B.S. L.309 J.D. [A Lord,B.&B.]
Wolfinsohn, Arthur A. '14 '37 C.999 A.A. L.209 LL.B. 111 W. Wash. St.
Wolfman, Scott '— '93 C.966 B.A. L.209 J.D. [S.B.Wolfman&Assoc.]
Wolfman, Scott B., & Associates 641 W. Lake Street, Suite 400
Wolf-McKenzie, Theresia E. '— '77 C.339 B.A. L.365 J.D. [C Arnstein&L.]
Wolford, Thomas C., (AV) '60 '86 C.1375 A.B. L.1066 J.D. [Neal,G.&E.]
Wolfsmith, John P. '73 '98 C.98 B.A. L.339 J.D. [A Jenner&B.]
Wolin, Harry S. '33 '58 C.475 B.A. L.597 J.D. [Cohon R.&R.]
Wolin, Jason '73 '00 C.37 B.A. L.365 J.D. [A Wolin&R.]
Wolin, Philip S., (AV) '43 '68 C.1016 B.S. L.206 J.D. [Wolin&R.]
Wolin & Rosen, Ltd., (AV) 55 West Monroe Street 36th Floor
Wolkoff, Robin L. '66 '90 C.339 B.S. L.597 J.D. [Fox,H.S.L.&C.]
Wollack, Steven E. '42 '66 C.339 B.S. L.597 J.D. 2452 N. Janssen Ave.
Wollin, Matthew K. '73 '98 C.879 B.A. L.209 J.D. [A Johnson&B.]
Woloshin, William, (AV) '— '59 C&L.209 J.D. [Beermann S.W.B.B.G.&L.]
Wolowitz, Jill A. '68 '94 C.966 B.A. L.209 J.D.
Associate Counsel, BlueCross BlueShield Assoc.
Wolpoff, Gregg, Law Office of '66 '91 C.352 B.A. L.146 J.D.
1025 West Webster Avenue
Wolter, Lindsay '78 '03 C.976 B.A. L.472 J.D. [A Seyfarth S.]
Woltjen, Maria '55 '87 C.339 B.S. L.424 J.D.
Chicago Lawyers' Comm. for Civil Rights
Wolven, Lauren J. '74 '99 C.347 B.A. L.339 J.D. [A Horwood M.&B.]
Wolz, Robert A. '59 '84 C.589 B.S. L.365 J.D. Asst. Coun.
Women's Legal Referral Service 205 West Wacker, Suite 2333
Wong, Benjamin W. '74 '00 C.339 B.S. L.146 J.D. 2615 N Sheffield Ave
Wong, Debbie '70 '97 C.910 B.A. L.966 J.D. PricewaterhouseCoopers, LLP
Wong, Patricia W. '69 '96 C.145 B.A. L.602 J.D. [A Baker&M.]
Wong, Philip, (AV) '51 '77 C.367 A.B. L.365 J.D. [Much S.F.D.A.&R.]
Wong, Winnie '75 '04 C.597 B.A. L.424 J.D., [A Seyfarth S.]
Woo, Hanna '74 '99 C.340 B.A. L.209 J.D.
Legal Counsel, HFR Asset Management, L.L.C.
Woo, Maryanne C. '— '99 C.999 B.A. L.178 J.D. [A Sachnoff&W.]
Wood, Andrea R. '73 '98 C.145 B.A. L.976 J.D. Atty., Chicago, M.R.O., S.E.C.
Wood, Bari D. '68 '93 C.475 B.A. L.339 J.D. [Chuhak&T.]
Wood, Dawn D. '70 '95 C.234 B.A. L.146 J.D. 105 West Madison St., Ste. 2000
Wood, Diane P. '50 '75 C&L.846 B.A., J.D. U.S. Cir. J.
Wood, Hal J. '68 '93 C&L.339 B.A., J.D. [Horwood M.&B.]
Wood, Marilyn J. '52 '84 C.339 B.A. L.365 J.D.
Asst. Chief Coun., Dept. of Children & Fam. Servs.
Wood, Mark D. '66 '90 C.339 B.S. L.477 J.D. [Katten M.R.]
Wood, Phillip S. '43 '78 C&L.1151 B.A., J.D. 130 E. Randolph Street
Wood, Phillip Shawn '68 '92 C.201 B.A. L.146 J.D. [Seyfarth S.]
Wood, Richard L., (AV) '35 '64
C.477 B.S.M.E. L.273 J.D. [Welsh&K.] (See Pat. Sect.) ⊙
Wood, Richard O., (AV) '48 '76 C.855 B.A. L.365 J.D. [Bell,B.&L.]
Wood, Spencer R. '71 '96 C.966 B.S. L.623 J.D. [C LeBoeuf,L.G.&M.]
Wood, Stephen A. '57 '92 C.273 B.A. L.424 J.D. [Kelley D.&W.]
Wood, William L. '72 '97 C.973 B.S. L.974 J.D. 30 North La Salle Street, Suite 4300

Wood, Phillips, Katz, Clark & Mortimer, (AV)
Citicorp Center, Suite 3800, 500 West Madison Street, 60661-2511
Telephone: 312-876-1800 Telecopier: 312-876-2020
Email: info@woodphillips.com URL: http://www.woodphillips.com
Members of Firm: Jeffrey L. Clark; Jeffery N. Fairchild; Stephen D. Geimer; Allen J. Hoover; Martin L. Katz; F. William McLaughlin; Dean A. Monco; John S. Mortimer; Lisa von Bargen Mueller; Paul M. Odell; Joel E. Siegel. Associate: Mark V. Polyakov (Not admitted in IL). Of Counsel: Richard S. Phillips; William A. Van Santen (Retired).
Intellectual Property and Unfair Competition Law.
See Professional Biographies, CHICAGO, ILLINOIS

Wood-Bill, Shantel D. '76 '01 C.338 B.S. L.209 J.D. [A Cassiday,S.&G.]
Woodford, Peter C., (AV) '50 '78 C.197 A.B. L.273 J.D. [Seyfarth S.]
Woodie, Tiffany '— '00 C.178 B.A. L.145 J.D. 2 N. LaSalle St.
Wooding, Carol A. '61 '91
C.209 B.S.C. L.424 J.D. Asst. Gen. Coun., National Futures Assn.
Woodley, Brenna B. '— '97 C&L.966 B.A., J.D. [Schiff H.]
Woodrow, Thomas R. '60 '85 C.276 A.B. L.424 J.D. [Holland&K.]
Woodruff, Casey (Kenneth) '62 '90 C.339 B.A. L.146 J.D. [C.Woodruff&Assoc.] ⊙

Woodruff, Casey, & Associates
155 N. Michigan Avenue, Suite 500, 60601 ⊙
Telephone: 630-585-2320 Fax: 630-585-2327
Email: cwoodruff@woodrufflawyers.com URL: http://www.woodrufflawyers.com
Casey (Kenneth) Woodruff. Associates: Jay Johnson; Mario C. Palermo.
Language: Spanish.
Workers Compensation, Personal Injury, Automobile Accidents, Social Security, Medical Malpractice, Products Liability.
Aurora, Illinois Office: Millennium Park Plaza, 75 Executive Drive, Suite 105, 60504. Telephone: 630-585-2320. Toll Free: 1-866-891-9211. Fax: 630-585-2327.
See Professional Biographies, CHICAGO, ILLINOIS

Woods, Beth B. '69 '98 C.145 B.A. L.472 J.D. [A Williams M.&J.]
Woods, Craig A. '69 '94 C.378 B.S.E.E. L.273 J.D. [Mayer,B.R.&M.]
Woods, Jeffrey D. '— '04 L.879 J.D. [A Ungaretti&H.]
Woods, Kendall E. '— '02 C.347 B.S. L.424 J.D. [A Chuhak&T.]
Woods, Susan E. '50 '76 C.597 B.A. L.424 J.D.
Assoc. Gen. Coun., Claims, Chicago Title Ins. Co.
Woods, Tamela M. '— '05 C.811 B.A. L.494 J.D. [A Mayer,B.R.&M.]
Woodward, Kathryn '— '03 C.966 B.A. L.146 J.D. [A Greene&L.]
Wool, Andrew L. '— '04 C.966 B.A. L.339 J.D. [A Chapman&C.]
Wool, Leon '37 '63 C.221 A.B. L.209 J.D. First Dep. Gen. Atty., Chicago Transit Auth.
Wooldridge, Robert R. '20 '51 8059 S. Wabash Ave.‡
Woolever, Michael H., (P.C.), (AV) '— '76 C.373 B.A. L.477 J.D. [Foley&L.]

Woollen, Michelle L. '70 '97 C.674 B.A. L.309 J.D. [A Sidley A.B.&W.]
Woolley, C. Randall, II '77 '03 C.209 B.S. L.424 J.D. [A Askounis&B.]
Woolley, Scott Laurence '53 '88 C.101 B.A. L.375 J.D. 5020 S. Lake Shore Dr.‡
Woolley, W. Allen '— '91 C.197 A.B. L.228 J.D. [Kirkland&E.]
Wootton, Robert R., (AV) '52 '79 C&L.976 B.A., J.D. [Sidley A.B.&W.]
Word, Ted M. '68 '98 C.864 B.A. L.424 J.D.
Sec. Coun., Capital Management Group Securities
Worker, Danny L. '63 '87 C&L.424 B.B.A., J.D. [Worker,S.&H.]

Worker, Sitko & Hoffman, LLC, (AV) BB
150 N. Wacker Drive, Suite 3100, 60606
Telephone: 312-345-1718 Fax: 312-345-1778
Email: dworker@wshlawfirm.com URL: http://www.wshlawfirm.com
Danny L. Worker; Mary F. Sitko; Stephen D. Hoffman (Not admitted in IL); James B. Tobin; Damon LaPorte;—Eric Alvine; Bonnie Bernadette Bijak; James J. Chandler; Marc Anthony Cervantes; Michael Schnitzer. Of Counsel: Gary W. Leydig.
Insurance Defense, Civil Litigation, Coverage Litigation, Medical Malpractice, Appellate Practice. Civil and Commercial Litigation, Construction Litigation, Franchise Litigation, Distribution Law.
Phoenix, Arizona Office: 101 N. 1st. Avenue, Suite 2075, 85003. Telephone: 602-840-6101. Fax: 602-840-6102.
See Professional Biographies, CHICAGO, ILLINOIS

Worm, Hollis D. '— '79 C.339 B.S. L.424 J.D. Admin Law J., Dept. of Rev.
Worsek, Richard D. '54 '79 C&L.339 B.A., J.D. [Worsek&V.]
Worsek & Vihon, P.C., (AV) 180 North La Salle Street Suite 3010
Worsley, David E. '— '74 C&L.352 B.A., J.D. [Chapman&C.]
Worstell, Jennifer L. '72 '99 C&L.1119 B.S., J.D. [Spitzer,A.S.&E.]
Wortel, William J. '— '96 C.339 B.S. L.209 J.D. [Bryan C.]
Worth, Susan H. '76 '01 C.210 B.A. L.347 J.D. 1366 Hoyne Avenue, Suite 3
Worthen, John S. '49 '75 C.339 B.A. L.209 J.D. [Gould&R.]
Wosik, Joseph M. '13 '39 C&L.209 LL.B. Ret. Cir. J.
Woulfe, Margaret F. '57 '82 C.338 B.S. L.339 J.D. [C Davis M.]
Woytek, Patrick J. '— '98 C&L.209 B.A., J.D. [A Freeborn&P.]
Wozniak, Robert J. '66 '00 C.477 B.A. L.212 J.D.
(adm. in DC; not adm. in IL) [A Much S.F.D.A.&R.]
Wray, Richard K., (AV) '— '74 C.340 B.A. L.880 J.D. [Sachnoff&W.]
Wren, Damien T., & Associates, (AV) '40 '67
C.602 B.A. L.145 J.D. 77 W. Washington St.
Wren, John L. '— '69 C.424 B.S. L.146 J.D. Suite 3400, 300 South Wacker Drive
Wrenn, Leo F. '25 '49 C.602 L.424 LL.B. 1328 Arthur St.
Wright, Amanda Helm '77 '01 C&L.339 B.A., J.D. [A Littler M.]
Wright, Derek L. '— '01 C.477 B.A. L.959 J.D. [A Foley&L.]
Wright, Elizabeth D. '71 '98 C.793 B.A. L.352 J.D. [Neal,G.&E.]
Wright, Frank M., Jr. '17 '49 C.309 M.B.A. L.146 LL.B. Cont'l Ill. Nat. Bk. & Tr. Co.
Wright, Gregory M. '80 '05 C&L.602 B.A., J.D. [A Dykema G.P.]
Wright, Heather Ann '— '01 C&L.424 B.A., J.D. [A Morgan,L.&B.]
Wright, Jason A. '73 '99 C.338 B.S. L.209 J.D. 191 N. Wacker Dr., Ste. 2400
Wright, John M. '— '02 C.228 B.A. L.893 J.D. [A Jones D.]
Wright, Joseph '64 '99 C.923 B.S. L.209 J.D. [A Hoogendoorn&T.]
Wright, Judith M. '44 '80 C.836 B.S. L.209 J.D. D'Angelo Law Libr.
Wright, Karla, (AV) '42 '74 C.352 L.146 J.D. [K.Wright]
Wright, Laurie A. '61 '87 C.339 B.A. L.477 J.D. V.P., The Northern Tr. Co.‡
Wright, Melissa E. '68 '00 C.338 B.S. L.365 J.D. Pub. Def. Off.
Wright, Melvin M., Jr. '— '91 C.705 B.A. L.776 J.D. [Sonnenschein N.&R.]
Wright, Michael D. '— '88 C.679 B.S. L.345 J.D. [Kirkland&E.]
Wright, Otis Charles '60 '98 C.477 B.A. L.365 J.D. [O.C.Wright&Assoc.]
Wright, Paul B., Jr. '69 '95 C.910 B.A. L.347 J.D. [Paul W.]
Wright, Robert T. '05 '35 C.118 B.A. L.597 J.D. 9021 S. Drexel Ave.‡
Wright, Timothy W. '55 '84 C.154 B.A. L.1068 J.D. [Burris,W.S.&T.]
Wright, Karla, Ltd., (AV) 11 S. La Salle St., Suite 1600
Wright, Otis C., & Associates 39 S. LaSalle, Ste. 900
Wrigley, Nicole E. '77 '02 C&L.339 B.S., J.D. [A Winston&S.]
Wrobel, Gregory G., (AV) '54 '78 C&L.145 B.A., J.D. [Vedder,P.K.&K.]
Wrobel, Joseph '48 '73 C.597 B.A. L.209 J.D. [J.Wrobel]

Wrobel, Joseph, Ltd.
105 West Madison Street, Suite 700, 60602
Telephone: 312-781-0996 Fax: 312-606-0413 URL: http://www.chicagobankruptcy.com
URL: http://www.chicagobankruptcylaw.com
Email: j.wrobel.ltd@chicagobankruptcy.com URL: http://www.chicagobankruptcylawfirm.com
Joseph Wrobel.
Bankruptcy including Personal Bankruptcy, Business Bankruptcy, Chapter 7, Chapter 11, Chapter 13, Foreclosures and Garnishments and Business Dissolutions.
See Professional Biographies, CHICAGO, ILLINOIS

Wrobleski, Theodore W., (AV) '46 '71
C.424 B.A. L.597 J.D. 111 West Washington Street, Suite 1420
Wrona, John R. '69 '97 C.339 B.S. L.146 J.D. [A Gardiner K.&W.]
Wrona, John S. '42 '70 C.679 B.S.M.E. L.424 J.D. 13333 S. Baltimore Ave.
Wrona, Patricia Ann '58 '83 C.597 B.A. L.209 J.D. 188 W. Randolph St., Ste. 2107
Wrona, Thomas J. '— '02 C.339 B.S. L.365 J.D. [A Brinks H.G.&L.] (See Pat. Sect.)
Wrona Eby, Dawn C. '— '92 C.674 B.S.E. L.1119 J.D. [Arnstein&L.]
Wruble, Stanley F., III '— '97 C.879 B.A. L.602 J.D. [A Krasnow S.C.]
Wu, Angela E. '74 '98 C.339 B.S. L.589 J.D. Asst. Corp. Coun.
Wu, Charles Qiong '72 '03 C.339 M.U.P. L.145 J.D. [A Mayer,B.R.&M.]
Wu, Derek A. '69 '96 C.339 B.A. L.589 J.D. [D.Wu]
Wu, Gregory M. '— '03 C.228 A.B. L.309 J.D. [A Jenner&B.]
Wu, Guohua '— '95 C.999 B.A. L.188 J.D.
(adm. in NY; not adm. in IL) [A Kirkland&E.]
Wu, Stephen Y. '74 '99 C.339 B.A./B.S. L.273 J.D. [A McDermott W.&E.]
Wu, Xiaoming '58 '94 C.999 B.A. L.352 J.D. 55 E. Monroe Street
Wu, Derek, P.C. 1333 N. Milwaukee Ave., 2nd Floor
Wulf, Julie Zitella '71 '97 C.473 B.S. L.365 J.D. [A Lowis&G.]
Wulfers, John M., (AV) '47 '76 C.966 B.A. L.802 J.D. [Lord,B.&B.]
Wulff, Richard A. '67 '97 C.870 B.S. L.846 J.D. [A Gardner C.&D.] (Pat.)
Wulfstat, Allan A., (AV) '39 '64 C&L.597 B.S., J.D. [Wildman,H.A.&D.]
Wunsch, John C., (AV) '56 '82 C.477 A.B. L.209 J.D. [J.C.Wunsch]
Wunsch, John C., P.C., Law Offices, (AV) 77 West Washington Street, Suite 1420
Wutscher, Ralph T. '70 '98 C.112 B.A. L.339 J.D. [A Noonan&L.]
Wyatt Zimmerman, Kathryn C. '58 '90 C.339 B.S. L.146 J.D. [A Pfeiffer&A.]
Wydajewski, Brian K. '66 '94 C.209 B.S. L.424 J.D. [Baker&M.]
Wyetzner, Linda '60 '87 C.339 B.A. L.588 J.D. Aftra
Wyland, Neil D. '68 '95 C.145 B.A. L.1068 J.D. [A Sidley A.B.&W.]
Wylie, John R. '54 '84 C.399 B.A. L.1068 J.D. [Susman,W.&W.]
Wylie, Joseph C., II '74 '99 C.112 B.A. L.276 J.D. [A Bell,B.&L.]
Wylie, Kenneth R., (AV) '51 '77 C.475 B.S.M.E. L.477 J.D.
10 S. Dearborn St., 48th Fl.
Wylie, Scott D., (BVⓉ) '57 '81 C.69 B.B.A. L.744 J.D. [Linebarger G.B.&S.]
Wyman, James M. '70 '95 Sr. Coun., Bank One Corp. (Law Dept.)

Wynacht, Peter T. '— '01 C.260 B.A. L.146 J.D. [Ⓐ Vedder,P.K.&K.]
Wynn, Mary Beth '73 '02 C.311 B.A. L.145 J.D. [Ⓐ Tabet D.&R.]
Wynn, Thomas J. '18 '42 C&L.209 A.B., J.D. Asso. Cir. J.
Wynne, Michael J. '59 '84 C.801 B.S. L.365 J.D. [Sonnenschein N.&R.]
Wyse, Joseph E., (AV) '27 '52 C&L.209 B.S., J.D. [Seyfarth S.] ‡
Wysocki, Kenneth R. '72 '96 C.347 B.S. L.893 J.D. [Ⓐ Clausen M.]
Wysoglad, Kenneth J. '42 '66 C.1024 B.A. L.477 LL.B. [K.J.Wysoglad&Assoc.]
Wysoglad, Kenneth J., & Associates 118 S. Clinton St.
Xue, Feng '67 '98 C.999 B.A. L.228 J.D. [Bell,B.&L.]
Yackel, Juliet M. '67 '92 C.679 B.A. L.861 J.D. 53 W. Jackson Blvd., Ste. 1544
Yacker, Julius Y., (AV) '25 '58 C&L.145 M.A., J.D. [Ⓑ DLPiper R.G.C.U.]
Yager, Anthony D. '— '89 C.477 B.B.A. L.339 J.D. [Chapman&C.]
Yagoda, Ryan E. '74 '99 C.339 B.A. L.146 J.D. [Ⓐ Kralovec,J.&S.]
Yahn, Kurt H. '54 '81 C.801 B.S. L.209 J.D. 2635 N. Kedzie Ave.
Yale, Debra B. '— '88 C.347 B.S. L.597 J.D. [Ⓑ Sonnenschein N.&R.]
Yalowitz, Jay A. '67 '93 C.477 B.A. L.910 J.D. [McGuirewoods]
Yamaguchi, Keith S. '61 '95 C.103 B.S. L.306 J.D. [Kaplan,v.&M.]
Yamaguchi, Vivian K., (AV) '56 '80 C.822 A.B. L.424 J.D.
Gen. Coun., Chicago Underwriting Group, Inc.
Yamamoto, Shinya '— '98 C.475 B.A. L.46 J.D. [Ⓐ Masuda,F.E.&M.]
Yamashiro, Maureen D., (BV) '60 '85 C.339 B.A. L.209 J.D. Chicago Transit Authority
Yamashiroya, Gary '65 '93 C.339 B.S. L.209 J.D. Commander‡
Yambert, Jon, (AV) '57 '83 C.801 B.S. L.339 J.D. 150 S. Wacker Dr.

Yanez, Philip P., Law Offices of '65 '90 C.339 B.S. L.477 J.D.
2400 N. Western Avenue, Suite 201, 60647
Telephone: 773-772-0844 Fax: 773-772-0845
Email: pyanezlaw@hotmail.com URL: http://www.pyanezlaw.com
Family Law, Criminal Law, Traffic, D.U.I., Residential Real Estate, Consumer Bankruptcy, Personal Injury, Slip and Fall, Auto Accidents, Dog Bites.
See Professional Biographies, CHICAGO, ILLINOIS

Yang, Qi (Alexander) '— '04 C.999 L.494 J.D.
(adm. in OH; not adm. in IL) [Ⓐ Kirkland&E.]
Yanibas, Aris F. '38 '70 C.293 A.B. L.365 J.D. 5026 N. Lincoln Ave.
Yankellow, Martin L., Jr., Law Offices of '76 '02
C.318 B.A. L.146 J.D. 407 S. Dearborn St., Ste. 1735
Yannella, Christopher F. '69 '96 C&L.910 B.A., J.D.
Personal Financial Counselor, Ernst & Young, LLP
Yanoff, David Lyon '63 '91 C.999 B.A. L.209 J.D. [Starr,Y.&R.]
Yanovsky, Jane D. '— '05 C.597 B.A. L.273 J.D. [Ⓐ Freeborn&P.]
Yant, Richard Demarest '55 '82 C.679 B.S. L.339 J.D. [Krasnow S.C.]
Yao, Wayne '— '04 L.597 J.D. [Ⓐ Wildman,H.A.&D.]
Yarber, Michelle R. '67 '91 C.145 A.B. L.146 J.D. 33 N. LaSalle
Yarbrough, Christopher K. '74 '00 C.674 B.A. L.424 J.D.
Legal Coun., Henderson Global Investors (North America) Inc.
Yarch, Rachel Edlinger '76 '01 C.475 B.A. L.209 J.D.
(adm. in GA; not adm. in IL) 150 N. Wacker Dr., Ste. 3000
Yardley, Thomas P. '— '91 C.477 B.A. L.436 J.D. [Arnstein&L.]
Yaross, Todd D. '78 '04 C.608 B.A. L.597 J.D. [Ⓐ Katten M.R.]

Yast, C. Joseph, (AV) '52 '77 C.860 B.A. L.145 J.D.
Willow Hill Executive Center, 540 Frontage Road Suite 2110 (Northfield), 60093-1224
Telephone: 847-441-0357; 847-507-2167 Fax: 847-441-0359
Email: joeyastlaw@comcast.net
Business and Commercial Litigation, Including Contracts, Leases, RICO, Partnership, Corporations, Fiduciary Litigation, Fraud, Franchise Litigation, Injunctions and Litigations, Non-Compete Litigation and Civil Appeals.
See Professional Biographies, CHICAGO, ILLINOIS

Yastrow, Joseph H., (AV) '54 '78 C.197 A.B. L.802 J.D. [Laner,M.D.B.L.&T.]
Yasuda, Ted K. '56 '82 C.976 B.A. L.1119 J.D. Off. of the Gen. Coun., Dept. of HHS
Yates, David R. '73 '01 C.976 B.A. L.16 J.D.
(adm. in GA; not adm. in IL) [Ⓐ Lord,B.&B.] (⊙Atlanta, GA)
Yates, Russell E., (AV) '45 '71 C.1262 B.A. L.208 J.D.
(adm. in CO; not adm. in IL) [Yates&L.] ⊙
Yates, Stephen R. '40 '68 C&L.145 B.A., J.D. Cir. J.
Yates & Leal, L.L.P., (AV) 333 S. Wacker Dr. (⊙Denver, CO)
Yatvin, Steven J. '73 '99 C.347 B.A. L.339 J.D. [Ⓐ Barack F.K.P.&N.]
Yavitz, Barry E. '44 '71 C.1016 B.S.B.A. L.339 J.D. 39 S. La Salle St.
Yavitz, David B., (AV) '44 '69 C.221 B.A. L.339 J.D. [Yavitz&L.]

Yavitz & Levey, LLP, (AV)
20 South Clark Street, Suite 2200, 60603
Telephone: 312-924-4400 Fax: 312-924-4411
URL: http://www.yldivorce.com
Members of Firm: David B. Yavitz; Ross S. Levey.
Family Law, Divorce, Premarital Counseling and Agreements, Paternity, Adoption Law, Child Custody, Matrimonial Law, Domestic Relations, Appellate Practice.
See Professional Biographies, CHICAGO, ILLINOIS

Yazici, Jody Meyer, (CV) '68 '94 C.597 B.A. L.188 J.D. [Ⓐ Davis F.Z.K.M.M.&R.]
Ybarra, John A., (AV) '61 '87 C.209 B.A. L.477 J.D. [Littler M.]
Yeager, Christina M. '72 '99 C&L.260 B.A., J.D. [Ⓐ Burke,W.M.&S.]
Yeager, Joshua D. '— '00 C.338 B.S. L.146 J.D. [Ⓐ Cremer,K.S.&S.]
Yeager, Mark L., (AV) '50 '75 C.477 B.A. L.597 J.D. [McDermott W.&E.]
Yearout, Jason E. '76 '02 C.900 B.A. L.945 J.D. [Ⓐ Jenner&B.]
Yee, Vicente C., Jr. '50 '88 C.999 B.S. L.209 J.D. Asst. State's Atty.
Yeley, Brian D. '74 '99 C.347 B.S. L.1119 J.D. [Ⓐ Hoogendoorn&T.]
Yelin, David B., (AV) '57 '86 C.8 B.S. L.930 J.D. [Duane M.]
Yellen, Larry I. '52 '77 C.477 B.A. L.597 J.D. WLS-TV
Yellin, C. Robert '30 '54 C&L.145 B.A., J.D. 77 W. Wash. St.
Yelton, Robert C., III, (AV) '51 '76 C.339 A.B. L.365 J.D. [Yelton&K.]
Yelton & Kehl, Ltd., (AV) One East Wacker Drive Suite 3720
Yen, David S. '50 '76 C.976 B.A. L.659 J.D.
Supervisory Atty., Legal Assistants Found.
Yetnikoff, Michael '— '88 C&L.145 B.A., J.D. [Ⓑ Schiff H.]
Yeung, Joseph M. '54 '90
C.490 B.A. L.494 J.D. Asst. Dist. Coun., U.S. Immig. & Nat. Serv.
Yi, Chae Uk '69 '02 C.860 B.A. L.424 J.D. [Ⓐ Mayer,B.R.&M.]
Yi, Theodore I., (AV) '57 '82 C.339 B.S.B.A. L.309 J.D. [DLPiper R.G.C.U.]
Yipp, Victor '44 '76 C.46 B.S. L.284 J.D. Asst. Atty. Gen.
Yochim, Elisa J. '53 '82 C.339 B.A. L.209 J.D. 77 W. Jackson Blvd., Ste. 2615
Yoder, Lowell D., (AV) '55 '82 C&L.339 B.S., J.D. [McDermott W.&E.]
Yohalem, Seth R. '— '04 C.31 B.A. L.178 J.D. [Ⓐ Kirkland&E.]
Yokich, Stephen A., (AV) '57 '82 C.597 B.A. L.477 J.D. [Cornfield&F.]
Yokoyama, Michelle '— '03 C.597 B.A. L.424 J.D. [Ⓐ Jones D.]
Yolles, Robert A., (AV) '— '65 C&L.597 B.A., J.D. [Ⓑ Jones D.]
Yonan, Jason A. '77 '02 C.338 B.A. L.339 J.D. U.S. Dist. Ct.
Yonan, Marcel Elia '56 '91 C.1183 B.A. L.339 J.D. 1 N. Lasalle St., Ste. 3100
Yonco, John, (AV) '10 '40 L.146 J.D. 77 West Wacker Drive, Suite 4400‡
Yondorf, Milton S. '22 '49 C.197 A.B. L.145 J.D. [M.Yondorf]
Yondorf, Milton 120 W. Madison St.
Yong, Barbara L., (BV) '58 '82 C.339 B.A. L.424 J.D. [Field&G.]
York, Ethan R. '— '99 C.477 B.A. L.602 J.D. [Ⓐ Winston&S.]
Yosick, Joseph A. '— '02 C&L.339 B.S.Ch.E., J.D.
[Ⓐ Brinks H.G.&L.] (See Pat. Sect.)
Yosowitz, Jeffrey S. '65 '91 C.477 A.B. L.930 J.D. Sr. Coun., Trans Union LLC
Youhas, Edward R. '22 '57 C.221 B.C.S. L.365 LL.B. 33 N. La Salle St.‡
Youkhana, Michelle C. '73 '99 C.700 B.A. L.365 J.D. [Youkhana&S.]
Youkhana & Skuja, Ltd. 205 West Randolph St., Suite 1600
Younes, Habib S. '32 '74 L.365 J.D. 22 W. Monroe
Younes, Joseph '58 '84 C.339 B.S. L.365 J.D. 22 W. Monroe Street, Suite 2102
Young, Alexander B. '— '00 C.367 B.A. L.276 J.D. [Ⓐ Schiff H.]
Young, Amy L. '78 '04 C.578 B.A. L.209 J.D. [Ⓐ Vedder,P.K.&K.]
Young, Andrew P. '— '04 C.276 B.A. L.494 J.D. [Ⓐ Schiff H.]
Young, Anthony E., (AV) '44 '69 C.641 B.A. L.128 J.D. [A.E.Young]
Young, Christine L. '60 '85 C.880 B.A. L.597 J.D. 311 W. Superior, Ste. 402
Young, Christy M. '— '03 C.63 B.A. L.893 J.D. [Ⓐ DLPiper R.G.C.U.]
Young, Harry A., Jr., (AV) '31 '58 C.293 B.A. L.309 LL.B. [Young,R.F.&S.]
Young, Heather J. '75 '01 C.628 B.S. L.1148 J.D. [Ⓐ Hall,P.&S.]
Young, James F., Jr. '49 '75 C.321 B.A. L.424 J.D. 53 W. Jackson Blvd.
Young, Jeffrey I. '77 '02 C.352 B.A. L.146 J.D. [Ⓐ Bollinger,R.&G.]
Young, Jenni L. '75 '00 C.259 B.S. L.209 J.D. [Ⓐ Stamos&T.]
Young, John W. '— '00 C.228 B.A. L.893 J.D. [Ⓐ Wildman,H.A.&D.]
Young, Jonathan W., (BV) '64 '90 C.976 B.A. L.597 J.D. [Wildman,H.A.&D.]
Young, Julie L. '75 '00 C&L.477 B.A., J.D. [Ⓐ Lord,B.&B.]

Young, Keith L., (AV) '53 '77 C.350 B.S. L.146 J.D.
333 West Wacker Drive, Suite 500, 60606
Telephone: 312-807-4777 Fax: 312-641-3004
Email: keithlyoung@prodigy.net URL: http://www.lawyers.com/kyounglaw
Personal Injury, Automobile Accidents and Injuries, Slip and Fall, Wrongful Death, Insurance Bad Faith, Medical Malpractice, Products Liability, Negligence, Civil Rights, Automotive Products Liability and Drug and Medical Device Litigation.
See Professional Biographies, CHICAGO, ILLINOIS

Young, Kevin J., (AV) '60 '86 C.339 B.A. L.365 J.D. [McGuirewoods]
Young, Lisa M. '66 '95 C.602 B.S.E.E. L.597 J.D.
Sr. Coun., Bank One Corporation (Law Dept.)
Young, Myla Barefield '72 '98 C&L.228 A.B., J.D. [Ⓐ DLPiper R.G.C.U.]
Young, Peter J. '— '02 C.136 B.A.A. L.1119 J.D. [Ⓐ Jenner&B.]
Young, Reginald G., Jr. '45 '72 C.118 B.A. L.477 J.D.
(adm. in MI; not adm. in IL) Dir. Intl. Tax Planning, Quaker Oats Co.
Young, Richard W., (AV) '56 '81 C.976 B.S. L.1119 J.D. [Gardner C.&D.] (Pat.)
Young, Rowland L. '22 '49 C.98 A.B. L.145 J.D. 6007 N. Sheridan Rd.‡
Young, Russell R. '71 '96 C.910 A.B. L.309 J.D. [Mayer,B.R.&M.]
Young, Samuel H., (AV) '22 '48 C&L.339 B.S., J.D. [Ⓑ Kamensky,R.H.&D.] ⊙
Young, Shane T. '73 '04 C.145 A.B. L.339 J.D. [Ⓐ Schwartz C.]
Young, Steedly '36 '71 C.347 A.B. L.1119 J.D.
(adm. in IN; not adm. in IL) Asst. Dist. Coun., I.R.S.
Young, Thomas H. '— '03 C.385 B.A. L.477 J.D. [Ⓐ Kirkland&E.]
Young, Timothy J., (AV) '58 '85 C.473 B.S. L.436 J.D. 150 S. Wacker Dr., Ste. 2400
Young, Todd M., (AV) '58 '83 C.197 A.B. L.145 J.D. [Hinshaw&C.]
Young, Todd S. '71 '97 C.293 B.A. L.477 J.D. [Ⓐ Sidley A.B.&W.]
Young, William T. '74 '04 C.338 B.A. L.1000 J.D. [Ⓐ Johnson&B.]
Young, Anthony E., Ltd., (AV) 330 N. Wabash Ave., Ste. 3208
Young Gottshall, Justine '69 '94 C.477 B.A. L.813 J.D. [Wildman,H.A.&D.]

Young, Rosen, Finkel & Silbert Limited, (AV)
33 North La Salle Street Suite 900, 60602
Telephone: 312-782-2555 Fax: 312-782-9360
Email: law@yrfs.com
Harry A. Young, Jr.; Alan Rosen; Norman T. Finkel; William R. Klein; Ronald G. Silbert. Associate: G. Terence Nader. Of Counsel: George E. Sang.
Civil litigation practice in all Trial and Appellate Courts, Corporate, Real Estate and Other Business Transaction Matters. Incorporation, Estate Planning, Probate and Tax Planning, and Real Estate Property Tax Reduction.
See Professional Biographies, CHICAGO, ILLINOIS

Youngerman, David A. '50 '79 C.696 B.A. L.145 J.D.
Chief Admin. Law J., Ill. Educ. Labor Relation Bd.
Youngerman, Jeffrey S. '61 '86 C.339 B.S. L.209 J.D. [Flaherty&J.]
Yount, Joshua D. '72 '98 C.340 B.A. L.145 J.D. [Ⓐ Mayer,B.R.&M.]
Yovits, Steven '— '98 C.477 B.S.E. L.893 J.D. [Ⓐ Sidley A.B.&W.]
Yowell, William R. '33 '59 C.174 B.A. L.597 J.D.
Assoc. Gen. Coun., Claims, Chicago Title Ins. Co.
Yu, Joonho '73 '99 C.145 B.A. L.424 J.D. [Ⓐ Fuchs&R.]
Yu, William '68 '96 C.604 B.A. L.365 J.D. [Ⓐ Hinshaw&C.]
Yudell, Carl R. '52 '78 C.674 A.B. L.145 J.D. 20 N. Clark St.
Yuen, David O. '68 '96 C.339 B.S. L.146 J.D. [Ⓐ Tressler,S.M.&P.]
Yuknis, Clifford E., (AV) '50 '74 C.209 B.A. L.309 J.D. [Hinshaw&C.]
Yun, Jin W. '67 '01 C.906 B.B.A. L.339 J.D. [Ⓐ Vedder,P.K.&K.]
Yura, Mark D., (AV) '53 '78 C&L.477 B.A., J.D. [DLPiper R.G.C.U.]
Yurchak, Patricia Anne '67 '93 C.309 B.A. L.145 J.D. [Mayer,B.R.&M.]
Yusim, Allan L. '45 '70 C&L.339 B.S., J.D. [Patzik,F.&S.]
Yusim, Bradley M. '76 '02 C.846 B.S.E.E. L.339 J.D. [Ⓐ Jenner&B.]
Yusim, Emily M. '73 '99 C.339 B.A. L.146 J.D. [Ⓐ Robbins,S.N.L.&T.]
Yusof, Maura '76 '02 C.276 B.S.L.A. L.910 J.D. [Ⓐ Foran G.P.&P.]
Zaander, Mark C., (AV) '— '76 C.339 B.S. L.145 J.D. [Schiff H.]
Zabel, Jay '49 '73 C.339 B.A. L.209 J.D. [J.Zabel&Assoc.]
Zabel, Sheldon A., (AV) '— '66 C.674 A.B. L.597 J.D. [Schiff H.]
Zabel, Jay, & Associates, Ltd. 55 W. Monroe St.
Zabelski, Richard E. '44 '79 C.339 E.E. L.589 J.D. 6153 N. Nettleton Ave.
Zabinski, Ellen J. '73 '99 C.424 B.S. L.209 J.D. [Ⓐ Bates&C.]
Zabinski, Lawrence E. '57 '81 C.98 B.S. L.597 J.D.
Sr. V.P. & Dir. of Claims, Attorneys' Liability Assurance Society, Inc.
Zaborsky, Richard J. '33 '58 C.339 B.S. L.365 J.D. 134 N. La Salle St.
Zabriskie, John F. '— '84 C&L.477 B.A., J.D. [Foley&L.]
Zabrosky, Alex W. '53 '78 C.145 A.B. L.273 J.D. [Gardner C.&D.]
Zac, Anthony '70 '98 C.424 B.A. L.209 J.D. [Reed,C.&Z.]
Zachar, Richard A., (AV) '42 '68 C.602 A.B. L.597 J.D. [Vedder,P.K.&K.] (Pat.)
Zacharias, James '12 '35 C&L.145 Ph.B., J.D. 4123 W. Peterson Ave.
Zachary, Jason K. '72 '99 C.839 B.B.A. L.146 J.D. [Ⓐ Seyfarth S.]
Zacks, JoEllen Bursinger '58 '87
C.966 B.A. L.365 J.D. Dir., Pub. Relations, Amer. Bar Assn.

Zaczek, Bert J., Law Office of '66 '93
C.966 B.A. L.146 J.D. 415 North LaSalle Street, Suite 300
Zadeik, Philip J., (BV) '58 '83 C.597 B.A. L.339 J.D. Gen. Coun., Turtle Wax, Inc.
Zadek, Robert F. '13 '44 C.137 L.209 LL.B. Asst. States Atty.
Zadina, Christopher W. '58 '83 C&L.93 B.A., J.D. U.S. Postal Serv.
Zaenger, Mark F. '54 '80 C.750 B.A. L.424 J.D. [Nisen&E.]
Zaengle, Edward P. '63 '99 C.1374 B.S. L.339 J.D. [Ⓐ Wildman,H.A.&D.]
Zaffere, Frank D., III, (AV) '48 '74 C.602 B.B.A. L.276 J.D. [Stejkowski&Z.]
Zafrani, André L. '73 '98 C.37 B.A. L.597 J.D. [Ⓐ Greenberg T.]
Zagel, James B. '41 '65 C.145 B.A. L.309 U.S. Dist. J.
Zagel, Margaret Maxwell, (AV) '49 '73
C.861 B.A. L.339 J.D. Gen. Coun., Grant Thornton, LLP
Zager, Pearl A. '55 '79 C.1086 B.S. L.966 J.D. [Vedder,P.K.&K.]
Zagon, Melissa L. '67 '92 C.477 B.A. L.309 J.D.
Assoc. Gen. Coun., True North Communications, Inc. (Legal Department)
Zahn, James K., (AV) '43 '90 C.339 B.A. L.146 J.D. [Sabo&Z.]
Zahn, Lisa Marie '67 '93 C.966 B.S. L.146 J.D. [Ⓐ W.G.Clark,Jr.&Assoc.]
Zahour, Nilgun Aykent '63 '89 C.597 B.A. L.436 J.D. [Sanchez&D.]
Zaideman, Robert J., (AV) '53 '78 C.339 B.A. L.597 J.D. [Zaideman&E.]

Zaideman & Esrig, P.C., (AV)
10 South Riverside Plaza, Suite 1020, 60606-3827
Telephone: 312-207-0005 Fax: 312-207-1332
Email: ze@zelaw.com
Robert J. Zaideman; Jerry A. Esrig.
Civil Trial and Appellate Practice in all courts. Commercial, Construction, Plaintiff Personal Injury, Medical Malpractice and Products Liability, Appeals.
See Professional Biographies, CHICAGO, ILLINOIS

Zajicek, David E., (AV) '39 '64 C.98 B.S. L.597 J.D. [Holland&K.]
Zak, Garry B. '68 '02 C.363 B.A. L.209 J.D. 150 S. Wacker Dr., Ste. 2400
Zakaras, Matthew R. '76 '01 C.436 B.A. L.209 J.D. [Ⓐ Levenfeld P.]
Zaknoen, Joseph J. '60 '91 C&L.347 B.A., J.D. [Winston&S.]
Zalas, Shelly A. '71 '99 C.424 B.A. L.365 J.D. TruServ Corp.
Zalenski, Cheryl M., (CVⓉ) '68 '93 C.999 B.A. L.802 J.D.
(adm. in MI; not adm. in IL) Asst. Staff Coun., ABA Ctr. for Pro Bono
Zalewa, James D., (AV) '47 '74 C.339 B.S. L.145 J.D.
[Leydig,V.&M.] (See Pat. Sect.)
Zalewski, Kathryn D. '— '97 C.679 B.S. L.477 J.D. [Schiff H.]
Zallar, Therese E. '58 '85 [Ⓐ Meyers&M.]
Zaluda, Jeffrey A., (AV) '60 '86 C.454 B.A. L.904 J.D. [Horwood M.&B.]
Zalutsky, Irwin L. '33 '57 C.339 B.A. L.209 J.C. [Zalutsky&P.]
Zalutsky & Pinski, Ltd. 20 N. Clark St.
Zamora, Javier E. '— '00 C.1494 B.A. L.209 J.D. [Ⓐ Hinshaw&C.]
Zampa, David J. '64 '90 C.597 B.A. L.602 J.D. [Sidley A.B.&W.]
Zandri, Robin M. '70 '97 C.339 B.S. L.589 J.D. [Ⓐ Anderson&Assoc.] ⊙
Zanfardino, Dominic P., (AV) '60 '90
C&L.424 B.S., J.D. [Brinks H.G.&L.] (See Pat. Sect.)
Zanger, Larry M., (AV) '— '70 C&L.597 B.S.B.A., J.D. [Holland&K.]
Zanzig, Blair R. '73 '00 C.260 B.S.B.A. L.477 J.D. [Ⓐ Jenner&B.]
Zanzola, Joan M. '58 '99 C.589 B.S. L.209 J.D. Off. of the Gen. Coun., Dept. of HHS
Zaper, Peter D. '56 '84 C.339 B.A. Asst. State's Atty.
Zapf, Matthew A.C. '62 '87 C.602 B.A. L.597 J.D. [Goldberg,K.B.B.R.&M.]
Zaphiriou, James A. '60 '86 C.912 B.A. L.477 J.D.
Lawyers Cooperative Publishing Co.
Zapp, Kirk '68 '94 C.36 B.A. L.424 J.D. [Clausen M.]
Zaraza, Mari-Kathleen Sarno '41 '71 C.734 B.S. L.424 J.D. 5634 N. Kerbs Ave. (Pat.)
Zarczynski, Kate L. '— '02 C.597 B.A. L.846 J.D. [Ⓐ Jones D.]
Zaremski, Miles J., (AV) '48 '73 C.339 B.S. L.930 J.D. [Kamensky,R.H.&D.] ⊙
Zaris, Steven N., (AV) '57 '81 C.178 A.B. L.477 J.D. [McCarthy D.]
Zarkos, Spiro G. '71 '97 C.966 B.S. L.146 J.D. [Ⓐ Kaplan P.&G.]
Zarkowsky, Aaron B. '70 '95 C.339 B.A. L.209 J.D. [Deutsch,L.&E.]
Zarlengo, Joseph A. '59 '85 C.1077 B.A. L.365 J.D. [Chuhak&T.]
Zarley, Kerry E. '— '01 C.587 B.A. L.339 J.D. [Ⓐ Chapman&C.]
Zaronias, Michael D. '65 '02 C.347 B.A. L.879 J.D. [Ⓐ Cook,A.M.M.C.&M.]
Zaroski, Laura R. '69 '94 C.608 B.A. L.851 J.D. 140 S. Dearborn, Ste. 700
Zarov, Herbert L., (AV) '45 '79 C.178 B.A. L.145 LL.B. [Mayer,B.R.&M.]
Zarski, David E. '58 '83 C.801 B.S. L.209 J.D. [Ⓒ Schuyler,R.&Z.]
Zarski, Michael J. '54 '79 C.801 B.A. L.209 J.D. Div. of Fed. Legis., Amer. Med. Assn.
Zartman, James N., (AV) '28 '53 C.210 B.A. L.309 LL.B. 840 W. Belden‡
Zaslavsky, Michael A. '53 '77 C.339 B.S. L.209 J.D. 180 N. Lasalle, Ste. 3220
Zaslavsky, Morton L. '15 '36 L.209 LL.B. 180 N. La Salle St.
Zatopa, James R. '44 '71 C.602 B.B.A. L.145 J.D.
Admin. Law J., Dept. of Employ. Sec.
Zaug, Mary E. '— '96 C.966 B.S.Ch.E. L.424 J.D. [Kirkland&E.]
Zavett, Errol, (AV) '38 '64 C.352 B.A. L.339 J.D. [Davis F.Z.K.M.M.&R.]
Zavis, Michael Wm., (P.C.), (AV) '37 '61 C.659 B.S. L.145 J.D. [Katten M.R.] ‡
Zavodnyik, Peter '69 '97 C&L.602 B.A., J.D. [Ⓐ Dowd&D.]
Zawarus, Gordon '42 '68 C&L.424 B.S., J.D. 5249 S. Parkside
Zazove, Daniel A., (AV) '47 '73 C.966 B.A. L.339 J.D. [Perkins C.]
Zdeb, Michael J., (AV) '— '76 C&L.424 A.B., J.D. [Arnstein&L.]
Zdravecky, Amy J. '70 '95 C&L.477 B.A., J.D. [Neal,G.&E.]
Zebovitz, Lisa S., (AV) '55 '80 C.393 B.A. L.209 J.D. [Neal,G.&E.]
Zeff, Stephen '69 '94 C.477 B.A. L.472 J.D.
Advertising Coun., The Interpublic Group of Companies, Inc.
Zehe, Jeffrey R. '54 '79 C.424 B.A. L.209 J.D. [Ellison,N.Z.&A.]
Zeiger, Jeanne M. '52 '79 C.352 B.S. L.910 J.D. [Ⓐ Kiesler&B.]
Zeiger, Jeffrey J. '— '01 C.902 B.A. L.477 J.D. [Ⓐ Kirkland&E.]
Zeigler, Janet E. '— '91 C.339 B.A. L.1119 J.D. [Foley&L.]
Zeisler, Karl '31 '54 C.145 Ph.B. L.309 J.D. St. Lukes Med. Center
Zeitler, Norma W. '— '95 C.801 B.S. L.424 J.D. [Ⓒ Barnes&T.]
Zeitlin, Charles E., (AV) '32 '56 C&L.309 A.B., J.D. [Ⓒ Aronberg G.D.&G.]
Zekich, Janeve Botica '67 '92 C.145 B.A. L.424 J.D. Atty.
Zeldin, Robin Jeffrey '52 '85 C.966 B.A. L.345 J.D. 111 E. Wacker Dr.‡
Zelechowski, Leon, (AV) '48 '75 C.801 B.S. L.597 J.D. [L.Zelechowski]

Zelechowski, Leon, Ltd., (AV)
111 West Washington Street, Suite 1437, 60602
Telephone: 312-609-0022 Fax: 312-609-0626
Email: lzelech@comcast.net
Leon Zelechowski.
Commercial Real Estate, Landlord and Tenant Law, Mortgages, Mechanics Liens, Breach of Contract, Creditors Rights, Collections, Buying and Selling of Businesses.
See Professional Biographies, CHICAGO, ILLINOIS

Zelek, Eugene F., Jr., (AV) '— '78 C.339 B.S. L.597 J.D. [Freeborn&P.]
Zeleny, Thomas D. '54 '80 C.589 B.S. L.365 J.D. Off. of Pub. Def.
Zelizer, Ethan G. '— '03 C&L.424 B.A., J.D. [Ⓐ Morgan,L.&B.]
Zelkowitz, Alan S., (BV) '64 '89 C.339 B.A. L.910 J.D. [Ⓐ Pretzel&S.]
Zell, Samuel '41 '66 C&L.477 B.A., J.D. 2 N. Riverside Plz.
Zeller, James P., (AV) '— '76
C.602 B.S.Ch.E. L.1119 J.D. [Marshall,G.&B.] (See Pat. Sect.)
Zeller, Patrick '70 '96 C.339 B.A. L.1000 J.D. [Ⓐ Seyfarth S.]
Zeller, Ryan S. '77 '04 C.347 B.A. L.209 J.D. [Ⓐ R.F.Coleman&Assoc.]
Zeller, Sheila '— '97 C.16 B.A. L.1000 J.D. [Ⓐ Freeborn&P.]
Zeller, Steven McMahon '67 '96 C.350 B.S. L.597 J.D. [Ⓐ Jenner&B.]
Zellermayer, Reuben J. '26 '50 C.339 L.209 LL.B. 205 W. Randolph St.
Zells, Heidi S. '69 '94 C.339 B.A. L.146 J.D. Cook Co. Pub. Guard. Off.
Zells, Martin B. '40 '65 C.801 B.S. L.339 LL.B. 20 N. Wacker Dr.
Zelmar, Stewart '46 '71 C.339 B.a. L.597 J.D. 200 N. LaSalle St., Ste. 2650
Zemel, Albert I. '19 '42 C&L.209 B.S., J.D. 134 N. La Salle St.
Zemm, Sandra P., (AV) '47 '75 C.339 B.S. L.259 J.D. [Seyfarth S.]
Zemnick, Scott R. '— '01 C.477 B.A. L.146 J.D. [Ⓐ Kirkland&E.]
Zeni, Ferdinand J., Jr. '24 '50 C&L.597 B.S., J.D.
Admin. Law J., State Dept. of Pub. Aid
Zenner, Sheldon T., (AV) '53 '78 C&L.597 B.A., J.D. [Katten M.R.]
Zenoff, A. J., (AV) '15 '37 C&L.436 J.D. [Zenoff&Z.]
Zenoff, Alan H., (AV) '48 '77 C.36 B.A. L.146 J.D. [Zenoff&Z.]
Zenoff & Zenoff, Chartered, (AV) 53 W. Jackson Blvd.
Zessar, Marjorie J. '67 '94 C.813 B.A. L.145 J.D. [Sonnenschein N.&R.]
Zettler, Nancy A. '58 '90 C.338 B.S. L.146 J.D. Two North La Salle Street
Zgliniec, Jason L. '— '01 C.477 A.B. L.188 J.D. [Ⓐ Schiff H.]
Zhang, Fan '— '04 L.178 J.D. [Ⓐ Latham&W.]
Zhao, Gary '— '03 C.477 B.a. L.910 J.D. [Ⓐ O'Hagan,S.&A.]
Zhao, Jia '40 '85 C.999 B.A. L.309 J.D. [Baker&M.]
Zhao, Lingzhi '72 '03 L.213 J.D. [Ⓐ Kiesler&B.]
Zibart, Christopher W. '— '84 C.473 A.B. L.339 J.D. [Foley&L.]
Zick, Steven J. '60 '85 C&L.209 B.A., J.D. Asst. State Atty.

Zickert, Lloyd L., (AV) '26 '53 C.679 B.S.M.E. L.273 J.D.
79 West Monroe Street, Suite 1100, 60603
Telephone: 312-236-1888 Fax: 312-236-1885
Email: zickert@compuserve.com
Patent, Trademark, Copyright and Unfair Competition Law.
See Professional Biographies, CHICAGO, ILLINOIS

Zidek, L. Charles '33 '65 C.597 B.S. L.146 J.D. 5265 N. Elston Ave.
Ziebarth, Christopher A. '— '00 C.478 B.A. L.228 J.D. [Ⓐ Kirkland&E.]
Ziebell, Gerald E. '— '96 C.145 B.A. L.146 J.D. [Ⓐ Karbal,C.E.S.&D.]
Ziebert, Paul C., (BV) '62 '90 C.902 B.A. L.273 J.D. [McGuirewoods]
Ziegelmueller, William P. '69 '94 C.896 B.A. L.597 J.D. [Stetler&D.]
Ziegler, Ann E. '58 '83 C.945 B.A. L.145 J.D. V.P., Corp. Develop., Sara Lee Corp.
Ziegler, James P. '52 '76 C.025 B.A. L.209 J.D. [Stone,P.&K.]
Ziegler, Richard G. '59 '88 C.602 B.A. L.477 J.D. [Ⓒ Mayer,B.R.&M.]
Zielinski, Kimberly M. '75 '04 C.393 B.A. L.146 J.D. [Ⓐ Mayer,B.R.&M.]
Zielinski, Robert T., (AV) '57 '82 C.309 B.A. L.569 J.D. [McGuirewoods]
Zielinski, Zane L. '— '02 C.145 B.A. L.146 J.D. [Ⓐ Frank/ G.]
Zielke, Brianna J. '75 '03 C.602 B.A. L.597 J.D. [Ⓐ McGuirewoods]
Ziemann, Jason R. '75 '02 C.98 B.S. L.365 J.D. [Ⓐ Heller&F.]
Zieske, William F. '— '97 C.910 B.A. L.602 J.D. [Ⓐ Bryan C.]
Zigman, Edward D. '46 '79 C.424 B.A. L.1151 J.D. 10540 S. Western Ave.
Zillmer, John R. '60 '03 C.339 B.A. L.146 J.D. [Ⓐ Kaplan,v.&M.]
Zima, Gary D., (AV) '54 '79 C.645 B.A. L.365 J.D. [Roddy,L.&Z.]
Zimbler, Jay H., (AV) '50 '75 C.477 B.A. L.309 J.D. [Sidley A.B.&W.]
Zimelis, Robert D., (AV) '50 '75 C&L.597 B.A., J.D. [Neal,G.&E.]
Zimmer, A. L. '40 '78 C.473 B.A. L.339 J.D. [Ⓒ Cosby,O.&B.]
Zimmer, Jeanette Sanniola '— '98 C.339 B.S.A. L.146 J.D. [Ⓐ Schiff H.]
Zimmer, Stephen C. '70 '95 C.436 B.S. L.146 J.D. Bk. of America
Zimmerman, Amy '63 '91 C.659 B.A. L.597 J.D. Legal Asst. Found. of Chicago
Zimmerman, Craig H. '62 '89 C.1036 B.A. L.276 J.D. [McDermott W.&E.]
Zimmerman, Dale G. '38 '63 C.578 B.A. L.966 LL.B.
(adm. in WI; not adm. in IL) Dir. of Hearings & App., R.R. Ret. Bd.
Zimmerman, Gifford R., (AV) '56 '82 C.339 B.A. L.477 J.D.
Mng. Dir., Assoc. Gen. Coun. & Asst. Secy., John Nuveen & Co., Inc.
Zimmerman, Jacalyn J., (AV) '52 '78
C.339 B.S. L.424 J.D. Gen. Coun., State Labor Rel. Bd.
Zimmerman, Mark C. '71 '01 C.436 B.S.E.E. L.209 J.D. [Grossman&F.] (Pat.)
Zimmerman, Mark W. '61 '93 C.801 B.S. L.209 J.D. [Clausen M.]
Zimmerman, Norman E. '36 '60 C.339 B.S. L.597 J.D. 120 W. Madison St.
Zimmerman, Robert J., (AV) '— '76 C.694 A.B. L.880 J.D. [Foley&L.]
Zimmerman, Sally J. '54 '91 C.750 B.S.N. L.589 J.D. [Cassiday,S.&G.] (⊙Rockford)
Zimmerman, Tony R. '56 '83 C.339 B.A. L.146 J.D. Sr. V.P., Heitman Properties Ltd
Zimmerman, Warren A. '54 '79 C.976 B.A. L.477 J.D. Asst. States Atty.
Zimmermann, Kent M. '72 '98 C.910 A.B. L.146 J.D. V.P. Gen Coun., Hubbard One
Zimring, Jon '67 '92 C.477 B.A. L.597 J.D. [Duane M.]
Zinanni, Meredith '— '03 C.910 B.A. L.228 J.D. [Ⓐ Kirkland&E.]
Zinder, David M., Law Office of '58 '85 C.966 B.B.A. L.472 J.D.
205 W. Wacker Drive
Zinder, Lawrence A. '30 '53 C&L.597 B.S., J.D. [Constantine,Z.&P.]
Zink, Christopher R. '— '98 C.118 B.A. L.424 J.D. [Ⓐ Hickey,M.&Assoc.]
Zinman, Lance A. '73 '98 C.475 B.A. L.597 J.D. [Ⓐ Katten M.R.]
Zinski, Christopher J. '— '87 C.436 B.S. L.276 J.D. [Schiff H.]
Zipprich, Reneé L. '70 '03 C.477 B.A. L.424 J.D. [Ⓐ Dykema G.P.]
Zirn, Alison N. '62 '94 C.477 B.A. L.1065 J.D. [DLPiper R.G.C.U.]
Zisook, Phillip J., (AV) '53 '78 C.339 B.A. L.146 J.D. [Deutsch,L.&E.]
Zitko, Robert R. '— '94 C&L.339 B.S., J.D. [Kirkland&E.]
Zito, Anthony S., Jr. '42 '67 C&L.930 B.A., J.D. Prof. of Law, John Marshall Law Sch.
Zito, Donald L. '29 '53 C.473 L.608 LL.B.
(adm. in OH; not adm. in IL) Gen. Servs. Admn.
Zito, Mark R. '72 '99 C.602 B.A. L.352 J.D. [Ⓐ Dykema G.P.]
Zito, William Francis, Jr. '64 '93 C.976 B.A. L.966 J.D. Acme World Sports, LLC
Zitzer, Dennis M. '46 '79 C.999 B.A. L.365 J.D. 3042 W. Cermak Rd.
Zivian, Bruce A. '59 '84 C.813 A.B. L.477 J.D. [Baker&M.]
Zivitz, Ellen Prince '72 '97 C.347 B.A. L.424 J.D. [Ⓐ Sonnenschein N.&R.]
Zlatic, Daniel J. '71 '97 C.894 B.A. L.879 J.D. [Ⓐ Johnson&B.] (⊙Highland, IN)
Zlotowicz, Barry M. '67 '94 C.1077 B.A. L.990 J.D.
(adm. in WA; not adm. in IL) Account Executive, Practicity
Zmigrocki, James J., (AV) '40 '64 C&L.602 B.A., J.D. [J.J.Zmigrocki]
Zmigrocki, James J., Chartered, (AV) 79 W. Monroe St. Ste. 1305
Zoll, Jeffery M. '54 '78 C&L.339 B.A., J.D. Touche Ross & Co.
Zolla, William A., (AV) '40 '65 C.477 B.A. L.145 J.D. [DLPiper R.G.C.U.]
Zolla, William A., II '68 '97 C.477 A.B. L.94 J.D. [Ⓐ Beermann S.W.B.B.G.&L.]
Zollar, Nikki M. '56 '81 C.367 B.A. L.276 J.D. Dir., State Dept. of Prof. Regulation
Zoller, Arie Ben '— '00 C.424 B.A. L.146 J.D. [Ⓐ Greenberg T.]
Zollner, Daniel J., (AV) '56 '81 C&L.339 B.S., J.D. [Ross,D.&B.]

Zolna, Bruce A. .... '48 '73 C.927 B.A. L.209 J.D. [Klein,T.&J.]
Zolna, Gladys C. .... '— '03 C.339 B.S. L.145 J.D. [🄰 Schiff H.]
Zolna, Jacie .... '— '02 C.489 B.A. L.209 J.D. [🄰 M.M.Cherry&Assoc.]
Zolner, Erica B. .... '77 '02 C.612 B.A. L.597 J.D. [🄰 Kirkland&E.]
Zolner, Michael Derek .... '73 '98 C&L.623 B.A., J.D. [🄰 Vedder,P.K.&K.]
Zolno, Mark S. .... '43 '78 C.589 B.S. L.365 J.D. [Katten M.R.]
Zontanos, Demetra .... '74 '99 C.424 B.A. L.209 J.D. 4633 N. Western
Zook, Ted H. .... '— '88 C.918 B.A. L.893 J.D. [Kirkland&E.]
Zordani, Jan M. '59 '85 C.966 B.B.A. L.436 J.D.
(adm. in WI; not adm. in IL) 333 W. Wacker Dr.‡
Zordani, Jennifer .... '— '94 C.145 B.A. L.146 J.D. [Ungaretti&H.]
Zorub, Grazia M. '— '03 C.228 B.A. L.276 J.D.
(adm. in NY; not adm. in IL) [🄰 Jones D.]
Zott, David J. .... '— '86 C.597 B.A. L.477 J.D. [Kirkland&E.]
Zoub, Burton I., (AV) .... '26 '52 C.339 B.A. L.597 J.D. 155 North Michigan Avenue
Zoufal, Donald R. .... '57 '83 C&L.339 B.A., J.D. State Dept. of Corrections
Zouras, James B. .... '70 '95 C.339 B.A. L.209 J.D. 161 N. Clark Street
Zubairi, Junaid A. '77 '02
C&L.424 B.B.A., J.D. Staff Atty., U.S. Secs. and Exchange Comm.
Zucker, Daniel N., (AV) .... '59 '84 C.494 B.S. L.597 J.D. [McDermott W.&E.]
Zuckerman, Allan C., (AV) .... '39 '64 C.966 B.S. L.597 J.D. 203 N. LaSalle St.
Zuckerman, Steven M. .... '55 '80 C.575 B.A. L.276 J.D. [Cohen,G.&R.]
Zuehl, James J., (AV) .... '47 '81 C.966 B.S. L.145 J.D. [Franczek S.]
Zuganelis, George M. .... '48 '78 C.477 B.S. L.589 J.D. [G.M.Zuganelis]

Zuganelis, George M., Attorney at Law, P.C.
3310 North Harlem Avenue, 60634
Telephone: 773-237-3516 Fax: 773-237-3518
Email: gmzlawpc@aol.com
George M. Zuganelis.
Criminal Defense, Real Estate, Personal Injury, Adoption, Workers Compensation.
See Professional Biographies, CHICAGO, ILLINOIS

Zuhn, Donald L. '62 '02 C.424 B.S. L.365 J.D.
[🄰 McDonnell B.H.&B.] (See Pat. Sect.)
Zukerman, Barbara .... '40 '87 C.597 B.A. L.424 J.D. 57 E. Delaware Pl.
Zukosky, Jamie L. .... '69 '96 C.330 B.A. L.1194 J.D. [Schottler&Z.]
Zulkey, Edward J., (AV) .... '48 '73 C.597 B.A. L.339 J.D. [Baker&M.]
Zulkey, Richard E., (AV) .... '41 '69 C.321 A.B. L.209 J.D. [R.E.Zulkey&Assoc.]
Zulkey, Richard E., and Associates, Chartered, (AV) ...79 West Monroe Street, Suite 1305
Zulkie, Paul L., (AV) .... '52 '77 C.589 B.A. L.339 J.D. [Zulkie]

Zulkie Partners LLC, (AV)
222 South Riverside Plaza, Suite 2300, 60606-6101
Telephone: 312-648-2244 Fax: 312-648-9848 URL: http://www.zulkiepartners.com
Email: pzulkie@zulkiepartners.com URL: http://www.lawyers.com/zulkiepartners
Paul L. Zulkie; Susan M. Maclean. Associates: Pamela Mick; Terri Barton Bragga (Not admitted in IL); Jennifer L. Simutis.
Immigration and Naturalization Law.
See Professional Biographies, CHICAGO, ILLINOIS

Zullo, Kelly M. .... '71 '02 C.339 B.A. L.276 J.D. [K.Zullo]
Zullo, Kelly .... 3349 N. Sheffield Ave.
Zummer, Anthony S., (AV) .... '29 '56 C.679 B.S. L.273 J.D. [Palmatier&Z.] (Pat.)
Zummo, John E. .... '69 '97 C.436 B.A. L.365 J.D. [🄰 Katten M.R.]
Zummo, Jos. L. .... '24 '53 C.597 B.S. L.209 J.D. 6049 W. Belmont St.
Zura, Peter '67 '97 C.1154 B.S.E.E. L.213 J.D.
(adm. in MI; not adm. in IL; Pat.) [🄰 Bell,B.&L.]
Zurawski, Mary Lou .... '48 '79 C.209 B.A. L.589 J.D. 6121 N. Northwest Hwy., Ste. 102
Zurek, Elizabeth A. .... '59 '87 C&L.424 B.S., J.D. Univ. of Chicago Hospitals
Zussman, Gary T. .... '57 '82 C.659 B.S.E. L.477 J.D. [Goldberg,K.B.B.R.&M.]
Zweig, Howard P., (AV) .... '54 '81 C.186 B.Arch. L.494 J.D. [Gardner C.&D.]
Zwick, Ann M. .... '— '89 C.339 B.S. L.597 J.D. [Freeborn&P.] ⊙
Zwick, Joseph A., (BV) .... '— '90 C.424 B.S. L.365 J.D. [Hennessy&R.]
Zwick, Mary Lou .... '— '95 C.602 B.B.A. L.424 J.D. [Sachnoff&W.]
Zwick, Susan, (AV) .... '55 '80 C&L.602 A.B., J.D. 1654 N. Newland Ave.
Zwirner, Richard T., (AV) .... '43 '68 C.477 B.A. L.597 J.D. [Schuyler,R.&Z.]
Zydeck, Jacqueline M. .... '63 '89 C.477 A.B. L.347 J.D. Dept. of HHS
Zygmuntowicz, Joseph A. .... '18 '42 C.424 Ph.D. L.597 J.D. 100 W. Monroe St.
Zyzda, Christine A. .... '61 '86 C&L.209 B.A., J.D. 19 S. LaSalle St.

ENGLISH LAWYERS RESIDENT IN CHICAGO

Abrahams, Darrow .... '73 '02 C&L.339 B.A. [🄰 Lovells] (⊙Chicago)
Ahlman, Jodi L. '75 '00 C&L.352 B.A., J.D.
(adm. in IA; not adm. in IL) [🄰 Lovells] (⊙Chicago)
Blackburn, Rachael .... '78 '02 C.339 B.A. L.966 J.D. [🄰 Lovells] (⊙Chicago)
Diffin, Ed .... '78 '03 C.827 B.A. L.145 J.D. [🄰 Lovells] (⊙Chicago)
Goodman, Adam B. .... '70 '95 C.691 B.A. L.145 J.D. [🄲 Lovells] (⊙Chicago)
Hawker, Alexis A. .... '75 '00 C.210 B.A. L.477 J.D. [🄰 Lovells] (⊙Chicago)
Hornish, Michele Lynn .... '75 '01 C&L.502 B.A., J.D. [🄰 Lovells] (⊙Chicago)

Lovells
One IBM Plaza, 330 North Wabash Avenue, Suite 1900, 60611 ⊙
Telephone: 312-832-4400 Fax: 312-832-4444
Email: information@lovells.com URL: http://www.lovells.com
Resident Partners: Thomas F. Bush, Jr.; Gail M. Goering; Eric A. Haab; David C. Linder (Not admitted in IL); Joseph T. McCullough IV; Neal J. Moglin; Kay E. Wilde. Of Counsel: Adam B. Goodman; John M. O'Bryan; Brad Ockene; Frank B. Slepicka; MaryBeth Wilkinson. Associates: Darrow Abrahams; Jodi L. Ahlman (Not admitted in IL); Rachael Blackburn; Ed Diffin; Robin C. Dusek; Jonathan R. Glusman; Alexis A. Hawker; Michele Lynn Hornish; Kris L. McCoy; R. Chad McCracken; Richard Alexander Nelson; Erin O'Brien; Peter B. Steffen; Mitchell B. Weiss.
Alternative Risk Transfer, Arbitration, Aviation, Banking, Banking Litigation, Building and Engineering, Capital Markets, China, Collective Investment Schemes, Commercial, Commodities, Competition and Trade Regulation, Computers, Construction, Consumer Financial Services, Corporate Finance, Corporate Law East-West Trade, EC, Employment, Energy, Environmental Law, Financial Services, Fraud and Asset Recovery, General Litigation, Insolvency, Insurance, Intellectual Property, Management Buy-Outs and Venture Capital, Media Law, Mergers and Acquisitions, Pensions, Planning, Product Liability, Property, Rating, Reinsurance, Shipping, Taxation, Trusts and Estate Planning.
Other Offices:
Alicante, Spain
Amsterdam, Netherlands
Beijing, Republic of China
Berlin, Germany
Brussels, Belgium
Budapest, Hungary Associated Office
Dusseldorf, Germany
Frankfurt, Germany
Hamburg, Germany
Ho Chi Minh City, Vietnam
Hong Kong
London, England
Madrid, Spain
Milan, Italy

(This Listing Continued)

Lovells (Continued)
Moscow, Russia
Munich, Germany
New York, N.Y.
Paris, France
Prague, Czech Republic
Rome, Italy
Shanghai, China
Singapore
Tokyo, Japan
Vienna, Austria Associated Office
Warsaw, Poland
Zagreb, Croatia Associated Office
Reviser of the Germany Law Digest for this Directory.
See Professional Biographies, LONDON, ENGLAND

McCracken, R. Chad .... '67 '99 C.976 B.A. L.846 J.D. [🄰 Lovells] (⊙Chicago)
Nelson, Richard Alexander .... '— '03 C.228 B.A. L.597 J.D. [🄰 Lovells] (⊙Chicago)
O'Brien, Erin .... '75 '00 C&L.339 B.A., J.D. [🄰 Lovells] (⊙Chicago)
O'Bryan, John M. .... '68 '97 C.188 A.B. L.597 J.D. [🄲 Lovells] (⊙Chicago)
Ockene, Brad .... '— '89 C.976 B.A. L.1365 J.D. [🄲 Lovells] (⊙Chicago)
Wilkinson, MaryBeth .... '72 '97 C.741 B.A. L.597 J.D. [🄲 Lovells] (⊙Chicago)

CHICAGO HEIGHTS, 32,776, *Cook Co.*

Anzelmo, August A. .... '52 '80 C.339 B.A. L.589 J.D. 311 S. Halsted St.
Brauer, David A., (AV) .... '46 '74 C.347 B.S. L.339 J.D. [McGrane,P.S.G.B.&R.]
Buttell, George J., III .... '25 '53 C&L.209 B.A., LL.B. 1515 Halstad St.
Chudada, Robert F. .... '49 '77 C.966 B.B.A. L.284 J.D. [Cifelli,S.C.&S.]
Ciambrone, Angelo A., (AV) .... '29 '55 C&L.209 B.S., J.D. [Wilczynski,W.&C.]
Cifelli, David J. .... '51 '81 C.174 B.S. L.209 J.D. [Cifelli,S.C.&S.]
Cifelli, John L. .... '23 '50 C.339 B.Litt. L.209 LL.B. [🄲 Cifelli,S.C.&S.]
Cifelli, Scrementi, Chudada & Spina, Ltd. .... 1700 South Halsted Street, Suite 201
Coniglio, George .... '30 '74 C.339 L.146 J.D. 100 1st National Plz., #201
Coppa, Peter J., (AV) .... '30 '62 C.339 B.S. L.209 B.L. 1515 Halsted St.
Foxley, John C. '49 '74 C.321 A.B. L.190 J.D.
(adm. in NE; not adm. in IL) Pres., Triangle Financial Corp.
Gerardi, Richard P., (AV) .... '43 '70 C.597 B.A. L.144 J.D. [McGrane,P.S.G.B.&R.]
Grupp, Charles J., Jr. .... '22 '50 C.339 B.S. L.146 LL.B. 844 N. Highland Dr.‡
Hopper, J. Brent .... '57 '86 C.999 B.A. L.365 J.D. 12 W. 15th St.

Kline, Mitchell A., Law Office of
(See Chicago)

Lamb, Natalie, Law Office of ... '63 '87 C.436 B.A. L.209 J.D. 20520 Hutchinson Avenue
McGrane, Perozzi, Stelter, Gerardi, Brauer & Ross, Ltd., (AV) .... 165 West 10th Street
Milord, Lisa L. .... '51 '83 C.976 B.A. L.1068 J.D. 336 Holbrook Cir.
Motter, Oliver W. .... '11 '44 C.339 B.S. L.146 LL.B. 3 Ellen Dr.
Perozzi, Joseph R., (AV) .... '30 '56 C.602 B.S. L.339 J.D. [McGrane,P.S.G.B.&R.]
Pigato, Joseph R., (BV) .... '37 '64 C.1151 B.S. L.209 LL.B. 20200 Ashland Ave.
Planera, Joseph L. .... '47 '78 C.999 B.A. L.1151 J.D. 222 Vollmer Rd.
Ritzler, Suzanne E. '65 '89 C.339 B.S. L.145 J.D.
Exec. V.P., Fin., Legal & Admn., Carmeuse North America Grp.
Ross, Andrew D., (AV) .... '48 '75 C.493 B.S. L.365 J.D. [McGrane,P.S.G.B.&R.]
Schroeder, Harry A. .... '50 '79 C.228 A.B. L.424 J.D. [H.A.Schroeder]
Schroeder, Harry A., PC, Law Offices of .... 1619 Western Ave.
Scrementi, Anthony C. .... '49 '74 C.339 B.S. L.209 J.D. [Cifelli,S.C.&S.]
Spina, Patrick H. .... '52 '77 C.209 B.S. L.801 J.D. [Cifelli,S.C.&S.]
Stelter, N. Richard, (BV) .... '36 '61 C.894 B.A. L.339 J.D. [McGrane,P.S.G.B.&R.]
Sulzbacher, Lawrence .... '26 '51 L.209 J.D. 71 E. Glengate Ave.‡
Wilczynski, Stanley A., Jr., (AV) .... '30 '53 C&L.209 J.D. [Wilczynski,W.&C.]
Wilczynski, Wilczynski & Ciambrone, Ltd., (AV) .... 1515 Halsted Street
Zerante, David M. .... '50 '80 C.177 B.A. L.365 J.D. 1492 Aberdeen Street

CHICAGO RIDGE, 14,127, *Cook Co.*

Panno, Frank J. .... '52 '77 C.339 B.S. L.424 J.D. 10549 S. Oak Park Ave.

Siwek, James J., Law Office of
(See Worth)

Tokar, Charles E. .... '53 '78 C.388 B.A. L.1151 J.D. Vil. Clk.

CHILLICOTHE, 5,959, *Peoria Co.*

Edmonds, John P., (BV) .... '49 '75 C.504 B.A. L.365 J.D. [J.P.Edmonds]
Edmonds, John P., Ltd., (BV) .... 220 Cloverdale Rd.
Jaeger, Philip L., (BV) .... '48 '73 C.927 B.A. L.339 J.D. [Safford,W.T.&J.] ⊙
Kehr, Thomas W., (BV) .... '20 '47 C.352 B.A. L.546 J.D. 1021 N. 4th St.
Laukitis, Richard V., (BV) .... '50 '76 C.210 B.A. L.365 J.D. 220 Cloverdale Rd.
Mahoney, Michael T., (BV) .... '54 '79 C&L.424 B.A., J.D. [M.T.Mahoney] ⊙

Mahoney, Michael T., Ltd., (BV)
1011 North Second Street, 61523 ⊙
Telephone: 309-274-5451 Fax: 309-274-5405
Email: mahoney@mchsi.com URL: http://www.mahoneyltd.com
Michael T. Mahoney.
Civil Litigation, Wills and Probate, Trusts and Estates, Estate Planning, Family Law, Personal Injury, Juvenile Law, DUI, Divorce, Adoptions, Child Support and Custody, Visitation Rights, Automobile Accidents, Dog Bites, Slip and Fall, Wrongful Death, Real Estate, Buying and Selling, Construction Law, Workers Compensation, Title and Insurance, Domestic Relations, Corporations.
References: First National Bank of Chillicothe; Chillicothe Foundation, Inc.
Peoria Office: 414 Hamilton Boulevard, Suite 300. Telephone: 309-673-0375.
See Professional Biographies, CHILLICOTHE, ILLINOIS

Safford, West, Tornow & Jaeger, (BV) .... P.O. Box 552 (⊙Peoria)
Tornow, Medley A., (BV) .... '40 '65 C.801 A.B. L.339 J.D. [Safford,W.T.&J.] ⊙
West, Stephen J., (BV) .... '55 '82 C.339 B.A. L.801 J.D. [🄰 Safford,W.T.&J.] ⊙

CICERO, 85,616, *Cook Co.*

Berkos, Christy S. .... '26 '52 L.146 LL.B. Ret. Cir. Ct. J.‡
Bidwell, Charles W., Jr. .... '28 '53 C&L.276 B.S., LL.B. Pres., National Jockey Club
Both, Dennis E. .... '57 '82 C.46 B.S. L.424 J.D. Town Atty.
Boyle, David R. .... '48 '96 C.326 B.S. L.796 J.D. [D.Boyle&Assoc.]
Boyle, Dave, & Associates .... 1831 S. Lombard Ave.
Carmell, David Laurence '57 '82
C.605 A.B. L.802 J.D. Pres., Blue & Grey Transp. Co., LCC

Christensen & Ehret, LLP
(See Chicago)

Davis, Gabrielle S., P.C.
(See Oak Park)

Dopierala, Walter C. .... '44 '69 C.145 A.B. L.424 J.D. Commerce Clearing House, Inc.
Drechen, Martin J. .... '38 '72 C.932 B.B.A. L.365 J.D. 2528 S. Austin Blvd.
Heelan, James R. .... '34 '62 C&L.209 LL.B. 5838 W. Cermak Road

Hovorka, Martha .... '38 '63 C.388 B.A. L.209 J.D. Central Fed. Svgs.

Karlin & Fleisher, L.L.C.
(See Chicago)

Kirsh, Calvin .... '36 '60 C&L.209 B.A., J.D. 5814 W. Cermak Rd.
Kolbuck, Frank J. .... '47 '75 C.475 B.A. L.424 J.D. 5934 W. 35th St.
Krafcisin, John R. (Jack) .... '61 '86 C.720 B.A. L.424 J.D. 5839 W. 35th St.
Kucera, Richard T., (BV) .... '31 '58 C.1016 B.A. L.209 J.D. [Mlade&K.]
Loula, Stanley D. .... '34 '59 C.98 B.S. L.597 J.D. 6000 W. Cermak Rd.
McNamara, William Zoller .... '33 '62 C.197 B.A. L.188 LL.B. 5046 W. 23rd Pl.‡
Merkel, Raymond W. .... '46 '71 C.201 B.S. L.1340 J.D. 3808 61st Ct.
Mlade, John M., Jr., (BV) .... '29 '59 C.339 B.A. L.209 J.D. [Mlade&K.]
Mlade & Kucera, (BV) .... 5744 W. Cermak Rd.
Podlesak, John C. .... '13 '47 C.597 B.S. L.209 J.D. 2319 S. 59th Ave.
Ptak, Sylvester J. .... '24 '53 C.1016 L.209 J.D. [Ptak&R.]
Ptak & Rooney .... 5717 W. 35th St.
Reiff, Robt. .... '13 '40 4706 W. Cermak Rd.
Rooney, Kimberly Ptak .... '57 '82 C.597 B.A. L.602 J.D. [Ptak&R.]
Sobotka, Frank J. .... '12 '38 C&L.209 LL.B. Pres., Family Fed. Svgs. & Loan Assn.
Spinasanta, Roxane .... '56 '88 C.209 B.A. L.424 J.D. 1617 S. Lombard Ave.
Vosahlik, Ladd Joseph .... '16 '40 C&L.339 A.B., J.D. 2108 S. Austin Blvd.‡

Wallenstein Wagner & Rockey, Ltd.
(See Chicago)

Walner, Harvey L., & Associates, Ltd.
(See Chicago)

Wlodek, Walter M. .... '40 '65 C.578 B.S. L.146 J.D. 5814 W. Cermak Rd.

CISSNA PARK, 805, *Iroquois Co.*

Hamrick, Terry D., (CV) .... '50 '81 C.1044 B.A. L.347 J.D. P.O. Box 428
Tungate, James L., (BV) .... '47 '79 C.340 B.S. L.339 J.D. [Tungate] ⊙
Tungate Law Offices, Ltd., (BV) .... Railroad Ave. & 3rd St. (⊙Onarga, Watseka)

CLARENDON HILLS, 7,610, *DuPage Co.*

Aldini, Louis J., (AV) .... '55 '80 C.209 B.A. L.424 J.D. 115 W. 55th St., Ste. 400
Becker, Eugene J., (AV) .... '28 '53 C&L.209 LL.B. 115 55th St.
Blair, John R. .... '15 '51 L.365 LL.B. 4 Algonquin Rd.‡
Blair, Ronald E. .... '31 '58 C.238 L.365 LL.B. 95220 Frontage Rd.

Byrne, Michael T., (AV) '56 '82 C.339 B.S. L.365 J.D.
115 West 55th Street, Suite 400, 60514
Telephone: 630-654-8333 Fax: 630-654-0150
Email: michaeltbyrne@aol.com
Criminal Law, Driving While Intoxicated, Drug Crimes, Felonies, Homicide, Sexual Assault, Traffic Violations and Probation Violations.
See Professional Biographies, CLARENDON HILLS, ILLINOIS

Caplan, Robert L. .... '41 '66 C.339 L.365 LL.B. [R.L.Caplan]
Caplan, Robert L., P.C. .... 444 Naperville Rd.
Cray, Daniel K., (AV) .... '56 '81 C.338 B.S. L.339 J.D. [Iwan C.H.H.&V.] ⊙
Dickey, Thomas L. .... '53 '99 C.339 B.S. L.365 J.D. 146 Naperville Rd.
Ekl, Terry A., (AV) .... '48 '73 C.597 B.A. L.339 J.D. 115 W. 55th St.
Faletti, Barbara L. .... '24 '47 C&L.585 B.A., J.D. 326 Park Ave.‡
Faletti, Richard J. .... '22 '49 C&L.339 B.S., J.D. 326 Park Ave.‡
Fawell, Harris W., (AV) .... '29 '52 C.578 L.146 J.D. (M.C.)
Fee, Terence M. .... '52 '77 C&L.602 B.B.A., J.D. 18 Mohawk Dr.
Gorman, Earl J., Jr. .... '41 '73 C.871 B.S. L.365 J.D. 283 Stonegate Rd.‡
Hayman, William '27 '53 C.434 L.923 LL.B.
(adm. in WV; not adm. in IL) 6425 ClarendonHills Rd.‡

Iwan Cray Huber Horstman & VanAusdal LLC, (AV)
115 West 55th Street, Suite 400, 60514 ⊙
Telephone: 630-789-8200
Email: attorneys@iwancray.com URL: http://www.iwancray.com
Daniel K. Cray.
Litigation Practice. Product Liability, Insurance Coverage, Complex Commercial, Professional Liability, Medical Malpractice, Transportation Liability, Premises Liability, Hospital Liability Defense, Environmental Litigation and Civil Appeals.
Chicago, Illinois Office: 303 West Madison Street, Suite 2200, 60606-3315. Telephone: 312-332-8450. Fax: 312-332-8451.
See Professional Biographies, CLARENDON HILLS, ILLINOIS

Kelly, Therese A. .... '61 '86 C.339 B.A. L.424 J.D. 133 Ann St.
Macomber, Martha D. .... '60 '87 C.597 B.S. L.1119 J.D. 345 Ridge Ave.
Mann, John M., (AV) .... '24 '53 C.174 B.S. L.276 J.D. 41 Golf Ave. (Pat.)‡
McNamara, Suzanne Muslin .... '62 '87 C.477 B.A. L.424 J.D. 219 Holmes‡
Moy, Patricia Dwyer .... '31 '85 C.597 B.S. L.146 J.D. 160 Burlington Ave.
Oexeman, Robert J. .... '41 '68 C.801 B.A. L.477 J.D. 58 Portwine Rd.
Piaskowy, Walter A., Jr. .... '50 '77 C.339 B.S. L.365 J.D. 61 Ogden Ave., Ste. 100
Plachek, Edgar J. .... '19 '49 L.209 LL.B. 104 Chicago Ave.
Provenzale, Patrick L. .... '69 '94 C.93 B.A. L.209 J.D. 115 W. 55th St.
Reiland, Robert N. .... '50 '75 C.684 B.A. L.339 J.D. 27 Waverly Ave.
Rock, Martin J. .... '19 '48 C&L.602 A.B., LL.B. 317 Park‡
Ruggiero, Vincent C., (BV) .... '58 '84 C.339 B.S. L.146 J.D. [Ruggiero F.L.]
Ruggiero Family Law, (BV) .... 115 West 55th Street, Suite 400
Williams, Patrick J. .... '56 '81 C.339 B.A. L.424 J.D. 115 W. 55th St.

CLIFTON, 1,347, *Iroquois Co.*

Razzano, A. William, (AV) .... '35 '59 C&L.339 B.S., J.D. [Razzano&K.] (⊙Watseka)
Razzano & Kinzer, (AV) .... 1st Nat. Bk. Bldg. (⊙Watseka)

CLINTON, * 7,437, *DeWitt Co.*

Bryan, Garry W., (BV) .... '53 '80 C.1151 B.A. L.365 J.D. [Moss,B.&M.]
Calvin, William C. .... '23 '49 C&L.339 B.S., J.D. Ret. Cir. J.
Davis, John L. .... '42 '67 C.357 B.S. L.734 J.D. Cir. J.
Junkert, Dodie L. .... '63 '98 C.338 B.S. L.1187 J.D. [D.Junkert]
Junkert, Dodie, Law Office of .... 216 S. Grant St.
Kuntz, Stephanie L. .... '75 '00 C.357 B.A. L.201 J.D. [Taylor,K.R.&Assoc.]
Lamkin, Phillip R., (BV) .... '52 '78 C&L.339 B.A., J.D. [Lamkin&L.]
Lamkin, Thomas M., (BV) .... '34 '60 C&L.339 B.S., LL.B. [Lamkin&L.]

Lamkin & Lamkin, P.C., (BV)
200 South Monroe Street, P.O. Box 597, 61727
Telephone: 217-935-3186 Fax: 217-935-8033
Raymond W. Lamkin (1923-2001); Thomas M. Lamkin; Phillip R. Lamkin.
General Civil Practice. Trials. Real Estate, Taxation, DUI/DWI, Traffic Violations, Felonies, Criminal, Wills and Probate Law. Title Policies. Family Law, Debtor and Creditor, Estate Planning, Divorce, Adoptions, Child Support, Child Custody, Bankruptcy.
Representative Clients: First National Bank & Trust of Clinton; Wallace Business Forms, Inc.
See Professional Biographies, CLINTON, ILLINOIS

Moss, David M., (BV) .... '54 '83 C.462 B.A. L.365 J.D. [Moss,B.&M.]
Moss, Ray, (AV) .... '32 '59 C.339 B.S. L.365 LL.B. [Moss,B.&M.]

Moss, Bryan & Moss, P.C., (AV)
122 Warner Court, P.O. Box 655, 61727-0655
Telephone: 217-935-8341 Facsimile: 217-935-4416
Email: mbm@mbmpc.com
Ray Moss; Garry W. Bryan; David M. Moss.
Personal Injury, Workers Compensation and General Litigation.
See Professional Biographies, CLINTON, ILLINOIS

Myers, Stephen R., (BV) .... '49 '77 C.927 B.A. L.365 J.D. 202 West Adams Street
Olson, Richard J. '46 '75 C.698 A.B. L.734 J.D.
(adm. in MO; not adm. in IL) Revere Copper Brass
Peters, Stephen H. .... '44 '75 C.234 B.S. L.365 J.D. Cir. J.
Rudasill, A. J., (AV) .... '19 '47 C&L.339 A.B., J.D. [Rudasill]
Rudasill Law Office, (AV) .... P.O. Box 478
Smith, Stephen J. .... '32 '59 C.339 B.A. L.365 LL.B. 117 S. Quincy St.
Smith, William B., (AV) .... '24 '52 C.339 L.996 LL.B. 211 S. Alexander‡
Taylor, Joseph B., (BV) .... '43 '69 C.801 B.S. L.972 J.D. [Taylor,K.R.&Assoc.]
Taylor, Kuntz, Rudasill & Associates, (BV) .... 216 S. Center St.
Waks, Randall D., (BV) .... '46 '74 C.801 B.A. L.500 J.D. 33 Manor Hill Dr., Ste. 1000

COAL CITY, 4,797, *Grundy Co.*

Fleming, James R., (BV) .... '36 '61 C.602 B.B.A. L.209 J.D. 105 S. Broadway
Longest, Gloria M., (BV) .... '54 '86 C.719 B.A. L.365 J.D. 385 Broadway Street
O'Brien, Mary K., (BV) .... '65 '94 C.927 B.A. L.339 J.D. 760 E. Division
Tira, James J., (BV) .... '50 '78 [Tira&T.]
Tira, John M., (BV) .... '50 '78 C.338 B.S. L.1151 J.D. [Tira&T.]
Tira & Tira, (BV) .... 285 S. Broadway

COAL VALLEY, 3,606, *Henry & RockIslands Cos.*

Bell, John L., (BV) .... '53 '83 C.499 B.S. L.1187 J.D. Assoc. Cir. J.

COLLINSVILLE, 24,707, *Madison & St. Clair Cos.*

Adams, Walter G. '60 '85
C.346 B.S. L.801 J.D. Assoc. Reg. Coun., Chicago Title Ins. Co.
Armstrong, Benton Tad, (AV) .... '51 '76 C&L.339 B.S., J.D. [Armstrong] ⊙
Armstrong Law Offices, (AV) .... 103 South Morrison (⊙Edwardsville)
Begian, Daniel R., (AVⓉ) .... '53 '78 C.957 A.B. L.801 J.D. [McMahon,B.H.L.C.&M.] ⊙
Berry, Thomas E. '62 '87 C.339 A.B. L.608 J.D.
(adm. in OH; not adm. in IL) [McMahon,B.H.L.C.&M.] ⊙
Berry, William L., (AV) .... '48 '73 C.357 B.A. L.910 J.D. [Dunham,B.&L.] ⊙
Bitzer, John L., (BV) .... '52 '79 C.339 B.S. L.365 J.D. [Dunham,B.&L.] ⊙
Blood, Curtis L., (BV) .... '52 '78 C&L.339 B.S., J.D. [Blood]
Blood Law Office, (BV) .... 1602 Vandalia
Boggs, Beth C., (BVⓉ) .... '67 '91 C.999 B.A. L.801 J.D. [Boggs,B.&B.] ⊙

Boggs, Boggs & Bates, LLC, (AVⓉ)
120 East Church Street, 62234 ⊙
Telephone: 618-343-0031 Fax: 618-343-0177
Email: bbblawyers.com
Beth C. Boggs.
Insurance Defense, Workers Compensation Defense, Professional Liability, Employment Law, Environmental, Insurance Coverage, Products Liability, Negligence Defense, Corporate Law, Civil Trial Practice, Negligence Defense, Medical Malpractice, Commercial Litigation, Collections, Subrogation, Fraud, Arson, Trial and Appellate, Health Law, Construction, Fire and Marine, General Business Litigation, Creditor's Rights, Insurance, Bad Faith Defense, Self Insured Defense, Life Insurance Defense, Health Care Liability, Legal Malpractice.
Kansas City, Missouri Office: 1300 N.W. Jefferson Court, Kansas City, 64105. Telephone: 816-472-5599. Fax: 816-472-0870.
Belleville, Illinois Office: 23 South First Street, 62220-2029. Telephone: 618-746-9540. Fax: 618-746-9541.
St. Louis, Missouri Office: 7912 Bonhomme, Suite 400, 63105-1912. Telephone: 314-726-2310. Fax: 314-726-2360.
See Professional Biographies, COLLINSVILLE, ILLINOIS

Brueggemann, Mark A., (BV) .... '58 '83 C.339 B.S. L.801 J.D. [🄰 M.A.Brueggemann]
Brueggemann, Mark A., Law Offices of, P.C., (BV) .... 2011 Mall St.
Brunton, Michael J., (CV) .... '61 '91 C.347 B.S. L.801 J.D. [M.J.Brunton]

Brunton, Michael J., Law Offices of, (CV)
100 E. Clay Street, Suite 200, 62234
Telephone: 618-343-0750 Fax: 618-343-0227
Email: mbrunton@ezl.com URL: http://www.bruntonlawoffice.com
Member of Firm: Michael J. Brunton.
Personal Injury, Automobile Accidents, Wrongful Death, Slip and Fall, Workers Compensation, Repetitive Stress Injuries, Industrial Accidents, Construction Accidents, Products Liability, Insurance Dispute, Employment, Wrongful Discharge, Breach of Contract, Warranty Law and Class Actions.
See Professional Biographies, COLLINSVILLE, ILLINOIS

Burroughs, Raymond H. .... '16 '40 C&L.190 B.S.C., J.D. 424 Vandalia
Cadagin, Colleen .... '66 '91 C.436 B.A. L.734 J.D. Asst. State Atty.
Cain, Michelle M. .... '58 '88 C.339 B.A. L.365 J.D. [McMahon,B.H.L.C.&M.] ⊙
Cain, Richard R., (BV) .... '38 '70 C.801 B.S. L.734 J.D. 1518 Vandalia
Chandler, Tamara R. .... '74 '01 C.999 B.S.N. L.801 J.D. [🄰 Dunham,B.&L.] ⊙
Cobb, Deborah Crouse, (BV) .... '54 '84 C.234 B.A. L.910 J.D. [Crouse C.&B.]
Cody, William W., (AVⓉ) '35 '65 C.436 B.S. L.734 J.D.
(adm. in MO; not adm. in IL) [🄲 McMahon,B.H.L.C.&M.] ⊙
Collins, Allen H., (CV) .... '59 '85 C&L.734 B.A., J.D. [Collins]
Collins Law Office, (CV) .... 1518 Vandalia
Corray, Jason W. .... '73 '01 C.339 A.B. L.801 J.D. [🄰 Dunham,B.&L.] ⊙
Correale, Michael G. .... '51 '85 C.801 D.D.S. L.734 J.D. 7610 W. Mill Creek Rd.
Crouse Cobb & Bays, (BV) .... 515 W. Main St. (⊙Charleston)

Dunham, Boman & Leskera, (AV)
300 West Clay Street, 62234 ⊙
Telephone: 618-344-7734 Telecopier: 618-344-3853
Email: dbl300@wberry.com
John W. Leskera; William L. Berry; Eric C. Young; John L. Bitzer. Associates: Jason W. Corray; Tamara R. Chandler; Harvey Taylor, Jr.; Kevin J. Newton.
General Civil Trial and Appellate Practice. Negligence and Products Liability, Medical Malpractice, Probate, Insurance, Family, Real Estate, Environmental, School, Criminal and Bankruptcy Law.
Attorneys for: Collinsville School District #10; Hanover Insurance Co.; Hartford Insurance Group; State Farm Insurance Cos.; Transamerica Insurance Group; The Travelers Indemnity Co.; Wausau Insurance Cos.; Nationwide Insurance Co.
Belleville Office: 208 N. High. Telephone: 618-235-7222. Telecopier: 618-236-2800; 618-236-1899.
See Professional Biographies, COLLINSVILLE, ILLINOIS

Evers, William C., III, (BV) .... '45 '72 C.1101 B.A. L.378 J.D. 2014 Ravenwood Drive
Ezra, D. Jeffrey, (AV) .... '56 '86 C.446 B.A. L.734 J.D. [Wendler&E.]
Foster, James N., Jr., (AVⓉ) '54 '79 C&L.734 B.A., J.D.
(adm. in MO; not adm. in IL) [McMahon,B.H.L.C.&M.] ⊙
Fox Schulze, Susan C. .... '75 '01 C.734 B.A. L.910 J.D. [🄰 McMahon,B.H.L.C.&M.] ⊙

Franklin, Corey L. '77 '02 C.473 B.A. L.1439 J.D.
(adm. in MO; not adm. in IL) [[A] McMahon,B.H.L.C.&M.] ⊙
Fritz, Daniel G. '77 '04 C.587 B.A. L.734 J.D.
(adm. in MO; not adm. in IL) [[A] McMahon,B.H.L.C.&M.] ⊙
Garland, Burton D., Jr. '70 '95 C.37 B.S.B.A. L.734 J.D.
[McMahon,B.H.L.C.&M.] ⊙
Giacoletto, Steven C., (BV) '65 '90 C.910 B.A. L.734 J.D. [Giacoletto]
Giacoletto Law Office, (BV) 1601 Vandalia St.
Gilbert, Geoffrey M., Jr. '66 '92 C.174 B.A. L.734 J.D.
(adm. in MO; not adm. in IL) [McMahon,B.H.L.C.&M.] ⊙
Gnavi, W. Michael, Jr., (BV) '51 '77 C.339 B.A. L.734 J.D. 1004 Vandalia
Hackmann, John S. '27 '55 C.910 A.B. L.734 LL.B. 3 Cypress Pt.‡
Hanna, Thomas M., (AVⓉ) '36 '60 C&L.862 B.S., LL.B.
(adm. in OK; not adm. in IL) [McMahon,B.H.L.C.&M.] ⊙

Harper, Julie
(See Alton)

Heinritz, Robert G., Jr., (CV) '45 '75 C.801 B.S. L.734 J.D. 230 S. Wilson Dr.
Hileman, Charles E., Jr. '51 '76 C.801 B.A. L.910 J.D. 1504 W. Main St.
Hudak, Frank R. '19 '51 C.338 B.E. L.734 J.D. 124 Westridge Court‡
Hustava, John Henry, (BV) '50 '81 C.801 B.S.B.A. L.734 J.D. P.O. Box 707
Johnston, Patrick Gerard '— '91 L.734 J.D. 1601 Vandalia
Jones, William B. '68 '97 C&L.602 B.A., J.D.
(adm. in MO; not adm. in IL) [McMahon,B.H.L.C.&M.] ⊙
Juen, Mary Sue '53 '90 C.801 B.A. L.734 J.D. 123 Mesa Dr.
Kahn, David M. '39 '62 C&L.910 A.B., LL.B. 1806 Ramada Blvd.
Katz, Michael A., (BV) '40 '64 C&L.910 A.B., LL.B. 1993 Vandalia St.
Kennedy, Ralph E., (AVⓉ) '19 '44 C.804 A.B. L.910 J.D.
(adm. in MO; not adm. in IL) [[B] McMahon,B.H.L.C.&M.] ⊙
Leskera, John H. '63 '88 C.339 L.A.S. L.734 J.D. [[A] Leskera]
Leskera, John W., (AV) '31 '55 C&L.339 A.B., J.D. [Dunham,B.&L.] ⊙
Leskera Law Firm 120 E. Church St.
Linihan, D. Michael, (AVⓉ) '41 '66 C.934 B.A. L.378 J.D.
(adm. in KS; not adm. in IL) [McMahon,B.H.L.C.&M.] ⊙
Lorenz, Kevin J., (AVⓉ) '55 '82 C&L.734 B.A., J.D. [McMahon,B.H.L.C.&M.] ⊙
Martin, Mary Carter '73 '98 C.502 B.S.B.A. L.280 J.D.
[[A] McMahon,B.H.L.C.&M.] ⊙
Mattea, Justin B. '77 '02 C.734 B.S. L.801 J.D. [Mattea]
Mattea Law Firm 115 E. Main St.
Maule, Stephen B. '70 '96 C.112 B.A. L.502 J.D.
(adm. in MO; not adm. in IL) [McMahon,B.H.L.C.&M.] ⊙
McCarthy, Thomas O., (AVⓉ) '47 '73 C&L.502 B.S.E.E., J.D.
(adm. in MO; not adm. in IL) [McMahon,B.H.L.C.&M.] ⊙
McFall, Patricia M., (AVⓉ) '51 '81 C&L.734 A.B., J.D.
(adm. in MO; not adm. in IL) [McMahon,B.H.L.C.&M.] ⊙

McMahon, Berger, Hanna, Linihan, Cody & McCarthy, A Professional Corporation, (AVⓉ)
400 N. Bluff Road, 62234 ⊙
Telephone: 618-345-5822 Fax: 618-345-6483
Email: lawfirm@mcmahonberger.com URL: http://www.mcmahonberger.com
Alan I. Berger (1933-1999); Thomas M. Hanna (Not admitted in IL); D. Michael Linihan (Not admitted in IL); Thomas O. McCarthy (Not admitted in IL); Robert W. Stewart (Not admitted in IL); James N. Foster, Jr. (Not admitted in IL); Daniel R. Begian; John B. Renick (Not admitted in IL); Patricia M. McFall (Not admitted in IL); Kevin J. Lorenz; Thomas E. Berry (Not admitted in IL); Stanley G. Schroeder (Not admitted in IL); Geoffrey M. Gilbert, Jr. (Not admitted in IL); Michelle M. Cain; Stephen B. Maule (Not admitted in IL); Robert D. Younger (Not admitted in IL); Burton D. Garland, Jr.; William B. Jones (Not admitted in IL).
Mary Carter Martin; Corey L. Franklin (Not admitted in IL); Susan C. Fox Schulze; Charles H. Morgan (Not admitted in IL); Christopher M. Sanders (Not admitted in IL); Laura B. Staley (Not admitted in IL); Daniel G. Fritz (Not admitted in IL); Stacie A. Owens (Not admitted in IL). Of Counsel: William W. Cody (Not admitted in IL); Ralph E. Kennedy (Not admitted in IL).
Labor Relations, Civil Rights and Administrative Law, Employment Litigation in all Courts.
Representative Clients: AmerenUE; Emerson Electric Co.; Mallinckrodt Inc.; Edward Jones; ATC/ Vancom; Nordyne, Inc.; Intier Automotive; Prairie Farms Dairy; Ralston Purina; Silgan Plastics.
St. Louis, Missouri Office: 2730 N. Ballas Road, Suite 200, 63131-3039, PO Box 31901. Telephone: 314-567-7350. Fax: 314-567-5968.

See Professional Biographies, COLLINSVILLE, ILLINOIS

Morgan, Charles H. '70 '02 C.1069 B.A. L.986 J.D.
(adm. in MO; not adm. in IL) [[A] McMahon,B.H.L.C.&M.] ⊙
Mundorf, Barney R. '64 '91 C.1348 B.A. L.734 J.D. [[A] Robbins,S.N.L.&T.]
Nalefski, Andrew T., (BV) '52 '80 C.801 B.A. L.45 J.D. 1014 Eastport Plaza Dr.
Newton, Kevin J. '75 '04 C.339 B.A. L.734 J.D. [[A] Dunham,B.&L.] ⊙
Owens, Stacie A. '74 '03 C.225 B.A. L.502 J.D.
(adm. in FL; not adm. in IL) [McMahon,B.H.L.C.&M.] ⊙
Porter, Wendy B. '56 '81 C&L.339 B.A., J.D. #2 Crestmont
Rafaelle, John B., Law Firm, (BV) '33 '60 C&L.734 J.D. 401 St. Louis Rd.
Rekowski, John J., (BV) '51 '79 C.801 B.S. L.734 J.D. [Rekowski&Assoc.]
Rekowski & Associates, (BV) 801 W. Main
Renick, John B. '45 '70 C&L.502 B.A., J.D.
(adm. in MO; not adm. in IL) [McMahon,B.H.L.C.&M.] ⊙
Richard, Douglas W., (CV) '55 '80 C.589 B.S. L.365 J.D. [Satter,B.B.&G.]
Robbins, Schwartz, Nicholas, Lifton & Taylor, Ltd., (AV)
230 Regency Ctr. (⊙Chicago, Decatur, Macomb)
Rubin, Thea F., (BV) '67 '92 C.801 B.A. L.339 J.D. 2011 Mall St.
Runge, H. Carl, Jr., (BV) '32 '62 C.293 B.A. L.966 J.D. [H.C.Runge,Jr.] ⊙
Runge, H. Carl, Jr., Ltd., Law Offices of, (BV) 1711 Keebler (⊙Greenville)
Ruth, Dennis R., (BV) '61 '86 C.191 B.S. L.734 J.D. 1014 Eastport Plaza Dr.
Sanders, Christopher M. '73 '03 C&L.734 B.S.B.A., J.D.
(adm. in MO; not adm. in IL) [[A] McMahon,B.H.L.C.&M.] ⊙
Satter, Beyer, Bertram & Gabor, (AV) 311 Collinsville Ave. (⊙Pontiac)
Schroeder, Stanley G. '52 '80 C&L.734 B.S., J.D.
(adm. in MO; not adm. in IL) [McMahon,B.H.L.C.&M.] ⊙
Smith, Sarah D. '76 '02 C.357 B.A. L.1339 J.D. [[A] Wendler&E.]
Staley, Laura B. '77 '02 C&L.502 B.A., J.D.
(adm. in MO; not adm. in IL) [[A] McMahon,B.H.L.C.&M.] ⊙
Stewart, G. Michael '65 '95 C.801 B.S. L.209 J.D. [[A] Rekowski&Assoc.]
Stewart, Robert W., (AVⓉ) '51 '75 C&L.734 B.S.C., J.D.
(adm. in MO; not adm. in IL) [McMahon,B.H.L.C.&M.] ⊙
Taylor, Dwight, (BV) '32 '58 C&L.910 LL.B. 1962 Vandalia St.
Taylor, Harvey, Jr. '77 '03 C&L.339 B.A., J.D. [[A] Dunham,B.&L.]
Thomason, Larry D., Jr. '69 '00 C&L.801 B.S., J.D. 100 Lanter Ct.
VanKavage, Elise Ann, (BV) '56 '84 C.234 B.S. L.734 J.D. 51 Odom
Welch, Paul A., (BV) '45 '70 C.339 B.S. L.502 J.D. [Welch]
Welch, Thomas M. '39 '65 C.339 B.S. L.502 J.D. Appl. Ct. J.
Welch Law Office, (BV) 1234 St. Louis Rd.
Wendler, Brian M., (AV) '61 '87 C&L.801 B.A., J.D. [Wendler&E.]
Wendler & Ezra, P.C., (AV) 850 Vandalia St., Ste. 310-320
Williams, W. Dakin, (CV) '19 '42 C&L.910 A.B., J.D. 97 Dewey Dr.‡
Winnett, R. Dan, (BV) '53 '84 C&L.801 B.A., J.D. 1711 Keebler
Wulff, Karl Joseph '67 '96 C.1291 B.A. L.615 J.D.
(adm. in MO; not adm. in IL) 1997 Vandalia
Young, Eric C., (AV) '50 '75 C.1182 B.A. L.339 J.D. [Dunham,B.&L.] ⊙
Younger, Robert D., (AVⓉ) '65 '92 C.502 B.S.B.A. L.734 J.D.
(adm. in MO; not adm. in IL) [McMahon,B.H.L.C.&M.] ⊙

COLUMBIA, 7,922, *Monroe Co.*

Adams, Tom D., (BV) '43 '68 C.291 B.S. L.734 J.D. 321 Wedgewood Sq.

Brown & Associates
(See Belleville)

Buser, Stephen C., (AV) '53 '78 C.378 B.S. L.734 J.D. [S.C.Buser]
Buser, Stephen C., Ltd., Law Office of, (AV) 108 Edelweiss Drive
Crowder, Floyd E., (AV) '33 '57 C&L.910 B.A., J.D. [Crowder&S.]

Crowder & Scoggins, Ltd., (AV)
121 West Legion Avenue, P.O. Box 167, 62236
Telephone: 618-281-7111 Fax: 618-281-7115
Email: lawyers@crowderscoggins.com URL: http://www.crowderscoggins.com
Floyd E. Crowder; Mark C. Scoggins; Mark S. Rohr; Timothy A. Gutknecht; Andrea Crowder Khoury; Gregory J. Hickel; Clay B. St. Clair.
Trial and Appellate Practice in State and Federal Courts. Personal Injury, Workers Compensation, Commercial, Banking, Municipal, Corporate, Tax, Estate Planning and Family, Criminal and Real Estate Law.
Counsel for: First Bank, Columbia; Columbia Quarry Co.; Luhr Bros., Inc.; Monroe County Title Co.; Chicago Title Co.; Illinois Excavators, Inc.; Rogers Redi-Mix, Inc.; Gateway FS, Inc.

See Professional Biographies, COLUMBIA, ILLINOIS

Gutknecht, Timothy A., (BV) '68 '93 C.31 B.A. L.910 J.D. [Crowder&S.]
Hickel, Gregory J. '73 '98 C.938 B.A. L.910 J.D. [Crowder&S.]
Khoury, Andrea Crowder '73 '98 C.734 B.A. L.910 J.D. [Crowder&S.]
Morris, Arthur W., (BV) '58 '83 C&L.734 B.S., J.D. [Traughber,R.&M.]
Reitz, Kris F., (BV) '61 '86 C&L.339 B.S., J.D. [Traughber,R.&M.]
Rohr, Mark S., (BV) '56 '81 C.1101 B.A. L.734 J.D. [Crowder&S.]
St. Clair, Clay B. '75 '00 C.999 B.S. L.910 J.D. [Crowder&S.]
Scoggins, Mark C., (AV) '52 '77 C.801 B.S. L.862 J.D. [Crowder&S.]
Stanley, Ronald D., (AV) '33 '70 C.234 B.S. L.734 J.D. 207 N. Main St.
Stumpf, Alan E., (CV) '51 '77 C.339 B.S. L.801 J.D. 222 S. Main St.
Traughber, Arlie E., (AV) '48 '73 C&L.339 B.A., J.D. [Traughber,R.&M.]
Traughber, Reitz & Morris, Ltd., (AV) 217 South Main Street

CORTLAND, 2,066, *DeKalb Co.*

Hathaway, Sarah L. '49 '74 C.238 B.A. L.280 J.D. Power Equipment Co.

COUNTRY CLUB HILLS, 16,169, *Cook Co.*

Ruffin, Trina K. '70 '99 C.1365 B.A. L.1000 J.D. 18055 Lavergne Avenue
Ward, James J. '34 '59 C&L.424 B.S., J.D. 17974 Amherst Ct.‡

COUNTRYSIDE, 5,991, *Cook Co.*

Bushmaker, Larry W. '48 '73 C.927 B.A. L.209 J.D.
Midwest Operating Engrs. Fringe Benefit Funds
Dvorak, Edwin A. '12 '35 L.146 LL.B. 6660 Brainard Ave.
Klocke, Wayne M. '52 '79
C&L.352 B.G.S., J.D. Ill. Fraternal Order of Pol. Labor Council
Przyborski, Thomas G. '18 '47 C.393 L.365 J.D. 6700 S. Brainard Ave. #329‡
Wilson, James T. '20 '50 C.385 A.B. L.597 J.D. [Wilson&W.]
Wilson, William S. '54 '83 C.846 B.A. L.597 J.D. [Wilson&W.]
Wilson & Wilson Law Offices
1023 W. 55th St. (⊙Redwood City, CA; Enid, OK; Salt Lake City, UT)

CRESTWOOD, 11,251, *Cook Co.*

Craig, Barbara J., Law Office of '72 '03
C.801 B.S. L.823 J.D. 12817 Carriage Lane, Suite 6

CRETE, 7,346, *Will Co.*

Blair, W. Robert '30 '54 C&L.923 A.B., LL.B. 1406 Main
Bransky, Philip L., (AV) '35 '61 C.597 B.S. L.145 J.D. 353 Milburn‡
Feeley, Raymond A., (BV) '47 '73 C.339 B.S. L.365 J.D. [R.A.Feeley]
Feeley, Raymond A., Ltd., (BV) 575 W. Exchange
Hobbs, Richard A. '50 '88 C.999 B.A. L.381 J.D. [R.A.Hobbs]
Hobbs, Richard A., P.C. 1395 C Main
Lantz, Leanne M., (BV) '56 '84 C.424 B.A. L.209 J.D. 1008 N. Main St. (⊙Joliet)
Mierzwa, Frederick S. '47 '73 C.339 B.S. L.146 J.D. [F.S.Mierzwa]
Mierzwa, Fred S. 26538 S. Murray Drive
Page, Kimberly M. '— '94 C.339 B.S.N. L.879 J.D. 23827 S. Candice Ct.
Rosiek-Cardin, Mary E., (CV) '56 '82 C.339 B.A. L.46 J.D. 1008 N. Main St.
Schwieters, Janet L. '47 '96 C.494 B.A. L.209 J.D. 1328 Main St.
Teykl, James S. '54 '80 C.339 B.A. L.597 J.D. [J.S.Teykl]
Teykl, James S., P.C., Law Offices of P.O. Box 283
VanDrunen, Linda Rietveld '66 '91 C.210 B.A. L.347 J.D. 1755 Rietveld Drive

CREVE COEUR, 5,448, *Tazewell Co.*

Anderson, William M., IV, (CV) '53 '78 C.894 B.A. L.734 J.D. [Anderson]
Anderson Law Offices, (CV) 625 S. Main
Reardon, Carl F., (BV) '38 '65 C&L.339 A.B., LL.B. [[B] Anderson]
Wilhelm, Kenneth A., (BV) '51 '79 C&L.209 B.A., J.D. 304 Rainbow Dr.

CRYSTAL LAKE, 38,000, *McHenry Co.*

Alexander, Meaghan '78 '04 C.187 B.A. L.589 J.D. [[A] Campion,C.D.&L.]
Arado, Thomas D. '68 '01 C.879 B.A. L.589 J.D. [[A] Campion,C.D.&L.]
Attapit, Sirat K. '76 '02 C.339 B.S. L.146 J.D. [[B] Matuszewich K.&M.]
Baranko, Thomas W. '69 '94 C.679 B.A. L.879 J.D.
(adm. in IN; not adm. in IL) V.P. & Trust Off., Home State Bk. N.A.
Barrett, Michael T. '64 '89 C&L.589 B.S., J.D. [M.T.Barrett]
Barrett, Michael T., P.C., Law Offices of 20 North Walkup Ave.
Bishop, James F., (BV) '40 '66 C.1024 B.S. L.146 J.D. [Bishop,J.F.&Assoc.]
Bishop, James F. & Associates, James F. Bishop & Associates, (BV)
550 Woodstock Street
Blackwell, Susan Cullen '53 '89 C.589 B.A. L.845 J.D.
(adm. in TX; not adm. in IL) 4517 Amy Dr.

Brewer, Donald R., (AV) '44 '74 C.352 B.S.E.E. L.365 J.D. [BB]
10 W. Terra Cotta Avenue, 60014
Telephone: 815-356-6900 Fax: 815-459-1573
Email: luvtojogsz@aol.com, URL: http://www.mchenryinjurylaw.com
Personal Injury including Catastrophic Injury, Wrongful Death, Automobile Accidents and Injuries, Head, Neck and Back Injury, Brain Injuries. Medical Malpractice including Failure to Diagnose or

(This Listing Continued)

Brewer, Donald R. (Continued)

Misdiagnosis, Hospital Malpractice, Nursing Malpractice, Birth Trauma, Obstetric Malpractice, Nursing Home Abuse and Neglect, Elder Abuse, Malnutrition and Dehydration. Verbal and Sexual Abuse, Assault, Medication Errors and Burns, Products Liability, Defective Products and Patent Litigation.

See Professional Biographies, CRYSTAL LAKE, ILLINOIS

Briscoe, Cynthia J., (BV) .... '61 '84 C.340 B.S. L.589 J.D. [Briscoe]
Briscoe Law Office, (BV) .... 210 N. Walkup Ave.
Brody, Steven J. .... '61 '91 C.36 B.S. L.424 J.D. [S.J.Brody&Assoc.]

Brody, Steven J., & Associates, LTD
101 N. Virginia Street Suite 110, 60014
Telephone: 815-479-8800 Fax: 815-479-8880 URL: http://www.sjbrodylaw.com
Email: steve@sjbrodylaw.com URL: http://www.stevenjbrody.com
Steven J. Brody.
Family Law including Divorce, Separation Agreements, Child Custody, Child Support, Visitation Rights, Spousal Support, Restraining Orders, Paternity, Adoptions, Pre-nuptial / post-nuptial Agreements, Bankruptcy including Chapter 7 & 13, Consumer Bankruptcy, Small Business Bankruptcy, Foreclosures, Repossessions.

See Professional Biographies, CRYSTAL LAKE, ILLINOIS

Bruning, Kevin W. .... '61 '88 C.424 B.A. L.209 J.D. [Bruning&Assoc.]
Bruning & Associates, P.C. .... 333 Commerce Dr., Ste. 900
Callas, Perry G., (BV) .... '29 '51 C&L.339 B.S., J.D. 108 N. Walkup Ave.
Campbell, Raymond W. '52 '80 C.592 B.A. L.602 J.D.
(adm. in IN; not adm. in IL; Pat.) Patent Counsel, Beloit Corporation
Campion, James A., (AV) .... '47 '72 C.746 B.A. L.597 J.D. [Campion,C.D.&L.]

Campion, Curran, Dunlop & Lamb, P.C., (AV)
8600 US Highway 14, Suite 201, 60012
Telephone: 815-459-8440 Fax: 815-455-8134
Email: contact@ccdllaw.com URL: http://www.ccdllaw.com
James A. Campion; Daniel F. Curran; Charles A. Dunlop; Cynthia D. Lamb;—Lee C. Lockwood; Thomas A. Vaclavek; Lori E. Fulton; Thomas D. Arado; Meaghan Alexander.
General Practice, Corporate Law, Trusts and Estate, Real Estate Law, Zoning, Planning and Land Use, Criminal Law, Appellate Practice, Insurance, Family Law, Labor and Employment, Administrative Law, Environmental Law, Personal Injury, Workers Compensation.

See Professional Biographies, CRYSTAL LAKE, ILLINOIS

Capuzzi, Michael A., Law Offices of '64 '93 C.37 B.A. L.1148 J.D.
6314 N. Wyndwood Drive (⊙Las Vegas, NV)
Carlson, John S., (BV①) .... '51 '79 C.966 B.A. L.838 J.D. 111 Erick St., Ste. 105
Carrol, Thomas J. .... '63 '88 C.352 B.S. L.209 J.D. 50 Virginia St.
Carroll, Thomas J. .... '60 '88 C.720 B.A. L.146 J.D. 10 W. Terra Cotta Ave.

Carroll & Carroll
(See Woodstock)

Clark, Charles W., (BV) .... '54 '80 C.746 B.A. L.365 J.D. [Clark&M.]
Clark & McArdle, P.C., (BV) .... 75 E. Crystal Lake Ave.
Coen, Patrick D., (BV) .... '51 '76 C.602 B.A. L.339 J.D. [Militello,Z.&C.]
Coonen, Martin J., (BV) .... '59 '84 C.352 B.A. L.339 J.D. [Coonen&R.]
Coonen & Roth, Ltd., (BV) .... 454 W. Virginia St.
Cooney, Melissa J., (BV) .... '48 '91 C.381 B.G.S. L.339 J.D. [Zukowski,R.F.&M.]
Coppedge, Michael E., (BV) .... '62 '87 C.719 B.A. L.589 J.D. [Cowlin,N.C.&C.]
Covey, Robert O. .... '21 '48 C.966 B.A. L.597 J.D. 467 Crystal Lake Ave.‡
Cowlin, John L., (AV) .... '37 '68 C.477 B.A. L.912 J.D. [Cowlin,N.C.&C.]
Cowlin, William J., (BV) .... '31 '56 C&L.477 B.B.A., J.D. [W.J.Cowlin]
Cowlin, Naughton, Curran & Coppedge, (AV) .... 20 Grant Street
Cowlin, William J., Law Offices of, (BV) .... 41 N. Virginia St.
Curran, Daniel F., (BV) .... '49 '74 C.424 B.B.A. L.209 J.D. [Campion,C.D.&L.]
Curran, Richard J., Jr., (BV) .... '49 '75 C.210 B.A. L.879 J.D. [Cowlin,N.C.&C.]
Dean, Edward F., (BV) .... '47 '74 C.424 B.S. L.365 J.D. 17 E. Crystal Lake Ave.
Duffy, Emery L., (BV) .... '30 '60 L.999 10 W. Terra Cotta Ave.
Dunlop, Charles A., (BV) .... '47 '81 C.591 B.A. L.365 J.D. [Campion,C.D.&L.]
Einstein, Carol Wind '53 '78 C.1111 B.A. L.326 J.D.
(adm. in TX; not adm. in IL) 9600 Partridge Lane‡

Ellis, H. Case, The Law Office of, (AV) '50 '76 C.679 B.S. L.46 J.D.
108 North Walkup Avenue, 60014
Telephone: 815-459-1001 Fax: 815-459-1249
Email: hcase@mc.net
Civil Practice, Arbitration/Mediation.

See Professional Biographies, CRYSTAL LAKE, ILLINOIS

English, Steven Gregory, (BV) .... '59 '87 C.801 B.S. L.365 J.D. 20 N. Walkup Ave.
Favaro, Dennis R. .... '61 '86 C.340 B.A. L.879 J.D. [Favaro&G.] ⊙
Favaro & Gorman, Ltd. .... 9510 Turnberry Trail (⊙Palatine)
Fisher, Christene A. .... '73 '00 C.1236 B.A. L.365 J.D. 50 N. Virginia St.
Fishman, Jack B. .... '61 '86 President, Novare, Inc.
Fishman, Jack B. & Associates, P.C. .... 824 S. Main St., Suite 202
Flood, Richard G., (AV) .... '49 '76 C.339 B.A. L.146 J.D. [Zukowski,R.F.&M.]
Fox, Robert T. .... '59 '85 C.339 B.S. L.146 J.D. Asst. Pub. Def.

Franks, Gerkin & McKenna, P.C., The Law Firm of
(See Marengo)

Franz, Donald F. .... '66 '93 C.597 B.A. L.146 J.D. [Ⓐ W.J.Cowlin]
Freund, Andrew T., (CV) .... '58 '84 C.339 B.S. L.365 J.D. 94 Dole Ave.
Fulton, Lori E. .... '58 '02 C.209 B.A. L.424 J.D. [Ⓐ Campion,C.D.&L.]
Garman, M. Edwin .... '47 '74 C.589 B.S.E. L.146 J.D. 3408 Route 176
Garry, Rita W., (BV) .... '57 '83 C.393 B.A. L.94 J.D. [Garry]

Garry Law Firm, The, PC, (BV)
27 Grant Street, 60014
Telephone: 815-356-8581 Fax: 815-356-8484
Email: rgarry@garrylaw.com URL: http://www.garrylaw.com
Rita W. Garry;—Carey E. Schulze.
Business/Corporate Law, Entity Planning Formation, Ownership Agreements, Business Transactions; Mergers/Acquisitions/Divestitures, U.S. and International Joint Ventures, Strategic Alliances and Partnerships, Commercial and Employment Contracts, Franchise Law, Conventional and SBA Financing, Private Placement Securities Law, Leasing, Commercial and Residential Real Estate Transactions, Land Use and Zoning, Estate Planning, Wills, Trusts, Probate, Business Succession Planning.

See Professional Biographies, CRYSTAL LAKE, ILLINOIS

Garry & Marek, Ltd., (BV) .... 27 Grant St.

Gervais, David R., Law Offices of, (BV) '53 '81 C.105 B.A. L.146 J.D.
4 East Terra Cotta Avenue, 60014
Telephone: 815-459-2844 815-459-2848
Email: drglaw@sbcglobal.net
Associates: Mary M.L. Spiegel; Thomas J. Leahy; David L. Stretch. Of Counsel: Scott A. Nolan.
Business Law and Contracts, Business Formation, Commercial Law and Litigation, Real Estate Law and Litigation, Municipal Law, Land Use, Zoning, Divorce, Child Custody, Child Support, Visitation Rights, Spousal Support, Post Judgment Matters, Adoption, Guardianship, Misdemeanor and Felony Criminal Defense, Traffic Matters, Estate Planning, Probate and Probate Litigation, Bankruptcy.

See Professional Biographies, CRYSTAL LAKE, ILLINOIS

Gorman, Patrick J. .... '58 '83 C.723 B.A. L.424 J.D. [Favaro&G.] ⊙
Gosch, Adrian M. .... '75 '00 C.590 B.S. L.793 J.D. [Ⓐ Militello,Z.&C.]
Gosch, Gillian .... '75 '00 C.493 B.A. L.793 J.D. [Ⓐ Waggoner]
Gottemoller, Joseph, (BV) .... '57 '82 C.339 B.A. L.30 J.D. [Madsen,S.&G.]
Gravenor, John P. .... '45 '73 C.390 B.A. L.146 J.D. 6903 Hillcrest Dr.

Gummerson & Rausch
(See Woodstock)

Harman, Floyd B. .... '13 '46 C.46 B.S. L.146 LL.B.,J.D 406 McHenry Ave.‡
Harris, Sharon I. .... '49 '83 C&L.589 B.A., J.D. [S.I.Harris&Assoc.]
Harris, S. I., & Associates, LLC .... P.O. Box 764
Hellyer, William, (BV) .... '— '85 L.365 J.D. [W.Hellyer]
Hellyer, William, Ltd., (BV) .... 10 W. Terra Cotta Ave.

Hinshaw & Culbertson LLP, (AV)
Hinshaw & Culbertson LLP is an Illinois registered limited liability partnership that has elected to be governed by the Illinois Uniform Partnership Act (1997)
500 Coventry Lane Suite 205, 60014-7504 ⊙
Telephone: 815-459-5123 Facsimile: 815-459-5223. Telex: 880248
Email: kfox@hinshawlaw.com URL: http://www.hinshawlaw.com
Partners: Jennifer L. Johnson; Gregory T. Snyder. Associates: Matthew F. Logan; Michelle J. Rozovics; David Ian Walters. Of Counsel: William O. Shank (Also at Chicago, Illinois Office).
Appellate, Banking & Financing, Bankruptcy & Creditors' Rights, Class Action Litigation, Civil Rights Defense, Commercial Litigation, Corporate, Construction Law, Director & Officer Liability, Employee Benefits, Environmental, Fidelity & Surety, General Liability Litigation, Government, Health Care, Insurance Coverage, Insurance and Reinsurance, Labor & Employment, Legal Malpractice, Medical Malpractice, Mergers & Acquisitions, Municipal Liability, Personal Injury Defense, Public Law, Products Liability Litigation, Professional Liability, Regulatory, Real Estate, School Law, Securities, Taxation, Transportation, White Collar Crime and Workers' Compensation Defense.
Other Office Locations: Chicago, Illinois; Appleton, Wisconsin; Belleville, Illinois; Boston, Massachusetts; Champaign, Illinois; Edwardsville, Illinois; Fort Lauderdale, Florida; Jacksonville, Florida; Joliet, Illinois; Lisle, Illinois; Los Angeles, California; Miami, Florida; Milwaukee, Wisconsin; Minneapolis, Minnesota; New York, New York; Peoria, Illinois; Phoenix, Arizona; Portland, Oregon; Providence, Rhode Island; Rockford, Illinois; St. Louis, Missouri; San Francisco, California; Schererville, Indiana; Springfield, Illinois; Tampa, Florida; Waukegan, Illinois.

See Professional Biographies, CRYSTAL LAKE, ILLINOIS

Horeled, John J., (BV) .... '51 '76 C.602 B.A. L.879 J.D. 651 W. Terra Cotta Ave.
Huls, James D. .... '50 '76 C.98 B.S. L.365 J.D. 530 Rockland Road
Jackson, Richard H. .... '53 '85 C.932 B.A. L.365 J.D. 137 S. Crandall Avenue
Jerrick, Ronald M., (AV) .... '— '70 C.602 A.B. L.209 J.D. [Querrey&H.] (⊙Chicago)
Johnson, Jennifer L., (CV①) .... '— '96 C.1216 B.A. L.347 J.D. [Hinshaw&C.]
Keating-Howard, Catherine .... '44 '72 C.339 B.A. L.209 J.D. [Ⓐ Militello,Z.&C.]
Kelly, James P. .... '— '91 C.116 B.A. L.146 J.D. [Matuszewich K.&M.]
Knowlton, Harold M. .... '20 '45 C&L.966 Ph.B., J.D. 4107 Sherwood Dr.‡
Krol, Casimar T. '18 '54 C.722 B.A. L.273 LL.B.
(adm. in DC; not adm. in IL) P.O. Box 295‡
Labaj, Susan .... '52 '81 C.347 A.B. L.345 J.D. 665 Greenbrier Lane
Lamb, Cynthia D., (CV) .... '62 '88 C.339 B.A. L.209 J.D. [Campion,C.D.&L.]
Leahy, Thomas J., (BV) .... '47 '72 C.436 B.S. L.146 J.D. [Ⓐ D.R.Gervais]
Lechner, Michael J. .... '— '03 C.339 B.S. L.209 J.D. 50 Virginia St.
Lockwood, Lee C. .... '70 '99 C.123 B.A. L.209 J.D. [Ⓐ Campion,C.D.&L.]
Logan, Matthew F. .... '73 '99 C.339 B.A. L.365 J.D. [Ⓐ Hinshaw&C.]
Lowrimore, Larry .... '45 '85 C.446 B.S. L.365 J.D. V.P., Human Res., Aptargroup, Inc.
Lucas, Mia M. .... '— '93 C.259 B.S. L.208 J.D. [Querrey&H.]

Madsen, Sugden & Gottemoller, (BV)
1 North Virginia Street, 60014
Telephone: 815-459-5152 Fax: 815-459-0290
Partners: Henry H. Sugden, III; Joseph Gottemoller. Associate: Keith D. Sloan.
Real Estate Law including Land Use, Zoning, Condemnation/Eminent Domain, Commercial Real Estate, Retail Development, Real Property Issues, Criminal Defense, Felonies, Misdemeanors, White Collar Criminal Defense, Fraud, Forgery, Assault and Battery, Manslaughter, Murder, Sex Crimes, Weapons Charges, Drugs and Narcotics, Parole and Probation Issues, Driving Under the Influence (DUI), Personal Injury, Automobile Accidents and Injuries, Workers Compensation, Head, Neck, Back and Shoulder Injuries, Repetitive Stress Injuries, Products Liability/Defective Products.

See Professional Biographies, CRYSTAL LAKE, ILLINOIS

Maher, Debra M. .... '57 '84 C.339 B.A. L.209 J.D. 3210 Open Gate Rd.‡
Majewski, Jerome C., (BV) '54 '79
C.602 B.A. L.339 J.D. 101 N. Virginia Street, Suite 150
Marek, Valeree D., (BV) .... '58 '83 C.957 B.B.A. L.146 J.D. [Garry&M.]
Matthews, Douglas E. .... '53 '86 C.371 B.A. L.966 J.D. 50 Virginia St.
Matuszewich, Lewis F., (AV) .... '— '66 C.210 B.A. L.597 J.D. [Matuszewich K.&M.] ⊙
Matuszewich Kelly & Mckeever, LLP, (AV) ... 453 Coventry Lane, Suite 104 (⊙Chicago)
McArdle, David W., (BV) .... '56 '81 C.347 A.B. L.365 J.D. [Zukowski,R.F.&M.]
McArdle, Steven J., (BV) .... '55 '80 C.965 B.S. L.339 J.D. [Clark&M.]
McGrath, Joseph D. .... '42 '68 C.378 B.A. L.276 J.D. 238 Lincolnshire Dr.‡
McKeever, Maura K. .... '— '90 C.602 B.A. L.93 J.D. [Ⓒ Matuszewich K.&M.]
Melei, Samuel S. .... '74 '99 C.93 B.A. L.209 J.D. 454 W. Virginia St.

Michling Hofmann Vinton Plaza & Wick, P.C.
(See Woodstock)

Militello, James G., (AV) .... '43 '68 C.436 B.S.B.A. L.209 J.D. [Militello,Z.&C.]
Militello, James G., III, (BV) .... '66 '91 C.436 B.S. L.365 J.D. [Militello,Z.&C.]

Militello, Zanck & Coen, P.C., (AV) BR
40 Brink Street, 60014
Telephone: 815-459-8800 FAX: 815-459-8429
URL: http://www.mzc.com
James G. Militello; Thomas C. Zanck; Patrick D. Coen; James L. Wright; Mark S. Saladin; James G. Militello, III;—Nancy Stingle Perkoski; David G. Phoenix; Jill J. Struck; Catherine Keating-Howard; Jeremy W. Shaw; Adrian M. Gosch.
Trial Practice in all State and Federal Courts, Banking, Business Acquisitions, Corporation and Partnership, Employment Law, Environmental, Insurance Defense, Probate and Guardianship, Real Estate, Wills and Trusts and Zoning and Land Planning.
References: American Community Bank & Trust; Home State Bank of Crystal Lake.

See Professional Biographies, CRYSTAL LAKE, ILLINOIS

Miller, Jeanne M. .... '— '98 C.530 B.A. L.424 J.D. [Ⓐ Querrey&H.]
Moreau Newby, Rachel Anne .... '77 '03 C&L.352 B.A., J.D. [R.A.MoreauNewby]
Moreau Newby, Rachel A., The Law Offices of .... 481 Windham Cove Dr.
Mueller, George A., & Associates, (BV) '56 '81 C.339 B.A. L.209 J.D.
101 N. Virginia St.
Mueller, Venus D., (BV) .... '56 '83 C.339 A.B. L.209 J.D. 1 N. Virginia St.
Murphy, Maureen T. .... '64 '91 C.602 B.A.B.S. L.209 J.D. 50 Virginia St.
Naughton, Richard P., (P.C.), (BV) .... '47 '72 C.597 B.A. L.209 J.D. [Cowlin,N.C.&C.]
Nolan, Scott A., (BV) .... '50 '80 C.339 B.A. L.365 J.D. [Ⓒ D.R.Gervais]
Paluch, Doreen T., (BV) .... '66 '91 C&L.339 A.B., J.D. [Ⓐ C.P.Rehberg]

Payton, Garry A., Law Offices of
(See Waukegan)

Perbohner, Julene M., (CV) '63 '88 C.339 B.A. L.146 J.D.
60B W. Terra Cotta Ave., #281

Phoenix, David G., (BV) '64 '89 C.339 B.A. L.589 J.D. [Ⓐ Militello,Z.&C.]
Pitluck, Haskell M. '42 '67 C&L.352 B.A., J.D. Cir. J.‡

Pollock, Meyers, Eickstaedt & Pulak, Ltd.
(See Marengo)

Prather, Ronald W. '50 '75 C&L.802 B.A., J.D. Pres., Prudential First Realty

Querrey & Harrow, Ltd., (AV)
651 West Terra Cotta Avenue, Suite 221, 60014 ⊙
Telephone: 815-479-1929 Fax: 815-479-1978
Email: rjerrick@querrey.com URL: http://www.querrey.com
Ronald M. Jerrick; Mia M. Lucas (Resident);—Jeanne M. Miller.
General Practice and Trial Practice.
Chicago, Illinois Office: 175 West Jackson Boulevard, Suite 1600. Telephone: 312-540-7000. Fax: 312-540-0578.
Wheaton, Illinois Office: 310 South County Farm Road, Third Floor. Telephone: 630-653-2600. Fax: 630-653-0178.
Waukegan, Illinois Office: 415 West Washington Street, Suite 205. Telephone: 847-249-4440. Fax: 847-249-4932.
Joliet, Illinois Office: 2 Rialto Square, Suite 401, 116 North Chicago Street. Telephone: 815-726-1600. Fax: 815-726-1674.
Merrillville, Indiana Office: 8585 Broadway, Suite 510. Telephone: 219-738-1820. Fax: 219-738-1821.
New York, N.Y. Office: 120 Broadway, Suite 2800. Telephone: 212-233-0130. Fax: 212-233-0172.
London, England Office: 141-142 Fenchurch Street, Fifth Floor. Telephone: 207-929-6670. Fax: 207-929-6671.
See Professional Biographies, CRYSTAL LAKE, ILLINOIS

Reder, Kathleen V. E. '69 '97 C.108 B.F.A. L.209 J.D. 201 Ridge Ave.★

Rehberg, Curt P., (BV) '64 '89 C.234 B.A. L.589 J.D.
64 East Terra Cotta Avenue, 60014
Telephone: 815-444-1050 Fax: 815-444-1060
URL: http://www.rehberglawoffice.com
Associate: Doreen T. Paluch.
Real Estate, including Commercial and Residential, Contracts, Closings, Land Acquisition and Sales, Land Trusts, Development, Investment, Joint Ventures, Partnerships; Wills, Trusts and Estate Planning, including Family Trusts, Living Trusts, Powers of Attorney, Business Succession Planning, Retirement Planning, Wealth Preservation; Business Law, including Contracts, Business Formation, Sole Proprietorships, Partnerships, Business Incorporation, Joint Ventures, Business Fraud, Buy-Sell Agreements.
See Professional Biographies, CRYSTAL LAKE, ILLINOIS

Robertson, Phillip J. '67 '92 C.436 B.A.J. L.589 J.D. 8600 Rte. 14, Ste. 201
Rodriguez, Richard R. '66 '97 C.1086 B.A. L.589 J.D. 210 N. Walkup Avenue
Rogers, H. David, (AV) '42 '69 C&L.802 B.B.A., J.D. [Zukowski,R.F.&M.]
Rosenberg, James E., (CV) '46 '82 C.338 B.A. L.365 J.D. 11 W. Paddock St.
Rosenthal, Rhonda L. '69 '95 C.436 B.A. L.589 J.D. [R.L.Rosenthal]
Rosenthal, Rhonda L., P.C. 20 N. Walkup Ave.
Roth, Jason A. '76 '03 C.98 B.S. L.589 J.D. 454 W. Virginia St.
Rozovics, Michelle J. '71 '96 C&L.477 A.B., J.D. [Ⓐ Hinshaw&C.]
Saladin, Mark S., (BV) '58 '83 C.750 B.A. L.365 J.D. [Militello,Z.&C.]
Santeler, John Jeremy '69 '00 C.589 B.A. L.365 J.D. 454 W. Virginia St.
Schmidt, Ryan J., (CV) '72 '97 C.57 B.A. L.209 J.D. [Cowlin,N.C.&C.]
Schulze, Carey E. '77 '02 C.589 B.S. L.146 J.D. [Ⓐ Garry]
Shank, Karen B. '51 '80 C.632 B.M. L.1243 J.D. 1006 Sheffield Dr.‡
Shank, William O., (AV) '24 '51 C.473 A.B. L.976 J.D. [Ⓒ Hinshaw&C.] (⊙Chicago)
Shaw, Jeremy W. '75 '02 C.123 B.A. L.221 J.D. [Ⓐ Militello,Z.&C.]
Sherman, John Howland, (AV) '25 '53 C.453 B.S. L.146 LL.B. 707 Bedford Dr. (Pat.)‡
Simko, John M., (BV) '51 '76 C.145 B.A. L.424 J.D. 6210 Lou Ave.
Sloan, Keith D. '70 '05 C.679 B.A. L.589 J.D. [Ⓐ Madsen,S.&G.]
Smoron, Michael J., (BV) '66 '91 C.602 B.A. L.146 J.D. [Zukowski,R.F.&M.]
Snyder, Gregory T., (BV) '59 '93 C.801 B.S. L.209 J.D. [Hinshaw&C.]
Spiegel, Mary M.L. '66 '92 C.741 B.A. L.879 J.D. [Ⓐ D.R.Gervais]
Spiesman, Audrey '56 '86 C.966 B.A. L.424 J.D. 1484 Blue Heron Dr.
Stingle Perkoski, Nancy, (CV) '71 '96 C.352 B.B.A. L.879 J.D. [Ⓐ Militello,Z.&C.]
Stretch, David L. '46 '78 C.976 B.A. L.1065 J.D. [Ⓐ D.R.Gervais]
Struck, Jill J. '72 '00 C.36 B.A. L.209 J.D. [Ⓐ Militello,Z.&C.]
Sugden, Henry H., III, (BV) '49 '75 C.36 B.S. L.365 J.D. [Madsen,S.&G.]
Thoms, Jeannine A., (BV) '— '84 C.589 B.A. L.146 J.D. [Zukowski,R.F.&M.]
Torchalski, Michael J., Law Office of, (BV) '55 '81
C.339 B.A. L.146 J.D. 820 E. Terra Cotta Ave., Ste. 207
Ungvarsky, Michael A., Jr., (AV) '44 '68 C.602 B.B.A. L.424 J.D. 40 Brink Street‡
Vaclavek, Thomas A. '74 '00 C.37 B.S. L.146 J.D. [Ⓐ Campion,C.D.&L.]
Vineyard, Wendi N. '— '03 C.556 B.A. L.589 J.D. [Ⓐ Matuszewich K.&M.]
Waggoner, David L., (BV) '50 '76 C.350 B.S. L.146 J.D. [Waggoner]
Waggoner, Gregory L., (BV) '52 '77 C.352 B.A. L.190 J.D. [Waggoner]
Waggoner, Lisa M., (BV) '58 '86 C.1016 B.S. L.145 J.D. [Waggoner]
Waggoner Law Firm, The, P.C., (BV) 4 N. Walkup Ave.
Walters, Barbara J., (AV) '28 '69 C.911 B.A. L.436 J.D. 101 N. Virginia Street
Walters, David Ian '74 '02 C.123 B.A. L.209 J.D. [Ⓐ Hinshaw&C.]
Weber, Gary '46 '73 C.589 B.A. L.424 J.D. 651 W. Terra Cotta Ave.
Whitlock, Holly C., (CV) '71 '97 C.57 B.A. L.589 J.D. 64 E. Crystal Lake Ave.
Wilbrandt, Laurence A., (BV) '52 '86 C.339 B.U.P. L.365 J.D. [Ⓐ R.A.Wilbrandt]
Wilbrandt, Robert A., (BV) '50 '75 C.339 B.A. L.597 J.D. [R.A.Wilbrandt]
Wilbrandt, Robert A., Sr. '17 '42 C.339 A.B. L.209 J.D. [R.A.Wilbrandt,Sr.] ‡
Wilbrandt, Robert A., Ltd., (BV) 65 S. Virginia St.
Wilbrandt, Robert A., Sr., Ltd. 65 S. Virginia St.
Wright, James L., (AV) '55 '80 C&L.339 B.A., J.D. [Militello,Z.&C.]
Zambon, James J. '46 '71 C&L.436 B.S., J.D.
(adm. in WI; not adm. in IL) Sr. V.P. & Tr. Offr., Home State Bk. N.A.
Zanck, Thomas C., (AV) '44 '68 C.177 B.A. L.276 J.D. [Militello,Z.&C.]
Zukowski, Edwin F., (AV) '13 '36 C&L.145 A.B., J.D. 50 Virginia St.

Zukowski, Rogers, Flood & McArdle, (AV) BB
50 Virginia Street, 60014-4126
Telephone: 815-459-2050 Facsimile: 815-459-9057
Email: zrfm@stans.com URL: http://www.zrfmlaw.com
Partners: H. David Rogers; Richard G. Flood; David W. McArdle; Jeannine A. Thoms; Melissa J. Cooney; Michael J. Smoron.
General Practice, Banking and Finance, Bankruptcy, Commercial, Construction, Corporation, Environmental, Family, Government, Insurance, Labor and Employment, Litigation, Personal Injury and Torts, Probate, Trust and Estate, Real Property, Vehicle Warranty, Fraud Litigation.
See Professional Biographies, CRYSTAL LAKE, ILLINOIS

DANVILLE, * 33,828, *Vermilion Co.*

Anderson, Curtis A., (BV) '51 '79 C.98 B.S. L.285 J.D. [C.A.Anderson]
Anderson, Curtis A., P.C., (BV) 7 E. Harrison St.

Asher, Smith & Isaf
(See Paris)

Barney, Edwin C., Jr. '74 '99 C.1101 B.A. L.734 J.D. [Saikley,G.C.&B.]
Bergschneider, Gaye Ann, (CV) '54 '79 C.1105 B.A. L.734 J.D. Asst. Pub. Def.
Blakely, Steven L., (CV) '64 '91 C.210 B.A. L.1119 J.D. 11 E. North St.

Blan, Kennith William, Jr., (BV) '46 '72 C&L.339 B.S., J.D.
712 West Fairchild Street, P.O. Box 1995, 61834-1995
Telephone: 217-443-5400 Facsimile: 217-443-5155
Email: ken@blanlaw.com URL: http://www.blanlaw.com
Medical and Legal Malpractice and Personal Injury, Negligence, and Worker's Compensation Law.
Reference: Old National Bank.

Borbely, James K. '47 '72 C&L.339 A.B., J.D. Assoc. Cir. J.
Bott, Wilford L. '54 '94 C.338 B.S.N. L.801 J.D. [Ⓐ Doyle&L.]
Brittingham, Francis M., (AV) '21 '47 C&L.339 A.B., J.D. 415 N. Gilbert St.
Brougher, James L., (BV) '43 '72 C.679 B.S. L.502 J.D. [Kesler,L.G.B.L.&T.]
Brown, Daniel D., (CV) '56 '84 C.927 B.S. L.365 J.D. [D.Brown]
Brown, Daniel, Law Office of, (CV) 819 Sherman
Christoff, Mark S. '62 '90 C&L.347 B.S., J.D. [Kapella&C.]
Clapper, Jeffrey K., (BV) '49 '77 C.338 B.S. L.365 J.D. [Clapper&C.]
Clapper, Kerry R., (BV) '54 '83 C.338 B.S. L.365 J.D. [Clapper&C.]
Clapper & Clapper, Professional Corporation, (BV) 15B East Liberty Lane
Clary, Michael D., (CV) '54 '79 C.339 B.S. L.801 J.D. Co. Ct. J.
Colombo, Kevin M., (BV) '53 '82 C.339 B.A. L.146 J.D. [Saikley,G.C.&B.]
Davis, Jerry A., (BV) '46 '74 C.339 B.A. L.8 J.D. [Davis&D.]
Davis & Delanois, P.C., (BV) 800 Oak St.
DeArmond, Craig H., (BV) '50 '75 C.352 B.A. L.365 J.D. Cir.J.
Delanois, Barbara L. '55 '91 C.234 B.S. L.801 J.D. [Davis&D.]
Devens, Charles J., (BV) '52 '77 C&L.339 B.A., J.D. [Manion,D.M.S.&S.] ⊙

Dobbins, Fraker, Tennant, Joy & Perlstein, A Professional Corporation
(See Champaign)

Donahue, William T., (BV) '57 '83 C.339 A.B. L.209 J.D.
1133 N. Walnut, 61832
Telephone: 217-446-6403 217-446-6403
Email: bill@donahueweb.com URL: http://www.donahueweb.com
General Practice. Juvenile, Adoption, Criminal Law, Personal Injury, Labor and Employment, Business Law and Civil Rights. Wills.
See Professional Biographies, DANVILLE, ILLINOIS

Doyle, Richard J., (BV) '40 '69 C.1191 B.A. L.146 J.D. [Doyle&L.] ⊙
Doyle & Lehman, P.C., (BV) 1022 North Vermilion Street (⊙Hoopeston)
Dukes, Carroll W., (AV) '30 '59 C.234 B.S. L.1017 J.D. [Ⓒ Dukes,R.M.F.F.&G.]
Dukes, Ryan, Meyer, Fahey, Freed & Goodwin, Ltd., (BV) 146 Vermilion
Fahey, Thomas J. '42 '73 C.98 B.S. L.146 J.D. Cir. J.
Foreman, Jonathan W. '70 '97 C.188 B.S. L.338 J.D. [Ⓐ Doyle&L.]
Freed, Kelly M., (CV) '56 '94 C.338 B.S. L.589 J.D. [Dukes,R.M.F.F.&G.]
Garman, Gill M., (BV) '43 '68 C.339 B.A. L.352 J.D. [Kesler,L.G.B.L.&T.]
Garrison, William L., (AV) '42 '67 C&L.339 A.B., J.D. [Saikley,G.C.&B.]
Gerlach, Bradley C. '59 '84 C.589 B.A. L.365 J.D. Asst. States Atty.
Girton, Derek J., (BV) '63 '93 C.645 B.S. L.607 J.D. [Ⓐ Smith,M.M.&O.]
Hall, Charles C., (AV) '47 '73 C.339 A.B. L.37 J.D. [Hall]
Hall Law Firm, (AV) 1018 North Vermilion Street
Hubbard, Fred L., (BV) '40 '63 C&L.339 B.S., J.D. 16 W. Madison Street
Hussmann Rogers, Liya J. '73 '00 C.98 B.S. L.365 J.D. [Ⓐ Kesler,L.G.B.L.&T.]
Jacobs, Darrel D., (BVⓉ) '38 '68 C.136 B.A. L.912 J.D. 417 W. Conron Avenue
Jenkins, John B., (AV) '36 '61 C&L.339 B.S., J.D. 15 Westwood Pl.‡
Johnson, Nancy S., (CV) '57 '88 C.340 B.A. L.801 J.D. [Dukes,R.M.F.F.&G.]
Kapella, Arthur J., (BV) '56 '81 C.1151 B.A. L.365 J.D. [Kapella&C.]
Kapella & Christoff, (BV) 419 N. Gilbert St.
Kesler, Robert E. '28 '52 C&L.339 B.S., LL.B. 2002 N. Gilbert St.‡
Kesler, William R., (AV) '28 '52 C&L.339 B.S., J.D. [Kesler,L.G.B.L.&T.]
Kesler, Laury, Garman, Brougher, Lietz & Townsley P.C., (AV) 220 N. Vermilion
Kirk, David H., (BV) '44 '75 C.339 B.S.B.A. L.365 J.D. 1022 Vermilion St.
Krapf, Alan F., (BV) '59 '86 C.339 B.S. L.796 J.D. First Appraisal Co. of Danville, Inc.
Kurth, Richard F., (CV) '49 '77 C.108 B.S. L.1194 J.D. [Kurth]
Kurth Law Office, (CV) P.O. Box 746
Lakey, Randy A. '67 '92 C.679 B.A. L.190 J.D. Asst. State's Atty.
Laury, Everett L., (AV) '32 '59 C.210 A.B. L.597 J.D. [Kesler,L.G.B.L.&T.]
Lehman, Mark A. '57 '97 C.054 B.A. L.339 J.D. [Doyle&L.]
Lietz, Gregory G., (BV) '47 '73 C.339 B.S. L.502 J.D. [Kesler,L.G.B.L.&T.]
Manion, Paul T., (BV) '40 '64 C.602 B.B.A. L.209 J.D. [Manion,D.M.S.&S.] ⊙
Manion, Devens, McFetridge, Spiros & Schum, Ltd., (BV)
24 E. North St. (⊙Hoopeston)

Marszalek, John E.
(See Chicago)

Martin, John F., (BV) '47 '72 C.210 B.A. L.339 J.D. [Meachum&M.]
McFetridge, John D., (BV) '50 '78 C.57 B.A. L.339 J.D. [Manion,D.M.S.&S.] ⊙
McNamara, William B., (BV) '37 '63 C&L.966 B.B.A., LL.B. 414 West North St.
Meachum, Bruce, (AV) '49 '76 C&L.339 B.A., J.D. [Meachum&M.]
Meachum, Clyde, (AV) '20 '48 C.338 B.Ed L.339 J.D. [Meachum&M.]
Meachum & Martin, (AV) 110 N. Vermilion Street
Mellen, Thomas J., II, (BV) '45 '71 C.388 B.A. L.339 J.D. 1020 Vermilion St.
Merlie, Donald L., (BV) '22 '51 C&L.339 B.S., LL.B. [Merlie&M.]
Merlie, Michael J., (BV) '49 '74 C.339 B.A. L.221 J.D. [Merlie&M.]
Merlie & Merlie, (BV) 114 N. Walnut St.
Meyer, Christopher P., (CV) '54 '85 C.339 B.S. L.589 J.D. [Dukes,R.M.F.F.&G.]
Meyer, John P., (AV) '20 '47 C&L.602 B.S., LL.B. 809 1/2 N. Gilbert St.
Meyer, Thomas B., (BV) '44 '69 C.473 B.A. L.424 J.D. [Smith,M.M.&O.]
Miles, Terrence, (CV) '61 '88 C.1024 B.A. L.1187 J.D. [Ⓐ Smith,M.M.&O.]
Miller, Phillip S., (BV) '49 '74 C.338 B.S. L.339 J.D. [Smith,M.M.&O.]
Mockbee, Charles D., III, (BV) '47 '75 C.589 B.S. L.365 J.D. 711 N. Gilbert St.
Mulholland, Frank M. '72 '02 C.801 B.S. L.339 J.D. [Ⓐ Manion,D.M.S.&S.] ⊙
O'Brien, Michael J., (BV) '48 '73 C&L.339 B.A., J.D. 15 N. Vermilion
O'Rourke, John P. '33 '61 C.707 B.A. L.276 J.D. Cir. J.‡
O'Shaughnessy, Thomas M., (BV) '57 '82 C.894 A.B. L.801 J.D. [Smith,M.M.&O.]
Parker, Leon S. '61 '98 C.1128 B.S. L.1187 J.D. [Young&P.]
Pea, Janice Farrell '49 '97 C&L.339 B.S., J.D. Law Clk., Ct. App.
Peck, Judd C. '54 '78 C.338 B.S. L.339 J.D. Pres., Danville Metal Stamping Co., Inc.

Phebus & Koester
(See Urbana)

Phipps, John T., Law Offices, P.C.
(See Champaign)

Quigley, Charlene A., (CV) '53 '80 C.927 B.S. L.339 J.D. Staff Atty., U.S.Dist. Cts.
Ryan, David J., (BV) '51 '76 C.424 A.B. L.339 J.D. [Dukes,R.M.F.F.&G.]
Saikley, Gilbert H., (AV) '48 '73 C&L.339 B.S., J.D. [Saikley,G.C.&B.]

Saikley, Garrison, Colombo & Barney, LLC, (AV)
208 West North Street, P.O. Box 6, 61834-0006
Telephone: 217-442-0244 Fax: 217-442-0582
Email: sgclaw@sbcglobal.net
Albert Saikley (1912-1987); William L. Garrison; Gilbert H. Saikley; Kevin M. Colombo; Edwin C. Barney, Jr.

(This Listing Continued)

Saikley, Garrison, Colombo & Barney, LLC (Continued)

General Civil Practice. Tort, Bankruptcy, Commercial, Corporation, Taxation, Probate, Real Estate, Domestic Relations and Criminal Law.
References: First Midwest Bank; Old National Bank; First National Bank of Danville.

See Professional Biographies, DANVILLE, ILLINOIS

Schiro, Nicholas M., (BV) '62 '90 C.357 B.A. L.300 J.D. [Tuggle&S.]
Schum, Todd E., (BV) '61 '87 C.339 B.S. L.801 J.D. [Manion,D.M.S.&S.] ⊙
Simpson, Deborah L. '58 '84 C.209 B.A. L.365 J.D. 1st Asst. States Atty.
Skowronski, Joseph P., Jr. '44 '69 C&L.339 A.B., J.D. Assoc. Cir. J.
Smith, Thomas R., (AV) '39 '64 C.210 A.B. L.339 LL.B. [Smith,M.M.&O.]
Smith, Timothy O., Law Offices, (BV) '48 '73 C&L.339 A.B., J.D. 2 E. Main St.
Smith, Meyer, Miller & O'Shaughnessy, (AV) 11 E. N. St.
Solava, Lawrence T. '65 '97 C.209 B.A. L.365 J.D. Asst. States Atty.
Stepke, Kenneth E., Law Office of, (CV) '50 '76 C&L.339 B.S., J.D. 1007 1/2 N. Vermilion
Thorlton, Timothy J. '58 '85 C.234 B.A. L.879 J.D. Law Clk., U.S. Bkrptcy. J.
Townsley, William L., (BV) '42 '74 C.339 B.S. L.365 J.D. [Kesler,L.G.B.L.&T.]
Tuggle, David A., (BV) '64 '91 C&L.339 B.A., J.D. [Tuggle&S.]
Tuggle & Schiro, (BV) 616 North Vermilion
Underhill, Frederick H., Jr., (BV) '46 '72 C.228 A.B. L.339 J.D. 414 West North St.
Wolgamot, John P., (AV) '44 '74 C.339 B.A. L.365 J.D. 11 E. North St.
Wright, M. Eugene, Law Office of, (BV) '41 '67 C.234 B.S. L.861 J.D. 211 N. Walnut St.
Young, William A., (BV) '32 '58 C&L.339 B.S., J.D. [Young&P.]
Young & Parker, (BV) 408 North Vermilion Street

DARIEN, 22,860, *DuPage Co.*

Claes, Robert M. '51 '76 C.1082 B.A. L.424 J.D. 1306 Plainfield Rd.
Cotter, William J., (AV) '52 '78 C.679 B.A. L.209 J.D. [Cotter&Assoc.]
Cotter & Associates, LLC, (AV) 8182 South Cass Avenue
Crifase, Philip A. '24 '51 7623 Sussex Creek Dr.
Douvas, Augustus G. '23 '49 C.546 B.S. L.309 LL.B. 1606 Coachmans Rd.
Forgue, Charles F. '16 '55 C.999 L.365 LL.B. 714 Walnut Dr., #110‡
Glimco, Joseph P., III '60 '85 C.221 L.707 J.D. 8340 Lemont Rd.
Kellough, Berner '20 '53 C.238 B.A. L.209 LL.B. 1614 Old Oak Pl.
Klumpner, George H. '47 '74 C.145 B.A. L.365 J.D. 1617 Holly Ave.
Marshall, Katherine A. '65 '94 C.178 B.A. L.424 J.D. [Ⓐ M.Overmann]
McKay, Paula F. '58 '85 C.700 B.A. L.146 J.D. 1409 Darien Club Dr.
Overmann, Michael '66 '95 C.679 B.S. L.734 J.D. [M.Overmann]

Overmann, Michael, Ltd.
7702 South Cass Avenue, Suite 135, 60561
Telephone: 630-810-0316 Fax: 630-810-1984
Email: molawltd@aol.com URL: http://www.lawyers.com/overmann
Michael Overmann;—Katherine A. Marshall.
Estate Planning, Trust and Estate Administration; Probate, Guardianship, Estate Litigation.

See Professional Biographies, DARIEN, ILLINOIS

Sauer, Charles William '56 '88 C.339 B.S.Ph. L.146 J.D. Natl. Pharmacists Assn.‡
Sodipe, Olukayode A. '58 '92 C.107 B.A. L.803 J.D. [Sodipe&Assoc.]
Sodipe & Associates, Law Offices of P.O. Box 2731
Vogel, Richard A. '29 '67 C.339 B.S. L.1003 J.D. 18 West 113-71st Street‡
Wallace, Scott E. '62 '88 C.228 A.B. L.145 J.D. Pres. & CEO, Eichrom Industries, Inc.

DECATUR, * 81,860, *Macon Co.*

Abraham, Jason F., (BVⓉ) '67 '92 C.966 B.A. L.436 J.D. [M.F.Hupy&Assoc.] ⊙
Abraham, Teena M., (BVⓉ) '62 '97 C.1172 B.S. L.436 J.D. [Ⓐ M.F.Hupy&Assoc.] ⊙
Alling, James W., (AV) '36 '64 C.347 B.S. L.146 J.D. 225 North Water Street, Suite 301‡
Atteberry, Dennis R. '72 '01 C.1101 B.A. L.801 J.D. [Ⓐ Shay&P.]
Baird, Donald G. '17 '41 C.357 A.B. L.597 J.D. 214 Cobb Ave.‡
Balsley, Heidi R., (CV) '71 '96 C.357 B.A. L.801 J.D. [Kehart,P.&B.]
Barr, John, (BV) '49 '76 C.339 B.S. L.280 J.D. [Barr&B.]
Barr, Julie D., (CV) '57 '90 C&L.339 B.A., J.D. [Barr&B.]
Barr & Barr, (BV) 1301 E. Mound Rd.
Basola, Joseph W., (BV) '42 '72 C.801 B.A. L.146 LL.B. [Brown,H.B.&M.]
Bateman, Philip L., (BV) '52 '80 C.339 B.S.Ch.E. L.597 J.D. 555 S. Seigel St. (Pat.)

Beavers, Graham & Fines
(See Taylorville)

Bickes, Kurt B., (BV) '60 '85 C.477 B.B.A. L.801 J.D. [Bickes,W.&M.]
Bickes, Wayne L., (AV) '32 '58 C&L.339 B.S., LL.B. [Bickes,W.&M.]
Bickes, Wilson & Moss, (AV) 101 South Main Street, Suite 600
Bolen, T. G., (AV) '34 '60 C&L.339 B.S., LL.B. [Ⓒ Bolen,R.&E.]
Bolen, Robinson & Ellis, (AV) 132 South Water Street, Suite 330
Boles, Jos. E. '16 '39 L.209 LL.B. 423 S. Ewing Ave.‡
Bollinger, Robert C., (CV) '71 '96 C.338 B.A. L.801 J.D. [Ⓐ Erickson,D.M.J.G.&W.]
Booth, Edward, (AV) '26 '54 C.347 A.B. L.309 LL.B. [Kehart,P.&B.]
Bourey, Alan D., (BV) '52 '76 C.575 B.A. L.339 J.D. 101 S. Main St., Ste. 501
Bowers, Phoebe S. '78 '03 C.357 B.S. L.801 J.D. [Ⓐ Samuels,M.S.J.&S.]
Bradley, Christopher K., (CV) '57 '92 C.339 A.B. L.801 J.D. [Bradley]
Bradley Law Office, Ltd., (CV) 132 S. Water Street
Brilley, Donald E., (CV) '57 '81 C.357 B.A. L.734 J.D. [Brilley]
Brilley Law Office, (CV) P.O. Box 1550
Brinkoetter, James P., Jr., (BV) '50 '75 C.1151 B.S. L.146 J.D. 250 N. Water St., Ste. 310
Brown, Britt A., (BV) '58 '83 C.339 B.A. L.801 J.D. [Brown,H.B.&M.]
Brown, Rex L., (BV) '30 '57 C.338 B.S.Ed. L.339 J.D. [Brown,H.B.&M.] ⊙
Brown, Hawkins, Basola & Mattingley, (BV) 234 S. Franklin St. (⊙Maroa)
Burger, Walter F., Jr., (BV) '24 '51 C&L.734 B.S., LL.B. 228 S. Franklin St. (⊙Cerro Gordo)
Burton, R. Nicholas, (AV) '48 '73 C&L.339 B.S., J.D. 132 South Water Street
Byers, Frank H., II, (BV) '52 '77 C&L.339 B.S., J.D. [F.H.Byers II]
Byers, Frank H., II, Ltd., (BV) 3795 N. Woodford St., Ste. 100
Casteel, Keith W., (BV) '50 '75 C.679 B.S.I.E. L.339 J.D. [Samuels,M.S.J.&S.] ⊙
Castleman, Linda M., (BV) '49 '77 C.339 B.A. L.502 J.D. [Parish&C.]
Cleave, Scott W., Jr., (BV) '19 '43 C&L.339 B.S., J.D. Millikin Ct. Bldg.
Clemens, Randy W. '49 '74 C.608 B.S. L.477 J.D. (adm. in OH; not adm. in IL) Corp. Coun., Ill. Power Co.
Coale, James A. '50 '75 C.927 B.A. L.339 J.D. [Heavner,H.&S.]
Cobb, John S., (AV) '46 '71 C&L.339 B.S., J.D. [Samuels,M.S.J.&S.]
Cole, Robert L., (AV) '29 '53 C&L.339 B.S., J.D. P.O. Box 403 B‡
Coryell, James R., (BV) '46 '71 C.209 B.A. L.146 J.D. 253 E Wood St
Costa, Edward Q., (BV) '58 '84 C.734 B.A. L.190 J.D. [Samuels,M.S.J.&S.]
Couter, John W., (BV) '49 '74 C.602 B.A. L.1119 J.D. Corp. Coun.
Craddock, Jason R. '70 '97 C.893 B.A. L.352 J.D. Asst. States Atty.
Craig, Carol Diane '57 '82 C.340 B.A. L.910 J.D. First National Bank of Decatur
Cunningham, Lee R., (AV) '50 '79 C&L.339 B.A., J.D. Corp. Counsel - Environmental, Archer-Daniels-Midland Company Inc.
Current, Richard A. '53 '78 C&L.339 A.B., J.D. Asst. State's Atty.
Custer, Cynthia M. '58 '05 C.1563 B.S.N. L.146 J.D. [Kehart,P.&B.]
Davis, Garry E., (AV) '40 '66 C&L.1119 J.D. [Erickson,D.M.J.G.&W.]
Davison, Jeffrey K. '41 '66 C&L.502 A.B., J.D. 47 Eastmoreland Ct.
Downing, William T., (AV) '30 '57 C.228 A.B. L.602 LL.B. [Downing&U.]
Downing & Uhl, (AV) 295 N. Franklin St. 3rd Fl.
Duffield, Thomas A. '25 '56 C&L.215 A.B., J.D. (adm. in MI; not adm. in IL) 4666 Faries Pkwy.
Dunn, John F., (BV) '36 '61 C&L.602 B.S., J.D. 330 Millikin Ct. (Pat.)
Eller, Martha O. '47 '75 C&L.339 B.A., J.D. Asst. State Atty.
Ellis, Christopher M. '75 '01 C.340 B.A. L.276 J.D. [Bolen,R.&E.]
Erickson, Frederick P., (AV) '41 '66 C.1106 B.A. L.597 J.D. [Erickson,D.M.J.G.&W.]
Erickson, Jonathan P. '73 '00 C.338 B.S. L.801 J.D. 225 S. Main St.
Erickson, Roy L. '23 '61 C.494 B.B.A. L.1035 J.D. (adm. in MN; not adm. in IL) 4666 Faries Pkwy.
Erickson, Davis, Murphy, Johnson, Griffith & Walsh, Ltd., (AV) ... 225 South Main Street
Featherstun, Glen A., (AV) '41 '66 C&L.910 B.S.B.A., J.D. [Winters,F.G.P.S.&F.]
Fichter, Lawrence R., (BV) '36 '63 C.388 B.A. L.209 LL.B. States Atty.
Fick, John E. '32 '65 C.339 A.B. L.309 J.D. 225 North Water Street, Suite 301‡
Fitzgerald, Peter D. '33 '58 C&L.424 B.S., J.D. Citizens Natl. Bk.
Flynn, Edward F., (BV) '57 '86 C.337 B.S. L.365 J.D. [Winters,F.G.P.S.&F.]
Fombelle, Gregory D., (BV) '65 '91 C.339 B.S. L.623 J.D. 228 S. Franklin St.
Fombelle, Michael J., (BV) '61 '88 C.357 B.S. L.1187 J.D. 228 S. Franklin St.
Fombelle, Norman J., (BV) '36 '60 C&L.339 B.S., LL.B. 228 S. Franklin St.
Fossier, Daniel P. '67 '95 C.339 B.S. L.910 J.D. [Ⓐ Hughes,H.&T.]
Fuller, Glenn O., (AV) '30 '60 C.338 B.S. L.477 J.D. [Fuller,H.&Q.]

Fuller, Hopp & Quigg, (AV)
1301 East Mound Road, P.O. Box 3220, 62526
Telephone: 217-875-7171 Telecopier: 217-875-7237
Email: lquigg@fhq.biz
Glenn O. Fuller; Richard W. Hopp; Leo W. Quigg, Jr.
Trial Practice. General, Civil, Criminal, Personal Injury, Auto Accidents; Probate, Family, Adoptions; Divorce; Real Estate, Corporation, Taxation, Estate Planning, Bankruptcy, Banking Law and Collections.

Funderburg, Stuart E. '63 '88 C&L.339 B.S., J.D. Corp. Counsel, Archer-Daniels-Midland Company Inc.
Fuson, James E., II, (CV) '35 '64 C.357 B.A. L.339 LL.B. 2554 S. Nantucket Dr.
Garwood, Scott E. '76 '02 C&L.339 B.S., J.D. [Ⓐ Samuels,M.S.J.&S.]
Gaumer, Daniel L., (AV) '50 '76 C.98 B.S. L.801 J.D. [Winters,F.G.P.S.&F.]
Geisler, Asher O., (BV) '25 '56 C.546 B.Sc. L.597 LL.B. [Geisler]
Geisler, Gary F., (BV) '50 '76 C.339 B.A. L.477 J.D. [Geisler]
Geisler, Jeffrey S., (BV) '60 '86 C.801 B.S. L.836 J.D. [Geisler]
Geisler Law Offices, (BV) 241 S. Main St.
Gibson, Mark D., (BV) '57 '82 C.340 B.A. L.352 J.D. [Ⓒ Hughes,H.&T.]
Golden, L. Warren '33 '57 C.602 A.B. L.209 J.D. P.O. Box 1470
Gollings, James R., (CV) '45 '78 C.357 B.A. L.365 J.D. [Gollings&G.]
Gollings & Gollings, P.C., (CV) 1668 W. Riverview Ave.
Greanias, Basil G., (CV) '28 '52 C&L.339 B.S., LL.B. 3 Lincoln Pl.
Greanias, Gus T., (AV) '15 '39 C.339 B.A. L.424 J.D. 31 Oakridge Dr.‡
Greanias, John K. '43 '67 C&L.339 B.A., J.D. Cir. J.
Griffith, Thomas E., (BV) '58 '85 C.357 B.A. L.862 J.D. [Erickson,D.M.J.G.&W.]
Gunn, Jonathan S., (CV) '59 '94 C.221 B.A. L.365 J.D. [Ⓐ Hughes,H.&T.]
Hair, Brian T. '70 '01 C.318 B.A. L.339 J.D. [Ⓐ Samuels,M.S.J.&S.]
Handegan, Nancy M., Law Office of, (BV) '57 '83 C&L.339 B.S., J.D. 202 S. Franklin, Suite 102

Harrington & Tock
(See Champaign)

Hawkins, Elmer C., (BV) '29 '55 C&L.339 B.S., LL.B. [Brown,H.B.&M.] ⊙
Hawkins, Jeffery J., (CV) '68 '94 C.339 B.A. L.801 J.D. [Brown,H.B.&M.]
Heavner, Richard L., (AV) '52 '77 C&L.339 B.S., J.D. [Heavner,H.&S.]
Heavner, Handegan & Scott, (AV) 111 East Main Street
Heinz, Rhonda L., (CV) '64 '91 C&L.339 B.S., J.D. [Samuels,M.S.J.&S.]
Hill, Bettye J. '62 '97 C.805 B.B.A. L.1049 LL.M. Dir. Compliance in Employment, Archer Daniels Midland Company
Hill, Gregory Q., (BV) '62 '89 C.338 B.S. L.365 J.D. [Hughes,H.&T.]
Hogan, Bridget C. '61 '97 C.698 B.S./B.A. L.734 J.D. [Samuels,M.S.J.&S.]

Holley & Rosen
(See Springfield)

Hopkins, Richard A., (CV) '63 '90 C.339 B.F.A. L.801 J.D. [Willoughby,L.&H.]
Hopp, Richard W., (BV) '45 '72 C.347 B.A. L.339 J.D. [Fuller,H.&Q.]
Hostetler, Thomas K. '28 '52 C&L.339 B.S., LL.B. Bennett & Spade Ins. Agcy.
Houchen, Vernon H., (AV) '25 '54 C&L.145 B.A., J.D. 1650 W. William St.
Hourigan, William E., Attorney at Law '— '74 C.1082 B.A. L.424 J.D. 1632 N. Union St.
Hubbard, Erick F. '68 '03 C.357 B.A. L.801 J.D. [Ⓐ Winters,F.G.P.S.&F.]
Hughes, Charles C., (AV) '53 '78 C.383 B.B.A. L.228 J.D. [Hughes,H.&T.]
Hughes, Hill & Tenney, L.L.C., (AV) 236 North Water Street, Suite 400
Hupy, Michael F., (AVⓉ) '46 '72 C&L.436 B.A., J.D. [M.F.Hupy&Assoc.] ⊙
Hupy, Michael F., & Associates, S.C., (AVⓉ) 2645 North Oakland Avenue, Suite B (⊙Normal, Peoria, IL; Appleton, Madison, Milw., WI)
Jack, David C. '25 '52 C.357 A.B. L.910 J.D. First Natl. Bk. of Decatur‡
Jackson, James T., (BV) '61 '88 C.937 B.A. L.174 J.D. [Samuels,M.S.J.&S.]
Jackson, Jerald E., (AV) '22 '49 C.927 B.S. L.145 J.D. [Samuels,M.S.J.&S.]
Jackson, Mark E., (AV) '49 '74 C.399 B.A. L.339 J.D. [Samuels,M.S.J.&S.]
Jankowicz, James A., (BV) '55 '80 C&L.339 A.B., J.D. 101 S. Main St.
Johnson, Evan H., (AV) '43 '68 C.701 Ch.E. L.339 J.D. [Erickson,D.M.J.G.&W.]
Johnson, James W., (BV) '44 '69 C.388 B.A. L.339 J.D. [Johnson,S.&W.]
Johnson, S. Greg '55 '80 C.339 B.S. L.801 J.D. [Moore,S.M.&W.]
Johnson, Stricklin & Waller, (BV) 412 S. Franklin St.
Jones, Deanne F., (CV) '63 '91 C.339 B.S. L.801 J.D. Atty., Archer-Daniels-Midland Company
Jones, Steven G., (CV) '66 '92 C.234 B.A. L.801 J.D. Asst. Corp. Coun.

Justice, Jeffry A., (BV) '51 '78 C.339 B.S. L.365 J.D.
Suite 515 Millikin Court, 132 South Water Street, 62523
Telephone: 217-422-9800 Fax: 217-428-9742
Email: jeff@jeffryjustice.com
Commercial Litigation, Uniform Commercial Code & Banking, Bankruptcy including Chapter 11 Cases, Commercial & Construction Litigation.

See Professional Biographies, DECATUR, ILLINOIS

Kahn, Orville S., Law Offices of, (CV) '22 '50
C&L.339 B.S., LL.B. 2890 Wildwood Drive
Kanoski, Ronald J., (BV) ....'47 '74 C.234 B.S. L.424 J.D. [Kanoski&Assoc.] ⊙
Kanoski & Associates, (BV)
363 South Main, Suite 180 (⊙Bloomington, Macomb, Peoria, Quincy, Rushville, Springfield)
Kehart, Michael J., (AV) ....'42 '67 C.337 A.B. L.477 J.D. [Kehart,P.&B.]

Kehart, Peckert & Booth, (AV)
A Partnership including a Professional Corporation
132 South Water Street, Suite 200, P.O. Box 860, 62525-0860
Telephone: 217-428-4689 Telecopier: 217-422-7950
Email: mjk@kehart.com URL: http://www.kehart.com
Edward Booth; Michael J. Kehart; James E. Peckert; Heidi R. Balsley; William D. Trimble; Jason B. Small; (Ms) Cynthia M. Custer. Of Counsel: Robert W. Ohlsen.
Litigation, Business Litigation, Commercial Litigation, Corporate Litigation, Class Actions, Banking Law, Banking Institutions, Business Transactions, Domestic Relations, Estate Planning, General Civil and Trial Practice, Lenders Rights, Labor and Employment, Real Estate Transactions, Medical Malpractice Defense, Insurance Defense, Municipal Law, Probate Law, Workers Compensation.
Representative Clients: Archer-Daniels-Midland Co.; A.E. Staley Manufacturing Co.; Mueller Co.; Illinova Resource Recovery, Inc.; Aetna Casualty & Surety Co.; Illinois State Medical Insurance Services; Richland Sales Corp.; Lincoln Diagnostics; Hickory Point Bank & Trust.
See Professional Biographies, DECATUR, ILLINOIS

Kehoe, Kevin L., (CV) ....'55 '81 C.178 B.A. L.734 J.D. Community Investment Corp.
Kenney, Frederic Lee, (AV) '58 '83 C.207 B.A. L.477 J.D.
Corp. Coun., Archer-Daniels-Midland Company
Kinser, Kenneth ....'17 '41 C&L.339 A.B., J.D. 439 Millikin Ct.
Kohr, Charles W., (CV) ....'43 '68 C&L.339 B.S., J.D. 1122 Buckeye Lane
Kreblin, Chad A. '76 '01 C.966 B.A. L.1410 J.D.
[⊡ M.F.Hupy&Assoc.] (⊙Normal, Peoria, IL; Appleton, Madison, WI)
Lakshmanan, Joseph L. '61 '88
C.112 B.A. L.1218 J.D. Sr. Corp. Coun., CLO, Ill. Power Co.
Langhoff, Steven C. ....'65 '96 C&L.801 B.S., J.D. IL Pollut. Control Bd.
Larmore, Kelly A. ....'77 '03 C.966 B.A. L.436 J.D. [⊡ M.F.Hupy&Assoc.] ⊙
Larson, Marc W., (BV) '53 '78 C.297 B.A. L.494 J.D.
Corp. Coun., A. E. Staley Mfg. Co.
Lucas-Durham, Jayne Ann '62 '88
C.801 B.A. L.500 J.D. Land of Lincoln Legal Asst. Foundation, Inc.
Malvestuto, Louis A. ....'37 '85 C.475 B.S. L.339 J.D. 2402 S. Lost Bridge Rd.‡
Massey, David Lee, (CV) ......'55 '85 C.801 B.A. L.710 J.D. 250 N. Water St., Ste. 310
Mattingley, Gregory A., (BV) ....'49 '75 C.339 B.S. L.221 J.D. [Brown,H.B.&M.]
McCarthy, D. Douglas, (BV) ....'53 '79 C.338 B.S. L.801 J.D. [McCarthy,R.&F.]
McCarthy, Kitty M., (AV) ....'53 '79 C.927 B.A. L.801 J.D. Cir. J.
McCarthy, Robert W. ....'24 '47 C&L.339 LL.B. [McCarthy,R.&F.]
McCarthy, Rowden & Faber, (BV) ....243 S. Water St.
McCarty, Colette L. ....'66 '91 C&L.339 B.A., J.D. [⊡ Robbins,S.N.L.&T.]
McGraw, Angela E. '75 '00 C.958 B.S. L.436 J.D.
[⊡ M.F.Hupy&Assoc.] (⊙Normal, Peoria, IL; Appleton, Madison, WI)
McKinley, Jack B. ....'22 '52 C.357 B.S. L.336 LL.B. 4 Peggy Ann Dr.‡
McNutt, William A., (BV) ....'47 '73 C.734 A.B. L.425 J.D. [Moore,S.M.&W.]
Metnick, Cherry, Frazier & Sabin, L.L.P.
(See Springfield)
Meurlot, Karl E. ....'33 '95 C.339 B.S. L.801 J.D. 420 Millikin Court
Miller, Kameron A. ....'55 '84 C.961 B.A. L.615 J.D. Asst. State's Atty.
Miller, Reeder C. ....'27 '55 C&L.347 B.S., J.D. 333 Greenway Lane‡
Mohan, J. Patrick '48 '73 C.608 B.S. L.767 J.D.
Exec. V.P., Admn., Gen. Coun. & Secy., A. E. Staley Mfg. Co.
Moore, Daniel M., Jr., (AV) ....'28 '53 C.910 A.B. L.339 J.D. [⊡ Moore,S.M.&W.]
Moore, Susler, McNutt, & Wrigley, L.L.C., (BV) ....3071 N. Water St.
Moorehead, Susan Foley ....'60 '85 C&L.339 B.A., J.D. Asst. State's Atty.
Morey, Walter T., (BV) ....'18 '47 C.339 B.S. L.309 J.D. [Morey&S.]
Morey & Shade, An Association of Sole Practioners, (BV) ....132 South Water Street
Morthland, Donald ....'26 '51 227 S. Water St.
Morthland, Mark Stephen, (BV) ....'58 '85 C&L.801 B.A., J.D. 227 S. Water St.
Morthland, Richd. F., (BV) ....'22 '49 C.357 B.S. L.339 J.D. 227 S. Water St.
Moss, Thom W., (AV) ....'48 '75 C.339 B.S. L.365 J.D. [Bickes,W.&M.]
Moss, Bryan & Moss, P.C.
(See Clinton)
Murphy, W. Scott, (AV) ....'45 '73 C&L.339 B.A., J.D. [Erickson,D.M.J.G.&W.]
Neiers, Nicholas J., (AV) ....'— '60 C&L.602 A.B., J.D. [⊡ Samuels,M.S.J.&S.]
Neill, Frederick W. ....'13 '38 C.578 A.B. L.309 LL.B. 1451 W. Decatur St.‡
Nicholas, Everett E., Jr., (BV) ....'41 '66 C.937 A.B. L.339 J.D. [Robbins,S.N.L.&T.]
Ohlsen, Robert W., (AV) ....'31 '57 C.98 B.S. L.339 J.D. [⊡ Kehart,P.&B.]
Owen, Robert M., (AV) ....'52 '80 C&L.477 A.B., J.D. 136 South Main Street
Paine, Theodore E. ....'52 '78 C&L.339 B.S., J.D. Cir. J.
Parish, Darrel F., (BV) ....'50 '75 C&L.339 B.S., J.D. [Parish&C.]
Parish & Castleman, Ltd., (BV) ....132 S. Water Street, Suite 429
Patton, Jerry L. ....'43 '69 C.801 B.A. L.500 J.D. Cir. J.
Peckert, James E., (BV) ....'62 '86 C.357 B.S. L.801 J.D. [Kehart,P.&B.]
Penn, James W. ....'32 '65 C.339 B.S. L.146 J.D. First of America Trust Co.
Perbix, Steven W., (BV) ....'62 '86 C.36 B.A. L.1049 J.D. [Shay&P.]
Postlewait, R. Samuel, (BV) ....'56 '85 C.234 B.S. L.615 J.D. [Winters,F.G.P.S.&F.]
Preiksaitis, Michelle K. ....'66 '91 C&L.339 B.A., J.D. 2843 Jockisch Road‡
Quigg, Leo W., Jr., (BV) ....'53 '80 C.357 B.A. L.862 J.D. [Fuller,H.&Q.]
Rathbun, Kent A., (BV) ....'48 '73 C.209 B.A. L.339 J.D. [K.A.Rathbun]
Rathbun, Kent A., P.C., (BV) ....250 N. Water St., Ste. 320
Rathmann, Dennis T., (AV⊤) ....'48 '74 C&L.734 B.S., J.D. [Rathmann&O.] ⊙
Rathmann & O'Brien, L.L.C., (AV⊤)
3130 North Susan Drive (⊙North Little Rock, AR; Springfield, St. Louis, MO)
Rau, Bradford A. ....'58 '83 C.340 B.A. L.910 J.D. 227 S. Water St.
Regan, John F., Jr. ....'11 '37 C.339 L.208 LL.B. [Regan&T.] ‡
Regan & Tueth, (BV) ....113 N. Main St.
Reising, Richard P. '44 '70 C.813 B.A. L.502 J.D.
Sr. V.P., Archer-Daniels-Midland-Co.
Rice, William M. ....'10 '34 C&L.339 B.S., J.D. 225 North Water Street, Suite 301‡
Riley, Bradley E. '70 '94 C.927 B.S. L.339 J.D.
Sr. Atty., Archer-Daniels-Midland Company Inc.
Robbins, Schwartz, Nicholas, Lifton & Taylor, Ltd., (AV)
420 Millikin Ct. (⊙Chicago, Collinsville, Macomb)
Roberts, Robert H., (AV) ....'28 '55 C.357 B.S. L.502 J.D. [Roberts]
Roberts, Scott Alan, (BV) '60 '84 C&L.190 B.S.B.A., J.D.
Asst. Gen. Coun. & Asst. Sec., Archer-Daniels-Midland-Co., Inc.

Roberts Law Office, Ltd., (AV)
Suite 300, Millikin Court, 132 South Water Street, 62523-1399
Telephone: 217-428-4385 Fax: 217-428-4387
Email: attybobob@aol.com URL: http://www.lawyers.com/robertrobertslaw
(This Listing Continued)

Roberts Law Office, Ltd. (Continued)
Robert H. Roberts.
Estate Planning, Wills, Probate, Trusts, Real Estate, Agricultural Law, Business Law.
See Professional Biographies, DECATUR, ILLINOIS

Robinson, Jon D., (AV) ....'46 '71 C.339 B.A. L.838 J.D. [Bolen,R.&E.]
Roney, Scott Allen, (CV) '64 '89 C.338 B.A. L.477 J.D.
Corp. Coun., Archer-Daniels-Midland Company Inc.
Root, Karen L., (CV) ....'55 '96 C.1247 B.A. L.339 J.D. [Moore,S.M.&W.]
Rowden, Hugh H., Jr., (BV) ....'47 '72 C.339 A.B. L.352 J.D. [McCarthy,R.&F.]

Samuels, Miller, Schroeder, Jackson & Sly, LLP, (AV)
225 North Water Street, Suite 301, P.O. Box 1400, 62525 ⊙
Telephone: 217-429-4325 Telecopier: 217-425-6313
Email: law@smsjslaw.com URL: http://www.smsjslaw.com
Members of Firm: Jerald E. Jackson; Guy E. Williams; John S. Cobb; Mark E. Jackson; Keith W. Casteel; Darrell A. Woolums; John E. Sanner; Edward Q. Costa; James T. Jackson; Rhonda L. Heinz; Bridget C. Hogan. Associates: Brian T. Hair; Scott E. Garwood; Phoebe S. Bowers. Of Counsel: Nicholas J. Neiers.
General Civil Trial and Appellate Practice, Personal Injury, Auto Accidents, Medical Malpractice, Workers Compensation, Corporate, Commercial, Employment, Banking, Finance, Mergers and Acquisitions, Health Care, Real Estate and Environmental, Trusts, Estates, Wills and Estates Planning.
Representative Clients: Illinois Power Company; Norfolk Southern Corporation; Decatur Memorial Hospital; Millikin University; Kemper Group; Gallagher-Bassett.
Arthur, Illinois Office: 131 B South Vine Street, 61911. Telephone: 217-543-3403.
See Professional Biographies, DECATUR, ILLINOIS

Sanner, John E., (BV) ....'59 '84 C&L.801 B.A., J.D. [Samuels,M.S.J.&S.]
Schelwat, Timothy W. ....'70 '98 C.312 B.A. L.221 J.D. [⊡ M.F.Hupy&Assoc.] ⊙
Schroeder, E. Wayne, (AV) '15 '38
C.357 A.B. L.597 J.D. 225 North Water Street, Suite 301‡
Scott, J. Gregory, (BV) ....'62 '87 C.339 B.S. L.801 J.D. [Heavner,H.&S.]
Scott, Rodney A. ....'15 '39 C&L.339 B.S., LL.B. Cir. J., Chf. J.‡
See, Milo J., Jr. ....'26 '66 C&L.339 A.B., LL.B. 2991 S Bentley Ct.‡
Shade, Thomas M., (BV) ....'49 '75 C.197 B.A. L.273 J.D. [Morey&S.]
Shafter, A. James, (AV) '47 '72 C.801 B.A. L.339 J.D.
V.P. & Asst. Gen. Coun., Archer-Daniels-Midland Company Inc.
Shay, Timothy M., (BV) ....'61 '86 C.339 B.S. L.502 J.D. [Shay&P.]

Shay & Perbix, (BV)
260 East Wood Street, 62523
Telephone: 217-425-5900 Fax: 217-425-5901
Email: shayperb@insightbb.com URL: http://www.shayandperbix.com
Timothy M. Shay; Steven W. Perbix. Associate: Dennis R. Atteberry.
Plaintiffs Personal Injury, Workers Compensation, Medical Malpractice, Products Liability.
See Professional Biographies, DECATUR, ILLINOIS

Small, Jason B. ....'73 '99 C.210 B.A. L.976 J.D. [Kehart,P.&B.]
Smith, David J., (BV) '55 '80 C.927 B.Bus. L.365 J.D.
Exec. V.P., Secy. & Gen. Coun., Archer-Daniels-Midland Co., Inc.
Snider, Andrew J. ....'58 '85 C.910 B.A. L.502 J.D. 412 S. Franklin St.
Spence, David A., (BV) ....'54 '82 C.339 B.S. L.801 J.D. States Atty.
Statzer, Darrell E., Jr., (BV) '50 '81
C.1083 B.A. L.365 J.D. 132 South Water Street, Suite 340
Stocks, Jerrold H., (BV) ....'64 '89 C.339 B.A. L.221 J.D. [Winters,F.G.P.S.&F.]
Stricklin, Jessica A., (BV) ....'49 '75 C.210 B.A. L.273 J.D. [Johnson,S.&W.]
Susler, Marshall A., (AV) ....'30 '55 C.357 A.B. L.145 J.D. [⊡ Moore,S.M.&W.]
Swick, Wilbur Kenneth ....'35 '70 L.107 J.D. [Swick]
Swick Law Office ....72 Colorado Drive
Taylor, Jeffrey C., (BV) ....'37 '63 C.357 B.S. L.339 LL.B. [⊡ Robbins,S.N.L.&T.]
Tenney, Carl J., (BV) ....'57 '82 C.340 B.A. L.801 J.D. [Hughes,H.&T.]
Tenney, Harold F., (AV) ....'33 '57 C&L.339 B.S., LL.B. 2437 Brooks Dr.
Tibbs, Philip J. ....'70 '99 C&L.801 B.A., J.D. [⊡ Geisler]

Tietz, Christopher M., (AV) '52 '76 C&L.339 B.S., J.D.
132 S. Water Street, Suite 444, 62523
Telephone: 217-425-4910
Email: cmt@tietzlaw.com URL: http://www.lawyers.com/tietz
Civil Litigation. Business Transactions, Real Estate, Corporate, Commercial, International, Employment, Construction, Technology, Insurance Defense, Products Liability, Professional Liability, Estate Planning, Trust and Probate Law.
See Professional Biographies, DECATUR, ILLINOIS

Trimble, William D. ....'69 '98 C.293 B.A. L.339 J.D. [Kehart,P.&B.]
Tueth, James E., (BV) ....'50 '76 C.338 B.Sc. L.339 J.D. [Regan&T.]
Uhl, James A., (AV) ....'30 '54 C&L.602 A.B., LL.B. [Downing&U.]
Venturelli, Donald M., (CV) ....'28 '56 C&L.339 J.D. 132 S. Water St.
Vigneri, Joseph W., (BV) ....'56 '83 C.357 B.A. L.734 J.D. [J.W.Vigneri]

Vigneri, Joseph W., Ltd. A Professional Corporation, (BV)
136 W. Washington Street, 62522
Telephone: 217-422-9992 Fax: 217-422-8669
Email: jvigneri@earthlink.net
Joseph W. Vigneri.
Criminal Defense.
See Professional Biographies, DECATUR, ILLINOIS

Waks, Amy M. ....'68 '98 C.927 B.A. L.546 J.D. Asst. States Atty.
Walker, Carol L. Evans ....'49 '83 C&L.589 B.S., J.D. Asst. State's Atty.
Waller, Ruth A. Warden, (CV) ....'— '87 C.1247 B.A. L.801 J.D. [Johnson,S.&W.]
Walsh, Michael A., (BV) ....'55 '85 C.1044 B.S. L.1338 J.D. [Erickson,D.M.J.G.&W.]
Watts, Jay M., (BV) ....'50 '75 C.339 B.S. L.45 J.D. P.O. Box 1136
Webber, Albert G., IV, (BV) ....'55 '81 C.340 B.A. L.910 J.D. Cir.J.
Weedman, Dennis L. ....'65 '93 C.339 B.A. L.801 J.D. [⊡ Robbins,S.N.L.&T.]
Wetzel, Joseph R. ....'80 '04 C.357 B.A. L.801 J.D. [⊡ Winters,F.G.P.S.&F.]
Wheeler, Thomas M., (BV) ....'41 '67 C.291 B.S.B.A. L.146 J.D. [T.M.Wheeler]
Wheeler, Thomas M., Ltd., A Prof. Corp., (BV) ....363 South Main St.
White, Lisa Holder, (BV) ....'68 '93 C.1151 B.A. L.339 J.D. 250 N. Water St., Ste. 310
Whitmer, Robert L. ....'46 '73 C.597 B.A. L.608 J.D. Decatur Title Company, L.L.C.
Wierman, Wm. L., (CV) ....'15 '41 C&L.339 B.A. P.O. Box 1435
Williams, Guy E., (AV) ....'40 '65 C&L.339 B.S., J.D. [Samuels,M.S.J.&S.]
Williams, Roy L. ....'70 '98 C.154 B.A. L.424 J.D. [⊡ M.F.Hupy&Assoc.] ⊙
Willoughby, Stephen O., (BV) ....'47 '73 C.801 B.A. L.734 J.D. [Willoughby,L.&H.]
Willoughby, Latshaw & Hopkins, P.C., (BV) ....502 W. Prairie
Wilson, Kirtley E., (AV) ....'35 '60 C&L.339 B.S., LL.B. [Bickes,W.&M.]
Winters, Robert D., (AV) ....'26 '50 C.679 B.S. L.477 J.D. [⊡ Winters,F.G.P.S.&F.]

Winters, Featherstun, Gaumer, Postlewait, Stocks & Flynn, (AV)
225 N. Water Street, Suite 200, P.O. Box 1760, 62525-1760
Telephone: 217-429-4453; 429-5213 Telecopier: 217-425-8892
URL: http://www.lawyers.com/wfgpsf
Members of Firm: Robert P. Vail (1877-1964); Walker H. Mills (1893-1962); Thos. H. Armstrong (1897-1981); Roswell C. Prince (1919-1994); Glen A. Featherstun; Daniel L. Gaumer; R. Samuel Postlewait; Jerrold H. Stocks; Edward F. Flynn. Associates: Erick F. Hubbard; Joseph R. Wetzel. Of Counsel: Robert D. Winters.
(This Listing Continued)

Winters, Featherstun, Gaumer, Postlewait, Stocks & Flynn (Continued)

General Practice. Trials. Insurance Defense, Legal and Medical Malpractice, Workers Compensation, Probate, Real Estate, Corporations, Labor Strikes.
Representative Clients: Allstate Insurance Co.; Bridgestone/Firestone, Inc.; USF&G Co.; The Cincinnati Insurance Co.; Brotherhood Mutual Insurance Co.; Pekin Insurance Co.; Archer-Daniels-Midland Co.; Northland Insurance Cos.; Employers Mutual Cos.
See Professional Biographies, DECATUR, ILLINOIS

Woolums, Darrell A., (BV) . . . . '47 '76 C.338 B.S. L.365 J.D. [Samuels,M.S.J.&S.]
Wrigley, Robert I., (BV) . . . . '43 '73 C.357 B.S. L.734 J.D. [Moore,S.M.&W.]
Zachry, James E., (BV) . . . . '49 '76 C.234 B.S. L.365 J.D. 228 S. Franklin St.

DEERFIELD, 18,420, *Cook & Lake Cos.*

Ablin, Rachel Beth . . . . '— '95 C.1036 B.A. L.424 J.D. Sr. Atty., Walgreen Co.
Alden, John R. . . . . '19 '41 C&L.900 B.A., LL.B. 441 Kelburn Rd.‡
Aldrich, Thomas L. '48 '73 C&L.597 B.A., J.D.
Assoc. Gen. Coun. & Chf. Lit. Coun., Baxter International, Inc.
Antonio, Alyson M. . . . . '66 '93 C.424 B.A. L.802 J.D. [Ⓐ Grobart&L.]
Atlas, Renee . . . . '58 '84 C.339 B.A. L.146 J.D. 845 Deerpark Ln.
Barrett, Joseph B. '59 '90 C.623 B.S. L.365 J.D.
Asst. Chf. Pat. Coun., Baxter Healthcare Corp.
Battle, Dorothy F. . . . . '14 '39 L.209 J.D. 300 Waukegan Rd.‡
Beermann & DeBruyne
(See Libertyville)
Belgrade, Mary N. . . . . '— '78 C.999 B.A. L.424 J.D. Asst. Gen. Coun., MMI Cos., Inc.
Benziger, Robert A. '42 '68
C&L.339 B.S., J.D. Assoc. Gen. Coun., Baxter International, Inc.
Berks, Melvyn H. . . . . '39 '66 C&L.209 A.B., J.D. [Berks&S.] (⊙Waukegan)
Berks & Sinton, LTD . . . . 111 Pfingsten Road
Berman, Elizabeth K. . . . . '41 '77 C&L.597 B.A., J.D. Clark Boardman Callaghan
Berman, Herbert M., (Ltd.) . . . . '36 '61 C.347 B.S. L.421 LL.B. P.O. Box 350
Berzon, Martha W. . . . . '56 '84 C.597 B.A. L.911 J.D. 48 Kenmore Ave.‡
Birg, Yuri M. . . . . '66 '91 C.339 B.A. L.209 J.D. [Birg&M.]
Birg & Meltser . . . . 570 Lake Cook Rd., Ste. 318
Blackburn, William R. '48 '74 C.350 B.A. L.352 J.D.
V.P. & Chf. Coun., Corp. Envir., Health & Safety, Baxter Intl. Inc.
Blair, Marla . . . . '— '97 C.302 B.A. L.910 J.D. Atty., Walgreen Co.
Bloom, Bruce E. . . . . '56 '88 C.339 B.S. L.146 J.D. 1449 Wincanton Dr.
Boehm, Brett L. . . . . '71 '99 C.347 B.A. L.365 J.D. 520 Lake Cook Road
Bolton, Michael J. '63 '88 C.339 B.A. L.477 J.D.
Corp. Coun., Baxter International, Inc.
Bonsen, Corinna Zur '59 '85 L.060
(adm. in Munich; not adm. in IL) Sr. Coun., Baxter Int'l.
Borecki, Thomas S. '58 '87
C.453 B.S.Ch.E. L.424 J.D. Sr. Coun., Baxter International, Inc. (Pat.)
Borre, Leslie A. . . . . '70 '99 C.209 B.A. L.146 J.D. Atty., Walgreen Co.
Bradley, Stephanie G. '— '78 C&L.597 B.S., J.D.
V.P., Employee Relations & Asst. Gen. Coun., Baxter Intl. Inc.
Brandt, Robert R. . . . . '69 '94 C.352 B.A. L.209 J.D. P.O. Box 208
Brekke, Deirdre C. . . . . '59 '84 C.1365 B.A. L.280 J.D. UNext
Buonaiuto, Mark J., (AV) '59 '84 C&L.597 B.A., J.D.
Assoc. Gen. Coun., Baxter International, Inc. (Pat.)
Bure, John P., (BV) . . . . '36 '60 C.602 A.B. L.477 LL.B. 700 Deerfield Rd. W.
Burge, Edward L. '48 '75
C.728 B.S. L.831 J.D. V.P. & Atty., Assocs. Com. Solutions, Inc.
Butterfield, Evan M. . . . . . '58 '92 C.339 M.A. L.209 J.D. Lawyers Cooperative Publishing
Byrd, Deidra L. . . . . '62 '87 C&L.209 B.A., J.D. Dir., Employ. Law, Walgreens, Co.
Cabay, Gina G.A. . . . . '— '00 C.1016 B.S. L.146 J.D. 10 Parkway N.
Campbell, Mary Jo . . . . '53 '78 C.741 B.A. L.424 J.D. Walgreen Co.
Caron, Michael M. . . . . '55 '80 C&L.339 B.S., J.D. [Lyon&C.]
Carter, Jason S. . . . . . . '75 '01 C.831 B.A. L.966 J.D. Corp. Coun., Baxter Healthcare Corp.
Casey, Daniel P. . . . . '42 '70 C.424 B.B.A. L.209 J.D. Gaylord Container Corp.
Cena, Celia Mamon '36 '77 C&L.662 B.S.J., LL.B.
Editorial Dir./Coord., Lawyers Cooperative Publishing
Cepla, Mary Joan '57 '87 C.741 B.A. L.146 J.D.
Editor, Lawyers Cooperative Publishing
Chan, Cindy H. . . . . . . '— '93 C.339 B.S. L.146 J.D. Corp. Coun., Baxter International, Inc.
Chao, Dorothy Chung . . . . '57 '81 C.339 B.S. L.309 J.D. Tax Coun., Baxter Intl. Inc.
Cheskey, Alan E. '57 '82 C.665 B.A. L.229 J.D.
(adm. in PA; not adm. in IL) The Ayco Corp.
Choroski, Edmund P. '44 '74 C.339 B.S. L.146 J.D.
Loss Prevention Manager, Pharmacy Operations, Walgreen Co.
Circle, Brent L. '45 '75 C.347 B.S. L.796 J.D.
(adm. in GA; not adm. in IL) Sr. Real Estate Mgr., Walgreen Co.
Clark, Barry L. . . . . '33 '62 C.597 B.S.M.E. L.273 J.D. 1759 We-Go Trail (Pat.)
Clifford, Marcia L. '56 '82 C.339 B.A. L.436 J.D.
(adm. in WI; not adm. in IL) Lawyers Coop. Pub. Midwestern State Products
Cohen, Sara Jane . . . . '55 '81 C.347 B.S. L.472 J.D. Callaghan & Co.
Cohn, Lauren Weiner . . . . '64 '89 C.966 B.A. L.146 J.D. Sr. Atty., Walgreen Co.
Collina, Mary Robbins '— '75
C.188 B.A. L.365 J.D. Editor, Lawyers Cooperative Publishing
Dahlen, Jane H. . . . . '60 '85 C.424 B.A. L.146 J.D. Sr. Corp. Atty., Astellas US LLC
Davis, Symeon K. . . . . '— '98 Atty., Walgreen Co.
Dawson, Suzanne S., (AV) '41 '65
C.436 B.A. L.424 J.D. Sr. Coun., Baxter International, Inc.
DeBoice, Geraldine S. . . . . '23 '76 C.339 B.A. L.146 J.D. 1145 Norman Ln.‡
Delaney, Robert R., Jr. . . . . '54 '79 C.46 B.S. L.146 J.D. Sr. Atty., Walgreen Co.
DeMoor, Laura J. . . . . . . '— '94 C.608 B.S.Ch.E. L.145 J.D. Baxter Healthcare Corp. (Pat.)
Derdiger, Jan Alan . . . . '49 '79 C.679 B.S.M.E. L.146 J.D. P.O. Box 484
Drell, Jill Leslie '47 '72 C.966 B.A. L.30 J.D.
Dir., Walgreens Health Initiatives, Walgreens, Co.
Duerinck, Kevin F. '56 '81 C.742 B.A. L.589 J.D.
Editor, Lawyers Cooperative Publishing
Eisenstadt, Jodi . . . . '61 '88 C.228 A.B. L.813 J.D. 98 Larkdale East, Suite 100
Eleff, Susan, (AVⓉ) . . . . '55 '78 C&L.659 B.A., J.D. 770 Lake Cook Road, Suite 150
Etienne, Peter . . . . '61 '89 C.999 B.A. L.339 J.D. Sr. Coun., Baxter Intl., Inc.
Evazians, Ramina E. . . . . '71 '96 C.339 B.S. L.146 J.D. Staff Atty., Walgreen Co.
Faraci, C. Joseph '57 '89 C.588 B.S. L.1209 J.D.
(adm. in VA; not adm. in IL; Pat.) Baxter International, Inc.
Felix, Daniel P., (BV) . . . . '56 '84 C.339 B.A. L.424 J.D. 1320 Meadow Street
Ferguson, Karen J. . . . . '59 '94 C.013 B.S.N. L.146 J.D. Sr. Atty., Walgreen Co.
Fields, Marshall G. . . . . '31 '55 C&L.597 B.S., LL.B. 1433 Laurel St.‡
Fine, Howard R. . . . . '63 '88 C&L.339 B.S., J.D. 108 Wilmot Road, Suite 330
Finkelstein, Ira D. '66 '98 C&L.477 B.S., J.D.
Corp. Coun., Baxter Healthcare Corp. (Pat.)
Finne, Fredric R. . . . . '21 '48 C.339 B.A. L.597 J.D. P.O. Box 396‡
Finnegan, John J. '28 '68 C.339 B.S. L.345 J.D.
(adm. in IN; not adm. in IL) 1650 Village Green Ct.‡
Finocchiaro, Peter D. . . . . '62 '87 C.602 B.B.A. L.424 J.D. [Pachter,G.&F.]
Fischer, Lawrence '44 '69 C.339 B.A. L.209 J.D.
V.P. & Gen. Coun., Real Estate Investment Partners, Inc.
Fitzsimmons, J. Patrick '59 '84
C.174 B.S. L.424 J.D. Corp. Coun., Baxter International, Inc.
Fox, William Bradley . . . . '66 '92 C.477 B.A. L.228 J.D. [Lyon&C.]
Frank, Todd G. . . . . '62 '87 C&L.477 B.B.A., J.D. Real Estate Mgr., Walgreen Co.
Friedman, Linda Fleisher '58 '83
C.339 B.S.W. L.597 J.D. V.P. & Gen. Coun., Fujisawa USA, Inc.
Gale, Christine D. . . . . '71 '97 C&L.352 B.A., J.D. Atty Editor, West Group
Gang, Paulette R. '50 '75 C&L.879 B.A., J.D.
Editorial Dir./Coor., Lawyers Cooperative Publishing
Gerstenberger, Katherine L. '48 '73 C&L.477 B.A., J.D. P.O. Box 456
Glickman, Michael '57 '82 C.339 B.A. L.424 J.D.
Chf. Fin. Offr. & Legal Coun., Mullin Consulting, Inc.
Glieberman, Scott L. '57 '81 C.339 B.A. L.146 J.D. 914 Wilmot Rd.,
Glynn, William B. '53 '84 C.932 B.A. L.879 J.D.
(adm. in IN; not adm. in IL) Lawyers Cooperative Publishing
Goble, Patricia A. '52 '77 C.339 B.A. L.365 J.D.
Editor, Lawyers Cooperative Publishing
Golden, Michelle L. . . . . '73 '01 C.1119 B.A. L.146 J.D. 102 Wilmot Rd., Ste. 410
Goldsmith, Larry G. . . . . '54 '87 C.339 B.S. L.365 J.D. Goldsmith Law Group
Goodman, Bruce D., (AV) . . . . '54 '79 C.674 A.B. L.813 J.D. [Ⓐ Grobart&L.]
Goodman, Roberta Wilensky '60 '88 C.659 B.S.E. L.597 J.D.
Coun., Amer. Brands, Inc.
Gore, Andrew M. . . . . '— '79 C.602 B.B.A. L.209 J.D. Tax Coun., Baxter Int'l.
Greco, Robert M. '46 '74 C.1033 B.S. L.128 J.D.
Assistant Vice President & Associate Counsel, First Reinsurance Company of Hartford
Green, Dana I. . . . . '49 '74 C.347 B.A. L.1119 J.D. V.P. Human Res., Walgreens, Co.
Greenberg, Martin L., Law Office of '47 '73
C.475 B.S. L.276 J.D. 790 Estate Dr., Ste. 150
Gregory, Patricia Baldwin . . . . '60 '87 C.433 B.S. L.597 J.D. [Pachter,G.&F.]
Grobart, David L. . . . . '61 '86 C.347 B.A. L.424 J.D. [Grobart&L.]
Grobart & Levick, LLC . . . . 770 Lake Cook Rd.
Groskopf, John E. . . . . '45 '76 C.932 B.B.A. L.365 J.D. Sr. V.P., MMI Cos., Inc.
Gruber, Kathryn '71 '98 C&L.260 B.A., J.D.
Sr. Trademark Paralegal/Admin., Baxter International Inc.
Gruchot, Thaddeus J. . . . . '30 '59 C&L.209 B.S., J.D. 35 Revere Ct.
Gullo, George M. '66 '91 C.424 A.B. L.209 J.D.
Editor, Lawyers Cooperative Publishing
Hahn, Ronald E. . . . . '40 '70 C.424 B.B.A. L.365 J.D. 1132 Green Tree Ave.
Hatton, Gregory M. . . . . '55 '85 C.1169 B.A. L.1049 J.D. [Hatton,P.&S.A.] ⊙
Hatton, Petrie & Stackler APC . . . . 108 Wilmot, Suite 330 (⊙Malibu, Newport Beach, CA)
Heller, Todd A., & Associates, Law Offices of '53 '78
C.367 B.A. L.209 J.D. 102 Wilmot Road, Suite 530 (⊙Chicago)
Henry, Patricia S. '49 '83
C.1101 B.A. L.146 J.D. Sr. Editor, Lawyer's Cooperative Publishing
Hershman, Janet C. '54 '94 C.597 B.A. L.424 J.D.
Labor & Employ. Coun., Baxter Int'l.
Higuera, Albert A. . . . . . . '53 '78 C.597 B.A. L.192 J.D. Mgr., Shand Morahan & Co., Inc.
Hodge, Garrick J. . . . . '62 '87 C.578 B.A. L.589 J.D. Dir., Walgreens, Co.
Hoff, Nanette H. '58 '84 C&L.339 B.S., J.D.
Asst. Gen. Coun., APAC Customer Services, Inc.
Houpt, Barbara Ann . . . . '42 '87 C.589 B.S. L.424 J.D. Dir. of Community Develop.
Iida, Kristine E. '64 '96 C.694 B.A. L.146 J.D. Sr. Atty., Walgreen Co.
Jaconetty, Kenneth '59 '88 C.339 B.S. L.273 J.D.
(adm. in PA; not adm. in IL) Corp. Coun., Baxter International, Inc.
Jakimcius, Irene P. '— '90 C.477 B.S. L.424 J.D.
Corp. Coun., Baxter International, Inc.
Jimenez, Arthur . . . . '72 '97 C.98 B.A. L.424 J.D. Atty., Walgreen Co.
Jimenez, Juan Fernando '64 '88
(adm. in Colombia; not adm. in IL) Corp. Coun., Baxter Int'l.
Johnson, Alan Anthony '62 '92
C.424 B.A. L.209 J.D. Editor, Lawyers Cooperative Publishing
Johnston, Steven L. . . . . '69 '98 C.293 B.A. L.910 J.D. Coun., Jim Beam Brands Co.
Kamerlink, Lydia Gross, (BV) . . . . . . '53 '80 C.347 B.A. L.365 J.D. [Kamerlink,S.&M.] ⊙
Kamerlink, Stark & McCormack, (AV) . . . . 790 Estate Dr., Ste. 180 (⊙Chicago)
Kanehl, Beth '46 '83 C.1044 B.A. L.180 J.D.
(adm. in DC; not adm. in IL) Editor, Lawyers Cooperative Publishing
Karolewski, Edmund T. . . . . '11 '42 C.597 L.209 LL.B. 1719 Christopher Dr.‡
Karpel, Jodi L. '69 '94 C.1077 B.A. L.221 J.D.
(adm. in CA; not adm. in IL) Sr. Atty., Walgreen Co.
Kaseff, Fred E. '57 '84 C.347 B.S. L.569 J.D.
(adm. in NY; not adm. in IL) Exec VP & CFO, Brann Worldwide
Katt, Faye L. '52 '90 C.502 B.S. L.910 J.D.
V.P., Employee Serv. & Corp. Coun., Baxter Intl. Inc.
Kaun, Glenn W. . . . . '61 '85 C.352 B.B.A. L.209 J.D. Sr. Atty., Walgreen Co.
Kelly, Paula J.F. '67 '92 C.1342 B.S. L.1018 J.D.
Corp. Cnsl. V, Baxter Healthcare Corporation
Kenesey, John W., (AV) '43 '68
C.363 A.B. L.608 J.D. Dir., Employ. Rel., Walgreens, Co.
Kern, Michelle Ann . . . . . . '60 '87 C&L.597 B.A., J.D. Sr. Coun., Baxter International, Inc.
King, Edward H. '46 '73 C&L.862 B.A., J.D.
(adm. in OK; not adm. in IL)
Dir., Govt. & Community Rel., & Asst. Secy., Walgreens, Co.
Klaus, Roger D. '45 '72
C.339 A.B.Econ. L.146 J.D. V.P., Editorial, Clark Boardman Callaghan
Klott, Richard S. . . . . '52 '79 C.339 B.A. L.910 J.D. 1556 Gordon Ter.
Kogan, Edward . . . . '74 '02 C.339 B.Acct. L.146 J.D. [Kogan]
Kogan Law Offices, Ltd. . . . . 1020 N. Milwaukee Ave., Ste. 124
Kohn, Richard F. . . . . '33 '57 C&L.477 A.B., J.D. 681 Smoke Tree Rd.
Kolesar, Edward M. '62 '88 C.528 B.S. L.930 J.D.
(adm. in OH; not adm. in IL) Deloitte
Koplow, Laurence N. '67 '93 C.260 B.A. L.228 J.D.
(adm. in FL; not adm. in IL) West Grp.
Koranda, Kenneth A. '53 '84
C&L.424 B.B.A., J.D. Corporate Counsel, Alliant Foodservice, Inc.
Kowalik, Francis C.M. '63 '92
C.696 B.A. L.365 J.D. Sr. Attorney, Intel. Prop., Walgreen Co.
Kramer, Pamela O. . . . . '56 '85 C.37 B.A. L.365 J.D. [P.Kramer]
Kramer, Pamela . . . . 856 Oxford Rd.

Kraus, Elena .... '62 '90 C.846 B.A. L.209 J.D. Sr. Staff Atty., Walgreen Co.
Kroloff, Steven J. '— '84
C.221 B.S. L.365 J.D. Dir., Loss Prevention Operati, Walgreen Co.
Kuczek, Theodore D. .... '57 '84 C.965 B.A. L.365 J.D. [Kuczek&Assoc.]
Kuczek & Associates .... P.O. Box 208
Kunstman, Gregory T. .... '77 '02 C.959 B.S. L.436 J.D. Attorney, Walgreen Co.
Lampert, Susan M. .... '64 '92 C.339 B.A. L.146 J.D. [Ⓐ Berks&S.] (⊙Waukegan)
Leff, Barbara J. .... '52 '77 C.477 B.B.A. L.276 J.D. Callaghan & Co.
Leithner, George E. .... '24 '53 C.425 L.365 LL.B. 1020 Milwaukee Ave.
Lennox, Edwin Cornell .... '— '65 C&L.597 B.A., J.D. Sr. Tax Coun., Baxter Intl. Inc.
Levenson, Steven S. .... '59 '83 C&L.339 B.S., J.D. Sr. Atty., Walgreen Co.
Levick, Michael J. .... '— '94 C.477 B.A. L.280 J.D. [Grobart&L.]
Levin, Jack K. .... '50 '74 C&L.145 J.D. West Grp.
Levin, Joel H. .... '33 '57 C&L.424 B.S.C., J.D. 200 Wilmot Rd.
Levin, Susan R. .... '58 '83 C&L.347 B.S., J.D. 505 Carriage Way‡
Levitan, Judith Nisenbaum .... '58 '83 C.339 B.S. L.597 J.D. Callaghan & Co.
Levitt, Catherine B. ..... '65 '91 C&L.339 B.S., J.D. Corp. Coun., Baxter International, Inc.
Lirtzman, Steven M. .... '62 '87 C.339 B.S. L.245 J.D. 809 Castlewood Ln.
Lyon, Jeffrey S., (AV) .... '49 '75 C.221 B.A. L.209 J.D. [Lyon&C.]

Lyon & Caron LLP, (AV)
790 Estate Drive, Suite 180, 60015
Telephone: 847-945-8810 Fax: 847-945-8812
URL: http://www.lc-law.com
Members of Firm: Michael M. Caron; Jeffrey S. Lyon; William Bradley Fox. Associate: Mary T. Manthy.
Business Law, Corporate Law, Partnership Law, Limited Liability Companies, Private Placements, Taxation, Real Estate and Estate Planning.
See Professional Biographies, DEERFIELD, ILLINOIS

Maher, Mary Brigid .... '71 '97 C.700 B.A. L.365 J.D. Atty. Editor, West Group
Mandler, James E. .... '22 '49 C&L.477 A.B., LL.B. 1547 Crabtree Ln.‡
Manthy, Mary T. .... '— '95 C.424 B.A. L.146 J.D. [Ⓐ Lyon&C.]
Margolis, Harvey .... '45 '72 C.966 B.B.A. L.209 J.D. 102 Wilmot Rd.‡
McCormack, Beth Fawver, (AV) .... '64 '92 C.338 B.A. L.365 J.D. [Kamerlink,S.&M.] ⊙
McDonald, Timothy M. '59 '86 C.477 B.S. L.912 J.D.
(adm. in MI; not adm. in IL) V.P., Taxation, Baxter Int'l.
McDonough, Jeanette Bourey '57 '87
C.429 B.A. L.365 J.D. Sr. Claims Atty., Markel Corporation
McKee, David C. '47 '73 C.623 B.A. L.309 J.D.
Corp. V.P. & Dep. Gen. Coun., Baxter International, Inc.
McShane, Maureen M. '57 '83
C.597 B.A. L.145 J.D. Asst. Gen. Coun., Fujisawa Healthcare Inc.
McVickar, Michael B. '63 '89 C.323 B.S. L.879 J.D.
Assoc. Gen. Coun., APAC Customer Services, Inc.
Meier, Marvin O. .... '35 '73 C.1016 B.A. L.209 J.D. Editor, Thomson Legal Publishing
Mella, Jenina .... '62 '90 C.339 B.A. L.347 J.D. Lawyers Cooperative Publishing
Meltser, Gene .... '74 '99 C&L.209 B.A., J.D. [Birg&M.]
Meltser, Yevgeny .... '74 '99 C&L.209 B.A., J.D. 570 Lake Cook Road
Menacker, Mark E. .... '61 '86 C.36 B.S. L.801 J.D. 500 Indian Hill Rd.★
Mendelson, Cheryl Lee '62 '93 C.339 B.S. L.436 J.D.
(adm. in WI; not adm. in IL) 1135 Prairie Ave.
Merrill, Richard Walter, Jr. .... '57 '87 C.339 B.S. L.146 J.D. Sr. Atty., Walgreen Co.
Merten, Laura Keller .... '60 '84 C.679 B.S. L.339 J.D. Dir., WHI Legal, Walgreen Co.
Metrick, Kimberly Grossman ...... '68 '93 C.477 B.A. L.146 J.D. Sr. Atty., Walgreen Co.
Mihevc, Chad .... '70 '96 C&L.339 B.A., J.D. Sr. Atty., Walgreen Co.
Millett, Katherine T. .... '52 '89 C.1307 B.A. L.145 J.D. TCI Great Lakes, Inc.
Millewich, Paul H. .... '50 '77 C.869 B.S. L.273 J.D. Baxter Intl. Inc.
Montgomery, William A., Jr. ...... '60 '87 C.269 B.A. L.910 J.D. Sr. Atty., Walgreen Co.
Moran, Matthew S. .... '60 '93 C.145 B.A. L.146 J.D. Sr. Atty., Walgreen Co.
Morrison, Andrew S. .... '62 '88 C.339 B.A. L.1066 J.D. 356 Warwick Road
Mulcrone, Jennifer F. .... '73 '98 C.339 B.A. L.146 J.D. Atty., Walgreen Co.
Murphy, Timothy J., (AVⓉ) .... '63 '88 C.966 B.B.A. L.436 J.D. Baxter Intl. Inc.
Neubauer, Michael C. '58 '84 C.597 B.A. L.339 J.D.
Citigroup Inc., Citi Commerce Solutions Div.;
Newcomb, Jonathan B. .... '58 '82 C&L.597 B.A., J.D. Div. Coun., TCI Great Lakes, Inc.
Nichols, Jeffrey C. '56 '91
C.420 B.S.M.E. L.365 J.D. Corp. Coun., Baxter International, Inc. (Pat.)
Niehus, Grant R. .... '54 '80 C.339 B.S. L.365 J.D. [G.R.Niehus]
Niehus, Grant R., Ltd., P.C. .... 1550 Stratford Rd.
Nigro, Joseph A., Jr '43 '68 C.145 B.A. L.986 J.D.
V.P. & Corp. Coun., Dade Behring Inc.
Oettinger, Julian A. '39 '64 C.339 B.S. L.597 J.D.
Sr. V.P., Gen. Coun. & Corp. Secy., Wallgreen Co.
Oettinger, Mike .... '66 '93 C.339 B.S. L.145 J.D. Walgreen Co.
Oliszewicz, Sandra D. ..... '58 '83 C&L.424 B.S., J.D. Sr. Coun., Baxter International, Inc.
Olswang, Daniel H. ...... '70 '96 C.966 B.A. L.146 J.D. [Ⓐ Weltman,W.&R.] (⊙Chicago)
Ordaz, Steven P. .... '57 '85 C.56 B.A. L.352 J.D. Sr. Atty., Deutsche Fin. Servs.
Osmond, Darin V. .... '68 '95 C.101 B.A. L.94 J.D. Sr. Atty., Lit., Walgreen Co.
Pachter, Larry H., (AV) .... '57 '82 C&L.477 B.B.A., J.D. [Pachter,G.&F.]

Pachter, Gregory & Finocchiaro, P.C., (AV)
790 Estate Drive, Suite 150, 60015
Telephone: 847-317-7350 Fax: 847-317-7355
Larry H. Pachter; Patricia Baldwin Gregory; Peter D. Finocchiaro; Barbara C. Raffaldini.
Real Estate Finance, Real Estate Development and Commercial Litigation.
See Professional Biographies, DEERFIELD, ILLINOIS

Palay, Linda Coren .... '57 '83 C.1365 B.A. L.597 J.D. 820 Fox Hunt Trail
Palmer, John J. .... '56 '83 C.174 B.A. L.597 J.D. Lawyers Cooperative Publishing Co.
Palys, Peter G. .... '49 '81 C.178 A.B. L.209 J.D. Sr. Atty., Deutsche Fin. Servs.
Parmacek, Jacqueline Morris .... '60 '86 C.477 B.A. L.597 J.D. 728 Fox Hunt Trail
Pearson, Louise S. ..... '55 '84 C.911 B.A. L.326 J.D. Gen. Coun., Dade Behring Inc. (Pat.)
Perlin, Daniel .... '70 '95 C.339 B.A. L.209 J.D. Atty., Walgreen Co.

Perrelli, Anthony '— '05 C.999 B.S. L.365 J.D.
510 Lake Road, Suite 105, 60015
Telephone: 847-317-1451 847-236-9901
Email: perrelli@ameritech.net
Business Corporate, Small Business, Contracts, Business Planning, Real Estate, Commercial Litigation and Taxation.
See Professional Biographies, DEERFIELD, ILLINOIS

Persky, Marla S. '56 '82
C.597 B.S. L.910 J.D. Assoc. Gen. Coun., Baxter International, Inc.
Peters, Gary Arthur, (AV) .... '52 '83 C.972 B.S. L.602 J.D. Sr. Atty., Walgreen Co.
Peterson, David D., Jr. '59 '84 C.95 A.B. L.597 J.D.
Sr. Coun., Baxter International, Inc.
Petrie, Arthur R., II .... '59 '92 C.112 B.A. L.1137 J.D. [Hatton,P.&S.A.] ⊙

Phoebus, Edgar W. '41 '79 C.1027 B.S. L.365 J.D.
Sr. V.P., Secy. & Gen. Coun., Shand Morahan & Co., Inc.
Pinon, Dwayne A. .... '67 '96 C.966 B.S. L.209 J.D. Sr. Atty., Walgreen Co. (Pat.)
Poczatek, Donna M. .... '65 '90 C&L.209 B.A., J.D. Princ. Atty. Editor, West Grp.
Polikoff, Alan M. .... '42 '70 C.477 B.S. L.209 J.D. 407 Milford Rd.
Polster, John C. '59 '85 C.145 B.A. L.602 J.D.
Asst. V.P. & Assoc. Gen. Coun., Meridian Leasing Corporation
Powell, Andrew K. '57 '86 C.575 B.A. L.813 J.D.
(adm. in CA; not adm. in IL) Assoc. Gen. Coun., Baxter Intl., Inc.
Prebish, Ronald F. .... '40 '64 C.339 B.A. L.597 J.D. 1455 Rosewood Ave.
Price, Bradford R. L. '52 '77
C.597 B.S. L.339 J.D. Sr. Coun., Baxter International, Inc. (Pat.)
Pritz, Jerome L. ...... '27 '51 C.339 L.365 J.D. Mng. Editor, Clark Boardman Callaghan‡
Prodromos, Debra .... '56 '83 C.966 B.A. L.365 J.D. 636 Ambleside Dr.
Pucin, John S. .... '66 '92 C.973 B.A. L.117 J.D. [Weltman,W.&R.] (⊙Chicago)
Raffaldini, Barbara C. .... '62 '87 C&L.276 B.S.F.S., J.D. [Pachter,G.&F.]

Rapaport, Steven I., Law Offices of
(See Northbrook)

Rapp, Kristine A. '52 '76
C.477 B.A. L.597 J.D. Assoc. Gen. Coun., Baxter International, Inc.
Raskin, Fred B. .... '39 '64 C.112 B.A. L.597 J.D. 753 Grouse Court‡
Redstone, Michael G. .... '64 '91 C&L.477 B.A., J.D. Sr. Atty., Walgreen Co.
Reed, Jan Stern '59 '84 C.477 B.A. L.597 J.D.
Corp. Secy. & Assoc. Gen. Coun., Baxter International, Inc.
Reichard, Mary Hammer .... '62 '88 C.225 A.B. L.734 J.D. 1222 Dartmouth Lane‡
Resnick, Allan M. .... '46 '72 C&L.608 B.A., J.D. Div. V.P., Walgreens, Co.
Rieman, Gary H. '39 '65 C&L.966 B.B.A., J.D.
Dir. of IDAPP, Capital Develop., Illinois Student Assistance Comm.
Rockwell, Amy L. H. '58 '86 C.741 B.S. L.365 J.D.
Asst. Gen. Coun., Baxter International, Inc. (Pat.)
Rohn, Richard M. .... '15 '47 C.145 B.A. L.146 LL.B. William M. Mercer Inc.
Rubin, Jeffrey O. .... '55 '80 C.339 B.A. L.146 J.D. Coun., Shand Morahan & Co., Inc.
Rumbaugh, James .... '38 '63 C.1016 B.A. L.145 J.D. Coun., Globs Corporation
Rybak, Cynthia A. ..... '— '91 C&L.339 B.S., J.D. Corp. Coun., Baxter International, Inc.
Sampras, Chris C. .... '57 '83 C.339 B.A. L.146 J.D. 506 Longfellow Ave.
Schencker, Richard L. .... '53 '80 C.589 B.S. L.365 J.D. 1161 Lake Cook Rd.
Schmidt, Richard F. .... '73 '99 C.477 B.A. L.146 J.D. Atty., Walgreen Co.
Schneider, Bryan A. .... '67 '92 C.854 B.S. L.966 J.D. Sr. Atty., Walgreen Co.
Schohl, Joseph ...... '68 '93 C.339 B.S. L.178 J.D. Corp. Coun., Baxter International, Inc.
Serewicz, Denise Markham '63 '92
C.401 B.S. L.262 J.D. Corp. Coun., Baxter International, Inc. (Pat.)
Shell, Dawn McGowen .... '52 '99 C.1183 B.S. L.365 J.D. 433 Birchwood Ave.
Shlensky, Steven A., (AV) '61 '86 C&L.966 B.B.A., J.D.
APAC Customer Serv(s)., Inc.
Siew, Ambrose Chua Hai '62 '88
(adm. in Singapore; not adm. in IL) Corp. Coun., Asia, Baxter Intl., Inc.
Silverglade, Christine Cohan .... '68 '93 C&L.339 A.B., J.D. 1470 Gordon Terr.
Silverman, Howard R. '41 '67 C.966 B.A. L.209 J.D.
Pres., Monarch Pork Processors, Inc.
Silverman, Jeffrey D. .... '55 '80 C.339 B.S. L.365 J.D. 790 Estate Dr., Ste. 100
Silverman, Robert M. '55 '80
C.339 B.A. L.221 J.D. Div. VP, Real Estate Law, Walgreen Co.
Sinclair, Wayne A. .... '46 '71 C&L.923 A.B., J.D. Sr. V.P. & Gen. Coun., MMI Cos., Inc.
Sinton, Scott J. .... '64 '89 C.339 A.B. L.209 J.D. [Berks&S.] (⊙Waukegan)
Sjostrom, Susan D. .... '45 '77 C.347 B.A. L.146 J.D. Callaghan & Co.
Slade, Eugene E. '46 '72 C&L.966 B.A., J.D.
(adm. in WI; not adm. in IL) Sr. Atty., Walgreen Co.
Slater, Rochelle Price '58 '84
C.188 B.A. L.477 J.D. Gen. Coun., Meridian Leasing Corporation
Slavney, John D. '61 '88 C.966 B.A. L.1119 J.D.
(adm. in WI; not adm. in IL) Editor, Lawyers Cooperative Publishing
Slivnick, Bruce A. .... '56 '81 C.597 B.A. L.339 J.D. [Ⓐ T.A.Heller&Assoc.]
Smith, Craig M. .... '50 '80 C.424 B.B.A. L.209 J.D. Jim Beam Brands Co.
Smith, Edward J. '44 '75 C.648 B.A. L.228 J.D.
(adm. in NC; not adm. in IL) Clark Boardman Callaghan
Spear, James A. .... '42 '70 C.347 B.A. L.146 J.D. Berger, Goldstein & Co.
Stark, H. Allan .... '39 '68 C.72 B.A. L.966 J.D. Sr. Labor Coun., Walgreen Co.
Stark, Vincent J., (BV) .... '62 '88 C.338 B.S. L.365 J.D. [Kamerlink,S.&M.] ⊙
Staubitz, Arthur F. '39 '64 C.918 A.B. L.659 J.D.
Senior Vice President & General Counsel, Baxter International Inc.‡
Steer, Marc H. .... '58 '83 C.339 B.A. L.94 J.D. P.O. Box 22
Stein, Miriam B. .... '60 '85 C.659 B.S. L.813 J.D. 780 Smoke Tree Rd.‡
Steiner, Richard N. .... '67 '93 C.966 B.S. L.146 J.D. Sr. Atty., Walgreen Co.
Stern, Asher .... '30 '55 C.966 B.B.A. L.597 LL.B. 1745 Portage Pass
Stern, Jerome H., (AV) '24 '59 C.597 M.B.A. L.209 J.D.
610 Robert York Ave., Apt. 406
Sternlieb, Lynne R. .... '— '87 C.966 B.A. L.46 J.D. Monsanto Bus. Servs.-Law
Svalina, Nicholas B. '54 '79
C.339 B.A. L.209 J.D. Resch. Atty., Clark Boardman Callaghan
Tanaka, David F. '50 '81
C.477 B.A. L.209 J.D. V.P. & Gen. Coun., Gaylord Container Corp.
Tavitian, Katherine R. .... '58 '84 C.679 B.S. L.976 J.D. Walgreen Co.
Timm, Theodore R. .... '60 '85 C&L.209 B.S.C., J.D. [Ⓐ Grobart&L.]
Toal, Patrick J. .... '— '72 C.339 B.S. L.424 J.D. 1516 Stratford Road
Tolan, Paula A. '55 '81 C&L.424 B.A., J.D.
Assoc. Gen. Coun., Shand Morahan & Co., Inc.
Toran, Janice A. '48 '75 C.788 B.A. L.588 J.D.
V.P., Compl., Fujisawa Healthcare, Inc.
Tortorello, Robert J. '49 '76 C.339 B.S. L.146 J.D.
V.P., Gen. Coun. & Secy., Woodhead Ind., Inc.
Tselepis, James T. .... '67 '93 C.393 B.A. L.365 J.D. Editor, West Group
Tyrell, Mary P. ..... '52 '78 C.1151 B.A. L.209 J.D. V.P. & Publisher, Lawyers Coop. Pub.
Van Swearingen, Cynthia S. '35 '77
C.788 B.A. L.365 J.D. Editor, Lawyers Cooperative Publishing
Wasinunec, Myron W. .... '60 '86 C.98 B.A. L.365 J.D. Callaghan & Co.
Waskowski, Patricia '49 '83
C.1101 B.A. L.46 J.D. Editor, Lawyers Cooperative Publishing
Wattley, Mark A. .... '65 '91 C.209 B.A. L.602 J.D. Sr. Atty., Walgreen Co.
Weber, Dawn M. .... '67 '93 C.280 B.A. L.145 J.D. Corp. Coun., Baxter Int'l.
Weigand, Kenneth R. '57 '82
C.339 B.S. L.880 J.D. Div. V.P. - Employ. Rel., Walgreens, Co.
Weinstein, Anne Spencer .... '52 '81 C.856 B.A. L.276 J.D. Callaghan & Co.

Weltman, Weinberg & Reis Co., L.P.A.
1419 Lake Cook Road (⊙Chgo., IL; Troy, MI; Burlington, NJ; Cin., Cleve., Columbus, OH; Phila., Pitts., PA)
Wersyn, John S. '48 '76
C.339 B.S.E. L.209 J.D. Sr. Claims Atty., Shand Morahan & Co., Inc.
Wertjes, Catherine J. '55 '80
C.493 B.A. L.494 J.D. Assoc. Gen. Coun., Fujisawa Healthcare, Inc.
Wikoff, Larry R., (AV) .... '43 '68 C.477 B.A. L.209 J.D. 423 Elm St., Apt. 5B
Williams, Richard J. .... '30 '53 C.339 L.209 LL.B. A.S. Hansen, Inc.
Williams, Robert J. .... '31 '57 C.874 B.S. L.659 J.D. 1349 Woodland Dr.‡
Winter, Gretchen A. .... '57 '83 C.339 B.A. L.145 J.D. V.P. & Coun., Baxter Int'l.
Wise, Steven H. .... '57 '83 C.597 B.A. L.910 J.D. P.O. Box 1016
Witte, Linda R. '52 '78 C.114 B.A. L.477 J.D.
Senior Vice President, General Counsel & Secy., Beloit Corporation
Zaleski, Kenneth G. .... '49 '85 C.350 B.S. L.146 J.D. Clark Boardman Callaghan
Zambreno, John '41 '73 C.597 B.S. L.209 J.D.
Asst. Dir., Tax Admn./Tax Coun., Walgreen Co.
Zeid, Aaron M. .... '76 '02 C.174 B.A. L.146 J.D. [A.M.Zeid]
Zeid, Aaron M., LTD. .... 102 Wilmot Road, Suite 400
Ziemba, Daniel E., (BV) .... '43 '68 C.602 B.A. L.597 J.D. 747 Deerfield Rd.
Zimring, Michael .... '35 '60 C.221 B.A. L.209 J.D. 102 Wilmot

DeKALB, 39,018, *DeKalb Co.*

Alfini, James J. .... '43 '73 C.178 A.B. L.597 J.D. Northern Ill. Univ. Coll. of Law.
Anderson, Rolf Allan .... '74 '00 C.36 B.S. L.146 J.D. P.O. Box 711
Andrzejewski, Abram A. '72 '97 C.589 B.A. L.309 J.D.
Pres., American Marketing & Publishing, LLC

Boyle, Cordes, Witheft & Brown, LLC, (AV)
301 East Lincoln Highway, 60115-3307
Telephone: 815-756-6328 Fax: 815-756-8842 URL: http://www.boylelawdekalb.com
URL: http://www.bcwblaw.com
Members of Firm: John G. Boyle (1907-1996); Gary W. Cordes; Charles G. Brown; David J. Witheft (Board Certified Specialist in Real Property Law-Business, Commercial and Industrial Transactions, North Carolina State Board of Legal Specialization).
General Civil Trial Practice in State and Federal Courts. Probate, Corporate, Trust and Estate Planning, Real Estate, Zoning and Planning, Secured Lending.
Representative Clients: DeKalb Park District; Castle Bank, N.A.; National Bank and Trust Company of Sycamore.
References: Castle Bank, N.A.; National Bank and Trust Company of Sycamore.
See Professional Biographies, DEKALB, ILLINOIS

Brady, Gregory A. .... '76 '02 C&L.589 B.S., J.D. Northern Ill. Univ.
Brennan, Bruce A. .... '55 '86 C.340 B.S. L.589 J.D. 112 Orchard Lane
Brown, Charles G., (BV) .... '51 '76 C.339 B.S. L.424 J.D. [Boyle,C.W.&B.]
Burns, Russell E., (BV) .... '41 '65 C&L.846 B.B.A., J.D. 224 N. Second Street
Carlson, Robert P., (BV) .... '51 '76 C.679 B.A. L.365 J.D. 317 E. Locust St.
Cebula, Colleen .... '55 '94 C.238 B.S. L.589 J.D. [Cebula]
Cebula Law Offices .... 913 S. 4th St., Ste. 204

Cliffe, Foster, Corneille, Buick & Buick, LLC, (BV)
151 West Lincoln Highway, 60115 ⊙
Telephone: 815-758-6616
URL: http://www.cfcbb.com
Members of Firm: Keith L. Foster; Kevin E. Buick (Resident, Sycamore Office); Marcy L. Buick (Resident, Sycamore Office). Associate: Heather M. Fritsch.
General Civil and Criminal Practice. Probate, Real Estate, Family Law, Municipal Law, Business and Estate Planning, Commercial Law, Personal Injury, Insurance and Corporation Law. Practice in all State and Federal Courts, including Federal Trial Practice.
Sycamore, Illinois Office: 331 West State Street. Telephone: 815-895-7411.
Shabbona, Illinois Office: 110 West Comanche. Telephone: 815-824-2258.
Waterman, Illinois Office: 200 West Lincoln. Telephone: 815-264-3340.
Hinckley, Illinois Office: 165 Lincoln. Telephone: 815-286-3501.
See Professional Biographies, DEKALB, ILLINOIS

Coles, Kathleen L. '49 '78 C.945 B.A. L.145 J.D.
(adm. in NY; not adm. in IL) 4 Miller Court
Cordes, Gary W., (AV) .... '33 '62 C&L.352 B.S.C., J.D. [Boyle,C.W.&B.]
Cosentino, Christian Joseph .... '74 '00 C&L.589 B.A., J.D. [Cosentino]
Cosentino Law Firm, The .... 213 S. 2nd St.
Countryman, John W. .... '44 '70 C.589 B.A. L.146 J.D. 1528 Sleepy Hollow
Cronauer, Charles E.
(See Sycamore)
Davidson, Kenneth L. '45 '70 C&L.862 B.S.B.A., J.D.
Bd. of Trustee Parliam & Assoc. V.P. & Gen. Coun., Northern Ill. Univ.
de Seife, Rodolphe J. A. '25 '55
C.999 B.A. L.128 J.D. Prof., Northern Ill. Univ. Coll. of Law
Desmuke Hawkins, Odele S. .... '69 '96 C.914 B.A. L.339 J.D. [A Gillio&Assoc.]
Diedrich, Edward F., (BV) .... '30 '60 C.711 A.B. L.209 J.D. 126 Oak St.
Doherty, Thomas L., (CV) .... '45 '86 C&L.589 B.S., J.D. 125 N. 1st St.
Erwin, Scott R., (BV) .... '55 '80 C.338 B.S.Ed. L.339 J.D. [S.Erwin]
Erwin, Scott, (BV) .... 211 N. 1st St.
Foster, Keith L., (BV) '50 '79
C.589 B.A. L.146 J.D. [Cliffe,F.C.B.&B.] (⊙Hinckley, Shabbona)
Fritsch, Heather M. .... '75 '00 C.339 B.A. L.146 J.D. [A Cliffe,F.C,B.&B.]
Gilbert, Norden S., (BV) '49 '74 C.855 A.B. L.145 J.D.
Univ. Coun., Northern Ill. Univ.
Gillio, Vickie A., (AV) .... '48 '74 C.746 B.A. L.339 J.D. [Gillio&Assoc.]
Gillio & Associates, (AV) .... 210 Thornbrook Rd.
Groark, Edward Michael .... '53 '94 C&L.589 B.A., J.D. [M.Groark]
Groark, Mike, Law Office of .... 137 E. Lincoln Hwy.
Harrison, Keith Michaele '56 '81
C.1320 B.A. L.145 J.D. Asst. Prof. of Law, Northern Ill. Univ.
Iskowich, Charles H., (BV) .... '44 '70 C.966 B.S. L.146 J.D. Pub. Guard.
Kauffman, S. Blair '48 '75 C&L.502 B.S., J.D.
(adm. in MO; not adm. in IL) 630 Grove St.‡
Krupp, James C. .... '73 '00 C.966 B.A. L.436 J.D. [A Krupp&K.]
Krupp, Robert J. .... '43 '68 C.589 B.S. L.424 J.D. [Krupp&K.]
Krupp, Thomas J. .... '43 '68 C.589 B.S. L.424 J.D. [Krupp&K.]
Krupp & Krupp .... 3281 Commerce Dr.
Larsen, Robert A., (BV) .... '59 '86 C.927 B.A. L.589 J.D. 536 W. Lincoln Hwy.
Leifheit, John A. .... '20 '48 C.339 B.A. L.966 J.D. 125 Mattek Ave.‡
Lothson, Gary E., (CV) .... '58 '86 C&L.589 B.A., J.D. [G.Lothson]
Lothson, Gary, Law Office of, (CV) .... 203 Grove St.
Mandell, Leonard .... '50 '76 C.184 B.A. L.93 J.D. Northern Ill. Univ. Coll of Law
Nolan, Robert P. .... '50 '76 C.927 L.146 J.D. 913 S. 4th St., Ste 204
Obrzut, Mary Clover '38 '92
C.429 B.A. L.589 J.D. Northern Illinois University College of Law
Parness, Jeffrey A. '48 '75
C.164 B.A. L.145 J.D. Prof., Northern Ill. Univ. College of Law

Paul, Bernard Z., (BV) .... '44 '69 C.339 B.A. L.146 J.D. 231 S. 4th St.
Pollock, Meyers, Eickstead & Pulak, Ltd.
(See Marengo)
Rettig, S. Kathleen .... '60 '92 C.57 A.B. L.589 J.D. Northern Ill. Univ.
Richgels, Mary .... '49 '91 C.966 B.A. L.589 J.D. 231 S. 4th St.
Riefler, Charlene L. .... '— '98 L.589 J.D. 1220 School St.
Rissman, Harold A., (BV) .... '17 '49 C&L.879 A.B., LL.B. Grove & S. Second Sts.
Roman, Robert E., Jr. .... '52 '77 C.177 B.A. L.339 J.D. 227 Forsythe Lane
Rosenow, Brian Thomas ... '73 '99 C.802 B.B.A. L.146 J.D. Rosenow-Franzene Develop.
Schmall, Lorraine A. .... '50 '81 C.339 B.A. L.273 J.D. Prof. of Law, Northern Ill. Univ.
Schneider, Daniel M. .... '48 '73 C.910 A.B. L.150 J.D. Prof. of Law, Northern Ill. Univ.
Shneider, Gordon B. .... '33 '74 C.597 B.S. L.209 J.D. Prof. of Law, Northern Ill. Univ.
Swift, Joel H. '39 '63 C.895 B.A. L.659 LL.M.
(adm. in NY; not adm. in IL) Prof. of Law, Northern Ill. Univ.
Tarallo, Michelle .... '57 '84 C.424 B.A. L.589 J.D. Ill. Pollution Control Bd.
Taylor, David .... '53 '81 C.228 B.A. L.910 J.D. Prof. of Law, Northern Ill. Univ.
Thompson, Lamont, Flaherty & Masur, A Professional Corporation
(See Aurora)
Ullrich, Deborah L., Law Offices of '65 '93
C.221 B.S.B.A. L.424 J.D. 125 N. 1st St., Ste. B
Walter, James R. .... '71 '97 C.339 B.S. L.221 J.D. Mgr., Walter Farms
Walton, John A. '54 '87 C.338 B.S. L.597 J.D.
(adm. in CO; not adm. in IL) Assoc. Prof., Northern Ill. Univ.
Williams, Leigh A. .... '53 '80 C.530 B.A. L.46 J.D. Northern Ill. Univ.
Witheft, David J., (AVⓉ) .... '45 '71 C.589 B.A. L.339 J.D. [Boyle,C.W.&B.]

DELAVAN, 1,825, *Tazewell Co.*

Allen, Mark E. .... '50 '75 C.339 B.S. L.910 J.D. 306 N. Locust St.
Culbertson, Robert M., Jr., (BV) .... '32 '56 C.340 L.339 LL.B. 306 N. Locust St.

DE PUE, 1,842, *Bureau Co.*

Wimbiscus, William J., Jr., (BV) '26 '50
C.339 B.S. L.209 J.D. 222 W. 4th St. (⊙Spring Valley)

DES PLAINES, 58,720, *Cook Co.*

Adams, Wayne A. .... '43 '79 C.1151 B.S. L.589 J.D. 570 N.W. Hwy.
Amin, Daksha '51 '89 C.339 B.A. L.770 J.D.
(adm. in CA; not adm. in IL) 555 S. River Rd.
Bartel, Raymond P. .... '46 '76 C.424 B.A. L.365 J.D. 1420 Miner Street, 4th Floor‡
Baxter, Margaret C., (AV) .... '18 '47 C.209 L.597 J.D. 1011 S. 6th Ave.
Bernstein, Robert T. .... '40 '67 C.424 B.S.B.A. L.209 J.D. 200 Howard Ave.
Bevan, Richard E. '59 '83 C&L.999 B.A., J.D.
(adm. in England; not adm. in IL) Sr. Reg. Coun., UOP LLC
Braun, Jeffrey W. '54 '81
C.966 B.S. L.146 J.D. Proj. Mgr., RDI Software Technologies, Inc.
Broadie, Stephen W. '52 '79 C.937 B.S. L.800 J.D.
V.P., Fin. Legislation & Regul., Natl. Assn. of Independent Insurers
Brodl, Raymond F. .... '24 '51 C.337 L.424 J.D. 366 W. Lance Dr.‡
Brown, Glenn L. '54 '79 C.960 B.S. L.966 J.D.
(adm. in WI; not adm. in IL) Fed. Aviation Admin.
Brown, Marc L., The Law Offices of
(See Park Ridge)
Camodeca, Frank R. .... '44 '69 601 Lee St.
Cerone, Jack P. .... '40 '64 C.750 B.A. L.209 J.D. 770 Lee St., Ste. 201
Chromek, Paul G. '47 '73 C&L.339 B.A., J.D.
Asst. Gen. Coun., Gas Technology Institute
Cipolla, Vincent C. .... '43 '74 C.424 B.S. L.365 J.D. [Kurnik&C.]
Cirignani Heller Harman & Lynch LLP
(See Chicago)
Cleasby, Donald S. '60 '85 C&L.966 B.A., J.D.
Asst. V.P. & Asst. Gen. Coun., Natl. Assn. of Independent Insurers
Coghlan, John Shea .... '55 '80 C.393 B.A. L.209 J.D. 420 Lee St.
Collins, Barry G. .... '42 '67 C.399 B.A. L.597 J.D. [Tuttle,V.&C.]
Comiskey, Edwin Joseph .... '30 '63 C.424 B.S.C. L.146 J.D. 1847 Algonquin Road‡
Cory, Donald W. .... '26 '55 C.238 A.B. L.209 LL.B. 2600 River Road‡
Craven, Susan J. .... '52 '76 C&L.879 B.A., J.D. [Maloney&C.]
Currie, M. Cecelia .... '54 '79 C.326 B.S. L.209 J.D. Asst. Gen. Coun.
Cutler & Associates, LTD.
(See Skokie)
Cutts, John G., Jr. .... '41 '76 C&L.46 B.S.Che., J.D. Pat. Atty., UOP LLC (Pat.)
D'Agostino, Carlo G. .... '68 '93 C.339 B.A. L.209 J.D. 420 Lee St.
Dail, Gurmit S. '64 '90 C&L.999 B.A., J.D.
(adm. in England; not adm. in IL) Reg. Coun., UOP LLC
Daubaras, Jeanette B. .... '44 '81 C.339 B.S. L.365 J.D. Gen. Atty.
Davis, Larry A. .... '50 '76 C.597 B.A. L.209 J.D. 960 Rand Rd., Ste. 210
Day, Paul R., Law Offices of .... '60 '00 C.339 B.S. L.146 J.D. 1454 Miner St.
Dienes, Mary Ellen, (AV) .... '42 '69 C.424 B.S. L.597 J.D. 9250 Hamilton Court
Dowd, Daniel J. .... '52 '78 C&L.209 B.A., J.D. [Dowd,D.&M.]
Dowd, Joseph P. .... '50 '87 C.209 B.A. L.615 J.D. 880 Lee St., Ste. 100
Dowd, Dowd & Mertes, Ltd. .... 701 Lee Street, Suite 790
Dvorin, Shirley R. .... '56 '81 C&L.597 B.S.J., J.D. 9240 Aspen Lane
Eisenstein, Irving .... '10 '31 C.339 A.B. L.145 J.D. 8815 Golf Rd.
Epton, Michael R. .... '48 '73 C&L.597 B.S., J.D. 960 Rand Rd., Ste. 210
Erickson, Rick J. .... '52 '77 C.339 B.S. L.365 J.D. [R.J.Erickson]
Erickson, Rick J., Ltd. .... 716 Lee St.
Fagan, Joseph M. .... '46 '69 C.339 L.209 J.D. 960 Rand Rd., Rm. 210
Fagan, Steven H. .... '73 '98 C.339 B.A. L.146 J.D. 960 Rand Rd., Ste. 210
Ferraro, Anthony B., The Law Offices of
(See Rosemont)
Fischer, Gerry R. .... '62 '01 C.339 B.S. L.365 J.D. Advantage Law Group
Foutris, Basileios J. .... '75 '00 C.597 B.A. L.424 J.D. [A Kurnik&C.]
Fuelling, Michael L. ... '67 '93 C.679 B.S.E. L.347 J.D. Asst. Div. Coun., UOP LLC (Pat.)
Furman, Mitch A. .... '70 '00 C.176 B.A. L.365 J.D. 8710 A Gregory Lane
Gerstein, Michael D., (AV) .... '44 '73 C.1016 B.A. L.146 J.D. 800 Lee St.
Goldberg, Mark '53 '78 C.659 B.A. L.446 J.D.
(adm. in MD; not adm. in IL; Pat.) Div. Pat. Coun., UOP LLC
Gooding, Arthur E. '54 '00 C.111 L.146 J.D.
(adm. in MI; not adm. in IL; Pat.) Pat. Atty, UOP LLC
Grabowski, Paul A. .... '58 '84 C.867 B.S. L.365 J.D. 2800 S. River Road
Greene, Neil J. .... '61 '86 C.966 B.S. L.910 J.D. 2800 S. River Road

Halleen, Otis H., (AV) '34 '63
C.937 A.B. L.597 J.D. V.P., Secy. & Gen. Coun., United Stationers
Hart, Patrick S., Attorney at Law '53 '81
C.339 B.A. L.209 J.D. 1585 Ellinwood Ave., Ste. 105
Hartrick, Kathryn M., (AV) '61 '86
C.477 B.B.A. L.930 J.D. Asst. Gen. Coun., United Stationers
Heidorn, David L. .... '54 '81 C&L.879 B.A., J.D. 2600 River Rd.
Holmgren, R. Bruce .... '20 '50 C.597 B.A. L.146 LL.B. Packaging Engg.
Hoppe, Charles C., Jr. .... '53 '78 C.1106 B.A. L.146 J.D. [Knight,H.F.&K.]
Hurns, Robert J. '55 '92
C.1183 B.A. L.209 J.D. Coun., Natl. Assn. of Independent Insurers
Huston, Steven C. '54 '80 C.337 B.A. L.365 J.D.
VP Gen Coun., Symons Corporation (⊙Dayton, OH)
Jacobs, Emil .... '10 '34 C.145 L.209 LL.B. 9209 Potter Rd.‡
Jacobs, William R., II .... '27 '53 C&L.597 B.S., J.D. 601 Lee St.
James, Mark E. .... '52 '82 C.597 B.S.Che. L.589 J.D. Sr. Grp. Coun., UOP LLC
Jenkins, Neil E. .... '49 '81 C.103 A.B. L.424 J.D. Corp. Atty., Lawson Products, Inc.
Jensen, Kathleen N. '59 '92 C.436 B.S. L.146 J.D.
Ins. Svcs. Coun., Natl. Assn. of Independent Insurers
Just, Lawrence E. .... '52 '79 C.339 B.A. L.146 J.D. Graph/Sphere Corp.
Kaiser, Neil J. .... '61 '86 C.1144 B.A. L.209 J.D. 688 Lee St.
Knight, Byron D. .... '50 '76 C.234 B.S. L.365 J.D. [Knight,H.F.&K.]
Knight, Elizabeth A. .... '53 '78 C&L.209 B.A., J.D. [Knight,H.F.&K.]
Knight, Hoppe, Fanning & Knight, Ltd. .... 2860 S. River Rd., Ste. 400
Kogut, A. Charles .... '52 '78 C.339 B.S. L.365 J.D. 2590 E. Devon
Kogut, Anthony J. .... '16 '44 L.365 LL.B. 2590 E. Devon St.
Koziol, Michael G. '55 '80 C&L.424 A.B., J.D.
Sr. Dir. & Coun., Natl. Assn. of Independent Insurers
Krajewski, Jeffrey Gerald .... '71 '96 C.587 B.A. L.209 J.D. 2600 River Road
Kupietz, Perry A. '50 '75 C.401 B.A. L.273 J.D.
(adm. in DC; not adm. in IL) FAA
Kurnik, William W., (AV) .... '46 '75 C.46 B.S. L.365 J.D. [Kurnik&C.] (⊙Indpls., IN)
Kurnik & Cipolla, Ltd., (AV) .... 2860 S. River Rd.
LaCost, Gregory W. '67 '95 C.340 B.A. L.365 J.D.
Coun., Property Casualty Insurers Association of America
Lester, Debra Ritt .... '56 '81 C&L.424 B.B.A., J.D. 516 Anita St.
Ligocki, Raymond J., (AV) .... '45 '69 C&L.424 B.B.A., J.D. Div. Coun., UOP LLC
Locks, David H., Law Offices of
(See Chicago)
Lockwood, James M. .... '54 '79 C&L.861 B.A., J.D. 340 Dover Dr.
Lucking, John T., (BVⓉ) '53 '79 C&L.93 A.B., J.D.
(adm. in NY; not adm. in IL) V.P. & Gen. Coun., UOP LLC
Maas, Maryann .... '64 '92 C.339 B.S. L.365 J.D. Div. Pat. Coun., UOP LLC (Pat.)
Maloney, E. William, Jr. .... '51 '76 C.776 A.B. L.879 J.D. [Maloney&C.]
Maloney & Craven, P.C. .... 2093 Rand Rd.
Mandarino, Samuel A. .... '69 '94 C.209 B.S. L.966 J.D. 2340 River Rd., Ste. 300
Marcis, Steve J. .... '51 '81 C.46 B.S. L.209 J.D. 3158 S. River Rd., Ste. 116
Mason, David E. .... '39 '64 C.299 A.B. L.145 J.D. Krasberg Corp.
McCabe, John F. .... '57 '84 L.608 J.D. 1924 Birch St.
McGuire, Monika Lussnig '66 '91 C.339 B.A. L.424 J.D.
Asst. Gen. Coun., Natl. Assn. of Independent Insurers
Mckibben, Scott D. .... '69 '94 C.209 L.966 J.D. 2340 River Rd., Ste. 300
McKinley, Michael F. .... '52 '82 C.215 B.A. L.365 J.D. Gen. Atty., Fed. Aviation Admin.
McLain, John R. .... '61 '86 C&L.477 B.A., J.D. Sr. Coun. Trade Reg., UOP LLC
McNally, Patrick J., Jr. .... '33 '61 C&L.424 B.S., J.D. 2600 River Rd.
McSweeney, Patrick F. .... '55 '80 C.339 B.A. L.424 J.D. Div. Coun., UOP LLC
Mertes, Drake D. .... '51 '76 C.597 B.A. L.209 J.D. [Dowd,D.&M.]
Molinaro, Frank S. '51 '90 C.424 B.S. L.209 J.D.
Dep. Chief Pat Coun., UOP LLC (Pat.)
Montgomery, Robt. C. .... '16 '47 C.597 L.146 LL.B. 740 E. Golf Rd.‡
Moore, Michael A. .... '56 '96 C.205 B.S. L.424 J.D. Div. Pat. Coun., UOP LLC (Pat.)
Moran, John Jos. .... '15 '48 C.999 L.424 LL.B. 404 Tracy Terr.
Moran, Timothy P. .... '63 '88 C.339 B.A. L.46 J.D. DoAll Co.
Moriarty, Joseph T. .... '60 '85 C.30 B.A. L.365 J.D. 770 Lee St.
Morris, Daniel M., (AV) .... '41 '66 C.473 B.S. L.597 J.D. 1111 E. Touhy Ave.
Mulhern, Thomas F. .... '27 '52 C&L.209 J.D. Sr. Atty., Chicago Motor Club Ins. Co.
Munden, Robin G. '47 '73
C.208 B.A. L.597 J.D. V.P. & Gen. Coun., DSC Logistics, Inc.
Munsterman, Herbert F. .... '59 '85 C.350 B.S. L.221 J.D. Div. Coun., UOP LLC (Pat.)
Nedeau, Nicholas J. .... '56 '81 C.475 B.A. L.436 J.D. Asst. Gen. Coun., UOP LLC
Norten, Candace R. .... '63 '88 C.679 B.S. L.146 J.D. Fed. Aviation Admn.
Novak, Carla T. '55 '82 C.1016 B.A. L.365 J.D.
Dir., Support Chain Support, DSC Logistics, Inc.
Nudo, Dennis S., (AV) .... '41 '67 C&L.209 LL.B. [Nudo,P.&S.]
Nudo, Potteracki & Salabes, P.C., (AV) .... 1700 E. Higgins Road
O'Laughlin, Thomas C. '49 '75 C.602 B.A. L.146 J.D.
Gen. Coun. & Secy., Gas Technology Institute
Orfei, Pierangela '55 '85 C.659 B.A. L.589 J.D.
Staff Atty., Health Care, ASB Meditest
Parry, Robert W. .... '18 '55 C.597 B.S. L.424 J.D. P.O. Box 2352
Paschall, James C., (AV) '65 '90
C.502 B.S. L.16 J.D. Sr. Grp. Pat. Coun., UOP LLC (Pat.)
Peterson, Charles T. .... '37 '62 C.339 B.S. L.209 J.D. 254 N. Laurel Ave.‡
Pinsof, Michael W. .... '54 '79 C.352 B.A. L.209 J.D. 960 Rand Rd., Ste. 210
Pluymert, James H. .... '56 '81 C.114 B.A. L.209 J.D. [Robinson,P.P.M.&A.] ⊙
Pope, Derwin B. .... '65 '90 C&L.734 B.A., J.D. Enforce. Atty.
Port, Sidney L. .... '11 '36 C.339 B.A. L.209 J.D. Lawson Products Inc.
Poteracki, Lee .... '50 '75 C.602 B.A. L.209 J.D. [Nudo,P.&S.]
Prock, Charles R. .... '47 '72 C&L.424 B.A., J.D. Federal Aviation Admn.
Ptasinski & Smith, P.C.
(See Niles)
Radek, Thomas N. .... '64 '91 C.339 B.A. L.997 J.D. 856 Pearson St.
Ramirez, Jack, (AVⓉ) '39 '64 C.174 B.S. L.900 J.D.
(adm. in KS; not adm. in IL) Pres., Natl. Assn. of Independent Insurers
Robinson, Pluymert, Piercey, MacDonald & Amato, Ltd, (BVⓉ)
733 Lee Street, Suite 100 (⊙Hoffman Estates)
Rozner, Irwin D. .... '33 '57 C.1016 L.209 LL.B. 2093 Rand Rd.
Salabes, George R. .... '45 '82 C.707 B.A. L.365 J.D. [Nudo,P.&S.]
Salon, Richard L. .... '50 '77 C.1016 B.S.B.A. L.365 J.D. 960 Rand Rd., Ste. 210
Schellenberg, Carl B. '40 '69 C.605 A.B. L.37 J.D.
(adm. in AZ; not adm. in IL) Reg. Coun., Fed. Aviation Admin.
Schoeneman, Jenna Lynn .... '55 '81 C.108 B.S. L.365 J.D. [Knight,H.F.&K.]
Schroeder, Nancy M. '49 '79 C.502 B.A. L.146 J.D.
Asst. V.P., Workers' Comp., Natl. Assn. of Independent Insurers

Schwartz, Daniel M. .... '50 '81 C.674 B.A. L.94 J.D. Ulmer Bros., Inc.
Scott, Randall W. '45 '73 C.123 B.A. L.309 J.D.
(adm. in DC; not adm. in IL) 780 Lee St.
Seidman Law Offices
(See Chicago)
Sheldon, James S. .... '30 '59 C&L.339 B.S., LL.B. 445 Kinkaid Ct.
Shuldiner, Paul R., Law Offices of, (BV) '53 '80
C.454 B.A. L.851 J.D. 420 Lee St. (⊙Chicago)
Skeen, Oliver '67 '95 C&L.999 B.A., LL.M.
(adm. in England; not adm. in IL) Reg. Coun., UOP LLC
Slutzky, Jay A.
(See Niles)
Snyder, Eugene I. .... '33 '78 C.831 B.S. L.424 J.D. 25 E. Algonquin Rd. (Pat.)
Sotos, Sarah Hansen .... '53 '77 C.473 A.B. L.424 J.D. [Ⓐ Knight,H.F.&K.]
Standefer, Mark C. .... '54 '80 C.339 B.A. L.146 J.D. United Stationers, Inc.
Stephenson, Harley A. .... '27 '52 C&L.912 B.A., LL.B. 1417 Ashland
Strazzante, Salvatore R. .... '40 '64 C&L.339 B.A., LL.B. 9231 Twin Oaks
Suderman, Verlyn L. '66 '92
C.659 B.S. L.209 J.D. Dir., Asst. Gen. Coun., DSC Logistics, Inc.
Sumberg, Alan .... '34 '58 C&L.339 B.S., LL.B. Dep. Asst. Chief Coun., FAA
Tolomei, John G. .... '53 '83 C.46 M.S. L.146 J.D. Chf. Pat. Coun., UOP LLC (Pat.)
Tuttle, Milton H. .... '14 '36 C.597 B.S. L.146 J.D. [Tuttle,V.&C.] ‡

Tuttle, Vedral & Collins PC
733 Lee Street, Suite 210, 60016
Telephone: 847-824-0124 Fax: 847-824-7905
URL: http://www.tvclaw.com
Milton H. Tuttle (Retired); Barry G. Collins; William D. Vedral.
Residential and Commercial Real Estate, Foreclosures, Banking Law, Trust and Estate Planning, Probate, Family Law, Divorce, Equitable Distribution, Corporate Law.
See Professional Biographies, DES PLAINES, ILLINOIS

Tyrpin, Terry E. '51 '76
C.238 B.A. L.146 J.D. Sr. V.P., Natl. Assn. of Independent Insurers
Van de Kerckhove, Michael E. '42 '68 C.707 B.A. L.339 J.D.
Asst. Gen. Coun., UOP LLC
Vedral, William D. .... '43 '68 C&L.339 B.A., J.D. [Tuttle,V.&C.]
Waldherr, David P. '57 '85 C.966 B.S. L.146 J.D.
Pres., Cambridge Educational Services
Weg, Stuart M. .... '61 '98 C.1349 B.A. L.146 J.D. 2860 River Rd.
Wheeler, William C., Jr. '45 '79 C.31 B.A. L.880 J.D.
(adm. in MI; not adm. in IL) Dir., Educ., Amer. Soc. of Safety Engrs.
Whelan, Michael C. .... '62 '87 C.436 B.S. L.190 J.D. 770 Lee St., Suite 202
Wills, Thomas R. '52 '77 C.477 B.S.Ch.E. L.912 J.D.
Asst. Gen. Coun., UOP LLC (Pat.)
Winton, Glen P., (AV) .... '30 '69 C.597 B.S. L.365 J.D. 9501 N. Terrace Pl.‡
Witek, J. Thomas .... '69 '95 C.976 B.A. L.339 J.D. [Witek]
Witek Law Offices .... 950 Lee St., Ste. 103
Wrighte, Andre D. '70 '96
(adm. in VT; not adm. in IL) 9319 W. Ballard Rd.
Yearwood, Ellen A. .... '55 '86 C.1365 B.S. L.209 J.D. 856 Pearson St.
Young, Thomas, Law Firm
(See Palatine)
Zeman, Robert L. '60 '85 C&L.424 B.A., J.D.
Sr. V.P., State Govt. Affrs., Natl. Assn. of Independent Insurers
Zurales, Chris G. .... '53 '79 C.339 B.A. L.365 J.D. F.A.A. Reg. Coun. Off.

DIXMOOR, 3,934, *Cook Co.*

Loewer, Robert E. .... '68 '95 C.700 B.A. L.1000 J.D. National Railway Equipment Co.

DIXON, * 15,941, *Lee Co.*

Ackert, Jacquelyn D Craig .... '67 '92 C.798 B.S. L.801 J.D. [Ackert]
Ackert Law Office .... P.O. Box 735
Badger, David W., (BV) .... '54 '79 C.357 B.A. L.339 J.D. [Ehrmann G.B.&L.]
Beckman, Charles T., (BV) .... '49 '75 C.234 B.S.Ed. L.365 J.D. Asso. Cir. J.
Considine, Dana M. .... '79 '03 C.927 B.B. L.221 J.D. [Ⓐ Ehrmann G.B.&L.]
Dixon, Henry S., (AV) .... '34 '63 C.602 B.A. L.365 J.D. [Dixon&G.] (⊙Amboy)
Dixon, Henry Sherwood, Jr., (BV) .... '67 '97 C.339 B.S. L.365 J.D. [Dixon&G.]
Dixon, James E., (AV) .... '39 '67 C.602 B.A. L.365 J.D. P.O. Box 408
Dixon, Mary Pat T. .... '69 '00 C.424 B.B.A. L.365 J.D. 114 E. Everett St.

Dixon & Giesen, (AV)
121 East First Street, P.O. Box 389, 61021
Telephone: 815-284-2288 Fax: 815-284-1338
Email: lag@hsdixonlaw.com URL: http://www.hsdixonlaw.com
Henry S. Dixon; Linda A. Giesen; Henry Sherwood Dixon, Jr.
General Civil, Criminal Trial and Appellate Practice in all State and Federal Courts. Banking, Corporation, Insurance, Workers Compensation and Family Law. Personal Injury. Probate and Estate Planning, Municipal and Environmental Law.
See Professional Biographies, DIXON, ILLINOIS

Downey, Michael C., (CV) .... '52 '84 C.98 B.S. L.201 J.D. 420 West 2nd St.
Ehrmann, Rolfe F., (BV) .... '49 '75 C.1183 B.A. L.209 J.D. [Ehrmann G.B.&L.]

Ehrmann Gehlbach Badger & Lee, (BV)
Commerce Towers Suite 100, 215 E. First Street, 61021
Telephone: 815-288-4949 Fax: 815-288-3068
URL: http://www.egbbl.com
Members of Firm: Rolfe F. Ehrmann; Gary R. Gehlbach; David W. Badger; Douglas E. Lee; Warren H. Badger (1911-2005). Associates: Megan G. Heeg; Dana M. Considine.
Criminal and Civil Litigation. Personal Injury, Corporate, Family, Insurance Defense, Real Estate, Estate Planning, Banking, Probate Law, Bankruptcy/Creditor's Rights Law and Worker's Compensation.
Representative Clients: AMCORE Bank N.A., Dixon; Bradford Mutual Insurance Co.
See Professional Biographies, DIXON, ILLINOIS

Feofanov, Dmitry .... '57 '94 C.999 L.146 J.D. 1639 Branywine Lane
Fish, Daniel A., (BV) .... '54 '81 C.927 B.S. L.365 J.D. States Atty.
Foulker, Darla A. .... '78 '03 C&L.589 B.A., J.D. [Ⓐ Ward&W.]
Fritts, David T. .... '48 '76 C.602 B.A. L.597 J.D. 309 S. Galena Ave., Ste. 410
Gehlbach, Gary R., (BV) .... '49 '78 C.388 B.A. L.146 J.D. [Ehrmann G.B.&L.]
Giesen, Linda A., (BV) .... '51 '91 C.801 B.A. L.352 J.D. [Dixon&G.]
Heeg, Megan G., (BV) .... '56 '90 C.697 B.S. L.589 J.D. [Ⓐ Ehrmann G.B.&L.]
Hill, Martin D. .... '40 '65 C.174 B.S. L.339 LL.B. Assoc. Cir. J.
Hornsby, Thomas E. .... '36 '64 C.339 B.A. L.365 J.D. 309 S. Galena Ave., Ste. 410
Jacobson, Ronald M., (BV) .... '57 '82 C.937 B.A. L.879 J.D. 302 S. Galena Ave.
Johnson, Harry E. .... '30 '80 C.339 A.B. L.589 J.D. 7182 Rock Nation Rd.‡
Keller, Bruce E., (BV) .... '51 '87 C.427 B.A. L.589 J.D. [Keller]
Keller, J. Richard, (AV) .... '24 '50 C&L.339 B.S., LL.B. [Keller] ⊙

Keller Law Office, (AV) … 119 West First Street (⊙Ashton)
Lathe, Douglas E., (BV) … '59 '84 C&L.339 B.A., J.D. 115 West First Street
Lee, Douglas E., (BV) … '62 '87 C.339 B.A. L.999 J.D. [Ehrmann G.B.&L.]
Magdich, Tomas M. … '39 '64 C.694 A.B. L.597 J.D. Cir. J.
Mandrgoc, David W., (BV) … '47 '73 C&L.424 J.D. [Mandrgoc]
Mandrgoc Law Office, (BV) … 221 E. 2nd St.
Nichols, Myra W. … '14 '38 C&L.145 A.B., J.D. 421 E. Everett St.‡
Payne, John E. … '48 '74 C.424 B.A. L.597 J.D. Assoc. Cir. J.
Thompson, Robert J., Law Office of … '66 '94 C.259 B.S. L.589 J.D. P.O. Box 1016
Ward, Kelly P., (CV) … '66 '91 C.589 B.A. L.500 J.D. [Ⓐ Ward&W.]
Ward, Nancy Ann, (CV) … '43 '91 C.927 B.A. L.589 J.D. [Ward&W.]
Ward, Patrick E., (BV) … '43 '70 C.602 A.B. L.365 J.D. [Ward&W.]
Ward & Ward, (BV) … 316 S. Peoria Ave.
Williams, Al Henry, (CV) … '48 '85 C.98 B.A.S. L.589 J.D. 2181/2 S. Ottawa Ave.
Williamson, David R., (BV) … '37 '64 C&L.966 B.S., LL.B. 1307 Burchell Ct.

DOLTON, 25,614, *Cook Co.*

Adams, Jean A., Law Offices of '52 '80
C.741 B.A. L.209 J.D. 1350 E. Silbey Blvd., Ste. 400
Conroy, John T. … '28 '57 C&L.209 B.S., J.D. [J.T.Conroy]
Conroy, John T., P.C. … P.O. Box 27
Essary, Jean … '21 '70 C.339 B.S. L.365 J.D. 15115 Hastings Dr.‡
Mortimer, J. Stirling, (Ltd.), (AV) … '18 '42 C.602 B.S. L.209 J.D. 1350 E. Sibley Blvd.
Sharkey, Edward, V. … '55 '85 C.339 B.S. L.365 J.D. 14105 Lincoln Ave.

DONGOLA, 728, *Union Co.*

Fike, Sara L., (BV) … '47 '85 C.435 B.A. L.801 J.D. 102 Elm St.

DOWNERS GROVE, 48,724, *DuPage Co.*

Angileri, Michael Anthony … '71 '98 C.750 M.B.A. L.365 J.D. [Angileri&Assoc.]
Angileri & Associates … 6900 Main St., Ste. 210
Argianas, Charles G. … '55 '86 C.238 B.S. L.365 J.D. 5509 Belmont Rd.
Baker, E. Clifford … '14 '38 C&L.209 LL.B. 5134 Main St.
Baker, Susan D. '53 '82 C.578 B.A. L.209 J.D.
VP, Sect'y & General Counsel-Mngt. Services, ServiceMaster Company L.P.
Beck, Darren Barber '69 '00 C.800 B.A. L.596 J.D.
Assoc. Corp. Coun., Heartland Home Finance, Inc.
Beggs, Gregory B., Law Offices of, (AV) '29 '56
C.976 B.A. L.145 J.D. 5100 Fairview Avenue (Pat.)
Blasi, David … '69 '96 C.375 B.A. L.146 J.D. Dir./Assoc. Coun., First Health Group Corp.
Bordyn, Dennis R. … '51 '82 C.602 B.A. L.209 J.D. 532 65th St.
Borla, Robert V. … '42 '67 C.602 B.B.A. L.339 J.D. [Borla,N.&Assoc.]
Borla, North & Associates, P.C. … 6912 S. Main St.
Bratzel, Andrew D. '59 '84 C.475 B.A. L.209 J.D.
V.P. & Sr. Legal Coun., The ServiceMaster Co.
Bromet, Michael G. … '73 '99 C&L.880 B.A., J.D. Corp. Coun., Hub Group, Inc.
Brower, Scott A. … '70 '95 C.624 B.A. L.589 J.D. Litig. Coun., Servicemaster Co., The
Bruce, Robert R. '58 '83 C&L.602 B.A., J.D.
V.P. & Labor Rel. Coun., The ServiceMaster Co.
Carney, Clifford M. … '26 '52 C.475 B.A. L.339 LL.B. 1121 Warren Ave.‡
Carroll, Walter B. … '19 '48 C&L.339 B.A., LL.B. 800 Ogden Ave.
Carrozza, Lori N. … '77 '02 C.339 B.A. L.734 J.D. [Ⓐ Momkus M.M.M.M.&S.]
Clark, George R., Law Offices of … '23 '53 C.339 B.S. L.209 J.D. 1021 Mistwood Lane
Cline, Jeffrey Ted … '55 '00 C.339 B.S. L.365 J.D. 9 S. 307 Florence Avenue
Cochran, David S., (BV) … '35 '67 C.597 Ph.B. L.424 J.D. 921 Curtiss St.
Coffey, John E. … '25 '51 C&L.209 LL.B. 902 Maple Ave.
Coffey, Mary Cox … '— '90 C.741 B.B.A./B.A. L.365 J.D. [Ⓐ McJoynt&K.]
Colber, Douglas W. '60 '87
C.937 B.A. L.597 J.D. V.P. & Legal Coun., The ServiceMaster Co.
Coleman, Gary Lee, (BV) … '45 '78 C.475 B.A. L.424 J.D. [L.Coleman]
Coleman, Lee, P.C., Law Office of, (BV) … 3051 Oak Grove Rd., Ste. 200

Collins, Mary L. '55 '80 C.966 B.A. L.436 J.D.
6912 S. Main Street, Suite 200, 60516
Telephone: 630-969-3903 Fax: 630-969-3931 URL: http://www.marycollinsdisabilitylaw.com
URL: http://www.collinsdisabilitylaw.com
Social Security Disability, Real Estate, Wills, Medicare, Medicaid, Elder Law.
See Professional Biographies, DOWNERS GROVE, ILLINOIS

Corbin, Kathy J. '64 '89 C&L.352 B.A., J.D.
Assoc. Coun. & Dir., First Health Group Corp.
Cotton, Jacqueline Ann, (BVⓉ) '60 '85 C.477 B.A. L.912 J.D.
(adm. in MI; not adm. in IL) 3500 Lacey Rd., Ste. 1040
Covey, Maude … '08 '65 C.393 L.365 LL.B. 4820 Bryan Pl.‡
Davis, Kimberly A. … '65 '97 C.801 B.S. L.146 J.D. [Momkus M.M.M.M.&S.]
DePew, David L., II, Law Offices of '59 '84
C.578 B.A. L.1292 J.D. 1007 Curtiss St., Ste. 3
Dillon, Erika … '68 '95 C.914 B.A. L.145 J.D. Sara Lee Food & Beverage
Dispensa, Paul C. … '52 '82 C.208 B.S.B.A. L.589 J.D. Liability Ins. Resch. Bureau
Douglas, Robert E. … '57 '82 C.339 B.A. L.209 J.D. Ill. St. Toll Hwy. Auth.
Dudley, Mary K. McMahon '59 '83
C.597 B.A. L.424 J.D. V.P. & Legal Coun., The ServiceMaster Co.
Dunne, Edward J. … '42 '71 C.339 B.S. L.209 J.D. 436 Ridgview St.
Dunworth, Robert E. … '36 '73 C.339 B.S. L.146 J.D. 921 Curtiss St.
Ekker, Steven B. … '66 '93 C.477 B.A. L.589 J.D. [Momkus M.M.M.M.&S.]
Fallon-Houle, Nancy … '56 '86 C.1016 B.S.B.A. L.146 J.D. [N.Fallon-Houle]

Fallon-Houle, Nancy, P.C.
5449 Bending Oaks Place, 60515-4456
Telephone: 630-963-0439 URL: http://www.nfhlaw.com
Email: nfallon@nfhlaw.com URL: http://www.lawyers.com/nfallon
Nancy Fallon-Houle.
Entrepreneur, Entrepreneurship, Starting a Business, Incorporation, Corporation, Corporations, *Limited Liability* Company, *Limited Liability* Companies, LLC, Entity, Partnership, Partnerships, Business Enterprises, Start-Up, Start Up, Early Stage, Early-Stage, Small Business, Business, Emerging Growth, Emerging Company, Corporate, Corporate Law, Corporate Lawyer.
Venture Capital, Raising Capital, Investor, Investing, Angel Investor, Seed Capital, Regulation D, Form D, Rule 506, Rule 504, SCOR, U-7, Form U-7, Business Plan, Business Planning, Disclosure, Due Diligence, Securities Disclosure, Private Placement, Private Offering, Private Offering Memo, Private Offering Memorandum, Private Placement Memo, Private Placement Memorandum, PPM, Subscription Agreement, Investor Agreement, Equity, Equity Financing, Financing, Stock, Shares, Stock Option, Option, Options, Warrants, Stock Offering.
Securities Law, Securities Offering, Securities Exemption, Exemption, Exempt Offering, SEC, Securities and Exchange Commission, Securities Registration, Securities Regulation, Registration, Compliance, Reg D, Blue Sky, Blue Sky Law, State Securities, State Securities Law, State Registration, Federal Securities, Regulation A, Regulation SB, IPO, NASDAQ, Securities Lawyer, Securities and Investments.
Investment Adviser, Investment Advisor, Financial planner, Financial Planning, IARD, ADV, Form ADV, WebCRD, CRD, NASD, Finder, Money Finder, Private Placement Broker, NFA, Managed

(This Listing Continued)

Fallon-Houle, Nancy, P.C. (Continued)

Funds, Hedge Fund, Trading Fund, Securities Fund, Futures Fund, Commodities Fund, Commodity Trading Advisor, CTA, Commodity Pool, CPO, Futures, Fund, Funds, CFTC, Disclosure Document, Compliance Audits, Regulatory Audits.
Business Law, Business Lawyer, Contract, Contracts, Agreement, Stockholder, Shareholder; Shareholder Agreement, Stockholder Agreement, LLC Agreement, Operating Agreement, Executive Agreement, Stock Option Agreement, Nondisclosure Agreement, Confidentiality Agreement, Closely-held, Closely held, Closely Held Businesses, Officers, Directors, Resolutions, Minute Book, Stock Ledger, Corporate Maintenance, Qualification, State Qualification, Business License, Annual Report.
Venture, Joint Venture, Joint Ventures, Strategic Alliance, Strategic Alliances, Film Financing.
See Professional Biographies, DOWNERS GROVE, ILLINOIS

Fernandez, Eduardo J. … '73 '03 C.339 L.146 J.D. 6900 Main St., Ste. 210
Fitzgerald, Eileen R., Law Office of '59 '85 C.209 B.S. L.879 J.D.
1561 Warren Avenue
Fleming, Edward L. … '35 '61 C.424 A.B. L.597 J.D. 902 Maple Ave.
Galloway, Norval B. … '50 '83 C.98 B.S. L.966 J.D. Sr. Coun., Vysis Inc. (Pat.)
Gaspar, James J., Law Offices of … '55 '91 C.339 B.S. L.365 J.D. 6555 Berrywood Lane
Gaston, Karen Marie … '69 '95 C.424 B.A. L.365 J.D. Sr. Atty., First Health Group Corp.
Genck, Heather L. … '71 '97 C.679 B.A. L.365 J.D. [Ⓒ Momkus M.M.M.M.&S.]
Goltermann, Neil T., (BV) … '55 '80 C.210 B.A. L.209 J.D. [Ⓐ Momkus M.M.M.M.&S.]
Greenwood, Craig H. … '46 '73 C&L.339 A.B., J.D. 4100 Lindley St.
Gyongyos, David G. '44 '73 C.611 B.A. L.930 J.D.
(adm. in OH; not adm. in IL) Serv. Systems Corp.
Hanson, Kurt E., (BV) … '61 '92 C.801 B.S. L.365 J.D. 1000 Maple Avenue
Harkness, James S. … '71 '96 C&L.879 B.A., J.D. [Ⓐ Momkus M.M.M.M.&S.]
Harper, Daniel R. … '— '87 C.884 B.A. L.209 J.D. Sr. Atty., Spiegel, Inc.
Hirsh, Richard L., & Associates, P.C.
(See Hinsdale)
Hoel, J. Richard, Jr. '48 '76 C.165 B.A. L.37 J.D.
V.P., Intl. Coun., The ServiceMaster Co., L.P.
Hudzik, Richard F. … '52 '78 C&L.339 B.A., J.D. [Wiedel,H.&R.]
Hultman, Alan C., (AV) … '24 '50 C&L.339 B.S., LL.B. [Hultman&J.]
Hultman and Johnson, P.C., (AV) … 1303 Ogden Avenue
Isaacs, Rosalie … '48 '85 C.331 B.A. L.767 J.D. 4803 Saratoga Ave.‡
Johnson, Douglas A. '43 '71 C&L.352 B.A., J.D.
Vice President & General Counsel, Pettibone, L.L.C. (Legal Department)
Johnson, George W., (AV) … '38 '63 C.504 B.A. L.146 J.D. [Hultman&J.]
Jones, Robert E., (BV) … '37 '65 C.238 B.A. L.365 LL.B. 5100 Fairview Ave.
Kaput, Jim L. '60 '87 C.659 B.S. L.188 J.D.
Sr. V.P. & Gen. Coun., ServiceMaster Company, The
Keyser, Paul T. … '50 '78 C&L.436 J.D. Claims Supvr., Wausau Insurance Co.
Kiser, Michael Lee … '48 '92 C.347 B.A. L.209 J.D. 4713 Seeley Avenue
Kleber, Dale Elliott … '56 '83 C&L.880 B.A., J.D. Finial Properties, LLC
Kogl, Cristen L. … '66 '91 C.393 B.A. L.966 J.D. 2500 Warrenville Rd
Kristufek, Lynne, (BV) … '50 '89 C.801 B.S. L.365 J.D. [McJoynt&K.]
Krone, Thomas R. … '31 '55 C&L.436 B.S., LL.B. 921 Curtiss St.
Lackner, Richard J. … '46 '72 C.339 B.A. L.209 J.D. 921 Curtiss St.
Landau, Eliot A. … '42 '67 C.145 B.A. L.209 J.D. 515 Ogden Ave., Ste. 101
Lane, Robert Thomas … '61 '93 C.338 B.S. L.365 J.D. Asst. Atty. Gen., IL Tollway
Lifka, Daniel … '63 '95 C.98 B.S. L.146 1551 Warren Ave.
Lunardini, Christopher Michael '75 '00
C&L.209 B.A., J.D. [Ⓐ Momkus M.M.M.M.&S.]
Lyons, R. Daniel … '— '86 C.209 B.A. L.146 J.D. 928 Warren Ave.
Mallin, Thomas W. '52 '77
C.339 B.S. L.597 J.D. Pres. & CEO, Property Loss Research Bur.
Marich, John G. … '56 '84 C.123 B.A. L.990 J.D. 1600 Chicago Ave
Marsh, James P. … '61 '88 C.234 B.A. L.365 J.D. [Momkus M.M.M.M.&S.]
Martan, Joseph R. '49 '77 C.339 B.A. L.146 J.D.
Staff Coun., Alliance of Amer. Insurers
Mayer, William E. … '— '99 C.999 B.A. L.589 J.D. Atty., Spiegel, Inc.
McCluskey, James F., (AV) … '54 '79 C.238 B.S. L.589 J.D. [Momkus M.M.M.M.&S.]
McCormick, William T. '59 '88
C.602 B.A. L.424 J.D. V.P. & Legal Coun., The ServiceMaster Co.
McCracken, Peggy A. … '51 '83 C&L.589 B.S.Ed., J.D. 6912 S. Main St.
McDonnell Hilligoss, Karen T. '71 '96
C.339 B.S. L.365 J.D. [Ⓐ Momkus M.M.M.M.&S.]
McGarr, Frank J., (AV) … '21 '50 C&L.424 A.B., J.D. 4146 Venard Rd.
McGinty, Rory K. … '53 '78 C.234 B.A. L.846 J.D. [R.K.McGinty]
McGinty, Rory K., P.C., Law Offices of … 5202 Washington, Suite 5
McJoynt, Timothy J., (BV) … '51 '77 C.927 B.S. L.365 J.D. [McJoynt&K.]

McJoynt & Kristufek, P.C., (BV)
1131 Warren Avenue, 60515
Telephone: 630-971-0100 Fax: 630-960-0263 URL: http://www.mcjoyntlaw.com
URL: http://www.mcjoyntkristufek.com
Timothy J. McJoynt; Lynne Kristufek;—Mary Cox Coffey.
General Civil Practice, Litigation, Criminal, Matrimonial, DUI, Real Estate, Probate, Estate Planning, Corporate and Transactional and Small Business Law.
See Professional Biographies, DOWNERS GROVE, ILLINOIS

Momkus, Edward J., (AV) … '53 '77 C.238 B.A. L.597 J.D. [Momkus M.M.M.M.&S.]

Momkus McCluskey Moltzen Monroe Marsh & Spyratos, LLC, (AV)
3051 Oak Grove Road, Suite 220, 60515 ⊙
Telephone: 630-434-0400 Fax: 630-434-0444
URL: http://www.momlaw.com
Members of Firm: Edward J. Momkus; James F. McCluskey; Mark W. Monroe; James P. Marsh; John D. Purdy, Jr.; E. Angelo Spyratos; Kimberly A. Davis; Steven B. Ekker. Of Counsel: Mary Caffrey Morrissy; Craig S. Stevens; Heather L. Genck. Associates: Lori N. Carrozza; Neil T. Goltermann; James S. Harkness; Christopher Michael Lunardini; Karen T. McDonnell Hilligoss; Edward R. Psenicka; James K. Theisen.
General Civil Practice, Corporate Practice with particular expertise in Corporate and Transactional Law, Civil Litigation, Commercial Litigation, Product Liability Defense, Insurance Defense and Coverage, Personal Injury and Property Damage, Appeals, Mediation, Arbitration, Commercial and Residential Real Estate, Tax-Based Transactions, Employment Law, Environmental Law, Construction, Collections, Financing, Estate Planning, Catastrophic Injuries, Intellectual Property and Covenants Not to Compete, Premises Liability, Injunctive Remedies, and Real Property Owner Disputes.
Representative Clients: Sunbeam Corporation; Allied Signal Inc.; USAA; Liberty Mutual Insurance Co.; Crawford & Co.; National Union Fire Insurance; Insurance Company of Illinois; Wal-Mart Stores Inc.; DPIC Companies; State Farm Insurance.
Chicago, Illinois Office: 33 North LaSalle Street, 34th Floor, 60606. Telephone: 312-279-1940. Fax: 312-279-1941.
See Professional Biographies, DOWNERS GROVE, ILLINOIS

Monroe, Mark W. … '55 '86 C.1376 B.S. L.589 J.D. [Momkus M.M.M.M.&S.]
Morrissy, Mary Caffrey … '51 '77 C.1291 B.A. L.910 J.D. [Ⓒ Momkus M.M.M.M.&S.]
Mosby, Mark A. '60 '86 C.893 B.A. L.910 J.D.
Dir. & Assoc. Coun., First Health Group Corp.
Munchak, Jo-Elle … '68 '96 C.145 A.B. L.209 J.D. Sr. Atty., First Health Group Corp.
Murphy, Leonard E. … '63 '94 C.608 B.S.I.E. L.365 J.D. The Prop. Loss Research Bur.

Murray, William E. .... '— '83 C.880 B.A. L.862 J.D. Sr. Coun., Vysis, Inc. (Pat.)
Naughton, William S. .... '24 '52 C.734 L.472 LL.B. 1141 55th St.‡
North, John C. ....'53 '78 C.388 B.A. L.146 J.D. [Borla,N.&Assoc.]

North, William C., (BV) '45 '71 C.694 A.B. L.339 J.D.
947 Maple Avenue, 60515-4930
Telephone: 630-960-1242 Fax: 630-960-3760
Email: williamnorth@wcnorth.com URL: http://www.lawyers.com/williamnorth
Personal Injury, Automobile Accidents, Medical Malpractice, Business Litigation, Employment Law, Human Rights, Discrimination, Divorce.
See Professional Biographies, DOWNERS GROVE, ILLINOIS

Olszewski, Paul J. ....'54 '85 C.424 B.S. L.365 J.D. Sr. Asst. Atty. Gen.
Olszowka, Joseph A., Jr. .... '59 '85 C.209 B.A. L.365 J.D. 6900 S. Main St., Ste. 204
Orticelli, Samuel A. ....'53 '78 C.436 B.S. L.209 J.D. 5623 Fairview Ave.
Passolt, James C., Jr. '44 '72 C.847 B.B.A. L.793 J.D.
(adm. in NE; not adm. in IL) Real Estate Mgr., United Parcel Serv.
Paulson, Thor ....'66 '91 C.118 B.A. L.597 J.D. Sr. Leg. Coun., Caremark RX, Inc.
Pegler, Laurie A. .... '59 '85 C.589 B.A. L.365 J.D. Alliance of Amer. Insurers
Perry, Julian S. ....'14 '42 C&L.209 LL.B. 5109 DeWitt Ln.
Pollard, C. William ....'38 '63 C.937 A.B. L.597 J.D. 2300 Warrenville Rd.
Porush, David S. ....'73 '00 C.999 B.A. L.146 J.D. 1901 Butterfield Rd.
Prost, David J. .... '64 '92 C.234 B.S. L.365 J.D. Private Business, Inc.
Provenzale, Linda L. ....'63 '93 L.209 J.D. [L.Provenzale]
Provenzale, Linda, Attorney at Law ....4085 Douglas Rd.
Psenicka, Edward R. ....'70 '98 C.589 B.A. L.339 J.D. [Momkus M.M.M.M.&S.]
Purdy, John D., Jr., (AV) ......'41 '66 C.976 B.A. L.145 J.D. [Momkus M.M.M.M.&S.]
Raduenz, Gary A. ..... '55 '86 C.679 B.A. L.365 J.D. Asst. Gen. Coun., Pettibone, L.L.C.
Randick, Richard Matthew ....'45 '70 C.424 B.S. L.365 J.D. 5300 Main St.
Reddish, Carin S. ....'61 '93 C.339 B.A. L.209 J.D. Sr. Atty., First Health Group Corp.
Reed, Sally A., Law Office of ....'57 '82 C.238 B.A. L.209 J.D. 1261 Brookside Lane
Rehnquist, Ralph L. ....'24 '53 C.339 L.365 LL.B. 5533 Lyman Ave.
Rosenfeld, David J. ....'62 '90 C.424 B.A. L.365 J.D. Sp. Asst. Atty Gen.
Russ, James F., Jr. ....'60 '85 C&L.436 B.S., J.D. [Wiedel,H.&R.]
Salstone, Sande L. ....'47 '78 C.188 B.A. L.146 J.D. Property Loss Research Bur.
Schamber, Mary Amanda ....'74 '99 C&L.424 B.A., J.D. 1533 George St.
Schneid, Jennifer E. .....'68 '95 C.578 B.A. L.146 J.D. Sr. Atty., First Health Group Corp.
Schwemm, John B., (AV) ....'34 '59 C.31 A.B. L.477 J.D. 2 Turvey Ln.‡
Siedlecki, Nancy T. ....'54 '80 C.339 L.146 J.D. 5300 Main St.
Sisul, Thomas J. ....'43 '67 C&L.209 B.A., J.D. 902 Maple Ave.
Smith, Patrick J., Attorney at Law ....'58 '85 C.742 B.A. L.209 J.D. 5116 Forest Ave.
Smyth, John M. .....'15 '40 C.674 A.B. L.597 J.D. Chmn. of the Bd., John M. Smyth Co.
Sorensen, Robert H. '46 '75 C.280 A.B. L.245 J.D.
(adm. in GA; not adm. in IL) V.P., Gen. Coun. & Secy., Spiegel, Inc.
Spears, Stephen D. ....'61 '87 C.951 B.A. L.145 J.D. Div. Legal Leader, Acxiom
Spyratos, E. Angelo, (BV) ......'66 '91 C.238 B.A. L.879 J.D. [Momkus M.M.M.M.&S.]
Stevens, Craig S. ....'47 '74 C.347 B.S. L.345 J.D. [Momkus M.M.M.M.&S.]
Stevens, Joan Gress ....'61 '87 C.679 B.A. L.339 J.D. [Hultman&J.]
Talley, John S. '53 '88 C.937 B.A. L.365 J.D.
V.P. & Legal Coun., The ServiceMaster Co.
Tandle, Stephen D. ....'54 '83 C.145 A.B. L.146 J.D. 3051 Oak Grove Rd., Ste. 200
Tedrowe, Justin J. ....'45 '71 C.424 B.S. L.602 J.D. 5300 Main St.
Theisen, James K. ....'70 '03 C.927 B.S. L.801 J.D. [Momkus M.M.M.M.&S.]
Thollander, David C. ....'61 '89 C.339 B.A. L.209 J.D. 1048 Ogden Ave., Ste. 200
Thompson, Barbara S. ....'41 '80 C.679 B.S. L.365 J.D. 4924 Oakwood Ave.‡
Torres, John F. ....'48 '77 C.238 B.A. L.365 J.D. 4336 Saratoga Avenue, Suite 201
Turacek, Heidi A. ....'74 '00 C.339 B.A. L.146 J.D. Legal Coun., Service Master Co.
Walsh, Thomas M., (BV) ....'47 '72 C&L.190 B.A., J.D. 921 Curtiss St.
Watts, Patrick ....'56 '81 C.510 B.A. L.383 J.D. Asst. V.P., Alliance of Amer. Insurers
Weinberger, James W. ....'32 '65 C.352 B.S. L.221 J.D. 1506 62nd St.
Wells, Christy L. ....'78 '02 C.424 B.B.A. L.910 J.D. 1048 Ogden Ave., Ste. 200
White, Frances J. .... '39 '78 C.339 B.A. L.1151 J.D. 5100 Main St.
Wiedel, Michael C., (BV) ....'42 '66 C&L.424 B.S., J.D. [Wiedel,H.&R.]
Wiedel, Hudzik & Russ, (BV) ....4915 Main Street
Wight, Mark T. ....'52 '80 C.685 B.A. L.602 J.D. Exec. V.P., Wight & Co.
Williams, Trevor T. ....'46 '75 C.694 A.B. L.146 J.D. 6912 Main St., 2nd Fl.
Wilson, Thomas E. '59 '85 C.339 B.A. L.365 J.D.
V.P. & Gen. Coun., Mgmt. Servs., The ServiceMaster Co.
Wilt, Vera A. ....'52 '82 C.339 B.A. L.365 J.D. Mgr., Washington Mutual

Wimmer, John R., (BV) '54 '79 C.188 B.A. L.339 J.D.
928 Warren Avenue, 60515
Telephone: 630-810-0005 Fax: 630-960-5852
Email: JWimmerLaw@aol.com URL: http://www.johnwimmer.com
Trials and Appeals in all State and Federal Courts, Civil Rights, Discrimination, Criminal, Felonies and Misdemeanors, Juvenile, Personal Injury and Commercial Disputes.
See Professional Biographies, DOWNERS GROVE, ILLINOIS

Woodward, Michael J. '51 '86 C.1024 B.S. L.365 J.D.
Spec. Asst. Atty. Gen., Ill. St. Toll Hwy. Auth.
Worrell, Andrea Leigh ....'63 '99 C.597 B.S.G.S. L.424 J.D. [A.L.Worrell]
Worrell, Andrea L., Law Office of ....619 Franklin St.
Yokom, Andrew Patrick '— '85 C.477 A.B. L.215 J.D.
Asst. Gen. Coun., Spiegel, Inc.
Zapf, Mark H. ....'60 '89 C.602 B.A. L.215 J.D. 1431 Pous Place

DUNDEE, —, *Kane Co.*

Baudin, W. Randal, (BV) ....'48 '75 C.339 B.S. L.209 J.D. [Baudin&B.]
Baudin, W. Randal, II ....'71 '97 C.999 B.A. L.365 J.D. [Baudin&B.]
Baudin & Baudin, (BV) ....P.O. Box 845
Harlovic, Nicholas J. ....'46 '71 C.973 B.S. L.424 J.D. [Harlovic&P.]
Harlovic, Richard P., (BV) ....'63 '92 C.339 B.S. L.365 J.D. [Harlovic&P.]
Harlovic & Perko ....116 W. Main St.
Husted, Richard W. ....'20 '50 C.337 A.B. L.996 LL.B. Route 1‡
Jablonowski, Katherine Ann ....'47 '75 C.966 B.A. L.146 J.D. [Jablonowski,K.A.]
Jablonowski, Katherine A. ....P.O. Box 526
McCarthy, Richard C. .... '25 '51 C&L.339 B.S., B.L. 36 W. 296 Hickory Hollow Dr.‡
Perko, Phyllis J. ....'46 '71 C&L.424 A.B., J.D. [Harlovic&P.]
Peterson, James R. ....'45 '79 C.801 B.S. L.589 J.D. 161 Hilltop Ln.
Peterson, Mark F., Law Office of, (BV) '52 '78
C.763 B.S. L.1137 J.D. 825 Village Quarter Rd., Ste A-4
Scarpelli, Frank J. ....'29 '53 C&L.424 B.S., J.D. 651 Oakridge Rd.
Schwarz, Benedict, II, (BV) '42 '71
C.966 B.S. L.365 J.D. The Simonds House, 303 W. Main St.
Seesser, Karl H. '40 '65 C&L.352 B.A., LL.B.
(adm. in IA; not adm. in IL) 218 W. Main St.‡

DUNLAP, 851, *Peoria Co.*

Barrett, Aline Cole '48 '88 C.860 B.S. L.285 J.D.
(adm. in WA; not adm. in IL) 12604 N. Colony Rd.‡

DUPO, 3,933, *St. Clair Co.*

Dupont, Mark P., (AVⓅ) ....'58 '84 C.424 B.S. L.910 J.D. 123 S. Main St.

DU QUOIN, 6,448, *Perry Co.*

Atkins, Aaron Ardene, (CV) ....'60 '85 C&L.801 B.A., J.D. [A.A.Atkins]
Atkins, Aaron A., (CV) ....18 N. Oak St.
Bastien, Robert E. ....'27 '59 C&L.800 B.S., LL.B. Ret. Cir. J.‡

Hart and Hart
(See Benton)

Maclin, J. Mark, (BV) ....'47 '72 C.221 B.A. L.339 J.D. 6 S. Division
Naumer, Walter W., Jr. .... '35 '62 C&L.477 B.B.A., J.D. Capital Management Grp.
Peek, R. K. ....'25 '50 C&L.339 B.S., LL.B. 20 N. Washington St.‡
Rose, Joseph W. ....'76 '02 C.209 B.A. L.801 J.D. 104 E. Main St.
Smith, Jerry B., (BV) ....'43 '68 C.339 B.S. L.345 J.D. 217 S. Washington St.

DURAND, 1,100, *Winnebago Co.*

Altham, James F., Jr. '46 '74 C.1252 B.A. L.184 J.D.
(adm. in CT; not adm. in IL) P.O. Box 398
Coplan, Robert G. ....'36 '61 C&L.339 A.B., LL.B. 13161 Farm School Road
Flores, Barbara K. '45 '72 C&L.705 B.A., J.D.
(adm. in NJ; not adm. in IL) 15813 Anderson Rd.‡
Huber, Paul J. ....'52 '86 C.339 B.A. L.589 J.D. P.O. Box 351

DWIGHT, 4,363, *Livingston Co.*

Masching, Irvin L., (BV) ....'50 '75 C.338 B.S. L.879 J.D. 105 E. Chippewa St.
Neville, Gary M., (BV) ....'50 '76 C.339 B.S. L.260 J.D. 146 East Main Street
Tock, Stephen J. ....'55 '86 C.801 B.S. L.910 J.D. 310 S. Prairie Ave.

EARLVILLE, 1,778, *La Salle Co.*

Deobler, Eric B., (BV) .... '45 '72 C&L.339 B.A., J.D. [White,M.A.M.D.&G.] (⊙Ottawa)
Marsh, Alan B., (AV) ....'39 '66 C.388 A.B. L.365 J.D. [White,M.A.M.D.&G.] (⊙Ottawa)
White, Marsh, Anderson, Martin Vickers, Deobler & Goode, (AV)
201 S. Ottawa St. (⊙Leland, Ottawa)

EAST ALTON, 6,830, *Madison Co.*

Berg, Leonard F., (BV) .... '52 '77 C.388 B.A. L.910 J.D. 625 S. Bellwood (IL Route 111)
Bono, Randall A., (BV) ....'51 '76 C.357 B.A. L.421 J.D. [SimmonsCooper]
Boyle, Patrick O., (AVⓅ) '35 '60
C&L.910 B.S., J.D. 210 Smith Avenue (⊙Florissant, MO)
Bradford, Glenn E., (BV) ....'47 '74 C.801 B.S. L.245 J.D. [Pratt&T.]
Bruegger, John A. ....'75 '01 C.502 B.A. L.734 J.D. [SimmonsCooper]
Carey, James R., (BV) ....'33 '78 C.782 B.S. L.421 J.D. [Pratt&T.]
Cooper, Jeffrey S., (BV) ....'69 '95 C.209 B.A. L.734 J.D. [SimmonsCooper]
Delaney, John M., Jr., (BV) ....'56 '81 C&L.734 A.B., J.D. 346 West St. Louis Avenue
Ebert, James A. ....'58 '90 C.959 B.A. L.910 J.D. [Pratt&T.]
Fishbein, Susan G. ....'58 '94 C.339 B.S. L.910 J.D. Coun., Olin Corp.
Gianaris, Ted N. ....'64 '96 C.140 B.A. L.801 J.D. [SimmonsCooper]
Gregory, Robert H., (AV) .... '52 '78 C.357 B.A. L.339 J.D. 2 Terminal Drive, Suite 17A
Griffin, Steven D., (CV) ....'63 '88 C&L.801 B.A., J.D. 346 W. St. Louis Ave.
Hylla, David A., (BV) ....'58 '85 C.801 B.A. L.734 J.D. [Pratt&T.]
Jansky, S. Martin ....'68 '95 C.861 B.A. L.734 J.D. [SimmonsCooper]
Kelley, Dorothy J. ....'25 '50 C&L.339 B.S., LL.B. 427 N. Shamrock Ave.
Kelly, James F. '65 '96 C.770 B.S. L.862 J.D.
(adm. in OK; not adm. in IL) [SimmonsCooper]
Kohlburn, William A. '58 '87 C.339 B.A. L.910 J.D.
(adm. in MO; not adm. in IL) [SimmonsCooper]
Phillips, Robert W. ....'69 '98 C&L.45 B.A., J.D. [SimmonsCooper]
Pollock, Jo Anna ....'75 '00 C.412 B.A. L.734 J.D. 707 Berkshire Blvd.
Pratt & Tobin, P.C., (BV) ....Rte. 111 at Airline Dr.
Raichle, Marcus E., Jr. ....'65 '92 C.910 B.A. L.862 J.D. [SimmonsCooper]
Schmieder, Christie R. .... '70 '97 C&L.801 B.A., J.D. Route 111 at Airline Drive
Simmons, John D. .... '67 '94 C.801 B.S. L.802 J.D. [SimmonsCooper] (⊙Savannah, GA)
SimmonsCooper, LLC, (BV) ....707 Berkshire Boulevard
Tobin, Gregory M., (BV) ....'60 '86 C.337 B.S. L.734 J.D. [Pratt&T.]
Unsell, Edward W., (BV) ....'51 '79 C.801 B.A. L.615 J.D. [E.Unsell]
Unsell, Jane E. Wolf, (BV) ....'52 '79 C.1147 B.A. L.616 J.D. 55 S. 9th St.
Unsell, Edward, (BV) ....69 S. 9th St.
Weaver, Lon D., (BV) ....'53 '81 C.801 B.A.B.S. L.1137 J.D. 346 E. St. Louis Ave.
Weishaupt, Jeffrey C., (BV) ....'62 '89 C.801 B.S. L.862 J.D. [J.Weishaupt]
Weishaupt, Jeffrey, (BV) ....82 E. Airline Dr.
Wolf, Jane E. ....'52 '79 C.1147 B.A. L.615 J.D. 55 S. 9th
Zimmermann, Theodore A. '64 '89 C&L.734 B.S., J.D.
Dep. Gen. Coun. and V.P., Metals and Winchester, 427 N. Shamrock

EAST DUBUQUE, 1,914, *Jo Daviess Co.*

Sprengelmeyer, Victor V. .... '42 '66 C.177 L.352 LL.B. Assoc. Cir. J.

EAST DUNDEE, 2,955, *Kane Co.*

Strom, Bruce D., (CV) ....'65 '90 C.371 B.A. L.339 J.D. Administer Justice

EAST MOLINE, 20,333, *Rock Island Co.*

Chickris, Greg G., (BV) ....'50 '76 C.927 B.B.A. L.209 J.D. [Phares&C.]
DeDoncker, David ....'32 '56 C.707 B.A. L.339 J.D. 460 43rd Avenue Ct.‡
DiMario, Salvatore D. '58 '87 C.178 B.A. L.1040 J.D.
(adm. in NY; not adm. in IL) Ill. Racing Bd.
Haytcher, Gary L., (CV) ....'46 '73 C.352 B.A. L.339 J.D. 912 15th Ave.
Hobert, Mark "Marcus" V., (CV) '55 '79
C&L.352 B.B.A., J.D. V.P. & Gen. Coun., Metrobank
Jackson, Mark A., (CV) ....'59 '85 C.499 B.A.B.S. L.500 J.D. [Jackson]
Jackson Law Office, (CV) ....922 15th Ave. (⊙Columbia, SC)
Lee, Graham J., (BV) ....'45 '71 C.339 B.A. L.146 J.D. 844 15th Ave.
Lytton, Julius M. ....'13 '35 C&L.209 B.S., J.D. 1608 8th St.
Phares, William T., (P.C.), (AV) ....'43 '69 C.339 B.S. L.424 J.D. [Phares&C.]
Phares & Chickris, (AV) ....4500 Kennedy Dr.
Ryan, Francis J., (BV) ....'23 '50 C.707 A.B. L.424 J.D. 920 15th Ave.
Silliman, Rich'd G. ....'22 '49 C.187 B.A. L.597 J.D. 4817 6th St. Ct.‡
Sutton, Dean L., (BV) ....'48 '75 C.57 A.B. L.879 J.D. [D.L.Sutton]

Sutton, Dean L., PC, (BV)
1608 Eighth Street, 61244
Telephone: 309-755-5239 Fax: 309-755-0966
Email: deansutton@dlsuttonpc.com URL: http://www.dlsuttonpc.com

(This Listing Continued)

Sutton, Dean L., PC (Continued)

Dean L. Sutton.
General Practice, Bankruptcy, Zoning and Land Use, Business Law, Starting a Business, Corporate and Small Business, Buying and Selling a Business, Business Planning, Contracts, Buying and Selling a Home, Eminent Domain, Guardianships, Social Security Disability, Commercial and Residential Real Estate, Wills and Probate, Trusts and Estates, Estate Planning, Municipal Law.
See Professional Biographies, EAST MOLINE, ILLINOIS

VandeWiele, Mark A., (BV) ....'59 '84 C.339 B.S. L.862 J.D. 844 15th Ave.
Zimmer, Richard A., (BV) ....'64 '89 C.57 B.A. L.589 J.D. [R.A.Zimmer]
Zimmer, Richard A., P.C., (BV) ....1608 8th Street

EAST PEORIA, 22,638, *Tazewell Co.*

Burrier, George M., Jr. ....'43 '75 C.589 B.A. L.146 J.D. 257 E. Washington St.
Bush, Stephen W., (BV) ....'53 '81 C.98 B.S. L.365 J.D. P.O. Box 2512
Culberson, Eugene B. ....'31 '59 C.138 L.260 J.D. 231 Castle Lane‡
James, R. L. ....'13 '39 C.339 Ph.B. L.734 LL.B. 500 Centennial Dr.‡
Moushon, Clayton W., (BV) ....'59 '86 C.424 B.S. L.990 J.D. 1009 Illini Dr.
Musgrove, Paul B. ....'11 '41 C.339 L.146 500 Centennial Dr.
Ohanesian, Nicholas Mihran '73 '00 C.932 B.S. L.945 J.D.
(adm. in MI; not adm. in IL) 81 N. Riverview Drive
O'Hara, Harold N. ....'12 '60 C.388 A.B. 617 Highview Rd.‡
Ohaver, Jane E., P.C., (BV) ....'61 '91 C.338 B.S. L.339 J.D. 111 W. Washington
Paluska, Larry G., (BV) ....'50 '80 C.339 B.S. L.209 J.D. 217 Springfield Rd.
Rickgauer, D. Michael, (BV) '62 '87
C.221 B.S.B.A. L.801 J.D. 252 E. Washington St., Ste. B
Taylor, Luke P. ....'65 '96 C.1090 B.S. L.589 J.D. [Ⓐ D.L.Williams&Assoc.]
Webster, Jami B. ....'74 '01 C&L.801 B.A., J.D. 200 Anna St.
Williams, Dick B. ....'69 '96 C.352 B.A. L.589 J.D. [Ⓐ D.L.Williams&Assoc.]
Williams, Dick L. ....'41 '65 C&L.339 B.S., J.D. [D.L.Williams&Assoc.]
Williams, Dick L., and Associates, P.C. ....139 East Washington Street
Winston, Robt. W. ....'10 '38 L.477 J.D. 1040 Fondulac Dr.‡

EAST ST. LOUIS, 31,542, *St. Clair Co.*

Allen, Beverly Ann '65 '90 C.22 B.A. L.734 J.D.
Land of Lincoln Legal Assistance Foundation, Inc.
Althardt, Carole ....'— '94 C.801 B.A. L.734 J.D. Dist. Ct. Law Clk.
Anderson, Donna M. ....'65 '97 C.450 B.S.N. L.734 J.D. [Rex C.]
Anderson, Ross T., (BV) ....'52 '78 C&L.339 A.B., J.D. [Rex C.]
Binetsch, Joan M. ......'54 '84 C.966 B.S. L.734 J.D. Staff Atty., U.S. Bkrptcy. Ct.
Bloom, Allen J., (AVⓉ) '30 '57
C.910 B.S.B.A. L.734 LL.B. 406 Missouri Ave. (☉St. Louis, MO)

Burroughs, Hepler, Broom, MacDonald, Hebrank & True, LLP
(See Edwardsville)

Bush, Pearson C. J. ....'45 '74 C.801 B.A. L.734 J.D. [P.Bush]
Bush, Pearson, Law Office, Ltd ....523 Missouri Ave.
Carr, Rex, (AV) ....'26 '50 C&L.339 A.B., J.D. [Rex C.] ☉
Cohn, Gerald B. ....'39 '65 C.337 B.A. L.145 J.D. P.O. Box 2587‡
Doles, Sarah Shoemake ....'71 '96 C.502 B.A. L.734 J.D. Law Clk., U.S Dist Ct.

Edwards, Benjamin F. '— '76 C.734 B.A. L.910 J.D.
The 1st Illinois Bank Building, 327 Missouri Avenue, Suite 402, 62201
Mailing Address: Post Office Box 306, East St Louis, IL 62202
Telephone: 618-274-3063 Fax: 618-875-5241
Email: bedwa10613@yahoo.com URL: http://www.bedwardslaw.com
The Edwards' Law Office provides legal services in the following areas of practice: Bankruptcy, Real Estate, Probate, Guardianship, Wills, Powers of Attorney, Family Law, Divorce, Traffic Violations, Automobile Accidents and Injuries and General Practice.
See Professional Biographies, EAST ST. LOUIS, ILLINOIS

Finan, Margaret A. '59 '84 C&L.734 A.B., J.D.
Law Clerk, U.S. Dist Ct., Southern Dist.
Firestone, Frederick R. ....'52 '81 C.502 B.S.Ed. L.734 J.D. 406 Missouri Ave.
Fix, Julie A. ....'59 '84 C&L.734 B.A., J.D. Sr. Law Clk. to U.S. Dist. Ct. J.
Glass, Mark, (AV) ....'— '74 C.339 B.S. L.734 J.D. [Glass&K.]

Glass & Korein, LLC, (AV)
412 Missouri Avenue, 62201
Telephone: 618-274-0434 Fax: 618-274-8369
Members of the Firm: Mark Glass; Michael H. Korein.
Workers Compensation, Personal Injury.
See Professional Biographies, EAST ST. LOUIS, ILLINOIS

Goldenhersh, David H., (BV) '18 '57
C&L.734 LL.B. 406 Missouri Ave. (☉St. Louis, MO)‡

Goldstein and Price, L.C.
(See St. Louis, Missouri)

Hardge, Andrew, (BV) ....'38 '79 C.410 B.A. L.325 J.D. 1st Ill. Bk. Bldg.
Heady, Brian David ....'56 '89 C.338 B.S. L.801 J.D. Law Clk. to U.S. Dist. Ct.
Herndon, David R. ....'53 '77 C&L.801 B.A., J.D. U.S. Dist. J.

Hoagland, Fitzgerald, Smith & Pranaitis
(See Alton)

Hoffman, Katherine Lynn ....'71 '96 C.500 B.A. L.734 J.D. Law Clk., U.S. Dist. Ct.
Hoffmann, Donald '37 '79 C.999 B.A. L.146 J.D.
Land of Lincoln Legal Assistance Found., Inc.
Korein, Michael H., (BV) ....'64 '91 C.37 B.S. L.910 J.D. [Glass&K.]
Kunin, Joel A., (AV) ....'38 '62 C&L.910 B.S.M.E., J.D. [Kunin]
Kunin, Michelle A., (BV) ....'67 '93 C.94 B.A. L.502 J.D. [Kunin]

Kunin Law Office, LLC, (AV)
412 Missouri Avenue, 62201
Telephone: 618-274-0434 Fax: 618-274-8369
Joel A. Kunin; Michelle A. Kunin; Mark M. Silvermintz. Associate: Steven M. Wallace.
Bankruptcy, Commercial and Debtors & Creditor Rights Law.
See Professional Biographies, EAST ST. LOUIS, ILLINOIS

Lucco, Brown, Threlkeld & Dawson, LLP
(See Edwardsville)

Marker, Michael B., (BV) ....'57 '90 C.836 B.A. L.910 J.D. [Rex C.]
Meyers, Kenneth J. ....'44 '69 C.234 B.S. L.347 J.D. Chief U.S. Bkrptcy. J.
Montroy, Christian G. ....'77 '04 C.276 B.A. L.597 J.D. 412 Missouri Ave.
Montroy, Gerald L., (AV) ....'39 '73 C.999 B.A. L.339 J.D. 412 Missouri Avenue
Pirtle, Alan G., (BV) ....'65 '91 C.234 B.A. L.734 J.D. [Rex C.]
Proud, Clifford J. ....'45 '72 C&L.734 A.B., J.D. U.S. Dist. Ct.
Reagan, Michael J. ....'54 '80 C.98 B.S. L.734 J.D. U.S. Dist. J.
Rebeschini, Nancy D., (BV) ....'56 '90 C&L.801 B.S., J.D. Law Clk., U.S. Mag. J.

Rex Carr Law Firm, LLC, The, (AV) 🅱🅱
412 Missouri Avenue, 62201 ☉
Telephone: 618-274-0434 800-333-5297 Fax: 618-274-8369 URL: http://www.rexcarr.com
URL: http://www.lawyers.com/rexcarr

(This Listing Continued)

Rex Carr Law Firm, LLC, The (Continued)

Members of Firm: Rex Carr; Staci M. Yandle; Ross T. Anderson; Paul G. Schoen; Troy E. Walton; Alan G. Pirtle; Michael B. Marker; Donna M. Anderson. Of Counsel: Lawrence Alan Waldman (Resident).
Railroad, Medical Malpractice, Product Liability, Toxic Torts, Nursing Home Negligence, General Negligence, Trial Practice, Workers Compensation, Class Actions, Complex Litigation, Automobile Litigation.
St. Louis, Missouri Office: 1 Metropolitan Square, 211 North Broadway, Suite 2970, 63102. Telephone: 1-800-333-5297.
Belleville, Illinois Office: 7012 West Main Street, 62223. Telephone: 618-397-9191.
See Professional Biographies, EAST ST. LOUIS, ILLINOIS

Ross, Samuel F., Jr., (BV) ....'25 '52 C&L.734 J.D. 110 N. Main St.
Schoen, Paul G., (BV) ....'45 '70 C.801 B.S. L.339 J.D. [Rex C.]
Silvermintz, Mark M., (BV) ....'52 '78 C.910 B.A. L.273 J.D. [Kunin]
Stewart, William R. ....'51 '87 C.1291 B.A. L.734 J.D. Law Clk., U.S. Mag.
Stiehl, William D. ....'25 '49 C.575 L.734 LL.B. U.S. Dist. J.
Turner, John P. ....'51 '78 C.801 B.A. L.800 J.D. Ill. Dept. of Employ. Security
Waldman, Lawrence Alan, (BV) ....'37 '62 C&L.910 B.S.B.A., J.D. [Ⓒ Rex C.]
Wallace, Steven M., (AV) ....'59 '88 C&L.734 A.B., J.D. [Ⓐ Kunin]
Walton, Troy E. ....'75 '00 C.339 B.A. L.734 J.D. [Rex C.]
Wilkerson, Donald G. ....'51 '93 C.338 B.S. L.734 J.D. U.S. Mag.
Williamson, Irvin N., (CV) '58 '85 C.338 B.S. L.734 J.D.
Reg. Coun., State Dept. of Child. & Fam. Servs.
Wood, Lois J. '49 '74 C.475 B.A. L.309 J.D.
Land of Lincoln Legal Assistance Found., Inc.
Yandle, Staci M., (BV) ....'61 '87 C.339 B.S. L.880 J.D. [Rex C.]
Younge, Wyvetter H. '30 '55 C.302 B.S. L.734 LL.B.
(adm. in MO; not adm. in IL) Ill. State Legislator
Zazove, Linda L., (BV) '52 '80
C.352 B.A. L.424 J.D. Land of Lincoln Legal Assist. Found. Inc.

EDWARDSVILLE, * 21,491, *Madison Co.*

Althardt, Laura L. ....'76 '02 C.465 B.B.A. L.734 J.D. [Ⓐ Heyl,R.V.&A.]
Anderson, Karen A. ....'60 '89 C.546 B.A. L.190 J.D. [Johnson&A.]
Anderson, Roy D. ....'55 '94 C.937 B.A. L.733 J.D. [Ⓐ Reed,A.G.M.&M.]
Antognoli, David L., (BV) ....'53 '80 C.339 A.B. L.801 J.D. 2227 S. State Rte. 157
Armstrong, Benton Tad, (AV) ....'51 '76 C&L.339 B.S., J.D. [Armstrong] ☉
Armstrong, Harry C., (AV) ....'32 '55 C&L.339 B.S., J.D. [Reed,A.G.M.&M.]

Armstrong Law Offices, (AV)
South Main and Schwarz Street, P.O. Box 565, 62025 ☉
Telephone: 618-656-6770 Facsimile: 618-656-6808 URL: http://www.tadarmstrong.com
Email: tad@armstronglaw.net URL: http://www.armstronglaw.com
Benton Tad Armstrong.
Personal Injury, Medical Malpractice, Products Liability, General Civil Trial Practice, Wrongful Death, Dog Bites, Slip and Fall, Automobile Accidents.
See Professional Biographies, EDWARDSVILLE, ILLINOIS

Armstrong Teasdale LLP, (AV)
A Partnership including Professional Corporations
241 North Main Street, 62025 ☉
Telephone: 618-650-7087 Facsimile: 618-655-4004
Email: armstrongteasdale@armstrongteasdale.com URL: http://www.armstrongteasdale.com
Members of Firm: Karen A. Baudendistel; Mark A. Boatman; David W. Braswell; Ann E. Buckley; Michael A. Chivell; Clark H. Cole; O. Kirby Colson, III; William M. Corrigan, Jr.; Glenn E. Davis; Richard W. Engel, Jr.; Raymond R. Fournie; Timothy J. Gearin; David L. Going; Robert C. Graham, III; Frank N. Gundlach (P.C.) (Not admitted in IL); Robert A. Kaiser; Patrick J. Kenny; Anita M. Kidd; David G. Loseman; Philip G. Louis, Jr.; Andrew B. Mayfield; Timothy R. McFadden; Connie McFarland-Butler; Jeffery T. McPherson; James E. Mello; Daniel C. Nelson; John J. O'Brien; Julie Emmerich O'Keefe; Daniel K. O'Toole; David G. Ott (P.C.); Patrick W. Rasche; John Talbot Sant, Jr., (P.C.); Robert G. Schwendinger (Chairman of the Health Care Practice Group) (Resident, St. Louis, Missouri Office); Amit B. Shah; Dean D. Small; Mark D. Sophir (P.C.); James L. Stockberger; Mark L. Stoneman; John L. Sullivan; Wilbur L. Tomlinson (P.C.); Therese Rolufs Trelz; Timothy J. Tryniecki; James J. Virtel; George M. von Stamwitz; Thomas B. Weaver; Michael E. Whittle; Lisa M. Wood; Jason Zellers. Associates: Mary L. Bordner; Kristin D. Byrd; Dori B. Detherow; Daniel M. Fitzgerald; Jovita M. Foster; Tyler J. Frank; Virginia H. Howell; Gregory A. Iken; Michael S. Jefferies; David B. Jennings; Jeffrey H. Kass; Michael B. Kass; Michael H. Kauffman; Heidi P. Klosterman; Scott K. G. Kozak; Bruce D. LeMoine; Jacqueline P. Ulin Levey; Mary M. Machon; Laura L. McLaughlin; Craig G. Moore; Harry M. (Mark) Murray, IV; Bryan D. Nicholson; Todd R. Nissenholtz; Susan K. Olsen; Jill M. Palmquist; Cynthia A. Petracek; Steven E. Pozaric; Matthew J. Reh; Russell C. Riggan; Anna T. Selby; Jarrod H. Sharp; Matthew S. Shorey; John H. Stockman; Joy L. Vokac; Roger A. Walker; Deanna M. Wendler Modde; LeeAnn R. Zigler. Of Counsel: Susan Bradley Buse; Theodore H. Hellmuth (P.C.); Thomas W. Kelty; Robert G. Raleigh; Melanie B. Tamsky. Senior Counsel: Donald U. Beimdiek.
General Civil Practice. Administrative Law, Agricultural Law, Alternative Dispute Resolution, Antitrust and Trade Regulation Law, Appellate Practice, Banking and Financial Services, Biotechnology/ Life Sciences, Business Law, Civil Rights, Class Actions, Communications Law, Computer, Constitutional Law, Construction Law, Corporate Compliance and Governance, Corporate Law, Corporate Finance, Education Law, Eminent Domain, Employee Benefits, Employment and Labor, Energy, Entertainment & Sports, Environmental Law, Financial Restructuring, Reorganization and Bankruptcy, Distribution and Franchise, Government Contracts, Governmental Relations, Health Care, Immigration and Naturalization, Insurance Coverage/Reinsurance and Extracontractual Liability, International Law, International Trade, Internet Law, Investments, Litigation, Medical Malpractice, Mergers & Acquisitions, Natural Resources, Occupational Safety & Health Administration, Patent, Trademark and Intellectual Property, Pension and Executive Compensation, Personal Injury, Products Liability, Professional Liability, Public Law and Finance, Real Estate, Securities, Taxation, Technology and Science, Toxic Torts, Transportation, Trusts and Estates, White Collar Crime, Workers Compensation and Zoning, Planning & Land Use and Development.
St. Louis, Missouri Office: One Metropolitan Square, Suite 2600, 63102. Telephone: 314-621-5070. Facsimile: 314-621-5065.
Kansas City, Missouri Office: 2345 Grand Boulevard, Suite 2000, 64108. Telephone: 816-221-3420. Facsimile: 816-221-0786.
Jefferson City, Missouri Office: 3405 West Truman Blvd., Suite 210, 65109-5713. Telephone: 573-636-8394. Facsimile: 573-636-8457.
Washington, D.C. Office: 1747 Pennsylvania Avenue, N.W., Suite 300, 20006. Telephone: 202-454-2800. Facsimile: 202-454-2805.
Springfield, Illinois Office: 3201 Pleasant Run, Suite A, P.O. Box 13317, 62791-3317. Telephone: 217-726-8200. Facsimile: 217-726-8300.
Belleville, Illinois Office: 23 South First Street, 62220. Telephone: 618-397-4411.
Overland Park, Kansas Office: 7400 West 132nd Street, Suite 200, 66213.
Henderson, Nevada Office: 701 North Green Valley Parkway, Suite 200, 89074. Telephone: 702-678-5070. Facsimile: 702-990-3003.
Sydney, Australia Office: C/Clayton Utz, Level 31, No. 1 O'Connell Street, Sidney, NSW 2000, Australia. Telephone: 61-29-262-6700. Facsimile: 61-29-262-3263.
New York, New York Office: 230 Park Avenue, Suite 2300, 10169. Telephone: 212-867-9500. Facsimile: 212-599-1759.
Shanghai, China Office: 1376 Nan Jing Xi Lu, Shanghai Center - Suite 718, Shanghai 200040, P.R. China. Telephone: 011-8621-6279-8808. Facsimilie: 011-8621-6279-8866.
See Professional Biographies, EDWARDSVILLE, ILLINOIS

Assouad, E. Timothy '76 '02 C.502 B.A. L.45 J.D.
(adm. in MO; not adm. in IL) [Ⓐ Burroughs,H.B.M.H.&T.]
Babb, Kevin J., (BV) ....'62 '87 C&L.339 B.A., J.D. 321 Hillsboro Ave.
Barberis, John B. ....'67 '96 C.338 B.S. L.734 J.D. 201 E. Vandalia St., Ste. B
Bash, Jeffrey T. ....'77 '03 C.339 B.A. L.734 J.D. [Ⓐ Heyl,R.V.&A.]

Bates, Brent A. '61 '86 C.707 B.A. L.352 J.D.
(adm. in IA; not adm. in IL) Sr. V.P. & Dir. of Claims, Florist Mutual Insurance Co.
Bauer, Beth A. ...... '75 '00 C.910 B.S. L.734 J.D. [🄰 Burroughs,H.B.M.H.&T.]
Baum, Brenda G., (AVⓉ) ...... '63 '88 C.293 B.A. L.910 J.D. [Burroughs,H.B.M.H.&T.]
Bauman, Mark D., (BV) ...... '59 '84 C.734 B.A. L.801 J.D. [Hinshaw&C.] (⊙Belleville)
Beasley, Jarrod P. ...... '76 '01 C.339 B.A. L.801 J.D. [🄰 Burroughs,H.B.M.H.&T.]
Bedesky, Michael J., (BV) ...... '66 '91 C.424 B.A. L.339 J.D. [Reed,A.G.M.&M.]
Beger, Brandy R. ...... '75 '00 C&L.910 B.A., J.D. [🄰 Burroughs,H.B.M.H.&T.]
Behnen, Nicole Cress, (BVⓉ) '67 '93 C.801 B.A. L.1439 J.D.
[Polsinelli S.W.S.] (⊙Kansas City, St. Louis, MO)
Belcher, Steven R. ...... '70 '02 C.375 B.S. L.801 J.D. [🄰 Burroughs,H.B.M.H.&T.]
Benecke, Kurt Christian '75 '02 C.502 B.A. L.910 J.D.
(adm. in MO; not adm. in IL) [🄰 Burroughs,H.B.M.H.&T.]
Bennett, Candice D. ...... '— '02 C&L.801 B.S., J.D. [🄰 Burroughs,H.B.M.H.&T.]
Bentivoglio, James J. ...... '55 '95 C.766 B.S. L.801 J.D. [🄲 Heyl,R.V.&A.]
Berg, Eric D. ...... '76 '04 C&L.339 B.S., J.D. [🄰 Thomson]
Bilbrey, Michael R., Law Office of, (BV) '54 '80 C.801 B.S. L.734 J.D.
8724 Pin Oak Rd.

Blackwell Sanders Peper Martin LLP
(See St. Louis, Missouri)

Blair, W. Wylie ...... '79 '05 C.339 B.A. L.801 J.D. [🄰 Heyl,R.V.&A.]
Blunt, David L., (BV) ...... '52 '77 C&L.502 B.A., J.D. [Blunt&Assoc.]
Blunt & Associates, Ltd., (BV) ...... 60 Edwardsville Professional Park
Boardman, Jane M. ...... '65 '93 C.134 B.S. L.734 J.D. [🄲 Heyl,R.V.&A.]
Boatman, Mark A., (BVⓉ) '58 '94
C.1347 B.G.S. L.734 J.D. [Armstrong T.] (⊙St. Louis, MO)
Bode, Dale L., (AV) ...... '45 '76 C.801 B.A. L.502 J.D. [Walker&W.] ⊙
Bornhofen, John H. ...... '71 '03 C.207 B.A. L.910 J.D. [🄰 Burroughs,H.B.M.H.&T.]
Bozarth, Troy A., (CV) ...... '69 '96 C.340 B.A. L.221 J.D. [Burroughs,H.B.M.H.&T.]
Bradley, Elizabeth A. ...... '71 '97 C.234 B.A. L.801 J.D. [🄰 Knapp,O.&G.]
Briddick, Thomas Patrick ...... '74 '00 C.589 B.S. L.801 J.D. [🄰 Burroughs,H.B.M.H.&T.]
Broom, Gordon R., (AV) ...... '44 '69 C&L.339 A.B., J.D. [Burroughs,H.B.M.H.&T.]
Brown, Joseph R., Jr., (AV) ...... '49 '74 C.861 B.A. L.339 J.D. [Lucco,B.T.&D.]
Bruegge, Robert T., (BV) ...... '49 '74 C.339 B.S. L.326 J.D. 400 St. Louis Street, Suite 2
Brummund, Matthew P., (BVⓉ) ...... '70 '95 C.827 B.A. L.477 J.D. 931 Surrey Court
Bryant, Aaron J. ...... '75 '01 C.999 L.502 J.D. [🄰 Heyl,R.V.&A.]
Buckley, Kathleen A., (BV) ...... '63 '89 C&L.801 B.A., J.D. 216 N. Main
Burkart, Karen ...... '61 '85 C.801 B.A. L.734 J.D. Sr. Law Clk., Appl. Ct.
Burnworth, Michael G., (BV) ...... '58 '84 C.339 B.S. L.734 J.D. [🄰 Blunt&Assoc.]

Burroughs, Hepler, Broom, MacDonald, Hebrank & True, LLP, (AV)
Two Mark Twain Plaza, Suite 300, 103 West Vandalia Street, P.O. Box 510, 62025-0510 ⊙
Telephone: 618-656-0184 Telecopier: 618-656-1364
Email: firm@ilmolaw.com URL: http://www.ilmolaw.com
Members of Firm: G. Gordon Burroughs (1909-2000); Larry E. Hepler; Gordon R. Broom; Theodore J. MacDonald, Jr.; Jeffrey S. Hebrank; Gary E. True; Stephen R. Kaufmann; Gerard T. Noce; Michael Reda (Resident); Paul W. Johnson; John D. Wendler; Lisa K. Franke; Brenda G. Baum; Daniel W. Farroll; Thomas Scott Stewart; Troy A. Bozarth; Wayne D. Skigen; Anne B. Schmidt. Associates: Paul B. Hunker, Jr. (Not admitted in IL); William L. Hanks; Joseph F. Grabowski; Kenneth E. Dick; George A. Kiser; Carl P. McNulty, II; Musette H. Vogel; Gregg A. Kinney; David Laurent; Gary A. Meadows; Stephen C. Morgan (Not admitted in IL); Robert H. Sands; Sean P. Sheehan; Michael J. Chessler; Anna R. Grabowski; W. Jason Rankin; Katherine M. Smith; Kristen Lynn Dieterich; Jennifer J. Scheibal; J. Phillip Steinman; Cassandra J. Hansell; Laura A. Hoffstetter (Not admitted in IL); Rebecca A. Nickelson; Matthew W. Potter; Bharat Varadachari (Not admitted in IL); Gretchen Wallace (Not admitted in IL); Beth A. Bauer; Brandy R. Beger; Thomas Patrick Briddick; Amanda M. Mueller; Nicholas V. Voswinkel (Not admitted in IL); Regina Lynn Lewis Wells; Jarrod P. Beasley; Candice D. Bennett; Dallas W. Cupp; James R. Grabowski; Eric P. Hall; Brian J. Huelsmann; Marc Jacob; Thomas H. Marrs; Noel L. Smith, Jr.; Allison Sonneveld; Erin Lyn Weber; E. Timothy Assouad (Not admitted in IL); Steven R. Belcher; Kurt Christian Benecke (Not admitted in IL); Douglas J. McCarty; Edna L. McLain; Kevin N. Mellick; Rachel D. Silger; Patrick W. Stufflebeam; Jill R. Sundberg; Michael L. Young; Dede K. Zupanci; John H. Bornhofen; Matthew B. Champlin; Peter A. Corsale; Carolyn M. Husmann; Kelly M. Plummer; Benjamin W. Powell; Eric D. Rosser; Dougglas A. Stultz; J. Michael Ward; Michael R. Wesley; Olga Camp; Amy L. Gervich (Not admitted in IL); Michael P. Murphy; Kathleen M. Nester; Michael C. Schroer (Not admitted in IL); Carol L. Sparks; Michael T. Harvath (Not admitted in IL).
General Civil Trial and Appellate Practice. Personal Injury, Negligence, Products Liability, Structural Work Act, Admiralty, Professional Malpractice, Insurance, Employment Law, Environmental, Asbestos and Toxic Tort, School, Municipal, Corporate, Tax, Real Estate and Probate Law.
Representative Clients: Ameritech; Travelers Insurance Co.; Bituminous Insurance Co.; BJC Health Systems; Cincinnati Insurance Co.; Illinois State Bar Association Mutual Insurance Co.; Kemper Insurance Co.; Ladede Gas Co.; Bondex; Prairie Farms; Amerenue.
St. Louis, Missouri Office: 1010 Market Street, Suite 500, 63101. Telephone: 314-355-6160.
See Professional Biographies, EDWARDSVILLE, ILLINOIS

Byron, Nicholas G. ...... '29 '58 C.367 A.B. L.910 J.D. Cir. J.
Cain, Scott Carl, (CV) ...... '58 '84 C.801 B.S. L.502 J.D. 515 St. Louis St.
Callis, Ann E. ...... '64 '90 C&L.734 B.S., J.D. Co. J.

Callis, Papa, Hale, Szewczyk, Rongey & Danzinger, P.C.
(See Granite City)

Camp, Olga ...... '77 '04 C&L.339 B.S., J.D. [🄰 Burroughs,H.B.M.H.&T.]
Carlson, Eric Jon ...... '70 '95 C.339 B.A. L.801 J.D. [Carlson&C.]
Carlson, Jon G., (AV) ...... '43 '67 C&L.339 A.B., J.D. [Carlson&C.] (⊙Chicago)

Carlson & Carlson, P.C., (AV) 🄱🄱
90 Edwardsville Professional Park, P.O. Box 527, 62025
Telephone: 618-656-0066 Fax: 618-656-0009 URL: http://www.carlsoninjurylaw.com
Email: ecarlson@mcleodusa.net URL: http://www.lawyers.com/carlson&carlson
Jon G. Carlson; Eric Jon Carlson. Of Counsel to: Mullen & Minnella, Chicago, Illinois.
Personal Injury. Trial Practice. Federal Employers Liability. Toxic Torts. Products Liability, Premises Liability, Medical Malpractice, Car and Truck Accident Litigation, Civil Litigation, and Aviation Law.
See Professional Biographies, EDWARDSVILLE, ILLINOIS

Carrion, Elizabeth Nicole ...... '76 '02 C.69 B.A. L.209 J.D. 241 N. Main St.
Carrow, Martin T., II ...... '65 '91 C.502 B.A. L.607 J.D. P.O. Box 425

Cates, Kurowski, Bailey & Shultz, LLC
(See Belleville)

Champlin, Matthew B. ...... '78 '03 C.798 B.S. L.1439 J.D. [🄰 Burroughs,H.B.M.H.&T.]
Chandler-Peneston, Sheri L. ...... '71 '01 C&L.502 B.A., J.D. 216 North Main
Chapman, Morris B., (AV) ...... '19 '42 C&L.734 J.D. 201 EA. Vandalia
Chessler, Michael J. ...... '67 '95 C.273 B.A. L.365 J.D. [🄰 Burroughs,H.B.M.H.&T.]
Clark, Michael D., (BV) ...... '50 '84 C.801 B.A. L.589 J.D. [🄲 Heyl,R.V.&A.]
Clark, Stephen R., (AVⓉ) '66 '91 C.602 B.A. L.734 J.D.
[Polsinelli S.W.S.] (⊙Kansas City, St. Louis, MO)
Clayborne, James F., Jr., (BV) '63 '88
C.832 B.S. L.472 J.D. [Hinshaw&C.] (⊙Belleville)
Coffey, Gary R., (AV) ...... '32 '55 C&L.339 B.S., J.D. [Coffey]
Coffey, Gregory W., (AV) ...... '59 '85 C.339 B.S. L.589 J.D. [Coffey]

Coffey Law Firm, Professional Corporation, (AV)
125 North Buchanan Street, P.O. Box 247, 62025-0247
Telephone: 618-656-2244 Fax: 618-656-1307
Email: info@midwestlawfirm.com URL: http://www.midwestlawfirm.com
Gary R. Coffey; Gregory W. Coffey; John W. McCracken;—Sandra J. Tatoian; Danielle Angelique La Chance-Yates.
Business Law, Corporate Law, Contracts, Mergers, Acquisitions and Divestitures, Trusts and Estates, Wills and Probate, Real Estate.
See Professional Biographies, EDWARDSVILLE, ILLINOIS

Cole, Clark H., (AVⓉ) '55 '80 C.420 B.A. L.502 J.D.
[Armstrong T.] (⊙Belleville, IL; St. Louis, MO)
Corsale, Peter A. ...... '78 '03 C.910 B.A. L.339 J.D. [🄰 Burroughs,H.B.M.H.&T.]
Cox, Tori L. ...... '78 '03 C.337 B.A. L.801 J.D. [🄰 Reed,A.G.M.&M.]
Cox, William M., (BV) ...... '23 '49 C.782 L.910 LL.B. 1010 St. Louis St.
Craig, John C., (BV) ...... '62 '91 C.339 B.S. L.734 J.D. [🄰 Heyl,R.V.&A.]
Cross, Andrew J. ...... '66 '93 C.602 B.A. L.734 J.D. [Polsinelli S.W.S.]
Crowder, Barbara L., (AV) ...... '56 '81 C&L.339 A.B., J.D. 155 N. Main St.
Cupp, Dallas W. ...... '76 '01 C.502 B.A. L.910 J.D. [🄰 Burroughs,H.B.M.H.&T.]
Daniels, Michael F. ...... '52 '90 C.93 B.A. L.1049 J.D. [🄰 Heyl,R.V.&A.]
Davis, Glenn E., (AVⓉ) '56 '82 C.210 B.A. L.910 J.D.
[Armstrong T.] (⊙Belleville, IL; St. Louis, MO)
Dawson, Curtis M. ...... '67 '95 C.234 B.A. L.801 J.D. [Lucco,B.T.&D.]
Dick, Kenneth E., (AVⓉ) ...... '49 '89 C&L.734 B.A., J.D. [🄰 Burroughs,H.B.M.H.&T.]
Dickey, Aaron Kenneth '74 '01 C.910 B.A. L.734 J.D.
(adm. in MO; not adm. in IL) 2227 S. State Rte. 157
Dieterich, Kristen Lynn ...... '72 '98 C&L.221 B.S.B.A., J.D. [🄰 Burroughs,H.B.M.H.&T.]

Dixon & Johnston, P.C.
(See Belleville)

Dobbels, Dennis J., (AVⓉ) '57 '82
C.976 B.A. L.1065 J.D. [Polsinelli S.W.S.] (⊙Kansas City, MO)
Dods, Sandra J., (CV) ...... '52 '80 C&L.801 B.A., J.D. 100 N. Main St., Suite 6
Donaho, Maureen Ann ...... '65 '91 C.339 B.S. L.801 J.D. Chicago Title Ins. Co.
Duff, Ellar ...... '49 '82 C&L.502 B.S., J.D. Assoc. Cir. J.
Dye, William J., Jr., (BVⓉ) ...... '47 '72 C&L.910 A.B., J.D. [🄲 Heyl,R.V.&A.]
Edwards, George R. ...... '35 '68 C.98 B.S. L.146 J.D. 4799 N. State Route 157
Eisele, Philip M., (AVⓉ) ...... '53 '79 C&L.502 B.A., J.D. [🄲 Heyl,R.V.&A.]
Elovitz, Robert L., Law Office of, (CV) ...... '62 '89 C.346 B.S. L.801 J.D. 216 St. Louis St.
Ess, John A., (BV) ...... '50 '75 C.801 B.A. L.221 J.D. Gen. Coun., R.P. Lumber Co. Inc.
Fahrenkamp, David M., The Law Office of, (BV) '53 '78
C.98 B.S. L.734 J.D. 205 N. Second
Farroll, Daniel W. ...... '66 '92 C.755 B.A. L.801 J.D. [Burroughs,H.B.M.H.&T.]
Felton-Armouti, Veronica ...... '63 '97 C.801 B.S. L.734 J.D. State Farm Ins. Co.
Ferguson, Edward C. ...... '44 '68 C.597 B.A. L.339 J.D. Cir. J.
Flanigan, Frank L., (BV) ...... '35 '61 C.388 B.A. L.1119 J.D. [Flanigan]
Flanigan Law Office, (BV) ...... 120 N. Main St.
Foppe, Patrick E. ...... '78 '04 C&L.734 B.S., J.D. [🄰 Heyl,R.V.&A.]
Foreman, Jonathan W. ...... '70 '97 C.188 B.S. L.339 J.D. [🄲 Thomson]
Fournie, Raymond R., (AVⓉ) '51 '79 C.339 B.S. L.734 J.D.
[Armstrong T.] (⊙Belleville, IL; St. Louis, MO)
Franke, Lisa K., (BV) ...... '57 '82 C&L.801 B.S., J.D. [Burroughs,H.B.M.H.&T.]
Garcia, Christopher M. ...... '— '04 C.608 B.S. L.861 J.D. [🄰 Reed,A.G.M.&M.]
Gerber, David J., (BV) ...... '67 '92 C.338 B.S. L.734 J.D. 241 N. Main Street
Gervich, Amy L. '75 '04 C&L.734 B.S.B.A., J.D.
(adm. in MO; not adm. in IL) [🄰 Burroughs,H.B.M.H.&T.]
Gibbons, John P. ...... '37 '76 C&L.734 B.S., J.D. 220 St. Louis St.
Gilbert, John L., (AV) ...... '50 '75 C.339 B.A. L.910 J.D. [Hinshaw&C.] (⊙Belleville)
Glass, Jeffrey R., (AV) ...... '53 '78 C&L.734 B.A., J.D. [Hinshaw&C.] (⊙Belleville)
Gori, Randy Lee ...... '72 '98 C&L.734 B.A., J.D. 2227 S. State Route 157
Gorman, James E., (AV) ...... '30 '56 C.707 B.A. L.339 J.D. [🄲 Lucco,B.T.&D.]
Graber, Dennis J., (BV) ...... '59 '84 C.337 B.A. L.801 J.D. [Hinshaw&C.] (⊙Belleville)
Grabowski, Anna R. ...... '62 '95 C.801 B.S. L.734 J.D. [🄰 Burroughs,H.B.M.H.&T.]
Grabowski, James R. ...... '75 '01 C&L.801 B.S., J.D. [🄰 Burroughs,H.B.M.H.&T.]
Grabowski, Joseph F., (CV) '63 '88 C.339 B.S. L.801 J.D.
[🄰 Burroughs,H.B.M.H.&T.]
Graham, Timothy A. ...... '55 '84 C.338 B.S. L.910 J.D. [🄲 Heyl,R.V.&A.]
Green, L. David, (BV) ...... '60 '86 C&L.801 B.S., J.D. [Knapp,O.&G.]
Gundlach, Frank N., (P.C.), (AVⓉ) '38 '63 C.165 A.B. L.910 J.D.
(adm. in MO; not adm. in IL) [Armstrong T.] (⊙St. Louis, MO)
Hackett, James ...... '51 '78 C&L.734 B.A., J.D. State Ct. J.
Hagans, Theresa A. '67 '92 C&L.734 B.A., J.D.
(adm. in MO; not adm. in IL) State Attys. Off.
Hahn, Dorothy Kuhns ...... '19 '49 C&L.339 B.S., J.D. 1149 Bermuda Holliday Shores‡
Haine, William R., (BV) ...... '44 '74 C&L.734 A.B., J.D. State's Atty.
Hall, Eric P. ...... '74 '01 C.339 B.A. L.801 J.D. [🄰 Burroughs,H.B.M.H.&T.]
Hanks, William L. ...... '41 '78 C.801 B.A. L.734 J.D. [🄰 Burroughs,H.B.M.H.&T.]
Hansell, Cassandra J. ...... '71 '99 C.352 B.A. L.801 J.D. [🄰 Burroughs,H.B.M.H.&T.]

Harper, Julie
(See Alton)

Harrison, Clarence W. ...... '64 '89 C&L.802 B.B.A., J.D. Assoc. Cir. J.
Harvath, Michael T. '78 '03 C.698 B.A. L.734 J.D.
(adm. in MO; not adm. in IL) [🄰 Burroughs,H.B.M.H.&T.]
Hawkins, Deborah A. ...... '56 '00 C.357 B.A. L.734 J.D. [🄰 Heyl,R.V.&A.]
Haynes, John C., (CV) ...... '48 '78 C.801 B.A. L.365 J.D. 6925 State Rt. 140
Hebrank, Jeffrey S., (AV) ...... '57 '82 C.201 B.A. L.734 J.D. [Burroughs,H.B.M.H.&T.]
Heinsz, Christine A. ...... '50 '05 C.801 B.S. L.910 J.D. [🄰 Heyl,R.V.&A.]
Heise, Douglas R., (BV) ...... '58 '83 C.234 B.S. L.365 J.D. [🄲 Heyl,R.V.&A.]
Hennessey, Robert P. ...... '41 '68 C.801 B.A. L.734 J.D. Asso. Cir. J.
Hepler, Larry E., (AV) ...... '43 '68 C.105 A.B. L.902 J.D. [Burroughs,H.B.M.H.&T.] ⊙

Heyl, Royster, Voelker & Allen, Professional Corporation, (AV)
Suite 100, Mark Twain Plaza II, 103 West Vandalia Street, P.O. Box 467, 62025 ⊙
Telephone: 618-656-4646 Telecopier: 618-656-7940
Email: firm@hrva.com URL: http://www.hrva.com
Partners: Robert H. Shultz, Jr.; Kent L. Plotner; Richard K. Hunsaker; James A. Telthorst; Joseph P. Whyte; Michael T. Kokal. Of Counsel: Edward E. Johnston; Timothy A. Graham; William J. Dye, Jr.; Philip M. Eisele; Douglas R. Heise; Michael D. Clark; Michael D. Schag; James J. Bentivoglio; Jane M. Boardman. Associates: Christine M. McClimans; John C. Craig; Michael F. Daniels; Aaron J. Bryant; Deborah A. Hawkins; Gray M. Magee, III; Laura L. Althardt; Mary Jo Kuca; Jeffrey T. Bash; Patrick E. Foppe; W. Wylie Blair; Christine A. Heinsz; Matthew J. Morris.
General Civil Trial and Appellate Practice in all Courts, Insurance Defense, Workers' Compensation Defense, Professional Liability Defense, Truck Accidents, Construction Law, Railroad Accidents and Injuries, Insurance Coverage, Self Insured Defense, Products Liability Defense, Civil Rights, Asbestos Defense, Class Action Defense, Corporate Law, Health Care, Banking, Government, Employment, Environmental, Probate, Elder Law, Agribusiness, Immigration, Religious Institutions, Nonprofit and Charitable Organizations, College and University Law, and Real Estate.
Peoria, Illinois Office: Suite 600, Chase Building, 124 S.W. Adams, 61602. Telephone: 309-676-0400. Telecopier: 309-676-3374.

(This Listing Continued)

Heyl, Royster, Voelker & Allen, Professional Corporation (Continued)

Springfield, Illinois Office: Suite 575, National City Center, P.O. Box 1687, 62705. Telephone: 217-522-8822. Telecopier: 217-523-3902.
Urbana, Illinois Office: Suite 300, 102 East Main Street, P.O. Box 129, 61803-0129. Telephone: 217-344-0060. Telecopier: 217-344-9295.
Rockford, Illinois Office: Second Floor, National City Bank Building, 120 West State Street, P.O. Box 1288, 61105-1288. Telephone: 815-963-4454. Telecopier: 815-963-0399.

See Professional Biographies, EDWARDSVILLE, ILLINOIS

Higgins, Mary Beth ....'57 '99 C.741 B.A. L.801 J.D. 157 N. Main St.
Hill, M. Joseph, (BV) ....'42 '67 C.707 B.A. L.734 J.D. 511 Saint Louis St.

Hinshaw & Culbertson LLP, (AV)
Hinshaw & Culbertson LLP is an Illinois registered limited liability partnership that has elected to be governed by the Illinois Uniform Partnership Act (1997)
156 North Main Street Suite 206, 62025 ⊙
Telephone: 618-655-0342 Facsimile: 618-655-0467
Email: kfox@hinshawlaw.com URL: http://www.hinshawlaw.com
Partners: Mark D. Bauman (Also at Belleville, Illinois Office); James F. Clayborne, Jr.; John L. Gilbert; Jeffrey R. Glass; Dennis J. Graber; Charles A. Pierce; John E. Sabo; Dawn A. Sallerson.
Appellate, Banking & Financing, Bankruptcy & Creditors' Rights, Class Action Litigation, Civil Rights Defense, Commercial Litigation, Corporate, Construction Law, Director & Officer Liability, Employee Benefits, Environmental, Fidelity & Surety, General Liability Litigation, Government, Health Care, Insurance Coverage, Insurance and Reinsurance, Labor & Employment, Legal Malpractice, Medical Malpractice, Mergers & Acquisitions, Municipal Liability, Personal Injury Defense, Public Law, Products Liability Litigation, Professional Liability, Regulatory, Real Estate, School Law, Securities, Taxation, Transportation, White Collar Crime and Workers' Compensation Defense.
Other Office Locations: Chicago, Illinois; Appleton, Wisconsin; Belleville, Illinois; Boston, Massachusetts; Champaign, Illinois; Crystal Lake, Illinois; Fort Lauderdale, Florida; Jacksonville, Florida; Joliet, Illinois; Lisle, Illinois; Miami, Florida; Milwaukee, Wisconsin; Minneapolis, Minnesota; New York, New York; Peoria, Illinois; Phoenix, Arizona; Portland, Oregon; Providence, Rhode Island; Rockford, Illinois; St. Louis, Missouri; San Francisco, California; Schererville, Indiana; Springfield, Illinois; Tampa, Florida; Waukegan, Illinois.

See Professional Biographies, EDWARDSVILLE, ILLINOIS

Hoagland, Fitzgerald, Smith & Pranaitis
(See Alton)

Hobin, Michael ....'70 '00 C.98 B.S. L.801 J.D. [Ⓐ Reed,A.G.M.&M.]
Hoffstetter, Laura A. '73 '99 C.910 B.A. L.734 J.D.
(adm. in MO; not adm. in IL) [Ⓐ Burroughs,H.B.M.H.&T.]
Hopkins, John J., & Associates, (BV) '51 '77
C.734 B.A. L.862 J.D. 1120 S. State Rte. 157, Ste. 200
Huelsmann, Brian J. .... '74 '01 C.698 B.A. L.801 J.D. [Ⓐ Burroughs,H.B.M.H.&T.]
Humes, Jack H., Jr., (BV) ....'52 '85 C.801 B.A. L.734 J.D. [Humes]

Humes Law Office, (BV)
515 St. Louis Street, P.O. Box 201, 62025
Telephone: 618-656-0616 Fax: 618-656-3166
URL: http://www.jackhumeslaw.com
Jack H. Humes, Jr.
Municipal, Public Finance, Construction, Corporate, Real Estate, Wills and Probate, Trusts and Estates, Commercial and Residential Real Estate, Buying and Selling a Home, Buying and Selling a Business.

See Professional Biographies, EDWARDSVILLE, ILLINOIS

Hunker, Paul B., Jr., (AVⓉ) '38 '66 C.934 B.A. L.910 J.D.
(adm. in MO; not adm. in IL) [Ⓐ Burroughs,H.B.M.H.&T.]
Hunsaker, Richard K., (AV) ....'60 '86 C.339 B.A. L.910 J.D. [Heyl,R.V.&A.]
Husmann, Carolyn M. ....'78 '03 C&L.734 B.A., J.D. [Ⓐ Burroughs,H.B.M.H.&T.]
Isbell, Jonathan, (BV) ....'50 '76 C.910 A.B. L.734 J.D. 1720-A N. Main St.
Jackstadt, Robert L., (AV) ....'60 '85 C.339 B.S. L.734 J.D. [Tueth,K.C.M.&J.]
Jacob, Marc ....'76 '02 C.1372 B.A. L.188 J.D. [Ⓐ Burroughs,H.B.M.H.&T.]
Jenkins, Rhonda K. ....'56 '96 C.999 B.A. L.801 J.D. P.O. Box 959
Jensen, Keith A., (BV) ....'51 '77 C.340 B.A. L.910 J.D. [Jensen]
Jensen Law Office, The, (BV) ....5323 Smith Drive
Johnson, Billie L., (BV) ....'47 '86 C.898 B.A. L.190 J.D. [Johnson&A.]
Johnson, Paul W., (BV) ....'60 '85 C&L.502 B.A., J.D. [Burroughs,H.B.M.H.&T.]

Johnson & Anderson, (BV)
201 Hillsboro Avenue, 62025
Telephone: 618-659-1400 Fax: 618-659-1700 URL: http://www.johnsonandersonlaw.com
URL: http://www.j-a-law.com
Billie L. Johnson; Karen A. Anderson.
Appellate Practice, Bankruptcy, Probate, Estate Planning, Estate Administration, Trusts and Estates, Asset Protection, Guardianship, General Civil, Family Law, Adoptions, Child Custody, Child Support, Domestic Violence, Divorce, Personal Injury, Wrongful Death, Medical Malpractice, Auto Accidents, Sexual Abuse, DWI, Drug Crimes, Juvenile Crimes, White Collar Crime, Traffic Violations, Elder Law, Parole Violation/Probation, Real Estate, Buying and Selling a Home.

See Professional Biographies, EDWARDSVILLE, ILLINOIS

Johnston, Edward E., (BV) ....'60 '86 C.339 B.A. L.910 J.D. [Ⓒ Heyl,R.V.&A.]
Jones, Stephanie E. ....'76 '02 101 West Vandalia, Ste. 210
Kalb, Brian R. ....'73 '02 C&L.801 B.A., J.D. 8 Donna Ct.
Kardis, Phillip John ....'42 '71 C.339 B.S. L.273 J.D. Cir. J. (Pat.)
Kaseberg, William G. ....'45 '74 C.934 B.A. L.930 J.D. 2110 Troy Rd.‡
Kassin, Alan R. ....'44 '70 C&L.339 B.A., J.D. 30 Edwardsville, Professional Park
Kaufmann, Stephen R., (AV) '52 '78 C.388 B.A. L.597 J.D.
[Burroughs,H.B.M.H.&T.]
Kelleher, Joseph T., Jr. ....'28 '53 C&L.734 LL.B. 332 S. Buchanan, Ste. D‡
Kelty, Thomas W. ....'45 '71 C.190 B.A. L.502 J.D. [Ⓒ Armstrong T.] (⊙Springfield)
Kidd, Anita M. .....'60 '89 C.424 B.S.R.N. L.426 J.D. [Armstrong T.] (⊙St. Louis, MO)
King, Charles W., (BV) ....'34 '63 C.602 B.A. L.734 J.D. 1507 Troy Rd.
Kinney, Gregg A. ....'67 '92 C.612 B.S. L.623 J.D. [Ⓐ Burroughs,H.B.M.H.&T.]
Kiser, George A., (AVⓉ) '61 '89 C&L.502 B.S.B.A., J.D.
[Ⓐ Burroughs,H.B.M.H.&T.]
Knapp, William J., (AV) ....'60 '85 C.1281 B.A. L.801 J.D. [Knapp,O.&G.]

Knapp, Ohl & Green, (AV)
6100 Center Grove Road, P.O. Box 446, 62025
Telephone: 618-656-5088 Fax: 618-656-5466
Email: wjk@knappohlgreen.com
Members of Firm: William J. Knapp; Donald J. Ohl; L. David Green. Associates: Elizabeth A. Bradley; Michael S. Prater; Carla C. Storm; John Joseph Lee.
Negligence, Products Liability, Insurance Coverage, Personal Injury, Workers Compensation, School Law, Municipal Law, Admiralty, Consumer Law, Medical Malpractice, Toxic Torts.

See Professional Biographies, EDWARDSVILLE, ILLINOIS

Koester, Jessica J. ....'77 '02 C.339 B.A. L.602 J.D. [Ⓐ Lucco,B.T.&D.]
Kokal, Michael T., (BV) ....'65 '92 C.602 B.S.E.E. L.502 J.D. [Heyl,R.V.&A.]
Kuca, Mary Jo ....'72 '03 C.801 B.S.N. L.734 J.D. [Ⓐ Heyl,R.V.&A.]
La Chance-Yates, Danielle Angelique ....'72 '99 C.999 B.A. L.801 J.D. [Ⓐ Coffey]

Lakin Law Firm, The, P.C.
(See Wood River)

Lauber, Paul H., (BV) '53 '78 C&L.879 B.A., J.D.
3B Club Centre Court, 62025-3519
Telephone: 618-692-9080 Fax: 618-692-9105
Email: plauber@cbnstl.com URL: http://www.lauberlaw.com

(This Listing Continued)

Lauber, Paul H. (Continued)

Business and Real Estate Transactions, Wills, Trusts, Estate Planning and Probate, Commercial and Business Litigation, Estate Planning.

See Professional Biographies, EDWARDSVILLE, ILLINOIS

Laurent, David, (CV) ....'68 '92 C.339 A.B. L.801 J.D. [Ⓐ Burroughs,H.B.M.H.&T.]
Lee, John Joseph ....'71 '97 C.587 B.A. L.910 J.D. [Ⓐ Knapp,O.&G.]
Levy, Elizabeth Levine R., (BV) ......'48 '74 C.331 B.A. L.910 J.D. 220 S. Buchanan St.
Levy, Mark A., (BV) ....'49 '77 220 S. Buchanan St.
Lowery, Ronald Dean ....'54 '79 C.801 B.A. L.734 J.D. R.P. Lumber Co., Inc.
Lucco, J. William, (AV) ....'47 '72 C&L.339 A.B., J.D. [Lucco,B.T.&D.]

Lucco, Brown, Threlkeld & Dawson, LLP, (AV) 🅱🅱
P.O. Box 539, 62025
Telephone: 618-656-2321 Fax: 618-656-2363
URL: http://www.lbtdlaw.com
Dick H. Mudge (1879-1952); Dick H. Mudge, Jr. (1919-1978); J. William Lucco; Joseph R. Brown, Jr.; Christopher P. Threlkeld; Curtis M. Dawson. Associates: Jessica J. Koester; Debra Kelly Zahalsky. Of Counsel: James E. Gorman.
General Civil and Criminal Litigation in State and Federal Courts. Federal Criminal Defense including White Collar Criminal Defense, Corporate Internal Investigations, and Health Care Fraud Defense; State Criminal Defense including all Felonies, DUI, Traffic and Juvenile Law.
Civil Litigation including Intellectual Property Litigation (Patents); Construction, Contracts, Corporations, Wrongful Death, Personal Injury, Workman's Compensation and UCC litigation.
Reference: Bank of Edwardsville, Edwardsville, Illinois.

See Professional Biographies, EDWARDSVILLE, ILLINOIS

MacDonald, Joyce Yulkey '52 '77 C.502 A.B. L.734 J.D.
(adm. in MO; not adm. in IL) 24 Camelot Dr.‡
MacDonald, Theodore J., Jr., (AV) '51 '78
C.659 B.A. L.734 J.D. [Burroughs,H.B.M.H.&T.]
Maddox, Lola P. ....'49 '75 C.338 B.S. L.228 J.D. Assoc. Cir. J.
Magee, Gray M., III ....'67 '95 C.836 B.A. L.734 J.D. [Ⓐ Heyl,R.V.&A.]
Mallott, Lewis E., (BV) ....'45 '73 C&L.734 B.S., J.D. Madison Cty Cthouse.
Marrs, Thomas H. ....'76 '01 C.810 B.A. L.744 J.D. [Ⓐ Burroughs,H.B.M.H.&T.]
Matoesian, A. Andreas ....'37 '65 C.339 B.A. L.910 J.D. Cir. J.
McCarthy, Edward T., Attorney at Law, (BV) '45 '73
C&L.910 B.S.B.A., J.D. P.O. Box 276
McCarty, Douglas J. ....'— '02 C&L.801 B.A., J.D. [Ⓐ Burroughs,H.B.M.H.&T.]
McClimans, Christine M., (BV) .....'61 '90 C.801 B.S.N. L.190 J.D. [Ⓐ Heyl,R.V.&A.]
McCord, John F.X. ....'63 '99 C.871 B.S. L.339 J.D. [Ⓐ Reed,A.G.M.&M.]
McCracken, John W. ....'67 '97 C.357 B.S. L.734 J.D. [Coffey]
McGuire, John P., (CV) ....'59 '84 C.910 B.S.B.A. L.801 J.D. Asst. State Atty.
McLain, Edna L. ....'77 '02 C.339 B.A. L.734 J.D. [Ⓐ Burroughs,H.B.M.H.&T.]

McMahon, Berger, Hanna, Linihan, Cody & McCarthy, A Professional Corporation
(See Collinsville)

McNamara, Edward D., Jr., (BV) ....'43 '68 C.734 B.S. L.339 J.D. [McNamara&E.] ⊙
McNamara & Evans, (BV) ....21 Glen-Ed Professional Park (⊙Springfield)
McNulty, Carl P., II ....'61 '90 C&L.260 B.A., J.D. [Ⓐ Burroughs,H.B.M.H.&T.]
Meacham, William J., (CV) ....'50 '89 C&L.801 B.S., J.D. [W.J.Meacham]
Meacham, William J., P.C., Law Office of, (CV) ....521 St. Louis Street
Meadows, Gary A., (CV) .....'63 '92 C.942 B.S. L.801 J.D. [Ⓐ Burroughs,H.B.M.H.&T.]
Meehan, Michael J. ....'51 '76 C.801 B.A. L.734 J.D. Assoc. Cir. J.
Mellick, Kevin N. ....'75 '02 C.436 B.A. L.734 J.D. [Ⓐ Burroughs,H.B.M.H.&T.]
Mendelsohn, Ralph J., (BV) ....'43 '68 C&L.339 B.A., J.D. 155 N. Main St.
Metz, Monica B. ....'74 '99 C.801 B.S. L.734 J.D. 157 N. Main St.
Metzger, Donald L., (AV) ....'38 '63 C&L.339 A.B., J.D. 517 St. Louis Street
Miller, William R., (CV) ....'67 '92 C.234 B.A. L.801 J.D. 2227 S. State Route 157
Moran, George J. ....'48 '74 C.801 B.S. L.734 J.D. Cir. J.
Moran, Mark B., (BVⓉ) ....'58 '87 C.502 B.S. L.734 J.D. [Ⓐ Reed,A.G.M.&M.]
Morgan, Stephen C. '67 '94 C.101 B.S. L.464 J.D.
(adm. in MO; not adm. in IL) [Ⓐ Burroughs,H.B.M.H.&T.]
Morris, Matthew J. ....'79 '05 C.98 B.S. L.734 J.D. [Ⓐ Heyl,R.V.&A.]
Morrison, Donna S. ....'66 '91 C.1182 B.A. L.734 J.D. 701 N. Main St.
Morrissey, Martin K., (AV) ....'59 '85 C.339 B.A. L.801 J.D. [Reed,A.G.M.&M.]
Mudge, Stephen C., (AV) ....'52 '77 C.707 B.A. L.734 J.D. [Reed,A.G.M.&M.]
Mudge, William A., (AV) ....'59 '85 C.338 B.S. L.734 J.D. States Atty.
Mueller, Amanda M. ......'75 '00 C.133 B.A. L.734 J.D. [Ⓐ Burroughs,H.B.M.H.&T.]
Murphy, Michael P. ....'79 '04 C.927 B.A. L.801 J.D. [Ⓐ Burroughs,H.B.M.H.&T.]
Musick, Robert Owens ....'66 '93 C&L.910 B.A., J.D. 2227 S. State Route 157
Nester, Kathleen M. ....'77 '04 C.190 B.A. L.734 J.D. [Ⓐ Burroughs,H.B.M.H.&T.]
Nickelson, Rebecca A. ....'74 '99 C&L.734 B.A., J.D. [Ⓐ Burroughs,H.B.M.H.&T.]
Noce, Gerard T., (AVⓉ) ....'51 '79 C&L.502 B.J., J.D. [Burroughs,H.B.M.H.&T.]

Noonan, Thomas J., P.C.
(See St. Louis, Missouri)

Ohl, Donald J., (AV) ....'63 '93 C.338 B.S. L.734 J.D. [Knapp,O.&G.]
O'Neill, Paul J. ....'46 '73 C.1024 B.A. L.734 J.D. Cir. J.
Pierce, Charles A., (BV) ....'66 '91 C.352 B.S. L.801 J.D. [Hinshaw&C.] (⊙Belleville)
Plotner, Kent L., (AV) ....'58 '85 C.338 B.S. L.734 J.D. [Heyl,R.V.&A.]
Plummer, Kelly M. ....'77 '03 C.927 B.S. L.734 J.D. [Ⓐ Burroughs,H.B.M.H.&T.]
Polinske, Brian L. ....'66 '92 C.121 B.S. L.734 J.D. 701 N. Main St.

Polsinelli Shalton Welte Suelthaus PC, (AVⓉ)
Mark Twain Plaza, Suite 225 101 West Vandalia Street, 62025 ⊙
Telephone: 618-655-9500 Fax: 618-655-9640
Email: pswslaw@pswslaw.com URL: http://www.pswslaw.com
Nicole Cress Behnen; Stephen R. Clark; Andrew J. Cross (Resident); Dennis J. Dobbels; Joseph T. Porter, Jr.; Eric M. Trelz.
Class Action Defense, Commercial Litigation, Employment Litigation, ERISA Litigation, Insurance, Mass Torts, Product Liability Defense, Toxic Torts, Toxic Torts Defense.
Kansas City, Missouri Office: 700 West 47th Street, Suite 1000. Telephone: 816-753-1000. Fax: 816-753-1536.
St. Louis, Missouri Office: 100 South Fourth Street, Suite 1100. Telephone: 314-889-8000. Fax: 314-231-1776.
Other St. Louis, Missouri Office: 7733 Forsyth Boulevard, Suite 1200. Telephone: 314-889-8000. Fax: 314-727-7166.
Overland Park, Kansas Office: 6201 College Boulevard, Suite 500. Telephone: 913-451-8788. Fax: 913-451-6205.
Topeka, Kansas Office: 555 Kansas Avenue, Suite 301. Telephone: 785-233-1446. Fax: 785-233-1939.
New York Office: 292 Madison Avenue, 17th Floor, 10017. Telephone: 212-684-0199. Fax: 212-684-0197.
Washington, D.C. Office: 555 Twelfth Street N.W., Suite 710, 20004. Telephone: 202-783-3300. Fax: 202-783-3535.

See Professional Biographies, EDWARDSVILLE, ILLINOIS

Porter, Joseph T., Jr., (AVⓉ) '52 '79 C.1347 B.S. L.734 J.D.
[Polsinelli S.W.S.] (⊙Kansas City, St. Louis, MO)
Potter, Matthew W. ....'73 '99 C.587 B.A. L.502 J.D. [Ⓐ Burroughs,H.B.M.H.&T.]
Powell, Benjamin W. ....'77 '03 C.999 B.A. L.1439 J.D. [Ⓐ Burroughs,H.B.M.H.&T.]
Prater, Michael S. ....'71 '01 C.1347 B.A. L.801 J.D. [Ⓐ Knapp,O.&G.]

Ramsey, Robert Brooks, (BVⓉ) ....'48 '80 C&L.734 B.A., J.D. [Ⓐ Blunt&Assoc.]
Rankin, W. Jason, (CV) ..... '71 '96 C.221 B.A. L.910 J.D. [Ⓐ Burroughs,H.B.M.H.&T.]
Reda, Michael, (BV) .... '56 '83 C.602 B.A. L.734 J.D. [Burroughs,H.B.M.H.&T.]

Reed, Armstrong, Gorman, Mudge & Morrissey, Professional Corporation, (AV)
115 North Buchanan Street, P.O. Box 368, 62025
Telephone: 618-656-0257 Facsimile: 618-692-4416
Email: info@reedarmstrong.com URL: http://www.reedarmstrong.com
Harry C. Armstrong; Stephen C. Mudge; Martin K. Morrissey; Michael J. Bedesky; Bryan L. Skelton; William B. Starnes, II;—Michael Hobin; Dominique N. Seymoure; John F.X. McCord; Stephen Michael Szewczyk; Tori L. Cox; Mark B. Moran; Christopher M. Garcia; Roy D. Anderson.
General Civil Trial and Appellate practice in all State and Federal Courts, including Missouri, Personal Injury, Negligence, Premises Liability, Products Liability, Insurance, Automobile, Construction, Commercial Litigation, Workers Compensation, Employment, Discrimination, Dram Shop/Liquor Liability, Marine/Water Recreational Boating, Wrongful Discharge, Extra Contractual Liability/Bad Faith, Property Damage, Fraud/Arson/Fire, Non-Vehicle General Liability, Eminent Domain, Civil Rights, Class Action, Environmental, Toxic Tort, School, Corporate, Probate, Estate Planning, Real Estate Law.
Representative Clients: State Farm Insurance Cos.; Country Companies; Standard Mutual Casualty Co.; General Casualty Co. of Wisconsin; Lloyds of London; Hawkeye Security Insurance Co.; Shelter Insurance Companies; Pekin Insurance Cos.; American International Adjusting Co.; Employers Reinsurance Corp.

See Professional Biographies, EDWARDSVILLE, ILLINOIS

Reeg & Nowogrocki, L.L.C.
(See St. Louis, Missouri)

Reilly, Erin E. .... '69 '94 C&L.734 B.A., J.D. 241 N. Main St., Ste. 100
Romani, Charles V., Jr. .... '47 '74 C.927 B.A. L.734 J.D. Cir. J.
Roosevelt, Greg E., (BV) .... '50 '76 C&L.339 B.S., J.D. [Roosevelt]
Roosevelt Law Office, (BV) .... 610 St. Louis Street
Rosser, Eric D. .... '76 '03 C.339 B.S. L.589 J.D. [Ⓐ Burroughs,H.B.M.H.&T.]
Rowland, Robert D., (BV) .... '62 '88 C.338 B.S. L.801 J.D. 2227 S. State Route 157
Sabo, John E., (BV) .... '57 '87 C.465 B.B.A. L.801 J.D. [Hinshaw&C.] (ⓄBelleville)
Sallerson, Dawn A., (BV) ..... '61 '86 C.739 B.A. L.734 J.D. [Hinshaw&C.] (ⓄBelleville)
Sands, Robert H. .... '67 '94 C.1077 B.S. L.1148 J.D. [Ⓐ Burroughs,H.B.M.H.&T.]
Sanford, William A. '33 '64 C&L.734 B.S., LL.B.
(adm. in MO; not adm. in IL) 4 Hidden Valley Lane
Schag, Michael D. .... '67 '94 C.339 B.S. L.616 J.D. [Ⓒ Heyl,R.V.&A.]
Scheibal, Jennifer J. .... '71 '98 C&L.801 B.S., J.D. [Ⓐ Burroughs,H.B.M.H.&T.]
Schmidt, Anne B. .... '54 '84 C.502 B.S. L.910 J.D. [Burroughs,H.B.M.H.&T.]
Schrimpf, Stephen P., (BV) ... '49 '74 C&L.45 B.A., J.D. Gen. Coun., Professional Offices
Schroer, Michael C. '78 '04 C.502 B.A. L.910 J.D.
(adm. in MO; not adm. in IL) [Ⓐ Burroughs,H.B.M.H.&T.]
Schuette, Maureen Nelson, (CV) .... '62 '89 C.801 B.S. L.678 J.D. [Schuette]
Schuette Law Office, (CV) .... 610 St. Louis St.
Seymoure, Dominique N. .... '76 '01 C&L.801 B.A., J.D. [Ⓐ Reed,A.G.M.&M.]
Sharrard, Richard F., (BV) .... '59 '84 C.98 B.S. L.734 J.D. [Ⓐ Blunt&Assoc.]
Shaw, Jennifer A. .... '71 '96 C&L.500 B.S., J.D. [J.A.Shaw]

Shaw, Jennifer A., P.C.
201 Hillsboro Avenue, 62025
Telephone: 618-655-0555 Fax: 618-659-1700
Email: j_a_shaw@yahoo.com URL: http://www.jashawlaw.com
Jennifer A. Shaw.
Family Law, Divorce, Child Custody, Child Support, Domestic Violence, Visitation Rights, Adoption Law, General Practice.

See Professional Biographies, EDWARDSVILLE, ILLINOIS

Sheehan, Sean P. .... '62 '94 C&L.734 B.S.B.A., J.D. [Ⓐ Burroughs,H.B.M.H.&T.]
Sherer, Barbara L., (CV) .... '62 '89 C&L.910 B.A., J.D. [B.Sherer]
Sherer, Barbara, (CV) .... 205 N. 2nd, Ste. 102
Shultz, Robert H., Jr., (AV) .... '52 '78 C&L.339 A.B., J.D. [Heyl,R.V.&A.]
Silger, Rachel D. .... '77 '02 C.801 B.S. L.734 J.D. [Ⓐ Burroughs,H.B.M.H.&T.]
Singer, Lucy A. .... '60 '91 C.804 B.S.W. L.734 J.D. 6904 Quail Walk
Skelton, Bryan L. .... '60 '93 C.1257 B.A. L.734 J.D. [Reed,A.G.M.&M.]
Skigen, Wayne D. .... '56 '81 C.170 B.A. L.276 J.D. [Burroughs,H.B.M.H.&T.]
Smith, Katherine M., (BV) ... '66 '96 C.801 B.S. L.734 J.D. [Ⓐ Burroughs,H.B.M.H.&T.]
Smith, Noel L., Jr. .... '76 '01 C.910 B.A. L.801 J.D. [Ⓐ Burroughs,H.B.M.H.&T.]
Sonneveld, Allison .... '78 '02 C.999 B.A. L.801 J.D. [Ⓐ Burroughs,H.B.M.H.&T.]
Sparks, Carol L. .... '79 '04 C.587 B.A. L.734 J.D. [Ⓐ Burroughs,H.B.M.H.&T.]
Stack, Daniel J. .... '50 '77 C.710 B.A. L.734 J.D. 155 N. Main St.
Stanton, Steven T. .... '58 '85 C.234 B.A. L.339 J.D. P.O. Box 615
Starnes, William B., II, (BV) .... '62 '89 C.378 B.S.B. L.986 J.D. [Reed,A.G.M.&M.]
Steele, Judy K. .... '68 '02 C.801 B.A L.734 J.D. Madison Co. State's Attys. Off.
Steiger, Frederick M., (AVⓉ) '51 '79
C.801 B.A. L.910 J.D. [Steiger] & [Ⓒ Menees,W.&B.]

Steiger Law Offices, (AVⓉ)
101 West Vandalia, Suite 150, 62025
Telephone: 618-656-2122 Fax: 618-656-2112
Email: steigerlaw@sbcglobal.net URL: http://www.steigerlawfirm.com
Frederick M. Steiger.
Domestic Relations, Child Custody, Divorce, Civil trial Practice, Business Litigation, Corporate Law.

See Professional Biographies, EDWARDSVILLE, ILLINOIS

Steinman, J. Phillip .... '68 '99 C.45 B.A. L.910 J.D. [Ⓐ Burroughs,H.B.M.H.&T.]
Stewart, Thomas Scott .... '63 '95 C.732 L.734 J.D. [Burroughs,H.B.M.H.&T.]
Stipes, Gale P., (BV) .... '54 '83 C.801 B.A. L.734 J.D. 220 S. Buchanan
Stockberger, James L., (AVⓉ) '58 '88
C&L.734 B.A., J.D. [Armstrong T.] (ⓄSt. Louis, MO)
Stockman, John H. ..... '64 '90 C.1213 B.S. L.982 J.D. [Ⓐ Armstrong T.] (ⓄSpringfield)
Storm, Carla C. .... '78 '03 C.339 B.S. L.734 J.D. [Ⓐ Knapp,O.&G.]
Strawn, Roy W., (AV) .... '31 '63 C.340 B.A. L.734 J.D. 60 Edwardsville Prof. Pk.
Stufflebeam, Patrick W. ...... '76 '02 C.927 B.A. L.734 J.D. [Ⓐ Burroughs,H.B.M.H.&T.]
Stultz, Dougglas A. .... '77 '03 C.1347 B.A. L.910 J.D. [Ⓐ Burroughs,H.B.M.H.&T.]
Sundberg, Jill R. .... '77 '02 C.10 B.A. L.734 J.D. [Ⓐ Burroughs,H.B.M.H.&T.]
Szewczyk, Stephen Michael, (BV) ..... '49 '82 C&L.734 A.B., J.D. [Ⓐ Reed,A.G.M.&M.]
Taliana, Lawrence O., (BV) .... '56 '81 C&L.339 B.A., J.D. 216 N. Main
Tatoian, Sandra J. .... '75 '02 C.999 B.S. L.801 J.D. [Ⓐ Coffey]
Telthorst, James A., (BV) .... '62 '92 C.502 B.S. L.734 J.D. [Heyl,R.V.&A.]
Thierstein, Joel P. '61 '91 C&L.823 B.S., J.D.
(adm. in PA; not adm. in IL) Southern Illinois Univ.
Thompson, Patricia .... '72 '97 C.1359 B.A. L.339 J.D. P.O. Box 959
Thomson, Stephen W., (AV) .... '46 '75 C.1070 B.S. L.1119 J.D. [Thomson]

Thomson Law Office, (AV)
A Professional Corporation
1 Sunset Hill Professional Centre Suite D, P.O. Box 538, 62025
Telephone: 618-692-0028 Telecopier: 618-692-0269
Email: firminfo@thomsonlaw.com URL: http://www.lawyers.com/thomsonlaw
Stephen W. Thomson;—Eric D. Berg. Of Counsel: Jonathan W. Foreman.
Insurance Defense Trial Law, Civil Trial, Personal Injury, Insurance Coverage.

See Professional Biographies, EDWARDSVILLE, ILLINOIS

Threlkeld, Christopher P. .... '68 '00 C.152 B.A. L.734 J.D. [Lucco,B.T.&D.]
Trelz, Eric M., (AVⓉ) '58 '87 C.133 B.A. L.734 J.D.
[Polsinelli S.W.S.] (ⓄKansas City, St. Louis, MO)
Trone, Robert E., (AV) .... '31 '55 C&L.339 B.S.L., J.D. Asst. State's Atty.
True, Gary E., (BV) .... '54 '91 C.801 B.S. L.734 J.D. [Burroughs,H.B.M.H.&T.]
Tryniecki, Timothy J., (AVⓉ) '56 '81
C.502 A.B. L.734 J.D. [Armstrong T.] (ⓄSt. Louis, MO)
Tueth, Keeney, Cooper, Mohan & Jackstadt, P.C., (AV)
101 West Vandalia Suite 210 (ⓄSt. Louis, MO)
Van Pelt, Wanda Kay .... '58 '87 C.589 B.S.Ed. L.339 J.D. Illinois Educ. Assn.
Varadachari, Bharat '72 '99 C.339 B.A. L.734 J.D.
(adm. in MO; not adm. in IL) [Ⓐ Burroughs,H.B.M.H.&T.]
Venker, Paul N., (AVⓉ) '55 '80
C&L.502 B.A., J.D. [Williams V.&S.] (ⓄSt. Louis, MO)
Virtel, James J., (AVⓉ) '44 '69 C.177 B.A. L.734 J.D.
[Armstrong T.] (ⓄBelleville, IL; St. Louis, MO)
Vogel, Musette H. .... '65 '91 C.339 B.A. L.209 J.D. [Ⓐ Burroughs,H.B.M.H.&T.]
Voswinkel, Nicholas V. '73 '02 C.575 B.A. L.734 J.D.
(adm. in MO; not adm. in IL) [Ⓐ Burroughs,H.B.M.H.&T.]
Vuagniaux, Earl L., (BV) .... '31 '56 C&L.734 B.Sc., J.D. [E.L.Vuagniaux]
Vuagniaux, Earl L., A Professional Corporation, (BV) .... 309 Hillsboro
Vucich, Jennifer Ann K. .... '75 '01 C.801 B.A. L.734 J.D. Madison Co. States Atty. Off.
Walker & Williams, Professional Corporation, (AV)
70 Edwardsville Professional Park (ⓄBelleville)
Wallace, Gretchen '66 '00 C.999 B.S. L.734 J.D.
(adm. in MO; not adm. in IL) [Ⓐ Burroughs,H.B.M.H.&T.]
Ward, J. Michael .... '78 '03 C&L.801 B.S., J.D. [Ⓐ Burroughs,H.B.M.H.&T.]
Weber, Don W. ... '48 '74 C.339 B.S. L.734 J.D. 20 Edwardsville Professional Pk., Ste. A
Weber, Erin Lyn .... '75 '01 C.862 B.A. L.221 J.D. [Ⓐ Burroughs,H.B.M.H.&T.]
Wells, Regina Lynn Lewis '— '00 C.910 B.A. L.1439 J.D.
[Ⓐ Burroughs,H.B.M.H.&T.]
Wendler, John D., (AV) .... '52 '77 C.801 B.A. L.734 J.D. [Burroughs,H.B.M.H.&T.]
Wesley, Michael R. .... '76 '03 C.261 B.A. L.801 J.D. [Ⓐ Burroughs,H.B.M.H.&T.]
Whyte, Joseph P., (BV) .... '62 '90 C.502 B.S. L.734 J.D. [Heyl,R.V.&A.]

Williams Venker & Sanders LLC, (AVⓉ)
111 E. Vandalia Street Suite 3, 62025 ⊙
Telephone: 618-659-9100 Fax: 618-659-9125
Email: wvs@wvslaw.com URL: http://www.wvslaw.com
Member of Firm: Paul N. Venker.
Aviation, Business Litigation, Employment Discrimination Litigation, Environmental Litigation, FELA, Health Care Litigation, Insurance Defense, Labor and Employment, Maritime, Medical Malpractice Defense, Occupational Disease Litigation, Premises Liability Defense, Product Liability Defense, Railroad Litigation, Toxic Torts, Transportation Litigation.
Belleville, Illinois Office: 23 South First Street, 62220. Phone: 314-345-5000. Fax: 314-345-5055.
St. Louis, Missouri Office: 10 South Broadway, Suite 1600, 63102. Phone: 314-345-5000. Fax: 314-345-5055.

See Professional Biographies, EDWARDSVILLE, ILLINOIS

Wood, Lisa M., (AVⓉ) ... '61 '89 C&L.734 B.A., J.D. [Armstrong T.] (ⓄSt. Louis, MO)
Young, Michael L. .... '76 '02 C.910 B.A. L.734 J.D. [Ⓐ Burroughs,H.B.M.H.&T.]
Zahalsky, Debra Kelly .... '— '01 C.801 B.S. L.910 J.D. [Ⓐ Lucco,B.T.&D.]
Zupanci, Dede K. .... '70 '02 C.801 B.A. L.734 J.D. [Ⓐ Burroughs,H.B.M.H.&T.]

EFFINGHAM, * 12,384, *Effingham Co.*

Austin, William W., (AV) .... '45 '70 C&L.339 B.S., J.D. [Siemer,A.R.F.&T.] ⊙
Berberich, Tracy A. .... '78 '03 C.999 L.801 J.D. [Ⓐ Taylor]
Berkbigler, Dennis L. .... '46 '72 C.801 B.A. L.339 J.D. 105 East Jefferson
Brummer, Richard H. .... '42 '67 C.1082 B.A. L.339 J.D. Cir. J.
Burkey, Bruce A., (BV) .... '45 '76 C.1070 B.S. L.801 J.D. [Taylor]

Craig & Craig
(See Mattoon)

Fuhr, Ronald E., (BV) .... '54 '84 C.136 B.S. L.801 J.D. [Siemer,A.R.F.&T.] ⊙
Graham, Christina Marie .... '70 '01 C.37 B.A. L.801 J.D. 207 N. Third St.
Harvey, James R. .... '49 '75 C.234 B.S. L.365 J.D. Assoc. Cir. J.

Heller, Holmes & Associates, P.C.
(See Mattoon)

Hortenstine, Matthew R. .... '67 '93 C.234 B.A. L.910 J.D. [Taylor]
Keller, K. Rick, (BV) .... '52 '76 C.234 B.A. L.146 J.D. [Keller&R.]
Keller & Runde, (BV) .... 214 W. Jefferson
Koester, Christopher A., (BV) .... '65 '90 C.234 B.A. L.801 J.D. [Taylor]
Koester, Kimberly G., (CV) .... '63 '88 C.473 L.910 J.D. 402 E. Virginia Avenue
Longwell, John E. .... '60 '85 C.234 B.A. L.879 J.D. 1000 Northwood Dr.
McDevitt, David A., (BV) .... '66 '92 C.234 B.S. L.734 J.D. [Taylor]

McMahon, Berger, Hanna, Linihan, Cody & McCarthy, A Professional Corporation
(See Collinsville)

Michaelree, Jack M. .... '25 '51 C&L.602 B.S., LL.B. Ret. Cir. J.
Orr, Twila Russell, (BV) .... '60 '84 C.927 B.S. L.734 J.D. [Schniederjon,W.&O.]
Parker, Kevin S., (CV) .... '59 '84 C.473 B.A. L.879 J.D. 409 S. Banker St., Ste. 105A
Phillips, Paula G., (BV) .... '39 '80 C.234 B.A. L.339 J.D. 105 East Jefferson
Resch, Marilyn B., (AV) .... '48 '73 C.970 B.A. L.347 J.D. [Siemer,A.R.F.&T.] ⊙
Runde, Richard A., (BV) .... '52 '77 C.339 B.A. L.365 J.D. [Keller&R.]

Ryan, Bennett & Radloff
(See Mattoon)

Schniederjon, Weber & Orr, (BV) .... 304 E. Jefferson
Seymour, Steven P. .... '46 '72 C&L.339 B.A., J.D. Res. Cir. J.

Sharp, Terry, P.C., Law Office of
(See Mount Vernon)

Siemer, Martin W., (CV) .... '67 '94 C.339 B.S. L.734 J.D. [Siemer,A.R.F.&T.] ⊙
Siemer, Q. Anthony, (BV) .... '44 '69 C.339 B.A. L.602 J.D. [Siemer,A.R.F.&T.] ⊙

Siemer, Austin, Resch, Fuhr & Totten, (AV)
307 North Third Street, P.O. Box 607, 62401-0607 ⊙
Telephone: 217-342-9291 Fax: 217-342-9295
Email: attorneys@psarf.com URL: http://www.lawyers.com/psarf
Members of Firm: Harry S. Parker (1871-1963); George H. Bauer (1895-1963); Howard S. Parker (1903-1978); James S. Parker (1933-1981); Q. Anthony Siemer; William W. Austin; Marilyn B. Resch; Ronald E. Fuhr; William B. Totten; Martin W. Siemer.
General Civil Practice, Real Estate, Corporate, Estate Planning, Probate, Insurance Defense, Banking, Family Law, Children, Commercial, Collections, Criminal Defense, Personal Injury Law, Social Security Law, Oil and Gas Law. Trial and Appellate Practice in all Courts.
Casey, Illinois Office: 14 North Central, Room 204. Telephone: 217-932-2158. Fax: 217-932-2159. Email: psarf@joink.com

See Professional Biographies, EFFINGHAM, ILLINOIS

Sutterfield, David W. .... '55 '80 C.578 B.A. L.339 J.D. [Sutterfield]

Sutterfield Law Offices, P.C. .... 208 S. 2nd St.

Taylor Law Offices, P.C., (BV)
122 East Washington, P.O. Box 668, 62401-0668
Telephone: 217-342-3925 Fax: 217-342-2341
Email: attorneys@taylorlaw.net URL: http://www.taylorlaw.net
Dale F. Wolff; Bruce A. Burkey; Lou J. Viverito; Matthew R. Hortenstine; David A. McDevitt; Christopher A. Koester;—Tracy A. Berberich.
Trial Practice in State and Federal Courts. Insurance, Personal Injury, Trusts, Probate, Estate Planning, Commercial, Municipal, Corporate, Bankruptcy, Real Estate, Oil and Gas, Criminal Law, Family Law, Collections, Utility, Energy and Power Generation Law, Land Use Law, Water Cooperatives.
Altamont, Illinois Office: 200 North Main Street, P.O. Box 350. Telephone: 618-483-6119. Fax: 618-483-5665.

See Professional Biographies, EFFINGHAM, ILLINOIS

Thompson, Maria G. ....'— '93 C.966 B.A. L.801 J.D. Pub. Def. Off.
Totten, William B., (BV) .... '60 '91 C.970 B.A. L.347 J.D. [Siemer,A.R.F.&T.] ⊙
Viverito, Lou J., (BV) .... '53 '82 C.234 B.S. L.365 J.D. [Taylor]
Weber, Rockney L., (BV) .... '47 '79 C.347 B.S. L.365 J.D. [Schniederjon,W.&O.]
Wolff, Dale F., (BV) .... '48 '75 C.339 B.S. L.879 J.D. [Taylor]
Young, Charles F., Law Offices of, (BV) '42 '85 C.234 B.A. L.801 J.D.
134 W. Jefferson

ELBURN, 2,756, *Kane Co.*

Bleifuss, Leslie G. ....'65 '94 C.801 B.S. L.589 J.D. 808 E. North St.
Bonk, Joseph J. '57 '83 C.475 B.A. L.912 J.D.
(adm. in MI; not adm. in IL) 648 Downing St.
Britz, Robert J., (BV) .... '49 '78 C.339 B.A. L.589 J.D. [Ottosen T.B.K.&C.]
Carlton, Howard A. .... '20 '49 C.976 B.A. L.309 LL.B. P.O. Box 600‡
Cooper, G. Robb .... '51 '87 C.628 B.S. L.424 J.D. [Ottosen T.B.K.&C.] ⊙
Gerity, John F. '08 '41 C&L.262 LL.B.
(adm. in NY; not adm. in IL) 41W100 High Woods Ct.‡
Gilbert, Thomas J., (AV) .... '49 '74 C.477 B.A. L.424 J.D. [Ottosen T.B.K.&C.] ⊙
Grabarek, William C. ....'39 '75 C.1016 B.A. L.365 J.D. 443 W. Pierce St. (Pat.)‡
Homola, Benjamin C. .... '26 '50 L.146 LL.B. 2N053 Grady Ct.
Kelly, John H. .... '51 '82 C.597 B.A. L.365 J.D. [Ottosen T.B.K.&C.] ⊙
Lourgos, James G. ....'53 '77 C.339 B.S. L.365 J.D. 3 N. 503 Townhall Rd.
Ottosen, Karl R. .... '60 '84 C.927 B.S. L.339 J.D. [Ottosen T.B.K.&C.] ⊙

Ottosen Trevarthen Britz Kelly & Cooper, Ltd., (AV)
303 North Main Street, 60119 ⊙
Telephone: 630-365-6441 Facsimile: 630-365-6451
URL: http://www.otbkc.com
Robert J. Britz; G. Robb Cooper; Thomas J. Gilbert; John H. Kelly; Karl R. Ottosen.
Fire Protection Districts, Municipal Law, School Law, Labor Law, Employment Law, Estate Planning and Probate, Insurance Defense, Family Law, General Business, Real Estate, Administrative Law, Zoning. Civil Trial Practice in all Courts.
Wheaton, Illinois Office: 300 South County Farm Road, Third Floor. Telephone: 630-682-0085. Facsimile: 630-682-0788.
Joliet, Illinois Office: Crystal Square Building, 81 North Chicago Street, Suite 204, 60432. Telephone: 815-723-0601. Fax: 815-723-2599.

See Professional Biographies, WHEATON, ILLINOIS

Pellegrini, Sheri ....'63 '91 C.679 B.S. L.597 J.D. 41 W. 75th, Oak Hills Court

ELDORADO, 4,536, *Saline Co.*

Aulgur, William E. ....'18 '48 C.503 A.B. L.502 LL.B. 1032 4th Street
Murphy, T. R., Jr., (BV) ....'48 '75 C.801 B.A. L.339 J.D. [Watson&M.]
Watson, C. Mart, (BV) ....'48 '73 C.801 B.A. L.339 J.D. [Watson&M.]
Watson and Murphy, (BV) ....1333 Locust St.

ELGIN, 94,487, *Cook & Kane Cos.*

Anderson, Donald T. .... '29 '63 C.589 B.S. L.365 J.D. 178 N. DuBois Ave.‡
Ariano, Frank V., (AV) ....'45 '70 C.966 B.S. L.146 J.D. [Ariano,H.N.J.R.&G.]

Ariano, Hardy, Nyuli, Johnson, Richmond & Goettel, P.C., (AV)
474 Summit Street, 60120 ⊙
Telephone: 847-695-2400 Telecopy: 847-695-8397
Email: aah@attorneys-illinois.com URL: http://www.attorneys-illinois.com
Ralph C. Hardy; Lisa M. Nyuli; Randy K. Johnson; Scott G. Richmond; Karrsten Goettel;—Jane Craddock Ryan; Todd E. Wallace; Celeste M. Walker. Of Counsel: Frank V. Ariano.
Languages: Spanish.
General Civil and Criminal Practice in all Courts. Banking, Probate, Real Estate, Corporation, Federal Taxation, Transactional, Employment, Family, Personal Injury, Collections, Creditor Bankruptcy, Foreclosures, Landlord and Tenant Law, Workers Compensation Law, Mediation, Zoning, Planning and Land Use.
Huntley, Illinois Office: 13300 Route 47, P.O. Box 487, 60142. Telephone: 847-669-5020.
Geneva Office: 22 S. 4th Street, Suite B, 60134.

See Professional Biographies, ELGIN, ILLINOIS

Arnold, Gerry R. ....'52 '77 C.234 B.S. L.546 J.D. States Attys. Appl. Prosecutors
Barnett, Shelley R.Z. ....'60 '85 C&L.339 B.A., J.D. 40 DuPage Ct., Ste. 306
Barry, Kevin R., (CV) ....'55 '80 C&L.589 B.S., J.D. 1070 Larkin Ave.
Bauer, Lawrence M. .... '50 '76 C.123 B.A. L.879 J.D. States Attys. Appl. Pros.
Beer, Fred J. ....'65 '90 C.879 B.S. L.365 J.D. [Brady&J.]
Bernhard, David A. ....'53 '85 C&L.589 B.A., J.D. States Atty. Off.
Bielsky, Hyman K. '54 '80
C&L.575 B.A., J.D. Gen. Coun. & Sr. V.P., Safety Kleen Corp.
Bingham, Richard P. .... '66 '92 C.339 B.A. L.893 J.D. [Juergensmeyer&Assoc.]
Blegen-McCoy, Leanne E. ....'60 '85 C.57 B.A. L.339 J.D. 2160 Niagara Ct.‡

Brady & Jensen, (AV) BB
2425 Royal Boulevard, 60123
Telephone: 847-695-2000 Fax: 847-695-3243
URL: http://www.bradylaw.com
Members of Firm: Wayne M. Jensen; Richard L. Heimberg; Roger K. Frandsen; Ronald E. Rasmussen; Alfred Y. Kirkland, Jr.; Glen T. Dobosz; Michael C. Deutsch; Keith A. Spong; Marios Nicholas Karayannis; Fred J. Beer. Associates: Brian L. Heimberg; Patrick J. Crimmins.
General Practice in all Courts. Trial and Appellate Practice. Corporation Law, Federal Taxation, Real Estate and Probate Law, Estate Planning, Personal Injury.
Representative Clients: Prudential Insurance Company of America; First Community Bank, Elgin; Union Insurance Group; Chicago Title Insurance Co.; Elgin Corrugated Box Co.; Hoffer Plastics Corp.; Lamp Construction Co.

See Professional Biographies, ELGIN, ILLINOIS

Brittain, John J., (AV) .... '31 '56 C.31 B.A. L.477 J.D. [Brittain&K.]

Brittain & Ketcham, P.C., (AV)
85 Market Street, 60123
Telephone: 847-742-6100 FAX: 847-742-6152
Email: jrif@msn.com
Lewis W. Terlizzi (Retired); William R. Ketcham (Retired); Randle E. Johnson (Retired); John J. Brittain (Retired); Leo M. Flanagan, Jr.; Jeff Rifken; Daniel Ervin Compton;—Patrick Flanagan.
General Civil Practice in all Courts. Probate, Estate Planning, Health Care Law, Collections, Chancery, Corporate, Banking and Insurance Law, Real Property, Municipal Law. Trials, Trusts. Domestic Relations. Elder Law, Family Law.

See Professional Biographies, ELGIN, ILLINOIS

Browers, William L. ....'50 '77 C.597 B.A. L.146 J.D. States Attys. Appl. Pros. Off.
Brown, F. Keith, (BV) .... '56 '82 C&L.221 B.A., J.D. 1382 Creekside Ct.

Brundage, Stephen A.
(See Wheaton)

Burns, Edward M., (BV) .... '51 '83 C&L.424 B.A., J.D. [O'Connell&Assoc.] ‡
Burns, Thomas J. ....'71 '96 C.363 B.A. L.424 J.D. [O'Connell&Assoc.]
Cahow, Bradley E., Law Office .... '51 '81 C&L.589 B.S., J.D. 1070 Larkin Ave.

Camic, Johnson, Wilson & McCulloch, P.C.
(See Sycamore)

Canning, Charles A. ....'59 '84 C.589 B.A. L.339 J.D. 40 N. Airlite St.
Carbary, Jonathan L., (BV) .... '49 '78 C.388 B.A. L.300 J.D. [J.L.Carbary]
Carbary, Warren E., (AV) .... '20 '49 C.309 S.B. L.477 J.D. 1815 Grandstand Pl.
Carbary, Jonathan L. LTD, (BV) ....1814 Grandstand Place
Carmody, Patrick M. .... '54 '80 C.234 B.A. L.365 J.D. 2010 Larkin Ave.
Castellanos, Diana ....'74 '00 [Lora,C.&C.]
Cavitt, Rodney D., (BV) .... '51 '78 C.597 B.A. L.1151 J.D. 23 Douglas Ave.
Chanthadouangsy, Wanchay ....'75 '00 C.57 B.A. L.209 J.D. [Lora,C.&C.]
Chase, Thomas D., (AV) ..... '41 '66 C.72 B.A. L.477 J.D. 574 North McLean Boulevard
Chesbrough, William C., (BV) ....'52 '80 C.589 B.S. L.365 J.D. 23 Douglas Ave.
Cohen, Gail '57 '83 C.881 B.A. L.472 J.D.
(adm. in MA; not adm. in IL) 150 Dexter Ct.
Compton, Daniel Ervin, (BV) ....'60 '87 C.879 B.S. L.365 J.D. [Brittain&K.]
Corr, Larry E. '30 '56 C.602 B.S.C. L.174 LL.B.
(adm. in CO; not adm. in IL) 154 Grand Blvd.‡
Crimmins, Patrick J., (BV) .... '61 '87 C.589 B.A. L.365 J.D. [Brady&J.]
Crisanti, Lawrence I., (AV) .... '43 '68 C.973 A.B. L.339 J.D. [Crisanti&Y.]
Crisanti & Young, P.C., (AV) ....85 Market St.
Dalton, Raymond F., Jr., (BV) ....'52 '79 C&L.602 B.B.A., J.D. [R.F.Dalton,Jr.]
Dalton, Raymond F., Jr., Law Offices of, P.C., (BV) ..... 1130 N. McLean Blvd., Ste. 201
Danielson, Barry K., (BV) ....'35 '64 C.57 B.S. L.502 J.D. 63 Douglas Ave., Ste. 200
Delk, Philip D., (BV) '48 '73 C.879 B.A. L.352 J.D.
V.P. & Dep. Gen. Coun., Montgomery Ward & Co., Inc.
Deutsch, Michael C., (BV) ....'54 '82 C.98 B.S. L.365 J.D. [Brady&J.]
DeWitt, Kim Marie ....'60 '85 C.338 B.S. L.209 J.D. Asst. Appl. Def.
Diaz, Marcelino ....'58 '01 C.339 B.A. L.262 J.D. [Diaz&R.]
Diaz & Rios, Law Offices of ....164 Division Street, Suite 210 (⊙Waukegan)
Dobosz, Glen T., (AV) ....'54 '79 C&L.879 B.S., J.D. [Brady&J.]
Doyen, Michael Charles ....'61 '87 C.602 B.A. L.734 J.D. 1815 Grandstand Pl.
Early, John F., (BV) .... '46 '71 C&L.339 B.A., J.D. [Early,C.T.R.W.&M.]
Early, Collison, Tousey, Regan, Wlodek & Morrow, (AV) ....2400 Big Timber Rd.
Ellingson, Janet Willerman, (CV) ....'58 '83 C.339 B.S. L.146 J.D. [J.W.Ellingson]
Ellingson, Janet W., (CV) ....1250 Larkin Ave.
Ellis, John A., Law Office of, (CV) '61 '88 C.238 B.A. L.589 J.D.
1130 N. McLean Blvd.
Feda, William A., Law Office of, (BV) '45 '74
C.177 B.A. L.365 J.D. 1418 Illinois Pkwy., Ste. B
Flanagan, Leo M., Jr., (AV) ....'42 '69 C.1151 B.A. L.209 J.D. [Brittain&K.]
Flanagan, Patrick .... '55 '99 C.339 B.A. L.146 J.D. [Brittain&K.]
Folarin, Olufemi O. ....'44 '83 C.943 B.S. L.589 J.D. Dir., City Human Resources
Fore, Scott E. '54 '78 C.347 A.B. L.1119 J.D.
(adm. in IN; not adm. in IL) Sr. V.P., Envir., Health & Safety, Safety-Kleen Corp.
Fosco, Gerard Carmen .... '60 '95 C&L.209 B.S., J.D. [O'Connell&Assoc.]
Frandsen, Roger K., (AV) ....'48 '74 C.210 B.A. L.339 J.D. [Brady&J.]
Franquelli, John L. ....'45 '78 C.597 B.S. L.598 J.D. [J.Franquelli]
Franquelli, John ....217 N. McLean Blvd.
Freeman, Bradley T., (BV) .... '45 '70 C&L.602 A.B., J.D. [Schnell,R.B.&F.]
Frett, Richard W. .....'51 '81 C.602 B.B.A. L.209 J.D. Dir., Legal Srvs., SKF USA INC.
Gashkoff, Geri A. ....'62 '91 C.720 B.S. L.365 J.D. Gen.Coun., DSM Desotech (Pat.)
Ginther, Lisa R. .... '66 '02 C&L.589 B.S., J.D. 40 N. Airlite, Suite 3
Glaser, Paul J., (BV) .... '52 '77 C.209 B.S.C. L.424 J.D. Off. of Appl. Def.
Goblirsch, Timothy G. ....'59 '84 C.734 A.B. L.339 J.D. 500 Redtail Rd.★
Goettel, Karrsten .... '71 '97 C.966 B.S. L.424 J.D. [Ariano,H.N.J.R.&G.] (⊙Geneva)
Gromer & Wittenstrom, P.C., (BV) ....75 Market St.
Grosch, Carla A. ....'55 '80 C.339 B.A. L.309 J.D. 24 Warwick Pl.‡
Habicht, F. Henry, II '53 '78 C.674 A.B. L.893 J.D.
(adm. in DC; not adm. in IL) Sr. V.P., Safety-Kleen Corp.
Hall, Jack H. .... '31 '62 C.688 B.Ch.E. L.273 LL.B. 709 Glen Ivy Dr.‡

Hanus, Richard, Law Offices of
(See Chicago)

Hardy, Ralph C., (AV) '43 '68 C.72 B.A. L.910 J.D.
[Ariano,H.N.J.R.&G.] (⊙Huntley)
Heimberg, Brian L. .... '70 '95 C.339 B.A. L.146 J.D. [Brady&J.]
Heimberg, Richard L., (AV) .... '41 '66 C&L.879 B.A., LL.B. [Brady&J.]
Heine, Spencer H. '42 '69 C.178 B.A. L.724 J.D.
(adm. in NY; not adm. in IL)
Exec. V.P., Secy. & Gen. Coun., Montgomery Ward & Co., Inc.
Hughes, Donald P., (BV) .... '43 '72 C.98 B.S. L.146 J.D. 1814 Grandstand Pl.
Iqbal, Mohammad '45 '98 C.910 Ph.D. L.589 J.D.
Gen. Coun. & Sr. V.P., Walker Parking Consultants
Jensen, Wayne M., (AV) .... '40 '64 C&L.879 B.A., LL.B. [Brady&J.]
Johnson, Randle E., (AV) ....'29 '54 C.98 B.S. L.339 J.D. [Brittain&K.] ‡
Johnson, Randy K., (AV) ....'52 '78 C.123 B.A. L.365 J.D. [Ariano,H.N.J.R.&G.]
Juergensmeyer, John E., (AV) '34 '63 C&L.339 A.B., J.D.
[Juergensmeyer&Assoc.] ⊙

Juergensmeyer and Associates, (AV)
1275 Davis Road, Suite 131, 60123-1304 ⊙
Telephone: 847-695-9800 Toll Free: 1-888-695-9822 FAX: 847-695-9818
Email: juerlaw@sbcglobal.net URL: http://www.juergensmeyerlawfirm.com
John E. Juergensmeyer. Associates: Richard P. Bingham; Danelle Wozniak Oilschlager.
Language: Spanish.
General, Civil Trial and Appellate Practice. Personal Injury, Governmental, Real Estate, Family, Workers Compensation Law, Municipal, Divorce, Chancery, Commercial, Insurance, Banking, Corporation, Trust and Probate Law.
Chicago, Illinois Office: 39 South La Salle Street, Suite 915. Telephone: 312-332-1114.

See Professional Biographies, ELGIN, ILLINOIS

Kalland, Michael E., (BV) ....'— '91 C&L.589 B.A., J.D. 167 E. Chicago St.
Karayannis, Marios Nicholas, (BV) ....'61 '86 C.339 B.S. L.365 J.D. [Brady&J.]
Kelly, Kerin E. ....'65 '91 C.339 B.S. L.365 J.D. [Steffen,K.&S.]
Ketcham, William R., (AV) .... '30 '55 C&L.339 LL.B. [Brittain&K.] ‡
Kirkland, Alfred Y., Jr., (AV) .... '44 '74 C.951 B.A. L.879 J.D. [Brady&J.]
Kirkland, James M., (CV) .... '47 '75 C.951 B.A. L.46 J.D. State Rep.
Kostelny, Marmarie J., (BV) ....'60 '85 C.937 B.A. L.209 J.D. [Zimmerman,S.&K.]
Kramer, Robert S., (BV) ....'50 '76 C.36 B.S. L.365 J.D. [R.S.Kramer]

Kramer, Robert S., P.C., (BV) .... 1250 Larkin Ave.
Larson, Diana S., (BV) .... '57 '85 C.958 B.S. L.146 J.D. [D.Larson]
Larson, Diana, Law Office of, (BV) .... 963 Stonehaven Dr.
Leahy, James P., Law Offices of '47 '76
C.339 B.S. L.424 J.D. 1275 Davis Road, Suite 131
Levine, Mark G. .... '50 '76 C.299 B.A. L.982 J.D. Off. of State Appl. Def.
Lilien, Thomas A. .... '53 '78 C&L.602 B.A., J.D. Asst. Def., State Appl. Def. Off.
Lora, Laura .... '73 '00 [Lora,C.&C.]
Lora, Chanthadouangsy & Castellanos LLC .... 606 Dundee Ave.
Lund, Clifford E. .... '51 '77 C.187 B.A. L.339 J.D. 30 Hamilton
Marblestone, Richard I., (BV) ...... '32 '59 C.910 B.S.B.A. L.339 LL.B. 1250 Larkin Ave.
Martin, James L., (AV) .... '31 '57 C&L.339 B.S., LL.B. 825 Douglas Ave.‡
Merrill, Raymond K. .... '16 '42 C.137 L.146 LL.D. 254 S. Clifton Ave.‡
Miles, Kenneth F., (AV) .... '27 '53 C&L.339 A.B., J.D. 11N333 Williamsburg Dr.
Miller, Howard S., (AV) .... '38 '61 C.339 L.209 J.D. [H.S.Miller&Assoc.]
Miller, Howard S., and Associates, P.C., (AV) .... 47 DuPage Ct.
Moltz, Martin P. .... '44 '71 C.339 B.A. L.623 J.D. State Atty. Appl. Pros., Dep. Dir.
Morrow, Robert J., (AV) .... '47 '73 C.190 B.A. L.339 J.D. [Early,C.T.R.W.&M.]
Mullally, James P. .... '50 '82 C.388 B.A. L.589 J.D. 164 Division
Muscarello, Mark J., (BV) .... '39 '63 C.602 B.B.A. L.339 J.D. 707-B Davis Rd.
Newman, John R. .... '53 '83 C.338 B.S. L.209 J.D. 216 Mosley St.
Nyuli, Lisa M., (BV) .... '64 '89 C.339 B.S. L.589 J.D. [Ariano,H.N.J.R.&G.] (⊙Geneva)
O'Connell, Daniel J. .... '54 '80 C.357 B.S. L.146 J.D. [O'Connell&Assoc.]
O'Connell & Associates PC .... 645 Tollgate Road, Suite 220
O'Hara, Sharon, Law Office of '— '94 C.1049 B.A. L.589 J.D.
920 Davis Road, Suite 302
Oilschlager, Danelle Wozniak '79 '05
C.352 B.A. L.1000 J.D. [⊡ Juergensmeyer&Assoc.]
Parikh, Dev Arya ... '69 '99 C.477 B.A. L.339 J.D. Asst. Def., Off. of the State Appl. Def.
Payton, Garry A., Law Offices of
(See Waukegan)
Pines, Judi Smith Solon .... '38 '74 C.97 B.S.Ed. L.117 J.D. Fireman's Fund Ins. Co.
Pintozzi, Barbara '63 '88 C.424 B.A. L.144 J.D.
Research Staff Atty., App. Ct., 2nd Dist.
Pointon, Louis R. '42 '86 C.690 A.B. L.900 J.D.
Sr. Resch. Staff Atty., 2nd Dist. Appl. Ct.
Rasmussen, Ronald E., (AV) .... '47 '74 C.588 B.A. L.146 J.D. [Brady&J.]
Regan, John E., (BV) .... '46 '74 C.597 B.S.E.E. L.424 J.D. [Early,C.T.R.W.&M.]
Repay, Henry, Law Offices of
(See Belvidere)
Richards, Van R., Jr., (AV) .... '30 '60 C.165 A.B. L.145 J.D. 1250 Larkin Ave.
Richmond, Scott G., (BV) '68 '95
C.475 B.A. L.146 J.D. [Ariano,H.N.J.R.&G.] (⊙Huntley)
Rifken, Ben, (AV) .... '16 '41 C.339 B.A. L.146 J.D. 85 Market St.‡
Rifken, Jeff, (BV) .... '46 '73 C&L.339 B.A., J.D. [Brittain&K.]
Rios, Rudy J. .... '— '00 C.589 B.A. L.339 J.D. [Diaz&R.] ⊙
Ritt, Norbert C., (BV) .... '40 '65 C&L.879 B.A., J.D. 1130 N. McLean Blvd.
Robinson, Mary T. .... '50 '75 C.339 B.A. L.800 J.D. 167 E. Chicago St.
Roeser, Ronald O., (BV) .... '50 '75 C.801 B.A. L.209 J.D. 920 Davis Rd.
Romano, Robert S. '55 '80 C.238 B.S. L.209 J.D.
V.P., Gen. Coun. & Corp. Secy., WMH Tool Group, Inc.
Ryan, Jane Craddock, (BV) ...... '60 '88 C.338 B.A. L.589 J.D. [⊡ Ariano,H.N.J.R.&G.]
Rydell, Thomas C., (BV) .... '36 '66 C.98 B.S. L.146 J.D. [Scheflow&R.]
Sadjadi, Shirley, Law Office of '64 '90
C.339 B.A. L.904 J.D. 100 E. Chicago St., Ste. 605
Salter, Richard J. .... '55 '81 C.209 B.S. L.146 J.D. 2400 Big Timber Rd., Ste. 200
Scheflow, Douglas J., (BV) .... '57 '83 C.447 B.S.E. L.339 J.D. [Scheflow&R.] (Pat.)
Scheflow, Richard S., (AV) .... '24 '53 C.72 B.A. L.339 LL.B. [Scheflow&R.]
Scheflow & Rydell, (AV)
Suite 200, 63 Douglas Avenue, 60120
Telephone: 847-695-2800 Telecopier: 847-695-4547
Email: scheflowrydell1@aol.com
Members of Firm: Richard S. Scheflow; Thomas C. Rydell; Douglas J. Scheflow.
General Practice, Litigation, Corporate Law, Banks and Banking, Business Law, Commercial Law, Partnership Law, Nonprofit and Charitable Organizations, Wills, Trusts and Estates, Probate, Estate Planning, Real Estate, Commercial Real Estate, Mortgage Foreclosure, Zoning, Planning and Land Use, Leases and Leasing, Municipal Law, Trademarks, Taxation, Bankruptcy, Collections, Family Law, Adoptions.
See Professional Biographies, ELGIN, ILLINOIS
Schnell, Theodore N., Jr., (AV) .... '30 '55 C.177 B.A. L.424 J.D. [Schnell,R.B.&F.]
Schnell, Richards, Brown & Freeman, P.C., (AV) .... 1250 Larkin Ave.
Seigle, Harry J. .... '46 '71 C.910 A.B. L.597 J.D. Pres., Jeigle's Home & Bldg. Ctrs.
Shriver, Donald P. .... '71 '96 C.388 B.A. L.910 J.D. 920 Davis Rd.
Skelnik, Josette M., (BV) .... '51 '78 C.339 B.A. L.597 J.D. [J.Skelnik]
Skelnik, Josette, Law Offices of, (BV) .... 167 E. Chicago St.
Slaw, Steven L. .... '56 '81 C.347 B.A. L.209 J.D. 2250 Point Blvd., Ste. 111
Slovacek, Gregory L. .... '52 '76 C.589 B.A. L.146 J.D. Staff Atty., State Atty. Appl. Pros.
Smith, Robert W., (BV) .... '48 '72 C&L.339 B.A., J.D. [Zimmerman,S.&K.]
Snell, Kenneth J. .... '57 '94 C.378 B.A. L.365 J.D. Assoc. Coun., Safety-Kleen Corp.
Spong, Keith A., (CV) .... '63 '88 C.350 B.S. L.352 J.D. [Brady&J.]
Steffen, F. John, Jr., (BV) .... '63 '89 C.339 B.A. L.365 J.D. [Steffen,K.&S.]
Steffen, Frederick J., (BV) .... '34 '62 C.339 B.S. L.365 J.D. [Steffen,K.&S.]
Steffen, Robert J. .... '65 '92 C.339 B.S. L.365 J.D. [Steffen,K.&S.]
Steffen, Kelly & Steffen, (BV) .... 17 Douglas Ave.
Stevens, Marshall M. .... '53 '79 C.58 B.A. L.339 J.D. States Attys. Appl. Pros.
Stiberth, Thomas J. .... '65 '90 C.97 L.8 J.D. 47 Dupage Ct.
Terlizzi, Lewis W. .... '24 '50 C&L.424 J.D. [Brittain&K.] ‡
Thompson, Bonne Harris .... '62 '88 C.800 B.A. L.1148 J.D. [⊡ Early,C.T.R.W.&M.]
Topol, Gary N., (BV) .... '50 '76 C&L.339 B.A., J.D. 1814 Grandstand Place
Tousey, Stephen D., (BV) .... '47 '80 C.339 B.A. L.365 J.D. [Early,C.T.R.W.&M.]
Travis, Richard E., Law Offices of, (BV) '45 '72 C.965 B.S. L.146 J.D.
2425 Royal Boulevard, 60123
Telephone: 847-289-3390 Fax: 847-695-3243
Email: richard@travislaw.net URL: http://www.richardtravislaw.com
General Practice in all Courts. Personal Injury, Wrongful Death, Commercial Litigation, Medical Malpractice, Products Liability and Worker's Compensation Law. Civil Litigation Practice, Automobile Accidents, Dog Bites, Slip and Fall.
See Professional Biographies, ELGIN, ILLINOIS
Vanek, Gary M., (BV) .... '55 '80 C.339 B.A. L.365 J.D. 1250 Larkin Ave.
Vietzen, Laurel A. .... '55 '81 C.679 B.A. L.146 J.D. Elgin Community Coll.
Vucha, Peter R., (BV) .... '49 '76 C.339 B.A. L.990 J.D. 920 Davis Rd., Ste. 100
Walker, Celeste M. .... '59 '00 C.221 B.A. L.589 J.D. [⊡ Ariano,H.N.J.R.&G.]
Wallace, Todd E. .... '75 '03 C.339 B.S. L.146 J.D. [⊡ Ariano,H.N.J.R.&G.]
Walters, John N., (BV) .... '52 '78 C.338 B.A. L.365 J.D. 1070 Larkin Ave.
Weaver, Donald J., (BV) .... '32 '61 C.339 B.S. L.365 LL.B. [D.J.Weaver]
Weaver, Donald J., PC, (BV) .... 100 N. McLean Blvd.
Wehrle, Donald L. .... '43 '92 C.424 B.S. L.365 J.D. Staff Atty.
Weller, G. Joseph .... '40 '66 C&L.280 B.B.A., J.D. Dep. Appl. Def.
Widerberg, Willard B., (BV) .... '42 '71 C.589 B.A. L.365 J.D. 225 N. McLean Blvd.
Wittenstrom, Clarence F., Jr., (BV) .... '32 '56 C.57 A.B. L.477 J.D. [Gromer&W.]
Wlodek, Michael A., (BV) .... '49 '76 C.238 B.A. L.146 J.D. [Early,C.T.R.W.&M.]
Young, Thomas P., (BV) .... '42 '73 C.801 B.S. L.879 J.D. [Crisanti&Y.]
Zimmerman, Charles M., (BV) .... '44 '70 C.118 B.A. L.365 J.D. [Zimmerman,S.&K.]
Zimmerman, Smith & Kostelny, (BV) .... 162 E. Chicago St.

ELIZABETH, 641, *Jo Daviess Co.*

Bush, Robert A., (AV) .... '42 '67 C.72 B.A. L.146 J.D. 200 Myrtle St.
Francomb, Lonn .... '53 '78 C.927 B.A. L.801 J.D. Pub. Def.
Nack, Louis A., Jr., (BV) .... '35 '66 C.321 B.S. L.339 J.D. [Nack,R.&N.] ⊙
Nack, Richardson & Nack, P.C., The Law Offices of, (AV)
Elizabeth State Bk. Bldg. (⊙Galena)

ELIZABETHTOWN, * 427, *Hardin Co.*

Baker, Larry O. .... '41 '73 C.801 B.A. L.836 J.D. Cir. J.
Jelliffe, Ferrell, Morris & Doerge
(See Harrisburg)
Lamar, Paul W., (BV) .... '58 '83 C.234 B.S. L.801 J.D. Corner of 1st & Main St.
Quarant, Jack L., & Associates .... '50 '78 C.801 B.A. L.365 J.D. RR 1 Box 500

ELK GROVE VILLAGE, 34,727, *Cook & DuPage Cos.*

Ambutas, Vytas P., (BV) '55 '80
C.932 B.S. L.424 J.D. V.P. Legal & Admin., National Material L.P.
Arezina, Mira D., (CV) .... '66 '91 C.339 B.A. L.424 J.D. Gen. Coun. for QT, Inc.
Barts, David G. .... '58 '89 C.1183 B.A. L.146 J.D. [D.Barts]
Barts, David .... 1325 Arlington Heights, Ste. 200
Bishop, Harold M. .... '55 '85 C.589 B.S. L.365 J.D. 84 Woodcrest Lane‡
Blake, K. Steven .... '64 '90 C&L.347 B.S., J.D. Gen. Coun., Aquion Partners, LP
Blake, Steve .... '64 '90 C.347 B.S. L.1119 J.D. Gen. Coun., Aquion Partners, LP
Bowden, Yvette J. .... '65 '91 C&L.1040 B.A., J.D. Corp. Atty., United Airlines
Busey, J. Craig, (AV) .... '47 '73 C&L.597 B.A., J.D. Sr. Coun., United Airlines
Carroll, Frances M. '54 '91 C.273 B.S. L.146 J.D.
Sys. Compliance Off., Alexian Bros. Health Sys., Inc.
Coyne, Jennifer A. .... '65 '90 C.352 B.S. L.145 J.D. Sr. Coun., United Airlines
Cutler & Associates, LTD.
(See Skokie)
DeMaertelaere, Ray J. .... '39 '67 C.424 L.365 J.D. [Garr&D.]
Durkin, Marian M., (AVⓇ) '54 '84
C.706 B.A. L.1035 J.D. Asst. Gen. Coun., United Airlines
Foster, Pamela A. ..... '67 '94 C.597 B.A. L.910 J.D. Assoc. Coun., National Material L.P.
Foster-Rice, Angela .... '— '97 C.691 B.A. L.597 J.D. Coun., United Airlines
Garr, Lee D. .... '43 '71 C.162 B.A. L.146 J.D. [Garr&D.]
Garr & DeMaertelaere, Ltd. .... 50 Turner Ave.
Glassenberg, Daniel R. .... '72 '97 C.339 B.A. L.597 J.D. Corp. Coun., United Airlines
Goolish, Stanley E. .... '73 '99 C.338 B.A. L.209 J.D. 240A University Lane
Hall, Janet L. .... '65 '94 C.589 B.S. L.339 J.D. Sr. Coun., United Airlines
Heineman, Steven .... '40 '71 C.861 B.A. L.597 J.D. Gen. Atty., United Airlines
Hindman, Donald deForest ...... '65 '90 C.478 B.A. L.347 J.D. Pres., Clark National Inc.
Hines, Frank M. .... '27 '58 C.340 Ph.B. L.365 J.D. 31 Park & Shop Center
Keegan, Raymond H. .... '23 '61 C.424 B.S. L.209 LL.B. 911 Lonsdale Rd.‡
Keywell, Bradley Alan '69 '93 C&L.477 B.B.A., J.D.
Pres., Brandon Apparel Group, Inc.
Klein-Kurland, Pamela M. '— '77 C.530 B.A. L.209 J.D.
Sr Contracts Dir, Motorola, Inc.
Klejwa, Padmavati G. .... '65 '90 C.188 B.A. L.659 J.D. 1569 Gibson Dr.
Klest Law Firm
(See Schaumburg)
Lanphier, James R. .... '48 '84 C.190 B.A. L.589 J.D. 817 Spring Creek La.‡
Leyden, Michael R. .... '36 '65 C.602 B.S. L.424 J.D. 554 Exmoor‡
Midgett, John T. .... '67 '94 C&L.597 B.S., J.D. Coun., United Airlines
Newcomb, Brent K. .... '70 '99 C.804 B.A.B.S. L.623 J.D. 945 Huntington Drive
Nicholson, John D. '49 '73
C.339 B.A. L.597 J.D. Mgr. Govt. and Milit. Mkt., United Airlines
Olaussen, David B. .... '55 '80 C.399 B.A. L.145 J.D. Sr. Coun., United Airlines
Osmundsen, Robert C. '51 '75 C&L.339 B.S., J.D.
V.P. & Gen. Coun., INX International Ink Co.
Pappalardo, Carla F. .... '58 '83 C.746 B.A. L.146 J.D. United Airlines
Par, Matthew T. .... '67 '92 C.473 B.A. L.146 J.D. Coun., Mid-Arc, Inc.
Patterson, Todd David .... '70 '97 C.385 B.A. L.966 J.D. Corp. Coun., United Airlines
Petropoulos, Anthony N. .... '52 '79 C.190 B.A. L.589 J.D. Gen. Coun.
Pettersen, Scott P. .... '62 '86 C&L.339 A.B., J.D. United Airlines
Robin, Daniel K., LTD
(See Arlington Heights)
Sawyer, Stephen P. ...... '39 '66 C&L.569 B.A., LL.B. Asst. Gen. Coun., United Airlines
Schlueter, David R. .... '59 '86 C.999 B.A. L.424 J.D. 50 Turner Ave.
Schumann, Ralph J., Law Offices of '54 '83
C.589 B.A. L.146 J.D. 901 Biesterfield Rd., Ste. 107
Schumm, Gilbert C. .... '52 '77 C.339 B.S. L.365 J.D. 836 S. Arlington Heights Road
Simpson, Colin C. E. .... '43 '70 C.1183 B.A. L.365 J.D. 1443 Worden Way
Stiefel, Reid A. .... '63 '88 C.1016 B.S.B.A. L.339 J.D. 1590 Louis Ave.
Swander, Richard C. .... '11 '35 C.339 L.146 Cinch Mfg. Co., Division of TRW, Inc.
Tang, Michael .... '54 '80 C.945 A.B. L.276 J.D. Vice Chmn., National Material Co.
Toman, Richard J. '56 '81 C.473 B.S. L.930 J.D.
(adm. in OH; not adm. in IL) Sr. Coun., United Airlines
Verret, Kathleen T. '62 '89 C.974 B.A. L.803
(adm. in LA; not adm. in IL) Reg. Dir. of Prop., Cendant Car Rental Group
Walker, Douglas M. '72 '97 C.668 B.A. L.902 J.D.
(adm. in WA; not adm. in IL) Coun., United Airlines
Wexley, Matthew H. .... '69 '97 C.477 B.A. L.978 J.D. Coun., United Airlines
Wit, Vania Montero .... '68 '93 C.597 B.A. L.309 J.D. Sr. Coun., United Airlines

ELKVILLE, 958, *Jackson Co.*

Daniels, Timothy E. .... '61 '99 C&L.801 B.S., J.D. [51 P.]
Dunham, Darrell W. .... '46 '71 C&L.950 B.A., J.D. [51 P.]
51 Place Law Offices .... U.S. Route 51

ELMHURST, 42,762, *DuPage Co.*

Acker, Andrew Y. .... '61 '91 C.207 B.A. L.1187 J.D. [Kubiesa,S.G.&A.]
Amato, Theresa A. .... '64 '90 C.309 A.B. L.569 J.D. Citizen Advocacy Ctr.

Andrews, George J. ....'49 '77 C.339 B.A. L.146 J.D. P.O. Box 886
Barnes-Euresti, Norma L. ....'67 '92 Keebler Company (Legal Department)
Bastianoni, Lebert D. ....'38 '73 C.339 B.S. L.365 J.D. 379 N. Addison Ave.
Bates, Alben F., Jr. ....'17 '46 C.188 L.597 J.D. 105 S. York St.
Bates, Henry G., (BV) ....'22 '50 C.188 A.B. L.146 LL.B. 120 Robert T. Palmer Dr.
Bauer, James G., (AV) ....'33 '58 C.966 A.B. L.209 J.D. [J.G.Bauer]
Bauer, James G., PC, (AV) .... 298 S. Chandler Ave.
Bryan, C. Clark ....'10 '35 C.293 A.B. L.309 J.D. 400 W. Butterfield Rd.‡
Caluwaert, John M., (BV) ....'44 '71 C.707 B.A. L.365 J.D. [Caluwaert&P.]
Caluwaert, Kristen R. .... '72 '97 C.339 B.A. L.365 J.D. 579 W. North Ave., Ste. 201
Caluwaert & Panegasser, (AV) .... 579 W. North Ave.
Cardey, Keith R. '24 '52 C.966 B.S. L.383 LL.B.
(adm. in KY; not adm. in IL) 460 Oriole Ave.‡
Chipain, Chris G. .... '66 '91 C.36 B.S. L.309 J.D. 100 W. Butterfield Rd., Suite 501
Crowley, Maureen A. ....'58 '83 C.769 B.A. L.1522 J.D. Staff Atty.
Daniels, Albert L. ....'17 '50 C.475 B.S. L.146 J.D. 180 W. Park Ave.‡
Dano, Mary Bartz '62 '88 C.746 B.A. L.424 J.D.
Dir., Risk Mgmt., & Corp. Compl. Offr., Elmhurst Memorial Hosp.
Eils, Robert C. ....'19 '47 C.597 B.A. L.146 J.D. 160 Arlington St.
Esposito, Kathleen C. ....'50 '76 C&L.424 B.S., J.D. 382 Prospect
Ferry, Carolyn O'Connor, (BV) '56 '85 C.602 B.B.A. L.966 J.D.
V.P. & Gen. Coun., Elmhurst Memorial Hosp.
Filkin, David L. ....'63 '88 C&L.339 B.S., J.D. Gen. Coun., Duchossois Industries, Inc.

Fleming, Michael W., Attorney at Law '59 '84 C.339 B.S. L.1000 J.D.
360 W. Butterfield, Suite 200, 60126
Telephone: 630-833-8400 Fax: 630-941-2852
Email: mfleminglaw@sbcglobal.net URL: http://www.fleminglaw-firm.com
Criminal Defense Litigation, Felonies, Misdemeanors, DUI and Juvenile Law.
See Professional Biographies, ELMHURST, ILLINOIS

Forgue, Brian A. ....'50 '75 C&L.424 B.A., J.D. [Forgue&F.]
Forgue & Forgue .... 925 S. Route 83
Galgan, Robert J., Jr., (BV) ....'48 '78 C.602 B.A. L.589 J.D. 340 W. Butterfield Rd.
Galvin, Jeanne, (CV) ....'65 '90 C.338 B.S. L.339 J.D. 579 W. North Ave.
Gaynor, Raymond R. .... '73 '04 C.347 B.S. L.146 J.D. [Ⓐ P.T.Sheehan&Assoc.]
Gildea, E. James, Attorney at Law, (AV) ....'37 '65 C&L.209 LL.B. 191 W. Fremont Ave.
Glasser, Michael A. ....'58 '84 C.696 B.A. L.365 J.D. P.O. Box 237
Gosselar, Barbara J. ....'46 '79 C.937 B.A. L.424 J.D. [Kubiesa,S.G.&A.]
Gouwens, Jean M. ....'— '82 C.339 B.A. L.1000 J.D. 520 S. York Street
Graves, Clarence K. ....'14 '43 C.137 L.146 LL.B. 400 W. Butterfield Road‡
Grothaus, Craig L. '41 '78 C.809 L.1137 J.D.
(adm. in CA; not adm. in IL) 200 Berteau‡
Hines, Judith M. ....'55 '81 C.430 B.S. L.365 J.D. 262 South St.‡
Honig, Robert N. ....'67 '93 C.339 B.A. L.146 J.D. [R.Honig]
Honig, Robert ....180 W. Park Ave., Ste. 130
Johnson, Terrence M. ....'52 '78 C&L.602 A.B., J.D. 200 E. Cayuga
Kelly, John R. ....'78 '03 C&L.339 B.S., J.D. [Ⓐ Kubiesa,S.G.&A.]
Kim, Edward T. '67 '93 C.112 B.A. L.221 J.D.
(adm. in PA; not adm. in IL) Spec. Coun., Nextel Communications, Inc.
Kleeman, Robert G. ....'62 '87 C&L.339 B.S., J.D. 360 W. Butterfield Rd.
Kordik, Daniel J., Attorney at Law, (BV) '59 '84 C&L.339 B.S., J.D.
276 N. Addison Ave.
Kowalkowski, Jeffrey N. ....'63 '89 C.338 B.S. L.209 J.D. [Lanphier&K.]
Kraus, Grace, (BV) ....'— '83 C.238 B.S. L.424 J.D. 269 N. Oaklawn Ave.
Krause-Stetson, Diane '57 '82 C.957 B.A. L.966 J.D.
Vice President - Human Resources, Duchossois Industries, Inc.
Kubiesa, Kenneth T., (BV) ....'50 '75 C.966 B.A. L.424 J.D. [Kubiesa,S.G.&A.]

Kubiesa, Spiroff, Gosselar & Acker, P.C., (BV)
533 W. North Avenue Suite 204, 60126
Telephone: 630-516-1800 Fax: 630-516-1808 URL: http://www.ksgalaw.net
Email: thefirm@ksgalaw.com URL: http://www.ksgaklaw.com
Kenneth T. Kubiesa; Harlan J. Spiroff; Barbara J. Gosselar; Andrew Y. Acker;—Joan E. Mullins; Margaret M. O'Connell; John R. Kelly; Mia S. Mcpherson; Jonathan P. Stringer. Of Counsel: Donald S. Nathan.
Municipal Law, Business Law, General Civil and Trial Practice in all Courts, Public Finance, Land Use Law, Administrative Law, Employment Law, Corporate Law, Civil Litigation, Appeals, Real Estate, General Practice, Criminal Law, Eminent Domain.
See Professional Biographies, ELMHURST, ILLINOIS

Lanphier, E. Paul, (AV) ....'38 '63 C.1082 B.A. L.209 J.D. [Lanphier&K.]
Lanphier & Kowalkowski, Ltd., (AV) .... 568 Spring Rd.
Law, Fred H., Jr. ....'22 '50 C.188 A.B. L.659 J.D. 14 Manchester Ln.‡
Levine, Adam R. ....'76 '02 C.696 B.A. L.910 J.D. [Ⓐ P.T.Sheehan&Assoc.]
Lewis, S. Keith ....'38 '72 C.578 B.A. L.365 J.D. 220 Claremont St.‡
Maciejewski, Michael A. ....'65 '92 C.145 B.A. L.424 J.D. [M.A.Maciejewski]
Maciejewski, Michael A., Ltd. .... 945 Oaklawn Ave.
McBride, Robert C. '26 '54 C.339 B.S. L.910 LL.B.
(adm. in MO; not adm. in IL) 677 Larch Ave.‡
McHugh, Kenneth A. ....'44 '71 C.602 B.B.A. L.146 J.D. DePaul Univ.
McHugh, Timothy P. ....'58 '84 C.339 B.S. L.146 J.D. [T.P.McHugh]
McHugh, Timothy P., Ltd. .... 360 West Butterfield, Suite 200
McKean, R. T. ....'31 '58 C&L.209 B.S., J.D. 447 Arlington Ave.‡
McMahon, Susan B. ....'50 '83 C.430 B.S. L.365 J.D. Self-Sufficiency Tr. of Ill.
Mcpherson, Mia S. ....'73 '98 C.679 B.A. L.209 J.D. [Ⓐ Kubiesa,S.G.&A.]
Messerschmidt, Fred A. ....'17 '41 C&L.145 A.B., J.D. 235 Claremont‡
Morrison, Michael S. ....'53 '82 C.339 B.S. L.1000 J.D. 110 East Schiller, Suite 205
Mullins, Joan E. ....'— '91 C.742 B.A. L.209 J.D. [Ⓐ Kubiesa,S.G.&A.]
Nathan, Donald S., (BV) ....'45 '75 C.339 B.A. L.424 J.D. [Ⓒ Kubiesa,S.G.&A.]
Norris, Wayne F. ....'41 '76 C.339 B.S. L.146 J.D. 111 N. Larch Ave., Suite 403
O'Connell, Margaret M. ....'64 '91 C.98 B.S. L.365 J.D. [Ⓐ Kubiesa,S.G.&A.]
Osborn, Jo E. ....'47 '79 C.838 B.A. L.589 J.D. Sr. Coun., Keebler Co.
Ostling, Peter W. ....'59 '84 C.879 B.A. L.339 J.D. P.O. Box 807
Panegasser, John, (AV) ....'45 '71 C.209 B.S.C. L.146 J.D. [Caluwaert&P.]
Peterson, Danette L. ....'70 '95 C.966 B.A. L.146 J.D. 386 N. York Rd., Ste. 204
Pontrelli, James A. ....'76 '02 C.188 B.A. L.602 J.D. State Atty. Off.
Pope, Anthony J. ....'42 '77 C.424 B.B.A. L.365 J.D. 185 N. York Rd.
Pope, Elizabeth A. ....'70 '99 C.741 L.1187 J.d. [Caluwaert&P.]
Postula, James E. ....'22 '50 C.238 B.A. L.209 J.D. 244 Eggleston‡
Rowe, Robt. S. ....'14 '41 C.188 L.213 LL.B. 400 W. Butterfield Rd.‡
Rozboril, Leopold S. ....'16 '60 L.209 J.D. 627 Saylor Ave.‡
Rush, Robert M. ....'74 '00 C.424 B.A. L.209 J.D. [Ⓐ P.T.Sheehan&Assoc.]
Schultz, Wilbert R., (AV) ....'17 '41 C&L.879 LL.B. 818 Saylor
Seifert, Joerg ....'69 '98 C.339 B.A. L.424 J.D. [J.Seifert]
Seifert, Joerg, Ltd. .... 263 North York Road, Suite 201
Sexner, Richard E., Law Offices of '68 '94
C.597 B.A. L.339 J.D. 679 W. North Ave., Ste. 206
Sheehan, Patrick T. ....'62 '87 C.589 B.S. L.424 J.D. [P.T.Sheehan&Assoc.]
Sheehan, Patrick T., & Associates, Attorneys At Law, P.C. .... 314 N. York Road
Shukas, Socrates N. ....'31 '55 C&L.209 B.S., J.D. 905 Washington St.‡
Spatz, Joanne ....'51 '85 C.339 B.A. L.424 J.D. Sr. Coun., Keebler Co.
Spiroff, Harlan J. ....'52 '82 C.1016 B.A. L.589 J.D. [Kubiesa,S.G.&A.]
Stringer, Jonathan P. ....'75 '01 C.97 B.A. L.365 J.D. [Ⓐ Kubiesa,S.G.&A.]
Tellefsen, Ralph F., III ....'54 '79 C.902 A.B. L.896 J.D. 126 South York
Urbik Kern, Laura M., L.L.C., Law Offices of ....386 N. York Rd., Ste. 204
Urbik-Kern, Laura M. ....'— '84 C.710 B.S. L.61 J.D. [L.M.UrbikKern]
Ventrelle, Michael J. ....'48 '81 C.1183 B.A. L.589 J.D. 15W459 Grand Place
Watkins, Natalie M. ....'61 '98 C.294 B.A. L.1000 J.D. 386 N. York Rd.
Watschke, David R., (BV) ....'— '78 C&L.339 B.A., J.D. 110 E. Schiller St.
Wier, Robert H., (BV) ....'33 '59 C.238 B.A. L.145 J.D. 120 Robert T. Palmer Dr.
Wilson, Ervin F. ....'20 '46 C&L.597 B.S., J.D. 180 W. Park Ave.

ELMWOOD, 1,945, *Peoria Co.*

Potts, Matthew C., (BV) ....'68 '94 C.339 B.S. L.209 J.D. [Whitney&P.]
Potts, Robert L., (BV) ....'44 '70 C&L.339 B.S., J.D. [Whitney&P.]
Whitney & Potts, Ltd., (BV) .... 118 W. Main Street

ELMWOOD PARK, 25,405, *Cook Co.*

Albano, Frank ....'28 '52 C.339 L.365 LL.B. 1833 N. 79th Ct.
Connell, William J. ....'39 '64 C&L.424 B.S., J.D. 7904 W. Cortland St.
Del Medico, Frank J. .....'70 '98 C.338 B.S. L.365 J.D. 7504 West Grand Avenue, Suite 1
DiGiovanni, Felicia M. ....'73 '98 C.220 B.A. L.365 J.D. [Spina,M.&O.]

Favia, Michael V.
(See Chicago)

Hopp, Edgar C. ....'29 '55 L.209 LL.B. 7804 W. Sunset Dr.‡
McGuire, James T. ....'49 '76 C.339 B.A. L.365 J.D. [Spina,M.&O.]
Okal, Timothy H. ....'50 '76 C.424 B.A. L.365 J.D. [Spina,M.&O.]
Platt, James R. ....'23 '52 C.602 B.S. L.209 J.D. 7914 Fullerton Ave.‡
Sarolas, George I., Law Office of '63 '92
C.999 B.A. L.1187 J.D. 7234 W North Avenue, Suite 210
Spina, Anthony F., (AV) ....'37 '62 C.424 B.S. L.209 J.D. [Spina,M.&O.]
Spina, John D. ....'63 '88 C&L.424 B.A., J.D. [Spina,M.&O.]

Spina, McGuire & Okal, A Professional Corporation, (AV) BB
7610 W. North Avenue, 60707-4195
Telephone: 708-453-2800 FAX: 708-452-5088
Email: spinalaw@aol.com URL: http://www.lawyers.com/spinamcguire&okal
Anthony F. Spina; James T. McGuire; Timothy H. Okal; John D. Spina; Felicia M. DiGiovanni.
Civil (State and Federal) Litigation, Commercial and Corporate Law, Family Law, Real Estate (Commercial and Residential), Real Estate Development, Family Law, Trusts, Estate and Probate, Union Labor Law, Appellate Practice, Personal Injury (including Product Liability).
See Professional Biographies, ELMWOOD PARK, ILLINOIS

EL PASO, 2,695, *Woodford Co.*

Leiken, Larry M., (BV) ....'38 '63 C&L.339 A.B., LL.B. P.O. Box 97 (ⓄEureka)
Leiken, Richard W., (BV) ....'41 '67 C.339 B.A. L.879 J.D. 37 E. Front St. (ⓄEureka)
Stoller, James J., (BV) ....'49 '74 C&L.339 B.S., J.D. 15 W. Front St.
Stoller, Justin J. ....'76 '02 C&L.339 B.S., J.D. [Stoller]
Stoller Law Office ....15 W. Front St.

ELSAH, 635, *Jersey Co.*

Gentry, Gary R. '48 '73 C.675 B.A. L.1049 J.D.
(adm. in CA; not adm. in IL) Principia Coll.

ERIE, 1,572, *Whiteside Co.*

Burns, Stephen R. ....'47 '72 C.388 B.A. L.597 J.D. Village Sq.

EUREKA, * 4,871, *Woodford Co.*

Baner, Richard M. ....'36 '65 C.98 B.S. L.365 LL.B. Resident Cir. J.
Faupel, Mary E., (BV) ....'56 '84 C.927 B.A. L.365 J.D. [Faupel]
Faupel Law Offices, Ltd., (BV) ....117 W. Center St.
Freese, John P. ....'47 '72 C.338 B.S. L.477 J.D. Assoc. Cir. J.
Harrod, Daniel M., (BV) ....'45 '75 C.248 B.A. L.365 J.D. [Harrod]
Harrod Law Firm, P.C., (BV) ....107 E. Eureka Street, Suite 2
Knapp, Gregory C., (BV) ....'52 '81 C.339 B.A. L.1119 J.D. 1952 S. Main St.
Lankton, Andrew John ....'66 '93 C.350 B.B.A. L.365 J.D. [Leiken-Lankton]
Leiken, Larry M., (BV) .... '38 '63 C&L.339 A.B., LL.B. [Ⓒ Leiken-Lankton] (ⓄEl Paso)
Leiken, N. Ned, (BV) ....'47 '73 C.339 B.S. L.228 J.D. [Leiken-Lankton]
Leiken, Richard W., (BV) .... '41 '67 C.339 B.A. L.879 J.D. 120 S. Main St. (ⓄEl Paso)‡
Leiken-Lankton, L.L.C., (BV) ....120 S. Main St.

Lynch and Bloom, P.C.
(See Peoria)

Riley, G. Patrick, (BV) ....'40 '74 C.340 B.S. L.221 J.D. [Ⓒ Harrod]

Westervelt, Johnson, Nicoll & Keller, LLC
(See Peoria)

EVANSTON, 74,239, *Cook Co.*

Abrams, Melvyn A. ....'42 '68 C&L.339 B.A., J.D. 2751 Prairie Ave.
Acker, William L. ....'15 '40 C.659 B.S. L.309 J.D. 2009 Harrison St.‡
Adams, Ann K. ..... '— '93 C.393 B.A. L.145 J.D. Assoc. Gen. Coun., Northwestern Univ.
Addelson, Laura S. ....'55 '80 C.966 B.A. L.424 J.D. 500 Davis St.‡
Alexander, Ellen J. ....'— '75 C.477 B.A. L.209 J.D. [Alexander]
Alexander, James N. ....'45 '71 C&L.339 B.A., J.D. [Alexander&Assoc.]
Alexander Associates ....2129 Central Park Ave.

Alexander Law Office
1603 Orrington Avenue, 60201
Telephone: 847-475-5010 Fax: 847-328-1928
Email: argalexander@earthlink.net
Member of Firm: Ellen J. Alexander.
Real Estate, Zoning, Arbitration and Mediation.
See Professional Biographies, EVANSTON, ILLINOIS

Alter, June M. ....'29 '80 C.37 B.S. L.146 J.D. 9221 N. Drake Ave.‡

Asher, Gittler, Greenfield & D'Alba, Ltd.
(See Chicago)

Atkins, Robert S., (AV) ....'31 '56 C.966 B.S. L.597 J.D. 2005 Orrington Ave.
Atkinson, Dale J. ....'58 '87 C.63 B.S. L.596 J.D. [Atkinson&A.]
Atkinson, John F., (AV) ....'32 '59 C.696 B.A. L.608 J.D. [Atkinson&A.]

Atkinson & Atkinson, (AV)
1603 Orrington Avenue, Suite 2080, 60201
Telephone: 847-864-0070 Facsimile: 847-864-0588
Email: AandA@ameritech.net URL: http://www.lawyers.com/atkinson&atkinson

(This Listing Continued)

Atkinson & Atkinson (Continued)

Members of Firm: John F. Atkinson; Dale J. Atkinson; Julia C. Works.
Association Law, Business Law including Corporate, Real Estate, Estate Planning, Estate and Trust Administration, Labor and Employee Benefits, Professional Associations, Professional Licensure and Certification, Administrative, Tax and Litigation related to these areas of practice.
A list of Representative Clients will be furnished upon request.

See Professional Biographies, EVANSTON, ILLINOIS

Audy, Anne M. .... '47 '72 [Audy&Assoc.]
Audy & Associates .... 1560 Sherman Ave., Ste. 310
Austin, William C. '72 '97 C.136 B.S. L.150 J.D.
(adm. in OH; not adm. in IL) 1421 Greenleaf★
Azar, Kathleen Livingston .... '62 '89 C.741 B.A. L.665 J.D. 1456 Oak Ave.‡
Bailey, Dexter M. .... '44 '70 C.264 A.B. L.128 J.D. 2246 Ridge Ave.
Bain, Gary .... '52 '79 C.339 B.A. L.146 J.D. 2001 Orrington Avenue
Banzuly, Robert D. .... '34 '58 C&L.597 B.A., J.D. 3501 Arcadia Pl.
Barefield, H. Russell .... '44 '75 C&L.597 B.S., J.D. 737 Ridge Ave.
Barker, Charles L. .... '52 '77 C.477 A.B. L.569 J.D. Conflict Mgmt. Inc.
Barkley, Alison, (AV) .... '49 '77 C.339 B.S. L.209 J.D. [Schuyler,R.&Z.] ⊙
Bartlett, Lynne E. .... '52 '80 C&L.378 B.A., J.D. 1221 Greenwood
Bassel, Elizabeth D. H. .... '54 '80 C.104 B.A. L.145 J.D. 2430 Orrington Ave.
Beck, Richard Alfred, (AV) .... '11 '35 C.347 A.B. L.309 LL.B. 1707 Chancellor St.‡
Bell, Brigitte Schmidt, (AV) .... '48 '79 C.821 B.A. L.145 J.D. [B.S.Bell] ⊙
Bell, Brigitte Schmidt, P.C., (AV)
500 Davis Street, Suite 1006 (⊙Chicago, Lake Forest)
Berger, Harold J. .... '11 '34 L.800 LL.B. 8936 Ewing St.
Berland, Howard .... '44 '72 C.477 A.B. L.209 J.D. 820 Church St.
Bermak, Jacqueline N. .... '53 '78 C.696 B.A. L.910 J.D. 2315 Pioneer Rd.
Bernstein, Steven J., Law Offices of .... '46 '71 C.339 B.S. L.209 J.D. 513 Chicago Ave.
Berti, Nancy A. .... '53 '93 L.146 J.D. 2609 Ridge Ave.
Billingsley, Jennifer L. '63 '88
C.477 B.B.A. L.309 J.D. Contracts Manager, ZS Associates, Inc.
Black, C. Robert .... '51 '89 C.597 B.M. L.209 J.D. [⊡ M.D.Poulos]
Blumenthal, Marc N., Law Office of
(See Chicago)
Bogdan, Joseph J. '63 '88 C.339 B.A. L.800 J.D.
COO & Gen. Coun., Cognitive Concepts, Inc.
Bohm, Martin .... '13 '38 C.999 L.365 J.D. 1731 South Blvd.‡
Bonges, Robert C. .... '40 '66 C.597 B.S.B.A. L.477 J.D. NASD Arbitrator
Bordes, John L., (AV) .... '05 '31 C&L.209 LL.B. 2501 Central St.‡
Bosselman, Fred P., (AV Ⓣ) .... '34 '59 C.174 A.B. L.309 LL.B. 2715 Woodbine Ave.
Bowler, Bonnie A. .... '52 '85 C.36 B.S. L.589 J.D. [B.Bowler]
Bowler, Bonnie .... 860 Hinman, Ste. 426
Bowlus, John M., (AV) .... '26 '56 C.25 A.B. L.145 J.D. 725 Hillman Ave.
Box, Murray L. .... '30 '59 C.102 B.A. L.597 J.D. 1007 Church St.
Breen, Leo M. .... '22 '55 C.339 B.S. L.209 J.D. 1555 Oak Ave.‡
Brenniman, Kathleen F. .... '42 '85 C.136 B.A. L.589 J.D. Asst. Corp. Coun.
Bridges, Steven J. .... '64 '89 C.340 B.S. L.339 J.D. Northwestern Univ.
Brooks, Allyn A., (Mr.) '43 '69
C.339 B.S. L.146 J.D. Admin. Law J., Ofc. of Hearings & Appeals
Brooks, Alvin G. .... '15 '46 C.597 M.A. L.209 J.D. 1924 Asbury Ave.
Brown, James B., (BV Ⓣ) '37 '66 C.20 A.B. L.128 J.D.
(adm. in MI; not adm. in IL) 2511 Princeton Ave.
Burzawa, Susan Kay .... '56 '83 C.597 B.A. L.424 J.D. 1629 Asbury Ave.
Campbell, Julie L. .... '74 '01 C.473 B.A. L.146 J.D. [⊡ M.D.Poulos]
Cardinal Law Group, Ltd., (AV) ⊙
1603 Orrington Avenue, 60201 ⊙
Telephone: 847-905-7111 Fax: 847-905-7113 URL: http://www.cardinallawgroup.com/lawyers/cook/
Email: info@cardinallawgroup.com URL: http://www.cardinallawgroup.com
Frank C. Nicholas.
Technology and Intellectual Property Law Including U.S. and International Patents, Patent Preparation, Patent Prosecution, Patent Litigation, Intellectual Property Licensing, Intellectual Property Litigation, Trademark, Copyright, Trade Dress, Trade Secret, Unfair Competition, Antitrust, Cyberlaw, Biotech, Mechanical, Electrical, Computer and Software Patents.
Chicago, Illinois Office: 720 South Dearborn Street, Suite 503, 60605. Telephone: 847-905-7111. Fax: 847-905-7113. URL: http://www.cardinallawgroup.com

See Professional Biographies, EVANSTON, ILLINOIS

Carrington, Jerrold B. .... '57 '83 C.183 B.A. L.1068 J.D. Inroads Capital Partners, L.P.
Cedarbaum, Daniel G. .... '— '84 C&L.309 A.B., J.D. [⊡ Levin&S.] ⊙
Check, Lewis A. .... '57 '88 C.477 B.A. L.424 J.D. [⊡ M.D.Poulos]
Clark, Cynthia S. .... '57 '82 C.970 B.A. L.188 J.D. 9549 Monticello Ave.‡
Clayton, Djenne B. .... '72 '97 C&L.597 B.A., J.D. Corp. Coun., Rotary Intl.
Cline, Thomas G. '54 '80 C.976 B.A. L.597 J.D.
V. P. & Gen. Coun., Northwestern Univ.
Cohan, Harvey A. .... '41 '66 C.966 B.S. L.597 J.D. 2113 W. Greenfeaf
Colker, David, (BV) '51 '82 C&L.893 B.S., J.D.
(adm. in OH; not adm. in IL) 1145 Judson Ave.
Cooley, John W., (AV) '43 '73 C.870 B.S. L.602 J.D.
2106 Orrington Avenue, 60201-2914
Telephone: 847-328-7285 Fax: 847-864-1586
Arbitrator-Mediator.

See Professional Biographies, EVANSTON, ILLINOIS

Craig, Martin Z. .... '54 '78 C.339 B.A. L.365 J.D. 2020 Dempster Plz.‡
Cravens, Richard J. .... '32 '57 C.976 B.A. L.309 LL.B. 2521 Marcy Ave.‡
Crohn, Linda R., (BV) .... '49 '76 C.339 B.A. L.365 J.D. 9003 Lincolnwood Dr.
Cubbage, Richard T. .... '13 '37 C&L.221 A.B., LL.B. 8912 Ewing‡
Culpepper, David A.
(See Chicago)
Cutler & Associates, LTD.
(See Skokie)
Davis, Beth Boosalis .... '48 '74 C.118 B.A. L.145 J.D. Exec. Dir., Natl. Lekotek Center
Davis, Kevin R. .... '— '91 C&L.597 B.A., J.D. Auction Science
Davis, Maxwell S., Jr. .... '48 '72 C.197 A.B. L.309 J.D. 1119 Michigan Ave.
DeWoskin, Linda J. .... '46 '85 C&L.597 B.S., J.D. 1121 Dobson St.
Deyoung, Constance .... '48 '76 C.475 B.A. L.477 J.D. 2734 Lawndale Ave.‡
Dial, Justine R. .... '59 '85 C.645 B.A. L.665 J.D. 2537 Prospect Ave.‡
Dick, John C. '47 '82 C.927 B.A. L.420 J.D.
(adm. in LA; not adm. in IL) 800 Hinman Ave.‡
Donohue, John M., (AV) .... '37 '66 C&L.339 A.B., LL.B. 1007 Church St., Ste. 311
Drumke, Ronald A., (AV) .... '41 '66 C&L.597 B.A., J.D. 222 Main St., Suite204
Duclos, Todd A. .... '61 '92 C&L.352 B.A., J.D. 2744 March Ave.‡
Durham, R. Gregory .... '12 '39 C.309 A.B. L.976 LL.B. 20 Calvin Circle‡
Eisendrath, Margaret M., (Mrs.) .... '27 '52 C.383 A.B. L.209 J.D. 1010 Maple Ave.‡

Evan Law Group, LLC
(See Chicago)
Evanston Main Law Office
One Rotary Center, 1560 Sherman Avenue, Suite 301, 60201
Telephone: 847-475-4474 Fax: 847-475-0286
Email: EvanstonMainLaw@sbcglobal.net URL: http://www.evanstonmainlaw.com
Roger H. Simon.
Bankruptcy, Consumer Bankruptcy, Family, Divorce, Child Custody, Child Support, Premarital Agreements, Spousal Support, Corporate, Business, Contract, Wills, Trusts, Estate Planning, Probate, Criminal, Driving While Intoxicated, Traffic Violations, Misdemeanors, Felonies and Civil Litigation Practice.

See Professional Biographies, EVANSTON, ILLINOIS

Ezra, Sidney .... '42 '66 C&L.339 B.A., J.D. 9317 Crawford Ave.
Feeney, Joseph D. .... '24 '50 C&L.597 B.S., J.D. 9360 Ridgeway‡
Felch, Patricia A., (AV) .... '47 '87 C.208 B.A. L.424 J.D. 1510 Main Street (Pat.)
Feldman, Stuart A.
(See Wilmette)
Fernandez, Fe, (Ms.) .... '53 '78 C.424 B.A. L.209 J.D. Evanston Community Def. Off.
Fiffer, Steven J. .... '50 '76 C.976 B.A. L.145 J.D. 2722 Hartzell
Firestone, H. Barney .... '50 '74 C.1019 B.A. L.597 J.D. 1606 Hinman Ave.
Fitzgerald, Richard B., (AV) .... '36 '60 C&L.597 B.A., J.D. 820 Davis St.
Flaherty, Kathleen M. .... '51 '77 C.339 B.A. L.597 J.D. 1138 N. Maple‡
Foster, Leila M. .... '29 '53 C&L.597 B.S., J.D. 1585 Ridge Ave.
Fredericks, Jomarie B. '61 '90
C.339 B.A. L.46 J.D. Asst. Gen. Coun., Rotary International
Freeman, Janette .... '45 '80 C.473 B.A. L.424 J.D. Asst. Corp. Coun.
Frenzel, Mary Naphin .... '44 '80 C.93 B.A. L.424 J.D. 9330 Lawndale
Friedman, Philip S. .... '54 '79 C&L.597 B.A., J.D. Pres., Lake Shore Props., Ltd.
Friedman, Suzanne C. .... '64 '92 C.1365 B.A. L.1206 J.D. 513 Chicago Ave.
Gaede, Lee A. .... '47 '84 C.999 B.A. L.910 J.D. 635-5 Chicago Ave.
Gagen, Franklin C. .... '16 '41 C.611 A.B. L.976 LL.B. 82 Salem Lane‡
Gallagher, Paul H. .... '10 '39 C.597 L.209 LL.B. 2530 Crawford Ave. (Pat.)
Garavaglia, Mark A. .... '58 '84 C.800 B.A. L.861 J.D. Asst. Gen. Coun., Rotary Intl.
Gautier, Harold W., Jr. .... '21 '58 2219 Central St.‡
Gilford, Anne Johnson .... '52 '91 C.536 M.S. L.425 J.D. 1600 Dodge Ave.‡
Ginocchio, Frank .... '43 '93 C.597 B.A. L.339 J.D. 1856 Sheridan Rd.
Girard, Richard E. .... '31 '55 C.209 B.S.C. L.602 J.D. 1028 Austin Street‡
Glazer, Myron .... '33 '58 C.1016 B.A. L.597 J.D. 1500 Chicago Ave.‡
Glazer, Sharon B., (AV) .... '45 '72 C.477 B.A. L.209 J.D. 414 Greenleaf St.
Godwin, Peter C. .... '67 '92 C.145 B.A. L.188 J.D. [Godwin L.]
Godwin Law, P.C. .... 1315 Chicago Ave., 1st Fl.
Goldberg, Benj. B. .... '07 '33 C.999 L.365 LL.B. 9201 N. Drake Ave.
Graham, Donald M., (AV) .... '13 '36 C&L.597 A.B., J.D. 3240 Park Pl.‡
Graham, Stephanie M. '65 '90
C.339 B.A. L.145 J.D. Dep. Gen. Coun., Northwestern Univ.
Gray-Keeler, Karen R. .... '55 '81 C.910 A.B. L.347 J.D. 9421 Springfield Ave.
Greenberg, Freddi L. '46 '75 C.477 B.A. L.424 J.D.
1603 Orrington Avenue Suite 1050, 60201
Telephone: 847-864-4010 Fax: 847-864-4037
Email: flgreenberg@flglaw.com
Energy Law, Non-Utility Electric Generation and Power Marketing, Landfill Gas and Natural Gas, Public Utility Law, Municipal Electric Utilities, Business Law.

See Professional Biographies, EVANSTON, ILLINOIS

Greenberger, Ellen L. .... '60 '87 C.674 B.A. L.597 J.D. Northwestern Univ.
Greenebaum, Ben I., Jr., (AV) .... '05 '29 C&L.145 Ph.B., J.D. 422 Davis St.‡
Greig, Richard A. .... '30 '62 C.597 B.S. L.209 J.D. 2731 Elgin Rd.
Hall, Suzanne L. .... '50 '86 C.1016 B.S. L.597 J.D. 1618 Orrington Ave., Ste. 320
Harjani, Priya Jenveja '75 '00 C.339 B.S. L.597 J.D.
Asst. Gen. Coun., Northwestern Univ., Off. of Gen. Coun.
Harmon, Susan Barton .... '53 '79 C.927 B.S. L.339 J.D. 2809 Grant St.
Harris, Mary DePoy .... '52 '78 C.882 B.A. L.902 J.D. 1500 Asbury Avenue
Harrison, Lolla M. .... '59 '85 C.228 B.A. L.910 J.D. 2507 Hurd Ave.‡
Hart, David C., (AV) .... '40 '65 C.597 B.A. L.309 LL.B. 2311 Lawndale Ave.‡
Hazard, William R. .... '29 '58 C.338 B.S. L.146 J.D. Northwestern Univ.
Hector, Louis G. .... '28 '56 C.424 Ph.B. L.597 J.D. 2530 Crawford Ave.
Heintzelman, Jonathan R. '47 '72 C.1106 B.A. L.597 J.D.
Assoc. V.P., Northwestern Univ.
Heise, Carol R. .... '42 '92 C.720 B.S.N. L.365 J.D. 929 Elmwood Ave.
Heisler, Marc H. '44 '75 C.597 B.A. L.424 J.D.
2820 Lincoln Street, 60201-2045
Telephone: 847-328-2238 Fax: 847-328-7795 Mobile: 847-971-4492
Email: counselmhh@aol.com URL: http://www.heislernet.com
Real Estate, Residential Real Estate, Buying and Selling a Home, Commercial Real Estate, Condominium Law and Mortgages. Business, Small Business, Partnership, Family Business and Buying and Selling a Business. Probate and Wills. Adoption Law. Civil Litigation, Chancery Practice, Collections, Personal Injury and Automobile Accidents.

See Professional Biographies, EVANSTON, ILLINOIS

Hellner, Mark, (AV) .... '51 '77 C.338 B.S. L.339 J.D. [⊡ M.D.Poulos]
Hill, Herbert D. .... '46 '72 C.454 B.A. L.93 J.D. 1st Asst. Corp. Coun.
Hill, Terrence M. .... '63 '91 C.347 B.S. L.209 J.D. 944 Michigan Ave.‡
Hillman, Jordan J., (AV) .... '24 '50 C&L.145 M.A., J.D. Northwestern Univ.
Hirsen, Sarah S. '51 '81 C.477 B.A. L.209 J.D.
Associate General Counsel, General Board of Pension & Health Benefits
Hirsh, Solomon I. .... '32 '55 C&L.145 A.B., J.D. 530 Forest Ave.
Hoag, Donald W., (AV) .... '22 '48 C&L.966 B.A., LL.B. 1410 Chicago Ave.
Hoffman, David B., (AV) .... '18 '42 C.188 L.597 4 Calvin Circle
Holton, Jas. T. .... '23 '50 C.705 B.S.C. L.145 J.D. 500 Davis St.
Holtsberg, C. Edw., Jr. .... '12 '41 C.145 A.B. L.910 LL.B. 2929 Central St.
Hoskins, Craig R. '52 '76 C.597 B.A. L.339 J.D.
Gen. Coun. & Asst. Gen. Secy., United Methodist Church
Howard, April R. .... '50 '82 C.1168 B.A. L.209 J.D. Staff Atty., U.S. Dept. of HHS
Howell, C. David .... '41 '67 C.893 B.A. L.884 LL.B. 912 Sheridan Rd.
Hudson, Barbara .... '40 '91 C.352 B.A L.405 J.D. 1414 Hinman Ave.
Hupert, Jeffrey D., (AV) .... '48 '78 C.475 B.A. L.209 J.D. [Hupert R.&W.]
Hupert Richards & Wood, (AV) .... 500 Davis St., Ste. 512
Hurley, McKenna & Mertz
(See Chicago)
Hurwich, Saul .... '29 '56 C&L.597 B.S., J.D. 1410 Rosalie St.‡
Jackson, William R., Jr. .... '50 '74 C.1034 B.S. L.597 J.D. 2521 Gross Point Rd., Ste. 1
Jacobson, Lise K. .... '56 '81 C.645 B.A. L.597 J.D. 824 Judson Ave.
Johnson, Carol, Law Offices of '46 '78
C.339 B.A. L.146 J.D. 1601 Sherman Ave., Ste. 200
Johnson, Charles E. .... '47 '72 C.207 B.A. L.910 J.D. 307 Wesley Ave.

Jonas, Alan L. ....'31 '54 C.339 L.209 J.D. Admin. Law J., Soc. Sec. Admn.
Kaiser, Steven P. ....'57 '84 C.966 B.A. L.629 J.D. 3140 Harrison Street
Karns, M. Elizabeth ....'— '04 C.685 B.A. L.1252 J.D. 2210 Colfax Street
Kellman, Hope B. ....'52 '89 C.339 B.A. L.184 J.D. 2610 Grant St.
Kennedy, John T., Law Office of ....'51 '79 C.823 B.A. L.365 J.D. 820 Davis St., Ste. 520
Kenny, James K. ....'67 '92 C.363 B.A. L.424 J.D. [A M.D.Poulos]
Kisor, Colin Abbott ....'69 '99 C.855 B.A. L.94 J.D. U.S. Navy
Knecht, Wm. C. ....'16 '42 C.477 B.A. L.309 LL.B. 2423 Harrison St.‡
Kolen, William A. ....'57 '82 C.352 B.A. L.188 J.D. Legal Asst. Foundation
Kornfeld, N. David, The Law Offices of '56 '81 C.339 B.A. L.94 J.D.
1718 Sherman Avenue, Suite 203 (⊙Chicago)
Kowitt, Arthur J., (AV) ....'33 '58 C.966 B.B.A. L.597 J.D. 9448 N. Drake Ave.‡
Kull, Alexander E. ....'14 '51 C.209 L.365 LL.B. 2639 Eastwood Ave.‡
Laiblin, William W. ....'18 '42 C&L.145 A.B., J.D. 2613 Central St.‡
LaKind, Steven M. ....'61 '86 C.475 B.A. L.477 J.D. 2740 Marcy Ave.
Lamberis, Anthony B., (AV) ....'41 '70 C&L.912 B.A., J.D. [A.B.Lamberis]
Lamberis, Anthony Byron, Ltd., (AV) .... 2956 Central St.
Landesman, Robert .... '24 '47 P.O. Box 563‡
Landsman, Warren P. ....'19 '47 C.209 L.597 J.D. 234 Greenwood St.

Larson, Keil M.
(See Chicago)

Lencioni, Allen S. ....'51 '78 C.424 B.A. L.146 J.D. Nat. Bk. of No. Evanston
Leone, Dolores A., Attorney at Law .... '— '95 C.1138 B.A. L.1051 J.D. 237 Custer Ave.

Lesavich High-Tech Law Group, PC
(See Chicago)

Lesser, Herbert, (AV) ....'19 '42 C&L.145 B.A., J.D. 917 Seward St.
Levin & Schreder, Ltd, (AV) ....500 Davis Street, Suite 812 (⊙Chicago)
Lippitz, Charles A., (AV) ....'26 '51 C&L.145 Ph.B., J.D. 917 Edgemere Ct.
Livingston, Lionel J. ....'15 '36 C&L.209 J.D 1611 Chicago Ave.‡
Lloyd, J. Vernon ....'19 '50 C.451 B.A. L.976 J.D. 1020 Grove St.‡
Logan, Mary K. ....'54 '81 C.383 B.A. L.966 J.D. 1200 Davis St.
Love, Emily ....'63 '93 C.311 B.A. L.424 J.D. [E.Love]

Love, Emily, P.C., Law Office of
621 Madison Street, 60202-2202
Telephone: 847-492-1612 Facsimile: 847-492-1618
Email: emily@emilylove.com URL: http://www.emilylovelaw.com
Emily Love.
Language: Spanish.
Immigration and Naturalization

See Professional Biographies, EVANSTON, ILLINOIS

Luczak, Ronald L. '38 '67 C&L.910 B.S., J.D.
(adm. in MO; not adm. in IL) 1103 Madison St.
Luecke, Mary R. ....'49 '79 C.700 B.A. L.209 J.D. 3330 Lake St.
Lyon, Elliott M. ....'34 '59 C.951 B.A. L.309 LL.B. Pres., Paladin Assocs., Inc.

Maciorowski, Sackmann & Ulrich
(See Chicago)

Mandell Menkes LLC
(See Chicago)

Marshall, Charles B. ....'30 '69 C.352 B.A. L.597 J.D. 2726 Princeton Ave.

Matek Law Offices, P.C.
(See Chicago)

Mayber, Amy D. '58 '83 C.347 B.A. L.146 J.D.
Assoc. Gen. Coun., Northwestern Univ.
McCourt, James P. ....'24 '53 C.623 B.A. L.209 J.D. Ret. Cir. J.‡
McCue, William M. ....'63 '91 C.1505 B.A. L.851 J.D. P.O. Box 5729
McCulloch, Hugh B. ....'21 '50 C.207 B.A. L.597 24 Calvin Circle‡
McDonald, Andrew G., Jr. '62 '89
C.101 B.A. L.477 J.D. Asst. Gen. Coun., Rotary International
McGirr, William J. ....'37 '70 C.188 A.B. L.309 J.D. V.P., Bank One‡
McGovern, John N. ....'53 '89 C.560 B.A. L.424 J.D. Nat. Lekotek Center
McLean, Louis A. ....'10 '34 C&L.339 A.B., LL.B. 1616 Hinman Ave.
McMurray, Sara J., (CVⓉ) ....'63 '91 C.494 B.A. L.209 J.D. [S.J.McMurray]
McMurray, Sara J., Attorney at Law, P.C., (CVⓉ) .... 1234 Elmwood Ave.
Melbinger, Karen M. ....'59 '84 C.602 B.A. L.339 J.D. 1800 Sherman Ave., Ste. 100
Melin, Della Rae ....'41 '71 C.597 B.A. L.424 J.D. 2515 Central St.
Metzler, Claude G. ....'18 '47 C.976 A.B. L.597 J.D. One Arbor Lane, #406‡
Metzler, Monica M. ....'64 '91 C.597 B.S. L.228 J.D. Sesquicentennial Dir.
Mierswa, David P., & Associates ....'— '00 8831 Gross Point Road, Suite 205
Miller, Richard A., (AV) ....'36 '62 C.674 B.A. L.477 J.D. P.O. Box 1307
Mills, Laura A. ....'62 '87 C&L.477 A.B., J.D. 2501 Prairie‡
Molitor, Thomas R. ....'57 '85 C.338 B.S. L.365 J.D. 820 Davis Street, Suite 520
Moring, Douglas T., (AV) ....'42 '71 C.339 B.S.C.E. L.424 J.D. 914 Ridge Court
Morris, Rick G. ....'59 '85 C.339 A.B. L.378 J.D. Northwestern Univ.

Morris & Stella
(See Chicago)

Morrison, John H., (AV) ....'33 '62 C.560 B.B.A. L.309 J.D. 2717 Lincoln St.‡
Mosolygo, Carol ....'47 '79 C.424 B.S. L.209 J.D. 935 Elmwood
Munos, Jane Schulteis '52 '77 C.475 B.A. L.215 J.D.
(adm. in MI; not adm. in IL) 1501 Oak Ave.‡
Murray, Francis J. '26 '70 C.884 A.B. L.1017 LL.B.
(adm. in NJ; not adm. in IL) 828 Oakton St.
Murray, James T., Law Offices of, (AV) '41 '66 C&L.424 A.B., J.D.
1033 University Pl.
Myers, Martin W. ....'41 '68 C&L.378 A.B., J.D. 2146 Central Pk. Ave.
Nicholas, Frank C., (AV) ....'61 '89 C.436 B.S.M.E. L.966 J.D. [Cardinal] (Pat.) ⊙
Ninneman, Maureen A. '62 '91
C.602 B.L. L.966 J.D. Asst. Gen. Coun., Rotary International
O'Malley, *Katherine S., Office, (BV)* ......'56 '89 C.966 B.S. L.209 J.D. 1528 Lincoln St.
O'Shaughnessy, Francis A. ....'19 '49 C.424 Ph.B. L.209 J.D. 2727 Eastwood Ave.‡
Oxman, Michelle L. ....'53 '78 C.339 B.A. L.424 J.D. 925 Hinman Avenue
Pabst, Edmund G., (AV) ....'16 '40 C&L.597 B.S.L., LL.B. 425 Grove St.‡
Pantoga, Robert ....'— '80 C.900 B.A. L.209 J.D. P.O. Box 6460
Pappert, Edward B. ... '47 '73 C.597 B.S. L.339 J.D. Admin. Law J., US Soc. Sec. Admn.
Parks, William L. ....'44 '69 C.375 B.A. L.145 J.D. 820 Davis Street, Suite 520
Patino, Susan G. ....'55 '87 C.352 B.A. L.365 J.D. 2409 Brown Avenue
Peters, Scott V. ....'49 '75 C.429 B.A. L.910 J.D. Ill. Institute of Technology
Pfeifer, George S. ....'46 '75 C.339 A.B. L.146 J.D. 701 Main Street, 2nd Floor
Phenner, Michael E., (P.C.), (AV) ....'— '62 C&L.602 B.A., J.D. 2049 Ridge Ave.‡
Phillips, Barbara W. ....'46 '83 C&L.966 B.A., J.D. Shand, Morahan & Co., Inc.
Piltz, Ira I. ....'73 '02 C.978 B.A. L.209 J.D. [Piltz&Assoc.]
Piltz & Associates, P.C. .... 1601 Sherman Ave., Ste. 200
Pink, Karen M. ....'60 '85 C.741 B.A. L.128 J.D. 732 Hinman Ave.
Pohn, Kendra B. '73 '99 C.174 L.146 J.D.
Program Officer, Great Lakes Protection Fund
Poulos, Michael D. ....'56 '80 C.694 B.A. L.424 J.D. [M.D.Poulos]
Poulos, Michael D., P.C. .... 1724 Sherman Ave.
Raoul, Kwame Y. ....'64 '93 1900 Asbury Ave.
Rausch, Frederick A. ..... '49 '83 C.352 B.A. L.365 J.D. 2nd V.P. & Tr. Offr., NBD Bank
Reams, Anne Sprecher, Attorney at Law ... '52 '77 C.207 B.A. L.597 J.D. 2910 Colfax St.
Redwine, Jack T. ....'19 '47 C&L.477 A.B., J.D. 2444 Central Park‡
Reeder, Robert H. '30 '60 C&L.900 A.B., J.D.
(adm. in KS; not adm. in IL) 800 Hinman Ave.‡
Reilly, Francis X. ....'16 '41 C.197 A.B. L.309 J.D. 1555 Oak Ave.‡
Reinke, Joan Mary ....'53 '87 C.297 B.A. L.146 J.D. 3528 Davis St.
Richman, Irvin F. ....'14 '37 L.209 J.D. 2601 Central St.
Romano, Frank J., Jr. ....'22 '49 C&L.602 A.B., LL.B. 1916 Keeney St.‡
Romano, Henry S. ....'24 '49 C.424 L.602 LL.B. 1916 Keeney
Rose, Barry A. .... '51 '77 C.589 B.A. L.146 J.D. Cook Co. Legal Assist. Found.
Rosen, Janet '60 '85 C.1349 B.A. L.569 J.D.
(adm. in NY; not adm. in IL) 2604 Noyes St.
Rosic, George S., (AV) ....'51 '77 C.388 B.A. L.145 J.D. 1603 Orrington, Suite 800
Routburg, Steven Z. ..... '63 '88 C.659 B.S. L.477 J.D. Gen. Coun., Rotary International
Russell, Joseph P. ....'61 '92 C.679 B.S. L.347 J.D. 1211 Mulford‡
Rutherford, David L. ....'50 '79 C.589 B.A. L.209 J.D. 2102 Harrison St.
Ruttenberg, Fred S. ....'33 '57 C&L.339 LL.B. 9337 Lincolnwood Dr.‡
Schaafsma, Marjorie B. '49 '75 C.477 L.912 J.D.
(adm. in MI; not adm. in IL) Northwestern University‡
Schaffer, Donald L. ....'23 '49 C&L.923 B.A., LL.B. 2658 Sheridan Rd.‡
Schneider, Linda A. ....'53 '78 C.910 B.A. L.145 J.D. 2700 Broadway

Schoenberg, Fisher, Newman & Rosenberg, Ltd.
(See Chicago)

Schreiber, Margaret S. ....'— '95 Pres., Schreiber Staffing, Inc.
Schultz, Barry A. ....'55 '80 C&L.339 B.A., J.D. [B.A.Schultz]
Schultz, Nancy J. ....'59 '85 C.436 B.A. L.94 J.D. 2311 Prospect Ave.
Schultz, Barry A., P.C., The Law Office of .... 1609 Sherman Ave., Ste. 205

Schuyler, Roche & Zwirner, a professional corporation, (AV)
Suite 2050, 1603 Orrington Avenue, 60201 ⊙
Telephone: 312-565-2400
URL: http://www.srzlaw.com
Shareholder: Alison Barkley.
General Practice: Estate Management: Estate Planning and Administration, Trusts, Probate and Trust Litigation, Estate and Transfer Taxation, Wealth and Health Planning; General Corporate; Tax; Commercial and Residential Real Estate.
Chicago, Illinois Office: One Prudential Plaza, Suite 3800, 130 East Randolph Street. Telephone: 312-565-2400. Facsimile: 312-565-8300.

See Professional Biographies, EVANSTON, ILLINOIS

Scott, Halsted & Babetch, P.C.
(See Chicago)

Segall, Leo, (AV) ....'11 '35 C&L.145 Ph.B., J.D. 1131 Sheridan Rd.‡
Shanker, Lawrence H. ....'54 '78 C&L.339 B.S., J.D. 1421 Sherman Ave., Ste. 101

Shaw Gussis Fishman Glantz Wolfson & Towbin LLC
(See Chicago)

Shuldiner, Alizon J. ....'55 '83 C.293 B.A. L.145 J.D. 1413 Wesley Ave.
Silvers, G. Matthew ....'66 '92 C&L.861 B.A., J.D. 2619 Lincolnwood Dr.
Simon, Jordan O. ....'23 '49 C.145 A.B. L.597 J.D. 606 Florence Ave.
Simon, Roger H. ....'44 '70 C&L.424 B.A., J.D. [Evanston M.]
Sloane, Emily A. ....'26 '74 C.1016 B.G.S. L.146 J.D. 1032 Ridge Ct.

Smith, Jeff, Law Offices of '56 '83 C.597 B.A. L.309 J.D.
1603 Orrington, Suite 800, 60201
Telephone: 847-372-9324 Fax: 847-332-1171
Email: jsmith@jefflaw.com
Computer Law, Internet Law, Business Law, E-Commerce, Contract Litigation, Intellectual Property, Estate Planning, Domestic Relations, Municipal Law, Employment Law and Real Estate.

See Professional Biographies, EVANSTON, ILLINOIS

Smith, Gary H., P.C., Law Offices of
(See Chicago)

Snell, Thaddeus S., (AV) ....'19 '48 C.597 B.S. L.976 LL.B. 402 Trinity Ct.‡
Snyder, Franklin Bliss, (AV) ....'16 '46 C.309 A.B. L.597 J.D. 422 Davis St., #405‡
Solomon, Steven G. '51 '77 C.502 B.J. L.986 J.D.
(adm. in MO; not adm. in IL) 1301 Lincoln St.
Solovy, Susan M. ....'49 '77 C.188 B.A. L.209 J.D. 2511 Princeton Ave.‡

Sternberg, David M.
(See Chicago)

Stevens, Thomas L., (AV) ....'30 '55 C.210 A.B. L.347 J.D. 1727 Hinman Ave.
Stillerman, Irving ....'22 '47 C.309 M.B.A. L.209 LL.B. Adm. Law J.
Stillerman, Richard ....'30 '53 C&L.145 B.A., J.D. 2530 Crawford Ave.
Stratigakis, Pamela J. ....'76 '01 C.424 B.S. L.209 J.D. [A Hupert R.&W.]
Streeky-Genet, Heidi ....'54 '81 C.238 B.A. L.365 J.D. Shand, Morahan & Co., Inc.
Suekoff, Raymond I., (AV) ....'10 '32 C&L.597 B.A., J.D. 422 Davis St.‡
Sultan, Gregory ....'51 '78 C.335 B.A. L.146 J.D. 1601 Sherman Ave., Ste. 200
Sultan, Larry A. ....'49 '73 C.347 B.S. L.273 J.D. 1601 Sherman Ave., Ste. 200
Syska, Mark R. ....'61 '87 C&L.339 B.S., J.D. Northwestern Univ. Sch. of Law
Thomas, Andrew M. '50 '78 C.1150 A.B. L.421 J.D.
(adm. in KY; not adm. in IL) 2405 Lincolnwood Dr.‡
Thomas, Nancy Bausch ....'37 '63 C.477 A.B. L.597 J.D. 1911 Sherman Ave.

Thompson, Michael
(See Chicago)

Thorne, Michele H. '65 '90 C&L.597 B.A., J.D.
Gen. Coun. on Finance & Admin., United Methodist Church

Tishler & Wald, Ltd.
(See Chicago)

Tower, John C. ....'32 '57 C.597 B.S. L.477 J.D. 995 N. Main St.‡
Vanneman, Edgar, Jr., (AV) ....'19 '47 C&L.597 B.S.B.A., J.D. 715 Monticello Place‡
Voeks, Howard A. ....'45 '86 C.182 B.A. L.365 J.D. [H.A.Voeks]
Voeks, Howard A., P.C., Law Offices of .... 1516 Hinman Avenue, Suite 801
Waldron, Brian M. ....'44 '73 C&L.424 B.S., J.D. [Witwer&W.]
Wallace, David C. ....'55 '79 C&L.879 B.A., J.D. 820 Davis St.

Wallenstein Wagner & Rockey, Ltd.
(See Chicago)

Ward, William A. ....'48 '80 C.1133 B.S. L.424 J.D. 2347 Ridge Ave.
Warner, Scott L. ....'71 '96 C&L.477 A.B., J.D. Northwestern Univ.

Weil & Associates
(See Northbrook)

Weitzman, Sharon M. ....'46 '83 C.910 B.A. L.597 J.D. 2737 Harrison St.
Welcome, Marcia D. Banas ....'45 '81 C.999 B.A. L.997 J.D. 643 Sheridan Road
Werb, Roseanne Malka '53 '91 C.02 B.A. L.035 LL.B.
(adm. in ON; not adm. in IL) 9200 Ridgeway Ave.
Werth, Andrew D. ....'61 '87 C&L.861 B.A., J.D. 2822 Central Street
West, Arthur H. ....'14 '43 C.679 L.146 LL.B. 1 Calvin Circle‡
Westcott, Barbara J. ....'44 '82 C.72 B.A. L.174 J.D. 380 Ridge Ave., #14-3‡
Weston, Michael C. ....'38 '64 C.103 A.B. L.477 J.D. 3231 Park Place‡
White, Francis L. ....'52 '77 C.372 B.A. L.146 J.D. 805 Dempster St., Ste. 2W
Whitney, Kenneth A., (BV) ....'47 '72 C.329 B.A. L.597 J.D. Sr. Atty.
Wightman, David F. ....'52 '78 C.20 B.A. L.215 J.D. 2704 Broadway Ave.
Williams-Sulkin, Alayne ....'58 '83 C.966 B.A. L.300 J.D. 1511 Sherman‡
Wilson, Dennis W. ....'51 '77 C.221 B.A. L.273 J.D. 2621 Park Place
Wilson, Myroslava F. ....'54 '78 C.424 A.B. L.339 J.D. 2nd V.P., Tr. Div., NBD Bank
Winter, Arthur, (AV) ....'55 '80 C.477 A.B. L.1066 J.D. 1800 Sherman Ave., Ste. 208
Witwer, Samuel W., Jr., (AV) ....'41 '67 C.216 A.B. L.477 J.D. [Witwer&W.]

Witwer & Waldron, LLC, (AV)
1603 Orrington Avenue, Suite 2080, 60201
Telephone: 847-332-2020 Fax: 847-332-2002
URL: http://www.lawyers.com/witwer&waldron
Samuel W. Witwer, Jr.; Brian M. Waldron.
Wills, Trusts, Probate, Estate Planning, General Litigation, First Amendment and Religious Law, Municipal, Government, Corporate, Real Estate.
See Professional Biographies, EVANSTON, ILLINOIS

Woehrel, Marilyn D. ....'50 '84 C.608 B.A. L.365 J.D. 2319 Marcy Ave.
Wood, Matthew W. ....'58 '83 C.694 B.A. L.1218 J.D. [Hupert R.&W.]
Works, Julia C. ....'67 '96 C.659 B.A. L.184 J.D. [Atkinson&A.]
Wynne, Melissa A. ....'56 '87 C.228 B.A. L.597 J.D. 1130 Hinman Ave.‡
Zak, Leonard E., (AV) ....'29 '54 C.118 B.A. L.597 J.D. 2738 Woodbine

EVERGREEN PARK, 20,874, *Cook Co.*

Brogan, Geo. E., (AV) ....'26 '50 C&L.424 Ph.B., J.D. 2400 W. 95th St.
Campbell, Ronald E. ....'48 '74 C.1157 B.A. L.879 J.D. 2940 W. 95th St.
Cardinal, Joseph John ....'54 '80 C.424 B.A. L.146 J.D. [J.Cardinal]
Cardinal, Joseph ....3960 W. 95th St., 2nd Fl.
Cleary, Joan M. '63 '89 C.209 B.S. L.365 J.D.
Trust Atty., First. Natl. Bk. of Evergreen Park
Collins, Michael W. ....'15 '40 C&L.209 LL.B. V.P., Heritage Bancorp., Inc.
Delprincipe, Yvonne ....'49 '91 C.339 B.A. L.365 J.D. [Prendergast&D.]
Drugas, Constantine G. ....'30 '55 C&L.597 B.S.L., LL.B. 9357 S. Harding Ave.‡

Forst Law Offices
(See Oak Lawn)

Freburg, Cynthia A. ....'66 '91 C.339 B.A. L.597 J.D. 3318 W. 95th St.
Gately, James T. ....'62 '90 C.742 B.A. Acct. L.365 J.D. 3101 W. 95th Street
Gutgsell, John A., Jr. ....'18 '46 C.137 L.365 LL.B. 9758 S. Ridgeway Ave.‡
Hamill, Steven Owen ....'59 '85 C.446 B.S. L.365 J.D. 3843 W. 95th St., Ste. 2
Johnson, James E. ....'20 '50 C.209 L.365 LL.B. 9237 S. Mozart St.
Kelley-Bergerson, Suellen, Law Offices of — '78
C.201 B.A. L.146 J.D. 3319 W. 95th St.
Lepore, Anthony J. ....'37 '65 C.249 B.A. L.146 J.D. 2940 W. 95th St.
Lewis, Lynette, Law Office of ....'61 '94 C.209 B.A. L.146 J.D. 3502 W. 95th St.
Lord, Bernard F. ....'52 '78 C.234 B.S. L.146 J.D. 2940 W. 95th St.
Marovitch, Joseph A. '56 '81 C&L.597 B.A., J.D.
Gen. Coun. & Pres., First Atty. Consultants, Ltd.
McGovern, Joseph M. ....'54 '81 C.770 B.S. L.424 J.D. 2940 West 95th Street
Odelson, Burton S. ....'47 '72 C.339 L.146 J.D. 3318 W. 95th St.
Peacock, Hiram R. ....'72 '00 C&L.209 B.S., J.D. 9551 S. Maplewood Ave. (Pat.)
Philbin, Joseph M. ....'12 '38 C&L.209 B.S., J.D. 9252 S. Richmond
Prendergast, Gerald A. ....'42 '76 C.1191 B.A. L.365 J.D. [Prendergast&D.]
Prendergast & DelPrincipe ....3540 W. 95th St.
Rugai, Ado L. ....'44 '85 C.424 B.S. L.365 J.D. 3319 W. 95th St.
Scheurich, Anne M. '57 '82
C.338 B.S. L.146 J.D. Tr. Offr., First Natl. Bk. of Evergreen Park
Siss, Gregory A. '52 '77
C.363 A.B. L.209 J.D. V.P & Tr. Offr., First Natl. Bk. of Evergreen
Sullivan, Michael F. ....'34 '62 C&L.424 B.S., J.D. 3316 W. 95th St.
Sullivan, Thomas J. ....'46 '73 C.424 B.A. L.178 J.D. 9135 S. Sacramento
Utz, John E. ....'46 '78 C.424 B.B.A. L.1000 J.D. [Utz&Assoc.]
Utz & Associates ....9149 South Mozart Avenue

FAIRBURY, 3,968, *Livingston Co.*

Ahlemeyer, David G., (BV) ....'40 '66 C&L.879 B.A., J.D. Pub. Def.
Goold, John J., (CV) ....'46 '79 C.234 B.S. L.1187 J.D. 111 W. Locust St.
Kinate, Gordon M., (BV) ....'46 '75 C.338 B.S. L.365 J.D. [Kinate&M.]
Kinate & Morgan, P.C., (BV) ....111 W. Locust Street
Mason, Paul G., (BV) ....'47 '77 C&L.339 B.A., J.D. 404 E. Oak St.
Morgan, Randell S., (BV) ....'52 '77 C.338 B.S. L.790 J.D. [Kinate&M.]
Traub, Harvey S., (AV) ....'30 '59 C&L.339 B.S., J.D. 110 1/2 West Locust Street
Trezise, Walwyn M. ....'38 '62 C&L.339 B.S., J.D. 319 W. Locust, Suite A-2

FAIRFIELD, * 5,439, *Wayne Co.*

Cochran, Richard C., (BV) ....'30 '57 C&L.880 B.A., J.D. 302 E. Main St.
Elliott, Christopher Shawn ....'71 '96 C.339 B.A. L.420 J.D. [C.Elliott]
Elliott, Chris, Law Office of ....207 E. Main
Fyie, Jay H., (BV) ....'48 '78 C.339 B.S. L.910 J.D. [Fyie&H.]
Fyie & Hawkins, (BV) ....115 North East Third Street
Harrison, David E., (CV) ....'64 '94 C.383 B.S. L.500 J.D. [Harrison]
Harrison, Joe ....'36 '65 C&L.383 B.A., LL.B. Cir. J.
Harrison Law Office, (CV) ....118 E. Main St.
Hawkins, Robert J., (BV) ....'45 '71 C.531 B.S. L.45 J.D. [Fyie&H.]
Laws, Marvin Neal, Jr., (BV) ....'49 '75 C.339 B.A. L.425 J.D. 221 E. Main
Molt, Michael J., Law Office of, (BV) ....'48 '74 C.339 B.S. L.500 J.D. 601 S. 1st St.
Quindry, Gerald T. ....'22 '52 C.801 L.996 LL.B. 115 N. E. 3rd St.‡
Robison, John C., Jr., (AV) ....'43 '69 C&L.339 A.B., J.D. 204 Southeast Third Street
Vaughn, Matthew E. ....'67 '93 C&L.801 B.S., J.D. [Vaughn]
Vaughn Law Office ....108A Northeast 2nd St.
Williams, David M., Law Office of, (BV) ....'48 '74 C.846 B.J. L.45 J.D. 308 E. Main St.
Ziegler, Harry L. ....'19 '52 C.150 A.B. L.734 LL.B. Ret. Cir. J.

FAIRVIEW HEIGHTS, 15,034, *St. Clair Co.*

Adams, John J. ....'33 '70 C&L.424 B.S.C., J.D. Zeigler Coal Co.
Adams, Norvan E. ....'20 '51 C.782 L.734 LL.B. 16 Cozy Lane
Adams, Richard T. ....'53 '84 C.801 B.A. L.734 J.D. 16 Cozy Lane‡
Baldwin, Tiffany L. '71 '97 C.30 B.A. L.910 J.D.
(adm. in MO; not adm. in IL) P.O. Box 1806
Bisping, Peggy Sue ....'63 '90 C.910 B.A. L.273 J.D. [Cordell&C.]
Clark, Stephen B., (BV) ....'48 '84 C&L.734 B.A., J.D. Asst. U.S. Atty.
Coonan, William Edward, (BV) '63 '90 C.597 B.A. L.910 J.D.
9 Executive Dr., Ste. 300
Cordell & Cordell, P.C. ....333 Salem Place, Suite 235 (©Kansas City, St. Louis, MO)
Crowe, James E., III '74 '00 C.602 B.A L.734 J.D.
(adm. in MO; not adm. in IL) Asst. U.S. Atty.
Cunningham, Allison ....'74 '00 C.249 B.S. L.734 J.D. [Ⓐ Cordell&C.]
Donovan, James K. ....'52 '77 C.801 B.S. L.734 J.D. IL Appl Ct., 5th Dist., Appl. Ct. J.
Douglas, Dennis O., (AV) ....'47 '75 C.801 B.A. L.734 J.D. [Ⓐ Keefe&D.]
Dowling, B. Jay, (BV) ....'60 '88 C.191 B.S. L.734 J.D. 6 Canty Lane
Erdmann, Richard O., Law Office, (BV) '47 '72
C&L.339 B.S., J.D. 10800 Lincoln Trial, Ste. 10
Friederich, Ralph M., (BV) ....'47 '76 C&L.801 B.A., J.D. Asst. U.S. Atty.
Garrison, Suzanne M., (BV) ....'66 '91 C.205 B.A. L.910 J.D. Asst. U.S. Atty.
Giffhorn, Neil Anthony ....'76 '01 C.801 B.A. L.734 J.D. 2 Executive Dirve
Greathouse, Michael D. ....'61 '87 C&L.801 B.S., J.D. Law Clk. to Ct. of App.

Harper, Julie
(See Alton)

Harrison, Moses W. ....'32 '58 C.170 B.A. L.910 J.D. Supm. Ct. Jus.
Hotto, William R. ....'27 '51 L.339 J.D. 10230 Lincoln Trail
Hurwitz, Diana M. '54 '83 C&L.910 B.A., J.D.
(adm. in MO; not adm. in IL) Sr. Appl. Law Clk. to Appl. J.
Jones, Laura Jeanne, (AV) '56 '80 C.531 B.A. L.146 J.D.
Asst. U.S. Atty., Chf. Civil Div.
Kammann, Philip H. ....'42 '74 C.339 B.A. L.734 J.D. 144 Parr Ave.‡
Keefe, James K., (AV) ....'55 '80 C.1082 B.A. L.734 J.D. [Keefe&D.]
Keefe, Michael F., (BV) ....'64 '98 C&L.734 B.A., J.D. 2 Executive Dr.
Keefe, Patrick M., (AV) ....'54 '88 C.602 B.A. L.734 J.D. [Ⓐ Keefe&D.]
Keefe, Thomas Q., (AV) ....'15 '53 C.1082 A.B. L.734 LL.B. [Ⓑ Keefe&D.]
Keefe & DePauli, P.C., (AV) ....2 Executive Drive
Keltner, Gregory S., (BV) ....'62 '87 C.927 B.S. L.801 J.D. [Ⓐ Keefe&D.]
Kuergeleis, Thomas H., (AV) ....'47 '73 C.339 B.S. L.910 J.D. [Keefe&D.]
Leggans, Thomas E., (AV) ....'63 '89 C.357 B.S. L.801 J.D. Asst. U.S. Atty.
Lemp, William, (AV) .....'57 '84 C.502 B.A. L.734 J.D. [Ⓐ Keefe&D.] (©St. Louis, MO)
Lloyd, Richard H. ....'48 '74 C.329 B.A. L.597 J.D. US Atty's Off., Southern Dist. Il.
Massey, Randy G., (AV) ....'54 '79 C.801 B.A. L.339 J.D. Asst. U.S. Atty.
McGovern, Richard W. ....'30 '57 C.711 B.A. L.734 LL.B. Ill. Fed. Svgs. & Loan Assn.
Merkel, Joel V., (BV) ....'45 '73 C.339 B.A. L.734 J.D. Asst. U.S. Atty.
Miller, B. Stephen, III ....'55 '81 C.910 B.A. L.309 J.D. Sr. Atty., State Supm. Ct.
Morrissey, Kit Renae, (BV) ....'61 '86 C.234 B.S. L.801 J.D. Asst. U.S. Atty.
Netzel, Quin W. ....'64 '89 C.339 B.A. L.801 J.D. State Farm Fire & Cas. Co.
Neubauer, Terry J., (BV) ....'47 '73 C.801 B.S. L.190 J.D. 955 Lincoln Hwy.
Price, James David '54 '85 C&L.846 B.A., J.D.
(adm. in AK; not adm. in IL) I.R.S.
Reppert, Bruce E., (AV) ....'51 '76 C&L.117 B.A., J.D. Asst. U.S. Atty.
Rich, Thomas C., (BV) ....'57 '83 C.723 B.A. L.209 J.D. 6 Executive Dr., Ste. 3
Risse, Richard H., (CV) ....'49 '85 C.999 A.B. L.734 J.D. [Ⓐ Keefe&D.]
Short, Darren K., (BV) ....'65 '92 C&L.801 B.A., J.D. [Ⓐ Keefe&D.]
Shy, David G. '48 '74 C&L.502 B.S., J.D.
(adm. in MO; not adm. in IL) Illini Fed. Svgs. & Loan
Simpkins, Robert L., (BV) ....'46 '72 C&L.923 B.S., J.D. 1st Asst. U.S. Atty.
Sterling, Harry J., (AV) ....'45 '70 C.339 B.S. L.146 J.D. [H.J.Sterling]
Sterling, Harry J., P.C., (AV) ....#6 Canty Lane
Sullivan, Kelly C., (BV) ....'66 '91 C&L.801 B.S., J.D. 10230 Lincoln Trail
Thompson, H. Michael, (BV) ....'51 '76 C.597 B.A. L.339 J.D. U.S. Atty.
White, Scott A. ....'64 '90 C.465 B.A. L.733 J.D. [Ⓐ Keefe&D.]

FARMER CITY, 2,114, *DeWitt Co.*

Drake, Stuart B. ....'55 '80 C.339 B.S. L.801 J.D. Pres., Farmer City State Bk.
Gammage, Bruce W., (BV) ....'48 '75 C.340 B.A. L.339 J.D. States' Atty. [Gammage]
Gammage Law Office, P.C., (BV) ....223 S. Main St.
Peithmann, Ortheldo A., (AV) ....'17 '48 C&L.339 B.S., J.D. [Peithmann]
Peithmann, William A., (AV) ....'54 '78 C.416 B.A. L.208 J.D. [Peithmann] (©Joliet)

Peithmann Law Office, The, (AV)
111 South Main Street, P.O. Box 228, 61842-1453
Telephone: 309-928-3390 Fax: 309-928-2731
Email: peithmannlawoffice@excite.com
Ortheldo A. Peithmann; William A. Peithmann.
Wealth Management, Asset Protection, Basic, Intermediate and Advanced Estate Planning, Trust and Estate Administration, Contested Estates, Elder Law, Closely Held Businesses, Farm and Commercial Real Estate, Gift, Estate and Income Taxation of all types.
See Professional Biographies, FARMER CITY, ILLINOIS

FARMERSVILLE, 698, *Montgomery Co.*

Bawden, Ralph E., (BV) ....'46 '71 C.424 B.A. L.339 J.D. [R.E.Bawden]
Bawden, Ralph E., Ltd., (BV) ....110 S. Cleveland St.

FARMINGTON, 2,535, *Fulton Co.*

Maas, Thomas C., (BV) ....'50 '76 C.960 B.A. L.146 J.D. 165 E. Fort St.
Potter, John C., (BV) ....'38 '72 C.630 B.S. L.339 J.D. 165 E. Fort St.
Toohill, Jos. V., (BV) ....'08 '31 C&L.734 J.D. [Ⓑ Toohill,T.&T.]
Toohill, Joseph V., Jr., (BV) ....'42 '70 C.707 B.A. L.190 J.D. [Toohill,T.&T.]
Toohill, Judith A., (CV) ....'41 '75 C.352 B.A. L.365 J.D. [Toohill,T.&T.]
Toohill, Toohill & Toohill, (BV) ....74 E. Fort St.

FINDLAY, 787, *Shelby Co.*

Bast, Kenneth L. ....'27 '75 C.234 B.S. L.345 J.D. P.O. Box 235‡

FISHER, 1,647, *Champaign Co.*

Helle, Susan Hanes ....'54 '78 C.106 B.A. L.352 J.D. P.O. Box 517‡

FLORA, 5,054, *Clay Co.*

Bright, Barry D. ....'54 '97 C.339 B.S. L.801 J.D. 434 W. North Ave.
Brissenden, James L., (BV) ....'43 '71 C.357 B.S. L.910 J.D. [Brissenden]
Brissenden Law Office, (BV) ....100 W. 6th St.
Coble, Robert G., (BV) ....'56 '82 C.234 B.A. L.616 J.D. [Coble&M.]
Coble & Milone, (BV) ....832 W. North Ave.
Klobnak, Michael W., (BV) ....'51 '76 C.221 B.A. L.607 J.D. 100 N. Main
Milone, Gary E., (CV) ....'58 '83 C&L.801 B.S., J.D. [Coble&M.]
Riggle, Paul T., (AV) ....'11 '36 C&L.339 A.B., J.D. 100 N. Main‡
Todd, William R. ....'27 '53 C&L.339 B.S., J.D. Cir. J.

Todd, William R., (BV) ....'48 '73 C.339 B.A. L.502 J.D. 130 E. North Ave.
Tungate, Mark J., (BV) ....'52 '77 C.234 B.A. L.862 J.D. 400 North Main

FLOSSMOOR, 9,301, *Cook Co.*

Armstrong, F. Dean ....'52 '77 C.221 B.A. L.602 J.D. [F.D.Armstrong]
Armstrong, F. Dean, P.C. .... 1324 Dartmouth Rd.
Bainbridge, Jack G. ....'52 '78 C.123 B.A. L.1151 J.D. 1835 Dixie Hwy.
Brannigan, John M. ....'68 '95 C.602 B.A. L.209 J.D. 19511 Governors Hwy.
Braun, Paul S. ....'54 '80 C.894 B.A. L.365 J.D. [Braun&E.]
Braun & Edwards .... 19630 Governors Highway
Butler, Robert J., (AV) '37 '70 C&L.424 B.S., J.D.
19511 Governors Hwy., Kedzie Ave.
Carey, Patrick T. ....'52 '80 C.589 B.A. L.365 J.D. 2630 Flossmoor Rd.
DiLuia, Edward A. ....'56 '83 C.602 B.B.A. L.209 J.D. 2333 Carroll Pkwy.
Dropkin, Lauren A. ....'73 '99 C.1036 B.A. L.339 J.D. [Ⓐ Braun&E.]
Edwards, Thomas C. ....'57 '91 C.927 B.A. L.365 J.D. [Braun&E.]
Garrison, Ray H. ....'22 '50 C.929 A.B. L.145 J.D. 848 Braemar Rd.
Gevers, Marcia B. ....'46 '80 C.536 B.A. L.209 J.D. 19710 Governors Hwy., Ste. 8
Herbstman, Janet S. ....'56 '81 C.681 A.B. L.145 J.D. 3018 Bonnie Brae Crescent‡
Huyck, Steven Michael ....'50 '79 2035 Hutchison Rd.
Irons, Spencer E., (AV) ....'17 '41 C.145 A.B. L.477 J.D. 1760 Western Ave.‡
Klimas, Elizabeth J. ....'47 '76 C.339 B.A. L.365 J.D. [Klimas&K.]
Klimas, Michael J. ....'47 '74 C.801 B.A. L.146 J.D. [Klimas&K.]
Klimas & Klimas ....2625 Flossmoor Rd.
LaCien, Richard A. ....'34 '62 C&L.209 B.S., LL.B. Asso. Cir. J.
LaPorte, MariJo C. ....'51 '99 C.844 B.S. L.209 J.D. [LaPorte]
LaPorte Law Offices, P.C. .... 2809 Wallace Dr., Ste. 100
LeBold, Sandra J. ....'48 '78 C.347 B.A. L.209 J.D. 2303 Hutchison Rd.
Loeb, Stephen H. ....'46 '71 C.339 B.A. L.597 J.D. 2117 Hagen Lane
Maher, Frank J., Jr., (BV) ....'41 '71 C.973 B.S. L.424 J.D. 19501 S. Governers Hwy.
Miller, Geoffrey C. ....'43 '68 C&L.339 B.S., J.D. 19630 Governors Hwy.
Odom, Timijanel B. ....'63 '90 C.927 B.S. L.146 J.D. Asst. Cook Co. Pub. Def.
Pappas, James, (Ltd.), (BV) ....'27 '52 C&L.966 J.D. [Ⓒ Braun&E.]
Pisani, Stanley, (AV) ....'24 '51 C.209 L.365 LL.B. 2635 Flossmoor Rd.
Pratt, Donald R., Jr. '49 '75 C.112 B.A. L.546 J.D.
(adm. in CA; not adm. in IL) 19710 Governors Hwy.
Reed, Michael A. '47 '77 C&L.502 B.S., J.D.
(adm. in MO; not adm. in IL) 1370 Dartmouth Rd.‡
Roseberry, Stanley L. ....'33 '60 C&L.352 B.S.C., J.D. 2712 Emelia Ct.‡
Schultz, Alyssa Marcel ....'73 '99 C.999 B.A. L.365 J.D. 3114 Bonnie Brae
Scully, George F., Jr. ....'52 '81 C.589 B.S. L.365 J.D. 850 Travers Lane
Sims, Murray W., Jr., (AV) ....'32 '59 C.1024 A.B. L.365 LL.B. 2630 Flossmoor Rd.
Smaron, Carolyn Ann ....'48 '79 C.339 B.A. L.146 J.D. 635 Argyle Ave.
Smith, Linda Suzanne ....'53 '81 C.597 B.A. L.245 J.D. 2405 Braeburn Ave.
South, Leslie Elaine ....'49 '78 C.424 B.A. L.597 J.D. 1412 Heather Hill Crescent
Tiernan, Marion G., (BV) ....'16 '52 C.801 B.S.L. L.339 2633 Flossmoor Rd.
Tyler, Thomas A., Jr. ....'50 '80 C.801 B.A. L.365 J.D. V.P., MEAS, Inc.
Yogore, Mariano G., III ....'46 '89 L.365 J.D. Pres., Pathology Servs., Ltd.

FOREST PARK, 15,688, *Cook Co.*

Bohlen, Reiner D. ....'35 '64 C&L.879 B.A., J.D. Site Dir., Operation ABLE
Buffardi, Louis J. ....'14 '39 C.597 L.146 Ferrara Candy Co.
Coleman, Mary Lynch ....'26 '52 C.530 B.A. L.424 J.D. P.O. Box 579
Gerst, William S. ....'53 '82 C.339 B.S. L.209 J.D. 517 Circle Ave.
Karlin, Leonard ....'15 '40 C.145 B.A. L.424 J.D. 7201 Adams‡
Katsis, Kevin G. ....'55 '79 C.339 B.A. L.424 J.D. 7346 W. Madison St.
O'Shea, Edward B., Jr., (BV) ....'27 '51 C.602 L.424 LL.B. [O'Shea&Q.]
O'Shea, Sharon A. ....'54 '80 C.1082 B.S. L.365 J.D. 7346 Madison St.
O'Shea and Quan, (BV) ....7346 Madison St.
Platt, Jos. C. ....'14 '39 C.137 M.A. L.209 LL.B. 7515 W. Madison St.
Quan, John J., (BV) ....'27 '51 C&L.209 LL.B. [O'Shea&Q.]
Rice, Daniel J., Law Office of ....'49 '76 C.424 B.S. L.365 J.D. 1001 S. Harlem Ave.
Senechalle, Robert E., Jr. ....'47 '73 C.750 B.A. L.209 J.D. 7423 Madison St.

FORRESTON, 1,469, *Ogle Co.*

James, Thomas H. ....'60 '86 C&L.585 B.B.A., J.D. [James&Assoc.]

James & Associates
412 S. 2nd Avenue, P.O. Box 398, 61030-9536
Telephone: 815-938-3241
Email: jameslaw1@aol.com URL: http://www.jamesandassociateslaw.com
Member of Firm: Thomas H. James.
Family Law, Civil Litigation, Professional Liability, Divorce, Debtor and Creditor, Tax Lien, Real Estate.
See Professional Biographies, FORRESTON, ILLINOIS

Miller, Donald J., (BV) ....'26 '62 C&L.145 B.A., J.D. P.O. Box 627

FOX LAKE, 9,178, *Lake Co.*

Grant, Michael S., (BV) ....'49 '77 C.293 B.A. L.146 J.D. [M.S.Grant]
Grant, Michael S., Ltd., (BV) ....28 East Grand Avenue

Idlas, Paul R., Law Office of
(See Grayslake)

Johnson, R. Gilman, (AV) ....'38 '63 C.393 B.A. L.146 J.D. [Soffietti,J.T.P.O.&M.]
Morozin, Christopher B., (BV) ......'64 '90 C.436 B.A. L.209 J.D. [Soffietti,J.T.P.O.&M.]
Ortiz, Jorge L., (BV) ....'62 '90 C.424 B.A. L.365 J.D. [Soffietti,J.T.P.O.&M.]
Phillips, Paul P., (BV) ....'49 '74 C&L.424 B.S., J.D. [Soffietti,J.T.P.O.&M.]
Soffietti, Johnson, Teegen, Phillips, Ortiz & Morozin, Ltd., (AV)
74 E. Grand Ave. Suite 100
Teegen, Howard R., (AV) ....'46 '71 C.57 A.B. L.209 J.D. [Soffietti,J.T.P.O.&M.]

FOX RIVER GROVE, 4,862, Lake & McHenry Cos.

Fins, Theodore S. ....'40 '67 C&L.966 B.S., J.D. P.O. Box 484

Wagner, James C., (BV) '50 '76 C.234 L.365 J.D.
Stone Hill Center of Cary-Grove, 960 Route 22, Suite 210, P.O. Box 23, 60021
Telephone: 847-639-1800 Fax: 847-516-0325
Email: jamescwagner@yahoo.com
Criminal Law, Personal Injury, Family Law, Bankruptcy, Real Estate, Wills, Estate Planning.

FRANKFORT, 10,391, *Will Co.*

Chin, Davis, (AV) ....'47 '74 C.701 B.S.E.E. L.64 J.D. 10281 W. Lincoln Hwy. (Pat.)
Clavio, John C. ....'69 '97 C.1151 B.A. L.365 J.D. 10479 Yankee Ridge Drive
Dennis, Peter R. '38 '64 C&L.966 B.S., LL.B.
(adm. in WI; not adm. in IL) Pres., Hazardnet, Inc./Geomar, Inc.‡

Dobbs and Hutchison
(See Chicago)

Donovan, Thomas B., Law Offices, (AV) '42 '70 C&L.424 A.B., J.D.
518 Aberdeen Rd.
Dutton, Barbara Jacobson ....'59 '84 C.339 B.S. L.146 J.D. 10325 W. Lincoln Hwy.
Gottschalk, Arthur R. ....'25 '50 C&L.339 B.A., J.D. 10642 Brookridge Dr.‡
Gowen, Ernest L. ....'43 '69 C.705 B.A. L.209 J.D. 19550 S. Harlem Ave., Ste. 2
Grey, Kenneth A., (BV) ....'51 '83 C.927 B.A. L.365 J.D. [McKeown,F.Z.B.H.&R.] ⊙
Jordan, Michael W. '54 '87 C.651 B.A. L.678 J.D.
(adm. in WA; not adm. in IL) 22054 Caroline Ct.
Karos, Demetrius J. ....'59 '89 C.347 B.S. L.365 J.D. [D.J.Karos]
Karos, Demetrius J., Ltd. ....1 Old Frankfort Way
Koonce, Dennis Dale ....'59 '86 C.234 B.S. L.61 J.D. [D.D.Koonce]
Koonce, Dennis D. ....11255 Patrick Court
Kraut, Barbara Fox ....'67 '93 C.999 B.A. L.209 B.A. 609 Prestwick Dr.‡
Littleton, Kathleen A. ....'59 '84 C.339 B.S. L.209 J.D. 7735 Coventry Lane‡

Malysa, Theresa M.
(See Orland Park)

Mansker, William H. ....'49 '75 C.197 B.A. L.145 J.D. 21252 Georgetown Road

McKeown, Fitzgerald, Zollner, Buck, Hutchison & Ruttle, (AV)
28 Kansas Street, 60423 ⊙
Telephone: 815-469-2176 Fax: 815-469-0295
URL: http://www.mckeownlawfirm.com
Kenneth A. Grey. Of Counsel: George E. Sangmeister.
General Civil, Trial and Appellate Practice. Corporation, Municipal, Probate, Estate Planning, Real Estate, Taxation, Employment, Healthcare, School and Personal Injury Law.
Joliet Office: 2455 Glenwood Avenue. Telephone: 815-729-4800. Fax: 815-729-4711.
See Professional Biographies, FRANKFORT, ILLINOIS

Novander, Kenneth L. ....'34 '65 C.210 B.A. L.146 J.D. 24515 S. 80th Ave.

Peters, William J., (BV) '49 '78 C&L.339 B.A., J.D.
237 South LaGrange Road, 60423
Telephone: 815-469-1399 Fax: 815-469-0822
Email: wjplaw@aol.com URL: http://www.lawyers.com/wjplaw
Trusts and Estates, Estate Planning, Asset Protection, Estate Litigation, Estate and Gift Taxation, Charitable Giving, Wills, Real Estate, Residential Real Estate, Commercial Real Estate, Condominium, Landlord and Tenant, Business, Small Business, Business Formations, Limited Liability, Buying and Selling of Businesses, Zoning and Land Use, Elder and Elder Care Law.
See Professional Biographies, FRANKFORT, ILLINOIS

Sangmeister, George E., (AV) '31 '60
C.238 A.B. L.365 J.D. [Ⓒ McKeown,F.Z.B.H.&R.] ⊙
Santoro, August J., (BV) ....'36 '60 C.1101 B.A. L.365 LL.B. 112 Kansas St.
Singer, Joseph H. ....'33 '59 C.1016 A.B. L.146 J.D. 811 Glenegales Ct.‡
Whitten, Michael C. ....'48 '75 C.420 B.A. L.146 J.D. 239 Oregon St.

FRANKLIN PARK, 19,434, *Cook Co.*

Aufox, Jerry M., (AV) '42 '74
C.390 B.S.E.E. L.365 J.D. Corp. Coun. & Secy., A. M. Castle & Co.
Blanchard, Eric A. ....'56 '81 C.477 B.B.A. L.309 J.D. Pres., Dairy Div., Dean Foods Co.
Bluthardt, Edw. E. ....'16 '50 C.337 A.B. L.365 J.D. 9758 W. Grand Ave.
Bolger, Shawn M., The Law Office of '59 '84
C.208 B.S.B.A. L.209 J.D. 10009 Grand Ave., Ste. 2051
Corwine, David B. ....'37 '69 C.393 B.A. L.209 J.D. Atty., Dean Foods Co
Deighan, Kathleen J. ....'56 '81 C&L.339 B.S., J.D. Atty., Dean Foods Co.
Douglas, Kenneth J. ....'22 '50 C.339 L.146 LL.B. 3600 N. River Rd.
Drickey, Steven L. ......'51 '87 C.546 B.A./B.S. L.597 J.D. Gen. Coun., Life Fitness Div.
Ernst, Mark S. ....'49 '80 C.1151 B.A. L.209 J.D. Nabisco Brands, Lifesavers Div.
Franklin, Randy W., (AV) ....'45 '72 C.98 B.S. L.999 J.D. 9240 Belmont Ave., 2nd Fl.
Kamide, James A. ....'57 '85 C.209 B.A. L.365 J.D. 10241 Panoramic Dr.
Mann, Stuart Jay ....'37 '62 C.587 L.365 LL.B. 9758 W. Grand Ave.
Pascale, Daniel, (AV) ....'40 '66 C.309 A.B. L.145 J.D. Sr. Coun., Dean Foods Co.
Pedersen, Barrett F., Attorney at Law ....'57 '90 C.238 L.146 9701 Grand Ave.
VanHouten, Peter J. ....'51 '80 C.937 B.A. L.352 J.D. V.P., St. Paul Fed. Bk.

FREEBURG, 3,872, *St. Clair Co.*

Nold, Gregory C., (BV) ....'57 '82 C.465 B.B.A. L.339 J.D. [Nold&N.]
Nold, Norman L., (BV) ....'27 '55 C&L.734 LL.B. [Ⓒ Nold&N.]
Nold & Nold, Ltd., (BV) ....P.O. Box 99
Parker, Rosemarie Heidenreich ....'— '94 C.502 B.A. L.734 J.D. [R.H.Parker]

Parker, Rosemarie Heidenreich, Law Office of
P.O. Box 125, 62243
Mailing Address: P.O. Box 125, Freeburg, IL 62243
Telephone: 618-539-9956 Fax: 618-539-9954
Email: parkerrobtrosie@juno.com URL: http://www.parkerlawoffice.net
Rosemarie Heidenreich Parker.
Real Estate, Wills, Trusts, Probate Estates, Bankruptcy, Small Business Law, Water Law, General Practice.
See Professional Biographies, FREEBURG, ILLINOIS

FREEPORT, * 26,443, *Stephenson Co.*

Anderson, Barry ....'44 '73 C.293 B.A. L.424 J.D. Cir. J.
Bald, Michael P., (BV) ....'56 '81 C.177 B.A. L.424 J.D. State's Atty.
Bauer, Nicole M. ....'71 '96 C.436 B.A. L.959 J.D. [Plager,K.&B.]
Brooks, Steven E. ....'68 '02 C.1245 B.S. L.589 J.D. [Ⓐ Hasting]
Brown, W. Neil, (CV) ....'40 '68 C.98 B.S. L.365 J.D. 222 W. Exchange St.
Burt, Woodruff A., (AV) ....'33 '63 C.339 B.S. L.597 J.D. [Ⓒ Snow,H.W.&F.] ‡
Celichowski, Mark R. ....'75 '03 C&L.966 B.B.A., J.D. [Ⓐ R.E.Elliott]
Cox, Steven A., (CV) ....'69 '94 C&L.339 B.S., J.D. [Shockey&C.] (⊙Lena)
Eden, Robert E., Law Offices, (BV) ......'47 '79 C.427 B.A. L.352 J.D. 722 Santa Fe Dr.
Elliott, Ralph E., (BV) ....'56 '81 C&L.339 B.S., J.D. [R.E.Elliott]

Elliott, Ralph E., A Professional Corporation, Law Offices of, (BV)
1005 West Loras Drive, P.O. Box 1149, 61032
Telephone: 815-233-1022 Telecopier: 815-233-1988
Email: ree.elliottlawfirm@insightbb.com URL: http://www.lawyers.com/elliottlaw
Ralph E. Elliott; Mark R. Celichowski.
General Civil and Criminal Trial and Appellate Practice in State and Federal Courts. Commercial, Business, Personal Injury, Wills, Trusts, Estate Planning, Estate Administration, Real Estate, Financial Institutions, Collections, Agriculture, Bankruptcy and Family Law.
See Professional Biographies, FREEPORT, ILLINOIS

Fagan, Robert M., (BV) ....'56 '92 C.1120 B.S. L.589 J.D. [R.M.Fagan] ⊙
Fagan, Robert M., Ltd., The Law Offices of, (BV)
10 North Galena Avenue (⊙Fountain Hills, AZ; Northbrook, IL)
Fishburn, Dan G., (BV) ....'52 '77 C.477 B.A. L.910 J.D. [Snow,H.W.&F.] ⊙

Gilbert, John
(See Rockford)

Hartman, Charles R. ....'45 '70 C.424 B.S. L.209 J.D. Cir. J.

Hartman, Howard J. '44 '76 C.81 B.S. L.378 J.D. 500 Economy Ct.
Hasting, H. Duane, (BV) '43 '69 C.350 B.S. L.352 J.D. [Hasting]
Hasting Law Offices, (BV) 50 West Douglas Street, Suite 300
Hauser, James M., (BV) '63 '88 C.352 B.A. L.436 J.D. [Mahoney&H.]
Hauser, Richard J., Jr., (BV) '59 '84 C&L.190 B.A., J.D. [Mahoney&H.]
Jeffrey, David L. '53 '79 C&L.339 B.A., J.D. Cir. J.
Knowlton, Dexter A. '25 '53 C.339 B.S. L.966 LL.B. Ret. Asso. Cir. J.
Koehler, George A. '20 '51 C&L.966 B.S., J.D. 844 W. American St.‡
Kroeger, Wilbur L., (BV) '14 '40 C.350 B.S.C.E. L.352 J.D.
208 West Stephenson Street
Krug, Lyle A., (BV) '47 '72 C&L.966 B.B.A., J.D. [Plager,K.&B.]
Laughlin, Shirl B., (CV) '29 '53 C.187 B.A. L.339 LL.B. P.O. Box 703
Madden, James G., (BV) '33 '60 C.162 B.A. L.477 LL.B. [Madden&S.]
Madden and Sisler, (BV) 218 W. Exchange St.
Mahoney, Francis X. '22 '48 C.93 A.B. L.597 J.D. [Ⓒ Mahoney&H.]
Mahoney, Timothy S., (BV) '67 '92 C.707 B.A. L.589 J.D. [Mahoney&H.]

Mahoney & Hauser, Ltd., (BV)
204 West Stephenson Street, P.O. Box 158, 61032
Telephone: 815-235-1515 Fax: 815-235-9657
Email: t.s.mahoney@prodigy.com
Richard J. Hauser, Jr.; Timothy S. Mahoney; James M. Hauser. Of Counsel: Francis X. Mahoney.
Civil Litigation, Personal Injury, Workers Compensation, Probate, Wills, Automobile Accidents, Wrongful Death, DUI, Juvenile Crimes, Divorce, Child Custody, Family and Real Estate Law, Criminal, Corporate.
See Professional Biographies, FREEPORT, ILLINOIS

Manus, Randall J., (CV) '48 '78 C.862 B.A. L.300 J.D. [Manus]
Manus Law Office, (CV) P.O. Box 864
McPherson, Heather '76 '01 C.72 B.A. L.436 J.D. [McPherson]
McPherson, Malcolm C., (BV) '45 '72 C.966 B.A. L.352 J.D. 1720 Hance Dr.
McPherson Law Offices 1720 Hance Dr.
Mitchell, John F. '52 '77 C.429 A.B. L.221 J.D. 224 W. Stephenson St.
Plager, Robert B., (AV) '40 '67 C.589 B.S. L.339 J.D. [Ⓐ Plager,K.&B.]
Plager, Krug & Bauer, Ltd., (AV) 10 North Galena Avenue, Suite 300
Prestwich, Howard H., (CV) '42 '68 C.611 B.A. L.966 J.D. 216 W. Stephenson St.
Shockey, David D., (BV) '56 '83 C&L.339 B.S., J.D. [Shockey&C.]
Shockey & Cox, (BV) 208 W. Stephenson Street, Suite 101
Sisler, William E., (BV) '43 '68 C.352 B.A. L.339 J.D. [Madden&S.]
Slattery, Robert K., (BV) '53 '81 C.339 B.A. L.365 J.D. 24 W Stephenson St.
Smith, Lawrence A., Jr. '36 '61 C&L.339 B.S., J.D. Ret. Cir. J.‡
Snow, Hunter, Whiton & Fishburn, Ltd., (BV) 8 East Stephenson Street (⊙Lena)
Thruman, Judd D. '73 '99 C.927 B.S. L.589 J.D. [Ⓐ Snow,H.W.&F.]
Ursin, Theresa L., (BV) '56 '82 C.966 B.A. L.589 J.D. Co. Assoc. Cir. J.
Vogt, John H., (BV) '50 '76 C.98 B.S. L.1003 J.D. P.O. 55
Weimer, A. R. '09 '33 L.436 J.D. 1712 W. Stephenson St.‡
Whiton, John B., (BV) '46 '74 C.473 B.A. L.145 J.D. [Snow,H.W.&F.] ⊙

FULTON, 3,881, *Whiteside Co.*

Holesinger, Russell J., (BV) '51 '76 C.114 B.A. L.339 J.D.
1405 14th Ave. (⊙Morrison)
Senneff, Thomas H., (BV) '50 '75 C.589 B.A. L.365 J.D. 408 11th St.

GALATIA, 983, *Saline Co.*

Barnes, Curtis R., (CV) '43 '84 C&L.801 B.A., J.D. 990 Johnston City Rd

GALENA, * 3,460, *Jo Daviess Co.*

Cox, John W., Jr., (BV) '47 '75 C.961 B.S. L.365 J.D. 612 Spring St.
Hammer, David L., (AVⓉ) '29 '56 C.293 B.A. L.352 J.D. [Hammer,S.&J.] ⊙
Hammer, Simon & Jensen, (AV) 303 N. Bench (⊙Dubuque, IA)
Hartz, Tracey W. '59 '84 C.339 B.A. L.326 J.D. P.O. Box 325
Jackman, Philip A., The Law Office of, (BV) '51 '76
C.429 B.A. L.425 J.D. 323 Spring St.
Jensen, Paul T., (CVⓉ) '50 '97 C.1106 B.A. L.352 J.D. [Ⓐ Hammer,S.&J.] ⊙
Jensen, Philip F., (BV) '59 '84 C.338 B.S. L.546 J.D. [Hammer,S.&J.] ⊙
Kelly, William A. '45 '71 C.812 B.A. L.209 J.D. Chf. Cir. J.
Knapp, Stacey '67 '03 C.352 B.A. L.362 J.D. P.O. Box 243
Mark, Julie B., (CV) '61 '89 C.338 B.S. L.365 J.D. 612 Spring St.
Nack, James J., (AV) '40 '64 C.602 B.A. L.477 J.D. [Nack,R.&N.]
Nack, Joseph E., (BV) '63 '89 C.812 B.S. L.190 J.D. [Nack,R.&N.]
Nack, Louis A., Jr., (BV) '35 '66 C.321 B.S. L.339 J.D. [Nack,R.&N.] ⊙
Nack, Thomas J. '65 '96 C.339 B.A. L.190 J.D. [Nack,R.&N.]

Nack, Richardson & Nack, P.C., The Law Offices of, (AV)
106 North Main Street, P.O. Box 336, 61036 ⊙
Telephone: 815-777-1218; 777-1219 Fax: 815-777-2609
Email: offices@nack.com URL: http://www.nack.com
Jos. M. Nack (1865-1939); Louis A. Nack (1901-1981); James W. Richardson (1925-1988); Louis A. Nack, Jr.; James J. Nack; Joseph E. Nack; Thomas J. Nack.
General Civil and Criminal Trial and Appellate Practice, Personal Injury, Corporate, Banking, Real Estate, Estate Planning and Probate, Family, Municipal. Creditor's Rights, Insurance Defense, DUI and Commercial Collections, Divorce, Custody, Adoption.
Elizabeth, Illinois Office: Elizabeth State Bank Building. Telephone: 815-858-3712. Fax: 815-858-2671.
See Professional Biographies, GALENA, ILLINOIS

Rose, Charles G. '58 '91 C.174 B.A. L.589 J.D. Asst. State Atty.
Roth, Robert R., (BV) '38 '63 C.177 B.A. L.352 LL.B. [Vincent,R.&T.]
Simon, Angela C., (AV) '49 '85 C.177 B.A. L.352 J.D. [Hammer,S.&J.] ⊙
Vincent, James B., (BV) '26 '53 C&L.352 B.S.C., LL.B. [Vincent,R.&T.] ⊙
Vincent, Roth & Toepfer, P.C., (BV) 122-1/2 N. Main St. (⊙Warren)
Ward, Kevin J., (BV) '65 '91 C&L.339 B.S., J.D. 612 Spring St.

GALESBURG, * 33,706, *Knox Co.*

Alcorn, Daniel S., (BV) '66 '91 C.338 B.A. L.221 J.D. [Stoerzbach M.]
Ball, Jack P., (BV) '54 '85 C.547 B.S. L.190 J.D. [J.P.Ball]
Ball, Jack P., P.C., (BV) 190 S. Kellogg St.
Barash, Barry M., (BV) '38 '63 C.188 B.A. L.145 J.D. [Barash&E.]

Barash & Everett, LLC, (AV)
256 S. Soangetaha Road Suite 108, 61401 ⊙
Telephone: 309-341-6010 Fax: 309-341-1945
URL: http://www.barashlaw.com
Members of Firm: Barry M. Barash; Reynolds M. Everett. Associates: Keith A. Luymes; Clinton A. Block; Grant R. Gulovsen; Thomas A. Hill; Maya P. Parekh.
Agricultural Law, Bankruptcy, Commercial Law, Probate, Real Estate, Workers Compensation, Computers and Internet, Corporate and Business, Estate Planning and Administration, Family Law and Child Custody, Personal Injury and Title Insurance Law.
Galva, Illinois Office: Yocum Bank Building, 110 N. Exchange Street, P.O. Box 165, 61434. Telephone: 309-932-2001. Fax: 309-932-3151.
Kewanee, Illinois Office: 211 W. 2nd Street, 61443. Telephone: 309-852-5555. Fax: 309-853-8135.
See Professional Biographies, GALESBURG, ILLINOIS

Barber, Richard E., (BV) '52 '79 C.339 B.S. L.862 J.D. [Hanlon&B.]
Blake, James David, (CV) '61 '98 C.504 B.A. L.365 J.D. [Blake]
Blake, John J., (BV) '23 '50 C.339 L.546 J.D. [Blake]
Blake Law Office, (BV) 303-5 Hill Arcade Building
Block, Clinton A. '59 '01 C.339 B.S. L.589 J.D. [Ⓐ Barash&E.] (⊙Kewanee)
Bulkeley, Harry C. '49 '74 C.846 B.B.A. L.146 J.D. Co. J.
Butts, C. William, Jr., (CV) '54 '79 C.336 B.S. L.733 J.D. Spec. Asst. Atty. Gen.
Conolly, Dawn A., (BV) '52 '78
C&L.801 B.A., J.D. Prairie St., Weinberg Arcade, Ste. 216
Everett, Reynolds M., (AV) '46 '73 C.339 B.S. L.424 J.D. [Barash&E.] (⊙Galva)
Graham, Mark M. '68 '01 C.388 B.A. L.352 J.D. Assist.State's Atty.
Gulovsen, Grant R. '68 '98 C.859 B.A. L.339 J.D. [Ⓐ Barash&E.]
Hanlon, John M., (BV) '51 '77 C.57 B.A. L.862 J.D. City Atty. [Hanlon&B.]
Hanlon, John W. '21 '49 C.339 A.B. L.477 LL.B. 1350 N. Academy St.‡
Hanlon & Barber, (BV) 250 East Main Street
Hattery, John J., (AV) '35 '61 C.350 B.A. L.339 J.D. [Hattery,S.&W.]
Hattery, Patricia A., (CV) '49 '98 C.388 B.A. L.339 J.D. [Ⓐ Hattery,S.&W.]
Hattery, Simpson & West, (AV) Suite 402 Hill Arcade (⊙Monmouth, Roseville)
Henning, William H. '24 '49 C.103 B.S. L.477 LL.B. 2314 N. Broad St.‡
Henson, Christopher, (BV) '68 '96
C.484 B.A. L.801 J.D. 1865 North Henderson Street, Suite 11B
Hill, Thomas A. '78 '03 C.747 B.A. L.494 J.D. [Ⓐ Barash&E.]
Johnson, Karl Arvid '59 '89 C.57 A.B. L.801 J.D. P.O. Box 1428
Kanthak, Christopher W., (CV) '50 '81 C.589 B.A. L.365 J.D. 161 S. Cherry, Ste. 102
Karlin, Jeremy S., (CV) '69 '94 C.823 B.A. L.424 J.D. [Stoerzbach M.]
Kimbell, Raymond G., III, (BV) '42 '67 C.597 B.A. L.276 J.D. States Atty.
King, Robert E. '67 '93 C.340 B.A. L.146 J.D. 311 E. Main St.
Lawson-Sanchez, Sherry Ruth '67 '94 C.338 B.A. L.589 J.D. [Lawson-Sanchez]
Lawson-Sanchez Law Office 64 S. Prairie St., Ste. 219
Lindstrom, Robert, (BV) '48 '75 C.162 B.A. L.221 J.D. [Mustain L.&H.]
Luymes, Keith A., (BV) '49 '74 C.350 B.S. L.339 J.D. [Ⓐ Barash&E.] (⊙Galva)
Mangieri, Paul L., (CV) '59 '84 C.162 B.A. L.734 J.D. Knox Co. State's Atty.
Mathers, Stephen C. '46 '74 C.597 B.A. L.339 J.D. Cir. J.
McCrery, David N., III '57 '93 C.339 B.S. L.801 J.D. 153 E. Main St.
McDonald, David R., (BV) '36 '63 C.378 B.A. L.597 J.D. Weinberg Arcade, Ste. 216
McLaughlin, Robert E., (BV) '15 '40 C.388 A.B. L.339 LL.B. Ste. 402 Hill Arcade
Mergener, Tracey L., (CV) '60 '86
C.966 B.A. L.589 J.D. West Central Ill. Legal Assistance
Morrison, Dwayne I., (AV) '47 '73 C&L.339 B.S., J.D. [Stoerzbach M.]
Mustain, Douglas D., (AV) '45 '74 C.339 B.S. L.352 J.D. [Mustain L.&H.]

Mustain Lindstrom & Henson, (AV)
1865 North Henderson Street, Suite 11B, 61401
Telephone: 309-344-5252 Facsimile: 309-344-3939
Members of Firm: Douglas D. Mustain; Robert Lindstrom; Ronald Henson (1942-2004).
General Civil Practice in State and Federal Courts, Trials and Appeals, Personal Injury, Workers Compensation, Real Estate, Insurance, Corporation, Commercial Law, Bankruptcy and Probate Law.
References: The Farmers and Mechanics Bank; Wells Fargo Bank, N.A.; First Bank, Farmers State Bank of Western Illinois; McGladrey and Pullen, LLP.
See Professional Biographies, GALESBURG, ILLINOIS

Olson, Barney, II, (Ltd., A Prof. Service Corp.), (CV) '44 '70
C.473 B.S. L.339 J.D. 208 Weinberg Arcade
Parekh, Maya P. '78 '04 C.424 B.A. L.494 J.D. [Ⓐ Barash&E.]
Pepmeyer, John T., (BV) '51 '76 C.340 B.A. L.365 J.D. [Pepmeyer&P.]
Pepmeyer, Thomas L., (CV) '56 '81 C.340 B.S. L.365 J.D. [Pepmeyer&P.]
Pepmeyer & Pepmeyer, P.C., (BV) 41 E. Simmons St.

Prusak, Winne & Gorman, Ltd.
(See Peoria)

Rehn, John R., (BV) '67 '95 C.339 B.S. L.602 J.D.
311 E. Main Street, Suite 412, 61401-4867
Telephone: 309-342-4200 Fax: 309-341-2462
URL: http://www.johnrehn.com
Criminal Law, Personal Injury and Insurance Litigation.
See Professional Biographies, GALESBURG, ILLINOIS

Richardson, William K. '13 '37 C.388 A.B. L.477 LL.B. Ret. Cir. J.‡
Robertson, John W., (AV) '46 '75 C.694 A.B. L.339 J.D. [Stoerzbach M.]
Schlake, Jonathon T., (CV) '55 '82 C.589 B.S. L.365 J.D. Asst. State's Atty.
Schumann, Roxy M., (CV) '43 '78 C.388 L.107 J.D. P.O. Box 671
Simpson, Carol Masden, (BV) '51 '79 C.57 B.A. L.1035 J.D. [Hattery,S.&W.]
Simpson, S. David, (AV) '45 '75 C.927 B.A. L.900 J.D. 250 East Main Street
Skinner, Jim, Law Office of, (CV) '68 '95 C.98 B.S. L.150 J.D. 20 W. Main St.
Smallwood, Richard L. '46 '72 C&L.339 B.S., J.D. Tr. Offr., Norwest Bk.

Stansell, Whitman & Baber
(See Monmouth)

Statham, H. Wayne, (BV) '60 '86 C.338 B.S. L.339 J.D. [Ⓐ Stoerzbach M.]
Stoerzbach, Daniel B., (BV) '58 '83 C.340 B.S. L.339 J.D. [Stoerzbach M.]
Stoerzbach, Robert C., (AV) '23 '49 C&L.339 B.S., J.D. [Stoerzbach M.]

Stoerzbach Morrison P.C., (AV)
139 South Cherry Street, P.O. Box 1328, 61402-1328
Telephone: 309-341-6000 Telecopier: 309-343-7500
URL: http://www.galesburglaw.com
Robert C. Stoerzbach; Dwayne I. Morrison; Daniel B. Stoerzbach; John W. Robertson; Pamela S. Wilcox; Daniel S. Alcorn; Jeremy S. Karlin;—H. Wayne Statham.
General Trial and Appellate Practice in State and Federal Courts. Corporation, Estate Planning, Estate Administration, Real Estate, Bankruptcy, Family Law, Personal Injury, Workers Compensation, Insurance Law.
Representative Clients: Auto-Owners Insurance Co.; City of Knoxville, Illinois; Columbia Insurance Co.; Knox College; Marquette Bank; Community School District No. 208; Grinnell Mutual Insurance Co.; Metropolitan Property & Casualty Co.; Pekin Farmers Insurance Co.; State Farm Ins. Cos.
See Professional Biographies, GALESBURG, ILLINOIS

Stoffel, Donald L. '32 '60 C.388 A.B. L.477 LL.B. Asso. Cir. J.
Watts, Steven R., (CV) '49 '74 C.340 B.A. L.352 J.D. P.O. Box 221
West, Thomas G., (BV) '40 '66 C.597 B.B.A. L.145 J.D. [Hattery,S.&W.]
Westjohn, Karla '62 '91 C.339 B.A. L.801 J.D. Asst. State's Atty.
Wilcox, Pamela S., (BV) '54 '89 C.338 B.A. L.802 J.D. [Stoerzbach M.]
Williamson, Roger L., (BV) '39 '64 C.597 B.S. L.339 J.D. [Hattery,S.&W.]

GALVA, 2,742, *Henry Co.*

Barash & Everett, (AV) 110 N. Exchange Street (⊙Galesburg, Kewanee)
Everett, Reynolds M., (AV) '46 '73 C.339 B.S. L.424 J.D. [Barash&E.] (⊙Galesburg)
Luymes, Keith A., (BV) '49 '74 C.350 B.S. L.339 J.D. [Ⓐ Barash&E.] (⊙Galesburg)
Massie, Michael E., (BV) '47 '72 C&L.339 A.B., J.D. 115 N.W. 3rd Ave.

GENESEO, 6,480, *Henry Co.*

Ames-Cutkomp, Stephanie, Law Office of '70 '97 C.589 B.A. L.1187 J.D. 208 S. State St.
Bean, John W., (BV) '51 '76 C.57 B.A. L.879 J.D. [Nash N.B.&F.]
Brown, Mabel W., (AV) '16 '41 C.604 B.A. L.145 J.D. [Brown&R.]

Brown and Ray, (AV)
115 North State Street, P.O. Box 238, 61254-1345
Telephone: 309-944-5115 Fax: 309-944-5261
Email: bandr@netexpress.net
Members of Firm: Harry E. Brown (1872-1944); Mabel W. Brown; Roger Ray.
General Civil Practice. Real Estate, Estate Planning and Probate, Drainage and Levee, Family and Taxation Law, Domestic Relations, Divorce, Wills and Trusts.
References: Central Trust & Savings Bank, Geneseo, Illinois; Farmers National Bank of Prophetstown, Geneseo Banking Center.
See Professional Biographies, GENESEO, ILLINOIS

Farber, John W., (BV) '49 '74 C.927 B.A. L.221 J.D. [Farber]
Farber Law Office, (BV) P.O. Box 257
Ford, Curtis J., (BV) '67 '93 C.350 B.B.A. L.589 J.D. [Nash N.B.&F.]
Jones, Theresa L., (BV) '63 '89 C.226 B.A. L.339 J.D. 208 South State St.
Nash, James H., (BV) '48 '73 C.57 B.A. L.879 J.D. [Nash N.B.&F.]
Nash, Robert N., (BV) '50 '76 C&L.339 B.S., J.D. [Nash N.B.&F.]

Nash Nash Bean & Ford, LLP, (BV)
445 U.S. Highway 6 East, P.O. Box 63, 61254-0063
Telephone: 309-944-2188 Fax: 309-944-3960
Email: info@nashbeanford.com URL: http://www.nashbeanford.com
Members of Firm: James H. Nash; Robert N. Nash; John W. Bean; Curtis J. Ford.
Trusts and Estates, Workers Compensation, Real Estate, Probate, Wills, Banking Law, Business Law, Corporate Law, Elder Law, Federal/State Civil Practice, Municipal Law, Personal Injury, Public School Law and Social Security.
References: Geneseo Community School District #228; Geneseo Fire Protection District; Blackhawk State Bank; Central Bank Illinois.

Palmgren, Nadine R., (CV) '54 '93 C.589 B.S. L.221 J.D. [Stone&P.]
Ray, Roger, (BV) '48 '74 C.299 B.A. L.365 J.D. [Brown&R.]
Stone, Edward J., (AV) '16 '42 C.57 B.A. L.339 J.D. 121 W. Frank St.‡
Stone, Richard A., (BV) '44 '69 C.399 B.A. L.597 J.D. [Stone&P.]
Stone & Palmgren, (BV) 211 S. State St.

GENEVA, * 19,515, *Kane Co.*

Allen, Ami F. '14 '38 C&L.145 B.A., J.D. Chmn. & Pres., A.L. Allen & Sons, Realtors

Ariano, Hardy, Nyuli, Johnson, Richmond & Goettel, P.C., (AV)
22 S. 4th Street, Suite B,, 60134 ⊙
Telephone: 847-695-2400
Email: aah@attorneys-illinois.com URL: http://www.attorneys-illinois.com
Lisa M. Nyuli; Karrsten Goettel.
General Civil and Criminal Practice in all Courts. Banking, Probate, Real Estate, Corporation, Federal Taxation, Transactional, Employment, Family, Personal Injury, Collections, Creditor Bankruptcy, Foreclosures, Landlord and Tenant Law, Workers Compensation Law and Mediation.
Huntley, Illinois Office: 13300 Route 47, P.O. Box 487, 60142. Telephone: 847-669-5020.
Elgin, Illinois: 474 Summit Street. Telephone: 847-695-2400. Telecopy: 847-695-8397.
See Professional Biographies, GENEVA, ILLINOIS

Bell, Theodore B. '66 '93 C.477 B.A. L.215 J.D. [Kowalczyk&B.]
Black, Gerald J. '46 '72 C.424 B.A. L.597 J.D. Pres., ClientFocus, Inc.
Brawka, Judith M. '54 '78 C.209 B.A. L.597 J.D. Cir. J.

Brooks, Adams and Tarulis
(See Naperville)

Brown, Craig D. '65 '92 C.966 B.A. L.20 J.D. [Ⓐ Foote,M.M.&F.]
Brown, Daniel E. '64 '96 C.578 B.A. L.589 J.D. [Donahue,S.&B.] ⊙

Brown, Bruce A., Law Office of
(See Aurora)

Brundage, Stephen A.
(See Wheaton)

Butts, Edward A. '43 '67 C&L.339 B.A., J.D. 228 N. 2nd St.
Carter, Cynthia Lee '56 '95 C.578 B.A. L.589 J.D. 219 South Third Street
Cesario, John R. '58 '83 C.339 B.A. L.861 J.D. Asst. State's Atty.
Chippas, Stephen J. '68 '97 C.339 B.S.M.E. L.146 J.D. CRL Group, LLC
Christophersen, C. Eric '45 '70 C.188 B.A. L.347 J.D. (adm. in OH; not adm. in IL) 621 West Lane
Clancy, Gates W., (AV) '09 '38 C.679 B.S. L.365 J.D. 428 W. State St.‡
Clancy, Peter F. '58 '84 C.309 A.B. L.424 J.D. [Jones L.G.&C.]
Colwell, Michael J. '47 '72 C.177 B.A. L.209 J.D. 100 S. 3rd St.
Conarty, Paul F., (Ltd.) '42 '68 C.424 A.B. L.1065 J.D. 419 S. 2nd Street
Cooper, Richard L., (BV) '10 '38 C.801 B.Ed. L.276 J.D. 117 S. 2nd St.
Cooper, Stephen M., (AV) '44 '71 C.996 B.A. L.339 J.D. [Cooper&S.]
Cooper & Storm, (AV) 117 S. Second St.
Cutler, David P. '54 '79 C&L.880 B.A., J.D. [McGowan&H.] ⊙
Dahl, Jay L., (CV) '53 '79 C.339 B.A. L.365 J.D. [J.L.Dahl]
Dahl, Jay L., Ltd., (CV) P.O. Box 187
Dillon, Thomas W., (BV) '64 '91 C&L.589 B.A., J.D. [Konicek&D.]
Dixon, Patrick J. '41 '66 C&L.436 B.A., J.D. Cir. J.
Dolak, Ronald D., (BV) '69 '95 C.477 B.G.S. L.209 J.D. 410 E. State St.
Donahue, John F., (AV) '44 '71 C&L.424 B.S., J.D. [Donahue,S.&B.] ⊙

Donahue, Sowa and Brown, (AV)
216 Campbell Street, 60134 ⊙
Telephone: 630-232-1780 Fax: 630-232-9671
Email: gsowa@dsbb-law.com URL: http://www.lawyers.com/dsbblaw
John F. Donahue; Glenn M. Sowa; Daniel E. Brown.
Criminal Defense, DUI, Traffic, Drivers License Reinstatement, Appellate Law, Juvenile Law.
Lisle Office: 3030 Warrenville Road, Suite 215, 60532. Telephone: 630-505-5200. Fax: 630-505-4250.
See Professional Biographies, GENEVA, ILLINOIS

Doyle, James '50 '76 C.209 B.A. L.365 J.D. Assoc. Cir. J.

Drendel & Drendel, A Professional Corporation
(See Batavia)

Dunn, Melvin E. '33 '71 C.1016 L.146 J.D. Cir. J.
Edler, Jacqueline M., (CV) '64 '92 C.145 A.B. L.589 J.D. Old Second Nat. Bk.
Edmondson, Wiley W. '48 '75 C.238 B.A. L.365 J.D. Assoc. Cir. J.
Eichmeier, Roger W. '32 '57 C.210 B.A. L.597 J.D. Assoc. Cir. J.
Eilert, Benn E. G., (BV) '31 '58 C.705 A.B. L.976 LL.B. 310 Campbell St.
Elders, Vincent J., (BV) '67 '93 C&L.589 B.S., J.D. [Smith,L.S.&E.]
Fabian, Donald J. '47 '75 C.346 B.S. L.339 J.D. Assoc. Cir. J.
Fleming, Robert A. '52 '79 C.589 B.S. L.1151 J.D. 825 Winners Cup Ct.

Fleming, Michael W., Attorney at Law
(See Elmhurst)

Flowers, Peter J. '67 '92 C.424 B.B.A. L.209 J.D. [Foote,M.M.&F.]
Foote, Robert M., (AV) '54 '80 C.309 B.A. L.966 J.D. [Foote,M.M.&F.]
Foote, Meyers, Mielke & Flowers, L.L.C., (AV) 416 South Second Street
Gerbrecht, Arno E., (BV) '46 '73 1804 Gray St.
Goettel, Karrsten '71 '97 C.966 B.S. L.424 J.D. [Ariano,H.N.J.R.&G.] (⊙Elgin)
Gooding, R. Gary, (BV) '44 '72 C.966 B.S. L.365 J.D. [R.G.Gooding]
Gooding, R. Gary, Ltd., (BV) 1250 Executive Pl.
Graham, Christopher J. '58 '83 C.424 B.B.A. L.477 J.D. [Jones L.G.&C.]
Gubbins, Patricia Jane '46 '77 L.146 J.D. 325 West Ln.‡
Hallahan, James C. '11 '37 C&L.597 B.A., J.D. 208 S. River Ln.‡
Haythorne, Robert E., (AV) '15 '38 C&L.145 A.B., J.D. 207 S. 5th St.‡
Hess, Rachel J., Law Offices of, (CV) '69 '94 C.338 B.S. L.356 J.D. 1795 West State Street, Suite B
Hulce, Mary Ellen, (BV) '50 '75 C.597 B.A. L.602 LL.B. P.O. Box 769
Hull, Edwin J., III, (BV) '53 '79 C.893 B.A. L.880 J.D. [McGowan&H.] ⊙
Hurley, William F. '66 '91 C.339 B.A. L.209 J.D. 301 S. Cambridge Dr.
Jaeger, J. Patrick '53 '84 C.742 B.A. L.209 J.D. Spec. Asst. State's Atty.
Jensen, Pamela Kirkland '42 '79 C.879 B.A. L.589 J.D. Cir. J.
Jones, W. Clyde, III, (AV) '37 '67 C.976 B.A. L.597 J.D. [Jones L.G.&C.]

Jones Lemon Graham & Clancy LLP, (AV)
223 East State Street, 60134
Telephone: 630-208-0805 Fax: 630-208-4651
URL: http://www.joneslemon.com
W. Clyde Jones, III; Steven J. Lemon; Christopher J. Graham; Peter F. Clancy; Robert Paul Norman.
Special Counsel: Matthew J. Nielsen. Associate: Joseph P. Kelly.
Corporate Law, Litigation, Trusts and Estates, Environmental Law, Probate, Employment Law, Professional Liability, Insurance, Excess and Reinsurance, HealthCare, Medical Malpractice, Nursing Home Liability, Products Liability.
See Professional Biographies, GENEVA, ILLINOIS

Keane, Patrick J. '62 '93 C.770 B.S.C. L.1000 J.D. [Ⓐ Foote,M.M.&F.]
Kelly, Joseph P. '79 '04 C.339 B.S. L.146 J.D. [Ⓐ Jones L.G.&C.]
Klein, Kurt P. '43 '72 C.339 B.S. L.209 J.D. Co. J.
Konicek, Daniel F., (BV) '64 '90 C.679 B.A. L.146 J.D. [Konicek&D.]
Konicek & Dillon, P.C., (BV) 21 W. State Street
Kowalczyk, Ronald B. '71 '01 C.362 B.A. L.209 J.D. [Kowalczyk&B.] ⊙
Kowalczyk & Bell, P.C. 215 Campbell Street (⊙Chicago)
Krill, Karen E. '65 '89 C.914 B.A. L.802 J.D. [Krill&K.]
Krill, Scott Douglas '62 '89 C.608 B.S. L.597 J.D. [Krill&K.]
Krill & Krill 18 South Fifth Street
Landmeier, Allen L., (AV) '42 '67 C&L.879 B.S.E.E., J.D. [Smith,L.S.&E.]
LeFeber, Alfred C. '19 '50 C&L.608 B.A., J.D. (adm. in OH; not adm. in IL) 921 Hawthorne La.‡
Lemon, Steven J., (BV) '61 '90 C.1144 B.A. L.339 J.D. [Jones L.G.&C.]
Lewis, Casandra '61 '91 C.1016 B.A. L.365 J.D. Asst. State's Atty.
Lonergan, Susan M. '53 '83 C&L.801 B.S., J.D. P.O. Box 712
Lundberg, Paula J. '54 '79 C.1106 B.A. L.424 J.D. 115 Crissey Ave.
Malato, Thomas E. '46 '75 C.591 B.S. L.146 J.D. 314 Chalmers St.
Mann, Pamuella F. '40 '67 C.98 B.S. L.339 J.D. V.P. & Tr. Offr., Old 2nd Natl. Bk. of Aurora
McGowan, J. Geoffrey '55 '86 C.378 B.A. L.365 J.D. [McGowan&H.] ⊙
McGowan and Hull, (BV) 230 E. State Street (⊙Chicago)
McLaughlin, Walter V., Jr. '38 '66 C&L.309 A.B., J.D. 1914 Pepper Valley Dr.
Menozzi, Greg A. '62 '88 C.719 B.A. L.365 J.D. 1950 S. Batavia Ave.
Meyers, Ted August, (BV) '60 '86 C.602 B.A. L.801 J.D. [Foote,M.M.&F.]
Mielke, Craig S., (AV) '55 '80 C&L.339 B.S., J.D. [Foote,M.M.&F.]
Mitchell, Jeffrey T. '65 '98 C.238 B.A. L.209 J.D. [Ⓐ Konicek&D.]
Moline, Gary L. '52 '77 C.927 B.A. L.734 J.D. State Bank of Geneva

Mulherin, Rehfeldt & Varchetto, P.C.
(See Wheaton)

Mulligan-Ferry, Melita '54 '91 C.741 B.A. L.608 J.D. Arbitration Admr., Admin. Off. of Ill. Cts.
Myers, Fred T., (BV) '60 '85 C.209 B.A. L.597 J.D. 17 N 6th St.
Nelson, David J., (BV) '59 '84 C.578 B.A. L.339 J.D. Corp. Coun., Chicago Title Insurance Co.
Nielsen, Matthew J. '67 '94 C.589 B.S. L.801 J.D. [Ⓒ Jones L.G.&C.]
Niermann, Michele '66 '91 C.57 A.B. L.339 J.D. 100 S. Third St., 4th Fl.
Noble, John S., (BV) '40 '81 C.59 B.A. L.365 J.D. [Weiler&N.]
Norman, Robert Paul '53 '89 C.927 B.A. L.365 J.D. [Jones L.G.&C.]
Nottolini, Gene L. '44 '68 C&L.734 J.D. Cir. J.
Nyuli, Lisa M., (BV) '64 '89 C.339 B.S. L.589 J.D. [Ariano,H.N.J.R.&G.] (⊙Elgin)
O'Brien, Michael F. '37 '63 C.597 B.A. L.365 J.D. Cir. J.
O'Connell, Barbara J. H. '21 '50 C.383 L.365 LL.B. 113 S. Third St.‡
O'Connell, Daniel F., (BV) '55 '82 C.128 B.A. L.339 J.D. 13 South 7th Street

O'Hagan, Smith & Amundsen
(See St. Charles)

Ohlmann, Brent E., P.C., Law Office of
(See Naperville)

O'Neil, Timothy D., (CV) '56 '85 C.746 B.A. L.589 J.D. Assoc. J. [Ⓐ Foote,M.M.&F.]
Parkhurst, William J., (BV) '60 '87 C.27 B.A. L.879 J.D. 115 Campbell St.
Parsons, Daniel G., (BV) '51 '92 C.1077 B.A. L.426 J.D. 314 Hamilton
Perington, Lamont Lee, (BV) '42 '72 C.234 B.S. L.146 J.D. 301 Hamilton St.
Petersen, John L. '36 '61 C.339 A.B. L.209 LL.B. Assoc. Cir. J.
Pinkepank, William R. '54 '86 C&L.260 B.S., J.D. 1870 Eldorado Drive
Piscopo, Philip J. '71 '97 C.339 B.A. L.910 J.D. P.O. Box 388
Quetsch, James F. '33 '59 C.602 B.A. L.146 J.D. Cir. J.
Radovich, Charles A., (AV) '46 '74 C.399 B.A. L.339 J.D. City Atty. [Radovich&R.]
Radovich, Joseph, (AV) '21 '43 L.209 LL.B. [Radovich&R.]
Radovich & Radovich, (AV) 312 W. State Street

Rinella and Rinella, Ltd.
(See Chicago)

Ruark, Eugene H., (AV) '28 '56 C.976 B.S. L.273 LL.B. 230 E. State St.
Rudolph, Carl Wm. '34 '58 C.473 A.B. L.424 J.D. 1399 E. State St.
Rusin, John B. '12 '51 C.145 B.A. L.146 1520 Kaneville Rd.‡
Safanda, Carl F., (BV) '42 '67 C.597 B.A. L.339 J.D. [Safanda]
Safanda, Roy A., (AV) '39 '64 C.309 A.B. L.477 J.D. [Safanda]
Safanda Law Firm, (AV) 111 East Side Drive
Schaerli, John A. '41 '71 C.763 B.S. L.209 J.D. Corporate Counsel, Miner Enterprises Inc
Scherschel, Mary M. '54 '83 C.424 B.A. L.146 J.D. 2657 Cedar Ave.
Schmitt, John L. '33 '75 C.228 B.S.M.E. L.365 J.D. P.O. Box 656 (Pat.)
Schoen, Linda Lee '47 '96 C.1236 B.A. L.862 J.D. P.O. Box 430
Schroeder, John L., (BV) '42 '75 C&L.209 B.S.C., J.D. 1250 Executive Pl., Ste. 201
Sheaffer, John R., II '54 '85 C.339 B.A. L.146 J.D. [Sheaffer&S.]
Sheaffer, Mark D. '71 '99 C.57 B.A. L.146 J.D. [Sheaffer&S.]

Sheaffer & Sheaffer .... 337 Steven Street
Sheehan, Sharon B. .... '48 '97 C&L.589 B.G.S., J.D. [Sheehan]
Sheehan Law Office .... 13 S. 7th St.
Shivers, Susan D., Law Office of, (BV) .... '58 '86 C.473 B.A. L.365 J.D. 823 W. State St.
Skaar, James D., (AV) .... '54 '81 C.961 B.S. L.365 J.D. [Smith,L.S.&E.]
Skelton, Richard D. .... '52 '80 C.429 B.A. L.546 J.D. 115 Campbell St.
Smith, Howard E., Jr., (AV) .... '25 '51 C.966 B.S. L.309 LL.B. [⊠ Smith,L.S.&E.]
Smith, Landmeier, Skaar & Elders, P.C., (AV) .... 15 North Second Street
Sowa, Glenn M., (BV) .... '48 '83 C&L.589 B.S.Ed., J.D. [Donahue,S.&B.] ⊙
Spence, Robert B., (BV) .... '55 '80 C.827 B.S. L.365 J.D. Asst. States Atty.
Storm, Peter M., (BV) .... '56 '85 C.750 B.A. L.365 J.D. [Cooper&S.]

Swanson, Martin & Bell
(See Chicago)

Tabor, James A. .... '67 '95 C.589 B.S. L.424 J.D. 115 Campbell St., Ste. 1
Tatnall, Susan B., (BV) ...... '40 '80 C.703 B.A. L.383 J.D. 115 Campbell Street, Suite 1
Tegeler, Donald Maurice, Jr. .... '63 '90 C.393 B.A. L.146 J.D. [D.M.Tegeler,Jr.]
Tegeler, Donald M., Jr., P.C., Law Office of .... 204 W. State Street
Tyler, Lloyd J., (AV) .... '24 '51 C.72 B.A. L.477 J.D. 701 Fargo Blvd.‡
Van Der Snick, J. Brick, (BV) .... '— '80 C.123 B.A. L.365 J.D. [Van Der S.]

Van Der Snick Law Firm, Ltd., (BV)
1795 West State Street, Suite B, 60134
Telephone: 630-845-8200 Fax: 630-845-1060 URL: http://www.vandersnicklaw.com
Email: bvandersnick@vandersnicklaw.com URL: http://www.lawyers.com/vandersnicklaw
J. Brick Van Der Snick.
Family Law, DUI and Traffic Law. Trials and Appeals. Criminal and Civil Trials. Divorce, Child Custody, Child Support.

See Professional Biographies, GENEVA, ILLINOIS

Violante, Lynn M. .... '64 '91 C.339 B.A. L.801 J.D. Jud. Clk., Co. J.
Warlick, Douglas B. .... '56 '81 C.393 B.A. L.146 J.D. [D.B.Warlick&Assoc.]
Warlick, Douglas B., & Associates, P.A. .... 319 1/2 W. State St., Apt. D
Wechter, Lawrence D., (BV) .... '53 '78 C.477 B.A. L.352 J.D. 1770 S. Randall Road
Weiland, Richard F., (BV) .... '45 '70 C.750 B.A. L.424 J.D. [R.F.Weiland]
Weiland, Richard F., PC, Law Office of, (BV) .... 216 Campbell St.
Weiler, Rory T., (BV) .... '53 '79 C.589 B.S. L.365 J.D. [Weiler&N.]
Weiler & Noble, P.C., (BV) .... 425 Williamsburg Avenue
Winter, Linda R. .... '54 '87 C.313 B.A. L.146 J.D. 522 South St.
Zurek, Agnes H. .... '77 '02 C&L.424 B.A., J.D. [⊠ Konicek&D.]

GENOA, 4,169, *DeKalb Co.*

Becker, Robert C., Jr., (BV) .... '46 '75 C&L.339 B.S., J.D. 213 W. Main St.
O'Grady, James D., (BV) .... '36 '61 C.602 B.A. L.879 LL.B. [O'Grady]
O'Grady Law Office, (BV) .... 30700 Carolwood Drive

Pollock, Meyers, Eickstead & Pulak, Ltd.
(See Marengo)

GEORGETOWN, 3,678, *Vermilion Co.*

Stokes, Gary Joe, (BV) .... '57 '83 C.193 B.A. L.801 J.D. [G.J.Stokes]
Stokes, Gary J., Law Offices of, (BV) .... 5022 Olivet Rd.

GIBSON CITY, 3,396, *Ford Co.*

Benz, Arthur R. .... '18 '49 C&L.339 B.S., J.D. 905 N. Bell‡
Dueringer, William J., (BV) .... '46 '72 C.338 B.S. L.339 J.D. 110 E. Nineth St.
Eckhardt, Terry E., (BV) .... '46 '77 C.338 B.S. L.801 J.D. [⊠ Eckhardt&L.]
Eckhardt & Lee, (CV) .... 308 N. Sangaman
Lee, Ellen Moore, (CV) .... '55 '81 C.145 B.A. L.209 J.D. [Eckhardt&L.]
Summers, Philip A. .... '41 '69 C.801 B.S. L.365 J.D. 106 East 8th St.

GILLESPIE, 3,412, *Macoupin Co.*

Grandone, William J., (CV) .... '49 '76 C&L.734 B.A., J.D. 114 S. Macoupin
Katich, William M., (CV) .... '62 '92 C&L.910 A.B., J.D. 14620 Rte. 138
McGrady, Denis A., (BV) .... '21 '46 C&L.339 B.S., J.D. 104 Chestnut St.
McGrady, Denis A., Jr., (BV) .... '45 '70 C&L.339 B.S., J.D. 104 E. Chestnut St.
Polo, Kevin A. .... '68 '95 C.339 B.A. L.801 J.D. 207 N. Macoupin St.

GLEN CARBON, 10,425, *Madison Co.*

Andrew, Diane Maxine, (BV) .... '59 '84 C.861 B.S. L.910 J.D. [Baron&B.]
Baron & Budd, A Professional Corporation, (BV)
7-A Ginger Creek Village (⊙Baton Rouge, LA; Cleve., Monroe, OH; Dallas, TX)
Beatty, William S., (AV) .... '51 '76 C.502 B.A. L.734 J.D. [Peel B.M.&F.]
Calvo, Larry A., (BV) .... '48 '75 C.734 B.S. L.365 J.D. 12 Pembrooke Court
Douglas, Charles R., Action Law Offices of '50 '76
C.339 B.S. L.734 J.D. Butternut Lane, Suite 2
Foster, Ronald J., Jr. .... '70 '97 C.339 B.A. L.365 J.D. [Peel B.M.&F.]
Francis, Terryl W. .... '29 '58 C.378 A.B. L.910 J.D. 23 Foreman Dr.
Haller, James J. .... '66 '93 C.118 B.A. L.910 J.D. [Mueller&H.] ⊙
Maag, Gordon E. .... '51 '79 C.734 B.A. L.500 J.D. Appl. Ct. Jus.
Motil, Ronald S., (BV) .... '56 '83 C.801 B.S. L.734 J.D. [Peel B.M.&F.]
Mueller, William A., (BV) .... '59 '84 C.234 B.A. L.734 J.D. [Mueller&H.] ⊙
Mueller & Haller, LLC, Law Offices of, (BV)
5 Glen-Ed Professional Park (⊙Belleville)
Peel Beatty Motil & Foster, (AV) .... P.O. Box 730
Steele, Randall P. .... '63 '88 C.57 B.A. L.734 J.D. 200 W. Main

GLENCOE, 8,762, *Cook Co.*

Angst, Candace S. .... '53 '79 C.1236 B.A. L.146 J.D. 211 Maple Hill Rd.
Baer, Joseph Winslow, (AV) .... '17 '40 C&L.145 B.A., J.D. 1109 Old Elm Lane‡
Basile, William B. .... '11 '33 C&L.145 Ph.B., J.D. 148 Glencoe Rd.
Bell, Albert R. .... '11 '35 C&L.597 B.S., J.D. 1223 Fairfield Rd.‡
Besant, Wilson J. .... '27 '55 C.339 B.S. L.209 J.D. 635 County Ln.‡
Brody, Stanton .... '26 '49 C.339 L.209 LL.B. 812 Strawberry Hill‡
Carragher, Mary A. .... '60 '85 C.424 B.A. L.145 J.D. 115 Franklin Dr.
Chapman, Marvin S., (AV) .... '21 '48 C.352 B.A. L.976 LL.B. 190 Linden Ave.‡
Cohen, Christopher B., (AV) .... '42 '68 C&L.477 B.A., J.D. [Cohen]
Cohen Law Firm, (AV) .... 444 Greenleaf
De Frank, Camille, Law Offices of .... '50 '75 L.597 J.D. 600 Longwood Avenue
Elrad, Becky M. .... '67 '92 C.659 B.S. L.424 J.D. 235 Dennis Lane‡
Esser, Jane Gale .... '58 '83 C.813 B.A. L.597 J.D. 484 Monroe St.‡
Fisher, Paul R. .... '37 '65 C.424 B.S. L.365 LL.B. 795 Oak Dr.
Friedman, James J. .... '35 '60 C&L.339 A.B., LL.B. [J.J.Friedman] ‡
Friedman, James J., Law Office of, P.C. .... P.O. Box 286
Goldschmidt, Jill H. .... '61 '85 C.597 B.A. L.273 J.D. 736 Sycamore Lane‡
Greenbaum, Rachel K. .... '38 '62 C&L.912 A.B., J.D. 730 Bluff St.‡
Guenther, Nancy W. .... '61 '97 C.589 B.A. L.209 J.D. 470 Drexel Ave.
Harper, Jeanne Schick .... '49 '74 C&L.966 B.A., J.D. 861 Greenwood Ave.
Jaman, Burton B. .... '13 '35 L.144 LL.B. 690 Strawberry Hill
Kalik-Miller, Shari J. .... '67 '92 C.273 B.A. L.365 J.D. 324 Lincoln Avenue
Kelly, Bruce W. .... '51 '83 C.645 B.S.M.B.A. L.209 J.D. 172 Enclid Ave.
Kotler, Nancy .... '36 '77 C.145 B.A. L.424 J.D. 301 Keystone Ct.
Lederer, Paul R. .... '39 '64 C.339 B.A. L.597 J.D. 717 Redwood Lane
Lerman, Janet L., Law Office of .... '57 '82 C.846 B.A. L.809 J.D. 244 Hazel Ave.
Lieberman, Kalman S. .... '19 '46 C&L.597 B.S.L., LL.B. 480 Westly Rd.
McErlean, Carol A. .... '59 '84 C.812 B.S. L.734 J.D. 145 Montgomery St.
Morton, Herbert, (AV) .... '16 '38 C&L.597 B.S., J.D. 982 Eastwood Rd.‡
Nelson, Peggy A. .... '54 '81 C.103 A.B. L.569 J.D. 679 Bluff St.
Nesselson, Debra Helene .... '54 '78 C.477 B.A. L.597 J.D. 1065 Skokie Ridge Dr.
Newberger, Nancy A. .... '55 '81 C.659 B.A. L.597 J.D. 538 Monroe Ave.‡
Nyeste, James T. .... '55 '79 C.475 B.S. L.145 J.D. 258 Maple Hill Road
Paseltiner, Ellen Kettler '50 '75 C.477 B.A. L.273 J.D.
(adm. in MD; not adm. in IL) 212 Maple Hill Rd.‡
Perelman, Jeffrey S. .... '51 '78 C.339 B.A. L.146 J.D. 805 Grove St.
Ross, Steven H. .... '54 '79 C.339 B.A. L.597 J.D. 492 South Ave.
Rubens, Arnold E. .... '57 '83 C.861 B.A. L.424 J.D. Stone Container Corp.
Schram, Leonard, (AV) .... '09 '32 C.966 B.A. L.145 J.D. 11 Lakewood Dr.‡
Schuman, Stanton, (AV) .... '15 '39 C&L.477 A.B., J.D. 735 Brookvale‡
Shalowitz, Sidney .... '28 '51 C&L.597 B.S., J.D. 99 Hogarth Lane‡
Siegel, Linda Soreff .... '40 '79 C.518 B.A. L.589 J.D. 980 Cherry Tree Lane‡
Silver, Ralph D. .... '24 '52 C.145 B.S. L.209 J.D. 1124 Old Elm Lane
Sperling, Priscilla C. .... '53 '79 C.518 B.A. L.145 J.D. 862 Grove St.‡
Stonebraker, Deborah K. .... '57 '81 C.697 A.B. L.309 J.D. 920 Bluff St.
Swenson, John Forbes .... '29 '54 C.197 A.B. L.597 J.D. 245 Hawthorn Ave.‡
Thomas, Caren D., (AV) .... '50 '75 C.66 A.B. L.976 J.D. 423 Northwood Dr.
Thompson, Charles W. N. .... '24 '50 C.652 B.S. L.309 LL.B. 240 Randolph St.
Tobias, Jos. M. .... '13 '37 L.146 LL.B. 660 Orchard Lane
Urstadt, Lynn F. '41 '71 C.994 B.A. L.776 J.D.
(adm. in NJ; not adm. in IL) 174 Beach Rd.‡
Watts, Dey W., (AV) .... '23 '50 C.674 A.B. L.309 LL.B. 684 Greenleaf Ave.
Weinberg, Margot D. .... '51 '74 C.823 B.A. L.597 J.D. 340 Hawthorne Ave.‡
Weiss, Alfred M. .... '31 '61 C.597 B.S. L.424 J.D. 494 Park Ave.
Witcoff, Lulu Beth .... '56 '81 C.112 B.A. L.1066 J.D. 525 Drexel Ave.

GLENDALE HEIGHTS, 31,765, *DuPage Co.*

Chase, Scott T., (BV) .... '58 '83 C&L.879 B.S., J.D. [⊠ Nigro&W.]
Di Canio, Michael J. .... '47 '73 C.339 B.A. L.365 J.D. 2103 Bloomingdale Rd., Rm. A
Fanella, Francis M. .... '58 '85 C.436 B.A. L.339 J.D. 1771 Bloomingdale Rd.
Gaffney, Glenn R., (BV) ...... '56 '81 C.339 B.S.B.A. L.801 J.D. 1771 Bloomingdale Rd.
George, Calvin M. .... '18 '50 C.894 A.B. L.365 J.D. 1824 Harvest Ln.‡
Goluba, Christopher J. .... '73 '00 C.338 B.S. L.209 J.D. [C.J.Goluba]
Goluba, Christopher J., P.C. .... 399 Wall Street, Unit H
Gryska, Mark E., (BV) .... '59 '85 C.424 B.S. L.365 J.D. [⊠ Nigro&W.]
Leaton, Thomas U., II .... '49 '79 C.879 B.A. L.589 J.D. 1966 Aspen Ln.

Martucci, Gregory J., P.C., Law Office of
(See Roselle)

Nigro, Michael T., (BV) .... '48 '73 C&L.424 B.S., J.D. [Nigro&W.]
Nigro & Westfall, P.C., (BV) .... 1793 Bloomingdale Road
Schwerdtner, Frederick H., The Law Offices of '49 '89
C&L.424 B.S., J.D. 39 W. Wrightwood Ave.
Westfall, Craig C., (BV) .... '51 '76 C.210 B.A. L.424 J.D. [Nigro&W.]

GLEN ELLYN, 26,999, *DuPage Co.*

Abrahamson, Linda S., (CV) .... '55 '92 C.352 B.B.S. L.589 J.D. 2S675 Arboretum Rd.

Benshoof, Terrence J., (BV) '46 '71 C.339 B.A. L.209 J.D.
170 Spring Avenue, 60137
Telephone: 630-605-6684 Fax: 630-469-1835
Email: tbenshoof@earthlink.net URL: http://www.terrencebenshoof.com
Taxation, Federal Taxation, State Taxation, Tax Audits, Property Tax Appeals, Tax Planning, Tax Litigation, Estate Planning.

See Professional Biographies, GLEN ELLYN, ILLINOIS

Brady, Joan M., (BV) .... '58 '83 C.750 B.A. L.365 J.D. [⊠ J.F.Morreale&Assoc.]
Brucar, Wayne Eli .... '53 '83 C.424 B.A. L.146 J.D. [Brucar&Y.] ⊙

Brucar & Yetter, P.C.
500 Roosevelt Road, Suite 330, 60137 ⊙
Telephone: 630-858-8840 Fax: 630-858-5299
Email: brucaryetter@hotmail.com URL: http://www.brucarandyetter.com
Wayne Eli Brucar; John P. Yetter.
Language: Spanish.
Criminal Law, Federal Criminal Law, State Criminal Law, Appellate Practice, Drug Crimes, Drunk Driving, Extradition, Felonies, Homicide, Juvenile Criminal Law, Misdemeanors, Parole and Probation, Post Conviction Remedies, Search and Seizure, Traffic Violations.
Rolling Meadows, Illinois Office: 1600 Golf Road, Corporate Center, Suite 1200, 60008. Telephone: 847-490-9140.

See Professional Biographies, GLEN ELLYN, ILLINOIS

Byrne, Robert E. .... '41 '68 C&L.424 B.S., J.D. 500 Roosevelt, Ste. 300
Carmody, William F., (AV) ... '43 '70 C.326 B.A. L.146 J.D. 526 Crescent Blvd., Ste. 203
Caviale, Louis A., Jr. .... '22 '47 C&L.436 J.D. 1440 River Dr.
Cleal, Scott C., (BV) .... '57 '85 C&L.546 B.A., J.D. 800 E. Roosevelt Rd.
Cleary, Patrick F. .... '50 '76 C.927 B.A. L.146 J.D. [⊠ J.F.Morreale&Assoc.]
Cleaver, William D. .... '65 '93 C.352 B.B.A. L.378 J.D. Z-Axis Corp.
Coburn, John T., (AV) .... '25 '50 C&L.339 A.B., LL.B. 587 Riford Rd.‡
Coffey, Timothy J. .... '68 '94 C.589 B.S. L.365 J.D. [Coffey]

Coffey Law Office, The, P.C.
577 Pennsylvania Avenue, Suite 204, 60137
Telephone: 630-534-6300 Fax: 630-534-6400
Email: tcofflaw@sbcglobal.net URL: http://www.lawyers.com/timcoffeylaw
Timothy J. Coffey.
Employment Law, Real Estate Law, Contract Litigation.

See Professional Biographies, GLEN ELLYN, ILLINOIS

Coolidge, H. Calvin .... '24 '53 C.103 A.B. L.309 LL.B. Pres., H.Calvin Coolidge, Ltd.
Cronin, Timothy E., (BV) .... '49 '76 C.750 B.A. L.597 J.D. [T.E.Cronin]
Cronin, Timothy E., P.C., (BV) .... 799 Roosevelt Road, Suite 3-100
Culliton, Ellen Champagne .... '43 '89 C.770 B.A. L.146 J.D. 369 Ridgewood Ave.
Cwik, Julie E. .... '72 '04 C.347 B.A. L.365 J.D. [⊠ J.F.Morreale&Assoc.]
Daley, Stephen D. .... '37 '64 C&L.209 B.S., LL.B. 626 Forest Ave.‡
Danner, Therese A. .... '61 '86 C.741 B.A. L.339 J.D. 22W111 Sheffield Ct.‡
Davidson, Kathleen Fuller .... '57 '86 C.399 B.A. L.146 J.D. 22W738 Ahlstrand Rd.
Delveaux, Karen L. .... '59 '86 C&L.589 B.A., J.D. 800 E. Roosevelt Rd., Ste. 102
Devery, Gerald P. .... '12 '36 C&L.209 LL.B. 237 Glenwood Ave.‡
Dornblaser, David .... '57 '89 C.339 B.S. L.146 J.D. 326 Anthony St.
Eckhardt, Thomas A., Thomas A. Eckhardt Attorney at Law '44 '69
C&L.972 B.A., J.D. 493 Duane St., Ste. 102
Evrard, John T. .... '48 '80 C.339 B.A. L.209 J.D. 22 W. 274 Glen Park Rd.‡

Fairbank, William A. .... '48 '76 C.339 B.S. L.910 J.D. 254 Regent Street
Garrity, Richard E. .... '48 '75 C.686 B.A. L.365 J.D. 290 N. Park Blvd.
Garvy, Denise King .... '68 '93 C&L.339 B.A., J.D. [D.K.Garvy]
Garvy, Denise King, P.C., Law Office of .... 800 Roosevelt Rd., Ste. A-7
Genovese, Thomas M. .... '48 '73 C&L.339 B.A., J.D. 500 Roosevelt Rd., Ste. 200
Georgelos, Andrea, (CV) .... '68 '93 C.659 B.A. L.339 J.D. [Ⓒ D.K.Garvy]
Glass, James M. '30 '66 C.108 A.B. L.345 LL.B.
(adm. in IN; not adm. in IL) 1 S. 450 Sunnybrook St.‡
Grant, Haldon K. .... '37 '61 C.679 B.S. L.145 J.D. 191 Montclair Avenue‡
Heidorn, O. Chris .... '55 '83 C&L.589 B.A., J.D. 22 W 155 Valley View Dr.
Heikes, Graham, (AVⓉ) .... '37 '63 C&L.424 A.B., J.D. 1001 Cresent Blvd.
Henninger, Carl F. J. .... '30 '59 L.365 J.D. 876 Saddlewood Dr.
Heroux, Lisé M. .... '61 '89 C.473 B.S. L.209 J.D. 636 Carolyn
Hoppe, Donald N., (AV) .... '47 '73 C.103 B.A. L.339 J.D. 25546 Ashley Dr.
Horton, Jas. C. '30 '58 C.880 B.A. L.347 LL.B.
(adm. in TX; not adm. in IL) 533 Carlisle Ct.‡
Jegen, William E., (BV) .... '44 '70 C.679 B.S.M.E. L.365 J.D. [W.E.Jegen]
Jegen, William E., P.C., (BV) .... 536 Crescent Blvd., 2nd Fl.
Karones, John G., Law Offices of .... '31 '61 C&L.597 B.S., J.D. 547 Williamsburgh Road
Kotecki, Donna J., (BV) .... '52 '84 C.589 B.A. L.339 J.D. [Kotecki&K.]
Kotecki, Roger G. .... '53 '78 C.589 B.A. L.309 J.D. [Kotecki&K.]
Kotecki & Kotecki, (BV) .... 2N124 Mildred Ave.
Kuhn, Carl W., (CV) .... '27 '53 C&L.209 B.S., J.D. 490 Pennsylvania Ave.
Kwak, Kathleen J. .... '77 '05 C.347 B.A. L.879 J.D. [Ⓐ J.F.Morreale&Assoc.]
Lantermo, Deborah Ann, (BVⓉ) '53 '89 C.338 B.S. L.589 J.D.
Faculty, Criminal Justice Dept., College of Dupage
Larson, Ward J. .... '24 '51 C.578 B.A. L.309 LL.B. 822 Saddlewood Dr.‡
LaVere, Raymond L. .... '16 '41 C.405 L.209 LL.B. 448 Raintree Ct.
Lessuk, Gerald H. '26 '51 L.273 J.D.
(adm. in DC; not adm. in IL) 715 Highland Ave.‡
Lipschultz, Charles C. .... '26 '49 C.597 L.145 J.D. 799 Roosevelt Rd., Bldg. 6‡
Lyle, Delbert S., (BV) .... '36 '60 C&L.339 B.S., LL.B. 337 Spring Ave.
Mack, Steven M. .... '47 '78 C.339 B.A. L.1151 J.D. [Ⓐ J.F.Morreale&Assoc.]
Malone, Kari A. .... '77 '02 C&L.589 B.S., J.D. [Ⓐ J.F.Morreale&Assoc.]
Manak, James P. .... '35 '64 C&L.107 B.A., J.D. 421 Ridgewood Ave., Suite 100
Marco, Frank .... '65 '90 C.436 B.A. L.188 J.D. 22W455 McCarron Rd.
Marquardt, Robt. F. .... '14 '47 C.578 B.A. L.209 LL.B. 347 Lorraine Rd.‡
Maslowe, Richard H. .... '45 '74 C.966 B.S. L.146 J.D. 22 W. 320 Glen Valley Dr.
Matacio, Timothy P. .... '55 '82 C.243 B.A. L.30 J.D. 325 Alder Ln.‡
Mazza, Michael P., (AV) .... '64 '89 C.602 B.S. L.624 J.D. [M.P.Mazza] (Pat.)

Mazza, Michael P., LLC, (AV)
686 Crescent Boulevard, 60137
Telephone: 630-858-5071 Fax: 630-282-7123
URL: http://www.mazzalawfirm.com
Michael P. Mazza;—John M. Michalik. Of Counsel: Lawrence E. Thompson (Not admitted in IL).
See Professional Biographies, GLEN ELLYN, ILLINOIS

McKay, Brian D. '66 '99 C.608 B.S. L.146 J.D.
Corp. Dir. of Admin., Clark Products, Inc.
Michalik, John M. .... '— '03 C.276 B.S. L.602 J.D. [Ⓐ M.P.Mazza]
Morreale, John F., (AV) .... '39 '66 C.424 B.S. L.597 J.D. [J.F.Morreale&Assoc.]

Morreale, John F., & Associates, P.C., (AV)
Golf Place, 449 Taft Avenue, 60137-6209
Telephone: 630-790-6300 Fax: 630-790-1081
Email: Law@mmtpc.com URL: http://www.morrealelaw.com
John F. Morreale;—Steven M. Mack; Joan M. Brady; Kari A. Malone; Patrick F. Cleary; Julie E. Cwik; Kathleen J. Kwak.
National and International Relocation Real Estate, Estate Planning, Trusts and Estates, Wills and Probate, Estate Planning, Financial Planning, Family, Divorce and Small Business, Bankruptcy, Civil and Criminal Law.
See Professional Biographies, GLEN ELLYN, ILLINOIS

Nelligan, John J. .... '28 '53 C&L.424 J.D. 607 Main St.
Newton, Sally Hughes .... '50 '77 C.597 B.A. L.910 J.D. 254 Regent St.
Noel, John E. .... '46 '74 C.602 A.B. L.424 J.D. 500 Roosevelt Rd.
Norgaard, Steven K. .... '64 '90 C.339 B.S. L.145 J.D. [S.K.Norgaard]

Norgaard, Steven K., P.C.
493 Duane Street, Suite 400, 60137
Telephone: 630-545-1005 Fax: 630-545-1051
Email: sn@norgaardlaw.com URL: http://www.norgaardlaw.com
Steven K. Norgaard.
Real Estate, Estate Planning, Probate, Buying and Selling a Home, Commercial Real Estate, Trusts and Estates, Small Business Law, Wills, Probate.
See Professional Biographies, GLEN ELLYN, ILLINOIS

Owens, Joseph C., (AV) .... '18 '44 C.177 B.A. L.597 J.D. [J.C.Owens]
Owens, Joseph C., P.C., (AV) .... 106 Exmoor Ave.
Papke, William L. .... '23 '52 C.145 A.B. L.365 LL.B. 2 S. 651 Devonshire Lane
Peck, Sarah Dean .... '52 '81 C.183 B.A. L.589 J.D. 726 N. Park Blvd.‡
Peppin, Harry Edmund '09 '34 C&L.724 B.A., LL.B.
(adm. in NY; not adm. in IL) 60 N. Nicoll Way‡
Perretti, Patrick J. .... '49 '75 C.238 B.A. L.365 J.D. 799 Roosevelt Rd., Bldg. 3
Porter, G. William, (AV) .... '30 '57 C.388 B.A. L.208 J.D. 625 Highview Ave.‡
Rees, Walter L. .... '25 '61 C.871 B.S. L.365 LL.B. 366 Turner Ave. (Pat.)
Roadman, Jack W. .... '27 '65 C.339 B.S. L.734 J.D. 23 W. 231 Windsor Dr.‡
Rodriguez, Mark T. .... '51 '76 C.321 B.A. L.424 J.D. 364 Pennsylvania
Rose, Ashley S. .... '33 '78 C.950 B.A. L.589 J.D. 799 Roosevelt Rd.
St. Hilaire, Brian D. .... '49 '75 C.589 B.S. L.365 J.D. 364 Pennsylvania Avenue
Shapiro, Norman M., (AV) '26 '53
C.679 B.S.Ch.E. L.128 LL.B. 1198 Royal Glen Dr. (Pat.)‡
Spalo, William M. .... '53 '81 C.234 B.A. L.589 J.D. 800 Roosevelt Rd., Ste. E-400
Stoakley, Yvor E. .... '50 '84 C.293 B.A. L.597 J.D. P.O. Box 2264
Studzinski, Andrea .... '61 '86 C.357 B.A. L.339 J.D. 309 North Park Blvd.
Telander, Brad S. .... '58 '83 C.98 B.S. L.365 J.D. 45 S. Park Avenue
Thomas, Debra A. .... '50 '84 C&L.339 B.A., J.D. [D.A.Thomas]

Thomas, Debra A., P.C.
800 Roosevelt Road, Building B Suite 110, 60137
Telephone: 630-790-0800 Fax: 630-790-3480
Email: debra@thomaslaws.com URL: http://www.debrathomaslaws.com
Debra A. Thomas.
Medical Malpractice, Products Liability, Personal Injury and Commercial Litigation.
See Professional Biographies, GLEN ELLYN, ILLINOIS

Thompson, Lawrence E. '— '97 C.339 B.S.E.E. L.36 J.D.
(adm. in AZ; not adm. in IL; Pat.) [Ⓒ M.P.Mazza]
Trapp, Courtney Q. .... '64 '93 C.491 B.S. L.424 J.D. Golf Pl., 449 Taft Ave.
Ulrich, Werner .... '31 '85 C.178 B.S. L.424 J.D. 434 Maple St. (Pat.)
Volkman, William W. .... '25 '52 C&L.597 B.S., J.D. 675 Roosevelt Rd.‡

Wagner, Joanna C. .... '64 '91 C.352 B.B.A. L.893 J.D. 510 Linden‡
Woulfe, Michael P., (BV) .... '68 '93 C.569 B.S. L.209 J.D. 449 Taft Ave., Ste. 300
Yetter, John P. .... '71 '96 C.589 B.S. L.201 J.D. [Brucar&Y.] ⊙

GLENVIEW, 41,847, *Cook Co.*

Abraham, Robert L. .... '52 '77 C.339 B.A. L.365 J.D. 1150 Lincoln
Alfredson, David M. '33 '71 C.297 B.A. L.879 J.D.
(adm. in IA; not adm. in IL) 1119 Pine St.‡
Atlas, Richard I. .... '49 '77 C&L.209 B.S.C., J.D. 950 Milwaukee Ave., Ste. 224
Bailey, R. Emmett .... '25 '49 C.424 B.A. L.596 J.D. 2020 Chestnut Ave.‡
Bak, Mary M. .... '53 '78 C.424 B.A. L.209 J.D. Dir., Dept. of Dev., Spec. Coun.
Ball, Jessica R. .... '72 '97 C.98 B.A. L.424 J.D. 229 Neva Ave.
Baxter, Gary M. .... '44 '70 C.36 B.S. L.273 J.D. Pres., Baxter Group Inc.‡
Beart, Robert W. .... '17 '47 C.57 B.A. L.146 J.D. 3600 W. Lake‡
Becker, Alfred G. .... '22 '50 C&L.494 B.S., LL.B. 1535 Evergreen Terr.‡
Becker, Bruce A. .... '40 '66 C.966 B.S. L.209 J.D. 802 Prairie Lawn
Becker, Richard O. .... '39 '64 C.174 B.S. L.597 J.D. 916 Wedgewood Dr.
Bedoya, Consuelo E. .... '49 '77 C.58 B.A. L.209 J.D. 1453 Woodlawn Ave.
Berk, Lauren .... '60 '85 C.966 B.S. L.365 J.D. 3823 Chester
Berkman, Michael G., (AV) .... '17 '58 C.145 B.S. L.209 J.D. 939 Glenview Rd. (Pat.)
Blackman, Jeffrey H. .... '56 '82 C.339 B.S. L.146 J.D. 2130 Warwick Lane‡
Block, Dennis H. .... '47 '71 C.339 L.209 J.D. 3420 Springdale Rd.
Boros, Sally P. .... '— '91 C.031 B.A. L.365 J.D. 128 Washington
Boyles, Charles M. .... '16 '40 C.502 L.734 LL.B. 1416 E. Lake Ave.
Breh, Donald J. '44 '78 C.932 B.S. L.365 J.D.
Group Tech. Coun., Illinois Tool Works Inc. (Pat.)
Brill, Richard H. .... '35 '58 C&L.597 B.S., LL.B. 526 Short Lane‡
Brook, Byron .... '41 '68 C.339 B.S. L.209 J.D. V.P. Invest., A. G. Edwards

Brown, Marc L., The Law Offices of
(See Park Ridge)

Buyer, Dennis .... '43 '68 C.339 A.B. L.209 J.D. 234 Waukegan Rd.
Byrne, Frank O. .... '20 '52 C.776 B.S. L.365 LL.B. 2039 Glen Oak Dr.
Carney, Vincent J., (AV) .... '17 '41 C&L.424 LL.B. 2121 N. Ammer Ridge Ct.‡
Cernek, Jeffrey T. .... '58 '84 C.388 B.A. L.146 J.D. [Ⓐ T.P.Cernek]

Cernek, Thomas P., & Associates, (AV) '27 '53 C.339 L.365 J.D.
1701 East Lake Avenue, Suite 460, 60025
Telephone: 847-998-1400 Facsimile: 847-998-8690
Email: tpcernek@quixnet.net
—Jeffrey T. Cernek.
Trial and Appellate Practice in State and Federal Courts, Personal Injury, Negligence, Medical Malpractice, Criminal, Real Estate, Corporation and Probate Law.
See Professional Biographies, GLENVIEW, ILLINOIS

Cohen, Donald W., (AV) .... '34 '57 C.145 B.S.L. L.597 J.D. 1220 Brook Ln.
Connery, John M., (AV) .... '32 '53 C.363 B.S. L.597 J.D. 1275 Milwaukee Ave.
Coyle, Charlotte M. .... '27 '55 C.1016 L.365 LL.B. 1404 Estate Ln.‡
Cramer, Jennifer G. '67 '93 C.188 B.A. L.659 J.D.
(adm. in PA; not adm. in IL) 2846 Linneman St.
Croft, Manly R. .... '18 '39 C.339 L.365 J.D. 1701 Lake Ave.‡
Croll, Mark W. '53 '83 C.105 B.S.M.E. L.209 J.D.
V.P., Pat. & Tech., Illinois Tool Works Inc. (Pat.)
Cummings, Kerry D. .... '55 '80 C.317 B.A. L.146 J.D. 2320 Swainwood Dr.
Curran, Daniel S. .... '30 '59 C.966 B.B.A. L.209 J.D. 1924 W. Ridgewood St.
Dallosto, Philip S. '53 '78 C.424 A.B. L.597 J.D.
Assoc. Gen. Coun. & Asst. Secy., Illinois Tool Works Inc.
Diamond, Tami J. .... '62 '88 C.477 B.A. L.896 J.D. [Ⓐ K.E.Vragel]

Di Giacomo, Carol & Kathryn Somers, L.L.C.
(See Northfield)

Donovan, Paul F. '68 '95 C.436 B.S.M.E. L.300 J.D.
(adm. in WI; not adm. in IL; Pat.) Group Tech Coun., Illinois Tool Works, Inc.
Downing, Michael D., (AV) .... '44 '74 C.436 B.S.C.E. L.424 J.D. [Miller,F.&D.]
Downing, Robert J., (AV) .... '15 '42 C.190 B.S.C. L.424 J.D. 1275 Milwaukee Ave.
Edmier, Timothy J. .... '73 '01 C.339 B.S. L.999 J.D. [Ⓐ P.K.Hanson&Assoc.]
Fagan, Joseph D. '56 '82 C.884 B.S. L.1017 J.D.
(adm. in PA; not adm. in IL) Asst. Gen. Coun., Aon Corp.

Feldman, Stuart A.
(See Wilmette)

Feldstein, I. H. .... '20 '47 L.209 LL.B. 2561 Central Rd.‡
Fields, John R. '45 '71 C.477 M.B.A. L.813 J.D.
(adm. in WI; not adm. in IL) V.P., Fields Cadillac Inc.
Fogarty, Martin J. .... '63 '89 C.339 B.A. L.424 J.D. [M.J.Fogarty&Assoc.]
Fogarty, Martin J., & Associates, P.C. .... 2222 Chestnut Avenue
Foley-Klein, Jacquelina .... '50 '81 C.37 B.A. L.209 J.D. Continental Bk.
Forest, Alan John, (BV) .... '43 '69 C.424 B.S. L.597 J.D. [Miller,F.&D.]
Garippo, Louis B., (AV) .... '— '55 C.602 Ph.B. L.209 J.D. 1275 Milwaukee Ave.
Gayle, Richard L. .... '47 '72 C&L.209 B.S., J.D. [Robbins,S.&P.] ⊙
Gelfeld, Mark R. .... '45 '70 C.339 B.S. L.209 J.D. 2252 Strawberry Ln.
Geppert, James A. .... '32 '59 C.597 B.S. L.273 J.D. 120 Washington St. (Pat.)
Goldberg, Bruce L. .... '48 '74 C.801 B.A. L.209 J.D. 1701 Lake Ave.
Goldberger, Marvin L. .... '16 '40 C.424 L.146 J.D. 2000 Chestnut Ave.
Goldman, Dianna Lynn .... '63 '89 C.694 B.A. L.145 J.D. 1510 Topp Lane‡
Goldman, Lawrence A. .... '52 '88 C.966 B.A. L.365 J.D. Combined Specialty Grp.
Goodman, Adorea S., (AV) .... '26 '49 C.813 A.B. L.597 J.D. 309 Ferndale Rd.‡
Goodwin, Richard .... '— '97 C.1033 B.S. L.209 J.D. Coun., Aon Corp.
Grad, Karen A. .... '66 '92 C.352 B.S. L.209 J.D. [K.A.Grad]
Grad, Karen A., PC .... 1946 Lehigh Ave., Ste. E
Green, Maria C. '52 '78 C.659 B.A. L.94 J.D.
Assoc. Gen. Coun. & Asst. Secy., Illinois Tool Works Inc.
Greenwood, Katherine A. .... '58 '84 C&L.861 B.A., J.D. 918 Harlem Ave.
Gruzmark, Alexander .... '70 '97 C&L.424 B.A., J.D. 1701 E. Lake Ave.
Guyer, Leah Hamilton .... '40 '63 C&L.339 B.A., J.D. 1328 Pine St.‡
Haffner, Joseph G. .... '65 '91 C.436 B.A. L.365 J.D. [J.Haffner]
Haffner, Joseph .... 662 Waukegan Road
Hamblen, Michael G. '56 '83 C&L.836 B.A., J.D.
V.P., Employee Rel., Illinois Tool Works Inc.
Hanson, Per K., (AV) .... '40 '65 C.477 B.A. L.597 J.D. [P.K.Hanson&Assoc.]

Hanson, Per K., Associated, The Firm of, (AV)
2222 Chestnut Avenue, Suite 201, 60026
Telephone: 847-486-9960 Fax: 847-486-9970
Email: firm@pkhpc.com URL: http://www.pkhpc.com
Per K. Hanson. Associates: Mary A. Long; Timothy J. Edmier.
Estate Planning, Trusts, Asset Protection, Charitable Giving, Guardianship and Conservatorship, Wills and Probate, Corporate, Real Estate, Business Law, and Collections.
See Professional Biographies, GLENVIEW, ILLINOIS

Harrington, James E., (AV) ....'27 '53 C.602 B.S. L.209 J.D. 320 N. Branch Rd.‡
Harrison, Miriam E. ....'41 '77 C.1183 B.A. L.209 J.D. 1734 Henley St.
Hecht, Kenneth G. .... '12 '38 C&L.597 B.S.L., J.D. 1452 Estate Lane‡

Heisler, Marc H.
(See Evanston)

Hertline, Everitt W. ....'07 '47 L.365 J.D. 908 Wagner Rd.
Hofstetter, Daniel F. ....'55 '83 C.352 B.A. L.365 J.D. [D.F.Hofstetter]
Hofstetter, Daniel F., Ltd., Law Offices of ....2400 Ravine Way, Suite 200
Hogan, Robert V., (AV) ....'17 '47 C&L.209 LL.B. 1925 Tanglewood Dr Apt 1C
Kail, Jack '46 '74 C.339 B.S.E.E. L.1340 J.D.
Assoc. Pat. Coun., Zenith Electronics Corp. (Pat.)
Karm, Howard N. .... '44 '69 800 Waukegan Rd., Rm. 202
Karp, Bruce A. ....'51 '79 C.910 B.A. L.365 J.D. 1304 Heatherfield Lane
Kesselman, Irwin M. ....'45 '73 C.221 B.S. L.146 J.D. 906 Lenox Rd.
Koprowski, Wayne M. ...'47 '76 C.734 B.S. L.209 J.D. Sr. Atty., Zenith Electronics Corp.
Krivitzky, Richard A. '52 '77 C.393 B.A. L.910 J.D.
Mgr. Compl., Guarantee Trust Life
Ladha, Shermin N. ....'73 '00 C.94 B.A. L.823 J.D. Gen. Coun., Fields Auto Group
Lamey, Wm. L. .... '14 '39 C&L.424 Ph.B., J.D. 921 Harlem Ave.
Laurent, Paul Andre ....'73 '01 C.801 B.S. L.339 J.D. 1411 Plymouth Lane‡
Lazerwith, Mark A. ....'36 '62 C.145 B.A. L.146 J.D. 207 Michael Manor
Leary, Jane S. '52 '84 C.436 B.A. L.1340 J.D.
Chief Coun., Meals & Pizza, Kraft Foods, Inc.
Leer, Mary Anne ....'50 '77 C.347 B.A. L.1119 J.D. Sr. Coun., Aon Corp.
Liu, Jean C. ....'— '95 C.339 B.S. L.424 J.D. Coun., Aon Corp.

Locke, Barry, & Associates, LTD.
(See Chicago)

Long, Mary A. .... '35 '85 C.1183 B.A. L.365 J.D. [Ⓐ P.K.Hanson&Assoc.]
Lynch, Kevin J. '50 '77 C.309 B.A. L.93 J.D.
(adm. in MA; not adm. in IL) V.P., Zenith Corp.
Mackie, Charles L., (BVⓉ) .... '51 '76 C&L.861 B.A., J.D. 2514 Osage Dr.
Maki, William O. ....'48 '73 C.597 B.A. L.209 J.D. 2721 Sunflower Ct.
Mancuso, Gregory J. '45 '73 C.893 B.Ch.E. L.326 J.D.
Assoc. Gen. Coun & Asst. Secy., Illinois Tool Works, Inc. (Pat.)
Markovits, Ronald D. '43 '69 C.491 B.A. L.585 J.D.
Assoc. Gen. Coun., Ins. Co. Law & Regul., Aon Corp.
Marmet, G. John, Law Office of ... '46 '70 C.763 B.S. L.597 J.D. 950 Milwaukee Avenue
Matik, Paul, Jr. ....'54 '79 C.339 B.S. L.424 J.D. 850 Prairie Lawn Rd.
McGee, Leonard F., Jr. ....'29 '54 C.221 B.A. L.597 J.D. 6158 Willowhill Rd.‡
McGrath, Alan T. .... '62 '00 C.589 B.S. L.365 J.D. [A.McGrath]
McGrath, Alan, P.C., Law Offices of .... 4400 West Lake Avenue, Suite 201B
Miller, Larry ....'37 '63 C.472 A.B. L.597 J.D. 1912 Wyndham Circle‡
Miller, Martin L., (AV) .... '38 '66 C.1016 B.S.B.A. L.365 J.D. [Miller,F.&D.]
Miller, Forest and Downing, Ltd., (AV) ....1275 Milwaukee Ave.
Mortimer, James K. ....'20 '49 C.165 A.B. L.477 J.D. 1721 Delogier Dr.
Nagy, Stephen J., (AV) .... '31 '58 C.210 B.A. L.597 J.D. 1820B Wildberry Dr.
Naselli, Carolyn ....'44 '82 C.991 B.A. L.146 J.D. 1503 Winnetka Ave.‡
Neben, Michael E. ....'49 '76 C.339 B.S. L.477 J.D. Sr. Coun., Aon Corp.
Nelson, Gayle Lynn ....'69 '94 C.966 B.A. L.209 J.D. 1628 Blackthorn Dr.
Neuson, Bridget A. ....'63 '94 C.424 B.S.N. L.146 J.D. [B.A.Neuson]
Neuson, Bridget A., Ltd., Law Offices of .... 1701 E. Lake Ave., Ste. 410
Nolan, Thomas L. ....'46 '73 C.339 B.S. L.347 J.D. 1704-B Weldberry
O'Brien, Arthur R., (AV) ....'24 '53 C&L.424 Ph.B., J.D. 969 Waukegan Rd.
O'Gara, Carolynn ....'66 '92 C.755 B.A. L.494 J.D. 2216 Larkdale Dr.
Olfson, Herbert B., (AV) ....'32 '57 C&L.309 A.B., LL.B. 1 IBM Plaza‡
Orphan, Jas. G. ....'18 '47 C.424 L.209 LL.B. 2000 Chestnut Ave.
Pappo, Donna Neudecker ....'54 '86 C.145 B.A. L.146 J.D. 1415 Baffin Rd.‡
Patt, Stephen P. .... '39 '64 C.209 B.S.C. L.365 J.D. [Robbins,S.&P.] ⊙
Peters, James H. ....'27 '51 C.674 B.A. L.659 J.D. 2060 Norwich Ct.
Pilarski, John H., (BV) '60 '87 C.436 B.S.M.E. L.966 J.D.
(adm. in WI; not adm. in IL; Pat.) Group Tech. Coun., Illinois Tool Works Inc.
Prasil, Linda A. ....'47 '77 C&L.30 B.A., J.D. 1320 Pleasant Ln.
Prince, Loretta ....'— '00 C.424 B.S. L.365 J.D. Coun., Aon Corp.
Provenza, James C. ....'56 '80 C.339 B.S. L.365 J.D. [J.Provenza]
Provenza, James, PC ....1701 E. Lake Ave.
Puzzo, Edward L. ....'51 '80 C.339 B.A. L.209 J.D. [E.L.Puzzo]
Puzzo, Edward L., Ltd. ....P.O. Box 381
Ramirez, Robert B. ....'56 '83 C.963 L.209 J.D. [R.B.Ramirez]
Ramirez, Robert B., P.C. ....1141 Waukegan Rd.
Randall, Jeffrey M. ....'42 '69 C.1016 B.S.B.A. L.365 J.D. [Robbins,S.&P.] ⊙
Rank, John T., (AV) ....'47 '72 C.602 B.A. L.813 J.D. 1320 Pleasant Lane
Reed, Kimberly ....'57 '87 C.210 B.S.N. L.365 J.D. [Reed]
Reed Law Associates, P.C. ....2516 Waukegan Road, Suite 321
Rice, James B. ....'23 '49 C&L.602 B.S., J.D. 969 Waukegan Rd.
Robbins, Salomon & Patt, Ltd., (AV) .......................P.O. Box 437 (⊙Chicago)
Rosen, Elliot D. ....'37 '64 C.98 B.S.B.A. L.209 LL.B. 1483 Kittyhawk Lane
Rosenblat, Michael C. .... '60 '85 C.339 B.A. L.365 J.D. [M.C.Rosenblat]

Rosenblat, Michael C., P.C.
2400 Ravine Way, Suite 200, 60025
Telephone: 847-657-0006 Fax: 847-657-7776
Email: MikeRLaw@msn.com URL: http://www.rosenblatlaw.com
Michael C. Rosenblat.
Criminal Law, Civil Practice, Qui Tam Litigation, False Claims Act, Whistleblower Litigation, White Collar Crimes, Drug Crimes, Parole and Probation, Juvenile Crimes, Driving While Intoxicated.
See Professional Biographies, GLENVIEW, ILLINOIS

Roth, John W., Jr. ....'50 '82 C.57 B.A. L.209 J.D. 2934 Peachgate Ct.
Rubenstein, Morton C. ....'28 '52 C.339 L.365 LL.B. 1701 Lake Ave.‡
Rudnit, Phyllis Miriam ....'— '91 C.339 B.A. L.365 J.D. 236 Waukegan Rd.
Rueckert, Thomas E. ....'40 '73 C.1106 B.A. L.146 J.D. 410 Huber Lane
Ryan, Richard R. ....'54 '79 C.1200 B.S.B.A. L.884 J.D. 938 Glenayre Dr.
Sarnat, Barry Marc ....'58 '94 C.112 B.A. L.209 J.D. 124 Cornell Ct.
Scherb, Louis H., Law Office .... '39 '67 C&L.424 B.B.A., J.D. 234 Waukegan Rd.
Schuman, Gary, (AV) ....'48 '75 C.24 B.A. L.602 J.D. Sr. Coun., Aon Corp.
Schy, Ronald A., (AV) ....'58 '83 C.339 B.S. L.145 J.D. 1618 Glenview Rd
Seidman, Susan E. ....'54 '80 C.339 B.S. L.209 J.D. 3454 Bellwood Lane
Sherman, Fred Ross .... '47 '72 C&L.209 B.S., J.D. 800 Waukegan Rd., Ste. 204

Shults, David M., Law Offices of
(See Northbrook)

Sindelar, Charles J. .... '37 '64 C.679 B.S. L.209 J.D. Zenith Electronics Corp. (Pat.)
Smith, Thomas E., Firm of, (AV) '28 '56 C.502 B.S. L.273 J.D.
1400 Executive Ct. (Pat.)
Soltis, Lisa M. '— '95 C.477 B.S.E. L.209 J.D.
Group Technology Coun., Illinois Tool Works, Inc.

Sparer, William J. ...... '52 '80 C.209 B.A. L.608 J.D. Asst. Gen. Coun., Fin., Aon Corp.
Spiegel, Mary Ann '64 '92 C.338 B.S. L.188 J.D.
Asst. Gen. Coun. & Asst. Secy., Illinois Tool Works, Inc.
Stavins, Ralph L. ....'34 '58 C.339 B.S. L.209 LL.B. 701 Forum Sq.
Stec, John M. ....'54 '85 C.339 B.S. L.209 J.D. 250 N. Branch Rd.
Stein, Sylvia A. .... '66 '92 C.597 B.A. L.477 J.D. Sr. Coun., Kraft Foods Global, Inc.
Swan, Jeffrey A. ....'52 '90 C.473 B.S. L.365 J.D. 960 Harlem Ave.
Taksin, Aaron .... '46 '72 C&L.209 B.S., J.D. 2222 Chestnut Ave., Ste. 202
Tews, Theisen & Theisen, (AV) ....1701 E. Lake Ave. (⊙Chicago)
Theisen, Kenneth F., (AV) ....'46 '77 C.1016 B.A. L.1187 J.D. [Tews,T.&T.] ⊙
Tyk, Roger E. ....'49 '80 C.976 B.A. L.846 J.D. 644 Echo Lane
Verges, Conrad G. .... '24 '54 L.424 LL.B. 1813 E. Wildbury
Vierneisel, Gail M. ....'53 '92 L.365 J.D. 2245 Covert Road
Vitkus, Richard F. '39 '66 C.966 B.B.A. L.477 J.D.
Sr. V.P. & Gen. Coun., Zenith Electronics Corp.
Vito, James C. ....'42 '74 C.707 B.A. L.146 J.D. Zenith Electronics Corp.
von Thury, Geza ....'18 '63 C&L.999 J.D. 840 Becker Rd.‡
Vragel, Kurt E., Jr. ....'48 '76 C.597 B.A. L.1294 J.D. [K.E.Vragel]
Vragel, Kurt E., P.C. ....1701 E. Lake Ave.
Wasik, Raymond ....'16 '42 L.365 J.D. 3208 Knollwood Lane‡
Weber, Stephen K. .... '42 '76 C.150 A.B. L.424 J.D. Zenith Electronics Corp.
Wetta, Jeanne M. '53 '77 C&L.546 B.A., J.D.
(adm. in NE; not adm. in IL) Kraft, Inc.
White, Jacqueline A. '— '94 C.569 B.A. L.309 J.D.
Assoc. Gen. Coun. & Asst. Secy., Illinois Tool Works Inc.
Wilson, Kent A. ....'50 '75 C.589 B.A. L.208 J.D. 938 Glenavre Drive
Winand, John H. .... '50 '75 C.339 B.S. L.209 J.D. 800 Waukegan Rd., Rm. 202
Winton, Thomas W. ....'05 '32 C.339 B.S. L.365 J.D. 2010 Fir St.
Witt, Linda Kreer ....'50 '75 C.228 B.A. L.424 J.D. [Witt&Assoc.]
Witt & Associates, Ltd. ....2005 Sunset Ridge Rd.
Woody, Russell, (AV) ....'42 '68 C&L.378 B.A., J.D. 2305 Swainwood Drive
Wooten, James H., Jr. '48 '82 C.339 B.A. L.145 J.D.
V.P., Gen. Coun. & Sec., Illinois Tool Works Inc.
Wurman, Barbara I. ....'51 '81 C.477 B.A. L.910 J.D. 1005 Barton Court‡
Wyckoff, Beverly A. ... '56 '81 C.976 B.A. L.472 J.D. Sr. Coun., Zenith Electronics Corp.
Zimmerman, Robert M. '33 '63
C&L.800 B.S., LL.B. Human Res. Dept., Zenith Electronics Corp.

GLENWOOD, 9,000, *Cook Co.*

Kane, William B. ....'12 '49 L.209 LL.B. Ret. Cir. J.
Mathieu, John R. ....'26 '61 C&L.209 LL.B. 747 Strieff Lane‡

GODFREY, 16,286, *Madison Co.*

Campbell, Timothy F., (BV) .... '47 '72 C.210 B.A. L.339 J.D. [Campbell&M.]
Campbell & McGrady, (BV) ....3017 Godfrey Rd.
Farrell, John A., (AV) .... '29 '61 C.339 B.S. L.734 J.D. [Farrell,H.H.&J.]
Farrell, Hunter, Hamilton & Julian, P.C., (AV) ....1310 D'Adrian Professional Park
Gainer, John J. ....'14 '38 C.602 A.B. L.910 J.D. 2200 Oakview Dr.‡
Hamilton, Phillip H. ....'64 '89 C.477 B.G.S. L.802 J.D. [Ⓐ Farrell,H.H.&J.]
Hoefert, John W., (AV) ....'27 '52 C.436 L.910 J.D. P.O. Box 5215
Hoefert, John W., Jr., (BV) ....'55 '80 C&L.190 B.S.B.A., J.D. P.O. Box 5215
Hunter, Christopher B., (BV) ....'53 '78 C.430 B.A. L.734 J.D. [Farrell,H.H.&J.]
Tracy, Julia M., (AVⓉ) '58 '91 C.339 B.S. L.1065 J.D.
(adm. in CA; not adm. in IL) [Tracy]
Tracy Law Offices, (AVⓉ) .... 5216 Willis Ave.
West, Stacy L. '60 '85 C.208 B.S.B.A. L.801 J.D.
(adm. in MO; not adm. in IL) 3324 Quail Run

GOLCONDA, * 823, *Pope Co.*

Flynn, Charles L. P. ....'70 '97 C&L.339 B.A., J.D. State's Atty.

Jelliffe, Ferrell, Morris & Doerge
(See Harrisburg)

Turner, Frederick, Jr., (BV) .... '— '78 C&L.801 B.A., J.D. P.O. Box 512

GOLF, 454, *Cook Co.*

Johnson, Donald D. '35 '62 C&L.966 B.S., J.D.
(adm. in WI; not adm. in IL) Exec. Dir., Western Golf Assn.
Tatara, Irene '60 '85 C&L.597 B.A., J.D.
(adm. in WI; not adm. in IL) P.O. Box 202‡

GRAND RIDGE, 546, *La Salle Co.*

Hinterlong, James E. .... '41 '72 C.750 B.S. L.365 J.D. P.O. Box 236

GRAND TOWER, 624, *Jackson Co.*

McCormick, Robert J. ....'51 '76 C.801 B.A. L.862 J.D. P.O. Box 283‡

GRANITE CITY, 31,301, *Madison Co.*

Albers, George H. .... '66 '01 C&L.734 B.A., J.D. [Ⓐ Roth&E.]
Allen, Dick ....'25 '62 C.337 L.734 J.D. 2945 Madison Ave.
Andrews, Laura R., (CV) .... '67 '92 C.801 B.S. L.589 J.D. 2862 Madison Avenue
Ashmore, Dale .... '37 '63 C.801 B.A. L.339 LL.B. 2569 Straford Ln.‡
Bacon, Susan E. ....'50 '88 C.1249 B.A. L.365 J.D. City Atty.
Becker, Gregory A., (BV) ....'55 '82 C.801 B.S. L.734 J.D. [Becker,G.&S.]
Becker, Galanti & Schroader, P.C., (BV) ....3673 Highway 111
Blasi, Peter S. ....'74 '00 C.734 B.A. L.365 J.D. [Ⓐ Roth&E.]
Bosslet, Robert W., Jr., (AV) ....'49 '76 C&L.502 B.S., J.D. [Bosslet&O.] ⊙
Bosslet and O'Leary, Ltd., (AV) .... 1406 Niedringhaus Avenue (⊙St. Louis, MO)
Brandt, Dennis A. ....'45 '73 C&L.339 B.A., J.D. 1517 20th St.

Brunton, Michael J., Law Offices of
(See Collinsville)

Callis, Lance, (AV) .... '35 '59 C&L.734 B.S., J.D. [Callis,P.H.S.R.&D.]

Callis, Papa, Hale, Szewczyk, Rongey & Danzinger, P.C., (AV)
1326 Niedringhaus Avenue, P.O. Box 1326, 62040
Telephone: 618-452-1323; 1-800-851-3105 Fax: 618-452-8024
Lance Callis; John T. Papa (Resident); Rand S. Hale; Edward J. Szewczyk; Robert W. Rongey, II; Kenneth P. Danzinger. Associate: Todd A. Neilson. Of Counsel: George Filcoff, Jr.; Philip J. Rarick.
General Civil, Trial and Appellate Practice. Federal Employers Liability Law, Negligence, Labor and Personal Injury, Workers Compensation, Probate, Estate Planning, Municipal and School, Criminal Law, Family Law.
Reference: Bank of Alton, Alton, Illinois.
See Professional Biographies, GRANITE CITY, ILLINOIS

Chapman, Matthew R. .... '73 '99 C.801 B.A. L.734 J.D. [Ⓐ Becker,G.&S.]
Chapman, Thomas W., (BV) ....'67 '92 C.338 B.A. L.734 J.D. 1517 20th St.
Danzinger, Kenneth P. ....'72 '97 C.385 B.A. L.734 J.D. [Callis,P.H.S.R.&D.]

Doroghazi, Stephen Joseph, Jr. ... '53 '79 C&L.734 B.A., J.D. [S.J.Doroghazi,Jr.]
Doroghazi, Stephen J., Jr., Law Office of ... 1 Executive Park
Evans, Eric W. ... '68 '93 C.910 B.S. L.734 J.D. [Roth&E.]
Farmer, R. Lee, P.L.L.C. Law Offices of
3388-B Maryville Road (⊙Bald Head Island, Yanceyville, NC)
Filcoff, George, Jr. ... '34 '57 C&L.910 A.B., J.D. [🄲 Callis,P.H.S.R.&D.]
Galanti, David M. ... '64 '95 [Becker,G.&S.]
Gitchoff, John, (BV) ... '25 '51 C.734 L.502 J.D. 1561 Johnson Rd.
Hagopian, Harry H. ... '30 '64 C.339 B.S. L.734 LL.B. 26 Devon Hill Ln.‡
Hale, Rand S., (BV) ... '51 '76 C.502 B.A. L.862 J.D. [Callis,P.H.S.R.&D.]
Hildebrand, Thomas E., Jr., (BV) ... '51 '76 C.801 B.A. L.339 J.D. 2709 Madison Ave.
Holder, Linda L. ... '60 '97 C.910 B.S.B.A. L.734 J.D. 3703 Nameoki Rd.
Kachigian, Amerik A., (CV) ... '33 '67 C.339 B.A. L.910 J.D. 2860 State St.
Knobbe, Edw. A. ... '22 '53 C.339 A.B. L.734 LL.B. 2 Frontenac Ln.‡
Konzen, Brian E., (BV) ... '59 '84 C.602 B.A. L.734 J.D. [Lueders,R.&K.]
Konzen, Leo H., (AV) ... '29 '53 C&L.734 B.S., J.D. [Lueders,R.&K.]
Kraus, Warren J. '20 '51 C&L.910 A.B., J.D.
(adm. in MO; not adm. in IL) 3144 Colgate Pl.‡
Lading, Philip J. ... '74 '99 C.340 B.A. L.734 J.D. [🄰 Roth&E.]

Lueders, Robertson & Konzen LLC, (AV) 🄱🅁
1939 Delmar Avenue, 62040
Telephone: 618-876-8500 Telecopier: 618-876-4534
Email: lrk@lrklaw.com URL: http://www.irkllc.com
Members of Firm: Wesley Lueders (1896-1957); Randall Robertson; Leo H. Konzen; R. Eric Robertson; Brian E. Konzen. Associates: Lauren K. Smith; Ryan E. Robertson.
General, Trial and Appellate Practice. Utility and Energy Law, Corporation and Banking and Trust Law, Estate, Probate, Real Estate and Administrative Law, Environmental Law, Municipal, Third Party Defense, Bankruptcy and Workers Compensation.
Representative Clients: Granite City Works; U.S. Steel Corp.; Allied Waste Industries, Inc.; Illinois Industrial Energy Consumers (IIEC) including Olin Corporation; Archers-Daniels-Midland Company; General Motors Corporation.
See Professional Biographies, GRANITE CITY, ILLINOIS

Massa, Mary E. ... '52 '85 C.801 B.S. L.910 J.D. [🄰 Becker,G.&S.]
Mateyka, William J., (BV) ... '36 '67 C.801 B.S. L.734 J.D. 1517 E. 20th St.
McGuire, Rosemary D., (BV) ... '60 '85 C.1182 B.A. L.734 J.D. Jud. Law Clk.
Mengarelli, Martin J., (BV) ... '64 '93 C.424 B.B.A. L.589 J.D. 2862 Madison Ave.
Meyers, Robert W., (BVⓉ) ... '48 '75 C.679 B.S. L.930 J.D. [🄲 Becker,G.&S.]
Miofsky, Andrew J., (CV) ... '54 '79 C&L.910 B.A., J.D. 2249 Pontoon Rd.
Neilson, Todd A. ... '77 '02 C.801 B.A. L.734 J.D. [🄰 Callis,P.H.S.R.&D.]
O'Leary, Dawn Kamadulski ... '69 '99 C.504 B.A. L.910 J.D. [🄰 Roth&E.]
O'Leary, Terrence V., (AV) ... '48 '73 C&L.734 A.B., J.D. [Bosslet&O.]
Orsey, Dennis J., (BV) ... '54 '80 C.339 B.A. L.801 J.D. [D.J.Orsey]
Orsey, Dennis J., P.C., (BV) ... 3388 Maryville Road
Papa, John T., (BV) ... '51 '76 C.602 B.A. L.339 J.D. [Callis,P.H.S.R.&D.]
Park, Shon A., (BV) ... '59 '85 C&L.339 B.S., J.D. [🄰 Becker,G.&S.]
Rarick, Philip J. ... '40 '66 C.801 B.A. L.734 J.D. [🄲 Callis,P.H.S.R.&D.]
Robertson, R. Eric, (AV) ... '46 '73 C.210 B.A. L.734 J.D. [Lueders,R.&K.]
Robertson, Randall, (AV) ... '20 '47 C&L.734 B.S., J.D. [Lueders,R.&K.]
Robertson, Ryan E. ... '76 '04 C&L.734 B.A., J.D. [🄰 Lueders,R.&K.]
Rollberg, Owen M. ... '35 '61 C&L.209 LL.B. One Bermuda Ln.
Rongey, Robert W., II, (BV) ... '60 '87 C&L.801 B.A., J.D. [Callis,P.H.S.R.&D.]
Rosch, Gilbert, (BV) ... '14 '38 C&L.910 J.D. 1420 20th St.‡
Roth, Ronald A., (BV) ... '53 '78 C.210 B.A. L.910 J.D. [Roth&E.]

Roth & Evans, (BV)
2421 Corporate Centre Drive Suite 200, 62040
Telephone: 618-931-5000 Fax: 618-931-6474
Email: rothlaw@rothlaw.com URL: http://www.rothlaw.com
Ronald A. Roth; Eric W. Evans. Associates: Philip J. Lading; Dawn Kamadulski O'Leary; Peter S. Blasi; George H. Albers.
General Civil Trial and Appellate practice in all State and Federal Courts, including Missouri.. Personal Injury, Negligence, Premises Liability, Products Liability, Insurance, Automobile, Construction, Commercial Litigation, Workers Compensation, Employment, Discrimination, Civil Rights, Class Action, Environmental, Toxic Tort, Municipal, Corporate, Probate, Real Estate Law.
See Professional Biographies, GRANITE CITY, ILLINOIS

Schooley, Thomas E., (BV) ... '57 '83 C.339 B.A. L.734 J.D. [🄰 W.W.Schooley]

Schooley, William W., (AV) '29 '61 C.870 B.S. L.734 J.D.
2038 Edison Avenue, P.O. Box 1289, 62040
Telephone: 618-877-2142; 452-7122 800-942-7122 Fax: 618-452-9612
Email: barnone@granitecity.com
—Thomas E. Schooley.
Plaintiff, Trial and Appellate Practice. Workers Compensation Law.
See Professional Biographies, GRANITE CITY, ILLINOIS

Schroader, Todd Jason ... '70 '96 [Becker,G.&S.]
Slate, Irvin C., Jr., (BV) ... '37 '63 C&L.910 A.B., J.D. [I.Slate,Jr.]
Slate, Irvin, Jr., (BV) ... 3600 Nameoki Rd., Ste. 205
Smith, Lauren K. ... '78 '03 C&L.801 B.S.W., J.D. [🄰 Lueders,R.&K.]
Spengler, Mark P., (BV) ... '61 '89 C.910 A.B. L.589 J.D. [M.P.Spengler]
Spengler, Mark P., P.C., (BV) ... 2001 State Street
Szewczyk, Edward J., (AV) ... '52 '76 C.602 B.S. L.339 J.D. [Callis,P.H.S.R.&D.]
Theis, Phillip A., Jr., (BV) ... '63 '89 C.98 B.S. L.45 J.D. [Theis]
Theis, Phillip A., Sr. ... '36 '62 C&L.910 B.A., J.D. 2145 Pontoon Rd.‡
Theis Law Firm, P.C., (BV) ... 2145 Pontoon Rd.
Walker, Alan D., (AV) ... '43 '69 C.801 B.A. L.339 J.D. [Walker]
Walker, Bill T. ... '48 '78 C.240 A.B. L.1194 J.D. [🄲 R.L.Farmer] (⊙Yanceyville, NC)
Walker Law Office, (AV) ... 1312 Niedringhaus
Waters, Robert G. ... '62 '89 C.802 B.B.A. L.502 J.D. 2350 Benton Ave.
Wilson, Robert W., (AV) ... '39 '63 C&L.502 A.B., LL.B. 1517 20th St.

GRANVILLE, 1,407, *Putnam Co.*

Helmig, Charles W., III, (BV) ... '37 '64 C&L.339 B.S., LL.B. 312 S. McCoy St. (⊙Peru)
Shore, Scott A. ... '52 '77 C.339 B.A. L.801 J.D. Cir. J.

GRAYSLAKE, 18,506, *Lake Co.*

Alexander, Lauren R. ... '73 '99 C.589 B.A. L.146 J.D. 270 S. Atkinson Rd.
Anderson, Elna M. '— '31 L.904 LL.B.
(adm. in DC; not adm. in IL) 34075 N. Wright Ave.‡

Anderson, Richard A. '52 '94 C.1183 B.A. L.436 J.D.
11 N. Slusser Street, 60030
Telephone: 847-223-7011 Fax: 847-223-7012
URL: http://www.richardandersonattorney.com
Criminal Law, Driving While Intoxicated, Misdemeanors, Felonies, Real Estate, Buying and Selling of Businesses, Juvenile Criminal Law.
See Professional Biographies, GRAYSLAKE, ILLINOIS

Baumgartner, John C., (AV) ... '33 '60 C.337 A.B. L.477 J.D. [Churchill,B.&Q.]
Benno, Edward L., (AV) ... '24 '50 C.145 B.S. L.597 J.D. 17960 W. Hwy. 120 (Pat.)
Brydges, Louis W., Sr., (AV) ... '32 '58 C.72 B.A. L.910 J.D. 30342 N. Imperial Court
Buckun, Anthony H. ... '66 '93 [Buckun&B.]
Buckun, Anthony T. ... '30 '62 C&L.424 B.S., J.D. [Buckun&B.]
Buckun & Buckun, P.C. ... 564 N. IL Rte. 83
Carlson, Richard D. '59 '84 C.118 B.A. L.221 J.D.
(adm. in IA; not adm. in IL) 452 Patricia Ct.
Churchill, Robert W., (BV) ... '47 '72 C.597 B.A. L.352 J.D. State Rep. [Churchill,B.&Q.]
Churchill, William A., (AV) ... '52 '77 C.221 B.A. L.472 J.D. [Churchill,B.&Q.]
Churchill, Baumgartner & Quinn, Ltd., (AV) ... 2 S. Whitney St.
Clark, William L., (BV) ... '36 '63 C.339 A.B. L.209 J.D. 236 Center St.
Frazin, James L. ... '45 '80 C.46 B.S. L.365 J.D. 100 N. Atkinson
Hamilton, Mark T., (AV) ... '52 '77 C.734 B.S.B.A. L.209 J.D. [Churchill,B.&Q.]

Idlas, Paul R., Law Office of '56 '82 C&L.339 B.S., J.D.
1099 North Corporate Circle, 60030
Telephone: 847-223-5555 Fax: 847-223-5583 URL: http://www.paulidlas.com
Email: pidlas@aol.com URL: http://www.idlas.com
Bankruptcy, Real Estate, Chapter 7 Bankruptcy, Real Estate Closings.
See Professional Biographies, GRAYSLAKE, ILLINOIS

Lindsay, Suzanne A., Law Offices of, (BV) '61 '87 C.589 B.S. L.365 J.D.
P.O. Box 235
McMahon, Richard J. '52 '81 C&L.546 M.B.A., J.D.
(adm. in NE; not adm. in IL) Gen. Mgr., State Oril Co.
Oleksak, Paul J. ... '54 '79 C.93 B.A. L.365 J.D. 100 N. Atkinson Rd., Ste. 110-F
Palmer-House, Gail E. ... '54 '90 C.502 B.A. L.1009 J.D. 270 S. Atkinson Rd.
Polster, Zvi ... '55 '82 C.381 B.A. L.146 J.D. 667 Lake St.
Quinn, John, (AV) ... '52 '78 C.339 B.A. L.146 J.D. [Churchill,B.&Q.]
Rapin, Charles E., (BV) ... '54 '86 C.209 B.A. L.365 J.D. 240 Commerce Dr., Ste. B
Richtman, John P., (AV) ... '58 '87 C.339 B.A. L.209 J.D. [Churchill,B.&Q.]
Rosen, Marc Shein ... '73 '99 C.339 B.A. L.378 J.D. 907 Manchester Circle★
Rubert, Ellen Blumberg '48 '76 C.112 B.A. L.146 J.D.
Prof. of Law, College of Lake Co.

Southern, Robert A., (AV) '30 '55 C&L.597 B.S., LL.B.
28 Bobolink Drive, 60030
Telephone: 919-969-8292 Fax: 919-969-8293
Email: rsouthern@nc.rr.com
Corporate, Securities and Finance.
See Professional Biographies, GRAYSLAKE, ILLINOIS

Straub, Peter J. '57 '82 C.36 B.S. L.1358 J.D.
Dept. of Navy, Naval Leg. Servs. N.C. Det.

GRAYVILLE, 1,725, *Edwards & White Cos.*

Walden, Jay D., (BV) ... '58 '84 C.347 B.A. L.339 J.D. 202 East North Street

GREAT LAKES, —, *Lake Co.*

Clady, John Edwin ... '66 '01 C.870 B.S. L.475 J.D. United States Navy
Digan, Thomas E. ... '58 '95 C.339 B.S. L.128 J.D. Atty.
Maye, Brian T. '71 '97 C.1458 B.A. L.7 J.D.
(adm. in NC; not adm. in IL) Navy JAG

GREENVILLE, * 6,955, *Bond Co.*

Bauer, Christopher J.T., (BV) ... '67 '93 C.934 B.S. L.734 J.D. [Schaufelberger-B.] ⊙
Buchmiller, James E., (BV) ... '30 '56 C&L.910 B.S.B.A., J.D. [J.E.Buchmiller]
Buchmiller, James E., Ltd., (BV) ... 102 E. Main
DeLaurenti, John L. ... '33 '61 C.339 A.B. L.879 J.D. Cir. J.
Kelsey, John W., (BV) ... '10 '38 C.597 B.S.L. L.144 J.D. 404 E. Harris Ave.
Knight, John ... '52 '81 C.291 B.S. L.910 J.D. State's Atty.
Marti, Douglas, (BV) ... '34 '57 C&L.339 B.S., LL.B. 218B North Second
Neumann, R. Randall, Attorney at Law, (BV) '48 '75
C.801 B.S. L.861 J.D. 115 E. College Ave.
Runge, H. Carl, Jr., (BV) ... '32 '62 C.293 B.A. L.966 J.D. [H.C.Runge,Jr.] ⊙
Runge, H. Carl, Jr., Ltd., Law Offices of, (BV) ... RR2 (⊙Collinsville)
Schaufelberger, Patrick F., (CV) ... '65 '92 C.291 B.S. L.801 J.D. [Schaufelberger-B.] ⊙
Schaufelberger-Bauer Law Offices, The, Ltd., (BV) ... 421 East Main (⊙Vandalia)
Stein, Lisa Marie ... '75 '01 C&L.801 B.A., J.D. Asst. State's Atty.
Stowe, Carl H. ... '20 '54 C.291 B.A. L.339 J.D. 611 Ward St.
Stowe, Charl K. ... '51 '81 C.291 B.A. L.801 J.D. 611 Ward
Sybert, Kevin Lewis ... '64 '98 C.291 B.S. L.836 J.D. Bond Co. Courthouse

GRIDLEY, 1,411, *McLean Co.*

Dalton, Richard J., (BV) ... '24 '51 C.337 L.972 LL.B. 208 E. Gridley Rd.

GURNEE, 28,834, *Lake Co.*

Bartolain, Paul L. ... '20 '48 C.145 M.B.A. L.209 J.D. 690 Chandler Rd.‡

Beermann & DeBruyne
(See Libertyville)

Bowen, Deanna J., Law Office of '69 '98
C.424 B.S. L.365 J.D. 401 North Riverside Drive, Suite 25
Cain, M. David, Jr. ... '60 '89 C.338 B.S. L.146 J.D. Milburn Cain Co.

Cartwright, Erin E.
(See Waukegan)

Cavanaugh, Michael T. '54 '00 C.628 B.S. L.589 J.D.
4193 Grove Avenue, 60031
Telephone: 847-263-8820 Fax: 847-336-2629
Email: mcavanaugh@cavanaughlawfirm.com URL: http://www.cavanaughlawfirm.com
Languages: Spanish and Italian interpreters are available.
Criminal Law.
See Professional Biographies, GURNEE, ILLINOIS

Ceckowski, Arthur F. ... '34 '80 C.215 B.S. L.365 J.D. 36141 N. Springbrook Lane‡
Ceckowski, Valerie Boettle ... '59 '83 C&L.801 B.S., J.D. 3873 Harper Ave.
Chancey, Matthew ... '53 '78 C.801 B.A. L.146 J.D. 314 Pilgrims Path
Christian, Richd. C. ... '25 '55 C.339 A.B. L.597 J.D. 924 Pine Grove St.
Daly, Dennis P., (BV) ... '47 '73 C.424 A.B. L.146 J.D. P.O. Box 241

Del Re, David R., A Professional Corporation, The Law Offices of
(See Waukegan)

Diambri, Walter, (BV) ... '58 '85 C.436 B.A. L.1187 J.D. [Diambri&V.]
Diambri & Vicari, P.C., (BV) ... 5101 Washington Street Suite 2A
Ferris, Saul, (BV) ... '59 '85 C.338 B.S. L.589 J.D. [Ferris,T.&Z.]

Ferris, Thompson & Zweig, Ltd., (BV)
103 South Greenleaf Avenue, Suite G, 60031
Telephone: 847-263-7770 Fax: 847-263-7771
Email: mzweig@injurylawyershotline.com URL: http://www.ftzlaw.net
Saul Ferris; Gary R. Thompson; Michael L. Zweig;—John Stergiou.

(This Listing Continued)

Ferris, Thompson & Zweig, Ltd. (Continued)

Languages: Spanish and Russian.
Personal Injury, Airplane Crashes, Medical Malpractice, Construction Site Accidents, Nursing Home Abuse and Neglect, Property Damage, Railroad Accidents and Injuries, Slip and Fall, Unsafe Products, Wrongful Death, Automobile Accidents, Workers Compensation, Criminal Defense, Drug Crimes, Drunk Driving, Felonies, Homicides, Juvenile Crimes, Misdemeanors, Parole and Probation, Traffic Violations.

See Professional Biographies, GURNEE, ILLINOIS

Glaeser, Tammy K. '63 '91 C.172 B.S. L.208 J.D. 495 N. Riverside Drive, Suite 209
Grace, Michael J. '20 '50 C&L.209 B.A., J.D. 3535A Grand Ave.
Gravel, Denis M., (BV) '62 '96 C.339 B.A. L.589 J.D. [D.M.Gravel&Assoc.]
Gravel, Denis M., & Associates, P.C., (BV) 5101 Washington Street, Suite 2R
Joslyn, D. Richard, (BV) '32 '58 C.58 B.A. L.365 LL.B. 5788 Regency Ct.

Kaplan, Matthew, & Associates
(See Libertyville)

Lazarus, Shelley N. '55 '82 C.959 B.A. L.436 J.D. 7583 Dada Dr.
Magna, Rudolph F., (AV) '49 '75 C.98 B.A. L.424 J.D. [Magna]
Magna Law Office, (AV) 495 N. Riverside Dr.
Magnuson, Lawrence Kenneth '56 '84 [L.K.Magnuson]
Magnuson, Lawrence K., P.C. 5250 Grand Ave., Ste. 14

May & Buege
(See Waukegan)

McCaffery, Joseph P., Attorney at Law
(See Aurora)

Neal, Janet M., (BVⓉ) '51 '84 C.121 B.S. L.436 J.D. Corp. Coun., Snap-on Credit LLC
Sagartz, Andrew P. '67 '98 C.1433 B.S. L.608 J.D. [A.Sagartz] (ⓒColumbus, OH)
Sagartz, Andrew, Law Offices of, LLC 5465 Grand Avenue, Suite 100
Shumaker, Wilbur A. '30 '56 C&L.378 A.B., LL.B. (adm. in KS; not adm. in IL) State Farm Ins. Co.
Siegel, Brent M. '48 '73 C.339 B.S. L.145 J.D. P.O. Box 269
Sinclair, Daniel K. '49 '73 C.393 B.A. L.597 J.D. 4170 Grand Ave.
Stergiou, John '72 '01 C.209 B.S. L.1187 J.D. [⊡ Ferris,T.&Z.]
Swanson, Barbara J., (BV) '54 '83 C.234 B.S. L.146 J.D. 4473 Grand Ave.
Swanson, W. Howard '23 '51 C.339 L.146 LL.B. 684 Dunham Rd.‡
Thompson, Gary R., (BV) '61 '87 C.352 B.A. L.589 J.D. [Ferris,T.&Z.]
Vicari, Anne Marie, (BV) '60 '85 C&L.879 B.S., J.D. [Diambri&V.]
Young, John S. '63 '91 C.209 B.A. L.801 J.D. Jud. Law Clk., Ct. App
Zweig, Michael L., (BV) '58 '85 C.36 B.S. L.61 J.D. [Ferris,T.&Z.]

HAMEL, 530, *Madison Co.*

Burkart, Thomas W., (BV) '60 '85 C.973 B.A. L.734 J.D. 130 West State Street (ⓒMaryville)

HAMILTON, 3,029, *Hancock Co.*

Morris, Stephen B., (BV) '54 '84 C.927 B.A. L.801 J.D. [S.B.Morris]
Morris, Stephen B., PC, Law Office of, (BV) 1040 Bwy.

HAMMOND, 527, *Piatt Co.*

Hull, A. Lewis, (AV) '16 '39 C&L.502 J.D. 208 E. 150 N. Rd.

HAMPSHIRE, 2,900, *Kane Co.*

Prindiville, Dale J. '33 '60 C&L.436 B.S.B.A., LL.B. (adm. in WI; not adm. in IL) 817 Bruce Robert Lane‡
Slayton, R. Duane '39 '67 C.937 B.A. L.146 J.D. 452 S. State Street
Witaske, Raymond A., Law Office of '46 '73 C.742 B.A. L.146 J.D. 124 S. State St.

HANNA CITY, 1,013, *Peoria Co.*

Honegger, Michael J., (BV) '57 '92 C.98 B.S. L.879 J.D. [M.J.Honegger]
Honegger, Michael J., PC, (BV) 12900 W. Farmington Rd.

HANOVER PARK, 38,278, *Cook & DuPage Cos.*

Binninger, James W. '51 '76 C.589 B.S. L.801 J.D. Vil. of Hanover Park
Chen, Cynthia S. T. '63 '89 C.1441 LL.B. L.276 LL.M. (adm. in NY; not adm. in IL) 820 Turnberry Ct.
Engel, James, Attorney at Law '50 '80 C.339 B.A. L.880 J.D. 2071 Irving Park Rd., Ste. 101

Heidelberger, Elliot, Law Offices of '42 '67 C&L.339 A.B., J.D.
7225 Longmeadow Lane, 60133
Telephone: 630-289-4000 Fax: 630-289-3444 URL: http://www.heidelbergerlaw.com
Email: elliot@heidelbergerlaw.com URL: http://www.lawyers.com/eheidelberger
Family Law, Divorce, Child Custody, Child Support, Premarital Agreements, Spousal Support, Parentage, Real Estate Closings.
Chicago, Illinois Office: 20 North Clark Street, Suite 1725, 60602-4101. Telephone: 312-443-8003.

See Professional Biographies, HANOVER PARK, ILLINOIS

Klest Law Firm
(See Schaumburg)

Marek, Anna D. '28 '54 C.339 B.A. L.365 LL.B. 27 W 242 Ontarioville Rd.

Martucci, Gregory J., P.C., Law Office of
(See Roselle)

Roloff, Earl J. '54 '79 C.238 B.A. L.365 J.D. 1060 Lake St.

HARDIN, * 959, *Calhoun Co.*

Burch, Charles H., (BV) '46 '71 C&L.734 B.A., J.D. States Atty.
Greenlief, Richard D. '49 '83 C.927 B.A. L.801 J.D. Cir. J.

HARRISBURG, * 9,860, *Saline Co.*

Beggs, Samuel G., (BV) '53 '90 C.801 B.S. L.90 J.D. [Lambert&B.]
Bittle, Todd P., (CV) '66 '96 C.234 B.S. L.801 J.D. Part-Time Pub. Def.
Brown, Nina Williams, (CV) '56 '81 C.801 B.A. L.221 J.D. 15 E. Poplar St.
Cape, Grant '56 '81 C&L.339 B.S., J.D. 105 S Commercial St
Doerge, Michal, (BV) '58 '84 C.531 B.S. L.801 J.D. [Jelliffe,F.M.&D.]
Ferguson, Charles M. '36 '61 C.339 B.A. L.221 J.D. 317 E. Poplar St.‡
Ferrell, Donald V., (AV) '44 '69 C.339 B.S. L.16 J.D. [Jelliffe,F.M.&D.]
Fornes, Timothy L., (BV) '46 '75 C.734 A.B. L.1049 J.D. 617 East Church Street, Suite 3
Hauptmann, David W., (CV) '47 '73 C.801 B.A. L.339 J.D. 617 East Church Street
Henshaw, Michael J. '44 '71 C.801 B.A. L.146 J.D. Cir. J.
Hines, Douglas E., (CV) '64 '93 C.249 B.S. L.801 J.D. [D.E.Hines]
Hines, Douglas E., P.C., Law Offices of, (CV) 317 E. Popular

Howerton, Dorris & Stone
(See Marion)

Jelliffe, Charles R., (AV) '25 '53 C&L.339 B.S., J.D. [⊡ Jelliffe,F.M.&D.] ‡

Jelliffe, Ferrell, Morris & Doerge, (AV) ⊞
108 East Walnut Street, P.O. Box 406, 62946
Telephone: 618-253-7153; 253-7647 Telecopier: 618-252-1843
Email: jfmdf@neondsl.com
Retired: Charles R. Jelliffe (Retired). Members of Firm: Donald V. Ferrell; Walden E. Morris; Michal Doerge. Associate: Kelly R. Phelps.
Insurance Law, Negligence and Personal Injury, Litigation, Workers' Compensation Law, and Employment Law. Commercial Collection and DUI's. General Civil Practice in State and Federal Courts. Trials and Appeals.
Representative Clients: Auto-Owners Insurance; Country Cos; Ohio Casualty Group; Standard Mutual Insurance Co.; State Farm Cos.

See Professional Biographies, HARRISBURG, ILLINOIS

Lambert, Todd D., (BV) '62 '90 C&L.801 B.S., J.D. [Lambert&B.]
Lambert & Beggs, (BV) 317 East Poplar Street, Suite B
Lockwood, Brocton D., (AV) '44 '69 C.604 B.A. L.880 J.D. P.O. Box 797
McGowan, Debra S., (CV) '68 '92 C.234 B.A. L.339 J.D. [⊡ Lambert&B.]

Mitchell & Mitchell
(See Marion)

Morris, Walden E., (AV) '49 '76 C.801 B.A. L.862 J.D. [Jelliffe,F.M.&D.]
Murphy, Glenn A., (BV) '55 '81 C&L.801 B.A., J.D. [G.Murphy]
Murphy, Glenn, (BV) P.O. Box 349
Myers, Paul L., Jr., (CV) '53 '79 C&L.801 B.S., J.D. 1 S. Main St.
Nelson, C. David, Law Office of, (BV) '41 '76 C.309 A.B. L.801 J.D. 117 West Poplar Street
Oshel, Michael V., (BV) '51 '76 C.339 A.B. L.801 J.D. [M.V.Oshel]
Oshel, Michael V., P.C., (BV) 317 East Poplar-Suite C
Phelps, Kelly R., (CV) '70 '95 C.339 B.A. L.801 J.D. [⊡ Jelliffe,F.M.&D.]
Rath, Robert H., (BV) '41 '66 C.801 B.A. L.339 J.D. 11 E. Poplar St.
Stewart, Bruce D. '52 '76 C&L.801 B.S., J.D. Cir. J.
Taylor, Charles D., (CV) '23 '82 L.801 J.D. 327 W. Poplar St.
Tison, Gloria, Attorney at Law '— '90 C.788 B.A. L.910 J.D. 206 E. Poplar
Tison, Krystal S., (BV) '52 '80 C&L.801 B.S.M.S., J.D. 15 E. Poplar St.
White, Frank R. '05 '40 C.337 A.B. L.339 J.D. 1620 May St.‡
Wilson, Robert C., (BV) '50 '75 C&L.339 B.S., J.D. 105 South Commercial

HARVARD, 7,996, *McHenry Co.*

Beeson, Charles J. '55 '86 C.508 B.A. L.146 J.D. 8501 White Oaks Rd.
Berg, Joel D., (BV) '67 '94 C.589 B.S. L.146 J.D. 105 1/2 E. Sumner St.
Bishop, James W. '01 '32 L.144 LL.B. 601 N. Lincoln St.‡
Bishop, James W. '31 '60 C.339 B.S. L.365 LL.B. 601 N. Lincoln St.‡
Carlson, Arthur B. '38 '63 C.1016 A.B. L.365 LL.B. P.O. Box 764
Carlson, Dale Alan, (BV) '59 '86 C.340 B.A. L.589 J.D. 35-1/2 N. Ayer
Elman, William, (AV) '32 '59 C.293 B.A. L.309 J.D. [Elman&E.]

Elman & Ehardt, Ltd., (AV) ⊞
100 South Ayer Street-Unit E, 60033-2900
Telephone: 815-943-4051 Fax: 815-943-4086
Email: elman@owc.net
William Elman.
General Practice. Trials, Negligence Law, Worker's Compensation, Real Estate and Probate. Mediation.

See Professional Biographies, HARVARD, ILLINOIS

Haugh, Stephen M., (BV) '49 '82 C.589 B.S.Ed. L.146 J.D. [S.M.Haugh]
Haugh, Stephen M., P.C., (BV) 60 N. Ayer St.
Papp, Bernard K., (AV) '52 '78 C.560 B.A. L.424 J.D. [B.K.Papp]
Papp, Bernard K., P.C., (AV) 62 N. Ayer St.

Pollock, Meyers, Eicksteadt & Pulak, Ltd.
(See Marengo)

Seegers, Carolyn B. '45 '79 C.63 B.S. L.209 J.D. Harvard Community Mem. Hosp.
Summers, Scott K. '49 '86 C.339 A.B. L.589 J.D. P.O. Box 430
Weir, Jas. H., (AV) '18 '42 C&L.339 B.S., LL.B. 35-1/2 N. Ayer St.

HARVEY, 30,000, *Cook Co.*

Flemister, Peter L. '50 '75 C.589 B.S. L.597 J.D. General Counsel, Allied Tube & Conduit Corporation, A Tyco Intl. Ltd. Co.
Jacoby, Diane Gilbert '58 '88 C.575 B.A. L.574 J.D. General Counsel, Ingalls Health System

HARWOOD HEIGHTS, 8,297, *Cook Co.*

Favia, Michael V.
(See Chicago)

Johns, Timothy J. '52 '80 C.363 A.B. L.589 J.D. 7151 W. Gunnison
Lampert, Jeffrey M. '41 '65 C.339 L.209 J.D. CEO, Har Technologies
Plotke, Thomas L. '55 '91 C.339 B.A. L.365 J.D. 6422 W. Gunnison
Schreiber, Berthold H. '36 '60 C.879 B.A. L.146 LL.B. Parkway Bk. & Tr. Co.

HAVANA, * 3,610, *Mason Co.*

Becker, Eldon H., (AV) '41 '66 C.98 B.A. L.339 LL.B. [Grosboll,B.&T.] (ⓒPetersburg)
Boggs, Don P., (AV) '37 '62 C.388 A.B. L.215 LL.B. [Boggs,K.&L.]
Boggs, Knuppel & Lindner, P.C., (AV) 124 W. Market St.
Brownfield, Thomas L. '49 '76 C.927 B.B. L.208 J.D. Cir. J.
Butler, Linda M. '56 '82 C&L.801 B.S., J.D. V.P. & Sr. Tr. Offr., Havana Natl. Bk.
Eaton, Clyde L. '15 '52 C.339 B.S. L.996 LL.B. 205 W. Market St.‡
Grosboll, Becker & Tice, (AV) 420 S. Promenade (ⓒPetersburg, Virginia)
Knuppel, William H., (AV) '39 '67 C.801 B.A. L.339 J.D. [Boggs,K.&L.]
Lindner, Blake, (CV) '70 '95 C.337 B.S. L.801 J.D. [Boggs,K.&L.]
Morgan, Steven B., (BV) '57 '85 C.504 B.A. L.879 J.D. [Perbix&M.]
Perbix, James L., (AV) '34 '58 C&L.879 B.A., J.D. [Perbix&M.]
Perbix and Morgan, (AV) 115 South Orange Street
Thomson, Roger Brian '67 '92 C.234 B.A. L.801 J.D. [Thomson,R.B.]
Thomson, Roger B. P.O. Box 135
Tucker, Alan D., (BV) '52 '78 C.339 B.A. L.472 J.D. State's Atty.
White, H. S. '15 '40 C.337 B.A. L.339 LL.B. 129 S. Orange St.‡

HAWTHORN WOODS, 6,002, *Lake Co.*

Abbott, Marny Joy '70 '97 C.1036 B.A. L.209 J.D. IFC Credit Corp.
Allen, Susan J. '52 '78 C.473 B.A. L.209 J.D. 32 Acorn Drive
Leyden, Kathleen L. '64 '91 C.424 B.B.A. L.602 J.D. 51 Lynn Drive
Lowry, Donald M. '29 '53 C&L.436 Ph.B., LL.B. 79 Mark Dr.‡
McGuan, Patrick J. '34 '62 C&L.424 B.S., J.D. 16 Elm
Miller, David C. '20 '45 C.025 B.A. L.276 J.D. 34 Steeplechase Dr.‡
Paulsen, Diane Margosian '58 '85 C.1217 B.S.B.A. L.213 J.D. (adm. in MI; not adm. in IL) 12 Arrowwood Dr.‡

HAZEL CREST, 14,816, *Cook Co.*

Bushnell, Richard, (AV) '26 '52 C.679 B.S. L.273 J.D.
3504 Lakeview Dr., Apt. 311 (Pat.)
Ellison, Sheila A. ... '61 '89 C.436 B.S.N. L.339 J.D. [Miller&E.]
Gurion, Henry B. '50 '75 C.339 B.A. L.424 J.D.
Vice President & General Counsel, MJMC, Inc.
Harris, Kirk E. ... '57 '85 C.705 B.A. L.1137 J.D. 3712 River Road
Lorsch, Ronald B. ... '54 '80 C.339 B.S. L.146 J.D. 1829 W. 170th St.
Miller, Steven R. ... '59 '84 C.597 B.A. L.339 J.D. [Miller&E.]
Miller & Ellison ... 17508 S. Carriageway Dr.
Murphy, William King ... '23 '50 C&L.209 LL.B. 1730 W. 170th St.‡

HEBRON, 1,038, *McHenry Co.*

Kelly, Richard C., (BV) ... '41 '67 C.755 B.A. L.209 J.D. [Kelly&K.]
Kelly, Richard C., Jr., (CV) ... '65 '92 C.755 B.A. L.209 J.D. [Kelly&K.]
Kelly and Kelly, (BV) ... 10008 Main St.

HENNEPIN, * 669, *Putnam Co.*

Bolin, Roger C., (BV) ... '54 '80 C.927 B.A. L.802 J.D. [Boyle&B.]
Boyle, Walter Durley, (AV) ... '13 '36 C&L.339 A.B., J.D. [Boyle&B.]
Boyle & Bolin, (AV) ... 227 E. Court St.
Bumgarner, James M. ... '19 '46 C&L.339 A.B., J.D. Cir. J.
Goldsmith, Linn C., (AV) ... '34 '64 C.679 B.S. L.145 J.D. [Ⓒ Boyle&B.]
Korba, Steven J. ... '46 '74 C.473 B.S. L.150 J.D. LTV Steel Corp.

Leynaud & Leynaud, A Prof. Corp., Law Offices of
(See Peru)

Mack, James A. ... '65 '95 C.338 B.S. L.589 J.D. State's Atty.
Raffety, Norman K., (BV) ... '49 '75 C.338 B.A. L.146 J.D. States Atty.

HENRY, 2,591, *Marshall Co.*

Swartz, Eric S., (BV) ... '50 '80 C.98 B.S. L.352 J.D. 611 2nd St.
Wosik, John J. ... '24 '51 L.365 LL.B. P.O. Box 191

HERRIN, 11,298, *Williamson Co.*

Bartelsmeyer, David L., (CV) ... '62 '92 C.339 L.801 J.D. [Craig&B.]
Bleyer, Kenneth A., (CV) ... '63 '88 C.734 B.A. L.801 J.D. City Atty.
Brandon, Donald R., (CV) ... '44 '75 C.801 M.S. L.146 J.D. 206 N. 14th St.
Craig, David R., (BV) ... '37 '73 C&L.339 B.S.C.E., J.D. [Craig&B.]
Craig & Bartelsmeyer, P.C., (BV) ... 203 N. Park Ave.

Hart and Hart
(See Benton)

Sneed, Carl D., (BV) ... '09 '36 C&L.339 B.A., J.D. 501 S. 16th St.

HEYWORTH, 2,431, *McLean Co.*

De Pew, James R., (AV) ... '19 '48 C.338 B.E. L.339 LL.B. Vil. Atty. [De Pew,G.&D.] ⊙
De Pew, Grimes & De Pew, (AV) ... 104 W. Main St. (⊙Bloomington)
Musick, Vicky L. '55 '85 C.1300 B.S. L.420 J.D.
(adm. in LA; not adm. in IL) 806 Tomahawk
Toohill, Clement M. ... '17 '44 C&L.734 LL.B. R.R. 2, Box 107‡

HICKORY HILLS, 13,926, *Cook Co.*

Andrews, George, (BV) ... '58 '85 C.339 B.A. L.1187 J.D. [G.Andrews&Assoc.]
Andrews, George, & Associates, PC, (BV) ... 8855 S. Roberts Road
Battaglia, Mark Anthony ... '74 '00 C.589 B.S. L.365 J.D. 7667 W. 95th St.
Davenport, Jack B. ... '44 '74 C.339 B.A. L.209 J.D. 7667 W. 95th St., Ste. 303
Doorhy, Martin ... '55 '85 C.209 B.A. L.424 J.D. 9231 S. Roberts Rd.
Family Law Association, Ltd. ... 8200 W. 95th St.
Fasone, Peter J. ... '36 '64 C.560 B.B.A. L.146 J.D. 7667 W. 95th St.
Gomolinski, William E. ... '59 '86 C.424 L.365 J.D. [Gomolinski&P.]
Gomolinski & Philipps, Ltd. ... 8855 S. Roberts Road
Kwit, Thomas J. ... '48 '77 C.1183 B.A. L.209 J.D. 9207 S. Kean
Lucente, Debra Jean ... '57 '82 C.339 B.A. L.146 J.D. Sr. Staff Coun., Correll Co.
Philipps, David J. ... '62 '87 C.424 B.A. L.339 J.D. [Gomolinski&P.]
Philipps, Mary E. ... '61 '88 C.597 B.A. L.339 J.D. [Ⓐ Gomolinski&P.]
Reidy, Robert E. ... '46 '76 C.602 A.B. L.209 J.D. 7667 W. 95th St., Ste. 202
Riley, Daniel A. ... '48 '75 C.1151 B.A. L.365 J.D. 9211 S. 85th Ct.
Riley, James G. ... '54 '82 C.1151 B.S. L.365 J.D. 9240 S. 82nd Ave.
Salah, A., & Associates ... '68 '97 C.339 B.S. L.365 J.D. 7667 West 95th Street, Suite 304
Sals, Terrence A. ... '51 '76 C.339 B.A. L.365 J.D. 7667 W. 95th St.
Tristano, Ceil A. ... '51 '75 C.339 B.S. L.209 J.D. [Family]
Tristano, Michael T. ... '47 '82 C.999 B.A. L.209 J.D. [Family]
Vakulskas, Brian Blane ... '75 '01 C.351 B.A. L.793 J.D. 1721 Jackson St.
Wunder, Michael J. ... '38 '70 C.209 B.S. L.365 J.D. 7667 W. 95th St.
Zumbakis, S. Paul ... '37 '69 C.424 B.S.C. L.365 J.D. 7667 W. 95th St.

HIGHLAND, 8,438, *Madison Co.*

Geismann, John P., (P.C.), (BV) ... '40 '68 C&L.734 B.S.C., J.D. 1019 Broadway

Hill, Thomas A., (BV) '48 '75 C.339 B.S. L.365 J.D.
100 Executive Drive, P.O. Box 141, 62249
Telephone: 618-654-9787; 654-6551 Fax: 618-654-4827
Email: hill-law@highlandil.com
Real Estate, Trusts and Estates, Business Law, Civil Practice, Corporate Law, Personal Injury.
A list of Representative Clients and References will be provided upon request.
See Professional Biographies, HIGHLAND, ILLINOIS

Homann, Matthew W., (CV) ... '68 '93 C.339 B.A. L.910 J.D. 12616 Route 143, Ste. 200
Johannes, Donald R., (BV) ... '44 '75 C.1082 B.A. L.734 J.D. [Johannes&M.]
Johannes & Marron, P.C., (BV) ... 1320 Bwy.
Johnson, Gregg N., (BV) ... '57 '85 C.927 B.S. L.801 J.D. 1320 Laurel Street
Koch, Dennis L., (CV) ... '47 '73 C&L.339 B.S., J.D. 1007 Lindenthal St.
Levi, Harry J., (AV) ... '19 '42 C&L.145 A.B., LL.B. 1566 Eastwood Ave.
Marron, George E., III, (BV) ... '55 '81 C&L.734 A.B., J.D. [Johannes&M.]
Potter, Edwin L., (CV) ... '57 '82 C.339 B.A. L.421 J.D. 1000 Pine St.

HIGHLAND PARK, 31,365, *Lake Co.*

Arnold, Leonard C., (AV) ... '21 '65 C.597 B.S. L.365 J.D. [L.C.Arnold]
Arnold, Leonard C., Ltd., (AV) ... 1900 Watercress Way
Arnson, Craig S. ... '60 '85 C.477 B.A. L.94 J.D. International Airport Centers
Bain, Howard M., (BV) ... '48 '78 C.339 B.S. L.589 J.D. [Emalfarb,S.&B.]
Baizer, Robert S., (AV) ... '46 '72 C.339 B.A. L.597 J.D. [Baizer&K.]

Baizer & Kolar, P.C., (AV)
513 Central Avenue, Fifth Floor, 60035
Telephone: 847-433-6677 Fax: 847-433-6735
Email: bk@baizlaw.com URL: http://www.baizlaw.com

(This Listing Continued)

Baizer & Kolar, P.C. (Continued)
Robert S. Baizer; Joseph E. Kolar;—Beth Greenberg Prager; Brian J. Lewis.
Plaintiff's Personal Injury, Medical Malpractice and Aviation Negligence Trials.
See Professional Biographies, HIGHLAND PARK, ILLINOIS

Barezky, Lawrence R., (AV) '37 '63
C.1016 B.S.B.A. L.597 J.D. [Beermann S.W.B.B.G.&L.] ⊙
Barrett, Edward J., (AV) ... '21 '50 C&L.597 B.A., J.D. 630 Onwentsia Ave.
Bartelstein-Foster, Terri Lynn ... '59 '85 C.174 B.A. L.276 J.D. 199 Cary Ave.‡
Becker, Martin I. ... '45 '72 C.966 B.B.A. L.174 J.D. 513 Central Ave., 5th Fl.
Beermann Swerdlove Woloshin Barezky Becker Genin & London, (AV)
1700 Greenbay Road (⊙Chicago)
Bellile, Kenneth W. ... '15 '42 C&L.966 B.A., J.D. 600 Central Ave.‡
Berlinsky, Joyce S. ... '50 '77 C.477 B.A. L.912 J.D. 513 Central Ave., 5th Fl.
Berman, C. Corey S., (BV) ... '65 '90 C.597 B.A. L.347 J.D. [Ⓒ Schiffman&J.]
Berman, Sue E. ... '58 '83 C.280 B.B.S. L.910 J.D. [S.Berman]
Berman, Sue ... 3023 Greenwood Ave.
Bernfield, Glen R., (AV) ... '35 '59 C.339 B.S. L.597 J.D. 2070 Partridge Lane
Bierig, Steven M., (AV) ... '56 '84 C.339 B.A. L.146 J.D. P.O. Box 438
Blumberg, Morris B. ... '17 '67 C.309 B.A. L.1119 J.D. 1025 Deerfield Park‡
Bonamarte, Michael F., III, (BV) '56 '81 C.388 B.A. L.209 J.D.
777 Central Ave., Ste. 9
Braithwaite, Susan W. ... '49 '80 C.339 B.A. L.209 J.D. 266 Sumac Rd.
Broderick, William J. ... '70 '03 C.436 B.A. L.146 J.D. [Ⓐ Emalfarb,S.&B.]
Brooks, Jerome M., (AV) ... '13 '37 C.339 B.A. L.209 J.D. 1831 Cavell Ave.‡
Brown, Kenneth H., (AV) ... '49 '76 C.966 B.S. L.209 J.D. [Brown&B.]
Brown, Roberta S. ... '49 '76 C.966 B.A. L.209 J.D. [Brown&B.]
Brown & Brown, P.C., (AV) ... 513 Central Ave., 5th Fl.
Buckman, Deborah F. ... '58 '83 C.367 B.A. L.94 J.D. 67 Ravinoaks Lane
Bush, Alvin B., (BV) ... '30 '55 C.1016 B.S. L.339 LL.B. 990 Coventry Lane
Carani, Joseph J. ... '30 '56 C.209 B.S. L.365 J.D. 1076 Court Ave.
Cascino, Mary Dory ... '49 '94 C&L.424 A.B., J.D. [Pasquesi]
Caspi, Melanie L. ... '72 '01 C.378 B.A. L.30 J.D. [Ⓐ Chausow S.]
Chaet, Tracy M. ... '64 '89 C.347 B.A. L.904 J.D. Broker, Coldwell Banker‡
Chamberlin, John B. ... '10 '34 C.197 A.B. L.597 J.D. 735 Baldwin Road
Channick, Herbert S. ... '29 '54 C.339 B.A. L.976 J.D. 3535 Patten Road
Chausow Shafer, P.C., (BV) ... 734 Central Avenue Suite 200
Chausow Shafer, Nancy, (BV) ... '55 '80 C.339 B.A. L.589 J.D. [Chausow S.]
Coan, Craig S. ... '61 '86 C.260 B.S. L.597 J.D. 203 Green Bay Rd.‡
Cohen, Arthur M. '49 '74 C.30 B.A. L.982 J.D.
(adm. in NY; not adm. in IL) 2660 Priscilla Ave.
Cohen, Nancy J. ... '62 '87 C&L.424 B.A., J.D. 617 Broadview‡
Coletta, Joseph Michael, (BV) ... '58 '83 C.221 B.A. L.900 J.D. One York Plz.
Cummings, Michael L. ... '59 '95 C.589 B.A. L.146 J.D. [Ⓐ Emalfarb,S.&B.]
Denenberg, Jay D. ... '55 '80 C.339 B.S. L.424 J.D. 1835 Elmwood‡
Dub, Allen W., (AV) ... '53 '78 C.273 B.A. L.1003 J.D. [Klein D.&H.] ⊙
Echt, Jeffrey D. ... '66 '91 C&L.347 B.S., J.D. 680 Sheridan Rd.
Edidin, Gary R. ... '45 '69 C.659 B.S. L.145 J.D. 600 Central Ave.
Eisenberg, Jos. L. '10 '35 C&L.608
(adm. in OH; not adm. in IL) 2906 Arlington Ave.‡
Eisenberg, Marc R. ... '66 '92 C.966 B.A. L.365 J.D. 1458 Sherwood Rd.
Emalfarb, Hal A., (AV) ... '52 '77 C.352 B.A. L.424 J.D. [Emalfarb,S.&B.]

Emalfarb, Swan & Bain, (AV)
440 Central Avenue, 60035
Telephone: 847-432-6900 Fax: 847-432-8950
Members of Firm: Hal A. Emalfarb; Peter G. Swan; Howard M. Bain. Associates: William J. Broderick; Michael L. Cummings; Fred Shestopal; Tara A. Moran.
Construction Law, Mechanics Liens, Construction Defects, Bankruptcy, Creditor Rights, Real Estate Law, Zoning Law, Contracts.
See Professional Biographies, HIGHLAND PARK, ILLINOIS

Emer, Steven D. ... '57 '82 C.339 B.S. L.146 J.D. 1695 Lake Cook Rd.
Esserman, Norman S. ... '25 '49 C&L.339 B.S., J.D. 522 Green Bay Rd.‡
Feinstein, Linda Maiman ... '52 '79 C.966 B.A. L.597 J.D. 960 Stonegate Dr.‡
Fieger, Joseph L. ... '37 '75 C.1016 B.S.B.A. L.146 J.D. [J.L.Fieger]
Fieger, Joseph L., Ltd. ... 983 Harvard Ct.
Fishleder, Martin S. ... '21 '49 C&L.209 B.S., J.D. 1271 Lynn Ter.
Fishman, Ross H. ... '60 '85 C.339 B.A. L.245 J.D. Pres., Ross Fishman Marketing, Inc.
Fiss, Jodi S. ... '62 '88 C.339 B.A. L.209 J.D. 1138 Lincoln Ave. S.‡
Ford, Robert H. ... '24 '50 C&L.494 B.S.L., J.D. 762 Exmoor Oaks Dr.‡
Fred Rothenberg & Associates, PC ... 426 Park Avenue East
Freeman, Barry J., (AV) ... '33 '57 C&L.597 B.S.L., LL.B. 235 Moraine Road
Frost, Jack P. ... '16 '40 C&L.597 B.S., J.D. 1386 Orleans Circle
Garland, Lee Rachel ... '74 '00 C.966 B.S. L.365 J.D. 440 Central Ave.
Goldman, Harold L. ... '21 '47 C.339 B.S. L.145 J.D. 953 Wildwood Ln.‡
Goldsmith, Earl A. ... '39 '65 C&L.597 B.S., J.D. P.O. Box 1653
Goodman, Wayne M. ... '46 '72 C.339 B.S. L.209 J.D. 230 Hastings Ave
Gorenstein, Edward A. ... '05 '28 C.339 A.B. L.145 J.D. 406 Woodland Rd.‡
Goslins, Miriam H. ... '49 '73 C.112 B.A. L.800 J.D. Miriam's Inc.

Grant and Grant, Professional Corporation
(See Chicago)

Gray, Robert L. ... '68 '94 [Ⓐ J.R.Grodner&Assoc.]
Grey, Beth Eiseman ... '62 '88 C.339 B.A. L.276 J.D. 571 Pleasant Ave.
Grodner, Jay R., (BV) ... '52 '78 C.966 B.A. L.365 J.D. [J.R.Grodner&Assoc.] ⊙
Grodner, Jay R., & Associates, P.C., (BV)
1893 N. Sheridan Rd., Ste. 215 (⊙Buffalo Grove, Chicago)
Gunnarsson, Gunnar B. ... '58 '88 C.145 A.B. L.339 J.D. 2755 Marl Oak Drive
Gurian, Jeffrey B., (AV) ... '56 '82 C.319 B.A. L.365 J.D. 513 Central Ave.
Haight, Edward A., (AV) ... '10 '34 C.966 A.B. L.309 LL.B. 267 Sumac Rd. (Pat.)
Hamity, Karen L. ... '49 '77 C.976 B.A. L.597 J.D. 90 Lakewood Pl.
Harris, Daniel M. ... '46 '71 C.339 B.S. L.597 J.D. 2345 Maple Lane

Harris Kessler & Goldstein LLC
(See Chicago)

Hattis, Russell E., (AV) '24 '50 C.339 B.S.E.E. L.273 LL.B.
1640 Jasmine Court (Pat.)‡

Heisler, Marc H.
(See Evanston)

Henry, Kenneth A.
(See Chicago)

Heymann, Idrienne L. ... '23 '45 C.680 L.575 LL.B. 2248 Linden Ave. (⊙Chicago)
Hoffman, S. David ... '22 '55 C.976 B.E.E. L.724 J.D. 603 Hillside Dr. (Pat.)
Holleb, Joshua D., (AV) ... '57 '83 C.478 B.A. L.146 J.D. [Klein D.&H.] ⊙
Jacobs, Michael S., (BV) ... '67 '92 C.966 B.A. L.365 J.D. [Schiffman&J.]
Jacobson, Ralph E. ... '18 '42 C&L.597 B.S.L., LL.B. 1801 Clifton‡

Jimmerson, J. Michael '56 '86 C.36 B.A. L.37 J.D.
(adm. in AZ; not adm. in IL) P.O. Box 220
Kalal, Patricia A., Law Offices of ... '57 '84 C.393 B.A. L.146 J.D. 426 Park Avenue East
Kantoff, Sheldon L. .... '36 '64 C.46 B.C.E. L.424 J.D. V.P., Leisure Care, Inc.
Kaplan, Harry '12 '40 C.415 B.A. L.1009 LL.B.
(adm. in NY; not adm. in IL) 2020 St. Johns Ave., #309‡
Katz, Edwin M. .... '09 '36 C&L.145 Ph.B., J.D. 1688 Green Bay Road
Kaufman, Amy R. .... '58 '86 C.228 B.A. L.145 J.D. 570 Lyman Ct.
Kaufman, Wm. S. .... '32 '58 C.477 B.A. L.145 J.D. 2860 Arlington Ave.‡
Klein, Robert M., (AV) .... '57 '82 C&L.966 B.B.A., J.D. [Klein D.&H.] ⊙

Klein Dub & Holleb, Ltd., (AV)
660 La Salle Place, Suite 100, 60035 ⊙
Telephone: 847-681-9100 Fax: 847-681-1600
Email: info@labor-law.com URL: http://www.labor-law.com
Robert M. Klein; Allen W. Dub; Joshua D. Holleb; Michael Paull. Of Counsel: Lawrence A. Reich.
Private and Public Sector Labor Law, Employment Law, Employment Discrimination and Affirmative Action. Litigation in State and Federal Courts and before Administrative Agencies in all listed practice areas.
Chicago, Illinois Office: 222 North La Salle Street, Suite 1900, 60601. Telephone: 312-464-9400.
See Professional Biographies, HIGHLAND PARK, ILLINOIS

Klow, Gary J. .... '41 '78 C.339 B.S.M.E. L.365 J.D. 1984 Sunset St.‡
Kolar, Joseph E., (AV) .... '60 '85 C.338 B.S. L.589 J.D. [Baizer&K.]
Krakowsky, Robert L. '45 '73 C.563 B.E. L.818 J.D.
(adm. in MA; not adm. in IL) Pres., Kropp Forge Co.
Kravitz, Morris A. .... '32 '60 C.339 L.365 LL.B. 2705 Bently Rd.
Kreiter, Shelley M. .... '50 '79 C.910 B.A. L.424 J.D. 525 Hillside‡
Kurland, Stuart A. .... '57 '82 C&L.978 B.A., J.D. 1860 Eastwood
Leiderman, Hermine S. '46 '71 C.1036 B.A. L.94 J.D.
(adm. in NY; not adm. in IL) 2896 Twin Oaks Drive‡
Leoris, Drake .... '21 '52 C.209 L.365 J.D. 622 Laurel Ave.
Leoris, Drake J., Jr. .... '55 '81 C.591 B.S. L.365 J.D. 622 Laurel Ave.
Levy, Francine F. .... '51 '75 C.966 B.A. L.597 J.D. 1850 Ridgelee Rd.

Lewinthal, Sklamberg & Associates
(See Northbrook)

Lewis, Brian J. .... '71 '97 C.477 B.A. L.339 J.D. [🄰 Baizer&K.]
Lewis, F. Raymond .... '30 '59 C&L.597 B.S., J.D. 703 Kincaid St.
Liebenson, Harold A. .... '17 '41 C.340 L.146 LL.B. 3311 Brook Rd.
Light, Kenneth B. '32 '57 C&L.569 B.S., LL.B.
(adm. in NY; not adm. in IL) 1825 Cavell Ave.‡
Lissa, Anna A. .... '57 '84 C.338 B.S. L.209 J.D. 646 Rice St.‡
Llanes, Andres M. .... '39 '82 C.999 LL.B. 85 Hemlock Lane
Logan, Robert I. .... '18 '47 C.103 A.B. L.597 J.D. 1162 Wade St.
Luskin, Bert L., (AV) .... '11 '33 L.209 LL.B. 1534 Mcoaniels Ave.

Manson, Lawrence A., (AV) '48 '74 C.880 B.A. L.178 J.D.
1445 St. Johns Avenue, 60035-3428
Telephone: 847-681-8734 Fax: 847-681-8735
Health Care Law, Litigation, Corporate Law.
See Professional Biographies, HIGHLAND PARK, ILLINOIS

Marder, Marvin A., (BV) .... '23 '48 C&L.209 B.S., J.D. 513 Central Ave.
McCarthy, Daniel T. .... '63 '88 C.339 B.A. L.589 J.D. 622 Laurel Ave.

Miller, Alan Benjamin, (AV) '44 '68 C.339 A.B. L.597 J.D.
1954 First Street Suite 245, 60035
Telephone: 847-721-5050 Fax: 847-831-9902
Email: alanlaw@TheRamp.net URL: http://www.lawyers.com/alanmiller
Business Litigation, Non-Consumer Collections, Probate Litigation, Insurance Fraud, Securities Fraud, Estate Planning and Administration, Real Estate, Small Business, Personal Injury.
See Professional Biographies, HIGHLAND PARK, ILLINOIS

Miller, Kirk L. .... '55 '80 C&L.801 B.A., J.D. 1910 First St.
Mitchell, Alan V. .... '36 '61 C.1016 B.S. L.365 J.D. 1700 Meadow Blvd.
Mokotoff, David .... '48 '83 C.623 B.A. L.818 J.D. 425 Park Ave.
Moos, A. Jerome .... '15 '40 C.137 L.146 LL.B. 1988 Green Bay Rd.
Moran, Tara A. .... '67 '94 C.607 B.A. L.365 J.D. [🄰 Emalfarb,S.&B.]
Moss, Edward J. .... '15 '39 C.966 B.S. L.597 LL.B. 410 Braeside Rd.‡
Moss, Scott A. '62 '87 C.347 B.S. L.692 J.D.
(adm. in VA; not adm. in IL) 1373 Oakwood Ave.‡
Mullin, Janis L., (Ms.) .... '46 '85 C.597 B.S. L.146 J.D. 1499 Chantilly Ct.‡
Murphy, Raymond T., (AV) '45 '72
C.1229 B.S. L.1003 J.D. 1510 Old Deerfield Road, Suite 230
Neiman, Erwin B. .... '32 '56 C&L.174 B.S., J.D. 2068 Old Briar Rd.
Olian, Terri R. .... '58 '83 C.118 B.A. L.424 J.D. 85 Oakmont Rd.
Orner, Seymour B. .... '13 '36 C.339 L.597 LL.B. 519 Hillside
Pasquesi, Theodore A., (AV) .... '30 '58 C&L.597 B.S.L., LL.B. [Pasquesi]
Pasquesi, Thomas A., (AV) .... '56 '82 C.597 B.A. L.365 J.D. [Pasquesi]
Pasquesi Associates, P.C., (AV) .... 460 Central Avenue
Patinkin, Debra L. .... '56 '83 C.339 B.A. L.365 J.D. [Patinkin&P.]
Patinkin, Richard E. .... '56 '84 C.339 B.A. L.365 J.D. [Patinkin&P.]
Patinkin & Patinkin .... 89 Lincolnwood Road
Paull, Donald, Law Offices of '28 '74 C.46 Ph.D. L.146 J.D.
619 Glenview Ave., Apt. 104
Paull, Michael, (AV) .... '61 '86 C.339 B.S. L.597 J.D. [Klein D.&H.] ⊙
Phillips, Gene M., (Ltd.) .... '26 '58 C.886 B.S. L.597 J.D. 1921 St. Johns Ave.
Pomrenze, Bonnie H. .... '50 '82 C.339 B.S. L.597 J.D. 3463 Summit Ave.‡
Prager, Beth Greenberg .... '60 '86 C.477 B.S.E. L.339 J.D. [🄰 Baizer&K.]
Regan, Peter J. '42 '70 C.433 B.Ch.E. L.262 J.D.
(adm. in NY; not adm. in IL) 1457 St. Tropez Ct.‡
Reich, Lawrence A., (AV) .... '37 '74 C.813 A.B. L.365 J.D. [⊡ Klein D.&H.] ⊙
Resnick, Gary A. .... '47 '73 C.966 B.B.A. L.339 J.D. 225 N. Deere Pk., E.‡
Rochell, Lawrence H. .... '35 '59 C.1016 B.S. L.209 LL.B. 119 Pierce Rd.‡
Roth, Michael J. .... '57 '82 C.145 B.A. L.146 J.D. 846 Virginia Rd.
Rothenberg, Fredrick .... '43 '74 C.174 B.A. L.424 J.D. [Fred R.&Assoc.]
Rubin, Leonard .... '21 '54 C.1016 B.A. L.365 LL.B. 1695 Sherwood Rd.
Ruder, Susan M. .... '39 '83 C.991 B.A. L.597 J.D. 325 Orchard Ln.‡
Ruffer, Galya B. '64 '89 C.659 B.A. L.597 J.D.
(adm. in PA; not adm. in IL) 224 Park Ave.‡
Ryan, Joseph D. .... '60 '86 C.966 B.S. L.146 J.D. [J.D.Ryan]
Ryan, Joseph D., P.C., Law Offices of .... 1896 Sheridan Rd.
Saks, Jori E., Law Office, (BV) .... '54 '79 C&L.339 B.A., J.D. 799 Central Ave., Ste. 300
Samuels, Henry B., (AV) .... '58 '83 C.339 B.S. L.146 J.D. 491 Laurel Ave.
Samuels, Michael D. '53 '77
C.221 B.A. L.770 J.D. Gen. Coun., DiamondSchreiber Homes, Inc.
Samuels, Robert E., (AV) .... '13 '39 C.145 A.B. L.365 J.D. 1601 Oakwood Ave.‡
Sandlow, Lisa I. .... '68 '93 C.846 B.A. L.424 J.D. 513 Central Avenue, 5th Floor
Savin, Bernard, (AV) .... '10 '35 L.209 LL.B. 1846 Rosemary Rd.‡

Schechter, Beth E. .... '70 '95 C.477 B.S. L.424 J.D. 192 S. Deere, Pk. Drive
Scheinbaum, Alan C. .... '47 '72 C&L.597 B.A., J.D. 1020 Carlyle Terrace
Schiffman, Reena J. .... '— '85 C.800 B.A. L.365 J.D. [Schiffman&J.]

Schiffman & Jacobs, P.C., (BV)
660 LaSalle Place, Suite 100, 60035
Telephone: 847-433-4300 Fax: 847-433-4328
Email: msjlaw4334300@aol.com URL: http://www.sjlawoffices.com
Reena J. Schiffman; Michael S. Jacobs. Of Counsel: C. Corey S. Berman.
Commercial Litigation, Family Law, Divorce, Real Estate, Franchise Law, Condominium Law, Corporate Transactions, Construction Defects, Child Rights, Criminal Defense, Driving While Intoxicated, Secretary of State License Reinstatements, Appellate Work.
See Professional Biographies, HIGHLAND PARK, ILLINOIS

Schulman, Harry, (AV) .... '16 '38 C&L.145 B.A., J.D. 1535 Forest Ave.‡
Schulman, Mark L. .... '70 '95 C.966 B.A. L.339 J.D. 1191 Beech Lane
Schuster, Alan G. .... '55 '80 C.966 B.S. L.146 J.D. 1866 Sheridan Rd., Ste. 213
Schwartz, Tammy W. '62 '87 C.1044 B.S. L.1009 J.D.
(adm. in NY; not adm. in IL) 1735 Sundrop Cir.
Segenreich, George R., (Ltd.) .... '50 '75 C.861 B.A. L.209 J.D. 1055 North Ave.
Senescu, Stuart .... '47 '73 C.339 B.S. L.1119 J.D. Princ., Independent Inside Counsel
Senk, Neil J. .... '51 '77 C.611 B.A. L.146 J.D. 546 Green Bay Rd.
Serlin, Lawrence I. .... '48 '74 C.910 B.S.B.A. L.209 J.D. [L.I.Serlin]
Serlin, Lawrence I., LTD .... 3218 Skokie Valley Rd.
Shaw, Michael S. .... '41 '68 C.605 A.B. L.597 J.D. 833 Rice St.
Shestopal, Fred .... '77 '02 C.209 B.A. L.365 J.D. [🄰 Emalfarb,S.&B.]
Shimberg, Jonathan E., (BV) .... '49 '74 C.72 B.A. L.46 J.D. 9003 Lincolnwood Drive
Shulman, Daniel S. .... '33 '56 1460 Glencoe Ave.

Shults, David M., Law Offices of
(See Northbrook)

Singer, Alvin Ira .... '31 '56 C.210 B.A. L.597 J.D. Ret. Assoc. Cir. J.
Smith, Rick E. .... '61 '86 C.339 B.A. L.597 J.D. 1690 Park Ave. W.
Soble, Elaine K. .... '55 '84 C&L.477 B.A., J.D. 215 Lakeside Pl.
Speisman, Albert .... '48 '81 C.424 B.A. L.365 J.D. [A.Speisman&Assoc.]
Speisman, Albert, & Associates, P.C. .... 3500 Western Ave.
Steiger, Zev .... '39 '64 C.46 B.S. L.145 J.D. 3209 University Ave.
Stoll, Christopher J. .... '51 '84 C.89 B.A. L.589 J.D. 622 Laurel Ave.
Swan, Peter G., (BV) .... '59 '84 C.339 B.A. L.424 J.D. [Emalfarb,S.&B.]
Tabin, Seymour, (AV) .... '18 '40 C&L.145 A.B., J.D. 1148 Lincoln Ave.‡
Takiff, Sanford .... '37 '60 C.339 B.S. L.597 J.D. P.O. Box 546‡
Terry, Eugene .... '34 '56 C&L.145 B.A., J.D. 450 Central Ave.‡
Thalman, Richard .... '35 '67 C.339 B.S. L.209 LL.B. I.R.S.
Toback, Neal R., (AV) .... '38 '62 C&L.597 B.S., J.D. 2471 Augusta Way
Vickman, Lee J., (AV) .... '32 '54 C&L.145 A.B., J.D. 1346 Sheridan Rd.

Weil & Associates
(See Northbrook)

Weiner, Barbara A. .... '48 '75 C.446 B.S. L.209 J.D. [B.Weiner]
Weiner, Samuel K. .... '25 '51 C&L.145 Ph.B., J.D. 1740 Heather Lane‡
Weiner, Barbara .... 513 Central Ave., 5th Fl.
Wertheimer, H. Douglas .... '48 '73 C.966 B.A. L.209 J.D. 1050 Carlyle Terrace
Wilensky, Roberta L. .... '60 '88 390 Moraine Rd.
Winter, Leland S. .... '14 '41 C.145 B.A. L.365 J.D. 3121 Greenwood Ave.‡
Wolf, Bertram J. .... '24 '56 C.145 M.B.A. L.209 J.D. P.O. Box 1548
Wolff, Allan I., Jr., (AV) .... '10 '37 C.197 A.B. L.597 J.D. 564 Braeside Rd.
Yablon, Alfred B. .... '37 '70 C.209 B.S.C. L.365 J.D. 274 Charal Lane‡

HIGHWOOD, 4,143, *Lake Co.*

Bradner, James H., Jr. .... '41 '67 C.95 B.A. L.608 J.D. P.O. Box 415
Caravello, Michael J., (BV) .... '55 '82 C.339 B.S. L.146 J.D. 300 Green Bay Rd.
Diambri, Paul P., (AV) .... '55 '80 C.436 B.A. L.365 J.D. 300 Green Bay Rd.
Dorado, Maria I. .... '60 '86 C.668 B.A. L.1068 J.D. 53 Holabird Cir.
Minorini, Theodore J. .... '49 '76 C.973 A.B. L.365 J.D. 295 Michigan
Ori, Nello .... '13 '45 C.393 L.597 LL.B. Highwood Ave.
Solomon, Julius E. .... '07 '30 L.146 LL.B. 634 Sheridan Rd.‡

HILLSBORO, * 4,400, *Montgomery Co.*

Adams, Barbara Paddock, (BV) .... '52 '77 C.967 B.A. L.910 J.D. 109 S. Main St.
Bullington, John T., (AV) .... '18 '42 C&L.339 B.A., LL.B. [⊡ Bullington,W.M.J.&E.] ‡
Bullington, White, McPhail, Jarman and Evans, P.C., (BV) .... 127 N. Main St.
Cullison, Stephen R., (BV) .... '52 '77 C.927 B.A. L.801 J.D. 405 S. Main St.
Dobrinic, Kathryn Slepicka, (BV) .... '54 '79 C&L.546 B.A., J.D. State's Atty.
Evans, John E., (BV) .... '47 '72 C&L.339 B.A., J.D. [Bullington,W.M.J.&E.]
Flowers, Stephanie L. .... '70 '98 C.357 B.S. L.339 J.D. [🄰 Bullington,W.M.J.&E.]
Huber, Dennis M. .... '47 '72 C&L.339 B.S., J.D. Cir. J.
Huber, Gerald Patrick, (CV) .... '43 '73 C.734 B.S. L.767 J.D. 225 S. Main St.
Jarman, Douglas L., (BV) .... '57 '85 C.234 B.A. L.801 J.D. [D.L.Jarman]
Jarman, Douglas L., P.C., (BV) .... 127 N. Main St.
Joy, Mark M. .... '48 '76 C.234 B.A. L.424 J.D. Asso. Cir. J.
Long, Kelly D., (BV) .... '44 '69 C.339 B.S. L.910 J.D. Cir.J.
McPhail, Raymond E., (BV) .... '35 '80 C.766 B.A. L.801 J.D. [Bullington,W.M.J.&E.]
Roberts, James L., (BV) .... '61 '86 C.234 B.A. L.801 J.D. 109 S. Main St.
Schroeder, Neil Thomas .... '66 '93 C&L.801 B.S., J.D. Asst. State's Atty.
Vandever, Ralph A., (AV) .... '17 '44 C.339 L.996 LL.B. 205 S. Oak St.‡

HILLSIDE, 8,155, *Cook Co.*

Conley, Edward J. .... '27 '53 L.146 LL.B. 323 Oakridge Ave.‡
English, Noel Ann .... '54 '79 C.339 B.A. L.597 J.D. Proviso Assn. for Retarded Citizens
Ferrill, Scott T. .... '58 '83 C.1288 B.S. L.365 J.D. 4100 Madison St.
Machroli, Vincent C. .... '50 '80 C.1016 B.A. L.365 J.D. [V.C.Machroli]
Machroli, Vincent C., P.C., Law Offices of .... 4415 W. Harrison St., Ste. 213
McGah, Edward R. .... '25 '78 C.602 B.S.C. L.1151 J.D. 4837 Butterfield Rd.
McGah, Joseph P., Jr. .... '52 '85 C.321 B.A. L.146 J.D. 4837 Butterfield Rd.
Ryan, James W. .... '35 '66 C&L.424 B.S.C., J.D. 96 Wolf Rd.‡
Weinstein, Marc H. .... '47 '74 C.589 B.S. L.146 J.D. [Weinstein&Assoc.]
Weinstein & Associates .... 4415 W. Harrison St., Ste. 234

HINCKLEY, 1,994, *DeKalb Co.*

Cliffe, Foster, Corneille, Buick & Buick, LLC, (BV)
165 Lincoln St. (⊙De Kalb, Shabbona, Sycamore, Waterman)
Foster, Keith L., (BV) '50 '79
C.589 B.A. L.146 J.D. [Cliffe,F.C.B.&B.] (⊙De Kalb, Shabbona)
Freriks, David R. .... '50 '80 C.339 B.A. L.146 J.D. 161 Maple St.
Lasswell, Roy S. .... '24 '52 C&L.597 B.S. 430 Prairie View Ln.
Schopp, David W. .... '64 '91 C.58 B.A. L.879 J.D. 600 Louise Dr.

HINES, —, *Cook Co.*

Atkinson, Bonnie H. '61 '88 C.338 B.S. L.146 J.D.
Staff Atty., Guardianship & Advocacy Comm.
Kokinda, Dennis A. '42 '80 C.347 B.A. L.1119 J.D. Dist. Coun., Vet. Admn.
Noel, Melbourne A., Jr., (AV) '43 '68 C.602 B.A. L.597 J.D.
U.S. Dept. of Vets. Affairs- Sr. Contract Atty.
Pellizzari, William F. '31 '57 C.999 B.A. L.365 J.D. Dept. of Vet. Affs.

HINSDALE, 17,349, *Cook & DuPage Cos.*

Alongi, Allan C., Law Offices of, (BV) '55 '85
C.352 B.G.S. L.146 J.D. 19 North Grant Street
Anglin, Mary C. '41 '66 C.713 B.A. L.597 J.D. 24 E. Ayers St.
Anthony, Debra '52 '79 L.966 J.D. 111 S. Adams St.
Atkenson, Charmaine E. '60 '86 C.339 B.S. L.209 J.D. 727 W. 6th St.
Avgeris, George N. '39 '64 C.578 B.A. L.339 LL.B. 29 E. 1st St.
Barnas, Daniel R. '49 '75 C.339 B.S. L.46 J.D. 22 Orchard Pl
Barnes, Robert D., (AV) '22 '50 C.791 B.S. L.597 J.D. 403 Chantileer Ln.‡
Beck, Lowell R. '34 '60 C.98 B.S. L.597 J.D. 17 East Walnut St.‡
Benner, Kathleen A. '67 '96 C.589 B.S. L.365 J.D. 619 S. Monroe St.
Biggert, Judith Borg '37 '63 C.813 B.A. L.597 J.D. 425 E. 6th St.
Boyle, Christine A. '54 '94 C.700 B.A. L.365 J.D. 201 E. Odgen Ave., Ste. 116
Cahill, Miles P. '59 '84 C.339 B.A. L.209 J.D. [Spiegel&C.]
Casper, Kenneth Michael '63 '87 C&L.259 B.A., J.D.
(adm. in FL; not adm. in IL) 38 S. Quincy St.
Cesario, Joseph T., (P.C.), (BV) '42 '68 C.436 B.S. L.597 J.D. [Cesario&W.]
Cesario & Walker, (BV) 211 West Chicago Avenue, Suite 118
Chawla, Tarran Paul S. '66 '91 C.339 B.A. L.910 J.D. [Chawla]

Chawla Group, The, LTD.
15 Spinning Wheel Road Suite 126, 60521
Telephone: 630-325-5557 Fax: 630-325-6666
URL: http://www.chawlagroup.com
Members of Firm: Tarran Paul S. Chawla; Craig Carnell Cunningham; Andrew B. Spiegel.
Entertainment Law, Corporate Law, Civil Practice, Domestic Relations, Personal Injury, Medical Malpractice.

See Professional Biographies, HINSDALE, ILLINOIS

Cochran, Wilbur P., III '39 '64 C&L.352 B.A., J.D. 505 Pamela Circle
Connolly, Stephen J. '46 '71 C.602 B.B.A. L.209 J.D. 119 Springlake Ave.
Coules, Peter, Jr. '61 '86 C.339 B.A. L.209 J.D. [Donatelli&C.]
Cummings, John R. '26 '53 C&L.209 B.S., LL.B. 21 Spinningwheel Rd.
Cunningham, Craig Carnell '65 '94 C.112 B.A. L.145 J.D. [Chawla]
Cunningham, Thomas J. '42 '67 C.36 B.S. L.930 J.D. 35 S. Garfield Ave.
Cusack, Richard W. '47 '73 C.893 B.A. L.146 J.D. 320 S. Garfield Ave.‡
Deppe, John W., Jr. '48 '75 Pres., Prof. Mgt. Res., Inc.
DeRose, John P. '43 '68 C&L.424 B.A., J.D. 15 Spinning Wheel Rd., Ste. 428
Diamant, William '28 '55 C&L.665 B.B.A., LL.B. 930 N. York Road
DiGrazia, Anthony A. '12 '39 L.209 LL.B. 105 E. 1st St.‡
Donatelli, Mark R. '58 '86 C.339 B.S. L.209 J.D. [Donatelli&C.]
Donatelli & Coules, Ltd. 15 Salt Creek Lane, Suite 312
Duggan, Michael J. '56 '83 C.679 B.S. L.365 J.D. 731 Town Place
Duhig, Michael J. '58 '83 C.801 B.A. L.209 J.D.
Asst. V.P. & Coun., Coldwell Banker Residential Real Estate
Ekroth, Robert R. '42 '69 C.105 B.S.B.A. L.339 J.D. [Ekroth&O.]
Ekroth & Osborne, Ltd. 15 Salt Creek Lane, Suite 122
Fitzgerald, Joseph E., The Law Offices of '45 '72
C&L.424 B.S., J.D. 105 E. 1st St., Ste. 203
Fronczak, Stanley W. '47 '89 C.424 B.S. L.365 J.D. 20 E. Ogden Ave.
Fry, Marcia L. '54 '81 C.339 B.S. L.365 J.D. 53 S. Lincoln St.
Garay, Martin R., III '49 '76 C&L.309 B.A., J.D. 621 Harding Rd.
Goodson, David M. '42 '75 C.959 B.S. L.146 J.D. 313 W. Fourth St.
Griffin, Nancy Hunter '46 '83 C.783 B.S. L.424 J.D. 1401 Burr Oak Rd., Apt. 1168
Groselak, Bradley S. '58 '83 C.999 B.A. L.221 J.D. 105 E. First St., Ste. 203
Grossmann, Robert M. '22 '50 C.145 Ph.B. L.146 J.D. 105 E. First St.
Hallett, Corinne '27 '76 C.145 B.A. L.365 J.D. 1401 Burr Oak Rd.
Hirsh, Richard L. '51 '76 C.1505 B.A. L.146 J.D. [R.L.Hirsh&Assoc.]

Hirsh, Richard L., & Associates, P.C.
15 Spinning Wheel Road Suite 128, 60521
Telephone: 630-655-2600 Fax: 630-655-2636 URL: http://www.bankruptcy-dupage.com
URL: http://www.hirshlawfirm.net
Richard L. Hirsh.
Bankruptcy, Personal Bankruptcy, Debtor and Creditor, Foreclosures and Buy-Sell Agreements.

See Professional Biographies, HINSDALE, ILLINOIS

Holbrook, H. Michael '36 '62 C.878 B.S. L.880 J.D. 6723 Kingswood Rd.
Hommel, John G. '49 '76 C&L.602 A.B., J.D. 4 N. Madison St.
Howell, Kathryn R. '— '96 C.344 B.A. L.705 J.D. 718 N. Elm St.‡
Hriszko, Robert W. '42 '68 C.742 B.A. L.597 J.D. 115 Oak Ridge Dr. E.‡
Irpino, Mark A. '60 '89 C.589 B.S. L.146 J.D. 35 S. Garfield Ave.
Joy, Harry J. '15 '39 C&L.424 LL.B. 305 Chanticleer Ln.‡
Keating, Charles J. '23 '50 C.999 L.365 LL.B. 21 Spinning Wheel Rd.‡
Kelly, Terrence F. '46 '74 C.321 A.B. L.262 J.D. 645 Lakeside Dr.
Kivela, Leo E. '28 '75 C.477 B.B.A. L.146 J.D. 225 E. 7th St.‡
Kopp, Angela Johnson '61 '87 C.323 B.A. L.1119 J.D. 348 The Lane‡
Koranda, Hugo '15 '41 C&L.597 B.S., LL.B. 6675 Shady Lane‡
Lenckos, Daniel J. '45 '70 C.201 B.S. L.597 J.D. V.P., The First Natl. Bank of Chicago
Lowenthal, Jody A. '48 '80 C.597 B.S.S. L.146 J.D. 208 Racquet Club Ct.
Mahay, Michael E. '59 '90 C.750 B.A. L.1000 J.D. [⊠ Spiegel&C.]
Main, Louis R., (AV) '30 '57 C.72 B.A. L.145 J.D. 115 E. First St.
Maltezos, Jill G. '52 '79 C.30 B.A. L.146 J.D. 303 Perk Clarengeon
Mancini, Dominic J. '50 '75 C.112 B.A. L.209 J.D. [D.J.Mancini]
Mancini, Dominic J., Law Offices of, P.C. 133 Fuller Rd.
Marchi, Louis R. '57 '83 C.679 B.S.I.E. L.424 J.D. LaSalle Bank‡
Markey, Howard T. '20 '50 C.37 L.424 LL.B.
Honorable, Americana Monticello Manor Care
Marsh, Nora H. '54 '79 C.339 B.A. L.424 J.D. 105 E. First St., Ste. 203
Martoccio, John F. '46 '73 C.597 B.A. L.365 J.D. 15 N. Lincoln St.
McGurren, Henry, (AV) '11 '35 C.188 A.B. L.477 LL.B. 201 E. Odgen‡
McNaney, Robert T. '34 '59 C&L.424 B.S., J.D. 1409 Burr Oak Road
Meyer, J. Robert '46 '71 C.477 B.S. L.309 J.D. 833 Merrill Woods Rd.
Miller, Barbara Matusik '39 '63 C&L.209 J.D. Value Mark Investment Services, Inc.
Mitzner, Scott L. '50 '77 C.589 B.S.Ed. L.365 J.D. [S.L.Mitzner]
Mitzner, Scott L., Ltd. P.O. Box 677
Morrison, Nancy J. '50 '77 C.967 B.S. L.200 J.D. 606 W. 56th St.‡
Nizamuddin, Azam, Law Office of '— '96 C.424 B.A. L.862 J.D. 15 N. Lincoln St.
Norris, William E. '44 '69 C.1016 B.A. L.365 J.D. 125 W. 2nd St.
Nuellen, James E. '35 '79 C.339 B.S. L.146 J.D. 1409 Burr Oak Rd.
Osborne, Rodney W. '46 '71 C.208 B.A. L.597 J.D. [Ekroth&O.]
Owens, Deborah W. '52 '86 C.700 B.A. L.424 J.D. 120 E. Ogden Ave.
Owens, Susan Brown '66 '92 C&L.802 B.S., J.D.
(adm. in MO; not adm. in IL) 827 S. Lincoln Street
Pieczynski, Linda S. '51 '77 C&L.209 B.A., J.D. 125 W. 2nd St.
Popuch, Steven L. '48 '77 C.309 B.A. L.424 J.D. 15 Spinning Wheel Road
Rediehs, Carol Ann '57 '82
C&L.802 B.B.A., J.D. Corp. Coun. & Secy., Chief Express, Inc.
Renno, Maureen '63 '89 C&L.209 B.A., J.D. Asst. States Atty.
Rio, Linda M. '63 '88 C.597 B.A. L.1068 J.D. 604 S. Stough St.
Roth, Sandra Z. '56 '86 C.289 B.A. L.30 J.D.
(adm. in PA; not adm. in IL) 604 W. Maple St.‡
Schaller, Robert V., & Associates '60 '85 C.339 B.S. L.209 J.D.
249 Meadowbrook Lane
Smith, Athena Platis '60 '85 C.813 B.A. L.597 J.D. 241 Meadowbrook Lane
Spiegel, Andrew B. '49 '74 C.339 B.A. L.424 J.D. [Chawla]
Spiegel, Martin Ted, (AV) '58 '83 C.473 B.A. L.1340 J.D. [Spiegel&C.]
Spiegel & Cahill, P.C., (AV) 15 Spinning Wheel Road, Suite 107
Theophilos, Theodore J., (AV Ⓣ) '53 '79 C.597 B.A. L.145 J.D. 535 Woodside Avenue
Ubatuba, Mary Chenoweth '49 '76 C.221 B.A. L.365 J.D. 645 Dalewood Lane‡
Vesely, Edward G., Jr. '48 '75 C.966 B.B.A. L.365 J.D. 930 N. York Rd., E.
Walker, Dan, Jr., (P.C.) '49 '74 C.770 B.A. L.597 J.D. [Cesario&W.]
Wilson, Deanna Shaw, Attorney at Law '— '98 C.963 B.A. L.966 J.D. 333 S. Elm St.
Witham, Richard T. '52 '76 C.63 B.S. L.801 J.D. 101 Burr Ridge Pkwy., Ste. 200
Wojciechowski, Stanley W. '49 '83
C.209 B.M. L.424 J.D. Asst. V.P., Liberty Fed. Svgs. Bk.
Zott, Elizabeth J. '62 '87 C.597 B.A. L.146 J.D. 810 S. Olay

HOFFMAN ESTATES, 49,495, *Cook Co.*

Alexander, Deborah R. '70 '96 C.477 A.B. L.309 J.D. Coun., Ameritech Corporation
Altier, Michael J. '48 '76 C.884 A.B. L.831 J.D.
(adm. in PA; not adm. in IL) Sr. Coun., Sears, Roebuck and Co.
Amato, Brent L. '49 '75 C.477 B.A. L.365 J.D. [Robinson,P.P.M.&A.]
Angelidis, Ellenore '66 '94
C.424 B.A. L.145 J.D. Asst. Gen. Coun., Sears, Roebuck and Co.
Ardito, Laurie A. '56 '81 C.700 B.A. L.589 J.D.
Asst. Gen. Coun., Sears, Roebuck & Co.

Arnstein & Lehr LLP, (AV)
2800 West Higgins Road, Suite 425, 60195-5224 ⊙
Telephone: 847-843-2900 Fax: 847-843-3355
Email: mail@arnstein.com URL: http://www.arnstein.com
Members of Firm: J. William Braithwaite; Lawrence E. Grelle; Nancy S. Harbottle.
General Practice.
Chicago, Illinois Office: Suite 1200, 120 South Riverside Plaza, 60606-3910. Telephone: 312-876-7100. Fax: 312-876-0288. Internet: mail@arnstein.com.
Boca Raton, Florida Office: 2424 North Federal Highway, Suite 462, 33431. Telephone: 561-322-6900. Fax: 561-322-6940.
Miami, Florida Office: Miami Center, 201 South Biscayne Boulevard, Fourth Floor, 33131. Telephone: 305-374-3330. Fax: 305-374-4744.
Tampa, Florida Office: 300 South Hyde Park Avenue, Suite 180, 33606. Telephone: 813-259-9964. Fax: 813-259-9724.
West Palm Beach, Florida Office: 515 North Flagler Drive, Suite 600, 33401-4323. Telephone: 561-833-9800. Fax: 561-655-5551.
Milwaukee, Wisconsin Office: 7161 North Port Washington Road, 53217. Telephone: 414-351-2440. Fax: 414-352-6901.

See Professional Biographies, HOFFMAN ESTATES, ILLINOIS

Atkins, Regina F. '62 '89
C.602 B.B.A. L.597 J.D. Asst. Gen. Coun., Sears, Roebuck and Co.
Beers, Michael P. '42 '68 C&L.339 A.B., J.D. 1936 Oakdale St.
Berghel, Victoria S., (AV) '52 '78 C&L.446 B.A., J.D.
(adm. in MD; not adm. in IL) Assoc. Gen. Coun., Sears, Roebuck and Co.
Block, Janice L., (AV) '— '88 C.674 B.A. L.178 J.D.
Sr. V.P., Gen. Coun. & Corp. Secy., Career Education Corp.
Bonina, Diane I. '63 '89 C.197 B.A. L.477 J.D.
Reg. Gen. Coun., Great Lakes, Cellula Wireless
Boone, Anthony '49 '74 C.238 B.A. L.608 J.D.
Assoc. Gen. Coun., Sears, Roebuck & Co.
Boone, Lynn Hudson '53 '78
C.604 B.A. L.276 J.D. Asst. Gen. Coun., Sears, Roebuck & Co.
Boston, Karyn D. '66 '92 C.302 B.S. L.213 J.D.
Asst. Gen. Coun., Escalated Customer Complaints, Sears, Roebuck and Co. (Legal Department)
Boyer, Daniel J. '42 '67 C.72 A.B. L.339 J.D. Sears, Roebuck & Co.
Boyle, Raymond E. '62 '87 C.174 B.S. L.339 J.D.
Associate General Counsel-Tax, Sears, Roebuck and Co.
Braithwaite, J. William, (AV) '— '56
C.184 B.A. L.178 LL.B. [Arnstein&L.] (⊙Chicago)
Browning, Julie A. '59 '86 C.597 B.A. L.145 J.D.
Asst. Gen. Coun., IT/Online, Sears, Roebuck and Co.
Bruce, James W. '46 '75 C.340 B.S. L.146 J.D. Atty., SAFECO Prop. & Cas. Ins. Co.
Burke, John Phillip '53 '78 C&L.339 B.A., J.D. Sr. Coun., Sears, Roebuck and Co.
Calabrese, Nicholas L. '55 '80
C.339 B.A. L.424 J.D. Sr. Coun., Transamerica Finance Corp.
Caywood, Christopher J. '60 '86 C&L.477 A.B., J.D. Sears, Roebuck and Co.
Cohan, Thomas J. '53 '81 C.424 B.A. L.589 J.D.
Asst. Gen. Coun., Transamerica Finance Corp.
Cohen, Laurence M. '67 '95 C.424 B.S. L.1187 J.D. 1033 W. Golf Road
Collins, Cary J., Law Offices of '47 '79
C.347 B.S.B.A. L.365 J.D. 2200 West Higgins Road, Suite 145
Cook, Steven M. '58 '83 C.589 B.A. L.339 J.D.
Dep. Gen. Coun., Sears, Roebuck and Co.
Crandall, Frith C. '61 '89
C.299 B.A. L.597 J.D. Asst. Gen. Coun., Sears, Roebuck and Co.
Crosby, Margaret M. '65 '96 C.550 B.A. L.365 J.D. [⊠ Pauley P.&E.] (Pat.)
d'Ambrosio, Thomas A. '62 '88 C.894 A.B. L.880 J.D.
Sr. Corp. Coun., Automatic Data Processing, Inc.
Darrow, V. Alexandra, (BV Ⓣ) '58 '89 C.228 B.A. L.575 J.D.
(adm. in GA; not adm. in IL) Corp. Coun., ADP
Di Lorenzo, Maria F. '64 '90
C.988 B.A. L.339 J.D. Asst. Gen. Coun., Sears, Roebuck & Co.
DiLorenzo, Sarah M. '68 '95 C.734 B.A. L.1119 J.D.
Sr. Coun., Sears, Roebuck and Co.
Dimaggio, Dominick T. '63 '89 C&L.209 B.A., J.D. 2200 W. Higgins, Ste. 145
Dziezak, Judie D. '55 '94 C.1216 B.S. L.424 J.D. [Dziezak] (Pat.)

Dziezak Law Firm, P.C.
2300 North Barrington Road, Suite 400, 60195
Telephone: 847-490-5370 Fax: 847-490-5378
Email: jdziezak@dziezak-law.com
Judie D. Dziezak.
Intellectual Property Law, including Patent, Trademark, Trade Secret, and Copyright Law, Licensing, and Unfair Competition.
See Professional Biographies, HOFFMAN ESTATES, ILLINOIS

Ealey Devens, Doris J. '65 '92 C.339 B.A. L.209 J.D. Assoc. Gen. Coun., Citicorp Credit Servs. Inc.
Edwards, Sandra ....'42 '75 C.347 A.B. L.228 J.D. 1566 W. Algonquin Rd., PMB-120
Elder, Sara E. .....'66 '91 C.910 A.B. L.209 J.D. Asst. Gen. Coun., Sears, Roebuck & Co.
Engfer, Victoria L. '62 '89 C.575 B.A. L.896 J.D. (adm. in CA; not adm. in IL) Asst. Gen. Coun., Sears, Roebuck and Co.
Erickson, Kevin D. ....'69 '95 C.352 B.S.M.E. L.365 J.D. [Pauley P.&E.] (Pat.)
Fanning, Robin Craig ...'51 '81 C.801 B.A. L.209 J.D. Sr. Coun., Sears, Roebuck and Co.
Farkas, Drew Eugene ....'62 '90 C.477 B.M. L.276 J.D. Sr. Coun., Sears, Roebuck & Co.
Feinstein, Scott D. '53 '78 C&L.93 B.S., J.D. (adm. in MA; not adm. in IL) Asst. Gen. Coun., Sears, Roebuck & Co.
Ferris, F. Henry, IV '68 '94 C.902 B.A. L.896 J.D. (adm. in SC; not adm. in IL) 3333 Beverly Rd., C4-196b‡
Filice, Eugene J. '50 '76 C.221 B.A. L.424 J.D. Asst. Gen. Coun., Sears, Roebuck and Co.
FitzSimon, Jean K., (AVⓉ) '51 '76 C.722 B.A. L.602 J.D. V.P. & Chf. Compl. Offr., Sears, Roebuck and Co.
Fleming, Daniel E., III, (CVⓉ) '58 '84 C.178 B.A. L.93 J.D. (adm. in PA; not adm. in IL) Sr. Coun., Sears. Roebuck & Co.
Gabe, Caryl Jacobs, & Associates, Inc., Law Offices of
(See South Barrington)
Gerak, Justin A. '62 '87 C&L.477 A.B., J.D. Assoc. Gen. Coun.-Online & Cust. Dir., Sears, Roebuck and Co.
Gladish, Kenneth J. '64 '89 C.597 B.A. L.339 J.D. Asst. Gen. Coun./V.P., Dealer Servs. Grp., Automatic Data Processing, Inc.
Glatz, David P. '68 '99 C.209 B.S. L.424 J.D. Asst. Gen. Coun., Sec. & Governance, Sears, Roebuck and Co.
Grace, Thomas E. ....'54 '79 C.338 B.A. L.365 J.D. Counsel, Ameritech Corporation
Grain, Peter S. ....'54 '84 C.575 B.S. L.146 J.D. [P.S.Grain&Assoc.]
Grain, Peter S., Law Offices of, & Associates, Ltd. ....2200 N. Stonington Ave.
Grelle, Lawrence E., (AV) ......'— '68 C.597 B.S. L.339 J.D. [Arnstein&L.] (⊙Chicago)
Griffin, Kimberly A. ....'64 '89 C.502 A.B. L.602 J.D. Sr. Coun., Sears, Roebuck and Co.
Hagener, Maria N. '42 '75 C.025 B.A. L.208 J.D. Assoc. Gen. Coun., Sears, Roebuck and Co.
Haley, Donald S. '53 '78 C.927 B.A. L.424 J.D. Asst. Mng. Atty., SAFECO Prop. & Cas. Ins. Co.
Haliuni, Isaiah '66 '93 C&L.178 B.A., J.D. (adm. in NY; not adm. in IL) Lead Coun., Sears, Roebuck and Co.
Harbottle, Nancy S. ....'— '87 C.589 B.A. L.46 J.D. [Arnstein&L.]
Heberton, Craig, IV '57 '82 C.228 A.B. L.910 J.D. Asst. Gen. Coun., Transamerica Finance Corp.
Heller, Amy Cohen .....'52 '83 C.260 B.A. L.365 J.D. Sr. Coun., Sears, Roebuck and Co.
Hickey, Timothy S. '68 '93 C&L.339 B.S., J.D. Sr. Coun., Info. Tech., Sear, Roebuck & Co.
Hilborn, Andrea G. '70 '96 C.1365 B.A. L.347 J.D. (adm. in VA; not adm. in IL) Sears, Roebuck and Co.
Hillery, Vincent E. '59 '84 C&L.145 B.A., J.D. Sr. V.P., Gen. Coun. & Secy., Transamerica Finance Corp.
Hodge, Heather R. '68 '94 C.339 B.S. L.347 J.D. Sr. Paralegal, Transamerica Finance Corporation (Pat.)
Hornacek, Thomas K. '61 '86 C.477 B.B.A. L.339 J.D. Sr. Coun., Sears, Roebuck and Co.
Hudson, Dennis L. ....'52 '80 C.107 B.A. L.365 J.D. 3333 Beverly Rd.
Jaynes, Lawrence C. ....'47 '73 C&L.424 B.S., J.D. 2300 N. Barrington Rd.
Jeannero, Jane M. '59 '84 C.477 B.A. L.1187 J.D. Senior Counsel, Sears, Roebuck and Co.
Keane, James G. '61 '92 C.309 A.B. L.597 J.D. Assoc. Gen. Coun., Sears, Roebuck and Co.
Kelly, Anastasia D., (AVⓉ) '49 '81 C.856 B.A. L.276 J.D. (adm. in DC; not adm. in IL) Exec. V.P. & Gen. Coun., Sears, Roebuck & Co.
Kemp, Kathryn M. '62 '88 C.602 B.A. L.424 J.D. Gen. Atty., Human Resources & Labor, Ameritech Corp.
Kier, Michael W. ....'63 '92 C.602 B.S. L.930 J.D. Sr. Coun., Sears, Roebuck and Co.
Klest Law Firm
(See Schaumburg)
Kottis, Nick C. ....'58 '84 C.679 B.S.Ch.E. L.846 J.D. [Pauley P.&E.] (Pat.)
Kreye, Jeffrey W. ....'63 '98 C.174 B.A. L.146 J.D. 2300 Barrington Rd., Ste. 220
Lennarson, Marvin R. ....'22 '50 C.352 B.A. L.597 J.D. 696 Scarbrough Cr.‡
Levitt, Michael ....'44 '70 C.910 B.A. L.209 J.D. GE Coml. Distribution Fin. Corp.
Lyman, Cynthia R. ....'62 '90 C.105 B.S. L.145 J.D. Sr. Coun., Sears, Roebuck & Co.
MacDonald, Gregory A. ....'58 '84 C.339 B.S. L.365 J.D. [Robinson,P.P.M.&A.]
Maring, Elizabeth Vogelzang, (BV) '58 '84 C.610 B.S.J. L.117 J.D. 2300 Barrington Rd.
Martin, Mary Anne O'Connor '63 '88 C.293 B.A. L.339 J.D. Sr. Coun., Sears, Roebuck and Co.
McKeough, Brendan J. '66 '92 C.339 B.A. L.1068 J.D. (adm. in IN; not adm. in IL) Asst. Gen. Coun., Sears, Roebuck and Co.
McKeown, Glenn E. '61 '92 C.178 A.B. L.309 J.D. Assoc. Gen. Coun., Sears, Roebuck & Co
McPartlin, Michael A. ....'53 '85 C.602 B.S. L.424 J.D. [Ⓐ C.J.Collins]
Merritt, David D. '63 '89 C&L.352 B.S., J.D. Asst. Gen. Coun., Sears, Roebuck and Co.
Metz, Walter R., Jr., (BVⓉ) '56 '81 C&L.546 B.A., J.D. (adm. in NE; not adm. in IL) Sr. Coun., Sears, Roebuck and Co.
Moderson, Janine A. ....'65 '02 C.963 B.S. L.589 J.D. [Ⓐ Pauley P.&E.] (Pat.)
Moran, Joyce E. '48 '72 C.788 B.A. L.976 J.D. V.P., Corp. Secy., Sears, Roebuck and Co.
Murphy, Leanne Ebert '64 '91 C.589 B.S. L.365 J.D. Sr. Coun., Sears, Roebuck and Co.
Myren, Matthew T. '67 '92 C&L.352 B.B.A., J.D. Asst. Gen. Coun., Sears, Roebuck and Co.
Narimatsu, Susan M. '49 '91 C.339 B.S.N. L.209 J.D. Sr. Coun., Sears, Roebuck and Co.
Nieslawski, Steven E., (AV) '59 '84 C.339 A.B. L.146 J.D. Sears, Roebuck and Co. (Legal Department)
Norris, Roland W. ....'54 '88 C.234 B.S. L.879 J.D. [Ⓐ Pauley P.&E.] (Pat.)
O'Brien, Pierce J. '53 '93 C.209 B.A. L.365 J.D. Mgr.of Investigation, AP Div., Sears, Roebuck and Co. (Legal Department)
Pauley, Douglas H., (AV) ....'59 '87 C.679 B.S.M.E. L.424 J.D. [Pauley P.&E.] (Pat.)
Pauley Petersen & Erickson, (AV) ....2800 West Higgins Road, Suite 365 (Pat.)
Payne, Richmond A., (BVⓉ) '62 '87 C.934 B.A. L.734 J.D. [Robinson,P.P.M.&A.] (⊙Cape Girardeau, MO)
Perry, John A. ....'31 '63 C.1016 B.S.C. L.597 J.D. 1550 Fairfield Lane
Petersen, Maxwell J., (AV) ....'56 '87 C.350 B.S. L.424 J.D. [Pauley P.&E.] (Pat.)
Phelan, John M. ....'65 '92 C.188 B.S. L.209 J.D. SBC Midwest
Pierce, Deborah R. '53 '78 C&L.659 B.A., J.D. (adm. in PA; not adm. in IL) Sears, Roebuck and Co.
Piercey, Rodney H. ....'46 '73 C.347 B.A. L.1119 J.D. [Robinson,P.P.M.&A.]
Pines, Richard Thomas ....'45 '70 C&L.209 B.Sc., J.D. Sears, Roebuck & Co.
Pluymert, James H. ....'56 '81 C.114 B.A. L.209 J.D. [Robinson,P.P.M.&A.] ⊙
Pursel, David F. ....'47 '78 C.911 B.S. L.623 J.D. Sr. Coun., Sears, Roebuck and Co.
Quane, Terrence J. '53 '81 C.589 B.A. L.365 J.D. Atty., SAFECO Prop. & Cas. Ins. Co.
Quist, Richard J., Jr. ....'60 '86 C.98 B.A. L.589 J.D. Gen. Atty., SBC
Rauch, Mary Ruffolo '67 '92 C.123 B.A. L.879 J.D. Sr. Coun., Transamerica Finance Corp.
Rauch, Melanie I. ....'73 '99 C.1154 B.S. L.365 J.D. [Ⓐ Pauley P.&E.] (Pat.)
Regenbogen, Ellis A., (AVⓉ) '46 '71 C.197 A.B. L.178 J.D. Asst. Gen. Coun., Corp. & Sec., Sears, Roebuck and Co. (Legal Department)
Robinson, Russel G. ....'57 '82 C.999 B.A. L.585 J.D. [Robinson,P.P.M.&A.]

Robinson, Pluymert, Piercey, MacDonald & Amato, Ltd, (BVⓉ)
2300 Barrington Road, Suite 220, 60195-2034 ⊙
Telephone: 847-310-0025 Fax: 847-310-0054
Email: info@rppmalaw.com URL: http://www.rppmalaw.com
Members of Firm: Russel G. Robinson; James H. Pluymert; Rodney H. Piercey; Gregory A. MacDonald; Brent L. Amato; Richmond A. Payne; Ronald J. Senechalle.
Business Law, Corporate Law, Banking Law, Estate Planning, Charitable Planning, Probate and Trust Administration, Family Law, Commercial Real Estate, Residential Real Estate, Condominium Law, Church Law, Non Profit Law, Litigation, Mediation and Arbitration.
Des Plaines Office: 733 Lee Street, Suite 100, 60016-6405. Telephone: 847-298-5030. Fax: 847-298-0169.
See Professional Biographies, HOFFMAN ESTATES, ILLINOIS

Rosenthal, Richard A., Jr. '51 '81 C.589 B.A. L.1119 J.D. Sr. Coun., Transamerica Finance Corp.
Rowley, Marilyn A. ....'62 '92 C.339 L.209 J.D. 2300 N. Barrington Rd., Ste. 400
Russell, Susan .....'60 '85 C.209 B.A. L.339 J.D. Senior Counsel, Sears, Roebuck and Co.
Schneider, Pamela Rolnick '59 '84 C.659 B.A. L.145 J.D. Gen. Coun. Sears Home Servs. & Home Stores Grp., Sears, Roebuck and Co.
Senechalle, Ronald J. ....'58 '86 C.339 B.A. L.424 J.D. [Robinson,P.P.M.&A.]
Siena, John J. '36 '76 C.209 B.S.C. L.424 J.D. Asst. Gen. Coun., Sears, Roebuck and Co.
Sitley, Stephen Langdon '63 '88 C.93 B.A. L.276 J.D. Sr. Coun., Sears, Roebuck and Co.
Smith, Gary M. '47 '73 C.367 B.A. L.273 J.D. (adm. in NC; not adm. in IL) Assoc. Gen. Coun., Credit, Sears, Roebuck and Co.
Speckman, Thomas W., (AV) .....'25 '63 C.597 Ph.B. L.365 J.D. [Ⓒ Pauley P.&E.] (Pat.)
Stanczak, Michael P., (BV) '55 '86 C.927 B.A. L.209 J.D. 2800 W. Higgins Rd., Ste. 510
Swanson, Mark D. ....'74 '02 C.999 B.S. L.365 J.D. [Ⓐ Pauley P.&E.] (Pat.)
Thompson, Amanda Pecchioni '— '00 C.1298 B.A. L.329 J.D. Sr. Coun., Sears, Roebuck and Co. (Legal Department) (Pat.)
Tietze, Fred B. ....'54 '80 C&L.339 B.A., J.D. Sr. Coun., Sears, Roebuck and Co.
Tolchin, Marsha A. '58 '85 C.475 B.A. L.213 J.D. Assoc. Coun., Sears, Roebuck and Co. (Legal Department)
Tortorice, Mary Elizabeth '63 '91 C.494 B.A. L.209 J.D. Asst. Gen. Coun., Sears, Roebuck and Co.
Tyndall, Candace Tillman '70 '95 C.112 B.A. L.1066 J.D. Sr. Coun., E-Commerce, Sears, Roebuck and Co.
Ulbrich, Sheila G. '71 '96 C.339 B.S. L.146 J.D. Sr. Coun., Sears, Roebuck and Co. (Legal Department)
Utley, W. David .....'46 '79 C.734 B.S. L.209 J.D. Atty., SAFECO Prop. & Cas. Ins. Co.
Walpole, James R. '44 '69 C.363 A.B. L.930 J.D. Asst. Gen. Coun., Sears, Roebuck and Co.
Weinstock, Pamela J. '58 '83 C.456 B.S. L.1048 J.D. Asst. Gen. Coun., Sears, Roebuck & Co.
Weiss, Arthur R. ....'55 '81 C.378 B.S. L.900 J.D. Sr. Coun., Sears, Roebuck and Co.
Williams, Richard N. ....'43 '69 C.207 B.A. L.7 J.D. Corp. Coun.
Wolonsky, Joseph P. ....'47 '73 C.179 B.S. L.424 J.D. V.P., Fin., Borg-Warner Ins. Servs.
Zopp, Andrea L., (AV) '57 '81 C&L.309 B.A., J.D. Gen. Coun., Sears, Roebuck and Co.

HOMER, 1,264, *Champaign Co.*

Lee, Marilyn K. ....'42 '75 C.494 B.S.B. L.1035 J.D. 999 County Rd. 2500 E.

HOMEWOOD, 19,543, *Cook Co.*

Andrews, Anthony D., Law Office ....'70 '95 17450 Halsted St., Ste. 260
Barron, Michael J., Jr. '64 '95 C.602 B.A. L.477 J.D. Coun., Canadian National/Illinois Central Railroad Company
Beaman, Ralph P. ....'21 '62 C.390 B.A. L.146 J.D. 1844 Sycamore Rd.‡
Beemsterboer, Matthew J. ....'35 '60 C.976 B.A. L.597 J.D. 1048 186th St.
Bergmann, Cynthia A. '61 '85 C.208 B.S.B.A. L.365 J.D. Coun. U.S. Corp., Canadian National/Illinois Central Railroad Company
Braverman, William C. ....'46 '71 900 Maple AVe.
Briones, Samuel ....'— '79 C&L.209 B.S.C., J.D. [Briones,H.&T.]
Briones, Harvey & Trevino ....1912 Ridge Road
Bryan, William J. ....'53 '78 C.965 B.B.A. L.43 J.D. 17926 Dixie Hwy.
Butcher, Robert J., (BV) ....'34 '65 C.424 B.S. L.365 LL.B. 2044 Ridge Road
Butcher, William P. ....'13 '45 C&L.209 A.B., LL.B. 17450 S. Halsted St.
Castellarin, Peter F. '57 '85 C.209 B.S. L.365 J.D. Chf. Fin. Offr., M & O Insulation Co.
Catullo, Anthony G., (BV) ....'44 '70 C.801 B.A. L.365 J.D. 18141 Dixie Highway
Coghlan, Martin D., (AV) ....'40 '64 C.436 L.209 LL.B. [M.D.Coghlan]
Coghlan, Martin D., P.C., (AV) ....18161 Morris Ave.
Cummings, Christopher J. ....'57 '84 C.108 B.S. L.209 J.D. [Cummings&D.]
Cummings, Walter D., (AV) ....'31 '55 C&L.209 B.S., J.D. [Ⓐ Cummings&D.]
Cummings & Duda, Ltd., (BV) ....2024 Hickory Rd., Ste. 300
Dietch, Henry X. ....'13 '37 C.999 L.365 J.D. 18161 Morris Ave.‡
Donley, Donald E. '34 '84 C.477 M.H.A. L.424 J.D. Sr. V.P./Leg. Cnsl, Advance Bancorp, Inc.
Doody, John T., Jr., (BV) ....'45 '74 C.750 B.A. L.365 J.D. P.O. Box 1392
Duda, James T., (BV) ....'49 '74 C.602 B.A. L.424 J.D. [Cummings&D.]

du Sartel, Alexandre F. '72 '99 C.999 M.L. L.146 LL.M. Dir., Legal Affs., Silliker Group Corp.
Foster, Chester H., Jr. .... '48 '78 C.1183 B.A. L.365 J.D. 3825 192nd St.
Gardiner, Edward Donald .... '58 '91 C.339 B.S. L.209 J.D. 2300 Maple Rd.
Gasperec, Louis S., (BV) .... '45 '70 C.602 B.A. L.339 J.D. 18350 S. Kedzie Ave.
Gilbert, Janet H. '47 '78 C.94 B.A. L.818 J.D. Canadian National/Illinois Central Railroad Company
Goldberg, Philip L., (BV) '63 '88 C.966 B.A. L.339 J.D. Gen. Coun., Simborg Development, Inc.
Gray, Melvin .... '32 '56 C.502 B.A. L.309 LL.B. 1 Graycor Dr.
Greenberg, Daniel M. .... '55 '79 C.339 B.S. L.209 J.D. [D.M.Greenberg]
Greenberg, Daniel M., Chartered, Law Offices .... 17900 Dixie Hwy.
Gyarmathy, Joseph A. .... '45 '78 C.63 B.S. L.365 J.D. 920 175th St., Ste. 5
Hamman, James S. .... '50 '87 C.720 B.A. L.365 J.D. 900 Maple Ave.
Hannigan, Michael P. '57 '85 C.734 B.S. L.146 J.D. Coun. - U.S. Lit., Canadian National/Illinois Central Railroad Company
Harvey, Ronald E. .... '— '86 C.597 B.A. L.146 J.D. [Briones,H.&T.]
Kral, Dennis G., Law Office of .... '46 '73 C.589 B.S. L.146 J.D. 18100 Harwood Ave.
Le Vert, Dwight W. .... '52 '81 C.864 B.S.M.E. L.365 J.D. 19025 Jodi Ter.
Lowe, Randall L. .... '55 '85 C.182 B.A. L.365 J.D. Mgr., Real Estate, Ill. Central R.R.
Moore, Don A. .... '28 '50 C.999 L.365 LL.B. 18225 Morris Ave.
Moore, Stephen W. .... '47 '73 C&L.879 B.A., J.D. 18141 Dixie Hwy.
Morrissey, Wm. F., (AV) .... '11 '37 C&L.424 B.S.C., J.D. 2311 W. 183rd St.‡
Nagel, Ronald G. .... '41 '79 C.679 B.A. L.365 J.D. 930 175th St.
Nagel, Sandra Bernardi .... '47 '80 C.436 B.A. L.209 J.D. 920 W. 175th St., Ste. 5
Olsen, George H. .... '45 '74 C.339 B.S. L.209 J.D. [G.H.Olsen]
Olsen, George H., Ltd. .... 18022 Cherrywood Lane
Overgaard, Mitchell J., (AV) .... '31 '57 C&L.145 A.B., J.D. 17450 Halsted St.
Patch, Sabrina M. .... '56 '94 C.999 B.A. L.424 J.D. 3011 W. 183rd St.
Pearlman, Elyse G. .... '49 '84 C.339 B.A. L.365 J.D. Counsel, Graycor Services, L.L.C.
Pebworth, Donald A. .... '40 '67 C.347 A.B. L.345 J.D. 18104 S. Park St.
Peterson, Ross D. .... '52 '80 C.879 B.A. L.300 J.D. 18442 California
Ryan, Charles T. .... '62 '88 C&L.589 B.S., J.D. 18141 Dixie Hwy.
Schafer-Lewers, Therese, Law Office of '64 '89 C.339 B.S.W. L.424 J.D. 18500 Riegel Road
Seely, Philip E. .... '25 '60 C.339 B.S. L.209 J.D. Admin. Law J.
Shore, Anita C. .... '56 '85 C.339 B.S. L.209 J.D. 1315 W. 191st St.‡
Silverman, Clifford A., (AV) .... '44 '69 C.339 L.209 J.D. 900 Maple (⊙Chicago)
Spina, James B. .... '53 '79 C.357 B.S. L.146 J.D. [J.B.Spina]
Spina, James B., Law Offices of, Ltd. .... 17900 Dixie Highway, Suite 12
Stander, Roena Mae '20 '54 C.612 B.S. L.862 LL.B. (adm. in OK; not adm. in IL) 2301 W. 183rd St.‡
Styx, Dorothy A., Law Office of .... '53 '92 C.999 B.A. L.146 J.D. 18141 Dixie Highway
Szymanski, Lawrence A., (BV) .... '56 '82 C.424 B.B.A. L.209 J.D. [L.A.Szymanski]
Szymanski, Lawrence A., P.C., Law Office of, (BV) .... 17900 Dixie Highway, Suite 14
Thompson, Mary C. .... '40 '81 C.339 B.S. L.589 J.D. 18115 Dixie Hwy.
Thomsen, Kristina L. '69 '94 C&L.602 B.B.A., J.D. Coun., Canadian National/Illinois Central Railroad Company
Trevino, Marcos P. .... '69 '95 C&L.801 B.A., J.D. [Briones,H.&T.]
Verkler, Richard A., (AV) '59 '84 C.339 B.A. L.190 J.D. Coun. - U.S. Environ., Canadian National/Illinois Central Railroad Company
Zimmerman, Joel C. .... '57 '82 C.347 B.S. L.146 J.D. 2024 Hickery Rd., 2nd Fl.
Ziolkowski, Leon A. .... '27 '70 C.597 B.B.A. L.365 J.D. 18803 King Rd.‡

HOOPESTON, 5,871, *Vermilion Co.*

Devens, Charles J., (BV) .... '52 '77 C&L.339 B.A., J.D. [Manion,D.M.S.&S.] ⊙
Doyle, Richard J., (BV) .... '40 '69 C.1191 B.A. L.146 J.D. [Doyle&Assoc.] ⊙
Doyle & Associates, (BV) .... 211 East Main Street (⊙Danville)
Manion, Paul T., (BV) .... '40 '64 C.602 B.B.A. L.209 J.D. [Manion,D.M.S.&S.] ⊙
Manion, Devens, McFetridge, Spiros & Schum, Ltd., (BV) 216 S. Market St. (⊙Danville)
McFetridge, John D., (BV) .... '50 '78 C.57 B.A. L.339 J.D. [Manion,D.M.S.&S.] ⊙
Mulholland, Frank M. .... '72 '02 C.801 B.S. L.339 J.D. [[A] Manion,D.M.S.&S.] ⊙
Nelson, William E., (BV) .... '41 '66 C.927 B.A. L.339 J.D. [Nelson&S.]
Nelson & Stipp, Professional Corporation, (BV) .... 112 E. Main St.
Schum, Todd E., (BV) .... '61 '87 C.339 B.S. L.801 J.D. [Manion,D.M.S.&S.] ⊙
Spiros, James .... '68 '94 C.679 B.A. L.365 J.D. [Manion,D.M.S.&S.]
Stipp, Gordon R., (BV) .... '47 '75 C.234 B.S. L.472 J.D. [Nelson&S.]
Wall, Karen E. .... '72 '97 C.338 B.A. L.365 J.D. [Manion,D.M.S.&S.]

HUBBARD WOODS, —, *Cook Co.*

Rashman, Lydia L. .... '16 '38 C&L.145 A.B., J.D. 196 Sheridan Rd.‡
Shuster, Lynn A. .... '42 '69 C&L.966 B.S., J.D. 249 Mary St.

HUNTLEY, 5,730, *Kane & McHenry Cos.*

Adams, Hubert A. .... '25 '57 C.602 Ph.B. L.209 J.D. 12348 Winding Creek Loop

Ariano, Hardy, Nyuli, Johnson, Richmond & Goettel, P.C., (AV)
13300 Route 47, P.O. Box 487, 60142 ⊙
Telephone: 847-669-5020
Email: aah@attorneys-illinois.com URL: http://www.attorneys-illinois.com
Ralph C. Hardy; Scott G. Richmond.
General Civil and Criminal Practice in all Courts. Banking, Probate, Real Estate, Corporation, Federal Taxation, Transactional, Employment, Family, Personal Injury, Collections, Creditor Bankruptcy, Foreclosures, Landlord and Tenant Law, Workers Compensation Law and Mediation.
Geneva Office: 13 S. 7th Street, 60134. Telephone: 630-208-0674.
Elgin, Illinois: 474 Summit Street. Telephone: 847-695-2400. Telecopy: 847-695-8397.
See Professional Biographies, HUNTLEY, ILLINOIS

Cole, Robert P., (AV) .... '13 '41 C.477 A.B. L.365 J.D. 13515 Marengo Rd.‡
Fickler, Debra J. .... '— '99 C.546 B.S. L.508 J.D. [Firm of D.J.Fickler]
Fickler, Debra J., Law Firm of .... 12525 Grandview Drive
Fleck, Michael J., (CV) .... '65 '95 C.339 B.S. L.146 J.D. [M.J.Fleck]

Fleck, Michael J., P.C., Law Office of, (CV)
10771 Route 47, P.O. Box 992, 60142
Telephone: 847-669-2558 Fax: 847-669-2564
Email: michaelfleck@earthlink.net URL: http://www.flecklawoffice.com
Michael J. Fleck.
Real Estate, Estate Planning, Estate Administration, Wills, Probate Law, Trusts and Estates, Corporate Law, Business Law, General Practice.
See Professional Biographies, HUNTLEY, ILLINOIS

Hardy, Ralph C., (AV) .... '43 '68 C.72 B.A. L.910 J.D. [Ariano,H.N.J.R.&G.] (⊙Elgin)

Militello, Zanck & Coen, P.C.
(See Crystal Lake)

Reiter, Marvin C. .... '31 '55 C.898 B.A. L.352 J.D. 13006 Brookwood Dr.‡
Richmond, Scott G., (BV) '68 '95 C.475 B.A. L.146 J.D. [Ariano,H.N.J.R.&G.] (⊙Elgin)
Stopka, Richard W. .... '38 '70 C.145 B.S. L.365 J.D. 6216 Lakeview
Von Keudell, Nils .... '63 '90 C.347 L.365 11614 Algonquin Road

INDIAN CREEK, 247, *Lake Co.*

Yanow, Paulette B. .... '59 '86 C.597 B.A. L.209 J.D. 48 Valley Rd.

INDIAN HEAD PARK, 3,685, *Cook Co.*

Hriljac, Michael J. '50 '99 C.999 D.P.M. L.365 J.D. School College of Podiatric Medicine
Matkovich, John A. .... '51 '84 C.383 B.A. L.589 J.D. General Motors Corp.
Schied, Leann G. .... '56 '83 C.339 B.A. L.589 6470 Thunderbird Drive
Stamat, Paul N. .... '24 '51 C&L.424 LL.B. 125 Aracia Circle
Swiess, John J. .... '47 '80 C.1016 B.A. L.589 J.D. 11333 Arrowhead Tr.

INGLESIDE, 1,621, *Lake Co.*

D'Andrea, Dana Marie .... '62 '92 C.338 B.S. L.862 J.D. P.O. Box 58
Reese, Norman G. .... '32 '58 C&L.472 B.B.A., J.D. 25620 W. Long Beach Dr.
Weber, Ronald .... '64 '89 C.339 B.S. L.589 J.D. 36654 Fairfield Rd.
Wehde, Christin J., (BV) .... '59 '85 C.339 B.A.S. L.146 J.D. 35478 N. Donald Ct.

INVERNESS, 6,749, *Cook Co.*

Allen, Gerald F. .... '44 '71 C.357 B.A. L.146 J.D. 137 Strome Ln.
Angelina, Michael J. .... '65 '90 C.602 B.B.A. L.405 J.D. [Angelina&P.]

Angelina & Palmer, P.C.
A Professional Corporation
1626 W. Colonial Parkway, 60067-4724
Telephone: 847-359-0010 Fax: 847-359-0011
Email: info@apclaw.com URL: http://www.apclaw.com
Directors: Michael J. Angelina; Raiford D. Palmer. Attorneys: Kyle F. Fraccaro; Jason M. Chmielewski; Ashley Harris Coles; Leslie Anne Slomka.
Family Law, including Divorce, Child Support, Child Custody, Alimony/Maintenance, Division of Property and Debt, Parentage, Grandparents' Rights, Visitation, Post Decree/Post Divorce Disputes, Separation, Uncontested Divorce, Divorce Settlements. Commercial Real Estate and Residential Real Estate Transactions, including Contract Drafting and Negotiation, Real Estate Closings, Real Estate and Construction Litigation, Zoning, Commercial and Residential Landlord/Tenant, Evictions, Commercial Lease Negotiation and Drafting. Business Law, including Formation of Corporations, Limited Liability Companies (LLC), and Limited Liability Partnerships (LLP). Advice for Business Legal Problems and Business Litigation. Employment Law, Executive Employment Agreements, Buy-Sell Agreements, Operating Agreements, Partnership Agreements, Asset Sales, Sales of Business.Estate Planning, including Wills, Trusts, Power of Attorney, Health Care Power of Attorney, Living Will, Special Needs Trust, Tax Avoidance Trust, Irrevocable Trust, Codicil, Probate.Criminal Law, including Criminal Defense, Felony, including Unlawful Use of Weapons, Battery, Theft, Burglary, Assault, DUI, Driving Under the Influence, Drug Possession, Drug Manufacture, Misdemeanor, Traffic, Ordinance Violation. Personal Injury for Serious Injuries and Wrongful Death.
See Professional Biographies, INVERNESS, ILLINOIS

Armstrong, Robert A., Jr. .... '46 '71 C.694 B.A. L.146 J.D. 1605 Colonial Parkway
Cannon, Douglas C., Law Offices of '49 '74 C.339 B.A. L.209 J.D. 1627 Colonial Pkwy., Ste. 302
Carlson, Nancy Lee, Law Offices of .... '54 '85 C.591 B.S. L.1187 J.D. 926 Braeburn Rd.
Chmielewski, Jason M. .... '74 '02 C.160 B.A. L.209 J.D. [Angelina&P.]
Coles, Ashley Harris .... '78 '04 C.612 B.A. L.623 J.D. [Angelina&P.]
Doss, Owen L., (AV) .... '23 '50 C.1106 L.339 J.D. [O.L.Doss]
Doss, Owen L., P.C., (AV) .... 101 Halkirk Cir.
Even, John T. .... '54 '83 C.424 B.B.S. L.146 J.D. [Roberts,S.&E.]
Felt, James H. .... '20 '48 C.339 B.S. L.309 J.D. Ret. Cir. J.
Fitton, Pamela J. .... '55 '83 C.927 B.A. L.365 J.D. 1659 W. Baldwin Rd.‡
Fraccaro, Kyle F. .... '73 '04 C.72 B.A. L.146 J.D. [Angelina&P.]
Hollis, Robert .... '50 '80 C.339 B.A. L.365 J.D. 1642 Colonial Pkwy.
Kightlinger, John D. .... '33 '68 C.502 B.J. L.365 J.D. 1642 W. Colonial Pkwy.‡
Lancaster, Deborah M. '53 '78 C.589 B.A. L.1151 J.D. 1642 Colonial Pkwy. (⊙Marco Island, FL)
Malleris, Leonidas C. .... '49 '78 C.870 B.S. L.424 J.D. 1627 Colonial Parkway
McElwain, Warren .... '52 '83 C.589 B.A. L.365 J.D. Pres., Inverness Develop., Inc.
Nash, Barbara Jean .... '46 '00 C.589 B.G.S. L.209 J.D. 125 Duntrune Ln.
Palmer, Raiford D. .... '69 '94 C.339 B.A. L.424 J.D. [Angelina&P.]
Pinter, Kristen M. .... '67 '92 C.339 B.A. L.146 J.D. [[A] Roberts,S.&E.]
Roberts, Bruce K. .... '40 '68 C.473 A.B. L.597 J.D. [Roberts,S.&E.]
Roberts, Simon & Even, Ltd. .... 1620 Colonial Pkwy.
Ross, Robert J., (AV) '56 '80 C.339 B.A. L.209 J.D. 1622 West Colonial Parkway, Suite 201
Schnur, Jacob J. .... '23 '49 C&L.209 LL.B. 194 Old Wick Ln.‡
Simon, James L. .... '48 '77 C.339 B.F.A. L.209 J.D. [Roberts,S.&E.]
Slomka, Leslie Anne .... '78 '04 C.755 B.A. L.209 J.D. [Angelina&P.]
Stafford, John J., (P.C.) .... '17 '39 C&L.209 J.D. 1547 Shire Cir.‡

ISLAND LAKE, 8,153, *Lake & McHenry Cos.*

MacFarlane, Bonnie L., (CV) .... '48 '90 C.589 B.S. L.146 J.D. 27979 N. Converse Road
Wiejaczka, Michelle G. .... '58 '83 C.801 B.S. L.910 J.D. 215 E. State Rd.

ITASCA, 8,302, *DuPage Co.*

Abbott, Kerry S. '60 '87 C.276 B.S.B.A. L.597 J.D. Senior Coun., AJG Financial Servs, Inc.
Alsop, Robert C. '23 '50 C.309 B.S. L.893 LL.B. (adm. in MA; not adm. in IL) 225 Windsor Dr.
Arends, Thomas F. .... '— '84 C.602 B.B.A. L.209 J.D. [R.M.Colombik&Assoc.]
Argento, Vincent C., Law Offices of, (CV) '56 '84 C.209 B.A. L.589 J.D. 1100 N. Arlington Heights Rd., Ste. 510
Beeler, Stephen C. '40 '66 C.1119 A.B. L.309 J.D. (adm. in IN; not adm. in IL) [[A] R.M.Colombik&Assoc.]
Bersani, Michael D., (BV) .... '63 '88 C.339 B.A. L.365 J.D. [Hervas,S.C.&B.]
Broad, Matthew R., (BVⓉ) '60 '85 C.112 B.A. L.1065 J.D. (adm. in ID; not adm. in IL) Exec. VP & Gen. Coun., OfficeMax Inc.
Carson, Steven L. .... '63 '89 C.373 B.A. L.347 J.D. 1789 Norwood Ave.
Colombik, Richard M. .... '53 '80 C.174 B.S. L.365 J.D. [R.M.Colombik&Assoc.]
Colombik, Richard M., & Associates, PC .... 1 Pierce Pl., Ste. 460 E.
Combs, Kim M. '67 '95 C.339 B.S. L.209 J.D. Assoc. Gen. Coun., OfficeMax Incorporated
Condon, Michael W. .... '59 '86 C.436 B.A. L.365 J.D. [Hervas,S.C.&B.]
Conley, Joseph M. '45 '72 C.1075 B.S. L.1049 J.D. Vice Pres., Asst. Secty & Dep. General Counsel, Signature Group
Dingel, Michael M., (CVⓉ) '69 '96 C&L.336 B.S., J.D. (adm. in ID; not adm. in IL) Assoc. Gen. Coun., OfficeMax Incorporated (⊙Boise, ID)
Divis, Deborah B. '— '84 C.679 B.S. L.209 J.D. Assoc. Gen. Coun., OfficeMax Incorporated
Dunavan, Dylan M. '71 '97 C.796 B.A. L.209 J.D. Atty., NEC Solutions (America), Inc.
Durden, Mildred Frances .... '— '86 Gen. Coun., Enesco Group, Inc.

Ekl, Elizabeth A. ....'71 '97 C.74 B.A. L.209 J.D. 333 Pierce Rd., Ste. 195
Faermark, Byron L., (BV) ....'51 '79 C.801 B.A. L.1151 J.D. [Mindel&F.]
Fasig, Carl E. ...'57 '82 C&L.339 B.S., J.D. Asst. Gen. Coun., Arthur J. Gallagher & Co.
Gasinski, David M. ....'58 '87 C.589 B.S. L.424 J.D. [D.M.Gasinski]
Gasinski, David M., PC ....320 W. Irving Park Rd.
Gray, Brian V. '48 '79 C.999 B.S. L.365 J.D.
Assoc. Gen. Coun. & Chf. Litig. Coun., Arthur J. Gallagher & Co.
Griffin, Molly ...'— '94 C&L.602 B.A., J.D. Assoc. Gen. Coun., OfficeMax Incorporated
Hageli, Alexander M. ....'75 '01 C.477 B.A. L.424 J.D. [⊡ R.M.Colombik&Assoc.]
Hanner, Jerome S. '57 '82
C.276 A.B. L.209 J.D. Asst. Gen. Coun., Arthur J. Gallagher & Co.
Hansen, Kindra L., (BVⓉ) '63 '94 C.906 B.A. L.336 J.D.
(adm. in ID; not adm. in IL) Assoc. Gen. Coun., OfficeMax Incorporated (⊙Boise, ID)
Herron, Stacie L. ...... '— '02 C.862 B.S.B.A. L.597 J.D. Coun., OfficeMax Incorporated
Hervas, Charles E. ....'58 '83 C.92 B.A. L.209 J.D. [Hervas,S.C.&B.]
Hervas, Sotos, Condon & Bersani, P.C., (AV) ....333 W. Pierce Rd., Ste. 195
Johnson, Kerilyn M. ....'— '95 C.57 B.A. L.209 J.D. Asst. Gen. Coun., Midas, Inc.
Kashian, Jeremy S. ....'70 '97 C.112 B.A. L.464 J.D. NEC Solutions (America), Inc.
Kloempken, John W. ....'52 '77 C.339 B.S. L.365 J.D. 865 West Irving Park Rd.
Lopatka, Arthur J., Jr. ....'— '76 C&L.209 B.A., J.D. Corp. Coun., Midas, Inc.
Marr, Alvin K. '— '90 C.145 B.A. L.477 J.D.
Sr. V.P., Gen. Coun. & Secy., Midas, Inc.
McKenna, Richard J. '47 '81
C.1041 B.B.A. L.1040 J.D. Exec. V.P., Gallagher Bassett Servs., Inc.
Mensching, Jack E. ....'52 '78 C.317 B.S. L.861 J.D. Pres., Itasca Bk. & Tr. Co.
Mindel, Norbert M. ....'52 '78 C&L.146 B.S., J.D. [Mindel&F.]
Mindel & Faermark, (BV) .... 105 E. Irving Park Rd.
Neumeyer, Jeffrey D., (AVⓉ) '63 '90 C.172 B.S. L.336 J.D.
(adm. in ID; not adm. in IL) Assoc. Gen. Coun., OfficeMax Incorporated
Oneale, Tracy R., (AVⓉ) '64 '92 C&L.972 B.A., J.D.
(adm. in WY; not adm. in IL) Assoc. Gen. Coun., OfficeMax Incorporated
Pankau, A. J., Jr., (BV) ....'46 '85 C.679 B.S. L.146 J.D. 105 E. Irving Pk.
Radocha, Dennis L., (BVⓉ) '55 '89 C.640 B.S. L.336 J.D.
(adm. in ID; not adm. in IL) Assoc. Gen. Coun., OfficeMax Incorporated
Reedy, Lenore D. '67 '96 C.339 B.S. L.365 J.D.
Assoc. Coun., Arthur J. Gallagher & Co.
Rose, Jason W. ....'66 '91 C.339 B.S. L.209 J.D. [⊡ Hervas,S.C.&B.]
Rosengren, John C. '46 '72 C.177 B.A. L.93 J.D.
(adm. in NY; not adm. in IL) V.P., Gen. Coun. & Secy., Arthur J. Gallagher & Co.
Schirott, James R. ....'42 '71 C.1159 B.S.M.E. L.365 J.D. 105 E. Irving Park Rd.
Shapiro, Steven H. '58 '84 C.178 B.A. L.145 J.D.
Exec. V.P. & Corp. Secretary, First Midwest Bancorp, Inc.
Sitter, J. Gerard ....'18 '42 L.365 LL.B. 401 E. Washington St.
Sotos, James G., (AV) ....'57 '86 C.62 B.A. L.365 J.D. [Hervas,S.C.&B.]
Stineman, Kevin M. '65 '92 C&L.770 B.Sc., J.D.
(adm. in CA; not adm. in IL) VP of Claims, Insurance Corporation of Hannover
Tixier, Joseph C. ..... '63 '88 C.878 B.S. L.326 J.D. Sr. Coun., Arthur J. Gallagher & Co.
VanHole, William R., (AVⓉ) '48 '76 C.172 B.S. L.336 J.D.
(adm. in ID; not adm. in IL) Assoc. Gen. Coun., OfficeMax Incorporated
Wagner-Fleming, Susan '68 '94 C&L.477 B.A., J.D.
V.P., Corp. Secy. & Assoc. Gen. Coun., OfficeMax Incorporated
Waltenburg, Audrey Z. ......'— '98 C.339 B.S. L.597 J.D. Asst. Gen. Coun., Midas, Inc.
Walter, Duane G. ....'26 '54 C.999 L.146 LL.B. Ret. Assoc. Cir. J.‡
Weber, Charles R. ....'50 '77 C.339 B.S. L.424 J.D. Pres., Dodi Management, LLC
White, Andy '— '96 C.608 B.S. L.117 J.D.
(adm. in OH; not adm. in IL) Assoc. Gen. Coun., OfficeMax Incorporated
Woodward, David R. '70 '01 C.1375 B.A. L.767 J.D.
(adm. in CA; not adm. in IL) Atty., NEC Solutions (America), Inc.

JACKSONVILLE, * 18,940, *Morgan Co.*

Applebee, Alan W., (BV) ....'48 '73 C.303 A.B. L.597 J.D. 211 W. State St.
Beard, Daniel J., (BV) ....'54 '79 C.234 B.A. L.339 J.D. [Bellatti,F.B.&B.]
Bellatti, John E., (AV) ....'18 '47 C.337 A.B. L.309 J.D. [⊡ Bellatti,F.B.&B.]
Bellatti, Walter R., (AV) ....'15 '39 C.337 B.A. L.309 LL.B. [Bellatti,F.B.&B.]
Bellatti, Fay, Bellatti & Beard, (AV) .... 333 West State Street
Bone, J. David ....'41 '71 C.597 A.B. L.362 J.D. Cir. J.
Bonjean, Robert V., III ....'71 '98 C.337 B.A. L.801 J.D. [⊡ Bonjean]
Bonjean Law Office .... 309 W. State
Bradney, Robert E., (AV) ....'— '50 C.337 B.A. L.309 LL.B. [⊡ Rammelkamp B.]
Brown, John M. ....'23 '52 C&L.421 B.A., J.D. 33 Sunset Dr‡

Carpenter, Eddie, (AV) '48 '80 C.337 B.A. L.339 J.D.
305 West State Street, P.O. Box 871, 62651
Telephone: 217-245-7015 FAX: 217-243-7725
Real Estate, Probate Law. Collections, Trusts, General Civil Practice.
See Professional Biographies, JACKSONVILLE, ILLINOIS

Cline, Gary L., (BV) ......'— '81 C&L.339 B.A., J.D. [Rammelkamp B.] (⊙Springfield)
Colburn, B. G. ....'29 '53 C&L.597 A.B., LL.B. 104 N. West St.‡
Colburn, Charles M. ....'59 '84 C.210 B.A. L.910 J.D. State's Atty.
Dahman, Marc, (AV) ....'38 '63 C&L.339 B.A., J.D. 1A West Central Park Plaza
DelGiorno, Anthony J. ....'— '02 C.337 B.A. L.30 J.D. [⊡ Rammelkamp B.]
Fay, William L., (AV) ....'14 '38 C.337 A.B. L.309 J.D. [⊡ Bellatti,F.B.&B.]
Flynn, J. Edward, (BV) ....'34 '62 C.337 B.A. L.734 J.D. [Flynn&F.]
Flynn, Larry J., (AV) ....'35 '60 C.337 L.734 J.D. [Flynn&F.]
Flynn & Flynn, (AV) .... 222 W. State St.
Freeman, Richard R., (BV) ....'— '88 C.98 B.S. L.910 J.D. [Rammelkamp B.]
Fritsche, Barbara, (BV) ....'— '77 C.161 B.A. L.209 J.D. [Rammelkamp B.]
Gonzalez, Maria M., (BV) ....'— '87 C.357 B.A. L.339 J.D. [Rammelkamp B.]
Henriksen, Kay E. ....'49 '76 C.912 B.S. L.383 J.D. MacMurray College
Hurst, Jonathan D. ....'62 '88 C.880 B.A. L.801 J.D. Asst. State Atty.
Jackson, Amy L. ....'— '93 C.340 B.A. L.734 J.D. [⊡ Rammelkamp B.]
Keaton, Forrest G., (AV) ....'— '77 C.98 B.A. L.339 J.D. [Rammelkamp B.]
Kesinger, G. Ronald, (BV) ....'39 '66 C.337 235 North West
Kuster, Larry D., (AV) ....'— '73 C.57 B.A. L.352 J.D. [Rammelkamp B.]
Lindsay, Nancy, (BV) '— '83 C.337 B.A. L.734 J.D.
[Rammelkamp B.] (⊙Springfield)
McNeely, Charles E., (BV) ....'49 '74 C.337 B.S. L.339 J.D. [Thomson,M.&T.]
Olson, Tim Phillip ....'54 '80 C.339 B.A. L.383 J.D. Assoc. Cir. J.
Pirtle, Harry C. ....'26 '50 C.801 A.B. L.339 J.D. 1481 W. Walnut St.‡
Rammelkamp, Theodore C., (AV) '19 '48 C.337 A.B. L.477 J.D.
232 West State Street‡
Rammelkamp, Theodore C., Jr., (AV) '45 '78
C.337 B.A. L.477 J.D. Davel Communications Group, Inc.

Rammelkamp Bradney, P.C., (AV)
232 West State Street, P.O. Box 550, 62651 ⊙
Telephone: 217-245-6177 Fax: 217-243-7322
Email: info@rblawyers.net URL: http://www.rammelkamplaw.com
Larry D. Kuster; Forrest G. Keaton; Barbara Fritsche; Nancy Lindsay; Maria M. Gonzalez; Richard R. Freeman; H. Allen Yow; Gary L. Cline; Bradley W. Wilson;—Amy L. Jackson; Anthony J. DelGiorno. Of Counsel: Robert E. Bradney; Richard E. Mann (Resident, Winchester Office).
General Practice. Insurance, Municipal, Probate, Estate Planning, Trusts, Tax, Real Estate and Corporation Law.
Representative Clients: Country Mutual Insurance Co.; State Farm Mutual Auto Insurance Co.; American States Insurance; Pekin Insurance Co.; Pleasant Plains State Bank; EMI Manufacturing; Tenneco Packaging; Soyland Power Cooperative, Inc.
Springfield, Illinois Office: 520 East Allen Street. 62703. Telephone: 217-522-6000. Fax: 217-522-6018.
Winchester, Illinois Office: 46 South Hill Street, 66666. Telephone: 217-742-5215. Fax: 217-742-3537.
See Professional Biographies, JACKSONVILLE, ILLINOIS

Robinson, David E., (BV) ....'37 '62 C.337 A.B. L.339 LL.B. 313 W. State St.
Rowe, Fredk. H. ....'23 '50 C.337 A.B. L.597 J.D. 1152 W. State St.‡
Ruppel, Timothy E., (BV) ....'61 '88 C.98 B.S. L.589 J.D. [Bellatti,F.B.&B.]
Smith, C Matthew A., (BV) ....'53 '78 C.963 B.S. L.801 J.D. [Bellatti,F.B.&B.]
Soltermann, Jeffrey L., (BV) ....'69 '94 C.357 B.A. L.339 J.D. [Bellatti,F.B.&B.]
Symons-Jackson, Amy Lynne ....'68 '93 C.340 B.A. L.734 J.D. 232 W. State St.
Thomson, Ralph, (AV) ....'22 '47 C&L.339 B.S., J.D. [Thomson,M.&T.]
Thomson, McNeely & Tobin, P.C., (AV) .... 226 W. State St.
Tobin, Jeffrey E. ....'61 '87 C.337 B.S. L.1187 J.D. [Thomson,M.&T.]
Veith, Thomas L., (BV) ....'64 '89 C.337 B.A. L.575 J.D. [Bellatti,F.B.&B.]
Wilson, Bradley W., (BV) ....'— '98 C.339 B.S. L.146 J.D. [Rammelkamp B.]
Woodruff, David B., (CV) ....'46 '77 C.1247 B.A. L.801 J.D. [D.Woodruff]
Woodruff, David, Law Offices of, (CV) .... 257 Finley St.
Yow, H. Allen, (BV) ....'— '89 C.894 A.B. L.801 J.D. [Rammelkamp B.] (⊙Winchester)

JERSEYVILLE, * 7,984, *Jersey Co.*

Cooper, Anita G., (AV) ....'49 '74 C.914 B.A. L.94 J.D. [Cooper&M.]
Cooper & McDonald, (AV) ....105 N. State St.
Davis, Claude J. ....'22 '48 C.674 A.B. L.339 LL.B. Cir. J.
Goetten, Norbert J., (AV) ....'40 '67 C.801 B.S. L.365 J.D. States Atty.
Guntren, John W., (BV) ....'55 '82 C.337 B.A. L.201 J.D. 1110 S. State St.

Harper, Julie
(See Alton)

Kirback, Mary E., (BV) ....'67 '92 C.1203 B.B.A. L.734 J.D. 123 W. Pearl
McDonald, Michael J., (BV) ....'47 '72 C.711 B.A. L.734 J.D. [Cooper&M.]
Mondhink, Harry R. ....'22 '49 C&L.339 A.B., LL.B. 1830 McClusky Rd.‡
Moore, Philip D., (BV) ....'31 '61 C.234 B.S. L.734 LL.B. 103 N. State St.
Pistorius, Eric S., (BV) ....'59 '84 C.927 B.S. L.801 J.D. 116 W. Pearl St.
Plummer, Lee J., Attorney at Law, (BV) '50 '76 C.1082 B.A. L.734 J.D.
100 S. State St.
Ringhausen, Richard J., (BV) ....'59 '84 C.801 B.A. L.128 J.D. States Atty.
Russell, Thomas G. ....'48 '78 C.813 B.A. L.169 J.D. Cir. J.
Ryder, W. Thomas, (BV) ....'49 '75 C.589 B.A. L.902 J.D. [W.T.Ryder]
Ryder, W. Thomas, Ltd., A Prof. Corp., (BV) ....100 S. State St.
Strang, William H. ....'50 '79 C.234 B.S. L.911 J.D. 108 N. Lafayette St.
Wittman, George P., (AV) ....'41 '70 C&L.734 A.B., J.D. 123 W. Pearl St.

JOLIET, 106,221, *Kendall & Will Cos.*

Adair, Patricia C. Grimes ....'45 '99 C.719 B.S. L.589 J.D. [⊡ Block,B.&K.]
Adler, Daniel J., Law Offices, (CV) '54 '79 C.602 A.B. L.339 J.D.
1616 W. Jefferson St.
Allen, J. Jeffrey ....'51 '76 C.597 B.A. L.209 J.D. Assoc.
Allen, James J., (BV) '51 '76 C.597 B.A. L.209 J.D.
Mng. Atty., Will Co. Legal Assistance Prog., Inc.
Andreano, Frank P., (BV) ....'64 '90 C.602 B.A. L.209 J.D. [Dunn,M.&M.]
Andreano, Samuel J., (BV) ....'38 '66 C.177 B.A. L.365 LL.B. Pub. Def.
Archambeault, Dinah Lennon, (BV) '52 '88 C.1151 B.A. L.365 J.D.
[⊡ Spesia,A.&A.]
Ardaugh, John R. "Jack", (BV) ....'59 '86 C.338 B.S. L.365 J.D. [Spesia,A.&A.]
Ayers, E. Kent, (AV) ....'42 '69 C.894 A.B. L.585 J.D. [Spesia,A.&A.]
Baker, Gregory R. ....'60 '94 C.959 B.B.A. L.209 J.D. 58 N. Chicago St.
Baron, Robert J. ....'39 '64 C.177 B.A. L.597 J.D. Cir.J.
Barrett, Brian E. ....'73 '99 C.209 B.A. L.146 J.D. Co. State's Atty. Off.
Baskin, James M., Attorney at Law '68 '93
C.339 B.A. L.597 J.D. 1504 Woodbridge Rd., Ste. 3A
Beaudry, Terry G. ...... '48 '77 C.589 B.A. L.365 J.D. Pres., First Midwest Tr. Co., N.A.‡
Beck, Alexander H. ....'63 '88 C.145 B.A. L.146 J.D. [Sabuco,B.H.&S.]
Beck, David A., (AV) ....'54 '79 C.339 B.A. L.365 J.D. [Kiesler&B.]
Bednarek, Theodore J., (BV) ....'49 '74 C&L.734 A.B., J.D. 63 W. Jefferson St.
Belford, Scott L. ....'49 '74 C.112 B.S. L.597 J.D. 5 W. Cass St.

Berdelle, Richard L., Jr., P.C.
(See Chicago)

Bertani, Amy M. ....'57 '85 C.744 B.A. L.1187 J.D. Cir. J.
Block, Michael D., (AV) ....'47 '70 C.1016 B.A. L.365 J.D. [Block,B.&K.]
Block, Winston J. ....'42 '65 C.1016 B.A. L.365 J.D. [Block,B.&K.]
Block, Block & Klukas, P.C., (AV) .... 19 W. Jefferson St.
Boetto, Dominic F., (BV) ....'22 '50 C.602 B.A. L.209 J.D. [Boetto&B.]
Boetto, Paul V., (BV) ....'56 '81 C.884 B.S. L.589 J.D. [Boetto&B.]
Boetto & Boetto, (BV) ....58 N. Chicago St.
Bolden, Raymond A. ....'33 '62 C&L.339 B.S., LL.B. [Mitchell,B.&M.]
Bolos, Michael L., (BV) .... '48 '74 C.347 B.A. L.365 J.D. [M.L.Bolos]
Bolos, Michael L., Ltd., Law Office of, (BV) ....116 N. Chicago St., Ste. 555
Bonds, Alexander, (BV) ....'42 '69 C.1151 B.A. L.209 J.D. [Codo,B.Z.&K.]
Boyack, Robert M., (BV) ....'42 '68 C.424 B.B.A. L.365 J.D. 3104 W. Glenwood Ave.
Boyer, Andrew Ben, (CV) ...... '58 '86 C.187 B.S.S. L.879 J.D. 71 N. Ottawa St., Ste. 216
Brady, James M., (BV) ....'43 '81 C.436 B.A. L.365 J.D. [J.M.Brady]
Brady, Sean D., (BV) ....'70 '97 C.234 B.A. L.339 B.A. [Mahoney,S.&C.]
Brady, James M., Ltd., (BV) .... 1403 Essington Road Suite 400
Braun, Bennett J., (BV) ..... '59 '87 C.339 B.A. L.362 J.D. 116 N. Chicago St., Ste. 555

Brenner, Ford, Monroe & Scott, Ltd.
(See Chicago)

Brenner & Moltzen, Ltd., (AV) ....57 West Jefferson, Suite 508-C (⊙Chicago)
Bretz, Charles L. ....'57 '82 C.999 B.A. L.339 J.D. [C.Bretz&Assoc.]

Bretz, Chuck, & Associates, P.C.
58 North Chicago Street, 2nd Floor, 60432
Telephone: 815-740-1545 Fax: 815-740-1546
Email: cbretz@bretzlawoffice.com URL: http://www.bretzlawoffice.com
Charles L. Bretz;—Cosmo J. Tedone; Erin W. O'Sullivan.
Trial Practice, Criminal Defense, Family Law, and Complex Personal Injury Law. DUI/DWI, White Collar Crime, Felonies, Murder, Homicide, Misdemeanors, Traffic, Suspended License, Drug Crimes,

(This Listing Continued)

Bretz, Chuck, & Associates, P.C. (Continued)
Juvenile Law, Divorce, Contested and Uncontested Divorce, Child Custody, Child Support, Visitation, Post Decree, Orders of Protection, Domestic Violence, Automobile Accidents, Wrongful Death and Medical Malpractice.
See Professional Biographies, JOLIET, ILLINOIS

Brick, Lyndean Lenhoff '59 '84
C.20 B.A. L.608 J.D. Heatlh Care Atty., Mirror Consulting Inc.
Brumund, James R., (BV) ....'48 '79 C.57 B.A. L.589 J.D. [Brumund,J.H.&D.]
Brumund, Robert P., (BV) ....'44 '71 C.801 B.A. L.365 J.D. 14 W. Jefferson St.

Brumund, Jacobs, Hammel & Davidson, LLC, (AV)
Executive Centre, Suite 200, 58 East Clinton Street, 60432-4193
Telephone: 815-723-0628 FAX: 815-723-1371
Email: garykdavidson@aol.com URL: http://www.lawyers.com/brumund&jacobs
Members of Firm: Paul F. Brumund (1916-2000); Myles L. Jacobs; James R. Brumund; Ted P. Hammel; Gary K. Davidson.
The firm has a general practice with individual lawyers specializing in specific areas of the law, including Commercial and Residential Real Estate, Land Use and Zoning, Condominium and Homeowners Association Law, Contract Law, Personal Injury, Commercial Litigation, Corporate Law, Criminal Law, Aggravated Traffic, including DUI, Collection Law, Probate and Estate Planning, Family, Divorce, Adoptions and Juvenile Law, Landlord and Tenant Law.
Representative Clients: Allstate Insurance Co.
Reference: First Midwest Bank/Illinois.
See Professional Biographies, JOLIET, ILLINOIS

Buck, Carl R. ....'68 '97 C.152 B.A. L.365 J.D. [Rathbun,C.&K.] (⊙Plainfield)
Burkey, Franklin, (BV) ....'37 '66 C.589 A.B. L.209 LL.B. 911 Buell AVe. St.
Burrows, Quentin C. ....'72 '97 C.589 B.A. L.879 J.D. [Burrows&Assoc.]
Burrows & Associates, P.C. ....2101 Graystone Drive
Byers, Frank S. ....'55 '89 C.339 B.A. L.597 J.D. Asst. State Atty.
Byrne, James C. ....'34 '61 C&L.424 B.S.C., J.D. 815 N. Larkin Ave.
Campbell, Matthew W. ....'65 '93 C.338 B.S. L.1187 J.D. [Ⓐ Dykema G.P.]
Carey, Thomas E., (BV) ....'44 '75 C.589 B.S. L.365 J.D. 24 W. Class St., 5th Fl.
Carlson, Kenneth A., (BV) ....'60 '86 C.339 B.A. L.356 J.D. [Tracy,J.&W.]
Cassian, William R. ....'69 '94 C.338 B.S. L.365 J.D. [Hinshaw&C.]

Castagnoli, Susan G., P.C., Law Offices of
(See Naperville)

Cernugel, Joseph M., (BV) ....'50 '75 C.597 B.A. L.339 J.D. [Krockey,C.C.C.&P.]
Cerri, Vincent J. ....'45 '70 C.209 B.S. L.365 J.D. 68 N. Chicago St., Ste. 243

Cetina & Jacques, P.C.
(See Oakbrook Terrace)

Chastain, Lisa Gray ....'72 '99 C.839 B.B.A. L.61 J.D. [Ⓐ Rathbun,C.&K.]

Chicago Internet Attorneys
(See Chicago)

Chopra, Kavita '76 '02
C.1182 B.A. L.146 J.D. Asst. States Atty., Will Co. State Atty. Off.
Cirricione, John F. ....'26 '52 C.999 L.365 LL.B. Assoc. Cir. J.
Clark, Timothy A., (CV) ....'62 '89 C.1277 B.A. L.589 J.D. [Krockey,C.C.C.&P.]
Clayton, Troy D. ....'70 '96 C.209 B.A. L.879 J.D. 58 N. Chicago St., Ste. 309
Clemens, Barbara A., (BV) ...'40 '83 C.1151 B.A. L.589 J.D. 24 W. Cass Street, 5th floor
Codo, Bonds, Zumstein & Konzelman, A Professional Corporation, (BV)
60 N. Chicago St.

Collins, Mary L.
(See Downers Grove)

Cooper, G. Robb ....'51 '87 C.628 B.S. L.424 J.D. [Ottosen T.B.K.&C.] ⊙

Corbett, John J., & Associates
(See Chicago)

Corboy & Demetrio, P.C.
(See Chicago)

Corlew, Gary L. ....'52 '77 C.589 B.A. L.146 J.D. 815 N. Larkin Ave., Ste. 107
Cowgill, Thomas E., (BV) ....'46 '75 C.182 B.M. L.365 J.D. [Krockey,C.C.C.&P.]
Cross, Thomas H., III, (BV) ....'58 '83 C.340 B.A. L.192 J.D. [Mahoney,S.&C.]
Cservenyak, Frank S., Jr., (BV) ....'63 '88 C.340 B.A. L.221 J.D. [Rathbun,C.&K.]
Dach, Richard A. ....'21 '48 C.999 L.209 LL.B. Chi. T. & T. Co.
Dallner, Daniel K., (CV) '65 '90 C.1151 B.A. L.589 J.D.
Asst. V.P. & Tr. Offr., First Midwest Tr. Co., N.A.‡
Davidson, Gary K. ....'73 '99 C.337 B.A. L.589 J.D. [Brumund,J.H.&D.]
Davis, L. Park, (AV) ....'39 '65 C.337 B.A. L.339 J.D. [Davis,D.H.&J.] ‡

Davis, Dystrup, Hoster & Jarot, P.C., (AV)
181 North Hammes Avenue, 60435
Telephone: 815-744-6550 Fax: 815-744-4518
Email: ddho@davis-dystrup-law.com URL: http://www.davis-dystrop-law.com
L. Park Davis (Retired); Andrew C. Dystrup; Scott Hoster; Edward J. Jarot, Jr.
Administrative Law, Banking Law, Business Law. Civil Litigation before all courts, departments and administrative agencies. Commercial Law, Construction Law, Corporations, Criminal Defense, Employee Benefits and Executive Compensation, Employment Law, Environmental Law; Estates, Trusts and Financial Planning, Mergers and Acquisitions, Partnership Law, Real Estate Law, Rezoning and Land Use, Taxation Law.
See Professional Biographies, JOLIET, ILLINOIS

DeBoer, Douglas G. '62 '87 C.578 B.A. L.146 J.D.
54 North Ottawa Street, Suite 260, 60432
Telephone: 815-724-1807 Fax: 815-727-5458
Email: dtdeboer@comcast.net URL: http://www.deboerlaw.com
Criminal Defense, Driving While Intoxicated, Homicide, Drug Crimes, Felonies, Juvenile Law, Misdemeanors, Sexual Assault, Traffic Violations, Personal Injury, Auto Accidents, Wrongful Death.
See Professional Biographies, JOLIET, ILLINOIS

Donahue, John W. ....'19 '70 C.597 L.365 J.D. 2821 Wilshire Blvd.
Doyle, Daniel L., (BV) ....'45 '76 C.1151 B.S. L.146 J.D. 58 N. Chicago St., Ste. 404
Drell, Lea Armstrong, (CV) ....'34 '85 C.536 B.A. L.365 J.D. [Stuhr&D.]
Duffy, Joseph E., (AV) ....'40 '65 C.602 B.A. L.597 J.D. [Schenk]
Dunn, Thomas A. ....'42 '72 C.707 B.A. L.209 J.D. Cir. J.
Dunn, Martin & Miller, Ltd., (BV) ....15 West Jefferson Street, Suite 300

Dykema Gossett PLLC, (AV)
111 North Ottawa Street, 60432 ⊙
Telephone: 815-727-4511 Facsimile: 815-727-1586
URL: http://www.dykema.com
Members of Firm: Robert R. Gorbold; James D. Grumley; Richard J. Kavanagh; Bryan W. Kopman. Of Counsel: William T. Kaplan; George J. Vosicky. Associates: Matthew W. Campbell; Pamela Davis Gorcowski; Paul J. Richards.
Antitrust and Trade Regulation, Automotive, Banking and Financial Services, Bankruptcy, Biotechnology and Life Sciences, Casino Gaming, Class Action Defense, Computer and Software Law, Construction, Consumer Financial Services, Corporate Finance, E-Commerce, Emerging Business and Technology, Employee Benefits, Entertainment and Sports, Environmental Law, Family Law, Franchise Law and Regulation, Government Contracts, Government Policy and Practice, HealthCare,
(This Listing Continued)

Dykema Gossett PLLC (Continued)
Indian Law, Insurance, Intellectual Property, International Law, Labor and Employment, Litigation and Dispute Resolution, Mergers and Acquisitions, Products Liability Defense, Public Finance, Real Estate, Retail Law, Securities, Taxation and Estates, Trade Associations.
Ann Arbor, Michigan Office: 2723 South State Street, Suite 400, 48104. Telephone: 734-214-7660. Fax: 734-214-7696.
Aurora, Illinois Office: 2 Hankes Road. Telephone: 630-844-2200. Facsimile: 630-844-2277.
Bloomfield Hills, Michigan Office: 39577 Woodward Avenue, Suite 300, 48304-2820. Telephone: 248-203-0700. Fax: 248-203-0763.
Chicago, Illinois Office: 10 South Wacker Drive, Suite 2300. Telephone: 312-876-1700. Fax: 312-876-1155.
Detroit, Michigan Office: 400 Renaissance Center, 48243-1668. Telephone: 313-568-6800. Fax: 313-568-6545.
Grand Rapids, Michigan Office: Suite 700, 300 Ottawa Avenue, N.W., 49503-2306. Telephone: 616-776-7500. Fax: 616-776-7573.
Lansing, Michigan Office: 124 W. Allegan Street, Suite 800, 48933-1742. Telephone: 517-374-9100. Fax: 517-374-9191.
Lisle, Illinois Office: 4200 Commerce Court, Suite 300. Telephone: 630-245-0400. Facsimile: 630-245-0140.
Los Angeles, California Office: 333 South Grand Avenue, Suite 2100, 90071. Telephone: 213-457-1800. Fax: 213-457-1850.
Washington, D.C. Office: Franklin Square, Suite 300 West, 1300 I Street, N.W., 20005-3353. Telephone: 202-906-8600. Fax: 202-906-8669.
See Professional Biographies, JOLIET, ILLINOIS

Dystrup, Andrew C., (BV) ....'45 '70 C&L.339 B.S., J.D. [Davis,D.H.&J.]
Egner, Charles A., (BV) ....'68 '95 C.98 B.S. L.1000 J.D. [Ⓐ Hinshaw&C.]
Ewert, Thomas M. ....'46 '71 C.589 B.S. L.339 J.D. [Ⓒ Spesia,A.&A.]
Fabrizio, James R., (BV) ....'49 '76 C.339 B.A. L.146 J.D. [Fabrizio,H.P.&K.]

Fabrizio, Hanson, Peyla & Kawinski, P.C., (BV)
Two Rialto Square, 116 N. Chicago Street, Suite 301, 60432
Telephone: 815-727-5445 Fax: 815-727-1224
Email: mhanson-fhandp@attglobal.net
George M. O'Brien (1917-1986); James R. Fabrizio; Mark E. Hanson; Gregory L. Peyla; Mr. Mark Kawinski;—Mr. Jeremiah K. O'Connor. Of Counsel: Lawrence E. Morrissey.
General Civil and Trial Practice. Insurance Defense, Personal Injury, Automobile Accidents, Products Liability, Wrongful Death, Construction Accidents, Workers Compensation, Corporate, Business, Probate, Real Estate, Health Care and Construction Litigation.
Representative Clients: The Hartford Insurance Company; Nationwide Insurance Co.; Continental National American Group.
Reference: The First National Bank of Joliet.
See Professional Biographies, JOLIET, ILLINOIS

Farmans, Janet M. ....'— '82 C.927 B.A. L.589 J.D. [Querrey&H.]
Feehan, Thomas, (AV) ....'26 '53 C&L.424 B.S., J.D. 111 N. Ottawa St.
Felton, John R., (BV) ....'63 '90 C.123 B.S. L.146 J.D. [Hinshaw&C.]
Fitzgerald, Joseph C., (AV) ....'33 '57 C&L.339 B.S., J.D. [McKeown,F.Z.B.H.&R.] ‡
Fitzgerald, Michael J. ....'68 '95 C.234 B.A. L.209 J.D. 350 Houbolt Rd., Ste. 210

Fleming, Michael W., Attorney at Law
(See Elmhurst)

Ford, William R., (BV) ....'49 '74 C.388 B.A. L.117 J.D. [Schenk]
Frano, Andrew J. ....'53 '82 C.98 B.S.C.E. L.46 J.D. T.J. Lambrecht Construction, Inc.
Fredin, Justin M. ....'77 '04 C.101 B.S. L.352 J.D. [Ⓐ Mahoney,S.&C.]
Friefeld, Bruce N. ....'48 '74 C.421 B.A. L.209 J.D. Spec. Exec. Asst., Co. of Will
Furlane, Emil A., (BV) ....'42 '70 C.589 L.365 J.D. 5 E. Van Buren St.
Gahan, Michael, (AV) ....'53 '78 C.1151 B.A. L.602 J.D. [Hinshaw&C.]
Gallo, John S., (BV) ....'58 '85 C.1151 B.A. L.424 J.D. [Tracy,J.&W.]
Gibson, Requel, Esq. ....'70 '97 C.197 B.A. L.602 J.D. 1862 Terry Drive
Gilbert, Thomas J., (AV) ....'49 '74 C.477 B.A. L.424 J.D. [Ottosen T.B.K.&C.] ⊙
Gillen, Suzanne, (BV) ....'61 '87 C.393 B.A. L.146 J.D. [Mangan,L.G.&L.] ⊙
Goldstein, Ira B., (AV) ....'46 '74 C.475 B.S. L.146 J.D. [I.B.Goldstein]
Goldstein, Ira B., Ltd., (AV) ....2701 Black Road
Gorbold, Robert R., (BV) ....'52 '79 C.937 B.A. L.365 J.D. [Dykema G.P.]
Gorcowski, Michael N., (CV) ....'56 '81 C&L.339 B.A., J.D. [M.N.Gorcowski]
Gorcowski, Pamela Davis, (BV) ....'56 '81 C.430 B.A. L.339 J.D. [Ⓐ Dykema G.P.]

Gorcowski, Michael N., P.C., (CV)
8 West Cass Street, 60432
Telephone: 815-740-5900 Fax: 815-740-5903
Email: mngorcow@sbcglobal.net URL: http://www.gorcowskilaw.com
Michael N. Gorcowski.
Language: Spanish.
Landlord and Tennant Law, Family, Divorce, Child Custody, Child Support, Adoption, Traffic Violations, Driving While Intoxicated, Misdemeanors, Wills, Estate Planning, Commercial Real Estate, Residential Real Estate, Real Estate Closings, Personal Injury, Automobile Accidents, Workers Compensation.
See Professional Biographies, JOLIET, ILLINOIS

Gordon, Careen M. ....'72 '98 C.339 B.A. L.365 J.D. Asst. States Atty
Gorman, Tiffany R. ....'78 '03 C.339 B.A. L.424 J.D. [Ⓐ McKeown,F.Z.B.H.&R.]
Gould, Donald J., (BV) ....'63 '89 C.679 B.A. L.589 J.D. 307 Moen Ave.
Gould, Rachael ....'76 '02 C.188 B.S. L.273 J.D. [Ⓐ McKeown,F.Z.B.H.&R.]
Grabiec, Edwin B. ....'41 '68 C.750 B.A. L.209 J.D. Assoc. Cir. J.
Gray, Lawrence C., (BV) ....'44 '71 C.388 B.A. L.209 J.D. Assoc. Cir. J.
Gray, Sara J. ....'74 '00 C&L.589 B.A., J.D. [Gray&I.]

Gray & Idris, P.C., Law Offices of
54 N. Ottawa Street, Suite B80, 60640
Telephone: 815-723-4543 Fax: 815-723-4922
URL: http://www.grayidrislaw.com
Sara J. Gray; Kayode R. Idris.
General Practice.
See Professional Biographies, JOLIET, ILLINOIS

Greenberg, Lorraine M., and Associates '52 '81 C.174 B.A. L.365 J.D.
57 West Jefferson, Suite 508 (⊙Chicago, Lisle)
Grey, Kenneth A., (BV) ....'51 '83 C.927 B.A. L.365 J.D. [McKeown,F.Z.B.H.&R.] ⊙
Grumley, James D., (BV) ....'50 '76 C.602 B.B.A. L.424 J.D. [Dykema G.P.]
Guess, Norma J., (BV) ....'54 '78 C&L.1151 B.A., J.D. 1313 Mayfield Avenue
Haase, Herman S. ....'42 '70 C.1101 B.A. L.597 J.D. Chief Judge Cir. Ct.
Hammel, Ted P., (CV) ....'63 '89 C.436 B.S. L.365 J.D. [Brumund,J.H.&D.]
Haney, Steven C., Law Office of, (BV) '60 '85
C.317 B.S. L.365 J.D. 116 N. Chicago St., Ste. 302
Hansen, Michael W., (BV) ....'51 '76 C.602 B.B.A. L.221 J.D. [M.W.Hansen]
Hansen, Michelle, (CV) ....'56 '83 C.338 B.S. L.365 J.D. [Sabuco,B.H.&S.]

Hansen, Michael W., P.C., (BV)
320 Waterstone Way, Suite 200, 60431
Telephone: 815-744-9500 Fax: 815-744-4515
Email: mikehansen@core.com
Michael W. Hansen;—Colleen M. Wengler.
Corporate, Real Estate, Estate Planning, Zoning, Planning and Land Use, Gaming Law, Closely Held Business Law, Limited Liability, Buying and Selling Businesses, Business Formation, Joint Ventures.
See Professional Biographies, JOLIET, ILLINOIS

Hanson, Eric P., (BV) .... '69 '97 C.339 B.A. L.365 J.D. [Mahoney,S.&C.]
Hanson, Mark E., (BV) .... '52 '77 C.602 B.A. L.424 J.D. [Fabrizio,H.P.&K.]
Harris, Jane E., (CV) .... '59 '84 C.927 B.A. L.61 J.D. P.O. Box 888
Hart, Angela E. .... '75 '04 C.1236 B.A. L.352 J.D. [Mahoney,S.&C.]
Harvey, James B., (BV) .... '55 '80 C.1151 B.A. L.365 J.D. [McKeown,F.Z.B.H.&R.]
Heathcock, Douglas E. .... '68 '93 C.339 B.A. L.146 J.D. [Dunn,M.&M.]
Hess, Anastasia L. .... '67 '99 C.339 B.A. L.879 J.D. [Ⓐ Mangan,L.G.&L.]

Hinshaw & Culbertson LLP, (AV)
Hinshaw & Culbertson LLP is an Illinois registered limited liability partnership that has elected to be governed by the Illinois Uniform Partnership Act (1997)
57 North Ottawa Street Suite 314, 60432 ⊙
Telephone: 815-726-5910 Facsimile: 815-726-0353 Telex: 880248
Email: kfox@hinshawlaw.com URL: http://www.hinshawlaw.com
Partners: William R. Cassian; John R. Felton; Michael Gahan; Scott E. Nemanich; Peter G. Panno; Daniel P. Slayden; Daniel J. Softcheck. Associates: Charles A. Egner; Michael J. Vines; Tammy S. Warden.
Appellate, Banking & Financing, Bankruptcy & Creditors' Rights, Class Action Litigation, Civil Rights Defense, Commercial Litigation, Corporate, Construction Law, Director & Officer Liability, Employee Benefits, Environmental, Fidelity & Surety, General Liability Litigation, Government, Health Care, Insurance Coverage, Insurance and Reinsurance, Labor & Employment, Legal Malpractice, Medical Malpractice, Mergers & Acquisitions, Municipal Liability, Personal Injury Defense, Public Law, Products Liability Litigation, Professional Liability, Regulatory, Real Estate, School Law, Securities, Taxation, Transportation, White Collar Crime and Workers' Compensation Defense.
Other Office Locations: Chicago, Illinois; Appleton, Wisconsin; Belleville, Illinois; Boston, Massachusetts; Champaign, Illinois; Crystal Lake, Illinois; Edwardsville, Illinois; Fort Lauderdale, Florida; Jacksonville, Florida; Lisle, Illinois; Los Angeles, California; Miami, Florida; Milwaukee, Wisconsin; Minneapolis, Minnesota; New York, New York; Peoria, Illinois; Phoenix, Arizona; Portland, Oregon; Providence, Rhode Island; Rockford, Illinois; St. Louis, Missouri; San Francisco, California; Schererville, Indiana; Springfield, Illinois; Tampa, Florida; Waukegan, Illinois.
See Professional Biographies, JOLIET, ILLINOIS

Hoster, Scott, (BV) .... '60 '85 C.92 B.A. L.209 J.D. [Davis,D.H.&J.]

Hughes Socol Piers Resnick & Dym, Ltd.
(See Chicago)

Idris, Kayode R. .... '63 '00 C.339 B.A. L.589 J.D. [Gray&I.]
Jacobs, Myles L., (AV) .... '32 '60 C.197 A.B. L.569 J.D. [Brumund,J.H.&D.]
Jarot, Edward J., Jr. .... '71 '96 C.346 B.A. L.424 J.D. [Davis,D.H.&J.]
Jonker, Donald P. .... '57 '84 C.339 B.A. L.1187 J.D. [Ⓐ Rathbun,C.&K.]
June, David A., (BV) .... '56 '81 C.221 B.A. L.352 J.D. [June,P.&R.]
June, Ford C., III, (BV) .... '47 '72 C.504 A.B. L.352 J.D. [June,P.&R.]

June, Prodehl & Renzi, L.L.C., (BV)
1861 Black Road, 60435
Telephone: 815-725-8000 Fax: 815-725-6126 URL: http://www.jprllc.com
Email: main@jprlaw.net URL: http://www.lawyers.com/jprllc
Members of Firm: David A. June; Ford C. June, III; Steven J. Prodehl; John C. Renzi;—Marilyn L. Wysocki; Jennifer M. Lynch.
General Civil and Trial Practice. Elder Law, Family, Divorce, Child Custody, Real Estate, Tax, Estate Planning, Personal Injury, Automobile Accidents, Criminal.
See Professional Biographies, JOLIET, ILLINOIS

Kahn, Glenn J. .... '65 '91 C.393 B.A. L.146 J.D. [Kipnis&K.] (⊙Chicago)
Kallan, Kathleen Glenney .... '49 '75 C.530 B.A. L.424 J.D. Assoc. Cir. J.
Kaplan, William T., (BV) .... '40 '66 C.293 B.A. L.910 J.D. [Ⓒ Dykema G.P.]
Kapsos, Kim M. .... '71 '02 C.959 B.S. L.424 J.D. [Ⓐ McKeown,F.Z.B.H.&R.]
Kaschak, Lawrence M. .... '66 '91 C.589 B.S. L.365 J.D. [Ⓐ Rathbun,C.&K.]
Kavanagh, Richard J., (AV) .... '44 '74 C.276 B.S. L.424 J.D. [Dykema G.P.]
Kawinski, Mark, (BV) .... '64 '91 C.623 B.A. L.146 J.D. [Fabrizio,H.P.&K.]
Kelly, John H. .... '51 '82 C.597 B.A. L.365 J.D. [Ottosen T.B.K.&C.] ⊙
Kennedy, Daniel L., (BV) .... '32 '56 C.602 A.B. L.145 J.D. 54 N. Ottawa St.
Kennedy, Daniel Lennon, (CV) .... '60 '86 C.755 B.A. L.190 J.D. [D.L.Kennedy&Assoc.]
Kennedy, Daniel L., & Associate, (CV) .... 54 N. Ottawa St., Ste. 260
Kennison, Victoria McKay .... '69 '96 L.365 J.D. 5 W. Jefferson St., Ste. 200
Kenol, Jean A. .... '76 '01 C.602 B.A. L.339 J.D. [Ⓐ McKeown,F.Z.B.H.&R.]
Kettelson, Ernest S., (AV) .... '24 '55 C.597 B.S. L.146 J.D. [Kettelson] (Pat.)
Kettelson Law Offices, Ltd., (AV) .... Wynderidge Pl. (Pat.)
Kielian, Gerald G., (AV) .... '47 '75 C.339 B.A. L.879 J.D. 23 West Jefferson Street

Kiesler & Berman, (AV)
57 North Ottawa Street Suite 210, 60432 ⊙
Telephone: 815-723-2755 FAX: 815-723-2763
Email: info@thekillerbees.com URL: http://www.kieslerberman.com
Partner: David A. Beck. Associate: Edwin J. Olson.
General Civil Trial and Appellate Practice. Insurance, Construction Litigation, Corporation, Real Estate and Probate Law. Asbestos Litigation, Civil Rights Law, Estate Planning, Insurance Coverage, Insurance Defense Law, Medical Malpractice Law, Police Misconduct, RICO, Surety and Fidelity Bond Law, Tort Law, Toxic Substances Law and Toxic Torts, Lanham Act Litigation, Condemnation Litigation, Arbitration.
Chicago Office: 70 West Madison, Suite 4200. Telephone: 312-332-2840. Fax: 312-332-4547.
See Professional Biographies, JOLIET, ILLINOIS

Kinney, Gerald R. .... '50 '75 C.801 B.A. L.424 J.D. Cir. J.
Kipnis & Kahn, Ltd. .... 54 N. Ottawa, Suite 305 (⊙Chicago, New Lenox)
Klepec, Jos. A. .... '20 '46 L.209 LL.B. Chicago Title & Trust Co.
Klukas, Elizabeth A., (BV) .... '63 '89 C.339 B.A. L.589 J.D. [Block,B.&K.]
Knick, Michael J. .... '59 '88 C.339 B.S.M.E. L.209 J.D. Asst. State Atty.
Konzelman, Bruce M., (BV) .... '45 '74 C.98 B.S. L.365 J.D. [Codo,B.Z.&K.]
Kopman, Bryan W., (BV) .... '70 '95 C.597 B.A. L.602 J.D. [Dykema G.P.]
Kozlowski, David R., (BV) .... '42 '70 C.679 A.B. L.1119 J.D. 1012 Plainfield Rd.
Kozol, William V., (BV) .... '53 '78 C.339 B.A. L.424 J.D. [Rathbun,C.&K.]
Krockey, Robert S., (AV) .... '40 '66 C.339 B.S.C. L.209 J.D. [Krockey,C.C.C.&P.]

Krockey, Cernugel, Cowgill, Clark & Pyles, (AV)
3100 Theodore Street, Suite 101, 60435
Telephone: 815-729-3600 Fax: 815-729-4280
URL: http://www.kcccp.com
Members of the Firm: Robert S. Krockey; Joseph M. Cernugel; Thomas E. Cowgill; Timothy A. Clark; Gary Scott Pyles.
Corporate and Tax, Probate, Estate Planning, Real Estate, Banking, Municipal, Family, Divorce, Child Support, Child Custody, Domestic Violence, Visitation Rights, Adoption, Workers Compensation, Personal Injury Law, Auto Accidents, Dog Bites, Sexual Abuse, Slip and Fall, Wrongful Death, Buying and Selling a Home, Construction, Eminent Domain, Environmental Law, Landlord and Tenant, Zoning and Land Use.
See Professional Biographies, JOLIET, ILLINOIS

Krzak, Susan E. .... '67 '92 C.177 B.A. L.339 J.D. 167 N. Chicago St.
Kucinic, William E., (BV) .... '43 '86 C.719 B.S. L.365 J.D. 151 Springfield Avenue
Kuhar, Ludwig J. .... '42 '66 C&L.339 B.S., J.D. Assoc. Cir. J.
Kuzma, Robert E. '57 '82
C.339 B.A. L.365 J.D. Dir. of Develop., University of St. Francis
LaFrance, Michael R. .... '38 '62 C&L.190 LL.B. 201 Union Street
Lagousakos, Athanasia .... '65 '91 C.339 B.A. L.46 J.D. Asst. St. Atty.
Langhenry, John G., III, (AV) .... '58 '85 C.602 A.B. L.424 J.D. [Mangan,L.G.&L.] ⊙

Lantz, Leanne M., (BV) '56 '84
C.424 B.A. L.209 J.D. 116 N. Chicago St., Ste. 302 (⊙Crete)
Latus, Lisa L. .... '65 '91 C.589 B.A. L.209 J.D. Asst. State's Atty.
LeBaron, Elizabeth Z. .... '55 '80 C.473 B.A. L.1119 J.D. [Ⓐ Rathbun,C.&K.]
Leinweber, Kurt A., (CV) .... '50 '76 C.46 B.S. L.424 J.D. 63 W. Jefferson St., Ste. 101

Lenard, George D., (AV) '57 '84 C.338 B.S. L.1187 J.D. ▣
Crystal Square Building, 81 North Chicago Street, Suite 206, 60432
Telephone: 815-723-9016 Fax: 815-723-7119
Email: LenardLaw@aol.com URL: http://www.lawyers.com/lenardlaw
Criminal Defense, Felonies, Homicide, Sexual Assault, Drug Crimes, Misdemeanors, Driving While Intoxicated, Traffic Violations and Juvenile Law.
See Professional Biographies, JOLIET, ILLINOIS

Lenard, Louis G. .... '20 '52 C&L.597 B.S., J.D. 1305 Mayfiekd Ave.‡
Lichtenwalter, Mark A. .... '70 '03 C.339 B.S. L.365 J.D. [Ⓐ Spesia,A.&A.]
Lisy, Deborah L. .... '60 '97 C.473 B.S. L.365 J.D. 514 Western Ave.
Long, James M., Jr. .... '76 '02 C.741 B.A. L.629 J.D. Wall Co. Atty. Off.
Lorz, Robert C. .... '50 '75 C.589 B.S.Ed. L.597 J.D. Assoc. Cir. J.
Loughran, Edward M., (CV) .... '37 '79 C.707 B.A. L.589 J.D. 58 N. Chicago St.
Lund, Cory D., (BV) .... '57 '82 C.589 B.A. L.801 J.D. [Ⓐ Tracy,J.&W.]
Lundquist, Troy A. .... '67 '92 C.339 B.A. L.365 J.D. [Mangan,L.G.&L.] ⊙
Lynch, Jennifer M. .... '73 '01 C.339 B.S.W. L.146 J.D. [Ⓐ June,P.&R.]
Maher, Teresa R., (BV) .... '55 '90 C.602 B.S. L.46 J.D. [Brenner&M.]
Mahoney, George F., III, (AV) .... '49 '74 C.1151 B.A. L.209 J.D. [Mahoney,S.&C.]

Mahoney, Silverman & Cross, Ltd., (AV) ▣
822 Infantry Drive, Suite 100, 60435
Telephone: 815-730-9500 Fax: 815-730-9598
URL: http://www.mscltdlaw.com
George F. Mahoney, III; David J. Silverman; Thomas H. Cross, III; Eric P. Hanson; James A. Murphy; Sean D. Brady; Walter J. Yurkanin; Kevin D. Yusman; Angela E. Hart; Justin M. Fredin. Counsel: William A. Peithmann.
Administrative Law; Appellate Practice; Banking Law; Business Law, including Business Formation, Maintenance and Planning, Financing, Acquisitions, Licensing and Business Transactions; Civil Litigation in State and Federal Courts, including Commercial, Construction, Personal Injury, Eminent Domain, Alternative Dispute Resolution, Zoning and Land Use; Construction Law; Land Use Law, including Zoning, Planning and Land Development; Local Governmental Law, including cities, villages, townships, fire protection, library and park districts, and governmental financing including tax increment financing districts; Real Estate Law; Tax Law; Traffic Law; Estate Planning; Trust Administration; Estate Administration; Contested Trusts and Estates; Elder Law; Gift, Estate and Income Tax Law.
See Professional Biographies, JOLIET, ILLINOIS

Maloney, Katherine L., (BV) '67 '94
C.589 B.A. L.273 J.D. [Rathbun,C.&K.] (⊙Plainfield)
Mangan, Jerald M. .... '57 '82 C.378 B.A. L.209 J.D. [Mangan,L.G.&L.] ⊙
Mangan, Langhenry, Gillen & Lundquist, (AV)
18 W. Cass Street, Suite 200 (⊙Chicago, Rockford, Wheaton)
Manning, Melanie D. .... '75 '01 C.339 B.A. L.365 J.D. [Ⓐ Tracy,J.&W.]
Markese, Bart P., Law Office of, (BV) '48 '75
C.338 B.S. L.365 J.D. 58 N. Chicago St., Ste. 305
Martin, Michael J., (BV) .... '50 '77 C.589 B.A. L.209 J.D. [Dunn,M.&M.]
Mason, Rick A., (BV) .... '51 '76 C&L.879 B.A., J.D. 81 N. Chicago Street
Masters, Edward F. .... '46 '72 C.221 B.A. L.146 J.D. 2701 Black Road
Mazzone, Joseph R., (BV) .... '50 '79 C.339 B.A. L.365 J.D. [Schenk]
McAsey, Christine .... '— '95 C.57 B.A. L.879 J.D. [Querrey&H.]
McFerrin, Philip N. '42 '67 C.197 A.B. L.893 J.D.
(adm. in VA; not adm. in IL) V.P., First Midwest Tr. Co., N.A.‡
McGarry, John J., (AV) .... '26 '52 C.999 L.424 LL.B. [Ⓒ Stefanich,M.&O.]
McKeown, Douglas J., (BV) '49 '74 C.927 B.B.A. L.146 J.D.
[McKeown,F.Z.B.H.&R.]

McKeown, Fitzgerald, Zollner, Buck, Hutchison & Ruttle, (AV)
2455 Glenwood Avenue, 60435 ⊙
Telephone: 815-729-4800 Fax: 815-729-4711
URL: http://www.mckeownlawfirm.com
Members of Firm: Charles J. McKeown (1908-1985); Paul O. McKeown (1913-1982); Richard T. Buck (1936-1992); Douglas P. Hutchison (1939-1998); Stewart C. Hutchison (1912-2002); Joseph C. Fitzgerald (Retired); David L. Ruttle; Douglas J. McKeown; James B. Harvey; Kenneth A. Grey; Christopher N. Wise; Nicholas E. Sakellariou; Arthur J. Wilhelmi; Christopher S. Ward. Of Counsel: George E. Sangmeister; Max E. Zollner (Retired). Associates: Kim M. Kapsos; Jean A. Kenol; Rachael Gould; Tiffany R. Gorman.
General Civil, Trial and Appellate Practice. Corporate, Business, Municipal, Probate, Estate Planning, Real Estate, Taxation, Employment, Healthcare, School and Personal Injury.
Representative Clients: Silver Cross Hospital; Villages of: Plainfield and Mokena; Southwest Agency for Risk Management; Joliet Junior College; Cornerstone Services, Inc.; Joliet Public Grade Schools District 86; Lewis University; Merchants and Manufacturers Bank; DTE Energy Services, Inc.; Joliet Arsenal Development Authority.
Frankfort Office: 28 Kansas Street. Telephone: 815-469-2176. FAX: 815-469-0295.
See Professional Biographies, JOLIET, ILLINOIS

McMenamin, William G. .... '46 '72 C.363 A.B. L.339 J.D. Assoc. Cir. J.
McNamara, Patrick J., (AV) .... '42 '70 C&L.209 Ph.B., J.D. [Schenk]
McSherry, William P., Jr., (BV) .... '46 '74 C.477 B.A. L.339 J.D. [W.P.McSherry]
McSherry, William P., Attorney at Law, (BV) .... 54 N. Ottawa St., Ste. 10
McSteen, Harry C., (BV) .... '37 '65 C.602 B.B.A. L.424 J.D. [McSteen]
McSteen, Raymond P., (BV) .... '65 '96 C.436 B.B.A. L.365 J.D. 71 N. Ottawa Street
McSteen Law Firm, The, (BV) .... 71 N. Ottawa St., Ste. 200
Meader, Raymond E., (BV) .... '47 '79 C.72 B.A. L.1151 J.D. [Tracy,J.&W.]
Melton, Amy .... '69 '98 C.966 B.A. L.589 J.D. [Mitchell,B.&M.]
Messamore, Kristen N. .... '67 '98 C.339 B.S. L.365 J.D. 58 E. Clinton St., Ste. 200

Meszaros, Patrick A., Law Office of '67 '97 C.719 B.A. L.209 J.D.
1256 West Jefferson Street, 60435
Telephone: 815-722-4001 Fax: 815-722-4007
URL: http://www.meszaroslaw.com
Personal Injury, Automobile Accidents and Injuries, Slip and Fall and Real Estate Law.
See Professional Biographies, JOLIET, ILLINOIS

Miller, Randal J., (BV) .... '52 '78 C.1151 B.A. L.365 J.D. [Dunn,M.&M.]
Mitchell, Eric A. .... '71 '98 C.679 B.A. L.347 J.D. [Mitchell,B.&M.]

Mitchell, Bolden & Melton, P.C.
54 North Ottawa Street, Suite 245, 60432
Telephone: 815-723-2895 Fax: 815-723-5136
Email: attorneymitchell@aol.com URL: http://www.mgblawoffices.com
Eric A. Mitchell; Raymond A. Bolden; Amy Melton.
Criminal Law, Civil Law, Traffic Violations, Real Estate, Employment Law, Family Law.
See Professional Biographies, JOLIET, ILLINOIS

Monahan, Thomas M. .... '28 '60 C.385 A.B. L.365 J.D. 58 N. Chicago St.
Morrissey, Lawrence E., (AV) '36 '64
C.339 B.S. L.365 LL.B. [Ⓒ Fabrizio,H.P.&K.] (⊙Chicago)

Moss and Bloomberg, Ltd.
(See Tressler, Soderstrom, Maloney & Priess)

Murer, Michael A., (BV) ....'43 '68 C.679 B.A. L.276 J.D. 58 N. Chicago St. 7th fl
Murphy, David .... '17 '41 C&L.209 J.D. Road Dist. Atty.
Murphy, James A., (AV) .... '60 '87 C.388 B.A. L.146 J.D. [Mahoney,S.&C.]
Murphy, Joel P. ....'78 '04 C&L.801 B.A., J.D. [Ⓐ Tracy,J.&W.]
Naal, Mary M., (BV) .... '62 '87 C.742 B.A. L.734 J.D. 57 W. Jefferson, Ste. 501

Nadler, Pritikin & Mirabelli, L.L.C.
(See Chicago)

Nash, Raymond A. .... '— '86 C&L.879 B.A, J.D. 71 N. Ottawa St., Ste. 216
Naughton, Thomas P., Law Offices of, (BV) '43 '80
C.1016 B.S.B.A. L.146 J.D. 57 W. Jefferson Street, Suite 505
Neal, Dave, and Associates, (BV) '55 '80
C.1151 B.A. L.589 J.D. 116 N. Chicago St., Ste. 602
Nemanich, Scott E., (BV) .... '52 '78 C.1151 B.A. L.597 J.D. [Hinshaw&C.]
Niznik, Gilbert L. .... '31 '55 C&L.339 B.S.L., LL.B. Assoc. Cir. J.
Nofal, Mohammed A. .... '77 '01 C.339 B.A. L.146 J.D. [Ⓐ Mangan,L.G.&L.]
Nolan, Thomas C., (BV) .... '46 '72 C&L.339 B.A., J.D. [Phelan&N.]
Norling, Dennis ......'48 '76 C.57 B.A. L.339 J.D. Sr. V.P., First Midwest Tr. Co., N.A.‡
O'Connell, Daniel F., (CV) .... '51 '82 C.1151 B.A. L.589 J.D. 69 N. Chicago Street
O'Connor, Jeremiah K. .... '69 '94 C.338 B.A. L.589 J.D. [Ⓐ Fabrizio,H.P.&K.]
Okrei, Roman R., (AV) .... '49 '77 C.1183 B.A. L.365 J.D. [Stefanich,M.&O.]
Olson, Edwin J. .... '— '94 C.475 B.A. L.146 J.D. [Ⓐ Kiesler&B.]
O'Meara, Wm. F., Jr. .... '33 '58 C.177 B.A. L.424 J.D. 50 W. Jefferson St.
Orenic, Gabriel G. .... '67 '03 C.1278 B.A. L.365 J.D. [Ⓐ Spesia,A.&A.]
Orloff, Richard B., (BV) .... '45 '71 C.339 B.S. L.424 J.D. [Reich&O.]
Osterberger, Thomas R. .... '65 '93 C&L.339 A.B., J.D. 333 N. Hammes Ave., Ste. 101
O'Sullivan, Erin W. .... '78 '04 C.1151 B.A. L.209 J.D. [Ⓐ C.Bretz&Assoc.]
Ottosen, Karl R. .... '60 '84 C.927 B.S. L.339 J.D. [Ottosen T.B.K.&C.] ⊙
Ottosen Trevarthen Britz Kelly & Cooper, Ltd., (AV)
81 North Chicago Street, Suite 204 (⊙Elburn, Wheaton)
Ozmon, Laird M., (BV) .... '54 '79 C.1151 B.A. L.424 J.D. [L.M.Ozmon]

Ozmon, Laird M., Ltd., (BV)
54 North Ottawa Street, Suite B-5, 60432
Telephone: 815-727-7700 FAX: 815-727-7800
Email: injury@ozmonlaw.com URL: http://www.ozmonlaw.com
Laird M. Ozmon.
Civil Trial Law, State and Federal Courts with emphasis on Serious Personal Injury, Products Liability, Wrongful Death and Medical Negligence.
Reference: First Midwest Bank/Joliet.
See Professional Biographies, JOLIET, ILLINOIS

Panno, Peter G., (BV) .... '54 '79 C.339 B.S. L.424 J.D. [Hinshaw&C.]
Parker, John L., (AV) .... '29 '55 C.602 B.S.Ch.E. L.209 J.D. 1900 Douglas St. (Pat.)‡
Peithmann, William A., (AV) '54 '78
C.416 B.A. L.208 J.D. [⊡ Mahoney,S.&C.] (⊙Farmer City)

Petersen, Cynthia L.
(See Blue Island)

Petrungaro, Barbara N. ....'67 '91 C.1151 B.A. L.879 J.D. Asst. States Atty.
Peyla, Gregory L., (BV) .... '53 '80 C&L.861 B.A., J.D. [Fabrizio,H.P.&K.]

Phalen, Stephen S., LLC, Law Offices of
(See Chicago)

Phelan, M. Thomas, (BV) .... '35 '67 C.679 B.S.M.E. L.365 J.D. [Phelan&N.]
Phelan, William J., (AV) .... '47 '73 C.1024 B.A. L.209 J.D. [Schenk]
Phelan & Nolan, (BV) .... 57 W. Jefferson St.
Pistilli, Louis V. ....'26 '57 C.209 M.A. L.424 J.D. 54 N. Ottawa St.
Polito, Joseph C., (AV) .... '43 '68 C.436 B.A. L.424 J.D. [J.C.Polito]
Polito, Joseph C., Ltd., (AV) ....23 West Jefferson Street

Pool, Leigh & Fabricius
(See Ottawa)

Porick, Dennis B., (BV) .... '44 '82 C.338 B.S. L.365 J.D. [D.B.Porick]
Porick, Dennis B., Ltd., (BV) ....63 W. Jefferson
Portlock, Vince G., (BV) ....'64 '89 C.679 B.A. L.589 J.D. [Shutts,S.&P.]
Prehn, John C., Jr., (BV) ....'56 '80 C.393 B.A. L.365 J.D. Pub. Def.
Prodehl, Steven J., (BV) ....'53 '80 C.1151 B.A. L.589 J.D. [June,P.&R.]
Pyles, Gary Scott, (BV) .... '65 '91 C.338 B.S. L.589 J.D. [Krockey,C.C.C.&P.]

Querrey & Harrow, Ltd., (AV)
2 Rialto Square Suite 401, 116 North Chicago Street, 60432 ⊙
Telephone: 815-726-1600 Fax: 815-726-1674
Email: jfarmans@querrey.com URL: http://www.querrey.com
Janet M. Farmans (Resident); Michael B. Stillman (Resident); Christine McAsey (Resident);—Richard J. Turiello (Resident).
General Practice and Trial Practice.
Chicago, Illinois Office: 175 West Jackson Boulevard, Suite 1600. Telephone: 312-540-7000. Fax: 312-540-0578.
Crystal Lake, Illinois Office: 651 West Terra Cotta Avenue, Suite 221. Telephone: 815-479-1929. Fax: 815-479-1978.
Waukegan, Illinois Office: 415 West Washington Street, Suite 205. Telephone: 847-249-4440. Fax: 847-249-4932.
Wheaton, Illinois Office: 310 South County Farm Road, Third Floor. Telephone: 630-653-2600. Fax: 630-653-0178.
Merrillville, Indiana Office: 8585 Broadway, Suite 510. Telephone: 219-738-1820. Fax: 219-738-1821.
New York, N.Y. Office: 120 Broadway, Suite 2800. Telephone: 212-233-0130. Fax: 212-233-0172.
London, England Office: 141-142 Fenchurch Street, Fifth Floor. Telephone: 207-929-6670. Fax: 207-929-6671.
See Professional Biographies, JOLIET, ILLINOIS

Rambo, John E. .... '63 '93 C.1151 L.146 J.D. [J.Rambo]
Rambo, John .... 3041 Theodore St.
Ratajczyk, Walter W. ....'53 '99 C.94 M.A. L.1005 J.D. Asst. State's Atty.
Rathbun, Timothy J., (AV) .... '50 '74 C&L.861 B.A., J.D. [Rathbun,C.&K.] (⊙Mokena)

Rathbun, Cservenyak & Kozol, LLC, (AV)
3260 Executive Drive, 60431 ⊙
Telephone: 815-730-1977 Fax: 815-730-1934
Email: webmail@rcklawfirm.com URL: http://www.rcklawfirm.com
Members of Firm: Timothy J. Rathbun; Frank S. Cservenyak, Jr.; William V. Kozol; Carl R. Buck; Katherine L. Maloney. Associates: Eric Swanson; Kevin Malcolm Rosner; Elizabeth Z. LeBaron; Lisa Gray Chastain; Lawrence M. Kaschak; Donald P. Jonker.
Civil Practice. Insurance Defense, Commercial Litigation, Personal Injury, Labor and Employment, Construction Law, Workers' Compensation, Criminal Law, Education Law, FELA, Real Estate, Family Law, Estate Planning, Bankruptcy, Medical Malpractice, Zoning, Planning and Land Use, Wills, Immigration.
Plainfield, Illinois Office: 618 West Main Street, 60544. Telephone: 815-577-9763. Fax: 815-577-9769.
Mokena Office: 9450 Enterprise Drive, 60448. Telephone: 708-479-9949. Fax: 708-479-0503.
See Professional Biographies, JOLIET, ILLINOIS

Reed, John A., (BV) ....'47 '74 C.339 B.A. L.1049 J.D. [J.A.Reed]
Reed, John A., Ltd., (BV) .... 63 W. Jefferson St.
Reich, Scott R., (BV) .... '51 '77 C.430 B.A. L.365 J.D. [Reich&O.]
Reich & Orloff, (BV) ....116 N. Chicago St.
Renzi, John C. .... '54 '79 C.339 B.S. L.273 J.D. [June,P.&R.]
Richards, Paul J., (BV) ....'70 '95 C.424 B.A. L.879 J.D. [Ⓐ Dykema G.P.]
Richardson, Marzell L., (BV) .... '54 '80 C.338 B.S. L.339 J.D. 14 W. Jefferson St.

Rinella and Rinella, Ltd.
(See Chicago)

Rosner, Kevin Malcolm .... '70 '01 C.05 B.A. L.146 J.D. [Ⓐ Rathbun,C.&K.]
Rouskey, Chris D., (BV) ....'52 '79 151 Springfield Ave.
Rozak, Daniel J. ....'51 '76 C.338 B.S. L.424 J.D. Assoc. Cir. J.
Rudman, Martin, (AV) ....'37 '62 C&L.339 J.D. 5 West Jefferson Street
Ruttle, David L., (AV) .... '45 '71 C.210 B.A. L.846 J.D. [McKeown,F.Z.B.H.&R.]

Ryan and Ryan
(See Chicago)

Sabuco, Roy A., (BV) .... '48 '73 C.234 B.A. L.339 J.D. [Sabuco,B.H.&S.]
Sabuco, Beck, Hansen & Schrock, P.C., (BV) .... 350 Houbolt Road
Sakellariou, Nicholas E. ....'46 '74 C.339 B.S. L.209 J.D. [McKeown,F.Z.B.H.&R.]
Sangmeister, George E., (AV) '31 '60
C.238 A.B. L.365 J.D. [⊡ McKeown,F.Z.B.H.&R.] ⊙

Sawyier, Michael T., Law Offices of
(See Chicago)

Schall, Jennifer J. .... '62 '87 C.589 B.A. L.8 J.D. Murer Grp.
Schenk, Robert H., (AV) .... '40 '65 C.347 A.B. L.1119 J.D. [Schenk]
Schenk Law Firm, (AV) .... 24 W. Cass Street, 5th Fl.
Schimanski, Scott A., Law Office of '66 '97 C.719 B.B.A. L.146 J.D.
360 W. Jefferson St.
Schoenstedt, Richard C. ....'32 '64 C&L.209 J.D. 81 N. Chicago St.‡
Schoenstedt, Richard Carl, (BV) .... '56 '81 C.436 B.A. L.209 J.D. 81 N. Chicago St.
Schrock, John Vernon, (CV) .... '64 '89 C.234 B.A. L.146 J.D. [Sabuco,B.H.&S.]
Seaborg, Dorothy A. W. .... '36 '79 C&L.1151 B.A., J.D. 81 W. Jefferson St.‡
Shanahan, Martin J., Jr. ....'— '98 C.719 B.A. L.365 J.D. [Ⓐ Spesia,A.&A.]
Shutts, Eugene C., (BV) ....'17 '42 C&L.477 A.B., LL.B. [⊡ Shutts,S.&P.]
Shutts, Robert D., (BV) ....'48 '74 C&L.378 B.A., J.D. [Shutts,S.&P.]
Shutts, Shutts and Portlock, (BV) .... 323 Springfield Avenue
Siegel, Richard J. ....'52 '82 C.719 B.M. L.589 J.D. Cir. J.
Silverman, David J., (BV) .... '52 '88 C.1151 B.A. L.365 J.D. [Mahoney,S.&C.]

Skubisz, Gregory R.
(See Calumet City)

Slayden, Daniel P., (BV) .... '61 '87 C.238 B.A. L.801 J.D. [Hinshaw&C.]
Smith, Brian D. '62 '88
C.338 B.S. L.589 J.D. Off. of Secy. of State, Admin. Hearings Div.
Snyder, Robert A., (BV) .... '37 '71 C.1016 B.A. L.365 J.D. 71 N. Ottawa Street
Softcheck, Daniel J., (CV) .... '54 '84 C.312 B.A. L.424 J.D. [Hinshaw&C.]
Spesia, Christian G., (BV) ....'68 '94 C.170 B.A. L.208 J.D. [Spesia,A.&A.]
Spesia, Douglas F., (AV) .... '40 '65 C.339 B.S. L.602 LL.B. [Spesia,A.&A.]
Spesia, John M., (AV) .... '67 '93 C.352 B.A. L.208 J.D. [Spesia,A.&A.]

Spesia, Ayers & Ardaugh, (AV) BB
Two Rialto Square, 116 North Chicago Street, Suite 200, 60432
Telephone: 815-726-4311 Fax: 815-726-6828
URL: http://www.spesia-ayers.com
Members of Firm: Douglas F. Spesia; E. Kent Ayers; John R. "Jack" Ardaugh; John M. Spesia; Christian G. Spesia; Jeffrey S. Taylor. Associates: Martin J. Shanahan, Jr.; Mark A. Lichtenwalter; Gabriel G. Orenic. Of Counsel: Dinah Lennon Archambeault; Thomas M. Ewert.
General Trial and Appellate Practice in State and Federal Courts. Insurance, Medical Malpractice, Corporate, Personal Injury, Real Estate Taxation, Probate, Municipal Law.
Counsel for: Alliance Pipeline, L.P.; Ameritech; Commonwealth Edison Co.; Indiana Consolidated Ins. Co.; Lakehead Pipeline Co.; Liberty Mutual Ins. Co.; Mickey Oil Companies; Natural Gas Pipeline Co. of America; Northern Illinois Gas Co.; Villages of New Lenox, Manhattan, Minooka and Rockdale.
See Professional Biographies, JOLIET, ILLINOIS

Stefanich, Matthew W., (AV) .... '14 '38 C&L.339 B.S., J.D. [⊡ Stefanich,M.&O.]
Stefanich, McGarry & Okrei, Ltd., (AV) .... P.O. Box 1246

Stevenson, James P., (BV) '53 '84 C.999 L.146 J.D.
54 North Ottawa Street, Suite 260, 60432
Telephone: 815-727-7879 Fax: 815-727-5458
General Civil Trial and Appellate Practice, State and Federal Courts with emphasis on Personal Injury, Automobile Accidents, Slip and Fall, Wrongful Death, Municipal Law, Zoning, Insurance Disputes, Construction Disputes.
See Professional Biographies, JOLIET, ILLINOIS

Stewart, Robert C. .... '41 '67 C&L.352 LL.B. Pres., LaVallie & Assoc., Inc.
Stiff, Michael R., (BV) .... '62 '88 C.1151 B.A. L.424 J.D. 111 North Ottawa Street
Stillman, Michael B. ....'— '94 C.98 B.A. L.209 J.D. [Querrey&H.]
Stubbs, Michael D., (CV) ...... '44 '78 C.339 B.S. L.589 J.D. 151 Springfield Ave., Ste. 8
Stuhr, George M., (CV) ....'37 '84 C.776 B.A. L.365 J.D. [Stuhr&D.]

Stuhr & Drell, (CV)
54 N. Ottawa Street, Suite 200, 60432
Telephone: 815-722-2252 Fax: 815-722-3809
Email: stuhr_drell@earthlink.net URL: http://www.struhrdrell.com
Members of Firm: George M. Stuhr; Lea Armstrong Drell.
Family Law, Aviation and Aerospace Law, Criminal Law, Juvenile Law, Real Estate, Bankruptcy, Business Law, Juvenile, Guardianship and Adoptions.
See Professional Biographies, JOLIET, ILLINOIS

Swanson, Eric .... '68 '93 C&L.879 B.A., J.D. [Ⓐ Rathbun,C.&K.]
Taylor, Jeffrey S., (AV) ....'67 '95 C.172 B.A. L.365 J.D. [Spesia,A.&A.]
Teas, Richard H., (AV) ....'30 '60 C&L.339 A.B., LL.B. [Tracy,J.&W.]
Tedone, Cosmo J. ....'66 '99 C.1213 B.S. L.1187 J.D. [Ⓐ C.Bretz&Assoc.]
Thomas, Charles E. .... '52 '77 C.589 B.A. L.910 J.D. 54 N. Ottawa St.
Thomas, Robert W., (AV) .... '06 '31 C.393 A.B. L.309 LL.B. 111 N. Ottawa St.

Tracy, Johnson & Wilson, (AV) BB
First Community Bank Building, 2801 Black Road, 2nd Floor, 60435
Telephone: 815-723-8500 Fax: 815-727-4846
Email: jolietlaw@tracylawfirm.com
Richard H. Teas; Raymond E. Meader; A. Michael Wojtak; Kenneth A. Carlson; John S. Gallo. Associates: Richard E. Vogel; Cory D. Lund; Melanie D. Manning; Joel P. Murphy.
General Civil and Appellate Practice in all Courts, Corporation, Business, Pension and Profit Sharing, Banking, Commercial, Bankruptcy, Probate, Estate and Tax Planning, Real Estate, Real Estate Taxation, Personal Injury, Workers' Compensation, Employment, Eminent Domain, Municipal, Land Development, Zoning and Governmental Law.
Representative Clients: Chicago Title Insurance Co.; Harris Bank Joliet, N.A.; Vulcan Materials Company; Dow Chemical, U.S.A.; Marathon Oil Co.; The Copley Press, Inc.; Citizens Utilities Co.; Empress River Casino Corporation; First Community Bank of Joliet; Bill Jacobs Automotives Group.
See Professional Biographies, JOLIET, ILLINOIS

Troha, George P., (AV) .... '34 '64 C.1024 B.A. L.209 J.D. 71 N. Chicago St.
Troha, Philip A., (BV) ....'42 '74 C.589 B.S. L.424 J.D. 63 West Jefferson Street

Troka, William G. .... '48 '82 C.927 B.S. L.589 J.D. 520 S. Midland Ave.
Troy, Steven P., (BV) .... '53 '78 C.340 B.A. L.146 J.D. [Troy&Assoc.]
Troy and Associates, (BV) .... 5 E. Van Buren St., Ste. 306
Turiello, Richard J. .... '— '01 C.999 B.P.S. L.146 J.D. [🄰 Querrey&H.]
Turner, Misty L., (CV) .... '64 '91 C&L.589 B.S., J.D. Asst. States Atty.

Turner, Phillip A., Law Offices of
(See Chicago)

Vargo, Stephen G. .... '25 '50 C.999 L.146 LL.B. 68 N. Chicago St.‡
Vargo-Lewandowski, Diana L. '62 '89 C.94 B.A. L.424 J.D.
68 N. Chicago St., Ste. 332

Varsek, Lawrence E., (BV) '42 '67 C.957 B.A. L.339 J.D.
1403 Essington Road, Suite 400, 60431
Telephone: 815-744-3323 Fax: 815-744-3325
Email: Kesrav@aol.com URL: http://www.lawyers.com/lawrenceevarsek
Estate Planning, Probate, Wills, Trusts and Estates, Guardianships, Corporate Law, Business Law, Family Business Law, Contested Trusts and Estates, Business Succession Planning.
See Professional Biographies, JOLIET, ILLINOIS

Vines, Michael J. .... '70 '03 C.589 B.A. L.1000 J.D. [🄰 Hinshaw&C.]
Vogel, Richard E. .... '70 '95 C&L.339 B.S., J.D. [🄰 Tracy,J.&W.]
Vosicky, George J., (BV) .... '55 '79 C.602 B.A. L.209 J.D. [⊡ Dykema G.P.]
Ward, Christopher S. .... '70 '97 C.723 B.A. L.365 J.D. [McKeown,F.Z.B.H.&R.]
Warden, Tammy S. .... '73 '98 C.719 B.A. L.424 J.D. [🄰 Hinshaw&C.]
Welz, Robert J., (CV) .... '55 '80 C.1151 B.A. L.209 J.D. 151 Springfield Ave.
Wengler, Colleen M. .... '65 '01 C.339 B.S. L.209 J.D. [🄰 M.W.Hansen]
Wilhelmi, Arthur J. .... '68 '93 C.424 B.A. L.146 J.D. [McKeown,F.Z.B.H.&R.]
Wise, Christopher N., (CV) .... '61 '86 C.57 B.A. L.879 J.D. [McKeown,F.Z.B.H.&R.]
Wisniewski, Robert F., (CV) .... '52 '78 C&L.1151 B.A., J.D. [Wisniewski]
Wisniewski Law Office, (CV) .... 81 N. Chicago St., Ste. 206
Wojtak, A. Michael, (BV) .... '55 '80 C.1151 B.A. L.424 J.D. [Tracy,J.&W.]
Wols, John F., (AV) .... '41 '67 C.424 B.S. L.209 J.D. 116 N. Chicago St.
Wood, Thomas B. .... '20 '53 C.846 B.B.A. L.273 LL.B. V.P., Joliet Pattern Inc.

Wrobel, Joseph, Ltd.
(See Chicago)

Wunderlich, Gary L., (BV) .... '57 '82 C.1151 B.A. L.365 J.D. [Wunderlich]
Wunderlich Law Offices, Ltd., (BV) .... 54 North Ottawa Street, Suite B-60
Wysocki, Marilyn L. .... '63 '88 C.339 B.S. L.589 J.D. [🄰 June,P.&R.]
Yurkanin, Walter J. .... '65 '94 C.720 B.A. L.365 J.D. [Mahoney,S.&C.]
Yusman, Kevin D. .... '72 '98 C.378 B.A. L.802 J.D. [Mahoney,S.&C.]
Zegart, Lesley R., (CV) .... '44 '87 C.339 B.S. L.589 J.D. Asst. Atty. Gen.
Ziech, Douglas L., (BV) .... '44 '73 C.388 B.A. L.365 J.D. 1861 Black Road
Zollner, Max E., (AV) .... '38 '63 C.388 A.B. L.339 J.D. [⊡ McKeown,F.Z.B.H.&R.] ‡
Zumstein, Bruce L., (BV) .... '46 '72 C.339 B.S. L.597 J.D. [Codo,B.Z.&K.]

JONESBORO, * 1,853, *Union Co.*

Clutts, Rodney A. .... '48 '73 C.801 B.A. L.425 J.D. Assoc. Cir. J.

Feirich/Mager/Green/Ryan
(See Carbondale)

Plesko, Jeffrey M. .... '48 '77 C.339 B.A. L.801 J.D. Dir.‡
Wilkins, H. Wesley .... '55 '80 C.801 B.A. L.192 J.D. State's Atty.

JUSTICE, 12,193, *Cook Co.*

Chadwick & Lakerdas, Law Offices of
(See Chicago)

Sira, Stephen N. .... '13 '47 C.339 L.51 LL.B. 7940 S. 87th Ave.

KANKAKEE, * 27,575, *Kankakee Co.*

Ackman, Richard L., (AV) .... '27 '50 C.378 B.S. L.339 J.D. [⊡ Ackman,M.M.&B.]

Ackman, Marek, Meyer & Boyd, Ltd., (AV)
Suite 400, One Dearborn Square, 60901
Telephone: 815-933-6681 Fax: 815-933-6623
Email: ammb@amb-ltd.com
J. Dennis Marek; John J. Boyd; Dana M. Meyer;—Michael T. Jeneary. Of Counsel: Richard L. Ackman; Robert W. Boyd.
General Civil and Trial Practice. Probate, Real Estate, Insurance, Medical Malpractice, Workers Compensation and Corporation Law.
Representative Clients: American States Insurance Co.; Auto Owners Insurance Co.; Consumers Illinois Water Co.; Country Mutual Insurance Co.; Farmers Insurance Group; Medical Protective Co.; Economy Fire & Casualty Co.; Union Insurance Co.
See Professional Biographies, KANKAKEE, ILLINOIS

Albrecht, Adrienne W., (BV) .... '55 '79 C&L.339 B.A., J.D. [Sacks,A.C.H.&S.]
Anderson, Charles E., Jr. .... '25 '52 C.174 B.S. L.209 J.D. 1080 Justine Dr.‡
Barmann, Glen R., (BV) .... '43 '69 C.589 B.S. L.339 J.D. [Barmann,B.&W.]

Barmann, Bohlen & Woodruff, P.C., (AV) BB
Suite 602, 200 East Court Street, P.O. Box 1787, 60901
Telephone: 815-939-1133 Fax: 815-939-0994
Email: law@bbwlaw.net
Glen R. Barmann; Christopher W. Bohlen; Deborah A. Woodruff.
General Practice. Trial, Probate, Estate Planning, Taxation, Real Estate, Corporate and Commercial Law, Health Law, Municipal, Appellate Practice in all Courts.
See Professional Biographies, KANKAKEE, ILLINOIS

Baron, Dennis J., (BV) .... '51 '77 C.339 B.A. L.477 J.D. [Deck&B.]
Benson, Roger A. .... '32 '58 C.597 B.B.A. L.209 J.D. Assoc. Cir. J.
Berz, Michael R., (BV) .... '37 '66 C.339 B.A. L.221 J.D. 701 S. Harrison Ave.
Bohlen, Christopher W., (AV) .... '49 '73 C.339 B.A. L.597 J.D. [Barmann,B.&W.]
Boyd, John J., (BV) .... '62 '89 C.234 B.A. L.365 J.D. [Ackman,M.M.&B.]
Boyd, Robert W., (BV) .... '33 '66 C.531 L.365 J.D. [⊡ Ackman,M.M.&B.]

Brenner, Ford, Monroe & Scott, Ltd.
(See Chicago)

Burnett, Mary Elise, (BV) .... '53 '84 C.880 B.A. L.502 J.D. [Cunnington&B.]
Burns, Patrick M. .... '32 '62 C.707 A.B. L.209 J.D. Cir. J.
Butz, Vernon G., (AV) .... '05 '27 C&L.340 LL.B. 1250 Cobb Blvd., Suite 208
Carr, Fred S., Jr. .... '36 '87 C.326 B.S. L.365 J.D. Cir. J.
Claudio, Brenda L., (CV) .... '71 '96 C.339 B.A. L.209 J.D. Asst. States Atty.
Cooper, Cynthia Y. .... '73 '98 C.597 B.S. L.146 J.D. 275 E. Court Street, Suite 201
Copeland, Kenneth Edward, (CV) ...... '62 '87 C.339 A.B. L.112 J.D. [Sacks,A.C.H.&S.]
Cunnington, Thomas W., (BV) .... '54 '81 C.340 B.A. L.365 J.D. [Cunnington&B.]
Cunnington and Burnett, (BV) .... 1 Dearborn Square, Suite 429
Danhausen, Martha J., (BV) .... '39 '88 C.624 A.B. L.146 J.D. 2 Dearborn Sq., Ste. 2
Deck, Gregory A., (BV) .... '50 '75 C&L.879 B.A., J.D. [Deck&B.]

Deck & Baron, (BV)
200 East Court Street Suite 408, P.O. Box 693, 60901-5133
Telephone: 815-939-7373 Fax: 815-939-3737
URL: http://www.pdrblaw.com

(This Listing Continued)

Deck & Baron (Continued)
Gregory A. Deck; Dennis J. Baron.
General Civil Practice. Banking, Real Estate, Wills, Probate, Estate and Gift Taxation, Trust, Living Wills, Elder Law, Nursing Home Abuse, Estate Planning, Administration, Corporate and Commercial Law. Commercial Personal Injury Litigation.
See Professional Biographies, KANKAKEE, ILLINOIS

Delaney, Doris White .... '51 '00 C.209 B.S. L.879 J.D. States' Atty. Off.
Dietchweiler, Michael L., (BV) .... '53 '87 C.221 B.S. L.365 J.D. [LaBeau D.&Assoc.]
Dunn, Patrick .... '68 '94 C.340 B.A. L.209 J.D. 701 South Harrison Avenue
Dunn, Patrick T., Attorney at Law, (BVⓉ) '68 '93
C.340 B.A. L.209 J.D. 200 E. Court St., Ste. 700
Dusenbury, Marshall R., (CV) .... '58 '83 C.880 B.A. L.209 J.D. [Dusenbury&Assoc.]
Dusenbury, Ronald J. .... '34 '59 C.801 B.A. L.880 J.D. 111 S. Schuyler Ave.‡
Dusenbury & Associates, P.C., (CV) .... 111 S. Schuyler Ave.
Erickson, Clark '48 '76 C&L.339 B.S., J.D.
Chf. J., Circuit's Clerk Kankakee Co. Courthouse Off.

Fabrizio, Hanson, Peyla & Kawinski, P.C.
(See Joliet)

Farmer, Karren Simone, (CV) .... '60 '98 C.999 B.A. L.801 J.D. [K.S.Farmer]
Farmer, Karren S., Law Office of, (CV) .... 2 Dearborn Sq., Ste. 201
Fuhrmann, Kathleen C. .... '57 '02 C.999 B.A. L.146 J.D. Asst. State's Atty.
Gorski, Brenda L., (CV) '57 '82
C&L.879 B.A., J.D. Chf. Coun., Civil Div., Co. of Kankakee
Gould, Daniel W. .... '44 '68 C.589 B.S. L.339 J.D. Assoc. J.
Gubbins, Matthew T., (P.C.), (BV) ..... '62 '88 C.339 B.S. L.424 J.D. 275 E. Court Street
Henry, Charles O., (BV) .... '33 '59 C.339 B.S. L.365 LL.B. 230 S. Harrison

Hooks Law Offices, P.C.
(See Chicago)

Householter, J. Gregory '45 '73 C.602 B.A. L.879 J.D.
Cir. J., Kankakee Co. Courthouse
Huber, Fredrick E., (BV) .... '33 '62 C.174 B.S.Ch.E. L.365 LL.B. 580 E Merchant St

Jaffe, David M., (AV) '41 '66 C.347 A.B. L.1119 J.D.
200 East Court Street, Suite 212, 60901
Telephone: 815-936-9186 Fax: 815-936-9765 URL: http://www.davidmjaffelaw.com
Email: jaffelaw@keynet.net URL: http://www.davidjaffelaw.com
Probate, Real Estate, Estate Planning, Trusts and Estates, Elder Law, Corporate and Commercial Law, Banking Law, Business Law, Land Use.
See Professional Biographies, KANKAKEE, ILLINOIS

Jeneary, Michael T. .... '70 '95 C.340 B.A. L.209 J.D. [🄰 Ackman,M.M.&B.]
Kezdy, John F. .... '59 '91 C.597 B.A. L.209 J.D. Asst. State's Atty.
Kick, Michael J., (BV) .... '53 '85 C.339 B.A. L.365 J.D. State's Atty.
LaBeau, Robert B., (BV) .... '47 '80 C.234 B.S. L.1218 J.D. [LaBeau D.&Assoc.]
LaBeau Dietchweiler & Assoc., P.C., (BV) .... 701 S. Harrison Avenue
Landwehr, Dawn L., (CV) .... '61 '85 C.624 B.A. L.365 J.D. 1 Dearborn Sq., Ste. 429
Leshen, Kenneth A., (BV) .... '50 '76 C.145 B.A. L.770 J.D. [Leshen,K.A.]
Leshen, Kenneth A., P.C., (BV) .... 1 Dearborn Square
Marek, J. Dennis, (AV) .... '43 '67 C.210 B.A. L.597 J.D. [Ackman,M.M.&B.]
McIntire, Edward A. .... '18 '47 C&L.339 A.B., LL.B. Ret. Assoc. Cir. J.
Meyer, Dana M., (CV) .... '72 '97 C&L.879 B.A., J.D. [Ackman,M.M.&B.]
Mungo, Derek A. '58 '87 C.893 B.A. L.1066 J.D.
(adm. in VA; not adm. in IL) 240 S. Warren Ave.‡
Norden, Dennis A., (AV) .... '45 '69 C&L.339 A.B., J.D. 3449 W. Rt. 115

Olton, Tina M.
(See Momence)

Palladino, Karin M. .... '74 '02 C.347 B.S. L.879 J.D. Asst. States Atty.

Parkhurst, Lindsay A., Law Offices of '— '89 C.339 B.A. L.146 J.D.
1 Dearborn Square, Suite 320, 60901-3957
Telephone: 815-933-0114 Fax: 815-933-7658
Email: parkhurstlaw@yahoo.com URL: http://www.parkhurstlaw.com
Language: English.
Family Law, Personal Injury, Bankruptcy, Traffic, Employment Law, Health Law, Social Security Disability, Real Estate, Small Business, Criminal.
See Professional Biographies, KANKAKEE, ILLINOIS

Power, L. Patrick, (BV) .... '41 '70 C.750 A.B. L.365 J.D. 956 N. 5th Ave.
Reagan, Sheldon W. .... '35 '66 C.797 L.365 J.D. Assoc. Cir. J.
Ridge, John P. .... '43 '84 C.209 L.146 J.D. 777 N. Kennedy Dr.
Sacks, Judy A., (CV) .... '43 '91 C.259 B.S. L.365 J.D. [Sacks,A.C.H.&S.]
Sacks, Leonard F., (AV) .... '41 '65 C.108 B.S. L.209 J.D. [Sacks,A.C.H.&S.]
Sacks, Albrecht, Copeland, Herzog & Sacks, (AV) .... 275 East Court Street
Serene, Larry D., (BV) .... '48 '79 C.339 B.S. L.365 J.D. 1 Dearborn Sq., Ste. 440

Smietanski, Alan F.
(See Bradley)

Smith, Edward D., (BV) .... '43 '74 C.234 B.S. L.365 J.D. States Atty., Kankakee Cty.
Smith, Valerie Michelle, (CV) '68 '93 C.836 B.A. L.339 J.D.
1 Dearborn Square, Ste. 320
Stanfa, Michael A. .... '49 '74 C&L.424 A.B., J.D. Kankakee Fed. Svgs. Bank
Steffen, Mark R., (BV) .... '53 '77 C.234 B.S. L.146 J.D. 605 South Fifth Avenue

Strough, Dale, Attorney at Law
(See Watseka)

Swaim, George T., (AV) .... '22 '53 C.339 B.S. L.861 J.D. [⊡ Swaim&S.]
Swaim, J. Scott, (AV) .... '46 '72 C.970 B.A. L.861 J.D. [Swaim&S.]
Swaim & Swaim, Ltd., (AV) .... One Dearborn Square

Swanson, Martin & Bell
(See Chicago)

Thacker, Lester L. .... '38 '69 C.234 B.S. L.209 J.D. 701 S. Harrison St.‡
Vogt, Edward G., (CV) .... '31 '58 C.602 A.B. L.424 J.D. 239 E. Court St.
Wenzelman, Kendall O. .... '54 '79 C.234 B.A. L.733 J.D. Chief J., Ct. of App.
Woodruff, Deborah A., (BV) .... '57 '85 C&L.801 B.S., J.D. [Barmann,B.&W.]
Yurgine, Joseph R., (BV) .... '40 '65 C.589 B.S. L.339 LL.B. [J.R.Yurgine]
Yurgine, Joseph R., Professional Corporation, Law Offices, (BV)
One Dearborn Square, Suite 500

KARNAK, 619, *Pulaski Co.*

Kruger, Henry & Hunter
(See Metropolis)

KEMPTON, 219, *Ford Co.*

Herr, James J., (BV) ... '30 '54 C&L.602 Ph.B., LL.B. Bank Bldg. (⊙Chatsworth, Pontiac)

KENILWORTH, 2,402, *Cook Co.*

Baker, Donald, (AVⓉ) '29 '55 C.999 L.145 J.D. 544 Earlston Rd.‡
Brown, David E. '26 '53 C.339 B.S. L.424 J.D. (adm. in LA; not adm. in IL) 509 Park Dr.
Grimes, Russell C., Jr. '52 '76 C.611 B.A. L.910 J.D. 639 Brier St.‡
Kahn, Laurence S. '55 '81 C.477 B.A. L.209 J.D. 78 Robsart Rd.
Kennedy, Sheila Berner '62 '89 C.93 B.A. L.597 J.D. 158 Melrose Ave.
Lane, James R. '69 '96 C.165 B.A. L.597 J.D. 157 Kenilworth Ave.
McKittrick, William W., (AV) '15 '39 C.210 A.B. L.597 J.D. 232 Essex Rd.‡
Meyers, Gail E. '52 '80 C.208 B.A. L.365 J.D. 517 Cumnor Rd.
Perdomo, Saul Anthony '36 '62 C.472 B.A. L.327 LL.B. Cir. J.
Salmeron, Barbara Doolittle '39 '80 C.597 B.A. L.146 J.D. 420 Greenbay Rd.
Sherman, John W. '18 '39 C&L.64 J.D. 411 Ridge Rd.‡
Spindell, Robert F., (AV) '05 '31 C&L.309 A.B., LL.B. 326 Essex Rd.‡
Thompson, Vicki A. '47 '75 C.187 B.A. L.339 J.D. 333 Leicester‡
Weber, Gay Morris '62 '86 C.880 B.A. L.16 J.D. 527 Abbotsford Rd.‡
Wehrenberg, Ralph A. '35 '64 C.597 B.S.B.A. L.209 J.D. 132 Tudor Place‡

KEWANEE, 12,969, *Henry Co.*

Andrews, Harper, (AV) '07 '32 C.388 B.A. L.309 J.D. 211 W. 2nd St.‡
Andrews & Eastman, A Ptnship. incl. a Prof. Corp., (BV) 211 W. 2nd St.
Barash & Everett, (AV) 211 W. 2nd Street (⊙Galesburg, Galva)
Blachinsky, Charles W., (AV) '14 '39 C&L.424 A.B., J.D. 224 W 2nd St.
Blachinsky, John M., (BV) '47 '76 C.488 B.A. L.365 J.D. [Blachinsky]
Blachinsky Law Offices, (BV) 224 W 2nd St.
Block, Clinton A. '59 '01 C.339 B.S. L.589 J.D. [⊠ Barash&E.] (⊙Galesburg)
Clemens, Scott E., (BV) '42 '73 C.357 B.A. L.221 J.D. 108 W. 1st St.
DeWulf, Martin G., Law Office, (BV) '55 '83 C.927 B.S. L.801 J.D. 108 E. Division St.
Eastman, Charles D., (BV) '52 '76 C&L.896 B.A., J.D. [Andrews&E.]
Fulton, Anne Elizabeth '47 '83 C.118 B.A. L.228 J.D. [A.E.Fulton]
Fulton, Anne E., Attorney at Law 214 S. Chestnut St.
Kerr, Tym J., (BV) '53 '79 C.357 B.S. L.365 J.D. 101 N. Tremont St.
McRae, Don J., (AV) '26 '51 C&L.597 B.S., J.D. [D.J.McRae&Assoc.]
McRae, Don J., and Associates, (AV) 419 S. Chestnut St.
Stewart, William E., (BV) '34 '64 C.339 B.S. L.276 J.D. City Atty. (⊙Annawan)
Stockton, Eugene L., (BV) '53 '78 C.57 B.A. L.201 J.D. [⊠ D.J.McRae&Assoc.]
Waugh, Sharon Pearse, (BV) '57 '83 C.323 B.A. L.339 J.D. [⊠ D.J.McRae&Assoc.]
Welch, R. Sheridan, (AV) '19 '46 C.813 A.B. L.339 J.D. 205 W. 1st St.
Woller, Edward A., (BV) '54 '79 C.177 B.A. L.801 J.D. 211 W. First St.

KILDEER, 3,460, *Lake Co.*

Finegan, Byron P. '22 '53 C.597 B.S. L.146 LL.B. 21298 N. Andover Rd.
Forrest, George W. '43 '67 C.293 B.A. L.145 J.D. Pres., Production Metal Products Co., Inc.
Womack, James W., (AV) '30 '60 C.804 B.S. L.597 J.D. 21218 Highwood Rd.

KNOXVILLE, 3,243, *Knox Co.*

Mathers, Max E. '19 '50 C.339 B.S. L.912 J.D. Ret. Lt. Col., U.S. Air Force‡

LACON, * 1,986, *Marshall Co.*

Beck, Elizabeth A., (BV) '59 '85 C.98 B.A. L.1187 J.D. 310 5th St.
Galley, Kevin R., (BV) '54 '80 C.339 B.A. L.734 J.D. Cir.J.
Knuckey, Donald D., (BV) '48 '73 C.927 B.A. L.424 J.D. States Atty.

Mahoney, Michael T., Ltd.
(See Chillicothe)

Meierkord, Brian G. '53 '81 C.338 B.S. L.990 J.D. 116 S. Main St.
Paolucci, Peter J. '26 '55 C.98 B.S. L.734 LL.B. Ret. Chf. Cir. J.

Westervelt, Johnson, Nicoll & Keller, LLC
(See Peoria)

LAFOX, 250, *Kane Co.*

Day, Ann M., Law Office of, (CV) '57 '89 C.339 B.A. L.589 J.D. P.O. Box 30
Gilmartin, David J. '62 '88 C.339 B.S. L.602 J.D. V.P., Richardson Electronics, Ltd.
Seils, William G., (AV) '35 '59 C&L.477 A.B., J.D. Sr. V.P., Gen. Coun. & Secy., Richardson Electronics, Ltd.

LA GRANGE, 15,608, *Cook Co.*

Bonnette, Steve '48 '79 C.965 B.A. L.589 J.D. 1332 W. 55th St.
Brejcha, Roger J. '45 '70 C.742 B.A. L.209 J.D. 512 W. Burlington
Brenson, Ian '56 '89 C.050 B.A. L.424 J.D. 1030 S. La Grange Rd., Ste. 14
Brockmeier, Warren G. '26 '52 C.46 B.S. L.209 J.D. 600 S. Stone Ave.‡
Brown, Joachim J. '48 '74 C.424 A.B. L.209 J.D. Pres., First Natl. Bk.
Burkey, Lee M., Jr., (AV) '42 '68 C.221 B.A. L.878 J.D. 516 Banyon Lane
Burrows, Robert E. '52 '91 C.927 B.A. L.365 J.D. 47 S. 6th
Butler, Joseph '29 '57 C.210 B.A. L.477 LL.B. Chmn. of the Bd. & CEO, First Ill. Bk. of La Grange
Carden, Terrence S., III, (BV) '63 '90 C.436 B.S. L.424 J.D. 230 S. Peck Avenue
Caruso, Barbara Gariepy '— '63 C.966 B.A. L.597 J.D. 718 S. Spring Ave.
Casper, Charles R. '38 '67 C.477 B.A. L.659 J.D. 521 S. LaGrange Rd.
Castator, Alan B., (AV) '44 '71 C.339 B.S. L.146 J.D. 502 W. Burlington Avenue
Combs, Laurence A. '07 '36 C.137 A.B. L.365 LL.B. 6508 Blackhawk Trail‡
Cooke, Raymond C. '33 '59 C.1016 B.S. L.209 LL.B. 26 S. LaGrange Rd.
Dixon, G. Grant, III '65 '91 C.347 B.S. L.365 J.D. [Dixon]
Dixon Law Office L.L.C. 1415 West 55th Street, Suite 104
Downey, John J. '59 '88 C.177 B.A. L.365 J.D. 72 S. La Grange, Ste. 6
Fitzgerald, Robert E., III '65 '93 C.861 B.S. L.1000 J.D. [R.E.Fitzgerald,III]
Fitzgerald, Robert E., III, PC, Law Office of 714 W. Burlington Ave.
Franzese, Victoria '53 '79 C.937 B.A. L.879 J.D. 220 S. 9th Ave.
French, Judith Kay '43 '81 C.339 B.S. L.424 J.D. Tr. Offr., La Grange Bk. & Tr. Co.
Graham, Mary M. '23 '45 C&L.145 B.A., J.D. 76 Dover St.‡
Harrison, David C. '49 '81 C.98 B.S. L.365 J.D. 6325 W. Joliet Rd.
Hutchison, Robert N. '39 '63 C.475 L.209 J.D. 547 South La Grange Rd.
Jacobs, Christopher '— '67 C.311 B.S. L.145 J.D. 719 S. Ashland St.
Jardine, Charles M. '40 '66 C.276 L.424 J.D. 106 W. Bullington St.
Jardine, Jeanne L. '44 '80 C.424 B.S. L.209 J.D. 106 W. Burlington
Johnson, Donn E. '22 '53 C.504 B.A. L.339 LL.B. 47 S. 6th Ave.
Karey, Kevin J. '49 '75 C.750 B.A. L.146 J.D. 1415 W. 55th St., Rm. 201
Kenney, John Matthew, Jr. '68 '93 C.385 B.A. L.1000 J.D. 5 S. 6th Ave.
Kerr, Judith Mottl '42 '69 C.966 B.S. L.597 J.D. 709 S. Stone Ave.
Krepps, Elizabeth M. '59 '90 C.597 B.A. L.424 J.D. 430 S. Waiola Ave.
Lake, C. William '47 '72 C.188 B.A. L.208 J.D. 110 W. Burlington
Lanciloti, Michael-Anne '69 '94 C.57 B.A. L.879 J.D. 47 S. 6th Ave., Ste. 100
Landry, Diane K. '47 '80 C.339 B.S. L.365 J.D. 47 S. 6th Ave.
LeMieux, Louis H. '28 '53 C&L.436 Ph.B., LL.B. 140 S. 7th Ave. (Pat.)
Lies, Mary Beth '59 '87 C.1101 B.A. L.209 J.D. 437 S. Spring
Lubiniecki, Elizabeth J. '59 '86 C.339 B.A. L.365 J.D. 340 S. Catherine Ave.
Lusson, Karen L. '59 '86 C.347 B.A. L.209 J.D. 349 S. Kensington Ave.
Lynch, Michael J., Law Office of '58 '88 C.436 B.A. L.209 J.D. 512 W. Burlington Avenue, Suite 10
Martin, Bernard T., Jr., Law Offices of '51 '76 C.424 B.A. L.861 J.D. 716 W. Burlington Ave.
Matiasek, Melanie J. '57 '82 C.209 B.A. L.146 J.D. 2001 60th St. Ave.
McCrery, Michael J., Law Offices of '— '87 C.608 B.S. L.117 J.D. 411 W. Hillgrove Ave.
McNichols, John J. '27 '53 C&L.424 Ph.B., J.D. 501 Lake Hinsdale Drive‡
McVicker, Paul W. '50 '77 C.340 B.S. L.146 J.D. 47 6th Ave.
Mossner, Alfred E., Jr. '29 '66 C.339 B.A. L.146 J.D. 221 W. Harris Ave.‡
Murray, William D. '40 '67 C.679 B.S. L.1119 J.D. 744 S. Spring Ave.
Musa, Majdel S. '76 '04 C.339 B.A. L.1187 J.D. [Musa]
Musa Law Offices, PC 112 Calendar Avenue
Nasenbenny, Mary Blake '63 '93 C.602 B.A. L.146 J.D. Asst Dir. & Coun., The Hartford Financial Services Group, Inc.
Peck, Robert F. '39 '64 C.98 A.B. L.146 LL.B. 47 6th Ave.
Power, Scott H. '63 '88 C.57 B.A. L.365 J.D. 521 South LaGrange Road, Suite 201
Raddatz, Peggy M. '54 '88 C.1016 B.A. L.365 J.D. 47 S. 6th Ave., Ste. 112
Reed, Kim D. '54 '86 C.966 B.S. L.744 J.D. V.P., La Grange Memorial Hosp.
Rogal, Ira A. '51 '76 C&L.339 B.S., J.D. 547 S. La Grange Rd.
Scafuri, Frank A. '49 '76 C&L.424 B.A., J.D. 80 S. LaGrange Rd.
Schwappach, Harold R. '25 '69 C.597 B.S.Ch.E. L.46 J.D. 717 Terry Lane‡
Sheils, Paul C. '44 '73 C.339 A.B. L.365 J.D. 110 W. Burlington Ave.
Snyder, Bernard A. '10 '39 C&L.424 LL.B. 64 N. Peck Ave.‡
Steinmeyer, Patricia E. '67 '92 C.976 B.A. L.145 J.D. 317 S. Spring Ave.
Tutt, Ronald '45 '72 C.339 B.S. L.209 J.D. 722 N. Kensington Ave.
Vacco, Philip J. '56 '81 C&L.221 B.A., J.D. 1415 W. 55th St., Ste. 201

LA GRANGE PARK, 13,295, *Cook Co.*

Braasch, George H. '36 '65 C.436 B.S. L.365 LL.B. 340 Dover
Challos, Letitia '— '75 C.339 B.A. L.146 J.D. 703 Sherwood Road
Emery, William R. '09 '37 C&L.145 B.A., J.D. 74 Brewster Lane‡
Emmett, Daniel J. '42 '69 C.238 B.S. L.365 J.D. 1519 Blanchan Ave.‡
Esford, Dennis F. '57 '04 C.201 L.146 J.D. [D.Esford]
Esford, Dennis, Law Office of 1525 Robinhood Lane
Kosin, Donald G. '32 '59 C&L.597 B.S., J.D. 729 S. Barnsdale Rd.
Kudia, Frank S. '45 '71 C.424 B.S. L.146 J.D. 605 N. LaGrange Rd.
Masterson, Michael J., Sr. '59 '97 C.742 B.A. L.365 J.D. 1626 Forest Road
Riden, Joseph '26 '51 C&L.208 B.S., J.D. 813 N. Brainard Ave.
Sbertoli, Dennis M. '53 '81 C.1151 B.A. L.589 J.D. 330 North Park Road
Smerz, Mary Jo '53 '81 C&L.209 B.A., J.D. 745 N. Waiola Avenue
Thompson, William P. '18 '42 C.467 A.B. L.145 J.D. (adm. in KS; not adm. in IL) 98 Brewster Ln.‡
Westrick, Robert C. '30 '55 C&L.602 B.S.C., J.D. 748 N. Kensington Ave.

LAKE BARRINGTON, 4,757, *Lake Co.*

Barish, Raymond S., (AV) '13 '39 C.339 L.146 J.D. 471C Valley View Rd.‡
Corbett, Diane K. '64 '89 C.347 B.S. L.209 J.D. 20 W. River's Bend Court
Jordt, Jeffery P. '55 '85 C.208 B.A. L.146 J.D. Alexander & Alexander Consulting Gp.
Thompson, Carol A. '53 '84 C.105 B.A. L.705 J.D. 106 Hunt Trl.
Wilkinson, John B. '42 '68 C.976 B.A. L.813 J.D. 280 Woodview Road

LAKE BLUFF, 6,056, *Lake Co.*

Avgerin, Nicholas C. '30 '56 C&L.597 B.S., J.D. 7 E. Washington Ave.
Barkhausen, David N. '50 '76 C.674 B.A. L.801 J.D. 714 E. Prospect Ave.
Blanda, Alisun Smith '47 '81 C.690 B.S. L.723 J.D. (adm. in NY; not adm. in IL) 27 Warrington Dr.‡
Browning, Warren W. '27 '52 C.813 A.B. L.597 J.D. 699 Bluff Rd.‡
Dorge, Carol L. '53 '81 C.188 B.S. L.602 J.D. 315 E. Sheridan Rd.
Fingerhut, Kristie C. '77 '03 C.800 B.A. L.424 J.D. 21 N. Skokie Hwy.
Homor, Emery J. '27 '67 C.1016 B.S.B.A. L.424 J.D. 900 N. Shore Dr.
Hurley, Michael James '44 '77 L.365 J.D. 235 Buckminster Court
Kakish, William J. '52 '96 C.602 B.A. L.365 J.D. 28540 Oakhaven Court
Kelly, Ellen '46 '71 C.706 A.B. L.893 J.D. 150 Norwich Ct.
Kirby, Tammy L. '59 '83 C&L.879 B.S.B.A., J.D. 115 Huntington St.
Michael, Leslie W. '38 '66 C.976 B.A. L.309 J.D. 544 Ravine Ave.
Pollack, Gerald L. '32 '63 C.339 B.S. L.365 J.D. Pres., Triple Net Realty
Rives, Stephanie K. '35 '85 C.801 B.S. L.146 J.D. 116 Ravine Avenue
Scott, Kendrick L., (BV) '47 '78 C.393 B.A. L.365 J.D. 21 N. Skokie Hwy.
Springer, Clement F., (AV) '05 '29 C&L.145 Ph.B., J.D. 541 E. Blodgett Ave.‡
Steadman, Hollis S. '57 '82 C.610 B.A. L.365 J.D. 110 E. Sheridan Rd.
Still, Jonathan W. '47 '77 C.145 B.S. L.976 J.D. 231 E. Prospect Ave.
Storms, R. Lawrence, (AV) '22 '50 C.399 B.A. L.477 J.D. 718 Birch Rd.‡
Turek, Anton '14 '43 C.597 B.S. L.424 J.D. 467 Pine Ct.‡
White, Roger A. '38 '64 C.393 B.A. L.209 LL.B. 21 N. Skokie Hwy.
Wick, Lawrence S., (AV) '45 '71 C.597 B.A. L.178 J.D. [Wick]
Wick Law Office, (AV) 317 Rothbury Court
Wilheim, Julian R., (AV) '09 '38 C&L.178 A.B., J.D. 405 E. Sheridan Rd.
Williamson, Carol Gleich '52 '88 L.365 J.D. [C.Williamson]
Williamson, Carol 208 N. Waukegan Rd.

LAKE FOREST, 20,059, *Lake Co.*

Abler, Julius '14 '37 L.724 LL.B. 351 Little Melody Ln.
Adams, Alan W. '— '93 C.164 B.A. L.472 J.D. Exec. V.P., Gen. Coun., Baytree Natl. Bk. & Tr. Co
Ader, Mary '45 '71 C.999 LL.B. L.597 LL.M. Trustmark Insurance Company (Legal Department)
Anderson, William B. '72 '97 C.378 B.A. L.309 J.D. Senior Attorney, W. W. Grainger, Inc.
Auburn, Stephen T. '55 '81 C.1044 B.A. L.823 J.D. Asst. Gen. Coun., Pactiv Corp.
Balsamo, Joseph S. '27 '53 C&L.145 Ph.B., J.D. 582 Oakwood Ave.
Barasa, Robert A. '51 '77 C.612 B.S. L.209 J.D. 736 N. Western Ave.
Barnes, Jay S. '58 '84 C.1457 B.A. L.659 J.D. Div. Coun., Tenneco Packaging, Inc.
Barr, Kenneth Charles '24 '50 C&L.209 B.A., LL.B. 120 Pembroke Dr.‡
Bass, Donna Kempler '41 '66 C.477 B.A. L.597 J.D. 1160 Arbor Lane
Bates, Edwin R., (AV) '19 '48 C.31 A.B. L.477 J.D. [Speranza&B.]
Bedward, Royce R. '66 '91 C.746 B.B.A. L.339 J.D. V.P. Legal, Hospira Inc.
Bell, Brigitte Schmidt, (AV) '48 '79 C.821 B.A. L.145 J.D. [B.S.Bell] ⊙
Bell, Brigitte Schmidt, P.C., (AV) One Westminster Place (⊙Chicago, Evanston)
Bockelman, C. William, Jr., (AV) '43 '70 C.209 B.S.C. L.146 J.D. [O'Neill&B.]
Bollman, Robert M., (AV) '32 '56 C.20 A.B. L.597 J.D. [⊠ Bollman,L.&M.]

Bollman, Lesser & McGlynn, LLP, (AV)
582 North Oakwood Road Suite 100, 60045
Telephone: 847-295-8800 Fax: 847-295-8886 URL: http://www.BOLLMAN-LESSER.COM
URL: http://www.bollman-lesser.com
Members of Firm: Fredric Bryan Lesser; Edmund R. McGlynn, Jr. Associates: David M. Lutrey; Mark T. Chavin; Jennifer J. Howe; Elizabeth L. Holland. Of Counsel: Albert L. Hall; Robert M. Bollman; Richard B. Kuseski.
Probate, Probate Litigation, Estate Planning, Trusts and Estates, Wills, Federal Estate and Gift Taxation, Guardianship, Commercial Law, Labor and Employment, Real Estate.
See Professional Biographies, LAKE FOREST, ILLINOIS

Bowers, Ralph E. .... '10 '35 C.800 A.B. L.309 LL.B. 1100 Pembridge Dr.‡
Bresler, Catherine M. ....'62 '93 C.589 B.S. L.365 J.D. Trustmark Ins. Co.
Bryant, Carina E. .... '61 '86 C&L.94 B.S., J.D. 829 Lane Lorraine St.‡
Buhler, Violetta Kapsalis ....'56 '80 C.209 B.S. L.597 J.D. 660 Rockefeller Road
Bunta, Andrew W., (AV) .... '10 '40 C&L.597 B.S., LL.B. 920 Grandview Lane
Burger, Emily S. ....'53 '79 C.1349 B.A. L.107 J.D. 120 Pembroke Dr.
Carlson, Susan M. ....'— '75 C.530 B.A. L.597 J.D. [© Schiff H.]
Carter, Lynn J. .... '50 '81 C.234 B.A. L.339 J.D. Sr. Atty., Pactiv Corp.
Casey, Thomas J. ....'11 '36 C.424 L.209 J.D. 701 Forest Hill Rd.‡
Caslione, John A. ....'53 '84 C.107 L.146 J.D. Andrew-Ward Intl., Inc.
Chandra, Rashmi ....'— '96 C.999 B.A. L.178 J.D. W. W. Grainger, Inc.
Chatfield, Lloyd C., II, (BVⓉ) '68 '93 C.825 B.A. L.383 J.D.
(adm. in KY; not adm. in IL) Dep. Gen. Coun., Brunswick Corporation
Chavin, Mark T. ....'70 '00 C.597 B.A. L.209 J.D. [Ⓐ Bollman,L.&M.]
Chronister, Wendy L. ....'— '92 C.197 A.B. L.339 J.D. Waud Capital Partners, L.L.C.
Coleman, Kristin M. '68 '93
C.228 A.B. L.477 J.D Assoc. Gen. Coun, Brunswick Corporation
Conzelman, Murray R., (AV) ....'29 '53 C.393 B.A. L.597 J.D. 410 Lexington Dr.

Covington, George M., (AV) '42 '67 C.976 A.B. L.145 J.D. BR
500 North Western Avenue Suite 204, 60045
Telephone: 847-735-8764 Fax: 847-735-8770
Email: gcovington@sbcglobal.net
Real Estate, Land Use and Zoning Law, Conservation Law.
See Professional Biographies, LAKE FOREST, ILLINOIS

Covington, John R. ....'13 '38 C.339 B.S. L.309 LL.B. 1100 Pembridge Dr.‡
Cox, Laura Picchietti .... '57 '88 C.473 B.A. L.209 J.D. 470 Michgamme Lane
Crabb, Michael R., (BVⓉ) '58 '93 C.350 B.S. L.221 J.D.
(adm. in IA; not adm. in IL; Pat.) Corp. Coun., Hospira, Inc., Dept. NLEG
Cummins, Michael J., Law Office of, (AV) '39 '68
C&L.424 B.S.C., J.D. 20 E. Westleigh Rd.
Dapier, Mark E. ..... '47 '75 C.201 B.S. L.365 J.D. 222 East Wisconsin Avenue, Suite 210
Dixon, LaVerne A. .... '09 '37 C.393 B.A. L.365 LL.B. 1230 N. Western Ave.‡
Donovan, Timothy R. '55 '81 C.608 B.S. L.117 J.D.
Exec. V.P. & Gen. Coun. & Mng. Dir. of Intl. Grp., Tenneco Automotive Inc.
Dorfman, David Allen .... '54 '84 C.36 B.S. L.365 J.D. 1540 Littlefield Ct.‡
Draa, H. Vincent, III '56 '84 C.259 B.A. L.280 J.D.
(adm. in GA; not adm. in IL)
Asst. Gen. Coun., Tenneco Automotive Inc. (Legal Department)
Drake, George T. '48 '74
C.966 B.B.A. L.209 J.D. Sr. V.P., Northern Tr. Bk./Lake Forest N.A.
Duggan, James G. ....'23 '50 C.72 A.B. L.597 J.D. 958 Waveland Rd.‡
Dykhouse, Richard R. '64 '89 C.624 B.S. L.347 J.D.
(adm. in IN; not adm. in IL) Sr. Coun., CNH Global N.V.

Eckert, Roland A., Law Office of '46 '76 C.339 B.S. L.930 J.D.
222 East Wisconsin Avenue, Suite 210, 60045-1721
Telephone: 847-615-1474 Fax: 847-615-1476
Email: r.eckert@eckertlawfirm.com URL: http://www.eckertlawfirm.com
General Business Practice, Corporate, Contracts, Zoning, Planning and Land Use, Environmental, Hazardous Materials and Substances, Hazardous Materials Management, Hazardous Materials Transportation, Construction Defects, Mechanics Liens, Buying and Selling of Businesses, Family Business, Limited Liability Company, Partnership, Small Business, Real Estate, Commercial Real Estate, Condominium and Mortgages.
See Professional Biographies, LAKE FOREST, ILLINOIS

Emerson, William H. ....'28 '56 C&L.188 A.B., LL.B. 593 Greenvale Rd.‡
Engel, Nathan A. ....'— '99 C.910 A.B. L.966 J.D. [Ⓐ Schiff H.]
Ensing, William A., (BV) ... '51 '85 C.393 B.A. L.146 J.D. 191 E. Deerpath Rd., Ste. 305
Farquer, Thomas L. '51 '78 C.1208 B.S. L.851 J.D.
Assoc. Gen. Coun., W. W. Grainger, Inc. (Pat.)
Faulkner, James V., Jr., (AV) '44 '71 C&L.276 A.B., J.D.
(adm. in NY; not adm. in IL) V.P., Gen. Coun. & Secy., Pactiv Corp.
Feather, Sharon S. ....'47 '73 C&L.846 B.A., J.D. 478 E. Westleigh Rd.‡
Fenley, Robert A. .... '57 '99 C.502 B.S. L.436 J.D. CNH Global
Finitzo, Nicole ....'— '75 C&L.597 B.S., J.D. [© Schiff H.]
FitzSimons, Edward J. .... '40 '66 C.393 B.A. L.597 J.D. 500 N. Western Ave.
Fleck, Charles J., (AV) ....'40 '67 C.597 B.A. L.879 J.D. [Schiller,D.&F.]
Ford, Donald J. '30 '56 C&L.629 LL.B.
(adm. in OR; not adm. in IL) V.P., Allstate Ins. Co.
Fox, Lisa N. .... '72 '98 C.475 B.A. L.213 J.D. Staff Atty., MFN Financail Corp.
Fratianni, Joann Marie, (BV) .... '54 '80 C.339 B.A. L.589 J.D. P.O. Box 825
Frueh, Anne E. '63 '90 C.801 B.A. L.146 J.D.
Corp. Coun., Tenneco Automotive Inc. (Legal Department)

Fullin Legal Services LLC
(See Libertyville)

Gaffigan, Lynn A. .... '55 '90 C.174 B.A. L.245 J.D. 736 N. Western Ave.
Galassini, Julie .... '62 '87 C.174 B.A. L.145 J.D. 311 Whytegate Ct.
Galatz, Henry F. '47 '79
C.37 B.A. L.464 J.D. Sr. Human Res. Atty., W. W. Grainger, Inc.
Gellersted, Richard H. ....'61 '88 C.494 B.S. L.209 J.D. 736 N. Western Ave., Box 231
Georgevich, Margaret M.G. '52 '79
C.991 B.A. L.146 J.D. V.P., Northern Tr. Bk./Lake Forest N.A.
Golden, Michael D. '66 '91 C.746 B.A. L.436 J.D.
(adm. in WI; not adm. in IL) Atty., Brunswick Corp.
Goodman, William H. ....'66 '91 C.103 B.A. L.597 J.D. Prototype Equipment Corp.‡
Gottschalk, Robert ....'11 '35 C.012 B.E. L.732 LL.B. 1416 N. Green Bay Rd. (Pat.)
Grabowski, Donald W. .... '40 '75 C.339 B.S. L.209 J.D. 1757 S. Wilson Dr.
Gramm, Frank G. '44 '75 C.339 B.A. L.424 J.D.
Sr. V.P., Gen. Coun. & Corp. Secy., Trustmark Ins. Co.
Greisman, Kenneth D. '60 '85 C.589 B.A. L.424 J.D.
VP & Chief Legal Coun., TAP Pharmaceutical Prod., Inc.
Grimm, Phyllis E. .... '58 '86 C.597 B.A. L.1119 J.D. Sr. Coun., CNH Global N.V.
Grisamore, C. W. .... '32 '60 C.234 L.352 LL.B. 410 Onwentsia Rd.
Grossman, Richard, (AV) ...'10 '33 C.145 Ph.B. L.309 LL.B. 1260 N. Western Ave.
Gruen, Aaron Nathaniel ....'63 '99 C.145 B.A. L.209 J.D. 282 Dover Circle
Hakes, John M. .... '40 '67 C&L.352 B.A., J.D. V.P., Northern Tr. Co.‡
Hale, George E., (AV) .... '13 '38 C.976 A.B. L.309 LL.B. 1100 Pembridge Dr.‡
Hall, Albert L., (AV) .... '26 '55 C.339 B.S. L.597 J.D. [© Bollman,L.&M.]
Hallagan, Kevin J. .... '36 '66 C&L.209 B.Sc., J.D. 1511 White Oak Rd.
Hamann, Walter C. .... '21 '44 C.999 L.365 J.D. 511 Beverly Pl.‡
Hanson, David S. '52 '78 C.339 B.A. L.424 J.D.
Assoc. Gen. Coun., W. W. Grainger, Inc.
Harvey, Bennet B., Jr., Law Offices of, (AV) '34 '60
C.674 A.B. L.309 LL.B. One Westminster Pl., Suite 100 (⊙Chicago)
Herron, Donna Jean ....'35 '98 C.937 B.A. L.146 J.D. 711 W. Old Elm Rd.
Hinton-Kedo, Jane Carol '53 '85
C.1024 B.A. L.365 J.D. Risk Manage. Coun., W. W. Grainger, Inc.
Hirsen, Mary W. .... '48 '82 C.597 B.A. L.209 J.D. 105 Surrey Lane
Hogan, Philip J. .... '15 '41 C&L.209 A.M., LL.B. 1720 S. Surrey Lane
Holland, Elizabeth L. .... '63 '02 C.967 B.A. L.1018 J.D. [Ⓐ Bollman,L.&M.]
Holt, Robert W. '49 '76
C.475 B.A. L.365 J.D. Sr. V.P., Northern Tr. Bk./Lake Forest, N.A.
Howard, John L. '57 '82 C&L.347 B.S., J.D.
(adm. in IN; not adm. in IL) Sr. V.P. & Gen. Coun., W. W. Grainger, Inc.
Howe, Jennifer J. ....'65 '92 C.602 B.A. L.215 J.D. [Ⓐ Bollman,L.&M.]
Hughes, John W., (AV) .... '19 '48 C.309 A.B. L.893 J.D. 71 Stonegate Rd.
Hutchen, Bridget W., (BV) ....'49 '74 C.450 B.A. L.424 J.D. 191 East Deerpath Suite 202
Hynes, Mary Ann '— '71 C.424 L.365 J.D.
Sr. V.P., Gen. Coun. & Asst. Secy., IMC Global Inc.
Jackson, Mary Dahlberg .... '52 '77 C&L.597 A.B., J.D. 229 Brampton Ln.‡
Jacobs, Frieda P. ....'53 '80 C.276 B.S. L.477 J.D. 280 Overlook Dr.‡
Jansson, Peter N., (AVⓉ) ......'— '69 C.119 B.S. L.893 J.D. [Jansson,S.M.&A.] (Pat.) ⊙
Jansson, Shupe, Munger & Antaramian, Ltd., (AVⓉ)
207 East Westminster, Suite 205 (Pat.) (⊙Racine, WI)
Jensen, Carl M., Jr. ....'18 '47 C&L.597 B.S., J.D. 485 E. Westleish Rd.‡
Johannesen, Michael B. .... '65 '90 C.339 B.A. L.477 J.D. Hospira, Inc., Dept. NLEG
Johnson, Mary Barb ....'— '44 C&L.659 B.S., LL.B. 971 N. Hawthorne Pl.
Julian, John W. '57 '83 C.339 B.A. L.1119 J.D.
Ass't. Gen. Coun., W. W. Grainger, Inc.
Kaeding, Robert H. .... '43 '74 C.276 A.B. L.809 J.D. 1301 N. Western Ave.
Kalebic, Charlene Q. ....'— '99 C.57 B.A. L.424 J.D. [Ⓐ Schiff H.]
Kaplan, Karen Stone ....'57 '82 C.788 A.B. L.597 J.D. 450 E. Wisconsin Ave.
Kearns, Virginia L. '41 '70 C.586 B.A. L.796 J.D.
(adm. in TX; not adm. in IL) 500 N. Field Dr.‡
Kelley, Stephen W. .... '64 '89 C.602 B.A. L.477 J.D. Gen. Coun., Verizon Avenue
Kelly, James A. C., (AV) .... '06 '32 C.210 A.B. L.146 LL.B. 1100 Pembridge Dr.‡
Kennedy, Kathryn G. .... '66 '92 C.951 B.A. L.145 J.D. 150 Field Dr.
Kintz, Susanna Truax ....'60 '87 C.800 B.A. L.146 J.D. 610 Newcastle Dr.
Kirby, John P., Jr. ....'38 '68 C.870 B.S. L.602 J.D. 155 Danbury Court (Pat.)
Koch, Marilyn A. .... '51 '76 C.228 A.B. L.802 J.D. P.O. Box 190
Kokkines, George C. '67 '92 C.477 A.B. L.309 J.D.
Assoc. Sr. Coun., Lit., TAP Pharmaceutical Products Inc.
Kolasa, Robert J., Law Office ....'57 '83 C&L.215 B.S., J.D. 582 Oakwood Ave., Ste. 200
Kreml, Melanie Ann ....'53 '79 C.597 B.A. L.424 J.D. 595 E. Longwood Dr.
Kuseski, Richard B., (BV) ....'37 '63 C.340 B.S. L.365 J.D. [© Bollman,L.&M.]
Kwakye, Benjamin .... '67 '93 C.197 B.A. L.309 J.D. Sr. Coun., Hospira, Inc.
Laundry, Melburn E. .... '31 '64 C.870 B.S. L.146 J.D. 410 Circle Ln. (Pat.)
Lesser, Fredric Bryan, (AV) ....'55 '80 C.339 B.A. L.477 J.D. [Bollman,L.&M.]
Lester, Raymond J. '54 '84
C.339 B.S. L.365 J.D. V.P., Assoc. Gen. Coun., Trustmark Ins. Co.
Levy, Katherine J. .... '— '80 C&L.209 B.S., J.D. [© Schiff H.]

Lewinthal, Sklamberg & Associates
(See Northbrook)

Linehan, Colleen Megan ....'73 '98 C.966 B.A. L.436 J.D. 450 Turicum Rd.
Linn, Anne Conzelman, (AV) ....'56 '81 C.675 B.A. L.910 J.D. 410 Lexington Dr.
Livingstone, Geo. D. .... '10 '46 C.145 Ph.B. L.209 J.D. P.O. Box 391
Lutrey, David M., (BV) ....'68 '96 C.339 B.S. L.209 J.D. [Ⓐ Bollman,L.&M.]
Lyczko, Catherine ("Cait") M. .... '59 '89 C.424 B.A. L.339 J.D. 400 Field Drive
Marcyan, Carlton R., (AV) .... '55 '81 C.209 B.S.C. L.365 J.D. [Schiller,D.&F.]
Mardoian, Jack C., (AV) ....'52 '79 C.602 A.B. L.692 J.D. [J.C.Mardoian]
Mardoian, Jack C., Ltd., (AV) ....450 Butler Dr.
Marlatt, William C., Jr. ....'42 '69 C.210 A.B. L.208 J.D. 207 E. Westminster St.
Marquardt, Gilbert H., Jr., (AV) ....'38 '63 C.976 B.A. L.597 J.D. 1 Westminister Pl.
McDaniel, Stephen J. '49 '83
C.894 B.A. L.424 J.D. Assoc. Gen. Coun., Trustmark Ins. Co.
McFarlin, Wm. F. '15 '39 C.293 B.A. L.352 J.D.
(adm. in IA; not adm. in IL) 1230 N. Western Ave.‡
McGlynn, Edmund R., Jr. ....'48 '77 C.46 B.S. L.365 J.D. [Bollman,L.&M.]
McLucas, Don H., (AV) ....'10 '35 C&L.597 B.S., J.D. 390 N. Green Bay Rd.‡
Melroy, Theresa A. '58 '83
C.375 B.A. L.146 J.D. Assoc. Gen. Coun., W. W. Grainger, Inc.
Mieling, Michael J. .... '54 '80 C&L.339 B.S., J.D. 227 Northgate
Miller, Elizabeth K., Law Offices of '54 '99
C.1083 B.S. L.365 J.D. 50 East Old Mill Road
Moss, John D., Jr. ....'41 '68 C&L.424 B.S., J.D. 1045 W. Old Mill Rd.
Mueller, David G., (BVⓉ) ...'58 '83 C.477 B.S. L.209 J.D. Sr. Coun., CNH Global N.V.
Nee, Katherine L. '60 '86 C.339 B.A. L.209 J.D.
Assoc. Gen. Coun., W.W. Grainger, Inc.
Nielsen, Walter W. .... '40 '71 C.210 B.A. L.597 J.D. 546 Timber Ln.
Nolan, Aimee Merriman '69 '94
C.475 B.A. L.215 J.D. Sr. Corp. Coun., W. W. Grainger, Inc.
O'Brien, M. Kathleen .... '53 '79 C.188 B.A. L.365 J.D. 1452 Edgewood Rd.
Olsen, John R. ....'49 '74 C.878 B.A. L.178 J.D. Packaging Corp. of America
Olson, Laura H. '49 '82
C.1121 B.S.B.A. L.589 J.D. Wintrust Asset Management Company
Olson, Roy A. .... '30 '55 C&L.585 B.A., J.D. 81 W. North Ave.
O'Neill, Robert E., (AV) ....'46 '74 C.879 B.S.E.E. L.64 J.D. [O'Neill&B.]
O'Neill & Bockelman, P.C., (AV) ....250 E. Illinois Rd.
Padgett, James L. ....'54 '82 C.586 B.B.A. L.145 J.D. 260 Pembroke Drive
Pedersen & Houpt, A Professional Corporation, (AV) ......1 Westminister Pl. (⊙Chicago)
Pence, Robert J., (AV) ....'— '75 C&L.339 B.A., J.D. Trans. Coun., IMC Global Inc.
Perkins, Randolph M., (AV) ....'— '82 C.338 B.S. L.339 J.D. [Schiff H.]
Potts, Robert E. ....'27 '55 C&L.424 B.S., J.D. 203 E. Niles Ave.‡
Przybyszewski, Sandra J. '63 '88 C.424 B.B.A. L.146 J.D.
Sec. V.P. & Assoc. Gen. Coun., Trustmark Ins. Co.
Quall, Matthew J. .... '59 '84 C.339 B.S. L.209 J.D. 469 E. Westleigh Rd.
Rand, Joseph L. ....'41 '66 C.477 B.B.A. L.597 J.D. 60 S. Ahwahnee Rd.
Ravich, Marshall ....'31 '59 C.1016 B.S.C. L.365 LL.B. 251 Sussex Lane‡
Reece, Donald B. '41 '65 C&L.623 B.B.A., J.D.
(adm. in OK; not adm. in IL) Northwestern Mutual Life Ins. Co.

Reid, Stuart A., Law Offices of '70 '97 C&L.352 B.A., J.D.
222 East Wisconsin Avenue, Suite 305, 60045
Telephone: 847-295-0566 Fax: 847-295-0577
Email: reidlaw@comcast.net URL: http://www.reidlawoffice.com
Matrimonial Law, Family Law, Domestic Relations, Divorce/Dissolution of Marriage, Child Custody, Child Support, Visitation Rights, Spousal Support/Alimony/Maintenance, Juvenile Law.
See Professional Biographies, LAKE FOREST, ILLINOIS

Revord, Matthew J., (AV) '63 '89
C.602 B.A. L.339 J.D. Dep. Gen. Coun., Brunswick Corporation
Ring, Dan F. ....'11 '37 C&L.209 J.D. 1351 Everett Rd.‡
Rodriguez, Paul L. .... '70 '94 C.228 B.S.E.E. L.145 J.D. Pactiv Corporation (Pat.)
Romeiser, Ellen R. .... '45 '70 C.706 B.A. L.597 J.D. 294 E. Rose Terr.

Schiff Hardin LLP, (AV)
A Limited Liability Partnership Including Professional Corporations
Founded in 1864
One Westminster Place, 60045 ⊙
Telephone: 847-295-9200 Facsimile: 847-295-7810
Partner: Randolph M. Perkins. Of Counsel: Susan M. Carlson; Nicole Finitzo; Katherine J. Levy; Richard L. Verkler. Associates: Nathan A. Engel; Charlene Q. Kalebic.
General Practice.
See Professional Biographies, LAKE FOREST, ILLINOIS

Schiller, DuCanto and Fleck, (AV) BB
Suite 300, 207 East Westminster Avenue, 60045-1857 ⊙
Telephone: 847-615-8300 Fax: 847-615-8284
Email: schillerducantoandfleck@sdflaw.com URL: http://www.sdflaw.com
Partners: Charles J. Fleck; Carlton R. Marcyan; Eric L. Schulman; Mario R. Ventrelli. Resident Associates: Neal A. Simon; Mary A. Zambreno.
Family Law, Complex Domestic Relations Issues, Divorce/Dissolution of Marriage, Prenuptial Agreements/Premarital Agreements, Child Custody and Visitation, Spousal Support/Alimony/Maintenance, Matrimonial Law and Litigation, Appeals, Mediation-Family/ Divorce, Marital Settlement Agreements, Separation Agreements, Property Rights, Financial Discovery and Analysis Related to Divorce, and Tax Considerations Related to Divorce.
Chicago, Illinois Office: 200 North La Salle Street, 30th Floor. Telephone: 312-641-5560. Fax: 312-641-6361.
Wheaton, Illinois Office: 311 South County Farm Road, Suite G. Telephone: 630-665-5800. Fax: 630-665-6082.
See Professional Biographies, LAKE FOREST, ILLINOIS

Schulman, Eric L. .... '71 '97 C.352 B.A. L.365 J.D. [Schiller,D.&F.]
Seeds, Robert G., Jr. .... '52 '77 C.221 B.A. L.146 J.D. 282 Kimberly LN
Seki, Hoken S., Law Offices of, (AV) '— '65
C.178 A.B. L.309 LL.B. 225 E. Deerpath Rd., Ste. 224
Semmelman, Andrew A., (AV) ......'31 '59 C.393 B.A. L.339 LL.B. [Semmelman&S.]
Semmelman, David A., (BV) ......'57 '83 C.966 B.S. L.365 J.D. [Semmelman&S.]

Semmelman & Semmelman, Ltd., (AV)
191 East Deerpath, Suite 301, 60045
Telephone: 847-234-4438 Fax: 847-234-4674
URL: http://www.semmelmanlaw.com
Andrew A. Semmelman; David A. Semmelman;—Kimberly Smoron Wisneski.
Estate Planning, Wills, Trusts, Probate, Real Estate and Business Matters.
Counsel For: Rondont Rockland Corp.
Representative Clients: Rondont Rockland Corp.
References: Northern Trust Bank/Lake Forest; Lake Forest Bank & Trust.
See Professional Biographies, LAKE FOREST, ILLINOIS

Shandor, Lidia Boyduy '55 '82 C.976 B.A. L.93 J.D.
(adm. in NY; not adm. in IL) 1504 N. Waukegan Rd.
Shannahan, Joan C. .... '57 '84 C.695 B.A. L.1202 J.D. 10 S. Green Bay Rd.
Sibbernsen, Richard D. ......'48 '75 C.436 B.A. L.190 J.D. Packaging Corp. of Amer.
Siegel, Steven Paul ......'51 '76 C&L.339 B.S., J.D. 1085 Mt. Vernon Ave.
Simon, Neal A. .... '78 '03 C.339 B.S. L.209 J.D. [A Schiller,D.&F.]
Sloan, James B., (AV) .... '34 '62 C&L.424 A.B., J.D. [▣ Pedersen&H.]
Smith, Marschall I. '44 '74
C.674 A.B. L.893 J.D. V.P. & Gen. Coun., Brunswick Corporation
Speranza, Carmen V., (AV) ......'35 '62 C&L.424 B.S., J.D. [Speranza&B.]
Speranza, Peter A., (BV) .... '60 '86 C.723 B.A. L.209 J.D. 1401 N. Western Ave.
Speranza and Bates, (AV) ....1401 N. Western Ave.
Springer, Clement F., Jr., (AV) .... '35 '60 C.31 B.A. L.597 J.D. 1152 Lynette Lane‡
Stuart, Robert D., Jr. '16 '46 C.674 B.A. L.976 LL.B.
Pres., North Star Investments, Inc.
Thompson, David F., (AV) ......'42 '70 C.424 B.S. L.597 J.D. 1051 Valley Rd.
Thullen, Henry M., (AV) ......'15 '39 C&L.608 A.B., LL.B. 1054 Franz Dr.‡
Torf, Jeffrey S. .... '— '71 C.1016 B.S.B.A. L.597 J.D. Litig. Coun., IMC Global Inc.
Tramel, Charles W. '54 '79
C.894 B.A. L.339 J.D. V.P. & Tr. Offr., Bank One, Illinois, N.A.‡
Treacy, William P. ....'20 '45 C&L.597 B.A., LL.B. 70 E. Laurel Ave.
Trusdell, Laurence M. '— '82
C.1090 B.A. L.145 J.D. Assoc. Gen. Coun., W.W. Grainger, Inc.
Turek, Marliss E. .... '46 '80 C.672 B.F.A. L.146 J.D. 196 Atteridge Rd.
Uhrig, Daniel J. ....'06 '33 C.597 B.S. L.146 LL.B. 1100 Pembridge Dr.‡
Ventrelli, Mario R. .... '68 '95 C&L.209 B.A., J.D. [Schiller,D.&F.]
Verkler, Richard L., (AV) .... '— '62 C.339 B.S. L.966 J.D. [▣ Schiff H.]
Waldo, C. Ives, Jr., (AV) .... '11 '36 C.976 B.A. L.597 J.D. 912 Barkclay Circle
Warco, Terry A. '54 '86 C.896 B.A. L.229 J.D.
(adm. in PA; not adm. in IL) V.P. & Assoc. Gen. Coun., CNH Global N.V.
Ward, James F., (AV) ......'24 '50 C&L.597 B.S.B.A., J.D. 135 E. North Ave.‡
Whipple, Jeffrey T. ......'45 '70 C&L.802 B.A., J.D. 222 E. Wisconsin, Ste. 105
Wilbur, Richard Sloan ......'24 '91 C.813 M.D. L.365 J.D. 985 N. Hawthorne Pl.
Wisneski, Kimberly Smoron .... '72 '97 C.352 B.A. L.146 J.D. [A Semmelman&S.]
Zambreno, Mary A. ......'78 '04 C.597 B.A. L.209 J.D. [A Schiller,D.&F.]
Zapinski, Robert P. '60 '85 C.98 B.S. L.339 J.D.
Corp. Coun., Tenneco Automotive Inc. (Legal Department)
Zellner, Robert J. .... '22 '67 C.746 B.A. L.146 J.D. 648 Highview Terr.‡
Zimmerman, J. Jeffrey '59 '84 C.207 B.A. L.597 J.D.
Asst. Gen. Coun., Tenneco Automotive Inc. (Legal Department)

LAKE IN THE HILLS, 23,152, *McHenry Co.*

Grier, Carol J. .... '54 '84 C.375 B.S. L.589 J.D. 9 Pebble Beach Ct.
Talbot, Kevin Howard ......'71 '98 C.966 J.B.S. L.1035 J.D. [K.H.Talbot]
Talbot, Kevin H. ....1301 Pyott Rd., Ste. 200

LAKE VILLA, 5,864, *Lake Co.*

Blacher, Louis A. ....'37 '63 C.339 A.B. L.910 J.D. 95 W. Grand Ave.
Brown, David R. .... '50 '78 C.475 B.A. L.145 J.D. 1319 Benton Rd.

DeRose, David
(See Lindenhurst)

Frantell, Diane M. .... '55 '86 C.801 B.S. L.910 J.D. 313 Hampton Court, Ste. 200
Samuelson, Don S. '41 '67 C.197 A.B. L.145 J.D.
Pres., DSSA Real Estate Development & Management
Venturi, Daniel B. ....'57 '84 C&L.801 B.S., J.D. P.O. Box 1107

LAKE ZURICH, 18,104, *Lake Co.*

Babcock, Andrew Dag .... '64 '99 [Babcock,I.]
Babcock IP, LLC ....24154 Lakeside Dr.
Dukor, Alexander A. .... '63 '00 L.146 J.D. [A.Dukor&Assoc.]
Dukor, Alexander, and Associates, P.C. .... 22960 N. Quentin Road
Extrom, Daniel M. ....'55 '81 C.927 B.A. L.365 J.D. 1323 Thorndale Lane
Fortelka, Lorraine V. .... '— '83 C.338 B.S. L.146 J.D. Coun., McDonald's Corp.
Hammer, Paul T. ....'47 '78 C.424 A.B. L.589 J.D. Hammer Properties
Heidenfelder, Randy S. ....'52 '81 C.30 B.A. L.904 J.D. 480 Surryse Rd.
Miller, Joel S. ....'54 '83 C.879 B.S. L.365 J.D. 75 S. Old Rand Rd.
Minarik, Irwin J. ....'17 '40 L.209 LL.B. 17 Elm St.‡
Salvi, Albert S., (AV) ....'24 '51 C.602 B.S. L.597 J.D. [Salvi,S.&W.]
Salvi, Joseph V., (BV) ....'66 '91 C.388 B.A. L.146 J.D. [A Salvi,S.&W.]
Salvi, Michael J., (BV) ....'59 '84 C.742 B.A. L.365 J.D. [Salvi,S.&W.]
Salvi, Salvi & Wifler, P.C., (AV) .... 335 Chancery Lane
Talbett, Michael S. ....'52 '85 C.645 B.S. L.879 J.D. 1245 Stratford Court
Thompson, Ruth P. .... '62 '87 C&L.352 B.A., J.D. P.O. Box 1106
Wifler, Catherine M., (BV) .... '56 '89 C.436 B.A. L.365 J.D. 335 Chancery Ln.
Wifler, Peter J., (BV) ....'56 '86 C.436 B.S. L.365 J.D. [Salvi,S.&W.]
Wood, Ann Bernard ....'56 '85 C.879 B.S.M.E. L.365 J.D. 25275 N Marilyn Ln

LANARK, 1,584, *Carroll Co.*

Meyers, Kipp E., (BV) .... '66 '91 C.339 B.A. L.209 J.D. P.O. Box 114
Mitchell, Edward J., (BV) .... '49 '74 C.187 B.A. L.930 J.D. 110 North Broad Street

LANSING, 28,332, *Cook Co.*

Adduci, James J., Jr., (BV) .... '47 '74 C.1157 B.A. L.209 J.D. 3056 Ridge Rd.
Anderson, Dale A., (AV) ......'37 '62 C.234 B.A. L.879 LL.B. [D.A.Anderson&Assoc.]
Anderson, Dale A., & Associates, Ltd., (AV) ....18225 Burnham Ave.
Appel, Peter T., (BV) ....'24 '49 L.209 LL.B. [Appel&A.]
Appel, Thomas A. ....'56 '82 C.317 B.A. L.602 J.D. [Appel&A.]
Appel & Appel, Ltd., (BV) ....18607 Torrence Ave.
Becker, Bobbie F. .... '— '80 C.339 B.A. L.146 J.D. [Becker&S.]
Becker & Silverman ....3243 Ridge Rd.
Bergstrom, Barry C., (AV) ....'46 '71 C.57 A.B. L.879 J.D. [B.C.Bergstrom]
Bergstrom, Barry C., Ltd., (AV) .... 3330 181st Pl., Suite 104
Biederman, Robt. A. .... '25 '50 C&L.209 LL.B. 18107 Torrence St.
Buoscio, F. Ronald, (AV) .... '27 '51 C&L.145 Ph.B., J.D. 17130 Torrence Ave., Ste. 400
Canalia, Peter B., (AV) ....'42 '70 C.701 B.S.M.E. L.365 J.D. [Canalia&V.]
Canalia & Valerius, P.C., (AV) ....18525 Torrance Ave.
Clark, David G. '56 '90 C&L.879 B.S., J.D.
(adm. in IN; not adm. in IL) First Natl. Bk.
Clegg, Marcia L. .... '54 '79 C.532 B.A. L.608 J.D. 16781 Torrence Ave.
Gardberg, Jerome M. '36 '71
C.1016 B.S. L.146 J.D. V.P. & Tr. Offr., 1st Chicago Tr. Co. of Ill.
Gianopolus, Dennis G., Law Offices of '59 '90
C.1191 B.A. L.209 J.D. 18511 Torrence Ave.
Hill, Philip ....'17 '68 C.339 A.B. L.365 J.D. 3256 Ridge Rd.‡
Kelly, Timothy M., (AV) ..... '— '83 C.57 B.A. L.209 J.D. 18607 Torrence Ave., Ste. 2A
Kiedaisch, Ronald A., (AV) ....'33 '57 C&L.879 B.A., LL.B. 3330 181st Pl.
Matuga, Richard J., (BV) .... '40 '65 C.966 B.S. L.347 J.D. [R.J.Matuga]
Matuga, Richard J., Ltd., (BV) ....3256 Ridge Rd., Suite 211
Mennella, Vincent .... '25 '52 C&L.209 B.S., LL.B. 18414 Oakwood‡
Molenaar, James E., (AV) ....'37 '64 C&L.339 A.B., LL.B. 3546 Ridge Rd.
Pagorek, Stanley W. .... '47 '72 C.1024 B.A. L.209 J.D. 18525 Torrence Avenue
Panichi, Thomas P. .... '48 '73 C.801 B.S. L.146 J.D. 18143 Greenwood St.
Perry, Joan E. '46 '83 C.966 Ph.D. L.345 J.D.
(adm. in WI; not adm. in IL) 18448 Roy St.
Rhed, Drew C. '67 '99 C.679 B.S. L.879 J.D.
(adm. in IN; not adm. in IL) [A Appel&A.]
Richter, Harold, (BV) ....'24 '52 C.477 B.S.E. L.309 J.D. 18525 Torrence Ave.
Sager, John F. .... '45 '76 L.146 J.D. [Sager&Assoc.]
Sager & Associates, Ltd. .... 3232 Ridge Rd., Ste. 7
Silverman, Norman H. ....'54 '79 C.597 B.S. L.910 J.D. [Becker&S.]
Valerius, Margaret L. ....'47 '90 C.516 B.S. L.1338 J.D. [Canalia&V.]
Vlasek, William A., (AV) .... '46 '73 C.742 B.A. L.209 J.D. [W.A.Vlasek]
Vlasek, William A., P.C., (AV) ....3256 Ridge Rd., Suite 201
Wheaton, Scott R. .... '62 '91 C.339 B.S. L.209 J.D. 18143 Greenwood St.

LA SALLE, 9,717, *La Salle Co.*

Aplington, Kaufman, McClintock, Steele & Barry, Ltd., (BV) ....160 Marquette St.

Armstrong & Surin
(See Ottawa)

Banich, William R., (BV) .... '51 '76 C.339 B.A. L.623 J.D. Asoc. J,
Barry, Patrick A., (BV) ....'53 '78 C.723 B.A. L.589 J.D. [Aplington,K.M.S.&B.]
Barry, Tobias G. .... '24 '52 C.436 Ph.B. L.602 J.D. [Aplington,K.M.S.&B.]
Bichl, Francis G., Jr. .... '33 '66 C.436 B.S. L.209 LL.B. 1132 North Marquette Street
Duncan, John S., III, (AV) '48 '73
C.363 B.S.B.A. L.424 J.D. [Herbolsheimer,L.H.D.&R.]
Eiten, Gary R., (BV) ....'54 '80 C.339 B.S. L.146 J.D. [Herbolsheimer,L.H.D.&R.]
Eiten, Karen C., (BV) .... '58 '83 C.927 B.A. L.209 J.D. [Herbolsheimer,L.H.D.&R.]
Ennenbach, Joseph P., (CV) .... '48 '80 C.339 B.S. L.365 J.D. [J.P.Ennenbach]
Ennenbach, Jos P., Law Offices, (CV) .... P.O. Box 1771
Gearhart, Gary L., (CV) .... '47 '72 C.340 B.A. L.276 J.D. [Gearhart&Assoc.]
Gearhart & Associates, (CV) ....951 5th St.
Gift, Douglas A., (BV) ......'50 '75 C.338 B.S. L.339 J.D. [Herbolsheimer,L.H.D.&R.]
Guido, Scott R., (CV) .... '58 '84 C.339 B.A. L.1000 J.D. Spec. Asst. Atty. Gen.
Henson, T. Donald, (AV) ......'42 '67 C&L.339 B.S., J.D. [Herbolsheimer,L.H.D.&R.]

Herbolsheimer, Lannon, Henson, Duncan and Reagan, P.C., (AV) BB
State Bank Building, Suite 400, 654 First Street, P.O. Box 539, 61301 ⊙
Telephone: 815-223-0111 Fax: 815-223-5829
George L. Herbolsheimer (1911-1992); R. James Lannon, Jr.; T. Donald Henson; John S. Duncan, III; Michael T. Reagan (Resident, Ottawa Office); Douglas A. Gift; Gary R. Eiten; Karen C. Eiten; Michael C. Jansz (Resident, Ottawa Office);—Jill W. Klein; Todd L. Martin; William P. Hintz; Stephen M. Osborne.
Corporate Law, Business Law, Criminal Law, DWI/DUI, Juvenile Law, Employment Law, Administrative Law, Employment Termination, Sexual Harassment, Estate Planning, Probate, Tax Planning, Wills and Trusts, Family Law, Divorce, Adoption, Prenuptial Agreements, Health Care, Civil Litigation, Insurance Defense, Products Liability, Insurance, Subrogation, Real Estate, Boundary Disputes, Easements.
Attorneys for: St. Paul Fire and Marine Insurance Co.; State Farm Insurance Co.; La Salle State Bank; Eureka Savings Bank; Illinois Valley Community Hospital; Community Hospital of Ottawa; Commonwealth Edison, Co.; Sentry Insurance; Cincinnati Ins.; General Casualty.

(This Listing Continued)

Herbolsheimer, Lannon, Henson, Duncan and Reagan, P.C. (Continued)

Ottawa, Illinois Office: First Federal Savings Bank Building, 633 La Salle Street, Suite 409. Telephone: 815-434-1400. Fax: 815-434-2423.

See Professional Biographies, LA SALLE, ILLINOIS

Hintz, William P., (BV) ...... '58 '83 C&L.209 B.A., J.D. [[A] Herbolsheimer,L.H.D.&R.]
Kaufman, Fremont M., (AV) ..... '08 '32 C&L.145 Ph.B., J.D. [[B] Aplington,K.M.S.&B.] ‡
Kelly, Kevin D., (BV) .... '12 '42 C.1082 L.365 LL.B. 505 1st St.
Klein, Jill W., (BV) .... '67 '92 C.338 B.S. L.589 J.D. [[A] Herbolsheimer,L.H.D.&R.]
Lannon, R. James, Jr., (AV) ..... '34 '60 C&L.339 B.S., J.D. [Herbolsheimer,L.H.D.&R.]

Leynaud & Leynaud, A Prof. Corp., Law Offices of
(See Peru)

Martin, Todd L., (CV) .... '65 '94 C.801 B.A. L.1187 J.D. [[A] Herbolsheimer,L.H.D.&R.]
McClintock, Thomas L., (BV) ...... '48 '74 C.589 B.S. L.879 J.D. [Aplington,K.M.S.&B.]
Osborne, Stephen M., (CV) '61 '86 C.339 A.B. L.801 J.D.
[[A] Herbolsheimer,L.H.D.&R.]
Sammons, Melinda G., (CV) .... '58 '97 C.339 B.S. L.801 J.D. 160 Marquette
Schwamberger, Leo J., (BV) .... '20 '50 C&L.209 J.D. [L.J.Schwamberger]
Schwamberger, Leo J., Ltd., (BV) .... 149 Gooding Street
Stanmar, Reginald S., (CV) .... '48 '86 C.707 B.A. L.365 J.D. [Stanmar]
Stanmar Law Firm, (CV) .... 206 Marquette St., Ste. 204
Steele, Robert B., (BV) .... '49 '74 C&L.339 B.S., J.D. [Aplington,K.M.S.&B.]
Terrando, Stephen G., (CV) .... '47 '74 C.338 B.A. L.796 J.D. 206 Marquette St.

LAWRENCEVILLE, * 4,745, *Lawrence Co.*

Benefiel, Philip B. .... '23 '49 C&L.339 J.D. Ret. Cir. J.
Blakeslee, Rebecca M. .... '65 '89 C.339 B.A. L.801 J.D. 1115 State St.
Bolmarcich, Gene .... '57 '90 C.893 B.S. L.273 J.D. 33109 Elm Ct.
Borden, John F., (BV) .... '45 '70 C.291 B.A. L.339 J.D. [Gosnell,B.E.&S.]

Brainard Law Offices, The
(See Charleston)

Cunningham, Roscoe D., (Ltd.) .... '23 '48 C&L.339 LL.B. Eleventh & State St.

Emison Doolittle Kolb & Roellgen
(See Vincennes, Indiana)

Enloe, Douglas A., (AV) .... '48 '73 C.234 B.S. L.339 J.D. [Gosnell,B.E.&S.]
Gosnell, Maurice E., (AV) .... '11 '34 C&L.339 B.S., J.D. [[B] Gosnell,B.E.&S.]

Gosnell, Borden, Enloe & Sloss, Ltd., (AV)
815 12th Street, P.O. Box 737, 62439-2496
Telephone: 618-943-2338 Fax: 618-943-2080
Email: gbes@midwest.net URL: http://www.lawyers.com/gbes
John F. Borden; Douglas A. Enloe; Larry N. Sloss, Jr.;—Darin K. Rice. Of Counsel: Maurice E. Gosnell.
General Practice. Insurance Defense. Trials. Probate Law. Oil and Gas Law. Personal Injury, Family Law.
General Counsel for: First Bank of Lawrence County; Peoples National Bank.
Local Counsel for: Hartford Accident & Indemnity Co.; Aetna Casualty & Surety Co.; Texaco, Inc.; Country Mutual Insurance Co.; State Farm Insurance Co.; St. Paul Fire & Marine Insurance Co.; Continental Insurance Co.; Crum & Forster Group.

See Professional Biographies, LAWRENCEVILLE, ILLINOIS

Hart Bell LLC
(See Vincennes, Indiana)

Hopkins, Robert M., (BV) ...... '51 '83 C.338 B.A. L.339 J.D. Lawrence Co. Cir. J.'s Off.
Large, Allen W., (CV) .... '47 '74 C.346 B.S. L.500 J.D. 715 12th St.
Neal, James M., (CV) .... '56 '83 C.801 B.A. L.245 J.D. 11th & State
Rice, Darin K. .... '74 '00 C.999 B.A. L.801 J.D. [[A] Gosnell,B.E.&S.]
Shinkle, Daniel B., (CV) .... '61 '87 C.291 B.S. L.1119 J.D. P.O. Box 833
Sloss, Larry N., Jr., (BV) .... '62 '87 C&L.801 B.A., J.D. [Gosnell,B.E.&S.]
Strange, William P., (BV) .... '47 '73 C&L.734 A.B., J.D. State's Atty.

LEBANON, 3,523, *St. Clair Co.*

Church, Harrison L. '41 '73 C&L.339 B.S., J.D.
(adm. in ND; not adm. in IL) P.O. Box 126‡
Clayton, Sally J., (BV) .... '27 '80 C.339 A.B. L.734 J.D. 939 Belleville St.
Ptacek, Anthony W. .... '— '61 C&L.966 B.S., J.D. 120 Merrill Dr.‡

LELAND, 970, *La Salle Co.*

Anderson, Mark E. .... '63 '94 C.58 B.A. L.365 J.D. [White,M.A.M.V.D.&G.] (⊙Ottawa)
Brouwer, Gerard .... '47 '75 C.46 B.S. L.880 J.D. 210 E. Gensessee St.‡
White, Marsh, Anderson, Martin Vickers, Deobler & Goode, (AV)
175 N. Main St. (⊙Earlville, Ottawa)

LEMONT, 13,098, *Cook Co.*

Antonopoulos, John P. .... '45 '71 C.424 B.B.A. L.209 J.D. 221 E. 127th St.
Bianucci, Alfred P. .... '36 '62 C.1024 B.S. L.424 J.D. [A.P.Bianucci]
Bianucci, Alfred P., Ltd., Law Offices of, The .... 12 S. 442 Christopher Dr.

Chawla Group, The, LTD.
(See Hinsdale)

Dystrup, Alderman .... '07 '31 C&L.145 5 E. Logan St.
Graver, Nancy J. .... '51 '76 C.156 B.A. L.365 J.D. 1035 Blacksmith Lane
Grenda, Ronald T., Attorney at Law, (BV) ... '47 '79 C.347 B.A. L.1000 J.D. 22 115th St.
Hoster, Jeffrey M. .... '59 '83 C.1151 B.A. L.339 J.D. 13 Woodland Drive (Pat.)
Kirk, Frank H. .... '12 '43 C.339 L.365 LL.B. 8 Illinois St.‡
Kompare, Bernard J. .... '43 '74 C.602 A.B. L.597 J.D. 1024 119th St.
Loeffler, Richard J., (AV) .... '44 '69 C.210 B.A. L.365 J.D. 13922 Steepleview Ln.
McEntee, Steve '14 '54 C.973 L.1340 LL.B.
(adm. in OH; not adm. in IL) Trailmobile Inc.
Pastor, James F. .... '57 '90 L.365 J.D. Secure Law Ltd.
Raines, William Burnett .... '59 '93 C.1073 B.A. L.284 J.D. [Shestokas,R.&S.]
Schochat, Joanne W. '53 '82
C.338 B.A. L.209 J.D. Asst. Supt. for HR, Troy Sch. Dist. 30C
Shestokas, David J. .... '52 '87 C.98 B.A. L.1000 J.D. [Shestokas,R.&S.]
Shestokas, Raines & Spiwak .... 114 East Illinois
Spiwak, Phillip .... '— '92 C.145 B.A. L.1187 J.D. [Shestokas,R.&S.]

Takiguchi, Masaru K.
(See Oak Brook)

Virtel, Lee T. .... '52 '77 C.339 B.S. L.734 J.D. 15419 127th St.

LENA, 2,887, *Stephenson Co.*

Cox, Steven A., (CV) .... '69 '94 C&L.339 B.S., J.D. [[A] Snow,H.W.&F.] (⊙Freeport)
Fishburn, Dan G., (BV) .... '52 '77 C.477 B.A. L.910 J.D. [Snow,H.W.&F.] ⊙
Rodkey, F. Stanley, (CV) .... '30 '57 C.813 B.A. L.146 LL.B. 122 E. Railroad
Snow, Hunter, Whiton & Fishburn, Ltd., (BV) .... 102 W. Main St. (⊙Freeport)

Whiton, John B., (BV) .... '46 '74 C.473 B.A. L.145 J.D. [Snow,H.W.&F.] ⊙

LeROY, 3,332, *McLean Co.*

Henderson, Hunt, Attorney at Law, (BV) ..... '48 '73 C&L.339 B.S., J.D. 112 E. Center St.
Henderson, Stephen H. .... '48 '73 C&L.339 B.S., J.D. [H.Henderson]
Henderson, Hunt .... 112 E. Center St.

LEWISTOWN, * 2,572, *Fulton Co.*

Bordner, Steven R. .... '55 '80 C.337 A.B. L.801 J.D. Assoc. Admin. J.
Claudon, Kost, Barnhart & Beal, Ltd., (AV) .... 200 N. Main St. (⊙Canton)
Collins, Ted G., (BV) .... '51 '76 C.338 B.S. L.221 J.D. [Collins&J.]
Collins & Johnson, P.C., (BV) .... 177 W. Lincoln Ave.
Davis, William C., Jr., (BV) .... '48 '75 C&L.339 B.S., J.D. 257 W. Lincoln St.
Ewing, Thomas B., (BV) .... '48 '78 C.855 B.A. L.930 J.D. [Ewing&S.]
Ewing & Scott, (BV) .... 190 N. Adams St.
Johnson, Andrewe W., (CV) .... '70 '95 C.339 B.A. L.575 J.D. [Collins&J.]
Johnson, Stephanie S., (CV) .... '71 '96 C&L.575 B.A., J.D. [Collins&J.]
Kost, Oral C., (AV) .... '29 '53 C.504 A.B. L.339 J.D. [Claudon,K.B.&B.] ⊙
Scott, Joan C., (BV) .... '47 '78 C.706 B.A. L.930 J.D. [Ewing&S.]
Toner, Hugh, III .... '58 '82 C.700 B.A L.424 J.D. Asst. State's Atty.
Walton, Patricia A.V. .... '60 '85 C.323 B.A. L.879 J.D. Assoc. Cir. J.

Westervelt, Johnson, Nicoll & Keller, LLC
(See Peoria)

Wilhelm, Charles H. .... '35 '62 C.98 B.S. L.879 LL.B. Ret. Cir. J.‡

LIBERTY, 541, *Adams Co.*

Holloway, Joseph W. .... '30 '58 C.679 B.S. L.1119 LL.B. 8832 White Oak Rd. (Pat.)

LIBERTYVILLE, 20,742, *Lake Co.*

Abbott, Cynthia Photos '62 '86 C.276 B.S.F.S. L.597 J.D.
Sr. Litig. Coun., Motorola, Inc.
Ahern, Archibald M. C., Jr. .... '49 '76 C.986 A.B. L.285 J.D. 600 N. U.S. Highway 45

Ashman Law Offices, LLC
(See Chicago)

Balos, Gregory G. .... '66 '91 C.679 B.A. L.146 J.D. [[A] Dudley&L.]
Beermann, Jon L., (BV) .... '39 '64 C.966 B.B.A. L.145 J.D. [Beermann&D.]
Beermann, Marc J. .... '71 '02 C.966 B.S. L.209 J.D. [[A] Beermann&D.]

Beermann & DeBruyne, (BV)
728 Florsheim Drive, 60048
Telephone: 847-680-7070 Fax: 847-816-6122
URL: http://www.beermanndebruyne.com
Jon L. Beermann; Kathy J. Debruyne;—Marc J. Beermann.
Family Law, Divorce, Adoption, Separation Agreements, Child Custody, Child Support, Domestic Violence, Visitation Rights, Family Mediation Adoption Law, Juvenile Law, Real Estate.

See Professional Biographies, LIBERTYVILLE, ILLINOIS

Benjoya, Marc F., (BV) ... '58 '83 C.589 B.A. L.146 J.D. [Cassiday,S.&G.] (⊙Rockford)
Berglund, James A. .... '61 '86 C.221 B.A. L.146 J.D. [[A] Cassiday,S.&G.]
Bickley, John H., Jr., (AV) .... '29 '52 C.999 L.146 LL.B. 1641 N. Milwaukee Ave.
Bond, Thaddeus M., Jr., (CV) ..... '66 '91 C.57 B.A. L.365 J.D. [T.M.Bond,Jr.&Assoc.] ⊙
Bond, Thaddeus M., Jr., & Associates, P.C., Law Offices of, (CV)
1641 N. Milwaukee Avenue (⊙Waukegan)
Borcia, John M. .... '66 '92 C.589 B.S. L.365 J.D. P.O. Box 447
Bose, Thomas L. .... '44 '69 C.108 B.A. L.1119 J.D. 319 E. Winchester Rd.
Boyd, Michael J., (AV) .... '46 '73 C.694 B.A. L.339 J.D. [Flannery,H.&B.]
Brennan, Margaret J. '52 '78
C.700 B.A.M.A. L.424 J.D. Asst. V.P. & Tr. Offr., First of Amer. Tr. Co.
Brown, Margaret Scanlan .... '52 '77 C.741 B.A. L.424 J.D. 313 Camelot Lane
Burke, John M., (AV) .... '41 '65 C&L.424 B.B.A., J.D. [[B] Dudley&L.]
Carlin, Christine F. '— '91 C.763 B.S. L.209 J.D.
Dir. Risk Mgr., Condell Medical Ctr.‡
Case, Alan E. ...... '48 '73 C.880 B.A. L.597 J.D. Senior Division Counsel, Motorola Inc.

Cassiday, Schade & Gloor, LLP, (AV)
1870 West Winchester Road Suite 148, 60048-5353 ⊙
Telephone: 847-932-6922 Fax: 847-932-6947
URL: http://www.cassiday.com
Members of Firm: Marc F. Benjoya (Also at Rockford); John R. Davis; John J. Reid. Associates: James A. Berglund; Andrew T. Fleishman; Jamie H. Goldstein; Robin B. Levin; Daniel E. Wiesch. Of Counsel: Tami J. Reding-Brubaker.
General Practice. Civil Trial Practice, Civil Appellate Practice, Insurance Coverage, Environmental, Medical and Professional Malpractice, Products Liability, Structural Work Act, Railroad, Employment, Corporate and Health Care Law, Commercial Litigation, Construction, Workers Compensation, Intellectual Property, Municipalities, Transportation, Patent Law.
Chicago, Illinois Office: 20 North Wacker Drive, Suite 1040, 60606-2903. Telephone: 312-641-3100. Fax: 312-444-1669.
Naperville, Illinois Office: 1230 East Diehl Road, Suite 202, 60563-9362. Telephone: 630-328-2970. Fax: 630-328-2979.
Rockford, Illinois Office: 120 West State Street, Suite 401, 61101-1159. Telephone: 815-962-8301. Fax: 815-962-8401.

See Professional Biographies, LIBERTYVILLE, ILLINOIS

Cerretani, John L., (AV⊤) .... '53 '78 C.477 B.A. L.912 J.D. Motorola, Inc.
Chen, Sylvia .... '69 '94 C.339 B.S. L.477 J.D. Intel. Prop. Coun., Motorola, Inc. (Pat.)
Christy, James O. .... '45 '70 C.339 B.A. L.424 J.D. P.O. Box 400‡
Coleman, Lindsay B. ... '78 '02 C.473 B.A. L.502 J.D. 1635 N. Milwaukee Ave., Apt. 103
Dailey, Kirk W. .... '65 '94 C.477 B.S.E.E. L.209 J.D. 600 N. U.S. Hwy. 45
Davis, John R., (AV) .... '51 '83 C.339 B.S. L.365 J.D. [Cassiday,S.&G.]
Debruyne, Kathy J. .... '— '93 C.536 B.A. L.424 J.D. [Beermann&D.]
DeSanto, James J., P.C., (AV) '43 '69
C.339 B.A. L.209 J.D. [DeSanto,M.&M.A.&Assoc.]

DeSanto, Morgan & Mittelman, An Assoc. of Prof. Corps., (AV) [BB]
An Association of Professional Corporations
712 Florsheim Drive, 60048-5270
Telephone: 847-816-8100 Facsimile: 847-816-8126
Email: desanto@iconnect.net URL: http://www.lawyers.com/desantolaw
James J. DeSanto, P.C.; Vernon E. Morgan, P.C.; Richard S. Mittelman, P.C.
Plaintiff's Personal Injury, Automobile Accidents and Injuries, Slip and Fall, Wrongful Death, Insurance Bad Faith, Products Liability, Commercial Litigation, Employment Litigation, Discrimination, Harassment, Wrongful Termination.

See Professional Biographies, LIBERTYVILLE, ILLINOIS

Dolin, Albert H. .... '13 '43 C.597 B.S. L.424 LL.B. 640 Kathryn Ct.‡
Dudley, J. Matthew, (BV) .... '67 '93 C.499 B.S. L.861 J.D. [Dudley&L.]

Dudley & Lake LLC, (BV)
100 East Cook Avenue, 2nd Floor, 60048
Telephone: 847-362-5385 Fax: 847-362-5386
URL: http://www.dudleylake.com
J. Matthew Dudley; Thomas M. Lake. Associates: Jacquelyn Dolores Melius; Gregory G. Balos; Peter M. Schlax. Of Counsel: Thomas M. Schippers; John M. Burke.

(This Listing Continued)

Dudley & Lake LLC (Continued)

Personal Injury, Wrongful Death, Medical Malpractice, Products Liability, Workers' Compensation, Construction Litigation.

See Professional Biographies, LIBERTYVILLE, ILLINOIS

Dyslin, Daniel R. ....'59 '91 C.1183 B.S. L.209 J.D. 1580 South Milwaukee, Suite 530
Eger, Charles L. '52 '77 C&L.37 B.A., J.D.
(adm. in AZ; not adm. in IL) Assoc. Gen. Atty., Motorola, Inc.
Emerson, John W., Law Office of '49 '83
C.207 B.A. L.365 J.D. 111 E. Church St., Ste. 202
Farish, Stephen E. '59 '85 C.10 B.A. L.280 J.D.
(adm. in GA; not adm. in IL) 1190 Winchester Rd.‡
Fato, Gildo E. ....'28 '60 C.46 B.S. L.209 J.D. 515 Ash St. (Pat.)
Flannery, Hoover & Boyd, (AV) ....1580 S. Milwaukee Ave., Ste. 600
Fleishman, Andrew T. ... '68 '01 C.569 B.A. L.146 J.D. [Ⓐ Cassiday,S.&G.] (⊙Chicago)
Fogle, Andrew R. ....'52 '81 C.966 B.A. L.365 J.D. 1580 S. Milwaukee Ave.
Friestedt, Betsy Wolf, (BV) ....'56 '83 C.350 B.A. L.602 J.D. [Ray&G.]
Fullin, Timothy J. ....'66 '01 C.737 B.S. L.365 J.D. [Fullin] (Pat.)

Fullin Legal Services LLC
711 North Milwaukee Avenue, 60048
Telephone: 847-573-9880 Fax: 847-573-9882
Email: tjfullin@fullinlegal.com
Timothy J. Fullin.
Patents, Trademarks, Licensing, Copyrights, Trade Secrets.

See Professional Biographies, LIBERTYVILLE, ILLINOIS

Geiger, Donald H., (BV) ....'45 '71 C.927 B.S. L.597 J.D. 1308 Kempton Dr.
Geiger, Fred A. ....'43 '68 C.210 B.A. L.339 J.D. Jus., Appl. Ct.
Glick, Kenneth J., (AV) ....'33 '56 C&L.339 B.S., LL.B. [Ⓒ Ray&G.]
Glick, Sidney A., (BV) ....'59 '84 C&L.339 B.S., J.D. [Ray&G.]
Goldstein, Jamie H. ....'79 '04 C.966 B.S. L.146 J.D. [Ⓐ Cassiday,S.&G.] (⊙Chicago)
Goles, David S. '72 '98
C.30 B.A. L.589 J.D. [Ⓐ Swanson,M.&B.] (⊙Chicago, Waukegan)
Gordon, David S., & Associates ......'60 '85 C&L.339 B.S., J.D. 731 N. Milwaukee Ave.
Graham, Michael R., (AV) ....'47 '72 C.436 B.A. L.424 J.D. [Graham,G.&S.]
Graham, William M., (AV) ....'35 '63 C.177 B.A. L.436 J.D. [Graham,G.&S.]
Graham, Graham & Sbertoli, Ltd., (AV) ....140 South Milwaukee Ave.

Hart, Patrick J. '49 '72 C&L.209 B.A., J.D.
728 Florsheim Drive, 60048-2015
Telephone: 847-680-7240 Fax: 847-816-6122
URL: http://www.patrickhartlaw.com
General Practice, Bankruptcy, Family Law, Estate Planning, Taxes, Real Estate.

See Professional Biographies, LIBERTYVILLE, ILLINOIS

Helander, Willard R., (Mrs.) '52 '78
C.500 B.A. L.838 J.D. Exec. Dir., TMA of Central Lake Co.
Hermann, James J., Jr., (AV) '36 '61
C.424 L.209 LL.B. [Hermann&H.] (⊙Gainesville, FL)
Hermann, James R., (BV) ....'58 '86 C.276 B.S. L.209 J.D. [Hermann&H.]
Hermann, Jennifer M. ....'65 '90 C.339 B.A. L.145 J.D. [Hermann&H.]
Hermann & Hermann, P.C., (AV) ....516 North Milwaukee Avenue
Heuberger, Steven R. ....'42 '69 C.339 B.S. L.209 J.D. P.O. Box 7110
Hoover, Earl L., (AV) ....'43 '71 C.399 B.A. L.597 J.D. [Flannery,H.&B.]
Johnson, Kevin Ross ....'59 '87 C.579 B.A. L.585 J.D. [Ⓐ G.L.Schlesinger]
Johnston, Jay J., (AV) ....'42 '67 C.436 B.S. L.602 LL.B. 516 N. Milwaukee Ave.
Jones, William J. ....'41 '70 C.252 B.S.Ph. L.365 J.D. 611 S. Milwaukee Ave.‡
Kahn, Donald W., Law Office of, (AV) '46 '74 C.589 B.S. L.365 J.D.
728 Florsheim Dr.

Kaplan, Matthew, & Associates, (BV) '48 '79 C.393 B.A. L.146 J.D.
611 S. Milwaukee Avenue, Suite 5, 60048
Telephone: 847-918-7077 Fax: 847-918-0974
Email: matt@mkaplanlaw.com URL: http://www.matthewkaplanlawfirm.com
—Sara L. Roberts.
Family Law, Divorce, Adoptions, Child Custody, Child Support, Domestic Violence, Spousal Support.

See Professional Biographies, LIBERTYVILLE, ILLINOIS

Kearns, Michael P. ....'36 '69 C.57 B.A. L.597 J.D. 1223 Deer Trail Ln.
Kessler, Jerald A., (BV) '47 '73 C&L.145 B.A., J.D.
14047 W. Petronella Dr., Ste. 202B
Kuhlman, Michone J., (BV) '67 '96
C.350 B.S. L.1059 J.D. [Ⓐ Swanson,M.&B.] (⊙Waukegan)
Lake, Thomas M., (BV) ....'64 '89 C.357 B.A. L.365 J.D. [Dudley&L.]

Lang, Howard M., (AV) '45 '74 C.589 B.A. L.146 J.D.
Werchek Professional Centre, Suite 11, 700 Florsheim Drive, 60048-3253
Telephone: 847-367-4460 FAX: 847-367-0090
Email: howardmlang@cs.com URL: http://www.hlanglaw.com
Business and Estate Planning, Estate Administration, Probate.

Larson, Steven L., (AV) '52 '77
C.339 B.A. L.910 J.D. [Swanson,M.&B.] (⊙Chicago, Waukegan)
Leaf, Sharon A. ....'61 '86 C.339 B.A. L.146 J.D. Sr. Corp. Coun., Hollister Incorporated
Lee, Robert E., Jr. ....'57 '85 C.602 B.S. L.424 J.D. 1411 Allyson Ct.
Levin, Robin B. ....'68 '99 C.339 B.S. L.365 J.D. [Ⓐ Cassiday,S.&G.]
Llamzon, Georgia Cullen '45 '80
C.813 A.B. L.424 J.D. Sr. Corp. Coun., Hollister Incorporated
Loftus, Cole ....'53 '96 C.1016 B.S.B.A L.972 J.D. 114 W. Lake St.
LoMonaco, Peter F., (BV) ....'52 '77 C.801 B.S. L.146 J.D. [P.F.LoMonaco]
LoMonaco, Peter F., P.C., (BV) ....200 N. Milwaukee Ave.
Lonchar, Donald M., Jr., (AV) '23 '55
C.597 B.S. L.209 J.D. 901 Florsheim Dr., Apt. 364‡
Lotysz, Joseph ....'47 '82 C.209 B.S. L.365 J.D. 1116 Trevor Circle
Madden, Carole ....'48 '76 C.339 B.A. L.365 J.D. 1117 S. Milwaukee Ave., Ste. A-13
Marcus, Steven J. ....'63 '88 C.339 B.S. L.597 J.D. [Ray&G.]

Martinovich, Bogdan, (AV) '50 '74 C.1183 B.A. L.209 J.D.
611 S. Milwaukee Avenue, 60048
Telephone: 847-970-3845 Fax: 847-680-9756
Email: martinovichlaw@earthlink.net URL: http://www.bogdanmartinovich.com
Personal Injury, Automobile Accidents, Dog Bites, Nursing Home Abuse, Slip and Fall, Products Liability, Wrongful Death, Medical Malpractice, Head and Spinal Injuries, Commercial Litigation.

See Professional Biographies, LIBERTYVILLE, ILLINOIS

McCollum, Steven P., P.C., Law Offices of
(See Waukegan)

McNeil, James D. '38 '69 C.815 B.S. L.851 J.D.
(adm. in OH; not adm. in IL; Pat.) 657 Sedgwick Dr.
Melius, Jacquelyn Dolores ....'74 '00 C.597 B.A. L.365 J.D. [Ⓐ Dudley&L.]
Mittelman, Richard S., P.C. '51 '83 C.339 B.A. L.146 J.D.
[DeSanto,M.&M.A.&Assoc.]
Monahan, Peter R., (AV) ....'38 '63 C.215 A.B. L.477 J.D. 4491 Westchester Lane
Morgan, Vernon E., P.C. ....'47 '77 C.339 B.A. L.221 J.D. [DeSanto,M.&M.A.&Assoc.]
Nader, Burl F., (BV) ....'21 '49 C.191 B.A. L.477 LL.B. 262 Florence Ct.
Nelson, Scott M. ....'62 '93 C.339 B.A. L.365 J.D. 746 Seventh Ave.
Newland, Charles T. ....'62 '88 C.339 B.S. L.365 J.D. [Newland,N.&N.] ⊙
Newland, Gary A. ....'68 '93 C&L.424 B.S., J.D. [Newland,N.&N.] ⊙
Newland, Stephen S. ....'66 '91 C.339 B.A. L.209 J.D. [Newland,N.&N.] ⊙

Newland, Newland & Newland
1512 Artaivs Parkway, 60048 ⊙
Telephone: 847-549-0000 Fax: 847-549-1908
Email: newlandglaw@aol.com URL: http://www.newlandlawfirm.com
Gary A. Newland; Charles T. Newland; Stephen S. Newland.
General Practice, Personal Injury, Slip & Fall, Auto Accidents.

See Professional Biographies, LIBERTYVILLE, ILLINOIS

O'Malley, John G. ....'63 '90 C.276 B.S. L.339 J.D. Sr. Corp. Coun., Hollister Inc.
Orlando, P. Leonard, Sr. ....'12 '38 C.529 Ph.B. L.128 LL.B. 1580 S. Milwaukee Ave.
Padnos, Joy I. ....'74 '00 C.1168 B.A. L.365 J.D. [Ⓐ Swanson,M.&B.] (⊙Waukegan)
Palmieri, Vincent L., (AV) ....'50 '75 C.339 B.S. L.597 J.D. [Ray&G.]
Pardys, David F., (BV) '57 '82
C.339 B.A. L.146 J.D. [Swanson,M.&B.] (⊙Chicago, Waukegan)

Perrelli, Anthony
(See Deerfield)

Preves, Gregory P. '69 '94 C.118 B.A. L.424 J.D.
Law Clk. to Hon. Fred A. Geiger, Ill. App. Ct., 2nd Dist.
Provenzano, William J., Law Offices of '49 '75
C.589 B.A. L.365 J.D. 1580 S. Milwaukee Ave.
Rallo, Douglas, (BV) ....'53 '79 C.555 B.A. L.365 J.D. [D.Rallo]
Rallo, Douglas, PC, Law Offices of, (BV) ....611 S. Milwaukee Ave.
Ranney, Geo. A., (AV) ....'12 '39 C&L.976 B.A., LL.B. 17370 W. Casey Rd.‡
Rawles, Frederick D., (BV) ....'42 '68 C.602 B.A. L.339 J.D. [F.D.Rawles]
Rawles, Frederick D., P.C., (BV) ....P.O. Box 6250
Ray & Glick, Ltd., (AV) ....611 S. Milwaukee Avenue
Reding-Brubaker, Tami J., (BV) .....'58 '83 C.578 B.A. L.146 J.D. [Ⓒ Cassiday,S.&G.]
Reid, John J., (BV) ....'71 '96 C.597 B.A. L.146 J.D. [Cassiday,S.&G.]
Reid, John L., (BVⓉ) ....'54 '79 C.502 B.A. L.846 J.D. P.O. Box 7164

Richards, Ralph & Schwab, Chartered
(See Veronon Hills)

Roach, Michael L., (AV) ....'41 '66 C.210 B.A. L.339 J.D. 516 N. Milwaukee Ave.
Roberts, Sara L. ....'73 '01 C.338 B.S. L.146 J.D. [Ⓐ M.Kaplan&Assoc.]
Ryan, Dennis P., Jr., (BV) ....'71 '97 C.1375 B.S. L.146 J.D. [Ryan]
Ryan, Dennis P., Sr. ....'40 '66 C.339 B.A. L.597 J.D. [Ryan]
Ryan, Lois B. ....'41 '66 C&L.597 B.A., J.D. [Ryan]
Ryan Law Office, Ltd., (BV) ....1580 S. Milwaukee Ave., Suite 410
Sachs, George M. ....'47 '79 C.339 B.A. L.146 J.D. 712 Florsheim Dr.
Saxon, Jerome A. ....'48 '75 C.597 B.A. L.146 J.D. V.P., Law, Hollister Inc.
Sbertoli, Thomas L., (AV) ....'46 '76 C.1151 B.A. L.146 J.D. [Graham,G.&S.]
Schiever, Carey J., (BV) ....'48 '73 C.210 B.A. L.910 J.D. [C.J.Schiever]

Schiever, Carey J., Ltd., (BV)
1512 Artaius Parkway, Suite 300, 60048
Telephone: 847-680-1123 FAX: 847-680-1124
Email: cjschiever@ameritech.net URL: http://www.lawyers.com/schieverlaw
Carey J. Schiever.
General Business Practice. Corporate, Estate Planning, Business Planning, Real Estate, Construction, Probate and Financial Institutions and Foreclosure.

See Professional Biographies, LIBERTYVILLE, ILLINOIS

Schippers, Thomas M. ....'60 '93 C.591 B.S. L.424 J.D. [Ⓒ Dudley&L.]
Schlax, Peter M., (BV) ....'59 '86 C.112 B.A. L.339 J.D. [Ⓐ Dudley&L.]

Schlesinger, Gary L., (AV) '45 '71 C.424 B.S. L.597 J.D. BB
Suite 300, 1512 Artaius Parkway, P.O. Box 6229, 60048
Telephone: 847-680-4970 Fax: 847-680-5459
Email: glschles@lawoffice.com URL: http://www.lawyers.com/schlesingerlaw
Associate: Kevin Ross Johnson.
Trials and Appeals of Divorce, Custody, Support, Paternity, Adoption, Family Law and Domestic Relations.

See Professional Biographies, LIBERTYVILLE, ILLINOIS

Schrum, Betty-Jane, (AV) ....'52 '83 C.390 B.S.N. L.823 J.D. 920 Burridge Court
Schwager, Michael L. ....'43 '86 C.597 B.S. L.146 J.D. App. Offr., I.R.S.
Schwartzman, Eva ....'08 '31 C&L.823 B.A., LL.B. 1590 S. Milwaukee Ave., 3rd Fl.
Shaul, John P. '— '91 C.107 B.A. L.851 J.D.
(adm. in MI; not adm. in IL) 31217 Prairie Ridge Rd.‡
Sieman, Michael M., (BV) ....'40 '69 C.742 B.A. L.146 J.D. [M.Sieman]
Sieman, Michael, (BV) ....130 E. Church St.
Snow, Mark H. ....'50 '77 C.436 A.B. L.146 J.D. 1216 Virginia Ave.
Solms, Evon S. ....'52 '85 C.339 B.A. L.424 J.D. DRH Cambridge Home
Spring, Linda E., (BV) '45 '83
C.494 B.S. L.424 J.D. [Swanson,M.&B.] (⊙Chicago, Waukegan)
Steffens, John L. ....'21 '50 C.424 B.A. L.597 J.D. 755 So. Milwaukee Ave.
Stutzman, Stacey L., (BV) ....'52 '79 C.339 B.S. L.209 J.D. 1242 Deer Trail Lane.
Surdyk, Thomas M. ....'49 '78 C.801 B.A. L.1151 J.D. 1200 Amy Ln.

Suskin, Marlon T. '71 '96
731 N. Milwaukee Avenue, 60048
Telephone: 847-680-1902
Email: msk@yahoo.com URL: http://www.marlonsuskinlawoffice.com
Real Estate, Collection, Family Law.

See Professional Biographies, LIBERTYVILLE, ILLINOIS

Sutter, David W., (BV) ....'37 '83 C.177 B.A. L.1209 J.D. 339 N. Milwaulkee Ave.

Swanson, Martin & Bell, (AV)
1860 West Winchester Road, Suite 201, 60048 ⊙
Telephone: 847-949-0025 Fax: 847-247-0555
URL: http://www.smbtrials.com
Partners: Steven L. Larson; David F. Pardys; Linda E. Spring; John A. Terselic. Associates: David S. Goles; Michone J. Kuhlman; Joy I. Padnos.
Class Action Lawsuits, Commercial Litigation, Construction Litigation/Disputes, Consumer and Warranty Law, Creditor's Rights, Drugs & Medical Devices, Employment Litigation, Environmental Law, Equipment Leasing, General Tort Liability, Healthcare, Insurance Coverage, Intellectual Property, Medical Negligence, Municipal Law, Product Liability, Professional Negligence, Real Estate Development/Zoning, Real Estate Litigation, Toxic and Mass Tort Litigation, and White Collar Criminal Defense.
Chicago, Illinois Office: 330 North Wabash, Suite 3300, 60611. Telephone: 312-321-9100. Fax: 312-321-0990.
Waukegan, Illinois, Satellite Office: 415 Washington Street, Suite 1B, Waukegan, Illinois, 60085. Telephone: 847-949-0025. Fax: 847-247-0555.
DuPage County, Illinois Office: 2525 Cabot Drive, Lisle, Illinois, 60532. Telephone: 630-799-6900. Fax: 630-799-6901.

See Professional Biographies, LIBERTYVILLE, ILLINOIS

Terselic, John A. '67 '92 C.801 B.A. L.209 J.D. [Swanson,M.&B.] (©Chicago, Waukegan)
Thompson, Paul E., (AV) '37 '61 C.945 L.339 LL.B. Gen. Coun., Aldridge Electric, Inc.
Thut, C. Jeffrey, (BV) '59 '84 C.338 B.S. L.879 J.D. 516 N. Milwaukee Ave.

Vanderwoude, Robbin D., (BV) '54 '81 C.1183 B.A. L.365 J.D.
1580 South Milwaukee Avenue, Suite 403, 60048
Telephone: 847-680-8508 Fax: 847-680-8878
URL: http://www.lawyers.com/rvanderwoude
Family Law, Divorce, Child Support, Child Custody, Visitation Rights, Legal Separation, Alimony, Post Divorce Modification.
Know Your Rights! Caring Female Attorney Concentrating in all Areas of Family Law.
See Professional Biographies, LIBERTYVILLE, ILLINOIS

Voegtle, Clayton P., (BV) '42 '71 C.801 B.A. L.209 J.D. 14047 West Petronella Drive
Wagener, Robert R. '23 '52 C.424 L.365 J.D. 811 Maywood Ct.‡
Warren, Raymond J. '57 '83 C&L.623 B.S.E.E., J.D. Dir., Motorola Law Dept. (Pat.)
Watanabe, Hisashi David '67 '93 C.910 B.S.E.E. L.424 J.D. (adm. in PA; not adm. in IL; Pat.) Pat. Atty., Motorola, Inc.
Weathers, Doyle M. '30 '53 C&L.502 A.B., LL.B. Sr. V.P., First of Amer. Tr. Co.
Weppler, Terry L., (BV) '51 '91 C.927 B.S. L.365 J.D. [T.Weppler]
Weppler, Terry, (BV) 121 W. Church St.
Wiesch, Daniel E. '75 '01 C.597 B.A. L.339 J.D. [Cassiday,S.&G.]
Williams, Lalita '62 '94 C.329 B.S.E.E. L.273 J.D. Motorola, Inc. (Pat.)
Winn, Michael C. '36 '64 C.424 B.S. L.209 J.D. Hollister Inc.

LINCOLN, * 15,418, *Logan Co.*

Barry, Robert J. '47 '72 C.303 A.B. L.221 J.D. 227 Delavan St.
Bates, William B., (AV) '54 '79 C.934 B.A. L.221 J.D. [Woods&B.] (©Springfield)
Blanford, Frederick L., (CV) '41 '67 C&L.339 A.B., J.D. 131 N. Logan St.
Burgrabe, Nick F., (BV) '57 '81 C&L.801 B.A., J.D. 419 Pulaski Street
Coogan, David L. '43 '68 C.927 B.A. L.339 J.D. Cir. J.
Dehner, Gerald G. '42 '72 C.880 B.A. L.910 J.D. Cir. J.
Fulton, E. M., Jr., (BV) '33 '56 C.586 B.A. L.846 J.D. [Harris&H.] (©Springfield)

Funk, Thomas W., The Law Office of, (BV) '59 '84 C.234 B.S. L.347 J.D.
427 Pulaski Street, 62656
Telephone: 217-735-1000 Fax: 217-735-5752 URL: http://www.tfunklaw.com
Email: tfunk@verizon.net URL: http://www.funklaw.com
Family Law, Adoption Law, Criminal Law, Real Estate, Probate, Bankruptcy, Social Security Disability, Wills, Trusts, Estates.
See Professional Biographies, LINCOLN, ILLINOIS

Gehlbach, John R., (BV) '20 '49 C.118 B.A. L.597 J.D. 529 Pulaski St.
Harris, Homer B., Jr., (AV) '26 '50 C.477 B.A. L.339 J.D. [Harris&H.]
Harris, Thomas M., (AV) '23 '49 C&L.597 J.D. [Harris&H.]

Harris & Harris, (AV)
9-11 Griesheim Building, 62656
Telephone: 217-732-8484; 732-6544 Fax: 217-732-3912
Members of Firm: Homer B. Harris (1896-1959); Thomas M. Harris. Of Counsel: Homer B. Harris, Jr.; Charles W. Nauts; E. M. Fulton, Jr.
Real Estate, Wills, Trusts and Commercial Law.
Representative Clients: Lincoln College; Farmers Bank of Mount Pulaski; State Bank of Latham; Middletown State Bank; Bank of Chestnut; New Holland-Middletown School District; Logan County Housing Authority.
Reference: State Bank of Lincoln.

Huyett, Timothy J. '56 '86 C&L.801 B.A., J.D. State's Atty.
Klink, Darrell E., Attorney at Law, (BV) '27 '53 C&L.339 B.A., J.D. 1 Lincoln Professional Park
McCullough, John T. '31 '55 L.339 LL.B. App. Ct. J.
Miller, Burke, (AV) '23 '46 C.118 B.A. L.145 J.D. [Miller&M.] ‡
Miller, Stephen L., (CV) '51 '78 C.597 B.A. L.146 J.D. [Miller&M.]
Miller and Miller, (CV) 105 N. Kickapoo St.
Mills, Edwin C., III '55 '92 C.801 B.S. L.107 J.D. (adm. in NY; not adm. in IL) 513 Broadway St.
Montalvo, Phillip A. '46 '70 C&L.436 A.B., J.D. 529 Pulaski St.
Muck, Douglas A., (BV) '53 '79 C.339 B.S. L.910 J.D. 207 S. Mclean St.
Muck, Laurie E., (CV) '54 '80 C.94 B.A. L.910 J.D. Century Bldg., Ste. 2
Nauts, Charles W. '30 '56 C&L.145 A.B., J.D. [Harris&H.]
Peacock, Aaron Michael '65 '98 C.679 B.S. L.589 J.D. Asst. States Atty.
Peters, Warren, (BV) '29 '54 C&L.339 B.S., J.D. 515 Bway.
Shumaker, Robert Thomas '74 '00 C.338 B.S. L.801 J.D. Law Clk., Appl. Ct.
Van Hook, Thomas L., Law Offices of '63 '95 C.589 B.S. L.1339 J.D. P.O. Box 305

Woods & Bates, (AV)
306 Clinton Street, 62656
Telephone: 217-735-1234 Fax: 217-735-1236
Email: bilbates@ccaonline.com
William B. Bates.
General Practice. Probate, Trusts and Estates, Wills, Real Estate and Collections.
Representative Clients: Illico Incorporated; The Abraham Lincoln Memorial Hospital; Lincoln Firemen's Pension Fund; Mt. Pulaski Products; Lincoln Christian College and Seminary; Lincoln Police Pension Fund; Construction Equipment Federal Credit Union; City of Lincoln.
See Professional Biographies, LINCOLN, ILLINOIS

LINCOLNSHIRE, 6,108, *Lake Co.*

Ahrendt, Lorraine B. '58 '83 C.114 B.A. L.347 J.D. 100 Half Day Rd.
Bach, Mark C. '66 '92 C.597 B.A. L.424 J.D. Corp. Atty., Intell. Prop., Snap-On Technologies (Pat.)
Ballentine, Andrew V. '48 '78 C.174 B.A. L.468 J.D. Corp. Coun., Sauer-Danfoss Inc.
Baugh, David A., (AV) '54 '79 C.280 B.B.A. L.838 J.D. [Mora,B.W.&U.] ©
Bergin, Roderick J. '69 '97 C.209 B.A. L.770 J.D. Takeda Pharmaceuticals North America
Blecher, M. David '46 '80 C.999 B.A. L.46 J.D. Hewitt Associates
Brandwein, Michael K. '53 '78 C.339 B.A. L.145 J.D. 5 Coventry Lane
Brown, L. Sheldon '11 '36 C&L.597 B.S., J.D. 53 Lincolnshire Dr.‡
Campbell, Lee A. '43 '69 C.976 B.A. L.339 J.D. [L.A.Campbell]
Campbell, Lee A., P.C. 175 Olde Half Day Rd.
Chao, Mark '62 '96 C.339 Ph.D. L.365 J.D. Intel. Property Coun., Takeda Pharmaceuticals North America, Inc. (Pat.)
Clark, Steven W. '70 '95 C.932 B.B.A. L.477 J.D. (adm. in MI; not adm. in IL) Hewitt Assocs.
Cohen, Barry Jerol '40 '74 C.1016 B.S.B.A. L.146 J.D. 514 Rivershire Pl.
Composto, Dennis V., Law Office of '64 '91 C.209 B.A. L.365 J.D. 100 Village Green Dr., Ste. 200
Condo, Joseph D. '66 '91 C.112 B.A. L.800 J.D. Sr. Coun., Calpine Corp.
Connolly, C. Lawrence, III '47 '72 C.602 B.B.A. L.309 J.D. Gen. Coun., Hewitt Assocs.
Contreni, Rachel A. '69 '94 C.347 B.A. L.424 J.D. Coun., Fortune Brands, Inc.
Cook, Marguerite D. '22 '72 C.862 B.A. L.424 J.D. Hewitt Assoc.
D'Angelo, Arnold F., Jr. '59 '86 C.1156 B.S. L.273 J.D. Assoc. Gen. Coun., Takeda Pharmaceuticals North America, Inc.
D'Arcy, Anita M. '57 '82 C&L.424 A.B., J.D. 100 Half Day Rd.
Dubas, Marlene C. '51 '76 C.475 B.A. L.145 J.D. Gen. Coun. & Secy., Takeda Pharmaceuticals North America, Inc.
England, John M., Jr. '49 '89 C.174 B.S. L.128 J.D. (adm. in PA; not adm. in IL; Pat.) 420 Barclay Blvd.
Fleisher, Marianne Savaiano '51 '85 C.1183 L.365 321 Rivershire Ct.
Foster, Julia Anne '60 '85 C.477 B.A. L.861 J.D. 45 Berkshire Lane
Freund, Charles G. '23 '56 C.999 B.S. L.365 LL.B. 30 Plymouth Ct.‡
Gardner, John D. '47 '74 C.367 B.A. L.608 J.D. (adm. in IN; not adm. in IL) Hewitt Assoc.
Gilford, Ronald M., (Ltd.) '27 '51 C&L.209 J.D. 205 Rivershire Lane
Grundei, August A. '33 '59 L.424 J.D. 44 Oxford Dr.
Hasegawa, Nancy L. '47 '78 C&L.339 B.A., J.D. Hewitt Assoc.
Healy, Christopher R. '54 '79 C.31 B.A. L.184 J.D. 100 Half Day Road
Herst, Michael A. '55 '80 C.339 B.S. L.424 J.D. 27 Berkshire Ln.‡
Hoos, John O. '44 '69 C.165 A.B. L.228 J.D. Hewitt Assoc.
Hubley, Ralph I., III '46 '73 C.454 B.A. L.597 J.D. V.P., Gen. Coun., Sec., Gateway Advisors, Inc.
Jain, Stasha '71 '98 C.145 B.A. L.477 J.D. Hewitt Associates LLC
Johnston, Jeffrey S. '61 '86 C.339 B.S. L.209 J.D. 250 Parkway Dr.
Kendrick, Matthew J. '62 '87 C.973 B.S.B.A. L.607 J.D. (adm. in IN; not adm. in IL) V.P. Gen. Coun., Mitsubishi Lithographic Presses
Kohn, Amy H. '67 '93 C.477 B.A. L.597 J.D. Hewitt Assocs.
Lane, Elizabeth Rourke '66 '91 C.93 B.A. L.597 J.D. Fortune Brands Inc.
Leon, Jack J., Law Offices of '46 '71 C.339 B.A. L.209 J.D. P.O. Box 814
Lewis, Jay Michael '75 '00 C.339 B.S. L.1119 J.D. 100 Half Day Road
Liebman, David L. '54 '83 C.165 A.B. L.209 J.D. CB Commercial Real Estate Group Inc.
Loewenstein, Pamela B. '56 '80 C.597 B.S. L.910 J.D. 4 Anglican Ln.‡
Long, George E. '23 '51 C&L.352 B.A., J.D. Hewitt Assoc.
Luxenberg, Steven B. '55 '81 C.339 B.A. L.800 J.D. (adm. in CA; not adm. in IL) 66 Riverwoods Rd.‡
Maddock, Raymond R., Jr. '51 '76 C.686 B.A. L.597 J.D. 100 Half Day Rd.
Matter, Monica R. '75 '01 C.264 B.A. L.912 J.D. Corp. Coun., Takeda Pharmaceuticals North America, Inc.
Mills, John W. '31 '59 C.674 A.B. L.309 LL.B. 100 Tri-State Intl.
Milstead, Cynthia W. '58 '87 C.339 A.B. L.228 J.D. 100 Half Day Rd.
Mohr, Rachel '68 '94 C&L.879 B.A., J.D. 100 Half Day Road
Moody, Marvin '24 '48 C.350 B.S.E.E. L.352 J.D. 20 Melrose Lane (Pat.)
Mora, Steven H., (AV) '44 '68 C.1036 B.A. L.309 J.D. [Mora,B.W.&U.] ©
Mora, Baugh, Waitzman & Unger, (AV) 250 Parkway Drive, Suite 130 (©Chicago)
Morrow, Stanley D. '38 '70 C.494 B.S. L.146 J.D. Hewitt Assoc.
Nelson, Andrew F. '70 '96 C.210 B.A. L.424 J.D. [D.M.Nelson]
Nelson, David M., (AV) '37 '62 C.813 B.A. L.597 J.D. [D.M.Nelson]
Nelson, David M., LLC, (AV) 7 Court of Wilmington
Novy, Michael "Ted" '72 '97 C.602 B.B.A. L.209 J.D. General Counsel, Hewitt Assocs.
Para, Gerard A. '53 '77 C&L.209 B.A., J.D. P.O. Box 450
Patterson, G. Douglas '58 '84 C.880 B.S. L.597 J.D. V.P. & Gen. Coun., Ivex Packaging Corp.
Press, Alan R. '— '93 C.276 B.S.B.A. L.424 J.D. 250 Parkway Dr.
Ramesh, Elaine M. '62 '97 C.107 B.S. L.146 J.D. Patent Coun., Takeda Pharmaceuticals, NA, Inc.
Ricaurte, Michael E. '71 '96 C.57 B.A. L.424 J.D. Design Consult., Hewitt Associates LLC‡
Rivkin, Larry R. '67 '94 C.813 B.A. L.145 J.D. [Rivkin&R.]
Rivkin, Michele '68 '94 C.373 B.A. L.597 J.D. [Rivkin&R.]
Rivkin & Rivkin, LLC 185 Milwaukee Ave.
Roche, Mark A. '54 '80 C.893 B.A. L.188 J.D. (adm. in NY; not adm. in IL) Sr. V.P., Gen. Coun. & Secy., Fortune Brands
Roque, Francisco A. '59 '84 C.339 B.A. L.276 J.D. 100 Half Day Rd.
Rose, Kenton R. '57 '84 C.399 B.A. L.94 J.D. (adm. in CT; not adm. in IL) Vice President & Associate General Counsel, Fortune Brands, Inc.
Ross, Peter E. '59 '84 C.339 B.S. L.597 J.D. Hewitt Assocs.
Schaper, David E. '53 '82 C.475 B.A. L.477 J.D. 11 Oxford Dr.
Schulte, Kathleen B. '60 '88 C&L.93 B.A., J.D. Coun., American Brands, Inc.
Schwanke Hallee, Michele L. '68 '00 C&L.209 B.A., J.D. Hewitt Assocs.
Simmons, John P. '62 '93 C.549 B.S. L.128 J.D. Assoc. Gen. Coun., Takeda Pharmaceuticals North America, Inc., Employ.
Stein, Judith Lynn '56 '90 C.393 B.A. L.424 J.D. Coun., Hewitt and Assoc., LLC
Steinberg, Allen T. '54 '79 C.659 B.A. L.597 J.D. Hewitt Associates
Sterling, Michael J. '— '76 L.146 J.D. [M.J.Sterling]
Sterling, Michael J., P.C. P.O. Box 258
Stern, Barbara L. '37 '79 C.679 B.S. L.365 J.D. Hewitt Assos.
Strange, Gerald '46 '79 C.339 B.A. L.365 J.D. 32 Essex Ln.
Sundberg, Paul A. '69 '95 C.802 B.S. L.861 J.D. Sr. Coun., Takeda Pharmaceuticals North America, Inc.
Tashma, Lauren S. '66 '91 C.597 B.A. L.424 J.D. 300 Tower Pkwy.
Thomas, John J. '44 '84 C.879 B.A. L.424 J.D. Pres., First Union Rail Corp.

Tressler, Soderstrom, Maloney & Priess
(See Chicago)

Unger, Linda E., (AV) '54 '79 C.339 B.A. L.146 J.D. [Mora,B.W.&U.] ©
Van Duzer, John B., Jr. '56 '80 C.399 B.A. L.597 J.D. Gen. Coun., Hewitt Assocs.
Waitzman, Gary R. '52 '80 C.339 B.S. L.365 J.D. [Mora,B.W.&U.] ©
Whitehead, Matthew J., II '40 '66 C.860 B.A. L.329 J.D. (adm. in NY; not adm. in IL) Vice President & Executive Counsel, Motient Corporation
Wunsch, Gerald E. '46 '71 C.197 A.B. L.276 J.D. 100 Half Day Rd.
Yamaya, Julie M. '55 '83 C.339 B.S. L.597 J.D. 100 Half Day Rd.
Zammuto, Carmela T. '51 '80 C.741 B.A. L.209 J.D. Dep. Gen. Coun., Takeda Pharmaceuticals North America, Inc.

LINCOLNWOOD, 12,359, *Cook Co.*

Abrams, Max A. '20 '47 C.999 L.209 LL.B. 6676 N. Lincoln Ave.
Adler, Ericka L. '71 '96 C.787 B.S. L.209 J.D. [Kamensky,R.H.&D.] ©
Alter, Michael '61 '87 C.309 B.A. L.145 J.D. The Alter Grp.
Aufrecht, Michael D. '40 '65 C.339 B.S. L.597 J.D. [Aufrecht E.]
Aufrecht Enterprises 3924 West Devon
Axelrad, Norman D. '29 '54 C.477 B.A. L.597 J.D. 6727 N. Lema 1
Baron, Joseph M. '12 '34 C&L.145 Ph.B., J.D. 6700 N. Nokinos Ave.‡
Batler, Michael D. '43 '69 C.1016 B.S.B.A. L.209 J.D. [Kamensky,R.H.&D.] ©

Ben Zeev, Jason Y. . . . . '60 '87 C.813 B.A. L.174 J.D. 6939 Keating Ave.
Bezkorovainy, Anatoly . . . . . '35 '77 C.339 Ph.D. L.146 J.D. 4242 W. Touhy Ave.‡
Bieber, Martin S. . . . . '20 '51 C&L.597 B.S., J.D. 4448 W. Pratt
Blustin, L. Sanford . . . . . '13 '37 L.365 J.D. 6431 N. Cicero Ave.
Boue, Adelqui J. . . . . '70 '96 C.339 B.A. L.365 J.D. 4433 W. Touhy Ave., Ste. 555
Boyance, Jennifer . . . . . '67 '99 C&L.209 B.S., J.D. 4433 W. Touhy Avenue Suite 301
Brody, Barry T. . . . . . '43 '68 C.477 B.B.A. L.597 J.D. 6444 N. Kolmar Ave.
Brohman, Michael B., (AV) . . . . . '54 '79 C.339 B.A. L.597 J.D. [Kamensky,R.H.&D.] ⊙
Butler, Adrienne . . . . . '51 '04 C.103 A.B. L.424 J.D. [A Kamensky,R.H.&D.]
Carroll, Howard W., (AV) '42 '67
C.1016 B.S.B.A. L.209 J.D. [C Kamensky,R.H.&D.] ⊙
Chotalia, Tushar . . . . . '57 '89 C.999 B.Com. L.365 J.D. [T.Chotalia]
Chotalia, Tushar, PC . . . . . 6512 N. Nokomis Ave.

Cutler & Associates, LTD.
(See Skokie)

DeKelaita, Robert W., The Law Office of '62 '97
C.339 B.A. L.424 J.D. 6600 North Lincoln Avenue, Suite 200
Delott, Avery, (AV) . . . . . '47 '72 C.339 B.S. L.597 J.D. [Kamensky,R.H.&D.] ⊙
Erens, Michael G., (AV) . . . . . '44 '69 C.966 B.S. L.209 J.D. [Kamensky,R.H.&D.] ⊙
Ericsson, Robert D. . . . . . '29 '58 C.57 A.B. L.146 LL.B. 6822 Knox
Feehan, Jean Grommes . . . . . '41 '66 C.597 B.A. L.146 J.D. 6525 N. Nokomis
Ghezzi, Sheryl R., (BV) . . . . . '55 '84 C.393 B.A. L.365 J.D. [S.R.Ghezzi]

Ghezzi, Sheryl Rae, (BV)
4433 West Touhy, Suite 301, 60712
Telephone: 847-675-7570 Fax: 847-673-0948
Email: ghezziatlaw@aol.com URL: http://www.ghezzilaw.com
Sheryl R. Ghezzi.
Languages: Romanian, English, Aramic and Italian.
Civil Litigation, Family Law, Child Custody, Divorce, Premarital Agreements, D.U.I., Drug Crimes, Juvenile Crimes, Misdemeanors, Traffic, DUI Defense, Immigration, Wills and Probate, Divorce, Child Support, Visitation Interference, Visitation Abuse, Personal Injury Defense, Property Damage Defense, Estate Planning, Real Estate Litigation.
See Professional Biographies, LINCOLNWOOD, ILLINOIS

Gimbel, Stuart M., (BV) . . . . . '61 '86 C.597 B.S. L.893 J.D. [Kamensky,R.H.&D.] ⊙
Grandi, Michael M. . . . . . '59 '86 C&L.424 B.S., J.D. 7101 N. Cicero, Ste. 110
Greenstein, Charles A. '27 '53
C&L.424 B.S., J.D. Sr. V.P., The First Natl. Bk. of Lincolnwood
Grossman, Raymon A. . . . . . '45 '73 C.1016 B.A. L.146 J.D. [R.A.Grossman&Assoc.]
Grossman, Raymon A., & Associates, P.C. . . . . . 7101 N. Cicero Avenue
Gryll, Charles R. . . . . . '51 '77 C.861 B.A. L.365 J.D. [C.R.Gryll]
Gryll, Charles R., Ltd. . . . . . 6703 N. Cicero Avenue
Gussin, Alan . . . . . '57 '82 C.910 A.B. L.145 J.D. 7010 E. Prairie Rd.
Hochman, David J., (AV) . . . . . '46 '73 C.502 B.A. L.339 J.D. [Kamensky,R.H.&D.] ⊙
Kagan, Andrew B. . . . . . '49 '80 C.823 B.A. L.1292 J.D. 7358 N. Lincoln, Ste. 130
Kamensky, Marvin, (Ltd.), (AV) '39 '66 C.339 B.S. L.209 J.D.
[Kamensky,R.H.&D.] ⊙

Kamensky, Rubinstein, Hochman & Delott, LLP, (AV)
An LLP Including Professional Corporations
Suite 200, 7250 North Cicero Avenue, 60712-1693 ⊙
Telephone: 847-982-1776 Telecopier: 847-982-1676
URL: http://www.kr-law.com
Marvin Kamensky (Ltd.); Sherwin R. Rubinstein; Michael G. Erens; Ben M. Roth; Michael B. Brohman; David J. Hochman; Avery Delott; Roger B. Mandel; Stuart M. Gimbel; Miles J. Zaremski; Dorothy Voss Ward; James K. Shaw; Lee J. Levin; John B. Waters; Ericka L. Adler. Associates: Alon Stein; Adrienne Butler. Of Counsel: Howard W. Carroll (Also with Carroll & Sain); Kenneth W. Sain (Also with Carroll & Sain); Samuel H. Young; Joseph L. Matz; Michael D. Batler.
Health Care, Taxation, Corporate Real Estate, Pension and Employee Benefits, Estate Planning and Probate, Bankruptcy, and Commercial Litigation.
Chicago, Illinois Office: Suite 4300, 30 North LaSalle Street, 60602. Telephone: 312-368-1776; 312-807-3960. Telecopier: 312-807-3652. (By Appointment Only)

Klein, Jane K. . . . . . '58 '82 C.339 B.A. L.146 J.D. 3940 Arthur Ave.
Kolnick, Alice . . . . . '19 '45 C&L.209 M.A., J.D. 4760 Devon Ave.
Kotin, Merritt R. . . . . . '24 '48 C&L.597 B.S.L., J.D. 3819 W. Jarlath Ave.‡
Kritikos, Nicholas J. . . . . . '56 '82 C.339 B.A. L.424 J.D. 3940 W. Touhy Ave.
Levin, Lee J. . . . . . '61 '86 C&L.339 B.A., J.D. [Kamensky,R.H.&D.] ⊙
Liebman, Jeffrey R., (AV) '46 '73 C.210 B.A. L.910 J.D.
Gen. Coun., Bk. of Lincolnwood
Liss, Cindy Rae . . . . . '56 '85 C.966 B.S. L.146 J.D. 6526 N. Keating Avenue
Locker, Charles . . . . . '35 '59 C.339 L.365 LL.B. 4433 W. Touhy Ave.
Mandel, Roger B., (AV) . . . . . '39 '66 C.339 B.S. L.146 J.D. [Kamensky,R.H.&D.] ⊙
Matz, Joseph L., (AV) . . . . . '29 '54 C&L.339 B.A., J.D. [C Kamensky,R.H.&D.] ⊙
Meyer, Morton H. . . . . . '18 '41 L.209 J.D. 3832 Chase Ave.‡
Milburn, Joe R. . . . . . '52 '77 C.589 B.S. L.424 J.D. 7366 N. Lincoln Avenue, Suite 206
Miller, Charles D. '40 '64 C&L.966 B.B.A., J.D.
Fin. & Estate Planner, The Lubin-Bergman Organization, Inc.
Motel, Harold . . . . . '21 '46 L.365 4433 W. Touhy Ave.
Motel, Robert A. . . . . . '51 '76 C.339 B.A. L.424 J.D. 4433 W. Touhy Ave.
Novak, Harold Z. . . . . . '15 '39 L.209 J.D. 7000 N. McCormick Blvd.‡
Ochsner, William J. . . . . . '69 '97 C.190 B.A. L.986 J.D. Intl. Sanitary Supply Assn.
Resnick, Carlton R. . . . . . '37 '91 C.188 A.B. L.209 J.D. 6739 N. St. Louis Ave.
Rosengarten, Paul Jay . . . . . '60 '87 C.352 B.A. L.940 J.D. 4560 W. Touhy Ave.
Roth, Ben M., (AV) . . . . . '50 '75 C.339 B.S. L.146 J.D. [Kamensky,R.H.&D.]
Rubinstein, Sherwin R., (AV) . . . '47 '73 C.339 B.A. L.209 J.D. [Kamensky,R.H.&D.] ⊙
Sain, Kenneth W., (AV) . . . . . '37 '66 C.424 B.S. L.880 J.D. [C Kamensky,R.H.&D.] ⊙
Sargis, Marc W. . . . . . '54 '81 C.339 B.A. L.365 J.D. 7366 N. Lincoln Avenue
Schachter, Samuel . . . . . '13 '38 C.999 L.365 J.D. 6676 N. Lincoln Ave.‡
Schwartz, Lawrence Y. . . . . . '45 '73 C.1016 B.A. L.424 J.D. [L.Y.Schwartz]
Schwartz, Lawrence Y., Ltd. . . . . . 7358 N. Lincoln, Ste. 130
Shaw, James K. . . . . . '54 '82 C.339 B.S. L.424 J.D. [Kamensky,R.H.&D.] ⊙
Sherman, Marc D. . . . . . '61 '86 C.339 B.A. L.209 J.D. [M.Sherman]
Sherman, Marc, P.C. . . . . . 3700 W. Devon Ave., Ste. E
Silberman, Renee Birnberg . . . . . '58 '83 C.339 B.S. L.146 J.D. 6951 N. Kedvale‡
Smiley, Gary A. . . . . . '51 '78 C.339 A.B. L.365 J.D. 7250 N. Keeler Ave.
Stein, Alon . . . . . '— '02 C.339 B.A. L.966 J.D. [A Kamensky,R.H.&D.] ⊙
Swidler, Louis, (AV) . . . . . '15 '36 L.365 LL.B. 6440 Christiana Ave.‡
Taylor, Joseph J. '51 '77 C.589 B.S. L.365 J.D.
Gen. Coun., Bell & Howell Financial Services Company
Thompson, John E. . . . . . '46 '73 C.826 B.A. L.365 J.D. 6542 N. Kolmar Ave.‡
Tierney, Gerald M., Jr. '47 '73 C.674 A.B. L.893 J.D.
(adm. in NY; not adm. in IL) 4433 W. Touhy Avenue
Vidakis, Irene '65 '90 C.1278 B.A. L.1206 J.D.
(adm. in FL; not adm. in IL) 7014 N. Keeler
Ward, Dorothy Voss, (BV) . . . . . '49 '81 C.239 B.A. L.146 J.D. [Kamensky,R.H.&D.] ⊙
Warso, Sherman . . . . . '28 '52 C&L.597 B.S., J.D. 6552 N. Christiana Ave.‡
Waters, John B. . . . . . '63 '91 C.350 B.S. L.336 J.D. [Kamensky,R.H.&D.] ⊙
Watson, G. Andrew . . . . . '58 '83 C.197 A.B. L.597 J.D. [Watson&Assoc.]
Watson & Associates . . . . . 7366 N. Lincoln Ave., Suite 305
Westover, Elizabeth M. . . . . . '73 '97 C.999 B.A. L.209 J.D. [E.Westover]
Westover, Elizabeth, Law Offices of . . . . . 4433 W. Touhy, Ste. 301
Wilson, Millard S. . . . . . '22 '48 C.339 L.597 LL.B. 6818 Lowell St.‡
Young, Samuel H., (AV) . . . . . '22 '48 C&L.339 B.S., J.D. [C Kamensky,R.H.&D.] ⊙
Zaremski, Miles J., (AV) . . . . . '48 '73 C.339 B.S. L.930 J.D. [Kamensky,R.H.&D.] ⊙
Zelden, Jerome J., (AV) . . . . . '34 '59 C.339 B.S. L.597 J.D. 4433 Touhy Ave.

LINDENHURST, 12,539, *Lake Co.*

DeRose, David A., (BV) . . . . . '56 '81 C.339 B.A. L.365 J.D. [D.DeRose]

DeRose, David, (BV)
2592 Grand Avenue, Suite 201, 60046
Telephone: 847-265-6700 Fax: 847-265-6701
David A. DeRose.
Personal Injury, Real Estate, Estate Planning, Wills, Corporate Law, Evictions, Foreclosures.
See Professional Biographies, LINDENHURST, ILLINOIS

McGowen, Darrell, (AV) . . . . . '32 '65 C.547 B.A. L.1009 J.D. 331 Poplar Ct.
Romanski, Henry . . . . . '48 '73 C.424 A.B. L.209 J.D. 2217 E. Sand Lake Rd.
Scheurer, William C. '50 '76 C&L.107 B.A., J.D.
(adm. in NJ; not adm. in IL) Pres., Welcome America Retail Marketing Corp.

LISLE, 21,182, *DuPage Co.*

Andrews, Gregory H., (BV) . . . . . '58 '92 C.427 B.A. L.46 J.D. [Andrews K.&P.]

Andrews Koehler & Passarelli, P.C., (BV)
4343 Commerce Court, Suite 615, 60532
Telephone: 630-505-9939 Fax: 630-505-9969
URL: http://www.akplaw.com
Gregory H. Andrews; Renée Koehler; Ronald J. Passarelli;—Isham R. Jones, III; Kerry L. Davidson.
Representing Employers in Labor and Employment Law; Employment Discrimination and Employment-Related Litigation.
See Professional Biographies, LISLE, ILLINOIS

Anthoney, Suzanne Nyhan '61 '91 C&L.424 B.A., J.D.
Pres. & Gen. Coun., Damien Corp.
Aprati, Robert L. '44 '68 C&L.209 B.A., J.D.
Exec V.P., Gen. Coun. & Secy., Budget Rent A Car Corp.
Athas, Leo J., (AV) . . . . . '43 '73 C.339 B.S. L.146 J.D. [Hinshaw&C.] (⊙Chicago)
Bartolotta, Ross W. . . . . . '69 '94 C.339 B.A. L.589 J.D. [A Swanson,M.&B.] (⊙Chicago)
Beck, Dawn M. '56 '82 C.959 B.A. L.300 J.D.
Asst. Gen. Coun., DaimlerChrysler Services NA LLC
Bellisario, Paul . . . . . '50 '80 C.424 B.A. L.1151 J.D. [Bellisario&Assoc.]
Bellisario and Associates . . . . . 1440 Maple Ave.
Bergerson, J. Steven . . . . . '42 '68 C&L.494 B.A., J.D. 2285 Pebble Creek Dr.‡
Bolger, Vincent J. . . . . . '23 '51 C&L.209 B.A., LL.B. 1700 Ogden Ave.
Bonds, Suzanne M. . . . . . '50 '94 C.339 B.A. L.146 J.D. [A Hinshaw&C.]
Boren, Steven C. . . . . . '49 '02 C.339 B.S. L.146 J.D. [C Chitkowski]
Bose, Romi N. . . . . . '65 '94 C.679 B.S.E.T. L.146 J.D. Pat. Coun., Molex Inc. (Pat.)
Branda, James E. . . . . . '50 '75 C.504 B.A. L.900 J.D. V.P., Budget Rent A Car Corp.
Bressler, David J. . . . . . '57 '82 C.494 B.A. L.424 J.D. [Dykema G.P.]
Brown, Daniel E. . . . . . '64 '96 C.578 B.A. L.589 J.D. [Donahue,S.&B.] ⊙
Butt, Edward T., Jr., (AV) '47 '71
C.399 B.A. L.477 J.D. [C Swanson,M.&B.] (⊙Chicago)
Cahill, David J., (AV) . . . . . '55 '81 C.339 B.A. L.46 J.D. [Swanson,M.&B.]
Caldwell, Stacey E. . . . . . '62 '91 C.339 B.S. L.146 J.D. Pat. Coun., Molex Inc. (Pat.)
Casey, Thomas Bernard . . . . . '64 '94 C.339 B.S. L.1049 J.D. Molex Inc.
Cassidy, Thomas B., (AV) . . . . . '44 '69 C&L.424 B.S., J.D. [Dykema G.P.]
Cherwin, Jerrold L., Jr. . . . . . '76 '01 C.352 B.S. L.378 J.D. [A Dykema G.P.]
Chitkowski, John J., (BV) . . . . . '63 '91 C.879 B.A. L.365 J.D. [Chitkowski]

Chitkowski Law Offices, (BV)
801 Warrenville Road, Suite 620, 60532
Telephone: 630-824-4808 Facsimile: 630-824-4809
URL: http://www.chitkowskilaw.com
John J. Chitkowski;—Corey B. Stern; Jason M. Loebach; Joseph D. Perrotta. Of Counsel: Steven C. Boren.
Business, Construction, Transportation, Corporate, Labor and Employment and Real Estate, Litigation and Transactions.
See Professional Biographies, LISLE, ILLINOIS

Chroust, David J. . . . . . '55 '80 C.293 B.A. L.178 J.D. [A Wildman,H.A.&D.]
Cohen, Charles S. . . . . . '60 '85 C.679 B.S.M.E. L.146 J.D. Pat. Coun., Molex Inc.
Coman, Daniel G., (AV) . . . . . '67 '90 C.518 B.A. L.339 J.D. 2525 Cabot Dr., Ste. 300
Comrie, John W. '48 '77 C&L.012 B.A., LL.B.
(adm. in SK; not adm. in IL) Secy. & Coun., IPSCO Enterprises, Inc.
Crowley, Timothy J. . . . . . '54 '79 C.209 B.S.C. L.589 J.D. [T.Crowley]
Crowley, Timothy, The Law Office of . . . . . 1025 Ogden Ave., Ste. 207
Davidson, Kerry L. . . . . . '72 '02 C&L.879 B.A., J.D. [A Andrews K.&P.]
DiBenedetto, James L. . . . . . '54 '79 C.363 B.S.B.A. L.589 J.D. 1440 Maple Ave.
Dickson, Barbara Beck . . . . . '51 '81 C.383 B.S.N. L.1340 J.D. 6568 Shagbark
Donahue, John F., (AV) . . . . . '44 '71 C&L.424 B.S., J.D. [Donahue,S.&B.] ⊙

Donahue, Sowa and Brown, (AV) BB
Suite 215, Lisle Executive Center, 3030 Warrenville Road, 60532 ⊙
Telephone: 630-505-5200 Fax: 630-505-4250
Email: gsowa@dsbb-law.com URL: http://www.lawyers.com/dsbblaw
John F. Donahue; Glenn M. Sowa; Daniel E. Brown. Associate: Patricia Magana.
Criminal Defense, DUI, Traffic, Drivers License Reinstatement, Appellate Law, Juvenile Law.
Geneva Office: 216 Campbell Street, 60134. Telephone: 630-232-1780. Fax: 630-232-9671.
See Professional Biographies, LISLE, ILLINOIS

Durbin, Elizabeth E. . . . . . '65 '93 C.352 B.A. L.209 J.D. 4200 Commerce Ct.
Durkin, James B., (AV) . . . . . '61 '90 C.338 B.S. L.365 J.D. [Wildman,H.A.&D.]

Dykema Gossett PLLC, (AV)
4200 Commerce Court Suite 300, 60532 ⊙
Telephone: 630-245-0400 Facsimile: 630-245-0140
URL: http://www.dykema.com
Members of Firm: David J. Bressler; Thomas B. Cassidy; George N. Gilkerson, Jr.; Bruce L. Goldsmith; Scott M. Hardek; John J. Mangan. Of Counsel: Richard L. Williams. Associates: Jerrold L. Cherwin, Jr.; Kimberly D. Fahrbach; Gregory L. Lacey; Dennis P. Lindell; Daniel J. Peters.
Antitrust and Trade Regulation, Automotive, Banking and Financial Services, Bankruptcy, Biotechnology and Life Sciences, Casino Gaming, Class Action Defense, Computer and Software Law, Construction, Consumer Financial Services, Corporate Finance, E-Commerce, Emerging Business and Technology, Employee Benefits, Entertainment and Sports, Environmental Law, Family Law, Franchise Law and Regulation, Government Contracts, Government Policy and Practice, HealthCare, Indian Law, Insurance, Intellectual Property, International Law, Labor and Employment, Litigation and Dispute Resolution, Mergers and Acquisitions, Products Liability Defense, Public Finance, Real Estate, Retail Law, Securities, Taxation and Estates, Trade Associations.
Ann Arbor, Michigan Office: 2723 South State Street, Suite 400, 48104. Telephone: 734-214-7660. Fax: 734-214-7696.
Aurora, Illinois Office: 2 Hankes Road. Telephone: 630-844-2200. Facsimile: 630-844-2277.
Bloomfield Hills, Michigan Office: 39577 Woodward Avenue, Suite 300, 48304-2820. Telephone: 248-203-0700. Fax: 248-203-0763.

(This Listing Continued)

Dykema Gossett PLLC (Continued)

Chicago, Illinois Office: 10 South Wacker Drive, Suite 2300. Telephone: 312-876-1700. Fax: 312-876-1155.
Detroit, Michigan Office: 400 Renaissance Center, 48243-1668. Telephone: 313-568-6800. Fax: 313-568-6545.
Grand Rapids, Michigan Office: Suite 700, 300 Ottawa Avenue, N.W., 49503-2306. Telephone: 616-776-7500. Fax: 616-776-7573.
Joliet, Illinois Office: 111 North Ottawa Street. Telephone: 815-727-4511. Facsimile: 815-727-1586.
Lansing, Michigan Office: 124 W. Allegan Street, Suite 800, 48933-1742. Telephone: 517-374-9100. Fax: 517-374-9191.
Los Angeles, California Office: 333 South Grand Avenue, Suite 2100, 90071. Telephone: 213-457-1800. Fax: 213-457-1850.
Washington, D.C. Office: Franklin Square, Suite 300 West, 1300 I Street, N.W., 20005-3353. Telephone: 202-906-8600. Fax: 202-906-8669.

See Professional Biographies, LISLE, ILLINOIS

Fahrbach, Kimberly D. .... '71 '96 C.238 B.S. L.146 J.D. [Ⓐ Dykema G.P.]
Ficarelli, Anthony .... '52 '78 C.686 B.S. L.276 J.D. [Hinshaw&C.]
Fisher, Hazel S. '42 '80 C.563 B.A. L.597 J.D. Chief Corporate Counsel, Delta Dental Plan of Illinois
Fitch, Suzanne M. .... '75 '01 C.339 B.S. L.589 J.D. [Ⓐ Swanson,M.&B.]
Forkins, James M. "Marc", Jr., (BV) .... '51 '85 C.378 B.A. L.424 J.D. [Hinshaw&C.]
Fortier, Robert F. .... '49 '75 C&L.339 A.B., J.D. 5515 E. Lake Dr.
Friede, Arnold I. '49 '73 C.665 B.S. L.273 J.D. (adm. in CA; not adm. in IL) V.P. & Gen. Coun., Van Den Bergh Foods Co.
Gentry, Henry L. .... '48 '75 C.339 B.A. L.424 J.D. Liberty Mut. Ins. Co.
Georgell, Holly Ann '68 '93 C.209 B.A. L.966 J.D. Labor Coun. & Dir., Employ. Compl., Wallace Computer Services
Gilkerson, George N., Jr., (AV) .... '45 '70 C&L.339 B.S., J.D. [Dykema G.P.]
Gleason, Timothy G. .... '72 '01 C.339 B.S. L.597 J.D. [Ⓐ Swanson,M.&B.]
Goldsmith, Bruce L., (AV) .... '45 '71 C.597 B.A. L.145 J.D. [Dykema G.P.] (⊙Aurora)
Gonzalez, Maria Elena .... '57 '82 C.209 B.A. L.146 J.D. 2395 Peppertree Ct.
Grant, Capper C. .... '46 '76 C.378 B.A. L.365 J.D. Liberty Mutual Ins. Grp.
Greenberg, Lorraine M., and Associates '52 '81 C.174 B.A. L.365 J.D. 4513 Lincoln Avenue, Suite 105A (⊙Chicago, Joliet)
Gustafson, Barbara A. '48 '83 C.801 B.Mus. L.145 J.D. Corp. Coun., GKN North America Services, Inc.
Haley, Clifton E. .... '31 '62 C.215 L.213 LL.B. 4225 Naperville Rd.
Hardek, Scott M., (AV) .... '64 '90 C&L.602 B.A., J.D. [Dykema G.P.]
Hecht, Louis A. .... '44 '69 C&L.339 B.S., J.D. Secy. & Gen. Coun., Molex Inc. (Pat.)
Hight, David H., (BV) .... '55 '85 C.357 B.A. L.209 J.D. [Wildman,H.A.&D.]

Hinshaw & Culbertson LLP, (AV)
Hinshaw & Culbertson LLP is an Illinois registered limited liability partnership that has elected to be governed by the Illinois Uniform Partnership Act (1997)
4343 Commerce Court, Suite 415, 60532-1099 ⊙
Telephone: 630-505-0010 Facsimile: 630-505-0959 Telex: 880248
Email: kfox@hinshawlaw.com URL: http://www.hinshawlaw.com
Partners: Leo J. Athas (Also at Chicago, Illinois Office); Anthony Ficarelli; James M. "Marc" Forkins, Jr.; Alice K. Kush; Joseph H. McMahon; Mark C. Metzger; Daniel M. Purdom; Maureen Lennon Zeeb. Associates: Suzanne M. Bonds; Christy L. Hoop.
Appellate, Banking & Financing, Bankruptcy & Creditors' Rights, Class Action Litigation, Civil Rights Defense, Commercial Litigation, Corporate, Construction Law, Director & Officer Liability, Employee Benefits, Environmental, Fidelity & Surety, General Liability Litigation, Government, Health Care, Insurance Coverage, Insurance and Reinsurance, Labor & Employment, Legal Malpractice, Medical Malpractice, Mergers & Acquisitions, Municipal Liability, Personal Injury Defense, Public Law, Products Liability Litigation, Professional Liability, Regulatory, Real Estate, School Law, Securities, Taxation, Transportation, White Collar Crime and Workers' Compensation Defense.
Other Office Locations: Chicago, Illinois; Appleton, Wisconsin; Belleville, Illinois; Boston, Massachusetts; Champaign, Illinois; Crystal Lake, Illinois; Edwardsville, Illinois; Fort Lauderdale, Florida; Jacksonville, Florida; Joliet, Illinois; Los Angeles, California; Miami, Florida; Milwaukee, Wisconsin; Minneapolis, Minnesota; New York, New York; Peoria, Illinois; Phoenix, Arizona; Portland, Oregon; Providence, Rhode Island; Rockford, Illinois; St. Louis, Missouri; San Francisco, California; Schererville, Indiana; Springfield, Illinois; Tampa, Florida; Waukegan, Illinois.

See Professional Biographies, LISLE, ILLINOIS

Hoop, Christy L. .... '70 '95 C.347 B.A. L.209 J.D. [Ⓐ Hinshaw&C.]
Jacobson, Matthew D. .... '68 '93 C&L.352 B.S., J.D. [Swanson,M.&B.]
Jardine, William S. '60 '85 C&L.339 B.S., J.D. Sr. V.P. & Gen. Coun., Nike Securities LP
Jaros, Robert G. .... '34 '58 C&L.209 LL.B. 1621 W. Ogden Ave.
Johnson, Richard C. .... '57 '82 C.209 B.A. L.365 J.D. [Wildman,H.A.&D.]
Jones, Isham R., III .... '69 '97 C.338 B.S. L.502 J.D. [Ⓐ Andrews K.&P.]
King, Patricia Mallick .... '41 '80 C.293 B.A. L.209 J.D. CEO, Gen. Resch. & Servs. Corp.
Koehler, Renée .... '66 '91 C.589 B.A. L.365 J.D. [Andrews K.&P.]
Krane, David J. .... '44 '74 C&L.424 B.S., J.D. 1045 Burlington Lisle
Krebs, Michael G. '60 '88 C&L.597 B.A., J.D. Sr. Corp. Atty. & Asst. Secy., Budget Rent a Car Corp.
Kush, Alice K., (BV) .... '51 '81 C.959 B.S.N. L.46 J.D. [Hinshaw&C.]
Lacey, Gregory L. .... '67 '93 C.910 B.A. L.352 J.D. [Ⓐ Dykema G.P.]
Lande, R. Christopher '62 '91 C.478 A.B. L.437 J.D. (adm. in IA; not adm. in IL) CGU Insurance
Laterza, Nancy R. '62 '87 C.210 B.S. L.424 J.D. V.P. & Sr. Coun., Computer Associates Intl., Inc.
Lawrence, Zachary, (BV) .... '49 '78 C.1222 B.A. L.146 J.D. [Lawrence]
Lawrence Law Firm, P.C., (BV) .... 4614 Main St., Ste. 1
Leffelman, Dean J., (AV) .... '53 '80 C.589 B.S. L.365 J.D. [Wildman,H.A.&D.]
Lento, Thomas J. .... '61 '92 C.209 B.A. L.365 J.D. P.O. Box 3229
Lindell, Dennis P. .... '73 '01 C.679 B.A. L.879 J.D. [Ⓐ Dykema G.P.]
Loebach, Jason M. .... '76 '01 C.578 B.A. L.589 J.D. [Ⓐ Chitkowski]
Lynch, George P., (AV) .... '32 '62 C.339 B.S. L.209 J.D. 3030 Warrenville Rd.
Magana, Patricia .... '71 '01 C.927 B.A. L.589 J.D. [Ⓐ Donahue,S.&B.]
Mangan, John J., (AV) .... '51 '76 C.378 B.A. L.365 J.D. [Dykema G.P.] (⊙Chicago)
Mankus, Tony .... '39 '86 C.1046 B.A. L.365 J.D. [Mankus&M.]

Mankus & Marchan, Ltd.
5950-E. Lincoln Avenue, Suite 500, 60532
Telephone: 630-960-0500 Fax: 630-960-0601
Email: tman@irstax.com URL: http://www.irstax.com
Tony Mankus; Margarita Marchan-Mankus.
Languages: Spanish and Lithuanian.
Tax Controversies, Bankruptcy, Social Security Disability, Real Estate, Family Law.

See Professional Biographies, LISLE, ILLINOIS

Marchan-Mankus, Margarita .... '45 '70 C&L.677 B.S., J.D. [Mankus&M.]
May, Frank B., Jr. '45 '79 C.569 B.A. L.365 J.D. Sr. Corp. Atty., Budget Rent a Car Corp.
McElravey, C. Dirk '65 '90 C.347 B.A. L.846 J.D. Asst. Gen. Coun., T-Systems North America, Inc.
McElvain, Carol K. .... '63 '89 C&L.966 B.A., J.D. Wausau Ins. Co.
McKillip, Elizabeth A. .... '— '04 C.339 B.A. L.424 J.D. [Ⓐ Wildman,H.A.&D.]
McMahon, Joseph H., (AV) .... '66 '92 C.352 B.B.A. L.365 J.D. [Hinshaw&C.]
Metzger, Mark C. .... '64 '89 C.340 B.A. L.801 J.D. [Hinshaw&C.]
Miller, Amy R. .... '74 '99 C.357 B.A. L.339 J.D. [Ⓐ Swanson,M.&B.]
Miller, Laurie M. .... '68 '95 C.966 B.A. L.146 J.D. [Ⓐ Wildman,H.A.&D.]
Milne, Murray F. .... '06 '30 C&L.436 J.D. 1700 Robin Lane‡
Murphy, Bart T., (AV) .... '56 '81 C.742 B.A. L.424 J.D. [Wildman,H.A.&D.]
Myers, Daniel N. '42 '76 C.623 B.A. L.276 J.D. Exec. V.P., Gen. Mgr. & Gen. Coun., National Propane Gas Assn.
Newman, Carol A. '61 '97 C.589 B.S. L.365 J.D. Gen. Coun., Intrinsic Technologies, L.L.C.
Nortell, Bruce .... '46 '71 C.94 A.B. L.145 J.D. P.O. Box 3130
Nosek, Ronald R. .... '45 '71 C.363 A.B. L.424 J.D. 3030 Warrenville Rd.‡
Passarelli, Ronald J. .... '63 '90 C.589 B.A. L.209 J.D. [Andrews K.&P.]
Paulius, Thomas David, (AV) '54 '82 C.602 B.S.C.E. L.146 J.D. Assoc. Gen. Coun., Molex Inc. (Pat.)
Perrotta, Joseph D. .... '72 '99 C.209 B.S. L.424 J.D. [Ⓐ Chitkowski]
Persin, Milton F. .... '26 '63 C.1016 B.M.E. L.209 LL.B. USF&G Ins. Co.
Peters, Daniel J. .... '69 '00 C.475 B.S. L.146 J.D. [Ⓐ Dykema G.P.]
Peterson, Judith Bakes '— '85 C.720 B.A. L.209 J.D. V.P., Sr. Corp. Atty. & Asst. Secy., Budget Rent A Car Corp.
Pines, Dennis S. '43 '73 C.124 B.S. L.1046 J.D. (adm. in OH; not adm. in IL) Corp. Coun., Lucent Technologies Inc.
Placek, Robert L. '45 '73 C.346 B.S. L.347 J.D. (adm. in IN; not adm. in IL) 2361 Barkridge Ct.‡
Purdom, Daniel M. .... '52 '78 C.338 B.S. L.801 J.D. [Hinshaw&C.] (⊙Chicago)
Riski, David J. .... '75 '00 C.589 B.S. L.209 J.D. [Ⓐ Swanson,M.&B.]
Rodriguez, Ana G. .... '67 '95 C.1042 B.A. L.477 J.D. Assoc. Gen. Coun., Molex Inc.
Rosenberg, David W. .... '44 '69 C.339 B.S. L.365 J.D. [D.W.Rosenberg]
Rosenberg, David W., P.C. .... 2867 Ogden Avenue
Roth, Michael M. .... '54 '80 C.339 B.S. L.365 J.D. [Wildman,H.A.&D.]
Rummer, Patricia K., Law Offices of '— '94 C.190 B.A. L.146 J.D. 5950 E Lincoln Avenue
Saunders, Gilbert O., Jr. '61 '00 C.1119 B.A. L.1029 J.D. Staff Atty., Primacy Relocation, LLC
Shaw, John C., Jr. '46 '75 C.800 B.A. L.999 J.D. (adm. in CA; not adm. in IL) 2215 Pebble Creek Dr.‡
Singer, Eric L., (AV) .... '64 '88 C.339 B.A. L.145 J.D. [Wildman,H.A.&D.]
Skwarek, Wayne M. '59 '84 C.424 B.B.A. L.365 J.D. Pres. & CEO, Outside Legal Counsel Ltd.
Sladek, Marti J. .... '46 '94 C.381 B.S. L.424 J.D. [M.J.Sladek]
Sladek, M.J. .... P.O. Box 564
Smith, Stephen R. '57 '82 C.937 B.A. L.145 J.D. Gen. Coun., GKN N. Amer. Srvcs., Inc.
Snorf, Lowell D., Jr., (AV) .... '19 '47 C&L.597 B.S., J.D. Pres., Warner Ins. Grp.
Snyder, James M. .... '59 '87 C&L.608 B.S., J.D. [Wildman,H.A.&D.]
Sowa, Glenn M., (BV) .... '48 '83 C&L.589 B.S.Ed., J.D. [Donahue,S.&B.] ⊙
Spencer, Dean R. .... '21 '48 C&L.209 B.S., J.D. 2010 Carriage Hill Rd.‡
Stern, Corey B. .... '72 '00 C.589 B.S. L.209 J.D. [Ⓐ Chitkowski]
Straub, Jenee M. .... '73 '99 C.98 B.S. L.589 J.D. [Ⓐ Wildman,H.A.&D.]
Stroh, Steven E. .... '35 '64 C.339 B.S. L.146 LL.B. 2183 Oak Hill Dr.‡
Sullivan, Christian A. .... '74 '02 C.339 B.A. L.589 J.D. [Ⓐ Swanson,M.&B.]
Summers, Diana Brodman '49 '93 C.1016 B.S.B.A. L.209 J.D. 3333 Warrenville Rd., Ste.200
Swanson, Lenard C., (AV) '37 '67 C&L.339 B.S., J.D. [Ⓒ Swanson,M.&B.] (⊙Chicago)

Swanson, Martin & Bell, (AV)
2525 Cabot Drive, Suite 204, 60532 ⊙
Telephone: 630-799-6900 Fax: 630-799-6901
URL: http://www.smbtrials.com
Partners: David J. Cahill; Matthew D. Jacobson; Bruce S. Terlep. Associates: Ross W. Bartolotta; Suzanne M. Fitch; Timothy G. Gleason; Amy R. Miller; David J. Riski; Christian A. Sullivan. Of Counsel: Lenard C. Swanson; Edward T. Butt, Jr.
Class Action Lawsuits, Commercial Litigation, Construction Litigation/Disputes, Consumer and Warranty Law, Creditor's Rights, Drugs & Medical Devices, Employment Litigation, Environmental Law, Equipment Leasing, General Tort Liability, Healthcare, Insurance Coverage, Intellectual Property, Medical Negligence, Municipal Law, Product Liability, Professional Negligence, Real Estate Development/Zoning, Real Estate Litigation, Toxic and Mass Tort Litigation, and White Collar Criminal Defense.
Chicago, Illinois Office: 330 North Wabash, Suite 3300, 60611. Telephone: 312-321-9100. Fax: 312-321-0990.
Lake County, Illinois Office: 1860 West Winchester Road, Suite 201, Libertyville, Illinois, 60048. Telephone: 847-949-0025. Fax: 847-247-0555.
Waukegan, Illinois Office: 415 Washington Street, Suite 1B, Waukegan, Illinois, 60085. Telephone: 847-949-0025. Fax: 847-247-0555.

See Professional Biographies, LISLE, ILLINOIS

Tarnow, William M. '46 '71 C&L.734 B.A., J.D. Reg. Coun., Prudential Ins. Co. of Amer.
Terlep, Bruce S., (BV) .... '58 '85 C.210 B.A. L.602 J.D. [Swanson,M.&B.]
Thomas, Kaye A. .... '51 '80 C.107 B.A. L.309 J.D. 4414 Middleton Place
Tirva, Algis A. .... '33 '71 C.339 B.S. L.424 J.D. Pat. Coun., Molex Inc.‡
Valrose, Corrie E. .... '— '00 C.63 B.L.A. L.146 J.D. [Ⓐ Wildman,H.A.&D.]
Vera, Jorge J., Law Offices of '70 '98 C.602 B.A. L.424 J.D. 1025 Ogden Ave., Ste. 202
Vitullo, Louis P., (AV) .... '44 '69 C.363 B.A. L.424 J.D. [Ⓒ Wildman,H.A.&D.] ⊙
Waddington, Croft C. .... '40 '66 C.337 A.B. L.339 LL.B. 4614 Main St., Ste. 1
Weiss, Stephen Z. .... '47 '73 C.339 B.S. L.209 J.D. Pat. Coun., Molex Inc. (Pat.)
Wesolowski, Frank, (BV) .... '29 '52 C.742 L.209 LL.B. 1621 W. Ogden Ave.‡

Wildman, Harrold, Allen & Dixon LLP, (AV)
2300 Cabot Drive, Suite 455, 60532 ⊙
Telephone: 630-955-0555 Fax: 630-955-0662
Email: info@wildmanharrold.com URL: http://www.wildmanharrold.com
Partners: James B. Durkin; David H. Hight; Richard C. Johnson; Dean J. Leffelman; Bart T. Murphy; Michael M. Roth; Eric L. Singer; James M. Snyder. Associates: David J. Chroust; Elizabeth A. McKillip; Laurie M. Miller; Jenee M. Straub; Corrie E. Valrose. Of Counsel: Louis P. Vitullo.
General Civil, Trial and Appellate Practice, Commercial Litigation, Corporate and Business Law, Government, Medical Malpractice, Municipal Finance, Probate and Estate Planning, Real Estate, Tax, Telecommunications.
Chicago, Illinois Office: 225 West Wacker Drive, Suite 3000. Telephone: 312-201-2000. Fax: 312-201-2155.

See Professional Biographies, LISLE, ILLINOIS

Williams, Richard L. .... '70 '95 C.339 B.A. L.589 J.D. [Ⓒ Dykema G.P.]
Wilson, Robert A. '40 '83 C.910 B.S. L.999 J.D. (adm. in CA; not adm. in IL) Budget Rent a Car Corp.
Zaruba, Carleton J. '62 '88 C.867 B.A. L.982 J.D. (adm. in CT; not adm. in IL) Sr. Div. Coun., Mercedes-Benz Credit Corp.
Zeeb, Maureen Lennon .... '64 '90 C.363 B.A. L.365 J.D. [Hinshaw&C.]
Zeitler, Robert J. .... '61 '94 C.474 B.S. L.424 J.D. Assoc. Gen. Coun., Molex Inc. (Pat.)

LITCHFIELD, 6,883, *Montgomery Co.*

Adams, Jay W., (AV) ... '51 '76 C.339 B.S. L.910 J.D. [J.W.Adams]
Adams, Jay William, P.C., (AV) ... 314 N. Monroe St.
Batty, Brett W. ... '70 '98 C.801 B.S. L.213 J.D. [Batty]
Batty Law Firm, LTD ... 423 N. State St.
Floreth, Frederick D., (CV) '56 '82
C.801 B.S. L.734 J.D. Montgomery Co. Pub. Guard. & Admr.
Hanafin, John C. ... '48 '73 C.801 B.A. L.734 J.D. Publisher, Litchfield News-Herald
Hantla, Christopher B. ... '74 '99 C.502 B.A. L.801 J.D. [Hantla&H.]
Hantla, G. Bradley, (AV) ... '47 '73 C.500 B.B.A. L.734 J.D. [Hantla&H.]
Hantla & Hantla, Ltd., (AV) ... 413 North State Street
Lober, Maureen Macy, (CV) ... '27 '52 C.259 A.B. L.996 LL.B. 118 W. Ryder St.
White, Michael B. '44 '73
C.910 B.S. L.339 J.D. V.P. & Corp. Coun., Bailey & Assocs., Inc.

LOCKPORT, 15,191, *Will Co.*

Caneva, Ronald L., (BV) ... '48 '74 C.589 B.A. L.424 J.D. [Luzbetak&C.]
Henderson, Angela D. ... '— '97 C&L.209 B.S., J.D. [Ⓐ McCarthy]
Klunk, John F., Law Office of ... '51 '85 [J.F.Klunk]
Klunk, J.F., Law Office of ... 936 S. State Street
Korst, Eugene J., (BV) ... '27 '59 C.339 B.S. L.365 LL.B. 800 S. State St.
Korst, Michael J., (BV) ... '62 '87 C.436 B.A. L.365 J.D. 800 S. State St.
Luzbetak, Stephen B., (BV) ... '37 '62 C&L.424 B.S., J.D. [Luzbetak&C.]
Luzbetak & Caneva, (BV) ... 1000 S. Hamilton St.

Malysa, Theresa M.
(See Orland Park)

McCarthy, Jeffrey M. ... '65 '92 C.597 B.S. L.424 J.D. [McCarthy]
McCarthy Law Office ... 136 East 9th Street
Podgorny, James A. ... '68 '00 C&L.424 B.S., J.D. P.O. Box 573
Rudolph, Donald Patrick '31 '66
(adm. in NY; not adm. in IL) 14940 Will-Cook Rd.
Varraveto, Dominick, Jr. ... '13 '37 C.602 B.A. L.209 J.D. 1234 Prodehl Dr.‡
Walin, Karen ... '57 '86 C&L.209 B.S.C., J.D. 13161 W. 143rd St.
Ward, Bernard D. ... '56 '82 C.339 B.A. L.589 J.D. [B.D.Ward]
Ward, Bernard D., Attorney at Law, PC ... 15420 Douglas Pkwy.
Woock, Sally Ann ... '33 '79 C.966 B.S. L.1151 J.D. 1000 S. Hamilton‡

LOMBARD, 42,322, *DuPage Co.*

Anderson, David G. '52 '79 C.696 B.A. L.982 J.D.
(adm. in NY; not adm. in IL) Sr. V.P. Admin. & Gen. Coun., Snecma USA, Inc.
Baiocchi, Mark J. ... '56 '84 C.1183 B.A. L.146 J.D. Legal Coun., United States Can Co.
Baker, Georgetta J. '— '81 C.1011 B.S. L.276 J.D.
(adm. in FL; not adm. in IL) Asst. Gen. Coun., Kinder Morgan Inc.
Beresoff, Alex J. ... '44 '72 C.393 B.A. L.339 J.D. 1702 S. Meyers Rd.
Calcagno, Joseph ... '70 '97 C.178 B.A. L.146 J.D. Asst. State Atty.
Carroll, Thomas '54 '91 C.1191 B.S. L.146 J.D.
V.P. Secy. & Dep. Gen. Coun., Snecma USA, Inc.
Catanese, John N. ... '54 '79 C.424 B.S. L.365 J.D. Royal Mgmt.
Cedarquist, Wayland B., (AV) ... '16 '41 C.339 A.B. L.309 LL.B. 556 Harmony Lane‡
Chaban, Marvin ... '26 '59 C.679 B.S. L.209 J.D. 1067 Apple Ln.‡
Cordts, Julianne ... '58 '84 C.357 B.A. L.801 J.D. Hyatt Legal Servs.
Cosgrove, Patricia M. '61 '86 C.734 B.S. L.339 J.D.
Asst. Gen. Coun., United States Can Company
Costello, Bradley H. ... '60 '86 C.801 B.S. L.365 J.D. State Farm Fire & Casualty Co.
Csink, Kevin Ann ... '63 '96 C.893 B.A. L.146 J.D. Mortice Kern Systems
Dahlgren, Becky L. ... '50 '76 C.57 B.A. L.879 J.D. [B.L.Dahlgren]
Dahlgren, Becky Lynn, Ltd., The Law Offices of ... 477 E. Butterfield Road, Suite 202
Davis, H. A. ... '06 '32 C.608 B.S. L.209 J.D. 127 S. Charlotte St.‡
DeCook, Brian F. ... '61 '93 C.539 B.A. L.209 J.D. 555 E. Butterfield Rd. (ⓒMonee)
Elliott, Robert A., (AV) ... '15 '40 C&L.477 B.S., J.D. 555 Foxworth Blvd.
Elsner, Rita E. ... '51 '76 C.578 B.A. L.209 J.D. Village Atty.
Erwin & Associates, L.L.C., (BV) ... 477 East Butterfield Road, Suite 101 (ⓒChicago)
Ewoldt, Valerie A. ... '64 '93 C.339 B.S. L.365 J.D. 252 N. Martha
Foley, Molly M. ... '68 '97 C.966 B.A. L.285 J.D. 2233 S. Highland Ave. Ste. 1509
Frank, Carl J. ... '46 '70 C&L.602 B.A., J.D. 720 E. Butterfield Rd.
Fry, Howard A., (BV) ... '49 '77 C.338 B.S. L.209 J.D. P.O. Box 1234
Gajda, James E. ... '47 '79 C.679 B.S. L.146 J.D. Natural Gas Pipeline Midcon
Goodman, Elliott I., (AV) ... '34 '58 C&L.597 B.S., J.D. ATI Carriage House, Inc.
Greene, Renez ... '56 '81 C.855 B.S. L.597 J.D. Asst. Gen. Coun., Kinder Morgan Inc.
Gust, Ralph J., Jr. ... '41 '67 C&L.597 B.S., J.D. 929 S. Main St.
Harms, Julie A. '68 '93 C.1365 B.A. L.861 J.D.
Sr. Legal Coun., Natl. Accts., Waste Management, Inc.
Haynes, Daniel J. ... '51 '75 C.209 B.A. L.365 J.D. 330 E. Roosevelt Rd., Ste. G6B
Hennings, Ronald J. ... '59 '84 C.597 B.A. L.146 J.D. [Pellettieri&H.]
Holt, Laura C.W. ... '78 '03 C.74 B.S. L.365 J.D. [Ⓐ Pellettieri&H.]
Hunt, James M. ... '60 '86 C.424 B.S. L.589 J.D. Coun., K N Energy, Inc.
Jardine, Andrea M. ... '74 '01 C.347 B.A. L.1202 J.D. [Erwin&Assoc.]
Jeffry, William A. '49 '76 C.37 B.S. L.365 J.D.
Sr. Legal Counsel, Midwestern Group, Waste Management, Inc.
Koykar, Frank J. ... '43 '72 C.177 B.A. L.365 J.D. [F.J.Koykar]
Koykar, Frank J., P.C. ... 151 E. 22nd Street, Ste. 100W
Lester, William A. ... '35 '74 C.750 B.A. L.209 J.D. [W.A.Lester]
Lester, William A., Ltd., Law Offices of ... 115 W. Ash Street
Lewis, Elizabeth E., (AV) '64 '89 C.105 B.A. L.477 J.D.
General Counsel, Corona Optical Systems, Inc.
Lietzke, Randolph C. ... '40 '65 C.347 B.S. L.1119 J.D. 576 Cedar Lane
Long, Robert W. ... '47 '74 C.208 B.A. L.169 J.D. 203 Yorktown
Loss, Joseph J. ... '49 '78 C.338 B.S. L.1151 J.D. [Loss,P.&O.]
Loss, Pavone & Orel, (AV) ... 1920 South Highland Ave., Suite 333
Mallory, Paul W. ... '46 '72 C.911 B.A. L.145 J.D. Asst. Gen. Coun., Kinder Morgan Inc.
McCabe, Michael H. ... '59 '85 C.350 B.A. L.339 J.D. The Coun. of State Gov.
McGinnis, Joseph J. ... '44 '70 C.339 B.S. L.146 J.D. 151 E. 22nd St.
McNicholas, Dennis J. ... '47 '74 C.742 B.A. L.602 J.D. [D.J.McNicholas]
McNicholas, Dennis J., Ltd. ... 425 S. Main St.
Mevorah, Steven H., & Associates '54 '79
C.1139 B.S. L.589 J.D. 900 E. Roosevelt Road (ⓒBloomingdale)
Orel, James D., (AV) ... '54 '83 C.338 B.S. L.365 [Loss,P.&O.]
O'Shea, Patrick J., (BV) ... '50 '79 C.339 B.S.E.E. L.365 J.D. 10 W. Saint Charles Rd.
Pavone, Louis V. ... '53 '79 C.504 B.A. [Loss,P.&O.]
Pellettieri, Carl A., Jr. ... '56 '81 C.300 B.A. L.365 J.D. [Pellettieri&H.]
Pellettieri & Hennings, P.C. ... P.O. Box 189
Perkins, R. Ben., Jr. ... '25 '72 C.945 A.B. L.146 J.D. 21 W. 273 Drury Ln.

Prato & Associates, P.C.
(See Oak Brook)

Price Tunney Reiter, A Professional Corporation
(See Chicago)

Rodriguez, Carlos M. ... '62 '92 C.339 B.A. L.146 J.D. [C.M.Rodriguez]
Rodriguez, Carlos M., P.C. ... 55 W. 22nd St., Ste. 109
Rooney, Mary F. ... '52 '81 C.436 B.A. L.365 J.D. Coun., Waste Mgmt., Inc.
Rotche, Phillip J. ... '37 '63 C.477 B.A. L.597 J.D. 320 Westmore Meyers Road
Sobol, Paul R. ... '30 '70 C.234 B.S. L.365 J.D. 1011 Hunter St.
Telleen, Philip R. ... '46 '74 C.57 A.B. L.477 J.D. Asst. Gen. Coun., Kinder Morgan Inc.

Traub, A., & Cádiz
(See Schaumburg)

Vlach, Thomas J. ... '68 '93 C.910 B.A. L.146 J.D. [T.J.Vlach]
Vlach, Thomas J., P.C., Law Office of ... 477 E. Butterfield Rd., Ste. 103
Weber, Ann M. '59 '87 C.424 B.A.A. L.365 J.D.
Govt. Affs. Coun., American Family Insurance Group
Weinert, Frank X. ... '74 '99 C.602 L.146 J.D. 900 E. Roosevelt Road
Wilt, Dennis M. '49 '76 C.24 B.A. L.215 J.D.
(adm. in MI; not adm. in IL) V.P. & Group Gen. Coun., Waste Management, Inc.
Zigterman, Bonnie L. ... '55 '81 C.114 B.A. L.339 J.D. 355 W. Ann St.‡

LONG GROVE, 6,735, *Lake Co.*

Arezina, Alexander I. ... '71 '98 C.945 B.B.A. L.1209 J.D. Kemper Ins. Cos.
Barnard, Douglas C. ... '58 '82 C.453 B.S. L.494 J.D. CF Industries, Inc.
Beatty, Donald C. '45 '75 C.901 A.B. L.776 J.D.
Assoc. Gen. Coun., Kemper Insurance Companies
Boznos, William P. ... '58 '84 C.260 B.A. L.365 J.D. Sr. Coun., Kemper Nat'l Ins. Cos.
Brewer, Brian S. ... '75 '01 C.238 B.A. L.365 J.D. [Ⓐ Pinzur,C.&K.]
Briody, Geo. M. ... '27 '55 C.602 B.A. L.209 J.D. Pres., Fairfield Svgs. & Loan Assn.
Cohen, Laura E. ... '64 '96 C.339 B.S. L.424 J.D. [Pinzur,C.&K.]
Condon, James G. '30 '55 C.424 B.S.C. L.597 LL.B.
Audit Attorney, Kemper Insurance Companies
Conner, Stephanie Bass ... '69 '96 C.354 B.A. L.424 J.D. 1250 Antietam Street
Dickman, Martin J. ... '44 '69 C.339 B.A. L.209 J.D. 5731 Hampton Dr.
Divito, Angela C. ... '68 '94 C.209 B.A. L.879 J.D. Kemper Insurance Companies
Eckardt, Peter J. ... '64 '91 C.966 B.A. L.436 J.D. 1 Kemper Dr.
Feder, Steven L. ... '51 '76 C.339 B.S. L.818 J.D. 3727 RFD‡
Fisher, Joy D. ... '52 '76 C&L.339 B.A., J.D. 4180 RFD Route. 83, Suite 208
Harding, Chas. F., III ... '15 '44 C.309 B.A. L.145 J.D. Rte. 22, R.F.D., Box 4322‡
Kerr, Megan Laura ... '73 '98 C.339 B.A. L.209 J.D. [Pinzur,C.&K.]
Liuzzi, Robert C. '44 '69 C.321 A.B. L.893 LL.B.
(adm. in NY; not adm. in IL) Pres. & CEO, CF Industries, Inc.
Marcus, Richard J. '52 '77 C.339 B.A. L.424 J.D.
Chf. Underwriting & Claim Coun., Kemper Reinsurance Co.
McGowan, Karen J. '64 '90 C.801 B.S. L.146 J.D.
National Litigation Coordinating Attorney, Kemper Insurance Companies
McGregor, John M. ... '68 '93 C&L.339 B.S., J.D. Sr. Coun., Kemper Ins. Cos.
McGuire, Thomas F. '39 '74
C.749 B.S. L.347 J.D. Box 4180 RFD, Long Grove Exec. House
Meehan, William P., (BVⓉ) '41 '73 C.1252 B.S. L.818 J.D.
(adm. in CT; not adm. in IL)
Eastern Region Litigation Officer, Kemper Insurance Companies
Merfeld, Brian R. ... '78 '03 C.446 B.A. L.209 J.D. [Ⓐ Pinzur,C.&K.]
Novak, Jerald ... '57 '87 C.1183 B.A. L.365 J.D. 6418 RFD
Obert, Paul R., (AV) '28 '54
C.276 B.S. L.665 J.D. V.P., Gen. Coun. & Secy., CF Indus., Inc.
Pikulin, David ... '63 '90 C.763 A.B. L.1049 J.D. 1 Kemper Dr.
Pinzur, Robert S. ... '53 '78 C.339 B.A. L.597 J.D. [Pinzur,C.&K.]

Pinzur, Cohen & Kerr, Ltd.
4180 RFD Route 83 Suite 208, 60047
Telephone: 847-821-5290 Fax: 847-821-5293
Email: info@pckltdlaw.com URL: http://www.pinzurcohenkerr.com
Robert S. Pinzur; Laura E. Cohen; Megan Laura Kerr;—Brian S. Brewer; Brian R. Merfeld.
Languages: English.
Administrative Matters, Adoption Law, Annexation, Appellate Practice, Arbitration, Asset Acquisitions and Sales, Banking and Loan Documentation, Banking Law, Business Law, Business Litigation, Business Planning and Formation, Business Successions, Buying and Selling of Businesses, Child Custody, Child Support, Civil Litigation in State and Federal Courts, Civil Rights, Class Actions, Closings, Collections, Commercial and Residential Development, Commercial Litigation, Commercial Real Estate, Community Association Law, Condemnation, Condominium Law, Contractual Disputes, Construction Law, Construction Arbitration, Construction Defects, Construction Litigation, Consumer Law, Contested Wills, Contracts, Cooperative Housing Law, Copyrights, Corporate Law, Corporations, Creditors Rights, Debtor and Creditor, Developer Disputes, Discrimination, Divorce, Domestic Violence, Elder Law, Employment Agreements, Employment Law, Entrepreneurial Ventures, Environmental Law, Equipment Leasing, Equitable and Injunctive Remedies, Estate Planning, Family Law, Family Business Law, Forcible Eviction Law, Foreclosures, Franchise Law, General Practice, Guardianship, Harassment, Homeowner's Association Law, Incorporation, Institutional Lending, Insurance Regulations, Workouts, Insurance, Land Development and Zoning, Landlord and Tenant Law, Leases and Leasing, Limited Liability Companies, Litigation, Matrimonial Law, Mechanics Liens, Mergers and Acquisitions, Mortgages, Municipal, Partnership Law, Personal Injury, Premarital Agreements, Probate Law, Real Estate, Real Estate Finance, Real Estate Litigation, Real Estate Tax Appeals, Real Estate Tax Assessment, Residential Real Estate, Sales Acquisitions, School Law, Secured Transactions, Small Business Law, Social Security, Spousal Support, Stock Acquisitions and Sales, Trademarks, Trusts and Estates, Uniform Commercial Code, Wills, Zoning, Planning and Land Use.

See Professional Biographies, LONG GROVE, ILLINOIS

Pluard, Gerald C., Jr. ... '58 '83 C&L.209 B.A., J.D. Kemper Insurance Companies
Raczkowski, Dale J. '51 '80 C.238 B.S. L.209 J.D.
Assistant General Counsel, Kemper Insurance Companies
Rill, Peter P., Jr. '56 '82 C.597 B.A. L.209 J.D.
Assoc. Gen. Couns., Kemper Life Insurance Companies
Schoenig, Bridget Healy ... '68 '93 C.645 B.S. L.602 J.D. 1 Kemper Dr.
Scott, John J. '50 '75 C.976 B.A. L.145 J.D.
Asst. Gen. Coun. & Asst. Secy., CF Indus., Inc.
Syc, Allan R. ... '47 '73 C.927 B.A. L.209 J.D. Asst. Gen. Coun., Kemper Ins. Cos.
Taylor, James H. ... '47 '74 C.766 B.A. L.1065 J.D. Kemper Nat. P. & C. Cos.
Vaccarella, Louis F. '48 '73 C.415 B.A. L.564 J.D.
Vice President & Chief Litigation Officer, Kemper Insurance Companies

LOUISVILLE, * 1,242, *Clay Co.*

Bayler, H. Carroll ... '15 '40 L.327 J.D. 152 S. Church St.
Brant, Marilyn Dawkins, (BV) ... '52 '77 C.234 B.A. L.801 J.D. 125 East Broadway Street
Buck, Alan, (BV) ... '48 '81 C.339 B.A. L.146 J.D. State's Atty.
Tungate, Sherri L. E. ... '53 '79 C.362 B.A. L.801 J.D. Assoc. Cir. J.

LOVES PARK, 20,044, *Boone & Winnebago Cos.*

Balsley, William L., (BV) ... '43 '68 C&L.339 B.A., J.D. [Balsley,K.&D.]
Balsley, Koonmen & Dahlberg, (BV) ... 5130 N. Second St.

Beattie, James M., Jr. '60 '89 C.352 B.G.S. L.300 J.D.
(adm. in MN; not adm. in IL) Legal Coun., Windsor Lakes Companies
Beese, Matthew C. ....'71 '03 C.1310 B.S. L.589 J.D. 535 Loves Park Dr.
Clark, Robert H., (AV) ....'54 '79 C.37 B.S. L.221 J.D. [Clark,J.&Z.]
Clark, Justen & Zucchi, Ltd., (AV) .... 7320 N. Alpine Rd.
Dahlberg, Jeffry A., (CV) ....'63 '91 C.339 B.A. L.589 J.D. [Balsley,K.&D.]
Frew, Stephen A., (CV) ....'46 '71 C&L.339 B.S., J.D. P.O. Box 15665
Holmstrom, John, III, (AV) '49 '74 C&L.339 B.S., J.D.
Gen. Coun., William Charles, Ltd.
Jagielski, Timothy H., (CV) '57 '96
C.840 B.F.A. L.589 J.D. Assistant Counsel, William Charles, Limited
Justen, Kevin P., (CV) ....'— '98 C.597 B.S. L.1000 J.D. [Clark,J.&Z.]
Koonmen, Karl C., (CV) ....'58 '84 C.697 B.S. L.589 J.D. [Balsley,K.&D.]
Lasparro, Michael Frank ....'76 '01 C.697 B.S. L.436 J.D. U.S. Atty. Off.
Maloney, James A., (CV) ....'67 '92 C.339 B.S. L.436 J.D. [Maloney]
Maloney Law Offices, (CV) .... P.O. Box 15052
Milani, Thomas E., Jr., (CV) ....'56 '81 C.221 B.A. L.352 J.D. 535 Loves Park Dr.
Petro, Nerino J., Jr., Attorney at Law, (BV) '63 '88
C&L.589 B.A., J.D. 349 E. Riverside Blvd.
Schuler, Paul G. '44 '73 C.436 B.S.M.E. L.339 J.D.
General Counsel, Secretary & Treasurer, Siebe Barber-Colman Company
Sommer, D. Kevin, (CV) '58 '83
C.338 B.S. L.734 J.D. Gen. Coun., Don Carter Lanes, Inc.
Zack, Sherry K. ....'63 '92 C.801 B.A. L.1187 J.D. 5294 Sand Piper Pl.
Zucchi, Jeffrey J., (BV) ....'66 '92 C.746 B.A. L.589 J.D. [Clark,J.&Z.]

LYNN CENTER, —, *Henry Co.*

Peterson, John W. ....'45 '71 C&L.339 B.S., J.D. Rural Rte. 1

LYONS, 10,255, *Cook Co.*

Jenks, James K., III ....'42 '73 7941 Ogden Ave., 1st Fl.
Malek, Francine ....'47 '80 C.339 B.A. L.146 J.D. 8041 42nd Ct.‡
Matz, Kevin D. ....'47 '79 C.472 B.A. L.365 J.D. 8643 Ogden Ave.
Pearson, William G., Law Office of '46 '78 C.209 B.A. L.365 J.D.
7337 W. Ogden Ave.
Petrucci, Judith B. ....'41 '83 C.1151 B.A. L.589 J.D. 7201 W. Ogden, Suite 200
Walsh, Kathleen Marie, LTD '52 '88 C.209 B.S. L.146 J.D.
7201 W. Ogden Ave., Suite 2
Walsh, Michael F. ....'51 '78 C&L.1151 B.A., J.D. 7714 45th Place

MACKINAW, 1,452, *Tazewell Co.*

McGrath, Mark J., (BV) ....'53 '78 C.273 B.A. L.801 J.D. [M.J.McGrath]
McGrath, Mark J., P.C., (BV) ....113 S. Main St.

MACOMB, * 18,558, *McDonough Co.*

Apfelbaum, Larry A., (BV) '61 '87 C.338 B.S. L.339 J.D.
[Ⓐ Kanoski&Assoc.] (ⒸBloomington, Peoria, Quincy, Rushville, Springfield)
Ashenhurst, A. Anthony, (AV) ...'54 '80 C.927 B.A. L.221 J.D. [Ⓑ Westervelt,J.N.&K.]
Bain, Florence, (BV) '42 '78 C.350 B.S. L.36 J.D.
[Ⓐ Kanoski&Assoc.] (ⒸBloomington, Peoria, Quincy, Rushville, Springfield)

Barash & Everett, LLC
(See Galesburg)

Benson, Heidi A., (BV) ....'72 '97 C.388 B.A. L.339 J.D. [Flack,M.&S.]
Biagini, Bruce J., (BV) ....'46 '72 C.723 B.S. L.339 J.D. [Flack,M.&S.]
Bracey, Earl, (CV) ....'50 '79 C.999 B.A. L.801 J.D. 2012 W. Adams
Carper, Gayle Tronvig, (BV) ....'50 '83 C.927 B.A. L.209 J.D. 315 E. Jackson St.
Carter, John Allen, (BV) ....'57 '82 C.338 B.S. L.910 J.D. Pub. Def. Off.
Clerkin, John R. ....'51 '77 C.597 B.A. L.365 J.D. Assoc. Cir. J.
Collins, Josiah W. ....'32 '62 C.871 B.S. L.273 LL.B. 1177 W. Jackson St.
Cook, Richard G., Jr., (BV) ....'59 '85 C.504 B.A. L.424 J.D. Atty. Gen.
DeJoode, Jeffrey W., (BV) ....'61 '89 C.350 B.S. L.352 J.D. 402 E. Jackson
Dye, Thomas W. ....'33 '61 C&L.339 B.A., LL.B. 141 S. Lafayette St.‡
Edmiston, Charles N., II, (BV) '54 '80 C.339 B.S. L.352 J.D.
[Ⓐ Kanoski&Assoc.] (ⒸBloomington, Peoria, Quincy, Rushville, Springfield)
Flack, Charles Haynes, (AV) ....'27 '54 C&L.597 B.S., J.D. [Ⓑ Flack,M.&S.]

Flack, McRaven & Stephens, (BV)
32 West Side Courthouse Square, 61455
Telephone: 309-837-5000 Fax: 309-836-2335
Email: maclaw@macomb.com
Of Counsel: J. Dixson McRaven; Charles Haynes Flack; Richard D. Stephens. Members of Firm: Lawrence J. Kwacala; Bruce J. Biagini; James Patrick Murphy (1948-1997); Heidi A. Benson. Associate: Matthew P. Kwacala.
General Civil and Criminal Practice in all Courts. Probate, Estate Planning, Real Estate, Corporation, Personal Injury, Higher Education, Family Law.
Representative Clients: Citizens National Bank of Macomb; MidAmerica National Bank; Western Illinois University; NTN-Bower; Macomb Public Building Commission; First Federal Bank; Chicago Title & Trust Co.; Macomb Clinic, Ltd.; McDonough County Chapter of the American Red Cross.

Glidden, John R., (AV) ....'36 '61 C.162 B.A. L.352 LL.B. [Hartzell,G.T.&H.] ⊙
Hartzell, Franklin M., (AV) ....'23 '50 C&L.339 B.S., LL.B. [Hartzell,G.T.&H.] ⊙
Hartzell, Thomas F., (AV) ....'59 '84 C.340 B.S. L.801 J.D. [Hartzell,G.T.&H.] ⊙

Hartzell, Glidden, Tucker and Hartzell, (AV)
Old Bailey House, 100 South Campbell Street, 61455 ⊙
Telephone: 309-833-3121
Email: firm@adams.net
Members of Firm: Franklin M. Hartzell; John R. Glidden; Stanley L. Tucker; Thomas F. Hartzell.
General Civil Trial and Appellate Practice in all State and Federal Courts. Real Estate, Estate Planning and Probate, Banking Law, Taxation, Personal Injury and Family Law.
Carthage, Illinois Office: Williams Building. Telephone: 217-357-3121. FAX: 217-357-2027.

See Professional Biographies, MACOMB, ILLINOIS

Heiser, Larry W. ....'45 '71 C&L.339 B.S., J.D. Asso. Cir. J.
Henderson, William D. ....'44 '68 C&L.352 B.A., J.D. Cir. J.
Kanoski, Ronald J., (BV) ....'47 '74 C.234 B.S. L.424 J.D. [Kanoski&Assoc.] ⊙
Kanoski & Associates, (BV)
127 N. Randolph (ⒸBloomington, Decatur, Peoria, Quincy, Rushville, Springfield)
Kwacala, Lawrence J., (BV) ....'44 '70 C&L.424 B.S., J.D. [Flack,M.&S.]
Kwacala, Matthew P. ....'75 '00 C.734 B.A. L.423 J.D. [Ⓐ Flack,M.&S.]
Leezer, Patsy, (BV) ....'53 '83 C.339 B.A. L.1288 J.D. Asst. Atty. Gen.
Leighty, Ellis E., (AV) ....'17 '51 C.339 B.S. L.209 J.D. 104 Oakland Lane‡
Lucie, Jim D., (BV) ....'43 '70 C.927 B.S. L.339 J.D. 315 East Jackson
McMillan, John D., (BV) ....'50 '75 C.388 B.A. L.362 J.D. 402 E. Jackson St.
McRaven, J. Dixson, (AV) ....'21 '51 C.339 B.S. L.996 LL.B. [Ⓑ Flack,M.&S.]
Melton, Robt. A. ....'25 '51 C.927 L.365 LL.B. 221 S. Randolph St.‡
O'Donnell, Joseph C. ....'51 '83 C.602 B.A. L.365 J.D. [O'Donnell]
O'Donnell Law Office ....127 S. Lafayette St.

Olivero, Kathy A., (CV) '56 '82 C.339 B.S. L.801 J.D.
[Ⓐ Kanoski&Assoc.] (ⒸBloomington, Peoria, Quincy, Rushville, Springfield)
Poncin, William E., (BV) ....'54 '80 C.927 L.365 J.D. State's Atty.
Randolph, William L. ....'25 '53 C&L.339 B.A., LL.B. Ret. Cir. J.
Rittenmeyer, Steven D., (CV) ....'46 '78 C.966 B.A. L.678 J.D. [Ⓑ Robbins,S.N.L.&T.]
Robbins, Lyle W. ....'10 '46 C.340 A.B. L.339 LL.B. 1001 Bobby Ave.‡
Robbins, Schwartz, Nicholas, Lifton & Taylor, Ltd., (AV)
616 Beverly Ave. (ⒸChicago, Collinsville, Decatur)
Simshauser, John V., (AV) ....'23 '55 C.340 Ph.B. L.996 50 S. Yorktown Rd.‡
Slater, Kent ....'45 '75 C.339 B.S. L.365 J.D. 3rd District of Appellette
Smith, Barney M., Jr. '21 '54 C&L.846 B.B.A., LL.B.
(adm. in TX; not adm. in IL) 1129 Maple Ave.‡
Stambaugh, Susan L. ....'69 '95 C.927 B.A. L.801 J.D. 127 S. Lafayette, Ste. 2
Stauffer, Scott ....'66 '91 C.339 B.A. L.365 J.D. Judicial Clk.
Stephens, Richard D., (BV) ....'27 '57 C.927 B.S. L.597 J.D. [Ⓑ Flack,M.&S.]
Tucker, Stanley L., (BV) ....'42 '70 C&L.339 B.S., J.D. [Hartzell,G.T.&H.] ⊙
Waldman, John J., (CV) '62 '88 C.801 B.A. L.339 J.D.
[Ⓐ Kanoski&Assoc.] (ⒸBloomington, Peoria, Quincy, Rushville, Springfield)

Westervelt, Johnson, Nicoll & Keller, LLC, (AV)
MidAmerica Banking Center, 130 North Side Square, Suite 202, 61435 ⊙
Telephone: 309-836-2900 Fax: 309-836-2844
URL: http://www.wjnklaw.com
A. Anthony Ashenhurst.
General Civil Trial and Appellate Practice in State and Federal Courts, Insurance Defense, Health and Health Care, Labor Relations, Employment Discrimination and Affirmative Action, Products Liability Litigation, ERISA and Benefits Plans, Corporate, Agricultural, Bankruptcy, Creditors' Rights, Banking, Real Estate, State and Federal Taxation, Estate Planning, Trusts and Probate, Workers Compensation, Environmental, Commercial.
Peoria, Illinois Office: 14th Floor, 411 Hamilton Boulevard, 61602; Telephone: 309-671-3550. Fax: 309-671-3588.

See Professional Biographies, MACOMB, ILLINOIS

Weston, C. Don, (BV) ....'33 '61 C.388 B.A. L.276 J.D. 120 N. Dudley St.

MADISON, 4,629, *Madison Co.*

Gilliard, Allen F., Jr. ....'43 '71 C.976 B.A. L.659 LL.B. 801 Greenwood St.
Vasileff, Nick D., (BV) ....'18 '50 C.339 L.734 LL.B. 404 Madison Ave.

MAHOMET, 4,877, *Champaign Co.*

Morrison, Robert W. ....'21 '44 C.309 B.A. L.339 J.D. P.O. Box 278
Van Hagey, William, (AV) ....'46 '72 C&L.339 A.B., J.D. 801 S. Jody Dr.

MAKANDA, 404, *Jackson Co.*

Adams, Steven Maynard '48 '00 C&L.575 B.A., J.D.
(adm. in NC; not adm. in IL) [Adams,S.M.]
Adams, Steven M. ....816 Hartline Rd.

MANHATTAN, 3,330, *Will Co.*

Carriere, Louise Stearns ....'15 '39 C&L.339 B.A., J.D. 26811 S. Kankakee St.‡
McGrath, Timothy J. ....'61 '86 C.190 B.S.B.A. L.365 J.D. 440 South State St.
Naughton, Michael R., (BV) ....'56 '81 C.209 B.A. L.365 J.D. [M.R.Naughton]
Naughton, M. R., (BV) .... 155 W. North St.
Tourlakes, Alexander James, II ....'62 '98 L.365 J.D. 160 Market Place

MANTENO, 6,414, *Kankakee Co.*

Bergdahl, David Earl ....'68 '93 C.339 B.A. L.801 J.D. [D.E.Bergdahl]
Bergdahl, David E., Law Office of ....269 S. Main St.
Smith, William F. ....'66 '91 C.602 B.A. L.209 J.D. Homestar Financial Group
Sweeney, Sandra Lin ....'63 '00 C.679 B.A. L.146 J.D. [S.Sweeney]
Sweeney, Sandra, Law Office of ....33 N. Main St., Ste. 2

MAPLE PARK, 765, *DeKalb & Kane Cos.*

MacTavish, David '— '99 C.209 B.A. L.365 J.D.
8N341 Thomas Road, 60151
Telephone: 630-365-2613 Fax: 630-365-9012
Email: david@mactavish-law.com URL: http://www.mactavish-law.com
Copyrights, Trademarks, Trade Names, Entertainment Law, Art Law, Internet, Cyberspace, Cyberpiracy, Domain Names, Idea Protection, Licensing, Trade Secrets, Unfair Competition, Computer Law.

See Professional Biographies, MAPLE PARK, ILLINOIS

Nickels, John L. ....'31 '61 C.589 B.S. L.209 J.D. Ret. Suprm.Ct. J.‡

MAPLETON, 255, *Peoria Co.*

LaSorsa, Peter M. ....'61 '03 C.98 B.S. L.365 J.D. [P.M.LaSorsa]
LaSorsa, Peter M., P.C., The Law Offices of .... 7109 S. Ridgebrook Dr.
Molchin, Cathy A., (BV) ....'58 '88 C.234 B.A. L.574 J.D. [C.A.Molchin]
Molchin, Cathy A., P.C., (BV) ....4909 Sir Lionel Court

MARENGO, 6,355, *McHenry Co.*

Conklin, Timothy J. ....'— '04 C&L.589 B.S., J.D. [Ⓐ Pollock,M.E.&P.]
Courier, Michelle J. ....'73 '98 C.339 B.S. L.589 J.D. [Ⓐ Firm of Franks,G.&M.]
del Granado, Juan J. ....'— '94 C.145 B.A. L.597 J.D [Ⓐ Firm of Franks,G.&M.]
Eicksteadt, Richard W., (BV) ....'35 '66 C.339 B.S. L.146 J.D. [Pollock,M.E.&P.]
Filler, Jay K., Jr., (BV) ....'54 '78 C.221 B.A. L.424 J.D. 3901 N. Rte. 23
Franks, Herbert H., (AV) ....'34 '61 C.1016 B.S. L.904 J.D. [Firm of Franks,G.&M.]
Franks, Jack D., (BV) ....'63 '89 C.966 B.A. L.904 J.D. [Firm of Franks,G.&M.]

Franks, Gerkin & McKenna, P.C., The Law Firm of, (AV) BR
19333 East Grant Highway, P.O. Box 5, 60152-0005
Telephone: 815-923-2107 Fax: 815-923-2114
Email: franklaw@mc.net URL: http://www.famlaw.com
Herbert H. Franks; Peggy D. Gerkin; Terrence J. McKenna; Jack D. Franks. Associates: Stephanie A. Kasten; David N. Rechenberg; Michelle J. Courier; Juan J. del Granado.
Languages: Spanish.
General, Civil & Criminal Trial Practice, Banking, Business Law, Commercial Real Estate, Corporate Law, Criminal Law, Debt Collections, Family Law, Personal Injury, Real Estate, Trusts & Estates, Immigration, Wills, Workers Compensation, Municipal Law, Traffic, Zoning, Planning and Land Use.

See Professional Biographies, MARENGO, ILLINOIS

Gerkin, Peggy D., (BV) ....'62 '88 C.338 B.S. L.589 J.D. [Firm of Franks,G.&M.]
Kasten, Stephanie A. ....'75 '00 C.293 B.A. L.589 J.D. [Ⓐ Firm of Franks,G.&M.]
Koch, Patrice E. ....'— '05 C.371 B.A. L.589 J.D. [Ⓐ Pollock,M.E.&P.]
Looney, Daniel C. ....'45 '70 C.602 B.B.A. L.339 J.D. 23519 Kishwaukee Valley Road
McKenna, Terrence J., (BV) ....'64 '89 C.589 B.S. L.209 J.D. [Firm of Franks,G.&M.]
Meyers, Harvey A., (BV) ....'34 '65 C.589 B.S. L.146 J.D. [Pollock,M.E.&P.]
Meyers, Kimberly A. ....'— '05 C.339 B.S. L.589 J.D. [Ⓐ Pollock,M.E.&P.]
Pollock, Norman J., (AV) ....'35 '65 C.589 B.S. L.146 J.D. [Pollock,M.E.&P.]

Pollock, Meyers, Eicksteadt & Pulak, Ltd., (AV)
100 West Washington Street, 60152
Telephone: 815-568-8071 FAX: 815-568-0003 URL: http://www.lawyers.com/pollockmeyerseicksteadt
Email: law@marengolaw.com URL: http://www.marengolawfim.com

(This Listing Continued)

Pollock, Meyers, Eickstead & Pulak, Ltd. (Continued)

Norman J. Pollock; Harvey A. Meyers; Richard W. Eickstead. Associates: Timothy J. Conklin; Patrice E. Koch; Kimberly A. Meyers.
General Trial Practice, Appellate Practice, Estate Planning, Probate Law, Trust Law, Real Estate, Banking Law, Bankruptcy Law, Personal Injury, Workers Compensation, Administrative Law, Corporate Law, Contracts, Civil Litigation, Trusts and Estates, Real Estate Law.
Representative Clients: Harris Bank/Marengo; Harris Bank/Woodstock; Woodstone Co.; Marengo Steel Co.; Marengo Disposal Co.; Key Development Co.; Agrinetics, Inc.; Compost Enterprises; McGill Metal Products Co.; Cardinal Savings and Loan Association.

See Professional Biographies, MARENGO, ILLINOIS

Rechenberg, David N., (CV) ...... '61 '87 C&L.589 B.S., J.D. [🄰 Firm of Franks,G.&M.]
Schmitt, Thomas W., (BV) .... '46 '75 C.597 B.S. L.146 J.D. 3901 N. Route 23
Schwartzman, Wayne A. '41 '70
C.966 B.S. L.365 J.D. Pres. & Gen. Coun., McGill Metal Products

MARION, * 16,035, *Williamson Co.*

Armstrong, William A., (AV) .... '41 '66 C&L.339 A.B., J.D. [🄲 Armstrong&G.] ‡

Armstrong & Green, (BV)
400 North Market Street, 62959
Telephone: 618-993-6072 Fax: 618-993-1194
Email: sgreen@midamer.net
Of Counsel: William A. Armstrong (Retired). Member of Firm: Stephen R. Green.
Insurance Defense, Personal Injury, School Law, Municipal Law, Workers Compensation, Commercial Law.

See Professional Biographies, MARION, ILLINOIS

Austin, Paul Thomas, (BV) .... '43 '71 C.801 B.A. L.836 J.D. 709 N. Carbon St.
Basi, Bart A. '40 '69 C.823 B.A. L.421 J.D.
Pres., Ctr. for Financial, Legal & Tax Planning
Bleyer, Brad K., (AV) .... '56 '83 C&L.801 B.S., J.D. 400 West Jackson Suite A
Bleyer, James B., (AV) .... '28 '55 C.801 B.A. L.602 J.D. [Bleyer&B.]
Bleyer, Joseph A., (BV) .... '61 '86 C&L.801 B.S., J.D. [Bleyer&B.]
Bleyer, Knute Rockne .... '53 '97 C&L.801 B.S, J.D. [🄰 Bleyer&B.]

Bleyer and Bleyer, (AV)
601 West Jackson Street, P.O. Box 487, 62959-0487
Telephone: 618-997-1331 FAX: 618-997-6559
Email: bleyer@bleyerlaw.com URL: http://www.lawyers.com/josephbleyer
James B. Bleyer; Joseph A. Bleyer; Knute Rockne Bleyer.
General and Trial Practice. Insurance Defense, Workers Compensation and Local Government Torts and Civil Rights.
Representative Clients: Country Mutual Insurance Co.; Allstate Insurance Co.; New Hampshire Insurance Group; Hartford Insurance Group; Carterville State & Savings Bank.

See Professional Biographies, MARION, ILLINOIS

Bradley, John E., (CV) .... '71 '96 C.846 B.A. L.339 J.D. [🄲 Mitchell&M.]
Brame, Linda J. .... '76 '02 C.734 B.A. L.801 J.D. [🄰 Winters,B.C.&S.]
Brenner, Daniel W., (CV) .... '57 '91 C&L.801 B.S., J.D. Asst. Atty. Gen.
Brewster, John S., (AV) .... '50 '76 C.823 B.A. L.801 J.D. [Winters,B.C.&S.]
Broeking, Lawrence E., (BV) .... '50 '77 C&L.801 B.A., J.D. Pub. Def.

Bryant & Kautz, PC
4501 West De Young, Suite B-2, 62959 ⊙
Telephone: 618-993-1468 Fax: 618-993-1329
Joseph M. Leberman.
General Civil and Criminal Practice. Trials and Appeals, State and Federal Courts. Personal Injury, Criminal, Real Estate, Corporation, Family Law, Trusts and Estates.
Paducah, Kentucky Office: 601 Washington Street, P.O. Box 1876, 42002-1876. Telephone: 270-442-1422. Fax: 270-443-8788.
Metropolis, Illinois Office: 222 Ferry Street, 62960. Telephone: 618-524-5671. Fax: 618-524-9671.

See Professional Biographies, MARION, ILLINOIS

Clayton, John H., Jr. .... '17 '49 C.801 B.Ed. L.339 1900 Suzanne Dr.‡
Crosby, Thomas F., III, (BV) .... '53 '81 C&L.801 B.A., J.D. [Winters,B.C.&S.]
Degen, Margaret J. .... '65 '91 C.352 B.B.A. L.801 J.D. Asst. State's Atty.
Dorris, Douglas N., (AV) .... '54 '81 C&L.801 B.S., J.D. [Howerton,D.&S.]
Drew, Robert A. .... '42 '72 C.801 B.A. L.45 J.D. 903 N. Market St.

Feirich/Mager/Green/Ryan
(See Carbondale)

Fine, Alexander M., (CV) .... '56 '83 C&L.801 B.S., J.D. Pub. Def.
Flan, Jeffrey V. '48 '82 L.1008 LL.B.
(adm. in CA; not adm. in IL) P.O. Box 1807‡
Franklin, Christine Pappelis '54 '81
C&L.801 B.A., J.D. Dept. of Children & Family Servs.
Garnati, Charles R., (BV) .... '52 '78 C&L.801 B.A., J.D. State's Atty.
Garrison, James T., (BV) .... '41 '66 C.801 B.A. L.146 J.D. 612 North Market
Gott, Amanda B. .... '75 '99 C.338 B.S. L.801 J.D. [Gott,A.B.]
Gott, Amanda Byassee .... P.O. Box 1743
Green, Stephen R., (BV) .... '63 '89 C&L.801 B.S., J.D. [Armstrong&G.]
Gustavson, Gregory E. .... '46 '88 C.37 B.S. L.362 J.D. [🄰 Howerton,D.&S.]
Hampson, Theodore J. .... '71 '00 C.339 B.S. L.801 J.D. 907 N. Market
Hardin, Jay A. .... '62 '91 C.338 B.S. L.801 J.D. State Farm Ins. Co.

Harris, Lambert, Howerton & Dorris
(See Howerton, Dorris & Stone)

Hart and Hart
(See Benton)

Howell, Synder .... '21 '50 C.801 B.S. L.339 Cir. J.
Howerton, Robert H., (AV) .... '43 '68 C.801 B.A. L.597 J.D. [Howerton,D.&S.]

Howerton, Dorris & Stone, (AV) BR
300 West Main Street, 62959
Telephone: 618-993-2616 Fax: 618-997-1845 URL: http://www.hdsplaw.lawoffice.com
Email: hds@neondsl.com URL: http://www.lawyers.com/hlh&d
Members of Firm: Robert H. Howerton; Douglas N. Dorris; Stephen W. Stone. Associate: Gregory E. Gustavson.
***Plaintiff's Personal Injury*, Workers Compensation Law, Insurance Bad Faith, Breach of Contract, Criminal Defense, Medical Malpractice, General Civil and Trial Practice.**

See Professional Biographies, MARION, ILLINOIS

Hubler, Kenneth T. .... '21 '50 C.801 B.A. L.910 J.D. 1807 Dorothy Lane‡

Jelliffe, Ferrell, Morris & Doerge
(See Harrisburg)

Keller, John Timothy .... '64 '94 C&L.801 B.S., J.D. 108 W Jackson St
Kibler, Keith W., (CV) .... '57 '81 C.801 B.A. L.734 J.D. 208 N. Market St.
Kochan, Mark, Law Office of .... '70 '99 C.801 B.A. L.146 J.D. P.O. Box 56
Krantz, Edw. G. .... '14 '40 C&L.597 B.A., J.D. 1810 Testa Dr.‡
Lauterjung, Larry Edward .... '54 '88 C&L.801 B.A., J.D. Director
Lawler, Bridget Ann .... '75 '00 C.734 B.A. L.801 J.D. P.O. Box 1773
Lawler, Raymond, (BV) .... '42 '72 C.999 B.A. L.469 J.D. 3003 Oak Court

Leberman, Joseph M. ..... '59 '88 C.531 B.S. L.801 J.D. [🄰 Bryant&K.] (⊙Paducah, KY)
Leech, Dean J. '48 '79 C.125 A.B. L.796 J.D.
(adm. in TX; not adm. in IL) P.O. Box 2000‡
Lewis, Brian D., (BV) .... '54 '80 C&L.801 B.S., J.D. 411 1/2 N. Court
Machicao, Dorothy L., (CV) .... '41 '89 C.249 B.S.N. L.801 J.D. 207 S. Market St.
Malkovich, Thomas Stephen .... '69 '94 C.339 B.A. L.801 J.D. P.O. Box 966
Maurizio, Michael W., (BV) .... '48 '84 L.801 J.D. 1903 West Main Street
McGarry, Brian P., (BV) .... '50 '76 C.801 B.A. L.1194 J.D. [B.McGarry]
McGarry, Brian, (BV) .... 500 N. Market St.
McNeill, Andrea Lynn, (CV) .... '68 '92 C&L.801 B.A., J.D. 503 W. Jackson St.
Mitchell, Bruce W., (BV) .... '50 '82 C.801 B.A. L.862 J.D. [Mitchell&M.]
Mitchell, J. C., (AV) .... '25 '49 C.597 L.339 LL.B. [Mitchell&M.]

Mitchell & Mitchell, (AV) BR
404 North Monroe, P.O. Box 488, 62959-2328
Telephone: 618-993-2134 Telecopier: 618-993-8702
Email: mail@mitchell-lawfirm.com URL: http://www.lawyers.com/mmb
J. C. Mitchell; Bruce W. Mitchell. Of Counsel: John E. Bradley.
General Trial and Appellate Practice. Insurance, Personal Injury, Medical Malpractice, Products Liability, Commercial Law, Litigation and Divorce.
Representative Clients: St. Paul Fire & Casualty Insurance Company; Liberty Mutual Insurance Company; Shelter Insurance Company; Atlantic Mutual Insurance Company; Farmer's Insurance Exchange; United States Fidelity and Guarantee Company; Horace Mann Insurance.

See Professional Biographies, MARION, ILLINOIS

Mitchell, Sam C., & Associates
(See West Frankfort)

Murphy, Paul S. .... '47 '72 C.276 A.B. L.93 J.D. Cir. J.‡
Narusis, Stanley W., (BV) .... '23 '51 C.801 B.A. L.734 LL.B. P.O. Box 95
Novick, William J., (AV) .... '21 '53 C.801 L.734 J.D. [Novick]
Novick, William P., (BV) .... '52 '82 C.339 B.A. L.801 J.D. [Novick]
Novick Law Office, (AV) .... 300 N. Monroe St.
Olson, Jason A. .... '69 '97 C&L.801 B.S., J.D. [Olson,J.A.]
Olson, Jason A. .... 1616 W. Main Street
Osman, Ronald E., & Associates, (AV) ...... '46 '79 C.339 B.S. L.801 J.D. P.O. Box 939
Palmer, Phillip G. .... '59 '84 C&L.801 B.S., J.D. Cir.J.
Patchett, John R. (Randy), (BV) .... '49 '78 C&L.801 B.A., J.D. 104 West Calvert
Paul, Bernard A., (BV) .... '36 '68 C&L.339 B.S., J.D. 806 W. DeYoung St.
Powless, Kenneth B. .... '17 '40 C&L.339 B.S., J.D. 905 N. Van Buren St.‡
Sanders, J. Lawrence, (BV) .... '56 '81 C.340 B.S. L.801 J.D. [Sanders&S.]
Sanders, John W., (CV) .... '62 '88 C.339 B.A. L.801 J.D. [Sanders&S.]
Sanders & Sanders, (BV) .... 208 North Market Street
Schafer, Paul Jason, (BV) .... '67 '94 C&L.801 B.S., J.D. [Winters,B.C.&S.]
Shore, Jeffrey A. .... '63 '93 C.34 B.S.C.J. L.801 J.D. 517 South Court Street
Smoot, Carolyn Bailey, (BV) .... '53 '83 C.624 B.A. L.801 J.D. 1471 Nassau Lane
Stone, Stephen W., (BV) .... '65 '90 C&L.801 B.A., J.D. [Howerton,D.&S.]
Tetzlaff, Glenn R., (BV) .... '48 '77 C&L.801 B.S., J.D. [G.Tetzlaff]
Tetzlaff, Glenn, (BV) .... 106 W. Jackson
Throgmorton, Winston C., Attorney at Law, (CV) '54 '85
C.801 B.S. L.678 J.D. 304 N. Monroe
Winkler, Michael B. .... '64 '96 C.801 B.S. L.1187 J.D. 806 W. De Young Street

Winters, Brewster, Crosby and Schafer LLC, (AV) BR
111 West Main, P.O. Box 700, 62959
Telephone: 618-997-5611 Fax: 618-997-6522
Email: winlaw@winterslaw.com URL: http://www.lawyers.com/winlaw
Members of Firm: Charles D. Winters (1917-1992); John S. Brewster; Thomas F. Crosby, III; Paul Jason Schafer. Associate: Linda J. Brame.
General Practice. Trials in State and Federal Courts. Plaintiffs Personal Injury, Workers' Compensation. Probate, Estate Planning, Real Estate, Corporation, Environmental Law, Wills, Trusts, Estates, Probate and Class Actions.

See Professional Biographies, MARION, ILLINOIS

Wolf, Thomas J., Jr., (BV) .... '51 '76 C&L.602 B.B.A., J.D. [T.J.Wolf,Jr.]
Wolf, Thomas J., Jr., P.C., (BV) .... 400 Tower Sq.
Woodcock, Barbara L., (CV) .... '48 '84 C.927 B.A. L.801 J.D. 905 N. Court St.
Zuber, Kelley V. .... '65 '99 C&L.801 B.S., J.D. 803 E. DeYoung

MARISSA, 2,141, *St. Clair Co.*

Becker-Roscow, Jennifer M. .... '69 '94 C&L.801 B.A., J.D. 112 North Main Street
Clendenin, John F., (BV) .... '46 '72 C.339 B.S. L.352 J.D. [Conn,C.&N.] ⊙
Conn, Clendenin & Norton, (BV) .... 112 N. Main St. (⊙Sparta)
Norton, William C., (BV) .... '53 '78 C.798 B.A. L.801 J.D. [Conn,C.&N.] ⊙

MARKHAM, 12,620, *Cook Co.*

Boyle, Janet E. .... '53 '78 C.339 B.A. L.146 J.D. Pub. Defs. Off.
Carey, Philip J. .... '18 '49 C.812 B.S.C. L.365 J.D. Cir. J.
Carroll, Lawrence W. .... '23 '50 C.339 L.424 J.D. Assoc. Cir. J.
Clifford, Robert J. .... '50 '79 C.1151 B.A. L.146 J.D. Asst. States Atty.
Copp, Gary T. .... '55 '80 C.424 B.B.A. L.589 J.D. Asst. Pub. Def.
Corsino, Joseph C. .... '52 '80 C.338 B.S. L.209 J.D. Asst. Pub. Def.
Daly, Noreen M. .... '55 '80 C.1024 B.S. L.424 J.D. Asst. States Atty.
Danielian, Jason Frank .... '64 '89 C.818 B.A. L.209 J.D. Asst. State's Atty.
Dohm, Dennis M. .... '41 '69 C&L.209 B.A., J.D. Cir. J.
Dooling, Deborah M. .... '53 '78 C.339 B.A. L.146 J.D. Asst. States Atty.
Evans, Michael Paul .... '76 '01 C.473 B.A. L.209 J.D. 15610 S. Kedzie
Gainer, Thomas V., Jr. .... '49 '77 C.424 B.S. L.365 J.D. Asst. States Atty.
Gavin, Marvin E. .... '31 '55 C.210 B.A. L.309 LL.B. Cir. J.
Gierach, Will E. .... '23 '45 C.966 B.A. L.209 J.D. Asso. Cir. J.
Gladney, Shari L. .... '— '98 C.22 B.A. L.1463 J.D. Asst. Pub. Def.
Houtsma, Cornelius J., Jr. .... '29 '59 C&L.424 LL.B. Assoc. Cir. J.
Lipinski, Marcella C. .... '42 '80 C.1191 B.A. L.365 J.D. Asst. Pub. Def.
Lynn, Alan Hugh .... '58 '83 C.720 B.A. L.209 J.D. Asst. States Atty.

Maramba & Associates, LLC
(See Arlington Heights)

McDonough, Martin E. .... '34 '59 C&L.424 B.S., J.D. Asso. Cir. J.
McNally, Martin J. .... '49 '74 C.750 B.A. L.424 J.D. 16327 S. Pulaski
Morris, Penelope .... '59 '97 C.424 B.A. L.209 J.D. Asst. Co. Pub. Def.
Muse, Elliott, Jr. .... '37 '76 C.1016 B.S.B.A. L.209 J.D. Cir. J.
Nichols, James .... '51 '80 C.339 B.A. L.209 J.D. Asst. States Atty.
Niesen, Debra S. .... '50 '80 C.347 B.A. L.879 J.D. Asst. Pub. Def.
Nikolic, Daniel P. .... '66 '91 C.424 B.A. L.365 J.D. Asst. State's Atty.
Perry, Paul E. .... '44 '71 C.276 B.A. L.128 J.D. Asst. States Atty.
Rago, Frank R. .... '49 '75 C.339 B.A. L.365 J.D. Asst. Pub. Def.
Thakkar, Shital Hasmukhbhai .... '— '00 C.339 B.A. L.146 J.D. Cook Co. State Atty. Off.
Willis, Camile E. .... '58 '84 C.339 B.S. L.608 J.D. Cir. Ct. J.

MAROA, 1,602, *Macon Co.*

Brown, Rex L., (BV) .... '30 '57 C.338 B.S.Ed. L.339 J.D. [Brown,H.B.&M.] ⊙
Brown, Hawkins, Basola & Mattingley, (BV) .... 115 W. Main St. (⊙Decatur)

Hawkins, Elmer C., (BV) .... '29 '55 C&L.339 B.S., LL.B. [Brown,H.B.&M.] ⊙

MARSEILLES, 4,655, *La Salle Co.*

Guerrini, Joseph T., (BV) ....'10 '33 C&L.424 J.D. 483 N. Main St.
Guerrini, Timothy J., (BV) .... '52 '78 C.424 B.S. L.801 J.D. 483 N. Main St.
Mason, S. Michael, (CV) .... '49 '83 C.1151 B.A. L.365 J.D. [M.Mason]
Mason, Michael, Attorney at Law, (CV) ....101 E. Bluff

MARSHALL, * 3,771, *Clark Co.*

Bennett, Schroeder & Wieck, (BV)
517 Locust Street, P.O. Box 98, 62441
Telephone: 217-826-8051 Fax: 217-826-5011
URL: http://www.lawyers.com/bennettschroederwieck
Members of Firm: Grendel F. Bennett (1900-1987); Joseph R. Schroeder; Paul E. Wieck.
General Civil and Criminal Trial Practice. Personal Injury, Workers Compensation, Domestic Relations, Family, Probate, Business/Contract, Wills/Estate Planning, Income Tax, Social Security Disability, Real Estate, Bankruptcy Law, Collections and Traffic.
See Professional Biographies, MARSHALL, ILLINOIS

Bernardoni, Richard J., (BV) ....'51 '76 C.339 B.S. L.436 J.D. [Meehling&B.]

Brainard Law Offices, The
(See Charleston)

Heller, Holmes & Associates, P.C.
(See Mattoon)

Hoth, Sandra L. ....'66 '93 C.339 B.Mus. L.734 J.D. Asst. State's Atty.
Lewis, David W., (BV) ....'52 '78 C.234 B.A. L.365 J.D. Assoc. Cir. Jud
Meehling, William F., (AV) .... '23 '49 C&L.339 B.S., J.D. [⊡ Meehling&B.]
Meehling & Bernardoni, (BV) ....115 S. 6th St.
Resch, Tracy W. ....'49 '73 C.970 B.A. L.339 J.D. Cir. J.; Clark Co. Cir. Ct.
Rich, Randolph M., (BV) ....'48 '74 C.37 B.S. L.879 J.D. 516 Archer Ave.
Schroeder, Joseph R., (BV) ....'50 '75 C.347 A.B. L.365 J.D. [Bennett,S.&W.]
Shawler, Omer T., (AV) ....'26 '50 C.346 B.S. L.339 J.D. [O.T.Shawler]
Shawler, Omer T., Law Office, (AV) ....220 S. 6th St.
Simonton, Dennis E., (BV) .... '55 '80 C.234 B.A. L.734 J.D. 19344 N. 1020th Street
Wieck, Paul E., (BV) ....'56 '81 C.339 B.A. L.146 J.D. [Bennett,S.&W.]

MARYVILLE, 4,651, *Madison Co.*

Beljanski, Kenneth B. .... '69 '96 C&L.801 B.S., J.D. 2135 N. Center
Burkart, Thomas W., (BV) ....'60 '85 C.973 B.A. L.734 J.D. [Burkart] ⊙
Burkart Law Offices, (BV) ....2135 N. Center St. (⊙Hamel)
Huffman, Brian A., Law Office of ....'67 '92 C.734 B.A. L.502 J.D. 2225 N. Center

MASCOUTAH, 5,659, *St. Clair Co.*

Binsbacher, Valroy, (BV) ....'46 '72 C.133 B.A. L.502 J.D. [V.Binsbacher]
Binsbacher, Valroy, P.C., (BV) ....36 W. Main St.
Connolly, Robert J., (BV) ....'51 '81 C.502 B.S. L.862 J.D. [Schroeder,S.&C.]
Degen, Richard A., (CV) ....'38 '63 C&L.734 B.S., LL.B. 5533 Brickyard Rd.
Moore, Dwight A. ....'46 '77 C.377 B.S. L.900 J.D. 1136 Widgeon Drive★
Schroeder, Mary T., (BV) ....'54 '80 C.57 B.A. L.734 J.D. [Schroeder,S.&C.]
Schroeder, Meryl T., (AV) ....'21 '49 C.801 B.Ed. L.910 J.D. 223 E. Main St.‡
Schroeder, Schroeder & Connolly, (BV) ....223 E. Main St.

MASON CITY, 2,558, *Mason Co.*

Kirby, Phillip M., (CV) ....'56 '83 C.927 B.S. L.734 J.D. 115 N. Tonica St.
McCreery, William M. '44 '69 C.340 B.S. L.362 J.D.
(adm. in FL; not adm. in IL) P.O. Box 127
McNeil, Charles L., (CV) ....'49 '77 C.339 B.S. L.221 J.D. 33735 Old Route 29

MATTESON, 12,928, *Cook Co.*

Barr, David R. ....'48 '73 C.309 B.A. L.145 J.D. 21322 Kildare Ave.
Buchholz, Diane K. ....'49 '84 C.339 B.A. L.365 J.D. 3632 W. 216th Pl.
Doeringer, John H. ....'33 '60 C&L.976 B.A., LL.B. 21141 Governors Hwy.‡
Dujsik, Lawrence, Law Office of '50 '91
C.720 M.F.A. L.879 J.D. 4440 W. Lincoln Hwy., Ste. 205
Fennell, Michael J. ....'47 '73 C.190 B.A. L.597 J.D. 3805 W. 216th St.

Gray & Idris, P.C., Law Offices of
(See Joilet)

Junge, Henry J. '38 '63 C.602 B.A. L.190 J.D.
(adm. in NE; not adm. in IL) 3750 W. 215th St.‡
Manestar, Cynthia ....'— '87 C.339 B.S. L.209 J.D. 4440 Lincoln Hwy.
McDermott, David D. ....'74 '98 L.365 J.D. [McDermott&M.]
McDermott, David G. ....'49 '79 C.234 B.A. L.365 J.D. [McDermott&M.]
McDermott, Deborah D. ....'51 '86 L.365 J.D. [McDermott&M.]
McDermott, Stacey Ames '75 '99 C.234 B.A. L.339 J.D.
4343 W. Lincoln Hwy., Ste. 303
McDermott & McDermott, Ltd. ....600 Holiday Plaza Dr., Ste. 500
Planera, Thomas, II ....'59 '89 C.424 A.B. L.146 J.D. 4440 Lincoln Hwy., Ste. 301
Regalado, Jose ....'23 '78 C.346 M.S. L.1151 J.D. 4123 Oakwood Ln.
Sahu, Pradip K. ....'71 '00 C.966 B.S. L.589 J.D. [Sahu&Assoc.]
Sahu & Associates ....3123 Holden Circle
Spence, Keith L. ....'64 '99 C.801 B.S. L.365 J.D. 33 Denise Ct.
Starks, Isaac J. ....'38 '80 C.661 B.A. L.209 J.D. 5704 Woodgate Dr.
Ward, Anderson J. ....'41 '86 C.45 Ph.D. L.1243 J.D. 21456 Main Street
Wigell, Raymond G. ...'49 '75 C.339 A.B. L.365 J.D. 4749 Lincoln Mall Drive, Suite 505

MATTOON, 18,291, *Coles Co.*

Armstrong, John H., (AV) ....'34 '60 C&L.339 B.A., J.D. [Armstrong&G.]

Armstrong & Grove, (AV)
1400 Charleston Avenue, P.O. Box 1425, 61938
Telephone: 217-234-2872 Fax: 217-234-2533
Email: aglaw@armstronggrove.com URL: http://www.armstronggrovelaw.com
Members of Firm: John H. Armstrong; Janet L. Grove.
Estate Planning, Probate, Trusts, Wills, Mineral Law, Drainage and Levee Law.
See Professional Biographies, MATTOON, ILLINOIS

Barger, John L., (BV) .... '58 '84 C.234 B.A. L.45 J.D. [Craig&C.]
Bennett, James A., (BV) ....'40 '65 C.711 A.B. L.128 J.D. [Ryan,B.&R.]
Bovard, Mark E. ....'72 '97 C.234 B.A. L.347 J.D. [Ⓐ Heller,H.&Assoc.]

Brainard Law Offices, The
(See Charleston)

Corn, Stephen L., (AV) ....'44 '69 C&L.339 B.A., J.D. [Craig&C.]

Craig & Craig, (AV)
1807 Broadway, P.O. Box 689, 61938-0689 ⊙
Telephone: 217-234-6481 Telecopier: 217-234-6486; 258-8292
Email: mattoon@craiglaw.net URL: http://www.lawyers.com/craig&craiglawoffices
(This Listing Continued)

Craig & Craig (Continued)
Members of Firm: Richard F. Record, Jr.; Stephen L. Corn; Robert G. Grierson; Gregory C. Ray; Paul R. Lynch (Resident, Mount Vernon Office); Kenneth F. Werts (Resident, Mount Vernon Office); John L. Barger; Julie A. Webb (Resident, Mount Vernon Office); John F. Watson; R. Sean Hocking. Associates: Sarah D. Moskowitz; Sarah B. Holsapple-Miller; J. Patrick Lee. Of Counsel: John P. Ewart (Retired).
General Practice in State and Federal Courts. Coal, Oil, Gas, Mining, Oil and Gas Transportation, Insurance, Drainage and Levee Law, Environmental, Corporation, Labor Relations, Workers Compensation and Real Estate Law. Estate Planning, Probate and Bankruptcy Law. Trials and Appeals.
Representative Clients: Marathon Oil Company; CN/ICRR; First Federal Savings and Loan Association of Mattoon, Illinois; The Medical Protective Co.; Illinois Consolidated Telphone Company; D-CO Laundry Villages, Inc.; Mattoon Enterprise Park, L.L.C.; Lake Land College; Consolidated Communications, Inc.; Mattoon Township Park District of Coles County.
Mount Vernon, Illinois Office: 115 North 7th Street. Telephone: 618-244-7511. Telecopier: 618-244-7628. Email: mtvernon@craiglaw.net.
See Professional Biographies, MATTOON, ILLINOIS

Crowder, Jason M., (CV) .... '70 '96 C.679 B.A. L.424 J.D. [Ⓐ Heller,H.&Assoc.]

Dilsaver & Nelson, (AV)
1500 Broadway, P.O. Box 649, 61938-0649
Telephone: 217-235-5651 Telecopier: 217-235-5255
Email: dnelson@dilsaver-nelson.com URL: http://www.dilsaver-nelson.com
Members of Firm: Jewell I. Dilsaver (1902-1991); David C. Nelson. Associate: Ernest Lee Waite, II.
Banking and Finance, Bankruptcy, Business Law, Criminal, Family Law, Litigation, Personal Injury, Real Estate, Trusts and Estates, Wills and Probate.
Representative Clients: Allstate Insurance Co.; First Mid-Illinois Bank & Trust; Rural King Supply, Inc.; B&M Construction; Curry Construction; Unique Home Properties; Heritage Builders; Anamet Electrical, Inc.; Parrish Carpets; Wells Fargo Bank.
See Professional Biographies, MATTOON, ILLINOIS

Dotson, L. Stanton, (BV) ....'38 '64 C.339 B.S. L.146 J.D. 1617 Wabash Ave.
Dunst, Robert Alan, (BV) ....'56 '82 C.648 B.A. L.339 J.D. [B.Dunst]
Dunst, Bob, Law Offices of, (BV) .... 421 N. 19th Street
Eberspacher, David Y., (AV) ....'53 '78 C.339 B.A. L.838 J.D. [Hefner,E.&T.]
Ewart, John P., (AV) ....'36 '61 C&L.339 J.D. [⊡ Craig&C.] ‡
Ferguson, Mark E., (BV) ....'54 '81 C.234 B.A. L.221 J.D. [M.E.Ferguson]
Ferguson, Mark E., Ltd., (BV) ....712 Broadway
Fuqua, Karen, (CV) ....'44 '80 C.339 B.A. L.589 J.D. 1617 Wabash Ave.
Glenn, Ralph D., (AV) ....'29 '53 C&L.339 B.S., J.D. [Glenn&L.]
Glenn & Logue, (AV) .... 901 Charleston Ave.
Grierson, Robert G., (AV) ....'50 '75 C.98 B.S. L.339 J.D. [Craig&C.]
Grove, Janet L., (BV) ....'55 '85 C.679 B.S. L.1119 J.D. [Armstrong&G.]
Hayden, Richard C., (AV) ....'42 '73 C.339 B.S. L.575 J.D. 201 East Richmond
Hefner, M. John, Jr., (AV) ....'43 '78 C.801 B.A. L.734 J.D. [Hefner,E.&T.]
Hefner, Eberspacher & Tapella, (AV) ....215 S. 17th Street
Heller, H. Kent, (AV) ....'52 '77 C&L.339 B.S., J.D. [Heller,H.&Assoc.]
Heller, Harlan, (AV) ....'28 '51 C&L.339 B.S., J.D. [Heller,H.&Assoc.]

Heller, Holmes & Associates, P.C., (AV)
1101 Broadway, P.O. Box 889, 61938-0889
Telephone: 217-235-2700 FAX: 217-235-0743
Email: hhlawoff@aol.com URL: http://www.hhlawoff.com
Harlan Heller; Brent D. Holmes; H. Kent Heller;—David Stevens; Fred Johnson; Jason M. Crowder; Mark E. Bovard; Gina R. Vonderheide.
General Civil and Trial Practice in all State, Federal and Appellate Courts. Personal Injury, Medical Negligence, Criminal Defense, Insurance, Litigation, Probate, Workers Compensation, Corporation, Commercial, Family Law, Oil and Gas.
Representative Clients: Quantum Chemical Co.; First National Bank of Effingham.
References: First National Bank, Mattoon, Ill.; Central National Bank of Mattoon.
See Professional Biographies, MATTOON, ILLINOIS

Hocking, R. Sean ....'73 '99 C.339 B.S. L.801 J.D. [Craig&C.]
Holmes, Brent D., (AV) ....'53 '78 C&L.339 B.S., J.D. [Heller,H.&Assoc.]
Holsapple-Miller, Sarah B. .... '80 '04 C.234 B.A. L.801 J.D. [Ⓐ Craig&C.]
Horsley, Jack E., (AV) ....'15 '39 C&L.339 A.B., J.D. 913 N. 31st
Johnson, Fred, (BV) ....'56 '81 C.57 B.A. L.801 J.D. [Ⓐ Heller,H.&Assoc.]
Jones, Daniel C., (CV) ....'68 '93 C.339 B.A. L.801 J.D. [Ⓐ Hefner,E.&T.]
Kaye, Carolyn A. ....'60 '85 C.674 B.A. L.1119 J.D. 2 Kent Fields‡
Lee, J. Patrick ....'74 '02 C.234 B.A. L.339 J.D. [Ⓐ Craig&C.]
Logue, Thomas J., (AV) ....'30 '56 C&L.339 B.A., LL.B. [Glenn&L.]
McGrath, William D., (CV) ....'55 '82 C&L.339 B.A., J.D. [Ⓐ B.Dunst]
Monippallil, Matthew M., (CV) ......'38 '84 C.424 M.B.A. L.801 J.D. 1521 Wabash Ave.
Moskowitz, Sarah D. ....'76 '02 C.352 B.A. L.801 J.D. [Ⓐ Craig&C.]
Nelson, David C., (AV) ....'46 '72 C.589 B.S. L.146 J.D. [Dilsaver&N.]
Owen, Joseph Preston ....'68 '98 C.357 B.S. L.801 J.D. 201 N. Logan
Radloff, Michael K., (BV) ....'54 '83 C.234 B.A. L.339 J.D. [Ryan,B.&R.]
Ray, Gregory C., (AV) ....'52 '76 C.801 B.S. L.339 J.D. [Craig&C.]
Record, Richard F., Jr., (AV) ....'37 '63 C.276 B.S. L.273 LL.B. [Craig&C.]
Roska, John '55 '83 C.118 A.B. L.477 J.D.
Land of Lincoln Legal Assistance Foundation, Inc.
Roytek, F. James, III, (CV) ....'50 '88 C.755 B.A. L.734 J.D. 921 Broadway Ave.
Ryan, Michael D., (AV) ....'50 '76 C.207 A.B. L.365 J.D. [Ryan,B.&R.]
Ryan, Stephen R., (AV) ....'46 '74 C.338 B.S. L.352 J.D. [Ryan,B.&R.]

Ryan, Bennett & Radloff, (AV)
300 Richmond East, P.O. Box 629, 61938-0629
Telephone: 217-234-2000 Fax: 217-234-2001
URL: http://www.lawyers.com/rbrkolaw
Members of Firm: Willis P. Ryan (1911-1983); James A. Bennett; Stephen R. Ryan; Michael D. Ryan; Michael K. Radloff.
General, Civil and Criminal Practice. Trials in all Courts. Insurance Defense, Workers Compensation, Negligence, Corporation, Probate, Estate Planning, Bankruptcy, Taxation and Oil and Gas Law. Domestic Relations, Divorce, Child Custody and Adoption Law.
Counsel For: State Farm Insurance Cos.; American States Insurance Co.; Auto-Owners Insurance Co.; Country Cos.; Economy Fire and Casualty Co.; Bituminous Insurance Cos.; Farmland Insurance; Millers Mutual Insurance; Horace Mann Insurance Co.
Reference: First Mid-Illinois Bank & Trust, Mattoon, Ill.
See Professional Biographies, MATTOON, ILLINOIS

Stevens, David, (BV) ....'47 '93 C.475 B.A. L.801 J.D. [Ⓐ Heller,H.&Assoc.]
Tapella, William R., (BV) ....'59 '94 C.801 B.A. L.339 J.D. [Hefner,E.&T.]
Tennyson, Connie Mouser '55 '99 C&L.801 B.A., J.D.
Land of Lincoln Legal Assistance Found., Inc.
Torbeck-Livesay, Judy ....'52 '92 C.234 B.A. L.801 J.D. [Winter-Black&L.] ⊙
Vonderheide, Gina R. ....'76 '04 C.357 B.S. L.734 J.D. [Ⓐ Heller,H.&Assoc.]
Waite, Ernest Lee, II ....'73 '00 C&L.801 B.S., J.D. [Ⓐ Dilsaver&N.]
Watson, John F., (CV) ....'67 '93 C.98 B.S.M.E. L.365 J.D. [Craig&C.]
Winter-Black, Janett S., (BV) ......'54 '79 C.234 B.A. L.801 J.D. [Winter-Black&L.] ⊙

Winter-Black & Livesay, Law Offices of, (BV)
201 North Logan Street, P.O. Box 835, 61938 ⊙
Telephone: 217-235-3400 Fax: 217-235-3402
URL: http://winter-blacklivesaylaw.com
Members of Firm: Janett S. Winter-Black; Judy Torbeck-Livesay.
(This Listing Continued)

Winter-Black & Livesay, Law Offices of (Continued)
Family Law, Foreclosures, Collections, Probate and Wills, Real Estate Contracts and Closings, Estate Planning, Bankruptcy, Appellate Practice.
Toledo, Illinois Office: 102 S. Meridian, 62468. Telephone: 217-849-2700. Fax: 217-849-2569.
See Professional Biographies, MATTOON, ILLINOIS

Zielke, Susan L. '72 '97 C&L.339 B.A., J.D.
Staff Atty., Land of Lincoln Legal Assistance Foundation, Inc.

MAYWOOD, 26,987, *Cook Co.*

Bailey, Barbara A. ... '66 '91 C.190 B.A. L.365 J.D. Asst. States Atty.
Beadle, Steven R. ... '54 '93 C.1156 B.S. L.1000 J.D. Asst. State's Atty.
Brander, Mike C. ... '43 '72 C.209 B.A. L.365 J.D. [Brander,S.&Assoc.]
Brander, Serpe & Associates, Law Office of ... 1317 South First Avenue
DeBoni, Frank ... '49 '74 C&L.209 B.S., J.D. Assoc. Cir. J.
Dixon, Donald R. ... '59 '95 C.347 A.S.N. L.879 J.D. Loyola Univ. Health Sys.
Etchingham, James P. ... '52 '78 C.746 B.A. L.589 J.D. Circuit Ct. J
Farina, Joseph A. ... '25 '52 C.209 L.365 LL.B. 110 S. 5th Ave.
Finney, Joseph C. '27 '72 C.880 B.A. L.981 LL.B.
(adm. in CA; not adm. in IL) Loyola Univ.
Fitzgibbons, Ryan C. ... '74 '00 C.589 B.A. L.801 J.D. 1701 S. 1st Ave., Ste. 300
Gamberdino, Nello P. ... '24 '61 C&L.209 A.B., J.D. Assoc. Cir. J.
Giralamo, John P. ... '73 '99 C.339 B.S. L.365 J.D. Asst. State's Atty.
Grossi, Colleen Tierney ... '53 '81 C.339 B.A. L.365 J.D. Asst. States Atty.
Harris, Gregory A. ... '65 '90 C.339 B.S. L.146 J.D. [G.Harris]
Harris, Gregory, Law Offices ... 1701 S. 1st Ave., Ste. 300
Karnezis, Themis N. ... '42 '70 C.215 B.Ch.E. L.365 J.D. Cir. J.
Kipperman, Carol A. ... '42 '66 C&L.659 B.A., J.D. Assoc. Cir. J.
Koppel, Jill Marie '67 '92 C.608 B.S. L.179 J.D.
Asst. Gen. Coun., Loyola Univ. Health System
Love, Noreen V. ... '51 '89 C.339 A.S. L.424 J.D. Asst. Pub. Def.
Mather, James S. ... '53 '81 C.207 B.A. L.365 J.D. Staff Atty., Cook Co. Pub. Def.

Mitchell Hoffman & Wolf LLC
(See Chicago)

Mondry, Karen M. ... '64 '90 C.339 B.S. L.46 J.D. 1300 Maybrook Dr., Ste. 101
Murphy, James V., II ... '46 '74 C.742 B.A. L.209 J.D. Assoc. Cir. J.
O'Brien, Maureen ... '59 '84 C.741 B.A. L.146 J.D. Asst. State's Atty.
Rappis, Jill M., (AV) ... '58 '84 C.383 B.A. L.436 J.D. Loyola Univ. Health Sys.
Reed, James L., Jr. '67 '93
C.473 B.A. L.1119 J.D. Asst. Gen. Coun., Loyola Univ. Health Sys.
Reiter, Charles E., III, (AV) '54 '81 C.94 B.A. L.472 J.D.
V.P. & Gen. Coun., Loyola Univ. Health Sys.
Ritchie, Meredith Emerson ... '64 '91 C.299 B.A. L.209 J.D. Asst. States Atty.
Scheffler, Henry E. ... '36 '62 C&L.209 A.B., J.D. Dep. Chf., Pub. Def.
Serpe, Ferdinand P. ... '55 '84 C.707 B.A. L.365 J.D. [Brander,S.&Assoc.]
Sorrentino, John M. ... '40 '65 C&L.209 B.S., J.D. Assoc. Cir. J.
Stratton, Karyn D. ... '53 '84 C.589 B.A. L.146 J.D. Asst. States Atty.
Tenuto, V. James ... '49 '78 C.339 B.S. L.1151 J.D. Asst. States Atty.
Terrell, Lawrence W., Sr. ... '50 '76 C.340 B.A. L.880 J.D. Cir. J.
Velasco, Xavier G. ... '46 '72 C.424 B.S. L.209 J.D. Dir., Suburbon Opers., Pub. Def.Off.
Walters, William O. ... '52 '77 C.339 B.A. L.146 J.D. 1500 Maybrook Dr.

Weaver Law Group, LLC
(See Chicago)

Welfeld, Jack A. ... '12 '39 C&L.597 B.S., LL.B. Assoc. Cir. J.
Zafiratos, James A. ... '18 '48 C.137 L.365 J.D. Cir. J.

McHENRY, 21,501, *McHenry Co.*

Alexander, Bud R. ... '52 '77 C&L.339 B.S., J.D. 3201 Terrace Dr.
Basford, Alan E. ... '55 '81 C.339 B.A. L.365 J.D. 5400 W. Elm St., Ste. 211
Bentley, Scott A., (BV) ... '60 '85 C&L.801 B.S., J.D. 3425 West Elm Street
Boudreau, Paul ... '64 '90 C.707 B.A. L.190 J.D. 4302-C. W. Crystal Lake Rd.
Brammer, Scott W., (CV) ... '66 '92 C.340 B.A. L.793 J.D. [Taradash&B.]
Bruce, Lori L. ... '61 '92 C.1333 B.S. L.146 J.D. [Mohr,B.H.&N.]
Brzezenski, Thomas J. ... '56 '84 C.273 B.A. L.861 J.D. Tr. Offr., McHenry State Bk.
Buxton, Renee A., (CV) '69 '97 C.966 B.A. L.209 J.D.
4314 W. Crystal Lake Rd., Ste. G
Casey, Robert F. ... '43 '75 C.602 B.A. L.209 J.D. 403 N. Country Club Dr.
Cowlin, James S., (BV) ... '56 '82 C.966 B.A. L.879 J.D. [Cowlin&C.]
Cowlin, Thomas L., (BV) ... '60 '87 C.966 B.A. L.365 J.D. [Cowlin&C.]
Cowlin & Cowlin, (BV) ... 5447 Bull Valley Rd.
Cunabaugh, Linda A., (BV) ... '52 '85 C.446 B.A. L.221 J.D. [McAndrews&C.]
Diamond, Samuel J., (BV) ... '42 '69 C.208 B.S. L.146 J.D. [Diamond&L.]
Diamond & LeSueur, P.C., (BV) ... 3431 W. Elm Street
Feetterer, Michael W., (BV) ... '65 '90 C.424 B.B.A. L.209 J.D. [Roth&F.]

Franks, Gerkin & McKenna, P.C., The Law Firm of
(See Marengo)

Gealow, Jon Carl ... '37 '66 C.339 B.S. L.273 J.D. 2903 N. Bayview Lane (Pat.)
Gilmore, Carl W., (BV) ... '65 '94 C.339 B.S. L.966 J.D. 3402 W. Elm St.
Godek, Laura Moore, (CV) ... '59 '84 L.146 J.D. 913 N. Curran Rd.
Green, Lance M. ... '48 '74 C.966 B.A. L.365 J.D. 818 S. Rte. 31
Hawkinson, Thomas N. '44 '74 C.627 B.A. L.190 J.D.
(adm. in NE; not adm. in IL) McHenry State Bk.
Hiera, Scott A. ... '63 '03 C.801 B.S. L.146 J.D. [A T.J.Popovich]
Hill, Carol L. ... '— '93 C&L.589 B.A., J.D. [Mohr,B.H.&N.]
Johnston, Janice Metros ... '36 '76 C.145 B.A. L.424 J.D. 7412 Saddle Creek Trail‡
Kasny, Roger R. ... '48 '75 C.679 B.S. L.365 J.D. 4310 W. Crystal Lake Rd., Ste. A
King, Philip S. ... '40 '69 C&L.477 A.B., LL.B. McHenry State Bk.‡
Kornak, John A., (BV) ... '56 '86 C.339 A.B. L.879 J.D. [A T.J.Popovich]
LeSueur, David C., (BV) ... '53 '80 C.172 B.A. L.146 J.D. [Diamond&L.]
Licastro, John T. ... '23 '55 C.999 L.365 LL.B. 1603 N. North Ave.‡
MacMeekin, Colin D. ... '48 '78 C.801 B.A. L.589 J.D. [C.MacMeekin]
MacMeekin, Colin, Law Offices of ... 5010 W. Elm St.
Malecki, Melinda S. ... '55 '92 C.424 B.A. L.365 J.D. 1509 N. Riverside Dr.
Mangiamele, Suzanne C., (BV) ... '58 '83 C.801 B.S. L.365 J.D. 3400 West Elm Street
Mast, Hans A. ... '62 '91 C.338 B.S. L.46 J.D. [A T.J.Popovich]
McAndrews, Patrick J., (BV) ... '51 '76 C.177 B.A. L.190 J.D. [McAndrews&C.]
McAndrews & Cunabaugh, P.C., (BV) ... 4314 West Crystal Lake Rd.
McClellan, Mary E. ... '— '04 C.999 B.S. L.365 J.D. 3014 S. Bergman Drive
McIntee, James M. ... '24 '54 3436 W. Elm St.‡

Michling Hofmann Vinton Plaza & Wick, P.C.
(See Woodstock)

Miller, James L. ... '48 '73 C.951 B.A. L.902 J.D. P.O. Box 1501
Missimer, David R., (BV) '59 '85
C.350 B.S. L.221 J.D. 4314 W. Crystal Lake Rd., Suite G
Mohr, Terry R., (BV) ... '42 '71 C.350 B.S.I.E. L.260 J.D. [Mohr,B.H.&N.]
Mohr, Bruce, Hill & Nader, (BV) ... 3402 W. Elm Street
Nader, Mary H. ... '— '94 C&L.424 B.A., J.D. [Mohr,B.H.&N.]
Orlowski, Jay R., (AV) ... '61 '87 C&L.424 B.B.A., J.D. [A T.J.Popovich]
Popovich, Kimberly A. ... '68 '93 C.123 B.A. L.436 J.D. [A T.J.Popovich]
Popovich, Thomas J., (BV) ... '64 '90 C.338 B.S. L.209 J.D. [T.J.Popovich]

Popovich, Thomas J., P.C., Law Offices of, (BV)
3416 West Elm Street, 60050
Telephone: 815-344-3797 Fax: 815-344-5280
Email: tkpopovich@aol.com URL: http://www.popovichlaw.com
Thomas J. Popovich;—Kimberly A. Popovich; Hans A. Mast; John A. Kornak; Jay R. Orlowski; Scott A. Hiera.
Catastrophic Personal Injury including Wrongful Death, Medical Malpractice including Birth Injuries, Cancer, Failure to Diagnose or Misdiagnosis, Obstetric, Surgical, Cardiac, Orthopedic and Nursing Malpractice, Automobile Accidents and Injuries, Head, Brain, Back and Neck Injuries, Motorcycle Accidents and Injuries, Construction Accidents and Injuries, Product Liability, Unsafe Product Injuries, Workers Compensation.
See Professional Biographies, MCHENRY, ILLINOIS

Reilly, Charles T., Law Office, (BV) '50 '79
C.602 B.A. L.365 J.D. 1303 N. Richmond Rd.
Rosario, Richard R. ... '62 '99 C&L.589 B.A., J.D. 5010 W. Elm St.
Roth, John A., (BV) ... '59 '84 C.597 B.A. L.424 J.D. [Roth&F.]
Roth & Feetterer, P.C., (BV) ... 607 North Front Street
Short, Richard J. ... '31 '57 L.365 J.D. [R.J.Short]
Short, Richard J., Ltd. ... 3604 N. Chapel Hill Rd., Johnsburg
Stone, David N., (AV) ... '43 '68 C.339 B.A. L.966 J.D. 3805 Grove Ave.
Taradash, Mary K., (BV) ... '49 '80 C.589 B.S. L.146 J.D. [Taradash&B.]
Taradash, Randall M., (BV) ... '47 '79 C.502 B.J. L.64 J.D. [Taradash&B.]
Taradash & Brammer, (BV) ... 908 S. Rte. 31
Theis, Peter F. ... '37 '75 C.976 B.E.E.E. L.146 J.D. 3203 Bay View Ln.‡
Truckenbrod, Donald W., (AV) '31 '66
C.589 B.S.Ed. L.146 J.D. 4108 W. Crystal Lake Rd.
Zadeikis, Donna, (CV) ... '62 '85 C.339 B.S. L.146 J.D. 818 S. Rte. 31

McLEANSBORO, * 2,945, *Hamilton Co.*

Bonan, F. William, (BV) ... '46 '73 C.339 B.A. L.383 J.D. N. Side Sq.
Daily, John D. ... '13 '37 C&L.339 B.S., LL.B. Ret. Cir. J.
Downen, Alan C., Law Offices of, (BV) '47 '74
C.801 B.A. L.209 J.D. 204 N. Washington St.

Hart and Hart
(See Benton)

Jelliffe, Ferrell, Morris & Doerge
(See Harrisburg)

Jones, Charles E. ... '24 '50 C&L.339 B.S., LL.B. Ret. Appl. Ct. J.‡
Minton, Bernard L., (BV) ... '13 '52 C.340 A.B. L.339 LL.B. 210 E. Main St.
Morris, Donald Wayne, (BV) ... '55 '80 C.234 B.A. L.339 J.D. States Atty.
Underwood, David L. ... '45 '76 C.1188 B.A. L.61 J.D. Cir. J.
Van Winkle, James L., (BV) ... '54 '79 C.597 B.A. L.273 J.D. [Van Winkle&V.]
Van Winkle, Theodore, (BV) ... '25 '58 C.801 B.S. L.734 LL.B. [Van Winkle&V.]
Van Winkle & Van Winkle, (BV) ... P.O. Box 337
Vaughan, Barry L., (BV) ... '62 '88 C&L.801 B.A., J.D. Resident Circuit Judge

MEDINAH, —, *DuPage Co.*

Johnston, Paul L. ... '47 '72 C&L.339 B.A., J.D. P.O. Box 488★

MELROSE PARK, 23,171, *Cook Co.*

Boldizsar, Laszlo ... '34 '71 C.209 B.A. L.424 J.D. Alberto-Culver Co.
Bruno, Gregory D. ... '54 '79 C.424 B.A. L.209 J.D. 1807 Broadway
Butcher, William C. ... '24 '52 C.339 L.356 LL.B. 10800 W. Barry
Cossident-Italia, Cathleen, Attorney at Law '58 '84
C.999 A.S. L.365 J.D. 1807 N. Broadway
Daleo, Vito ... '22 '53 C&L.209 B.S. 2210 W. North Ave.
DeSimone, Patricia M. '66 '98 C.21 B.S. L.659 J.D.
Intellectual Property Coun., Alberto-Culver Co.
Dickens, John F. ... '46 '75 C.57 A.B. L.477 J.D. Sr. Atty., Alberto-Culver Co.
Goggin, Terrence J., (AV) ... '49 '76 C.750 B.A. L.365 J.D. 501 W. North Ave.
Guerine, George N. ... '12 '48 L.989 J.D. 1300 Augusta‡
Hughes, Mary D. ... '23 '61 C&L.209 A.B., J.D. 253 Winters Dr.‡
McCaffery, Michael J. ... '62 '91 C&L.352 B.B.A., J.D. Sr. Atty., Alberto-Culver Co.
Mentone, Ronald J. ... '56 '82 C.424 B.A. L.209 J.D. 1807 N. Broadway
Mirones, Juan B. ... '32 '80 L.589 J.D. 1616 N. 19th Ave.
Morford, Richard G. ... '55 '95 C&L.209 B.M., J.D. Gen. Coun., Enviro Tech Intl. Inc.
Novak, Robert J. ... '28 '51 C&L.472 B.B.A., J.D. 2300 W. Lake Street
Schlax, Donald R. ... '53 '79 C&L.339 B.S., J.D. Tax Atty., Jewel-Osco
Schmidt, Gary P. '51 '76 C.473 B.A. L.7 J.D.
Sr. V.P., Gen. Coun. and Secy., Alberto-Culver Co.
Serpico, Ronald M., Sr. ... '52 '77 C.338 B.S. L.209 J.D. 1807 N. Bway.
Sewell, J. Roger ... '35 '60 C.966 L.209 LL.B. 1835 Bway.
Shonfeld, Willard L. ... '31 '55 C&L.339 B.A., LL.B. Handy Button Machine Co.
Spira, James M. ... '63 '90 C.347 B.S. L.424 J.D. Sr. Atty., Alberto-Culver Co.
Volkman, Steven B. ... '54 '83 C.123 B.A. L.365 J.D. V.P., Cochrane Compressor Co.‡
Zubik, Sandra J. ... '— '87 C.477 B.A. L.365 J.D. Albertson's, Inc.

MENDOTA, 7,272, *La Salle Co.*

Engels, Bernard L., (BV) ... '50 '80 C.424 A.B. L.215 J.D. 704 Jefferson St.
Guilfoyle, Michael S., (BV) ... '49 '75 C.338 B.S. L.424 J.D. 1316 Meriden St.

Holland, Troy D., (CV) '68 '94 C.927 B.A. L.365 J.D.
812 Washington Street, P.O. Box 177, 61342
Telephone: 815-539-3711 Fax: 815-538-2660
Probate, Wills, Trusts and Estates, Real Estate, Civil Litigation, Corporate Law, Municipal Law and Collections.

Kaleel, David M., (CV) ... '58 '83 C.597 B.A. L.273 J.D. 806 Jefferson St.

Leynaud & Leynaud, A Prof. Corp., Law Offices of
(See Peru)

Troupis, Christ T., (AV) ....'23 '49 C.597 L.309 J.D. 806 Jefferson St.

METAMORA, 2,700, *Woodford Co.*

Baldwin, Scott M., Attorney at Law ....'67 '93 C.339 B.S. L.930 J.D. P.O. Box 469
Hayes, Thomas M., (BV) ....'41 '70 C.339 A.B. L.424 J.D. 18 Coral Bank Road
Kelly, William R., Law Offices of, (BV) '41 '66
C.98 B.S. L.597 J.D. 416 Main St., Suite 832
Perley, Barbara ....'60 '91 C.98 B.A. L.339 J.D. V.P., Perley Cable Construction, Inc.‡
Williams, Maureen, Law Office of '— '91 C.190 B.S. L.300 J.D.
(adm. in MN; not adm. in IL) P.O. Box 747

METROPOLIS, * 6,482, *Massac Co.*

Abell, Rick W., (BV) ....'59 '84 C.339 B.S. L.801 J.D. [▣ Kruger,H.&H.]
Bryant, Brenda G., (CV) ....'49 '79 C.383 B.A. L.801 J.D. 103 E. 5th St.

Bryant & Kautz, PC
222 Ferry Street, 62960 ⊙
Telephone: 618-524-5671 Fax: 618-524-9671
Allison N. Kidd. Of Counsel: Joseph M. Leberman.
General Civil and Criminal Practice. Trials and Appeals, State and Federal Courts. Personal Injury, Criminal, Real Estate, Corporation, Family Law, Trusts and Estates.
Paducah, Kentucky Office: Bryant & Kautz, PC, 601 Washington Street, P.O. Box 1876, 42002-1876. Telephone: 270-442-1422. Fax: 270-443-8788.
Marion, Illinois Office: 4501 West De Young, Suite B-2, 62959. Telephone: 618-993-1468. Fax: 618-993-1329.
See Professional Biographies, METROPOLIS, ILLINOIS

Chase, Robert H., (AV) ....'13 '38 C&L.339 B.S., J.D. 508 Market St.
Foster, Terry J. ....'48 '72 C.801 B.A. L.339 J.D. Cir. J.
Helm, Milton M., (AV) ....'23 '51 C&L.339 B.S., LL.B. Jones Bldg.‡
Henry, Paul F., (BV) ....'50 '79 C&L.801 B.A., J.D. [Kruger,H.&H.]
Hunter, Mark C., (BV) ....'58 '83 C.339 B.A. L.734 J.D. [Kruger,H.&H.]
Jackson, Joseph J., (BV) ....'44 '79 C.801 B.A. L.838 J.D. 775 Mount Mission Rd.
Johnson, Dolores J. ....'30 '53 C.339 L.209 LL.B. [Johnson&J.]
Johnson, Louis P. ....'24 '52 C&L.209 B.S.C., LL.B. [Johnson&J.]
Johnson & Johnson ....205 W. 6th St.
Kidd, Allison N. ....'71 '96 C.339 B.S. L.801 J.D. [▣ Bryant&K.]
Kruger, Richard, (BV) ....'45 '71 C&L.339 A.B., J.D. [Kruger,H.&H.]

Kruger, Henry & Hunter, (BV)
110 West 5th, P.O. Box 568, 62960
Telephone: 618-524-9302 Fax: 618-524-9305
URL: http://www.lawyers.com/khhlaw
Members of Firm: Richard Kruger; Paul F. Henry; Mark C. Hunter. Of Counsel: Rick W. Abell.
Civil and Criminal Trial and Appellate Practice. Negligence, Product Liability, Wrongful Death, Workman's Compensation, Criminal, Family, Real Estate, Corporate, Probate, Bankruptcy, Divorce, Driving While Intoxicated.
Representative Clients: Mermet Grain Co.; Metropolis Builder's Supply; J.M. Walters & Son, Inc. (Electrical Contractor); Village of Joppa; Southgate Health Care, Inc.; Mid-South Towing Co.
References: City National Bank, Metropolis, Illinois; National State Bank, Metropolis, Illinois.
See Professional Biographies, METROPOLIS, ILLINOIS

Leberman, Joseph M. ....'59 '88 C.531 B.S. L.801 J.D. [▣ Bryant&K.]
Mac Leberman, Joseph ....'59 '88 C.531 B.S. L.801 J.D. 106 W. 5th Street
Neely, Joseph J., (BV) ....'50 '76 C.801 B.S. L.365 J.D. [Neely]
Neely, Robert J., (BV) ....'23 '56 C.801 L.986 J.D. P.O. Box 428 (⊙Vienna)

Neely Law Firm, The, (BV)
P.O. Box 428, 62960-0428
Telephone: 618-524-2642 Fax: 618-524-2433
Email: jjn@hcis.net URL: http://www.lawyers.com/neelylaw
Member of Firm: Joseph J. Neely.
General Trial and Appellate Practice. Probate, Real Estate, Family, Corporate, Personal Injury, Municipal and Criminal Law.
Reference: MidCountry Bank, Metropolis, Illinois.
See Professional Biographies, METROPOLIS, ILLINOIS

Peters, Leslie J. ....'— '93 C.530 B.A. L.365 J.D. 600 Market Street
Terry, Ken B. ....'63 '91 C.531 B.S. L.801 J.D. P.O. Box 428
Windhorst, Leonard Patrick ...'75 '00 C.339 B.S. L.801 J.D. Massac Co. State Atty.'s Off.

MIDLOTHIAN, 14,372, *Cook Co.*

Buck, Michael A. ....'49 '75 C&L.209 B.A., J.D. [▣ J.R.Sullivan]
Sullivan, John R. ....'35 '60 C&L.602 B.S., LL.B. 4610 W. 147th St.

MILAN, 5,348, *Rock Island Co.*

Collinson, Kenneth M., (BV) ....'39 '64 C.57 B.A. L.597 J.D. 225 E. 1st St.
Swanson, Robert P. ....'46 '85 C.927 B.A. L.589 J.D. 520 W. 14th Ave.‡

MILFORD, 1,369, *Iroquois Co.*

Rose, Lori Ann ....'70 '97 C.63 B.S. L.201 J.D. In-House Coun., CTB Inc.
Sunderland, Louis B., (AV) ....'30 '58 C.894 A.B. L.597 J.D. [Sunderland,S.J.&T.] ⊙
Sunderland, Spenn, Johnson and Thompson, (AV) ....7 South Axtel (⊙Watseka)
Witt, Kevin Bruce ....'57 '84 C.339 B.A. L.800 J.D. 223 Walnut Street

MILLEDGEVILLE, 1,076, *Carroll Co.*

Ward, Murray, Pace & Johnson, P.C., (AV) .... 323 N. Main St. (⊙Sterling)
Zumdahl, Mark E., (AV) ....'50 '75 C.937 B.A. L.339 J.D. [Ward,M.P.&J.] ⊙

MINONK, 2,168, *Woodford Co.*

Janssen, Thomas L., (BV) ....'54 '79 C&L.339 B.S., J.D. 474 Chestnut St.
Riely, James A., (BV) ....'31 '58 C.602 A.B. L.209 J.D. 474 Chestnut St.‡

MINOOKA, 3,971, *Grundy & Will Cos.*

Lab, Charles E., (BV) ....'52 '79 C.679 B.A. L.146 J.D. 26001 Canal Rd., N.
Shadwell Keller, Julie A. ....'63 '90 C.234 B.A. L.339 J.D. Asst. Pub. Def., Will Co.

MOKENA, 14,583, *Will Co.*

Babbington, John M. ....'44 '72 C.424 B.B.A. L.209 J.D. 19906 S. Wolf Rd.
Bosco, James A. ....'70 '03 C.436 B.S. L.146 J.D. Gen. Coun., Penn Media
Celani, Franklin A., Jr., (BV) '49 '74
C.209 B.A. L.365 J.D. 19065 Hickory Creek Dr., Ste. 210
Christensen, Hans F. ....'60 '99 C.1171 B.S. L.146 J.D. C & C Partnership Inc.
Conley, Martin J. ....'35 '63 C&L.424 B.S., J.D. 19628 Scarth Lane
Eckert, Paul J. ....'65 '91 C.339 B.S. L.146 J.D. 9400 Bormet Dr., Ste. 7
Gerrity, John E. ....'39 '79 C.209 Ph.B. L.365 J.D. 18909 Creekview Ln.
Hankins, Shawn K. ....'55 '80 C.234 B.S. L.365 J.D. 10031 W. 191st St.
Maday, Timothy ....'— '86 C.801 B.S. L.365 J.D. 19224 Schoolhouse Rd.

Malysa, Theresa M.
(See Orland Park)

Pech, Jerry ....'09 '36 C.339 B.A. L.424 J.D. 11862 Josephine Dr.‡

Rakich, Steven D., (AV) ....'43 '70 C.373 B.A. L.912 J.D. [Rakich]
Rakich Law Office, (AV) .... 8519 West 191st Street, Suite 29
Rathbun, Timothy J., (AV) ....'50 '74 C&L.861 B.A., J.D. [Rathbun,C.&K.] (⊙Joliet)
Rathbun, Cservenyak & Kozol, LLC, (AV) ..... 9450 Enterprise Drive (⊙Joliet, Plainfield)
Repenning, Betty J. ....'41 '72 C.209 B.A. L.365 J.D. 19827 Greenview
Smart, William D., Jr. ... '60 '85 C&L.339 B.A., J.D. Glenbrook Properties, Group, L.L.C.
Weber, Kerry Anne ....'69 '96 C.741 B.A. L.879 J.D. [Weber]
Weber Law Office ....19229 Schoolhouse Road

MOLINE, 43,768, *Rock Island Co.*

Adam, Joseph N. ....'56 '89 C.707 B.A. L.352 J.D. Sr. Atty., Deere & Company
Alvine, Robert H., (BV) ....'44 '68 C&L.221 B.A., J.D. [Sandholm,A.&R.]
Anderson, Richard E. '47 '74 C.57 B.A. L.383 J.D.
Asst. Gen. Coun., Deere & Company

Andich & Andich
(See Rock Island)

Archer, John H., Jr. ....'72 '98 C.340 B.A. L.801 J.D. Atty., Deere & Co.

Barash & Everett, LLC
(See Galesburg)

Barnes, Mark A. ....'50 '76 C.210 B.A. L.339 J.D. Mgr., Deere & Co.
Batcher, Richard M., (AV) ....'41 '67 C.350 B.S.M.E. L.352 J.D. [Bozeman,N.P.&N.] ⊙
Becht, James H. .....'53 '79 C.228 B.A. L.608 J.D. Assoc. Gen. Coun., Deere & Company
Blade, Thomas A., (BV) ....'43 '69 C.57 B.A. L.145 J.D. 620 17th St.
Boeye, Robert P., (AV) ....'34 '59 C.399 B.A. L.352 J.D. [Califf&H.] ⊙
Bozeman, Virgil, (AV) ....'12 '37 C.339 L.802 LL.B. [▣ Bozeman,N.P.&N.]

Bozeman, Neighbour, Patton & Noe, LLP, (AV)
1630 5th Avenue, P.O. Box 659, 61266-0659 ⊙
Telephone: 309-797-0850 Fax: 309-764-1371
URL: http://www.bnpn.com
John V. Patton (1922-1993). Members of Firm: Robert J. Noe; James D. Mowen; Richard M. Batcher; John P. Harris; Gary L. Sissel; James R. Patton; Mark R. McLaughlin; William L. Cleaver (Also at Davenport Office); J. Sue Myatt; William P. Rector; Jeffrey D. Martens; Mark A. Tarnow. Associates: Benjamin J. Samuelson; Heather G. Rouleau. Of Counsel: Virgil Bozeman; Hubbard B. Neighbour; Daniel P. Ellard.
General Practice in State and Federal Courts. Appellate Practice, Bankruptcy, Banks and Banking, Business Law, Civil Practice, Civil Rights, Commercial Law, Commercial Real Estate, Constitutional Law, Construction Law, Contracts, Corporate Law, Debtor and Creditor, Disabilities, Employee Benefits, Environmental Law, Family Law, Fidelity and Surety, Finance, Guardianship and Conservatorship, Health Care, Hospital Law, Housing Law, Insurance, Insurance Defense, Labor and Employment, Leases and Leasing, Legal Ethics and Professional Responsibility, Litigation, Medical Malpractice, Mergers, Acquisitions and Divestitures, Mortgages, Municipal Law, Negligence, Personal Injury, Probate, Products Liability, Professional Liability, Real Estate, Taxation, Torts, Trusts and Estates, Wills, Workers' Compensation.
Representative Clients: Deere & Company; Allstate Insurance Co.; Fireman's Fund American Group; Royal Insurance Group; St. Paul Insurance Group; Continental Insurance Cos.; State Farm Mutual Automobile Insurance Co.; Wausau Insurance Co.; Crum & Forster Group.
Davenport, Iowa Office: 4300 E. 53rd Street, Suite 103, 52807. Telephone: 563-449-1037. Fax: 309-764-1371.
See Professional Biographies, MOLINE, ILLINOIS

Byram, Tamara J. '64 '90 C.221 B.A./B.A. L.800 J.D.
(adm. in CA; not adm. in IL) John Deere Health Care, Inc.
Cady, Thomas E., (CV) ....'65 '96 C.927 B.S. L.589 J.D. [Katz,H.&F.]

Califf & Harper, P.C., (AV)
6th Floor First Midwest Bank Building, 506 Fifteenth Street, P.O. Box 719, 61266-0719 ⊙
Telephone: 309-764-8361 Facsimile: 309-764-8394
URL: http://www.califf.com
Robert P. Boeye; Dennis R. Fox; John A. Slover, Jr.; Thomas A. Harper; Jeffrey B. Moorhouse; Roger L. Strandlund; Arthur W. Eggers; Harvey A. Levin; James S. Zmuda; Jonathon C. Fox; Franklin S. Mitvalsky;—Karla C. Steele. Of Counsel: James A. Harper.
Corporate, Commercial, Civil Litigation in all State and Federal Courts, Labor, Employment, Banking, Governmental, School, Administrative (including N.L.R.B.), Products Liability, Insurance, Taxation, Estate Planning and Probate Law, Real Estate, Land Development and Zoning, Business Enterprises, Closely Held Business, Limited Liability Companies, Partnerships, Small Business, Buying or Selling a Business, Collections, Employee Benefits, Employment Contracts, Human Resources, Contracts, Business Lawsuits, Internet Law, E-Commerce, Commercial Leasing, Landlord and Tenant; Buying or Selling a Home; Tax Planning and Asset Protection.
Representative Clients: First Midwest Bank/Western Illinois, N.A.; Associated Employers of the Quad Cities; Iowa-Illinois Gas & Electric Co.; Metropolitan Airport Authority of Rock Island County; Travelers Insurance Co.
Wheaton, Illinois Office: 123 West Front Street, Suite 200, 60187. Telephone: 800-764-4999. Facsimile: 630-871-1347.
See Professional Biographies, MOLINE, ILLINOIS

Carpentier, Jos. G. ....'15 '48 C.707 B.S. L.352 J.D. 3721 35th St.‡
Carter, Joel S. ....'49 '78 C&L.339 B.S.E.E., J.D. Sr. Pat. Coun., Deere & Company (Pat.)
Cartwright, Max D., (BV) ....'50 '76 C&L.801 B.A., J.D. 1725 40th Street Ct.
Choudhry, Ray ....'45 '75 C.1097 B.A. L.597 J.D. [Mid A.]
Churchill, Daniel, (AV) ....'43 '69 C.57 B.A. L.339 J.D. [Churchill&C.]
Churchill, Mark D. ....'77 '02 C.108 B.S. L.339 J.D. [Churchill&C.]

Churchill & Churchill, P.C., (AV)
1610 Fifth Avenue, 61265
Telephone: 309-762-3643; 762-3644 FAX: 309-762-4690
Email: cclaw@churchillfirm.com URL: http://www.churchilllawfirm.com
Members of Firm: J. B. Oakleaf (1886-1930); J. L. Oakleaf (1905-1958); Cyrus Churchill (1903-1999); Daniel Churchill; Mark D. Churchill.
General Civil Trial Practice in State and Federal Courts. Corporation, Business Law, Commercial, Banking, Real Estate, Probate and Bankruptcy Law, Trusts and Estates, Wills, Estate Planning, Taxation.
Representative Clients: First Moline Financial Corp.; First Federal Savings Bank of Moline; Builders Sales & Service Co.; Moline Board of Education; The Moline Daily Dispatch.
See Professional Biographies, MOLINE, ILLINOIS

Clarke, Wade P., Jr. '40 '65 C.602 B.A. L.477 J.D.
V.P., Govt. Affs., Deere & Company
Cleaver, William L., (AV) ....'49 '74 C.57 B.A. L.352 J.D. [Bozeman,N.P.&N.]
Cooney, Thomas O. ....'44 '69 C&L.352 B.B.A., J.D. Sr. Mgr., Deere & Co.
Coordes, Duane A. '45 '74
C.339 B.S.E.E. L.904 J.D. Sr. Pat. Coun., Deere & Company (Pat.)
Cravero, Joseph P. ....'41 '73 C.262 B.S. L.30 J.D. Deere & Co.‡
Dailey, David N., Attorney at Law, (BV) ....'47 '74 C.162 B.A. L.365 J.D. 1528 6th Ave.
Dailey, William H., (AV) ....'38 '63 C.162 B.A. L.309 LL.B. [W.H.Dailey]
Dailey, William H., Ltd., (AV) .... 1528 Sixth Avenue
Dalton, Wm. L. ....'27 '52 C.597 B.S. L.339 LL.B. 1465 41st St.‡
Davies, Todd E. ....'60 '86 C.339 B.A. L.146 J.D. Coun., Deere & Company
Denger, Peter ....'16 '60 C.57 L.339 LL.B. 1630 5th Ave.
Dixon, William Michael '63 '94 C.271 B.A. L.7 J.D.
(adm. in OH; not adm. in IL) Pat. Atty., Deere & Co.
Doak, John F., (BV) ....'65 '90 C.57 B.A. L.339 J.D. [Katz,H.&F.]

Eagle, Suzanne E. '64 '89 C&L.589 B.A., J.D.
Trademark Spec., John Deere, Corp. Brand Mgmt.
Edwards, Frank R., (AV) ....'31 '58 C.602 B.A. L.339 LL.B. [Katz,H.&F.]
Eggers, Arthur W., (BV) ....'52 '77 C.352 B.A. L.190 J.D. [Califf&H.] ⊙
Ellard, Daniel P., (AV) '55 '80
C.880 B.S. L.280 J.D. [▣ Bozeman,N.P.&N.] (⊙Davenport, IA)
Fackel, Joseph F. ....'39 '63 C.351 B.A. L.352 LL.B. [VanHooreweghe&F.]
Fieweger, Peter C., (AV) ....'34 '62 C.602 B.S. L.597 J.D. [Katz,H.&F.]
Fieweger, Stephen T., (BV) ....'61 '87 C.602 B.B.A. L.589 J.D. [Katz,H.&F.]
Fox, Dennis R., (AV) ....'39 '65 C.339 B.S. L.597 J.D. [Califf&H.] ⊙
Fox, Jonathon C., (BV) ....'69 '96 C.347 B.A. L.1161 J.D. [Califf&H.] ⊙
Frankel, Steven R. ....'45 '71 C.347 A.B. L.352 J.D. Asst. Gen. Coun., Deere & Company
Geuther, Christine A. ....'71 '96 C.352 B.A. L.589 J.D. [Katz,H.&F.]
Gibson, Kathleen R. ....'51 '76 C.339 A.B. L.597 J.D. Sr. Coun., Deere & Co.
Glockhoff, Roy H., (BV) ....'12 '37 C&L.339 B.A., LL.B. 5308-23rd Ave.
Gorsline, Monique C., (CVⓉ) ....'69 '94 C&L.352 B.B.A., J.D. Atty., Deere & Co.

Gosma, Tarbox & Associates, P.L.C.
(See Davenport, Iowa)

Grafton, B. Craig ....'47 '73 C.57 B.A. L.352 J.D. [B.C.Grafton]
Grafton, B. Craig, P.C. ....3610 25th St.
Graham, Charles T. ....'57 '85 C.339 B.S. L.912 J.D. Gen. Pat. Coun., Deere & Co. (Pat.)
Graves, Victoria J. '61 '89 C&L.339 B.A., J.D.
V.P. & Gen. Coun., John Deere Health Care, Inc.
Haake, Dale G., (BV) ....'52 '79 C.57 B.A. L.339 J.D. [Katz,H.&F.]
Hancks, Derek L., (BV) ....'64 '89 C.352 B.A. L.589 J.D. [D.L.Hancks]
Hancks, Marvin L. ....'28 '63 C.707 B.A. L.904 LL.B. 1308 34th Ave. A‡
Hancks, Derek L., P.C., (BV) ....1504 7th St., Ste. 2

Hanna, Steve, Attorney at Law, (BV) '54 '90 C.707 B.A. L.734 J.D.
418 Sixteenth Street, 61265
Telephone: 309-797-9000 Fax: 309-762-0177
Email: steve@hanna-law.com URL: http://www.hanna-law.com
Criminal Law, Driving While Intoxicated, Drug Crimes, Juvenile Criminal Law, Parole and Probation, Traffic Violations. Illinois, Iowa, Federal Practice.
See Professional Biographies, MOLINE, ILLINOIS

Harper, James A., (AV) ....'17 '42 C&L.477 A.B., J.D. [▣ Califf&H.] ⊙
Harper, Thomas A., (BV) ....'50 '76 C&L.221 B.S., J.D. [Califf&H.] ⊙
Harring, Michael A. '50 '75 C.339 B.A. L.424 J.D.
Corp. Sec. & Assoc. Gen. Coun., Deere & Company
Harris, John P., (BV) ....'55 '80 C&L.352 B.A., J.D. [Bozeman,N.P.&N.] ⊙
Harvey, Daniel A. ....'58 '83 C.350 B.S. L.352 J.D. Asst. Gen. Coun., Deere & Company
Hill, Thomas C. ....'46 '75 C.894 A.B. L.879 J.D. H & R Accounts, Inc.
Hlavaty, Michael C. '42 '73
C.350 B.S.I.E. L.352 J.D. Asst. Gen. Coun., Deere & Company (Pat.)
Howe, Linda E. ....'44 '00 C.378 B.S. L.801 J.D. 1531 47th Ave., Ste. 2
Howze, Marc A. '63 '95 C&L.477 A.B., J.D.
(adm. in MI; not adm. in IL) Atty., Deere & Co.
Huntoon, H. Karl, (AV) ....'49 '75 C&L.339 B.S., J.D. [Katz,H.&F.]
Jackson, Julia Bunton, (BVⓉ) '67 '92 C.347 B.A. L.1119 J.D.
Oper. Coun., KONE Inc.
Jenkins, James R., (AVⓉ) '45 '73
C&L.477 B.A., J.D. Sr. V.P. & Gen. Coun., Deere & Company
Johnson, Kirk D. '73 '98 C.293 B.A. L.477 J.D.
(adm. in MI; not adm. in IL) Coun., KONE Inc.
Jones, Mary K. W. ....'68 '93 C.587 B.A. L.352 J.D. Sr. Atty., Deere & Company
Katz, Martin H., (AV) ....'37 '62 C.57 B.A. L.597 J.D. [Katz,H.&F.]

Katz, Huntoon & Fieweger, P.C., (AV)
1000 36th Avenue, 61265-7126
Telephone: 309-797-3000 Facsimile: 309-797-3330
Email: attorneys@katzlawfirm.com URL: http://www.katzlawfirm.com
Isador I. Katz (1905-1996); Martin H. Katz; Peter C. Fieweger; Frank R. Edwards; H. Karl Huntoon (Resident); Dale G. Haake; Frank L. Nowinski (Resident); Brian S. Nelson; Stephen T. Fieweger; John F. Doak; Thomas E. Cady; Christine A. Geuther (Resident).
Civil Trial and Appellate Practice. Personal Injury, Insurance, Commercial, Banking, Bank and Savings and Loan Failures, Bankruptcy, Corporation, Probate, Real Estate, Labor Relations, Taxation, Professional Malpractice, Products Liability, Workers Compensation, Employment, Administrative, Public, School and Municipal Law and Business Crimes.
Attorneys for: Augustana College; O'Rourke Bros, Inc.; International Limousines, Ltd.; Reynolds State Bank.
Local Attorneys for: Aetna Casualty & Surety Co.; Maryland Casualty Co.; Liberty Mutual Insurance Co.; CIGNA Cos.; Country Mutual Insurance Co.; Cincinnati Insurance Co.
See Professional Biographies, MOLINE, ILLINOIS

Koenig, Philip E.
(See Rock Island)

Kraft, Steven R. ....'60 '85 C&L.352 B.A., J.D. Sr. Atty., Deere & Company
Lareau, Hector L., (CV) ....'63 '93 C.339 B.A. L.221 J.D. [Lareau]

Lareau Law Office, (CV)
3551 7th Street, Suite 206, 61265
Telephone: 309-764-0775 Fax: 309-764-0975
URL: http://www.lareaulaw.com
Hector L. Lareau.
See Professional Biographies, MOLINE, ILLINOIS

Larson, Andrew M. ....'71 '00 C&L.352 B.A., J.D. 611 35th Avenue, Suite 2
Lester, Jeffrey D., (BV) ....'60 '86 C&L.352 B.S., J.D. City Atty.
Levin, Harvey A., (BV) ....'43 '71 C.475 B.A. L.597 J.D. [Califf&H.] ⊙
Long, D. Jamieson, Jr., (CV) ....'53 '79 C.597 B.A. L.339 J.D. 1531 47th Ave., Ste. 2
Long, Durward J., Sr., (BV) ....'27 '53 C.57 A.B. L.339 J.D. 3820-27th St.
Lytton, Tom M. ....'43 '68 C&L.597 B.A., J.D. Appl. Ct. J.
Martens, Jeffrey D., (BV) ....'69 '94 C.57 B.A. L.966 J.D. [Bozeman,N.P.&N.]
McCallister, J. Wilson, (BV) '42 '69
C.259 B.A. L.352 J.D. Assoc. Gen. Coun., Deere & Company

McCarthy, Callas, Fuhr & Ellison, P.C.
(See Rock Island)

McCraw, Lisa J. ....'63 '89 C.587 B.S. L.37 J.D. Deere & Co.
McLaughlin, Mark R., (BV) ....'60 '88 C.352 B.A. L.734 J.D. [Bozeman,N.P.&N.]
McLaughlin, Raymond L. ....'31 '55 C.93 L.734 LL.B. Pres., McLaughlin Holding Co.
McManus, Todd E. '72 '01 C&L.352 B.A., J.D.
(adm. in IA; not adm. in IL) Comm. Coun., KONE Inc.
Meersman, H. Moss ....'23 '51 C.707 B.A. L.352 LL.B. Pub. Guard. for the Co.‡
Meier, David W., (BV) ....'51 '77 C.350 B.S. L.339 J.D. Sr. Coun., Deere & Company
Mid America Law Offices, Ltd. ....1630 Fifth Ave., Ste. 200
Mihm, Michael W., (BV) '63 '89
C.436 B.S.Civ.E. L.589 J.D. Asst. Gen. Coun., Deere & Company (Pat.)

Milnamow, John P., (AV) '36 '64 C.436 B.S.M.E. L.365 LL.B.
[Rockey,M.&K.] (Pat.) ⊙
Mitvalsky, Franklin S., (CV) ....'72 '98 C.597 B.A. L.352 J.D. [Califf&H.] ⊙
Moens, Thomas O., (CV) ....'61 '92 C&L.352 B.S., J.D. [Moens]
Moens Law Offices, Chartered, (CV) ....1601 52nd Avenue, 2nd Floor
Moorhouse, Jeffrey B., (BV) ....'45 '72 C&L.352 B.B.A., J.D. [Califf&H.] ⊙
Moriarty, Kevin J. '52 '81 C.446 B.S. L.128 J.D.
(adm. in VA; not adm. in IL; Pat.) Asst. Gen. Coun., Deere & Company
Morrison, Deborah ....'55 '81 C.643 B.A. L.665 J.D. Sr. Coun., Deere & Company
Moss, Timothy E. ....'58 '86 C.879 B.S. L.365 J.D. First Midwest Bank-Trust Div.
Mowen, James D., (BV) ....'43 '68 C.350 B.S. L.424 J.D. [Bozeman,N.P.&N.]
Murphy, Derek D. ....'— '93 C.352 B.A. L.276 J.D. Atty., Deere & Company
Murray, Wm. A. ....'24 '48 C.339 B.S. L.7 LL.B. 3205 15th St.‡
Myatt, J. Sue, (BV) ....'63 '89 C.351 B.A. L.352 J.D. [Bozeman,N.P.&N.]

Nash Nash Bean & Ford, LLP
(See Geneseo)

Neighbour, Hubbard B., (AV) ... '25 '50 C&L.597 B.S.M.E., J.D. [▣ Bozeman,N.P.&N.]
Nelson, Brian S., (BV) ....'61 '86 C.57 B.A. L.879 J.D. [Katz,H.&F.]
Noe, Gregory R., (BV) ....'66 '91 C.602 B.A. L.424 J.D. Sr. Coun., Deere & Company
Noe, Robert J., (AV) ....'39 '63 C.707 B.A. L.602 J.D. [Bozeman,N.P.&N.]
Nolan, John M. '32 '57 C&L.602 B.S., LL.B.
(adm. in IA; not adm. in IL; Pat.) John Deere Rd.‡
Nowinski, Frank L., (BV) ....'55 '80 C.57 B.A. L.424 J.D. [Katz,H.&F.]
Oaks, Jimmie R. '40 '68
C.560 B.S.M.E. L.128 J.D. Sr. Pat. Coun., Deere & Company (Pat.)
O'Shea, John Donald ....'41 '65 C&L.602 B.A., J.D. 3113 2nd St‡

Pappas & Schnell, P.C.
(See Rock Island)

Parsons, Henry W., (BV) ....'10 '35 C.604 L.597 Secy., Rock Island Co. Bar Assn.
Pastrnak, Thomas J., (BVⓉ) ....'59 '84 C.145 B.A. L.221 J.D. [Pastrnak] ⊙
Pastrnak Law Firm, P.C., (BVⓉ) ....1535-47th Ave. (⊙Davenport, IA)
Patramanis, Mike G. '34 '59 C.162 B.A. L.352 J.D.
Asst. Chief Coun., U.S. Army Ind. Oper. Comm.
Patton, James R., (BV) ....'54 '84 C.57 B.A. L.589 J.D. [Bozeman,N.P.&N.]
Plagenz, Jodi Kay Obrecht ....'67 '92 C&L.339 B.A., J.D. 1 John Deere Place

Pulsifer, Sharon L., (CV) '— '80 C.707 B.A. L.339 J.D.
3325 Avenue of the Citius, 61265
Telephone: 309-762-6831 Fax: 309-736-3034
Email: slpattorney@sbcglobal.net URL: http://www.attorneypulsifer.com
Family Law, Bankruptcy, Adoptions, Child Custody, Child Support, Divorce, Domestic Violence, Visitation Rights, Divorce, Real Estate, Wills and Probate.
See Professional Biographies, MOLINE, ILLINOIS

Rector, William P., (BV) ....'62 '87 C.896 B.A. L.352 J.D. [Bozeman,N.P.&N.] ⊙
Riggs, Maureen E. ....'72 '99 C.602 B.A. L.339 J.D. Dep. City Atty.
Rinden, Gerry M., (AV) ....'39 '65 C&L.352 LL.B. 3637 23rd Ave.‡
Rockey, Milnamow & Katz, Ltd., (AV)
1630 5th Avenue (Pat.) (⊙Chgo., IL; Arlington, VA)
Rouleau, Heather G. ....'76 '01 C.339 B.A. L.589 J.D. [▣ Bozeman,N.P.&N.]
Rowe, Jody R. '63 '91 C.591 B.S. L.352 J.D.
(adm. in IA; not adm. in IL) Blackhawk Title Co.
Ruud, Robert R., (BV) ....'51 '76 C.56 B.A. L.1218 J.D. [Sandholm,A.&R.]
Samuelson, Benjamin J. ....'74 '00 C.352 B.A. L.424 J.D. [▣ Bozeman,N.P.&N.]
Sandholm, Alvine & Ruud, (BV) ....501 15th Street
Schwiebert, Lloyd A. ....'13 '37 C.57 B.A. L.352 J.D. [▣ Schwiebert&S.] ‡
Schwiebert, Mark W., (BV) ....'50 '75 C.57 A.B. L.221 J.D. [Schwiebert&S.]
Schwiebert & Schwiebert, (BV) ....501 15th Street
Servine, Don J. ....'48 '75 C.118 B.A. L.339 J.D. L. B. Benefits, Inc.
Sissel, Gary L., (BV) ....'48 '73 C&L.352 B.A., J.D. [Bozeman,N.P.&N.] ⊙
Sloat, Bonnie Kerwin ....'61 '92 C&L.352 B.S., J.D. Jud. Law Clk., Appl. Ct.
Slover, John A., Jr., (BV) ....'44 '69 C&L.339 B.A., J.D. [Califf&H.] ⊙
Small, Len R. ....'42 '67 C.813 A.B. L.339 J.D. Pres., Small Newspaper Grp.‡

Snyder, Park & Nelson, P.C.
(See Rock Island)

Stanley, Lande & Hunter, A Professional Corporation
(See Davenport, Iowa)

Steele, Karla C. ....'70 '02 C.763 B.A. L.352 J.D. [▣ Califf&H.] ⊙
Steenlage, Keith E. ....'70 '98 C.958 B.S. L.1292 J.D. In House Coun., Deere & Company
Stepaniak, Kurt E. '58 '84 C&L.912 B.A., J.D.
Sr. V.P., Law & Bus. Dev. & Gen. Coun., KONE Inc.
Strandlund, Roger L., (BV) ....'55 '81 C.350 B.S. L.352 J.D. [Califf&H.] ⊙
Tackett-Hunt, Cristy ....'67 '97 C.352 B.A. L.589 J.D. Rock River Trust Co.
Tarnow, Mark A., (BV) ....'59 '84 C.927 B.A. L.352 J.D. [Bozeman,N.P.&N.]
Thompson, Linnea E., (BV) ....'53 '79 C.707 B.A. L.910 J.D. 5030 38th Ave.
Trevor, Curtis L., (BV) ....'28 '54 C.57 A.B. L.477 LL.B. 501 15th St.
Van Hooreweghe, Francis R. ....'40 '67 C&L.339 B.A., J.D. [VanHooreweghe&F.]
Van Hooreweghe & Fackel ....1718 8th Ave.
Whalen, Kirk E., (BVⓉ) '58 '85 C.846 B.B.A. L.260 J.D.
(adm. in FL; not adm. in IL) Gen. Coun., Heart of America
Wilczynski, A. Paul ....'57 '84 C.57 B.A. L.352 J.D. Asst. Gen. Coun., Deere & Company

Winstein, Kavensky & Wallace
(See Rock Island)

Zmuda, James S., (BV) ....'64 '89 C.352 B.B.A. L.589 J.D. [Califf&H.] ⊙

MOMENCE, 3,171, *Kankakee Co.*

Nutting, Mary P., (BV) ....'25 '52 C.741 A.B. L.347 J.D. 27 N. Dixie
Ogibovic, Richard S., II, (CV) ......'67 '94 C.338 B.S. L.734 J.D. 123 W. Washington St.

Olton, Tina M., (BV) '56 '81 C.63 B.S. L.347 J.D.
114 N. Dixie Street, P.O. Box 39, 60954
Telephone: 815-472-2417 Fax: 815-472-2477
Email: oltonlaw@aol.com URL: http://www.tinaolton.com
Real Estate, Social Security Disability, Family Law, Divorce, Child Custody, Bankruptcy, Wills, Probate.
See Professional Biographies, MOMENCE, ILLINOIS

Zeglis, Donald D. ....'17 '42 C.98 B.S. L.339 LL.B. 103 N. Dixie St.‡

MONEE, 2,924, *Will Co.*

DeCook, Brian F. '61 '93
C.539 B.A. L.209 J.D. 6212 W. Monee Manhattan Rd. (⊙Lombard)
McGrane, Joseph J., (AV) ....'10 '39 C.339 L.209 J.D. 25736 S. Mccorkle Ave.‡

MONMOUTH, * 9,841, *Warren Co.*

Baber, James G., (BV) ....'61 '86 C&L.801 B.A., J.D. [Stansell,W.&B.]

Barash & Everett, LLC
(See Galesburg)

Beal, Pratt & Pratt, (AV)
57 Southeast Public Square, P.O. Box 200, 61462-0200
Telephone: 309-734-3193 Telecopier: 309-734-7279
Email: attys@bealprattlaw.com
Members of Firm: Edward B. Love (1906-1972); Marion L. Beal (1922-1999); Channing L. Pratt; Jane Hartley Pratt.
General Civil and Trial Practice. Probate, Estate Planning, Real Estate, Insurance, Personal Injury, Corporation and Municipal Law.
Representative Clients: State Farm Mutual Insurance Co.; Western States Insurance; Wolverine Insurance; Aetna Life and Casualty; General Casualty Company of Wisconsin; Hawkeye Security Insurance; CNA Insurance.
See Professional Biographies, MONMOUTH, ILLINOIS

Bour, Elmer F. ... '13 '41 C.128 A.B. L.339 LL.B. Natl. Bk. Bldg.‡
Brinkmann, George H., (CV) ... '45 '72 C.597 B.A. L.585 J.D. 92 Square
Butler, Ralph D., (BV) ... '31 '60 C.339 B.S. L.477 J.D. 510 E. 1st Ave.
Clark, David Reid, (BV) ... '46 '75 C.801 B.A. L.352 J.D. P.O. Box 797
Hattery, Simpson & West, (AV) ... 1025 East Broadway (⊙Galesburg, Roseville)
Hawkins, Dennis P. ... '45 '00 C.268 B.S. L.900 J.D. 1000 W. Harlem Avenue
Hultgren, David R. ... '51 '78 C.57 B.A. L.575 J.D. Cir. J.
Klukos, Scott I. ... '21 '50 C.790 L.339 LL.B. Cir. J.
Pratt, Channing L., (BV) ... '29 '54 C.504 A.B. L.1119 J.D. [Beal,P.&P.]
Pratt, Jane Hartley, (AV) ... '30 '55 C.265 A.B. L.1119 J.D. [Beal,P.&P.]
Sanderson, Keith ... '20 '44 C&L.339 B.S., B.L. 1601 E. Broadway‡
Shipplett, Scott, (CV) ... '60 '93 C&L.339 B.A., J.D. 304 S. Main St., Ste. 105
Siegel, Thomas R. ... '77 '03 C.504 B.A. L.589 J.D. [🄰 Stansell,W.&B.]
Spears, Larry L., (BV) ... '37 '62 C.801 B.A. L.339 LL.B. 201 W. Bway.
Standard, James R., (BV) ... '43 '69 L.365 J.D. P.O. Box 646
Stansell, Theodore L., (AV) ... '19 '42 C.210 A.B. L.597 J.D. [Stansell,W.&B.] ‡

Stansell, Whitman & Baber, (AV)
203 East Broadway, P.O. Box 408, 61462
Telephone: 309-734-7926 Fax: 309-734-7929
Email: swb@lawyer.com URL: http://www.lawyers.com/swb
Members of Firm: Theodore L. Stansell (Retired 2002); Kenneth E. Critser (1928-1983); Mr. Richard L. Whitman, Sr.; Mr. James G. Baber;—Mr. Thomas R. Siegel.
Personal Injury, Banking, Bankruptcy, Collections, Criminal, Divorce, Probate and Wills, Real Estate, Workers Compensation Law. Civil Litigation.
Representative Clients: The National Bank of Monmouth; Pekin Insurance Co.
See Professional Biographies, MONMOUTH, ILLINOIS

Stombaugh, Ronald D., (BV) ... '48 '74 C.338 B.S. L.345 J.D. [Hattery,S.&W.]
Tenold, Ronald C. ... '46 '71 C&L.352 B.A., J.D. Cir. J.
Whitman, Richard L., Sr., (AV) ... '47 '72 C.234 B.A. L.597 J.D. [Stansell,W.&B.]
Youngquist, Andrew L., The Law Office of '64 '00 C.385 B.A. L.146 J.D.
P.O. Box 284

MONTGOMERY, 5,471, *Kane & Kendall Cos.*

Marcum, Donald C. ... '54 '80 C.827 B.A. L.209 J.D. Wheatland Title Guaranty Co.
O'Brien, James M., Law Offices of '47 '75
C&L.209 B.A., J.D. 1655 Timberlane Drive, Ste. 100
Schwager, Bradley J. ... '48 '73 C&L.879 B.A., J.D. 215 Boulder Hill Pass
Shilts, Gary L. ... '43 '74 C.589 B.A. L.365 J.D. 23 Boulder Hill pass

MONTICELLO, * 5,138, *Piatt Co.*

Ayers, James L., (BV) ... '48 '72 C.339 B.S. L.862 J.D. [Shonkwiler,A.&R.]

Beckett & Webber, P.C.
(See Urbana)

Braun, Brian A. ... '47 '75 C.339 B.S. L.209 J.D. [Miller,T.B.F.&M.]
Clark, Stanley H., Jr. ... '41 '67 C&L.174 B.A., J.D. Coun., Kaiser Abstract Co.
Finson, Hugh ... '47 '72 C.210 B.A. L.339 J.D. [Finson]
Finson Law Office ... 110 W. Washington St.
Foltz, John W., (BV) ... '48 '73 C.338 B.S. L.339 J.D. [Glasgow&F.]
Funk, S. Jeff ... '59 '85 C&L.339 B.A., J.D. [Miller,T.B.F.&M.]
Glasgow, William C., (BV) ... '47 '72 C.340 B.S. L.339 J.D. [Glasgow&F.]
Glasgow & Foltz, P.C., (BV) ... 114 E. Wash. St.
Guenther, Megan ... '56 '89 C&L.339 B.A., J.D. [🄲 Miller,T.B.F.&M.]
Hays, L. Keith, Jr., (CV) ... '38 '73 C&L.339 B.S., J.D. 202 W. Main St.
Hutson, Keith E. ... '25 '49 C&L.339 Pres., Monticello Business Servs., Inc.
Keller, Henry R., (CV) ... '29 '55 C.319 B.A. L.145 J.D. 121 N. State

Meyer Capel, A Professional Corporation
(See Champaign)

Miller, J. Christian ... '67 '92 C.339 B.A. L.61 J.D. [Miller,T.B.F.&M.]
Miller, Thomas R., (BV) ... '43 '73 C.870 B.S. L.339 J.D. [Miller,T.B.F.&M.]
Miller, Tracy, Braun, Funk & Miller, Ltd., (BV) ... 316 S. Charter St.
Rhoades, Dana ... '70 '95 C.338 B.S. L.424 J.D. [Shonkwiler,A.&R.]
Rumery, Leonard R. ... '48 '89 C.112 B.A. L.339 J.D. Asst. St. Atty.
Shonkwiler, John P. ... '33 '62 C.339 B.A. L.597 J.D. Chf. Cir. J.

Shonkwiler, Ayers & Rhoades, (BV)
114 South Charter Street, 61856
Telephone: 217-762-3661 Fax: 217-762-8199
Email: ayers@prairienet.net URL: http://www.lawyers.com/sarlaw
Members of Firm: James L. Ayers; Dana Rhoades.
General Civil Trial Practice. Probate, Real Estate, Tax, Estate Planning, Corporate and Family Law.
Representative Clients: Bank One of Monticello; First State Bank of Monticello; Hammond State Bank; State Bank of Bement; Central Illinois Manfacturing Co.
See Professional Biographies, MONTICELLO, ILLINOIS

Simpson, Roger A., (BV) ... '48 '75 C.1183 B.S. L.365 J.D. States Atty.
Tracy, William F., II, (BV) ... '47 '72 C.734 A.B. L.597 J.D. [Miller,T.B.F.&M.]
Wells, Suzanne J. ... '61 '87 C.339 B.A. L.209 J.D. 104 South Charter Street
Wilson, T. J., (BV) ... '51 '77 C.123 B.A. L.339 J.D. [🄰 Miller,T.B.F.&M.]

MOOSEHEART, —, *Kane Co.*

Solfa, Leonard J., Jr., (BV) '48 '77 C.755 B.A. L.209 J.D.
Gen. Coun., Moose Intl., Inc.

MORRIS, * 11,928, *Grundy Co.*

Bates, Johnathan Michael ... '70 '00 C.953 B.A. L.1187 J.D. 105 1/2 W. Washington St.
Bates, Susan O. ... '49 '96 C.280 B.A. L.896 J.D. Grundy Co. State Atty. Off.
Belt, Scott M., (BV) ... '62 '90 C.801 B.S. L.1187 J.D. 105 1/2 W. Washington St.
Bertani, Matthew G., (BV) ... '61 '88 C.221 B.A. L.37 J.D. [Rigazio&B.]
Black, August B., (AV) ... '15 '40 C&L.339 A.B., J.D. [🄲 Black&B.]
Black, Donald F., (AV) ... '48 '77 C.1151 B.S. L.365 J.D. [Black&B.]
Black, Frank J., (AV) ... '49 '74 C.1151 B.A. L.339 J.D. [Black&B.]
Black, George R., (AV) ... '46 '72 C.1151 A.B. L.339 J.D. [Black&B.]
Black, Richard J., (AV) ... '60 '88 C.1151 B.A. L.37 J.D. [Black&B.]
Black, Timothy J. ... '78 '03 C.927 A.B. L.365 J.D. [🄰 Black&B.]
Black & Black Lawyers, (AV) ... 201 Liberty St., Ste. 211
Bolen, Virginia R. ... '37 '61 C.881 B.A. L.208 LL.B. P.O. Box 490‡

Brenner, Ford, Monroe & Scott, Ltd.
(See Chicago)

Bzdill, Anne Hynds, (BV) ... '70 '95 C.597 B.A. L.221 J.D. 105 W. Main St.
Bzdill, David, (BV) ... '68 '94 C.351 B.A. L.221 J.D. 105 W. Main St.
Condon, John W., (AV) ... '45 '70 C.477 B.A. L.262 J.D. 211 E. Jefferson St.‡
Cortina, Frank J., Jr., (BV) ... '56 '81 C.340 B.A. L.589 J.D. 124 W. Washington Street
Dobbs, Gary A., (BV) ... '56 '81 C.589 B.S. L.209 J.D. Pub. Def.
Ellis, Ronald S., (BV) ... '52 '77 C.339 B.A. L.424 J.D. Asst. State Atty.

Fabrizio, Hanson, Peyla & Kawinski, P.C.
(See Joliet)

Flood, James D., (BV) ... '51 '77 C.602 B.A. L.209 J.D. 111 E. Washington St., Rm. 29
Frobish, Eric P. ... '70 '96 C.339 B.S. L.365 J.D. 124 W. Washington St.
Garretson, Gary R., (BV) ... '52 '77 C.338 B.S. L.910 J.D. 1802 Division St., Ste. 201
Geiger, Robert E., (BV) ... '55 '80 C.221 B.A. L.339 J.D. [Malmquist&G.]
Gomien, Roger B., (AV) ... '34 '62 C&L.339 B.S., LL.B. [Gomien&H.]
Gomien & Harrop Law Offices of, (AV) ... 220 W. Main St.
Hanson, Ellen Chamberlain ... '41 '67 C.36 B.A. L.910 J.D. [Hanson&H.]
Hanson, John V., (BV) ... '44 '69 C.231 B.A. L.910 J.D. [Hanson&H.]
Hanson and Hanson, Attorneys at Law, P.C., (BV) ... 1802 N. Division St.
Harrop, Joan N., (BV) ... '54 '95 C.338 B.S. L.146 J.D. [Gomien&H.]
Hoffman, Leonard ... '18 '40 C&L.145 A.B., J.D. Ret. Cir. J.
Holsinger, Russelle L., (BV) ... '71 '97 C.719 B.A. L.879 J.D. [Holsinger&Assoc.]
Holsinger & Associates, (BV) ... 101 W. Illinois Ave., Ste. 1
Hynds, John W., (AV) ... '39 '64 C.602 B.A. L.597 J.D. 105 W. Main St.
Jesiolowski, Karen K., (BV) ... '59 '84 C.424 B.A. L.589 J.D. Asst. States Atty.
Jorstad, Diane Yohnka, (BV) ... '56 '81 C&L.339 B.A., J.D. 105 W. Main St.
Klingner, Harold W., (AV) ... '20 '50 C.597 L.146 LL.B. P.O. Box 766 (⊙Wilmington)

Leynaud & Leynaud, A Prof. Corp., Law Offices of
(See Peru)

Malmquist, Robert W., (AV) ... '— '48 L.145 J.D. 415 Liberty St.‡
Malmquist, Timothy P., (BV) ... '54 '79 C.338 B.S. L.339 J.D. [Malmquist&G.]
Malmquist & Geiger, (BV) ... 415 Liberty St.
Marsaglia, Robert C. ... '56 '83 C.597 B.A. L.209 J.D. Assoc. Cir. J.
Massino, Michael H., (BV) ... '58 '85 C.472 B.B.A. L.1187 J.D. 405 Liberty St.
Mattingly, Michael A., (BV) ... '59 '87 C.338 B.S. L.424 J.D. 105 W. Main St.
McFarland, Wayne W., Jr., (BV) ... '54 '80 C.1151 B.A. L.146 J.D. [Peacock&M.]
Montgomery, Christopher S. ... '76 '02 C.234 B.A. L.146 J.D. [🄰 Hanson&H.]
Mueller, Joseph A., (BV) ... '51 '77 C.1183 B.S. L.209 J.D. 124 W. Washington Street
Peacock, James L. ... '29 '53 C&L.339 B.S., LL.B. [🄲 Peacock&M.] ‡
Peacock, John D., (BV) ... '63 '89 C.234 B.S. L.589 J.D. [Peacock&M.]
Peacock & McFarland, P.C., (BV) ... 101 1/2 W. Washington St.
Rigazio, Mark W., (BV) ... '55 '81 C.801 B.S. L.589 J.D. [Rigazio&B.]
Rigazio & Bertani, (BV) ... 220 West Main Street
Rooks, John N., (AV) ... '48 '73 C.210 B.A. L.910 J.D. 105 W. Main St.
Russo, Robert J., (AV) ... '58 '84 C.597 B.A. L.209 J.D. 211 E. Jefferson St.
Sheahan, Phyllis C. ... '33 '79 C.519 B.A. L.589 J.D. 3955 Sawmill
Sheedy, Amanda ... '50 '77 C.289 B.A. L.930 J.D. 2250 N. Verona Rd.
Yard, Keith Elliott, (BV) ... '61 '89 106 W. Washington

MORRISON, * 4,363, *Whiteside Co.*

Buckwalter-Schurman, Michelle B., (CV) '69 '95 C.338 B.S. L.589 J.D.
[Weinstine,S.&B.]
Burch, William A., (AV) ... '49 '75 C.339 A.B. L.910 J.D. [Ludens P.B.&M.] ⊙
Coplan, Ronald F., (BV) ... '37 '65 C&L.339 A.B., LL.B. 114 E. Main St.
Deckro, Stephen A., (BV) ... '40 '64 C&L.879 B.A., J.D. 101 E. Main St.
Dunagan, Danny A. ... '46 '75 C.801 B.A. L.339 J.D. Cir. J.
Hauptman, John L. ... '53 '78 C.927 B.A. L.365 J.D. Assoc. Cir. J.
Heuerman, James F., (BV) ... '67 '93 C.961 B.S. L.589 J.D. 114 E. Main St.
Holesinger, Russell J., (BV) ... '51 '76 C.114 B.A. L.339 J.D. 105 E. Main St. (⊙Fulton)
Huffman, Daniel A. ... '71 '99 C.1175 B.A. L.589 J.D. [Nelson,K.R.&H.]
Kilgus, Walter C., (AV) ... '40 '66 C.123 B.A. L.339 LL.B. [Nelson,K.R.&H.]
Leemon, John A., (AV) '28 '52 C&L.339 B.S., LL.B.
301 E. Main St. (⊙Mount Carroll)
Ludens Potter Burch & Melton, (AV) ... 409 North Cherry (⊙Rock Island)
McNeal, William S., (BV) ... '59 '83 C.747 B.A. L.365 J.D. First Asst. States Atty.
Melton, M. Tod, (BV) ... '66 '92 C.589 B.S. L.902 J.D. [Ludens P.B.&M.] ⊙
Mennenoh, John D. ... '28 '58 C.98 B.S. L.365 LL.B. Pres., H. B. Wilkinson Co.‡
Nelson, L. Willard, (AV) ... '21 '47 C&L.352 B.A., J.D. [Nelson,K.R.&H.]
Nelson, Kilgus, Richey & Huffman, (AV) ... 209 East Main Street
Potter, Robert H., (AV) ... '18 '46 C.597 B.S. L.477 LL.B. [Ludens P.B.&M.]
Potter, Thomas J., (BV) ... '51 '76 C.118 B.A. L.352 J.D. [Ludens P.B.&M.] ⊙
Richey, Lon M., (BV) ... '47 '77 C.802 B.A. L.339 J.D. [Nelson,K.R.&H.]
Shirk, William R., (BV) '52 '77
C.927 B.A. L.801 J.D. [Weinstine,S.&B.] (⊙Mount Carroll)
Slavin, Timothy J. ... '51 '76 C.602 B.A. L.93 J.D. Res. Cir. J.
Spencer, Gary L., (BV) ... '49 '79 C.338 B.S. L.221 J.D. States Atty.
Steines, Stanley B., (CV) ... '64 '90 C&L.352 B.S., J.D. [🄲 Ludens P.B.&M.]

Turner, Harold L., Law Offices of
(See Rockford)

Weinstine, Lester S., (BV) '36 '64
C.339 A.B. L.365 J.D. [Weinstine,S.&B.] (⊙Mount Carroll)
Weinstine, Shirk and Buckwalter-Schurman, P.C., (BV) ... 301 E. Main Street

MORTON, 15,198, *Tazewell Co.*

Bush, Michael L., (BV) ... '49 '76 C.248 B.A. L.365 J.D. [Bush,S.&Assoc.]
Bush, Snyder & Associates, (BV) ... 225 N. Main St.
Butler, Susan Hickman, (BV) ... '52 '77 C.836 B.A. L.221 J.D. 100 S. Main St.
Davies, Thomas E., (BV) ... '50 '75 C.339 B.S. L.146 J.D. Village Atty. [T.E.Davies]
Davies, Thomas E., P.C., (BV) ... 403 N. Main Street
Dluski, Peter Robert ... '72 '01 C.338 B.S. L.879 J.D. 14 Pennsylvania Court
Helmuth, Kenneth L. ... '50 '83 C.467 B.A. L.900 J.D. Gen. Atty., Caterpillar Inc.
Krieg, Thomas A., (CV) ... '54 '80 C.118 B.A. L.339 J.D. [Mason&K.]
LaKemper, Daniel A. ... '57 '82 C.98 B.S. L.190 J.D. P.O. Box 185
Mason, Ramon H., (BV) ... '18 '49 C&L.339 B.S., J.D. [Mason&K.]
Mason and Krieg, (BV) ... 200 South First Avenue
Snyder, Marikay L. ... '62 '88 C.98 B.A. L.424 J.D. [Bush,S.&Assoc.]
Sommer, Roger A. ... '43 '68 C.98 B.A. L.893 LL.B. Chf. Jus., Claims Ct.
Wanless, Annette L., (CV) ... '56 '87 C.597 B.S. L.734 J.D. [Wanless]

Wanless, Frank M., (BV) .... '19 '51 C.679 B.S. L.996 LL.B. Asst. Atty. Gen.
Wanless Law Office, (CV) .... 118 W. Jefferson St.

MORTON GROVE, 22,408, *Cook Co.*

Abrahamson, Maurice F. .... '19 '48 C.145 B.A. L.793 LL.B. 9218 Marmora St.
Alm, David W., (BV) .... '45 '75 C.231 B.A. L.879 J.D. [Brenner,M.&A.]
Anastos, Themis N. .... '12 '46 C&L.597 B.A. 5501 Madison St.
Apcel, Edmund J. .... '16 '51 C&L.424 LL.B. 8544 Morton Ave.‡
Bellows, Shael .... '41 '67 C.978 B.A. L.209 J.D. Pres., First Health Care Assn., Ltd.
Berrafato, Gabriel S. .... '28 '53 C&L.209 B.S., J.D. 8720 Ferris Ave.
Block, Joel Jay .... '52 '87 C.1183 B.A. L.365 J.D. 8832 N. Osceola Ave.
Braeseke, John O. .... '26 '53 C.393 L.209 LL.B. 6055 Dempster St.
Brenner, Nathan G., Jr., (AV) .... '28 '56 C&L.339 B.S., J.D. [Brenner,M.&A.]
Brenner, Mavrias & Alm, (AV) .... 8720 Ferris Ave.

Cutler & Associates, LTD.
(See Skokie)

Davis, Edward R. .... '35 '61 C.221 B.A. L.209 J.D. 5901 W. Lincoln Ave.
Diamond, Roy S. .... '23 '49 C.337 B.S. L.339 LL.B. 6200 Lincoln Ave.
Flynn, Thomas W. .... '36 '73 C.801 B.S. L.146 J.D. 8700 N. Waukegan Rd.
Friedman, Herbert S. .... '24 '51 C&L.966 LL.B. 5506 Lincoln Ave.
Friedman, Nathaniel .... '20 '41 C.339 L.144 LL.B. 8916 N. Moody Ave.
Friedman, Robert L. .... '52 '76 C.589 B.S. L.1000 J.D. 8700 Waukegan Rd., Ste. 135
Graf, Carl N., Jr., (BV) .... '42 '69 C.641 B.S. L.424 J.D. [C.N.Graf,Jr.&Assoc.]
Graf, Carl N., Jr. and Associates, (BV) .... 6032 N. Lincoln Ave.
Hofeld, Anthony R., (AV) .... '59 '88 C.221 B.S. L.365 J.D. 8724 Ferris Avenue
Hynan, Jas. F. .... '12 '36 C&L.209 Ph.B., J.D. 6600 Maple St.
Kachoyeanos, Gail M. .... '37 '92 C.597 B.A. L.365 J.D. 5617 West Dempster
Kahn, Sanford C., (AV) ..... '51 '76 C.959 B.A. L.365 J.D. 8700 Waukegan Rd., Ste. 140
Klapman, Sander A. .... '41 '67 C.1016 B.S. L.209 J.D. 9235 N. Menard St.
Mavrias, James G. .... '44 '68 C.145 B.A. L.424 J.D. [Brenner,M.&A.]
Mehlman, Lester .... '23 '49 C.405 E.E. L.209 LL.B. Mat Assoc. Consulting Corp.‡
Meyer, Jeffrey Scott '53 '79 C.817 B.S.M.E. L.436 J.D.
Director, Legal, John Crane, Inc.
Mooradian, Arthur .... '27 '55 C.999 L.146 LL.B. 7928 N. Lotus St.
Pilson, Robert Michael '39 '91
C.446 B.S. L.823 J.D. V.P., Compl., Pennex Pharmaceuticals, Inc.
Renier, Edith A. .... '15 '39 C.339 L.146 LL.B. 5807 Theobald Rd.
Rothenberg, Phillip .... '22 '51 C.209 B.S. L.365 J.D. 7733 W. Maple St.
Russ, Cary .... '48 '73 C.208 B.S.B.A. L.46 J.D. U.S. Treas. Dept.
Sander, Nancy N. .... '51 '77 C&L.209 B.A., J.D. 8532 School St.

Slutzky, Jay A.
(See Niles)

Walter, Neal C. .... '44 '70 C.1016 B.A. L.146 J.D. 8720 Ferris Ave.
Zalosh, Harry H. .... '19 '49 C.273 B.S. L.209 J.D. 9005 McVickers Ave.‡

MOUND CITY, * 765, *Pulaski Co.*

Kruger, Henry & Hunter
(See Metropolis)

Oros, George .... '39 '67 C&L.339 B.S., LL.B. Cir. J.
Thurston, William J. .... '63 '00 C.531 B.S. L.801 J.D. Cir.J., Pulaski Co.
Waite, Loren H., Jr. .... '36 '77 C&L.801 B.A., J.D. City Atty.

MOUNT CARMEL, * 7,982, *Wabash Co.*

Bramlet, Eric, (BV) .... '60 '86 C.249 B.S. L.801 J.D. [Koger&B.]
Easton, William, Jr. .... '64 '02 C.801 B.S. L.585 J.D. [Ⓐ Rhine,E.&V.]
Ernest, Stanton D., (BV) .... '50 '77 C.339 B.S. L.300 J.D. [Rhine,E.&V.] ⊙
Farrar, John P., (BV) .... '57 '82 C.249 B.A. L.421 J.D. 734 Market St.
Fowler, Jack D., (AV) .... '41 '67 C.801 B.A. L.383 J.D. 2201 College Dr.
Greenlee, Melissa J. '78 '04 C.339 B.S. L.1119 J.D.
(adm. in IN; not adm. in IL) [Ⓐ Rhine,E.&V.]
Hudson, William C. .... '78 '04 C.339 B.A. L.801 J.D. 120 E. Fifth St.
Illingworth, William C. .... '73 '99 C.999 B.S. L.585 J.D. [Rhine,E.&V.]
Keenan, Robert M., Jr. .... '36 '72 C.346 B.S. L.879 J.D. Cir. J.
Kline, Richard L., (BV) .... '44 '74 C.801 B.S. L.838 J.D. [Woodcock&K.]
Koger, Leonard M., Jr., (BV) .... '24 '53 C.378 B.A. L.339 J.D. Pub. Def. [Koger&B.]
Koger & Bramlet, P.C., (BV) .... 316 1/2 Market St.
Nolan, John M. '52 '79 C.602 B.B.A. L.851 J.D.
(adm. in OH; not adm. in IL) 801 West 9th St.
Price, Shannon L. .... '79 '04 C.293 B.A. L.339 J.D. [Ⓐ Rhine,E.&V.]
Price, Thomas E., (BV) ..... '44 '72 C.929 B.S. L.383 J.D. 801 W. 9th St., Suites 100-108
Renner, Brandon S. .... '74 '04 C.801 B.A. L.365 J.D. [Ⓐ Rhine,E.&V.]
Rhine, John E., (AV) .... '52 '77 C.801 B.A. L.339 J.D. [Rhine,E.&V.]

Rhine, Ernest & Vargo, (AV)
631 Market Street, 62863-1489 ⊙
Telephone: 618-262-8611 Fax: 618-262-7145
Email: information@rhinelaw.com URL: http://www.rhinelaw.com
Members of Firm: John E. Rhine; Stanton D. Ernest; Joseph F. Vargo; William C. Illingworth. Associates: William Easton, Jr.; Brandon S. Renner; Shannon L. Price; Christine St. John; Melissa J. Greenlee (Not admitted in IL).
Coal, Oil and Gas Law, Real Estate, Corporate, Civil Trial Practice, Wills and Estates, Environmental Law.
Representative Clients: Sahara Coal Co.; R & R Coal, Inc.; Green River Coal Co., Inc.; Illinois Coal Association; Old Ben Coal Co.; Zeigler Coal Co.; Security Bank and Trust Co.
Evansville, Indiana Office: Old National Place, One Main Street, Suite 600, 47708. Telephone: 812-759-0600. Fax: 812-759-0601.
See Professional Biographies, MOUNT CARMEL, ILLINOIS

Sadlek, Lawrence A., Jr. .... '31 '57 C&L.597 B.S., J.D. Pres., Lawrence Oil Company
St. John, Christine .... '56 '91 C.1115 B.S.B.A. L.923 J.D. [Ⓐ Rhine,E.&V.]
Sawyer, Steve .... '53 '79 C.234 B.Mus. L.339 J.D. Assoc. Cir. J.
Vargo, Joseph F., (CV) .... '54 '89 C.383 B.S.C.E. L.801 J.D. [Rhine,E.&V.]
Witters, C. Michael, Attorney at Law, (BV) '46 '72 C.801 B.A. L.880 J.D.
P.O. Box 129
Woodcock, George W., (AV) .... '30 '57 C.929 A.B. L.383 J.D. [Woodcock&K.]
Woodcock & Kline, (AV) .... P.O. Box 400

MOUNT CARROLL, * 1,832, *Carroll Co.*

Brinkmeier, Scott Lee .... '67 '92 State Atty., The Carroll Co. States Atty.
DeMoss, Richard E. .... '41 '68 C&L.900 B.A., J.D. Assoc. Cir. J.
Gunnarsson, Val, (BV) .... '55 '80 C.880 B.A. L.339 J.D. State's Atty.
Joyce, John F., (BV) .... '47 '73 C.755 B.A. L.424 J.D. 309 E. Benton St.
Kallemeyn, Ronald P. .... '68 '98 C.589 B.S. L.546 J.D. [Kallemeyn]
Kallemeyn Law Office .... 104 1/2 W. Market St.
Kane, J. Jerry, (BV) .... '66 '92 C.338 B.S. L.190 J.D. P.O. Box 112

Leemon, John A., (AV) '28 '52 C&L.339 B.S., LL.B.
1021/2 E. Market St. (⊙Morrison)
Rapp, John W., Jr. .... '40 '65 C&L.424 A.B., J.D. Appl. Ct. Jus.
Shirk, William R., (BV) '52 '77 C.927 B.A. L.801 J.D.
1021/2 E. Market St. (⊙Morrison)
Weinstine, Lester S., (BV) '36 '64
C.339 A.B. L.365 J.D. 1021/2 E. Market St. (⊙Morrison)
Weissmiller, David W., (BV) .... '60 '87 C.340 B.A. L.339 J.D. [Ⓐ Weissmiller]
Weissmiller, Robert W., (AV) .... '18 '47 C.210 A.B. L.597 J.D. [Weissmiller]
Weissmiller Law Office, (AV) .... 310 North Main Street

MOUNT MORRIS, 2,919, *Ogle Co.*

Augsburger, Constance, (CV) .... '58 '84 C.63 B.A. L.306 J.D. 111 E. Hitt St.
Buzard, Brian L., (BV) .... '57 '92 C.178 B.A. L.589 J.D. 111 E. Hill St.
Hanson, Robert T., (BV) .... '55 '80 C.352 B.B.A. L.221 J.D. [Smith,H.H.M.&F.]
McGuire, Craig Eugene, (BV) .... '39 '63 C&L.339 B.S., J.D. 305 S. Lowell Park Rd.
Minnis, Robin Van Dien, (BV) .... '55 '85 C.963 B.S. L.589 J.D. 111 E. Hitt St.
Smith, Hanson, Hahn, Morrow & Floski, P.C., (BV)
One North Wesley Avenue (⊙Oregon)

MOUNT PROSPECT, 56,265, *Cook Co.*

Beatty, Gerald E. .... '43 '72 C.966 B.A. L.597 J.D. Chicago Title Ins. Co.
Bell, Samuel K. ...... '47 '73 C.339 B.A. L.209 J.D. 479 E. Business Center Dr., Ste. 108
Bootz, Andrew J. .... '28 '55 C&L.923 B.S.M.E., J.D. 504 S. Albert St. (Pat.)
Broucek, F. J., Jr. .... '14 '38 L.146 LL.B. 302 N. Maple St.‡
Burns, Michael J. .... '64 '98 C.746 B.A. L.146 J.D. 9 North Pine St.
Busch, Raymond W. .... '28 '52 C.118 B.A. L.145 J.D. 907 S. Maple Dr.‡
Calimafde, George J. '20 '50 C&L.724 B.B.A., J.D.
(adm. in NY; not adm. in IL) 1699 Wall St.
Camasto, Nicholas A., (Ltd.) '30 '57
C.46 B.S.E.E. L.365 J.D. 1800 W. Central Rd. (Pat.) (⊙River Forest)
Chickerneo, Carey Laurence .... '52 '86 C.705 B.A. L.365 J.D. [Chickerneo&F.]
Chickerneo & Fosco .... 350 W. Kensington, Ste. 120
Cipriano, John E. '— '76 C&L.477 B.A., J.D.
Asst. Gen. Coun., Mitsubishi Electric & Electronics USA, Inc.
Cohn, Bradley M. .... '53 '78 C.352 B.A. L.472 J.D. [Thrun,T.&C.]
Cutts, Anita S. .... '46 '76 C.966 B.S. L.146 J.D. 613 S. Emerson St.
Czekala, David E. .... '37 '62 C&L.597 B.S., J.D. 1700 S. Elmhurst Rd.
Downs, Edward J. .... '37 '65 C.424 B.S.C. L.209 J.D. 1600 W. Golf Rd.
Driscoll, J. P. .... '14 '39 C&L.424 J.D. 1189 S. Linneman Rd.‡
Duffy, William J., (BV) .... '34 '58 C&L.424 B.C.S., J.D. 101 S. Pine St.
Ehlman, Paul M. .... '34 '58 C.339 B.S. L.597 J.D. 501 W. Shabonee Tr.
Fosco, Paul .... '55 '86 C.209 B.S. L.365 J.D. [Chickerneo&F.]
Georgi, Richard H. .... '19 '50 C.966 Ph.B. L.597 J.D. 617 N. Pine St.‡

Glasgow, Thomas, Ltd., The Law Offices of
(See Schaumburg)

Griffin, John E. .... '44 '78 C.339 B.S. L.365 J.D. 980 E. Northwest Hwy.
Grossi, William A. .... '53 '79 C.436 B.S. L.146 J.D. 1919 E. Burr Oak Drive
Haas, John C. .... '50 '75 C&L.339 B.A., J.D. 115 S. Emerson St.
Healy, John Francis '63 '88 C.602 B.B.A. L.1522 J.D.
Pres., Arron Road Construction Co.
Howard, Robert L. .... '18 '46 C&L.966 B.A., J.D. 600 W. Shabonee Trail‡
Johnson, Charles W. .... '17 '48 C&L.209 B.S., J.D. 902 S. Lancaster St.‡
Karras, Angelo W. .... '26 '51 L.365 LL.B. 205 W. Hiawatha Trl.
Kiselstein, Bruce, Law Offices of '52 '78
C.184 B.A. L.365 J.D. 930 East Northwest Highway
Krause, Carolyn H., (BV) .... '38 '66 C.966 B.A. L.146 J.D. State Rep. [Krause&K.]
Krause, David S., (BV) .... '35 '67 C.205 B.S. L.146 J.D. [Krause&K.]
Krause & Krause, (BV) .... 200 E. Evergreen Ave. (⊙New York, NY)
Kuntz, Donald W. .... '29 '60 C.150 B.B.A. L.365 J.D. [Kuntz&K.]
Kuntz, Scott C. .... '59 '84 C.589 B.S. L.146 J.D. [Kuntz&K.]
Kuntz & Kuntz .... 900 E. Northwest Hwy.
Kurtz, Norman I. .... '50 '74 C.831 B.A. L.989 J.D. 32 W. Busse Ave.
Leffler, Ruth L., (AV) .... '17 '48 C&L.597 B.S., J.D. 701 W. Central Rd.‡
Lombardo, Anthony M. .... '53 '79 C.746 B.A. L.1151 J.D. [A.M.Lombardo]
Lombardo, Anthony M., Ltd. .... 401 E. Prospect Ave., Ste. 113
Longo, Joseph A. .... '57 '83 C.436 B.A. L.734 J.D. 2100 W. Haven
Lotsoff, Terry L. .... '51 '77 C.347 A.B. L.339 J.D. 440 W. Bob O. Link Rd.
Luby, William J., Law Office of .... '66 '94 C.93 B.S. L.424 J.D. 830 E. Rand Rd., Ste. 6
Lucas, Catherine Ann .... '53 '78 C&L.424 B.A., J.D. 1202 W. Green Acres Ln.‡
McDermott, William J. .... '27 '53 C&L.602 Ph.B., J.D. 1208 W. Lonnquist Blvd.‡
Meersman, Maureen P., (BV) '61 '86
C.201 B.S. L.209 J.D. 16 West Northwest Highway, 2nd Floor
Meinhardt, Paul W. .... '37 '68 C.894 A.B. L.365 J.D. 923 S. Emerson
Murphy, Kathleen Meersman, Law Offices of '56 '80
C.436 B.A. L.209 J.D. 16 West Northwest Highway
Myers, Douglas W. .... '46 '74 C.1265 B.Ph. L.365 J.D. NBD Mortgage Co.
Nagle, Joseph J. .... '28 '51 L.209 LL.B. 104 S. Elmhurst Ave.‡
Natoli, Gloria A. .... '34 '81 C.530 B.A. L.365 J.D. 712 S. Louis St.
Oleson, Debra Ann .... '57 '84 C.274 B.S.B.A. L.424 J.D. 719 S. Chris Lane
Pechette, Jean Marie R. '57 '80 C.347 B.A. L.1119 J.D.
Assoc. Gen. Coun., GE Healthcare
Petrucelli, Leonard J. .... '42 '73 C.1016 B.A. L.146 J.D. 980 E. N.W. Hwy.
Ritt, James W. .... '42 '67 C&L.424 B.S., J.D. 1824 Cree Lane

Robin, Daniel K., LTD
(See Arlington Heights)

Seyring, Gerhard W. .... '14 '55 C.597 L.209 LL.B. 11 S. William St.‡
Shaffer, Jane E., Attorney at Law .... '54 '88 C.477 B.B.A. L.424 J.D. 217 College Dr.
Singer, Robert W. .... '29 '53 C&L.597 B.A., J.D. 1320 W. Northwest Hwy.

Sodos, Saul R. '57 '84 C.957 B.B.A. L.221 J.D.
300 West Golf Road, Suite 201, 60056
Telephone: 847-398-3052 Fax: 847-398-3054
Email: TXMAVN@aol.com URL: http://www.lawyers.com/sodos
Taxation, Trusts and Estate Planning, Wills and Probate, Residential and Commercial Real Estate, Consumer Bankruptcy, Consumer Law, Contracts, Corporations, Light Trespass.
See Professional Biographies, MOUNT PROSPECT, ILLINOIS

Stelk, Roger W., Law Offices of
(See Arlington Heights)

Storey, Richard A., Jr. '48 '87
C.123 B.A. L.589 J.D. Coml. Underwriter, Chicago Title Ins. Co.
Tallman, John E. .... '52 '77 C.424 B.A. L.472 J.D. [Thrun,T.&C.]
Thatcher, K. Blake '59 '87 C.101 B.A. L.597 J.D.
General Counsel, NTNUSA Corporation

Thorsen, Richard P. ... '45 '71 C&L.597 B.S., J.D. Pres., FNW Capital, Inc.
Thrun, Howard A., Jr. ... '45 '73 C&L.879 B.S.B.A., J.D. [Thrun,T.&C.]
Thrun, Tallman & Cohn, Ltd. ... 111 E. Busse Ave.
Tumbarello, Gregory L. ... '26 '53 C&L.339 B.S., J.D. 110 S. I-Oka Ave.‡
Wasiak, Robert J. ... '56 '91 C.209 M.B.A. L.213 J.D. 907 South Nawata
Watychowicz, Mark John ... '75 '02 C.1182 B.A. L.365 J.D. 115 S. Emerson St.
Williams, Don E. ... '28 '65 C.597 B.S. L.146 LL.B. 1011 W. Lincoln St.
Wohlmuth, Edmund J. ... '42 '69 C.742 B.A. L.966 J.D. [E.Wohlmuth]
Wohlmuth, Edmund ... 115 S. Emerson St.
Ziemba, Andrew A. ... '46 '71 C.1024 B.A. L.209 J.D. 900 E. Golfview Dr.

MOUNT STERLING, * 2,070, *Brown Co.*

Alsup, John W., Jr. ... '42 '69 C&L.734 J.D. 124 W. Main St.
Hooker, Jerry Joe ... '63 '88 C.338 B.S. L.607 J.D. Brown Co. State Atty.
Lagoski, Diane M. ... '50 '79 C.430 B.A. L.424 J.D. Assoc. J.
Leonard, John B., (BV) ... '47 '76 C.339 B.S. L.365 J.D. State's Atty.
Slocum, David K. ... '41 '71 C.1082 B.A. L.339 J.D. Cir. J.
Tucker, Edward B. ... '39 '65 C.801 B.S. L.339 J.D. 111 W Washington Ste C
Turner, Edward D. ... '28 '56 C.337 A.B. L.339 J.D. Ret. Cir. J.
Utter, Robert E., (BV) ... '27 '53 C&L.339 B.S., J.D. 118 N. Capitol St.

MOUNT VERNON, * 16,269, *Jefferson Co.*

Alling, Kathleen M. ... '50 '76 C.855 B.A. L.602 J.D. Assoc. Cir. J.
Anderson, Edwin J. ... '58 '84 C.347 B.S. L.1119 J.D. Asst. Def.
Antonik, Douglas A., (BV) ... '57 '85 C.57 B.A. L.801 J.D. [Antonik]
Antonik Law Office, (BV) ... 411 Main St.
Bahn, Peter R. ... '50 '84 C.311 B.S. L.472 J.D. RR2 Box 239A (Pat.)
Ballard, Mark J., (AV) ... '53 '78 C.339 B.A. L.39 J.D. [Campbell,B.C.H.B.&M.]
Black, Terry R., (AV) ... '45 '70 C.340 B.A. L.228 J.D. [Campbell,B.C.H.B.&M.]
Blades, Rhonda K. ... '71 '01 C&L.801 B.S.Ed., J.D. [A Harvey&B.]
Borek, Thomas J. '54 '80 C&L.569 B.A., J.D.
Land of Lincoln Legal Assist. Found., Inc.
Bradley, Joshua M. ... '74 '99 C.500 B.A. L.801 J.D. [Harvey&B.]
Campbell, David A., (AV) ... '44 '69 C.934 A.B. L.339 J.D. [Campbell,B.C.H.B.&M.]

Campbell, Black, Carnine, Hedin, Ballard & McDonald, P.C., (AV) BB
108 South Ninth Street, P.O. Drawer C, 62864
Telephone: 618-242-3310 Fax: 618-242-3735
Email: frontdesk@illinoisfirm.com URL: http://www.illinoisfirm.com
David A. Campbell; Terry R. Black; Roy L. Carnine; Craig R. Hedin; Mark J. Ballard; Jerome E. McDonald; Howard W. Campbell (1911-1980); John E. Jacobsen (1922-1985); Glenn E. Moore (1911-1991); David E. Furnall (1905-1993);—Fred R. Mann; Aaron S. Carnine; C. Stephen Swofford; Shane M. Carnine.
General Civil Practice in State and Federal Courts. Mining, Oil and Gas, Insurance, Workers Compensation, Corporation, Family, Probate, Real Estate and Trust Law. Trials and Appeals.
Representative Clients: Country Mutual Insurance Co.; Southern Illinois Stone Co; Rend Lake Conservancy District; Consolidation Coal Co.; Illinois State Medical Insurance Services; State Farm Automobile Insurance Co.
See Professional Biographies, MOUNT VERNON, ILLINOIS

Carnine, Aaron S. ... '69 '98 C.339 B.A. L.801 J.D. [A Campbell,B.C.H.B.&M.]
Carnine, Meagan N. ... '79 '04 C&L.801 B.S., J.D. [A Mitchell]
Carnine, Roy L., (AV) ... '49 '73 C.234 B.S. L.500 J.D. [Campbell,B.C.H.B.&M.]
Carnine, Shane M. ... '77 '03 C.234 B.A. L.801 J.D. [A Campbell,B.C.H.B.&M.]
Chapman, Melissa A. ... '51 '83 C.801 B.A. L.734 J.D. Dist. Ct. J.
Costa, Sharon S., (BV) ... '51 '77 C&L.801 B.A., J.D. 2001 Bwy.

Craig & Craig, (AV)
115 North 7th Street, P.O. Box 1545, 62864 ⊙
Telephone: 618-244-7511 Telecopier: 618-244-7628
Email: mtvernon@craiglaw.net URL: http://www.lawyers.com/craig&craiglawoffices
Resident Personnel: Paul R. Lynch (Resident); Kenneth F. Werts (Resident); Julie A. Webb (Resident).
General Practice in State and Federal Courts. Coal, Oil, Gas, Mining, Insurance, Drainage and Levee Law, Environmental, Corporation, Labor Relations, Workers Compensation and Real Estate Law. Estate Planning and Probate. Trials and Appeals.
Mattoon, Illinois Office: 1807 Broadway. Telephone: 217-234-6481. Telecopier: 217-234-6486. Email: mattoon@craiglaw.net
See Professional Biographies, MOUNT VERNON, ILLINOIS

Curry, Ellen Jenkins, (BV) ... '57 '86 C.339 B.A. L.801 J.D. 2929 Broadway St., Ste. 7
Dowell, Nobel Y., Jr., Law Office of, (CV) '52 '76 C.801 B.A. L.793 J.D.
1509 Triangle
Flood, John J., (BV) ... '53 '78 C.234 B.A. L.801 J.D. Appl. Ct.
Gamber, Terry H. ... '47 '73 C.597 B.A. L.209 J.D. Cir. J.
Gibson, Larry D., (BV) ... '51 '78 C&L.801 B.A., J.D. [L.D.Gibson]
Gibson, Larry D., Law Office of, P.C., (BV) ... 2012 Broadway
Given, Charles M. ... '44 '69 C&L.339 A.B., J.D. State Bd. of Educ.
Griffeth, Julie R. ... '75 '99 C.130 B.A. L.910 J.D. 206 S. Ninth Ave.
Hanagan, Michael J., (AV) ... '51 '76 C.686 A.B. L.734 J.D. [Hanagan&D.]
Hanagan, Steven F., (BV) ... '58 '84 C.801 B.S. L.734 J.D. [Hanagan&D.]
Hanagan, William D., (AV) ... '27 '53 C.742 B.A. L.276 J.D. [Hanagan&D.]
Hanagan & Dousman, (AV) ... Ninth & North Street
Hannebaum, Nancy Hall, (BV) ... '47 '76 C.339 B.A. L.424 J.D. 3 Parker Drive
Hanson, Leslie James, (AV) ... '52 '83 C&L.801 B.S., J.D. [Neubauer&H.]

Hart and Hart
(See Benton)

Harvey, Morris Lane, (AV) ... '50 '75 C.531 B.S. L.383 J.D. [Harvey&B.]

Harvey & Bradley, Law Offices of, (AV) BB
2029 Broadway, 62864
Telephone: 618-244-9544 Fax: 618-244-9344
Email: lhlaw@mvn.net URL: http://www.lawyers.com/morrisharvey
Morris Lane Harvey; Joshua M. Bradley. Associate: Rhonda K. Blades.
Litigation. Negligence, Personal Injury, Domestic Relations, Insurance Law, Oil and Gas. Trials and Appeals.
See Professional Biographies, MOUNT VERNON, ILLINOIS

Hassakis, Mark D., (AV) ... '51 '76 C.597 B.A. L.734 J.D. [Hassakis&H.]

Hassakis & Hassakis, P.C., (AV)
Suite 201, Boston Building, 206 South Ninth Street, P.O. Box 706, 62864-0706
Telephone: 618-244-5335 Telefax: 618-244-5330
Email: mhass@hassakislaw.com URL: http://www.hassakislaw.com
Mark D. Hassakis.
Concentrated in Civil Trial Practice, Negligence, Workers Compensation, Insurance, Medical and Nursing Home Malpractice.
See Professional Biographies, MOUNT VERNON, ILLINOIS

Hedin, Craig R., (AV) ... '50 '75 C.210 B.A. L.862 J.D. [Campbell,B.C.H.B.&M.]
Henson, James H., (BV) ... '48 '75 C.357 B.S. L.146 J.D. Pub. Def.
Hofmann-Mullett, Sarah '56 '81
C.699 B.A. L.1218 J.D. Land of Lincoln Legal Assist. Found., Inc.

Howard, G. W., III, (AV) ... '35 '59 C&L.339 A.B., J.D. [Howard,L.P.&H.]
Howard, Jeffrey G., (BV) ... '63 '90 C&L.339 B.A., J.D. [Howard,L.P.&H.]

Howard, Leggans, Piercy & Howard, LLP, (AV) BB
1008 Main, P.O. Drawer U, 62864
Telephone: 618-242-6594 Fax: 618-244-7197
URL: http://www.lawyers.com/hlph
Members of Firm: George W. Howard, Jr. (1907-1994); G. W. Howard, III; David R. Leggans; David L. Piercy; Jeffrey G. Howard.
General Practice in all Courts. Probate and Estate Planning. Tax, Corporation, Municipal and Real Estate Law.
Representative Clients: Integra Bank, N.A.; First State Bank of Dix; Tri-County Electric Cooperative; Hamilton County Telephone Co-op., City of Mt. Vernon; Mt. Vernon Township; Texico State Bank.
See Professional Biographies, MOUNT VERNON, ILLINOIS

Hundley, John T., (AV) ... '48 '79 C.339 B.S. L.209 J.D. [T.Sharp] ⊙
Irish, Ellen Eder ... '45 '86 C.999 B.A. L.801 J.D. Staff Atty., 5th District Appellate Court
Irvin, Donald E. ... '40 '69 C.801 B.A. L.365 J.D. 1203 Salem Rd.
Kalo-Keistler, Zari Ann ... '57 '83 C&L.801 B.A., J.D. Chf. Reg. Hearing Off.

Kerley & Associates, P.C., Law Office of
(See Springfield)

Kirwan, Daniel M., (AV) '50 '74
C.347 B.A. L.1119 J.D. Dep. Def.; Off. of State Appl. Def.
Krause, Lehman D. ... '25 '64 C.910 B.S.Ch.E. L.339 J.D. Ret. Cir. J.‡
Langenstein, Sharee S. '70 '98
C.804 B.A. L.801 J.D. Staff Atty., Off. of State Atty. Appl. Pros.
Leggans, David R., (BV) ... '55 '79 C.801 B.A. L.339 J.D. [Howard,L.P.&H.]
Lynch, Paul R., (AV) ... '52 '77 C.424 B.A. L.339 J.D. [Craig&C.]
Mann, Fred R., (CV) ... '52 '85 C.339 B.S. L.801 J.D. [A Campbell,B.C.H.B.&M.]
Marshall, Trent M. ... '71 '99 C.338 B.S. L.801 J.D. State Atty. App. Pros.
Martin, Curtis W., (BV) ... '64 '89 C.339 B.S. L.801 J.D. [Shaw&M.]
Mastrangelo, Vito A., (BV) '53 '80 C&L.801 B.S., J.D.
Staff Atty., Appl. Ct. Resch. Dept.
Maynor, Walter H. ... '14 '40 C.339 L.146 LL.B. P.O. Box 1297‡
McDonald, Jerome E., (AV) ... '55 '80 C.221 B.A. L.339 J.D. [Campbell,B.C.H.B.&M.]
McHaney, Michael D., (BV) ... '57 '82 C&L.801 B.A., J.D. 411 Main St.

McMahon, Berger, Hanna, Linihan, Cody & McCarthy, A Professional Corporation
(See Collinsville)

Mitchell, A. Ben, (AV) ... '41 '66 C.862 B.S. L.339 J.D. [Mitchell]

Mitchell Law Office, P.C., (AV) BB
2020 Broadway, P.O. Box 1088, 62864
Telephone: 618-242-0705 Fax: 618-242-4820
Email: abenlaw@charter.net
A. Ben Mitchell;—Meagan N. Carnine.
General Civil Practice.
See Professional Biographies, MOUNT VERNON, ILLINOIS

Musick, Donald G., (AV) ... '31 '56 C&L.910 A.B., J.D. 1006 Main Street
Neubauer & Hanson, P.C., (AV) ... 123 S. 10th St., 6th Fl.

Noonan, Thomas J., P.C.
(See St. Louis, Missouri)

Norris, Stephen E., (BV) ... '41 '78 C.665 Ph.D. L.910 J.D. Dep. Dir., State Appl. Pros.
Overstreet, David K., (BV) ... '66 '91 C.1064 B.S. L.838 J.D. [Neubauer&H.]
Parrish, Troy J. ... '73 '00 C.798 B.S. L.801 J.D. [T.J.Parrish]
Parrish, Troy J., LLC ... 123 S. 10th St., Ste. 601
Piercy, David L., (AV) ... '57 '82 C&L.339 B.A., J.D. [Howard,L.P.&H.]
Powell, Cheryl A., Law Office of, (BV) '63 '88
C&L.589 B.A., J.D. 1908 Broadway, Ste. 300
Quinn, Scott Russell ... '74 '01 C.339 B.S. L.910 J.D. Ste 204, 2208 Olive
Raymond, David, (BV) ... '— '76 C.338 B.S. L.602 J.D. 1908 Bway.
Renshaw, C. Kent, (CV) ... '53 '94 C&L.801 B.S., J.D. [Renshaw&Assoc.]
Renshaw & Associates, (CV) ... 1015 Broadway
Sharp, Terrell Lee, (AV) ... '44 '73 C&L.339 B.S., J.D. [T.Sharp] ⊙

Sharp, Terry, P.C., Law Office of, (AV) BB
1115 Harrison Street, P.O. Box 906, 62864 ⊙
Telephone: 618-242-0246 Fax: 618-242-1170
Email: law@lotsharp.com URL: http://www.lawyers.com/tsharp
Terrell Lee Sharp; John T. Hundley.
Bankruptcy, Creditor's Rights, Commercial, Banking, Real Estate, Corporate, Probate and Estate Planning Law. No small collections.
Representative Clients: Housing Authority of the City of Mt. Vernon; N.E. Mt. Vernon Water Co.; Peoples National Bank; South Pointe Bank; Centrue Bank; First Financial Bank; AgLease or Loan, LLC, States Resources Corp., Bombardier Capital.
Benton, Illinois Office: 105 North Main Street. Telephone: 618-435-5109. FAX: 618-242-1170.
See Professional Biographies, MOUNT VERNON, ILLINOIS

Shaw, Robert E., (BV) ... '43 '79 C.502 B.S. L.801 J.D. [Shaw&M.]

Shaw & Martin, P.C., (BV)
U.S. Bank Building, 123 South Tenth Street, Suite 302, P.O. Box 1789, 62864
Telephone: 618-244-1788 Fax: 618-244-2588 URL: http://www.shawmartin.com
Email: shawmartin@mvn.net URL: http://www.lawyers.com/shaw&martin
Robert E. Shaw; Curtis W. Martin.
Banking, Commercial Law, Creditors Rights, Wills, Trusts and Estates, Real Estate, Family Law, Civil Trials and Appeals.
See Professional Biographies, MOUNT VERNON, ILLINOIS

Strawn, Valery Paige Clark ... '72 '97 C.339 B.A. L.801 J.D. Off. of Appl. Def.
Swofford, C. Stephen, (BV) ... '52 '77 C&L.801 B.S., J.D. [A Campbell,B.C.H.B.&M.]
Timberlake, George W. ... '48 '77 C&L.339 B.A., J.D. Assoc. Cir. J.
Troutt, Michael D. ... '53 '77 C&L.801 B.S., J.D. P.O. Box 1703
Villani, Henry P., (BV) ... '65 '95 C.347 B.S. L.801 J.D. 320 South 11th Street
Webb, Julie A. ... '71 '96 C.339 B.S. L.801 J.D. [Craig&C.]
Wells, Larry R. ... '58 '82 C.234 B.A. L.801 J.D. Asst. Appel. Def.
Werts, Kenneth F., (AV) ... '57 '84 C.339 B.A. L.801 J.D. [Craig&C.]
Wexstten, James M. ... '50 '77 C&L.801 B.S., J.D. Cir. J.

Wham & Wham
(See Centralia)

MOUNT ZION, 4,845, *Macon Co.*

Sappington, Warren A. ... '28 '58 C.357 B.S. L.339 LL.B. Assoc. Cir. J.‡

MOWEAQUA, 1,923, *Shelby Co.*

Allison, Robert J., (CV) ... '50 '80 C.1247 B.S. L.365 J.D. [Allison&A.]
Allison, Stephen J., (CV) ... '44 '74 C.482 B.S. L.365 J.D. [Allison&A.]
Allison & Allison, (CV) ... 525 N. Main, # 1
Burris, Victoria Ehret ... '54 '79 C.234 B.A. L.734 J.D. 1756 N. 2525 East Rd.‡
Sanders, R. J. ... '14 '41 C&L.339 B.S., LL.B. 702 E. Warren St.‡

MUNDELEIN, 30,935, *Lake Co.*

Ackley, Robert O. ... '52 '88 C.589 B.A. L.365 J.D. [R.Ackley]
Ackley, Robert ... 500 N. Lake St.

Anderson, Richard A.
(See Grayslake)

Aubel, Bradley F. ... '64 '97 309 N. Lake St., Ste. 203
Besore, Thomas G. '65 '97 C.339 B.S. L.424 J.D.
(adm. in OH; not adm. in IL) [T.G.Besore]
Besore, Thomas G., Co., L.P.A. ... 27554 Turf Hill Dr.

Bruno, Randie, Law Offices of
(See Waukegan)

Clark, Larry M. ... '51 '80 C.589 B.S. L.209 J.D. 700 N. Lake St., Ste. 200
Deuster, Donald E. ... '29 '57 C.694 B.A. L.112 LL.B. 132 N. Sylvan Dr.
Elman, Anthony R. ... '66 '92 C.477 B.A. L.861 J.D. [Elman&E.]
Elman, Fred W. ... '37 '62 C&L.209 LL.B. [Elman&E.]

Elman & Elman, Law Offices of
700 N. Lake Street, Suite 205, 60060
Telephone: 847-949-8182 847-949-8185
Email: elmanlaw@aol.com URL: http://www.elmanlaw.com
Members of Firm: Fred W. Elman; Anthony R. Elman.
Bankruptcy, Personal Injury, Workers Compensation, Health Care, Litigation.
See Professional Biographies, MUNDELEIN, ILLINOIS

Gates, Kim Boman ... '52 '84 C.347 B.A. L.146 J.D. 128 Idlewild Ave.
Grady, Steven T. ... '65 '93 C.424 B.A. L.209 J.D. 505 E. Hawley, Ste. 240
Green, John G., (BV) '18 '49 L.209 J.D.
(adm. in FL; not adm. in IL) 464 N. Lake St.
Green, John G., III, (BV) ... '41 '70 C.1024 A.B. L.209 J.D. 464 N. Lake St.
Hannigan, Richard D., (AV) ... '47 '73 C.201 B.S. L.365 J.D. [R.D.Hannigan]
Hannigan, Thomas M., (BV) ... '22 '53 C&L.424 LL.B. 505 E. Hawley
Hannigan, Thomas M. P., (BV) ... '44 '69 C.201 B.A. L.424 J.D. 111 W. Maple Ave.
Hannigan, Richard D., Ltd., (AV) ... 505 E. Hawley
Hartel, Harry D., Jr. ... '36 '60 C&L.339 B.A., LL.B. Assoc. Cir. Ct. J.
Hayes, Jeffry M. ... '51 '88 C.1183 B.A. L.424 J.D. [J.Hayes]
Hayes, Jeffrey ... 505 E. Hawley St., Ste. 130
Liberman, Alex M. ... '64 '89 C.352 B.A. L.477 J.D. Gen. Coun., Medline Industries, Inc.

Martinovich, Bogdan
(See Libertyville)

Mendes, Meredith Wise '58 '83 C.103 B.A. L.309 J.D.
V.P. & Chf. Fin. Offr., Medline Industries, Inc.
Moree, Anthony I. '54 '82 C&L.436 B.A., J.D.
(adm. in WI; not adm. in IL) 26919 Long Meadow Cir.‡
O'Connor, Nancy M. ... '60 '91 C&L.209 B.A., J.D. 831 McKinley
Schiessle, Michael ... '31 '60 C&L.424 LL.B. P.O. Box 354
Wahlert, Jerome G. '44 '74 L.1026 J.D.
(adm. in CA; not adm. in IL) 1303 Dunleer Drive

MURPHYSBORO, * 13,295, *Jackson Co.*

Bailey, Joni Beth, (CV) ... '60 '84 C.339 B.S. L.801 J.D. 1008 Walnut St.
Blake, Richard L., (CV) ... '64 '92 C.801 B.A. L.1015 J.D. [🄰 Reed,H.M.&G.]
Burke, Rex G., Attorney at Law ... '51 '75 C.801 B.S. L.734 J.D. 907 Chestnut St.
Christenson, Paul ... '46 '84 C.357 B.A. L.801 J.D. 1009 Chestnut
Cripps, Gregory Brian ... '66 '02 C&L.338 B.A., J.D. State Atty.'s Off.
Doherty, Barbara Vogler ... '55 '80 C.880 B.A. L.801 J.D. First Bk. & Tr. Co.
Fiello, Michael A. ... '57 '84 C&L.339 B.S., J.D. Land of Lincoln Legal Asst. Found., Inc.
Frazier, Dana S. ... '63 '97 C.339 B.S. L.801 J.D. 818 Locust Street
Goffinet, Diane Marie ... '67 '92 C&L.801 B.S., J.D. Land of Lincoln Legal Assistance
Gross, Gene, (BV) ... '58 '83 C.801 B.A. L.910 J.D. [Reed,H.M.&G.]
Gross, Patricia ... '51 '83 C.801 B.A. L.284 J.D. Pub. Def.
Heikkinen, Ralph J. '42 '70 C.477 B.A. L.912 J.D.
(adm. in MI; not adm. in IL) RR 5 Box 35‡
Heller, Edward J., (BV) ... '46 '73 C.870 B.S. L.339 J.D. [Reed,H.M.&G.]

Howerton, Dorris & Stone
(See Marion)

Kimmel, E. Dan ... '37 '67 C&L.339 B.S., J.D. Assoc. Cir. J.
Kunce, Peyton H. ... '18 '42 C&L.339 B.S., J.D. 2301 Division St.‡
Lucio, Lydia Ann ... '56 '91 C.36 B.A. L.801 J.D. Land of Lincoln Legal Assistance, Inc.
Mansfield, Thomas W., (BV) ... '50 '78 C&L.801 B.A., J.D. [Reed,H.M.&G.]
Matalonis, Paul ... '58 '84 C&L.801 B.S., J.D. Land of Lincoln Legal Asst. Found., Inc.

McCann, Maurice J., (CV) '50 '86 C&L.801 Ph.D., J.D.
1331 Walnut Street, 62966-2026
Telephone: 618-684-5242
Email: mjmccann@globaleyes.net
Criminal Law, DUI, Probate, Personal Injury, Divorce.
See Professional Biographies, MURPHYSBORO, ILLINOIS

McDermott, John C., Attorney at Law, (CV) ... '57 '82 C.880 B.A. L.801 J.D. 105 S. 11th
McMeen, Herbert E., (CV) ... '48 '80 C&L.801 B.A., J.D. [Ridgeway&M.]
Miller, Gary T., Attorney at Law, (BV) ... '48 '76 C&L.801 B.S., J.D. P.O. Box 1503
Naumer, Helen T. ... '32 '83 C&L.801 B.A., J.D. 297 E. Lake Drive‡
Reed, Gerald S., (BV) ... '52 '77 C.339 B.A. L.801 J.D. [Reed,H.M.&G.]
Reed, Heller, Mansfield & Gross, (BV) ... 1100 Walnut St.
Reiman, Peggy L. ... '74 '99 C&L.801 B.A., J.D. [🄰 Reed,H.M.&G.]
Ridgeway, William G., (BV) ... '27 '52 C.801 A.B. L.339 J.D. [Ridgeway&M.]
Ridgeway & McMeen, (BV) ... 18 1/2 S. 10th St.
Schwartz, William G. ... '49 '76 C&L.801 B.A., J.D. Resident Cir. J.
Simon, Sheila Jeanne '61 '87 C.967 B.A. L.276 J.D. Asst. State's Att.
Stewart, John L. ... '15 '39 C&L.339 B.S., LL.B. 907 Chestnut St.‡
Strong, Guice G., III ... '51 '76 C.340 B.A. L.945 J.D. [G.G.Strong]
Strong, Guice G. ... 330-B North St.
Watt, David W., Jr. ... '43 '68 C.966 B.S. L.339 J.D. Presid. Cir. J.
White, Richard E., (AV) ... '34 '58 C.801 L.339 J.D. [R.E.White]
White, Richard E., Chartered, Law Offices of, (AV) ... 1003 Chestnut Street
Zirkelbach, Brian K. ... '69 '97 C.801 B.A. L.1119 J.D. [🄰 Reed,H.M.&G.]

NAPERVILLE, 128,358, *DuPage & Will Cos.*

Adams, Steven B., (BV) ... '59 '84 C.347 B.A. L.1119 J.D. [Brooks,A.&T.]
Albright, Paula A., (BV) '53 '84 C.210 B.A. L.146 J.D.
Assoc. Gen. Coun., Edward Health Services Corporation
Allison, Alexander C. ... '38 '63 C.31 B.A. L.145 J.D. 1844 Ferry Road

Ambrose & Cushing, P.C.
(See Chicago)

Amdall, Kenneth H. ... '25 '72 C.477 B.S.C.E. L.502 J.D. 24 W. 610 Parkview Ct.
Anderson, Mark D. ... '52 '77 C.338 B.A. L.424 J.D. [Coman&A.]

Anderson & Associates, P.C.
(See Schaumburg)

Anselmo, Thomas J. ... '54 '80 C.339 B.S. L.365 J.D. [Freedman,A.L.&R.]

Armstrong, Thea '41 '86 C.791 B.S. L.1000 J.D.
232 N. Washington Street, 60540
Telephone: 630-355-7680 Fax: 630-355-7684
Email: thea@thearmstrong.com URL: http://www.thearmstronglaw.com
Criminal Defense, Criminal Law, Driving While Intoxicated, Drug Crimes, Felonies, Homicide, Juvenile Law, Misdemeanors, Parole and Probation, Sexual Assault, Traffic Violations, Elder Law, Family Law, Adoptions, Child Custody, Child Support, Divorce, Domestic Violence, Premarital Agreements, Spousal Support, Visitation Rights, Commercial Real Estate, Residential Real Estate, Wills and Probate, Guardianship and Conservatorship, Business Formation, Buying and Selling Businesses, Small Business Law, Commercial Leasing.
See Professional Biographies, NAPERVILLE, ILLINOIS

Asmus, Ryan Wade ... '68 '93 C.1044 B.A. L.8 J.D. Claims Atty., Illinois Provider Trust
Babington, Thomas K. '46 '73 C.674 A.B. L.494 J.D.
(adm. in MN; not adm. in IL) National Marine Serv.

Baniak Pine & Gannon
(See Chicago)

Barlett, Jeanne M. '59 '91 C.30 B.A. L.273 J.D.
(adm. in PA; not adm. in IL) Vitalink Pharmacy Svcs., Inc.
Barrett, Donald F. ... '41 '73 C&L.424 B.B.A., J.D. 1520 Cascade Ct.
Bathas, Nicholas P. ... '53 '88 C.602 A.B. L.424 J.D. [Bathas&Assoc.]
Bathas & Associates ... 1304 Dunrobin Rd., Ste. 100
Benes, Cheryl Fernandez '70 '02
C.339 B.S. L.424 J.D. Staff Intell. Prop. Atty, Tellabs, Inc.
Berndtson, Scott Allen, (CV) ... '58 '87 C.339 B.A. L.146 J.D. 956 Creekside Cir.
Bernhard, Patti A. ... '54 '98 C.98 B.S. L.365 J.D. [🄰 Dommermuth,B.C.&W.]
Bertoux, Carol W. '47 '80
C.801 B.S. L.209 J.D. Assoc. Gen. Coun., Ill. Credit Union League
Betz, Richard L. ... '40 '65 C.589 B.S. L.597 J.D. 1004 Sheringham Dr.
Bialek, Mitchell R. ... '56 '83 C.337 A.B. L.365 J.D. 1724 Atwood Circle
Biskupic, Vincent J. ... '30 '53 C.347 L.424 LL.B. 1809 Clyde Dr.
Blaber, Leo B., Jr. ... '28 '57 C.602 B.S. L.209 J.D. Pres., Regency Savings Bk., F.S.B.
Black, Robert G., Law Offices of '59 '85
C.98 B.S. L.365 J.D. 300 East Fifth Avenue, Suite 365
Blevins, Jeffrey A., (AV) ... '55 '81 C.207 B.A. L.209 J.D. 2219 Sisters Ave., Ste. 1
Bobosky, W. Brand, (BV) ... '39 '65 C.602 B.S. L.339 J.D. 50 W. Chicago Ave.
Bohmer, John T. '60 '85 C&L.339 B.A., J.D.
Asst. V.P. & Assoc. Gen. Coun., Illinois Hospital & HealthSystems Assn.
Bollow, Jennifer A. ... '73 '98 C.338 B.S. L.424 J.D. [🄰 Cassiday,S.&G.]
Boyd-Obarski, Rebecca ... '58 '84 C.339 B.A. L.365 J.D. 1228 Millet St.
Braun, Richard A., (AV) ... '43 '68 C.473 B.A. L.146 J.D. P.O. Box 9411
Breininger, Thomas M. '45 '79 C.665 B.S. L.229 J.D.
Corp. Pat. & Trademark Coun., Nalco Co. (Pat.)
Brestal, Willard F., (AV) ... '41 '68 C.339 B.S. L.424 J.D. [Dommermuth,B.C.&W.]
Briggs, Alysha Sue '75 '00 C&L.589 B.A., J.D.
1155 South Washington Street, Suite 106
Broida, Ronald J., (AV) ... '43 '69 C&L.339 B.A., J.D. [Broida&T.]

Broida and Tullis, Ltd., (AV)
Naperville Corporate Center, Suite 108, 1250 East Diehl Road, 60563
Telephone: 630-245-1515 Fax: 630-245-1565
Email: broidatullis@aol.com
Members of Firm: Ronald J. Broida; Jeffrey A. Tullis. Associate: Joseph K. Nichele. Of Counsel: Fredric J. Grossman.
Civil Trial and Appellate Practice in State and Federal Courts, including Business and Commercial, Employment Discrimination, Labor, Corporate and Real Estate Litigation, Divorce and Family Law, Personal Injury, Municipal Representation, Arbitration and Mediation, General and Transactional Practice.
See Professional Biographies, NAPERVILLE, ILLINOIS

Broihier, John C. ... '45 '78 C.746 B.B.A. L.209 J.D. 1001 E. Chicago Ave.
Bromberek, James J., (BV) ... '62 '88 C.750 B.A. L.365 J.D. [Wyeth,H.&B.]
Brooks, Gerald J., (AV) ... '37 '66 C.801 B.A. L.424 J.D. [Brooks,A.&T.]

Brooks, Adams and Tarulis, (AV)
101 North Washington Street, 60540
Telephone: 630-355-2101 FAX: 630-355-7843
Email: info@napervillelaw.com URL: http://www.napervillelaw.com
Members of Firm: Gerald J. Brooks; Steven B. Adams; Richard J. Tarulis; David G. Wentz. Associates: John Raymond Wieser; Douglas C. Tibble; Timothy J. Hoppa; Nicole L. Karas. Of Counsel: David N. Schaffer.
General Practice including Trial and Appellate Litigation. General Business, Business/Commercial Litigation, Employment, Corporation, Municipal, School, Park, Condemnation, Real Estate, Environmental, Land Developments, Zoning, Probate, Wills, Trusts, Special Needs Trusts, Adoptions, Estate Planning, Banking, Commercial, Personal Injury, Condominium Law and Civil Rights Law, Consumer Protection, Consumer Fraud, Consumer Litigation, Family Law, Divorce, Matrimonial Law, Criminal/Traffic Defense, Juvenile Representation and School Law Matters.
See Professional Biographies, NAPERVILLE, ILLINOIS

Brumm, Margaret M. '57 '88 C.474 B.S.Ch.E. L.477 J.D.
(adm. in MI; not adm. in IL; Pat.) Pat. Atty. I, Nalco Co.
Brummond, David J. '50 '75 C.436 B.A. L.352 J.D.
Gen. Coun., Natl. Fraternal Congress of America

Bueche, Gregory J.
(See Warrenville)

Bufalino, Marie A. (Nanette) '56 '86
C.602 B.A. L.424 J.D. V.P. & Gen. Coun., Edward Hosp.
Burgess, Aubrey L. ... '22 '58 C.273 B.M.E. L.209 J.D. 1191 Banbury Cir.‡
Burnett, Robert W. ... '55 '81 C.339 B.S. L.209 J.D. 1300 Iroquois Dr.

Byrne, Michael T.
(See Clarendon Hills)

Cahill, Mary Denise, (BV) '— '76 C&L.424 B.A., J.D.
1155 South Washington Street, 60540
Telephone: 630-778-6500 Fax: 630-778-0722
Email: mdcahill@sbcglobal.net
Representing families with special needs children. Attention Deficit, Hyperactivity Disorder, Developmental Disabilities and Learning Disabilities. Family Law, School Law, Special Education, School Equal Protection, Disabled Rights, Class Action Defense, Employment Law, and Estate Planning Law, Mediation.
See Professional Biographies, NAPERVILLE, ILLINOIS

Calabrese Associates, A Professional Corporation
(See Wheaton)

Calvo, James W. ... '65 '90 C.98 B.S. L.589 J.D. [J.W.Calvo]
Calvo, James W., P.C. Law Offices of ... 1117 Briergate Dr.
Carey, Brook M. ... '78 '03 C.1151 B.A. L.424 J.D. [🄰 Cassiday,S.&G.]
Casey, Jacqueline J. ... '68 '98 C.209 B.A. L.1294 J.D. 804 N. Washington St.

Cassiday, Schade & Gloor, LLP, (AV)
1230 East Diehl Road, Suite 202, 60563-9362 ⊙
Telephone: 630-328-2970 Fax: 630-328-2979
URL: http://www.cassiday.com

(This Listing Continued)

Cassiday, Schade & Gloor, LLP (Continued)

Members of Firm: Brian J. Hickey; Therese S. Seeley; Douglas S. Strohm. Associates: Jennifer A. Bollow; Brook M. Carey; Jonathan P. Mincieli; Mark A. Sansone.
General Practice. Civil Trial Practice, Civil Appellate Practice, Insurance Coverage, Environmental, Medical and Professional Malpractice, Products Liability, Structural Work Act, Railroad, Employment, Corporate and Health Care Law, Commercial Litigation, Construction, Workers Compensation, Intellectual Property, Municipalities, Transportation, Patent Law, Intellectual Property.
Chicago, Illinois Office: 20 North Wacker Drive, Suite 1040, 60606-2903. Telephone: 312-641-3100. Fax: 312-444-1669.
Libertyville, Illinois Office: 1870 West Winchester Road, Suite 148, 60048-5353. Telephone: 847-932-6922. Fax: 847-932-6947.
Rockford, Illinois Office: 120 West State Street, Suite 401, 61101-1159. Telephone: 815-962-8301. Fax: 815-962-8401.

See Professional Biographies, NAPERVILLE, ILLINOIS

Cassioppi, Gerald A. '57 '82 C&L.339 B.S., J.D.
Gen. Coun., United Asset Coverage Inc.
Castagnoli, Susan G. '53 '79 C.504 B.A. L.589 J.D. [S.G.Castagnoli] ⊙

Castagnoli, Susan G., P.C., Law Offices of
1119 North Washington Street, 60563 ⊙
Telephone: 630-717-1594; TT4-630-566-5222 Fax: 630-717-1596
Email: susancastagnoli@scastagnolilaw.com URL: http://www.castagnolilaw.com
Susan G. Castagnoli.
Languages: Sign Language.
Bankruptcy, Commercial Bankruptcy, Consumer Bankruptcy, Foreclosures, Debt Management, Family, Divorce, Divorce Planning, Premarital Agreements, Custody, Adoptions, Child Support, Real Estate, Financial Planning, Wills and Probate, Estate Planning, Trusts and Estates, Equine Law.
Kane County Office: 1444 North Farnsworth Avenue, Suite 107, Aurora, Illinois, 60505. Telephone: 630-717-1594. Fax: 630-717-1596.

See Professional Biographies, NAPERVILLE, ILLINOIS

Cavenagh, Thomas D. '62 '87 C.999 B.A. L.209 J.D.
Assoc. Prof. & Dir., Dispute Resolution Ctr., North Central College

Cetina & Jacques, P.C.
(See Oakbrook Terrace)

Chicago Internet Attorneys
(See Chicago)

Cho, Lawrence M. '69 '94
C.188 B.S.E.E. L.494 J.D. Sr. Coun. - Intell. Prop., Tellabs (Pat.)

Christensen & Ehret, LLP
(See Chicago)

Cirignani Heller Harman & Lynch LLP
(See Chicago)

Clarke, Brian J. '59 '85 C&L.339 A.B., J.D. V.P. & Gen. Coun., U.S. Filter Corp.
Cline, Richard L. '42 '68 C.63 A.B. L.1119 J.D. 608 S. Washington St.
Cobine, Craig J., (BV) '48 '72 C.424 B.A. L.597 J.D. [Dommermuth,B.C.&W.]
Collander, Dan M., (BV) '54 '79 C.339 B.S. L.146 J.D. 568 S. Washington St.
Collander, Deborah H. '52 '79 C.86 B.A. L.146 J.D. Naperville Natl. Bk. & Tr. Co.
Collins, Shawn M., (AV) '57 '87 C.602 B.B.A. L.145 J.D. [Collins]
Collins Law Firm, The, P.C., (AV) 1770 N. Park St., Ste. 200
Coman & Anderson, P.C. 1979 N. Mill St., Ste. 211
Comstock, Gabriella '— '96 C&L.424 B.S., J.D. [A Knuckles&Assoc.]
Condron, Thomas John '51 '84 C.750 B.A. L.209 J.D. 1249 Arthur Rd.
Corrigan, Charles J., (AV) '60 '87 C.276 B.A. L.365 J.D. [A Dommermuth,B.C.&W.]
Coulter, Douglas Glen '52 '79 C&L.477 B.G.S., J.D. Tax Atty., BP America Inc.
Courney, Raymond J. '41 '65 C&L.424 LL.B. 336 S. Birchwood Dr.
Coyne, Kevin M. '75 '00 C.352 B.B.A. L.209 J.D. [Rogers&C.]
Crabill, Mary Jane, (BV) '45 '79 C.436 A.B. L.365 J.D. [Crabill&C.]
Crabill, Warren E., (BV) '43 '75 C.436 B.S.B.A. L.365 J.D. [Crabill&C.]
Crabill & Crabill, Ltd., (BV) 123 Water Street
Creel, Susan E., (BV) '50 '87 C&L.339 B.A., J.D. [Fay,F.&Assoc.]

Cremer, Kopon, Shaughnessy & Spina, LLC
(See Chicago)

Csukor, Karl A. '62 '87 C.578 B.A. L.365 J.D. 190 E. 5th Ave.
Daum, Mary A. '72 '98 C.339 B.A. L.770 J.D. Staff Atty., Tellabs
Davidson, Susan M. '42 '80 C.210 B.A. L.589 J.D. 798 E. Gartner Rd.
Dawidiuk, Robert L. '69 '04 C.1183 B.A. L.365 J.D. [A Collins]
Day, Scott M., (BV) '53 '81 C.339 B.F.A. L.424 J.D. [Day&R.]
Day & Robert, P.C., (BV) 300 E. 5th Ave.
Deaton, Mark D. '55 '80 C.8 B.A. L.7 J.D.
Sr. V.P. & Gen. Coun., Illinois Hospital & HealthSystems Assn.
DeBord, Eric J. '58 '84 C.347 B.A. L.345 J.D.
V.P., Gen. Coun. & Gen. Mgr., Bill Jacobs Motorsport, Inc.
DeLair, Sidney C. '51 '92 C.880 B.A. L.46 J.D. 1515 Welton Ct.
DelGeorge, Louis O. '47 '77 C.46 B.S. L.146 J.D. 542 Braemer Ave.‡
Dentz, Edward J. '21 '52 C.105 L.446 LL.B.
(adm. in MD; not adm. in IL) 851 Santa Maria Dr.‡
Desch, Theodore E., (AV) '31 '55 C&L.339 B.A., LL.B. 129 Springwood Dr.
Di Prima, John A. '24 '51 C.209 L.365 LL.B. Travelers Ins. Co.

Dommermuth, Brestal, Cobine and West, Ltd., (AV)
123 Water Street, P.O. Box 565, 60566-0565 ⊙
Telephone: 630-355-5800; 355-6001 Fax: 630-355-5976
Email: PLP@DBCW.com
Albin Dommermuth (1910-1998); Willard F. Brestal; Craig J. Cobine; Kathleen C. West; Robert G. Gibson; Edward J. Welch; Kevin M. Gensler; John F. Philipchuck;—Kevin M. Gallaher; Charles J. Corrigan; Russell G. Whitaker; James R. Sethna; Patti A. Bernhard; Vincent M. Rosanova.
General Civil Practice. Personal Injury, Worker's Compensation, Corporate, Banking, Municipal, Zoning and Development, Real Estate, Family and Probate Law, Litigation, Federal and State Taxation, Commercial Collection.
Aurora, Illinois Office: Old Second National Bank Building, 111 West Downer Place, Suite 300. Telephone: 630-892-5700.

See Professional Biographies, NAPERVILLE, ILLINOIS

Donath, Anita, Law Office of '— '78 C.801 B.A. L.146 J.D.
1300 Iroquois Ave., Suite 100
Dowd, Lynn D., Law Offices of, (AV) '58 '85
C.339 B.A. L.209 J.D. 421 East School Street
Doyle, John M. '28 '59 C.475 B.A. L.146 LL.B. 1151 Black Stallion Ct.

Dreyer, Foote, Streit, Furgason and Slocum, A Professional Association
(See Aurora, Illinois)

Dunning, Aldorah F. '28 '55 C&L.339 LL.B. 25W252 Plank Rd.

Erickson, Randall T., PC, The Law Office of
(See Wheaton)

Esp, Lynn W. '63 '89 C.93 B.A. L.146 J.D. Compl. Coun., Ill. Credit Union League
Fabbri, Daniel '69 '03 C.339 B.S. L.209 J.D. [Collins]
Fagan, Bernard J., Jr, (CV) '49 '78 C.424 B.S. L.209 J.D. 40 E. Jefferson Ave.
Farley, Robert H., Jr. '54 '79 C.424 B.A. L.597 J.D. 1155 S. Washington St.
Farrow, Mark R. '61 '90 C.589 B.A. L.339 J.D. [Fay,F.&Assoc.]

Fawell & Fawell, Ltd.
(See Wheaton)

Fay, John L. '— '79 [Fay,F.&Assoc.]
Fay, Farrow & Associates, P.C., (BV) 1730 Park St., Ste. 109

Feely, Elizabeth M., P.C.
(See Chicago)

Fein, Melvin J. '55 '80 C.339 B.S. L.146 J.D. 1155 S. Washington St.
Fenech, Joseph C. '50 '75 C.475 B.A. L.477 J.D. [Fenech P.W.]
Fenech Pachulski Welgat, P.C. 1656 Imperial Cir.
Fenelon, Terence M., Law Office of, (BV) '54 '80
C.578 B.A. L.589 J.D. 445 West Jackson Avenue, Suite 107
Fennell, Patricia M. '55 '85 C&L.589 B.A., J.D. 1844 Ferry Rd., Ste. 7W
Fewkes, David A., (AV) '35 '67 C.339 B.S. L.209 J.D. [Fewkes W.&S.] ‡

Fewkes Wentz & Strayer, (AV)
A Law Partnership of Professional Corporations
184 Shuman Boulevard Suite 250, 60563
Telephone: 630-527-8552 Fax: 630-527-8636
URL: http://www.businesslegalexperts.com
Members of Firm: David A. Fewkes (Retired); William H. Wentz; Jay B. Strayer.
Business, Corporate, Mergers and Acquisitions, Commercial Real Estate and Antitrust Law.

See Professional Biographies, NAPERVILLE, ILLINOIS

Fish, David J. '74 '99 C.338 B.S. L.589 J.D. 1770 N. Park Ave., Ste. 200
Fleming, William E. '47 '73 C&L.352 B.B.A., J.D.
(adm. in IA; not adm. in IL) Chicago Title Ins. Co.
Foreman, Donald D. '47 '72 C&L.793 B.S., J.D.
(adm. in SD; not adm. in IL) 225 Winding Creek Dr.‡
Fraser, Shannon Alexis Fox '74 '99
C.338 B.S. L.146 J.D. Staff Atty., Edward Hospital & Health Servs.
Fraum, Jeffrey S. '56 '83 C.311 B.A. L.552 J.D.
(adm. in NJ; not adm. in IL) Sr. Coun., Tellabs, Inc.
Freedman, Louis S., (AV) '54 '80 C.910 A.B. L.365 J.D. [Freedman,A.L.&R.]
Freedman, Anselmo, Lindberg & Rappe, (AV) 1807 West Diehl Road
Freeman, Deborah K. '49 '81 C.880 B.A. L.209 J.D. 608 South Washington, Suite 101
Gallaher, Kevin M. '63 '88 C.723 B.A. L.209 J.D. [A Dommermuth,B.C.&W.]
Garner, Bruce E. '65 '91 C.351 B.A. L.589 J.D. [A James,G.&T.]
Gensler, Kevin M., (BV) '57 '85 C.475 B.A. L.365 J.D. [Dommermuth,B.C.&W.]
George, Thomas E. '46 '71 C.228 B.A. L.245 J.D. 1801 N. Mill St., Ste. K
Getty, Kathleen J. '59 '95 C.339 B.S. L.146 J.D. P.O. Box 4806
Gibson, Robert G., (BV) '58 '83 C.602 B.A. L.339 J.D. [Dommermuth,B.C.&W.]
Gierach, Denice A. '— '76 L.146 J.D. 1755 Park St.
Gillen, Robert D., (CV) '54 '79 C.339 B.S. L.146 J.D. [R.D.Gillen] ⊙
Gillen, Robert D., Ltd., Law Offices of, (CV) 22 E. Chicago Avenue (⊙Scottsdale, AZ)
Goren, William D. '60 '85 C.881 A.B. L.1049 J.D. Assoc. Prof.
Gott, Dennis C. '48 '73 C.107 B.A. L.145 J.D.
V.P., Gen. Coun. & Secy., Conagra Foods Refrigerated Foods Co., Inc.
Graham, Edward P. '61 '87 C.602 B.A. L.607 J.D. [E.P.Graham]

Graham, Edward P., Ltd., Law Offices of
1112 South Washington Street, Suite 212, 60540
Telephone: 630-357-2333 Fax: 630-357-2393
Email: counselors@graham-law.com URL: http://www.graham-law.com
Edward P. Graham. Associate: Melissa A. Grahonya.
Adoptions, Bankruptcy, Business Formation and General Counsel, Collections, Criminal Defense, Divorce, Estate Planning, Wills and Trusts, General Litigation, Juvenile, Landlord - Tenant Relations, Municipal Law, Zoning and Land Use, Personal Injury, Workers Compensation, Probate and Guardianship, Real Estate Transactions, Traffic Prosecution and Defense.

See Professional Biographies, NAPERVILLE, ILLINOIS

Grahonya, Melissa A. '77 '02 C&L.339 B.A., J.D. [A E.P.Graham]

Gray & Idris, P.C., Law Offices of
(See Joilet)

Greenberg, E. Barry '49 '79 C.801 B.A. L.589 J.D. 47 E. Chicago Avenue
Grossman, Fredric J., (AV) '32 '56 C&L.597 B.S.L., LL.B. [© Broida&T.]
Grunyk, Danya A. '55 '87 C.477 B.A. L.776 J.D. [Firm of D.A.Grunyk]

Grunyk, Danya A., P.C., The Law Firm of
5th Avenue Station, 200 East Fifth Avenue, Suite 118, 60563
Telephone: 630-428-3300 Fax: 630-428-3313
Email: dgrunyk@aol.com URL: http://www.lawyers.com/grunyklaw
Danya A. Grunyk.
Divorce, Family Law, Litigation, Collaborative Law, Mediation, Child Custody, Child Support, Adoptions, Guardianship, Paternity.

See Professional Biographies, NAPERVILLE, ILLINOIS

Guill, John H., (AV) '49 '74 C.338 B.S. L.146 J.D. 816 Turnbridge
Gustafson, Steven D., (BV) '64 '91 C.338 B.S. L.365 J.D. [James,G.&T.]
Hafer, William L. '51 '83 C.874 B.A. L.339 J.D. 1256 Sandpiper Lane
Hagemann, Michael C. '79 '05 C.352 B.S.E. L.365 J.D. [M.Hagemann]
Hagemann, Michael 804 Corday Dr., Ste. 305
Hamilton, Scott B. '58 '84 C.228 B.A. L.339 J.D.
Regional Counsel, United States Filter Corporation

Hanauer, James W., The Law Office of
(See Wheaton)

Harris, Allyson B. '63 '94 C.209 B.A. L.146 J.D. [A S.B.Levy]
Harris, Susan Lauren '49 '90 C.1267 B.S. L.326 J.D.
(adm. in TX; not adm. in IL) Sr. Real Estate Rep., Shell Oil Co.
Heap, Robert A. '55 '83 C.589 B.S. L.146 J.D. 552 S. Washington St., Ste. 100
Heim, Jack L., (CV) '24 '57 C.578 L.245 J.D. 1827 Wehrli Rd.
Heitz, Russell J., (BV) '63 '89 C.339 B.A. L.365 J.D. [Wyeth,H.&B.]
Heller, Rosemarie A., (CV) '56 '83 C.339 B.A. L.589 J.D. 1625 Ambleside Cir.
Helm, Stephen D., (AV) '43 '68 C.357 B.S. L.339 J.D. 804 N. Washington St.
Hendrix, Ronald L. '51 '85 C.20 B.A. L.146 J.D. 2425 Rivermist Ct.
Hennessy, Donald J. '30 '53 C.424 L.209 J.D. ret. Assoc. Cir. J.
Heying, John R. '38 '75 C.743 M.A. L.424 J.D. 608 S. Washington
Heyl, Richard F. '25 '52 C&L.602 Ph.B., LL.B. 2147 Lancaster Circle‡
Hickey, Brian J., (BV) '63 '88 C.339 B.S. L.209 J.D. [Cassiday,S.&G.]
Higgins, Patricia M., (BV) '52 '77 C&L.602 B.A., J.D. [Nagle&H.]
Hinds, Melanie Markovic '59 '84 C.339 B.A. L.365 J.D.
Leg. Analyst, Natl. Fraternal Congress of America

Hirsh, Richard L., & Associates, P.C.
(See Hinsdale)

Hittle, Kathleen J. '49 '74 C.339 B.A. L.145 J.D. 15 W. Jefferson

Holloway, Sheryl Y.
(See Chicago)

Hoppa, Timothy J. ....'78 '03 C.121 B.S. L.589 J.D. [Ⓐ Brooks,A.&T.]
Hudetz, Joseph B. ....'47 '78 C.589 B.S. L.146 J.D. Solar Press, Inc.
Isaza, Catherine A. '60 '86 C.879 B.A. L.1119 J.D.
(adm. in KY; not adm. in IL) 3415 Scottsdale Circle
Ismond, R. L. ....'14 '38 C.999 A.A. L.146 LL.B. 411 Orleans Ave.
Jablonsky, Tracie A. ....'67 '02 C.999 B.A. L.365 J.D. 111 E. Jefferson Ave.
James, John D., (BV) ....'41 '66 C.879 B.A. L.146 J.D. [James,G.&T.]
James, Gustafson & Thompson, Ltd., (BV) .... 1001 East Chicago Avenue, Suite 103
Johnson, Douglas H. ....'64 '91 C.477 B.S. L.424 J.D. [Ⓐ K.T.Zellner&Assoc.]
Johnston, Timothy W. ....'56 '90 C.792 B.S. L.145 J.D. 923 Emerald Dr.
Joshi, Saily ....'67 '93 C.597 B.A. L.665 J.D. 1647 Prestwick Dr.
Kamerman, Richard A. ....'47 '76 C.339 B.A. L.365 J.D. Ill. Credit Union
Karalius, Audrone M. '52 '81 L.424 J.D.
Vice President, EH & S, Nalco Chemical Company‡
Karas, Nicole L. ....'70 '04 C.879 B.A. L.209 J.D. [Ⓐ Brooks,A.&T.]
Kas, Ronald M. ....'53 '78 C.234 B.A. L.846 J.D. [K.M.Lynch&Assoc.]
Kavvadias, Manos M., (BV) ....'58 '84 C.339 B.A. L.146 J.D. [Ryan&K.]
Kelly, Kathryn L., (BV) ....'29 '54 C&L.339 B.S., J.D. 505 Bernie Ct.
Kelly, Robert D. ....'27 '53 C.57 A.B. L.339 J.D. 505 Bernie Ct.‡
Kennedy, Charles W.L. ....'68 '95 C.94 B.A. L.802 J.D. Tellabs
Kenniff, T. Charles ....'38 '66 C.973 B.S. L.150 J.D. 1504 Maple Hills Ct.‡
Keough, Charles M. ....'67 '96 C.339 B.A. L.146 J.D. [Ⓐ Knuckles&Assoc.]
Klein, Daniel L. ....'57 '82 C.339 A.B. L.436 J.D. 931 Watercress
Klein, Richard D., & Associates, (BV) '50 '85
C.1350 B.A. L.146 J.D. 500 E. Ogden Avenue, Suite 200
Kmiotek, Thomas A. ....'54 '79 C&L.339 B.S.M.E., J.D. 30W152 Bruce Lane (Pat.)

Knell & Poulos, A Professional Corporation
(See Chicago)

Knobloch, John F., Law Offices of, (BV) '55 '84
C.750 B.A. L.424 J.D. 608 W. Washington St., Ste. 101
Knoll, Jeffrey G. ....'61 '92 C.339 B.S. L.146 J.D. Packer Engineering, Inc. (Pat.)
Knuckles, Jeffry J., (BV) ....'46 '73 C&L.339 B.A., J.D. [Knuckles&Assoc.]
Knuckles & Associates, (BV) .... 48 East Jefferson Street
Koback, Robert ....'55 '98 C.912 B.S. L.365 J.D. [Ⓐ R.G.Winick&Assoc.]
Kocsis, Brian Michael, (BV) ....'51 '80 C.338 B.S. L.365 J.D. 222 S. Mill St., Ste. 200
Kodiak, K. Thomas ....'50 '79 C.373 B.A. L.209 J.D. Sr. Atty., Nalco Co.
Kokoris, Nicholas P. ...'60 '86 C.339 B.S. L.146 J.D. Corp. Coun., Juristech Assoc. Ltd.
Koranda, Kenneth R. '49 '75
C.813 B.A. L.597 J.D. V.P., Mid-America Fed. Svgs. & Loan Assn.
Krula, David W., (BV) ....'58 '83 C.937 B.A. L.365 J.D. 804 N. Washington St.
Kuhn, Daniel L., (BV) ....'43 '68 C.750 B.A. L.597 J.D. [Kuhn,M.M.&L.]
Kuhn, Richard W., (BV) .... '53 '78 C.98 B.A. L.146 J.D. 552 S. Wash.
Kuhn, Mitchell, Moss & Lechowicz, P.C., (BV) .... 111 E. Jefferson Ave.
Landsman, Stephen N. '59 '84
C&L.339 A.B., J.D. V.P., Gen. Coun. & Corp. Sect., Nalco Co.
Lane, Kathleen S., Law Offices of '67 '94
C.424 B.B.A. L.209 J.D. 608 S. Washington Street
Larmon, Michael H. ....'43 '71 C.973 A.B. L.209 J.D. 1426 Druid Hills Court
Larson, Ellen Roucek ....'50 '75 C.475 B.A. L.352 J.D. 568 S. Washington St.
Larson, Mark E., Jr., (AV) ....'47 '73 C.339 B.S. L.597 J.D. [Larson,P.&W.]
Larson, Perry & Ward P.C., (AV) ....1212 S. Naper Blvd., Ste. 119-131
Latham, William C. ....'49 '76 C.46 B.S. L.146 J.D. Sr. Atty., Nalco Co.
Laz, Thomas J. ....'50 '75 C.750 B.A. L.209 J.D. 600 South Washington Street
Lechowicz, Alan E., (BV) ....'57 '85 C.339 B.S. L.365 J.D. [Kuhn,M.M.&L.]
Lee, Paula K. ....'61 '94 C.424 B.A. L.146 J.D. 846 Buttonwood Circle
Lemmenes, Michael L. '49 '79 C.694 L.966 J.D.
(adm. in WI; not adm. in IL) V.P., Firstar Bk. Illinois
Leonard, Allen J. ....'24 '50 C&L.209 LL.B. 1858 Princeton Cir.
Levin, Emily R. '53 '90 C.184 B.A. L.1029 J.D.
(adm. in CT; not adm. in IL) [Ⓐ R.D.Klein&Assoc.]
Levine, Howard P. ....'61 '88 C.339 B.A. L.209 J.D City of Naperville
Levy, Steven B., (AV) ....'54 '79 C.339 B.A. L.146 J.D. [S.B.Levy]

Levy, Steven B., Ltd., (AV)
650 East Diehl Road Suite 121, 60563
Telephone: 630-416-6300 Telefax: 630-245-0930 URL: http://www.lawyers.com/stevenblevy
Email: slevy@sblevyltdlaw.com URL: http://www.sblevyltdlaw.com
Steven B. Levy;—Allyson B. Harris.
Languages: Spanish.
Plaintiff's Personal Injury, Wrongful Death, Medical Malpractice, Automobile Accidents, Truck Accidents, Products Liability and Premises Liability Law.
See Professional Biographies, NAPERVILLE, ILLINOIS

Liebenson, Paul M. '51 '80 C.860 B.A. L.276 J.D.
Asst. Gen. Coun.-Transactions, Tellabs
Liimatainen, Robert Tor '71 '98 C.893 B.A. L.188 J.D.
(adm. in NY; not adm. in IL) Atty., Nalco Co.
Lindberg, Steven C. ....'55 '80 C.339 B.A. L.365 J.D. [Freedman,A.L.&R.]
Lipinsky, John ....'63 '91 C&L.339 B.S., J.D. 1979 N. Mill Street
Lohff, William ....'29 '61 C.494 B.Ch.E. L.209 J.D. 7 S. 450 Green Acres Dr.‡
Lord, Patricia Johnson ... '55 '81 C.340 B.A. L.1049 J.D. City of Naperville, Legal. Dept.
Lynch, Kevin M. ....'64 '90 C.339 B.S. L.209 J.D. [K.M.Lynch&Assoc.]
Lynch, Kevin M., & Associates, P.C. ....1300 Iroquois Avenue Suite 220A
Lyons, Cynthia R., Law Office of ....'46 '80 C.696 A.B. L.146 J.D. 1216 Brighton Rd.
Malm, John J. ....'66 '93 C.57 B.A. L.879 J.D. [J.J.Malm]
Malm, John J., P.C. ....1730 Park Street, Suite 210
Manjarres, David ....'62 '97 C.589 B.S. L.209 J.D. Nalco Co.
Mantell, Ross B. ....'75 '01 C.340 B.A. L.146 J.D. [Ⓐ James,G.&T.]
Manzke, Edward J. ....'67 '92 C&L.339 B.A., J.D. [Ⓐ Collins]
Martin, Michael B. ....'58 '92 C.966 B.S. L.209 J.D. Sr. Pat. Atty., Nalco Co.
Mathys, Mark W. ....'— '93 C.746 B.B.A. L.209 J.D. [M.W.Mathys&Assoc.]
Mathys, Mark W., & Associates, PC. .... 1730 Park Street, Suite 224
Matthews, K. Kyle ....'62 '88 C&L.101 B.A., J.D. Asst. Gen. Coun., Tellabs, Inc.
McCafferty, Robert Kevin ....'59 '93 521 E. Tanglewood Ln.

McCarthy, David H., III '49 '79 C.602 B.A. L.365 J.D.
1155 South Washington Street, Suite 102, 60540
Telephone: 630-357-4520 Fax: 630-355-5949
Email: dhm1649@aol.com URL: http://www.lawyers.com/dhmlaw
Personal Injury, Divorce and Family Law, Corporate and Employment Law, Elder Law and Probate, Real Estate.
See Professional Biographies, NAPERVILLE, ILLINOIS

McClellan, Sally L. '62 '87 C.339 B.S. L.910 J.D.
1555 Naperville/Wheaton Rd., Ste. 207

McJoynt & Kristufek, P.C.
(See Downers Grove)

McNamara, Daniel G. ....'— '92 C.338 B.S. L.365 J.D. Assoc. Gen. Coun., Nicor Gas Co.
Meyer, Karl V., (CV) ....'66 '94 C.98 B.S. L.339 J.D. [Ⓐ Freedman,A.L.&R.]
Mickelson, Steven R. ....'51 '77 C.119 B.S.E.E. L.146 J.D. 816 Pawnee Lane
Midkiff, Dawn ....'— '84 C&L.424 A.B., J.D. 215 Shuman Blvd.
Miller, Christopher J. ....'60 '86 C.597 B.S. L.424 J.D. 931 W. 75th Street, Suite 137
Miller, Mary Ann Jacoby ....'53 '80 C.976 B.A. L.472 J.D. 8 S. 492 Bell Dr.
Mincieli, Jonathan P. ....'71 '97 C.1458 B.A. L.724 J.D. [Ⓐ Cassiday,S.&G.]
Misiorowski, Mark R., (BV) ....'58 '85 C.72 B.A. L.209 J.D. 1755 Park St., Ste. 310
Mitchell, Janine Helen '64 '89 C&L.339 B.A., J.D.
IL Provider Trust, Risk Mgmt, Servs.
Mitchell, Paul M., (BV) ....'47 '73 C.210 B.A. L.209 J.D. [Kuhn,M.M.&L.]
Mohr, William W., (BV) ....'53 '80 C.966 B.S. L.365 J.D. 1300 Iroquois Dr.

Moline, Denise B. '48 '83 C.999 B.A. L.259 J.D.
1212 South Naper Boulevard, Suite 119-215, 60540
Telephone: 630-753-0112 Facsimile: 630-753-0137
Email: dbmoline@wowway.com
(Not admitted in IL).
Telecommunications Law, Mass Media, Wireless, Satellite.
See Professional Biographies, NAPERVILLE, ILLINOIS

Moore, Gary M., (BV) '52 '78 C&L.339 B.A., J.D.
535 South Washington Street, 60540-6662
Telephone: 630-357-6966 Fax: 630-357-1210; 630-839-3007
Email: garymoore@naperlaw.com URL: http://www.naperlaw.com
Real Estate, Trusts and Estates, Estate Planning, Bankruptcy, Taxation, Wills and Probate, Small Business, Corporate.
See Professional Biographies, NAPERVILLE, ILLINOIS

Moreno, Christopher P. '66 '99 C.453 B.S.E.E. L.365 J.D.
Sr. Patent Atty., Optobionioics Corporation (Pat.)
Moss, Jonathan Y., (BV) ....'49 '75 C.339 B.S. L.424 J.D. [Kuhn,M.M.&L.]
Mueller, Christine Charysh ....'58 '83 C&L.339 B.S., J.D. 2412 Modaff Rd.
Muer, Sandra E. ....'64 '93 C.339 B.A. L.966 J.D. Sr. Atty., Tellabs
Murphy, Michael P. ....'62 '94 C.338 B.S. L.209 J.D. Atty., Nalco Co.

Murzyn, Brenda L., Law Office of '54 '83 C.347 B.S. L.589 J.D.
1300 Iroquois Avenue, Suite 125, 60563 ⊙
Telephone: 630-961-1058 Fax: 630-961-1333
Email: brendamurzynlaw@ameritech.net URL: http://www.lawyers.com/murzyn
Associate: Edward F. Stetter.
Real Estate Closings, For Sale By Owner Investment Property, Foreclosure, Probate, Wills, Residential Real Estate, Commercial Real Estate, Real Estate Investment, Land Trusts, Land Sales, Real Estate Acquisitions, Real Estate Contracts.
Chicago Office: 1255 North State Parkway, 60610. Telephone: 312-330-3458. Fax: 312-266-5967.
See Professional Biographies, NAPERVILLE, ILLINOIS

Myers, John A., Jr., (Ltd.) ....'42 '71 C.347 B.S. L.363 J.D. 85360 College Rd.
Nadelhoffer, Carleton, (AV) ....'27 '56 C.118 B.A. L.145 J.D. [Ⓒ Kuhn,M.M.&L.] ‡
Naftzger, Jay R. ....'55 '82 C&L.352 B.B.A., J.D. 936 Sanctuary Lane
Nagle, Brian J., (BV) ....'49 '76 C&L.602 B.B.A., J.D. [Nagle&H.]
Nagle & Higgins, P.C., (BV) ....222 S. Mill Street

Nathe, Philip R., The Law Office of, (BV) '59 '88 C.927 B.A. L.365 J.D.
552 S. Washington, Suite 104, 60540
Telephone: 630-416-7600 Fax: 630-357-1922
Email: prnathe@aol.com URL: http://www.law-shack.com
Criminal Defense, Criminal Law, DUI, Traffic Violations, Juvenile Law, Civil Litigation.
See Professional Biographies, NAPERVILLE, ILLINOIS

Nawrocki-Verburgt, Marcia J. '66 '92
C.209 B.S. L.1187 J.D. Attorney, Nicor Gas Company
Newberry, James S. '21 '49 C.225 A.B. L.502 LL.B.
(adm. in MO; not adm. in IL) 1365 Stonegate Rd.‡
Newton, J. Michael ....'43 '73 C.932 B.B.A. L.209 J.D. Ondeo Nalco Center‡
Nichele, Joseph K. ....'80 '05 C.679 B.S. L.879 J.D. [Ⓐ Broida&T.]
Noble, Dennis J. ....'61 '89 C.589 B.S. L.365 J.D. 1979 N. Mill St., Ste. 211
Nodzenski, Thaddeus J. '56 '82 C.145 A.B. L.46 J.D.
Assoc. Gen. Coun., Illinois Hospital & HealthSystems Assn.
Nyberg, Ronald A. ....'53 '78 C.57 B.A. L.46 J.D. Ste 116, 200 E 5th Ave
O'Brien, Anne M., Attorney at Law '67 '91
C.339 B.S. L.1170 J.D. 1163 E. Ogden Ave., Suite 705-192 (Pat.)
Oddo, Thomas G. ....'65 '90 C.339 B.A. L.209 J.D. 222 S. Mill St.
O'Donnell, John M. '58 '83 C.145 B.A. L.659 J.D.
Associate General Counsel & Assistant Secretary, Interlake Corporate
Oei, Lorijean G. ....'64 '89 C.108 B.A. L.884 J.D. Sr. Mng. Atty., Tellabs
Ohlmann, Brent E., (BV) ....'64 '90 C.347 B.A. L.589 J.D. [B.E.Ohlmann]

Ohlmann, Brent E., P.C., Law Office of, (BV)
1730 Park Street, Suite 210, 60563
Telephone: 630-355-8008 Fax: 630-355-8068
Email: beo@beohlmann.com URL: http://www.beohlmann.com
Brent E. Ohlmann.
Trademarks, Copyrights, Business Transactions, S-Corporation and LLC Issues, Entertainment Contracts, Software Licensing, Confidentiality Agreements, Strategic Alliances, Business Succession Planning, Internet Law.
See Professional Biographies, NAPERVILLE, ILLINOIS

Olek, Donald H., Attorney at Law ... '52 '77 C.602 B.A. L.893 J.D. 639 S. Washington St.
Olson, Stephen R. '50 '77 C.747 B.A. L.352 J.D.
Exec. V.P., Gen. Coun. & CEO, Ill. Credit Union League
Pachulski, James G. ....'58 '83 C&L.477 B.A., J.D. [Fenech P.W.]
Page, William J. ....'39 '76 C.347 B.S. L.365 J.D. [W.J.Page]
Page, William J., P.C. .... 1801 N. Mill Street, Suite L
Palasz, Robert A. ....'62 '91 C.209 B.S.C. L.148 J.D. 1452 Baldwin Ct.
Peel, Joe W. '28 '55 C.377 A.B. L.900 LL.B.
Coun., Natl. Fraternal Congress of America‡

Perrelli, Anthony
(See Deerfield)

Peters, Kevin R.
(See Chicago)

Peyton, James P. ....'39 '65 C&L.966 B.S., J.D. Sr. Atty., Intl., Nalco Chem. Co.

Phalen, Stephen S., LLC, Law Offices of
(See Chicago)

Phelan, Donald M. ....'49 '80 C.589 B.S. L.209 J.D. 1155 S. Washington St., Ste. 105
Philipchuck, John F., (BV) ... '46 '78 C.963 B.S. L.365 J.D. [Dommermuth,B.C.&W.] ⊙
Pieroni, Charles M. ....'10 '36 C.63 L.602 LL.B. 1440 Crystal Ct.‡
Plauda, Daniel D. .... '46 '71 C&L.494 B.A., J.D. Pres. & CEO, Ill. Credit Union Sys.

Poeppel, Sarah L., (BV) ....'46 '79 C.188 B.S. L.589 J.D. 608 S. Washington St., Ste. 210
Prato & Associates, P.C.
(See Oak Brook)
Presperin, Thomas S. ....'60 '86 C.339 B.S. L.209 J.D. 15 N. Julian St.
Primozic, Eileen K. ....'58 '84 C.1074 B.S. L.424 J.D. 940 Pimpernel Ct.‡
Rabovsky, Barry R., The Law Office of '53 '83
C.339 B.A. L.209 J.D. 1355 S. Rte. 59, Ste. 1-A
Rapier, Aaron W. ....'73 '99 C.707 B.A. L.146 J.D. 1770 Park St., Ste. 200
Rappe, Robert H. ....'63 '89 C&L.209 B.A., J.D. [Freedman,A.L.&R.]
Rebeck, Gerald A. ....'— '82 C.63 B.S. 630 N. Washington
Rechenmacher, LeRoy L. ....'12 '42 C.351 L.1002 LL.B. 1103 N. Mill St.‡
Reed, Patricia Ann ....'57 '86 C.999 B.S. L.744 J.D. 821 Cardiff Rd.
Rekar, Pamela ....'53 '79 C&L.146 B.S., J.D. 2720 Wild Timothy Road
Reyes, Jay ....'74 '04 C.339 B.A. L.365 J.D. [Ⓐ Day&R.]
Ries, Tracy A. ....'— '04 [Fay,F.&Assoc.]
Robbins, Kenneth C. .... '42 '73 C.454 B.A. L.818 J.D. Pres., Illinois Hospital Association
Robert, Rachel Katherine ....'66 '92 C.879 B.A. L.208 J.D. [Day&R.]
Rogers, Susan R. ....'61 '91 C.937 B.A. L.589 J.D. [Rogers&C.]

Rogers & Coyne, LLC, Law Offices of
1700 Park Street, Suite 102, 60563-2902
Telephone: 630-579-0635 Fax: 630-579-0638
Email: susanrrogers616B@aol.com URL: http://www.lawyers.com/rogerslawfirm
Susan R. Rogers; Kevin M. Coyne.
Estate Planning, Trust and Estate Administration, Residential and Commercial Real Estate.
See Professional Biographies, NAPERVILLE, ILLINOIS

Rosanova, Vincent M. .... '77 '05 C.1151 B.A. L.589 J.D. [Ⓐ Dommermuth,B.C.&W.]
Roscich, Carolyn S., (CV) .... '44 '80 C.234 B.S. L.589 J.D. [Roscich&R.]
Roscich, John V., (BV) ....'43 '72 C.234 B.S. L.365 J.D. [Roscich&R.]
Roscich & Roscich, (BV) .... 214 1/2 S. Washington St.
Roth, Frederick E. ....'53 '79 C.339 B.S. L.365 J.D. [Roth]
Roth, John C., (BV) ....'64 '89 C.339 B.A. L.365 J.D. 2317 Keim Road
Roth Law Firm, LLC .... 47 East Chicago Avenue Suite 360
Roy, Sharmila, (CVⓉ) ....'46 '85 C.999 B.S. L.37 J.D. 3760 Celeste Lane
Rudofski, Kenneth J. '66 '91 C&L.477 B.S.E.E., J.D.
Asst. Gen. Coun. - Intell. Prop., Tellabs (Pat.)
Ruth, Timothy M. ....'64 '91 C.884 B.A. L.61 J.D. 123 Water St.
Ryan, James M. .... '70 '95 C.338 B.A. L.589 J.D. [Ryan&K.]
Ryan & Kavvadias, (BV) .... 1555 Bond Street, Suite 103
Sahakian, Curtis E. .... '51 '80 C.966 L.365 J.D. General Counsel, Rims
Sansone, Mark A. ....'75 '00 C.1024 B.S. L.879 J.D. [Ⓐ Cassiday,S.&G.]
Schaffer, David N., (AV) ....'58 '84 C.339 B.A. L.1119 J.D. [Ⓑ Brooks,A.&T.]
Sebesta, Glenn W. ....'— '91 C.340 B.A. L.339 J.D. [G.W.Sebesta]

Sebesta, Glenn W., P.C., Law Offices of
2503 Bar Harbor Court, 60564
Telephone: 630-922-5400 Fax: 630-922-5408
Email: sebestalawoffices@sbcglobal.net URL: http://www.sebestalawoffices.com
Glenn W. Sebesta.
Healthcare Provider Professional Rights, Healthcare Provider Defense in Licensing/Privileging Actions.
See Professional Biographies, NAPERVILLE, ILLINOIS

Seeley, Therese S., (BV) ....'55 '82 C.602 B.B.A. L.209 J.D. [Cassiday,S.&G.]
Sethna, James R. .... '74 '01 C.209 B.A. L.365 J.D. [Ⓐ Dommermuth,B.C.&W.]
Setzen, Joel A. ....'41 '81 C.112 B.A. L.365 J.D. 915 S. Charles St.
Shamburek, Peter A. ....'53 '78 C.966 L.1000 1801 N Mill St. Ste. J
Shamp, Larry D. '41 '78 C.267 B.A. L.1065 J.D.
(adm. in IN; not adm. in IL) Shell Pipeline Corp.
Shaw, M. Allan ....'40 '65 C.172 B.A. L.208 J.D. Pres., Aztec Corp.‡
Shaw Gussis Fishman Glantz Wolfson & Towbin LLC
(See Chicago)
Sheehan, James M. ....'63 '88 C&L.339 B.S., J.D. E.V.P., Gen Coun. & Sec., Tellabs
Sill, Bryan W. ....'65 '90 C.424 B.A. L.602 J.D. Sr. Atty., Nalco Co.
Sims, Bryan M. ....'— '96 C.1115 B.A. L.424 J.D. [Ⓐ James,G.&T.]
Smith, Kelli M. ....'61 '86 C.340 B.A. L.221 J.D. [Ⓐ Day&R.]
Spitzzeri, Alfred A., (BV) .... '54 '86 C.209 B.A. L.424 J.D. 1801 N. Mill St., Ste. J
Sprude, Frank L. ....'69 '99 C.339 B.A. L.813 J.D. 200 E. 5th Ave. Stn., Ste. 117A
Stangel, Maria E. .... '63 '88 C.914 B.A. L.424 J.D. 430 Redstart Rd.
Stephanides, Paul L. ....'65 '90 C&L.209 B.A., J.D. City of Naperville Legal Dept.
Stetter, Edward F. ....'79 '04 C.602 B.B.A. L.146 J.D. [Ⓐ B.L.Murzyn]
Stevenson, Julie Vick .... '57 '84 C&L.101 B.A., J.D. 2776 Willow Ridge Dr.‡
Stock, Carlson, Flynn & Associates
(See Wheaton)
Stowell, Frederick C. '43 '79 C.688 B.M.E. L.464 J.D.
Gen. Coun., MRC Polymers, Inc.
Strassman, Sandra E. ....'64 '90 C.260 B.A. L.145 J.D. [Ⓐ Collins]
Strayer, Jay B. ....'42 '70 C&L.378 B.A., J.D. [Fewkes W.&S.]
Streck, Kathie Y. .... '67 '95 C.339 B.S. L.424 J.D. Tax Atty., BP America, Inc.
Strohm, Douglas S. ....'64 '91 C&L.352 B.S., J.D. [Cassiday,S.&G.]
Strom, Robert M. ....'68 '98 C.999 B.A. L.910 J.D. 2767 Springdale Circle
Suich, Thomas J., The Law Offices of '— '00
C.589 B.S. L.339 J.D. 3088 Kentshire Circle
Sullivan, John P., Law Office of '50 '97
C.424 B.S. L.589 J.D. 40 Shuman Boulevard, Suite 160
Sunleaf, Robert S. .... '57 '82 C.339 B.A. L.209 J.D. Lawyers Title Ins. Corp.
Suzzi, Carolyn A. ....'46 '84 C.339 B.A. L.365 J.D. 1378 Green Trails Dr.
Sweders, Peter A. P., Sr. ....'48 '76 C.339 B.A. L.146 J.D. P.O. Box 5346
Swisher, Samuel D. '47 '75 C.477 B.B.A. L.912 J.D.
(adm. in MI; not adm. in IL) Director of Taxes, BP America Inc.
Tarantino, John M. '66 '99 C.473 B.A. L.851 J.D.
(adm. in MD; not adm. in IL) Hiring Atty., JurisClerks
Tarulis, Richard J., (BV) ....'58 '87 C.801 B.S. L.589 J.D. [Brooks,A.&T.]
Taylor, Danielle N. ....'76 '02 C.578 B.A. L.589 J.D. 124 S. Webster, Ste. 202
Theis, Roger A. '34 '58 C&L.966 B.B.A., LL.B.
(adm. in WI; not adm. in IL) 1104 Summit Hills Ave.‡
Thometz, Richard J. ....'75 '03 C.238 B.A. L.1000 J.D. Nicor Gas Company
Tibble, Douglas C., (AV) .... '52 '77 C.209 B.A. L.823 J.D. [Ⓐ Brooks,A.&T.]
Trendell, William P. '55 '82 C.999 B.A. L.209 J.D.
Tax Dir., NFC International Holdings (U.S.A.) Inc.
Tullis, Jeffrey A. ....'71 '97 C.424 B.A. L.365 J.D. [Broida&T.]
Uffelman, William R. '47 '76 C.205 B.A. L.596 J.D.
(adm. in IN; not adm. in IL) Managing Attorney, ASSIGNED COUNSEL Incorporated
Vaught, Kathleen, P.C.
(See Wheaton)
Verhage, George E. ....'23 '49 C.378 B.S. L.477 J.D. 221 E. 14th Ave. (Pat.)‡
Vlazny, Adalbert L., III, (BV) .... '44 '69 C&L.339 B.S., J.D. 608 Wash. St.
Wallenstein Wagner & Rockey, Ltd.
(See Chicago)
Walton, Ernest J. .... '57 '87 C.999 B.A. L.209 J.D. [Walton]

Walton Law Offices, LLC
608 S. Washington Street Suite 207, 60540
Telephone: 888-432-7792 Fax: 630-893-3586
Ernest J. Walton.
Divorce Law.
See Professional Biographies, NAPERVILLE, ILLINOIS

Ward, C. David, (CV) ....'47 '75 C.861 B.A. L.365 J.D. [Larson,P.&W.]
Warren, Charles L. '48 '78 C.838 B.S. L.365 J.D.
Corp. Coun., Lucent Technologies, Inc. (Pat.)
Watland, Ross T. ....'48 '80 C.579 B.S.E.E. L.585 J.D. A.T.&T. Bell Labs.
Watts, Mary S., (BV) ....'53 '88 L.209 J.D. 1001 E. Chicago Ave., Ste. 103
Wehrli, Win ....'54 '85 C.339 B.A. L.464 J.D. 104 S. Parkway Dr.
Welch, Edward J., (BV) ....'47 '72 C&L.602 A.B., J.D. [Dommermuth,B.C.&W.]
Welgat, Robin R. ....'75 '00 C.424 B.A. L.209 J.D. [Fenech P.W.]
Wentz, David G., (BV) ....'63 '89 C.57 B.A. L.339 J.D. [Brooks,A.&T.]
Wentz, William H., (AV) ....'45 '70 C.103 A.B. L.659 J.D. [Fewkes W.&S.]
West, Kathleen C., (BV) ......'51 '81 C.339 B.U.P. L.424 J.D. [Dommermuth,B.C.&W.]
Whitaker, Russell G. ....'78 '04 C.578 B.A. L.209 J.D. [Ⓐ Dommermuth,B.C.&W.]
Wieser, John Raymond ....'63 '92 C.578 B.A. L.146 J.D. [Ⓐ Brooks,A.&T.]
Wilhelm, Timothy S. ....'70 '96 C.966 B.B.A. L.146 J.D. [Ⓐ Day&R.]
Williams, James S., (BV) ....'47 '75 C.347 B.S. L.209 J.D. 608 S. Washington St.
Winick, Russel G. ....'55 '83 C.293 B.A. L.629 J.D. [R.G.Winick&Assoc.]

Winick, Russel G., & Associates, P.C.
1220 Iroquois Avenue, Suite 100, 60563
Telephone: 630-548-5800 Fax: 630-548-5568
Email: russwinlaw@sbcglobal.net URL: http://www.winicklaw.com
Russel G. Winick;—Robert Koback.
Business Law, Business Development, Business Formation, Business Litigation, Business Organization, Business Planning, Business Start-Ups, Business Transactions, Business Transfers, Buy-Sell Agreements, Buying and Selling of Businesses, Closely Held Business Law, Complex Business Litigation, Emerging Business Law, Entrepreneurial Business Law, Joint Ventures, Limited Liability Company Law, Small Business Law.
See Professional Biographies, NAPERVILLE, ILLINOIS

Witt, Thomas A. ....'50 '77 C.103 B.A. L.145 J.D. United States Filter Corp.
Wittenberg, Jody L. '52 '81 C.156 B.A. L.365 J.D.
Assoc. Gen. Coun., Illinois Hospital Association
Wood, Joseph P. ....'53 '91 C.339 M.D. L.145 J.D. Edward Hospital
Woodcock, Gerald Edward ....'33 '95 C.339 B.S. L.589 J.D. [Woodcock,G.E.]
Woodcock, Gerald E. ....11 South, 680 Lillian Court
Woodruff, Casey, & Associates
(See Chicago)
Wunderlich, Sandra Rybak .... '57 '82 C.234 B.A. L.146 J.D. 2430 Wendover Dr.
Wyeth, John Justin, (BV) ....'59 '84 C.339 B.S. L.365 J.D. [Wyeth,H.&B.]
Wyeth, Heitz & Bromberek, (BV) .... 300 East 5th Avenue, Suite 380
Yorke, Randall J. ....'47 '74 C.750 B.A. L.209 J.D. 1155 S. Washington St.
Zahay, Debra L. ....'55 '83 C.910 A.B. L.424 J.D. Pres., Zahay, Inc.
Zellner, Kathleen T., (AV) ....'56 '83 C.041 B.A. L.589 J.D. [K.T.Zellner&Assoc.]

Zellner, Kathleen T., & Associates, (AV) BR
1717 North Naper Boulevard Suite 203, 60563
Telephone: 630-955-1212 Facsimile: 630-955-1111 URL: http://www.kathleent.zellner.com
Email: k21234@aol.com URL: http://www.lawyers.com/zellnerlaw
Kathleen T. Zellner;—Douglas H. Johnson.
Medical Malpractice, Civil Rights, Premises Liability, Trials and Appeals in State and Federal Courts.
See Professional Biographies, NAPERVILLE, ILLINOIS

NASHVILLE, * 3,202, *Washington Co.*

Barkau, Brad, (BV) ....'51 '76 C.927 B.S. L.801 J.D. 124 E. St. Louis St.
Brown & Associates
(See Belleville)
Cross, Robert L., (BV) ....'29 '56 C.339 B.S. L.209 J.D. 124 E. St. Louis St.
DeMoss, Clarence W., (AV) ....'32 '57 C&L.339 B.S., J.D. [Hohlt,H.D.&E.]
DeMoss, William C., (BV) ....'58 '84 C.234 B.A. L.801 J.D. [Hohlt,H.D.&E.]
Endres, Frederick M. ....'40 '71 C.879 B.A. L.734 J.D. [F.Endres]
Endres, Frederick ....181 E. St. Louis St.
Epplin, Aaron M. ....'70 '95 C.234 B.Acct. L.801 J.D. [Hohlt,H.D.&E.]
Green, P. E. ....'12 '39 C.782 Ph.B. L.146 LL.B. 124 E. St. Louis St.‡
Hohlt, House, DeMoss & Epplin, (AV) .... Holston Bldg.
House, James Byron, (AV) ....'27 '55 C&L.339 B.S., J.D. [Ⓑ Hohlt,H.D.&E.] ‡
Jones, Kimberly Kuhlengel .... '70 '95 C&L.801 B.S., J.D. 238 E. Adams St.
Karmeier, Lloyd A. ....'40 '64 C&L.339 B.S., J.D. Cir. J.
Kozuszek, Julie Ann .... '70 '98 C&L.338 B.A., J.D. [Kozuszek,J.A.]
Kozuszek, Julie A. ....251 E. St. Louis
Maxwell, Francis E. ....'23 '49 C&L.339 LL.B. Ret. Cir. J.
Unverfehrt, Gary ....'56 '90 C.339 B.S. L.801 J.D. 239 E. St. Louis St.

NAUVOO, 1,108, *Hancock Co.*

Fehseke & Eschman Law Offices
(See Fort Madison, Iowa)
Literski, Nicholas S. ....'66 '99 C.877 B.S. L.589 J.D. 530 S. Gordon

NEOGA, 1,854, *Cumberland Co.*

Braden, Glenn A., (BV) ....'44 '73 C.801 B.A. L.325 J.D. 189 E. 6th St.

NEWARK, 840, *Kendall Co.*

Hughes, David R. ....'58 '88 C.879 B.S. L.339 J.D. 16045 Hughes Rd.‡

NEW BERLIN, 1,030, *Sangamon Co.*

Sheehan, Patrick J., (AV) ....'51 '77 C&L.734 B.A., J.D. [Sheehan&S.] ⊙
Sheehan, William J., (AV) ....'53 '78 C&L.734 B.A., J.D. [Sheehan&S.] ⊙
Sheehan and Sheehan, Lawyers, P.C., (AV) .... Illinois St. (⊙Springfield)

NEW LENOX, 17,771, *Will Co.*

Bruggeman, Alan R., (BV) .... '44 '74 C.871 B.S. L.861 J.D. [Bruggeman,H.&Assoc.]
Bruggeman, Hurst & Associates, Ltd., (BV) ...... 400 E. Lincoln Hwy. (⊙Chicago, Joliet)
Cladis, Mark D., (CV) ....'56 '84 C&L.879 B.A., J.D. [Ⓐ D.W.Schlak&Assoc.]
Cunico, Gerald J., (BV) ....'42 '67 C&L.339 A.B., J.D. 105 Forest St.
Dow, Carolyn ....'68 '01 [Ⓐ Bruggeman,H.&Assoc.]
Dvells-Lomeda, Jeanette Marie .... '60 '02 C.238 B.S. L.146 J.D. 400 E. Lincoln Highway

Dyrcz, William ....'55 '88 C.1016 B.S. L.365 J.D. 1108 Plaza Drive
Hurst, David C. ....'— '95 C.393 B.A. L.146 J.D. [Bruggeman,H.&Assoc.]
Loverude, Russell H., (BV) ....'48 '79 C.589 B.S. L.365 J.D. [R.H.Loverude]
Loverude, Russell H., L.L.C., Law Offices of, (BV) .... 1243 North Cedar Road
Manzella, Thomas J. ....'74 '01 C.1151 B.A. L.209 J.D. [[A] Bruggeman,H.&Assoc.]
Quigley, Daniel J., (BV) ....'47 '75 C.1151 B.A. L.365 J.D. 1234 N. Cedar Rd.
Schlak, Douglas W., (BV) ....'47 '74 C&L.879 B.A., J.D. [D.W.Schlak&Assoc.]
Schlak, Douglas W, & Associates, (BV) .... 321 W. Maple St (Rt 30), Ste 100
Seil, David G. ....'53 '78 C.1151 B.A. L.608 J.D. 205 W. Maple St.
Stan, Robert Paul ....'49 '87 500 W. Maple, Ste. 205
Truesdale, Daniel C. ....'59 '84 C.436 B.S. L.365 J.D. 1131 Marley Rd.
Welch, William C., (AV) ....'24 '51 C&L.339 B.S., J.D. 917 N. Cedar Rd.‡
Wennlund, Donald L., (BV) '41 '68
C.339 B.A. L.365 J.D. State Rep. [D.L.Wennlund&Assoc.]
Wennlund, Donald L., & Assoc., (BV) ....1234 N. Cedar Rd.
Wirt, James S., (AV) ....'32 '59 C.388 B.A. L.597 J.D. 1261 Wirt Rd.‡

NEWTON, * 3,154, *Jasper Co.*

Cox, Phillips, Weber, Tedford & Heap, P.C.
(See Robinson)

Hoffeditz, William R. ....'56 '92 C&L.801 B.A., J.D. P.O. Box 42
Kasserman, Geo. W., Jr. ....'21 '48 C&L.339 B.S., LL.B. Ret. Appl. Ct. J.
Quindry, Curtis G., (BV) ....'43 '68 C&L.383 B.S., J.D. 100 S. Lafayette St.
Tomaw, Patricia, (CV) ....'44 '71 C.234 B.S. L.339 J.D. City Atty.
Weber, Michael R. ....'47 '74 C.339 B.S. L.734 J.D. Courthouse

NILES, 30,068, *Cook Co.*

Blase, Nicholas B. ....'28 '51 C&L.602 B.Sc., LL.B. 8074 Milw. St.
Bobel, Anthony M. ....'18 '46 L.209 LL.B. 7117 Cleveland Ave.‡
Brown, David R. '54 '80 C.930 B.A. L.424 J.D.
Pres., A.L.P. Lighting & Ceiling Products, Inc.

Brown, Marc L., The Law Offices of
(See Park Ridge)

Chareas, Stephen Arthur ....'65 '02 C.347 B.S. L.1187 J.D. 8074 Milwaukee Ave.
Cohen, Kenneth J. ....'31 '55 C.339 L.209 LL.B. 8074 N. Milwaukee Ave.‡
Cohen, Mitchell A. ....'46 '74 C.339 B.A. L.209 J.D. 7749 N. Milwaukee Ave.
Cole, Robert J. ....'56 '81 C&L.879 B.A., J.D. Corp. Coun., Sportmart, Inc.
Compton, Nancy Kirk '45 '90 C.539 B.S. L.107 J.D.
(adm. in NY; not adm. in IL) Ft. Dearborn Co.

Cutler & Associates, LTD.
(See Skokie)

Daidone, Benj., (AV) ....'17 '43 L.146 LL.B. 7124 W. Touhy Ave.
Dennis, John C. ....'22 '50 C.209 L.365 LL.B. 8558 N. Oleander

Ferraro, Anthony B., The Law Offices of
(See Rosemont)

Gordon, Harvey C. ....'47 '72 C.910 B.A. L.597 J.D. Asst. Gen. Coun., BGE, Ltd.
Henderson, Susan A., (AV) ...'45 '69 C.813 B.A. L.145 J.D. Asst. Gen. Coun., BGE, Ltd.
Hochberg, Andrew S. ....'62 '87 C.659 B.S.E. L.597 J.D. Sr. V.P., Sportmart, Inc.
Hochberg, Larry J. ....'37 '60 C.966 B.S. L.597 LL.B. 7233 Dempster St.
Joshua, Jonathan S. '— '99 C.978 B.A. L.262 J.D.
(adm. in NY; not adm. in IL) Corp. Coun., Arrow Financial Servs. LLC
Juranek, Frank J. ....'30 '80 C.597 B.S. L.589 J.D. 5959 W. Howard St.
Kirk, Nancy J. '45 '90 C.540 B.S. L.107 J.D.
(adm. in NY; not adm. in IL) Fort Dearborn Co.‡
Lagioia, Salvatore M. ....'33 '58 C.339 B.S. L.597 J.D. Prov. Wash. Ins. Co.
Lerner, Jeffrey M. ....'46 '74 C.801 B.S. L.146 J.D. 6767 N. Milwaukee Ave.
Levine, Elliott B. ....'42 '70 C.1016 B.A. L.365 J.D. [Levine&Assoc.]
Levine & Associates, Ltd. ....8926 N. Greenwood Ave.
Lippman, Roger I. ....'36 '60 C.339 L.209 LL.B. 9030 N. Clifton
London, Howard M. ....'27 '53 C.339 B.S. L.597 J.D. 7400 N. Oak Park Ave.
Matthew, Norman L. ....'51 '76 C.339 B.A. L.424 J.D. 6440 Howard
Michelotti, Ronald F. ....'39 '65 C&L.209 A.B., J.D. 8539 N. Osceola Ave.
Newton, Robert M. ....'42 '66 C&L.477 B.A., J.D. 6125 W. Howard‡
Nicewick, Edward W., (AV) ....'27 '55 C.339 B.S. L.424 J.D. 9036 N. Chester‡
Novak, Julie Anne '74 '99
C.339 B.A. L.209 J.D. Corp. Coun., Arrow Financial Servs. LLC
Phillips, G. William ....'38 '66 C&L.347 B.S., J.D. Golf Mill State Bk.
Platt, Joel R. ....'46 '74 C.339 B.S. L.276 J.D. V.P. & Gen. Coun., BGE, Ltd.
Ptasinski, Lawrence J. ....'49 '79 C.602 B.B.A. L.365 J.D. [Ptasinski&S.]

Ptasinski & Smith, P.C.
241 Golf Mill Professional Building Suite 800, 60714
Telephone: 847-296-6631 Fax: 847-296-7503 URL: http://www.ptasinskismith.com
URL: http://www.lawyers.com/ptasinski-smith
Lawrence J. Ptasinski; Donald A. Smith.
Probate, Estate Planning and Administration, Trusts and Estates, Wills, Elder Law, Real Estate, Business Law, Divorce.
See Professional Biographies, NILES, ILLINOIS

Regenbogen, Howard W. ....'50 '76 C.473 B.A. L.365 J.D. [H.Regenbogen]
Regenbogen, Howard ....8121 N. Milwaukee
Reiss, Jacob ....'47 '73 C.339 B.A. L.209 J.D. 6767 N. Milwaukee Ave.
Robertson, Karl M. ....'50 '76 C.339 B.A. L.365 J.D. 8041 N. Octavia Ave.
Rog, Kathlyne M. '49 '89 C.339 B.A. L.597 J.D.
(adm. in MA; not adm. in IL) 7875 N. Caldwell Ave.
Rossi, Dominic ....'15 '38 C&L.209 J.D. 7636 N. Milwaukee Ave.
Sassan, Dennis D. ....'42 '65 C&L.209 J.D. 7788 N. Milwaukee Ave.
Scott, Larry R. ....'57 '82 C&L.339 B.S., J.D. Pres., Scott Stainless Steel
Sharp, L. Diane ....'55 '80 C&L.209 B.A., J.D. 9901 Wendy Way
Slutzky, Irving ....'17 '53 L.365 LL.B. 7749 N. Milwaukee Ave.

Slutzky, Jay A. '48 '74 C&L.209 B.A., J.D.
7749 North Milwaukee Avenue, 60714
Telephone: 847-967-7979 Fax: 847-967-7984
Email: jayslutzky@yahoo.com
Wills, Living Trusts, Estate Planning, Residential Real Estate, Commercial Real Estate, Divorce, Personal Injury, Bankruptcy Law, Elder Law, DUI, DWI, Business Law, Commercial Law, Commercial Litigation, Business Organization, Business Transactions, Business Counseling, Business Advice, Real Estate Law, Real Estate Litigation, Commercial Transactions, Contracts, Construction Law, Litigation, Motor Vehicle Accidents, Personal Injury Defense, Plaintiffs Personal Injury, Probate, Estate Administration, Trusts, By-Pass Trusts, Credit Shelter Trusts, Special Needs Trusts, Testamentary Trusts, Ancillar Administration, Durable Powers of Attorney, Medical Powers of Attorney, Living Wills, Pour-Over Wills, Marital Deduction Trusts, Beneficiary Designations, Irrevocable Life Insurance Trusts, Split Dollar Purchase Agreements, Crummey Trusts, Workers Compensation, Civil Litigation, Criminal Defense, Pre-Marital Agreements, Planning for Disabled Spouses, Planning for Disabled Children, Estate Tax Return Preparation, Second Marriage Issues, Contested Wills and Trusts, Partnerships, Corporations, Limited Liability Companies.
See Professional Biographies, NILES, ILLINOIS

Smith, Donald A. ....'58 '84 C.602 B.A. L.424 J.D. [Ptasinski&S.]
Stein, James ....'15 '38 C.999 L.365 LL.B. 9500 Wash. St.‡
Suchor, Debra L. ....'58 '84 C.339 A.B. L.365 J.D. DLS Consulting
Tralewski, Walter J. ....'46 '76 C.46 B.S.C.E. L.146 J.D. 8548 N. Oleander St.
Wilansky, Steven C. '61 '86 C.188 B.A. L.273 J.D.
(adm. in DC; not adm. in IL) V.P. & Chf. Legal Off., Arrow Financial Servs. LLC

NOKOMIS, 2,389, *Montgomery Co.*

Glenn, Michael R., (BV) ....'51 '78 C.801 B.A. L.502 J.D. 320 W. Central St.

NORMAL, 45,386, *McLean Co.*

Abraham, Jason F., (BVⓉ) ....'67 '92 C.966 B.A. L.436 J.D. [M.F.Hupy&Assoc.] ⊙
Abraham, Teena M., (BVⓉ) .....'62 '97 C.1172 B.S. L.436 J.D. [[A] M.F.Hupy&Assoc.] ⊙
Bowles, Charles E., Jr. '17 '40 C&L.902 A.B., LL.B.
(adm. in VA; not adm. in IL) 2 Lateer Dr.‡
Brady, Connolly & Masuda, P.C., (AV) .... 705 East Lincoln, Suite 202 (⊙Chicago)
Campbell, William D. ....'50 '76 C&L.339 A.B., J.D. Dir., Ill. State Univ.
Eggan, Christine A., (CV) ....'49 '85 C.338 B.S. L.339 J.D. 101 Anthony Dr.
Gordon, Donald R. ....'25 '62 C.427 B.A. L.146 LL.B. 2010 BramblewoodCt.‡
Hupy, Michael F., (AVⓉ) ....'46 '72 C&L.436 B.A., J.D. [M.F.Hupy&Assoc.] ⊙
Hupy, Michael F., & Associates, S.C., (AVⓉ)
211 Landmark Drive, Suite D-1 (⊙Decatur, Peoria, IL; Appleton, Madison, Milw., WI)
Kreblin, Chad A. '76 '01 C.966 B.A. L.1410 J.D.
[[A] M.F.Hupy&Assoc.] (⊙Decatur, Peoria, IL; Appleton, Madison, WI)
Larmore, Kelly A. ....'77 '03 C.966 B.A. L.436 J.D. [[A] M.F.Hupy&Assoc.] ⊙
Lugg, Elizabeth T. '59 '83 C&L.352 B.A., J.D.
(adm. in IA; not adm. in IL) EAF 327 Degarmo Hall, Campus Box 5900
Mahrt, Steven D., (BV) ....'53 '78 C.947 B.A. L.546 J.D. Corp. Coun.
McCarthy, Julia B. ....'60 '87 C.707 B.A. L.424 J.D. [Brady,C.&M.]
McGraw, Angela E. '75 '00 C.958 B.S. L.436 J.D.
[[A] M.F.Hupy&Assoc.] (⊙Decatur, Peoria, IL; Appleton, Madison, WI)
Miller, Scott T. ....'41 '68 C&L.421 B.A., J.D. 1016 Crooked Stick Ln.
Oliver, Wendell E. ....'12 '38 C.338 B.Ed. L.339 LL.B. 142 Eastview Dr.‡

Prior Law Firm, The, P.C.
(See Bloomington)

Rochelle, Victor C. ....'18 '48 C.846 B.A. L.178 LL.B. 27 Lateer Dr.‡
Romero, Ronald L. '53 '88 C.988 B.A.B.A. L.911 J.D.
(adm. in WA; not adm. in IL) P.O. Box 328
Schelwat, Timothy W. ....'70 '98 C.312 B.A. L.221 J.D. [[A] M.F.Hupy&Assoc.] ⊙
Shultz, Gary L. '48 '73 C.383 B.A. L.472 J.D.
V.P., Gen. Coun. & Secy., Mitsubishi Motor Manufacturing of Amer.‡
Sud, Suniti Rani ....'69 '94 C.340 B.A. L.966 J.D. Gen. Coun., Sud's Motor Car Co., Inc.
Townley, Wayne C., Jr. ....'29 '52 C.340 Ph.B. L.339 J.D. 906 Crestline Dr.‡
Varner, Carson H., Jr. ....'45 '75 C.473 A.B. L.623 J.D. Prof. of Law, Ill. State Univ.
Weeks, Lois Jean K. ....'28 '64 C.347 A.B. L.345 J.D. 208 Concord Dr.‡
Whiteman, Roy M. ....'21 '48 C.353 B.A. L.352 LL.B. 1570 Hunt St.‡
Williams, Roy L. ....'70 '98 C.154 B.A. L.424 J.D. [[A] M.F.Hupy&Assoc.] ⊙

NORRIDGE, 14,582, *Cook Co.*

Due, Brian G. ....'47 '72 C.589 B.A. L.365 J.D. 7615 W. Montrose Ave.

Favia, Michael V.
(See Chicago)

Ferraro, Anthony B., The Law Offices of
(See Rosemont)

Hirschenbein, Richard A. ....'45 '71 C.347 B.A. L.575 J.D. 4363 N. Harlem Ave.

NORRIS CITY, 1,057, *White Co.*

Heid, Christopher, Christopher Heid ....'50 '79 C.927 B.A. L.801 J.D. P.O. Box 24

NORTH AURORA, 10,585, *Kane Co.*

Booth, Robert P., (BV) ....'52 '78 C.36 B.S. L.365 J.D. [R.P.Booth]
Booth, Robert P., Ltd., (BV) ....149 S. Lincolnway
DeBroux, Carl H., (BV) ....'35 '76 C.58 B.A. L.424 J.D. 161 S. Lincolnway
Duggan, John P., (BV) ....'51 '76 C.209 B.A. L.339 J.D. [Duggan]
Duggan Law Offices, (BV) ....181 S. Lincolnway
Grometer, R. Peter ....'46 '73 C.475 B.S. L.339 J.D. Cir. J.
Lange, Kathleen P. ....'42 '80 C.801 B.A. L.589 J.D. 215 N. Lincolnway
Russo, Susan Schneider, (CV) '53 '84
C.578 B.A. L.339 J.D. 149 South Lincolnway, Suite 200
Swearingen, Brad M., (BV) '54 '79 C.927 B.S. L.801 J.D.
149 S. Lincolnway, Suite 200
Thelander, Fred G. ....'26 '59 C.58 B.S. L.345 J.D. 625 Lindsay Circle (Pat.)
Wyeth, Jay R., (BV) ....'61 '86 C.999 B.A. L.339 J.D. 149 S. Lincoln Way, Suite 200

NORTH BARRINGTON, 2,918, *Lake Co.*

Campbell, Julian C., Law Offices, (AV) ....'53 '78 C&L.221 B.A., J.D. 145 Haverton Way
DiCara, Mark Michael ....'61 '87 C.927 B.S. L.365 J.D. [Mallon&D.]
Mallon & DiCara, P.C. ....236 Shady Lane

NORTHBROOK, 33,435, *Cook Co.*

Abbey, G. Marshall ....'33 '57 C.696 B.A. L.188 J.D. 836 Skokie Boulevard
Abrams, Amy L. ....'54 '82 C.293 A.B. L.145 J.D. Allstate Ins. Co.
Addis, Wayne B. ....'53 '78 C&L.589 B.A., J.D. 707 Skokie Blvd., Ste. 540
Adler, Richard M. ....'40 '66 C&L.966 B.S., J.D. 4025 Crestwood
Agnew, Barbara J. ....'50 '80 C.597 B.S. L.146 J.D. 435 Lee Rd.
Ahern, Erika S. ....'72 '98 C.1021 B.A. L.801 J.D. Allstate Insurance Co.
Ahn, Soon Mo ....'41 '91 707 Skokie Blvd.
Allen, Martha M. '70 '00 C.473 B.A. L.424 J.D.
Corp. Sec. Investigator, Allstate Insurance Co.
AmericAsia Global Law, Ltd ....500 Skokie Blvd.
Anderson, Mark M., (AV) ....'51 '76 C.228 A.B. L.209 J.D. [O'Halloran,K.G.&C.]
Apter, David ....'39 '64 C&L.339 B.A., J.D. [Kantor&A.]
Arbus, Lee A., Ltd., (AV) ....'53 '78 C.339 B.S. L.146 J.D. [Levun,G.&C.]
Austriaco, Aurora ....'65 '91 C&L.209 B.S., J.D. [[B] Peck,B.A.&M.] ⊙
Avery, Martha J. .....'62 '89 C.602 B.A. L.209 J.D. Assoc.Coun., Allstate Insurance Co.
Babarik, Dan E. ....'48 '74 C.679 B.A. L.910 J.D. 1625 Shermer Rd.
Bach, Paul M., Law Offices of, (CV) '67 '92
C.98 B.S. L.221 J.D. 1955 Shermer Rd., Ste. 150
Baker, Neal A. '59 '94 C.477 B.A. L.209
V.P., Legal Serv. & Mng. Coun., Caremark Rx, Inc.
Balikov, Howard A., (AV) ....'57 '82 C.339 B.S. L.146 J.D. [H.A.Balikov]
Balikov, Howard A., Ltd., (AV) ....555 Skokie Blvd., Ste. 400
Banks, Sharon F. ....'41 '85 C.1183 B.A. L.365 J.D. 3710 Commercial Ave.

Banks, Vanita M. '55 '80
C.679 B.A. L.879 J.D. Coun., Corp. Law, Allstate Insurance Co.
Barnett, Steve M. .... '41 '66 C.118 A.B. L.145 J.D. Pres., C D C, Inc.
Basofin, Michael S. .... '45 '71 C.473 B.A. L.424 J.D. 3031 Commercial Ave.‡
Batman, Cynthia P. '54 '86 C.608 B.A. L.8 J.D.
(adm. in OH; not adm. in IL) Coun., Allstate Insurance Co.
Bauer, Bruce I. .... '42 '67 C.477 B.B.A. L.209 J.D. 555 N. Skokie Blvd.
Behnke, Peter R., (AV) .... '48 '77 C.966 B.A. L.365 J.D. 555 Skokie Boulevard
Bengston, John S. ......'65 '95 C.57 B.A. L.1000 J.D. Asst. Coun., Allstate Insurance Co.
Bennett, Susan E. '67 '92 C&L.352 B.M., J.D.
(adm. in IA; not adm. in IL) Culligan Ltd.
Bensing, Robert C. '22 '47 C&L.421 A.B., LL.B.
(adm. in KY; not adm. in IL) 1 Court of Harborside‡
Bentz, Diego E. '70 '96 C.878 B.S. L.352 J.D.
(adm. in WA; not adm. in IL) 666 Dundee Rd., Ste. 704
Bergman, Neil L. .... '33 '59 C.339 B.S. L.209 J.D. 650 Dundee Rd.
Bergstrom, Eldon W., Jr. .... '30 '64 C.339 B.S.B.A. L.1049 J.D. 875 Hawthorne Lane
Berkun, Susan J., (AV) .... '55 '80 C.339 B.S. L.424 J.D. [⊠ Levun,G.&C.]
Berlin, Arthur E. .... '27 '50 C&L.145 Ph.B., J.D. [Berlin&B.] ‡

Berlin & Braude, (AV)
Suite 456, 650 Dundee Road, 60062
Telephone: 847-412-1300 Telecopier: 847-412-1314
Arthur E. Berlin (Retired); Michael E. Braude; Louise S. Greenfield; Michael R. Goldfein.
Civil Practice in all State and Federal Courts. Commercial Real Estate Transactions, Corporations, Taxation, Employee Benefits, Labor and Employment, Estate Planning and Probate.
See Professional Biographies, NORTHBROOK, ILLINOIS

Berman, Alan S. .... '37 '65 C.209 B.A. L.365 LL.B. 900 Skokie Boulevard
Berman, Harvey, (AV) .... '29 '55 C.339 B.S. L.209 J.D. 4513 Lindenwood Ln.‡
Berns, Matthew H. '67 '92
C.339 B.S. L.477 J.D. Asst. Gen. Coun., Culligan International Co.
Bezark, Fred .... '33 '60 C.475 B.A. L.424 J.D. 3435 Carol Ln.
Birt, Maurice W., III .... '69 '99 C.291 B.S. L.424 J.D. [M.W.Birt,III]
Birt, Maurice W., III, LLC, Law Office of .... 5 Revere Drive Suite 200
Bishop, Karen .... C.705 B.A. L.1494 J.D. PotashCorp Legal

Block, Bradford E., Law Offices of, (AV) '46 '75 C.659 B.S.Ec. L.209 J.D.
1935 Shermer Road, Suite 350, 60062
Telephone: 847-559-0860 Fax: 847-509-8523
URL: http://www.blocklawoffices.com
Business Formation, Corporate Finance, Mergers and Acquisitions, Asset Based Finance, Securities Offerings, Corporate Contracts, Technology Contracts, Equipment Leasing, Computer Law.
See Professional Biographies, NORTHBROOK, ILLINOIS

Bloom, Kenneth M., (AV) .... '63 '88 C.339 B.S. L.146 J.D. [Peck,B.A.&M.] ⊙
Bloom, Philip M., (AV) ... '34 '58 C.339 L.209 LL.B. 650 Dundee Rd. (⊙Uniondale, NY)
Blum, David S. .... '56 '82 C.37 B.A. L.146 J.D. 4061 Applewood Lane
Blum, Seymour H. .... '16 '40 L.146 LL.B. P.O. Box 1026
Blumenthal, Jeffrey C. .... '53 '79 C.597 B.A. L.659 J.D. [J.C.Blumenthal]
Blumenthal, Jeffrey C., Chartered .... 2970 Maria Ave., Ste. 223
Bohlender, Hugh D. .... '51 '86 C.870 B.S. L.597 J.D. Coun., Allstate Insurance Co.
Bohrer, David .... '58 '85 C.339 B.S. L.589 J.D. [D.Bohrer]
Bohrer, D. .... 450 Skokie Blvd., Ste. 502
Bollinger, Denise A. .....'56 '02 C.209 B.A. L.365 J.D. Asst. Coun., Allstate Insurance Co.
Boodro, William J. ....'54 '81 C.454 B.A. L.425 J.D. Coun., Allstate Insurance Co.
Booker, Susan H. .... '60 '85 C.705 B.A. L.904 J.D. [⊠ Levun,G.&C.]
Born, Robert C. '44 '69 C.264 A.B. L.734 J.D.
(adm. in MO; not adm. in IL) Dir., Allstate Ins. Co.
Boutwell, Charles D., (AV) .... '45 '70 C.880 B.A. L.16 J.D. 3075 Plum Island Dr.
Bradley, Patrick F., (Ltd., P.C.) ...... '52 '77 C.973 B.S.B.A. L.209 J.D. 1130 Shermer Rd.
Braude, Michael E., (AV) .... '40 '65 C.659 B.S. L.145 J.D. [Berlin&B.]
Bremen, Ronald B. .... '42 '70 C.347 B.S. L.1119 J.D. 666 Dundee Rd.
Brenner, Gail V. '55 '80 C.339 B.S. L.146 J.D.
Coun., Corp. Law, Allstate Insurance Co.
Brenner, Leonard J. .... '57 '85 C.589 B.S. L.1049 J.D. [L.J.Brenner]

Brenner, Leonard J., Ltd.
555 Skokie Boulevard, Suite 500, 60062
Telephone: 847-480-1020 Fax: 847-480-0034
Email: ljbrenner@brennerlegal.com URL: http://www.leonardbrenner.com
Leonard J. Brenner.
Business and Corporate Law, Tax Controversies, Estate Planning and Probate.
See Professional Biographies, NORTHBROOK, ILLINOIS

Bronner, James R., (AV) ..... '43 '68 C.477 B.A. L.597 J.D. Chm., Speakers of Sport, Inc.
Brosk, Joel, (BV) .... '49 '74 C.339 B.S. L.174 J.D. 40 Skokie Blvd.
Brostoff, Sandra N., Law Office of '— '82
C.596 B.S. L.365 J.D. 707 Skokie Boulevard, Suite 420
Brown, Anthony O. .... '47 '73 C.604 B.A. L.930 J.D. 500 Skokie Boulevard
Brown, Beth A. .... '55 '80 C&L.879 B.A., J.D. Coun., Allstate Insurance Co.
Brown, Pamela Platt ....'49 '78 C.597 B.A. L.209 J.D. Coun., Allstate Insurance Co.
Brown, Robert A. .... '24 '65 C.477 B.S. L.146 J.D. 2530 Shannon Rd. (Pat.)
Brozosky, Martin M., (BV) .... '37 '61 C&L.339 B.S., LL.B. 40 Skokie Blvd.
Bruch, Julie A. .... '67 '93 C.597 B.A. L.424 J.D. [O'Halloran,K.G.&C.]
Brunner, Anne Marie L. .....'58 '83 C.118 B.A. L.910 J.D. Coun., Allstate Insurance Co.
Bryant, Doris '47 '85 C.339 B.A. L.146 J.D.
Asst. V.P. & Asst. Gen. Coun., Allstate Insurance Co.
Buchanan, John E. ..... '70 '98 C.589 B.S. L.365 J.D. Asst. Coun., Allstate Insurance Co.
Bulasko, Elizabeth E. .... '54 '91 C.1350 B.A. L.365 J.D. Andersen Consulting
Burnett, Malcolm W., Jr. .... '34 '63 C.602 B.B.A. L.597 J.D. 2700 Illinois Rd.
Burns, Kenneth J., Jr., (AV) .... '26 '51 C&L.597 B.S., J.D. 2315 Sanders Rd.
Burnstein, Harold R., (AV) .... '— '50 C.597 B.S. L.209 J.D. [⊠ Strauss&M.]
Butler, Cecile Anne Viau '55 '83 C.1107 B.A. L.575 J.D.
(adm. in MA; not adm. in IL) 3100 Sanders Road
Caplan, Alan M. .... '52 '77 C.339 B.S. L.145 J.D. 3000 Dundee Rd.
Carman, Fred, (AV) .... '25 '53 C&L.209 B.S., J.D. [F.Carman]
Carman, Fred, Ltd., (AV) .... 95 Revere Drive
Casson, George J., Jr. .... '47 '72 C.276 B.S.F.S. L.145 J.D. [⊠ O'Halloran,K.G.&C.]
Ceravolo, Anthony J. .... '43 '79 C.339 B.S. L.209 J.D. Coun., Allstate Insurance Co.
Citro, Marvin H. .... '41 '68 C.339 B.S. L.209 J.D. 2555 Cobblewood Dr.
Clark, Kelly A. ....'69 '94 C.477 A.B. L.209 J.D. Asst. Coun., Allstate Insurance Co.
Clausen, Glenn R. .... '39 '65 C.1024 B.A. L.339 LL.B. 3860 Mission Hills Rd.
Cleary, Lara A. .... '70 '98 C.502 B.S. L.209 J.D. [Whitted,C.&T.]
Cloch, Sandi R. .... '64 '90 C.339 B.A. L.424 J.D. [⊠ J.E.Fish]
Coe, Robert A., (AV) .... '37 '60 C&L.597 B.S.B.A., J.D. [R.A.Coe]
Coe, Robert A., Ltd. & Assoc., (AV) .... 555 Skokie Blvd.
Cohen, Bennett L. .... '52 '77 C&L.629 B.A., J.D. [Cohen S.&H.]
Cohen, Michael J., Ltd., (AV) .... '54 '81 C.659 B.S. L.146 J.D. [Levun,G.&C.] ⊙
Cohen Salk & Huvard, P.C. .... 630 Dundee Rd., Suite 120

Collins, Edward T. .... '60 '86 C&L.801 B.A., J.D. Coun., Allstate Insurance Co.
Collison, Edgar K., III, (BV) .... '47 '76 C.210 B.A. L.365 J.D. 1894 Techny Ct.
Conlon, Timothy J. '71 '96
C.363 B.A. L.209 J.D. Corp. Coun., Underwriters Laboratories Inc.
Conner, James R. '27 '61 C&L.229 B.A., LL.B.
(adm. in MO; not adm. in IL) Allstate Ins. Co.
Connolly, John C., III '62 '92
C.424 B.S. L.146 J.D. Assoc. Coun., Allstate Insurance Co.
Cook, Gerard W. .... '53 '78 C.597 B.A. L.365 J.D. [O'Halloran,K.G.&C.]
Cotler, Marcia G. .... '64 '89 C.339 B.M. L.276 J.D. 2940 Lake Placid Lane‡
Cox, John H., (LTD.) .... '55 '80 C.339 B.A. L.146 J.D. 3330 Dundee Road
Crane, Richard A. .... '48 '73 C.339 B.S. L.597 J.D. 707 Skokie Blvd.
Crimmins, William G. '52 '78 C.742 B.A. L.146 J.D.
V.P. & Dep. Gen. Coun., Allstate Insurance Co.
Crotty, Richard G., (BV) .... '45 '70 C&L.597 B.S.B.A., J.D. 650 Dundee Rd., 4th Fl.
Cruz, Lori A. .... '59 '92 C.98 B.A. L.146 J.D. Assoc. Coun., Allstate Insurance Co.
Cutler, Paul W., (AV) .... '06 '32 C.197 A.B. L.597 J.D. 1775 South Lane‡
Davidson, Denise G. .... '51 '77 C.339 B.S. L.424 J.D. 605 Dauphine Ct.
Deemer, Patricia L. .... '51 '94 C.424 B.S. L.209 J.D. [⊠ A.G.Orlowsky]
De Frank, Sam .... '53 '78 C.602 B.B.A. L.145 J.D. Asst. V.P., Tax
de Generes, Tasker O. .... '42 '72 C.112 A.B. L.209 J.D. 1845 Happ Rd.
Derrig, Deidre B. .... '57 '83 C.436 B.A. L.424 J.D. Coun., Allstate Insurance Co.
Di Giacomo, Carol & Kathryn Somers, L.L.C.
(See Northfield)
Dill, James R. .... '50 '75 C.339 B.A. L.209 J.D. Coun., Allstate Insurance Co.
Dilling, Kirkpatrick W. .... '20 '47 C&L.597 B.S. 1120 Lee Road
DiNovi, Mark '58 '87 C.299 B.A. L.1040 J.D.
(adm. in NY; not adm. in IL) Coun., Allstate Insurance Co.
Dixon, John W., (BV) '66 '92 C.732 B.A. L.365 J.D.
V.P. & Gen. Coun., First Insurance Funding Corp.
Domm, William A. .... '38 '63 C.72 B.A. L.597 J.D. [W.A.Domm]
Domm, William A., P.C. .... 149 Arrowwood Lane
Doughty, Maria S. '66 '92 C.1365 B.A. L.245 J.D.
Assoc. Coun., Allstate Insurance Co.
Dugan, Timothy R. '60 '90 C&L.502 B.B.A., J.D.
Assoc. Coun., Allstate Insurance Co.
Durrani, Waqas A. '71 '98 C.424 B.A. L.339 J.D.
Assoc. Coun., Corp. Law, Allstate Insurance Co.
Dzakovich, Angela Allegra .... '50 '83 C.436 B.A. L.209 J.D. 2336 Woodlawn Rd.
Eberhart, Caryn S. '— '90 C.424 B.A. L.146 J.D.
Assoc. Coun., Allstate Insurance Co.
Eich, Brian B. .... '69 '98 C.966 B.A. L.146 J.D. Unforgettable Price, Inc.
Elden, Douglas L., (AV) .... '47 '72 C.352 B.A. L.339 J.D. [Elden]
Elden, Robbin C. .... '61 '90 C.347 B.A. L.339 J.D. [Elden]
Elden Law Firm, The, (AV) .... 1033 Skokie Blvd., Ste. 640
Elizer, Steven H. .... '57 '83 C&L.910 B.A., J.D. [Elizer&M.]

Elizer & Meyerson, L.L.C.
900 Skokie Boulevard, Suite 208, 60062-4031
Telephone: 847-513-6600 Fax: 847-513-6692
URL: http://emlegal.lawoffice.com
Steven H. Elizer; David S. Meyerson.
Criminal Law, Felonies and Misdemeanors, DUI, DWI, Traffic Violations, Personal Injury, Automobile Accidents, Wrongful Death.
See Professional Biographies, NORTHBROOK, ILLINOIS

Elwart, Ralph J., Jr. .... '47 '78 C.472 B.A. L.365 J.D. Coun., Allstate Insurance Co.
Engerman, Allen C., Law Offices of, (AV) '34 '58 C.339 B.S. L.145 J.D.
666 Dundee Rd.
Erickson, David G. ... '65 '93 C.83 B.A. L.146 J.D. [Erickson-Papanek-Peterson-Erickson]
Erickson, Grant D., (AV) '37 '62
C.494 B.B.A. L.597 J.D. [Erickson-Papanek-Peterson-Erickson]
Erickson-Papanek-Peterson-Erickson, (AV) .... 1625 Shermer Road
Ewing Elmore, Maya '71 '97 C.801 B.A. L.424 J.D.
Asst. Coun., Corp. Law, Allstate Insurance Co.
Fabbrini, Richard R. '49 '75
C.927 B.A. L.421 J.D. Sr. V.P. & C.F.O., Lane Industries, Inc.
Fagan, Robert M., (BV) .... '56 '92 C.1120 B.S. L.589 J.D. [R.M.Fagan] ⊙
Fagan, Robert M., Ltd., The Law Offices of, (BV)
1319 Southwind Dr. (⊙Fountain Hills, AZ; Freeport, IL)
Faigus, Eugene M. '46 '74 C.473 B.S. L.1003 J.D.
(adm. in OH; not adm. in IL) Jack Jacobs & Co.
Falknor, G. Scott '53 '84 C.597 B.A. L.209 J.D.
Asst. VP, Asst. Gen. Coun. & Asst. Sec., Claim Lit, Allstate Insurance Co.
Felbinger, Karl L. .... '44 '70 L.209 J.D. [Felbinger&F.]
Felbinger, Karl L., Jr. .... '67 '92 C.966 B.A. L.174 J.D. [Felbinger&F.]
Felbinger & Felbinger .... 1314 Shermer Rd.
Feldman, Michael R. .... '55 '79 C.388 B.A. L.880 J.D. 3482B Milwaukee Ave.
Feldman, Robert K. .... '58 '83 C.378 B.S. L.365 J.D. 401 Huehl Rd., Ste. 1-A
Fenton, James S. '55 '80 C.339 B.A. L.273 J.D.
V.P. & Asst. Gen. Coun., Grubb & Ellis
Filler, Bernard M., (AV) '35 '63 C.339 B.S. L.813 LL.B.
Pres., Lidemara Enterprises, Inc.
Fiorini, Lloyd D. .... '66 '94 C.038 B.S. L.365 J.D. Sr. Legal Coun., Caremark Rx, Inc.
Fish, John E. .... '54 '83 C.339 B.S. L.209 J.D. [J.E.Fish]
Fish, John E., Ltd. .... 630 Dundee Rd., Ste. 200
Fishbein, Todd A. .... '68 '93 C.477 B.A. L.339 J.D. Pres., Red Seal Develop. Corp.‡
Fisher, Leo B. .... '12 '37 C.999 B.S. L.146 LL.B. 1280 Rudolph Dr.‡
Fjelde, Mark B., (BV⊕) '53 '79 C&L.585 B.A., J.D.
(adm. in ND; not adm. in IL) Coun., Allstate Insurance Co.
Flamporis, Georgia '64 '89 C.945 B.B.A. L.1017 J.D.
(adm. in NJ; not adm. in IL) Assoc. Coun., Allstate Insurance Co.
Flank, Arnold M., (AV) .... '42 '67 C&L.477 B.A., J.D. 555 Skokie Blvd., Ste. 500
Flitcraft, Gregg A. .... '56 '83 C.339 B.S. L.365 J.D. [Olson,G.&F.]
Fontana, Angela K. '68 '94
C.352 B.B.A. L.321 J.D. Assoc. Coun., Allstate Insurance Co.
Fox, Leon .... '51 '75 C.339 B.A. L.424 J.D. [Morgen&F.]
Fox, Sidney N., (AV) .... '27 '56 C.597 B.S. L.209 J.D. [S.N.Fox] (Pat.)
Fox, Sidney N., P.C., (AV) .... 555 Skokie Blvd. (Pat.)
Frank, Laura Sokolik '— '92
C.477 B.A. L.910 J.D. Assoc. Coun., Allstate Insurance Co.
Frank, Leonard J. .... '18 '54 C&L.209 LL.B. 1250 Rudolph Rd.‡
Fraser, Anne W. .... '— '69 C.813 A.B. L.94 J.D. Coun., Allstate Insurance Co.
Fredenburg, Lila D. .... '48 '73 C.012 B.A. L.1003 J.D. IMC Global Inc.
Freedman, Kenneth S. .... '46 '71 C.393 B.A. L.209 J.D. 40 Skokie Blvd., Ste. 630
Freibrun, Eric S. .... '— '83 C.339 B.S. L.910 J.D. [E.S.Freibrun]

Freibrun, Eric S., Ltd., Law Offices of
630 Dundee Road, Suite 120, 60062-2749
Telephone: 847-562-0099 Fax: 847-562-0033 URL: http://www.freibrun.com
Email: efreibrun@msn.com URL: http://www.lawyers.com/freibrun
Eric S. Freibrun.
Intellectual Property, Intellectual Property Licensing, Intellectual Property Litigation, Internet Intellectual Property, Internet Law, Trademark Law, Proprietary Rights, Computers and Software, Computer Contracts, Computer Law, Computer Security, Computer Software Law, Information Technology, Information Technology Contracts, Information Technology Licensing, International Computer Law, Software Copyright, Software Licensing, Software Protection, Software Publishing Technology, E-commerce.

See Professional Biographies, NORTHBROOK, ILLINOIS

Gage-Bernheimer, Victoria H. . . . . . . '63 '88 C&L.420 B.S., J.D. All State Ins. Co.
Gagerman, Paul A. . . . .'71 '97 C.174 B.A. L.365 J.D. Gen. Coun., Financial Clearing, Inc.
Garcia, Ruben M. . . . . . . '66 '94 C.339 B.S. L.365 J.D. [R.M.Garcia]
Garcia, Ruben M., P.C. . . . . . . 899 Skokie Boulevard, Suite 300
Garlousky, Hillard . . . . . . '39 '68 C.339 B.S. L.365 J.D. New England Financial
Gass, Stanford E., (AV) . . . . . . '36 '61 C&L.477 B.A., LL.B. [Gass&L.] ⊙
Gass and Lewis, Ltd., (AV) . . . . . . 707 Skokie Blvd. (⊙Chicago)
Gaston, Judith Y. '56 '92 C.63 B.S. L.209 J.D.
Coun., Corp. Law., Allstate Insurance Co.
Geitner, Neal P., (BV) . . . . . . '55 '82 C.801 B.S. L.280 J.D. [O'Halloran,K.G.&C.]
Geraghty, Robert C. . . . . . '47 '72 C.932 B.A. L.146 J.D. 707 Skokie Blvd., Ste. 420
Gerber, Marshall J. . . . . . . '41 '66 3240 Brookdale Lane‡
Gerstein, Leonard J. . . . . . . '39 '73 C.221 B.A. L.146 J.D. [L.J.Gerstein]
Gerstein, Leonard J., Ltd. . . . . . . 95 Revere Dr.

Gignilliat & Hymen, P.C., (AV)
500 Skokie Boulevard, Suite 530, 60062
Telephone: 847-564-7880 Fax: 847-564-7890
Email: gnh@earthlink.net URL: http://www.lawyers.com/g&hlaw
Leigh R. Gignilliat, III (1928-2005); Roger J. Hymen.
Corporate, Estate Planning, Trusts and Estates, Wills and Probate, Taxation and Real Estate Law, Commercial Real Estate.

See Professional Biographies, NORTHBROOK, ILLINOIS

Glaubinger, H. Jay . . . . . . '70 '99 C.347 B.S. L.910 J.D. [Ⓐ Strauss&M.]
Glickman, Mark R. . . . . . . '63 '88 C.339 B.S. L.424 J.D. 3100 Dundee Rd.
Glickstein, Daniel B. . . . . .'51 '77 C.424 B.A. L.365 J.D. Gen. Coun., Shell Vacations LLC
Gold, Joanne . . . .'60 '86 C.861 B.A. L.30 J.D. [Ⓐ Erickson-Papanek-Peterson-Erickson]
Gold, Phillip . . . . . . '37 '89 C.339 B.A. L.46 J.D. 3000 Dundee Road
Goldberg, Bruce R. . . . .'59 '84 C.424 B.A. L.365 J.D. Coun., Allstate Insurance Co.
Goldberg, Myrna B. . . . .'62 '87 C&L.477 B.A., J.D. 3605 Woodhead Dr., Ste. 108
Golden, John E., (AV) . . . . . . '13 '38 C&L.424 LL.B. 10 Timbe Lane
Goldfein, Michael R. . . . . . . '51 '80 C.339 B.S. L.424 J.D. [Berlin&B.]
Goldman, Bruce L. . . . . . . '57 '81 C.477 B.S. L.339 J.D. 1540 Grant Rd.
Goldstein, Berton Ira . . . . .'54 '81 C.589 B.S. L.146 J.D. 1500 Skokie Boulevard, Suite 430
Goldstein, Ilene F., (AV) . . . . . . '55 '79 C&L.424 A.B., J.D. [I.F.Goldstein]
Goldstein, Mark L. . . . . . . '40 '64 C.339 L.209 LL.B. 3710 Commercial Ave.
Goldstein, Ilene F., Chartered, Law Offices of, (AV) . . . . 425 Huehl Road, Suite 16B
Gontovnick, Bernard H. . . . . . . '39 '62 C.1016 B.A. L.209 LL.B. 206 Carter Ct.
Goode, Howard C. . . . . . . '40 '64 C&L.597 B.A., J.D. 633 Skokie Blvd.
Goodman, Lawrence S., Ltd., (AV) '42 '67 C.966 B.B.A. L.339 J.D.
[Levun,G.&C.] ⊙
Goodman, Michael D. . . . . . . '37 '62 C&L.309 A.B., LL.B. 1692 Longvalley Dr.
Gooze-Miller, Michelle H. . . . . . . '71 '97 C.597 B.A. L.145 J.D. [Ⓐ Strauss&M.]
Gordon, David J. . . . . '55 '82 C.174 B.A. L.209 J.D. Merrill Lynch Pierce Fenner & Smith
Gordon, Milton O. . . . . . . '15 '60 C.724 B.S. L.365 LL.B. 1621 Mission Hills Rd., Ste. 105
Gorman, Robert D. . . . . . . '62 '87 C.475 B.A. L.209 J.D. [Ⓐ Levun,G.&C.]
Gotkin, Michael S. '42 '68 C.178 B.S. L.880 J.D.
Sr. V.P. & Gen. Coun., Exclusive Trading Company
Gould, Ann . . . .'— '95 C.424 M.B.A. L.365 J.D. Asst. Coun., Allstate Insurance Co.
Grabill, Edward M., Jr. . . . . . . '35 '63 C.473 B.A. L.477 J.D. [Olson,G.&F.]
Grabill, Michael R. . . . . . . '66 '96 C.473 B.A. L.146 J.D. [Olson,G.&F.]
Grant, Burton F., (AV) . . . . . . '38 '62 C&L.209 B.A., J.D. [Grant&G.] ⊙
Grant, Joan C., (AV) . . . . . . '— '80 C.477 B.A. L.209 J.D. [Grant&G.] ⊙

Grant and Grant, Professional Corporation, (AV)
707 Skokie Boulevard, Suite 600, 60062 ⊙
Telephone: 847-291-4343
Email: info@grantandgrant.com URL: http://www.lawyers.com/grantandgrantlaw
Burton F. Grant; Joan C. Grant.
Complex Family Law including Divorce, Dissolution of Marriage, Marital Property Distribution including Retirement Benefits, Spousal Support, Alimony, Maintenance, Child Custody, Visitation, Child Support, Domestic Violence, Paternity, all phases of Matrimonial Litigation, Post Divorce Modification, Premarital Agreements, Separation Agreements, Marital Settlement Agreements, Postmarital Agreements and Appeals.
Chicago, Illinois Office: 30 North La Salle Street, 29th Floor, 60602. Telephone: 312-641-3600. Fax: 312-641-2723.

See Professional Biographies, NORTHBROOK, ILLINOIS

Grayson, Brad S. . . . . . . '60 '87 C.477 B.A. L.424 J.D. [Strauss&M.]
Green, Morris . . . . . . '28 '51 C&L.339 A.B., LL.B. 2810 Floral Dr.
Greenblatt, Philip J. . . . . . . '48 '76 C.347 B.S. L.424 J.D. [Greenblatt&Assoc.]
Greenblatt & Associates . . . . . . 1955 Raymond Dr. Ste. 111
Greene, David K. . . . .'62 '86 C.597 B.A. L.145 J.D. Assoc. Gen. Coun., Fannie Mae
Greene, William L. . . . . . . '43 '68 C.801 B.A. L.146 J.D. 330 Pfingsten Road
Greenfield, Louise S. . . . . . . '51 '77 C&L.339 B.A., J.D. [Berlin&B.]
Groen, Egbert B. . . . . . . '15 '40 C.388 B.A. L.339 J.D. 3741 Mission Hills Rd.‡
Grosh, Jason '73 '00 C&L.966 B.B.A., J.D.
(adm. in WI; not adm. in IL) 2814 Dundee Road
Gross, Dennis A., (AV) . . . . . . '40 '66 C.755 B.A. L.597 J.D. [Hill] (Pat.)
Grossman, Robert C. . . . . . . '43 '67 C.473 A.B. L.597 J.D. 910 Skokie Blvd.
Hager, Jennifer M. '59 '85
C.399 B.A. L.597 J.D. Coun., Corp. Law, Allstate Insurance Co.
Hairston, Yvette M. '— '97 C.339 B.S. L.146 J.D
Corp. Sec. Mgr., Allstate Insurance Co.
Hamer, Paul . . . . . . '25 '57 C.339 B.S. L.209 J.D. 1356 Shermer Rd.‡
Hanshaw, Kenneth J. '59 '86 C.338 B.S. L.966 J.D.
Assoc. Coun., Corp. Law, Allstate Insurance Co.

Hanson, Per K., Associated, The Firm of
(See Glenview)

Heald, David L. . . . . . . '43 '70 C.207 B.A. L.880 J.D. Consulting Fiduciaries, Inc.
Hedien, Colette J. . . . . . . '— '81 C.966 B.S. L.209 J.D. 2531 Shannon Rd.
Hedrick, John R. '50 '75 C&L.339 B.S., J.D.
Coun., Corp. Law, Allstate Insurance Co.

Heisler, Marc H.
(See Evanston)

Hergott, Jay S. . . . .'46 '72 C.801 B.A. L.146 J.D. Pres., Castlewood Development Co.
Herling-Tighe, Lynn . . . . . . '47 '88 C.1016 B.S. L.365 J.D. 1253 1st Street
Herman, Arthur . . . . . . '15 '39 L.209 LL.B. 1721 Mission Hills Rd.‡
Hernández, René '64 '94 C.1222 B.A. L.966 J.D.
(adm. in WI; not adm. in IL) Assoc. Coun., Allstate Insurance Co.
Herst, William S. . . . . . . '55 '82 C.347 A.B. L.339 J.D. 555 Skokie Blvd., Ste. 500
Hertzberg, Sandra L. . . . . . . '47 '80 C.339 B.A. L.209 J.D. Coresource
Herzberg, Steven . . . . . . '57 '01 C.597 B.A. L.365 J.D. [S.I.Rapaport]

Hill Firm, The, (AV)
666 Dundee Road, Suite 1201, 60062
Telephone: 847-509-0250 Fax: 847-509-0255
Email: dagross@hillfirm.com
Member of Firm: Dennis A. Gross.
Intellectual Property Law, Patent, Copyright, Trade Secrets, Unfair Competition, Trademark and Technology Agreements.

See Professional Biographies, NORTHBROOK, ILLINOIS

Hirsch, Timothy E. . . . . . . '69 '98 L.424 J.D. 1033 Skokie Blvd., Suite 250
Hodapp, James D. . . . . . . '32 '56 C&L.424 B.S.C., J.D. 3100 Sanders Rd.
Hodges, Elaine . . . . . . '57 '82 C.859 B.A. L.477 J.D. 149 Avon‡
Hodges, Sheryl L. '— '85
C.597 B.A. L.910 J.D. Coun., Corp. Law, Allstate Insurance Co.
Hoffman, David A. . . . . . . '42 '67 C.98 L.209 B.L. Chmn., Red Seal Develop. Corp.

Horwood Marcus & Berk, Chartered
(See Chicago)

Hulme, Michael E. '61 '86 C.112 B.A. L.800 J.D.
(adm. in CA; not adm. in IL) V.P. & Gen. Coun., U.S. Filter Corp.
Huvard, Bruce K. . . . . . . '56 '81 C.170 B.A. L.145 J.D. [Cohen S.&H.]
Hymen, Roger J., (AV) . . . . . . '51 '75 C.339 B.A. L.424 J.D. [Gignilliat&H.]
Ihm, Stephen L. . . . . . . '62 '88 C.123 B.A. L.589 J.D. Coun., Allstate Insurance Co.
Jackson, Gayle A. . . . . . . '48 '73 C.991 B.A. L.597 J.D. 1145 Jeffrey Ct. N.
Jacobs, Marjorie C. . . . . . . '— '86 C.861 B.A. L.910 J.D. Alternative Strategies, Inc.
Jacobson, David M. . . . . . . '13 '36 C&L.597 B.S.L., J.D. 716 York Court‡
Jann, Irwin G., (BV) . . . . . . '42 '66 C&L.209 J.D. [I.G.Jann&Assoc.]
Jann, Irwin G., & Associates, P.C., (BV) . . . . . . 465 Central Ave.
Jasilli, Barry A. . . . .'46 '77 C.262 B.S. L.724 J.D. Sr. Legal Coun., Caremark Rx, Inc.
Jensen, Cynthia L. '56 '81 C.504 B.A. L.209 J.D.
[Ⓐ Erickson-Papanek-Peterson-Erickson]
Johnson, Brian E. . . . . . . '60 '86 C.477 B.A. L.602 J.D. PotashCorp Legal
Johnson, Donna J. . . . . . . '55 '83 C.475 B.A. L.574 J.D. Coun., Allstate Insurance Co.
Johnson, Joseph C. . . . . . . '44 '69 C.210 B.A. L.912 J.D. [J.C.Johnson]
Johnson, Rodney K. . . . . . . '37 '61 C&L.597 B.S., J.D. 333 Skokie Blvd.
Johnson, Joseph C., P.C. . . . . . . 1205 Shermer Road
Joyce, Sally O. . . . . . . '64 '94 C.436 B.S. L.424 J.D. [Ⓐ O'Halloran,K.G.&C.]
Judge, Thomas C., (AV) . . . . . . '58 '83 C.188 B.A. L.477 J.D. 544 Greenwood Road
Jurkash, Carole Randolph '61 '85
C.145 A.B. L.976 J.D. V.P., & Asst. Gen. Coun., Grubb & Ellis
Justesen, Kristina J. . . . . . . '68 '93 C&L.879 B.A., J.D. 3100 Dundee Rd.
Kalkowski, Michael J. . . . . . . '58 '83 C.209 B.A. L.424 J.D. 4201 Lake Cook Rd.
Kantor, Myron . . . . . . '40 '65 C.352 B.A. L.209 LL.B. [Kantor&A.]
Kantor & Apter, Ltd. . . . . . . 650 Dundee Rd.
Kaplan, Jack S., (BVⓉ) . . . . . . '53 '79 C.221 B.A. L.146 J.D. 1331 Church St.‡
Kasperson, Richard W. . . . . . . '27 '58 C.475 B.A. L.597 J.D. 1339 Eastwood Dr.‡
Katz, David . . . . . . '47 '71 C.339 B.S. L.209 J.D. [D.Katz]
Katz, David, Ltd. . . . . . . 3175 Commercial Ave.
Kaufman, David A. . . . . . . '62 '87 C.339 B.S. L.424 J.D. 555 Skokie Blvd.
Keating, William M. . . . . . . '53 '78 C.339 B.S. L.424 J.D. Lane Industries Inc.
Keiler, Louis C., (AV) . . . '47 '71 C.424 A.B. L.597 J.D. 555 Skokie Boulevard, Suite 500
Keleher, Brendan J., (BV) . . . . '54 '80 C&L.424 B.A., J.D. 555 Skokie Blvd., Ste. 500
Kelly, Timothy G. . . . . . . '60 '87 C.700 B.A. L.365 J.D. Allstate Ins. Co.
Kennedy, Llewellyn . . . . . . '68 '98 C.940 B.A. L.146 J.D. [Ⓐ Weil&Assoc.]
Kierig, Paul N. '52 '77 C&L.339 B.A., J.D.
Asst. V.P., Asst. Secy. & Asst. Gen. Coun., Allstate Insurance Co.
King, Angela Marie '68 '95 C.475 B.A. L.276 J.D.
(adm. in FL; not adm. in IL) Assoc. Coun., Allstate Insurance Co.
King, James P. . . . . . . '49 '76 C.339 B.A. L.146 J.D. Coun., Allstate Insurance Co.
Klasky, Bennett R., & Associates . . . '57 '84 C.801 B.A. L.146 555 Skokie Blvd., Ste. 500
Knox, Michael S. '59 '85 C.352 B.A. L.494 J.D.
Sr. V.P. & Claims Atty., C.R. Vince and Assoc., Inc.
Koenig, Ray J., III . . . . . . '73 '99 C.475 B.A. L.209 J.D. [Ⓐ Peck,B.A.&M.] ⊙
Kolehmainen, Philip M., (AV) . . . . '38 '64 C.976 B.S. L.597 J.D. [Mason,K.R.&W.] (Pat.)
Kosky, Kenneth A. . . . . . . '58 '85 C.339 B.A. L.365 J.D. [Strauss&M.]
Koslow, Alan J. . . . . . . '49 '76 C.910 B.S.B.A. L.209 J.D. 3501 Prestwick Lane‡
Kosoff, Clifford G. . . . . . . '54 '78 C.446 B.A. L.365 J.D. [O'Halloran,K.G.&C.]
Kramer, Jeremy J. . . . . . . '71 '96 C.347 B.A. L.365 J.D. [Ⓐ Strauss&M.]
Krieger, Joseph, (AV) . . . . . . '44 '69 C&L.477 B.S.E.E.E., J.D. [Mason,K.R.&W.] (Pat.)
Krisor, Alphons S., Jr. . . . . . . '12 '43 C.999 L.365 LL.B. 1032 Shermer Rd.
Kron, JoAnne L. . . . . . . '56 '81 C.339 B.A. L.365 J.D. Coun., Allstate Insurance Co.
Krumpelt, Andrew '66 '93 C.145 B.A. L.910 J.D.
Sr. Corp. Coun., Underwriters Laboratories, Inc.
Lampel, Justin Kyle . . . . . . '73 '01 C.338 B.S. L.365 J.D. [Lampel&Assoc.]
Lampel & Associates, P.C. . . . . . . 555 Skokie Blvd., Ste. 500
Landau, Beth A. . . . . . . '65 '90 C.1036 B.A. L.94 J.D. 3644 Dauphine Ave.
Langtry, Alfred L., III '67 '93
C.477 B.A. L.209 J.D. Gen. Counsel, Banner Property Managment
Lapham, Elizabeth (Beth) J. '— '91
C.37 B.S. L.477 J.D. Coun., Corp. Law, Allstate Insurance Co.
Lapin, Harvey I., (AV) . . . . . . '37 '63 C&L.597 B.S., J.D. 2592 Chedworth Ct.
LaVarre, Donald J. . . . . . . '34 '60 C.424 B.S. L.209 J.D. 650 Dundee Rd.
Lavin, Donald S. . . . . . . '43 '68 C.966 B.S. L.209 J.D. 95 Revere Dr.
Lazaroff, Cathy A. Glaser '50 '78 C.529 A.B. L.262 J.D.
(adm. in MI; not adm. in IL) Asst. V.P., Allstate Ins. Co.
Leavitt, William S. '52 '77 C&L.477 A.B., J.D.
Pres., Leavitt Financial Consultants, Inc.
Lee, Wei . . . '— '04 C.339 B.A. L.209 J.D. Corp. Sec. Investigator, Allstate Insurance Co.
Lees, Susan LeSueur '57 '87 C.103 A.B. L.623 J.D.
Asst. V.P., Asst. Gen. Coun. & Asst. Secy., Allstate Insurance Co.
Leonard, David R. '41 '71 C.1057 A.B. L.818 J.D.
(adm. in ME; not adm. in IL) 2775 Sanders Rd.
Lerner, Jerome . . . . . . '20 '50 C&L.424 LL.B. 1250 Rudolph Dr.‡
Leston, Kristine E. '48 '85
C.339 B.S. L.597 J.D. Coun., Corp. Law, Allstate Insurance Co.
Levinson, Cara B. . . . . . . '56 '90 C.788 B.A. L.146 J.D. 500 Skokie Boulevard
Levit, Louis W., (AV) . . . . . . '23 '47 C&L.145 B.S., J.D. 555 Skokie Blvd., Ste. 500
Levun, Charles R., Ltd., (AV) . . . . . . '44 '70 C.339 B.S. L.145 J.D. [Levun,G.&C.] ⊙

Levun, Goodman & Cohen, LLP, (AV)
Comprised of Professional Corporations
500 Skokie Boulevard Suite 650, 60062 ⊙
Telephone: 847-509-7700 Fax: 847-509-7709
Email: lgc@lgclaw.com URL: http://www.lgclaw.com
Lawrence S. Goodman, Ltd.; Charles R. Levun, Ltd.; Michael J. Cohen, Ltd.; Gary B. Shulman, Ltd.; Jeffery S. Taylor, Ltd.; Lee A. Arbus, Ltd. Associates: Susan J. Berkun; Susan H. Booker; Vasili D. Russis. Of Counsel: Robert D. Gorman; Charles L. Mervis.
General Business and Tax Practice including Federal and State Taxation, Corporate Law, Partnership Law, Employee Benefits and Executive Compensation, Real Estate, Estate Planning, Estate and Trust Administration, and Commercial Litigation.
Chicago, Illinois Office: One North LaSalle Street, Suite 1920. Telephone: 312-263-4661.
See Professional Biographies, NORTHBROOK, ILLINOIS

Levy, Irving H. . . . '30 '56 C.228 B.A. L.309 LL.B. 60 Avon Rd.
Levy, Joyce A. . . . '55 '81 C.976 B.A. L.880 J.D. [Strauss&M.]
Lewinthal, Robert A. . . . '51 '76 C.208 B.A. L.146 J.D. [Lewinthal,S.&Assoc.]

Lewinthal, Sklamberg & Associates
633 Skokie Boulevard, Suite 410, 60062
Telephone: 847-480-0110 Fax: 847-480-0156
Email: lewinthal@comcast.net URL: http://www.adignifieddivorce.com
Members of Firm: Robert A. Lewinthal; Sandra H. Sklamberg.
Family Law, Divorce, Child Custody, Child Support, Spousal Support, Domestic Relations, Alimony, Matrimonial, Palimony, Paternity, Premarital Agreements and Separation Agreements, Divorce Tax Considerations.
See Professional Biographies, NORTHBROOK, ILLINOIS

Lewis, Geoffrey A. '48 '75 C.98 B.A. L.365 J.D.
Mng. Corp. Coun.-Litig. Servs., Underwriters Labs. Inc.
Lewis, Philip S. . . . '39 '64 C.477 B.B.A. L.309 LL.B. [Gass&L.] ⊙
Lieberman, Richard L. . . . '57 '83 C.966 B.B.A. L.146 J.D. 175 Fairview Ln.
Lihosit, Steven '64 '89 C.339 B.S. L.365 J.D.
Coun., Claim Litig., Allstate Insurance Co.
Limperes, Donna '50 '79 C.589 B.S. L.424 J.D.
Asst. V.P. & Asst. Gen. Coun., Allstate Insurance Co.
Lipman, Philip '70 '99 C.813 B.S. L.309 J.D.
(adm. in NY; not adm. in IL) 1416 Hemlock Knoll Ter.
Locandro, Diane S. '53 '79
C.504 B.A. L.424 J.D. Gen. Coun., Focused Health Solutions, Inc.
Locascio, Mark A. . . . '57 '83 C.927 B.S. L.209 J.D. 450 Skokie Blvd.

Locke, Barry, & Associates, LTD.
(See Chicago)

Longeway, Christopher T. . . . '67 '95 C.602 B.B.A. L.589 J.D. Allstate Insurance Co.
Lowe, Jung Y. . . . '— '58 C.162 B.A. L.976 J.D. [AmericAsia G.L.]
Lowry, Thomas F., III . . . '52 '77 C&L.339 B.S., J.D. Dir. of Taxes, Lane Industries, Inc.
Lumicao, Benjamin E. . . . '66 '91 C&L.228 A.B., J.D. Coun., Allstate Insurance Co.
Lyons, Richard . . . '25 '57 C.569 M.B.A. L.262 J.D. 3851 Mission Hills Road
MacKay, Jon C. '45 '70 C.602 B.A. L.477 J.D.
Asst. V.P., Asst. Sec. & Asst. Gen. Coun., Allstate Insurance Co.
Madigan, John E. . . . '— '87 C.602 B.A. L.880 J.D. 2801 Fern Ave.
Magas, Amy . . . '77 '05 C.350 B.S. L.1000 J.D. 1751 Shawnee Trail
Maharaj, Dhana S. . . . '64 '87 C&L.999 LL.B., L.E.C. 1101 Skokie Boulevard
Malk, Arnold B. . . . '47 '72 C.339 B.A. L.209 J.D. [Strauss&M.]
Maloney-Knauff, Patrice '59 '85 C.589 B.A. L.1000 J.D.
Coun., Allstate Insurance Co.
Mangan, Joseph R. (Casey), Jr. '54 '81
C.800 B.A. L.597 J.D. Coun., Corp. Law, Allstate Insurance Co.
Mantilla, Felix A. '55 '80 C&L.966 B.B.A., J.D.
Asst. V.P. & Asst. Gen. Coun., Allstate Insurance Co.
Markovitz, Michael J. . . . '52 '77 C.608 B.A. L.146 J.D. Pres., Ferris Auto Leasing
Marsh, Christyl L. . . . '70 '96 [Ⓐ Cohen S.&H.]
Marziani, Rula '67 '92 C.339 B.A. L.365 J.D.
Sr. Corp. Coun., Underwriters Labs. Inc.
Masia, Jacqueline Rothbart '66 '91 C.477 B.A. L.146 J.D.
Atty., Rothbart Construction Co.
Mason, Kolehmainen, Rathburn & Wyss, (AV) . . . 853 Sanders Road, # 330 (Pat.)
Mathews, John R. . . . '52 '77 C&L.602 B.B.A., J.D. Coun., Allstate Life Insurance Co.
May, Jane M. . . . '66 '91 C.145 B.A. L.93 J.D. [Ⓐ O'Halloran,K.G.&C.]
Mayer, Lynn Rosenthal '52 '82 C.801 B.A. L.1000 J.D.
Legal Coun., Caremark Rx, Inc.
Mazer, Jeffrey A. '58 '84 C.604 A.B. L.94 J.D.
(adm. in NY; not adm. in IL) Portfolio Mgr., Allstate Ins. Co.
McAllister, Harl L., Jr. . . . '30 '60 C.209 L.365 LL.B. 1843 Milton Ave.‡
McCabe, Michael J. '45 '71 C.173 B.S. L.128 J.D.
(adm. in DC; not adm. in IL) Sr. V.P. & Gen. Coun., Allstate Ins. Co.
McClelland, Michael P. . . . '48 '78 C.424 A.B. L.1151 J.D. 1487 Shermer Rd.
McDonnell, Timothy D. '46 '71
C&L.209 B.A., J.D. V.P. & Gen. Coun., Trailmobile Corp.
McElvain, Peter A. . . . '62 '88 C.473 B.A. L.966 J.D. Coun., Allstate Insurance Co.
McEnroe, Megan E. '59 '84 C.201 B.A. L.365 J.D.
Asoc. Coun., Corp. Law, Allstate Insurance Co.
McGinn, Mary J. '47 '70 C.999 B.A. L.734 J.D.
V.P. & Dep. Gen. Coun., Allstate Insurance Co.
McGuire, David A., (AV) . . . '46 '74 C.1016 B.S.B.A. L.209 J.D. [Stone,M.&S.] ⊙
McHale, David A., (BVⓉ) '61 '87 C.767 B.A. L.464 J.D.
(adm. in CA; not adm. in IL) Allstate Insurance Company (⊙Rancho Cordova, CA)
McKenna, Michael R., (AV) '48 '76 C.339 B.S.M.E. L.146 J.D.
666 W. Dundee Rd., Ste. 1706 (Pat.) (⊙Kailua-Kona, HI; Chgo., IL)
McLaughlin, John A. . . . '59 '85 C.339 B.A. L.365 J.D. Coun., Allstate Insurance Co.
Meister, Barry P. . . . '54 '79 C.339 B.S. L.597 J.D. 1200 Shermer Rd.
Melgares, Gregory J. . . . '66 '96 C.190 B.S.B.A. L.424 J.D. [Ⓐ O'Halloran,K.G.&C.]
Mellon, Jane M. '— '89 C.238 B.S. L.365 J.D.
Coun., Corp. Law, Allstate Insurance Co.
Mervis, Charles L., (AV) . . . '41 '67 C.31 B.A. L.424 J.D. [Ⓒ Levun,G.&C.]
Meyerson, David S. . . . '63 '89 C.339 B.A. L.862 J.D. [Elizer&M.]
Miller, Darren K., Law Offices of '61 '91 C&L.209 B.A., J.D.
3000 Dundee Rd., Ste. 306
Mills, Kendall Richelle '71 '97 C.339 B.S. L.365 J.D.
Corp. Sec. Investigator, Allstate Insurance Co.
Millsaps, Joseph Reed . . . '57 '85 C.597 B.S. L.146 J.D. [J.R.Millsaps]
Millsaps, J. Reed, Law Offices of . . . 3100 Dundee Rd., Ste. 501
Minkus, April A. . . . '65 '90 C.966 B.A. L.209 J.D. Assoc. Coun., Allstate Insurance Co.
Mitchell, D. Rebecca . . . '53 '80 C.823 B.A. L.107 J.D. [Peck,B.A.&M.] ⊙
Mitchell-Fox, Debra F. . . . '56 '85 C.378 B.A. L.36 J.D. 630 Dundee Rd., Ste. 125
Molay, Mark D. . . . '68 '94 C.352 B.A. L.436 J.D. [Ⓐ Wiczer&Z.]
Moon, Sun Jin . . . '71 '98 C.31 B.A. L.477 J.D. Asst. Coun., Allstate Insurance Co.
Moran, Edward J. . . . '45 '73 C.728 B.S. L.831 J.D. Coun., Allstate Ins. Co.
Moran, Mary E. . . . '55 '83 C.381 B.A. L.161 J.D. The Child & Fam. Law Ctr.
Moran, Patrick Booth . . . '73 '01 C.1172 B.A. L.1187 J.D. Platinum Legal Services, P.C.
Morgen, Perry M. . . . '53 '78 C.597 B.A. L.146 J.D. [Morgen&F.]
Morgen & Fox . . . 555 Skokie Blvd., Ste. 595
Morita, Carol Hiromi '64 '90 C.597 B.S.J. L.608 J.D.
Mng. Corp. Coun.-Intl., Underwriters Labs. Inc.
Morris, Karen S. . . . '60 '85 C.742 B.A. L.339 J.D. Coun., Allstate Insurance Co.
Mortge, Barry I., (BV) . . . '60 '85 C.269 B.A. L.469 J.D. [Ⓐ Cohen S.&H.]
Morton, Kent J. '61 '88 C.1027 B.S. L.976 J.D.
(adm. in VA; not adm. in IL) Proj. Dir., SkyGen Energy
Moynihan, John F. . . . '61 '86 C.608 B.A. L.424 J.D. Sen. Atty., General Binding Corp.
Mulvihill, Meghan Orr '63 '90 C.289 B.A. L.64 J.D.
(adm. in MD; not adm. in IL) Assoc. Coun., Allstate Insurance Co.
Mulvihill, Michael F. '53 '83 C.686 B.S. L.1137 J.D.
(adm. in CA; not adm. in IL) Coun., Allstate Insurance Co.
Murphy, Michael A. . . . '48 '75 C.985 B.A. L.190 J.D. Coun., Allstate Insurance Co.
Nadell, Glenn A. . . . '52 '77 C.446 B.A. L.705 J.D. 3906 Bordeaux Ct.
Nadig, David G. '60 '85 C.339 B.S. L.424 J.D.
Asst. V.P. & Asst. Gen. Coun., Allstate Insurance Co.
Nebolsky, Shannon L. . . . '65 '96 C.339 B.Sc. L.597 J.D. [Pioneer] (Pat.)
Nemeth, George G. . . . '42 '68 C&L.569 B.A., J.D. Pollio Dairy Products
Nickow, Hy . . . '19 '50 C.597 B.S. L.424 J.D. Pres., General Loose Leaf Bindery Co., Inc.
Noeth, Lawrence A. '23 '51 C&L.930 B.B.A., LL.B.
(adm. in OH; not adm. in IL) 1849 Walnut Cir.‡
Notaro, Frank J. . . . '63 '89 C.107 B.S.E.E. L.145 J.D. V.P., G.C., Sec., IDEX Corp.
Oakes, Christopher D. . . . '61 '87 C.966 B.A. L.146 J.D. 3330 Dundee Rd., Ste. S-3
O'Halloran, James E., Jr., (AV) . . . '38 '65 C.165 B.A. L.597 J.D. [O'Halloran,K.G.&C.]

O'Halloran, Kosoff, Geitner & Cook, P.C., (AV)
Edens Corporate Center, Fourth Floor, 650 Dundee Road, 60062
Telephone: 847-291-0200 Fax: 847-291-9230
URL: http://www.okgc.com
James E. O'Halloran, Jr.; Clifford G. Kosoff; Neal P. Geitner; Gerard W. Cook; Mark M. Anderson; Julie A. Bruch;—George J. Casson, Jr.; Sally O. Joyce; Jane M. May; Stacy M. Overby; Gregory J. Melgares; Elisha S. Rosenblum.
Civil Trial and Appellate Practice in Federal and State Courts. Complex and Multi-District Litigation, Civil Rights and Government Tort Liability, Municipal Liability Defense, Construction, Insurance, Product Liability Defense, Securities, Estate Planning, Real Estate, Corporate, Commercial Transactions and Business Law.
See Professional Biographies, NORTHBROOK, ILLINOIS

Olsen, Donald G. . . . '62 '89 C.339 B.A. L.911 J.D. [D.G.Olsen]
Olsen, Donald G., P.C. . . . 5 Revere Dr., Ste. 200
Olson, Norman L., Jr., (AV) . . . '27 '56 C.951 A.B. L.339 J.D. [Olson,G.&F.]
Olson, Grabill & Flitcraft, (AV) . . . 707 Skokie Boulevard, Suite 420
Omura, Kenneth I. . . . '59 '84 C.339 B.A. L.188 J.D. Coun., Allstate Insurance Co.
O'Regan, James J. '44 '75 C.436 B.A. L.146 J.D.
Tax Coun., Wolters Kluwer U.S. Corp.
Orlowsky, Alan G. . . . '49 '75 C.339 B.S. L.146 J.D. [A.G.Orlowsky]
Orlowsky, A.G., Ltd. . . . 630 Dundee Road, Suite 125
Orzoff, Stewart C. . . . '43 '66 C.1016 B.A. L.209 J.D. 450 Skokie Blvd.
Overby, Stacy M. . . . '65 '90 C.1365 B.B.A. L.659 J.D. [Ⓐ O'Halloran,K.G.&C.]
Padilla, Jesse Paul . . . '77 '04 C.436 B.A. L.966 J.D. Asst. Coun., Allstate Insurance Co.
Page, Deborah G. . . . '53 '78 C&L.477 B.A., J.D. 1417 Kingsport Ct.‡
Palmer, L. Guy . . . '51 '79 C.859 B.A. L.215 J.D. [Palmer&Assoc.] ⊙

Palmer and Associates LLC
Two Northbrook Place, 60 Revere Drive, Suite 600, 60062 ⊙
Telephone: 847-272-6900 Fax: 847-272-6905
Email: gpalmer@palmerlaw.net
L. Guy Palmer.
Taxation, Estate and Gift Taxation, ERISA, Real Estate and Business Law, General Commercial Practice.
Frederick, Maryland Office: 615 West Patrick Street, 21701. Telephone: 301-695-0700; 800-732-7907. Fax: 301-695-0701.

Panarese, Nicholas D. . . . '56 '82 C.259 B.S. L.589 J.D. 2750 Waters Ave.
Papanek, Samuel, III, (AV) '45 '70
C.597 B.S.B.A. L.146 J.D. [Erickson-Papanek-Peterson-Erickson]
Papastratakos, Nick . . . '59 '86 C.173 B.S. L.146 J.D. Coun., Allstate Insurance Co.
Parmly, Jeffrey A. '62 '90
C.339 B.S. L.589 J.D. Sr. Corp. Coun., Underwriters Labs. Inc.
Patinkin, Howard P. . . . '32 '77 C.1016 B.S. L.209 J.D. 1713 Sunnyside Circle
Pavich, Megan M. . . . '78 '03 C.473 B.A. L.424 J.D. Asst. Coun., Allstate Insurance Co.
Pawlan, Mitchell D., (BV) . . . '57 '82 C.338 B.S. L.365 J.D. [M.D.Pawlan]
Pawlan, Mitchell D., Ltd., (BV) . . . 650 Dundee Rd., Ste. 250
Pearlman, Alan . . . '46 '74 C.209 B.M. L.365 J.D. [A.Pearlman]
Pearlman, Alan, Ltd. . . . 707 Skokie Blvd., Suite 600
Peck, Kerry R., (AV) . . . '52 '78 C.589 B.S.Ed. L.146 J.D. [Peck,B.A.&M.] ⊙
Peck, Bloom, Austriaco & Mitchell, LLC, (AV) . . . 601 Skokie Boulevard (⊙Chicago)
Pehlke, Robert E. . . . '47 '76 C.339 B.S. L.365 J.D. Coun., Allstate Insurance Co.
Perellis, Florie Shertzer '57 '82 C.1044 B.A. L.273 J.D.
Asst. V.P., Asst. Gen. Coun. & Asst. Secy., Allstate Insurance Co.
Perlik, Stuart . . . '47 '93 C&L.424 B.S., J.D. 4028 Dundee Rd.

Perrelli, Anthony
(See Deerfield)

Perry, Joy Ann (Jan) '56 '80 C.338 B.S. L.1048 J.D.
(adm. in CT; not adm. in IL) Allstate Plaza
Perry, Sheldon '38 '65 C.176 B.A. L.1009 J.D.
(adm. in NY; not adm. in IL) Pres., Take a Meeting Productions, Inc.
Pestine, Ronald G. . . . '47 '73 C.347 B.S. L.209 J.D. 555 Skokie Blvd., Rm. 595
Peterson, Julie A. '58 '83 C.1106 B.A. L.300 J.D.
[Erickson-Papanek-Peterson-Erickson]
Peterson, Richard F. . . . '25 '51 C&L.209 B.S., J.D. 425 Huehl Rd.
Phillips, Mary Ann . . . '61 '87 C.339 B.S.W. L.209 J.D. Coun., Allstate Insurance Co.
Pieper, Mark Eric . . . '71 '00 C.477 B.A. L.597 J.D. Assoc., SFX Baseball

Pinsel, David L., P.C., Law Offices of
(See Rolling Meadows)

Pioneer Patent, LLC
1334 Shermer Road, Suite 220, 60062
Mailing Address: P.O. Box 128, Northbrook, IL 60065-0128
Telephone: 847-412-0073 Fax: 847-412-0074 URL: http://www.Pioneer-Patent.com
Email: NEBOLSKY@Pioneer-Patent.com URL: http://www.lawyers.com/pioneerpatent
Shannon L. Nebolsky.
Intellectual Property, Patent, Trademark, Copyright, Licensing Agreements and Trade Secrets. Entertainment Law.
See Professional Biographies, NORTHBROOK, ILLINOIS

Plunkett, Kevin M. . . . '65 '90 C.299 B.A. L.424 J.D. Sr. Legal Coun., Caremark Rx, Inc.

Podwika, Joseph A. '62 '88 C.107 B.A. L.597 J.D.
(adm. in NY; not adm. in IL) Sr. Legal Coun., PotashCorp Legal
Poli, Carl E. ... '52 '78 C.424 A.B. L.209 J.D. [Stone,M.&S.] ⊙
Pollak, Jay M., (AV) ... '37 '62 C.473 B.S. L.597 J.D. [Pollak]
Pollak, Michael E., (AV) ... '41 '66 C.473 B.S. L.424 J.D. [Pollak]
Pollak Law Firm, P.C., The, (AV) ... Suite 301 1200 Shermer Road
Pollard, Beth ... '66 '91 C.339 B.A. L.879 J.D. Coun., Allstate Insurance Co.
Poole, Anthony (Tony) '54 '81
C.674 A.B. L.93 J.D. Coun., Corp. Law, Allstate Insurance Co.
Pozin, Mendy L., Ltd. ... '56 '84 C.339 B.A. L.424 J.D. 853 Sanders Rd.
Pringle, Homer S. ... '30 '62 C&L.188 B.S., J.D. 333 Pfingsten Rd.‡
Prousis, Michael T. ... '48 '73 C.339 B.A. L.436 J.D. Div. Chf., Sp. Asst. Atty. Gen.
Quinn, Gerald T. ... '58 '85 C&L.623 B.A., J.D. [G.T.Quinn]
Quinn, Mary Jo ... '55 '88 C.957 B.S. L.1065 J.D. Coun., Allstate Insurance Co.
Quinn, Gerald T., Chartered ... 1240 Neadow Rd.
Radogno, Joseph A., (AV) '58 '84 C.339 B.A. L.146 J.D.
Coun., Allstate Insurance Co.
Rakowski, L. Steven ... '64 '90 C.339 B.A. L.365 J.D. 899 Skokie Boulevard, Suite 300
Rapaport, Steven I. ... '58 '84 C.228 A.B. L.910 J.D. [S.I.Rapaport]

Rapaport, Steven I., Law Offices of
630 Dundee Road, Suite 120, 60062-9280
Telephone: 847-559-9270 Fax: 847-559-9280
Email: raplaw@ameritech.net
Steven I. Rapaport; Steven Herzberg.
Workers Compensation, Personal Injury, Automobile Accidents, Construction Accidents, Criminal Law, Traffic Violations, DWI, Insurance, Legal Malpractice, Estate Planning.
See Professional Biographies, NORTHBROOK, ILLINOIS

Rath, Joseph P., (AVⓉ) '49 '74 C.737 B.A. L.602 J.D.
(adm. in OH; not adm. in IL) Asst. V.P. & Asst. Gen. Coun., Allstate Insurance Co.
Rawson, Jerold S. ... '47 '74 L.209 J.D. [Rawson&Assoc.]
Rawson & Associates ... 1935 Shermer Rd., Ste. 220
Reed, Allen R., (BV) ... '59 '84 C.339 B.S. L.347 J.D. Assoc. Coun., Allstate Ins. Co.
Rego, Charles A. '70 '96 C.93 B.S. L.209 J.D.
Sr. Corp. Coun., Underwriters Laboratories Inc.
Reid, Colleen M., (AV) ... '60 '85 C&L.339 B.A., J.D. Coun., Allstate Insurance Co.
Reinert, John E., (AV) ... '36 '66 C.378 B.S. L.597 J.D. 4 The Court of Cobblestone
Reinfranck, James D. ... '62 '88 C.339 B.S. L.209 J.D. Coun., Allstate Insurance Co.
Reingold, Gordon A. ... '57 '82 C.910 A.B. L.904 J.D. Atty., The Reingold Co.
Reingold, Sara L. ... '54 '78 C.477 B.A. L.424 J.D. 899 Skokie Hwy.
Reinstein, Philip T., (AV) ... '37 '62 C.339 B.S. L.209 J.D. [Reinstein&S.]
Reinstein & Sherman, (AV) ... 910 Skokie Boulevard, Suite 109
Resnick, Myron J. ... '31 '56 C.659 B.S. L.477 J.D. Sr. V.P. & Treas., Allstate Ins. Co.
Ridge, Kieran T. ... '31 '58 C&L.93 B.S.B.A., LL.B. 2275 Sanders Rd.
Rippin, Joseph P., III ... '59 '86 C.560 B.A. L.339 J.D. Coun., Allstate Insurance Co.
Rissman, Lawrence E. ... '54 '79 C.976 B.S. L.477 J.D. [🄾 S.C.Weiss]
Roberts, Colleen M. ... '58 '00 C.136 B.A. L.424 J.D. Legal Coun., Caremark Rx, Inc.
Rochester, Richard R. ... '31 '59 C.339 B.S. L.146 LL.B. 3817 Eastwind Ct.‡
Rohlfing, Gregory C. ... '59 '85 C.340 B.A. L.365 J.D. Coun., Allstate Insurance Co.
Romano, Henry S., Jr. ... '48 '77 C&L.602 B.A., J.D. Health Cost Controls, Inc.
Rosborough, Susan L. '— '81
C.879 B.A. L.228 J.D. Coun., Corp. Law, Allstate Insurance Co.
Rose, Heather J. '75 '00 C.323 B.A. L.365 J.D.
[🄰 Erickson-Papanek-Peterson-Erickson]
Rosemarin, Carey S., (AV) ... '50 '78 C.477 B.S. L.838 J.D. [C.S.Rosemarin]

Rosemarin, Carey S., P.C., Law Offices of, (AV) [BR]
500 Skokie Boulevard, Suite 510, 60062
Telephone: 847-897-8000 Fax: 312-896-5786
Email: csr@rosemarinlaw.com URL: http://www.rosemarinlaw.com
Carey S. Rosemarin.
Environmental Law.
See Professional Biographies, NORTHBROOK, ILLINOIS

Rosemeyer, Donna Cox '58 '82
C.357 B.A. L.339 J.D. Legal Director, Allstate Insurance Co.
Rosenbaum, David G., (BVⓉ) '56 '84 C.293 B.A. L.146 J.D.
[Rosenbaum&Assoc.] (Pat.)
Rosenbaum & Associates, P.C., (BVⓉ) ... 650 Dundee Road, Suite 380 (Pat.)
Rosenbloom, Eric J. '62 '89 C.477 B.A. L.1068 J.D.
V.P. & Gen. Coun., Hillco Trading Company, Inc.
Rosenbloom, Jay A. ... '57 '82 C.339 B.S. L.146 J.D. 3914 Raintree Lane
Rosenblum, Elisha S. ... '69 '94 C.424 B.B.A. L.146 J.D. [🄰 O'Halloran,K.G.&C.]
Rosenfeld, Sheldon S. ... '34 '59 C&L.352 LL.B. 340 Wainwright Dr.
Rosenman, Robert O., (AV) ... '31 '56 C&L.477 B.B.A., J.D. [🄾 Strauss&M.]
Rosenthal, Ryan M., & Associates ... '74 '99 C.966 B.A. L.146 J.D. 1034 Cobblestone Ct.
Rosner, Julie E. ... '57 '84 C.477 B.G.S. L.209 J.D. 920 Huckleberry Lane‡
Ross, Mark A. ... '50 '77 C.339 B.A. L.209 J.D. Allstate Ins. Co.
Rothbart, Gary B. '46 '72 C.966 B.B.A L.1065 J.D.
V.P., Rothbart Construction Co., Inc.
Rothenbaum, Norman L., (AV) ... '33 '57 C&L.597 B.S.L., J.D. [N.L.Rothenbaum]
Rothenbaum, Norman L., P.C., (AV) ... 555 Skokie Blvd.
Ruben, Kristen ... '65 '91 C.339 B.S. L.146 J.D. 3605 Woodhead Dr.
Rubin, Edward M. ... '54 '79 C.339 B.A. L.424 J.D. 4224 Yorkshire Lane‡
Rubin, Gerald M. ... '30 '54 C.46 B.S. L.209 J.D. 1800 Mission Hills Rd., E.
Rubin, Steve '47 '72 C.352 B.A. L.209 J.D.
V.P., Secy. & Gen. Coun., General Binding Corp.
Ruchim, Mitchell B. ... '60 '86 C.477 B.S. L.146 J.D. 3000 Dundee Rd.
Rudd, Terri L. ... '57 '83 C.477 A.B. L.569 J.D. 2148 Clover Road
Ruiz, James E. '43 '82 C.477 B.Arch. L.1119 J.D.
V.P. & Claims Atty., C.R. Vince & Assocs., Inc.
Ruskin, Howard M. ... '31 '55 C&L.209 LL.B. 555 Skokie Blvd.‡
Russis, Vasili D. ... '66 '95 C.339 B.S. L.146 J.D. [🄰 Levun,G.&C.]
Sabin, Robert L. ... '51 '76 C.339 B.S. L.597 J.D. 650 Dundee Rd., Ste. 250
Saeks, Jerrold N. ... '38 '64 C&L.209 B.S.C., J.D. 3956 Dundee Rd.
Sales, Charlene K. ... '51 '76 C.339 B.S. L.597 J.D. 1450 Coral Pkwy.
Salk, Bruce A. ... '54 '79 C&L.352 B.A., J.D. [Cohen S.&H.]
Schechter, Stewart F. ... '53 '79 C.339 B.S. L.424 J.D. [Schechter&Assoc.]
Schechter & Associates ... 555 Skokie Boulevard, Suite 260
Scheinman, Andrew '60 '02 C.339 B.S. L.61 J.D.
(adm. in NC; not adm. in IL; Pat.) [🄰 Rosenbaum&Assoc.]
Schiller, Arthur J. '54 '80 C.118 B.A. L.339 J.D.
V.P., Secy. & Gen. Coun., Lane Industries, Inc.
Schloss, William K. ... '54 '81 C.339 B.S. Acctg. L.146 1458 Kingsport Ct.‡
Schorsch, Martin B. ... '63 '90 C.36 B.S. L.365 J.D. 601 Skokie Blvd., Ste. 101
Schreiber, Eliot B. ... '56 '81 C.103 B.A. L.597 J.D. 990 Skokie Blvd.
Schroeder, Edward H. ... '05 '29 C.937 L.144 957 Suffield Ter.‡
Schulze, Eric W. '— '97 C.338 B.S. L.436 J.D.
Asst. Coun., Corp. Law, Allstate Insurance Co.
Schuman, John G. ... '62 '97 C.999 B.Mus.Ed. L.145 J.D. Cyber Tech.
Schuman, Robert A., Law Offices of ... '51 '76 C.352 B.B.A. L.146 J.D. 555 Skokie Blvd.
Schuster, Philip A. ... '52 '80 C.602 A.B. L.930 J.D. Coun., Allstate Insurance Co.
Sennett, Carolyn S. '67 '92
C.103 A.B. L.597 J.D. Sr. Corp. Coun., Underwriters Labs. Inc.
Sennett, Richard S. ... '23 '48 L.597 J.D 555 Skokie Blvd.
Sernett, Richard P. ... '38 '63 C&L.352 B.B.A., J.D. 2579 Fairford Lane‡
Shah, Sheetal R. ... '79 '03 C.209 B.S. L.966 J.D. [🄰 Kantor&A.]
Shandles, H. Martin ... '57 '85 C&L.966 B.B.A., J.D. Coun., Allstate Insurance Co.
Shandling, Fred I. ... '44 '68 C.339 B.A. L.209 J.D. 2409 The Strand
Shapera, Louis M. ... '19 '42 C&L.145 A.B., J.D. 801 Skokie Blvd.
Shapiro, Bruce K., (BV) ... '57 '82 C.477 B.G.S. L.146 J.D. [B.Shapiro]
Shapiro, Bruce, Law Office of, (BV) ... 555 N. Skokie Blvd., Ste. 500
Sharp, Robert W., (AV) ... '22 '50 C&L.477 A.B., LL.B. 1520 Grant Rd.‡
Sheffey, Steven R. ... '60 '86 C&L.597 B.A., J.D. Coun., Allstate Insurance Co.
Sherman, Burton A. ... '36 '63 C&L.209 B.S., J.D. [Reinstein&S.]
Sherman, Sidney S. ... '09 '33 L.209 LL.B. 1831 Mission Hills Rd.‡
Shifris, Donald S. ... '35 '59 C&L.209 J.D. 3170 Commercial
Shimkus, Alexander R. '62 '93
C.190 B.S.B.A. L.801 J.D. Assoc. Coun., Allstate Insurance Co.
Shulman, Gary B., Ltd., (AV) ... '55 '80 C.339 B.A. L.365 J.D. [Levun,G.&C.]

Shults, David M., Law Offices of '73 '03 C&L.209 B.S., J.D.
555 Skokie Boulevard, Suite 500, 60062
Telephone: 847-480-1020 Fax: 847-480-7859
Email: lawdms@yahoo.com
Commercial Law, Civil Litigation, Real Estate, and Family Law.
See Professional Biographies, NORTHBROOK, ILLINOIS

Siegel, Michael L., (AV) ... '50 '75 C.293 B.A. L.339 J.D. [Stone,M.&S.] ⊙
Silver, Barry Stewart ... '49 '74 C.339 B.S. L.209 J.D. [B.S.Silver]
Silver, David W. ... '62 '87 C.347 B.S. L.146 J.D. 155 Trailwood Lane
Silver, Barry S., P.C. ... 707 Skokie Blvd.
Silverman, David J. '47 '78 C.912 B.A. L.215 J.D.
(adm. in MI; not adm. in IL) Legal Dir., Allstate Ins. Co.
Silverman, Steven E. ... '49 '75 C.339 B.A. L.209 J.D. 630 Dundee Rd.
Silvertrust, Raymond H. R. ... '46 '77 C.597 B.A. L.823 J.D. 1227 Alleghany Lane
Simmons, Robert L. ... '— '90 C.588 B.S. L.209 J.D. Reg. Coun., Allstate Insurance Co.
Simonaitis, William E. '68 '93
C.436 B.A. L.209 J.D. Assoc. Coun., Allstate Insurance Co.
Simpson, G. Northrup, Jr. ... '29 '59 C.31 B.A. L.146 LL.B. P.O. Box 424‡
Singer, Shelvin ... '31 '60 C.589 B.S.E. L.209 J.D. Cir. J.
Sitz, David N. ... '66 '95 C.488 B.A. L.61 J.D. Assoc. Coun., Allstate Insurance Co.
Sklamberg, Sandra H. ... '53 '81 C.339 B.A. L.146 J.D. [Lewinthal,S.&Assoc.]
Smith, Charles M. ... '70 '95 C.352 B.S. L.902 J.D. Assoc. Coun., Allstate Insurance Co.
Smith, Diane Stern ... '56 '81 C.910 A.B. L.30 J.D. 1800 Larkdale‡
Smith, Katherine A. ... '60 '99 Asst. Coun., Corp. Law, Allstate Insurance Co.

Snow & Snow, Ltd.
(See Chicago)

Sobel, Alan P. ... '43 '69 C.339 B.A. L.209 J.D. 2801 Shannon Rd.
Soloway, Brett D. '68 '93
C.477 B.A. L.339 J.D. V.P. & Gen. Coun., Red Seal Develop. Corp.
Spitz, David M. ... '48 '75 C.477 B.A. L.597 J.D. 3330 Dundee Road
Staab, Michael J., (BV) '55 '81 C.263 B.A. L.221 J.D.
V.P., Legal Servs. & Mng. Coun., Caremark Rx, Inc.
Stasica, Richard, V ... '77 '02 C&L.602 B.B.A., J.D. Coun., Shell Vacations LLC
Steele, Thomas P. '47 '77
C.1105 B.A. L.945 J.D. Coun., Corp. Law, Allstate Insurance Co.
Stein, Mark S. ... '54 '79 C.339 B.A. L.146 J.D. 95 Revere Dr., Ste. J
Stern, Hamilton ... '29 '54 C&L.597 B.B.A., J.D. 1544 B. Shermer
Stevens, Jason Blake ... '— '03 C.338 B.S. L.365 J.D. 900 Skokie Blvd., Ste. 208
Stewart, Charles L., Jr., (AV) ... '19 '48 C.339 A.B. L.145 J.D. 2525 Mayapple Ct.‡
Stiles, William Robert ... '41 '96 C.309 A.B. L.424 J.D. 1500 Sherner Rd.
Stone, Howard L., (AV) ... '41 '72 C.1016 B.S.B.A. L.209 J.D. [Stone,M.&S.] ⊙

Stone, McGuire & Siegel, (AV) [BR]
801 Skokie Boulevard, Suite 200, 60062 ⊙
Telephone: 847-239-7555 FAX: 847-239-7556
URL: http://www.stonemcguire.com
Members of Firm: Howard L. Stone; David A. McGuire; Michael L. Siegel; Carl E. Poli.
Federal and State Taxation, IRS Circular 230, Administrative Law, General Corporate and Commercial Law, Healthcare, Business Acquisitions and Dispositions, General Securities, Computer Fraud and Employee Embezzlement Law, Probate, Not-For-Profit Governance, Criminal Tax Law, Criminal and Civil Trial and Appellate Practice in all State and Federal Courts.
See Professional Biographies, NORTHBROOK, ILLINOIS

Strauss, Benton C., (AV) ... '47 '72 C.339 B.A. L.424 J.D. [Strauss&M.]
Strauss, Michael S. ... '70 '98 C.966 B.S. L.146 J.D. [🄰 Strauss&M.]

Strauss & Malk LLP, (AV)
A Limited Liability Partnership including Professional Corporations
135 Revere Drive, 60062
Telephone: 847-562-1400 Chicago: 312-441-0900 Fax: 847-562-1422
Email: straussmalk@straussmalk.com URL: http://www.straussmalk.com
Arnold B. Malk; Benton C. Strauss; Joyce A. Levy; Kenneth A. Kosky; Brad S. Grayson;—Michael S. Strauss; H. Jay Glaubinger; Michelle H. Gooze-Miller; Jeremy J. Kramer. Of Counsel: Robert O. Rosenman; Harold R. Burnstein.
Estate Planning, Wealth Preservation, Probate, Business Succession Planning, Corporate Law, Business Acquisitions and Sales, Real Estate Acquisition and Development, Business and Real Estate Financing, ERISA, Executive Compensation, Professional Service Businesses, Tax Law, Litigation including Commercial, Business Transactions, Real Estate, Trusts and Estates and Torts.
See Professional Biographies, NORTHBROOK, ILLINOIS

Stremler, Darrell J. ... '59 '86 C.114 B.A. L.178 J.D. 2215 Sanders Rd.
Szuter, Gregory P., (AVⓉ) '45 '73 C.363 B.A. L.930 J.D.
500 Skokie Boulevard, Suite 350 (⊙Cleve., OH)
Tarver, Benjamin A. '54 '85 C.570 B.S.I.E. L.564 J.D.
(adm. in NJ; not adm. in IL) Asst. V.P., Allstate Insurance Co.
Taxe, Stephen M., Law Offices of ... '41 '67 C&L.209 B.S.C., LL.B. 2159 Valencia
Taylor, Jeffery S., Ltd., (AV) ... '56 '81 C.347 B.A. L.365 J.D. [Levun,G.&C.]
Teichner, Bruce A. '— '85 C.352 B.A. L.209 J.D.
Assoc. Coun., Allstate Insurance Co.
Temple, Marvin W., (AV) ... '28 '51 C.145 Ph.B. L.597 LL.B. 555 N. Skokie Blvd.
Thursby, W. Gerald, (AV) ... '32 '61 C.813 A.B. L.477 LL.B. 1 Ct. of Chapelwood‡
Timothy, Michael C. ... '57 '85 C.966 B.A. L.146 J.D. 4201 Lake Cook Rd.
Tish, Elyse M., (BV) '61 '87
C.339 B.A. L.597 J.D. V.P. & Asst. Gen Coun., Grubb & Ellis
Tolmatsky, Alexander ... '61 '91 C.1183 B.S. L.365 J.D. [A.Tolmatsky]

Tolmatsky, Alexander, Ltd., Law Office of 3000 Dundee Rd., Ste. 320
Topol, Morris '25 '50 C.1016 L.209 LL.B. 3 Court of Harborside
Torf, Philip R. '52 '84 C.339 B.S. L.365 J.D. [Torf]
Torf Law Firm 2210 Ash Lane
Trabaris, Kevin E. '62 '88 C.339 B.A. L.228 J.D. Coun., Allstate Insurance Co.
Tressel, Harry K. '43 '73 C.95 A.B. L.597 J.D. 2785 Shannon
Umbrarescu, Dimitrie B., Law Office of '75 '02
C.424 B.A. L.209 J.D. 555 Skokie Blvd., Ste. 500
Vainikos, Efie M. '73 '99 C.597 B.A. L.146 J.D. Asst. Coun., Allstate Insurance Co.
Vainisi, William A. '57 '82 C.339 B.A. L.209 J.D.
Asst. V.P., Asst. Secy. & Asst. Gen. Coun., Allstate Insurance Co.
Vavra, Richard J. '58 '83 C&L.209 B.S.C., J.D. Coun., Allstate Insurance Co.
Velotta, Michael J. '46 '73 C.68 B.A. L.117 J.D.
(adm. in OH; not adm. in IL) Sr. V.P., Secy. & Gen. Coun., Allstate Insurance Co.
Vlamis, Georgia L. '60 '85 C.339 B.S. L.209 J.D. Sr. Litig. Coun., Motorola, Inc.
Vogel, Howard J. '50 '76 C.589 B.S. L.365 J.D. 3000 Dundee Rd.
Vogelman, Richard P. '42 '69 C.589 B.S. L.597 J.D. 2775 Sanders Rd.
Vold, Michael '41 '80 C.966 B.S. L.209 J.D. 1535 Lake Cook Rd.
Walton, Anne M. '64 '01 C.347 B.S. L.209 J.D. Asst. Coun., Allstate Insurance Co.
Wanger, Anthony L. '68 '93 C.1365 B.A. L.94 J.D. Asst. Gen. Coun., Sterling Capital
Wathen, Charles F. '19 '52 C.801 B.A. L.734 LL.B.
(adm. in MO; not adm. in IL) Allstate Ins. Co.
Weber, Lesley R. '75 '00
C.475 B.A. L.424 J.D. Asst. Coun. II, Allstate Insurance Company
Weil, Sandra M. '44 '79 C&L.502 B.A., J.D. [Weil&Assoc.]

Weil & Associates
60 Revere Drive, Suite 888, 60062
Telephone: 847-509-0015 Fax: 847-509-0021
Email: weil@weilassoc.com URL: http://www.weilassociates.com
Sandra M. Weil. Associate: Llewellyn Kennedy.
Family Law, Divorce, Collaborative Law, Adoptions, Child Custody, Child Support, Divorce, Domestic Violence, Premarital Agreements, Spousal Support.
See Professional Biographies, NORTHBROOK, ILLINOIS

Weingart, Scott '60 '85 C&L.339 B.S., J.D. Chunowitz, Teitelbaum & Baerson
Weinstock, Lawrence W. '37 '63 C.339 B.S. L.597 J.D. 910 Skokie Blvd. Ste. 109
Weinstock, Louis A. '53 '77 C.339 B.A. L.146 J.D. 490 Banyan Dr.
Weis, LeRoy, (AV) '04 '27 C.339 B.S. L.477 J.D. 1250 Rudolph Rd.‡
Weisenberg, Scott A. '70 '96
C.378 B.A. L.339 J.D. Assoc. Gen. Coun., Red Seal Develop. Corp.
Weiss, Howard J. '51 '78 C.801 B.A. L.146 J.D. 3400 Dundee Rd., Ste. 310

Weiss, Steven C., Law Offices of, (AV) '56 '79 C&L.146 B.S., J.D. BR
One Northbrook Place, 5 Revere Drive, Suite 200, 60062
Telephone: 312-782-3415 Fax: 312-782-3421
Email: scweiss@msn.com URL: http://www.lawyers.com/weisslawfirm
Of Counsel: Lawrence E. Rissman.
Logistics and Supply Chains, Third Party Supplier Contracting, Freight Forwarding, Freight Brokers, Admiralty and Maritime Law, Business Transactions, Corporate Law, Inland Marine Law, Marine Cargo, Air Cargo, Freight Loss and Damage, Insurance Coverage Disputes, Interstate Commerce, Motor Carrier Defense, Motor Carrier Liability, Shipping Regulation, Surface Transportation.
See Professional Biographies, NORTHBROOK, ILLINOIS

Weiszmann, Fred, Jr. '21 '49 C&L.597 B.S., J.D. 1356 Shermer Ave.
Wenc, Stephen H. '66 '91 C.602 B.A. L.276 J.D.
Actg. Gen. Coun., Underwriters Laboratories Inc.
Whitlock, Lyndon J. '30 '56 C&L.597 B.S., J.D. 2840 Sugar Pine Circle
Whitted, Brooke R., (AV) '46 '78 C.612 B.S. L.365 J.D. [Whitted,C.&T.]
Whitted, Linda Murakishi '57 '82 C.477 B.A. L.424 J.D.
(adm. in WI; not adm. in IL) 3000 Dundee Road‡
Whitted, Cleary & Takiff, (AV) 3000 Dundee Rd., Ste. 303
Wiczer, Bernard, (AV) '37 '62 C.597 B.S.B.A. L.145 J.D. [Wiczer&Z.]
Wiczer, Elliot Scott '65 '91 [Wiczer&Z.]
Wiczer & Zelmar, LLC, (AV) 500 Skokie Boulevard
Willemsen, Lisette S. '— '02 C.769 B.A. L.464 J.D.
Asst. Coun., Allstate Insurance Co.
Wilson, Candice '— '94 C.103 A.B. L.424 J.D. Allstate Insurance Company
Wilson, Jodi Givner '54 '87 C.763 B.A. L.800 J.D. 630 Dundee Rd., Ste. 125
Wintroub, Alene P. '55 '80 C.910 B.A. L.209 J.D. 4317 Oak Knoll Ct.
Wippman, Tom David '59 '84 C&L.339 A.B., J.D. 1033 Skokie Boulevard
Wise, Frank J. '43 '68 C.659 B.S. L.150 J.D. Allstate Ins. Co.
Wiseman, Debra Ann '— '87 C.339 B.S. L.365 J.D. 2561 Anne Lane
Wisniewski, Mark B. '67 '93 C.424 L.190 555 Skokie Blvd., Ste. 500
Wochner, James J. '45 '71 C&L.734 A.B., LL.B. [Wochner]
Wochner Law Firm 707 Skokie Blvd., Ste. 500
Wojciechowski, Margaret C. '52 '84
C.801 B.S.W. L.365 J.D. Sr. Corp. Coun., Underwriters Labs. Inc.
Yang, Frank Z. '60 '95 C.339 B.S. L.597 J.D. [Rosenbaum&Assoc.] (Pat.)
Yang, Luke D. '76 '03 C.339 B.S. L.424 J.D.
Corp. Sec. Investigator, Allstate Insurance Co.
Young, Terry R. '60 '93 C.612 B.B.S. L.325 J.D. Assoc. Coun., Allstate Insurance Co.
Zelmar, Michael A. '42 '67 C.339 B.S. L.209 J.D. [Wiczer&Z.]
Zigterman, Paul '57 '83 C.114 B.A. L.339 J.D. Coun., Allstate Insurance Co.
Zilberstein, Seymour R. '44 '69 C.339 A.B. L.424 J.D.
Prin., Consulting Fiduciaries, Inc.
Zimmerman, Frank '46 '75 C.339 B.S. L.365 J.D. 2100 Valencia Dr.‡
Zimmerman, Gerald L., Jr. '66 '93 C.966 B.A. L.190 J.D.
Coun., Allstate Insurance Co.
Zivin, Lee R., (AV) '10 '35 C.597 B.S. L.146 LL.B. 3330 Dundee Rd.
Zucker, Susan M. '57 '83 C&L.424 A.B., J.D. 3585 Pleasant St.
Zukowski, Janet M. '— '82
C.221 B.A. L.352 J.D. Coun., Corp. Law, Allstate Insurance Co.
Zwirn, Sherwood M. '41 '67 C.221 B.S. L.146 LL.B. [S.M.Zwirn&Assoc.]
Zwirn, Sherwood M., & Associates, Ltd. 910 Skokie Blvd.

NORTH CHICAGO, 35,918, *Lake Co.*

Albrecht, James L. '32 '64 C.388 B.A. L.209 J.D. Sr. Atty., Abbott Labs.‡
Anderson, Robert J. '— '93 L.818 J.D.
(adm. in MA; not adm. in IL) Sr. Coun., Abbott Labs.
Baruffi, Stephen L. '51 '87 C.98 B.S. L.180 J.D.
(adm. in MA; not adm. in IL) Sr. Coun., Abbott Labs.
Becker, Cheryl L. '64 '90 C.446 B.S. L.930 J.D. Sr. Coun., Abbott Labs. (Pat.)
Bergeson, Patricia T., (AV) '51 '76 C.475 B.A. L.602 J.D.
Gen Coun., Finch Univ. of Health Sci./The Chicago Med. Sch.
Berman, Clifford E. '59 '85 C.477 B.S.Pharm. L.424 J.D. Sr. Coun., Abbott Labs.
Berry, John A. '52 '77 C.597 B.A. L.424 J.D.
Div. V.P., Legal, Secs. & Benefits, Abbott Labs.
Breitkopf, Laurel D. '53 '79 C.914 B.A. L.209 J.D. Abbott Laboratories
Buchbinder, Lysle V. '— '01 C.1375 B.A. L.112 J.D.
(adm. in CA; not adm. in IL) Coun., Abbott Labs.
Chavez, Margarita Isabel Misa '— '97 C&L.770 B.S., J.D.
(adm. in CA; not adm. in IL) Coun., Abbott Labs.
Chen, Portia '72 '97 C.339 B.S. L.990 J.D. Coun., Abbott Labs. (Pat.)
Collins, Kathryn Shaw '— '91 C.197 B.A. L.976 J.D. Sr. Coun., Abbott Labs.
Corbin, Johanna M. '75 '02 C.602 B.S. L.209 J.D. Coun., Abbott Labs. (Pat.)
Dean, Clifford A. '27 '53 C&L.477 B.S.E., J.D. Sr. Pat. Atty., Abbott Labs. (Pat.)
Deane, Dana D., (AV) '59 '86 C.1229 B.A. L.477 J.D. Sr. Coun., Abbott Labs.
DeBerardine, Robert '58 '83 C.390 B.S. L.188 J.D.
(adm. in CA; not adm. in IL; Pat.) Div. V.P., Chf. Patent &, Abbott Labs.
Dezelan, Deborah E. '— '98 C.475 B.S. L.602 J.D. Coun., Abbott Labs.
Downing, Paul A. '20 '50 L.209 LL.B. V.P., Kenosha Svgs. & Loan Assn.
Egan, James J. '50 '75 C.276 B.S.F.S. L.770 J.D. Assoc. Div. Coun., Abbott Labs.
Felician, Nicole L. '— '99 C.597 G.S.J. L.966 J.D. Coun., Abbott Labs.
Ferrari-Dileo, Gabryleda '— '02 C.999 B.S. L.424 J.D. Coun., Abbott Labs.
Fishman, David S. '— '83 C.339 B.A. L.424 J.D. Div. V.P., Abbott Labs.
Foley, Michael J. '32 '61 C.885 B.A. L.923 LL.B.
(adm. in WV; not adm. in IL) V.P., Abbott Laboratories
Frekko, Matthew T. '72 '00 C.165 B.A. L.276 J.D.
(adm. in MD; not adm. in IL) Coun., Abbott Labs.
Gersten, Steven N. '62 '89
C&L.94 B.S.B.A., J.D. Div. V.P., Legal Regulatory, Abbott Labs.
Gherlein, David G. '— '90 C.608 B.S. L.1003 J.D. Coun., Abbott Labs.
Goldberg, Honey Lynn '— '82 C.103 A.B. L.309 J.D.
Div. V.P., Dom. Legal Oper. & Asst. Secy., Abbott Labs.
Goller, Mimi C. '66 '93 C&L.436 B.S., J.D.
(adm. in WI; not adm. in IL) Coun., Abbott Labs.
Gorman, Edward H., Jr. '38 '77 C.446 B.S. L.262 J.D.
(adm. in IN; not adm. in IL; Pat.) V.P. & Assoc. Gen. Coun., Abbott Labs.
Grundin, Katherine M. '60 '84 C.597 B.A. L.46 J.D. Sr. Atty., Abbott Labs
Gunther, Laurie T. '— '91 C.188 A.B. L.597 J.D. Sr. Coun., Abbott Labs.
Hale, Karen L. '68 '93 C.228 B.A. L.945 J.D. Sr. Coun., Abbott Labs.
Hannum, David C. '53 '82 C.597 B.S.Che. L.424 J.D. Abbott Laboratories
Hickey, Nicole Vickroy '70 '95 C.473 B.A. L.930 J.D.
(adm. in OH; not adm. in IL; Pat.) Abbott Laboratories
Holden, Thomas P. '49 '78 C.679 B.S. L.365 J.D. Abbott Laboratories
Husami, Mateen I. '66 '95 C.790 B.S. L.146 J.D. Coun., Abbott Labs.
Jonaus, Laura J. '63 '88 C.602 B.B.A. L.966 J.D. Abbott Laboratories, Abbott Park
Jursich, John T. '28 '50 C.339 L.209 J.D. 1500 Sheridan Rd.
Kim, Nancy M. '71 '96 C.340 B.A. L.602 J.D. Sr. Coun., Abbott Labs.
Klein, Michael J. '— '94 C&L.339 B.A., J.D. Coun., Abbott Labs.
Koenen, Deborah K. '70 '95 C&L.339 B.S., J.D. Coun., Abbott Labs.

Lasky & Rifkind, Ltd.
(See Chicago)

Lee, Lisa I. '— '97 C.597 B.S. L.145 J.D. Coun., Abbott Labs.
Levitan, Lara M. '69 '94 C.429 B.A. L.569 J.D.
Sr. Coun., Abbott Laboratories (Legal Department)
Lussen, John F. '42 '67 C&L.262 B.S., J.D.
(adm. in NY; not adm. in IL) Abbott Laboratories

Mandell Menkes LLC
(See Chicago)

Martinez, Rita L., (AV) '50 '81 C.530 B.S. L.424 J.D. Sr. Coun., Abbott Labs.
McCann, Michael E., (AV Ⓣ) '72 '97 C.602 B.B.A. L.276 J.D. Coun., Abbott Labs.
McElroy, Marian Frances '53 '81 C.329 B.A. L.597 J.D. 1700 20th St.
Michael, Edward L. '57 '82 C.347 A.B. L.1119 J.D. Div. Coun., Abbott Labs.

Novak, Paul B.
(See Waukegan)

Orleski, Gregory M.C. '— '89 C.982 B.A. L.012 LL.B.
(adm. in QU; not adm. in IL) Sr. Coun., L.A./Canada, Intl. Legal Opers., Abbott Labs.
Pappamichiel, Melissa L. '65 '88 C.424 B.S. L.339 J.D. 2834 Green Bay Rd.
Parker, Lisa J. '— '95 C.393 B.A. L.734 J.D. Coun., Abbott Labs.
Parker, Neal B. '64 '92 C.893 B.A. L.273 J.D. Sr. Coun., Abbott Labs.
Parks, Michelle Ann '74 '99 L.146 J.D. 100 Abbott Park Rd.
Petros, Peter P. '68 '95 C.347 B.A. L.879 J.D. Coun., Abbott Labs.
Porembski, Priscilla E. '— '87 C.339 B.S. L.146 J.D. Sr. Coun., Abbott Labs.
Poulos, Nicholas A., (AV) '54 '80 C.679 B.S.C.E. L.145 J.D.
Div. V.P., Pat., Pharma Products, Abbott Labs. (Pat.)
Qazi, Sulaiman M. '72 '00 C.339 B.S. L.365 J.D. Coun., Abbott Labs.
Risher, Jeff C. '73 '99 C.197 B.A. L.1068 J.D.
(adm. in CA; not adm. in IL) Coun., Abbott Labs.
Rivera, Jose E. '66 '90 C.93 B.A. L.309 J.D. Div. V.P., Litig., Abbott Labs.
Roge, Paul E. '42 '67 C&L.339 B.S., J.D.
Assoc. Gen. Coun., Domestic Oper., Abbott Labs.
Rogers, Rick L. '53 '86 C.238 B.S. L.424 J.D. Abbott Labs
St-Gelais, Marie-Claude '— '94 L.018 LL.L
(adm. in QU; not adm. in IL) Coun., Intl. Legal Opers., Abbott Labs.
Sazdanoff, Catherine A. '56 '81 C.602 B.A. L.597 J.D. Sr.Coun., Abbott Laboratories
Schodin, David J. '65 '01 C.388 B.A. L.146 J.D. Pat. Coun., Abbott Labs. (Pat.)
Schumacher, Laura Jonaus '63 '88 C.602 B.B.A. L.966 J.D.
Sr. V.P., Sec. & Dep. Gen. Coun., Corp. Legal Div., Abbott Labs.
Sommers, Mary K. '52 '81 C.694 B.A. L.436 J.D. Abbott Laboratories
Sprague, Henry H. (Hal) '57 '85 C.951 B.A. L.174 J.D. Coun., Abbott Labs.
Steele, Gregory W. '53 '88 C.801 B.S. L.352 J.D.
(adm. in IA; not adm. in IL; Pat.) Sr. Coun., Abbott Labs.

Sternberg, David M.
(See Chicago)

Trimble, Thomas D. '47 '72 C.967 B.A. L.851 J.D. Div. Coun., Abbott Labs.
Tunick, Bonnie I. '59 '85 C.339 B.S. L.597 J.D. Sr. Atty., Abbott Labs.
Van Stan, Rana Abbasi '73 '98 C.597 B.A. L.424 J.D. Coun., Abbott Labs.
Velasco, Juan Pablo Malfavón-Ruiz '75 '98
(adm. in Mexico; not adm. in IL) Legal & Prices Mngr., Abbott Labs.
Veoukas, April T. '67 '95 C.424 B.S. L.209 J.D.
Sr. Regulatory Compliance Proj. Mgr., Abbott Laboratories
Vlahos, Georgia '59 '85 C.607 B.A. L.597 J.D. Naval Training Ctr. Great Lakes
Vrioni, Beth A. '— '94 C.350 B.S. L.589 J.D. Coun., Abbott Labs. (Pat.)
Ward, Michael J. '— '96 C.423 B.S. L.146 J.D. Coun., Abbott Labs.
Ward, Shane M. '74 '02 C.893 B.A. L.276 J.D. Coun., Abbott Labs.
Wardell, David A. '54 '83 C.674 A.B. L.930 J.D. Div. V.P., Int'l Legal, Abbott Labs.
Wark, Allen W. '56 '81 C.475 B.S. L.912 J.D.
(adm. in MI; not adm. in IL; Pat.) Sr. Coun., Abbott Labs.
Weinstein, David L. '— '75 C.679 B.S. L.502 J.D. Coun., Abbott Labs. (Pat.)

Weishaar, Henry A. '46 '75 C.1070 B.S. L.209 J.D.
Div. V.P., Pers., Abbott Laboratories
Well, Sarah .... '69 '95 C.881 B.A. L.145 J.D. Coun., Abbott Labs.
Wilcox, James L. '51 '80 C.97 B.S. L.851 J.D.
(adm. in OH; not adm. in IL; Pat.) Assoc. Div. Coun., Abbott Labs.
Winburn, Mary L. .... '— '69 C&L.339 B.A., J.D. Coun., Abbott Labs.
Wittenberg, Kenneth A., (AVⓉ) '65 '90
C&L.477 B.A., J.D. Sr. Coun., Legal Regulatory, Abbott Labs.
Yee, Stephanie Kim .... '61 '88 C.893 B.A. L.276 J.D. Abbott Labs.

NORTHFIELD, 5,389, *Cook Co.*

Bailey, Richard A. '49 '76 C&L.028 B.A., LL.B.
(adm. in ON; not adm. in IL) Sr. V.P. & Dep. Gen. Coun., NA, Kraft Foods Global, Inc.
Banks, Theodore L. '51 '76
C.72 B.A. L.208 J.D. Assoc. Gen. Coun., Kraft Foods Global, Inc.
Barthel, Tara Klena .... '70 '96 C.57 B.A. L.339 J.D. 211 Waukegan Rd.
Bass, Howard I. .... '38 '60 C.339 B.S. L.597 LL.B. 550 Frontage
Biagi, Richard B. .... '70 '01 C.339 B.M. L.209 J.D. [A Neal&M.]
Bley, Kenneth W. .... '49 '79 C.393 B.A. L.146 J.D. 2014 Suffork Road
Blumenthal, Martin A. .... '52 '81 C.1183 B.S. L.146 J.D. 1 Northfield Plz., Ste. 300
Brandstrader, Thomas C., (AV) '49 '79
C.763 B.A. L.1137 J.D. 181 Waukegan Road, Suite 306 (☉Chicago)
Bright, Steven .... '55 '80 C.597 B.S. L.209 J.D. [Levenfeld P.] ☉
Brown, Charles B. '56 '82
C.276 B.S.B.A. L.988 J.D. Founder/Princ., CorpLaw Associates
Burke, Jerome J. .... '— '62 C.602 B.S. L.276 J.D. Pres., Burke Enterprises, Inc.
Bynoe, Carol A. .... '— '90 C.879 B.A. L.146 J.D. Sr. Atty., Stepan Co.
Carnow, Donald S. .... '42 '67 C.1016 B.S.B.A. L.365 J.D. 778 Frontage Rd.
Caudill, Kathryn Lind .... '58 '83 C.710 B.A. L.352 J.D. 790 Frontage Rd.

Chatzky, Paul, Law Offices of, (AV) '58 '83 C&L.260 B.A., J.D. BB
790 West Frontage Road, Suite 212, 60093
Telephone: 847-441-4288 Fax: 847-441-4289
Email: pc@chatzkylaw.com URL: http://www.chatzkylaw.com
General Practice, Divorce, Family Law, Criminal Defense, Felonies, Driving While Intoxicated, Real Estate, Business Law, Estate Planning, Wills, Personal Injury and Civil Litigation.
See Professional Biographies, NORTHFIELD, ILLINOIS

Chernoff, Michael G., (AV) '35 '59 C&L.145 B.A., LL.B.
Suite 300, One Northfield Plaza
Cherry, Douglas W. '60 '89 C.929 B.S. L.477 J.D.
Sr. Trademark Coun., Kraft Food Holings Inc.
Christman, Deirdre A. .... '— '79 C.121 B.A. L.597 J.D. [D.B.Kahn&Assoc.]
Condon, Kevin J. .... '53 '79 C.339 B.A. L.209 J.D. 1869 Stockton Dr.
Dallmeyer, Suzanne Beman ...... '47 '77 C.881 B.A. L.365 J.D. 466 Central Ave., Ste. 47
Daly, James J. '55 '83 C.690 B.S. L.424 J.D.
Sr. Tax Coun., Philip Morris Management Corp.
Damon, Robert J. C. .... '30 '54 C.197 B.A. L.966 J.D. 2323 Pebble Fork Ln.
Di Giacomo, Carol A. .... '52 '82 C.339 B.A. L.146 J.D. [C.&K.S.DiGiacomo]

Di Giacomo, Carol & Kathryn Somers, L.L.C.
211 Waukegan Road, Suite 105, 60093
Telephone: 847-784-8900 Fax: 847-784-8929
URL: http://www.digiacomo-somersllc.com
Carol A. Di Giacomo; Kathryn M. Somers.
Family Law, Divorce, Collaborative Law, Child Custody, Child Support, Spousal Support, Visitation, Adoption, Mediation and Complex Family Law relating to Valuation and Tax Considerations, Estate Planning, Real Estate, Contract and Bankruptcy Law.
See Professional Biographies, NORTHFIELD, ILLINOIS

Divorce Mediation Institute of the North Shore .... 466 Central Road
Doherty, Christopher J. '56 '84 C.602 B.A. L.477 J.D.
Chf. Coun., Lit., Kraft Foods Global, Inc. (☉New York, NY)
Dubbs, John W. .... '16 '42 C.602 B.S. L.597 J.D. 540 W. Frontage Rd.
Dubbs, Rita K. .... '18 '45 C&L.597 B.A., J.D. 2329 Winnetka Ct.‡
Duperier, Laurie Plessala '64 '90 C.1096 B.A. L.276 J.D.
VP & Assoc. Gen. Coun., Altria Corporate Services, Inc.;
Dwyer, Christopher D. .... '67 '92 C.676 B.A. L.930 J.D. [C.Dwyer]

Dwyer, Christopher, Law Offices of
788 W. Frontage Road Suite 109, 60093
Telephone: 847-784-8606 Fax: 847-919-3821
Email: christopher_dwyer@yahoo.com
Christopher D. Dwyer.
Estate Planning, Estate Administration, Business Succession Planning, Income Tax Planning and Retirement Planning.
See Professional Biographies, NORTHFIELD, ILLINOIS

Eberts, F. Samuel, III '59 '85 C.424 B.S. L.94 J.D.
Gen. Coun., Secy., & V.P., Stepan Co.
Eisner, Seth A. '45 '76 C.597 B.A. L.145 J.D.
V.P. & Assoc. Gen. Coun., Corp. &. U.S. Sales, Kraft Foods Global, Inc.
Eklund, Roger P., (AV) .... '31 '56 C&L.309 A.B., LL.B. P.O. Box 8487
Endres, Krista A. '67 '92 C.914 B.A. L.178 J.D.
Dep. Corp. Secy. & Sr. Coun., Corp. & Secs., Kraft Foods Global, Inc.
Field, Henry F., (AV) .... '— '65 C.309 B.A. L.145 J.D. [D.B.Kahn&Assoc.]
Firestone, Marc S. ...... '59 '85 Exec. V.P., Gen. Coun. & Corop. Sect., Kraft Foods, Inc.
Friedman, Andrea E. .... '57 '85 C.339 B.A. L.145 J.D. [B Neal&M.]
Frohling, Susan Hanaway '64 '95 C.352 B.B.A. L.145 J.D.
Sr. Trademark Coun., Kraft Foods Holdings Inc.
Fuller, James '55 '80 C.269 B.A. L.260 J.D.
Labor Coun., Labor & Employ., Kraft Foods Global, Inc.
Fullerton, David S. .... '46 '72 C.207 B.A. L.339 J.D. 1775 Maple St.
Galvin, Deborah L. '51 '76 C.339 L.209 J.D.
Chf. Coun., Sales Strategy, Kraft Foods Global, Inc.
Gelfman, Paul M. .... '25 '53 C.209 L.365 J.D. [Gelfman&G.]
Gelfman, Stuart G. .... '59 '84 C.339 B.S. L.365 J.D. [Gelfman&G.]
Gelfman & Gelfman .... 550 Frontage Road, Suite 2720
Giller, Thomas M. '55 '83 C.311 B.A. L.1065 J.D.
Sr. Envir. & Worker Safely Coun., Kraft Foods Global, Inc.
Greenswag, Richard A. .... '54 '79 C.165 B.A. L.352 J.D. [Kaplan&G.]
Gregorcy, Philip D. '62 '87 C.697 B.S. L.589 J.D.
Sr. Tax Coun., Altria Corporate Services, Inc.
Harris, Morton J., (AV) .... '16 '39 C&L.145 B.A., J.D. [B Kwiatt&S.]
Herst, Robert L. '55 '80 C.339 B.A. L.424 J.D.
V.P., Assoc. Gen. Coun., Global Supply Chain, Kraft Foods Global, Inc.
Hielscher, William J. .... '60 '85 C.473 B.A. L.209 J.D. 550 W. Frontage Rd., Ste. 2700
Hurlbutt, James E. .... '53 '79 C.174 B.S. L.208 J.D. 2135 Northgate Rd.
Iverson, Lisa A. .... '63 '88 C&L.966 B.A., J.D. [Neal&M.]

Jaffe, Maria J. '— '02 C.424 B.S. L.365 J.D.
1 Northfield Plaza, Suite 300, 60093 ☉
Telephone: 847-441-1814
URL: http://www.mariajaffelawfirm.com
Adoption, Child Support, Criminal Law, Custody and Visitation, Debtor/Creditor, Divorce, Family Law, Immigration Law, Landlord/Tenant, Mediation, Medical Malpractice, Motor Vehicle Accidents, Plaintiff Personal Injury, Real Estate.
Chicago, Illinois Office: 8 South Michigan Avenue, Suite 3200, 60603. Telephone: 312-641-1052. Fax: 312-641-1052.
See Professional Biographies, NORTHFIELD, ILLINOIS

Jarett, Andrew R. .... '53 '80 C.494 B.E.S. L.1000 J.D. 466 Central Ave., Ste 34
Jesser, Steven H., (AV) ...... '48 '74 C.597 B.A. L.46 J.D. 790 Frontage Road, Suite 110
Kahn, David B., (AV) .... '— '67 C.910 B.A. L.309 J.D. [D.B.Kahn&Assoc.]
Kahn, Sharon N. .... '— '80 C.966 B.A. L.146 J.D. [D.B.Kahn&Assoc.]
Kahn, David B., & Associates, Ltd., (AV) .... One Northfield Plaza Suite 100
Kaplan, Daniel S. .... '58 '90 C.36 B.S. L.424 J.D. [Kaplan&G.] ☉

Kaplan & Greenswag LLC
181 Waukegan Road, Suite 205, 60093 ☉
Telephone: 847-501-5300 Fax: 847-501-5325
Email: firm@kaplangreenswag.com URL: http://www.kaplangreenswag.com
Daniel S. Kaplan; Richard A. Greenswag;—Jordon S. Steinway.
Commercial Litigation, Trial Practice, Dispute Resolution, Franchise Law, Bankruptcy Litigation, Business Law, Contracts, Unfair Competition, Covenants Not to Compete, Noncompetition and Non-Solicitation Agreements, Restrictive Covenants, Business Fraud, Deceptive Trade Practices, Trade Secrets, Estate Planning, Commercial Real Estate.
Chicago Office: 600 W. Jackson Boulevard, Suite 200, 60661.
See Professional Biographies, NORTHFIELD, ILLINOIS

Kehoe, Barbara Speer, Law Offices of '44 '77
C.911 B.A. L.838 J.D. 1855 Old Willow Road, Ste. 315
Kelly, William B. .... '63 '94 C.339 B.A. L.46 J.D. Cook Cty. St. Atty.
King, Mark E., (BV) .... '— '85 C.597 B.A. L.146 J.D. [D.B.Kahn&Assoc.]
Klauke, Joseph M. '— '95 C.339 B.A. L.145 J.D.
Bus. Coun., Kraft Foods Global, Inc.
Kohn, Sharon Elise '65 '90 C.103 B.A. L.477 J.D.
Coun., Mkting. & E-Commerce, Kraft Foods Global, Inc.
Kwiatt, Kenneth L., (AV) .... '36 '66 C.424 B.S. L.365 J.D. [Kwiatt&S.]
Kwiatt & Silverman, Ltd., (AV) .... 211 Waukegan Road
Lackner, Wolfram Sebastian '69 '01
Coun., Global Supply Chain, Kraft Foods Global, Inc.
Leimer, Jacqueline A. '51 '81 C&L.879 B.A., J.D.
Chf. Trademark Coun., Kraft Foods Holdings, Inc.

Levenfeld Pearlstein, LLC, (AV)
211 Waukegan Road, Suite 300, 60093 ☉
Telephone: 847-441-7676 Facsimile: 847-441-9976
Email: lplegal@lplegal.com URL: http://www.lplegal.com
Members of Firm: Steven Bright; Philip E. Ruben; William S. Schwartz. Associate: Steven M. Weiss. Corporate Law, Mergers, Acquisitions and Divestitures, Banks and Banking, Financial Institutions Law, Finance, Secured Lending, Federal Taxation, State Taxation, Securities, Bankruptcy, Workouts, Estate Planning, Employment Law.
Chicago Office: 2 North LaSalle Street, Suite 1300, 60602. Telephone: 312-346-8380. Facsimile: 312-346-8434.
See Professional Biographies, NORTHFIELD, ILLINOIS

Lynch, Joseph B. .... '17 '45 271 Crestwood
Marcouiller, Sheryl A. '50 '82 C.741 B.S. L.424 J.D.
Sr. Coun., Food Law, Kraft Foods Global, Inc.
Mattenson, David M., (AV) .... '45 '72 C.1016 B.M. L.146 J.D. One Northfield Plaza
McAllister, Robert W. .... '29 '80 C&L.93 B.S., J.D. [R.W.McAllister]
McAllister, Robert W., Ltd. .... 13 The Landmark
McDevitt, Kevin J. .... '65 '90 C.679 B.A. L.823 J.D. [Neal&M.]
McMurray, John W., (AV) .... '27 '53 C.1027 B.S. L.597 J.D. 1703 D Northfield Sq.‡
Miller, Debra H. .... '64 '89 C.477 B.A. L.966 J.D. [D.B.Kahn&Assoc.]
Nathan, Allan I., (AV) .... '43 '68 C.477 B.A. L.597 J.D. Two Northfield Plaza, Suite 340
Neal, Susan Somers .... '49 '82 C&L.209 B.A., J.D. [Neal&M.]

Neal & McDevitt
1776 Ash Street, 60093
Telephone: 847-441-9100 Fax: 847-441-0911
Email: info@nealmcdevitt.com URL: http://www.lawyers.com/nealmcdevitt
Members of Firm: Susan Somers Neal; Kevin J. McDevitt; Lisa A. Iverson;—Richard B. Biagi. Of Counsel: Andrea E. Friedman.
Intellectual Property Practice (including Trademarks, Copyrights, Unfair Competition, Licensing and Litigation).
See Professional Biographies, NORTHFIELD, ILLINOIS

Neylan, John F. .... '29 '55 C.276 B.S. L.178 LL.B. 2031 Old Willow Rd.
O'Day, Patrick C. .... '41 '65 C&L.339 B.A., J.D. [Divorce M.I.S.]
Parrish, Pam D. '— '82 C.575 B.A. L.146 J.D.
Sr. Coun., Employment Law, Kraft Foods Global, Inc.
Passis, Dennis P. ..... '42 '69 C.1016 B.S.B.A. L.209 J.D. Pres., Transworld Exhibits, Inc.
Pell, Wilbur F., III '45 '71
C.347 B.S. L.1119 J.D. Chf. Coun., Litig., Kraft Foods Global, Inc.
Peltz, Howard M. .... '28 '55 C.1016 A.B. L.145 J.D. 1780 Maple St.
Peters, Mildred G. .... '— '52 C&L.145 A.B., J.D. 540 Frontage Rd., Ste. 2320
Platt, John H., Jr. .... '23 '50 C&L.477 A.B., LL.B. 7 Old Hunt Rd.‡
Porter, Helen Viney .... '35 '61 C.347 A.B. L.421 J.D. 225 Maple Row
Rabyne, Milton .... '32 '61 C.339 B.S. L.209 J.D. 1 Northfield Plaza
Reiter, Burton L. '48 '73 C&L.477 B.A., J.D.
Chf. Coun., Labor & Benefits, Kraft Foods Global, Inc.
Rohner, James T. .... '40 '65 C&L.976 B.A., LL.B. The Instrumentalist
Rosenbloom, Sandra M. .... '41 '92 C.1016 B.A. L.424 J.D. 1 Northfield Plz., Ste. 300
Ruben, Philip E. .... '58 '83 C.339 B.S. L.146 J.D. [Levenfeld P.] ☉
Schwartz, William S. .... '65 '90 C.339 B.A. L.146 J.D. [Levenfeld P.] ☉
Silverman, Michael, (AV) .... '38 '66 C.1016 B.A. L.365 J.D. [Kwiatt&S.]
Snyder, Dean E. .... '46 '72 C.679 B.S. L.477 J.D. [D.E.Snyder&Assoc.]
Snyder, Dean E. & Associates, P.C. .... 189 Happ Rd.
Soler, Laurie Peard .... '60 '91 C.339 B.S. L.424 J.D. 211 Waukegan Rd.
Somers, Kathryn M. .... '53 '81 C.597 B.A. L.209 J.D. [C.&K.S.DiGiacomo]
Spak, David G. .... '62 '87 C.477 B.G.S. L.597 J.D. 2 Northfield Plaza
Spear, Kathleen Kelly '49 '79 C.788 A.B. L.597 J.D.
Sr. V.P. & Dep. Gen. Coun., North America, Kraft Foods Global, Inc.
Steinway, Jordon S. .... '79 '04 C.94 B.A. L.424 J.D. [A Kaplan&G.]
Sullivan, Dudley R., (AV) '16 '47
C.103 A.B. L.309 LL.B. 540 Frontage Rd., Willow Hill Exec. Ctr.
Thompson, J. Edward '42 '68 C&L.339 A.B., J.D.
Chf. Food Law Coun., Kraft Foods Global, Inc.
Ward, Kristin Lynn .... '74 '99 C.339 B.S. L.424 J.D. 790 Frontage Road
Weiner, Robert N. .... '51 '82 C.339 B.A. L.365 J.D. [R.N.Weiner]
Weiner, Robert N., P.C. .... 466 Central Ave., Ste. 34

Weinstein, Alvin I., (Ltd.) .... '16 '39 C&L.145 B.A., J.D. One Northfield Plaza‡
Weintraub, Gary A. .... '52 '76 C.597 B.A. L.146 J.D. 465 Central Ave.
Weiss, Steven M. .... '73 '02 C.846 B.A. L.146 J.D. [Ⓐ Levenfeld P.] ⊙
Wright, Debbie K., (AV) '55 '83
C.925 B.S. L.575 J.D. Chf. Pat. Coun., Kraft Foods, Inc. (Pat.)
Zimmerman, Hugh A. .... '34 '62 C.855 A.B. L.178 LL.B. 1 Northfield Plaza
Zuiker, Sharon S. '66 '92 C.339 B.S. L.309 J.D.
Sr. Real Estate & Bus. Coun., Kraft Foods Global, Inc.

NORTHLAKE, 11,878, *Cook Co.*

Berns, Favil D. .... '26 '52 C.46 B.S. L.365 J.D. 30 E. North Ave.
Berns, Louis A. .... '59 '84 C.36 B.S. L.365 J.D. 30 E. North Ave.
Harmon, Baron David .... '60 '84 C.1183 B.S. L.365 J.D. 30 E. North Ave.
Henker-Mattiessen, Jean .... '58 '84 C.209 B.A. L.365 J.D. 21 Macarthur Dr.
Miller, Glenn J. .... '61 '86 C&L.260 B.A, J.D 404 E North Avenue
Nussbaum, Howard J. .... '56 '82 C.339 B.S. L.146 J.D. 165 W. Lake St.
Ogisaka, James H. .... '16 '48 C.112 A.B. L.597 J.D. 213 S. Prater Ave.
Pauletto, James M. .... '54 '80 C&L.209 B.A., J.D. 220 E. North Ave
Russell, Lee H. .... '41 '79 58 E. North Ave.
Sherwin, Jeffrey T. .... '53 '78 C.1183 B.A. L.146 J.D. 220 E. North Ave.

NORTH RIVERSIDE, 6,688, *Cook Co.*

DiNatale, Joseph N. .... '42 '68 C.209 A.B. L.597 J.D. [DiNatale]
DiNatale Law Office .... 2501 Des Plaines Ave., Ste. A
Don, Robert E. '36 '62 C.174 B.S.B.A. L.145 J.D.
Chmn. of the Bd. & CEO, Edward Don & Co.
Dvorak, Liberty P. .... '17 '40 C.339 L.146 J.D. 2900 Lincoln Ave.‡
Giuliano, Vincent F. .... '45 '70 C.209 B.S. L.146 J.D. 7222 W. Cermak Rd.
Monaco, George M., Law Offices of, (AV) '43 '68 C.388 A.B. L.365 J.D.
P.O. Box 1364
Orehek, Frederick A. .... '49 '75 C.363 B.A. L.209 J.D. 2924 Des Plaines Ave.
Skryd, David A. .... '61 '86 C.424 B.S. L.146 J.D. 8933 W. Cermak Rd.
Skryd, Paul J. .... '57 '82 C.424 B.S. L.146 J.D. 8933 W. Cermak Rd.

OAK BROOK, 8,702, *DuPage Co.*

Abear, Anthony .... '— '92 C.339 B.A. L.209 J.D. 1010 Jorie Blvd., Ste. 337
Adel, Bryan R. .... '63 '88 C.477 A.B. L.966 J.D. 2915 Jorie Boulevard
Angelini, Philip M. .... '59 '85 C.339 B.A. L.209 J.D. 1900 Spring Rd., Ste. 500
Anjam, S. Naseem .... '54 '83 C.339 B.A. L.209 J.D. Coun., McDonald's Corp.
Arbetter, Charles M. .... '37 '72 C.209 B.S.C. L.365 J.D. 1200 Harger Road
Artman, Daniel J. .... '71 '97 C&L.209 B.A., J.D. [Ⓐ Power&C.]
Aument, Robert C. .... '59 '89 C.338 B.S. L.146 J.D. [Daspin&A.]
Bailey, Christopher M. '70 '99 C.1024 B.S. L.1119 J.D.
(adm. in IN; not adm. in IL) Coun., McDonald's Corp.
Bales, Richard F. .... '51 '86 C.337 B.A. L.589 J.D. Ticor Title Ins.
Baloga, Mark A. '63 '88 C.597 B.A. L.494 J.D.
(adm. in MN; not adm. in IL) 1220 Oak Brook Rd.‡
Barhydt, David K., Law Office of ...... '58 '86 C.405 B.A. L.146 J.D. 2901 Butterfield Rd.
Barnes, Karen Kay .... '50 '78 C.879 B.A. L.209 J.D. Mng. Coun., McDonald's Corp.
Barrette, Matthew P. .... '76 '01 C&L.602 B.A., J.D. [Ⓐ Sullivan H.&C.]
Bartlett, David F. .... '71 '96 C.963 B.S. L.209 J.D. Coun., McDonald's Corporation
Bass, Richard S. .... '56 '85 L.365 J.D. 2021 Midwest Rd.
Bauer, H. Dan .... '49 '77 C.927 B.B.A. L.365 J.D. 2901 Butterfield Rd.
Baum, Robert H. '43 '67 C.966 B.S. L.597 J.D.
Executive Vice President & General Counsel, Inland Real Estate Group, Inc.
Bedell, Mary Lynn '55 '91 L.424 J.D.
Sr. Coun., Mktg./Advertising, McDonald's Corp.
Bedrava, E. William, (AV) .... '41 '66 C.589 B.S. L.146 J.D. [Bedrava&L.]
Bedrava & Lyman, (AV) .... 1301 W. 22nd St.
Bellock, Charles J., (AV) .... '46 '73 C.215 B.S. L.436 J.D. [Manetti&G.]
Benedetto, Michael A., (BV) '44 '72 C.339 B.S. L.424 J.D.
1900 Spring Road, Suite 500
Bennett, Margaret A., (AV) .... '50 '76 C.112 A.B. L.424 J.D. [M.A.Bennett]

Bennett, Margaret A., P.C., Law Offices of, (AV) BR
1200 Harger Road, Suite 718, 60523-1908
Telephone: 630-573-8800 Fax: 630-573-9810
Email: mbennetlaw@aol.com URL: http://www.lawyers.com/mabennett
Margaret A. Bennett;—Anne V. Swanson; Richard G. Rius, Jr.
Family Law, Divorce, Domestic Relations, Marital Property Law, Child Custody, Child Support, Visitation Rights, Alimony, Spousal Support, Legal Separation, Equitable Distribution, Marital Agreements, Marital Property Settlements, Separation Agreements, Matrimonial Law, Post Divorce, Real Property.

See Professional Biographies, OAK BROOK, ILLINOIS

Berman, Adam E. .... '63 '88 C.339 B.A. L.597 J.D. Great Lakes REIT, Inc.
Bernstein, Ira P. '51 '77 C.994 B.A. L.851 J.D.
(adm. in NY; not adm. in IL) Mng. Coun., Labor Rel., McDonald's Corp.
Berres, Roger E. '48 '74 C.755 B.A. L.221 J.D.
(adm. in IA; not adm. in IL) WMX Technologies, Inc.
Bigoness, Nicholas M. .... '57 '85 C.1004 B.A. L.365 J.D. [Powers&B.]
Bishop, Robert B. .... '44 '69 McDonald's Corp.
Bishop and Bishop, A Professional Corporation, Law Office of ...... 100 Oakbrook Center

Bishop, Rossi & Scarlati, Ltd.
(See Oakbrook Terrace)

Bishop-Papp, Dilene .... '61 '88 C&L.174 B.A., J.D. 100 Oakbrook Ctr., Ste. 24
Bittourna, Bert K. .... '57 '82 C.209 B.A. L.339 J.D. 2901 Butterfield Rd.
Block, Bradley S., (BV) '62 '87
C.674 B.A. L.309 J.D. Managing Coun., McDonalds's Corporation
Blomberg, Philip D., (AV) .... '55 '81 C.477 B.A. L.365 J.D. 1200 Jorie Boulevard
Boksa, Mary Lou Anne .... '59 '89 C.209 B.S. L.424 J.D. Lions Clubs Intl. Found.

Bormes, James X., P.C., Law Office of
(See Chicago)

Botti, Aldo E., (AV) .... '36 '66 C.698 A.B. L.734 J.D. [Botti,M.&D.] ⊙
Botti, Stephen R., (BV) .... '54 '80 C&L.692 B.S., J.D. [Botti,M.&D.] ⊙

Botti, Marinaccio & DeLongis, Ltd., (AV) BR
720 Enterprise Drive, 60523 ⊙
Telephone: 630-573-8585 Fax: 630-573-8586
URL: http://www.lawyers.com/bottimaridellaw
Aldo E. Botti; Lee A. Marinaccio; Stephen R. Botti; Peter M. DeLongis; Jean Lasics-Wessels;—Carla Labunski; Paige M. McClelland-Theobald; Jamie Lynn Ryan.
Trial and Appellate Practice in State and Federal Courts, Civil, Criminal, Personal Injury, Family, Zoning, Corporation, Probate, Commercial and Government Litigation.
Wheaton, Illinois Office: Suite 402 The Ticor Title Building, 330 Naperville Road. Telephone: 630-653-2100.

See Professional Biographies, OAK BROOK, ILLINOIS

Boyd, William J., P.C. .... '29 '57 C&L.209 B.A., J.D. 2021 Midwest Rd.‡

Brethauer, Troy M. ..... '64 '90 C.339 B.S.E.E. L.477 J.D. Sr. Coun., McDonald's Corp.
Bronson, Cynthia '— '82
C.679 B.S. L.352 J.D. Asst. Gen. Coun., Metropolitan Life Ins. Co.
Burgess, M. Katherine .... '60 '93 C.118 B.A. L.285 J.D. 1919 Midwest Rd.
Caldarazzo, Richard J. .... '48 '75 C.477 A.B. L.209 J.D. 2311 W. 22nd St.
Callahan, Eugene G. .... '42 '67 C.177 B.A. L.146 LL.B. 1200 Jorie Blvd.
Callahan, John P., Jr. .... '63 '88 C.436 B.S. L.146 J.D. [Ⓐ Sullivan H.&C.]
Cameron, Jill A. .... '68 '94 C.347 B.S. L.365 J.D. Sr. Coun., McDonald's Corp.
Canulli, Michael D., (BV) .... '53 '78 C.1082 B.S. L.209 J.D. 1301 W. 22nd St., Ste. 1012
Cappetta, Frederick C. .... '40 '66 C.602 B.B.A. L.209 LL.B. [Cappetta&S.]
Cappetta & Shadle, Ltd. .... 1900 Spring Road, Suite 102
Carey, K. Kristann ...... '70 '97 C.966 B.A. L.424 J.D. Coun., McDonald's Corporation
Carlson, Eric J. .... '— '98 C.123 B.A. L.966 J.D. McDonald's Corporation
Carlson, W. Roger, Jr. .... '61 '86 C.339 B.S. L.146 J.D. 2805 Butterfield Rd., Ste. 150
Caro, Jodi J. .... '65 '89 C.436 B.A. L.46 J.D. Looking Glass Networks
Cavallaro, Carlo F. '65 '92 C.589 B.S. L.365 J.D.
Dir., Franchising & Govt. Affs., AT&T Broadband and Internet Services
Cerne, Wence F. .... '31 '56 C.1365 B.B.A. L.597 J.D. 18 Cambridge Dr.‡
Chapello, Margaret E. ..... '57 '81 C.589 B.S. L.285 J.D. Ombudsman, McDonald's Corp.
Cheung, Kenneth N. .... '74 '99 C.339 B.S. L.209 J.D. 46 Kingston Drive
Chimenti, Norman V. .... '40 '67 C&L.976 B.A., LL.B. [Martin,C.C.&S.]
Chmura, Martin W. .... '58 '84 C.234 B.S. L.146 J.D. Mng. Coun., McDonald's Corp.
Christou, William M. .... '59 '88 C.209 B.A. L.424 J.D. Ace Hardware Corp.
Ciecko, Thomas L. .... '54 '84 C.1016 B.A. L.365 J.D. McDonald's Corp.
Cisar, Thomas J. .... '48 '73 C.339 B.A. L.365 J.D. 1550 Spring Rd., Ste. 210
Cohn, Steven P. .... '54 '79 C.1044 B.A. L.659 J.D. McDonald's Corp.
Condara, Christie .... '55 '84 C&L.326 B.A., J.D. 261 Williamsburg Court
Conniff, Anthony J. .... '50 '78 C.424 A.B. L.589 J.D. 1900 Spring Rd.
Conroy, David S. .... '69 '93 C.338 B.A. L.339 J.D. Sr. Coun., McDonald's Corp.
Conway, John J. .... '61 '93 C.338 B.S. L.209 J.D. [Sullivan H.&C.]
Coogan, Kimberly S. .... '61 '93 C.339 B.S. L.146 J.D 1110 Jorie Blvd., Ste. 210
Coppin, Darrell G. .... '52 '78 C.602 B.A. L.424 J.D. McDonald's Corp.
Cordero, Jeannine M. '59 '90 C.172 B.A. L.602 J.D.
Director of Legal Affairs, XO Communications, Inc.
Cornelison, Kari L. .... '71 '96 C.475 B.A. L.365 J.D. [Ⓐ J.R.Kulerski]
Cowen, Sandra E. '48 '80 C.966 B.A. L.209 J.D.
Asst. Gen. Coun., Evangelical Health Systems
Cronin, Daniel J., (BV) .... '59 '86 C.597 B.A. L.424 J.D. [Power&C.]
Cunningham, Woodrow M. '37 '74 C.339 B.A. L.424 J.D.
2 South 600 Avenue Vendome‡
Curran, Desmond Patrick .... '67 '92 C&L.602 A.B., J.D. [Ⓐ Sullivan H.&C.]
Custer, Russell R., Jr. .... '49 '76 C.742 B.A. L.365 J.D. [Lillig&T.]
Dalmaso, Roseann .... '— '85 C.436 B.A. L.209 J.D. Sr. Coun., Metropolitan Life Ins. Co.

Daspin & Aument, LLP, (AV)
210 W. 22nd Street, Suite 102, 60523 ⊙
Telephone: 630-928-0430 Fax: 630-928-0392
Robert C. Aument; Jefferson Perkins. Of Counsel: John T. Huntington.
Real Estate, Commercial Real Estate Development, Estate Planning, Business Succession Planning, Tax Planning, Trust Administration, Estate Administration, Corporate Law and Financial Services Law. Intellectual Property including Patents, Trademarks, Copyrights and Computer Law.
Chicago Office: 10 South Riverside Plaza, Suite 1220, 60606. Telephone: 312-258-1600. Fax: 312-258-1955.

See Professional Biographies, OAK BROOK, ILLINOIS

Deely, Martin J. .... '68 '94 C.597 B.A. L.1065 J.D. [Ⓐ Power&C.]
DeFranco, Leonard S., & Associates, (AV) '53 '78
C.436 B.S. L.365 J.D. 2311 West 22nd Street, Suite 217
Del Medico, Michael L. .... '59 '91 C.209 B.S.C. L.365 J.D. [Kemp&G.]
DeLongis, Peter M., (AV) .... '56 '82 C.589 B.S. L.146 J.D. [Botti,M.&D.] ⊙
Demma, Michael B. .... '49 '78 C.363 B.A. L.209 J.D. 2S674 Ave. Normandy E.
De Sio, Isabel R. .... '53 '78 C.1077 B.A. L.809 J.D. McDonald's Corp.
Dewyer, William P. .... '63 '91 C.338 B.S. L.365 J.D. [Ⓐ Power&C.]
Diersen, Daniel A. .... '34 '61 C.293 B.A. L.365 LL.B. McDonald's Corp.
Discipio, Francis J., (AV) .... '61 '88 C.338 B.S. L.1029 J.D. [F.J.Discipio] ⊙
Discipio, Francis J., Ltd., (AV) .... 1200 Harger Road, Suite 500 (⊙Chicago)
Domansky, Edward C. '63 '89 C.602 B.A. L.851 J.D.
(adm. in OH; not adm. in IL) Dir., System Pub. Rel. Advocate Health Care‡
Dougherty, Jill A. .... '58 '83 C.951 B.A. L.339 J.D. Labor Rel. Coun., McDonald's Corp.
Drumheller, Scott '71 '98
C.305 B.A. L.209 J.D. Gen. Coun., The Intl. Assn. of Lions Clubs
Duda, Anthony G. .... '44 '69 McDonald's Corp.
Dudgeon, Thomas C. .... '52 '77 C.57 A.B. L.221 J.D. 1200 Harger Rd.
Eckhardt, Lana .... '53 '84 C.357 B.A. L.339 J.D. Federal Signal Corp.
Elmore, David G. .... '34 '58 C.347 B.S. L.1119 J.D. 2809 Butterfield Rd.
Evangelou, Alina M. .... '— '97 C.259 B.S. L.1202 J.D. Sr. Coun., Met Life
Evans, Gary R. .... '57 '86 Cisar and Mrotka, Ltd.

Farnell, Alan S.
(See Chicago)

Farrell, Shirley A. '58 '87
C.589 B.S. L.365 J.D. Sr. Coun., Real Estate, McDonald's Corp.
Fassola, John P. .... '67 '92 C.589 B.A. L.339 J.D. [Power&C.]
Fata, Gregory J. '59 '87 C.927 B.A. L.221 J.D.
Assoc. Gen. Coun., Dominick's Finer Foods, Inc.
Ferrigno, Penelope .... '74 '03 C.497 B.A. L.146 J.D. Coun., McDonald's Corp.

Fewkes Wentz & Strayer
(See Naperville)

Fine, Steven E. '51 '79 C.339 B.A. L.424 J.D.
Sr. Coun., Labor Rel., McDonald's Corp.
Flaherty, Mary Pat, Law Office of .... '61 '86 C.424 B.A. L.893 J.D. 3824 York Rd.
Forgas, Brian J. .... '71 '97 C.1175 B.A. L.128 J.D. Coun., McDonald's Corp.
Forman, Lee P. .... '41 '65 C.339 B.A. L.209 J.D. 1301 W. 22nd St., Ste. 603
Fox, Jonathan J. .... '64 '95 C.801 B.A. L.365 J.D. [Oldfield&F.]
Fox, Sean .... '41 '80 C.999 B.S.Ed. L.589 J.D. 900 Jorie Blvd.
Freeland, Eric A. .... '59 '86 C.608 B.A. L.339 J.D. [Ⓐ Lorenzini&Assoc.]
Gallender, Eric W. .... '68 '93 C&L.339 B.S., J.D. Sr. I.P. Coun., McDonald's Corp.

Garofalo, Schreiber, Hart & Storm, Chartered
(See Chicago)

Godfrey, Linda .... '47 '02 C.589 B.S. L.365 J.D. Health Sci. Tech. LLC
Gonzalez, Felix Manuel .... '74 '99 C&L.339 B.A., J.D. [Ⓐ F.J.Discipio]
Graff, Stuart I., (AV) '63 '87 C.597 B.S. L.424 J.D.
Grp. VP & Gen. Coun., Sanford Brands (Pat.)‡
Grauer, Corey H. '65 '90 C.339 B.A. L.424 J.D.
V.P., Gen. Coun. & Sec., Ion Beam Applications
Grazian, Lawrence L. .... '66 '90 C.339 A.B. L.94 J.D. Ste. 200, 1900 Spring Rd.

Griffin, Catherine A. '56 '81 C.750 B.A. L.424 J.D.
U.S. Gen. Coun.; V.P., Gen. Coun., Partner Brands, McDonald's Corp.
Griffith, Gary W. ....'47 '74 C.707 B.A. L.209 J.D. [Manetti&G.]
Gross, W. B. Martin, (AV) .... '36 '61 C.31 B.A. L.309 LL.B. [Martin,C.C.&S.]
Grosso, Samuel T. ....'45 '74 C.589 B.S. L.146 J.D. Pres., New Beginning Tours, Inc.
Grzelakowski, Edward J. ....'53 '82 C.597 B.A. L.209 J.D. [Kemp&G.]
Guthrie, James Walter ....'60 '88 C.112 A.B. L.209 J.D. Financial Serv.
Hands, Daniel O. ....'49 '75 C.932 B.B.A. L.879 J.D. [D.O.Hands]
Hands, Daniel O., P.C., Law Office of .... 1301 West 22nd Street, Suite 603
Hannon, James R. ....'48 '73 C&L.209 B.S.C., J.D. [Hannon&S.]
Hannon & Scalzo .... 1301 West 22nd Street
Hanzal, Marilyn E. '61 '86 C.679 B.S. L.347 J.D.
Dir. Legal Services, Univ. HealthSystem Consortium
Harris, Bradley J. .... '46 '72 C.339 B.S. L.146 J.D. 1301 W. 22nd St., Ste. 914
Harry, Kathryn L. .... '— '91 C.357 B.S. L.209 J.D. 1200 Harger Rd., Ste. 412
Hasan, Zainab Fatima '— '01 C.145 B.A. L.146 J.D.
Of Coun., GJ & P Enterprises, Ltd.
Hasbrouck, Gail Durham '45 '75 C.112 A.B. L.597 J.D.
V.P., Gen. Coun. & Corp. Secy., Advocate Health Care Network
Hassan, Gwendolyn L. ... '66 '97 C.966 B.A. L.209 J.D. Corp. Atty., Federal Signal Corp.
Healy, Donald J., Jr. '— '80
C.801 B.A. L.365 J.D. Ass. Gen. Coun., Metropolitan Life Ins. Co.
Heintz, Janet R. '63 '89 C.679 B.A. L.347 J.D.
Asst. Coun. & V.P., The Inland Real Estate Grp., Inc.
Hemmer, Daniel J. '69 '96 C.477 B.A. L.309 J.D.
(adm. in XX; not adm. in IL) Centerpoint Property Trust
Henry, Paul M., (AVⓉ) .... '61 '88 C.659 B.S. L.665 J.D. 1415 W. 22nd St., Ste. 1100
Higgins, Robert G. '52 '77 C.602 A.B. L.424 J.D.
V.P., Oper. Off. Gen. Coun. & Secy., Banyan Management Corp.
Hilgers, Danielle L. ....'— '00 C.339 B.S.N. L.209 J.D. 1200 Harger Rd., Ste. 209
Hincks, Patrick M. ....'64 '89 C.742 B.A. L.424 J.D. [Sullivan H.&C.]
Hochman, James A. '49 '77
C.103 A.B. L.94 J.D. Sr. V.P. & Sr. Coun., CB Richard Ellis, Inc.
Hois, Laura L. ....'58 '84 C.339 B.A. L.209 J.D. Sr. Coun., McDonald's Corp.
Hollins, Mitchell L., (AV) '47 '71 C.930 B.A. L.569 J.D.
Sr. V.P., Chf. Legal. Offr. & Secy., Oak Brook Bank
Holzhueter, Michael R. .... '— '95 C&L.424 B.A., J.D. Advocate Health Care Network
Honesty, Edward F. ....'54 '79 C.976 B.A. L.597 J.D. C McDonald's Corporation
Horne, Denise A. ...'— '88 C.436 B.S. L.339 J.D. Mng. Coun., Corp., McDonald's Corp.
Houpt, Richard V., (AV) '26 '52
C.145 A.B. L.339 LL.B. 3003 Butterfield Rd. (⊙Chicago)
Hoy, Michael J. '54 '80 C.602 B.S. L.436 J.D.
V.P., Treas. Servs., Advocate Health Care Network

Hucek, Jeffrey M., (AV) '55 '83 C.893 B.S.C. L.494 J.D. [BB]
1900 Spring Road Suite 200, 60523
Telephone: 630-586-9600 Fax: 630-586-9610
Email: huceklaw@aol.com URL: http://www.lawyers.com/huceklaw
Estate Planning, Family Wealth Transfers, Wills, Trusts and Estates, Estate and Gift Taxation, Charitable Gift Planning, Contested Trusts and Estates, Premarital Agreements, Real Estate.
See Professional Biographies, OAK BROOK, ILLINOIS

Huebsch, Jeffrey B. ....'58 '84 C.578 B.A. L.146 J.D. [Power&C.]
Huntington, John T., (BV) ....'50 '75 C.207 B.A. L.146 J.D. [[C] Daspin&A.]
Hussain, Mahrukh S. ....'— '96 C.145 B.A. L.339 J.D. Coun., McDonald's Corp.
Hutson, Kristin E. ....'67 '92 C.802 B.A. L.424 J.D. McDonald Corp.
Hyink, Benjamin P., (BV) ....'52 '79 C.1247 B.A. L.209 J.D. [Hyink]
Hyink Law Firm, (BV) .... 1100 Jorie Boulevard Suite 258
Invergo, Anne Smilansky '65 '91 C.339 B.A. L.1338 J.D.
Sr. Coun., McDonald's Corp.
Jalili, Mahir ....'44 '77 C.999 B.Sc. L.424 J.D. [M.Jalili] ⊙
Jalili, Mahir, P.C., Law Offices of
1200 Harger Road, Suite 718 (⊙Virginia Water, England)
Jamieson, Adele M. '54 '89 C.339 B.A. L.209 J.D.
Dir., Off. of the Chmn. & Asst. Secy., McDonald's Corp.
Jaros, Arthur G., Jr. ....'50 '75 C.297 B.A. L.145 J.D. [Richter,J.&R.]
Jaynes, Gordon L. '29 '54 C.939 A.B. L.911 LL.B.
(adm. in WA; not adm. in IL) [[C] M.Jalili] ⊙
Jenkins, David M. ....'66 '92 C.967 B.A. L.365 J.D. 721 Enterprise Dr., Ste. 200
Jenkins, Michele A. ....'63 '89 C.436 B.S. L.209 J.D. Coun., McDonald's Corp.
Jennings, Amy Remington ....'62 '87 C&L.339 B.A., J.D. 1900 Spring Rd., Suite 200
Jerak, John W. ....'47 '81 C.339 B.S. L.209 J.D. [[C] Kemp&G.]
Johnson, Robert ......'68 '93 C.388 B.A. L.339 J.D. Sr. Coun., McDonald's Corporation
Jones, H. Susan ....'49 '89 C.970 B.A. L.146 J.D. 1900 Spring Rd., Suite 200
Joyce, James M. ....'59 '93 C.1268 B.A. L.146 J.D. [[A] Lillig&T.]
Kamenear, Elliot B. ....'46 '73 C.98 B.A. L.209 J.D. 2901 Butterfield Rd.
Kaminky, Mark D. '65 '90 C.966 B.A. L.424 J.D.
V.P., Pres. & Gen. Coun., Sendai Publishing Group, Inc.
Kane, Jeffrey W. .... '43 '69 C.25 B.S. L.966 J.D. Asst. Secy., System Capital Corp.‡
Karl, Steven R. ....'69 '94 C.209 B.S. L.801 J.D. Sr. Coun., McDonald's Corp.
Karp, Steven C. ....'— '86 C.861 B.A. L.339 J.D. Sr. Coun., Metropolitan Life Ins. Co.
Kayner, David J., (AV) ....'38 '63 C.339 B.S. L.477 J.D. Inland Real Estate Corp.
Keating, Cathleen M. ....'55 '80 C&L.339 B.A., J.D. [Martin,C.C.&S.]
Kemp, James J., Jr., (BV) ....'46 '72 C.424 B.A. L.209 J.D. [Kemp&G.]
Kemp & Grzelakowski, Ltd., (AV) .... 1900 Spring Rd., Ste. 500
Kenny, William E., Law Office of, (AV) '48 '74
C.755 B.A. L.209 J.D. 2210 Midwest Road, Suite 212
Kerger, Cary J. '58 '83 C&L.190 B.S.B.A., J.D.
General Counsel, Anvan Midwest Realty Management Co.
Kerns, Michael Edwin '58 '84 C.966 B.B.A. L.424 J.D.
Assoc. Gen. Coun., Advocate Health Care Network
King, Maurice L. ....'46 '77 C.339 B.S. L.597 J.D. McDonald's Corp.
King, Richard C. ....'32 '57 C.597 B.S. L.477 J.D. Spiegel, Inc.
Knee, William F. ....'— '95 C.174 B.A. L.589 J.D. [W.F.Knee]

Knee, William F., Ltd.
1900 Spring Road, Suite 204, 60523
Telephone: 630-571-7777 Fax: 630-954-1984 URL: http://www.kneelawoffice.com
URL: http://www.williamfknee.com
William F. Knee.
Family Law and Child Custody Law.
See Professional Biographies, OAK BROOK, ILLINOIS

Knudsen, William K. '38 '65 C&L.597 B.S., J.D.
Sr. V.P. & Gen. Coun., Mutual Tr. Life Ins. Co.
Kocinski, Julita ....'71 '02 C.339 B.A. L.209 J.D. [Kocinski]
Kocinski Law Offices, LLC ....1919 Midwest Rd., Ste. 212
Kolby, Walter A. ....'10 '34 C.602 A.B. L.209 J.D. 2 Oak Brook Club Dr.‡
Kosiba, Louis W. '50 '77 C.589 B.A. L.339 J.D.
Dir., Mbr. Servs. & Legal, Ill. Mun. Retire. Fund
Kostich, Nada ....'53 '82 C.347 A.B. L.589 J.D. 211 Saint Michael Ct.
Kotel, Kathryn M. ....'59 '86 C.339 B.S. L.365 J.D. Mng. Coun., McDonald's Corp.
Kraft, Michael A. '59 '88 C.57 B.A. L.1000 J.D.
Corp. Coun., United Financial Mortgage Corp.
Kramer, James M. '46 '75
C.177 B.A. L.365 J.D. V.P., Intl. Franchising, McDonald's Corp.
Krzyminski, Edward J. '57 '82
C.234 B.A. L.365 J.D. Sr. Coun., Real Estate, McDonald's Corp.
Kujawa, John A. ....'59 '84 C.98 B.S. L.339 J.D. McDonald's Corp.
Kulerski, J. Richard ....'40 '63 C.1182 L.209 J.D. [J.R.Kulerski]

Kulerski, J. Richard, P.C.
1200 Harger Road, Suite 320, 60523
Telephone: 630-928-0600 Fax: 630-928-0670
Email: rk@familylawdupage.com URL: http://www.illinoisdivorceinfo.com
J. Richard Kulerski;—Kari L. Cornelison; Matthew M. Williams.
Divorce, Mediation, Custody, Collaborative Divorce, Family Law, Alimony.
See Professional Biographies, OAK BROOK, ILLINOIS

Kuta, Kathleen M. ....'— '76 C.424 B.S. L.209 J.D. Mng. Coun., McDonald's Corp.
Labunski, Carla ....'— '02 C.597 B.S.J. L.424 J.D. [[A] Botti,M.&D.]
LaKoma, Matthew W. ....'53 '78 C.1183 B.A. L.209 J.D. 1200 Jorie Blvd., Ste. 329
Lanzel, Marvin G. ....'44 '71 C.106 B.A. L.146 J.D. 800 Enterprise Dr., Ste. 100
LaPetina, Gary M. '55 '80
C.424 B.S. L.365 J.D. Gen. Coun., The Intl. Assn. of Lions Clubs
Lasics-Wessels, Jean ....'68 '95 C.879 B.A. L.1187 J.D. [Botti,M.&D.] ⊙
Lasser, Alyse I. ....'59 '84 C.339 B.A. L.597 J.D. Dir., Kensington Intl.‡
League, David W. '39 '70 C.37 B.A. L.365 J.D.
Vice President & General Counsel, Ace Hardware Corporation‡
Leggett, Maria '64 '94 C.1218 B.S. L.1206 J.D.
(adm. in FL; not adm. in IL) Gen. Coun., Latin Ame. & Canada, McDonald's Corp.
Lehr, Sheila '59 '84 C&L.339 B.A., J.D.
Mng. Coun., Mktg./Advertising, McDonald's Corp.

Leiter, Irwin E., (AV) '49 '77 C.339 B.A. L.146 J.D.
1301 W. 22nd Street, Suite 210, 60523
Telephone: 630-571-7767 Fax: 630-573-0460
Email: lionelir@sbcglobal.net
Real Estate Development, Condominium Law, Estate Planning.
See Professional Biographies, OAK BROOK, ILLINOIS

Lepping-Pool, Sharon '67 '92
C.205 B.A. L.776 J.D. Atty., Labor Rel., McDonald's Corp.
Leurck, John G. ....'69 '98 C.436 B.A. L.347 J.D. Sr. Coun., McDonald's Corp.
Levy, Pauline, (AV) ....'64 '89 C&L.339 B.A., J.D. Sr. Coun., McDonald's Corp.
Lewis, Elliot R., (BVⓉ) '60 '87 C.347 B.S. L.1119 J.D.
(adm. in IN; not adm. in IL) Gen. Coun., E.L.R. International, Inc.
Liddle, Rob, (AV) '50 '77 C.999 B.A. L.475 J.D.
(adm. in NY; not adm. in IL) Asst. V.P., Labor Rel., McDonald's Corp.
Lillig, Martin J. ....'40 '66 C.742 B.S. L.146 J.D. [Lillig&T.]

Lillig & Thorsness, Ltd.
1900 Spring Road Suite 200, 60523-1495
Telephone: 630-571-1900 Telecopy: 630-571-1042
Email: lt@lilliglaw.com
Martin J. Lillig; William W. Thorsness; Russell R. Custer, Jr.; Gregory F. Smith;—Francesco Roselli; David R. Stallter; James M. Joyce; Karyn R. Vanderwarren; Joseph P. Wleklinski, Jr.
Business, Corporate, Civil Litigation and Appeals in State and Federal Courts. Commercial, Contracts, Construction, Arbitration and Alternate Dispute Resolution. Estate Planning, Probate, Real Estate, Financial Institutions, Computer Consulting, Title Insurance, Common Law and Securities Fraud, Labor and Employment, Employee Benefits and Tax Law.

Limon, Leticia Isela ....'— '96 C.843 B.B.A. L.597 J.D. Coun., McDonald's Corp.
Lindgren, Karin J., (AV) '60 '85 C.874 B.S. L.809 J.D.
Gen. Coun. & Corp. Coml. Offr., University HealthSystem Consortium
Liska, G. R. ....'74 '02 C.352 L.1000 J.D. 900 Jorie Boulevard, Suite 122
Liss, Michael R. ....'55 '80 C.339 B.A. L.424 J.D. [M.R.Liss]
Liss, Michael R., P.C. .... 1301 West 22nd Street, Suite 709
Lloyd, William P. ....'49 '77 C.597 A.B. L.146 J.D. 1200 Harger Road

Locke, Barry, & Associates, LTD.
(See Chicago)

Longwell, Marilyn F., (AV) ....'43 '73 C.608 B.A. L.209 J.D. [Longwell] ⊙
Longwell Associates, Chartered, (AV) ..... 1301 West 22nd. Street, Suite 914 (⊙Chicago)
Lorenzen, John C. ....'54 '86 C.898 B.A. L.209 J.D. [J.C.Lorenzen]
Lorenzen, John C., Ltd. .... Ste. 603, 1301 W. 22nd St.
Lorenzini, Ronald N., Jr. ....'59 '84 C.602 B.A. L.209 J.D. [Lorenzini&Assoc.]
Lorenzini & Associates, Ltd. ....1900 Spring Road, Suite 501
Lundeen, William T. ....'56 '85 C.37 B.S.B.A. L.893 J.D. 1301 W. 22nd St., Suite 1100
Lundin, Molly Ashenhurst '55 '79
C.208 B.A. L.273 J.D. Coun., Real Estate, McDonald's Corp.
Lyman, William D., (AV) .... '40 '70 C.589 B.S. L.424 J.D. [Bedrava&L.]
Mackie, Douglas B. ....'52 '78 C.896 B.A. L.589 J.D. Great Lakes International Inc.
Malec, Sheri Anne '75 '00 C.339 B.S. L.145 J.D.
Dir. of Records Info. Mgmt., McDonald's Corp., Records Info. Mgmt.
Malter, Melvin C. ....'21 '56 L.365 LL.B. P.O. Box 3697
Manetti, Mark D., (AV) ....'47 '73 C.436 B.A. L.209 J.D. [Manetti&G.]
Manetti & Griffith, Ltd., (AV) .... 2311 West 22nd Street, Suite 217
Marchetti, Marilyn H., (AV) ....'47 '79 C.347 B.A. L.146 J.D. Great Banc Trust Company
Marinaccio, Lee A., (AV) ....'44 '71 C.238 B.A. L.424 J.D. [Botti,M.&D.] ⊙
Marks, Karl L. '29 '64 C.339 B.S. L.174 J.D.
(adm. in DC; not adm. in IL) 3 Oakbrook Dr.‡

Martin, Craig, Chester & Sonnenschein, (AV)
2215 York Road, Suite 550, 60523
Telephone: 630-472-3400 Fax: 630-472-0048
Email: firm@mccslaw.com URL: http://www.mccslaw.com
Members of Firm: W. B. Martin Gross; Norman V. Chimenti; Cathleen M. Keating; Mark D. Toljanic; Stephen R. Paul.
General Practice including: business organization and operations, acquisitions and divestitures, federal, state and local taxation, real estate and real estate finance, employee benefits, employment law, labor relations, not-for-profit and charitable organizations, municipal law, administrative proceedings, estate planning, probate and trust, family foundations and environmental law.
See Professional Biographies, OAK BROOK, ILLINOIS

Martineau, Theodore J. '36 '64 C.966 B.S. L.309 LL.B.
(adm. in DC; not adm. in IL) 156 Saddle Brook Dr.‡
Martinez, Ramon, Jr. ....'49 '77 C.589 B.S. L.597 J.D. Sr. Coun., McDonald's Corp.
Matthews, Mary S. '59 '90
C&L.477 B.S.N., J.D. Staff Coun., Advocate Health Care Network

Matthews, Patricia C. '53 '77 C.30 B.A. L.276 J.D.
(adm. in DC; not adm. in IL) McDonald's Corp.
McClellan, Charles E. .... '36 '66 C.339 B.S. L.209 J.D. 2215 York Rd.‡
McClelland-Theobald, Paige M. .... '76 '04 C.221 B.A. L.589 J.D. [Ⓐ Botti,M.&D.]
McKay, Daniel C., (AV) .... '32 '60 C.209 B.A. L.424 J.D. 32 Briarwood South
McVickers, John K. .... '62 '87 C.339 B.A. L.146 J.D. Ste. 200, 1900 Spring Rd.
Medina, Rafael '— '77 C.860 B.A. L.659 J.D.
(adm. in PA; not adm. in IL) Mng. Coun., Labor Rel., McDonald's Corp.
Melroy, Robert L. .... '31 '63 C.375 B.S. L.146 LL.B. Wheelabrator Water Tech. Inc.‡
Merck, Hal B. .... '66 '92 C.937 B.A. L.309 J.D. Sr. Coun., McDonald's Corp.
Mezik, Kimberly A. .... '74 '99 C.475 B.A. L.477 J.D. [Ⓐ Power&C.]
Miller, Lesa K. .... '— '92 L.146 J.D. P.O. Box 5084
Miller, Ralph W., Jr. .... '31 '56 C&L.597 B.S., J.D. Comr., State Indus. Comn.
Mills, W. David '44 '71 C&L.209 B.A., J.D.
Coun. & Asst. Secy., Mutual Tr. Life Ins. Co.
Mlsna, Kathryn K. '52 '77 C&L.597 B.A., J.D.
Mng. Coun., Mktg./Advertising, McDonald's Corp.
Moeller, Raymond H. ...... '33 '95 C.339 B.S. L.424 J.D. 120 Oakbrook Center, Suite 204
Molloy, Padraic G. '65 '04 C.999 L.424 J.D.
Reg. Coun., McDonald's USA, LLC, U.S. Legal Dept.
Montgomery, Janet Rae, (AV) .... '51 '76 C.800 A.B. L.813 J.D. [Pokorny&Assoc.]
Moran, Kathleen M. '60 '87
C&L.966 B.A., J.D. Sr. Atty., Labor Rel., McDonald's Corp.
Morgan, James P. .... '27 '53 C&L.910 B.S.B.A., J.D. 1200 Harger Rd.
Mudd, Anne Chestney .... '44 '98 C.421 B.A. L.365 J.D. 2803 Butterfield Rd.
Mueller, Anne L. .... '50 '83 C.746 B.S. L.209 J.D. [Ⓐ Longwell]
Napolski, Paul T. .... '48 '73 C.602 B.A. L.424 J.D. 800 Enterprise Dr., Ste. 100
Nelson, Alan H. .... '50 '95 C.339 B.S.E. L.46 J.D. [Trott N.]
Nestor, Justin T. .... '76 '04 C.63 B.A. L.879 J.D. [Ⓐ Power&C.]
Neumann, Bruce A. .... '67 '91 C.338 B.S. L.352 J.D. Sr. Coun., McDonald's Corp.
Niew, Stanley E. .... '40 '72 C.1016 B.S.B.A. L.365 J.D. 900 Jorie Blvd.
O'Brien, Walter J., II, (AV) .... '— '65 C.602 B.B.A. L.597 J.D. [O'Brien&Assoc.]
O'Brien & Associates, P.C., (AV) .... 1900 Spring Road Suite 501
Oldfield, E. Lawrence, (AV) .... '44 '73 C.589 B.A. L.209 J.D. [Oldfield&F.]

Oldfield & Fox, P.C., (AV) BR
Suite 201, 2021 Midwest Road, 60523
Telephone: 630-495-3377 Facsimile: 630-495-2774 URL: http://www.oldfieldfox.com
Email: eloesq@oldfieldfox.com URL: http://www.lawyers.com/eloesq
E. Lawrence Oldfield; Jonathan J. Fox. Of Counsel: Michael R. Panter; Robert J. Ross.
General Civil Litigation. Commercial Transactions, Business Law, Family Law, Real Estate, Personal Injury, Probate, Wills and Trusts, Misdemeanor Criminal, Mediation, Arbitration and Livestock Insurance Defense.
Representative Clients: Hartford Fire Insurance Co.; Fireman's Fund; Star Insurance Co.; Mid-Way Supply, Inc.; Dupage Credit Union; Earthwise Environmental, Inc.; National Cattlemen's Beef Association; Medical Applications Specialists, Inc.; Energy Associates, Inc; Leo Construction, Inc.
Chicago, Illinois Office: 30 North La Salle Street, Suite 1524, 60602. Telephone: 312-782-0933. Fax: 312-782-4474.
Inverness, Illinois Office: 1622 Colonial Parkway, Suite 201, 60067. Telephone: 847-358-5757. Fax: 847-358-7706.
See Professional Biographies, OAK BROOK, ILLINOIS

O'Malley, Jennifer A. ... '— '93 C.012 B.A. L.597 J.D. Sr. I.P. Coun., McDonald's Corp.
Orenic, Paul M. .... '59 '86 C.1278 B.A. L.365 J.D. [Cappetta&S.]
Ortiz-Olinger, Haydee '58 '83 C&L.209 B.S.C., J.D.
Mng. Coun., Global Corp. Comp. Dir., McDonald's Corp.
Ostis, Algird R. .... '31 '65 C.446 B.S. L.209 J.D. 5 Oakbrook Club Dr. (Pat.)‡
Padnos, Norman B. .... '39 '64 C.221 B.A. L.146 LL.B. McDonald's Corp.
Panno, John Arthur .... '63 '89 C.999 B.S. L.200 J.D. CBI Industries, Inc.
Papp, Dilene Bishop .... '61 '88 C&L.174 B.A., J.D. [Bishop&B.]
Paquette, Tammy A. .... '73 '03 C.424 B.A. L.209 J.D. [Ⓐ Power&C.]
Pate, Lorenzo .... '70 '96 C&L.339 B.S., J.D. Gen. Coun., Oak Brook Bank
Paul, Stephen R. .... '66 '93 C.188 B.S. L.589 J.D. [Martin,C.C.&S.]
Pavone, Ronze J. .... '67 '94 C.339 B.S. L.146 J.D. [Ⓐ Manetti&G.]
Payton, Koreen A. .... '65 '93 C.347 B.S./B.A. L.879 J.D. Coun., McDonald's Corp.
Pechter, Gary .... '51 '77 C.339 B.S. L.365 J.D. 2901 Butterfield Rd.
Peña, Amy J. ...... '72 '00 C.35 B.S. L.589 J.D. Staff Atty., The Intl. Assn. of Lions Clubs
Penicook, Mary Ellen .... '59 '87 C&L.339 B.A., J.D. 1415 W. 22nd St.
Perkins, Jefferson, (AV) .... '55 '83 C.339 B.S.E.E. L.365 J.D. [Daspin&A.] (Pat.) ⊙
Platek, David F. .... '53 '80 C.209 B.S. L.365 J.D. 2210 Midwest Rd.
Platt, Robert J. .... '52 '82 C.436 B.S. L.589 J.D. Mostardi Platt Environmental
Pochowicz, Jeffrey J. .... '77 '02 C.659 B.S. L.597 J.D. Coun., McDonald's Corp.
Pokorny, William H. .... '17 '41 C&L.424 A.B., J.D. [Pokorny&Assoc.]
Pokorny, William H., Jr., (AV) .... '47 '72 C.276 A.B. L.424 J.D. [Pokorny&Assoc.]
Pokorny & Associates, Limited, (AV) ....1000 Jorie Boulevard, Suite 260
Porter, Cecil Earl, III .... '75 '02 C.337 B.A. L.589 J.D. [Ⓐ Power&C.]
Power, John F., III .... '50 '76 C.861 B.S. L.146 J.D. [Power&C.]
Power & Cronin, Ltd., (BV) ....900 Commerce Drive, Suite 300
Powers & Bigoness, P.C. .... 1010 Jorie Blvd., Ste. 222
Poznak, James L., (AV) .... '53 '79 C.597 B.A. L.1202 J.D. [Poznak]
Poznak Law Firm Ltd., (AV) ....2210 Midwest Road, Suite 212
Prato, Jack Vincent .... '54 '95 C&L.209 B.A., J.D. [Prato&Assoc.]

Prato & Associates, P.C.
2725 35th Street, 60523
Telephone: 630-570-5299 Fax: 630-570-5298 URL: http://members.aol.com/PRATOLAW/index.html
Email: pratolaw@aol.com URL: http://www.lawyers.com/pratolaw
Jack Vincent Prato.
Languages: Spanish and Italian.
Real Estate Transactions, Bankruptcy, Small Businesses, Corporate, Criminal, DUI, Personal Injury and Immigration Law.
See Professional Biographies, OAK BROOK, ILLINOIS

Prokes, Lori Ann, (AV) '63 '88
C.879 B.A. L.365 J.D. Sr. Reg. Coun., Newell Rubbermaid
Rawitz, Brett G. '63 '88 C.659 B.A. L.800 J.D.
Mng. Coun. - Labor Relations, McDonald's Corp.
Redick, Jeffrey B. .... '69 '94 C.234 B.A. L.221 J.D. [Power&C.]
Richter, Robert I. .... '44 '69 C&L.145 A.B., J.D. [Richter,J.&R.]
Richter, Jaros & Robinson .... 1200 Harger Rd.
Rieser, Richard M., Jr. '43 '69
C.103 A.B. L.145 J.D. Pres., First Oak Brook Bancshares, Inc.
Rius, Richard G., Jr. .... '78 '04 C.340 B.A. L.124 J.D. [Ⓐ M.A.Bennett]
Robinson, Robert G. .... '56 '82 C.927 B.S. L.424 J.D. [Richter,J.&R.]
Rodek-Quick, Adriana M. '70 '96 C.339 B.A. L.209 J.D.
V.P. & Coun., Oak Brook Bank
Roselli, Francesco .... '61 '86 C&L.209 B.S., J.D. [Ⓐ Lillig&T.]
Ross, Vivian .... '49 '74 C.477 B.A. L.424 J.D. V.P., Labor Rel., McDonald's Corp.

Roti, Thomas D. '45 '70 C&L.424 B.S., J.D.
V.P. & Gen. Coun., Dominick's Finer Foods, Inc.
Rudnik, Eugene J., Jr. .... '48 '74 C.602 B.B.A. L.209 J.D. [Kemp&G.]
Ryan, Jamie Lynn .... '77 '02 C.339 B.S. L.146 J.D. [Ⓐ Botti,M.&D.]
Sale, Edwin W., (AV) .... '12 '37 C.597 B.S. L.339 J.D. 2021 Spring Rd.‡
Santona, Gloria '50 '77
C.475 B.S. L.477 J.D. Gen. Coun. & Exec. V.P., McDonald's Corp.
Sarna, Richard F. .... '47 '73 C.424 B.A. L.209 J.D. 1900 Spring Road
Sayvetz, Ann, (BVⓉ) '50 '76 C&L.174 B.A., J.D.
Assoc. Gen. Coun., Advocate Health Care Network
Scalzo, Michael J. .... '48 '73 C.210 B.A. L.930 J.D. [Hannon&S.]
Schaefer, Peter L. .... '59 '89 C.477 B.A. L.424 J.D. Dir., Safety, McDonald's Corp.
Shadle, Ronald E. .... '50 '76 C.589 B.S. L.597 J.D. [Cappetta&S.]
Sheinfeld, Meyer .... '23 '68 C.209 B.S. L.146 J.D. Treas. & Secy., Spiegel, Inc.
Shelton, Susan B. .... '59 '84 C.937 B.A. L.209 J.D. Portillo's Hot Dogs Inc.
Sherman, Jennifer .... '64 '89 C&L.477 B.B.A., J.D. Corp. Atty., Federal Signal Corp.
Shiner, Kenneth S. '54 '82
C.339 B.A. L.424 J.D. Sr. Coun., Real Estate, McDonald's Corp.
Simpson, Craig A. .... '55 '81 C.339 B.S. L.209 J.D. McDonalds Corp.
Skelding, David L. '58 '83 C.145 A.B. L.188 J.D.
Vice President & General Counsel, Christian Brothers Investment
Skokos, Soula .... '— '02 C.597 B.S. L.424 J.D. [Skokos]

Skokos Law Group, LLC
1100 Jorie Boulevard, Suite 220, 60523
Telephone: 630-368-1699 Fax: 630-368-3586 URL: http://www.skokoslawgroup.com
Email: sskokos@aol.com URL: http://www.soulaskokoslawfirm.com
Soula Skokos.
Intellectual Property, Patents, Trademarks, Copyrights.
See Professional Biographies, OAK BROOK, ILLINOIS

Slattery, Timothy J. .... '66 '93 C.339 B.A. L.210 J.D. Coun., McDonald's Corp.
Smedstad, Heather Labadot '71 '95 C.145 B.A. L.228 J.D.
Sr. Coun., McDonald's Corp.
Smith, Gregory F. .... '54 '80 C.973 B.S.B.A. L.365 J.D. [Lillig&T.]
Smith, Robert C., Jr. '46 '73 C.339 B.S. L.209 J.D.
Sr. V.P., Secy. & Gen. Coun., White Hen Pantry, Inc.
Smyth, Daniel T., Jr. .... '46 '76 C.436 A.B. L.339 J.D. [D.T.Smyth,Jr.]
Smyth, Daniel T., Jr., Ltd. .... 1900 Spring Rd.
Solomon, Barry .... '60 '87 C&L.145 B.A., J.D. Exec.V.P., Interface Software, Inc.
Souers, P. Eric '43 '72 C&L.145 B.A., J.D.
(adm. in CA; not adm. in IL) Waste Mgt. International Inc.
Spada, David M. .... '71 '98 C.424 B.A. L.365 J.D. 1200 Harger Rd.
Speiser, Matthew B. .... '77 '02 C.340 B.A. L.209 J.D. [Ⓐ Sullivan H.&C.]
Stallter, David R. .... '62 '90 C&L.879 B.S., J.D. [Ⓐ Lillig&T.]
Stein, Judith V. .... '45 '87 C.339 B.S. L.424 J.D. 3216 Mulberry Ln.
Stein, Stanley R. .... '42 '67 C.94 B.A. L.93 LL.B. Exec. V.P., Mgmt., McDonald's Corp.
Stenn, Edgar H. .... '18 '42 C&L.145 A.B., J.D. 1200 Harger Rd.‡
Stepnicka, Craig D. .... '49 '74 C&L.339 B.S., J.D. JMG Financial Group
Sullivan, Daniel C. .... '40 '67 C.375 A.B. L.900 J.D. [Sullivan H.&C.]
Sullivan, James R. .... '35 '70 C&L.424 B.B.A., J.D. 2021 Midwest Rd.
Sullivan, Joseph A. '68 '93
C&L.477 A.B., J.D. V.P. & Gen. Coun., White Hen Pantry, Inc.

Sullivan Hincks & Conway, Law Offices of
A Partnership of Professional Corporations
122 West 22nd Street, Suite 100, 60523
Telephone: 630-573-5021 Fax: 630-573-5130 URL: http://www.shlawfirm.com
Email: dansullivan@shlawfirm.com URL: http://www.lawyers.com/sullivan&hincks
Daniel C. Sullivan; Patrick M. Hincks; John J. Conway. Associates: John P. Callahan, Jr.; Desmond Patrick Curran; Matthew P. Barrette; Matthew B. Speiser.
Corporate and Business Law, Civil Litigation, Real Estate, Logistics, Transportation, Taxation, Administrative, Environmental, Employment and Related Litigation, Insurance Coverage, Insurance Regulatory Matters, Commercial Law, Equine Law.
See Professional Biographies, OAK BROOK, ILLINOIS

Summers, Anthony W., III .... '43 '67 C.424 B.S. L.597 J.D. 1301 W. 22nd St.
Sundheim, George M., (AV) '26 '53 C.597 B.A. L.365 J.D.
210 W. 22nd St. (⊙Chicago)
Swanson, Anne V. .... '54 '81 C.57 B.A. L.365 J.D. [Ⓐ M.A.Bennett]
Swanson, James A. .... '35 '70 C.589 B.S.E. L.365 J.D. 1301 W. 22nd Street
Switzer, Robert L. '54 '79 C&L.339 B.S., J.D.
V.P., Assoc. Gen. Coun., Corp., McDonald's Corp.

Takiguchi, Masaru K. '55 '86 C.424 B.A. L.365 J.D.
1415 West 22nd Street, Tower Floor, 60523
Telephone: 630-645-3833 Fax: 630-645-3834
URL: http://www.mastakiguchilaw.com
Real Estate, Probate and Estate Planning, Civil Litigation, Commercial Transactions.
See Professional Biographies, OAK BROOK, ILLINOIS

Talarico, Alphonse A., Ltd., Law Offices of '48 '83
C.424 B.S.B.A. L.1000 J.D. 1010 Jorie Boulevard, Suite 326
Tameling, Eva W., (BV) .... '48 '79 C.238 B.S. L.209 J.D. [Tameling&Assoc.]
Tameling & Associates, P.C., (BV) .... 1010 Jorie Boulevard Suite 337
Tasch, Martin D. .... '60 '85 C.927 B.Bus. L.339 J.D. [M.D.Tasch]

Tasch, Martin D., P.C., Law Offices of
1200 Jorie Boulevard, Suite 329, 60523
Telephone: 630-571-9000 Fax: 630-571-9009
Email: mtasch@taschlaw.com URL: http://www.taschlaw.com
Martin D. Tasch.
Commercial Litigation, Contract Disputes, Collection, Construction Disputes, Mechanics Lien Disputes, Real Estate Litigation, Business, Corporate, Mergers and Acquisitions, Arbitration, Mediation, Franchise Disputes, Negligence, Partnership Disputes, Shareholders Disputes, Mortgage Foreclosures, Collections.
See Professional Biographies, OAK BROOK, ILLINOIS

Tatar, Jerome A. .... '49 '79 C.388 B.A. L.424 J.D. 1200 Harger Rd., Ste. 830
Tate-Mathis, Jacqueline D. '— '94 C&L.836 B.B.A., J.D.
(adm. in TN; not adm. in IL) McDonald's Corp.
Teglia, Karin N. '68 '95 C.347 B.S. L.309 J.D.
Asst. V.P., Int'l. Tax, McDonald's Corp.
Thorsness, William W. .... '47 '73 C.98 B.A. L.209 J.D. [Lillig&T.]
Tiesenga, Edward N. .... '60 '84 C.323 B.A. L.30 J.D. 1200 Harger Rd., Ste. 830

Tighe, Frank P., III
(See Chicago)

Toljanic, Mark D. .... '61 '86 C.347 B.S. L.477 J.D. [Martin,C.C.&S.]
Tolva, Donald E. .... '41 '65 C.436 B.S.B.A. L.424 J.D. 2625 Butterfield Rd.
Toussaint, Bernard J., III .... '58 '83 C.750 B.A. L.209 J.D. 2805 Butterfield Rd., Ste. 150
Trott, Gregory K. .... '68 '96 C.610 B.S. L.117 J.D. [Trott N.]

Trott Nelson, P.C.
1550 Spring Road, Suite 225, 60523
Telephone: 630-530-4161 Fax: 630-214-5351
Email: alan@trottnelson.com URL: http://www.trottnelson.com
Gregory K. Trott; Alan H. Nelson.
Construction Law, Mechanics Lien, Construction Contracts, Construction Litigation.
See Professional Biographies, OAK BROOK, ILLINOIS

Tu, James .... '71 '96 C.339 B.S. L.589 J.D. Sr. Coun., McDonald's Corp.
Tucker, Todd O., (AV) '59 '85
C.951 B.A. L.309 J.D. V.P. & Gen. Coun., McDonald's Corp.
Valdez, Henry R. ....'53 '91 C.881 B.A. L.477 J.D. McDonald's Corp.
Van Arkel, Erin E. ....'77 '02 C.10 B.A. L.365 J.D. Staff Atty., Oak Brook Bank
Vanderwarren, Karyn R. .... '— '03 C.720 B.A. L.146 J.D. [Ⓐ Lillig&T.]
Van Epps, Robert F., (AV) '39 '71
C.162 B.A. L.818 J.D. 1301 W. 22nd Street, Suite 914 (Pat.)‡
Van Poucke, Michael J., (BV) '66 '92 C.578 B.A. L.209 J.D.
Coun., McDonald's Corp.
Van Zeyl, John J. .... '35 '63 C.734 B.S. L.209 J.D. Ace Hardware Corp.
Vertovec, Edward J., (AV) ... '23 '50 C.238 L.209 LL.B. 2021 Midwest Road, Suite 1105
Vix, Carol A. ....'41 '88 C.209 B.S. L.365 J.D. Counsel, McDonald's Corporation
von Ebers, David P. .... '62 '87 C&L.339 B.A., J.D. 2805 Butterfield Rd., Ste. 150
Waldman, Valerie R. ....'65 '90 C.668 B.A. L.1066 J.D. Ty Inc.
Walker, Jon C. ....'78 '04 C.05 B.A. L.339 J.D. [Ⓐ Power&C.]
Waters, Thomas Wilson, (AV) ....'47 '78 C.861 B.A. L.365 J.D. [Kemp&G.]
Weber, Christopher J. ....'75 '00 C.1182 B.A. L.734 J.D. Coun., McDonald's Corp.
Weidenfeld, David ....'51 '77 C.264 B.A. L.365 J.D. Mng. Coun., McDonald's Corp.
Weinstein, Michael B. ....'49 '73 C&L.339 B.A., J.D. State Mun. Retire. Fund
Whisler, Barbara J. '64 '89 C.273 B.A. L.597 J.D.
V.P. & Assoc. Gen. Coun., Van Kampen Investments, Inc.
White, Patrick M. ..... '64 '92 C.477 B.S.A. L.209 J.D. Coun., McDonald's Corporation
Williams, Geneace '— '88
C&L.339 B.S., J.D. Mng. Coun., Bus. Coun., McDonald's Corp.
Williams, Matthew M. ....'— '03 C.1183 B.A L.589 J.D [Ⓐ J.R.Kulerski]
Wilton, Scott W. .... '60 '85 C.339 B.S. L.424 J.D. 2901 Butterfield Rd.
Winter, Michael J. ....'52 '78 C.339 A.B. L.734 J.D. Pres., Autoline Industries, Inc.
Wleklinski, Joseph P., Jr. .... '53 '84 C.172 B.A. L.345 J.D. [Ⓐ Lillig&T.]
Wuttke, Stephen ....'52 '77 C.927 B.A. L.339 J.D. 19W063 Normandy South
Young, Sandra ....'76 '03 C.589 B.S. L.365 J.D. Gen. Coun., Tristar Title, LLC

OAKBROOK TERRACE, 2,300, *DuPage Co.*

Anderson, Laureen R. '72 '02 C.338 B.S. L.352 J.D.
Policy Consultant, Paragon Resources
Andrews, Harold G. ....'26 '52 C&L.597 B.S., J.D. 2 Mid America Plaza
Antoniou, Andreas A. ....'54 '82 C.966 B.S. L.424 J.D. The Anvan Corp.
Bianchi, Sal M. '38 '63 C.424 B.S. L.209 J.D.
Exec. Dir., Intergovernmental Risk Mgmt. Agcy.
Bishop, Lucy M. ....'34 '58 C.966 B.A. L.893 LL.B. [ⓒ Bishop,R.&S.] ‡
Bishop, Rossi & Scarlati, Ltd., (AV)
Two TransAm Plaza, Suite 200, 60181
Telephone: 630-916-0123 Telecopier: 630-916-0567
Email: brs@bishoprossi.com
Raymond E. Rossi; Frank S. Scarlati Jr.; Robert A. Hall; George F. LaForte, Jr. Of Counsel: Leslie R. Bishop (1928-1997); Lucy M. Bishop (Retired); Richard C. Ernst (Ltd.) (1935-2004).
Federal and State Taxation, Commercial Litigation and Personal Injury, Business Law, Corporate Law, Real Estate Law, Commercial Transactions, Private Charitable Foundation Law, Trusts and Estates, Probate Law and Banking.
See Professional Biographies, OAKBROOK TERRACE, ILLINOIS

Bowman, John J. ....'30 '59 C.339 B.S. L.365 LL.B. Appl. Ct. J.
Boyne, James J. '66 '91 C.589 B.S. L.146 J.D.
Sr. V.P. & Dep. Gen. Coun., Van Kampen Investments
Braselton, Debra J. ....'— '94 C.999 B.S. L.424 J.D. [Braselton&M.]
Braselton and Millard ....One Tower Lane, Suite 1700
Bressler, Harold J., (AV) '43 '67 C.339 A.B. L.597 J.D.
General Counsel, Joint Comm. on Accreditation of Healthcare Organizations
Carpenter, Henry A. '50 '75 C&L.339 B.S., J.D.
Asst. Gen. Coun., BCS Financial Corp.
Cason, Marilynn J. '43 '69 C.813 B.A. L.477 J.D.
Sr. V.P., Gen. Coun. & Corp. Secy., De Vry Inc.
Cetina, Michael S., (AV) ....'60 '85 C.293 B.A. L.910 J.D. [Cetina&J.]
Cetina & Jacques, P.C., (AV)
1S450 Summit Avenue Suite 140, 60181
Telephone: 630-953-8200 Fax: 630-953-0866
Email: mcetina@cetina-jacques.com URL: http://www.cetinaandjacquespc.com
Michael S. Cetina; Charles T. Jacques.
Personal Injury, Personal Injury Appeals, Personal Injury Arbitration, Personal Injury Defense, Personal Injury Mediation, Plaintiffs Personal Injury, Medical Malpractice, Nursing Home Abuse and Neglect, Driving While Intoxicated, Drug Crimes, Traffic Violations.
See Professional Biographies, OAKBROOK TERRACE, ILLINOIS

Chivilo, James P. .... '75 '00 C.750 B.A. L.1000 J.D. [Ⓐ Holland&K.] (☉Chicago)
Dahlquist, John W. '70 '96 C.339 B.A. L.365 J.D.
Assoc. Corp. Coun., Prof. Servs. Industries, Inc.
DeLuca, Paul ....'53 '79 C.424 B.B.A. L.1151 J.D. 1 South 443 Summit Ave., Ste. 303
Denten, Raymond T. ....'29 '55 C&L.424 B.S., J.D. 1901 S. Meyers Rd.‡
Didier, Alfred L. ....'32 '67 C.424 B.S. L.597 J.D. Two Transam Plaza, Ste. 200
Dolci, Dominick P. ....'37 '62 C.742 B.A. L.209 J.D. 17W662 Buttwerfield Rd.
Donner, James M. ....'50 '78 C.424 B.A. L.1151 J.D. 17W 220 22nd Street, Suite 200
Dubnick, Harry L., (AV) '59 '84
C.145 B.A. L.910 J.D. Claims Coun., ComEd An Exelon Company
Duffy, Robert M. ....'44 '71 C.742 L.424 J.D. 1 S. 376 Summit
Freedman, Larry S. ....'63 '88 C.94 B.S. L.1068 J.D. 1901 S. Meryers Road, Ste. 600
Garvey, Donald B., & Associates, The Law Offices of '50 '75
C.424 B.A. L.597 J.D. 1 S. 376 Summit Ave., Ste. 3C
Greene, Dennis R. ..... '39 '76 C.589 B.S.E. L.146 J.D. Admin. Law J., Soc. Sec. Admin.
Hall, Robert A. ....'42 '73 C.340 B.A. L.365 J.D. [Bishop,R.&S.]
Hitt, Stephanie A. '64 '91 C.914 B.A. L.893 J.D.
(adm. in NY; not adm. in IL) Staff Atty., IBM Corp.

Holland & Knight LLP, (AV) BR
Suite 1000, One Mid America Plaza, 60181 ☉
Telephone: 630-954-2100 Fax: 630-954-2112
URL: http://www.hklaw.com
Oakbrook Terrace Member: Carl A. Neumann (Also at Chicago Office). Associate: James P. Chivilo (Also at Chicago Office).
Litigation, Government Law, Business Law, Real Estate Law and Private Wealth Services.
Annapolis, Maryland Office: State Circle Building, 47 State Circle, Suite 400, 21401. Telephone: 410-263-7800. Fax: 410-263-3768.
Atlanta, Georgia Office: One Atlantic Center, 1201 West Peachtree Street, N.E., Suite 2000, 30309. Telephone: 404-817-8500. Fax: 404-881-0470.

(This Listing Continued)

Holland & Knight LLP (Continued)
Beijing, China Office: No. 33, 14th Floor, IBM Tower, Pacific Century Place, 2 A Workers Stadium Road North, Chaoyang District, 100027. Telephone: 86-10-653-91232. Fax: 86-10-653-91060.
Bethesda, Maryland Office: 3 Bethesda Metro Center, Suite 800, 20814. Telephone: 301-654-7800. Fax: 301-656-3978.
Boston, Massachusetts Office: 10 St. James Avenue, 11th Floor, 02116. Telephone: 617-523-2700. Fax: 617-523-6850.
Bradenton, Florida Office: Bradenton Financial Center, 1401 West Manatee Avenue, Suite 1200, 34205. Telephone: 941-748-7076. Fax: 941-747-9774.
Chicago, Illinois Office: 131 South Dearborn Street, 30th Floor, 60603. Telephone: 312-263-3600. Fax: 312-578-6666.
Fort Lauderdale, Florida Office: One East Broward Boulevard, Suite 1300, 33301. Telephone: 954-525-1000. Fax: 954-463-2030.
Jacksonville, Florida Office: 50 North Laura Street, Suite 3900, 32202. Telephone: 904-353-2000. Fax: 904-358-1872.
Lakeland, Florida Office: 92 Lake Wire Drive, 33815. Telephone: 863-682-1161. Fax: 863-688-1186.
Los Angeles, California Office: 633 West Fifth Street, 21st Floor, 90071. Telephone: 213-896-2400. Fax: 213-896-2450.
Mexico City, Mexico Office: Holland & Knight - Gallastegui y Lozano, S.C., Edificio Arcos Bosques Corporativo, Paseo de los Tamarindos 400-B, Piso 2, Delegación Cuajimalpa, Bosques de las Lomas, 05120. Telephone: 525-55-261-1866. Fax: 525-55-261-1867.
Miami, Florida Office: 701 Brickell Avenue, Suite 3000, 33131. Telephone: 305-374-8500. Fax: 305-789-7799.
New York, New York Office: 195 Broadway, 24th Floor, 10007. Telephone: 212-513-3200. Fax: 212-385-9010.
Northern Virginia: 1600 Tysons Boulevard, Suite 700, McLean, Virginia, 22102. Telephone: 703-720-8600. Fax: 703-720-8610.
Orlando, Florida Office: SunTrust Building, Suite 2600, 200 South Orange Avenue, 32801. Telephone: 407-425-8500. Fax: 407-244-5288.
Portland, Oregon Office: 2300 U.S. Bancorp Tower, 111 Southwest Fifth Avenue, 97204. Telephone: 503-243-2300. Fax: 503-241-8014.
Providence, Rhode Island Office: One Financial Plaza, Suite 1800, 02903. Telephone: 401-751-8500. Fax: 401-553-6850.
Rancho Santa Fe, California Office: 6050 El Tordo, 92067. Telephone: 858-756-4410. Fax: 858-756-4386.
Sacramento, California Office: 1215 K Street, 17th Floor, 95814. Telephone: 916-503-1695. Fax: 916-503-2401.
San Antonio, Texas Office: 112 East Pecan Street, Suite 2700, 78205. Telephone: 210-229-3000. Fax: 210-229-1194.
San Francisco, California Office: 50 California Street, Suite 2800, 94111. Telephone: 415-743-6900. Fax: 415-743-6910.
Seattle, Washington Office: 2600 Pike Tower, 520 Pike Street, 98101. Telephone: 206-340-1825. Fax: 206-623-4363.
St. Petersburg, Florida Office: 200 Central Avenue, Suite 1600, 33701. Telephone: 727-896-7171. Fax: 727-822-8048.
Tallahassee, Florida Office: 315 South Calhoun Street, Suite 600, 32301. Telephone: 850-224-7000. Fax: 850-224-8832.
Tampa, Florida Office: 100 North Tampa Street, Suite 4100, 33602. Telephone: 813-227-8500. Fax: 813-229-0134.
Tokyo, Japan Office: Akasaka Tokyu Building, 7th Floor, 2-14-3 Nagatacho, Chiyoda-Ku, Tokyo, 100-0014. Telephone: 03-3539-5881. Fax: 03-3503-1033.
Washington, D.C. Office: 2099 Pennsylvania Avenue, N.W., Suite 100, 20006. Telephone: 202-955-3000. Fax: 202-955-5564.
West Palm Beach, Florida Office: 222 Lakeview Avenue, Suite 1000, 33401. Telephone: 561-833-2000. Fax: 561-650-8399.
Representative Offices:
Caracas, Venezuela Office: Tinoco, Travieso, Planchart & Núñez, Avenida Francisco De Miranda, Torre Country Club, Pisos 1 y 2, Chacaito, 1050. Telephone: 582-12-952-9033 (Master). Fax: 582-12-953-1053/8365/7583.
Helsinki, Finland Office: Holland & Knight Oy, Pohjoisesplanadi 33, FIN-00100. Telephone: 358-9-684-1520. Fax: 358-9-6841-5252.
Tel Aviv, Israel Office: Haim Samet, Steinmetz, Haring & Co. Advocates, 23 Begin Road, 66814. Telephone: 972-3-567-0100. Fax: 972-3-567-01010.
See Professional Biographies, OAKBROOK TERRACE, ILLINOIS

Imhoff, Herbert F., Jr. '50 '76 C&L.221 B.S., J.D.
V.P. & Gen. Coun., General Employ. Enterprises, Inc.
Jacques, Charles T., (CV) ....'59 '88 C.861 B.A. L.365 J.D. [Cetina&J.]
Johnston, Kimberly Anne .... '56 '94 C.339 B.S. L.589 J.D. 1 Tower Lane, Ste. 1700
Kohlstedt, James A. ....'49 '76 C.597 B.A. L.1119 J.D. 2100 Clearwater Dr.

Kubiesa, Spiroff, Gosselar & Acker, P.C.
(See Elmhurst)

LaForte, George F., Jr. ....'70 '96 C.589 B.S. L.365 J.D. [Bishop,R.&S.]
Letizia, Daniel P. ....'52 '76 C.339 B.S. L.209 J.D. [Letizia&L.]
Letizia, David D. ....'56 '80 C&L.209 B.S.C., J.D. [Letizia&L.]
Letizia & Letizia, Ltd. ....Two TransAm Plaza Dr.

Lubin, Peter S., (AV) '57 '83 C.197 A.B. L.145 J.D.
17 W. 220 22nd Street, Suite 200, 60181 ☉
Telephone: 630-333-0000 Facsimile: 630-333-0333
Email: psl@ditommasolaw.com URL: http://www.lawyers.com/peterslubin
General Business Lawsuits, Small Business Lawsuits, Employment Law, Employment Discrimination, Sexual Harassment, Wrongful Termination, Consumer, Consumer Fraud, Unsafe Products, Warranties, Class Actions, Consumer Class Actions, Legal Malpractice, Franchises, Business Law, Business Litigation, Business Fraud.
See Professional Biographies, OAKBROOK TERRACE, ILLINOIS

Maher, Deborah A. '69 '94
C.30 B.A. L.597 J.D. Corp. Dir. of Human Resources, DeVry Inc
Marsh, Robert L. .... '42 '68 C.124 B.S. L.607 J.D. [Patnaude,V.&M.]

McBride Baker & Coles
(See Holland & Knight LLC)

McMillan, Ian, (AV) '35 '66 C&L.879 B.A., J.D.
1 S 376 Summit Avenue, Unit C, 60181
Telephone: 630-620-5990 Fax: 630-932-0758
Contracts, Trusts, Estates, Wills, Probate, Guardianship.
Representative Clients: A.O. Smith Corp.; English District of the Lutheran Church - Missouri Synod.
References: Chicago Title & Trust Co.; Northern Trust Co.
See Professional Biographies, OAKBROOK TERRACE, ILLINOIS

Meier, Henry N., Jr. '48 '77 C.589 B.S. L.365 J.D.
V.P., Sequest Health Care System, Inc.
Millard, Isabel Marie .... '— '99 C.1101 B.A. L.146 J.D. [Braselton&M.]
Mitchell, Elisa '69 '95 C.446 B.A. L.64 J.D.
(adm. in MD; not adm. in IL) V.P. & Assoc. Gen. Coun., Van Kampen Investments
Morrissey, Walter W., (AV) ....'42 '72 C.602 B.A. L.209 J.D. [Morrissey&R.]
Morrissey & Robinson, (AV) ....1 Oakbrook Terrace
Nelson, Elizabeth '67 '92 C&L.339 B.S., J.D.
V.P. & Assoc. Gen. Coun., Van Kampen Invests.
Neumann, Carl A., (AV) ...... '— '68 C.959 B.A. L.966 J.D. [Holland&K.] (☉Chicago)
Nicolls, Keith K., (AV) ....'22 '49 C&L.477 B.S., J.D. 1 S. 376 Summit Ave. (Pat.)
Patnaude, Edmond T., (AV) ....'26 '55 C.688 B.S. L.273 J.D. [Patnaude,V.&M.] (Pat.)
Patnaude, Videbeck & Marsh, (AV) .... 1 S. 376 Summit Ave. (Pat.)
Robinson, Joseph M. ....'44 '71 C.602 B.A. L.339 J.D. [Morrissey&R.]
Rossi, Raymond E., (AV) ....'53 '80 C.578 B.A. L.365 J.D. [Bishop,R.&S.]
Scarlati, Frank S., Jr., (AV) ....'61 '87 C.209 B.S.C. L.589 J.D. [Bishop,R.&S.]

Schulman, Jerry A., (AV) '44 '73
C.46 B.S.Ch.E. L.424 J.D. 1 S. 376 Summit Ave., Court C
Sherman, Barry H. ....'44 '69 C.339 B.S. L.178 J.D. 1 S. 376 Summit Ave.
Smith, Garrett A. '73 '00 C.424 B.A. L.608 J.D.
Assoc. Corp. Coun., Prof. Servs. Industries, Inc.
Stavropoulos, Steven Dean ......'76 '01 C&L.209 B.A., J.D. Gen. Coun., Comat Properties
Stewart, Charles A. ....'58 '84 C.339 B.A. L.1119 J.D. Sr. Coun., De Vry Inc.
Stewart, Kenneth E. ....'39 '64 C.878 B.A. L.477 J.D. Admin. Law J., Soc. Sec. Admn.
Stillo, Adam N., Jr. ....'53 '78 C.219 B.A. L.589 J.D. [A.N.Stillo,Jr.]
Stillo, Adam N., Jr., P.C., Law Offices of ....1 S 443 Summit Ave., Ste. 303
Sullo, Nicholas John ....'76 '01 C.424 B.B.A. L.146 J.D. [N.J.Sullo]
Sullo, Nicholas J., P.C. ....17W695 Butterfield Rd., Ste. D
Thorne, Frederick ....'50 '86 C.681 B.A. L.589 J.D. Compl. Atty., BCS Ins.
Turner, William P. ....'49 '78 C.338 B.S. L.801 J.D. The Northern Trust Co.
Videbeck, James N. ....'45 '73 C.339 B.S.M.E. L.1119 J.D. [Patnaude,V.&M.] (Pat.)
Wagner, Eleanor R. '41 '70 C.94 A.B. L.424 J.D.
Dir., Legal Affs., Joint Comm. on Accreditation of Healthcare Organizations
Walsh, Chas. G., Jr. ....'24 '51 C.329 L.365 LL.B. Admin. Law J., Soc. Sec. Admn.
Weiland, Mark B. '56 '81 C.339 B.A. L.146 J.D.
Gen. Coun., Prof. Servs. Industries, Inc.
Wells, Henry M., III '45 '83 C.418 B.S. L.215 J.D.
Sr. V.P., Human Res., Dental Network of Amer.‡
Westermeyer, Michael T. '49 '77 C.755 B.A. L.300 J.D.
(adm. in MN; not adm. in IL) V.P. & Gen. Coun., BCS Financial Corp.
Willis, Douglas A. '63 '88 C.337 B.A. L.209 J.D.
Assoc. Corp. Coun., Prof. Servs. Industries, Inc.
Zavislak, John L. ....'46 '71 C.363 A.B. L.424 J.D. 1 S. 280 Summit Court, C-2

OAK FOREST, 28,051, *Cook Co.*

Ashack, James T. ....'56 '82 C.424 B.S. L.209 J.D. [Elmore&D.]
Burt, Edward J. ....'48 '73 C.602 B.B.A. L.209 J.D. [Urban&B.]
Daudish, Joseph E. ....'60 '85 L.424 J.D. [Elmore&D.]
DeMichael, Joseph J. ....'44 '68 C&L.209 B.A., J.D. [Elmore&D.]
Ehrenstrom, Jon E. ....'58 '94 C.720 B.A. L.1000 J.D. [Ryan&E.]
Elmore, Elbert F. ....'32 '57 C.999 L.209 LL.B. [Elmore&D.]
Elmore & DeMichael ....15507 S. Cicero Ave.
Eyestone, Linda L. ....'— '83 C.339 B.A. L.209 J.D. 14511 S. Central Ct., PH 1
Hook, Brenda S. ....'59 '85 C.999 B.A. L.339 J.D. 15440 Arroyo Dr.
Jesk, Robin P. ....'49 '76 C.1016 B.S. L.146 J.D. [R.P.Jesk&Assoc.]
Jesk, Robin Philip, and Associates ....15150 S. Cicero Ave.
Jurus, John A. ....'29 '62 C.259 B.S. L.365 J.D. [J.A.Jurus]
Jurus, John A., Ltd. ....15340 Central St.
Kelly, Bernard J. ....'32 '82 C.452 B.E. L.146 J.D. 15332 Maple Dr.
Moskal, Mary I. ....'49 '85 C.999 B.A. L.365 J.D. [Moskal&Assoc.]
Moskal & Associates, Ltd. ....15601 S. Cicero Ave., Ste. 101
Narko, Medard M. ....'41 '66 C.424 B.S. L.597 J.D. [M.M.Narko]
Narko, Medard M., Associates, P.C. ....15000 S. Cicero Ave.
Ryan, Christine M. ....'61 '02 C.719 B.S. L.365 J.D. [Urban&B.]
Ryan, Frank J. ....'56 '81 C.589 B.A. L.365 J.D. [Ryan&E.]
Ryan & Ehrenstrom, Ltd. ....4849 167th Street
Ryder, Sandra L. ....'47 '84 L.365 J.D. 5039 W. 151st St.
Sender, R. Scott ....'64 '89 C.208 B.S.B.A. L.910 J.D. [Sender&Assoc.]
Sender Associates, Charter ....15601 Cicero Ave., Ste. 101
Smith, Raymond S., (AV) ....'46 '73 C.339 B.S. L.209 J.D. [Urban&B.]
Toolis, Thomas W. ....'71 '99 C.339 B.S. L.146 J.D. [Urban&B.]
Urban, Edmund G. ....'27 '52 C.145 B.S. L.209 J.D. [Urban&B.]
Urban, Edmund G., III ....'57 '82 C.98 B.S. L.209 J.D. [Urban&B.]
Urban & Burt, Ltd. ....5320 W. 159th St.
Zeleznak, Cheryl C. ....'52 '91 C.1191 B.S. L.365 J.D. [Urban&B.]

OAK LAWN, 55,245, *Cook Co.*

Behling, Geo. A., Jr. ....'24 '49 C&L.145 Ph.B., J.D. 5210 W. 95th St.
Burke, Joseph J. ....'48 '78 9333 S. Sproat Ave.‡
Conroy, John T., (BV) ....'39 '65 C.1024 B.A. L.146 J.D. 4544 W. 103rd St.
Daoud, Nawal Abueid ....'75 '00 C.339 B.S. L.146 J.D. [N.A.Daoud]
Daoud, Nawal A., P.C. ....4815 W. 103rd St.
Drury, Patrick G. ....'59 '89 C.339 B.A. L.365 J.D. 8938 S. Ridgeland
Dunn, William R. ....'35 '58 C.145 B.A. L.597 LL.B. 4544 W. 103rd St., 2nd Fl.
Ebner, Henry F. ....'23 '52 C&L.597 B.S., J.D. 9209 S. 55th Court‡
Ellis, John P. ....'36 '67 C.145 B.A. L.365 LL.B. 9211 S. Keeler
Fanelli, Joseph C. '42 '68 C.424 B.S. L.597 J.D.
Sr. V.P. & Tr. Offr., First Natl. Bk. of Evergreen Pk.
Farrell, Thomas J. ....'35 '61 C&L.424 B.S., J.D. 5170 W. 95th St.
Fegan, Thomas H., Sr. ....'10 '40 C&L.424 LL.B. 10513 S. Lawler Ave.‡
Fifer, Gregory ....'57 '83 C.750 B.S. L.146 J.D. 9000 S. Cicero
Finegan, Thomas F., Jr. ....'40 '72 C.602 B.A. L.424 J.D. Asst. Pub. Def.
Forst, Richard J. ....'58 '83 C.424 B.A. L.146 J.D. [Forst]

Forst Law Offices
9150 South Cicero Avenue, Suite 204, 60453
Telephone: 708-499-2560 Fax: 708-499-2560
Email: forstlaw@sbcglobal.net
Richard J. Forst.
Divorce, Debtor Bankruptcy.
See Professional Biographies, OAK LAWN, ILLINOIS

Gardner, William G. ....'35 '60 C.742 L.209 LL.B. 4931 W. 95th
George J. Witous, P.C. ....10600 S. Cicero Ave.
Gierach, James E., Law Offices of, (BV) '44 '69
C.479 B.A. L.209 J.D. 9759 Southwest Highway
Gliege, Gerhardt J. ....'20 '50 C.339 B.A. L.365 LL.B. 4219 W. 95th St.
Goggin, Richard E. ....'29 '61 C.597 Ph.B. L.146 LL.B. 10741 Kenneth Ave.
Groebe, Charles L. ....'61 '88 C.339 B.A. L.365 J.D. 5041 W. 95th St.
Hallenbeck, Stephen M., (AV) '41 '66
C.174 B.S. L.424 J.D. Exec. V.P., First Natl. Bk. of Evergreen Pk.
Haney, Gerald J. ....'32 '58 C&L.424 B.S.C., J.D. 5210 W. 95th St.
Jach, Virginia A. V. ....'40 '65 C.339 B.S. L.146 J.D. 5016 W. Lamb Dr.
Johnson, Arvid C. ....'35 '59 C&L.424 B.S., J.D. 4700 W. 99th Place‡
Johnson, Ronald O. ....'28 '54 C&L.209 B.A., J.D. 10613 S. Kolin St.‡
Jurgens, Roland J., (BV) ....'32 '57 C.339 L.209 LL.B. 10200 S. Cicero Ave.
Karno, Earle S. ....'30 '55 C.339 L.209 LL.B. 9629 Southwest Hwy.
Kennedy, Robert J., (AV) ....'21 '52 C.209 B.A. L.365 LL.B. 4001 W. 95th St.
Kenny, Robert E., Jr. ....'32 '61 C.424 B.S.C. L.209 LL.B. 5210 W. 95th St.
Kenny, William W. ....'64 '92 C.602 B.B.A. L.424 J.D. 5210 W. 95th St.
Lablaiks, Marilyn R. ......'52 '01 C.999 B.S.N. L.365 J.D. University of Chicago Hospitals
Litton, Michael L. ....'54 '79 C&L.209 B.A., J.D. 4550 W. 103rd St.
Lynch, Thomas W. ....'55 '87 C.209 B.S. L.365 J.D. [T.W.Lynch]

Lynch, Thomas W., P.C.
9231 S. Roberts Road, 60457
Telephone: 708-598-5999 Fax: 708-598-6299
Email: twlpc@worldnet.att.net URL: http://www.thomaswlynchpc.com
Thomas W. Lynch.
Federal Taxation, IRS and State Representation including Collections Division, Audits, Appeals, Tax Court and State or US District Court, State Taxation, Tax Appeals and Real Estate.
See Professional Biographies, OAK LAWN, ILLINOIS

Marcus, Lillian (Polisky) ....'23 '45 L.209 LL.B. 9221 S. Keeler‡
McCarthy, Michael T. '30 '66 C.424 B.S. L.365 LL.B.
9620 S. Komensky Ave., Apt. 201
McGlynn, Terrence R. ....'58 '86 C.424 B.A. L.365 J.D. 9236 Kedvale Avenue
McKay, Richard S. ....'36 '63 C.424 B.S.C. L.146 J.D. 8732 S. 49th Ct.
McNamara, Lawr. J. ....'29 '53 L.365 J.D. 4219 W. 95th St.
Montgomery, Lee ....'48 '73 C.98 B.S. L.365 J.D. 4550 W. 103rd St., Ste. 201
Novotny, Thomas F. ....'48 '81 C.1151 B.A. L.146 J.D. 4550 W. 103rd St.
O'Connor, John J. ....'39 '67 C.1024 B.S. L.146 J.D. 4544 W. 103rd St.
Phelan, Maurice E., (Ltd.) ....'38 '62 C.424 L.209 LL.B. 9759 Southwest Hwy.
Phelps, Frank K. ....'37 '67 C.436 B.S. L.146 J.D. P.O. Box 816
Roche, Jean M., & Associates ....'55 '79 C.339 B.S. L.146 J.D. 10735 S. Cicero Ave.
Sajewski, Edmund N. ....'35 '62 C.973 A.B. L.424 J.D. [E.N.Sajewski]
Sajewski, Edmund N., P.C. ....10200 S. Cicero
Scheibel, James R. ....'56 '81 C.339 B.A. L.424 J.D. [J.R.Scheibel]
Scheibel, James R., Ltd., Law Office of ....5013 W. 95th St.
Scheidt, Richard C. ....'27 '52 C.602 L.221 LL.B. 5840 W. 104th St.‡
Schussler, Edward G. ....'43 '71 C.210 B.A. L.339 J.D. 9759 S.W. Hwy.
Scott-Rudnick, Clifford '48 '78
C.388 B.A. L.146 J.D. Trust Offr., Suburban Bank & Trust Co.

Siwek, James J., Law Office of
(See Worth)

Sutera, Stephen M. ....'59 '86 C.424 B.B.A. L.365 J.D. [S.Sutera]
Sutera, Stephen ....4927 W. 95th St.
Tschetter, Duane D. ....'38 '70 C&L.209 B.S.C., J.D. 9850 S. Cicero Ave.
Tucker, Berry K. ....'46 '72 C.589 B.S. L.424 J.D. 5210 W. 95th St.
Urbut, Patrick J., Law Office ....'45 '73 C.424 B.S. L.146 J.D. 4931 W. 95th St.
Voorn, Barry N. '56 '82
C.999 B.S. L.365 J.D. Gen. Coun., First Natl. Bk. of Evergreen Pk.
Witous, Daniel William ....'69 '98 C.602 B.A. L.1187 J.D. [George J.W.]
Witous, George J. ....'31 '58 C.602 B.A. L.209 J.D. [George J.W.]
Wojcik, William S. ....'52 '80 C.589 B.S. L.365 J.D. 10312 S. Cicero Ave., 2nd Fl.
Zegar, Sam S. ....'64 '91 C.339 B.A. L.1187 J.D. 8938 Ridgeland Ave., Ste. 103
Zimmer, Jason N. ....'71 '97 C.339 B.S. L.365 J.D. First Natl. Bk. of Evergreen Park
Zubek, Matthew F. ....'— '81 C.339 B.A. L.365 J.D. 8855 S. Ridgeland

OAK PARK, 52,524, *Cook Co.*

Alexander, Kevin F. ....'59 '84 C.700 B.A. L.146 J.D. 137 N. Oak Park Ave.
Armstrong, Gene L., (AV) ....'40 '67 C.966 B.S. L.813 J.D. [G.L.Armstrong&Assoc.]
Armstrong, Gene L., & Associates, P.C., (AV) ....1111 South Boulevard

Ash, Anos, Freedman & Logan, L.L.C.
(See Chicago)

Baker, Geoffrey A. ....'65 '96 C.659 B.S.E. L.966 J.D. [Dowell B.] (Pat.)
Berardi, Matthew J., (BV) ....'42 '72 C.209 B.S.C. L.146 J.D. 715 Lake St.
Berman, Edward J., (BV) ....'48 '74 C.966 B.A. L.209 J.D. 901 N. Marion
Boutet, Simone M. ....'63 '89 C.436 B.S. L.209 J.D. Asst. Village Atty.
Brauneis, Geraldine A. ....'30 '78 C.813 A.B. L.146 J.D. 1125 Rosell
Byrne, Paul V., Jr., (BV) ....'46 '72 C.676 B.A. L.597 J.D. 1016 South Kenilworth
Caragher, Thomas J. '28 '55 C&L.436 B.S., LL.B.
(adm. in WI; not adm. in IL) 1000 S. Grove St.‡
Carlson, David B., (AV) ....'45 '70 C.339 B.S. L.365 J.D. 1140 Lake Street, Suite 403
Carson, Bruce L., (AV) ....'21 '48 C&L.597 B.S., J.D. 1020 S. Grove‡
Cederoth, Lisa J. ....'60 '85 C.98 B.S. L.339 J.D. 422 N. Scoville Ave.‡
Cheeks, Dansby G. ....'43 '74 C.352 B.A. L.146 J.D. 108 Madison St.

Chittenden, Murday & Novotny, LLC
(See Chicago)

Christopher, Walter A. ....'11 '36 C&L.879 B.A., LL.B. 931 N. Grove Ave.‡
Coburn, Violet M. ....'16 '42 C&L.209 LL.B. 6821 North Ave.‡
Conniff, Lyn C. ....'51 '87 C.999 B.A. L.424 J.D. [L.C.Conniff]
Conniff, Lyn C., P.C. ....1010 Lake St.
Coplan, Gregory F., (BV) ....'66 '92 C.339 B.A. L.589 J.D. 1101 Lake St., Ste. 200
Cornelius, Linda S. ....'56 '81 C.293 B.A. L.477 J.D. Cook Co. Legal Assistance Found.
Crane, Benjamin A. ....'75 '01 C.746 B.A. L.1000 J.D. 1101 Lake St., Ste. 200
Crawford, Mary Hazel ....'— '35 C&L.209 LL.B. 705 Lyman
Cristiano, Maria A. ....'62 '87 C&L.209 B.A., J.D. 6817 W. North Ave.
Cuda, Anthony, (AV) ....'54 '80 C.238 B.A. L.589 J.D. 1146 Westgate
Davis, Gabrielle S. ....'55 '83 C.388 B.A. L.146 J.D. [G.S.Davis]

Davis, Gabrielle S., P.C.
1011 Lake Street, Suite 424, 60301
Telephone: 708-660-9164 Fax: 708-358-1335
URL: http://www.gabrielledavislaw.com
Gabrielle S. Davis.
Family Law.
See Professional Biographies, OAK PARK, ILLINOIS

DeBoer, Michael J., (AV) ....'58 '86 C.208 B.S. L.146 J.D. [Goedert,H.&D.]
De'Medici, Bruce E., (BV) '54 '80
C.477 B.A. L.912 J.D. 1011 Lake Street, Suite 205 (©Chicago)
Doheny, Peggy Ann, Law Office of '59 '86 C.339 B.A. L.146 J.D.
711 South Blvd., Ste. 6
Doll, Donald K. ....'67 '93 C.209 B.A. L.146 J.D. [D.Doll]
Doll, Donald, Law Office of ....830 S. Wenonah

Dowell Baker
229 Randolph Street, 60302 ⊙
Telephone: 708-660-1413 Fax: 312-873-4466
Member of Firm: Geoffrey A. Baker.
General Practice.
Lafayette, Indiana Office: 1001 Main Street, 47901. Telephone: 765-429-4004. Telephone: 765-429-4114.
See Professional Biographies, OAK PARK, ILLINOIS

Downs, Barbara A. ....'39 '84 C.611 B.A. L.209 J.D. [Downs]
Downs, Robert K., (AV) ....'35 '65 C.293 B.A. L.362 J.D. [Downs] ⊙
Downs Law Offices, P.C., (AV) ....1010 Lake Street, Suite 620 (©Chicago)
Duncan, Jon A., (BV) ....'54 '80 C.210 B.A. L.209 J.D. [G.L.Armstrong&Assoc.]
Esposito, Stephen C. ....'52 '87 C.873 B.A. L.365 J.D. 7120 W. Roosevelt Rd.

Farley, William F. '42 '69 C.95 B.A. L.93 J.D.
(adm. in MA; not adm. in IL) Chmn. of the Bd., Farley Industries, Inc.
Fee, Russell J., III .... '47 '75 C.945 B.A. L.365 J.D. 721 Belleforte Avenue
Fein, Eileen L. .... '46 '80 C.589 B.A. L.146 J.D. [Fein&S.]
Fein & Seeskin .... 818 Harrison St.
Finder, Gary N. '56 '89 C.1036 B.A. L.659 J.D.
(adm. in GA; not adm. in IL) 333 S. Oak Park Ave. Unit 2-S‡
Fisher, Ward P., (AV) .... '25 '52 C.597 B.S. L.145 J.D. 1033 N. Euclid
Gamboney, William G., Jr., (AV) .... '50 '77 C.339 B.S. L.146 J.D. [W.Gamboney]
Gamboney, William, (AV) .... 216 S. Marion St.
Georgiou, George .... '20 '74 C.145 M.B.A. L.209 J.D. 314 S. East Ave.‡
Gerrity, Edw. M. .... '15 '53 C&L.424 B.S.C. 1111 Ontario St.‡
Gibson, Eric .... '45 '77 C.238 B.A. L.209 J.D. 814 S. Taylor Ave.
Gilbert, David G. .... '46 '76 C.912 B.A. L.424 J.D. 1005 N. Elmwood Ave.
Goedert, John P., (AV) .... '13 '39 C&L.424 A.B., J.D. 1011 Lake Street, Suite 303

Goedert, Huntington & DeBoer, (AV)
1011 Lake Street Suite 303, 60301-1138
Telephone: 708-848-6066 Fax: 708-848-6067 URL: http://www.ghdlaw.com
Email: ghd@ameritech.net URL: http://www.lawyers.com/gh&dlaw
Members of Firm: Robert A. Huntington; Michael J. DeBoer.
Business Law, Corporate Law, Mergers and Acquisitions, Contracts, Employee Benefits, Taxation, Trusts and Estates, Wills, Decedents Estates, Probate, Elder Law, Nonprofit and Charitable Organizations, Real Estate.
See Professional Biographies, OAK PARK, ILLINOIS

Goode, Wendy M. .... '— '96 C.339 B.A. L.801 J.D. Estate Tax Atty.
Gottardo, David A., Attorney at Law '— '99
C.339 B.S.M.E. L.365 J.D. 918 S. Kenilworth Ave., Ste. 01 (Pat.)
Goulding, Regina A. .... '54 '85 C&L.424 B.A., J.D. 401 S. Grove‡
Gradel, Joyce Ford .... '43 '75 C.1016 B.S. L.209 J.D. 115 S. Marion St.
Green, Colby M. .... '70 '95 C.145 B.A. L.424 J.D. 801 North Woodbine Avenue
Gross, Evelyn C. .... '53 '78 C.679 B.A. L.365 J.D. 410 Lake St.
Hanrahan, Edward V., (AV) .... '21 '49 C.602 B.S.C. L.309 LL.B. 901 Lake St.
Hansen, John C. .... '70 '97 C.201 B.A. L.861 J.D. [J.C.Hansen]
Hansen, Thomas R. .... '46 '75 C.589 B.S. L.365 J.D. 1010 Lake St.
Hansen, John C., LLC .... 805 S. Scoville Ave.
Heffernan, Linda F., Law Office .... '46 '82 C.753 B.S. L.365 J.D. 730 S. Kenilworth
Herrick, Walter D., (AV) .... '09 '34 C.145 Ph.B L.477 J.D. 1010 Lake St.‡
Hesik, George A. .... '46 '74 C.209 B.A. L.146 J.D. [G.A.Hesik&Assoc.]
Hesik, George A., & Associates, Ltd. .... 821 Garfield St.
Hlava, John Jeffrey .... '70 '96 C.112 B.A. L.426 J.D. 1226 Forest Ave.
Holmquest, Thomas K. .... '28 '58 C&L.309 A.B., LL.B. 320 Wisconsin‡
Houha, Leonard J. .... '30 '53 L.209 LL.B. 1034 1/2 Lake St.
Howard, Ronald C. .... '47 '76 C.879 B.S.B.A. L.365 J.D. 845 Washington St.
Hoy, David E. .... '48 '83 C.238 B.S.B.A. L.589 J.D. 1100 Lake St., Ste. 245
Huebner, Harold C., Jr. .... '18 '42 C.436 L.209 LL.B. 212 S. Maple Ave.

Hughes Socol Piers Resnick & Dym, Ltd.
(See Chicago)

Huntington, Robert A., (AV) .... '46 '72 C&L.436 B.S., J.D. [Goedert,H.&D.]

Igoe, Philip A., The Law Offices of
(See Chicago)

Johnsen, Robert E., Jr. .... '29 '55 C.339 B.S. L.597 J.D. 1026 N. Marion St.
Jones, Herbert D., Jr. .... '13 '39 C.209 L.365 LL.B. 1221 N. Edmer Ave.
Judge, William J. ..... '52 '81 C.162 B.A. L.589 J.D. 803A N. Harlem, Ste. 2N #1
Justice, Marina C. '45 '77 C.347 A.B. L.1162 J.D.
(adm. in DC; not adm. in IL) 1133 Linden Ave.‡
Karr, Jennifer K. .... '— '91 C.966 M.S. L.209 J.D. 1131 Lake St., Ste. 133
Kennelly, John M. .... '49 '78 C.1207 B.A. L.424 J.D. 1010 Lake St.
Ketchum, Amy E., Attorney at Law '58 '84 C.475 B.A. L.424 J.D.
524 S. Kenilworth Ave.
Kiefer, Lesa Struck .... '66 '92 C.424 B.S. L.365 J.D. 1145 Westgate
Kloak, Richard C. .... '54 '79 C&L.424 B.A., J.D. 224 S. Marion St.

Kopecky, James L., P.C.
(See Chicago)

Krebs, Thomas G. .... '48 '76 C.339 B.A. L.146 J.D. 1111 Westgate Street
Maganzini, Paul J. .... '48 '73 C.742 B.A. L.602 J.D. 1111 South Blvd.
Maliszewski, Edward J., Jr. .... '55 '80 C.209 B.A. L.365 J.D. [Meyer&M.]
Marmer, Sandra S. .... '42 '75 C.47 B.A. L.209 J.D. 137 S. Scoville
Martin, William J., (AV) .... '36 '62 C&L.424 B.S., J.D. [W.J.Martin]
Martin, William J., Ltd., (AV) .... 1011 Lake St., Ste. 201
McMahon, James E. .... '48 '74 C.973 B.S. L.602 J.D. 1111 South Blvd.
Meek, Fredric W. .... '42 '69 C.191 B.A. L.209 J.D. 1st Bk. of Oak Pk.
Mertz, Richard A. .... '64 '89 C.475 B.A. L.477 J.D. 1220 N. Grove Ave.
Merz, Mary Catherine .... '62 '89 C.1060 B.A. L.1065 J.D. 1140 Lake St.
Meyer, James S. .... '51 '79 C&L.589 B.A., J.D. [Meyer&M.]
Meyer & Maliszewski .... 840 S. Oak Park Ave.
Meyerson, Pamela McLean, Law Office of '59 '83
C.209 B.S. L.145 J.D. 151 N. Harvey Ave.
Middleton, Martha .... '— '80 L.209 J.D. 708 Clarence
Morley, Richard K. ...... '63 '91 C.209 B.S.C. L.146 J.D. 137 N. Oak Park Ave., Ste. 201
Motz, Anton .... '26 '55 C&L.966 B.A., LL.B. 728 N. Elmwood‡
Murphy, Marianne C. .... '37 '76 C.530 B.A. L.424 J.D. 165 N. Kenilworth Ave.
Murr, Rita C. .... '74 '02 C.1016 B.A. L.365 J.D. 1146 Westgate, Ste. 4
Nesburg, Kathryn S. .... '48 '73 C.700 B.A. L.424 J.D. 415 N. East Ave.‡

Oak Park Legal Clinic
114 Chicago Avenue, 2nd Floor, 60304
Telephone: 708-524-1181 Fax: 708-524-1346
URL: http://www.lawyers.com/oakparklegal
Member of Firm: Robert Rattler.
Bankruptcy, Real Estate, Criminal Law, Divorce, Accidents, Social Security.
See Professional Biographies, OAK PARK, ILLINOIS

Osga, Kristi A. .... '44 '70 C.424 B.S. L.597 J.D. 535 N. Taylor Ave.
Ostrander, Joel W. .... '49 '75 C.424 A.B. L.365 J.D. 617 S. Wesley Ave.
Pearsall, Henry B. .... '34 '61 C.31 A.B. L.477 J.D. 721 Ontario‡
Pellegrini, Frank .... '53 '76 C&L.209 B.S.C., J.D. 6817 W. North Ave.
Peregrine, Moore W., (AV) .... '26 '53 C.679 B.S. L.424 J.D. 1010 Lake St.
Petrich, Gail Sears .... '48 '82 C.608 M.A. L.424 J.D. 212 S. Humphrey
Proteau, Paul J. .... '31 '62 C.424 B.S. L.209 J.D. 115 S. Marion St.
Ransom, Robt. M. .... '22 '50 C&L.597 B.S., LL.B. 711 South Blvd.
Rattler, Robert .... '— '87 C.238 B.S. L.146 J.D. [Oak P.]
Ravin, Andrea .... '58 '84 C.976 B.A. L.276 J.D. 322 South Lombard‡

Rieck, Charles '— '78 C.602 B.A. L.813 J.D.
100 Forest Place, Suite 405, 60301
Telephone: 630-399-7751 Fax: 708-386-3728
Email: mitstnfnd@aol.com

(This Listing Continued)

Rieck, Charles (Continued)
Computer, Electronics and Software Patents, Patent Applications, Patent Infringement, Patent Prosecution. Intellectual Property Law, Licensing Agreements.
See Professional Biographies, OAK PARK, ILLINOIS

Rifis, Jordan B. .... '45 '71 C.1016 B.A. L.209 J.D. [J.Rifis]
Rifis, Jordan, P.C. .... 218 Lake St.
Rohlfing, Harold T. .... '33 '72 C.597 B.M.E. L.365 J.D. [H.T.Rohlfing]
Rohlfing, Harold T., P.C. .... 1010 Lake St., Ste. 612
Roupas, Geoffrey T. '44 '68 C.966 B.S. L.597 J.D.
Assoc. Reg. Coun., Dept. of Housing & Urban Develop.
Sahlas, Colleen Lynette .... '71 '00 C.1144 B.A. L.365 J.D. 1100 Lake St., Ste. 245
Samuelson, C. Lois .... '23 '49 C.145 Ph.B. L.146 LL.B. 203 N. Kenilworth Ave.‡
Schaefer, William Dee ... '50 '81 C.674 B.S.E. L.46 J.D. Controller, Farley Industries, Inc.
Schelthoff, John W. .... '25 '53 C&L.209 LL.B. 1225 Linden Ave.
Schoen, Constance B. .... '52 '81 C.136 B.S.Ed. L.1187 J.D. 846 Gunderson Avenue
Schoenmeyer, Joel A. .... '— '96 C.475 B.A. L.477 J.D. 1101 Lake St., Ste. 403
Schroeder, Robert L. .... '48 '79 C.560 B.A. L.365 LL.B. [Schroeder,R.L.]
Schroeder, Robert L., Ltd. .... P.O. Box 1494
Seeskin, Morris A. .... '43 '78 C&L.597 B.A., J.D. [Fein&S.]
Simkunas, Michael J. .... '63 '90 C&L.209 B.A., J.D. 1111 South Boulevard
Sims, Iris K. .... '— '86 C.597 B.S. L.145 J.D. Attorney, BP Amoco Corporation
Singler, Mark R. .... '77 '02 C.352 B.A. L.365 J.D. 104 N. Oak Park Ave.
Smith, Gregory L. .... '48 '75 C.966 B.A. L.209 J.D. 115 S. Marion St.
Spagat, David .... '24 '51 C.1016 B.A. L.146 J.D. 945 N. Elmwood Ave.‡
Spira, Maurice H. .... '10 '35 C.145 L.209 J.D. 100 Forest Pl.‡
Stephenson, Robert .... '71 '02 L.608 J.D. [R.M.Stephenson]

Stephenson, R.M., LLC
801 South Boulevard, Suite 3, 60302
Telephone: 708-434-1267 Fax: 708-434-0784
Email: info@rmstephenson.com URL: http://www.rmstephenson.com
Robert Stephenson.
Appellate Practice, Criminal Defense, Family Law, Wills, Trusts and Estates, Civil Litigation, Business Law, Real Estate Law.
See Professional Biographies, OAK PARK, ILLINOIS

Stepnowski, Edward L. .... '24 '50 C.339 L.209 J.D. 1515 N. Harlem Ave.
Stern, Adam M. .... '69 '94 C.94 B.A. L.879 J.D. 137 N. Oak Park Ave., Ste. 400
Stewart, Thomas M. .... '44 '78 C.174 B.A. L.365 J.D. 1010 Lake St., Ste. 612
Stickler, Paul .... '18 '42 C&L.597 B.S., J.D. 1031 N. Grove Ave.
Stuart, Rhonda .... '64 '93 C.293 B.A. L.339 J.D. 711 S. Blvd., Ste. 10
Suber, Beverly S. .... '54 '82 C.473 B.A. L.597 J.D. 1127 W. Augusta
Sullivan, Mason D. .... '34 '62 C&L.602 Ph.B., LL.B. 625 S. Kenilworth Ave.
Sullivan, William B. .... '66 '92 C.339 B.A. L.209 J.D. 1101 Lake St., Ste. 405

Takiguchi, Masaru K.
(See Oak Brook)

Tamari & Blumenthal, LLC
(See Chicago)

Tibbetts, Jack H. .... '54 '79 C&L.597 B.A., J.D. Asst. Village Atty.
Triner, Jeanne E. .... '50 '75 C.57 A.B. L.339 J.D. 646 N. Euclid Ave.
Troelstrup, John .... '39 '68 C.502 B.A. L.923 J.D. [Troelstrup]
Troelstrup Law Office .... 1140 Lake Street, Suite 300

Tyma, Stephen L., P.C.
(See Chicago)

Veldenz, Russell P., (AV) .... '57 '82 C.357 B.S. L.365 J.D. 429 S. Scoville
Wakenight, Mark T. .... '56 '88 C.145 B.A. L.378 J.D. 1146 Westgate St.
Wallick, Sandra M. .... '42 '75 C.47 B.A. L.209 J.D. 137 S. Scoville Ave.
Walsh, Christopher G., Jr., (AV) '48 '76
C.424 A.B. L.569 J.D. 1111 South Boulevard (⊙Chicago)
Walsh, Mary J. .... '54 '80 C.700 B.A. L.602 J.D. 827 Linden Ave.
Williams, Anthony C. .... '62 '91 C.339 B.A. L.209 J.D. 824 N. Ridgeland Ave.★
Winkler, Donald J. .... '47 '76 C.98 B.S. L.209 J.D. 308 Madison St.
Yannias, Kathleen C., Attorney at Law '48 '76
C.339 B.S. L.597 J.D. 174 N. Elmwood Ave.
Zissimopoulos, Dina V. .... '68 '94 C.339 B.A. L.228 J.D. 605 Wenonah Ave.

OBLONG, 1,616, *Crawford Co.*

Cox, Phillips, Weber, Tedford & Heap, P.C.
(See Robinson)

O'FALLON, 21,910, *St. Clair Co.*

Belsheim, Harold G., II, (BV) ...... '48 '78 C.182 B.A. L.910 J.D. Ste 100, 1002 E Wesley
Benedick, Thomas F., (BV) .... '50 '74 C.801 B.A. L.734 J.D. [Benedick]
Benedick Law Office, (BV) .... 1004 S. Lincoln Ave., Ste. 12
Bernstein, Dina L. '67 '92 C.846 B.B.A. L.744 J.D.
(adm. in TX; not adm. in IL) 637 Wintergreen Dr.
Bradley, Daniel L., (BV) .... '65 '97 C&L.801 B.A., J.D. [Ⓐ DeFranco]
Bruckert, Terry Ivan, (CV) ... '59 '93 C.357 B.S. L.801 J.D. 1002 E. Wesley Dr., Ste. 100
Dacosse, Lori E., (CV) .... '74 '99 C.339 B.A. L.1117 J.D. 772 Wall Street
DeFranco, James E., (BV) .... '56 '81 C.338 B.S. L.801 J.D. [DeFranco]
DeFranco Law Firm, P.C., (BV) .... 785 Wall Street, Suite 200
Evans, Paul J., (BV) .... '60 '88 C&L.801 B.S., J.D. [Evans]
Evans Law Firm, (BV) .... 6 Eagle Ctr. #3, Ste. 10
Faust, Dana L. Holtmeier '69 '98 L.734 J.D.
Dir. Plan Servs., Great-West Life & Annuity Ins. Co.
Fleming, Timothy P., (BV) .... '47 '73 C.711 B.A. L.30 J.D. 100 S. Lincoln
Funk, Brian M. .... '76 '02 C.339 B.S. L.734 J.D. 807 W. Hwy. 50
Glassl, Norbert Jakob Josef, (BV) ...... '60 '92 C&L.734 B.S., J.D. 784 Wall St., Ste. 100
Green, Joel P. .... '75 '01 C.98 B.S. L.734 J.D. 784 Wall St., Ste. 100
Gruenke, Douglas C. .... '77 '02 C&L.801 B.A., J.D. Ste 100, 1002 E Wesley Dr
Juliano, PC, (BV) .... 772 Wall St.
Juliano, Rand, (BV) .... '55 '88 C.357 B.A. L.734 J.D. [Juliano]
Kasten, Chadwick, (BV) .... '67 '92 C.352 B.A. L.734 J.D. [Kasten&N.]
Kasten & Norsigian, (BV) .... 784 Wall Street
Koebel, Delmar O., (AV) .... '26 '53 C.465 A.B. L.910 J.D. 6 Joshua Dr.‡
Kujawski, John P., (AV) .... '48 '73 C&L.734 A.B., J.D. [Kujawski&N.] ⊙

Kujawski & Nowak, P.C., (AV)
1331 Park Plaza Drive, Suite 2, 62269-1764 ⊙
Telephone: 618-622-3600 Fax: 618-622-3700
John P. Kujawski; Michael K. Nowak;—Angel Von Bokel.
Federal Employers Liability. Negligence, Maritime Negligence, Workers Compensation, Products Liability Law and Medical Malpractice. General and Trial Practice.
Approved Attorneys for: Local 520, International Union of Operating Engineers; International Brotherhood of Firemen & Oilers; International Brotherhood of Locomotive Engineers.

(This Listing Continued)

Kujawski & Nowak, P.C. (Continued)

Reference: West Pointe Bank and Trust Co., Belleville, Illinois.
North Little Rock, Arkansas Office: 201 W. Broadway, Suite E. Telephone: 501-372-8047.

Lindauer, Curt C., (BV) .... '31 '54 C&L.910 A.B., J.D. [Lindauer&W.]
Lindauer & Welch, (BV) .... 784 Wall St., Ste. 100
Norsigian, Hrant "Hud", Jr., (BV) .... '63 '88 C&L.910 B.A., J.D. [Kasten&N.]
Nowak, Michael K., (BV) .... '59 '85 C.234 B.A. L.589 J.D. [Kujawski&N.]
Pinjuh, Joseph M. '66 '92 C.823 B.A. L.880 J.D.
(adm. in TN; not adm. in IL) 1009 E. 3rd St.★
Rosen, Rick E., (BV) .... '47 '75 C.178 B.A. L.365 J.D. [Rosen]
Rosen Law Firm, (BV) .... 1669 Windham Way
Sawyer, Jacob D. .... '78 '03 C.612 B.S. L.910 J.D. [A DeFranco]
Stauder, Cindy .... '61 '87 C.1288 B.A. L.734 J.D. Diversified Coatings Ltd.
Ulkus, David H., (BV) .... '52 '78 C.801 B.A. L.339 J.D. 100 S. Lincoln
Vetri, Kristi Maurine .... '54 '97 C.443 B.S. L.734 J.D. P.O. Box 548
Von Bokel, Angel .... '68 '96 C.338 B.S. L.801 J.D. [A Kujawski&N.]
Welch, Kay A., (BV) .... '41 '81 C.234 B.S. L.910 J.D. [Lindauer&W.]

Wiltsie, Timothy S.
(See Belleville)

OGLESBY, 3,619, *La Salle Co.*

Brolley, Vincent D., (CV) .... '57 '82 C.602 B.A. L.339 J.D. [Perona]
Day, David C., (BV) .... '47 '76 C.98 B.S. L.910 J.D. [Perona]
Hunter, Gerald M., (BV) .... '45 '72 C.112 B.A. L.146 J.D. [G.M.Hunter]
Hunter, Gerald M., Ltd., (BV) .... 129 W. Walnut St.
Kelly, Kevin M. .... '59 '84 C.436 B.A. L.209 J.D. 18 Park Rd.
Perona Law Offices, (BV) .... 170 E. Walnut St/ (⊙Peru)
Peterlin, Gary L., (BV) .... '49 '80 C.589 B.S. L.365 J.D. [Perona]

OHIO, 540, *Bureau Co.*

Knuth, Conrad J., Attorney at Law, (CV) '49 '78 C.424 A.B. L.146 J.D.
203 N. Main St.

OKAWVILLE, 1,274, *Washington Co.*

Moehle, Walter E., (BV) .... '16 '41 C.910 B.S. L.221 LL.B. P.O. Box 41
Schmale, Arnold A., Attorney at Law ...... '54 '83 C.465 B.A. L.365 J.D. 606 N. Front St.

OLNEY, * 8,664, *Richland Co.*

Arnold, Laurence L. .... '16 '47 C&L.309 A.B., J.D. Ret. Cir. J.
Bowen, William C., (CV) .... '41 '70 C.531 B.S. L.383 J.D. P.O. Box 633
Bruce, Terry L. .... '44 '69 C&L.339 B.S., J.D. IL Eastern Community Coll.
Burke, Patrick M., (BV) .... '51 '76 C.209 B.S. L.365 J.D. 2001 E. Main St.
Clark, John A., (BV) .... '48 '76 C.589 B.A. L.146 J.D. [Croegaert,C.&H.]
Croegaert, Paul A., Sr., (AV) .... '38 '63 C.57 B.A. L.209 J.D. 305 East Main Street‡
Croegaert, Clark & Hough, Ltd., (BV) .... 305 East Main Street

Fleming, Jeffrey E., (BV) '46 '71 C&L.339 B.S., J.D.
420 Whittle Avenue, P.O. Box 598, 62450-0598
Telephone: 618-395-8491 Fax: 618-392-3174
Email: humor8@midwest.net
Probate, Estate Planning, Real Estate, Corporate, Oil and Gas, Federal Income, Estate and Gift Taxation, Commercial and Banking Law.
References: First National Bank in Olney; The Peoples State Bank of Newton.

Hart Bell LLC
(See Vincennes, Indiana)

Heller, Holmes & Associates, P.C.
(See Mattoon)

Hough, Stephen J., (BV) .... '57 '86 C.339 B.A. L.734 J.D. [Croegaert,C.&H.]
Hyde, David A. .... '58 '86 C.339 A.B. L.500 J.D. 418 S. Morgan‡
Murvin, Jane L. .... '60 '84 C.210 B.A. L.208 J.D. 1712 S. Whittle Ave.
Roberts, Charles, (CV) .... '54 '80 C.339 A.B. L.801 J.D. [C.C.Roberts]
Roberts, C.C., Ltd., The Law Offices of, (CV) .... 504 Main St.
Shumaker, J. Claire .... '23 '49 C&L.339 B.S., LL.B. 208 N. Walnut St.
Stein, Thomas M. '59 '91 C.108 B.S. L.345 J.D.
(adm. in IN; not adm. in IL) 1702 Linda Ln.
Taylor, Larry P., (CV) .... '50 '77 C.999 B.A. L.845 J.D. City Atty.
Vaughn, Charles Bradley, (BV) .... '48 '77 C.357 B.A. L.300 J.D. 309 E. Main St.
Vaughn, Charles R. .... '22 '48 C.357 B.S. L.339 LL.B. 408 Douglas Dr.‡
Vaughn, Ray Weber, (BV) .... '57 '82 C&L.801 B.A., J.D. 308 S. Kitchell Ave.
Weber, Tom L., (BV) .... '46 '72 C.339 A.B. L.910 J.D. 101 S. Elliott
Welch, Mary Beth .... '70 '95 C.346 B.S. L.339 J.D. [A Croegaert,C.&H.]

OLYMPIA FIELDS, 4,732, *Cook Co.*

Anagnost, Yvonne .... '49 '75 C.424 B.A. L.365 J.D. I.C.C.
Bader, D. James .... '39 '65 C&L.339 B.S., LL.B. 20200 Governors Dr. (Pat.)
Barrett, Barbara Anne .... '43 '79 C.578 B.A. L.424 J.D. 23 Graymoor Ln.
Barrows, William E. .... '40 '68 C.911 B.A. L.145 J.D. 1020 Evergreen Circle
Cochrane, Gordon A. .... '44 '70 C.429 B.A. L.352 J.D. 20000 Governors Park Dr.
Dirksen, Lawrence G., (AV) .... '37 '67 C.927 B.S. L.146 J.D. 3612 West 211th St.
Ebers, Earl S., Jr., (AV) .... '30 '56 C.597 B.S. L.209 J.D. 1 Wysteria Dr.
Gubbins, Michael D., (BV) .... '35 '61 C&L.424 B.S., LL.B. 3612 W. Lincoln Hwy.
Hampton, Charisse L. .... '64 '91 C.597 B.S. L.477 J.D. 2440 Saint Andrews Drive
Hankins, Kenneth L. .... '20 '50 C.337 A.B. L.365 LL.B. 842 Highview St.
Harley, DeWitt C. .... '33 '78 C.1016 B.S.B.A. L.146 J.D. 2555 West 211th Street
Harrington, Cornelius J., Jr., (AV) .... '24 '49 C.602 L.209 LL.B. 3 Wysteria Dr.‡
Klose, Jerome B., (AV) .... '23 '50 C&L.339 B.S., J.D. 20414 Achilles Ave. (Pat.)
LaForte, George F., (BV) .... '41 '67 C.1016 L.365 J.D. 20180 Governors Hwy.
O'Rourke, Edward M. .... '27 '51 C.602 A.B. L.597 J.D. 2800 County Club Dr.‡
Perel, Marshall, (AV) .... '27 '53 C.16 B.S. L.209 J.D. P.O. Box 35
Potter, Alton W., (AV) .... '21 '50 C.597 B.S. L.477 J.D. 3633 Breakers Dr.‡
Ryza, Willis S., (AV) .... '21 '49 C&L.597 B.S., J.D. 20040 Western Ave.‡
Sax, Leonard B. .... '17 '42 C&L.597 B.S.C., J.D. 3421 Woodland Dr.‡
Snyder, Peter W. .... '48 '77 C.970 B.A. L.365 J.D. Asst. Reg. Coun., U.S. DOT
Stewart, Ardis L. .... '64 '93 C.927 B.A. L.879 J.D. Assoc. Coun., Francorp, Inc.
Treichel, Richard L. .... '43 '68 C&L.879 B.A., J.D. 20000 Governors Park Dr.
Wilkes, James T., Jr. .... '32 '56 C.575 B.S. L.597 LL.B. 20280 Governors Hwy.

ONARGA, 1,438, *Iroquois Co.*

Tungate, James L., (BV) .... '47 '79 C.340 B.S. L.339 J.D. [Tungate] ⊙
Tungate Law Offices, Ltd., (BV) .... 109 N. Chestnut St. (⊙Cissna Park, Watseka)

ONEIDA, 752, *Knox Co.*

Dickinson, Maureen Mahoney, (CV) .... '63 '91 C.339 B.S. L.146 J.D. P.O. Box 452

OQUAWKA, * 1,442, *Henderson Co.*

Stansell, Whitman & Baber
(See Monmouth)

OREGON, * 4,060, *Ogle Co.*

Baccam, Vongchouane M. .... '72 '01 C&L.352 B.A., J.D. Asst. State's Atty

Boyle, Cordes, Witheft & Brown, LLC
(See De Kalb)

Cargerman, Alan W., (AV) .... '45 '70 C.339 L.209 LL.B. [C Fearer,N.&C.] ⊙
Chadwick, Paul E. .... '— '04 C.602 B.A. L.589 J.D. [A Fearer,N.&C.] ⊙
Chadwick, Robert T., (BV) .... '48 '82 C.1070 B.S. L.602 J.D. [Fearer,N.&C.] ⊙

Cwynar, Daniel A.
(See Rockford)

Ellis, Deborah E., (CV) .... '57 '97 L.589 J.D. Asst. States Atty.
Fearer, William P., II, (BV) .... '32 '65 C.210 B.A. L.146 J.D. [Fearer,N.&C.]
Fearer, William P., III, (BV) .... '59 '84 C.36 B.A. L.802 J.D. [Fearer,N.&C.]

Fearer, Nye & Chadwick, (AV)
209 South Fifth Street, P.O. Box 256, 61061 ⊙
Telephone: 815-732-6113 Fax: 815-732-3193
Email: fearz@essex1.com URL: http://www.fearer-nye.com
Members of Firm: William P. Fearer, II; William P. Fearer III; Philip H. Nye, Jr.; Robert T. Chadwick. Associate: Paul E. Chadwick. Of Counsel: Alan W. Cargerman.
General Practice including Corporate, Business, Workers Compensation, Insurance, Insurance Defense, Probate, Estate Planning, Wills, Zoning, Tax, Real Estate, Family, Divorce, Personal Injury, Automobile Accidents, Medical Malpractice, Products Liability, Criminal, Driving While Intoxicated and Trial Practice.
Rochelle, Illinois Office: 420 Fourth Avenue, 61068. Telephone: 815-562-2156. Fax: 815-562-2158.

Floski, Douglas Porter .... '56 '81 C.388 B.A. L.339 J.D. [Smith,H.H.M.&F.]

Gilbert, John
(See Rockford)

Houser, Kimberly A. .... '62 '87 C.846 B.B.A. L.339 J.D. 412 W. Washington St.
Howarter, Wendy S., (BV) .... '66 '91 C&L.339 B.S., J.D. [Williams&M.]
James, Sheila Jo, (CV) .... '65 '91 C.966 B.A. L.678 J.D. Asst. State's Atty.
Kauffmann, Kathleen O. .... '55 '91 C&L.589 B.S., J.D. U.S. Cir. J., 15th Jud. Cir.
Krahenbuhl, Kim D., (AV) .... '50 '75 C&L.802 B.B.A., J.D. [Williams&M.]
Lenz, F. Lawrence .... '25 '50 C&L.602 LL.B. Cir. J.
Lindsey, Clayton L., (BV) .... '59 '84 C.338 B.S. L.365 J.D. [Williams&M.]
Madsen, Melanie A. .... '61 '02 C&L.589 B.G.S., J.D. [M.A.Madsen]
Madsen, Melanie Alexandrine, Attorney at Law .... 201 N. Third St., Ste. 217
Moehle, Robert C., (AV) .... '20 '47 C&L.910 B.S.B.A., J.D. [C Smith,H.H.M.&F.]
Morrow, Eric D., (CV⊤) .... '75 '00 C.927 B.S. L.801 J.D. [Smith,H.H.M.&F.]
Nieman, Timothy P., (BV) .... '50 '75 C.121 B.A. L.339 J.D. Cir.Ct. J.
Nye, Philip H., Jr., (AV) .... '36 '61 C.597 B.A. L.339 J.D. [Fearer,N.&C.] ⊙
Pemberton, Stephen C. .... '50 '75 C&L.339 B.S., J.D. Cir. J.
Riley, Dennis J., Law Office, (BV) '51 '77 C.589 B.S. L.424 J.D.
412 W. Washington St.
Smith, David A., (AV) .... '42 '73 C.589 B.S. L.945 J.D. [Smith,H.H.M.&F.]
Smith, Hanson, Hahn, Morrow & Floski, P.C., (AV)
129 South Fourth Street (⊙Mount Morris)

Williams & McCarthy, A Professional Corporation, (AV) BB
607 Washington Street, P.O. Box 339, 61061 ⊙
Telephone: 815-732-2101 Fax: 815-732-2289
Kim D. Krahenbuhl; Clayton L. Lindsey; Wendy S. Howarter.
General Civil and Trial Practice. Administrative Law, Advertising and Media Law, Banking, Bankruptcy and Commercial Work Outs, Business Litigation, Closely-held Business, Commercial Lending, Condemnation and Zoning, Construction Law, Education Law, Employee Benefits, Employers' Liability, Environmental Law, Family Law, Health Care and Hospital Law, Insurance Coverage, Insurance Defense, International Law, Labor and Employment (Management), Municipal Finance, Probate, Trust Law and Estate Planning, Products Liability, Real Estate, Taxation, Unfair Competition, Workers' Compensation (Management).
Representative Clients: Aircraft Gear Corp.; Anderson Industries, Inc.; Gallagher Bassett Insurance Co.; Liberty Mutual Insurance Co.; Atwood Industries, Inc.; The Travelers; American Mutual Insurance Co.; Rockford Health Systems; West Bend.
Rockford, Illinois Office: 321 West State Street, P.O. Box 219. Telephone: 815-987-8900. Fax: 815-968-0019.

See Professional Biographies, OREGON, ILLINOIS

Zaffer, Philip J. .... '47 '75 C&L.209 B.S., J.D. 410 N. Washington Street

ORION, 1,713, *Henry Co.*

Ames, John G., (BV) .... '35 '61 C&L.352 B.A., J.D. [J.Ames]
Ames, Steven C. .... '62 '96 C&L.589 B.A., J.D. [Ames]
Ames, John, (BV) .... 1000 Third St.
Ames Law Offices .... 1000 3rd St.

ORLAND HILLS, 6,779, *Cook Co.*

Lebold, Sheldon L., & Associates, (AV) '38 '60
C&L.145 A.B., J.D. 16061 South 94th Avenue
Tanquilut, Eric J. .... '72 '98 C.339 B.A. L.1000 J.D. [Tanquilut&Assoc.]
Tanquilut & Associates, Ltd. .... 16406 Pepperwood Trl.

ORLAND PARK, 51,077, *Cook Co.*

Barrett, Gabriel J., (AV) .... '27 '52 L.209 LL.B. 14300 S. Ravinia Ave.
Barry, Carroll A., (BV) .... '— '80 C.274 B.S. L.589 J.D. [Feinberg&B.] ⊙
Beaudreau, Albert J. .... '63 '94 C.1151 B.A. 9439 W. 144th Place
Beranek, Robert J. .... '39 '63 C.602 B.A. L.597 J.D. 7021 West 153rd St.
Blanchfield, Thomas M. .... '42 '72 C.424 B.B.A. L.209 J.D. 10749 Winterset Dr.
Burke, Kelly M. .... '66 '92 C.339 B.A. L.365 J.D. [A T.E.Grotta&Assoc.]
Burke, Richard E. .... '52 '76 C.339 B.A. L.146 J.D. [Wolfenson,S.&B.]
Cachey, Theodore J. .... '33 '58 C.477 B.B.A. L.424 J.D. 9961 W. 151st St.
Canna, John F., (BV) .... '52 '77 C.602 B.A. L.597 J.D. 10703 W. 159th St.
Canna, Thomas J. .... '56 '81 C.602 B.A. L.209 J.D. 10703 W. 159th St.
Carroll, Michael F. .... '63 '95 C.589 B.A. L.365 J.D. 9031 W. 151st Street, Suite 206
Croke, Jerome P. .... '33 '60 C.424 B.S.C. L.209 J.D. 15252 S. Harlem
Datlow, Lesly F. .... '61 '87 C.477 B.A. L.209 J.D. [A T.E.Grotta&Assoc.]

Daudell, David, The Law Offices of
(See Chicago)

DeBruyn, Harry E. .... '31 '54 C.999 L.597 LL.B. 15252 S. Harlem
Devine, Therese M. .... '62 '87 C.543 B.A. L.436 J.D. 14003 Blackhawk Lane
Dolinick, Karen J., Law Offices of '— '87
C.720 B.A. L.209 J.D. 15774 S. LaGrange Rd., Suite 387
Drugas, Peter T. .... '61 '86 C.958 B.S. L.365 J.D. 15127 S. 73rd Ave.
Dunneback, James F. .... '49 '75 C&L.209 B.A., J.D. [J.F.Dunneback]

Dunneback, James F., P.C.
14535 John Humphrey Drive, Suite 101, 60462
Telephone: 708-460-4000 Fax: 708-460-6967
Email: jdunneback@dunnebacklaw.com URL: http://www.lawyers.com/dunnebacklaw
James F. Dunneback; Anne M. Kelly;—John M. Galich.

(This Listing Continued)

Dunneback, James F., P.C. (Continued)

Corporate, Business, Contracts, Estate Planning, Probate, Probate Litigation, Real Estate and Real Estate Development.

See Professional Biographies, ORLAND PARK, ILLINOIS

Feinberg, Joy M., (AV) ....'52 '77 C.339 B.A. L.209 J.D. [Feinberg&B.] ⊙
Feinberg & Barry, P.C., (AV) ....14315 South 108th Avenue, Suite 222 (⊙Chicago)
Felicetti, Gary F. ....'48 '74 C.589 B.A. L.146 J.D. 14475 John Humphrey Drive
Fera, Peter A. ....'42 '69 14305 Vintage Ct.
Flynn, Patricia A. ....'57 '87 C.338 B.S. L.365 J.D. 10919 Atwood Ct.
Fotopoulos, John S. ....'71 '00 C.339 B.S. L.1000 J.D. 15030 S. Ravinia Ave., Ste. 30
Friel, James A. ....'47 '79 C.339 B.S. L.209 J.D. [J.Friel]
Friel, James, Law Office of ....1500 Ravinia Pl.
Frigo, Paul A. ....'70 '97 C.352 B.A. L.190 J.D. [Ⓐ T.E.Grotta&Assoc.]
Galich, John M. ....'63 '88 C.208 B.A. L.209 J.D. [Ⓐ J.F.Dunneback]
Gaspardo, Carol A. ....'43 '81 C.339 B.S. L.365 J.D. 17125 Deer Run Dr.
Gentile, Paul V. ....'50 '80 C.927 B.A. L.589 J.D. 14300 S. Ravinia, Ste. 302
Glennon, Owen G. ....'53 '83 C&L.424 B.S., J.D. 14210 Woodward Dr.
Grochocinski, David E. ....'51 '76 C.339 B.A. L.365 J.D. [Grochocinski,G.&L.]
Grochocinski, Mark S. ....'55 '80 C.339 B.S. L.424 J.D. [Grochocinski,G.&L.]
Grochocinski, Grochocinski & Lloyd, Ltd. .... 800 Ravinia Place
Grotta, Thomas E. ....'46 '75 C.1191 B.S. L.146 J.D. [T.E.Grotta&Assoc.]
Grotta, Thomas E., & Associates, P.C. .... 10775 163rd Pl.
Guimaraes, Cintya ....'66 '00 C&L.999 B.A., J.D. Andrew Corp.
Harty, Richard B. ....'24 '50 C.197 L.209 LL.B. 15100 S. LaGrange Rd.
Hauser, Richard J. ....'62 '88 C&L.209 B.S.C., J.D. 8636 W. Flint Ln.
Hevrdejs, Richard J. ....'33 '69 C&L.209 B.S.C., J.D. 13930 S. Blackhawk Lane
Hoenig, Ronald J. ....'48 '73 C.93 A.B. L.597 J.D. 14744 Pinetree Rd.
Holkeboer, Dirk J. '55 '80 C.114 B.A. L.912 J.D.
(adm. in MI; not adm. in IL) Barnabas Foundation
Huguelet, Michael T. ....'54 '79 C.602 B.B.A. L.365 J.D. 10749 Winterset Dr.
Jablonski, James J., (Ltd.) ....'54 '81 C.339 B.S. L.365 J.D. 8000 West 159th St.
Johnson, Marilyn Grant ....'50 '79 C.339 B.A. L.424 J.D. [Johnson&J.]
Johnson, Wayne L. ....'45 '76 C.424 B.A. L.146 J.D. [Johnson&J.]
Johnson & Johnson, Ltd. ....14300 S. Ravinia Ave., Suite 301
Katsenes, Chris W., (BV) ....'51 '75 C.1191 L.365 J.D. [Katsenes]
Katsenes, Gary ....'54 '81 C.1151 B.A. L.1000 J.D. 14310 S. Jefferson
Katsenes Law Office, (BV) ....14310 S. Jefferson Ave.
Kelly, Anne M. ....'— '82 C.338 B.S. L.146 J.D. [J.F.Dunneback]
Knight, Thomas R. ....'54 '83 C.589 B.S. L.365 J.D. 14813 Oak Creek Ct.
Krydynski, Vincent J. ....'63 '89 C.742 B.A. L.365 J.D. [T.E.Grotta&Assoc.]
Lloyd, David P. ....'58 '82 C&L.209 B.A., J.D. [Grochocinski,G.&L.]
Lockie, Thomas F. ....'28 '60 C.424 Ph.B. L.365 J.D. 14614 Creekview Dr.
Loritz, Richard F. ....'41 '66 C.750 B.A. L.209 J.D. [Loritz&Assoc.]
Loritz & Associates, Ltd. ....1100 Ravinia Pl.
Lozano-Netzel, Aleida F. ....'57 '82 C&L.209 B.A., J.D. 10833 Crystal Springs Lane

Lynch, Thomas W., P.C.
(See Oak Lawn)

MacTaggart, Philip A., (BVⓉ) .... '— '84 C&L.352 B.A., J.D. 11253 Melrose Court

Malysa, Theresa M. '42 '84 C.472 B.B.A. L.365 J.D.
Landmark Atrium Building, Suite 303, 9501 West 144th Place, 60462
Telephone: 708-403-1550 Fax: 708-403-1556
Email: ldyloyr@prodigy.net URL: http://www.lawyers.com/idyloyr
Family Law, Divorce, Tax Considerations, Retirement Benefits, Child Custody, Parenting Time, Visitation, Child Support, Domestic Violence, Paternity, Matrimonial Litigation, Premarital Agreements.

See Professional Biographies, ORLAND PARK, ILLINOIS

Marks, Kelly ....'76 '01 C.589 B.A. L.146 J.D. [Ⓐ T.E.Grotta&Assoc.]
Mazian, Gary J. ....'56 '81 C&L.339 B.A., J.D. [Sokol&M.]
McCormick, Michael J. ....'60 '88 C.927 B.S. L.365 J.D. Asst. State Atty.
Miller, Stephen J. ....'50 '84 C.209 B.A. L.589 J.D. 8253 Highgate Ct.
Mohan, Robert P. ....'51 '76 C.589 B.A. L.602 J.D. Andrew Corp.
Moy, Albert ....'48 '82 C.46 B.S. L.146 J.D. Asst. Secy., CNA Insurance‡
Murphy, Thomas L. ....'45 '71 C.238 B.A. L.209 J.D. 1100 Ravinia Pl
Noga, John T. ....'47 '73 C&L.424 B.A., J.D. 15220 Timber Ridge Ct.
O'Brien, Therese L. .... '63 '99 C.720 B.A. L.209 J.D. 15020 S. Ravinia Ave., Ste. 20
O'Connell, George L. ....'27 '61 C.339 B.S. L.146 J.D. 10600 W. 143rd St.
Petelle, James F. '50 '75 C.602 B.A. L.477 J.D.
Corporate Secretary & General Attorney, Andrew Corporation
Postweiler, John G. ....'47 '72 C.597 B.S. L.879 J.D. 10600 143rd St.
Rodger, Ronald A. ....'44 '81 C&L.589 B.S., J.D. [R.A.Rodger]
Rodger, Ronald A., Ltd. ....9501 W. 144th Place
Rummler, Arthur ....'65 '91 C.477 B.B.A. L.146 J.D. [Ⓐ Grochocinski,G.&L.]
Schoen, Edward J., Jr. ....'58 '91 C&L.424 B.B.A., J.D. 15030 S. Ravinia Ave., Ste. 30
Schouten, Paul R. ....'50 '76 C&L.209 B.A., J.D. [Wolfenson,S.&B.]
Schreiber, Paul R., (AV) ....'08 '30 C&L.339 LL.B. 14425 Raneys Lane‡
Sheehy, Edward F. ....'29 '63 C&L.209 B.S. 9946 Constitution Ct.‡
Smith, Herbert F., Jr., & Associates .....'58 '91 C.720 B.A. L.365 J.D. 9935 W. 151st St.
Sokol, Ronald P. ....'50 '75 C&L.339 B.A., J.D. [Sokol&M.]
Sokol & Mazian .... 60 Orland Square Dr.
Stortzum, Jim L. ....'51 '76 C.801 B.A. L.365 J.D. 10723 W. 159th Street
Sullivan, Thomas B. ....'37 '62 C&L.209 A.B., J.D. [Ⓒ Grochocinski,G.&L.]
Taylor, Stephen W. ....'50 '75 C.357 B.S. L.879 J.D. 15252 S. Harlem Ave.
Tracy, James E. ....'24 '54 C.46 B.S.E.E. L.209 J.D. 7913 Woodruff Dr.‡
Vaci, Henry A. ....'47 '74 C&L.209 B.A., J.D. 14535 John Humphrey Dr.
Voom, Barry N. '— '82 L.365 J.D.
(adm. in KS; not adm. in IL) 16616 South 107th Co
Walczak, Joseph J. ....'60 '88 C.720 B.A. L.365 J.D. [J.J.Walczak]
Walczak, Joseph J., P.C. .... 14045 S. 88th Ave.
Williams, Jim ....'77 '01 C.1024 B.S. L.879 J.D. [J.Williams]
Williams, Jim, LLC .... 16555 S. 108th Ave.
Wolfenson, James W. ....'50 '76 C.602 B.A. L.146 J.D. [Wolfenson,S.&B.]
Wolfenson, Schouten & Burke ....1435 John Humphrey Dr.
Wrobel, Eugene R. ....'39 '67 C&L.209 B.S., J.D. 10412 San Luis Lane
Youdelman, Robert A. '42 '69 C.930 B.B.A. L.569 LL.B.
(adm. in NY; not adm. in IL) Exec. V.P. & CFO, Allen Telecom Inc.

OSWEGO, 13,326, *Kendall Co.*

Caulfield, John J. ....'31 '59 C&L.424 B.S., J.D. 2 Abbeyfeale Drive

Dreyer, Foote, Streit, Furgason and Slocum, A Professional Association
(See Aurora, Illinois)

Mahoney, Silverman & Cross, Ltd.
(See Joliet)

Peterson, Pamela Luella ....'68 '94 [P.L.Peterson]
Peterson, Pamela L., P.C., Law Office of ....14F Stonehill Rd.
Sackmann, John P. ....'63 '89 C&L.801 B.A., J.D. 605 Arbor Court
Sharrard, Anne Elizabeth ....'64 '90 C.690 B.A. L.383 J.D. 418 Burr Oak Dr.
Swanson, Laurence A., (CV) ....'41 '85 C.94 B.M. L.589 J.D. P.O. Box 1040

OTTAWA, * 18,307, *La Salle Co.*

Agostinelli, Robert J., (BV) ......'46 '73 C.201 B.A. L.229 J.D. Dep. Def., App. Def. Off.
Anderson, Mark E. ...'63 '94 C.58 B.A. L.365 J.D. [White,M.A.M.V.D.&G.] (⊙Leland)

Armstrong & Surin, (BV)
724 Columbus Street, 61350
Telephone: 815-431-1234 Fax: 815-434-5338 URL: http://www.lawyers.com/armstrongsurinandassociates
Email: aslaw@mchsi.com URL: http://www.armstrongsurin.com
Members of Firm: Craig M. Armstrong (1927-1996); William T. Surin.
Personal Injury, Workers Compensation, Corporation, Probate, Real Estate, Negligence, Family Law, Bankruptcy, Criminal, Traffic, Wills and Trusts.

See Professional Biographies, OTTAWA, ILLINOIS

Balestri, William P. ....'51 '77 C.723 B.A. L.734 J.D. Assoc. Cir. J.
Barton, Marilyn S., (CV) ....'35 '70 C.1191 B.Ed. L.365 J.D. 1606 Champlain St.
Baxter, Lawrence W., (BV) ....'46 '71 C&L.339 B.S., J.D. 417 W. Madison St.
Benson, Floyd L. ....'16 '40 C&L.339 B.A., LL.B. 222 W. Madison St.‡
Berkland, Duane A. ....'74 '02 C.801 B.S. L.589 J.D. 227 W. Madison St.
Berry, Richard J., (BV) ....'52 '77 C.880 B.A. L.602 J.D. [Myers,B.O.&K.] ⊙
Bonecutter, Max H. '51 '01 C.597 B.M. L.431 J.D.
Research Atty., Illinois Appellate Ct., 3rd Dist.
Breslin, John X., (BV) ....'44 '73 C.215 A.B. L.424 J.D. Dep. Dir., State Appl. Pros.
Breslin, Peg ....'46 '71 C&L.424 B.S., J.D. Ret. Appellate Jus.
Brown, Kenneth D. ....'48 '84 C.339 B.S. L.146 J.D. Asst. Def., State App. Def. Off.
Brusatte, James L. ....'52 '77 C.221 B.A. L.339 J.D. Co. Ct. J.
Bryson, Kerry Jeanne ....'73 '98 C.578 B.A. L.209 J.D. Asst. Def.
Bute, Daniel J., (AV) ....'51 '77 C.339 B.S. L.365 J.D. 628 Columbus St.
Cantlin, John L., (AV) ....'48 '77 C.339 B.S. L.365 J.D. 760 E. Etna Rd.
Cantlin-Vanwiggeren, Christina Maria ....'76 '01 C.339 B.S. L.589 J.D. 760 E. Etna Road
Carter, Nancy Rink, (BV) '42 '74 C.436 A.B. L.339 J.D.
Off. of State's Atty's Appl. Pros.
Carter, Robert L. ....'45 '76 C.801 B.S. L.879 J.D. Chf. J., Cir. Ct.
Carusona, Peter A., (BV) ....'52 '78 C.012 B.A. L.146 J.D. Asst. Def.
Clydesdale, Thomas R., (AV) ....'13 '38 C.388 A.B. L.477 J.D. [Ⓒ P.F.Ferracuti]
Creedon, Timothy J., III, (CV) ....'52 '77 C.339 B.S. L.190 J.D. [Hoffman,M.&C.]
Daugherity, Eugene P. ....'45 '73 C.424 B.A. L.209 J.D. Co. Ct. J.
Deobler, Eric B., (BV) '45 '72 C&L.339 B.A., J.D.
[White,M.A.M.V.D.&G.] (⊙Earlville)
Eschbach, Robert M., Attorney at Law, (BV) '52 '77
C.338 B.S. L.339 J.D. 728 Columbus St.
Fabricius, Raymond P., (P.C.), (BV) ....'59 '88 C.209 B.S. L.365 J.D. [Pool,L.&F.]
Fedorow, Bradley T. ....'48 '77 C&L.339 B.S., J.D. 504 Courtney St.
Ferracuti, Peter F., (AV) ....'26 '53 C&L.339 A.B., J.D. [P.F.Ferracuti]
Ferracuti, Peter F., P.C., Law Offices of, (AV) ....110 E. Main Street
Fitzpatrick, Jeanne M., (BV) ....'50 '88 C.338 B.A. L.589 J.D. Asst. Atty. Gen.
Fleshman, Gist ....'57 '85 C.338 B.S. L.209 J.D. Clk. of the Ct., 3rd Dist. Appl. Ct.
Flood, Thomas R. ....'26 '49 C.602 L.424 LL.B. Cir. J.
Gnidovec, Gary F. ....'51 '77 C.201 B.A. L.365 J.D. State Appl. Pros.
Goode, Gina E., (CV) ....'67 '96 C.719 B.A. L.365 J.S. [White,M.A.M.V.D.&G.]
Hansen, Robert M., (BV) '49 '74
C.338 B.S. L.339 J.D. Staff Atty., State's Atty. Appl. Pros.
Hardesty, William E. '72 '00 C.801 B.S. L.589 J.D.
Tr. Offr., First Natl. Bk. of Ottawa IL

Herbolsheimer, Lannon, Henson, Duncan and Reagan, P.C., (AV)
First Federal Savings Building, 633 La Salle Street, Suite 409, 61350 ⊙
Telephone: 815-434-1400 Fax: 815-434-2423
Michael T. Reagan; Michael C. Jansz (Resident, Ottawa Office).
General Civil Practice and Trials in all Courts. Insurance, Real Estate, Probate, Corporation, Federal, Tax and School Law.
La Salle, Illinois Office: State Bank Building, Suite 400, 654 First Street, P.O. Box 539. Telephone: 815-223-0111. FAX: 815-223-5829.

See Professional Biographies, OTTAWA, ILLINOIS

Hoffman, Melvin H. ....'48 '73 C.801 B.S. L.339 J.D. [Hoffman,M.&C.]
Hoffman, Mueller & Creedon, P.C., (BV) ....501 State Street
Homer, Thomas J. ....'47 '74 C.339 B.A. L.146 J.D. Appl. Ct. J.
Howarter, Alan R., Law Office of, (CV) '52 '77
C.801 B.A. L.339 J.D. 628 Columbus St., Ste. 204
Hupp, George C., (AV) ....'24 '49 C.473 L.546 J.D. [Ⓒ Hupp,L.I.&M.]
Hupp, Lanuti, Irion & Martin, P.C., (AV) ....227 W. Madison
Jansz, Michael C., (BV) ......'63 '88 C.177 B.A. L.589 J.D. [Herbolsheimer,L.H.D.&R.]
Johnson, Linda Kristina '57 '83 C.210 B.A. L.339 J.D.
Resch. Dir., Third Dist. Appl. Ct.
Kalnitz, Robert W. ....'77 '03 C.339 B.A. L.146 J.D. 3rd Dist. Appl. Ct. Res Dept.
Keely, James Leo ....'47 '73 C.339 A.B. L.502 J.D. Co. J.
Keene, William K., (CV) ....'65 '90 C.338 B.A. L.801 J.D. [Keene]
Keene Law Offices, (CV) .... 417 W. Madison, Ste. 20
Kelly, Edward P. '35 '60 C.103 A.B. L.262 J.D.
(adm. in NY; not adm. in IL) 3000 Columbus St
Kelly, Judith Z., (BV) ....'49 '74 C.910 A.B. L.339 J.D. Off. of State's Atty's. App. Pros.
Koenig, Jennifer H. ....'71 '98 C.477 B.A. L.209 J.D. [Ⓐ Pool,L.&F.]
Kuleck, Edward J., (BV) ....'48 '74 C.424 B.S. L.365 J.D. 403 W. Norris Dr.
Kuzma, Sheryl H., (BV) ....'65 '90 C.589 B.A. L.966 J.D. [Myers,B.O.&K.] ⊙
Langer, H. Robert, (BV) ....'29 '59 C.388 B.A. L.221 LL.B. 628 Columbus St.
Lanuti, James A. ....'48 '77 C.339 B.S. L.146 J.D. Assoc. Cir. J.
Lanuti, Joseph E., (AV) ....'17 '41 C&L.339 B.S., J.D. [Hupp,L.I.&M.]

Leynaud & Leynaud, A Prof. Corp., Law Offices of
(See Peru)

Lindig, James R., (BV) ....'61 '90 C&L.589 B.S., J.D. [Ⓐ Pool,L.&F.]
Marche, Carrie Brooke ....'72 '98 C.763 B.A. L.209 J.D. Asst. State Def.
Marsh, Alan B., (AV) '39 '66
C.388 A.B. L.365 J.D. [White,M.A.M.V.D.&G.] (⊙Earlville)
Martin, Paul V., (AV) ....'43 '73 C.589 B.S. L.365 J.D. [White,M.A.M.V.D.&G.]
McCabe, Catherine Geralyn ....'61 '01 C.424 B.A. L.589 J.D. Appl. Ct. Clk.
McEvoy, Kenneth R., The Law Office of, (CV) '63 '87
C.424 B.S. L.146 J.D. 628 Columbus St., Ste. 107
Meinz, Verlin R., (BV) ....'50 '75 C.597 B.A. L.424 J.D. Asst. Appl. Def.
Meredith, Christy L. ....'70 '96 C&L.339 B.S., J.D. [Stephens&M.]
Mertel, Rita Kennedy ....'48 '74 C.234 B.S. L.339 J.D. States Attys. Appl. Pros. Atty.
Mueller, George, (BV) ....'50 '76 C.589 B.S. L.339 J.D. [Hoffman,M.&C.]
Myers, Stephen C., (BV) ....'46 '71 C.602 A.B. L.597 J.D. [Myers,B.O.&K.] ⊙

Myers, Berry, O'Conor & Kuzma, Ltd., (BV)
130 East Madison Street, 61350 ⊙
Telephone: 815-434-6206 Fax: 815-434-6203
John A. Berry (1912-1986); Andrew J. O'Conor (1919-1998); Stephen C. Myers; Richard J. Berry; Sheryl H. Kuzma.
General Civil and Trial Practice in all Courts. Banking, Commercial and Corporate Law, Government and School Law, Estate Planning and Probate, Real Estate, Health Care Law.
Representative Clients: Auto Owners Ins., Co.; Union Bank; First Nat'l. Bank of Ottawa; Union Bancorp Inc.; First State Bank; First Midwest Bank; Allied Ins. Group; St. Mary's Hosp.; General Casualty Ins., Co.
Streator, Illinois Office: 7 Northpoint Drive, 61364. Telephone: 815-672-3116. Fax: 815-672-0738.

See Professional Biographies, OTTAWA, ILLINOIS

Omolecki, Stephen H. ......'51 '79 C.589 B.A. L.146 J.D. Asst. Def., State App. Def. Off.
Perona, Louis J. ....'28 '51 C&L.209 LL.B. Cir. J.

Pool, Leigh & Fabricius, (BV)
An Association of Professional Corporations
Central Life Building, 628 Columbus Street, Suite 208, 61350
Telephone: 815-434-0097 Fax: 815-434-0270
Email: plflaw@theramp.net
Member of Firm: Raymond P. Fabricius (P.C.);—Jennifer H. Koenig; James R. Lindig.
General Civil Trial and Appellate Practice in all Courts, Insurance, Real Estate and Family Law.

See Professional Biographies, OTTAWA, ILLINOIS

Raccuglia, Anthony C., (AV) '33 '59 C.339 B.S. L.365 J.D.
[A.C.Raccuglia&Assoc.] ⊙
Raccuglia, Cynthia M. ..... '56 '81 C.741 B.A. L.589 J.D. Co. J., LaSalle Co. Courthouse

Raccuglia, Anthony C., & Associates, P.C., (AV)
633 La Salle Street, 61350 ⊙
Telephone: 815-434-2003
Email: raccuglialaw@insightbb.com
Anthony C. Raccuglia.
General Civil and Trial Practice in all State and Federal Courts. Personal Injury, Medical Malpractice, Products Liability, Workers Compensation, Probate, Real Estate, Construction Accidents, Structural Work Cases, Business Litigation.
References: La Salle National Bank; Citizens First National Bank of Peru, Illinois.
Peru, Illinois Office: 1200 Maple Drive. Telephone: 815-223-0230.

See Professional Biographies, OTTAWA, ILLINOIS

Ralph, Frank W. ....'48 '77 C.602 B.A. L.424 J.D. State Appl. Def.
Reagan, Michael T., (AV) '47 '72 C.679 B.S.M.E. L.276 J.D.
[Herbolsheimer,L.H.D.&R.]
Reilly, James T., (BV) ....'50 '79 C.339 B.A. L.424 J.D. 1516 Birchlawn
Rice, Elizabeth Jane, (BV) ....'49 '80 C.340 B.A. L.146 J.D. 760 E. Etna Rd.
Ryan, Howard C., Jr. ....'57 '84 C.338 B.S. L.365 J.D. Cir. J.
Seigler, Darrell K., (BV) ....'54 '79 C.801 B.A. L.339 J.D. [D.K.Seigler]
Seigler, Darrell K., Ltd., (BV) .... 434 Pearl Street
Siena, Leila Elizabeth Christie '73 '99 C.966 B.A. L.209 J.D.
Prairie State Legal Serv(s).
Silvern, Sherry R. ....'58 '89 C.1165 B.S. L.1398 J.D. Asst. Appl. Def.
Stephens, Kyle L. ....'63 '88 C.1288 B.A. L.589 J.D. [Stephens&M.]
Stephens & Meredith .... 712 LaSalle Street
Surin, William T., (BV) ....'49 '75 C.339 B.A. L.146 J.D. [Armstrong&S.]
Thompson, Wendell L. ....'15 '40 C.145 L.146 LL.B. Ret. Cir. J.
Ursini, Gerald ....'60 '85 C&L.339 B.A., J.D. Resch. Dir., Appl. Ct.
Vescogni, Michelle A. ....'73 '98 C.578 B.A. L.146 J.D. 116 W. LaFayette Street, Suite 5
Vickers, John F., (BV) ....'47 '78 C.201 B.A. L.424 J.D. [White,M.A.M.V.D.&G.]
Wagner, Fred P. ....'23 '54 C.999 L.209 J.D. Ret. Cir. J.
Warren, Harland D., (BV) .... '16 '41 C.339 B.A. L.793 LL.B. [H.D.Warren&Assoc.]
Warren, Harland D., & Associates, P.C., (BV) .... 633 La Salle St.
West, Stephen J., (CV) .... '48 '75 C.339 B.A. L.365 J.D. 628 Columbus St.

White, Marsh, Anderson, Martin, Vickers, Deobler & Goode, (AV) BR
511 East Etna Road, 61350 ⊙
Telephone: 815-434-2000 Fax: 815-434-0564
Email: wmavd@aol.com URL: http://www.wmavd.com
Thomas M. Anderson, Jr. (1934-1988); Thomas M. Anderson, Sr. (1904-1989). Members of Firm: Robert E. White (1933-2004); Alan B. Marsh; Paul V. Martin; John F. Vickers; Eric B. Deobler; Mark E. Anderson; Gina E. Goode.
General Civil and Trial Practice, Automobile Accidents, Wrongful Death, Personal Injury, Workers Compensation, Insurance Defense, Probate, Estate Planning, Wills and Trusts, Real Estate, Zoning Law, Municipal Law, Corporate Law, Banking, Commercial, Criminal and Appellate Practice.
References: National Bank of Earlville; First National Bank of Grand Ridge, Illinois; First National Bank of Ottawa; UnionBank, Ottawa, Illinois.
Earlville, Illinois Office: 201 S. Ottawa Street. Telephone: 815-246-8121.

See Professional Biographies, OTTAWA, ILLINOIS

PALATINE, 65,479, *Cook Co.*

Adler Law Offices, Ltd.
(See Arlington Heights)

Allen, James M. .... '56 '82 C.339 L.A.S. L.801 J.D. 1642 Colonial Pkwy., 2nd Fl.
Alloy, Stephen E. .... '56 '82 C.352 B.A. L.424 J.D. 800 E. Northwest Hwy.

Angelina & Palmer, P.C.
(See Inverness)

Asher, Mitchell F. ....'43 '67 C.339 B.S. L.597 J.D. 157 N. Brockway St.
Ayres, James J. ....'54 '84 C.339 B.A. L.209 J.D. [J.J.Ayres]
Ayres, James J., P.C., The Law Offices of .... 800 E. Northwest Highway, Suite 700
Badiano, Gerardo ....'71 '96 C.424 B.A. L.146 J.D. 20063 N. Rand Rd.
Bauer, Susan R. ....'57 '85 C.589 B.A. L.365 J.D. [Favaro&G.]
Berg, Robert J. ....'66 '92 C.339 B.A. L.209 J.D. 210 N. Hale
Berger, Newmark & Fenchel P.C., (AV) ... 100 West Palatine Road, Suite 200 (⊙Chicago)
Boldt, Melvin W. ....'42 '68 C.602 A.B. L.893 LL.B. 1111 N. Blackburn Dr.
Bramwell, M. Russell ....'23 '52 C.340 B.S. L.365 LL.B. 800 E. Northwest Hwy.
Calabrese, James A. .... '47 '72 C&L.209 B.S., J.D. 1278 N. Wellington Drive
Cassato, Victor J. ....'14 '38 C&L.209 LL.B., J.D. 142 Imperial Ct.‡
Ciura, Bruce F. .... '55 '81 C.339 B.A. L.424 J.D. 1935 S. Plum Grove Rd.
Cohan, Brian J. .... '55 '81 C.37 B.A. L.209 J.D. 800 E. Northwest Hwy.
Cohen, Ira J. ....'55 '83 C&L.209 B.Sc., J.D. 675 N. North Ct.
Cohen, Stuart D. .... '49 '76 C.589 B.S. L.209 J.D. 4501 Fairfax Ave.
Conklin, Richard C., (AV) .... '29 '58 C.339 B.S. L.597 J.D. 1271 S. Falcon Dr.★
Copeland, Victor G. '56 '81 C.228 B.A. L.245 J.D.
Asst. Gen. Coun. & Asst. Secy., Square D Company
Corbett, David J. .... '62 '89 C.1169 L.209 800 E. Northwest Hwy.
Cremerius, Edward P. .... '33 '57 C.742 B.S. L.209 J.D. 236 E. Northwest Hwy.
Cremerius, Kathryn M. .... '59 '85 C.339 B.A. L.424 J.D. 236 E. Northwest Hwy.
Daeschner, R. Wilbur '17 '41 C.246 B.S. L.900 LL.B.
(adm. in KS; not adm. in IL) 1700 Appleby Rd.‡
Davidson, Winn C. .... '38 '67 C.597 B.S.B.A. L.365 J.D. Bk. of Palatine
Davies, Paul J. ....'54 '80 C&L.339 B.S., J.D. 639 Braeburn Rd.
Di Mucci, Salvatore, Jr. .... '33 '62 C.966 B.S. L.365 LL.B. 100 W. Dundee Rd.
Driscoll, Rodney E. .... '65 '97 C.375 B.S. L.365 J.D. [A Favaro&G.]
Etchingham, Joseph M. ....'67 '92 C.746 B.A. L.365 J.D. 425 Creekside Drive
Evans, Steven G., Law Offices .... '59 '85 C.130 B.A. L.801 J.D. 1627 Colonial Pkwy.
Falkenberg, Charles V., Jr. ....'30 '55 C.602 A.B. L.597 J.D. 517 E. Warwick Rd.
Farrell, Neal F. ....'34 '69 C.209 B.S.C. L.365 J.D. 1392 Shire Circle
Favaro, Dennis R. .... '61 '86 C.340 B.A. L.879 J.D. [Favaro&G.] ⊙

Favaro & Gorman, Ltd.
835 Sterling Avenue, Suite 100, 60067 ⊙
Telephone: 847-934-0060 Fax: 847-934-6899
URL: http://www.favarogorman.com
Dennis R. Favaro; Patrick J. Gorman; Susan R. Bauer; Andrew H. Haber;—Patricia L. Jochum; Rodney E. Driscoll.
Employment Law, Civil Litigation, Business Law, Commercial Litigation.
Crystal Lake, Illinois Office: 9510 Turnberry Trail, 60014. Telephone: 815-477-1110. Fax: 815-477-1165.

See Professional Biographies, PALATINE, ILLINOIS

Femal, Michael J. '47 '73 C.436 B.S.E.E. L.46 J.D.
Sr. Pat. & Intl. Trade Atty., Square D Co. (Pat.)
Flotow, William J. .... '41 '67 C.347 B.S. L.1119 J.D. 800 E. Northwest Highway
Foersterling, Fredk. J. ....'16 '39 C.339 A.B. L.879 J.D. 861 N. Sterling Rd.‡
Frano, Stephen P. ..... '62 '91 C.1106 B.A. L.424 J.D. Commercial Interior Specialists Co.
Gardner, Mary E. ....'— '85 C.801 B.S. L.209 J.D. 1278 W. Northwest Hwy., Ste. 903
Geocaris, James A. .... '65 '91 C.424 L.365 J.D. 425 S. Creekside Dr.
Glorch, Robert H., Law Offices of ....'42 '67 C.388 B.A. L.339 J.D. 616 North Court
Golden, Larry I. ...... '51 '77 C.339 B.S. L.146 J.D. Gen. Pat. Coun., Square D Co. (Pat.)

Good, Neil H. '60 '86 C.589 B.S. L.146 J.D.
800 E. Northwest Highway, Suite 814, 60074 ⊙
Telephone: 847-577-4476 Fax: 847-934-7292
Email: neil@neilgood.com URL: http://www.neilgoodlawfirm.com
Social Security Disability, Personal Injury, Medical Malpractice, Plaintiffs Personal Injury.
Chicago, Illinois Office: 30 N. La Salle, Suite 3400, 60602. Telephone: 312-629-1212.

See Professional Biographies, PALATINE, ILLINOIS

Gorman, Patrick J. .... '58 '83 C.723 B.A. L.424 J.D. [Favaro&G.] ⊙
Gottlieb, Jeffrey R. ....'74 '00 C.339 B.S. L.209 J.D. 616 North Ct., Ste. 160
Guttman, Richard T. '37 '64 C.477 B.S.E. L.1003 J.D.
(adm. in OH; not adm. in IL; Pat.) Retired
Haber, Andrew H. ....'54 '88 C.357 B.M. L.339 J.D. [Favaro&G.]
Harris, Keith E. ....'45 '78 C.494 B.A. L.589 J.D. [K.E.Harris]
Harris, Keith E., P.C. ....345 N. Quentin Road
Hartwell, Janice K. ....'55 '81 C&L.477 B.A., J.D. Asst. Gen. Coun., Square D Co.
Heinze, Robert W. .... '23 '50 C.393 B.A. L.597 LL.B. 422 Comfort Lane
Hershenhorn, Robert G. '43 '68 C.910 A.B. L.146 J.D.
Pres. & Chmn. of the Bd., First Bk. & Tr. Co. of Ill.
Irfan, Kareem M. ....'60 '89 C.999 B.S.E.E. L.209 J.D. Asst. Gen. Coun., Square D Co.
Japlon, Howard E. '52 '79 C.262 B.A. L.339 J.D.
Dep. Gen. Coun. & Asst. Secy., Square D Company
Jochum, Patricia L. ....'65 '91 C.339 B.A. L.365 J.D. [A Favaro&G.]
Kaiser, Kenneth E. ....'51 '78 C.424 A.B. L.365 J.D. 502 N. Plum Grove Rd.

Kanabay, Roberta K., The Law Offices of
(See Schaumburg)

Kaplan, Robert M. ....'60 '87 C&L.260 B.B.C., J.D. Gen. Coun.& CFO, Propheteer Intl.
Kathe, Steven R. .... '65 '92 C.493 B.S. L.365 J.D. 1601 W. Colonial Pkwy., Suite H
Keating, Martin J. W., (AV) ...... '27 '55 C&L.339 B.S., LL.B. One E. Northwest Hwy.‡
Keaton, Michael J. ....'65 '91 C.339 B.A. L.365 J.D. [Keaton&Assoc.]
Keaton & Associates, P.C. ....1278 W. Northwest Hwy.
Kemp, Dennis W., Attorney at Law '47 '73
C.589 B.S. L.146 J.D. 1 E. Northwest Hwy., Ste. 101

Klest Law Firm
(See Schaumburg)

Knott, Paul H. ....'35 '61 C.174 A.B. L.209 J.D. 218 E. Hicks Pl.
Kolodz, Thomas J. .... '41 '86 C.208 B.A. L.365 J.D. 835 Sterling Ave.
Kopeny, Sean T. ....'76 '01 C&L.339 B.A., J.D. 751 E. Pompano Ln.
Kos, Michael R. ....'40 '65 C&L.339 LL.B. 1153 Pepper Tree Drive
Koukios, Steven S. .... '58 '86 C.589 B.S. L.209 J.D. 800 E. Northwest Hwy.
Kurczewski, Walter W. '43 '70
C.339 A.B. L.477 J.D. V.P., Gen. Coun. & Secy., Square D Co.
Leavitt, Ira D. ....'48 '74 C.339 B.S. L.209 J.D. [I.D.Leavitt]
Leavitt, Ira D., Ltd. .... P.O. Box 1907
Lennon, James K., Law Office of '48 '74
C.201 B.A. L.424 J.D. 345 N. Quentin Rd., Ste. 201
Link, Thomas H. .... '33 '64 C&L.8 B.S., J.D. 1244 Borders Dr. (Pat.)
Litchfield, Stephen A. '53 '79
C.339 B.S. L.365 J.D. Asst. Gen. Coun., Square D Co. (Pat.)
Manno, Ronald S. ....'48 '83 C.424 B.S. L.589 J.D. 345 N. Quentin Road, Suite 404
Mason, James R. .... '25 '51 L.209 LL.B. 1231 E. Thurston Dr.
McLean, Mary Ann F. '57 '86 C.741 B.B.A. L.424 J.D.
Asst. Gen. Coun., Square D Co.
McWilliams, Paul A. ....'26 '56 C.716 A.B. L.724 LL.B. 157 N. Brockway St.
Meschino, Michael A., Law Offices of '55 '82
C.1183 B.A. L.365 J.D. 800 E. Northwest Highway, Suite 503
Miner, Steven A. .... '55 '80 C.339 B.A. L.365 J.D. 100 W. Dundee
Miranti, Richard F. ....'54 '81 C.1100 B.A. L.365 J.D. 926 South Elm Street
Molohon, Patrick J. .... '31 '58 C.363 B.S. L.424 J.D. 616 N. Court
Mugalian, Richard A., (AV) .... '22 '47 C&L.145 B.A., J.D. 579 1st Bank Dr.
Newsom, Larry J. ....'46 '74 C.959 B.A. L.365 J.D. 414 S. Lauder Ln.
Patterson, James R., (AV) ....'43 '68 C.193 A.B. L.365 J.D. 1133 E. Prati, Ste. 201
Pinderski, Jerome W., Jr. ....'57 '81 C.436 B.A. L.424 J.D. [Pinderski&P.]
Pinderski, Paul C. ....'59 '84 C.234 B.A. L.365 J.D. [Pinderski&P.]
Pinderski, Polly J. ....'67 '92 C.339 B.A. L.209 J.D. [Pinderski&P.]

Pinderski & Pinderski, Ltd.
115 West Colfax, 60067-5086
Telephone: 847-358-5220 FAX: 847-358-4506
Email: PinderLaw@aol.com URL: http://www.pinderski.com
Louis Pinderski (1883-1943); Jerome W. Pinderski (1925-1993); Paul C. Pinderski; Jerome W. Pinderski, Jr.; Polly J. Pinderski.
General Practice. Litigation. Corporate and Business Transactions, Securities, Estate Planning, Probate, Real Estate Development, Bankruptcy, Intellectual Property, Immigration, Family Law.
Representative Clients: Clean Air Engineering; Total Marketing Associates; Royal American Bank; IL & P Enterprises; Harris Bank Palatine, N.A.
References: Royal American Bank; Harris Bank Palatine, N.A.

See Professional Biographies, PALATINE, ILLINOIS

Quarles, Mary McCarthy '50 '83 C.1154 B.G.S. L.912 J.D.
Real Estate Atty., Pace Membership Warehouse, Inc.
Resnick, Thomas D. ....'54 '84 C.927 B.B. L.146 J.D. [T.D.Resnick]

Resnick, Thomas D., P.C. .... 345 N. Quentin Rd.
Richter, Kurt A. .... '60 '86 C.589 B.A. L.209 J.D. 800 E. Northwest Hwy.
Robeznieks, John O. .... '57 '84 C.112 B.A. L.209 J.D. 840 N. Clark St.
Ross, Jonathan '53 '80 C.881 A.B. L.831 J.D.
(adm. in PA; not adm. in IL) 1415 S. Roselle Rd.‡
Ryan, William J. .... '23 '49 C&L.209 LL.B. 819 N. Quentin Rd.
St. Pierre, Duane, Law Office of ..... '50 '83 C.801 B.S. L.146 J.D. 853 N. Quentin Road
Schmalz, Eric .... '44 '74 C.966 B.S. L.124 J.D. 165 E. Palatine Rd.
Schmalz, Henry E. .... '44 '74 C.966 B.S. L.124 J.D. [Schmalz,E.]
Schmalz, Eric .... 165 E. Palatine Rd.

Schneider, Linda K., and Associates '48 '87 C.655 B.S. L.146 J.D.
1627 Colonial Parkway, Suite 204, 60067
Telephone: 847-359-9202 Fax: 847-359-9605
URL: http://www.lindakschneider.com
Adoption, Child Support, Custody and Visitation, Divorce, Family Law.
See Professional Biographies, PALATINE, ILLINOIS

Schnitzer, Herbert .... '21 '52 C.1016 A.B. L.597 300 E Northwest Hwy
Schuman, Thomas R. .... '41 '66 C.734 B.S. L.930 J.D. 106 Belle Ave.
Shapiro, Julius H., (AV) .... '34 '59 C.339 B.S. L.597 J.D. [Berger,N.&F.] ⊙
Stacey, David R. '49 '88 C.880 B.E. L.838 J.D.
(adm. in TN; not adm. in IL) Sr. Intell. Prop. Atty., Square D Co.

Stelk, Roger W., Law Offices of
(See Arlington Heights)

Stemwedel, Charles G. '37 '62
C.321 A.B. L.309 LL.B. V.P. & Secy., Suburban Bancorp, Inc.
Tauchert, Patricia A. .... '55 '79 C.801 B.A. L.597 J.D. Sr. Atty., Square D Company
Thill, Bruce G. .... '48 '73 C.963 B.S. L.146 J.D. 117 West Slade Street Suite 201
Tris, Mary Severson '50 '87
C.494 B.A. L.424 J.D. Sr. Benefits Coun., Square D Company
Tyrrell, Thomas J., (AV) .... '46 '76 C.1151 B.A. L.146 J.D. 425 S. Creekside Dr.
Wardell, John W., (AV) .... '29 '56 C&L.339 B.A., J.D. 675 N. Court
Welker, Kenneth R. .... '47 '72 C.1101 B.A. L.597 J.D. 4880 Euclid Avenue
Wesley, Lynda .... '56 '82 C.1183 B.A. L.146 J.D. 800 E. Northwest Hwy., Ste. 821
Young, Thomas C. .... '43 '79 C.209 B.A. L.589 J.D. [T.Young]

Young, Thomas, Law Firm
350 N. Eric Drive, 60067
Telephone: 847-359-8999 Fax: 847-359-9234
Email: thomascyou@aol.com URL: http://www.thomasyounglaw.com
Thomas C. Young.
Real Estate, Civil Practice.
See Professional Biographies, PALATINE, ILLINOIS

PALOS HEIGHTS, 11,260, *Cook Co.*

Alberts, John '50 '89 C.388 B.A. L.365 J.D.
Chairman, Payan, Alberts & Thompson, Ltd.
Andringa, John P. .... '28 '58 C&L.424 B.S., J.D. 7330 College Dr.
Arnold, George J., II .... '67 '91 C.339 B.A. L.424 J.D. [Sosin L.&A.]
Barrett, Michael B. .... '66 '91 C.352 B.A. L.424 J.D. 6446 W. 127th St.
Bellah, Kenneth D., Law Offices, (AV) '55 '80 C.57 B.A. L.146 J.D.
12750 South Harlem Avenue (⊙Chgo., IL; Sanderson, TX)
Bozich, Bruce M. .... '52 '77 C.188 B.A. L.209 J.D. 11800 S. 75th Ave., Ste. 301
Brady, Nona B. .... '45 '86 C.1016 B.S. L.326 J.D. [N.Brady]
Brady, Nona, P.C. .... 11801 Southwest Highway, Suite 25
Courtney, Thomas F., (BV) .... '42 '73 C.339 A.B. L.365 J.D. 7000 W. 127th St.
Daly, Patrick F. .... '43 '69 C.602 B.B.A. L.597 J.D. [P.F.Daly]
Daly, Patrick F., P.C. .... 6400 W. College Dr.
Delaney, Michael S. .... '68 '99 C.339 B.A. L.596 J.D. [DeLaney]
DeLaney Law Offices, Ltd. .... 12416 S. Harlem, Ste. 103
Devine-Mannix, Colleen .... '60 '93 C.589 B.A. L.801 J.D. P.O. Box 117
Duda, John Joseph .... '47 '76 C.339 B.A. L.146 J.D. [J.Duda]
Duda, John .... 12820 S. Ridgeland, Ste. C
Economou, Diane .... '47 '71 C&L.209 B.S., J.D. 7909 Beacon Dr.
Evans, Carl Lauras, Jr. .... '66 '93 C.1183 B.S. L.365 J.D. [C.L.Evans,Jr.]
Evans, Carl L., Jr., Law Offices of .... 12616 South Harlem Ave.
Farrell, Daniel J. .... '43 '69 C&L.424 B.S., J.D. [Farrell&Assoc.]
Farrell & Associates, Ltd. .... 7250 W. College Dr., Ste. 2 N.W.
Freireich, Lydia Anne .... '56 '81 C.339 B.S. L.146 J.D. 13012 Comanche Dr.‡
Garlanger, James W., (BV) ...... '48 '76 C.589 B.S. L.365 J.D. 11800 South 75th Avenue
Garrison-Barrett, Bernadette .... '65 '91 C.209 B.S. L.424 J.D. 6446 W. 127th St.
Gausselin, Edwin A. .... '36 '65 C.602 B.A. L.209 LL.B. 7804 College Drive
Grimm, Robert William .... '37 '88 C.597 B.S.J. L.365 J.D. 7910 Oak Knoll Lane
Groebe, William C., III .... '48 '73 C.339 B.S. L.209 J.D. [W.Groebe]
Groebe, WmC., & Co., Inc., Realtors .... 7250 W. College Drive
Healy, Patrick F., (AV) .... '33 '61 C.602 A.B. L.424 J.D. 13466 Westview Dr.‡
Jasinski, George J., Law Offices of '54 '79
C.98 B.S. L.365 J.D. 7330 W. College Dr., Ste. 101
Kezelis, Robert A., (AV) '57 '86
C.597 B.A. L.365 J.D. 6151 West 125th Place, Suite B (⊙Chicago)
Korn, Joseph Arthur .... '68 '93 C.804 B.S. L.209 J.D. [Ⓐ B.M.Bozich]
Kredens, Kenneth A. .... '52 '81 C.339 B.A. L.801 J.D. [K.A.Kredens]
Kredens, Ken A. .... 11800 S. 75th Ave., Ste. 100
Lawler, Timothy G. .... '56 '81 C.976 B.A. L.339 J.D. [Sosin L.&A.]
Malatt, Raymond E. .... '26 '50 L.424 LL.B. 6410 W. 127th St.
Marszalek, Joseph D. '55 '80 C.927 B.S.B.A. L.365 J.D.
Asst. V.P., Palos Bk. & Tr. Co.
Matug, Alexander P., (BV) .... '46 '72 C.742 B.A. L.424 J.D. [A.P.Matug]
Matug, Alexander P., P.C., (BV) .... 7250 W. College Drive
McGuinness, Thomas P. .... '30 '59 C.424 B.S. L.365 LL.B. 7735 Foresthill Ln.
Mclaughlin, William John .... '67 '93 C.720 B.A. L.546 J.D. [W.J.McLaughlin]
McLaughlin, William J. .... 7227 W. 127th St.
Morrone, John M. .... '58 '83 C.720 B.A. L.365 J.D. [J.M.Morrone]
Morrone, John M., P.C. .... 12820 S. Ridgeland Ave., Ste. C
Mulvaney, Bernard P., Sr. .... '49 '83 C.1151 B.A. L.209 J.D. 7001 W. 127th St., Ste. 201
O'Donnoghue, Kelly B. .... '77 '02 [Ⓐ Sosin L.&A.]
O'Meara, Arthur C., (AV) .... '11 '33 C&L.145 Ph.B., J.D. 7711 W. Oak Ridge Ct.‡
Palmisano, James A., (AV) .... '48 '73 C.339 B.A. L.146 J.D. [J.A.Palmisano]
Palmisano, James Anthony, Ltd., (AV) .... 11800 S. 75th Avenue, Suite 101
Pasquinelli, James R. .... '35 '67 C.339 B.S. L.209 J.D. 12210 Cheyenna Dr.
Prendergast, Jeanne J. .... '63 '01 C.339 L.146 7250 College Dr., Ste. 2NW
Sarna, Cheryl L.S. .... '50 '82 C&L.424 B.A., J.D. [C.L.Sarna]
Sarna, Cheryl L. .... 6420 W. 127th St., Ste. 210
Schmit, Robert J. .... '54 '79 C.424 B.A. L.597 J.D. 11800 S. 75th Ave., Ste. 101
Schuster, Naomi H. .... '51 '78 C.589 B.S. L.209 J.D. 7480 W. College Dr., Ste. 101

Siwek, James J., Law Office of
(See Worth)

Slaughter, Percy C. .... '34 '70 C.209 B.A. L.365 J.D. N.Y. Life Ins. Co.
Sosin, David B. .... '47 '72 C.339 B.S. L.597 J.D. [Sosin L.&A.]
Sosin Lawler & Arnold, L.L.C. .... 11800 S. 75th Street
Sramek, Gerald J., Attorney at Law, (AV) '46 '73
C.339 B.A. L.365 J.D. 6446 W. 127th St.
Strzelecki, Stanley A., Jr., (BV) .... '43 '68 C.602 B.S. L.424 J.D. [S.Strzelecki]
Strzelecki, Stanley, (BV) .... 6446 W. 127th St.
Svanascini, Kathy .... '64 '95 C&L.209 B.A., J.D. 7309 W. Choctaw Rd.
Taylor, Joseph H., (BV) .... '34 '65 C&L.424 B.S., J.D. 7330 W. College Drive, Suite 101
Toscas, Angelo J., Law Offices of ... '66 '92 C.424 B.A. L.365 J.D. 12616 S. Harlem Ave.
Toscas, John Z., Law Offices of '56 '90 C.339 B.A. L.365 J.D.
12616 South Harlem Ave.
Wideikis, John R. .... '39 '70 C.424 B.S. L.209 J.D. 6446 W. 127th St.
Zarzecki, Charles M. .... '57 '83 C.720 B.A. L.209 J.D. [Ⓐ Sosin L.&A.]

PALOS HILLS, 17,665, *Cook Co.*

Azulay, Horn & Seiden, LLC, Law Offices of, (AV)
10005 S. Roberts Road (⊙Chgo., IL; New York, NY)
Cervas, Joseph C., (BVⓉ) .... '25 '68 C.912 L.213 J.D. 11143B Northwest Rd.
De Young, David A. .... '59 '85 C.1191 B.A. L.365 J.D. Ntnl Insurance Crime Bureau
Georgis, Thomas J. .... '32 '63 C.339 L.365 LL.B. 11020 S. Roberts Rd.
Gosewisch, Kevin P., Law Office of ... '59 '91 C.750 B.A. L.365 J.D. 9944 S. Roberts Rd.
Griffin, John C. .... '51 '76 C.602 B.B.A. L.209 J.D. 10001 S. Roberts Rd.
Griffin, Jos. P. .... '16 '38 C&L.209 LL.B. 10001 S. Roberts Rd.
Griffin, Patrick J. .... '56 '83 C.602 B.B.A. L.209 J.D. 10001 S. Roberts Rd.
Hertz, James G., (AV) '56 '80 C&L.801 B.A., J.D.
Assoc. Gen. Coun., National Insurance Crime Bureau
Houha, Ann Marie .... '73 '01 C.587 B.A. L.146 J.D. 10001 S. Roberts Rd.
Javior, Gerald J. .... '35 '75 C.742 B.A. L.365 J.D. 8150 W. 111th St.
Khalaf, Vivian R. .... '66 '92 C.339 B.A. L.46 J.D. [Azulay,H.&S.] (⊙Chicago)
Landenberger, Eugen K. .... '27 '52 C&L.585 B.S.C., LL.B. 10710 S. Roberts Rd.
Moore, Thomas A. .... '52 '81 C.927 B.A. L.365 J.D. 10001 S. Roberts Rd.
Mulderink, Rudy Alan .... '42 '84 C.339 B.A. L.365 J.D. City Clk.
Najib, Omar M. .... '43 '77 L.209 J.D. 8116 W. 111th St.
Pecko, Joseph E. .... '55 '81 C&L.424 B.S., J.D. 8901 W. 95th St.
Simcoe, Edward F. .... '14 '52 C&L.424 J.D. 8515 Broadmoor Drive‡

Siwek, James J., Law Office of
(See Worth)

Small, John F. .... '45 '82 C.339 B.A. L.209 J.D. 7808 W. College Dr., Ste. 2-W
Vaccarello, Anthony M. .... '49 '76 C.1024 B.A. L.424 J.D. 9959 S. Roberts Rd.
Vlcek, David M. .... '— '87 L.424 J.D. 9944 S. Roberts
Wallace, Terry .... '63 '89 C.208 B.A. L.190 J.D. 7836 W. 103rd. St.
Walsh, Michael D. .... '53 '77 C.424 B.A. L.209 J.D. [M.D.Walsh]

Walsh, Michael D., PC
10001 South Roberts Road, 60465
Telephone: 708-599-7500
Email: mdwalsh53@netscape.net URL: http://www.lawyers.com/michaelwalshlawfirm
Michael D. Walsh.
Family Law, Divorce, Personal Injury, Workers Compensation, Real Estate, Child Custody, Child Support, Premarital Agreements, Spousal Support, Visitation Rights, Automobile Accidents, Medical Malpractice, Dog Bites, Head and Spinal Injuries, Nursing Home Litigation, Railroad Accidents, Sexual Abuse, Slip and Fall, Truck Accidents, Wrongful Death, Traffic Violations, Driving While Intoxicated, Commercial Leasing, Zoning and Land Use, Eminent Domain, Union Contractor Benefit Contributions.
See Professional Biographies, PALOS HILLS, ILLINOIS

Wittenmeier, Fred J. .... '13 '41 C.137 B.A. L.209 J.D. 8246 Holly Ct.‡

PALOS PARK, 4,689, *Cook Co.*

Butler, Francis P. .... '21 '52 C&L.424 Ph.B., J.D. Ret. Assoc. Cir. J.
Chisholm, Richard A. .... '39 '67 C.589 B.A. L.146 J.D. 9700 W. 131st St.
Dohm, Mark D. .... '47 '78 C.1191 B.S.E. L.209 J.D. [M.Dohm]
Dohm, Mark, Law Office of .... 10120 Creek Rd.
Gallagher, George V. .... '18 '48 C.93 A.B. L.309 LL.B. 12715 Farmhill Lane‡
Hett, Thomas A. .... '35 '60 C&L.209 LL.B. Cir. J.
King, John M., & Associates .... '48 '78 C.1151 B.A. L.424 J.D. 9700 W. 131 St.
Kosinski, George R. .... '45 '77 C.46 B.S. L.365 J.D. 9700 W. 131st St., Ste. 2ND

Malysa, Theresa M.
(See Orland Park)

McCarthy Duffy, (AV) .... 8102 West 119th Street, Suite 800 (⊙Chicago)
Milovich, Nicole D. .... '68 '98 C.966 B.S. L.365 J.D. 11617 S. Highwood Dr.
Panos, George E. .... '34 '78 C.1016 B.A. L.589 LL.B. 12800 S. 81st Ct.
Rafferty, Donal .... '12 '38 P.O. Box 126
Rohe, George J., (AV) .... '24 '54 C&L.209 A.B., LL.B. 13050 S. 83rd Ct.
Schaps, Joel P. .... '38 '65 C.339 B.S. L.209 J.D. 9700 W. 131st St.
Sims-Taylor, Lynne A. .... '— '78 C.145 B.A. L.146 J.D. 2 Partridge Ln.
Singletary, Kathleen H. .... '46 '97 L.424 J.D. 9302 W. 122nd St.
Smith, Jay L. .... '18 '46 C&L.339 B.S., LL.B. 9003 W. 126th St.‡

PANA, 5,614, *Christian Co.*

Amling, William H., (BV) ...... '21 '49 C&L.339 A.B., LL.B. City Atty., City of Pana, IL
Farr, William E., (CV) .... '59 '85 C.340 B.A. L.589 J.D. 148 S. Locust
Franklin, Daniel M., (BV) .... '59 '84 C.339 L.365 J.D. [Franklin]
Franklin Firm, (BV) .... 123 E. 3rd St.
Freitag, Robert H. .... '36 '67 C.339 B.S. L.365 J.D. 808 E. Seventh St.
Fribley, Joseph L. .... '32 '58 C&L.339 B.S., J.D. Ret. Cir. J.
Gregory, William L. .... '69 '98 C.209 B.A. L.424 J.D. 123 E. Third St.
Henschen, Sharon M. .... '49 '89 C&L.339 B.A., J.D. [S.Henschen]
Henschen, Sharon .... 110 E. Third St.
Kahl, Kevin H. .... '54 '80 C.801 B.S. L.339 J.D. 123 E. 3rd St.
Slater, Bill J. .... '22 '49 C&L.339 LL.B. Ret. Cir. J.

PARIS, * 8,987, *Edgar Co.*

Anderson, E. Robert, (BV) .... '60 '85 C.234 B.A. L.339 J.D. [Kreckman&A.]
Andrews, H. Dean .... '45 '71 C&L.339 A.B., J.D. Assoc. Cir. J.
Asher, Jack O'Hair, (AV) .... '30 '57 C.339 B.S. L.861 J.D. [Asher,S.&I.]
Asher, Jane F. .... '29 '57 C.112 L.861 J.D. P.O. Box 667

Asher, Smith & Isaf, (AV)
236 West Court Street, P.O. Box 340, 61944-0340
Telephone: 217-465-6444 Fax: 217-463-2486
URL: http://www.asilaw.net

(This Listing Continued)

Asher, Smith & Isaf (Continued)

Members of Firm: Ward E. Dillavou (1909-1987); Jack O'Hair Asher; S. Craig Smith; Mark R. Isaf. Of Counsel: Ralph S. Pearman.
General Practice in all Courts. Trials and Probate Law. Corporation, Insurance and Commercial Banking Law and Workers Compensation Law, Personal Injury and Negligence Litigation. Divorce, Child Custody, Child Support.
Representative Clients: Kansas State Bank; Edgar County Bank & Trust Co., Paris, Illinois; Citizens National Bank of Paris; Wolfe's Auto Supply; The Morgan Co.; Illinois Insurance Co.
See Professional Biographies, PARIS, ILLINOIS

Baber, Bruce, (CV) ... '54 '80 C.210 B.A. L.145 J.D. 216 East Wood Street
Baker, George H., (AVⓉ) '44 '70 C.318 B.A. L.477 J.D.
(adm. in IN; not adm. in IL) [© Kreckman&A.]
Bell, Allen A., Jr., (BV) ... '51 '80 C.210 B.A. L.345 J.D. 209 N. Central Ave.
Bitterman, Amy M., (CVⓉ) '67 '92 C.966 B.A. L.589 J.D.
(adm. in IN; not adm. in IL) 202 East Crawford Street

Brainard Law Offices, The
(See Charleston)

Burkybile, Karen L., (CV) ... '56 '83 C.346 B.S. L.801 J.D. 15175 U.S. Hwy. 150
Dole, George V. ... '14 '39 C.197 A.B. L.309 J.D. 117 E. Wash. St.‡
Dole, Peter T., (BV) ... '44 '72 C.197 A.B. L.880 J.D. [Dole]
Dole Law Offices, (BV) ... 117 E. Washington

Fruin, Garst & Kash, (AV)
129 North Central Avenue, 61944-1783
Telephone: 217-465-4196 Fax: 217-466-1213
Email: fgk@comwares.net URL: http://www.fruingarstkash.com
Members of Firm: Steven L. Garst; Richard M. Kash, Jr.; Roger J. Fruin (1915-2002).
General Practice, Probate and Estates, Trusts, Taxation, Elder and Family Law, Corporations, Criminal Law, Trials, DWI, Drug Crimes, Elder Abuse, Bankruptcy, Municipal, Drainage, Adoption, Divorce, Custody, Child Support, Visitation.
References: Edgar County Bank & Trust Co.; The Citizens National Bank; State Bank of Chrisman; First National Bank of Chrisman; First Federal Bank, FSB, of Paris.
See Professional Biographies, PARIS, ILLINOIS

Garst, Steven L., (AV) ... '49 '74 C.338 B.A. L.339 J.D. [Fruin,G.&K.]
Gibson, Robert L., (AV) ... '20 '49 C.210 A.B. L.477 J.D. [© Kreckman&A.]
Isaf, Mark R., (BV) ... '63 '91 C.299 B.A. L.589 J.D. [Asher,S.&I.]
James, Richard L., (BV) ... '47 '73 C.339 B.S. L.1119 J.D. 328 North Central
Jones, Larry B., (BV) ... '53 '78 C.339 B.A. L.801 J.D. [Jones&J.]
Jones, Wayne S., (AV) ... '21 '48 C&L.339 B.A., LL.B. [Jones&J.]
Jones & Jones Law Offices, P.C., (AV) ... 110 E. Washington St.
Kash, Richard M., Jr., (CV) ... '53 '78 C&L.339 B.S., J.D. [Fruin,G.&K.]
Kreckman, Alfred H., Jr., (AV) ... '41 '70 C.446 B.S. L.477 J.D. [Kreckman&A.]
Kreckman and Anderson, (AV) ... 908 North Main Street
Lolie, Allan F., Jr., (CV) ... '66 '91 C.927 B.S. L.801 J.D. State's Atty.
Pearman, Ralph S. ... '29 '53 C&L.339 B.S., J.D. [© Asher,S.&I.]
Ping, James R. ... '69 '00 C.999 B.A. L.347 J.D. [Ⓐ Kreckman&A.]
Piper, John A., (CV) ... '47 '74 C.701 B.S. L.347 J.D. [Piper]
Piper Law Offices, (CV) ... 112 East Washington
Rowe, Max L., (AV) ... '21 '47 C.145 M.B.A. L.339 J.D. [© Jones&J.] (©Springfield)
Scott, Richard E. ... '41 '66 C&L.339 B.S., J.D. Cir. J.
Smith, S. Craig, (AV) ... '49 '76 C.16 B.S. L.192 J.D. [Asher,S.&I.]
Stanfield, James Caleb, (BV) ... '23 '49 C&L.902 A.B., J.D. 227 W. Court St.
Sullivan, Matthew L. ... '69 '94 C&L.339 B.S., J.D. States Atty.

PARK FOREST, 23,462, *Cook & Will Cos.*

Abramovitz, Naomi Gil ... '67 '92 C.339 B.S. L.569 J.D. Gen. Coun., Gil and Associates
Colson, George L. '35 '64 C&L.469 A.B., LL.B.
(adm. in GA; not adm. in IL) 219 Nauvoo St.‡
Gregerson, Lloyd G. ... '31 '54 C&L.190 LL.B. 415 Stanton‡
Hall, Richard W. ... '23 '51 C.37 B.S. L.365 J.D. 274 Rich Rd.
Havlicek, Glenn T. ... '54 '82 C.339 B.S. L.209 J.D. Deloitte Haskins & Sells
Maker, Walter S. ... '24 '50 L.145 J.D. 33 Braeburn‡
Medhurst, Ralph C. ... '28 '62 C.504 B.S. L.365 J.D. 416 Illinois St. (Pat.)
Mitchell, Terrance ... '32 '55 C&L.339 J.D. 310 Gentry St.‡
Pryor, Vikki L. ... '53 '79 C&L.107 B.A., J.D. 180 Park Rd.
Simons, James F. ... '29 '62 C.171 M.S. L.174 J.D. 108 Chestnut St. (Pat.)
Smith, Richard B. '32 '61 C.347 A.B. L.1119 LL.B.
(adm. in IN; not adm. in IL) 103 Monee Rd.‡

PARK RIDGE, 37,775, *Cook Co.*

Aberman, Sheldon J. ... '69 '94 C.978 B.A. L.146 J.D. 1030 W. Higgins Road, Suite 365
Adamowski, Gilbert L. ... '15 '38 C&L.209 LL.B. 10 N. Summit Ave., #158‡
Albarello, Margherita M. ... '57 '84 C.339 B.S. L.146 J.D. [Di Monte&L.]
Allegretti, James L., (AV) ... '49 '78 C.424 B.A. L.365 J.D. [Allegretti&Assoc.]
Allegretti & Associates, (AV) ... 617 West Devon
Alms, David E. ... '52 '77 C.597 B.A. L.365 J.D. 1420 Renaissance Dr.
Anderlik, Kathryn James, (AV) ... '57 '83 C.927 B.A. L.365 J.D. [© Judge,J.&K.]
Anderson, Mark S. ... '58 '83 C.602 B.A. L.880 J.D. 542 S. Washington Avenue

Annes, Scott M., Law Offices of '63 '91 C.339 B.S. L.209 J.D.
2 West Talcott, 60668
Telephone: 847-292-0105 Fax: 847-292-0113
Email: smalaw@aol.com URL: http://www.scottannesattorney.com
Commercial Litigation with focus on Small Business Law, Small Business Litigation, Family Business Law, Partnership Law, Breach of Contract, Employment Law and Wrongful Termination, Elder Law and Real Estate.
See Professional Biographies, PARK RIDGE, ILLINOIS

Ansani, Daniel R. ... '50 '74 C&L.209 B.A., J.D. 1411 W. Peterson St., Ste. 202
Ansani, Theodore J. ... '40 '64 C&L.209 B.A., J.D. 1411 W. Peterson St.
Arena, David T. ... '68 '96 C.424 B.A. L.1003 J.D. [Di Monte&L.]
Barnett, Russell Marc ... '69 '94 C.339 B.A. L.209 J.D. [Raysa&Z.]
Bartosch, Edward A., Jr. ... '28 '56 C.209 L.365 LL.B. 123 S. Northwest Hwy.
Bartoshuk, Karen ... '50 '83 C&L.209 B.S., J.D. 511 N. Seminary Ave.‡
Bellas, George S., (AV) ... '48 '73 C&L.424 B.S., J.D. [Bellas&W.]
Bellas & Wachowski, (AV) ... 15 North Northwest Highway
Beyer, Gerald D., Jr. ... '47 '77 C.339 B.S. L.365 J.D. 754 N. Merrill
Bielski, John N., II ... '72 '97 C.750 B.A. L.209 J.D. [Pembroke,B.&Assoc.]
Black, Bryan L. ... '75 '00 C.999 B.A. L.900 J.D. [Ⓐ DiFranco&Assoc.]
Blazej, Agnes H. ... '77 '02 C&L.424 B.A., J.D. [Ⓐ Larsen&E.]
Blondin, Daniel P., (CV) ... '52 '81 C.238 B.A. L.589 J.D. [Raysa&Z.]
Bode, Keith F., (AV) ... '31 '55 C&L.597 B.S., J.D. 174 E. Edgemont Ln.‡
Bremer, William B. ... '16 '40 C&L.597 A.B., J.D. 816 S. Crescent Ave.‡
Brennan, John F. ... '47 '73 C.728 B.S. L.597 J.D. [J.F.Brennan]

Brennan, John F., P.C.
422 N. Northwest Highway, Suite B2, 60068-3272
Telephone: 847-292-0032 Fax: 847-292-0153
Email: jbrennanlaw@sbcglobal.net

(This Listing Continued)

Brennan, John F., P.C. (Continued)

John F. Brennan.
Civil Litigation, Insurance Defense, Insurance Coverage, First Property, Reinsurance, Subrogation.
See Professional Biographies, PARK RIDGE, ILLINOIS

Brown, Marc L., The Law Offices of '52 '86 C.340 B.S. L.146 J.D.
422 N. Northwest Highway, 60068
Telephone: 847-825-1900 Fax: 847-825-1979
Email: marclbrown@sbcglobal.net
Elder Law, Real Estate, Trusts and Estates, Wills, Probate, Living Trusts, Guardianship, Nursing Home Abuse and Neglect, Health Care.
See Professional Biographies, PARK RIDGE, ILLINOIS

Brustein, Abraham E., (BV) ... '50 '76 C.597 B.A. L.209 J.D. [Di Monte&L.]
Carpenter, Richard W. ... '23 '48 C.436 L.209 J.D. 44 Park Lane (Pat.)
Cawley, Thomas P. ... '36 '61 C&L.424 LL.B. 1217 Talcott Rd.
Cello, Michael M. ... '— '91 C.209 B.S. L.424 J.D. Pollina Corp. Real Estate, Inc.
Cloney, John E. ... '24 '52 C&L.209 LL.B. 101 Summit Ave.
Collins, Ellen K. ... '54 '78 C&L.209 B.A., J.D. 901 S. Aldine
Condo, Amy Pinkerman ... '69 '95 C.36 B.A. L.221 J.D. Warrior Insurance Group, Inc.
Conlon, Jerome W. ... '39 '65 C&L.424 B.B.A., J.D. 1026 S. Knight
Cook, Kara L. ... '52 '78 C.339 B.A. L.424 J.D. 400 S. Rose Ave.‡
Cummings, George T., Law Office of '26 '61 C.424 A.B. L.365 J.D.
1420 Renaissance Dr.
Cupp, Cathy L., Law Offices of ... '57 '82 C.679 B.A. L.879 J.D. 925 S. Vine Ave.
Curtis, Philip J., (AV) ... '18 '47 C.686 A.B. L.276 J.D. 1858 Habberton St.‡

Cutler & Associates, LTD.
(See Skokie)

Di Franco, Frank R. ... '61 '87 C.424 B.A. L.146 J.D. [DiFranco&Assoc.]

Di Franco & Associates, P.C.
617 Devon Avenue, 60068
Telephone: 847-825-7744 Fax: 847-825-7746
Email: difrancolaw@aol.com URL: http://www.difrancolaw.com
Frank R. Di Franco;—Lawrence M. Lykowski; Katrina M. Maglaya; John A. Lewert; Bryan L. Black.
Criminal Defense, Civil Litigation.
See Professional Biographies, PARK RIDGE, ILLINOIS

Di Monte, Eugene A., (AV) ... '36 '61 C&L.209 B.S.C., J.D. [Di Monte&L.]
Di Monte, Riccardo A., (AV) ... '60 '85 C.801 B.S. L.209 J.D. [Di Monte&L.]

Di Monte & Lizak, (AV) BB
216 West Higgins Road, 60068
Telephone: 847-698-9600 Fax: 847-698-9623
Email: firm@dimonteandlizak.com
Members of Firm: Margherita M. Albarello; David T. Arena; Abraham E. Brustein; Eugene A. Di Monte; Riccardo A. Di Monte; Paul A. Greco; Linscott R. Hanson; Chester A. Lizak; Jeffrey S. McDonald; Robert S. Minetz; Jane Kaminski Simers; Alan L. Stefaniak. Associates: Francis J. Ferraro, IV; Julia E. Jensen; Sarah Lappin; Richard W. Laubenstein.
Construction and Real Estate Development (Zoning, Mechanics' Lien, etc.), Banking, Bankruptcy and Insolvency, Corporate Law, Estate Planning, Probate and Trust Litigation, Employment Law, Health Care Law, Civil Litigation Trials and Appeals.
See Professional Biographies, PARK RIDGE, ILLINOIS

Donlan, John F. ... '32 '56 C&L.209 B.S.C., J.D. 821 S. Seminary Ave.‡
Dorff, Charles A., Jr. ... '57 '84 421 N. Western Avenue
Dudley, Robert W. ... '28 '62 C.597 B.S.M.E. L.209 J.D. 634 N. Overhill (Pat.)‡
Edlund, Curtis E. ... '45 '77 C.339 B.A. L.424 J.D. [Larsen&E.]
Edlund, Jennifer L. ... '74 '99 C.473 B.A. L.424 J.D. [Ⓐ Larsen&E.]
Elder, Debra Oswald ... '54 '82 C.209 B.A. L.424 J.D. 1946 Manor Ln.‡
Elmer, George R. ... '23 '51 C.597 L.146 LL.B. 2400 Archbury Lane
Erickson, Charles B. ... '32 '60 C&L.502 A.B., LL.B. 15 N. Northwest Hwy.
Fanchi, Louis A. ... '29 '60 C&L.209 B.S.C., J.D. 611 Wisner St.
Ferraro, Francis J., IV ... '78 '03 C.347 B.A. L.209 J.D. [Ⓐ Di Monte&L.]

Ferraro, Anthony B., The Law Offices of
(See Rosemont)

Fink, Richd. J. ... '17 '41 C&L.597 B.S., J.D. 349 Austin Ave.‡
Fio Rito, Deborah J. ... '59 '84 C.927 B.A. L.146 J.D. [Firm of Karris&F.R.]
Flaa, Cynthia J. ... '56 '83 C.747 B.A. L.424 J.D. Staff Coun., Lutheran Gen. Hosp.
Gallo, Judith L. ... '58 '89 C.1322 B.A. L.365 J.D. 31 S. Home Ave.‡
Gann, Gregory S. ... '53 '78 C.840 B.A. L.146 J.D. [Gann&P.]
Gann & Parker, P.C. ... 1480 Renaissance Drive Suite 201
Gibbons, David J., (AV) ... '29 '54 C&L.424 B.S., J.D. 834 S. Cumberland‡
Gierum, John E., Jr., (AV) ... '50 '76 C.424 B.A. L.365 J.D. [Gierum&M.]
Gierum & Mantas, (AV) ... 1030 West Higgins Road Suite 220
Glennon, Helen L. ... '19 '43 C&L.339 B.A., LL.B. 301 W. Touhy Ave.‡
Gonzalez, Vicki M. ... '56 '92 C.589 B.A. L.365 J.D. [Ⓐ Bellas&W.]
Greco, Paul A. ... '69 '95 C.732 B.A. L.146 J.D. [Di Monte&L.]
Greco, Philip G., JR '64 '94 C.209 B.A. L.365 J.D.
1580 N. Northwest Hwy., Ste. 223 B
Green, William R. ... '45 '74 C.339 B.A. L.424 J.D. 845 Brookline‡
Greene, Paul M. ... '52 '77 C.424 B.A. L.801 J.D. V.P., Bank One
Haley, William H., Law Offices of ... '47 '72 C.190 B.A. L.339 J.D. 36 Main St., Ste. 107
Hall, Kenneth R. '55 '85 C.44 B.S.E. L.1243 J.D.
(adm. in AR; not adm. in IL)
Contract Mgr. & Reinsurance Coun., Amer. Agricultural Ins. Co.
Hansen, Thomas J. ... '51 '89 C.209 M.S.T. L.365 J.D. [T.J.Hansen]
Hansen, Thomas J., Ltd. ... 444 N. Northwest Hwy., Ste. 205
Hanson, Linscott R., (AV) ... '37 '61 C&L.477 B.A., J.D. [Di Monte&L.]
Harrington, Philip E. ... '45 '71 C.436 B.S. L.597 J.D. 1220 N. Hamlin Ave.

Harris Kessler & Goldstein LLC
(See Chicago)

Harth, Charles C. ... '60 '87 C.927 B.S. L.365 J.D. [C.C.Harth&Assoc.]
Harth, Charles C., PC, & Associates ... 422 N. Northwest Hwy., Ste. 100
Hegarty, Mary F. ... '50 '75 C&L.209 B.A., J.D. 301 W. Touhy Ave.
Herting, Claireen M. ... '29 '60 C.339 B.S. L.365 J.D. 1281 Northwest Hwy.‡
Hester-Tone, Mary M., (BV) ... '53 '78 C.30 B.A. L.339 J.D. 750 Wisner St.
Hintz, Werner E. ... '51 '76 C&L.424 B.A., J.D. [W.E.Hintz&Assoc.]
Hintz, Werner E., & Associates ... 1625 S. Ashland
Hopkinson, Brian L., (BV) '56 '83
C.1082 B.S. L.365 J.D. Suite 220 1030 West Higgins Road
Jancovic, Bruce M. ... '45 '71 444 N. Northwest Hwy., Suite 205
Jensen, Julia E. ... '75 '00 C.339 B.A. L.424 J.D. [Ⓐ Di Monte&L.]
Johnston, Frederick P., Sr. ... '31 '58 C.393 B.A. L.597 J.D. 444 N. Northwest Hwy.‡
Judge, Jay S., (AV) ... '40 '70 C.436 B.S. L.365 J.D. [Judge,J.&K.]
Judge, James & Kujawa, LLC, (AV) ... 422 N. Northwest Highway, Suite 200
Jung, Lorraine A. ... '21 '47 C.339 B.S. L.209 J.D. 1704 S. Ashland Ave.
Kamowski, Norbert R. ... '24 '50 C&L.209 B.S., J.D. 1340 S. Knight Ave.‡

Karris, Assunta A. .... '71 '96 C.339 B.A. L.146 J.D. [Firm of Karris&F.R.]
Karris and Fio Rito, Law Firm of .... 8 W. Devon Ave.
Keating, James T. J., (AV) ....'43 '72 C.339 B.A. L.209 J.D. 22 Park Ln., Unit 410
Kelly, Edward J. ....'19 '42 C&L.602 B.A., LL.B. 8765 W. Higgins Rd.‡
Kidston, Marlowe A. .... '30 '55 C.604 A.B. L.597 J.D. 401 Ascot‡
Kinnel, R. Jackson .... '30 '58 C&L.477 B.B.A., J.D. 1309 S. Fairview Ave.
Kirchberg, Charles R. .... '39 '69 C.697 B.A. L.146 J.D. 1710 Greendale
Kozicki, Steven A., The Law Offices of '60 '85
C.687 B.S. L.424 J.D. 15 North Northwest Highway
Krause, Richard L. '46 '74
C.276 B.A. L.477 J.D. Asst. Coun., Amer. Farm Bur. Federation
Kujawa, Michael E. .... '67 '98 C.927 B.S. L.365 J.D. [Judge,J.&K.]
Kukla, Robert J. .... '32 '57 C&L.597 B.S., J.D. Admin. J.
LaDolce, Deborah L. .... '50 '75 C.339 B.A. L.597 J.D. 133 N. Wisner St.
LaJone, Lynne M. .... '54 '79 C.399 B.A. L.966 J.D. 706 N. Wisner Av.
Lamont, Karen A. ....'51 '76 C.589 B.A. L.209 J.D. 1824 W. Stewart Ave.
Lappin, Sarah ....'77 '02 C.338 B.S. L.209 J.D. [Ⓐ Di Monte&L.]
Larsen, Richard G., (AV) .... '46 '70 C.597 B.A. L.424 J.D. [Larsen&E.]
Larsen & Edlund, (AV) .... 444 N. Northwest Highway, Suite 155
Laubenstein, Richard W. ....'60 '86 C.999 B.A. L.146 J.D. [Ⓐ Di Monte&L.]
Lees, Carolyn Victoria J. ....'78 '03 C.145 B.A. L.770 J.D. [Ⓐ Raysa&Z.]
Lesak, Robert L. ....'43 '69 C.98 B.S. L.146 J.D. 1111 S. Prospect
Lewert, John A. ....'77 '02 C.340 B.A. L.209 J.D. [Ⓐ DiFranco&Assoc.]
Linderman, Abe M. ....'21 '50 C.597 L.365 LL.B. 1301 Touhy‡
Lizak, Chester A., (BV) .... '36 '63 C&L.209 B.S., J.D. [Di Monte&L.]
Lock, Robert K., Jr.
(See Chicago)
Lofthouse, Wayne T. ....'48 '75 C.424 B.A. L.146 J.D. 1420 Renaissance Dr.
Logan, Michael G. ....'48 '73 C.209 B.A. L.597 J.D. 1442 Bonita Dr.
Loutos, Peter A., (Ltd.), (AV) ....'32 '64 C.339 B.S. L.209 LL.B. 1410 W. Higgins
Luchtenburg, Russell J. ....'51 '83 C.209 B.A. L.365 J.D. 646 Busse Hwy.
Lykowski, Lawrence M. ....'50 '76 C.174 B.A. L.146 J.D. [Ⓐ DiFranco&Assoc.]
Lynn, Gary A., (BV) ....'50 '77 C.424 B.A. L.365 J.D. [Judge,J.&K.]
Maglaya, Katrina M. ....'75 '01 C.L.209 B.A., J.D. [Ⓐ DiFranco&Assoc.]
Manrose, Susan M. ....'47 '79 C.769 B.A. L.477 J.D. 1731 Pavilion Way, Unit 407
Mantas, William J. .... '61 '87 C.339 B.A. L.365 J.D. [Gierum&M.]
Maramba & Associates, LLC
(See Arlington Heights)
Marchionna, Sal B., & Associates ....'47 '83 C.1151 B.A. L.589 J.D. 1809 Wash.
Marquis, Catherine Bjork .... '50 '80 C.966 B.A. L.146 J.D. 120 N. Dee Rd.
Marsh, Angela ....'61 '87 C.1214 B.A. L.273 J.D. 505 Grand Blvd‡
Matthias, Russell H., Jr. '34 '62 C.674 A.B. L.597 J.D.
Secy. & Gen. Coun., Protection Mutual Insurance Company
Mayfield, C. David '45 '70 C.210 B.A. L.546 J.D.
Secy. & Assoc. Gen. Coun., Amer. Farm Bur. Federation
McCarthy, Michael S. .... '53 '80 C.276 B.A. L.424 J.D. Chmn. & CEO, The Parkside Co.
McDonald, Jeffrey S. ....'58 '87 C.602 B.S. L.365 J.D. [Di Monte&L.]
Mermel, Michael G. ....'51 '76 C.801 L.365 J.D. Mermel Realty
Milano, Carmen R. ....'25 '52 C&L.339 B.S., LL.B. 315 Grant Place‡
Miller, Joseph A. ....'55 '91 C.1335 B.S. L.1243 J.D. American Farm Bureau
Miner, Barnhill & Galland, P.C.
(See Chicago)
Minetz, Robert S., (AV) ....'46 '73 C.209 B.A. L.339 J.D. [Di Monte&L.]
Nelson, Milton E., Jr. ....'37 '63 C.976 A.B. L.145 J.D. 715 N. Merrill St.
Nuccio, Teresa, (BV) .....'48 '81 C.1183 B.A. L.424 J.D. 1460 Renaissance Dr., Ste. 105
O'Donnell, Kevin Michael, (BV) .... '61 '88 C&L.209 B.S.C., J.D. [K.M.O'Donnell]
O'Donnell, Kevin M., Ltd., (BV) ....250 S. Northwest Hwy., Ste. 301
Oskandy, James M. ....'— '79 C&L.589 B.S., J.D. [Oskandy&Assoc.]
Oskandy and Associates ....1504 S. Vine Ave.
Osran, Thomas Neil ....'61 '90 C.339 B.S. L.589 J.D. [Ⓐ Judge,J.&K.]
Otto, Frederick J., (BV) ....'48 '73 C&L.546 B.S., J.D. [Otto&Assoc.]
Otto & Associates, (BV) ....3 South Prospect Avenue Suite 206
Owens, Denis J., (AV) ....'40 '64 C.602 B.S. L.209 J.D. [Owens,O.&R.]
Owens, John E., (AV) ....'36 '62 C.424 B.S.C. L.209 J.D. [Owens,O.&R.]
Owens, John V., (AV) ....'62 '87 L.602 J.D. [Ⓒ Owens,O.&R.]
Owens, Patrick D. ....'71 '96 C.602 B.B.A. L.209 J.D. [Owens,O.&R.]

Owens, Owens & Rinn, Ltd., (AV)
444 N. Northwest Highway, P.O. Box 578, 60068
Telephone: 847-825-2128; Chicago: 773-693-3565 Fax: 773-693-3567
Email: office@owensowensrinn.com URL: http://www.owensowensrinn.com
John E. Owens, Sr. (1894-1966); Thomas L. Owens (1898-1948); Vincent G. Rinn (1905-1996); Samuel W. Miller (1907-1979); John E. Owens; Denis J. Owens; Patrick D. Owens;—Ursula Szczepanski. Of Counsel: John V. Owens.
Estate Planning, Probate, Taxation, Real Estate, Zoning, and Corporate Law. General Civil Trial and Appellate Practice in Federal and State Courts.
See Professional Biographies, PARK RIDGE, ILLINOIS

Parker, Deborah G. ....'61 '86 C.679 B.A. L.146 J.D. [Gann&P.]
Pavelko, Thomas M., (BVⓉ) '58 '83 C.436 B.A. L.910 J.D.
Contracts & Regulatory Atty., American Agricultural Insurance Company
Pembroke, John J., (AV) ....'50 '79 C.339 B.S. L.597 J.D. [Pembroke,B.&Assoc.]

Pembroke, Bielski and Associates, LLC, (AV)
A Limited Liability Company of Attorneys
Suite 150 422 North Northwest Highway, 60068
Telephone: 847-696-0060; 847-825-1900 Facsimile: 847-696-0950
URL: http://www.pembrokelaw.com
John J. Pembroke; John N. Bielski II.
Corporate Law, Federal and State Income, Estate and Gift Tax, Commercial Litigation, Wills, Trusts, Estate Planning, General Commercial Law, Elder Law, Probate, Real Estate and Financial Planning.
See Professional Biographies, PARK RIDGE, ILLINOIS

Pietrzyk ....422 N. Northwest Hwy., Ste. 150
Pietrzyk, George ....'52 '77 C.424 B.A. L.146 J.D. [Pietrzyk]
Pontarelli, Michael L. ....'49 '77 C.659 B.S. L.146 J.D. 1216 South Western Ave.
Ponticelli, Michael I. ....'41 '75 C.424 B.S. L.146 J.D. 1480 Renaissance Dr., Ste. 209
Ptasinski & Smith, P.C.
(See Niles)
Rademacher, John '44 '69 C.1151 B.A. L.209 J.D.
General Counsel, American Farm Bureau Federation & Affiliated Co.
Rago, Matteo ..... '52 '83 C.1183 B.A. L.589 J.D. 1550 N. Northwest Highway, Suite 311
Rathbun, Harold J. ....'11 '39 C.930 B.S.E.E. L.1003 J.D. 1892 De Cook Ave.‡
Raysa, Richard G. ....'07 '31 C&L.424 LL.B. 22 South Washington Street
Raysa, William G. ....'45 '74 C.300 B.A. L.424 J.D. [Raysa&Z.]

Raysa & Zimmermann, LLC, (CV)
22 South Washington Avenue, 60068
Telephone: 847-268-8600 Fax: 847-268-8614

(This Listing Continued)

Raysa & Zimmermann, LLC (Continued)
John J. Zimmermann; Michael F. Zimmermann; William G. Raysa; Russell Marc Barnett; Daniel P. Blondin;—Carolyn Victoria J. Lees.
Local Government Law, Zoning, Real Estate, Probate, Trusts, Wills, Estate Planning, General Civil Trial Practice, Insurance Defense and Subrogation.
See Professional Biographies, PARK RIDGE, ILLINOIS

Regas, William T. ....'29 '55 C&L.209 B.A., J.D. 123 S. Northwest Hwy.
Risner, Gerald C., (AV) ....'32 '58 C&L.424 B.S.C., J.D. [G.C.Risner]
Risner, Gerald C., P.C., (AV) .... 521 Oakton St.
Ryan, Peter N., Law Offices of ....'50 '83 C.454 B.A. L.365 J.D. P.O. Box 652
Schlake, Richard J. ....'23 '60 C.879 A.B. L.146 LL.B. 1400 Renissance Dr.‡
Schmidt, Wayne W. '41 '66 C.560 B.A. L.616 J.D.
Exec. Dir. & Supervising Coun., Amer. for Effective Law Enforcement, Inc.
Schreiber, Karla A. ....'59 '85 C.339 B.A. L.145 J.D. [Ⓐ K.M.O'Donnell]
Shire, Clark C. ....'24 '52 C.339 L.146 LL.B. [Shire&S.]
Shire, Richard K. ....'55 '82 C.145 A.B. L.46 J.D. [Shire&S.]
Shire & Shire ....2140 Glenview Avenue
Silver, Robert D. ....'27 '52 C&L.966 B.S., J.D. 125 E. Kathleen Dr. (Pat.)
Simers, Jane Kaminski ....'54 '85 C.589 B.S. L.209 J.D. [Di Monte&L.]
Slutzky, Jay A.
(See Niles)
Smith, Albert W. ....'33 '70 C.46 B.S. L.146 J.D. 506 N. Root St.‡
Smith, Charles B. ....'25 '59 C.597 B.A. L.146 LL.B. P.O. Box 63‡
Smith, Jeff, Law Offices of
(See Evanston)
Stefaniak, Alan L. ....'47 '73 C.597 B.A. L.339 J.D. [Di Monte&L.]
Stewart, Russell J. ....'49 '79 C.209 B.S.C. L.589 J.D. 805 Touhy Ave.
Stientjes, Michael J. '39 '64 C&L.221 B.S., LL.B.
(adm. in IA; not adm. in IL) Asst. Coun., Amer. Farm Bur. Federation
Studenroth, David L. ....'61 '87 C.831 B.A. L.365 J.D. [D.Studenroth]
Studenroth, David ....617 Devon Ave.
Sullivan, John M., (BV) ....'32 '58 C&L.424 B.S., LL.B. 22 South Washington Ave.
Summerfield, John A. ....'33 '58 C.103 B.A. L.597 J.D. 1580 N. Northwest Hwy.
Szczepanski, Ursula ....'75 '01 C.700 B.A. L.365 J.D. [Ⓐ Owens,O.&R.]
Tighe, Marybeth Schumar ....'57 '83 C.475 B.S. L.365 J.D. 646 Busse Highway
Tobin, Mitchell H. .....'57 '83 C.597 B.S.J. L.910 J.D. Amer. Assn. of Nurse Anesthetists
Toulon, Leon J. ....'33 '64 C&L.209 J.D. 1411 W. Peterson
Tuttle, Vedral & Collins PC
(See Des Plaines)
Upton, Ellen L. ....'52 '78 C.339 B.S. L.477 J.D. 317 N. Meacham Ave.‡
Uzemack, Marilyn V. ....'47 '77 C.589 B.S. L.365 J.D. 15 S. Prospect, 2nd Fl.
Wachowski, Peter C. ....'65 '90 C.424 B.S. L.365 J.D. [Bellas&W.]
Wasko, Steven E. ....'54 '79 C.187 B.S. L.146 J.D. 1580 Northwest Hwy., Ste. 212
Weissman, Benj. L. ....'08 '33 C&L.597 B.S. 614 Wesley Dr.
Werderitch, Jerome J. '43 '68
C&L.424 B.S., J.D. Sr. Asst. Coun., Amer. Farm Bur. Federation
Whamond, Wilbur O. ....'13 '40 C.303 L.365 LL.B. 1005 N. Northwest Hwy.
Whitney, Larry A. .....'44 '82 C.350 B.S.C.E. L.146 J.D. 422 N. Northwest Hwy., Ste. B1
Wiemerslage, Frank R. ....'43 '70 C&L.339 B.S., J.D. [F.R.Wiemerslage] ‡
Wiemerslage, Frank R., Ltd. ....711 S. Seminary
Wietecha, Ronald W. ....'42 '72 C.742 B.A. L.424 J.D. 301 W. Touhy Ave.
Witanen, John E. ....'60 '85 C.597 B.A. L.209 J.D. 1030 W. Higgins Rd., Ste. 365
Wojcicki, Christopher J. ....'64 '02 C.209 B.S.C. L.365 J.D. [C.J.Wojcicki]
Wojcicki, Christopher J., P.C., Law Offices of .... 1580 N. Northwest Highway, Ste. 222
Zelek, Robert M., Law Offices of, (BV) .....'57 '83 C&L.209 B.A., J.D. 110 Higgins Rd.
Zimmermann, John J. ....'39 '67 C&L.209 A.B., J.D. [Raysa&Z.]
Zimmermann, Michael F. ....'69 '94 C.436 B.A. L.209 J.D. [Raysa&Z.]
Zukowski, John ....'09 '35 C&L.209 LL.B. 1229 Courtland‡

PAWNEE, 2,647, *Sangamon Co.*

Rhodes, Jerry S. ....'32 '62 C.339 A.B. L.146 LL.B. 3520 Alvies Rd.‡

PAXTON, * 4,525, *Ford Co.*

Dilks, Sidney H., (AV) ....'06 '31 L.734 J.D. [Ⓒ Dilks,R.&G.] ‡
Dilks, Rodeen & Gibson, Ltd., (BV) ....146 N. Market St.
Gibson, Sue A., (BV) ....'50 '76 C.339 B.A. L.146 J.D. [Dilks,R.&G.]
Johnson, Kamalen K., (BV) ....'58 '85 C.338 B.S. L.801 J.D. Co. Cir. Clk.
Kaye, George ....'30 '57 C&L.145 A.B., J.D. Kaye Bldg.
Lee, Anthony A., (CV) ....'53 '79 C.388 B.A. L.146 J.D. Off. of State Atty.
Luebchow, Kevin H., (CV) ....'68 '93 C.340 B.A. L.339 J.D. [Martensen,N.&L.]
Martensen, Robert E., (AV) ... '37 '61 C&L.339 B.S., LL.B. City Atty. [Martensen,N.&L.]
Martensen, Niemann & Luebchow, (AV) .... 140 N. Taft St.
Niemann, Jerry L., (BV) ....'48 '77 C.338 B.S. L.339 J.D. [Martensen,N.&L.]
Pacey, Charles W., (BV) ....'46 '74 C.339 B.S. L.146 J.D. [Pacey&P.]
Pacey, Stephen R. ....'48 '74 C&L.339 B.A., J.D. 200 W. State St.
Pacey & Pacey Lawyers, P.C., (BV) .... 125 W. State St.
Rodeen, Gerald P., (BV) ....'47 '73 C.347 B.S. L.1119 J.D. [Dilks,R.&G.]
Strough, Dale, Attorney at Law
(See Watseka)

PECATONICA, 1,997, *Winnebago Co.*

Fuenty, Janet D., Law Offices of ....'64 '90 C.339 B.A. L.589 J.D. 519 Main

PEKIN, * 33,857, *Tazewell Co.*

Addy, Brian A., (BV) ....'54 '81 C.98 B.S. L.910 J.D. 342 St. Mary St.
Bagley, John R., (AV) ....'37 '62 C.502 B.A. L.477 J.D. [Bagley&M.]

Bagley & Miller, (AV)
6 South Fourth Street, P.O. Box 669, 61554
Telephone: 309-346-2161 Fax: 309-346-6387
Email: bagleymillerlaw@grics.net
Members of Firm: John R. Bagley; Louis E. Miller.
General Civil Practice. Banking, Corporation, Probate, Real Estate, Public Utility and Real Property Taxation Law. No Collections under $3,000.

Bernardi, Frederick A., (AV) '50 '75
C&L.602 B.B.A., J.D. 100 North 5th Street, Suite 230
Bernardi, John A., (AV) ....'45 '71 C.602 B.B.A. L.734 J.D. Pub. Def.
Birner, Donald K., (BV) ....'45 '74 C.1042 B.A. L.900 J.D. 2613 Mayflower Dr.
Bode, Kirk W., (BV) ....'53 '78 C.340 B.A. L.339 J.D. 110 N. 5th St., Ste. 205
Bosich, Susan ....'53 '96 C.184 B.S. L.1040 J.D. [Ⓐ Elliff,K.O.&D.]
Brewer, Thomas K., (BV) ....'67 '94 C.338 B.S. L.190 J.D. [Moehle,S.&U.]
Carmichael, H. Wayne, (BV) ....'37 '66 C&L.339 B.S., J.D. 110 N. 5th Street
Cassidy, Elizabeth K., (CV) ....'39 '65 C.1082 B.A. L.339 LL.B. 6 S. Fourth

Clevenger, Robert V., (AV) .... '21 '47 C&L.339 A.B., J.D. 1011 Monroe St.‡
Dancey, Burt L., (BV) .... '48 '77 C.197 B.A. L.588 J.D. [Elliff,K.O.&D.]

Elliff, Keyser, Oberle & Dancey, P.C., (AV)
109 South Fourth Street, P.O. Box 873, 61554
Telephone: 309-346-4148 Fax: 309-346-0633
John T. Elliff (1872-1960); Nathan T. Elliff (1905-1993); Patrick E. Oberle; Burt L. Dancey; William P. Streeter; Ronald L. Keyser (Retired). Associate: Susan Bosich.
General Practice. Business, Estate Planning, Probate, Banking, Municipal and Real Estate Law, Civil Trial and Appellate Practice, No Collections under $3000.00.
Representative Clients: City of Pekin; Central Illinois Dock.
Local Counsel for: Pekin Hospital.
See Professional Biographies, PEKIN, ILLINOIS

Hayes, Richard G., (BV) .... '37 '67 C.801 B.A. L.900 J.D. 331 S. Fourth St.
Johnson, Kevin E., (BV) ...... '60 '86 C.98 B.S. L.900 J.D. Tazewell Co. State Atty. Off.
Kelly Law Offices, P.C., (AV) .... 236 Broadway (⊙Bloomington)
Keyser, Ronald L., (AV) ..... '33 '57 C.98 L.339 J.D. [Elliff,K.O.&D.] (⊙Phoenix, AZ)‡
Kuhfuss, W. Thad, (AV) .... '45 '72 C.339 B.S. L.910 J.D. [Kuhfuss&P.]

Kuhfuss & Proehl, P.C., (AV)
342 Elizabeth Street, P.O. Box 1068, 61555-1068
Telephone: 309-347-4164 Fax: 309-347-7872
Members of Firm: Harold H. Kuhfuss (1909-1993); W. Thad Kuhfuss; Jason W. Proehl.
General Civil Practice in all Courts. Trials, Probate and Real Estate Law, Banking.
Attorneys for: Pekin National Bank; First Farmers State Bank of Minier; Pekin Savings Bank.
General Counsel for: Pekin Insurance Cos.
See Professional Biographies, PEKIN, ILLINOIS

Leuck, John F., (CV) .... '39 '89 C&L.190 B.S.B.A., J.D. 408 Court Street
Luke, Fred J. .... '49 '75 C.98 B.S. L.146 J.D. V.P., Pekin Abstract & Title Co.

Lynch and Bloom, P.C.
(See Peoria)

Madison, Angela Perucca .... '58 '83 C.679 B.A. L.1194 J.D. [A.P.Madison]
Madison, Angela P., Attorney at Law .... 110 N. 5th St., Ste. 201
Mara, Wayne .... '55 '79 C.597 B.A. L.902 J.D. Asst. State's Atty.
Maxey, Wayne E. .... '44 '91 C.1247 B.A. L.1339 J.D. Asst. State's Atty.
McCoy, Richard D., (BV) .... '55 '80 C.340 B.A. L.339 J.D. Assoc. Cir. J.
Metzler, Robert L., (CV) .... '36 '66 C&L.339 B.S., LL.B. 1114 S. 18th Street
Miller, Louis E., (BV) .... '55 '80 C&L.339 B.A., J.D. [Bagley&M.]
Moehle, Edward C., (BV) .... '25 '56 C&L.910 B.S.B.A., J.D. [Moehle,S.&U.]
Moehle, Swearingen & Umholtz, Ltd., (BV) .... 410 Broadway (⊙Washington)
Newlin, Jackson P. .... '18 '42 C.37 A.B. L.339 LL.B. Assoc. Cir. J.

Nicoara & Steagall
(See Peoria)

Oberle, Patrick E., (AV) .... '46 '75 C&L.221 B.S.B.A., J.D. [Elliff,K.O.&D.]
Ogolin, William J., Jr., (BV) .... '50 '76 C&L.339 B.S., J.D. Chf. Asst. States Atty.
Oltman, Bernard L., (BV) .... '26 '58 C.208 A.B. L.221 LL.B. 901 Bdway.
Proehl, Jason W. .... '76 '03 C.339 B.S. L.589 J.D. [Kuhfuss&P.]

Prusak, Winne & Gorman, Ltd.
(See Peoria)

Reardon, William J. .... '22 '48 C&L.339 A.B., J.D. Ret. Assoc. Cir. Ct. J.
Rossi, Mark F., (BV) .... '58 '84 C.340 B.A. L.209 J.D. [Kelly]
Sarff, Brandon Michael .... '75 '01 C.338 B.S. L.801 J.D. 331 S. 4th Street
Sheehan, Dennis M., (BV) .... '44 '69 C&L.424 B.S., J.D. [D.Sheehan]
Sheehan, Dennis, (BV) .... 406 Court St.
Smith, Gerald W., (P.C.), (BV) .... '24 '56 C&L.339 B.S., J.D. 410 Elizabeth St.
Streeter, William P., (BV) .... '62 '89 C.813 B.S. L.1068 J.D. [Elliff,K.O.&D.]

Strodel, Robert C., Ltd.
(See Peoria)

Thomas, Charles R., (BV) .... '37 '63 C&L.339 A.B., J.D. [C.R.Thomas]
Thomas, Charles R., PC, (BV) .... 417 Court St.
Umholtz, Stewart J., (AV) .... '59 '85 C.339 B.S. L.589 J.D. States Atty.
Umholtz, Valerie Moehle, (BV) '60 '85
C.339 B.S. L.589 J.D. Spec. Asst. Atty. Gen. [Moehle,S.&U.]
Wherry, Richard P., (BV) .... '37 '65 C.504 A.B. L.365 J.D. 2980 Court St.
Yontz, Ivan L. .... '21 '49 C.340 B.A. L.339 LL.B. Ret. Cir. Ct. J.‡

Zuckerman, Richard W.
(See Peoria)

PEORIA, * 112,936, *Peoria Co.*

Abraham, Jason F., (BVⓉ) .... '67 '92 C.966 B.A. L.436 J.D. [M.F.Hupy&Assoc.] ⊙
Abraham, Teena M., (BVⓉ) ..... '62 '97 C.1172 B.S. L.436 J.D. [🄰 M.F.Hupy&Assoc.] ⊙

Adams, Hall, LLC, Law Offices of
(See Chicago)

Alexandre-Strong, Dominique .... '70 '97 C.340 B.A. L.879 J.D. [Strong]
Allen, Jamison J. .... '74 '02 C.346 B.S. L.339 J.D. [Miller,H.&T.]
Allen, Lyle W., (AV) .... '24 '50 C.597 B.S. L.966 J.D. [🄲 Heyl,R.V.&A.]
Altenberger, William V. .... '35 '63 C&L.339 B.S., LL.B. U.S. Bkrptcy. J.
Ames, Henry T. .... '45 '71 C.174 B.A. L.178 J.D. Assoc. Gen. Coun., Caterpillar Inc.
Anderson, D. Phillip '53 '81 C.476 B.S. L.339 J.D.
Atty.-Adv., Office of the U.S. Trustee‡
Anderson, Kent V. .... '65 '91 C.549 B.A. L.1067 J.D. Sr. Staff Atty., Fed. Def. Off.
Anderson, Mark K. .... '66 '95 C.188 B.A. L.145 J.D. Corp. Atty., Caterpillar Inc.
Anderson, Sean M., (CV) .... '67 '97 C.105 B.A. L.1066 J.D. [Sutkowski&R.]
Apfelbaum, Larry A., (BV) '61 '87 C.338 B.S. L.339 J.D.
[🄰 Kanoski&Assoc.] (⊙Bloomington, Macomb, Quincy, Rushville, Springfield)
Ault, J. Peter .... '46 '71 C&L.879 B.A., J.D. Assoc. Cir. J.
Babcock, Bret S., (AV) '46 '71
C.966 B.S. L.339 J.D. 411 Hamilton Boulevard, Suite 1720
Bach, Robert W., (BV) .... '52 '78 C.98 B.A. L.734 J.D. 414 Hamilton Blvd.
Bain, Florence, (BV) '42 '78 C.350 B.S. L.36 J.D.
[🄰 Kanoski&Assoc.] (⊙Bloomington, Macomb, Quincy, Rushville, Springfield)

Baker, Baker & Krajewski, LLC
(See Springfield)

Ball, R. Lawrence .... '13 '37 C&L.339 B.A., LL.B. 5807 N. Briarwood Lane‡
Ballor, Jeanne Wysocki, (BV) .... '51 '88 C&L.339 B.A., J.D. 227 N.E. Jefferson St.

Barash & Everett, LLC
(See Galesburg)

Barbee, Lisa R. .... '— '03 C.57 B.A. L.124 J.D. [🄰 Hasselberg,W.G.S.&B.]
Barnes, D. James '— '02 C.160 B.S.M.E. L.790 J.D.
(adm. in NY; not adm. in IL; Pat.) Caterpillar Inc.
Barnes, Robert A., Jr. .... '42 '66 C&L.339 A.B., J.D. Assoc. Cir. J.‡
Barnhart, Nancy L. .... '72 '97 C.388 B.A. L.365 J.D. [🄰 Davis&C.]
Barra, John A. .... '49 '74 C.339 B.S. L.734 J.D. Cir. J.
Bartley, Joseph F., Jr., (AV) .... '16 '41 C&L.477 A.B., LL.B. 3027 N. Bigelow‡
Becker, Bruce R., (BV) .... '41 '65 C.697 B.A. L.339 LL.B. 411 Hamilton Blvd.
Becker, Robert B., (BV) .... '68 '93 C.473 B.A. L.221 J.D. 331 Fulton St.
Beckman, William A. '74 '03
C.597 B.S.M.E. L.146 J.D. Intell. Prop. Atty., Caterpillar Inc.
Behrends, F. Louis, (AV) .... '32 '59 C&L.339 B.S., LL.B. [Behrends]
Behrends Law Offices, (AV) .... 331 Fulton Street
Bell, Allison N., (CV) .... '71 '97 C.293 B.A. L.352 J.D. [🄰 Quinn,J.H.&P.]
Bell, Gregory S., (AV) .... '48 '75 C&L.339 B.A., J.D. [Hasselberg,R.B.&K.]
Benassi, A. Lou, (AV) .... '42 '68 C.339 B.S. L.1066 J.D. [Benassi&B.]
Benassi, Patricia C., (AV) .... '43 '69 C.1077 B.A. L.1066 J.D. [Benassi&B.]

Benassi & Benassi, P.C., (AV)
300 Northeast Perry, 61603
Telephone: 309-674-3556 FAX: 309-674-7989 URL: http://www.benassi.com
Email: lawfirm@benassi.com URL: http://www.lawyers.com/benassi&benassi
A. Lou Benassi; Patricia C. Benassi;—Athena M. Papachronis Herman.
Civil and Trial Practice. Administrative, Personal Injury, Workers Compensation, Family, Employment Discrimination, Civil Rights, Labor and Employee Benefits Law, Divorce, Child Custody.
See Professional Biographies, PEORIA, ILLINOIS

Benckendorf, David A., (BV) .... '56 '81 C.98 B.S. L.339 J.D. [Benckendorf&B.]
Benckendorf, Glenn E., (BV) .... '29 '57 C.248 B.A. L.910 J.D. [Benckendorf&B.]
Benckendorf, James W., (BV) .... '62 '88 C&L.589 B.A., J.D. [Benckendorf&B.]
Benckendorf & Benckendorf, P.C., (BV) .... 101 N.E. Randolph Ave.
Bender, Paul E. .... '51 '76 C.357 B.A. L.300 J.D. Chic. Title Ins. Co.
Benjamin, Hollis W., (AV) .... '25 '54 C.98 B.S. L.339 J.D. 411 Hamilton Boulevard‡
Bennett, Robert M., (BV) .... '68 '93 C.338 B.S. L.339 J.D. [🄰 Heyl,R.V.&A.]
Bernstein, Michael J. .... '47 '74 C.927 B.S. L.904 J.D. Admin. Law J., Soc. Sec. Admn.
Bertschy, Nicholas J., (AV) .... '56 '81 C.339 B.S. L.966 J.D. [Heyl,R.V.&A.]
Bertschy, Timothy L., (AV) .... '52 '77 C.339 A.B. L.273 J.D. [Heyl,R.V.&A.]
Bianchi, David J. .... '68 '93 C&L.602 B.A., J.D. Intell. Prop. Coun., Caterpillar Inc.
Billimack, SueAnn Sage, (BV) .... '— '94 C.388 B.A. L.339 J.D. [Husch&E.]
Binkele, Lynne Marie, (CV) .... '72 '96 C&L.339 B.A., J.D. [🄰 Benckendorf&B.]
Birdsall, Sandra J., (BV) .... '— '82 C.927 B.S. L.146 J.D. [Hasselberg,W.G.S.&B.]
Bishop, Erin L. .... '— '96 C.578 B.A. L.861 J.D. Attorney, Caterpillar Inc.
Black, Bruce W. .... '44 '71 C.98 A.B. L.339 J.D. Cir. J.‡
Blake, William L. .... '38 '66 C.339 B.S. L.276 J.D. [🄲 Westervelt,J.N.&K.]
Blanc, Erik I. .... '47 '75 C.98 B.S. L.339 J.D. Co. J.
Blumenshine, J. Wesley '62 '86 C.98 B.S. L.589 J.D.
Gen. Coun., Caterpillar Inc. (Pat.)
Bluth, Thomas J. '67 '92 C.350 B.S.E.E. L.597 J.D.
(adm. in VA; not adm. in IL; Pat.) 100 NE Adams St.
Bode, C. Brett .... '39 '68 C&L.339 B.A., J.D. Assoc. Cir. J.
Boos, John F., (BV) .... '43 '72 C.734 B.S. L.146 LL.B. [J.Boos]
Boos, Jack, P.C., (BV) .... 933 Commerce Bank Bldg.
Borden, Stuart P. .... '51 '77 C.98 A.B. L.801 J.D. Assoc. Cir. J.
Borsberry, Joseph M., (BV) .... '68 '93 C.338 B.S. L.209 J.D. [🄰 Reynolds,M.&Assoc.]
Bourne, Sumner A., (BV) .... '68 '94 C.339 B.S. L.94 J.D. [Rafool&B.]
Bowles, James E., (AV) .... '44 '69 C.98 B.A. L.339 J.D. [Goldfine&B.]
Bradshaw, Paul G. .... '32 '73 C.98 B.S. L.146 J.D. 413 W. Main St.
Brady, Gerald W., Jr., (BV) .... '49 '81 C.98 B.S. L.733 J.D. 1133 N. North St.
Brady, John C., (BV) .... '45 '71 C.436 A.B. L.339 J.D. [Vonachen,L.T.&S.]
Brady, John T., (BV) .... '45 '77 C.128 B.A. L.339 J.D. 411 Hamilton Blvd., Ste. 1102
Brannon, James S., (BV) .... '29 '58 C&L.477 A.B., LL.B. 207 Main St.
Braskich, Keith J. .... '56 '81 C.201 B.A. L.209 J.D. [Davis&C.]
Brennan, Kevin W. .... '66 '91 C&L.339 B.S., J.D. Litig. Coun., Caterpillar Inc.
Broadway, James D., (AV) .... '44 '68 C.861 B.A. L.802 J.D. [Sorling,N.H.C.&C.] ⊙
Broderick, Thomas F., (BV) .... '52 '80 C&L.339 B.S., J.D. Central Ill. Light Co.

Brown, Joel E., Attorney at Law '65 '92 C.910 A.B. L.734 J.D.
416 Main Street, Suite 625, 61602
Telephone: 309-673-4357 Fax: 309-673-6119
Email: jebrownlaw@aol.com URL: http://www.jebrownlaw.com
Personal Injury, Medical Malpractice, Criminal Law.
See Professional Biographies, PEORIA, ILLINOIS

Brown, William K., (BV) .... '50 '76 C.861 B.S. L.339 J.D. [🄰 Goldfine&B.]
Bruhn, Barry R. .... '42 '68 C.225 A.B. L.910 J.D. Prairie State Legal Servs.
Brunton, Scott A., (CV) .... '63 '92 C.679 B.S.M.E. L.339 J.D. [Miller,H.&T.]
Brush, Beth A. .... '55 '90 C.338 B.S. L.911 J.D. Chicago Title Ins. Co.
Bryson, Laraine Graves .... '55 '87 C.98 B.S. L.734 J.D. Tri-County Urban League
Buck, Byron G., II '68 '95 C.277 B.E.E. L.796 J.D.
China Coun., Caterpillar Inc. (Pat.)
Buck, Stephen M., (BV) .... '66 '92 C&L.734 B.A., J.D. [Husch&E.]
Buda, James B. '47 '73 C.63 B.A. L.602 J.D.
V.P., Gen. Coun. & Secy., Caterpillar Inc.
Bunce, James H., (AV) .... '40 '66 C.98 A.B. L.276 J.D. [Johnson,B.&N.]
Burke, Bridget A. .... '64 '89 C.686 B.A. L.37 J.D. 408 W. Morningside Dr.
Butler, Bradly M., (BV) .... '68 '95 C.388 B.A. L.734 J.D. Sr. Atty., Caterpillar Inc.
Calkins, Robert S. .... '15 '40 C.98 A.B. L.276 J.D. 3900 N. Stable Ct.‡
Callanan, Timothy J. '65 '93 C.602 B.A. L.1051 J.D.
(adm. in OR; not adm. in IL) Sr. Corp. Atty., Caterpillar Inc.
Campbell, William H., (AV) .... '51 '76 C.401 B.S. L.665 J.D. [Davis&C.]
Canterbury, Ross E., (AV) .... '42 '68 C&L.976 B.A., J.D. [Westervelt,J.N.&K.]
Caras, Peter J., Jr. .... '47 '75 C.346 B.S. L.345 J.D. Admin. Law J., OHA, SSA
Carter, James R., (BV) .... '53 '78 C.347 B.A. L.365 J.D. [Carter]

Carter Law Offices, (BV)
Commerce Bank Building, Suite 529, 61602
Telephone: 309-673-3517 Facsimile: 309-673-3318 URL: http://www.jcarterlaw.com
Email: jcarter@jcarterlaw.com URL: http://www.lawyers.com/carterlaw
Member of Firm: James R. Carter. Associates: Laura Ostrowski; Brian Allen Kuehn.
Products Litigation including Asbestos and Toxic Tort Litigation, Medical Malpractice, Appellate Law, Wrongful Death, Birth Trauma. Tort Litigation, Insurance, Employment and Civil Rights Litigation. Commercial Litigation.
See Professional Biographies, PEORIA, ILLINOIS

Casey, James J., Jr. '63 '90 C.965 B.A. L.200 J.D.
(adm. in WI; not adm. in IL) 117 Bradley Hall, 1501 W. Bradley Ave.
Cassidy, Andrew D., (BV) .... '61 '89 C.436 B.S. L.589 J.D. [Cassidy&M.]
Cassidy, Christopher F., (BV) .... '56 '94 C.338 B.S. L.801 J.D. [Cassidy&M.]
Cassidy, John E., III, (BV) .... '54 '83 C.686 B.S. L.734 J.D. [Cassidy&M.]
Cassidy, Timothy J., (AV) .... '55 '83 C.686 B.S. L.734 J.D. [Cassidy&M.]

Cassidy & Mueller, (AV) BB
323 Commerce Bank Building, 416 Main Street, 61602
Telephone: 309-676-0591 Fax: 309-676-8036
Email: c_m@mtco.com URL: http://www.cassidymueller.com

(This Listing Continued)

Cassidy & Mueller (Continued)

Members of Firm: John E. Cassidy, Sr. (1896-1984); John E. Cassidy, Jr. (1924-2003); David B. Mueller; John E. Cassidy, III; Timothy J. Cassidy; Andrew D. Cassidy; Christopher F. Cassidy; Gay Nell G. German; Jennifer L. Wolfe.
General, Civil, Trial and Appellate Practice. Product Liability, Asbestos, Medical Malpractice, Drug and Medical Device and Commercial, Employment, Federal Civil Rights and Insurance Litigation. Banking, Business, Insurance, Officers, Directors and Professional Liability, Probate, Real Estate and Worker's Compensation Law.
Representative Clients: Aetna Casualty & Surety Co.; Atchison, Topeka & Santa Fe Railroad Co.; Chicago Motor Club Ins. Co.; Continental Oil Company; E.I. DuPont-DeNemours & Company; Hartford Accident & Indemnity Company; Illinois-American Water Company; Lake States Insurance Company; John P. Pearl & Associates, Ltd.; Liberty Mutual Insurance Co.
See Professional Biographies, PEORIA, ILLINOIS

Caviness, John P. .... '62 '91 C.1169 B.A. L.1049 J.D. Tax Coun., Caterpillar, Inc.
Cerulo, Gregory A., (AV) ....'54 '79 C.502 B.A. L.339 J.D. [Quinn,J.H.&P.]
Chaddock, Adam P. ....'76 '01 C&L.339 B.A., J.D. [Ⓐ Quinn,J.H.&P.]
Chamberlain, Kathy ....'75 '00 C.339 B.A. L.146 J.d. [Ⓐ Howard,H.&M.]
Chambers, David A. ....'— '02 C.98 B.A. L.339 J.D. [Ⓐ Husch&E.] (See Pat. Sect.)
Chambers, Patrick T., (BV) ....'51 '78 C.339 B.A. L.146 J.D. [P.Chambers]
Chambers, Patrick, Law Office of, (BV) ....411 Hamilton Blvd.
Charlton, Diana L. ....'60 '00 C.98 B.S. L.734 J.D. Sr. Intell. Prop. Atty., Caterpillar Inc.
Cheek, John J. '69 '94 C.894 A.B. L.201 J.D.
(adm. in OH; not adm. in IL; Pat.) Sr. Intell. Prop. Atty., Caterpillar Inc.
Chenevert, Donald J., Jr. .....'67 '93 C.496 B.A. L.245 J.D. Corp. Atty., Caterpillar Inc.
Cheng, Karen Mei-Yee '73 '99 C.112 B.A. L.61 J.D.
(adm. in CA; not adm. in IL) Atty., Caterpillar Inc.
Christensen, Elizabeth Wiese, (BV) ....'61 '85 C.927 B.S. L.339 J.D. 124 S.W. Adams
Christison, William H., (AV) ....'36 '61 C.597 B.A. L.352 LL.B. 401 Main St.‡
Clark, Gary L., (AV) ....'38 '63 C.707 B.A. L.339 LL.B. 433 Hamilton Blvd.
Clayton, Roger R., (AV) ....'53 '78 C.98 B.A. L.801 J.D. [Heyl,R.V.&A.]
Codevilla, David A. '— '96 C.1375 B.A. L.1209 J.D.
(adm. in VA; not adm. in IL) Atty., Caterpillar Inc.
Coe, Rocky L. ....'50 '76 C&L.339 B.A., J.D. NLRB
Coletta, Robert J. ....'60 '85 C.172 B.A. L.900 J.D. [Davis&C.]
Collier, Glenn H. ....'50 '76 C&L.339 B.A., J.D. Cir. J.
Collins, David Blair, (BV) ....'60 '89 C.352 B.A. L.589 J.D. [Quinn,J.H.&P.]
Comfort, Julie P., (BV) ....'57 '83 C&L.36 B.S., J.D. 6017 N. Wickwood Rd.
Compton, LeRoy A., (AV) ....'58 '84 C.927 B.S. L.801 J.D. [Ⓐ Goldfine&B.]
Conatser, Tammie L. ....'65 '90 C.138 B.A. L.383 J.D. 227 E. Jefferson St.
Connor, William C., (BV) ....'62 '87 C.98 B.S. L.801 J.D. [Ⓐ Leiter]
Cooper, Duncan B., III, (AV) ....'40 '68 C.339 B.S. L.190 J.D. [Ⓒ Heyl,R.V.&A.]
Corrigan, Mary A., (BV) ....'60 '85 C.504 B.A. L.365 J.D. [Vonachen,L.T.&S.]
Coulter, Christopher R. .....'72 '97 C.57 B.A. L.602 J.D. Corp. Coun., Peoria Disposal Co.
Couri, Charles, (BV) ....'56 '82 C.338 B.S. L.801 J.D. [Westervelt,J.N.&K.]
Couri, David M., (BV) '51 '76 C.734 B.A. L.900 J.D.
414 Hamilton Boulevard, Suite 100
Courson, Donald C. ....'44 '70 C.602 B.B.A. L.365 J.D. Cir. J.
Cover, David L., (BV) ....'49 '74 C.339 B.S. L.209 J.D. 124 S.W. Adams St.
Covey, Charles A. ....'33 '60 C.282 B.A. L.339 J.D. Assoc. Cir. J.
Covey, Charles E., (BV) ....'53 '78 C.339 B.A. L.879 J.D. 416 Main St.
Covey, William I., (AV) ....'57 '83 C.339 B.S. L.801 J.D. [Heyl,R.V.&A.]
Cruz, Donna Wamack, (BV) ....'60 '86 C&L.339 B.A., J.D. Asst. States Atty.
Cummings, James A. ....'31 '56 C&L.339 B.S., LL.B. Commerce Bk. Bldg.‡
Cusack, Daniel P., (P.C.), (BV) ....'49 '77 C.707 B.A. L.329 J.D. [Cusack,F.G.&O.]
Cusack, Fleming, Gilfillan & O'Day, (BV) ....124 S.W. Adams, Ste. 520
Dailey, Floyd, (CV) ....'60 '87 C.801 B.A. L.300 J.D. 124 N.E. Madison Ave.
Davies, Kenneth E., (BV) ......'— '97 C.970 B.A. L.801 J.D. [Ⓐ Hasselberg,W.G.S.&B.]
Davis, David, Jr., (CV) ....'42 '67 C.801 B.S. L.1119 J.D. 6135 N. Oak Point Ct.
Davis, Ralph D., (BV) ....'49 '87 C.145 M.B.A. L.597 J.D. [Ⓐ Janssen]
Davis, Roy G. ....'48 '73 C.98 B.S. L.273 J.D. [Davis&C.]
Davis, Thomas R., (BV) ....'52 '86 C.339 B.S. L.209 J.D. [Miller,H.&T.]

Davis & Campbell L.L.C., (AV)
401 Main Street, Suite 1600, 61602-1241 ⊙
Telephone: 309-673-1681 Fax: 309-673-1690
Email: info@dcamplaw.com URL: http://www.dcamplaw.com
Roy G. Davis; William H. Campbell; J. Reed Roesler; Keith J. Braskich; David G. Lubben; Robert J. Coletta;—Janet L. Jannusch; James R. Jorgensen; Nancy L. Barnhart; Richard A. Russo; Jeremy M. Pelphrey. Of Counsel: Carlos M. Recio (Not admitted in IL); Jonathan G. Bunge.
Management Labor Law, Corporate Law, Trial Practice, Employee Benefits, Mergers and Acquisitions, Employer Rights, Local Government Rights, Employment Law, Commercial Law, Commercial Litigation, Complex Litigation, Intellectual Property, Securities Regulation, Antitrust, Immigration and Naturalization, Real Estate, Zoning Planning and Land Use, Tax Law, Estate Planning, Probate.
Chicago, Illinois Office: 161 N. Clark, Suite 4700, 60601. Telephone: 312-523-2120. Fax: 312-523-2121.
Washington, D.C. Office: 1828 L Street N.W., Suite 660. Telephone: 202-293-5690. Fax: 202-296-5706.
See Professional Biographies, PEORIA, ILLINOIS

Dawson-Tibbits, Susan, (BV) '54 '79
C.338 B.A. L.477 J.D. 411 Hamilton Blvd., Ste. 1102
Day, Robt. G., Sr., (BV) ....'14 '39 C&L.339 B.S. 1021 Peoria Savings Plaza
De Armond, Maureen R. ....'73 '04 C.351 B.A. L.352 J.D. [Ⓐ Heyl,R.V.&A.]
de Blank, Andrew S., (BV) ....'64 '89 C.94 B.A. L.259 J.D. [Ⓐ Knell&K.]
Dekker, Christopher F. ....'68 '93 C.477 B.A. L.209 J.D. Sr. Atty., Caterpillar Inc.
Dersch, Wilbur D., (AV) ....'12 '38 C.98 B.A. L.793 LL.B. Commerce Bk. Bldg.‡
DeVary, Allen L. ....'71 '99 C.338 B.S. L.801 J.D. [Ⓐ Hinshaw&C.]
Dewey, Robert V., Jr., (AV) ....'44 '69 C.103 B.A. L.966 J.D. [Heyl,R.V.&A.]
Dixon, Jas. S., (BV) ....'26 '50 C.98 A.B. L.910 J.D. 1st. Com. Bk. Bldg.
Dluski, Thomas J. ....'73 '00 C.338 B.S. L.879 J.D. [Ⓐ Heyl,R.V.&A.]
Dorsey, Michael D., (BV) '49 '80
C&L.339 B.S., J.D. Sr. Compensation Atty., Caterpillar Inc.
Doscotch, Christopher R., (BV) ....'69 '94 C.388 B.A. L.801 J.D. [Ⓐ Janssen]
Dundas, John G., (CV) ....'74 '00 C&L.339 B.S., J.D. [Ⓐ J.B.VanFleet]
Dunham, Bradley W., (AV) ....'44 '69 C&L.339 B.A., J.D. [Quinn,J.H.&P.]
Dunlap, Blake E. ....'— '01 C.1101 B.A. L.801 J.D. [Prusak,W.&G.]
Dunn, Joseph W., (BV) ....'65 '95 C.339 B.S. L.801 J.D. [Ⓐ Janssen]
Dura, Maribeth Egert, (BV) ....'61 '87 C.697 B.A. L.365 J.D. [M.E.Dura]
Dura, Maribeth E., (BV) ....4516 N. Sterling Ave., Ste. 350
Durree, Edward R., (AV) ....'49 '75 C.339 A.B. L.221 J.D. [Kingery D.W.&R.]
Dvorak, David A., (BV) ....'40 '71 C.98 B.A. L.339 J.D. [Orr,D.&Assoc.]
Eagleton, Richard E. ....'30 '58 C.976 B.A. L.339 J.D. [Ⓒ Hinshaw&C.]
Earle, Kevin Christopher '76 '04
C.339 B.S. L.365 J.D. Intell. Prop. Atty., Caterpillar Inc.
Eathington, Kenneth R., (AV) ....'61 '91 C&L.339 B.S., J.D. [Husch&E.]
Ebel, Thomas G. ....'41 '70 C.750 A.B. L.602 J.D. Courthouse, 324 Main St.‡
Edmiston, Charles N., II, (BV) '54 '80 C.339 B.S. L.352 J.D.
[Ⓐ Kanoski&Assoc.] (⊙Bloomington, Macomb, Quincy, Rushville, Springfield)
Eggert, Michelle R. ....'70 '94 C.477 B.A. L.209 J.D. 106 E. Morningside
Eissfeldt, Theodore L., (AV) ....'50 '76 C&L.339 B.S., J.D. [Howard&H.]
Elder, Kevin L., (BV) ....'65 '90 C.339 B.A. L.734 J.D. [Ⓐ Goldfine&B.]
Elias, Cynthia Lee ....'53 '78 C.473 B.A. L.309 J.D. [Ⓒ Elias,M.R.&S.]
Elias, John S., (AV) ....'51 '79 C.197 A.B. L.309 J.D. [Elias,M.R.&S.]

Elias, Meginnes, Riffle & Seghetti, P.C., (AV)
416 Main Street, Suite 1400, 61602
Telephone: 309-637-6000 Facsimile: 309-637-8514
URL: http://www.emrslaw.com
John S. Elias; Brian J. Meginnes; Robert M. Riffle; Michael R. Seghetti; Troy N. Pudik;—David N. Schellenberg; Janaki Nair; Sonya A. Pasquini. Of Counsel: Cynthia Lee Elias.
Tax, Corporate, Real Estate, Litigation, Environmental, Intellectual Property, Municipal, Estate Planning, Probate, Health Care.
See Professional Biographies, PEORIA, ILLINOIS

Elward, Brad A., (BV) ....'64 '89 C.339 B.S. L.804 J.D. [Heyl,R.V.&A.]
Enyeart, Curtis W. ....'40 '64 C.293 B.A. L.178 LL.B. 205 N. Kickapoo
Estes, Paul C., (AV) ....'55 '80 C.234 B.A. L.893 J.D. [Hinshaw&C.]
Etrick, Mary B. ....'48 '91 C.375 B.S. L.477 J.D. V.P., Natl. City Bank‡
Fahey, Robert F., Law Offices of, (AV) '39 '65
C.339 B.S. L.209 J.D. 903 W. Kensington Drive
Faletto, Jon S., (BV) ....'56 '83 C.339 B.S. L.146 J.D. [Howard&H.]
Feehan, Joseph G., (AV) ....'61 '88 C.338 B.S. L.589 J.D. [Heyl,R.V.&A.]
Ferrero-Patten, Rhonda J. ....'65 '92 C.346 B.S. L.589 J.D. [Hinshaw&C.]
Fiddes, Gordon M. ....'59 '86 C.338 B.S. L.1000 J.D. [Stephens,F.M.&Assoc.]
Fifield, Jordan A., (AV) ....'31 '58 C.388 B.A. L.309 J.D. [Ⓒ Kavanagh,S.S.W.&F.]
Fisher, Deborah A. '50 '75 C&L.339 B.S., J.D.
(adm. in WI; not adm. in IL) N.L.R.B.
Flaherty, Voni D., (BV) ....'61 '89 C.508 B.S. L.146 J.D. The Commerce Trust Co.
Fleming, John P., (BV) ....'59 '84 C.357 B.A. L.339 J.D. [Schmidt&F.]
Fleming, Michael A., (P.C.), (BV) ....'49 '74 C.210 B.A. L.339 J.D. [Cusack,F.G.&O.]
Foster, Rhonda J. ....'— '91 C.737 B.A. L.608 J.D. P.O. Box 6056
Franklin, Eloise A. '32 '83 C.98 B.S. L.273 J.D.
Off. of Hearings & Appeals, Soc. Sec. Admn.
Fredericksen, Chris L., (BV) ....'51 '77 C.589 B.A. L.879 J.D. Assoc. J.
Fritz, Everett, II, (CVⓉ) '51 '79 C.502 B.S. L.900 LL.B.
(adm. in KS; not adm. in IL) 2449 W. Imperial Drive
Fuller, Chester C., (BV) ....'47 '76 C.338 B.S. L.365 J.D. [C.Fuller]
Fuller, Chester, Law Firm, (BV) ....124 S.W. Adams, Ste. 348
Gaede, Donovan W., (CV) ....'68 '94 C.597 B.A. L.801 J.D. [Ⓐ Janssen]
Galassi, Julie L., (BV) ....'59 '88 C.228 B.S. L.589 J.D. [Hasselberg,R.B.&K.]
Gallatin, Howard P., (BV) '45 '74 C&L.352 B.B.A., J.D.
V.P. & Tr. Coun., Commercial Natl. Bk. of Peoria
Garrett, Angela K., (CV) ....'— '94 C.98 B.S. L.910 J.D. P.O. Box 3738
Garrett, Scott E., (BVⓉ) '64 '95 C.734 B.A. L.273 J.D.
(adm. in NY; not adm. in IL) Atty., Caterpillar Inc.
Garrigues, Shinobu K. '69 '98 C.174 B.A. L.494 J.D.
(adm. in MN; not adm. in IL) Atty., Caterpillar, Inc.
Gasick, Gery R., (BV) ....'49 '74 C.98 B.S. L.209 J.D. 411 Hamilton Blvd., Ste. 1600
Gehlbach, Kurt F. ....'57 '82 C.339 B.A. L.477 J.D. Gen. Atty., Caterpillar Inc.
Gentry, Richard N., Jr., (BV) ......'44 '69 C.477 B.A. L.339 J.D. 456 Fulton St., Ste. 425
German, Gay Nell G. ....'69 '96 C.339 B.A. L.174 J.D. [Cassidy&M.]
Ghiglieri, Bernard J., Jr., (AV) '22 '50
C.602 A.B. L.276 J.D. 615 Commerce Bk Bldg. (⊙Toluca)
Gibson, Darcy K. ....'77 '02 C.339 B.S. L.801 J.D. [Ⓐ Knell&K.]
Gifford, Michael D., (BV) .....'52 '81 C&L.801 B.A., J.D. 411 Hamilton Blvd., Ste. 1102
Giftos, Alexander C., (BV) '67 '94
C.550 B.A. L.734 J.D. Sr. Labor Rel. Atty., Caterpillar Inc.
Gilfillan, Joseph P., (AV) ....'50 '75 C.878 B.S. L.602 J.D. 415 Hamilton Blvd.
Gilfillan, Paul P., (AV) ....'57 '82 C.338 B.S. L.879 J.D. [Quinn,J.H.&P.]
Ginzel, Jonathan D., (BV) '69 '97 C.98 B.S. L.910 J.D.
Sr. Corp. Atty., Caterpillar, Inc.
Goldfine, Morton S. ....'37 '62 C.209 L.339 J.D. [Goldfine&B.]
Goldfine & Bowles, P.C., (AV) ....124 S.W. Adams St.
Gorman, John A. ....'42 '67 C.340 B.A. L.339 J.D. U.S. Mag. J.
Grandstaff, Douglas S. ....'60 '91 C.546 B.A. L.188 J.D. Litig. Coun., Caterpillar Inc.
Grawey, Richard E. ....'48 '73 C.602 B.A. L.94 J.D. Cir. J.
Gray, Laura L. ....'66 '92 C.339 B.A. L.221 J.D. 124 S.W. Adams St., Ste. 415
Grebe, James R., (BV) ....'— '80 C.999 B.A. L.339 J.D. [Hasselberg,W.G.S.&B.]
Greek, Elaine ....'36 '79 C.98 B.A. L.339 J.D. 416 Main Street
Greenberg, Arthur G. ....'29 '57 C.339 A.B. L.477 J.D. Cir. J.
Greening, Jay E., (BV) ....'68 '95 C.98 B.S. L.589 J.D. [Miller,H.&T.]
Griffin, Douglas G., (CV) ....'66 '91 C.338 B.S. L.801 J.D. [Miller,H.&T.]
Griminger, Larry B. '47 '76
C.98 B.A. L.1051 J.D. Reg. Coun., Dept. of Children & Fam. Servs.
Groh, Danielle A. ....'79 '05 C.234 B.A. L.607 J.D. [Ⓐ Hinshaw&C.]
Gruber, Dexter Rowe ....'64 '95 C.958 B.S. L.589 J.D. [Ⓐ Kavanagh,S.S.W.&F.]
Gury, Elmer F., (AV) ....'13 '39 C.602 B.C.S. L.339 LL.B. 820 W. Loire Ct., Apt. 111
Gwillim, Brent H., (AV) ....'46 '71 C.98 B.A. L.986 J.D. [Heyl,R.V.&A.]
Gwillim, Todd C. ....'72 '99 C.923 B.S.B.A. L.734 J.D. Tax Atty., Caterpillar Inc.
Habecker, Edward T., (BV) ....'53 '81 C.500 B.A. L.300 J.D. [Howard,H.&M.]
Hafele, James L., (AV) ....'36 '64 C&L.339 B.A., LL.B. [Hafele,S.S.&G.]
Hafele, Schmidt, Stephens & Glancy, P.C., (AV) ....416 Main St.
Hall, Robert C., (AV) ....'48 '73 C.98 B.S. L.339 J.D. [Miller,H.&T.]
Halliday, Ronald E., (BV) ....'50 '76 C.339 B.S. L.838 J.D. [Parker&H.]

Hallihan Intellectual Property Law, Ltd.
(See Chicago)

Hamm, Ronald L., (AV) '41 '68 C.98 L.365 J.D.
415 Hamilton Boulevard, 61602
Telephone: 309-671-9701 Fax: 309-637-5788
Email: rhamm@cfgolaw.com
Personal Injury, Criminal Law, Workers Compensation.
See Professional Biographies, PEORIA, ILLINOIS

Hamm & Hanna, Ltd., A Professional Corporation, (AV)
411 Hamilton Boulevard Suite 1004, 61602
Telephone: 309-676-3608 Fax: 309-676-3219
Email: hammhanna@sbcglobal.net URL: http://www.hammhanna.com
Ronald Hanna;—Ronald Len Hanna.
General Civil Trial and Appellate Practice. Workers Compensation, Personal Injury, Airplane Crash Litigation, Products Liability, Medical Malpractice, Criminal Law, Driving Under the Influence. Practice in State and Federal Courts.
See Professional Biographies, PEORIA, ILLINOIS

Haney, Mark A., (CV) ....'70 '95 C.992 B.A. L.339 J.D. 227 N.E. Jefferson St.
Hanley, Steven M. '64 '00 C.112 B.S.M.E. L.989 J.D.
(adm. in IN; not adm. in IL) Intell. Prop. Atty., Caterpillar Inc.
Hanna, Ronald, (AV) ....'46 '72 C.338 B.S. L.339 J.D. [Hamm&H.]

Hanna, Ronald Len .... '76 '01 C.339 B.A. L.801 J.D. [Hamm&H.]
Hanold, Wayne L., (AV) ....'32 '57 C.801 B.S. L.339 LL.B. 411 Hamilton Boulevard‡
Hansen, Mark D., (BV) .... '69 '94 C.589 B.S. L.339 J.D. [Heyl,R.V.&A.]
Hardesty, Theresa Rahe, (AV) .... '51 '77 C.339 B.S. L.209 J.D. 7513 N. Regent Pl.
Harman, K. Mark '49 '75
C.317 A.B. L.930 J.D. V.P., Human Res., Fleming Packaging Corp.
Harmon, Edmund F. .... '30 '59 C.707 B.A. L.339 LL.B. 219 E. Embert St.‡
Hartshorn, Donald M., (AV) .... '44 '69 C&L.339 B.A., J.D. [Swain,H.&S.]
Harvel, Thomas G., (AV) .... '46 '72 C.98 B.A. L.221 J.D. [Westervelt,J.N.&K.]
Harvey, R. Wayne, (BV) .... '42 '70 C&L.339 B.A., J.D. [Harvey&S.]
Harvey & Stuckel, Chartered, (AV) .... 331 Fulton Street
Hasinger, Ronald W. .... '66 '03 C.651 B.A. L.339 J.D. [Westervelt,J.N.&K.]
Hasselberg, Eric E., (AV) .... '50 '75 C&L.352 B.A., J.D. [Hasselberg,R.B.&K.]
Hasselberg, Michael R., (AV) .... '— '75 C.339 B.A. L.365 J.D. [Hasselberg,W.G.S.&B.]

Hasselberg, Rock, Bell & Kuppler LLP, (AV)
Suite 200, Associated Bank Building, 4600 North Brandywine Drive, 61614
Telephone: 309-688-9400 Fax: 309-688-9430
URL: http://www.hrbklaw.com
Members of Firm: Eric E. Hasselberg; Jeffrey B. Rock; Charles M. Rock; Gregory S. Bell; Karl B. Kuppler; Julie L. Galassi; Danny L. Schroeder, Jr. Associate: Marci M. Shoff.
General Civil and Trial Practice. Corporate, Business, Real Estate and Development, Estate Planning, Trusts and Probate, Taxation, Municipal, Construction, Landlord and Tenant Law, Debtor and Creditor, Replevin, Employment and Family Law. Commercial and Civil Litigation, Personal Injury and Workers' Compensation.
See Professional Biographies, PEORIA, ILLINOIS

Hasselberg, Williams, Grebe, Snodgrass & Birdsall, (AV)
Bank One Building, Suite 360, 124 S.W. Adams Street, 61602-1320
Telephone: 309-637-1400 Telecopier: 309-637-1500
URL: http://www.hwgsb.com
Michael R. Hasselberg; Raymond C. Williams; James R. Grebe; Kenneth M. Snodgrass, Jr.; Charles J. Urban; Sandra J. Birdsall; David L. Wentworth, II. Associates: Kenneth E. Davies; Alison E. McLaughlin; Boyd O. Roberts, III; Megan R. Russo; Lisa R. Barbee.
General Practice, Litigation, Wills, Trusts and Estates, Probate, Elder Law, Estate Planning, Federal Taxation, Insurance, Insurance Defense, Real Estate, Personal Injury, Workers Compensation, Agricultural Law, Corporate Law, Governmental Law, Administrative Law, Commercial Law, Criminal Law, Driving While Intoxicated, Traffic Violations, Labor and Employment, Family Law, Adoption Law, Bankruptcy, Zoning, Planning and Land Use and Real Estate Title Insurance.
See Professional Biographies, PEORIA, ILLINOIS

Hassiepen, John P. ..... '57 '85 C.602 A.B. L.228 J.D. Gen. Atty., Geneva, Caterpillar Inc.
Hatcher, James, (BV) .... '34 '65 C.309 B.A. L.178 J.D. [Hatcher&R.]
Hatcher & Rose, (AV) .... 321 Main St.
Haugens, Edward E. .... '21 '49 C&L.339 B.S., J.D. 215 E. Hines Pl.‡
Hawley, Jonathan E. .... '71 '97 C.339 B.A. L.209 J.D. Appel. Div. Chief
Hefflefinger, Matthew S., (AV) .... '62 '89 C.98 B.S. L.801 J.D. [Heyl,R.V.&A.]
Heine, Stephen J., (AV) .... '55 '81 C.338 B.S. L.801 J.D. [Heyl,R.V.&A.]
Heiple, James D. .... '33 '57 C.98 B.S. L.421 J.D. Supm. Ct. Jus.
Heiple, Jeremy H., (BV) .... '62 '87 C.20 B.A. L.339 J.D. [Heiple]
Heiple, Jonathan J., (BV) .... '64 '92 C.20 A.B. L.893 J.D. [Heiple]
Heiple, Rae C., II .... '29 '53 C.98 B.S. L.339 J.D. Commerce Bank Bldg.

Heiple Law Offices, (BV)
9121 N. Industrial Road, Suite A, 61615-1549
Telephone: 309-691-7263 Fax: 309-691-7266 URL: http://www.heiple.com
Email: heiple@earthlink.net URL: http://www.lawyers.com/heiplelaw
Members of Firm: Jeremy H. Heiple; Jonathan J. Heiple. Of Counsel: John A. Schellenberg.
Christian firm with diverse General Civil Trial and Appellate Practice including: Workers' Compensation, Personal Injury, Guardianship, Advance Directives, Business and Corporate, Real Estate, Wills and Trust/Estate Planning, and Probate.
See Professional Biographies, PEORIA, ILLINOIS

Heller, Michael W. .... '24 '51 C.597 B.S. L.813 J.D. Com. Bk. Bldg.
Heming, William B. '51 '77
C&L.546 B.S.M.E., J.D. Gen. Pat. Coun., Caterpillar Inc. (Pat.)
Henderson, R. Michael, (AV) .... '44 '69 C.339 B.S. L.424 J.D. [Quinn,J.H.&P.]
Hendricks, Clyde Bertram .... C.98 B.A. L.339 J.D. First American Title Insurance Co.
Henry, Thomas M., (BV) .... '53 '78 C.338 B.S. L.801 J.D. Commerce Bank
Herring, William H., (BV) .... '30 '54 C.98 B.S. L.339 J.D. 124 N.E. Madison
Heth, Georgia Kay, (CV) .... '56 '81 C.357 B.A. L.813 J.D. Asst. Atty Gen.

Heyl, Royster, Voelker & Allen, Professional Corporation, (AV)
Suite 600, Chase Building, 124 S.W. Adams, 61602 ⊙
Telephone: 309-676-0400 Telecopier: 309-676-3374
Email: firm@hrva.com URL: http://www.hrva.com
Managing Partner: Robert V. Dewey, Jr. Partners: Brent H. Gwillim; Rex K. Linder; Timothy L. Bertschy; Gary D. Nelson; David R. Sinn; Roger R. Clayton; Bradford B. Ingram; Nicholas J. Bertschy; Stephen J. Heine; Karen L. Kendall; Craig S. Young; William I. Covey; Christopher P. Larson; James M. Voelker; Joseph G. Feehan; Matthew S. Hefflefinger; David A. Perkins; Lisa A. LaConte; Brad A. Elward; James J. Manning; Timothy W. Kirk; Mark D. Hansen; Debra L. Stegall; Craig L. Unrath. Associates. Robert M. Bennett; Tobin J. Taylor; Mark A. Ludolph; Thomas J. Dluski; Andrew J. Keyt; Carol J. Perkins; Adam J. Lagocki; Gregory J. Rastatter; Maureen R. De Armond; John M. Redlingshafer; John K. Kim. Retired Of Counsel: Lyle W. Allen; Duncan B. Cooper III; Clarence W. Heyl (1884-1968); Richard N. Molchan; Gary M. Peplow; John H. Royster (1907-1985); William J. Voelker, Jr. (1917-1993).
General Civil Trial and Appellate Practice in all Courts, Insurance Defense, Workers' Compensation Defense, Professional Liability Defense, Truck Accidents, Construction Law, Railroad Accidents and Injuries, Insurance Coverage, Self Insured Defense, Products Liability Defense, Civil Rights, Asbestos Defense, Class Action Defense, Corporate Law, Health Care, Banking, Government, Employment, Environmental, Probate, Elder Law, Agribusiness, Immigration, Religious Institutions, Nonprofit and Charitable Organizations, College and University Law, and Real Estate.
Springfield, Illinois Office: Suite 575, National City Center, P.O. Box 1687, 62705. Telephone: 217-522-8822. Telecopier: 217-523-3902.
Urbana, Illinois Office: Suite 300, 102 East Main Street, P.O. Box 129, 61803-0129. Telephone: 217-344-0060. Telecopier: 217-344-9295.
Rockford, Illinois Office: Second Floor, National City Bank Building, 120 West State Street, P.O. Box 1288, 61105-1288. Telephone: 815-963-4454. Telecopier: 815-963-0399.
Edwardsville, Illinois Office: Suite 100, Mark Twain Plaza II, 103 West Vandalia Street, P.O. Box 467, 62025. Telephone: 618-656-4646. Telecopier: 618-656-7940.
See Professional Biographies, PEORIA, ILLINOIS

Higgins, Thomas, (BV) '64 '90 C.98 B.S. L.365 J.D.
Dir. of Paralegal Studies, Illinois Central Coll.
Higgs, David L., (AV) .... '51 '81 C.927 B.S. L.801 J.D. [Husch&E.]
High, Lance W. '66 '93 C.197 B.A. L.945 J.D.
(adm. in VA; not adm. in IL) Sr. Atty., Caterpillar Inc.

Hinshaw & Culbertson LLP, (AV)
Hinshaw & Culbertson LLP is an Illinois registered limited liability partnership that has elected to be governed by the Illinois Uniform Partnership Act (1997)
456 Fulton Street Suite 298, 61602-1220 ⊙
Telephone: 309-674-1025 Facsimile: 309-674-9328 Telex: 880248
Email: kfox@hinshawlaw.com URL: http://www.hinshawlaw.com
Partners: Paul C. Estes; Rhonda J. Ferrero-Patten; David E. Jones; Douglass A. Marshall; L. Lee Smith. Associates. Allen L. DeVary; Danielle A. Groh; James LeFante; Garth C. K. Madison; Patricia J. Naylor; Timothy J. Newlin; Tamara A. Paul-Reeff; Christopher J. Spanos. Of Counsel: Richard E. Eagleton.

(This Listing Continued)

Hinshaw & Culbertson LLP (Continued)
Appellate, Banking & Financing, Bankruptcy & Creditors' Rights, Class Action Litigation, Civil Rights Defense, Commercial Litigation, Corporate, Construction Law, Director & Officer Liability, Employee Benefits, Environmental, Fidelity & Surety, General Liability Litigation, Government, Health Care, Insurance Coverage, Insurance and Reinsurance, Labor & Employment, Legal Malpractice, Medical Malpractice, Mergers & Acquisitions, Municipal Liability, Personal Injury Defense, Public Law, Products Liability Litigation, Professional Liability, Regulatory, Real Estate, School Law, Securities, Taxation, Transportation, White Collar Crime and Workers' Compensation Defense.
Other Office Locations: Chicago, Illinois; Appleton, Wisconsin; Belleville, Illinois; Boston, Massachusetts; Champaign, Illinois; Crystal Lake, Illinois; Edwardsville, Illinois; Fort Lauderdale, Florida; Jacksonville, Florida; Joliet, Illinois; Lisle, Illinois; Los Angeles, California; Miami, Florida; Milwaukee, Wisconsin; Minneapolis, Minnesota; New York, New York; Phoenix, Arizona; Portland, Oregon; Providence, Rhode Island; Rockford, Illinois; St. Louis, Missouri; San Francisco, California; Schererville, Indiana; Springfield, Illinois; Tampa, Florida; Waukegan, Illinois.
See Professional Biographies, PEORIA, ILLINOIS

Hinton, Eric F. .... '68 '97 C.877 B.A. L.101 J.D. Corp. Atty., Caterpillar Inc.
Hockaday, Rex D. '63 '93
C.628 B.S., B.S. L.1051 J.D. Sr. Intell. Prop. Atty., Caterpillar Inc.
Hoehne, Thomas V., (BV) .... '45 '72 C.589 B.A. L.365 J.D. 124 N. Madison
Hoffman, Steven C. .... '52 '77 C&L.339 A.B., J.D. Assoc. Gen. Coun., Caterpillar Inc.
Holcombe, Nick G. '71 '99 C.101 B.A. L.910 J.D.
(adm. in NY; not adm. in IL) Atty., Caterpillar Inc.
Holdridge, William E. .... '48 '80 C.339 Ph.D. L.801 J.D. Appl. Ct. Jus.
Holman, William K., (BV) .... '49 '74 C&L.339 B.S., J.D. 124 N.E. Madison
Holzgrafe, Roger E., (AV) .... '48 '73 C.602 B.A. L.276 J.D. [Westervelt,J.N.&K.]
Homa, Eric James, (CV) .... '59 '00 C.234 B.A. L.589 J.D. [E.J.Homa]
Homa, Eric James, PC, Law Office of, (CV) .... 1122 North Ellis Street
Honegger, Andrew A., (BV) .... '— '94 C.339 B.A. L.94 J.D. [Husch&E.]
Hoos, Jodi Melinda .... '74 '00 C.543 B.S. L.546 J.D. State's Atty. Off.

Horn, Jerold I., (AV) '41 '66 C.674 A.B. L.976 J.D.
124 S.W. Adams Street, Suite 515, 61602-1355
Telephone: 309-676-2778 Fax: 309-676-2779
Email: JIHORN@AOL.COM
Estate Planning, Trusts and Estates, Taxation, Business Law and Real Estate.
Reference: National City Bank
See Professional Biographies, PEORIA, ILLINOIS

Howard, John W., (BV) .... '49 '74 C.813 B.A. L.339 J.D. [Howard,H.&M.]
Howard, Timothy J., (AV) .... '50 '76 C.674 A.B. L.602 J.D. [Howard&H.]

Howard, Habecker & Morris, LLC, (BV)
456 Fulton Street, Suite 398, 61602
Telephone: 309-671-4555 Fax: 309-671-4556
URL: http://www.hhmlaw.com
Members of Firm: John W. Howard; Edward T. Habecker; Stephen M. Morris;—Kathy Chamberlain.
Insurance Defense, Civil Litigation, Workers Compensation, Torts.
See Professional Biographies, PEORIA, ILLINOIS

Howard & Howard Attorneys, P.C., (AV)
One Technology Plaza, Suite 600, 211 Fulton Street, 61602-1350 ⊙
Telephone: 309-672-1483 Fax: 309-672-1568
URL: http://www.h2law.com
Theodore L. Eissfeldt; Jon S. Faletto; Timothy J. Howard; Frank W. Ierulli; Diana M. Jagiella; Michael Robert Lied; Tracy C. Litzinger; Janice M. Powell; Leonard W. Sachs; Michael S. Seneca; Jeffrey G. Sorenson; Sandra M. Traicoff.
Administrative, Business, Commercial, Corporate, Creditors Rights, Education, Employee Benefits, Environmental, Financial Institutions, Government Relations, Immigration, Intellectual Property (Patents, Trademarks, Copyrights, and Gaming), Labor and Employment, Litigation, Probate, Public Finance, Real Estate, Securities, Taxation (Federal, State and Local), Trusts and Estates.
Representative Clients: National City Bank of Michigan/Illinois; Marion Memorial Hospital; Caterpillar, Inc.; Greater Peoria Airport Authority; Central Illinois Light Co.; DaimlerChrysler Corporation; Princeton National Bancorp, Inc.; MidAmerica National Bank; Methodist Medical Center of Illinois; Archer Daniels Midland.
Kalamazoo, Michigan Office: Comerica Building, Suite 800, 151 Rose Street. Telephone: 269-382-1483. Telecopier: 269-382-1568.
Bloomfield Hills, Michigan Office: The Pinehurst Office Center, Suite 101, 39400 Woodward Avenue. Telephone: 248-645-1483. Telecopier: 248-645-1568.
Ann Arbor, Michigan Office: One North Main, Suite 300, 101 North Main Street. Telephone: 734-222-1483. Fax: 734-761-5957.
See Professional Biographies, PEORIA, ILLINOIS

Hubler, Katherine Gorman, (BV) .... '68 '93 C.339 B.S. L.801 J.D. [Prusak,W.&G.]
Huff, Raymond L., (BV) .... '48 '73 C&L.339 A.B., J.D. [Huff]
Huff Law Offices, (BV) .... 2000 W. Pioneer Pkwy., Ste. 20
Hunt, David A., (BV) .... '64 '89 C&L.339 B.A., J.D. [Goldfine&B.]
Hunt, Robert E. .... '16 '41 C.339 B.S. L.966 J.D. 2725 N. Rockwood Dr.‡
Hunziker, Gregory A., (BV) .... '65 '90 C.98 B.S. L.734 J.D. [Hunziker&W.]
Hunziker & Walton L.L.C., (BV) .... 416 Main
Hupy, Michael F., (AV(T)) .... '46 '72 C&L.436 B.A., J.D. [M.F.Hupy&Assoc.] ⊙
Hupy, Michael F., & Associates, S.C., (AV(T))
7501 North University, Suite 221-B (⊙Decatur, Normal, IL; Appleton, Madison, Milw., WI)
Hurst, J. Michael '73 '98 C.228 B.S. L.150 J.D.
(adm. in CA; not adm. in IL) Trademark Atty., Caterpillar, Inc.

Husch & Eppenberger, LLC, (AV)
401 Main Street, Suite 1400, 61602-1241 ⊙
Telephone: 309-637-4900 FAX: 309-637-4928
URL: http://www.husch.com
Members of Firm: SueAnn Sage Billimack; Stephen M. Buck; Kenneth R. Eathington; David L. Higgs; Andrew A. Honegger; Christopher A. Nichols; Brian W. Ruddell; Jeffrey A. Ryva; Charles H. Young. Associates: David A. Chambers; Tyler Petersen; Kimberly A. Sutton Sarff.
Administrative Law, Agricultural Law, Alternative Dispute Resolution, Antitrust, Appellate Practice, Asset Protection, Bankruptcy, Banks and Banking, Business Law, Casinos and Gambling, Children, Civil Practice, Class Action, Commercial Law, Commercial Real Estate, Communications and Media, Complex and Multi District Litigation, Computers and Software, Constitutional Law, Construction Law, Consumer Law, Contracts, Copyrights, Corporate Finance, Corporate Law, Debtor and Creditor, Education Law, Election, Campaign and Political Law, Eminent Domain, Employee Benefits, Entertainment Law, Environmental Law, Estate Planning, Family Law, Fidelity and Surety, Finance, Government, Guardianship and Conservatorship, Health Care, Hospital Law, Immigration and Naturalization, Insurance, Insurance Defense, Intellectual Property, International Law, International Trade, Investments, Labor and Employment, Litigation, Medical Malpractice, Mergers, Acquisitions and Divestitures, Municipal Law, Nonprofit and Charitable Organizations, Occupational Safety and Health, Partnership Law, Patents, Probate, Products Liability, Property Law, Real Estate, Securities, Taxation, Technology and Science, Torts, Toxic Torts, Trade Secrets, Trademarks, Trusts and Estates, Wills, Worker's Compensation, Zoning, Planning and Land Use.
Jefferson City, Missouri Office: 235 East High Street, Monroe House, Suite 300, P.O. Box 1251. Telephone: 573-635-9118. FAX: 573-634-7854.
Kansas City, Missouri Office: 1200 Main, Suite 2300. Telephone: 816-421-4800. FAX: 816-421-0596.
St. Louis, Missouri Office: 190 Carondelet Plaza, Suite 600. Telephone: 314-480-1500. FAX: 314-480-1505.
Springfield, Missouri Office: 1949 E. Sunshine Street, Suite 2-300. Telephone: 417-862-6726. FAX: 417-862-6948.
Chattanooga, Tennessee Office: 736 Georgia Avenue, Suite 300. Telephone: 423-266-5500. FAX: 423-266-5499.

(This Listing Continued)

Husch & Eppenberger, LLC (Continued)

Memphis, Tennessee Office: One Memphis Place, 200 Jefferson Avenue, Suite 1450, 38103. Telephone: 901-523-1123. FAX: 901-523-7472.
Nashville, Tennessee Office: 2525 West End Avenue, Suite 1400, 37203. Telephone: 615-963-2200. FAX: 615-963-3611.

See Professional Biographies, PEORIA, ILLINOIS

Iben, Chas. W. . . . . . . '18 '49 C.31 B.A. L.976 LL.B. Ret. Cir. J.
Ierulli, Frank W. . . . . . . '66 '92 C.424 B.A L.190 J.D. [Howard&H.]
Ingram, Bradford B., (AV) . . . . . . '54 '80 C&L.221 B.A., J.D. [Heyl,R.V.&A.]
Inman, Arthur J., (BV) . . . . . .'42 '68 C.340 B.A. L.339 J.D. 411 Hamilton Blvd., Ste. 1302
Jackson, Donald R., (BV) . . . . . . '38 '74 C.98 B.S. L.339 J.D. 456 Fulton St.
Jacobs, Randall M., Attorney at Law '44 '69
C.98 B.S. L.145 J.D. 3101 W. Harmon Hwy., Ste. B
Jaeger, Philip L., (BV) . . . . . . '48 '73 C.927 B.A. L.339 J.D. [Safford,W.T.&J.] ⊙
Jagiella, Diana M., (AV) . . . . . .'59 '87 C.679 B.A. L.209 J.D. [Howard&H.]
Jannusch, Janet L. . . . . . . '51 '76 C.589 B.A. L.879 J.D. [Ⓐ Davis&C.]
Janovetz, James M., (BV) . . . . . . '54 '79 C.742 B.A. L.339 J.D. [Ⓐ Stephens,F.M.&Assoc.]
Jans, Peggy L., Attorney at Law, (BV) . . . . . . '53 '88 C.927 B.S. L.801 J.D. P.O. Box 5459
Janssen, Jay H., (AV) . . . . . .'37 '61 C.98 B.S. L.339 J.D. [Janssen]

Janssen Law Center, (AV) [BB]
Janssen Building Main and Jefferson, 333 Main Street, 61602
Telephone: 309-676-2341 Fax: 309-676-7678 URL: http://www.jjlaw.com
Email: jay@jjlaw.com URL: http://www.lawyers.com/janssen
Jay H. Janssen;—Ralph D. Davis; Christopher R. Doscotch; Joseph W. Dunn; Donovan W. Gaede; Patrick S. Oshaughnessy.
Personal Injury, Automobile Accidents, Dog Bites, Sexual Abuse, Slip and Fall, Wrongful Death, Airplane Crashes, Maritime Injuries, Nursing Home Abuse, Unsafe Products, Products Liability, Litigation, Medical Malpractice, Pharmaceutical Malpractice, Workers Compensation, Health, Civil Rights.

See Professional Biographies, PEORIA, ILLINOIS

Jennetten, Peter R., (BV) . . . . . . '69 '96 C.339 B.S. L.276 J.D. [Quinn,J.H.&P.]
Jennetten, Robert H., (AV) . . . . . .'45 '72 C.1082 B.A. L.339 J.D. [Quinn,J.H.&P.]
Jensen, Elizabeth L., (BV) . . . . . . '68 '94 C.20 B.A. L.424 J.D. Law Clk.
Johns, Daniel L., (AV) . . . . . .'46 '71 C&L.339 B.A., J.D. [Westervelt,J.N.&K.]
Johnson, Carroll F., (AVⓉ) '11 '36 C&L.352 B.A., J.D.
(adm. in IA; not adm. in IL) 2919 W. Gilbert‡
Johnson, E. Richard '31 '60 C.388 A.B. L.1119 J.D.
2632 W. Willowlake Dr., Apt. 623‡
Johnson, Frederick A., (AV) . . . . . .'44 '68 C&L.339 B.S., J.D. [Johnson,B.&N.]
Johnson, Frederick D., (AV) . . . . . . '27 '53 C.174 B.A. L.477 J.D. 411 Hamilton Blvd.‡
Johnson, James P., (BV) . . . . . . '53 '78 C&L.339 A.B., J.D. [Johnson,B.&N.]

Johnson, Bunce & Noble, P.C., (AV) [BB]
Executive Offices - Parkway Plaza, 7800 N. Sommer Street, Suite 425, 61615-1994
Telephone: 309-691-9650 Fax: 309-691-9651
Email: info@peorialawyers.com URL: http://www.peorialawyers.com
James H. Bunce; Kent A. Noble; Frederick A. Johnson; James P. Johnson; Matthew P. Jones;—Lester W. Vicary, Jr.
General Civil and Trial Practice in all Courts. Corporation, Banking, Municipal, Commercial, Probate, Taxation, Real Estate, Estate Planning, Collections, Eminent Domain, Family Law, Title Insurance.
Representative Clients: The Greater Peoria Sanitary District; Traders Realty Corporation; Northern Border Pipeline Company.

See Professional Biographies, PEORIA, ILLINOIS

Johnston, W. Thomas, (AV) . . . . . .'41 '66 C.927 B.A. L.339 J.D. [Ⓒ Quinn,J.H.&P.]
Jones, David E., (AV) . . . . . . '47 '80 C.69 B.M. L.339 J.D. [Hinshaw&C.]
Jones, Matthew P., (CV) . . . . . .'65 '91 C&L.339 B.S., J.D. [Johnson,B.&N.]
Jones, Robt. H. . . . . . .'25 '51 C.98 B.S. L.477 J.D. Commerce Bk. Bldg.
Jorgensen, James R. . . . . . . '68 '97 C.679 B.S. L.209 J.D. [Ⓐ Davis&C.]
Joseph, Richard M., (BV) . . . . . .'60 '85 C.602 B.B.A. L.436 J.D. [Miller,H.&T.]
Judd, Laurie M., (BV) . . . . . .'52 '83 C.339 B.A. L.801 J.D. [Quinn,J.H.&P.]
Kahler, H. Richard '47 '77 C.645 B.A. L.276 LL.B.
(adm. in DC; not adm. in IL) Caterpillar Inc.
Kamin, John F., (BV) . . . . . . '65 '90 C.98 B.S. L.801 J.D. [Quinn,J.H.&P.]
Kane, James F., (AV) . . . . . . '51 '76 C.338 B.S. L.339 J.D. [Winget&K.]
Kanoski, Ronald J., (BV) . . . . . .'47 '74 C.234 B.S. L.424 J.D. [Kanoski&Assoc.] ⊙
Kanoski & Associates, (BV)
331 Fulton St., Ste. 410 (⊙Bloomington, Decatur, Macomb, Quincy, Rushville, Springfield)
Kanuru, Rajendra K. '70 '97 C.88 B.S. L.16 J.D.
(adm. in AL; not adm. in IL) Sr. Atty., Caterpillar Inc.
Kauffman, Robert J. . . . . . . '35 '59 C&L.436 LL.B. U.S. Mag. J.
Kavanagh, Scully, Sudow, White & Frederick, P.C., (AV)
301 S.W. Adams Street, Suite 700
Keen, Joseph W. '47 '75
C.339 B.S.M.E. L.831 J.D. Sr. Intell. Prop. Coun., Caterpillar Inc. (Pat.)
Keers-Sanchez, Allison R. . . . . . . '74 '04 C.340 B.A. L.801 J.D. [Miller,H.&T.]
Keller, Homer W., (AV) . . . . . .'17 '43 C.336 B.S. L.339 LL.B. [Westervelt,J.N.&K.]
Kelly, James Michael, (CV) . . . . . .'69 '94 C.676 B.A. L.190 J.D. 416 Main Street Suite 832
Kelly, Stephen P., (BV) . . . . . . '64 '90 C.707 B.A. L.365 J.D. [Knell&K.]
Kendall, Karen L., (AV) . . . . . .'45 '81 C&L.801 B.A., J.D. [Heyl,R.V.&A.]
Keyt, Andrew J. . . . . . . '74 '02 C.338 B.S. L.589 J.D. [Ⓐ Heyl,R.V.&A.]
Kibby, Steven G. . . . . . .'63 '94 C.610 B.S. L.128 J.D. Sr. Intell. Prop. Atty., Caterpillar Inc.
Kim, John K. . . . . . . '78 '05 C.938 B.A. L.904 J.D. [Ⓐ Heyl,R.V.&A.]
Kim, Tracie . . . . . .'74 '01 C.705 B.A. L.94 J.D. Atty., Caterpillar Inc.
King, Michael S. . . . . . .'74 '03 C.1335 B.S. L.1049 J.D. Intell. Prop. Atty., Caterpillar Inc.
Kingery, Arthur R., (AV) . . . . . .'42 '66 C&L.339 B.S., J.D. [Kingery D.W.&R.]

Kingery Durree Wakeman & Ryan, Assoc., (AV) [BB]
Commerce Bank Building, 416 Main Street, Suite 915, 61602
Telephone: 309-676-3612 FAX: 309-676-1329 URL: http://www.kdwrlaw.com
Email: KDWRyan@sbcglobal.net URL: http://www.lawyers.com/kingerydurree
Arthur R. Kingery; Edward R. Durree; Steven A. Wakeman; Christopher P. Ryan; Philip M. O'Donnell; James P. Lawson; Michael S. McKinley.
General Civil and Trial Practice, Products Liability, Workers Compensation, Personal Injury, Medical and Professional Malpractice Law, Automobile Accidents, Wrongful Death, Dog Bites, Slip and Fall.
Reference: Commerce Bank of Peoria.

See Professional Biographies, PEORIA, ILLINOIS

Kinskey, Tim M. '65 '90 C.699 A.B. L.880 J.D.
(adm. in NC; not adm. in IL) Sr. Corp. Atty., Caterpillar Inc.
Kirk, Timothy W., (BV) . . . . . . '56 '81 C.338 B.S. L.221 J.D. [Heyl,R.V.&A.]
Kleczek, Andrew J. . . . . . . '42 '68 C.145 A.B. L.365 J.D. 321 NE Madison Ave.
Klock, Diane R. . . . . . . '51 '85 C.791 B.S. L.589 J.D. Clk., App. Ct.
Knauss, Darilynn J., (BV) . . . . . . '52 '76 C.98 B.A. L.146 J.D. First Asst. State's Atty.
Knell, Charles D., (AV) . . . . . . '50 '76 C.339 B.A. L.802 J.D. [Knell&K.]

Knell & Kelly, L.L.C., (AV) [BB]
504 Fayette, 61603
Telephone: 309-655-1530 Fax: 309-655-1535
Email: law@knell-kelly.com URL: http://www.lawyers.com/knellkelly
Members of Firm: Charles D. Knell; Stephen P. Kelly;—Andrew S. de Blank; Darcy K. Gibson.
General Practice.

See Professional Biographies, PEORIA, ILLINOIS

Koehler, Denise A. . . . .'62 '89 C.339 B.A. L.39 J.D. Staff Coun., RLI Insurance Company
Koehler, Julie Ann . . . . . . '— '97 401 S.W. Water Street, Suite 409
Koepke, Bryon L. '72 '00 C.880 B.S. L.900 J.D.
(adm. in KS; not adm. in IL) Securities Atty., Caterpillar Inc.

Koepke & Hiltabrand, P.C.
(See Springfield)

Kohlhase, William R., (AV) . . . . . . '50 '75 C.966 B.A. L.273 J.D. [Miller,H.&T.]
Konishenko, Angela C., (BV) . . . . . .'65 '90 C&L.801 B.A., J.D Asst. Atty. Gen.
Konrath, Richard P. . . . . . . '61 '86 C.608 B.A. L.851 J.D. Gen. Atty., Caterpillar Inc.
Konsky, James E., (BV) . . . . . .'47 '75 C.801 B.A. L.352 J.D. [Vonachen,L.T.&S.]
Kouri, Stephen A., (BV) . . . . . . '57 '82 C.190 B.A. L.339 J.D. [Vonachen,L.T.&S.]
Koziner, Pablo M. '72 '99 C&L.93 B.A., J.D.
(adm. in NY; not adm. in IL) Sr. Atty., Capterpillar, Inc.
Kraft, Michael A., (BV) . . . . . .'68 '93 C&L.339 A.B., J.D. [Quinn,J.H.&P.]

Krajewski, J. Phillip
(See Baker, Baker & Krajewski, LLC)

Kreblin, Chad A. '76 '01 C.966 B.A. L.1410 J.D.
[Ⓐ M.F.Hupy&Assoc.] (⊙Decatur, Normal, IL; Appleton, Madison, WI)
Kroger, James A. '73 '98 C&L.602 B.A., J.D.
(adm. in MI; not adm. in IL) Atty., Caterpillar Inc.
Krumpe, Jeffrey E., (BV) . . . . . . '68 '95 C.894 B.A. L.339 J.D. [Miller,H.&T.]
Kuehn, Brian Allen, (CV) . . . . . . '53 '80 C.932 B.A. L.339 J.D. [Ⓐ Carter]
Kumar, Jaiprakash P. '72 '97 C.197 B.A. L.846 J.D.
(adm. in TX; not adm. in IL) Lit. Atty, Caterpillar, Inc.
Kuper, Debra E. '65 '97 C.999 B.A. L.436 J.D.
(adm. in WI; not adm. in IL) Sec. Coun., Caterpillar Inc.
Kuppler, Karl B., (AV) . . . . . .'56 '81 C.578 B.A. L.339 J.D. [Hasselberg,R.B.&K.]
Lacey, Michelle . . . . . . '— '91 C.504 B.A. L.190 J.D. RLI Corp.
LaConte, Lisa A., (AV) . . . . . . '64 '88 C.339 B.S. L.910 J.D. [Heyl,R.V.&A.]
Lagocki, Adam J. . . . . . . '77 '03 C.74 B.S. L.339 J.D. [Ⓐ Heyl,R.V.&A.]
Langenfeld, Clifford J. . . . . . . '49 '86 C&L.339 B.S., J.D. 2624 W. Eugenia Ave.
Larmore, Kelly A. . . . . . . '77 '03 C.966 B.A. L.436 J.D. [Ⓐ M.F.Hupy&Assoc.] ⊙
Larson, Christopher P., (AV) . . . . . . '59 '84 C.98 B.S. L.339 J.D. [Heyl,R.V.&A.]
LaSaine, Dorian B. . . . . . .'46 '77 C.801 B.S. L.365 J.D. 456 Fulton
Lawless, J. Martin, (AV) . . . . . .'26 '50 C&L.339 B.S., J.D. [Ⓒ Vonachen,L.T.&S.]
Lawson, James P., (BV) . . . . . .'70 '95 C.339 B.S. L.801 J.D. [Kingery D.W.&R.]
LeFante, James . . . . . . '71 '96 C.927 B.A. L.365 J.D. [Ⓐ Hinshaw&C.]
Leiter, Thomas E., (BV) . . . . . . '44 '69 C.597 B.S. L.339 J.D. [Leiter]
Leiter Group, The, Attorneys and Counselors, P.C., (BV) . . . . . . 309-A Main Street
Lenzini, Phillip B., (AV) . . . . . .'49 '76 C&L.801 B.A., J.D. [Kavanagh,S.S.W.&F.]
Leuba, Sean P. '70 '97 C.446 B.A. L.902 J.D.
(adm. in MD; not adm. in IL) Corp. Atty., Caterpillar Inc.
Lied, Michael Robert, (AV) . . . . . . '53 '83 C.339 B.S. L.477 J.D. [Howard&H.]
Linder, Rex K., (AV) . . . . . . '48 '74 C.98 B.S. L.900 J.D. [Heyl,R.V.&A.]
Lindley, Doreen M. Hichey . . . . . . '57 '83 C.339 B.S.N. L.209 J.D. Chicago Title Ins. Co.‡
Litterst, Roland N., (BV) . . . . . .'36 '62 C.894 A.B. L.1119 LL.B. [Litterst]
Litterst Law Office, Ltd., (BV) . . . . . . 331 Fulton St., Ste. 416
Litzinger, Tracy C., (BV) . . . . . . '67 '94 C.1347 B.S. L.734 J.D. [Howard&H.]
Long, Cheryl Jean . . . . . . '58 '83 C.578 B.A. L.146 J.D. 809 W. Detwiller Drive‡
Long, Suzette M. '65 '99 C&L.36 B.S., J.D.
(adm. in AZ; and limited adm. in IL) Atty., Caterpillar Inc.
Lubben, David G. . . . . . . '63 '90 C.339 B.A. L.813 J.D. [Davis&C.]
Lucas, Susan K., (BV) . . . . . . '50 '76 C.339 B.A. L.910 J.D. 411 Hamilton Blvd.
Lucas, Zane L., Jr., (BV) '61 '87
C.98 B.S. L.608 J.D. 411 Hamilton Boulevard, Suite 1808
Ludolph, Mark A., (BV) . . . . . .'70 '97 C.234 B.A. L.339 J.D. [Ⓐ Heyl,R.V.&A.]
Luncsford, Lori S. . . . . . .'56 '96 C.338 B.S. L.615 J.D. Prairie State Legal Services
Lundquist, Steve D. . . . . . .'53 '03 C.98 B.S.E.E. L.734 J.D. Pat. Atty., Caterpillar Inc.
Lynch, David M., (AV) . . . . . .'47 '74 C.504 B.A. L.339 J.D. [Lynch&B.]

Lynch and Bloom, P.C., (AV)
411 Hamilton Boulevard, Suite 1300, 61602
Telephone: 309-673-7415 Fax: 309-673-3189
Email: dlynch4780@aol.com URL: http://www.lynchbloom.com
David M. Lynch; Prescott E. Bloom (1942-1986).
Matrimonial and Family Law, Divorce, Adoptions, Child Support, Child Custody, General Civil Litigation. Personal Injury Law.

See Professional Biographies, PEORIA, ILLINOIS

Lyons, Kevin W., (AV) . . . . . . '56 '81 C.999 B.A. L,221 J.D. State's Atty.
Madison, Garth C. K. . . . . . . '77 '02 C&L.228 B.S., J.D. [Ⓐ Hinshaw&C.]
Magill, James L., (BV) . . . . . .'47 '73 C&L.339 B.S., J.D. Asst. U.S. Trustee
Maher, Jerelyn D. . . . . . .'52 '77 C.98 B.A. L.424 J.D. Assoc. J.
Mahoney, Michael T., (BV) . . . . . .'54 '79 C&L.424 B.A., J.D. [M.T.Mahoney] ⊙

Mahoney, Michael T., Ltd., (BV)
414 Hamilton Boulevard, Suite 300, 61602 ⊙
Telephone: 309-673-0375 Fax: 309-274-5405
Email: mahoney@mchsi.com URL: http://www.mahoneyltd.com
Michael T. Mahoney.
Civil Litigation, Wills and Probate, Trusts and Estates, Estate Planning, Family Law, Personal Injury, Juvenile Law, DUI, Divorce, Adoptions, Child Support and Custody, Visitation Rights, Automobile Accidents, Dog Bites, Slip and Fall, Wrongful Death, Real Estate, Buying and Selling, Construction Law, Workers Compensation, Title and Insurance, Domestic Relations.
Chillicothe Office: 1011 North Second Street, 61523. Telephone: 309-274-5451.

See Professional Biographies, PEORIA, ILLINOIS

Makovic, William T., (BV) . . . . . . '21 '50 C.98 B.S.S. L.339 LL.B. 606 E. High Pt. Terr.
Manning, James J., (BV) . . . . . .'67 '92 C.602 B.B.A. L.734 J.D. [Heyl,R.V.&A.]
Manning, Robert E., Jr. . . . . . . '31 '60 C.98 B.S. L.602 J.D. Cir. J.
Marincic, Michael T., (CV) . . . . . .'69 '97 C.338 M.S. L.801 J.D. [Ⓐ Goldfine&B.]
Marshall, Douglass A., (AV) . . . . . .'48 '82 C.927 B.A. L.734 J.D. [Hinshaw&C.]
Mathis, J. Michael, (BV) . . . . . .'37 '59 C.169 L.339 LL.B. [Mathis]
Mathis, Joseph Michael, Jr., (BV) . . . . . .'55 '83 C.1111 B.A. L.801 J.D. [Ⓐ Mathis]
Mathis Law Firm, The, (BV) . . . . . . 7707 N. Knoxville Avenue
Maver, Thomas B., Jr. . . . '58 '84 C.197 B.A. L.339 J.D. Caterpillar Financial Servs. Corp.
Mayer, Richard A. '27 '52 C&L.352 B.A., LL.B.
(adm. in IA; not adm. in IL) Caterpillar Tractor Co.
Mayer, Thomas C., (AV) . . . . . .'40 '65 C.821 B.A. L.665 LL.B. 100 N.E. Adams Street‡

McCarthy, David H., Law Offices of, (BV) '45 '73
C.338 B.S.Ed. L.734 J.D. 411 Hamilton Boulevard, Suite 1820
McCarthy, Timothy D., (CV) ....'74 '99 C.347 B.A. L.365 J.D. [Ⓐ D.H.McCarthy]
McConnaughay, Thomas A., (BV) .....'60 '86 C&L.339 A.B., J.D. [Westervelt,J.N.&K.]
McCord, Robert A. ....'20 '48 C&L.145 B.A., J.D. 510 E. High Point Pl.‡
McDade, Joe Billy ....'37 '63 C.98 B.S. L.477 J.D. U.S. Dist. J.
McDade, Mary Wheeler, (BV) ....'39 '84 C.477 B.A. L.339 J.D. State of IL Cts.
McGill, Norman L. ....'61 '86 C.98 B.S. L.801 J.D. [Stephens,F.M.&Assoc.]
McGowan, Andrew J. '59 '93 C.910 B.A. L.900 J.D.
(adm. in KS; not adm. in IL) Fed. Public Def.'s Off.
McGraw, Angela E. '75 '00 C.958 B.S. L.436 J.D.
[Ⓐ M.F.Hupy&Assoc.] (⊙Decatur, Normal, IL; Appleton, Madison, WI)
McGuire, Michael Andrew ....'72 '99 C.602 B.A. L.893 J.D. Atty., Caterpillar Inc.
McKenzie, Vanessa R. ....'73 '99 C.154 B.A. L.910 J.D. Atty., Caterpillar, Inc.
McKessy, Sean X. '67 '92 C.602 B.A. L.273 J.D.
(adm. in VA; not adm. in IL) Securities Coun., Caterpillar Inc.
McKinley, Michael S., (BV) ....'68 '93 C.812 B.S. L.801 J.D. [Kingery D.W.&R.]
McLaughlin, Alison E. ......'— '98 C.1044 B.A. L.1019 J.D. [Ⓐ Hasselberg,W.G.S.&B.]
McPherson, William B., III '61 '96
C.277 B.S.E.E. L.734 J.D. Sr. Intell. Prop. Atty., Caterpillar Inc.
Meginnes, Brian J., (AV) ....'53 '78 C.602 B.A. L.339 J.D. [Elias,M.R.&S.]
Melie, Michael D. ....'51 '77 C.860 B.A. L.64 J.D. 100 N.E. Adams St.
Michalec, Scott L. ....'64 '89 C.339 B.A. L.589 J.D. Asst. Atty. Gen.
Mihm, Michael M. ....'43 '67 C.177 B.A. L.734 J.D. Dist. J.
Miller, Michele A., (BV) ....'69 '00 C.338 B.S. L.801 J.D. [Ⓐ Westervelt,J.N.&K.]
Miller, Nathan R., (BV) ....'57 '82 C&L.339 B.A., J.D. [Miller,H.&T.]
Miller, Robert Hollis, (AV) ....'26 '50 C.679 B.S. L.339 J.D. 416 Main St.‡

Miller, Hall & Triggs, (AV)
416 Main Street, Suite 1125, 61602
Telephone: 309-671-9600 Fax: 309-671-9616
URL: http://www.mhtlaw.com
Robert C. Hall; Dennis R. Triggs; William R. Kohlhase; Patrick A. Murphey; Michael J. Tibbs; Richard M. Joseph; Thomas R. Davis; Nathan R. Miller; Jay E. Greening; Scott A. Brunton; Douglas G. Griffin; Jeffrey E. Krumpe; M. Curt Richardson; Jamison J. Allen; Allison R. Keers-Sanchez.
General Civil Practice, School and Local Government, Real Estate, Corporations, Probate, Labor, Banking, Taxation, Litigation and Title Insurance (ATGF).
See Professional Biographies, PEORIA, ILLINOIS

Milman, Kelsey L. .... '69 '97 C&L.339 B.S., J.D. Intell. Prop. Atty., Caterpillar Inc.
Mitchell, Charles Philip .... '61 '86 C&L.339 B.S., J.D. Prairie State Legal Serv., Inc.
Mitchell, Clifton J., (BV) ....'50 '75 C.98 B.A. L.339 J.D. Corp. Coun. City of Peoria
Mitchell, John E., (BV) ....'46 '74 C.963 B.S. L.365 J.D. 415 N.E. Jefferson Ave.
Molchan, Richard N., (AV) ....'32 '56 C.707 B.A. L.339 J.D. [Ⓒ Heyl,R.V.&A.]
Moore, Shelley Lynne ....'74 '01 C.475 B.A. L.365 J.D Peoria County Courthouse
Moos, Patrick T., (BV) ....'48 '73 C.910 B.A. L.339 J.D. [Moos,S.&O.]
Moos, Schmitt & O'Brien, P.C., (BV) ....311 Fulton St.
Mooty, Brian D., (BV) ....'60 '86 C.234 B.A. L.801 J.D. [Kavanagh,S.S.W.&F.]
Moran, Barbra J. ..... '65 '95 C.98 B.S./M.B.A. L.1040 J.D. Corp. Atty., Caterpillar Inc.
Morgan, Robert D. ....'12 '37 C.98 A.B. L.145 J.D. Ret. U.S. Dist. Ct. J.
Morris, Gary L. ....'50 '76 C.339 B.S. L.365 J.D. 1010 Savings Center Tower
Morris, Stephen M., (CV) ....'71 '96 C&L.190 B.A., J.D. [Howard,H.&M.]
Morrison, James R., (BV) ....'45 '71 C.352 B.A. L.339 J.D. [Westervelt,J.N.&K.]
Mueller, David B., (AV) ....'41 '66 C.623 B.A. L.477 LL.B. [Cassidy&M.]
Murphey, Patrick A., (AV) ....'50 '77 C.218 B.A. L.879 J.D. [Miller,H.&T.]
Murphy, G. Edward, (BV) ....'62 '87 C.352 B.A. L.589 J.D. [Reynolds,M.&Assoc.]
Murphy, Theresa Brodeur, (BV) '62 '88 C.1024 B.S. L.589 J.D.
[Ⓒ Reynolds,M.&Assoc.]
Mytich, Ketra A., The Law Office of, (BV) '— '72
C.734 B.A. L.436 J.D. 6809 N. Knoxville Ave., Ste. B
Nair, Janaki ....'78 '02 C.145 B.A. L.339 J.D. [Ⓐ Elias,M.R.&S.]
Napoli, Joseph R., Ltd., (BV) ....'34 '64 C.98 B.S. L.365 J.D. 1820 First Financial Plz.
Natonek, Louise M., (BV) ....'55 '80 C.927 B.S. L.339 J.D. [Ⓐ Cusack,F.G.&O.]
Naylor, Patricia J. ....'78 '03 C.339 B.A. L.589 J.D. [Ⓐ Hinshaw&C.]
Nebel, Mary Beth, (BV) '56 '80
C&L.801 B.S., J.D. V.P. & Gen. Coun., RLI Insurance Company
Neff, Robert J. ....'38 '34 C.801 B.S. L.339 J.D. 301 S.W. Adams St., Ste. 800
Nelson, Gary D., (AV) ....'50 '77 C&L.339 B.A., J.D. [Heyl,R.V.&A.]
Nemenoff, Brian M. ....'47 '74 C.473 B.A. L.339 J.D. Assoc. Cir. J.
Newell, John C., Jr., (AV) ....'15 '40 C.894 B.A. L.477 LL.B. 227 N.E. Jefferson St.
Newlin, Timothy J., (BV) ....'52 '78 C&L.802 B.A., J.D. [Ⓐ Hinshaw&C.]
Nichols, Christopher A., (BV) ....'62 '88 C.210 B.A. L.347 J.D. [Husch&E.]
Nicoara, John P., (AV) ....'48 '75 C.477 A.B. L.339 J.D. [Nicoara&S.]

Nicoara & Steagall, (AV) BB
Commerce Bank Building, 416 Main Street, Suite 815, 61602-1103
Telephone: 309-674-6085 Fax: 309-674-6032 URL: http://www.nicoara.com
Email: nicsteag@mtco.com URL: http://www.lawyers.com/nicoaralaw
Members of Firm: John P. Nicoara; Richard L. Steagall.
Languages: Romanian.
General Civil Trial and Appellate Practice in State and Federal Courts. Personal Injury and Insurance Law, Civil Rights Litigation, Employment Discrimination, Auto Accidents, Aviation Law, Legal Malpractice, Medical Malpractice, Products Liability, Sex Offenses. Arbitration and Mediation Services.
Representative Clients: Founders Insurance Co.
Reference: Commerce Bank.
Affiliated With: Katz, Friedman, Eagle, Eisenstein & Johnson. 77 W. Washington Street, 20th Floor, Chicago, Illinois, 60602. Telephone: 312-263-6330.
See Professional Biographies, PEORIA, ILLINOIS

Nicol, William C., (AV) ....'11 '40 C&L.339 B.S., LL.B. 227 N.E. Jefferson St.
Noble, Kent A., (AV) ....'43 '68 C&L.339 B.S., J.D. [Johnson,B.&N.]
Noe, Stephen L. ....'47 '86 C.338 B.S. L.912 J.D. 100 N.E. Adams Street (Pat.)‡
Noetzel, Henry D., (AV) ....'22 '49 L.597 LL.B. [H.D.Noetzel&Assoc.] ‡
Noetzel, Henry D., & Associates Ltd., (AV) ....816 W. Fairlawn Lane
Nordwall, Michael A., (BV) ....'60 '91 C&L.589 B.S., J.D. [M.A.Nordwall]
Nordwall, Michael A., Ltd., (BV) .... 910 W. Glen Ave.
Norton, Larry '50 '75 C.934 B.A. L.623 J.D.
(adm. in OK; not adm. in IL) 2517 Madison Ave., N.E.‡
O'Brien, Daniel R., (BV) ....'51 '76 C.589 B.S. L.910 J.D. [Moos,S.&O.]
O'Brien, E. Michael, (BV) ..... '30 '61 C.942 A.B. L.602 LL.B. Courthouse, 324 Main St.
O'Connor, Kevin R. ....'69 '96 C.36 B.S. L.61 J.D. Corp. Atty., Caterpillar Inc.
O'Day, Daniel G., (BV) ....'55 '81 C.98 B.S. L.339 J.D. 415 Hamilton Blvd.
O'Donnell, Philip M., (BV) ....'69 '94 C.339 B.S. L.378 J.D. [Kingery D.W.&R.]
Olivero, Kathy A., (CV) '56 '82 C.339 B.S. L.365 J.D.
[Ⓐ Kanoski&Assoc.] (⊙Bloomington, Macomb, Quincy, Rushville, Springfield)
O'Neal, Thomas W., (AV) ....'55 '80 C.388 B.A. L.802 J.D. [Westervelt,J.N.&K.]
Orr, Gary E., (BV) ....'54 '77 C.234 B.A. L.365 J.D. [Orr,D.&Assoc.]
Orr, Dvorak and Associates, Ltd., (BV) ....124 SW Adams Street
Oshaughnessy, Patrick S. ....'71 '96 C.98 B.S. L.597 J.D. [Ⓐ Janssen]

Ostrowski, Laura, (CV) ....'73 '00 C&L.589 B.A., J.D. [Ⓐ Carter]
Ott, Kenneth L., (CV) ....'24 '51 C.910 L.734 LL.B. 3618 N. Sterling Ave.
Papachronis Herman, Athena M. ....'72 '97 C.98 B.S. L.339 J.D. [Ⓐ Benassi&B.]
Parker, Drew, (BV) ....'51 '76 C.339 B.S. L.146 J.D. [Parker&H.]
Parker & Halliday, (BV) ....414 Hamilton Blvd.
Parsons, Richard H., (BV) ....'36 '63 C.98 B.S. L.902 LL.B. Fed. Pub. Def.
Pasquini, Sonya A. ....'77 '02 C.910 B.A. L.339 J.D. [Ⓐ Elias,M.R.&S.]
Paul-Reeff, Tamara A. ....'74 '04 C.338 B.S. L.823 J.D. [Ⓐ Hinshaw&C.]
Paulsen, Scott R., (BV) ....'63 '90 C.338 B.S. L.352 J.D. [Ⓐ Kavanagh,S.S.W.&F.]
Pelphrey, Jeremy M. ....'76 '04 C.234 B.A. L.1017 J.D. [Ⓐ Davis&C.]
Penn, Thomas J., (BV) ....'43 '67 C.98 B.S. L.339 J.D. [T.J.Penn,Jr.]
Penn, Thomas J., Jr., LTD, Law Offices of, (BV) ....416 Main St.
Peplow, Gary M., (AV) ....'40 '66 C.98 B.A. L.339 J.D. [Ⓒ Heyl,R.V.&A.]
Perkins, Carol J. ....'58 '00 C.63 B.S. L.602 J.D. [Ⓐ Heyl,R.V.&A.]
Perkins, David A., (AV) ....'57 '87 C.339 B.A. L.352 J.D. [Heyl,R.V.&A.]
Perkins, S. Linn, (BV) ....'61 '90 C.430 B.S. L.339 J.D. [Ⓐ Vonachen,L.T.&S.]
Perkins, Thomas L., (BV) ....'58 '84 C.352 B.B.A. L.347 J.D. Bkrptcy. Ct.
Perry, Sandra J., (CV) ....'54 '79 C.98 B.S. L.801 J.D. Prof., Bradley Univ.
Petersen, Laura A., (BV) ....'73 '98 C&L.339 B.S., J.D. [Ⓐ Quinn,J.H.&P.]
Petersen, Tyler, (BV) ....'— '99 C&L.339 B.S., J.D. [Ⓐ Husch&E.]
Petesch, Sabrina M. (Doll) '62 '87 C.210 B.A. L.1119 J.D.
(adm. in WI; not adm. in IL) 401 Main St., Ste. 1100
Phelps, Barbara G. ....'56 '02 C.339 B.A. L.862 J.D. [Ⓐ C.E.Walker&Assoc.]
Pierce, William F., Jr. '43 '76 C.882 B.A. L.818 J.D.
(adm. in PA; not adm. in IL) Pres. & CEO, OSF HealthPlans, Inc.
Pollock, Philip M. ....'46 '74 C.339 B.A. L.560 J.D. 1715 Savings Center Tower
Poltz, Judith T. ....'49 '77 C.1350 B.A. L.339 J.D. N.L.R.B.
Poteat, Thena G. ....'67 '91 C.911 A.B. L.976 J.D. 1114 W. Oakglen Dr.‡
Powell, Janice M., (BV) ....'58 '83 C&L.339 B.A., J.D. [Howard&H.]
Pretorius, Murvel, Jr., (AV) ....'46 '71 C.388 B.A. L.339 J.D. [Quinn,J.H.&P.]
Prusak, Maximilian M., (AV) .... '43 '68 C&L.339 B.S., J.D. [Prusak,W.&G.]

Prusak, Winne & Gorman, Ltd., (AV) BB
403 N.E. Jefferson Street, 61603-3725
Telephone: 309-674-4222 Fax: 309-674-9701
Email: mprusak@mtco.com URL: http://www.lawyers.com/prusak&winne
Maximilian M. Prusak; Joseph E. Winne; Katherine Gorman Hubler; Blake E. Dunlap.
General Practice. Trial, Insurance, Workers Compensation, Personal Injury, Probate, Corporate, Construction Litigation, Fire Loss, Professional Liability, Real Estate Law, Automobile Liability Defense, Insurance Coverage, Uninsured and Underinsured Motorists Arbitration, Products Liability Defense, Professional Liability Defense.
See Professional Biographies, PEORIA, ILLINOIS

Pudik, Troy N., (BV) ....'68 '93 C.339 A.B. L.221 J.D. [Elias,M.R.&S.]
Pugh, Robert E. ....'77 '04 C.834 B.S. L.801 J.D. Asst. State's Atty.
Purham, Albert L., Jr., (BV) ....'57 '83 C.910 A.B. L.494 J.D. Asst. State's Atty.
Pusey, John R., (AV) ....'42 '69 C&L.602 A.B., J.D. [Vonachen,L.T.&S.]

Quinn, Johnston, Henderson & Pretorius, Chartered, (AV)
(Formerly McConnell, Kennedy, Quinn & Johnston)
227 N. E. Jefferson Street, 61602 ⊙
Telephone: 309-674-1133 Telecopier: 309-674-6503
Email: quinnlaw@qjhp.com URL: http://www.qjhp.com
Lowell R. McConnell (1911-1971); Golden A. McConnell (1914-1974); Joseph A. Leimkuehler (1931-1974); Thomas B. Kennedy, Sr. (1912-1988); Richard E. Quinn (1928-2000); R. Michael Henderson; Murvel Pretorius, Jr.; Bradley W. Dunham; Robert H. Jennetten; Gregory A. Cerulo; Paul P. Gilfillan; Laurie M. Judd; David Blair Collins; John F. Kamin; Matthew B. Smith; Peter R. Jennetten; Michael A. Kraft; Jonathan A. Stump; Laura A. Petersen; Jo Tewes Wetherill; Adam P. Chaddock; Allison N. Bell; Melinda Rowe. Of Counsel: W. Thomas Johnston.
Trial Practice in all Courts. Personal Injury, Professional Negligence, Admiralty, Insurance Law, Workers Compensation Law, Banking, Commercial and Bankruptcy Law. Real Estate, Corporate and Probate Law.
Representative Clients: Allstate Insurance Co.; American International Insurance Co.; Bituminous Casualty Corp.; General Motors; Illinois State Medical Insurance Services, Inc.; Pekin Insurance; Peoria Journal Star, Inc.; St. Paul Insurance Co.
Springfield, Illinois Office: 205 South Fifth Street, Suite 900, 62701. Telephone: 217-753-1133. Fax: 217-753-1180.
See Professional Biographies, PEORIA, ILLINOIS

Radley, David B., (AV) ....'41 '66 C.174 B.A. L.339 J.D. [D.B.Radley]

Radley, David B., P.C., (AV)
700 Commerce Bank Building, 416 Main Street, Suite 700, 61602-1180
Telephone: 309-674-8125 Fax: 309-674-8149
Email: Radleydb@prodigy.net
David B. Radley.
General Civil Practice, Appellate Practice, State and Federal Commercial and Civil Litigation, Real Estate, Probate, Arbitration, Securities Fraud, Trusts and Estates, Construction, Buying and Selling a Home, Commercial Real Estate, Buying and Selling of Businesses, Commercial Leasing, Business Law, Contracts, Lawsuits, Small Business Law, Personal Injury, Automobile Accidents, Wills and Probate, Estate Planning.
See Professional Biographies, PEORIA, ILLINOIS

Rafool, Gary T., (AV) ....'35 '60 C.98 B.S. L.362 J.D. [Rafool&B.]
Rafool & Bourne, (AV) ....411 Hamilton Blvd.
Rastatter, Gregory J. ....'74 '03 C.98 B.A. L.339 J.D. [Ⓐ Heyl,R.V.&A.]
Ray, Randall P., (BV) ....'52 '77 C&L.339 B.A., J.D. Corp. Coun., City of Peoria
Redlingshafer, John M. ....'79 '04 C.98 B.A. L.209 J.D. [Ⓐ Heyl,R.V.&A.]
Renner, Franklin L., (BV) ....'45 '71 C.352 B.A. L.339 J.D. 1007 River Valley Plaza
Reynolds, James D. ....'24 '51 C.531 L.209 LL.B. [Ⓒ Reynolds,M.&Assoc.]
Reynolds, Murphy & Associates, P.C., (BV) .... 411 Hamilton Blvd., Ste. 1510
Rhoads, Dean B., (BV) ....'49 '76 C&L.339 B.S., J.D. [Sutkowski&R.]
Rhode, Robert H., (BV) ....'62 '89 C&L.339 B.S., J.D. [Sutkowski&R.]
Richardson, M. Curt ....'77 '02 C.234 B.A. L.801 J.D. [Miller,H.&T.]
Riddell, Rebecca S. ....'50 '79 C.338 B.A. L.910 J.D. Assoc. Cir. J.
Riddle, John D. ....'38 '64 C.357 B.A. L.339 LL.B. 2204 N. Bigelow‡
Riffle, Robert M., (BV) ....'59 '85 C.339 B.S. L.878 J.D. [Elias,M.R.&S.]
Ririe, Andrew J. '— '02 C.1335 B.S. L.273 J.D.
(adm. in VA; not adm. in IL; Pat.) In-house Coun., Caterpillar Inc.
Rivera, Isabel C. '66 '95 C.94 B.S. L.276 J.D.
(adm. in MA; not adm. in IL) Atty., Caterpillar Inc
Roberson, Keith P. '67 '97 C.98 B.S.M.E. L.880 J.D.
Corp. Atty., Solar Turbines Inc., Caterpillar Inc.
Roberts, Boyd O., III, (BV) ... '— '97 C.339 B.A. L.209 J.D. [Ⓐ Hasselberg,W.G.S.&B.]
Roberts, Troy I., (BV) ....'62 '93 C.339 B.A. L.347 J.D. [T.I.Roberts]

Roberts, Troy I., PC, Law Office of, (BV)
Peoria Professional Building, 207 Main Street, Suite 500, 61602
Telephone: 309-655-3003 Fax: 309-672-2201
Email: troyroberts@ameritech.net
Troy I. Roberts.
Family Law, Civil Litigation, Civil Appeals, Personal Injury Law, Workers Compensation, Criminal Law.
See Professional Biographies, PEORIA, ILLINOIS

Rochford, James M., (CV) ....'54 '83 C.177 B.A. L.365 J.D. [Rochford&Assoc.]
Rochford & Associates, (CV) .... 124 S.W. Adams
Rock, Charles M., (BV) ....'54 '80 C.339 B.S. L.910 J.D. [Hasselberg,R.B.&K.]
Rock, Jeffrey B., (AV) ....'52 '77 C.339 B.A. L.910 J.D. [Hasselberg,R.B.&K.]
Roesler, J. Reed ....'54 '79 C.172 B.A. L.339 J.D. [Davis&C.]
Rooney, James M. .... '66 '92 C&L.339 B.S., J.D. Litig. Coun., Caterpillar Inc.
Rose, Mark A., (AV) ....'48 '74 C.679 B.A. L.734 J.D. Asst. Pub. Def. [Hatcher&R.]
Roth, Charles G., (AV) ....'40 '66 C.98 B.S. L.1119 J.D. [Kavanagh,S.S.W.&F.]
Rowe, Melinda .... '71 '03 C&L.589 B.S., J.D. [Ⓐ Quinn,J.H.&P.]
Ruddell, Brian W., (AV) ....'49 '74 C.339 B.S. L.602 J.D. [Husch&E.]
Russo, Megan R. .... '— '02 C.63 B.A. L.339 J.D. [Ⓐ Hasselberg,W.G.S.&B.]
Russo, Richard A. .... '78 '03 C.57 B.A. L.339 J.D. [Ⓐ Davis&C.]
Rutherford, William L., (AV) ....'14 '37 C.98 A.B. L.145 J.D. 5823 N. Forest Pk. Dr.
Ryan, Christopher P., (AV) ....'59 '84 C&L.339 B.A., J.D. [Kingery D.W.&R.]
Ryva, Jeffrey A., (BV) ....'55 '80 C.339 B.A. L.365 J.D. [Husch&E.]
Sachs, Leonard W., (BV) .... '64 '89 C.597 B.S. L.339 J.D. [Howard&H.]
Sack, Kevin M. ....'69 '98 C.338 B.S. L.589 J.D. [Ⓐ Stephens,F.M.&Assoc.]
Safford, West, Tornow & Jaeger, (BV) ....416 Main Street, Suite 727 (⊙Chillicothe)
Sahn, John G., (BV) '46 '75 C.742 B.A. L.46 J.D.
Chf. Exec. Offr., John C. Proctor Endowment
Sandoval, J. Robert '56 '89 C.424 B.A. L.477 J.D.
(adm. in NY; not adm. in IL) Sr. Corp. Atty., Caterpillar Inc.
Sandy, John .... '59 '87 C.347 B.A. L.146 J.D. RLI Insurance Company
Sarff, Kimberly A. Sutton ....'— '01 C.531 B.A. L.801 J.D. [Ⓐ Husch&E.]
Schellenberg, David N., (CV) .... '61 '90 C.98 B.S. L.801 J.D. [Ⓐ Elias,M.R.&S.]
Schellenberg, John A., (BV) ....'65 '90 C.98 B.S. L.801 J.D. [Ⓑ Heiple]
Schelwat, Timothy W. .... '70 '98 C.312 B.A. L.221 J.D. [Ⓐ M.F.Hupy&Assoc.] ⊙
Schertz, Ronald B., (BV) '36 '68
C.288 B.A. L.339 J.D. 411 Hamilton Boulevard, Suite 1900
Schleef, Eric Lee .... '76 '01 C.357 B.S. L.339 J.D. Clk., U.S. Bkrptcy. Ct.
Schlehuber, Thomas E., (CV) ... '34 '58 C.98 B.S. L.209 J.D. 1600 Associated Bank Plz.‡
Schlicksup, Harold A., Attorney at Law, (BV) '57 '82
C.589 B.S. L.365 J.D. 411 Hamilton Blvd., Ste. 1720
Schmidt, Daniel L., (AV) ....'51 '83 C.339 B.A. L.910 J.D. [Schmidt&F.]
Schmidt, Gary E., (BV) ....'52 '78 C.207 B.A. L.802 J.D. [Kavanagh,S.S.W.&F.]
Schmidt & Fleming, (AV) ....411 Hamilton Boulevard
Schmitt, Henry A., II, (BV) ....'51 '76 C.337 A.B. L.910 J.D. [Moos,S.&O.]
Schneider, Clifford E., (AV) ....'17 '43 C.340 A.B. L.339 J.D. 214 W. Crestwood Dr.‡
Schneider, Kevin D., (BV) .... '53 '83 C.98 B.A. L.221 J.D. [Westervelt,J.N.&K.]
Schroeder, Danny L., Jr., (BV) .....'56 '82 C.340 B.A. L.801 J.D. [Hasselberg,R.B.&K.]
Schroen, Derek A. .... '74 '01 C.679 B.A. L.146 J.D. [Ⓐ Cusack,F.G.&O.]
Schwenger, Lawrence E., Jr., (BV) ......'44 '70 C.98 B.S. L.734 J.D. [Vonachen,L.T.&S.]
Scott, Robert W., Jr., (AV) ....'47 '73 C.628 B.S. L.339 J.D. [Swain,H.&S.]
Seghetti, Michael R., (BV) .... '61 '86 C.339 B.S. L.602 J.D. [Elias,M.R.&S.]
Seneca, Michael S., (BV) ....'75 '00 C&L.801 B.S., J.D. [Howard&H.]
Serck, Duane L. ....'37 '65 C&L.502 B.A., J.D. Pres., Ill. Title Servs., Inc.
Sergey, James A. ....'49 '83 C.937 B.A. L.209 J.D. Soc. Sec. Admin.
Serritella, Gerard A., (BV) ....'44 '69 C&L.424 J.D. 124 S.W. Adams, Ste 700
Serritella, Judith A. .... '76 '01 C.339 B.A. L.801 J.D. [Ⓐ Westervelt,J.N.&K.]
Shadid, James E., (BV) ....'57 '83 C.98 B.S. L.365 J.D. Co. J.
Shah, Shital A. '71 '97 C&L.150 B.S., J.D.
(adm. in OH; not adm. in IL; Pat.) Caterpillar Inc.
Shoff, Marci M. ....'77 '02 C&L.339 B.S., j.d. [Ⓐ Hasselberg,R.B.&K.]
Shostrom, Stephen S. ....'42 '67 C.430 B.A. L.339 J.D. Reg. Atty., N.L.R.B.
Sielaff, Dale L. '46 '71 C&L.477 A.B., J.D.
(adm. in MI; not adm. in IL) Banc One Ill. Corp.
Silberstein, Robert L. .... '37 '63 C.339 B.S. L.421 LL.B. 333 Main St.
Simpson, Francis L. R. ....'44 '71 C.340 B.A. L.910 J.D. Caterpillar Tractor Co.
Sinn, David R., (AV) .... '50 '76 C.927 B.S. L.838 J.D. [Heyl,R.V.&A.]
Skarvan, Dennis C. '60 '92
C.1229 B.S.M.E. L.347 J.D. Asst. Gen. Pat. Coun., Caterpillar Inc. (Pat.)
Slayton, Douglas S., (BV) '62 '88
C&L.339 A.B., J.D. Citizens Equity Federal Credit Union
Slevin, John A., (AV) ....'35 '60 C&L.602 Ph.B., LL.B. [Vonachen,L.T.&S.]
Sloan, John F., (AV) ....'11 '36 C.602 B.C.S. L.597 J.D. 1202 N. Underhill St.‡
Smith, Adam R. '72 '99 C.94 B.A. L.1045 J.D.
(adm. in TN; not adm. in IL) Atty., Caterpillar Inc.
Smith, James R. ....'65 '97 C&L.336 B.S.M.E., J.D. Intell. Prop. Atty., Caterpillar Inc.
Smith, L. Lee, (AV) .... '53 '78 C.339 B.A. L.801 J.D. [Hinshaw&C.]
Smith, Matthew B., (BV) .... '67 '93 C&L.339 B.S., J.D. [Quinn,J.H.&P.]
Snodgrass, Kenneth M., Jr., (BV) '— '81 C&L.339 B.A., J.D.
[Hasselberg,W.G.S.&B.]
Solls, Joseph J. ....'30 '57 C.340 B.A. L.421 LL.B. 1101 Peoria Savings Plaza
Sorenson, Jeffrey G., (BV) .... '64 '89 C.473 B.A. L.339 J.D. [Howard&H.]

Sorling, Northrup, Hanna, Cullen and Cochran, Ltd., (AV)
Formerly Sorling, Catron and Hardin
401 S.W. Water Street Suite 301, 61602 ⊙
Telephone: 309-674-1144 Telecopier: 309-671-4368
Email: businessdevelopment@sorlinglaw.com URL: http://www.sorlinglaw.com
James D. Broadway.
General Civil Practice including Administrative Law, Agricultural Law, State and Federal Appellate Practice, Banking and Finance, Banking, Bankruptcy, Business Law, Civil Rights Defense, Commercial Law, Communications, Construction Law, Contract Preparation and Litigation, Corporate Law, Education Law, Elder Law, Election Law, Employee Benefits, Energy Law including Public Utilities, Environmental Law, Family Law, Illinois Governmental Advocacy and Representation, Health and Hospital Law, Insurance Regulation and Defense; Intellectual Property Rights, Labor and Employment Law, General State and Federal Litigation, News Media Representation, Mergers and Acquisitions, Municipal and Local Governmental Law, Natural Resources, Not for Profit Organizations, Personal Injury and Torts, Probate, Estate and Trust, Professional Liability and Disciplinary Defense, Products Liability, Real Estate, Securities, Taxation, Telecommunications, Trade and Professional Association Representation, Transportation Law, Workers Compensation, Zoning Planning and Land Use.
Counsel for: AmerenServices; Bank One; Illini Dairy Queen, Inc.; Springfield Airport Authority.
Representative Clients: CIGNA Insurance; WICS-TV, Inc.
Springfield Office: 800 Illinois Building, 607 East Adams Street, P.O. Box 5131, 62705. Telephone: 217-544-1144. Telecopier: 217-522-3173.
See Professional Biographies, PEORIA, ILLINOIS

Spanos, Christopher J., (BV) ....'63 '95 C.338 B.S. L.879 J.D. [Ⓐ Hinshaw&C.]
Spears, Christopher C., (CV) '68 '94
C.77 B.A. L.383 J.D. Gen. Coun., Asia-Pacific, Caterpillar Inc.
Sposato, Michael G. '64 '89 C&L.276 B.A., J.D.
(adm. in PA; not adm. in IL) Gen. Coun., Caterpillar Fin. Servs. Corp., Caterpillar Inc.
Springer, James W., (BV) ....'45 '86 C&L.339 A.B., J.D. [Kavanagh,S.S.W.&F.]
Stanley, Jason J. ..... '74 '00 C.98 B.S.C.E. L.339 J.D. Intell. Prop. Atty., Caterpillar Inc.
Steagall, Richard L., (AV) .... '53 '77 C.340 B.A. L.280 J.D. [Nicoara&S.]
Stefanik, Debra L. '57 '83 C.608 B.S. L.602 J.D.
(adm. in OH; not adm. in IL) Natl. Labor Relations Bd.
Stegall, Debra L., (BV) ....'55 '91 C.339 B.A. L.801 J.D. [Heyl,R.V.&A.]
Stensland, Craig W., (BV) '59 '85 C.98 B.S. L.436 J.D.
Corp. Secy., Central Ill. Light Co.
Stephens, G. Douglas, (BV) ...... '51 '77 C.589 B.A. L.365 J.D. [Stephens,F.M.&Assoc.]
Stephens, Fiddes, McGill, & Associates, P.C., (BV) .... 456 Fulton
Stockton, Pamela Steadley, (CV) '55 '80 C.475 B.A. L.424 J.D.
V.P. of Foster Care, Children's Home Assn. of Illinois
Stoffer, Christiane M. ....'59 '86 C.198 B.A. L.575 J.D. 211 Fulton St.
Straub, Marcia F., Attorney at Law '55 '78
C.1151 B.A. L.339 J.D. 411 Hamilton Blvd., Ste. 1936
Straub, Phillip B. '67 '96 C.679 B.S. L.734 J.D.
Corp. Atty., Solar Turbines, Inc., Caterpillar Inc.
Strodel, Robert C., (AV) ....'30 '55 C.597 B.S. L.477 J.D. [R.C.Strodel]

Strodel, Robert C., Ltd., (AV) ▣
927 Commerce Bank Building, 61602
Telephone: 309-676-4500 Fax: 309-676-4566 URL: http://www.attorneylocate.com
Email: stro927@aol.com URL: http://www.lawyers.com/strodellaw
Robert C. Strodel.
General Practice. Personal Injury Claims, with specialty in Medical Malpractice.
See Professional Biographies, PEORIA, ILLINOIS

Strong, Todd A., (CV) ....'68 '94 C.340 B.A. L.879 J.D. [Strong]
Strong Law Offices, (CV) ....3618 N. Sterling
Stuckel, David W., (AV) ....'47 '74 C.98 B.S. L.945 J.D. [Harvey&S.]
Stump, Jonathan A., (BV) ....'70 '96 C.1154 B.A. L.339 J.D. [Quinn,J.H.&P.]
Stumpe, Karen M., (AV) ....'54 '79 C.927 B.B. L.339 J.D. [Kavanagh,S.S.W.&F.]
Sudow, Joseph Z., (AV) ....'14 '38 C.477 A.B. L.309 LL.B. [Kavanagh,S.S.W.&F.]
Sullivan, Kevin F., (BV) .... '62 '88 C.436 B.A. L.221 J.D. 110 S.W. Jefferson
Sutkowski, Edward F., (AV) .... '39 '63 C.966 B.B.A. L.339 LL.B. [Sutkowski&R.]
Sutkowski & Rhoads Ltd., (AV) ....416 Main Street Suite 400
Swain, Tim, (AV) ....'39 '63 C&L.339 B.A., J.D. [Swain,H.&S.]
Swain, Hartshorn & Scott, (AV) ....411 Hamilton Boulevard, Suite 1812
Szydlowski, Roberta L. ....'40 '76 C.136 B.A. L.365 J.D. Asst. States Atty.
Taseff, George F., (BV) ....'55 '81 C.338 B.S. L.801 J.D. Fed. Pub. Def.
Taylor, Bret E. ....'67 '93 C.352 B.B.A. L.190 J.D. 456 Fulton St., Ste. 265
Taylor, Tobin J., (CV) .... '71 '96 C.98 B.S. L.910 J.D. [Ⓐ Heyl,R.V.&A.]
Teplitz, Jack B. .....'43 '69 C.339 B.S. L.209 J.D. V.P. & Gen. Coun., Cohen Develop. Co.
Thieneman, Kevin R. ....'63 '90 C.347 B.S. L.228 J.D. 100 N.E. Adams St.
Thomas, Dale Robert ....'58 '86 C.1106 B.A. L.365 J.D. Asst. State's Atty.
Thomas, Howard Vincent .... '44 '74 C.490 B.A. L.190 J.D. [H.V.Thomas]
Thomas, Howard V. ....110 S.W. Jefferson St., Ste. 530
Thompson, Bert M. ....'28 '53 C&L.966 B.S., LL.B. V.P. & Gen. Coun., RLI Corp.
Thompson, Clay ....'67 '93 C.132 B.A. L.352 J.D. Asia-Pacific Coun., Caterpillar Inc.
Thornton, Robert R., (AV) .... '26 '53 C.276 A.B. L.178 LL.B. 3715 Linden Lane‡
Tibbs, Michael J., (BV) ....'49 '75 C.339 B.S. L.734 J.D. [Miller,H.&T.]
Tomlin, James M., (BV) ....'42 '67 C&L.339 B.S., J.D. 5823 N. Forest Pk. Dr.
Toohill, Donald J., (BV) ....'45 '72 C.707 B.A. L.734 J.D. Asst. State's Atty.
Tornow, Medley A., (BV) .... '40 '65 C.801 A.B. L.339 J.D. [Safford,W.T.&J.] ⊙
Trager, Thomas H., (AV) ....'31 '59 C.197 A.B. L.339 J.D. [Vonachen,L.T.&S.]
Traicoff, Sandra M., (BV) ....'44 '78 C.378 B.A. L.209 J.D. [Howard&H.]
Triggs, Andrew C. '72 '98 C.118 B.A. L.477 J.D.
(adm. in MN; not adm. in IL) Atty., Caterpillar Inc.
Triggs, Dennis R., (AV) .... '44 '70 C.1070 B.S. L.276 J.D. [Miller,H.&T.]
Tucker, Charles E., Jr. .... '56 '82 C.602 B.A. L.209 J.D. Staff Atty., Natl. Labor Rel. Bd.
Ullman, Richard David ....'69 '94 C.473 B.S. L.734 J.D. 211 Hanover Place
Umland, Scott E., (BV) ....'60 '93 C.340 B.A. L.365 J.D. [Hafele,S.S.&G.]
Unrath, Craig L., (BV) ....'55 '91 C.1100 B.A. L.339 J.D. [Heyl,R.V.&A.]
Urban, Charles J., (BV) .... '— '89 C.339 B.S. L.801 J.D. [Hasselberg,W.G.S.&B.]
Vallejo, Estella .... '60 '85 C.221 B.S.B.A. L.352 J.D. Gen. Atty., Caterpillar Inc.
VanFleet, Joseph B., (AV) ....'64 '90 C&L.339 B.S., J.D. [J.B.VanFleet]

VanFleet, Joseph B., L.L.C., Law Office of, (AV)
Peoria Professional Building, 207 Main Street, Suite 500, 61602
Telephone: 309-672-2200 Facsimile: 309-672-2201
Email: jvanfleet@vanfleetlaw.com URL: http://www.lawyers.com/vanfleet
Member of Firm: Joseph B. VanFleet. Associate: John G. Dundas.
Commercial Litigation, Corporate Investigations, White Collar Criminal Defense, Real Estate Litigation, Real Estate Development, Real Estate Disputes, Alternative Dispute Resolution, Business Law.
See Professional Biographies, PEORIA, ILLINOIS

Varda, John M. .... '44 '73 C.424 B.B.A. L.213 J.D. Sr. Corp. Atty., Caterpillar Inc.
Venezky, Julian B. ....'09 '31 C.446 L.273 [Ⓑ Kavanagh,S.S.W.&F.]
Vermylen, Robert T. C. '72 '00 C&L.276 B.A., J.D.
(adm. in NY; not adm. in IL) Sr. Atty., Caterpillar, Inc.
Vespa, Joe R. .... '48 '77 C.98 B.S. L.365 J.D. Cir. J.
Vespa, John P., (BV) ....'57 '91 C.1247 B.S. L.801 J.D. 124 S.W. Adams Street, Suite 500
Vicary, Henry, III, (BV) ....'67 '94 C.98 B.S. L.221 J.D. [Ⓑ Schmidt&F.]
Vicary, Lester W., Jr., (CV) ....'52 '78 C.337 B.S. L.801 J.D. [Ⓑ Johnson,B.&N.]
Viets, Robert O. '43 '69 C.900 B.A. L.910 J.D.
(adm. in MO; not adm. in IL) Central Ill. Light Co.‡
Voelker, James M., (AV) .... '61 '86 C.339 B.S. L.352 J.D. [Heyl,R.V.&A.]
Vogel, Steven H., (BV) .... '47 '73 C.347 B.A. L.188 J.D. 416 main St., Ste. 1000
Vonachen, Donald F., (AV) ....'25 '50 C&L.339 B.S., J.D. [Ⓑ Vonachen,L.T.&S.]
Vonachen, Lawless, Trager & Slevin, (AV) .... 456 Fulton Street
Wakeman, Steven A., (AV) ....'53 '77 C.98 B.A. L.339 J.D. [Kingery D.W.&R.]
Waldman, John J., (CV) '62 '88 C.801 B.A. L.339 J.D.
[Ⓐ Kanoski&Assoc.] (⊙Bloomington, Macomb, Quincy, Rushville, Springfield)

Walker, C. Edwin, & Associates, (BV) '55 '82 C.801 B.A. L.339 J.D.
411 Hamilton, Suite 1710, 61602
Telephone: 309-674-3740 Fax: 309-674-3743
Email: ewalker627@aol.com URL: http://www.lawyers.com/walker
Associate: Barbara G. Phelps.
General Civil Practice, Commercial Law, Collections, Credit Law, Bankruptcy and Construction Law.
See Professional Biographies, PEORIA, ILLINOIS

Walters, Brent A., (BV) .....'64 '91 C.98 B.S. L.801 J.D. Sr. Corp. Atty., Caterpillar Inc.
Walton, Mark D., (CV) ....'67 '95 C.338 B.S. L.589 J.D. [Hunziker&W.]
Walvoord, David J., (AV) ....'40 '67 C.597 A.B. L.209 J.D. [Kavanagh,S.S.W.&F.]
Washkuhn, Wilson C., (AV) '42 '69 C.357 B.S. L.339 J.D.
124 S.W. Adams St., Ste. 560‡
Waters, M. Michael, (BV) .... '51 '79 C.338 B.S. L.365 J.D. [Ⓐ Vonachen,L.T.&S.]
Weaver, Charles E. ....'56 '83 C.98 B.S. L.209 J.D. Weaver Foods
Welsh, Kevin L. '63 '90 C.902 B.A. L.1017 J.D.
(adm. in PA; not adm. in IL) Corp. Atty., Singapore, Caterpillar Inc.
Wentworth, David L., II, (BV) ... '— '93 C.20 B.A. L.215 J.D. [Hasselberg,W.G.S.&B.]
West, Stephen J., (BV) .... '55 '82 C.339 B.A. L.801 J.D. [Ⓐ Safford,W.T.&J.] ⊙

Westervelt, Johnson, Nicoll & Keller, LLC, (AV)
14th Floor, 411 Hamilton Boulevard, 61602 ⊙
Telephone: 309-671-3550 Fax: 309-671-3588
URL: http://www.wjnklaw.com
Members of Firm: Frank T. Miller (1873-1948); O. P. Westervelt (1887-1970); Eugene R. Johnson (1899-1981); David A. Nicoll (1913-1993); Homer W. Keller; Ross E. Canterbury; Thomas G. Harvel; Roger E. Holzgrafe; Daniel L. Johns; Kevin D. Schneider; James R. Morrison; Thomas W. O'Neal; Charles Couri; Thomas A. McConnaughay. Associates: Michele A. Miller; Judith A. Serritella; Ronald W. Hasinger. Of Counsel: William L. Blake.
General Civil Trial and Appellate Practice in State and Federal Courts, Insurance Defense, Health and Health Care, Labor Relations, Employment Discrimination and Affirmative Action, Products Liability Litigation, ERISA and Benefits Plans, Corporate, Agricultural, Bankruptcy, Creditors' Rights, Banking, Real Estate, State and Federal Taxation, Estate Planning, Trusts and Probate, Workers Compensation, Environmental, Commercial.
Representative Clients: Allstate Insurance Cos.; Bituminous Insurance Companies; Caterpillar Inc.; Citizens Equity First Credit Union; Eureka College; Hertz Corporation; John Deere Co.; Metropolitan Life Insurance Co.; Perry Memorial Hospital; State Farm Insurance Cos.
Macomb, Illinois Office: MidAmerica Banking Center, 130 North Side Square, Suite 202, 61435. Telephone: 309-836-2900. Fax: 309-836-2844.

See Professional Biographies, PEORIA, ILLINOIS

Wetherill, Jo Tewes ... '71 '97 C&L.352 B.S., J.D. [Ⓐ Quinn,J.H.&P.]
White, Eugene L., (AV) ... '17 '42 C.602 L.424 J.D. [Ⓒ Kavanagh,S.S.W.&F.]
Whitney, John A. ... '21 '49 C.894 A.B. L.477 LL.B. Ret. Assoc. Cir. J.‡
Wilbur, R. Carl, Jr. '62 '91 C.216 B.S. L.352 J.D.
Sr. Corp. Atty., Caterpillar Inc. (Pat.)
Williams, Harry M., (BV) ... '57 '82 C.338 B.S. L.734 J.D. 414 Hamilton Blvd., Ste. 210
Williams, Raymond C., (BV) '— '80 C.357 B.M.E. L.339 J.D.
[Hasselberg,W.G.S.&B.]
Williams, Roy L. ... '70 '98 C.154 B.A. L.424 J.D. [Ⓐ M.F.Hupy&Assoc.] ⊙
Williams, Sonni Choi ... '69 '99 C.352 B.A. L.589 J.D. City of Peoria
Williamson, Nile J., (BV) ... '47 '72 C.352 B.A. L.221 J.D. 1926 Associated Bank Plz.
Wilson, Lisa, (BV) '62 '88
C.339 B.A. L.589 J.D. Mng. Atty., Praire State Legal Servs., Inc.
Winget, Walter W., (AV) ... '36 '62 C.674 A.B. L.477 J.D. [Ⓒ Winget&K.]
Winget & Kane, (AV) ... 411 Hamilton Boulevard, Suite 1711
Winne, Joseph E., (AV) ... '— '76 C.707 B.A. L.300 J.D. [Prusak,W.&G.]
Wisdom, Michael J., (BV) '54 '79
C.927 B.A. L.813 J.D. V.P. & Gen. Coun., The Joseph Co.
Wise, Michael J. ... '73 '99 C.665 B.A. L.201 J.D. Caterpillar Inc.
Wolfe, J. Kevin, (BV) ... '60 '86 C.339 B.A. L.1292 J.D. 331 Fulton St., Ste. 900
Wolfe, Jennifer L. ... '74 '99 C.339 B.A. L.589 J.D. [Cassidy&M.]
Wombacher, William C., (AV) '54 '79 C.602 B.A. L.352 J.D.
416 Main Streeet, Suite 700
Woods, Michael L. '72 '02 C.174 B.S.M.E. L.273 J.D.
Patent Atty., Caterpillar Inc. (Pat.)
Wyant, John M. ... '46 '94 C.473 B.S. Ed. L.851 J.D. Illinois Central College
Young, Charles H., (AV) ... '48 '73 C.57 A.B. L.339 J.D. [Husch&E.]
Young, Craig S., (AV) ... '60 '85 C.98 B.A. L.339 J.D. [Heyl,R.V.&A.]
Zabek, Samuel B. ... '74 '02 C.37 B.S. L.424 J.D. 309-A Main St.
Zhu, Jiming, (BVⓉ) ... '61 '91 C&L.585 M.A., J.D. Sr. Corp. Atty., Caterpillar Inc.
Zmugg, Leslie '69 '94 C.1349 B.A. L.262 J.D.
(adm. in NJ; not adm. in IL) Corp. Atty., Caterpillar Inc.

Zuckerman, Richard W., (AV) '51 '76 C.98 B.S. L.365 J.D.
415 Hamilton Boulevard, 61602
Telephone: 309-637-3732 Fax: 309-637-5788
Email: rwzuckermanesq@insightbb.com
Family Law, Divorce, Post-Divorce, Mediation, Appeals, Paternity, Child Custody, Child Support, Visitation Rights, Adoption Law.

See Professional Biographies, PEORIA, ILLINOIS

Zundel, Jurg ... '53 '88 L.966 J.D. Mng. Atty., Caterpillar Inc.

PEORIA HEIGHTS, 6,635, *Peoria & Woodford Cos.*

Broers, Lynette Alaine ... '70 '95 C.347 B.A. L.352 J.D. 1717 E. Terrace Ct.

PEOTONE, 3,385, *Will Co.*

Coleman, Robert L. ... '15 '63 C.339 B.S. L.146 LL.B. 122 N. 2nd St.‡
Knuth, Thomas J., Law Offices of, (BV) ... '60 '85 C.339 B.A. L.424 J.D. 103 E. Main St.
Roberts, Evan D. ... '30 '61 C.339 B.S. L.146 J.D. 119 N. Second St. (Pat.)‡

PERU, 9,835, *La Salle Co.*

Andreoni, James A., (BV) ... '54 '79 C.98 B.S. L.734 J.D. [Perona]
Brandt, Jonathan F., (BV) ... '58 '88 C.338 B.S. L.365 J.D. [Duncan&B.]
Duncan & Brandt, P.C., (BV) ... 1800 Fourth Street
Fisher, John W., (CV) ... '53 '91 C.234 B.S. L.365 J.D. 925 Shooting Park Rd., Ste. 1
Ganassin, Scott J. ... '61 '87 C.589 B.A. L.365 J.D. [Schweickert&G.]
Hannigan, Henry Jay ... '41 '88 C.846 B.B.A. L.589 J.D. 1627 Shooting Park Rd.
Helmig, Charles W., III, (BV) '37 '64 C&L.339 B.S., LL.B.
1824 Fourth St. (⊙Granville)

Herbolsheimer, Lannon, Henson, Duncan and Reagan, P.C.
(See La Salle)

Lasorella, William T., (BV) ... '50 '75 C.424 B.S. L.339 J.D. 1611 5th St.
Leynaud, George G., (BV) ... '58 '83 C.98 B.S. L.1187 J.D. [Leynaud&L.]
Leynaud, Rebecca M., (BV) ... '65 '90 C.98 B.S. L.589 J.D. [Leynaud&L.]

Leynaud & Leynaud, A Prof. Corp., Law Offices of, (BV)
1200 38th Street, 61354-2005
Telephone: 815-224-4700 Fax: 815-224-4703 URL: http://www.leynaudlaw.com
Email: george@leynaudlaw.com URL: http://www.lawyers.com/leynaud&leynaud
George G. Leynaud; Rebecca M. Leynaud.
General Civil and Trial Practice, Personal Injury, Mediation, Worker's Compensation, Real Estate, Criminal, Landlord/Tenant and Family Law. Business/Banking Litigation, DUI and Traffic. Insurance, General Practice, Medical Malpractice, Zoning and Land Use. Bad Faith, Drug Crimes, Juvenile Crimes, White Collar, Adoptions, Child Custody, Divorce, Child Support, Visitation Rights, Domestic Violence. Auto Accidents, Dog Bites, Slip and Fall, Wrongful Death, Buying and Selling, Wills and Probate.
References: Peru Federal Savings & Loan Association, Peru; Union Bank, Peru; La Salle National Bank, La Salle, Illinois; Amcore Bank; First State Bank.

See Professional Biographies, PERU, ILLINOIS

McPhedran, James A., (BV) ... '50 '75 C.589 B.S. L.365 J.D. [Ⓐ A.C.Raccuglia&Assoc.]
Olivero, Douglas B. ... '54 '79 C.339 B.S. L.221 J.D. 1615 Fourth St.
Olivero, John, (BV) ... '24 '50 C.597 L.339 LL.B. 1211 5th St. (⊙Tonica)
Olivero, Lisa M., (BV) ... '57 '82 C&L.339 B.S., J.D. 1611 5th St.
Olivero, Louis E. ... '32 '60 C&L.339 B.S., J.D. [L.E.Olivero&Assoc.]
Olivero, Louis E., & Associates ... 1615 Fourth St.
Perona, Michael James ... '75 '00 C.602 B.A. L.424 J.D. 4110 Progress Blvd.
Perona, Paul D., (BV) ... '38 '63 C.602 B.A. L.597 J.D. 4110 Progress Blvd.
Perona Law Offices, (BV) ... 4110 Progress Blvd. (⊙Oglesby)
Popurella, Brad ... '76 '01 C.339 B.A. L.589 J.D. [Ⓐ A.C.Raccuglia&Assoc.]
Raccuglia, Anthony C., (AV) '33 '59 C.339 B.S. L.365 J.D.
[A.C.Raccuglia&Assoc.] ⊙

Raccuglia, Anthony C., & Associates, P.C., (AV) BR
1200 Maple Drive, 61354 ⊙
Telephone: 815-223-0230
Email: raccuglialaw@insightbb.com URL: http://raccuglialawoffice.lawoffice
Anthony C. Raccuglia. Associates: James A. McPhedran; Brad Popurella.
General Civil and Trial Practice in all State and Federal Courts. Personal Injury, Medical Malpractice, Products Liability, Workers Compensation, Probate, Real Estate, Construction Accidents, Structural Work Cases, Business Litigation.
References: La Salle National Bank; Citizens First National Bank of Peru, Illinois.
Ottawa, Illinois Office: 633 La Salle Street. Telephone: 815-434-2003.

See Professional Biographies, PERU, ILLINOIS

Schley, Gregory R. ... '70 '99 C.352 B.B.A. L.589 J.D. [Ⓐ Duncan&B.]
Schweickert, Douglas J., (BV) '52 '77 C.98 B.S. L.339 J.D.
City Atty. [Schweickert&G.]
Schweickert and Ganassin, (BV) ... 2101 Marquette Rd.
Zukowski, Walter J., (BV) ... '54 '80 C.1247 B.A. L.602 J.D. 817 Peoria St.

PETERSBURG, * 2,261, *Menard Co.*

Baumgarten, Kenneth R., (BV) ... '58 '85 C&L.801 B.S., J.D. State Atty.
Becker, Eldon H., (AV) ... '41 '66 C.98 B.A. L.339 LL.B. [Grosboll,B.&T.] (⊙Havana)
Blane, Samuel S., (AV) ... '20 '49 C.388 A.B. L.339 J.D. 102 E. Jackson St.
Germeraad, John H., (BV) ... '45 '69 C.340 B.A. L.802 J.D. 113 N. 7th St.
Grosboll, John E., (AV) ... '18 '48 C.339 B.S. L.477 J.D. [Grosboll,B.&T.]
Grosboll, Becker & Tice, (AV) ... 101 E. Douglas (⊙Havana, Virginia)
Lewis, Jefferson, (AV) ... '13 '36 C&L.339 A.B., J.D. 148 Beech Dr.‡
Lipe, Lyle E. ... '32 '59 C&L.339 B.S., LL.B. Cir. J.

Lipsky, Nolan, Law Offices of, (AV) '44 '69 C.339 B.S. L.146 J.D. BR
106 East Jackson Street, 62675 ⊙
Telephone: 217-632-2612 Toll Free: 888-662-2612 Fax: 217-632-2450
URL: http://www.nolanlipsky.com
Family Law, Divorce, Custody, Paternity, Personal Injury, Criminal.
Springfield Office: 1100 South 5th Street, 62703. Telephone: 217-789-1607.

See Professional Biographies, PETERSBURG, ILLINOIS

Pope, M. Carol ... '54 '79 C.339 B.S. L.209 J.D. Cir. J.
Smith, Charles K., (BV) ... '54 '79 C.340 B.A. L.733 J.D. 101 E. Douglas
Tice, Homer J., (BV) ... '40 '66 C&L.339 B.S., LL.B. [Grosboll,B.&T.] (⊙Virginia)
Tippey, Kevin D. ... '74 '02 C.248 B.A. L.801 J.D. 101 E. Douglas

PINCKNEYVILLE, * 5,464, *Perry Co.*

Bigham, Donald, (BV) ... '53 '78 C.801 B.A. L.339 J.D. [Johnson,S.&B.]
Boester, Kevin L. ... '61 '93 C.234 B.S. L.801 J.D. 1 N. Main
Campanella, James W., (BV) ... '50 '75 C.338 B.S. L.365 J.D. Co. J.

Hart and Hart
(See Benton)

Johnson, Don E., (AV) ... '39 '61 C.357 A.B. L.339 LL.B. [Johnson,S.&B.]

Johnson, Seibert & Bigham, (AV)
One North Main, P.O. Box 467, 62274
Telephone: 618-357-2178 Fax: 618-357-3314
Email: jsbattorneys@midamer.net URL: http://www.lawyers.com/js&b
Members of Firm: Don E. Johnson; Roger H. Seibert; Donald Bigham.
General Civil Practice, Probate, Trust, Estate Planning, Real Estate, Oil and Gas and Coal Law, Federal and State Taxation, Banking, Corporate, Negligence, Municipal, School and Family Law, Trial and Appellate Practice.

See Professional Biographies, PINCKNEYVILLE, ILLINOIS

Pyatt, Gayl Simonds, (BV) ... '42 '76 C.339 A.B. L.801 J.D. One W. Laurel St.
Saigh, Jennifer Phipps ... '74 '98 C&L.801 B.A., J.D. Asst. States Atty.
Seibert, Roger H., (BV) ... '46 '74 C&L.879 B.S., J.D. [Johnson,S.&B.]
Stanton, David N. ... '58 '91 C.504 B.A. L.801 J.D. Asst. State's Atty.

PITTSFIELD, * 4,231, *Pike Co.*

Burrows, Cecil J. ... '22 '52 C.932 B.S. L.597 J.D. Ret. Cir. J.
Filbert, Walker R., Law Office of, (BV) '60 '92 C.339 B.S. L.910 J.D.
112 W. Washington
Grigsby, Professional Corporation, (AV) ... 130 South Monroe Street
Grigsby, Lewis M., Sr., (AV) ... '21 '48 C&L.339 A.B., J.D. [Grigsby]
Grote, Paul F., (BV) ... '11 '37 C&L.339 B.A., LL.B. 127 1/2 Madison St.
Hollahan, Michael J., (BV) ... '51 '77 C.338 B.S. L.424 J.D. [Hollahan]
Hollahan Law Office, (BV) ... 109 E. Wash. St.
Irving, Brett, (CV) ... '55 '81 C.927 B.S. L.221 J.D. [Irving&I.]
Irving, Michael Brett ... '55 '81 C.927 B.A. L.221 J.D. 118 E. Adams St.
Irving & Irving, P.C., (CV) ... 118 E. Adams Street
Lowry, William E., (BV) ... '43 '70 C&L.500 B.B.A., J.D. [W.Lowry]
Lowry, William, (BV) ... 130 S. Madison
Roseberry, Michael R., (CV) ... '54 '79 C.927 B.S. L.910 J.D. Co. Courthouse
Shaw, David B., Attorney at Law, (CV) ... '50 '81 C.502 B.S. L.1187 J.D. 303 E. Adams

PLAINFIELD, 13,038, *Will Co.*

Avril, Gary L. '52 '79 C.339 B.S. L.365 J.D.
Asst. Gen Coun, Chicago Bridge & Iron Co.
Buck, Carl R. ... '68 '97 C.152 B.A. L.365 J.D. [Rathbun,C.&K.] (⊙Joliet)
Cann, Martin J. ... '67 '92 C.339 B.A. L.608 J.D. 13422 S. Columbine Cir.
Clark, Sandra R. ... '69 '94 C&L.589 B.A., J.D. 23101 W. Lincoln Highway
Cowgill, Sandra Cirricione ... '50 '77 C.338 B.S. L.365 J.D. 106 N. Sunshine Cir.

Fogelman, Jerry A. '56 '81 C.347 B.S. L.1119 J.D.
13122 Merganser Cove, 60544
Telephone: 815-685-3538 Fax: 815-254-6917
Email: jerryfogelman@att.net URL: http://www.fogelmanlawoffice.com
Litigation, Business Law, Corporate Law, Family Law, Divorce, Child Custody, Personal Injury and Medical Malpractice, Real Estate, General Practice.

See Professional Biographies, PLAINFIELD, ILLINOIS

Graney, James J. ... '58 '83 C.210 B.A. L.365 J.D. 25428 Blakely Dr.
Gruber, Patricia T. ... '67 '92 C.339 B.S. L.966 J.D. [Gruber]
Gruber, Priscilla H. ... '39 '78 C.801 B.A. L.1151 J.D. 23214 W. Lincoln Hwy.
Gruber Law Office ... 23214 W. Lincoln Hwy.
Helenhouse, Pennie Marie ... '60 '92 C.1151 B.S. L.146 J.D. 401 West Lockport
Kinealy, Paul V. ... '70 '96 C.861 B.S. L.146 J.D. [Kinealy,W.&W.]
Kinealy, Wilkens and Wilkens ... 10061 Clow Creek Road
Kramer, Robert F. ... '67 '93 C&L.589 J.D. 23101 W. Lincoln Hwy.
Maloney, Katherine L., (BV) '67 '94 C.589 B.A. L.273 J.D.
[Ⓐ Rathbun,C.&K.] (⊙Joliet)
Marker, Jason A. ... '75 '01 C.338 B.S. L.365 J.D. 13040 Meadow Ln.

Meszaros, Patrick A., Law Office of
(See Joliet)

Patterson, Lawrence F. ....'42 '68 C&L.424 B.S., J.D. 21518 W. Douglas Ct.
Plachta, Kevin F., The Law Office of '63 '89 C.424 B.A. L.365 J.D.
16125 Vintage Drive
Rathbun, Cservenyak & Kozol, LLC, (BV) ....618 West Main Street (☉Joliet, Mokena)
Rickmon, Roger D., (BV) ..... '53 '80 C.1151 B.A. L.365 J.D. 530 Lockport St., Ste. 208
Schielke, Kent J. ....'52 '78 C.339 B.A. L.477 J.D. Chicago Bridge & Iron Co.
Whitley, Robert G., Jr., (BV) .... '44 '70 C.340 B.S. L.352 J.D. 704 N. Des Plaines St.
Wilkens, Mary Frances ....'66 '01 [Kinealy,W.&W.]
Wilkens, W. Scott ....'68 '95 C.234 B.A. L.146 J.D. [Kinealy,W.&W.]
Wright, Craig T., (AV) ....'31 '60 C&L.352 B.A., LL.B. 23160 W. Lincoln Hwy.

PLANO, 5,633, *Kendall Co.*

Joyner, Wade R. .... '64 '88 C.679 B.A. L.823 J.D. 275 Ash Road (☉Aurora)
Krentz, Peter L., (BV) ....'32 '56 C&L.879 B.A., J.D. [Krentz&K.]
Krentz, Stephen L., (BV) ....'65 '90 C&L.879 B.A., J.D. [Krentz&K.]
Krentz & Krentz, P.C., (BV) ....100 W. Main St.
Rea, Charles R. ....'57 '85 C.894 B.A. L.365 J.D. 105 E. South St.

PLEASANT PLAINS, 745, *Sangamon Co.*

Aldridge, Shayne L. ....'64 '97 C.589 B.S.Ed. L.801 J.D. 113 Sycamore

POLO, 2,514, *Ogle Co.*

Suits, M. Thomas ....'50 '90 C&L.589 B.A., J.D. [M.T.Suits]
Suits, M. Thomas, Law Offices of, P.C. ....114 W. Mason St.

PONTIAC, * 11,864, *Livingston Co.*

Babb, David J., Jr. ....'59 '87 C.340 B.A. L.801 J.D. 303 W. Madison St.
Bauknecht, Jennifer H. ....'67 '94 C.339 L.365 J.D. [Strong,B.S.&B.]
Bertram, William H., (BV) ....'61 '88 C.1082 B.A. L.734 J.D. [Satter,B.B.&G.]
Beyer, John A., (AV) ....'45 '70 C.589 B.S. L.339 J.D. [Satter,B.B.&G.]
Blakeman, C. Thomas, (BV) ....'49 '75 C&L.339 B.A., J.D. [Strong,B.S.&B.]
Brown, Thomas John, (BV) ....'53 '82 C.338 B.S. L.851 J.D. State's Atty.
Casson, James A., (BV) ....'56 '81 C.338 B.S. L.424 J.D. Asst. States Atty.
Caughey, Robert R., (BV) ....'40 '66 C&L.339 B.S., J.D. [Caughey,L.&F.] ☉
Caughey, Legner & Freehill, (BV) ....204 N. Main St. (☉Chenoa)
Clay, Alonzo W., (BV) ....'16 '40 C.388 B.A. L.477 J.D. 306 N. Plum
Fellheimer, Mark A. ....'72 '97 C.36 B.S. L.879 J.D. [Ⓐ Fellheimer]
Fellheimer, Ronald K., (AV) ....'38 '64 C.339 B.S. L.365 J.D. [Fellheimer]
Fellheimer Law Firm, (AV) ....210 North Main Street
Follmer, Robert P., (BV) ....'50 '80 C.339 B.S. L.365 J.D. 210 North Main Street
Frank, Charles H. ....'48 '77 C.338 B.S. L.365 J.D. Assoc. Cir. J.
Freehill, John A., (BV) ....'48 '77 C.339 B.A. L.800 J.D. [Caughey,L.&F.] ☉
Frobish, Harold J. ....'43 '68 C&L.339 B.A., J.D. Cir. J.
Gabor, Brian M. ....'73 '98 C.339 B.A. L.209 J.D. [Satter,B.B.&G.]
Glennon, Charles E. ....'42 '66 C&L.339 B.A., J.D. Ret. Cir. J.‡
Herr, James J., (BV) '30 '54
C&L.602 Ph.B., LL.B. 103 N. Main St. (☉Chatsworth, Kempton)
Herr, Thomas E., (BV) ....'66 '92 C.602 B.A. L.146 LL.B. 103 N. Main St.
Jackson, Daniel Clark ....'51 '01 C.72 B.A. L.339 J.D. Asst. State Atty.
Johnson, Taylor F., (BV) ....'47 '72 C.597 B.A. L.339 J.D. [Johnson&T.]

Johnson & Taylor, (AV)
Formerly Ortman, Johnson & Taylor
109 North Mill Street, P.O. Box 497, 61764-0497
Telephone: 815-844-7151 Fax: 815-844-7539
Members of Firm: F. A. Ortman (1882-1955); J. Kenneth Johnson (1912-2000). Partners: John A. Taylor; Taylor F. Johnson.
General Practice. Probate, Estate Planning, Tax and Real Estate Law.
Attorneys For: Flanagan State Bank; Good Samaritan Home of Flanagan; Villages of Flanagan and Long Point; Flanagan-Graymont and Reddick and Long Point Fire Districts; CAPS and Flanagan Park Districts; Evenglow Lodge; Oliver Trusts.
See Professional Biographies, PONTIAC, ILLINOIS

Legner, Edward J., (BV) ....'47 '73 C.707 B.A. L.365 J.D. [Caughey,L.&F.]
Loy, Rodney H., (BV) ....'43 '69 C.388 A.B. L.339 J.D. 300 N. Ladd St.
Luckman, Carey J., (BV) ....'53 '79 C.339 B.A. L.424 J.D. 214 W. Washington St.
Malin, Michael Eveland ....'73 '01 C&L.801 B.S., J.D. Asst. State's Atty.
Myers, Curtis W., (CV) ....'43 '73 C&L.339 B.S., J.D. 200 W. Madison St.
Satter, John G., (AV) ....'33 '59 C.793 B.A. L.145 J.D. [Ⓒ Satter,B.B.&G.]
Satter, Beyer, Bertram & Gabor, (AV) ....402 N. Plum St. (☉Collinsville)
Schrock, Alan M., (BV) ....'56 '81 C.338 B.S. L.339 J.D. [Strong,B.S.&B.]
Smith, Sidney E. ....'25 '51 C&L.339 B.S., J.D. 117 N. Mill
Steffen, Johnathan E. ....'72 '02 C.338 B.A. L.589 J.D. [Ⓐ Caughey,L.&F.]
Stodd, Walter L. ....'25 '51 C.98 L.209 J.D. 529 E. Indiana Ave.‡
Strong, Kenneth L., (AV) ....'28 '52 C.894 B.A. L.597 J.D. [Strong,B.S.&B.]
Strong, Blakeman, Schrock & Bauknecht, Ltd., (AV) ....307 W. Washington St.
Taylor, John A., (AV) ....'25 '50 C&L.597 B.S., J.D. [Johnson&T.]
Travers, Robert M., (AV) ....'49 '77 C.339 B.A. L.879 J.D. [Fellheimer]

POPLAR GROVE, 1,368, *Boone Co.*

Koller, Nancy Paterson ... '53 '80 C.112 B.A. L.597 J.D. 214 Tamarack Hollow St., S.W.‡
Walsh, Richard P. ....'52 '84 C&L.209 B.S., J.D. 1008 Candlewick Dr., N.E.‡

POSEN, 4,730, *Cook Co.*

Spangler, Walter L. '41 '75 C.932 B.S. L.969 J.D.
(adm. in GA; not adm. in IL) Interlake Steele, Inc.

PRAIRIE VIEW, —, *Lake Co.*

Peth, Fred J. ....'30 '57 C&L.209 A.B., LL.B. 30323N. Clarice Ave.

PRINCETON, * 7,501, *Bureau Co.*

Anderson, Daniel C. .... '— '04 C.927 B.A. L.801 J.D. [Ⓐ Russell,E.S.&B.]
Angel, Roger K., (AV) ....'43 '74 C&L.339 B.S., J.D. [Angel,I.&T.]
Angel, Isaacson & Tracy, (AV) ....111 Park Avenue East
Beneke, William S., (BV) ....'53 '79 C.187 B.A. L.623 J.D. [Russell,E.S.&B.]
Bernabei, Marc P., (AV) ....'54 '81 C.1151 B.A. L.589 J.D. Cir. J.
Caffarini, Geno J. ....'61 '87 C.589 B.A. L.1187 J.D. Asst. State's Atty.
Carlson, Wayne S. ....'51 '79 C.339 B.S. L.801 J.D. 1019 S. 5th St.★
Comba, Alan R. ....'42 '67 C.37 B.A. L.352 J.D. [Comba]
Comba Law Firm ....777 S. Main St., Ste. C
English, Michael L., (BV) ....'53 '78 C.347 B.A. L.494 J.D. [Russell,E.S.&B.]
Gunning, Stephen H., (BV) ....'44 '69 C.477 A.B. L.339 J.D. 714 S. Pleasant St.
Henneberry, Michael L., (CV) ....'55 '81 C.338 B.A. L.209 J.D. [M.L.Henneberry]
Henneberry, Michael L., PC, (CV) ....408 S. Main St.
Herrmann, Patrick J., (BV) ....'59 '84 C.339 B.A. L.589 J.D. Resident Cir. J.
Hornbaker, Richard R. ....'49 '74 C.597 B.S. L.339 J.D. Rte. 4, Box 235A‡
Isaacson, John C., (BV) ....'48 '77 C.589 B.S. L.339 J.D. [Angel,I.&T.]

Leynaud & Leynaud, A Prof. Corp., Law Offices of
(See Peru)

Maloney, Matthew A., (BV) ....'45 '73 C.712 B.S. L.734 J.D. [Pierson,M.&R.]
Martin, Donald C., (AV) ....'25 '52 C.502 A.B. L.352 LL.B. [Ⓒ Russell,E.S.&B.]
Pierson, Maloney & Rayfield, (BV) ....620 South Main Street

Raccuglia, Anthony C., & Associates, P.C.
(See Peru)

Rayfield, Donald R., (BV) ....'53 '78 C&L.339 B.S., J.D. [Pierson,M.&R.]
Roush, Gary Richard ....'41 '87 C.927 B.A. L.1029 J.D. R.R. 4
Russell, Daniel K., (AV) ....'44 '69 C.927 B.A. L.339 J.D. [Russell,E.S.&B.]
Russell, Robert F., (BV) ....'48 '74 C.813 A.B. L.339 J.D. [Russell,E.S.&B.]

Russell, English, Scoma & Beneke, P.C., (AV)
(Formerly, Johnson, Martin, Russell, English, Scoma & Beneke, P.C.)
Ten Park Avenue West, 61356
Telephone: 815-875-4555 Fax: 815-875-2211
Email: tenpark@theramp.net
Daniel K. Russell; Robert F. Russell; Michael L. English; Paul M. Scoma; William S. Beneke;—Daniel C. Anderson. Of Counsel: Donald C. Martin.
General Civil, Trial and Appellate Practice. Probate, Real Estate, Insurance, Corporation, Governmental, Taxation, Employment and Family Law.
See Professional Biographies, PRINCETON, ILLINOIS

Scoma, Paul M., (BV) ....'52 '82 C.589 B.A. L.424 J.D. [Russell,E.S.&B.]
Straub, Donald A. ....'33 '58 C.46 B.S. L.209 J.D. Exec. Consultant, Dor-O-Matic Inc.
Tracy, Daniel F., (BV) ....'49 '79 C.658 B.S. L.425 J.D. [Angel,I.&T.]
Trimble, Howard B., (BV) ....'19 '51 C.484 B.A. L.500 J.D. 111 Park Ave.
Wampler, C. Howard ....'33 '58 C.340 B.S. L.339 LL.B. Cir. J.
Wimbiscus, James J. ....'37 '61 C&L.209 B.S., J.D. Assoc. Cir. J.

PRINCEVILLE, 1,621, *Peoria Co.*

Cordis, Kerry R., (BV) ....'43 '70 C.339 B.A. L.365 J.D. [K.R.Cordis]
Cordis, Kerry R., Ltd., (BV) ....112 E. Main St.
Gilles, Mark E., (BV) ....'66 '91 C.338 B.A. L.339 J.D. 129 N. Walnut

PROPHETSTOWN, 2,023, *Whiteside Co.*

Copeland, Rod W., (BV) ....'48 '77 C.350 B.S. L.801 J.D. 107 E. 3rd St.
Sipe, Donald L., (BV) ....'18 '42 C.513 L.209 107 E. 3rd St.

PROSPECT HEIGHTS, 17,081, *Cook Co.*

Adams, James A. '64 '94 C.475 B.A. L.1187 J.D.
(adm. in MI; not adm. in IL) Sr. Coun., HSBC Finance Corp.
Arias, Elizabeth De Paula '61 '87 C.129 B.A. L.128 J.D.
(adm. in NJ; not adm. in IL) Assoc. Gen. Coun., HSBC Finance Corp.
Bak, Mary E. ....'62 '92 C.339 B.A. L.146 J.D. Coun., HSBC-North America
Black, Kenneth W. '30 '59 C&L.734 B.S., LL.B.
(adm. in MO; not adm. in IL) 207 Tully Pl.‡
Bouc, David C. '55 '83 C.399 B.A. L.615 J.D.
Assoc. Gen. Coun., HSBC-North America
Bromley, Nancy Johnson '55 '81
C.1106 B.A. L.424 J.D. Gen. Coun., HSBC Financial Corp.
Budish, Andrew M. '62 '87
C.339 B.A. L.46 J.D. Assoc. Gen. Coun., HSBC Finance Corp.
Burak, Janet L. '56 '81 C.264 B.A. L.564 J.D.
(adm. in NY; not adm. in IL) Asst. Gen. Coun. Reg., HSBC North America
Burke, Aimee L. ....'61 '86 C.339 A.B. L.597 J.D. Sr. Coun., Household Finance Corp.
Buschardt-Pisarczyk, Karen '68 '95 C&L.734 B.S., J.D.
Sr. Coun., HSBC Finance Corp.
Cantu, Kristin L. '65 '97
C.475 B.A. L.145 J.D. Sr. Coun., Household Mortgage Servs., Inc.
Carlson, Michael M., (AV) '46 '72 C.424 A.B. L.597 J.D.
Ass't Gen. Coun.- Benefits, HSBC Finance Corp.
Davenport, Julie A. '60 '85 C.750 L.365 J.D.
Gen. Coun., Household Retail Servs., USA
Davis, Tiffany R. .... '72 '98 C&L.597 B.S., J.D. Coun., HSBC-North America
Dubinski, Leon E. ....'46 '80 210 Fairway Ct.
Farber, Luke '61 '90 C.569 B.A. L.564 J.D.
(adm. in NY; not adm. in IL) Assoc. Gen. Coun., HSBC North America
Ferguson, Paula S. '58 '83
C.393 B.A. L.93 J.D. Gen. Coun., Household Credit Servs., Inc.
Forde, Michael J. '61 '87 C.477 B.A. L.845 J.D.
(adm. in TX; not adm. in IL) Assoc. Gen. Coun., HSBC Finance Corp.
Gudgeon, Le Roy W. ....'22 '49 C&L.424 A.B., J.D. 79 Country Club Dr.‡
Hollevoet, Cecile '55 '81 C&L.999 B.A., J.D.
(adm. in NY; not adm. in IL) Assoc. Gen. Coun., HSBC North America
Jefferson, Thomas S. '50 '77 C.207 B.A. L.245 J.D.
Assoc. Gen. Coun., Household Mortgage Servs., Inc.
Jewell, Susan B. '55 '79 C.659 A.B. L.597 J.D.
Dep. Gen. Coun., Opers., HSBC Finance Corp.
Juffernbruch, Dale I. '63 '90 C.112 B.A. L.273 J.D.
(adm. in VA; not adm. in IL) Coun., Household Bk.
Kirschner, Ian M. '55 '80 C.1349 B.A. L.94 J.D.
(adm. in NY; not adm. in IL) Assoc. Gen. Coun., HSBC North America
Leggette, Lemire '49 '74 C.411 B.A. L.597 J.D.
Assoc. Gen. Coun., HSBC Finance Corp.
Leopold, Mark F. '50 '75 C.30 B.A. L.424 J.D.
Ass't Gen. Coun.- Litig. & Emp., HSBC Finance Corp.
Levy, Judd A. '68 '93 C.347 B.S. L.365 J.D.
Dep. Gen. Coun., Household Mortgage Servs., Inc.
Litman, Helena '48 '81 C&L.569 A.B.D., J.D.
(adm. in NY; not adm. in IL) Assoc. Gen. Coun., HSBC North America
Mancini, Rose C. '55 '80 C.339 B.S. L.146 J.D.
Grp. Gen. Coun., HSBC Finance Corp.
Marks, Donna L. '62 '91
C.209 B.S.C. L.365 J.D. Assoc. Gen. Coun., HSBC Finance Corp.
Mattenson, Laurie S. '58 '84
C.339 B.A. L.146 J.D. Assoc. Gen. Coun., HSBC Finance Corp.
McKnight, Michael K. '68 '96 C.1275 B.A. L.209 J.D.
Sr. Coun., HSBC Finance Corp.
Melcer, David ....'56 '81 C.339 B.A. L.1068 J.D. Sr. Coun., HSBC-North America
Miller, Victor H. ....'64 '93 C.511 B.A. L.1035 J.D. Sr. Coun., HSBC Finance Corp.
Montenaro, Daniel L. '73 '98 C.209 B.A. L.1003 J.D.
(adm. in OH; not adm. in IL) Coun., HSBC Finance Corp.
Moorshead, Kathryn D. '66 '00 C.238 B.S. L.146 J.D.
Coun., Household Mortgage Serv.

Pampel, Martha Anne '66 '92 C.893 B.A. L.945 J.D.
Assoc. Gen. Coun. & Ass't. Sec., HSBC-North America
Platzer, Ann R. '57 '82 C.821 B.A. L.145 J.D.
Assoc. Gen. Coun., HSBC Finance Corp.
Previn, Matthew P. '70 '97 C.976 B.A. L.276 J.D.
(adm. in NY; not adm. in IL) Sr. Coun., HSBC Finance Corp.
Radzik, Donna L. '63 '88 C&L.339 B.S., J.D.
Assoc. Gen. Coun., HSBC Finance Corp.
Randolph, Kenneth V. (Ted), III '— '00 C.923 B.S. L.309 J.D.
(adm. in NY; not adm. in IL) HSBC-North America
Robin, Kenneth H. '47 '72 C.645 B.S. L.831 J.D.
(adm. in PA; not adm. in IL)
Sr. Exec. V.P., Gen. Coun. & Corp. Sec., HSBC-North America
Rotzien, William A. '47 '73 C.477 B.A. L.1119 J.D.
(adm. in IN; not adm. in IL) Sr. Coun., HSBC Finance Corp.
Santee, John C. .... '53 '78 C.784 B.A. L.221 J.D. 200 E. Evergreen Ave.
Schwartz, Patrick D. '57 '84 C.602 B.A. L.767 J.D.
Ass't Gen. Coun., Corp., Chief Gov. Off. & Ass't, HSBC Finance Corp.
Segrato, Glen D. '71 '97 C.840 B.S. L.846 J.D.
(adm. in TX; not adm. in IL) Sr. Coun., Household Retail Servs.
Shank, Allison '54 '79 C&L.597 B.A., J.D.
Gen. Coun., Tech. Servs., Household Retail Servs., USA
Siegel, Abra C. .... '63 '88 C.339 B.S. L.597 J.D. Sr. Coun., HSBC Finance Corp.
Stern, Laurence R., (AVⓉ) '42 '66 C.4 B.A. L.823 LL.B.
(adm. in NY; not adm. in IL) Assoc. Gen. Coun., HSBC North America
Stevenson, Raymond H. .... '27 '60 C.221 B.S. L.146 J.D. Pres., Stevenson Intl. Inc.
Tunstall, Mercedes Kelley '73 '99 C.210 B.M. L.477 J.D.
(adm. in VA; not adm. in IL) Coun., Household Intl., Inc.
Upton, Roland C., (AV) ..... '23 '50 C&L.597 B.A., LL.B. 417 N. Prospect Manor Mount
White, David .... '52 '80 C.339 A.B. L.801 J.D. P.O. Box 7011
Wood, Jeffrey B. .... '59 '84 C.945 B.A. L.597 J.D. Gen. Coun., Auto Companies
Woodrow, Tracy S. '— '98 C.1044 B.A. L.94 J.D.
(adm. in MA; not adm. in IL) HSBC-North America

QUINCY, * 40,366, *Adams Co.*

Adams, Donald G., (BV) .... '31 '55 C&L.339 B.S., LL.B. 522 Vermont
Adams, John F., Attorney at Law, (AV) .... '32 '60 C&L.879 B.A., LL.B. P.O. Box 116
Adrian, Robert K., (BV) .... '57 '83 C.357 B.A. L.801 J.D. [Adrian&D.]
Adrian & Dunn, P.C., (BV) .... 510 Main St.
Anastas, Terrence J., (BV) .... '58 '83 C.801 B.S. L.339 J.D. [Mays,W.&A.]
Apfelbaum, Larry A., (BV) '61 '87 C.338 B.S. L.339 J.D.
[Ⓐ Kanoski&Assoc.] (⊙Bloomington, Macomb, Peoria, Rushville, Springfield)
Awerkamp, Gena J., (AV) .... '47 '82 C&L.502 B.S., J.D. [Schmiedeskamp,R.N.&M.]
Awerkamp, Mary Lucinda, (BV) .... '49 '76 C.1082 B.A. L.734 J.D. [Awerkamp&M.]
Awerkamp & McClain, P.C., (BV) .... 701 Broadway
Bain, Florence, (BV) '42 '78 C.350 B.S. L.36 J.D.
[Ⓐ Kanoski&Assoc.] (⊙Bloomington, Macomb, Peoria, Rushville, Springfield)
Barnard, Jonathan H., Law Offices of, (AV) '50 '75
C.57 B.A. L.836 J.D. 316 North Sixth Street
Bertoglio, Raymond A. .... '16 '42 C&L.339 B.S., LL.B. 901 York St.‡
Bickhaus, Michael A., (CV) '68 '94 C.1082 B.S. L.502 J.D.
[Schmiedeskamp,R.N.&M.]
Bier, Barney S. .... '62 '87 C.339 B.S. L.910 J.D. [Ⓐ Goehl,S.&C.]
Bier, Betsy .... '56 '88 C.63 L.339 J.D. [Bier&B.]
Bier, Byron S., (BV) .... '62 '87 C.339 B.A. L.910 J.D. States Atty.
Bier, Robert J., (BV) .... '35 '63 L.339 LL.B. [Bier&B.]
Bier and Bier, (BV) .... 529 Hampshire St.
Bilderback, Stering G. '11 '42 C.191 L.733 LL.B.
(adm. in MO; not adm. in IL) 2130 Harrison‡

Boshardy, John V., & Associates, P.C.
(See Springfield)

Brennan, Babette L., (BV) '61 '88 C.502 B.S. L.734 J.D.
[Ⓐ Schmiedeskamp,R.N.&M.]
Brennan, Jerry L., (AV) ...... '36 '67 C.502 B.S. L.339 J.D. [Schmiedeskamp,R.N.&M.]
Brenner, Talmadge G., (BV) .... '62 '87 C.293 A.B. L.879 J.D. [Staff,B.&S.]

Cameron, Anthony B., (AV) '42 '73 C.339 B.A. L.352 J.D.
529 Hampshire, Suite 511, 62301
Telephone: 217-228-8669 Fax: 217-228-2225
Email: dacamara@adams.net URL: http://www.abclawoffice.com
Professional Discipline. Employment, Environmental Litigation. Administrative Law (State and Federal). Civil Litigation. Licensing. Municipal Law.
See Professional Biographies, QUINCY, ILLINOIS

Cashman, Andrew K. .... '74 '99 C.339 B.S. L.374 J.D. [Ⓐ Schmiedeskamp,R.N.&M.]
Cashman, Dennis K. .... '45 '70 C.339 B.S. L.146 J.D. Pres. Cir. J.
Cashman, J. Devin, (BV) .... '59 '84 C.338 B.S. L.424 J.D. [Cashman&K.]
Cashman & Kuhlman, (BV) .... 520 N. 30th St., Ste. 23
Cassens, Mark A., (BV) .... '52 '80 C.927 B.A. L.801 J.D. [Goehl,S.&C.]
Clark, E. John .... '62 '87 C.191 B.S. L.801 J.D. 529 Hampshire St., Ste. 501
Cook, Robert W. .... '43 '68 C&L.339 A.B., J.D. App. Ct. Jus.
Deege, John P., (BV) .... '16 '44 C&L.339 A.B., J.D. 518 Vermont St.
Depke, Daniel J., (CV) .... '68 '94 C.339 B.S. L.365 J.D. 2540 Broadway St.
Dieterich, Wm. J. .... '15 '39 C.893 B.A. L.145 J.D. State Bk. Bldg.‡
Dittmeyer, Edward B. .... '19 '43 C.1082 L.436 LL.B. Ret. Cir. Ct. J.‡
Downey, Edward K. '41 '73 C.701 B.S. L.7 J.D.
(adm. in OH; not adm. in IL) Co. Pub. Def.
Drummond, Mark A., (BV) .... '56 '80 C.927 B.S. L.339 J.D. Assoc. J.
Duesterhaus, Joseph A., (BV) .... '53 '83 C.293 B.A. L.352 J.D. [Scholz,L.P.S.&D.]
Dunn, Lonnie R., (CV) .... '64 '91 C.1082 B.A. L.801 J.D. [Adrian&D.]
Edmiston, Charles N., II, (BV) '54 '80 C.339 B.S. L.352 J.D.
[Ⓐ Kanoski&Assoc.] (⊙Bloomington, Macomb, Peoria, Rushville, Springfield)
Erwin, Drew T., (BV) .... '66 '91 C.934 B.A. L.862 J.D. 608 Vermont St.
Evans, Christina B. '50 '75 C&L.378 B.S., J.D.
(adm. in MO; not adm. in IL) 9 Barclay Dr.‡
Eyler, Todd R. .... '73 '99 C.1082 B.A. L.801 J.D. 300 N. 6th St.
Farha, Gary L., (BV) .... '58 '84 C.191 B.A. L.502 J.D. [Leeper&F.]
Geise, Henry B., (BV) .... '36 '64 C.1082 B.S. L.339 J.D. 314 N. 6th St.
Goehl, Russell R., (BV) .... '35 '60 C.1082 A.B. L.209 J.D. [Goehl,S.&C.]

Goehl, Schuering & Cassens, (BV)
506 Vermont Street, 62301
Telephone: 217-224-2555; 224-5556 Fax: 217-224-2569
Email: rrg@gsclawnet.com URL: http://www.gsclawnet.com
Members of Firm: Russell R. Goehl; Donald R. Schuering; Mark A. Cassens; Christopher D. Schuering. Associate: Barney S. Bier.

(This Listing Continued)

Goehl, Schuering & Cassens (Continued)
Civil Practice, Trial Practice in all Courts. Personal Injury, Family Law, Trusts and Estates, Real Estate, Workers Compensation, Product Liability, Corporate Law, Reinsurance and Criminal Law.
References: Mercantile Trust and Savings Bank; Town & Country Bank of Quincy.

Gorman, Brett K., (BV) .... '66 '92 C&L.339 B.A., J.D. [Schmiedeskamp,R.N.&M.]
Gorman, Dennis W., (AV) .... '42 '67 C&L.339 B.A., J.D. [Schmiedeskamp,R.N.&M.]
Hansen, James A., (CV) ...... '70 '97 C.927 B.B. L.734 J.D. [Schmiedeskamp,R.N.&M.]
Heck, F. Donald, Jr., (BV) .... '47 '73 C.1082 B.A. L.734 J.D. 300 N. 6th St.
Hellyer, Donald R. .... '24 '50 L.347 LL.B. 3 Brentwood
Henze, Holly J. .... '62 '02 C.391 B.S. L.502 J.D. [Schnack]
Holley, Cheri T. '47 '91 C.912 B.S.B.A. L.213 J.D.
(adm. in MI; not adm. in IL) General Counsel, Titan International, Inc.
Hunter, Robert S., (AV) .... '19 '42 C&L.597 B.S.L., LL.B. 4132 Coachlight Ct.‡
Hurley, Delores R. .... '65 '91 C&L.801 B.A., J.D. Asst. State's Atty.
Hutmacher, Matthew A., (BV) .... '40 '65 C.734 B.S. L.597 J.D. [Hutmacher&R.]
Hutmacher & Rapp, P.C., (AV) .... 428 N. Sixth Street
Ingham, James R., (BV) .... '49 '79 C.1082 B.S. L.607 J.D. [Inghram&I.]
Ingham, John T., IV, (BV) .... '45 '71 C.1082 B.A. L.836 J.D. [Inghram&I.]
Inghram & Inghram, (BV) .... 529 Hampshire Street, Suite 409
Kabrick, Larry E. .... '43 '71 C.587 L.45 J.D. 522 Vermont St.
Kanoski, Ronald J., (BV) .... '47 '74 C.234 B.S. L.424 J.D. [Kanoski&Assoc.] ⊙
Kanoski & Associates, (BV)
2540 Broadway (⊙Bloomington, Decatur, Macomb, Peoria, Rushville, Springfield)
Keefe, James N., (AV) .... '21 '47 C.1082 A.B. L.339 J.D. 316 N. Sixth St.‡
Keller, William G., Jr., (AV) '49 '74 C.339 B.S. L.879 J.D.
[Schmiedeskamp,R.N.&M.]
Kuhlman, Denette C., (CV) .... '65 '90 C.191 B.S. L.339 J.D. [Cashman&K.]
Lannerd, Amy C. .... '76 '01 C.37 B.S. L.1410 J.D. [Ⓐ Lewis&L.]
Leeper, Thomas K., (BV) .... '44 '78 C.339 B.S. L.896 J.D. [Leeper&F.]
Leeper & Farha, P.C., (BV) .... P.O. Box 1201
Lewis, George J., (AV) .... '30 '58 C&L.339 B.S., J.D. [Lewis&L.]
Lewis & Longlett, (AV) .... 435 Hampshire Street
Little, David C., (BV) .... '43 '68 C.191 B.S. L.502 J.D. [D.Little]
Little, David, (BV) .... 535 Main St., Ste. 5
Longlett, John R., (BV) .... '47 '72 C.339 B.S. L.502 J.D. [Lewis&L.]
Madison, Melinda S. .... '64 '99 C.1082 B.S. L.801 J.D. [Ⓐ Schmiedeskamp,R.N.&M.]
Madsen, Harold L. .... '20 '49 C&L.339 B.S., LL.B. Ret. Assoc. Cir. J.
Madsen, Robert L. .... '47 '75 C.339 A.B. L.378 J.D. 800 W.C.U. Bldg.
Mays, William O., Jr., (BV) .... '53 '81 C.879 B.S.E.E. L.365 J.D. [Mays,W.&A.]
Mays, Wm. Owen, (BV) .... '20 '49 C&L.477 A.B., J.D. [Mays,W.&A.]
Mays, Walden & Anastas, (BV) .... 636 Hampshire St., Ste 101
McClain, Michael F., (BV) .... '47 '77 C.711 B.A. L.734 J.D. [Awerkamp&M.]
McCleery, William M., Jr., (BV) '55 '81
C.880 B.A. L.276 J.D. [Schmiedeskamp,R.N.&M.]
Mitchell, Delmer R., Jr., (AV) '41 '66 C.801 A.B. L.339 J.D.
[Schmiedeskamp,R.N.&M.]
Neu, Richard B., (AV) ...... '36 '62 C&L.339 A.B., LL.B. [Schmiedeskamp,R.N.&M.] ‡
Niemann, Ted M., (BV) ...... '57 '83 C.339 B.A. L.209 J.D. [Schmiedeskamp,R.N.&M.]
Nissen, William F., (BV) .... '26 '52 L.365 J.D. 522 Vermont St., Ste. 2
Oakley, Harold B., (BV) ..... '68 '93 C.934 B.A. L.502 J.D. [Schmiedeskamp,R.N.&M.]
Oakley, Lisa Smith .... '56 '83 C.999 B.S. L.923 J.D. 529 Hampshire St., Suite 700‡
O'Connell, Richard P., (AV) .... '28 '55 C.910 A.B. L.597 J.D. [R.P.O'Connell]
O'Connell, Richard P., Ltd., (AV) .... 608 Vermont St.
Olivero, Kathy A., (CV) '56 '82 C.339 B.S. L.801 J.D.
[Ⓐ Kanoski&Assoc.] (⊙Bloomington, Macomb, Peoria, Rushville, Springfield)
Pagliara, Tracy D. '63 '89 C&L.339 B.S., J.D.
VP, Gen. Coun. & Secy., Gardner Denver, Inc.
Palmer, James L., (AV) .... '48 '73 C.1082 B.B.A.A. L.339 J.D. [Scholz,L.P.S.&D.]
Parsell, Ellecia L. .... '77 '02 C&L.339 B.S., J.D. App. Ct. Law Clk.
Penn, David G., (BV) .... '69 '94 C&L.93 B.A., J.D. [Schmiedeskamp,R.N.&M.]
Pezman, Alfred L. .... '18 '45 C&L.339 A.B., LL.B. Ret. Cir. J.‡
Pratt, Gregory A. .... '72 '99 C.1082 B.A. L.339 J.D. [Schmiedeskamp,R.N.&M.]
Prizy, Randall R., (CV) .... '54 '84 C.927 B.S. L.1187 J.D. 304 1/2 N. 6th St., Ste. 1
Rapp, James A., (AV) .... '49 '74 C.339 B.S. L.910 J.D. [Hutmacher&R.]
Robertson, E. Mont, (BV) .... '45 '70 C.277 B.S.I.M. L.910 J.D. 510 Main Street
Rodriguez, Anita M. .... '56 '81 C&L.900 B.A., J.D. Asst. State Atty.; Adams Co.
Rodriguez, Norman J. '55 '80 C.1082 B.A. L.900 J.D.
(adm. in KS; not adm. in IL) 1236 N. 10th St.‡
Sandness, Lawrence K. '48 '75 C.475 B.A. L.309 J.D.
(adm. in CT; not adm. in IL) Dyneer/Dynamic

Schmiedeskamp, Robertson, Neu & Mitchell, (AV)
525 Jersey, P.O. Box 1069, 62306
Telephone: 217-223-3030 Fax: 217-223-1005
Email: srnm@srnm.com URL: http://www.srnm.com
Members of Firm: George H. Wilson (1866-1949); Richard W.S. Neu (1905-1951); Carl G. Schmiedeskamp (1898-1987); Sam G. Jenkins (1907-1989); John T. Robertson (1916-1995); Theodore Grant House (1930-1980); Richard B. Neu (Retired); Delmer R. Mitchell, Jr.; Dennis W. Gorman; Jerry L. Brennan; William G. Keller, Jr.; William M. McCleery, Jr.; Ted M. Niemann; Gena J. Awerkamp; Brett K. Gorman; Harold B. Oakley; Michael A. Bickhaus; David G. Penn; James A. Hansen; Gregory A. Pratt;—Babette L. Brennan; Andrew K. Cashman; Melinda S. Madison.
General Practice. General Civil and Appellate Practice. Corporate, Mergers and Acquisitions, Federal Taxation, Banking and Insurance Law, Real Estate, Commercial, Bankruptcy, Estate Planning and Probate, Employment and Labor Law, Education Law.
Representative Clients: Mercantile Trust & Savings Bank; Allied Property & Casualty Insurance Co.; CNA Insurance; Illinois State Medical Insurance Services, Inc.; Knapheide Mfg. Co.; Harris Corp.; Bituminous Casualty Corp.; Quincy Compressor Division of Colt Industries, Inc.; Culver-Stockton College.
See Professional Biographies, QUINCY, ILLINOIS

Schnack, Andrew C., III, (AV) .... '49 '74 C.57 B.A. L.879 J.D. [Schnack]
Schnack, Andrew C., Jr., (AV) .... '23 '49 C&L.879 J.D. 510 Vermont St.‡
Schnack, Kent R., (BV) .... '53 '78 C&L.879 A.B., J.D. [Schnack]
Schnack, Loren E. .... '26 '50 C&L.879 J.D. Assoc. Cir. J. [Ⓖ Schnack]
Schnack Law Offices, (AV) .... 510 Vermont St.
Schneidman, Sam .... '15 '42 C.352 B.S.C. L.339 J.D. 2168 Wilmar Ct.‡
Scholz, Charles A., (AV) .... '26 '50 C.790 L.469 LL.B. [Scholz,L.P.S.&D.]
Scholz, Christopher G., (BV) .... '57 '87 C.927 B.A. L.469 J.D. [Scholz,L.P.S.&D.]
Scholz, Richard F., (BV) .... '28 '53 C.339 L.469 LL.B. 529 Hampshire St., Ste. 700

Scholz, Loos, Palmer, Siebers & Duesterhaus, (AV) BB
625 Vermont Street, 62301
Telephone: 217-223-3444 Fax: 217-223-3450
Email: slpsd@rnet.com URL: http://www.slpsd.com
Members of Firm: Richard F. Scholz, Sr. (1901-1975); Delbert Loos (1909-1993); Charles A. Scholz; James L. Palmer; Steven E. Siebers; Joseph A. Duesterhaus; Christopher G. Scholz; Jennifer A. Winking; William L. Siebers.
General Civil and Trial Practice in all Courts. Probate, Real Estate, Banking, Insurance Defense and Corporation Law, Tax, Bankruptcy, Commercial Law and Employment Law, Wills and Trusts.

(This Listing Continued)

Scholz, Loos, Palmer, Siebers & Duesterhaus (Continued)

Representative Clients: Sunset Home; Quincy Notre Dame Foundation; First Bankers Trust Company, N.A.; Quincy Newspapers, Inc.; Niemann Foods, Inc.; Quincy Broadcasting Co.; United State Bank; First Federal Bank.

See Professional Biographies, QUINCY, ILLINOIS

Schuering, Christopher D., (CV) ... '71 '96 C.602 B.B.A. L.339 J.D. [Goehl,S.&C.]
Schuering, Donald R., (BV) ... '45 '71 C.711 B.A. L.602 J.D. [Goehl,S.&C.]
Schuering, Mark A. ... '53 '78 C.1082 B.A. L.734 J.D. Cir. J.
Shair, David K. A., (CV) ... '49 '76 C.197 A.B. L.339 J.D. 1025 1/2 Kentucky Street
Siebers, Steven E., (AV) ... '54 '79 C.927 B.B. L.339 J.D. [Scholz,L.P.S.&D.]
Siebers, William L., (CV) ... '71 '96 C.1082 B.S. L.879 J.D. [Scholz,L.P.S.&D.]
Smith, Mark Damon ... '61 '97 C.1082 B.A. L.378 J.D. Pub. Def.
Snowden, Howard L., (AV) ... '27 '55 C&L.339 B.S., J.D. [Snowden&S.] ⊙
Snowden, James H., (CV) ... '57 '82 C.999 B.A. L.145 J.D. [Snowden&S.] ⊙
Snowden & Snowden, (AV) ... 237 N. 6th St. (⊙La Grange, MO)
Staff, Andrew W. ... '69 '99 C.339 B.A. L.365 J.D. [Staff,B.&S.]
Staff, Hubert G., (BV) ... '39 '68 C&L.339 B.S., J.D. [Staff,B.&S.]
Staff, Brenner & Staff, (BV) ... 237 North Sixth Street, Suite 200
Steele, Jeremy T. '72 '00 C.101 B.S. L.228 J.D.
Sr. Coun. & Asst. Secy., Gardner Denver, Inc.
Stone, Jason P., (CV) ... '71 '96 C&L.339 A.B., J.D. [🄰 Lewis&L.]
Thomas, Kenneth C. '48 '74
C.46 B.S. L.146 J.D. Hearing Referee, Dept. of Employment Sec.
Tracy, Jil Walker, (BV) ... '56 '80 C&L.801 B.A., J.D. Dir., Atty. Gen. Off.
Vahle, Chet W. ... '50 '77 C.1082 B.A. L.879 J.D. Asso. Cir. J.
Venvertloh, Dale J., (BV) ... '49 '74 C.602 B.B.A. L.339 J.D. 607 Vermont
Walden, Scott H. ... '53 '78 C.675 B.A. L.879 J.D. Cir. Ct. J.
Waldman, John J., (CV) '62 '88 C.801 B.A. L.339 J.D.
[🄰 Kanoski&Assoc.] (⊙Bloomington, Macomb, Peoria, Rushville, Springfield)
Weinberg, Donald L. ... '44 '77 C.1082 B.A. L.61 J.D. W.C.U. Bldg.‡
Winking, Jennifer A., (BV) ... '66 '96 C.1082 B.A. L.502 J.D. [Scholz,L.P.S.&D.]
Wooleyhan, John C. ... '49 '75 C.945 A.B. L.910 J.D. Assoc. Cir. J.

RALEIGH, 305, *Saline Co.*

Kuppart, Roman P. ... '70 '02 C.280 B.A. L.801 J.D. P.O. Box 217

RANTOUL, 12,857, *Champaign Co.*

Allen & Korkowski & Associates, (BV)
123 North Garrard Street, 61866
Telephone: 217-893-1401 Fax: 217-893-4788 URL: http://www.ak-lawoffice.com
Email: bscott@mchsi.com URL: http://www.aklaw.com
Members of the Firm: William R. Scott; Craig R. Hunt.
Business Law, Real Estate, Estate Planning, Administrative Law, Family Law, Bankruptcy and Commercial Collections.
Representative Clients: Bank of Rantoul; Hicks Oils; Hicksgas, Inc.; Rantoul First Bank; Rantoul Park District.
References: Bank of Rantoul, Rantoul, Illinois.

See Professional Biographies, RANTOUL, ILLINOIS

Finney, Kathleen A. ... '53 '90 C.1182 B.A. L.436 J.D. [K.A.Finney]
Finney, Kathleen A., A P.C., Law Office of ... 121 N. Garrard, Ste. A
Gambill, John E., (AV) ... '26 '53 C&L.966 B.S., LL.B. 123-125 N. Garrard St.‡
Hunt, Craig R., (BV) ... '58 '83 C.234 B.S. L.365 J.D. [Allen&K.&Assoc.]
Korkowski, Donald J., (AV) ... '23 '51 C&L.339 B.S.L., LL.B. 777 Oakcrest Dr.‡
Lanto, Reino C., Jr., (BV) ... '43 '68 C&L.339 B.A., J.D. Col., USAFR (Ret.)

Meyer Capel, A Professional Corporation
(See Champaign)

Opsahl, Richard B., (AV) ... '37 '63 C.427 B.A. L.339 LL.B. 425 E. Champaign Ave.
Schurter, Brian T. ... '71 '96 C.679 B.A. L.851 J.D. 425 East Champaign Avenue
Schurter, Neill ... '43 '68 C.430 A.B. L.339 J.D. 214 S. Garrard
Scott, William R., (BV) ... '50 '75 C&L.339 B.A., J.D. [Allen&K.&Assoc.]
Wilson, Paul R., Jr., (BV) ... '49 '74 C.221 B.A. L.339 J.D. 300 S. Garrard

RAYMOND, 927, *Montgomery Co.*

Polston, Ronald W. ... '31 '59 C.234 B.S. L.339 LL.B. P.O. Box 20‡

RED BUD, 3,422, *Randolph Co.*

Becker, Carl H. ... '27 '55 C&L.879 J.D. Ret. Cir. J.‡

Brown & Associates
(See Belleville)

Cooper, Richard C., (BV) ... '50 '76 C.801 B.A. L.734 J.D. [Rau&C.]
Fricke, Rayburn A., (BV) ... '39 '77 C.502 B.S. L.365 J.D. 1114 Alan Dr. (⊙Chester)
Rau, David P., (BV) ... '44 '73 C.999 B.A. L.733 J.D. [Rau&C.]
Rau & Cooper, (BV) ... 205 E. Market St.
Sachtleben, Earl H., (BV) ... '33 '64 C.339 B.A. L.910 LL.B. 140 W. Market St.

RICHMOND, 1,016, *McHenry Co.*

Easterberg, John C. ... '18 '47 C.902 A.B. L.597 J.D. 8809 N. Solon Rd.‡
Simes, Joanne Schnurr ... '31 '93 C.966 B.S. L.589 J.D. 10604 Main St.
Stinespring, Donald C., Jr. ... '— '97 C.747 B.A. L.365 J.D. 10604 Main St.

RICHTON PARK, 12,533, *Cook Co.*

Hawkins, Charles W. ... '41 '75 C.1191 B.S. L.209 J.D. 4424 Imperial Dr.
Robinson, Natasha L. ... '74 '99 C.352 B.A. L.966 J.D. 22320 Piccadilly Court

RIVERDALE, 15,055, *Cook Co.*

Larson, Donald R. '31 '73 C.867 A.B. L.161 J.D.
(adm. in MI; not adm. in IL) Exec. V.P., House-O-Lite Corp.
Lynch, John T. ... '58 '86 C.145 B.A. L.209 J.D. Asst. Gen. Coun., Acme Metals Inc.
Weber, Edward P., Jr. '37 '64
C.610 B.S.C. L.930 J.D. V.P., Gen. Coun. & Secy., Acme Metals Inc.

RIVER FOREST, 11,669, *Cook Co.*

Adamik, James B. ... '49 '77 C.927 B.B.A. L.209 J.D. [J.B.Adamik]
Adamik, James B., P.C. ... 426 Franklin Ave.
Bruno, Bernard J. ... '22 '47 C&L.209 LL.B. 1541 Clinton Pl.
Bryant, Beverly C. ... '71 '95 C.446 B.A. L.146 J.D. [🄰 Owens&Assoc.]
Burns, Sandra K., (Ltd.) ... '43 '75 C.927 B.A. L.209 J.D. 348 Lathrop Ave.
Camasto, Nicholas A., (Ltd.) '30 '57
C.46 B.S.E.E. L.365 J.D. 545 Thatcher St. (Pat.) (⊙Mount Prospect)
Claps, Joseph M., (AV) ... '48 '73 C.424 B.S. L.146 J.D. Assoc. Cir. J.
Esposito, Michael R. ... '48 '73 C&L.602 B.B.A., J.D. 834 Forest Ave.
Fiedler, Edward H., Jr., (AV) ... '32 '60 C.350 B.S. L.424 J.D. One Gale Ave.‡
Geldner, JuliAnn ... '59 '90 C&L.339 B.A., J.D. 1345 Ashland Ave.
Haraburd, Suzanne ... '54 '85 C.999 B.A. L.424 J.D. 633 Bonnie Brae Place
Hardin, John W., III ... '51 '76 C.177 B.A. L.602 J.D. 7320 Lake St.
Higgins, Colin O. ... '18 '49 C.210 B.A. L.597 J.D. 107 Keystone Ave.
Kogut, Donna Gagliardo ... '55 '83 C.201 B.S. L.365 J.D. 7375 W. North Ave.

Kopecky, James L., P.C.
(See Chicago)

Krueger, Kathryn L. ... '51 '85 C.473 B.A. L.146 J.D. P.O. Box 5523
Latchford, George P., (AV) ... '24 '55 C&L.425 J.D. 417 Lathrop Ave.
Lauber, Daniel M. ... '49 '85 C.145 B.A. L.597 J.D. 7215 Oak Avenue
Lee, Robert Emmett ... '24 '51 C.602 B.S. L.209 J.D. 531 Lathrop Ave.
Marino, Patricia A. ... '47 '85 C.107 B.A. L.209 J.D. 1515 Ashland Ave.
McCarthy, Rita J. '57 '91 C.715 B.A. L.776 J.D.
(adm. in NJ; not adm. in IL) 110 Keystone St.‡
McCullough, Chester C. ... '17 '48 C.72 B.A. L.146 LL.B. 314 Forest Ave.‡
McGuire, William L. ... '14 '38 C&L.424 Ph.B., J.D. 1435 Bonnie Brae Pl.‡
Mennes, Mark H. ... '47 '74 C.747 B.B.A. L.365 LL.B. 1549 Clinton Pl.
Montino, Paul J. ... '36 '61 C&L.339 B.A., LL.B. 7623 Lake St.
Moriarty, Edward '14 '38 C&L.190 B.A., LL.B.
(adm. in NE; not adm. in IL) 7200 W. Divison St.‡
O'Connell, Daniel F. ... '20 '53 C.339 B.S. L.424 J.D. 407 Ashland Ave.‡
Organ, Marcia M. ... '58 '84 C.339 B.A. L.424 J.D. 1213 Park Ave.
Owens, Lori A. ... '57 '82 C&L.221 B.A., J.D. [Owens&Assoc.]
Owens & Associates of Illinois, P.C. ... P.O. Box 521
Patsavos, Estelle C. ... '56 '81 C.914 B.A. L.472 J.D. 800 Lathrop Ave.
Pelafas, Peter G., (AV) ... '28 '56 C&L.339 A.B., LL.B. 7610 W. Madison St.
Ragalie, Gregg Stephen ... '58 '85 C.700 B.A. L.365 J.D. 906 Jackson Ave.
Ratcliff, Richard S. ... '31 '55 C&L.477 B.A., J.D. Village Atty.‡
Rees, Lynn Modica ... '61 '87 C.190 B.S.B.A. L.145 J.D. 330 Gale Ave.‡
Ricks, Yolanda L. ... '66 '00 C.713 B.A. L.494 J.D. [🄰 Owens&Assoc.]
Sabatello, Mary L. ... '25 '48 L.209 J.D. 1535 Forest Ave.‡
Simon, Elizabeth C. ... '52 '83 C.881 B.A. L.424 J.D. 234 Franklin
Simons, Raymond B. '48 '79
C.46 B.S. L.365 J.D. Gen. Mgr., Methode Technical Components
Stathos, Michael ... '31 '59 C.1016 B.A. L.597 J.D. P.O. Box 5425‡
Tatter, Sarah Jane ... '49 '74 C.604 B.A. L.146 J.D. 239 Ashland Ave.
Trombetta, Carmine V. ... '56 '83 C.589 B.A. L.365 J.D. 7369 North Ave.
Walters, Helen M. ... '37 '62 C.209 L.365 LL.B. 518 Bonnie Brae‡
Wesolowski, Karen ... '53 '78 C.959 B.A. L.945 J.D. 542 Thatcher‡
Wolfman, Paul I. ... '49 '75 C.966 B.A. L.365 J.D. 719 N. Franklin Ave.

RIVER GROVE, 10,668, *Cook Co.*

Doctor, David H. ... '40 '01 C.1106 B.S. L.365 J.D. 2636 N. Haymond St.
McMahon, Dennis A. '54 '78
C.339 B.A. L.145 J.D. V.P., Gen. Coun. & Secy., Follett Corp.
O'Hara, Alison E. ... '63 '88 C.170 B.A. L.174 J.D. Sr. Coun., Follett Corp.
Rickert, Edward D. ... '59 '89 C.352 B.S. L.146 J.D. [Smith,R.&S.]
Smith, Bart A. ... '61 '88 C.174 B.A. L.146 J.D. [Smith,R.&S.]
Smith, Harry J., Jr. ... '35 '60 C.177 B.A. L.424 J.D. [Smith,R.&S.]
Smith, Rickert & Smith ... 8259 Grand Ave.
Walsh, Suzanne M. ... '— '93 C.700 B.A. L.602 J.D. Counsel, Follett Corp.

RIVERSIDE, 8,895, *Cook Co.*

Boeger, Elmore L. ... '14 '38 C&L.879 B.A., LL.B. 2914 S. Harlem Ave.
Boeger, Heerwagen, Lusthoff & Brendemuhl, P.C. ... 2914 Harlem Ave.
Brendemuhl, James L. ... '50 '75 C.188 L.879 [Boeger,H.L.&B.]
Brendemuhl, Ruth Anne ... '52 '77 C&L.879 B.A., J.D. [Boeger,H.L.&B.]
Campagna, Thomas B. ... '55 '91 C.338 B.S. L.1148 J.D. 3034 Harlem Avenue
Cihak, Jerome E. ... '39 '64 C.1016 B.S. L.365 J.D. [Hennessy&C.]
Collins, David A., Law Office of ... '59 '92 C.597 B.A. L.424 J.D. 680 Selborne Rd.
Dages, Patrick T. ... '62 '94 C.339 B.A. L.424 J.D. 100 Lincoln Avenue
Donovan, Brendan ... '58 '87 C.602 B.S.C.E. L.424 J.D. 361 Nuttall Rd.
Dvorak, Joseph M., III ... '47 '73 C.934 B.A. L.146 J.D. 1 Riverside Rd., Ste. C
Gieseman, Albert W., Jr. ... '55 '87 C.602 B.B.A. L.597 J.D. 294 Gatesby Road
Gorman, Michael C. ... '51 '79 C.927 B.Bus. L.597 J.D. 195 Maplewood Rd.
Groll, Jonathan D. ... '69 '96 C&L.879 B.A., J.D. [🄰 Boeger,H.L.&B.]
Heerwagen, Kurt ... '38 '64 C.879 B.A. L.208 J.D. [Boeger,H.L.&B.]
Hennessy, Michael J., (AV) ... '36 '64 C.958 B.S. L.365 J.D. [Hennessy&C.]
Hennessy & Cihak, P.C., (AV) ... 2501 Desplaines Avenue
Kamm, Melvin J. ... '37 '63 C&L.424 A.B., J.D. [M.J.Kamm]
Kamm, Melvin J., Ltd. ... P.O. Box 105
Kemp, Wallace B., (AV) ... '12 '37 C.388 A.B. L.477 LL.B. 306 Northwood Rd.‡
Kolar, Edward J., Jr. ... '35 '60 C&L.597 B.S., J.D. 266 Northwood Rd.‡
Krubel, Frederick J. ... '21 '48 C.339 B.S. L.273 J.D. 289 Shenstone Rd. (Pat.)
Kubiczky, Stephen R., (AV) ... '47 '72 C.602 B.S. L.597 J.D. P.O. Box 85
Lusthoff, Craig W. ... '47 '74 C.879 B.A. L.209 J.D. [Boeger,H.L.&B.]
Muldoon, John E. ... '19 '42 C&L.209 LL.B. IRS
Newman, David C. ... '35 '59 C&L.228 A.B., LL.B. 1 Riverside Rd.

Niemi, Frederick C. '38 '64 C.339 B.A. L.146 J.D.
362 East Burlington, 60546
Telephone: 708-442-0635 Fax: 708-442-6884
Email: niemiatlaw@sbcglobal.net URL: http://www.niemilaw.com
Wills and Probate, Real Estate, Trusts and Estates, Guardianships, Alternatives to Probate.

See Professional Biographies, RIVERSIDE, ILLINOIS

Norbut, Alex S. ... '20 '47 L.209 LL.B. [Norbut&Assoc.]
Norbut, Nancy Ann ... '57 '84 C.966 B.S. L.589 J.D. 362 E. Burlington
Norbut & Associates ... 362 E. Burlington St.
Suriano, William P. ... '53 '78 C.475 B.A. L.94 J.D. 280 Shenstone Rd.
Tourek, James M. ... '32 '57 C.750 B.A. L.209 LL.B. 3034 S. Harlem Ave. (⊙Chicago)
Wier, Donald E. ... '37 '77 C.472 B.A. L.209 J.D. 86 Lincoln Ave.‡

RIVERWOODS, 3,843, *Lake Co.*

Arden, John W. ... '54 '80 C.723 B.A. L.209 J.D. Assoc. Pub., CCH Inc.
Ashman, Kenneth J., (AV) ... '61 '90 C.36 B.A.E. L.94 J.D. [Ashman] ⊙
Ashman Law Offices, LLC, (AV)
2801 Orange Brace Road (⊙Chgo., IL; New York, NY)
Bianco, Kathleen M. ... '69 '98 C.339 B.A. L.365 J.D. 2700 Lake Cook Rd.
Bock, Harvey N., (AVⓉ) '50 '75 C&L.976 B.A., J.D.
Deputy General Counsel/Senior Vice President, Dean Witter, Discover & Co.
Braun, Sheldon L. ... '54 '79 C.339 B.S. L.424 J.D. [Braun,B.&Assoc.]
Braun, Browne & Associates, P.C. ... 300 Saunders Road
Browne, Glenn A. ... '64 '89 C&L.339 B.A., J.D. [Braun,B.&Assoc.]
Chamberlain, Cheryl D. ... '59 '89 C.339 B.A. L.146 J.D. 2760 Riverwoods Rd.
Chhabria, Sameer ... '73 '99 C.94 B.A. L.424 J.D. [🄰 S.H.Peck]
Chiron, Linda J. '52 '80 C.188 B.S. L.352 J.D.
V.P., Discover Financial Services, Morgan Stanley

Clugston, William H. '50 '81 C.573 B.A. L.46 J.D.
Coun., Discover Financial Services, Morgan Stanley
Corley, Kathryn McNamara '60 '89 C.800 B.A. L.1209 J.D.
(adm. in VA; not adm. in IL)
Sr. V.P. & Gen. Coun., Discover Financial Services, Morgan Stanley
Daily, Steven C. '63 '88 C.569 B.A. L.893 J.D.
Senior Coun., Discover Financial Services, Morgan Stanley
Dean, MaryAnn E. '60 '90 C.1208 B.A. L.930 J.D.
(adm. in SC; not adm. in IL) 2700 Lake Cook Rd.
Fleishman, Wendy K. '66 '93 C.31 B.A. L.145 J.D.
Sr. Coun., Discover Financial Services, Morgan Stanley
Fletcher, L. John .... '43 '68 C&L.221 B.S.B.A., J.D. [Fletcher]
Fletcher Law Office .... 600 Portwine Road
Foley, Leann M. .... '73 '00 C.340 B.A. L.94 J.D. Leg. Work, CCH INCORPORATED
Foley, Thomas A. .... '62 '87 C.793 B.A. L.602 J.D. CCH Incorporated
Graber, Tony D., (CVⓉ) '64 '92 C.347 B.A. L.607 J.D.
(adm. in IN; not adm. in IL) 2700 Lake Cook Road
Granat, Kenneth H. .... '45 '70 C.477 B.B.A. L.339 J.D. 470 White Oak Ln.
Graziano, Bruno L. .... '52 '77 C&L.424 B.A., J.D. CCH Incorporated
Greco, Joseph A. '— '94
C.569 B.A. L.724 J.D. Coun., Morgan Stanley Discover Fin. Servs.
Greenspan, Sandra L. '— '86 C.477 B.A. L.365 J.D.
Coun., Discover Financial Services, Morgan Stanley
Gresham, John Sanford '58 '84 C.893 B.A. L.469 J.D.
(adm. in GA; not adm. in IL) CCH, Inc.
Hartigan, Michael J., Jr. '51 '78 C.602 B.A. L.339 J.D.
(adm. in OH; not adm. in IL)
V.P. & Assoc. Gen. Coun., Discover Financial Services, Morgan Stanley
Horwitz, Sara L. '59 '85 C.494 B.A. L.1035 J.D.
Coun., Discover Financial Services, Morgan Stanley
Jacksack, Susan M. .... '60 '84 C&L.339 A.B., J.D. CCH Inc.
Jensen, Dennis .... '52 '83 C.347 B.A. L.209 J.D. Analyst, CCH, Inc.
Jensen, E. Beth .... '55 '81 C.477 B.A. L.146 J.D. CCH Inc.
Kareken, John A. '51 '76 C&L.339 B.A., J.D.
Capital Changes Coun., CCH INCORPORATED
Koutouzos, Georgia D. '55 '80 C.339 A.B. L.221 J.D.
(adm. in IA; not adm. in IL) Editor of Law Books, CCH Inc.‡
LaMantia, Victor A. .... '57 '81 C.597 B.S.J. L.602 J.D. 2500 Lake Cook Rd.
Lauletta, Thomas K. .... '50 '75 C&L.209 B.A., J.D. CCH Inc.
Lichten, Earl B., (AV) .... '23 '58 C.46 B.S.M.E. L.424 J.D. 1800 Trillium Lane‡
Mallinger, Larry A. '47 '74 C.475 B.A. L.477 J.D.
V.P., Discover Financial Services, Morgan Stanley
Montgomery, Heather Love ..... '70 '97 C.893 B.A. L.607 J.D. Commerce Clearing House
Nelson, Mark S. .... '69 '97 C.238 B.A. L.365 J.D. CCH Inc.
Notaro, Karen Anne .... '54 '80 C.424 B.A. L.209 J.D. CCH inc.
Nudelman, Brian H. '69 '94
C.966 B.A. L.365 J.D. Writer/Analyst, State Tax Dept., CCH Inc.
Old, John E. .... '64 '88 C.339 B.A. L.145 J.D. Writer/Analyst, CHH, Inc.
Ostapiuk, Sharon M. .... '— '97 C.339 B.A L.146 J.D. 2700 Lake Cook Rd.
Peck, Steven H. '57 '82 C.309 B.A. L.93 J.D.
300 Saunders Road, Suite 100 (⊙Uniondale, NY)
Quere-Barrionuevo, Alexandra '68 '95
C.145 A.B. L.94 J.D. Product Mgr., Legal Markets, CCH, Inc.
Rudolph, Stephen Bert .... '53 '97 C.597 B.S. L.209 J.D. CCH, Inc.
Sacks, Avram L. .... '54 '81 C.347 A.B. L.930 J.D. Commerce Clearing House
Sandler, Stacey J. '64 '88
C.339 B.A. L.424 J.D. Coun., Morgan Stanley Discover Fin. Servs.
Schott, Jennifer K. '73 '98 C.339 B.S. L.146 J.D.
Asst. Coun., Morgan Stanley Discover Fin. Servs.
Sennott, Justine McWilliams '73 '98 C&L.436 B.A., J.D.
(adm. in WI; not adm. in IL) 2700 Lake Cook Rd.
Simon, Sandra R. .... '73 '97 C.597 B.A. L.209 J.D. 304 Saunders Rd.
Slovin, Stanford R. .... '64 '90 C.339 B.S. L.1000 J.D. 2500 Lake Cook Rd.
Solomon, Beth J. '63 '89 C.477 B.A. L.910 J.D.
Coun., Discover Financial Services, Morgan Stanley
Stachura, Joseph T. '43 '69
C.597 B.S.B.A. L.424 J.D. Assoc. Coun., CCH INCORPORATED
Stroka, Geraldine S. .... '46 '87 C.424 B.S.N. L.365 CCH INCORPORATED
Sulkes, Carol F. '53 '78 C&L.477 A.B., J.D.
V.P. & Sr. Coun., Discover Financial Servs., Inc.
Swift, James P. '53 '78 C.597 B.S. L.424 J.D.
Exec. Dir., Discover Financial Services, Morgan Stanley
Szuberla, Geraldine C. .... '47 '75 C.627 B.S. L.424 J.D. CCH Inc.
Tierney, Laura A. '62 '88 C.1350 B.A. L.1019 J.D.
(adm. in NY; not adm. in IL) CCH, Inc.
Traisman, Kenneth Neil .... '58 '83 C&L.424 A.B., J.D. Commerce Clearing House
Trautmann, Theodore W. ...... '64 '89 C.20 B.A. L.966 J.D. Sr. Writer/Analyst, CCH Inc.‡
Villalba, A. J. .... '66 '91 C.339 B.A. L.425 J.D. 2500 Lake Cook Rd.
Vollen, Robert J., (AV) .... '40 '64 C.477 A.B. L.145 J.D. 2 Kingswood Ct.
Vydra, Frank N. '52 '81 C&L.339 B.S., J.D.
Sr. Coun., Discover Financial Services, Morgan Stanley
Ware, Dyahanne ....'— '84 C.339 A.B. L.365 J.D. Assoc. Coun., CCH INCORPORATED
White, Thomas F. .... '46 '72 C&L.424 B.A., J.D. Pres., Morgan Stanley Credit Corp.
Wilson, Anita J. '70 '96 C.589 B.A. L.339 J.D.
Asst. Coun., Morgan Stanley Discover Financial Services, Inc.
Wilson-Freelon, Sheila '— '85 C.500 B.A. L.597 J.D.
V.P. & Sr. Coun., Discover Financial Services, Morgan Stanley

ROBINSON, * 6,740, *Crawford Co.*

Anderson, Jon C., Attorney at Law, (CV) ... '47 '73 C.801 B.S. L.500 J.D. 107 W. Walnut

Brainard Law Offices, The
(See Charleston)

Correll, David M. .... '46 '74 C.679 B.A. L.1119 J.D. Cir. J.

Cox, Phillips, Weber, Tedford & Heap, P.C., (AV)
216 South Cross Street, P.O. Box 250, 62454-0250
Telephone: 618-544-8661 Fax: 618-544-3003
Email: cpwth@midwest.net
M.E. Cox (1880-1958); Carroll T. Cox (1912-1976); Frank J. Weber; Max L. Tedford; William G. Heap; Thomas R. Wiseman; Christopher L. Weber; Craig O. Weber. Of Counsel: G. Kent Phillips.
General Civil, Trial and Appellate Practice. Probate, Real Estate, Title Insurance, Municipal, Taxation, Corporation, Estate Planning, Workers Compensation, Oil and Gas Law, Collections, and Matrimonial Law.

(This Listing Continued)

Cox, Phillips, Weber, Tedford & Heap, P.C. (Continued)
Representative Clients: Regions Bank; First National Bank, Olney; First Robinson Savings & Loan, F.A., Robinson; Robinson Daily News; Robinson-Palestine Water Commission; Willow Hill Grain, Inc.; Mont Eagle Mills, Inc.; Mary Heath Foundation; Crawford Hospital District.
See Professional Biographies, ROBINSON, ILLINOIS

Darnold, Michael W., Attorney at Law, (CV) '51 '78 C.234 B.S. L.801 J.D.
P.O. Box 595
Douglas, Robert L., (Ltd.) '36 '65 C.234 B.S. L.339 LL.B.
103 Old Indian Boundary Rd.
Heap, William G., (BV) .... '48 '79 C.346 B.S. L.365 J.D. [Cox,P.W.T.&H.]

Heller, Holmes & Associates, P.C.
(See Mattoon)

Hill, James V. .... '44 '74 C.966 B.S. L.838 J.D. Assoc. Cir. J.
Holtzhouser, Jay R., (BV) .... '57 '91 C.502 B.S. L.862 J.D. Crawford Co. State's Atty.
Jones, A. H. .... '12 '40 C&L.339 A.B. Ret. Cir. J.
Lane, James William, Jr., (BV) .... '53 '92 C.234 B.S. L.862 J.D. 209 South Franklin
Phillips, G. Kent, (AV) .... '13 '57 C.339 [⊡ Cox,P.W.T.&H.]
Price, E. H., (BV) .... '18 '46 C&L.339 B.S., LL.B. 505 W. Walnut St.
Sanders, Kevin E., (CV) .... '60 '91 C.346 B.S. L.339 J.D. 309 N. Howard St.
Shaner, Mark L., (BV) .... '56 '81 C.234 B.A. L.339 J.D. 11828 N. 1150th St.

Stout, James D., Law Offices of, (BV) '— '74 C.801 B.A. L.339 J.D.
309 South Jefferson, P.O. Box 714, 62454 ⊙
Telephone: 618-546-5404 Fax: 618-544-3659
Email: jds1@shawneelink.net URL: http://www.lawyers.com/stoutholtzhouser
Associate: Lindsey D. Floyd (Resident, Bridgeport Office).
General Civil Practice. Trials. Corporation, Real Estate, Oil and Gas, Probate and Estate Planning Law, Family Law, Creditor Bankruptcy.
§§.
Bridgeport, Illinois Office: 324 North Main Street. Telephone: 618-945-2911. Fax: 618-945-3941.
See Professional Biographies, ROBINSON, ILLINOIS

Tedford, Max L., (BV) .... '52 '77 C.234 B.A. L.801 J.D. [Cox,P.W.T.&H.]
Wapner, Andrew J., (CV) .... '47 '74 C.381 B.A. L.365 J.D. S. Side Sq.
Weber, Christopher L., (BV) .... '69 '94 C&L.339 B.S., J.D. [Cox,P.W.T.&H.]
Weber, Craig O. .... '72 '97 C.339 B.S. L.801 J.D. [Cox,P.W.T.&H.]
Weber, Frank J., (AV) .... '44 '69 C.234 B.S. L.339 J.D. [Cox,P.W.T.&H.]
Weber, Mark R., (Chartered), (BV) .... '42 '66 C&L.339 B.A., J.D. P.O. Box 696
Wiseman, Thomas R., (CV) .... '62 '87 C.339 B.A. L.801 J.D. [Cox,P.W.T.&H.]

ROCHELLE, 9,424, *Ogle Co.*

Ahlberg, James G., Attorney at Law, (BV) '51 '78
C.1106 B.A. L.339 J.D. 516 Fourth Ave.
Cargerman, Alan W., (AV) .... '45 '70 C.339 L.209 LL.B. [⊡ Fearer,N.&C.] ⊙
Chadwick, Paul E. .... '— '04 C.602 B.A. L.589 J.D. [⊡ Fearer,N.&C.] ⊙
Chadwick, Robert T., (BV) .... '48 '82 C.1070 B.S. L.602 J.D. [Fearer,N.&C.] ⊙
Cole, Charles Patrick .... '51 '00 C.589 B.A. L.365 J.D. [C.P.Cole,Jr.]
Cole, Charles P., Jr. .... P.O. Box 24
Cooper, Alan H., (BV) .... '45 '74 C.198 A.B. L.846 J.D. 400 May Mart Dr.
Dietrich, Adam Thomas .... '69 '00 C&L.589 B.S., J.D. 6972 S. Sarah Ave.

Fearer, Nye & Chadwick, (AV) BR
420 Fourth Avenue, P.O. Box 117, 61068 ⊙
Telephone: 815-562-2156 Fax: 815-562-2158
Email: fnaclaw@rochelle.net
Members of Firm: William P. Fearer, II (Resident, Oregon, Illinois Office); William P. Fearer III (Resident, Oregon, Illinois Office); Philip H. Nye, Jr.; Robert T. Chadwick. Associate: Paul E. Chadwick. Of Counsel: Alan W. Cargerman.
General Practice including Corporate, Business, Workers Compensation, Insurance, Insurance Defense, Probate, Estate Planning, Wills, Zoning, Tax, Real Estate, Family, Divorce, Personal Injury, Automobile Accidents, Medical Malpractice, Products Liability, Criminal, Driving While Intoxicated and Trial Practice.
Represent: Kishwaukee College; First National Bank & Trust; Flagg-Rochelle Community Park District; Rochelle Community Hospital; Rochelle High School; Lincoln State Bank; Holcomb State Bank.
Oregon, Illinois Office: 209 South Fifth Street, P.O. Box 256, 61061. Telephone: 815-732-6113. Fax: 815-732-3193.

Guest, David K., (AV) .... '28 '53 C.72 B.A. L.597 J.D. [Guest]
Guest, Thomas D., (BV) .... '59 '86 C.393 B.A. L.679 J.D. [Guest]

Guest Legal, P.C., (AV)
316 Lincoln Highway, P.O. Box 150, 61068
Telephone: 815-562-5568 Fax: 815-562-7963
Email: guestlaw@rochelle.net
David K. Guest; Thomas D. Guest.
Estate Administration, Estate Planning, Real Estate Law and Tax Law.
Reference: First National Bank and Trust Company of Rochelle.

Hewitt, Dennis R., (BV) .... '52 '84 C&L.589 B.S., J.D. [Hewitt]
Hewitt Law Office, (BV) .... 1124 Lincoln Hwy.
Mallon, Michael T., (BV) .... '48 '77 C.589 B.S. L.365 J.D. [Roe,M.&T.]
Nye, Philip H., Jr., (AV) .... '36 '61 C.597 B.A. L.339 J.D. [Fearer,N.&C.] ⊙
Roe, John B., (BV) .... '42 '67 C.138 A.B. L.339 J.D. [Roe,M.&T.]
Roe, Mallon and Tess, (BV) .... 1090 N. Seventh St.
Tess, David D., (BV) .... '53 '82 C.965 B.B.A. L.589 J.D. [Roe,M.&T.]

ROCHESTER, 2,893, *Sangamon Co.*

Atkins, Michael W. .... '32 '59 C.612 B.S. L.623 LL.B. 11600 Pheasant Dr.

ROCK FALLS, 9,654, *Whiteside Co.*

Blodgett, Donald E., (AV) .... '16 '40 C.123 L.146 LL.B. 319 1st Ave.
Mertes, James William .... '68 '93 C&L.589 B.S., J.D. 102 E. Route 30
Mertes, Magen J. .... '79 '04 C.340 B.A. L.30 J.D. 102 E. Rte. 30
Pignatelli, Louis F., (BV) .... '46 '71 C.602 J.D. L.339 J.D. 102 E. Rte. 30

ROCKFORD, * 150,115, *Winnebago Co.*

Abate, Alex M., (BV) .... '47 '74 C&L.339 B.S., J.D. [Abate&S.]

Abate & Smith, (BV)
6072 Brynwood Drive, Suite 201, 61114
Telephone: 815-282-8228 Fax: 815-282-6620
URL: http://www.abatateandsmith.com
Alex M. Abate; Michael J. Smith.
Family Law including Divorce, Child Custody, Child Support, Spousal Support, Alimony, Visitation Rights, Distribution of Property, Paternity, Adoption Law, Personal Injury including Automobile Accidents and Injuries, Real Estate, Contracts.
See Professional Biographies, ROCKFORD, ILLINOIS

Agnew, Harris H. .... '36 '73 C.589 B.S. L.365 J.D. 129 S. Phelps Ave.
Agnew, Patrick H., (BV) .... '60 '87 C.352 B.B.A. L.589 J.D. [Agnew]
Agnew Law Office, (BV) .... 129 S. Phelps, Ste. 801
Aiello, Mark F., (BV) .... '57 '86 C.436 B.A. L.365 J.D. Asst. Pub. Def.

Albert, John R. . . . . '57 '91 C.623 B.B.A. L.862 J.D. 363 Financial Ct., Ste. 100
Alexander, Charles P., (BV) . . . . '69 '93 C.339 B.S. L.589 J.D. [Cicero&F.]
Alexander, Peter, (BV) . . . . '42 '66 C.697 L.339 LL.B. [P.Alexander]
Alexander, Peter, Ltd., (BV) . . . . One Court Place
Allen, James M., (BV) . . . .'72 '99 C.338 B.S. L.1000 J.D. [Hinshaw&C.]
Altamore, A. F., (CV) . . . . '52 '87 C.801 B.A. L.61 J.D. [Thorsen A.&S.]
Altamore, Albert, (BV) . . . . '56 '82 C.697 B.A. L.365 J.D. 308 W. State St., Ste. 420
Anderson, Karen M. . . . . '58 '82 C.104 A.B. L.145 J.D. Prairie State Legal Servs., Inc.
Anderson, La Verne E. . . . . '22 '47 C&L.339 A.B., LL.B. 724 Broadway
Anderson, Russell D., (BV) . . . . '46 '71 C&L.339 B.A., J.D. [Williams&M.]
Anderson, Terry D., (AV) . . . .'45 '76 C.697 B.A. L.339 J.D. [Williams&M.]
Antonacci, Brad A. . . . . '77 '02 C.339 B.A. L.589 J.D. [Ⓐ Heyl,R.V.&A.]
Arntz, W. Charles . . . .'42 '70 C&L.767 B.A., LL.B. Wash. Nat. Tr. Co.
Austin, Lynne B. . . . . '52 '80 C.945 B.A. L.8 J.D. 5815 El Paso Cir.‡
Bagley, H. Jim, (BV) . . . .'41 '73 C&L.280 A.B.J., J.D. 1600 N. Main St.
Bailey, Carol N. . . . . '53 '77 C.209 B.S. L.734 J.D. [Williams&M.]
Balogh, Stephen E., (AV) . . . . '56 '87 C.446 B.S. L.339 J.D. [Williams&M.]
Balsley, Stephen G., (BV) . . . . '47 '72 C.961 B.S. L.339 J.D. [Barrick,S.L.B.&V.]
Baluch, Laura A. . . . . '77 '03 C.589 B.S. L.1187 J.D. [Ⓐ Barrick,S.L.B.&V.]
Barbosa, Manuel . . . . '47 '77 C.750 B.A. L.365 J.D. U.S. Bankrptcy. J.
Barch, Ronald A., (BV) . . . . '64 '92 C.927 B.S. L.365 J.D. [Cicero&F.]
Barenbaum, Jerrod L., (BV) . . . . '69 '94 C.393 B.A. L.209 J.D. [Hinshaw&C.]
Barrett, Gregory E., (AV) . . . . '49 '74 C.999 B.A. L.546 J.D. [Barrett&G.]

Barrett & Gilbert LLP, (AV) [BR]
1645 Temple Lane, 61112
Telephone: 815-332-9600 Fax: 815-332-9646 Email: gbarrett@barrettandgilbert.com
Email: dtbarrett@barrettandgilbert.com URL: http://www.barrettandgilbert.com
Members of Firm: Gregory E. Barrett; Daniel T. Gilbert;—Susan M. Brazas.
Medical Malpractice, Catastrophic Personal Injury, Law Enforcement Litigation, Products Liability, Commercial Motor Vehicle Safety, General Litigation, Transportation, Automobile Accidents, Dog Bites, Slip and Fall, Wrongful Death, International Law.
See Professional Biographies, ROCKFORD, ILLINOIS

Barrick, Switzer, Long, Balsley & Van Evera, (AV)
6833 Stalter Drive, First Floor, 61108
Telephone: 815-962-6611 Facsimile: 815-962-0687
Email: info@bslbv.com
Members of Firm: Stephen G. Balsley; Richard K. Van Evera; James E. Stevens; Thomas A. Green; Robert C. Pottinger; Jason H. Rock; Douglas R. Henry;—Tyler A. Moore; Laura A. Baluch; Stacy K. Shelly; Adam S. Long; Charlotte A. LeClercq. Of Counsel: William H. Barrick (1916-2003); Peter S. Switzer; Joseph L. Long; Armour T. Beckstrand.
Insurance Defense Litigation: Products Liability, Environmental Law, Premises Liability, Age Discrimination in Employment, Sex Discrimination, Race Discrimination, Dram Shop Liability, Professional Malpractice, Automobile, Construction and Fire, Business Law, Real Estate, Family Law, Probate, Civil Trial in All State and Federal Courts.
Representative Clients: Auto Owners Ins.; USF&G Ins.; State Farm Fire & Casualty; Stillman Valley National Bank (Illinois); Village of Cherry Valley.
See Professional Biographies, ROCKFORD, ILLINOIS

Bates, George D., (CV) . . . .'63 '90 C.209 B.S. L.46 J.D. 5823 Inverness Drive
Beck, Jeffrey, (BV) . . . . '57 '86 C.893 B.A. L.150 J.D. 6845 Weaver Rd., Ste. 203
Beckstrand, Armour T., (BV) . . . .'28 '56 C.123 B.S. L.902 LL.B. [Ⓒ Barrick,S.L.B.&V.]
Beger, Jerrold R., (BV) . . . .'44 '70 C.339 B.S. L.352 J.D. [J.R.Beger&Assoc.]
Beger, Jerrold R., & Associates, Limited, (BV) . . . . 910 2nd Ave., Ste. 110
Benjoya, Marc F., (BV) '58 '83 C.589 B.A. L.146 J.D.
[Cassiday,S.&G.] (⊙Libertyville)
Bergstrom, Jeremy P. . . . . '76 '01 C.339 B.A. L.209 J.D. [Ⓐ Faulkner&J.]
Berman, Richard A., (AV) . . . .'44 '74 C.340 B.A. L.879 J.D. [Williams&M.]
Bernsten, Benjamin W. . . . .'75 '02 C.399 B.A. L.966 J.D. [Ⓐ Williams&M.]
Beu, William R., (BV) . . . . '40 '66 C&L.879 B.A., J.D. 401 W. State St., Ste. 509
Beynon, Kathleen T., (CV) . . . . '63 '91 C.339 B.A. L.589 J.D. P.O. Box 6706
Bidzinski, Zenon J. . . . . '53 '80 C&L.602 B.A., J.D. 826 Roland Ave.
Bischoff, Kathryn A., Law Offices of, (BV) '59 '85
C.958 B.S. L.589 J.D. 405 W. State St.
Bivens, Jeffrey Alan . . . .'— '92 [J.A.Bivens]
Bivens, Jeffrey A., PC . . . . .5844 Elaine Dr.
Black, James F., (BV) . . . .'53 '85 C.339 B.A. L.734 J.D. 202 W State St Ste 1000
Blair, Brent D. . . . . '59 '91 C&L.589 B.A., J.D. [Martenson B.&R.]
Bond, David R. . . . . '28 '52 C&L.339 B.A., LL.B. 4571 Cinnamon Lane‡
Boreen, John M., (BV) . . . .'45 '75 C.999 B.A. L.365 J.D. [J.M.Boreen]
Boreen, John M., Ltd., (BV) . . . . 321 West State Street, Suite 1100
Boswell, Thomas H., (AV) . . . .'50 '80 C.870 B.S. L.801 J.D. [Hinshaw&C.]
Bowman, Louis C. . . . . '45 '74 C.589 B.S. L.209 J.D. 401 W. State Street, Room 600
Box, Charles E. . . . .'51 '76 C.197 A.B. L.477 J.D. Mayor
Boyd, Scott M., Law Office, (CV) . . . . '48 '73 C&L.966 B.A., J.D. 1 Court Pl., Ste. 302
Brady, Jana L. . . . . '78 '03 C.465 B.A. L.589 J.D. [Ⓐ Heyl,R.V.&A.]
Brandt, Frederic T., III, (BV) . . . . '48 '72 C.694 B.A. L.339 J.D. [Kostantacos&R.]
Brassfield, David James, (BV) . . . .'62 '87 C.879 B.S. L.793 J.D. [Brassfield,K.&R.]
Brassfield, Krueger & Ramlow, Ltd., (BV) . . . . 1491 S. Bell School Road
Braun, Patrick E., (CV) . . . . '57 '83 C.338 B.S. L.589 J.D. 401 W. State St.
Brazas, Susan M., (BV) . . . . '59 '90 C.98 B.S. L.339 J.D. [Ⓐ Barrett&G.]
Bresnahan, Angela Connelly . . . . '76 '01 C.589 B.S. L.339 J.D. [Ⓐ Holmstrom&K.]
Bretscher, John T. . . . . '58 '99 C.145 B.A. L.146 J.D. [Ⓐ Leydig,V.&M.] (⊙Chicago)
Brooks, Aaron W., (BV) . . . . '69 '96 C.1329 B.A. L.339 J.D. [Holmstrom&K.]
Brown, David J., (CV) . . . .'57 '83 C.339 B.S. L.589 J.D. 216 N. Court St.
Bruce, Joseph J., (BV) . . . . '52 '77 C.399 B.A. L.273 J.D. [Bruce,J.J.]
Bruce, Joseph J., P.C., (BV) . . . . 321 W. State St.
Bruscato, Joseph Peter, (BV) . . . . '62 '87 C&L.436 B.A., J.D. 1 Court Place

Buchanan, Tomiko L., Law Office of '72 '97 C.589 B.S. L.879 J.D.
555 N. Court Street, Suite 10, 61103-6898
Telephone: 815-961-8760
Email: Tomikolaw@sbcglobal.net URL: http://www.tomikolaw.com
Criminal Law, Expungements, DWI, Juvenile Law, Personal Injury, Automobile Accidents, Child Support, Expungements.
See Professional Biographies, ROCKFORD, ILLINOIS

Bueschel, Thomas A., (BV) . . . . '52 '78 C.98 B.S. L.285 J.D. [Conde K.B.&C.]
Butera, Lucia . . . . '63 '89 C.927 B.A. L.1187 J.D. [Butera]
Butera, Richard M., (CV) . . . . '56 '82 C.57 B.A. L.365 J.D. [Butera]
Butera Law Offices, P.C., (CV) . . . . 728 N. Main St.
Cacciatore, William T., (BV) . . . . '40 '73 C.597 B.S. L.365 J.D. 321 West State Street
Cacciatore, William T., Jr., (BV) . . . . '69 '98 C.697 B.S. L.365 J.D. [Ⓐ W.T.Cacciatore]
Cain, Daniel J., (AV) . . . . '48 '75 C.339 B.S. L.146 J.D. [Sreenan&C.]
Calgaro, Robert A., (BV) . . . .'54 '78 C.597 B.A. L.339 J.D. [Conde K.B.&C.]
Canavesi, Karl J., Law Office '31 '62 C.697 B.A. L.966 J.D.
321 W. State St., Ste. 1114
Canfield, Elizabeth F. . . . .'— '50 C.187 L.981 LL.B. 202 W. State St.
Canfield, Robert E. . . . . '47 '78 C&L.494 B.A., J.D. 910 2nd Ave.
Cannariato, Sam J., (BV) . . . . '19 '49 C&L.339 B.S., J.D. 924 Nassau Pkwy.
Carlson, Ann-Marie . . . .'43 '88 C.1183 B.A. L.589 J.D. 501 7th Street
Carpenter, Jacob M. . . . .'— '03 C.210 B.A. L.469 J.D. [Ⓐ Williams&M.]
Carpenter, Paul A., Law Office of '— '01
C.339 B.A. L.589 J.D. 2222 E. State St. Suite G2
Casey, Kim M., (AV) . . . . '57 '81 C.338 B.S. L.339 J.D. [Holmstrom&K.]
Caskey, David H. . . . .'31 '57 C.311 B.A. L.966 J.D. Rock Valley College
Cassel, Jamie J. Swenson, (BV) . . . . '60 '86 C&L.972 B.S., J.D. [Reno&Z.]

Cassiday, Schade & Gloor, LLP, (AV)
120 West State Street, Suite 401, 61101-1159 ⊙
Telephone: 815-962-8301 Fax: 815-962-8401
URL: http://www.cassiday.com
Members of Firm: Marc F. Benjoya (Also at Libertyville); William W. Ranard (Also at Chicago Office); Sally J. Zimmerman (Also at Chicago Office). Associate: Ronald D. Fiet (Also at Chicago Office).
General Practice. Civil Trial Practice, Civil Appellate Practice, Insurance Coverage, Environmental, Medical and Professional Malpractice, Products Liability, Structural Work Act, Railroad, Employment, Corporate and Health Care Law, Commercial Litigation, Construction, Workers Compensation, Intellectual Property, Municipalities, Transportation, Patent Law.
A list of Representative Clients will be made available upon request.
Chicago, Illinois Office: 20 North Wacker Drive, Suite 1040, 60606-2903. Telephone: 312-641-3100. Fax: 312-444-1669.
Libertyville, Illinois Office: 1870 West Winchester Road, Suite 148, 60048-5353. Telephone: 847-932-6922. Fax: 847-932-6947.
Naperville, Illinois Office: 1230 East Diehl Road, Suite 202, 60563-9362. Telephone: 630-328-2970. Fax: 630-328-2979.
See Professional Biographies, ROCKFORD, ILLINOIS

Castegnaro, David R. . . . . '49 '80 C.602 B.A. L.209 J.D. 211 E. State St., Ste. A
Castree, Samuel J., Jr., (BV) . . . .'61 '87 C&L.339 B.A., J.D. Staff Mgmt. Inc.
Cheney, Greg A., (BV) . . . . '50 '76 C.338 B.A. L.801 J.D. 4320 Spring Creek Road
Chostner, Chester R., Jr., (CV) . . . . '51 '76 C.589 B.A. L.801 J.D. [C.R.Chostner,Jr.]
Chostner, Chester R., Jr., P.C., (CV) . . . . 1 Court Pl., Suite 202
Cicero, Mathew P. . . . . '20 '49 C&L.339 B.S., J.D. 1903 Boscobel Ct.‡
Cicero, Paul R., (AV) . . . .'49 '74 C.339 B.A. L.910 J.D. [Cicero&F.]

Cicero & France, A Professional Corporation, (AV) [BR]
6323 East Riverside Boulevard, 61114
Telephone: 815-226-7700 Fax: 815-226-7701
URL: http://www.cicerofrancelaw.com
Paul R. Cicero; John W. France; Ronald A. Barch; Charles P. Alexander.
Insurance Defense, First and Third Party Insurance Defense, Property and Casualty Defense, Automobile Insurance Defense, Business Law and Litigation including Family Owned Businesses, Fraud, Contracts, Employment Agreements, Business Sales and Acquisitions, Commercial Litigation, Family Law including Divorce, Child Custody, Child Support, Spousal Support, Alimony, Adoptions, Visitation Rights, Separation Agreements and Parenting Plans.
See Professional Biographies, ROCKFORD, ILLINOIS

Clark, Gregory H., (CV) . . . .'47 '75 C.697 B.A. L.221 J.D. 401 W. State St.
Close, Henry J., (AV) . . . . '36 '61 C.686 A.B. L.424 J.D. [Ⓒ Oliver,C.W.W.&G.]
Cocoma, Christopher J., (BV) . . . . '68 '93 C.72 B.A. L.1194 J.D. [McGreevy W.]
Conde, Dale F., (AV) . . . . '22 '48 C.339 L.597 J.D. [Conde K.B.&C.]

Conde Killoren Bueschel & Calgaro, (AV)
120 West State Street, Suite 400, 61101
Telephone: 815-987-4000 Fax: 815-987-9889
Members of Firm: Dale F. Conde; Thomas A. Killoren; Thomas A. Bueschel; Robert A. Calgaro.
Estate Planning including Probate, Trusts, Charitable Giving, Business Succession Planning, Wealth Preservation, Taxation, Commercial Law, Corporate Law, Business Law and Litigation, School Law, Residential and Commercial Real Estate, Contracts, Leases, Land Use, Zoning.
See Professional Biographies, ROCKFORD, ILLINOIS

Cowan, Alfred W., (BV) . . . . '36 '63 C.72 B.A. L.339 LL.B. P.O. Box 5143
Cox, Gregory E., (BV) . . . .'60 '85 C.694 B.A. L.589 J.D. [Ⓐ Nicolosi&Assoc.]
Crosby, Michael S. . . . . '51 '76 C.375 B.S. L.986 J.D. [Crosby&Assoc.]
Crosby & Associates, P.C., A Law Office of . . . . .475 Executive Parkway
Crowe, Lawrence E. . . . .'— '97 C.339 B.S. L.365 J.D. [Reinhart B.V.s.c.]
Crowell, Lynsey A. . . . . '80 '05 C.339 B.A. L.589 J.D. [Ⓐ Heyl,R.V.&A.]
Crowley, Thomas P. . . . .'70 '02 C.999 L.589 J.D. [Ⓐ Heyl,R.V.&A.]
Currier, Thomas E., (BV) . . . .'38 '67 C.976 B.E. L.273 LL.B. 124 N. Water St.

Cwynar, Daniel A. '53 '79 C&L.209 J.D.
One Court Place, Suite 100, 61101
Telephone: 815-964-4601 Fax: 815-964-3932
Email: dac53golf@aol.com URL: http://www.rockfordbankruptcylaw.com
Bankruptcy including individual and small business, foreclosures, repossessions, chapter 7, chapter 13; Residential and Commercial Real Estate, Buying and Selling, Contracts, Criminal Defense, DUI, Traffic, Misdemeanors.
See Professional Biographies, ROCKFORD, ILLINOIS

Cyrs, Michael T., (BV) . . . .'69 '94 C.602 B.B.A. L.436 J.D. [Williams&M.]
Dailing, Joseph A. '43 '74
C.602 B.A. L.352 J.D. Exec. Dir., Prairie State Legal Servs., Inc.
Daugherty, Anthea Riley . . . . '65 '00 C.1248 B.S. L.365 J.D. 5848 Crampton Ct.
Davenport, Tara D. . . . . '74 '01 C.1348 B.A. L.589 J.D. 4615 E. State St., Ste. 203
Davitt, David L., (BV) . . . . '56 '82 C.1144 B.A. L.221 J.D. [Schlueter E.O.M.&D.]
Davitt, Vern L., (CV) . . . . '29 '53 C&L.221 LL.B. 504 N. Church St.
Day, Lisa A. '61 '86 C.187 B.A. L.352 J.D.
2nd V.P. & Asst. Gen. Coun., Conseco Services, L.L.C.
Dean, Samuel L., Jr. . . . . '21 '49 L.94 LL.B. 317 Mulberry St.
DeGunther, Richard N. . . . . '33 '61 C.352 B.A. L.339 LL.B. U.S. Bkrptcy. J.
Delia, Debra A., (BV) . . . . '62 '87 C.436 B.A. L.339 J.D. [Oliver,C.W.W.&G.]
Dempsey, Ann T., (BV) . . . .'65 '90 C&L.339 B.A., J.D. [Oliver,C.W.W.&G.]
Denning, Michael J. . . . . '77 '02 C.98 B.S. L.589 J.D. [Ⓐ Heyl,R.V.&A.]
DeRango, Christopher A., (BV) . . . . '64 '94 C&L.589 B.A., J.D. [Ⓐ Sreenan&C.]
Devine, James P., (BV) . . . .'56 '81 C.234 B.A. L.339 J.D. [Williams&M.]
Dicaprio, Joseph A. . . . .'48 '90 C.999 A.B. L.1183 J.D. 6281 Valley Knoll
Dietrich, William H. '— '97 C.792 B.S. L.793 J.D.
(adm. in SD; not adm. in IL) [Ⓐ Reinhart B.V.s.c.]
Dittmar, Ann Marie, (BV) . . . .'58 '89 C.589 B.S.,M.S. L.339 J.D. [McGreevy W.]
Doar, Michael '55 '84 C.674 A.B. L.245 J.D.
(adm. in GA; not adm. in IL) The Ingersoll Milling Machine Co.
Dodson, Christopher William, (BV) . . . . '67 '96 C&L.589 B.S., J.D. [C.W.Dodson]
Dodson, Christopher W., Attorney at Law, (BV) . . . . .4855 E. State St.
Doepke, Nancy L., (CV) . . . .'66 '94 C.136 B.A. L.1187 J.D. [McGreevy W.]
Doherty, Eugene G., (BV) . . . . '61 '89 C&L.589 B.S., J.D. [Holmstrom&K.]
Dohm, Jerome E. '27 '51 C.688 L.436 LL.B.
(adm. in WI; not adm. in IL) Rockford Title Co.
Donahue, Daniel M., (BV) . . . . '51 '79 C&L.339 B.A., J.D. [McGreevy W.]
Donohue, James L., (AV) . . . .'36 '64 C&L.352 B.A., J.D. One Court Place
Ecklund, Carl A., (BV) . . . .'64 '90 C.937 B.A. L.966 J.D. [Williams&M.]
Ecklund, Gary L., (BV) . . . . '36 '63 C.937 B.A. L.339 J.D. [Schlueter E.O.M.&D.]
Edgren, Idalis O., (CV) . . . . '64 '97 C.1090 B.S. L.972 J.D. 3821 E. State St.

Ellis, Stephen A., (BV) ....'36 '64 C.894 A.B. L.309 LL.B. [Ellis&E.]
Ellis & Ellis, (BV) .... 321 W. State St. (⊙Fairport, NY)
Emmert, William D., (BV) .... '54 '80 C.697 B.S. L.900 J.D. Asst. States Atty.
Engelsma, Fernando L., (BV) ....'54 '79 C.697 B.A. L.146 J.D. Asst. Pub. Def.
Enichen, Edward J., (AV) ....'29 '54 C.162 B.A. L.339 J.D. [Guyer&E.]
Epstein, Laura Ann, & Associates ... '69 '94 C.966 B.A. L.339 J.D. [L.A.Epstein&Assoc.]
Epstein, Laura A., & Associates .... 4011 N. Mulford Road
Eubank, Franklin J., Jr., (CV) .... '— '92 C.339 B.A. L.365 J.D. 126 N. Church St.
Fabiano, Anthony R., (BV) .... '27 '54 C&L.339 B.A., J.D. [Fabiano]
Fabiano Law Offices, (BV) .... 321 West State Street
Fahy, Edward J., (AV) ....'11 '36 C&L.276 A.B., J.D. [Ⓒ Reno&Z.]
Faulkner, David P., (AV) .... '55 '81 C.800 B.A. L.339 J.D. [Faulkner&J.]
Faulkner & Jensen LLC, (AV) .... 6832 Stalter Drive
Fennell, Debra D., (BVⓉ) .... '59 '84 C.967 B.A. L.117 J.D. 6922 Wicksbury Lane
Ferguson, Ray Alan, (BV) .... '50 '80 C.697 B.A. L.365 J.D. 216 N. Court St.
Ferolie, Lawrence J., (AV) .... '22 '70 C.339 B.A. L.365 LL.B. [Ferolie,P.&W.]
Ferolie, Perrecone & White, Ltd., (AV) .... 321 West State Street
Fiet, Ronald D. .... '66 '96 C.56 B.A. L.879 J.D. [Ⓐ Cassiday,S.&G.] (⊙Chicago)
Flanagan, Maureen ....'45 '99 C.182 B.S. L.1051 J.D. [Ⓐ Hinshaw&C.]
Flanders, Gary C., (BV) .... '52 '81 C.697 B.S. L.990 J.D. Bankruptcy Clinic
Foley, John H., Jr. .... '26 '52 C&L.966 B.S., LL.B. 1128 Scottswood Rd.
Fong, Patricia N. Wong '55 '81
C.339 B.S. L.352 J.D. V.P. & Tr. Offr., AMCORE Investment Grp.
Fore, Allen G. ....'65 '91 C.248 B.A. L.879 J.D. Asst. Atty. Gen.
Forsythe, Stacy Lynn ....'72 '97 C.339 B.A. L.846 J.D. Stat's Atty. Off.
Fox, Pamela S., (AV) .... '51 '77 C&L.1165 B.A., J.D. [Hinshaw&C.]
France, John W., (AV) ....'46 '75 C.966 B.S. L.146 J.D. [Cicero&F.]
Frankfort, Philip R., (AV) ....'48 '74 C&L.37 B.S., J.D. [Holmstrom&K.]

Frantz, Keith '55 '93 C.350 B.S.M.E. L.589 J.D.
401 West State Street, Suite 200, 61101
Telephone: 815-987-9820 Fax: 815-987-9869 Email: Keith_Frantz@msn.com
Email: KeithFrantz@aol.com
Intellectual Property Law including Patents, Trademarks, Trade Secrets, Trade Dress, Unfair Competition, Franchise Matters, Computer Law and related litigation and licensing matters with an emphasis in the Electrical, Mechanical, Chemical, Pharmaceutical and Biotechnology areas.
See Professional Biographies, ROCKFORD, ILLINOIS

Fredrickson, Robert A., (AV) ....'45 '71 C&L.966 B.B.A., J.D. [Reno&Z.]
Freedle, Brette E. ....'— '98 C.597 B.A. L.365 J.D. [Ⓐ O'Hagan,S.&A.]
French, Robert J. ....'30 '59 C.337 A.B. L.209 J.D. Ret. Assoc. Cir. J.
Frost, Kevin J. .... '67 '95 C&L.339 B.S., J.D. 7320 N. Alpine Rd.
Fulbright, Shawn C., (BV) .... '70 '96 C.475 B.S. L.221 J.D. [Guyer&E.]
Gaines, Richard D., (AV) ....'44 '69 C.210 B.A. L.339 J.D. [Holmstrom&K.]
Galluzzo, Gino, (CV) ....'71 '97 C.589 B.S. L.365 J.D. [Nicolosi&Assoc.]
Gamm, Stacey M. ....'74 '01 C.502 B.S.Ed. L.589 J.D. [Ⓐ Reno&Z.]
Ganschow, Jaime R. '77 '02
C.339 B.A. L.589 J.D. Pub. Def., Winnebago Co. Pub. Def. Off.
Gaziano, Angelo N., (CV) ....'22 '50 C&L.339 B.S.L. 321 W. State St.
Gaziano, Mary J., (BV) ....'57 '83 C&L.339 B.A., J.D. Co. Pub. Admr. & Pub. Guard.

Gaziano, Paul E., (AV) '49 '75 C.755 B.A. L.1035 J.D.
311 Seventh Street, 61104
Telephone: 815-964-7933 Fax: 815-964-6189
Criminal Litigation. Criminal Appeals in Federal and State Courts, Traffic, DUI, Juvenile.
See Professional Biographies, ROCKFORD, ILLINOIS

Geissler, Burkhard, (BV) ....'43 '69 C.339 B.A. L.352 J.D. [Geissler]

Geissler Law Office, P.C., (BV)
6845 Weaver Road, Suite 100, 61114
Telephone: 815-633-2500 Fax: 815-633-2516
Email: geissler@geisslerlaw.com
Burkhard Geissler.
Business Law and Litigation including corporate, Limited Liability Companies (LLC's), Partnerships, Mergers, Acquisitions, Dissolutions, Contracts, Business Formation, Employment Agreement, Real Estate Law including, Contracts, Leases, Like-Kind Exchanges, Estate Planning including Gift and Estate Tax Advisement, Simple and Complex Trusts, Charitable Gift Planning, Business Succession Planning, Probate and Trust Administration.
See Professional Biographies, ROCKFORD, ILLINOIS

Gesmer, James Andrew, (CV) ....'60 '86 C.388 B.A. L.1119 J.D. [Gesmer]
Gesmer, Jason N., (BV) .... '29 '53 C&L.597 B.A., J.D. [Gesmer]
Gesmer Law Offices, P.C., (BV) ....630 N. Church St., Ste. 201
Gibbs, Patricia E., (CV) '64 '92
C.697 B.A. L.589 J.D. Asst. Gen. Coun., First Rockford Group
Gilbert, Daniel T., (BV) .... '54 '80 C.697 B.S. L.365 J.D. [Barrett&G.]

Gilbert, John '— '95 C.927 B.A. L.1187 J.D.
202 West State Street, 61101
Telephone: 815-877-2500 Fax: 815-877-2300
Email: attygilb1@aol.com URL: http://www.jgilbertlawfirm.com
Criminal Law, DUI/DWI, Drug Crimes, Parole and Probation, Juvenile Law, Traffic Violations, Bankruptcy, Real Estate, Criminal Leasing, Residential, Family Law, Child Custody, Child Support, Divorce, Visitation Rights, Domestic Violence, Adoption, Wills and Probate, Trusts and Estates, Estate Planning, Business Law, Business Planning, Contracts, Business Litigation, Business Enterprises.
See Professional Biographies, ROCKFORD, ILLINOIS

Gilbert, Louis R., (BV) .... '24 '52 C.884 L.436 LL.B. 3106 N. Rockton Ave.
Gilbert & Lowe ....3400 North Rocton Avenue
Gill, Timothy R. .... '47 '72 C.589 L.436 J.D. Assoc. Cir. J.
Gillen, Suzanne, (BV) ....'61 '87 C.393 B.A. L.146 J.D. [Mangan,L.G.&L.] ⊙
Glazer, Jeffrey M. ....'— '04 C.851 B.B.A. L.146 J.D. [Ⓐ Reno&Z.]
Glidden, Victoria R., (BV) ....'57 '88 C&L.347 B.A., J.D. [Hinshaw&C.]
Goddard, Alpheus John, III ....'36 '61 C.31 A.B. L.309 LL.B. 1639 N. Alpine Rd.
Godlewski, Paul S., Law Office of, (BV) '50 '76
C.339 B.A. L.365 J.D. 1 Court Pl., Ste. 103
Goff, William M., (BV) ....'56 '84 C.927 B.A. L.221 J.D. [Ⓐ Mateer&Assoc.]
Golian, Gary J., (CV) ....'52 '84 C.629 B.S. L.589 J.D. Sr. Reg. Legal Coun.
Gosdick, Robert W., (AV) ......'33 '58 C.602 B.A. L.597 J.D. 4615 E. State St. (⊙Byron)
Gottfred, William E., (BV) ....'56 '82 C.1144 B.A. L.616 J.D. [Ⓐ Reese&R.]
Gravino, Marc C., (BV) ....'62 '88 C.589 B.G.S. L.966 J.D. [Williams&M.]
Green, Mary Linn, (BV) ....'52 '92 C.753 B.S. L.589 J.D. [Hinshaw&C.]
Green, Thomas A., (BV) .... '57 '84 C.957 B.A. L.589 J.D. [Barrick,S.L.B.&V.]
Greene, Herbert I., (BV) .... '39 '63 C&L.209 B.S., J.D. 401 W. State St.
Greenlee, Cheri N., (BV) .... '49 '75 C.98 B.A. L.365 J.D. [Greenlee&K.]
Greenlee & Kreitlow, P.C., (BV) .... One Court Pl.
Greenwald, Thomas E., (AV) ..... '45 '70 C.220 B.A. L.436 J.D. [Oliver,C.W.W.&G.] ⊙
Greg Tuite & Associate, (BV) .... 119 N. Church St.
Grimme Schilling, Nancy, (CV) ....'69 '97 C.72 B.A. L.966 J.D. [Ⓐ Reno&Z.]
Gulley, Gwyn, (CV) .... '64 '91 C.338 B.S. L.325 J.D. 202 W. State Street, Suite 400
Gustafson, Rogert H. .... '76 '03 C.338 B.S. L.589 J.D. [Ⓐ Faulkner&J.]

Guth, Gregory P., (AV) .... '47 '76 C.589 B.A. L.146 J.D. [Guth M.]
Guth Mediations Inc., (AV) .... 555 N. Court St., Ste. 203

Guyer & Enichen, P.C., (AV) BR
2601 Reid Farm Road, Suite B, 61114
Telephone: 815-636-9600 Fax: 815-636-9666 URL: http://www.guyerlaw.com
Email: guyer@guyerlaw.com URL: http://www.guyerlawfirm.com
Stanley H. Guyer (1903-1986); Edward J. Enichen; G. Michael Scheurich; James E. Tuneberg; Edward M. Maher; Shawn C. Fulbright;—Melissa S. Oulavong; Thomas R. Jakeway; Timothy A. Muldowney.
Real Estate Law and Litigation including Land Use and Zoning, Real Estate Valuation, Commercial and Residential Real Estate, Property Assessment Challenge, Land Development, Municipal Law, Estate Planning, Wealth Preservation, Charitable Giving, Business Succession Planning, Trusts, Estate, Taxation, Probate, Probate Litigation, Business, Corporate, Environmental Law, Commercial Litigation, Creditors Rights, Bankruptcy, Mechanics Liens, Private and Agency Adoptions.
Reference: Amcore Bank N.A. of Rockford, Ill.
See Professional Biographies, ROCKFORD, ILLINOIS

Haggestad, Troy E., (BV) .... '68 '95 C.589 B.S. L.602 J.D. [Williams&M.]
Haines, Victoria M. '58 '89 C.346 B.S. L.146 J.D.
Asst. Gen. Coun., Hamilton Sundstrand Corp.
Hallsten, Dawn, (BV) ....'51 '93 C.697 B.A. L.966 J.D. [Ⓐ Mateer&Assoc.]
Hammer, Natalie Marie ....'70 '97 C&L.589 B.A., J.D. Law Clk., U.S. Dist. Ct.

Hampilos, George P., (CV) '67 '92 C.801 B.A. L.823 J.D.
308 West State Street Suite 210, 61101 ⊙
Telephone: 815-962-0044 Fax: 815-962-6250 URL: http://www.lawyers.com/sm&h
Email: GEORGEHAMP@AOL.COM URL: http://www.smhlawoffice.com
Commercial Collections and Creditors Rights.
See Professional Biographies, ROCKFORD, ILLINOIS

Hampilos, George P., (CV) '67 '92 C.801 B.A. L.823 J.D.
[Schirger,M.&H.] (⊙Rockford)
Harlan, Sherry L., (BV) .... '61 '87 C.340 B.A. L.966 J.D. [Ⓐ Hinshaw&C.]
Harris, Jeffrey L. '52 '78 C.494 B.A. L.352 J.D.
(adm. in IA; not adm. in IL) 1523 S. Central Ave.★
Hartline, Carol A., (CV) ....'72 '99 C.339 B.A. L.589 J.D. [Ⓐ Picha&S.]
Hawley, Christine J., (CV) .... '55 '84 C.602 B.A. L.589 J.D. 6448 Willowick Court
Hayes, Patrick W., (BV) .... '63 '88 C&L.589 B.S., J.D. 425 E. State Street
Healy, Bernard F., (BV) .... '32 '56 C&L.424 B.S.C., J.D. 6067 Strathmoor Drive
Heaslip, Patrick L., (BV) .... '53 '82 C.589 B.S. L.221 J.D. 400 West State Street
Heckinger, John F., Jr. ....'48 '75 C.707 B.A. L.734 J.D. P.O. Box 1492
Hedeen, Michael J., (BV) ....'53 '88 C&L.801 B.S., J.D. [Soderberg&Assoc.]
Heinisch, Andrew J., (BV) .... '— '97 C&L.339 B.S., J.D. [Reinhart B.V.s.c.]
Helsten, Charles F., (BV) ....'50 '79 C.248 B.A. L.221 J.D. [Hinshaw&C.]
Hennelly, Collis M. ....'28 '53 C&L.209 B.S., J.D. 504 N. Church St.
Henry, Douglas R., (BV) .... '61 '95 C.477 B.A. L.851 J.D. [Barrick,S.L.B.&V.]
Hess, James M., (BV) .... '41 '71 C.602 B.A. L.352 J.D. 201 S. Madison St.
Hevrin, Matthew M., (CV) ....'73 '98 C.339 B.S. L.589 J.D. [Hinshaw&C.]

Heyl, Royster, Voelker & Allen, Professional Corporation, (AV)
Second Floor, National City Bank Building, 120 West State Street, P.O. Box 1288, 61105-1288 ⊙
Telephone: 815-963-4454 Telecopier: 815-963-0399
Email: firm@hrva.com URL: http://www.hrva.com
Partners: Douglas J. Pomatto; Kevin J. Luther; Mark J. McClenathan. Of Counsel: Brent A. Swanson; Scott G. Salemi; Kathleen M. Stockwell; Charles E. Timmerwilke. Associates: Jill I. Rogers-Manning; Brad A. Antonacci; Thomas P. Crowley; Michael J. Denning; Andrew J. Roth; Lori E. McGirk; Jana L. Brady; Lynsey A. Crowell.
General Civil Trial and Appellate Practice in all Courts, Insurance Defense, Workers' Compensation Defense, Professional Liability Defense, Truck Accidents, Construction Law, Railroad Accidents and Injuries, Insurance Coverage, Self Insured Defense, Products Liability Defense, Civil Rights, Asbestos Defense, Class Action Defense, Corporate Law, Health Care, Banking, Government, Employment, Environmental, Probate, Elder Law, Agribusiness, Immigration, Religious Institutions, Nonprofit and Charitable Organizations, College and University Law, and Real Estate.
Peoria, Illinois Office: Suite 600, Chase Building, 124 S.W. Adams, 61602. Telephone: 309-676-0400. Telecopier: 309-676-3374.
Springfield, Illinois Office: Suite 575, National City Center, P.O. Box 1687, 62705. Telephone: 217-522-8822. Telecopier: 217-523-3902.
Urbana, Illinois Office: Suite 300, 102 East Main Street, P.O. Box 129, 61803-0129. Telephone: 217-344-0060. Telecopier: 217-344-9295.
Edwardsville, Illinois Office: Suite 100, Mark Twain Plaza II, 103 West Vandalia Street, P.O. Box 467, 62025. Telephone: 618-656-4646. Telecopier: 618-656-7940.
See Professional Biographies, ROCKFORD, ILLINOIS

Hilden, Joseph F. ..... '41 '68 C.424 A.B. L.209 J.D. Asst. V.P., Conseco Services, L.L.C.

Hinshaw & Culbertson LLP, (AV) BR
Hinshaw & Culbertson LLP is an Illinois registered limited liability partnership that has elected to be governed by the Illinois Uniform Partnership Act (1997)
100 Park Avenue, P.O. Box 1389, 61105-1389 ⊙
Telephone: 815-490-4900 Facsimile: 815-490-4901 Telex: 880248
Email: kfox@hinshawlaw.com URL: http://www.hinshawlaw.com
Partners: James M. Allen; Jerrod L. Barenbaum; Thomas H. Boswell; Pamela S. Fox; Victoria R. Glidden; Mary Linn Green; Charles F. Helsten; Matthew M. Hevrin; Lori L. Hoadley; Gary R. Kardell; James W. Keeling; Penelope M. Lechtenberg; Thomas J. Lester; Frank P. Maggio; Stephen T. Moore (Co-Chair, Health Care Specialty Practice Group); Marcia L. Mueller; James R. Pirages; Richard S. Porter; Richard M. Schilling; D. Reneé Schroeder; Jeffry S. Spears; Charles F. Thomas. Associates: Maureen Flanagan; Sherry L. Harlan; Kenya A. Jenkins; Erik W. Lindberg; Timothy J. Leake; Carol A. Lockwood; Lisa R. Munch; Alyson R. Rumshas.
Appellate, Banking & Financing, Bankruptcy & Creditors' Rights, Class Action Litigation, Civil Rights Defense, Commercial Litigation, Corporate, Construction Law, Director & Officer Liability, Employee Benefits, Environmental, Fidelity & Surety, General Liability Litigation, Government, Health Care, Insurance Coverage, Insurance and Reinsurance, Labor & Employment, Legal Malpractice, Medical Malpractice, Mergers & Acquisitions, Municipal Liability, Personal Injury Defense, Public Law, Products Liability Litigation, Professional Liability, Regulatory, Real Estate, School Law, Securities, Taxation, Transportation, White Collar Crime and Workers' Compensation Defense.
Other Office Locations: Chicago, Illinois; Appleton, Wisconsin; Belleville, Illinois; Boston, Massachusetts; Champaign, Illinois; Crystal Lake, Illinois; Edwardsville, Illinois; Fort Lauderdale, Florida; Jacksonville, Florida; Joliet, Illinois; Lisle, Illinois; Los Angeles, California; Miami, Florida; Milwaukee, Wisconsin; Minneapolis, Minnesota; New York, New York; Peoria, Illinois; Phoenix, Arizona; Portland, Oregon; Providence, Rhode Island; St. Louis, Missouri; San Francisco, California; Schererville, Indiana; Springfield, Illinois; Tampa, Florida; Waukegan, Illinois.
See Professional Biographies, ROCKFORD, ILLINOIS

Hoadley, Lori L., (CV) ....'62 '99 C&L.589 B.A., J.D. [Hinshaw&C.]
Hohe, Sara M. .... '59 '89 C.927 B.S. L.146 J.D. Asst. State Atty., State Atty.'s Off.
Holevas, John J., (AV) ....'61 '86 C.352 B.A. L.879 J.D. [Williams&M.]
Holliman, Ronda ....'71 '00 C.927 B.A. L.339 J.D. Winnebago Cty State Attny Off
Holmgren, Janet Clark ....'55 '85 C.208 B.A. L.589 J.D. Cir. J.
Holmstrom, John, Jr., (AV) ....'20 '48 C&L.339 B.S., J.D. [Holmstrom&K.]

Holmstrom & Kennedy, P.C., (AV) BR
800 North Church Street, P.O. Box 589, 61105
Telephone: 815-962-7071 Fax: 815-962-7181
Email: mail@holmstromlaw.com URL: http://www.holmstromlaw.com
John Holmstrom, Jr.; Richard D. Gaines; Philip R. Frankfort; Donald L. Moore; Bradley T. Koch; Kim M. Casey; Roberta L. Holzwarth; Michael J. Schappert; Michael Jon Shalbrack; Eugene G. Doherty; Alexander J. Mezny; Aaron W. Brooks; Kristine Pihl Youman;—Suzanne R. Lukas; James C. Lukas; Angela Connelly Bresnahan; Erin E. Walsh.

(This Listing Continued)

Holmstrom & Kennedy, P.C. (Continued)

General Civil, Trial and Appellate Practice in State and Federal Courts, Complex Litigation, Administrative, Professional Malpractice Defense, Creditor's Rights and Bankruptcy, Health Care, Labor and Employment, Corporate and Business, Tax, Technology, Computer and Telecommunications, Real Estate, Estate Planning and Probate, Mediation and Arbitration.

See Professional Biographies, ROCKFORD, ILLINOIS

Holzwarth, Roberta L., (AV) ... '58 '83 C.813 B.A. L.339 J.D. [Holmstrom&K.]
Honzel, Donna R., (BV) ... '65 '91 C.134 B.S. L.339 J.D. [[A] Mateer&Assoc.]
Horne, Andrea L. '65 '91 C&L.597 B.A., J.D.
V.P., Corp. Develop., Newell Rubbermaid, Inc.
Horning, Timothy F., (BV) ... '59 '89 C.958 B.A. L.365 J.D. 3400 N. Rockton Ave.
Huffman, Barbara L., (BV) ... '53 '91 C.25 B.A. L.589 J.D. [McGreevy W.]
Hyzer, Keith, (AV) ... '31 '58 C.388 B.A. L.339 J.D. [Hyzer,H.&J.]
Hyzer, Nancy, (BV) ... '39 '84 C.966 B.S. L.589 J.D. [Hyzer,H.&J.]

Hyzer, Hyzer & Jacobs, (AV)
855 North Madison Street, 61107-3095
Telephone: 815-965-3600 Fax: 815-965-3636
Email: hyzerlawfirm@ameritech.net
Keith Hyzer; Nancy Hyzer; Erik K. Jacobs.
Residential Real Estate, Commercial Real Estate, Condominium Development, Business Law, Corporate Law, Trusts and Estates, Civil Litigation and Appellate Practice.

See Professional Biographies, ROCKFORD, ILLINOIS

Jackson, William C. ... '26 '52 C&L.339 B.S., J.D. 725 Tamarack Ln.‡
Jacobs, Erik K., (BV) ... '65 '91 C.352 B.B.A. L.589 J.D. [Hyzer,H.&J.]
Jakeway, Thomas R. ... '78 '04 C&L.589 B.S., J.D. [[A] Guyer&E.]
Jenkins, Kenya A. ... '78 '03 C.879 B.A. L.589 J.D. [[A] Hinshaw&C.]
Jenkins, Michael ... '46 '77 C.221 B.A. L.801 J.D. Dept. of Community Develop.
Jensen, Lisa A. ... '62 '87 C.338 B.S. L.146 J.D. [Faulkner&J.]
Johnson, Thomas S., (AV) ... '42 '67 C.697 A.B. L.309 LL.B. [Williams&M.]
Joike, Rebecca Ann ... '42 '80 C.339 A.B. L.1035 J.D. 5620 Coachman Ct.
Kalivoda, Fredrick F., (BV) ... '20 '48 C.504 L.209 J.D. [Kalivoda&S.]
Kalivoda & Shelton, (BV) ... 321 W. State St.
Kapala, Frederick J. ... '50 '76 C.436 A.B. L.339 J.D. Cir. J.
Kaplan, Lewis B., (BV) ... '42 '68 C.966 B.A. L.339 J.D. P.O. Box 1254
Kardell, Gary R., (BV) ... '47 '73 C&L.339 B.S., J.D. [Hinshaw&C.]
Kastberg, Erin E. ... '— '04 C.350 B.S. L.352 J.D. [[A] Reno&Z.]
Katz, Stephen G., (AV) '49 '73 C&L.966 B.A., J.D.
Gen. Coun., Rockford Pub. Schools
Keeling, James W., (AV) ... '48 '74 C.399 B.A. L.174 J.D. [Hinshaw&C.]
Keys, Marvin L. ... '73 '98 C.258 B.A. L.589 J.D. Asst. Gen. Coun., First Rockford Group
Kielty, Arthur G., (BV) ... '66 '91 C&L.339 A.B., J.D. [Reno&Z.]
Killoren, Thomas A., (AV) ... '31 '59 C&L.339 B.A., J.D. [Conde K.B.&C.]
King, Daniel ... '37 '64 C.668 B.A. L.339 LL.B. 401 W. State St., Ste. 201
Kleitsch, Rodney W. ... '76 '01 C&L.352 B.A., J.D. [[A] Reno&Z.]
Kleppin, Fred C. ... '11 '35 C.339 L.146 LL.B. 1903 Bradley Rd.‡
Kney, Kevin J. '56 '81 C.573 B.B.A. L.990 J.D.
Asst. Gen. Coun., Hamilton Sundstrand Corp.
Knight, William D., Jr. ... '25 '53 C.197 A.B. L.597 J.D. 4764 N. Main St.‡
Koch, Bradley T. ... '51 '76 C.352 B.A. L.190 J.D. [Holmstrom&K.]
Kosek, Joseph Benjamin ... '61 '86 C.597 B.A. L.209 J.D. 405 W. State St.
Koski, David D. ... '44 '69 C.679 B.A. L.339 J.D. First Dep. States Atty.
Kostantacos, Charles P., (BV) ... '54 '81 C.477 B.A. L.365 J.D. [Kostantacos&R.]
Kostantacos, Peter C., (AV) ... '24 '52 C.72 B.A. L.477 J.D. [Kostantacos&R.]
Kostantacos & Reuterfors, P.C., Law Offices of, (AV) ... 321 W. State St., Ste. 212
Kovanda, Gary L., (BV) ... '54 '79 C&L.879 B.A., J.D. Asst. States Atty.
Krause, Richard A., (CV) ... '57 '93 C&L.589 B.A., J.D. 400 W. State St.
Kreitlow, Margaret L., (BV) ... '— '86 C&L.589 B.S., J.D. [Greenlee&K.]
Krueger, Matthew K., (BV) ... '65 '91 C.937 B.A. L.879 J.D. [Brassfield,K.&R.]
Kurlinkus, David J., (BV) ... '51 '92 C.339 B.A. L.424 J.D. [Nicolosi&Assoc.]
Kurtz, Kate C. ... '77 '02 C&L.339 B.A., J.D. Winnebago Co. Dist. Atty. Off.
Lafayette, Gerald W., (BV) ... '40 '69 C.801 L.365 J.D. 126 N. Church St.
Lambert, J. Laird, (BV) ... '51 '81 C.910 B.A. L.365 J.D. 2425 Charles St.
Landon, Michelle L. ... '79 '04 C.597 B.A. L.608 J.D. [[A] Picha&S.]
Langhenry, John G., III, (AV) ... '58 '85 C.602 A.B. L.424 J.D. [Mangan,L.G.&L.] ⊙
Lanpher, John D., (BV) ... '50 '91 C.375 B.S. L.365 J.D. 4615 E. State St.
Larkin, Brian K., Attorney at Law, (CV) '57 '84
C.589 B.S. L.365 J.D. 1 Court Pl., Ste. 301
Larson, Wendy Lisa Coretz, (CV) '52 '91
C.339 B.A. L.589 J.D. Supvr., Felony Trial Team
Laughlin, Everett E. ... '15 '39 C.187 B.A. L.339 LL.B. 6401 Newburg Rd.‡
Laughlin, Thomas E., (BV) ... '47 '72 C.352 B.A. L.339 J.D. [Ritz&L.]
Lawrence, Jason A. ... '71 '96 C.57 B.A. L.589 J.D. [[A] Reese&R.]
Leahy, Dennis L. ... '50 '76 C.589 B.S.Ed. L.607 J.D. [D.L.Leahy]
Leahy, Dennis L., PC ... 1 Court Pl., Ste. 203
Leake, Timothy J. ... '77 '02 C.427 B.A L.1000 J.D. [[A] Hinshaw&C.]
Lechtenberg, Penelope M., (BV) ... '— '93 C.228 A.B. L.146 J.D. [Hinshaw&C.]
LeClercq, Charlotte A. ... '70 '04 C.293 B.A. L.589 J.D. [[A] Barrick,S.L.B.&V.]
Lester, Thomas J., (BV) ... '53 '85 C.201 B.S. L.365 J.D. [Hinshaw&C.]
Lewandowski, Daniel A. ... '72 '00 C.57 B.A. L.365 J.D. [[A] O'Brien,H.&Z.]

Leydig, Voit & Mayer, Ltd., (AV) BB
6815 Weaver Road, Suite 300, 61114-8018 ⊙
Telephone: 815-963-7661 Telecopier: 815-963-7664
Email: mail@leydig.com URL: http://www.leydig.com
Associate: John T. Bretscher. Of Counsel: Charles S. Oslakovic (Resident).
Patent, Trademark, Copyright, Unfair Competition and Related Antitrust and International Trade Law. Trials and Appeals.
Chicago, Illinois Office: Two Prudential Plaza, 180 North Stetson Avenue, Suite 4900. Telephone: 312-616-5600. Telecopier: 312-616-5700.
Washington, D.C. Office: Leydig, Voit & Mayer, 700 Thirteenth Street, N.W., Suite 300. Telephone: 202-737-6776. Telecopier: 202-737-6776.
Seattle, Washington Office: 1420 Fifth Avenue, Suite 2200. Telephone: 206-521-5985. Telecopier: 206-224-3557.

See Professional Biographies, ROCKFORD, ILLINOIS

Liebovich, Theodore, (BV) ... '50 '76 C.339 B.A. L.209 J.D. [Liebovich&W.]
Liebovich & Weber, P.C., (BV) ... 421 S. Mulford Rd., Suite 204
Light, Edward A., (BV) ... '53 '81 C.930 B.A. L.801 J.D. Asst. Pub. Def.
Lindberg, Erik W. ... '74 '01 C.473 B.S. L.734 J.D. [[A] Hinshaw&C.]
Lindberg, Wesley E., (BV) ... '34 '59 C&L.339 B.S., LL.B. [Reno&Z.]

Lindstedt, Norman, (AV) '42 '69 C&L.879 B.A., J.D. BB
One Court Place, Suite 300, 61101
Telephone: 815-965-4412 Fax: 815-967-0783
Family Law, Complex Domestic Relations Issues, Divorce, Dissolution of Marriage, Prenuptial Agreements, Premarital Agreements, Child Custody, Visitation Rights, Spousal Support, Alimony, Maintenance, Matrimonial Law, Litigation, Mediation, Marital Settlement Agreements, Separation Agreements, Property Rights, Financial Discovery and Analysis Related to Divorce, Tax Consideration related to Divorce.

(This Listing Continued)

Lindstedt, Norman (Continued)

See Professional Biographies, ROCKFORD, ILLINOIS

Lindvall, Robert J. ... '48 '75 C.57 A.B. L.879 J.D. Praire State Legal Servs.
Linnabary, Ian K. ... '73 '02 C.999 B.A. L.589 J.D. [[A] Reno&Z.]
Livingston, Jeffrey E., (BV) ... '63 '89 C&L.966 B.S., J.D. 401 W. State St., Ste. 300
Lockwood, Carol A. ... '62 '01 C.597 B.A. L.339 J.D. [[A] Hinshaw&C.]
Logli, Christopher T. ... '77 '03 C&L.352 B.A., J.D. [[A] McGreevy W.]
Logli, Paul A., (AV) ... '49 '74 C.177 B.A. L.339 J.D. State Atty., State Atty. Off.
Long, Adam S. ... '79 '04 C.339 B.A. L.383 J.D. [[A] Barrick,S.L.B.&V.]
Long, Joseph L., (BV) ... '36 '63 C&L.339 B.S., LL.B. [[C] Barrick,S.L.B.&V.]
Lowe, Robert D. ... '62 '03 C.801 B.S. L.589 J.D. [Gilbert&L.]
Lubben, Thomas C. '59 '84 C.114 B.A. L.339 J.D.
Assoc. Coun., Pioneer Life Insurance Company of Illinois
Lucas, John E. '59 '85 C.437 B.B.A. L.8 J.D.
(adm. in OH; not adm. in IL) Pension Consultant, McGladrey & Pullen
Luchetti, Thomas D., (BV) ... '48 '75 C.697 B.A. L.424 J.D. [T.D.Luchetti]
Luchetti, Thomas D., P.C., (BV) ... 6838 E. State St.
Lukas, James C., (CV) ... '68 '97 C.966 B.B.A. L.339 J.D. [[A] Holmstrom&K.]
Lukas, Suzanne R., (CV) ... '73 '98 C.209 B.A. L.339 J.D. [[A] Holmstrom&K.]
Lundquist, Troy A. ... '67 '92 C.339 B.A. L.365 J.D. [Mangan,L.G.&L.] ⊙
Luther, Kevin J., (AV) ... '59 '84 C.1101 B.A. L.910 J.D. [Heyl,R.V.&A.]
Lyon, Faye Marie, (CV) ... '57 '87 C.1288 B.S. L.999 J.D. 4615 E. State St.
MacCloskey, Kim, Law Office of, (BV) '51 '89
C.1028 B.A. L.589 J.D. 202 West State Street, Suite 1000
Maddox, Jay R. '36 '62 C.645 A.B. L.665 LL.B.
(adm. in PA; not adm. in IL) Exec. V.P. & T.O., Amcore Investment Grp. N.A.
Maggio, Frank P., (AV) ... '37 '63 C.686 A.B. L.602 J.D. [Hinshaw&C.]
Mahaffey, Kenneth A. ... '67 '98 C.338 B.S. L.421 J.D. [Brassfield,K.&R.]
Maher, Brendan A., (BV) ... '70 '97 C.57 B.A. L.879 J.D. [Williams&M.]
Maher, Edward M., (BV) ... '49 '75 C.966 B.A. L.424 J.D. [Guyer&E.]
Mahoney, P. Michael ... '46 '71 C.707 B.A. L.339 J.D. U.S. Mag.
Makeever, Jeffery J., (BV) '— '97 C.607 B.S.E.E. L.365 J.D.
[Reinhart B.V.s.c.] (Pat.)
Mangan, Jerald M. ... '57 '82 C.378 B.A. L.209 J.D. [Mangan,L.G.&L.] ⊙
Mangan, Langhenry, Gillen & Lundquist, (AV)
6785 Weaver Rd. (⊙Chicago, Joliet, Wheaton)
Manning, Donald Q., (BV) ... '61 '87 C.966 B.S. L.365 J.D. [McGreevy W.]

Maramba & Associates, LLC
(See Arlington Heights)

Markley, Kristen M., (CV) ... '72 '98 C.339 B.A. L.801 J.D. Asst. States Atty.
Martenson, David L. ... '34 '60 C.357 B.A. L.145 J.D. [Martenson B.&R.]
Martenson Blair & Raridon, P.C., (BV) ... One Court Place, Suite 404
Martin, Kenneth D. '44 '71 C.665 B.S. L.229 J.D.
(adm. in PA; not adm. in IL) Asst. Gen. Coun., Sundstrand Corp.
Martinez, Francis M., (BV) ... '57 '83 C.910 A.B. L.589 J.D. 311 7th St.
Mateer, Don M., (AV) ... '45 '71 C.477 B.A. L.339 J.D. [Mateer&Assoc.]

Mateer & Associates, (AV) BB
401 West State Street, Suite 400, 61101
Telephone: 815-965-7745 Fax: 815-965-7749
Member of Firm: Don M. Mateer. Associates: William M. Goff; Dawn Hallsten; Donna R. Honzel.
Insurance Defense including Automobile Casualty and Fire, Products Liability and Professional Malpractice.

See Professional Biographies, ROCKFORD, ILLINOIS

Matlaw, Leslie V., P.C.
(See Chicago)

Matschullat, Dale L. '45 '70 C&L.813 A.B., J.D.
(adm. in NY; not adm. in IL) V.P. & Gen. Coun., Newell Rubbermaid Inc.
(⊙Janesville, WI)
Mayer, Lee R. '46 '71 C.430 A.B. L.339 J.D.
Ex. V.P. & Tr. Offr., Amcore Investment Grp.
Mayfield, David E., (BV) ... '44 '69 C.357 B.A. L.879 J.D. [Schlueter E.O.M.&D.]
McCabe, Eileen J. ... '66 '91 C&L.589 B.A., J.D. [[A] W.T.Cacciatore]
McCarty, Stephen W., (CV) ... '47 '73 C.801 B.S. L.339 J.D. 308 W. State St., Ste. 120
McClenathan, Mark J., (BV) ... '62 '87 C.957 B.A. L.300 J.D. [Heyl,R.V.&A.]
McCumber, Lloyd R., (BV) ... '63 '88 C.801 B.A. L.589 J.D. [Picha&S.]
McGirk, Lori E. ... '60 '03 C&L.589 B.A., J.D. [[A] Heyl,R.V.&A.]
McGrail, Daniel J., (BV) ... '57 '85 C.589 B.A. L.494 J.D. [McGrail&Assoc.]
McGrail & Associates, (BV) ... 321 W. State St., Ste 602
McGraw, Joseph G., (BV) ... '55 '85 C.339 B.A. L.589 J.D. [J.G.McGraw]
McGraw, Joseph G., Ltd., The Law Office of, (BV) ... P.O. Box 1451

McGreevy • Williams, P.C., (AV)
6735 Vistagreen Way, P.O. Box 2903, 61132-2903
Telephone: 815-639-3700 Fax: 815-639-9400
Michael T. McGreevy (1930-1993); Raymond E. Johnson (1939-2001); Daniel T. Williams, Jr.; Michael F. O'Brien; Bruce Ross-Shannon; Daniel M. Donahue; William A. Reilly II; Donald Q. Manning; Ann Marie Dittmar; Christopher J. Cocoma; Nancy L. Doepke; Barbara L. Huffman; Christopher T. Logli; Scott P. Robinson; Jeffrey P. Orduno.
General Civil, Trial and Appellate Practice in all Courts. Business Litigation, Insurance, Real Estate, Corporation, Tax, Commercial, Environmental, Bankruptcy, Collection, Family Law, Probate and Estate Planning.

See Professional Biographies, ROCKFORD, ILLINOIS

McNamara, Edward J. '47 '72 C.1151 B.A. L.424 J.D.
2nd V.P., Conseco Services, L.L.C.
McNamara, John F. ... '39 '64 C.602 B.A. L.477 LL.B. Mayor
McNeely-Johnson, Kathy A., (BV) ... '57 '94 C.98 B.S. L.589 J.D. Asst. Pub. Def.
McWilliams, Robert R., (AV) ... '44 '70 C.966 B.S. L.209 J.D. [Kostantacos&R.]
Meyer, Thomas O., (BV) ... '51 '76 C.338 B.S. L.365 J.D. 3400 N. Rockton Avenue
Mezny, Alexander J., (BV) ... '67 '92 L.339 J.D. [Holmstrom&K.]
Mican, Stephen George '50 '81 C.339 B.S.E.E. L.365 J.D.
Asst. Intellectual Prop. Coun., Hamilton Sundstrand Corp. (Pat.)
Miller, Timothy A., (BV) ... '61 '88 C.177 B.A. L.16 J.D. [Oliver,C.W.W.&G.]
Mindrup, Nancy H., (BV) ... '46 '80 C.20 A.B. L.209 J.D. 111 N. Court St., Suite 101
Misevich, M. Allyson, (CV) ... '55 '86 C.317 B.A. L.589 J.D. 1378 S. Alpine Rd. #L-1
Monteleone, David F., (CV) ... '63 '91 C.352 D.D.S. L.1049 J.D. [Schirger,M.&H.]
Montgomery, Robert ... '47 '73 L.146 J.D. 234 E. Riverside Blvd.
Moore, Donald L., (AV) ... '48 '74 C.927 B.A. L.339 J.D. [Holmstrom&K.]
Moore, Stephen T., (AV) ... '49 '74 C.927 B.S. L.221 J.D. [Hinshaw&C.]
Moore, Tyler A. ... '76 '01 C.57 B.A. L.589 J.D. [[A] Barrick,S.L.B.&V.]
Moore, William D., Jr. ... '51 '76 C.697 B.A. L.190 J.D. 4023 Charles St.‡
Moran, Sharon T. ... '70 '97 C.679 B.A. L.300 J.D. Off. of Pub. Def.

More, Angus S., Jr. .... '39 '67 C.339 A.B. L.30 J.D. Assoc. Cir. J.
Morris, Wade F., (CV) .... '61 '93 L.589 J.D. 1508 Sweetclover Lane
Morrison, Michael R. .... '44 '70 C.965 B.B.A. L.146 J.D. Assoc. Cir. J.
Morrissey, Joseph A., (BV) .... '29 '58 C.707 B.S. L.339 J.D. 127 N. Wyman St.
Morrissey, Lawrence J., (CV) .... '69 '95 C.602 B.A. L.339 J.D. 127 N. Wyman St.
Mueller, Marcia L., (BV) .... '53 '78 C.502 B.A. L.365 J.D. [Hinshaw&C.]
Muldowney, Timothy A. .... '55 '97 C.966 B.S.N. L.986 J.D. [Ⓐ Guyer&E.]
Munch, Lisa R., (CV) .... '66 '99 C.790 B.S. L.589 J.D. [Ⓐ Hinshaw&C.]
Naill, Timothy P., (CV) .... '— '99 C.339 B.S. L.589 J.D. [Ⓐ Reese&R.]
Nash, Steven M. .... '52 '80 C.697 B.A. L.339 J.D. Assoc. Cir. J.
Nash, Thomas L., (BV) .... '51 '80 C.589 B.S. L.221 J.D. 2425 Charles
Nash, William R. .... '24 '51 C.339 B.S. L.146 J.D. 5426 Rudgate Ct.‡
Natale, Bernard J., (BV) .... '51 '77 C.338 B.S. L.365 J.D. 308 West State Street
Nelson, John M. .... '51 '76 C.747 B.A. L.861 J.D. 1318 E. State St.
Nelson, Lawrence A., (BV) .... '48 '75 C.589 B.S. L.424 J.D. Asst. Atty. Gen.
Nelson, Oliver W. .... '46 '76 C&L.339 B.A., J.D. [O.W.Nelson]
Nelson, Oliver W., P.C. .... 6885 Vistagreen Way, Ste. 4

Netzel & Associates, P.C.
(See Chicago)

Nicolosi, Paul S., (CV) .... '64 '91 C.424 B.S. L.589 J.D. [Nicolosi&Assoc.]
Nicolosi, Philip A. .... '23 '48 C&L.339 B.A., LL.B. [Nicolosi&Assoc.]
Nicolosi, Philip J., (CV) .... '59 '85 C.340 B.A. L.589 J.D. [Nicolosi&Assoc.]
Nicolosi & Associates, (BV) .... 363 Financial Ct., Ste. 100
Nolte, Peter B., (BV) .... '49 '74 C.381 B.A. L.146 J.D. [Ⓐ Sreenan&C.]
Nordquist, Steven L., (BV) .... '51 '77 C.339 B.S. L.300 J.D. [Nordquist]
Nordquist, Stuart B. .... '15 '46 C&L.339 B.S., LL.B. 1612 Greenley‡
Nordquist Law Offices, Ltd., (BV) .... P.O. Box 71
North, David A., (BV) .... '29 '58 C.37 A.B. L.339 J.D. 216 N. Court St.
O'Brien, Michael F., (AV) .... '44 '69 C.210 B.A. L.228 J.D. [McGreevy W.]

O'Brien, Healy & Zuba, (BV)
6067 Strathmoor, 61107
Telephone: 815-397-7000 Fax: 815-397-1834
URL: http://www.zubalaw.com
Members of Firm: James T. Zuba; Linda M. Zuba. Associate: Daniel A. Lewandowski.
Family Law including Divorce, Child Custody, Child Support, Visitation Rights, Spousal Support, Alimony, Paternity, Adoption Law, Qualified, Domestic Orders, QDRO's, Criminal Defense including White Collar, Criminal Defense, Felonies, Fraud, Litigation.
See Professional Biographies, ROCKFORD, ILLINOIS

O'Connell, Laura A., (BV) .... '45 '83 C.424 B.S. L.146 J.D. [Picha&S.]
O'Connell, Robert M. .... '45 '71 C.424 B.A. L.326 J.D. [Picha&S.]

Odling, Mary Alice, (CV) '52 '93 C.339 B.A.B.S. L.589 J.D.
401 West State Street, Suite 201, 61101
Telephone: 815-961-2663 Fax: 815-965-2601
Email: maodling@yahoo.com URL: http://www.odlinglaw.com
Family Law, Child Custody, Divorce, Juvenile Law, Traffic Violations, Probate, Adoption, Child Support, Spousal Support, Visitation Rights, Domestic Violence.
See Professional Biographies, ROCKFORD, ILLINOIS

O'Hagan, Smith & Amundsen, (AV)
Stewart Square, 308 West State Street, Suite 320, 61101-1140 ⊙
Telephone: 815-987-0441 Fax: 815-987-9891
URL: http://www.osalaw.com
Member of Firm: Ruth E. Robinson. Associate: Brette E. Freedle.
Commercial; Commercial Transportation; Appellate; Complex Litigation; Construction; Corporate Transactions; Employment; Extra-Contractual/Insurance Litigation; Healthcare; Insurance Coverage; Personal Lines; Product Liability; Professional Liability; Property Litigation.
Chicago, Illinois Office: 150 North Michigan Avenue, Suite 3300, 60601. Telephone: 312-894-3200. Fax: 312-894-3210.
St. Charles, Illinois Office: 3815 E. Main Street, Suite A-1, 60174-2488. Telephone: 630-587-7910. Fax: 630-587-7960.
Waukegan, Illinois Office: 415 West Washington Street, Suite 204, 60079-0410. Telephone: 847-599-9503. Fax: 847-599-9525.
Woodstock, Illinois Office: 666 Russel Court, 60098. Telephone: 815-337-4900. Fax: 815-337-4910.
Milwaukee, Wisconsin Office: 4811 South 76th Street, Suite 305, 53220. Suite 117, 53406-3770. Telephone: 414-282-7103. Fax: 414-282-1803.
See Professional Biographies, ROCKFORD, ILLINOIS

Ohlander, Jan H., (AV) .... '54 '79 C.339 B.S. L.436 J.D. [Reno&Z.]
Ohlson, Larry E., (BV) .... '33 '61 C&L.339 A.B., J.D. 4308 Saint Annes Way
Oldenburg, Susan Kay .... '54 '89 C.597 B.A. L.93 J.D. 2323 Glenwood Ave.
Oliver, Robert J., (AV) .... '32 '56 C&L.597 B.S., J.D. [Oliver,C.W.W.&G.]

Oliver, Close, Worden, Winkler & Greenwald LLC, (AV)
Suite 300, Waterside Center, 124 North Water Street, P.O. Box 4749, 61110-4749 ⊙
Telephone: 815-968-7591 Facsimile: 815-968-7507
Email: attorneys@rockfordlaw.com URL: http://www.rockfordlaw.com
Members of Firm: Robert J. Oliver; Curtis D. Worden; Karl F. Winkler; Thomas E. Greenwald; John Rearden, Jr.; Ann T. Dempsey; Timothy A. Miller; Debra A. Delia. Of Counsel: Henry J. Close. Associate: Bradley A. Rightnowar.
Business Transactions, Corporate and Commercial Real Estate, Banking, Labor and Employment, Probate and Estate Planning, Civil Trial and Appellate Practice in all State, Federal, and Bankruptcy Courts, and General Practice.
Counsel for: First National Bank and Trust Co. of Rockford; Aqua-Aerobics Systems, Inc.; Rockford Coatings Corp.; Rockford Public Library; Smith Oil Corp.
Local Counsel for: Northern Illinois University; Hesston Corp.; Melvin Simon & Associates.
See Professional Biographies, ROCKFORD, ILLINOIS

Olsen, Joseph D., (BV) .... '55 '80 C.602 B.B.A. L.209 J.D. [Yalden,O.&W.]
Olson, John L., (BV) .... '49 '74 C.339 B.S. L.862 J.D. [Schlueter E.O.M.&D.]
O'Neill, Joyce A., (CV) .... '48 '86 C.378 B.S. L.339 J.D. 401 W. State St., Ste. 701
Orduno, Jeffrey P. .... '70 '04 C.697 B.A. L.365 J.D. [Ⓐ McGreevy W.]
Orth, Daniel A., III '37 '67 C.436 B.S. L.597 J.D.
V.P. & Gen. Coun., Wash. Nat. Ins. Co.
Oslakovic, Charles S., (AV) '41 '73
C.46 B.S.E.E. L.209 J.D. [Ⓒ Leydig,V.&M.] (See Pat. Sect.)
Oulavong, Melissa S. .... '78 '03 C.597 B.A. L.1494 J.D. [Ⓐ Guyer&E.]
Owano, Keith R. .... '58 '84 C.339 B.A. L.221 J.D. Asst. States Atty.
Paddock, David S., (AV) .... '24 '52 C&L.174 B.A., J.D. 850 N. Church St.
Palmer, William E., (BV) .... '28 '52 C&L.477 A.B., LL.B. 1323 Radcliffe Ct.

Pavalon, Gifford, Laatsch & Marino
(See Chicago)

Pease, Ernest V., Jr. '50 '75 C.375 B.S. L.900 J.D.
(adm. in KS; not adm. in IL) 3015 S. 4th St.‡
Perrecone, Frank A., (AV) .... '56 '81 C.589 B.A. L.221 J.D. [Ferolie,P.&W.]
Pfau, John E., (AV) .... '48 '73 C&L.339 B.S., J.D. [Williams&M.]
Pfister, R. Jerome, (AV) .... '36 '61 C.57 B.A. L.339 J.D. [Reno&Z.]
Picha, George J., (AV) .... '38 '63 C.578 B.A. L.597 J.D. [Picha&S.]

Picha & Salisbury, (AV)
Edgebrook Court Building, 1639 North Alpine, Suite 300, 61107-1449
Telephone: 815-227-4300 Fax: 815-227-4330
URL: http://www.pichasal.com

(This Listing Continued)

Picha & Salisbury (Continued)

Members of Firm: George J. Picha; Jeffrey L. Salisbury; Lloyd R. McCumber; Robert M. O'Connell (Board Certified, Labor and Employment Law, Texas Board of Legal Specialization); Laura A. O'Connell. Associates: Carol A. Hartline; Michael P. Williams; Michelle L. Landon.
Workers Compensation Defense, Civil Trial, Employers Liability, Insurance Defense, Labor and Employment (Management); Environmental Law, Real Estate.
Representative Clients: General Casualty Companies; Liberty Mutual Insurance Group; Westfield Companies; Zurich-American Insurance Company.
See Professional Biographies, ROCKFORD, ILLINOIS

Pillote, Vernon J., (AV) .... '25 '52 C&L.966 B.S.E.E., LL.B. 310 7th St. (Pat.)
Pirages, James R., (AV) .... '55 '80 C.697 B.A. L.801 J.D. [Hinshaw&C.]
Pirrello, Ronald L., (CV) .... '48 '81 C.338 B.A. L.300 J.D. Co. J.
Polito, Joseph L., (CV) .... '45 '73 C.697 B.A. L.339 J.D. 1 Court Pl., Ste. 401
Pomatto, Douglas J., (AV) .... '52 '77 C.98 B.S. L.192 J.D. [Heyl,R.V.&A.]
Porter, J. Daniel, (BV) .... '60 '85 C.338 B.S. L.589 J.D. [Ⓐ Mangan,L.G.&L.]
Porter, Richard S., (BV) .... '66 '92 C.338 B.S. L.801 J.D. [Hinshaw&C.]
Pottinger, Robert C., (BV) .... '66 '90 C.69 B.A. L.146 J.D. [Barrick,S.L.B.&V.]
Pratt, Eric C. .... '64 '93 C.697 B.S. L.365 J.D. 185 Buckley Dr.
Price, Joyce Combest '45 '84 C.852 B.S. L.209 J.D.
Dir. of Desegregation, Rockford Bd. of Educ.
Prochaska, J. Edward, (BV) .... '53 '87 C.57 B.A. L.326 J.D. Winnebago Co. Cthse.
Proctor, Eleanor M. .... '— '92 C.589 B.A. L.365 J.D. [Ⓐ Crosby&Assoc.]
Prorok, Charles J., (BV) .... '51 '77 C.190 B.A. L.365 J.D. Dep. States Atty.
Ramlow, Todd A., (BV) .... '63 '94 C.697 B.S. L.436 J.D. [Brassfield,K.&R.]
Ranard, William W., (BV) '66 '92 C.597 B.A. L.502 J.D.
[Cassiday,S.&G.] (ⒸChicago)
Raridon, Michael W., (BV) .... '55 '81 C.604 B.A. L.910 J.D. [Martenson B.&R.]
Ray, Donald E., (CV) .... '65 '94 C&L.589 B.S., J.D. One Court Place, Suite 301
Rearden, John, Jr., (BV) .... '56 '84 C.234 B.A. L.245 J.D. [Oliver,C.W.W.&G.]
Reese, Bernard P., Jr., (BV) .... '25 '55 C&L.339 B.S., J.D. [Reese&R.]
Reese, Brian P., (BV) .... '54 '85 C.999 B.S. L.336 J.D. [Reese&R.]
Reese, Gary Stephen, (BV) .... '47 '86 C.999 B.A. L.1187 J.D. [Reese&R.]
Reese, Randall K., (BV) .... '49 '74 C.338 B.S. L.910 J.D. [Reese&R.]
Reese & Reese, (BV) .... 979 North Main Street
Reidenbach, Thomas R., (BV) '62 '90
C.965 B.B.A. L.966 J.D. Gen. Coun., Rubloff Development Group
Reilly, William A., II, (BV) .... '58 '83 C.177 B.S. L.352 J.D. [McGreevy W.]
Reinhard, David J., (BV) .... '72 '97 C.339 B.S. L.589 J.D. Asst. States Atty.
Reinhard, Philip G. .... '41 '64 C&L.339 A.B., J.D. U.S. Dist. J.

Reinhart Boerner Van Deuren s.c., (BV)
Suite 7 483 North Mulford Road, 61107-5191 ⊙
Telephone: 815-484-1900 Fax: 815-484-1032
URL: http://www.reinhartlaw.com
Lawrence E. Crowe; Andrew J. Heinisch; Jeffery J. Makeever; Kevin L. Wingate;—William H. Dietrich (Not admitted in IL).
General Practice. Litigation, Corporation, Securities, Real Estate, Taxation, Banking, Bankruptcy, Estate Planning, Probate, Labor/Employment, Admiralty, Employee Benefits, Environmental Law, Health Care, Intellectual Property, International Law, Patent Trademark, Copyright Law and related Litigation, OSHA, Telecommunications and Energy, Insurance.
Milwaukee, Wisconsin Office: 1000 North Water Street, P.O. Box 2965, 53201-2965. Telephone: 414-298-1000. Facsimile: 414-298-8097.
Madison, Wisconsin Office: 22 East Mifflin Street, P.O. Box 2018, 53701-2018. Telephone: 608-229-2200. Fax: 608-229-2100.
Greenwood Village, Colorado Office: 8400 Prentice Avenue, The Penthouse, 80111. Telephone: 303-843-6042. Fax: 303-721-1083.
Waukesha, Wisconsin Office: W233 N2080 Ridgeview Parkway, P.O. Box 2265. Telephone: 262-951-4500. Fax: 262-951-4690.
See Professional Biographies, ROCKFORD, ILLINOIS

Remencius, Leonard C. .... '36 '64 C.697 B.A. L.966 LL.B. 943 Bluecrest Drive
Reno, Roger, (AV) .... '24 '50 C.118 A.B. L.976 LL.B. [Ⓒ Reno&Z.]

Reno & Zahm LLP, (AV)
2902 McFarland Road, Suite 400, 61107
Telephone: 815-987-4050 Fax: 815-987-4092
URL: http://www.renozahm.com
Shelby L. Large (1911-1960); Guy B. Reno (1917-1972); Ralph S. Zahm (1935-1984); H. Emmett Folgate (1954-1993); William B. Powell (1913-2003); Wesley E. Lindberg; R. Jerome Pfister; Robert A. Fredrickson; Jack D. Ward; Jan H. Ohlander; John H. Young; Jamie J. Swenson Cassel; Craig P. Thomas; Arthur G. Kielty. Associates: Nancy Grimme Schilling; Rodney W. Kleitsch; Ian K. Linnabary; Stacey M. Gamm; Erin E. Kastberg; Jeffrey M. Glazer. Counsel: Roger Reno; Edward J. Fahy.
General Civil and Trial Practice. Corporation, Banking, Creditors' Rights, Real Estate, Insurance, Taxation, Labor, Employee Benefits, Estate Planning, Probate, Workers Compensation, Trusts and Estates.
See Professional Biographies, ROCKFORD, ILLINOIS

Resh, John A. .... '14 '50 C.72 B.A. L.597 J.D. 2136 Churchview Dr.‡
Reuterfors, Robert E., (BV) .... '46 '72 C.937 B.A. L.339 J.D. [Kostantacos&R.]
Reynolds, Thomas G.Reynolds, Thomas G. '63 '89 C.317 B.A. L.477 J.D.
(adm. in MI; not adm. in IL) AMCORE Investment Grp.
Riggs, Bradner C. .... '24 '52 C&L.273 LL.B. Ret. Cir. J.‡
Rightnowar, Bradley A. .... '74 '04 C.339 B.S. L.589 J.D. [Ⓐ Oliver,C.W.W.&G.]
Ring, Gordon C. .... '52 '77 C.352 B.S. L.365 J.D. 2425 Charles St.
Ritts, Catherine M. .... '50 '83 C.665 B.A. L.209 J.D. Prairie State Legal Servs., Inc.
Ritz, Kenneth F., (AV) .... '35 '59 C.851 B.B.A. L.339 LL.B. [Ritz&L.]

Ritz & Laughlin, Ltd., (AV)
728 North Court Street, 61103
Telephone: 815-968-1807 Fax: 815-961-1917
Email: kenritz@aol.com
Kenneth F. Ritz; Thomas E. Laughlin.
Commercial Law, emphasizing Creditors Rights, Commercial Collections and Bankruptcy Law, in the U.S. District Court in Rockford, Illinois and in State Courts throughout Northwestern Illinois.
See Professional Biographies, ROCKFORD, ILLINOIS

Robinson, Mark A., (CV) '60 '92
C.966 B.B.A. L.339 J.D. Rubloff Development Grp., Inc.
Robinson, Ruth E., (BV) .... '— '91 C.589 B.S. L.146 J.D. [O'Hagan,S.&A.]
Robinson, Scott P. .... '76 '03 C.589 B.A. L.339 J.D. [Ⓐ McGreevy W.]
Rock, Jason H., (BV) .... '69 '94 C.160 B.A. L.221 J.D. [Barrick,S.L.B.&V.]
Rogers-Manning, Jill I., (CV) .... '68 '99 C.697 B.S. L.589 J.D. [Ⓐ Heyl,R.V.&A.] (Pat.)
Rollins, Timothy J., (AV) .... '59 '85 C.339 B.A. L.309 J.D. [Williams&M.]
Ross-Shannon, Bruce, (AV) .... '51 '77 C.813 B.A. L.800 J.D. [McGreevy W.]
Roszkowski, Stanley J. .... '23 '55 C&L.339 B.S., J.D. Sr. U.S. Dist. J.‡
Roth, Andrew J. .... '74 '03 C.927 B.S. L.589 J.D. [Ⓐ Heyl,R.V.&A.]

Rouleau, Mark, (BV) '58 '83 C.801 B.A. L.209 J.D.
5301 E. State Street Suite 215D, 61108-2392
Telephone: 815-229-7246 Fax: 815-229-7251
Email: rouleau-law@afo.net URL: http://www.rouleaulaw.com

(This Listing Continued)

Rouleau, Mark (Continued)

Catastrophic Personal Injury including Wrongful Death, Automobile Accidents and Injuries, Motorcycle Accidents, Trucking Accidents. Medical Malpractice including Surgical Malpractice, Failure to Diagnose/Misdiagnosis, Hospital Malpractice, Nursing Malpractice, Pharmaceutical Malpractice.

See Professional Biographies, ROCKFORD, ILLINOIS

Rudy, Sharon R., (CV) ....'55 '82 C.118 B.A. L.424 J.D. 405 W. State St.
Rumshas, Alyson R. ....'73 '05 C.1175 B.A. L.209 J.D. [A Hinshaw&C.]
Ruud, Thomas G., (BV) ....'59 '84 C.697 B.A. L.221 J.D. 216 N. Court St.
Sahlstrom, Craig ....'54 '79 C.221 B.S. L.365 J.D. Assoc. Cir. J.
Salemi, Scott G., (BV) ....'66 '92 C.210 B.A. L.589 J.D. [C Heyl,R.V.&A.]
Salisbury, Jeffrey L., (BV) ....'53 '83 C.446 B.A. L.339 J.D. [Picha&S.]
Sandquist, Thomas P., (BV) ....'63 '88 C.697 B.A. L.339 J.D. [Williams&M.]
Savaiano, Anthony A., (BV) ....'52 '77 C.248 B.A. L.365 J.D. 535 Loves Park Drive
Savitski, Peter A., (BV) ....'51 '77 C.338 B.S. L.1009 J.D. [P.Savitski]
Savitski, Peter, (BV) .... 1600 N. Main St.
Schafer, Debra D. ....'66 '91 C.338 B.S. L.339 J.D. [A Sreenan&C.]
Schappert, Michael J., (BV) ....'55 '80 C.602 B.B.A. L.436 J.D. [Holmstrom&K.]
Scheurich, G. Michael, (AV) ....'47 '72 C.424 A.B. L.597 J.D. [Guyer&E.]
Schilling, Richard M. ....'37 '62 C.966 B.S. L.309 J.D. [Hinshaw&C.]
Schirger, William E., (BV) ....'35 '63 C.749 B.S. L.602 LL.B. [Schirger,M.&H.]
Schirger, Monteleone & Hampilos, (BV) .... 308 West State Street
Schlueter, Charles D., (BV) ....'53 '79 C.937 B.A. L.365 J.D. [Schlueter E.O.M.&D.]
Schlueter Ecklund Olson Mayfield & Davitt, (BV) .... 4023 Charles Street
Schmidt, Derrick J. '76 '02 C&L.879 B.A., J.D.
Asst. Pub. Def., Winnebago Co. Pub. Def.
Schmidt, John N. ....'29 '58 C.385 A.B. L.597 J.D. 201 S. Madison St.
Schreiber, Bradley J., (CV) ....'63 '93 C.927 B.S. L.1148 J.D. [Schreiber]
Schreiber Law Firm, The, (CV) .... One Court Place
Schroeder, D. Reneé, (BV) ....'60 '85 C.338 B.S. L.589 J.D. [Hinshaw&C.]
Schroeder, Jean H., (CV) ....'— '95 C.98 B.A. L.904 J.D. [A Faulkner&J.]
Schroeder, Michele S., (BV) ....'61 '91 Asst. U.S. Atty.
Schuman, Robert L. ....'63 '89 C.347 B.A. L.365 J.D. 400 W. State St., Ste. 619
Scoville, Thomas H. '47 '74
C&L.339 B.S., J.D. V.P. & Tr. Offr., AMCORE Investment Grp.
Selander, Bryan G., (BV) ....'58 '84 C.697 B.S. L.365 J.D. P.O. Box 1835
Shalbrack, Michael Jon, (BV) ....'59 '84 C.966 B.B.A. L.209 J.D. [Holmstrom&K.]
Shapiro, Bernard H. '42 '67
C.339 B.S. L.597 J.D. Dir. of Litig., Prairie State Legal Servs., Inc.
Shappert, Amy E., (BV) ....'64 '89 C.802 B.B.A. L.424 J.D. 4615 E. State St., Ste. 101
Shelden, Jas. W. ....'23 '50 C.477 C.L.339 LL.B. 1701 National Ave.‡
Shelly, Stacy K. ....'78 '03 C.399 B.A. L.477 J.D. [A Barrick,S.L.B.&V.]
Shelton, Gerald B., Jr., (BV) ....'53 '79 C.589 B.A. L.910 J.D. [Kalivoda&S.]
Shepherd, John L., (BV) ....'47 '75 C.339 B.A. L.365 J.D. [Williams&M.]
Shore, Brian Dean, (BV) ....'58 '83 C.338 B.S. L.801 J.D. Cir. J.
Shriver, Donald L., (BV) ....'42 '67 C.388 B.A. L.910 J.D. 401 W. State St., Ste. 701
Siegfried, Ruth L. '47 '72 C.954 A.B. L.608 J.D.
(adm. in OH; not adm. in IL) 206 Guard St.‡
Silvestri, Amy L. ....'65 '92 C.937 B.A. L.117 J.D. 4615 E. State St., Ste. 203
Simpson, William John ....'35 '78 C.597 B.A. L.976 J.D. 2524 Country Club Terr.‡
Slates, Michael D., (BV) ....'60 '85 C.357 B.A. L.589 J.D. 6000 E. State St.
Small, Benjamin F. '47 '72 C.347 B.A. L.1119 J.D.
Asst. Gen. Counsel, Sundstrand Corp.
Smith, Andrew T. ....'68 '93 C.338 B.A. L.801 J.D. [A T.D.Luchetti]
Smith, Barbara W. ....'30 '79 C.339 B.S. L.146 J.D. [Thorsen A.&S.]
Smith, David F. ....'34 '59 C&L.339 J.D. Ret. Cir. J.‡
Smith, Loren M. '29 '54 C.339 A.B. L.966 LL.B.
(adm. in WI; not adm. in IL) United Bk. of Ill.
Smith, Michael J., (BV) ....'55 '80 C.927 B.A. L.801 J.D. [Abate&S.]
Smith, Sally Ann ....'48 '76 C.472 B.A. L.424 J.D. 5094 Severson Rd.‡
Snively, William H., (BV) ....'35 '60 C.174 B.A. L.339 LL.B. 401 W. State St.
Soderberg, Darlene D., R.N., (CV) '48 '95 C.697 B.S.N. L.589 J.D.
[Soderberg&Assoc.]

Soderberg & Associates, P.C., (BV)
1330 East State Street, 61104
Telephone: 815-964-0100 Fax: 815-964-6151
Email: DSoderberg@htslawyers.com URL: http://www.soderberglaw.com
Darlene D. Soderberg, R.N.; Michael J. Hedeen.
Medical Malpractice including Wrongful Death, Birth Injuries, Failure to Diagnose or Misdiagnosis, Obstetric, Surgical, Cardiac, Orthopedic and Nursing Malpractice.
See Professional Biographies, ROCKFORD, ILLINOIS

Sorensen, Karen L., (BV) ....'48 '74 C.679 B.A. L.209 J.D. Pub. Def.
Sosnowski, Roxanne M. ....'80 '04 C&L.589 B.A., J.D. 363 Financial Ct., Ste. 100
Spears, Jeffry S. ....'56 '81 C.927 B.A. L.339 J.D. [Hinshaw&C.]

Sreenan & Cain, P.C., (AV)
Suite 700, 321 West State Street, 61101
Telephone: 815-962-5490 Telefax: 815-962-2755
Email: dcain@sreenan-cain.com URL: http://www.sreenan-cain.com
Patrick H. Sreenan (1930-1994); Daniel J. Cain;—Randy Wilt; Debra D. Schafer; Christopher A. DeRango; Peter B. Nolte; Anne M. Vecchio.
Criminal and Civil Trial Practice in Federal and State Courts, Felonies, Misdemeanors, DUI, Traffic, Family, Negligence, General Practice. Personal Injury, Workers Compensation, Medical Malpractice.
See Professional Biographies, ROCKFORD, ILLINOIS

Stevens, James E., (BV) ....'54 '80 C.339 B.A. L.285 J.D. [Barrick,S.L.B.&V.]
Stockwell, Kathleen M., (CV) ....'68 '93 C&L.339 B.A., J.D. [C Heyl,R.V.&A.]
Strauss, Marc J., (BV) '53 '79 C&L.597 B.A., J.D.
Gen. Coun., First Rockford Grp., Inc.
Stravinskas, Lisa '59 '87 C&L.339 B.S.N., J.D.
V.P. Corp. Compl., Rockford Health Systems
Street, Thomas A., (AV) ....'15 '40 C&L.339 A.B., LL.B. 1802 Birchwood Lane
Sullivan, Donald, Law Office of, (CV) ....'51 '87 202 W. State St., Ste. 1100
Sullivan, Scott C., (AV) ....'54 '79 C&L.602 B.B.A., J.D. [Williams&M.]
Swain, Robert E. ....'72 '98 C.602 B.A. L.339 J.D. Law Clk., U.S. Mag.
Swanson, Arthur R., (BV) ....'44 '70 C.589 B.S.Ed. L.339 J.D. [A.Swanson]
Swanson, Brent A., (BV) ....'52 '77 C&L.879 B.A., J.D. [C Heyl,R.V.&A.]
Swanson, Arthur, Attorney at Law, (BV) .... 311 7th St.

Swanson, Martin & Bell
(See Chicago)

Sweet & Maier, S.C.
(See Elkhorn, Wisconsin)

Switzer, Ann Elizabeth, (CV) '64 '89 C&L.174 B.S., J.D.
Staff Atty., Northern IL Coll. of Law, Zeke Georgi Legal Clinic
Switzer, Peter S., (AV) ....'38 '63 C.339 B.A. L.966 LL.B. [C Barrick,S.L.B.&V.]
Sype, John E. ....'16 '39 C&L.145 B.A., J.D. 117 Douglas St.‡
Szeto, Aaron ....'77 '04 C.339 B.S. L.589 J.D. 363 Financial Ct., Ste. 100
Szymanski, Karl A., (BVⓉ) '52 '82
C.259 B.S. L.260 J.D. [SzymanskiKorollLitigationGroup] ⊙
Szymanski Koroll, Cynthia J. '59 '01
C&L.589 B.S.N., J.D. [SzymanskiKorollLitigationGroup] ⊙

Szymanski Koroll Litigation Group, The, (BVⓉ)
One Court Place, Suite 102, 61101-1007 ⊙
Telephone: 815-639-9000 Fax: 815-639-9066
Email: sklg@sklg.com URL: http://www.szymanskikoroll.com
Karl A. Szymanski; Cynthia J. Szymanski Koroll.
Personal Injury, Wrongful Death, Medical Malpractice including Birth Injuries, Cancer, Failure to Diagnose and Misdiagnosis, Bar iatric Weight Loss Surgery, Obstetric, Surgical, Cardiac, Orthopedic, Nursing Malpractice, Nursing Home Abuse and Neglect including Bedsores, Malnutrition, Falls, Physical Abuse, Medication Errors, Automobile Accidents and Injuries, Head, Neck and Back Injuries, Burns.
Lake Worth, Florida Office: 6894 Lake Worth Road, Suite 203, 33467. Telephone: 561-686-9444. Fax: 561-968-7988.
See Professional Biographies, ROCKFORD, ILLINOIS

Talley, Randall C., (BV) ....'49 '74 C.339 B.S. L.352 J.D. 120 W. State St., Ste. 206
Tarara, Mario J., (CV) ....'73 '98 C.339 B.A. L.477 J.D. [M.J.Tarara]

Tarara, Mario J., P.C., Law Office of, (CV)
3600 East State Street Suite 315, 61108
Telephone: 815-399-6090 Facsimile: 815-397-2907
Email: mjtarara@sbcglobal.net URL: http://www.tararalaw.com
Mario J. Tarara.
Real Estate, Real Estate Development, Zoning and Land Use, Construction Disputes, Business Law, Corporate Law and Contracts, Mechanics Liens.
See Professional Biographies, ROCKFORD, ILLINOIS

Taylor, Mark A. '50 '77 C.750 B.A. L.365 J.D.
Asst. Exec. Dir., Prairie State Legal Servs., Inc.
Teeter, James O., Jr., (CV) '64 '97 C.352 B.B.A. L.589 J.D.
Coun., Star Develpm't LLC
Thomas, Charles F., (AV) ....'34 '60 C&L.276 B.S., J.D. [Hinshaw&C.]
Thomas, Craig P., (BV) ....'64 '89 C.72 B.A. L.339 J.D. [Reno&Z.]
Thomas, William R. ....'— '91 C.57 B.A. L.879 J.D. [A Crosby&Assoc.]
Thompson, James C. ....'64 '88 C.697 B.A. L.339 J.D. 401 W. State St., Ste. 701
Thorsen, Robert L., (BV) ....'41 '66 C&L.597 B.A., J.D. [Thorsen A.&S.]
Thorsen Altamore & Smith, (BV) .... 401 W. State Street
Timmerwilke, Charles E., (BV) ....'66 '91 C.123 B.A. L.879 J.D. [C Heyl,R.V.&A.]
Torbert, Robert C. ....'74 '99 C.57 B.A. L.339 J.D. 363 Financial Ct., Ste. 100
Trost, Jay S., (BV) ....'50 '76 C.234 B.A. L.790 J.D. 1 Court Pl., Ste. 103
Tsao, Fred ....'64 '89 C.145 B.A. L.477 J.D. Prairie State Legal Servs.
Tuite, Gerald F., (BV) ....'28 '58 C.276 L.146 J.D. [Greg T.&Assoc.]
Tuite, Gregory E., (BV) ....'55 '80 C.174 B.A. L.146 J.D. [Greg T.&Assoc.]
Tuneberg, James E., (AV) ....'58 '84 C.697 B.S. L.221 J.D. [Guyer&E.]

Turner, Harold L., Law Offices of, (AV) '43 '67 C.352 L.339 J.D. BB
1330 East State Street, P.O. Box 4504, 61110-4504
Telephone: 815-964-0100 Fax: 815-964-6151
Email: hturner@htslawyers.com URL: http://www.haroldturnerlaw.com
Personal Injury including Automobile Accidents and Injuries, Head, Neck and Back Injuries, Medical Malpractice including Misdiagnosis and Failure to Diagnose, Birth Injuries, Cancer, Obstetric, Surgical, Cardiac, Orthopedic and Nursing Malpractice, Nursing Home Abuse and Neglect including Bedsores, Malnutrition, Dehydration, Wandering, Falls, Fractures, Physical, Verbal and Sexual Abuse and Assault, Legal Ethics and Professional Responsibility including Professional Malpractice, Legal Malpractice, Mediation and Arbitration.
See Professional Biographies, ROCKFORD, ILLINOIS

Tyson, Cleveland A. ....'46 '76 C.209 L.424 J.D. Blue Cross-Blue Shield
Van Evera, Richard K., (AV) ....'48 '78 C.162 B.A. L.192 J.D. [Barrick,S.L.B.&V.]
Vecchio, Anne M. ....'80 '04 C.339 B.A. L.36 J.D. [A Sreenan&C.]
Vecchio, Kelly A. ....'76 '01 C.339 B.S. L.589 J.D. 321 W. State Street, Suite 1204
Vecchio, Steven G., (BV) ....'51 '76 C.339 B.S. L.436 J.D. 4772 Will Ann Dr.
Vella, Frank P., Jr. ....'43 '68 C.1146 B.A. L.436 J.D. 401 W. State St., Ste. 300
Verseman, Scott Arthur, (AV) ....'63 '88 C&L.734 B.S., J.D. U.S. Atty. Off.
Vidal, Richard W. ....'48 '73 C.210 A.B. L.910 J.D. Cir. J.
Wade, Ronald T., (BV) ....'44 '69 C.934 B.A. L.802 J.D. 6833 Stalter Drive, Suite 201
Walsh, Erin E. ....'78 '03 C.352 B.B.A. L.436 J.D. [A Holmstrom&K.]
Wanner, James A. ....'43 '70 C.679 B.S.M.E. L.213 J.D. Dir. Lic., Sundstrand Corp. (Pat.)
Ward, Jack D., (AV) ....'52 '78 C&L.101 B.S., J.D. [Reno&Z.]
Weber, Gerald H., Jr. ....'55 '81 C.37 B.S. L.424 J.D. [C Liebovich&W.]
Werderich, Walter G. '73 '00 C.999 B.A. L.879 J.D.
Northern IL Univ. College of Law, Zeke Giorgi Legal Clinc
Wham, Fred L., III, (BV) ....'37 '64 C&L.339 B.S., LL.B. 1111 S. Alpine Road, Suite 509
Whitcher, John D. ....'54 '79 C&L.802 B.A., J.D. Pres., The Viking Grp., Ltd.
White, Francine Buscemi, (BV) ....'56 '82 C.424 B.A. L.365 J.D. [Ferolie,P.&W.]
White, Ronald J. ....'48 '79 C.338 B.S. L.1151 J.D. Assoc. Cir. J.
Wilkins, Daniel T., Law Office of, (BV) '70 '94
C.338 B.A. L.424 J.D. 202 West State Street, Suite 410
Willette, Craig A., (BV) ....'52 '77 C.927 B.S. L.339 J.D. [Yalden,O.&W.]
Willette, Rose A. ....'62 '91 C.424 B.A. L.146 J.D. Prairie State Legal Services., Inc.
Williams, Daniel T., Jr., (AV) ....'46 '71 C&L.339 B.A., J.D. [McGreevy W.]
Williams, Michael P., (CV) ....'73 '98 C.72 B.A. L.365 J.D. [A Picha&S.]

Williams & McCarthy, A Professional Corporation, (AV) BB
321 West State Street, P.O. Box 219, 61105-0219 ⊙
Telephone: 815-987-8900 Fax: 815-968-0019
Email: mail@wilmac.com URL: http://www.wilmac.com
Thomas S. Johnson; Russell D. Anderson; John E. Pfau; Richard A. Berman; John L. Shepherd; Terry D. Anderson; Kim D. Krahenbuhl (Resident Partner, Oregon, Illinois Office); Scott C. Sullivan; Carol N. Bailey; James P. Devine; John J. Holevas; Timothy J. Rollins; Clayton L. Lindsey (Resident Partner, Oregon, Illinois Office); Stephen E. Balogh; Marc C. Gravino; Thomas P. Sandquist; Carl A. Ecklund; Wendy S. Howarter (Resident Partner, Oregon, Illinois Office); Michael T. Cyrs; Troy E. Haggestad; Brendan A. Maher;—Benjamin W. Bernsten; Jacob M. Carpenter.
Karl C. Williams (1934-1984); Edward R. Telling, III (1970-2004).
General Civil and Trial Practice. Administrative Law, Advertising and Media Law, Banking, Bankruptcy and Commercial Work Outs, Business Litigation, Closely-held Business, Commercial Lending, Condemnation and Zoning, Construction Law, Education Law, Employee Benefits, Employers' Liability, Environmental Law, Family Law, Health Care and Hospital Law, Insurance Coverage, Insurance Defense, International Law, Labor and Employment (management), Municipal Finance, Probate, Trust Law and Estate Planning, Products Liability, Real Estate, Taxation, Unfair Competition, Workers' Compensation (management).
Representative Clients: Aircraft Gear Corp.; Anderson Industries, Inc.; Gallagher Bassett Insurance Co.; Liberty Mutual Insurance Co.; Atwood Industries, Inc.; The Travelers; American Mutual Insurance Co.; Rockford Health Systems; West Bend.
Oregon, Illinois Office: 607 Washington Street. P.O. Box 339. Telephone: 815-732-2101. Fax: 815-732-2289.
See Professional Biographies, ROCKFORD, ILLINOIS

Wilt, Randy, (BV) ....'56 '80 C.608 B.A. L.424 J.D. [A Sreenan&C.]
Wingate, Kevin L., (CV) ....'— '98 C.339 B.S. L.365 J.D. [Reinhart B.V.s.c.]
Winkler, Karl F., (BV) ....'42 '69 C.197 A.B. L.339 J.D. [Oliver,C.W.W.&G.]

Worden, Curtis D., (AV) .... '36 '61 C&L.966 B.S., J.D. [Oliver,C.W.W.&G.]
Yalden, Raphael E., II, (BV) .... '48 '73 C.177 B.A. L.597 J.D. [Yalden,O.&W.]
Yalden, Olsen & Willette, (BV) .... 1318 East State Street
Youman, Kristine Pihl, (BV) .... '71 '97 C&L.339 B.A., J.D. [Holmstrom&K.]
Young, John H., (BV) .... '60 '85 C.999 B.A. L.221 J.D. [Reno&Z.]
Zeglis, James D., & Associates, (CV) '55 '80
C.679 B.S. L.345 J.D. 202 W. State St., Ste. 510
Zenoff, Kathryn E., (BV) .... '46 '72 C.813 B.A. L.178 J.D. Cir. Ct. J.
Zimmerman, Nick E., (CV) '73 '00 C.961 B.S. L.589 J.D.
400 W. State Street, Suite 340
Zimmerman, Sally J. ...... '54 '91 C.750 B.S.N. L.589 J.D. [Cassiday,S.&G.] (⊙Chicago)
Zimmerman, Steven P., (AV) .... '55 '81 C.339 B.A. L.280 J.D. 1707 East State Street
Zuba, James T., (BV) .... '58 '86 C.36 B.S. L.209 J.D. [O'Brien,H.&Z.]
Zuba, Linda M. .... '59 '01 C.36 B.A. L.966 J.D. [O'Brien,H.&Z.]

ROCK ISLAND, * 39,684, *Rock Island Co.*

Anderson, Keirsten G. .... '72 '97 C.57 B.A. L.879 J.D. Prairie State Legal Servs. Inc.
Anderson, Pamela M., (BV) .... '49 '80 C.846 B.A. L.352 J.D. [Ⓒ Snyder,P.&N.]
Andich, David W., (AV) .... '47 '75 C.589 B.S. L.365 J.D. [Andich&A.]
Andich, Marvin S. .... '22 '52 C.57 B.A. L.352 J.D. [Ⓒ Andich&A.] ‡
Andich, Stephen G., (BV) .... '49 '75 C.589 B.S. L.365 J.D. [Andich&A.]

Andich & Andich, (AV)
Safety Building, Suite 404, 1800 Third Avenue, 61201
Telephone: 309-788-9337 Facsimile: 309-788-9332
URL: http://www.andichlaw.com
Members of Firm: David W. Andich; Stephen G. Andich. Of Counsel: Marvin S. Andich.
Commercial Law, Business Litigation, Consumer Litigation, Creditor's Rights, Media, Bankruptcy, Employment, Domestic Relations, Real Estate, Probate, Civil Trial and Appeals, Wills, Estates, Family Law, Divorce, Child Custody, Child Support, Adoption.
See Professional Biographies, ROCK ISLAND, ILLINOIS

Bailey, Pamela S. '50 '79 C.339 B.A. L.209 J.D.
Atty.-Advsr., U.S.A. TACOM-RI, Off. of Coun.

Barash & Everett, LLC
(See Galesburg)

Barrows, Karen J. .... '69 '01 C.352 B.S. L.221 J.D. [Ⓐ Pappas&S.]
Bartsh, Allison E. .... '78 '03 C.602 B.A. L.352 J.D. [Ⓐ Brooks&T.]
Beane, C. Ernest '40 '65 C.231 B.A. L.352 J.D.
Gen. Coun., Modern Woodmen of Amer.
Beatty, Joseph F. .... '48 '74 C.707 B.A. L.733 J.D. Cir. J.
Benson, Peter J., (BV) .... '57 '82 C.597 B.A. L.352 J.D. [Lane&W.] ⊙
Bert, Jeffrey D., (BVⓉ) .... '67 '92 C.350 B.A. L.352 J.D. [Brooks&T.]

Betty, Neuman & McMahon
(See Davenport, Iowa)

Blackwood, Alan G., (BV) .... '45 '73 C.339 B.S. L.734 J.D. 210 15th St.
Blais, William E., (CV) .... '57 '87 C.145 A.B. L.146 J.D. [Ⓐ Nelson K.K.]
Bohnert, Lester L., (BV) ...... '62 '88 C.801 B.S. L.365 J.D. Modern Woodmen of Amer.
Borden, Henry G. .... '14 '49 C&L.339 B.S., J.D. 423 Seventheenth St.‡

Bozeman, Neighbour, Patton & Noe, LLP
(See Moline)

Brinn, Michael P. .... '48 '76 C.707 B.A. L.339 J.D. Asso. Cir. J.
Brooks, Jack L., (AV) .... '50 '75 C.197 B.A. L.221 J.D. [Brooks&T.]

Brooks & Trinrud, A Professional Corporation, (AV)
3725 Blackhawk Road, P.O. Box 3487, 61204-3487 ⊙
Telephone: 309-786-4900 Fax: 309-786-4940
Email: info@btlawpc.com URL: http://www.BTLawPC.com
Jack L. Brooks; Richard J. Trinrud; Jeffrey C. McDaniel; Bernard J. Hofmann; Jeffrey D. Bert; Milissa K. Hofmann;—Derek G. Jones; Kathleen E. Mesich; Henry W. Latham, II (Not admitted in IL); Brian T. Fairfield; Allison E. Bartsh; Jason P. Butt.
General Practice, Civil Litigation, Workers Compensation, Bankruptcy, Estate Planning, Trusts and Probate, Business Law (including Corporations, Partnerships), Family Law, Commercial Collections, Real Estate Foreclosure, Real Estate, Commercial Real Estate.
Davenport, Iowa Office: 220 Emerson Place, 52801. Telephone: 563-326-4900. Fax: 563-326-4944.
See Professional Biographies, ROCK ISLAND, ILLINOIS

Buckrop, Bruce A., (BV) .... '52 '77 C.707 B.A. L.300 J.D. 329 18th Street, Suite 500
Burch, William A., (AV) .... '49 '75 C.339 A.B. L.910 J.D. [Ludens P.B.&M.] ⊙
Butt, Jason P. .... '75 '01 C.352 B.A. L.36 J.D. [Ⓐ Brooks&T.]

Califf & Harper, P.C.
(See Moline)

Callas, Darcy G., (BV) '58 '83 C.339 B.A. L.146 J.D.
Asst. Gen. Coun., Modern Woodmen of Amer.
Callas, John S., (BV) .... '57 '82 C.339 B.A. L.146 J.D. [McCarthy,C.F.&E.]
Camp, Gary L. .... '40 '63 C&L.221 B.S.B.A., LL.B. Royal Neighbors of Amer.
Cartwright, Janet M. .... '47 '90 C.1016 B.A. L.589 J.D. 1612 Second Avenue
Castro, Patricia, (CV) .... '71 '97 C.57 B.A. L.221 J.D. Asst. States Atty.
Church, Peter W., (BV) .... '67 '93 C.350 B.A. L.352 J.D. [McCarthy,C.F.&E.]

Churchill & Churchill, P.C.
(See Moline)

Ciaccio, Karin McLaughlin, Ltd. .... '47 '75 C.801 B.S. L.209 J.D. Reg. Coun.
Conklin, Raymond J., (BV) .... '49 '75 C&L.352 B.A., J.D. 115 17th St.
Conway, Martin E., Jr. .... '42 '66 C&L.602 B.A., J.D. Cir. J.
Corbi, Anne '50 '89 C.262 B.A. L.352 J.D.
(adm. in IA; not adm. in IL) Project Now, Inc.
Coryn, James J., (AV) .... '32 '56 C&L.602 B.S., LL.B. [Coryn,W.&M.]
Coryn, Walker and Meehan, (AV) .... 1515 4th Ave.
Coyle, Francis J., Jr., (BV) .... '47 '73 C.352 B.A. L.221 J.D. [Coyle,G.&S.I.]
Coyle, Gilman & Stengel, Including a Prof. Corp., (AV) .... 100 17th St.
Craig, Dana M., (AV) .... '50 '75 C.350 B.S. L.477 J.D. [Lane&W.] ⊙
Crane, Thomas F. .... '32 '59 C&L.352 B.A., J.D. Dist. Coun., U.S. Army Corps of Engrs.
Cunningham, David L., (BV) .... '62 '89 C&L.221 B.A., J.D. [Winstein,K.&W.]
Cunningham, John .... '11 '36 C.707 A.B. L.276 J.D. Assoc. Cir. J.
Cyr, Mark F., (BV) .... '51 '79 C.742 B.A. L.146 J.D. 115 17th St.
Darrow, Clarence A., (BV) .... '40 '71 C.177 B.S. L.146 J.D. 1515 4th Ave., Ste. 200
Darrow, Clarence Michael .... '70 '99 C.436 B.A. L.339 J.D. [C.Darrow]
Darrow, Clarence, Law Offices of .... 1515 Fourth Ave., Ste. 200
Davidson, Richard A., (BVⓉ) .... '59 '84 C&L.221 B.S.B.A., J.D. [Lane&W.] ⊙
De Porter, Dennis A. .... '45 '72 C.589 B.A. L.339 J.D. Cir. J.
Deutsch, Joel A., (BV) .... '46 '73 C.966 B.A. L.339 J.D. [Deutsch&D.]
Deutsch & Deutsch, (BV) .... 1825 3rd Avenue
Doyle, Peter C., (CV) .... '57 '86 C.338 B.S. L.589 J.D. Modern Woodmen of Amer.
Doyle, Shea .... '68 '93 C.93 B.A. L.352 J.D. Modern Woodman of Amer.
Eagle, Edw. L., Jr., (AV) .... '17 '41 C&L.339 B.A., J.D. [Eagle&E.]
Eagle, Elizabeth, (BV) .... '50 '78 C.378 B.A. L.285 J.D. [Eagle&E.]
Eagle, Robert A., (AV) .... '22 '47 C&L.339 A.B., LL.B. [Eagle&E.]
Eagle & Eagle, (AV) .... Rock Island Bank Bldg.
Elles, Charles F. '47 '73 C&L.546 B.S., J.D.
(adm. in NE; not adm. in IL) Bituminous Ins. Cos.
Evans, Lane A. .... '51 '78 C.57 B.A. L.276 J.D. (M.C.)
Fairfield, Brian T. .... '69 '94 C&L.190 B.A., J.D. [Ⓐ Brooks&T.]
Faust, Dennis M., (BV) .... '40 '65 C.504 A.B. L.339 LL.B. Asst. States Atty.
Feeney, Timothy M., (BV) .... '67 '93 C&L.352 B.S., J.D. [McCarthy,C.F.&E.]
Flynn, Patrick J., (BV) .... '48 '74 C.207 B.A. L.880 J.D. [Pappas&S.]
Fogle, Gary L. '51 '81 C.477 B.S.E. L.424 J.D.
Sr. Claims Legal Coun., Bituminous Casualty Corporation
Friederich, John A. '56 '81 C.350 B.A. L.352 J.D.
(adm. in IA; not adm. in IL) Asst. Gen. Coun., Royal Neighbors of America
Fuhr, Frank R., (BV) .... '55 '80 C.801 B.A. L.966 J.D. [McCarthy,C.F.&E.]
Fuhr, Mary Lynn Kenney, (BV) '58 '85
C.927 B.S. L.589 J.D. SIORI-GC, Rock Island Arsenal
Galvin, Frank J., Jr., (BV) .... '30 '55 C.707 B.A. L.339 J.D. 311 Safety Bldg.
Galvin, Michael J., (CV) .... '59 '84 C.57 B.A. L.879 J.D. 1800 3rd Ave., Ste. 311
Gillies, William G., Jr., (BV) .... '50 '77 C.429 B.A. L.61 J.D. [W.G.Gillies,Jr.]
Gillies, W.G., Jr., Attorney At Law, P.C., (BV) .... 329 Eighteenth Street
Gillman, Bernard C., (BV) .... '28 '53 C.707 B.A. L.339 LL.B. City Atty.
Gilman, Samuel M., (AV) .... '20 '48 C.145 B.A. L.309 J.D. [Coyle,G.&S.I.]

Gosma, Tarbox & Associates, P.L.C.
(See Davenport, Iowa)

Grushon, Matthew G. '75 '03 C.610 B.S. L.608 J.D.
(adm. in IA; not adm. in IL) [Ⓐ Winstein,K.&W.]
Hamilton, Jennifer L. .... '75 '02 C.846 B.B.A. L.352 J.D. [Ⓐ Lane&W.]

Hamilton, Jay R., PLC, Law Office of
(See Davenport, Iowa)

Hancks, Rian William .... '— '84 C.945 B.A. L.339 J.D. Clock Tower Bldg.
Hancock, Melissa A. .... '76 '02 C.177 B.A. L.352 J.D. [Ⓐ Pappas&S.]

Hanna, Steve, Attorney at Law
(See Moline)

Hass, James W. .... '43 '68 C&L.352 B.B.A., J.D. Pres., Valley Grp., Inc.
Heller, Michelle L. .... '77 '02 C&L.352 B.A., J.D. [Ⓐ Nepple L.] ⊙

Heninger and Heninger, Professional Corporation
(See Davenport, Iowa)

Hewitt, Adrienne D. '55 '83 C.197 B.A. L.276 J.D.
(adm. in DC; not adm. in IL) 4709 44th St.‡
Hoffman, David C. .... '44 '69 C.197 A.B. L.597 J.D. 1504 Third Ave.
Hofmann, Bernard J., (BV) .... '66 '93 C.352 B.A. L.221 J.D. [Brooks&T.]
Hofmann, Milissa K., (BVⓉ) .... '68 '93 C.57 B.A. L.221 J.D. [Brooks&T.]
Horack, Bruce M., (AVⓉ) '47 '72 C.228 B.A. L.861 J.D.
(adm. in VT; not adm. in IL)
Sr. V.P. Claims & Sr. Claims Legal Coun., Bituminous Casualty Corp.
Howard, Douglas B. '55 '81 C&L.221 B.A., J.D.
(adm. in IA; not adm. in IL) Sr. Claims Legal Coun., Bituminous Casualty Corporation
Ishibashi, Peter .... '55 '84 C.57 A.B. L.352 J.D. Asst. State's Atty.
Jarrell, Reginald D. .... '57 '88 C.30 B.A. L.352 J.D. Prairie State Legal Servs., Inc.
Johnson, Gary C. ...... '43 '68 C&L.352 B.A., J.D. Gen. Coun., Royal Neighbors of Amer.
Jones, Derek G., (CV) .... '72 '97 C&L.352 B.A., J.D. [Ⓐ Brooks&T.]
Jung, Jay .... '72 '03 C&L.352 B.A., J.D. [Ⓐ Nepple L.] ⊙

Katz, Huntoon & Fieweger, P.C.
(See Moline)

Kavensky, Craig L., (BV) .... '57 '82 C.339 B.S. L.46 J.D. [Winstein,K.&W.]
Kavensky, Harrison H., (AV) .... '28 '52 C&L.339 B.S.L., J.D. [Winstein,K.&W.]
Kay-Decker, Courtney M., (CV) .... '73 '97 C.597 B.A. L.352 J.D. [Lane&W.] ⊙
Keefe, Edward .... '28 '58 C.743 A.B. L.339 J.D. Cir. J.
Keleher, Michael J. .... '60 '86 C.1247 B.A. L.589 J.D. Asst. State's Atty.
Kennerly, Pamela J. .... '69 '97 C.504 B.A. L.801 J.D. [Ⓐ McCarthy,C.F.&E.]
Keys, Amy Lynn .... '75 '00 C.98 B.S. L.352 J.D. [Ⓐ Snyder,P.&N.]
Keys, Christine A., (BV) .... '62 '92 C.707 B.A. L.209 J.D. [Nelson K.K.]
Keys, Richard, (BV) .... '64 '91 C.57 B.A. L.365 J.D. [Nelson K.K.]
Kilbride, Thomas L. .... '53 '81 C.742 B.A. L.1162 J.D. Supm. Ct. Jus.
Klein, Alissa D. .... '78 '04 C.351 B.A. L.352 J.D. [Ⓐ Lane&W.]
Klockau, Christopher J., (BV) .... '47 '73 C.339 B.A. L.879 J.D. [Klockau,M.&S.]
Klockau, Marquis & Skorepa, P.C., (BV) .... 1808 Third Avenue

Koenig, Philip E., (BV) '49 '75 C.801 B.A. L.809 J.D.
1515 Fourth Avenue, 61201
Telephone: 309-786-3313 Fax: 309-786-0061
Email: pkoenig@qconline.com URL: http://www.lawyers.com/koeniglaw
Wills and Probate, Estate Planning, Real Estate, Business Organization, Tax, Bankruptcy, Commercial Real Estate, Commercial Bankruptcy, Trusts and Estates and General Civil Practice, including Trials and Appeals.
See Professional Biographies, ROCK ISLAND, ILLINOIS

Konecky, John P., (BV) .... '46 '71 C.347 B.S. L.477 J.D. 1515 4th Ave., Ste. 300
Kopp, Frederick P. .... '49 '74 C&L.352 B.A., J.D. 329 18th Street
Kutsunis, Theodore G., (AV) .... '56 '82 C.57 B.A., B.S. L.1187 J.D. [Kutsunis&W.]
Kutsunis & Weng, P.C., (AV) .... 1515 Fourth Avenue, Suite 301
Landwehr, Rebecca Norton, (BV) .... '60 '90 C.351 B.A. L.352 J.D. P.O. Box 2004

Lane & Waterman LLP, (AV) BB
224 18th Street, Suite 500, 61201 ⊙
Telephone: 309-786-1600 Fax: 309-786-1794
URL: http://www.l-wlaw.com
Members of Firm: Charles E. Miller; Dana M. Craig; Robert V. P. Waterman, Jr.; Peter J. Benson; John D. Telleen; Richard A. Davidson; Jason J. O'Rourke; Courtney M. Kay-Decker; Diane M. Reinsch. Associates: Alissa D. Klein; Jennifer L. Hamilton.
General Civil Practice.
Davenport, Iowa Office: 220 North Main Street, Suite 600. Telephone: 563-324-3246. Fax: 563-324-1616.
See Professional Biographies, ROCK ISLAND, ILLINOIS

Latham, Henry W., II '64 '91 C.707 B.A. L.352 J.D.
(adm. in IA; not adm. in IL) [Ⓐ Brooks&T.]
Lazenby, Robert Franklin, II .... '49 '86 L.1187 J.D. US Army Corps of Eng.
Lefstein, Lori R. .... '58 '83 C.339 B.F.A. L.575 J.D. Cir. J.
Lefstein, Stuart R., (AV) .... '34 '58 C.57 B.A. L.477 J.D. [Ⓒ Pappas&S.]
Leiby, Jack L., Sr. .... '42 '77 C&L.339 B.A., J.D. 2915 21st Avenue
Lewarne, John R., (BV) .... '41 '67 C&L.352 B.A., J.D. 121 16th St.
Leyshon, Robert Kelly, (CV) .... '69 '94 C&L.352 B.A., J.D. [Winstein,K.&W.]
Lousberg, Peter H., (AV) .... '31 '56 C.976 B.A. L.602 J.D. [Ⓒ McCarthy,C.F.&E.]
Ludens Potter Burch & Melton, (AV) .... 226-17th Street, Suite Nine (⊙Morrison)

Maginas, Stephen P. '— '90 C&L.861 B.A., J.D.
(adm. in LA; not adm. in IL) Claims Legal Coun., Bituminous Casualty Corporation
Mahoney, Michael P. ... '53 '83 C.602 B.A. L.589 J.D. U.S. Army
Marquis, G. Trent, (BV) ... '45 '72 C.339 B.S. L.879 J.D. 400 16th Street
Marquis, George C. ... '13 '36 L.502 LL.B. 47 Woodley Rd.‡
Marsh, C. Stephan, (AV) ... '52 '79 C.339 B.A. L.146 J.D. [Ruud,S.&M.]
Martin, Terri L. ... '52 '99 C.375 B.S. L.365 J.D. [Pappas&S.]
McAuley, Donan B. ... '46 '74 C&L.494 B.A., J.D. [McAuley]
McAuley Law Office ... 1800 3rd Ave., Ste. 415
McCarthy, Richard W., (AV) ... '22 '49 C.707 L.209 J.D. [McCarthy,C.F.&E.]

McCarthy, Callas, Fuhr & Ellison, P.C., (AV)
The Law Centre, 329 18th Street, 61201
Telephone: 309-788-2800 Fax: 309-793-4090
Email: mcfe@thelawcentre.com URL: http://www.mcfe-law.com
Richard W. McCarthy; John S. Callas; Frank R. Fuhr; Peter W. Church; Timothy M. Feeney;—Pamela J. Kennerly. Of Counsel: Peter H. Lousberg.
Divorce, Commercial and Residential Real Estate, Labor Law, Labor Relations, Labor Arbitration, Commercial Litigation, Criminal Defense, Probate and Probate Administration, Inheritance, Dram Shop Law, Liquor Liability, Casualty Insurance, Medical Negligence, Debtor/Creditor Bankruptcy, ERISA, Personal Injury, Wrongful Death, Maritime Accidents, Products Liability, Traffic Violations.
See Professional Biographies, ROCK ISLAND, ILLINOIS

McClean, John Richard, Jr. ... '48 '75 C.686 B.A. L.365 J.D. Assoc. Cir. J.
McDaniel, Jeffrey C., (BV) ... '68 '93 C&L.352 B.A., J.D. [Brooks&T.]
McGuire, Bernadine Feller '50 '77 C.187 B.M.E. L.352 J.D.
(adm. in IA; not adm. in IL) U.S.A. Armament, Munitions & Chemical Command
Meehan, Gerald J., (AV) ... '49 '74 C.816 B.ENG L.1000 J.D. [Coryn,W.&M.]
Meersman, F. Michael, (BV) ... '55 '82 C.472 B.B.A. L.365 J.D. Pub. Def.
Melaas, Ira J., Jr., (BV) ... '32 '59 C.427 B.A. L.879 LL.B. 2607-36th St.
Melbourne, Barbara J. '63 '88
C.190 B.A. L.378 J.D. Sr. Development Officer, Planned Giving‡
Melton, M. Tod, (BV) ... '66 '92 C.589 B.S. L.902 J.D. [Ludens P.B.&M.] ⊙
Mesich, Kathleen E. ... '76 '02 C.339 B.S. L.801 J.D. [[A] Brooks&T.]
Miller, Charles E., (AV①) ... '45 '73 C.597 A.B. L.352 J.D. [Lane&W.] ⊙
Miller, Stephen C. ... '15 '38 C&L.602 A.B., LL.B. 1337 21st Ave.‡
Nelson, Brett Andrew, (CV) ... '67 '93 C&L.221 B.S.B.A., J.D. [Nelson K.K.]
Nelson, Steven L., (BV) ... '48 '77 C.927 B.A. L.221 J.D. [Snyder,P.&N.]
Nelson•Keys•Keys, P.C., (BV) ... 1830 Second Avenue, Suite 250
Neppl, James L., (AV) ... '42 '67 C.177 B.A. L.352 J.D. 1600 4th Ave., Ste. 450
Nepple, James A., (AV) ... '45 '70 C.190 B.A. L.352 J.D. [Nepple L.] ⊙

Nepple Law, P.L.C., (AV)
American Bank Building, 1515 4th Avenue, Suite 300, 61201 ⊙
Telephone: 309-732-1230 Toll Free: 877-888-0675 Telecopier: 309-786-0061
Email: tax@nepplelaw.com URL: http://www.nepplelaw.com
James A. Nepple;—Jay Jung; Michelle L. Heller.
Taxation, Estate Planning, Trust and Estate Administration, Wills and Probate Administration, Nonprofit and Charitable Organizations, Businesses and Corporations, Pension and Profit Sharing Plans, Real Estate, and Farms.
Muscatine, Iowa Office: Hershey Professional Center, 216 Sycamore Street, Suite 500, 52761-3809. Telephone: 563-264-6840. Toll Free: 877-888-0675. Telecopier: 563-264-6844.
Davenport, Iowa Office: Wells Fargo Bank Building, 4300 E. 53rd Street, Suite 103, 52807. Telephone: 563-355-6841. Toll Free: 877-888-0675. Telecopier: 563-355-6842.

O'Connor, Edward F. '18 '42 C&L.352 B.A., J.D.
(adm. in IA; not adm. in IL) Asst. Dist. Coun., U.S. Army Corps of Engrs.
O'Connor, Jeffrey W. ... '49 '74 C.602 B.B.A. L.365 J.D. Chf. Cir J.
Olberts, Mark A. ... '54 '82 C.339 B.A. L.378 J.D. 4409 37th Ave.‡
O'Rourke, Jason J., (BV) ... '73 '98 C&L.190 B.A., J.D. [Lane&W.] ⊙
Osborn, Margaret Ann ... '56 '82 C.707 B.A. L.734 J.D. Asst. State's Atty.
Panousis, Christ T. ... '33 '66 C&L.352 B.S., LL.B. 610 Safety Bldg.‡
Pappas, Matthew P., (BV) ... '62 '88 C.339 B.A. L.879 J.D. [Pappas&S.]

Pappas & Schnell, P.C., (BV)
Paddock Building, 1617-2nd Avenue, Suite 300, P.O. Box 5408, 61204-5408
Telephone: 309-788-7110 Fax: 309-788-2773
Email: pslaw@pappasandschnell.com URL: http://www.pappasandschnell.com
Matthew P. Pappas; Molly O'Meara Schnell; Patrick J. Flynn; Terri L. Martin. Of Counsel: Roy W. Van Der Kamp; Stuart R. Lefstein;—Karen J. Barrows; Melissa A. Hancock.
Labor and Employment, Litigation, Trusts and Estates, Probate, Taxation, Corporate, Business Law, Real Estate, Education.
See Professional Biographies, ROCK ISLAND, ILLINOIS

Park, Robert T., (BV) ... '46 '73 C&L.339 B.A., J.D. [Snyder,P.&N.]
Patton, Frederick P. ... '23 '53 C.293 B.A. L.352 LL.B. Asso. Cir. J.
Paulus, Lori S. '61 '85 C.504 B.S. L.352 J.D.
Claims Legal Coun. & V.P., Bituminous Casualty Corporation
Peterson, Bruce, (BV) '52 '78
C&L.339 B.A., J.D. Asst. Gen. Coun., Royal Neighbors of Amer.

Pool, Leigh & Fabricius
(See Ottawa)

Potter, Frederick H. ... '12 '42 C.339 A.B. L.793 LL.B. 311 Safety Bldg.‡
Potter, Thomas J., (BV) ... '51 '76 C.118 B.A. L.352 J.D. [Ludens P.B.&M.] ⊙

Pulsifer, Sharon L.
(See Moline)

Ramirez, Phillip T. ... '66 '91 C&L.352 B.A., J.D. 1800 3rd Ave.
Reinsch, Diane M., (BV) ... '58 '96 C.350 B.A. L.352 J.D. [Lane&W.] ⊙
Rink, Paul E. ... '16 '41 C.707 B.A. L.209 LL.B. Ret. Cir. J.
Robertson, Donovan S., (BV) ... '56 '82 C.57 A.B. L.880 J.D. 115 17th St.
Roche, James M., (CV) ... '61 '87 C.436 B.A. L.424 J.D. [VanDerGinst R.&W.]
Rock, John A. ... '35 '64 C.221 B.S.B.A. L.352 J.D. Atty. Advsr., AMCCOM, U.S. Army
Rothert, Ronald H. '38 '74 C.707 B.A. L.352 J.D.
(adm. in IA; not adm. in IL) Gen. Atty., Army Corps of Engrs.
Runnels, Dee Ann, (BV) ... '50 '80 C.427 B.A. L.352 J.D. [Snyder,P.&N.]
Ruud, Glenn F., (BV) ... '45 '75 C.352 B.A. L.365 J.D. [Ruud,S.&M.]
Ruud, Scovil & Marsh, (AV) ... 2009 9th Ave.
Ryan, Eric ... '75 '01 C.339 B.S. L.589 J.D. [[A] Winstein,K.&W.]
Sauser, Frank '46 '85 C.94 B.S.B.A. L.352 J.D.
(adm. in IA; not adm. in IL) Claims Legal Coun., Bituminous Casualty Corporation
Schick, William Gerald, (BV) '47 '72
C.57 B.A. L.836 J.D. 423 Seventeenth Street, Second Floor
Schnell, Molly O'Meara, (BV) ... '64 '89 C.352 B.B.A. L.430 J.D. [Pappas&S.]
Schoede, Edw. C., (BV) ... '15 '39 C.57 B.A. L.477 J.D. 1800 3rd Ave.‡
Schultz, Herbert F., Jr., (BV) ... '59 '87 C.352 B.S. L.1187 J.D. [Schultz&S.]
Schultz, Herbert F., Sr., (BV) ... '25 '52 C.707 L.339 J.D. [Schultz&S.]
Schultz, James H., (BV) ... '55 '80 C.339 B.A. L.221 J.D. [J.H.Schultz]
Schultz, James H., P.C., (BV) ... 329 Eighteenth Street
Schultz & Shearer, (BV) ... 224 18th St.
Schwartz, Jack A. ... '58 '84 C.388 B.A. L.862 J.D. 1800 3rd Ave.
Sconyers, Anthony B. ... '51 '81 C.424 A.B. L.209 J.D. U.S. Army
Scott, Robert G., (BV) ... '23 '48 C.57 A.B. L.339 LL.B. 1800 3rd Ave.
Scovil, Douglas C., (BV) ... '52 '77 C.602 B.B.A. L.365 J.D. [Ruud,S.&M.]
Shearer, Robert C., (BV) ... '39 '64 C&L.352 B.B.A., J.D. [Schultz&S.]
Shields, Thomas J., (AV①) '47 '72 C.945 A.B. L.345 J.D.
(adm. in IN; not adm. in IL) U.S. Dist. Ct.
Skorepa, Thomas A., (BV) ... '52 '80 C.589 B.A. L.801 J.D. [Klockau,M.&S.]
Snyder, William J., (BV) ... '42 '67 C&L.352 B.A., J.D. [Snyder,P.&N.]

Snyder, Park & Nelson, P.C., (BV)
1600 Fourth Avenue, Suite 200, P.O. Box 3700, 61204-3700
Telephone: 309-786-8497 Telefax: 309-786-0463
Email: lawfirm@snyderpark.com URL: http://www.snyderpark.com
William J. Snyder; Robert T. Park; Steven L. Nelson; Dee Ann Runnels; Joseph N. Van Vooren;—Amy Lynn Keys. Of Counsel: Pamela M. Anderson.
Banking, Bankruptcy, Commercial, Corporation, General Civil Litigation in all State and Federal Courts, Insurance, Labor Law, Probate, Real Estate, Taxation, Estate Planning, Trials, Employment Law, Workers Compensation, Construction and Commercial Litigation and Administrative Law.
See Professional Biographies, ROCK ISLAND, ILLINOIS

Soble, Peter M. ... '41 '64 C&L.339 LL.B. 226-17th St.
Sosalla, Theresa L. ... '62 '94 C.162 B.A. L.352 J.D. [[A] M.J.Warner&Assoc.]

Stanley, Lande & Hunter, A Professional Corporation
(See Davenport, Iowa)

Steckel, John, (CV) ... '71 '97 C.174 B.A. L.190 J.D. [VanDerGinst R.&W.]
Stengel, Bridget Ann ... '59 '84 C&L.339 B.A., J.D. U.S. Army
Stengel, William R., Jr., (BV) ... '47 '72 C.339 B.S. L.352 J.D. [Coyle,G.&S.I.]
Stephens, B. Douglas, (BV) ... '48 '75 C.966 B.A. L.424 J.D. 1800 3rd Avenue, Suite 608
Stojan, Clark J., (BV) ... '54 '79 C.589 B.S. L.339 J.D. [Wessels&S.]
Taber, Ronald C. ... '41 '67 C.57 B.A. L.352 J.D. Cir. J.
Tappa, James L., (BV) ... '44 '69 C.707 L.352 LL.B. First of America Bldg., Ste. 300
Telleen, John D., (BV) ... '58 '84 C.57 B.A. L.352 J.D. [Lane&W.] ⊙
Telleen, John M. ... '22 '50 C.57 A.B. L.339 LL.B. Cir. J.
Tephly, Annette M. ... '69 '95 C&L.352 B.A., J.D. Asst. Coun., Royal Neighbors of Amer.
Teros, James T. ... '45 '73 C.57 B.A. L.879 J.D. Cir. J.
Terronez, Jeff, (BV) ... '71 '97 C.927 B.S. L.879 J.D. 1515 4th Ave.
Theisen, Christopher Thomas ... '64 '89 C.172 B.S. L.209 J.D. [VanDerGinst R.&W.]
Trinrud, Richard J., (BV) ... '50 '81 C.747 B.A. L.300 J.D. [Brooks&T.]
VanDerGinst, Dennis A., (BV) ... '62 '89 C.589 B.A. L.209 J.D. [VanDerGinst R.&W.]
VanDerGinst Roche & Westensee, LTD, (BV) ... 400 16th Street
Van Der Kamp, Roy W., (AV) ... '19 '43 C.132 B.A. L.352 J.D. [[C] Pappas&S.]
Van Vooren, Joseph N., (CV) ... '70 '96 C.338 B.S. L.589 J.D. [Snyder,P.&N.]
Walker, William M., (BV) ... '42 '68 C.228 B.A. L.144 J.D. [Coryn,W.&M.]
Wallace, Barbara K., (BV) ... '70 '97 C.57 B.A. L.352 J.D. [Winstein,K.&W.]
Wallace, Franklin S., (BV) ... '27 '53 C.1027 B.S. L.477 J.D. [Winstein,K.&W.]
Walton, Robert W. ... '30 '59 C.57 B.A. L.352 J.D. 4041-25th Ave.‡
Warner, Michael J., (AV) ... '45 '71 C.339 B.S. L.146 J.D. [M.J.Warner&Assoc.]

Warner, Michael J., & Associates, (AV)
1600 4th Avenue, Suite 410, P.O. Box 3544, 61204-3544
Telephone: 309-794-1660 Fax: 309-794-1454
Email: warner@mjwlaw.com URL: http://www.mjwlaw.com
Michael J. Warner. Associate: Theresa L. Sosalla.
Personal Injury, Wrongful Death, Medical Malpractice, Products Liability, Workers Compensation.
See Professional Biographies, ROCK ISLAND, ILLINOIS

Wassell, Michael L., (BV) ... '53 '85 C.707 B.A. L.589 J.D. [VanDerGinst R.&W.]
Waterman, Robert V. P., Jr., (AV) ... '55 '81 C.597 B.A. L.352 J.D. [Lane&W.] ⊙
Welling, John J. ... '50 '75 C.602 B.A. L.190 J.D. Rock Island Arsenoll
Weng, Michael J., (BV) ... '54 '81 C.57 B.A. L.146 J.D. [Kutsunis&W.]
Wessels, Pete M., (AV) ... '49 '76 C.351 B.A. L.190 J.D. [Wessels&S.] ⊙
Wessels & Stojan P.C., (AV) ... 423 Seventeenth Street, Suite 101 (⊙Waterloo, IA)
Westensee, John H., (BV) ... '47 '73 C.350 B.S. L.879 J.D. [J.H.Westensee]
Westensee, John H., P.C., (BV) ... 400 16th St.
Whitmore, Charles H. ... '14 '37 C.293 B.A. L.352 J.D. 1800 3rd Ave.‡
Winstein, Arthur R., (BV) ... '63 '88 C.352 B.G.S. L.910 J.D. [Winstein,K.&W.]
Winstein, Stewart R., (AV) ... '14 '39 C.57 B.S. L.145 J.D. [Winstein,K.&W.]

Winstein, Kavensky & Wallace, (AV) [BB]
4th Floor, U.S. Bank Building, 224 18th Street, P.O. Box 4298, 61201
Telephone: 309-794-1515; 800-747-1527 Fax: 309-794-9929
URL: http://www.wkwlawyers.com
Members of Firm: Stewart R. Winstein; Harrison H. Kavensky; Franklin S. Wallace; Craig L. Kavensky; Arthur R. Winstein; David L. Cunningham; Robert Kelly Leyshon; Barbara K. Wallace. Associates: Eric Ryan; Matthew G. Grushon (Not admitted in IL).
General Civil Practice in all State and Federal Courts. Trial and Appellate Practice. Personal Injury, Products Liability, Labor, Workers Compensation, Matrimonial, Criminal, Bankruptcy, Probate, Real Estate and Commercial Litigation Law.
Local Regional Counsel for: United Auto Workers.
Reference: Mercantile Bank, Midwest.
See Professional Biographies, ROCK ISLAND, ILLINOIS

Young, D.W. ... '29 '53 C&L.352 B.A., J.D. 3626 38th St.‡

ROCKTON, 5,296, *Winnebago Co.*

Cook, Jack R., (BV) ... '26 '51 C.966 L.972 J.D. 1116 Cannell Ct.
Cook, Jack R., Jr., (CV) ... '49 '77 C.697 B.A. L.365 J.D. 1116 Cannell Ct.
Wheeler, Thomas R. ... '19 '48 C&L.339 A.B., J.D. 765 Salem St.‡

ROLLING MEADOWS, 24,604, *Cook Co.*

Adams, Jennifer Perry ... '70 '95 C.608 B.A. L.896 J.D. Kimball Hill, Inc.
Aghion, Victor ... '56 '84 C.293 B.A. L.221 J.D. Sr. Coun., 3Com Corporation
Amirante, Sam L. ... '48 '74 C&L.424 B.S., J.D. Assoc. Cir. J.
Anderson, Shelly ... '66 '91 C.747 B.A. L.209 J.D. State Atty. Off.

Angelina & Palmer, P.C.
(See Palatine)

Brown, Jason L. ... '73 '98 C&L.329 B.A., J.D. Dir., PepsiAmericas, Inc.
Brucar, Wayne Eli ... '53 '83 C.424 B.A. L.146 J.D. [Brucar&Y.] ⊙
Brucar & Yetter, P.C. ... 1600 Golf Road Corporate Center, Suite 1200 (⊙Glen Ellyn)
Chessick, Judy ... '48 '83 C.339 B.A. L.260 J.D. [Sullivan]

Cosley, Christopher M. '71 '99 C.388 B.A. L.146 J.D.
1931 Rohlwing Road, Suite C, 60008
Telephone: 847-809-0625 Fax: 847-253-3434
URL: http://www.cosleylawfirm.com
Criminal Law, Divorce, Real Estate, Bankruptcy, Driving While Intoxicated, Drug Crimes, Traffic Violation, Misdemeanors, Felonies, Juvenile Crimes, Parole and Probation.
See Professional Biographies, ROLLING MEADOWS, ILLINOIS

Cosley, Donald J. ... '69 '94 C.210 B.A. L.1000 J.D. 1931 Rohlwing Road, Suite C
Crandell, Rosaland M. ... '23 '58 C.597 B.S. L.146 LL.B. Assoc. Cir. J.

DeRemer, Richard L. ....'48 '79 C.187 B.A. L.145 J.D. Apollo Travel Servs.
Downing, James S. '47 '74 C.347 B.S. L.1119 J.D. (adm. in IN; not adm. in IL) Div. Gen. Coun., Bridgestone/Firestone, Inc., Retail Opers.
Fahlgren, Daniel J. ....'62 '89 C.339 B.A. L.365 J.D. Asst. State Atty.
Fink, Howard Lewis ....'35 '60 C.966 B.S. L.309 LL.B. Assoc. Cir. J.
Fogg, Jason A. '67 '97 C.700 B.A. L.209 J.D. Managing Claims Atty., Monitor Liability Managers, Inc.
Fortney, Chandra Lin ....'74 '00 C.741 B.A. L.884 J.D. 2121 Euclid Ave.
Geocaris, James A. ....'30 '53 C.145 B.A. L.209 J.D. Presid. Cir. J.
Gilpin, Susan Lea '54 '83 C.234 B.A. L.365 J.D. CEO, The Foundation for Rehab. Ed. & Resrch.

Glasgow, Thomas, Ltd., The Law Offices of
(See Schaumburg)

Glazier, Donald A. ....'59 '84 C.966 B.A. L.365 J.D. V.P., Monitor Liability Mgrs., Inc.

Gleason & MacMaster, LLC
(See Chicago)

Glowacki, Frank E., (AV) ....'28 '56 C.293 B.A. L.209 J.D. 2121 Euccid Ave.
Goldman, Elliot '60 '85 C.339 B.A. L.424 J.D. Labor & Employ. Atty., PepsiAmericas, Inc.
Goldman, Joel, Law Office .....'47 '73 C.339 B.S. L.597 J.D. 5105 Tollview Dr., Ste. 199
Grigonis, Albert ....'50 '81 C.1183 B.A. L.589 J.D. Sr. Corp. Coun., 3Com Corporation
Hageman, Paul Henry Kivett .....'56 '83 C.679 B.A. L.117 J.D. [P.H.K.Hageman&Assoc.]
Hageman, Paul H. K., & Associates, Ltd. .... 5005 Newport Drive
Hamilton, Ann M. ....'60 '86 C&L.339 B.A., J.D. Asst. Gen. Coun., Kimble Hill, Inc.
Holland, Sherry L. '49 '81 C.339 B.A. L.209 J.D. Sr. Real Estate & Fin. Coun., Kimble Hill, Inc.
Howard, Michael L. ....'59 '84 C&L.602 B.S., J.D. Vice Pres., PepsiAmericas, Inc.
Janura, Arthur L., Jr. ....'49 '75 C.966 B.B.A. L.209 J.D. Assoc. Cir. J.
Jordan, Horace W., Jr. '62 '88 C.860 B.S. L.597 J.D. V.P., Gen. Coun. & Secy., Relational, LLC
Jurczyk, Richard A. ....'65 '91 C.597 B.A. L.424 J.D. Monitor Liability Mgrs., Inc.
Kaplan, Nancy G. ....'62 '88 C.861 B.A. L.146 J.D. Asst. States Atty.
Karahalios, Pamela G. ....'52 '78 C&L.1151 B.A., J.D. Assoc. Cir. J., Cir. Ct.
Karwaczka, Richard George ....'76 '01 Cook Co. State Atty. Off.
Kinigson, Andrew M. '— '83 C.1133 B.S. L.365 J.D. V.P., Employee Rel., PepsiAmericas, Inc.

Klest Law Firm
(See Schaumburg)

Kowalski, Robert J. ....'47 '73 C.846 B.S. L.46 J.D. Cir. J.
Kumar, Sandeep ....'69 '04 C.339 B.A. L.365 J.D. Staff Atty., MYR Group Inc.
Lake, Ronald M. ....'48 '73 C.209 B.S. L.146 J.D. 1941 Rohlwing Rd.
Levine, Jennifer Dienstag '69 '94 C.339 B.A. L.966 J.D. Claims Atty., Monitor Liability Mgrs., Inc.
Loftus, Brian A., (AV) '42 '66 C.674 A.B. L.569 LL.B. Sr. V.P., Gen. Coun. & Sec., Kimble Hill, Inc.
Lombardi, John R. ....'54 '89 C.1183 B.A. L.365 J.D. Asst. States Atty.
MacKinnon, Charles '51 '79 C.208 B.S.E.E. L.879 J.D. Asst. Gen. Coun., UTStarcom, Inc. (Pat.)

Maramba & Associates, LLC
(See Arlington Heights)

McGoey, Michael E. ....'56 '82 C.910 A.B. L.424 J.D. Borg-Warner Financial Servs., Inc.
Meltzer, Neil V. ....'51 '77 C.910 B.A. L.669 J.D. V.P., Assoc. Agencies, Inc.
Michaels, Wayne H. ...'48 '79 C.188 A.B. L.146 J.D. Sr. Corp. Coun., 3Com Corporation
Miller, Gayle L. ....'63 '89 C.339 B.A. L.46 J.D. Asst. Pub. Def.
Moran, Kristin L. '65 '94 C.352 B.A. L.424 J.D. V.P. & Gen. Coun., Intl. Truck Finance Grp.
Nathan, Joshua J. '61 '86 C.966 B.A. L.424 J.D. Gen. Coun./Comm. Dir., NEG Micon USA, Inc.
Nehs, W. Scott '66 '91 C.597 B.A. L.966 J.D. Vice Pres., Legal & Chf. Compl. Offr., PepsiAmericas, Inc.
Nicol, Nancy J. ....'49 '78 C.201 B.S. L.209 J.D. [Sullivan]
Orndahl, Michael L. '62 '88 C.589 B.S. L.424 J.D. Assistant General Counsel, MYR Group, Inc.
Osajda, Michael C. ....'47 '76 C.276 B.S.F.S. L.597 J.D. Reg. Coml. Mgr., Motorola, Inc.
Paese, James P. ....'50 '76 C&L.209 B.A., J.D. Asst. Pub. Def.
Palac, Lynn T. ....'74 '99 C.424 B.S. L.209 J.D. State Atty. Off.
Palmer, John F. ....'28 '56 C.645 B.A. L.276 J.D. Whitman Corp.

Paynter, Bruce D., The Law Offices of
(See Arlington Heights)

Perilli, Marc A. ....'48 '74 C.339 B.A. L.424 J.D. Dep. Chf., Off. of Pub. Def.
Pinsel, David L. ....'59 '85 C&L.339 B.S., J.D. [D.L.Pinsel]

Pinsel, David L., P.C., Law Offices of
3701 Algonquin Road, Suite 750, 60008
Telephone: 847-818-8700 Fax: 847-818-8226
Email: dpinsel@aol.com URL: http://www.lawyers.com/pinsel
David L. Pinsel.
Divorce, Family, Child Custody, Child Support, Visitation Rights, Paternity, Real Estate, Landlord and Tenant Law, Commercial Collections, Debtor and Creditor Law.
See Professional Biographies, ROLLING MEADOWS, ILLINOIS

Podkowirow, Waleri ....'52 '84 C.597 B.A. L.365 J.D. Asst. Pub. Def.
Pomaro, Nicholas T. ....'37 '65 C.209 B.S.C. L.365 LL.B. Assoc. Cir. J.
Pope, Michael J. ....'43 '74 C.209 B.S. L.365 J.D. Assoc. Cir. J.
Porcellino, Charles E. ....'41 '72 C&L.209 B.S.C., J.D. Assoc. Cir. J.
Pulcanio, Michael J. '73 '99 C.589 B.S. L.365 J.D. Labor & Employ. Coun., PepsiAmericas, Inc.
Rajaram, V. ....'48 '91 C.966 Ph.D. L.146 J.D. PRC Envir. Mgt., Inc.
Reichard, David P. '— '69 C.980 B.A. L.607 J.D. (adm. in OH; not adm. in IL) Asset Mgr. & Asst. Secy., Bridgestone/ Firestone, Inc.‡
Ruttenberg, Marvin H. ....'17 '41 C&L.597 B.S., J.D. Assoc. Cir. J.
Ryan, James T. ....'34 '59 C.390 B.S. L.966 J.D. Cir. Ct. J.
Sadlier, Susan '52 '89 C.456 B.S. L.1202 J.D. Off of Chief Judge, Cir Ct of Cook Cty, 3rd Mun Dist
Sager, James S. '62 '91 C.347 B.S. L.424 J.D. Sr. Real Estate Atty., Bridgestone/Firestone, Inc.-Retail Opers.
Schneid, Mark T. ....'71 '96 C.209 B.S. L.146 J.D. 3701 Algonquin Rd., Suite 760
Sheerin, John G. '61 '94 C.46 B.S.C.E. L.146 J.D. Envir. Mgr., Bridgestone/Firestone, Inc.-Retail Opers.
Shifrin, Alan H. ....'50 '75 C.352 B.A. L.365 J.D. [A.H.Shifrin&Assoc.]
Shifrin, Alan H., & Associates, LLC ....3315 Algonquin Road
Shroff, Ketki M. ....'66 '91 C.339 B.A. L.365 J.D. Asst. State Atty.
Slaw, Terry D. ....'57 '82 C.502 B.J. L.146 J.D. [[A] A.H.Shifrin&Assoc.]

Slonim, Scott ....'50 '81 C&L.861 B.A., J.D. 2121 Euclid Ave., Ste. 141
Spain, Richard C., (AV) '50 '75 C.399 B.A. L.930 J.D. [Spain,S.&V.] (⊙Chgo., Schaumburg, IL; Northborough, MA)
Spain, Spain & Varnet, P.C., (AV) 1600 Golf Road, Suite 450 (⊙Chgo., IL; Northborough, MA)
Spitzig, John R. '61 '86 C.597 B.A. L.424 J.D. Div. Gen. Coun., Employ., Bridgestone/Firestone, Inc.
Stephenson, James W. '54 '79 C.927 B.A. L.221 J.D. Sr. Coun. II, Northrop Grumman Corp., Defensive Systems Div.
Sullivan, Denise M. ....'64 '89 C.589 B.S. L.365 J.D. 4290 W. Kirchoff‡
Sullivan, Michael D. ....'40 '65 C&L.602 B.B.A., J.D. [Sullivan]
Sullivan, Terry ....'43 '68 C.1024 B.S. L.424 J.D. [Sullivan]

Sullivan Firm, The, Ltd.
The Meadows Corporate Center-East Tower, 2550 West Golf Road, Suite 101, 60008-4501
Telephone: 847-228-1100 Fax: 847-228-5199
Email: thesullivanfirm@aol.com URL: http://www.lawyers.com/thesullivanfirm
Terry Sullivan; Michael D. Sullivan; Nancy J. Nicol; Judy Chessick.
Litigation, Criminal Law, Family Law, Employment Law, Business Law, DWI and Real Estate.
See Professional Biographies, ROLLING MEADOWS, ILLINOIS

Szarkowicz, Edward A., Jr. '56 '83 C.347 B.S. L.326 J.D. Gen. Coun., First Source Financial, Inc.
Tarnaris, Napoleon P. ....'55 '85 C.1106 B.A. L.1187 J.D. [N.P.Tarnaris]
Tarnaris, Napoleon P., Ltd. ....3701 Algonquin, Ste. 750
Vienuzis, Edward V. ....'48 '74 C.966 B.A. L.365 J.D. Asst. State Atty.
Wagner, David A. '73 '99 C&L.966 B.A., J.D. Claims Atty., Monitor Liability Managers, Inc. (Legal Department)
Wanca, Brian J. ....'54 '79 C.705 B.A. L.345 J.D. 3701 Algonquin Rd., Ste. 760
Woloshin, Michael ....'47 '80 C.339 B.A. L.146 J.D. Asst. Pub. Def.
Yetter, John P. ....'71 '96 C.589 B.S. L.201 J.D. [Brucar&Y.] ⊙
Zagone, Nicholas S. ....'31 '54 C.999 L.365 J.D. Cir. J.

ROMEOVILLE, 21,153, *Will Co.*

Meegan, Owen D. .....'42 '92 C.742 B.A. L.424 J.D. One University Parkway, Suite 1114

Meszaros, Patrick A., Law Office of
(See Joliet)

ROSCOE, 6,244, *Winnebago Co.*

Kobussen, Sheryl L., (CV) ....'64 '89 C.741 B.B.A. L.436 J.D. 9191 River View Trail
Lutz, Jerome J. ....'29 '69 C.966 B.B.A. L.146 J.D. 11232 Bayberry Dr.‡

ROSELLE, 23,115, *Cook & DuPage Cos.*

Bassitt, Janet L.H. ....'41 '81 C.339 B.A. L.365 J.D. P.O. Box 72277
Carroll, John C. ....'45 '77 C.602 A.B. L.46 J.D. Asst. Atty. Gen.
Coleman, Selwyn ....'16 '41 C&L.597 B.S., LL.B. 205 Pinecrof
Dobra, Charles W. ....'44 '75 C.209 B.A. L.365 J.D. [C.W.Dobra]
Dobra, Charles W., Ltd. .... 675 E. Irving Park Rd.

Gailan & Najera, P.C.
(See Addison)

Haugh, Scott C. ....'57 '88 C.500 B.A. L.597 J.D. 525 Dee Lane
Hipskind, Alexander N. ....'66 '91 C&L.424 B.A., J.D. 510 Sycamore Ave.
Jaile, Mercedes ....'57 '02 C.999 B.S. L.365 J.D. [M.Jaile]
Jaile, Mercedes, LLC .... 400 West Lake Street
Kal, Darwin P., (BV) ....'31 '58 C.145 B.A. L.146 LL.B. 725 E. Irving Park Road
Kardon, Robin D. ....'59 '83 C.569 B.A. L.904 J.D. 613 N. Plum Grove Rd.‡
Koeppel, Calvin E. ....'45 '74 C.108 B.S. L.365 J.D. 701 E. Irving Pk.
Kwiatkowski, Anthony J., (BVⓉ) ....'46 '77 C.46 B.S. L.616 J.D. P.O. Box 725148
Lanciloti, Richard F. ....'42 '81 C.339 B.S. L.209 J.D. 205 Pinecroft Dr.
Lanciloti, Rick M., Jr., (BV) ....'66 '94 C.388 B.A. L.1187 J.D. [Lanciloti]
Lanciloti Law Offices, (BV) .... 205 Pinecroft Dr.
Lundeen, Gary S. ....'55 '80 C&L.589 B.A., J.D. 806 E. Nerge Rd.
Martucci, Gregory J. ....'57 '83 C.238 B.A. L.365 J.D. [G.J.Martucci]

Martucci, Gregory J., P.C., Law Office of
1150 W. Lake Street, Suite B, 60172
Telephone: 630-980-8333 Fax: 630-980-8404
URL: http://www.martuccilaw.com
Gregory J. Martucci.
Bankruptcy, Criminal Law, Driving While Intoxicated, Juvenile Criminal Law, Traffic Violations, Domestic Violence, Personal Injury, Automobile Accidents and Injuries, Slip and Fall, Workers Compensation.
See Professional Biographies, ROSELLE, ILLINOIS

Mraz, Edward S., (AV) ....'33 '57 C&L.602 A.B., LL.B. 111 E. Irving Park Rd.
Pistorio, Francis T., (BV) ....'47 '72 C&L.209 B.A., J.D. [F.T.Pistorio]
Pistorio, Francis T., P.C., (BV) .... 601 E. Irving Park Rd.
Price, Edward A. ....'46 '79 C.337 B.A. L.365 J.D. [E.A.Price]
Price, Edward A., Ltd. ....1030 Summerfield Dr.
Rindal, Ellen J. ....'50 '76 C.352 B.A. L.146 J.D. [E.J.Rindal]
Rindal, Ellen J., P.C. .... 344 Ventura Club Dr.
Robinson, Richard P. ....'26 '59 C.602 B.S. L.1119 J.D. 2 Forest Ave.‡
Shockey, Russell C. '30 '54 C&L.879 B.A., LL.B. (adm. in IN; not adm. in IL) V.P. & Tr. Offr., Harris Bk. Roselle‡
Simons, Elizabeth A. ....'63 '88 C.36 B.S. L.365 J.D. [[A] F.T.Pistorio]
Tumminaro, Peter M. ....'52 '81 C.1082 B.S. L.424 J.D. 330 S. Prospect St.

ROSEMONT, 4,224, *Cook Co.*

Allen, Martin ....'43 '71 C.339 B.S. L.1119 J.D. Phillips Mfg. Co.
Bastian, Thomas M. ....'53 '84 C.209 B.A. L.365 J.D. [[A] Storino,R.&D.]
Baugh, Brian W. ....'65 '91 C&L.589 B.S.Acct., J.D. [[A] Storino,R.&D.]
Berliner, Brad R. '67 '95 C.347 B.S. L.365 J.D. Atty., Central States Health & Welfare & Pension Funds
Berry, Bryan J. ....'61 '87 C.97 B.S. L.209 J.D. [[C] Storino,R.&D.]
Bishop, Kerry C. ....'71 '97 C.339 B.S. L.209 J.D. Corp. Coun., Comdisco, Inc.
Carey, Francis J. '42 '68 C&L.602 B.A., J.D. Supvr., Benefits Litig., Central States Health & Welfare & Pension Funds
Casale, Anthony J., (BV) ....'54 '80 C.209 B.S. L.589 J.D. [[A] Storino,R.&D.]
Chapman, Kathryn Ann '50 '78 C.112 B.S. L.1049 J.D. V.P./ Legal & Intl. Legal Dir., Comdisco, Inc.
Charney, Shawna F. ....'55 '85 C.339 B.A. L.146 J.D. Chf. Coun.-IT CAP, Comdisco, Inc.
Chikkalingaiah, Rathna '70 '97 C.459 B.A. L.424 J.D. Staff Atty., Central States Health & Welfare & Pension Funds
Clancy, Joseph P. '44 '69 C.276 A.B. L.262 J.D. Sr. V.P., Opus Designers Builders Developers, Inc.
Coco, Robert Anthony '60 '87 C.209 B.A. L.365 J.D. Staff Atty., Central States Health & Welfare & Pension Funds

Condon, James P. '52 '80 C.705 B.A. L.597 J.D.
Dep. Gen. Coun., Central States Health & Welfare & Pension Funds
Conley, Gregory A. '55 '84
C.679 B.S.E.E. L.276 J.D. V.P. & Gen. Coun., Galileo Intl. Partnership
Connolly, Mary K. .... '49 '75 C.665 B.A. L.128 J.D. [Ⓐ Storino,R.&D.]
Conwell, Roberta C. .... '54 '96 C.801 B.S. L.365 J.D. Sprint PCS
Cribaro-Mello, Camille A. '66 '99
C.338 B.S. L.424 J.D. Asst. Corp. Coun., Comdisco, Inc.

Cutler & Associates, LTD.
(See Skokie)

Dell, David H. '42 '68 C.604 B.A. L.339 J.D.
Tax Mgr., Wolf, Weis & Horowitz, LLC, CPA's
DelMarto, Angelo F. .... '51 '85 C.209 B.S. L.365 J.D. [Ⓐ Storino,R.&D.]
DiMartino, Lisa T. ......'71 '96 C.339 B.A. L.276 J.D. Prop. Specialist, Crown Castle USA
Diorio, Leonard P. .... '45 '70 C.339 B.S. L.597 J.D. [Ⓒ Storino,R.&D.]
Doerr, Thomas M. '42 '83 C.1151 B.A. L.146 J.D.
V.P./Legal & Assoc. Gen. Coun., Comdisco, Inc.
Donald, Daryl M. '— '95 C&L.339 B.S., J.D.
Licensing Atty., Business Objects Americas
Durkin, Michael K. .... '53 '78 C.339 B.A. L.146 J.D. [Storino,R.&D.]
Evola, Elizabeth Muraca .... '59 '86 C&L.424 B.S., J.D. [Evola&E.]
Evola, Vito M. .... '51 '79 C.424 B.A. L.300 J.D. [Evola&E.]
Evola & Evola .... 9501 W. Devon Ave., Ste. 603
Fahrenbach, Margaret M. '54 '81 C.602 B.Arch. L.424 J.D.
Central States Health & Welfare & Pension Funds

Ferraro, Anthony B., The Law Offices of '51 '83 C&L.209 B.S., J.D.
5600 North River Road Suite 764, 60018
Telephone: 847-292-1220 Fax: 847-292-1221
Email: abfcpalaw@aol.com URL: http://www.lawyers.com/ferraro
Wills, Trusts, Estates, Estate Planning, Estate Taxation, Probate and Trust Administration, Medicaid, Guardianship, Elder Law, and Trust and Estate-Related Commercial Transactions including Business Acquisitions and Real Estate, Commercial Arbitration.
See Professional Biographies, ROSEMONT, ILLINOIS

Fitzgerald, Jeremiah M. '53 '78
C.973 B.S.B.A. L.424 J.D. V.P. & Chf. Legal Offr., Comdisco, Inc.
Franczyk, John J., Jr. '68 '94 C.597 B.A. L.146 J.D.
Staff Atty., Central States Health & Welfare & Pension Funds
Frankel, Dean A. '57 '82 C.597 B.A. L.209 J.D.
V.P./Legal & Assoc. Gen. Coun., Comdisco, Inc.
Gagliardo, Donna J. .... '57 '87 C.550 B.S. L.880 J.D. Coun., Galileo Intl.
Garstka, Kenneth E. .... '57 '82 C&L.209 B.A., J.D. Sr. Coun., Comdisco, Inc.
Giampietro, Nicholas L. '62 '87 C.602 B.B.A. L.597 J.D.
Sr. Vice Pres., Gen. Coun. & Secy., Reyes Holdings, LLC
Gillin, Leon S. .... '29 '53 C.228 A.B. L.209 J.D. 9801 W. Higgins Rd.
Glavin, Kristin Olds '62 '90 C.597 B.S. L.424 J.D.
Assoc. Gen. Coun., Corp. Legal Affs., Amer. Academy of Orthopaedic Surgeons
Harvey, Harold Scott .... '54 '80 C.502 B.S. L.365 J.D. 6111 N. River Rd.
Harvey, Scott S. '— '80 C.502 B.A. L.365 J.D.
V.P./Legal & Dep. Gen. Coun., Comdisco, Inc.
Hoffman, Scott V. .... '60 '85 C.597 B.A. L.209 J.D. 5290 N. Pearl St.
Jaffe, Donald S. .... '32 '57 C&L.339 B.S., LL.B. 10275 Higgins Rd.
Jones, Kelly G. ..... '60 '85 C.57 B.A. L.146 J.D. Assoc. Gen. Coun., Kanbay Incorporated
Krakowski, Mary F. '56 '82 C.424 B.A. L.589 J.D.
Gen. Coun., Transamerica Business Credit Corporation
Kusper, Joseph G. .... '54 '79 C.602 B.B.A. L.589 J.D. [Ⓒ Storino,R.&D.]
Lebow, Joan Moeckel, (AV) '53 '78 C.1168 B.A. L.146 J.D.
Gen. Coun. & Corp. Secy., Ibex Healthdata Systems
Lee, Charles H. .... '70 '96 Central States Health & Welfare & Pension Funds
Lester, Richard A. ....'47 '72 C.375 B.S. L.378 J.D. V.P. & Gen. Coun., Riddell Inc.
Macholl, James E. .... '57 '83 C.209 B.S.C. L.365 J.D. [Ⓐ Storino,R.&D.]
Madden, Albert M. '53 '80 C.339 B.A. L.209 J.D.
Staff Atty., Central States Health & Welfare & Pension Funds
McKenzie, Donald W. .... '34 '60 C.602 B.S. L.424 J.D. 6111 N. River Rd.
Miroballi, Melissa A. .... '72 '97 C&L.424 B.A., J.D. [Ⓐ Storino,R.&D.]
Movish, Glenn Alan ....'58 '83 C.475 B.A. L.910 J.D. Tucker Assocs.-HL Fin. Grp.
Nellis, William J. '37 '61 C&L.424 A.B., J.D.
Secy. to the Bd., Central States Health & Welfare & Pension Funds
Nichols, Robert H., (AV) ....'41 '67 C.976 A.B. L.145 J.D. Air Line Pilots Assn. Intl.
Nyhan, Thomas C. '52 '77 C.424 B.S., Econ. L.209 J.D.
Gen. Coun., Central States Health & Welfare & Pension Funds
Pacione, Peter A. .... '74 '99 C.436 B.A. L.365 J.D. [Ⓐ Storino,R.&D.]
Pascucci, Vincent J. .... '31 '55 C&L.424 B.S., J.D. 9801 W. Higgins Rd.
Paul, Lyssa Kaye '60 '93 C.763 B.A. L.767 J.D.
(adm. in CA; not adm. in IL) V.P. Legal & Chf. Coun.-Commu. Capital, Comdisco, Inc.
Pazol, Judith Armstrong .... '61 '87 C.221 B.S. L.146 J.D. Sr. Coun., Comdisco, Inc.
Peppers, Nicholas S. .... '60 '85 C.118 B.A. L.209 J.D. [Storino,R.&D.]
Petersen, Patricia J. .... '58 '83 C.597 B.A. L.424 J.D. CMP Financial Servs., Inc.
Peterson, Richard N. '60 '91 C.886 B.S. L.1209 J.D.
(adm. in VA; not adm. in IL)
General Counsel, American Academy of Orthopaedic Surgeons
Peterson, Richard N. '55 '81 C.293 B.A. L.910 J.D.
Gen. Coun., Amer. Academy of Orthopaedic Surgeons
Ramello, Richard J. .... '54 '79 C.98 B.S. L.209 J.D. [Storino,R.&D.]
Rath, Cathy Lynn '64 '01 C.347 B.S. L.146 J.D.
Staff Atty., Central States Health & Welfare & Pension Funds
Reuter, Timothy C. '74 '03 C.436 B.A. L.146 J.D.
Staff Atty., Central States Health & Welfare & Pension Funds
Rose, Donald M., (AV) .... '31 '59 C&L.209 B.S., J.D. [Ⓐ Storino,R.&D.]
Scott, Joseph R. '58 '93 C&L.209 B.S., J.D.
Staff Atty., Central States Health & Welfare & Pension Funds
Sheade, Ronald R. .... '50 '78 C.589 B.S. L.146 J.D. 6111 N. River Rd.
Simmons, Joan P. ....'48 '79 C.362 B.A. L.472 J.D. 9377 W. Higgins Rd., 10th Fl.
Small, Richard D., Jr. '53 '78
C.347 B.A. L.1119 J.D. Exec. V.P. & Gen. Coun., AHI Intl. Corp.
Snyder, Robert A. .... '46 '73 C.339 B.A. L.145 J.D. 6111 N. River Rd.
Stephens, Mark R. .... '59 '89 C&L.209 B.S., J.D. [Ⓒ Storino,R.&D.]
Sterling, Victoria J. .... '54 '80 C.150 B.A. L.201 J.D. 6133 N. River Road
Storino, Donald J., (AV) .... '47 '73 C.602 A.B. L.209 J.D. [Storino,R.&D.]
Storino, Donald J., II .... '73 '98 C.602 B.A. L.209 J.D. [Ⓒ Storino,R.&D.]

Storino, Ramello & Durkin, (AV)
9501 West Devon Avenue, Eighth Floor, 60018
Telephone: 847-318-9500 Telecopier: 847-318-9509
URL: http://www.srd-law.com

(This Listing Continued)

Storino, Ramello & Durkin (Continued)
Members of Firm: Donald J. Storino; Michael K. Durkin; Richard J. Ramello; Nicholas S. Peppers;—Donald M. Rose; Thomas M. Bastian; Angelo F. DelMarto; James E. Macholl; Mary K. Connolly; Brian W. Baugh; Melissa A. Miroballi; Peter A. Pacione; Anthony J. Casale. Of Counsel: Joseph G. Kusper; Mark R. Stephens; Bryan J. Berry; Donald J. Storino II; Leonard P. Diorio.
General Civil Trial and Appellate Practice. Real Estate, Corporation, Tort and Commercial Litigation, Municipal Law and Revenue Bonds.
See Professional Biographies, ROSEMONT, ILLINOIS

Sturino, Michael J. .... '66 '98 C.205 B.A.A.S. L.365 J.D. 9501 W. Devon
Weithers, Thomas M. '55 '86 C.424 B.A. L.209 J.D.
Staff Atty., Central States Health & Welfare & Pension Funds
Williams, Robert A. ....'62 '91 C.8 B.S. L.7 J.D. V.P. & Gen. Coun., Kanbay Incorporated
Ziegler, Frank J. '49 '75 C.93 A.B. L.966 J.D.
V.P. Legal & Assoc. Gen. Coun., Comdisco, Inc.

ROSEVILLE, 1,151, *Warren Co.*

Hattery, Simpson & West, (AV) .... 130 N. Main Street (ⓞGalesburg, Monmouth)
Hennenfent, George M., (BV) .... '54 '79 C.927 B.S. L.339 J.D. [Hattery,S.&W.]

ROUND LAKE, 5,842, *Lake Co.*

Anderson, Richard A.
(See Grayslake)

Browne, Henry H. .... '33 '71 C.37 B.S.B.A. L.209 J.D. 210 W. Forest Ave.‡

Idlas, Paul R., Law Office of
(See Grayslake)

Kegel, Thomas M. '61 '87 C.959 B.B.A. L.436 J.D.
(adm. in WI; not adm. in IL) 513 W. Highplains Road‡
Lancaster, Kristina Geister ....'70 '97 C.340 B.A. L.589 J.D. 2009 W. Windsor Drive
Magee, James T., (BV) .... '46 '71 C.424 A.B. L.339 J.D. [Magee,N.&Assoc.]
Magee, Thomas L. .... '11 '34 C&L.209 LL.B. 444 N. Cedar Lake
Magee, Negele & Associates, (BV) .... 444 N. Cedar Lake Rd.
Negele, Hilary J., (BV) .... '46 '79 C&L.424 B.S., J.D. [Magee,N.&Assoc.]
Primack, Jordan .... '37 '63 C.1016 B.S.B.A. L.146 J.D. 21 W. Rollins Rd.

ROUND LAKE BEACH, 25,859, *Lake Co.*

Harter, Jeremy S. .... '72 '01 C.589 B.A. L.339 J.D. [Harter&S.]
Harter & Schottland, P.C. .... 625 W. Rollins Road, Suite F
Schottland, Bruce D. .... '73 '01 C&L.339 B.A., J.D. [Harter&S.]

RUSHVILLE, * 3,229, *Schuyler Co.*

Apfelbaum, Larry A., (BV) '61 '87 C.338 B.S. L.339 J.D.
[Ⓐ Kanoski&Assoc.] (ⓞBloomington, Macomb, Peoria, Quincy, Springfield)
Bain, Florence, (BV) '42 '78 C.350 B.S. L.36 J.D.
[Ⓐ Kanoski&Assoc.] (ⓞBloomington, Macomb, Peoria, Quincy, Springfield)
Burton, Charles A., (BV) ....'50 '75 C.339 B.A. L.365 J.D. 114 W. Lafayette St.
Butler, Scott J., (BV) .... '54 '81 C.234 B.S. L.801 J.D. South Side of Sq.
Edmiston, Charles N., II, (BV) '54 '80 C.339 B.S. L.352 J.D.
[Ⓐ Kanoski&Assoc.] (ⓞBloomington, Macomb, Peoria, Quincy, Springfield)
Jones, Robert A., Law Office, (BV) ..... '52 '79 C.927 B.A. L.365 J.D. 211 W. Wash. St.
Kanoski, Ronald J., (BV) ....'47 '74 C.234 B.S. L.424 J.D. [Kanoski&Assoc.] ⓞ
Kanoski & Associates, (BV)
129 S. Congress St. (ⓞBloomington, Decatur, Macomb, Peoria, Quincy, Springfield)
Klitz, Carson D. .... '38 '69 C.927 L.365 J.D. Cir. J.
Mc Millen, Alesia A. .... '54 '80 C.57 B.A. L.209 J.D. Cir.J.
Miller, Edward P. ....'44 '68 C.1062 B.A. L.339 J.D. 508 W. Lafayette St.
Olivero, Kathy A., (CV) '56 '82 C.339 B.S. L.801 J.D.
[Ⓐ Kanoski&Assoc.] (ⓞBloomington, Macomb, Peoria, Quincy, Springfield)
Strong, Arthur R. .... '43 '68 C.107 A.B. L.339 J.D. Assoc. Cir. J.
Vincent, Mark L., (CV) .... '60 '92 C.927 B.A. L.801 J.D. Co. Atty.
Waldman, John J., (CV) '62 '88 C.801 B.A. L.339 J.D.
[Ⓐ Kanoski&Assoc.] (ⓞBloomington, Macomb, Peoria, Quincy, Springfield)

ST. CHARLES, 27,896, *DuPage & Kane Cos.*

Agrella, Raymond F., (AV) .... '37 '67 C.393 B.A. L.424 J.D. [Shearer&A.]
Ammarell, Scott William .... '60 '85 C.350 B.A. L.276 J.D. 6N969 Whispering Trail‡
Bailey, Earl P. '42 '71 C.610 B.B.A. L.1003 J.D.
(adm. in OH; not adm. in IL) [Wessels&P.]
Bayer, Christine Cloud ....'65 '94 C.597 B.S.Ed. L.339 J.D. Asst. State Atty.
Bayer, Karl E. ....'— '96 C.388 B.A. L.365 J.D. [Ⓐ O'Hagan,S.&A.]
Beaghan, John Joseph '66 '92 C.602 B.B.A. L.424 J.D.
(adm. in CA; not adm. in IL) 55 Lakewood Circle
Belford, Craig R. .... '70 '95 C.339 B.A. L.145 J.D. Assoc. Clk, Ill Sup. Ct.
Bettag, Jerome L., (BV) .... '62 '94 C.750 B.A. L.589 J.D. [Ⓐ Shearer&A.]
Biallas, John S., Attorney at Law ...... '48 '75 C.801 B.A. L.365 J.D. 3N918 Sunrise Lane
Boles, Susan Clancy, (BV) ....'65 '90 C.880 B.A. L.879 J.D. [Clancy]
Bollero, Jennifer Leisner ....'63 '88 C.597 B.A. L.424 J.D. 1011 S. 3rd St.
Boose, Jerry D., (BV) ....'42 '68 C&L.339 B.S., J.D. 4N645 School Road
Brannen, George W., (P.C.), (AV) .... '40 '68 C.197 B.A. L.228 J.D. [Casey,B.&R.]
Bree, Debra Lynn .... '74 '99 C.999 B.S. L.209 J.D. King Co. Atty.
Brewe, Franklin D., (BV) .... '47 '76 C.339 B.A. L.597 J.D. J., Kane Co.
Brizuela, M. Caroline, (BV) ....'68 '93 C.339 B.A. L.589 J.D. [Ⓐ Griffin&H.]
Brodner, Joseph M. .... '64 '91 C.679 B.S. L.990 J.D. 602 N. 12th St.

Brundage, Stephen A.
(See Wheaton)

Burke, John S. .... '60 '92 C.363 B.A. L.1003 J.D. [Higgins&B.]
Caruso, Anthony J., Jr., (AV) ....'47 '75 C.134 B.S. L.838 J.D. [Ⓐ Wessels&P.]
Casey, Robert F., (P.C.), (AV) .... '21 '49 C&L.339 B.S., LL.B. [Casey,B.&R.]

Casey, Brannen & Romag, (AV)
A Partnership of Professional Corporations
Timbers Professional Center, 240 W. River Drive, 60174-5535
Telephone: 630-513-0066 Fax: 630-513-0109
Email: caseylaw@lawyers.com URL: http://www.cbrlaw.net
Members of Firm: Robert F. Casey (P.C.); George W. Brannen (P.C.); James J. Romag.
Personal Injury Litigation, Truck Accidents, Motorcycle Accidents, Boat Accidents, Construction Accidents, Aircraft Accidents, and other Major Accidents and Injuries, Medical Malpractice, Nursing Home Negligence, Wrongful Death, Products Liability, Premises Liability, Dram Shop Liability, Insurance Defense, Insurance Coverage Law, Uninsured and Underinsured Motorists.
See Professional Biographies, ST. CHARLES, ILLINOIS

Catella, Alvin L., (BV) ....'38 '65 C.647 B.S. L.365 LL.B. 801 E. Main St.
Cavallo, Lynn C., Law Offices of .... '52 '91 L.424 J.D. 2400 East Main Street
Cherny, William D. .... '55 '97 C.608 B.S. L.365 J.D. Asst. Public Def.
Clancy, Michael W., (AV) ....'59 '85 C.31 B.A. L.93 J.D. [Clancy]
Clancy, Wendell W., (P.C.), (AV) ....'38 '63 C.228 B.A. L.146 J.D. [Clancy]

Clancy Law Offices, (AV)
7 South Second Avenue, 60174
Telephone: 630-584-7666 Fax: 630-584-1649
URL: http://www.clancylaw.com
Wendell W. Clancy (P.C.); Michael W. Clancy; Susan Clancy Boles.
Personal Injury, Medical Malpractice, Professional Malpractice, Catastrophic Injury, Products Liability, Business Transactions, Partnership Law.

See Professional Biographies, ST. CHARLES, ILLINOIS

Cooke, James F., Law Office of, (BV) ......'54 '80 C.388 B.A. L.146 J.D. 215 Illinois St.
Crane, William B. ....'— '02 C.424 B.A. L.209 J.D. [B] O'Hagan,S.&A.]
Cuscaden, Douglas R., (BV) ....'61 '88 C.238 B.A. L.365 J.D. [Hoscheit,M.M.&C.]
Denker, Michael J. ....'70 '95 C.800 B.A. L.597 J.D. [Denker&M.]

Denker & Muscarello, LLC
4N701 School Road, 60175
Telephone: 630-513-9191 Fax: 630-524-9146
Email: info@denkermuscarello.com URL: http://www.denkermuscarello.com
Michael J. Denker; Charles V. Muscarello.
Business Law, Business and Commercial Litigation, Corporate Law, Commercial Law, Information Technology Law, Computer and Internet Law, Intellectual Property Law, Health Care Law, Real Estate Law, Family Law.

See Professional Biographies, ST. CHARLES, ILLINOIS

Di Marzio, Philip L. ....'49 '73 C.589 B.A. L.339 J.D. Cir. J.
Dwyer, Timothy P., (CV) ....'62 '90 C.339 B.S.W. L.365 J.D. 240 West River Dr.
Fitzpatrick, Mary Agrella, (BV) ....'63 '88 C.339 B.A. L.589 J.D. [Shearer&A.]
Gajewski, Megan K. '66 '96 C.966 B.A. L.776 J.D.
(adm. in NJ; not adm. in IL) 103 N. 11th Ave., Suite 101
Galante, Gail A. ....'— '84 C.597 B.A. L.424 J.D. [B] O'Hagan,S.&A.]
Gitchell, Rita Lowery ....'— '85 C.338 B.S. L.146 J.D. [O'Hagan,S.&A.]
Golden, Patricia Piper, (BV) ....'50 '75 C.339 B.S. L.823 J.D. Assoc. Cir. J.
Gomoll, Jennifer M., (CV) ....'70 '95 C.339 B.A. L.209 J.D. [Gomoll]
Gomoll Law Office, A Professional Corporation, (CV) ........................P.O. Box 465
Gorecki, Robert L., (BV) ....'28 '56 C.339 B.S. L.365 J.D. 801 E. Main St.
Green, Ellen L. ....'— '88 C.413 B.A. L.339 J.D. [O'Hagan,S.&A.]
Griffin, Patrick M., (BV) ....'68 '95 C.339 B.S. L.589 J.D. [Griffin&H.]

Griffin & Hoskins LLC, (BV)
40W320 LaFox Road, Suite E, 60175
Telephone: 630-584-6327 Fax: 630-584-6403
URL: http://www.griffinhoskinsbrizuela.com
Members of Firm: Patrick M. Griffin; Gregory W. Hoskins. Associates: Kenneth L. Kaergard; M. Caroline Brizuela.
Real Estate Sales and Acquisitions, Development and Zoning, Buying and Selling a Home, Buying and Selling of Businesses, Corporate, Business Planning and Litigation, Municipal Law, General Civil Litigation, Appeals in State and Federal Courts.
Representative Clients: Balck Electric Corp.; Valley Ambulatory Surgery Center; B & B Enterprises; Fox Mill Limited Partnership; Valley Community Bank; Taut, Coilform Co.; Independent Publishing Co.; Kane County Fair; Valley Medical Inn.

See Professional Biographies, ST. CHARLES, ILLINOIS

Grove, Terry F. ....'40 '66 C.589 L.365 LL.B. 311 N. Second St.‡
Gustafson, C. Donald ....'30 '67 C.57 B.A. L.365 J.D. 1401 Walnut Hill‡
Hallock, James C., (CV) ....'51 '78 C.233 B.S. L.1151 J.D. J.
Hamilton, Walter H., Law Office of, (BV) '46 '75
C.473 B.A. L.365 J.D. 711 Mosedale St.
Harriett, Kathleen M. ....'60 '87 C.602 B.B.A. L.209 J.D. 4N077 Arbor Creek Rd.
Hartman, Raymond V. ....'40 '64 C&L.424 B.B.A., J.D. V.P., Tax, BCI Holdings Corp.
Hatch, Jack G. ....'19 '46 C.578 B.S. L.339 LL.B. 915 S. 6th St.
Haule, R. James ....'47 '73 C.932 B.A. L.1000 J.D. 2020 Dean St.
Hauptman, Nancy M. ....'52 '79 C.347 B.A. L.345 J.D. 2280 Persimmon Drive
Higgins, John B., (BV) ....'55 '80 C.228 A.B. L.209 J.D. [Higgins&B.]
Higgins & Burke, P.C., (BV) ....Seven South Second Avenue
Hlavin, Joseph R., Jr. ....'29 '59 C.424 B.S. L.209 J.D. 2035 Foxfield Drive‡
Hoscheit, John J., (BV) ....'59 '84 C&L.339 B.S., J.D. [Hoscheit,M.M.&C.]

Hoscheit, McGuirk, McCracken & Cuscaden, P.C., (AV)
1001 East Main Street, Suite G, 60174
Telephone: 630-513-8700 630-513-8799
Email: johnm@hmcpc.com URL: http://www.hmcpc.com
John J. Hoscheit; John M. McGuirk; Kate L. McCracken; Douglas R. Cuscaden.
General Civil Practice including, Personal Injury, Workers Compensation, Real Estate, Corporate, Commercial Litigation, Estate Planning and Criminal Law, Construction, Buying and Selling, Landlord Tenant, Zoning and Land Use, DWI, Traffic, Drug Crimes, Juvenile Law, White Collar, Family, Divorce, Child Custody, Child Support, Adoptions, Commercial Leasing, Business Law, Franchise, Limited Liability, Contracts, Starting a Business, Auto, Dog Bites, Slip and fall, Wrongful Death.

See Professional Biographies, ST. CHARLES, ILLINOIS

Hoskins, Gregory W. ....'63 '95 C.352 B.B.A. L.589 J.D. [Griffin&H.]
Huang, Gerald C. ....'— '00 C&L.339 B.S., J.D. [B] O'Hagan,S.&A.]
Hudson, Donald C. ....'49 '75 C.209 B.A. L.365 J.D. 1209 Winners Cup Circle
Jacobs, Stephen M. ....'64 '89 C&L.589 B.S., J.D. [Shaw,J.&Assoc.]
James, Matthew Scott ....'75 '01 C.145 B.A. L.352 J.D. Kane Co. State Atty. Off.
Janes, Robert L. ....'49 '74 C.1151 B.A. L.209 J.D. 37W777 Route 38
Joerg, Nancy E. ....'45 '85 C.319 B.A. L.589 J.D. [Wessels&P.]
Johnson, Keith A. ....'— '95 C.339 B.A. L.589 J.D. [B] O'Hagan,S.&A.]
Kaergard, Kenneth L., (BV) ....'50 '77 C.46 B.S. L.365 J.D. [B] Griffin&H.]
Kennedy, John Thomas ....'59 '84 C.589 B.S. L.365 J.D. 5N893 Mill Stone Drive
Kliment, David P., (BV) ....'59 '84 C.338 B.S. L.589 J.D. Co. Pub. Def.
Lane, Jamie Sean ....'— '91 C&L.209 B.S., J.D. [O'Hagan,S.&A.]
Larson, Richard J. ....'35 '61 C.898 B.A. L.339 LL.B. Assoc. Cir. J.
Larson, Richard J. ....'58 '83 C.210 B.A. L.339 J.D. Assoc. Cir. J.
Larson, Scott P., (BV) ....'61 '94 C.339 B.S. L.589 J.D. 37W777 Rt. 38, Ste. 300
Lee, Tonda ....'— '03 C.970 B.A. L.146 J.D [B] O'Hagan,S.&A.]
Leonard, Glenn Daniel ....'57 '00 C.927 B.S. L.1000 J.D. 24 Foxwood Ct.
Loudon, Clayton B. ....'41 '79 C.338 B.S. L.589 J.D. Asst. Pub. Def.
Marchi, John R. '21 '49 C.33 L.477 LL.B.
(adm. in MT; not adm. in IL) 45 Whittington Course‡
McArdle, David A. ....'— '87 C&L.145 B.A., J.D. P.O. Box 64‡
McArdle, Joyce L. ....'60 '88 C.597 B.A. L.145 J.D. 1600 E. Main St.
McCracken, Kate L. ....'59 '86 C.966 B.A. L.678 J.D. [Hoscheit,M.M.&C.]
McGuirk, John M., (AV) ....'48 '75 C.201 B.A. L.209 J.D. [Hoscheit,M.M.&C.]
Mills, Brian R. ....'77 '02 C.350 B.S. L.424 J.D. 1505 C Indiana Street
Moravcik, George C. ....'42 '67 C.424 B.B.A. L.365 J.D. 42 W. 225 Silver Glen Rd.
Mular, Wayne L., (CV) ....'44 '71 C.46 B.S.M.E. L.365 J.D. [W.Mular]
Mular, Wayne, Law Offices of, (CV) ....1121 E. Main St., Ste. 300
Muscarello, Charles V. ....'70 '95 C.473 B.S. L.910 J.D. [Denker&M.]
Newman, Laura M. ....'68 '95 C.339 B.S. L.146 J.D. [B] Wessels&P.]

O'Hagan, Smith & Amundsen, (AV)
3815 E. Main Street, Suite A-1, 60174-2488 ⊙
Telephone: 630-587-7910 Fax: 630-587-7960
Email: choffice@osalaw.com URL: http://www.osalaw.com

(This Listing Continued)

O'Hagan, Smith & Amundsen (Continued)

Members of Firm: Rita Lowery Gitchell; Ellen L. Green; Jamie Sean Lane; Michael J. Pavlisin; Thomas P. Scherschel; H. Evan Williams, IV. Associates: Karl E. Bayer; William B. Crane; Gail A. Galante; Gerald C. Huang; Keith A. Johnson; Tonda Lee; Bradley G. Rausa; Jennifer Anne Seidler; Warren Wilkosz.
Commercial; Commercial Transportation; Appellate; Complex Litigation; Construction; Corporate Transactions; Employment; Extra-Contractual/Insurance Litigation; Healthcare; Insurance Coverage; Personal Lines; Product Liability; Professional Liability; Property Litigation.
Chicago, Illinois Office: 150 North Michigan Avenue, Suite 3300, 60601. Telephone: 312-894-3200. Fax: 312-894-3210.
Rockford, Illinois Office: Stewart Square, 308 West State Street, Suite 320, 61101-1140. Telephone: 815-987-0441. Fax: 815-987-9891.
Waukegan, Illinois Office: 415 West Washington Street, Suite 204, 60079-0410. Telephone: 847-599-9503. Fax: 847-599-9525.
Woodstock, Illinois Office: 666 Russell Court, 60098. Telephone: 815-337-4900. Fax: 815-337-4910.
Milwaukee, Wisconsin Office: 4811 South 76th Street, Suite 305, 53220. Telephone: 414-282-7103. Fax: 414-282-1830.

See Professional Biographies, ST. CHARLES, ILLINOIS

Pavlisin, Michael J. ....'— '82 C.927 B.B. L.365 J.D. [O'Hagan,S.&A.]
Proscia, Julie ....'75 '03 C.234 M.A. L.589 J.D. [B] Wessels&P.]
Puklin, Barry E. ....'36 '61 C.597 B.A. L.339 LL.B. Cir. J.

Quinn, John M., & Associates, Ltd.
(See Bloomingdale)

Rausa, Bradley G. ....'— '98 C.597 B.A. L.94 J.D. [B] O'Hagan,S.&A.]
Ravenscraft, Krista L. ....'56 '80 C.597 B.A. L.365 J.D. 39W 925 Cutwood Lane
Raysa, Richard J. '40 '65 C.293 B.A. L.950 J.D.
(adm. in OR; not adm. in IL) 3 N. 515 Lincoln Dr.‡
Richeson, Geroge, (BV) ....'58 '84 C&L.801 B.A., J.D. 1450 W. Main

Rinella and Rinella, Ltd.
(See Chicago)

Risch, Jeffrey A. ....'72 '98 C.338 B.S. L.862 J.D. [B] Wessels&P.]
Romag, James J. ....'64 '91 C&L.589 B.S., J.D. [Casey,B.&R.]
Rosensteel, Thomas E., (AV) '46 '73 C.755 B.A. L.146 J.D.
555 S. Randall Rd., Ste. 206
Ross, William Z. ....'— '75 C&L.339 B.A., J.D. 1121 E. Main St., Ste. 200
Sauber, Joseph P., Jr., (BV) ....'60 '85 C.339 B.S. L.146 J.D. [Shearer&A.] (Pat.)
Scherschel, Thomas P., (AV) ....'— '83 C.801 B.S. L.146 J.D. [O'Hagan,S.&A.]
Schuster, Theodore G., (AV) ....'21 '51 C&L.966 B.S., LL.B. 240 W. River Dr.‡
Seaton, Debra Ann ....'60 '86 C&L.352 B.S., J.D. Asst. Pub. Def.
Seidler, Jennifer Anne ....'— '98 C.357 B.F.A. L.209 J.D. [B] O'Hagan,S.&A.]
Seraphin, Leonard J., (AV) ....'43 '68 C.602 B.B.A. L.597 J.D. [Seraphin&S.]
Seraphin, Scott L., (BV) ....'68 '94 C.723 B.A. L.589 J.D. [Seraphin&S.]
Seraphin & Seraphin, Ltd., (AV) ....2210 Dean Street, Suite P-2
Setzen, Leah D. ....'— '00 C&L.339 B.A., J.D. Asst. State's Atty.
Shaw, Matthew G., (BV) ....'60 '86 C.337 B.A. L.589 J.D. [Shaw,J.&Assoc.]
Shaw, Jacobs & Associates, P.C., (BV) ....555 S. Randall Rd., Ste. 205

Shearer & Agrella, (AV)
Established in 1929 as Hempstead & Green
4N701 School Road, 60175
Telephone: 630-584-3142 Fax: 630-584-4198 URL: http://www.shearerandagrella.com
URL: http://www.lawyers.com/shearer&agrella
Members of Firm: Richard Shearer (1916-1994); Raymond F. Agrella; Joseph P. Sauber, Jr.; Mary Agrella Fitzpatrick. Associate: Jerome L. Bettag.
General Practice, Civil Litigation, Probate, Estate Planning, Real Estate, Corporate Litigation, Personal Injury, Family Law, Construction Litigation.
Representative Client: Harris Bank, St. Charles.

See Professional Biographies, ST. CHARLES, ILLINOIS

Sheldon, Timothy Q. ....'46 '75 C.965 B.B.A. L.365 J.D. Cir. J.
Sheridan, Patricia Martin ....'39 '82 C.238 B.A. L.589 J.D. 6N857 Maple Ave.‡
Spivy, Sara D. ....'74 '03 C.145 B.A. L.228 J.D. Cook Cty. Pub. Def.
Stanfa, Anne Casey, (BV) ....'57 '82 C.157 B.A. L.424 J.D. Asst. States Atty.
Webb, James B. ....'60 '85 C&L.352 B.B.A., J.D. Coun., Universal Sports Assoc., Inc.
Wessels, Richard H., (AV) '39 '67
C.388 B.A. L.209 J.D. [Wessels&P.] (⊙Davenport, IA)

Wessels & Pautsch, P.C., (AV)
Dunham Center, 2035 Foxfield Drive, 60174 ⊙
Telephone: 630-377-1554 Fax: 630-377-1653
Email: wessels@stch.w-p.com URL: http://www.w-p.com
Richard H. Wessels; Earl P. Bailey (Not admitted in IL); Nancy E. Joerg. Senior Attorneys: Anthony J. Caruso, Jr.; Jeffrey A. Risch; Laura M. Newman;—Julie Proscia.
Representing Employers in Labor and Employment Law Matters. NLRA, RLA, all Federal and State Employment Discrimination Laws, Federal and State Disability Laws, Wrongful Discharge, Employment Contracts, Collective Bargaining Negotiations and Arbitrations, Employee Substance Abuse, Safety and Health, Unemployment Insurance, Benefits Law, Wage and Hour, and Employment-Based Immigration Matters. Litigation before all Federal and State Courts and Agencies, Trial and Appellate Practice.
Representative Clients: Ace Hardware Corp.; Claire's Stores, Inc.; Edward Hines Lumber Co.; Jay Foods, L.L.C.; Patten Industries, Inc.; Power Packaging Inc.; Tractor Supply Co.
Milwaukee, Wisconsin Office: Two Plaza East, 330 East Kilbourn Avenue, Suite 1475. Telephone: 414-291-0600. Fax: 414-291-0200.
Chicago, Illinois Office: Chicago Bar Association Building, 321 South Plymouth Court, Suite 900. Telephone: 312-461-0500. Fax: 312-461-0595.
Davenport, Iowa Office: Northwest Bank Building, 101 W. Second Street, Suite 307. Telephone: 563-333-9102. Fax: 563-333-9105.
Minneapolis, Minnesota Office: MoneyGram Tower, 1550 Utica Avenue South, Suite 450. Telephone: 952-746-1700. Fax: 952-746-1704.
Indianapolis, Indiana Office: Market Tower, 10 West Market Street, Suite 1770. Telephone: 317-656-8800. Fax: 317-656-8855.

See Professional Biographies, ST. CHARLES, ILLINOIS

Wilkosz, Warren ....'— '04 C.436 B.S. L.339 J.D. [B] O'Hagan,S.&A.]
Williams, H. Evan, IV, (BV) ....'— '76 C.339 B.S.M.E. L.146 J.D. [O'Hagan,S.&A.]
Wittenstrom, John T. ....'67 '92 C.966 B.S. L.146 J.D. 5N057 W. Woods Dr.
Wixted, Kevin M. ....'67 '92 C.352 B.A. L.209 J.D. 1904 Forrest Blvd.‡
Yu, Thomas Sung ....'74 '00 C.339 B.A. L.589 J.D. State Atty. Off.

ST. ELMO, 1,473, *Fayette Co.*

Day, Richard J., (CV) ....'51 '76 C&L.339 B.S., J.D. Asst. State's Atty.

SALEM, * 7,909, *Marion Co.*

Albright, Robert D., (BV) ....'35 '59 C&L.910 A.B., J.D. 210 W. Schwartz St.‡

Campbell, Black, Carnine, Hedin, Ballard & McDonald, P.C.
(See Mount Vernon)

Craig & Craig
(See Mount Vernon)

Creason, James W., (BV) ....'51 '77 C&L.801 B.S., J.D. States Atty.
Ferguson, Curt W. ....'65 '89 C.106 B.A. L.846 J.D. [C.W.Ferguson]
Ferguson, Curt W., PC ....P.O. Box 418

Forgue, Vernon ....'19 '50 L.365 J.D. 310 E. Jennings‡
Garner, David E., (BV) ....'42 '67 C.210 B.A. L.597 J.D. [Pfaff,G.&T.]
Hillis, Paul H., Jr., (BV) ....'47 '75 C.338 B.S.B.A. L.339 J.D. State's Atty.
Johnston, Stanley M. ....'29 '66 C.465 A.B. L.365 J.D. 503 Willow Pl.‡
Matoush, Robert W., (BV) ....'53 '78 C.801 B.A. L.734 J.D. 202 W. Schwartz St.
Milner, Bill J., (BV) ....'60 '86 C&L.801 B.S., J.D. 109 E. Main St.
Pfaff, Garner & Terlizzi, (AV) .... 202 W. Schwartz St.
Quinn, Steve W., (BV) ....'50 '86 C.234 B.S.Ed. L.801 J.D. Pub. Def.
Temple, Harry C. '12 '38 C&L.339 B.S., LL.B.
Chmn. of the Bd. & CEO, Shakespeare Oil Co., Inc.
Terlizzi, Eric L., (AV) ....'51 '76 C&L.339 B.S., J.D. [Pfaff,G.&T.]

Wham & Wham
(See Centralia)

Wilzbach, Scott, Attorney at Law, (BV) ....'47 '72 C&L.339 B.A., J.D. 215 E. Main St.
Woodruff, Hubert W., II ....'23 '50 C.98 B.S. L.339 LL.B. Drawer 370

SANDWICH, 6,509, *DeKalb Co.*

Farmer, David A. ....'67 '92 C.58 B.A. L.879 J.D. [Wiegman&F.]
Groat, James G., Jr., (BV) ....'47 '73 C.801 B.A. L.365 J.D. 222 E. Railroad St.
Morrissey, Edward P. ....'— '74 C.93 A.B. L.190 J.D. 820 N. Lafayette St.
Neuendorf, Louis E. ....'23 '49 C&L.436 LL.B. 208 East Railroad St. (⊙Yorkville)
Stockley, Dale L. ....'40 '84 C.339 B.S. L.209 J.D. [D.L.Stockley]
Stockley, Dale L., Inc. ....222 E. Railroad St.
Wiegman and Farmer, P.C. .... 1025 Suzy St.

SAUK VILLAGE, 10,411, *Cook Co.*

Banks, Kimberly ....'— '98 C.339 B.S. L.146 J.D. 1636 E. 217th St.

SAVANNA, 3,542, *Carroll Co.*

LeComte, John R., (BV) ....'48 '75 C&L.339 B.S.Ch.E., J.D. [J.LeComte]
LeComte, John, Law Office, (BV) .... 322 Main St.
Smith, Richard K., (CV) ....'29 '60 C.339 B.A. L.966 J.D. 311 3rd St.

SCHAUMBURG, 75,386, *Cook & DuPage Cos.*

Abrahams, Philip S. .... '53 '78 C.339 B.S. L.597 J.D. Senior Attorney, AT&T Corp.
Adelman, David A. ....'67 '92 C.339 B.A. L.365 J.D. [Adelman]
Adelman Law Offices, P.C. .... 1320 Tower Rd., Ste. 114
Alesia, Michael J., & Associates '65 '91 C.339 B.A. L.365 J.D.
1111 Plaza Dr., Ste. 450
Allen, Dillis V., (AV) .....'37 '64 C.966 B.S.M.E. L.273 LL.B. [D.V.Allen&Assoc.] (Pat.)
Allen, D.V. & Associates, (AV) ....105 S. Roselle Rd., Ste. 101 (Pat.)
Anderson, Jonathan G. ....'53 '81 C.966 B.A. L.260 J.D. [Anderson&Assoc.] ⊙

Anderson & Associates, P.C.
1701 East Woodfield Road, Suite 1050, 60173 ⊙
Telephone: 847-995-9999 Fax: 847-995-0117
URL: http://www.andersonandassociatespc.com
Jonathan G. Anderson;—Robin M. Zandri; Andrea C. Lawrence; Christopher J. Maurer; Mia Do.
Family Law, Bankruptcy, Real Estate Litigation and Transactions, Estate Planning and Probate.
Chicago Office: 166 W. Washington Street, Suite 640. Telephone: 312-236-5599.
Wheaton Office: 400 S. County Farm Road, Suite 120. Telephone: 630-653-9400. Fax: 630-653-9450.
See Professional Biographies, SCHAUMBURG, ILLINOIS

Andrulis, Paul A. '65 '96 C.475 B.S. L.365 J.D.
V.P. & Corp. Coun., Affiliated Computer Serv.
Angelakos, Angelo, Ltd. Law Offices of '63 '95
C.339 B.S. L.201 J.D. 830 E. Higgins Rd., Ste. 111S

Angelina & Palmer, P.C.
(See Inverness)

Arnold, Lester N. .... '39 '68 C.420 B.S.E.E. L.208 J.D. 1409 Wright Blvd. (Pat.)
Aronberg Goldgehn Davis & Garmisa, (AV)
10 North Martingale Road, Fourth Floor (⊙Chicago)
Bahr, Rita T. ....'57 '85 C.659 B.A. L.260 J.D. Senior Counsel, Motorola Inc.
Bainbridge, Harry B. ....'25 '56 C.388 B.A. L.365 J.D. [▣ Pancratz,R.&S.] ⊙‡
Balk, Allen C. ....'— '96 C.424 B.B.A. L.146 J.D. [Ⓐ Meltzer,P.&S.]
Bane, Keith J. ....'39 '68 C.98 B.S. L.597 J.D. 1303 E. Algonquin Rd.

Barrett & Gilbert LLP
(See Rockford)

Bartusiak, Paul J. ....'— '01 C.834 B.S.E.E. L.146 J.D. 1303 E. Algonquin Road
Basch, Margaret M., (AV) ....'62 '85 C.338 B.A. L.146 J.D. 1111 Plaza Dr., Ste. 405
Bauer, Steven M. '63 '88 C.309 A.B. L.424 J.D.
Asst. V. P., Specialty Claims, Zurich U.S.
Beauregard, Michael R. '63 '89 C.477 B.A. L.665 J.D.
(adm. in PA; not adm. in IL) V.P., Strategic Planning, N.A., Sunbeam Corp.
Becker, Henry P. ....'43 '68 C.659 B.S. L.339 J.D. V.P., Bufka & Rodgers
Beeler, Stephen T. '71 '00 C.339 B.A. L.209 J.D.
Assoc. Gen. Coun., GE Consumer Finance, Partnership Marketing Grp.
Bencik, Deborah L. ....'69 '94 C.473 B.S. L.477 J.D. Sr. Coun., Motorola Inc.
Berg, Michael E. '67 '92 C.597 B.S. L.477 J.D.
Coun., Midwest Area, Verizon Wireless
Bianchi, LeRoy L. ....'42 '73 C.339 B.A. L.365 J.D. P.O. Box 68452

Bolon, Laurence J.
(See Chicago)

Boron, Sandra '56 '80 C.339 B.A. L.146 J.D.
V.P. & Asst. Gen. Coun., Zurich-Amer. Ins. Grp.
Bowers, David Alan '46 '73 C&L.608 B.S., J.D.
Exec. V.P. & Gen. Coun., Zurich-Amer. Ins. Grp.
Breslin, Warren J., (AV) ....'49 '79 C.209 B.A. L.424 J.D. [W.J.Breslin]

Breslin, Warren J., Law Offices, (AV) ▣
10 N. Martingale Road, Suite 400, 60173-2418
Telephone: 847-934-7070 Fax: 847-934-5551 URL: http://www.breslinlaw.com
Email: warren@breslinlaw.com URL: http://www.lawyers.com/breslin
Warren J. Breslin.
Criminal Law (All Felonies & Misdemeanors); DUI & All Traffic Violations (Major & Minor); Revoked & Suspended Licenses, Driver's License Reinstatement; Petitions for Executive Clemency (Governor Pardons); Expungements (Clearing Criminal & Traffic Arrest Records).
See Professional Biographies, SCHAUMBURG, ILLINOIS

Bresnahan, Victoria C. .... '70 '95 C.339 B.A. L.365 J.D. [Ⓐ Meltzer,P.&S.]
Bressler, Stuart L. ....'59 '87 C.339 B.A. L.365 J.D. 1535 W. Schaumburg Rd.
Brown, Jeffrey A. ....'— '93 C.597 B.S.I.E. L.145 J.D. Corp. Coun., Motorola Inc.
Bryan, Kathleen A. '52 '81 C.454 B.A. L.588 J.D.
(adm. in MA; not adm. in IL)
Corporate VP & Director of Litigation Management, Motorola Inc.

Buczyna, John R., Law Office of '43 '70
C.405 B.A. L.365 J.D. 1450 American Ln., Ste. 1925
Buetow, Herbert R. ....'55 '88 C.1183 B.A. L.146 J.D. [H.Buetow]

Buetow, Herbert, Law Offices of
11 E. Schaumburg Road, 2nd Floor, 60194
Telephone: 847-584-2264 Fax: 847-584-2258
Email: hbuetow@msn.com
Herbert R. Buetow.
Bankruptcy, Real Estate, Civil Litigation.
See Professional Biographies, SCHAUMBURG, ILLINOIS

Burkart, Jeffery M. '64 '90 C.589 B.A. L.365 J.D.
Sr. Staff Atty., Amer. Fam. Ins. Grp.
Bussert, Deborah S. ....'— '84 C.424 B.B.A. L.597 J.D. [Meltzer,P.&S.]
Byanna, Malini M. ....'68 '03 C.339 B.A. L.146 J.D. [M.M.Byanna]

Byanna, Malini M., LLC
869 East Schaumburg Road, # 352, 60194
Telephone: 847-923-1706 Facsimile: 847-923-1707
Email: malini@creativefamilylaw.com URL: http://www.creativefamilylaw.com
Malini M. Byanna.
Domestic Relations, Mediation, Collaborative Law, Family Law, Divorce, Guardianship, Child Custody, Child Support, Visitation Rights, Domestic Violence.
See Professional Biographies, SCHAUMBURG, ILLINOIS

Cádiz, Carol ....'70 '96 C.339 B.S. L.209 J.D. [A. .&C.Traub]
Cahalan, James L. '57 '82 C&L.352 B.B.A., J.D.
Exec. V. P. - Legal Affairs, Roanoke Companies
Callahan, John W. ....'70 '97 C.339 B.S. L.209 J.D. [M.T. .&J.W.C.Norris]
Carter, James W., Jr. ....'43 '72 C.932 B.S. L.339 J.D. 150 N. Martingale Rd.‡
Cartwright, Patricia G. ....'73 '01 C.339 B.S. L.209 J.D. [Ⓐ J.R.Buczyna]
Caruso, F. Willis, Jr., (AV) ....'66 '90 C.966 B.A. L.597 J.D. AT&T Corp.
Casbarian, Paul W. ....'43 '76 C.801 B.A. L.424 J.D. 215 Clearbrook Ct.
Cerny, Frank J., Jr. '43 '81 C.46 B.S.E.E. L.424 J.D.
Motorola Corp. Research & Development Ctr. (Pat.)
Chessick, Cary Steven ....'66 '91 C.339 B.S. L.209 J.D. [Ⓐ K.Chessick]
Chessick, Kenneth C. ....'44 '84 C.339 B.S. L.589 J.D. [K.Chessick]
Chessick, Kenneth, Law Office of ....1870 N. Roselle Rd., Ste. 104
Clar, Christine Helen ....'64 '89 C&L.424 B.A., J.D. 302 Pleasant Dr.
Clark, J. Anthony '52 '80
C.302 B.A. L.145 J.D. Coun., Montgomery Ward Enterprises, Inc.
Clery, Jeffrey M. ....'48 '73 C.602 A.B. L.608 J.D. [Clery&C.]
Clery, John T. ....'54 '79 C.339 B.A. L.201 J.D. [Clery&C.]
Clery & Clery ....1111 N. Plaza Dr., Ste. 580
Clutts, Raymond E., (AV) ....'57 '84 C.339 B.A. L.209 J.D. [R.E.Clutts]
Clutts, Raymond E., P.C., (AV) .... 830 North Meacham, Suite 114
Coffing, James ....'62 '96 C.46 B.S. L.146 J.D. Dir. Tech. Assets and Portfolio Mgmt.
Cohen, Jeffrey M., Law Offices of '60 '87 C.589 B.A. L.146 J.D.
11 E. Schaumburg Rd.
Combs, Eva B. ....'49 '83 C.339 B.A. L.365 J.D. [▣ Pancratz,R.&S.]
Cooper, Miriam, Law Office of '50 '88
C.1183 B.A. L.365 J.D. 14500 E. American Ln., Ste. 1925

Cosley, Christopher M.
(See Rolling Meadows)

Cothran, Elaynne B. ....'49 '87 C.937 B.A. L.659 J.D. Zurich-Amer. Ins. Grp.
Cowhey, Carrie Niblack '72 '97
C.679 B.A. L.823 J.D. Coverage Coun., Zurich North America
Cozzi, Paul C. '60 '87 C.578 B.S. L.339 J.D.
Vice President & Division Counsel, Fidelity National Title Insurance Co.
Cua, Simeon S. '57 '90 C&L.999 B.S., LL.B.
(adm. in NY; not adm. in IL) 1340 Remington Rd.‡
Curtis, Charles R. ....'69 '95 C.388 B.A. L.879 J.D. 2300 Barrington Rd., Ste. 400
Czapla, Edward Adam ....'63 '89 C.339 B.A. L.365 J.D. [Ⓐ P.W.Grauer&Assoc.]
Dallmeyer, R. Ford '47 '74 C.197 A.B. L.145 J.D.
Sr. V.P. & Gen. Coun., Nielsen Media Research Intl.
DeGrazia, Joel J. ....'56 '82 C.238 B.A. L.589 J.D. 1515 Woodfield Dr., Ste. 880
Devinger, David W. '63 '89
C.339 B.A. L.209 J.D. Account Specialist, Zurich Amer. Ins. Grp.
Do, Mia ....'— '04 C.339 B.A. L.146 J.D. [Ⓐ Anderson&Assoc.] ⊙
Dodd, David W. ....'60 '93 C.589 B.S. L.365 J.D. Asst. Gen. Coun., GE Fin.
Dohrer, Thomas A. ....'69 '94 C.339 B.A. L.209 J.D. Zurich Insurance

Doyle, Joseph P. '76 '03 C.424 B.S. L.607 J.D.
105 S. Roselle Road, Suite 203, 60193
Telephone: 847-985-1100 Fax: 847-985-1126
URL: http://www.joedoylelaw.com
Bankruptcy.
See Professional Biographies, SCHAUMBURG, ILLINOIS

Dreimann, Ingrid A. '63 '90 C&L.352 B.A., J.D.
(adm. in NY; not adm. in IL) Chf. Reg. Coun., N.A., ACNielsen (US), Inc.
Duker, Ann '50 '79 C.339 B.U.P. L.424 J.D.
Sr. V.P. & Gen. Coun., Dovenmuehle Mortgage, Inc.
Dunn, Michael A., (AV) .... '40 '64 C&L.597 B.S.L., J.D. 120 W. Golf Rd., Ste. 106
Ellis, Gregory J. ....'54 '80 C.339 B.A. L.146 J.D. [G.J.Ellis]
Ellis, Gregory J., Esq., Ltd. ....999 Plaza Dr., Ste. 777
Epstein, Stephen J. .... '39 '64 C.339 B.S. L.597 J.D. 1920 Thoreau Dr., N.
Erton, Linda H. ....'53 '83 C.597 B.A. L.209 J.D. Motorola, Inc.
Euwema, John B. ....'51 '77 C.114 B.A. L.879 J.D. Sr. V.P., GE Fin. Assurance
Falduto, Thomas F. ....'47 '71 C.226 B.A. L.188 J.D. State Dept. of Transp.
Falkner, Robert F. '40 '66 C.72 B.A. L.597 J.D.
Corp. Vice President & Asst. General Counsel, Motorola Inc.
Farion, Marta ....'47 '80 C.424 B.A. L.146 J.D. Pres., Redex Packaging Co.
Feldman, Jeffrey S. '46 '72 C.4 B.S. L.724 J.D.
(adm. in NY; not adm. in IL) 854 E. Algonquin Rd.‡
Field, Ann Lederer ....'65 '91 C.429 B.S. L.879 J.D. Reinsurance Mgr., Zurich U.S.
Fisher, Scott M. .... '48 '73 C.339 B.A. L.597 J.D. 1505 Coventry Rd.
Fisk, John W., (CV) ....'55 '81 C.927 B.A. L.146 J.D. [Ⓐ K.Chessick]
Flexman, Steven J. ....'57 '82 C&L.339 B.S., J.D. 1821 Walden Office Sq., Ste. 447
Flosi, Leone .... '41 '66 C&L.209 B.A., J.D. Quest Consultants Int'l.
Forsyte, Carol H. ....'62 '89 C.551 B.A. L.1065 J.D. Motorola Inc.
Forte, Steven J. ....'66 '96 C.347 B.S. L.365 J.D. 1005 W. Wise Rd., 2nd Fl.
Fortune, Anne O., (AVⓉ) '49 '78 C.546 B.F.A. L.490 J.D.
(adm. in NE; not adm. in IL) Atty., Zurich American Insurance Group
Foster, John J. '49 '75 C.201 B.S. L.46 J.D.
Sr. V.P. & Chf. Coun., Fidelity Natl. Title Ins. Co.
Fox, William C. ....'29 '52 C&L.209 J.D. 1303 E. Algonquin Rd.
Freeman, John J. ...'60 '87 C.589 B.S. L.146 J.D. Coverage Coun., Zurich North America

Funai, Bryan Y. .... '— '81 C.589 B.S. L.1187 J.D. [Masuda,F.E.&M.] (⊙Chicago)
Funai, Masaru .... '— '57 C.312 B.A. L.597 J.D. [Masuda,F.E.&M.] (⊙Chicago)
Gabe, Allen S. .... '46 '74 C.475 B.A. L.365 J.D. 1821 Valden Office Sq.

Gabe, Caryl Jacobs, & Associates, Inc., Law Offices of
(See South Barrington)

Gaber, Kathleen M. .... '— '85 C.477 B.B.A. L.245 J.D. [Masuda,F.E.&M.] (⊙Chicago)
Galer, Roger P. .... '71 '03 C.350 B.S. L.365 J.D. [Galer]
Galer Firm, The, P.C. .... 900 Dighton Lane
Gamrat, Theodore ...... '53 '80 C.209 B.S.C. L.365 J.D. Montgomery Ward Life Ins. Co.
Gillman, James W. .... '33 '64 C.871 B.S. L.339 J.D. Motorola Inc. (Pat.)
Gitles, Alan E. .... '56 '82 C&L.477 B.A., J.D. CEO, Landmark Merchant Solutions
Glasgow, Thomas T. .... '67 '94 C.500 B.A. L.146 J.D. [T.Glasgow]

Glasgow, Thomas, Ltd., The Law Offices of
1834 Walden Office Square, Suite 500, 60173
Telephone: 847-654-0650 Fax: 847-654-0520
Email: glasgowlaw_TG@hotmail.com URL: http://www.glasgowlaw.net
Thomas T. Glasgow. Associates: Nichole M. Waltz; Jacqueline Lacy.
Languages: Spanish, German and Portuguese.
Criminal, Federal, State, Felony, Misdemeanor, DUI, Traffic, Drunk Driving, Revoked and Suspended License, Murder, Drug Offense, Weapons Charge, Civil, Contracts Litigation, Administrative, Divorce, Family Law.

See Professional Biographies, SCHAUMBURG, ILLINOIS

Goldman, Joy S., (AV) .... '52 '77 C&L.597 B.A., J.D. [▣ Meltzer,P.&S.]
Goldy, Jill A. .... '51 '82 C.788 B.A. L.178 J.D. Motorola, Inc.‡
Goodman, Stephen E. .... '44 '69 C&L.339 B.S., J.D. [▣ Meltzer,P.&S.]
Graft, William C., (AV) .... '61 '86 C.190 B.A. L.209 J.D. [Graft&J.]

Graft & Jordan, (AV) ▣
1900 East Golf Road, Suite 600, 60173-5006
Telephone: 847-330-2423 Fax: 847-330-1652
Email: law@graftjordan.com URL: http://www.lawyers.com/graftjordan
Members of Firm: William C. Graft; Thomas E. Jordan.
Languages: English and Mandarin (Chinese).
Land Use Entitlement and Zoning, Commercial Real Estate, Mergers and Acquisitions, Complex Corporate Planning, Corporate Law and Commercial Loan Documentation.
Burr Ridge Office: (By Appointment) 7420 County Line Road, 80527. Telephone: 630-325-2255.

See Professional Biographies, SCHAUMBURG, ILLINOIS

Grauer, Paul W., & Associates '43 '71
C.854 B.S.M.E. L.339 J.D. 1300 Woodfield Road, Suite 205
Greco, Joseph F., (AV) .... '41 '70 C&L.209 B.A., J.D. [Greco&T.]

Greco and Tarallo L.L.P., Attorneys and Counsellors at Law, (AV)
MB Financial Bank Building, 200 West Higgins Road, Suite 300, 60195-3718
Telephone: 847-843-8850 Fax: 847-843-2583
Email: gretarlaw@aol.com URL: http://www.lawyers.com/greco&tarallo
Members of Firm: Joseph F. Greco; Phillip S. Tarallo. Of Counsel: David E. Ruedlin.
Corporate and Transactional Law. Commercial and Residential Real Estate. Civil Trial and Appellate Practice in all State and Federal Courts. Family, Divorce, Matrimonial and Estate Planning Law. Employment and Civil Rights Litigation.

See Professional Biographies, SCHAUMBURG, ILLINOIS

Grinde, William J., (AV) .... '47 '75 C.966 B.B.A. L.813 J.D. [Meltzer,P.&S.]
Gudmundson, Scott D. .... '58 '85 C.145 B.A. L.424 J.D. [Meltzer,P.&S.]
Guthrie, James M. .... '34 '59 C.504 B.A. L.339 LL.B. 105 S. Roselle Rd.
Harlos, Christopher L. '52 '91 C.385 B.A. L.564 J.D.
(adm. in NM; not adm. in IL) IBM Global Servs.
Harold, Susan Kott '49 '86 C.597 B.A. L.424 J.D.
V.P., Asst. Gen. Coun. & Corp. Secy., Zurich-Amer. Ins. Grp.
Harrod, Samuel G., IV .... '65 '91 C.248 B.A. L.339 J.D. [Meltzer,P.&S.]

Heidelberger, Elliot, Law Offices of
(See Hanover Park)

Hennig, Richard Paul '45 '70 C.723 B.A. L.365 J.D.
V.P. & Asst. Gen. Coun., Zurich-Amer. Ins. Grp.
Hixson, David F. '43 '71 C.674 A.B. L.178 LL.B.
(adm. in NY; not adm. in IL) Vice President - Antitrust, Motorola Inc.
Hoffman, James '45 '75
C.1106 B.A. L.365 J.D. Assoc. Gen. Coun., Amer. Fam. Ins. Grp.
Hoogland, Kay Ann, (AV) '56 '81 C.878 B.A. L.893 J.D.
Sr. Communications Enterprise Coun., Motorola, Inc.
Horn, Raymond J., III .... '67 '92 C.221 B.A. L.339 J.D. [Meltzer,P.&S.]

Hunt, Thaddeus, Law Offices Of
(See Chicago)

Hwang, David S. .... '— '98 C.339 B.A. L.910 J.D. [▣ Masuda,F.E.&M.] (⊙Chicago)
Irish, Ruthann Wendel .... '59 '87 C.276 B.S.F.S. L.424 J.D. 707 Valley View‡
Jackson, Timothy Bryce .... '75 '01 C.299 B.A. L.146 J.D. 931 N. Plum Grove Road
Janko, Michael M. .... '51 '85 C.602 B.B.A. L.365 J.D. Janko Financial Group
Johns, Richard B. '46 '71 C.36 B.S. L.37 J.D.
(adm. in AZ; not adm. in IL) Dir. of Risk Mgmt., Motorola, Inc.
Johnson, Lloyd T. '46 '72 C.550 B.A. L.588 J.D.
Sr. Coverage Coun., Claims-Legal, Zurich North America‡
Joppa, Glenn L. '43 '69 C.589 B.S. L.339 J.D.
Sr. V.P., Gen. Coun. & Secy., GE Financial Assurance
Jordan, Thomas E. .... '64 '96 C.339 B.S. L.146 J.D. [Graft&J.]
Joyce, Kevin J. .... '70 '98 C.966 B.A. L.796 J.D. [▣ Meltzer,P.&S.]
Julian, Frank J., Jr. '52 '78 C&L.339 B.S., J.D.
Sr. V.P. & Assoc. Gen. Coun., Zurich Life
Kaiser, Marcia T. .... '54 '79 C.597 B.A. L.339 J.D. Coun., Progressive Cas. Ins.
Kakuda, Eldon H. .... '— '86 C&L.276 B.S.F.S., J.D. [Masuda,F.E.&M.] (⊙Chicago)

Kanabay, Roberta K., The Law Offices of '53 '97 C.209 B.A. L.146 J.D.
1920 Thoreau Drive, Suite 171, 60173
Telephone: 847-925-1007 Fax: 847-925-1012
Email: kanabaylaw@sbcglobal.net URL: http://www.lawyers.com/kanabay
Family, Divorce, Child Custody, Child Support, Criminal, Driving While Intoxicated, Traffic and Commercial Litigation.

See Professional Biographies, SCHAUMBURG, ILLINOIS

Kaplan, Alan M., (AV) ... '— '80 C.597 B.S.E. L.209 J.D. [Masuda,F.E.&M.] (⊙Chicago)
Karnick, Jerome A. '69 '93
C.472 B.B.A. L.309 J.D. Coun., Midwest Area, Verizon Wireless
Kasenter, Robert A. '68 '94 C.294 B.A. L.665 J.D.
Corp. Coun., G.E. Partnership Marketing Group
Keane, James C. '61 '87
C.742 B.A. L.365 J.D. Sr. Staff Atty., American Family Ins. Group
Kelley, John P., (AV) .... '31 '58 C&L.424 B.S.C., J.D. [Kelley,K.&K.] ⊙
Kelley, Martin C. .... '66 '92 C.424 B.S. L.1187 J.D. [Kelley,K.&K.] ⊙
Kelley, Matthew X. .... '59 '93 C.338 B.S. L.1187 J.D. [Kelley,K.&K.] ⊙
Kelley, William F., (AV) .... '55 '80 C&L.424 B.A., J.D. [Kelley,K.&K.] ⊙
Kelley, Kelley & Kelley, (AV) .... 1535 West Schaumburg Road (⊙Chicago)
Kennedy, Terence P., (AV) .... '53 '84 C.602 B.A. L.262 J.D. [Meltzer,P.&S.]
Kerley, Sidney Lamon '74 '00 C.10 B.A. L.880 J.D.
V.P. & Gen. Coun., Insurance Auto Auctions, Inc.
Khosravi, Kourosh Cyrus .... '63 '92 C.339 B.S.E.E. L.365 J.D. Motorola Inc.
Klest, Joseph G., (BV) .... '53 '82 C.1183 L.365 J.D. [Klest]

Klest Law Firm, (BV)
1701 East Woodfield Road, Suite 909, 60173-5137
Telephone: 847-969-9510 Fax: 847-969-9514 URL: http://www.lawyers.com/klest
Email: info@josephklest.com URL: http://www.chicagotriallaw.com
Joseph G. Klest.
Personal Injury, Medical Malpractice, Products Liability, Legal Malpractice, Construction Accidents, Airplane Crash Litigation, Insurance Bad Faith, Automobile Accidents, Motorcycle Accidents, Birth Trauma, Sexual Abuse, Child Abuse and Neglect, Slip and Fall, Wrongful Death, Dog Bites, Railroad Accidents and Injuries, Automobile Products, Liability and Drug and Medical Device Litigation, Trial Practice.

See Professional Biographies, SCHAUMBURG, ILLINOIS

Kline, Angela P. .... '50 '82 C.36 B.A. L.146 J.D. 1515 Woodfield Rd.
Knack, Robert H. .... '26 '52 C.999 L.209 J.D. 1318 Hampton Lane‡
Kojelis, Daina E. '— '85 C.696 B.A. L.424 J.D.
V.P. & Dir., Claims-Legal, Zurich North America
Kopidlansky, Victor R. .... '31 '64 C.746 B.A. L.365 J.D. Motorola, Inc.
Kroll, Steven L., (AV) '59 '84 C.197 B.A. L.477 J.D.
V.P. & Gen. Coun., Corp. Sec., Cancer Treatment Ctr. of America (⊙Chicago)
Kulat, Randall S. .... '55 '80 C&L.339 B.A., J.D. [Meltzer,P.&S.]
Lacy, Jacqueline .... '— '03 C.927 B.S. L.365 J.D. [▣ T.Glasgow]
Lagattuta, John M. .... '60 '85 C&L.209 B.S., J.D. 1515 E. Woodfield Rd., Ste. 880
Lampel, Carey .... '71 '97 C.589 B.A. L.146 J.D. 2111 Primrose
Laporte, Eugene F. .... C&L.209 [E.F.Laporte]
Laporte, Eugene F., LTD .... 1014 E. Algonquin Rd., Ste. 165
Laurich, Linda L. '45 '86
C.352 B.A. L.378 J.D. State Govt. Affs. Dir., Amer. Fam. Ins. Co.
Lawrence, Andrea C. .... '72 '97 C.589 B.A. L.209 J.D. [▣ Anderson&Assoc.] ⊙
Lawrence, Ann .... '59 '92 C.112 B.A. L.365 J.D. 1821 Walden Off. Sq.
Lawson, A. Peter '46 '72 C.197 A.B. L.178 J.D.
Exec. V.P. & Gen. Coun., Motorola Inc.
Layer, George L. ... '52 '81 C.608 B.S.B.A. L.365 J.D. Mng. Atty., Amer. Fam. Ins. Grp.
Lee, Laura Dickinson .... '56 '82 C.793 B.S. L.602 J.D. Coun., Advantis
LeFevour, Mark L. .... '58 '83 C.687 B.A. L.424 J.D. [Kelley,K.&K.] ⊙
Lewycky, Alexandra B. .... '65 '92 C.339 B.S. L.879 J.D. [A.Lewycky]
Lewycky, Alexandra .... 545 W. Wise Rd., Suite 200B1
Life, Travis .... '74 '03 C.352 B.A. L.146 J.D. [▣ K.Chessick]
Lowe, Charmaine M. '68 '96 C.597 B.S. L.365 J.D.
Assoc. Claims Coun., Stewart Title Guaranty Co.
Lysaught, Thomas F. '60 '85 C&L.209 B.A., J.D.
Asst. V.P. & Dir., Envir. Claims, Zurich-American Insurance Group
MacPhail, Douglas F. ...... '40 '65 C.197 A.B. L.228 J.D. General Attorney, Motorola Inc.
Malak, Michael P. '61 '86 C.259 B.A. L.597 J.D.
V.P., & Asst. Gen. Coun., Corp. Law, Zurich American Ins. Grp.
Marcus, Gerald I. .... '46 '70 C.1019 B.B.A. L.365 J.D. [G.I.Marcus]
Marcus, Gerald I., Ltd. .... 1350 Remington Rd.
Marder, Robert M. .... '47 '72 C.589 B.A. L.146 J.D. 1076 S. Roselle Rd.

Martucci, Gregory J., P.C., Law Office of
(See Roselle)

Massey, Kathleen M., (AV©) '55 '81 C.373 B.A. L.966 J.D.
(adm. in WI; not adm. in IL) V.P., Litig., Motorola Inc.
Masuda, Funai, Eifert & Mitchell, Ltd., (AV)
Suite 800, 1475 E. Woodfield Rd. (⊙Torrance, CA; Chgo., IL)
Maurer, Christopher J. .... '72 '97 C.339 B.S. L.424 J.D. [▣ Anderson&Assoc.] ⊙
McAllister, Marcia '51 '76
C.157 B.A. L.145 J.D. V.P. Gov. Affairs, Ins. Auto Auctions, Inc.
McCoy, James .... '56 '82 C.750 B.A. L.209 J.D. 518 Kenilworth Dr.
McGrath, Terrence K. .... '57 '87 C.720 B.A. L.365 J.D. Zurich-American
McJoynt, Jeanne L. '34 '83 C.519 B.A. L.215 J.D.
(adm. in MI; not adm. in IL) Motorola, Inc.
McLean, Pamela L. .... '66 '92 C.893 B.A. L.602 J.D. [▣ Meltzer,P.&S.]
McLellan, Donald F. .... '65 '90 C&L.145 B.A., J.D. Counsel, Motorola Inc.
McNabb-Stange, Brenda A. '— '86 C.97 B.A. L.796 J.D.
(adm. in TT; not adm. in IL) Sr. Coun., GE Fin. Assurance
McNichols, Edwin J. '56 '84 C.746 B.A. L.966 J.D.
Asst. Gen. Coun., GE Financial Assur., Ptnrshp. Mktg. Grp.
Melamed, Mitchell J., (AV) .... '43 '68 C&L.339 B.S., J.D. [Aronberg G.D.&G.] ⊙
Melamed, Phillip H. .... '43 '78 C.339 B.S.E.E. L.209 J.D. Motorola Inc. (Pat.)
Meltzer, Brian .... '44 '69 C.188 A.B. L.309 J.D. [Meltzer,P.&S.]

Meltzer, Purtill & Stelle LLC, (AV)
Second Floor, 1515 East Woodfield Road, 60173-5431
Telephone: 847-330-2400 Fax: 847-330-1231
Email: mps@mpslaw.com
Members of Firm: Deborah S. Bussert; William J. Grinde; Scott D. Gudmundson; Samuel G. Harrod IV; Raymond J. Horn III; Terence P. Kennedy; Randall S. Kulat; Brian Meltzer; William J. Mitchell; Thomas R. Palmer; John F. Purtill; Mark R. Raymond; Roger T. Stelle; Michael J. Wolfe. Associates: Allen C. Balk; Victoria C. Bresnahan; Kevin J. Joyce; Shannon R. Silverman. Of Counsel: Pamela L. McLean; Joy S. Goldman; Stephen E. Goodman.
Business and commercial transactions, real estate transactions, commercial finance, financial institution regulatory matters and commercial litigation, with emphasis in asset-based and construction lending, sales and purchases of business, representation of land developers and builders, and general business representation.

See Professional Biographies, SCHAUMBURG, ILLINOIS

Miller, Eileen Norton '64 '89 C.347 B.S. L.209 J.D.
Coverage Coun., Zurich-American Insurance Group (Legal Department)
Mitchell, William J. .... '62 '88 C.757 B.A. L.146 J.D. [Meltzer,P.&S.]
Moglia, Alejandro D. .... '55 '82 C.276 B.S.F.S. L.145 J.D. 1325 Remington Rd.
Moore, Jeffrey C. '61 '87 C.473 B.S. L.608 J.D.
(adm. in NY; not adm. in IL) Coun., Advantis
Moyer, Lyman C. '34 '60 C.494 L.1035 LL.B.
(adm. in MN; not adm. in IL) 200 N. Martingale Rd.
Murray, Nancy '44 '80 C.700 B.A. L.365 J.D.
Sr. Coverage Coun., Claims-Legal, Zurich North America
Myers, Dennis L. '47 '72 C.388 B.A. L.339 J.D.
Area Gen. Coun., Midwest Area, Verizon Wireless
Nalepka, Timothy J. '55 '83 C.339 B.A. L.597 J.D.
V.P., Gen. Coun. & Secy., Motor Coach Industries International, Inc.
Neis, Robert W. .... '46 '79 C.1151 B.A. L.589 J.D. [Thilmany&N.]
Norris, Michael T. .... '44 '71 C&L.209 B.A., J.D. [▣ M.T. .&J.W.C.Norris]

Norris, Michael T., Ltd. & John W. Callahan, Ltd.
One Woodfield Place, 1701 E. Woodfield Road, Suite 1101, 60173
Telephone: 1-877-FELONY-3; 1-877-335-6693 Fax: 847-605-0440
Email: callahanjw@sbcglobal.net URL: http://www.chicagofelonylaw.com
John W. Callahan; Michael T. Norris.
Murder, Rape, Armed Robbery, Bank Robbery, Burglary, Predatory Criminal Sexual Assault, Aggravated Criminal Sexual Abuse, Aggravated Criminal Sexual Assault, Child Pornography, Delivery of a Controlled Substance, All Narcotics Offenses, including multi-kilo possession and delivery charges. Aggravated Battery, Unlawful Restraint, White Collar Crimes, Aggravated Felony, DUI, Reckless Homicide, Aggravated Driving While License Revoked. DWI, Traffic Violations, Drivers License Issues, Formal and Informal Secretary of State Hearings.
See Professional Biographies, SCHAUMBURG, ILLINOIS

O'Connell, Thomas M. .... '58 '86 C.602 B.A. L.190 J.D. 947 N. Plum Grove Road
O'Connor, Michael J., Sr. '60 '87
C.339 B.A. L.146 J.D. Sr. Staff Atty., American Family Ins. Grp.
O'Donnell, Kevin ....'47 '73 C.884 A.B. L.424 J.D. 1515 E. Woodfield, Ste. 880
Onixt, David T. .... '39 '63 C.339 B.S. L.597 S.J.D. 1635 W. Wise Rd.
Osborne, Richard W. ....'59 '84 C.209 B.A. L.365 J.D. Atty., Intercargo Ins. Co.
Palmer, Thomas R. .... '53 '79 C&L.209 B.A., J.D. [Meltzer,P.&S.]
Pancratz, James E., (AV) .... '52 '83 C.966 B.S. L.365 J.D. [Pancratz,R.&S.] ⊙
Pancratz, Riffner & Scott, LLP, (AV) .... 1920 North Thoreau Drive Suite 100 (⊙Chicago)
Parisi, Joseph S. ....'— '75 C.339 B.S. L.424 J.D. [Masuda,F.E.&M.] (⊙Chicago)
Pastika, Maureen A. ....'61 '91 C&L.424 B.B.A., J.D. 1821 Walden Office Sq.
Patton, Denise J., Law Office of ...... '66 '96 C.589 B.S. L.209 J.D. 401 Woodcroft Lane
Patton, Jesse M., Jr. '— '92
C.679 B.A. L.1119 J.D. Sr. Staff Atty., American Family Insurance

Paynter, Bruce D., The Law Offices of
(See Arlington Heights)

Perkins, Y. Jacqueline
(See Arlington Heights)

Perrelli, Anthony
(See Deerfield)

Peters, Kevin R.
(See Chicago)

Peterslie, Trudy L., (BVⓉ) '53 '84 C.966 B.A. L.221 J.D.
(adm. in IA; not adm. in IL) Environmental Claims, Zurich U.S.‡
Polach, Raymond F. .... '50 '76 C.339 B.S. L.146 J.D. 1111 N. Plaza Dr.
Poskozim, Judy H. '51 '80 C.339 B.A. L.146 J.D.
V.P., Asst. Secy. & Dep. Gen. Coun., The Signature Grp.
Priestley, James E., (BV) '55 '83
C.884 B.S. L.424 J.D. Sr. Staff Atty., Amer. Fam. Ins. Grp.
Proctor, Stephen M. ....'— '82 C.347 B.A. L.1119 J.D. [Masuda,F.E.&M.] (⊙Chicago)
Puccio, Mark V. .... '54 '81 C.243 B.S. L.146 J.D. Zurch North America
Purtill, John F., (BV) .... '50 '76 C.597 B.A. L.424 J.D. [Meltzer,P.&S.]
Quello, Sandra G. .... '54 '95 C.209 B.A. L.365 J.D. 1821 Walden Office Sq.
Rasmussen, Kurt S., (BV) '45 '82 C&L.146 B.S., J.D.
Sr. Staff Atty., Am. Fam. Ins. Grp.
Raymond, Mark R. ....'64 '91 C.591 B.S. L.424 J.D. [Meltzer,P.&S.]
Reilly, Edgar Bourke ... '65 '95 C.602 B.B.A. L.145 J.D. Gen. Coun., Wight Realty Group
Reinhold, Charleen A. ...... '57 '82 C&L.424 B.S., J.D. Sr. Coun., Hewlett-Packard Co.
Reis, John C. .... '35 '71 C.339 B.S.E.E. L.365 J.D. [J.C.Reis]
Reis, John C., PC .... 1053 Glouchester Hbr.
Rezabek, Debra P. '56 '81 C.597 B.S. L.209 J.D.
Exec. V.P., Gen. Coun. & Corp. Secy., Zurich Life
Riffner, Robert G. ....'58 '84 C.589 B.S. L.352 J.D. [Pancratz,R.&S.]
Ritter, Andrew K. '59 '86 C.1044 B.A. L.564 J.D.
(adm. in NY; not adm. in IL) Coun., Advantis

Robin, Daniel K., LTD
(See Arlington Heights)

Rose, Steven J. ....'62 '89 C.123 B.A. L.146 J.D. Sr. Staff Atty., Am. Fam. Ins. Grp.

Rosenfeld Hafron Shapiro & Farmer, (AV)
Suite 570, 1111 Plaza Drive, 60173 ⊙
Telephone: 847-330-9800 Fax: 847-330-0600
Email: ed@shapiro-lawyers.com URL: http://www.lawyers.com/shapiro-lawyers
Resident Partner: Edwin H. Shapiro.
Commercial and Civil Litigation. Real Estate, Mortgages, Business, Contracts, Corporate, Partnership, Family, Divorce, Child Custody, Child Support and Matrimonial Litigation. Personal Injury. Chicago, Illinois Office: 221 North La Salle Street, Suite 1763. Telephone: 312-372-6058. Fax: 312-641-3139.
See Professional Biographies, SCHAUMBURG, ILLINOIS

Rowden, Todd A., The Law Offices of, (AV) '64 '89
C.477 B.A. L.966 J.D. 1834 Walden Off. Sq.
Royston, Jonathan W. '57 '82 C.103 A.B. L.845 J.D.
Southwestern Bell Mobile Systems
Ruedlin, David E. .... '43 '69 C.98 B.S. L.851 J.D. [Ⓒ Greco&T.]
Ruggirello, Gaspare G. '57 '82
C.475 B.A. L.215 J.D. General Counsel, Insurance Auto Auctions
Ryan-Reinking, Mary E. '54 '83
C.686 B.S. L.424 J.D. Senior Corporate Counsel, Motorola Inc.
Sadowski, Donald L., Jr. ....'58 '83 C.424 B.B.A. L.607 J.D. [D.L.Sadowski]
Sadowski, Donald L., P.C. .... 1515 Woodfield Rd.
Santana, Daniel J. .... '64 '98 C.927 B.A. L.146 J.D. 849 S. Phensant Walk
Sarli, Anthony J., Jr. '40 '68 C.645 B.S.E.E. L.273 J.D.
(adm. in VA; not adm. in IL; Pat.) V.P. & Dir., Motorola Inc.
Schaffner, Theodore W. ....'46 '71 C.608 B.A. L.309 J.D. Motorola, Inc.
Schechtman, David '52 '76 C.339 B.S. L.608 J.D.
Sr. Coun., Motor Coach Industries International, Inc.
Schechtman, Melvin A. ....'49 '84 C.597 M.S.E.E. L.425 J.D. Motorola Inc. (Pat.)
Scott, Edward A., III .... '47 '76 C.37 B.A. L.365 J.D. [Pancratz,R.&S.]
Sedlmayer, G. F. .... '24 '55 C.424 B.S. L.146 LL.B. Montgomery Ward-Life Ins.
Seidler, Irving J. ....'49 '74 C.999 B.A. L.146 J.D. 1076 S. Roselle Rd.
Seifert, John D. .... '63 '91 C.436 B.S. L.146 J.D. Zurich American Insurance Co.
Selby, George W., Jr. '48 '73 C.1365 B.A. L.260 J.D.
(adm. in FL; not adm. in IL) General Attorney, Motorola Inc.
Shapiro, Edwin H., (AV) .... '38 '63 C.339 B.S. L.597 J.D. [Rosenfeld H.S.&F.]
Shaykin, Steven M. .... '56 '82 C.424 B.A. L.365 J.D. 2227 Hammond Drive
Silhavy, Jack C. '56 '81 C.602 B.A. L.424 J.D.
V.P. & Gen. Coun., Amer. Pharmaceutical Partners. Inc.
Silverman, Shannon R. .... '71 '97 C.477 B.A. L.212 J.D. [Ⓐ Meltzer,P.&S.]
Sjoholm, John J. .... '45 '71 C.855 B.A. L.597 J.D. 308 Stock Port Ln.
Slater, Robert C. .... '38 '71 C.475 B.S. L.209 J.D. P.O. Box 681186
Smith, Janet K. ....'65 '97 C.473 B.S.B.A. L.477 J.D. Sr. Coun., Motorola, Inc.
Snoke, Stephen Dow '52 '78 C.945 B.A. L.910 J.D.
Exec. V.P. & Gen. Coun., Hitachi High Technologies America, Inc.

Spain, Richard C., (AV) '50 '75 C.399 B.A. L.930 J.D.
1821 Walden Square, Suite 400 (⊙Chgo., Rolling Meadows, IL; Northborough, MA)
Sprague, Karen A. .... '62 '96 C.424 B.A. L.146 J.D. Sr. Coun., Zurich Life
Stagno, Anthony .... '48 '91 C.339 B.S. L.365 J.D. 1870 N. Roselle Rd.
Stanis, John B. .... '— '88 C.338 B.S. L.339 J.D. [Masuda,F.E.&M.] (⊙Chicago)
Stark, Carol A. ....'64 '89 C.338 B.S. L.365 J.D. Zurich-Amer. Ins. Grp.
Staubitz, Sheldon H. .... '37 '58 C.597 B.S. L.424 J.D. 2125 Frost Rd.
Stavropoulos, Thomas C. .... '61 '88 C.209 B.S. L.365 J.D. Coun., One Life Insurance Co.
Stelle, Roger T. .... '44 '70 C.597 B.S. L.1119 J.D. [Meltzer,P.&S.]
Stewart, Gretchen Wehrenberg ....'60 '85 C.597 B.S.J. L.1119 J.D. [Ⓐ Adelman]
Strauss, David L. '66 '93 C.228 B.A. L.966 J.D.
Vice Pres. & Asst. Gen. Coun., Experian

Sullivan Firm, The, Ltd.
(See Rolling Meadows)

Sutkowski, Michael A. .... '63 '89 C&L.209 B.S.C., J.D. 2227A Hammond Dr.
Swiss, Susan M. '54 '79 C.976 B.A. L.145 J.D.
(adm. in CA; not adm. in IL) 1245 Cranbrook Dr.
Takayanagi, Yuichiro '57 '88 L.424 J.D.
V.P. & Gen. Coun., Omron Management Center of America, Inc.
Tarallo, Phillip S. .... '60 '85 C&L.209 B.A., J.D. [Greco&T.]
Thilmany, Mary Ann .... '53 '81 C.750 B.A. L.365 J.D. [Thilmany&N.]
Thilmany & Neis ....999 N. Plaza Dr.
Thomas, Juanita M. '55 '81 C.587 B.A. L.502 J.D.
V.P. & Asst. Gen. Coun., Zurich Life
Thomas, Judith Thomson .... '52 '77 C.914 B.A. L.101 J.D. Motorola Inc.
Thompson, William J. '35 '62 C&L.352 B.A., J.D.
Sr. V.P., Secy. & Gen. Coun., The Signature Grp.
Tornatore, Salvatore J. .... '49 '75 C.209 B.S.C. L.365 J.D. 1450 American Ln., Ste. 1650
Townsend, Patricia A. ....'57 '83 C.597 B.A. L.365 J.D. 200 N. Martingale
Tracy, Keith M. ....'47 '81 C.238 B.S. L.589 J.D. 1699 E. Woodfield Rd.
Traub, Angel M. ....'71 '01 C.589 B.A. L.365 J.D. [A. .&C.Traub]

Traub, A., & Cádiz
1305 Remington Road Suite O, 60173
Telephone: 847-839-4590 Fax: 847-839-4591
Email: atraub@atclaw.com URL: http://www.atclaw.com
Angel M. Traub; Carol Cádiz.
Language: Spanish.
General Practice, Litigation, Family Law, Adoption, Child Custody/Support, Divorce, Estate Planning, Wills and Probate, Landlord and Tenant, Bankruptcy, Real Estate: Residential, Guardianship, Traffic.
See Professional Biographies, SCHAUMBURG, ILLINOIS

Valentine, James S. '37 '63 C.357 B.S. L.365 LL.B.
Sr. V.P. & Gen. Coun., USLife Credit Life Ins. Co.
Valentine, Linda Bryant '50 '75
C.477 B.A. L.276 J.D. Sr. V.P. & Asst. Gen. Coun., Motorola, Inc.
Van Wormer, Brandon ....'73 '98 C.477 B.A. L.209 J.D. XL Design Professional
Verona, David A., Sr. '54 '85 C.63 B.S. L.146 J.D.
Coverage Coun., Claims-Legal, Zurich North America
Waid, A. Clark, III, (BVⓉ) '42 '73 C.674 A.B. L.930 J.D.
Asst. Gen. Coun., Pioneer Financial Services, Inc.

Wallenstein Wagner & Rockey, Ltd.
(See Chicago)

Waltz, Nichole M. .... '— '01 C.352 B.A. L.209 J.D. [Ⓐ T.Glasgow]
Wenzel, Arthur W. .... '45 '70 C.694 B.A. L.880 J.D. 1111 N. Plaza Dr., Ste. 405
West, Livia Solange '70 '97 C.37 B.A. L.209 J.D.
(adm. in NY; not adm. in IL) A.C. Nielsen
White, Douglas B. '48 '76 C.339 B.S.E.M. L.365 J.D.
1901 N. Roselle Rd., Ste. 802 (Pat.)
White, Robert S., (AV) .....'— '93 C.602 B.A. L.146 J.D. [Masuda,F.E.&M.] (⊙Chicago)
Whited, Richard H. .... '37 '62 C.210 B.A. L.339 J.D. General Attorney, Motorola Inc.
Wilson, Jeffrey S. .... '62 '87 C.339 B.S. L.597 J.D. 1821 Walden Office Sq.
Wise, Howard J. ....'68 '97 C.37 B.F.A. L.1187 J.D. [Ⓐ W.H.Wise&Assoc.] ⊙

Wise, William H., & Associates, Law Offices of, (AV) '40 '65 C.1016 A.B. L.365 J.D.
1821 Walden Office Square, 4th Floor, 60173 ⊙
Telephone: 847-397-1112 Fax: 847-272-4255
Email: wise4444@aol.com URL: http://www.wiseattorneys.net
Associate: Howard J. Wise.
Criminal Law, Driving While Intoxicated, Traffic Violations, Juvenile Law, Expungement, Parole and Probation, Drug Crimes, Felonies, Homicide, Misdemeanors, Secretary of State Drivers License Revocation, White Collar Crime, Personal Injury, Automobile Accidents, Constitutional Law and Workers Compensation.
Chicago, Illinois Office: 134 North LaSalle Street, Suite 1515, 60602. Telephone: 312-346-4555. Fax: 847-272-4255.
See Professional Biographies, SCHAUMBURG, ILLINOIS

Wolfe, Michael J., (BV) .... '60 '86 C.201 B.A. L.1003 J.D. [Meltzer,P.&S.]
Wright, Alan W. '42 '68 C.812 B.S. L.472 J.D.
(adm. in FL; not adm. in IL) 1105 Tall Timbers Rd.
Wybrow-Albano, Theresa '— '97
C.494 B.A. L.801 J.D. Staff Atty., American Family Insurance

Young, Thomas, Law Firm
(See Palatine)

Zandri, Robin M. .... '70 '97 C.339 B.S. L.589 J.D. [Ⓐ Anderson&Assoc.] ⊙
Zeigler, David R. .... '68 '94 C.276 A.B. L.861 J.D. Zurich North America
Zuhlke, James R. ....'46 '71 C&L.966 B.B.A., J.D. Intercargo Corp.

SCHILLER PARK, 11,850, *Cook Co.*

Betancourt, Glenn ....'66 '94 C.424 B.A. L.209 J.D. [Rogoff&B.]
Corbin, Keith S. .... '32 '60 C.597 B.S. L.365 J.D. 3860 N. 25th Ave.
Rogoff, Scott D. ....'67 '93 C.966 B.A. L.146 J.D. [Rogoff&B.]
Rogoff & Betancourt ....9611 Soreng Ave.
Rubic, Mark Joseph '59 '85 C.923 B.S. L.352 J.D.
U.S. Dept. Homeland Sec., Transp. Sec. Admin.
Tuerk, Robert D., (AV) ....'46 '71 C.276 B.S.B.A. L.273 J.D. 5060 River Rd.
Weiler, Roger A. '29 '52 C.339 B.S. L.145 J.D.
Chmn., Intaglio Vivi-Color Alliance, Ltd.

SEATON, 221, *Mercer Co.*

Seaton, John C., Jr. '18 '47 C&L.352 B.S.C., J.D.
Pres. & Chmn. of the Bd., State Bk. of Seaton

SESSER, 2,087, *Franklin Co.*

Szczeblewski, Gary J. ....'49 '74 C.340 B.S.Ed. L.45 J.D. 111 E. Franklin St.

SHABBONA, 897, *DeKalb Co.*

Cliffe, Foster, Corneille, Buick & Buick, LLC, (BV)
110 W. Comanche St. (⊙De Kalb, Hinckley, Sycamore, Waterman)

Foster, Keith L., (BV) '50 '79
C.589 B.A. L.146 J.D. [Cliffe,F.C.B.&B.] (⊙De Kalb, Hinckley)

SHAWNEETOWN, * 1,410, *Gallatin Co.*

Foster, Thomas J., (BV) .... '61 '88 C&L.339 B.S., J.D. States's Atty.
Franklin, Keely Dobbs ....'73 '98 C.339 B.A. L.801 J.D. 450 N. Lincoln Blvd. East

Jelliffe, Ferrell, Morris & Doerge
(See Harrisburg)

Smith, James H., (AV) .... '46 '73 C&L.421 B.A., J.D. [J.H.Smith]
Smith, James H., P.C., (AV) .... 131 W. McClernand

SHELBYVILLE, * 4,943, *Shelby Co.*

Baker, John J., Jr., (AV) ....'28 '52 C&L.339 A.B., J.D. 132 N. Broadway

Brainard Law Offices, The
(See Charleston)

Broverman, Robert Lee ....'31 '57 C.801 B.A. L.339 LL.B. 123 W. Main St.
Davis, H. Glenn, (BV) .... '51 '79 C&L.339 B.S., J.D. 150 N. Morgan St.
Dove, Franklin E., (BV) ....'36 '64 C.611 A.B. L.597 J.D. 151 S. Morgan St.
Eberspacher, Edward C., III, (BV) .... '49 '74 C&L.339 B.A., J.D. P.O. Box 647
Eversole, David E., (BV) ....'49 '75 C.338 B.S. L.734 J.D. 161 N. Morgan
Finks, Thomas O. ....'58 '84 C.210 B.A. L.801 J.D. Asst. States Atty.
Freeman, John V., (BV) ....'48 '74 C.234 B.S. L.339 J.D. 220 N. Morgan St.
Hardy, Whitney D., (BV) ....'36 '61 C.473 A.B. L.339 LL.B. [Hardy]
Hardy Law Offices, (BV) ....304 E. Main St.
Kiley, Michael P. ....'51 '77 C.339 B.A. L.365 J.D. Co. J.
Plummer, Belle A. ....'52 '76 C.339 B.S. L.209 J.D. [Plummer]
Plummer, Vernon L., II ....'50 '75 C.339 B.A. L.146 J.D. [Plummer]
Plummer Law Offices ....404 N. Douglas St.

Tietz, Christopher M.
(See Decatur)

Turner, Philip L., II, (BV) .... '36 '63 C&L.339 A.B., LL.B. 225 E. First St.
Turner, William L., (AV) .... '25 '50 C&L.339 A.B., LL.B. 125 N. Bway.

SHELDON, 1,232, *Iroquois Co.*

Bolling, Rodger A. ....'45 '71 C.927 B.B. L.260 J.D. 1741 N. 2580E Rd.‡
Sumner, Jessie J., (Miss) ....'— '23 C.788 L.051 Pres., Sumner Natl. Bk.
Sygulla, Richard J., (BV) .... '36 '71 C.1134 B.S.A. L.339 J.D. 125 E. Grove St.

SHERMAN, 2,871, *Sangamon Co.*

Tolbert, Victor P. '18 '49 C.339 L.1119 LL.B.
(adm. in IN; not adm. in IL) 109 Stardust‡

SHOREWOOD, 7,686, *Will Co.*

Aeschliman, Keith M., (BV) ....'49 '75 C.497 B.A. L.365 J.D. 619 Rollingwood Dr.
Belom, John A. ....'28 '52 C.999 L.209 LL.B. 701 S. Raven‡

McKeown, Fitzgerald, Zollner, Buck, Hutchison & Ruttle
(See Joliet)

Washburn, William C., Jr., (BV) ...... '49 '77 C.497 B.A. L.365 J.D. [W.C.Washburn,Jr.]
Washburn, William C., Jr., PC, (BV) ....619 Rollingwood Dr.

SILVIS, 7,269, *Rock Island Co.*

Balk, Steven E., (CV) .... '70 '97 C&L.352 B.S.E., J.D. [Ⓐ McGehee,B.W.O.&P.]
DeWulf, James N. ....'36 '61 C.424 B.S. L.209 1110 17th Ave.
McGehee, John L., (BV) .... '61 '89 C.57 B.A. L.221 J.D. [McGehee,B.W.O.&P.]
McGehee, Boling, Whitmire, Olson & Pepping, Ltd., (BV) ....105-7th St.
Olson, Douglas G., (BV) .... '46 '72 C&L.339 B.S., J.D. [McGehee,B.W.O.&P.]
Payson, Earl A., (BV) .... '40 '66 C.57 B.A. L.352 J.D. [McGehee,B.W.O.&P.]
Pepping, Jerry J., (BV) .... '58 '84 C.352 B.B.A. L.339 J.D. [McGehee,B.W.O.&P.]

SKOKIE, 63,348, *Cook Co.*

Angelo, William V. .... '49 '81 C.424 B.a. L.209 J.D. [Denkewalter&A.]
Arnstein, Albert E. .... '18 '47 C.209 B.S. L.365 LL.B. [Arnstein&Z.]
Arnstein & Zeller ....9933 N. Lawler St.
Aronson, Harold ....'13 '56 C&L.209 B.S., J.D. 5126 Fargo Ave.‡
Augustus, Howard ....'— '71 C.910 A.B. L.424 J.D. [Augustus]
Augustus Law Office .... 9933 Lawler Avenue, Suite 100
Baker, David A., (AV) ....'14 '40 C.103 A.B. L.94 J.D. 9530 Lamon St.‡
Baker, Keith B. ....'56 '82 C&L.339 B.S., J.D. [K.B.Baker]
Baker, Keith B., Ltd., The Law Offices of .... 9933 Lawler Avenue, Suite 514
Barbour, Alyssa R. '— '95 C.260 B.S. L.128 J.D.
Director of Legal Affairs, OMNA Medical Partners
Bartnik, Casimir J. ....'53 '78 C.424 B.A. L.597 J.D. Asst. State's Atty.
Becker, Max J. ....'10 '33 C&L.597 B.S., J.D. 5150 Carol St.
Bentivenga, Vincent E., Jr. ....'41 '60 C.424 B.S. L.209 J.D. Cir. J.
Berg, Gershon S. ....'35 '60 C.347 B.S. L.209 J.D. 4350 W. Oakton
Berg, Harold ....'31 '54 C.339 L.209 LL.B. 5301 W. Dempster
Berkson, Irving L. ....'13 '36 C&L.597 B.S., LL.B. 9240 Gross Point Rd.
Binstock, Deana M. ....'58 '84 C.66 B.A. L.861 J.D. Asst. Pub. Def.
Bogomolny, Robert L. '38 '63
C&L.309 A.B., LL.B. Chf. Pharma Law Strategist, Monsanto Co.
Boumstein, Mark N., (BV) ....'50 '80 C.801 B.S. L.365 J.D. Asst. States Atty.
Boyer, Alan I. ....'26 '50 C.209 L.146 J.D. 5550 W. Touhy Ave.
Boyles, John W. ....'43 '77 C.1016 B.S.B.A. L.365 J.D. [J.W.Boyles]
Boyles, John W., P.C. ....5225 Old Orchard Rd.
Britt-Handy, Veda L. '— '83 C.881 A.B. L.893 J.D.
VP & Deputy Gen. Coun., Rand McNally & Company
Brown, Adolph A. ....'11 '37 L.365 J.D. 8955 N. Kildare Ave.‡

Bruno, Randie, Law Offices of
(See Waukegan)

Butbul, David .... '61 '91 L.146 J.D. 4051 Old Orchard Rd.
Carini, Daniel J. '69 '97 C.436 B.A. L.365 J.D.
Opers. Mgr. & Corp. Coun., Biasco-Baldwin Piano
Carini, Joseph B., Jr. ....'34 '61 C&L.424 7919 N. Lincoln Ave.
Carlton, Frank A. ....'49 '74 C.976 B.A. L.309 J.D. Rand McNally
Carvalho, Amarante M. ....'— '77 C.999 B.A. L.597 LL.M. 8923 N. Bronx Ave.
Casey, Robert ....'21 '50 C&L.597 B.S., LL.B. Hirsh Co.

Cece, Frank, Jr.
(See Chicago)

Chaet, Louis ....'11 '35 C.999 L.209 LL.B. 5253 Mulford St.‡

Chatzky, Paul, Law Offices of
(See Northfield)

Cirignani Heller Harman & Lynch LLP
(See Chicago)

Cohen, Lynn A. ....'45 '82 C.339 B.A. L.365 J.D. [Delman&C.]
Collens, Mark B., Law Offices of ....'44 '71 C.801 B.S. L.365 J.D. 5550 West Touhy
Connelly, James P., (AV) ....'24 '51 C.884 B.A. L.424 J.D. 8114 Kildare Ave.
Crowley, Catherine T. ....'54 '82 C.597 B.A. L.424 J.D. State Attys. Off.
Curtiss, Jeffrey E. ....'48 '72 C&L.546 B.S.B.A., J.D. G.D. Searle & Co.
Cutler, David H. ....'64 '90 C.1357 B.S. L.472 J.D. [Cutler&Assoc.]

Cutler & Associates, LTD.
5550 W. Touhy Avenue, 4th Floor, 60077
Telephone: 847-673-8600 Fax: 847-673-8636
Email: David@CutlerLtd.com URL: http://www.dhclegal.com
David H. Cutler.
Bankruptcy, Consumer Bankruptcy, Bankruptcy Chapter 7, Foreclosures, Small Business, Buying and Selling of Businesses, Family Business, Limited Liability, Partnership, Corporate, Contract, Breach of Contract, General Practice, Debtor and Creditor, Collections, Creditors, Rights and Civil Litigation.
See Professional Biographies, SKOKIE, ILLINOIS

Dallas, Nickolas ....'51 '76 C.589 B.S. L.146 J.D. [N.Dallas]
Dallas, Nickolas, P.C. ....8415 Karlov Ave.
Delman, Dennis A. ....'46 '74 C.502 B.A. L.209 J.D. [Delman&C.]
Delman & Cohen ....4711 Golf Road
Denenberg, Brian S. ....'66 '91 C&L.339 B.S., J.D. [Ⓐ Denkewalter&A.]
Denkewalter, Kim R., Mr. ....'48 '74 C.424 A.B. L.146 J.D. [Denkewalter&A.]
Denkewalter & Angelo ....5215 Old Orchard Road, #1010
Denny, James M. '32 '63 C.494 B.A. L.276 J.D.
(adm. in NY; not adm. in IL) Sr. V.P., G.D. Searle & Co.
diLiscia, Eleonora R. ....'59 '88 C.477 B.A. L.966 J.D. [E.diLiscia]
diLiscia, Eleonora ....9239 Gross Pt., Ste. 202A
DiVincenzo, Anthony S., (AV) '52 '76
C.424 B.A. L.597 J.D. [Ⓑ Lustig&Assoc.] (⊙Chicago)
Domash, Richard Alan '52 '77 C.1183 B.A. L.1049 J.D.
9933 N. Lawler Avenue, Suite 100 (⊙Skokie)
Domash, Richard Alan ....'52 '77 C.1183 B.A. L.1049 J.D. [Ⓢ J.Schachter&Assoc.]
Dordek, David ....'54 '79 C.339 B.A. L.146 LL.B. 8424 Skokie Blvd.
DuBoe, Burton V. ....'34 '60 C.1016 B.S. L.597 J.D. 5301 W. Dempster St.
Dubrow, Herbert B. ....'42 '67 C.98 B.A. L.146 J.D. 4711 Golf Rd., Ste. 807
Dul, John A. ...... '61 '86 C.472 B.B.A. L.597 J.D. Gen. Coun., Anixter International, Inc.
Emanuel, Bertram .... '30 '57 C.1016 B.A. L.209 J.D. 4220 W. Greenwood

Emerick, Julie T., Ltd., Law Offices of
(See Chicago)

Epstein, James R., (AV) ....'53 '78 C&L.597 B.A., J.D. Cir. Ct. J.

Evanston Main Law Office
(See Evanston)

Evonitz, Richard ....'67 '03 C.945 B.A. L.209 J.D. 7420 Kenneth Ave.
Fallmer, William F. ....'33 '71 [Fallmer&F.]
Fallmer & Friedman ....5005 W. Touhy Ave.
Federer, Richard E. ....'54 '79 C&L.734 B.S., J.D. Dir. of Taxes, G.D. Searle & Co.

Feldman, Stuart A.
(See Wilmette)

Fiala, Edward M., Jr. .... '28 '57 C.1016 A.B. L.209 J.D. Assoc. Cir. J.
Fohrman, Seymour F. '16 '39
C.597 B.S. L.209 LL.B. Chmn. of the Bd., Milmour Products, Inc.
Frankston, Lawrence ....'64 '90 C.597 B.A. L.880 J.D. 4125 Enfield
Freedman, Carl ....'14 '35 C.999 L.209 5200 Oakton St.‡
Friedland, Charles ....'51 '81 C.339 A.B. L.146 J.D. 8717 Gross Point Rd.
Friedman, David M. ....'52 '75 C.978 B.A. L.597 J.D. [Fallmer&F.]
Friedman, Earl .... '55 '03 C.597 1977 L.589 J.D. 3924 Keeney St.

Froman, Michael S., (AV) '50 '76 C.339 B.A. L.209 J.D.
Suite 322, Westmoreland Building, 9933 Lawler Avenue, 60077-3703
Telephone: 847-677-1555 Fax: 847-677-1080
Email: mfromanlaw@aol.com URL: http://www.lawyers.com/michaelsfroman
Insurance Defense, General Liability Claims Defense, Subrogation, Workers Compensation Defense, Personal Injury. Arbitration and Alternative Dispute Resolution. Corporate and Business Litigation. Probate and Estate Planning. Legal Audit and Claims Review Services.
Reference: Citibank, N.A., Skokie, Illinois.
See Professional Biographies, SKOKIE, ILLINOIS

Fulk, Winton D. ....'38 '70 C.46 B.S.E.E. L.146 J.D. 9451 N. Kostner Ave.‡
García, Christa ....'71 '02 C.347 B.A. L.146 J.D. [Ⓐ Immigration&Assoc.]

Ghezzi, Sheryl Rae
(See Lincolnwood)

Gladkowski, Mary Ann ....'54 '89 C.700 B.A. L.365 J.D. 10024 Skokie Blvd.
Glait, Marshall B. ....'36 '60 C.1016 L.146 J.D. 8545 N. Monticello Ave.
Goldmeier, Norman P. ....'52 '77 C.209 B.A. L.424 J.D. [N.Goldmeier]
Goldmeier, Norman ....5225 Old Orchard Rd., Ste. 50
Gopman, Howard Z., (AV) ....'40 '65 C&L.966 B.S., J.D. [H.Z.Gopman&Assoc.]
Gopman, Howard Z., & Associates, Ltd., (AV) ....5225 Old Orchard Road, Suite 24B
Gordon, M. Scott, Law Offices of '62 '95
C.999 B.S. L.146 J.D. 4709 W. Golf Rd., Ste. 475
Greenwood, Glenn ....'35 '60 C.477 B.A. L.597 J.D. 9131 Kenneth Ave.
Griffiths, L. Gene, Jr. '40 '65 C.695 A.B. L.902 LL.B.
(adm. in VA; not adm. in IL) Sr. V.P., Louis Melind Co.
Grossman, Phillip, (AV) ....'37 '62 C&L.597 B.S., J.D. 8707 North Skokie Boulevard
Grussel, Susan Ruscitti ....'47 '79 C.927 B.A. L.365 J.D. Cir.J.
Gutof, Richard S., (BV) ....'40 '64 C.339 B.A. L.209 J.D. 9933 Lawler Ave.
Hanley, J. Patrick ....'55 '85 C.337 B.A. L.209 J.D. 5127 Oakton Street
Harris, Peter H. '63 '90 C.597 B.A. L.309 J.D.
Sr. Vice President & General Counsel, OMNA Medical Partners
Harrison, Howard R. '40 '64 C.674 A.B. L.178 J.D.
(adm. in CT; not adm. in IL) G.D. Searle & Co.
Hartigan, Michael R. ....'75 '00 C.436 B.A. L.209 J.D. 4616 Washington St., Apt. G
Haskell, Dean S. '51 '76 C.431 B.A. L.1048 J.D.
Sr. V.P. & Chf. Admn. Off., Rand McNally & Company

Heisler, Marc H.
(See Evanston)

Hoffman, Manuel S. ....'18 '42 L.146 J.D. 9933 N. Lawler Ave.
Hoffman, R. Thomas '51 '77
C.801 B.S. L.209 J.D. V.P. & Gen. Coun., Forsythe Tech., Inc.
Immigration Law Associates, P.C. ....8930 Gross Point Road, Suite 500
Jacobson, Leonard H. ....'32 '62 C.16 B.S. L.209 LL.B. 9656 Crawford St.
Jaffe, Nancy Oddi ... '54 '85 C.339 B.S. L.209 J.D. Legal Off. of Rush N Shore Med. Ctr.

Jennings, James Patrick '50 '99
C&L.209 B.A., J.D. Asst. State Atty., Cook Co. State Atty.
Johnson, Karl A. .... '69 '97 C.339 L.365 J.D. Law Office of Karl A. Johnson
Jordan, Michael S. .... '42 '66 C.966 B.S. L.209 J.D. Cir. J.
Kahn, Bert L. .... '38 '64 C&L.966 B.B.S., J.D. 8707 Skokie Blvd.
Kanter, William .... '64 '92 C.999 B.H.L. L.209 J.D. 7135 N. Carpenter Rd.
Kaplan, Alexey Y. .... '74 '00 C.393 B.A. L.146 J.D. [Kaplan]
Kaplan Law Offices, P.C. .... 4043 Dempster Street
Keenan, Matthew David .... '62 '89 C.72 B.A. L.424 J.D. [M.Keenan]
Keenan, Matt, Law Offices of .... 9239 Gross Pt., Ste. 202 A
Kersch, Robert S. .... '28 '53 C&L.494 B.S.L., J.D. 9644 Lawler
Kingsley, Ronald E. .... '57 '84 C&L.424 B.B.A., J.D. Tax Coun., G.D. Searle & Co.
Kirschbaum, Gerald A. .... '47 '80 C.966 B.A. L.46 J.D. Asst. Co. Pub. Def.
Kleper, Dennis M. .... '48 '74 C.597 B.A. L.209 J.D. 9933 Lawler Ave.

Kopecky, James L., P.C.
(See Chicago)

Koppel, Irving .... '20 '43 L.209 LL.B. 9045 N. Kostner St.
Korshak, Ted A. .... '35 '60 C&L.597 B.S., J.D. 8950 Gross Point Rd. H
Krackenberger, Mary P. .... '45 '73 C.746 B.S. L.365 J.D. 4449 Concord La.
Kransen, Harry J. .... '32 '66 C.1016 B.A. L.146 J.D. 8424 Skokie Blvd.
Krucks, William N., (AV) '49 '76 C.861 B.A. L.500 J.D.
V.P., Secy. & Gen. Coun., Rauland-Borg Corp. (⊙Chicago)
Lapidos, Manny M. .... '45 '70 C&L.339 B.A., J.D. [Simon,L.&S.]
Lavin, Michael H. .... '37 '61 C&L.209 B.S., J.D. 9933 N. Lawler
Lerner, Jonathan E. .... '49 '75 C.477 B.A. L.339 J.D. Asst. State's Atty.
Levin, Henry H. .... '24 '50 C.46 B.S. L.365 J.D. 9411 Kolmar Ave.
Levin, Jerome S. .... '27 '53 C&L.209 B.S., J.D. [Levin&R.]
Levin & Rosen, Ltd. .... 4051 Old Orchard Rd.
Levy, Donald A. .... '44 '69 C&L.339 B.S., J.D. 4711 Golf Road
Levy, Harry H. .... '07 '28 L.146 LL.B. 9558 Gross Pt. Rd.‡

Lewis, Barry Michael
(See Chicago)

Lichtenstein, Aviva Z. .... '55 '81 C.339 B.A. L.46 J.D. 3648 W. Grove‡
Lieberman, Ronald M. .... '45 '70 C.801 B.S. L.365 J.D. Asst. States Atty.
Lipsky, Lawrence J. '26 '55
C.597 B.B.A. L.424 J.D. Pres., North Shore Tax Consultants, Ltd.
Livas, George G. .... '54 '96 C.209 B.A. L.146 J.D. 9933 N. Lawler Ave., Ste. 540
Lopata, Lester .... '33 '68 C.209 B.S.C. L.146 J.D. 8800 Lowell Ter.

Lusky, Barbara E., (BV) '53 '82 C.347 B.A. L.365 J.D.
Suite 322, Westmoreland Building, 9933 Lawler Avenue, 60077-3703
Telephone: 847-676-2575 Fax: 847-677-1080
Email: luskylaw@sbcglobal.net URL: http://www.lawyers.com/luskylaw
Concentration in Family Law, Divorce, Child Custody, Child Support. Also available to practice in Probate, Estate Planning, Civil Litigation.
See Professional Biographies, SKOKIE, ILLINOIS

Lustig, Sheldon M., (AV) .... '51 '78 C.589 B.S.B.A. L.146 J.D. [Lustig&Assoc.]
Lustig & Associates, (AV) .... 4711 Golf Rd.
Lyon, Michael T. '43 '70 C&L.813 B.A., J.D.
(adm. in CA; not adm. in IL) Pres., Amazing Svgs. of Ill.
Maclin, A. D. .... '58 '86 C.1036 B.A. L.477 J.D. Pres., Blue Pencil Inc.
Magence, Meyer .... '48 '79 C.424 B.A. L.146 J.D. 8320 Skokie Blvd.
Mahon, Francis J. .... '16 '41 C&L.734 A.B., LL.B. Cir. J.

Mandell Menkes LLC
(See Chicago)

Maramba & Associates, LLC
(See Arlington Heights)

Margolies, Michael Z., Attorney at Law '55 '80
C.910 A.B. L.276 J.D. 4709 W. Golf Road, Ste. 475

Matek Law Offices, P.C.
(See Chicago)

Mendelson, Arthur B. .... '28 '50 C&L.209 B.S., J.D. 3832 Enfield Ave.
Merel, Ronald H. .... '48 '75 C.339 B.A. L.146 J.D. 5225 Old Orchard Road
Mermall, Neal .... '32 '60 C.145 M.B.A. L.146 LL.B. 8310 Kenton Ave.
Missirlian, Harry .... '41 '68 C.912 B.A. L.365 J.D. 9933 Lawler Ave.
Mitchell, Sheldon .... '31 '56 C&L.597 B.S.L., J.D. 4239 Main St.
Mohr, Elaine G. .... '31 '55 C&L.145 B.A., J.D. 4934 Church St.‡

Mojarad, Azita M.
(See Chicago)

Moran, Dorothy D. .... '57 '83 C.477 B.G.S. L.146 J.D. Monsanto Co.
Moran, Thomas M. '64 '91 C.436 B.A. L.879 J.D.
(adm. in NJ; not adm. in IL) 9933 N. Lawler Ave., Ste. 540
Morris, Ellen J. .... '52 '77 C.289 A.B. L.365 J.D. 4711 Golf Road, Ste. 807
Morris, Mary C. .... '55 '86 C.477 A.B. L.209 J.D. Asst. State's Atty.
Mueller, Henry E. .... '46 '73 C&L.339 B.S., J.D. The Vil. of Skokie Corp. Coun. Off.
Murnane, Catherine W. '67 '92
C.347 B.A. L.146 J.D. Asst. Gen. Coun., Anixter International, Inc.
Murray, Anthony J., Jr. .... '40 '67 C.424 B.S. L.209 J.D. 9039 La Crosse Ave., Apt. 2N
Naumann, Adrienne B., Law Office of '49 '84 C.145 B.A. L.146 J.D.
8210 N. Tripp (Pat.)
Neuman, Glen .... '52 '78 C.339 B.A. L.424 J.D. [Lustig&Assoc.]
Newman, Michael J. .... '61 '87 C.347 B.S. L.146 J.D. 8833 Gross Point Rd., Ste. 204
Nix, Robert F. .... '36 '61 C.363 B.S.B.A. L.276 J.D. Cir. J.
O'Connell, John R. '24 '50 C.707 B.A. L.424 J.D.
Chmn. of the Bd., Skokie Fed. Svgs. & Loan Assn.
O'Gara, Thomas F., (AV) .... '39 '72 C.424 B.A. L.146 J.D. Asst. Pub. Def.
Orr, Marcia B. .... '46 '72 C&L.477 B.A., J.D. Asso. Cir. J.
Parad, Boris .... '46 '79 C.999 M.S.M.E. L.365 J.D. 4711 Golf Road Suite 705

Patton & Ryan LLC
(See Chicago)

Pauletto, Anthony J., (AV) .... '37 '59 C&L.339 B.S., LL.B. 9933 Lawler
Peck, Herbert I., (AV) '37 '60 C&L.145 A.B., J.D.
Assoc. Gen. Coun., Anixter International, Inc.
Perkal, M. Jay .... '— '50 C.597 L.365 LL.B. 8344 Niles Ctr. Rd.
Peronti, Gino M. .... '48 '74 C&L.424 B.S., J.D. Chief Pub. Def.
Phemister, Bonnie B. .... '45 '76 C.475 B.A. L.597 J.D. Asst. States Atty.

Pinsel, David L., P.C., Law Offices of
(See Rolling Meadows)

Piper, Harry C. .... '41 '74 C.597 B.A. L.209 J.D. 4234 Bobolink Terr.

Plotnick, Paul W., Attorney At Law, (AV) '47 '74 C.801 B.A. L.209 J.D.
9933 Lawler Avenue Suite 312, 60077
Telephone: 847-675-2660 Fax: 847-675-2661 Email: 9933212@SBCGlobal.net
Email: lawfun@msn.com URL: http://www.lawyers.com/plotnicklaw

(This Listing Continued)

Plotnick, Paul W., Attorney At Law (Continued)
Language: Romanian.
Real Estate, Real Estate Litigation, Family Law, Divorce, Criminal Law, Driving While Intoxicated, Felonies, Business Law, Corporate Law, Personal Injury.
See Professional Biographies, SKOKIE, ILLINOIS

Richter, Marshall, (BV) .... '57 '88 C.339 B.S. L.424 J.D. [M.T.Richter]
Richter, Marshall T., (BV) .... 5225 Old Orchard Rd., Ste. 29
Robbins-Ost, Harriet Beth .... '55 '85 C.1183 B.A. L.209 J.D. 8940 Kilbourn Ave.
Roberti, Stephen R. .... '— '86 C.339 B.A. L.910 J.D. Gen. Coun., MPC Products Corp.
Rochford, Mary K. .... '54 '79 C&L.602 B.B.A., J.D. Assoc. Cir. J.
Romanoff, Robert Arthur .... '38 '64 C.477 B.B.A. L.597 J.D. [R.A.Romanoff]
Romanoff, Robert A., Law Offices of .... 9933 Lawler Ave., Ste. 312
Rosen, Edw. I. .... '31 '54 C.1016 L.146 LL.B. [Levin&R.]
Rubin, Albert G. .... '24 '51 C&L.209 B.S., J.D. [A.G.Rubin&Assoc.]
Rubin, Albert G., & Associates, Ltd. .... 10024 Skokie Blvd.
Ruffer, Lowell L. .... '29 '54 C.999 B.S. L.209 J.D. 5301 W. Dempster
Rusnak, Anthony F. .... '50 '76 C.927 B.A. L.146 J.D. Asst. Pub. Def.
Sabora, Marilyn G. .... '44 '97 C.597 B.S. L.365 J.D. 5600 Old Orchard Rd., Ste. 263
Sanes, David P. .... '30 '53 C.1016 L.209 LL.B. 4711 Golf Rd., Ste. 807
Schachter, Jerome .... '37 '62 C.145 L.339 LL.B. [J.Schachter&Assoc.]
Schachter, Jerome, & Associates, LTD .... 9933 N. Lawler Avenue, Suite 100

Schoenberg, Fisher, Newman & Rosenberg, Ltd.
(See Chicago)

Schultz, Lori .... '59 '85 C.339 B.A. L.365 J.D. Asst. States Atty.
Serlin, Howard R. .... '39 '69 C.597 B.S.B.A. L.365 J.D. 9933 N. Lawler Ave.
Shapiro, Frieda Shulamis .... '76 '00 C&L.424 B.A., J.D. [🄰 Immigration&Assoc.]
Shapiro, Gayle M. .... '52 '80 C.339 B.A. L.589 J.D. Asst. Pub. Def.

Shaw Gussis Fishman Glantz Wolfson & Towbin LLC
(See Chicago)

Siegel, Elaine K. B. .... '49 '82 C.112 A.B. L.1119 J.D. [E.K.B.Siegel&Assoc.] ⊙
Siegel, Elaine K. B., & Assoc., P.C. .... 5005 Touhy Avenue (⊙Chicago)
Silverman, Carol G. .... '— '85 C.339 B.A. L.146 J.D. [🄰 L.J.Wasserman]
Simon, Earl L. .... '44 '69 C.339 B.S. L.209 J.D. [Simon,L.&S.]
Simon, Stephanie D. .... '— '98 C.339 B.S. L.966 J.D. [Simon,L.&S.]

Simon, Lapidos & Simon, LLC
4709 West Golf Road, Suite 475, 60076
Telephone: 847-329-7878 Facsimile: 847-329-9450
Email: earlsimon44@hotmail.com URL: http://www.lawyers.com/simonlapidos&simonllc
Earl L. Simon; Manny M. Lapidos; Stephanie D. Simon.
Commercial Litigation, Residential and Commercial Real Estate, Business Transactions including Acquisitions and Mergers, Contracts, Taxation, Probate, Estate Planning including Guardianship and Elder Law, Landlord and Tenant Law, General Practice, Corporate Debtor and Creditor Reorganization and Bankruptcy, Pension and Profit Sharing Plans.
See Professional Biographies, SKOKIE, ILLINOIS

Sitrick, David H., (AV) '50 '80
C.339 B.S.E.E. L.802 J.D. 8340 N. Lincoln Ave., Ste. 201 (Pat.)

Slutzky, Jay A.
(See Niles)

Soskin, Rollin J. .... '52 '79 C.339 B.S. L.424 J.D. 9933 Lawler Ave.
Spector, Lawrence H. .... '45 '72 C.339 B.A. L.209 J.D. Asst. States Atty.
Spector, Solomon R. .... '— '35 C&L.145 Ph.B., J.D. 9450 Keeler St.
Springer, Barry A., (BV) .... '51 '78 C.339 B.S. L.209 J.D. [B.A.Springer]
Springer, Barry A., PC, (BV) .... 4350 Oakton St
Stein, Jack G. .... '25 '50 C&L.339 B.S. Cir. Ct.
Steinberg, Barbara A. .... '42 '79 C.966 B.S. L.146 J.D. Asst. Pub. Def.
Steinberg, Richard A. .... '51 '79 C.209 B.A. L.365 J.D. 8350 N. Kimball

Sternberg, David M.
(See Chicago)

Sullivan, Harold W. .... '26 '51 C.424 B.A. L.209 J.D. Cir. J.
Sutker, Calvin R. .... '23 '50 C&L.145 A.B., J.D. Co. Comm.
Tepper, Michael A. .... '60 '85 C.589 B.S. L.209 J.D. [M.A.Tepper&Assoc.]
Tepper, Michael A., & Associates, P.C. .... 7870 N. Lincoln Ave.
Terpinas, William, Jr. .... '66 '92 C.1183 B.A. L.61 J.D. [Tuzzolino&T.]
Traynor, William Michael .... '63 '89 C.966 B.S. L.46 J.D. Asst. State's Atty.
Turek, Gerald L. .... '30 '57 C.1016 A.B. L.365 J.D. 9139 Kedvale Ave.
Tuzzolino, Sam .... '66 '91 C.339 B.S. L.209 J.D. [Tuzzolino&T.]
Tuzzolino and Terpinas .... 8930 Gross Point Road Suite 600
Valenti, Linda P. .... '50 '77 C.569 B.A. L.209 J.D. Chicago Title & Tr. Co.
Valentine, Andrew J., Esq., Law Office of '— '80
C.871 B.S. L.976 LL.M. 5215 Old Orchard, Ste. 900
Victorson, Larry .... '43 '68 C.912 B.A. L.477 J.D. Asst. States Atty.
Vlay, Burton B. .... '32 '56 C&L.339 B.S., LL.B. 8338 Kenton St.
Wagman, Harold L. .... '33 '57 5301 W. Dempster St.
Walder, Elizabeth M. .... '59 '89 C.367 B.A. L.124 J.D. [Immigration&Assoc.]

Wasserman, Laurie J., Law Offices of, (AV) '— '79 C.145 B.A. L.597 J.D. 🄱🄱
Westmoreland Building, 9933 Lawler Avenue, Suite 122, 60077-3703
Telephone: 847-674-7324 Fax: 847-674-6684
Email: ljw@webemploymentlaw.com URL: http://www.lawyers.com/wassermanlaw
Associate: Carol G. Silverman.
Employment, Employment Discrimination, Employee and Employer Rights, Sexual Harassment, Americans With Disabilities Act, Family and Medical Leave Act, Whistle Blower Cases, Severance Agreements, Non-Compete Agreements, Retaliation.
See Professional Biographies, SKOKIE, ILLINOIS

Weisman, Nancy E. '53 '83 C.930 B.A. L.146 J.D.
Gen. Coun., Rush N. Shore Med. Ctr.
Weiss, Earl W. .... '55 '80 C.472 B.B.A. L.209 J.D. 4051 Old Orchard Rd.
Weitzman, Daniel M. ...... '58 '83 C&L.339 B.S., J.D. Frost Ruttenberg and RothblattPC
White, John J. .... '19 '55 C.976 B.S. L.365 J.D. Midland Mfg. Corp.
Wolter, Wm. Dennis .... '39 '71 C.602 B.A. L.365 J.D. State's Atty. Off.
Worster, William .... '72 '02 C.378 B.A. L.146 J.D. [🄰 Immigration&Assoc.]
Zaitseva, Flora B. .... '60 '04 C.999 Ph.D. L.365 J.D. [F.Zaitseva]
Zaitseva, Flora, Esq. .... 5229 W. Crain St.
Zeller, David J. .... '46 '73 C.927 B.A. L.209 J.D. [Arnstein&Z.]
Zeman, Francis J., Jr. .... '50 '75 C&L.424 B.A., J.D. [F.J.Zeman]
Zeman, Francis J., Attorney at Law .... 9933 Lawler Ave., Ste. 533
Zimmerman, Maurice .... '06 '29 C&L.597 J.D. 8448 Harding Ave.
Ziporyn, Charlotte W. .... '31 '60 C.627 B.S. L.365 J.D. 4711 Golf Rd.‡

SMITHTON, 2,248, *St. Clair Co.*

Hummel, Carole M., (BV) .... '57 '83 C.378 B.S. L.734 J.D. 4065 Bur Oak St.
Keeley, Anne Fohne, (BV) .... '56 '84 C.339 B.A. L.734 J.D. 5350 Wild Oak Ln.

SOMONAUK, 1,295, *DeKalb & La Salle Cos.*

Fuertges, Edmund J., (CV) ... '53 '78 C.338 B.S. L.365 J.D. 440 E. Market (Rt. 34)
Marshall, Charles E., (BV) ... '39 '63 C.339 B.S. L.146 J.D. [Marshall&M.]
Marshall, Howard ... '12 '40 C.339 B.S. L.146 LL.B. [🄰 Marshall&M.] ‡
Marshall & Marshall, Ltd., (BV) ... 121 W. DeKalb St.
Shogren, Linnea A. '64 '93 C.209 B.A. L.879 J.D.
(adm. in TX; not adm. in IL) 640 Rustic Rour

SOUTH BARRINGTON, 3,760, *Cook Co.*

Berres, Karen Arndt ... '49 '80 C.436 B.S. L.209 J.D. [Fuller&B.]
Caldwell, Henry H. ... '11 '35 C&L.597 B.A., J.D. 48 N. Liberty Dr.‡
Chapman, Judith A. ... '58 '89 C.705 B.A. L.300 J.D. 49 Revere Dr.
Cillick, Martin P. ... '60 '88 C.879 B.A. L.776 J.D. Asst. Coun., Allstate Insurance Co.‡
Dybala, Ray A. ... '48 '81 C.1016 B.S.B.A. L.209 J.D. 14 Wescott Lane
Fuller, Warren R. ... '42 '67 C&L.424 B.B.A., J.D. [Fuller&B.]
Fuller & Berres ... 69 S. Barrington Rd.
Gabe, Caryl Jacobs ... '— '76 C.102 B.A. L.365 J.D. [C.J.Gabe&Assoc.]

Gabe, Caryl Jacobs, & Associates, Inc., Law Offices of
33 West Higgins Road, Suite 620, 60010
Telephone: 847-551-3751 Fax: 847-551-3791
Email: CGABE7129@aol.com URL: http://www.lawyers.com/gabe
Caryl Jacobs Gabe.
Family, Divorce, Paternity, Mediation, Child Custody, Child Support, Matrimonial Law, Domestic Relations, Orders of Protection, Prenuptial Agreements, Adoptions, and Injunctions.
See Professional Biographies, SOUTH BARRINGTON, ILLINOIS

Hoffman, Nancie Hudell ... '54 '81 C.205 B.A. L.589 J.D. Coun., Allstate Ins. Co.
James, Henry F., Jr. ... '46 '83 C.58 B.A. L.589 J.D. [H.James,Jr.]
James, Henry, Jr., The Law Office of ... 33 W. Higgins Rd., Ste. 4090
Jennings, Robyn E. '49 '85
C.472 B.A. L.146 J.D. Coun., Specialty Lines, Allstate Ins. Co.
Koivun, David W. ... '45 '76 C.36 B.S. L.365 J.D. 69 S. Barrington Road
Levine, Gary L. ... '64 '97 C.1147 B.A. L.616 J.D. Asst. Coun., Allstate Insurance Co.
Lewis, Thadd J. ... '70 '00 C.350 B.S. L.365 J.D. 33 W. Higgins Rd., Ste. 1060
Lucey, Gerald P. ... '35 '58 C&L.424 B.S.C., J.D. 38 Watergate Dr.
Maslov, Edward I. ... '51 '76 C.339 B.A. L.910 J.D. Coun., Allstate Ins. Co.
Noone, John T. ... '55 '80 C.188 B.A. L.228 J.D. Coun., Allstate Ins. Co.
Ryske, Paul R. ... '55 '81 C.339 B.A. L.365 J.D. Assoc. Coun., Allstate Ins. Co.
Sporleder, James G. '51 '76 C.578 B.A. L.146 J.D.
Asst. V.P. & Asst. Gen. Coun., Allstate Ins. Co.
Swanson, Sue A. ... '52 '79 C.424 B.A. L.146 J.D. 51 W. Higgins Rd.
Taheny, Dennis G. ... '45 '71 C.208 B.S.B.A. L.145 J.D. 19 Watergate

SOUTH BELOIT, 5,397, *Winnebago Co.*

Thiede, Steven Michael, A Law Office of '66 '01
C.999 B.S. L.589 J.D. 214 South 8th Street

SOUTH CHICAGO HEIGHTS, 3,970, *Cook Co.*

Tristan, Ana B., Law Offices of ... '— '93 C.339 B.A. L.146 J.D. 25 W. Sauk Trail

SOUTH ELGIN, 16,100, *Kane Co.*

Hartwell, Thomas M. ... '59 '85 C.57 B.A. L.352 J.D. Kane Co. Bd. Mbr.
Klein, Robert J. ... '68 '93 114 N. La Fox St.
Michniewicz, Kenneth E., (BV) ... '44 '72 C.46 B.S. L.209 J.D. 1116 La Fayette Dr.

SOUTH HOLLAND, 22,105, *Cook Co.*

Abbott, Gardner ... '11 '36 C.145 Ph.B. L.146 LL.B. Carrier-Oehler‡
Anthony, Stephen C. ... '47 '76 C.207 B.A. L.365 J.D. Pres., Chicago-Wilcox Mfg. Co.
Bobak, Thomas R. ... '34 '58 C&L.734 B.S.C., J.D. [🄰 Hiskes,D.O.M.&L.]
Dalenberg, Jack ... '46 '78 C.210 B.S. L.146 J.D. V.P., South Holland Tr. & Svgs. Bk.
De Graff, Randy W. ... '52 '80 C.339 B.S. L.146 J.D. S. Holland Tr. & Savings Bk.
Dillner, J. David ... '38 '65 C.36 B.A. L.365 LL.B. [Hiskes,D.O.M.&L.]
Dillner, Scott ... '66 '92 C.36 B.S. L.365 J.D. [🄰 Hiskes,D.O.M.&L.]
Fortner, Marjorie ... '60 '87 C.209 B.A. L.424 J.D. P.O. Box 623
Gilley, Dennis C. ... '46 '71 C.597 B.S. L.209 J.D. 15525 S. Park Ave.
Gilley, George D. ... '22 '48 C.221 B.C.S. L.209 J.D. 525 E. 162nd St.
Godbolt, W. Terrance ... '51 '98 C&L.124 B.A., J.D. [W.T.Godbolt]
Godbolt, W. T., Esq., LTD ... 16233 S. Wausan
Heaney, Chris J., (AV) ... '44 '74 C.1157 B.S. L.365 J.D. [🄰 Hiskes,D.O.M.&L.]
Hiskes, John A. ... '51 '76 C.114 B.A. L.424 J.D. [Hiskes,D.O.M.&L.]
Hiskes, Dillner, O'Donnell, Marovich & Lapp, Ltd. ... 16231 Wausau Ave.
Kurc, Gary M. ... '49 '75 C.339 B.A. L.146 J.D. 16162 Ellis Avnue.
Lanting, James ... '49 '75 C.114 B.A. L.879 J.D. [Lanting&P.]
Lanting & Paarlberg, Ltd. ... 16230 Louis Ave.
Lapp, Timothy C. ... '59 '90 C&L.209 B.S., J.D. [Hiskes,D.O.M.&L.]
Mahon, Patricia R. ... '64 '98 C.98 B.A. L.209 J.D. Dir.
Marion, Stanley W. ... '11 '46 C.145 L.365 J.D. 227 E. 165th St.‡
Marovich, Michael J. ... '60 '85 C.339 B.S. L.424 J.D. [Hiskes,D.O.M.&L.]
Movsisian, Korean ... '12 '36 C&L.209 LL.B. 16342 Woodlawn E. Dr.
O'Donnell, John J. ... '59 '84 C.927 B.B.A. L.879 J.D. [Hiskes,D.O.M.&L.]
Paarlberg, Russell T. ... '56 '80 C.323 B.A. L.1119 J.D. [Lanting&P.]
Phelps, Alfred S. ... '58 '85 C.302 B.S. L.879 J.D. 15557 S. State St.
Russell, John R. ... '59 '89 C.340 B.M.E. L.365 J.D. 16924 S. Park Ave.
Scott, Edward A., Jr., (AV) ... '23 '50 C&L.209 B.A., LL.B. 15330 S. Greenwood Rd.
Stanula, Edward F. ... '35 '66 C.209 B.S.C. L.365 J.D. 15906 Avalon Ave.
Thuftedal, Dennis L. ... '34 '58 C&L.494 B.S., J.D. 460 E. 162nd St.
Tobin, William H. ... '46 '73 C.309 A.B. L.145 J.D. 453 E. 166th Street
Tunelius, Edward J. ... '52 '00 L.146 J.D. 17000 South Park Ave.
Vitiritti, Angelo ... '64 '90 C.504 B.A. L.209 J.D. [🄰 Hiskes,D.O.M.&L.]
Voorn, John C. ... '44 '73 C.323 A.B. L.879 J.D. [🄰 Hiskes,D.O.M.&L.]
Walberg, Leonard D., (BV) ... '34 '58 C.339 B.A. L.880 LL.B. 15525 S. Park Ave.

SPARTA, 4,486, *Randolph Co.*

Brown & Associates
(See Belleville)

Clendenin, John F., (BV) ... '46 '72 C.339 B.S. L.352 J.D. [Conn,C.&N.] ⊙
Conn, Clendenin & Norton, (BV) ... P.O. Box 315 (⊙Marissa)
Farris, Alan R., (BV) ... '54 '79 C.504 B.A. L.221 J.D. 221 South Market Street
Heaton, Beth M., (CV) ... '64 '90 C.339 B.A. L.801 J.D. 1501 N. Market St., Suite 2
Howell, Michael R. ... '58 '83 C&L.801 B.S., J.D. Exec. V.P. & Treas., Charter Bank
Kelley, James W., (CV) ... '61 '87 C.234 B.A. L.284 J.D. 314 W. 3rd Street
Norton, William C., (BV) ... '53 '78 C.798 B.A. L.801 J.D. [Conn,C.&N.] ⊙

SPEER, 90, *Stark Co.*

Campbell, Charles W. ... '18 '48 C.504 A.B. L.665 LL.B. R.R. 2‡

SPRINGFIELD, * 111,454, *Sangamon Co.*

Abbott, Randall, (BV) ... '46 '80 C&L.339 A.B., J.D. [Abbott]
Abbott Law Offices, (BV) ... 528 S. Fifth St., Ste. 210
Abrell, John ... '49 '81 C.234 B.S. L.365 J.D. Ill. Dept. of Health
Accettura, Michael V. '54 '79
C.874 B.A. L.365 J.D. Asst. Chief Coun., State Dept. of Transp.
Ackerman, James W., (BV) ... '61 '86 C.57 B.A. L.879 J.D. 230 W. Carpenter St.
Adami, Paul E., (BV) ... '50 '75 C&L.339 B.S., J.D. [Mohan,A.P.&A.]
Albers, John D. ... '72 '97 C.338 B.A. L.339 J.D. Hearing Exam.
Alewelt, Edward J., (AV) ... '32 '68 C.339 B.S. L.734 J.D. [Mohan,A.P.&A.] ‡
Allen, R. Lee, (BV) ... '63 '94 C&L.339 B.S., J.D. [Sorling,N.H.C.&C.]
Alvarez, R. John, Attorney at Law, (BV) '47 '76
C.927 B.A. L.365 J.D. 975 S. Durkin Dr., Ste. 103
Anderson, Elizabeth W., (BV) ... '63 '89 C&L.802 B.F.A., J.D. [🄰 Brown,H.&S.]
Anderson, Michelle L. ... '71 '97 C.927 B.A. L.801 J.D. State of IL
Andreasen, Bryon C. '56 '84 C.877 B.A. L.188 J.D.
(adm. in NY; not adm. in IL) 7796 Ponderosa Dr.‡
Apfelbaum, Larry A., (BV) '61 '87 C.338 B.S. L.339 J.D.
[🄰 Kanoski&Assoc.] (⊙Bloomington, Macomb, Peoria, Quincy, Rushville)
Armitage, Julie K. ... '63 '88 C.98 B.S. L.801 J.D. Asst. Coun., Ill. E.P.A.

Armstrong Teasdale LLP, (AV)
A Partnership including Professional Corporations
3201 Pleasant Run, Suite A, P.O. Box 13317, 62791-3317 ⊙
Telephone: 217-726-8200 Facsimile: 217-726-8300
Email: armstrongteasdale@armstrongteasdale.com URL: http://www.armstrongteasdale.com
Associate: John H. Stockman. Of Counsel: Thomas W. Kelty.
General Civil Practice. Administrative Law, Agricultural Law, Alternative Dispute Resolution, Antitrust and Trade Regulation Law, Appellate Practice, Banking and Financial Services, Biotechnology/ Life Sciences, Business Law, Civil Rights, Class Actions, Communications Law, Computer, Constitutional Law, Construction Law, Corporate Compliance and Governance, Corporate Law, Corporate Finance, Education Law, Eminent Domain, Employee Benefits, Employment and Labor, Energy, Entertainment & Sports, Environmental Law, Financial Restructuring, Reorganization and Bankruptcy, Distribution and Franchise, Government Contracts, Governmental Relations, Health Care, Immigration and Naturalization, Insurance Coverage/Reinsurance and Extracontractual Liability, International Law, International Trade, Internet Law, Investments, Litigation, Medical Malpractice, Mergers & Acquisitions, Natural Resources, Occupational Safety & Health Administration, Patent, Trademark and Intellectual Property, Pension and Executive Compensation, Personal Injury, Products Liability, Professional Liability, Public Law and Finance, Real Estate, Securities, Taxation, Technology and Science, Toxic Torts, Transportation, Trusts and Estates, White Collar Crime, Workers Compensation and Zoning, Planning & Land Use and Development.
St. Louis, Missouri Office: One Metropolitan Square, Suite 2600, 63102. Telephone: 314-621-5070. Facsimile: 314-621-5065.
Kansas City, Missouri Office: 2345 Grand Boulevard, Suite 2000, 64108. Telephone: 816-221-3420. Facsimile: 816-221-9786.
Washington, D.C. Office: 1747 Pennsylvania Avenue, N.W., Suite 300, 20006. Telephone: 202-454-2800. Facsimile: 202-454-2805.
Jefferson City, Missouri Office: 3405 West Truman Blvd., Suite 210, 65109-5713. Telephone: 573-636-8394. Facsimile: 573-636-8457.
Belleville, Illinois Office: 23 South First Street, 62220. Telephone: 618-397-4411.
Overland Park, Kansas Office: 7400 West 132nd Street, Suite 200, 66213.
Edwardsville, Illinois Office: 241 North Main Street, 62025. Telephone: 618-650-7087. Facsimile: 618-655-4004.
Henderson, Nevada Office: 701 North Green Valley Parkway, Suite 200, 89074. Telephone: 702-678-5070. Facsimile: 702-990-3003.
Sydney, Australia Office: C/Clayton Utz, Level 31, No. 1 O'Connell Street, Sidney, NSW 2000, Australia. Telephone: 61-29-262-6700. Facsimile: 61-29-262-3263.
New York, New York Office: 230 Park Avenue, Suite 2300, 10169. Telephone: 212-867-9500. Facsimile: 212-599-1759.
Shanghai, China Office: 1376 Nan Jing Xi Lu, Shanghai Center - Suite 718, Shanghai 200040, P.R. China. Telephone: 011-8621-6279-8808. Facsimilie: 011-8621-6279-8866.
See Professional Biographies, SPRINGFIELD, ILLINOIS

Aronfeld, Mandel L. ... '14 '37 C.405 L.209 LL.B. Pros. Atty., Off. of Secy. of State
Arthur, Elizabeth E., (BV) ... '54 '79 C.385 B.A. L.339 J.D. Franklin Sq.
Ascher, Jennifer M. ... '78 '03 C.339 B.S. L.734 J.D. [🄰 Sorling,N.H.C.&C.]
Bagby, Benault ... '51 '77 C&L.801 B.A., J.D. State of IL Metro Mgmt.
Bagley, Kelly ... '63 '94 C.338 B.S. L.801 J.D. Admin. J.
Bailey, Gary Lee ... '60 '86 C.597 B.A. L.146 J.D. State Labor Relations Bd.
Bailey, Velma Neal ... '38 '86 C&L.801 B.S., J.D. 1901 Jeanette Ln., Apt. 3‡
Bain, Florence, (BV) '42 '78 C.350 B.S. L.36 J.D.
[🄰 Kanoski&Assoc.] (⊙Bloomington, Macomb, Peoria, Quincy, Rushville)
Baker, James P., (BV) ... '45 '71 C.303 B.A. L.208 J.D. [Baker,B.&K.]
Baker, John A., (CV) ... '71 '98 C.502 B.A. L.365 J.D. [Baker,B.&K.]

Baker, Baker & Krajewski, LLC, (AV)
415 South Seventh Street, 62701
Telephone: 217-522-3445 Telecopier: 217-522-8234
Email: bakerlaw@sbcglobal.net
James P. Baker; John A. Baker; J. Phillip Krajewski.
Labor and Employment Discrimination Law. General Civil, Trial and Appellate Practice before State and Federal Courts and Administrative Agencies. Estate Planning, Probate, Real Estate, Corporate, Tax, Railroad Law, Labor Relations, Healthcare Compliance Law.
References: First National Bank of Springfield; Warren Boyton State Bank, New Berlin, Ill.
See Professional Biographies, SPRINGFIELD, ILLINOIS

Baker-Bowen, Kathy M. ... '59 '00 C.339 B.S. L.801 J.D. [McWard] ⊙
Bapst, Lawrence J. ... '54 '79 C.339 B.S. L.1292 J.D. State Appl. Defs. Off.

Barber Segatto Hoffee and Hines, (AV) BR
Formerly Barber & Barber
Monroe at Ninth, P.O. Box 79, 62705-0079
Telephone: 217-544-4868 Telecopier: 217-544-5225
URL: http://www.barberlaw.com
Members of Firm: John A. Barber (1870-1939); Clayton J. Barber (1879-1970); Charles F. Barber (1904-1988); Henry R. Barber (1910-1991); Alton G. Hall (1904-1991); Bernard G. Segatto (1931-1994); Carl O. Hoffee; Barry O. Hines; Bernard G. Segatto, III; R. Kurt Wilke; Randall W. Segatto.
Associates: Matthew J. Cate; John Charles Milhiser.
Banking, Condemnation, Contract, Corporation, Estate Planning, General Civil Trial and Appellate Practice in State and Federal Courts, Media, Negligence Law, Probate, Real Estate, Taxation and Workers Compensation, Bankruptcy, Business Law, land Use and Zoning.
Representative Clients: The Copley Press; International Harvester Co.; Rochester State Bank; Wemple State Bank.
Waverly, Illinois Office: 176 West State Street. Telephone: 217-435-7241.
See Professional Biographies, SPRINGFIELD, ILLINOIS

Barewin, Robert D., (BV) ... '45 '71 C.1016 B.A. L.209 J.D. [R.Barewin]
Barewin, Robert, Attorney at Law, (BV) ... 915 S. 2nd St.
Barris, R. Gerald, (BV) ... '40 '69 C.207 B.A. L.910 J.D. [Sorling,N.H.C.&C.]
Barton, Michael G., (AV) ... '55 '83 C&L.339 B.S., J.D. [Bellatti,B.H.&C.]
Bass, Timothy A., (BV) ... '63 '94 C.339 B.S. L.734 J.D. Asst. U.S. Atty.
Bates, William B., (AV) '54 '79
C.934 B.A. L.221 J.D. [🄰 Sorling,N.H.C.&C.] (⊙Lincoln)
Beard, Peter C. ... '69 '97 C.98 B.A. L.801 J.D. [🄰 Holley&R.]
Beard, Peter Crenshaw ... '70 '97 1836 S. Walnut St.

Beavers, Graham & Fines
(See Taylorville)

Becker, Alvin G. ....'38 '62 C.339 A.B. L.145 J.D. Ill. Nat. Bk. of Spr.
Becker, Michael W. .... '45 '73 C.57 A.B. L.339 J.D. Chf. Bur. of Admin. Hearing
Beeman, Bruce A., (BV) ....'47 '75 C.801 B.S. L.365 J.D. [Wolter,B.&L.]
Behnke, Dawn D., (CV) ....'51 '98 C&L.801 B.S., J.D. [Ⓐ LaBarre&Y.]

Bellatti, Barton, Hamill & Cochran, LLC, (AV)
944 Clock Tower Drive Suite A, 62704
Telephone: 217-793-9300 Fax: 217-793-9301
Email: lawyers@bellatti-barton.com
Members of Firm: Robert M. Bellatti (1948-2005); Michael G. Barton; Mark S. Cochran; Thomas G. Hamill.
Estate Planning, Business Planning, Agricultural Law, Wills, Probate, Trust, Real Estate and Federal Income, Estate, Gift Taxation and Environmental Law.
See Professional Biographies, SPRINGFIELD, ILLINOIS

Belz, John W., (BV) .... '64 '90 C.339 B.A. L.734 J.D. First Asst. State's Atty.
Beneze, Lee, (BV) '50 '85
C.927 B.A. L.801 J.D. Legal Servs. Developer, Ill. Dept. on Aging
Bennett, Allen F., (CV) .... '43 '68 C.339 B.S. L.838 J.D. 1820 S. MacArthur St.
Benoit, Joel A., (BV) ....'63 '92 C.339 B.S. L.801 J.D. [Mohan,A.P.&A.]
Benson, Fredric, (BV) .... '48 '72 C.966 B.A. L.339 J.D. [Feldman,W.D.&B.]
Bentley, Melinda '75 '01 C.57 B.A. L.879 J.D.
First Asst. Coun., Illinois State Bar Assn.
Berg, Steven W., (BV) ....'52 '78 C.339 A.B. L.801 J.D. [Berg&R.]
Berg & Robeson, P.C., (BV) .... 1217 South 6th Street
Bergschneider, David P. '51 '76 C.337 B.A. L.436 J.D.
Off. of the State Appellet Defender
Bialorucki, Bruce R. .... '59 '00 C.97 B.S. L.146 J.D. IL Troopers, Lodge 41
Bian, Eugene N. .... '50 '79 C.424 B.A. L.300 J.D. Legal Advsr., State Secs. Dept.
Bickel, Roger H., (AV) ....'— '89 C.347 B.A. L.424 J.D. [Freeborn&P.] ⊙
Biggins, Keleigh Lynn ....'76 '99 C&L.801 B.A., J.D. Asst. State Def.
Bilinsky, Matthew D., (CV) ....'68 '93 C.20 B.A. L.339 J.D. Asst. Atty. Gen.
Billington, John A., (BV) ....'40 '66 C.357 B.S. L.339 J.D. [Billington&B.]
Billington, Thomas R., (BV) ....'44 '71 C.339 B.A. L.365 J.D. [Billington&B.]
Billington and Billington, (BV) .... 915 South Sixth Street
Bima, Kenneth S. .... '70 '95 C.339 B.A. L.190 J.D. [Livingstone,M.O.&D.]
Bingaman, Charles C. '41 '68 C.210 B.A. L.145 J.D.
Exec. Dir., Illinois Institute for Continuing Legal Education
Biswell, Christian D. ....'71 '01 C&L.801 B.A., J.D. [Ⓐ Drake,N.&M.]
Blackburn, Michelle L. .... '71 '01 C.234 B.S. L.365 J.D. [Ⓐ Feldman,W.D.&B.]
Blalock, Howard R. .... '18 '48 L.996 LL.B. 1820 Dial Ct.‡
Bleakley, William M. '34 '67 C.999 B.A. L.436 J.D.
(adm. in WI; not adm. in IL) Ill. Legislative Research Unit
Blodgett, D. Bradley, (AV) .... '37 '62 C&L.339 B.S., LL.B. [Hinshaw&C.]
Blue, Randy E., (BV) .... '51 '76 C.347 A.B. L.1119 J.D. [Sgro,H.&B.]
Bobbitt, Loren M. .... '16 '47 C.337 A.B. L.996 LL.B. 11 Turnberry Place‡
Bochenek, Stephen J., (AV) ....'51 '77 C.734 A.B. L.608 J.D. [Sorling,N.H.C.&C.]
Bodewes, Herman G., (BV) .... '37 '64 C&L.734 B.S., J.D. [Giffin,W.C.&B.]
Bomher, John T. ....'60 '85 C&L.339 B.A., J.D. Staff Atty., Dept. of Pub. Aid
Bonczyk, Bruce S., (BV) .... '51 '85 C.502 B.S.C.E. L.801 J.D. 601 W. Monroe St.
Booker, Matthew R., (BV) .... '73 '00 C.340 B.S.N. L.801 J.D. [Ⓐ Heyl,R.V.&A.]
Borah, Gary L., (AV) .... '49 '75 C.339 B.S. L.851 J.D. [Heyl,R.V.&A.]
Borland, James Andrew, (BV) ....'66 '91 C.1082 B.A. L.990 J.D. [Quinn,J.H.&P.]
Boshardy, John V., (BV) ....'65 '91 C.209 B.A.S. L.365 J.D. [J.V.Boshardy&Assoc.]

Boshardy, John V., & Associates, P.C., (BV)
1610 South 6th Street, 62703
Telephone: 217-544-8000 Fax: 217-544-8063
John V. Boshardy.
Workers Compensation, Personal Injury, On the Job Injuries, Automobile Accidents, Medical Malpractice, Wrongful Death.
See Professional Biographies, SPRINGFIELD, ILLINOIS

Bown, Paul, (AV) ....'49 '76 C.57 B.A. L.801 J.D. [Brown,H.&S.]
Boyle, Kenneth R., (BV) ....'37 '63 C&L.339 A.B., J.D. 1123 S. Second St.
Bozarth, Keith S., (BVⓉ) '51 '81 C&L.502 B.A., J.D.
(adm. in MO; not adm. in IL) Exec. Dir., IL Teachers' Retirement Sys.
Brand, Corinne L. ....'59 '85 C.339 B.A. L.221 J.D. Franklin Sq.
Braverman, Howard H. .... '22 '50 C.103 A.B. L.564 LL.B. 2621 Idlewild Dr.‡
Bredemeyer, Arthur C. '58 '83 C.337 B.S. L.900 J.D.
(adm. in KS; not adm. in IL) 3421 S. Douglas★
Bresney, Todd A. .... '70 '96 C.338 B.S. L.146 J.D. [Ⓐ Kanoski&Assoc.]
Brickman, Kenneth A. '40 '70
C.191 B.S. L.502 J.D. Dep. Dir., Admin., Dept. of The Lottery
Briggle, Charles G., Jr., (BV) ....'11 '33 C.337 A.B. L.597 J.D. 2312 Wiggins Ave.
Brigman, Myron W. .... '42 '77 C.145 B.A. L.365 J.D. Ill. Dept. of Public Aid
Broadway, James D., (AV) .... '44 '68 C.861 B.A. L.802 J.D. [Sorling,N.H.C.&C.] ⊙
Broeker, Gerard William ....'70 '99 C&L.339 B.A., J.D. 427 E. Monroe
Brown, Gary A., (BV) ....'47 '77 C.339 B.S. L.910 J.D. [Sorling,N.H.C.&C.]

Brown, Hay & Stephens, LLP, (AV) BR
205 South Fifth Street, Suite 700, P.O. Box 2459, 62705-2459
Telephone: 217-544-8491 Fax: 217-544-9609
URL: http://www.bhslaw.com
Members of Firm: Robert A. Stuart, Jr.; J. Patrick Joyce, Jr.; Eric L. Grenzebach; Jeffery M. Wilday; Paul Bown; Almon A. Manson, Jr.; Dwight H. O'Keefe, III; Donald R. Tracy; Emmet A. Fairfield; Denise M. Druhot; Harvey M. Stephens; James W. Bruner; Lorilea Buerkett; Thomas R. Lamont; Amy K. Schmidt; Scott C. Helmholz; Thomas P. Schanzle-Haskins, III; Hugh F. Drake. Counsel: Elizabeth W. Anderson; Claire A. Manning. Associates: Roland R. Cross; James L. Nichelson; Robert M. Shupenus; Daniel K. Wright; Jennifer L. Parker. Of Counsel: Harvey B. Stephens; Edward J. Cunningham; Simon L. Friedman; Charles A. Chapin; Saul J. Morse; Donald L. Woods.
General Civil Trial and Appellate Practice in State and Federal Courts. Health Law, Real Estate, Probate, Insurance, Banking, Environmental, Governmental, School Law, Corporation, Family Law, Administrative Proceedings, Injunctions, Public Utilities, Labor Law, Chancery Practice and Oil and Gas Law.
See Professional Biographies, SPRINGFIELD, ILLINOIS

Bruner, James W., (BV) .... '67 '94 C.98 B.S. L.1187 J.D. [Brown,H.&S.]
Brunsman, John J., (AV) ....'50 '75 C.813 B.A. L.276 J.D. Atty. Gen.
Bucher, Bradley Roger, (BV) ....'64 '93 C.338 B.S. L.61 J.D. State Atty. Gen. Off.

Bucklin, Bradford C., (BV) '54 '80 C.339 B.A. L.801 J.D.
230 West Carpenter Street, P.O. Box 2346, 62705
Telephone: 217-544-5441 Toll Free: 888-646-3600 Fax: 217-789-1210
Email: bucklin@prodigy.net URL: http://www.bucklinlaw.com
Automobile Accidents, Personal Injury, Wrongful Death, Workers Compensation, Social Security.
See Professional Biographies, SPRINGFIELD, ILLINOIS

Buell, Linda Moscato .... '51 '76 C.822 A.B. L.209 J.D. Commerce Comm.
Buerkett, Lorilea, (BV) ....'56 '93 C&L.585 E.D., J.D. [Brown,H&S.]
Bullard, Jacqueline L. ....'61 '97 C&L.339 B.A., J.D. Asst. Def.

Cadigan, Patrick J., (AV) .... '36 '61 C.910 B.A. L.339 LL.B. 2130 Sylvan Rd.‡
Cahnman, Samuel J. ....'54 '78 C&L.339 B.S.B.A., J.D. 915 S. Second Street
Capitano, Nelson Joseph '12 '41 C&L.569 B.A., J.D.
(adm. in NY; not adm. in IL) 2601 Montvale Dr.‡
Cardosi, Julie A., (BV) ....'60 '86 C.338 B.S. L.221 J.D. [J.A.Cardosi]
Cardosi, Julie A., P.C., Law Office of, (BV) ....3040 Spring Mill Drive, Suite B
Carlisle, Thomas J. ....'45 '79 C.427 B.A. L.365 J.D. State Dept. of Nuclear Safety
Carlson, Bruce L. ....'52 '78 C.427 B.A. L.352 J.D. Ill. Environ. Protection Agcy.
Carter, Joyce E. ....'48 '85 C.1247 B.A. L.734 J.D. Asst. State's Atty.
Casey, John J., (BV) ....'32 '59 C&L.734 J.D. [Casey&C.]
Casey & Casey, (BV) .... 1231 S.Eighth St.
Casper, Donald J., (BV) ....'37 '63 C.1151 B.S. L.339 LL.B. [D.J.Casper]
Casper, Donald J., P.C., (BV) ....2206 Watson Road
Castle, Creighton R. ....'66 '93 C.338 B.S. L.365 J.D. [Giffin,W.C.&B.]
Cate, Matthew J., (BV) .... '75 '00 C.927 B.A. L.801 J.D. [Ⓐ Barber S.H.&H.]
Cavanagh, C. Joseph ....'32 '61 C&L.276 B.S., LL.B. 605 Williams Blvd.
Cavanagh, Peter C. .... '70 '97 C.338 B.S. L.365 J.D. [Cavanagh&M.]
Cavanagh, William K., Jr., (AV) .... '52 '79 C.276 A.B. L.365 J.D. [Cavanagh&O.]
Cavanagh & Madonia, (CV) .... 403 East Adams Street
Cavanagh & O'Hara, (AV) .... 407 E. Adams Street
Cavanaugh, Jerry D. ...... '60 '85 C.338 B.S. L.801 J.D. Sr. State Comr. of Bks. & Tr. Cos.
Chapin, Charles A., (AV) ....'21 '50 C.118 A.B. L.477 J.D. [Ⓒ Brown,H.&S.]
Cherry, Diana N., (BV) ....'52 '76 C.289 B.A. L.128 J.D. [Metnick,C.F.&S.]
Chesley, Patrick J., (BV) ....'49 '74 C&L.339 B.S., J.D. Asst. U.S. Atty.
Chipman, James W. ..... '57 '82 C.337 A.B. L.801 J.D. Exec. Dir., IL Prop. Tax App. Bd.
Ciaccio, Joseph, (CV) .... '51 '80 C.734 B.A. L.589 J.D. Pres., Ill. Railroad Assn.
Ciaccio, Joseph J., Sr. ....'22 '56 C.999 L.996 LL.B. 1638 S. MacArthur
Cicci, Raymond J., (BV) ....'45 '73 C&L.221 B.S., J.D. 415 S. 7th St.
Cinotto, James V. .... '56 '81 C&L.339 B.A., J.D. Law Clk., U.S. Bkrptcy. Ct.
Claggett, W. Stephen ....'38 '63 C&L.339 A.B., LL.B. Ill. St. Com. Comm.
Clarke, Marylynn McGuire '49 '89
C.416 A.B. L.209 J.D. Ill. Hospital & Health Sys. Assn.
Clary, Joseph P. ....'59 '90 C.1105 B.A. L.602 J.D. P.O Box 10083
Cline, Gary L., (BV) '56 '81 C&L.339 B.A., J.D.
[Rammelkamp,B.K.K.F.&L.] (⊙Jacksonville)
Cochran, Mark S. ....'52 '77 C.679 B.S. L.74 J.D. [Bellatti,B.H.&C.]
Cohen, Robert Lawrence ....'54 '79 C.209 B.A. L.365 J.D. Legis. Ref. Bur.
Cohen, Robert S., (AV) ....'32 '59 C.339 B.S. L.910 J.D. [Ⓒ Giffin,W.C.&B.]
Coleman, Edward G., (BV) ....'22 '50 C.999 L.602 J.D. 21 Hawthorne Ln.
Collins, Elizabeth L., (BV) ....'46 '74 C&L.339 A.B., J.D. Asst. U.S. Atty.
Collins, Gregory D., (BV) ....'54 '79 C.339 B.S. L.801 J.D. Levi, Ray, & Shoup
Collins, William E., (AV) ....'16 '39 C&L.339 B.A., LL.B. 2424 Manchester Dr.‡
Colliton, Edward O. ....'20 '51 C.755 L.748 LL.B. 4101 W. Iles Ave., Apt. 110‡
Cona, Roberta Pilant ....'36 '78 C.225 B.A. L.502 J.D. 1608 Noble Ave‡
Cona, Robin Pilant, (CV) '36 '78
C.225 B.A. L.502 J.D. Asst. Legal Adv., State Bd. of Educ.
Connelly, Claudia Ausdal ....'59 '85 C&L.339 B.A., J.D. 3920 Stone Bridge Rd.
Connelly, Michael C. .... '57 '85 C&L.339 B.S., J.D. [Sorling,N.H.C.&C.]
Connor, Kevin J., (AV) '62 '87 C.339 B.A. L.146 J.D.
Gen. Coun. & Dir. of Bus. Regul., Gov. Exec. Off., Off of Mgmt. and Budg.
Connor, William J., (BV) .... '64 '90 C.339 B.A. L.801 J.D. [Connor]
Connor Law Offices, (BV) ....2160 South 6th Street
Cornell, Arthur B., Jr., (BV) '56 '81 C.597 B.A. L.910 J.D.
The Honorable Jeanne E. Scott Chambers, U.S. Dist. Ct., IL Central Dist.
Corr, Kevin R. '55 '80 C.339 B.A. L.424 J.D.
Supvr. Spec. Agent/Chf. Div. Coun., F.B.I.
Corrigan, Terence J., (BV) ....'55 '85 C.338 B.S. L.801 J.D. Asst. Atty. Gen.
Costello, Michael J., (AV) ....'34 '62 C.98 B.S. L.146 J.D. 820 S. 2nd St., Ste. 1
Covington, James R., III ....'54 '79 C.234 B.A. L.623 J.D. State Bar Assn.
Cox, J. Randall, (BV) ....'66 '91 C.388 B.A. L.801 J.D. [Feldman,W.D.&B.]

Craig & Craig
(See Mattoon)

Craven, Donald M., (BV) ....'56 '81 C.747 B.A. L.801 J.D. [D.M.Craven]
Craven, James C., (AV) ....'25 '50 C&L.339 B.A., J.D. 1005 North 7th Street

Craven, Donald M., P.C., (BV)
1005 North 7th Street, 62702-3918
Telephone: 217-544-1777 Fax: 217-544-0713
URL: http://www.cravenlawoffice.com
Donald M. Craven;—Scott B. Sievers.
Media and First Amendment, Libel Defense, Intellectual Property, Commercial Transactions, Commercial Litigation, Appellate Practice and Legislative Law.
See Professional Biographies, SPRINGFIELD, ILLINOIS

Cross, Roland R. ....'65 '01 C.207 B.A. L.734 J.D. [Ⓐ Brown,H.&S.]
Cudmore, Byron G. ....'52 '77 C.339 B.S. L.801 J.D. U.S. Mag. J.
Cullen, Mark K., (BV) ....'62 '88 C.597 B.A. L.339 J.D. [Sorling,N.H.C.&C.]
Cunningham, Edward J., (AV) ....'33 '60 C.976 A.B. L.145 J.D. [Ⓒ Brown,H.&S.]
Cunningham, Joseph F., Jr. ....'24 '52 C.201 A.B. L.910 J.D. 7014 Piper Glen Dr.‡
Curtis, William T. '47 '79 C.57 B.A. L.146 J.D.
Sutheran Child and Family Servs. of Ill.
Darby, Karen S. '47 '80 C.117 B.A. L.608 J.D.
(adm. in OH; not adm. in IL) 2395 W. Jefferson Street
David, Roger E. '45 '86 C.801 B.A. L.339 J.D.
Asst. Legal Advsr., Ill. State Brd. of Educ.
Davis, Thomas E., (BV) ....'54 '79 C.838 B.A. L.1292 J.D. State of IL, Atty. Gen. Off.
Davlantis, Daniel J., (BV) ....'63 '88 C.339 B.A. L.801 J.D. [Ⓐ Scott&S.]
Davlin, Kevin J., (BV) ....'59 '83 C.338 B.S. L.425 J.D. [Ⓒ Livingstone,M.O.&D.]
Dees, Brian J., (CV) ....'60 '89 C.357 B.A. L.339 J.D. [Dees]

Dees Law Office, (CV)
1035 South Second Street, 62704
Telephone: 217-528-9226 Fax: 217-528-6837 URL: http://www.deeslawoffice.com
Email: brian@deeslawoffice.com URL: http://www.lawyers.com/dees-law
Brian J. Dees.
Divorce, Family Law, Child Custody, Child Support, Bankruptcy, Workers Compensation, Driving While Intoxicated, Personal Injury.
See Professional Biographies, SPRINGFIELD, ILLINOIS

Deffenbaugh, Robert W., (AV) .... '20 '48 C&L.339 B.A., J.D. 955 S. Durkin Dr.
Dehen, Robert E. ....'16 '53 C.999 L.996 LL.B. 2108 Kenwood‡
Demeroukas, Christopher .... '64 '90 C&L.339 J.D. 1021 North Grand Avenue, E
Denes, Jane N., (BV) ....'51 '84 C.788 B.A. L.910 J.D. [Posegate&D.]
Denney, Shawn W., (AV) .... '51 '76 C.430 B.A. L.339 J.D. Sr. Coun. to the Atty. Gen.
De Saint Phalle, Alexandra, (BV) .... '51 '77 C.145 B.A. L.1119 J.D. [Londrigan,P.&R.]
Dinardo, E. Zachary, (CV) ....'73 '99 C.338 B.A. L.734 J.D. [Ⓐ Sorling,N.H.C.&C.]
Doctors, Rachel .... '62 '88 C.477 B.A. L.665 J.D. 1021 N. Grand Ave. E.
Dove, Paulette F., (BV) ....'71 '97 C.1044 B.A. L.904 J.D. [Drake,N.&M.]

Drake, David L., (AV) ....'48 '73 C.927 B.A. L.146 J.D. [Drake,N.&M.]
Drake, Hugh F., (BV) ....'70 '99 C&L.339 B.A., J.D. [Brown,H.&S.]
Drake, James M., (BV) ....'28 '56 C&L.477 A.B., LL.B. 1300 S. 8th St.

Drake, Narup & Mead, P.C., (AV)
107 East Allen Street, 62704
Telephone: 217-528-9776 Telecopier: 217-528-9401
URL: http://www.dnmpc.com
David L. Drake; Richard H. Narup; Randall A. Mead; Kirk W. Laudeman; Paulette F. Dove;—Christian D. Biswell; Steven C. Ward.
Insurance Defense, General Civil and Trial Practice in all Courts, Professional Liability, Personal Injury, Probate, Real Estate, Legal Malpractice, Medical Malpractice Law, Arbitration and Mediation.
See Professional Biographies, SPRINGFIELD, ILLINOIS

Draper, Carl R., (BV) ....'55 '81 C.98 B.S. L.339 J.D. [Feldman,W.D.&B.]
Dratler, Owen ....'50 '75 C.24 B.A. L.982 J.D. Sr. Labor Rel. Atty.
Draznin, Anne L. ....'45 '71 C.231 B.A. L.339 J.D. Prof., Univ. of IL-Springfield
Driver, N. LaDonna, (BV) .... '— '94 C.806 B.A. L.801 J.D. [Hodge D.Z.]
Druhot, Denise M., (BV) ....'— '87 C.880 B.A. L.801 J.D. [Brown,H.&S.]
Duggan, Timothy E., (BV) ....'52 '80 C&L.801 B.A., J.D. [Stine,G.&D.]
Dunn, James S., (BV) ....'51 '79 C.340 B.A. L.801 J.D. [Dunn&M.]
Dunn & McMenamin, (BV) ....212 S. 2nd St.
Durbin, Richard J. ....'44 '69 C&L.276 B.S., J.D. P.O. Box 1949
Durr, Michael M., (BV) ....'65 '92 C.338 B.S. L.801 J.D. [Rabin,M.&H.]
Dutton, Marcilene ....'61 '90 C.357 B.A. L.420 J.D. 2020 Timberbrook Drive
Dwyer, Edward W., (AV) ....'— '88 C.37 B.A. L.801 J.D. [Hodge D.Z.]
Eack, Kevin D. .... '58 '84 C.927 B.S. L.801 J.D. IL State Police, Off. of the Dir.
Easum, Nancy G. ....'56 '81 C.340 B.A. L.879 J.D. Dep. Gen. Coun. to Secy. of State
Ebert, William B. '28 '54 C&L.352 B.S., J.D.
(adm. in IA; not adm. in IL) Asst. V.P. & Sr. Tr. Offr., First Natl. Bk. of Springfield‡
Edmiston, Charles N., II, (BV) '54 '80 C.339 B.S. L.352 J.D.
[Ⓐ Kanoski&Assoc.] (ⓒBloomington, Macomb, Peoria, Quincy, Rushville)
Edwards, David O., (BV) ....'70 '95 C&L.339 B.S., J.D. [Giffin,W.C.&B.]
Edwards, Richard C., (BV) ....'44 '74 C&L.339 A.B., J.D. Legislative Refer. Bur.
Eggers, Robert J. ....'44 '75 C.339 B.S. L.365 J.D. Assoc. Cir. J.
Egizii, Mary Jo, (BV) ....'47 '89 C.338 B.A. L.365 J.D. 1 Horace Mann Plz.
Ellis, Jon K., (BV) ....'52 '86 C.927 B.A. L.734 J.D. 1035 S. Second St.
Elmore, James E., (BV) ....'58 '83 C&L.801 B.A., J.D. [Elmore&R.]
Elmore & Reid, (BV) ....808 S. 2nd Street
England, Stephen J. '51 '76 C.339 A.B. L.94 J.D.
Chief Legal Coun., State Dept. of Nuclear Safety
Enlow, James R., (BV) ....'63 '88 C.339 B.A. L.801 J.D. [Scott&S.]
Enlow, William R., (BV) ....'47 '79 C.339 B.A. L.146 J.D. [Sorling,N.H.C.&C.]
Enoex, Robert N., Jr., (BV) '49 '77 C.813 B.A. L.734 J.D.
Chief Coun., Ill. Dept. of Ins.
Ervin, Cynthia ....'66 '91 C.98 B.S. L.910 J.D. 1 N. Old State Capitol Plz., Ste. 325
Essenburg, Sheryl K., (BV) ....'53 '78 C.114 B.A. L.339 J.D. Asst. State Atty.
Essig, Lawrence J. ....'53 '83 C.338 B.S. L.46 J.D. Asst. Dep. Def.
Estep, Thomas B., Sr. ....'07 '39 C.502 A.B. L.477 J.D. Invest. Trustee‡
Evans, Charles H. ....'22 '49 C&L.339 A.B., J.D. U.S. Mag. J.
Evans, Verne H. ....'37 '63 C.937 B.S. L.597 J.D. [ⓒ McNamara&E.]
Eveloff, Steven, (BV) ....'41 '71 C&L.910 B.S.B.A., J.D. 1300 S. 8th St.
Ewart, Stephen C. ....'48 '77 C.197 B.A. L.209 J.D. Dep. Coun., E.P.A.
Fahey, James G., (BV) ....'61 '97 C.750 B.A. L.734 J.D. [Ⓐ Sorling,N.H.C.&C.]
Fain, Cynthia M. '62 '88 C&L.352 B.A., J.D.
Sr. Asst. Gen. Coun., Teachers' Retirement Sys. of Ill.
Fairfield, Emmet A., (AV) ....'58 '81 C&L.339 B.S., J.D. [Brown,H.&S.]
Farrand, Walter F. ....'22 '55 L.365 J.D. 8 Timberline Dr.
Feldman, Howard W., (AV) .... '46 '73 C.679 B.S. L.1119 J.D. [Feldman,W.D.&B.]

Feldman, Wasser, Draper & Benson, (AV)
1307 South Seventh Street, P.O. Box 2418, 62705
Telephone: 217-544-3403 Facsimile: 217-544-1593
Email: feldwass@feldwass.com URL: http://www.feldman-wasser.com
Members of Firm: Howard W. Feldman; Stanley N. Wasser; Carl R. Draper; Fredric Benson; J. Randall Cox. Associates: Kelli Ellen Hillis; Michelle L. Blackburn; James J. Rammelkamp. Of Counsel: Thomas J. Immel.
Administrative Law, Civil Litigation and Appeals, Civil Rights, Construction Law, Criminal Defense, Domestic Relations, General Practice.
Representative Clients: Williams Brothers Construction Co.; Illinois Capital Development Board. Medical Equipment Co.;
Reference: Town & Country, Springfield, Illinois.
See Professional Biographies, SPRINGFIELD, ILLINOIS

Ferguson, Mark H., (BV) ....'53 '78 C&L.339 B.A., J.D. [ⓒ Sorling,N.H.C.&C.]
Fathauer, Emily B. ....'80 '05 C.340 B.A. L.734 J.D. [Ⓐ Sorling,N.H.C.&C.]
Feuer, I. J. ....'19 '43 L.996 LL.B. P.O. Box 11080
Feurer, William E., (BV) ....'34 '71 C.502 B.J. L.339 J.D. [W.E.Feurer]
Feurer, William E., Ltd., (BV) ....919 S. 8th St.
Finne, Bruce J. ....'42 '67 C.238 B.A. L.209 J.D. Exec. Dir., State Civil Serv. Comm.
Finnell, Matthew J. ....'55 '79 C.221 B.A. L.861 J.D. Ct. Admr., Ill. Ct. of Claims
Fitzgerald, Mary K. ....'58 '84 C&L.734 B.A., J.D. [Fitzgerald&F.]
Fitzgerald, Patrick W. ....'53 '87 C&L.734 B.A., J.D. [Fitzgerald&F.]
Fitzgerald & Fitzgerald, Ltd. ....2916 Interlacken Drive
Floren, Arleen ...... '50 '91 C.1183 B.A. L.801 J.D. Admin. Law J., Educ. Labor Rel. Bd.
Flynn, Neil F., (AV) ....'54 '80 C.927 B.A. L.734 J.D. 1035 S. 2nd St.
Fodor, Troy A., (BV) ....'66 '91 C.645 B.S., B.A. L.801 J.D. [T.A.Fodor]
Fodor, Troy A., P.C., (BV) ....913 South Sixth Street
Fornoff, Chad D. ....'67 '93 C.430 B.A. L.339 J.D. [Ⓐ R.E.Wagner&Assoc.]
Foust, Jeffrey D., (BV) ....'50 '75 C.347 A.B. L.1119 J.D. Asst. Appl. Def.
Frazier, Richard D., (BV) ....'61 '86 C.234 B.A. L.801 J.D. [Metnick,C.F.&S.]

Freeborn & Peters LLP, (AV)
217 E. Monroe Street Suite 202, 62701 ⊙
Telephone: 217-535-1060 Fax: 217-535-1069
URL: http://www.freebornpeters.com
Partners: Roger H. Bickel; Ann M. Zwick. Associate: Jennifer L. Milos.
Corporate Counseling and Transactions; Litigation and Alternative Dispute Resolution; Compliance with Regulations by Government Agencies.
Chicago, Illinois Office: 311 South Wacker Drive, Suite 3000, 60606. Telephone: 312-360-6000. Fax: 312-360-6520.
See Professional Biographies, SPRINGFIELD, ILLINOIS

Friedman, Simon L., (AV) ....'21 '44 C&L.339 A.B., J.D. [ⓒ Brown,H.&S.]
Fuller, Edwin F. ....'13 '52 C.273 A.B. L.734 LL.B. 510 E. Monroe St., 3rd Fl.‡
Fulton, E. M., Jr., (BV) ....'33 '56 C.586 B.A. L.846 J.D. [ⓒ T.A.Fodor] (ⓒLincoln)
Fultz, Daniel L. ....'68 '04 C.234 B.A. L.734 J.D. [Fultz]

Fultz Law Offices
524 East Capitol Avenue, 62701
Telephone: 217-492-1560 Fax: 217-492-1562
Email: danfultz@sbcglobal.net URL: http://www.brunsfultz.com

(This Listing Continued)

Fultz Law Offices (Continued)
Member of Firm: Daniel L. Fultz.
Criminal Defense, Family Law, Estate Planning, Real Estate, Governmental Affairs.
See Professional Biographies, SPRINGFIELD, ILLINOIS

Funk, Donald H., (AV) ....'37 '63 C&L.597 B.A., J.D. [Van Meter,O.&F.]
Fyans, Angela Marie ....'74 '02 C.879 B.A. L.347 J.D. Asst. State Atty.
Gaffney, Elizabeth R. .... '72 '04 C.788 B.A. L.424 J.D. [Ⓐ Giffin,W.C.&B.]
Gain, E. Frederick C., (CV) ....'40 '65 C&L.910 B.S.E., J.D. 1731 S. Park Ave.
Gainer, Irene H. ....'47 '91 C.719 B.S. L.365 J.D. 607 E. Adams St.
Ganski, Linda S. ....'51 '76 C.339 B.A. L.209 J.D. Staff Atty., Dept. of Mental Health
Gardner, Albert J. ....'48 '74 C.339 B.S. L.734 J.D. A.G. Edwards & Sons, Inc.
Gates, Gordon W., (BV) ....'61 '86 C.352 B.B.A. L.589 J.D. [Gates,W.&S.]

Gates, Wise & Schlosser, P.C., (AV)
1231 South 8th Street, 62703
Telephone: 217-522-9010 Fax: 217-522-9020
URL: http://www.gwspc.com
Gordon W. Gates; D. Peter Wise; Frederick J. Schlosser;—Bradley B. Wilson; Todd M. Goebel.
Criminal Defense, Federal Criminal Law, Business Transactions, Commercial Litigation, Real Estate Transactions, Corporate Law, Personal Injury, Civil Rights, General Litigation and Appeals.
See Professional Biographies, SPRINGFIELD, ILLINOIS

Gehman, Larry K. ....'43 '68 C.937 B.A. L.597 J.D. Exec. Dir., Merit Commission
Germann, Carl Clark, (BV) ....'45 '72 C.337 B.S. L.339 J.D. [Sorling,N.H.C.&C.]
Gibson, Michael O., (CV) ....'42 '70 C.750 B.A. L.339 J.D. Ill. Nat. Bk.
Giffin, William M., (BV) ....'18 '48 C.339 L.597 U.S. Mag.

Giffin, Winning, Cohen & Bodewes, P.C., (AV)
1 West Old State Capitol Plaza, Suite 600 Myers Building, P.O. Box 2117, 62705
Telephone: 217-525-1571 Facsimile: 217-525-1710
Email: gifwinlaw@gifwinlaw.com URL: http://www.gifwinlaw.com
D. Logan Giffin (1890-1980); Montgomery S. Winning (1892-1966); C. Terry Lindner (1903-1987); Alfred F. Newkirk (1904-1980); James M. Winning (Retired); Herman G. Bodewes; John L. Swartz; R. Mark Mifflin; David A. Herman; Michael Joseph Mannion; David O. Edwards; Creighton R. Castle;—Philip C. Kaufmann; Kent Gray; Christopher E. Sherer; Elizabeth R. Gaffney; Kristina E. Mony. Of Counsel: Robert S. Cohen; Ronald W. Periard; Carolyn Taft Grosboll.
General Civil Trial and Appellate Practice in Federal and State Courts. Corporation, Bankruptcy, Banking and Financial Institutions, Commercial Law, Employment Law, Real Estate, Taxation, Probate and Estates, Legislative Affairs and Administrative Law.
Representative Clients: Grinnell Mutual Reinsurance Co.; Illinois League of Financial Institutions; Great Central Insurance Cos.; Prime Panels Inc.; Family Video Inc.
See Professional Biographies, SPRINGFIELD, ILLINOIS

Giganti, Adam, (BV) ....'63 '90 C.339 B.A. L.734 J.D. [Stratton,G.S.&K.]
Giganti, Francis J., (AV) ....'50 '76 C.352 B.A. L.1000 J.D. 85 Old State Capitol Plz.
Gjerde, Ronald L. ....'53 '80 C.338 B.S. L.339 J.D. Legal Coun., Off. of Lt. Gov.
Goebel, Todd M. ....'75 '01 C.339 B.S. L.801 J.D. [Ⓐ Gates,W.&S.]
Goldman, Alan L. ....'49 '74 C.339 B.A. L.94 J.D. P.O. Box 1180
Gonzalez, Catherine Jane, (CV) ....'58 '83 C.339 B.S. L.36 J.D. [Presney,K.&P.]
Gorman, Mary P., (AV) ....'51 '77 C.700 B.A. L.339 J.D. U.S. Bkrptcy. J.
Gottfried, Theodore A. ....'40 '66 C.1016 B.A. L.365 LL.B. State Appl. Def.
Gower, Edward R. ....'55 '80 C.210 B.A. L.893 J.D. [Hinshaw&C.]
Graham, Hugh J., III, (AV) .... '37 '61 C&L.339 B.A., LL.B. [Graham&G.]

Graham and Graham, Ltd., (AV) BB
1201 South Eighth Street, 62703
Telephone: 217-523-4569 Fax: 217-523-4656
James M. Graham (1851-1945); James J. Graham (1880-1965); Hugh J. Graham (1877-1972); Hugh J. Graham, Jr. (1910-1994); Hugh J. Graham, III;—Richard J. Wilderson; Nancy Eckert Martin; Bradley E. Huff; Ryan R. Wilson; Nathan L. Wetzel.
General Civil Practice in all Courts of Record and Commissions. Health Care and Hospital Law. Probate and Real Estate Law. Trials.
Counsel for: Hospital Sisters Health System.
Representative Clients: Illinois and Midland Railway; SPCSL Railway; St. Anthony's Memorial Hospital, Effingham; St. Mary's Hospital, Decatur; St. John's Hospital, Springfield.
See Professional Biographies, SPRINGFIELD, ILLINOIS

Gray, Kent ....'70 '02 C.424 B.B.A. L.734 J.D. [Ⓐ Giffin,W.C.&B.]
Gray, Thomas Stewart, (BV) '51 '86
C&L.801 B.S., J.D. Gen. Coun., Teachers' Retirement Sys. of Ill.
Gray, Thomas W. ....'18 '53 C.801 A.B. L.996 LL.B. 2512 Somerton Rd.‡
Green, Edward R., (BV) ....'50 '75 C.388 B.A. L.352 J.D. [Hinshaw&C.]
Green, Martin, (BV) ....'64 '97 C.927 B.A. L.734 J.D. Exec. Asst. Atty. Gen.
Greer, Daniel J., (BV) ....'41 '66 C.611 B.A. L.339 J.D. [Stine,G.&D.]
Gregory, Charles W. '21 '51 C&L.923 B.S., LL.B.
(adm. in WV; not adm. in IL) 2308 Bates Ave.‡
Grenzebach, Eric L., (BV) ....'44 '73 C.207 B.A. L.424 J.D. [Brown,H.&S.]
Grigg, Erritt Hill ....'70 '00 State's Atty., Sangomon Co.
Grischow, Raylene DeWitte ....'72 '99 C.338 B.S. L.910 J.D. [Ⓐ Hinshaw&C.]
Grohne, James A., (BV) ....'46 '73 C.174 B.S. L.339 J.D. Asst. States Atty.
Grosboll, Carolyn Taft ....'61 '88 C&L.801 B.A., J.D. [ⓒ Giffin,W.C.&B.]
Grummon, Richard R., Law Offices of '18 '50
C.187 A.B. L.996 LL.B. 1000 First Natl. Bk. Bldg.‡
Gulley, Roy O. ....'24 '48 C&L.339 B.S., J.D. 1st of America Center, Ste.575
Gunnarson, Charles W. '65 '90 C&L.339 A.B., J.D.
Asst. Coun., IL Envir. Protec. Agcy., Legal Coun. Div.
Hack, Susanne Meredith ....'74 '00 C&L.339 B.A., J.D. 406 State House
Haddock, Gary L. ....'41 '66 C&L.339 A.B., LL.B. 245 N. 5th St.
Hagan, Deborah, (BV) ....'56 '82 C.473 B.A. L.201 J.D. Asst. Atty. Gen.
Hagen, Henry C., (BV) ....'45 '70 C.357 B.A. L.879 J.D. [Loewenstein,H.&S.]
Hahn, Fredrick W. ....'56 '81 C.339 B.A. L.801 J.D. Chf. Coun.
Hairston, Leslie A. ....'61 '91 C.966 B.A. L.424 J.D. State's Atty. App, Pros.
Hall, David Patrick, (CV) ....'63 '93 C&L.1119 B.S., J.D. 1119 South Sixth Street
Hall, Robert T. ....'52 '80 C.430 B.S. L.801 J.D. Assoc. Cir. J.
Hamill, Thomas G. ....'68 '93 C&L.339 B.A., J.D. [Bellatti,B.H.&C.]
Haning, Carissa A. ....'75 '03 C.504 B.A. L.801 J.D. [Ⓐ Londrigan,P.&R.]
Hanken, W. Scott, (BV) ....'63 '89 C.436 B.A. L.190 J.D. [Rabin,M.&H.]
Hanley, William S., (AV) '39 '64
C.602 A.B. L.145 J.D. [ⓒ Sorling,N.H.C.&C.] (ⓒBlue Hill, ME)
Hanlon, James A., (BV) '54 '79
C.339 B.A. L.910 J.D. Asst. Chief Coun., Ill. Dept. of Pub. Health
Hanlon, John J. ....'57 '83 C.339 B.A. L.896 J.D. Asst. Def., Off. of State Appl. Def.
Hanna, Philip E., (AV) .... '20 '45 C.187 A.B. L.477 LL.B. [Sorling,N.H.C.&C.] ‡
Hanrahan, Donald J., (BV) ....'57 '82 C&L.339 B.A., J.D. [Sgro,H.&B.]
Hardy, William P., (BV) .... '61 '89 C.1247 B.A. L.801 J.D. [Hinshaw&C.]
Harless, Adrian E., (AV) ....'56 '82 C.339 B.S. L.734 J.D. [Heyl,R.V.&A.]
Harmon, Jacqueline P., (BV) ....'61 '94 C.444 B.S. L.801 J.D. 230 West Carpenter
Harms, Lisa M., (AV) ....'53 '78 C.578 B.A. L.904 J.D. 4600 Wildcat Run
Harris, David K., (BV) ....'51 '76 C.436 A.B. L.365 J.D. [D.Harris]
Harris, David, (BV) ....1307 S. 7th St., Ste. 1
Hart, Richard E., (AV) ....'42 '67 C&L.339 A.B., J.D. [Hart,S.&W.]

Hart, Southworth & Witsman, (AV)
One North Old State Capitol Plaza Suite 501, 62701-1323
Telephone: 217-753-0055 Telecopier: 217-753-1056
Richard E. Hart; Mike Southworth; Samuel J. Witsman; Timothy Rigby. Associate: Amy D. Sanders.
Public Finance, Municipal Bonds, Banks and Banking, Creditor Rights, Real Estate, Commercial Real Estate, Construction Law, Commercial Law, Business Law, Corporate Law, Probate, Trusts and Estates, Estate Planning, Employment Law, Insurance Law.
See Professional Biographies, SPRINGFIELD, ILLINOIS

Harvatin, Theodore J., (BV) .... '56 '81 C.388 B.A. L.339 J.D. [Harvatin]
Harvatin Law Offices, P.C., (BV) .... 1100 South Fifth Street
Haschemeyer, Delbert D. .... '41 '69 C.927 B.S. L.879 J.D. Asst. Atty. Gen.
Hastings, Michael W. '60 '87
C.379 B.A. L.900 J.D. Coun., Association of Ill. Elec. Cooperatives
Hawes, Hardin W. .... '45 '70 C.597 B.A. L.339 J.D. U.S. Bkrptcy. Clk.
Haxel, Martin J., (BV) .... '55 '81 C.801 B.S. L.734 J.D. [Livingstone,M.O.&D.]
Hayes, John G., (BV) .... '32 '59 C&L.339 B.A., LL.B. 13 McLean Ln.
Hayes, Patricia L. .... '58 '86 C.699 B.A. L.896 J.D. [Hayes]
Hayes Law Office .... 915 S. 4th St., Ste. 1
Heaton, Jeanne B. .... '— '88 C.339 B.A. L.1119 J.D. [Ⓐ Hodge D.Z.]
Hedges, Robert O. .... '22 '51 C.339 A.B. L.1119 J.D. 2317 Grinnell Dr.‡
Hedinger, Stephen F., (BV) .... '59 '88 C&L.801 B.A., J.D. [Hedinger]

Hedinger Law Office, (BV)
2601 South Fifth Street, 62703
Telephone: 217-523-2753 Facsimile: 217-523-4366
Email: hhlaw@cityscape.net URL: http://www.lawyers.com/hedingerlaw
Stephen F. Hedinger.
Environmental Law, Civil Litigation, Construction Law, Consumer Rights and Mediation.
See Professional Biographies, SPRINGFIELD, ILLINOIS

Hefti, Jan M. .... '46 '74 C.347 B.A. L.1119 J.D. 625 S College St.
Helmholz, Scott C., (BV) .... '53 '78 C.221 B.A. L.910 J.D. [Brown,H.&S.]
Helmich, Terry O. .... '38 '62 C&L.339 A.B., LL.B. Legislative Ref. Bureau

Hennessy & Roach, P.C., (AV)
2501 Chatham Road, Suite 220, 62704 ⊙
Telephone: 217-726-0037 Fax: 217-726-0137
Email: hennroach@hennessyroach.com URL: http://www.hennessyroach.com
Managing Partner: Stephen J. Klyczek;—Chrissie L. Peterson; Emilie A. Miller.
Workers Compensation Defense, including litigation, mediation and arbitration; Liability Defense, including insurance defense, construction accidents, post-structured work act; Employer Liability, retaliatory discharge; Premises Liability, industrial machinery, auto and truck, consumer products; Insurance Coverage, Transportation, Property Damage, Fire Loss, Motor Vehicle Accidents, Industrial Accidents; Civil, State and Federal Appeals, Industrial Commission Appeals.
Chicago, Illinois Office: Marquett Building, 140 S. Dearborn, Suite 520, 60603. Telephone: 312-346-5310. Fax: 512-346-5330.
St. Louis, Missouri Office: 720 Olive Street, Suite 2222, 63101. Telephone: 314-231-0770. Fax: 314-231-0990.
See Professional Biographies, SPRINGFIELD, ILLINOIS

Henriksen, John C. '52 '79 C.659 B.A. L.383 J.D.
Dep. Exec. Dir., State Assoc. of Aggregate Products
Herman, David A., (BV) .... '66 '92 C.338 B.S. L.589 J.D. [Giffin,W.C.&B.]
Hess, Lawrence J., (AVⓉ) .... '50 '75 C&L.734 B.A., J.D. [Ⓐ Kanoski&Assoc.]

Heyl, Royster, Voelker & Allen, Professional Corporation, (AV)
Suite 575, National City Center, P.O. Box 1687, 62705 ⊙
Telephone: 217-522-8822 Telecopier: 217-523-3902
Email: firm@hrva.com URL: http://www.hrva.com
Partners: Frederick P. Velde; Gary L. Borah; Gary S. Schwab; Adrian E. Harless; Scott D. Spooner; Daniel R. Simmons; Theresa M. Powell. Of Counsel: Sarah J. Pratt. Associates: April G. Troemper; Matthew R. Booker; John O. Langfelder; Peter E. Naylor.
General Civil Trial and Appellate Practice in all Courts, Insurance Defense, Workers' Compensation Defense, Professional Liability Defense, Truck Accidents, Construction Law, Railroad Accidents and Injuries, Insurance Coverage, Self Insured Defense, Products Liability Defense, Civil Rights, Asbestos Defense, Class Action Defense, Corporate Law, Health Care, Banking, Government, Employment, Environmental, Probate, Elder Law, Agribusiness, Immigration, Religious Institutions, Nonprofit and Charitable Organizations, College and University Law, and Real Estate.
Peoria, Illinois Office: Suite 600, Chase Building, 124 S.W. Adams, 61602. Telephone: 309-676-0400. Telecopier: 309-676-3374.
Urbana, Illinois Office: Suite 300, 102 East Main Street, P.O. Box 129, 61803-0129. Telephone: 217-344-0060. Telecopier: 217-344-9295.
Rockford, Illinois Office: Second Floor, National City Bank Building, 120 West State Street, P.O. Box 1288, 61105-1288. Telephone: 815-963-4454. Telecopier: 815-963-0399.
Edwardsville, Illinois Office: Suite 100, Mark Twain Plaza II, 103 West Vandalia Street, P.O. Box 467, 62025. Telephone: 618-656-4646. Telecopier: 618-656-7940.
See Professional Biographies, SPRINGFIELD, ILLINOIS

Hillis, Kelli Ellen, (BV) .... '73 '98 C.339 B.S. L.801 J.D. [Ⓐ Feldman,W.D.&B.]
Hiltabrand, Lori Poppe, (BV) .... '69 '97 C.340 B.A. L.801 J.D. [Koepke&H.]
Hines, Barry O., (AV) .... '47 '72 C&L.339 B.S., J.D. [Barber S.H.&H.]

Hinshaw & Culbertson LLP, (AV) BB
Hinshaw & Culbertson LLP is an Illinois registered limited liability partnership that has elected to be governed by the Illinois Uniform Partnership Act (1997)
400 South Ninth Street, Suite 200, 62701-1908 ⊙
Telephone: 217-528-7375 Facsimile: 217-528-0075 Telex: 880248
Email: kfox@hinshawlaw.com URL: http://www.hinshawlaw.com
Partners: D. Bradley Blodgett; Edward R. Gower; Edward R. Green; William P. Hardy; James M. Lestikow; John E. Nolan; Andrew M. Ramage; Russell L. Reed; J. William Roberts (Also at Chicago, Illinois Office); Charles R. Schmadeke. Associate: Raylene DeWitte Grischow.
Appellate, Banking & Financing, Bankruptcy & Creditors' Rights, Class Action Litigation, Civil Rights Defense, Commercial Litigation, Corporate, Construction Law, Director & Officer Liability, Employee Benefits, Environmental, Fidelity & Surety, General Liability Litigation, Government, Health Care, Insurance Coverage, Insurance and Reinsurance, Labor & Employment, Legal Malpractice, Medical Malpractice, Mergers & Acquisitions, Municipal Liability, Personal Injury Defense, Public Law, Products Liability Litigation, Professional Liability, Regulatory, Real Estate, School Law, Securities, Taxation, Transportation, White Collar Crime and Workers' Compensation Defense.
Other Office Locations: Chicago, Illinois; Appleton, Wisconsin; Belleville, Illinois; Boston, Massachusetts; Champaign, Illinois; Crystal Lake, Illinois; Edwardsville, Illinois; Fort Lauderdale, Florida; Jacksonville, Florida; Joliet, Illinois; Lisle, Illinois; Los Angeles, California; Miami, Florida; Milwaukee, Wisconsin; Minneapolis, Minnesota; New York, New York; Peoria, Illinois; Phoenix, Arizona; Portland, Oregon; Providence, Rhode Island; Rockford, Illinois; St. Louis, Missouri; San Francisco, California; Schererville, Indiana; Tampa, Florida; Waukegan, Illinois.
See Professional Biographies, SPRINGFIELD, ILLINOIS

Hodge, Katherine D., (AV) .... '— '86 C.259 B.S. L.801 J.D. [Hodge D.Z.]

Hodge Dwyer Zeman, (AV)
3150 Roland Avenue, P.O. Box 5776, 62705-5776
Telephone: 217-523-4900 Facsimile: 217-523-4948
URL: http://www.hdzlaw.com
Members of Firm: Edward W. Dwyer; Katherine D. Hodge; Christine G. Zeman; N. LaDonna Driver; Thomas G. Safley. Associates: Gale W. Newton; Jeanne B. Heaton; Monica T. Rios; Ryan E. Mohr. Of Counsel: James R. Schick.
Environmental Law.
See Professional Biographies, SPRINGFIELD, ILLINOIS

Hoffee, Carl O., (AV) .... '34 '58 C&L.339 LL.B. [Barber S.H.&H.]
Hoffmann, Frederick B., (BV) .... '41 '68 C.145 Ph.B. L.339 J.D. [Sorling,N.H.C.&C.]
Hogan, Michael W. .... '26 '54 C.225 A.B. L.861 LL.B. 425 S. 7th St.‡
Hogan, William James .... '61 '86 C&L.209 B.S.C., J.D. Admin. Law J., IL Dept. of Rev.
Holley, Grady E., (AV) .... '46 '70 C&L.339 B.S., J.D. [Holley&R.]

Holley & Rosen, (AV) BB
440 West South Grand Avenue, 62704
Mailing Address: P.O. Box 5036, Springfield, IL 62705
Telephone: 217-544-3368; Toll Free: 1-888-828-9037 Fax: 217-544-5262 URL: http://www.holleyrosenlaw.com
Email: hr@holleyrosenlaw.com URL: http://www.lawyers.com/holleyrosen
Members of Firm: Grady E. Holley; Steven J. Rosen. Associate: Peter C. Beard.
General Civil Trial and Appellate Practice in State and Federal Courts, Plaintiff Personal Injury, Insurance Defense, Plaintiffs Medical Malpractice, Employment Discrimination, Mediation/Arbitration, Workers Compensation, Automobile Accidents, Dog Bites, Slip and Fall, Wrongful Death.
See Professional Biographies, SPRINGFIELD, ILLINOIS

Hollis, Richard A., (BV) .... '32 '57 C&L.339 B.A., LL.B. 522 E. Monroe
Holman, Sandra J. '52 '76 C.910 B.A. L.94 J.D.
Assoc. Gen. Coun., Ill. Educ. Assn.-NEA
Holmes, Roger W. .... '51 '76 C&L.339 B.S., J.D. Assoc. Cir. J.
Holt, Michael J., (BV) .... '62 '90 C.35 B.S. L.365 J.D. [Quinn,J.H.&P.]
Hornyak, Juleann .... '48 '79 C.201 B.A. L.146 J.D. Clerk, Supm. Ct.
Horsley, G. William .... '10 '35 C.339 L.996 LL.B. 2615 Baronne Dr.
Horstman, Michael G., Jr. .... '72 '97 C.339 B.A. L.910 J.D. [Ⓐ Sorling,N.H.C.&C.]
Hosteny, John M., (BV) '55 '80 C&L.424 B.S., J.D.
Trooper's Lodge #41, Fraternal Order of Police
Howard, L. Joseph .... '49 '75 C.234 B.S.Ed. L.339 J.D. Asst. Atty. Gen.

Howard & Howard Attorneys, P.C.
(See Peoria)

Huebner, Roger D. L. .... '56 '83 C.234 B.A. L.365 J.D. Gen. Coun.
Huff, Bradley E., (BV) .... '64 '91 C.339 A.B. L.801 J.D. [Ⓐ Graham&G.]
Hughes, Patrick J., Jr., (AV) .... '35 '60 C&L.424 B.Sc., J.D. First Asst. Appl. Def.
Huntley, Edward W., (BV) .... '51 '76 C.855 B.A. L.659 J.D. 217 E. Monroe
Immel, Thomas J., (BV) .... '43 '68 C.597 B.A. L.424 J.D. [Ⓒ Feldman,W.D.&B.]
Immke, Keith H. .... '53 '78 C.339 A.B. L.801 J.D. Off. of the State Fire Marshal
Ingersoll, William D. .... '50 '81 C.338 B.S. L.464 J.D. E.P.A.
Ishmael, Joshua J. .... '78 '04 C.339 B.A. L.801 J.D. [Ⓐ Koepke&H.]
Jackson, Dean W., (BV) .... '55 '83 C.352 B.B.A. L.801 J.D. [Jackson]
Jackson, Thomas L. .... '56 '83 C.234 B.A. L.339 J.D. U.S. Small Bus. Admn.
Jackson Law Office, (BV) .... 264 N. Koke Mill Rd.
Jarrico, Bill '40 '78 C.685 B.A. L.426 J.D.
(adm. in CA; not adm. in IL) Tech. Consultant, Metamor Info. Servs.
Johansson, Tracy Ann .... '71 '00 C.338 B.S. L.801 J.D. Asst. Corp. Coun.
Johnson, David R. .... '47 '72 C&L.339 B.A., J.D. Staff Atty., Leg. Ref. Bur.
Johnson, Jo E., (CV) .... '66 '92 C.191 B.A. L.339 J.D. Senate Republican Staff
Jones, Lance T., (BV) .... '58 '84 C.234 B.A. L.209 J.D. 1100 South Fifth Street
Jones, Larry M. .... '47 '74 C.1082 B.A. L.339 J.D. Ill. Com. Comm.
Joyce, J. Patrick, Jr., (AV) .... '47 '72 C&L.424 B.A., J.D. [Brown,H.&S.]
Joyce, Joshua A. .... '74 '99 C.927 B.A. L.93 J.D. Asst. State's Atty.
Jurgens, Jeffrey R. .... '75 '00 C.338 B.S. L.30 J.D. [Ⓐ Sorling,N.H.C.&C.]
Kanoski, Ronald J., (BV) .... '47 '74 C.234 B.S. L.424 J.D. [Kanoski&Assoc.] ⊙
Kanoski & Associates, (BV)
2730 South MacArthur Boulevard (⊙Bloomington, Decatur, Macomb, Peoria, Quincy, Rushville)
Kappel, James L. '40 '64 C.734 B.S. L.339 J.D.
Spec. Asst. Chief Coun., Dept. of Transp.
Kassem, Jamiela Theresa, (CV) '74 '00 C.234 B.A. L.801 J.D.
200 S. 9th Street, Rm. 402
Kasten, Walter H., (BV) .... '34 '64 C.339 B.S. L.502 LL.B. 844 S. 2nd St.
Kauerauf, John A., (BV) .... '61 '86 C.340 B.A. L.339 J.D. [Sorling,N.H.C.&C.]
Kaufmann, Philip C. .... '73 '01 C.337 B.A. L.339 J.D. [Ⓐ Giffin,W.C.&B.]
Keith, John R., (BV) .... '48 '74 C.234 B.A. L.69 J.D. [Keith]
Keith Law Office, (BV) .... 217 E. Monroe St., Ste. 100
Kelley, Patrick W., (BV) .... '58 '83 C.98 B.S. L.188 J.D. Cir. J.
Kelly, James D., (BV) .... '47 '72 C.1151 B.A. L.339 J.D. [Presney,K.&P.] ⊙
Kelty, Thomas W. .... '45 '71 C.190 B.A. L.502 J.D. [Ⓒ Armstrong T.] (⊙Edwardsville)

Kelty Law Offices
(See Armstrong Teasdale LLP)

Kelty Law Offices, P.C. .... 3201 Pleasant Run, Suite A
Kenney, George W., (BV) .... '37 '64 C.357 B.A. L.365 J.D. [Kenney&P.]
Kenney & Pearson, (BV) .... 401 W. Monroe, Ste. 2
Kent, Marylou Lowder .... '51 '79 C.1247 B.A. L.801 J.D. Ill. State Bar Assn.
Kepner, Daniel E., (BV) .... '57 '82 C.339 B.S. L.352 J.D. [Kepner&R.]
Kepner & Reiser, (BV) .... 1028 S. Grand Ave., W.
Kerley, John E., (BV) .... '60 '89 C&L.801 B.S., J.D. [Kerley&Assoc.]

Kerley & Associates, P.C., Law Office of, (BV)
2131 W. White Oak Drive, Suite B2, 62704
Telephone: 217-698-0007 Fax: 217-726-0006
Email: lawyerjohn@aol.com URL: http://www.johnkerleylawfirm.com
John E. Kerley.
Collections, Estate Planning, Probate, Employment, Contested Estates, Business Advise, Financial Planning, Commercial Litigation, Insurance Coverage, Insurance Defense, Business Law, Commercial Law, Insurance, Real Estate Agents and Brokers Errors and Omissions, Personal Injury, Real Estate.
See Professional Biographies, SPRINGFIELD, ILLINOIS

Kerr, Gary E., (BV) .... '48 '74 C.589 B.A. L.597 J.D. [G.E.Kerr]
Kerr, Gary E., Ltd., (BV) .... 1020 S. 7th St.
Kim, Richard, (BV) .... '69 '94 C&L.896 B.A., J.D. [Ⓐ Metnick,C.F.&S.]
King, Gary P. .... '52 '77 C&L.879 B.S.C.E., J.D. Ill. Envir. Protection Agcy.
Kinion, Steve W. .... '65 '95 C.619 B.A. L.862 J.D. [Z.Stamp]
Kirn, Kim L. .... '60 '85 C.502 B.A. L.602 J.D. Asst. Legal Coun., Ofc. of Comptr.
Klein, Andrew J. .... '57 '84 C&L.801 B.S.B.A., J.D. E. Old State Cap. Plz.
Klingler, Gwenn .... '44 '81 C.611 B.A. L.273 J.D. State Rep.
Klyczek, Stephen J., (BV) .... '— '90 C&L.589 B.A., J.D. [Hennessy&R.]
Knuppel, Shelly Davis, (CV) '60 '86 C&L.339 B.A., J.D.
Reg. Coun., IL Dept. of Children & Family Servs.
Koepke, Kurt M., (BV) .... '61 '88 C.927 B.A. L.801 J.D. [Koepke&H.]

Koepke & Hiltabrand, P.C., (BV)
2050 West Iles, Suite G, 62704
Telephone: 217-726-8646 Fax: 217-726-8861
Kurt M. Koepke; Lori Poppe Hiltabrand;—Joshua J. Ishmael.
General Civil Trial and Appellate Practice in all Courts, Insurance Defense, Workers' Compensation Defense, Professional Liability Defense, Insurance Coverage, Self Insured Defense, Employment/ Discrimination Defense.
See Professional Biographies, SPRINGFIELD, ILLINOIS

Kopec, A. Michael, (BV) .... '50 '75 C.339 B.S. L.347 J.D. [Stratton,G.S.&K.]
Kopecky, Frank J. .... '42 '67 C&L.339 B.A., J.D. Sangamon State Univ.
Korte, R. Frederick .... '45 '81 C.801 B.S. L.1187 J.D. Admn. Law J.
Krajec, William A. .... '41 '68 C&L.339 A.B., J.D. 837 S. 4th St.
Krajewski, J. Phillip, (AV) .... '43 '69 C&L.339 B.A., J.D. [Baker,B.&K.]
Kreidler, Amy Strack .... '73 '99 C.74 B.S. L.201 J.D. Staff Atty.
Kroack, Laurel L. .... '59 '87 C.381 B.S. L.145 J.D. 1021 N. Grand Ave., E.
Kueper, Marilyn A., (BV) '52 '77
C.338 B.A. L.910 J.D. Chief, Asbestos Div., Atty. Gen. Off.
LaBarre, Alfred B. "Pete", (AV) .... '43 '68 C&L.339 B.S., J.D. [LaBarre&Y.]
LaBarre & Young, (AV) ....1300 South Eighth Street, Suite Two
Lahr, Guy M., III, (BV) ....'44 '73 C.465 B.A. L.734 J.D. [Kelty]
Lamar, Cynthia J. Stephenson '60 '97 C.1247 B.A. L.734 J.D.
V.P. & Asst. Gen. Coun., Reinsurance Assoc. of America
LaMarca, William, (BV) .... '53 '79 C.209 B.A. L.589 J.D. [LaMarca]
LaMarca Law Office, (BV) .... 1119 S. 6th St.
Lamont, Thomas R., (BV) .... '47 '73 C.338 B.S. L.339 J.D. [Brown,H.&S.]
Lang, James A. '61 '92 C.56 B.A. L.801 J.D.
Asst. Corp. Coun., City of Springfield (Legal Department)
Langfelder, John O. .... '56 '02 C.927 B.S. L.179 J.D. [Heyl,R.V.&A.]
Langley, Patricia A. ....'47 '75 C.157 B.A. L.215 J.D. Univ. of Ill.
Larson, Roma B., (BV) .... '55 '85 C&L.352 B.A., J.D. [Scott&S.]
Laudeman, Arthur N., (BV) ....'36 '67 C.339 B.S. L.365 J.D. [A.N.Laudeman]
Laudeman, Kirk W., (BV) ....'65 '90 C.339 B.A. L.365 J.D. [Drake,N.&M.]
Laudeman, Arthur N., Ltd., (BV) .... 107 E. Allen St.
Laughridge, Kristen C. .... '77 '04 C.1375 B.S. L.339 J.D. Asst. Atty. Gen.
Lawless, John J. .... '16 '39 C&L.734 LL.B. P.O. Box 2459
Layzell, Thomas D. '38 '66 C.357 B.A. L.339 J.D.
Chan., Bd. of Gov's. of State Colleges & Univ.
Leahy, John P., (BV) .... '68 '95 C.339 B.S. L.589 J.D. 403 E. Adams
Leahy, Mary L. C. .... '40 '66 C.424 B.S. L.145 J.D. 308 E. Canedy
Leblang, Theodore R. '49 '74 C.645 B.A. L.339 J.D.
Southern Ill. Univ. Sch. of Medicine
Lee, Mark N., The Law Offices of, (CV) '62 '90
C.357 B.A. L.336 J.D. 1101 S. Second Street
Leja, Carolyn H. .... '46 '83 C.209 B.A. L.146 J.D. Admin. Off. of the Ill. Cts.
Lesniak, James A. ....'46 '73 C.339 B.S. L.209 J.D. Pres., James A. Lesniak & Co.
Lessen, Larry L. .... '39 '62 C&L.339 A.B., LL.B. U.S. Bkrptcy. J.‡
Lestikow, James M., (AV) .... '48 '73 C.589 B.S. L.339 J.D. [Hinshaw&C.]
Levin, Tracy Ann '71 '00 C.338 B.S. L.801 J.D.
Asst. Corp. Coun., City of Springfield (Legal Department)
Lewis, James A. '40 '67 C.976 B.A. L.145 J.D.
(adm. in MS; not adm. in IL) Asst. U.S. Atty., Chief Civil Div.
Libby, Judith L., (BV) .... '48 '77 C.1016 B.A. L.365 J.D. State Appl. Def.
Lierman, Owen Donald .... '25 '51 L.339 J.D. 316 Cartwright Dr.‡
Lindahl, Norman C. .... '22 '57 C.57 A.B. L.209 J.D. 9 Whippoorwill Rd.‡
Lindsay, Nancy, (BV) '— '83 C.337 B.A. L.734 J.D.
[Rammelkamp,B.K.K.F.&L.] (⊙Jacksonville)
Lippa, Charles S. .... '33 '61 C.1191 B.Ed. L.209 J.D. P.O. Box 7592

Lipsky, Nolan, Law Offices of, (AV) '44 '69 C.339 B.S. L.146 J.D.
1100 S. 5th Street, 62703 ⊙
Telephone: 217-789-1607 Toll Free: 888-662-2612
URL: http://www.nolanlipsky.com
Family Law, Divorce, Custody, Paternity, Personal Injury, Criminal.
Petersburg Office: 106 East Jackson Street, 62675. Telephone: 217-632-2612. Fax: 217-532-2450.
See Professional Biographies, SPRINGFIELD, ILLINOIS

Livingstone, Mueller, O'Brien and Davlin, P.C., (AV) ....620 East Edwards Street
LoBue, Donald A., The Law Offices of, (BV) '46 '75
C.339 B.A. L.146 J.D. 1020 S. 7th St.
Locher, Bruce D., Law Office of, (BV) .....'41 '68 C.393 A.B. L.424 J.D. 1212 South 7th
Loewenstein, Ralph H., (AV) ....'48 '73 C.339 B.S. L.273 J.D. [Loewenstein,H.&S.]
Loewenstein, Hagen and Smith, P.C., (AV) .... 1204 South Fourth Street
Logan, Michael J., (BV) .... '43 '72 C.430 B.A. L.365 J.D. [M.J.Logan]

Logan, Michael J., Ltd., Law Office of, (BV)
837 S. 4th Street, P.O. Box 3163, 62708
Telephone: 217-522-8880 Fax: 217-522-8887
URL: http://www.lawyers.com/mikelogan
Michael J. Logan.
Personal Injury, Workers Compensation, General Practice.
See Professional Biographies, SPRINGFIELD, ILLINOIS

Londrigan, James T., (AV) .... '25 '50 C.339 L.146 J.D. [Londrigan,P.&R.] ‡
Londrigan, Thomas F., (AV) ....'37 '62 C.602 A.B. L.339 LL.B. [Londrigan,P.&R.]
Londrigan, Thomas F., Jr., (BV) .... '67 '92 C.152 B.A. L.602 J.D. [Londrigan&L.]
Londrigan, Timothy J., (BV) .... '57 '83 C&L.801 B.S., J.D. [Londrigan,P.&R.]
Londrigan & Londrigan, (BV) ....1227 S. 7th Street

Londrigan, Potter & Randle, P.C., (AV)
1227 South 7th Street, P.O. Box 399, 62705
Telephone: 217-544-9823 Telecopier: 217-544-9826 URL: http://www.lprpc.com
Email: lpr@lprpc.com URL: http://www.lawyers.com/lprpc
Thomas F. Londrigan; James R. Potter; Craig A. Randle; Alexandra De Saint Phalle; Timothy J. Londrigan;—Douglas J. Quivey; Carissa A. Haning. Of Counsel: James T. Londrigan.
General, Trial and Appellate Practice. Insurance, Negligence, Products Liability, Medical Malpractice, Employment Discrimination, Corporation and Antitrust Law.
See Professional Biographies, SPRINGFIELD, ILLINOIS

Loro, Marc C. ....'52 '77 C.338 B.A. L.910 J.D. Asst. States Atty.
Lott, Richard L., (BV) .... '35 '63 C.174 B.S. L.966 LL.B. [Lott&S.]
Lott and Surman, P.C., (BV) ....452 S. Grand Ave. W.
Lowe, Mary Lloyd ....'48 '80 C.388 B.A. L.365 J.D. Staff Coun., Ill. Dept. of Pub. Health
Lowery, Rosalie Howard ....'— '96 L.801 J.D. Asst. Atty. Gen.
Lowy, Barry G. ....'60 '87 C.393 B.A. L.861 J.D. 500 S. 2nd St.
Luke, Michael J. ....'51 '78 C&L.339 B.A., J.D. Sr. Asst. Atty. Gen., Atty. Gen. Off.
Lynch, Francis J., (BV) ....'59 '83 C&L.801 B.A., J.D. [Wolter,B.&L.]
Maddox, Joseph W. .... '23 '52 L.996 LL.B. 1019 S. 6th St.‡
Maddox, Matthew J., (BV) .... '56 '83 C.339 B.S. L.300 J.D. [Quinn,J.H.&P.]
Maddox, Nathan P. .... '51 '85 C.1247 B.A. L.801 J.D. Admin. Off. of the Ill. Cts.
Madonia, John M., (CV) ....'70 '97 C&L.339 B.A., J.D. [Cavanagh&M.]
Maher, Daniel L., Law Offices of, (BV) '57 '84 C.597 B.A. L.801 J.D.
926 South 7th St.
Malany, LeGrand L. .... '41 '70 C&L.339 B.S., J.D. 600 S. Rosehill
Manning, Claire A. .... '53 '79 C.98 B.A. L.424 J.D. [Brown,H.&S.]
Manning, Jennifer Mings ... '72 '98 C.234 B.A. L.589 J.D. Sr. Coun., Levi, Ray, & Shoup
Mannion, Michael Joseph, (BV) ....'67 '92 C.436 B.S. L.365 J.D. [Giffin,W.C.&B.]
Manson, Almon A., Jr., (BV) ....'49 '78 C.273 B.A. L.734 J.D. [Brown,H.&S.]
Manuel, Scott A. .... '60 '89 C.234 B.A. L.801 J.D. Appl. Pros.
Manuele, Anthony J. ....'15 '39 C&L.339 B.S., J.D. 939 S. 8th St.‡
Manuele, Peter J., (CV) .... '46 '85 C.1247 B.A. L.1187 J.D. [Manuele]
Manuele Law Office, (CV) ....939 S. 8th St.
Marcus, Julie M. .... '70 '94 C.339 B.A. L.801 J.D. [R.E.Wagner&Assoc.]
Martin, Nancy Eckert, (BV) .... '60 '85 C.339 B.S. L.801 J.D. [Graham&G.]
Martinez, Frank S., (CV) '62 '94 C&L.352 B.B.A., J.D.
Asst. Corp. Counsel, City of Springfield, Off. of Corp. Coun.
Mathewson, Mark S. .... '55 '85 C.966 B.A. L.339 J.D. Ill. Bar Journal
Matrisch, Steve ....'— '98 L.734 J.D. Asst. Atty. Gen.
Maxwell, Madalyn .... '26 '51 C&L.339 B.S., M.A. Asst. Atty. Gen.
May, Dirk A., (BV) ....'57 '83 C.339 B.S. L.734 J.D. Legal Services Support Ctr.
McAnulty, Dorothea F. .... '09 '32 L.996 1700 W. Washington St.‡
McCay, Jean A. .... '55 '80 C.221 B.A. L.339 J.D. Legis. Ref. Bur.
McClain, Linda S., (BV) ...... '57 '83 C.801 B.A. L.734 J.D. State's Atty. Appl. Pros. Off.
McComb, Susan S. .... '55 '87 C.176 B.A. L.365 J.D. 155 Pinehurst Dr.
McCullough, Mark E. .... '67 '98 C.612 B.S. L.862 J.D. Asst. Atty. Gen.
McDermott, Kevin N., (BV) '56 '87
C.339 B.S. L.734 J.D. 15 South Old State Capitol Plaza, Suite 103
McFadden, Amy L. .... '73 '98 C&L.339 B.S., J.D. Asst. Atty. Gen.
McFadden, Kevin J., (BV) .... '66 '92 C&L.339 B.A., J.D. [Z.Stamp]
McIntosh, Michael D. .... '56 '91 C.624 B.A. L.589 J.D. Dep. Chf. Legal Coun.
McMenamin, Joseph E., (BV) ....'53 '79 C.339 A.B. L.801 J.D. [Dunn&M.]
McNamara, Edward D., Jr., (BV) .... '43 '68 C.734 B.S. L.339 J.D. [McNamara&E.] ⊙

McNamara & Evans, (BV)
931 South Fourth Street, P.O. Box 5039, 62705 ⊙
Telephone: 217-528-8476 Telecopier: 217-528-8480
Email: mcnamara.evans@springnetl.com URL: http://www.mcnamaraevens.com
Member of Firm: Edward D. McNamara, Jr. Of Counsel: Verne H. Evans.
General Civil, Trial and Appellate Practice in State and Federal Courts. Administrative Practice before Governmental Agencies. Corporation, Insurance, Probate and Real Estate Law. Administrative and Governmental Law. Computer, Environmental, Franchise and Health Law. Public Utilities, Motor Carrier and Interstate Commerce Law.
Edwardsville, Illinois Office: 21 Glen-Ed Professional Park. Telephone: 618-656-3511; Telecopier: 618-656-3534.
See Professional Biographies, SPRINGFIELD, ILLINOIS

McNaught, Karen L., (BV) .... '60 '89 C&L.221 B.A., J.D. Asst. Atty. Gen.
McQuillan, Phillip, (BV) .... '52 '78 C.338 B.S. L.339 J.D. Asst. Atty. Gen.
McWard, Monroe D., (CV) ....'59 '85 C.339 B.S. L.879 J.D. [McWard] ⊙
McWard Law Office, (CV) ....1100 South Fifth Street (⊙Taylorville)
Mead, Randall A., (BV) ....'56 '81 C.927 B.A. L.801 J.D. [Drake,N.&M.]
Mehlick, John A. ....'51 '76 C.339 B.A. L.734 J.D. Sangamon Co. Cir. Ct.
Menninger, Karl A., II .... '50 '75 C.145 A.B. L.900 J.D. 100 South Grand Avenue East
Messina, Robert A. '73 '98 C.339 B.A. L.801 J.D.
Chief Legal Coun., Illinois Environmental Protection Agency
Metnick, Michael B., (AV) ....'47 '75 C.623 B.A. L.365 J.D. [Metnick,C.F.&S.]

Metnick, Cherry, Frazier & Sabin, L.L.P., (AV)
Second Floor, Myers Building, 1 West Old State Capitol Plaza, P.O. Box 12140, 62791
Telephone: 217-753-4242 Telefax: 217-753-4642 URL: http://www.springfieldlawfirm.com
Email: info@springfieldlawfirm.com URL: http://www.lawyers.com/springfieldlawfirm
Members of Firm: Michael B. Metnick; Diana N. Cherry; Richard D. Frazier; Scott A. Sabin. Associates: Richard Kim; Christopher G. Perrin.
General Trial and Appellate Practice. Criminal Defense, Workers Compensation, Personal Injury, Family Law, Labor and Employment Law, Estate Planning, Business Law.
See Professional Biographies, SPRINGFIELD, ILLINOIS

Mifflin, R. Mark, (BV) ....'51 '78 C.927 B.A. L.801 J.D. [Giffin,W.C.&B.]
Milhiser, John Charles ....'70 '97 C.1369 B.S. L.339 J.D. [Barber S.H.&H.]
Miller, David R. .... '52 '77 C.880 B.A. L.976 J.D. IL Legislative Research Unit
Miller, Emilie A. .... '— '04 C.234 L.801 J.D. [Hennessy&R.]
Miller, Joseph S., (BV) ....'50 '76 C.234 B.S. L.365 J.D. 526 E. Allen
Milligan, Daniel L. .... '41 '65 C&L.966 B.S., J.D. I.R.S.
Mills, Richard Henry ....'29 '57 C.337 B.A. L.469 J.D. U.S. Dist. J.
Milos, Jennifer L. ....'— '01 C.477 B.A. L.339 J.D. [Freeborn&P.]

Mohan, Alewelt, Prillaman & Adami, (AV)
Suite 325, 1 North Old Capitol Plaza, 62701-1323
Telephone: 217-528-2517 Telecopier: 217-528-2553
URL: http://www.mohanlaw.com
Members: James T. Mohan (1927-2004); Fred C. Prillaman; Paul E. Adami; Cheryl S. Neal; Patrick D. Shaw; Joel A. Benoit. Associate: Christopher D. Oswald. Retired Partner: Edward J. Alewelt.
General Commercial, Contract and Construction Litigation. Environmental Law. Corporation Law, Federal and State Taxes, Estate Planning and Real Estate Law and Tax. Personal Injury. Bankruptcy. Matrimonial Law.
See Professional Biographies, SPRINGFIELD, ILLINOIS

Mohr, Ryan E. .... '— '05 C.801 B.A. L.734 J.D. [Hodge D.Z.]
Mony, Kristina E. .... '72 '99 C.373 B.A. L.912 J.D. [Giffin,W.C.&B.]
Mool, Deanna Seward, (BV) .... '— '90 C&L.339 B.A., J.D. P.O. Box 8624
Mool, Robert G. .... '64 '90 C.340 B.A. L.339 J.D. St. Atty., Ill. Dept. of Natl. Res.
Moran, William F., III, (BV) ....'60 '85 C&L.801 B.S., J.D. [Stratton,G.S.&K.]
Moreno, Lisa Elin ....'47 '78 C.388 B.A. L.910 J.D. Ill. Environ. Protection Agcy.
Morgan, James L., (BV) .... '57 '82 C.249 B.S. L.339 J.D. IL Atty. Gen. Off.
Morphew, James M., (BV) ....'54 '83 C.1151 B.A. L.424 J.D. [Sorling,N.H.C.&C.]
Morris, Gloria A. ....'— '94 [Kanoski&Assoc.]
Morris, Stanley L., (BV) ....'39 '71 C.593 B.S. L.502 J.D. [Quinn,J.H.&P.]
Morse, Saul J., (AV) ....'48 '73 C&L.339 B.A., J.D. [Brown,H.&S.]
Mote, David B., (CV) ....'59 '90 C.338 B.A. L.801 J.D. Asst. Fed. Def.
Mueller, Allen C., (BV) ....'58 '84 C.399 B.A. L.300 J.D. [Livingstone,M.O.&D.]
Mueller, L. Robert, (AV) .... '48 '79 C.399 B.A. L.801 J.D. [Livingstone,M.O.&D.]
Mueller, Robert L., (AV) ....'22 '53 C.339 B.S. L.996 LL.B. [Livingstone,M.O.&D.]
Mueller, Sue ....'53 '78 C.338 B.A. L.589 J.D. Dept. of Children & Family Servs.
Munoz, Karen L., (BV) ....'50 '75 C.929 B.A. L.734 J.D. Asst. State Appl. Def.
Murphy, D. Scott, (BV) .... '62 '94 C.430 B.S. L.1187 J.D. [Livingstone,M.O.&D.]
Murray, William Allen '48 '76 C.430 A.B. L.910 J.D.
Regulatory Affs. Mgr., City Water, Light & Power
Myers, John M., (AV) ....'51 '80 C.530 B.S. L.597 J.D. [Rabin,M.&H.]
Myers, Michael A., (BV) ....'45 '70 C.861 B.A. L.910 J.D. [Sorling,N.H.C.&C.]
Myerscough, Sue E. ....'51 '80 C&L.801 B.A., J.D. App. Ct.J.
Nafziger, George H. .... '36 '62 C.340 B.A. L.880 J.D. Admin. Law J., Ill. Dept. of Rev.
Narup, Richard H., (BV) .... '56 '81 C.1101 B.A. L.801 J.D. [Drake,N.&M.]
Naylor, Peter E. ....'79 '05 C.337 B.A. L.734 J.D. [Heyl,R.V.&A.]
Neal, Cheryl S., (BV) .... '53 '84 C.999 B.A. L.339 J.D. [Mohan,A.P.&A.]
Nelson, Daniel T. .... '66 '02 C.801 B.S. L.589 J.D. Legal Advsr.
Nessler, Frederic W. ....'51 '77 C.339 B.S. L.146 J.D. 536 N. Bruns Lane
Newman, Bradley Jay '57 '83 C.37 B.S. L.213 J.D.
(adm. in MI; not adm. in IL) Assoc. Gen. Coun., Amer. Gen. Corp.
Newton, Gale W. .... '— '01 C.999 B.A. L.1556 J.D. [Hodge D.Z.]

Nichelson, James L. ... '75 '01 C.357 B.S. L.801 J.D. [🄰 Brown,H.&S.]
Noe, Margaret A. '47 '00 C.248 B.A. L.801 J.D.
Assoc Chancellor Aeo, 1 University Plz
Nolan, John E., (BV) ... '66 '91 C.802 B.A. L.734 J.D. [Hinshaw&C.]
Noll, Jon G., (BV) ... '48 '75 C.870 B.S. L.339 J.D. [Noll]
Noll Law Office, (BV) ... 802 S. 2nd St.
Northrup, Charles H., (AV) ... '14 '39 C.340 A.B. L.339 J.D. [Sorling,N.H.C.&C.] ‡
Northrup, Charles J., (BV) ... '60 '88 C.694 B.A. L.801 J.D. [Sorling,N.H.C.&C.]
O'Brien, Dennis S., (BV) ... '53 '78 C.700 B.A. L.424 J.D. [Livingstone,M.O.&D.]
O'Brien, James L. ... '39 '68 C.999 A.B. L.339 J.D. 1625 W. Cook St.
O'Brien, Joseph H. ... '43 '67 C&L.734 B.S., J.D. Program Dir., Ill. Com. Comm.
Oehlert, Allen J., (AV) ... '47 '76 C.589 B.S.Ed. L.801 J.D. 225 E. Cook St.
O'Hara, Michael W., (BV) ... '52 '78 C&L.339 B.A., J.D. [Cavanagh&O.]
O'Hara, Patrick J., (BV) ... '52 '79 C&L.339 B.A., J.D. [🄰 Cavanagh&O.]
O'Keefe, Dwight H., III, (BV) ... '43 '70 C.802 B.A. L.339 J.D. [Brown,H.&S.]
Olivero, Kathy A., (CV) '56 '82 C.339 B.S. L.801 J.D.
[🄰 Kanoski&Assoc.] (⊙Bloomington, Macomb, Peoria, Quincy, Rushville)
Olson, D. P. '22 '47 L.208 LL.B.
(adm. in CO; not adm. in IL) Teachers Ins. Co.
Omoniyi, A. Olusanjo ... '59 '96 C&L.801 B.A./B.S., J.D. [Omoniyi]
Omoniyi Law Firm ... 4030 Millstone Drive
O'Neill, Dan ... '38 '71 C.276 B.A. L.365 J.D. Asst. Atty. Gen.
O'Shea, Robert S. ... '25 '50 C&L.347 A.B., J.D. 2170 Sylvan Rd.‡
Oswald, Christopher D. ... '77 '02 C.339 B.S. L.589 J.D. [🄰 Mohan,A.P.&A.]
Otwell, Brian T., (AV) ... '58 '84 C.338 B.S. L.801 J.D. Chief Pub. Def.
Oxtoby, Robert B., (AV) ... '21 '49 C.118 A.B. L.597 J.D. [Van Meter,O.&F.]
Panichi, William T., Law Office, (BV) ... '44 '69 C&L.339 B.A., J.D. 808 S. 2nd St.
Pappas, James A., (CV) ... '53 '79 C.339 B.A. L.589 J.D. 915 S. 2nd St.
Papushkewych, Gerri, (BV) ... '49 '74 C.436 B.A. L.339 J.D. [Wolfson&P.]
Parker, Jennifer L. ... '71 '05 C.268 B.A. L.879 J.D. [🄰 Brown,H.&S.]
Parkinson, Edwin R. '45 '71 C.98 A.B. L.365 J.D.
(adm. in TN; not adm. in IL) Chief Legal Coun., Dept. of Conservation
Patino, Robert M. ... '76 '04 C.352 B.S.E. L.209 J.D. 1 W. Old State Capital, Ste. 505
Patton, Lynn E. ... '65 '90 C.801 B.A. L.339 J.D. 500 S. Second Street
Patton, Samuel C., (BV) ... '23 '52 L.996 LL.B. 814 E. Edwards
Paul, Denise M. ... '51 '76 C.339 A.B. L.801 J.D. Off. of State Appl. Def.
Pearson, Thomas Y., (BV) ... '42 '68 C.861 B.A. L.365 J.D. [Kenney&P.]
Pecoraro, Giacomo A., Sr. '49 '82
C.1016 B.G.S. L.365 J.D. Secy. of State, Dept. of Pol./Dir.
Periard, Ronald W., (AV) ... '43 '68 C&L.477 B.S., J.D. [🄲 Giffin,W.C.&B.]
Perrin, Christopher G., (BV) ... '60 '88 C.602 B.A. L.801 J.D. [🄰 Metnick,C.F.&S.]
Perzan, Christopher P. '66 '92 C.388 B.A. L.910 J.D
Asst. Coun., Ill. Envir. Protec. Agcy.
Peters, Howard A., IV ... '75 '01 C.302 B.S. L.801 J.D. [🄰 Scott&S.]
Peters, Michael W. '62 '88 C.339 B.A. L.900 J.D.
(adm. in KS; not adm. in IL) Association of Ill. Elec. Cooperatives
Petersen, Kirk H. ... '52 '79 C.589 B.A. L.365 J.D. [Z.Stamp]
Peterson, Chrissie L. ... '— '03 C.388 L.801 J.D. [🄰 Hennessy&R.]
Peterson, David E. ... '49 '74 C&L.339 A.B., J.D. Ill. State Dept. of Human Servs.
Petrilli, Lisa ... '77 '03 C.339 B.A. L.365 J.D. [🄰 Sorling,N.H.C.&C.]
Petry, Amy Jo ... '72 '98 C.339 B.A. L.801 J.D. 500 S. 2nd St.
Pfeifer, Frank M. ... '08 '34 C.46 L.996 LL.B. 2-B Lawrence Square‡
Pinelo, Armando J. ... '54 '82 C.393 B.A. L.597 J.D. Ofc. of the Atty. Gen.
Pittman, Nancy Sue Short, (BV) '62 '88 C.339 B.A. L.910 J.D.
Chf.Labor Rel. Coun.,State Dept. Central Mgmt. Servs.
Plawer, Henry J., (BV) ... '49 '76 C.1082 B.A. L.339 J.D. 201 Buckhorn Dr.
Pogge, Mariann, (BV) ... '54 '82 C.1082 B.A. L.339 J.D. 1001 Durkin Drive
Posegate, Carol Hansen, (AV) ... '49 '73 C.182 B.A. L.276 J.D. [Posegate&D.]

Posegate & Denes, P.C., (AV)
111 North 6th Street, Suite 200, 62701
Telephone: 217-522-6152 Fax: 217-522-6184
Email: jane@posegate-denes.com URL: http://www.lawyers.com/posegate&denes
Carol Hansen Posegate; Jane N. Denes.
General Civil Litigation, Employment Law, Estate Planning, Taxation, Business Law, College and University Law, Administrative Law.
See Professional Biographies, SPRINGFIELD, ILLINOIS

Potter, James R., (AV) ... '40 '66 C.388 B.A. L.352 J.D. [Londrigan,P.&R.]
Potts, Claude H. ... '43 '69 C&L.502 B.S. in B.A., J.D. Asst. Atty. Gen.
Powell, Theresa M., (BV) ... '69 '95 C.234 B.A. L.801 J.D. [Heyl,R.V.&A.]
Powers, Robert B., (BV) ... '49 '80 C.927 B.A. L.209 J.D. 3001 S. 2nd
Pratscher, Darryl D. ... '51 '79 C.340 B.A. L.801 J.D. 201 W. Monroe St.
Pratt, Sarah J., (BV) ... '60 '85 C.337 B.A. L.339 J.D. [🄲 Heyl,R.V.&A.]
Preckwinkle, George W. '56 '81
C&L.802 B.B.A., J.D. V.P., Bishop Hardware & Supply Co.
Presney, Paul E., (AV) ... '34 '57 C&L.339 B.A., J.D. [Presney,K.&P.]
Presney, Paul E., II, (BV) ... '57 '82 C.339 B.A. L.146 J.D. [Presney,K.&P.]
Presney, Kelly and Presney, (AV) ... 726 S. 2nd St. (⊙Chatham)
Pressnall, Christopher R. '71 '97
C.801 B.A. L.339 J.D. Asst. Coun., State Envir. Protec. Agcy.
Prillaman, Fred C., (AV) ... '42 '68 C.855 B.A. L.597 J.D. [Mohan,A.P.&A.]
Proctor, Michelle Lee ... '67 '96 C.339 B.S. L.362 J.D. P.O. Box 13317
Puclik, Mark S. '55 '80 C.98 B.S. L.45 J.D.
(adm. in AR; not adm. in IL) Univ. of Illinois

Quinn, Johnston, Henderson & Pretorius, Chartered, (AV)
(Formerly McConnell, Kennedy, Quinn & Johnston)
205 South Fifth Street, Suite 900, 62701 ⊙
Telephone: 217-753-1133 Fax: 217-753-1180
Email: quinnlaw@qjhp.com URL: http://www.qjhp.com
Stanley L. Morris; James Andrew Borland; Michael J. Holt; Matthew J. Maddox. Associate: John A. Wolters.
Trial Practice in all Courts. Personal Injury, Professional Negligence, Admiralty, Insurance Law, Workers Compensation Law, Banking, Commercial and Bankruptcy Law. Real Estate, Corporate and *Probate Law.*
Representative Clients: Allstate Insurance Co.; American International Insurance Co.; Bituminous Casualty Corp.; General Motors; Illinois State Medical Insurance Services, Inc.; Pekin Insurance; Peoria Journal Star, Inc.; St. Paul Insurance Co.
Peoria, Illinois Office: 227 N. E. Jefferson Street, 61602. Telephone: 309-674-1133.
See Professional Biographies, SPRINGFIELD, ILLINOIS

Quivey, Douglas J. ... '65 '94 C.234 B.A. L.339 J.D. [🄰 Londrigan,P.&R.]
Rabin, A. Mark, (BV) ... '41 '65 C.927 B.S. L.365 J.D. [Rabin,M.&H.]
Rabin, Myers & Hanken, P.C., (AV) ... 1300 S. Eighth St.
Rader, James ... '39 '64 C.855 B.A. L.221 LL.B. Dept. of Pub. Aid
Radkey, William A., (BV) ... '50 '79 C&L.339 B.A., J.D. [Stratton,G.S.&K.]
Rahn, Steven C., (BV) ... '59 '84 C.734 B.A. L.339 J.D. IICLE
Ramage, Andrew M., (BV) ... '71 '98 C.234 B.A. L.801 J.D. [Hinshaw&C.]
Rammelkamp, James J. ... '78 '04 C&L.339 B.A., J.D. [🄰 Feldman,W.D.&B.]
Rammelkamp, Bradney, Kuster, Keaton, Fritsche & Lindsay, P.C., (AV)
520 East Allen Street (⊙Jacksonville, Winchester)
Randle, Craig A., (BV) ... '49 '74 C.801 B.A. L.339 J.D. [Londrigan,P.&R.]
Read, Jeffrey A. ... '62 '88 C.63 B.S. L.801 J.D. Dept. of Prof. Regulation
Reardon, Timothy J., (AV) ... '35 '66 C.477 B.B.A. L.213 J.D. 520 South Douglas Avenue
Redlich, James W. ... '52 '77 C.339 B.S. L.818 J.D. Ill. State Police, Chf. Coun.
Reed, R. Phillip, (BV) ... '52 '77 C.734 A.B. L.339 J.D. 1129 S. Seventh St.
Reed, Russell L., (BV) ... '61 '87 C.338 B.S. L.589 J.D. [Hinshaw&C.]
Reichle, Lou Ann ... '51 '84 C.388 B.A. L.424 J.D. Asst. Clk., Supm. Ct.
Reid, William D., (BV) ... '58 '83 C.338 B.S. L.801 J.D. [Elmore&R.]
Reilly, Patrick V., (BV) ... '39 '63 C.602 B.B.A. L.597 J.D. [🄲 Sorling,N.H.C.&C.]
Reisch, Lawrence W., Jr. ... '28 '54 C.502 A.B. L.910 J.D. 131 Doral Dr.
Reiser, Craig J., (BV) ... '64 '90 C.339 B.S. L.801 J.D. [Kepner&R.]
Rendleman, Dennis A., (BV) ... '56 '81 C&L.339 B.A., J.D. Gen. Coun., State Bar Assn.
Reynolds, Brian E. ... '53 '78 C.201 B.A. L.339 J.D. Exec. Dir., State Labor Rel. Bd.
Rhode, Rebekah A. ... '63 '89 C.338 B.S. L.339 J.D. Research Atty., Supm. Ct.
Ridings, Craig A. ... '20 '47 C.362 L.421 LL.B. P.O. Box 4265‡
Rigby, Timothy, (BV) ... '69 '94 C.234 B.S. Bus. L.801 J.D. [Hart,S.&W.]
Rios, Monica T. ... '— '04 C.136 B.S. L.30 J.D. [🄰 Hodge D.Z.]
Rippe, Lawrence C. '43 '72 C.966 B.S. L.339 J.D.
Gen. Atty., U.S. Small Business Admn.
Rishel, George Fox ... '44 '79 C.339 B.A. L.365 J.D. Staff Atty., Legis. Research Unit
Roberts, J. William, (AV) ... '— '68 C.340 B.A. L.910 J.D. [Hinshaw&C.] (⊙Chicago)
Robeson, J. Jay ... '38 '68 C.932 B.A. L.209 J.D. [Berg&R.]
Robinson, John T. ... '56 '83 C.339 B.A. L.146 J.D. Dept. Of Revenue, Dep. Couns.
Robinson, Sarah M. '73 '00 C.234 B.A. L.801 J.D.
Sr. Trust Ofr., Asst. Legal Coun., United Community Bank
Rogers, Barbara Kilduff '50 '75 C.741 B.A. L.734 J.D.
(adm. in MO; not adm. in IL) Ill. Com. Comm.
Rogers, Melissa A., (BV) '69 '94 C&L.801 B.S., J.D.
Asst. Corp. Coun., City of Springfield (Legal Department)
Rogers, Robert M. ... '45 '69 C.801 B.A. L.339 J.D. Corp. Coun., City of Springfield
Rolf, Alice J. ... '61 '87 C&L.339 B.A., J.D. 1718 S. Bates Ave.‡
Rolf, David A., (BV) ... '62 '87 C&L.339 B.S., J.D. [Sorling,N.H.C.&C.]
Roncone, John M. ... '32 '58 C.602 Ph.B. L.209 J.D. 1045 Outer Pk. Dr.
Rosen, Steven J., (BV) ... '65 '90 C.339 B.A. L.910 J.D. [Holley&R.]
Roth, Stephan J., (CV) ... '66 '93 C.1247 B.A. L.589 J.D. Secy. of State Off.
Rotman, Pamela F. ... '56 '79 C&L.339 B.A., J.D. State Environ. Protection Agcy.
Rotskoff, Peter L. '58 '86 C.880 B.A. L.365 J.D.
Sr. Coun., Atty. Regis. & Disciplinary Comm.
Roubitchek, Michael S. '76 '01 C.347 B.S. L.146 J.D.
Asst. Coun., Envir. Protec. Agcy., Div. of Legal Servs.
Rowe, Max L., (AV) ... '21 '47 C.145 M.B.A. L.339 J.D. 49 Inverness Rd. (⊙Paris)
Rundblom, James C. ... '57 '84 C.339 B.S. L.801 J.D. Franklin Sq.
Rutherford, Roger L., (BV) ... '48 '75 C.339 B.S. L.879 J.D. [Rutherford]
Rutherford Law Offices, (BV) ... 2041 W. Iles Avenue, Ste. A
Rutz, J. Nicole '71 '97 C.69 B.B.A. L.326 J.D.
Coun., State Dept. of Central Mgmt. Servs.
Ryan, Margaret (Peggy) J., (BV) ... '61 '90 C.502 B.J. L.801 J.D. [Sorling,N.H.C.&C.]
Ryan, Michelle Marie ... '68 '92 C.477 B.A. L.339 J.D. E.P.A.
Ryder, Sterling M. ... '39 '71 C.627 B.A. L.339 J.D. Asst. Coun., State Gaming Bd.
Saavedra, Richard A., Jr. ... '49 '74 C.238 B.A. L.424 J.D. State Dept. of Pub. Aid
Sabin, Scott A., (BV) ... '67 '92 C.477 B.A. L.910 J.D. [Metnick,C.F.&S.]
Safley, Thomas G., (BV) ... '— '95 C.502 B.A. L.352 J.D. [Hodge D.Z.]
Salus, Babette P. ... '60 '85 C.880 B.S. L.910 J.D. [Schwing&S.]

Samuels, Miller, Schroeder, Jackson & Sly, LLP
(See Decatur)

Sanchez, Esteban F., (AV) ... '53 '79 C&L.734 A.B., J.D. Asst. U.S. Atty.
Sanders, Amy D. ... '79 '04 C&L.339 B.S., J.D. [🄰 Hart,S.&W.]
Sargent, Rosalind A. '78 '03
C.98 B.A. L.221 J.D. Staff Atty., State of Illinois Legis. Serv. Bur.
Saunderson, Christina M., (CV) ... '58 '83 C.339 B.A. L.209 J.D. Asst. Atty. Gen.
Schafer, George M. ... '29 '53 C&L.502 A.B., J.D. Dept. of Comm. & Community Affairs
Schall, Gary K. ... '43 '73 C.340 B.A. L.879 J.D. I.R.S.
Schanzle-Haskins, Ellen J. ... '50 '76 C.234 B.S. L.801 J.D. Dir. & Dep. Clk.
Schanzle-Haskins, Thomas P., III, (AV) ... '46 '76 C&L.801 B.A., J.D. [Brown,H.&S.]
Schechter, Gary ... '48 '74 C&L.910 A.B., J.D. 1825 S. Whittier
Schempp, Dale A., (CV) ... '42 '97 C.871 B.S. L.734 J.D. [Schempp]
Schempp Law Office, PC, (CV) ... 2520 S. Grand Ave. E.
Schick, James R. ... '— '75 C&L.339 B.A., J.D. [🄲 Hodge D.Z.]
Schiedel, Charles M., (AV) ... '46 '76 C&L.477 A.B., J.D. State Appl. Def.
Schlosser, Frederick J., (BV) ... '63 '92 C.602 B.B.A. L.801 J.D. [Gates,W.&S.]
Schmadeke, Charles R., (BV) ... '52 '77 C.589 B.A. L.365 J.D. [Hinshaw&C.]
Schmidt, Amy K., (BV) ... '65 '90 C.1288 B.S. L.862 J.D. [Brown,H.&S.]
Schmidt, Maria Richter '56 '82
C&L.339 A.B., J.D. Asst. Exec. Dir., Illinois Health Care Assoc.
Schmidt, Thomas M., (BV) ... '52 '78 C.103 B.A. L.352 J.D. [Livingstone,M.O.&D.]
Schmit, John P., (BV) '42 '81
C.424 B.A. L.589 J.D. Sr. Asst. Corp. Coun., City of Springfield
Schoenbaum, Edward J. '42 '68 C.472 B.S. L.930 J.D.
Admin. Dir., Lutheran High School
Schroeder, Susan J. ... '49 '80 C.589 B.A. L.209 J.D. 2200 Churchill Rd.
Schuering, Daniel P. ... '54 '91 C.1247 B.A. L.734 J.D. [Schuering&Assoc.]
Schuering & Associates ... 3050 Montvale Drive, Suite B
Schumacher, Daniel J. ... '42 '93 C.1044 B.S. L.365 J.D. 259 Wisteria Dr.
Schwab, Gary S., (AV) ... '56 '81 C.340 B.A. L.352 J.D. [Heyl,R.V.&A.]
Schwartz, Brian D., Law Offices of ... '67 '94 C.927 B.A. L.190 J.D. 2940 Baker Drive
Schwing, Eric M. ... '48 '82 C.475 B.A. L.1187 J.D. [Schwing&S.]
Schwing & Salus, P.C. ... 1100 S. 5th St.
Scott, Angela ... '67 '00 C&L.801 B.S., J.D. 600 E. Monroe
Scott, Gregory A., (AV) ... '51 '77 C.338 B.S. L.365 J.D. [Scott&S.]
Scott, Jeanne E. ... '48 '73 C.98 B.A. L.597 J.D. U.S. Dist. J.
Scott, R. Stephen, (AV) ... '50 '77 C.436 B.S. L.146 J.D. [Scott&S.]
Scott, Robert F., (BV) ... '15 '47 L.996 LL.B. 611 East Monroe, Suite 200
Scott & Scott, P.C., (AV) ... 611 East Monroe, Suite 200
Seeder, Robert D. ... '59 '84 C.339 B.S. L.146 J.D. Asst. Appl. Def.
Segatto, Bernard G., III, (AV) ... '60 '85 C.602 B.A. L.801 J.D. [Barber S.H.&H.]
Segatto, Randall W., (BV) ... '61 '86 C.72 B.A. L.801 J.D. [Barber S.H.&H.]
Seiple, Stephen W. ... '49 '74 C.504 A.B. L.339 J.D. Ill. Dept. of Central Mgt. Serv.(s)
Sgro, Gregory P., (BV) ... '61 '86 C.597 B.S. L.910 J.D. [Sgro,H.&B.]
Sgro, Hanrahan & Blue, L.L.P., (BV) ... 1119 South Sixth Street
Shafer, Terry C. ... '56 '95 C.999 B.A. L.862 J.D. Hearing Offr.
Sharpe, Robert C. ... '48 '77 C.197 A.B. L.339 J.D. Environmental Protection Agcy.
Shaw, Patrick D., (BV) ... '68 '93 C.339 B.A. L.861 J.D. [Mohan,A.P.&A.]

Shea, Gerald W., (BV) ....'31 '60 C.339 B.S. L.209 LL.B. 421 W. Edwards St.
Sheehan, Patrick J., (AV) ....'51 '77 C&L.734 B.A., J.D. [Sheehan&S.] ⊙
Sheehan, William J., (AV) ....'53 '78 C&L.734 B.A., J.D. [Sheehan&S.] ⊙
Sheehan and Sheehan, Lawyers, P.C., (AV) .... 1214 S. 8th Street (⊙New Berlin)
Sherer, Christopher E. ....'75 '00 C.798 B.S. L.986 J.D. [[A] Giffin,W.C.&B.]
Shiffman, Stuart H. ....'48 '74 C.597 B.A. L.209 J.D. J.
Shull, John ....'51 '79 C.234 B.A. L.221 J.D. Leg. Ref. Bur.
Shupenus, Robert M., (CV) ....'71 '96 C.210 B.A. L.221 J.D. [[A] Brown,H.&S.]
Siebert, William Newell
(See Chicago)
Sievers, Scott B. .... '68 '01 C.492 B.S. L.339 J.D. [[A] D.M.Craven]
Simhauser, Val C., (CV) '54 '80
C.350 B.A. L.365 J.D. Asst. Atty. Gen., IL Atty. Gen. Off.
Simmons, Daniel R., (AV) ....'59 '85 C.57 B.A. L.352 J.D. [Heyl,R.V.&A.]
Simpson, John R., (BV) ....'51 '76 C&L.339 B.A., J.D. Sr. Asst. Atty. Gen.
Sinclair, E. David .... '— '94 C.173 B.A. L.1370 J.D. House Republican Staff.
Sinder, Janet L. ....'55 '79 C.188 A.B. L.477 J.D. Asst. State Appl. Def.
Sisk, George M. ....'69 '97 C.249 B.A. L.1340 J.D. Chief Legal Counsel
Smith, Gary L., (AV) ....'51 '76 C.589 B.A. L.801 J.D. [Loewenstein,H.&S.]
Smith, Valjean R., (Mr.) .... '28 '53 C.999 L.996 LL.B. 124 Cypress Point Dr.‡
Smoot, Sean M. '69 '95 C.534 B.S. L.1106 J.D.
Chief Legal Counsel, PB&PA of Illinois
Somers, Allan C. '47 '74 C&L.221 B.A., J.D.
(adm. in IA; not adm. in IL) 5th & Adams‡
Sorensen, George C. ....'45 '74 C.589 B.A. L.146 J.D. Ill. Dept. of Rev.

Sorling, Northrup, Hanna, Cullen and Cochran, Ltd., (AV) [BB]
Formerly Sorling, Catron and Hardin
800 Illinois Building, 607 East Adams Street, P.O. Box 5131, 62705 ⊙
Telephone: 217-544-1144 Telecopier: 217-522-3173
Email: businessdevelopment@sorlinglaw.com URL: http://www.sorlinglaw.com
Members of Firm: Carl A. Sorling (1896-1991); B. Lacey Catron, Jr. (1912-1959); John H. Hardin (1909-1978); George William Cullen (1917-1986); Thomas L. Cochran (1916-1994); R. Gerald Barris; Stephen A. Tagge; Michael A. Myers; Carl Clark Germann; Gary A. Brown; Frederick B. Hoffmann; William R. Enlow; Michael C. Connelly; John A. Kauerauf; James M. Morphew; Stephen J. Bochenek; David A. Rolf; Margaret (Peggy) J. Ryan; Mark K. Cullen; Thomas H. Wilson; Todd Michael Turner; R. Lee Allen; Charles J. Northrup; James D. Broadway;—Elizabeth A. Urbance; E. Zachary Dinardo; James G. Fahey; Jeffrey R. Jurgens; Michael G. Horstman, Jr.; Jennifer M. Ascher; Lisa Petrilli; Emily B. Fathauer. Of Counsel: Patrick V. Reilly; William S. Hanley; William B. Bates; Mark H. Ferguson. Retired: Charles H. Northrup (Retired, 2004); Philip E. Hanna (Retired, 2004).
General Civil Practice including Administrative Law, Agricultural Law, State and Federal Appellate Practice, Banking and Finance, Banking, Bankruptcy, Business Law, Civil Rights Defense, Commercial Law, Communications, Construction Law, Contract Preparation and Litigation, Corporate Law, Education Law, Elder Law, Election Law, Employee Benefits, Energy Law including Public Utilities, Environmental Law, Family Law, Illinois Governmental Advocacy and Representation, Health and Hospital Law, Insurance Regulation and Defense; Intellectual Property Rights, Labor and Employment Law, General State and Federal Litigation, News Media Representation, Mergers and Acquisitions, Municipal and Local Governmental Law, Natural Resources, Not for Profit Organizations, Personal Injury and Torts, Probate, Estate and Trust, Professional Liability and Disciplinary Defense, Products Liability, Real Estate, Securities, Taxation, Telecommunications, Trade and Professional Association Representation, Transportation Law, Workers Compensation, Zoning Planning and Land Use.
Counsel for: AmerenServices; Bank One; Illini Dairy Queen, Inc.; Springfield Airport Authority.
Representative Clients: CIGNA Insurance; WICS-TV, Inc.
Peoria Office: 401 S.W. Water Street, Suite 301, 61602. Telephone: 309-674-1144. Telecopier: 309-671-4368.
See Professional Biographies, SPRINGFIELD, ILLINOIS

Southworth, Mike, (AV) ....'54 '83 C.976 B.A. L.910 J.D. [Hart,S.&W.]
Spooner, Scott D., (AV) ....'52 '81 C.927 B.A. L.221 J.D. [Heyl,R.V.&A.]
Staats, Keith W. ....'54 '80 C.357 B.A. L.46 J.D. Gen. Coun., Ill. Dept. of Rev.
Stamp, Zack, (BV) ....'53 '80 C.504 B.A. L.801 J.D. [Z.Stamp]
Stamp, Zack, Ltd., (BV) ....601 West Monroe Street
Steele, Karen J., (BV) ....'53 '80 C.234 B.S. L.276 J.D. Asst. Atty. Gen.
Steere, Robert D. ......'54 '78 C.475 B.A. L.477 J.D. Gen. Coun., State Bureau of Budget
Steinhour, Paul E. '44 '72 C&L.339 B.S., J.D.
Dir., Civil Penalty Program, Ill. Commerce Comm.
Stephens, Harvey B., (AV) ....'34 '60 C.95 A.B. L.145 J.D. [[C] Brown,H.&S.]
Stephens, Harvey M., (BV) ....'63 '88 C.385 A.B. L.910 J.D. [Brown,H.&S.]
Stephenson, Mack ....'14 '43 C.339 A.B. L.996 LL.B. 42 Fox Mill Ln.‡
Stine, Robert E., (BV) ....'39 '68 C.234 B.S. L.352 J.D. [Stine,G.&D.]
Stine, Greer & Duggan, (BV) .... 426 South 5th Street
Stitt, Susan B. .....'62 '87 C.602 B.A. L.339 J.D. Air Quality Mgr., State Dept. of Transp.
Stockman, John H. ... '64 '90 C.1213 B.S. L.982 J.D. [[A] Armstrong T.] (⊙Edwardsville)
Stoller, H. L., Jr. ....'44 '69 C&L.339 B.A., J.D. Commerce Comm.
Stone, Frederick H. ....'21 '48 C&L.228 A.B., J.D. 2031 Briarcliff‡
Stone, Ronald J., (BV) ....'52 '77 C.97 B.A. L.801 J.D. [Stratton,G.S.&K.]
Stratton, Bruce, (BV) ....'38 '65 C.388 B.A. L.146 LL.B. [Stratton,G.S.&K.]
Stratton, Giganti, Stone & Kopec, (BV) ....725 S. 4th St.
Stuart, Robert A., Jr., (AV) ....'48 '73 C.95 B.A. L.339 J.D. [Brown,H.&S.]
Studach, Guy A., (BV) .... '58 '83 C&L.801 B.A., J.D. 575 1st of America Ctr.
Surman, John K., (BV) ....'44 '69 C&L.339 A.B., J.D. [Lott&S.]
Svoboda, Joseph E. ....'47 '73 C.559 B.A. L.560 J.D. Ill. Environ. Protection Agcy.
Swartz, John L., (AV) ....'45 '71 C.339 A.B. L.145 J.D. [Giffin,W.C.&B.]
Sweeten, Patrick K. '71 '97 C.846 L.744
(adm. in TX; not adm. in IL) 1 S.E. Old State Capitol Plaza
Tagge, Stephen A., (AV) ....'44 '69 C.388 A.B. L.145 J.D. [Sorling,N.H.C.&C.]
Tanner, Peggy H. ....'49 '97 C.234 B.S. L.589 J.D. 2004 Fairway Dr.
Taylor, John P. ....'48 '98 C.999 B.A. L.734 J.D. 8220 Hunt Rd.
Taylor, William M., (BV) ....'46 '85 C.1347 B.A. L.734 J.D. 939 S. 8th
Tharp, John F. '24 '51 C.151 L.1340 LL.B.
(adm. in OH; not adm. in IL) Exec. V.P., Ill. Tele. Assn.
Thetford, Gale S., (BV) .... '52 '84 C&L.801 B.S., J.D. Gen. Coun., State Dept. on Aging
Thielen, Mark D. ....'63 '88 C.793 B.S. L.801 J.D. [[A] Scott&S.]
Tinch, Patricia Phillips ....'55 '82 C.339 B.S. L.616 J.D. 4513 Barrington Dr.
Tinkham, George W., (CV) .... '47 '74 C.339 B.S. L.879 J.D. Pres., Tax Law Ctr., Ltd.
Tracy, Donald R., (AV) ....'50 '76 C.36 B.S. L.836 J.D. [Brown,H.&S.]
Traynor, Duane L., (BV) ....'10 '34 C&L.585 B.A., J.D. 510 E. Monroe St., 3rd Fl.
Trigillo, Tracey .... '61 '87 C.1247 B.S. L.192 J.D. Secretary of State Legal Representative
Troemper, April G., (BV) ....'72 '98 C.234 B.A. L.801 J.D. [[A] Heyl,R.V.&A.]
Turner, Chad E. ....'70 '98 C&L.999 B.S., J.D. [Turner]
Turner, Todd Michael, (BV) ....'65 '92 C.927 B.A. L.339 J.D. [Sorling,N.H.C.&C.]

Turner Law Office
1 West Old State Capital Plaza, Suite 810, 62701
Telephone: 217-525-7008 Fax: 217-525-7056 URL: http://www.chadturnerlaw.com
Email: cturner@chadturnerlaw.com URL: http://www.chadturnerlawfirm.com
Chad E. Turner.
Criminal Defense, Driving While Intoxicated, Driving Under the Influence, Traffic Violations, Felonies, Misdemeanors, Drug Crimes, Appeals, Forfeiture, Search and Seizure, Sex Crimes.
See Professional Biographies, SPRINGFIELD, ILLINOIS

Tweedt, Jon E. ......'50 '78 C&L.801 B.A., J.D. Dep. Chief Coun., State Dept. of Transp.
Ungaretti & Harris, (AV)
400 East Jefferson Street, Suite 1200 (⊙Wash., DC; Chgo., IL)
Urbance, Elizabeth A., (BV) ....'62 '87 C.927 B.A. L.502 J.D. [[A] Sorling,N.H.C.&C.]
van Dijk, Margaret Louise '64 '89 C.629 B.S. L.910 J.D.
Dept. of Child. & Family Serv.'s
Van Huis, William A., (BV) '66 '93 C.339 A.B. L.801 J.D.
Dept. of Central Mngt. Srvs.
Van Lieshout, David L. ....'49 '80 C.959 B.A. L.1035 J.D. State Dept. of Ins.
Van Meter, A. D., Jr., (AV) ....'22 '49 C.1027 B.A. L.597 J.D. [Van Meter,O.&F.]
Van Meter, Oxtoby & Funk, (AV) .... 625 S. College St.
Van Ostrand, Shannie Bibie, (BV⊤) ..... '45 '75 C.339 B.S. L.345 J.D. 217 E. Monroe St.
Van Scyoc, Wilma ....'53 '86 C.63 B.S. L.345 J.D. Teachers Retirement Sys. of Ill.
Velde, Frederick P., (AV) ....'46 '72 C.210 B.A. L.838 J.D. [Heyl,R.V.&A.]
Vespa, Robert F., (BV) ....'24 '51 C.339 B.A. L.734 J.D. 319 E. Madison
Vinson, Sam, (AV) .... '— '79 C.197 B.A. L.276 J.D. [Ungaretti&H.] (⊙Chicago)
Vonnahmen, Michael H., (BV) .... '52 '77 C&L.801 B.A., J.D. 105 W. Allen St.
Waggoner, Steven M. '56 '85 C.338 B.S. L.801 J.D.
Chf. Hearing Off., State Property Tax App. Bd.
Wagner, Robert E., (BV) ....'52 '81 C.927 B.S. L.383 J.D. [R.E.Wagner&Assoc.]
Wagner, Robert E., and Associates, P.C., (BV) .... 3029 Newport Dr.

Walbaum, Robert C., (AV) '33 '61 C.339 B.S. L.910 J.D.
Barrister Building, 1231 South Eighth Street, 62703
Telephone: 217-789-0911 Fax: 217-789-0913
Email: walbaumlaw@sbcglobal.net
General Civil Practice. Probate, Trusts, Wills, Estate Planning. Real Estate, Banking and Corporation Law.
Representative Clients: Pleasant Plains State Bank; Brandt Consolidated, Inc.; Springfield Plastics, Inc.; Springfield Park District.
Reference: Pleasant Plains State Bank.
See Professional Biographies, SPRINGFIELD, ILLINOIS

Waldman, John J., (CV) '62 '88 C.801 B.A. L.339 J.D.
[[A] Kanoski&Assoc.] (⊙Bloomington, Macomb, Peoria, Quincy, Rushville)
Waligore, John Philip ....'58 '86 C&L.477 B.A., J.D. Asst. Coun., E.P.A.
Wallace, Michael L. ....'52 '77 C.347 B.A. L.146 J.D. Ill. State Employees Assn.
Ward, Steven C., (BV) ....'56 '83 C.210 B.A. L.146 J.D. [[A] Drake,N.&M.]
Warrington, Richard C., Jr. '49 '79 C.999 M.A. L.339 J.D.
Ill. Environ. Protection Agcy.
Warwick, Linda M. ....'73 '99 C.57 B.A. L.801 J.D. 217 East Monroe Street
Wasser, Stanley N., (BV) ....'50 '75 C.645 B.A. L.128 J.D. [Feldman,W.D.&B.]
Watson, Charles S., (BV) ...... '56 '83 C.339 B.S. L.221 J.D. 427 East Monroe, Suite 301
Weber, Raymond P. ....'49 '75 C.339 B.A. L.146 J.D. #1 Franklin Sq.
Wells, Christopher K. ....'63 '90 C.531 B.S. L.801 J.D. Asst. Atty. Gen.
Wendt, John W. ....'51 '86 C&L.801 B.A., J.D. 1101 S. Second St.
Wermcrantz, Steven Eric, Law Offices of '44 '69 C&L.879 B.A., J.D.
925 S. Spring Street
Wetzel, Nathan L. ....'78 '04 C.170 B.A. L.146 J.D. [[A] Graham&G.]
White, David V., (BV) ....'64 '89 C.339 B.S. L.383 J.D. [Stratton,G.S.&K.]
White, Rebecca Lyn ....'55 '82 C.339 B.S. L.365 J.D. State Attys Appl. Prosecutors
White, William Stanley, (BV) ....'47 '72 C.311 B.A. L.339 J.D. 817 S. 4th St.
Wilday, Jeffery M., (AV) ....'52 '77 C.976 B.A. L.910 J.D. [Brown,H.&S.]
Wilderson, Richard J., (AV) .... '48 '78 C&L.734 B.A., J.D. [[A] Graham&G.]
Wilgenbusch, Shirley Kathryn '— '82
C&L.801 B.A., J.D. Research Dir., 4th Dist. App. Ct.
Wilke, R. Kurt, (AV) ....'59 '85 C.339 B.S. L.1119 J.D. [Barber S.H.&H.]
Williams, Anita '48 '78 C.798 B.S.Ed. L.910 J.D.
Asst. Gen. Coun., State Dept. of Human Servs.
Williams, Deborah J. '71 '97
C.597 B.A. L.146 J.D. Asst. Coun., State Envir. Protec. Agcy.
Wilson, Bradley B. ....'65 '96 C.502 B.A. L.589 J.D. [[A] Gates,W.&S.]
Wilson, David M. ....'15 '45 C.339 A.B. L.996 LL.B. 8220 Hunt Rd.
Wilson, Ryan R. ....'79 '04 C.927 B.S. L.801 J.D. [[A] Graham&G.]
Wilson, Thomas H., (BV) ....'64 '89 C.1062 B.A. L.801 J.D. [Sorling,N.H.C.&C.]
Winning, James M., (AV) ....'21 '49 C.210 A.B. L.477 LL.B. [Giffin,W.C.&B.] ‡
Wise, D. Peter, (AV) ....'59 '84 C.861 B.A. L.365 J.D. [Gates,W.&S.]
Wise, Rodney Alan ....'56 '81 C&L.339 B.A., J.D. State Legislative Reference Bureau
Witsman, Samuel J., (BV) ....'58 '86 C.338 B.S. L.339 J.D. [Hart,S.&W.]
Wolfson, Henry A., (AV) ....'47 '75 C&L.339 B.A., J.D. [Wolfson&P.]
Wolfson, Jerome F. ....'19 '42 C&L.339 B.A., LL.B. 2405 Wiggins
Wolfson & Papushkewych, (AV) .... 2904 Greenbriar Drive
Wolter, Randall A., (BV) ....'50 '74 C.589 B.A. L.339 J.D. [Wolter,B.&L.]
Wolter, Beeman & Lynch, (BV) ....413 South Seventh Street
Wolters, John A., (CV) ....'55 '99 C.801 B.A. L.209 J.D. [[A] Quinn,J.H.&P.]
Wood, Donald E. '52 '79 C&L.339 B.A., J.D.
Dir. Gov't Rel., Association of Ill. Elec. Cooperatives
Wood, Harlington, Jr. ....'20 '48 C&L.339 A.B., J.D. U.S. Ct. of App. J.‡
Wood, John M. ....'57 '82 C&L.339 B.A., J.D. Ill. Human Rights Dept.
Woodruff, Clarke ....'34 '57 C&L.339 B.S., LL.B. Security Bk.
Woods, Donald L. ....'50 '83 C.1101 B.A. L.801 J.D. [[C] Brown,H.&S.]
Workman, William G., (CV) '58 '89 C.1247 B.A. L.801 J.D.
Asst. Corp. Coun., City of Springfield (Legal Department)
Wright, Daniel K. ....'79 '04 C.337 B.A. L.734 J.D. [[A] Brown,H.&S.]
Yonkauski, Stanley, Jr. ....'52 '83 C.1102 B.A. L.365 J.D. IL Dept. of Nat. Res.
Young, Duane D., (BV) ....'45 '73 C&L.339 B.S., J.D. [LaBarre&Y.]
Yung, R. Dale ....'31 '55 C&L.339 B.S., LL.B. Ill. Dept. of Rev.
Zalar, Charles R., (BV) ... '47 '72 C&L.339 A.B., J.D. Spec. Pros., States Attys App. Pros.
Zeman, Christine G., (AV) ....'— '79 C.339 B.A. L.801 J.D. [Hodge D.Z.]
Zenge, Lorraine .... '59 '84 C.340 B.A. L.339 J.D. Tr. Offr., First Natl. Bk. of Springfield
Zwick, Ann M. ....'— '89 C.339 B.S. L.597 J.D. [Freeborn&P.] ⊙

SPRING GROVE, 3,880, *McHenry Co.*

Abramson, Jane A. ....'49 '97 C.927 B.A. L.146 J.D. P.O. Box 461
Hoyt, N. Landon, IV ....'50 '78 C.188 A.B. L.94 J.D. 10701 Red Hawk Lane
Perry, Robin L. ....'64 '97 C.209 B.S. L.365 J.D. [Perry&Assoc.]

Perry & Associates
3309 Cardinal Lane, 60081
Telephone: 815-678-4920 Fax: 501-634-0943 URL: http://www.perrylaws.com
Email: perryr@core.com URL: http://www.perryassociateslaw.com
Robin L. Perry.
Land Use, Zoning, Municipal Law, Government, Employment Law, Civil Rights.
See Professional Biographies, SPRING GROVE, ILLINOIS

Stinespring, Donald C. ......'49 '73 C.747 B.A. L.365 J.D. 3209 Oxfordshire (⊙Chicago)

SPRING VALLEY, 5,398, *Bureau Co.*

Fiocchi, Richard C., (BV) ....'53 '79 C.723 B.A. L.1151 J.D. 201 E. St. Paul St.
Hollerich, Cornelius J., (BV) ....'49 '76 C.276 B.S. L.209 J.D. 116 N. Greenwood St.
Tonozzi, Thomas A., Law Offices of, (BV) '47 '72
C.602 B.A. L.339 J.D. 222 E. St. Paul St.
Wimbiscus, William J., Jr., (BV) '26 '50 C.339 B.S. L.209 J.D.
102 E. Paul St. (⊙De Pue)

STANDARD, 260, *Putnam Co.*

Grivetti, John A., Jr. .... '46 '70 C&L.424 B.B.A., J.D. P.O. Box 50

STAUNTON, 5,030, *Macoupin Co.*

Denby, Meno, Bloomer & Denby, (AV) .... 108 South Union (⊙Benld, Carlinville)
Drummond, Peter C., (BV) ....'47 '74 C.388 B.A. L.339 J.D. [Drummond]
Drummond Law Office, (BV) ....425 W. Main St.
Meno, J. Richard, (BV) ....'48 '73 C&L.734 B.S., J.D. [Denby,M.B.&D.] ⊙

STEGER, 9,682, *Cook & Will Cos.*

Brenner, Steven A. ....'59 '91 L.1187 J.D. 33 W. 36th St.

STERLING, 15,132, *Whiteside Co.*

Arnold, William E., (AV) ....'33 '60 C.602 B.A. L.477 LL.B. 15 E. 3rd St.‡
Besse, Kennard J., (AV) ....'14 '39 C.72 B.A. L.477 LL.B. 15 E. 3rd St.‡
Branson, Robert E., (BV) ....'49 '74 C.221 B.A. L.245 J.D. [Ward,M.P.&J.]
Burall, Theron William ....'73 '00 C.338 B.S. L.1439 J.D. 2203 22nd Ave.
Bush, Trent L. ....'73 '99 C.132 B.A. L.1035 J.D. [🄰 Ward,M.P.&J.]
Dillon, Roberta S. ....'44 '96 C.707 B.A. L.352 J.D. [🄰 Ward,M.P.&J.]
Feldman, Wallace ....'27 '57 L.339 J.D. 32 W. 3rd St.
Friel-Draper, Theresa, (CV) '59 '89
C.352 B.S.N. L.46 J.D. Gen. Coun., CGH Medical Ctr.
Frye, L. Vernon, (AV) ....'20 '49 C&L.597 B.S., J.D. 15 E. 3rd St.
Gillespie, James W. '18 '67 C.910 B.A. L.365 J.D.
(adm. in IN; not adm. in IL) 1312 Riverview Rd.‡
Gretler, William E. ....'29 '57 C&L.597 B.S., J.D. [Haglund&G.] ‡
Guzzardo, John A., (BV) ....'57 '83 C.436 B.A. L.146 J.D. [Ward,M.P.&J.]
Haglund, Alexander L., (AV) ....'14 '39 C&L.339 B.S., LL.B. [Haglund&G.]
Haglund and Gretler, (AV) .... 224 E. 3rd St.
Hawkins, Daniel C., (BV) ....'65 '90 C.339 B.A. L.589 J.D. [Ward,M.P.&J.]
Heaton, Joseph E., Jr., (BV) ....'49 '75 C.347 B.S. L.365 J.D. [Ward,M.P.&J.]
Helm, Rolf L. ....'27 '50 C.747 L.221 LL.B. 803 First Ave.‡
Johnson, Laurence F., (BV) ....'46 '73 C&L.339 B.S., J.D. [Ward,M.P.&J.]
Lancaster, Michael A., (BV) ....'56 '81 C.57 B.A. L.880 J.D. [Miller,L.&W.]
LeSage, Robert T., III ....'71 '96 C.597 B.A. L.146 J.D. [🄰 Ward,M.P.&J.]
Linkowski, Carol P., (BV) ....'50 '78 C.700 B.A. L.209 J.D. Asst. State's Atty.
Lopez, Vincent, Jr. ....'52 '85 C.927 B.A. L.1162 J.D. Asst. Pub. Def.
Lovaas, Ivan ....'25 '53 L.1035 LL.B. Ret. Asso. Cir. J.‡
Miller, John E., (BV) ....'49 '74 C&L.339 B.A., J.D. [Miller,L.&W.]
Miller, Lancaster & Walker, P.C., (BV) ....15 East Third Street
Murray, David E., (AV) ....'36 '60 C&L.339 A.B., LL.B. [🄱 Ward,M.P.&J.]
Osborn, Paul A., (BV) ....'55 '80 C.679 B.S.I.M. L.339 J.D. [Ward,M.P.&J.]
Pace, Ole Bly, III, (AV) ....'39 '66 C.340 A.B. L.339 J.D. [Ward,M.P.&J.]
Palmer, Richard A., (AV) ....'51 '76 C&L.339 B.S., J.D. [Ward,M.P.&J.]
Reese, James L., (AV) ....'43 '67 C.1101 B.A. L.339 J.D. [Ward,M.P.&J.]
Ripley, Marvin G. ....'47 '75 C.446 B.A. L.424 J.D. 302 1st Ave.
Sanders, Thomas, (BV) ....'54 '85 C.927 B.S. L.339 J.D. [Ward,M.P.&J.]
Say, James K. ....'54 '79 C.546 B.A. L.477 J.D. 608 W. 10th St.
Schott, Gregory F., (BV) ....'54 '79 C.697 B.A. L.365 J.D. 205 3rd Ave.
Sefton, Kevin D. ....'68 '98 C.504 B.A. L.589 J.D. [Miller,L.&W.]
Treviranus, Lisa A., (BV) ....'56 '87 C.339 B.S. L.589 J.D. [Ward,M.P.&J.]
Walker, Kelli D., (CV) ....'66 '91 C.697 B.A. L.424 J.D. [Miller,L.&W.]
Ward, Philip H., Jr., (AV) ....'31 '55 C&L.339 A.B., J.D. [Ward,M.P.&J.]
Ward, Murray, Pace & Johnson, P.C., (AV) .... 202 East Fifth Street (⊙Milledgeville)
Zollinger, Timothy B., (BV) ....'67 '92 C.338 B.S. L.589 J.D. [Ward,M.P.&J.]
Zumdahl, Mark E., (AV) ....'50 '75 C.937 B.A. L.339 J.D. [Ward,M.P.&J.] ⊙

STOCKTON, 1,871, *Jo Daviess Co.*

Nagel, Harold D. ....'20 '47 C.226 B.A. L.597 J.D. Ret. Cir. J.
Paja, Ronald P., (BV) ....'52 '79 C.602 B.A. L.589 J.D. [R.Paja]
Paja, Ronald, Law Office of, (BV) ....P.O. Box 124

STREAMWOOD, 36,407, *Cook Co.*

Davies, William T. ....'32 '63 C.339 B.S. L.365 LL.B. 525 Bartlett Rd.
Lyons, Redmond J. .... '42 '67 C.927 B.A. L.209 J.D. 279 Butternut Ln.
Teitelbaum, William Richard, Jr. ....'45 '01 C.1183 B.A. L.1187 J.D. [W.R.Teitelbaum]
Teitelbaum, William Richard ....253 Acorn Drive

STREATOR, 14,190, *La Salle & Livingston Cos.*

Bennett, Dale L. '41 '89 C.1101 B.A. L.312 J.D.
(adm. in HI; not adm. in IL) 1215 N. Bloomington St.‡
Berry, Richard J., (BV) ....'52 '77 C.880 B.A. L.602 J.D. [Myers,B.O.&K.] ⊙
Dixon, June Marie ....'33 '56 L.339 LL.B. 205 W. 1st St.‡
Drendel, Gerald A., (BV) ....'43 '68 C.187 B.A. L.339 J.D. 511 E. Main St.
Gulo, M. G., (BV) ....'22 '50 C&L.339 A.B., J.D. 123 S. Monroe St.
Gulo, Michael F., (BV) ....'52 '77 C.221 B.A. L.365 J.D. [M.G.Gulo&Assoc.]
Gulo, M. G., and Associates, Ltd., (BV) .... 123 S. Monroe St.
Guyon, Emmanuel F., (CV) ....'38 '73 C.339 B.S.M.E. L.436 J.D. 5 E. Bridge
Harrison, Frank J., (BV) ....'19 '42 C&L.145 A.B., J.D. 114 N. Bloomington St.

Herbolsheimer, Lannon, Henson, Duncan and Reagan, P.C.
(See La Salle)

Kuzma, Sheryl H., (BV) ....'65 '90 C.589 B.A. L.966 J.D. [Myers,B.O.&K.] ⊙
Mohan, John J., (CV) ....'18 '42 C&L.339 B.S., J.D. [Mohan,J.&R.]
Mohan, Richd. A., (CV) ....'22 '49 C&L.339 B.S., LL.B. [Mohan,J.&R.]
Mohan, John & Richard, (CV) .... 112 S. Park St.
Myers, Stephen C., (BV) ....'46 '71 C.602 A.B. L.597 J.D. [Myers,B.O.&K.] ⊙

Myers, Berry, O'Conor & Kuzma, Ltd., (BV)
7 Northpoint Drive, 61364 ⊙
Telephone: 815-672-3116 Fax: 815-672-0738
John A. Berry (1912-1986); Stephen C. Myers; Richard J. Berry; Andrew J. O'Conor (1919-1998); Sheryl H. Kuzma.
General Civil and Trial Practice in all Courts. Banking, Commercial and Corporate Law, Government and School Law, Probate, Real Estate, Health Care Law, Mediation and Arbitration.
Ottawa, Illinois Office: 130 East Madison Street, 61350. Telephone: 815-434-6206. Fax: 815-434-6203.
See Professional Biographies, STREATOR, ILLINOIS

Wheeler, Richard K. '46 '76 C.72 B.A. L.1003 J.D.
(adm. in OH; not adm. in IL) V.P. & Tr. Offr., Union Natl. Bk.

STRONGHURST, 799, *Henderson Co.*

Fort, Lyman R., (AV) ....'22 '49 C.98 L.597 J.D. [Fort&N.]
Fort & Neff, (AV) ....109 S. Bway.
Neff, Michael L., (BV) ....'46 '74 C.340 B.A. L.880 J.D. [Fort&N.]

SUGAR GROVE, 3,909, *Mercer Co.*

Durrenberger, Bill, (BV) ....'49 '81 C&L.339 B.S., J.D. 330 Division St.
Janota, David L. ....'51 '76 C.209 B.A. L.365 J.D. American Heartland Bank and Trust
Lindner, Patricia Reid, (BV) ....'39 '81 C.597 B.S. L.589 J.D. State Legis.
Motta, Robert M., II ....'69 '01 C.234 B.A. L.146 J.D. [Reiss&M.]
Parker, Eugene F. ....'33 '59 C&L.339 LL.B. 3 S. 928 Lake Wood Dr.‡
Reiss, Alison H. '74 '01 C.1376 B.A L.146 J.D.
(adm. in PA; not adm. in IL) [Reiss&M.]
Reiss & Motta, L.L.P. ....935 Stamford Pl.
Sanmiguel, Ruben D. ....'59 '91 C&L.424 B.A., J.D. [R.Sanmiguel]

Sanmiguel, Ruben, Law Offices of
330 N. Division Drive, Suite C, 60554
Telephone: 630-466-8400 Fax: 630-466-8401
Email: rubensanmiguel@comcast.net URL: http://www.lawsanmiguel.com
Ruben D. Sanmiguel.
Language: Spanish.
Criminal Law, Real Estate, Business Development.
See Professional Biographies, SUGAR GROVE, ILLINOIS

Stampolis, Marjorie Friedl ....'42 '68 C&L.352 B.B.A., J.D. P.O. Box 1169
White, James F., Law Office of '63 '89 C.347 B.A. L.365 J.D.
330 Division Drive, Suite E

SULLIVAN, * 4,354, *Moultrie Co.*

Brainard Law Offices, The
(See Charleston)

Elder, Oliver D. ....'46 '73 C.234 B.S. L.339 J.D. [Elder&E.]
Elder, Robert V. ....'40 '65 C&L.339 B.S., LL.B. [Elder&E.]
Elder & Elder ....101 W. Harrison St.
Flannell, Danny L. ....'52 '77 C&L.339 B.A., J.D. Cir. J.
Florini, Joseph V., (BV) ....'41 '65 C&L.339 B.S., J.D. [McLaughlin&F.]
Freese, Chris E. ....'52 '78 C.339 B.S. L.421 J.D. Co. Ct. J.
Johnson, Susan O'Neal, (CV) .... '57 '90 C.338 B.A. L.365 J.D. 805 S. Washington Street
Kranz, Worthy B. ....'17 '50 C.339 B.S.L. L.365 LL.B. Ret. Cir. J.
Mayberry, Steven W. ....'63 '89 C.357 B.A. L.607 J.D. [Wood&M.]

McLaughlin and Florini, Ltd., (AV) BB
16 South Washington Street, P.O. Box 228, 61951
Telephone: 217-728-7325 Fax: 217-728-8122
Email: twtignor@one-eleven.net
Joseph L. McLaughlin (1884-1963); James M. McLaughlin (1918-2005); Joseph V. Florini.
Probate, Real Estate, Estate Planning, Corporation and Tax Law. Trials. General Civil Practice.
Representative Clients: Scott State Bank, Bethany, Ill.; State Bank of Arthur, Ill.; First Mid-Illinois Bank & Trust.
See Professional Biographies, SULLIVAN, ILLINOIS

Powers, Arthur, Jr. ....'39 '78 C.234 B.S.Ed. L.801 J.D. Assoc. Cir. J.
Stone, Paul ....'15 '42 C&L.339 B.S., J.D. 303 E. Harrison St.‡
Werner, Kristin Denise ....'69 '94 C.477 A.B. L.851 J.D. 18 Seth Dunscomb Drive
Wood, Steven K., (BV) ....'40 '71 C.336 B.A. L.339 J.D. [Wood&M.]
Wood & Mayberry, (BV) ....200 W. Harrison St.
Wright, R. Glen, (CV) ....'48 '77 C.339 A.B. L.801 J.D. Asst. States Atty.

SUMMIT, 10,637, *Cook Co.*

Balich, Jos. C. ....'25 '53 C.118 B.A. L.477 LL.B. 7336 W. 63 St., Argo
Bojanowski, Thaddeus J. ....'34 '62 C&L.424 B.S.C., J.D. 6145 S. 75th Ave.
Dineff, Beverly E. ....'44 '72 C&L.37 B.A., J.D. Asst. Real Estate Comr.
Martell, Matthew T., Law Offices of '72 '99
C.145 B.A. L.959 J.D. 7557 W. 63rd Street (⊙Chicago)
Pitts, Frances M. '59 '85 C.436 B.A. L.879 J.D.
Exec. V.P. & Gen. Coun., Umbrella Bancorp, Inc.

SWANSEA, 10,579, *St. Clair Co.*

Babka, Brian A., (BV) ....'54 '82 C.801 B.S. L.734 J.D. [Chatham&B.]
Chatham, Grey, (BV) ....'54 '80 C.234 B.S. L.365 J.D. [Chatham&B.]
Chatham & Babka, (BV) ....4010 N. Illinois St.
Hazlett, Kevin M., Attorney at Law, (BV) '55 '87
C.837 B.S. L.734 J.D. 209 W. Pointe, Ste. C
Livingston, Penni S. ....'61 '87 C&L.589 B.A., J.D. 4972 Benchmark Centre
Lopinot, Vincent J., (AV) ....'53 '78 C.338 L.734 2902 Polo Court
McLaughlin, Daniel M. .... '— '94 C.1082 B.A. L.801 J.D. 1609 North Illinois Street
Mealey, Allen George ....'62 '95 C.420 B.S. L.861 J.D. Gateway Bankruptcy Group
Miller, Doreen H. '57 '83
C.339 B.S.N. L.209 J.D. Title Coun., First American Title Ins. Co.
Schlichter, Jerome J., (AV) ....'48 '72 C.339 B.S. L.1068 J.D. [Schlichter,B.&D.] ⊙

Schlichter, Bogard & Denton, (AV)
2661 N. Illinois, Suite 187, 62226 ⊙
Telephone: 618-632-3329
URL: http://www.lawyers.com/sbd
Member of Firm: Jerome J. Schlichter.
Personal Injury, Railroad Personal Injury, Maritime Personal Injury, Medical Malpractice, Products Liability, Toxic Tort Law.
St. Louis, Missouri Office: 100 South Fourth Street, Suite 900. Telephone: 314-621-6115.
See Professional Biographies, SWANSEA, ILLINOIS

SYCAMORE, * 12,020, *DeKalb Co.*

Boies, John H. '44 '70 C.197 B.A. L.339 J.D.
Exec.V.P. & Tr. Offr., The National Bk. & Tr. Co. of Sycamore
Brown, Kathryn J. '— '86 C&L.589 B.A., J.D.
V.P. & T.O., The National Bk. & Tr. Co. of Sycamore
Buck, James R., (BV) ....'46 '74 C.399 B.A. L.339 J.D. [Klein,S.B.W.&L.]
Buick, Kevin E., (BV) ....'64 '90 C.174 B.A. L.597 J.D. [Cliffe,F.C.B.&B.]
Buick, Marcy L. ....'64 '90 C.339 B.S. L.589 J.D. [Cliffe,F.C.B.&B.]
Camic, David E., (AV) ....'— '87 C.58 B.A. L.365 J.D. [Camic,J.W.&M.]

Camic, Johnson, Wilson & McCulloch, P.C., (AV) BB
207 W. State Street, 60178
Telephone: 815-899-0155
Email: administrator@cjwm.com URL: http://www.lawyers.com/cjwm
David E. Camic; Gary V. Johnson; Thomas O. McCulloch.
Languages: Spanish.

(This Listing Continued)

Camic, Johnson, Wilson & McCulloch, P.C. (Continued)
Criminal Trial Practice, including Assault, Batter, Burglary, Driver's License Suspension, Driving While Intoxicated (DUI), Forfeiture, Fraud, Death Penalty, Felonies, Forgery, Manslaughter, Misdemeanors, Murder, Parole and Probation, Post-Conviction Remedies, Search and Seizure, Sex Crimes, Theft, Traffic Violations, and Weapons Charges. Expungements and Secretary of State hearings. Family Practice, including Child Custody and Visitation, Divorce, Child Support and Adoption. Real Estate.
See Professional Biographies, SYCAMORE, ILLINOIS

Campbell, Calvin C., (BV) .... '63 '91 C.301 B.A. L.589 J.D. [Campbell]
Campbell Law Firm, The, (BV) .... 921 Berkshire Court
Chuffo, Victoria ..... '65 '91 C.720 B.A. L.146 J.D. Pub. Def., DeKalb Co. Pub. Def. Off.
Cliffe, Foster, Corneille, Buick & Buick, LLC, (BV)
331 West State Street (⊙De Kalb, Hinckley, Shabbona, Waterman)
Coghlan, Michael P. .... '58 '83 C.339 B.A. L.146 J.D. [Smith&T.]

Cronauer, Charles E., (BV) '45 '74 C.602 B.A. L.365 J.D.
1101 DeKalb Avenue, 60178
Telephone: 815-895-8585 FAX: 815-895-4070
Email: cronauerlaw@aol.com URL: http://www.cronauerlaw.com
General Civil Trial and Appellate Practice in State and Federal Courts. Real Estate, Zoning Planning, Land Use, Business, Corporation, Commercial, Probate, Estate Planning, Trust, Personal Injury, Products Liability, Workers Compensation, Insurance, and National and International Franchising and Agricultural Law, Elder Law, Business Law, Environmental Law.
References: National Bank & Trust Company of Sycamore; De Kalb Bank; First National Bank in De Kalb; The American Bank of De Kalb.
See Professional Biographies, SYCAMORE, ILLINOIS

Dombek, James J. '55 '81 C.589 B.S. L.46 J.D.
V.P. & T.O., The National Bk. & Tr. Co. of Sycamore
Donnelly, James ....'44 '74 C.589 B.S. L.146 J.D. Co. J.
Florschuetz, Diane M. '51 '89 C&L.589 B.S., J.D.
V.P. & Secy., The National Bk. & Tr. Co. of Sycamore
Hoenig, Lesley A. .... '77 '02 C.339 B.S. L.589 J.D. P.O. Box 273
Jenkins, Robert C. .... '25 '53 C.339 L.146 J.D. Assoc. Cir. J.
Johnson, Gary V., (AV) .... '— '78 C.340 B.A. L.221 J.D. [Camic,J.W.&M.]

Kinnally, Krentz, Loran, Hodge & Herman, P.C.
(See Aurora)

Klein, Ronald G., (AV) .... '39 '63 C&L.339 B.S., LL.B. [Klein,S.B.W.&L.]

Klein, Stoddard, Buck, Waller & Lewis, LLC, (AV)
2045 Aberdeen Court, 60178
Telephone: 815-748-0380 Fax: 815-748-4030
Email: info@ksbwl.com URL: http://www.ksbwl.com
Ronald G. Klein; James A. Stoddard; James R. Buck; Bradley J. Waller; Jeffrey L. Lewis.
General Civil and Trial Practice. Appeals, Probate, Real Estate, Bankruptcy, Banking, Corporate, Commercial, Estate Planning Law, Elder Law, Personal Injury, Divorce, Adoption, and Family Law.
Representative Clients: The National Bank and Trust Co.; Resource Bank; Squaw Grove and Pierce Township; Cortland and Sycamore Fire Protection District; Kishwaukee Community Hospital; DeKalb Area Association of Realtors; DeKalb County Building Authority; Village of Hinckley; Conserv FS, Inc.
See Professional Biographies, SYCAMORE, ILLINOIS

Krasner, Jeffrey M., (BV) '49 '77 C.894 A.B. L.146 J.D.
407 West State Street, Suite 4, 60178-1455
Telephone: 815-899-8436 Fax: 815-895-1700
Email: krasnerlaw2001@yahoo.com URL: http://www.lawyers.com/krasnerlaw
Language: German.
General Practice. Real Estate, Estate Planning, Bankruptcy, Debtors and Creditor Rights, Business Law, Litigation, Wills, Trusts, Estates, Collections.
Representative Clients: 1st American Title Insurance Company; Welsh Industries; Star Properties; S & H Builders; U.A.G., Inc.; T.Q.M., Inc.; Bygone Era; 407 West State Associates.
See Professional Biographies, SYCAMORE, ILLINOIS

Larson, Richard D., (BV) ....'44 '69 C&L.339 B.A., J.D. 111 East Elm Street
Lewis, Jeffrey L. ....'69 '99 C&L.589 B.S., J.D. [Klein,S.B.W.&L.]

Leynaud & Leynaud, A Prof. Corp., Law Offices of
(See Peru)

Manning, Mary K. .... '36 '87 C.157 B.S. L.146 J.D. Asst. State's Atty.
Marshall, James K. .... '26 '53 C.602 B.S. L.146 J.D. Ret. Assoc. Cir. J.
McCulloch, Thomas O., (AV) .... '— '74 C.207 B.A. L.365 J.D. [Camic,J.W.&M.]
Meilinger, Rex F. .... '21 '50 C.339 B.S. L.597 J.D. Cir. J.
Mogren, Linda G. '59 '85 C.183 B.A. L.174 J.D.
(adm. in CO; not adm. in IL) 204 S. Walnut St.‡
Moudry, Ladimir J. .... '12 '39 C&L.477 B.A., J.D. 625 Parkside Dr.‡
Rice, Philip M., (CV) .... '62 '88 C.589 B.A. L.339 J.D. Chicago Title Co.
Rove-Williams, Lisa May .... '— '89 C&L.589 B.S., J.D. 114 W. State Street
Slingerland, Jack C., (BV) ....'50 '77 C.589 B.S. L.424 J.D. 114 W. State St.
Smith, Alexander J. ....'70 '98 C.679 B.A. L.209 J.D. [Smith&T.]
Smith, Peter Thomas, (BV) .... '46 '71 C.424 B.S. L.273 J.D. [Smith&T.]

Smith & Tucker, (AV)
1958 Aberdeen Court, 60178
Telephone: 815-787-7033 Fax: 815-748-1020
URL: http://www.smithtucker.com
Members of Firm: Peter Thomas Smith; Watson B. Tucker; Alexander J. Smith; Michael P. Coghlan. From its offices in Sycamore, Illinois, Smith & Tucker provides services to its clients in the following core areas: civil litigation, corporate and business law, municipal and non-profit law, real estate development (including zoning, land use, and planning), commercial and residential real estate sale and leasing transactions, employer labor law, banking practices and loan review, creditor's rights and bankruptcy, collections and mortgage foreclosures, wills and trusts, estate planning and health care directives, probate, personal injury law, employment law, civil rights law, election law and criminal litigation.
Reference: The National Bank & Trust Company of Sycamore.
See Professional Biographies, SYCAMORE, ILLINOIS

Stoddard, James A., (BV) ....'51 '76 C&L.339 B.S., J.D. [Klein,S.B.W.&L.]
Stuckert, Robbin J., (BV) ....'53 '90 C&L.589 B.A., J.D. 114 W. State St.
Tucker, Watson B., (AV) ....'40 '65 C&L.597 B.S., J.D. [Smith&T.]
Turner, Richard L., Jr., (BV) '55 '81 C.589 B.S.Ed. L.209 J.D.
107 West Exchange Street
Waller, Bradley J., (BV) ....'61 '88 C&L.589 B.S., J.D. [Klein,S.B.W.&L.]
Walsh, James M., (BV) ....'49 '89 C.589 B.S. L.209 J.D. Asst. State Atty.

TAYLOR SPRINGS, 670, *Montgomery Co.*

Pretnar, Alan A., (BV) ....'57 '82 C.234 B.A. L.900 J.D. 510 Hillsboro

TAYLORVILLE, * 11,427, *Christian Co.*

Alexander, Hal, (BV) ....'42 '76 C.801 B.A. L.910 J.D. Pub. Def.
Austin, Daniel W., (AV) ....'49 '74 C.357 B.A. L.910 J.D. [Meyer,A.&R.]
Baker-Bowen, Kathy M. ....'59 '00 C.339 B.S. L.801 J.D. [McWard] ⊙
Barra, Raymond P., (BV) ....'25 '52 C&L.352 B.A., LL.B. 210 S. Main St.
Beavers, James O., (AV) ....'34 '64 C.234 B.S. L.734 J.D. [Beavers,G.&F.]

Beavers, Graham & Fines, (AV)
221 West Main Cross, P.O. Box 320, 62568
Telephone: 217-824-3341 Facsimile: 217-824-3842
URL: http://www.lawyers.com/bg&flaw
Members of Firm: Charles Evans Bliss (1906-1986); Richard G. Hershey (1916-1991); James O. Beavers; Edward T. Graham, Jr.; David R. Fines; Beth E. Brotherton; Michelle M. Coady.
Civil Trial Law, Probate, Real Estate, Taxation, Personal Injury Defense, Insurance Law, Domestic Relations, Appellate Practice, Banking Law.
Attorneys for: U.S. Bank of Taylorville; First National Bank Taylorville; Peoples Bank & Trust.
See Professional Biographies, TAYLORVILLE, ILLINOIS

Brotherton, Beth E. ....'65 '97 C.357 B.A. L.734 J.D. [Beavers,G.&F.]
Broverman, P.C., (BV) ....113 E. Main Cross
Broverman, Quinn M. ....'71 '97 C.337 B.A. L.801 J.D. [Broverman]
Broverman, Robert, (BV) .... '40 '65 C.337 B.A. L.339 LL.B. [Broverman]
Coady, John P. ....'52 '77 C.339 B.A. L.608 J.D. Cir. J.
Coady, Michelle M. ....'76 '03 C.801 B.S. L.502 J.D. [Beavers,G.&F.]
Cooper, J. Robert ....'52 '78 C.880 B.A. L.802 J.D. Breeze Printing Co.
DePaepe, Louis A., (BV) .... '65 '91 C&L.339 B.A., J.D. 222 West Market Street
Doyle, Thomas E., (BV) .... '50 '76 C.339 B.S. L.365 J.D. [Doyle&F.]
Doyle & Fraley, (BV) ....123 S. Washington St.
Ess, Gerry A., The Law Offices of ...'69 '94 C.339 B.A. L.734 J.D. 215 West Main Cross
Fines, David R., (AV) ....'62 '87 C&L.339 B.S., J.D. [Beavers,G.&F.]
Fraley, Vance L., (BV) ....'34 '58 C&L.339 B.S., J.D. [Doyle&F.]
Fry, Alicia M. ....'78 '02 C.291 B.A. L.734 J.D. 101 S. Main St.
Givens, Hartzell ....'12 '39 C.248 A.B. L.424 J.D. Christian Co. Title Co.
Graham, Edward T., Jr., (BV) ....'52 '82 C.958 B.S. L.365 J.D. [Beavers,G.&F.]
Grigsby, Gregory B., (BV) ....'51 '77 C.1101 B.A. L.744 J.D. States Atty.
Lacy, Thomas William .... '52 '79 C.734 B.A. L.201 J.D. 209 S. Washington St.
McWard, Monroe D., (CV) ....'59 '85 C.339 B.S. L.879 J.D. [McWard] ⊙
McWard Law Office, (CV) ....210 South Webster Street (⊙Springfield)
Meyer, William J., Jr., (AV) ....'29 '53 C.339 B.S. L.146 LL.B. [Meyer,A.&R.] ‡

Meyer, Austin & Romano, P.C., (AV)
210 South Washington Street, P.O. Box 140, 62568-0140
Telephone: 217-824-4931 Telecopier: 217-824-8892
Clark H. Miley (1905-1985); Daniel W. Austin; Rocci L. Romano; William J. Meyer, Jr. (Retired).
General Civil and Criminal Trial and Appellate Practice in State and Federal Courts. Insurance Defense, Personal Injury, Workers Compensation, Real Estate, Probate, Estate Planning, Family, Business and Municipal Law.
Reference: First Trust and Savings Bank of Taylorville.
See Professional Biographies, TAYLORVILLE, ILLINOIS

Paisley, Bradley T., (BV) ....'69 '94 C.339 B.S. L.734 J.D. Christian Co. State's Atty.
Reese, Daniel G., (CV) ....'28 '54 C.339 B.S. L.145 J.D. [Reese&R.]
Reese, Lindsey E., (Mr.), (CV) ....'59 '84 C.388 B.A. L.801 J.D. [Reese&R.]
Reese & Reese, (CV) ....205 S. Wash.
Romano, Rocci L., (AV) ....'49 '74 C.234 B.S. L.910 J.D. [Meyer,A.&R.]
Rosborough, Amy R. ....'72 '97 C.339 B.S. L.801 J.D. Asst. States Atty.
Spears, Ronald D. ....'51 '77 C.339 B.A. L.801 J.D. Cir. J.
Sweeney, Brenda, (BV) ....'13 '38 C.910 L.996 LL.B. P.O. Box 767
Taylor, Sam M. ....'10 '35 C.197 B.A. L.996 LL.B. 123 S. Wash. St.‡
Tipsword, Rolland F. ....'25 '51 C.336 A.B. L.597 LL.B. Ret. Cir. J.‡
Traynor, Stuart J. .... '19 '50 C&L.734 LL.B. 302 E. Market

TEUTOPOLIS, 1,559, *Effingham Co.*

Siemer, Richard C. ....'49 '75 C.339 B.A. L.228 J.D. Siemer Milling Co.

TINLEY PARK, 48,401, *Cook & Will Cos.*

Anders, David L. ....'59 '84 C.339 B.A. L.209 J.D. [Hutchison,A.&H.]
Bettenhausen, Donald I. '53 '81 C.1049 B.A. L.209 J.D.
17400 S. Oak Park Ave., Ste. 1W
Busch-Rubalcava, Rachel .... '56 '86 C.424 B.B.A. L.365 J.D. 1032 West Taylor Street
Cannonito, Christopher E. ....'68 '92 C.57 B.A. L.209 J.D. [C.Cannonito]
Cannonito, Christopher .... 15930 S. 75th Ct., Ste. 100
Corbett, J. J. ....'15 '41 C&L.209 LL.B. Group 4 Ins. Agcy.
Cossidente, John G., Jr. ....'57 '83 C&L.209 B.Sc., J.D. 7777 159th St., Ste. B
Donkel, Kenneth J. ....'56 '82 C.589 B.S. L.146 J.D. 7220 W. 194th St., Ste. 105
Dzik, Robert B. ....'43 '73 C&L.161 B.S.E.E., LL.B. Hyatt Legal Servs.
Fankhauser, John T. ....'22 '77 C.352 B.A. L.209 J.D. Group 4 Ins. Agcy.
Gaynor, Edward T. .... '43 '71 C&L.209 B.S.C., J.D. 17307 S. 84th Ave.
Gordan, Elias M. ....'62 '94 C.597 B.S.C.E. L.365 J.D. 16335 S. Harlem Ave. (Pat.)
Hickey, Lynn M. ....'66 '91 C.339 B.S.B.A. L.209 J.D. [Hutchison,A.&H.]
Horn, John E. ....'51 '76 C.1275 B.A. L.178 J.D. 16710 Oak Park Ave.
Hutchison, Richard L. ....'39 '67 C&L.339 B.A., J.D. [Hutchison,A.&H.]
Hutchison, Anders and Hickey .... 16860 S. Oak Park, Ste. 101
Jarman, Gregg W. ....'54 '87 C.339 B.S.Ed. L.365 J.D. 17400 S. Oak Park Ave.
Johnson, James J. ....'43 '69 C.742 B.A. L.209 J.D. 17400 Oak Park Ave.
Kenny, Mary Alice ....'61 '88 C.338 B.S. L.209 J.D. [M.A.Kenny]
Kenny, Mary Alice, Ltd. .... 16335 Harlem Ave., Ste. 400
Kleszynski, Linda C. ....'— '87 C.424 B.S. L.146 J.D. [R.N.Primack]
Kueltzo, Gary S. .... '49 '72 C.589 B.S. L.209 J.D. 17650 Heather Lane
Lanigan, John J., Law Office of .... '64 '93 C.339 B.S. L.146 J.D. P.O. Box 1245
Larson, Orval A., (Ltd.) .... '19 '48 L.424 LL.B. 17659 Oak Park Ave.
Lechner, Paul A. ....'47 '80 C.1024 B.S. L.209 J.D. Mng. Partner, TLG Ltd.
Leonard, Edward J. ....'55 '87 C.801 B.S. L.365 J.D. 6743 181st Street
Maher, George A. ....'25 '49 C.502 L.209 J.D. 16860 S. Oak Park Ave.
McCann, Robert A. ....'64 '91 C.107 B.S. L.982 J.D. Pat. Atty., Panduit Corp. (Pat.)
McGinnis, Suzanne Duggan .... '50 '80 C.741 B.A. L.365 J.D. 16431 Leslie Ann
Morehouse, Carolyn L. .... '74 '99 C.880 B.A. L.347 J.D. [R.N.Primack]
Palmisano, Nancy A. ....'54 '85 C.339 B.A. L.146 J.D. Hyatt Legal Servs.
Parchem, Robert P. ....'44 '81 C.801 B.S. L.365 J.D. 8630 W. Carriage Ln.
Price, Jill K. '— '97 C.260 B.A. L.472 J.D.
(adm. in FL; not adm. in IL) 18120 66th Ct., Apt. 103
Primack, Ronald N. ....'55 '81 C.966 B.S. L.209 J.D. [R.N.Primack]

Primack, Ronald N., L.L.C., Law Offices of
18401 Maple Creek Drive Suite 100, 60477
Telephone: 708-444-0277 Fax: 708-444-4149
Email: rnplaw@earthlink.net
Member of Firm: Ronald N. Primack. Associates: Linda C. Kleszynski; Carolyn L. Morehouse.
General Practice including Banking, Real Estate, Commercial Litigation, Business and Municipal Law.
See Professional Biographies, TINLEY PARK, ILLINOIS

Richardson, Edwin J. ....'29 '53 C.711 L.209 LL.B. 17556 Mulberry
Saltzman, Jay A. ....'68 '93 C.339 B.S. L.477 J.D. Pat. Atty., Panduit Corp. (Pat.)
Shore, Marvin P. ....'25 '53 L.209 J.D. 9325 W. 178th St.
Stone, Ollie E. ....'19 '49 C&L.209 LL.B. 16411 Mark Ln.
Weimar, John A. ....'51 '97 C.238 B.S. L.365 J.D. 8811 159th St., Ste. 3D

Wentzel, Charles R. ....'41 '68 C&L.477 B.S.E., J.D. 17301 Ridgeland Ave.
Williams, Gary R. ....'43 '70 C.589 B.A. L.365 J.D. [G.R.Williams&Assoc.]
Williams, Gary R., & Associates .... 16710 Oak Park Ave.

TOLEDO, * 1,199, *Cumberland Co.*

Cutright, John O., (BV) ....'42 '67 C&L.339 A.B., J.D. E. Side of Sq.
Prather, William C., (AV) ....'21 '47 C&L.339 A.B., J.D. 142 Courthouse Sq
Torbeck-Livesay, Judy ....'52 '92 C.234 B.A. L.801 J.D. [Winter-Black&L.] ⊙
Winter-Black, Janett S., (BV) ....'54 '79 C.234 B.A. L.801 J.D. [Winter-Black&L.] ⊙
Winter-Black & Livesay, Law Offices of, (BV) ....102 S. Meridian (⊙Mattoon)

TOLONO, 2,605, *Champaign Co.*

Sweeney, Thomas P., (BV) ....'45 '76 C.436 B.A. L.339 J.D. 409 Pamela Drive

TOLUCA, 1,315, *Marshall Co.*

Ghiglieri, Bernard J., Jr., (AV) '22 '50 C.602 A.B. L.276 J.D.
Citizens Nat. Bk. (⊙Peoria)
Ryan, Earle V., (BV) ....'33 '59 C.707 B.A. L.339 LL.B. 115 N. Main St.

TONICA, 715, *La Salle Co.*

Olivero, John, (BV) ....'24 '50 C.597 L.339 LL.B. 250 S. LaSalle St. (⊙Peru)

TOULON, * 1,328, *Stark Co.*

Rennick, James A., (BV) ....'47 '72 C.339 B.S. L.365 J.D. P.O. Box 430
Rennick, Robert H., Sr., (BV) ....'42 '67 C&L.339 B.S., J.D. 117-119 W. Court St.
Wilson, Charles M. ....'16 '40 C&L.339 A.B., LL.B. 113 N. Wash.‡

TOWER LAKES, 1,333, *Lake Co.*

Glazov, Jordan E. ....'42 '67 C.339 B.S. L.597 J.D. 24714 Nodding Flower Ct

TREMONT, 2,088, *Tazewell Co.*

Cullinan, Michael N. ....'48 '73 C.597 B.A. L.339 J.D. Pres., R.A. Cullinan & Sons
Kepple, Eugene C., (BV) ....'49 '74 C.894 B.A. L.339 J.D. 320 W. Pearl St., Ste. D

TRENTON, 2,610, *Clinton Co.*

Callahan, James P. ....'49 '76 C&L.378 B.A., J.D. [J.P.Callahan]
Callahan, J. Patrick, P.C. ....215 E. Bway.
Moran, George J., (AV) ....'13 '38 C.734 L.273 LL.B. P.O. Box 115

TROY, 8,524, *Madison Co.*

Donavon, Michelle L. ....'68 '97 C.35 B.A. L.734 J.D. 1112 Antler Drive
Downs, Alicia J. ....'73 '00 C.340 B.A. L.146 J.D. [Downs]
Downs Law Office ....535 Edwardsville Rd., Suite 120
Drazen, James M., (CV) ....'57 '82 C.502 B.A. L.734 J.D. [Drazen]
Drazen Law Office, (CV) .... 108 S. Kimberlin
Goodwin, Neil W. ....'56 '81 C.234 B.S. L.734 J.D. 33 Autumn Circle
Leonard, Mark R. ....'54 '00 C.801 B.S. L.734 J.D. [Leonard&Assoc.]
Leonard & Associates ....503 Buckeye Dr.
Levo, Bonnie Moeller ....'42 '90 C&L.801 B.S., J.D. [B.Levo&Assoc.]
Levo, Bonnie, & Associates ....200 E. Market St.
Swenson, Rebecca P. '55 '89 C.589 B.S. L.117 J.D.
(adm. in OH; not adm. in IL) 981 Weathervane Ln.‡
Trone, Doane Kent, (AV) ....'34 '60 C.927 L.339 J.D. 943 Olde Farm Rd.‡
Wendler, Arthur F., (BV) ....'22 '50 C&L.339 B.S., J.D. 200 E. Market St.

TUSCOLA, * 4,448, *Douglas Co.*

Baer, Tammy Lynn ....'70 '98 C.339 B.S. L.1439 J.D. 401 S. Main St.

Brainard Law Offices, The
(See Charleston)

Broch, Richard L., Jr. ....'56 '82 C.234 B.A. L.616 J.D. [Broch&N.]
Broch & Nolan .... 107 West South Central
Carroll, Michael G., (BV) ....'47 '75 C.234 B.S. L.339 J.D. 401 S. Main St.
Garrett, Jeannine, (CV) ....'47 '78 C&L.801 B.A., J.D. [T.J.Garrett]
Garrett, T. Jeannine, (CV) ....106 W. Sale
Lee, James D., (BV) ....'54 '80 C.339 A.B. L.174 J.D. [Lee&L.]
Lee and Lee Ltd., (BV) ....................P.O. Box 317
Lincoln, Frank W. ....'38 '64 C.210 A.B. L.339 J.D. Cir. J.
McCown, Harrison J., (AV) ....'22 '48 C&L.260 J.D. [Nichols,J.&M.]

Meyer Capel, A Professional Corporation
(See Champaign)

Moore, Emerson L., (BV) ....'43 '68 C.103 A.B. L.339 J.D. 401 S. Main St.
Murphy, Lloyd A. .....'56 '82 C.98 B.S. L.339 J.D. Pres. & Gen. Coun., Tuscola Natl. Bk.

Nichols, Jones & McCown, (AV)
104 East North Central Avenue, P.O. Box 258, 61953
Telephone: 217-253-2342 Fax: 217-253-3441
George E. Nichols (1893-1974); Harold C. Jones (1907-1965); Harrison J. McCown.
Probate, Estate Planning, Real Estate, Corporate Law and Family Farm Estate Planning..
Attorneys for: First State Bank of Newman; Villa Grove State Bank; Conrail; Illinois Central Railroad; Baltimore & Ohio Railway Co.; Murdock Township; Newman Fire Protection District.

Nolan, Kevin P. ....'65 '91 C.589 B.A. L.365 J.D. [Broch&N.]
Price, Darrell S., (CV) ....'52 '77 C.339 B.A. L.733 J.D. Asst. States Atty.
Sipich, Diane Rader ....'46 '85 C&L.339 B.S., J.D. State's Atty., Douglas Co.

UNIVERSITY PARK, 6,662, *Cook & Will Cos.*

Long, Andrew J. '70 '96 C.338 B.S. L.879 J.D.
Mng. Corp. Coun., Applied Systems, Inc.

URBANA, * 36,344, *Champaign Co.*

Auler, Robert I. ....'40 '66 C&L.339 B.A., J.D. 202 W. Green St.
Baker, Harold A. ....'29 '56 C&L.339 B.A., LL.B. U.S. Dist. J.
Balbach, S. Byron, Jr., (BV) ....'45 '70 C.691 B.A. L.339 J.D. [Balbach&F.]
Balbach, Stanley B., (AV) ....'19 '42 C&L.339 B.S., J.D. [Balbach&F.]
Balbach & Fehr, P.C., (AV) ....102 East Main, Suite 301
Bautch, Sheryl A. ....'57 '86 C.293 B.A. L.339 J.D. 202 Lincoln Sq.‡
Beattie, Ellen M., (CV) ....'60 '93 C.339 B.S. L.146 J.D. 110 W. Main St.
Beckett, Chad S., (CV) ....'72 '98 C&L.339 B.A., J.D. [Beckett&W.]
Beckett, J. Steven, (AV) ....'48 '73 C&L.339 B.A., J.D. [Ⓒ Beckett&W.]

Beckett & Webber, P.C., (BV)
508 South Broadway, P.O. Box 17160-61803, 61801-7160
Telephone: 217-328-0263 Fax: 217-328-0290
URL: http://www.lawyers.com/beckettwebberlaw
Roger B. Webber; Chad S. Beckett;—Peter T. Borich; Brett N. Olmstead; Carol A. Dison; Andrew W. B. Bequette; Barbra Ann Webber. Of Counsel: J. Steven Beckett.
General, Trial, Appellate and Federal Practice, Criminal, Personal Injury, Family, Probate and Estate Planning Law, DWI, Traffic Violations, Wills, Child Support, Divorce, Child Custody, Adoption, Workers Compensation, Real Estate, Elder Law.
See Professional Biographies, URBANA, ILLINOIS

Bequette, Andrew W. B. ....'76 '01 C&L.339 B.S., J.D. [Ⓐ Beckett&W.]
Berg, Mark E. ....'57 '82 C.597 B.A. L.339 J.D. Asst. Pub. Def.
Berns, Michael Andrew ....'68 '93 C.339 B.S.C.E. L.910 J.D. 135 W. Main St.
Bernthal, David G. ....'50 '76 C&L.339 A.B., J.D. U.S. Mag. J.
Betz, Thomas E. ......'54 '81 C.932 B.S. L.912 J.D. Univ. of Ill., Student Legal Serv. Plan
Blockman, Arnold F. ....'47 '73 C.1015 B.S. L.339 J.D. Cir. J.
Bonds, Bruce L., (AV) ....'57 '82 C.339 B.A. L.910 J.D. [Heyl,R.V.&A.]
Borich, Peter T., (CV) ....'61 '92 C.339 B.S. L.209 J.D. [Ⓐ Beckett&W.]
Bruno, Thomas A., & Associates, (BV) .....'54 '80 C&L.339 B.A., J.D. 301 W. Green St.
Bryan, George G., (AV) ....'39 '64 C.234 B.S. L.1119 J.D. [Tummelson B.&K.]
Burgard, Warren E. ....'27 '54 L.734 LL.B. 1202 E. McHenry‡
Carson, John D., (CV) ....'20 '46 C&L.339 B.A., LL.B. 714 W. Iowa
Casady-Trimble, Carolyn, (BV) ....'43 '85 C.352 B.A. L.339 J.D. P.O. Box 443
Causeman, Sue D. ....'51 '81 C.1247 B.A. L.801 J.D. Staff Atty., Appl. Ct.
Clem, Harry Earl ....'46 '72 C&L.339 B.A., J.D. Cir. J.
Clemons, Holly Fujiye ....'57 '84 C.393 B.A. L.209 J.D. Assoc. Co. J.
Clower, Laura D., (AV) '59 '88 C.893 B.A. L.339 J.D.
Assoc. Univ. Coun., Univ. of IL, Univ. Coun. Off.

Craig & Craig
(See Mattoon)

Cribbet, John E. ....'18 '47 C.340 A.B. L.339 J.D. Prof. of Law Emeritus, Univ. of Ill.
Davis, Francis J., (BV) ....'39 '71 C.357 B.S. L.339 J.D. [Maloney&D.]
Dedman, James C., (CV) ....'48 '75 C.234 B.S. L.339 J.D. 102 W. Main
De La Mar, John R. ....'45 '70 C&L.339 B.A., J.D. Cir. J.
Dison, Carol A., (CV) ....'61 '91 C.808 B.A. L.339 J.D. [Ⓐ Beckett&W.]

Dobbins, Fraker, Tennant, Joy & Perlstein, A Professional Corporation
(See Champaign)

Dobrovolny, James L., (BV) ....'48 '75 C.339 B.S. L.365 J.D. P.O. Box 686
Dunbar, Florence W. ....'23 '46 C.145 B.A. L.209 J.D. 2001 S. Lindcoln Ave.
Einhorn, Ann Adler ....'38 '79 C.914 B.A. L.339 J.D. Assoc. Cir. J.
Elder & Disability Law Firm, (BV) ....................P.O. Box 905

Erwin, Martinkus & Cole, Ltd.
(See Champaign)

Everson-Donnelly, Wanda Yvette ....'75 '00 L.339 J.D. Asst. State Atty.
Facer, Thorpe, (BV) ....'57 '88 C&L.101 B.A., J.D. [Elder&D.]
Fallon, Laurence J. ....'61 '91 C.436 B.A. L.424 J.D. V.P., The Carle Foundation
Fehr, E. Thomas, (BV) ....'47 '71 C.802 B.A. L.339 J.D. [Balbach&F.]
Fehrenbacher, Jeffrey L. ....'54 '78 C.339 B.S. L.477 J.D. Univ. of Ill.
Finch, Robert M., (CV) ....'47 '74 C&L.339 B.A., LL.B. [Finch]
Finch Law Office, (CV) ....2203 Combes St.
Fitz-Gerald, Roger M. ....'35 '61 C&L.339 B.S., J.D. 1104 S. Orchard St.‡
Flodstrom, John D., (BV) ....'61 '86 C.339 B.A. L.589 J.D. [Heyl,R.V.&A.]

Flynn, Palmer & Tague
(See Champaign)

Follmer, Clive, (AV) ....'31 '58 C&L.339 B.S., J.D. P.O. Box 97
Ford, Jeffrey B. ....'51 '76 C&L.339 B.S., J.D. Assoc. Cir. J.
Forrester, Gary D. ....'46 '75 C.234 B.S. L.339 J.D. [Ⓐ Phebus&K.]
Frederick, Jeffrey D., (CV) ....'57 '82 C.589 B.A. L.146 J.D. [Frederick&H.]
Frederick, Robert G., (AV) '48 '72 C.589 B.S. L.339 J.D.
Ct. of Claims J. [Frederick&H.]
Frederick & Hagle, (AV) ....129 W. Main St.
Frooman, Hilary W., (CV) ....'54 '81 C&L.339 B.A., J.D. Asst. U.S. Atty.
Fruehling, Keith E., (BV) ....'68 '93 C.339 B.S. L.365 J.D. [Heyl,R.V.&A.]
Garrett, Mark ....'55 '81 C.930 B.A. L.1068 J.D. 1207 East Florida Avenue
German, Greg J., (BVⓉ) '61 '91 C.340 B.A. L.845 J.D.
(adm. in TX; not adm. in IL) [Tepper,M.&G.]
Gerstein, Marvin I. ....'40 '64 C.339 B.S. L.209 J.D. 803 S. Grove St.
Gibala, Edw. S. ....'23 '52 C&L.339 B.S., J.D. 506 Burkwood Ct., E‡
Grandone, Helen F., (CV) ....'47 '95 C&L.339 B.A., J.D. [Ⓐ Tummelson B.&K.]
Green, Frederick S. ....'23 '51 C&L.339 B.S., LL.B. [Ⓒ Tummelson B.&K.]
Grossman, Margaret R. ....'47 '79 C&L.339 B.Mus., J.D. Prof., Agric. Law, Univ. of IL
Guyette, Joseph K. ....'79 '04 C.97 B.S. L.339 J.D. [Ⓐ Heyl,R.V.&A.]
Hagle, James J., (BV) ....'54 '80 C.589 B.A. L.339 J.D. [Frederick&H.]
Hanlon, Patrick J. ....'69 '94 C.1082 B.S. L.910 J.D. [Frederick&H.]

Harrington & Tock
(See Champaign)

Harris, Duke C., (CV) ....'56 '81 C.977 B.A. L.300 J.D. 101 E. Main St.
Heinrich, Fred K., (BV) ....'60 '86 C&L.339 B.A., J.D. 102 E. Main St., Ste. 300
Helle, Steven J. ....'54 '79 C&L.352 B.S., J.D. Univ. of Ill.
Henss, Mark D., (BV) .....'57 '82 C.339 B.S. L.208 J.D. Assoc. Univ. Coun., Univ. of Ill.
Hessee, Susan Y., (CV) ....'49 '82 C.477 A.B. L.339 J.D. Univ. of Ill.

Heyl, Royster, Voelker & Allen, Professional Corporation, (AV)
Suite 300, 102 East Main Street, P.O. Box 129, 61803-0129 ⊙
Telephone: 217-344-0060 Telecopier: 217-344-9295
Email: firm@hrva.com URL: http://www.hrva.com
Partners: James C. Kearns; Edward M. Wagner; Michael E. Raub; Bruce L. Bonds; John D. Flodstrom; Bradford J. Peterson; Keith E. Fruehling. Associates: Toney J. Tomaso; Jay E. Znaniecki; Keith B. Hill; Kingshuk K. Roy; Monica H. Sholar; Joseph K. Guyette.
General Civil Trial and Appellate Practice in all Courts, Insurance Defense, Workers'' Compensation Defense, Professional Liability Defense, Truck Accidents, Construction Law, Railroad Accidents and Injuries, Insurance Coverage, Self Insured Defense, Products Liability Defense, Civil Rights, Asbestos Defense, Class Action Defense, Corporate Law, Health Care, Banking, Government, Employment, Environmental, Probate, Elder Law, Agribusiness, Immigration, Religious Institutions, Nonprofit and Charitable Organizations, College and University Law, and Real Estate.
Peoria, Illinois Office: Suite 600, Chase Building, 124 S.W. Adams, 61602. Telephone: 309-676-0400. Telecopier: 309-676-3374.
Springfield, Illinois Office: Suite 575, National City Center, P.O. Box 1687, 62705. Telephone: 217-522-8822. Telecopier: 217-523-3902.
Rockford, Illinois Office: Second Floor, National City Bank Building, 120 West State Street, P.O. Box 1288, 61105-1288. Telephone: 815-963-4454. Telecopier: 815-963-0399.
Edwardsville, Illinois Office: Suite 100, Mark Twain Plaza II, 103 West Vandalia Street, P.O. Box 467, 62025. Telephone: 618-656-4646. Telecopier: 618-656-7940.
See Professional Biographies, URBANA, ILLINOIS

Hicks, Sharon A., (CV) ....'62 '88 C&L.608 B.A., J.D. 401 West Elm
Higgins, Byron H. ....'38 '62 C&L.912 A.B., LL.B. Univ. Coun., Univ. of Ill.
Hill, Keith B. ....'77 '02 C.16 B.A. L.339 J.D. [Ⓐ Heyl,R.V.&A.]
Hoff, David H., (AV) ....'50 '75 C.339 B.S. L.365 J.D. Asst. U.S. Atty.
Holland, Roger W. '67 '97
C.339 A.B. L.801 J.D. Res. & Law Libr., Champaign Co. Law Libr.
Holz, Stephen Joachim ....'59 '92 C&L.339 B.F.A., J.D. City Atty.
Ingersoll, Mark Eugene ....'75 '01 C.999 B.B.A. L.879 J.D. 507 S. Broadway Avenue
Ivy, Alfred D., III, Attorney at Law ....'71 '02 C&L.339 B.A., J.D. 202 W. Green St.

Kaczor, Mark A. '53 '84 C.602 B.A. L.1048 J.D.
(adm. in NY; not adm. in IL) University of Illinois, College of Engineering
Karplus, Wayne .... '56 '83 C&L.339 B.A., J.D. Asst. Pub. Def.
Kearns, James C., (AV) .... '44 '75 C.602 B.A. L.339 J.D. [Heyl,R.V.&A.]
Keller, Robert O., (BV) .... '43 '71 C.531 B.S. L.383 J.D. 210 N Broadway Ave
Knox, E. Phillips, (AV) .... '46 '71 C.473 B.S. L.339 J.D. [Tummelson B.&K.]
Koester, Thomas F., (BV) .... '56 '82 C.352 B.A. L.221 J.D. [Phebus&K.]
Krause, Harry D. .... '32 '59 C&L.477 B.A., J.D. 903 Silver St.‡
Ladd, Heidi .... '56 '82 C&L.339 B.A., J.D. Asst. States Atty.
Landsman, Spencer J. .... '54 '79 C.861 B.A. L.209 J.D. 2021 Boudreau‡
Lenik, Diana S. .... '52 '77 C.597 B.A. L.801 J.D. 202 W. Green

Lietz, Banner & Ford
(See Champaign)

Loeb, Sandra Kay .... '72 '99 C&L.339 A.B., J.D. [⊠ Frederick&H.]

Maatuka, Shayla, Law Office of '— '04 C&L.339 B.A., J.D.
306 W. Green Street, 61801
Telephone: 217-337-0700 Fax: 217-337-0707
Email: maatukalaw@insightbb.com URL: http://www.maatukalaw.com
Real Estate: Litigation, Residential, Commercial, Contracts, Closings, Land Trusts, Landlord Tennant, Evictions, Foreclosures; Business Law including Contracts, Incorporations, LLC's, Small Business, Advertisement, Corporate; Taxation; Family Law & Divorce; Immigration.
See Professional Biographies, URBANA, ILLINOIS

Madigan, Timothy O. .... '43 '67 C&L.339 B.S., J.D. Dep. Coun., Univ. of Ill.
Maloney, John E., (BV) .... '44 '73 C.436 B.S. L.424 J.D. [Maloney&D.]
Maloney & Davis, (BV) .... 135 W. Main Street
Mann, Arthur L., (BV) .... '45 '70 C&L.339 B.S., J.D. [Tepper,M.&G.]
Marsh, Roger A., (BV) .... '46 '74 C.589 B.S. L.339 J.D. [Pavia&M.]
McClellan, Michael B., (BV) .... '46 '74 C&L.339 B.S., J.D. 102 E. Main St., Ste. 301
McCuskey, Michael P. .... '48 '75 C.338 B.S. L.734 J.D. Chief J.
McGavran, Jacqueline A., (CV) .... '57 '82 C.234 B.A. L.61 J.D. 2403 Burlison Dr.

Meyer Capel, A Professional Corporation
(See Champaign)

Moore, David R., (BV) .... '59 '83 C.108 B.A. L.345 J.D. [Prillaman&M.]
Mulcahey, Robert W. '50 '87
C.339 B.A. L.146 J.D. V.P. & Gen. Coun., Stratum Med, Inc.
Novak, Anthony E., (BV) .... '50 '77 C.293 A.B. L.339 J.D. 130 W. Main Street
Olmstead, Brett N. .... '68 '94 C&L.339 B.A., J.D. [⊠ Beckett&W.]
Parkinson, Donald R. .... '46 '72 C&L.339 B.A., J.D. 135 W. Main
Pavia, Joseph D. .... '52 '77 C&L.339 B.S., J.D. [Pavia&M.]
Pavia & Marsh, Attys. at Law, A Prof. Corp., (BV) .... P.O. Box 987
Peak, Philip W. .... '76 '02 C.340 B.A. L.339 J.D. [⊠ Frederick&H.]
Pennacchi, Marjorie Lawler '60 '93 C.659 B.A. L.339 J.D.
Staff Atty., City of Ubana IL
Perrero, Bryan M., (CVⓉ) '68 '93 C.339 B.A. L.879 J.D.
Asst. Univ. Coun., Univ. of IL
Peterson, Bradford J., (BV) .... '62 '87 C.338 B.S. L.801 J.D. [Heyl,R.V.&A.]
Petit, Charles E. .... '— '95 C.910 A.B., A.B. L.339 J.D. 1012 N. Busey
Phebus, Joseph W., (AV) .... '40 '68 C&L.339 B.S., J.D. [Phebus&K.]

Phebus & Koester, (AV)
136 West Main Street, 61803-2797
Mailing Address: P.O. Box 1008, Urbana, IL 61803-1008
Telephone: 217-337-1400 Telecopier: 217-337-1607
URL: http://www.phebuslaw.com
Members of Firm: Joseph W. Phebus; Thomas F. Koester;—Gary D. Forrester; Daniel J. Pope; Helen Pope.
Civil trial practice in all courts, including class actions, mass torts, personal injury, including products liability, medical malpractice, automobile accidents, slip and fall, and railroad.
Representative Clients: Furnished upon request.
See Professional Biographies, URBANA, ILLINOIS

Phipps, John T., Law Offices, P.C.
(See Champaign)

Piland, John C., (BV) .... '61 '87 C&L.339 B.S., J.D. State's Atty.
Pope, Daniel J., (AV) .... '48 '75 C.424 B.A. L.365 J.D. [⊠ Phebus&K.]
Pope, Helen .... '— '91 C&L.339 B.A., J.D. [⊠ Phebus&K.]
Power, Lisa M., (BVⓉ) '58 '96 C.347 B.G.S. L.260 J.D.
In-House Compliance Coun., Carle Clinic Association
Prillaman, Roger L., (BV) .... '52 '80 C.339 B.S. L.345 J.D. [Prillaman&M.]
Prillaman & Moore, Ltd., (BV) .... 220 W. Main St.
Raub, Michael E., (BV) .... '52 '77 C&L.801 B.A., J.D. [Heyl,R.V.&A.]
Rawles, Margaret O'Donoghue, (BV) '56 '83
C&L.339 B.S.W., J.D. Asst. Univ. Coun., Univ. of Ill.

Rawles, O'Byrne, Stanko & Kepley, P.C.
(See Champaign)

Reisman, Carl H. .... '61 '96 C&L.339 B.A., J.D. [Reisman]

Reisman Law Office
212 W. Green Street, P.O. Box 395, 61803
Telephone: 217-344-1000 Fax: 217-344-1010
Email: creisman61@yahoo.com URL: http://www.reismanlaw-firm.com
Member of Firm: Carl H. Reisman.
Personal Injury, Automobile Accidents, Slip and Fall, Workers Compensation, Wrongful Death.
See Professional Biographies, URBANA, ILLINOIS

Rice, Louis W., III '51 '77 C.797 B.A. L.469 J.D.
(adm. in GA; not adm. in IL) Univ. of Ill. Found.
Riley, Nancy M. .... '29 '72 C.388 B.A. L.560 J.D. Parkland Coll.
Rose, Thomas Chapin, II '73 '00
C&L.339 B.A., J.D. Champaign County State's Atty. Office
Rosenbaum, Randall B. .... '64 '92 C.597 B.S. L.339 J.D. B-8 Lincoln Square
Rotunda, Marcia A. .... '46 '71 C.879 B.A. L.309 J.D. Assoc. Coun., Univ. of Ill.
Roy, Kingshuk K. .... '78 '02 C&L.339 B.S., J.D. [⊠ Heyl,R.V.&A.]
Ryan, Gregory L., (CV) .... '56 '84 C.927 B.A. L.900 J.D. [G.L.Ryan]
Ryan, Gregory L., Law Offices, (CV) .... 123 W. Main St., Suite 210
Sholar, Monica H. .... '79 '04 C.339 B.S. L.945 J.D. [⊠ Heyl,R.V.&A.]
Silkwood, Larry R., (BV) .... '47 '75 C.801 B.S. L.339 J.D. P.O. Box 67
Silverman, Brian C. .... '43 '71 C.1016 B.A. L.209 J.D. 102 W. Main St.
Solberg, Kristin R., (CV) .... '59 '91 C.103 A.B. L.339 J.D. 130 W. Main St.
Steigmann, Robert J. .... '44 '68 C&L.339 B.S., J.D. State of IL, 4th Dist. Appl.
Stone, Victor J. .... '21 '49 C.604 A.B. L.178 LL.B. 1804 Pleasant Circle‡
Sullivan, Ramona Mary .... '71 '96 C&L.339 B.A., J.D. Pub. Def.
Summers, Holten D., (BV) .... '38 '83 C.446 B.A. L.339 J.D. [Webber&T.]
Tan-Sanchez, Charisma T. .... '71 '95 C.112 B.S. L.1066 J.D. Sr. Asst. States Atty.
Taylor, John C., (AV) .... '53 '79 C.145 B.A. L.339 J.D. 2105 S. Zuppke
Tepper, Michael, (BV) .... '41 '67 C.339 B.S. L.477 J.D. [Tepper,M.&G.]
Tepper, Mann & German, P.C., (BV) .... P.O. Box 548
Thies, David C., (AV) .... '55 '80 C&L.339 B.A., J.D. [Webber&T.]
Thies, John E., (AV) .... '62 '88 C.347 B.A. L.339 J.D. [Webber&T.]
Thies, Richard L., (AV) .... '31 '55 C&L.339 B.A., J.D. [Webber&T.]

Thomas, Mamer & Haughey, LLP
(See Champaign)

Threlkeld, A. Brian '60 '02 C.678 B.A. L.178 J.D.
(adm. in SC; not adm. in IL) Pub. Def.
Tomaso, Toney J., (BV) .... '70 '95 C.339 B.A. L.420 J.D. [⊠ Heyl,R.V.&A.]
Townsend, John G. .... '48 '75 C.246 B.A. L.339 J.D. Cir. J.
Tummelson, Hurshal C., (AV) .... '23 '50 C&L.339 J.D. [⊡ Tummelson B.&K.]

Tummelson Bryan & Knox, (AV)
115 North Broadway, 61801-0099
Mailing Address: P.O. Box 99, Urbana, IL 61803-0099
Telephone: 217-367-2500 Fax: 217-367-2555
Email: info@tbklaw.com URL: http://www.tbklaw.com
Partners: George G. Bryan; E. Phillips Knox; Allen E. Verchota III. Associate: Helen F. Grandone. Of Counsel: Hurshal C. Tummelson; Frederick S. Green.
General Practice in all Courts including Trials and Appeals, Insurance, Workers' Compensation, Corporation, Administrative, Probate, Banking, Real Estate, Creditor's Rights and Mortgage Law.
See Professional Biographies, URBANA, ILLINOIS

Ucherek, David M., Law Offices of .... '69 '95 C.59 B.A. L.365 J.D. 103 N. Race St.
Uchtmann, Donald L. .... '46 '74 C.339 B.S. L.161 J.D. Univ. of Ill.
Vallandigham, Paul H., (CV) .... '47 '72 C&L.339 B.A., J.D. 2006 Vawter Street, #1
Van Den Bussche, Richard A. .... '56 '80 C.98 B.S. L.365 J.D. 129 W. Main St.
Van Ness, Phillip R., (BV) .... '46 '75 C.508 B.S. L.365 J.D. [Webber&T.]
Veazie, Steven A. .... '50 '75 C.399 B.A. L.802 J.D. Univ. Coun., Univ. of Ill.
Verchota, Allen E., III, (BV) .... '61 '88 C.339 B.A. L.356 J.D. [Tummelson B.&K.]
Wagner, Edward M., (AV) .... '51 '80 C.436 B.A. L.190 J.D. [Heyl,R.V.&A.]
Weaver, Blake .... '50 '75 C.339 B.S. L.734 J.D. 130 W. Main St.
Webber, Barbra Ann .... '72 '97 C.340 B.A. L.339 J.D. [⊠ Beckett&W.]
Webber, Carl M., (AV) .... '44 '74 C.597 B.S. L.339 J.D. [Webber&T.]
Webber, Roger B., (BV) .... '58 '83 C.338 B.S. L.209 J.D. [Beckett&W.]

Webber & Thies, P.C., (AV)
P.O. Box 189, 61803-0189
Telephone: 217-367-1126 Fax: 217-367-3752
Craig R. Webber (1936-1998); Charles M. Webber (1903-1991); Richard L. Thies; Carl M. Webber; David C. Thies; Holten D. Summers; John E. Thies; Phillip R. Van Ness.
General, Appellate, Trial and Federal Practice, Complex Litigation, Probate, Trust, Family, Corporation, Labor/Employment (Management), Taxation, Real Estate, Zoning, Environmental, Health, Banking and Intellectual Property Law.
See Professional Biographies, URBANA, ILLINOIS

Weisiger, Gene D., (BV) .... '14 '38 C&L.339 B.S., J.D. 1 Northwood Dr.
Welch, Harvey C., Law Offices of, (CV) ... '55 '80 C.659 B.A. L.339 J.D. 401 W. Elm St.
Wozniak, John T. .... '70 '96 C.116 B.A. L.339 J.D. 108 E. Anthony Dr.
Young, Jane O'Leary .... '45 '77 L.339 J.D. 109 W. Illinois Street, Apt. 512
Znaniecki, Jay E., (BV) .... '56 '97 C&L.339 B.S., J.D. [⊠ Heyl,R.V.&A.]
Zopf, Michael J. .... '53 '80 C&L.339 B.S., J.D. P.O. Box 991

VANDALIA, * 6,975, *Fayette Co.*

Bauer, Christopher J.T., (BV) .... '67 '93 C.934 B.S. L.734 J.D. [Schaufelberger-B.] ⊙

Burnside, Johnston, Choisser & Sheafor, (AV)
First National Bank Building, 62471
Telephone: 618-283-3260 Fax: 618-283-2851
Email: bjcs@bjcs-law.com
Members of Firm: J. G. Burnside (1873-1969); Robert G. Burnside (1913-2005); Jack B. Johnston; Dale F. Choisser; M. Don Sheafor; J. Marc Kelly.
General, Civil and Trial Practice in all Courts, Banking, Real Estate, Estate Planning and Probate Law, Personal Injury, Family Law, Municipal Law, Criminal Defense.
General Counsel for: First National Bank; The First State Bank of St. Peter; State Bank of Farina; South-Central Regional Planning And Development Commission; S&S Urethane, Inc.
See Professional Biographies, VANDALIA, ILLINOIS

Choisser, Dale F., (BV) .... '53 '78 C.880 B.A. L.365 J.D. [Burnside,J.C.&S.]
Groves, C. Kenneth '09 '43 C.910 L.986 LL.B.
(adm. in MO; not adm. in IL) Route 2‡
Irvin, Rodney D. .... '65 '91 C.337 B.S. L.801 J.D. [Irvin]
Irvin Law Offices .... 522 West Gallatin Street
Johnston, Jack B., (AV) .... '37 '62 C.210 B.A. L.339 LL.B. [Burnside,J.C.&S.]
Kelly, J. Marc .... '73 '00 C.801 B.A. L.1000 J.D. [Burnside,J.C.&S.]
Lawinger, Jane M., (BV) .... '60 '91 C.961 B.S. L.209 J.D. [Lawinger]
Lawinger Law Office, (BV) .... 106 South 5th St.
LeFevre, Larry L., (BV) .... '47 '74 C.578 B.A. L.365 J.D. [LeFevre O.&M.]
LeFevre Oldfield and Meyers, Law Group, Ltd., (BV) .... 303 S. 7th Street
Myers, James R. .... '67 '94 C.475 B.A. L.589 J.D. [⊠ LeFevre O.&M.]
Oldfield, David A. .... '52 '79 C.339 B.A. L.880 J.D. [LeFevre O.&M.]
Payne, Troy G. .... '73 '00 C.150 B.A. L.801 J.D. [⊠ LeFevre O.&M.]
Schaufelberger, Patrick F., (CV) .... '65 '92 C.291 B.S. L.801 J.D. [Schaufelberger-B.] ⊙
Schaufelberger-Bauer Law Offices, The, Ltd., (BV)
107 South Fourth Street (⊙Greenville)
Schwarm, S. Gene .... '55 '81 Cir. J.
Sheafor, M. Don, (BV) .... '55 '81 C.234 B.A. L.1187 J.D. [Burnside,J.C.&S.]

Taylor Law Offices, P.C.
(See Effingham)

Thoele, Pamela J. .... '74 '99 C&L.801 B.S., J.D. [⊠ LeFevre O.&M.]

VERNON HILLS, 20,120, *Lake Co.*

Bathelt, Ed .....'— '89 C.188 B.S. L.94 J.D. Assoc. Gen. Coun., Komatsu America Corp.
Boyle, William E. .... '65 '91 C.602 B.A. L.424 J.D. American Hotel Register Co.
Carroll, Bartlett J., Jr. .... '40 '66 C&L.209 B.A., J.D. Pub. Def. Off.

Eckert, Roland A., Law Office of
(See Lake Forest)

Elfant, Noel '60 '85 C.112 B.A. L.597 J.D.
V.P. & Gen. Coun., Zebra Technologies Corp.
Foss, Richard E. '65 '90
C.694 B.A. L.424 J.D. Sr. Staff Atty., Amercian Family Insurance

Fullin Legal Services LLC
(See Libertyville)

Gruca, Kathleen M. .... '60 '84 C.589 B.S. L.209 J.D. V.P., Heller Financial, Inc.
Halpin, Thomas P. .... '27 '51 C&L.597 B.S., J.D. 1327 Cromwell Ct.‡
Heim, Ross C. .... '47 '77 C.475 B.A. L.823 J.D. [R.C.Heim]
Heim, Ross C., P.C. .... 1014 Cumberland Court

Hendricks, Frank W. '23 '56 C.214 B.S. L.213 J.D.
(adm. in MI; not adm. in IL) V.P., Intl. Div., Rust-Oleum Corp.
Jensen, Maria D. .... '60 '85 C.424 B.A. L.365 J.D. Sr. Staff Atty., Amer. Fam. Ins. Grp.
Lehmann, Thomas G. '58 '85 C.424 B.B.A. L.339 J.D.
V.P. & Gen. Coun., Washington Mutual Mortg. Sec. Corp.
Lenhardt, Eileen R. '— '82 C.339 B.A. L.365 J.D.
Mng. Atty., Amer. Fam. Claim Atty.
Litwin, Michael J. ... '47 '76 C.927 B.A. L.365 J.D. Sr. Group Pres., Heller Financial, Inc.
Marshak, Bruce S. .... '53 '80 C.339 B.S. L.146 J.D. Washington Mutual Bk.
McClain, James E., (AVⓉ) '51 '77 C.38 B.B.A. L.802 J.D.
(adm. in AR; not adm. in IL) V.P. & Gen. Couns., Tetra Pak Inc.
Moorman, Helen D. .... '40 '73 C.145 A.B. L.910 J.D. Sr. Asst. Pub. Def.
Murphy, Michael T. .... '46 '77 C.801 B.A. L.365 J.D. Corp. Coun., RPM, Inc. (Pat.)
Nardo, David D. '42 '69 C.446 B.A. L.276 J.D.
V.P. & Gen. Coun., Komatsu American Corp.
O'Connor, Kathleen A. '60 '85
C.679 B.S. L.424 J.D. Sr. Coun., Zebra Technologies Corp.
Ralph, Michael L., Jr. .... '74 '99 C.347 B.A. L.146 J.D. [Ⓐ Richards,R.&S.] ⊙
Ralph, Michael L., Sr., (AV) .... '47 '72 C.123 B.A. L.436 J.D. [Richards,R.&S.] ⊙
Richards, Alan E., (AV) .... '49 '76 C.123 B.A. L.436 J.D. [Richards,R.&S.] ⊙

Richards, Ralph & Schwab, Chartered, (AV) BB
One Hawthorn Place, 175 East Hawthorn Parkway, Suite 345, 60061 ⊙
Telephone: 847-367-9699 Fax: 847-367-9621
Email: attorney@rrs-chtd.com URL: http://www.lawyers.com/richardandschwab
Michael L. Ralph, Sr.; Alan E. Richards; David J. Schwab;—Michael L. Ralph, Jr.; Lauren B. Schreeder.
Corporate and Business. Banking and Finance. Bankruptcy and Creditors' Rights. Real Estate. Commercial Litigation.
Chicago, Illinois Office: 39 South LaSalle Street, Suite 905, 60603. Telephone: 312-641-6696. Fax: 847-367-9621. Email: attorney@rrs-chtd.com.
See Professional Biographies, VERNON HILLS, ILLINOIS

Samson, Howard ..... '49 '76 C.172 B.A. L.209 J.D. Office Coun., Chicago Title Ins. Co.
Schlesinger, Gary L.
(See Libertyville)
Schreeder, Lauren B. .... '70 '95 C.1365 B.A. L.861 J.D. [Ⓐ Richards,R.&S.] ⊙
Schwab, David J., (BV) .... '63 '90 C.347 B.S. L.209 J.D. [Richards,R.&S.] ⊙
Singer, Michael I. '40 '68 C.732 B.A. L.94 LL.B.
(adm. in DC; not adm. in IL)
V.P. & Gen. Coun., Global Mining Mkt. Div., Komatsu America Corp.
Wellek, Jeffrey A. .... '61 '86 C.339 B.S. L.597 J.D. V.P., Heller Financial, Inc.
White, George H., (AV) .... '13 '39 C&L.209 J.D. 335 Cherrywood Ct.‡
Wilgus, Jeffery L., Law Offices of '64 '98 C.589 B.S. L.146 J.D.
392 W. Sycamore Street
Wilson, Robert S. '64 '92
C.234 B.A. L.1187 J.D. Sr. Staff Atty., American Family Insurance
Zidek, James F. .... '46 '75 C.1151 B.A. L.146 J.D. 76 Sterling Heights Rd.

VIENNA, * 1,234, *Johnson Co.*

Cain, Tambra K., Attorney at Law .... '71 '03 C&L.801 B.A., J.D. P.O. Box 1311
Herbert, Marcus H., Attorney at Law .... '64 '92 C.339 B.A. L.801 J.D. P.O. Box 275
Jelliffe, Ferrell, Morris & Doerge
(See Harrisburg)
Kruger, Henry & Hunter
(See Metropolis)
Neely, Robert J., (BV) .... '23 '56 C.801 L.986 J.D. 504 W. Main St. (⊙Metropolis)
Porter, Robert B. .... '14 '38 C&L.339 B.A., LL.B. Courthouse Sq.‡
Rudert, William J. M. .... '48 '84 C&L.801 B.S., J.D. Fifth St. at Vine
Webb, Mary Jane R. .... '35 '70 C.37 B.S. L.339 J.D. P.O. Box 66‡
Williamson, James R. .... '45 '75 C.210 B.A. L.45 J.D. Cir. J., Johnson Co. Cir. Ct.

VILLA GROVE, 2,553, *Douglas Co.*

Keller, Chester R., (BV) .... '42 '68 C&L.339 B.S., J.D. 7 N. Main
Sherrick, James N., (AV) .... '18 '50 C.234 B.Ed. L.339 LL.B. 104 Vine St.‡

VILLA PARK, 22,075, *DuPage Co.*

Cain, Donna Craft, (CV) .... '63 '88 C.339 B.S. L.146 J.D. [Cain]
Cain Law Offices, (CV) .... 124 West St. Charles Road, Suite 1
Catrambone, Gregory .... '54 '80 101 E. St. Charles Rd.
Craft, Lewis John .... '27 '64 C.339 B.S.E.E. L.146 J.D. 250 East St. Charles Road
Emery, Charles W. .... '42 '76 C.492 B.A. L.424 J.D. [C.W.Emery]
Emery, Charles W., Ltd. .... 227 Highland Ave.
Haas, Glenn R. .... '42 '66 C.339 B.S. L.146 J.D. 25 E. Park Blvd.
Jacobs, Kenneth S., (BV) '31 '57
C&L.339 A.B., J.D. 408 N. Ardmore Ave. (⊙Waupaca, WI)
Kalkanian, Gerald S., Jr., (CV) '51 '78
C.589 B.S. L.365 J.D. 336 E. Central Blvd., Rm. 100
Librizzi, Joseph J., (AV) .... '29 '53 C&L.209 LL.B. 1046 S. Rand Rd.‡
Mack, John R. .... '49 '82 C.927 B.S. L.589 J.D. 128 W. St. Charles Rd.
Madden, Gregory L. .... '73 '99 C.352 B.B.A. L.589 J.D. 1901 S. Meyers Rd.
May, Daniel E. .... '51 '82 C.589 B.S. L.365 J.D. 259 E. Division
McNamara, Daniel Gerard .... '59 '92 C.338 B.S. L.365 J.D. 104 E. Jackson St.
Payne, Gordon D. .... '50 '79 C.264 A.B. L.146 J.D. 15226 Danby St.
Raudabaugh, Robert L. .... '18 '42 C&L.608 B.A., LL.B. 422 E. Highland Ave.
Reichardt, James L., (BV) .... '49 '77 C.273 B.A. L.146 J.D. 27 West Park Boulevard
Rudnik, Thomas H. .... '39 '64 C.209 B.A. L.365 LL.B. 128 W. Saint Charles Rd.
Schamberger, Hermann M., Jr. ..... '38 '68 C.393 B.A. L.146 J.D. Schamberger Bros. Inc.
Stege, Charles E. .... '11 '36 C.197 A.B. L.145 J.D. P.O. Box 10
Tancredi, Mary Brady .... '48 '78 C.1120 B.A. L.678 J.D. 1214 S. Summit Ave.

VIRDEN, 3,488, *Macoupin & Sangamon Cos.*

Deihl, Kenneth R., (BV) .... '56 '82 C.1101 B.A. L.801 J.D. P.O. Box 290
Dubosh, Anthony P., (CV) .... '22 '53 C.339 B.S. L.209 J.D. 113 N. Springfield St.

Moore, Kim L., Law Office of '55 '03 C.872 L.589 J.D.
121 N. Springfield Street, 62690
Telephone: 217-965-3772 Fax: 217-965-3778
URL: http://www.kimmoorelaw.com
Family Law, Divorce, Spousal Support, Child Support, Domestic Violence, Alimony, Real Estate, Title, Contracts, Business Law, Corporate Law, Estate Planning, Litigation, Commercial.
See Professional Biographies, VIRDEN, ILLINOIS

Murphy, Lucile J. .... '08 '40 C.739 A.B. L.339 J.D. 105 S. Finis St.‡
Nichelson, William C. .... '70 '96 C.357 B.S. L.801 J.D. 1330 N. Springfield St.
Woolley, Reed A. .... '37 '62 C.340 B.S. L.192 LL.B. P.O. Box 290

VIRGINIA, * 1,767, *Cass Co.*

Brannan, Thomas J., (AV) .... '43 '73 C.339 B.S. L.1119 J.D. [McClure,B.&H.] ⊙
Dahlem, John F., (BV) .... '50 '75 C.430 B.A. L.910 J.D. States Atty.
Grosboll, Becker & Tice, (AV) .... 134 Beardstown St. (⊙Havana, Petersburg)
Mays, Matthew C., (BV) .... '55 '80 C.1222 B.A. L.801 J.D. 240 E. Beardstown St.
McClure, George S., (AV) .... '47 '75 C&L.339 B.S., J.D. [McClure,B.&H.] ⊙
McClure, L. Milton, (AV) .... '41 '66 C&L.339 B.S., J.D. [McClure,B.&H.] ⊙
McClure, Brannan & Hardwick, (AV) .... South Side Sq. (⊙Beardstown)
Reither, Fred W. .... '24 '50 C&L.339 B.S., J.D. Cir. J.
Tice, Homer J., (BV) .... '40 '66 C&L.339 B.S., LL.B. [Grosboll,B.&T.] (⊙Petersburg)
Welch, Robert .... '41 '72 C.801 B.A. L.339 J.D. Cir. J.

WADSWORTH, 3,083, *Lake Co.*

Cashin, Maurice Matthew .... '59 '86 C&L.424 B.A., J.D. 13885 21st St.‡

WARREN, 1,550, *Jo Daviess Co.*

DeMar, Eric S. .... '25 '50 C.72 L.339 J.D. Ret. Cir. J.
Hay, Rodger K., (BV) .... '47 '72 C&L.339 B.S., J.D. [R.K.Hay]
Hay, Rodger K., Ltd., (BV) .... 157 E. Main St.
Horton, Mary M. Vincent, (CV) .... '54 '83 C.352 B.S. L.589 J.D. [Vincent,R.&T.]
Vincent, James B., (BV) .... '26 '53 C&L.352 B.S.C., LL.B. [Vincent,R.&T.] ⊙
Vincent, Roth & Toepfer, P.C., (BV) .... 125 East Main Street (⊙Galena)

WARRENVILLE, 13,363, *DuPage Co.*

Battaglia, Richard J. .... '46 '73 C.597 B.A. L.339 J.D. Sr. Atty., BP America, Inc.
Beck, Douglas G. .... '66 '92 C.339 B.A. L.597 J.D. Sr. Coun., Navistar Intl. Corp.
Beck, Staci S. .... '67 '92 C.321 B.A. L.145 J.D. Atty., BP America Inc.
Borkus, Randall H. .... '59 '01 C.589 B.S. L.365 J.D. [Borkuslaw]
Borkuslaw, Ltd. .... 2 South 061 Salem Court
Brilliant, Neil L. .... '56 '84 C&L.659 B.A., J.D. Sr. Atty., BP America, Inc.
Brown, Sharon Booker '— '92
C.800 B.A. L.494 J.D. Sr. Coun., Intl. Truck & Engine Corp.

Bueche, Gregory J. '60 '86 C&L.477 B.A., J.D.
27475 Ferry Road, 60555
Telephone: 630-717-2962 Fax: 630-717-3556
Email: gbueche7035@wowway.com URL: http://www.lawyers.com/gbueche
General Civil Litigation, Corporate and Business Law, Employment Matters, Estate Planning and Probate.
See Professional Biographies, WARRENVILLE, ILLINOIS

Cabreré, Eleanor P. '68 '93
C.597 B.S. L.347 J.D. Sr. Counsel, Intl. Truck & Engine Corp.
Calfa, Jeffrey P. '59 '92
C.1350 B.S. L.818 J.D. Sr. Coun., Intl. Truck & Engine Corp. (Pat.)
Calhoun, Mildred L. .... '54 '78 C.597 B.A. L.345 J.D. Sr. Atty., BP America, Inc.
Casey, Mary Louise, (BV) .... '50 '81 C.597 B.A. L.209 J.D. Atty., BP America, Inc.
Covey, Steven K. '51 '77
C.339 B.A. L.209 J.D. Sr. V.P. & Gen. Coun., Navistar Intl. Corp.
Cue, Brandon .... '70 '98 C.123 B.A. L.339 J.D. Atty., BP America Inc.
Dash, Jeffrey L. .... '61 '93 C.339 B.S. L.801 J.D. Sr. Coun., Intl. Truck & Engine Corp.
D'Cruz, Sheila .... '67 '92 C.339 B.A. L.145 J.D. Atty., BP America, Inc.
Douglas, Edwin L. .... '14 '40 C.999 L.146 LL.B. Ret. Cir. J.
Duffin, Robert James '47 '77 C&L.424 B.A., J.D.
Reg. Coun., First Amer. Title Ins. Co.
Dwyer, William K., Jr. .... '46 '70 C.602 B.A. L.424 J.D. Sr. Atty., BP America, Inc.
Everhardus, John C., (BVⓉ) .... '67 '92 C&L.477 B.S., J.D. BP America Inc.
Fernando, Raymond M. .... '70 '96 C.436 B.S. L.365 J.D. Sr. Coun., Navistar Intl. Corp.
Filippi, Roland K., (AV) '53 '79 C.57 B.A. L.365 J.D.
Assoc. Gen. Coun., Corp. & Region-WH, BP America Inc.
Freeman, Lisa D. .... '65 '90 C.597 B.A. L.477 J.D. Sr. Atty., BP America, Inc.
Fuchs, Elsa Theile '46 '76
C.339 B.F.A. L.424 J.D. Asst. Reg. Coun., First Amer. Title Ins. Co.
Funtowitz, Joel M. '52 '79 C.1183 B.A. L.365 J.D.
Sr. Coun., Intl. Truck & Engine Corp.
Gabala, James A., (AV) '43 '78
C.46 B.S. L.424 J.D. Sr. Patent Atty., BP America Inc. (Pat.)
Ganim, Ronald J., (AV) .... '47 '73 C.696 B.A. L.597 J.D. Sr. Atty., BP America, Inc.
Gase, Karen K. '62 '87 C.112 B.A. L.273 J.D.
(adm. in CA; not adm. in IL) BP America Inc.
Georgetown, Michelle L. .... '— '01 C.325 B.A. L.803 J.D. BP America Inc.
Goblet, Meg E. .... '58 '87 C.424 B.S. L.345 J.D. P.O. Box 579
Goetsch, Richard J. .... '42 '67 C.103 A.B. L.145 J.D. Sr. Atty., BP America, Inc.
Gonzalez, Jessica L. .... '73 '98 C.674 A.B. L.813 J.D. Atty., BP America Inc.
Goudeau, W. Bernard, III '69 '96
C&L.326 B.S., J.D. Real Estate Atty., BP America Inc.
Hall, Jennifer M. .... '63 '90 C.930 B.S.Ch.E. L.273 J.D. Atty., BP America, Inc.
Harris, Jonathan W. .... '59 '84 C.1036 B.A. L.597 J.D. Sr. Atty., BP America, Inc.
Hensley, Stephen L. '52 '76
C.347 B.S. L.930 J.D. Gen. Pat. Atty., BP America, Inc. (Pat.)
Hernandez, Steven .... '56 '81 C.961 B.A. L.966 J.D. Atty., BP America Inc.
Herrin, M. Gwen, (BV) .... '55 '80 C&L.339 B.S., J.D. Sr. Atty., BP America, Inc.
Hipp, Stephanie S. .... '73 '98 C.276 B.A. L.477 J.D. BP America Inc.
Holstein, Mark, (BV) .... '61 '87 C.339 B.A. L.209 J.D. Sr. Atty., BP America, Inc.
Hutchings, Debra L. '— '02 C.578 B.A. L.365 J.D.
Indep. Contractor, Int'l Truck & Engine Corp.
Hutchinson, John L. .... '20 '52 C.446 B.S. L.276 J.D. 2 S. 667 Pierre Curie (Pat.)
Jackson, Rochelle H. .... '55 '89 C.937 B.A. L.209 J.D. Sr. Atty., BP America, Inc.
Jarrick, Michael A. '51 '77
C.927 B.A. L.339 J.D. Gen. Atty., Intl. Truck & Engine Corp.
Jerzy, Sandra L. '60 '85 C.98 B.A. L.209 J.D.
Asst. Reg. Coun., First Amer. Title Ins. Co.
Johnson, Douglas W., (AV) .... '49 '74 C&L.208 B.A., J.D. Mng. Atty., BP America, Inc.
Kanady, Mary Jo, (AV) '42 '80 C.801 B.A. L.146 J.D.
Pat. Atty., BP America, Inc. (Pat.)
Kim, Patrick J. .... '70 '01 C.808 B.S. L.425 J.D. Patent Atty., BP America Inc.
Klewin, Jane E. .... '57 '83 C.966 B.A. L.597 J.D. Sr. Atty., BP America, Inc.
Klovanich, John G. .... '68 '96 C.454 B.B.A. L.209 J.D. Tax Atty., BP America Inc.
Knapp, Donald C., Jr. '59 '88 C.30 B.A. L.904 J.D.
Sr. Trademark & Copyright Atty., BP America Inc.
Kramer, Curt A. '68 '96 C.472 B.B.A. L.1252 J.D.
Sr. Coun., Intl. Truck & Engine Corp.
LaFleur, Frances P., (BV) ...... '62 '90 C.234 B.S. L.597 J.D. Sr. Atty., BP America Inc.
Lasics-Parker, Julie .... '59 '91 C&L.209 B.S.N., J.D. 3S080 Barkley
Lebowitz, Stephen E. '64 '91 C.882 B.A. L.273 J.D.
(adm. in DC; not adm. in IL) BP America Inc.
Lee, Stephen C. .... '71 '96 C.645 B.S. L.930 J.D. BP America Inc.
Lewis, Roberta S., (AV) .... '64 '91 C.293 B.A. L.424 J.D. Sr. Atty., BP America Inc.
Lucari, James L. .... '62 '89 C.339 B.A. L.146 J.D. Sr. Atty., BP America, Inc.

Lukasik, Susan L. '— '95
C.46 B.S.E.E. L.424 J.D. Atty., Intl. Truck & Engine Corp. (Pat.)
Mavrin, Robert J. .... '60 '85 C.339 B.A. L.209 J.D. Atty., BP America, Inc.
Mayer, Gary A., (BV) .... '58 '84 C.399 B.A. L.209 J.D. 30 W. 181 Foxboro Ct.
McDermed, Marguerite E. '51 '76 C.783 B.A. L.209 J.D.
Mng. Atty., Mktg., Trading, Coml. Real Estate, BP America, Inc.
McDonald, Scott P., (AV) '54 '89
C.339 B.S. L.597 J.D. Sr. Pat. Atty., BP America, Inc. (Pat.)
McGurn, George W., (AV) ....'14 '38 C.160 L.146 J.D. 29 W. 140 Butterfield Rd.‡
McLain, Janice M. ....'50 '85 C.477 B.S. L.851 J.D. Sr. Atty., BP America, Inc. (Pat.)
Merzon, Melvin S., (AV) '33 '72 C.912 B.A. L.215 J.D.
Sr. Coun., Litig. & Ins., Intl. Truck & Engine Corp.
Moorehead, Timothy L. ....'57 '81 C.801 B.A. L.893 J.D. Sr. Atty., BP America, Inc.
Mulligan, Stephen E. '51 '78 C.276 A.B. L.262 J.D.
Gen. Atty., Corp. Opers., Intl. Truck & Engine Corp.
Nahrstadt, Debra L. ....'67 '92 C.352 B.B.A. L.339 J.D. Atty., BP America, Inc.
Neath, James J. ....'57 '82 C.436 B.A. L.659 J.D. Asst. Gen. Coun., BP America, Inc.
Nemo, Thomas E. ....'53 '89 C.867 B.S. L.209 J.D. Sr. Pat. Atty., BP America, Inc. (Pat.)
Noble, William J. ....'53 '80 C.339 B.A. L.477 J.D. Sr. Atty., BP America, Inc.
Nolan, James A., Jr., (AV) '60 '86 C.436 B.A. L.347 J.D.
Mng. Atty., BP America, Inc.
Novack, Paul J. ....'59 '84 C.339 B.S. L.447 J.D. BP-Amoco
O'Neill, Thomas S., (AV) '63 '89 C.339 B.A. L.602 J.D.
Lead Coun. Exelon Nuclear & Assoc. Gen. Coun., Exelon Business Services Co.
Osadjan, Marie Frances ......'61 '86 C.477 B.S. L.209 J.D. Sr. Atty., BP America, Inc.
Patel, Nirav ....'76 '02 C.1062 B.S. L.365 J.D. Pat. Atty., BP America Inc.
Perna, Robert J. '64 '88 C.645 B.S. L.273 J.D.
Gen. Atty. & Corp. Secy., Intl. Truck & Engine Corp.
Pickett, James D. ....'50 '76 C.118 B.A. L.69 J.D. Sr. Atty., BP America, Inc.
Piech, David A. .....'59 '92 C.602 B.S. L.210 J.D. Sr. Coun., Intl. Truck & Engine Corp.
Pinkert, Daniel B. '45 '73 C.477 B.S.E.E. L.145 J.D.
Asst. Gen. Coun., BP America, Inc.
Prange, Stacey L. ....'65 '90 C.347 B.A. L.188 J.D. Sr. Coun., Navistar Intl. Corp.
Price, William A. ....'53 '78 C.339 A.B. L.228 J.D. 28512 River Oaks Dr.
Rajagopal, Ravi ....'67 '96 C.27 B.A. L.862 J.D. Tax Atty., BP America Inc.
Reistroffer, Douglas J. ....'57 '82 C.339 B.S. L.477 J.D. Sr. Atty., BP America, Inc.
Rigney, Michael E., (AV) '50 '80
C.602 B.A. L.145 J.D. Asst. Gen. Coun., BP America, Inc.
Savine, Gary N. ....'71 '96 C.475 B.A. L.477 J.D. Sr. Coun., Navistar Intl. Corp.
Sawada, Suzanne R., (AV) '51 '77
C.696 B.A. L.145 J.D. Managing Atty., BP America, Inc.
Schoettle, Ekkehard '52 '82
C.477 B.S. L.209 J.D. Sr. Intell. Prop. Atty., BP America Inc.
Serwich, T. Gregory, II, (BVⓉ) '46 '84
C.871 B.S. L.861 J.D. Sr. Atty., BP America, Inc.
Sohl, Amy Courtin ....'71 '96 Atty., BP America, Inc.
Sroka, Frank J., (AV) '48 '74
C.679 B.S. L.424 J.D. Chf. Pat. Coun. U.S., BP America, Inc. (Pat.)
Stevens, Richard J. ....'58 '84 C.597 B.A. L.209 J.D. BP Products N.A., Inc.
Stevenson, Christine M. '69 '95 C.893 B.A. L.128 J.D.
(adm. in NJ; not adm. in IL) Sr. Atty., BP America Inc.
Sullivan, Dennis K. '42 '69 C.215 B.M.E. L.209 J.D.
Sr. Pat. & Trademark Coun., Intl. Truck & Engine Corp. (Pat.)
Tanaka, Aida Saracevic '64 '89
C.930 B.A. L.188 J.D. Gen. Atty., Intl. Truck & Engine Corp.
Tetlak, Thomas E. '49 '76 C.201 B.A. L.161 J.D.
(adm. in OH; not adm. in IL) BP America Inc.
Vaughan, Bernard F. ....'58 '88 C.161 B.A. BP Co.
Vyas, Himanshu A. ....'69 '03 C.879 B.S. L.365 J.D. BP America Inc.
Walsh-Madden, Diane C. ....'— '87 C&L.424 B.A., J.D. BP America Inc.
Weinbaum, Michael A. ....'55 '80 C.188 B.S. L.477 J.D. Mng. Atty., BP America, Inc.
Wessells, Paul D., Jr. ......'46 '73 C.802 B.A. L.846 J.D. Corp. Coun., BP America, Inc.
Weston, James K. ......'42 '68 C.750 B.A. L.597 J.D. First American Title Insurance Co.
Wilbur, Peter D. ....'54 '78 C.813 B.A. L.145 J.D. Sr. Atty., BP America, Inc.
Winters, Stephen R., (AV) '50 '75 C&L.378 B.A., J.D.
Assoc. Gen. Coun., Refing & Mktg, Global, BP America, Inc.
Wood, John L. '59 '87 C.36 B.S.Ch.E. L.1218 J.D.
(adm. in UT; not adm. in IL) Sr. Atty., BP America Inc.
Yassen, Thomas A. '58 '88
C.46 B.S.CH. Eng. L.146 J.D. Sr. Patent Atty., BP America, Inc.
Zigterman, Kent A., (AV) .....'51 '80 C.999 A.B. L.145 J.D. Sr. Atty., BP America, Inc.
Zwit, Joan Zaworski ....'53 '85 C.339 B.A. L.365 J.D. Sr. Atty., BP America, Inc.

WASHINGTON, 10,841, *Tazewell Co.*

Black, Kenneth L., (AV) ....'42 '74 C.98 B.S. L.421 J.D. [Black,B.&B.]
Black, Black & Brown, (AV) ....P.O. Box 270
Brown, David A., (BV) ....'64 '90 C.679 B.S. L.347 J.D. [Black,B.&B.]
Brown, Robert W., Jr., (BV) ....'60 '85 C.98 B.S. L.801 J.D. [Black,B.&B.]
Eirinberg, Keith W. '56 '82
C.477 B.A. L.472 J.D. Ctr. for Strategic & International Studies★
Essig, Dean R., (BV) ....'42 '74 C.98 B.A. L.339 J.D. 135 Washington Sq.
Heller, Brian ....'55 '81 C.98 B.S. L.339 J.D. P.O. Box 213
Heller, J. Brian, (BV) ....'55 '81 C.98 B.S. L.339 J.D. [J.B.Heller]
Heller, J. Brian, P.C., (BV) ....200 Walnut St.
Holtzman, John ....'15 '39 C&L.339 A.B., LL.B. RR #1, 1994 Highwood‡
Hosafros, F. Jean, (BV) ....'10 '60 C.430 A.B. L.477 M.A. 410 Monroe St.
Mescher, Gregory A., (BV) ....'54 '79 C.339 B.S. L.280 J.D. [Mescher]
Mescher Law Offices, PC, (BV) ....108 S. Wood St.
Moehle, Melvin O., (BV) ....'22 '48 C.910 B.S. L.502 LL.B. [Moehle S.&U.]
Moehle Swearingen & Umholtz, Ltd., (BV) ....118 Peoria St. (⊙Pekin)
Swearingen, Bradley W., (BV) ....'46 '76 C.927 B.A. L.146 J.D. [Moehle S.&U.]
Tavana, John P. '61 '84 C.340 B.A. L.352 J.D.
(adm. in IA; not adm. in IL) 110 S. Meadowview★
Teeven, Kevin M. ....'45 '71 C.234 B.S. L.339 J.D. Assoc. Prof., Bradley Univ.

WATERLOO, * 7,614, *Monroe Co.*

Brown & Associates
(See Belleville)

Buettner, Mary E. ....'63 '87 C&L.910 A.B., J.D. [M.E.Buettner]
Buettner, Mary E., P.C. ....836 North Market St.
Coffee, Richard J., II, (CV) ....'54 '78 C.801 B.S. L.339 J.D. [Ⓐ Rau&R.]

Crowder & Scoggins, Ltd.
(See Columbia)

Dunham, Boman & Leskera
(See Belleville)

Eberspecher, Kelly J. ....'68 '98 C.972 B.S. L.347 J.D. [Strellis&F.] (Pat.)
Faulbaum, Otto J., (BV) ....'51 '76 C.801 B.A. L.1209 J.D. 111 S. Main St., Ste. A
Field, Dennis M., (BV) ....'55 '86 C&L.801 B.S., J.D. [Strellis&F.]
Jacobsen, Dennis J. ....'43 '72 C&L.339 B.S., J.D. Cir. J.
Lewis, David Edward, Law Offices of ......'58 '93 C.801 B.S. L.734 J.D. 3201 Loehr Rd.
Murphy, Robert E. ....'38 '68 C&L.910 A.B., J.D. P.O. Box 151
Rau, C. Glennon, (BV) ....'42 '67 C&L.734 B.S., J.D. [Rau&R.]
Rau, Judith A. ....'41 '75 C&L.734 B.S.M.A., J.D. [Rau&R.]
Rau and Rau, (BV) ....119 E. Mill St.
Rosenfeld, Jonathan Alan ....'74 '01 C.401 B.A. L.146 J.D. [Strellis&F.]
Sondag, Victor H. ....'20 '48 C&L.734 B.S., J.D. State Bank Bldg.‡
Strellis, Gregg E. ....'72 '98 C.339 B.S. L.347 J.D. [Strellis&F.]
Strellis, Jack A., (AV) ....'44 '71 C.339 A.B. L.424 J.D. [Strellis&F.] (⊙Chicago)

Strellis & Field, Chartered, (AV)
115 East Mill Street, 62298 ⊙
Telephone: 618-939-3404 FAX: 618-939-3402
Email: lawyers@waterloolaw.com
Jack A. Strellis; Dennis M. Field; Gregg E. Strellis; Jonathan Alan Rosenfeld; Kelly J. Eberspecher.
General, Civil Trial Practice in all Courts. Personal Injury, Wrongful Death, Workers Compensation, Products Liability, Probate and Estate Planning, Real Estate, Family Law and Adoption, Trademark, Patent, Intellectual Property.
Reference: First National Bank of Waterloo.
Belleville, Illinois Office: 216 West Washington, 62220. Telephone: 618-235-8701. Fax: 618-235-8967.
Chicago, Illinois Office: 444 North Wells Street, Suite 202, 60610. Telephone: 312-201-0000. Fax: 312-201-0007.

See Professional Biographies, WATERLOO, ILLINOIS

Zimmer, Edgar O., (BV) ....'04 '31 C&L.339 B.S., J.D. 116 N. Main St.

WATERMAN, 1,224, *DeKalb Co.*

Cliffe, Foster, Corneille, Buick & Buick, LLC, (BV)
200 W. Lincoln (⊙De Kalb, Hinckley, Shabbona, Sycamore)
Evans, John R. ....'57 '88 C&L.589 B.S., J.D. 9632 Shabbona Grove Rd.

WATSEKA, * 5,670, *Iroquois Co.*

Boyer, Ronald E., (BV) ....'40 '65 C.339 B.A. L.145 J.D. [R.E.Boyer]
Boyer, Ronald E., P.C., (BV) ....600 E. Walnut St.
Dannehl, Robert L. ....'26 '50 C&L.339 J.D. [Ⓡ Razzano&K.]
Johnson, Kay Lawfer, (BV) ....'59 '84 C.906 B.S. L.365 J.D. [Sunderland,S.J.&T.]
Kinzer, James B., III, (BV) ....'52 '78 C.976 B.S. L.339 J.D. [Razzano&K.]
Looker, Ivan, (BV) ....'30 '57 C.357 B.S. L.339 LL.B. [Looker&L.]
Looker, Lynelle, (CV) ....'62 '87 C.679 B.A. L.879 J.D. [Looker&L.]
Looker and Looker, (BV) ....136 E. Walnut St.
Lustfeldt, Gordon L. ....'54 '79 C.234 B.A. L.339 J.D. Cir. J.
Markwalder, Dale W., (AV) ....'28 '51 C&L.339 B.S., J.D. 116 W. Jefferson Ave.‡
McGrew, Dwight W. ....'31 '59 C.465 B.A. L.910 J.D. Ret. Assoc. Cir. J.
McTaggart, Jane A., (AVⓉ) ....'45 '77 C.338 B.S. L.1035 J.D. 123 S. Fourth Street
Razzano, A. William, (AV) ....'35 '59 C&L.339 B.S., J.D. [Razzano&K.] (⊙Clifton)
Razzano & Kinzer, (AV) ....115 East Walnut Street (⊙Clifton)
Ripley, Scott R., (CV) ....'65 '90 C.338 B.S. L.221 J.D. Asst. States' Atty.
Simutis, Frank J., (AV) ....'46 '71 C&L.339 B.A., J.D. [F.J.Simutis]

Simutis, Frank J., P.C., Law Offices of, (AV) BR
123 South Fourth Street, 60970
Telephone: 815-432-5567 Fax: 815-432-5582
Email: fjslaw@earthlink.net
Frank J. Simutis.
General Civil Defense Law, Probate Law, Banking Law, Municipal Law, Corporate Law, Estate Planning, Personal Injury.

See Professional Biographies, WATSEKA, ILLINOIS

Spenn, Theodore R., (BV) ....'48 '73 C&L.339 B.S., J.D. [Sunderland,S.J.&T.]
Strough, Dale A., (BV) ....'52 '78 C.338 B.S. L.209 J.D. [D.Strough]

Strough, Dale, Attorney at Law, (BV)
216 East Walnut Street, 60970
Telephone: 815-432-4921 Fax: 815-432-6628
URL: http://www.daslaw.com
Dale A. Strough.
Bankruptcy, Family, Divorce, Adoption, Visitation Rights, Criminal, DWI, Drug Crimes, Juvenile Crimes, Traffic Violations, White Collar Crimes, Domestic Violence, Personal Injury, Medical Malpractice, Wrongful Death, Trusts and Estates, Estate Planning and Wills and Probate Law. General Practice.

See Professional Biographies, WATSEKA, ILLINOIS

Sunderland, Louis B., (AV) ....'30 '58 C.894 A.B. L.597 J.D. [Sunderland,S.J.&T.] ⊙
Sunderland, Spenn, Johnson and Thompson, (AV) ..............P.O. Box 407 (⊙Milford)
Thompson, Mark B., (BV) ....'50 '78 C.145 B.A. L.300 J.D. [Sunderland,S.J.&T.]
Tungate, James L., (BV) ....'47 '79 C.340 B.S. L.339 J.D. [Tungate] ⊙

Tungate Law Offices, Ltd., (BV)
744 East Walnut Street, P.O. Box 337, 60970 ⊙
Telephone: 815-432-4979 Fax: 815-432-4977
Email: tungate7733@sbcglobal.net URL: http://www.lawyers.com/tungate
James L. Tungate.
General Civil and Criminal Trial Practice in all State and Federal Courts. Personal Injury, Banking, Probate, Real Estate, Corporate, Taxation, Family, Commercial, School and Municipal Law.
Representative Clients: Sumner National Bank of Sheldon, Ill.; Cissna Park State Bank; Hicksgas; Federated Bank of Onarga; Citizens State Bank of Cropsey; Village of Onarga; Iroquois Mental Health Center.
References: Sumner National Bank of Sheldon, Ill.; Cissna Park State Bank; Village of Cissna Park.
Cissna Park, Illinois Office: Railroad Avenue at Third Street, P.O. Box 272, 60924. Telephone: 815-457-2723.
Onarga, Illinois Office: 109 North Chestnut Street. 60955. Telephone: 815-268-4979.

See Professional Biographies, WATSEKA, ILLINOIS

Ziegler, Steven D., (CV) ....'61 '86 C.123 B.A. L.365 J.D. Asst. State's Atty.

WAUCONDA, 9,448, *Lake Co.*

Brott, Donald J., (AV) ....'28 '57 C&L.966 B.S.E.E., J.D. 27075 Ivanhoe Ct.‡
Brown, Douglas R. ....'48 '76 C.221 B.S. L.146 J.D. 203 W. Church St.‡
De Laurentis, Dina M. '67 '93 C.436 B.A. L.809 J.D.
(adm. in CA; not adm. in IL) General Counsel, Prate Installations, Inc.
Gooch, Thomas W., The Law Offices of ....'48 '79 L.365 J.D. 209 South Main Street
Harris, George P. ....'51 '78 C.674 A.B. L.818 J.D. 209 Main Street

LoVerde, Vito P., The Law Office of '51 '91 C.1183 B.S. L.365 J.D.
729 Saddlewood Drive, 60084
Telephone: 847-487-4909 Fax: 847-487-4822
Email: vpl@loverdelaw.com
Litigation, Corporate Law, Alternative Dispute Resolution.

See Professional Biographies, WAUCONDA, ILLINOIS

Malik, Thomas W. '48 '73 C.597 B.A. L.228 J.D. 211 S. Main St.

Mitchell, Clay J. '59 '89 C.477 B.A. L.209 J.D.
121 East Liberty Street Suite 3, 60084-1929
Telephone: 847-487-7988 Fax: 847-526-9498
General Practice, Personal Injury, Insurance Law, Criminal Defense, Traffic and DUI and Real Estate Transactions.
See Professional Biographies, WAUCONDA, ILLINOIS

Nakon, Richard J. '49 '74 C&L.209 B.A., J.D. 121 E. Liberty St.
Waitzman, Martin J. '52 '83 C.1183 B.A. L.365 J.D. [M.J.Waitzman]
Waitzman, Martin J., Law Offices of, P.C. 368 West Liberty Street

WAUKEGAN, * 87,901, *Lake Co.*

Alexy, Brooke E. '63 '88 C&L.966 B.B.A., J.D. Corp. Coun., Cardinal Health
Anderson, William P., (BV) '53 '78 C.927 B.A. L.801 J.D. [🄰 Diver,G.Q.&M.]
Appelbaum, Larry A. '62 '87 C.339 B.A. L.146 J.D. [Linn&C.]
Applehans, Stephen G., (BV) '47 '76 C.30 B.A. L.146 J.D. [S.G.Applehans]
Applehans, Stephen G., Chartered, (BV) 1733 Washington
Apter, Kevin '65 '90 C&L.339 B.A., J.D. [🄰 Daniels,L.&P.]
Arezina, Vladimir I. '72 '97
C.893 B.S.M.E. L.1209 J.D. Intell. Prop. Coun., WMS Gaming Inc.

Argeros, Anthony G., L.L.C.
(See Chicago)

Argueta, Julio Cesar '74 '00 C.339 B.A. L.424 J.D. State's Atty. Off.
Arthurs, Timothy M., (CV) '69 '94 C.889 B.A. L.365 J.D. [🄰 W.C.Lindsay&Assoc.]
Baddeley, D. Jeffrey '38 '62 C&L.597 B.S., J.D. 100 Sea Horse Dr.
Bailey, John D. '65 '97 C&L.339 B.A., J.D. Asst. Pub. Def.
Bairstow, Richard R. '17 '47 C&L.339 A.B., J.D. Admin. Law J., State Dept. of Rev.
Bajko, Robert F. '39 '73 C.424 B.S. L.365 J.D. 325 Washington Street
Bakk, James C., Law Offices of, (AV) '53 '78 C.339 B.A. L.472 J.D. 200 N. Utica St.
Baron, Philip B., (BV) '53 '81 C.536 B.A. L.365 J.D. 25 North County Street
Barrientos-Duvall, Laura '77 '02 C.734 B.A. L.209 J.D. [Leibowitz]
Battaglia, Donald C. '53 '88 C.999 B.A. L.365 J.D. 3433 W. Sunset Avenue
Behr, Warren C. '21 '50 C&L.339 A.B., LL.B. 312 Grand Ave.‡
Belokon, Mark B. '54 '78 C.98 J.D. L.424 J.D. 25 N. Country Street
Berdenis, Lori Weiss '— '93 C.234 B.A. L.589 J.D. [🄰 T.M.Bond,Jr.&Assoc.]
Berks, Melvyn H. '39 '66 C&L.209 A.B., J.D. One N. County St. (⊙Deerfield)
Bernstein, Bruce W. '55 '99 [🄰 W.C.Lindsay&Assoc.]
Bird, Ronald Frank '45 '80 C.339 B.A. L.1241 J.D. Asst. States's Atty.
Blankstein, Michael J. '— '92 C&L.966 B.S.W.W., J.D.
Exec. Dir., Intell. Prop., WMS Gaming Inc. (Pat.)
Boches, Barry H., (BV) '55 '80 C.966 B.A. L.365 J.D. [B.H.Boches&Assoc.]
Boches, Barry H. & Associates, P.C., (BV) 409 Grand Ave.
Bond, Thaddeus M., Jr., (CV) '66 '91 C.57 B.A. L.365 J.D. [T.M.Bond,Jr.&Assoc.] ⊙
Bond, Thaddeus M., Sr. '40 '64 C&L.209 A.B., LL.B. Pres., Mid America Title Co.
Bond, Thaddeus M., Jr., & Associates, P.C., Law Offices of, (CV)
200 N. King Avenue, Suite 203 (⊙Libertyville)
Booras, James K. '52 '79 C&L.589 B.S., J.D. Cir. Ct. J.
Borcia, Margaret Morrison, (CV) '64 '89 C.927 B.S. L.146 J.D. 32 N. West St.
Brady, Paul E. '63 '99 C.927 B.S. L.365 J.D. [🄰 Johnson&B.] (⊙Chicago)
Brady, Terrence J. '40 '69 C.755 B.A. L.339 J.D. Assoc. Cir. J.
Brebner, Dennis A., (BV) '52 '83 C.339 B.A. L.209 J.D. [Brebner]
Brebner Law Firm, (BV) 860 S. Northpoint Boulevard

Brenner, Ford, Monroe & Scott, Ltd.
(See Chicago)

Briscoe, Thomas A., (AV) '53 '78 C.1157 B.A. L.46 J.D. [T.A.Briscoe]
Briscoe, Thomas A., P.C., (AV) 33 North County Street, Suite 203
Broderick, Mark P., (BV) '— '95 C.602 B.A. L.1187 J.D. [O'Hagan,S.&A.]
Brodsky, David Paul '60 '85 L.146 J.D. Lake Co. Public Defender
Bruno, Louis M. '56 '81 C&L.209 B.A., J.D. [© R.Bruno]

Bruno, Randie, Law Offices of, (BV) '— '85 C.347 B.A. L.365 J.D.
118 North Genesee Street, 60085
Telephone: 847-244-5002
Email: olb9239@yahoo.com
Of Counsel: Louis M. Bruno.
Criminal Law, Driving While Intoxicated, Drug Crimes, Felonies, Homicide, Juvenile, Misdemeanors, Parole and Probation, Sexual Assault, Traffic Violations, Family Law, Divorce, Child Custody, Child Support, Domestic Violence, Spousal Support.
See Professional Biographies, WAUKEGAN, ILLINOIS

Brydges, Louis W., Jr., (AV) '55 '80 C.1365 B.A. L.245 J.D. 1220 Grand Avenue
Buege, Robert M., (BV) '47 '83 C.589 B.S. L.365 J.D. [May&B.]
Burke, Thomas P. '— '84 C.757 B.A. L.424 J.D. [Querrey&H.]
Campe, Thomas D., Jr., (AV) '63 '89 C&L.339 B.S., J.D. [Linn&C.]
Canel, James H., (AV) '44 '68 C.910 B.A. L.209 J.D. [© Salvi,S.&P.] (⊙Chicago)
Canty, Steve C. '— '96 C.339 B.A. L.209 J.D. [Johnson&B.] (⊙Chicago)
Carlson, Mary M. '44 '89 C.424 B.A. L.365 J.D.
Dir., Licensing & Trademarks, WMS Gaming Inc.

Cartwright, Erin E. '77 '00
409 Grand Avenue, 60085
Telephone: 847-336-0710 Fax: 847-244-5399
Email: ecartwright@aol.com URL: http://www.erincartwrightlaw.com
General Practice.
See Professional Biographies, WAUKEGAN, ILLINOIS

Casey, Laureen Cahill '61 '86 C&L.424 B.A., J.D. Asst. Pub. Def.
Caton, Dewey J. '60 '84 C&L.339 B.A., J.D. Sr. Atty., Outboard Marine Corp.
Chadwick, Mary Ellen (Megan), (BV) '59 '85 C.338 B.S. L.365 J.D. [© Gibson&K.]

Chatzky, Paul, Law Offices of
(See Northfield)

Clark, Richard M. '— '75 C.321 B.A. L.813 J.D. [McKenna S.]
Clarke, Lewis D., (AV) '06 '32 C.197 A.B. L.146 LL.B. 1429 Hickory St.‡
Clarke, Lewis D., Jr., (BV) '36 '66 C.207 B.A. L.30 J.D. [Snyder,C.F.&Assoc.]
Clewis, Scott R. '65 '00 C.339 B.A. L.146 J.D. [🄰 Salvi,S.&P.]
Collins, Kelly A. '66 '91 C.339 B.A. L.276 J.D. Asst. State's Atty.
Cone, Norman F. '25 '52 C.477 L.424 LL.B. 3328 Chatham Rd.

Connelly Roberts & McGivney LLC
(See Chicago)

Conway, Michael J. '65 '92 C.339 B.A. L.1187 J.D. [M.J.Conway]

Conway, Michael J., Attorney at Law, L.L.C.
222 North Martin Luther King, Jr. Avenue, 60085
Telephone: 847-599-1969 Fax: 847-263-1258
Email: mjconwaylaw@ameritech.net URL: http://www.michaelconwaylaw.com
Michael J. Conway.

(This Listing Continued)

Conway, Michael J., Attorney at Law, L.L.C. (Continued)
Criminal Defense, Family Law, Parental Rights, Juvenile Law, Driving Under the Influence, Traffic Violations, Personal Injury.
See Professional Biographies, WAUKEGAN, ILLINOIS

Coulson, Robert Edwards '12 '36 C.197 A.B. L.145 J.D. 1031 Pacific St.‡
Crenshaw, John L. '56 '84 C.108 B.S. L.502 J.D.
Regulatory/Compl. Coun., Allegiance Healthcare Corp.
Culmer, Marjorie M. '12 '47 C.399 B.A. L.597 J.D. 9 N. County St.‡
Curler, Kathleen E. '69 '02 C.475 B.A. L.770 J.D. Asst. States Atty.
Curnyn, John '70 '98 C.57 B.A. L.146 J.D. [Stone&Assoc.]

Curran, Mark C., Jr., The Law Offices of, (AV) '63 '90 C.812 B.S. L.146 J.D.
235 North West Street, 60085
Telephone: 847-782-0200 Fax: 847-782-0600
Email: curranlaw@aol.com URL: http://www.curran-criminallawyer.com
Criminal Defense including State and Federal, Drugs, Narcotics, Search and Seizure, Trafficking, RICO, Conspiracy, Felonies, Misdemeanors, Sexual Misconduct, Sexual Offenses, Sexual Abuse and Sexual Assault, Internet Crimes, Pornography, Weapons, Traffic Violations, Driving While Intoxicated (DWI); Family Law including Divorce, Child Custody, Child Support, Visitation Rights, Spousal Support (Alimony), Personal Injury, Workers Compensation, Juvenile Matters.
See Professional Biographies, WAUKEGAN, ILLINOIS

Danforth, Michael A. '62 '95 C.589 B.A. L.1339 J.D. [🄰 Shaw&F.]
Danian, Michael S., (BV) '31 '74 C.1161 B.S. L.1340 J.D. [M.S.Danian]

Danian, Michael S., P.C., (BV)
Nine North County Street, 60085
Telephone: 847-662-8777 Fax: 847-662-8794
Email: danianmsdlaw@aol.com
Michael S. Danian.
General Civil, Criminal Trial and Appellate Practice. Personal Injury, Workers Compensation, Pharmaceutical, Corporation, Real Estate, Probate, Driving While Intoxicated Felonies and Family Law.
See Professional Biographies, WAUKEGAN, ILLINOIS

Daniels, Richard C. '57 '89 C.424 B.S. L.365 J.D. [Daniels,L.&P.]
Daniels, Long & Pinsel, (BV) 19 North County Street
Davis, Maer I. '44 '69 C&L.339 B.S., J.D. 226 N. Utica St.

Decker & Linn, Ltd.
(See Linn & Campe, Ltd.)

Del Re, David R. '71 '98 C.339 B.A. L.862 J.D. [D.R.DelRe]

Del Re, David R., A Professional Corporation, The Law Offices of
210 N. Martin Luther King, Jr. Avenue, 60085
Telephone: 847-625-9800 Fax: 847-625-9980 URL: http://www.delrelawfirm.com
Email: drd@delrelaw.net URL: http://www.daviddelrelaw.com
David R. Del Re.
Criminal Defense, Family Law.
See Professional Biographies, WAUKEGAN, ILLINOIS

Demosthene, Cliff '75 '01 C.608 B.A. L.879 J.D. [Joanem&D.]

DeSanto, Morgan & Mittelman, An Assoc. of Prof. Corps.
(See Libertyville)

Diaz, Marcelino '58 '01 C.339 B.A. L.262 J.D. [Diaz&R.]
Diaz & Rios, Law Offices of 2424 Washington Street, Suite 1-202 (⊙Elgin)

Diver, Grach, Quade & Masini, LLP, (AV) BB
Bank of Waukegan Building, 111 North County Street, 60085
Telephone: 847-662-8611 FAX: 847-662-2960
Email: divergrach@divergrach.com URL: http://www.divergrach.com
Members of Firm: Clarence W. Diver (1883-1962); Thomas W. Diver (1916-2000); Brian S. Grach; David R. Quade; Robert J. Masini; David L. Hazan; Donna-Jo Rodden Vorderstrasse. Associates: Gretchen A. Neddenriep; William P. Anderson.
General Litigation and Appellate Practice, Wills and Probate, Trusts and Estates, Municipal Law, Real Estate, Taxation, Commercial Litigation, Corporate Law, Family, Criminal, Financial Institutions.
A list of Representative Clients will be furnished upon request.
Reference: First Midwest Bank of Waukegan.
See Professional Biographies, WAUKEGAN, ILLINOIS

Douglas, Dwayne '65 '91 C.589 B.A. L.146 J.D. [Weinstein&D.]
Driscoll, John M. '50 '78 C.209 B.S.C. L.365 J.D. [J.M.Driscoll]
Driscoll, John M., P.C. 33 N. County Street Suite 500
Drobinski, Roderick Andrew '76 '01 C.602 B.A. L.276 J.D. Asst. State. Atty.
Drunken Driving Defense Lawyers of Illinois, Ltd., (AV)
25 North County Street 2nd Floor (⊙Chicago)
Dunn, W. Elliott, (BV) '36 '74 C.421 B.A. L.424 J.D. 38187 North Shore Ave.
Dunn, Wallace B. '40 '65 C.339 B.S. L.209 J.D. Assoc. Cir. J.
Ebener, Brian S., (BV) '— '87 C.1172 B.A. L.589 J.D. [🄰 O'Hagan,S.&A.]

Eckberg, David
(See Chicago)

Eckert, Roland A., Law Office of
(See Lake Forest)

Ehrmantraut, Jennifer '70 '96 C.475 B.A. L.910 J.D. Asst. States Atty., Civil Div.
Eiden, Raymond A. '14 '39 C&L.424 B.A., LL.B.
Chmn. of the Bd., Bank of Northern Ill., N.A.

Elizer & Meyerson, L.L.C.
(See Northbrook)

Evans, Timothy R., Law Office of, (BV) '62 '94
C.338 B.S. L.1000 J.D. 216 West Madison Street
Feather, William L. '46 '72 C&L.846 B.A., J.D.
Sr. V.P., Gen. Coun. & Secy., Cardinal Health
Fekete, Christopher J. '52 '79 C.980 B.A. L.07 J.D. [🄰 Griesheimer&Assoc.]★
Field, Daniel P. '49 '74 C&L.339 A.B., J.D. 209 W. Madison St., 3rd Fl.
Files, McLaurin Hill '69 '96 C.902 B.A. L.896 J.D. Staff Coun., WMS Gaming Inc.
Finn, Newton E. '48 '78 C.393 B.A. L.365 J.D. 3315 Victoria Ln.
Flanigan, Wayne B., (BV) '40 '64 C.973 A.B. L.339 LL.B. P.O. Box 771
Fluri, James E. '58 '85 C.207 B.A. L.734 J.D. 25 N. County St.‡
Foley, Gary N. '65 '96 C.424 B.A. L.589 J.D. [Shaw&F.]
Ford, Elizabeth E. '53 '80 C.597 B.S. L.365 J.D. Cardinal Health
Fouts, James S., (BV) '33 '62 C.393 A.B. L.209 J.D. [Snyder,C.F.&Assoc.]
Fox, Robert J., (BV) '45 '75 C.221 B.A. L.365 J.D. 9 S. County St.
Foy, Marykatherine '54 '97 C.436 B.S. L.424 J.D. Asst. States Atty.
Franke, Allyn J., (AV) '18 '42 C&L.145 A.B., LL.B. [Hinshaw&C.]
Franks, William Y., (BV) '48 '87 C.98 B.S. L.365 J.D. 216 W. Madison St.
Fritz, Michael J. '50 '76 C.121 B.S. L.365 J.D. Assoc. Cir. J.
Frost, William D., II '51 '84 C.871 B.S. L.228 J.D. [© Goldberg&K.]
Fuqua, Winter & Stiles, Ltd., (BV) Nine North County Street
Fusz, Michael J. '51 '77 C&L.146 B.S., J.D. Cir.J.

Ganfield, David R., II ....'59 '84 C.339 B.A. L.910 J.D. [Ryan,R.&L.]
Gerling, Robert K., (CV) ....'23 '51 C&L.966 LL.B. Outboard Marine Corp. (Pat.)
Gibson, Ellen E. ....'— '91 C.477 B.A. L.339 J.D. [Querrey&H.]
Gibson, Scott B., (AV) ....'57 '82 C.339 B.A. L.209 J.D. [Gibson&K.]

Gibson & Kopsick, Ltd., (AV)
415 West Washington Street, Suite 103, 60085
Telephone: 847-263-5100 Fax: 847-249-7588
Email: attorney@gibkop.com URL: http://www.gibsonkopsicklaw.com
Scott B. Gibson; Richard S. Kopsick. Of Counsel: Mary Ellen (Megan) Chadwick.
Personal Injury, Medical Malpractice, Automobile Accidents, Uninsured and Underinsured Motorist, Construction Accidents, Motorcycle Accidents, Vehicular Accidents, Lawyers Malpractice, Professional Negligence, Products Liability, Workers Compensation.
See Professional Biographies, WAUKEGAN, ILLINOIS

Gilbert, Ronald W., (CV) ....'52 '77 C.424 B.A. L.365 J.D. 1321 Grand Ave.
Gilleran-Johnson, Barbara ....'52 '78 C.209 B.A. L.146 J.D. Assoc. Cir. J.
Gingiss, Joel D. ....'42 '93 C.871 B.S. L.209 J.D. 1 N. County St.
Goldberg, Deborah L., (BV) ....'55 '84 C.604 A.B. L.365 J.D. [Goldberg&K.]
Goldberg & Kane, (BV) .... 813 Washington St.
Goles, David S. '72 '98 C.30 B.A. L.589 J.D.
[A] Swanson,M.&B.] (⊙Chicago, Libertyville)
Goshgarian, John R. ....'46 '72 C.597 B.A. L.339 J.D. Cir. J.
Goshgarian, Richard G., Attorney at Law '59 '92
C.436 B.A. L.365 J.D. 220 W. Washington St.
Goshgarian, Robert N., (AV) .... '56 '81 C.121 B.A. L.424 J.D. 220 W. Washington
Grach, Brian S., (AV) ....'45 '70 C&L.339 B.S., J.D. [Diver,G.Q.&M.]
Grange, David P., (BV) ....'63 '88 C.589 B.S. L.424 J.D. 33 N. County, Ste. 500
Greenblatt, Michael A., (BV) ....'41 '66 C.966 B.S. L.209 J.D. 1 N. Genesee St.
Griesheimer, Ronald E., (BV) .... '36 '61 C.339 L.802 LL.B. [Griesheimer&Assoc.]

Griesheimer & Associates, (BV)
321 Grand Avenue, 60085
Telephone: 847-244-3131 Fax: 847-244-0766
URL: http://www.goldenrulelaw.com
Ronald E. Griesheimer;—Christopher J. Fekete.
Family, Divorce, Child Custody, Personal Injury, Criminal, Driving While Intoxicated, Military, Probate, Bankruptcy and General Civil Trial Practice.
See Professional Biographies, WAUKEGAN, ILLINOIS

Grimes, G. Douglas, (BV) ....'47 '73 C&L.339 B.S., J.D. 221 Wash. St.
Gurewitz, Thomas M., (AV) ....'49 '75 C.72 B.A. L.365 J.D. 20 N. King Avenue
Hall, David M. ....'52 '76 C.123 B.A. L.424 J.D. Assoc. Cir. J.
Hall, Myron J., (BV) ....'33 '59 C.597 B.S. L.365 J.D. [Hall&J.]
Hall & Jensen, Ltd., (BV) ....33 N. County St.

Harris Kessler & Goldstein LLC, (AV)
404 Water Street, 60085 ⊙
Telephone: 847-263-1919
URL: http://www.hkgold.com
Richard N. Kessler.
General Business Practice including Litigation, Secured Lending, Real Estate, Health Care and Estate Planning.
Chicago, Illinois Office: 640 North LaSalle Street, Suite 590, 60610-3731. Telephone: 312-280-0111. Fax: 312-280-8232.
See Professional Biographies, WAUKEGAN, ILLINOIS

Hayes, Louise Bryant, (BV) ....'62 '89 C.679 B.A. L.365 J.D. Asst. States Atty.
Hazan, David L. ....'51 '77 C.36 B.A. L.365 J.D. [Diver,G.Q.&M.]
Henderson, Donna R. ....'43 '67 C&L.339 B.S., J.D. [Henderson&H.]
Henderson, J. John, (BV) ....'41 '66 C.378 B.A. L.339 J.D. [Henderson&H.]
Henderson & Henderson, (BV) .... 700 S. Lewis Ave.
Henrick, Michael F., (AV) ....'48 '74 C.424 B.S. L.365 J.D. [Hinshaw&C.]
Herrero, Van J. ....'49 '82 C.46 B.S. L.365 J.D. Asst. State's Atty.

Hinshaw & Culbertson LLP, (AV)
Hinshaw & Culbertson LLP is an Illinois registered limited liability partnership that has elected to be governed by the Illinois Uniform Partnership Act (1997)
110 North West Street, 60085-4330 ⊙
Telephone: 847-244-0551 Facsimile: 847-244-0579 Telex: 880248
Email: kfox@hinshawlaw.com URL: http://www.hinshawlaw.com
Partners: Allyn J. Franke; Michael F. Henrick; Thomas A. Morris, Jr.; Stacey L. Seneczko. Associates: Richard S. Kolodziej; Stephen A. Oakley.
Appellate, Banking & Financing, Bankruptcy & Creditors' Rights, Class Action Litigation, Civil Rights Defense, Commercial Litigation, Corporate, Construction Law, Director & Officer Liability, Employee Benefits, Environmental, Fidelity & Surety, General Liability Litigation, Government, Health Care, Insurance Coverage, Insurance and Reinsurance, Labor & Employment, Legal Malpractice, Medical Malpractice, Mergers & Acquisitions, Municipal Liability, Personal Injury Defense, Public Law, Products Liability Litigation, Professional Liability, Regulatory, Real Estate, School Law, Securities, Taxation, Transportation, White Collar Crime and Workers' Compensation Defense.
Other Office Locations: Chicago, Illinois; Appleton, Wisconsin; Belleville, Illinois; Boston, Massachusetts; Champaign, Illinois; Crystal Lake, Illinois; Edwardsville, Illinois; Fort Lauderdale, Florida; Jacksonville, Florida; Joliet, Illinois; Lisle, Illinois; Los Angeles, California; Miami, Florida; Milwaukee, Wisconsin; Minneapolis, Minnesota; New York, New York; Peoria, Illinois; Phoenix, Arizona; Portland, Oregon; Providence, Rhode Island; Rockford, Illinois; St. Louis, Missouri; San Francisco, California; Schererville, Indiana; Springfield, Illinois; Tampa, Florida.
See Professional Biographies, WAUKEGAN, ILLINOIS

Hoffert, Scott James ....'70 '00 C&L.339 B.A., J.D. 18 N. County Street
Hoffman, Matthew T. ....'71 '99 C.436 B.A. L.424 J.D. State Atty.
Hoffman, Mitchell L. ....'59 '84 C.170 B.A. L.339 J.D. Assoc. J.
Holmberg, Edward R., (AV) ....'22 '49 C.477 A.B. L.597 J.D. 20 S. Utica St.
Hoogasian, Claudia A. ....'43 '80 C.966 B.A. L.365 J.D. Chief Asst. State Atty.
Hoogasian, Jack ....'25 '58 C.339 B.S. L.365 J.D. Cir. J.

Hughes Socol Piers Resnick & Dym, Ltd.
(See Chicago)

Hutton, Brian D. '57 '83 C.966 B.A. L.285 J.D.
(adm. in WA; not adm. in IL) 1945 Hickory St.‡

Immigration Law Center, P.C.
(See Chicago)

Jacobson, Susan J. ....'66 '91 C.477 B.A. L.494 J.D. Corp. Coun., Cardinal Health
Jacquette, Mari-Jo ......'65 '95 C.1183 B.A. L.436 J.D. 415 Washington Street, Suite 203
Jeep, Markham M., (AV) ....'52 '79 C.589 B.A. L.424 J.D. [M.M.Jeep&Assoc.]
Jeep, Markham M., & Associates, P.C., (AV) ....450 N. Green Bay Rd.
Jensen, Michael R., (BV) ....'60 '91 C.294 B.A. L.365 J.D. [Hall&J.]
Joanem, John L. ....'66 '94 C.339 B.A. L.1117 J.D. [Joanem&D.]
Joanem & Demosthene, P.C. ....521 Clayton Street
Johnas, Lora J. '61 '89 C.960 B.S.N. L.436 J.D.
Gen. Coun. & Risk Mgr., Victory Health Servs.
Johnson, Julian, (AV) ....'20 '50 C&L.339 B.S., J.D. 325 Washington St., Ste. 401
Johnson, Nicholas ....'— '05 C.957 B.A. L.1187 J.D. [A] Querrey&H.]

Johnson & Bell, Ltd., (AV)
325 Washington Street Suite 200, 60085 ⊙
Telephone: 847-662-7458 Facsimile: 847-662-7366
Email: novys@jbltd.com URL: http://www.johnsonandbell.com

(This Listing Continued)

Johnson & Bell, Ltd. (Continued)
Shareholders: Steven B. Novy; Steve C. Canty. Associates: Paul E. Brady; Angela M. Kotsalieff; Jason Orleans.
Trial practice in state and federal courts, including national coordinating counsel. Appellate Law, Asbestos Litigation, Automotive Product Liability Litigation, Aviation Litigation, Benefits, Business Litigation and Practice, Complex Plaintiff Litigation, Construction Litigation, Corporate Health Care, Criminal Litigation, Employment Law, ERISA, Environmental Law, Financial Crimes, Financial Institution Representation, General Negligence and Premises Liability, Gun Litigation, Hospital Law and Medical Liability, Insurance Coverage, Intellectual Property, Long Term Care/Nursing Home Liability, Mass Tort, Medical Device Liability, Mold Litigation, Municipal Liability, National Coordinating Counsel, Probate, Product Liability, Professional Liability, Railroad Litigation, Toxic Tort and Trucking and Transportation.
Chicago, Illinois Office: Suite 4100, 55 East Monroe Street, 60603-5896. Telephone: 312-372-0770. Facsimile: 312-372-9818.
Highland, Indiana Office: 9000 Indianapolis Boulevard, Suite A, 46322. Telephone: 219-923-5250. Facsimile: 219-923-6170.
See Professional Biographies, WAUKEGAN, ILLINOIS

Jones, Alan, (BV) ....'60 '89 C.339 B.A. L.209 J.D. [A.Jones]
Jones, Alan, Attorney at Law, P.C., (BV) ....203 Greenwood Ave.
Kahn, Cheryl ....'62 '88 C.477 A.B. L.339 J.D. Corp. Coun., Cardinal Health
Kaiser, Paul W., Jr., (CV) ....'28 '58 C.339 B.S. L.208 LL.B. 32 N. West St.
Kane, Kevin M., (BV) ....'48 '78 C&L.339 B.A., J.D. [Goldberg&K.]
Keefe, David J., (BV) ....'43 '82 C.238 B.AS. L.146 J.D. Asst. Pub. Def.
Kenton, Jas. K. ....'23 '56 C&L.602 B.S.C., LL.B. 211 Wash. St.
Kessler, Richard N., (AV) ....'57 '82 C.339 B.A. L.146 J.D. [Harris K.&G.] ⊙

Kiesler & Berman
(See Chicago)

Kleinhubert, Daniel Joseph ....'60 '87 C.742 B.A. L.365 J.D. Asst. State's Atty.
Ko, Harper H. ....'73 '99 C.477 B.S. L.146 J.D. Staff Coun., WMS Gaming Inc.
Kober, Dale P. ....'39 '64 C&L.966 B.S., LL.B. 325 Washington St.
Kolodziej, Richard S. ....'71 '96 C.98 B.S. L.209 J.D. [A] Hinshaw&C.]
Komie, Stephen M., (AV) ....'49 '76 C.37 B.A., M.A. L.209 J.D. [Drunken D.D.o.I.]

Komie and Associates, Law Offices of
(See Chicago)

Kopsick, Richard S., (AV) ....'57 '82 C.477 B.A. L.209 J.D. [Gibson&K.]
Kotsalieff, Angela M. ....'— '00 C.339 B.S. L.146 J.D. [A] Johnson&B.] (⊙Chicago)
Krelina, Kate ....'— '02 C.209 B.A. L.146 J.D. [A] Shaw&F.]
Kristopek, Gloria Ann ....'— '00 C.999 B.A. L.879 J.D. Jud. Ct.
Kuderko, J. Ted, (BV) ....'55 '87 C.123 B.A. L.365 J.D. 9 N. County, Ste. 203
Kuhlman, Michone J., (BV) '67 '96
C.350 B.S. L.1059 J.D. [A] Swanson,M.&B.] (⊙Libertyville)
LaLuzerne, Lawrence, (BV) ....'— '85 C.602 B.B.A. L.424 J.D. [Smith&L.]
Lampert, Susan M. ....'64 '92 C.339 B.A. L.146 J.D. One N. County St. (⊙Deerfield)
Landa, Scott R., (BV) ....'60 '85 C.927 B.A. L.339 J.D. [Ryan,R.&L.]
Lang, E. Thomas ....'43 '69 C.300 B.A. L.424 J.D. Cir. J.
Larson, Steven L., (AV) '52 '77
C.339 B.A. L.910 J.D. [Swanson,M.&B.] (⊙Chicago, Libertyville)
Lee, Jerome E., (BV) ....'48 '73 C&L.339 B.S., J.D. [Smythe&L.]
Leech, Steven H. ....'80 '04 C.145 B.A. L.602 J.D. [A] Salvi,S.&P.]
Leibowitz, David P., (AV) ....'50 '74 C.597 B.A. L.424 J.D. [Leibowitz]

Leibowitz Law Center, (AV) [BB]
420 Clayton Avenue, 60085
Telephone: 847-249-9100 Fax: 847-249-9180 URL: http://www.lawyers.com/lakelaw
Email: dpl@lakelaw.com URL: http://www.lakelaw.com
David P. Leibowitz; Laura Barrientos-Duvall. Associate: Chaya D. Williams. Of Counsel: Allan G. Sweig.
Languages: Spanish and French.
Bankruptcy, Creditors Rights, Business and Real Estate, Litigation, Estate and Probate, Commercial Litigation, Elder Law, Consumer Protection.
See Professional Biographies, WAUKEGAN, ILLINOIS

Lidschin, Mark R., (BV) ....'31 '55 C.118 A.B. L.477 J.D. 128 Madison St.
Lindsay, William C., (BV) ....'58 '85 C.966 B.S. L.365 J.D. [W.C.Lindsay&Assoc.]
Lindsay, William C., & Associates, L.L.C., Law Offices of, (BV) .... 221 N. West St.
Linn, Craig M., (AV) ....'47 '76 C.747 B.A. L.365 J.D. [Linn&C.]

Linn & Campe, Ltd., (AV)
215 N. Martin Luther King, Jr. Avenue, 60085
Telephone: 847-249-4600 Fax: 847-249-9927
Craig M. Linn; Thomas D. Campe, Jr.; John J. Rizzo; Larry A. Appelbaum.
Plaintiff's Catastrophic Personal Injury, Construction Litigation, Professional Negligence, Automobile Accidents and Injuries, Wrongful Death Litigation, Workers' Compensation.
See Professional Biographies, WAUKEGAN, ILLINOIS

Loizzo, Thomas F., (BV) ...'50 '76 C.966 B.S. L.365 J.D. [A] Salvi,S.&P.] (⊙Woodstock)
Lombardo, D. Christopher, (BV) .... '— '91 C.210 B.A. L.734 J.D. [Lombardo&M.]
Lombardo & Mauro, P.C., (BV) ....325 W. Washington, Suite 405
Long, Robert J. ....'54 '81 C.339 B.A. L.209 J.D. [Daniels,L.&P.]
Lundquist, Donald C. ....'12 '43 C.597 B.S. L.365 J.D. 2021 Hickory St.‡
Lundquist, Julie A., (BV) ....'46 '78 C.747 B.A. L.365 J.D. [J.Lundquist]
Lundquist, Julie, Law Offices of, (BV) ....25 N. County St.
Macaluso, Steven P. '76 '02 C.976 B.A. L.145 J.D.
Staff Coun., Lic. & Trademarks, WMS Gaming Inc.
Maher, Michael E. ....'60 '85 C.177 B.A. L.209 J.D. [Salvi,R.&M.]
Maitland, Laura Jean ....'46 '03 C.1100 L.365 J.D. 325 Washington St., Ste. 301

Maramba & Associates, LLC
(See Arlington Heights)

Marder, Chris ....'45 '75 C.605 A.B. L.128 J.D. 9 N. County St., Ste. 100
Marks, Jason S. ....'76 '01 C.352 B.B.A. L.209 J.D. [A] Noonan,P.P.]
Marshall, Tamara A. ....'66 '02 C.112 B.A. L.589 J.D. Lake Co. Publ Def.
Martin, Stephen M., (BV) ....'46 '82 C.339 B.A. L.146 J.D. 216 Madison St.
Martin, Victoria L. ....'52 '80 C.473 B.S. L.146 J.D. Assoc. Cir. J.
Masini, Robert J. ....'51 '76 C.966 B.A. L.339 J.D. [Diver,G.Q.&M.]
Mauro, D. Dean, (BV) ....'65 '90 C.388 B.A. L.424 J.D. [Lombardo&M.]

May & Buege, (BV)
33 North County, Suite 500, 60085-4388
Telephone: 847-244-9100 Fax: 847-244-9298
Email: maybuegelaw@earthlink.net
Charles M. May (1924-1987); Robert M. Buege.
Personal Injury, Workers Compensation and Insurance Law. Litigation.
See Professional Biographies, WAUKEGAN, ILLINOIS

McCaffery, Joseph P., Attorney at Law
(See Aurora)

McCollum, Steven P., (BV) ....'53 '78 C&L.339 B.A., J.D. [S.P.McCollum]

McCollum, Steven P., P.C., Law Offices of, (BV)
415 Washington Street, Suite 103, 60085-5564
Telephone: 847-662-2474 Fax: 847-249-7588 URL: http://www.stevenmccollum.com
Email: stevenpmccollum@aol.com URL: http://www.lawyers.com/smccollumlaw

(This Listing Continued)

McCollum, Steven P., P.C., Law Offices of (Continued)
Steven P. McCollum.
Criminal Law, Felonies, White Collar Crime, Juvenile Law, Termination of Parental Rights, Misdemeanors, Driving While Intoxicated, Drug Crimes, Homicide, Parole and Probation, Sexual Assault, Traffic Violations, Domestic Violence, Assault and Battery, Grand Jury Practice, Capital Offences, Construction Accidents, Personal Injury, Products Liability, Wrongful Death, Automobile Accidents and Injuries, Sexual Abuse. General Practice.
See Professional Biographies, WAUKEGAN, ILLINOIS

McGee, Joyce A. ....'69 '99 C.999 B.A. L.1280 J.D. Prairie State Legal Serv., Inc.
McGowan, Melvin J. ....'22 '52 C.162 A.B. L.273 J.D. 1932 Chestnut St.‡
McJohn, Kathleen J. '59 '85
C.276 B.A. L.339 J.D. V.P. & Gen. Coun., WMS Gaming Inc.

McKenna Storer, (AV)
33 North County Street 6th Floor, 60085-4343 ⊙
Telephone: 847-249-1620 Fax: 847-249-8457
Email: postmaster-@mckenna-law.com URL: http://www.mckenna-law.com
Resident Partner: Richard M. Clark.
Administrative Hearings, Appellate, Banking and Lending, Bankruptcy, Civil Rights, Commercial, Construction, Employment, Estate Planning, Fidelity, Insurance Coverage, Legal Malpractice, Mediation Services, Medical Malpractice, National Coordination, Personal Injury, Products Liability, Professional Liability, Surety, Tax and Toxic Tort.
Chicago, Illinois Office: 33 N. LaSalle Street, 14th Floor, 60602-2610. Telephone: 312-558-3900. Fax: 312-558-8348.
Woodstock, Illinois Office: 666 Russel Court, Suite 303, 60098-2672. Telephone: 815-334-9690. Fax: 815-334-9697.
See Professional Biographies, WAUKEGAN, ILLINOIS

McKeown, Denis J., (AV) ....'47 '75 C.177 B.A. L.365 J.D. 415 Washington
McKoski, Raymond J. ....'47 '72 C.578 B.A. L.209 J.D. Cir. J.
McQueen, Robert K. ....'20 '50 C&L.273 A.B., J.D. 111 N. County St.‡
Melius, Michael M., (BV) ....'48 '80 C.589 B.A. L.365 J.D. 222 North Utica Street
Meuth, Patterson Carl, (CV) ......'53 '80 C.338 B.S. L.146 J.D. 111 N. County St., Ste. 7
Meyer, Marshall, (AV) ....'06 '28 C&L.339 B.S., J.D. 2041 North Ave.‡
Michel, Jeffrey E. '66 '93
C.860 B.A. L.424 J.D. Dir., Lic. & Trademarks, WMS Gaming Inc.

Miner, Barnhill & Galland, P.C.
(See Chicago)

Moe, Christine-Ann ....'52 '87 C.742 B.A. L.146 J.D. Asst. States Atty.
Moran, Dorothy Lupton ....'52 '78 C.991 B.A. L.424 J.D. 218 N. Utica St.‡

Morgan, Wendy R., The Law Firm of
(See Arlington Heights)

Morris, Thomas A., Jr., (AV) ....'47 '71 C.321 A.B. L.893 J.D. [Hinshaw&C.]
Morrison, Donald T., (AV) ....'28 '55 C&L.597 B.S.L., J.D. [Morrison&M.]
Morrison, Joseph T., (AV) ....'57 '82 C.388 B.A. L.209 J.D. [Morrison&M.]
Morrison & Morrison, P.C., (AV) ....32 N. West St.
Mueller, Catherine E., (BV) ......'61 '87 C.339 B.S. L.209 J.D. [Ⓐ W.C.Lindsay&Assoc.]
Mullen, Margaret Jean ....'56 '80 C.338 B.A. L.365 J.D. Cir. J.
Murphy, John Eugene ....'66 '97 C.93 B.A. L.146 J.D. Pub. Def.

Nadler, Pritikin & Mirabelli, L.L.C.
(See Chicago)

Nagel, Doris K. ....'57 '88 C.339 B.A. L.378 J.D. Intl. Coun., Cardinal Health
Neddenriep, Gary Glen ....'42 '72 C.544 B.S. L.209 J.D. Assoc. Cir. J.
Neddenriep, Gretchen A. ....'74 '99 C.234 B.A. L.365 J.D. [Ⓐ Diver,G.Q.&M.]
Nelson, Thomas B., (CV) ....'19 '51 C&L.602 LL.B. 103 N. Sumac Ave.
Noonan, Michael K., (AV) ....'46 '74 C.589 B.A. L.477 J.D. [Noonan,P.P.]

Noonan, Perillo, Polenzani, Ltd., (AV)
25 North County Street, 60085-4342
Telephone: 847-244-0111 FAX: 847-244-0513 URL: http://www.sullivansmithlaw.com
URL: http://www.lawyers.com/sulsmi
Michael K. Noonan; Michael J. Perillo, Jr.; Joseph E. Polenzani. Associate: Jason S. Marks. Of Counsel: Leo J. Sullivan, III; Richard J. Smith.
General Trial and Appellate Practice in State and Federal Courts. Negligence and Insurance Law. Workers Compensation, Commercial, Banking, Domestic Relations and Municipal Defense, Military Law, Civil Rights, Product Liability, Criminal Law and Traffic Law, Nursing Home Negligence.
Representative Client: Allstate Insurance Co.
Reference: First Midwest Bank of Waukegan.
See Professional Biographies, WAUKEGAN, ILLINOIS

Nordigian, Peter J., (AV) ....'31 '58 C&L.339 J.D. 110 N, West St.

Novak, Paul B. '71 '96 C.338 B.S. L.365 J.D.
210 North Martin Luther King Jr. Avenue, 60085
Telephone: 847-244-1399 Fax: 847-625-9980
Email: paul@novaklaw.net URL: http://www.paulnovaklaw.com
Criminal Law, Juvenile Law, Family Law.
See Professional Biographies, WAUKEGAN, ILLINOIS

Novy, Steven B., (AV) ....'47 '73 C.339 B.A. L.602 J.D. [Johnson&B.] (⊙Chicago)
Oakley, Stephen A. ....'70 '97 C.339 B.A. L.365 J.D. [Ⓐ Hinshaw&C.]
O'Brien, Mary Beth, (BV) ....'59 '84 C.741 B.B.A. L.209 J.D. [Ⓐ Ryan,R.&L.]

O'Hagan, Smith & Amundsen, (AV)
415 West Washington Street, Suite 204, 60079-0410 ⊙
Telephone: 847-599-9503 Fax: 847-599-9525
URL: http://www.osalaw.com
Member of Firm: Mark P. Broderick. Associate: Brian S. Ebener.
Commercial; Commercial Transportation; Appellate; Complex Litigation; Construction; Corporate Transactions; Employment; Extra-Contractual/Insurance Litigation; Healthcare; Insurance Coverage; Personal Lines; Product Liability; Professional Liability; Property Litigation.
Chicago, Illinois Office: 150 North Michigan Avenue, Suite 3300, 60601. Telephone: 312-894-3200. Fax: 312-894-3210.
Rockford, Illinois Office: Stewart Square, 308 West State Street, Suite 320, 61101-1140. Telephone: 815-987-0441. Fax: 815-987-9891.
St. Charles, Illinois Office: 3815 E. Main Street, Suite A-1, 60174-2488. Telephone: 630-587-7910. Fax: 630-587-7960.
Woodstock, Illinois Office: 666 Russel Court, 60098. Telephone: 815-337-4900. Fax: 815-337-4910.
Milwaukee, Wisconsin Office: 4811 South 76th Street, Suite 305, 53220. Suite 117, 53406-3770. Telephone: 414-282-7103. Fax: 414-282-1830.
See Professional Biographies, WAUKEGAN, ILLINOIS

O'Keefe, Paul F., (BV) ....'65 '90 C.321 B.A. L.339 J.D. [P.F.O'Keefe] ⊙

O'Keefe, Paul F., P.C., (BV)
32 N. West Street, Second Floor, 60085 ⊙
Telephone: 847-263-9262
Email: okeefelaw@msn.com URL: http://www.okeefelawoffice.com
Paul F. O'Keefe.
Languages: Spanish.
Arbitration, Business Law, Business Litigation, Complex Business Litigation, Federal Civil Practice, Commercial Law, Complex Commercial Litigation, Contracts, Breach of Contracts, Contract Litigation, Corporate Law, Corporate Litigation, Criminal law, Criminal Defense, Governmental Law, Labor and Employment, Employment Breach of Contract, Litigation, Civil Litigation, Complex

(This Listing Continued)

O'Keefe, Paul F., P.C. (Continued)
Litigation, Defense Litigation, Federal Litigation, Trial Practice, Medical Malpractice, Personal Injury, Probate, Ancillary Probate, Probate Administration, Probate Litigation, Criminal Taxation, Trusts and Estates, Contested Trusts and Estates, Decedents Estates, Estate Litigation, Estate Settlements, White Collar Crimes, White Collar Criminal Defense, Wills, Contested Wills, Inheritance, Decedents Estates, Estate Administration, Estate Litigation, Estate Planning, Internet Crimes, Felonies.
Chicago, Illinois Office: 20 North Clark Street, Suite 2550. 60602. Telephone: 312-263-9200. Fax: 312-263-6245.
See Professional Biographies, WAUKEGAN, ILLINOIS

Ollivier, Charles L. ....'46 '76 C.734 B.S. L.365 J.D. 321 N. Utica St.
Orleans, Jason ....'73 '99 C.339 B.A. L.146 J.D. [Ⓐ Johnson&B.] (⊙Chicago)
Padnos, Joy I. ....'74 '00 C.1168 B.A. L.365 J.D. [Ⓐ Swanson,M.&B.] (⊙Libertyville)
Panter, Michael R., & Associates, (BV) '52 '78
C.966 B.A. L.209 J.D. 312 Grand Avenue (⊙Chicago)
Pantsios, Joan L. ....'48 '75 C.66 B.A. L.365 J.D. Asst. Pub. Def.
Pardys, David F., (BV) '57 '82
C.339 B.A. L.146 J.D. [Swanson,M.&B.] (⊙Chicago, Libertyville)
Parikh, Shyama S. ....'78 '03 C&L.209 B.A., J.D. [Ⓐ Shaw&F.]
Pascucci, Danielle Mary '72 '98
C.338 B.S. L.365 J.D. Asst. State Atty., Lake Co. State Atty. Off.

Payton, Garry A., Law Offices of '58 '87 C.801 B.A. L.489 J.D.
325 Washington Street, Suite 201, 60085
Telephone: 847-625-9900 Fax: 847-625-8880
Email: payton@attorneygarrypayton.com URL: http://www.lawyers.com/gapayton
Criminal Defense, Personal Injury, Medical Malpractice, Products Liability, Automobile Accidents, Wrongful Death, Construction Site Accidents, Driving While Intoxicated, Drug Crimes, Felonies, Homicide, Juvenile, Misdemeanors, Sexual Assault and Traffic Violations.
See Professional Biographies, WAUKEGAN, ILLINOIS

Peavey, Mark B., (BV) ....'50 '87 C.536 B.A. L.424 J.D. [M.B.Peavey]
Peavey, Mark B., P.C., (BV) ....325 Washington St., Ste. 201
Perillo, Michael J., Jr., (BV) ....'55 '83 C.222 B.A. L.564 J.D. [Noonan,P.P.]
Peterson-Gleason, June M., (CV) '— '90 C.882 B.A. L.146 J.D.
[Ⓐ T.M.Bond,Jr.&Assoc.]
Phillips, John T. ....'47 '72 C.162 B.A. L.352 J.D. Assoc. Cir. J.
Pinsel, Elliot A., (BV) ....'66 '91 C.339 B.S. L.146 J.D. [Daniels,L.&P.]

Pinzur, Cohen & Kerr, Ltd.
(See Long Grove)

Place, Linda A. ....'54 '96 C.339 B.S. L.209 J.D. 704 W. Pacific Ave.
Plewe, Tara R. ....'78 '03 C.339 B.A. L.436 J.D. [Ⓐ Salvi,S.&P.]
Polenzani, Joseph E., (BV) ....'60 '87 C.338 B.S. L.365 J.D. [Noonan,P.P.]
Potkonjak, Theodore S. ....'56 '82 C.430 B.A. L.61 J.D. Assoc. J.
Pribyl, David G., (BV) ....'61 '88 C.966 B.A. L.365 J.D. [Salvi,S.&P.]
Puisis, Edward A., (Ltd.) ....'30 '56 C&L.209 LL.B. 300 Grand Ave.
Quade, David R., (AV) ....'41 '68 C.98 B.S. L.365 J.D. [Diver,G.Q.&M.]

Querrey & Harrow, Ltd., (AV)
Suite 205, 415 West Washington Street, 60085 ⊙
Telephone: 847-249-4440 Fax: 847-249-4932
Email: tburke@querrey.com URL: http://www.querrey.com
Thomas P. Burke (Resident); Ellen E. Gibson (Resident);—Nicholas Johnson; Lawrence A. Steingold (Resident).
General Practice and Trial Practice.
Chicago, Illinois Office: 175 West Jackson Boulevard, Suite 1600. Telephone: 312-540-7000. Fax: 312-540-0578.
Crystal Lake, Illinois Office: 651 West Terra Cotta Avenue, Suite 221. Telephone: 815-479-1929. Fax: 815-479-1978.
Joliet, Illinois Office: 2 Rialto Square, Suite 401, 116 North Chicago Street. Telephone: 815-726-1600. Fax: 815-726-1674.
Wheaton, Illinois Office: 310 South County Farm Road, Third Floor. Telephone: 630-653-2600. Fax: 630-653-0178.
Merrillville, Indiana Office: 8585 Broadway, Suite 510. Telephone: 219-738-1820. Fax: 219-738-1821.
New York, N.Y. Office: 120 Broadway, Suite 2800. Telephone: 212-233-0130. Fax: 212-233-0172.
London, England Office: 141-142 Fenchurch Street, Fifth Floor. Telephone: 207-929-6670. Fax: 207-929-6671.
See Professional Biographies, WAUKEGAN, ILLINOIS

Radosevich, John G. ....'45 '71 C.602 B.B.A. L.424 J.D. Assoc. Cir. J.
Rafferty, Alex T., III, (BV) ....'32 '60 C.602 B.S. L.424 J.D. 9 N. Country St.
Rappaport, Stuart N. ....'62 '88 C.966 B.A. L.339 J.D. [Ⓐ W.C.Lindsay&Assoc.]
Repp, Gordon '59 '86 C.927 B.A. L.589 J.D.
Sr. Coun. & Asst. Secy., Outboard Marine Corp.

Richards, Ralph & Schwab, Chartered
(See Vernon Hills)

Ridge, Scott G., (BV) ....'47 '73 C.547 B.A. L.221 J.D. [Ⓒ W.C.Lindsay&Assoc.]

Rinella and Rinella, Ltd.
(See Chicago)

Rios, Rudy J. ....'— '00 C.589 B.A. L.339 J.D. [Diaz&R.] ⊙
Rizzo, John J., (BV) ....'68 '94 C.424 B.A. L.190 J.D. [Linn&C.]
Rominski, Joseph R., (BV) ....'54 '81 C.602 B.B.A. L.365 J.D. 203 N. West St.
Rosing, William G., (AV) ....'39 '64 C&L.339 A.B., J.D. One N. County St.
Rossetti, Victoria Ann ....'52 '79 C.734 B.S. L.589 J.D. Assoc. J.
Rothnagel, Linda A., (BV) '56 '81
C.478 B.A. L.477 J.D. Mng. Atty., Prairie State Legal Servs. Inc.
Rozenberg, Helen ....'54 '79 C.477 B.A. L.215 J.D. Cir. Ct. J.
Ryan, Kathleen, (AV) ....'55 '83 C&L.424 B.S.N., J.D. [Ryan,R.&L.]
Ryan, Philip J., (AV) ....'54 '79 C&L.424 B.B.A., J.D. [Ryan,R.&L.]

Ryan and Ryan
(See Chicago)

Ryan, Ryan & Landa, (AV) ....209 W. Madison Street
Saalfeld, Harold M. ....'54 '96 C.262 B.S. L.365 J.D. 25 N. Gunty Street, Suite 2R
Sachs, Christopher R. '52 '77 C&L.436 B.S., J.D.
(adm. in WI; not adm. in IL) Outboard Marine Corp.
Salvi, Albert J., (BV) ....'60 '85 C.602 B.A. L.339 J.D. [Salvi,R.&M.]
Salvi, Patrick A., (AV) ....'53 '78 C.742 B.A. L.602 J.D. [Salvi,S.&P.] ⊙

Salvi, Roskam & Maher, L.L.C., (BV)
325 Washington Street, Suite 302, 60085 ⊙
Telephone: 847-662-3303 Fax: 847-662-3453
Email: srmtms@sbcglobal.net URL: http://www.salvi-law.com
Members of Firm: Albert J. Salvi; Peter J. Roskam (Resident, Wheaton Office); Michael E. Maher.
Personal Injury, Automobile Accidents and Injuries, Slips and Falls, Dog Bites, Construction Accidents, Wrongful Death, Medical Malpractice, Workers Compensation and Legal Malpractice.
See Professional Biographies, WAUKEGAN, ILLINOIS

Salvi, Schostok & Pritchard P.C., (AV) BB
Established 1982 as Law Offices of Patrick A. Salvi, P.C.
218 North Martin Luther King Jr. Avenue, 60085 ⊙
Telephone: 847-249-1227 Facsimile: 847-249-0138
Email: psalvi@salvilaw.com URL: http://www.salvilaw.com

(This Listing Continued)

Salvi, Schostok & Pritchard P.C. (Continued)

Patrick A. Salvi; Michael P. Schostok; David J. Pritchard (Resident, Chicago Office); David G. Pribyl; Donald R. McGarrah (Resident, Chicago Office); Mark N. Senak (Resident, Chicago Office);—Scott R. Clewis; Kathleen A. McGinty (Resident, Chicago Office); Matthew L. Williams; John S. Muir (Resident, Chicago Office); Tara R. Plewe; Steven H. Leech. Of Counsel: James H. Canel; Thomas F. Loizzo.
Concentration in representing Plaintiffs in personal injury, medical malpractice, wrongful death, transportation liability, aviation, product liability and commercial litigation.
References: First Midwest Bank, Waukegan, Illinois; Northern Trust Bank, Lake Forest, Illinois; Commercial Litigation Clients; Anderson Consulting, LLP.; Baxter Healthcare.
Chicago, Illinois Office: 181 West Madison, Suite 3800, 60602. Telephone: 312-372-1227. Telefax: 312-372-3720.

See Professional Biographies, WAUKEGAN, ILLINOIS

Santi, Emilio B. .... '47 '74 C.436 B.A. L.607 J.D. Cir. J.
Savaglio, Michael T. .... '65 '90 C.436 B.A. L.365 J.D. 118 N. Genesee St.
Scheller, Stephen J. .... '62 '89 C.339 B.A. L.365 J.D. 325 Washington St., Ste. 201

Schlesinger, Gary L.
(See Libertyville)

Schostok, Michael P., (BV) .... '61 '86 C.473 B.A. L.117 J.D. [Salvi,S.&P.]
Scoco, Priscilla Rellas '58 '83
C.188 B.S. L.64 J.D. Asst. Secy. & Sr. Coun., Cardinal Health
Scott, Charles F. .... '42 '67 C&L.597 B.A., J.D. Cir. J.
Scurto, Sherby Dianne .... '— '04 C.238 B.A. L.1000 J.D. [S.D.Scurto]

Scurto, Sherby Dianne, P.C., Law Office of
222 Washington Street, 60085
Telephone: 847-336-9755 Fax: 847-336-9765
URL: http://www.sherbyscurto.com
Sherby Dianne Scurto.
Discrimination, Sexual Harassment, Wrongful Discharge, Civil Rights, Gay and Lesbian Rights, Criminal Records, Real Estate Closing, Buyer and Seller, Personal Injury.

See Professional Biographies, WAUKEGAN, ILLINOIS

Seneczko, Stacey L., (BV) .... '64 '89 C&L.801 B.S., J.D. [Hinshaw&C.]
Shaw, Mark L. .... '61 '88 C.679 B.S. L.347 J.D. [Shaw&F.]
Shaw & Foley, L.L.C. .... 33 North County Street, Suite 302
Simonian, James K. .... '64 '89 C.210 B.A. L.347 J.D. Asst. State Atty.
Simonian, Stephen M., (BV) ..... '60 '85 C.118 B.A. L.146 J.D. 25 N. County St., 2nd Fl.
Sinton, Scott J. .... '64 '89 One N. County St. (⊙Deerfield)
Skonieczny, Conrad J., (CV) .... '57 '85 C&L.424 B.A., J.D. Asst. States Atty.
Smith, Charles W., (AV) .... '50 '75 C.93 B.A. L.734 J.D. [Smith&L.]
Smith, Perry S., Jr., (BV) .... '54 '85 C.424 B.S. L.146 J.D. [Wysocki&S.]
Smith, Richard J., (AV) .... '39 '66 C.57 B.A. L.477 J.D. [Noonan,P.P.]
Smith & LaLuzerne, LTD., (AV) .... One North County Street
Smythe, Terry J., (BV) .... '47 '72 C.162 B.A. L.880 J.D. [Smythe&L.]
Smythe & Lee, (BV) .... 207 N. M.L. King Jr. Ave.
Snarski, Eugene M. .... '27 '52 C.602 B.A. L.597 J.D. 1920 N. Sheridan Road‡
Snyder, Gerald C., Jr., (BV) .... '33 '62 C.855 A.B. L.966 J.D. [Snyder,C.F.&Assoc.]
Snyder, Clarke, Fouts & Associates, (BV) .... 700 S. Lewis Ave.
Sowinski-Fix, Patricia, (CV) .... '66 '91 C.339 B.S. L.424 J.D. Chf. Dep. States Atty.
Spring, Linda E., (BV) '45 '83
C.494 B.S. L.424 J.D. [Swanson,M.&B.] (⊙Chicago, Libertyville)
Stalter, Lisle A. .... '67 '97 C.352 B.A. L.589 J.D. Staff Atty., Cir. Ct.
Starck, Christopher C. .... '54 '79 C.121 B.S. L.424 J.D. Assoc. Cir. J.

Stein, Ray & Harris LLP
(See Chicago)

Steingold, Lawrence A. .... '— '03 C.1119 B.S. L.146 J.D. [Querrey&H.]
Stiles, Douglas W., (BV) .... '49 '76 C.951 B.A. L.188 J.D. [Fuqua,W.&S.]
Stone, Jed, (AV) .... '49 '76 C.393 B.A. L.146 J.D. [Stone&Assoc.]

Stone & Associates L.L.C., (AV) BB
415 Washington Street, Suite 107, 60085
Telephone: 847-336-7888; 312-943-7881 Fax: 847-336-0733
Email: jstone@jedstone.com
Jed Stone; John Curnyn.
Practice limited to Criminal Law including White Collar Crime, Capital Offenses, Narcotics and Drugs, Death Penalty, Murder, Homicide and Federal Criminal Law.

See Professional Biographies, WAUKEGAN, ILLINOIS

Strathmann, Ralph A., (CV) .... '62 '89 C.339 B.A. L.209 J.D. [R.P.Will,Jr.&Assoc.]
Suhadolnik, William L., (BV) .... '59 '85 C.339 B.A. L.209 J.D. 25 N. County St.
Sullivan, Leo J., III, (AV) .... '34 '58 C&L.734 J.D. [Noonan,P.P.]

Swanson, Martin & Bell, (AV)
415 Washington Street Suite 1B, 60085 ⊙
Telephone: 847-949-0025 847-247-0555
URL: http://www.smbtrials.com
Partners: Steven L. Larson; David F. Pardys; Linda E. Spring; John A. Terselic. Associates: David S. Goles; Michone J. Kuhlman; Joy I. Padnos.
Class Action Lawsuits, Commercial Litigation, Construction Litigation/Disputes, Consumer and Warranty Law, Creditor's Rights, Drugs & Medical Devices, Employment Litigation, Environmental Law, Equipment Leasing, General Tort Liability, Healthcare, Insurance Coverage, Intellectual Property, Medical Negligence, Municipal Law, Product Liability, Professional Negligence, Real Estate Development/Zoning, Real Estate Litigation, Toxic and Mass Tort Litigation, and White Collar Criminal Defense.
Chicago, Illinois Office: 330 North Wabash, Suite 3300. Telephone: 312-321-9100. Fax: 312-321-0990.
DuPage County, Illinois Office: 2525 Cabot Drive, Lisle, Illinois, 60532. Telephone: 630-799-6900. Fax: 630-799-6901.
Libertyville, Illinois Office: 1860 West Winchester Road, Suite 201. Telephone: 847-949-0025. Fax: 847-247-0555.

See Professional Biographies, WAUKEGAN, ILLINOIS

Sweig, Allan G., (AV) .... '35 '60 C&L.597 B.S.B.A., J.D. [Leibowitz]
Swett, Kathleen Claire, (CV) .... '50 '76 C.429 B.A. L.339 J.D. Ticor Title Ins. Co.
Terselic, John A. '67 '92
C.801 B.A. L.209 J.D. [Swanson,M.&B.] (⊙Chicago, Libertyville)
Theophilos, George D. .... '— '78 C.597 B.A. L.1410 J.D. [Daniels,L.&P.]
Tonigan, Henry C., III .... '50 '76 C.187 B.A. L.802 J.D. Cir. J.
Trobe, Peter M. .... '48 '75 C.339 B.S. L.424 J.D. 404 W. Water St.
Trull, Ethan E. .... '62 '89 C&L.424 B.B.A., J.D. Asst. Gen. Coun., Cardinal Health
Tukesbrey, James S., (BV) .... '54 '79 C.339 B.A. L.801 J.D. [J.S.Tukesbrey]
Tukesbrey, James Scot, The Law Offices of, (BV) .... 33 North County Street, Suite 403
Ukena, Jay W., (BV) .... '47 '79 C.393 B.A. L.365 J.D. 204 North West Street
Van Deusen, Lloyd A. .... '17 '48 C.393 A.B. L.597 J.D. 2130 Ash Ave.‡
Vogg, Mark J., Law Offices of '63 '88
C.357 B.S. L.339 J.D. 210 North Martin Luther King Jr. Avenue
Vorderstrasse, Donna-Jo Rodden, (BV) '56 '84 C.879 B.A. L.906 J.D.
[Diver,G.Q.&M.]
Waldeck, Joseph R., (BV) .... '52 '79 C.436 B.A. L.589 J.D. 18 North County Street
Waldmann, Larra Call .... '— '01 L.146 J.D. Staff Coun., WMS Gaming Inc.
Walker, Charvis R. .... '76 '02 C.98 B.A. L.209 J.D. 1 N. County St.
Waller, Jane D. .... '46 '73 C.856 B.A. L.339 J.D. Cir. J.
Waller, Michael J., (BV) .... '48 '73 C.602 A.B. L.339 J.D. Lake Co. State's Atty.
Weinstein, David S. .... '65 '91 C.347 B.A. L.472 J.D. [Weinstein&D.]

Weinstein & Douglas, P.C.
325 Washington Street, Suite 301, 60085-5572
Telephone: 847-336-4343 Fax: 847-336-4916
Email: contactus@weinsteinanddouglas.com URL: http://www.lawyers.com/weinsteinanddouglas
David S. Weinstein; Dwayne Douglas.
Criminal Defense, Family Law, Divorce, Adoptions, Child Custody, Child Support, Domestic Violence, Premarital Agreements, Spousal Support, Paternity, Juvenile Law, Personal Injury, Automobile Accidents, Traffic Violations, Driving While Intoxicated, Drug Crimes, Felonies, Homicide and Sexual Assault.

See Professional Biographies, WAUKEGAN, ILLINOIS

Wexler, Geoffrey M. .... '— '89 C.339 B.S. L.424 J.D. [Daniels,L.&P.]
Whyte, Charles L. .... '08 '32 C.477 A.B. L.597 J.D. 2132 North Ave.‡
Will, Robert P., Jr., (AV) .... '38 '62 C&L.339 B.A., J.D. [R.P.Will,Jr.&Assoc.]
Will, Robert P., Jr. & Associates, (AV) .... 7 South County Street
Willaert, Matthew T. .... '67 '92 C&L.352 B.B.A., J.D. Corp. Coun., Cardinal Health
Williams, Chaya D. .... '77 '04 C&L.339 B.S., J.D. [Leibowitz]
Williams, Matthew L. .... '73 '98 C.339 B.A. L.209 J.D. [Salvi,S.&P.]
Wilson, Charles S., III, (AV) .... '29 '60 C.393 B.A. L.209 J.D. 222 W. Washington St.
Winer, David J. .... '61 '88 C.352 B.A. L.146 J.D. [Winer&W.]
Winer, Evan J. .... '62 '88 C.352 B.A. L.424 J.D. [Winer&W.]
Winer, Harold H. .... '26 '60 C.823 B.A. L.365 LL.B. [Winer&W.]
Winer & Winer .... 9 North County Street
Winter, Bernard R., (BV) .... '30 '58 C.238 B.A. L.597 J.D. [Fuqua,W.&S.]
Winter, Bryan R., (BV) .... '59 '84 C&L.436 B.S., J.D. [Fuqua,W.&S.]

Wrobel, Joseph, Ltd.
(See Chicago)

Wysocki, Albert L. .... '50 '77 C.339 B.A. L.146 J.D. [A.L.Wysocki]
Wysocki, Bernard, (BV) .... '49 '74 C.339 A.B. L.910 J.D. [Wysocki&S.]
Wysocki, Albert L., A Professional Corporation .... 325 Washington Street, Suite 401
Wysocki & Smith, (BV) .... 403 Grand Ave.

Yanez, Philip P., Law Offices of
(See Chicago)

Yarc, Mary E. .... '64 '89 C.93 B.A. L.365 J.D. Asst. State Atty.
Zagoras, Hercules Paul, (BV) .... '31 '61 C.339 A.B. L.146 LL.B. [H.P.Zagoras]
Zagoras, Hercules Paul, Ltd., (BV) .... 25 N. County St.
Zeit, Douglas E., Law Offices of, (BV) .... '51 '79 C.560 B.A. L.589 J.D. 32 N. West St.

WAYNE, 2,137, *DuPage & Kane Cos.*

Bond, Richard C., Jr. '36 '63 C.31 A.B. L.976 LL.B.
(adm. in PA; not adm. in IL) 5N958 Surrey Rd.

WENONA, 1,065, *Marshall Co.*

Canty, Ross M. .... '19 '52 C.98 B.S. L.597 LL.B. 210 N. Chestnut St.‡
Zukosky, Edward .... '23 '53 C.801 L.339 LL.B. 136 Chestnut St.

WESTCHESTER, 16,824, *Cook Co.*

Casey, Richard J. .... '66 '93 C.674 A.B. L.201 J.D. Gen. Coun., KMS Energy, Inc.
Castellano, Christine '66 '90
C.174 B.A. L.477 J.D. Atty., Corn Products International., Inc.
Doane, Marcia E. '41 '76 C.210 B.M. L.424 J.D.
V.P. & Gen. Coun., Corn Products International, Inc.
Duda, Richard A. '— '99
C.339 B.S. L.424 J.D. Lit. Coun., Corn Products International, Inc.
Fischer, Harry A., Jr., (AV) .... '26 '51 C.966 B.B.A. L.597 J.D. 1333 Burr Ridge Pkwy.‡
Glorioso, Mauro .... '56 '97 C.720 B.A. L.365 J.D. 2917 Becket Ave.
Gorka, Paul F. .... '51 '80 C.589 B.S. L.365 J.D. 1817 Manchester St.
Grunnet, Roy D. .... '27 '50 C&L.339 B.S.L., LL.B. 10500 W. Cermak Rd.
Hoar, James C. '59 '85 C.262 B.A. L.1019 J.D.
(adm. in NY; not adm. in IL) Natl. Restaurant Enterprises, Inc.
Langefeld, Thomas A. '66 '92
C.352 B.B.A. L.209 J.D. Reg. Coun., PeopleSoft USA, Inc.
Levy, Michael N. '73 '98 C.273 B.A./B.S. L.597 J.D.
Atty., U.S./Canada Oper., Corn Products International, Inc.
Matuga, Edward A. .... '21 '47 C&L.209 B.A., LL.B. [E.A.Matuga]
Matuga, Edward A., Ltd. .... 1651 Westchester Blvd.
Mikuta, Richard J. .... '57 '84 C.801 B.S. L.146 J.D. 2850 Downing
Montegna, Joseph A. .... '23 '50 C&L.602 LL.B. 10526 W. 22nd St.
Moran, Patrick J. .... '38 '68 C.339 B.S. L.209 J.D. 1127 S. Mannheim Rd.
Murphy, Frederick F. .... '16 '43 C.93 L.818 LL.B. 1541 Manchester Ave.‡
O'Donnell, Michael .... '57 '82 C.750 B.A. L.146 J.D. 1127 S. Mannheim Rd.
Prempas, Louis J. .... '26 '58 C.597 B.S. L.365 LL.B. 10526 W. Cermak Rd.
Ryan, Richard F. '59 '94
C.589 B.A. L.146 J.D. Two Westbrook Corporate Center, Suite 400
Shouh, John G. .... '24 '55 C.339 B.S. L.146 LL.B. 1315 High Ridge Pkwy.‡
Spahn, Thomas J. .... '51 '77 C.602 B.B.A. L.209 J.D. [T.J.Spahn&Assoc.]
Spahn, Thomas J. & Associates, P.C. .... 10500 W. Cermak Rd.
Straw, Ann L. '— '78 C&L.347 B.A., J.D.
Asst. Gen. Coun., Corn Products International, Inc.
Teborek, James S. .... '33 '60 C.118 A.B. L.145 J.D. 22 Queens Court
Thomas, Roderick D. .... '62 '96 C.339 B.S.E. L.209 J.D. [R.D.Thomas]
Thomas, Roderick D., P.C. .... 9909 W. Roosevelt Road, Suite 101
Van Vlierbergen, Frank E. .... '44 '80 C.1151 B.A. L.146 J.D. 10055 W. Roosevelt Rd.
Walters, James P., Attorney at Law .... '54 '92 C.843 B.A. L.365 J.D. 1509 Norfolk Ave.

WEST CHICAGO, 23,469, *DuPage Co.*

Acevedo, Carmelo .... '50 '98 C.405 B.S. L.209 J.D. 100 Arbor Ave.
Deaver, John W. '53 '80 C&L.910 A.B., J.D.
(adm. in MO; not adm. in IL) 29W725 Waynewood Dr.
Edgerton, Michael P., (BV) .... '42 '66 L.339 J.D. 125 Wood St.
Greenwalt, Robert D. .... '40 '72 C.870 B.S. L.145 J.D. 100 Main St.
Hatfield, Patricia L. .... '48 '73 C.338 B.S. L.597 J.D. 125 Wood St.
Hellman, Joanne E. .... '57 '83 C&L.910 B.A., J.D. 726 Hillview Ave.
Houle, Patricia C., (CV) .... '— '79 C.597 B.S. L.146 J.D. 18275 Edgewood Walk
Kelsey, Bruce R. .... '48 '73 C.910 B.S.B.A. L.339 J.D. 27w722 Holly Court
Konewko, Michael R. .... '53 '78 C.174 B.A. L.589 J.D. [Konewko&Assoc.]
Konewko & Assoc., Ltd. .... 1213 South Joliet
Melcher, Timothy P. .... '61 '88 C&L.174 B.S., J.D. 1955 North Aviarion Ave.
Moody, Gerald W. .... '26 '54 C.393 L.339 LL.B. 716 Wendall Ave.‡
Peard Knasel, Laurie .... '60 '91 C.339 B.S. L.424 J.D. Jel Sert Co., The
Ryan, Donald J. .... '28 '54 C&L.209 LL.B. 1313 South Oak St.
Spelman, Harold J., (AV) .... '23 '48 C&L.145 A.B., J.D. 200 High St.

Thomas, George A. ....'47 '78 C.238 B.A. L.365 J.D. 1213 Joliet St., Ste. F
Ward, Patricia L. ....'48 '73 C.338 B.S. L.597 J.D. 1275 Roosevelt Rd., Suite 106

WEST DUNDEE, 5,428, *Kane Co.*

Bolz, James M., (BV) ....'50 '75 C.221 B.A. L.464 J.D. 895 W. Main St., Ste. 200
Buehler, Rance V. ....'43 '74 C.63 B.S. L.365 J.D. P.O. Box 571
Burstein, Ronald B., (BV) ....'36 '64 C.597 B.A. L.365 LL.B. 100 S. 1st St.
Faber, George E., & Associates '36 '64
C.234 B.S. L.146 LL.B. 510 Market Loop, Ste. 203
Gates, Boyd L. ....'45 '71 C.966 B.S. L.146 J.D. P.O. Box 26

Juergensmeyer and Associates
(See Elgin)

Kugia, Martin, V .... [M.V.Kugia]
Kugia, Martin V., Law Office of .... 510 Market Loop, Suite 203
McCarty, Kevin M., (BV) ....'52 '81 C.338 B.S.Ed. L.365 J.D. 895 W. Main St., Ste. 200
Schnag, Frank James ....'55 '81 C.589 M.S. L.365 J.D. V.P., First Amer. Bk.
Uteg, Mark D., (BV) ....'56 '85 C.339 B.A. L.209 J.D. 707 W. Main St.
Weiler, Daniel A., (BV) ....'48 '76 C.424 B.A. L.365 J.D. 303 W. Main St.
Wolff, Wallace J. ....'52 '78 C.207 B.A. L.365 J.D. Exec. V.P., First Amer. Bk.

WESTERN SPRINGS, 12,493, *Cook Co.*

Beck, Frederick W. ....'36 '67 C.674 A.B. L.184 J.D. 4204 Howard Ave.
Bryant, James R., Jr., (AV) ....'25 '54 C.502 B.A. L.145 J.D. 1022 Linden Lane‡
Butler, Joseph J., Jr., (AV) '43 '75 C.801 B.A. L.365 J.D.
(adm. in FL; not adm. in IL) 4933 Grand Avenue
Connors, Robert A. ....'31 '57 C.485 B.A. L.966 LL.B. 617-54th Place
Cosentino, Robert Anthony, Law Offices of '53 '78
C.339 B.S. L.734 J.D. 1000 Hillgrove Avenue
Davi, Umberto S. ....'50 '82 C.927 B.S. L.365 J.D. 1105 W. Burlington Ave.
Dudzik, Carol J. ....'50 '87 C.927 B.A. L.365 J.D. 4228 Garden Avenue
Frewert, William H. ....'30 '65 C.597 B.B.A. L.209 LL.B. 5712 Lawn Dr.
Gaudio, Frank J. ....'55 '81 C.339 B.S. L.146 J.D. 5234 Woodland Ave.
Gildea, Frank S. ....'— '84 C.98 B.S. L.146 J.D. 901 W. Burlington Ave.
Gralen, Kimberly Kentra ....'60 '85 C.741 B.A. L.339 J.D. 4047 Forest Ave.‡
Hanson, Heidi E. ....'54 '78 C&L.339 B.S., J.D. [H.E.Hanson]
Hanson, H.E., P.C. .... 4721 Franklin Ave.
Haugh, Thomas P. ....'23 '52 C&L.424 LL.B. 5204 Grand Ave.‡
Herman, Keith J. ....'60 '98 C.339 B.S.M.E. L.209 J.D. 901 W. Burlington Ave., Ste. 500
Klima-Martin, Carol L., Law Offices of '— '87 C.72 B.A. L.1000 J.D.
4721 Howard Ave.
Lambe, James F. ....'45 '72 C.339 B.S. L.209 J.D. Sr. V.P., Nalco Chem. (Pat.)‡
Martin, Carol L. K. ....'— '87 C.72 B.A. L.365 J.D. 4721 Howard Ave.
Mejda, James J. ....'12 '35 C.999 L.209 J.D. 5804-A Wolf Rd.‡
Parker, Donald J., (AV) ....'30 '55 C&L.424 B.S., J.D. 5317 Lawn Ave.
Peiss, John H. ....'54 '82 C.966 B.B.A. L.300 J.D. 3837 Lawn Ave.
Premo, John G. ....'27 '52 L.209 LL.B. 110 51st Place (Pat.)
Prendergast, Virginia A. ....'— '55 C.597 A.B. L.209 J.D. 5123 Caroline‡
Quinn, Daniel G. ....'60 '85 C&L.424 B.A., J.D. 4479 Central Ave.
Schuette, Debra S. ....'59 '84 C.475 B.A. L.477 J.D. 4837 Lawn Ave.
Sheen, Fulton J. ....'33 '61 C.424 A.B. L.146 LL.B. 820 Elm
Skarr, Ronald J., (AV) ....'49 '75 C.191 B.A. L.365 J.D. 4307 Western
Sonneborn, Thomas F., (BV) ....'50 '75 C.339 B.A. L.365 J.D. 5600 S. Wolf Rd.
Wallach, Kevin G. ....'56 '81 C.602 B.S. L.424 J.D. 5013 Woodland Ave.
Walsh, Cecilia ....'54 '91 C.741 B.B.A. L.424 J.D. 1108 Oak Ln.

WEST FRANKFORT, 8,196, *Franklin Co.*

Alexander, William A., (AV) ......'43 '73 C&L.339 B.S., J.D. [🄰 S.C.Mitchell&Assoc.]
Brown, Lance P. ....'77 '03 C&L.801 B.S., J.D. [🄰 S.C.Mitchell&Assoc.]
Brown, W. Campbell, (BV) ....'49 '76 C.339 B.S. L.801 J.D. 402 E. Main St.
Douglas, Steven R. ....'50 '84 C.801 B.A. L.117 J.D. 9980 State Hwy. 149

Hart and Hart
(See Benton)

Irish, Bruce D., (BV) ....'42 '73 C&L.910 B.S.B.A., J.D. [🄰 S.C.Mitchell&Assoc.]
Lucas, Don R., & Associates, Ltd., (AV) ......'35 '63 C.801 B.S. L.966 J.D. 404 S. Logan
Mitchell, Sam C., (AV) ....'39 '68 C.801 B.S. L.424 J.D. [S.C.Mitchell&Assoc.]

Mitchell, Sam C., & Associates, (AV) BB
115 1/2 East Main Street, P.O. Box 280, 62896
Telephone: 618-932-2772; 937-2662 Telecopier: 618-932-3456
URL: http://www.lawyers.com/samcmitchell
Sam C. Mitchell. Associates: Bruce D. Irish; William A. Alexander; Lance P. Brown.
Plaintiff Personal Injury and Workers Compensation cases only.
See Professional Biographies, WEST FRANKFORT, ILLINOIS

Riva, D. Michael, (BV) ....'48 '74 C.388 B.A. L.910 J.D. [D.M.Riva]
Riva, D. Michael, Ltd., (BV) ....226 E. Main St.
Vantrease, Susan A., (BV) ....'53 '83 C.388 B.A. L.801 J.D. 402 E. Main St.

WESTMONT, 24,554, *DuPage Co.*

Alexander, Bradley D. ....'63 '88 C.424 B.S. L.365 J.D. 407 Linden St.
Andrews, Todd Alan ....'69 '95 C.94 B.A. L.209 J.D. Legal Coun., Man Roland, Inc.
Arnold, Joel D. ....'47 '73 C.1106 B.A. L.365 J.D. [Fortunato,F.D.&A.]
Boucek, Joseph ....'11 '35 L.146 J.D. 1228 Williamsport Dr., Unit 1‡
Brady, Daniel J. ....'56 '83 C.187 B.A. L.352 J.D. Market Science Assoc., Inc.
Britz, Juliene A. '72 '98 C&L.597 B.A., J.D.
Chf. Admr., Industrial Gas Engineering Co., Inc.
Burkhardt, Gwenda M. '— '82
C.472 B.A. L.365 J.D. Sr. Labor & Employ. Coun., SIRVA, Inc.
Daly, J. Frank ....'29 '55 C.72 A.B. L.597 J.D. 640 Pasquinelli Dr.
Davenport, Linda E. ....'53 '78 C.174 B.A. L.209 J.D. [Fortunato,F.D.&A.]
Delker, Wilja ....'44 '81 C.589 B.A. L.146 J.D. 315 S. Williams St.
Eck, R. Paul ....'35 '62 C.373 B.A. L.597 J.D. 700 Oakmont Lane‡
Egan, James E., (BV) ....'45 '74 C.602 B.B.A. L.209 J.D. [J.E.Egan]
Egan, James E., Chartered, (BV) .... 6432 S. Cass Ave.
Engler, James W. ....'47 '74 C&L.378 B.A., J.D. Pres., EMJ Companies, The
Farrell, B. J. ....'49 '78 C.750 B.A. L.1151 J.D. [Fortunato,F.D.&A.]
Fortunato, Joseph R., Jr. ....'48 '73 C.589 B.A. L.365 J.D. [Fortunato,F.D.&A.]
Fortunato, Farrell, Davenport & Arnold, Ltd. ....4112 Cass Ave.
Gualano, Richard L., (BV) .....'45 '73 C.339 B.A. L.424 J.D. 6301 S. Cass Ave., Ste. 300
Hubeny, John R., & Associates ....'47 '82 C.209 B.S.C. L.365 J.D. 200 East Chicago Ave.

Johnson, Theresa V., Law Office of '51 '96 C.991 B.A. L.146 J.D.
200 East Chicago Avenue, Suite 200, 60559
Telephone: 630-321-1330 Fax: 630-321-1185
Email: theresavjohnson@prodigy.net URL: http://www.theresavjohnson.com
Foreign and Domestic Intellectual Property (IP) including Patents, Trademarks, Trade Secrets, Copyrights, Unfair Competition, Licensing, International IP Arbitration and Mediation, IP Litigation,

(This Listing Continued)

Johnson, Theresa V., Law Office of (Continued)
Madrid Protocol Trademark Filing and Consultation, Patent Cooperation Treaty and Paris Convention Filing, International Law, Immigration, Entertainment Law, Defamation, Title VII Discrimination/Retaliation, Family Medical Leave Act (FMLA), Americans with Disabilities Act (ADA), Personal Injury, Mechanics Liens, Replevin/Recovery of Engagement Ring, Probate, Estates.
See Professional Biographies, WESTMONT, ILLINOIS

Knobbe, Sharon Rita ....'76 '00 C.338 B.S. L.365 J.D. [🄰 Fortunato,F.D.&A.]
Kornichuk Emery, Ellen S. ....'56 '82 C.589 B.S. L.365 J.D. 202 Carlisle Ave.
Laz, David M., (BV) ....'57 '82 C.750 B.A. L.209 J.D. 32 W. Burlington Ave.
Marsik, J. Scott ....'50 '78 C.1109 B.A. L.589 J.D. 4112 Cass Ave.
McBride, Terry W. '42 '69 C.028 B.A. L.025 LL.B.
(adm. in BC; not adm. in IL) V.P. & Gen. Coun., UPM-Kymmeno, Inc.
Morrow, Brian T., (BV) ....'49 '77 C.734 A.B. L.365 J.D. 6301 S. Cass Ave.

Scurto, Sherby Dianne, P.C., Law Office of
(See Waukegan)

Serafin, Robert E. ....'55 '80 C.454 B.A. L.209 J.D. 214 N. Wilmette Ave.
Solon, Joseph I., Jr. ....'55 '85 C.339 B.A. L.365 J.D. [🄰 Fortunato,F.D.&A.]
Stein, Frederick W. ....'64 '91 C.723 B.S. L.146 J.D. Vice Pres. & Gen. Coun., EFMARK
Traynham, Wayne O. '50 '81
(adm. in MA; not adm. in IL; Pat.) Sr. Coun., SIRVA, Inc.
Wu, John L. ....'35 '80 C.999 B.A. L.589 J.D. 825 North Cass Avenue, Suite 203

WEST PEORIA, * 4,762, *Peoria Co.*

Groezinger, Linda S., (CV) ....'62 '99 C.98 B.A. L.589 J.D. [Lowe&G.]
Lowe, Kevin, (CV) ....'70 '95 C&L.339 B.A., J.D. [Lowe&G.]
Lowe & Groezinger, P.C., (CV) .... 2009 W. Ayres Ave.

WHEATON, * 55,416, *DuPage Co.*

Abraham, Kenneth A. ....'45 '70 C.339 B.A. L.209 J.D. Co. J.
Acker, David S., (AV) ....'46 '74 C.697 B.A. L.597 J.D. 416 E. Roosevelt Rd.
Adams, Gail Patricia ....'60 '85 C.339 B.F.A. L.589 J.D. 2050 Cromwell Dr.‡
Adkins, Russell A. ....'66 '91 C.339 B.S. L.209 J.D. 1755 S. Naperville Rd.
Adkins, Susan S. ....'66 '91 C.937 B.A. L.209 J.D. 1755 S. Naperville Road
Ahern, Janet Marie ....'52 '82 C.927 B.A. L.589 J.D. Asst. State's Atty.
Allen, Josette C. ....'67 '92 C.597 B.A. L.1119 J.D. Asst. Pub. Def.
Alspaugh, David W. ....'27 '63 C.339 L.146 LL.B. 102 N. Cross St.
Altimari, Jamie ....'55 '88 C.530 B.A. L.1049 J.D. Arbitration Admr.
Anderson, Jonathan G. ....'53 '81 C.966 B.A. L.260 J.D. [Anderson&Assoc.] ⊙
Anderson, Michael R. ....'52 '82 C.339 B.A. L.209 J.D. Chicago Title Ins. Co.
Anderson, Nancy Phillips ....'58 '83 C&L.209 B.A., J.D. 1426 Glencoe St.‡
Anderson, Pamela W. ....'57 '91 C.879 B.S. L.365 J.D. [🄰 C.R.Gessner]

Anderson & Associates, P.C.
400 S. County Farm Road, Suite 120, 60187 ⊙
Telephone: 630-653-9400 Fax: 630-653-9450
Jonathan G. Anderson;—Robin M. Zandri; Andrea C. Lawrence; Christopher J. Maurer; Mia Do.
Family Law, Bankruptcy, Real Estate Litigation and Transactions, Estate Planning and Probate.
Chicago Office: 166 W. Washington Street, Suite 640. Telephone: 312-236-5599.
Schaumburg Office: 1701 East Woodfield Road, Suite 1050. Telephone: 847-995-9999. Fax: 847-995-0117.
See Professional Biographies, WHEATON, ILLINOIS

Andrews, W. Anthony ....'66 '93 C.1151 B.A. L.209 J.D. [Norton,M.W.&D.] ⊙
Antas, Sarah Mahoney ....'60 '85 C.679 B.A. L.365 J.D. 1011 Robbins Ct.
Appelhans, Patricia F. '55 '83 C.339 B.A. L.589 J.D.
Exec. Dir., National Association of Bond Lawyers
Argentati, Patricia L., (BV) ....'53 '82 C.436 B.A. L.146 J.D. [Mulherin,R.&V.]
Armamentos, Steven David ....'58 '84 C.589 B.A. L.209 J.D. 128 S. Country Farm
Armstrong, Timothy A., (BV) ....'64 '89 C.208 B.A. L.365 J.D. 1776 B S. Naperville Rd.
Austin, C. Stanley ....'53 '79 C.339 B.A. L.209 J.D. Cir. Ct. J.
Bahr, Irene F. ....'49 '77 C.339 B.A. L.209 J.D. 1751 S. Naperville Rd., Ste. 209

Bailey & Bailey
(See Chicago)

Bakalis, George J. ....'41 '69 C.393 B.A. L.209 J.D. Cir. J.
Baker, Stephen W. ....'52 '78 C.927 B.A. L.424 J.D. Pub. Def.
Banahan, Brian J. ....'68 '98 C&L.589 B.S., J.D. 610 W. Roosevelt, Ste. B2
Banahan, Lillian M. ....'18 '44 C&L.424 Ph.B., J.D. 209 Naperville Rd.‡
Barclay & Damisch, Ltd., (BV) ....115 W. Wesley St.
Barger, Jonathan K. ....'76 '02 C.880 B.A. L.146 J.D. 1755 S. Naperville Rd., Ste. 200
Barrientes, Jesse V., Law Offices of '64 '91 C.424 B.A. L.365 J.D.
1650 Casa Solana Dr.
Bartler, John C., (AV) ....'31 '56 C&L.597 B.S., J.D. 2100 Manchester
Barton, Marilynn ....'75 '00 C.209 L.365 J.D. 1761 S. Naperville Road
Bartosiak, Harry E. ....'66 '92 C&L.424 B.A., J.D. [Tressler,S.M.&P.]
Bates, Elizabeth A. ....'55 '80 C.282 B.A. L.884 J.D. 1755 S. Naperville Road, Suite 200
Beck, Joseph M., (AV) ....'59 '85 C.339 B.S. L.365 J.D. [Beck,H.&S.]
Beck, Robert C., (BV) ....'67 '95 C.424 B.S. L.1187 J.D. [R.C.Beck]

Beck, Houlihan & Scott, P.C., (AV) BB
534 West Roosevelt Road, 60187
Telephone: 630-933-9220 Fax: 630-933-0220
Email: lawyers@bhsatlaw.com URL: http://www.lawyers.com/bhsatlaw
William J. Scott, Jr.; Joseph M. Beck; John P. Houlihan; Patricia A. Fox.
Trial Practice. Domestic Relations, Real Estate, General Practice, Criminal and Commercial Law, Bankruptcy, Estate Planning, Family Law Mediation.
See Professional Biographies, WHEATON, ILLINOIS

Beck, Robert C., P.C., The Law Office of, (BV) .... 534 West Roosevelt Road
Bell, Stephen K., (BV) ....'52 '80 C.339 B.S. L.381 J.D. 422 W. Wesley St.
Benda, Thomas J., (BV) '35 '65 C&L.339 B.A., J.D.
Suite 105, 416 East Roosevelt Road
Benzing, Deborah A. ....'62 '87 C.801 B.A. L.734 J.D. 104 E. Roosevelt Rd., Ste. 204
Best, Vanderlaan & Harrington, (AV) ......2100 Manchester Road, Suite 1420 (⊙Chicago)
Betz, Carole, (CV) ......'— '82 C.339 B.A. L.589 J.D. 2100 Manchester Road, Suite 1440
Birkett, Joseph E. ....'55 '81 C.578 B.A. L.365 J.D. Off. of State's Atty.
Bishop, Mark S. '71 '99 C&L.339 B.S., J.D.
1755 S. Naperville Rd., Suite 200 (⊙Wheaton)
Boersma, David J., The Law Office of '49 '81
C.999 B.A. L.879 J.D. 330 S. Naperville Rd., Ste. 300
Boeye, Robert P., (AV) ....'34 '59 C.399 B.A. L.352 J.D. [Califf&H.] ⊙
Bond, Patrick K., (BV) ....'60 '86 C.436 B.A. L.209 J.D. 203 E. Liberty
Bongiorno, Joseph S. ....'53 '79 C.238 B.A. L.589 J.D. Assoc. Cir. J.
Botti, Aldo E., (AV) ....'36 '66 C.698 A.B. L.734 J.D. [Botti,M.&D.] ⊙
Botti, Stephen R., (BV) ....'54 '80 C&L.692 B.S., J.D. [Botti,M.&D.] ⊙

Botti, Marinaccio & DeLongis, Ltd., (AV)
Suite 402 Ticor Title Building, 330 Naperville Road, 60187 ⊙
Telephone: 630-653-2100
URL: http://www.lawyers.com/bottimaridellaw

(This Listing Continued)

Botti, Marinaccio & DeLongis, Ltd. (Continued)
Aldo E. Botti; Lee A. Marinaccio; Stephen R. Botti; Peter M. DeLongis; Jean Lasics-Wessels.
Trial and Appellate Practice in State and Federal Courts, Civil, Criminal, Personal Injury, Family, Zoning, Corporation, Probate Law, Commercial and Government Litigation.
Oak Brook, Illinois Office: 720 Enterprise Drive. Telephone: 630-573-8585. Fax: 630-573-8586.
See Professional Biographies, WHEATON, ILLINOIS

Bouma, Ralph R., Jr. '42 '68 C.388 B.A. L.339 J.D. [Huck B.]
Boyer, Neil J. '41 '66 C.597 B.A. L.339 J.D. 1808 North Stoddard Avenue
Boylan, William E., (BV) '47 '76 C.424 B.S. L.597 J.D. 1701 Kay Rd.
Bradshaw, George M., (BV) '46 '72 C.238 B.A. L.365 J.D. [Huck B.]
Bravos, Zachary M., Law Office of '51 '78 C.238 B.A. L.1151 J.D. 600 W. Roosevelt Rd.
Bredlie, Kirsten R. '71 '97 C.182 B.A. L.494 J.D. State's Atty. Off.

Brenner, Ford, Monroe & Scott, Ltd.
(See Chicago)

Brinkman, Paul G., (BV) '50 '76 C.57 B.A. L.339 J.D. 115 West Wesley Street, Suite 4
Brisske, Heinz J., (BV) '49 '74 C.504 A.B. L.228 J.D. 1325 N. Main St.

Brodsky & Odeh
(See Chicago)

Brodzinski, William R. '73 '99 C.679 B.S. L.146 J.D. [⊡ Mulherin,R.&V.]
Bromann, Scott, (AV) '52 '77 C.802 B.A. L.879 J.D. 127 W. Willow Ave.
Brower, Karren '60 '89 C.851 B.B.A. L.1003 J.D. [K.Brower]
Brower, Karren, PC, Law Office of 104 E. Roosevelt Rd., Ste. 101
Brown, Edith Juanita, Law Offices of '42 '81 C.661 B.A. L.589 J.D. 1751 S. Naperville Rd.
Bruckner, Dale W., (BV) '52 '77 C.966 B.A. L.383 J.D. [Peregrine,S.N.R.&B.]

Brundage, Stephen A., (BV) '58 '90 C.1151 B.A. L.209 J.D.
1749 South Naperville Road, Suite 105, 60187
Telephone: 630-260-9647 Fax: 630-462-3767
Email: Sablaw@aol.com URL: http://www.lawyers.com/brundagelaw
Criminal Law, Driving While Intoxicated, Drug Crimes, Felonies, Homicide, Juvenile Law, Misdemeanors, Parole and Probation, Sexual Assault, Traffic Violations, Assault and Battery, Burglary, Criminal Defense, Drivers License Suspension, Forgery, Manslaughter, Search and Seizure, Sex Crimes, Theft, Juvenile Law, Family Law, Divorce, Child Custody, Child Support, Domestic Violence, Premarital Agreements, Spousal Support, Martial Agreements, Marital Property Distribution, Martial Property Law, Marital Property Settlements, Matrimonial Law, Paternity, Post Divorce Modification, Real Estate, Real Estate Sales, Residential Real Estate, Residential Real Estate Sales, Personal Injury, Automobile Accidents and Injuries, Dog Bites, Sexual Abuse, Slip and Fall and Wrongful Death Law.
See Professional Biographies, WHEATON, ILLINOIS

Burek, Alexander J., (AV) '16 '49 C.578 B.A. L.597 J.D. 100 N. Hale St.‡
Burke, Michael J. '58 '84 C.589 B.S. L.365 J.D. Asst. State's Atty.
Butkus, J. Steven '57 '82 C.221 B.A. L.209 J.D. [Guerard,K.&B.]

Byrne, Catherine M.
(See Chicago)

Byrne, Michael T.
(See Clarendon Hills)

Cahalan, Suzanne M. '57 '82 C.898 B.A. L.352 J.D. 909 S. Wheaton Ave.
Cahill, Thomas B., (AV) '57 '83 C.750 B.A. L.589 J.D. [Mulherin,R.&V.]
Calabrese, Michael J. '69 '93 L.209 J.D. [Calabrese&Assoc.]

Calabrese Associates, A Professional Corporation
310 South County Farm Road, Suite H, 60187
Telephone: 630-588-8010 Fax: 630-588-8070
Email: calabreseassoc@aol.com URL: http://www.lawyers.com/calabreseassociates
Michael J. Calabrese.
Family Law including Divorce Law, Child Custody, Visitation Rights, Support, Adoption Law, Paternity, Prenuptial Agreements and Appeals.
See Professional Biographies, WHEATON, ILLINOIS

Califf & Harper, P.C., (AV)
123 West Front Street, Suite 200, 60187 ⊙
Telephone: 800-764-4999 Facsimile: 630-871-1347
URL: http://www.califf.com
Robert P. Boeye; Dennis R. Fox; John A. Slover, Jr.; Thomas A. Harper; Jeffrey B. Moorhouse; Roger L. Strandlund; Arthur W. Eggers; Harvey A. Levin; James S. Zmuda; Jonathon C. Fox; Franklin S. Mitvalsky;—Karla C. Steele. Of Counsel: James A. Harper.
Corporate, Commercial, Civil Litigation in all State and Federal Courts, Labor, Employment, Banking, Governmental, School, Administrative (including N.L.R.B.), Products Liability, Insurance, Taxation, Estate Planning and Probate Law, Real Estate, Land Development and Zoning.
Representative Clients: First Midwest Bank/Western Illinois, N.A.; Associated Employers of the Quad Cities; Iowa-Illinois Gas & Electric Co.; Metropolitan Airport Authority of Rock Island County; Travelers Insurance Co.
Moline, Illinois Office: 6th Floor First Midwest Bank Building, 506 Fifteenth Street, P.O. Box 719. Telephone: 309-764-8361. Facsimile: 309-764-8394.
See Professional Biographies, WHEATON, ILLINOIS

Callow, Mary E., (AV) '45 '85 C.700 B.A. L.365 J.D. [Clingen C.&M.]
Callum, Thomas E. '44 '73 C.1024 B.A. L.146 J.D. Cir. J.
Canavan, R. Lawrence, (BV) '45 '79 C.339 B.S. L.589 J.D. [Lehrer,F.&C.]
Carder, Deborah A. '70 '95 C.339 B.A. L.209 J.D. [⊡ Schiller,D.&F.]
Carlson, Kurt A., (BV) '44 '71 C&L.209 J.D. [Stock,C.F.&Assoc.]
Carrara, Emily R. '71 '01 C.94 B.A. L.365 J.D. [⊡ Sullivan T.&G.]
Carrara, Kevin M. '69 '01 C.589 B.S. L.365 J.D. [⊡ Rathje&W.]
Carroll, Brenda Mary, (BV) '48 '86 C.424 B.A. L.146 J.D. DuPage Co. Bar Assoc., Legal Aid
Carroll, Mark J. '74 '01 C.317 B.A. L.589 J.D. [⊡ Guerard,K.&B.]
Carter, Andrew M. '— '99 C.860 B.A. L.1194 J.D. (adm. in VT; not adm. in IL) 401 S. Carlton St., Ste. 204
Carter, Doris Adkins '55 '80 C.339 B.S. L.424 J.D. [Carter&T.]
Carter & Tani 402 E.Roosevelt Rd., Ste.206
Caruso, Matthew T., (P.C.), (BV) '63 '88 C.339 B.A. L.365 J.D. [Fitzsimmons,R.P.&C.]
Cermak, Francis T. '75 '00 C.578 B.A. L.209 J.D. Asst. State Atty.
Cerne, Neal W., (BV) '60 '88 C.597 B.A. L.424 J.D. 311 South County Farm Road, Suite A

Cetina & Jacques, P.C.
(See Oakbrook Terrace)

Chapman, Mary Jane Forbes '45 '83 C.347 M.A. L.209 J.D. [M.J.Chapman]
Chapman, Mary Jane, Law Office 511 W. Wesley St., Ste. 3000

Chicago Internet Attorneys
(See Chicago)

Chiesa, Abigail M. '68 '93 C.810 B.A. L.273 J.D. [⊡ Schiller,D.&F.]
Chiles, Harry Ray, Jr., (BV) '49 '74 C&L.424 A.B., J.D. [H.Chiles&Assoc.]
Chiles, Harry, and Associates, (BV) 1737 S. Naperville Rd., Ste. 207
Chval, Craig J. '60 '84 C.602 B.B.A. L.146 J.D. Asst. State's Atty.
Clark, David W. '66 '92 C.347 B.A. L.424 J.D. [Peregrine,S.N.R.&B.]

Clark, William G., Jr., & Associates, LTD.
(See Chicago)

Clarke, Augusta R. '53 '89 C.783 B.A. L.365 J.D. DuPage Co State Attny's Off, Spec Victims Unit
Claud, R. Daniel, Jr. '39 '72 C.886 B.S. L.365 J.D. 1155 Shady Ln.

Clausen Miller P.C., (AV)
Building C, Suite 1700, 2100 Manchester Road, 60187-2402 ⊙
Telephone: 630-668-9100 Fax: 630-668-9169
Email: info@clausen.com URL: http://www.clausen.com
Thomas H. Ryerson; Michael L. Vittori; Michael E. Zidek;—Denis K. Sheehan.
General Civil Practice. Insurance, Corporations.
References: The First National Bank of Chicago; La Salle National Bank.
Chicago, Illinois Office: 10 South LaSalle Street, Suite 1600, 60603-1098. Telephone: 312-855-1010. Fax: 312-606-7777. Internet Email: clientservices@clausen.com.
European Affiliated Law Firm—Clausen Miller Europe: Tetaud-Lambard-Jami & Associés, 83, boulevard Raspail, 75006, Paris, France. Telephone: +33.1.45.48.62.63. Fax: +33.1.45.48.42.57. Studio Legale Corapi, Via Flaminia, 318 00196- Roma. Telephone: 39.06.32.18.563. Fax: 39.06.32.00.992. van Cutsem-Wittamer-Marnef & Partners, Avenue Louise 137/1, B-1050 Brussels, Belgium. Telephone: +32-2-543-02-00. Fax: +32-2-538-13-78.
European Affiliated Law Firm—Clausen Miller, L.L.P.: 148 Leadenhall Street, London, EC3V 4QT England. Telephone: +44.20.7648.8460. Fax: +44.20.7648.8461.
New York, N.Y. Office: One Chase Manhattan Plaza, 10005. Telephone: 212-805-3900. Fax: 212-805-3939.
Newark, New Jersey Office: One Gateway Center, Suite 2600, 07102-5397. Telephone: 973-645-0564. Fax: 973-622-3423.
Irvine, California Office: 2040 Main Street, Suite 500, 92614. Telephone: 949-474-3100. Fax: 949-474-3190.
See Professional Biographies, WHEATON, ILLINOIS

Clingen, Kenneth W. '60 '87 C&L.602 B.B.A., J.D. [Clingen C.&M.]

Clingen Callow & McLean, LLC, (AV)
2100 Manchester Road Suite 1750, 60187
Telephone: 630-871-2600 Fax: 630-871-9869
URL: http://www.ccmlawyer.com
Kenneth W. Clingen; Mary E. Callow; Timothy M. McLean; Paul M. Fullerton; Ross I. Molho; Kenneth J. Vanko. Associates: Deanna M. Quinn-McCollian; Deven S. Kane. Of Counsel: Delrose Ann Koch.
Banking, Commercial Litigation, Corporate, Employment Law, Estate Planning, Real Estate, Business Planning.
See Professional Biographies, WHEATON, ILLINOIS

Coco, Anthony V. '67 '93 C.347 B.A. L.46 J.D. Pub. Def.
Coffin, Margaret '25 '50 C.102 L.724 LL.B. Asst. States Atty.
Collins, Daniel R., Law Offices of '66 '98 C.1286 B.A. L.1187 J.D. 1725 S. Naperville Rd., Ste. 200
Conick, Harold W., (BV) '50 '80 C.424 A.B. L.589 J.D. [Conick&C.]
Conick, Marshall W., (BV) '55 '93 C.424 B.A. L.365 J.D. [Conick&C.]
Conick & Conick, Ltd., (BV) 321 S. Wheaton Ave.

Connelly Roberts & McGivney LLC
(See Chicago)

Conrad, Lynn R. '58 '86 C.418 B.S. L.424 J.D. [Piccione,K.&Assoc.]
Constantino, Mary C. '49 '92 C.530 B.S. L.365 J.D. Asst. State's Atty.
Cook, Christopher L. '63 '90 C.123 B.A. L.146 J.D. 1776 South Naperville Road, Suite 104A
Coolahan, Patrick M. '48 '73 C.339 B.A. L.209 J.D. 1594 Whitman Ln.
Coon, Carol A. '45 '82 C.739 B.A. L.589 J.D. 93 Kensington Circle
Cooper, G. Robb '51 '87 C.628 B.S. L.424 J.D. [Ottosen T.B.K.&C.] ⊙
Cores, Andrew P. '68 '93 C.363 B.A. L.597 J.D. 290 S. Country Farm Rd., Ste. M
Cornelius, Vincent F. '64 '89 C.717 B.B.A. L.589 J.D. Asst. State's Atty.
Corrigan, Barbara Ann '68 '93 C.340 B.A. L.209 J.D. [⊡ L.B.Haskin&Assoc.]
Costello, Patrick T. '67 '93 C.339 B.A. L.589 J.D. 128 S. County Farm Rd.
Cotteleer, Michael A., (BV) '44 '71 C.589 B.A. L.424 J.D. 207 N. Washington St.
Coughlin, Colleen D. '50 '84 C.339 A.B. L.424 J.D. Asst. State Atty.
Courter, Craig Earle, (AV⊤) '55 '86 C.234 B.A. L.1049 J.D. (adm. in CA; not adm. in IL) 1724 Stoddard Avenue
Cox, Robert A. '31 '59 C.123 L.879 J.D. 528 W. Roosevelt Rd.
Creswell, Kathryn E. '— '84 C.477 A.B. L.209 J.D. Assoc. Cir. J.
Cronin, Mary K., (BV) '53 '86 C.1191 B.S.Ed. L.365 J.D. Asst. States Atty.
Cuchna, Wayne M. '48 '73 C.602 B.B.A. L.209 J.D. [Pietsch&C.]
Cummings, Richard T. '61 '86 C&L.339 B.A., J.D. 1723 N. Summit St.‡
Cunningham, William F., (AV) '45 '71 C&L.209 B.A., J.D. [Cunningham M.&V.]
Cunningham Meyer & Vedrine, P.C., (AV) 2100 Manchester Road, Suite B-1050
Curshellas, Lisa '74 '99 C.424 B.A. L.1000 J.D. [⊡ Mangan,L.G.&L.]
Damisch, John W., (BV) '26 '50 C&L.597 B.S., J.D. [Barclay&D.]
Daniel, Mark W., (BV) '68 '94 C.339 B.S. L.365 J.D. [Rathje&W.]
Darnall, C. Jackson '34 '60 C&L.597 B.A., J.D. [⊡ Tressler,S.M.&P.]
Da Rosa, Ronald A., (BV) '43 '70 C.589 B.S. L.365 J.D. [Da Rosa&M.]
Da Rosa and Miller, (BV) 208 N. West St.
Daw, Timothy M., (BV) '59 '85 C.339 B.S. L.209 J.D. [Schiller,D.&F.]
DeAno, James L., (AV) '56 '81 C.927 B.A. L.365 J.D. [Norton,M.W.&D.] ⊙
Defalco, Marcelline '70 '97 C.1183 B.A. L.365 J.D. [⊡ Mulherin,R.&V.]
De La Mar, Cathleen Noelle '72 '01 C&L.339 B.A.S., J.D. DuPage Co. State Atty.'s Off.
Delis, Maria '74 '01 C.424 B.S. L.1000 J.D. State's Atty.'s Off.
DeLongis, Peter M., (AV) '56 '82 C.589 B.S. L.146 J.D. [Botti,M.&D.] ⊙
Demakis, Spyro J. '68 '93 C.424 B.A. L.273 J.D. [⊡ Cunningham M.&V.]
Demling, John W., (AV) '51 '77 C.532 B.A. L.146 J.D. 505 N. County Farm Rd.
DeSalvo, Frank J., (BV) '48 '74 C.801 B.A. L.365 J.D. 400 W. Roosevelt Rd., Ste. 2-E
Deutsch, Levy & Engel, Chartered, (AV) 620 West Roosevelt Road (⊙Chicago)
Devine, Michael J., (AV) '52 '78 C.363 B.S.B.A. L.365 J.D. [Deutsch,L.&E.] ⊙
DeYoung, Susan C. '53 '81 C.114 B.A. L.1292 J.D. 610 West Roosevelt Road, Suite C-2
Diamond, Brian J. '57 '82 C.602 B.A. L.339 J.D. Assoc. Judge
Diamond, Timothy J. '64 '89 C.602 B.A. L.436 J.D. Asst. State Atty.
Didzerekis, Paul P., (BV) '39 '64 C&L.424 B.B.A., J.D. Pub. Admr.
Dillon, William S., Jr. '47 '72 C.659 B.S.Econ. L.339 J.D. [W.S.Dillon]
Dillon, William S., Attorney at Law 1918 Clydesdale Dr.
Diver, Jeffrey R. '42 '67 C.367 A.B. L.178 J.D. 1749 S. Naperville Rd.
Do, Mia '— '04 C.339 B.A. L.146 J.D. [⊡ Anderson&Assoc.] ⊙
Dockery, Peter J. '50 '75 C.602 B.A. L.339 J.D. Assoc. Judge

Dommermuth, Brestal, Cobine and West, Ltd.
(See Naperville)

Downing, Thomas F. '56 '84 C.339 B.A. L.801 J.D. State's Atty.'s Off.

Doyle, Joseph P.
(See Schaumburg)

Drunken Driving Defense Lawyers of Illinois, Ltd.
(See Chicago)

Dudycha, Donald L., Law Offices of ...'47 '72 C.589 B.S. L.146 J.D. 419 E. Willow Ave.
Duncan, Edward R., Jr. ....'45 '72 C.188 B.A. L.339 J.D. Cir. J.
Dvorak, Amy L. ....'79 '04 C.473 B.S. L.365 J.D. 211 S. Wheaton Ave., Ste. 200
Dwyer, Mark W., (BV) ....'50 '75 C.602 B.A. L.209 J.D. 505 N. County Farm Rd.
Dyer, Lloyd E., Jr., (BV) ....'44 '69 C.970 B.A. L.597 J.D. [Mountcastle&D.]
Dyer, Robert E., (AV) ....'29 '53 C&L.597 B.S.L., LL.B. 300 E. Roosevelt Rd.
Eckhoff, Grant, (BV) ....'59 '85 C.475 B.S. L.146 J.D. [Eckhoff&M.]

Eckhoff & Massarelli, P.C., (BV)
330 South Naperville Road, Suite 408, 60187
Telephone: 630-510-0660 Fax: 630-682-4938 URL: http://www.lawyers.com/gelawoffices
Email: lawyers@gelawoffices.com URL: http://www.gelawoffices.com
Grant Eckhoff; Catherine M. Massarelli.
Civil Litigation including but not limited to Divorce, Collections, Personal Injury, Domestic Violence, Slip and Fall, Trucking and Automobile Accidents, Real Estate, Shareholders Disputes, Creditors Bankruptcy, Wills, Probate, Check Fraud, Corporate Litigation.
See Professional Biographies, WHEATON, ILLINOIS

Eggers, Arthur W., (BV) ....'52 '77 C.352 B.A. L.190 J.D. [Califf&H.] ⊙
Elliott, Timothy D. ....'71 '96 C.473 B.A. L.309 J.D. [Ⓒ Rathje&W.]
Equi, Rodney W. ....'48 '79 C.209 B.A. L.589 J.D. Cir. J.
Erickson, Randall T. ....'57 '89 C&L.339 B.S.M.E., J.D. [R.T.Erickson] (Pat.)

Erickson, Randall T., PC, The Law Office of
425 W. Wesley Street, Suite 1, 60187
Telephone: 630-665-9404 Fax: 630-665-9414
Email: randallerickson@sbcglobal.net URL: http://www.lawyers.com/randallericksonlaw
Randall T. Erickson.
Intellectual Property, Patents, Patent Prosecution, Trade Secrets, Trademarks, Trademark Prosecution, Unfair Competition.
See Professional Biographies, WHEATON, ILLINOIS

Esp, Douglas J. ....'56 '85 C.424 B.S. L.209 J.D. 290 S. Country Farm Rd., Ste. M
Faris, Francis W., Jr. ....'27 '50 C&L.802 B.B.A., LL.B. Assoc. Cir. J.
Fawell, Blanche Hill, (BV) ...... '55 '80 C.30 B.A. L.424 J.D. 505 N. County Farm Road
Fawell, Bruce R., (BV) ....'27 '52 C.578 L.146 LL.B. 2100 Manchester Rd.
Fawell, Jeffrey B., (BV) ....'52 '77 C.578 B.A. L.801 J.D. [Fawell&Assoc.]
Fawell, Terry, (BV) ....'50 '75 C.475 B.A. L.209 J.D. [Fawell&F.]
Fawell & Associates, (BV) ....2100 Manchester Rd.

Fawell & Fawell, Ltd., (BV)
2100 Manchester Road, Suite 945, 60187
Telephone: 630-871-2400 Fax: 630-871-2404
Email: tflaw622@aol.com URL: http://www.fawelllaw.com
Terry Fawell.
Family Law, Divorce Law, Child Custody, Child Support, Domestic Violence, Spousal Support, Premarital Agreements, Mediation and Adoptions.
See Professional Biographies, WHEATON, ILLINOIS

Fechner, Donovan S. ....'68 '94 211 S. Wheaton Ave.
Fedder, Arthur W. ... '36 '60 C&L.879 B.A., J.D. Asst. Reg. Coun., Chicago Title Ins. Co.
Felice, Richard D., (BV) ....'54 '79 C.424 B.A. L.589 J.D. [R.D.Felice]
Felice, Richard D., PC, (BV) ....511 W. Wesley St.
Fenili, William J., (BV) ....'52 '77 C.629 B.A. L.146 J.D. P.O. Box 151
Ferguson, William I. ....'49 '75 C.503 B.S. L.146 J.D. Assoc. J.
Fezzey, Thomas F. ..... '53 '95 C.476 B.S. L.213 J.D. 600 West Roosevelt Road, Suite B1
Field, Christine Moriarty, (CV) ....'56 '84 C.1183 B.A. L.365 J.D. 107 N. Pierce Ave.
Field, Harold G., (AV) ....'23 '52 C.36 B.S. L.146 J.D. [Ⓒ Schiller,D.&F.]
Fitzsimmons, Justin T. ....'71 '98 C.967 B.A. L.146 J.D. Asst. States Atty.
Fitzsimmons, Roberts, Paine & Caruso, (AV) .... 411 W. Wesley (⊙Chicago)
Flaherty, Maureen, (BV) ....'39 '78 [Lehrer,F.&C.]

Fleming, Michael W., Attorney at Law
(See Elmhurst)

Fliss, John J. ....'— '93 C.436 L.146 J.D. [J.J.Fliss]
Fliss, John J., P.C., The Law Offices of .... 1811 West Diehl Road, Suite 800
Flynn, John W. ....'40 '68 C.801 B.S. L.209 J.D. [Stock,C.F.&Assoc.]

Foran Glennon Palandech & Ponzi PC
(See Chicago)

Ford, Donald W., Law Offices of, (BV) '28 '57
C.475 B.A. L.209 J.D. 520 W. Roosevelt Rd.
Fox, Dennis R., (AV) ....'39 '65 C.339 B.S. L.597 J.D. [Califf&H.] ⊙
Fox, Jonathon C., (BV) ....'69 '96 C.347 B.A. L.1161 J.D. [Califf&H.] ⊙
Fox, Patricia A., (BV) ....'62 '90 C.338 B.S. L.365 J.D. [Beck,H.&S.]
Franklin, Alison S. ....'60 '88 C&L.339 B.S., J.D. [Piccione,K.&Assoc.]
Frederick, George S. ....'65 '98 C.36 B.S. L.589 J.D. [Ⓐ Mirabella&K.]
French, Dorothy F. ....'51 '78 C.475 B.S. L.146 J.D. Assoc. J.
Frontzak, Rosemarie .... '63 '88 C.424 B.A. L.146 J.D. [Ⓒ Roberts&Assoc.]

Fuchs & Roselli, Ltd.
(See Chicago)

Fullerton, Paul M. .... '58 '90 C.589 B.S. L.365 J.D. [Clingen C.&M.]
Gabric, Ralph A., (AV) ....'29 '55 C.98 B.S. L.365 LL.B. [Gabric,M.&O.]
Gabric, Millon & Ory, Chtd., (AV) .... 104 E.Roosevelt Rd.
Gaertner, Kent A., (BV) ....'52 '77 C.123 B.A. L.1206 J.D. [K.A.Gaertner]

Gaertner, Kent A., P.C., (BV)
400 South Country Farm Road, Suite 330, 60187
Telephone: 630-510-0000 Fax: 630-510-0004
URL: http://www.lawyers.com/gaertnerlaw
Kent A. Gaertner.
Bankruptcy, Business Reorganization, Business Formation and Real Estate Law, Bankruptcy Litigation.
See Professional Biographies, WHEATON, ILLINOIS

Gailan & Najera, P.C.
(See Addison)

Gaines, John W. ....'20 '51 C.383 B.S. L.912 J.D. 140 Fairway Lane (Pat.)‡
Galasso, Michael R. ....'36 '61 C.238 B.S.B.A. L.146 J.D. [Schiller,D.&F.]
Galasso, Nicholas J. ....'58 '83 C.340 B.A. L.209 J.D. Assoc. Cir. J.
Garrow, John F., (BV) ....'53 '79 C.927 B.A. L.221 J.D. [Rathje&W.]
Geraghty, James A., Law Office of ... '27 '52 C&L.424 B.S.C., J.D. 115 W. Wesley Street
Gessner, Connie R., (BV) ....'47 '81 C.238 B.A. L.365 J.D. [C.R.Gessner]
Gessner, Connie R., PC, (BV) ....373 S. County Farm Rd., Ste. 103
Gilbert, Thomas J., (AV) ....'49 '74 C.477 B.A. L.424 J.D. [Ottosen T.B.K.&C.] ⊙
Gillen, Suzanne, (BV) ....'61 '87 C.393 B.A. L.146 J.D. [Mangan,L.G.&L.] ⊙
Ginsburg, Scott L. ....'79 '04 C.210 B.A. L.910 J.D. [Ⓐ Norton,M.W.&D.]
Given, J. Randolph ....'55 '85 C.473 B.A. L.209 J.D. 1755 S. Naperville Road
Goetz, James D. ....'48 '75 C.352 B.A. L.365 J.D. Chf. Dep. Treas.
Gorski, Gerald M. ....'43 '70 C.578 B.A. L.209 J.D. 211 S. Wheaton Ave.
Graham, Edward T. ....'27 '65 C.209 B.Ph. L.365 LL.B. 217 W. Illinois St.

Graham, Edward P., Ltd., Law Offices of
(See Naperville)

Greene, Allen S., (AV) ....'24 '51 C.72 B.A. L.146 J.D. 1755 S. Naperville Rd.
Grotto, John J., (BV) ....'50 '79 C.424 B.A. L.589 J.D. [Grotto&V.]
Grotto & VanDerMolen, (BV) ....127 W. Willow Ave.

Grunyk, Danya A., P.C., The Law Firm of
(See Naperville)

Guerard, Richard M., (AV) ....'47 '75 C.589 B.S. L.365 J.D. [Guerard,K.&B.]

Guerard, Kalina & Butkus, (AV)
100 West Roosevelt Road, Suite A-1, 60187
Telephone: 630-665-9033 Telecopier: 630-690-9652
Members of Firm: J. Steven Butkus; Richard M. Guerard; Mark F. Kalina; Mary Krasner; John J. Pcolinski, Jr.; Mark G. Patricoski. Associate: Mark J. Carroll.
Real Estate Construction and Development, Banking and Commercial Finance, Mechanic Liens, Personal Injury, Workers Compensation, Creditor's Rights, Financial Services, Corporate and Commercial Law, Zoning and Land Use, Estate Planning and Probate, General Civil and Trial Practice.
See Professional Biographies, WHEATON, ILLINOIS

Guerin, Daniel Patrick, (AV) ....'64 '89 C.339 B.S. L.209 J.D. Asst. States Atty.
Guilde, Karen Johnson '58 '87
C&L.879 B.A., J.D. 1776 South Naperville Road, Suite 104A
Gumina, Juli A., (CV) ....'— '95 C.424 B.A. L.146 J.D. [Sullivan T.&G.]
Gustafson, Harriet A. Doheny, (BV) .....'55 '81 C.424 B.S. L.365 J.D. Sr. Asst. Pub. Def.
Gutzke, John D., (BV) ....'58 '84 C&L.339 B.A., J.D. [Rolewick&G.]
Haas, Douglas L., (BV) ....'44 '79 C.801 B.S. L.1151 J.D. [Haas&M.]
Haas & McLennan, (BV) ....209 S. Naperville Rd.
Hackett, David B. ....'49 '81 C.937 B.A. L.146 J.D. 1043B College
Hambrick-Stowe, Elizabeth Anne, (BVⓉ) '48 '84 C.914 B.A. L.64 J.D.
[Ⓒ Rathje&W.]
Hamer, Lissa L. ....'— '87 C.436 B.S. L.589 J.D. [Querrey&H.]

Hanauer, James W., The Law Office of '64 '96 C.58 B.A. L.365 J.D.
600 W. Roosevelt Road Suite B1, 60187
Telephone: 630-784-1800 Fax: 630-784-1806
Email: jameshanauerlaw@aol.com URL: http://www.jameshanauerlaw.com
Family Law, Divorce, Child Custody, Child Support, Real Estate and Personal Injury Law.
See Professional Biographies, WHEATON, ILLINOIS

Handler, Thayer & Duggan, LLC
(See Chicago)

Hannon, Dennis P. ....'60 '91 C.750 B.A. L.146 J.D. 1749 S. Naperville Rd.
Hanrahan, Barbara Kilroe '58 '85 C.339 B.A. L.209 J.D.
1751 S. Naperville Rd., Suite 209
Hansen, Edward D. ....'22 '48 C.378 A.B. L.986 LL.B. 1338 Shagbark Lane‡
Harper, James A., (AV) ....'17 '42 C&L.477 A.B., J.D. [Ⓒ Califf&H.] ⊙
Harper, Thomas A., (BV) ....'50 '76 C&L.221 B.S., J.D. [Califf&H.] ⊙
Harrington, Alison M. ....'71 '97 C.352 B.S. L.436 J.D. [Best,V.&H.] ⊙
Harrison, Dennis A. ....'50 '86 C.209 B.A. L.365 J.D. [Ⓐ Laraia&H.]
Harrison, Michael James ....'49 '00 C.999 B.A.S. L.365 J.D. State's Atty. Off.

Harrison Law Offices, P.C.
(See Woodstock)

Harvey, Michael F. ....'35 '65 C.424 B.S. L.862 J.D. 1 S. 615 Winfield Rd.
Haskin, Lyle B., & Associates, (BV) '40 '72
C.589 B.A. L.146 J.D. 290 South County Farm Road
Healy, Margaret M. ....'— '83 C.436 B.A. L.146 J.D. State's Atty. Off.
Helm, Beverly M. ....'54 '80 C.1154 B.A. L.213 J.D. [B.M.Helm]
Helm, Beverly M., PC .... 1213 Briarbrook Drive
Henry, John E. ....'63 '90 C.339 B.A. L.209 J.D. 109 N. Hale St.
Herndon, Laurel T. ....'57 '82 C.679 B.A. L.339 J.D. Chicago Title & Tr. Co.
Higgins, Michael J., (BV) ....'47 '78 C.1024 B.S. L.1151 J.D. 1603 Mayo Dr.
Hoffmann, William J. ....'67 '93 C.393 B.A. L.365 J.D. [Ⓐ Mulherin,R.&V.]
Holman, Ricky M. ....'53 '89 C.1356 B.S. L.1187 J.D. Pub. Def. Off.
Hone, Robert E. ....'12 '39 C&L.178 A.B., LL.B. 510 W. Evergreen St.‡

Hoornstra, Dennis W., Attorney, (BV) '44 '77 C.477 B.A.,M.B.A. L.424 J.D.
100 W. Roosevelt Road, Unit B-8, 60187
Telephone: 630-462-8100 Fax: 630-462-8127
URL: http://www.hoornstralaw.com
Real Estate, Dissolution of Marriage Law.
See Professional Biographies, WHEATON, ILLINOIS

Horwitz, Joseph H. ....'47 '73 C.589 B.S. L.209 J.D. 1776 S. Naperville Rd.
Houlihan, John P., (BV) ....'61 '86 C.293 B.A. L.221 J.D. [Beck,H.&S.]
Hoyt & Waller, P.C., (AV) .... 1275 E. Butterfield (⊙Chicago)
Hruby, Ralph R., (BV) .... '55 '82 C.719 B.A. L.365 J.D. 2100 Manchester Rd., Ste. 1015
Hubbard, Kenneth D., (AV) ....'54 '86 C.801 B.S. L.365 J.D. [Laraia&H.]
Huck, James M., Jr., (AV) ....'38 '63 C&L.339 B.S., LL.B. [Huck B.]
Huck, Kevin J., (AV) ....'46 '73 C.1150 B.A. L.146 J.D. 1755 S. Naperville Rd.

Huck Bouma PC, (AV)
1755 S. Naperville Road, Suite 200, 60187-8144
Telephone: 630-221-1755 Fax: 630-221-1756 URL: http://www.wp.com/HuckLaw/
Email: hucklaw@ix.netcom.com URL: http://www.huckbouma.com
James M. Huck, Jr.; Ralph R. Bouma, Jr.; John P. Martin; Robert E. Jones; George M. Bradshaw; Patrick B. Hurley; Kathleen R. Ryding; Lawrence A. Stein; William J. Strons.
Corporate Law, Business Law, Commercial Real Estate, Estate Planning, Taxation, Land Use, Civil Litigation, Business Litigation, Personal Injury, Estate Settlements, Banking.
See Professional Biographies, WHEATON, ILLINOIS

Hughes Socol Piers Resnick & Dym, Ltd.
(See Chicago)

Hundman, James E., (BV) .... '63 '88 C.338 B.S. L.1187 J.D. [Rice&H.]
Hurley, Patrick B. ....'68 '93 C&L.93 B.A., J.D. [Huck B.]
Huszagh, R. L., Law Offices of '29 '57
C.674 A.B. L.145 J.D. 330 Naperville Road, Suite 202
Hutchins, Cynthia Hayes, (BV) ....'58 '87 C.477 B.A. L.597 J.D. [C.H.Hutchins]

Hutchins, Cynthia Hayes, P.C., The Law Office of, (BV)
620 West Roosevelt Road, Suite C-1, 60187
Telephone: 630-510-0600 Fax: 630-510-0618
Email: chhutchins@aol.com URL: http://www.lawyers.com/hutchins
Cynthia Hayes Hutchins.
Estate Planning, Trust Law, Wills and Probate, Estate and Gift Taxation, Probate Administration, Probate Litigation, Contested Trusts and Estates, Guardianship, Elder Law.
See Professional Biographies, WHEATON, ILLINOIS

Hyde, John A. ....'24 '52 L.365 LL.B. 1224 Hoffman St.

Iwan Cray Huber Horstman & VanAusdal LLC
(See Chicago)

Jackson, Thomas A., (CV) ....'67 '92 C&L.339 B.A., J.D. [Piccione,K.&Assoc.]

Jaeschke, Danielle M. ....'— '87 C.473 B.S. L.209 J.D. [🄰 Roberts&Assoc.]
Jeep, Jeffery D. ....'58 '82 C.589 B.A. L.424 J.D. [Jeff,D.]
Jeff Dive Group, The, LLC .... 1749 S. Naperville Rd., Ste. 102
Jeffers, Frank E., III, (BV) ....'51 '77 C.226 B.S. L.190 J.D. 127 W. Willow Ave.
Jendryk, James S., (AV) ....'— '75 C.602 B.B.A. L.365 J.D. [Querrey&H.]
Jerz, James W. ....'41 '65 C&L.339 A.B., J.D. Assoc. Cir. J.
Jones, Robert E., (AV) ....'49 '74 C.937 B.A. L.880 J.D. [Huck B.]
Jones, Robert Edward ....'70 '98 C.339 B.A. L.365 J.D. 330 S. Naperville Rd.
Jorgensen, Ann Brackley ....'55 '80 C.424 B.A. L.209 J.D. Cir. J.
Kalina, Mark F., (BV) ....'54 '81 C.589 B.S. L.209 J.D. [Guerard,K.&B.]
Kalina, R. Terence, (AV) ....'47 '72 C.750 B.A. L.602 J.D. [Rathje&W.]
Kamstra, William H. ....'19 '52 C.114 A.B. L.477 J.D. 1205 Howard Cir. (Pat.)
Kane, Deven S. ....'75 '00 C.839 B.B.A. L.339 J.D. [🄰 Clingen C.&M.]
Karubas, Justin J. ....'73 '98 C.339 B.A. L.146 J.D. [🄰 Rolewick&G.]
Kasson, Tracy D., (BV) ....'61 '87 C.339 B.A. L.424 J.D. [Rathje&W.]
Kay, Robert T. C., (BV) ....'61 '86 C.937 B.A. L.209 J.D. [Peregrine,S.N.R.&B.]
Keay, David H., (BV) .....'51 '80 C.427 B.A. L.589 J.D. 128 S. County Farm Rd., Ste. D
Keeley, Patrick C., (AV) ....'52 '79 C.339 B.S. L.424 J.D. [Piccione,K.&Assoc.]
Kelleghan, Thomas C. ....'28 '57 C&L.602 LL.B.,J.D 217 S. Hale St.
Kelly, Emily J. ....'— '89 C&L.209 B.A., J.D. Asst. State's Atty.
Kelly, John H. ....'51 '82 C.597 B.A L.365 J.D. [Ottosen T.B.K.&C.] ⊙
Kelly, John P., (BV) ......'53 '79 C.210 B.A. L.424 J.D. 1725 S. Naperville Rd., Ste. 200
Kelly, Mary Jo ....'49 '78 C.1191 B.S. L.365 J.D. 1751 Naperville Rd., Ste. 209
Kelly, Roger H., (BV) ....'50 '83 C.238 B.S. L.365 J.D. [🄰 Z.M.Bravo]
Kennedy, John ....'56 '82 C&L.339 B.A., J.D. State's Atty.'s Ofc.
Kennelly, Eugene J. ....'54 '84 C&L.589 B.A., J.D. Asst. State's Atty.
Kenny, Michael H., (BV) ....'64 '89 C.436 B.S. L.46 J.D. [Kenny&K.]
Kenny, Thomas G., (BV) ....'57 '82 C.602 B.B.A. L.209 J.D. [Kenny&K.]
Kenny & Kenny, (BV) ....100 W. Roosevelt Rd.
Kienlen, J. Laurence ....'42 '73 C.801 B.A. L.365 J.D. 1776 South Naperville Road
Kightlinger, Stephen M. ....'63 '91 C.502 B.A. L.365 J.D. 25461 White Birch Lane
Kilander, Robert K., (AV) ....'43 '70 C.207 L.209 LL.B. First Asst. States Atty.
Kincaid, John B., (AV) ....'38 '63 C.598 B.S. L.146 J.D. [Mirabella&K.]
Kindorf, William A., III, (AV) '52 '77
C.339 B.S. L.477 J.D. [Tressler,S.M.&P.] (⊙Chicago)
King, David A. ....'65 '93 C.339 B.S. L.209 J.D. [Schiller,D.&F.]
King, John J. ....'66 '91 C.339 B.S.E.E. L.424 J.D. [J.J.King] (Pat.)
King, John J., PC, The Law Office of ..................................P.O. Box 1555 (Pat.)
Kinney, Helen C. ....'23 '59 C&L.209 A.B., J.D. Ret. Cir. J.
Kinsella, John J., (AV) ....'55 '81 C.927 B.A. L.589 J.D. Asst. States Atty.

Kinzy & Associates, P.C.
(See Chicago)

Knee, William F., Ltd.
(See Oak Brook)

Knell, Bradley C., (BV) ....'62 '88 C.234 B.A. L.607 J.D. [Knell&P.] ⊙
Knell & Poulos, A Professional Corporation, (AV) ....511 West Wesley (⊙Chicago)
Knight, Thomas L. ....'45 '70 C.430 B.A. L.339 J.D. [Walsh,K.K.&P.]
Knippen, James H., II, (AV) ....'52 '79 C.746 B.A. L.339 J.D. [Walsh,K.K.&P.]
Koch, Delrose Ann ....'56 '81 C.177 B.A. L.352 J.D. [🄲 Clingen C.&M.]

Komie and Associates, Law Offices of
(See Chicago)

Konetski, James J., (BV) ....'59 '84 C&L.339 B.A., J.D. 625 Robinwood Court
Koontz, Albert C. ....'29 '60 C.97 B.S.B.A. L.1003 J.D. 418 W. Union Ave.
Korstad, Dorothy C. ....'41 '78 C.274 B.A. L.1151 J.D. 511 W. Wesley‡
Kowalczyk, Mark E., (BV) ....'42 '70 C.750 L.365 J.D. 1607 Taft Ave.
Krasner, Mary, (BV) ....'52 '79 C.742 B.A. L.209 J.D. [Guerard,K.&B.]
Kreamer, John C. ....'73 '99 C.162 B.B.A. L.209 J.D. [🄰 Best,V.&H.] ⊙
Krumdick, Candace ....'58 '91 C.339 B.S. L.209 J.D. Dep. Ct. Admin.
Kruse, Adam C. ....'79 '04 C.502 A.B. L.1439 J.D. [🄰 Walsh,K.K.&P.]
Lanciotti, David J., (CV) ....'67 '93 Amer. Nat Bk.
Langhenry, John G., III, (AV) ....'58 '85 C.602 A.B. L.424 J.D. [Mangan,L.G.&L.] ⊙
Laraia, James J. ....'74 '01 C.750 B.A. L.589 J.D. [🄰 Laraia&H.]
Laraia, Joseph M., (AV) ....'37 '62 C&L.597 B.A., J.D. [Laraia&H.]

Laraia & Hubbard, P.C., (AV)
1761 S. Naperville Road Suite 203, 60187
Telephone: 630-690-6800 Fax: 630-690-0196
Email: laraiahubbardpc@ameritech.net URL: http://www.lawyers.com/laraia&hubbardpc
Joseph M. Laraia; Kenneth D. Hubbard;—James J. Laraia; Dennis A. Harrison.
Criminal Law, General Civil and Chancery Litigation, Personal Injury, Divorce and General Trial Practice.
See Professional Biographies, WHEATON, ILLINOIS

Larsen, Robert L. ....'64 '89 C.602 B.A. L.128 J.D. [🄰 Cunningham M.&V.]
Lasics-Wessels, Jean ....'68 '95 C.879 B.A. L.1187 J.D. [Botti,M.&D.] ⊙
Lass, Christina M. L. ....'67 '92 C.145 A.B. L.879 J.D. [Sheridan&L.]
Lassen, Brian D., Law Office of ......'55 '80 C.937 B.A. L.146 J.D. 400 W. Liberty Drive
Lawrence, Andrea C. ....'72 '97 C.589 B.A. L.209 J.D. [🄰 Anderson&Assoc.] ⊙
Lawrence, Roy F. ....'30 '74 C.674 A.B. L.145 J.D. Assoc. Cir. J.
Leach, Marie F., (CV) ....'45 '82 C.388 B.A. L.589 J.D. [🄰 Roberts&Assoc.]
Lee, A. Scott ....'53 '80 C.597 B.S.S. L.161 J.D. 25 W. 455 Carrol Gate Rd.
Lee, Jennifer H. ....'67 '92 C.339 B.A. L.365 J.D. 109 N. Hale St.
Leetz, Paul A., (BV) ....'33 '57 C.339 A.B. L.597 LL.B. 418 W. Union‡
Lehrer, Norman H., (BV) ....'46 '78 C.145 A.B. L.589 J.D. [Lehrer,F.&C.]
Lehrer, Flaherty & Canavan, (BV) ....429 W. Wesley St.
Leinenweber, Thomas More, (AV) ....'66 '92 C.473 B.A. L.365 J.D. 411 W. Wesley
Lemkau, Gary R. ....'42 '70 C.353 B.A. L.146 J.D. 330 S. Naperville Rd.
Leston, Patrick J. ....'48 '73 C.339 B.S. L.597 J.D. Assoc. Cir. J.
Levin, Harvey A., (BV) ....'43 '71 C.475 B.A. L.597 J.D. [Califf&H.] ⊙
Levine, Neil J. '58 '90 C.1044 B.S. L.276 J.D.
Du Page County Public Defenders Office

Levy, Steven B., Ltd.
(See Naperville)

Ley, Marshall F., (CV) ....'22 '51 C.339 B.S. L.424 J.D. P.O. Box 4492
Liber, Adrianna K., (BV) ....'59 '86 C.145 B.A. L.209 J.D. [🄲 Norton,M.W.&D.]

Lincoln Law Group, The, (AV) BB
Carlton Sentre, 300 South Carlton Avenue Suite 130, 60187
Telephone: 630-933-8400 Fax: 630-933-8432
Email: migloreatlaw@yahoo.com URL: http://www.lawyers.com/lincolnlawgroup
Salvatore C. Miglore.
Languages: English, Spanish, Polish and Italian.
Criminal Law, Felonies, Traffic Violations, Appeals, Driving While Intoxicated, Divorce, Family, Child Custody, Litigation, Commercial Litigation, Real Estate, Insurance Defense, Insurance Coverage and Estate Planning Law.
See Professional Biographies, WHEATON, ILLINOIS

Logan, Charles P. ....'20 '58 C.205 B.A. L.446 LL.B. 26W100 Durfee Rd.‡
Long, Thomas J. ....'58 '83 C.602 B.A. L.424 J.D. [Norton,M.W.&D.] ⊙
Loveless, R. Craig ....'48 '75 C.473 B.S. L.1119 J.D. 529 W. Roosevelt Rd.
Lowry, Mary M. ....'— '72 C.320 B.A. L.846 J.D. 305 Naperville Rd.
Lundquist, Troy A. ....'67 '92 C.339 B.A. L.365 J.D. [Mangan,L.G.&L.] ⊙
Lundy, Kara N. ....'77 '02 C.1203 B.A. L.494 J.D. [🄰 Norton,M.W.&D.]
Mackenzie, Harold B. ....'14 '40 C.937 B.A. L.597 J.D. 724 Howard St.‡
Mahoney, Harry T. ....'22 '51 C.238 B.A. L.597 J.D. 1110 Shady Ln.‡
Maidlow, Daniel B. ....'73 '00 C.610 B.S. L.851 J.D. [🄰 Peregrine,S.N.R.&B.]
Malartsik, Jon P. ....'69 '95 C.880 B.A. L.209 J.D. [🄰 Paulsen&M.]
Malec, Kenneth J. ....'52 '82 C.339 B.S. L.365 J.D. [Paulsen&M.]
Mancini, Lorenzo A., (AV) ....'46 '77 C.742 B.A. L.209 J.D. [Norton,M.W.&D.] ⊙
Mangan, Jerald M. ....'57 '82 C.378 B.A. L.209 J.D. [Mangan,L.G.&L.] ⊙
Mangan, Langhenry, Gillen & Lundquist, (AV)
311 South County Farm Road (⊙Chicago, Joliet, Rockford)
Mannina, Anthony ....'32 '61 C.424 B.S. L.365 LL.B. 1761 S. Napperville Rd.

Maramba & Associates, LLC
(See Arlington Heights)

Marcott, Robert S. ....'51 '81 C.927 B.A. L.508 J.D. [🄰 Roberts&Assoc.]
Marinaccio, Lee A., (AV) ....'44 '71 C.238 B.A. L.424 J.D. [Botti,M.&D.] ⊙
Marquardt, E. Clifford ....'25 '50 C&L.209 LL.B. 1617 Whitman Ln.‡
Martin, John P. ....'47 '72 C.339 B.A. L.494 J.D. [Huck B.]
Massarelli, Catherine M. ....'63 '90 C.352 B.S. L.146 J.D. [Eckhoff&M.]
Maurer, Christopher J. ....'72 '97 C.339 B.S. L.424 J.D. [🄰 Anderson&Assoc.] ⊙
McCann, John J. ....'36 '60 C&L.424 LL.B. V.P., Ticor Title Ins. Co.
McCarthy, Kathleen A. ....'57 '82 C.813 A.B. L.424 J.D. Asst. State's Atty.
McDonough, Robert ....'49 '75 C.339 B.A. L.365 J.D. 330 S. Naperville Rd., Ste. 40
McGowen, Thomas C. .....'66 '98 C.742 B.A. L.146 J.D. 1751 S. Naperville Rd., Ste. 101
McGrath, Robert L., (BV) ....'52 '79 C.208 B.A. L.365 J.D. [R.L.McGrath]
McGrath, William J., (AV) ....'25 '53 C.742 B.S.S. L.424 LL.B. 529 W. Roosevelt Rd.
McGrath, Robert L., P.C., (BV) ....520 W. Roosevelt Rd., Ste. 300
McKillip, Brian R., (BV) .....'46 '72 C&L.424 B.A., J.D. 330 S. Naperville Rd., Ste., 304
McLaren, Robert D. ....'44 '69 C.504 B.A. L.221 J.D. Cir. J.
McLaughlin, Colleen M. '55 '80 C.589 B.A. L.146 J.D.
1751 S. Naperville Rd., Ste. 209
McLean, Timothy M., (BV) ....'61 '88 C&L.602 B.A., J.D. [Clingen C.&M.]
McLennan, Mary L., (BV) ....'45 '80 C.436 B.A. L.589 J.D. [Haas&M.]
McNichols, Gerald F., (CV) ....'23 '55 C.424 L.209 LL.B. 115 W. Wesley St.
McSwain, Mary E., (BV) '54 '83 C.424 B.A. L.589 J.D.
311 S. County Farm Rd., Ste. A
McTigue, John P., & Associates, (BV) ....'49 '80 C.973 A.B. L.424 J.D. 108 West Liberty
Mehling, Ronald B. ....'42 '66 C&L.221 B.A., J.D. Cir. J.
Meyer, David P. ....'48 '74 C.338 B.A. L.352 J.D. 290 S. County Farm Rd., Ste. M
Meyer, Mark C., (BV) ....'59 '85 C.578 B.A. L.146 J.D. [Cunningham M.&V.]
Meyering, Jules V., Jr. ....'26 '50 C.602 B.S. L.424 J.D. 1584 Wadsworth Rd.‡
Miglore, Salvatore C., (AV) ....'53 '81 C.1151 B.A. L.209 J.D. [Lincoln]
Miller, Robin R., (BV) ....'51 '83 C.339 B.A. L.201 J.D. [Da Rosa&M.]
Millon, Kevin H., (BV) ....'59 '84 C.339 B.S. L.365 J.D. [Gabric,M.&O.]
Mirabella, Joseph F., Jr., (AV) ....'35 '64 C.339 A.B. L.146 LL.B. [Mirabella&K.]
Mirabella, Lynn M. ....'62 '87 C.339 L.A.S. L.146 J.D. [🄰 Mirabella&K.]

Mirabella & Kincaid, P.C., (AV)
1776 South Naperville Road,, P.O. Box 1029, 60187
Telephone: 630-665-7300 Fax: 630-665-7609
Email: mkpclaw@aol.com URL: http://www.mirabellakincaid.com
Joseph F. Mirabella, Jr.; John B. Kincaid;—George S. Frederick; Lynn M. Mirabella.
Trial Practice, Domestic Relations, Appellate Practice, Personal Injury, Real Estate, General Practice, Commercial Law, Mediation.
See Professional Biographies, WHEATON, ILLINOIS

Mirabile, Thomas K., (BV) ....'48 '75 C.589 B.A. L.616 J.D. [T.K.Mirabile]
Mirabile, Thomas K., P.C., (BV) .... 1751 S. Naperville, Ste. 203
Mitton, Jane Hird ....'— '83 C.494 B.A. L.589 J.D. Co. Ct. J.
Mitvalsky, Franklin S., (CV) ....'72 '98 C.597 B.A. L.352 J.D. [Califf&H.] ⊙
Mokosaik, Michael J. ....'69 '98 C.388 B.A. L.300 J.D. Asst. Pub. Def.
Molho, Ross I. ....'68 '93 C.429 B.A. L.930 J.D. [Clingen C.&M.]

Momkus McCluskey Moltzen Monroe Marsh & Spyratos, LLC
(See Downers Grove)

Montgomery, Philip G. ....'62 '87 C.234 B.A. L.221 J.D. [🄰 Fawell&Assoc.]
Moore, Kelly Marie ....'78 '04 C.339 B.A. L.365 J.D. [🄰 Sullivan T.&G.]
Moore, Maura W., (CV) ....'68 '93 C.602 B.A. L.424 J.D. [🄰 Cunningham M.&V.]
Moorhouse, Jeffrey B., (BV) ....'45 '72 C&L.352 B.B.A., J.D. [Califf&H.] ⊙
Moran, James P. ....'57 '82 C.602 B.B.A. L.146 J.D. [Mulherin,R.&V.]

Morgan, Wendy R., The Law Firm of
(See Arlington Heights)

Moss and Bloomberg, Ltd.
(See Tressler, Soderstrom, Maloney & Priess)

Motz, Donald Forrest, Jr. ....'43 '86 C.339 B.A. L.365 J.D. [D.F.Motz,Jr.]
Motz, Donald F., Jr., Attorney at Law ....526 S. Gables Blvd.
Mountcastle, David G., (AV) ....'32 '61 C.210 B.A. L.146 J.D. [Mountcastle&D.]
Mountcastle & Dyer, P.C., (AV) .... 1725 S. Naperville Rd.
Moy, Kenneth ....'33 '61 C.238 B.S. L.365 LL.B. Cir. J.
Mulherin, John M., (AV) ....'42 '67 C.339 A.B. L.597 J.D. [Mulherin,R.&V.]

Mulherin, Rehfeldt & Varchetto, P.C., (AV) BB
211 South Wheaton Avenue, 60187
Telephone: 630-653-9300 Fax: 630-653-9316; 630-653-0776
Email: mrv@mrvlaw.com URL: http://www.mrvlaw.com
John M. Mulherin; Louis A. Varchetto; Stephen A. Rehfeldt; Joseph G. Skryd; Ray H. Rittenhouse; James P. Moran; William J. Ulrich, Jr.; Patricia L. Argentati; Thomas B. Cahill;—Andrew R. Poyton; Marcelline Defalco; William J. Hoffmann; Kathleen A. Reid; Christine C. Perakis; William R. Brodzinski.
Commercial and Business Transactions, Health Care, Estate Planning, Litigation, Business, Tax, Employment, Insurance Defense, Medical Malpractice Defense and Employment Litigation.
See Professional Biographies, WHEATON, ILLINOIS

Munshi, Samin G. ....'73 '00 C.424 B.S. L.589 J.D. Co. States Atty.
Murdock, G. Steven ....'67 '94 C.98 B.S.M.E. L.589 J.D. [🄰 Gabric,M.&O.]
Murman, Ilyse D. ....'66 '91 C.103 A.B. L.276 J.D. 25 W. 772 Sunnyridge Court
Murphy, Francis P. ....'50 '78 C.436 B.S. L.1151 J.D. Ill. Dept. of Public Aid.
Murray, Patricia Gail ....'52 '86 C.700 B.A. L.365 J.D. 1607 Taft Ave.

Nadler, Pritikin & Mirabelli, L.L.C.
(See Chicago)

Nagle, James P., (BV) ....'62 '89 C.339 B.S. L.146 J.D. 529 W. Roosevelt Rd.
Nelson, Roger C., Jr. ....'46 '73 C.339 L.365 J.D. [Nelson]
Nelson Law Offices, PC ....528 W. Roosevelt Rd., Ste. 100

Newman, Thomas M., (AV) ....'45 '71 C.210 B.A. L.347 J.D. [Peregrine,S.N.R.&B.]
Nihill, Burke J. ....'78 '03 C.340 B.A. L.146 J.D. [A Tressler,S.M.&P.] (⊙Chicago)

Nolan, Carol A., (BV) '51 '96 C&L.589 B.A., J.D.
620 West Roosevelt Road Suite C-1, 60187
Telephone: 630-668-6600 Fax: 630-510-0618
Email: canolanlaw@aol.com URL: http://www.lawyers.com/canolan
Elder Law, Medicaid Planning, Estate Planning, Special Needs Trusts, Probate, Wills, Trust Law, Living Trusts, Guardianship, Contested Trusts and Estates, Powers of Attorney.
See Professional Biographies, WHEATON, ILLINOIS

Norton, John E., (AV) ....'49 '75 C.602 A.B. L.209 J.D. [Norton,M.W.&D.] ⊙

Norton, Mancini, Weiler & DeAno, (AV)
109 North Hale Street, P.O. Box 846, 60189-0846 ⊙
Telephone: 630-668-9440 Fax: 630-668-9489
Email: firm@nortonmancini.com
John E. Norton; Lorenzo A. Mancini; Thomas R. Weiler; James L. DeAno; Thomas J. Long; W. Anthony Andrews;—Kenneth C. Yuen; Kara N. Lundy; Mary T. Yong; Scott L. Ginsburg. Of Counsel: Adrianna K. Liber.
Trial Practice. Personal Injury, Malpractice, Products Liability, Environmental Law, Corporate Litigation, Commercial Litigation, Municipal Litigation, Insurance and Probate Law, Medical Malpractice.
Representative Clients: Aetna Life & Casualty; Allstate Insurance Company; Chicago Motor Club Insurance Company; County of DuPage; Frontier Insurance Co.; CNA Insurance Company; Hartford Insurance Company; Illinois State Medical Insurance Services, Inc.; St. Paul Insurance Company; Wausau Insurance Companies.
Chicago, Illinois Office: 111 West Washington Street, Suite 835. Telephone: 312-807-4999. Fax: 312-807-4998.
See Professional Biographies, WHEATON, ILLINOIS

Novack, Debra Falduto ....'59 '84 C.578 B.A. L.597 J.D. 1545 Wilmette St.
Nuckolls, Louisa J. ....'71 '96 C.339 B.A. L.209 J.D. Asst. States Atty., DuPage Co.
Nusgart, Cathy J. Nunziati ....'65 '92 C.347 B.A. L.61 J.D. Asst. State's Atty.
O'Brien, Michael A. ....'63 '93 C.338 B.S. L.589 J.D. [M.A.O'Brien]
O'Brien, Patricia Cadagin '60 '85 C.801 B.A. L.339 J.D.
1755 S. Naperville Rd., Ste. 200
O'Brien, Michael A., P.C. ....311 S. County Farm Road
O'Connor, John J. ....'— '86 C.338 B.A. L.365 J.D. [Knell&P.] ⊙

O'Connor, Thomas V., (AV) '41 '65 C&L.602 B.B.A., J.D.
Suite 300, Ticor Title Building, 330 South Naperville Road, 60187-5442
Telephone: 630-665-9400 Fax: 630-665-3011
General Trial Practice. Negligence Litigation, including Personal Injury, Real Estate, Contract and Family Law.
See Professional Biographies, WHEATON, ILLINOIS

O'Hagan, Smith & Amundsen
(See St. Charles)

O'Hallaren, Ann C. ....'71 '99 C.473 B.A. L.46 J.D. State Atty.
O'Hern, Tonya L. '54 '92 C.36 B.S. L.900 J.D.
(adm. in KS; not adm. in IL) Claims Coun., Media/Professional Ins. Agency, Inc.
O'Leary, Richard A. ....'25 '75 C.93 B.S.B.A. L.724 LL.B. 221 E. Illinois Stre‡

O'Leary, John J.
(See Chicago)

Olsen, Edward L. ....'32 '73 C.937 B.A. L.365 J.D. 800 Pinegrove Ct.‡
O'Reilly, John F. ....'67 '92 C.676 B.A. L.602 J.D. [O'Reilly]
O'Reilly, Molly M., (BV) ....'66 '91 C.93 B.A. L.146 J.D. [O'Reilly]
O'Reilly Law Offices, (AV) .... 1751 South Naperville Road, Suite 101
Ory, Christine M., (BV) ....'53 '86 C.578 B.A. L.365 J.D. [Gabric,M.&O.]
Ottosen, Karl R. ....'60 '84 C.927 B.S. L.339 J.D. [Ottosen T.B.K.&C.] ⊙

Ottosen Trevarthen Britz Kelly & Cooper, Ltd., (AV)
300 South County Farm Road, Third Floor, 60187 ⊙
Telephone: 630-682-0085 Facsimile: 630-682-0788
URL: http://www.otbkc.com
Robert J. Britz; G. Robb Cooper; Thomas J. Gilbert; John H. Kelly; Karl R. Ottosen.
Fire Protection Districts, Local Government Law, Municipal Law, Education Law, School Law, Public Finance, Public Pensions, Labor and Employment, Election Law, Estate Planning, Probate, Insurance Defense, Family Law, Commercial Litigation, Business Law, Real Estate, Administrative Law, Zoning Law. Civil Practice.
Elburn, Illinois Office: 303 North Main Street, 60119. Telephone: 630-365-6441. Fax: 630-365-6451.
Joliet, Illinois Office: Crystal Square Building, 81 North Chicago Street, Suite 204, 60432. Telephone: 815-723-0601. Fax: 815-723-2599.
See Professional Biographies, WHEATON, ILLINOIS

Pape, Arthur E., (AV) ....'39 '65 C.665 B.A. L.309 LL.B. [Pape]

Pape Law Firm, The, (AV)
100 West Roosevelt Road, Building A-3, Suite 102, 60187-5260
Telephone: 630-933-9300 Fax: 630-933-9301
Email: apape@papelaw.com URL: http://www.papelaw.com
Arthur E. Pape.
Real Estate Law, Construction Law.
See Professional Biographies, WHEATON, ILLINOIS

Patricoski, Mark G. ....'61 '89 C.258 B.S. L.365 J.D. [Guerard,K.&B.]
Paulsen, Harvey A., (BV) ....'53 '77 C.209 L.861 J.D. [Paulsen&M.]
Paulsen & Malec, Ltd., (BV) ....1761 S. Naperville Rd.
Paveza, Michelle M. ....'70 '96 C.37 B.A. L.209 J.D. [A Mangan,L.G.&L.]
Pawl, Michael P. ....'70 '97 C.861 B.A. L.128 J.D. Asst. States Atty.
Pcolinski, John J., Jr., (AV) ....'60 '86 C.578 B.A. L.339 J.D. [Guerard,K.&B.]
Peck, Reese J., (BV) ....'53 '82 C.353 B.A. L.221 J.D. [Rathje&W.]
Perakis, Christine C. ....'74 '00 C.589 B.S. L.365 J.D. [A Mulherin,R.&V.]
Peregrine, Roy I., (AV) ....'28 '56 C.118 B.A. L.146 J.D. [Peregrine,S.N.R.&B.]

Peregrine, Stime, Newman, Ritzman & Bruckner, Ltd., (AV)
221 East Illinois Street, P.O. Box 564, 60189
Telephone: 630-665-1900 Fax: 630-665-0407
Email: law@psnrb.com URL: http://www.psnrb.com
Hartman E. Stime (1927-1991); Roy I. Peregrine; Thomas M. Newman; Roger A. Ritzman; Dale W. Bruckner; Robert T. C. Kay; David W. Clark;—Daniel B. Maidlow; Elizabeth P. Schaffer.
General Civil Practice. Commercial Litigation, Corporations, Estate Planning, Trusts and Estates, Probate, Real Estate, Family Law, Personal Injury, Insurance, Worker's Compensation, Municipal Law, Banking Law, Library Law, Collections, Trials and Appeals, Condemnations.
See Professional Biographies, WHEATON, ILLINOIS

Perkins, Mark D., (BV) ....'65 '90 C.238 B.S. L.46 J.D. [Perkins&Z.]

Perkins & Zayed, P.C., (BV)
1751 South Naperville Road, Suite 203, 60187
Telephone: 630-665-2300 Toll Free: 1-877-TRUST.50 Facsimile: 630-665-4343
Email: pzlaw@att.net URL: http://www.lawyers.com/p&z
Mark D. Perkins; Dean K. Zayed.
Estate Planning Law, Tax Planning, Business Succession Planning, Wealth Preservation, Asset Protection and Charitable Planning.
See Professional Biographies, WHEATON, ILLINOIS

Perrelli, Anthony
(See Deerfield)

Pesch, Susan Marie, (CV) ....'— '91 C.589 B.S. L.424 J.D. [Pesch]

Pesch Law Office, (CV)
310 S. County Farm Road, Suite H, 60187-2409
Telephone: 630-462-9300 Fax: 630-462-0422
Email: peschlaw@aol.com URL: http://www.lawyers.com/peschlawoffice
Susan Marie Pesch.
Family, Divorce, Child Custody, Child Support, College Expenses, Post-Decree issues, Mediation, Child Representative, Guardian Ad Litem, Adoption, Guardianship, Name Change.
See Professional Biographies, WHEATON, ILLINOIS

Peskin, Mitchell M. ....'— '95 C.966 B.S. L.365 J.D. 104 E. Roosevelt Rd., Ste. 204
Pfeiffer, James M. '74 '00 C.679 B.S. L.589 J.D.
1776 South Naperville Road, Suite 104A
Piccione, John J., (AV) ....'42 '67 C.339 B.S. L.424 J.D. [Piccione,K.&Assoc.]

Piccione, Keeley & Associates Ltd., (AV)
122 S. County Farm Road, 60187-4594
Telephone: 630-653-8000 Fax: 630-653-8029
Email: info@pkalaw.com URL: http://pkalaw.lawoffice.com
John J. Piccione; Patrick C. Keeley; Mark W. Tader; Lynn R. Conrad; Alison S. Franklin; Thomas A. Jackson. Associate: Jason Singleton.
Civil Trial and Appellate Practice, Business Law and Complex Litigation, Mergers and Acquisitions, Negligence, Product and Aviation Litigation, Securities Law, Family Law, Real Estate, Probate Law, Zoning and Eminent Domain Law.
See Professional Biographies, WHEATON, ILLINOIS

Pieper, John N., (BV) ....'49 '76 C.339 B.S. L.365 J.D. 1761 South Naperville Road
Pietsch, Leigh R., (BV) ....'43 '72 C.898 B.A. L.146 J.D. [Pietsch&C.]
Pietsch & Cuchna, (BV) ....1776 Naperville Rd.
Pittinaro, Marc S. ....'71 '97 C.339 B.A. L.879 J.D. [A Mangan,L.G.&L.]
Pleviak, John A. ....'51 '78 C.339 B.A. L.146 J.D. Hofner & Hofner
Pointner, Scott E. ....'67 '96 C.347 B.S. L.809 J.D. [Rathje&W.]
Polachek, Michael J., (AV) '50 '76
C.339 B.A. L.146 J.D. [Tressler,S.M.&P.] (⊙Chicago)
Polick, Joseph M. ....'61 '90 C.589 B.A. L.424 J.D. 109 N Hale St.
Pollock, Bradley N. ....'70 '95 C.339 B.A. L.424 J.D. [Walsh,K.K.&P.]
Popejoy, Charley, (AV) ....'12 '39 C.679 B.S. L.365 J.D. 1 Wheaton Ctr.‡
Popejoy, Kenneth L. ....'50 '77 C.475 B.A. L.146 J.D. Assoc. Cir. J.
Poulos, David T., (AV) ....'67 '92 C.339 B.A. L.46 J.D. [Knell&P.] ⊙
Powell, Joanne I. ....'57 '84 C.339 B.A. L.146 J.D. 1315 Clifden Ct.
Poyton, Andrew R. ....'70 '96 C.174 B.A. L.209 J.D. [A Mulherin,R.&V.]
Pritchett, L. Bow ....'34 '64 C.350 B.A. L.209 J.D. 330 S. Naperville Rd.
Provenzale, Mary E. ....'— '77 C.530 B.A. L.209 J.D. Assoc. Cir. J.
Quaintance, Richard C. ....'26 '58 C.347 B.S. L.1119 LL.B. 1N149 Mission Court‡

Querrey & Harrow, Ltd., (AV)
310 South County Farm Road, Third Floor, 60187-5473 ⊙
Telephone: 630-653-2600 Fax: 630-653-0178
Email: jjendryk@querrey.com URL: http://www.querrey.com
James S. Jendryk; Lissa L. Hamer (Resident);—Cynthia D. Traynor.
General Practice and Trial Practice.
Chicago, Illinois Office: 175 West Jackson Boulevard, Suite 1600. Telephone: 312-540-7000. Fax: 312-540-0578.
Crystal Lake, Illinois Office: 651 West Terra Cotta Avenue, Suite 221. Telephone: 815-479-1929. Fax: 815-479-1978.
Joliet, Illinois Office: 2 Rialto Square, Suite 401, 116 North Chicago Street. Telephone: 815-726-1600. Fax: 815-726-1674.
Waukegan, Illinois Office: 415 West Washington Street, Suite 205. Telephone: 847-249-4440. Fax: 847-249-4932.
Merrillville, Indiana Office: 8585 Broadway, Suite 510. Telephone: 219-738-1820. Fax: 219-738-1821.
New York, N.Y. Office: 120 Broadway, Suite 2800. Telephone: 212-233-0130. Fax: 212-233-0172.
London, England Office: 141-142 Fenchurch Street, Fifth Floor. Telephone: 207-929-6670. Fax: 207-929-6671.
See Professional Biographies, WHEATON, ILLINOIS

Query, Henry C., Jr. ....'63 '88 C.339 B.S. L.424 J.D. 504 S. Pierce Ave.
Quinlan, Thomas F. ....'18 '53 C.602 B.S.C. L.982 LL.B. 1047 Oakview Dr.‡

Quinlan & Carroll, Ltd.
(See Chicago)

Quinn, John M., & Associates, Ltd.
(See Bloomingdale)

Quinn-McCollian, Deanna M. ....'68 '98 C.999 B.A. L.589 J.D. [A Clingen C.&M.]
Ramsell, Donald J. ....'58 '84 C.424 B.S. L.209 J.D. 128 S. County Farm Rd., Ste. F.
Rath, William W. .....'44 '78 C.446 B.A. L.1151 J.D. 600 West Roosevelt Road, Suite B-1
Rathje, S. Louis ....'39 '64 C.937 A.B. L.597 J.D. 300 East Roosevelt Road, Suite 300

Rathje & Woodward, (AV)
300 East Roosevelt Road, Suite 300, 60187
Telephone: 630-668-8500 Fax: 630-668-7350
Email: info@rathjewoodward.com URL: http://www.rathjewoodward.com
Members of Firm: R. Terence Kalina; Henry S. Stillwell, III; Gary L. Taylor; John F. Garrow; Reese J. Peck; Tracy D. Kasson; Mark W. Daniel; John R. Zemenak; Scott E. Pointner. Associates: Carol Anne Watkiss; Kevin M. Carrara. Of Counsel: Elizabeth Anne Hambrick-Stowe; Timothy D. Elliott.
General Civil and Appellate Practice. Commercial, Industrial and Residential Real Estate, Municipal, Zoning, Insurance, Probate, Estate Planning, Environmental, Eminent Domain, Corporate, Trademarks, Unfair Competition, Copyright, Family Law, Personal Injury, and Business Law.
See Professional Biographies, WHEATON, ILLINOIS

Reddick, Conrad R. '47 '75 C.659 B.A. L.477 J.D.
(adm. in MI; not adm. in IL) 1015 Crest St
Reed, Elizabeth ....'62 '89 C.339 B.A. L.365 J.D. Co. Pub. Def.
Rehfeldt, Stephen A. ....'48 '74 C.679 B.S. L.339 J.D. [Mulherin,R.&V.]
Reid, Kathleen A. ....'73 '98 C.339 B.A. L.365 J.D. [A Mulherin,R.&V.]
Reinke, Aaron H. ....'75 '00 C&L.424 B.A., J.D. State's Atty. Off.
Renfro, Robert L. ....'56 '90 1755 S. Naperville Rd., Ste. 200
Rice & Hundman, Ltd., A Professional Corporation, (BV)
300 South County Farm Road Suite G
Riggs, Thomas J., (AV) ....'43 '68 C.424 B.S. L.209 J.D. 606 Myrtlewood Ln.

Rinella and Rinella, Ltd.
(See Chicago)

Rittenhouse, Ray H., (AV) ....'53 '81 C&L.209 B.A., J.D. [Mulherin,R.&V.]
Ritzman, Roger A., (AV) ....'51 '76 C.477 B.A. L.339 J.D. [Peregrine,S.N.R.&B.]
Roberts, Keith E., Sr., (AV) ....'28 '53 C&L.339 B.S., J.D. [E Roberts&Assoc.]
Roberts, Keith E. (Chuck), Jr., (AV) '55 '83
C.701 B.S.M.E. L.589 J.D. [Roberts&Assoc.]

Roberts and Associates, P.C., (AV)
104 East Roosevelt Road, Suite 202, 60187
Telephone: 630-668-4211 Fax: 630-668-2076
URL: http://www.robertsandassoc.com

(This Listing Continued)

Roberts and Associates, P.C. (Continued)
Keith E. (Chuck) Roberts, Jr. Of Counsel: Keith E. Roberts, Sr.; Rosemarie Frontzak;—Marie F. Leach; Robert S. Marcott; Danielle M. Jaeschke; Kate M. Roxas.
Litigation, Family Law.
See Professional Biographies, WHEATON, ILLINOIS

Rogers & Coyne, LLC, Law Offices of
(See Naperville)
Rolewick, David F., (AV) . . . . . '46 '71 C&L.424 B.S., J.D. [Rolewick&G.]
Rolewick & Gutzke, P.C., (AV)
Danada West Professional Center, 1776 South Naperville Road, Suite 104A, 60187-8133
Telephone: 630-653-1577 Fax: 630-653-1579
Email: rg@rglawfirm.com URL: http://www.rglawfirm.com
David F. Rolewick; John D. Gutzke;—Justin J. Karubas.
General Practice with an emphasis on Estate Planning, Tax Planning, Real Estate, Business Law and Commercial Litigation.
See Professional Biographies, WHEATON, ILLINOIS

Roskam, Peter J., (BV) . . . . . '61 '89 C.339 B.A. L.46 J.D. [Salvi,R.&M.]
Roxas, Kate M. . . . . . '— '99 C.966 B.A. L.365 J.D. [[A] Roberts&Assoc.]
Russo, Anthony L., (AV) . . . . . '27 '55 C&L.209 LL.B. [Russo&R.]
Russo, Richard, (AV) . . . . . '52 '78 C.209 B.S.C. L.365 J.D. [R.D.Russo]
Russo, Richard D., (AV) . . . . . 1755 Naperville Rd., Ste. 206
Russo & Russo, Ltd., (AV) . . . . . 1761 S. Naperville Road (⊙Teaneck, NJ)
Ryan, Thomas M. . . . . . '26 '58 C&L.209 B.S., LL.B. 1005 Heathrow Ct.‡
Ryan and Ryan
(See Chicago)
Ryding, Kathleen R. . . . . . '56 '81 C&L.339 B.S., J.D. [Huck B.]
Ryerson, Thomas H., (AV) . . . . . '51 '76 C.597 B.A. L.424 J.D. [Clausen M.]
Rynning, Lawrence K. '55 '80 C.121 B.S. L.575 J.D.
Wheaton Office Center, 310 South County Farm Road, 60187
Telephone: 630-682-9500 Fax: 630-682-8107
Email: lkrlaw@ameritech.net
Insurance Coverage, Civil Litigation, General Civil Practice.
See Professional Biographies, WHEATON, ILLINOIS

Sadowski, Ronald W. . . . . . '52 '78 C.602 B.A. L.209 J.D. 1761 S. Naperville, Ste. 101
Salvi, Roskam & Maher, LLC, (BV) . . . . . 1755 S. Naperville Road (⊙Waukegan)
Sanchez, Manuel "Manny", (AV) . . . . . '47 '74 C.589 B.A. L.659 J.D. [Sanchez&D.] ⊙
Sanchez & Daniels, (AV) . . . . . 2100 Manchester Road (⊙Bloomington, Chicago)
Sandberg, Richard J. . . . . . '27 '53 C.436 Ph.B. L.424 J.D. 529 W. Roosevelt Rd.
Schaffer, Elizabeth P. . . . . . '58 '84 C.880 B.A. L.146 J.D. [[A] Peregrine,S.N.R.&B.]
Schauer, Patrick J. . . . . . '53 '79 C.597 B.S. L.345 J.D. P.O. Box 0881
Schiller, DuCanto and Fleck, (AV) [BR]
311 South County Farm Road, Suite G, 60187 ⊙
Telephone: 630-665-5800 Fax: 630-665-6082
Email: schillerducantoandfleck@sdflaw.com URL: http://www.sdflaw.com
Members: Timothy M. Daw; Michael R. Galasso; David A. King. Associates: Deborah A. Carder; Abigail M. Chiesa. Of Counsel: Harold G. Field.
Family Law, Complex Domestic Relations Issues, Divorce/Dissolution of Marriage, Prenuptial Agreements/Premarital Agreements, Child Custody and Visitation, Spousal Support/Alimony/Maintenance, Matrimonial Law and Litigation, Appeals, Mediation-Family/ Divorce, Marital Settlement Agreements, Separation Agreements, Property Rights, Financial Discovery and Analysis Related to Divorce, and Tax Considerations Related to Divorce.
Chicago, Illinois Office: 200 North La Salle Street, 30th Floor. Telephone: 312-641-5560. Fax: 312-641-6361.
Lake Forest, Illinois Office: Suite 300, 207 East Westminster Avenue. Telephone: 847-615-8300. Fax: 847-615-8284.
See Professional Biographies, WHEATON, ILLINOIS

Schroeder, Carl F., (AV) . . . . . '48 '73 C.879 B.A. L.424 J.D. [C.F.Schroeder]
Schroeder, Carl F., Ltd., (AV) . . . . . 2100 Manchester Road, Suite 503
Scidmore, S. Bruce . . . . . '20 '53 C.768 A.B. L.770 J.D. Ret. Assoc. Cir. J.
Scott, William J., Jr., (AV) . . . . . '48 '73 C.734 A.B. L.209 J.D. [Beck,H.&S.]
Scott, Halsted & Babetch, P.C.
(See Chicago)
Sexton, Elizabeth Walter . . . . . '54 '84 C.967 B.A. L.146 J.D. Assoc. Cir. J.
Sheehan, Denis K., (BV) . . . . . '63 '89 C.197 B.A. L.424 J.D. [[A] Clausen M.]
Sheen, Terence M., (BV) . . . . . '56 '81 C.424 B.A. L.1183 J.D. Co. Pub. Admr.
Sheridan, Gerald M., Jr., (AV) . . . . . '31 '60 C&L.209 B.S.C., J.D. [Sheridan&L.]
Sheridan & Lass, P.C., (AV)
315 Naperville Road, P.O. Box 572, 60189-0572
Telephone: 630-665-3900 Fax: 630-665-3912
Email: sheridanlaw@prodigy.net URL: http://www.lawyers.com/sheridanlass
Gerald M. Sheridan, Jr.; Christina M. L. Lass.
Business Law, Contracts, Collections, Bankruptcy, Civil Practice, Corporate Law, Litigation, Commercial Real Estate, Probate, Real Estate, Trusts and Estates, Wills.
See Professional Biographies, WHEATON, ILLINOIS

Shivers, Todd L., Attorney at Law '58 '83
C.990 B.S. L.365 J.D. 202 W. Willow Ave., Ste. 102
Sikorski, Laurie J. . . . . . '63 '88 C.347 B.S. L.879 J.D. Asst. States Atty.
Singleton, Jason . . . . . '75 '01 C&L.502 B.S.B.A., J.D. [[A] Piccione,K.&Assoc.]
Skiera, Audrey J. . . . . . '74 '02 C.93 B.S. L.424 J.D. 1755 S. Naperville Rd.
Skokos Law Group, LLC
(See Oak Brook)
Skryd, Joseph G., (BV) . . . . . '63 '88 C.679 B.A. L.365 J.D. [Mulherin,R.&V.]
Slover, John A., Jr., (BV) . . . . . '44 '69 C&L.339 B.A., J.D. [Califf&H.] ⊙
Smit, Justin M. . . . . . '72 '98 C.927 B.S. L.365 J.D. 1776 S. Naperville Rd., Ste. 202
Speer, Lloyd L., (AV) . . . . . '34 '61 C.475 B.S. L.339 LL.B. [Speer&Assoc.]
Speer & Associates, (AV) . . . . . 201 Naperville Rd.
Spencer, Charles W. . . . . . '33 '62 C.238 B.A. L.146 J.D. 625 Myrtlewood
Stacey, Paul H. . . . . . '52 '79 C.339 A.B. L.365 J.D. 202 W. Willow
Stahl, Charles S., Jr., (AV) . . . . . '48 '75 C.339 B.S. L.365 J.D. 703 Warrenville Road
Stamogiannos, George . . . . . '69 '03 C&L.801 B.S., J.D. 610 W. Roosevelt
Stauber, Raymond W., Jr., Law Office of '47 '73
C.363 B.A. L.339 J.D. 330 Naperville Rd., Suite 304
Steele, Karla C. . . . . . '70 '02 C.763 B.A. L.352 J.D. [[A] Califf&H.] ⊙
Stein, Lawrence A., (CV) . . . . . '65 '93 C.145 A.B. L.589 J.D. [Huck B.]
Stein, Ray & Harris LLP
(See Chicago)
Stephani, Otto C., Jr. . . . . . '43 '68 C.504 B.A. L.69 LL.B. 100 W. Roosevelt Rd.
Stillwell, Henry S., III, (BV) . . . . . '48 '75 C.339 B.S. L.365 J.D. [Rathje&W.]
Stock, John P., III, (BV) . . . . . '46 '75 C.504 B.A. L.209 J.D. [Stock,C.F.&Assoc.]
Stock, Carlson, Flynn & Associates, (BV)
124 S. County Farm Road, 60187
Telephone: 630-665-2500 Fax: 630-665-9427 URL: http://www.scfalaw.com
URL: http://www.dupagebusinesslaw.com

(This Listing Continued)

Stock, Carlson, Flynn & Associates (Continued)
John P. Stock, III; Kurt A. Carlson; John W. Flynn.
Business Organizations, Divorce, Elder Law, Estate Planning, Real Estate.
Representative Clients: West Chicago State Bank; Wheaton College.
See Professional Biographies, WHEATON, ILLINOIS

Stogsdill, William J., Jr., (BV) . . . . . '49 '74 C.965 B.B.A. L.365 J.D. [W.J.Stogsdill,Jr.]
Stogsdill, William J., Jr., P.C., Law Offices, (BV) . . . . . 1776 S. Naperville Rd., Ste. 202B
Strandlund, Roger L., (BV) . . . . . '55 '81 C.350 B.S. L.352 J.D. [Califf&H.] ⊙
Strobel, Joseph A. . . . . . '43 '68 C&L.209 B.S., J.D. Chicago Title Ins. Co.
Strons, William J. . . . . . '67 '93 C.339 B.A. L.209 J.D. [Huck B.]
Stull, Christopher J. . . . . . '63 '88 C.578 B.A. L.589 J.D. Dep. Pub. Def.
Suder, Caryn R. . . . . . '66 '94 C&L.424 B.S.N., J.D. [[A] Cunningham M.&V.]
Sulkson, Christopher M. . . . . . '— '02 C.339 M.B.A. L.365 J.D. 26 W. 353 Menomini Drive
Sullivan, Shannon S. . . . . . '63 '88 C.36 B.A. L.365 J.D. Law Clk., App. Ct. J.
Sullivan, Thomas F., Jr., LTD Law Offices of '47 '73
C.177 B.A. L.339 J.D. 1725 S. Naperville Rd., Ste. 200
Sullivan Taylor and Gumina, (BV)
1749 South Naperville Road Suite 106, 60187-8192
Telephone: 630-665-7676 Fax: 630-665-8630
Email: lawyers@stglaw.com URL: http://www.lawyers.com/sullivantaylor
Maureen Sullivan Taylor; Juli A. Gumina;—Emily R. Carrara; Kelly Marie Moore.
Family Law including Divorce, Child Custody, Child Support, Visitation Rights, Adoption Law, Paternity, Prenuptial Agreements and Mediation, Collaborative Law, Appellate Practice.
See Professional Biographies, WHEATON, ILLINOIS

Sutter, Ronald D. . . . . . '— '80 C.338 B.S. L.339 J.D. Co. J.
Sylvester, Warren G. . . . . . '— '93 C.1111 L.209 J.D. [[A] W.J.Stogsdill,Jr.]
Szatkowski, Peter J. . . . . . '54 '84 C.393 B.A. L.365 J.D. 2062 Creekside Dr.
Tader, Mark W., (CV) . . . . . '60 '85 C.937 B.A. L.339 J.D. [Piccione,K.&Assoc.]
Tameling, Connie M. . . . . . '72 '97 C.347 B.S. L.146 J.D. 1303 Aurora Way
Tameling, Gretta A. . . . . . '43 '84 C.938 A.B. L.146 J.D. Asst. State's Atty.
Tani, Christine K. . . . . . '49 '77 C.72 B.A. L.146 J.D. [Carter&T.]
Tatarelis, Kenneth P., Jr. . . . '75 '00 C.339 B.A. L.424 J.D. DuPage Co. State's Atty.'s Off.
Taylor, Gary L., (BV) . . . . . '51 '76 C.339 B.A. L.365 J.D. [Rathje&W.]
Taylor, Maureen Sullivan, (BV) . . . . . '42 '82 C.707 B.A. L.589 J.D. [Sullivan T.&G.]
Teschner, John S. . . . . . '35 '65 C.801 B.S. L.966 J.D. Ret. Cir. J.
Teune, David A. . . . . . '52 '77 C.937 B.A. L.365 J.D. Wheaton College
Thompson, Perry R. . . . . . '50 '75 C.385 A.B. L.902 J.D. Cir. J.
Thompson, William B. . . . . . '41 '65 C&L.623 B.B.A., J.D. 26 W 061 Tomahawk
Tobin, Mary H. Skoglund . . . . . '43 '82 C.713 B.A. L.589 J.D. Asst. State's Atty.
Toran, Ross P., (AV) . . . . . '28 '56 C&L.209 B.S., J.D. 2020 Glencoe St.
Traynor, Cynthia D. . . . . . '— '88 C.694 A.B. L.365 J.D. [[A] Querrey&H.] (⊙Chicago)
Tressler, Soderstrom, Maloney & Priess, (AV)
2100 Manchester Road, Suite 950, 60187-4532 ⊙
Telephone: 630-668-2800 Telecopier: 630-668-3003
URL: http://www.tsmp.com
Members: William A. Kindorf, III; Michael J. Polachek; Harry E. Bartosiak (Resident). Of Counsel: C. Jackson Darnall. Resident Associate: Burke J. Nihill.
General Civil Litigation and Trial Practice, Insurance, Reinsurance, Litigation, Insurance Bad Faith, Appellate Practice, Business Litigation, Business Transactions, Class Action Defense, Commercial Litigation, Complex Litigation, Directors and Officers Liability, Construction Law, Architects and Engineers, Fidelity and Surety, Real Estate Litigation and Transactions, Alternative Dispute Resolution, Product Liability, Intellectual Property, Internet Law, Electronic Commerce, Environmental Law, Asbestos Litigation, Health Care, ERISA, Labor and Employment, Technology Law, Securities Litigation, Health Care, Bankruptcy, Advertising Law, Personal Injury, Trusts and Estates, Contracts, Professional Liability, Regulatory, White Collar Crime, Corporate Law, Mergers and Acquisitions, Commodities, Condominium and Common Interest Community Law, Municipal Law.
Chicago, Illinois Office: 233 Wacker Drive, Sears Tower, 22nd Floor, 60606. Telephone: 312-627-4000. Fax: 312-627-1717.
Bolingbrook, Illinois Office: 305 West Briarcliff Road, Suite 201, 60440-0858. Telephone: 630-759-0800. FAX: 630-759-8504.
Newark, New Jersey Office: 744 Broad Street, Suite 1510, 07102. Telephone: 973-848-2900. Fax: 973-623-0405.
Los Angeles, California Office: 1901 Avenue of the Stars, Suite 450, 90067. Telephone: 310-203-4800. Fax: 310-203-4850.
Costa Mesa, California Office: 3070 Bristol Street, Suite 450, 92626. Telephone: 714-429-2900. Fax: 714-429-2901.
See Professional Biographies, WHEATON, ILLINOIS

Trinta, Edwin . . . . . '74 '02 C.339 B.A. L.589 J.D. 1737 S. Naperville Road, Suite 202
Ulrich, William J., Jr., (BV) . . . . . '49 '80 C.589 B.S. L.209 J.D. [Mulherin,R.&V.]
Utchen, Theodore M. . . . . . '29 '58 C.378 B.A. L.477 J.D. P.O. Box 140
Vanderlaan, Lori A. . . . . . '68 '95 L.365 J.D. [Best,V.&H.] ⊙
VanDerMolen, Harold H. . . . . . '49 '77 C.937 B.A. L.161 J.D. [Grotto&V.]
Van Dyke, Jeffrey R., (AV) . . . . . '64 '89 C.937 B.A. L.209 J.D. [J.R.Van Dyke]
Van Dyke, Jeffrey R., P.C., (AV) . . . . . 2100 Manchester Road
Vanko, Kenneth J. . . . . . '72 '97 C.608 B.S.B.A. L.339 J.D. [Clingen C.&M.]
Varchetto, Louis A., (AV) . . . . . '54 '79 C.339 B.A. L.365 J.D. [Mulherin,R.&V.]
Vaught, Kathleen . . . . . '48 '77 C.770 B.A. L.801 J.D. [K.Vaught]
Vaught, Kathleen, P.C.
600 West Roosevelt Road, Suite B-1, 60187
Telephone: 630-871-9100 Fax: 630-871-9200
URL: http://www.kathleenvaught.com
Kathleen Vaught.
Bankruptcy, Consumer Bankruptcy, Business Bankruptcy, Financial Planning, Litigation, Tort Litigation, Contract Litigation, Real Estate, Divorce, Family, Estate Planning, Probate Law, Arbitration, Mediation, Alternative Dispute Resolution, Debt Relief Agent.
See Professional Biographies, WHEATON, ILLINOIS

Vedrine, Kevin J., (BV) . . . . . '64 '89 C.339 B.A. L.209 J.D. [Cunningham M.&V.]
Veenstra, Richard J. . . . . . '78 '03 C.238 B.S. L.209 J.D. Asst. State's Atty.
Vess, Henry B., III, (AV) . . . . . '47 '72 C.385 B.A. L.597 J.D. [H.B.Vess,III]
Vess, Henry B., III, P.C., (AV) [BR]
2100 Manchester Road, Suite C1640, 60187
Telephone: 630-510-8220 Fax: 630-510-8250
Email: henry@vesslawfirm.com URL: http://www.vesslawfirm.com
Henry B. Vess, III.
Civil Trial Practice, Real Estate Litigation, Eminent Domain, Commercial Litigation, Personal Injury.
See Professional Biographies, WHEATON, ILLINOIS

Vittori, Michael L., (AV) . . . . . '57 '86 C.339 B.A. L.365 J.D. [Clausen M.]
Waller, William M. . . . . . '40 '73 C&L.209 B.S., J.D. [Hoyt&W.]
Walsh, Edward J., (AV) . . . . . '48 '73 C.162 B.A. L.424 J.D. [Walsh,K.K.&P.]
Walsh, Knippen, Knight & Pollock, Chartered, (AV)
601 West Liberty Drive, 60187
Telephone: 630-462-1980 Fax: 630-462-1984
Email: lawyers@wkkplaw.com URL: http://www.wkkplaw.com
Edward J. Walsh; James H. Knippen II; Thomas L. Knight; Bradley N. Pollock. Associate: Adam C. Kruse.
Trial Practice concentrated in representing plaintiffs in complex damage cases, including claims for wrongful death & personal injury arising out of transportation, medical negligence, legal negligence and product liability cases.

(This Listing Continued)

Walsh, Knippen, Knight & Pollock, Chartered (Continued)
References: City of Wheaton, Illinois; Northern Trust Bank, Naperville, Illinois.
See Professional Biographies, WHEATON, ILLINOIS

Ward, Edward T., Jr. '44 '73
C.165 M.A. L.209 J.D. 1776 South Naperville Road, Suite 200
Warren, Monique '64 '00 C.839 B.S. L.424 J.D. [M.Warren]
Warren, Monique, P.C. 2100 Manchester Rd., Ste. 1750
Watkiss, Carol Anne '67 '00 C.338 B.A. L.589 J.D. [A Rathje&W.]
Watson, Janet L., Law Offices of, (CV) '49 '82
C.937 B.A. L.589 J.D. 330 S. Naperville Rd., Ste. 400
Webb, J. Bradley '60 '85 C&L.352 B.B.A., J.D. 1830 Roosevelt Rd.
Webster, Hollis L. '55 '82 C.339 B.A. L.424 J.D. Cir. J.
Weiler, Thomas R., (BV) '58 '83 C.602 B.B.A. L.424 J.D. [Norton,M.W.&D.] ⊙
Wheaton, Bonnie M. '44 '78 C.118 B.A. L.1151 J.D. Cir. J.
Whited, Lynne Ann '63 '88 C.966 B.A. L.339 J.D. 25W780 Flint Creek Dr.

Wiedner & McAuliffe, Ltd.
(See Chicago)

Wiehle, Michael S. '67 '97 C&L.589 B.A., J.D. Asst. Pub. Def.
Wilkinson, Donald E., (BV) '41 '70 C.339 B.S. L.365 J.D. 330 Naperville Rd.
Williams, Raymond E. '42 '76 C.494 B.A. L.365 J.D. 202 W. Willow Ave.
Willits, George W. '32 '79 C.388 A.B. L.1151 J.D. 100 W. Roosevelt Rd.
Winfield, David L. '41 '68 C.475 B.A. L.146 J.D. 209 Napereville Rd.

Winick, Russel G., & Associates, P.C.
(See Naperville)

Wolfe, Michael A. '59 '85 C.436 B.S. L.365 J.D. Asst. State's Atty.
Wolfe, Nancy J. '51 '80 C.700 B.A. L.209 J.D. Sr. Asst. Pub. Def.
Woodward, Alfred E. '13 '39 C.604 B.S. L.597 J.D. Ret. App. J.
Yong, Mary T. '76 '01 C.578 B.A. L.365 J.D. [A Norton,M.W.&D.]
Yonke, A. Kent '43 '78 C.927 B.S. L.1151 J.D. 208 N. West St.
York, Jeffrey P. '59 '84 C&L.879 B.A., J.D. Ticor Title Ins. Co.
York, Jeffrey R. '71 '96 C&L.339 B.S., J.D. Sr. Asst. Pub. Def., Pub. Def. Off.
Young, Kenneth M., (AV) '42 '68 C.57 B.A. L.365 J.D. 209 N. Washington St.
Yuen, Kenneth C. '70 '95 C.145 B.A. L.146 J.D. [A Norton,M.W.&D.]
Zandri, Robin M. '70 '97 C.339 B.S. L.589 J.D. [A Anderson&Assoc.] ⊙
Zayed, Dean K. '72 '97 C&L.597 B.A., J.D. [Perkins&Z.]
Zemenak, John R. '68 '94 C.473 B.A. L.365 J.D. [Rathje&W.]
Zidek, Michael E., (AV) '61 '87 C.363 B.S. L.190 J.D. [Clausen M.]
Zimmerman, Howard J. '46 '80 C.347 B.S. L.365 J.D. P.O. Box 4678
Zmuda, James S., (BV) '64 '89 C.352 B.B.A. L.589 J.D. [Califf&H.] ⊙
Zotti, Robert J., Law Firm of, (BV) '53 '79
C.363 B.S. L.209 J.D. 1761 S. Naperville Rd., Ste 101

Zuganelis, George M., Attorney at Law, P.C.
(See Chicago)

WHEELING, 34,496, *Cook & Lake Cos.*

Adler Law Offices, Ltd.
(See Arlington Heights)

Baker, Michael D., Law of Offices of '63 '88
C.339 B.A. L.910 J.D. 1098 S. Milwaukee Ave, Ste. 306
Barton, Thomas K. '61 '01 C.961 B.S. L.146 J.D.
Treas. & Gen. Coun., U.S. Tsubaki, Inc.
Binder, Richard M. '41 '65 L.597 J.D. 190 Abbott Drive
Caspersen, F. W. '34 '65 L.767 LL.B.
(adm. in CA; not adm. in IL) 131 Mayer Ave.‡
Cherney, David T., (AV) '50 '82 C.339 B.S. L.209 J.D. [Stein&C.] ⊙
Crane, Michael A. '49 '74 C.162 B.A. L.146 J.D. United Buying Serv.
Fell, Jerry I. '48 '83 C.679 B.S.I.E. L.365 J.D. 1601 Blackhawk Trail‡
Gold, Sidney '25 '68 C.112 L.365 J.D. 1071 S. Wolf Rd.
Greenblatt, Ian L. '73 '99 C.597 B.S. L.209 J.D.
Sr. V.P. Bus. Affs., Broadbus Technologies, Inc.
Henning, Christopher F. '66 '01 C.755 B.A. L.94 J.D.
Gen. Coun., CEM Servs. Intl. Inc.
Holleb, David L. '36 '59 C.339 B.S. L.209 J.D. 395 Oak Creek Dr.
Jenen, Paul R. '49 '74 C.339 B.S. L.365 J.D. 433 N. Milwaukee Ave.
Kulinsky, Lois '46 '80 C.494 B.S. L.146 J.D. [L.Kulinsky&Assoc.]

Kulinsky, Lois, & Associates, Ltd.
395 E. Dundee Road, Suite 200, 60090
Telephone: 847-459-4448 Fax: 847-459-8548
Email: lois@kulinskylaw.com URL: http://www.lawyers.com/kulinskylaw
Lois Kulinsky. Staff Attorney: Eleanor M. Proctor.
Family Law, Divorce, Adoptions, Child Custody, Child Support, Real Estate, Domestic Violence, Visitation Rights, Buying or Selling a Home, Trusts and Estates, Estate Planning, Wills and Probate, Incorporation.
See Professional Biographies, WHEELING, ILLINOIS

Lederer, William J. '06 '31 C&L.597 B.S., J.D. 371 E. Norman Lane‡
Lewert, Adam E. '30 '59 C&L.880 A.B., LL.B.
(adm. in NY; not adm. in IL) 1071 S Wolf Rd N
Lopez, Viviana '75 '02 C.339 B.S. L.209 J.D. 860 Tanglewood Drive
Meleshko, Dmitriy '70 '00 C.209 B.S. L.424 J.D. 914 N. Milwaukee, Ste. 303
Moore, Robert F., (AV) '30 '57 C&L.209 B.A., J.D. 566 N. Wolf Rd.‡
Neiman, William L. '48 '73 C.477 B.A. L.94 J.D. North American Signal Company
Ostrov, Robert '49 '78 C.188 B.s. L.146 J.D. Sr. V.P. & Gen Coun., Wickes Furniture
Perry, Eric T. '60 '87 C.209 B.A. L.146 J.D. 1098 S. Milwaukee Ave., Ste. 306
Popek, Gregory M. '48 '91 L.365 J.D. 912 Wilshire Dr.
Proctor, Eleanor M. '51 '91 C.589 B.S. L.1000 J.D. [S L.Kulinsky&Assoc.]
Rhodes, James A. '51 '76 C.424 B.A. L.365 J.D. Village Atty.

Robin, Daniel K., LTD
(See Arlington Heights)

Shields, Georgia E. '42 '79 C.145 B.A. L.146 J.D. 1485 Chippewa Trl.‡
Spangenberg, William Charles '55 '81 C.339 B.A. L.365 J.D. 109 Wilshire Drive
Stein, Steven A., (AV) '55 '81 C.589 B.S. L.365 J.D. [Stein&C.] ⊙
Stein & Cherney, Ltd., (AV) 747 West Dundee (⊙Chicago)
Sternfield, Scott F. '40 '66 C&L.597 B.S.B.A., J.D.
V.P., Gen. Coun. & Secy., Joseph J. Freed & Assoc., Inc.
Tatooles, James P., (AV) '38 '64 C.58 B.A. L.365 J.D.
1098 S. Milwaukee Ave., Ste. 100
Taylor, Jeffrey W. '52 '77 C.154 B.S. L.597 J.D. Pres., Cole Taylor Bk.
Turner, Glenn Martin '60 '92 C.835 B.S. L.424 J.D. 317 Robert Avenue
Waller, Donald Lee '42 '78 C.1229 B.M.E. L.1187 J.D.
(adm. in MI; not adm. in IL; Pat.) Pres., Genesis I Tech., Ltd.
Weiner, Gary M. '55 '81 C.339 B.A. L.146 J.D. 9600 Capitol Dr.
Wilson, Woodrow P. '18 '41 2251 Foster Ave.

WHITE HALL, 2,629, *Greene Co.*

Hubbard, Lorenzo K., (BV) '16 '48 C&L.339 B.S., LL.B. 103 S. Main St.‡
Piper, Thomas H., (BV) '52 '77 C.927 B.A. L.734 J.D. 103 S. Main

WILLIAMSVILLE, 1,439, *Sangamon Co.*

Duncan, LeRoy E. '30 '59 C&L.339 B.S., J.D. 217 So. Elkhart St.
Greening, Alfred H., (BV) '21 '49 C.911 L.597 LL.B. 101 West Main St.

WILLOWBROOK, 8,967, *DuPage Co.*

Bobrowicz, Donna '— '84 C.339 B.S. L.146 J.D.
Pat. & Trademark Coun., Viskase Companies
Broderick, William A. '34 '75 C&L.209 B.A., J.D. 301 Lake Hinsdale Dr., Apt. 205
Courtney, William D. '27 '52 C&L.209 LL.B. 853 Cramer Ct.‡
Duttlinger, Kimberly K. '— '89 C.234 B.A. L.339 J.D. Gen. Coun., Viskase Companies
Flynn, James F., Law Office of '63 '97 C.1350 B.A. L.818 J.D.
7501 South Quincy Road
Hakes, Harold L. '29 '79 C.97 B.S. L.365 J.D. 202 MacArthur Dr.
Hansen, Leroy R. '36 '74 C.1016 B.Ed. L.146 J.D. 6262 Kingery Hwy.
Limjuco, Judy Rachelle '72 '98 C.750 B.A. L.365 J.D. 6646 Sheffield Lane
Linardakis, Christos Michalis '66 '00 C.1182 B.A. L.365 J.D. 201 Lake Hinsdale Dr.
McHargue, James P. '72 '97 C.424 B.A. L.146 J.D. 621 Planfield Rd.
Morris, Kim L. '59 '83 C.1038 B.S. L.146 J.D. V.P. & Gen. Coun., Midland Mgmt. Co.
Mosteller, James '68 '96 C.608 B.A. L.365 J.D. 6725 Kingery Hwy.
Mrizek, Jerry J. '42 '67 C.309 A.B. L.145 J.D. 132 Waterford Dr.

Walsh, Patrick W. '63 '89 C.347 B.S. L.365 J.D.
625 Plainfield Road, 60527
Telephone: 630-794-0300
Email: docs@walshdocs.com URL: http://www.walshdocs.com
Criminal Law.
See Professional Biographies, WILLOWBROOK, ILLINOIS

Zitzka, Kathleen I. '56 '81 C.352 B.A. L.589 J.D. 646 67th Pl.

WILLOW SPRINGS, 5,027, *Cook Co.*

Baukert, Joseph J. '— '79 C.589 B.A. L.1151 J.D. 1360 Prospect Ave.
Beckman, Scott H. '59 '84 C&L.424 B.A., J.D. 8618 Dory Lane
Kozlowski, Jos. J. '24 '50 C.838 L.273 LL.B. 8695 Archer Ave.
Levitske, John, Jr. '56 '91 C&L.229 B.S.B.A., J.D. 9001 Orchard St.
Selimos, Vasiliki Billie '54 '79 C.339 B.A. L.424 J.D. 8385 S. Archer Rd.

WILMETTE, 27,651, *Cook Co.*

Adelman, Charlotte '37 '63 C&L.145 B.A., J.D. 232 Lawndale‡
Albanese, Kathleen Witherspoon '53 '79 C&L.477 A.B., J.D. 727 Park Ave.
Alonzi, Saverio J. '19 '46 C.424 B.S. L.602 LL.B. P.O. Box 278‡
Armstrong, Paul R. '48 '76 C.238 B.A. L.209 J.D. 210 Catalpa Pl.
Atkinson, Jeff '48 '77 C.597 B.S. L.209 J.D. 3514 Riverside Dr.
Axelrood, Jack '22 '61 C.145 B.S. L.365 LL.B. 415 Sunset Dr. (Pat.)‡
Baker, Brian C. '54 '80 C.276 B.S.B.A. L.602 J.D. 1405 Lake Ave.
Berning-Peppey, Brooke '62 '89 C.966 B.S. L.569 J.D. 1325 Washington Ave.
Bohrer, Nancy King '50 '79 C.339 B.S. L.365 J.D. 214 Hibbard Road
Bonem, Robert E. '54 '79 C&L.339 A.B., J.D. 1616 Sheridan Rd.‡
Brady, Roger M. '11 '56 C&L.93 A.B., LL.B.
(adm. in MA; not adm. in IL) 825 Lake Ave.‡
Bridges, S. Powell, (AV) '32 '58 C.198 B.S. L.880 LL.B. 1129 Romona Rd.
Bright, Joseph '52 '77 C&L.209 B.S., J.D. 820 LaCrosse‡
Brocksmith, Carolyn Gallagher '56 '82 C.742 B.A. L.209 J.D. 427 Laurel Ave.
Broderick, Richard, Law Office of, The '64 '94 1000 Skokie Blvd., Ste. LL3
Brody, Bernard B. '08 '38 C.339 Ph.C. L.146 LL.B. 446 Beverly Dr.
Brody, Jeffrey A. '54 '79 C.589 B.A. L.1151 J.D. 825 Greenbay Rd.
Browder, William B., (AV) '16 '41 C&L.339 A.B., J.D. 1616 Sheridan Rd.‡
Canafax, Nancy M., Law Offices of '38 '68 C.623 B.S. L.276 J.D.
2214 Greenwood Ave.
Collins, H. Richard '35 '60 C.363 B.S. L.602 LL.B. 2145 Chestnut St.‡
Condit, D. Sidney, (AV) '38 '63 C.210 B.A. L.477 J.D. 914 Cherokee Road, Suite 100
Conrad, Warren T. '47 '72 C.352 B.S. L.16 J.D.
(adm. in IA; not adm. in IL) 511 Illinois Rd.★
Dana, David A. '63 '89 C&L.309 B.A., J.D.
(adm. in NY; not adm. in IL) 1323 Gregory Ave.
Davis, Earon S. '50 '75 C.339 B.A. L.910 J.D. Ecological Illness Law Rept.
Dreyfus, Donald '44 '70 C.339 B.S. L.209 J.D. 1009 Seneca Rd.‡
Dugan, John C. '25 '50 C.347 L.209 LL.B. 1000 Skokie Blvd.
Eidmann, Maryann '53 '82 C&L.208 B.A., J.D. 1103 Michigan Ave.‡
Elliott, Robert L., Jr., (AV) '07 '31 C.31 A.B. L.309 LL.B. 1148 Isabella St.‡
Epstein, Sheldon L., Law Office of '38 '64 C.453 B.E.E. L.178 J.D. P.O. Box 400 (Pat.)
Falkof, Ellen Lubarsky '54 '79 C.347 B.A. L.150 J.D. 2205 Greenwood Ave.

Feldman, Stuart A., (AV) '51 '76 C.966 B.B.A. L.276 J.D.
811 Westwood Lane, 60091-2162
Telephone: 847-256-9800 Fax: 847-256-5191
Email: sfeldman@northshore.net URL: http://www.stuartfeldmanlaw.com
Wills and Probate, Estate Planning, Trusts and Estates, Guardianships, Tax Planning, Taxation, IRS Audits, Business Planning, Small Business, General Business and Real Estate.
See Professional Biographies, WILMETTE, ILLINOIS

Field, Gerson B., (AV) '28 '51 C.339 L.209 LL.B. 110 Carriage Way‡
Fox, E. Frances '18 '43 C.477 A.B. L.209 J.D. 1221 Hunter Rd.‡
Frenzer, Timothy J. '58 '83 C&L.424 B.A., J.D. Corp. Coun.
Frick, Robert H. '24 '50 C&L.477 B.B.A., J.D. 921 Westerfield Dr.‡
Gass, Raymond W. '37 '63 C.679 B.S. L.339 LL.B. 1325 Greenwood Ave.
Geller, William A. '50 '75 C.107 B.A. L.145 J.D. [Geller&Assoc.]
Geller & Assoc. 2116 Thornwood Ave.
Gershon, Karyn G. '61 '86 C.188 B.S.I.L.R. L.597 J.D. 833 Greenwood Ave.‡
Goerth, Charles R. '32 '78 C.150 B.A. L.209 J.D. 825 Green Bay Rd., Ste. 210
Goldhirsh, Michael '65 '91 C.846 B.B.A. L.146 J.D. 3545 Lake Ave., Ste. 200
Green, Lesley D. '32 '86 C.050 B.A. L.146 J.D. 824 Lake Ave.‡
Gudmundsen, Robert F., (AV) '15 '41 C.339 L.146 J.D. 422 Fifth St.‡
Hamilton, Mary F. '27 '85 C.597 B.S. L.146 J.D. 1925 Lake Avenue

Heisler, Marc H.
(See Evanston)

Hellander, Martha E. '52 '78 C&L.494 B.A., J.D. 2517 Thornwood Ave.‡
Henderson, James B. '16 '46 C&L.477 A.B., J.D. 3034 Highland
Higgins, James E. '34 '60 C&L.597 B.S.B.A., J.D. 204 Ridge Rd.
Hoover, Rebecca L. '62 '87 C.188 B.S.S. L.276 J.D.
(adm. in VA; not adm. in IL) 301 Hibbard Rd.‡

Howard, Carter, Law Offices, (AV) '35 '61
C.951 A.B. L.597 J.D. 1000 Skokie Blvd., Ste. 270
Jacobs, Betty C. . . . '47 '72 C.30 B.A. L.145 J.D. 625 Maple
Jonscher, George V. . . . '34 '67 C.209 B.S. L.365 J.D. 1000 Skokie
Katlin, Andrew J. . . . '61 '87 C.472 B.A. L.339 J.D. Maurice Sporting Goods
Keating, Francis J. . . . '26 '50 C&L.602 LL.B. Mallinckrodt College
Keller, Paul D., (AV) . . . '27 '55 C.972 B.A. L.146 LL.B. 2240 Lake Ave.
Kelly, John T. . . . '25 '50 C&L.477 B.B.A., J.D. 2010 Beechwood St.‡
Kemper, Richard J. . . . '30 '58 C&L.597 B.S., J.D. 429 Pinecrest Ln.
Kempin, Pamela J. . . . '54 '79 C&L.597 B.A., J.D. 909 Ashland‡
Kepper, Kimberlee R. . . . '56 '82 C.367 B.A. L.339 J.D. 1120 Michigan Ave.
Kesselman, Paul R., The Law Firm of '56 '81
C.339 B.S. L.365 J.D. 1167 Wilmette Avenue
Kioutas, Anna Paniotte . . . '31 '62 C.999 LL.B. L.209 J.D. 1006 Michigan Ave.
Kite, Sherwin B. . . . '40 '64 3045 Lake Ave.‡
Klinge, Roland P. . . . '16 '51 C&L.209 J.D. 1062 Linden Ave.
Korbakes, Lee C. . . . '30 '56 C&L.597 B.S., J.D. 909 Ottawa Ln.

Kretchmar, S. Randolph '52 '01 C.597 B.A. L.209 J.D.
1170 Michigan Avenue, 60091
Telephone: 847-853-8106 Fax: 847-853-0114
Email: s_randolph@earthlink.net
Mental Health Law, Right to Refuse Psychiatry.
See Professional Biographies, WILMETTE, ILLINOIS

Lesser, Norman H. . . . '27 '52 C.1016 B.S. L.209 J.D. 326 Beverly Dr.
Lidman, James R. . . . '30 '55 C&L.597 B.S., J.D. 1127 Chestnut‡
Lieberman, Eugene . . . '18 '40 C&L.209 LL.B. 801 LeClaire Ave.
Lifton, Robert J. . . . '43 '68 C.228 B.A. L.477 J.D. 336 Gregory Ave.
Lillard, Thomas M., Jr. . . . '20 '50 C.378 A.B. L.900 LL.B. 809 Westerfield Dr.‡
Mangler, Robert J., (BV) . . . '30 '58 C.424 B.S. L.597 J.D. 103 Bwy.dwalle St.
Marcus, Richard H. . . . '50 '75 C.339 B.A. L.209 J.D. 421 Sandy Ln.
Marshall, William J., Jr., (AV) . . . '18 '49 C&L.597 LL.B. 827 Westerfield‡
McPhee, Sandra Ferguson . . . '51 '76 C.788 B.A. L.94 J.D. 825 Green Bay Rd., Ste. 270
Mehlman, Edward B. . . . '44 '68 C.910 A.B. L.339 J.D. 425 Beverly Dr.
Meloy, Nancy . . . '59 '87 C&L.352 B.A., J.D. 801 Ashland Ave.‡
Messner, Steven . . . '47 '78 C.339 B.S. L.365 J.D. 444 Skokie Blvd.
Mikula, Charles C. . . . '17 '48 C&L.424 Ph.B., J.D. 435 Ridge Rd.
Moore, Jo Gruidl '48 '78 C.190 B.A. L.1035 J.D.
(adm. in MN; not adm. in IL) 1222 Chestnut‡
Morse, J. Patrick . . . '46 '76 C.340 B.A. L.424 J.D. 1331 Maple
Murray, Daniel A. . . . '58 '83 C&L.477 B.A., J.D. 920 Linden Ave.‡
Murray, Sandra I. . . . '45 '70 C.881 A.B. L.597 J.D. 2811 Iroquois Rd.
Nahmod, Sonia L. . . . '— '76 C.145 B.A. L.229 J.D. V.P. & Mgr., Bank One, Chicago, NA
Najarian, David V. . . . '46 '73 825 Green Bay Rd., Rm. 10
Nanus, Arthur R. . . . '54 '84 C.339 B.S. L.424 J.D. 211 Valley View‡

Neal & McDevitt
(See Evanston)

Nemerovski, Leonard J. . . . '25 '49 C.477 A.B. L.209 J.D. 1440 Sheridan Rd.
Olk, Judith Kavanagh . . . '40 '84 C.436 B.A. L.215 J.D. [J.K.Olk]
Olk, Judith Kavanagh, Ltd. . . . 306 Lawndale Street
Oraham, Victor Kurish . . . '59 '83 C.472 B.M. L.259 J.D. [Oraham]
Oraham Law Firm PC . . . 1000 Skokie Blvd., Ste. 340
Park, Thomas G. . . . '— '87 C.674 A.B. L.597 J.D. 1000 Skokie Blvd., Ste. 255
Perkaus, Robt. P. . . . '10 '31 C.137 L.365 LL.B. 3812 Lake Ave.‡
Pernick, Steven L. . . . '41 '73 C.1016 B.A. L.209 J.D. 836 LaCrosse Ave.
Petersen, Linda Ann . . . '62 '87 C.602 B.A. L.477 J.D. 2218 Kenilworth Ave.‡
Price, Herbert T. . . . '10 '36 C.340 A.B. L.597 J.D. 1437 Wilmette Ave.
Quandt, Karen S. . . . '51 '76 C&L.966 J.B.A., J.D. 825 Green Bay Rd., Ste. 270
Quinn, William J. . . . '11 '35 C.755 B.A. L.494 J.D. 1420 Sheridan Rd.‡
Radjenovich, Rod . . . '— '91 C.597 B.A. L.347 J.D. [J.Strange&Assoc.]
Ramm, Walter C. . . . '26 '55 C.597 B.S. L.146 J.D. 444 Skokie Rd. (Pat.)‡
Rasmussen, Paul R. . . . '15 '40 C.597 B.S. L.365 J.D. 141 Green Bay Rd.‡
Rifken, Herold L., (AV) . . . '28 '56 C&L.339 B.S., LL.B. 405 W. Wilshire Blvd.‡

Roberg, Marilee, (AV) '52 '77 C.821 B.A. L.930 J.D.
121 6th Street, 60091-3435
Telephone: 847-853-1208 Fax: 847-853-9425
Email: mroberg@ameritech.net
Appellate Practice, Arbitration and Alternative Dispute Resolution.
See Professional Biographies, WILMETTE, ILLINOIS

Rodman, Mimi L., (AV) . . . '63 '89 C.145 B.A. L.597 J.D. 1709 Forest Ave.
Rothschild, Harriett Piper . . . '54 '80 C.788 A.B. L.597 J.D. 1046 Elmwood‡
Santacruz, J Steve . . . '61 '90 C&L.209 B.S., J.D. [Santacruz&Assoc.]
Santacruz Associates, LTD . . . 444 Skokie Blvd., Ste. 310
Scheiwe, Kenneth . . . '50 '76 C.339 B.S. L.365 J.D. 104 16th St.
Schmidt, Jerrold K. . . . '52 '77 C.477 B.B.A. L.209 J.D. 421 Brookside Dr.
Sebastian, Frances R. . . . '32 '66 C&L.477 B.A., J.D. 1500 Sheridan Rd.‡
Share, Alan M. . . . '51 '76 3545 W. Lake Ave., Ste. 200
Sharpe, Emily J. . . . '56 '82 C.914 B.A. L.276 J.D. 614 Laurel Ave.‡
Sheffield, Hope Reisman . . . '56 '80 C.681 A.B. L.309 J.D. 730 Lake Ave.
Shepp, Eugene L., (AV) . . . '29 '56 C.659 B.S. L.597 J.D. 3545 Lake Ave.
Shultz, Alan D. . . . '51 '76 C.46 B.S. L.146 J.D. 1187 Wilmette Ave.
Simon, Thelma Brook . . . '16 '40 C.339 B.A. L.145 J.D. 3119 Wilmette Ave.‡
Singer, Mark E. . . . '49 '77 C&L.597 B.A., J.D. 236 Valley View Drive
Smith, Bruce M., (AV) . . . '15 '39 C&L.477 A.B., LL.B. 910 Elmwood Ave.‡
Smith, Susan E. M. . . . '65 '91 C.966 B.A. L.365 J.D. 444 Skokie Blvd., Ste. 303
Solomon, Lois . . . '39 '61 C&L.145 A.B., J.D. 1318 Isabella
Sterman, Lynn R. . . . '46 '71 C.119 B.A. L.145 J.D. 303 Greenleaf Ave.‡
Stogin, John M. . . . '30 '62 C.46 B.S. L.424 J.D. 630 Lake Ave.
Stoker, Corinne Moore '54 '78 C.893 B.A. L.945 J.D.
(adm. in VA; not adm. in IL) 1212 Princeton Pl.‡
Stone, Michael L. . . . '36 '61 C&L.309 A.B., LL.B. 117 4th St.‡
Strange, Jeffrey . . . '52 '78 C.112 A.B. L.809 J.D. [J.Strange&Assoc.]
Strange, Jeffrey, & Associates . . . 717 Ridge Road
Suizzo, Anthony G., Law Offices of '53 '78
C.597 B.A. L.339 J.D. 3201 Old Glenview Rd., Ste. 225
Sullivan, James E. . . . '39 '67 C.602 B.A. L.339 J.D. 324 Central Ave.
Sylvester, Patrick Sean . . . '70 '00 C.742 B.A. L.300 J.D. [Sylvester] ⊙
Sylvester Law Firm, PC . . . 3545 Lake Ave., Suite 200 (⊙Milw., WI)
Theiss, Susan L. . . . '62 '87 C.197 A.B. L.145 J.D. 1046 Seneca Rd.
Thompson, Richard E. . . . '35 '61 C.385 A.B. L.145 J.D. Wilmette Pub. Library Dist.
Vogel, Robert C., (AV) . . . '17 '43 C.597 A.B. L.146 LL.B. 2025 Thornwood Ave.‡
Weinstein, Lawrence C. . . . '46 '73 C.475 B.A. L.145 J.D. 558 Hunter Rd.‡
Wilson, D. Stuart . . . '28 '56 C&L.608 B.A., J.D. 2210 Greenwood‡
Wilson, Norman E. . . . '35 '62 C.597 B.S. L.352 LL.B. 903 Ridge Rd., 3rd Fl.
Wingader, Thomas A. . . . '44 '69 C.388 B.A. L.339 J.D. 1510 Walnut Ave.
Young, Dawn K. . . . '73 '04 C.94 B.A. L.823 J.D. 340 Ridge Rd., Ste. 201
Young, William R. . . . '73 '02 C.140 B.A. L.823 J.D. 332 Ridge Rd.
Zissman, Marshall L. . . . '29 '53 C.339 B.A. L.309 LL.B. 802 Redbud Lane‡

WILMINGTON, 5,134, *Will Co.*

Fisher, Jeffrey L., (BV) . . . '57 '82 C.602 B.A. L.1003 207 S. Water St.
Greenway, Teresa Kosla . . . '61 '92 C.1016 B.S.B.A. L.365 J.D. 26065 Willow Ln.
Klingner, Harold W., (AV) '20 '50 C.597 L.146 LL.B.
6577 North Will Road (⊙Morris)

WINCHESTER, * 1,650, *Scott Co.*

Bell, Lois A. . . . '61 '85 C.801 B.S. L.339 J.D. Cir.J., Scott County
Cherry, David R., (P.C.) . . . '46 '73 C.339 B.S. L.500 J.D. Scott Co. State's Atty.
Coonrod, John D., Law Office, (BV) . . . '53 '79 C.927 B.A. L.500 J.D. 44 E. Side Square
Mann, Richard E. . . . '— '48 C&L.339 A.B., J.D. [Rammelkamp,B.K.K.F.&L.]
Rammelkamp, Bradney, Kuster, Keaton, Fritsche & Lindsay, P.C., (AV)
46 South Hill Street (⊙Jacksonville, Springfield)
Yow, H. Allen, (BV) '— '89 C.894 A.B. L.801 J.D.
[Rammelkamp,B.K.K.F.&L.] (⊙Jacksonville)

WINFIELD, 8,718, *DuPage Co.*

Arnolds, Laura Ann . . . '— '93 C.339 B.A. L.146 J.D. 26 W362 Pinehurst Dr.
Bianchi, Patricia E. . . . '47 '79 C.679 B.S. L.1151 J.D. 0S050 Page
Garlinger, Donald W., (AV) . . . '34 '62 C.210 B.A. L.477 J.D. 26 W. 576 Blair
Gorr, Kathleen H. . . . '45 '90 C.94 B.A. L.339 J.D. [K.H.Gorr]
Gorr, Kathleen H., P.C. . . . OS 125 Church St., 2nd Fl.
Grotto, Le Roy A. . . . '22 '68 C.46 B.S.A.B. L.365 J.D. 27 W. 385 Jewell Rd.‡
Guild, William L., III, (BV) . . . '51 '79 C.932 B.A. L.589 J.D. [W.L.Guild,III]
Guild, William L., III, P.C., (BV) . . . 1 N 141 County Farm Road Suite 230
Kollias, Daniel John . . . '75 '99 C.477 B.A. L.602 J.D. [D.J.Kollias]
Kollias, Daniel J., P.C., Law Offices of . . . 1N141 County Farm Road Suite 230
Markl, Steven R. '50 '82 C.339 B.S. L.365 J.D.
(adm. in CA; not adm. in IL; Pat.) P.O. Box 372
McAdams, Thomas O. . . . '59 '84 C.589 B.A. L.209 J.D. [T.O.McAdams]
McAdams, Thomas O., P.C. . . . 27W073 Jewell Road
McClow, Thomas A., (BV) . . . '44 '69 C.475 B.S. L.424 J.D. [T.A.McClow]
McClow, Thomas A., Ltd., (BV) . . . P.O. Box 522
Meyer, Edward B., Jr. . . . '55 '88 C.578 B.A. L.365 J.D. ONO32 Ambleside Drive
Mullen, Terence C., (BV) . . . '55 '80 C.589 B.A. L.221 J.D. [Mullen&W.]
Mullen & Winthers, P.C., (BV) . . . 1 N. 141 County Farm Rd.
Onken, Mary A. . . . '64 '89 C.347 B.A. L.339 J.D. Pres., Onken Consulting, Inc.
Pindel, Donna B. . . . '53 '83 C.339 B.S. L.365 J.D. 26 W. 291 Parkway Dr.‡
Stauber, Mark J., (BV) . . . '50 '77 C.424 B.A. L.365 J.D. 1N141 County Farm Rd.
Stime, Steven Paul, (CV) '58 '94 C.57 B.A. L.365 J.D.
27W130 Roosevelt Rd., Ste. 101
Volpe, James F., Law Offices of . . . '57 '93 C.338 B.S. L.209 J.D. 26 W. 172 Prestwick
Winthers, David J., (BV) . . . '56 '80 C.937 B.A. L.365 J.D. [Mullen&W.]

WINNETKA, 12,419, *Cook Co.*

Auerbach, Carl A. '15 '38 C.415 A.B. L.309 LL.B.
(adm. in NY; not adm. in IL) 1530 Tower Rd.‡
Bâby, Henry P., Jr. . . . '39 '64 C.602 B.B.A. L.597 J.D. 199 Birch St.‡
Baltz, William S. . . . '18 '48 C.976 B.A. L.309 LL.B. 98 Woodley Rd.
Barrett, Roger Spooner, (AV) . . . '11 '34 C&L.494 A.B., LL.B. 615 Cedar‡
Berwanger, John J. . . . '42 '67 C.674 A.B. L.145 J.D. 1067 Oak
Bishop, Lois C. . . . '33 '76 C.145 B.A. L.597 J.D. 1290 Scott Ave.
Bishop, M. Lee . . . '30 '56 C&L.339 B.S., J.D. [M.L.Bishop]
Bishop, M. Lee, P.C. . . . 722 Oak St.
Boge, Georgie C. . . . '67 '97 C.674 B.A. L.976 J.D. 1351 Scott Avenue
Bohrer, Mason L. . . . '23 '50 C&L.309 A.B., LL.B. P.O. Box 130
Brady, Cynthia Antonak . . . '59 '86 C.473 B.S. L.880 J.D. 615 Spruce St.
Burden, David G. . . . '36 '62 C.424 B.S. L.209 J.D. [Couri&C.]
Cannon, Robert H. . . . '43 '68 C.321 A.B. L.893 J.D. 555 Ash Street
Chensoff, Gary V. '52 '77 C.473 B.S. L.94 J.D.
(adm. in OH; not adm. in IL) 100 Indian Hill Rd.
Chiga, Ann '65 '93 C.813 A.B. L.1066 J.D.
(adm. in CA; not adm. in IL) 1001 Green Bay Rd.
Churchwell, Thomas L. . . . '42 '67 C.210 B.A. L.597 J.D. 1344 Sunview Ln.
Coburn, John H. . . . '11 '51 C&L.209 LL.B. 757 Locust St.
Cohen, Jeffrey D. . . . '52 '77 C.339 A.B. L.146 J.D. 1028 Cherry St.
Couri, Phillip A. . . . '69 '95 C.602 B.A. L.424 J.D. [Couri&C.]
Couri, Phillip E., (BV) . . . '37 '62 C.436 B.S. L.209 J.D. [Couri&C.]

Couri & Couri, (BV)
552 Lincoln Avenue, 60093
Telephone: 847-446-7372 Fax: 847-501-4858
Members of Firm: Phillip E. Couri; David G. Burden; Phillip A. Couri; George L. Plumb (1936-1992).
Civil Trial Practice. Civil Liability, Corporate, Banking, Probate, Estate Planning, Commercial Real Estate, Residential Real Estate, Family and Tax Law.
References: Harris Bank, Glencoe; Harris Bank, Winnetka.
See Professional Biographies, WINNETKA, ILLINOIS

Crowe, Robert W. . . . '24 '49 C&L.145 A.B., J.D. 1228 Westmoor Rd.
Davies, Mary M. . . . '61 '86 C.800 B.A. L.424 J.D. 861 Bryant Ave.
Davis, Britton A., (AV) . . . '36 '60 C&L.597 B.S.L., LL.B. 285 Linden St.‡
Davis, Chester R., Jr., (AV) . . . '30 '58 C.674 A.B. L.309 LL.B. [Davis]
Davis Law Office, (AV) . . . 670 Blackthorn Road
Deibert, Raymond H. '42 '86 C.339 B.S. L.87 J.D.
(adm. in AL; not adm. in IL) OCCUSAFE, Inc.
Dekoven, Seymour Samuel . . . '20 '42 C&L.597 B.S., J.D. 1757 Tower Rd.‡
Dini, Robert U., (AV) . . . '38 '63 C.602 B.A. L.145 J.D. 1056 Gage St., Hubbard Woods
Durning, Catherine M. . . . '63 '91 C.478 B.A. L.818 J.D. 838 Locust Rd.
Dussman, Dorothy S. . . . '17 '41 L.209 666 Garland St.
Ericksen, Keith C. . . . '44 '80 C.378 B.S.B.A. L.365 J.D. Sr. V.P., Harris Bk. Winnetka
Fawcett, Dwight W., (AV) . . . '27 '51 C.347 B.S. L.309 J.D. 711 Winter St.‡
Fields, Douglas A. '49 '77 C&L.259 B.S., J.D.
(adm. in FL; not adm. in IL) 570 Arbor Vitae‡
Fox, Kenneth A. . . . '57 '82 C.475 B.S. L.823 J.D. Sr. V.P., Invsts., R. W. Baird & Co.‡
Gavin, Alison L. . . . '60 '85 C.937 B.A. L.477 J.D. 191 Fuller Lane‡
Gibbons, William J. . . . '24 '56 C&L.309 A.B., LL.B. 1137 Tower Rd.‡
Goldstein, Joni L. . . . '58 '84 C.914 B.A. L.309 J.D. 260 Fairview‡
Greeley, Samuel S., (AV) . . . '14 '39 C&L.309 A.B., LL.B. 800 Tower Rd.‡
Harms, Mark R. . . . '46 '72 C.165 B.A. L.94 J.D. 558 Hill Ter.
Harsha, E. Houston, (AV) . . . '16 '41 C&L.145 A.B., J.D. 24 Warwick Rd.‡
Hecht, Marc L., (AV) . . . '44 '70 C.976 B.A. L.659 LL.B. 1096 Spruce St.

Heisler, Marc H.
(See Evanston)

Herman, Stephen M. . . . . '32 '57 C.597 A.B. L.309 LL.B. 1051 Cherry St.‡
Herst, Theodore J., (AV) . . . . '24 '50 C&L.145 A.B., J.D. 1319 Trapp Ln.‡
Hines, Lauren G. . . . . '56 '82 C.399 B.A. L.597 J.D. 1020 Spruce St.‡
Hintzke, Edward S. . . . . '37 '60 C&L.145 A.B., J.D. 416 Maple St.‡
Howe, Lawrence, (AV) . . . . '21 '48 C.309 A.B. L.145 J.D. 175 Chestnut St.
Istvan, Rudyard L. '50 '77 C&L.309 A.B., J.D.
(adm. in MA; not adm. in IL) 277 Chestnut St.‡
James, David F. . . . . '23 '63 C.424 Ph.B. L.209 LL.B. 1078 Spruce St.
Karabas, James J. . . . . '61 '91 C.424 B.B.A. L.365 J.D. 325 Fairview Ave.
Kenn, Edward J. . . . . '18 '42 C.563 B.S. L.178 LL.B. 220 Woodland Ave.‡
Knott, Thomas Andrew "Andy" . . . . '55 '87 C.838 B.S. L.1000 J.D. [T.A.Knott]
Knott, Thomas Andrew . . . . 1260 Ash Street
Knowlton, John M. . . . . '12 '37 C.293 A.B. L.145 J.D. 37 Longmeadow Rd.
Ley, Patricia B. . . . . '24 '65 C.966 B.A. L.209 J.D. 1472 Asbury Ave.‡
Ley, Robert J., (AV) . . . . '18 '42 C.339 A.B. L.209 J.D. 560 Green Bay Road, Suite 303
Mann, Basil P., (AV) . . . . '25 '56 C.976 B.E. L.424 J.D. 144 White Bridge Hill (Pat.)
Maurer, Otto H. . . . . '42 '67 C&L.262 A.B., LL.B. 615 Elm St.
McCarty, Franklin B., Jr. . . . . '24 '52 C.209 B.S. L.597 J.D. 462 Green Bay Rd.
McClain, Deborah A. . . . . '59 '83 C.207 B.A. L.209 J.D. 571 Hill Ter.
McMillen, Thomas R., (AV) . . . . '16 '41 C.674 A.B. L.309 LL.B. 231 Forest St.‡
Melander, Michael . . . . '— '03 C.610 B.A. L.339 J.D. [A Padgitt,P.&P.]
Menk, John C., (AV) . . . . '14 '39 C.339 L.365 J.D. 524 Hawthorn Lane‡
Micali, Thomas A. . . . . '14 '39 C&L.339 B.A., LL.B. 1301 Plum Tree Ln.‡
Montgomery, Frank R. . . . . '26 '49 C.437 L.923 LL.B. 1035 Willow Rd.
Mucci, Robert R. . . . . '53 '83 C.339 B.A. L.365 J.D. 1040 Tower Rd.
Nickow, Glenn S. . . . . . '56 '85 C.339 B.S. L.146 J.D. General Loose Leaf Bindery Co., Inc.
Nielsen, Marianne D. . . . . '44 '84 C&L.597 M.A., J.D. 200 De Windt Rd
Niemann, William L., (AV) . . . . '20 '48 C.123 A.B. L.597 J.D. 1243 Forest Glen N.‡
Olson, Kristine A. . . . . '52 '80 C.560 B.A.Sc. L.424 J.D. 574 Lincoln‡
Padgitt, D. Lee . . . . '60 '90 C.629 B.S. L.878 J.D. [Padgitt,P.&P.]
Padgitt, Donald L., (AV) . . . . '30 '59 C.388 A.B. L.145 J.D. [Padgitt,P.&P.]

Padgitt, Padgitt & Peppey Ltd., (AV)
Suite 100, 560 Green Bay Road, 60093-2260
Telephone: 847-446-2900 Facsimile: 847-446-2908
Email: info@ppp-ltd.com
Donald L. Padgitt; D. Lee Padgitt; Brooke L. B. Peppey;—Michael Melander.
General Practice. Corporate, Real Estate, Probate and Estate Planning Law.
See Professional Biographies, WINNETKA, ILLINOIS

Page, William H., II . . . . '30 '62 C.966 B.S. L.424 J.D. 786 Foxdale Ave.‡
Parmer, Carolyn J.N. . . . . '30 '80 C.700 B.A. L.209 J.D. 9 Woodley Rd.‡
Peppey, Brooke L. B. . . . . '62 '89 C.966 B.S. L.569 J.D. [Padgitt,P.&P.]
Peters, Victor S., Jr. . . . . '20 '49 C.597 B.S. L.145 J.D. 1205 Sunset Rd.‡
Proesel, Mark K. . . . . '52 '77 C.602 B.A. L.424 J.D. 3 Longmeadow Rd.‡
Redding, George H., Jr. . . . . '21 '49 C.901 A.B. L.597 J.D. 365 Chestnut St.‡
Reiman, James A. . . . . '55 '80 C.178 B.A. L.597 J.D. 1291 Asbury Ave.
Roin, Dan R., (AV) . . . . '27 '51 C&L.145 Ph.B., J.D. 1225 Westmoor Road
Rothschild, Tom A. . . . . '40 '65 C.188 B.A. L.145 J.D. Tar, Inc
Rouse, Barbara Rest . . . . '56 '83 C.788 B.A. L.893 J.D. 955 Old Green Bay Rd.
Rusin, Bron J. . . . . '10 '46 C.339 L.365 LL.B. 1086 Ash St.
Rusin, Thomas D., Attorney at Law . . . . '50 '77 C.472 B.S. L.365 J.D. 1086 Ash St.
Ryan, Robert J. . . . . '47 '73 C.602 B.B.A. L.424 J.D. 560 Green Bay Rd., Ste. 303
Samuels, Arthur M. . . . . '11 '36 C.339 L.209 1202 Ash St.
Schiff, Patricia Foisie . . . . '55 '81 C.309 A.B. L.94 J.D. 25 Locaust Rd.
Schrauth, David M. . . . . '64 '91 C.602 B.A. L.424 J.D. [Stephens&S.]
Severns, Todd Neil . . . . '73 '99 C&L.910 B.A., J.D. 741 Prospect Avenue
Sharp, Donald H. . . . . '18 '47 C.900 A.B. L.477 J.D. 1220 Hill Rd.‡
Shay, Elizabeth P. . . . . '56 '81 C.339 B.A. L.734 J.D. Prairie Legal Servs.
Shay, Paul R. '54 '79 C.602 B.A. L.734 J.D.
(adm. in CT; not adm. in IL) Mng. Dir., Shay & Shay
Shepard, John C., Offices of John C. Shepard '50 '75
C.597 B.S.E. L.209 J.D. 575 Sunset Rd. (Pat.)
Sido, Mary O'Neil . . . . '57 '85 C.915 B.A. L.365 J.D. 721 Lincoln Ave.
Silver, Jay Kit . . . . '56 '81 C.597 B.A. L.209 J.D., V.P., Bank One
Snyder, John B., (AV) . . . . '29 '57 C.951 A.B. L.309 LL.B. 592 Cherry St.‡
Sprowl, James A., (AVⓉ) . . . . '— '67 C&L.477 B.S.E.E., J.D. 416 Elder Lane (Pat.)
Stephens, Todd J. . . . . '61 '91 C.966 B.S. L.146 J.D. [Stephens&S.]
Stephens & Schrauth, P.C. . . . . 833 Elm Street, Suite 205 & 207
Stern, John N. . . . . '17 '42 C.604 A.B. L.309 LL.B. 640 Winnetka Mews‡
Sullivan, John P. . . . . '02 '26 C.602 B.A. L.352 J.D. 192 Church Rd.‡
Taslitz, Lauren . . . . '57 '84 C.674 B.A. L.309 J.D. 1210 Broadmeadow Rd.‡
Theis, William H., (AV) . . . . '45 '70 C.424 A.B. L.597 J.D. 841 Foxdale Avenue
Thonander, Robert V., (AV) . . . . '17 '48 C&L.597 B.S., J.D. 560 Green Bay Rd.
Turney, Mimi Lawton . . . . '57 '83 C.788 A.B. L.597 J.D. 854 Boal Pkwy.‡
Van Herik, Russell . . . . '49 '74 C.72 B.A. L.966 J.D. 133 Glenwood Ave.
Vogler, Linda Coffing, Law Offices of '52 '77 C.338 B.S. L.801 J.D.
1585 Hickory Lane
Walsh, Elmer Michael, Jr., (AV) . . . . '28 '57 C.145 B.A. L.276 J.D. P.O. Box 129
Weinberger, Daniel . . . . '28 '56 C.8 B.A. L.477 LL.B. 1492 Asbury St.‡
Williams, Robert C., (AV) . . . . '15 '46 C&L.477 A.B., LL.B. 134 Green Bay Rd.‡
Wirt, Pamela Cocalas . . . . '65 '90 C&L.339 B.S., J.D. 770 Bryant Ave.
Yntema, Elizabeth B. . . . . '58 '84 C.893 B.A. L.477 J.D. 165 Thorntree Lane‡

WINTHROP HARBOR, 6,670, *Lake Co.*

Ordonez-Mackey, Maria G. . . . . '— '00 C&L.436 B.S., J.D. 1812 Fourth St.

WONDER LAKE, 7,463, *McHenry Co.*

Lavin, Karen M., (CV) . . . . '57 '82 C.965 B.A. L.146 J.D. 8908 Highland Drive
Lewis, Evan W., (CV) . . . . '48 '74 C.966 B.A. L.405 J.D. [E.Lewis]
Lewis, Evan, Law Office, (CV) . . . . 7512 Hancock Dr.
Ruckoldt, Charmaine Guffa, (CV) . . . . . . '54 '85 C&L.589 B.A., J.D. 7610 Hancock Dr.
Wachholz, Nancy B. . . . . '42 '86 C.966 B.A. L.589 J.D. 7610 Hancock Dr.

WOOD DALE, 13,535, *DuPage Co.*

Foley, Timothy F. '61 '86 C.276 B.S.B.A. L.424 J.D.
Sr. Coun., Household Retail Servs.
Hornewer, John R. . . . . '60 '85 C.597 B.A. L.339 J.D. 312 Saint Andrews Dr.
Johnson, Kenneth P. . . . . '50 '76 C.827 B.A. L.209 J.D. 191 W. Irving Park Rd.
Kuenster, Richard A. . . . . '51 '78 C.602 B.A. L.365 J.D. [R.A.Kuenster&Assoc.]
Kuenster, Richard A., & Associates, Ltd. . . . . 386 W. Irving Park Rd.
Lucyshyn, Peter S., (AV) '35 '59 C&L.477 B.S.E.E., LL.B.
Pat. Coun. & Asst. Secy., Videojet Systems Intl., Inc. (Pat.)‡
McHugh, Guy M. . . . . '30 '60 C.420 B.S. L.209 J.D. 225 Jefferson Ln.
Mencini, Ana M. '69 '01 C.393 B.A. L.146 J.D.
345 Georgetown Square, Suite 206, 60191
Telephone: 630-616-3900 Fax: 630-616-3913
Email: amencini@mencinilaw.com URL: http://www.mencinilaw.com
Real Estate (Residential and Commercial), Landlord/Tenant, Business Law, Family Law, Estate Planning, Wills, Trusts, Powers of Attorney, Probate, Immigration.
See Professional Biographies, WOOD DALE, ILLINOIS

Nelson, Robert R., (BV) . . . . '30 '58 C&L.339 B.S., J.D. 467 Hiawatha Trail
Norris, John K., Jr., (AV) . . . . '54 '83 C.1111 B.A. L.146 J.D. [Rubin&N.] ⊙
Pulsifer, Howard A. '42 '71 C.349 B.S. L.818 J.D.
(adm. in MA; not adm. in IL) V.P., Gen. Coun. & Secy., AAR Corp.
Pulsifer, Jennifer L. . . . . '74 '99 C.340 B.A. L.365 J.D. Sr. Coun., AAR Corp.
Rubin, Donald T., (AV) . . . . '50 '80 C.339 B.A. L.365 J.D. [Rubin&N.] ⊙
Rubin & Norris, LLC, The Law Offices of, (AV) . . . . 189 North Cedar Avenue (⊙Chicago)
Trotto, Anthony J. . . . . '49 '76 C.201 B.S. L.365 J.D. 158 Murray Dr.
Vilim, Donald J. . . . . '62 '88 C.209 B.S.C. L.339 J.D. Asst. Gen. Coun., AAR Corp.
Zimmer, Terrance H. . . . . '— '76 C.339 B.A. L.365 J.D. 386 W. Irving Park Road

WOODHULL, 808, *Henry Co.*

Montgomery, Thomas W., (BV) '45 '72
C&L.339 B.S., J.D. 147 N. Division St. (⊙Cambridge)

WOODRIDGE, 30,934, *DuPage Co.*

Alexander, Roger L. '35 '74 C.235 B.S. L.1003 J.D.
(adm. in OH; not adm. in IL) 2932 Hickory Ct.‡
Amerine, Roy R. '45 '79 C.112 B.S. L.809 J.D.
(adm. in CA; not adm. in IL) 3 Williams Ct.
Baskin, Steven A. . . . . '58 '82 C.477 A.B. L.145 J.D. Gen. Coun., Al Baskin Co.
Brown, Cynthia A. . . . . '62 '88 C.589 B.S. L.146 J.D. 6527 Halsey Dr.ve.‡
Conti, Lee Ann '— '76 C.801 B.A. L.209 J.D.
Assoc Gen. Coun., Citizens Util. Co. of Ill.
Cox, Janice L. . . . . '53 '79 C&L.801 B.S., J.D. 3420 High Trail Dr.‡
Czepiel, Lawrence J. . . . . '47 '73 C.339 B.A. L.424 J.D. 7501 S. Lemont Rd., Ste. 20
Dietrich, Wolf C. '41 '71 C.976 B.A. L.1068 J.D.
(adm. in CA; not adm. in IL) 6819 Harvest Ave.‡
Erickson, Diane Q. . . . . '59 '85 C.339 B.S. L.879 J.D. 6413 Greene Rd.
Hardgrove, Nicholas A. '67 '92
C&L.339 B.S., J.D. Senior Attorney, Citizens Utilities Company
Hickey, Robert W. '48 '77 C.397 B.A. L.1209 J.D.
(adm. in VA; not adm. in IL) 1401 Davey Rd., Ste. 300

Hirsh, Richard L., & Associates, P.C.
(See Hinsdale)

Hull, Julius H. . . . . '19 '46 C.475 A.B. L.276 J.D. Gen. Coun., Wilton Enterprise, Inc.
Hunt, Sharon L. . . . . '61 '87 C.1111 B.A. L.46 J.D. 2386 Kildeer St.
Hymes, Richard W., Jr. '46 '82 C.1106 B.A. L.589 J.D.
6825 Hobson Valley Dr Ste 104
Kraft, Claire I. . . . . '48 '81 C.339 B.A. L.146 J.D. 6100 Allan Dr.
Lynch, John J., Law Offices of '58 '99 C.1222 B.A. L.1206 J.D.
3590 Hobson Road, Suite 103, 60517
Telephone: 630-253-2900 Fax: 630-968-5540 URL: http://www.johnjlynch.net
Email: jlynch@johnjlynchesq.com URL: http://www.johnjlynchesq.com
Bankruptcy, Wills and Trusts, Probate, Real Estate, Business Law.
See Professional Biographies, WOODRIDGE, ILLINOIS

Martin, James D. . . . . '34 '87 C.791 B.S. L.365 J.D. 7930 Everglade Ave.
Merican, Steven R., (AV) . . . . '— '82 C.1376 B.A. L.146 J.D. [S.R.Merican]

Merican, Steven R., P.C., (AV)
3840 Vardon Court Suite 200, 60517
Telephone: 630-579-6460 Fax: 630-579-6461 URL: http://www.lawyers.com/localcounsel
Email: merican@illinoislocalcounsel.com URL: http://www.illinoislocalcounsel.com
Steven R. Merican.
Appellate Practice, Civil Appeals, Criminal Appeals, Products Liability, Toxic Torts, Toxic Exposure, Commercial Litigation, Commercial Torts, Breach of Contract, Contract Litigation, Personal Rights, Election Law, Civil Litigation.
See Professional Biographies, WOODRIDGE, ILLINOIS

Pettit, George W. . . . . '25 '72 C.358 B.S. L.365 J.D. 6518 Maxwell Dr.‡
Renaldi, Michael E. . . . . '49 '77 C.679 B.S.I.M. L.424 J.D. 6612 Oak Tree Trail
Roseen, Kathryn L. . . . . '54 '80 C.78 B.A. L.94 J.D. Gen. Cinema Theatres
Thompson, John T., Jr. '38 '68 C&L.734 A.S., J.D.
(adm. in MO; not adm. in IL) 2661 Sumac St.‡
Treat, Paul H. '22 '51 C.800 A.B. L.910 LL.B.
(adm. in MO; not adm. in IL) 8111 Route 53
Wolfe, Marc D. '51 '76 C.208 B.A. L.365 J.D.
3550 Hobson Road, Suite 101 (⊙Chicago)

WOOD RIVER, 11,296, *Madison Co.*

Allen, Benjamin B., (BV) . . . . '40 '69 C.801 B.S. L.623 J.D. [C Lakin]
Armbruster, Charles W., III, (AV) . . . . '66 '92 C.477 B.A. L.910 J.D. [A Lakin]
Barr, Joseph J., (AV) . . . . '19 '43 C&L.602 A.B., LL.B. 7 N. Wood Ave.‡
Barton, Dennis J., III . . . . '73 '03 C.1119 B.S. L.910 J.D. [A Lakin]
Bassett, Merle C., (BV) . . . . '28 '52 C.210 A.B. L.910 LL.B. [Bassett]
Bassett Law Office, P.C., (BV) . . . . 16 W. Lorena Ave.
Blotevogel, Michael T. . . . . '72 '03 C.587 B.A. L.910 J.D. [A Lakin]
Burke, Richard J., Jr., (BVⓉ) . . . . '53 '78 C.388 B.A. L.910 J.D. [A Lakin]
Butler, Rene Bassett '70 '94 C.862 B.S. L.425 J.D.
(adm. in FL; not adm. in IL) [Bassett]
Caffey, Rodney D. . . . . '— '03 C.338 B.S. L.616 J.D. [A Lakin]
Chapman, Charles W. . . . . '42 '67 C.801 B.A. L.734 J.D. [C Lakin]
Cohen, Daniel J. . . . . '67 '92 C&L.910 B.A., J.D. [A Lakin]
Dripps, Roy C., (AV) . . . . '56 '82 C&L.734 A.B., J.D. [A Lakin]
Gibson, Richard W., (BV) . . . . '60 '85 C.1082 B.A. L.602 J.D. [R.Gibson]
Gibson, Ric, Law Office of, (BV) . . . . 200 N. Wood River Ave.
Hoffman, Jay, (BV) . . . . '— '86 C.338 B.S. L.734 J.D. [C Lakin]
Holland, Thomas W., (BV) . . . . '26 '51 C&L.910 A.B., J.D. 7 N. Wood River Ave.
Jensen, Craig J., (BV) . . . . '59 '88 C.424 B.S. L.365 J.D. [A Lakin]
Lakin, Bradley M., (BV) . . . . '70 '97 C.339 B.S. L.589 J.D. [Lakin]
Lakin, L. Thomas, (AV) . . . . '40 '70 C.801 B.S. L.421 J.D. [Lakin] ⊙

Lakin Law Firm, The, P.C., (AV) BB
300 Evans Avenue, P.O. Box 229, 62095-0027 ⊙
Telephone: 618-254-1127 Telecopier: 618-254-0193
Email: lakinlaw@com URL: http://www.lakinlaw.com
L. Thomas Lakin; Bradley M. Lakin. Associates: Roy C. Dripps; Richard J. Burke, Jr.; Marc W. Parker; Craig J. Jensen; Charles W. Armbruster, III; Gail Renshaw; John E. Winterscheidt; Daniel J. Cohen; Jeffrey A.J. Millar; Thomas G. Maag; Paul A. Marks; Michael T. Blotevogel; Gary E. Peel; Gerald R. Walters; Elizabeth A. Parker; Dennis J. Barton, III; Rodney D. Caffey; Robert W. Schmieder, II. Of Counsel: Benjamin B. Allen; Charles W. Chapman; Jay Hoffman.

(This Listing Continued)

Lakin Law Firm, The, P.C. (Continued)

General Trial Practice. Admiralty, Federal Employers Liability Act (FELA), Personal Injury and Workers Compensation.
St. Louis, Missouri Office: 1015 Locust Street, Suite 800. Telephone: 314-231-3138.
See Professional Biographies, WOOD RIVER, ILLINOIS

Maag, Thomas G. .... '75 '00 C.500 B.P.A. L.801 J.D. [▣ Lakin]
Mallon, Lance R., (BV) .... '49 '73 C.589 B.A. L.339 J.D. [Mallon]
Mallon Law Firm, Ltd., (BV) .... 515 Madison Ave.
Marks, Paul A. .... '— '99 C.338 B.S. L.734 J.D. [▣ Lakin]
Millar, Jeffrey A.J. .... '73 '99 L.215 J.D. [▣ Lakin]
Parker, Elizabeth A. .... '51 '01 C.932 B.S. L.36 J.D. [▣ Lakin]
Parker, Marc W., (BV) .... '65 '90 C.801 B.S. L.734 J.D. [▣ Lakin]
Peel, Gary E., (AV) .... '44 '68 C.801 B.A. L.45 J.D. [▣ Lakin]
Pitts, Rodney J., (BV) .... '48 '73 C.927 B.A. L.734 J.D. [Pitts,D.&D.]
Pitts, Dugan & Diaz, P.C., (BV) .... 200 N. Wood River Ave.
Renshaw, Gail, (AV) .... '— '76 C.502 B.A. L.276 J.D. [▣ Lakin]
Sachtleben-Green, Sue .... '— '82 C&L.801 B.S., J.D. 301 Evans Avenue‡
Schmieder, Robert W., II .... '71 '96 C.597 B.A. L.801 J.D. [▣ Lakin]
Sweet, Dean E., (CV) .... '47 '76 C.234 B.A. L.734 J.D. Asst. State Atty.
Walters, Gerald R., (BV) .... '47 '74 C&L.339 B.A., J.D. [▣ Lakin]
Washington, Janis A. '63 '89 L.608 J.D.
(adm. in MO; not adm. in IL) Shell Oil Co.
Winterscheidt, John E., (AV) .... '64 '90 C.56 B.A. L.910 J.D. [▣ Lakin]

WOODSTOCK, * 20,151, *McHenry Co.*

Andrle, James H., III .... '69 '99 C.589 B.S. L.1252 J.D. [▣ Weisz B.&G.]
Arnold, Ward S. .... '45 '73 C.339 B.S. L.365 J.D. Cir. J.
Baker, Thomas F. .... '42 '67 C&L.424 B.S., J.D. Assoc. Cir. J.
Berendt, Emily P. .... '48 '86 C.801 B.S. L.365 J.D. P.O. Box 1635
Berner, James E., (AV) .... '30 '57 C&L.209 Ph.B., J.D. [Caldwell,B.&C.]
Bolger, John D., (AV) .... '38 '63 C.602 B.B.A. L.145 J.D. 105 Van Buren St.
Botto, Francisco J. .... '60 '93 C.31 B.A. L.597 J.D. [Weisz B.&G.]

Bradshaw, M. Margaret, P.C.
454 West Jackson Street, 60098
Telephone: 877-SSD-ATTY or 815-206-2908 Fax: 877-773-9889
Email: margaret@SSDAtty.com URL: http://www.SSDAtty.com
Margaret Murray-Bradshaw.
Social Security, Social Security Disability.
See Professional Biographies, WOODSTOCK, ILLINOIS

Busche, Sara L. .... '71 '02 C.679 B.A. L.365 J.D. [▣ Gitlin,H.&K.]
Caldwell, Michael T., (AV) .... '39 '63 C&L.424 LL.B. State Assoc. J.
Caldwell, William I., Jr., (AV) .... '42 '67 C.436 B.A. L.424 J.D. [Caldwell,B.&C.]

Caldwell, Berner & Caldwell, (AV)
100 1/2 Cass Street, P.O. Box 1289, 60098
Telephone: 815-338-3300 Fax: 815-338-0015
Email: caldwell1@ameritech.net
Members of Firm: William I. Caldwell (1908-1971); James E. Berner; William I. Caldwell, Jr.; Jeffrey A. Rouhandeh; Sandra S. Kerrick; Cynthia A. Schaupp.
General Practice. Appellate, Insurance, Real Property, Zoning Law, Estate Planning, Probate, Administrative Law, Litigation. Agricultural Law. Negligence, Personal Injury, Products Liability, Family and Criminal Law, Business and Commercial Law.
Representative Clients: Amcore Bank N.A., Woodstock; Allstate Insurance Co.; American States Insurance Co.; Capitol Indemnity Corp.; Maryland Casualty Co.; Kemper Insurance Group; Northwestern National Insurance Group; C.N.A. Group; Universal Underwriters Insurance Co.; American Home Group.
See Professional Biographies, WOODSTOCK, ILLINOIS

Campion, Curran, Dunlop & Lamb, P.C.
(See Crystal Lake)

Carroll, Peter F., (BV) .... '53 '83 C.339 B.S. L.365 J.D. [Carroll&C.]
Carroll, William M., Jr., (AV) .... '22 '48 C.602 A.B. L.209 J.D. 1720 S. Eastwood Dr.

Carroll & Carroll, (BV)
107 Dean Street, 60098
Telephone: 815-337-4259 Fax: 815-337-2006
Email: pfcarrolllaw@sbcglobal.net URL: http://www.peterfcarroll.com
Peter F. Carroll.
Divorce, Custody, Paternity, Real Estate, Traffic, Criminal, Wills, Estate Planning, Probate.
See Professional Biographies, WOODSTOCK, ILLINOIS

Collins, Jane L., Law Office of '— '97
C.906 B.A. L.589 J.D. 13610 Kishwaukee Valley Rd.
Condon, Joseph P. .... '46 '72 C.436 A.B. L.424 J.D. Cir. J.
Cook, Mark G., (BV) .... '60 '86 C.589 B.S. L.365 J.D. 2200 N. Seminary Dr.
Cook, Sara E., (AV) .... '— '80 C.352 B.A. L.424 J.D. [McKenna S.]
Cowlin, Henry L. .... '24 '52 C.477 B.A. L.912 J.D. Cir. J.
Cross, Richard R., (BV) .... '22 '49 C&L.339 B.S., J.D. 235 Washington St.‡
Cuda, Steven J., (BV) .... '53 '78 C.723 B.A. L.602 J.D. [Hamer,S.&C.]
Dakin, Herbert W. .... '28 '52 C&L.966 B.S., LL.B. P.O. Box 729‡
Duffy, Dolores A. .... '57 '85 C.338 B.S. L.546 J.D. Co. State's Atty.'s. Off.
Facchini, Mark R. .... '77 '02 C.1183 B.A. L.146 J.D. State Atty., Mchenry Co.
Flavin, Raymond M., III .... '61 '92 C&L.801 B.S., J.D. 400 Russel Court

Fleck, Michael J., P.C., Law Office of
(See Huntley)

Floeter, Conrad F. .... '31 '61 C&L.424 A.B., J.D. Cir. J.

Franks, Gerkin & McKenna, P.C., The Law Firm of
(See Marengo)

Franz, James C. .... '32 '63 C.339 B.S. L.146 J.D. Cir. J.
Gable, R. Glenn .... '47 '87 C.1016 B.G.S. L.365 J.D. Asst. State's Atty., Chf., Civil Div.
Gaffney, John W. .... '64 '89 C.999 B.M. L.365 J.D. Asst. State Atty.
Gilbert, Theodore A., (AV) .... '48 '75 C.589 B.A. L.365 J.D. [Weisz B.&G.]
Gitlin, Gunnar J., (BV) .... '62 '87 C.385 B.A. L.424 J.D. [Gitlin]
Gitlin, H. Joseph, (AV) .... '— '59 C&L.209 LL.B. [Gitlin,H.&K.]
Gitlin, Haaff & Kasper, (AV) .... 111 Dean Street

Gitlin Law Firm, The, (BV)
663 East Calhoun Street, 60098-4262
Telephone: 815-338-9401 Fax: 815-338-9403
Email: susan@gitlinlawfirm.com URL: http://www.gitlinlawfirm.com
Gunnar J. Gitlin; Paulette M. Gray. Associate: Ericka B. Pavey.
Family Law, Divorce, Child Custody, Child Support and Matrimonial Law.
See Professional Biographies, WOODSTOCK, ILLINOIS

Goodwin, Camille A., (BV) .... '61 '86 C.221 B.S. L.365 J.D. 400 Russel Court
Gosser, Francis X., Attorney at Law, (BV) '53 '77
C.340 B.A. L.352 J.D. 105 Van Buren St.
Graham, Gordon E. .... '47 '77 C.932 B.A. L.365 J.D. Assoc. Cir. J.
Gray, Paulette M., (BV) .... '69 '96 C.494 B.A. L.365 J.D. [Gitlin]
Gray, Robert L. .... '68 '94 C.338 B.A. L.209 J.D. [▣ Gummerson&R.]
Gummerson, R. Mark, (AV) .... '55 '80 C.177 B.A. L.221 J.D. [Gummerson&R.]

Gummerson & Rausch, (AV)
101 S. Benton Street, Suite 201, 60098
Telephone: 815-337-7700 Fax: 815-337-7990
URL: http://www.lawgr.com
R. Mark Gummerson; Tom E. Rausch. Associates: Philip E. Wand; Robert L. Gray; Jamie Rae Wombacher; Christopher M. Kern.
Criminal Defense, Workers Compensation, Commercial Litigation, Family Law, Personal Injury, Medical Malpractice Defense, Zoning, Trusts and Estates, Corporate Law.
See Professional Biographies, WOODSTOCK, ILLINOIS

Haaff, Chris S., (BV) .... '72 '97 C.291 B.A. L.339 J.D. [Gitlin,H.&K.]
Hamer, Schuh & Cuda, (BV) .... 101 Van Buren Street
Hanrahan, James R., Jr., (AV) .... '29 '55 C.424 B.S.C. L.209 J.D. [O'Brien,H.&F.]
Harrison, James T. .... '58 '91 L.1000 J.D. [Harrison]

Harrison Law Offices, P.C.
684 S. Eastwood Drive (Rt. 47), 60098
Telephone: 815-338-7773 Fax: 815-338-7738
Email: jharrison@harrisonlawoffices.com URL: http://www.harrisonlawoffices.com
James T. Harrison.
Concentrating in Employment Law and Civil Rights, Employment Discrimination, Sexual Harassment, Disability, Gender, Race, Religion, Age, Civil Rights, Unemployment Compensation, Employers' Policy Manuals, Privacy Rights, Severance Agreements, Wrongful Discharge and Retaliatory Discharge, Employment Contracts, Restrictive Covenants, Non-competition Agreements, Wage and Hour Claims, Government Law, Pension Claims, Employment Handbooks, Employer/Employee Rights, Labor Unions, State and Federal Appeals, Professional License-holder Defense.
See Professional Biographies, WOODSTOCK, ILLINOIS

Hecht, James P., (AV) .... '35 '60 C.118 B.A. L.976 LL.B. 100 N. Benton St.
Helt, Gerald L. .... '48 '80 C.746 B.A. L.589 J.D. 1242 Dean St.
Hofmann, Daniel T., (BV) .... '54 '80 C.801 B.S. L.365 J.D. [Michling H.V.P.&W.]
Hoyt, Paige D. .... '— '03 C.350 B.A. L.589 J.D. [▣ Michling H.V.P.&W.]
Hutchinson, Susan Fayette .... '50 '77 C.1082 B.A. L.209 J.D. Cir. J.‡
Januszkiewicz, Edward J. .... '— '03 C.424 B.A. L.365 J.D. [▣ Weisz B.&G.]
Johnson, George E.Q., (AV) .... '17 '41 C&L.597 B.S., J.D. [▣ Mangum,S.&J.]
Johnson, Larry K., (BV) .... '48 '73 C.340 B.A. L.209 J.D. 2030 N. Seminary Ave.
Jones, Richard T., (BV) .... '41 '83 C.499 B.A. L.146 J.D. 138 Cass St.
Kasper, Ian S. .... '68 '98 C.1111 B.A. L.146 J.D. Co. Asst. Pub. Def.
Kasper, Thomas J., (BV) .... '68 '93 C.424 B.A. L.365 J.D. [Gitlin,H.&K.]
Kell, Vette E., (AV) .... '15 '40 C&L.352 B.A., J.D. 10431 Deerpath Rd.‡
Kern, Christopher M. .... '71 '01 C.961 B.A. L.823 J.D. [▣ Gummerson&R.]
Kerrick, Sandra S., (BV) .... '48 '74 C.339 A.B. L.608 J.D. [Caldwell,B.&C.]
Knapp, Peter G. .... '67 '93 C&L.190 B.A., J.D. 248 1/2 North Throop Street
Kraeger, Joyce E. .... '— '95 C.339 B.A. L.424 J.D. [O'Hagan,S.&A.]
Kraft, Patricia C. .... '— '85 C.589 B.S. L.424 J.D. [▣ McKenna S.]
Lancaster, Kelly L. .... '78 '03 C.123 B.A. L.1202 J.D. [▣ Weisz B.&G.]
Lennon, Mary H. .... '— '94 C&L.424 B.A., J.D. Asst. State's Atty.
Loizzo, Thomas F., (BV) '50 '76 C.966 B.S. L.365 J.D.
666 Russell Court, Suite 100A (⊙Waukegan)
Lowrimore, Dona S., (BV) .... '42 '91 C.512 B.A. L.365 J.D. 130 1/2 Cass Street
Madden, William M. .... '35 '61 C&L.424 B.S., J.D. 2019 Mallard Ln.
Mangum, Ronald Scott, (AV) .... '44 '68 C&L.597 B.A., J.D. [Mangum,S.&J.]
Mangum, Smietanka & Johnson, L.L.C., (AV) .... 15106 Pleasant Valley Rd.
Maxwell-Wickett, Janet K. .... '69 '97 C.477 B.B.A. L.209 J.D. Asst. States Atty.
McIntyre, Maureen P. .... '47 '76 C.262 B.A. L.146 J.D. Assoc. Cir. J.

McKenna Storer, (AV)
666 Russel Court Suite 303, 60098-2672 ⊙
Telephone: 815-334-9690 Fax: 815-334-9697
Email: postmaster@mckenna-law.com URL: http://www.mckenna-law.com
Resident Partner: Sara E. Cook. Associate: Patricia C. Kraft.
Administrative Hearings, Appellate, Banking and Lending, Bankruptcy, Civil Rights, Commercial, Construction, Employment, Estate Planning, Fidelity, Insurance Coverage, Legal Malpractice, Mediation Services, Medical Malpractice, National Coordination, Personal Injury, Products Liability, Professional Liability, Surety, Tax and Toxic Tort.
Chicago, Illinois Office: 33 N. LaSalle Street, 14th Floor, 60602-2610. Telephone: 312-558-3900. Fax: 312-558-8348.
Waukegan, Illinois Office: 33 North Country Street, 6th Floor, 60085-4343. Telephone: 847-249-1620. Fax: 847-249-8457.
See Professional Biographies, WOODSTOCK, ILLINOIS

McNerney, Michael J., (BV) .... '48 '74 C.973 B.A. L.424 J.D. 1320 N. Seminary Ave.
Mengeling, Daniel A., Law Offices of, (BV) .. '44 '71 L.365 J.D. 666 Russel Ct., Ste. 214
Michling, Peter D., (BV) .... '54 '82 C.791 B.S. L.365 J.D. [Michling H.V.P.&W.]

Michling Hofmann Vinton Plaza & Wick, P.C., (BV)
101 N. Throop Street, 60098
Telephone: 815-338-9600 Fax: 815-337-4005; 337-3611
Peter D. Michling; Daniel T. Hofmann; Norman D. Vinton; Edwin M. Plaza; Melissa A. Wick;—Angela C. Thuma; Paige D. Hoyt; Jenét González Pequeño.
Personal Injury, Workers Compensation, Criminal Law, Family Law, Civil Litigation, Corporate Law, Residential Real Estate, Commercial Real Estate, Landlord and Tenant Law, Wills and Trusts, Land Use and Development, Zoning, Appellate Practice.
See Professional Biographies, WOODSTOCK, ILLINOIS

Militello, Zanck & Coen, P.C.
(See Crystal Lake)

Murray-Bradshaw, Margaret .... '67 '94 C.347 B.S.P.A. L.982 J.D. [M.M.Bradshaw]
Neese, Michael T., (BV) .... '47 '74 C.98 B.A. L.424 J.D. V.P., Harvard Svgs. Bank
Nelson, Ruth L. .... '13 '56 C.339 L.365 LL.B. 467 Crescent Ct.‡
Nickels, Edward M. .... '30 '77 C&L.209 B.A., J.D. 10518 Shelley Ct.‡
Nuelle, Thomas D., (BV) .... '38 '68 C.791 B.S. L.734 J.D. 121 E. Calhoun St.
O'Brien, Hanrahan & Fay, (AV) .... 722 East Calhoun Streeat (⊙Chicago)

O'Hagan, Smith & Amundsen, (AV)
666 Russel Court, 60098 ⊙
Telephone: 815-337-4900 Fax: 815-337-4910
URL: http://www.osalaw.com
Members of Firm: Joyce E. Kraeger; Heather E. Shea; Elizabeth Felt Wakeman.
Commercial; Commercial Transportation; Appellate; Complex Litigation; Construction; Corporate Transactions; Employment; Extra-Contractual/Insurance Litigation; Healthcare; Insurance Coverage; Personal Lines; Product Liability; Professional Liability; Property Litigation.
Chicago, Illinois Office: 150 North Michigan Avenue, Suite 3300, 60601. Telephone: 312-894-3200. Fax: 312-894-3210.
Rockford, Illinois Office: Stewart Square, 308 West State Street, Suite 320, 61101-1140. Telephone: 815-987-0441. Fax: 815-987-9891.
St. Charles, Illinois Office: 3815 E. Main Street, Suite A-1, 60174-2488. Telephone: 630-587-7910. Fax: 630-587-7960.
Waukegan, Illinois Office: 415 West Washington Street, Suite 204, 60079-0410. Telephone: 847-599-9503. Fax: 847-599-9525.
Milwaukee, Wisconsin Office: 4811 South 76th Street, Suite 305, 53220. Suite 117, 53406-3770. Telephone: 414-282-7103. Fax: 414-282-1830.
See Professional Biographies, WOODSTOCK, ILLINOIS

Pack, Gary .... '50 '76 C.338 B.A. L.365 J.D. States Atty.
Pavey, Ericka B., (CV) .... '73 '99 C.234 B.A. L.1000 J.D. [A Gitlin]
Pequeño, Jenét González .... '— '04 [A Michling H.V.P.&W.]
Perez, Mario J. .... '35 '60 C.339 B.A. L.209 J.D. [M.Perez]
Perez, Mario .... 134 Cass St.
Plaza, Edwin M., (BV) .... '53 '78 C.436 B.A. L.146 J.D. [Michling H.V.P.&W.]
Poehlmann, Theodore A. E., (AV) .... '31 '62 C.339 B.A. L.597 J.D. [T.A.E.Poehlmann]

Poehlmann, Theodore A. E., P.C., Law Office of, (AV) BB
202 West South Street, P.O. Box 271, 60098-0271
Telephone: 815-337-3337 Fax: 815-337-3340
Theodore A. E. Poehlmann;—Philip A. Prossnitz.
General Civil and Trial Practice. Probate, Real Estate, Family, Corporation, Negligence and Zoning Law, Personal Injury.
See Professional Biographies, WOODSTOCK, ILLINOIS

Pollock, Meyers, Eicksteadt & Pulak, Ltd.
(See Marengo)

Poper, Michael C., (BV) .... '43 '68 C&L.339 B.S., J.D. 130 Cass Street
Prather, Sharon L. .... '44 '80 C&L.589 B.A., J.D. Assoc. Cir. J.
Pribla, Wesley R. .... '47 '75 C.801 B.S. L.365 J.D. 138 Cass St.
Prossnitz, Philip A. .... '55 '80 C.228 A.B. L.861 J.D. [A T.A.E.Poehlmann]
Rausch, Tom E., (AV) .... '50 '76 C.880 B.A. L.365 J.D. [Gummerson&R.]
Rech, Carolina A. .... '— '02 C&L.339 B.S., J.D. [A Weisz B.&G.]
Renteria, Jose Antonio .... '67 '00 C.999 B.A. L.339 J.D. [A Weisz B.&G.]

Rinella and Rinella, Ltd.
(See Chicago)

Rouhandeh, Jeffrey A., (BV) .... '58 '85 C&L.801 B.A., J.D. [Caldwell,B.&C.]
Schaupp, Cynthia A., (CV) .... '71 '97 C.352 B.A. L.365 J.D. [Caldwell,B.&C.]
Schermerhorn, Thomas A. .... '35 '72 C&L.424 B.S.C., J.D. Cir. J.
Shea, Heather E., (BV) .... '— '94 C.879 B.A. L.989 J.D. [O'Hagan,S.&A.]
Smietanka, Allan J., (AV) .... '12 '46 C.477 L.365 J.D. [C Mangum,S.&J.]
Stetler, Michael R. .... '78 '03 C&L.339 B.S., J.D. [A Gitlin,H.&K.]
Stevens, Brian K., (BV) .... '63 '91 C.339 B.S. L.209 J.D. 223 Main St.
Sullivan, Michael C. .... '64 '98 C.339 B.A. L.424 J.D. Co. J.
Sullivan, Michael J., (BVⓉ) .... '41 '66 C.177 B.A. L.602 J.D. 2200 Seminary Avenue

Swanson, Martin & Bell
(See Chicago)

Thuma, Angela C. .... '71 '96 C.339 B.S. L.589 J.D [A Michling H.V.P.&W.]
Vinton, Norman D., (BV) .... '58 '89 C.591 B.S. L.209 J.D. [Michling H.V.P.&W.]
Wakeman, Elizabeth Felt .... '— '93 C.339 B.S. L.209 J.D. [O'Hagan,S.&A.]
Wand, Philip E. .... '70 '95 C.589 B.A. L.494 J.D. [A Gummerson&R.]
Weech, Charles P., (BV) .... '57 '89 C.927 B.S. L.589 J.D. Assoc. Cir. J.
Weisz, Daniel L., (BV) ..... '25 '51 L.209 LL.B. 2030 North Seminary Avenue (Route 47)
Weisz, Mitchell R., (BV) .... '57 '81 C.597 B.A. L.146 J.D. [Weisz B.&G.]

Weisz Botto & Gilbert, P.C., (AV)
2030 North Seminary Avenue (Route 47), 60098
Telephone: 815-338-3838 Fax: 815-338-7817
Email: complaw@mc.net URL: http://www.weiszbottogilbert.com
Mitchell R. Weisz; Francisco J. Botto; Theodore A. Gilbert;—James H. Andrle, III; Carolina A. Rech; Edward J. Januszkiewicz; Kelly L. Lancaster; Jose Antonio Renteria.
Personal Injury, Workers Compensation, Family, Criminal Trial, Residential, Industrial and Commercial Real Estate, Zoning and Real Estate Development Law. Civil Litigation and Appellate Practice.
See Professional Biographies, WOODSTOCK, ILLINOIS

Wick, Melissa A. .... '63 '94 C.530 B.A. L.209 J.D. [Michling H.V.P.&W.]
Wilkins, Bruce G., (BV) .... '41 '78 C.589 B.A. L.1151 J.D. [A O'Brien,H.&F.]
Wombacher, Jamie Rae .... '78 '03 C&L.352 B.A., J.D. [A Gummerson&R.]
Zopp, Gerald Martin, Jr. .... '45 '70 C.424 B.S. L.339 J.D. Assoc. Cir. J.

Zukowski, Rogers, Flood & McArdle
(See Crystal Lake)

WORTH, 11,047, *Cook Co.*

Bilanzic, Peter J. .... '54 '80 C.1191 B.S. L.365 J.D. 11555 S. Harlem Ave., Ste. A
Choate, David L. .... '50 '74 C&L.209 B.A., J.D. 7000 W. 111th St.
Coakley, Joseph A. .... '40 '65 C.177 A.B. L.209 J.D. 7000 W. 111th St.
Coughlin, William C. .... '53 '79 C.589 B.A. L.365 J.D. 6844 W. 111th St.
Ebersohl, James L. .... '46 '73 C.339 B.A. L.802 J.D. 11212 S. Harlem St.
Land, James E. .... '28 '56 C.339 L.209 LL.B. 11452 S. Ridgeland Ave.‡
Manella, Samuel J. .... '59 '85 C&L.209 B.S., J.D. 11112 S. Depot St.
McDonnell, J. Brian .... '43 '75 C.424 B.S. L.146 J.D. 11555 S. Harlem Ave.
Meyer, Kurt G. .... '52 '78 C.589 B.A. L.365 J.D. [K.Meyer]
Meyer, Kurt .... 7000 W. 111th St., Ste. 102

Siwek, James J., Law Office of '53 '87 C.221 B.S. L.589 J.D.
6657 W. 111th Street, P.O. Box 367, 60482
Telephone: 708-448-5210; 708-429-3420 Fax: 708-448-7428
Email: siweklaw@comcast.net
Bankruptcy - Chapters 7 and 13, Consumer Fraud, Criminal Law, Misdemeanors and Felonies, Driving While Intoxicated, Drug Crimes, Juvenile Law, Parole and Probation, Family Law, Adoptions, Child Custody, Child Support, Divorce, Domestic Violence, Visitation Rights, General Practice, Real Estate, Buying or Selling a Home, Construction, Landlord and Tenant, Trusts and Estates, Land Trusts, Living Trusts, Guardianships, Powers of Attorney, Wills and Probate.
See Professional Biographies, WORTH, ILLINOIS

Venkus, Gerald A. .... '39 '67 C.339 L.209 J.D. 6965 W. 111th St.
Wojnarowski, Richard R. .... '53 '78 C.999 B.A. L.209 J.D. 11212 S. Harlem

WYOMING, 1,462, *Stark Co.*

Borden, Scott W., (BV) .... '48 '73 C.98 B.A. L.221 J.D. [Borden]
Borden Law Offices, (BV) .... 113 E. Williams St.
Eagelston, Mary Ellen .... '60 '85 C.98 B.S. L.61 J.D. 309 S. Galena
Fehrenbacher, Bruce P., (BV) .... '55 '80 C.338 B.S. L.30 J.D. [Fehrenbacher&F.]
Fehrenbacher, Richard G., (AVⓉ) ...... '52 '78 C.339 B.S. L.1188 J.D. [Fehrenbacher&F.]
Fehrenbacher & Fehrenbacher, P.C., (AVⓉ) ....101 West Williams Street
Rennick, Anne C., (BV) .... '51 '76 C.339 B.S. L.365 J.D. 120 E. William St.

YORKVILLE, * 6,189, *Kendall Co.*

Barliant, Samuel .... '15 '36 C.999 L.365 J.D. Pres., Barliant & Co.
Barnhart, Melissa S., (BV) .... '60 '86 C.338 B.A. L.365 J.D. [Pilmer&B.]

Dreyer, Foote, Streit, Furgason and Slocum, A Professional Association
(See Aurora, Illinois)

Grant, Thomas W., (BV) .... '46 '70 C&L.424 B.B.A., J.D. 200 Hillcrest
Ingemunson, Dallas C., (AV) .... '38 '65 C.339 B.S.E.E. L.209 J.D. States Atty.

Kinnally, Krentz, Loran, Hodge & Herman, P.C.
(See Aurora)

Konen, Jill K. .... '68 '02 C.851 B.S. L.589 J.D. 1107A S. Bridge Street
Kramer, Daniel J., Law Offices of, (BV) '51 '76
C.1024 B.S. L.365 J.D. 1107A S. Bridge St.
Larsen, Kristine Kay, Law Offices of '60 '85
C.36 B.S. L.209 J.D. 215 Hillcrest Ave., Ste. C
Maye, Melissa Ann .... '61 '91 C.686 B.S. L.1059 J.D. 602 Center Parkway
Myers, Gerald E. .... '14 '43 C.46 B.S. L.365 LL.B. 6650A Minkler Rd.‡
Neuendorf, Louis E. .... '23 '49 C&L.436 LL.B. 206 Bridge St. (⊙Sandwich)
Pilmer, Robert P., (BV) .... '58 '83 C.747 B.A. L.221 J.D. [Pilmer&B.]
Pilmer & Barnhart, P.C., (BV) .... 215 Hillcrest Ave., Ste. C
Walsh, Joseph F., Jr. .... '30 '55 C&L.209 B.S., J.D. P.O. Box 477
Wegner, Grant S. .... '52 '78 C.589 B.A. L.300 J.D. Cir. J.
Weis, Eric C. '72 '97 C.578 B.S. L.589 J.D.
Asst. State Atty., Kendall Co. State Atty. Off.
Wilson, James M. .... '45 '77 C.589 B.S. L.365 J.D. Cir. J.

ZION, 22,866, *Lake Co.*

Atsaves, Louis G., (AV) .... '55 '79 C.339 B.A. L.1151 J.D. [L.G.Atsaves] ⊙
Atsaves, Louis G., Ltd., (AV) .... 2613 Sheridan Road (⊙Chicago)
LaBelle, Clifford W. .... '25 '64 C.597 B.S. L.146 J.D. 3130 27th St.
Mitchell, Dorothy J., (BV) .... '39 '85 C.1172 B.A. L.146 J.D. 2610 Sheridan Rd.
Mitchell, Theodore A., (BV) .... '22 '50 C.597 B.S. L.309 J.D. 2610 Sheridan Rd.

INDIANA

CAPITAL: INDIANAPOLIS

Indiana State Bar Association
230 East Ohio Street,
4th Floor
Indianapolis, Indiana 46204
Telephone: 317-639-5465
Fax: 317-266-2588

Index of Towns and Cities Listed by County

*Indicates County Seat

Adams County
Berne
* Decatur

Allen County
* Fort Wayne
Grabill
Monroeville
New Haven
Woodburn

Bartholomew County
* Columbus
Edinburgh
Elizabethtown

Benton County
* Fowler

Blackford County
* Hartford City
Montpelier

Boone County
* Lebanon
Thorntown
Whitestown
Zionsville

Brown County
* Nashville

Carroll County
* Delphi
Flora

Cass County
* Logansport

Clark County
Charlestown
Clarksville
Henryville
* Jeffersonville
Marysville
Memphis
Sellersburg

Clay County
* Brazil

Clinton County
* Frankfort

Crawford County
* English

Daviess County
Odon
* Washington

Dearborn County
Aurora
* Lawrenceburg

Decatur County
* Greensburg

De Kalb County
* Auburn
Butler
Garrett
Waterloo

Delaware County
Albany
* Muncie
Yorktown

Dubois County
Ferdinand
Huntingburg
* Jasper

Elkhart County
Bristol
Elkhart
* Goshen
Middlebury
Nappanee
Wakarusa

Fayette County
* Connersville

Floyd County
Floyd's Knobs
Georgetown
* New Albany

Fountain County
Attica
* Covington
Hillsboro
Veedersburg

Franklin County
Batesville
* Brookville

Fulton County
Akron
* Rochester

Gibson County
Fort Branch
Oakland City
Owensville
* Princeton

Grant County
Gas City
* Marion

Greene County
* Bloomfield
Linton

Hamilton County
Arcadia
Carmel
Cicero
Fishers
* Noblesville
Sheridan
Westfield

Hancock County
Fortville
* Greenfield
McCordsville
New Palestine
Shirley

Harrison County
* Corydon
West Harrison

Hendricks County
Avon
Brownsburg
* Danville
Plainfield

Henry County
Knightstown
Middletown
* New Castle
Shirley

Howard County
* Kokomo

Huntington County
* Huntington
Markle
Roanoke
Warren

Jackson County
* Brownstown
Seymour

Jasper County
Demotte
Remington
* Rensselaer

Jay County
* Portland

Jefferson County
* Madison

Jennings County
North Vernon
* Vernon

Johnson County
Bargersville
Edinburgh
* Franklin
Greenwood
New Whiteland
Trafalgar

Knox County
Bicknell
* Vincennes

Kosciusko County
Nappanee
Syracuse
* Warsaw

LaGrange County
* LaGrange
Wolcottville

Lake County
* Crown Point
Dyer
East Chicago
Gary
Griffith
Hammond
Highland
Hobart
Lake Station
Lowell
Merrillville
Munster
St. John
Schererville
Whiting

La Porte County
* La Porte
Michiana Shores
Michigan City
Rolling Prairie
Westville

Lawrence County
* Bedford
Mitchell

Madison County
Alexandria
* Anderson
Chesterfield
Elwood
Pendleton

Marion County
Beech Grove
* Indianapolis
Speedway

Marshall County
Argos
Bremen
Culver
* Plymouth

Martin County
Loogootee
* Shoals

Miami County
* Peru

Monroe County
* Bloomington
Unionville

Montgomery County
* Crawfordsville

Morgan County
* Martinsville
Monrovia
Mooresville
Morgantown

Newton County
Goodland
* Kentland
Morocco

Noble County
* Albion
Kendallville
Ligonier
Rome City
Wolcottville
Wolflake

Ohio County
* Rising Sun

Orange County
French Lick
* Paoli

Owen County
* Spencer

Parke County
* Rockville

Perry County
* Cannelton
Tell City

Pike County
* Petersburg

Porter County
Beverly Shores
Chesterton
Hebron
Portage
Porter
* Valparaiso

Posey County
Cynthiana
* Mt. Vernon
New Harmony
Poseyville

Pulaski County
* Winamac

Putnam County
Bainbridge
Cloverdale
* Greencastle

Randolph County
Albany
Union City
* Winchester

Ripley County
Batesville
Milan
Osgood
Sunman
* Versailles

Rush County
* Rushville

St. Joseph County
- Granger
- Mishawaka
- New Carlisle
- North Liberty
- Notre Dame
- Osceola
- * South Bend

Scott County
- Austin
- * Scottsburg

Shelby County
- Edinburgh
- Fountaintown
- * Shelbyville

Spencer County
- Dale
- * Rockport
- Santa Claus

Starke County
- * Knox
- North Judson

Steuben County
- * Angola
- Fremont
- Orland

Sullivan County
- * Sullivan

Switzerland County
- * Vevay

Tippecanoe County
- * Lafayette
- West Lafayette

Tipton County
- * Tipton

Union County
- * Liberty
- West College Corner

Vanderburgh County
- * Evansville

Vermillion County
- Clinton
- * Newport

Vigo County
- Lewis
- * Terre Haute

Wabash County
- North Manchester
- * Wabash

Warren County
- * Williamsport

Warrick County
- * Boonville
- Newburgh

Washington County
- * Salem

Wayne County
- Cambridge City
- Centerville
- Hagerstown
- * Richmond

Wells County
- * Bluffton
- Markle
- Ossian

White County
- Brookston
- * Monticello
- Wolcott

Whitley County
- * Columbia City
- South Whitley

*Indicates County Seat

AKRON, 1,045, *Fulton Co.*

Tinkey, Byron L., (BV) '52 '79 C.432 B.S. L.1151 J.D. 10781 W. 900 S.

ALBANY, 2,368, *Delaware & Randolph Cos.*

Beasley, Robert C., (BV) '54 '80 C.894 B.A. L.345 J.D. Gen. Coun., Paws, Inc.

ALBION, * 2,284, *Noble Co.*

Hagen, Steven C., (BV) '51 '78 C.347 B.A. L.345 J.D. [Firm of Hagen&H.]
Hagen & Hagen, Law Firm of, (BV) 104 East Main Street
Kramer, Michael J. '55 '83 C.63 B.S. L.201 J.D. Noble Superior Court
Miller, Diane Marie '56 '89 C.679 B.S. L.285 J.D. [D.M.Miller]
Miller, Diane M. 100 W. Main St.
Prickett, James M., (BV) '46 '71 C.679 B.S. L.145 J.D. 117 West Jefferson Street (⊙Fort Wayne)
Probst, Robert C. '34 '60 C.20 A.B. L.879 LL.B. Sr. J.
Spindler, Stephen '43 '73 C&L.569 A.B., J.D. Supr. Ct. J.

ALEXANDRIA, 6,260, *Madison Co.*

Kirkwood, Leeanna K., Law Office of, (CV) '— '86 C.679 B.A. L.879 J.D. 111 W. Washington St.

ANDERSON, * 59,734, *Madison Co.*

Alger, David E., (CV) '48 '82 C.63 B.S. L.1119 J.D. 111 E. 9th St.
Alley, Edward B., (BV) '47 '73 C.63 B.S. L.345 J.D. 2 W. 8th St. (⊙Elwood)
Anderson, Harold J. '07 '36 C.347 A.B. L.1119 J.D. 602 Natl. City Bank Bldg.‡

Anderson, James O., (BV) '55 '80 C.1288 B.A. L.345 J.D.
800 Main Street Suite 210, 46016
Telephone: 765-643-3100 Fax: 765-643-0609
Email: jamand@indy.net URL: http://www.lawyers.com/janderson
Wills, Probate, Trusts and Estates, Estate Planning, Asset Protection, Guardianships, Banking, Real Estate, Estate Administration, Business Law, Business Planning, Contracts, Lawsuits, Debtor and Creditor, Collections, Entrepreneurial Business Law, Partnerships, Corporate Law, Limited Liability Company Law, Small Business, Real Estate Litigation, Probate Litigation, Taxation Law and Civil Trials in all Courts.
References: Community Bank; National City Bank.

See Professional Biographies, ANDERSON, INDIANA

Austin, Michael D., (BV) '51 '76 C.108 B.A. L.345 J.D. [Hulse,L.H.A.&S.]
Austin, Robert L., (AV) '18 '42 C.347 A.B. L.1119 J.D. [🄲 Busby,A.C.&F.]
Bagot, Free & Shearer, P.C., (BV) 522 Historic W. 8th St.
Bash, Richard M., Attorney at Law '45 '99 C.679 B.S. L.347 J.D. 33 W. 10th St., Ste. LL4
Baylor, Paul E. '71 '98 C.894 B.A. L.345 J.D. 1106 Meridian Plaza
Beeman, Thomas M., Attorney at Law, (BV) '60 '85 C.63 B.S. L.345 J.D. 33 W. 10th St., Ste. 200
Bennett, Mark A., (CV) '56 '82 C.679 B.A. L.347 J.D. 1106 Meridian Plza.

Bingham, Farrer & Wilson, A Professional Corporation
(See Elwood)

Blevins, John M., (BV) '47 '74 C.992 B.A. L.345 J.D. 205 Historic W. 8th St.
Braddock, Charles F., (BV) '40 '70 C.698 B.S. L.213 J.D. [C.Braddock]
Braddock, Charles, Law Office, (BV) 1106 Meridian Plz., Ste. 109
Brinkman, Jack L. '50 '75 C.347 B.S. L.345 J.D. Supr. Ct. J.
Broderick, Thomas J., Jr., (BV) '53 '78 C.63 B.S. L.345 J.D. 34 W. 8th St.
Brown, Katherine S. '75 '01 C.346 B.S. L.345 J.D. [🄰 Busby,A.C.&F.]
Builta, Jonathan R., (BV) '56 '81 C.894 A.B. L.345 J.D. 1001 Jackson St.
Burke, Thomas P., (BV) '45 '72 C&L.494 B.A., J.D. 410 W. Ninth St.
Burton, J. Bayne, (BV) '16 '52 L.345 LL.B. 459 Union Bldg., 1106 Meridian Plz.‡

Busby, Austin, Cooper & Farr, (BV)
800 Main Street, Suite 200, 46016-1564
Telephone: 765-644-2891 Fax: 765-644-2894
URL: http://www.bacf.com
Members of Firm: Lawrence M. Busby (1898-1983); John A. Farr, Jr. (1926-1990); Ralph E. Sipes; D. Eric Hall. Associate: Katherine S. Brown. Of Counsel: Robert L. Austin; Philip S. Cooper.
General Civil, Trial and Appellate Practice. Real Estate, Wills and Probate and Estate Planning, Trusts and Estates, Asset Protection, Guardianships, Corporation, Banking, Creditors Rights, Business Litigation, Business Planning, Business Law, Contracts, Lawsuits, Business Enterprises, Partnerships, Limited Liability Companies, Starting a Business, Buying and Selling a Business, Debt and Credit, Creditor Rights, Collections, Banking and Finance, Mediation.
General Counsel for: Saint John's Health System Corporation; Saint John's Medical Center; Warner Press, Inc.
Local Counsel for: National City Bank, Indiana; Brockway Glass Co.; The Continental Insurance Cos.; Commercial Union Insurance Group; General Motors Corp.; Ford Motor Company.

See Professional Biographies, ANDERSON, INDIANA

Bybee, Elizabeth Bashaw, (BV) '49 '84 C.347 L.345 LL.B. 130 W. 8th St.
Byer, C. William, Jr., (BV) '56 '85 C.347 B.S. L.1187 J.D. [Byer&B.]
Byer & Byer, (AV) Six W. Eighth St.
Cage, Christopher A., (BV) '71 '96 C.63 B.A. L.345 J.D. [🄰 Hulse,L.H.A.&S.]
Campbell, Craig B. '38 '64 C.210 A.B. L.1119 LL.B. [Howard&W.]
Carroll, Dennis D. '47 '74 C.992 B.A. L.345 J.D. Supr. Ct. J.
Chapin, Michael W. '57 '83 C.63 B.S. L.347 J.D. 940 Meridian Plaza
Clark, Sharon C., Law Office of, (BV) '43 '69 C.992 B.A. L.345 J.D. 632 Jackson Street
Clem, Thomas L. '52 '81 C.63 B.S. L.345 J.D. Co. Ct. J.
Clifford, William R. '30 '55 C.347 B.S. L.1119 J.D. 120 W. 10th St.‡
Coker, James R. '37 '61 C.602 S.J. L.255 A.M. 730 Glenwood Lane‡
Cooper, Philip S., (AV) '19 '48 C.347 B.S. L.345 J.D. [🄲 Busby,A.C.&F.]
Cotton, Jane G., (CV) '68 '93 C.347 B.A. L.1119 J.D. [J.G.Cotton]
Cotton, Jane G., P.C., (CV) 2 West Eighth Street
Cunningham, Patrick J., (BV) '38 '69 C.435 B.S. L.345 J.D. 931 Meridian Street, Suite 505

Davis, James E., Attorney at Law
(See Greenfield)

Davisson, Daniel S., (BV) '37 '62 C.347 B.S. L.1119 J.D. [Davisson&D.]
Davisson, Leslie A., (CV) '58 '84 C&L.221 B.S., J.D. 1111 Meridian Plz.
Davisson, Richard F., (AV) '30 '58 C.347 B.S. L.1119 J.D. [Davisson&D.]
Davisson, William C., (CV) '61 '88 C.347 B.A. L.879 J.D. [Davisson&D.]
Davisson & Davisson, Professional Corporation, (AV) 1111 Meridian Plaza
Decker, Philip G., II, (BV) '44 '70 C.210 B.A. L.1119 J.D. [Decker,L.&M.]
Decker, Lawyer & Maynard, (BV) 505 W. 9th St.

DeFur Voran LLP
(See Muncie)

DeLey, Lisa '69 '97 C.63 B.S. L.117 J.D. 403 W. 8th St.
Dickmann, Charles H., (BV) '19 '50 C.347 B.S. L.345 J.D. 1001 Jackson‡
Dickmann, John P. '30 '58 C.347 B.S. L.1119 J.D. 33 W. 10th St.‡
Dietzen, Gregory A., (CV) '46 '73 C.63 B.S. L.345 J.D. 111 E. 9th St.
Dixon, R. C., (CV) '— '87 C.63 B.S. L.345 J.D. P.O. Box 2682
Dudley, Mark K., (BV) '65 '90 C&L.347 B.A., J.D. 403 West Eighth Street
Eads, Kevin M., (BV) '55 '81 C.63 B.S. L.345 J.D. 405 W. 8th St.
Eisele, John E., (AV) '38 '68 C.347 A.B. L.345 J.D. 200 E. 11th St.
Flatt-Moore, Nancy J. '59 '98 C.63 B.A. L.345 J.D. Madison Co. Pros. Off.
Fortune, Kimberly D. '61 '89 C&L.347 B.A., J.D. UAW-GM Legal Servs. Plan
Fowler, Ronald K., (BV) '37 '61 C.347 B.S. L.1119 J.D. 1106 Meridian Street, Suite 401
Free, Wade H., Jr. '17 '40 C.347 B.S. L.1119 LL.B. [Bagot,F.&S.] ‡
Freeman, James E., Jr., (BV) '44 '69 C.885 B.A. L.1119 J.D. 1001 Jackson Street
Garman, John G., Jr., (CV) '62 '90 C.347 B.A. L.879 J.D. [Garman]
Garman Law Offices P.C., (CV) 109 E. 9th St.
Gaus, Charles F., (AV) '22 '48 C.346 B.S. L.1119 J.D. 4309 S. Layton Rd.
Goldy, Susan E. '54 '85 C.354 B.M. L.831 J.D. (adm. in PA; not adm. in IN) Sr. V.P. & Gen. Coun., Delco Remy International

Gonzalez, Jill A., Attorney At Law
(See Muncie)

Gustin, Robert L. '45 '73 C.63 B.S. L.36 J.D. National City Bank
Hall, D. Eric, (BV) '52 '77 C.992 B.A. L.345 J.D. [Busby,A.C.&F.]
Hamer, Thomas E., (BV) '53 '78 C.992 B.A. L.608 J.D. [T.E.Hamer]
Hamer, Thomas E., Law Office, (BV) 2101 E. 8th St.
Handley, E. Lee, (CV) '28 '85 C.1229 B.B.A. L.345 J.D. 940 Meridian Plaza
Hardacre, Stephen R., (BV) '50 '75 C.347 B.S. L.345 J.D. [Hulse,L.H.A.&S.]
Hasler, Samuel C., (CV) '60 '87 C.63 B.S. L.879 J.D. 916 Main Street
Hopper, David W. '49 '78 C.679 B.A. L.345 J.D. Co. Ct. J., Madison Co. Govt. Ctr.
Howard, Max, (AV) '39 '70 C.347 B.S. L.345 J.D. [Howard&W.]
Howard & Walker, (AV) 800 Main St., Suite 208
Hughel, George K. '19 '48 C.679 B.S. L.1119 J.D. 241 Somerville Rd.‡
Hulse, Thomas L., (BV) '39 '66 C.63 B.S. L.345 J.D. [Hulse,L.H.A.&S.]
Hulse, Lacey, Hardacre, Austin & Shine, P.C., (BV) 911 Meridian Plaza
Hurst, Donald H. '41 '96 C.347 L.345 J.D. 33 W. 10th Street
Julian, Leisa I. '59 '89 C.63 B.Sc. L.347 J.D. City Controller
Kelley, Kathryn '56 '81 C.249 B.A. L.345 J.D. UAW-GM Legal Servs. Plan
Kelley, Vincent F. '15 '38 L.383 LL.B. 403 Historic W. 8th St.‡
Kreegar, William C., (BV) '49 '75 C.347 A.B. L.192 J.D. 1424 East 8th Street
Lacey, Michael C., (BV) '48 '73 C.932 B.A. L.1119 J.D. [Hulse,L.H.A.&S.]
Lanane, Timothy S., (BV) '52 '77 C.63 B.S. L.345 J.D. City Atty.
Lawler, William F., Jr., (BV) '26 '56 C.679 B.S. L.345 J.D. 2219 Starlight Drive
Lawyer, Lynne H., (BV) '56 '82 C.347 B.S. L.345 J.D. [Decker,L.&M.]
Lockwood, Jeffrey A., (AV) '45 '74 C.63 B.S. L.345 J.D. 200 E. 11th St., Ste. 100A
Long, Douglas R., (BV) '49 '78 C.63 B.S. L.8 J.D. 403 Historical W. 8th St.
Longnaker, John W., III, (CV) '67 '93 C.894 A.B. L.347 J.D. [J.Longnaker]
Longnaker, John, Law Office of, (CV) 940 Meridian St.
Maynard, Mark D., (BV) '50 '81 C.347 A.B. L.345 J.D. [Decker,L.&M.]
McCarty, William D., (BV) '43 '79 C.894 B.A. L.345 J.D. 34 W. 8th St.
McNabney, Ronald L., (BV) '39 '76 C.63 M.A. L.345 J.D. 917 Meridian Street
Miller, Alan R., (BV) '60 '87 C.894 A.B. L.879 J.D. [Miller&M.]
Miller, Robert W., (AV) '31 '56 C.894 B.A. L.1119 J.D. [Miller&M.]
Miller & Miller, (AV) 522 W. 8th St., Ste. B
Motluck, Mark E. '57 '93 C.424 B.B.A. L.472 J.D. 3113 Wayside Ln.
Nave, Irma Hampton, (BV) '46 '76 C.63 B.A. L.345 J.D. 507 W. 9th St.
Newman, Thomas, Jr. '41 '72 C.30 B.A. L.345 J.D. Supr. Ct. J.
Nicholls, Jeffrey M. '53 '79 C&L.879 B.A., J.D. 3320 Main St., Ste. K
Norton, William J., (BV) '28 '54 C.602 B.S. L.276 J.D. 34 W. 8th St.
Pancol, G. George, (BV) '51 '77 [Pancol&P.]
Pancol, Geo. G., (BV) '26 '53 C.347 A.B. L.345 LL.B. [Pancol&P.]
Pancol & Pancol, (BV) 34 W. 8th St.
Peck & Peck 28 W. 9th St.
Phillippe, Donald R. '33 '64 C.63 B.S. L.345 J.D. 202 Mill Stream Lane
Puckett, David L., (BV) '47 '86 C.63 B.S. L.345 J.D. 16 East 9th Street
Quickel, Danl. D. '13 '38 C.165 B.A. L.345 J.D. 608 Central Way‡
Ramsey, Shawn D., Law Office of, (CV) '72 '95 C.63 B.A. L.345 J.D. 33 W. 10th Street
Rector, NiCale, Law Office of '75 '01 C.347 B.S. L.345 J.D. 1106 Meridian Plaza Suite 466
Reisert-Wehmueller, Mary Ann '62 '90 C.679 B.A. L.879 J.D. UAW-GM Legal Servs. Plan
Robbins, Larry W. '40 '76 C.63 B.S. L.345 J.D. Co. J.
Rock, Mary J. '59 '88 C.63 B.S. L.347 J.D. [🄲 Howard&W.]
Rock, Robert W., (BV) '61 '88 C&L.347 B.A., J.D. 34 W. 8th St.
Sabina, James M. '69 '97 C.999 B.S.E.E. L.345 J.D. UAW-GM Legal Servs. Plan
Saltzmann, Eric George, (CV) '68 '97 C.992 B.A. L.851 J.D. 403 W. 8th St.
Schuyler, Billie W. C., (AV) '21 '55 C.63 B.S. L.345 J.D. [Schuyler]
Schuyler, Stephen W., (BV) '53 '82 C.63 B.S. L.345 J.D. [Schuyler]
Schuyler Professional Corporation, (AV) 200 E. 11th St.
Scott, Daryl E., (BV) '28 '56 C&L.879 B.A., J.D. 1106 Meridian
Scott, John T., (BV) '35 '61 C.347 B.S. L.1119 LL.B. 931 Meridian St.
Shearer, William M., (BV) '50 '79 C.347 B.S. L.1137 J.D. [Bagot,F.&S.]
Shine, Gerald P., Jr., (BV) '42 '68 C.210 B.A. L.930 J.D. [Hulse,L.H.A.&S.]
Sipes, Ralph E., (BV) '53 '84 C.63 B.S. L.345 J.D. [Busby,A.C.&F.]
Smith, Steven C., (BV) '44 '78 C.641 B.A. L.1241 J.D. 936 Meridian Plaza

Smith, Theodore F., Jr., (AV) '51 '76 C&L.602 B.A., J.D.
215 Historic West 8th, 46016-1374
Telephone: 765-644-8410; 800-296-2290 Fax: 765-643-8613 URL: http://www.tedsmithlaw.com
Email: tsmith@tedsmithlaw.com URL: http://www.lawyers.com/tedsmithlaw
Social Security Disability, Personal Injury, Wrongful Death.

See Professional Biographies, ANDERSON, INDIANA

Sorg, Edward A., (CV) '64 '89 C&L.347 B.S., J.D. [🄰 C.Braddock]
Spencer, Fredrick R. '38 '71 C.63 B.S. L.345 J.D. Cir. J.
Spurgeon, Michael W., (CV) '53 '79 C.347 B.A. L.1119 J.D. Mng. Atty., UAW-GM Legal Servs. Plan
Taylor, Samuel D., (CV) '60 '90 C.679 B.A. L.347 J.D. 1001 Jackson Street
Walker, Richard B., (BV) '51 '77 C.347 L.345 J.D. [Howard&W.]
Warner, Angela Gayle '74 '99 C&L.347 B.A., J.D. 911 Meridian Plz.
Webb, Scott L., (CV) '52 '77 C.303 B.A. L.345 J.D. 412 W. 9th St.
Whitehead, Wm. Catlin '17 '41 C&L.477 A.B., J.D. 10 W. 8th St.‡
Wilson, Ardeth, (AV) '34 '82 C.303 B.A. L.345 J.D. 940 Meridian Plaza
Withers, Michael R., (CV) '52 '77 C.63 B.S. L.345 J.D. 33 W 10 St Ste 520
Woodruff, Randall L., (BV) '54 '85 C.347 B.A. L.345 J.D. 109 E. 9th St.
Woolbert, Marianne, (CV) '61 '87 C.108 B.A. L.201 J.D. 200 E. 11th St., Ste. 101

ANGOLA, * 7,344, *Steuben Co.*

Beech, Beth E. '54 '88 C.434 B.S. L.851 J.D. (adm. in OH; not adm. in IN) Pres., Norwest BK-Ind., N.A.

Benson, Craig T., (BV) '47 '72 C.861 B.A. L.846 J.D.
109 South Martha Street, 46703
Telephone: 260-665-6111 Fax: Available Upon Request
General Civil Practice. Estate Planning, Probate and Real Estate Law. Trials.
Representative Client: Steuben County Board of Aviation Commissioners.
See Professional Biographies, ANGOLA, INDIANA

Berger, John R. .... '29 '53 C.317 B.S. L.309 J.D. 112 S. Wayne St.
Bryan, William B., (BV) .... '47 '72 C&L.347 A.B., J.D. [Bryan]
Bryan Law Office, (BV) .... 215 W. Maumee Street

Burns, James W., (BV) '54 '79 C.347 A.B. L.1119 J.D.
213 W. Maumee Street, 46703-1424
Telephone: 260-665-6611 Fax: 260-665-2887
Email: burnsjw@hotmail.com
Criminal Law, Domestic Relations, Divorce, Civil Litigation and Probate, Business and Corporate Law.
See Professional Biographies, ANGOLA, INDIANA

Coffey, Randy, (BV) .... '55 '79 C.854 B.A. L.345 J.D. Mag. J., Supr. and Cir. Ct.s
Fee, William .... '54 '80 C.679 B.A. L.930 J.D. Supr. Ct. J.
Forbes, Randal S., (CV) .... '60 '87 C.210 B.A. L.345 J.D. [Forbes]
Forbes Law Office, (CV) .... P.O. Box 374
Gutstein, Alfred R., (BV) ..... '32 '58 C.976 B.A. L.597 J.D. 114 E. Maumee St., Ste. 101
Hendrickson, Angela L. .... '72 '02 C.679 L.607 J.D. Steuben Co. Pros. Atty.

Henry, David L., (CV) '48 '75 C.344 B.A. L.345 J.D.
1275 N. 290 West, 46703-9004
Telephone: 260-668-8868 Fax: 260-668-8868
Email: angolahenry@hotmail.com URL: http://www.dhenrylaw.com
Business Law, Corporate Law, Real Estate Law, Business litigation, Contracts, Wills and Probate, Elder Law, Trusts and Estates, Estate Planning, Social Security Disability, Civil Litigation.
See Professional Biographies, ANGOLA, INDIANA

Hess, Michael W., (BV) .... '52 '81 C.475 B.S. L.1187 J.D. Chf. Dep. Pros. Atty.
Kaiser, Brian W., (CVⓉ) .... '57 '83 C.5 B.A. L.851 J.D. 207 Hoosier Dr., Ste. 6B
Mayer, Steven C., (CV) .... '55 '81 C.381 B.S. L.608 J.D. 227 W. Maumee St.
Milliken, John C., (BVⓉ) '49 '74 C.608 B.A. L.851 J.D.
300 Lane 100A Pine Canyon Lk.
Morrissey, Michael L., (BV) .... '48 '74 C.347 B.S. L.345 J.D. 114 E. Maumee

Roebuck & Associates, P.C.
(See Ft. Wayne)

Shively, Donald P., (BV) .... '54 '81 C.679 B.A. L.1119 J.D. Olde Opera House Block
Shoup, Kim Elloitt, (BV) .... '51 '80 C.347 B.A. L.1187 J.D. 112 S. Wayne St.
Shoup, Wilson E., (BV) .... '15 '50 C.347 A.B. L.273 LL.B. 112 S. Wayne St.
Stout, Allen R., (BV) .... '44 '81 C.854 B.A. L.1187 J.D. [Stout,W.&Z.]

Stout, Wheeler & Zabona, (BV)
118 W. Maumee Street, 46703
Telephone: 260-665-5717 Fax: 260-665-1122
URL: http://www.swzlaw.com
Members of Firm: Allen R. Stout; Christopher J. Wheeler; Linda Ann Zabona.
General Practice, DUI, Driving While Intoxicated, Drug Crimes, Juvenile Crimes, Parole and Probation, Traffic Violations, White Collar Crime, Criminal Law, Domestic Violence, Adoptions, Child Custody, Child Support, Divorce, Domestic Violence, Visitation Rights, Prenuptial Agreements, Unmarried Couples, Guardianships, Automobile Accidents, Dog Bites, Head and Spinal Injuries, Nursing Home Abuse, Sexual Abuse, Slip and Fall, Trucking Accidents, Wrongful Death, Class Actions, Construction Accidents, Personal Injury, Railroad Accidents, Natural Disasters, Business Enterprises, General Business, Starting a Business, Buying or Selling a Home, Construction, Eminent Domain, Environmental, Landlord and Tenant, Zoning and Land Use, Neighbors and Pets, Natural Disasters, Asset Protection, Estate Planning, Wills and Probate.
See Professional Biographies, ANGOLA, INDIANA

Trennepohl, Donald L. .... '21 '51 C.347 B.S. L.1119 J.D. 802 S. Washington St.‡
Wheat, Allen N. .... '49 '76 C.347 B.S. L.345 J.D. Cir. J.
Wheat, Latriealle .... '48 '77 C&L.347 A.S., LL.B. 107 W. Maumee St.
Wheeler, Christopher J. .... '67 '95 [Stout,W.&Z.]
Wible, William R., (BV) .... '53 '79 C.679 B.A. L.345 J.D. 213 N. Martha St.

Wilson, Thomas E., (AV) '48 '73 C.303 B.A. L.1119 J.D.
109 South Martha Street, 46703-1916
Telephone: 260-665-5715 Fax: Available Upon Request
Probate and Estate Planning, and Real Estate Law.
Representative Client: First Federal Savings & Loan Assn. of Angola.
Reference: First Federal Savings & Loan Assn. of Angola.
See Professional Biographies, ANGOLA, INDIANA

Zabona, Linda Ann .... '67 '00 C.63 B.S. L.1187 J.D. [Stout,W.&Z.]

ARCADIA, 1,747, *Hamilton Co.*

Booker, Joe D. .... '32 '64 C.347 A.B. L.345 LL.B. Rte. 1‡

ARGOS, 1,642, *Marshall Co.*

Swihart, Beverly H. .... '30 '55 C&L.912 B.A., LL.B. 20001 Gumwood Rd.‡

ATTICA, 3,457, *Fountain Co.*

Barnhart, Keith E., (BV) .... '26 '50 C.210 A.B. L.597 J.D. [Barnhart&O.]
Barnhart & O'Connor, Law Office of, (BV) .... 121 West Main Street

Blackburn & Green
(See Fort Wayne)

Morrison, Stephen D., (BV) .... '41 '66 C.210 B.A. L.1119 LL.B. P.O. Box 128
O'Connor, Thomas P., (BV) .... '50 '76 C.339 B.A. L.345 J.D. [Barnhart&O.]

AUBURN, * 12,074, *De Kalb Co.*

Blackburn & Green
(See Fort Wayne)

Blythe, Neal R. .... '77 '03 C.347 B.A. L.1119 J.D. [Ⓐ Mefford&W.]
Bosworth, Eugene C., (CV) .... '53 '92 C.260 B.S.B.A. L.74 J.D. 129 S.Main Street
Brown, Monte L., Law Office of, (BV) .... '53 '78 C.932 B.A. L.345 J.D. 305 E. Ninth St.
Franzman, Terry '46 '78 C.112 B.A. L.770 J.D.
(adm. in CA; not adm. in IN) 316 Iwo St.
Grimm, John C. .... '42 '66 C.347 B.S. L.1119 LL.B. [Grimm&G.]
Grimm, Kurt Bentley, (BV) .... '60 '88 C.317 B.L.S. L.1187 J.D. [Grimm&G.]
Grimm & Grimm, P.C., (BV) .... 101 E. 9th St.
Hippensteel-Hines, Lee A. '58 '89
C.347 B.A. L.1119 J.D. V.P. and Tr. Off., Peoples Federal Svgs. Bk.
Kraus, Anthony L., (BV) .... '65 '90 C.679 B.A. L.347 J.D. [Likes&K.]
Kruse, Andrew D. .... '73 '98 C.679 B.A. L.1119 J.D. 143 E. 9th. St.
Kruse, David A., (BV) .... '43 '68 C.347 A.B. L.1119 J.D. 6808 County Road 31
Kruse, Derald D., (BV) '44 '69
C.347 B.A. L.1119 J.D. Corp. Coun., Ambassador Steel Corp.
Likes, Kevin L., (BV) .... '57 '83 C.347 B.S. L.345 J.D. [Likes&K.]
Likes & Kraus, (BV) .... 129 S. Main St.

McCanna, James P., (AV) '47 '74 C.276 A.B. L.345 J.D.
1320 South Grandstaff, P.O. Box 543, 46706
Telephone: 260-925-3787 FAX: 260-925-4884
Email: jpmccanna123@mchsi.com
Wills, Trusts and Estates, Real Estate, Banks and Banking, Corporate, Commercial, Elder Law, Civil and Family Mediation.
See Professional Biographies, AUBURN, INDIANA

Mefford, Donald T., (AV) .... '29 '56 C.894 B.A. L.347 J.D. [Mefford&W.]

Mefford and Weber, P.C., (AV)
130 East Seventh Street, 46706-1839
Telephone: 260-925-2300 Facsimile: 260-925-2610
URL: http://www.lawmw.com
Donald T. Mefford; W. Erik Weber;—Neal R. Blythe.
Personal Injury, Trial and Civil Practice. Banking, Commercial, Corporation, Probate and Estate Planning, Elder Law, Taxation, Real Estate, Environmental, Municipal and Zoning Law, Domestic Relations, Civil and Domestic Relations Mediation.
See Professional Biographies, AUBURN, INDIANA

Nugen, J. Bryan, (BV) .... '67 '93 C.347 B.A. L.1003 J.D. 221 S. Main St
Poff, Phyllis G., (BV) .... '30 '53 C.347 L.365 LL.B. 211 N. Cedar St.

Roebuck & Associates, P.C.
(See Ft. Wayne)

Romero, Frederic L., (BV) .... '31 '71 C.854 B.S. L.607 J.D. 110 W. 8th St.
Smith, John Charles Thompson .... '69 '98 C.63 B.S. L.879 J.D. P.O. Box 686
Smith, John Martin .... '39 '65 C&L.347 B.S., J.D. 12th & Jackson St.

Stout, Wheeler & Zabona
(See Angola)

Taylor, Hugh N., (BV) .... '47 '86 C.347 B.S. L.851 J.D. P.O. Box 728

Trotter Law Office
(See Fort Wayne)

Turner, Jeffrey L., (AV) '52 '77 C.63 B.S. L.345 J.D.
Vice President Administration & General Counsel, Metal Technologies, Inc.
VanHorne, Grant M., (AV) .... '37 '63 C.894 A.B. L.345 J.D. [G.VanHorne]

VanHorne, Grant, (AV)
112 South Cedar Street, 46706-0523
Telephone: 260-925-1966 Telecopier: 260-925-6166
Email: gvh@mchsi.com
Member of Firm: Grant M. VanHorne.
General Civil, Trial, Corporate, Employment, Probate, Environmental, Trucking Law.
Representative Clients: NUCOR Corporation; Herbert E. Orr Company; Cooper Tire & Rubber Company; Evans Trucking; Broadview Lumber Co., Inc.

Wallace, Kevin P. .... '52 '79 C.602 B.A. L.851 J.D. Supr. Ct. J.
Weber, W. Erik, (BV) .... '71 '98 C.1024 B.S. L.365 J.D. [Mefford&W.]

AURORA, 3,965, *Dearborn Co.*

Byers, Paul R. '52 '88 C.1032 B.A. L.336 J.D.
(adm. in ID; not adm. in IN) Natl. Legal Professional Assoc.
Denmure, Law Office, (BV) .... 402 Second Street
Denmure, Douglas R., (BV) .... '40 '66 C.347 B.S. L.345 J.D. [Denmure]
McGill, Arnold L., (BV) .... '45 '70 C.473 B.A. L.150 J.D. 437 2nd St.
Meyer, Anthony C. .... '33 '60 C.347 B.S. L.1119 LL.B. Ret. Sr. J.‡
Stratman, Jeffrey E. .... '71 '98 C.347 B.S. L.1119 J.D. [Ⓐ Denmure]
Willenborg, Edward F. '11 '41 C.973 L.1340 LL.B.
(adm. in OH; not adm. in IN) R.R. 2, Box 148C‡

AUSTIN, 4,727, *Scott Co.*

Campbell, Raleigh, Jr. .... '64 '00 C.235 B.A. L.1187 J.D. [Campbell]
Campbell Law Office .... P.O. Box 130
Payne, Joseph Leon, (BV) .... '58 '83 C.347 B.A. L.345 J.D. [J.L.Payne]
Payne, Joseph L., Law Office of, (BV) .... 377 W. Main St.

AVON, 6,248, *Hendricks Co.*

Baker, Rex E., (BV) '57 '87 C.303 B.A. L.1137 J.D.
7388 Business Center Dr., Ste. 480
Gregory, Susan B. .... '65 '91 C.679 B.S.B.A. L.339 J.D. 1433 Cherry Tree Rd.
Gundlach, Philip L. .... '60 '87 C.966 B.A. L.879 J.D. 7071 E. US Hwy. 36
Hubble, Harry M. .... '38 '68 C.679 B.S. L.345 J.D. 2237 Gray Birch Court
Webb, Russell M., III .... '— '01 L.345 J.D. [Webb&W.]
Webb, Russell M., Jr., (BV) .... '46 '74 C.347 B.A. L.345 J.D. [Webb&W.]
Webb & Webb, Attorneys at Law, (BV) .... 7386 Business Center Dr.

BAINBRIDGE, 682, *Putnam Co.*

Chappell, Bill G. '19 '64 C.420 L.362 LL.B.
(adm. in FL; not adm. in IN) R. R. 1, Box 114‡

BARGERSVILLE, 2,120, *Johnson Co.*

Buehl, Robert T., (BV) .... '29 '63 C.347 A.B. L.345 J.D. P.O. Box 515

BATESVILLE, 6,033, *Franklin & Ripley Cos.*

Burns, Debra L., (BV) '— '89 C.350 B.A. L.345 J.D.
V.P. & Sr. Lit. Coun., Hillenbrand Industries, Inc.
Craig, David W., (BV) .... '59 '85 C&L.347 B.S., J.D. P.O. Box 340
DeMaynadier, Patrick D., (AVⓉ) '60 '85 C&L.893 B.A., J.D.
(adm. in TX; not adm. in IN) V.P., Gen. Coun. & Sec., Hillenbrand Industries, Inc.
Dorenbusch, John F., Jr., (BV) .... '62 '87 C.210 B.A. L.602 J.D. 616 E. Pearl St.
Edison, Sheri H. '57 '83 C.800 B.A. L.597 J.D.
(adm. in OH; not adm. in IN) V.P. & Gen. Coun., Hill-Rom Co., Inc.
Fledderman, Lynnette M. .... '66 '92 C.679 B.S. L.347 J.D. 137-B S. Main St.
Gloyd, Carol A. .... '— '95 C.679 B.S. L.347 J.D. P.O. Box 340
Hoying, Joyce A. .... '74 '99 C.188 B.S. L.893 J.D. Corp. Coun., Hill-Rom Co., Inc.
Jones, Mark E., Law Offices, (BV) .... '56 '81 C.894 A.B. L.879 J.D. 616 E. Pearl St.
Junker, Martha E. .... '58 '84 C.276 B.S.F.S. L.150 J.D. Forethought Ctr.
Kellerman, Clay M. .... '72 '00 C&L.347 B.A., J.D. [Kellerman]
Kellerman, John L., (AV) .... '42 '67 C.347 A.B. L.1119 J.D. [Kellerman]
Kellerman, John L., II, (BV) .... '68 '93 C&L.347 B.A., J.D. [Kellerman]

Kellerman Law Firm, (AV)
105 East George Street, P.O. Box 116, 47006
Telephone: 812-934-4334 Fax: 812-934-6144
Email: kellerman@nalu.net
Members of Firm: Albert Wycoff (1875-1940); Paul V. Wycoff (1896-1973); William W. Greeman (1915-1993); John L. Kellerman; John L. Kellerman II; Clay M. Kellerman; Amy P. Streator.
Criminal Law, Family Law, Domestic Violence, Corporate, Real Estate Title, Trusts and Estates.
Representative Clients: Hillenbrand Industries, Inc.; Town of Sunman; Cinergy, Inc.; GE Lighting; Eagle Fire Co.; Ripley County Community Foundation; Roman Nobbe, Inc.; National City Bank; Fifth Third Bank.

Kelley, William J., II, (CV) .... '59 '85 C.1365 B.A. L.276 J.D. 1305 Tekulve Road
Leitten, Brian Joseph .... '49 '77 C.688 B.S.Ch.E. L.128 J.D. Hillenbrand Indus., Inc. (Pat.)

Lindenmeyer, Mark R., (BV) .... '47 '72 C&L.602 A.B., J.D. 10 E. Pearl Street
McGowan, Clarence J. .... '24 '53 C.477 B.A. L.178 LL.B. 10 Birchwood Court
Miller, Dwight L., (AV) '61 '86
C.210 B.A. L.145 J.D. Asst. Gen. Coun., Hill-Rom Co., Inc.
Morrison, William A. '60 '93 C.665 B.S. L.347 J.D.
Sr. Intell. Prop. Coun., Hill-Rom Co., Inc. (Pat.)
Mullen, David K. ......'66 '90 C.1118 B.A. L.150 J.D. Forethought Financial Services, Inc.
Pictor, Henry A., (BV) .... '38 '63 C.1024 B.A. L.597 J.D. 4 Village Dr.
Renfroe, Timothy R. .... '61 '86 C&L.383 B.S., J.D. Asst. Gen. Coun., Hill-Rom Co., Inc.
Rudolf, Steven G. '64 '89
C.347 B.S. L.94 J.D. Sr. Labor Coun., Hillenbrand Industries, Inc.
Schuerman, John P., (BV) .... '46 '72 C.679 B.S. L.347 J.D. [Schuerman]
Schuerman Law Firm, The, P.C., (BV) .... 507 N. Walnut St.
Shields, Jack R., (BV) .... '38 '64 C.347 A.B. L.1119 J.D. 10 W. Pearl St.
Streator, Amy P. .... '74 '00 C.347 B.A. L.209 J.D. [Kellerman]
Weiler, Kristen R. ....'72 '96 C&L.201 B.A., J.D. 24 Red Maple Ct.
Willoughby, Mark A. '48 '74 C.347 B.S. L.1119 J.D.
Government Relations Counsel, Forethought Group Inc.
Wilson, Douglas C., (BV) ....'54 '79 C&L.1161 B.S., J.D. 137-B S. Main St.
Wright, Judith L. '59 '84 C.679 B.A. L.345 J.D.
Vice President and General Counsel, Forethought Financial Services, Inc.
Zerkle, John R., (AV) '54 '82 C.992 B.A. L.880 J.D.
V.P. & Gen. Coun., Batesville Casket Co., Inc.

BEDFORD, * 13,817, *Lawrence Co.*

Burton, Christopher W., Law Office, (BV) ... '52 '77 C.346 B.S. L.1119 J.D. 1502 I Street

Chapman & Nelson, P.C.
(See Bloomington)

Donovan, Emery & Hewetson, (AV) .... 1501 "J" Street
Emery, Gordon K., (AV) ....'35 '61 C.477 A.B. L.1119 LL.B. [Donovan,E.&H.]
Gill, W. Brent, Law Offices of, (AV) ..... '50 '80 C.347 B.S. L.345 J.D. 1602 I St., Ste. 1
Hall, Charlene Ritter, (CV) '51 '81
C.347 B.S. L.1119 J.D. Compliance Officer, Dunn Memorial Hosp.
Haury, John C., (BV) ....'48 '75 C.918 B.A. L.1119 J.D. [Haury&W.]
Haury & Woodward, (BV) .... 1534 I Street
Henderson, Donald G., (AV) ....'45 '71 C.347 B.S. L.1119 J.D. [Henderson&H.]

Henderson & Henderson, (AV)
P.O. Box 909, 47421-0909
Telephone: 812-275-5644 Fax: 812-279-0423
Email: donaldghenderson@msn.com
Members of Firm: Gordon R. Henderson (1911-1995); Donald G. Henderson.
Business Law, Commercial Transactions, Property Law, Probate and Estates.
Representative Clients: The Stone City Bank of Bedford; Peoples Trust Company of Linton, Indiana; Indiana Limestone Co., Inc.; Architectural Stone Sales, Inc.; Elliott Stone Co., Inc.; Aztec Aviation, Inc.; Board of Aviation Commissioners; Monroe-Lawrence Farm Bureau Co-op.
References: The Stone City Bank of Bedford; NBD Bank, N.A.
See Professional Biographies, BEDFORD, INDIANA

Herthel, Nick J., (CV) ....'59 '85 C.347 B.S. L.345 J.D. 1012 16th St., Ste. 100
Hewetson, Bruce A., (BV) ....'51 '76 C.347 A.B. L.345 J.D. [Donovan,E.&H.]
Hickman, Donald J., (BV) ....'46 '76 C.347 B.A. L.1119 J.D. 1839 Stevens
Jones, Charles W. .... '35 '78 C.477 B.S.M.E. L.1119 J.D. 419 Northwood Dr.‡
Kern, Raymond ....'47 '80 C&L.347 A.B., J.D. Supr. Ct. J.

Mallor Clendening Grodner & Bohrer LLP
(See Bloomington)

McIntyre, Meredith L., (BV) .... '55 '80 C&L.347 B.A., J.D. [McIntyre&S.]
McIntyre, Richard D., Sr. .... '56 '81 C.174 B.E. L.1119 J.D. Cir. J.
McIntyre & Smith, (BV) .... 1522 I Street

McSoley, Darlene Steele, (CV) '33 '83 C.347 B.S. L.1119 J.D.
Masonic Temple, Room 1, 917 15th Street, P.O. Box 294, 47421
Telephone: 812-275-3978 Fax: 812-275-3983
Family, Domestic Relations, Adoptions, Probate, Estate Planning, Real Estate and Guardianship Law.

Pittman, James G., (CV) .... '70 '96 C.347 B.A. L.421 J.D. [Donovan,E.&H.]
Plummer, John M., III, (BV) ....'68 '96 C.347 B.A. L.1187 J.D. [Plummer]
Plummer, John M., Jr., (AV) ....'42 '68 C.347 B.A. L.1119 J.D. [Plummer]
Plummer Law Offices, (AV) .... Masonic Temple, Room 3
Robbins, Michael A., (BV) '44 '72
C.347 B.S. L.345 J.D. Gen. Coun., Conva-Care Servs., Inc.
Robison, Ray W., The Law Office of, (CV) ....'46 '71 C.347 A.B. L.1119 J.D. 1608 H St.
Short, Robt. W., (BV) '23 '51 C.347 A.B. L.1119 LL.B.
Pres., Bedford Fed. Svgs. & Loan
Sleva, William G. ....'52 '81 C.339 B.A. L.1119 J.D. Co. Ct. J.
Smith, David A., (BV) ....'57 '83 C.346 B.S. L.345 J.D. [McIntyre&S.]
Steele, Brent E., (BV) .... '47 '72 C.347 B.S. L.345 J.D. [Steele&S.]
Steele, Byron W., (AV) .... '41 '65 C.347 A.B. L.1119 J.D. [Steele&S.]
Steele & Steele, L.L.C., (AV) .... 1602 I Street
Wood, Richard J. ....'44 '71 C.347 A.B. L.1119 J.D. 1539 E. Oolitic Rd.
Woodward, Michelle L., (CV) ....'72 '96 C.347 B.A. L.201 J.D. [Haury&W.]

BEECH GROVE, 14,880, *Marion Co.*

Brown, Richard L., (AV) ....'32 '60 C.346 A.B. L.1119 J.D. City. Atty.
Byers, David L., (AV) ....'53 '80 C.347 B.A. L.345 J.D. [Holwager,B.&C.]
Caughey, James E., (BV) ....'46 '85 C.894 B.A. L.345 J.D. [Holwager,B.&C.]
Falcon, A. Michael .... '46 '80 C.63 B.S. L.345 J.D. 12019 Emory Dr.
Gerber, Katherine I., (BV) ....'49 '78 C.597 B.A. L.345 J.D. 380 Main St.
Gonzales, Marcia N. ....'66 '94 C&L.347 B.A., J.D. Indiana Heart Physicians, Inc.
Gray, Milo G., Jr., (BV) ....'40 '71 C.265 B.A. L.345 J.D. 380 Main St.
Holwager, William J., (AV) ....'55 '80 C&L.347 B.A., J.D. [Holwager,B.&C.]
Holwager, Byers and Caughey, A Professional Association, (AV) .... 1818 Main St.
Jones, Pamela J. ....'65 '95 C.679 B.A. L.347 J.D. 1600 Albany Street
Kitley, Gloria Jean, (BV) ....'52 '83 C.473 B.A. L.345 J.D. [Kitley]
Kitley, John A., (AV) ....'23 '54 C&L.347 A.B., J.D. [Kitley]
Kitley, John A., Jr., (AV) ....'57 '83 C.347 B.A. L.345 J.D. [Kitley]
Kitley Professional Corporation, (AV) .... 380 Main St.
Wolfe, Daniel H., (BV) ....'62 '87 C.347 B.A. L.1119 J.D. [Ⓒ Kitley]

BERNE, 4,150, *Adams Co.*

Agler, Jeffery A., (CV) ....'56 '82 C.63 B.S. L.607 J.D. 755 W. Main
Baumgartner, David N., (BV) ....'60 '85 C.91 A.B. L.345 J.D. [Baumgartner&B.]
Baumgartner, Howard E., (AV) .... '24 '50 C&L.347 B.S., J.D. [Ⓒ Baumgartner&B.] ‡
Baumgartner & Beitler, (AV) .... 110 South Jefferson Street
Beitler, James E., Jr., (AV) ....'47 '74 C.937 B.A. L.1119 J.D. [Baumgartner&B.]
Biberstein, Robert L., (BV) ....'39 '64 C.827 A.B. L.1119 LL.B. P.O. Box 385
Rybolt, Russell H. ....'51 '77 C.347 A.B. L.879 J.D. 1117 Westwind Trail
Sprunger, Rick L., (CV) ....'60 '85 C.827 B.A. L.345 J.D. 1218 W. Water Street

BEVERLY SHORES, 622, *Porter Co.*

Vance, Susan Margaret, (AVⓉ) .... '42 '76 C.477 B.A. L.209 J.D. 8 Beach Ave.‡

BICKNELL, 3,357, *Knox Co.*

Levell, James P. ....'47 '75 C&L.347 B.A., J.D. 214 North Washington St.

BLOOMFIELD, * 2,592, *Greene Co.*

Abbott, Jeffrey H., (BV) .... '49 '75 C.108 B.S. L.345 J.D. P.O. Box 266‡
Corn, R. Todd, Attorney at Law, (BV) ..... '56 '86 C.63 B.S. L.1119 J.D. 114 E. Main St.
Hartman, Marilyn A., (BV) ....'48 '85 C&L.1119 A.B., J.D. [Hartman&P.]
Hartman & Paddock, (BV) ....44 South Franklin Street
Holt, J. David ....'42 '67 C.347 A.B. L.1119 J.D. Supr. Ct. J.
Holtsclaw, Jarrod D. ....'73 '98 C&L.347 B.A., J.D. Green Co. Pros. Off.
Johnson, David K. ....'47 '73 C.347 B.S. L.345 J.D. Co. J.
Klein, Michael A. ....'41 '88 C.597 B.A. L.1119 J.D. Gen. Coun. Off., Indiana Univ.
Paddock, Mona A., (BV) .... '— '88 C.763 L.1119 J.D. [Hartman&P.]
Sullivan, Joseph A., (BV) ....'38 '66 C.1216 A.B. L.1119 J.D. 31 S. Washington St.

BLOOMINGTON, * 69,291, *Monroe Co.*

Abplanalp, Marc O. ....'69 '03 C&L.1119 B.S., J.D. [Abplanalp]
Abplanalp Law Office ....205 North College Ave., Suite 715
Affe, Robert B. ....'54 '81 C.276 A.B. L.569 J.D. 2117 Azalea Ln.
Allen, D. Michael ....'75 '00 C.347 B.A. L.1119 J.D. [Ⓐ Mallor C.G.&B.]
Allen, David Michael ....'75 '00 C.347 B.A. L.1119 J.D. 301 W. 7th St.
Aman, Alfred C., Jr. ....'45 '72 C.696 A.B. L.145 J.D. Univ. of Indiana Sch. of Law
Andree, Jamie, (BV) '55 '79 C&L.188 B.A., J.D.
Mgn. Atty., Legal Servs., Organization of Ind., Inc.
Andrews, William H., (AV) ....'34 '59 C.209 A.B. L.1119 J.D. [Andrews,H.M.&C.]
Andrews, Harrell, Mann & Coyne, A Professional Corporation, (AV)
4100 7th Street, Ste. 104
Applegate, K. Edwin ....'23 '49 C.347 B.S. L.1119 J.D. [Ⓒ Applegate,M.&K.] ‡
Applegate, McDonald & Koch, P.C., (BV) .... P.O. Box 2627
Ardery, Samuel R., (AV) ....'58 '84 C.210 B.A. L.1119 J.D. [Bunger&R.]
Arnold, Dean J., (BV) ....'64 '89 C.347 B.S. L.1119 J.D. [Ⓐ Nunn]
Bailey, Matthew W. ....'72 '99 C&L.347 B.A., J.D. 520 N. Walnut, Suite 200
Barker, Jane E. ....'59 '84 C.347 B.A. L.602 J.D. Juv. Ref. & Prob. Comr.
Barnhart, Frank A., (AV) ....'29 '57 C.347 B.S. L.1119 J.D. [Barnhart,S.&S.]

Barnhart, Sturgeon & Spencer, (AV)
313 North Lincoln, P.O. Box 1234, 47402-1234
Telephone: 812-332-9476 Fax: 812-331-8819
Members of Firm: Alfred Evens (1881-1949); Leroy Baker (1903-1989); Frank A. Barnhart; Suzanne Sturgeon; Michael J. Spencer.
General Civil Practice. Corporation, Probate and Estate Planning, Construction, Real Estate, Criminal Law, Guardianship, Municipal and Zoning Law, Trials and Personal Injury, Guardianship and Probate.
Approved Attorneys for: Lawyers Title Insurance Corp.
See Professional Biographies, BLOOMINGTON, INDIANA

Batalon, Carrie L. ....'71 '98 C&L.347 B.S., J.D. [Ⓐ Mallor C.G.&B.]
Baude, Patrick L. '43 '66 C&L.378 A.B., J.D.
(adm. in WI; not adm. in IN) Prof. of Law, Ind. Univ.
Bauer, Jawn J., (BV) ....'55 '81 C&L.347 B.A., J.D. [Bauer&D.]
Bauer & Densford, (BV) ....608 W. Third St.
Baugh, Paul D., (CV) ....'63 '90 C&L.347 B.S., J.D. 416 W. 11th St.
Baus, J. William .... '— '93 C.249 B.A. L.1119 J.D. 1210 West 8th Street
Beard, Ben A. ....'50 '82 C.347 B.S. L.146 J.D. 986 Hwy. 446
Beggs, William J., (BV) ....'67 '92 C.210 B.A. L.879 J.D. [Bunger&R.]
Belcher, Thomas J., (BV) ....'52 '80 C.347 B.A. L.1119 J.D. [Kelley,B.&B.]
Benckart, Judith Corcoran, (BV) ....'56 '85 C.63 B.S. L.345 J.D. [Ⓒ Jones,M.&B.]
Berry, Thomas A., (AV) .... '39 '65 C.608 B.S. L.1119 J.D. [Berry&D.]

Berry & Domer, (AV) BB
701 North Walnut Street, 47404
Telephone: 812-336-8300 Fax: 812-336-2343 URL: http://www.tomberry.com
Email: lawyer@tomberry.com URL: http://www.berry-law.com
Thomas A. Berry; Michelle Berry Domer. Associate: Debra Traylor Davis.
General Civil and Business Litigation. Personal Injury, Criminal Defense, Family Law and Estates.
See Professional Biographies, BLOOMINGTON, INDIANA

Bethel, Terry A. '46 '71 C&L.608 B.A., J.D.
(adm. in OH; not adm. in IN) Indiana University
Bingham, Lisa B. '55 '79 C.788 A.B. L.184 J.D.
(adm. in CT; not adm. in IN)
Asst. Prof., Indiana Univ. School of Pub. & Environmental Affairs
Bohrer, James F., (BV) .... '57 '82 C.347 B.s. L.1119 J.D. [Mallor C.G.&B.] ⊙
Boshkoff, Douglass G. ....'30 '55 C&L.309 A.B., LL.B. Ind. Univ.
Bowers, Caryl M., (CV) ....'54 '90 C.608 B.S. L.345 J.D. [Mallor C.G.&B.]
Bowers, Thomas '51 '80 C.608 B.S.B.A. L.569 J.D.
Dir., Sports & Entertainment Academy, Indiana Univ.
Boyd, Lindsay ....'56 '00 C.1110 B.A. L.1119 J.D. 3099 Bethel Avenue
Bridges, Douglas R. ....'35 '66 C.679 B.S.M.E. L.1119 J.D. Cir. J.
Brown, Barry Spencer, (BV) ....'45 '71 L.1119 J.D. 701 N. Walnut St.
Brown, Darla Sue, (BV) ....'63 '88 C&L.347 B.A., J.D. [Kelley,B.&B.]
Brugger, Vernon W. ....'10 '46 C.793 B.S. L.273 J.D. 104 North Overhill Drive
Bunger, Thomas, (BV) ....'51 '76 C.347 B.S. L.345 J.D. [Bunger&R.]

Bunger & Robertson, (AV) BB
226 South College Square, P.O. Box 910, 47402-0910
Telephone: 812-332-9295 Fax: 812-331-8808
Email: br@lawbr.com URL: http://www.lawbr.com
Members of Firm: Len E. Bunger, Jr. (1921-1993); Don M. Robertson; Thomas Bunger; Joseph D. O'Connor; James L. Whitlatch; Samuel R. Ardery; Margaret M. Frisbie; William J. Beggs; John W. Richards; Steven K. Emery;—Holly M. Harvey; Suzette Vandivier Sims; Kevin A. Halloran; Maryanne Pelic; Lara Cutshall.
General Practice, Civil Practice, Trial Practice, Corporate Law, Business Law, Banking Law, Wills and Probate, Trusts and Estates, Guardianships, Elder Law, Estate Planning, Insurance, Hospital Law, Health Care, Education Law, School Law, Real Estate, Land Use, Contracts, Lawsuits, Business Planning, Business Enterprises, Limited Liability Companies, Partnerships, Small Business.
Representative Clients: Aetna Insurance Companies; Bloomington Hospital; Commercial Union Group; Indiana Insurance Co.; Liberty Mutual Insurance; Medical Protective Co.; Monroe County Community School Corp.; Professional Golf Car, Inc.; Prudential Insurance Company of America; State Farm Automobile Insurance Co.
See Professional Biographies, BLOOMINGTON, INDIANA

Burchfield, Patricia A., (Mrs.) .... '29 '69 C.303 A.B. L.1119 J.D. 1702 S. High St.‡
Buxbaum, Hannah L. '66 '93 C&L.188 B.A., J.D.
(adm. in NY; not adm. in IN) Assoc. Prof. of Law, Indiana Univ.
Carmin, Michael L., (BV) ....'54 '80 C.347 B.A. L.1119 J.D. [Andrews,H.M.&C.]

Carson Boxberger LLP, (AV) BB
3100 John Hinkle Place, Suite 106, 47408 ⊙
Telephone: 812-333-1225 Fax: 812-333-1925
URL: http://www.carsonboxberger.com

(This Listing Continued)

Carson Boxberger LLP (Continued)

Members of Firm: Edward J. Liptak; Douglas A. Hoffman; Jeremy M. Dilts.
General Civil Trial and Appellate Practice in all State and Federal Courts. Corporate, Business Transactions, Financial Institutions, Health Care, Probate and Estate Planning, Family Law, Transportation Law and Administration, Civil Rights, Real Estate, Labor, Insurance, Medical and Professional Malpractice, Products Liability, Workers' Compensation, Commercial, Creditors Rights and Bankruptcy Law, Mediation, Municipal.
Representative Clients: Admiral Insurance Company; Allstate Insurance Company; American Insurance Adjusting Company; American Medical Insurance Exchange; Atlantic Mutual Insurance Company; Bituminous Insurance Company; Bliss-McKnight Group; Capital Indemnity Corp.; CIGNA Companies; CNA Insurance.
Fort Wayne, Indiana Office: 1400 One Summit Square. Telephone: 260-423-9411. Telecopier: 260-423-4329.

See Professional Biographies, BLOOMINGTON, INDIANA

Carter, C. Kent ... '29 '62 C.347 B.S. L.831 LL.B. 220 W 7th St., 1st Fl.‡
Carter, Sarah A., (BV) ... '51 '76 C&L.347 B.A., J.D. 615 North Walnut Street
Chang, Kun Young ... '69 '01 L.347 S.J.D. 1257 Basswood Cir. S.
Chapman, Ronald L., (AV) ... '42 '71 C.701 B.S.E.E. L.1119 J.D. [Chapman&N.]

Chapman & Nelson, P.C., (AV)
Graham Plaza, P.O. Box 521, 47404
Telephone: 812-333-9900 Fax: 812-333-9902
Email: shn@cnbloomington.com URL: http://www.cnbloomington.com
Members of Firm: Ronald L. Chapman; Susan H. Nelson.
Criminal Law, Driving While Intoxicated, Traffic Violations, Personal Injury, Litigation, Family Law, Dissolutions of Marriage, Adoption Law, Guardianship, Modification of Support and Visitation, Name Changes.

See Professional Biographies, BLOOMINGTON, INDIANA

Clendening, Gary J., (AV) ... '44 '68 C&L.347 A.B., J.D. [Mallor C.G.&B.] ⊙
Colman, David J., (BV) ... '45 '70 C.347 B.A. L.1119 J.D. [Colman]
Colman Law Offices, (BV) ... 114 S. Grant
Cotner, James R., (AV) ... '24 '52 C.477 B.S. L.1119 J.D. 1720 N Kinser Pike‡
Cotter, Colleen M. ... '65 '91 C.602 B.A. L.347 J.D. Legal Servs. Org.
Coyne, Lynn H., (AV) ... '44 '72 C.347 A.B. L.1119 J.D. [Andrews,H.M.&C.]
Craft, Edward O. ... '16 '40 C.347 A.B. L.1119 LL.B. 909 S. Highland Ave.‡
Crane, David G. ... '37 '69 C.317 A.B. L.1119 J.D. 802 S. Washington
Crosson, Cathy E. ... '53 '83 C&L.347 B.A., J.D. Ind. Univ. School of Law
Cutshall, Lara ... '76 '04 C.473 B.A. L.1119 J.D. [A] Bunger&R.]
Dau-Schmidt, Kenneth '56 '82 C.966 B.A. L.477 J.D.
(adm. in WI; not adm. in IN) Prof., Indiana Univ. School of Law
Davidson, Pamela J., (BV) '53 '79 C.347 B.A. L.345 J.D.
Charitable Gift Planner & Consultant, Davidson Gift Design
Davis, Debra Traylor ... '55 '04 C&L.347 B.A., J.D. [A] Berry&D.]
Densford, Thomas E., (CV) ... '59 '88 C.347 B.A. L.879 J.D. [Bauer&D.]
Diekhoff, Mary Ellen Stanzione, (BV) ... '58 '86 C.879 B.A. L.1119 J.D. Dep. Pros.
Dilts, Jeremy M. ... '75 '00 C.347 B.A. L.1119 J.D. [Carson B.]
Dilts, Jon Paul ... '45 '81 C.999 B.A. L.879 J.D. Ind. Univ.
Dixon, James M. ... '29 '60 C.347 A.B. L.1119 J.D. Sr. J.
Domer, Michelle Berry, (CV) ... '67 '92 C.966 B.A. L.347 J.D. [Berry&D.]
Drew, Kiply Suzanne, (BV) '61 '89 C.303 B.A. L.1119 J.D.
Off. of Leg. Coun., Indiana Univ., 211 Bryan Hall
Dworkin, Roger B. '43 '67 C.674 A.B. L.813 J.D.
(adm. in CA; not adm. in IN) Prof., Ind. Univ. Sch. of Law
Dworkin, Terry Morehead '— '76
C.813 A.B. L.1119 J.D. Chair Prof. of Bus. Law, Ind. Univ.
Eckes, Suzanne E. ... '72 '01 C&L.966 B.A., J.D. Asst. Prof., Indiana Univ.-Bloomington
Elliott, James M. '42 '69 C.347 B.S. L.1119 J.D.
(adm. in KY; not adm. in IN) [Elliott&Assoc.]
Elliott & Associates ... 230 Fountain Sq.
Emery, Steven K., (BV) ... '60 '87 C.347 B.S. L.1119 J.D. [Bunger&R.]
English, Terry L., (CV) ... '49 '79 C.347 A.B. L.1119 J.D. 820 N. College Ave.
Erickson, Morris H., (AV) ... '46 '74 C.347 B.A. L.1119 J.D. [M.Erickson]
Erickson, Morrie, A Professional Corporation, (AV) ... 810 Auto Mall Rd.
Evans, Stacee E., (CV) ... '69 '96 C.347 B.A. L.1119 J.D. [A] Andrews,H.M.&C.]
Fawcett, William A., (BV) ... '— '65 C&L.347 B.S., J.D. 409 S. Walnut Street
Ferguson, David L., (BV) ... '56 '81 C.347 B.S. L.1119 J.D. [Ferguson&F.]
Ferguson, James H. ... '28 '53 C.347 A.B. L.1119 J.D. [Ferguson&F.]
Ferguson, Matthew W., (CV) ... '66 '92 C.347 B.A. L.597 J.D. [A] Ferguson&F.]
Ferguson, Theodore J., (BV) ... '— '80 C.894 A.B. L.1119 J.D. [Ferguson&F.]
Ferguson & Ferguson, (BV) ... 403 E. 6th St.
Fitzgerald, Michael O. ... '49 '77 L.1119 3480 Inverness Farms Rd.
Foley, Colleen A. ... '61 '93 C.93 B.A. L.574 J.D. 205 North College Avenue
Foster, Justin '45 '75 C.347 B.A. L.245 J.D.
(adm. in GA; not adm. in IN) 1224 E. Maxwell Lane‡
Founds, Garry L. ... '67 '00 C.992 B.A. L.1119 J.D. [A] Mallor C.G.&B.]
Francis, Donald W., Jr., (CV) ... '64 '92 L.365 701 N. Walnut St.
Frank, Clarence C., (BV) ... '43 '82 C.338 B.S. L.1119 J.D. Dep. Pub. Def.
Franklin, Joseph A. ... '37 '63 C.347 B.S. L.1119 J.D. Dir., Fed. Rel., Ind. Univ.
Frapwell, Dorothy J. ... '47 '73 C.645 B.S. L.1119 J.D. Univ. Coun., Indiana Univ.
Frey, Bruce M. ... '43 '67 C.347 A.B. L.1119 J.D. 355 S. Madison St.
Frisbie, Margaret M., (BV) ... '50 '84 C.597 B.S.J. L.383 J.D. [Bunger&R.]
Frohman, Thomas M., (BV) ... '54 '84 C.347 B.S. L.1119 J.D. 242 West 7th Street
Gastineau, Michael B. ... '75 '02 C.347 B.A. L.276 J.D. 927 South Curry Pike‡
Ginger, Laura A. ... '54 '79 C.210 B.A. L.145 J.D. IN Univ. Sch. of Bus.
Gjerdingen, Kendra Gowdy, (BV) ... '50 '78 C.352 B.A. L.1035 J.D. [Mallor C.G.&B.]
Glass, George R. ... '29 '53 C.210 A.B. L.477 LL.B. 510 E. Lakewood Dr.
Gordon, Ann ... '67 '93 C.303 B.A. L.1119 J.D. 901 S. Rogers St., Suite C
Graham, Roy J. ... '55 '91 C&L.347 B.A., J.D. 3330 North Russell Road
Greene, Betsy K., (AV) ... '57 '82 C.347 B.A. L.1119 J.D. [Greene&S.]

Greene & Schultz Trial Lawyers, (AV)
320 W. 8th Street, Suite 100, 47401
Telephone: 812-336-4357 Fax: 812-336-5615
URL: http://www.greeneschultztriallawyers.com
Members of Firm: Betsy K. Greene; Fred Schultz.
Personal Injury, Automobile Negligence, Products Liability, Wrongful Death, Premises Liability, Wrongful Denial of Insurance, Tort Law, Insurance Disputes.

See Professional Biographies, BLOOMINGTON, INDIANA

Greenebaum, Edwin H. '36 '61 C&L.309 A.B., LL.B.
(adm. in IL; not adm. in IN) Prof. of Law, Ind. Univ., Sch. of Law
Gregory, Fred H., (CV) ... '25 '53 C.674 A.B. L.1119 LL.B. 205 S. Walnut St., Ste. 14‡
Grodner, Geoffrey M., (BV) ... '50 '75 C.347 A.B. L.1119 J.D. [Mallor C.G.&B.] ⊙
Guthrie, Philippa M. '60 '92
C.197 A.B. L.347 J.D. Gen. Coun., Indiana University Foundation
Haller, Lyndsay A. ... '78 '04 C.347 B.A. L.300 J.D. [A] Jones,M.&B.]
Halloran, Kevin A. ... '66 '92 C.347 B.A. L.1119 J.D. [A] Bunger&R.]
Hamilton, Mary J., (BV) ... '46 '90 C.713 B.A. L.1119 J.D. Dep. Pub. Def., Monroe Co.
Hamstra, Cynthia A., (BV) ... '61 '87 C.347 B.A. L.1119 J.D. [A] Ferguson&F.]

Hansen, Richard Arthur ... '62 '98 C.339 B.A. L.801 J.D. Dep. Pros. Atty.
Harrell, Harold A., (AV) ... '36 '61 C.347 A.B. L.1119 J.D. [Andrews,H.M.&C.]
Harvey, Holly M. ... '71 '97 C&L.347 B.A., J.D. [A] Bunger&R.]
Haseman, Christine Talley, (CV) ... '66 '95 C&L.347 B.S., J.D. [Haseman]
Haseman Law Office, (CV) ... 701 N. Walnut St.
Hayford, Stephen L. '49 '88 C.249 B.S.B.A. L.1119 J.D.
(adm. in FL; not adm. in IN) 4180 S. Downs Dr.‡
Hedges, Steven G. ... '— '82 C.63 B.S. L.1119 LL.B. P.O. Box 5085
Hill, Frances Gall ... '52 '80 C.679 B.S. L.1119 J.D. Consultant Juvenile & Family Law
Hoff, E. Michael ... '48 '75 C&L.347 A.B., J.D. Cir. J.
Hoffman, Douglas A., (BV) ... '65 '90 C.967 B.A. L.347 J.D. [Carson B.] ⊙
Howe-Fernandez, Karen, (BV) ... '— '94 C.477 B.S. L.347 J.D. [A] Ferguson&F.]
Huerta, Michael A. R. ... '51 '83 C.347 B.A. L.1119 J.D. Student Legal Serv.
Hunt, James B. ... '70 '95 C.339 B.S.G.E. L.365 J.D. Corp. Coun., Cook Group (Pat.)
Hunt, Michael E., (BV) ... '41 '69 C.347 A.B. L.1119 J.D. Pub. Def.
Johnson, Lonnie D. ... '57 '92 C&L.347 B.A., J.D. [Mallor C.G.&B.]
Jones, Robert Delano, (BV) ... '42 '68 C.347 A.B. L.1119 J.D. [Jones,M.&B.]

Jones, McGlasson & Benckart, P.C., (AV)
205 South Walnut Street, P.O. Box 279, 47402
Telephone: 812-332-4431 Fax: 812-332-0554
Email: jmbattys@bloomington.in.us URL: http://www.jmbattys.com
Robert Delano Jones; Thomas M. McGlasson;—Janet C. Stavropoulos; Marguerite R. Shreve; Lyndsay A. Haller. Of Counsel: Judith Corcoran Benckart; David Rogers.
General Civil and Trial Practice. Probate and Estate Planning and Administration, Real Estate, Title Insurance, Corporation, Commercial, Business, Creditors Rights, Bankruptcy, Taxation, Contracts, Construction Law, Banking, Personal Injury, Insurance, Non-profit Corporations and Motor Carrier Law.
Representative Clients: Workingmens ONB Bank; Woolery Stone Co., Inc.
Reference: Monroe County Bank.

See Professional Biographies, BLOOMINGTON, INDIANA

Kaiman, Beth R. ... '66 '91 C&L.347 B.S., J.D. Legal Servs. Organization of Indiana, Inc.
Kauble, Keith A. ... '35 '65 C.347 B.S. L.1119 LL.B. 1385 W. Allen St.
Kehr, Jeffrey A. ... '72 '97 C.347 B.A. L.1119 J.D. Dep. Pros. Atty.
Keith, John T. ... '70 '96 C.894 B.A. L.347 J.D. Indiana Univ. Foundation
Kellams, Marc R. ... '49 '78 C.347 A.B. L.1119 J.D. Cir. J.
Kelley, Joseph A., (CV) ... '50 '80 C.347 B.A. L.1119 J.D. 123 S. College Ave.
Kelley, Thaddeus Craig ... '73 '00 C.303 B.A. L.4210 J.D. [A] Kelley,B.&B.]
Kelley, William H., (AV) ... '46 '71 C.347 A.B. L.1119 J.D. [Kelley,B.&B.]

Kelley, Belcher & Brown, A Professional Corporation, (AV) [BB]
301 West Seventh Street, P.O. Box 3250, 47402-3250
Telephone: 812-336-9963 Telecopier: 812-336-4588
William H. Kelley; Thomas J. Belcher; Darla Sue Brown;—Shannon L. Robinson; Thaddeus Craig Kelley.
General Civil and Insurance, Personal Injury, Corporate, Banking and Probate Law.

See Professional Biographies, BLOOMINGTON, INDIANA

Kennedy, James L. ... '41 '68 C.347 B.S. L.1119 J.D. Dir., Police Dept., Indiana Univ.
Kenworthy, Phyllis Lea ... '47 '81 C.347 B.A. L.1119 J.D. Supr. Ct. J.
Kilmer, Herbert L., Law Office of, (CV) '47 '83
C.347 B.S. L.1119 J.D. 406 West Kirwood
Kincaid, Jennifer Uber ... '66 '96 C.602 B.A. L.262 J.D. 7322 W. Eller Rd.
Kinkead, Duncan, (CV) ... '42 '90 C.976 B.A. L.1119 J.D. 1011 Walnut St.
Koch, Eric Allan ... '64 '89 C.276 B.S.B.A. L.347 J.D. [Applegate,M.&K.]
Kubley, Deborah Davis, (CV) ... '50 '94 C&L.347 B.A., J.D. [A] Applegate,M.&K.]
Kulis, James M. '47 '73 C&L.424 B.S., J.D.
(adm. in IL; not adm. in IN) Liability Specialist, Great West Casualty Company
Lamb, Carl, & Associates ... '56 '84 C.347 B.A. L.345 J.D. 2613 E. Third Street
Lappin, Claudia Carroll, (CV) ... '51 '78 C.347 A.B. L.345 J.D. 1401 S. Walnut St.
Lauer, Gregory Scott '67 '93
C.303 B.A. L.347 J.D. Corp. Coun., Blackwell Construction, Inc.
LeBus, Betty V. '23 '48 C&L.911 B.S., LL.B.
(adm. in WA; not adm. in IN) 2455 Tamarack Trl.‡
Liell, Katharine C., (BV) ... '61 '89 C.347 B.A. L.1119 J.D. [Liell&M.]
Liell & McNeil, (BV) ... P.O. Box 2417 (Pat.)
Like, Lance D., (BV) ... '64 '90 C.249 B.S. L.1119 J.D. [Mallor C.G.&B.]
Liptak, Edward J., (AV) ... '54 '79 C.93 A.B. L.1119 J.D. [Carson B.]
Little, David W. '22 '49 C.197 A.B. L.597 J.D.
(adm. in IL; not adm. in IN) 3303 Browncliff Ln.‡
Lloyd, William C., (BV) ... '— '67 C.347 B.S.Bus. L.1119 J.D. 403 E. Sixth St.
Loftman, Guy R., Law Office of, (BV) '45 '74 C.347 B.A. L.1119 J.D.
532 N. Walnut St.
Lomax, Bernard J. '52 '84 C.763 B.S. L.1137 J.D.
(adm. in CA; not adm. in IN) ARM-Index Solutions, Inc.
Lotz, Arthur M. ... '31 '65 C.432 B.A. L.1119 J.D. Asst. Dean, Ind. Univ. Law Sch.
Mallor, Andrew C., (AV) ... '49 '74 C.347 B.A. L.1119 J.D. [Mallor C.G.&B.] ⊙
Mallor, Jane Pratt ... '50 '76 C&L.347 B.A., J.D. Univ. of Ind. Sch. of Bus.

Mallor Clendening Grodner & Bohrer LLP, (AV)
511 Woodscrest Drive, P.O. Box 5787, 47407-5787 ⊙
Telephone: 812-336-0200 Fax: 812-333-0083
Email: info@mcgb.com URL: http://www.mcgb.com
Partners of Firm: Andrew C. Mallor; Gary J. Clendening; Geoffrey M. Grodner; James F. Bohrer; Kendra Gowdy Gjerdingen; Caryl M. Bowers; Lance D. Like; Lonnie D. Johnson. Associates: Carrie L. Batalon; Garry L. Founds; D. Michael Allen; Janice L. Sterling; Stacy F. Thompson; Anthony J. Yorio, Jr.; Patrick Omilian.
Civil Litigation, Insurance Defense, Business Law, Wills, Trusts and Estates, Family Law, Personal Injury, Taxation, Corporate Law, Real Estate, Probate, Labor and Employment.
References: Monroe County Bank; Bank One, Bloomington, NA; Irwin Union Bank & Trust Company.
Indianapolis, Indiana Office: Suite 770 Market Square Center, 151 N. Delaware Street, 46204. Telephone: 317-453-2000. Fax: 812-333-0083.

See Professional Biographies, BLOOMINGTON, INDIANA

Mann, Elizabeth N. ... '47 '76 C.347 B.A. L.1119 J.D. Cir. J.
Mann, Robert D., (AV) ... '41 '66 C.210 A.B. L.1119 J.D. [Andrews,H.M.&C.]
Manns, Alphonso ... '41 '80 C.254 B.S. L.1119 J.D. 405 W. 6th St.
McAuley, Jason L. ... '72 '00 C.347 B.A. L.1119 J.D. [A] Bauer&D.]
McBride, Shelly K. ... '71 '00 C.347 B.A. L.1119 J.D. Co. Pros. Off.
McCoy, Douglas M. ... '61 '88 C&L.347 B.S., J.D. 512 Green Rd.‡
McCrea, David S., (BV) ... '43 '68 C&L.347 A.B., J.D. [McCrea&M.]
McCrea, Edward F., (BV) ... '46 '72 C.309 A.B. L.1119 J.D. [McCrea&M.]
McCrea & McCrea, (BV) ... 119 S. Walnut St.
McDonald, Thomas M., (BV) ... '37 '62 C.347 B.S. L.1119 J.D. [Applegate,M.&K.]
McGlasson, Thomas M., (AV) ... '43 '68 C.347 A.B. L.1119 J.D. [Jones,M.&B.]
McKinney, Barbara E. '59 '84 C.347 B.A. L.1119 J.D.
Dir., Bloomington Human Rights Comm., Legal
McNeil, Michael B. ... '62 '91 C.679 B.S.A.E. L.1119 J.D. [Liell&M.] (Pat.)
McSoley, Patrick S., (BV) ... '54 '80 C.347 A.B. L.345 J.D. 9507 South Lakeside Drive
Mendelson-Steigerwald, Anne ... '52 '77 C.347 B.A. L.276 J.D. 3309 Gosport Ct.‡

Miller, Joseph C. .... '38 '65 C.339 A.B. L.145 J.D. Ind. Univ.
Miller, Robert T., (BV) .... '52 '80 C.346 B.S. L.347 J.D. 205 N. College Ave.
Miller, Stephen G., (BV) '68 '94 C.679 B.S. L.347 J.D.
CEO & Gen. Coun., Pinnacle Asse Mgmt., Inc.
Mills, Daniel M., (BV) .... '47 '79 C.347 B.S. L.345 J.D. [Mills L.]
Mills Law, (BV) .... 701 N. Walnut St.
Minger, Tammy Miller .... '62 '88 C.346 B.A. L.1119 J.D. [Minger]
Minger Law Office .... 1408 South Walnut Street
Moberly, Stephen C., Law Office of, (AV) '41 '66
C.347 A.B. L.345 LL.B. 2638 E. Windermere Woods Dr.
Nardi, Barbara A., (BV) .... '51 '81 C.347 B.A. L.1119 J.D. 3779 E. Fulford Rd.
Nelson, Susan H., (BV) .... '48 '75 C&L.879 B.A., J.D. [Chapman&N.]
Niehoff, Benjamin L. .... '74 '00 C.347 B.A. L.1119 J.D. 400 W. 7th St., Ste. 104
Nolan, Val, Jr. .... '20 '49 C.347 A.B. L.1119 J.D. Prof. of Law, Emeritus, Ind. Univ.
Nordhoff, John Michael .... '47 '94 C.679 B.S.E.E. L.347 J.D. 8635 Rockport Road
Nunn, Kenneth L., (BV) .... '40 '67 C.347 B.S. L.1119 J.D. [Nunn]
Nunn Law Office, (BV) .... 104 Franklin Road
O'Connor, Joseph D., (AV) .... '53 '78 C.679 B.S. L.1119 J.D. [Bunger&R.]
Omilian, Patrick .... '73 '03 C.188 B.S. L.347 J.D. [Ⓐ Mallor C.G.&B.]
O'Neal, Sterling, Jr. '42 '82 C.382 B.A. L.1119 J.D.
(adm. in KY; not adm. in IN) South Central Community Mental Health Ctr.
Ortman, Gerald T. .... '49 '74 C.347 B.A. L.1119 J.D. 3504 Violet Lane
Palmer, James A. .... '39 '71 C.347 A.B. L.345 J.D. Resch. Atty., Indiana Univ.
Palmer, Judith G. .... '48 '74 C.347 A.B. L.345 J.D. V.P.& Chf. Fin. Offr., IN Univ.
Parker, Angela Foster, (BV) .... '60 '95 C&L.347 B.A., J.D. [Andrews,H.M.&C.]
Pauwels, Gerard W. .... '— '95 L.1119 J.D. P.O. Box 1506
Pelic, Maryanne .... '60 '86 C.347 B.S. L.1119 J.D. [Ⓐ Bunger&R.]
Penslar, Robin Levin '54 '84 C.1077 B.A. L.1066 J.D.
(adm. in PA; not adm. in IN) Indiana Univ.
Pepinsky, Harold E. '45 '68 C.477 B.A. L.309 LL.B.
(adm. in OH; not adm. in IN) Prof., Univ. of Ind.
Perin, James P. .... '47 '76 C&L.347 A.B., J.D. 2120 Azalea Ln.
Pettay, Lee .... '45 '70 C.62 B.A. L.1119 J.D. 1200 E. Rhorer Dr.
Plimpton, Thomas L. .... '34 '67 C.918 A.B. L.345 J.D. Bank One
Poer, DL, (CV) .... '55 '81 C.347 A.B. L.862 J.D. 737 S. Deer Trce.
Pratt, Donna F., (BV) .... '47 '88 C.347 B.S. L.1119 J.D. [Pratt&P.]
Pratt, Lewellyn H., (AV) .... '29 '58 C.347 B.S. L.1119 J.D. [Pratt&P.]

Pratt & Pratt, (AV)
4334 East Third Street Suite 100, P.O. Box 1284, 47402-1284
Telephone: 812-339-1661 Fax: 812-339-4521
Email: lpratt@iquest.net
Members of Firm: Lewellyn H. Pratt; Donna F. Pratt.
Trial and Appellate Practice, Family and Domestic Relations, Family Mediation, Probate, Real Property Law, Auto Accident and Personal Injury.

Price, Robert C. .... '50 '76 C.679 B.S. L.347 J.D./M.S. [Price&R.]
Price & Runnells, (BV) .... 1329 S. High St.
Ratliff, Wesley W., Jr. .... '25 '50 C.63 L.879 J.D. Sr. J.‡
Reichard, Cynthia J. '58 '84
C.679 B.A. L.1119 J.D. Lecturer in Law, IN Univ. Sch. of Law
Rice, Marjorie K. .... '68 '97 C.108 B.S. L.347 J.D. Co. Legal Dept.
Richards, John W., (BV) .... '64 '92 C&L.347 B.S., J.D. [Bunger&R.]
Riess, Theresa Ann '59 '86 C.339 A.B. L.1119 J.D.
V.P. & Gen. Coun., Advanced Designs Corporation
Robertson, Don M., (AV) .... '38 '65 C.679 B.S. L.1119 J.D. [Bunger&R.]
Robinson, Shannon L., (CV) .... '62 '90 C.249 B.S. L.347 J.D. [Ⓐ Kelley,B.&B.]
Robling, Kevin R. '62 '98 C&L.347 B.S., J.D.
Dean of Adm., Indiana Uni. School of Law
Rogers, David, (BV) .... '28 '55 C.347 A.B. L.345 J.D. [Ⓒ Jones,M.&B.]
Ruf, Catherine Thomas .... '55 '81 C.347 B.S. L.1119 J.D. PTS Corp.
Runnells, Mary M., (BV) .... '47 '75 C.347 B.A. L.705 J.D. [Price&R.]
Russell, Stephen W. .... '47 '75 C&L.846 B.S., J.D. 302 Sycamore Hall
St. Germain, Tonia P. .... '60 '87 C.938 B.A. L.1162 J.D. 403 E. 6th St.
St. Martin, Ronald F. .... '35 '62 C.347 A.B. L.345 J.D. 5050 E. Moores Creek Rd.‡
Sallee, Philip A., (BV) .... '48 '73 C.347 B.A. L.1119 J.D. 910 Pleasant Ridge
Salzmann, Carl A., (BV) .... '52 '81 C.347 B.S. L.345 J.D. Pros. Atty.
Saunders, Kathy J. .... '58 '87 C.375 B.A. L.1119 J.D. Fire Chf.
Savich, Rudolph Wm., (BV) '55 '80 C.347 B.A. L.1119 J.D.
205 N. College Ave., St. 315
Scarton, Michael T. .... '72 '00 C.63 B.S. L.345 J.D. Monroe County Prosecutor's Off.
Schornhorst, F. Thomas .... '34 '63 C.352 B.A. L.273 J.D. Prof. of Law, Ind. Univ.
Schultz, Fred, (BV) .... '69 '96 C.108 B.S. L.74 J.D. [Greene&S.]
Shapiro, Samuel S., (AV) .... '53 '79 C.347 B.A. L.345 J.D. 4334 E. 3rd St.
Shean, John H., (BV) .... '56 '81 C.154 B.A. L.426 J.D. [Shean]
Shean Law Offices, A Professional Corporation, (BV) .... 1114 North College Avenue
Sherman, Daniel .... '49 '87 C.347 B.A. L.1119 J.D. Atty. Admr.‡
Shreve, Gene R. .... '43 '69 C.623 B.A. L.309 LL.B. Indiana University
Shreve, Marguerite R., (BV) .... '46 '71 C.518 A.B. L.94 J.D. [Ⓐ Jones,M.&B.]
Shupe, Matthew T., (BVⓉ) '66 '91 C.587 B.S. L.352 J.D.
(adm. in IA; not adm. in IN) Regional Couns., Great West Casualty Company
Siefers, Jerry L., Jr. .... '65 '92 C.679 B.S. L.345 J.D. P.O. Box 6446
Simpson, Vi Sentman .... '46 '94 L.345 J.D. 4965 Westwoodland Drive
Sims, Suzette Vandivier, (BV) .... '63 '89 C.347 B.A. L.1119 J.D. [Ⓐ Bunger&R.]
Sirois, Saml. F. .... '10 '35 C.347 L.1119 LL.B. 117 1/2 W. Kirkwood‡
Slotegraaf, Eric P. .... '67 '96 C.625 B.A. L.215 J.D. 400 W. 7th St., Ste. 104
Smith, Bradford J. .... '67 '95 C.445 B.S. L.64 J.D. 123 S. College Ave.
Spencer, Michael J., (BV) .... '49 '73 C.347 B.S. L.1119 J.D. [Barnhart,S.&S.]
Stavropoulos, Janet C. .... '46 '95 C.282 B.A. L.1119 J.D. [Ⓐ Jones,M.&B.]
Steger, William K., (AV) .... '44 '69 C.894 A.B. L.1119 J.D. P.O. Box 1154
Stein, Carrie A. .... '71 '98 C.477 B.A. L.851 J.D. Indiana Univ. Found.
Sterling, Janice L. .... '72 '01 C.719 B.A. L.209 J.D. [Ⓐ Mallor C.G.&B.]
Stewart, Daniel C., (BV) .... '49 '78 C.347 B.S. L.1119 J.D. 409 S. College Ave., Ste. B
Stewart, Thomas U. '63 '92 C.679 B.S. L.347 J.D.
(adm. in KY; not adm. in IN) Reg. Atty., Great West Casualty Company
Straw, Andrew U. '69 '99 C.347 B.A. L.1119 J.D.
Asst. Dean, Internat'l Prog., Indiana U. School of Law
Sturgeon, Suzanne, (BV) .... '50 '83 C.346 B.A. L.1119 J.D. [Barnhart,S.&S.]
Swain, Paul W., Jr. .... '54 '82 C.347 B.A. L.1119 J.D. P.O. Box 1564
Tackitt, Sylvan W., (AV) '09 '31 C.347 B.S. L.1119 LL.B.
103 N. College Ave., Ste. 203
Taliaferro, Viola J. .... '28 '77 C.887 B.S. L.1119 J.D. Cir. J.
Tanford, James A. .... '50 '77 C.674 A.B. L.228 J.D. IN Univ. Sch. of Law
Tempel, Jeremy M. .... '75 '00 C.210 B.A. L.1119 J.D. 3406 Cedarwood Circle
Thompson, James F., (BV) .... '17 '67 C.347 A.B. L.1119 J.D. 314 W. 17th Street
Thompson, Stacy F. .... '77 '02 C&L.347 B.S., J.D. [Ⓐ Mallor C.G.&B.]
Todd, Kenneth G. .... '45 '70 C.347 A.B. L.1119 J.D. Cir. J.
Todd, Robert J., (CVⓉ) '51 '77 C.352 B.A. L.1048 J.D.
VP of Claims, Great West Casualty Company
Travis, Cliff K. .... '30 '57 C.347 B.A. L.1119 J.D. Univ. Coun., Indiana Univ.
Trubitt, Hillard J. .... '29 '59 C.339 A.B. L.1119 J.D. Prof., Ind. Univ.
Trulock, James R., II, (BV) .... '52 '79 C.880 B.S.M.E. L.1119 J.D. Co. Atty.
Vaughan, Ann R. .... '27 '77 C.914 A.B. L.1119 J.D. Dep. City Atty.
Veidlinger, Rebecca L. .... '70 '97 C.012 B.A. L.276 J.D. Adj. Prof., Indiana Univ.‡
Velasquez, Albert J., (BV) '44 '74 C.347 B.S. L.1119 J.D.
Gen. Coun., Mirwec Film Inc.

Vrana, Timothy J., LLC
(See Columbus)

Warf, Wayne J. .... '62 '03 C.728 B.S. L.347 J.D. [Warf]
Warf Law Office .... 750 E. Rhorer Road
Weeks, Stacy L. .... '63 '94 C&L.347 B.A., J.D. 1720 N Kinser Pike‡
Welch, David L. .... '51 '83 C.347 A.B. L.1209 J.D. Cir. J.
Wenzler, Marcy, (BV) '52 '81
C.347 B.A. L.845 J.D. Legal Servs. Organization of Ind., Inc.
Wertz, Mary H., (CV) .... '65 '90 C&L.347 B.A., J.D. Dep. Pros. Atty.
White, Paula Gordon, (BV) '36 '75
C.1036 B.A. L.1119 J.D. Assoc. Dir., Student Legal Servs.
Whitlatch, James L., (AV) .... '58 '84 C.210 B.A. L.1119 J.D. [Bunger&R.]
Wyle, Karen A. .... '55 '80 C.813 B.A. L.309 J.D. [K.A.Wyle]
Wyle, Karen A., Law Office .... 4475 N. Benton Ct.
Yonkman, Peter R. .... '72 '98 C&L.347 B.A., J.D. Gen. Counsel, Cook Group Inc.
Yorio, Anthony J., Jr. .... '72 '02 C.1103 B.A. L.347 J.D. [Ⓐ Mallor C.G.&B.]
York, Alvin Robert .... '44 '69 C.347 B.S. L.1119 J.D. Asst. Univ. Coun., Indiana Univ.
Zinman, Ira B. .... '46 '72 C.347 B.S. L.1119 J.D. 403 E. 3rd St.

BLUFFTON, * 9,536, *Wells Co.*

Antrim, Andrew K., (BV) .... '62 '88 C.303 B.A. L.469 J.D. 222 W. Market St.
Babcock, Timothy K. .... '73 '99 C.347 B.A. L.245 J.D. 1127 North Main Street
Brown, Jon M., (AV) .... '42 '67 C.347 B.S. L.1119 J.D. 222 W. Market St.
Brown-Stohler, Michelle, (BV) .... '67 '93 C.346 B.S. L.879 J.D. 222 W. Market St.
Carnall, Andrew J., (BV) .... '64 '93 C&L.347 B.A., J.D. [N.R.Carnall. A.J.Carnall]
Carnall, Ned R., (AV) .... '35 '60 C.347 B.S. L.1119 J.D. [N.R.Carnall. A.J.Carnall] ‡
Carnall, Ned R., Andrew J., P.C., (BV) .... 124 West Market Street
Crowell, Anthony O., (BV) .... '57 '84 C.347 B.A. L.345 J.D. 1427 N. Main St.
Dale, David C., (AV) .... '38 '62 C.347 B.S. L.1119 J.D. 1427 N. Main St.
Edris, John H., Jr., (AV) .... '27 '53 C.679 B.S. L.345 J.D. 222 W. Market St.‡
Feeback, David A., (BV) .... '51 '76 C.894 B.A. L.1119 J.D. City Atty.
Gallivan, Hamilton, Seese & Patterson, (BV) .... 125 S. Marion St., Ste 100 (ⓞOssian)
Gordon, Daniel R., (AV) .... '51 '76 C.63 B.A. L.309 J.D. [Gordon&Assoc.] ⓞ

Gordon & Associates, Professional Corporation, (AV)
119 East Oak Forest Drive, 46714 ⓞ
Telephone: 260-824-9377 Facsimile: 260-824-9675
Email: gordonassociates@parlorcity.com
Daniel R. Gordon.
Trusts and Estates, Business Law, Estate and Gift Taxation, Medicaid Planning, Agricultural Law. Huntington, Indiana Office: 2859 Northpark Avenue.

Goshorn, Everett E. .... '45 '70 C.679 B.S. L.1119 J.D. Supr. Ct. J.
Hanselman, David L. .... '45 '74 C.210 B.A. L.1119 J.D. Cir. J.
Holdman, Travis L., (BV) .... '50 '91 C.798 B.A. L.347 J.D. [Lautzenheiser&H.]
Huffman, Keith P., (BV) .... '51 '80 C.5 B.A. L.1119 J.D. 1427 N. Main St.
Johnson, Roy R., (BV) .... '50 '75 C.347 A.B. L.1119 J.D. 222 W. Market St.
Lautzenheiser, Michael W., (BV) '52 '78
C.63 B.S. L.607 J.D. Pros. Atty. [Lautzenheiser&H.]
Lautzenheiser & Holdman, (BV) .... P.O. Box 471
Mattern, Kenneth J. .... '62 '01 C.347 A.G.S. L.1187 J.D. 119 E. Oak Forest

Roebuck & Associates, P.C.
(See Ft. Wayne)

Seese, William D., (BV) .... '31 '59 C.303 B.A. L.1119 J.D. [Gallivan,H.S.&P.] ⓞ
Spear, Donna Mccoy '66 '91
C.679 B.A. L.879 J.D. Dep. Pros. Atty. [Ⓐ Lautzenheiser&H.]
Waters, Gregory K., Law Office Of, (CV) '53 '81 C.347 B.A. L.608 J.D.
201 Market Place

BOONVILLE, * 6,834, *Warrick Co.*

Ashley, Don R., (AV) .... '29 '54 C.347 A.B. L.1119 LL.B. 130 W. Locust St.
Aylsworth, Robert R. .... '53 '79 C.999 B.S. L.345 J.D. Supr. Ct. J., Warric Co. Jud. Ctr.
Aylsworth, Tony, (BV) .... '63 '91 C.999 B.S. L.421 J.D. Peoples Tr. & Svgs. Bk.

Bamberger, Foreman, Oswald and Hahn, LLP
(See Evansville)

Bruner, J. William, Law Office of, (BV) '45 '74 C.679 B.S. L.1119 J.D.
316 S. 2nd. Street
Campbell, Edward A. .... '36 '65 C.249 B.S.E.E. L.345 J.D. Sr. J.
Cosby, Julie Dersch '72 '97 C.249 B.A. L.1119 J.D.
Gen Coun., Compl. Offr., Peoples Tr. & Svgs. Bk.
Hendrickson, Donald G. .... '32 '56 C.249 A.B. L.1119 LL.B. Cir. J.
Hendrickson, J. Waldo .... '13 '37 C.210 A.B. L.477 LL.B. Peoples Tr. & Svgs. Bk.
Hendrickson, Mark Hart, (BV) .... '50 '77 C.210 B.A. L.300 J.D. P.O. Box 307

Kahn, Dees, Donovan & Kahn, LLP
(See Evansville)

Long, S. Anthony, (BV) .... '44 '70 C.210 A.B. L.347 J.D. 301 W. Main St.
Martin, Charles L., (BV) .... '38 '63 C.210 B.A. L.477 J.D. 125 S. 2nd St.
Meier, Keith A., (BV) .... '49 '76 C.346 B.A. L.345 J.D. Supr. Ct. J.
Neff, Mark E., (BV) .... '50 '75 C.347 A.B. L.1119 J.D. [M.E.Neff]
Neff, Mark E., Law Office, Inc., (BV) .... 224 W. Locust Street
Phillips, Mark K., (CV) .... '63 '93 C.209 B.A. L.347 J.D. 301 W. Main St.
Phillips, Michael K., (BV) .... '43 '69 C.210 B.A. L.345 J.D. 301 W. Main St.
Rideout, Robert H., (BV) .... '28 '57 C.249 A.B. L.1119 LL.B. 132 W. Locust St.

Rudolph, Fine, Porter & Johnson LLP
(See Evansville)

Scales, John B., (BV) .... '33 '61 C.249 B.S. L.1119 LL.B. 226 S. 3rd St.

Terrell, Baugh, Salmon & Born, LLP
(See Evansville)

Weyerbacher, John W., (BV) .... '52 '77 C.347 A.B. L.345 J.D. 130 S. 3rd St.
Zengler, David K., (BV) .... '49 '74 C.249 B.S. L.345 J.D. 106 S. 3rd St.

BRAZIL, * 8,188, *Clay Co.*

Akers, J. Blaine, (BV) .... '52 '84 C.346 B.S. L.347 J.D. 2092 E. County Road 900 N.
Baumunk, John M., (AV) .... '26 '57 C.346 B.S. L.1119 LL.B. 211 E. National Ave.‡

Berry, Margaret A., (BV) ....'50 '76 C.347 A.B. L.1119 J.D. 13 W. National Ave.
Brown, William G., (CV) .... '42 '68 C.346 B.S. L.1119 J.D. 711 E. Jackson St.

Hunt, Hassler & Lorenz LLP
(See Terre Haute)

Neal, Robert W. .... '24 '51 C.347 A.B. L.1119 J.D. Ret. App. Ct. J.
Pell, Robert A., (CV) ....'55 '80 C.347 A.B. L.345 J.D. Dep. Pros. Atty.
Reberger, B. Lee, Jr. ....'69 '95 C.346 B.A. L.1119 J.D. 211 East National Avenue
Simons, Sam J. '55 '81 C.1099 B.S. L.425 J.D.
(adm. in LA; not adm. in IN) 614 N. Meridian St.‡
Stelle, John P. ....'39 '71 C.346 B.S. L.1119 J.D. Supr. Ct. J.
Sumhile, Eric D., (CV) ....'52 '86 C.346 B.A. L.345 J.D. 711 E. Jackson
Thomas, Amos P., (AV) .... '30 '56 C.347 A.B. L.1119 J.D. [Thomas&T.]
Thomas, Andrew P., (CV) ....'60 '87 C.347 B.A. L.879 J.D. [Thomas]
Thomas, John J., (AV) .... '23 '48 C.347 L.1119 LL.B. [Thomas&T.]
Thomas Law Firm, (CV) .... 33 W. National Ave.
Thomas & Thomas, (AV) .... 33 W. National Ave.

Wilkinson, Goeller, Modesitt, Wilkinson & Drummy
(See Terre Haute)

Wyndham, Eric L. ....'46 '73 C.347 B.S. L.345 J.D. 115 E. National Ave.
Yelton, Ernest E. ....'48 '74 C.347 A.B. L.345 J.D. Cir. J.

BREMEN, 4,486, *Marshall Co.*

Holmes, David R., (BV) '43 '67
C.679 B.A. L.602 LL.B. Pros. Atty. [Holmes&W.] (⊙Plymouth)
Holmes & Walter, LLP, (BV) .... 116 W. Plymouth St. (⊙Nappanee, Plymouth)
Kizer & Neu, LLP, (AV) .... 1406 West Plymouth Street (⊙Plymouth)
Newcomb, Jon E., Law Office, (CV) '44 '72 C.210 B.A. L.1119 J.D.
2149 Hill Trail Rd.
Wagner, Mark E., (BV) ....'50 '75 C.999 B.A. L.345 J.D. [Kizer&N.]

BRISTOL, 1,333, *Elkhart Co.*

Muir, David J. ....'28 '68 C.265 A.B. L.345 J.D. 55535 State Rd. 15‡
Schmuhl, William J., Jr. '43 '67
C&L.602 B.B.A., LL.B. Pres. & CEO, Heywood Williams, Inc.

BROOKSTON, 1,804, *White Co.*

Little, Robert H., Law Office of, (BV) .... '51 '76 C.679 B.S. L.339 J.D. 600 S. Prairie St.
Trent, Rebecca A. .... '69 '94 C.679 B.S. L.347 J.D. [Ⓐ R.H.Little]

BROOKVILLE, * 2,652, *Franklin Co.*

Barrett, David P., (AV) .... '37 '62 C.347 A.B. L.1119 J.D. [Barrett&W.]
Barrett & Wilhelm, (AV) ....1 Bracken Hill
Bohland, Michael L., (AV) ....'13 '35 C&L.347 LL.B. 312 Franklin St.‡
McMillin, Lowell C., (BV) ....'49 '74 C.63 B.S. L.150 J.D. 814 Main St.
Mullin, James P. ....'07 '34 C.339 B.S. L.273 J.D. 814 Main St.‡
O'Connor, Thomas J., (BV) ....'31 '57 C.347 A.B. L.1119 LL.B. [O'Connor&S.]
O'Connor & Stewart, (AV) .... 601 Main St.
Rychener, Ronald K., (BV) ....'49 '74 C.610 A.B. L.150 J.D. 814 Main St.
Smith, Roger H., (AV) ....'31 '58 C.347 B.S. L.1119 J.D. Chf. Dep. Pros. Atty.
Stewart, Eugene A., (AV) .... '45 '70 C&L.383 B.S., J.D. [O'Connor&S.]

Thompson Law Office
(See Connersville)

Werner, Troy C., (BV) .... '69 '94 C.679 B.A. L.347 J.D. Chf. Dep. Pros.
Wilhelm, Melvin F., (BV) .... '49 '76 C.435 B.S. L.999 J.D. Pros. Atty. [Barrett&W.]
Wilhelm-Waggoner, Brenda L., Law Office of, (BV) '71 '97
C&L.347 B.C.J., J.D. 424 Court Street

BROWNSBURG, 14,520, *Hendricks Co.*

Bays, Donna J.
(See Indianapolis)

Blake, Harold W., (BV) .... '53 '79 C.63 B.S. L.345 J.D. P.O. Box 1021
Bracken, William L. ....'43 '90 C.1111 B.A. L.347 J.D. 16 Ashwood Cir.‡
Casey, Thomas A., (BV) ....'51 '81 C.1024 B.S. L.345 J.D. [Dunbar&C.]
Dorman, Jeffery S. ....'55 '84 C&L.347 B.S., J.D. 23 Motif Blvd., Ste. 101
Dunbar, D. Joseph, (BV) ....'51 '81 C.346 B.S. L.345 J.D. [Dunbar&C.]
Dunbar & Casey, (BV) ....21 N. Green
Engel, Charles C., Law Offices, (BV) '49 '74
C.347 B.S. L.1119 J.D. 41 Motif Blvd., Ste. A
Falvey, Charles L., (AV) .... '31 '56 C.436 A.B. L.345 J.D. 10821 E. County Rd. 750 N.‡
Gordon, Brian S. ....'61 '90 C&L.347 B.S., J.D. 9850 N. 950 E
Gordon, Susan W. .... '64 '90 C&L.347 B.S., J.D. 9850 N. 950 E.
Helfrich, Cynthia P. ....'71 '98 C&L.1119 B.A., J.D. [Ⓐ Dunbar&C.]
Hostetter, Charles E., (BV) ....'46 '76 C.347 B.A. L.910 J.D. [Hostetter&O.]
Hostetter & O'Hara, (BV) ....515 N. Green St., Ste. 200
Johnson, Brian J. ....'68 '97 C.347 B.A. L.345 J.D. [Ⓐ Hostetter&O.]
O'Hara, Mark S., (BV) ....'59 '85 C.608 B.S. L.345 J.D. [Hostetter&O.]
Stalcup, Wayne L. ....'21 '59 C.346 B.S. L.345 J.D. 7618 Burns Dr.‡
Sutherland, David J., (BV) ....'51 '84 C.885 B.A. L.345 J.D. 345 Rapid Rill Lane
Tucker, Mary Ann ....'— '73 C.579 B.S. L.345 J.D. [Tucker] (See Pat. Sect.)

Tucker Law Offices
61 Ridgeway Drive, 46112-1004
Telephone: 317-852-3291 Fax: 317-852-7537
Email: mtuckeresq@aol.com
Mary Ann Tucker.
Intellectual Property, Patent and Trademark Law.

See Professional Biographies, BROWNSBURG, INDIANA

Vorndran-Jones, MaCharri R. '60 '93
C.432 B.S. L.347 J.D. Corp. Coun., Eli Lilly & Co. (Pat.)
West, Robert D. .... '35 '73 C.210 B.A. L.345 J.D. 21 Augusta Dr.‡

BROWNSTOWN, * 2,978, *Jackson Co.*

Lambring, Ronald K., (BV) .... '47 '76 C.303 B.A. L.1340 J.D. 136 S. Main St.
Markel, Bruce S., III, (BV) .... '47 '74 C.575 A.B. L.421 J.D. [Markel&M.]
Markel, Joseph K., (BV) .... '52 '77 C.16 B.A. L.421 J.D. [Markel&M.]
Markel & Markel, (BV) .... 136 South Main Street
Nierman, Jeffrey A., (BV) .... '43 '68 C.347 B.S. L.1119 J.D. Co. Pros. Atty.

BUTLER, 2,725, *De Kalb Co.*

McNerney, Gerald M., (BV) .... '44 '73 C.932 B.S. L.345 J.D. Co. Coun. Atty.

CAMBRIDGE CITY, 2,091, *Wayne Co.*

Todd, Charles K., Jr., (BV) ....'62 '96 C.63 B.A. L.345 J.D. 15 N. Foote St.

CANNELTON, * 1,209, *Perry Co.*

Hay, Norman E. .... '34 '66 C.15 B.A. L.345 J.D. 201 East 7th Street
Waldschmidt, William H., (AV) .... '10 '34 C&L.347 A.B., J.D. P.O. Box 147‡

CARMEL, 37,733, *Hamilton Co.*

Abel, David R., (BV) .... '53 '78 C.265 B.S. L.345 J.D. [Dickinson&A.]
Abel & Lantis, P.C. .... 301 E. Carmel Dr.
Ailes, Thaddeus R. ....'71 '97 C.108 B.S. L.1119 J.D. [Ⓐ Harrison&M.]
Altman, Christine Crull, (BV) .... '54 '81 C.347 B.S. L.345 J.D. 1219 Hillcrest Dr.
Archer, Edward A. .... '59 '84 C.346 B.S. L.345 J.D. 390 Uxbridge Lane
Atherly, Harold E., (BV) ....'36 '68 C.976 B.A. L.813 LL.B. [Petit H.A.&P.]
Austgen, Priscilla Howell ....'50 '77 C.1264 B.A. L.1119 J.D. 356 W. 107th St.
Baber, Jeremy S. ....'73 '01 C.679 B.A. L.1187 J.D. 931 S. Rangeline Rd.
Back, Kathleen D. .... '62 '93 C&L.347 B.S., J.D. Sr. V.P. & Gen. Coun., Pedcor Bancorp
Bardach, Gail T. Z., (CV) .... '50 '75 C.347 B.A. L.345 J.D. City Ct. J.
Barker, David J., (BV) ....'62 '89 C.347 B.S. L.879 J.D. [D.J.Barker]
Barker, David J., P.C., (BV) .... 12588 Sandstone Run
Barr, Jerry M. .... '41 '67 C.976 A.B. L.145 J.D. [Krieg D.]
Beeman, Melissa K. ....'74 '01 C.973 B.A. L.345 J.D. Pedcor Bancorp
Bender, Wayne F. '55 '80 C&L.339 A.B., J.D.
(adm. in IL; not adm. in IN) Gen. Coun., BFS Diversified Products, Inc.
Berg, Alexis M., (BV) '46 '77 C.659 B.A. L.831 J.D.
(adm. in PA; not adm. in IN)
V.P. & Assoc. Gen. Coun., Conseco, Inc. (Legal Department)
Bernard, Ann Cassidy '61 '87
C.108 B.A. L.345 J.D. Gen. Coun., One Call Communications, Inc.
Blanck, Clinton E. ....'71 '96 C.347 B.A. L.345 J.D. [Ⓐ Maurer R.&H.]
Bober, John M. ....'60 '00 C.879 B.S.M.E. L.345 J.D. 12650 Hamilton Crossing Blvd.
Bower, Raymond C. ....'18 '41 C.756 L.602 LL.B. 8 W. Main St.
Bowman, Bruce J. .... '61 '88 C.679 B.S.E. L.607 J.D. [Bowman&Assoc.] (Pat.)
Bowman & Associates .... 1016 3rd Ave. S.W. (Pat.)
Briggs, James A., (BV) .... '32 '57 C.210 A.B. L.477 J.D. 10361 Towne Rd.
Bromund, Mark V. ....'64 '90 C.679 B.A. L.347 J.D. 4436 Blue Creek Dr.
Broyles, John A. ....'68 '97 C.210 B.A. L.347 J.D. [Broyles,K.&R.]
Broyles, Kight & Ricafort, LLP ....11595 North Meridian Street, Suite 300
Burkett, Robert E., Jr. '54 '81 C.679 B.A. L.1119 J.D.
Sr. V.P., Legal, Conseco, Inc. (Legal Department)
Buroker, Andrew B., (AV) .... '61 '90 C.210 B.A. L.1119 J.D. [Krieg D.]
Bussell, Donald D. ....'40 '68 C.679 B.A. L.345 J.D. [Bussell&B.]
Bussell, Ronald L. ....'40 '72 C.679 B.A. L.345 J.D. [Bussell&B.]
Bussell and Bussell ....703 Pro-Med Lane
Butcher, Curtis J., Law Offices .... '39 '71 C&L.347 B.S., J.D. 8 W. Main St.
Butler, Scott D., (AV) '55 '82
C.679 B.A. L.976 J.D. V.P. & Sr. Coun., Pedcor Investments, LLC
Campbell, Jamie Thompson .... '58 '84 542 Tulip Poplar Crst.

Campbell Kyle Proffitt LLP, (AV)
11595 N. Meridian, Suite 701, 46032 ⊙
Telephone: 317-846-6514 FAX: 317-843-8097
Email: ckplaw@ckplaw.com URL: http://www.ckplaw.com
Members of Firm: John D. Proffitt; Deborah L. Farmer; William E. Wendling, Jr.; Anne Hensley Poindexter; Michael A. Casati; Rodney T. Sarkovics. Associates: Scott P. Wyatt; Amy E. Higdon; N. Scott Smith.
Civil Practice. State and Federal Courts and Administrative Agencies, Domestic Relations, Family Law, Divorce, Adoptions, Personal Injury, Corporation, Business Law, Utility Law, Insurance, Wills and Probate, Trusts and Estates, Estate Planning and Elder Law, Real Estate, Zoning, Employment Law, Criminal Law. Contracts, Taxation, Real Estate, Commercial Litigation.
Representative Clients: PSI Energy, Inc.; Mobil Oil Corp.; Minnesota Mining & Manufacturing Co.; Buck Creek Utilities; Conseco Insurance Companies.
Noblesville Office: 198 South Ninth Street, P.O. Box 2020. Telephone: 317-773-2090. Fax: 317-776-5051.

See Professional Biographies, CARMEL, INDIANA

Carafiol, Laura Spitzberg .... '69 '94 C&L.347 B.A., J.D. 1363 Clay Springs Dr.

Carroll, Daniel R.
(See Indianapolis)

Cartmel, Thomas O., (BV) ....'33 '64 C.63 A.B. L.345 LL.B. 155 Audubon Dr.‡
Casati, Michael A. .... '59 '92 C&L.347 B.S., J.D. [Campbell K.P.]
Cassman, Ryan H. ....'75 '02 C.347 B.A. L.345 J.D. [Ⓐ Coots,H.&W.]
Chadd, Darren C. ....'69 '95 C.894 B.A. L.345 J.D. [Ⓐ Jennings T.&W.]
Christ, Dale Albert '59 '85 C.801 B.S. L.734 J.D.
(adm. in IL; not adm. in IN) 5973 Osage Dr.

Church, Church, Hittle & Antrim
(See Noblesville)

Clark, Kathleen L. ....'62 '93 C.679 B.S. L.74 J.D. [Clark&Assoc.]
Clark and Associates .... 9640 N. Augusta Dr., Ste. 412
Coleman, Charles S., II .... '71 '96 C.602 B.B.A. L.16 J.D. [Krieg D.] (⊙Indianapolis)
Colliflower, Michael A., (AVⓉ) '54 '79 C.1122 B.B.A. L.896 J.D.
(adm. in NC; not adm. in IN) Sr. V.P., Legal, Conseco, Inc. (Legal Department)
Conrad, Matthew E. .... '78 '03 C.827 B.S. L.1119 J.D. [Ⓐ Krieg D.] (⊙Indianapolis)
Coots, Daniel E. .... '72 '99 C&L.347 B.S., J.D. [Coots,H.&W.]
Coots, E. Davis, (AV) ....'44 '69 C.504 B.A. L.345 J.D. [Coots,H.&W.]

Coots, Henke & Wheeler, Professional Corporation, (AV)
255 East Carmel Drive, 46032
Telephone: 317-844-4693 Fax: 317-573-5385
URL: http://www.lawyers.com/chwlaw
E. Davis Coots; James K. Wheeler; Jay Curts; James D. Crum; Jeffrey S. Zipes; Elizabeth I. Van Tassel; Matthew L. Hinkle; J. Kathryn Jenkins; Daniel E. Coots;—Ryan H. Cassman; Laura E. Trulock; Erin Maloy. Of Counsel: Steven H. Henke.
General Civil and Criminal Practice. Litigation in all Courts. Corporate, Insurance, Probate and Estate Planning, Taxation, Real Estate and Zoning and Planning Law. Business Law, Personal Injury, Insurance Defense, Tort and Family Law, Divorce Law, Criminal Law, Domestic Relations.
Representative Clients: Thomas & Skinner, Inc.; MPD, Inc.; Silco Engineering Co., Inc.; Metro Bank.

See Professional Biographies, CARMEL, INDIANA

Correll, Philip R. ....'17 '45 C&L.347 A.B., LL.B. 111 Audubon Dr.‡
Crossen, Trevor J. .... '69 '95 C.674 A.B. L.347 J.D. [Wagner R.&C.]
Crum, James D., (BV) ....'61 '89 C.608 B.A. L.345 J.D. [Coots,H.&W.]
Cullem-Fiore, Meg '57 '92 C.262 M.B.A. L.362 J.D.
V.P., Assoc. Gen. Coun., Conseco, Inc. (Legal Department)
Curts, Jay, (BV) .... '63 '88 C.347 B.S. L.345 J.D. [Coots,H.&W.]
Cutter, G. Terry .... '39 '68 C.63 B.S. L.345 J.D. 11641 Eden Estates Dr.‡

DeLaney & DeLaney LLC
(See Indianapolis)

Dickinson, Curtis J. ....'59 '85 C.992 A.B. L.990 J.D. [Dickinson&A.]
Dickinson & Abel, A Professional Corporation, (BV) ........P.O. Box 306
Dilley, Daniel K. ....'— '01 C.1568 B.S. L.345 J.D. [Ⓐ Knowles&Assoc.]
Downs, Edward L., Jr. ....'51 '83 C.934 B.A. L.1137 J.D. P.O. Box 874
Draper, Monette E. ....'52 '80 C.679 B.A. L.345 J.D. 1352 W. 106th St.

Drewry Simmons Vornehm, LLP
(See Indianapolis)

Dutton & Associates, L.L.C.
(See Indianapolis)

Dziuba, Ann L., Law Office of '65 '90 C.602 B.A. L.424 J.D.
(adm. in IL; not adm. in IN) 14041 Settlers Ridge Trl.

Eichhorn & Eichhorn, (AV)
9640 North Augusta Drive Suite 412, 46032 ⊙
Telephone: 317-228-9670 Telecopier: 317-228-9569
Senior Associate: Michael Roth.
General Practice, Litigation in State and Federal Courts. Public Utility, Banking, Corporation, Health Care, Insurance, Commercial Transactions, Labor and Employment Law, Real Estate, Professional Liability and Tort Law. Mediation.
Hammond, Indiana Office: 200 Russell Street, P.O. Box 6328, 46325. Telephone: 219-931-0560. Fax: 219-931-5370.
See Professional Biographies, CARMEL, INDIANA

Elsner, Stephen E. .... '58 '83 C.347 B.S. L.345 J.D. 12463 Glendurgan Dr.
Elwood, Clark D., (AV) '60 '84 C.221 B.S.B.A. L.910 J.D.
Sr. V.P., Gen. Coun. & Secy., ITT Educational Servs., Inc.
Emerson, Jill M. .... '67 '95 C.679 B.A. L.347 J.D. [Ⓐ Schultz&P.]
Epstein, J. David .... '51 '78 C.1236 B.A. L.880 J.D. P.O. Box 305
Fairfield, Stephanie J. .... '65 '00 C.347 B.S. L.345 J.D. [Ⓐ Maurer R.&H.]
Farmer, Deborah L., (AV) .... '54 '83 C.108 B.S. L.345 J.D. [Campbell K.P.]
Fedder, Richard Scott .... '53 '00 C.103 L.801 State Atty. App. Pros.
Field, David G. .... '71 '97 C.347 B.S. L.345 J.D. [Ⓐ Schultz&P.]
Fineberg, M. J. .... '11 '36 C.347 B.A. L.1119 LL.B. 116 E. Carmel Dr.‡
Foster, Herman .... '29 '57 C.563 B.C.E. L.273 J.D. Consultant, Retired‡
Frank, Phillip B., (BV) '59 '84 C.347 B.S. L.345 J.D.
Asst. Gen. Coun. & Dir., Real Estate, ITT Educational Servs., Inc.
Fuson, Bradley S., (BV) .... '59 '86 C.210 B.A. L.345 J.D. [Krieg D.]
Galloway, Michael C. .... '47 '79 C.679 B.A. L.345 J.D. 891 Cedar Wood
Garino, Carla V. .... '73 '98 C.108 B.A. L.1119 J.D. [Ⓒ Schultz&P.]
Geisler, Stephan H. .... '61 '88 C.477 B.A. L.276 J.D. [Ⓐ Krieg D.]
Gillaspy, Joseph M. .... '27 '79 C.108 A.B. L.345 J.D. 5930 Bunty Lane‡
Goldberg, Paula S. .... '65 '91 C.477 B.A. L.1009 J.D. 10464 Windemere Dr.
Gowan, Darrin L. .... '66 '91 C.999 B.S. L.990 J.D. 703 Pro-Med Lane, Suite 202
Graber, Gale, (AV) .... '17 '40 C&L.347 B.A., J.D. 962 Lenox Lane‡
Green, Kelly J. .... '69 '04 C.63 B.S. L.345 J.D. [Ⓐ Krieg D.] (⊙Indianapolis)
Grooms, Thomas E., Jr. .... '63 '97 C.210 B.A. L.1187 J.D. [Ⓐ Dickinson&A.]
Gross, Stephen A., (BV) .... '44 '72 C.108 B.S. L.345 J.D. P.O. Box 328
Hahn, Stephanie J. .... '69 '95 C.992 B.A. L.879 J.D. [Kendall&H.]
Haley, Thomas R., III .... '61 '87 C.347 B.A. L.345 J.D. [Jennings T.&W.]
Hamm, Angela L. .... '74 '99 C.347 B.A. L.345 J.D. [Ⓐ Krieg D.] (⊙Indianapolis)
Haney, Douglas C., (BV) .... '56 '81 C&L.966 B.A., J.D. Asst. City Atty.
Hardy, Gregory A. '59 '86 C.967 B.A. L.276 J.D.
(adm. in DC; not adm. in IN)
V.P. & Assoc. Gen. Coun., Conseco, Inc. (Legal Department)
Hardy, Richard M., (BV) .... '38 '71 C.679 B.S. L.345 J.D. P.O. Box 3744‡
Harlow, Stephen A., (BV) .... '40 '68 C.679 B.S. L.1119 J.D. 2000 E. 116th St.
Harris, Wayne A. '63 '90 C.659 B.S. L.347 J.D.
Chf. Coun., ACES Power Marketing LLC

Harrison & Moberly, LLP, (AV)
11611 North Meridian Street Suite 150, 46032 ⊙
Telephone: 317-639-4511 Fax: 317-574-6055
Email: attorneys@h-mlaw.com URL: http://www.harrisonmoberly.com
Partners: Rory O'Bryan; Jeffrey W. Scripture. Senior Counsel: Robert J. Hoffman (Resident, Carmel Office). Associate: Thaddeus R. Ailes (Resident, Carmel Office).
Marion Office: 315 South Adams Street, 3rd Floor, Marion, Indiana, 46952. Telephone: 765-673-6499.
See Professional Biographies, CARMEL, INDIANA

Hatch, Millicent E. .... '— '78 C.999 B.A. L.347 J.D. [Knowles&Assoc.]
Hearn, David L. .... '61 '91 C&L.347 B.S., J.D. 5166 Woodside Court
Hearn, Jeffrey A., (AV) .... '56 '81 C.346 B.S. L.221 J.D. 2325 Pointe Parkway
Heck, Nancy S. .... '58 '96 C&L.347 B.A., J.D. 1 Civic Sq.
Helfrich, James C. '47 '79 C.800 M.A. L.37 J.D.
(adm. in AZ; not adm. in IN) [Ⓒ Dickinson&A.]
Henke, Steven H., (BV) .... '51 '77 C.347 B.S. L.345 J.D. [Ⓒ Coots,H.&W.]
Hess, Jennifer M. .... '78 '03 C&L.347 B.A., J.D. 2000 East 116th Street Suite 106
Hess, John L., (AV) .... '43 '68 C.347 A.B. L.1119 J.D. 2000 East 116th Street, Suite 106
Higdon, Amy E. .... '75 '99 C.63 B.S. L.345 J.D. [Ⓐ Campbell K.P.]
Hill, Sherwood P., (AV) .... '35 '70 C.347 B.S. L.345 J.D. [Maurer R.&H.]
Hinkle, Matthew L., (CV) .... '70 '96 C&L.347 B.A., J.D. [Coots,H.&W.]
Hiott, Angela D. .... '72 '97 C.317 B.A. L.347 J.D. [Ⓐ Jennings T.&W.]
Hirschman, Elizabeth Hurst .... '64 '89 C.1119 B.S. L.339 J.D. 10418 Bosahan Ct.
Ho, Peter Peck-Koh '37 '85
C.911 Ph.D. L.347 J.D. Gen. Coun. & Sr. V.P., Telamon Corporation
Hoffman, Frank A., (AV) .... '57 '83 C.210 B.A. L.345 J.D. [Krieg D.]
Hoffman, Robert J., (AV) .... '45 '74 C.347 A.B. L.345 J.D. [Ⓒ Harrison&M.]
Hollingsworth, Kena S. .... '74 '02 C.999 B.A. L.74 J.D. [Hollingsworth J.&Z.]
Hollingsworth Jocham & Zivitz, LLC .... 9650 N. Augusta Dr., Suite 532

Holt, Fleck & Romine
(See Noblesville)

Hopko, Dorothy J. .... '43 '86 C.935 B.A. L.790 J.D. Asst. Dir.
Hughes, David B., (AV) .... '39 '64 C.611 A.B. L.1119 J.D. 13762 Driftwood Dr.
Husman, Charles E. .... '42 '75 C.679 B.S. L.345 J.D. Tr. Offr., NBD Bank, N.A.
Irvin, Robert H. .... '52 '77 C.63 B.S. L.347 J.D. R.H. Irvin & Co., Inc.
Jackson, Ronald L. '48 '76 C.210 B.A. L.345 J.D.
V.P. & Assoc. Gen. Coun., Conseco, Inc. (Legal Department)
Jaques, Tracy L. .... '68 '96 C.347 B.A. L.1187 J.D. Atty., Ingersoll-Rand Co.
Jenkins, J. Kathryn, (BV) .... '44 '94 C.679 B.S. L.347 J.D. [Coots,H.&W.]
Jennings, Charles T., (BV) .... '48 '78 C.347 A.B. L.345 J.D. [Jennings T.&W.]
Jennings Taylor & Wheeler, P.C., (AV) .... 11711 N. Pennsylvania St., Suite 250
Jocham, Stephenie .... '68 '01 C.739 B.A. L.345 J.D. [Hollingsworth J.&Z.]
Johnston, Thomas M., (AV) .... '48 '74 C.347 B.S. L.345 J.D. [Ⓐ Maurer R.&H.]
Kagan, Harvey M., (CV) .... '40 '70 C.347 A.B. L.1119 J.D. 316 Meadow Lane
Kauffman, Mary K. '41 '91 C.475 B.S. L.1187 J.D.
(adm. in MI; not adm. in IN) Asst. V.P. & Coun., Conseco, Inc. (Legal Department)
Kendall, Michael C., (BV) .... '47 '75 C&L.602 B.A., J.D. [Kendall&H.]
Kendall & Hahn, (BV) .... 220 North Rangeline Road
Kenworthy, Kraig A., (BV) .... '61 '88 C.210 B.A. L.1148 J.D. P.O. Box 1241
Khairy, Ibrahim W. .... '— '02 C.30 B.A. L.347 J.D. 15219 Citation Rd.
Kight, Megan J. .... '73 '97 C.210 B.A. L.347 J.D. [Broyles,K.&R.]
Kindig, Karl W., (AV) '55 '80 C.347 B.S. L.228 J.D.
Senior Vice President, Legal, Conseco, Inc. (Legal Department)
Kite, Donald B., Sr., (BV) .... '60 '87 C.423 B.A. L.345 J.D. [Schultz&P.]
Knowles, William W., (AV) .... '— '69 C.347 A.B. L.345 J.D. [Knowles&Assoc.]

Knowles & Associates, LLC, (AV) BB
811 South Range Line Road, 46032
Telephone: 317-848-4360 Telecopier: 317-848-4363
Email: Firm@KnowlesAssociatesLLC.com URL: http://www.lawyers.com/knowles
William W. Knowles; Millicent E. Hatch;—Shawn M. Scott; Daniel K. Dilley.
Practice limited to Wills and Probate, Business Law, Business Planning, Starting a Business, Buying and Selling a Business, Elder Law, Estate Planning, Litigation, Trusts and Estates, Tax Planning, Medicaid Planning.
See Professional Biographies, CARMEL, INDIANA

Kochinski, James '64 '92 C.1111 B.A. L.1000 J.D.
V.P. & Asst. Gen. Coun., Conseco, Inc. (Legal Department)
Kooi, Jeffrey R. .... '76 '00 C.999 B.A. L.801 J.D. [Kooi]
Kooi Law Firm, LLC 11939
Kovacs, William P. '46 '74 C.894 B.A. L.352 J.D.
(adm. in IA; not adm. in IN)
V.P., Sr. Coun. & Chf. Compl. Offr., Conseco, Inc. (Legal Department)
Kozey, Stephen G. '50 '76 C.311 B.A. L.659 J.D.
(adm. in DC; not adm. in IN) Gen. Coun., Midwest ISO

Krieg DeVault LLP, (AV)
12800 North Meridian Street, Suite 300, 46032 ⊙
Telephone: 317-566-1110 Fax: 317-636-1507
Email: contact@kdlegal.com URL: http://www.kriegdevault.com
Partners: Bradley S. Fuson; Jeffrey C. McDermott; Frank A. Hoffman; Eric A. Manterfield; Andrew B. Buroker; Glenn T. Troyer; The Honorable Jerry M. Barr; Susan E. Ziel; Charles S. Coleman, II. Of Counsel: Edward R. Schmidt. Associates: Rodney S. Retzner; Robert S. Schein; Stephan H. Geisler; Matthew R. Strzynski; Matthew E. Conrad; Kelly J. Green; Angela L. Hamm; Nigel J. Riggins.
Acquisitions, Divestitures and Mergers, Antitrust, Appeals, Banking, Bankruptcy, Business and Commercial, Copyright, Corporations, Creditors'' Rights, Employee Benefits, Energy, Environmental, ERISA, Estate Planning and Probate, Family/Domestic Relations, Federal and State Taxation, Government Relations, Health Care, Hospital Law, Intellectual Property, Insurance, International, Labor and Employment, Legislative, Litigation, Patent, Public Finance, Public Utilities, Products Liability, Real Estate, Securities Law, Tax-Exempt and Nonprofit Organizations, Technology and E-Commerce, Trademark.
Indianapolis, Indiana Office: One Indiana Square, Suite 2800, 46204. Telephone: 317-636-4341. Fax: 317-636-1507.
Fort Wayne, Indiana Office: Krieg DeVault Lundy LLP, 825 Anthony Wayne Building, 203 East Berry Street, 46802. Telephone: 260-422-1534. Fax: 260-423-1590.
Hammond, Indiana Office: Krieg DeVault Galvin LLP, 5231 Hohman Avenue, 46320. Telephone: 219-933-0380. Fax: 219-933-0471.
See Professional Biographies, CARMEL, INDIANA

Kyle, Catherine L., (BV) .... '71 '96 C.575 B.A. L.1119 J.D. [Ⓐ Schultz&P.]
Lamberti, Ida C. .... '39 '92 C.190 B.A. L.1119 J.D. [Ⓐ Maurer R.&H.]
Lantis, Edgar R., III .... '59 '87 C.63 B.S. L.879 J.D. [Abel&L.]
Latimer, William P. '35 '64 C.951 B.A. L.309 LL.B.
(adm. in PA; not adm. in IN) 11825 N. Penn. St.
Leventhal, Barbara W. .... '49 '74 C.347 A.B. L.345 J.D. 225 E. Carmel Dr.
Linnemeier, Philip, (AV) .... '53 '79 C.347 B.A. L.879 J.D. [Smith&L.]
Lorenz, John T., (AV) .... '42 '68 C.602 A.B. L.1119 J.D. [Ⓐ Smith&L.]
Loveland, Gail M. .... '51 '76 C&L.477 B.A., J.D. 221 1st Ave., N.E.‡
Lund, Jeffrey L. .... '73 '00 C.373 B.A. L.879 J.D. [Ⓐ Schultz&P.]
Maier, Paula J. .... '64 '89 C&L.347 B.S., J.D. 14101 Warbler Way N.
Mallon, Michelle .... '69 '00 C.63 B.A. L.345 J.D. Corp. Coun., ADESA Corp.
Maloy, Erin .... '78 '04 C&L.347 B.A., J.D. [Ⓐ Coots,H.&W.]
Manterfield, Eric A., (AV) .... '47 '72 C.207 B.A. L.477 J.D. [Krieg D.]
Marshall, Julia J. .... '70 '97 2nd V.P. & Coun., Conseco, Inc. (Legal Department)

Marshall, Sheila A., (AV) '56 '86 C.265 B.A. L.345 J.D.
320 S. Rangeline Road, 46032
Telephone: 317-575-0320 Fax: 317-575-9570
Email: sam@mandmlawyers.com URL: http://www.smarshalllaw.com
Family Law, Divorce, Child Custody, Visitation Issues, Child Support, Prenuptial Agreements, Mediation.
See Professional Biographies, CARMEL, INDIANA

Maturi, Dheepa R. .... '70 '95 C.477 B.A. L.145 J.D. 10548 Chatham Ct.

Maurer Rifkin & Hill, P.C., (AV)
11550 North Meridian Street, Suite 115, 46032
Telephone: 317-844-8372 Fax: 317-573-5564
Email: rrifkin@mrhlaw.com URL: http://www.maurerrifkinandhill.com
Robert S. Rifkin; Sherwood P. Hill;—Clinton E. Blanck; Stephanie J. Fairfield; Ida C. Lamberti; Thomas M. Johnston.
Labor and Employment Law, Disability Accommodation, Discrimination, Employee Benefits, Wrongful Termination, Sexual Harassment, Civil Rights, Business Law, Business Planning, Contracts, Business Litigation, Business Enterprises, Small Business, Partnerships, Limited Liability Companies, Buying and Selling a Business, Starting a Business, Corporate Law, Family Law, Adoptions, Child Custody, Child Support, Divorce, Wills, Probate, Trusts and Estates, Estate Planning.
See Professional Biographies, CARMEL, INDIANA

Mautner, Kathie P. '53 '88
(adm. in DC; not adm. in IN)
V.P. & Asst. Gen. Coun., Conseco, Inc. (Legal Department)
McDermott, Jeffrey C., (AV) .... '61 '86 C.679 B.A. L.602 J.D. [Krieg D.]
Meiners, Louis M., Jr. '50 '76 C&L.421 B.S., J.D.
(adm. in KY; not adm. in IN) 1303 E. 126th St.‡
Metzger, A. Richard .... '65 '00 C.602 B.S. L.851 J.D. 3436 Briar Dr.

Meyer Law Office
(See Indianapolis)

Moyer, Kevin L. .... '62 '98 C.344 B.S. L.347 J.D. 12800 N. Meridian St.
Murphy, Donald S. .... '57 '91 C.679 B.A. L.74 J.D. 803 Cedar Wood
Nelson, John Woodrow .... '58 '00 C.347 B.S. L.345 J.D. P.O. Box 143
New, Leroy K., (BV) .... '20 '46 C.362 A.B. L.1119 LL.B. 1910 E. 106th

Newton Becker Bouwkamp
(See Indianapolis)

O'Brien, Colleen M. .... '64 '90 C.339 B.A. L.347 J.D. [Ⓐ Jennings T.&W.]
O'Bryan, Rory, (AV) .... '47 '72 C.347 A.B. L.1119 J.D. [Harrison&M.] ⊙
Paulus, Sharon Marie .... '49 '84 Sagamore Health Network, Inc.
Petit, Bruce E., (BV) .... '56 '82 C.679 B.S. L.345 J.D. [Petit H.A.&P.]
Petit, Maurice R., (BV) .... '24 '51 C.679 B.S. L.345 J.D. [Petit H.A.&P.]
Petit, Miriam L., (BV) .... '27 '83 C.679 B.S. L.345 J.D. [Petit H.A.&P.]
Petit Hess Atherly & Petit, P.A., (BV) ...... Suite 106, 2000 E. 116th St.
Pinnick, Jon M., (BV) .... '64 '90 C.303 B.A. L.1119 J.D. [Schultz&P.]
Pippin, Judy W. .... '65 '92 C.63 B.S. L.347 J.D. [Ⓐ Wagner R.&C.]
Pogue, Peter H., (AV) .... '61 '89 C.210 B.A. L.879 J.D. [Schultz&P.]
Poindexter, Anne Hensley .... '62 '88 C.63 B.S. L.345 J.D. [Campbell K.P.]
Pontarelli, Thomas '49 '74 C.602 B.A. L.424 J.D.
(adm. in IL; not adm. in IN) Exec. V.P., Washington Natl. Ins. Co.
Proffitt, John D., (AV) .... '32 '59 C.894 A.B. L.145 J.D. [Campbell K.P.]
Reese, Jason R. .... '71 '97 C.37 B.A. L.1119 J.D. [Wagner R.&C.]

Reifeis, Paul E. ....'53 '84 C.347 L.345 J.D. 11939 N. Meridian St.‡

Reis, Catherine H. ....'53 '79 C.602 B.A. L.345 J.D. 795 Hawthorne Dr.‡

Retzner, Rodney S. ....'68 '98 C.701 B.S.M.E. L.150 J.D. [Ⓐ Krieg D.]

Ricafort, Nissa M. ....'72 '99 C.210 B.A. L.345 J.D. [Broyles,K.&R.]

Rifkin, Robert S., (BV) ....'44 '72 C.339 B.A. L.1119 J.D. [Maurer R.&H.]

Riggins, Nigel J. .... '78 '05 C.210 B.A. L.345 J.D. [Ⓐ Krieg D.] (⊙Indianapolis)

Rigsbee, Christopher B. '65 '90
V.P. & Assoc. Gen. Coun., Conseco, Inc. (Legal Department)

Ritz, Stephen M. ....'62 '90 C.597 B.A. L.347 J.D. 12360 Pebblepointe Pass

Rivers, L. Alan ....'56 '85 C.420 B.L.E. L.861 J.D. 703 Pro-Med Ln., Ste. 202

Roach, Charles S., Jr., (BV) '67 '92
C.602 B.A. L.347 J.D. Assoc. Gen. Coun., ADESA Corp.

Robertson, Stephen W. '46 '76 C&L.546 B.S., J.D.
(adm. in NE; not adm. in IN) Sr. V.P., Gov. Rel., Conseco, Inc. (Legal Department)

Rogers, Clark Howard ....'63 '89 C.210 B.A. L.201 J.D. 16 Horseshoe Lane

Rose, Anthony J., (BV) '64 '90 C.477 B.A. L.347 J.D.
V.P., Gen. Coun. & Corp. Secy., Haverstick Consulting, Inc.

Roth, Michael ....'— '95 C&L.347 B.S., J.D. [Ⓐ Eichhorn&E.]

Rubenstein, Clifford T. ....'53 '88 C.696 B.A. L.345 J.D. 12307 Windsor Dr.

Sams, Steven
(See Indianapolis)

Sarkovics, Rodney T. ....'70 '96 C.116 B.S. L.607 J.D. [Campbell K.P.]

Schein, Robert S., (AV) ....'70 '97 C.347 B.A. L.345 J.D. [Ⓐ Krieg D.]

Schiering, John H. '46 '81 C.103 B.A. L.1202 J.D.
(adm. in MA; not adm. in IN) 5179 Carrington Circle

Schlegel, Robert E., III ....'45 '86 C.229 B.A. L.347 J.D. 301 East Carmel Drive

Schmidt, Edward R., (BV) ....'47 '72 C.820 B.S. L.602 J.D. [Ⓒ Krieg D.]

Schultz, Thomas R., (AV) ....'62 '87 C&L.347 B.A., J.D. [Schultz&P.]

Schultz & Pogue, LLP, (AV)
11611 North Meridian Street Suite 706, 46032
Telephone: 317-569-2570 Fax: 317-569-2580
URL: http://www.schultzpoguelaw.com
Thomas R. Schultz; Peter H. Pogue; Jon M. Pinnick; Donald B. Kite, Sr.;—Jill M. Emerson; David G. Field; Catherine L. Kyle; Jeffrey L. Lund; Charles S. Smith. Of Counsel: Carla V. Garino; Angela L. Southern.
Insurance Defense, Personal Injury, Medical Malpractice, Pharmacy Law, Drugs and Medical Devices, Health Care, Administrative Law, Appellate Practice, Government Liability, Products Liability, Construction Law, Labor and Employment.

See Professional Biographies, CARMEL, INDIANA

Schuman, Jack, (AV) ....'26 '53 C.563 B.Ch.E. L.564 J.D. 3762 Carmel Dr.

Scott, Shawn M. ....'— '04 C.303 B.A. L.365 J.D. [Ⓐ Knowles&Assoc.]

Scripture, Jeffrey W., (AV) ....'62 '87 C.894 B.A. L.345 J.D. [Harrison&M.] ⊙

Seketa, Gregory J. ..... '63 '89 C.210 B.A. L.1119 J.D. V.P. & Coun., 40/86 Advisors, Inc.

Shopiro, Paula B. '61 '86 C.339 B.S. L.209 J.D.
(adm. in IL; not adm. in IN) V.P. & Corp. Coun., Washington Natl. Ins. Co.

Shortle, Barbara B. '48 '76 C.184 B.A. L.1119 J.D.
2nd V.P. & Asst. Gen. Coun., Conseco, Inc. (Legal Department)

Sims, Eileen J. ....'50 '94 C.679 B.A. L.1119 J.D. [Ⓐ Jennings T.&W.]

Slater, George G. ....'47 '79 C.399 B.A. L.347 J.D. [Slater&Assoc.]

Slater, Nancy F. ....'50 '99 C.339 B.S. L.345 J.D. [Ⓐ Slater&Assoc.]

Slater & Associates ....301 East Carmel Dr., Bldg. G

Smith, Charles S. ....'72 '01 C.63 B.S. L.280 J.D. [Ⓒ Schultz&P.]

Smith, Joseph S., Law Office of ....'49 '76 C.346 B.S. L.345 J.D. 201 Greyhound Pass

Smith, N. Scott ....'76 '05 C.679 B.A. L.1119 J.D. [Ⓐ Campbell K.P.]

Smith, Paul G. ....'24 '52 C.347 A.B. L.345 LL.B. 10427 Connaught Dr.‡

Smith, Robert A., (AV) ....'44 '70 C.347 B.S. L.1119 J.D. [Smith&L.]

Smith & Linnemeier, (AV) ....12900 N. Meridian St., Ste. 100

Soder, Carrie J. ....'75 '00 C&L.1119 B.S., J.D. 11711 N. Pennsylvania St., Ste. 250

Southern, Angela L. ....'63 '88 C.210 B.A. L.1119 J.D. [Ⓒ Schultz&P.]

Stafford, Jeffrey J. '63 '89 C.679 B.S. L.910 J.D.
Vice President & Assistant General Counsel, Conseco, Inc.

Starbuck, Dane C. ....'56 '91 C.333 B.A. L.276 J.D. 11950 Pebblepointe Pass

Stein, Richard P., (BV) ....'25 '50 C.228 L.421 J.D. 12588 Gray Rd.

Stephenson, M. Susann ....'55 '99 C&L.74 B.S., J.D. 754 Woodview South Drive

Stewart, Darron S. ....'67 '98 C.108 B.A. L.1187 J.D. 931 S Range Line Rd.

Stewart, David Wayne ....'— '89 C.894 B.A. L.347 J.D. [Stewart&S.]

Stewart & Stewart ....931 South Rangeline Road

Strzynski, Matthew R. ....'76 '02 C.347 B.A. L.150 J.D. [Ⓐ Krieg D.]

Sullivan, John F., Jr., (BV) ....'37 '66 C.435 A.B. L.345 LL.B. P.O. Box 479

Swingler, Lana R., (CV) ....'57 '82 C.63 B.S. L.345 J.D. 13106 Cheval Ct.

Taylor, David L., (AV) ....'61 '86 C.894 B.A. L.345 J.D. [Jennings T.&W.]

Thompson, Paul Kevin '53 '84
C.347 M.A.B. L.345 J.D. V.P., Risk Mgmt., Mayflower Transit, Inc.

Toombs, James R. ....'58 '92 C.347 B.S. L.345 J.D. 959 Keystone Way

Trierweiler, Robert L. '51 '76 C.172 B.S. L.608 J.D.
Coun. & Mgr. Real Est., ITT Educational Services, Inc.

Troyer, Glenn T., (AV) ....'44 '75 C.967 B.A. L.117 J.D. [Krieg D.]

Trulock, Laura E. ....'78 '03 C&L.347 B.A., J.D. [Ⓐ Coots,H.&W.]

Turner, Karen Calhoun, (AV) '63 '88
C.347 B.S. L.477 J.D. V.P. & Gen. Coun., ADESA Corp.

Ty, Claire M. ....'70 '04 C.999 L.345 J.D. [C.Ty]

Ty, Claire, Law Offices of ....30 E. Main St.

Van Tassel, Elizabeth I., (BV) ....'59 '91 C.719 B.S. L.347 J.D. [Coots,H.&W.]

Vestermark, Gary D., (AVⓉ) ....'41 '72 C.112 A.B. L.273 J.D. P.O. Box 232

Wagner, Stephen M. ....'69 '94 C.602 B.A. L.347 J.D. [Wagner R.&C.]

Wagner Reese & Crossen, LLP
11939 North Meridian, 46032
Telephone: 317-569-0000; 800-792-0332 Fax: 317-569-8088 URL: http://www.InjuryAttorneys.com
Email: WRC@InjuryAttorneys.com URL: http://www.lawyers.com/wrclaw
Stephen M. Wagner; Jason R. Reese; Trevor J. Crossen. Associate: Judy W. Pippin.
Personal Injury, Wrongful Death, Premises Liability, Construction Accidents, Medical Malpractice, Legal Malpractice, Workers Compensation, Insurance Claims, Civil Rights, Class Actions.

See Professional Biographies, CARMEL, INDIANA

Walsh, David L., (AV) ....'48 '73 C.63 B.S. L.345 J.D. 12183 Teal Ln.

Walsh, Michael S., (AV) ....'50 '75 C.602 B.B.A L.228 J.D. [M.S.Walsh]

Walsh, Michael S., P.C., (AV)
11350 North Meridian Street Suite 420, 46032-4528
Telephone: 317-575-5700 Fax: 317-575-5704
Email: msw@mwalshprofcorp.com
Michael S. Walsh.
General Civil Practice. Commercial, Corporate, Trusts and Estates, Estate Planning and Administration, Real Estate, Civil Litigation, Business Law and Closely Held Business Law.
Representative Clients: Herff Jones, Inc.; Superb Sound, Inc.

See Professional Biographies, CARMEL, INDIANA

Walters, Robert P. ....'62 '89 C&L.347 A.B., J.D. 190 Twin Springs Ct.

Ware, Robert C. ....'34 '58 C&L.347 A.B., J.D. [Ware&Assoc.]

Ware & Associates, P.C. ....10840 Tam O Shanter Dr.

Wells, Michael W. ....'53 '79 C.679 B.S. L.345 J.D. Pres., REI Investments, Inc.

Wendling, William E., Jr., (BV) ....'50 '83 C.842 B.A. L.345 J.D. [Campbell K.P.]

Wheeler, James K., (BV) ....'45 '71 C.679 B.S.M.E. L.345 J.D. [Coots,H.&W.]

Wheeler, Stephen C., (BV) ....'63 '89 C.63 B.S. L.904 J.D. [Jennings T.&W.]

Williams, Jennifer E. ....'— '95 C&L.280 A.B., J.D. 931 S. Rangeline Rd

Williams, John Christopher '61 '99 C.894 A.B. L.345 J.D.
Sr. Contracts Specialist, Ingersoll-Rand Company

Williams, Kenneth J. ....'48 '75 C.210 B.A. L.879 J.D. 12868 Northants Cir.

Wolkoff-Beall, Sherrie L. ....'60 '89 C.347 B.A. L.201 J.D. 13238 Snow Owl Dr.

Wyatt, Scott P. ....'70 '98 C.587 B.A. L.347 J.D. [Ⓐ Campbell K.P.]

Young, Elisabeth L. '60 '84 C&L.421 B.A., J.D.
(adm. in KY; not adm. in IN) 12984 Andover Dr

Zanetis, John M., Jr. ....'45 '71 C.346 B.S. L.345 J.D. [Zanetis]

Zanetis Law Office, P.C. ....301 E. Carmel Dr., Ste. H250

Ziel, Susan E. ....'51 '91 C.999 B.S.M. L.790 J.D. [Krieg D.]

Zimmerman, Ralph H. ....'23 '53 C.999 B.A. L.365 LL.B. 11921 Forest Lane‡

Zimpfer, Matthew J. '67 '93 C.108 B.A. L.347 J.D.
V.P. & Asst. Gen. Coun., Conseco, Inc. (Legal Department)

Ziobron, Eugene G. ....'— '72 C.475 B.A. L.912 J.D. P.O. Box 4464

Zipes, Jeffrey S., (BV) ....'65 '90 C.861 B.A. L.345 J.D. [Coots,H.&W.]

CENTERVILLE, 2,398, *Wayne Co.*

Gethers, David D., (BV) ....'45 '71 C.347 B.S. L.345 J.D. 100 E. Main St.

CHARLESTOWN, 5,993, *Clark Co.*

Adams, Darrell, (CV) ....'47 '76 C.347 B.S. L.421 J.D. Indiana Dept. of Corrections

CHESTERFIELD, 2,969, *Madison Co.*

Kreegar, Richard E. ....'31 '62 C.63 A.B. L.345 J.D. 406 E. Main St.‡

CHESTERTON, 10,488, *Porter Co.*

Anderson, Malcolm E. ....'19 '51 C&L.879 B.A., LL.B. 111 S. Calumet Rd.‡

Babcock, Gregory T., Attorney at Law, (BV) '52 '79
C&L.879 B.A., J.D. 111 S. Calumet Rd.

Blumenthal, Jeanne B., & Associates, (BV) '52 '78
C.228 A.B. L.209 J.D. 179 B Calumet Rd.

Bose McKinney & Evans LLP, (AV)
P.O. Box 957, 46304 ⊙
Telephone: 219-983-1552 Facsimile: 219-983-1741
URL: http://www.boselaw.com
Monica J. Conrad.
General Civil Practice in all Courts including Agricultural Law, Antitrust, Appellate Practice, Capital Strategies, Civil Rights, Commercial Law, Communications and Media, Constitutional Law, Corporate Law, Creditors Rights, Creditors Rights in Bankruptcy, Debtor Bankruptcy, Education Law, Employee Benefits, Entertainment and the Arts, Entrepreneurial Services, Environmental Law, Finance, Financial Institutions Law, Government Contracts, Government Relations, High Technology, Insurance, Intellectual Property, International Law, Labor and Employment, Legislative Practice, Litigation, Mergers and Acquisitions, Municipal Finance, Municipal Law, Planning and Land Use, Probate, Real Estate, Regulated Industries, Regulatory Agency Practice, Securities, Taxation, Trusts and Estates, Utility Law, Wills and Zoning.
Indianapolis, Indiana Office: 2700 First Indiana Plaza, 135 North Pennsylvania Street, 46204. Telephone: 317-684-5000. Facsimile: 317-684-5173.
Indianapolis, Indiana North Office: 600 East 96th Street, Suite 500 46240. Telephone: 317-684-5300. Facsimile: 317-684-5316.
Washington, D.C. Office: 700 North One Lafayette Centre, 1120 20th Street, N.W., 20036. Telephone: 202-973-1229. Fax: 202-973-1212.
Crown Point, Indiana Office: 3577 West Lakeshore Drive, 46307. Telephone: 219-663-2968. Fax: 219-663-2969.
West Lafayette, Indiana Office: 3000 Kent Avenue. Telephone: 765-464-3200. Fax: 765-464-3225.

See Professional Biographies, CHESTERTON, INDIANA

Braje, Craig V., (AV) ....'49 '74 C.927 B.A. L.879 J.D. [Braje&N.] ⊙

Braje & Nelson, LLP, (AV)
1100 S. Calumet Road, Suite 3-C, 46304 ⊙
Telephone: 219-728-0100 Fax: 219-728-0123
Members of Firm: Craig V. Braje; William J. Nelson, Jr.; Kurt R. Earnst; Elizabeth Ann Flynn;—Christopher L. Willoughby; Carri N. Crider. Retired: C. T. Kitowski.
General Civil and Criminal Trial Practice. Commercial, Real Estate, Family, Domestic Relations, Personal Injury Law, Estate Planning, Probate and Bankruptcy.
Representative Clients: Northern Indiana Education Foundation.
Reference: NBD Bank, N.A.
Michigan City, Indiana Office: 126 West Fourth Street, P.O. Box 1006, 46361. Telephone: 219-872-2100. Fax: 219-873-9163.

See Professional Biographies, CHESTERTON, INDIANA

Chubb, Larry L., Law Office of, (CV) '57 '89
C.1086 B.A. L.1119 J.D. 348 Indian Boundary Rd.

Conrad, Monica J. ....'64 '94 C.346 B.S. L.879 J.D. [Bose M.&E.]

Crider, Carri N. ....'74 '99 C.347 B.A. L.879 J.D. [Ⓐ Braje&N.] ⊙

Dasari, Veda Praveen ....'— '02 C.679 B.S. L.879 J.D. [Ⓐ T.J.Scully,III]

Dyerly, Rodney B. ....'32 '58 C&L.378 A.B., LL.B. 7 Crest Dr., Dune Acres‡

Earnst, Kurt R., (CV) ....'70 '96 C.679 B.A. L.879 J.D. [Braje&N.] ⊙

Fleming, T. Clifford, (BV) .... '44 '73 C.879 B.S. L.602 J.D. [T.C.Fleming&Assoc.]

Fleming, T. Clifford & Associates, P.C., (BV) ....108 Wilson Street

Flynn, Elizabeth Ann ....'70 '95 C.249 B.A. L.879 J.D. [Braje&N.] ⊙

Gavagan, M. Anne ....'— '82 C.347 B.A. L.879 J.D. 1252 Trillium Drive

Granquist, Daniel W., (CV) ....'53 '83 C.937 B.S. L.879 J.D. P.O. Box 892

Harris, Michael C., (AV) ....'38 '64 C.347 B.S. L.345 LL.B. [Harris,W.&L.]

Harris, Welsh & Lukmann, (AV) BR
107 Broadway, 46304
Telephone: 219-926-2114 Fax: 219-926-1503
Email: hwl@hwllaw.com URL: http://www.hwllaw.com
Members of Firm: Michael C. Harris; Robert A. Welsh; L. Charles Lukmann, III; Charles F. G. Parkinson.
General Civil Practice in all State and Federal Courts. Corporation, Wills and Probate, Trusts and Estates, Estate Planning, Personal Injury, Automobile Accidents, Wrongful Death, Insurance, Real Property, Eminent Domain, Banking and Municipal Law. Trials.
Representative Clients: Northern Indiana Commuter Transportation District; Duneland School Corp.; Town of Burns Harbor, Indiana; Town of Chesterton; Paulson Oil Co.; Steel & Machinery Transport, Inc.; Porter Memorial Hospital; Centier Bank; Rediehs Transit Line, Inc.; Oak Management Company.

See Professional Biographies, CHESTERTON, INDIANA

Hiestand, Terry K., Law Office of, (BV) ... '46 '71 C.347 A.B. L.1119 J.D. 117 Broadway

Kitowski, C. T. ....'25 '52 C&L.879 LL.B. [Ⓒ Braje&N.] ⊙‡

Kohlhoff, Elizabeth S., (CV) ..... '62 '90 C.956 B.A. L.260 J.D. 348 Indian Boundary Rd.

Lasser, Herbert S., & Associates, P.C.
(See Merrillville)

Lawson, Sarah A. ....'73 '98 C.347 B.A. L.1119 J.D. 117 Broadway

Levenfeld, Andrew W., & Associates, Ltd.
(See Chicago, Illinois)

Livarchik, George R., (BV) ....'54 '79 C.303 B.A. L.879 J.D. 424 Broadway
Lukmann, L. Charles, III, (BV) ....'53 '79 C.602 B.A. L.345 J.D. [Harris,W.&L.]
Nelson, William J., Jr., (BV) ....'65 '92 C.827 B.A. L.879 J.D. [Braje&N.] ⊙
O'Toole, William H., (CV) ....'49 '80 C.145 A.B. L.1119 J.D. 802 Wabash Avenue
Parkinson, Charles F. G. ....'64 '98 C.1265 B.S. L.879 J.D. [Harris,W.&L.]
Philbrick, Suzanne N., (CV) ....'46 '76 C.320 B.A. L.365 J.D. [S.Philbrick]
Philbrick, Suzanne, (CV) .... 802 Wabash Avenue
Salinas-McClure, Cynthia ....'54 '00 C.347 B.A. L.209 J.D. 402 Grant Avenue
Savage, James S. ....'15 '38 C&L.879 B.A., LL.B. 83 East Rd.‡
Scully, Thomas J., III, (BV) '45 '73 C.831 B.A. L.1292 J.D.
372 Indian Boundary Road (⊙Chgo., IL; Munster, IN)
Shoffner, Jack Donald ....'33 '58 C.528 B.A. L.930 J.D. Bethlehem Steel Corp.‡
Welsh, Robert A., (AV) ....'43 '68 C.347 A.B. L.1119 J.D. [Harris,W.&L.]
Willoughby, Christopher L. ....'70 '02 C.578 B.A. L.879 J.D. [🄰 Braje&N.] ⊙
Young, Eugene V., Jr. ....'47 '80 C.346 B.S. L.1119 J.D. P.O. Box 2231

CICERO, 4,303, *Hamilton Co.*

Cook, J. Bradley, (BV) ....'55 '81 C&L.347 B.A., J.D. 22919 Overdorf Rd.

CLARKSVILLE, 21,400, *Clark Co.*

Coe, Spencer Brian '70 '95 C.383 B.S. L.421 J.D.
(adm. in KY; not adm. in IN) Coun., Gohmann Asphalt & Construction, Inc.

Colomb, Bart, Law Office of
(See New Albany)

Cooper, Kyle A., (BV) ....'59 '86 C.383 B.S. L.421 J.D. [Greene&C.] ⊙
Fifer, C. Gregory, (BV) ....'56 '81 C.880 B.A. L.421 J.D. Reynolds Grp.
Fratini, Pamela J. ....'50 '84 L.347 J.D. 965 Hazelwood Dr. (⊙Louisville, KY)‡
Greene, C. Joseph, (AVⓉ) ....'47 '79 C.421 B.A. L.383 J.D. [Greene&C.] ⊙
Greene & Cooper, (AVⓉ) .................................P.O. Box 398 (⊙Louisville, KY)
Gwin, Samuel K., (BV) ....'41 '67 C.347 A.B. L.1119 LL.B. 608 Gerald Dr.
Heubi, Magnus F., (AV) ....'21 '43 C&L.347 B.S., J.D. 2709 Wildwood Dr.

Mattox Mattox & Wilson
(See New Albany)

Mayer, John M., Jr., (BV) ....'43 '68 C.362 B.A. L.421 J.D. [J.M.Mayer,Jr.]
Mayer, John M., Jr., Law Offices of ....501 Eastern Boulevard
Prentice, R. J. ....'17 '41 C.347 L.345 LL.B. P.O. Box 2100‡

CLINTON, 5,040, *Vermillion Co.*

Antonini, Henry J., (BV) ....'28 '69 C.346 B.S. L.421 J.D. [Antonini&A.]
Antonini, Henry L., (BV) ....'64 '89 C.346 B.A. L.879 J.D. [Antonini&A.]
Antonini and Antonini, (BV) ....224 S. Main St.
Beardsley, Joe E., II, (AV) ....'38 '63 C.346 B.S. L.1119 J.D. 320 S. Main St.

Hunt, Hassler & Lorenz LLP
(See Terre Haute)

Thomas, Jeff M., (CV) ....'47 '77 C.346 B.S. L.345 J.D. [Thomas&T.]
Thomas, Larry C., (CV) ....'42 '75 C.346 B.S. L.345 J.D. Pros. Atty. [Thomas&T.]
Thomas & Thomas, (CV) .... 242 Mulberry St.

CLOVERDALE, 2,243, *Putnam Co.*

Gilmartin, Brian G. ....'46 '71 C.1041 B.A. L.564 J.D. 1315 E. County Road 1100 S‡

COLUMBIA CITY, * 7,077, *Whitley Co.*

Arnold, Jeffrey S., Attorney At Law .....'70 '97 C.679 B.S. L.347 J.D. 209 W. Van Buren

Blackburn & Green
(See Fort Wayne)

Bloom, Timothy J., (BV) ....'52 '78 C.347 B.S. L.345 J.D. [Bloom&W.]
Bloom, William M., (AV) ....'17 '42 C.347 A.B. L.1119 LL.B. [🄲 Bloom&W.] ‡
Bloom & Whiteleather, (AV) .... 119 South Main Street
Cowan, John D. ....'68 '96 C.347 B.A. L.879 J.D. [🄰 Bloom&W.]
Fleck, James R. ....'43 '69 C&L.347 A.B., J.D. 119 S. Main St.‡

Gates, Benton E., Jr., (AV) '29 '54 C&L.477 A.B., LL.B.
407 Pinecrest Drive, P.O. Box 251, 46725-0251
Telephone: 260-244-5175 Fax: 260-244-5177
Taxation, Probate and Estate Planning.
Attorney for: Furnished upon request.

Heuer, James R. ....'49 '74 C.679 B.S. L.1119 J.D. Cir. J.
Hockemeyer, Greggory William ....'62 '89 C.894 A.B. L.347 J.D. [Myers,T.H.&M.]
Kennedy, Julia S. ....'64 '90 C.347 B.S. L.608 J.D. 1253 N. Wilson Road
Linn, Jerry J. ....'58 '85 C.679 B.A. L.1119 J.D. 250 Claiborne Dr.★
McNagny, Marcia A., (BV) ....'64 '90 C.473 B.A. L.347 J.D. [Myers,T.H.&M.]
McNagny, Patricia Gates ....'26 '51 C.347 A.B. L.1119 J.D. 380 W. Gates Rd.
Meyers, Edw. J. ....'24 '51 C.347 B.S. L.1119 J.D. Cir. J.
Myers, Jonathan J., (BV) ....'60 '86 C.602 B.A. L.345 J.D. [Myers,T.H.&M.]
Myers, Soultana S., (BV) ....'61 '86 C.679 B.S. L.1119 J.D. [Myers,T.H.&M.]
Myers, Tison, Hockemeyer & McNagny, (BV) ....202 West Van Buren Street, Suite A
Nelson, Daniel E. ....'67 '92 C.210 B.A. L.1119 J.D. Dep. Prosecutor

Roebuck & Associates, P.C.
(See Ft. Wayne)

Rothberg Logan & Warsco LLP
(See Fort Wayne)

Rush, Michael D. ....'45 '73 C.303 B.A. L.879 J.D. Supr. Ct. J.
Sigler, Daniel J., (AV) ....'49 '74 C.265 B.A. L.879 J.D. [Bloom&W.]
Smith, Terry L., (BV) ....'45 '74 C.63 B.A. L.477 J.D. [T.L.Smith&Assoc.]
Smith, Terry L. & Associates, P.C., (BV) .... 116 N. Main St.
Tison, J. Earl, (BV) ....'65 '90 C.879 B.A. L.347 J.D. [Myers,T.H.&M.]
Whiteleather, John W., Jr., (AV) ....'40 '65 C.347 B.S. L.1119 LL.B. [Bloom&W.]

COLUMBUS, * 39,059, *Bartholomew Co.*

Able, Walter ....'32 '68 C.347 A.B. L.345 J.D. Columbus Medical Corp.
Anderson, Lisa Hensley ....'73 '00 C.347 B.A. L.345 J.D. [Sharpnack B.S.&W.]
Andrews, Scott C. ....'75 '00 C.679 B.A. L.776 J.D. 415 Washington St.
Arnholt, G. Gene, Law Office of, (CV) ... '45 '76 C.347 A.B. L.1119 J.D. 426 Fifth Street
Bartlett, Merlyn C., Law Office of ....'45 '75 C.473 B.S L.879 J.D. 1431 Hunter Pl.
Bigley, Thomas C., Jr., (AV) ......'39 '63 C.347 A.B. L.1119 J.D. [Sharpnack B.S.&W.]
Blackwell, Jean S., (AV) ....'54 '79 C.945 B.A. L.477 J.D. 500 Jackson St.
Boll, Cynthia A., (BV) ....'55 '81 C.347 B.A. L.345 J.D. [Deppe F.&B.] ⊙
Bush, R. Benjamin ....'28 '56 C.679 B.S. L.347 J.D. 1000 5th St.‡
Cain, Tanita Michelle ....'— '99 C.329 B.A. L.481 J.D. [T.Cain]
Cain, Tanita, Law Offices of ....500 Jackson St.
Carter, Pamela S., (AV) '49 '84 C.215 A.B. L.347 J.D.
V.P. & Gen. Coun., Cummins Engine Co., Inc.
Chambers, William D. '37 '66
C.347 B.S. L.1119 J.D. V.P., Secy. & Gen. Coun., Irwin Mgt. Co.
Cline, King & King, P.C., (AV) ....P.O. Box 250
Conner, William S., (BV) ....'44 '79 C.679 B.S.C.E. L.1000 J.D. 230 Franklin
Corbin-Beverly, Millie E. ....'68 '98 C&L.347 B.S., J.D. [M.Corbin-Beverly]
Corbin-Beverly, Millie ....2756 25th. St., Ste. 300
Coriden, Kathleen Tighe, (BV) ....'47 '72 C.440 B.A. L.851 J.D. Pros. Atty's. Off.
Crump, F. Jefferson, III, (BV) ....'42 '67 C.885 B.S. L.1119 J.D. [Jewell,C.A.&P.]
Cue, Molly J. ....'70 '97 C.475 B.A. L.880 J.D. Corp. Counsel
Curry, Norman D. ....'33 '72 C.108 B.S. L.472 J.D. Supr. Ct. J.
Dalmbert, Robert L., (BV) ....'30 '58 C.108 A.B. L.345 J.D. 320 Franklin St.

Deppe Fredbeck & Boll, (AV)
225 Washington Street, 47202 ⊙
Telephone: 812-378-5137 Fax: 812-378-5256
Member of Firm: Cynthia A. Boll (Resident). Associate: Kathryn D. Molewyk.
General, Civil, Criminal and Trial Practice. Probate and Estate Planning, Elder Law, Corporation and Real Property, Labor Relations, School, Health Care and Commercial Law.
Franklin, Indiana Office: Nine East Court, 46131. Telephone: 317-736-5138. Fax: 317-736-8268.

See Professional Biographies, COLUMBUS, INDIANA

Edwards, Donald S., Attorney at Law, (CV) .....'46 '80 C.347 B.S. L.345 J.D. 722 3rd. St.
Eynon, Richard S., (BV) ....'43 '69 C&L.879 B.A., J.D. [Eynon,H.R.&G.]
Eynon, Harmon, Rocker & Glover, P.C., (BV) ....555 First Street
Fairchild, Raymond F. ....'46 '71 C.339 B.A. L.345 J.D. 2501 E. South St.
Gamso, Stanley A., (BV) ....'53 '90 C.679 B.S.M.S. L.347 J.D. [Lawson,P.M.&G.]
Garber, William G., (BV) ....'41 '68 C.932 B.A. L.477 J.D. 431 Washington St.
Gerstle, Mark R., (BV) '55 '81 C.347 B.A. L.1119 J.D.
(adm. in NY; not adm. in IN) Cummins Engine Company, Inc. (Law Department)
Gifford, Gregory Carden '49 '82 C.347 A.B. L.1187 J.D.
(adm. in MI; not adm. in IN) P.O. Box 486
Glover, Dominic W. ....'71 '97 C.894 B.A. L.1119 J.D. [Eynon,H.R.&G.]
Graston, Maurice W. ....'11 '36 C.303 B.A. L.1119 LL.B. 2632 Meadowlark Ln‡
Green, J. Randolph ....'45 '79 C.446 B.S. L.602 J.D. 4253 E. Windsor Ln.

Greene & Schultz Trial Lawyers
(See Bloomington)

Grogg, Tim A., (BV) '47 '78
C.347 B.S. L.300 J.D. V.P. & Gen. Mgr., Strategic HR Grp., Inc.
Guthrie, Jason H. ....'71 '97 C.63 B.S. L.345 J.D. [Sharpnack B.S.&W.]
Hamilton, George O. ....'42 '67 C.118 B.A. L.477 J.D. Cosco Inc.
Hamilton, Peter B. '46 '72 C.674 A.B. L.976 J.D.
Cummins Engine Company, Inc. (Law Department)
Harmon, Landyn K., (BV) ....'56 '81 C.894 B.A. L.1119 J.D. [Eynon,H.R.&G.]
Heimann, Stephen R. ...... '54 '80 C.894 B.A. L.345 J.D. Cir. J., Bartholomew Co. Cir. Ct.
Holland, James W., (AV) ....'43 '68 C.303 A.B. L.1119 J.D. 201 Washington St.
Hunt, V. William ....'44 '69 C.347 A.B. L.1119 J.D. Arvin Industries, Inc.
Jackson, Jeffrey B. ....'58 '77 C&L.347 B.A., J.D. [Jackson]
Jackson Law Office, The .... 415 Washington Street, Suite 2C
Jewell, Ralph L., (BV) ....'30 '57 C.347 A.B. L.1119 J.D. [Jewell,C.A.&P.]

Jewell, Crump, Angermeier & Prall, (BV)
1325 Washington Street, P.O. Box 1061, 47202-1061
Telephone: 812-376-9751 Fax: 812-372-6384
Email: fjc@iquest.net URL: http://www.jcalaw.com
Members of Firm: Gerald G. Angermeier (1940-2005); F. Jefferson Crump, III; Jerry E. Prall.
Retired: Ralph L. Jewell.
General Civil and Criminal Trial Practice. Driving While Intoxicated, Drug Crimes, Juvenile Law, Parole and Probation, Traffic Violations, Personal Injury, Automobile Accidents, Slip and Fall, Wrongful Death, Wills and Probate, Trusts and Estates, Estate Planning, Taxation, Business Organizations, Commercial Law, Business Law, Business Litigation, Business Planning, Contracts, Buying and Selling a Business, Business Start-Ups, Debtor and Creditor, Collections, Business Enterprises, Corporate, Limited Liability Companies, Small Business, Partnerships, Family/Domestic Relations, Child Custody, Child Support, Divorce, Visitation Rights, Adoptions, Insurance Defense, Real Estate and Title Insurance Law.
Reference: Home Federal Savings Bank, Columbus, Indiana.

See Professional Biographies, COLUMBUS, INDIANA

Jones, Patterson & Tucker, Professional Corporation, (BV) .... 330 Franklin St.
King, Arthur D., (AV) ....'27 '52 C.347 B.S. L.1119 LL.B. [Cline,K.&K.]
King, J. Kevin, (BV) ....'59 '86 C.347 B.A. L.692 J.D. [Cline,K.&K.]
King, Peter C., (BV)..........................'54 '79 C.347 A.B. L.861 J.D. [Cline,K.&K.]
Koenig, Joseph R., (BV) ....'51 '76 C.344 B.A. L.345 J.D. Pros. Atty.
Kummerer, J. Michael, Law Office of '46 '72
C.347 B.A. L.1049 J.D. 433 1/2 Washington St.
Lawson, Paul D. ....'12 '44 C.344 B.S. L.345 LL.B. [🄲 Lawson,P.M.&G.]
Lawson, Pushor, Mote & Gamso, (AV) .... 426 Fourth Street

Loheide, Benjamin, Law Office of '74 '04 C.347 B.S. L.1119 J.D.
421 Washington Street, 47201
Telephone: 812-376-8135 Fax: 812-376-9286
Email: loheidelaw@sbcglobal.net URL: http://www.loheidelaw.com
Criminal Law, Family Law, Divorce, Bankruptcy.

See Professional Biographies, COLUMBUS, INDIANA

Long, James W. ....'36 '71 C.265 A.B. L.345 J.D. Ret. State Ct. J.‡
Malone, Paul W., II '68 '93
C.145 B.A. L.347 J.D. Corp. Coun., Cummins Engine Co., Inc.
Marshall, C. Richard, (AV) ....'40 '67 C&L.347 A.B., J.D. 430 Second Street
Marshall, William F. ....'34 '62 C&L.345 B.S., J.D. 435 3rd St.
Meek, Joseph W. '64 '89 C.344 B.A. L.607 J.D.
(adm. in OH; not adm. in IN) 225 Washington Street
Molewyk, Kathryn D., (BV) ....'56 '81 C.114 B.A. L.1119 J.D. [🄰 Deppe F.&B.]
Monroe, Chris D. ....'55 '80 C.347 B.A. L.861 J.D. Supr. Ct. J.
Mote, Thomas N., (BV) ....'37 '65 C.347 B.S. L.345 LL.B. [Lawson,P.M.&G.]
Mufson, Ellen Z. ....'49 '87 C.645 B.A. L.345 J.D. Inside Coun., Irwin Financial Corp.
Nash, William M. ....'64 '90 C.347 B.A. L.596 J.D. 330 Franklin St.
Nie, William L., (BV) '46 '74
C.894 B.A. L.345 J.D. Corp. Coun., Cummins Engine Co., Inc.
Norton, Daniel J. ....'49 '79 C.999 B.S. L.345 J.D. 3882W N. Wood Lake Dr.‡
Oller, Janet Petrey '52 '84 C.174 B.A. L.326 J.D.
Vice President/Compliance Attorney, Irwin Union Bank
Patterson, Dan A., (BV) ....'48 '74 C.679 B.A. L.861 J.D. [Jones,P.&T.]
Post, Charles C. ....'52 '80 C.722 B.A. L.309 J.D. Corp. Coun., Cummins Engine Co., Inc.
Prall, Jerry E., (CV) ....'56 '84 C&L.347 B.S., J.D. [Jewell,C.A.&P.]
Pushor, John A., (AV) ....'32 '57 C.585 Ph.B. L.378 LL.B. [Lawson,P.M.&G.]
Rivera, Miguel R. ....'60 '90 C&L.339 B.A., J.D. Sr. Coun., Cummins Inc.
Rocker, Jeffrey C., (CV) ....'70 '96 C.477 B.A. L.879 J.D. [Eynon,H.R.&G.]
Rose, Marya M. '62 '90 C.951 B.A. L.74 J.D.
V.P. & Gen. Coun., Cummins Engine Co., Inc.

Rubino, John A., III, (BV) '49 '87
C.321 A.B. L.1119 J.D. Corp. Coun., Cummins Engine Co., Inc.
Scattoloni, Rosann '70 '97 C.105 B.A. L.347 J.D.
(adm. in KY; not adm. in IN)
Quality Manager-Corp. Human Resources, Cummins Engine Co.
Schug, Otto F., (BV) .... '37 '64 C.894 B.A. L.345 LL.B. 1220 Washington St.

Sharpnack Bigley Stroh & Washburn LLP, (AV) BB
321 Washington Street, P.O. Box 310, 47202-0310
Telephone: 812-372-1553 Fax: 812-372-1567
Email: sbsw@sbswlaw.com
Members of Firm: Thomas C. Bigley, Jr.; John A. Stroh; Jeffrey S. Washburn; Lisa Hensley Anderson; Jason H. Guthrie.
Trials. Business, Corporation, Probate and Estate Planning, Elder Law, Real Estate, Family/Domestic Relations, Banking. General Practice.
Representative Clients: Irwin Union Bank and Trust Co.; Ameritech; State Farm Mutual Insurance Cos.; Home News Enterprises; Centra Credit Union; Richards Elevator, Inc.; Indiana Farmers Insurance; Glick Farms, Inc.
See Professional Biographies, COLUMBUS, INDIANA

Shelton, Angel Fleetwood '71 '96 C.160 B.A. L.339 J.D.
Corp. Coun., Cummins Engine Company, Inc. (Law Department)
Snyder, Ronald R., (AV) ..... '44 '69 C.347 B.S. L.1119 J.D. Gen. Coun., Arvin Ind., Inc.
Souza, Matthew F. .... '57 '83 C.347 B.A. L.1119 J.D. Irwin Financial Corporation
Stark, Dennis M., Law Office Of, (BV) '49 '81
C.679 B.S. L.1119 J.D. 201 Washington St.
Stevens, Barbara, (BV) ...... '46 '85 C.475 B.S. L.347 J.D. Gen. Coun., Impact Forge, Inc.
Stewart, Ann H. .... '63 '89 C.610 B.A. L.117 J.D. Corp. Coun., Cummins Engine Co., Inc.
Stone, William H., (BV) .... '49 '74 C.303 B.A. L.345 J.D. P.O. Box 750
Stoner, Richard B. .... '20 '48 C.347 B.S. L.309 LL.B. P.O. Box 290‡
Straub, F. Scott, (CVⓣ) '66 '98 C.1237 B.C.J. L.1243 J.D.
(adm. in AR; not adm. in IN) 1203 Chestnut St.
Stroh, John A., (BV) .... '46 '82 C.611 B.A. L.345 J.D. [Sharpnack B.S.&W.]
Terpstra, Jean M. .... '59 '86 C.118 B.S. L.494 J.D. 3210 Grove Pkwy.‡
Thomasson, Michael .... '45 '71 C.210 A.B. L.345 J.D. P.O. Box 2086
Thomasson, Sean G. .... '66 '95 C.610 B.A. L.607 J.D. 1526 N Meadowland Dr
Thompson, Joseph S., (AV) .... '27 '54 C.347 B.S. L.1119 J.D. 207 Washington Street
Tinsley, Arlette C. .... '66 '93 C&L.893 B.A., J.D. Human Rights Comm.
Tucker, J. Grant, (BV) .... '56 '82 C.265 B.A. L.345 J.D. [Jones,P.&T.]
Tupin-Crites, Joan E. .... '59 '91 C.205 B.A. L.1119 J.D. Irwin Union Bank & Trust Co.
Voelz, James K., (BV) .... '50 '75 C.303 B.A. L.345 J.D. 427 Washington St.
Vrana, Timothy J., (BV) .... '52 '82 C.228 A.B. L.74 J.D. [T.J.Vrana]

Vrana, Timothy J., LLC, (BV)
636 3rd Street, P.O. Box 527, 47202
Telephone: 812-375-9306 Toll-Free: 1-866-788-8270 Fax: 812-375-9304
Email: tim@timvrana.com URL: http://www.timvrana.com
Timothy J. Vrana.
Social Security Disability, Civil Litigation, Civil Appeals.
See Professional Biographies, COLUMBUS, INDIANA

Washburn, Jeffrey S., (BV) .... '57 '83 C.303 B.A. L.1119 J.D. [Sharpnack B.S.&W.]
Wells, Charles R. .... '19 '52 C.347 B.S. L.1119 J.D. P.O. Box 644‡
Whitted, Alan L., (BV) .... '55 '80 C.63 B.S. L.607 J.D. 431 Washington St.
Wilson, Robert C. .... '30 '58 C.265 A.B. L.345 J.D. 4332 Kennedy Court‡
Witte, R. Kent, (BV) .... '39 '63 C.303 A.B. L.345 J.D. 225 Washington St.
Wright, David C. '46 '76 C.608 B.S. L.607 J.D.
(adm. in OH; not adm. in IN) Corp. Coun., Cummins Engine Co., Inc.

CONNERSVILLE, * 15,411, *Fayette Co.*

Alexander, John W., (BV) .... '54 '79 C&L.347 B.A., J.D. [Tarvin&A.]
Baker, Jon D., (BV) .... '41 '68 C.63 B.S. L.345 J.D. [Baker&B.]
Baker and Bodwell, A Professional Corporation, (BV) .... 621 Central Ave., Ste. 1
Bodwell, John W., (BV) .... '46 '72 C.347 B.S. L.345 J.D. [Baker&B.]
Butsch, Beth A., (BV) .... '59 '86 C.347 B.A. L.345 J.D. 422 Central Avenue
Butsch, David R., (BV) .... '53 '79 C.347 B.A. L.201 J.D. [Butsch]
Butsch Law Office, (BV) .... 422 Central Ave.

Clarkson & Gulde, P.C.
(See Rushville)

Demkovich, Allen, (BV) .... '50 '76 C.347 A.B. L.345 J.D. Pros. Atty.
Heeb, Louis J. .... '41 '73 C.679 B.S. L.345 J.D. 1517 Virginia Ave.
Jones, Bette Jo, (CV) .... '70 '95 C.384 B.A. L.347 J.D. [B.J.Jones]
Jones, Bette J, (CV) .... 721 Willow Dr.
Kuntz, William H., (CV) .... '54 '89 C.679 B.A. L.347 J.D. [Ⓐ Baker&B.]
Pflum, Daniel L. .... '47 '75 C.347 A.B. L.345 J.D. Cir. J.
Shaw, Pete, (BV) .... '47 '75 C.184 B.S. L.1119 J.D. [Shaw&W.]
Shaw and Wilhoite, (BV) .... 126 W. 6th St.
Shull, Frederick H. .... '46 '73 C.347 A.B. L.1119 J.D. 424 N. Central Ave.
Smith, Gary E., (BV) .... '44 '72 C.63 B.S. L.345 J.D. 324 Central Ave.
Smith, Richard N., (BV) .... '36 '60 C.347 B.S. L.1119 J.D. 402 Central Avenue
Tarvin, Thomas L. .... '49 '75 C.235 A.B. L.150 J.D. [Tarvin&A.]
Tarvin & Alexander, P.C., (BV) .... 526 Central Avenue
Thompson, Thomas M. .... '— '93 C.602 B.A. L.1119 J.D. [Thompson]

Thompson Law Office
705 West 30th Street, 47331
Telephone: 765-827-3082 Fax: 765-827-6500
Email: info@tomthompsonlaw.com URL: http://www.tomthompsonlaw.com
Members and Associates: Thomas M. Thompson; Thomas T. Wellman.
Personal Injury, Debt Collection, Estate Planning, Criminal Law, Appellate Practice, Bankruptcy, Environmental Law, Family Law.
See Professional Biographies, CONNERSVILLE, INDIANA

Wellman, Thomas T. .... '75 '03 C.63 B.S. L.345 J.D. [Ⓐ Thompson]
Wilhoite, William A., (BV) .... '50 '81 C.63 B.S. L.1119 J.D. [Shaw&W.]

CORYDON, * 2,661, *Harrison Co.*

Austin, Maryland L., (CV) .... '41 '79 C.999 B.A. L.36 J.D. [M.Austin]
Austin, Maryland, (CV) .... 415 N. Capitol Ave.
Blair, Vernon W., II '45 '80 C.613 B.A. L.421 J.D.
(adm. in KY; not adm. in IN) 5551 E. Hwy. 62‡
Burgher, Marcus M., IV .... '70 '96 C.210 L.345 J.D. 210 E. Chestnut St.
Byrd, Christopher L. .... '68 '02 C.347 B.S. L.345 J.D. [Ⓐ H.E.Dillman]
Byrd, Dennis L., (BV) .... '59 '89 C.345 B.S. L.201 J.D. [Thompson&B.]
Davis, Roger D. .... '54 '82 C.347 B.S. L.345 J.D. Supr. Ct. J.
Davis, William H., (BV) .... '46 '71 C.473 B.S. L.1119 J.D. [Davis,D.&L.]
Davis, Davis & Layson, (BV) .... 102 North Capitol Avenue
Dillman, Harold E. .... '35 '69 C&L.421 B.S.C., J.D. 219 N. Capitol Avenue
Eskew, Curtis B. .... '44 '69 C.210 B.A. L.1119 J.D. Cir. J.
Fink, Leah S., (CV) .... '64 '91 C.347 B.A. L.421 J.D. 209 N. Capitol Ave.
Finke, E. Joe .... '57 '91 C.679 B.S.E.E. L.362 J.D. 209 N. Capitol Ave.
Ingle, Gordon D., (CV) .... '57 '86 C.347 B.A. L.1288 J.D. 209 N. Capitol Ave.
Layson, David A., (BV) .... '46 '72 C.347 A.B. L.345 J.D. [Davis,D.&L.]

Mattox Mattox & Wilson
(See New Albany)

Merkley Law Office
(See Jeffersonville)

Murphy, Charles R.
(See New Albany)

Pearcy, Marian M. .... '34 '82 C.914 B.A. L.845 J.D. 103 E. Beaver St.
Thompson, G. Patrick, (CV) .... '50 '77 C.201 B.A. L.1340 J.D. [Thompson&B.]
Thompson & Byrd, (BV) .... 303 North Capitol Avenue
Whitis, H. Lloyd, (BV) .... '46 '71 C.347 A.B. L.383 J.D. [Whitis]
Whitis Law Office, (BV) .... 223 E. Walnut St.
Wilson, S. Morris .... '13 '38 C.347 B.A. L.1119 LL.B. 328 Morris Ave.‡
Young, Barbara H. .... '47 '89 C&L.421 B.A., J.D. [B.Young]
Young, Barbara, P.C., Law Offices of .... 4625 Corydon Ridge Road N.E.

COVINGTON, * 2,565, *Fountain Co.*

Bunch, James R., (AV) .... '43 '69 C.108 B.S. L.345 J.D. [Wallace]
Campbell, Don P., (AV) .... '38 '64 C.210 B.A. L.347 LL.B. [Wallace]
Campbell, Stephanie S. .... '70 '96 C.108 B.S. L.347 J.D. [Wallace]
Grogg, Vincent F. .... '33 '58 C.894 A.B. L.1119 J.D. Ret. Cir. J.
Henderson, Susan D. Orr .... '58 '84 C.347 B.S. L.201 J.D. Co. J.
Holmes, Richard M. .... '45 '74 C.63 B.S. L.1119 J.D. 310 4th St.
Rennick, Richard L., Jr., (BV) .... '52 '78 C.894 B.A. L.796 J.D. [Wallace]
Shambach, John L., (BV) .... '46 '71 C.701 B.S.M.E. L.1119 J.D. [Wallace]
Wallace Law Firm, (AV) .... 303 Washington Street
White, Kipling N., (BV) .... '49 '72 C.210 B.A. L.1119 J.D. P.O. Box 98
Williams, Robert O., (BV) .... '35 '60 C.259 A.B. L.1119 J.D. [Williams&W.]
Williams & Williams, (BV) .... 1107 4th St.

CRAWFORDSVILLE, * 15,243, *Montgomery Co.*

Ault, David A. .... '48 '73 C.894 B.A. L.1119 J.D. Supr. Ct. J.
Ayers, Gwyneth A.E., (BVⓣ) '68 '97
C.347 B.S. L.174 J.D. [Ⓞ Wernle,R.&A.] (©Boulder, CO)
Ayers, James E., (AV) .... '41 '66 C.894 A.B. L.309 LL.B. [Wernle,R.&A.]
Baird, John K., (CV) .... '58 '86 C.207 B.A. L.347 J.D. Dep. Pros. Atty., Pros. Off.
Buser, Joseph R., (BV) '54 '79
C.894 A.B. L.880 J.D. Pros. Atty., Montgomery Co. Pros. Off.
Capper, John S., IV, (BV) .... '49 '74 C.63 B.S. L.345 J.D. [Capper,T.&R.]

Capper, Tulley & Reimondo, (AV)
131 North Green Street, P.O. Box 429, 47933
Telephone: 765-362-7340 Fax: 765-362-5023
Email: bctatty@sbcglobal.net
Andrew N. Foley (1877-1963); John R. Berry (1907-1986); Richard G. Tulley; John S. Capper, IV; Robert N. Reimondo.
General Civil and Probate Practice. Agricultural Law, Business Law and Litigation, Construction Law, Corporation, Real Estate, Family, Municipal, Environmental Law, Real Estate Development, Planning and Zoning Law, and Personal Injury Law. Trials.
Representative Clients: Elston Bank & Trust Co.; R. R. Donnelley & Sons Co. (Crawfordsville Division); Linden State Bank; City of Crawfordsville, Ind.
See Professional Biographies, CRAWFORDSVILLE, INDIANA

Carlson, Amy S. .... '70 '98 C.679 B.A. L.356 J.D. [Ⓐ Henthorn,H.&W.]
Collier, James D., (BV) .... '45 '74 C&L.347 B.S., J.D. [Collier,H.&S.]
Collier, Homann & Siamas, (AV) .... 200 Union Fed. Bldg.
Donaldson, S. Bryan, (CV) .... '63 '88 C&L.347 B.A., J.D. 134 W. Main St.
Flaningam, DeVon W. .... '16 '53 C.894 A.B. L.1119 J.D. 5992 Boulder Dr.‡
Goebel, William A., (BV) .... '58 '83 C.894 B.A. L.880 J.D. [Goebel,M.&S.]
Goebel, McGaughey & Sosbe, (BV) .... 127 E. Main St.
Green, William P. (Bill), (BV) .... '55 '80 C.679 B.S. L.345 J.D. [W.P.Green]
Green, William P., The Law Office of, (BV) .... 134 W. Main St.
Groves, Aquilla W. .... '10 '34 C.894 A.B. L.1119 LL.B. 808 W. Main St.‡
Harris, J. Lamont, (AV) .... '47 '76 C.679 B.S. L.345 J.D. [Henthorn,H.&W.]
Harris, Terry E., (AV) .... '34 '58 C.347 A.B. L.345 LL.B. [Harris,H.&P.]
Harris, Harvey & Peebles, LLC, (AV) .... 100 West Main Street
Harvey, Conrad G., (BV) .... '36 '59 C.679 B.S. L.1119 J.D. [Harris,H.&P.]
Hays, Will, Jr. .... '15 '40 C.894 A.B. L.976 LL.B. 208 Union Federal Bldg.‡
Henthorn, C. Rex, (AV) .... '37 '62 C.894 A.B. L.345 J.D. [Henthorn,H.&W.]
Henthorn, Carl F., (AV) .... '17 '41 C.347 L.345 LL.B. [Henthorn,H.&W.] ‡
Henthorn, Harris & Weliever, P.C., (AV) .... 122 East Main Street
Homann, Kurt R., (BV) .... '51 '78 C.894 B.A. L.345 J.D. [Collier,H.&S.]
Howard, Frank N., Jr., (BV) .... '24 '51 C.37 A.B. L.1119 LL.B. 100 W. Main St.‡

Justice, Elizabeth A., (BV) '58 '83 C.681 A.B. L.1119 J.D.
506 East Market Street, 47933-1817
Telephone: 765-364-1111 Facsimile: 765-364-1430 URL: http://www.justice-law.com
Email: elizabeth@justice-law.com URL: http://www.ejusticelaw.com
Estate Planning, Wills and Probate, Trusts and Estates, Guardianships, Real Estate, Business Law, Contracts, Family Law, Divorce, Child Support, Personal Injury and Litigation.
See Professional Biographies, CRAWFORDSVILLE, INDIANA

Kelly, Daniel W.
(See Terre Haut)

Kirtley, Raymond M. .... '52 '81 C.347 A.B. L.345 J.D. Co. Ct. J.
Lohorn, Peggy, (BV) .... '55 '82 C.679 B.A. L.345 J.D. Chief Dep. Pros. Atty.
McGaughey, Richard "Stoney", (CV) ...... '51 '87 C.894 B.A. L.345 J.D. [Goebel,M.&S.]
Miller, Gregory H., (BV) .... '61 '86 C.894 A.B. L.201 J.D. 132 East Main Street
Milligan, Suanne C., (CV) .... '41 '92 C.346 B.S. L.347 J.D. 100 W. Main St.
Milligan, Thomas K. .... '41 '66 C.894 A.B. L.1119 J.D. Cir. J.
Peebles, David S., (CV) .... '63 '93 C.385 A.B. L.347 J.D. [Harris,H.&P.]
Redmaster, Christopher V., (CV) .... '64 '90 C.679 B.A. L.345 J.D. Pub. Def.
Reimondo, Robert N. .... '70 '97 C.894 B.A. L.347 J.D. [Capper,T.&R.]
Ristine, Richard O., (AV) .... '20 '44 C.894 A.B. L.178 LL.B. [Wernle,R.&A.] ‡
Siamas, Harry A., (AV) .... '50 '77 C.347 B.A. L.345 J.D. [Collier,H.&S.]
Sosbe, Patricia McGaughey, (BV) .... '53 '86 C.347 B.A. L.345 J.D. [Goebel,M.&S.]
Tulley, Richard G., (AV) .... '32 '62 C.894 A.B. L.345 J.D. [Capper,T.&R.]
Weliever, Stuart K., (BV) .... '60 '87 C&L.347 B.S., J.D. [Henthorn,H.&W.]

Wernle, Ristine & Ayers, L.P.C., (AV)
309 Dubois Avenue, 47933
Telephone: 765-362-2640 Fax: 765-339-7852
Retired: Robert F. Wernle (1914-2005); Richard O. Ristine. Member of Firm: James E. Ayers. Of Counsel: Gwyneth A.E. Ayers.
General Civil Practice. Corporation, Construction, Contracts, Domestic Relations, Real Estate, Negligence, Insurance, Probate and Estate Planning. Trials.

(This Listing Continued)

Wernle, Ristine & Ayers, L.P.C. (Continued)
Representative Clients: Wabash College; Lincoln Federal Savings Bank; Tri-County Bank and Trust Co.; Ameritech, Inc.; North Montgomery Elementary School Building Corp.; Thrifty Wholesale Supply Inc.; United States Fidelity & Guaranty Co.; Ohio Casualty Co.
See Professional Biographies, CRAWFORDSVILLE, INDIANA

Wynne, Roland Brooks ....'16 '40 C.894 A.B. L.1119 J.D. 309 E. Wabash Ave.‡

CROWN POINT, * 19,806, *Lake Co.*

Abrahamson & Reed
(See Hammond)

Addison, Robert J., (AV) ....'18 '49 C.347 A.B. L.309 J.D. 3952 S. Lake Shore Dr.‡
Alvarez, Walter J., Prof. Corp. ....'47 '73 C.1082 B.A. L.879 J.D. [W.J.Alvarez]
Alvarez, Walter J., P.C. .... 1524 West 96th Avenue
Anderson, John C., IV ....'63 '90 C.679 B.A. L.879 J.D. Dep. Pros. Atty.
Antink, Karen E., Law Office of '44 '97 C.209 B.A. L.365 J.D.
(adm. in IL; not adm. in IN) 89 S. County Line Road
Arredondo, Lorenzo ....'41 '74 C.347 A.B. L.767 J.D. Cir. J.
Austgen, David M., (BV) ....'55 '81 C.602 B.A. L.365 J.D. [Austgen&D.]
Austgen & Decker, P.C., (BV) .... 130 North Main Street
Back, Michael W., (BV) ....'49 '79 C.679 B.S. L.365 J.D. 1 Professional Ctr.

Barber, Herman L., Jr., (BV) '41 '66 C.210 B.A. L.879 J.D.
130 North Main Street, 46307
Telephone: 219-663-5600 Fax: 219-662-3519
Email: hbarber@austgenlaw.com URL: http://www.hbarberlaw.com
Real Estate, Wills and Probate, Trusts and Estates, Estate Planning, Asset Protection, Guardianship, Elder Law, Family Law, Adoption, Child Custody, Child Support, Divorce, Visitation Rights.
See Professional Biographies, CROWN POINT, INDIANA

Barnard, Hannah ....'— '03 706 Merrillville Road

Beckman, Kelly & Smith
(See Hammond)

Bielefeld, James R., (CV) .... '37 '62 C.602 A.B. L.1119 LL.B. 100 S. Main St.

Bose McKinney & Evans LLP, (AV)
3557 West Lakeshore Drive, 46307 ⊙
Telephone: 219-663-2968 Facsimile: 219-663-2969
URL: http://www.boselaw.com
Of Counsel: Peter Lynn Goerges.
General Civil Practice in all Courts including Agricultural Law, Antitrust, Appellate Practice, Capital Strategies, Civil Rights, Commercial Law, Communications and Media, Constitutional Law, Corporate Law, Creditors Rights, Creditors Rights in Bankruptcy, Debtor Bankruptcy, Education Law, Employee Benefits, Entertainment and the Arts, Entrepreneurial Services, Environmental Law, Finance, Financial Institutions Law, Government Contracts, Government Relations, High Technology, Insurance, Intellectual Property, International Law, Labor and Employment, Legislative Practice, Litigation, Mergers and Acquisitions, Municipal Finance, Municipal Law, Planning and Land Use, Probate, Real Estate, Regulated Industries, Regulatory Agency Practice, Securities, Taxation, Trusts and Estates, Utility Law, Wills and Zoning.
Indianapolis, Indiana Office: 2700 First Indiana Plaza, 135 North Pennsylvania Street, 46204. Telephone: 317-684-5000. Facsimile: 317-684-5173.
Indianapolis, Indiana North Office: 600 East 96th Street, Suite 500 46240. Telephone: 317-684-5300. Facsimile: 317-684-5316.
Washington, D.C. Office: 700 North One Lafayette Centre, 1120 20th Street, N.W., 20036. Telephone: 202-973-1229. Fax: 202-973-1212.
Chesterton, Indiana Office: P.O. Box 957, 46304. Telephone: 219-983-1552. Fax: 219-983-1741.
West Lafayette, Indiana Office: 3000 Kent Avenue. Telephone: 765-464-3200. Fax: 765-464-3225.
See Professional Biographies, CROWN POINT, INDIANA

Burke, John J. ....'47 '73 C.108 B.S. L.879 J.D. Dep. Pros. Atty.
Cantrell, Julie N. ....'67 '93 C.679 B.S. L.862 J.D. Supr. Ct. J., Nick Supr. Ct. Div. III
Carroll, William F., (AV) ....'21 '50 C.174 B.A. L.1119 J.D. [Carroll&D.]
Carroll & Donaldson, (AV) .... 101 N. Main St.
Carter, Bernard A., (BV) ....'— '84 C.382 B.S. L.879 J.D. Dep. Co. Pros.
Clement, James L. ....'27 '56 C.472 B.A. L.879 LL.B. Crim. Ct. J.
Collins, Susan L., (BV) ....'61 '86 C.210 B.A. L.221 J.D. Chf. Dep. Pros.
Conroy, Richard J. ....'33 '63 C.436 A.B. L.209 J.D. Ret. Supr. Ct. J.
Corbin, Robert M., (AV) '50 '76 C.347 B.A. L.879 J.D.
V.P. & Gen. Coun., St. Anthony Medical Ctr.
Davis, John H. ....'57 '85 C.1246 B.S. L.1137 J.D. P.O. Box 43
Decker, Adam D., (CV) ....'69 '94 C.679 B.S.M.E. L.879 J.D. [Austgen&D.]
Dolin, Mark L., (AVⓉ) '— '91 C&L.851 B.S., J.D.
(adm. in MI; not adm. in IN) [Kopka,P.D.&E.] (⊙Farmington Hills, MI)
Donaldson, Marc H., Jr., (BV) ....'46 '74 C.347 A.B. L.1119 J.D. [Carroll&D.]
Dywan, Jeffery J. ....'49 '74 C.679 B.S.I.E. L.879 J.D. Chf. Supr. Ct. J.
Eads, John T., III, (AVⓉ) '— '90 C.317 B.A. L.692 J.D.
(adm. in MI; not adm. in IN) [Kopka,P.D.&E.] (⊙Farmington Hills, MI)
Galanis, Michael J., Law Office of '53 '79 C.347 B.A. L.472 J.D.
One Professional Center, #204, 2100 North Main Street
Galanos, George P., (BV) '61 '87
C.347 B.S. L.1187 J.D. One Professional Center, Suite 306
Gasparis, Irene C. ....'62 '93 C.879 B.A. L.146 J.D. 301 S. Main St.
Gastevich, Vladimir, Jr. '58 '85 C.145 B.A. L.597 J.D.
(adm. in IL; not adm. in IN) 1 Professional Ctr.‡
Gaudio-Graves, Ginamarie ....'64 '91 C.209 B.A. L.602 J.D. 4127 Augusta Drive
Giorgi, Andrew V., (AV) ....'29 '52 C.424 B.A. L.602 J.D. [Giorgi&G.]
Giorgi, Geoffrey G., (BV) '66 '91 C.473 B.A. L.345 J.D.
One Professional Center #204, 2100 North Main Street
Giorgi, Paul J., (AV) ....'35 '59 C&L.879 B.A., J.D. [Giorgi&G.]
Giorgi & Giorgi, (AV) ....2100 N. Main St.
Goerges, Peter Lynn ....'44 '69 C.249 A.B. L.1119 J.D. [Ⓒ Bose M.&E.]

Gonzalez, Marce, Jr.
(See Merrillville)

Greenberg, Thomas M., P.C.
(See Merrillville)

Greener, Michael ....'47 '74 C.347 A.B. L.421 J.D. Dep. Pros. Atty.

Grimmer, Edward P., (AV) '50 '76 C&L.602 A.B., J.D.
603 N. Main Street, 46307-3233
Telephone: 219-662-1661 Fax: 219-663-4151
Email: ed@grimmerlaw.com URL: http://www.grimmerlaw.com
Civil Litigation in all Courts. Commercial Litigation, Probate and Estate Planning, Trusts and Estates, Guardianship, Asset Protection, Real Estate, Corporate and Business, Contracts, Business Planning, Business Enterprises, Partnership Law, Limited Liability Company Law, Real Estate, Municipal and Zoning, Utility Law.
Representative Clients: Furnished Upon Request.
See Professional Biographies, CROWN POINT, INDIANA

Grimmer, Maureen Johns, (BV) .....'50 '76 C.679 B.A. L.602 J.D. 603 North Main Street
Gross, Derla R. ....'56 '89 C.347 B.S. L.879 J.D. Trail Supvr.

Hodges & Davis, P.C.
(See Merrillville)

Hoeppner Wagner & Evans LLP
(See Valparaiso)

Hoffman, Thomas K., (BV) ....'52 '77 C.309 B.A. L.879 J.D. Ste. 308, 1 Professional Ctr.
Hollandsworth, Teresa K. ....'69 '96 C&L.879 B.A., J.D. 2117 N. Main Street
Jackson, J. Thomas ....'43 '74 C.347 A.B. L.345 J.D. Dep. Pros. Atty.
Jacobs, Jacqueline L. ....'54 '98 C.679 B.A. L.879 J.D. 2293 N. Main St.

Jeffirs, Kent A., (BV) '67 '92 C.602 B.A. L.347 J.D.
104 West Clark Street, 46307
Telephone: 219-663-7781 Fax: 219-663-7820
Email: kent@jeffirslawoffice.com URL: http://www.jeffirslawoffice.com
Wills and Probate, Trusts and Estates, Estate Planning, Guardianship, Civil Litigation, Real Estate, Family Law, Adoptions.
See Professional Biographies, CROWN POINT, INDIANA

Johnson & Rappa, LLC
(See Merrillville)

Jones, Shawn P., (CVⓉ) ....'64 '94 C.912 B.S. L.213 J.D. 811 Alice St.
Katich, Nick, (BV) ....'47 '72 C.894 A.B. L.145 J.D. [Katich&S.T.]
Katich & Shappell Legal Team, LLP, (BV) .... 1201 North Main Street, Suite A

Kelly, Timothy F., and Associates
(See Dyer)

Knight, Kenneth E. ....'21 '44 C.210 B.A. L.1119 J.D. 385 Ellendale Pkwy.‡

Kopka, Pinkus, Dolin & Eads, (AVⓉ)
5240 Fountain Drive, 46307-1000 ⊙
Telephone: 219-794-1888 Fax: 219-794-1892 URL: http://www.kpdlawfirm.com
Email: gapkinkus@kopkalaw.com URL: http://www.kopkalaw.com
Gene A. Pinkus; Mark L. Dolin (Not admitted in IN); John T. Eads, III (Not admitted in IN); James E. O'Gallagher.
Insurance Defense, Product Liability, Professional Liability, Insurance Fraud, Workers Compensation, Transportation, Toxic Tort and Environmental Liability.
South Bend, Indiana Office: 227 South Main Street, Suite 200, 46601-2624. Telephone: 574-288-3270. Fax: 574-288-3280.
Farmington Hills, Michigan Office: 32605 West Twelve Mile Road, Suite 200, 48334-3339. Telephone: 248-324-2620. Fax: 248-324-2610.
Chicago, Illinois Office: 200 North LaSalle Street, Suite 2850, 60601. Telephone: 312-782-9920. Fax: 312-782-9965.
Buffalo Grove, Illinois Office: 100 Lexington Drive, Suite 100, 60089-6937. Telephone: 847-549-9611. Fax: 847-549-9636.
Indianapolis, Indiana Office: 10333 N. Meridian Street, Suite 475, 46290. Telephone: 317-818-1360. Fax: 317-818-1390.
See Professional Biographies, CROWN POINT, INDIANA

Kortenhoven, Marilyn H. ....'43 '78 C.145 B.A. L.879 J.D. Co. Pros. Off.
Kowalczyk, David J. ....'62 '88 C.679 B.A. L.879 J.D. 2293 N. Main St.
Kozlowski, Susan ....'52 '96 C.679 B.E. L.879 J.D. [Kozlowski]
Kozlowski Law Office ....P.O. Box 906
Kuiper, Timothy R. ....'76 '02 C&L.879 B.S., J.D. [Ⓐ Austgen&D.]
Kuzemka, Alice Ann, (CV) ......'56 '80 C.679 B.S. L.1119 J.D. Staff Atty., Lake Cir. Ct.
Kvachkoff, Douglas R., (CV) ....'59 '84 C.894 B.A. L.1119 J.D. 325 N. Main St.

Lambert, Michael
(Merrillville)

Lambka, Bruce A., Office, (CV) ....'55 '83 C.347 B.A. L.879 J.D. 120 1/2 S. Main St.
Letsinger, James E. ....'34 '62 C&L.879 B.A., J.D. Supr. Ct. J.
Lewis, Yolando Sherice ....'71 '99 C.302 B.A.S.W. L.424 J.D. Pros. Off.

Lucas, Holcomb & Medrea LLP
(See Merrillville)

Macalka, James Michael ....'63 '89 C.1024 B.S. L.879 J.D. 1524 W. 96th Ave.
Maroc, Richard W. ....'42 '68 C.1157 B.A. L.1119 J.D. Supr. Ct. J.
McPhee, Deborah M., (BV) ....'52 '77 C&L.879 B.A., J.D. 13022 Marshall Street
Mears, Darlene W. ....'46 '71 C&L.879 B.A., J.D. Sr. J. Supr. Ct.
Medved, Keith F., (BV) ....'52 '80 C.679 B.S. L.365 J.D. [K.F.Medved]
Medved, Keith F., PC, (BV) ....1 Professional Ctr.
Moore, David M. ....'42 '67 C.347 A.B. L.1119 J.D. Dept. Pros. Atty.
Moss, Sheila M. ....'56 '92 C&L.879 B.A., J.D. 2293 N. Main St.
Mullins, Thomas J. ....'46 '73 C.679 B.S. L.215 J.D. Dep. Pros. Atty.
Murphy, Benjamen W. ....'75 '98 C.347 B.S. L.879 J.D. 1524 West 96th Avenue
Murphy, Robert J. ....'17 '75 C.347 B.S. L.879 J.D. 9204 E. 93rd Ave.‡
Murray, Clarence D. ....'48 '86 C.832 B.S. L.879 J.D. Sup. Ct. J.
Nalbor, Sally S. ....'47 '74 C&L.190 B.A., J.D. 11625 W. Valley Dr.
Neff, D. Eric, (BV) ....'56 '82 C.697 B.S. L.851 J.D. [D.E.Neff]
Neff, D. Eric, P.C, (BV) ....270 North Main Street Suite 270A
Neumaier, Robert J. ....'51 '75 C&L.260 B.A., J.D. Dep. Pros. Atty.
Nicholls, David H., (BV) ....'42 '67 C.347 B.S. L.1119 J.D. [Nicholls&N.]
Nicholls, Steven P. ....'72 '00 C.63 B.S. L.879 J.D. [Nicholls&N.]
Nicholls & Nicholls, L.L.C., (BV) .... 117 1/2 West Joliet Street
O'Drobinak, John M., (AV) ... '35 '60 C.602 B.B.A. L.1119 J.D. 5240 Fountain Dr., Ste J
O'Gallagher, James E., (CV) ....'— '90 C.436 B.A. L.1119 J.D. [Kopka,P.D.&E.]
Osan, Ana Patricia ....'74 '00 C.999 B.A. L.879 J.D. [Ⓐ Austgen&D.]
Parry, Thomas K. ....'53 '80 C.679 B.S. L.879 J.D. P.O. Box 819

Patrick, George C., & Associates, (BV) '— '92 C.597 B.A. L.879 J.D.
706 Merrillville Road, 46307
Telephone: 219-662-7959 Fax: 219-226-9061
Email: george@georgepatrick.com URL: http://www.georgepatrick.com
Plaintiffs Worker's Compensation Litigation, Government Practice, Litigation.
See Professional Biographies, CROWN POINT, INDIANA

Pera, John R., (BV) ....'49 '75 C.347 A.B. L.879 J.D. 2293 N. Main St.
Phillips, Michael J., (BVⓉ) ....'54 '80 C.602 B.A. L.209 J.D. [Ⓐ Austgen&D.]

Pinkerton and Friedman, Professional Corporation
(See Munster)

Pinkus, Gene A. ....'— '89 C&L.851 B.A., J.D. [Kopka,P.D.&E.]
Postelli, Connie J. ....'55 '98 C.932 B.S. L.879 J.D. 2117 North Main St.
Pyle, Scott ....'— '04 706 Merrillville road
Reese, J. Michael ....'76 '00 C.209 B.S. L.184 J.D. Pros. Off.
Rominger, Anna S., (BV) ....'47 '72 C&L.94 A.B., J.D. [Ⓒ Sendak&S.]
Schiralli, Nicholas J. ....'48 '74 C.602 B.A. L.1119 J.D. Co. J.
Schlesinger, P. Jeffrey ....'51 '77 C.473 B.A. L.879 J.D. One Professional Ctr.
Schneider, Diane Kavadias ....'48 '82 C.679 B.A. L.879 J.D. Mag.
Schuster, Patrick A. ....'56 '78 C&L.879 B.A., J.D. 1920 N. Main St.
Sendak, Timothy R., (BV) ....'48 '73 C.879 B.A. L.345 J.D. [Sendak&S.]
Sendak & Stamper, (BV) .... 209 South Main Street
Shappell, Stephanie ....'69 '99 C.249 B.A. L.879 J.D. [Katich&S.T.]
Sievers, Elaine M. ....'46 '82 C.347 L.879 J.D. Trust Offr., Lake County Trusts Co.
Sorbello, John R., (BV) ....'39 '66 C.347 L.879 J.D. [J.R.Sorbello]
Sorbello, John R., P.C., (BV) .... 517 North Main Street

Spangler, Jennings & Dougherty, P.C.
(See Merrillville)

Stalmack, Joseph, & Associates, P.C.
(See Hammond)

Stamper, Peggy Jo, (CV) .... '55 '83 C&L.879 B.A., J.D. [Sendak&S.]
Stanko, Paul D., (CV) .... '55 '79 C.229 B.A. L.879 J.D. Asst. Pub. Def.
Sufana, Raymond C. .... '26 '54 C.347 B.S. L.345 LL.B. 1 Professional Center
Szczepanski, Deborah L., (BV) .... '58 '84 C.742 B.A. L.879 J.D. 138 S. Main St., Ste. 302
Tom, Frederick J. .... '52 '97 C.45 B.S.B.A. L.1000 J.D. Pros. Atty.
Von Willer, William H., Law Office of '44 '71
C&L.879 B.S.B.A., J.D. 117-1/2 W. Joliet St.
Wilson, David M., (BV) .... '40 '65 C.385 A.B. L.347 LL.B. 116 N. West St.
Wolf, Mark A. .... '50 '75 C.597 B.A. L.1119 J.D. Off. of the Pros. Atty.

CULVER, 1,404, *Marshall Co.*

Easterday, James E., (BV) .... '48 '73 C.347 B.S. L.1119 J.D. [Easterday&U.] ⊙
Easterday & Ummel, (BV) .... 212 N. Main St. (⊙Plymouth)
Ummel, T. Edward, (BV) .... '55 '80 C.999 B.A. L.879 J.D. [Easterday&U.] ⊙

CYNTHIANA, 669, *Posey Co.*

Nunn, Leslie E. '41 '67 C.249 B.A. L.208 J.D.
(adm. in CO; not adm. in IN) P.O. Box 98‡

DALE, 1,553, *Spencer Co.*

Cissna, Bruce E. .... '48 '74 C.63 B.S. L.345 J.D. 319 S. Washington St.
Howard, Deborah A., (CV) '50 '85 C.603 B.A. L.421 J.D.
Assoc. Prof. of Law, University of Evansville

DANVILLE, * 6,418, *Hendricks Co.*

Baldwin, Jeffrey K. .... '54 '79 C.63 B.S. L.345 J.D. 67 N. Cross St.
Baldwin, Patricia Ann, (BV) .... '55 '79 C.63 B.A. L.345 J.D. Co. Pros.
Boles, J. V. .... '41 '74 C.108 B.A. L.347 J.D. Cir. J.
Brenton, Thomas G., (BV) .... '51 '77 C.172 B.A. L.345 J.D. P.O. Box 227
Broderick, Amy Comer .... '68 '94 C.210 B.A. L.117 J.D. [Comer]
Burkert, Matthew .... '59 '95 C.679 B.S. L.347 J.D. [Burkert]
Burkert Law Office .... 97 S. Washington Street
Coleman, David H. '48 '74 C.346 B.S. L.345 J.D.
Sup. Ct. J., Hindercks Co. Courthouse
Comer, Ben D. .... '70 '96 C.210 B.A. L.879 J.D. [Comer]
Comer, Lee T. .... '46 '72 C.347 B.S. L.345 J.D. [Comer] ‡
Comer, Mary Lee .... '48 '81 C.347 B.S. L.345 J.D. Supr. Ct. J.
Comer Law Firm .... 71 West Marion Street
Conger, Suzanne X., (BV) .... '56 '83 C&L.923 B.A., J.D. 46 S. Tennessee
Cooper, Mary A. .... '56 '90 C&L.347 A.B., J.D. 897 W. Country Rd. 100 S.
Degan, Randall G. .... '76 '01 C.910 B.A. L.347 J.D. 2102 E. Main St.
Gibbs, J. Gordon, Jr., (BV) .... '39 '68 C.894 B.A. L.345 J.D. [Hinkle&G.]
Gooch, Jeremy P. .... '74 '01 C.347 B.A. L.345 J.D. [▣ Hinkle&G.]
Groover, Richard J., (AV) .... '23 '51 C.628 L.345 LL.B. 97 S. Washington St.‡
Hadley, Paul A. .... '64 '90 C.827 B.S.W. L.347 J.D. 97 S. Washington
Harrington, William O. .... '63 '89 C.894 A.B. L.1119 J.D. [W.O.Harrington]
Harrington, William O., P.C. .... 105 North Washington Street
Hinkle, Harlan H., (AV) .... '32 '62 C.347 B.S. L.345 J.D. [Hinkle&G.]
Hinkle, Kevin J., (BV) .... '56 '81 C.347 B.A. L.345 J.D. [Hinkle&G.]

Hinkle & Gibbs, (AV)
35 West Marion Street, 46122
Telephone: 317-745-5441 Fax: 317-745-0490 URL: http://www.h-glaw.com
Email: khinkle105@aol.com URL: http://www.lawyers.com/hinkle&gibbslaw
Members of Firm: Harlan H. Hinkle; Kevin J. Hinkle; J. Gordon Gibbs, Jr. Associate: Jeremy P. Gooch.
Civil and Criminal Trial Practice in all State and Federal Courts. Litigation, Bankruptcy, Personal Injury, Corporate, Probate and Estate Planning, Real Estate, Family, Domestic Relations and Banking Law.
Representative Clients: Hendricks Community Hospital; Town of Lizton; Town of Clayton; The North Salem State Bank; Hendricks County Bank and Trust Co.; Carson Chrysler-Plymouth, Inc.; Kiefer & Associates, Inc.; ERA Preston Realtors; Dayton Enterprises, Inc.
References: Hendricks County Bank and Trust Co.; The North Salem State Bank.
See Professional Biographies, DANVILLE, INDIANA

Howard, John M., Jr., (BV) .... '40 '67 C.108 B.A. L.345 J.D. 110 S. Washington St.

Kendall, Wood, Lowry & Kessinger, (BV)
1 South Washington Street, P.O. Box 8, 46122
Telephone: 317-745-4408 Fax: 317-745-0390
Members of Firm: John A. Kendall (1907-1993); Robert A. Wood; James L. Lowry; Terry M. Kessinger.
General Trial Practice in all Courts. Probate and Estate Planning, Personal Injury, Real Estate, School, Family, Domestic Relations and Criminal Defense Law.
Representative Clients: Mid State Bank of Hendricks County; Danville, Plainfield and Millcreek Community School Corp.; North West Hendricks School Corp.; Town of Coatesville.
Local Counsel for: Public Service Co. of Indiana, Inc.; Indiana Insurance Co.; Prudential Life Insurance Co.; Indiana Bell Telephone Co.
See Professional Biographies, DANVILLE, INDIANA

Kenninger, David E., Attorney at Law, (CV) '61 '87
C.894 B.A. L.345 J.D. 71 W. Marion St.
Kessinger, Terry M., (BV) .... '48 '76 C.838 B.S. L.345 J.D. [Kendall,W.L.&K.]
Lawson, David E., (BV) .... '37 '66 C.303 B.A. L.345 J.D. 110 S. Washington St.
Lewis, Seth B., (BV) .... '40 '66 C.108 A.B. L.345 J.D. 52G W. Main St.
Lind, Melvin R., (AV) .... '26 '57 C.347 B.S. L.345 J.D. 106 N. Washington St.
Love, Karen M. .... '57 '86 C.108 B.S. L.345 J.D. Hendricks Co.
Lowry, James L., (BV) .... '39 '66 C.108 B.A. L.345 J.D. [Kendall,W.L.&K.]
Lulich, Michael K., (BV) .... '57 '82 C.894 B.A. L.209 J.D. 2102 E. Main St.
Phillips, Constance Baker .... '72 '97 C.347 B.A. L.339 J.D. 101 Woodfield Place
Pierce, John E., (BV) .... '52 '77 C.347 B.A. L.345 J.D. 47 West Marion Street
Piercy, Starr, Law Office of, (CV) .... '48 '94 C.651 B.S.Ed. L.345 J.D. P.O. Box 408

Ruppert & Schaefer, P.C.
(See Indianapolis)

Stegemoller, Sharon E., (CV) .... '47 '84 C.624 B.A. L.345 J.D. Co. Pros. Off.
Steuerwald, Gregory E., (BV) .... '52 '81 C.346 B.S. L.345 J.D. 106 N. Washington St.
Stewart, Robert E., (BV) .... '35 '66 C.894 A.B. L.345 J.D. 71 W. Marion St.
Twait, Traci Justice .... '65 '90 C.879 B.A. L.347 J.D. 6437 Red Oak Dr.
Vandivier, John C., Jr., (AV) .... '28 '56 C.347 A.B. L.345 J.D. 97 S. Washington St.
Wheatley, Lawrence R., (BV) .... '55 '84 C.347 B.A. L.345 J.D. [L.R.Wheatley]
Wheatley, L. R., (BV) .... 594 W. Main St.
Witham, Herb D., (BV) .... '63 '94 C.265 B.A. L.490 J.D. 106 N. Washington St.
Wood, Gary L., (BV) .... '60 '84 C.210 B.A. L.345 J.D. 135 S. Washington St.
Wood, Robert A. .... '34 '63 C.591 L.213 Dist. J.
Wood, Robert A., (BV) .... '48 '74 C.346 A.B. L.345 J.D. [Kendall,W.L.&K.]

Zielinski, Daniel F., (BV) .... '63 '89 C.303 B.A. L.347 J.D. 106 N. Washington St.

DECATUR, * 9,528, *Adams Co.*

Ainsworth, Scott B., (BV) .... '62 '88 C.347 B.A. L.1119 J.D. [De Voss,J.B.&A.]
Baker, Timothy E., (BV) .... '53 '78 C.679 B.A. L.345 J.D. [De Voss,J.B.&A.]

Blackburn & Green
(See Fort Wayne)

Brown, Blair A., (CV) .... '48 '75 C.432 B.S. L.345 J.D. 107 S. 2nd Ave.
Brown, Jeremy W., (AV) .... '71 '96 C.679 B.A. L.1119 J.D. Pros. Off.
Burry, Daniel C., (BV) .... '43 '69 C.91 B.S.Bus. L.607 J.D. [Smith,B.H.&M.]
De Voss, Jay M., (AV) .... '42 '68 C.265 A.B. L.345 J.D. [De Voss,J.B.&A.]
De Voss, Johnson, Baker & Ainsworth, Professional Corporation, (AV)
147 South 2nd Street
Harvey, Christopher E., (BV) .... '60 '86 C.894 A.B. L.879 J.D. [Zurcher&H.]
Heimann, James A. .... '42 '67 C.1024 B.A. L.1119 J.D. Supr. Ct. J.
Herman, DuWayne W., (BV) .... '49 '75 C.679 B.S. L.1119 J.D. [Smith,B.H.&M.]
Johnson, Joseph M., II, (AV) .... '44 '71 C.347 B.S. L.345 J.D. [De Voss,J.B.&A.]
Miller, Adam T., (BV) .... '62 '88 C.999 B.B.A. L.607 J.D. [Smith,B.H.&M.]

Roebuck & Associates, P.C.
(See Ft. Wayne)

Schurger, Frederick A. .... '46 '72 C.894 A.B. L.1119 J.D. Cir. Ct. J.
Sheets, Thomas Wade, (CV) .... '56 '81 C.347 B.S. L.879 J.D. [T.W.Sheets]
Sheets, Thomas W., (CV) .... 157 North 2nd Street
Smith, Burry, Herman & Miller, P.C., (BV) .... 113 N. 2nd St.
Sullivan, Richard J., (BV) .... '34 '58 C.347 B.S. L.345 LL.B. 107 S. 2nd St.
Zurcher, Susan E. S., (BV) .... '51 '78 C.210 B.A. L.1119 J.D. [Zurcher&H.]
Zurcher & Harvey, P.C., (BV) .... 119 S. 2nd St.
Zwick, Zane R., (BV) .... '45 '70 C&L.879 B.A., J.D. Dep. Pros. Atty.

DELPHI, * 3,015, *Carroll Co.*

Blackburn & Green
(See Fort Wayne)

Carey, Joseph W. .... '26 '53 C.347 B.S. L.1119 LL.B. Judge
Currie, Donald E., (BV) .... '58 '87 C.879 B.A. L.345 J.D. Chf. Pros. Atty.
Emerson, Barry T., (BV) .... '51 '76 C.347 B.S. L.421 J.D. [Emerson&M.]
Emerson & Manahan, (BV) .... 112 W. Main St.
Fouts, Kurtis G., (CV) .... '69 '95 C.347 B.S. L.339 J.D. [Obear,O.H.R.&F.]
Hall-Justice, Susannah M. .... '68 '97 C.309 A.B. L.347 J.D. 312 E. Main St.
Huffer, James R., (BV) .... '45 '73 C.347 B.S. L.345 J.D. [Obear,O.H.R.&F.]
Isaacs, Fred W., (BV) .... '36 '72 C.679 B.S. L.345 J.D. 6975 West Crestwood Drive
Ives, Joseph T., Jr., (AV) .... '31 '59 C.210 A.B. L.1119 LL.B. [Ives&I.]
Ives, Robert T., (BV) .... '57 '82 C.210 A.B. L.347 J.D. [Ives&I.]
Ives and Ives, (AV) .... 113 W. Franklin St.
Justice, Courtney B. .... '41 '66 C.894 A.B. L.273 LL.B. 312 E. Main St. (⊙Logansport)
Manahan, Patrick F., (BV) .... '55 '92 C.172 B.S. L.208 J.D. [Emerson&M.]
Mullin, Lewis N., (BV) .... '17 '40 C.347 A.B. L.1119 LL.B. 117 S. Market St.
Obear, George W., (AV) .... '08 '33 C.210 B.A. L.352 J.D. [▣ Obear,O.H.R.&F.]
Obear, Overholser, Huffer, Rider & Fouts, (AV) .... 102 South Union Street
Overholser, Carl Dean, (AV) .... '28 '55 C.347 A.B. L.1119 J.D. [Obear,O.H.R.&F.]
Rider, Jeffrey C., (BV) .... '61 '88 C.130 B.A. L.326 J.D. [Obear,O.H.R.&F.]
Smith, Jeffrey R. .... '47 '72 C.894 A.B. L.1119 J.D. Supr. Ct. J.

DEMOTTE, 3,234, *Jasper Co.*

Burkhart, Glenn D. .... '58 '97 C.679 B.A. L.879 J.D. Pub. Def.
Campbell, Barbara A. '46 '95
C.679 B.A. L.146 J.D. V.P. & Trust Offr., Demotte State Bank
Gabrielse, Robert J., (BV) .... '52 '78 C.999 A.B. L.879 J.D. [R.J.Gabrielse]
Gabrielse, Robert J., Law Office, (BV) .... 109 S. Halleck St.

Lasser, Herbert S., & Associates, P.C.
(See Merrillville)

DYER, 13,895, *Lake Co.*

Baker, Andrew B., Jr. .... '42 '68 C.679 E.E. L.879 LL.B. Asst. U.S. Atty.
Bella, Daniel L., (BV) .... '52 '77 C.879 B.A. L.1119 J.D. Asst. U.S. Atty.
Bouwer, Greg A. .... '66 '92 C.114 B.A. L.347 J.D. [Koransky&B.]
Brown, Beth L. .... '77 '03 C&L.879 B.A., J.D. [▣ T.F.Kelly&Assoc.]
Capp, David, (AV) .... '50 '77 C.966 B.A. L.879 J.D. U.S. Atty. Off.
Crosmer, Andrew A., (CV) .... '62 '87 C&L.879 B.A., J.D. [Rubino,C.S.&S.]
Higginson, Robert K. .... '43 '74 C.597 B.B.A. L.146 J.D. 449 Sycamore Ave.
James, Richard F., (BV) .... '35 '60 C.347 L.879 J.D. [James,J.&M.]
James, James & Manning, P.C., (BV) .... 200 Monticello Dr.
Kelly, Timothy F., (AV) .... '47 '72 C.723 B.A. L.494 J.D. [T.F.Kelly&Assoc.]

Kelly, Timothy F., and Associates, (AV) BR
202 Joliet Street Suite 2A, 46311
Telephone: 219-322-0606 Fax: 219-322-0707
Email: tfklaw@tfklaw.net URL: http://www.tfklaw.net
Members of Firm: Timothy F. Kelly; Karl K. Vanzo. Associates: Michael P. Massucci; Beth L. Brown; Daniel Stephens.
General Practice, Commercial, Business Law, Business Planning, Contracts, Business Litigation, Business Enterprises, Wills and Probate, Trusts and Estates, Asset Protection, Guardianships, Estate Planning, Corporation, Real Estate, Labor and Employment, Trials and Appeals in all Courts, Insurance Defense, Automobile Accidents, Slip and Fall, Wrongful Death, Products Liability, Professional Liability and Medical Malpractice.
See Professional Biographies, DYER, INDIANA

Kohl, Jacquelyn M., (CV) .... '50 '81 C.347 B.A. L.1187 J.D. 202 Joliet Street
Koransky, Peter G., (AV) .... '44 '69 C.347 B.S. L.1119 J.D. [Koransky&B.]
Koransky & Bouwer, P.C., (AV) .... 425 Joliet Road, Suite 425
Kunstmanas, Raymond '56 '80 C.597 B.A. L.209 J.D.
(adm. in IL; not adm. in IN) 8000 Tapper Pl.‡
Manning, Kenneth A., (BV) .... '49 '74 C&L.879 B.S., J.D. [James,J.&M.]
Massucci, Michael P. .... '77 '02 C&L.436 B.A., J.D. [▣ T.F.Kelly&Assoc.]
Rubino, Terrence M., (BV) .... '50 '75 C.381 B.A. L.365 J.D. [Rubino,C.S.&S.]
Rubino, Crosmer, Smith & Sersic, (BV) .... 202 Joliet Street, Suite 201
Sersic, Steven J., (CV) .... '69 '94 C.145 B.A. L.347 J.D. [Rubino,C.S.&S.]
Smith, Kevin C., (CV) .... '69 '94 C.659 B.A. L.209 J.D. [Rubino,C.S.&S.]
Stephens, Daniel .... '— '00 C&L.879 B.A., J.D. [▣ T.F.Kelly&Assoc.]
Thanos, Mary Kay .... '61 '88 C.347 B.A. L.879 J.D. 202 Joliet Street
Van Wormer, Bernard L. .... '44 '92 C.966 B.S. L.879 J.D. Asst U.S. Atty.
Vanzo, Karl K., (BV) .... '57 '82 C.602 A.B. L.1119 J.D. [T.F.Kelly&Assoc.]
Wruck, Donald William, III, Law Offices of '74 '99
C.123 B.A. L.879 J.D. 275 U.S. Hwy. 30, Ste. 250

EAST CHICAGO, 32,414, *Lake Co.*

Beckman, Kelly & Smith
(See Hammond)

Cappas, Thomas S., (BV) .... '34 '59 C&L.879 B.A., LL.B. 1802 E. Columbus Dr.

Cayia, Robert V. '54 '84 C.1265 B.S. L.215 J.D.
(adm. in IL; not adm. in IN) Mgr. Union Rel., ISPAT Inland Inc.
Corona, Maria L., (BV) ...... '41 '81 C.347 B.A. L.1119 J.D. Dept. of Family & Children
Davis, William E. ....'48 '76 C.679 B.A. L.1119 J.D. Supr. Ct. J., Civ. Div.
Dawson, Rudolph V., (CV) .... '27 '58 C.347 A.B. L.1119 J.D. 3926 Main St.
Holcomb, Noah L., Jr. .... '43 '77 C.347 B.S. L.879 J.D. [Holcomb,N.L.]
Holcomb, Noah L. .... 1919 E. Columbus Dr.
Jeske, Marc R. '52 '79 C.339 B.A. L.597 J.D.
(adm. in IL; not adm. in IN) Gen. Coun., ISPAT
Kowalski, Wm. A., (BV) ....'32 '58 C.347 L.209 LL.B. 4704 Indianapolis Blvd.
Lesniak, Richard J., (BV) .... '39 '64 C.894 A.B. L.1119 LL.B. 1802 E. Columbus Dr.
McCarthy, Edward C. '47 '78 C&L.339 A.B., J.D.
(adm. in MN; not adm. in IN) Coun., ISPAT
Parker, Patrick D. ....'— '89 C.679 B.S. L.209 J.D. Sect. Manager, Ispat Inland Inc.
Randolph, Lonnie M., & Associates '49 '79
C.589 B.S. L.365 J.D. 1919 E. Columbus Drive
Ryan, Thomas D., (BV) ....'47 '74 C.1157 B.S. L.146 J.D. 4704 Indianapolis Blvd.
Sacha, Barbara A. '56 '81 C.424 B.A. L.365 J.D.
(adm. in IL; not adm. in IN) LTV Steel Co.
Scherschel, Mathew S. ....'52 '78 C.347 A.B. L.421 J.D. 3210 Watling St.
Silverman, Marvin E., (BV) ...... '34 '58 C.347 B.S. L.1119 LL.B. 620 W. Chicago Ave.
Waddy, Dujuana D., Law Office of .... '66 '97 C.352 B.A. L.879 J.D. 4922 Carey St.
Williams, Del-Marae, (CV) .... '41 '74 C.1016 B.A. L.209 J.D. City J.
Wooden, April Elizabeth .... '52 '87 C.63 B.S. L.365 J.D. Dept. of Bus. Dev. & Plan.

EDINBURGH, 4,505, *Bartholomew, Johnson & Shelby Cos.*

Kirtland, Robert E. .... '68 '97 C.879 B.A. L.209 J.D. Capt. U.S. Army JAG

ELIZABETHTOWN, 495, *Bartholomew Co.*

Guthrie, R. Keith, (BV) .... '53 '78 C.347 B.A. L.273 J.D. 13242 S 600 E.

ELKHART, 51,874, *Elkhart Co.*

Ahlemann, Elizabeth Bottorff '57 '83
C.210 B.A. L.477 J.D. Sr. Legal Coun., C.T.S. Corp.
Alick, Nafe S. '61 '89 C.477 B.A. L.276 J.D.
V.P., Alicks Home Medical Equipment, Inc.
Areaux, Daniel G., (BV) ....'55 '81 C.347 B.S. L.345 J.D. [Sanders P.]
Arko, Victor, (BV) ....'34 '59 C.347 B.S. L.602 J.D. 303 S. 3rd St.
Atwater, Vernon, (AV) ....'26 '55 C.347 B.S. L.1119 LL.B. 314 W. Lexington Ave.

Baker & Daniels LLP, (AV) BR
317 West Franklin Street, P.O. Box 507, 46515-0507 ⊙
Telephone: 574-296-6000 Fax: 574-296-6001
URL: http://www.bakerdaniels.com
Members of Firm: James R. Brotherson; Glenn E. Killoren; Kennard R. Weaver (Resident); Robert C. Whippo. Of Counsel: Robert A. Pfaff. Associates: Jennifer Elaine Greene; Jeremy D. Pfister; Christopher J. Spataro; Krista J. Zimmerman.
Antitrust, Bankruptcy, Business Planning, Commercial, Corporate Finance, Creditors Rights, Employee Benefits, Employment, Environment, Estate and Probate, Family, Financial, Food and Drug, Government Affairs, Health Care, Insurance, Intellectual Property, International, Legislative, Litigation, Medical Technology Regulation, Municipal, Nonprofit, Product Liability, Real Estate, Securities, Sports, Tax, Transportation, Utilities, Year 2000, Zoning and Land Use Law.
Representative Clients: Central Soya Co., Inc.; The Lutheran Hospital of Indiana, Inc.; Tokheim Corp.; General Motors Corp.; Eli Lilly and Co.
Indianapolis, Indiana Office: 300 North Meridian Street, Suite 2700, 46204. Telephone: 317-237-0300. Fax: 317-237-1000.
South Bend, Indiana Office: First Bank Building, 205 West Jefferson Boulevard, Suite 250, 46601. Telephone: 574-234-4149. Fax: 574-239-1900.
Fort Wayne, Indiana Office: 111 East Wayne Street, Suite 800, 46802. Telephone: 260-424-8000. Fax: 260-460-1700.
Indianapolis-96th Street, Indiana Office: Parkwood Six, 600 East 96th Street, Suite 600, 46240. Telephone: 317-569-9600. Fax: 317-569-4800.
Washington, D.C. Office: 805 15th Street, N.W., Suite 700, 20005. Telephone: 202-312-7440. Fax: 202-312-7460.
Qingdao, China Office: 4/F, Office Tower, Crowne Plaza Qingdao, No. 76 Hong Kong Middle Road, 266071. Telephone: +011-86-532-575-1051. Fax: +011-86-532-575-1055.
Beijing, China Office: Room 1919, Tower 2, China World Trade Center, No. 1 JianGuoMenWai Avenue, 100004. Telephone: +86-10-6505-7733. Fax: +86-10-6505-8730.
See Professional Biographies, ELKHART, INDIANA

Banik, Michael K., (CV) '57 '87 C.679 B.S.M.E. L.602 J.D.
Dep. Pros. Atty. [Banik&R.]
Banik & Renner, (BV) ....217 S. 4th St.

Barnes & Thornburg LLP, (AV) BR
121 West Franklin Street, Suite 200, 46516 ⊙
Telephone: 574-293-0681 FAX: 574-296-2535
URL: http://www.btlaw.com
Partners: Geoffrey K. Church; Samuel S. Thompson; Rand W. Nilsson; Richard W. Paulen; J. Scott Troeger; Brian J. Clark; Eric H. J. Stahlhut. Of Counsel: Robert G. Devetski; Timothy A. Weaver. Associates: Christopher Riley; Andrew M. Hicks; Andrew G. Helfrich.
Acquisitions and Divestitures, Ad Valorem Tax, Administrative Law, Affirmative Action, Agriculture Law, Americans with Disabilities Act, Antidumping, Antitrust, Antitrust and Trade Regulation, Appellate Practice, Attorney Grievances, Automotive Warranty Law, Aviation and Aerospace, Aviation Law, Banking Law, Banking Regulations, Bankruptcy, Bankruptcy Reorganization, Banks and Banking, Biochemical Patents, Biomedical Products Liability, Biomedical Technology, Biotechnology Patent Prosecution, Bond Law, Brain Injury, Breach of Warranty, Brown Fields Redevelopment, Business Immigration, Business Law, Business Litigation, Business Planning, Business Regulatory and Administrative, Business Start-ups, Business Succession Planning, Business Taxation, Business Torts, Business Transactions, Business Transfers, Buying and Selling of Businesses, Cable TV, Cargo Claims, Charitable Trusts and Foundations, Chemical Intellectual Property, Chemical Patent Prosecution, Chemical Patents, Chemical Products Liability, Civil Appeals, Civil Litigation, Civil Practice, Civil RICO, Class Action Defense, Clean Air Act, Clean Water Act, Closely Held Business Estate Planning, Closely Held Businesses, Closely Held Business Law, Closely Held Corporations, Collective Bargaining, Commercial Bankruptcy, Commercial Finance Law, Commercial Law, Commercial Leasing and Financing, Commercial Litigation, Commercial Conveyancing, Commercial Real Estate, Commercial Real Estate Acquisition, Commercial Real Estate Development, Commercial Real Estate Finance, Commercial Transactions, Commodities Fraud, Communications and Media, Complex Commercial Litigation, Complex Litigation, Computer and Software Patents, Computer Law, Computers and Software, Conflicts of Interest, Construction Labor Law, Construction Law, Consumer Credit, Contract Litigation, Cooperatives, Copyrights, Corporate Finance, Corporate Formation, Corporate Law, Corporate Taxation, Corporate Tax Planning, Countervailing Duties, Covenants Not To Compete, Creditors Rights, Creditors Rights in Bankruptcy, Criminal Defense, Criminal Law, Criminal Tax Audits, Customs Law, Dealer and Distributor Termination, Debt and Equity Finance, Decedents Estates, Defense Litigation, Design Patents, Disability Insurance Defense, Discrimination, Distribution, Drug and Medical Device Defense, Economic Development, Education Law, Elder Law, Election, Campaign and Political Law, Electric Power, Electric Utilities, Electrical Intellectual Property, Electrical Patents, Electro-mechanical Patents, Electronic Commerce, Electronic Patents, Eminent Domain, Employee Benefits, Employee Stock Ownership Plans, Employment Defense, Employment Discrimination, Employment Law, Employment Litigation, Energy, Energy Contracts, Energy Regulation, Environmental Administrative Law, Environmental Cleanup, Environmental Compliance, Environmental Criminal Defense, Environmental Law, Environmental Litigation, Environmental Permitting, Environmental Real Estate, Environmental Regulation, Environmental Risk Management, Equal Employment Opportunity Law, ERISA Litigation, Estate Administration, Estate and Gift Taxation, Estate Planning, Estate Planning and Taxation, Estate Planning and Administration, Estate Planning and Probate, Estate Planning for Parents of Handicapped Children, Estate Planning for Unmarried Individuals, Executive Compensation, Executive Severance Contracts, Export Regulation,

(This Listing Continued)

Barnes & Thornburg LLP (Continued)
Fair Employment Practices, Family and Medical Leave Act, Family Business Successions, Family Wealth Transfer, Federal and State Administrative Regulatory Practice, Federal and State Legislative Practice, Federal Civil Litigation, Federal Civil Practice, Federal Criminal Law, Federal Estate and Gift Taxation, Federal Litigation, Federal Tax Controversies, Federal Taxation, Fiduciary Income Tax, Finance, Financial Transactions, First Party Insurance, Foreign Investment in the United States, Freight Claims, Freight Loss and Damage, Gaming Law, Gaming Licensing, Gas Utilities, General Litigation, Government, Government Affairs, Government Agency Practice, Government Contracts, Government Investigations, Government Relations, Groundwater Contamination, Hazardous Materials and Substances, Hazardous Waste, Hazardous Waste Liability, Head Injury, Health Care, Health Care Corporate Law, Health Care Contracts, Health Care Fraud, Health Care Licensing, Health Care Litigation, Health Care Mergers and Acquisitions, Health Care Regulation, Health Care Reimbursement, Health Law, Heavy Equipment Products Liability, Immigration Law, Industrial Revenue Bond Law, Inheritance Tax, Initial Public Offerings, Insurance, Insurance Bad Faith, Insurance Coverage, Insurance Litigation, Insurance Regulation, Integrated Health Care Delivery Systems, Intellectual Property, Intellectual Property General Prosecution, Intellectual Property Infringement, Intellectual Property Licensing, Intellectual Property Litigation, Intellectual Property Procurement, Intellectual Property Protection, Intellectual Property Rights, International Business Law, International Intellectual Property, International Law, International Patents, International Trade, International Transportation Law, Internet Law, Internet Trademark Law, Joint Ventures, Labor and Employment, Labor Arbitration, Labor Law, Labor Relations, Land Use, Lease Law, Leasing, Legal Ethics and Professional Responsibility, Legal Malpractice Defense, Legislative Practice, Licensing, Life Insurance Defense, Limited Liability Company Law, Limited Partnerships, Liquor Licensing, Litigation, Loans, Lobbying, Local Government Law, Logistics, Long Term Care, Managed Care, Managed Care Contracts, Management Employment Law, Management Labor Law, Manufacturers Liability, Maritime Regulations, Mechanical Intellectual Property, Mechanical Patents, Media Law, Mediation, Medical Antitrust, Medical Intellectual Property, Medical Patents, Mental Health Law, Mergers, Acquisitions and Divestitures, Mergers and Acquisitions, Mineral Taxation, Molecular Biology Patents, Motor Carrier Law, Motor Carrier Regulation, Multi-Employer Pensions, Municipal Bonds, Municipal Bonds Taxation, Municipal Finance, Municipal Law, Municipal Leasing, Municipal Redevelopment, Municipal Securities, Municipal Taxation, National Labor Relations Act, Neurolaw, Nonprofit and Charitable Organizations, Nonprofit Organizations Law, North American Free Trade Agreement, Occupational Safety and Health, OSHA, Partnership Law, Partnership Taxation, Patent Infringement, Patent Interference Practice, Patent Litigation, Patent Prosecution, Patents, PCT Legal Export, Personal Injury, Personal Injury Defense, Pesticide Litigation, Pharmaceutical Intellectual Property, Pharmaceutical Patents, Physician Contracts, Physician Practices, Planning and Land Use, Power Line Contact Injury, Probate, Probate Litigation, Products Liability, Products Liability Defense, Professional Liability, Property Law, Property Tax, Property Tax Abatement, Property Tax Appeals, Psychological Injury, Public Finance, Public Sector Labor Relations, Public Utility Law, Railroad Law, Real Estate, Real Estate Acquisitions, Real Estate Contracts, Real Estate Development, Real Estate Finance, Real Estate Licensing, Real Estate Secured Lending, Real Estate Title Insurance, Real Property, Real Property Acquisitions, Real Property Finance, Reorganizations, Resource Conservation and Recovery Act (RCRA), Retirement Benefit Plans, School Law, Securities, Securities Litigation, Securitization, Semiconductor Technology, Sexual Harassment, Small Business Corporations, State Government Law, State Tax Controversies, State Taxation, Structured Finance, Succession Planning, Superfund, Tax Controversies, Tax Exempt Finance, Tax Exempt Organizations, Tax Increment Finance, Tax Law, Tax Litigation, Taxation, Technology and Science, Technology Law, Technology Licensing, Technology Transfers, Telecommunications Competition, Telecommunications Law, Theft of Trade Secrets, Title VII Discrimination, Title IX Discrimination, Tort Defense, Toxic Exposure, Toxic Tort Class Actions, Toxic Torts, Toxic Tort Defense, Trade Dress, Trade Secrets, Trademark Litigation, Trademarks, Trademark Prosecution, Trademark Protection, Trademark Registration, Transportation, Transportation Safety, Trial Practice, Trusts and Estates, Unfair Competition, Unfair Trade, Uniform Commercial Codes, Union Contract Negotiations, Union Elections, Utilities, Utility Law, Wage and Hour Law, WARN Act, Water Pollution, Water Quality, Water Utilities, Wetland Regulation, White Collar Crime, White Collar Criminal Defense, Wills, Workers Compensation, Workouts, World Trade Organization, Wrongful Death, Wrongful Termination, Wrongful Termination Defense, Zoning, Planning and Land Use.
Representative Clients: Bank One; Elkhart Community Schools; Elkhart General Hospital; KeyBank National Association; Partners National Health Plans of Indiana, Inc.; Rieth-Riley Construction Co., Inc.; Skyline Corporation; Truth Publishing Company, Inc.; United Musical Instruments USA, Inc.; Whirlpool Corporation.
Indianapolis, Indiana Office: 11 South Meridian Street, 46204. Telephone: 317-236-1313. FAX: 317-231-7433.
Fort Wayne, Indiana Office: 600 One Summit Square, 46802. Telephone: 260-423-9440. FAX: 260-424-8316.
South Bend, Indiana Office: 600 1st Source Bank Center, 100 North Michigan, 46601-1632. Telephone: 574-233-1171. FAX: 574-237-1125.
Chicago, Illinois Office: One North Wacker Drive, Suite 4400, 60606-2833. Telephone: 312-357-1313. FAX: 312-759-5646.
Washington, D.C. Office: Suite 900, 750 17th Street, N.W., 20006. Telephone: 202-289-1313. FAX: 202-289-1330.
Grand Rapids, Michigan Office: 300 Ottawa Avenue, N.W., Suite 500, 49503. Telephone: 616-742-3930. FAX: 616-742-3999.
See Professional Biographies, ELKHART, INDIANA

Becker, Vicki E., (CV) .... '72 '97 C.344 B.A. L.347 J.D. [A Cosentino&C.]
Beckman, Kelly & Smith
(See Hammond)
Bilbrew, Sharon L., (CV) ....'59 '85 C.112 B.A. L.329 J.D. Dep. Pub. Def.
Bonfiglio, David C. .... '54 '82 C.602 B.A. L.879 J.D. Supr. Ct. J.
Bowers, Stephen R., (BV) ....'53 '77 C.347 A.B. L.1119 J.D. 405 W. Lexington Ave.
Boyn, Gary D., (BV) ....'45 '72 C.182 B.A. L.879 J.D. [Warrick&B.]
Breckenridge, Franklin E., Sr. ....'40 '68 C.347 B.S. L.345 J.D. 1884 Miles Ave.‡
Brewer, Alice A. '47 '91 C.347 A.B. L.1340 J.D.
Sr. Pat. Coun., Bayer HealthCare,LLC, Diag. Div. (Pat.)
Brotherson, James R., (BV) ....'52 '78 C.228 B.A. L.1119 J.D. [Baker&D.]
Burggraf, Norman L., (CV) .... '58 '95 C.602 B.A. L.879 J.D. 221 W. Lexington Blvd.
Burton, Dean O., (BV) ....'60 '87 C.63 B.S. L.1187 J.D. 505 S. 3rd. St.
Butler, Rebecca F., (BV) .... '60 '83 C.347 B.S. L.602 J.D. 221 W. Lexington Ave.
Chester, Edward J., (BV) ....'53 '80 C.347 B.A. L.345 J.D. [Chester]
Chester, Willard H., (AV) ....'25 '52 C.347 A.B. L.209 J.D. 317 West Franklin Street

Chester Law Office, (BV)
230 N. Main, Suite 2, P.O. Box 1768, 46515
Telephone: 574-296-1515 Fax: 574-295-9316
Email: ed@chesterlawoffice.com
Edward J. Chester. Associate: Laura L. Ezzell.
Personal Injury, Civil Trials and Appeals in State and Federal Courts, including Employment and Commercial Litigation, Wrongful Death.
See Professional Biographies, ELKHART, INDIANA

Christofeno, Michael A., (BV) ....'59 '85 C.602 B.S. L.879 J.D. [Cosentino&C.]
Church, Geoffrey K., (AV) ....'— '71 C.197 B.A. L.1119 J.D. [Barnes&T.]
Cittadine, Jack P., (BV) ....'41 '66 C.210 B.A. L.597 J.D. 230 Waterfall Dr.
Clark, Brian J., (BV) ....'— '84 C.347 B.S. L.879 J.D. [Barnes&T.]
Cohen, William J., (BV) .... '50 '78 C.37 B.A. L.345 J.D. [Cohen]
Cohen Law Offices, (BV) ....401 West Bristol Street
Cosentino, Michael A., (AV) ....'36 '63 C.72 B.A. L.966 LL.B. [Cosentino&C.]
Cosentino & Christofeno, (AV) ....115 West Lexington Avenue
Cutter, Richard G., III '46 '71
C.63 B.S. L.150 J.D. V.P., Gen. Coun. & Secy., C.T.S. Corp.
Davis, Jeannine M., (BV) '48 '81
C.112 B.A. L.602 J.D. V.P., Gen. Coun. & Secy., CTS Corp.
Davis, Mary E., (BV) ....'48 '74 C.347 B.A. L.339 J.D. [Davis&D.]
Davis, Richard W., Jr., (BV) ....'45 '70 C.347 B.A. L.1119 J.D. [Davis&D.]
Davis & Davis, Prof. Corp., (BV) .... 400 W. High St.
Dean, Paul A. .... '75 '01 C.051 B.A. L.602 J.D. Suite 200, 121 West Franklin St.

DeBoer, David L., (BV) ....'50 '75 C.114 B.A. L.679 J.D. [Stutsman,M.&D.]
Devetski, Robert G., (BV) ....'— '88 C.347 B.A. L.1119 J.D. [Ⓒ Barnes&T.]

Doran • Blackmond LLP
(See South Bend)

Dorbin, John W., Jr., (CV) ......'71 '98 C.679 B.A. L.602 J.D. City of Elkhart Legal Dept.
Doty, Mark W., Law Office of, (CV) '60 '85
C.347 B.S. L.879 J.D. 409 W. Lexington Avenue
Duncan, Glenn L., (BV) ....'49 '75 C.347 B.A. L.345 J.D. [Thorne G.]
Eash, Paul D. ....'62 '87 C.63 B.S. L.345 J.D. 306 W. High Street
Eisele, Thomas Lee .... '49 '84 C.363 B.A. L.879 J.D. Gen. Coun. & Secy., NIBCO, INC.
Ellis, John F., Law Office of, (CV) .... '42 '72 C.679 B.A. L.602 J.D. 57685 C.R. 9 South
Ezzell, Laura L. ....'64 '03 C.679 B.A. L.879 J.D. [Ⓐ Chester]
Frechette, John R., (BV) ....'52 '75 C.347 A.B. L.1119 J.D. 315 W. Lexington Ave.
Fritz, Cassidy C., (BV) ....'57 '85 C.1052 B.A. L.879 J.D. 128 W. Lexington
Frost, Jacob S., (CV) ....'70 '96 C.602 B.A. L.345 J.D. [Ⓐ Thorne G.]
Gaydos, John J. ....'28 '60 C.679 B.S. L.424 J.D. 330 W. Lexington Ave. (Pat.)
Gillard, Cynthia Schaefer, (BV) ....'54 '82 C.373 B.A. L.602 J.D. [Warrick&B.]
Greene, Jennifer Elaine ....'— '05 C.679 B.A. L.910 J.D. [Ⓐ Baker&D.]
Greene, Michael S., (CV) .... '61 '94 C.184 B.A. L.347 J.D. 221 Lexington Ave.
Greenlee, Rosalind A. ....'— '98 C.880 B.S. L.280 J.D. 307 S. Main St., Ste. 301
Grodnik, Charles H., (AV) ....'44 '70 C&L.494 B.A., J.D. [Thorne G.]
Grolimund, J. Moritz, Jr., (CV) ....'31 '62 C.699 B.A. L.1119 LL.B. 212 W. Jefferson
Haut, William D., (BV) ....'61 '86 C.679 B.S. L.900 J.D. [Warrick&B.]
Helfrich, Andrew G. ....'— '04 C.432 B.A. L.879 J.D. [Ⓐ Barnes&T.]
Hengesbach, Theodor J. ....'66 '91 C.602 B.A. L.347 J.D. Law Clk., Supr. Ct. J.
Hesser, Randall G., (BV) ....'58 '83 C.347 B.A. L.93 J.D. [Warrick&B.]
Hicks, Andrew M. ....'— '02 C.1157 B.S. L.602 J.D. [Ⓐ Barnes&T.]
Hill, Curtis T., Jr., (BV) ....'61 '88 C.347 B.S. L.1119 J.D. 414 Vistula St.
Iemma, Anthony J., (CV) ....'43 '68 C.201 B.S.B.A. L.607 J.D. 212 S. 2nd St.
Jonas, John ....'22 '52 C.477 M.B.A. L.912 LL.B. 1520 Ash Dr., E‡
Jones, Donald W. ....'35 '60 C.346 A.B. L.1119 LL.B. Supr. Ct. J.

Katz, Bernard, (BV) '35 '64 C.98 B.S. L.602 J.D.
421 South Second Street, Suite 300, 46516
Telephone: 574-293-3597 Fax: 574-294-7224
General Civil Trial Practice in all Courts. Corporate, Business, Real Estate, Children, Family, Domestic Relations, Adoptions, Divorce, Child Custody, Child Support, Parenting Time Rights, Paternity, Personal Injury, Automobile Accidents, Slip and Fall, Wrongful Death, Trusts, Wills, Probate and Estate Planning Law.
References: Society Bank, Elkhart; NBD Bank, Elkhart, Ind.
See Professional Biographies, ELKHART, INDIANA

Kauffman, Gregory P. ....'71 '00 C.608 B.A. L.607 J.D. 301 North Nappanee
Kennedy, Sandra L. '70 '99
C.741 B.A. L.1119 J.D. Assoc. Coun., Coachmen Industries, Inc.
Killoren, Glenn E., (BV) ....'58 '83 C&L.602 B.B.A., J.D. [Baker&D.]
Kinsman, Eric E., (CV) ....'69 '98 C.1172 B.A. L.209 J.D. 216 W. High St.

Konopa, Reagan & Aigotti, P.C.
(See South Bend)

Lauer, Jay
(See South Bend)

Lavers, Richard M., (BVⓉ) '47 '72 C&L.477 B.A., J.D.
Exec. V.P., Secy. & Gen. Coun., Coachman Indus. (Pat.)
Lavery, William G., (BV) ....'57 '82 C.347 B.A. L.1119 J.D. [Whisler&L.]
Law, William L., III ....'78 '03 C.1175 B.A. L.602 J.D. [Ⓐ Warrick&B.]
Leazenby, Dean E., (CV) ....'72 '98 C.679 B.A. L.345 J.D. [Ⓐ Warrick&B.]
Lewis, P. Shawn, (BV) ....'67 '92 C.679 B.S. L.117 J.D. [Sanders P.]
Like, Steven K. .... '56 '81 C.210 B.A. L.1119 J.D. Patriot Homes Inc.
MacKenzie, Gordon G., (BV) ....'30 '55 C.347 B.S. L.1119 J.D. 414 W. High St.
May, George William ....'44 '89 C.999 B.A. L.339 J.D. P.O. Box 968

May Oberfell Lorber
(See Mishawaka)

McCaslin, James L., (BV) .... '37 '63 C.347 A.B. L.1119 LL.B. [McCaslin&M.]
McCaslin, Nancy A., (BV) .... '41 '81 C.347 B.S. L.879 J.D. [McCaslin&M.]

McCaslin & McCaslin, (BV)
228 West High Street, 46516
Telephone: 574-293-6033 Fax: 574-293-7012 URL: http://www.mccaslin-law.com
Email: jlmnam@aol.com URL: http://www.mccaslinlaw.com
James L. McCaslin; Nancy A. McCaslin.
Civil Trial Litigation and Appellate Practice in all State Courts. Wills and Probate, Trusts and Estates, Estate Planning, Elder Law, Corporate, Real Estate, Commercial, Family Law, Adoptions, Divorce.
See Professional Biographies, ELKHART, INDIANA

Mellinger, Lee F., (CV) ....'39 '64 C&L.347 A.B., LL.B. 216 W. High St.
Mengel, Marie W., (CV) ..... '38 '79 C.347 B.A. L.602 J.D. Elkhart Legal Aid Serv., Inc.
Metz, Michael A., (BV) ....'61 '87 C.894 B.A. L.201 J.D. 320 E. Bristol St.
Meyers, Penny J. ....'69 '00 C.317 B.A. L.879 J.D. [Ⓐ Sanders P.]
Miller, Lynn M., (BV) ....'46 '76 C.347 A.B. L.602 J.D. [Ⓒ Miller&M.]
Miller, Robert W., (BV) ....'42 '67 C.347 B.S. L.1119 J.D. [Miller&M.]
Miller and Miller, (BV) ....112 North 2nd Street
Mulvaney, Douglas A., (BV) ....'57 '83 C.323 B.A. L.1194 J.D. [Stutsman,M.&D.]
Murray, Charles L. .... '15 '40 C.679 B.S.E.E. L.1119 LL.B. 23072 Greenleaf Blvd.‡
Nilsson, Rand W., (BV) ....'— '74 C.894 B.A. L.228 J.D. [Barnes&T.]
Nofziger, Phyllis Kay ....'49 '97 C.608 B.S.N. L.879 J.D. Law Clk., Supr. Ct. J.
Noser, Richard C. ....'48 '73 C&L.602 B.A., J.D. 700 E. Beardsley
Nuttle, Thomas N., (CV) ....'55 '94 C.972 B.S. L.602 J.D. 216 S. Fourth St.
Nye, William J., (AV) ....'31 '55 C&L.602 A.B., J.D. 505 S 3rd. St.
Parker, R. Michael, (AV) .... '45 '70 C.894 A.B. L.802 J.D. 131 E. Franklin St.
Paulen, Richard W., (AV) ....'— '74 C.249 B.A. L.879 J.D. [Barnes&T.]
Petersen, Christopher J. ....'68 '95 C&L.879 B.A., J.D. 314 West High Street
Pfaff, Robert A., (AV) ....'33 '61 C.902 A.B. L.477 J.D. [Ⓒ Baker&D.]

Pfaff, Brotherson & Killoren, LLP
(See Baker & Daniels LLP)

Pfister, Jeremy D. ....'— '03 C.966 B.A. L.345 J.D. [Ⓐ Baker&D.]
Pianowski, Michael A., (AV) ....'47 '79 C.63 B.S. L.879 J.D. [Sanders P.]
Platt, Stephen E. ....'45 '70 C&L.879 B.A., J.D. Supr. Ct. J.
Pressler, Paul R., (BV) ....'21 '54 C.347 B.S. L.602 J.D. 405 W. Lexington Ave.‡
Quinn, Bridget Kerry '65 '93 C.477 B.A. L.602 J.D.
Coun. & Asst. Secy., C.T.S. Corp.
Ransel, J. Richard, (BV) ....'47 '74 C.473 B.A. L.602 J.D. [Thorne G.]
Renner, Tamara L., (BV) ....'56 '86 C.347 B.A. L.602 J.D. [Banik&R.]
Rieckhoff, James W. ....'40 '66 C.31 A.B. L.597 J.D. Supr. Ct. J.
Riley, Christopher ....'— '01 C.684 B.A. L.602 J.D. [Ⓐ Barnes&T.]

Rodino, Samuel J., (AV) ....'31 '54 C&L.602 A.B., J.D. 314 W. Lexington Ave

Rowe & Rowe, Law Offices
(See South Bend)

Samovitz, Kathy L. .... '71 '01 C.63 B.A. L.879 J.D. Assoc. Coun., Coachmen Industries
Sanders, Robert T., III, (AV) ....'49 '73 C.347 B.S. L.1119 J.D. [Sanders P.]

Sanders • Pianowski, LLP, (AV) BB
300 Riverwalk Drive, 46516
Telephone: 574-294-1499 Fax: 574-294-7277
Email: lawyers@riverwalklaw.com URL: http://www.riverwalklaw.com
Members of Firm: Philip E. Byron, Jr. (1911-1977); Robert C. Daniels (1928-1995); Robert T. Sanders, III; Michael A. Pianowski; James L. Todd; Matthew A. Yeakey; P. Shawn Lewis; Daniel G. Areaux. Associates: Jason G. Ward; Penny J. Meyers; Courtney G. Williams.
General Practice, Corporate, Business Law, Civil Litigation, Insurance, Bank Collection and Foreclosure, Commercial Litigation, Labor and Employment, Mergers and Acquisitions, Real Estate, Estate Planning, Trusts and Estates, Probate, Wills and Estate Administration, Environmental, Family Law, Adoption, Child Custody, Child Support, Divorce, Visitation Rights.
Representative Clients: Yoder Oil Co., Inc.; WSJV-TV; Tom Naquin Chevrolet, Inc.; Ascot Enterprises, Inc.; KeyBank National Association; WISE-TV; Carrige, Inc.; L.E. Technologies, LLC; Cardinal Buses, Inc.
See Professional Biographies, ELKHART, INDIANA

Schenk, Carie .... '77 '03 C.679 B.A. L.345 J.D. 212 South Second Street
Shelly, Timothy S., (BV) ....'60 '85 C.210 B.A. L.945 J.D. [Warrick&B.]
Skinner, Claire E. '54 '81 C.802 B.F.A. L.602 J.D.
(adm. in IL; not adm. in IN)
Chairman of Bd. and Chief Executive Officer, Coachmen Indsutries, Inc.‡
Spahn, Alphonse J., (AV) '19 '48
C.177 B.A. L.602 J.D. Gen. Coun., Holiday Rambler Corp.
Spataro, Christopher J., (CV) ....'71 '96 C.569 B.A. L.602 J.D. [Ⓐ Baker&D.]
Stahlhut, Eric H. J., (BV) ....'— '92 C.95 B.A. L.734 J.D. [Barnes&T.]
Stevens, James D., (BV) ....'43 '77 C.475 B.S. L.1136 J.D. 519 W. Franklin St.
Stuart, Edward C. ....'21 '49 C.347 B.S. L.309 LL.B. 910 Grove St.
Stutsman, David T., (BV) ....'40 '71 C.932 B.A. L.347 J.D. [Stutsman,M.&D.]

Stutsman, Mulvaney & DeBoer, (BV)
1300 Cassopolis Street, P.O. Box 1337, 46515-1337
Telephone: 574-266-8500 1-800-867-5907 Fax: 574-206-9215
URL: http://www.smdlawfirm.com
David T. Stutsman; Douglas A. Mulvaney; David L. DeBoer.
General Civil and Appellate Practice in all State and Federal Courts. Personal Injury, Automobile Accidents, Slip and Fall, Wrongful Death, Workers Compensation, Medical Malpractice, Corporate, Wills and Probate, Trusts and Estates, Asset Protection, Guardianships, Estate Planning, Real Estate, Internet Law.
Reference: Bankone, Elkhart, Ind.
See Professional Biographies, ELKHART, INDIANA

Talmage, Charles A. E., (CV) .... '49 '94 C.309 A.B. L.602 J.D. [Talmage]
Talmage Law Offices, P.C., (CV) .... 221 South Third Street
Thompson, Samuel S., (AV) ....'— '74 C.679 B.S.E. L.345 J.D. [Barnes&T.]
Thorne, W. Douglas, (BV) '59 '86 C.429 B.A. L.851 J.D.
Dir. Employee and Student Relations, Elkart Community Schools
Thorne, William A., (AV) ....'24 '49 C&L.879 J.D. [Thorne G.] ‡

Thorne • Grodnik, LLP, (AV)
228 West High Street, 46516-3176 ⊙
Telephone: 574-294-7473 FAX: 574-294-5390
Email: firm@tglaw.us URL: http://www.tglaw.us
Members of Firm: William A. Thorne (Retired); Charles H. Grodnik; J. Richard Ransel; Glenn L. Duncan; Steven L. Hostetler (Resident, Mishawaka Office); Michael A. Trippel (Resident, Mishawaka Office). Associates: Jacob S. Frost; Jamie C. Woods (Resident, Mishawaka Office); Jordan P. Williams. Of Counsel: Joseph C. Zakas.
Commercial and Civil Litigation, Creditors Rights, Bankruptcy, Banking and Bank Related Matters, Corporate and Commercial Transactions, Insurance Defense, Personal Injury, Automobile Accidents, Slip and Fall, Wrongful Death, Real Estate and Zoning, Wills and Probate, Trusts and Estates, Estate Planning, School Law and Family Law, Adoptions, Divorce, Child Custody, Child Support, Visitation Rights, Mediation.
Counsel for: Valley American Bank and Trust Co., Mishawaka, Indiana; NBD Bank.
Mishawaka, Indiana Office: 420 Lincoln Way West, P.O. Box 1210, 46544. Telephone: 574-256-5660. FAX: 574-674-6835.
See Professional Biographies, ELKHART, INDIANA

Todd, James L., (BV) ....'47 '79 C.871 B.S. L.879 J.D. [Sanders P.]
Tokar, Thomas, Law Office Of, (CV) '57 '82
C.347 B.A. L.1119 J.D. 1720 East Bristol Street
Troeger, J. Scott, (BV) ....'— '81 C.209 A.B. L.1119 J.D. [Barnes&T.]

Tuesley & Hall, LLP
(See South Bend)

Ward, Jason G., (CV) ....'— '97 C&L.347 B.A., J.D. [Ⓐ Sanders P.]
Warrick, Thomas E., (BV) ....'32 '60 C.347 B.A. L.477 LL.B. [Warrick&B.]

Warrick & Boyn, L.L.P., (BV)
Suite 400, 121 West Franklin Street, 46516-3278
Telephone: 574-294-7491 Fax: 574-294-7284
Email: thefirm@warrickandboyn.com URL: http://www.warrickandboyn.com
Members of Firm: Thomas E. Warrick; Gary D. Boyn; James V. Woodsmall; Cynthia Schaefer Gillard; Randall G. Hesser; Timothy S. Shelly; William D. Haut. Associates: Dean E. Leazenby; William L. Law, III.
General Civil Practice in all Courts. Corporation, Litigation, Real Estate, Environmental, Securities, Labor and Employment, EEOC, Bond Counsel, Probate and Estate Planning, Bankruptcy, Municipal and Zoning Law, and Banking Law. Federal Taxation, Elder Law, School Law.
Representative Clients: EFP Corp.; Elkhart Brass Manufacturing Co., Inc.; Fabwel, Inc.; Georgie Boy Mfg., Inc.; Jayco, Inc.; Juhl Advertising Agency, Inc.; Martin's Feed Mills, Inc.; Schult Homes Corp.
See Professional Biographies, ELKHART, INDIANA

Weaver, Kennard R., (BV) ....'40 '65 C.475 B.A. L.309 J.D. [Baker&D.]
Weaver, Timothy A. ....'— '90 C.210 B.A. L.597 J.D. [Ⓒ Barnes&T.]
Weseman, Steven D. '67 '96 C.474 B.S.C.E. L.424 J.D.
(adm. in IL; not adm. in IN; Pat.) Pat. Atty., C.T.S. Corp.
Weymouth, Ann G. ....'66 '93 C.893 B.A L.602 J.D. Legal Coun., CTS Corp.
Whippo, Robert C., (CV) ....'65 '91 C&L.879 B.A., J.D. [Baker&D.]
Whisler, Patrick J., (BV) ....'55 '80 C.347 B.A. L.1119 J.D. [Whisler&L.]
Whisler & Lavery, (BV) .... 600 South Main Street
Whitmer, J. A., (BV) ....'52 '82 C.303 B.A. L.602 J.D. 219 S. 4th St.
Wicks, Charles C., (BV) ....'45 '70 C.861 B.A. L.1119 J.D. 514 S. Main St.
Williams, Clifford R., (BV) .... '45 '79 C.347 A.B. L.1187 J.D. 115 1/2 E. Lexington Ave.
Williams, Courtney G. ....'76 '01 C.198 B.A. L.879 J.D. [Ⓐ Sanders P.]
Williams, Jordan P. ....'76 '01 C.210 B.A. L.879 J.D. [Ⓐ Thorne G.]
Wilson, Thomas S., Jr., (CV) ....'68 '93 C.436 B.S. L.602 J.D. [Wilson&Assoc.]
Wilson & Associates, (CV) .... 301 North Nappanee Street
Woodsmall, James V., (BV) ....'50 '78 C&L.597 B.A., J.D. [Warrick&B.]
Yeakey, Matthew A., (BV) ....'64 '90 C.602 B.A. L.1119 J.D. [Sanders P.]

Yoder, Ainlay, Ulmer & Buckingham, LLP
(See Goshen)

Zakas, Joseph C., (BV) ....'50 '80 C.339 B.A. L.602 J.D. [Ⓒ Thorne G.]

Zimmerman, Krista J. ....'— '01 C.288 B.A. L.602 J.D. [Ⓐ Baker&D.]

ELWOOD, 9,737, *Madison Co.*

Alley, Edward B., (BV) ....'47 '73 C.63 B.S. L.345 J.D. 213 N. 16th St. (⊙Anderson)

Bingham, Farrer & Wilson, A Professional Corporation, (BV)
1601 South Anderson Street, P.O. Box 494, 46036
Telephone: 765-552-9878 Fax: 765-552-5496
URL: http://www.bfwlawyers.com
Michael E. Farrer; James W. Wilson.
General Practice, Banking and Finance, Bankruptcy, Business Planning, Sales and Acquisitions, Consumer and Commercial Law, Consumer and Commercial Collections, Transactions and Litigation, Contracts, Corporate Law, Creditors Rights, Debtor-Creditor Law, Elder Law, Family Law, Domestic Relations, Adoption Law, Child Support, Custody, Dissolution/Divorce, Separation and Visitation, Government Relations, Zoning, Planning and Land Use, Municipal Law, Probate, Guardianship, Estate Planning, Wills and Trusts, Real Estate, Foreclosures, Mechanics Liens.
Representative Clients: Alexandria Housing and Economic Development Corp.; Avondale Federal Credit Union; Ball State Federal Credit Union; City of Alexandria, Indiana; City of Elwood, Indiana; Elwood Industrial Development Corp.; Finance Center Federal Credit Union; First Farmers Bank & Trust Co.; Madison County Council; Perfect Wireless, Inc.
See Professional Biographies, ELWOOD, INDIANA

Farrer, Michael E., (BV) ....'— '75 C.346 B.S. L.345 J.D. [Bingham,F.&W.]
Hailey, Anna C. ....'20 '60 L.345 LL.B. 1526 N. A St.
Simmons, Gary W. ....'56 '82 C.894 B.A. L.862 J.D. 2507 Main St‡
Tancey, Michael E. ....'11 '34 C.973 L.347 LL.B. 1326 Madison Rd.‡
Van Briggle, Larry W., (BV) ....'55 '83 C.63 B.S. L.990 J.D. [Van Briggle]
Van Briggle Law Office, (BV) ....1601 South Anderson Street
Wilson, James W., (BV) ....'— '76 C.63 B.S. L.190 J.D. [Bingham,F.&W.]

ENGLISH, * 614, *Crawford Co.*

Fowler, Michael R. '60 '86 C.197 B.A. L.309 J.D.
(adm. in MA; not adm. in IN) R.R. 2‡
Lopp, Kenneth Lynn ....'56 '84 C.347 B.A. L.421 J.D. Cir. Ct. J.
Shelton, Lester V., Law Office Of ... '49 '84 C&L.347 B.G.S., J.D. 502 South Court Street

EVANSVILLE, * 121,582, *Vanderburgh Co.*

Ahlers, Jeffrey W., (BV) ....'62 '87 C.210 B.A. L.879 J.D. [Kahn,D.D.&K.]
Allega, Gerald F., (BV) ....'53 '77 C.346 B.A. L.1119 J.D. [Statham A.&J.]
Allen, Ronald R., (AV) ....'38 '65 C.249 A.B. L.345 LL.B. [Ⓒ Fine&H.]

Allyn & Givens
(See Mt. Vernon)

Almon, S. Brent, (BV) .....'53 '78 C.208 B.A. L.347 J.D. 20 NW Fourth Street, Suite 708
Anderson, Edward B., (BV) ....'50 '77 C.346 B.S. L.1095 J.D. [Gerling]
Angermeier, Curt J., (BV) ....'53 '78 C.679 B.A. L.1119 J.D. 18 N.W. 4th St.
Angermeier, James W., (BV) ....'25 '51 C&L.436 B.S., J.D. 223 S.E. 2nd St.
Annakin, Joseph W., (AV) '39 '65
C.346 B.S. L.345 J.D. V.P. & Gen. Coun., Traylor Bros., Inc.
Appel, Stephen R. .... '49 '74 C.347 A.B. L.1119 J.D. V.P. & Tr. Offr., Citizens Natl. Bk.
Armstrong, David K., (AVⓉ) '56 '88 C&L.101 B.S., J.D.
Senior Vice President & General Counsel, Accuride Corporation
Armstrong, Russell S., (BV) '11 '41
C.800 A.B. L.16 LL.B. 312 N.W. Martin Luther King Jr. Blvd.
Armstrong, Sacha L. ....'75 '03 C.446 B.A. L.421 J.D. [Ⓐ Kightlinger&G.]
Arnaez, Ivan A. ....'72 '00 C.347 B.A. L.345 J.D. 123 N.W. 4th St.
Ashton, Brett J. '71 '00 C.63 B.S. L.1119 J.D.
State Rel.Offr., American International Group
Atkinson, Jerry A., (BV) ....'41 '69 C.63 B.S. L.345 J.D. [Atkinson]
Atkinson Law Office, (BV) ....123 N.W. 4th St.
Balser, Donald R. ....'32 '61 C.347 A.B. L.345 J.D. Sr. V.P., Old Natl. Tr. Co.

Bamberger, Foreman, Oswald and Hahn, LLP, (AV)
20 NW Fourth Street, Suite 708, 47708 ⊙
Telephone: 812-425-1591 Fax: 812-421-4936
URL: http://www.bamberger.com
Members of Firm: Robert H. Hahn (1925-2004); Robert M. Becker; Fred S. White; R. Thomas Bodkin; Terry G. Farmer; Henry C. Hudson; Jerry D. Stilwell; Thomas J. Kimpel; Donald J. Fuchs; Michele S. Bryant; Marc E. Hawley; John P. Broadhead; J. Herbert Davis; Marjorie M. Blalock; Catherine A. Nestrick; M. Beth Burger; Jason P. Lueking; Douglas A. Welp; Lori Yarbor Young; Laura A. Scott; Andrew C. Ozete; Christopher C. Wischer. Associates: Michael G. Smith; Heather H. Lacy; Shawn Rountree; D. Andrew Nestrick; James E. Gentry, Jr.; Adam J. Farrar; James C. Hall; Jennifer A. Elston. Senior Counsel: Charles E. Oswald, Jr.; K. Richard Hawley; Paull Michael Mitchell. Of Counsel: Gerald H. Evans; John Stuff Staser; Michael J. Cork; W. Trent Van Haaften; Kent A. Poulton.
Administrative Law, Antitrust Law, Appellate Practice, Arbitration, Banking Law, Bankruptcy Law, Business Law, Civil Rights, Civil Trial Practice, Commercial Law, Commercial Litigation, Communications Law, Construction Law, Corporate Law, Creditors' Rights, Elder Law, Energy Law, Environmental Law, Health Care Law, Insurance Defense, Intellectual Property Law, Labor and Employment Law, Land Use Law, Medical Malpractice, Mergers and Acquisitions, Product Liability Law, Public Utilities Law, Real Estate Law, Trademark, Copyright and Unfair Competition, Trusts and Estates, Wills and Probate.
Representative Clients: Aetna Life and Casualty Group; AT&T; CNB Bancshares Inc.; Dow Chemical Co.; Medical Protective Insurance Co.; Southern Indiana Gas and Electric Co.; St. Mary's Medical Center of Evansville, Inc.; State Farm Mutual Automobile Insurance Co.; Travelers Insurance Co.; Welborn Clinic/HMO.
Indianapolis, Indiana Office: Market Tower, Suite 2950, 10 West Market Street, 46204. Telephone: 317-464-1591. Fax: 317-464-1592. Toll Free: 888-994-7976.
Mt. Vernon, Indiana Office: 309 Main Street, 47620. Telephone: 812-838-4495. Fax: 812-838-9445.
Poseyville, Indiana Office: 178 South Lockwood, 47633. Telephone: 812-874-3365. Fax: 812-874-3366.
Princeton, Indiana Office: 302 N. Prince Street, 47670. Telephone: 812-386-6482. Fax: 812-386-6480.
See Professional Biographies, EVANSVILLE, INDIANA

Banks, Cole G. ....'47 '73 C.265 B.A. L.1119 J.D. 713 W. Buena Vista St.
Barber, Steve, (AV) ....'48 '74 C&L.347 A.B., J.D. [Barber,S.&S.]

Barber, Shoulders & Siesky, LLP, (AV) BB
123 N.W. Fourth Street, Suite 402, 47708
Telephone: 812-425-9211 Fax: 812-425-9216
Email: mail@barlegal.net URL: http://www.barlegal.net
***Steve Barber; Jeffrey T. Shoulders;* Lane C. Siesky.**
General Practice, Estates and Wills, Personal Injury, Social Security Claims, Business Law, Corporate Law, Family Law, Divorce, Insurance Claims, Criminal Defense.
See Professional Biographies, EVANSVILLE, INDIANA

Barfield, Daniel A., (CV) ....'70 '95 C.679 B.A. L.879 J.D. [Gerling]
Barnett, George C., Jr., (BV) ....'55 '80 C.347 B.A. L.1119 J.D. [Noffsinger B.]
Barrett, Barbara S., (BV) ....'50 '90 C.249 B.A. L.734 J.D. [Barrett]

Barrett Law Offices, P.C., (BV)
915 Main Street, Suite 205, P.O. Box 3052, 47730
Telephone: 812-424-4878; 800-380-4878 Fax: 812-424-8875
Email: bbarrettlaw@aol.com URL: http://www.bbarrettlaw.com
Barbara S. Barrett.
Personal Injury, Medical Malpractice, Wrongful Death, Wills, Trusts, Estates, Medicaid Planning.
See Professional Biographies, EVANSVILLE, INDIANA

Barringer, Stanley P., Jr. '56 '83 C.999 B.A. L.228 J.D.
(adm. in NC; not adm. in IN) Coun., Bristol-Myers Squibb Co.
Barron, Robert F. "Ted", II, (BV) ....'57 '97 C&L.347 B.A., J.D. [Kahn,D.D.&K.]
Barsumian, Todd C. ....'73 '98 C.303 B.A. L.221 J.D. [Kahn,D.D.&K.]
Bates, Claude H. ....'24 '53 C.249 B.S. L.1119 J.D. 3116 E. Morgan Ave.
Baugh, Jerry P., (AV) ....'33 '58 C.210 A.B. L.477 J.D. [Terrell,B.S.&B.] ‡
Becker, Robert M., (AV) ....'46 '71 C.347 A.B. L.477 J.D. [Bamberger,F.O.&H.]
Bender, Diane L. (Wolf), (AV) ....'55 '80 C&L.602 B.B.A., J.D. [D.L.Bender]

Bender, Diane L., (AV)
111 Southeast Third Street, Suite 402, P.O. Box 1536, 47706-1536
Telephone: 812-423-8558 Fax: 812-423-8559
Diane L. (Wolf) Bender.
General Civil Practice including Probate and Estate Planning Law.
Reference: Old National Bank in Evansville.
See Professional Biographies, EVANSVILLE, INDIANA

Berger, Charles L., (AV) ....'47 '72 C.249 B.A. L.345 J.D. [Berger&B.]

Berger and Berger, (AV) BB
313 Main Street, 47708-1485
Telephone: 812-425-8101 Toll Free: 800-327-0182 Fax: 812-421-5909
Email: berger@bergerlaw.com URL: http://www.bergerlaw.com
Members of Firm: Sydney L. Berger (1917-1988); Charles L. Berger; Sheila M. Corcoran; Mark W. Rietman. Associate: Jennifer Ulrich-Keppler. Of Counsel: William J. Brune.
Personal Injury, Admiralty, Labor and Employment, Municipal, Family Law, Probate, Business Law, Trials. General Civil in all State and Federal Courts.
References: Old National Bank, Evansville; Integra Bank, Evansville.
See Professional Biographies, EVANSVILLE, INDIANA

Bernhardt, Thomas R. ....'45 '81 C.347 B.S. L.1026 J.D. Kight Lbr. Co.
Biesecker, Kyle F. ....'74 '03 C.347 B.S. L.345 J.D. [Biesecker&D.]
Biesecker & Dutkanych ....317 S.E. Third St.
Black, Paul E., (AV) ....'45 '70 C.249 B.A. L.1119 J.D. [Bowers H.]
Blalock, Marjorie M., (BV) ....'66 '91 C.210 B.A. L.347 J.D. [Bamberger,F.O.&H.]
Blanton, Jean M. ....'78 '04 C.347 B.S. L.150 J.D. [Ⓐ Ziemer,S.W.&S.]
Bodkin, R. Thomas, (AV) ....'45 '73 C.347 B.S. L.345 J.D. [Bamberger,F.O.&H.]
Bohleber, Steven L., (BV) ....'50 '75 C.346 B.S. L.345 J.D. 123 N.W. 4th St.
Born, D. Timothy, (AV) ....'55 '81 C.346 B.S. L.990 J.D. [Terrell,B.S.&B.]
Bosse, Jeffrey A., (BV) ....'46 '73 C.880 B.A. L.597 J.D. [J.Bosse&Assoc.]
Bosse, Jeff, & Associates, (BV) ....915 Main St., Ste. 600
Bowers, F. Wesley, (AV) ....'— '51 C.347 A.B. L.1119 J.D. [Ⓒ Bowers H.]
Bowers, Scott R. ....'49 '76 C.347 A.B. L.326 J.D. Supr. Ct. J.

Bowers Harrison, LLP, (AV)
25 N.W. Riverside Drive, P.O. Box 1287, 47706-1287
Telephone: 812-426-1231 Fax: 812-464-3676
Email: web@bowersharrison.com URL: http://www.bowersharrison.com
Equity Partners: Joseph H. Harrison; Paul E. Black; Arthur D. Rutkowski; Paul J. Wallace; David L. Jones; David E. Gray; Thomas A. Massey; Keith E. Rounder. Non-Equity Partners: Greg A. Granger; Joseph H. Harrison, Jr.; Christopher L. Lucas; Gary K. Price; Jay A. Ziemer; Sara Harrison Zeidler. Associates: Kelly A. Lonnberg; Mark F. Warzecha; Cory A. Kuhlenschmidt. Of Counsel: F. Wesley Bowers; Keith M. Wallace; George A. Porch.
General Civil Practice and Litigation in all Courts, Banking, Corporation and other Business Entities, Railroad, Mineral, Environmental, Probate and Estate Planning, Real Estate, Taxation, Labor and Employment, Bankruptcy, Patent and Trademark.
Division Counsel in Indiana for: Southern Railway Co.
See Professional Biographies, EVANSVILLE, INDIANA

Brasseale, Kent A., II, (CV) ....'67 '93 C.679 B.S. L.347 J.D. [Kahn,D.D.&K.]
Breckenridge, J. B. '17 '46 C.947 A.B. L.228 LL.B.
(adm. in NY; not adm. in IN) 22 Johnson Pl.‡
Breedon, Allyson R. ....'75 '01 C.347 B.S. L.1119 J.D. [Ⓐ Ziemer,S.W.&S.]
Bressner, S. Earl ....'24 '51 C.347 A.B. L.1119 J.D. 11323 Seib Rd.‡

Bright, Lloyd D., (BV) '48 '80 C&L.383 B.S.G., J.D.
2321 West Delaware Street, 47712
Mailing Address: P.O. Box 6388, Evansville, IN 47719
Telephone: 812-423-6885 Fax: 812-423-6893
Email: ldbrightatty@sigecom.net
Oil and Gas, Coal, Real Estate, Title, Regulatory, Business and Probate.
See Professional Biographies, EVANSVILLE, INDIANA

Brinkerhoff Riley, Stephanie ....'72 '01 C.249 B.S. L.1119 J.D. [Brinkerhoff R.]

Brinkerhoff Riley LLC
400 Court Street, 47708
Telephone: 812-464-3966 Fax: 812-464-3968
Email: ssbrinkerhoff@yahoo.com URL: http://www.brinkerhoffrileylaw.com
Stephanie Brinkerhoff Riley.
Family Law, Child Custody, Divorce, Juvenile Matters, Criminal Defense, Felonies, Misdemeanors, Probation Violations, Small Claims, Contract Disputes, Medical Malpractice and Employment Law.
See Professional Biographies, EVANSVILLE, INDIANA

Brinkmeyer, Dennis L., (BV) ....'47 '75 C.249 B.A. L.421 J.D. 525 Sycamore St.
Briody, Douglas K., (CV) ....'69 '94 C.309 A.B. L.1119 J.D. [Ⓐ Noffsinger B.]
Broadhead, John P., (AV) '56 '81
C.249 B.S. L.345 J.D. [Bamberger,F.O.&H.] (⊙Poseyville)
Brown, Douglas R., (BV) '62 '87 C.136 B.S. L.801 J.D.
Chief Dep. Pros., Sanderburg Coun. Pros. Off.
Brown-Cox, Abigail ....'75 '01 C.249 B.S. L.179 J.D. [Ⓐ Rudolph,F.P.&J.]
Browning, Elizabeth A. ....'74 '02 C.383 B.A. L.347 J.D. [Ⓐ Kahn,D.D.&K.]
Brune, William J. ....'28 '62 C.249 A.B. L.345 LL.B. [Ⓒ Berger&B.]
Bryan, Thomas H., (AV) ....'44 '69 C.679 B.S.M.E. L.1119 J.D. [Fine&H.]
Bryant, Michele S., (BV) ....'63 '89 C.210 B.A. L.1119 J.D. [Bamberger,F.O.&H.]
Buente, Benjamin E., Jr., (BV) ....'24 '52 C.347 L.879 LL.B. 8250 Maple Lane
Bumb, Laurie Baiden, (BV) ....'55 '80 C.347 L.345 J.D. [Keating,B.V.&L.]
Bunner, David A., (BV) ....'50 '79 C.346 B.S. L.221 J.D. 123 N.W. 4th St., Ste. 518
Burger, M. Beth, (CV) ....'67 '93 C.249 B.S. L.347 J.D. [Bamberger,F.O.&H.]
Burkart, Robert L., (BV) ....'65 '92 C.303 B.A. L.245 J.D. [Ziemer,S.W.&S.]
Burke, John R., Jr., (AV) ....'35 '61 C.1024 B.S. L.1119 J.D. 7008 Monroe Ave.‡
Bussing, Wilfred C., III, (BV) ....'56 '81 C.249 B.S. L.602 J.D. 2709 Washington Ave.
Buthod, John J., (BV) ....'49 '76 C.347 B.A. L.1119 J.D. [Kinney,K.&B.]
Cain, Renee Allen, (BV) ....'— '97 C.338 B.S. L.801 J.D. Co. Pros. Off.
Caine, Jack E. ....'27 '53 C.249 L.345 LL.B. 2221 W. Franklin St.
Campbell, Elizabeth A. ....'66 '93 C.602 B.A. L.733 J.D. 425 Main Street
Canada, Robert, (BV) ....'58 '83 C.249 B.S. L.345 J.D. 5111 Lincoln Ave.
Capshaw, Tom D. '36 '61 C.616 B.S. L.623 LL.B.
Adm. Law. J., U.S. Dept. of Health & Human Servs.
Carithers, Robert P., (BV) ....'50 '76 C.249 B.A. L.345 J.D. [Ⓐ Trimble&J.]
Carroll, Brian K., (AV) ....'56 '82 C.347 B.S. L.345 J.D. [Johnson,C.N.K.&S.]
Carroll, John L., (AV) .... '22 '48 C.347 A.B. L.1119 J.D. [Ⓒ Johnson,C.N.K.&S.] ‡
Carwile, Dan J., (BV) ....'54 '83 C.432 B.A. L.1119 J.D. P.O. Box 868
Case, Gary R., (AV) ....'42 '73 C&L.37 B.S.Ch.E., J.D. Old National Bancorp
Casey, James P., (BV) ....'54 '80 C.347 B.S. L.345 J.D. [Ziemer,S.W.&S.]

Casey, S. Brian '47 '77 C.880 B.A. L.383 J.D.
(adm. in KY; not adm. in IN) Claims Rep., Seaboard Sys. R.R.
Chandler, Earl E., (CV) ... '39 '84 C.714 B.S. L.345 J.D. 301 Mary St.
Chapman, Neil Byron, (CV) ... '65 '94 C.800 B.A. L.602 J.D. [Danks&D.]
Christian, Ronald E. ... '58 '83 C.249 B.A. L.421 J.D. P.O. Box 209
Church, Steven A. ... '— '98 C.249 B.S.E.E. L.347 J.D. 1115 S. Stockwell Road (Pat.)
Cirignano, Kristi Prutow ... '75 '00 C.361 B.A. L.347 J.D. [Ⓐ Kahn,D.D.&K.]
Cirignano, Nick J. ... '71 '01 C.311 B.A. L.1119 J.D. [Ⓐ Ziemer,S.W.&S.]
Clark, David L., (BV) ... '49 '75 C.249 B.A. L.362 J.D. 1033 Mt. Pleasant Rd., Ste. H
Clouse, James R., Jr. ... '30 '56 C.473 B.A. L.607 J.D. 7716 Highland Ct.‡
Clouse, John D., (AV) ... '25 '52 C.249 A.B. L.1119 J.D. 123 NW 4th St.,
Cochren, Michael R., (CV) ... '68 '96 C&L.347 B.S., J.D. [Ⓐ R.John&Assoc.]
Collins, C. Richard, (BV) ... '50 '75 C.249 B.A. L.221 J.D. [Collins&Assoc.]
Collins & Associates, (BV) ... 101 Plaza East Boulevard, Suite 230
Compton, Charles A., (BV) ... '66 '92 C.210 B.A. L.880 J.D. [Ziemer,S.W.&S.]
Comstock, Allison K., (CV) ... '70 '94 C.1232 B.A. L.809 J.D. [Kahn,D.D.&K.]
Condict, Curtis D. ... '78 '03 C.210 B.A. L.345 J.D. [Ⓐ Kightlinger&G.]
Condict, Julia A. ... '78 '04 C.827 B.S. L.345 J.D. [Ⓐ Fine&H.]
Corcoran, Sheila M., (BV) ... '50 '79 C.249 B.A. L.345 J.D. [Berger&B.]
Cork, Michael J. ... '50 '77 C.123 B.A. L.879 J.D. [Ⓒ Bamberger,F.O.&H.]
Corn, Beverly K. ... '54 '83 C.249 B.A. L.347 J.D. 915 Main St.
Cory, Rick A., (BV) ... '59 '84 C&L.879 B.A., J.D. [Danks&D.]
Cox, John Coates, (BV) '41 '66
C.367 B.A. L.1119 J.D. 108 N.W. Martin Luther King Jr. Blvd.
Cox, Michael J., (BV) '65 '92
C.679 B.A. L.607 J.D. 108 N.W. Martin Luther King Jr. Blvd.

Craig, Randall K., Law Offices of, (AV) '50 '75 C.347 B.S. L.345 J.D. BB
5000 East Virginia Street, Suite 1, 47715
Telephone: 812-477-3337 Telefax: 812-477-3658
Email: rkcraig@dynasty.net URL: http://www.rkcraiglaw.com
Taxation, Probate, Estate Planning, Elder, Corporate, Business and Real Estate Law.
See Professional Biographies, EVANSVILLE, INDIANA

Cravens, Garland W., Jr., (BV) ... '53 '82 C.347 B.A. L.345 J.D. [Frick P.W.C.&S.]
Culley, Stephen E. ... '51 '77 C.894 B.A. L.347 J.D. Legal Servs. Organization of IN
Daly, R. Lawrence, (AV) ... '41 '71 C.880 B.A. L.1119 J.D. [Wright&D.]
Danks, Michael J., (BV) ... '51 '86 C.346 B.S. L.801 J.D. [Danks&D.]
Danks, Scott A., (BV) ... '59 '89 C.346 B.A. L.347 J.D. [Danks&D.]
Danks & Danks, (BV) ... 1010 Sycamore Street
Davis, J. Herbert, (BV) ... '66 '91 C&L.347 B.A., J.D. [Bamberger,F.O.&H.]
Deems, William W., (BV) ... '49 '75 C.347 A.B. L.1119 J.D. P.O. Box 4260
Deig, Glenn A., (CV) ... '62 '88 C.894 B.A. L.345 J.D. [Deig]
Deig, Steven K., (BV) ... '53 '78 C.249 B.A. L.345 J.D. 3319 Washington Avenue
Deig Law Office, (CV) ... 2804 N. 1st Ave.
DeLucio, Marco L., (BV) ... '59 '84 C.210 B.A. L.345 J.D. [Ziemer,S.W.&S.]
Devine, Jeffrey L., (CV) ... '66 '92 C.999 B.S. L.734 J.D. 8627 Elizabeth Ln.
Dietsch, Terry D. ... '32 '59 C.714 A.B. L.1119 LL.B. Supr. Ct. J.
DiRienzo, Michael E. ... '73 '01 C.1391 B.A. L.602 J.D. [Ⓐ Kahn,D.D.&K.]
Dix, Brendan B. ... '68 '94 C.367 B.S.C.E. L.665 J.D. 123 N.W. 4th St., Ste. 614 (Pat.)
Dix, Harold G. '39 '64
C.972 B.A. L.502 J.D. Asst. Gen. Coun., American Gen. Fin. Srvcs.
Dodd, Timothy R. ... '41 '66 C.197 A.B. L.1119 LL.B. 233 S.E. 3rd Street
Dodson, R. Jeff, (CV) ... '60 '86 C.347 B.S. L.201 J.D. 915 Main St., Ste. 208
Dooms, Tami L. ... '65 '91 C.999 B.A. L.801 J.D. V.P., TTT Christian Youth Ministries
Downs, Larry R., (AV) ... '48 '74 C.210 B.A. L.1119 J.D. [Kahn,D.D.&K.]
Dumes, Jill A., Attorney at Law ... '62 '93 C.37 B.A. L.61 J.D. 10800 Eagle Crossing Dr.
Dunlap, Roberta S., (BVⓉ) '56 '87 C.249 B.M. L.421 J.D.
123 N.W. Fourth St., Ste. 214
Dutkanych, Andrew, III ... '74 '02 [Biesecker&D.]

Early, Arnold & Ziemer, LLP
(See Ziemer, Stayman, Weitzel & Shoulders, LLP)

Edwards, Monica E. ... '72 '00 C.802 B.S. L.421 J.D. [Ⓐ Kahn,D.D.&K.]
Eisen, Jeffrey M. '55 '80 C.434 B.A. L.477 J.D.
(adm. in DC; not adm. in IN) Univ. of Evansville
Elston, Jennifer A. ... '— '04 C.249 B.S. L.347 J.D. [Ⓐ Bamberger,F.O.&H.]
Erkilla, Jack R. '59 '84 C.399 B.A. L.893 J.D.
(adm. in WI; not adm. in IN) Asst. Gen Coun, American Gen. Counsumer Finance
Ernest, Stanton D., (BVⓉ) ... '50 '77 C.339 B.S. L.300 J.D. [Rhine,E.&V.] ⊙
Ethridge, James W., Jr., (BV) ... '53 '83 C.999 B.A. L.1119 J.D. Dep. Pros. Atty.
Ethridge, Lani A., (BV) ... '54 '82 C.249 B.S. L.1119 J.D. [Ethridge]
Ethridge Law Office, (BV) ... 123 N.W. 4th St., Ste. 219
Evans, Gerald H., (BV) ... '37 '62 C.894 B.A. L.145 J.D. [Ⓒ Bamberger,F.O.&H.]
Evernham, Robin Michelle ... '78 '03 C.383 B.A. L.421 J.D. [Ⓐ Kahn,D.D.&K.]
Evernham, Scott J. '77 '03
C.679 B.S. L.421 J.D. Assoc. Gen. Coun., Old National Bancorp
Farmer, Terry G., (AV) ... '57 '81 C.347 B.S. L.1119 J.D. [Bamberger,F.O.&H.]
Farr, Donita F. M. ... '65 '91 C.910 B.A. L.365 J.D. 48 Oak Meadow Road
Farrar, Adam J. ... '— '04 C.1119 B.A. L.347 J.D. [Ⓐ Bamberger,F.O.&H.]
Faulkner, Robert R., Attorney at Law, (CV) '62 '95 C.999 A.S. L.347 J.D.
400 Court St.
Fields, James E., (BV) ... '33 '61 C.347 A.B. L.1119 J.D. 312 N.W. ML King Blvd.
Fiester, Max E. ... '77 '02 C&L.347 B.A., J.D. [Ⓐ Rudolph,F.P.&J.]
Fine, Marc D., (BV) ... '59 '84 C.347 B.S. L.339 J.D. [Rudolph,F.P.&J.]

Fine & Hatfield, A Professional Corporation, (AV)
520 N.W. Second Street, P.O. Box 779, 47705-0779
Telephone: 812-425-3592 Telecopier: 812-421-4269
Email: Fine@Fine-Hatfield.com URL: http://www.Fine-Hatfield.com
Isadore J. Fine (1897-1975); Joe S. Hatfield (1908-1993); James E. Marchand (1931-1999); Thomas H. Bryan; Thomas R. Fitzsimmons; Danny E. Glass; Todd I. Glass; John J. Kreighbaum; David D. Sanders; H. Linwood Shannon, III;—Jessica A. McCarthy; Daniel B. Gearhart; James D. Jones; Julia A. Condict. Of Counsel: Ronald R. Allen.
Bankruptcy, Commercial, Corporate and Business, Environmental, Health Care Law, Insurance, Labor and Employment, Probate and Estate Planning, Real Estate, Land Use, Federal Securities Litigation and Taxation Law. Defense of Professional Malpractice including Medical, Legal, Architects and Accounting, Products Liability, Trials in State and Federal Courts.
A List of Representative Clients Furnished Upon Request.
See Professional Biographies, EVANSVILLE, INDIANA

Fitzsimmons, Thomas R., (AV) ... '50 '75 C.597 B.A. L.345 J.D. [Fine&H.]
Flynn, James F., (AV) ... '40 '65 C&L.602 A.B., J.D. [Newman,T.L.F.&R.]
Folz, Frederick R., (AV) ... '51 '76 C.880 B.A. L.1119 J.D. [Keck&F.]
Foster, Mark A., (BV) ... '58 '83 C.346 B.S. L.345 J.D. [Foster,M.&O.]

Foster, Montgomery & O'Daniel, LLP, (BV)
3820 Oak Hill Road, 47711
Telephone: 812-424-8101 Toll Free: 888-280-8101 Fax: 812-437-8364
Email: tstatz@fmolaw.com URL: http://www.fmolaw.com
(This Listing Continued)

Foster, Montgomery & O'Daniel, LLP (Continued)
Mark A. Foster; Thomas L. Montgomery; Conor M. O'Daniel.
Criminal Defense, DWI, Bankruptcy, Family and Domestic Relations, Probate and Estates. Practice in all State and Federal Courts.
See Professional Biographies, EVANSVILLE, INDIANA

Frank, Shannon Scholz, (BV) ... '64 '90 C.347 B.S. L.1119 J.D. 5000 E. Virginia
Freel, Angela L. ... '73 '98 C.347 B.S. L.1119 J.D. [Rudolph,F.P.&J.]
Freson, Ronald J., (BV) ... '42 '70 C.420 B.S.E.E. L.326 J.D. 111 S.E. 7th St.
Freyberger, Greg J. ... '76 '01 C.346 B.S. L.74 J.D. [Ⓐ Kahn,D.D.&K.]

Frick Powell Whinrey Cravens & Schmitt, LLP, (AV)
223 S.E. Second Street, P.O. Box 1200, 47706
Telephone: 812-425-4687 Fax: 812-425-4690
URL: http://www.fpwcs.com
Members of Firm: Bernard A. Frick (1910-1967); William D. Powell (1927-1987); John B. Whinrey; Garland W. Cravens, Jr.; Reed S. Schmitt; David G. Harris.
General Civil Practice in all Courts. Corporate, Probate and Estate Planning, Family/Domestic Relations, Real Estate and Litigation in all State and Federal Courts.
Approved Attorneys for: Chicago Title Insurance Co.; Lawyers Title Insurance Corp.
Reference: The National City Bank of Evansville.
See Professional Biographies, EVANSVILLE, INDIANA

Fuchs, Donald J., (AV) ... '54 '79 C.894 B.A. L.345 J.D. [Bamberger,F.O.&H.]
Fuchs, Gerald G. ... '28 '53 C.249 A.B. L.1119 LL.B. Ninth & Vine Sts.
Fulcher, Jacob R. ... '76 '02 C.999 B.S. L.61 J.D. [Ⓐ Kahn,D.D.&K.]
Gager, Greg L. '64 '94 C.383 B.A. L.421 J.D.
Asst. Gen Coun., American Gen. Financial Services
Gannott, Peter M., (BVⓉ) '62 '86
C.339 B.A. L.904 J.D. [Mapother&M.] (⊙Louisville, KY)
Garnett, Britt Michelle ... '74 '00 C.679 B.A. L.200 J.D. 2221 W. Franklin St.
Garrison, Barbie Ann '54 '90 C.612 B.A. L.623 J.D.
(adm. in OK; not adm. in IN) Mgr., Off. of Hearings & Apps.
Gearhart, Daniel B. ... '75 '03 C.347 B.S. L.1119 J.D. [Ⓐ Fine&H.]
Gentry, James E., Jr. ... '— '03 C.383 B.S. L.801 J.D. [Ⓐ Bamberger,F.O.&H.]
George, Harry D., Jr. '49 '75 C.659 B.S. L.904 J.D.
Asst. Gen. Coun., American General Fin. Svcs.
Georges, Sean M., (CV) ... '61 '89 C.871 B.S. L.339 J.D. Shoe Carnival, Inc.
Gerling, Gary L., (AV) ... '37 '63 C.249 B.S. L.1119 J.D. [Ⓒ Gerling]

Gerling Law Offices, Professional Corporation, (AV)
519 Main Street, P.O. Box 3203, 47731
Telephone: 812-423-5251 Fax: 812-423-9928
Email: info@gerlinglaw.com URL: http://www.gerlinglaw.com
Gayle Gerling Pettinga; Edward B. Anderson; David G. Hatfield; Stephen Hensleigh Thomas; Daniel A. Barfield. Of Counsel: Gary L. Gerling.
Personal Injury, Wrongful Death, Negligence, Products Liability, Mediation, Arbitration, Medical Malpractice, Social Security Disability, Commercial Litigation and Workers Compensation Law. (Plaintiffs Only).
See Professional Biographies, EVANSVILLE, INDIANA

Gibson, Kevin D., (BV) ... '62 '86 C.249 B.S. L.1119 J.D. Legal Aid Soc. of Evansville
Glass, Danny E., (AV) ... '50 '77 C.303 B.A. L.345 J.D. [Fine&H.]
Glass, Todd I., (BV) ... '61 '88 C.894 A.B. L.201 J.D. [Fine&H.]
Goldman, Jon D., (AV) ... '51 '77 C.347 B.A. L.146 J.D. [Kahn,D.D.&K.]

Goodridge, John Andrew, Law Office '70 '96 C.894 B.A. L.879 J.D.
1904 E. Mulberry, 47714 ⊙
Telephone: 812-426-0482 Fax: 812-426-2211 URL: http://www.jaglofirm.com
Email: jgoodridge@jaglo.com URL: http://www.jaglo.com
Bankruptcy and Federal Criminal Law.
See Professional Biographies, EVANSVILLE, INDIANA

Graber, Thomas D., (AVⓉ) '56 '81 C.221 B.A. L.178 J.D.
(adm. in IL; not adm. in IN) Deputy Gen. Coun., American Gen. Counsumer Finance

Grampp, Glenn A., (AV) '48 '73 C.346 B.S. L.1119 J.D. BB
115 S.E. 4th Street, P.O. Box 3401, 47733
Telephone: 812-464-8800 Fax: 812-422-8832 URL: http://www.gramplaw.com
URL: http://www.lawyers.com/gramplaw
Civil and Criminal Trial Practice in all Courts. Personal Injury Litigation and Family/Domestic Relations.
Reference: Citizens National Bank.
See Professional Biographies, EVANSVILLE, INDIANA

Granger, Greg A., (BV) ... '56 '83 C.347 B.A. L.345 J.D. [Bowers H.]
Gray, David E., (AV) ... '51 '78 C.346 B.S. L.345 J.D. [Bowers H.]
Griffith, Charles C., (AV) ... '39 '66 C.679 B.S. L.1119 J.D. [Ⓒ Johnson,C.N.K.&S.] ‡
Grove, Rodney H., (BV) ... '39 '63 C.894 A.B. L.1119 J.D. [Grove]
Grove Law Office, (BV) ... 304 S.E. 1st St.
Guerrettaz, David A., (BV) ... '66 '91 C.1216 B.A. L.823 J.D. [Ziemer,S.W.&S.]
Gwinn, Malcolm S., (BV) ... '57 '83 C.249 B.S. L.347 J.D. [Shaw&G.]
Haas, Stephen C., (BV) ... '37 '63 C.347 B.S. L.345 J.D. 3300 Yale Dr.
Hahn, Steven K., (BV) ... '56 '81 C.347 B.A. L.345 J.D. [Ziemer,S.W.&S.]
Hall, James C. ... '— '04 C.1420 B.S. L.851 J.D. [Ⓐ Bamberger,F.O.&H.]

Hall, Partenheimer & Kinkle
(See Princeton)

Hambidge, Timothy J., (BV) ... '57 '82 C.679 B.A. L.345 J.D. [Olsen,W.&H.]
Hamilton, John A., (AV) ... '51 '78 C.999 B.S. L.1119 J.D. 311 N. Wabash Ave.
Hansen-davis, Evelyn ... '57 '93 C.249 B.S. L.347 J.D. 2221 W. Franklin St.
Hardy, Sarah Link, (BVⓉ) ... '62 '88 C.138 B.A. L.880 J.D. [Ziemer,S.W.&S.]
Harris, David G., (CV) ... '70 '96 C.346 B.S. L.347 J.D. [Frick P.W.C.&S.]
Harris, Stacy K., (CV) ... '71 '96 C.679 B.A. L.347 J.D. [Ⓐ Rudolph,F.P.&J.]
Harrison, Joseph H., (AV) ... '— '53 C&L.602 A.B., J.D. [Bowers H.]
Harrison, Joseph H., Jr., (BV) ... '59 '85 C.210 B.A. L.345 J.D. [Bowers H.]
Hartig, Sue Ann, (BV) '54 '79 C.249 B.S. L.345 J.D.
Exec. Dir., Legal Aid Soc. of Evansville, Inc.
Hatfield, David G., (BV) ... '54 '80 C.249 B.A. L.345 J.D. [Gerling]
Hawley, K. Richard, (AV) ... '27 '51 C.347 A.B. L.1119 J.D. [Ⓒ Bamberger,F.O.&H.]
Hawley, Marc E., (BV) ... '51 '81 C.679 B.S.E.E. L.1119 J.D. [Bamberger,F.O.&H.]
Hawley, Richard O., Jr., (BV) ... '65 '91 C.210 B.A. L.608 J.D. [Kightlinger&G.]
Hayden, Michael J., (BV) ... '47 '73 C.346 B.S. L.345 J.D. 2906 1st Ave.
Hayes, Philip H., (BV) ... '40 '67 C.347 A.B. L.345 J.D. [Hayes]
Hayes, Timothy M. '55 '81
C.321 A.B. L.802 J.D. Sr. VP and Gen Coun., American Intl. Group
Hayes Law Offices, (BV) ... 400 Court Street
Haynie, Kenneth G., Jr., (CV) ... '51 '75 C&L.347 A.B., J.D. P.O. Box 357
Heathcotte, Bruce R., (BV) ... '39 '72 C.347 A.B. L.345 J.D. 400 Ct. St.
Hegeman, John E., (BV) ... '48 '85 C.734 A.B. L.345 J.D. [Kahn,D.D.&K.]
Heldt, Carl A. ... '44 '69 C.879 B.A. L.1119 J.D. Cir. J.; Vanderburgh Cir. Ct.
Helfrich, Jeffrey K., (BV) ... '59 '85 C.347 B.S. L.345 J.D. [Kahn,D.D.&K.]
Henning, Jeffrey W., (CV) ... '68 '93 C.347 B.S L.734 J.D. [Rudolph,F.P.&J.]

Hermann, Nicholas G. ....'78 '04 C.63 B.S. L.345 J.D. 123 N.W. Fourth St., Ste. 614
Hewins, Daniel F., (BV) ....'45 '71 C.976 B.A. L.880 J.D. [Hewins&H.]
Hewins, Elvin H., (AV) ....'15 '38 C.347 B.A. L.597 J.D. [Hewins&H.]
Hewins and Hewins, (AV) ....123 N.W. 4th St., Ste. 210
Hoar, Steven S., (BV) ....'72 '97 C.210 B.A. L.347 J.D. [Kahn,D.D.&K.]
Hollonquest, Barbara J., (BV) '51 '78 C.679 B.A. L.597 J.D.
(adm. in IL; not adm. in IN) 601 NW 2nd St.
Hubert, Timothy J., (BV) ....'53 '79 C.347 A.B. L.345 J.D. [Ziemer,S.W.&S.]
Hudson, Henry C., (AV) ....'41 '66 C.347 A.B. L.1119 J.D. [Bamberger,F.O.&H.]
Hudson, Rebecca L. '71 '97 C.352 B.A. L.1187 J.D.
[Ⓐ Mapother&M.] (⊙Louisville, KY)
Humphrey, Mary Jane ....'54 '80 C.249 B.A. L.345 J.D. P.O. Box 18094‡
Hussmann, William G., Jr. ....'50 '76 C&L.879 B.A., J.D. U.S. Mag.
Jackson, Kelly J. ....'75 '00 C.929 B.A. L.345 J.D. [Ⓐ Rudolph,F.P.&J.]
Jeffries, Mathew ....'71 '01 C.347 B.S. L.801 J.D. 123 NW 4th Street, Suite 1
Jessen, Douglas V., (BV) ....'46 '81 C.350 B.S. L.1119 J.D. [Statham A.&J.]
Jewell, John J., (BV) ....'54 '79 C.347 A.B. L.1119 J.D. [Trimble&J.]
John, Robert, & Associates, (AV) '46 '72 C.347 B.S. L.345 J.D.
319 Northwest Martin Luther King Jr. Boulevard
Johns, Janice L. '54 '88 C.912 B.A. L.213 J.D.
(adm. in MI; not adm. in IN) Atty. Advsr., Dept. of Health. & Human Servs.
Johnson, Edward W., (AV) ....'44 '70 C.347 B.S. L.1119 J.D. [Johnson,C.N.K.&S.]
Johnson, James D., (BV) ....'60 '87 C.259 B.S. L.345 J.D. [Rudolph,F.P.&J.]
Johnson, R. Eugene, (AV) ....'29 '56 C&L.602 B.S., J.D. 19 Fourth Street

Johnson, Carroll, Norton, Kent & Straus, P.C., (AV)
2230 West Franklin Street, P.O. Box 6016, 47719-0016
Telephone: 812-425-4466 Telecopier: 812-425-4233
URL: http://www.jcglaw.com
Edwin W. Johnson (1922-2002); Edward W. Johnson; Brian K. Carroll; Thomas P. Norton; David W. Kent; J. August Straus. Retired: John L. Carroll (Retired); Charles C. Griffith (Retired).
General Civil and Trial Practice. Personal Injury, Condemnation, Probate and Estate Planning, Real Estate, Intellectual Property, Corporation and Mineral Law, Family Law, Divorce.
References: Old National Bank in Evansville; The Citizens National Bank of Evansville; The National City Bank of Evansville.
See Professional Biographies, EVANSVILLE, INDIANA

Jones, David L., (AV) ....'— '76 C.249 B.A. L.345 J.D. [Bowers H.]
Jones, James D. ....'73 '00 C.63 B.S. L.893 J.D. [Ⓐ Fine&H.]
Jones, Katharine Vanost, (CV) '48 '78 C.1109 B.A. L.1137 J.D.
123 N.W. 4th St., Ste. 304

Kahn, Dees, Donovan & Kahn, LLP, (AV)
Fifth Main Financial Plaza, Suite 305, P.O. Box 3646, 47735-3646
Telephone: 812-423-3183 Fax: 812-423-3841
Email: evvlaw@k2d2.com URL: http://www.k2d2.com
Members of Firm: Isidor Kahn (1887-1963); Harry P. Dees (1912-2004); Arthur R. Donovan (1910-2000); Robert Kahn (1918-1999); Alan N. Shovers; Thomas O. Magan; Larry R. Downs; Jon D. Goldman; Brian P. Williams; G. Michael Schopmeyer; John E. Hegeman; Jeffrey K. Helfrich; Jeffrey W. Ahlers; Kent A. Brasseale II; Christopher D. Lee; Mark S. Samila; Robert F. "Ted" Barron II; Allison K. Comstock; Steven S. Hoar; Todd C. Barsumian. Associates: Maria Talbert Worthington; Amy E. Steinhart; Kristi Prutow Cirignano; Monica E. Edwards; Michael E. DiRienzo; Greg J. Freyberger; Jacob R. Fulcher; Elizabeth A. Browning; Kevin R. Martin; Robin Michelle Evernham; Carrie M. Roelle.
General Civil Practice including Litigation, Environmental, Labor Management, Corporate, Pension, Banking, Hospital, Insurance Defense, Real Estate, Workers' Compensation, Tax, Construction, Immigration and General Civil Law.
Counsel for: Deaconess Hospital, Inc.; Keller Crescent Co., Inc.; Champion Laboratories, Inc.; Cresline Plastic Pipe Co., Inc.; University of Southern Indiana; Toyota Motor Corporate Services of North America, Inc.; AK Steel Corporation; North Park Cinemas, Inc.; Raben Tire Co., Inc.; AES Corporation.
See Professional Biographies, EVANSVILLE, INDIANA

Kasha, Rebecca T., (BV) ....'60 '85 C.347 B.S. L.608 J.D. [Kinney,K.&B.]
Keating, Michael C., (AV) ....'52 '77 C.894 B.A. L.345 J.D. [Keating,B.V.&L.]
Keating, Bumb, Vowels & LaPlante, P.C., (AV) ....915 Main Street Suite 100

Keck & Folz, (AV)
420 Main Street, Suite 1402, P.O. Box 3437, 47733-3437
Telephone: 812-424-5558 Fax: 812-428-6617
Email: keckfolz@evansville.net
Members of Firm: David M. Keck (1934-2002); Frederick R. Folz. Associate: Andrew S. Ward.
General Civil Practice in all State and Federal Courts. Probate Administration and Estate Planning, Corporation, Real Estate, Trials, Tax, Commercial and Administrative Law, General Litigation, Mediation, Labor and Employment.
Approved Attorneys for: Lawyers Title Insurance Corp.; Pioneer National Title Insurance Co.; Chicago Title Insurance Co.
References: Old National Bank in Evansville; The Citizens National Bank of Evansville.
See Professional Biographies, EVANSVILLE, INDIANA

Kent, David W., (CV) ....'66 '92 C.249 B.S. L.1187 J.D. [Johnson,C.N.K.&S.]
Kiely, James L. ....'32 '59 C.347 B.S. L.192 LL.B. 1357 Washington Ave.

Kightlinger & Gray, LLP, (AV)
7311 Eagle Crest Blvd., 47715 ⊙
Telephone: 812-474-4400 Telecopier: 812-474-4414
Email: info@k-glaw.com URL: http://www.k-glaw.com
Resident Partners: Brent R. Weil; Richard O. Hawley, Jr. Resident Associates: Sacha L. Armstrong; Curtis D. Condict; Chad M. Smith.
Civil Litigation, Commercial and Business Litigation, Drug and Medical Device Litigation, Environmental and Toxic Tort Litigation, Casualty, Surety and Life Insurance Law, General Litigation, Malpractice Litigation (Pharmacy, Medical, Legal, Architects and Engineers, Accountants, Insurance Agents, Real Estate Agents and School Boards), Products Liability Law, Trucking Defense Litigation, Construction Law, ICC Regulatory Law, Appeals (State and Federal), Worker's Compensation, Maritime Law, Civil Rights and Wrongful Discharge Law, All areas of Government Liability, including Law Enforcement Liability Litigation, Class Actions, Labor Law, Securities Litigation.
Indianapolis, Indiana Office: Market Square Center, Suite 600, 151 North Delaware Street, 46204. Telephone: 317-638-4521. Telecopier: 317-636-5917.
New Albany, Indiana Office: One Commerce Square, 4106 Charlestown Road, 47150. Telephone: 812-949-2300. Telecopier: 812-949-8556.
See Professional Biographies, EVANSVILLE, INDIANA

Kilcoyne, John M. '59 '89
C.712 B.S.Chem. L.276 J.D. Sr. Coun., Pats., Mead Johnson & Co. (Pat.)
Kimpel, Thomas J., (AV) ....'50 '76 C.108 B.A. L.365 J.D. [Bamberger,F.O.&H.]
King, Daniel J., (CV) ....'69 '94 C&L.861 B.A., J.D. [Terrell,B.S.&B.]
Kinney, Jeffrey R., (AV) ....'40 '67 C.679 B.S. L.345 J.D. [Kinney,K.&B.]
Kinney, Kasha & Buthod, LLP, (AV) .... 20 N.W. First St.
Knight, J. Douglas, Jr. '44 '69 C.347 B.A. L.192 J.D.
Supr. Ct. J.; Sandra Berke Supr. Ct.
Knoll, Raymond P. ....'32 '56 C&L.602 B.S., LL.B. 13900 Bickmeier Road
Koch, Jody L. McPherson, (CVⓉ) '59 '84 C.502 B.A. L.339 J.D.
(adm. in TX; not adm. in IN) 8201 Newburgh Rd.
Kolumbus, Alexander G. '61 '91 C.347 B.S. L.910 J.D.
(adm. in MO; not adm. in IN) Asst. Gen. Coun., American Gen. Fin. Srvcs.
Koontz, Patrick A. ....'73 '99 C.347 B.A. L.1119 J.D. P.O. Box 657

Kornblum, James A., (AV) ....'51 '77 C.249 B.A. L.345 J.D. [Lockyear K.&M.]
Kornblum, Kathryn L. ....'52 '00 C.249 B.S. L.345 J.D. [VanStone&K.]
Kreighbaum, John J. ....'52 '94 C.1044 B.S. L.347 J.D. [Fine&H.]
Krohn, R. Steven, (BV) ....'45 '70 C.347 B.S. L.1119 J.D. [Ⓒ Rudolph,F.P.&J.]
Kuhlenschmidt, Cory A. ....'— '01 C.347 B.A. L.1509 J.D. [Ⓐ Bowers H.]
Lacy, Heather H. ....'68 '03 C.249 B.S. L.347 J.D. [Ⓐ Bamberger,F.O.&H.]
Lamont, David W., (BV) ....'46 '79 C.210 B.A. L.365 J.D. 609 Main St.
Lantz, Jeffery L., (AV) ....'41 '67 C.347 B.S. L.345 J.D. 525 Sycamore Street
LaPlante, R. Stephen, (BV) ....'46 '73 C.602 A.B. L.347 J.D. [Keating,B.V.&L.]
Larner, Michael L., II '76 '02 C.929 B.A. L.347 J.D.
Law Clerk, U.S. Dist. Ct., Southern Dist. of Indiana
Laudeman, William D. '21 '62 C.339 A.B. L.1002 LL.B.
(adm. in MD; not adm. in IN) 2600 S. Ruston Ave.‡
Lavallo, Stephen S., (BV) .....'61 '86 C.207 B.A. L.910 J.D. 5000 E. Virginia St., Ste. 4
Lee, Christopher D., (CV) ....'66 '93 C.210 B.A. L.347 J.D. [Kahn,D.D.&K.]
Lensing, Robert W. ....'37 '63 C.602 B.S. L.879 LL.B. Supr. Ct. J.
Link, Stephen T., Law Office of, (BV) '55 '80
C.234 B.A. L.339 J.D. 1033 E. Mount Pleasant Rd., Ste. H.
Lloyd, Mary Margaret, (CV) ....'64 '91 C.249 B.S. L.1119 J.D. Dep. Pros. Atty.
Lockyear, Krista B., (BV) ....'66 '92 C&L.347 B.A., J.D. [Rudolph,F.P.&J.]
Lockyear, Thomas ....'33 '57 C&L.880 LL.B. Supr. Ct. J.

Lockyear Kornblum & Macer LLP, (AV)
555 Sycamore Street, P.O. Box 3515, 47734
Telephone: 812-422-1199 Fax: 812-426-0779
Email: info@lockyear-kornblum.com URL: http://www.lockyear-kornblum.com
Members of Firm: Theodore Lockyear (1929-2004); James A. Kornblum; B. Michael Macer.
Personal Injury Law and Trials. Class Actions. General Civil Practice in all State and Federal Courts. Appellate Practice.
See Professional Biographies, EVANSVILLE, INDIANA

Long, Nancy Hankins ....'51 '77 C.346 B.S. L.801 J.D. Supr. Ct. Mag.
Long, R. Edgar, (CV) ....'51 '81 C.231 B.A. L.345 J.D. Off. of Hearings and Appeals
Longest, Dennis B. ....'49 '75 C.249 B.A. L.345 J.D. V.P., Old Natl. Tr. Co.
Lonnberg, Kelly A., (BV) ....'63 '88 C.339 B.A.B.S. L.801 J.D. [Ⓐ Bowers H.]
Lopp, James D. ....'15 '36 C.347 L.345 LL.B. 18 S.E. 6th St.‡
Lopp, James D., Jr., (CV) ....'43 '68 C.472 A.B. L.362 J.D. 18 S.E. 6th St.
Lucas, Christopher L., (BV) ....'61 '87 C.346 B.S. L.1119 J.D. [Bowers H.]
Lynn, Claude B., (AV) ....'18 '52 C.347 A.B. L.1119 J.D. [Wright&D.] ‡
Macer, B. Michael, (CV) ....'72 '97 C.249 B.S. L.345 J.D. [Lockyear K.&M.]
Magan, Thomas O., (AV) ....'42 '70 C.210 A.B. L.1119 J.D. [Kahn,D.D.&K.]
Maier, Ruth E., (BV) ....'17 '40 C.249 A.B. L.1119 J.D. 115 W. Columbia St.‡
Mann, Mark R. ....'67 '98 C.446 B.A. L.1187 J.D. Law Clk., U.S. Dist. Ct.
Mapother, William R., (AV) ....'38 '63 C.602 A.B. L.893 J.D. [Mapother&M.] ⊙
Mapother & Mapother, P.S.C., (AV)
329 Main Street (⊙Lexington, Louisville, KY; Cin., OH; Huntington, WV)
Martin, James B. '22 '51 C.375 B.S. L.900 LL.B.
(adm. in KS; not adm. in IN) 1407 N. Ruston Ave.‡
Martin, Kevin R. ....'76 '01 C.347 B.S. L.1119 J.D. [Ⓐ Kahn,D.D.&K.]
Massey, Thomas A., (AV) ....'59 '84 C.679 B.S.M. L.879 J.D. [Bowers H.]
Maurer, Terrell, (BV) ....'60 '85 C.249 B.S. L.345 J.D. Vanderburgh Supr. Ct. Mag.
McCarthy, Jessica A. ....'76 '03 C.999 B.A. L.879 J.D. [Ⓐ Fine&H.]
McCray, Michael, (AV) ....'34 '61 C.339 A.B. L.1119 J.D. 5000 East Virginia Street
McDonald, Bruce D. ....'48 '74 C.347 B.A. L.345 J.D. 5200 Washington Ave.‡
McGinn, Daniel J., (AV) ....'49 '74 C.63 B.S. L.345 J.D. 519 Main St. Walkway‡
McMurray, James K. ....'64 '90 Asst. Gen. Coun., American Gen. Fin. Srvcs.
Meyer, Gregory G., (BV) ....'57 '82 C.347 B.S. L.345 J.D. 420 Main St.
Meyer, Michael L. ....'65 '97 C.999 B.S. L.421 J.D. 515 Beringer Drive
Miller, David V., (AV) ....'43 '69 C.477 A.B. L.345 J.D. [Ziemer,S.W.&S.]
Miller, Mark E., (BV) ....'57 '84 C.918 B.A. L.184 J.D. [Miller&Assoc.]
Miller, Verdelski V. ....'60 '89 C.355 B.S. L.45 J.D. Dep. Pros. Atty.
Miller, Wm. H. ....'26 '53 C.249 A.B. L.345 J.D. Sr. Cir. J.

Miller & Associates, (BV)
915 Main Street Suite 408, P.O. Box 3009, 47730-3009
Telephone: 812-425-1490 Toll Free: 1-888-279-0947 Fax: 812-425-3493
URL: http://www.indianalawonline.com
Mark E. Miller. Associate: Douglas S. Walton.
General Litigation, Small Business, Labor and Employment Law, Real Estate, Taxation, Collections, Debtor and Creditor Law, Federal Practice, Commercial Law, Personal Injury, Family Law, Estate Planning.
See Professional Biographies, EVANSVILLE, INDIANA

Mitchell, P. Michael, (AV) ....'36 '64 C.976 A.B. L.1119 LL.B. [Mitchell,S.&S.]
Mitchell, Paull Michael ....'36 '64 C.976 A.B. L.1119 LL.B. [Ⓒ Bamberger,F.O.&H.]
Mitchell, Staser and Shaw, (AV) .... 522 Main Street
Montgomery, Thomas L., (BV) ....'63 '90 C.249 B.S. L.347 J.D. [Foster,M.&O.]
Moore, Ralph E. ....'33 '63 C.502 A.B. L.1119 J.D. Supr. Ct. J.
Musgrave, Robert P., (BV) ....'55 '83 C.210 B.A. L.275 J.D. [Musgrave]
Musgrave Law Office, (BV) ....123 N.W. Fourth Street
Myrick, Diana Lorae '41 '95 C.421 B.A. L.1036 J.D.
101 Miliking Boulevard, Room 272
Nesmith, William D., (CVⓉ) '50 '88 C.249 B.A. L.383 J.D.
(adm. in KY; not adm. in IN) 123 N.W. 4th St., Ste. 214
Nestrick, Catherine A., (BV) ....'67 '93 C.303 B.A. L.347 J.D. [Bamberger,F.O.&H.]
Nestrick, D. Andrew ....'— '03 C.383 B.S. L.879 J.D. [Ⓐ Bamberger,F.O.&H.]
Newman, Trockman, Lloyd, Flynn & Rheinlander, (AV) .... 20 NW 6th S.
Niemeier, Paul J. ....'44 '78 C.249 B.S. L.365 J.D. 1103 N. 2nd Ave.‡
Noffsinger, Terry, (AV) ....'44 '69 C.347 B.S. L.1119 J.D. [Noffsinger B.]
Noffsinger • Barnett, LLP, (AV) ....101 N.W. First Street, Suite 116
Norton, Robert D., (AV) ....'22 '48 C.894 A.B. L.1119 J.D. 123 NW 4th St.‡
Norton, Thomas P., (BV) ....'52 '77 C.999 B.A. L.192 J.D. [Johnson,C.N.K.&S.]
O'Connor, Maurice C. ....'37 '63 C.1024 A.B. L.1119 LL.B. Supr. Ct. J.
O'Daniel, Conor M., (CV) ....'71 '96 C.894 A.B. L.345 J.D. [Foster,M.&O.]
Oeding, Jill M. ....'71 '00 C.347 B.S. L.345 J.D. 3507 Washington Avenue
Oliver, DanielLee, (BV) ....'48 '77 C.608 B.S. L.969 J.D. 7201 E. Virginia St.
Olsen, Ole J., Jr., (BV) ....'37 '61 C.249 B.S. L.880 J.D. [Olsen,W.&H.]

Olsen, White & Hambidge, LLP, (BV)
123 Locust Street, 47708-1488
Telephone: 812-423-3143 Fax: 812-429-0448
URL: http://www.thelawteam.net
Members of Firm: Ole J. Olsen, Jr.; Terry A. White; Timothy J. Hambidge; Jill Dewig Wesch.
Probate, Business Law, Family Law, Wills, Personal Injury, Criminal Law, Real Estate.
See Professional Biographies, EVANSVILLE, INDIANA

Ortmeyer, Edmund F., (AV) ....'12 '36 C.347 L.1119 LL.B. 9225 Hedden Rd.‡
Oswald, Charles E., Jr., (AV) '22 '48
C.347 B.S. L.1119 J.D. [Ⓒ Bamberger,F.O.&H.] (⊙Indianapolis)

Owen, Steven S., (AVⓉ) '65 '91 C.1375 B.A. L.112 J.D.
Gen. Coun., Traylor Bros., Inc.
Owens, Stephen H., (BV) '49 '82
C.249 B.S. L.347 J.D. 1 NW Martin Luther King Jr. Blvd.
Ozete, Andrew C., (CV) ....'70 '96 C.347 B.A. L.1119 J.D. [Bamberger,F.O.&H.]
Pamplin, Laura L. .... '70 '95 C.383 B.B.A. L.421 J.D. 20 N.W. Fourth Street
Peters, Kathryn D., Law Office of, (CV) '60 '85
C.347 B.A. L.1119 J.D. 1666 Lodge Avenue
Pettinga, Gayle Gerling, (CV) .... '61 '87 C.788 A.B. L.345 J.D. [Gerling]
Porch, George A., (AV) ....'43 '68 C.249 B.A. L.347 J.D. [Ⓒ Bowers H.]
Porter, L. Montgomery, (BV) .... '61 '86 C.249 B.S. L.347 J.D. [Rudolph,F.P.&J.]
Poulton, Karen T. .... '49 '91 C.608 B.S. L.900 J.D. [Ⓒ Bamberger,F.O.&H.]
Price, Gary K., (BV) ....'56 '90 C.1069 B.S. L.421 J.D. [Bowers H.] (Pat.)
Pulcini, Mary L. ....'66 '95 C.249 B.A. L.851 J.D. City Housing Auth.
Ratliff, Marilyn R., (BV) ....'48 '74 C.350 B.S. L.345 J.D. 123 NW 4th St.
Reisz, Bernard (Sonny), Law Offices of, (CV) '49 '86
C.346 B.S. L.1000 J.D. 915 Main St.
Retherford, Angila M., (CV) '65 '91
C.347 B.S. L.208 J.D. 20 NW Fourth Street, Suite 708
Rheinlander, Robert E., (BV) .... '41 '78 C.347 B.S. L.345 J.D. [Newman,T.L.F.&R.]

Rhine, Ernest & Vargo, (AVⓉ)
Old National Place, One Main Street, Suite 600, 47708 ⊙
Telephone: 812-759-0600 Fax: 812-759-0601
Email: information@rhinelaw.com
Stanton D. Ernest.
Coal, Oil and Gas Law, Real Estate, Corporate, Civil Trial Practice, Wills and Estates, Environmental Law.
Representative Clients: Sahara Coal Co.; R & R Coal, Inc.; Green River Coal Co., Inc.; Illinois Coal Association; Old Ben Coal Co.; Zeigler Coal Co.; Security Bank and Trust Co.
Mount Carmel, Illinois Office: 631 Market Street, 62863-1489. Telephone: 618-262-8611. Fax: 618-262-7145. URL: http://www.rhinelaw.com.
See Professional Biographies, EVANSVILLE, INDIANA

Rietman, Mark W., (BV) .... '51 '76 C.347 A.B. L.1119 J.D. [Berger&B.]
Ritz, Louis W. .... '15 '39 C.249 A.B. L.477 LL.B. Tamarack Petro. Co., Inc.
Robinson, Clark, (BV) '44 '82
C.231 A.B. L.1119 J.D. Staff Atty., Dept. of Health & Human Servs.
Robinson, David K., (AV) ....'52 '78 C.999 B.S. L.421 J.D. [Robinson]
Robinson Law Office, (AV) ....123 N.W. 4th Street, Suite 420
Roelle, Carrie M. ....'72 '01 C.347 B.S. L.208 J.D. [Ⓐ Kahn,D.D.&K.]
Rounder, Keith E., (BV) .... '59 '87 C.249 B.A. L.1119 J.D. [Bowers H.]
Rountree, Shawn ....'— '03 C.337 B.A. L.801 J.D. [Ⓐ Bamberger,F.O.&H.]
Rudolph, Ross E., (AV) ....'55 '80 C.473 B.A. L.345 J.D. [Rudolph,F.P.&J.]

Rudolph, Fine, Porter & Johnson LLP, (AV)
221 N.W. Fifth Street, P.O. Box 1507, 47706
Telephone: 812-422-9444 Fax: 812-421-7459
Email: rfpj@rfpj.com URL: http://www.rfpj.com
Members of Firm: Ross E. Rudolph; Marc D. Fine; L. Montgomery Porter; James D. Johnson; Krista B. Lockyear; Keith A. Sermersheim; Jeffrey W. Henning; Angela L. Freel. Associates: Stacy K. Harris; Brian E. Townsend; Kelly J. Jackson; Abigail Brown-Cox; Max E. Fiester; Ted C. Ziemer, IV. Of Counsel: R. Steven Krohn.
General Corporate Practice. Health Care Law, Commercial Litigation, Insurance Defense, Real Estate, Zoning and Land Use Law, Mediation and Arbitration, Bankruptcy Law, Mergers and Acquisitions. Probate and Estate Planning, Tax, Employment Law, Appeals, Banking. Trials in all State and Federal Courts.
References: Old National Bank; Bank of Evansville.
See Professional Biographies, EVANSVILLE, INDIANA

Russell, Charles E. '59 '85
C.249 B.A. L.1119 J.D. Dep. Gen. Coun., American Gen. Fin. Srvcs.
Rutkowski, Arthur D., (AV) ....'42 '67 C.347 B.S. L.1119 J.D. [Bowers H.]
Rybak, Katherine J. .... '54 '79 C.93 A.B. L.188 J.D. Legal Servs. Organization of IN
Rynder, Theodore L. ....'71 '97 C.851 B.B.A. L.339 J.D. 301 Belmont Drive‡
Salmon, Bradley J., (BV) .... '58 '83 C.346 B.S. L.879 J.D. [Terrell,B.S.&B.]
Samila, Mark S. .... '64 '89 C&L.502 B.S., J.D. [Kahn,D.D.&K.]
Sanders, David D., (CV) ....'62 '97 C.37 B.S. L.347 J.D. [Fine&H.]
Sanders, Timothy E. .... '51 '77 C.57 B.A. L.801 J.D. Legal Servs. Organization of Ind.
Sauvey, Marian Weilert, (BV) '53 '78 C.698 A.B. L.502 J.D.
General Counsel, Vice President & Corporate Sect'y, Atlas Van Lines, Inc.
Schaefer, Kirstin M. .... '68 '94 C.571 B.A. L.74 J.D. 1911 Linkin Ave.
Schiff, Mary Lee, (BV) .... '64 '89 C.973 B.S.B.A. L.150 J.D. [Ziemer,S.W.&S.]
Schiff, Wm. Michael, (AV) ....'53 '79 C.346 B.A. L.345 J.D. [Ziemer,S.W.&S.]
Schmidt, Richard D. '51 '85 C.485 B.A. L.1218 J.D.
(adm. in NY; not adm. in IN; Pat.) Coun.-Patents, Bristol-Myers Squibb Co.
(⊙New York, NY)
Schmitt, Reed S., (BV) ....'59 '84 C.679 B.A. L.345 J.D. [Frick P.W.C.&S.]
Schopmeyer, G. Michael, (AV) ....'58 '83 C.249 B.S. L.345 J.D. [Kahn,D.D.&K.]
Schroeder, W. Jack, (AV) .... '30 '55 C.597 B.S. L.347 J.D. [W.J.Schroeder]
Schroeder, W. Jack, P.C., (AV) ....P.O. Box 207
Schulte, Michael '67 '93
C.966 B.S. L.300 J.D. Asst. Gen. Coun., American Gen. Fin. Srvcs.
Schwentker, James M., Jr., (AV) '25 '52
C.347 A.B. L.1119 J.D. 123 N.W. 4th St., Ste. 414
Schymik, Kathryn D. ....'79 '04 C.679 B.A. L.1119 J.D. [Ⓐ Ziemer,S.W.&S.]
Scott, Laura A., (CV) ....'70 '95 C.347 B.S. L.345 J.D. [Bamberger,F.O.&H.]
Sermersheim, Keith A., (CV) .... '65 '94 C.679 B.S. L.347 J.D. [Rudolph,F.P.&J.]
Shannon, H. Linwood, III, (CV) ....'70 '95 C.138 B.A. L.421 J.D. [Fine&H.]
Shaw, David M., (BV) .... '49 '74 C.880 B.A. L.1119 J.D. [Mitchell,S.&S.]
Shaw, Toby D., (AV) ....'43 '68 C.347 A.B. L.1119 J.D. [Shaw&G.]
Shaw & Gwinn, P.C., (AV) .... 1911 Lincoln Avenue
Shearer, Lawrence E. ....'46 '71 C.347 B.S. L.345 J.D. Adm. Law J., Soc. Sec. Admn.
Sheets, F. Stephen, (CV) ....'49 '82 C.999 B.A. L.602 J.D. 417 N. Weinbach Ave.
Shirey, Daniel R. '42 '69 C&L.608 B.Met.E., J.D.
(adm. in OH; not adm. in IN) 611 Harriet St.
Shoulders, Jeffrey T., (BV) .... '67 '92 C.347 B.A. L.201 J.D. [Barber,S.&S.]
Shoulders, Patrick A., (AV) ....'53 '78 C.347 B.A. L.345 J.D. [Ziemer,S.W.&S.]
Shovers, Alan N., (AV) ....'39 '64 C&L.966 B.B.A., J.D. [Kahn,D.D.&K.]
Shrode, W. Scott, (BV) '52 '77
C.249 B.A. L.597 J.D. V.P. for Develop., Univ. of Evansville
Shrode, Willard C., (BV) ....'24 '49 C.210 A.B. L.309 J.D. 103 N.W. 10th St.
Siegel, Philip H., (AV) .... '34 '60 C.347 B.S. L.1119 J.D. 501 Main St.
Siesky, Lane C. ....'72 '98 C&L.1119 B.S., J.D. [Barber,S.&S.]
Simpkins, Robert L., (BV) ....'44 '71 C.249 B.A. L.1119 J.D. 4920 Lincoln Avenue
Smith, Chad M. .... '76 '02 C.347 B.S. L.345 J.D. [Ⓐ Kightlinger&G.]
Smith, Michael G. ....'68 '01 C.878 B.A. L.1119 J.D. [Ⓐ Bamberger,F.O.&H.]

Son, James R., Attorney at Law ....'44 '70 C.347 B.A. L.1119 J.D. 2821 St. George Rd.
Spaetti, Charles A., (BV) '48 '72 C.347 A.B. L.1119 J.D.
5011 Washington Avenue, Suite 103, 47715
Telephone: 812-477-6483 Fax: 812-477-1836
General Civil Practice including Bankruptcy, Collections and Insurance Law.
See Professional Biographies, EVANSVILLE, INDIANA

Stack, Jonna Leigh '— '97 C.36 B.S. L.208 J.D.
(adm. in CO; not adm. in IN) P.O. Box 4242
Stahl, Dirck H., (BV) .... '68 '93 C.894 A.B. L.347 J.D. [Ziemer,S.W.&S.]
Stalions, Stuart M. ....'50 '92 C.346 B.S. L.347 J.D. Tr. Admr., Natl. City Bk.
Standley, Barry L., (CV) .... '42 '76 C.249 B.A. L.1340 J.D. 3116 A E. Morgan Ave.
Staser, John Stuff, (AV) ....'45 '71 C.347 A.B. L.345 J.D. [Ⓒ Bamberger,F.O.&H.]
Statham, William E., (AV) ....'32 '56 C.249 A.B. L.345 J.D. [Statham A.&J.]

Statham Allega & Jessen, LLP, (AV)
915 Main Street, Suite 202, P.O. Box 3567, 47734-3567
Telephone: 812-425-5223 Facsimile: 812-421-4238
Email: sajr@statham-ajr.com URL: http://www.statham-ajr.com
Members of Firm: William E. Statham; Gerald F. Allega; Douglas V. Jessen.
Civil and Commercial Litigation, Insurance Law, Product Liability Law, Malpractice Defense, Trials.
See Professional Biographies, EVANSVILLE, INDIANA

Stayman, Robert F., (AV) ....'46 '73 C.210 B.A. L.477 J.D. [Ziemer,S.W.&S.]
Steedman, Richard B., (BV) '49 '78
C.249 B.A. L.345 J.D. 1033 East Mount Pleasant Road
Steinhart, Amy E., (CV) ....'72 '97 C&L.347 B.A., J.D. [Ⓐ Kahn,D.D.&K.]
Stephens, William D., (BV) ....'24 '51 C.249 B.S. L.1119 J.D. Sr. J.‡
Stone, Jack A., Law Offices of, (AV) '21 '48
C&L.309 B.S., J.D. 1400 Old National Bank Building
Stone, Scott S., (BV) ....'59 '90 C.801 B.S. L.339 J.D. 915 Main St., Ste. 404
Straus, J. August ....'74 '00 C.36 B.A. L.836 J.D. [Johnson,C.N.K.&S.]
Sullivan, Chad J., (CV) ....'72 '97 C.502 B.S.B.A. L.910 J.D. [Ziemer,S.W.&S.]
Sullivan, Kathryn A. ....'68 '95 C.711 L.347 J.D. Law Clk., U.S. Dist. Ct.
Sullivan, Shawn M., (BV) ....'64 '94 C.112 B.S. L.347 J.D. [Terrell,B.S.&B.]
Taylor, Erika N., (CV) ....'71 '97 C&L.347 B.A., J.D. Corp Coun, Brake Supply Co., Inc.
Taylor, Matthew J. ....'71 '99 C&L.347 B.S., J.D. Your PD&S Agent, Inc.
Taylor, William V. '52 '91
C.906 B.S.C.E. L.911 J.D. Asst. Gen. Coun., American Gen. Fin. Srvcs.
Terrell, Thomas H., (AV) ....'38 '68 C.347 B.S. L.1119 J.D. [Terrell,B.S.&B.]

Terrell, Baugh, Salmon & Born, LLP, (AV)
700 S. Green River Road, Suite 2000, 47715
Telephone: 812-479-8721 Fax: 812-474-6059
Email: bsalmon@tbslaw.com
Members of Firm: Thomas H. Terrell; Bradley J. Salmon; D. Timothy Born; Patricia Kay Woodring; Shawn M. Sullivan; Daniel J. King. Retired: Jerry P. Baugh.
General Civil Trial and Appellate Practice in State and Federal Courts. Insurance Defense, Commercial Transactions, Business Organizations, Employment, Construction, Bankruptcy, Probate and Estate Planning and Administration, Real Estate, Personal Injury, Environmental, Mediation, Zoning, Shopping Center Development and Leasing.
Representative Clients: Auto-Owners Insurance Company; Guaranty National Insurance Company; H.F.I.C. Management Company, Inc.; Physicians Insurance Company of Indiana; Central Industries, Inc.; Whirlpool Corp.; Modern Maid Food Products, Inc. Central Tower, Inc.; Regency Property Management, Inc.; Eades Properties.
Reference: Old National Bank in Evansville.
See Professional Biographies, EVANSVILLE, INDIANA

Thomas, Andrew D., Law Office of, (BV) '51 '76
C.602 A.B. L.1119 J.D. 2906 First Avenue
Thomas, Anne Cavanaugh ....'50 '76 C.347 B.A. L.1119 J.D. U.S. Admin. Law J.
Thomas, Ellen K. ....'32 '73 C.604 B.A. L.1119 J.D. Adm. Law J., Soc. Sec. Adm.
Thomas, Stephen Hensleigh, (AV) .... '51 '76 C&L.801 B.A., J.D. [Gerling]
Thread, Tracy L., (CV) ....'60 '90 C.999 B.S. L.347 J.D. IN Legal Servs., Inc.
Tornatta, Robert Jeffrey ....'59 '85 C.347 B.A. L.1119 J.D. Supr. Ct. J.
Townsend, Brian E. ....'68 '99 C&L.347 B.A., J.D. [Ⓐ Rudolph,F.P.&J.]
Trimble, Thomas V. ....'19 '43 C.249 A.B. L.345 LL.B. [Trimble&J.]
Trimble & Jewell, (BV) ....706 Court Street
Trockman, Howard P., (AV) ....'33 '58 C.347 A.B. L.1119 J.D. [Newman,T.L.F.&R.]
Trockman, Wayne S. ....'59 '85 C.346 B.S. L.345 J.D. Supr. Ct. J.
Tuley, Daniel J., (BV) ....'58 '86 C.346 B.S. L.1340 J.D. [Tuley]
Tuley Law Office, (BV) ....20 N.W. First Street, Suite 610
Turpin, H. Wayne, (BV) ....'42 '74 C.1077 B.A. L.879 J.D. 400 Ct. St.
Ulrich-Keppler, Jennifer ....'76 '01 C.347 B.A. L.1119 J.D. [Ⓐ Berger&B.]
Van Haaften, W. Trent ....'64 '90 C.393 B.A. L.221 J.D. [Ⓒ Bamberger,F.O.&H.]
VanStone, Jack N., (AV) ....'30 '53 C.347 B.S. L.1119 J.D. [VanStone&K.]
Van Stone & Kornblum, (AV) ....103 N.W. 10th
Vollmer, Susan Dayton ....'70 '96 C.63 B.A. L.201 J.D. [Ⓐ J.Bosse&Assoc.]
Volz, Gregory L. '50 '79 C.347 A.B. L.1119 J.D.
Legal Servs. Organization of Ind., Inc.
Vonderahe, Keith William .... '71 '99 C.249 B.S. L.862 J.D. [Ziemer,S.W.&S.]
Vowels, Donald R., (BV) ....'58 '87 C.999 B.S. L.607 J.D. [Keating,B.V.&L.]
Vreeland, Joseph A., (BV) '48 '80 L.1119 J.D.
Dept. of Health & Human Servs., Supvr. Atty.
Wade, James C., Jr. ....'29 '55 C.347 A.B. L.1119 J.D. P.O. Box 99
Wallace, Keith M., (CV) .... '56 '83 C.347 B.A. L.879 J.D. [Ⓒ Bowers H.]
Wallace, Paul J., (BV) ....'— '79 C.347 B.S. L.1119 J.D. [Bowers H.]
Walton, Douglas S. ....'73 '00 C.999 B.A. L.879 J.D. [Ⓐ Miller&Assoc.]
Ward, Andrew S., (CV) ....'61 '88 C.882 B.A. L.347 J.D. [Ⓐ Keck&F.]
Ward, Kelly Leigh .... '65 '90 C.249 B.A. L.421 J.D. Ct. Admr.
Warrum, Ronald, (BV) ....'41 '66 C.894 B.A. L.1119 J.D. 123 N.W. 4th St.
Warzecha, Mark F. ....'— '94 C.705 B.S. L.61 J.D. [Ⓐ Bowers H.]
Weil, Brent R., (AV) ....'60 '85 C.679 B.S. L.879 J.D. [Kightlinger&G.]
Weitzel, Stephan E., (AV) .... '49 '75 C.210 B.A. L.245 J.D. [Ziemer,S.W.&S.]
Welp, Douglas A., (CV) ....'69 '94 C.894 B.A. L.347 J.D. [Bamberger,F.O.&H.]
Wesch, Jill Dewig ....'77 '04 C.999 B.S. L.879 J.D. [Olsen,W.&H.]
Wever, Paul B., Jr. .... '30 '56 C.210 A.B. L.1119 J.D. V.P., Opers., Compu Let, Inc.
Whinrey, John B., (AV) ....'41 '66 C.970 B.A. L.477 J.D. [Frick P.W.C.&S.]
White, Fred S., (AV) .... '40 '72 C.679 B.S. L.345 J.D. [Bamberger,F.O.&H.]
White, Terry A., (BV) ....'53 '78 C.249 B.A. L.345 J.D. [Olsen,W.&H.]
Wilhite, Jeffrey A. .... '59 '84 C.347 B.A. L.1119 J.D. [Wilhite&Assoc.]
Wilhite and Associates ....One Mulberry Place
Williams, Brian P., (AV) ....'56 '81 C.347 A.B. L.1119 J.D. [Kahn,D.D.&K.]
Winternheimer, Kevin W., Law Offices of, (BV) '55 '80
C.249 B.A. L.345 J.D. 123 N.W. 4th St., Ste. 416
Wintner, Bernard G. ....'19 '55 C.249 B.S. L.1119 J.D. [Ⓐ Newman,T.L.F.&R.]
Wischer, Christopher C., (CV) .....'70 '96 C.853 B.A. L.383 J.D. [Bamberger,F.O.&H.]
Woll, David L. ....'48 '79 C.910 B.A. L.345 J.D. Pres., Woll Enterprises, Inc.
Woodring, Patricia Kay, (BV) ....'51 '87 C.63 B.S. L.1119 J.D. [Terrell,B.S.&B.]
Woods, J. Michael, (BV) ....'55 '82 C.346 B.S. L.347 J.D. [Woods&W.]

Woods, William P., (BV) .... '52 '90 C.347 B.A. L.801 J.D. [Woods&W.]
Woods & Woods, LLP, (BV) .... 123 N.W. 4th St., Ste. 618
Woodson, Russell T., (BV) .... '53 '78 C.347 B.S. L.608 J.D. 123 N.W. 4th. St.
Worthington, Maria Talbert, (CV) .... '71 '97 C.249 B.S. L.1119 J.D. [Ⓐ Kahn,D.D.&K.]
Wright, Donald R., (AV) .... '37 '61 C.347 B.S. L.1119 J.D. [Wright&D.]

Wright and Daly, (AV)
425 Main Street, 47708
Telephone: 812-424-3300 Fax: 812-421-5588
Email: WED-MainSt@MSN.Com URL: http://www.wrightdaly.com
Members of Firm: Claude B. Lynn (Retired); Donald R. Wright; R. Lawrence Daly.
General Civil Litigation, Civil Litigation, including Trials and Appeals in State and Federal Courts. Construction Law, Family Law, Insurance Law, including Automobile, Commercial, Life and Health, Liability and Property Law. Personal Injury Claims and Litigation. Products Liability Claims and Litigation. Social Security, Wills, Estates and Probate Law, including Litigation and Worker's Compensation.
Representative Clients: Browning-Ferris Industries of Indiana, Inc.; Castle Contracting Co., Inc.; Computing Solutions, Inc.; Need-A-Nurse, Inc.; Mills-Wallace and Associates, Inc. Design Professionals; Servicemaster of Evansville, Inc.; Siemers Glass Company, Inc.; Southwestern Indiana Mental Health Center, Inc.; Complete Environmental Services, Inc.
See Professional Biographies, EVANSVILLE, INDIANA

Young, Lori Yarbor, (CV) .... '70 '95 C.679 B.S. L.347 J.D. [Bamberger,F.O.&H.]
Young, Richard L. .... '53 '80 C.221 B.A. L.1209 J.D. U.S. Dist. J.
Zeidler, Sara Harrison, (CV) .... '65 '92 C.741 B.A. L.347 J.D. [Bowers H.]
Ziemer, Jay A., (CV) .... '65 '91 C.436 B.A. L.345 J.D. [Bowers H.]
Ziemer, Ted C., IV .... '77 '03 C&L.347 B.A., J.D. [Ⓐ Rudolph,F.P.&J.]
Ziemer, Ted C., Jr., (AV) .... '35 '62 C.734 B.S. L.1119 LL.B. [Ziemer,S.W.&S.]

Ziemer, Stayman, Weitzel & Shoulders, LLP, (AV) BR
(Formerly Early, Arnold & Ziemer)
One Riverfront Place, 20 N.W. First Street 9th Floor, P.O. Box 916, 47706-0916
Telephone: 812-424-7575 Telecopier: 812-421-5089 (9th Fl.); 812-421-5076 (7th Fl.)
URL: http://www.zsws.com
Members of Firm: John E. Early (1912-1983); Ted C. Ziemer, Jr.; Robert F. Stayman; Stephan E. Weitzel; Patrick A. Shoulders; David V. Miller; Wm. Michael Schiff; Marco L. DeLucio; Steven K. Hahn; James P. Casey; Timothy J. Hubert; Mary Lee Schiff; David A. Guerrettaz; Robert L. Burkart; Charles A. Compton; Sarah Link Hardy; Dirck H. Stahl; Chad J. Sullivan; Keith William Vonderahe.
Associates: Nick J. Cirignano; Allyson R. Breedon; Jean M. Blanton; Kathryn D. Schymik.
General Civil Practice. Litigation in Federal and State Courts. Banking, Bankruptcy and Business Reorganization, Business and Commercial Transactions, Construction, Corporation, Creditors Rights, Environmental Law, Hospital and Medical, Insurance, Negligence and Products Liability, Labor and Employment Discrimination, Oil and Gas and Mining, Probate, Estate Planning and Administration, Mergers and Acquisitions, Real Estate, and Workers Compensation. Environmental Law.
Reference: Old National Bank.
See Professional Biographies, EVANSVILLE, INDIANA

FERDINAND, 2,318, *Dubois Co.*

Gillie, Armon C., (BV) .... '47 '72 C.347 A.B. L.345 J.D. 631 Cardinal Dr.
Ippoliti, Victor J. .... '53 '99 C.262 B.A. L.74 J.D. [Ippoliti]
Ippoliti Law Office .... 530 Main Street
Lueken, Francis H., Jr., (CV) .... '49 '77 C.679 B.S. L.1119 J.D. [F.H.Lueken]
Lueken, Francis H., Law Office of, (CV) .... 223 West 10th Street

FISHERS, 37,835, *Hamilton Co.*

Ackman, Jacob D. .... '22 '50 L.150 J.D. 12010 Allisonville Rd.

Bays, Donna J.
(See Indianapolis)

Cagnassola, Gregory J. .... '62 '92 C.679 B.S. L.347 J.D. [Ⓐ DeFur V.]
Caldwell, Thomas K., (BV) .... '63 '89 C.475 B.A. L.1119 J.D. [Ⓐ Maddox H.&C.]

Campbell Kyle Proffitt LLP
(See Noblesville)

Carroll, Daniel R.
(See Indianapolis)

Church, Church, Hittle & Antrim
(See Noblesville)

Clapp, Sean M., (AV) .... '62 '88 C.879 B.A. L.1119 J.D. [S.M.Clapp]

Clapp, Sean M., LLC, (AV)
8766 South Street, Suite 220, 46038
Telephone: 317-578-9966 Fax: 317-578-9967
Email: sean@seanmclapp.com URL: http://www.clapplawfirm.com
Sean M. Clapp.
Commercial Real Estate, Residential Real Estate, Title Claims, Foreclosures, Landlord and Tenant Law, Mortgages, Eminent Domain, Real Estate Tax Law, Commercial Leasing, Construction Law, Business Litigation, Copyright and Trademark Law, Internet Law, Business Enterprises, Limited Liability Company Law, Professional Practices, Small Business Law, Closely Held Business, Corporate Law, Partnerships, Buying and Selling of Businesses, Collections, Creditor's Rights, Business Law, Business Planning, Contracts, Intellectual Property, Trade Secrets, Business Start-Ups.
See Professional Biographies, FISHERS, INDIANA

Cohen, Lester H., (AV) .... '44 '88 C.112 B.A. L.345 J.D. [Ⓒ DeFur V.]
Cooper, Michelle L. .... '73 '99 C.63 B.S. L.74 J.D. [Ⓐ DeFur V.] ⊙

DeFur Voran LLP, (AV)
8409 Fishers Centre Drive, 46038 ⊙
Telephone: 317-585-8085 Telecopier: 317-585-8858
Email: "atty's first initial, last name"@defur.com URL: http://www.defur.com
William H. Lutz;—Gregory J. Cagnassola; Michelle L. Cooper; Holly J. Wanzer. Of Counsel: Lester H. Cohen.
General Civil Practice. Business Organizations, Personal Planning, Education, Health, Personnel and Employment, Banking, Real Estate, Taxation, Employee Benefit/Retirement Plans, Creditor's Rights, Civil Litigation, Mediation, Intellectual Property, Family.
General Counsel for: Ball State University; Ball Memorial Hospital, Inc.; American National Bank and Trust Company; First Merchants Bank, N.A.; Community Care Centers, Inc.; Mount Pleasant Township Community School; Muncie Housing Authority; Agbest Co-op.
Muncie, Indiana Office: 201 East Jackson Street, Suite 400, 47305. Telephone: 765-288-3651. Telecopier: 765-288-7068.
See Professional Biographies, FISHERS, INDIANA

Fihn, Jeffrey G. .... '49 '77 C.910 B.S.B.A. L.112 J.D. 219 Orchard Blvd.
Galbraith, Brad A., (BV) .... '66 '94 C&L.347 B.S., J.D. [Galbraith&Assoc.] ⊙
Galbraith, Tracy J. .... '68 '94 C.347 B.A. L.1119 J.D. [Galbraith&Assoc.]
Galbraith & Associates, P.C., (BV) .... 10150 Lantern Road (⊙Naples, FL)
Goodman, Loren P., (BVⓉ) '30 '55 C.912 A.B. L.215 LL.B.
(adm. in MI; not adm. in IN) 622 Colbarn Dr.
Greenawald, Heather Cameron '71 '97
C.839 B.A. L.309 J.D. Asst. Gen. Coun., Sallie Mae, Inc.
Griffin, Keith L. .... '73 '00 C&L.347 B.A., J.D. [Ⓐ Maddox H.&C.]
Hamilton, Lisa T. .... '58 '82 C.604 B.A. L.1119 J.D. 12067 Sunrise Cir.‡
Hansen, Lawrence M., (BV) .... '63 '89 C.347 B.S. L.365 J.D. [Hansen]
Hansen Law Firm, LLC, (BV) .... 8405 Fishers Center Drive
Hargett, Thomas A. .... '58 '94 C&L.347 B.A., J.D. [Maddox H.&C.]
Hill, Aimee R. .... '72 '98 C.303 B.A. L.345 J.D. Assoc. Coun., Irwin Mortgage Corp.
Hoeg, Larry S. .... '41 '83 C.347 B.A. L.345 J.D. Pres., Hy-Pro Corp.
Hogan, Patrick James .... '51 '83 C.347 B.S. L.345 J.D. I.R.S.

Holt, Fleck & Romine
(See Noblesville)

Hunter, Susan M. .... '65 '97 C.303 B.A. L.1161 J.D. P.O. Box 6321
Hynes, Brian J. .... '62 '91 C.98 B.S. L.602 J.D. Chf. Privacy Offr., Sallie Mae, Inc.
Jackson, Larry R. .... '57 '86 C.63 B.A. L.345 J.D. [Jackson]
Jackson Law Firm, LLC .... 11671 Maple Street
Johnson, James W., III, (BV) .... '64 '91 C.347 B.S. L.1119 J.D. 8777 E. 116th Street
Kassebaum, Jeanette C., (BV) .... '62 '91 C.679 B.A. L.347 J.D. 11614 Maple St
Kielty, John J. .... '42 '67 C&L.776 B.A., J.D. 11987 Sunrise Cir.
Leatherman, John B., Jr. .... '39 '69 C.188 B.Ch.E. L.1119 J.D. 9995 Allisonville Rd.
Lutz, William H., (BV) .... '59 '91 C.879 B.S.W. L.734 J.D. [DeFur V.] ⊙
Maddox, Mark E., (AV) .... '61 '86 C.894 B.A. L.880 J.D. [Maddox H.&C.]

Maddox Hargett & Caruso, P.C., (AV)
10100 Lantern Road, Suite 150, 46037 ⊙
Telephone: 317-598-2040 Telefax: 317-598-2050
URL: http://www.investorprotection.com
Mark E. Maddox; Thomas A. Hargett; Steven B. Caruso (Resident, New York, N.Y. Office);—Thomas K. Caldwell; Keith L. Griffin; Barbara Quinn Smith (Not admitted in IN).
Mediation, Securities Arbitration, Securities Litigation.
Reference: Bank One, Indianapolis.
New York, N.Y. Office: 80 Broad Street, 5th Floor, 10004, Telephone: 212-837-7908. Telefax: 212-837-7998.
See Professional Biographies, FISHERS, INDIANA

Marcus, Cynthia A. .... '54 '95 C.63 B.S. L.347 J.D. [Marcus]

Marcus Law Firm, The
11978 Fishers Crossing Drive, 46038
Telephone: 317-845-4444 Fax: 317-284-0266
Email: cmarcus@marcus-law.com URL: http://www.marcus-lawfirm.com
Cynthia A. Marcus. Associate: Amber L. Small.
Healthcare Law, Elder Law, Personal Injury, Automobile Accidents, Slip and Fall, Wrongful Death, Legal Malpractice, Consumer Law, Medical Malpractice, Unsafe Products, Civil Rights, Employment law, Wrongful Termination, Discrimination, Harassment, Trial Practice, Family Law, Adoptions, Child Custody, Child Support, Divorce, Visitation Rights, Real Estate, Wills and Probate, Trusts and Estates, Estate Planning, Guardianships, Asset Protection, Business Law, Business Planning, Contracts, Lawsuits, Business Enterprises, Corporate, Limited Liability Companies, Partnerships, Buying and Selling a Business.
See Professional Biographies, FISHERS, INDIANA

Martens, William C., Jr. .... '33 '68 C.937 B.S. L.146 J.D. 7429 Glenvista Pl.‡

Meyer Law Office
(See Indianapolis)

Mitchell & Associates
(See Indianapolis)

Nicholson, Roy A. '48 '80 C.882 B.A. L.30 J.D.
(adm. in DC; not adm. in IN) Chmn. of the Bd. & CEO, United Student Aid Funds, Inc.
Olsen-Darst, Sandra A. .... '65 '93 C.347 B.S.N. L.345 J.D. MSC Holdings, Inc.
Parker, Todd W. .... '63 '99 C.63 B.S. L.347 J.D. 9740 Olympia Dr.
Risinger, Jeffery B., (AV) .... '56 '81 C.347 B.S. L.145 J.D. [J.B.Risinger]

Risinger, Jeffery B., P.C., (AV)
12985 Lantern Road, 46038
Telephone: 317-578-1801 Fax: 317-578-1480
Email: jbrfinlaw@aol.com URL: http://www.lawyers.com/risinger
Jeffery B. Risinger.
Business Law, Finance, Securities and Investments, Business Enterprises, Closely Held Business Law, Corporate, Franchises, Limited Liability Companies, Partnership Law, Small Business Law, Buying and Selling of Businesses, Business Planning, Contracts, Real Estate, Commercial Leasing, Business Start-Ups, Strategic Alliances, Joint Ventures, Mergers, Taxation, Tax Planning, Water Law, Sewer Utilities.
See Professional Biographies, FISHERS, INDIANA

Rogers, Emily M. .... '69 '92 C&L.436 B.A., J.D. 10864 Thistle Ridge‡
Small, Amber L. .... '76 '03 C.347 B.S. L.879 J.D. [Ⓐ Marcus]
Smith, Barbara Quinn '64 '91 C.363 B.A. L.930 J.D.
(adm. in OH; not adm. in IN) [Ⓐ Maddox H.&C.]
Speicher, John A. .... '54 '79 C.210 B.A. L.851 9620 Willowview Dr.
Strunk, Tommy L. .... '33 '70 C.347 B.S. L.1119 J.D. 6841 Cherry Blossom East Drive
Todderud, James C., Attorney at Law '45 '72
C.347 B.S. L.1119 J.D. 9929 E. 126th St., Ste. A
Wanzer, Holly J. .... '73 '99 C.63 B.S. L.345 J.D. [Ⓐ DeFur V.]

FLORA, 2,179, *Carroll Co.*

Bishop, Dick N., (AV) .... '31 '56 C.231 A.B. L.345 J.D. 19 S. Center St.
Bishop, Dick T., (AV) .... '52 '77 C.303 B.A. L.345 J.D. 19 S. Center St.
Briggs, Florence A. .... '34 '58 C.683 A.B. L.383 LL.B. 28 S. Center St.
Briggs, William J. .... '23 '54 C.210 A.B. L.383 LL.B. 28 S. Ctr. St.
Robeson, Miriam E. .... '64 '89 C.679 B.S. L.344 J.D. 1799 N. 200 E.‡

FLOYD'S KNOBS, —, *Floyd Co.*

Andrews, David Ashley .... '65 '90 C.902 B.A. L.347 J.D. 3114 Twin Circle Dr.
Brizendine, Paul A., (CV) .... '64 '95 C.326 B.S. L.862 J.D. 752 Highlander Point Dr.
Burdette, Evin M. '— '97 C.378 B.A. L.900 J.D.
(adm. in KS; not adm. in IN) 4401 Country View Dr.

FORT BRANCH, 2,320, *Gibson Co.*

Druley, Ray M., Law Office of, (BV) '41 '65 C.840 B.A. L.1119 J.D.
505 N. Church St.
Schleter, Nita D. .... '— '91 L.421 J.D. 107 N. McCreary St.

FORTVILLE, 3,444, *Hancock Co.*

Johnson, Walter R. .... '34 '72 C.475 B.S. L.345 J.D. P.O. Box 236‡
Moll, Kathryn A., (AV) .... '62 '88 C.347 B.A. L.930 J.D. [Nation S.M.]
Nation, Van A., (AV) .... '53 '81 C.347 B.A. L.345 J.D. [Nation S.M.]
Nation Schoening Moll, P.C., (AV) .... 721 E. Broadway
Norman-Moffatt, Nancy, (AV) .... '64 '89 C.201 B.A. L.347 J.D. [Ⓐ Nation S.M.]
Puterbaugh, David J., (CV) .... '49 '74 C.347 B.S.E.D. L.345 J.D. 6878 N. 50 E.
Schoening, Michael A., (BV) .... '57 '82 C.340 B.A. L.365 J.D. [Nation S.M.]
Taylor, Carol A., (AVⓉ) .... '45 '80 C.494 B.A. L.146 J.D. [Ⓐ Nation S.M.]

FORT WAYNE, * 205,727, *Allen Co.*

Adair, Heidi Bieberich, (BV) .... '69 '94 C&L.347 B.A., J.D. [Ⓐ Beers M.B.&S.]
Adair, Stephen W., (BV) .... '42 '67 C.347 A.B. L.1119 J.D. [Beers M.B.&S.]
Adams, Nicholas Alan .... '67 '03 C.347 B.A. L.879 J.D. [Ⓐ Steele,U.&M.]
Adelsperger, Douglas R., (BV) .... '62 '88 C.347 B.S. L.1119 J.D. [Skekloff,A.&K.]
Adolf, Anthony T. .... '70 '96 C.57 B.A. L.879 J.D. [A.T.Adolf]

Adolf, Anthony T., P.C., Law Office of ....912 South Calhoun Street
Aikman, Donald M., (BV) .... '40 '66 C.347 B.S. L.1119 J.D. P.O. Box 11381
Allen, Thomas C., (BV) .... '63 '88 C.347 B.S. L.1119 J.D. 202 W. Berry, Suite 0101
Allison, Loren K., (CV) ....'— '79 C.347 B.A. L.201 J.D. [L.Allison]
Allison, Loren, Law Offices of, (CV) ....519 Tennessee Avenue
Alter, Thomas E. .... '47 '72 C.602 A.B. L.1119 J.D. Catholic Cemetary Assn., Inc.
Amber, Cynthia Penn, (BV) .... '57 '89 C.347 B.S. L.879 J.D. Mag.
Anderson, Kathleen M., (BV) .... '— '92 C.303 B.A. L.347 J.D. [Barnes&T.]
Antalis, Gregory M., (BV) ....'52 '78 C.894 B.A. L.345 J.D. 233 W. Baker St.
Anzini, Albert, III .... '61 '90 C.679 B.A. L.945 J.D. [Ⓐ Arata]
Arata, Patrick J., (AV) .... '53 '79 C.347 B.A. L.464 J.D. [Arata]

Arata Law Firm, (AV)
Lincoln Tower - 14th Floor, 116 E. Berry Street, 46802
Telephone: 260-424-1010 Fax: 260-420-1406
Email: patarata@aol.com URL: http://www.thearatalawfirm.com
Patrick J. Arata;—Robert W. Gevers; Albert Anzini, III.
Civil and Criminal Litigation, Driving While Intoxicated, Personal Injury.
See Professional Biographies, FORT WAYNE, INDIANA

Ardington, Mary Jo .... '56 '81 C.210 B.A. L.345 J.D. Coun., Lincoln Natl. Corp.
Armstrong, Edward P. '35 '68 C.665 B.S. L.436 J.D.
(adm. in WI; not adm. in IN; Pat.) 9632 Woodstream Dr.
Arnold, Daniel T. ....'55 '80 C.602 B.B.A. L.345 J.D. 623 Airport Worth Office Pk.
Arnold, James Robert, (AV) .... '16 '40 C&L.347 A.B., J.D. 419 E. Wayne St.
Ashbridge, Margaret S. '42 '82 C.801 B.A. L.345 J.D.
V.P. & Regulatory and Compliance Mngr., Swiss Re Life & Health America, Inc.
Avery, David J., (AV) .... '51 '76 C.338 B.S. L.879 J.D. [Avery&V.]
Avery & Van Gilder, (AV) .... 202 W. Berry St.
Baach, Richard M. .... '36 '59 C.910 A.B. L.597 LL.B. [Komisarow&B.]
Bachman, Kurt Russell, (BV) .... '64 '89 C.432 B.S. L.344 J.D. [Beers M.B.&S.] ⊙
Backs, Charles W., (CV) .... '70 '96 C.347 B.A. L.879 J.D. [Beers M.B.&S.]
Backs, Vincent J., (AV) .... '40 '65 C.347 A.B. L.1119 J.D. [Beers M.B.&S.]
Baeverstad, Mark W., (AV) .... '56 '81 C.323 B.A. L.823 J.D. [Rothberg L.&W.]
Bailey, David E., (BV) .... '73 '99 C.473 B.S. L.347 J.D. [Eilbacher F.]
Baker, Carl L. '43 '68 C.1060 A.B. L.1119 J.D.
Vice President & Deputy General Counsel, Lincoln National Life Insurance Co.‡
Baker, Eric A., (CV) '67 '96 C.347 B.A. L.879 J.D.
Coun., North Amer. Van Lines, Inc.
Baker, Norman E. .... '35 '63 C.347 B.S. L.1119 LL.B. Allen Co., Sr. J.

Baker & Daniels LLP, (AV)
111 East Wayne Street, Suite 800, 46802 ⊙
Telephone: 260-424-8000 Fax: 260-460-1700
URL: http://www.bakerdaniels.com
Members of Firm: J. Stephen Bennett (Not admitted in IN); Jon A. Bomberger; John R. Burns, III; Timothy J. Haffner; Steven L. Hazelrigg; John F. Hoffman; David P. Irmscher; Steven L. Jackson; Michael L. James; Joseph W. Kimmell, II; David J. Kuker; Jeanne E. Longsworth; Robert D. Moreland; Michael J. Nader; Anthony Niewyk; Laura C. O'Donnell (Also at Indianapolis office); Maclyn T. Parker; Douglas Dormire Powers; David A. Scott; Lawrence E. Shine; Thomas M. Shoaff; N. Reed Silliman; Keith E. White. Counsel: Karen T. Moses. Resident Associates: Thomas R. Biehl, Jr. (Not admitted in IN); Betsy M. Brooks; Michael S. Burns; Scott C. Burns (Not admitted in IN); Abigail Marie Butler; Cynthia M. Cormany; Adam F. Cox; David P. Durm; Brian Thomas Geisler (Not admitted in IN); Jeffrey V. Gery; Jeffrey A. Goeglein; Shellie L. Goetz; Damian Gosheff; Jerome Byron Hayes; Julie Annette Hoffman; Jason A. Houser; Mark F. Juba; Thomas C. Kus; Martha M. Lemert; Jon L. Lindberg (Not admitted in IN); Shannon K. Reed; Patrick A. Scheiderer; Michael D. Schwartz; Matthew B. Skaggs; David D. Storey; Andrew J. Welborn; Mark A. Werling.
Antitrust, Bankruptcy, Business Planning, Commercial, Corporate Finance, Creditors Rights, Employee Benefits, Employment, Environment, Estate and Probate, Family, Financial, Food and Drug, Government Affairs, Health Care, Insurance, Intellectual Property, International, Legislative, Litigation, Medical Technology Regulation, Municipal, Nonprofit, Product Liability, Real Estate, Securities, Sports, Tax, Transportation, Utilities, Year 2000, Zoning and Land Use Law.
Indianapolis, Indiana Office: 300 North Meridian Street, Suite 2700, 46204. Telephone: 317-237-0300. Fax: 317-237-1000.
South Bend, Indiana Office: First Bank Building, 205 West Jefferson Boulevard, Suite 250, 46601. Telephone: 574-234-4149. Fax: 574-239-1900.
Elkhart, Indiana Office: 317 West Franklin Street, Suite 507, P.O. Box 507, 46515-0507. Telephone: 574-296-6000. Fax: 574-296-6001.
Indianapolis-96th Street, Indiana Office: Parkwood Six, 600 East 96th Street, Suite 600, 46240. Telephone: 317-569-9600. Fax: 317-569-4800.
Washington, D.C. Office: 805 15th Street, N.W., Suite 700, 20005. Telephone: 202-312-7440. Fax: 202-312-7460.
Qingdao, China Office: 4/F, Office Tower, Crowne Plaza Qingdao, No. 76 Hong Kong Middle Road, 266071. Telephone: +011-86-532-575-1051. Fax: +011-86-532-575-1055.
Beijing, China Office: Room 1919, Tower 2, China World Trade Center, No. 1 JianGuoMenWai Avenue, 100004. Telephone: +86-10-6505-7733. Fax: +86-10-6505-8730.
See Professional Biographies, FORT WAYNE, INDIANA

Barce, John C., (AV) .... '64 '89 C.347 B.S. L.1119 J.D. [Barrett&M.]
Barnard, Larry L., (BV) .... '62 '87 C.347 B.S. L.345 J.D. [Carson B.]

Barnes & Thornburg LLP, (AV)
600 One Summit Square, 46802 ⊙
Telephone: 260-423-9440 FAX: 260-424-8316
URL: http://www.btlaw.com
Partners: Michael A. Scheer; William T. (Tuck) Hopkins, Jr.; Dennis C. Becker; Bobby B. Gillenwater; M. Scott Hall; Stephen L. Fink; D. Randall Brown; Kathleen M. Anderson; Mark S. Kittaka; Dawn R. Rosemond; Gary C. Furst; Shaun E. Graham. Associates: Matthew M. Hohman; Gregory S. Cooper; Mark D. Scudder; Danel Michelle Nickels; Tiffany L. Gooden; Jason T. Clagg; Christopher M. Forrest; Robert R. Vass.
Acquisitions and Divestitures, Ad Valorem Tax, Administrative Law, Affirmative Action, Agriculture Law, Americans with Disabilities Act, Antidumping, Antitrust, Antitrust and Trade Regulation, Appellate Practice, Attorney Grievances, Automotive Warranty Law, Aviation and Aerospace, Aviation Law, Banking Law, Banking Regulations, Bankruptcy, Bankruptcy Reorganization, Banks and Banking, Biochemical Patents, Biomedical Products Liability, Biomedical Technology, Biotechnology Patent Prosecution, Bond Law, Brain Injury, Breach of Warranty, Brown Fields Redevelopment, Business Immigration, Business Law, Business Litigation, Business Planning, Business Regulatory and Administrative, Business Start-ups, Business Succession Planning, Business Taxation, Business Torts, Business Transactions, Business Transfers, Buying and Selling of Businesses, Cable TV, Cargo Claims, Charitable Trusts and Foundations, Chemical Intellectual Property, Chemical Patent Prosecution, Chemical Patents, Chemical Products Liability, Civil Appeals, Civil Litigation, Civil Practice, Civil RICO, Class Action Defense, Clean Air Act, Clean Water Act, Closely Held Business Estate Planning, Closely Held Businesses, Closely Held Business Law, Closely Held Corporations, Collective Bargaining, Commercial Bankruptcy, Commercial Finance Law, Commercial Law, Commercial Leasing and Financing, Commercial Litigation, Commercial Conveyancing, Commercial Real Estate, Commercial Real Estate Acquisition, Commercial Real Estate Development, Commercial Real Estate Finance, Commercial Transactions, Commodities Fraud, Communications and Media, Complex Commercial Litigation, Complex Litigation, Computer and Software Patents, Computer Law, Computers and Software, Conflicts of Interest, Construction Labor Law, Construction Law, Consumer Credit, Contract Litigation, Cooperatives, Copyrights, Corporate Finance, Corporate Formation, Corporate Law, Corporate Taxation, Corporate Tax Planning, Countervailing Duties, Covenants Not To Compete, Creditors Rights, Creditors Rights in Bankruptcy, Criminal Defense, Criminal Law, Criminal Tax Audits, Customs Law, Dealer and Distributor Termination, Debt and Equity Finance, Decedents Estates, Defense Litigation, Design Patents, Disability Insurance Defense, Discrimination, Distribution, Drug and Medical Device Defense, Economic Development, Education Law, Elder Law, Election, Campaign and Political Law, Electric Power, Electric Utilities, Electrical Intellectual Property, Electrical Patents, Electro-mechanical Patents, Electronic Commerce, Electronic Patents, Eminent Domain, Employee Benefits, Employee Stock Ownership Plans, Employment Defense, Employment

(This Listing Continued)

Barnes & Thornburg LLP (Continued)

Discrimination, Employment Law, Employment Litigation, Energy, Energy Contracts, Energy Regulation, Environmental Administrative Law, Environmental Cleanup, Environmental Compliance, Environmental Criminal Defense, Environmental Law, Environmental Litigation, Environmental Permitting, Environmental Real Estate, Environmental Regulation, Environmental Risk Management, Equal Employment Opportunity Law, ERISA Litigation, Estate Administration, Estate and Gift Taxation, Estate Planning, Estate Planning and Taxation, Estate Planning and Administration, Estate Planning and Probate, Estate Planning for Parents of Handicapped Children, Estate Planning for Unmarried Individuals, Executive Compensation, Executive Severance Contracts, Export Regulation, Fair Employment Practices, Family and Medical Leave Act, Family Business Successions, Family Wealth Transfer, Federal and State Administrative Regulatory Practice, Federal and State Legislative Practice, Federal Civil Litigation, Federal Civil Practice, Federal Criminal Law, Federal Estate and Gift Taxation, Federal Litigation, Federal Tax Controversies, Federal Taxation, Fiduciary Income Tax, Finance, Financial Transactions, First Party Insurance, Foreign Investment in the United States, Freight Claims, Freight Loss and Damage, Gaming Law, Gaming Licensing, Gas Utilities, General Litigation, Government, Government Affairs, Government Agency Practice, Government Contracts, Government Investigations, Government Relations, Groundwater Contamination, Hazardous Materials and Substances, Hazardous Waste, Hazardous Waste Liability, Head Injury, Health Care, Health Care Corporate Law, Health Care Contracts, Health Care Fraud, Health Care Licensing, Health Care Litigation, Health Care Mergers and Acquisitions, Health Care Regulation, Health Care Reimbursement, Health Law, Heavy Equipment Products Liability, Immigration Law, Industrial Revenue Bond Law, Inheritance Tax, Initial Public Offerings, Insurance, Insurance Bad Faith, Insurance Coverage, Insurance Litigation, Insurance Regulation, Integrated Health Care Delivery Systems, Intellectual Property, Intellectual Property General Prosecution, Intellectual Property Infringement, Intellectual Property Licensing, Intellectual Property Litigation, Intellectual Property Procurement, Intellectual Property Protection, Intellectual Property Rights, International Business Law, International Intellectual Property, International Law, International Patents, International Trade, International Transportation Law, Internet Law, Internet Trademark Law, Joint Ventures, Labor and Employment, Labor Arbitration, Labor Law, Labor Relations, Land Use, Lease Law, Leasing, Legal Ethics and Professional Responsibility, Legal Malpractice Defense, Legislative Practice, Licensing, Life Insurance Defense, Limited Liability Company Law, Limited Partnerships, Liquor Licensing, Litigation, Loans, Lobbying, Local Government Law, Logistics, Long Term Care, Managed Care, Managed Care Contracts, Management Employment Law, Management Labor Law, Manufacturers Liability, Maritime Regulations, Mechanical Intellectual Property, Mechanical Patents, Media Law, Mediation, Medical Intellectual Property, Medical Patents, Mental Health Law, Mergers, Acquisitions and Divestitures, Mergers and Acquisitions, Mineral Taxation, Molecular Biology Patents, Motor Carrier Law, Motor Carrier Regulation, Multi-Employer Pensions, Municipal Bonds, Municipal Bonds Taxation, Municipal Finance, Municipal Law, Municipal Leasing, Municipal Redevelopment, Municipal Securities, Municipal Taxation, National Labor Relations Act, Neurolaw, Nonprofit and Charitable Organizations, Nonprofit Organizations Law, North American Free Trade Agreement, Occupational Safety and Health, OSHA, Partnership Law, Partnership Taxation, Patent Infringement, Patent Interference Practice, Patent Litigation, Patent Prosecution, Patents, PCT Legal Export, Personal Injury, Personal Injury Defense, Pesticide Litigation, Pharmaceutical Intellectual Property, Pharmaceutical Patents, Physician Contracts, Physician Practices, Planning and Land Use, Power Line Contact Injury, Probate, Probate Litigation, Products Liability, Products Liability Defense, Professional Liability, Property Law, Property Tax, Property Tax Abatement, Property Tax Appeals, Psychological Injury, Public Finance, Public Sector Labor Relations, Public Utility Law, Railroad Law, Real Estate, Real Estate Acquisitions, Real Estate Contracts, Real Estate Development, Real Estate Finance, Real Estate Licensing, Real Estate Secured Lending, Real Estate Title Insurance, Real Property, Real Property Acquisitions, Real Property Finance, Reorganizations, Resource Conservation and Recovery Act (RCRA), Retirement Benefit Plans, School Law, Securities, Securities Litigation, Securitization, Semiconductor Technology, Sexual Harassment, Small Business Corporations, State Government Law, State Tax Controversies, State Taxation, Structured Finance, Succession Planning, Superfund, Tax Controversies, Tax Exempt Finance, Tax Exempt Organizations, Tax Increment Finance, Tax Law, Tax Litigation, Taxation, Technology and Science, Technology Law, Technology Licensing, Technology Transfers, Telecommunications Competition, Telecommunications Law, Theft of Trade Secrets, Title VII Discrimination, Title IX Discrimination, Tort Defense, Toxic Exposure, Toxic Tort Class Actions, Toxic Torts, Toxic Tort Defense, Trade Dress, Trade Secrets, Trademark Litigation, Trademarks, Trademark Prosecution, Trademark Protection, Trademark Registration, Transportation, Transportation Safety, Trial Practice, Trusts and Estates, Unfair Competition, Unfair Trade, Uniform Commercial Codes, Union Contract Negotiations, Union Elections, Utilities, Utility Law, Wage and Hour Law, WARN Act, Water Pollution, Water Quality, Water Utilities, Wetland Regulation, White Collar Crime, White Collar Criminal Defense, Wills, Workers Compensation, Workouts, World Trade Organization, Wrongful Death, Wrongful Termination, Wrongful Termination Defense, Zoning, Planning and Land Use.
Representative Clients: American General Realty Advisors; Bank One; Do it Best Corp.; EP Graphics, Inc.; Frick Services, Inc.; Group Dekko International; Karl Schmidt Unisia-Zollner Pistons Division; Liberty Homes, Inc.; Lincoln National Corporation; Wells Fargo Bank Indiana, N.A.
Indianapolis, Indiana Office: 11 South Meridian Street, 46204. Telephone: 317-236-1313. FAX: 317-231-7433.
South Bend, Indiana Office: 600 1st Source Bank Center, 100 North Michigan, 46601-1632. Telephone: 574-233-1171. FAX: 574-237-1125.
Elkhart, Indiana Office: 121 West Franklin Street, Suite 200, 46516. Telephone: 574-293-0681. FAX: 574-296-2535.
Chicago, Illinois Office: One North Wacker Drive, Suite 4400, 60606-2833. Telephone: 312-357-1313. FAX: 312-759-5646.
Washington, D.C. Office: Suite 900, 750 17th Street, N.W., 20006. Telephone: 202-289-1313. FAX: 202-289-1330.
Grand Rapids, Michigan Office: 300 Ottawa Avenue, N.W., Suite 500, 49503. Telephone: 616-742-3930. FAX: 616-742-3999.
See Professional Biographies, FORT WAYNE, INDIANA

Barranda, Michael A. .... '78 '05 C.602 B.A. L.424 J.D. [Ⓐ Miller M.&M.]
Barrett, James M., III, (AV) .... '24 '49 C&L.477 A.B., J.D. [Barrett&M.] ‡

Barrett & McNagny LLP, (AV)
215 East Berry Street, P.O. Box 2263, 46801-2263
Telephone: 260-423-9551 Telecopier: 260-423-8920
URL: http://www.barrettlaw.com
Partners: William F. McNagny (Retired); James M. Barrett, III (Retired); Ted S. Miller (Retired); J. Michael O'Hara (Retired); John M. Clifton, Jr.; Robert S. Walters; John F. Lyons; N. Thomas Horton, II; Richard D. Robinson; Patrick G. Michaels; Thomas M. Fink; Richard E. Fox; John P. Martin; Thomas P. Yoder; Thomas M. Kimbrough; Ronald J. Ehinger; Stephen L. Chapman; Thomas A. Herr; Thomas J. Markle; Michael P. O'Hara; Thomas M. Niezer; Anthony M. Stites; David R. Steiner; John C. Barce; Kevin K. Fitzharris; Cathleen M. Shrader; Dawn Snow Mattox; Samuel J. Talarico, Jr.; H. Joseph Cohen; Trisha J. Paul; Patrick G. Murphy. Of Counsel: Howard L. Chapman (Retired). Associates: Renee L. Riecke; Anne E. Simerman; Henry P. Najdeski; Tina M. Bell; Michael H. Michmerhuizen; Jeffrey M. Woenker; James J. O'Connor, Jr.; Joshua C. Neal; Janell M. Sprinkle; Charles C. Dubes; Zachary E. Klutz; Alisa L. Pearson.
Administrative, Alternative Dispute Resolution, Antitrust, Appellate, Business and Commercial, Commercial and Business Litigation, Computer, Copyright, Corporate, Creditors' Rights and Bankruptcy, E-Commerce; Employee Benefits, Environmental, ERISA and ERISA Litigation, Estate Planning and Administration, Federal and State Tax, Financial Institutions, Franchising and Licensing, Governmental Relations, Guardianship, Health Care and Hospital, Insurance, Labor and Employment, Media, Medical and Professional Malpractice, Mergers and Acquisitions, Mortgage Banking, Municipal Finance, Products Liability, Railroad, Real Estate, Securities, School Administration, Tax Exempt Organizations, Trademark, Worker's Compensation and Zoning and Land Use Law.
Counsel for: Al-Fe Heat Treating, Inc.; Do It Best Corp.; Fort Wayne Foundry Corp.; Franklin Electric Co., Inc.; National City Bank of Indiana; OmniSource Corp.; Parkview Health System; Steel Dynamics, Inc.; Towne Air Freight LLC; University of St. Francis.
See Professional Biographies, FORT WAYNE, INDIANA

Bash, Charles D., (BV) .... '49 '85 C.475 B.S. L.145 J.D. [Ⓐ Swift&F.]
Bauer, Diana C., (BV) .... '60 '87 C&L.879 B.A., J.D. [Carson B.]
Beadie, Thomas N. '27 '52 C&L.178 A.B., LL.B.
(adm. in NY; not adm. in IN) 4015 N. Washington Rd.‡
Beams, Glen J., (AV) .... '14 '39 C&L.347 A.B., LL.B. [Ⓒ Helmke,B.B.&W.]
Beams, John M., (BV) .... '48 '72 C.347 A.B. L.1119 J.D. 235 W. Creighton Ave.
Bechert, Chad B., (CV) .... '72 '97 C.347 B.S. L.1119 J.D. [Ⓐ Tremper,B.L.&T.]
Bechert, Robert S., (BV) ....'43 '72 C.347 B.S. L.345 LL.B. [Tremper,B.L.&T.]
Beck, Edward E., (AV) .... '49 '73 C.347 A.B. L.345 J.D. [Shambaugh,K.B.&W.]

Beck, Stephanie D. Shultz . . . . '72 '98 C.432 B.S. L.879 J.D. [Ⓐ Boeglin,T.&G.]
Becker, Dennis C., (AV) . . . .'— '79 C.347 B.S. L.276 J.D. [Barnes&T.]
Beckman, Frederick A., (AV) . . . . '23 '50 C.1024 A.B. L.1119 J.D. [Ⓒ Beckman L.]

Beckman Lawson, LLP, (AV)
800 Standard Federal Plaza, 46802
Telephone: 260-422-0800 Facsimile: 260-420-1013
URL: http://www.beckmanlawson.com
Partners: Jack W. Lawson; Howard B. Sandler; John H. Brandt; Robert L. Nicholson; Craig R. Patterson; Wendy W. Davis; Edward J. Ormsby; Patrick R. Hess; Mark E. Witmer; Matthew J. Elliott. Associates: Brian C. Heck; Mark E. Bloom; Michael D. Story; Andrea R. Dick; Jeremy L. Reidy. Of Counsel: William L. Sweet, Jr.; Gary D. Johnson; Frederick A. Beckman; Douglas E. Miller.
General Civil and Criminal Trial and Appellate Practice in all Federal and State Courts. Corporate, Bankruptcy, Family, Real Estate, Planning and Zoning, Probate and Estate Planning, Administrative, Health and Hospital, Personal Injury, Environmental, Employment and Labor Law, School Law.
Reference: National City Bank.
See Professional Biographies, FORT WAYNE, INDIANA

Beerbower, Douglas O., (BV) '50 '76
C.347 B.A. L.345 J.D. Sr. Coun., Lincoln Natl. Corp.
Beers, Richard E., (AV) . . . .'50 '76 C.347 B.S. L.345 J.D. [Beers M.B.&S.]

Beers Mallers Backs & Salin, LLP, (AV)
110 West Berry Street, Suite 1100, 46802 ⊙
Telephone: 260-426-9706 Fax: 260-420-1314
URL: http://www.beersmallers.com
Members of Firm: Vincent J. Backs; Stephen W. Adair; G. William Fishering; Richard E. Beers; Peter G. Mallers; James P. Posey; Kurt Russell Bachman; Roy F. Kiplinger; Kevin P. Bruns; John B. Bentz; Charles W. Backs; Laura L. Maser. Associates: Heidi Bieberich Adair; Lisa M. Bowen-Slaven; Joshua A. Burkhardt; Jonathan H. Nusbaum; Stacy K. Somers. Of Counsel: Daniel K. Leininger.
General Trial and Appellate Practice in all State and Federal Courts. Administrative Law, Bankruptcy, Banks and Banking, Business Law, Civil Rights, Collections, Commercial Law, Computers and Software, Construction Law, Contracts, Copyrights, Corporate Law, Debtor and Creditor, Elder Law, Environmental Law, Estate Planning and Administration, Franchising and Licensing, Government, Health Care, Insurance, Litigation, Mergers, Acquisitions and Divestitures, Municipal Law, Personal Injury, Probate, Products Liability, Public and Private Sector Labor and Employment (Management), Public Finance, Real Estate, Securities, Trademarks, Trusts and Estates, Zoning, Planning and Land Use.
LaGrange, Indiana Office: 108 West Michigan Street. Telephone: 260-463-4949. FAX: 260-463-4905.
See Professional Biographies, FORT WAYNE, INDIANA

Bell, Tina M., (BV) . . . .'74 '98 C.248 B.A. L.347 J.D. [Ⓐ Barrett&M.]
Bennett, J. Stephen '69 '95 C.339 B.A. L.273 J.D.
(adm. in IL; not adm. in IN) [Baker&D.]
Benson, H. Bixler '49 '74 C.477 A.B. L.446 J.D.
(adm. in MD; not adm. in IN) 11735 Woodstream Ridge Ct.‡
Benson, M. Robert . . . . '44 '71 C&L.347 B.S., J.D. [Benson,P.M.J.&L.]
Benson, Pantello, Morris, James & Logan, (BV) . . . . 3505 Lake Ave.
Bentz, John B., (BV) . . . . '69 '94 C.602 B.S. L.1119 J.D. [Beers M.B.&S.]
Berning, William A., (BV) . . . . '31 '55 C&L.879 B.A., LL.B. [Ⓒ Helmke,B.B.&W.]
Berta, T. Randall . . . . '53 '79 C.894 B.A. L.1119 J.D. 1421 Sevan Lake Ct.
Bertin, Michael V. '— '90
(adm. in NY; not adm. in IN) 1919 W. Cook Rd.‡
Bewley, George N., Jr., (AV) . . . . '47 '73 C.347 A.B. L.1119 J.D. [Bewley&K.]

Bewley & Koday, LLP, (AV)
110 West Berry Suite 2006, 46802
Telephone: 260-424-0566 Fax: 260-423-1325
Email: bewleykoday@bewleykoday.com URL: http://www.bewleykoday.com
George N. Bewley, Jr.; James Koday.
Probate and Estate Planning, Tax, Mediation, Employee Benefits and Corporate Law.
See Professional Biographies, FORT WAYNE, INDIANA

Biehl, Thomas R., Jr. '— '96 C.608 B.A. L.851 J.D.
(adm. in OH; not adm. in IN) [Ⓐ Baker&D.]
Biggs, Thomas W. '44 '69 C.347 B.S. L.1119 J.D.
Assoc. Gen. Coun., Magnavox Electronics Systems Co.
Bishop, David D. '46 '73 C.502 B.A. L.221 J.D.
(adm. in MO; not adm. in IN) 5001 U.S. Hwy. 30 W.‡
Bishop, Robert J., (CV) . . . .'65 '91 C.347 B.A. L.851 J.D. [Bishop]
Bishop Law Offices, (CV) . . . . .202 W. Berry St., Ste. 10E
Blachly, Tabor, Bozik & Hartman, (AV) . . . . 4656 West Jefferson, Suite 120 (⊙Valparaiso)
Blackburn, Thomas D., (BV) . . . . '51 '77 C.347 B.S. L.345 J.D. [Blackburn&G.]

Blackburn & Green, (BV)
3344 Mallard Cove Lane, 46804
Telephone: 260-422-4400; 800-444-1112 Telecopier: 260-436-4404
URL: http://www.lawyers.com/blackburn-green
Members of Firm: Thomas D. Blackburn; Raymond T. Green.
Litigation, Personal Injury Law.
See Professional Biographies, FORT WAYNE, INDIANA

Blee, Thomas J., (BV) . . . .'30 '75 C&L.347 A.B., J.D. [Ⓒ Burt,B.D.S.&B.]
Bloom, Allan E., (BV) . . . .'32 '56 C&L.879 A.B., J.D. [Ⓒ Burt,B.D.S.&B.]
Bloom, Alton Dale, (BV) . . . . '46 '71 C.347 B.S. L.879 J.D. [Burt,B.D.S.&B.]
Bloom, John S., (AV) . . . .'46 '73 C&L.347 A.B., J.D. [Shambaugh,K.B.&W.]
Bloom, Mark E. . . . .'— '01 C.679 B.A. L.345 J.D. [Ⓐ Beckman L.]
Bloom, Renee S. . . . .'75 '02 C.347 B.A. L.607 J.D. [Ⓐ Burt,B.D.S.&B.]
Blume, Ralph R., (AV) . . . . '30 '57 C&L.602 A.B., LL.B. [Ⓒ Blume,C.J.&S.]
Blume, Connelly, Jordan & Stucky, (AV) . . . . 110 W. Berry St.
Bobay, Craig J. . . . .'56 '91 C&L.347 B.A., J.D. Mag.
Boeglin, Troyer & Gerardot, PC, (BV) . . . . 7321 West Jefferson Boulevard
Bohdan, John C., II, (BV) '64 '89
C&L.347 B.A., J.D. 1900 Lincoln Tower, 116 East Berry Street
Bolinger, Samuel L. . . . .'58 '86 C.528 B.A. L.999 J.D. 126 W Columbia St. Ste. 300
Bolino Law Firm . . . . 323 W. Berry St.
Bomberger, Jon A., (BV) . . . .'59 '84 C.932 B.A. L.602 J.D. [Baker&D.]
Bonahoom, Joseph G., (BV) . . . .'60 '86 C&L.436 B.S., J.D. [Bonahoom&B.]
Bonahoom, Otto M., (AV) . . . .'30 '54 C&L.436 A.B., J.D. [Bonahoom&B.]
Bonahoom & Bonahoom, (AV) . . . . .110 West Berry Street
Borgmann, Daniel J., (AV) . . . .'50 '76 C.473 A.B. L.607 J.D. [Helmke,B.B.&W.]
Bowen-Slaven, Lisa M., (CV) . . . .'67 '93 C.679 B.S. L.879 J.D. [Ⓐ Beers M.B.&S.] ⊙
Bowman, Chester E., (BV) . . . .'17 '50 C&L.378 B.S., LL.B. [Bowman&M.]
Bowman & McEntee, (BV) . . . . .206 Paine Webber Bldg.
Boxberger, Bruce O., (BV) . . . . '48 '74 C.347 B.A. L.345 J.D. [Carson B.]
Boyer, Nancy Eshcoff . . . .'51 '76 C.210 B.A. L.345 J.D. Supr. Ct. J.
Boyer, R. David, (AV) . . . .'38 '64 C.827 A.B. L.659 J.D. [Helmke,B.B.&W.]
Boyer, R. David, II, (BV) . . . .'72 '98 C.827 B.A. L.345 J.D. [Ⓐ Helmke,B.B.&W.]
Boyer, Thomas P. . . . .'55 '80 C.894 B.A. L.1119 J.D. Mag.
Bradford, Steven J. . . . .'75 '01 C.999 B.A. L.879 J.D. [Ⓐ Kos&Assoc.]
Bragalone, Jon A., (BV) . . . . '52 '81 C.347 B.S. L.221 J.D. [Carson B.]
Brandt, John H., (AV) . . . . '49 '78 C.347 B.S. L.851 J.D. [Beckman L.]
Bredemeier, Melvin W., (BV) '50 '76
C.347 A.B. L.1119 J.D. V.P. & Coun., Norwest Bk.-Ind.

Briggs, William L. . . . .'37 '75 C.347 B.S. L.879 J.D. Supr. Ct. J.
Brine, Jeffrey A. '48 '91 C.94 B.S. L.818 J.D.
(adm. in CT; not adm. in IN) Asst. V.P. & Coun., Lincoln Natl. Corp.
Brogan, Kathryn A., (AV) . . . .'53 '80 C.347 B.A. L.1119 J.D. [Rothberg L.&W.]
Bronsdon, James F., Jr. '56 '87 C.478 A.B. L.818 J.D.
(adm. in CT; not adm. in IN) Sage Life Assurance of America Inc.
Brooks, Betsy M. . . . .'— '05 C.36 B.A. L.851 J.D. [Ⓐ Baker&D.]
Brophy, Daniel E., (BV) . . . . '56 '84 C.475 B.A. L.912 J.D. [D.E.Brophy]
Brophy, Daniel E., LLC, (BV) . . . . .126 West Columbia Street Suite 300
Brown, D. Randall, (AV) . . . . '— '90 C.432 B.S. L.1119 J.D. [Barnes&T.]
Brown, Dean A., Law Office of, (BV) . . . '38 '71 C.679 B.A. L.1119 J.D. 5675 St. Joe Rd.
Brown, Dennis R., (BV) . . . .'73 '98 C.432 B.S. L.345 J.D. 809 South Calhoun Street
Brown, Elizabeth M. . . . . '59 '84 C.602 B.S. L.352 J.D. 5701 Reed Rd.‡
Brown, Kristi L., (BV) . . . . '65 '91 C.679 B.A. L.879 J.D. Coun., Norwest Bk.-Ind.
Bruggeman, Patrick . . . .'48 '73 C.813 B.A. L.309 J.D. P.O. Box 11529‡
Bruns, Kevin P., (CV) . . . .'66 '93 C.347 B.A. L.989 J.D. [Beers M.B.&S.] ⊙
Buchholz, James P., (BV) . . . . '63 '88 C.967 B.A. L.347 J.D. [Carson B.]
Bullman, John P., (BV) . . . .'45 '73 C.347 A.B. L.879 J.D. 1014 Webster St.
Bunnell, Scott L., (AV) . . . .'54 '83 C.475 B.A. L.1187 J.D. [Hunt S.K.]
Burke, Brian . . . . '55 '85 C.608 B.A. L.851 J.D. Coun., Lincoln Natl. Corp.
Burke, Larry J., (AV) . . . . '29 '54 C.63 A.B. L.477 LL.B. 1010 Loch Lomond Dr.
Burkhardt, Joshua A. . . . . '— '01 C.1161 B.A. L.607 J.D. [Ⓐ Beers M.B.&S.]
Burns, Gerald A., (AV) '49 '74 C.347 A.B. L.345 J.D.
V.P. & Gen. Coun., Triple Crown Services Company
Burns, John R., III, (AV) . . . .'49 '74 C.63 A.B. L.602 J.D. [Baker&D.]
Burns, Michael S. . . . .'— '01 C.894 A.B. L.345 J.D. [Ⓐ Baker&D.]
Burns, Scott C. '76 '01 C.911 B.A. L.880 J.D.
(adm. in CA; not adm. in IN) [Ⓐ Baker&D.]
Burt, J. Philip, (AV) . . . . '35 '61 C&L.477 B.A., LL.B. [Burt,B.D.S.&B.]

Burt, Blee, Dixon, Sutton & Bloom, LLP, (AV)
200 East Main Street, Suite 1000, 46802
Mailing Address: P.O. Box 10810, Ft. Wayne, IN 46854-0810
Telephone: 260-426-1300 Fax: 260-422-2722
Email: info@burtblee.com
Members of Firm: Alton Dale Bloom; J. Philip Burt; Jeffrey A. Clark; Timothy L. Claxton; Gregory Martin Cole; Robert E. Doelling, Jr.; W. Michael Horton; John T. Menzie; Michael C. Moellering; Carol Bennett Rhodes; Suzan L. Rutz; Wesley N. Steury; Dennis D. Sutton. Associates: Renee S. Bloom; Robert C. Kruger; William C. Butler; Shane C. Mulholland; Jeremy J. Grogg; Emily S. Patterson; Stephen J. Shumlas. Of Counsel: Thomas J. Blee; Allan E. Bloom; Thomas J. Dixon.
Appellate Practice, Banking, Bankruptcy and Creditor Rights, Business Law and Business Litigation, Commercial and Agricultural Financing, Corporate, Elder Law, Probate and Estate Planning, Family Law and Domestic Relations, Personal Injury Litigation and Product Liability, Real Estate, Interstate Adoptions, Taxation, Estate and Gift Tax.
Representative Clients: Standard Federal Bank; LaSalle National Bank; Ossian State Bank; Peoples Federal Savings Bank; Midwest Pipe & Steel, Inc.; Our Sunday Visitor; Pretzels, Inc.; Attorneys Title Group, Inc.; ABN AMRO Mortgage Group, Inc.
See Professional Biographies, FORT WAYNE, INDIANA

Butler, Abigail Marie . . . . '75 '00 C.317 B.S. L.475 J.D. [Ⓐ Baker&D.]
Butler, William C. . . . .'74 '00 C.475 B.A. L.213 J.D. [Ⓐ Burt,B.D.S.&B.]
Butz, James A. . . . . '61 '86 C.347 B.S. L.930 J.D. [Dahm&E.]
Campbell, Johanna J. . . . .'70 '04 C.1400 B.A. L.1187 J.D. [Perry]
Campbell, Stanley L., (BV) . . . .'50 '76 C.63 B.S. L.1119 J.D. [Swanson&C.]
Carlile, Brett A., (BV) . . . .'43 '99 C&L.347 B.S., J.D. [Carson B.]
Carlile, Peggy A. . . . .'74 '00 C.502 B.A. L.879 J.D. [Ⓐ Rothberg L.&W.]
Carney, Anne, (BV) . . . .'62 '87 C.347 B.A. L.602 J.D. [Rothberg L.&W.]
Carson, Philip L., (AV) . . . .'42 '67 C.210 B.A. L.1119 J.D. [Carson B.]

Carson Boxberger LLP, (AV)
1400 One Summit Square, 46802-3173 ⊙
Telephone: 260-423-9411 Telecopier: 260-423-4329
URL: http://www.carsonboxberger.com
Members of Firm: Philip L. Carson; Bruce O. Boxberger; Paul B. McNellis; John J. Wernet; Richard P. Samek; Phillip A. Renz; Edward J. Liptak (Resident, Bloomington, Indiana Office); Robert T. Keen, Jr.; Jon A. Bragalone; Larry L. Barnard; Arthur E. Mandelbaum; Diana C. Bauer; James P. Buchholz; Douglas A. Hoffman (Resident, Bloomington Office); Karl J. Veracco; M. Randall Spencer; Timothy M. Pape; Brett A. Carlile; Grant A. Liston; Jeremy M. Dilts (Resident, Bloomington Office); Benjamin Ice; Jeremy V. Senk; Marcia M. Yoder; Kevin P. Podlaski.
General Civil Trial and Appellate Practice in all State and Federal Courts. Corporate, Business Transactions, Financial Institutions, Health Care, Probate and Estate Planning, Family Law, Transportation Law and Administration, Civil Rights, Real Estate, Labor, Insurance, Medical and Professional Malpractice, Products Liability, Workers' Compensation, Commercial, Creditors Rights and Bankruptcy Law, Mediation, Municipal.
Representative Corporate and Financial Clients: Advanced Machine & Tool Corporation; Ford Motor Credit Company; Wal-Mart Inc.
Representative Insurance Clients: Bliss-McKnight Group; Employer's Mutual Company; Employers Mutual of Wausau; General Accident Fire & Life Assurance Corp., LTD.
Bloomington, Indiana Office: 3100 John Hinkle Place, Suite 106. Telephone: 812-333-1225. Fax: 812-333-1925.
See Professional Biographies, FORT WAYNE, INDIANA

Chalwick, Jerome T., (BV) '49 '74 C&L.339 B.S., J.D.
(adm. in IL; not adm. in IN) Asst.Coun., Essex Group, Inc.
Chambers, Mark C., (BV) . . . .'— '75 C.63 B.S. L.861 J.D. [Haller&C.]
Chapman, Howard L., (AV) . . . .'34 '58 C&L.597 B.S., LL.B. [Ⓒ Barrett&M.] ‡
Chapman, Stephen L., (BV) . . . .'55 '81 C.210 B.A. L.345 J.D. [Barrett&M.]
Chickedantz, C. Erik, (AV) . . . . '41 '72 C.870 B.A. L.477 J.D. [Hawk,H.K.&C.]
Christoff, Catherine S., (BV) . . . .'60 '85 C.597 B.S. L.347 J.D. [Christoff&C.]
Christoff, Joseph, (AV) . . . . '29 '54 C.347 B.A. L.1119 J.D. [Ⓒ Christoff&C.]
Christoff, Joseph A., (BV) . . . .'63 '90 C&L.347 B.S., J.D. [Christoff&C.]
Christoff & Christoff, (BV) . . . . .130 W. Main St.
Chrzan, Linda Peters, Law Offices of, (BV) '60 '86
C.57 B.A. L.879 J.D. 110 W. Berry St., Ste. 1700
Churchward, Anthony S., (BV) . . . . . '69 '98 C.1159 B.S. L.851 J.D. [Ⓐ Tremper,B.L.&T.]
Clagg, Jason T. . . . .'— '03 C.679 B.S. L.345 J.D. [Ⓐ Barnes&T.]
Clagg, Thomas L. '43 '70 C.350 B.S. L.352 J.D.
V.P. & Assoc. Gen. Coun., Lincoln Natl. Corp.‡
Clark, Gregory A. . . . .'51 '79 C.1154 B.A. L.345 J.D. 1 Summit Sq.‡
Clark, Jeffrey A., (BV) . . . . '65 '95 C&L.347 J.D. [Burt,B.D.S.&B.]
Claxton, Timothy L., (BV) . . . . '64 '89 C.347 B.S. L.1119 J.D. [Burt,B.D.S.&B.]
Clifford, Donald R., (P.C.), (BV) '31 '55 C&L.436 B.S., LL.B.
127 W. Berry St., Ste. 40
Clifton, John M., Jr., (AV) . . . .'37 '63 C.347 B.S. L.1119 J.D. [Barrett&M.]
Cline, Connie J. . . . . '63 '02 C.999 B.S.M. L.607 J.D. 201 E. Rudisill, Ste. 100
Cohen, H. Joseph, (BV) . . . . '70 '96 C&L.347 B.S., J.D. [Barrett&M.]
Cole, Gregory Martin, (BV) . . . .'61 '86 C.63 B.A. L.345 J.D. [Burt,B.D.S.&B.]
Colvin, Sherrill Wm., (AV) . . . .'— '65 C.894 A.B. L.1119 J.D. [Haller&C.]
Connelly, Matthew J., (AV) . . . . '49 '74 C&L.602 B.A., J.D. [Blume,C.J.&S.]
Connor, Timothy J., (AV) . . . .'39 '64 C.1024 B.A. L.1119 LL.B. 3601 Hobson Rd.
Cooper, Gregory S. . . . . '— '98 C.679 B.S. L.229 J.D. [Ⓐ Barnes&T.] (See Pat. Sect.)
Corbat, Sara S., (CV) . . . . .'62 '91 C.347 B.S. L.879 J.D. Assoc. Coun., Lincoln Natl. Corp.

Cormany, Cynthia M., (BV) .... '65 '90 C&L.347 B.A., J.D. [Ⓐ Baker&D.]
Cornelius, Terry L., (BV) .... '48 '74 C.347 B.S. L.345 J.D. [Cornelius&W.]
Cornelius & Weingartner, (BV) .... 919 S. Harrison St.
Cornwell, David D., (BV) .... '50 '76 C.347 A.B. L.1119 J.D. [Snyder B.C.&M.] ⊙
Cosbey, Roger B. .... '50 '75 C.932 B.A. L.851 J.D. U.S. Mag. J.
Cox, Adam F. .... '74 '99 C.473 B.S. L.347 J.D. [Ⓐ Baker&D.] (See Pat. Sect.)
Crell, Marvin S., (BV) .... '32 '57 C.347 A.B. L.1119 LL.B. [Tourkow,C.R.&J.]
Criso, Anthony J. .... '36 '70 C.1044 B.Mar.E. L.184 J.D. Secy., Essex Grp., Inc. (Pat.)
Culp, King K. '46 '72 C&L.608 B.A., J.D.
(adm. in OH; not adm. in IN) V.P. & Gen. Coun., Magnavox Electronics Systems Co.
Custer, Jason C., (CV) .... '72 '97 C.347 B.A. L.879 J.D. [Ⓐ Hunt S.K.]
Dahm, Albert J., (AV) .... '58 '83 C.973 B.S.B.A. L.345 J.D. [Dahm&E.] ⊙

Dahm & Elvin, LLP, (AV) BR
9604 Coldwater Road, Suite 201, 46825 ⊙
Telephone: 260-497-6000 Fax: 260-497-6019
URL: http://www.dahmelvin.com
Albert J. Dahm; Michael S. Elvin; Matthew S. Elvin (Not admitted in IN); James A. Butz;—Sandy L. Morris (Not admitted in IN); Matthew R. Shipman.
Drug & Medical Device Litigation, Product Liability, Class Action Defense, Federal Civil Litigation, Complex and Multi-District Litigation, Business Litigation.
Chicago, Illinois Office: 161 North Clark Street, Suite 1750, 60601. Phone: 312-683-3900. Fax: 312-683-3911.

See Professional Biographies, FORT WAYNE, INDIANA

Daley, William E. '44 '80 C.339 B.A. L.365 J.D.
(adm. in IL; not adm. in IN) Gen. Coun. & Secy., Medical Protective Co.
Daly, Patricia A. '52 '77 C.201 B.A. L.1119 J.D.
V.P. & Assoc. Gen. Coun., Lincoln Natl. Corp.
Danehy, Jack D., (BV) .... '26 '52 C.973 B.S. L.1119 LL.B. 5705 Old Mill Rd.
Daniel, Stephen C., (BV) '45 '76
C.63 B.S. L.345 J.D. 2nd V.P. & Sr. Coun., Lincoln Natl. Corp.
Davis, Bertrand A. .... '23 '53 C.231 A.B. L.1119 J.D. 4917 Reed Rd.‡
Davis, Charles E., (BV) .... '— '78 C.870 B.S. L.259 J.D. [Ⓐ Swift&F.]
Davis, Wendy W. .... '66 '91 C.937 B.A. L.879 J.D. [Beckman L.]
Deam, Michael T., (BV) .... '64 '89 C&L.347 B.S., J.D. [Rothberg L.&W.]
DeCamp, Richard R. .... '27 '52 C.679 B.S. L.1119 LL.B. 1655 St. Joe Ctr. Rd.‡
DeGroote, Timothy W., (BV) .... '69 '95 C.436 B.A. L.879 J.D. [Hunt S.K.]
Deller, Gerald .... '23 '52 C&L.879 A.B., J.D. Ret. Admin. Law J.
Den Houter, Joy E. .... '55 '84 C.323 B.A. L.602 J.D. K & K Ins. Grp., Inc.
Dever, Stephen E., (BV) .... '67 '95 C&L.347 B.S., J.D. [Hunt S.K.]
Dick, Andrea R. .... '— '03 C.1024 B.S. L.1119 J.D. [Ⓐ Beckman L.]
Dirig, Lisa M., (CV) .... '67 '99 C.999 B.A. L.475 J.D. [Ⓐ Nakos]
Dirig, Timothy R. .... '54 '79 C.347 B.S. L.345 J.D. 111 E. Wayne St.
Dixon, Thomas J., (AV) .... '29 '59 C.707 B.A. L.602 J.D. [Ⓒ Burt,B.D.S.&B.]
Doelling, Robert E., Jr., (BV) .... '63 '89 C.679 B.S. L.879 J.D. [Burt,B.D.S.&B.]
Donovan, J. Rickard, (BV) .... '68 '93 C.108 B.A. L.879 J.D. [Rothberg L.&W.]
Doss, Matthew A. .... '69 '02 C.347 B.S. L.589 J.D. 6009 Stoney Creek
Doxsee, Donald D., (BV) .... '37 '63 C.347 B.A. L.1119 J.D. 323 W. Berry St.
Drier, John C. .... '65 '91 C.373 B.A. L.879 J.D. [Blume,C.J.&S.]
Dubes, Charles C. .... '77 '03 C.210 B.A. L.1119 J.D. [Ⓐ Barrett&M.]
Duechle, Gary P. '55 '81 C.1161 B.S. L.1340 J.D.
(adm. in OH; not adm. in IN) The Medical Protective Co.
Durm, David P., (CV) .... '70 '98 C.347 B.S. L.1119 J.D. [Ⓐ Baker&D.]
Dykhuizen, Dennis F., (BV) .... '55 '80 C.347 B.S. L.1119 J.D. [Rothberg L.&W.]
Ediger, Catherine C., (BV) '57 '84 C.321 B.A. L.862 J.D.
Sr. V.P., Corp. Servs., Parkview Health System
Ediger, Gerald D., (BV) '51 '83
C.1421 B.A. L.862 J.D. Assoc. Gen. Coun., Medical Protective Co.
Eherenman, Robert W., (BV) .... '— '92 C.210 B.A. L.347 J.D. [Haller&C.]
Ehinger, Ronald J., (BV) .... '56 '82 C.854 B.S. L.602 J.D. [Barrett&M.]
Eilbacher, Leonard E., (AV) .... '34 '65 C.347 B.S. L.1119 J.D. [Eilbacher F.]

Eilbacher Fletcher LLP, (AV)
803 South Calhoun Street, Suite 400, 46802
Telephone: 260-425-9777 Fax: 260-424-9177
Email: admin@eflawyers.com URL: http://www.eflawyers.com
Members of Firm: Martin T. Fletcher, Sr.; Daniel G. McNamara; David E. Bailey; Leonard E. Eilbacher; Alan VerPlanck; James P. Fenton; Patrick L. Proctor.
Business Litigation, Commercial Litigation, Securities Law, Litigation and Arbitration, Insurance Law, Civil Mediation and Commercial Arbitration.

See Professional Biographies, FORT WAYNE, INDIANA

Ekpo, Mweni .... '72 '98 C.852 B.A. L.1119 J.D. Assoc. Coun., Lincoln Natl. Corp.
Elliott, Matthew J., (BV) .... '69 '98 C.477 A.B. L.309 J.D. [Beckman L.]
Elvin, Matthew S. '67 '92 C.105 B.A. L.1017 J.D.
(adm. in IL; not adm. in IN) [Dahm&E.] ⊙
Elvin, Michael S., (CV) .... '63 '88 C.105 B.S.B.A. L.597 J.D. [Dahm&E.] ⊙
Emley, Glenn A., (BV) .... '52 '77 C.347 A.B. L.436 J.D. [Emley]
Emley Law Office, (BV) .... 116 E. Berry Street, Suite 1700
Engeler, Frank D. .... '14 '40 C.679 B.S. L.145 J.D. 2209 St. Joe Ctr. Rd.‡
Essex, Thomas D. .... '61 '87 C.182 B.A. L.1119 J.D. E.E.O.
Evans, Ernest E. '33 '61
C.347 A.B. L.345 J.D. V.P. Emeritus, Three Rivers Title Co., Inc.‡
Ewing, Thomas C., (AV) .... '50 '75 C.679 B.S. L.1119 J.D. [Hunt S.K.]
Fagan, William P., (AV) .... '31 '56 C&L.602 A.B., J.D. 116 E. Berry St.
Falls, Margaret S. .... '47 '85 L.345 J.D. 323 W. Berry St.
Farnbauch, David L., (BV) .... '60 '86 C.249 B.S. L.879 J.D. [Sweeney]
Farr, Melanie L., (CV) .... '— '98 C.203 B.S. L.851 J.D. [Haller&C.]
Federoff, James A., (AV) .... '47 '75 C&L.912 B.A., J.D. [Federoff]
Federoff, Scott M., (BV) .... '71 '97 C.347 B.A. L.896 J.D. [Federoff]

Federoff Law Firm, LLP, (AV)
904 South Calhoun Street, 46802
Telephone: 260-407-0920 Fax: 260-407-7005
URL: http://www.federoff-law.com
James A. Federoff; Scott M. Federoff; Jason M. Kuchmay.
Commercial and Residential Real Estate Transactions and Development, Land Use and Zoning, Business Organizations and Transactions, Business and Commercial Litigation, Real Estate and Construction Litigation, Probate Litigation, Trademark and Copyright Law.

See Professional Biographies, FORT WAYNE, INDIANA

Feighner, John O., (AV) .... '— '76 C.103 A.B. L.345 J.D. [Haller&C.]
Felger, Ronald D., (BV) .... '53 '82 C.679 B.S. L.345 J.D. [Shambaugh,K.B.&W.]
Fellrath, Abbie Franke '70 '97
C&L.602 B.A., J.D. Coun., Amer. Elect. Power Serv. Corp.
Felts, Thomas J. .... '54 '79 C.602 B.A. L.1119 J.D. Mag., Allen Cir. Ct., Fam. Rel.
Fennessy, Michelle M., (BV) .... '62 '88 C.802 B.A. L.347 J.D. [Ⓐ Schenkel T.&K.]
Fenton, James P., (AV) .... '49 '76 C.178 A.B. L.1119 J.D. [Eilbacher F.]
Fink, Stephen L., (BV) .... '— '88 C.679 B.S. L.345 J.D. [Barnes&T.]
Fink, Thomas M., (AV) .... '47 '73 C.602 B.B.A. L.419 J.D. [Barrett&M.]
Finlayson, Craig R., (AV) .... '46 '73 C.347 B.S. L.345 J.D. [Swift&F.]
Firestone, Susan Lorraine, (BV) .... '55 '91 C.932 B.S. L.494 J.D. [O'Malley&F.]
Fisher, Edwin H., Jr. .... '57 '82 C.576 B.A. L.213 J.D. The Medical Protective Co.
Fishering, G. William, (BV) .... '50 '75 C.317 B.A. L.345 J.D. [Beers M.B.&S.]
Fitzharris, Kevin K., (AV) .... '65 '90 C.679 B.A. L.602 J.D. [Barrett&M.]
Fletcher, Martin T., Sr., (AV) .... '43 '69 C.221 B.A. L.1119 J.D. [Eilbacher F.]
Fogel, Sam, (AV) '26 '48 C.347 A.B. L.1119 J.D.
1100 Commerce Building (⊙Grabill, Monroeville)
Ford, Ralph A. '46 '72 C.512 B.A. L.94 J.D.
(adm. in MD; not adm. in IN) Sr. V.P. & Gen. Coun., North Amer. Van Lines, Inc.
Forrest, Christopher M. .... '— '02 C.432 B.A. L.1119 J.D. [Ⓐ Barnes&T.]
Fox, Richard E., (AV) .... '48 '73 C.597 B.S. L.1119 J.D. [Barrett&M.]
Fox, William P., (CV) .... '43 '84 C.705 B.A. L.345 J.D. [Fox]
Fox Law Offices, (CV) .... 6727 Pawawna Dr.
Frederick, Elizabeth A. '51 '77
C.347 A.B. L.1119 J.D. V.P. & Dep. Gen. Coun., Lincoln Natl. Corp.
Frew, Donald J., (BV) .... '64 '92 C.63 B.S. L.607 J.D. [Ⓐ Helmke,B.B.&W.]
Furst, Gary C., (BV) .... '— '96 C.333 B.A. L.879 J.D. [Barnes&T.]
Gallmeyer, Thomas M., (AV) .... '47 '72 C.165 B.A. L.1119 J.D. [Ⓒ Hawk,H.K.&C.]

Gehring, Ronald K., (BV) '41 '67 C.347 A.B. L.1119 J.D.
Suite 321 Metro Building, 202 West Berry Street, 46802-2242
Telephone: 260-422-6912 Fax: 260-422-6764
General Civil Trial Practice in all Courts. Personal Injury, Commercial, Corporate, Business, Probate, Bankruptcy, Real Estate and Family Law. Probate, Wills, Trusts and Estates.

See Professional Biographies, FORT WAYNE, INDIANA

Geisler, Brian Thomas '— '03 C.980 B.E. L.8 J.D.
(adm. in OH; not adm. in IN; See Pat. Sect.) [Ⓐ Baker&D.]
Gerardot, Jane M., (BV) .... '46 '90 C.347 B.S. L.477 J.D. [Boeglin,T.&G.]
Gery, Jeffrey V., (CV) .... '67 '94 C&L.347 B.A., J.D. [Ⓐ Baker&D.]
Gevers, Robert W., (AV) .... '60 '85 C.597 B.A. L.347 J.D. [Ⓐ Arata]
GiaQuinta, Mark E., (BV) .... '— '79 C.347 B.A. L.1119 J.D. [Haller&C.]
Gillenwater, Bobby B., (AV) '— '83
C.838 B.S.E.E. L.93 J.D. [Barnes&T.] (See Pat. Sect.)
Glaser, Steven J. .... '63 '90 C.63 B.S. L.1119 J.D. 116 E. Berry, Suite 1900
Goeglein, Andrew M., (BV) .... '56 '82 C.347 B.S. L.345 J.D. [Nieter&G.]
Goeglein, Jeffrey A. .... '— '04 C.347 B.S. L.1119 J.D. [Ⓐ Baker&D.]
Goetz, Shellie L. .... '70 '04 C.347 B.A. L.1119 J.D. [Ⓐ Baker&D.]
Golden, Dennis G. .... '64 '02 C.347 B.S. L.1187 J.D. [Golden]
Golden Law Office .... 614 West Berry Street
Gooden, Tiffany L. .... '— '03 C&L.352 B.A., J.D. [Ⓐ Barnes&T.]
Gosheff, Damian .... '— '05 C.347 B.S. L.851 J.D. [Ⓐ Baker&D.]
Goshorn, Richard W. .... '21 '48 C.347 B.S. L.1119 J.D. 5023 Camden Dr.
Gould, Trina Glusenkamp, (BV) .... '57 '82 C&L.879 B.A., J.D. [Helmke,B.B.&W.]
Graham, Shaun E., (BV) .... '— '95 C.602 B.A. L.347 J.D. [Barnes&T.]
Graly, Daniel M., (BV) .... '49 '74 C.347 B.A. L.1119 J.D. 116 E. Berry St.
Grant, Robert E. .... '54 '80 C.894 B.A. L.1017 J.D. U.S. Bkruptcy J.
Green, Raymond T., (BV) .... '52 '77 C.346 B.S. L.345 J.D. [Blackburn&G.]
Griebel, Stephen P., (BV) .... '64 '90 C.347 B.A. L.477 J.D. 202 W. Berry St., Ste. 200
Grogg, Jeremy J. .... '77 '03 C.679 B.A. L.345 J.D. [Ⓐ Burt,B.D.S.&B.]
Grossman, James R., (AV) .... '27 '52 C.347 A.B. L.1119 J.D. [Grossman&L.]

Grossman & Litchin LLP, (AV)
1600 Lincoln Tower, 46802
Telephone: 260-422-4706 Fax: 260-422-4708
URL: http://www.gllawfirm.com
Members of Firm: James R. Grossman; Kent C. Litchin.
General Civil Practice. Personal Injury, Probate, Family/Domestic Relations, Real Estate, Bankruptcy, Creditor's Rights.

See Professional Biographies, FORT WAYNE, INDIANA

Grover, Ann C. '50 '75 C.477 A.B. L.1066 J.D.
(adm. in CA; not adm. in IN) Adm. Law J., Soc. Sec. Admn.
Grunden, April S. .... '69 '97 C.347 B.S. L.879 J.D. [Grunden]

Grunden Law Office
Building 3, 10355 Dawson's Creek Boulevard, Suite C, 46825
Telephone: 260-969-1177 Fax: 260-497-9747
URL: http://www.grundenlaw.com
April S. Grunden.
Estate Planning, Guardianship, Business Planning, Family Law, General Litigation.

See Professional Biographies, FORT WAYNE, INDIANA

Gulley, Jeffrey J. .... '63 '88 C.510 A.B. L.1119 J.D. V.P., SRA-USA
Haffner, Timothy J., (BV) .... '59 '85 C.894 B.A. L.1119 J.D. [Baker&D.]
Haist, David A., (AV) '51 '77 C.432 B.S. L.345 J.D.
Exec. V.P. & Corp. Oper. Offr., Do it Best Corp.
Hall, M. Scott, (BV) .... '— '86 C.1230 B.A. L.347 J.D. [Barnes&T.]
Haller, Robert W., (AV) .... '— '54 C.347 A.B. L.1119 J.D. [Haller&C.]

Haller & Colvin, P.C., (AV)
444 East Main Street, 46802
Telephone: 260-426-0444 Telefax: 260-422-0274
URL: http://www.hallercolvin.com
Robert W. Haller; Sherrill Wm. Colvin; Stephen E. Lewis; Vincent J. Heiny; John O. Feighner; Mark E. GiaQuinta; Mark C. Chambers; George Sistevaris; Cynthia P. Rockwell; Robert W. Eherenman; Suzanne Hampton Wagner; Charles J. Heiny; Martin E. Seifert; Melanie L. Farr;—Lori W. Jansen; Duane J. Snow.
Languages: Spanish, German.
Civil and Commercial Litigation in Federal and State Courts. Personal Injury, Wrongful Death, Products Liability, Land Use and Zoning, Domestic Relations, Employment Law, Real Estate Transactions, Taxation, Estate Planning and Administration, Hospital and Health Care, General Corporate Law, and Environmental Law, Bankruptcy and Creditor Rights.

See Professional Biographies, FORT WAYNE, INDIANA

Hammond, Randall J., (BV) .... '55 '81 C&L.879 B.S., J.D. [Tremper,B.L.&T.]
Hampshire, Sherie L., (AV) .... '57 '82 C.63 B.A. L.879 J.D. [Hampshire&Assoc.]

Hampshire & Associates, P.C., (AV)
803 South Calhoun, Suite 201, 46802
Telephone: 260-423-3637 Fax: 260-420-1182
Sherie L. Hampshire.
Family Law, Domestic Relations, Child Custody.
Reference: Wells Fargo Bank.

See Professional Biographies, FORT WAYNE, INDIANA

Hampton Wagner, Suzanne, (BV) .... '— '88 C.136 B.S. L.1187 J.D. [Haller&C.]
Hand, Steven S. .... '72 '02 C.347 B.A. L.879 J.D. [Ⓐ Hunt S.K.]
Harants, Stephen J., (BV) .... '69 '94 C.265 B.A. L.347 J.D. [Miller M.&M.]
Hardin, Thomas A., (BV) .... '70 '96 C.477 B.A. L.345 J.D. [Shine&H.]
Hardy, David Lott .... '44 '69 C.347 A.B. L.1119 J.D. 5625 Autumn Woods Trail
Hardy, Sherry F. .... '43 '76 C.679 B.S. L.345 J.D. Sr. Coun., Lincoln Natl. Corp.

Harlan, Jeffrey S., (BV) '59 '84 C.347 A.B. L.345 J.D.
V.P. & Coun., First Land Title Co.
Harmeyer, Michael D., (BV) '63 '88 C.249 B.S. L.602 J.D. [Harmeyer]
Harmeyer Law Firm LLC, (BV) 200 E. Main St., Ste. 630
Harris, William E., (AV) '38 '63 C.210 B.A. L.477 J.D. [Moss&H.]
Hart, Wayne A., (BV) '26 '52 C&L.793 B.S., LL.B. Metro Bldg.
Hartman, Georgia L., (CV) '62 '97 C.679 B.A. L.347 J.D. Legal Coun.
Havrilla-Lennox, Felicity '71 '96 C.679 B.S. L.1119 J.D. Legal Coun., PEJUS, Inc.
Hawk, David K., (BV) '48 '73 C.347 B.S. L.1119 J.D. [Hawk,H.K.&C.]
Hawk, Melissa Garland '75 '01 C.932 B.A. L.879 J.D. [A Hunt S.K.]
Hawk, Michael D., (BV) '74 '00 C.347 B.A. L.879 J.D. 803 S. Calhoun Street
Hawk Gutman, Carrie, (BV) '70 '95 C&L.347 B.A., J.D. [A Hawk,H.K.&C.]
Hawk, Haynie, Kammeyer & Chickedantz, (AV) 116 E. Berry St., Ste. 302
Hayes, Cornelius B. (Neil), (AV) '52 '80 C.347 B.S. L.1187 J.D. [Hayes&H.]
Hayes, Jerome Byron '— '05 C.303 B.A. L.1119 J.D. [A Baker&D.]

Hayes & Hayes, (AV)
Third Floor, Eight Ten Building, 810 South Calhoun Street, 46802
Telephone: 260-420-1800 Facsimile: 260-420-1809
Email: hayesneil@aol.com URL: http://www.hayesandhayeslaw.com
C. Byron Hayes (1891-1975); J. Byron Hayes (1920-1986); Cornelius B. (Neil) Hayes.
Family Law (all areas), Divorce, Dissolution of Marriage, Civil Trial Practice in all State and Federal Courts. General Practice.
See Professional Biographies, FORT WAYNE, INDIANA

Haynie, Gilmore S., Jr., (BV) '47 '73 C.347 B.S. L.1119 J.D. [Hawk,H.K.&C.]
Hazelrigg, Steven H., (BV) '52 '77 C.210 B.A. L.1119 J.D. [Baker&D.]
Heath, Daniel G., (BV) '53 '84 C&L.347 B.A., J.D. Supr. Ct. J.
Heck, Brian C. '— '99 C.494 B.S. L.1119 J.D. [A Beckman L.]
Heiney, John H., (AV) '34 '58 C.347 A.B. L.1119 J.D. [C Rothberg L.&W.]
Heiny, Charles J., (BV) '— '90 C.347 B.S. L.345 J.D. [Haller&C.]
Heiny, Vincent J., (AV) '— '76 C.347 A.B. L.345 J.D. [Haller&C.]
Helfrich, Leonard J., (BV) '54 '79 C&L.608 B.A., J.D. Sr. Coun., Lincoln Natl. Corp.
Helmke, Paul, (BV) '— '73 C.347 B.A. L.976 J.D. [C Helmke,B.B.&W.]
Helmke, Walter P., (AV) '27 '52 C.347 A.B. L.879 J.D. [Helmke,B.B.&W.]

Helmke, Beams, Boyer & Wagner, (AV) BR
202 W. Berry Street, Suite 300, 46802-2242
Telephone: 260-422-7422 Telecopier: 260-422-6764
URL: http://www.hbbwlaw.com
Members of Firm: Walter E. Helmke (1901-1976); Walter P. Helmke; R. David Boyer; Robert A. Wagner; J. Timothy McCaulay; Daniel J. Borgmann; Trina Glusenkamp Gould. Associates: R. David Boyer, II; Donald J. Frew. Of Counsel: Glen J. Beams; William A. Berning; Paul Helmke.
General Civil and Trial Practice. Indiana and Federal Courts, Corporate, Commercial, Insurance, Real Estate, Probate and Estate Planning, Insolvency and Municipal Law.
Representative Clients: Aalco Distributing Co., Inc.; Brotherhood Mutual Insurance Co.; Fremont Community Schools; Air-O-Mat, Inc.; Leo Distributors, Inc.; The City of Fort Wayne, Indiana; Foellinger Foundation, Inc.
See Professional Biographies, FORT WAYNE, INDIANA

Helstrom, W. Richard '22 '48 C.210 A.B. L.273 J.D.
(adm. in DC; not adm. in IN) 1728 Dunbarton Lane‡
Herr, Thomas A., (AV) '56 '82 C.784 B.A. L.221 J.D. [Barrett&M.]
Hess, Patrick R., (BV) '62 '96 C.679 B.S. L.150 J.D. [Beckman L.]
Higgins, G. Michael '50 '81
C.999 B.A. L.851 J.D. Asst. V.P. & Dir., Reinsurance Controls
Hill, E. Franklin, Jr. '40 '66 C.347 B.A L.477 J.D. [A Swift&F.]
Hockensmith, Robert R. '28 '71 C.347 L.345 LL.B. Supr. Ct. J.
Hofer, Alan K., (BV) '50 '81 C.347 A.B. L.1119 J.D. 203 W. Wayne St.
Hoffman, Douglas A., (BV) '65 '90 C.967 B.A. L.347 J.D. [Carson B.] ⊙
Hoffman, John E., (AV) '15 '39 C&L.228 A.B., J.D. 110 W Berry St.
Hoffman, John F., (AV) '47 '72 C.602 B.S. L.273 J.D. [Baker&D.] (See Pat. Sect.)
Hoffman, Julie Annette '74 '02 C.303 B.A. L.602 J.D. [A Baker&D.]
Hogan, Cynthia A., Law Office of '56 '03
C.854 B.S. L.1187 J.D. 110 W. Berry Street, Suite 1912
Hohman, Matthew M., (BV) '— '98 C.333 B.S. L.494 J.D. [A Barnes&T.]
Holleran, Clifford A., (BV) '43 '71 C.801 B.A. L.1119 J.D.
4630 W. Jefferson Boulevard
Hood, G. Stanley, (AV) '38 '66 C.347 B.S. L.345 J.D. [Roby H.&M.]
Hopkins, William T. (Tuck), Jr., (AV) '— '77 C.602 B.S.E.E. L.734 J.D. [Barnes&T.]
Horton, N. Thomas, II, (AV) '44 '70 C.347 A.B. L.477 J.D. [Barrett&M.]
Horton, W. Michael, (BV) '45 '73 C.347 B.A. L.1119 J.D. [Burt,B.D.S.&B.]
Houk, Phillip E. '61 '86 C.347 B.A. L.879 J.D. Supr. Ct.Mag.
Houser, Jason A. '77 '04 C.679 B.S.E.E. L.879 J.D. [A Baker&D.] (See Pat. Sect.)
Howard, James T., (CV) '60 '94 C.1070 B.S. L.1339 J.D. 1 E. Main Street, Room 940
Hubbard, Grant R. '30 '69 C.516 B.S. L.365 J.D. [G.R.Hubbard]
Hubbard, Grant R., P.C. P.O. Box 15307
Huffman, Jonathan R. '78 '05 C.879 B.S. L.347 J.D. [A Miller M.&M.]
Hultquist, Kerry M., (CV) '71 '98 C.125 B.A. L.190 J.D. [A Wyss&M.]
Hultquist, Roger W., (BV) '37 '66 C.475 B.A. L.502 J.D. 110 W. Berry St.

Hunt Suedhoff Kalamaros LLP, (AV)
803 South Calhoun Street, Ninth Floor, P.O. Box 11489, 46858-1489 ⊙
Telephone: 260-423-1311 Fax: 260-424-5396
URL: http://www.hsk-law.com
Members of Firm: P. Michael Miller; Robert E. Kabisch; David A. Stewart; Arthur G. Surguine, Jr.; Thomas C. Ewing; Michael D. Mustard; Branch R. Lew; James J. Shea, Sr.; Scott L. Bunnell; Dane L. Tubergen; Carolyn M. Trier; Kathleen A. Kilar; N. Jean Schendel; Timothy W. DeGroote; Stephen E. Dever; Linda A. Polley; Daniel J. Palmer. Associates: Jason C. Custer; Orfej Petar Najdeski; Melissa Garland Hawk; Andrew S. Williams; Steven S. Hand; Richard W. Karcher.
General Civil Trial and Appellate Practice. Insurance Defense Litigation. Commercial Real Estate Financing and Transactions. Corporate and Commercial Law. Probate and Estate Planning.
South Bend, Indiana Office: 120 West LaSalle Avenue, Twelfth Floor, P.O. Box 4156, 46634-4156. Telephone: 574-232-4801. Fax: 574-232-9736.
Indianapolis, Indiana Office: 6323 S. East Street, 46227. Telephone: 317-784-4966. Fax: 317-784-5566.
St. Joseph, Michigan Office: 608 S. Pleasant Street, P.O. Box 46, 49085-0046. Telephone: 269-983-4405. Fax: 269-983-5645.
See Professional Biographies, FORT WAYNE, INDIANA

Hunter, Jack D., (AV) '37 '61 C&L.477 B.B.A., LL.B.
Exec. V.P. & Gen. Coun., Lincoln Natl. Corp.‡
Ice, Benjamin '76 '01 C.63 B.S. L.347 J.D. [Carson B.]
Irmscher, David P., (BV) '56 '82 C.197 A.B. L.477 J.D. [Baker&D.]
Jackson, Melissa M. '63 '88 C.347 B.A. L.602 J.D. Lincoln Life Ins. Co.
Jackson, Steven L., (AV) '51 '78 C.679 B.A. L.1119 J.D. [Baker&D.]
James, Donald E. '58 '85 C.763 B.A. L.1065 J.D. Legal Servs. Corp.
James, Michael L., (BV) '51 '77 C.249 B.A. L.1119 J.D. [Baker&D.]
James, Ronald E., (BV) '54 '79 C.347 A.B. L.1119 J.D. [Benson,P.M.J.&L.]
Jansen, Lori W. '— '96 C.679 B.S. L.879 J.D. [A Haller&C.]
Jarjour, Samuel W., (BV) '61 '90 C.63 B.S. L,879 J.D. [Snow&S.]
Jaubert, Nicole T. T. '67 '96 C.217 B.A. L.861 J.D. [N.Jaubert]
Jaubert, Nicole 202 W. Berry St.
Johnson, Gary D., (BV) '66 '91 C.347 B.S. L.345 J.D. [C Beckman L.]
Johnson, Tandra S., (CV) '54 '98 C.347 B.S.N. L.345 J.D. [T.S.Johnson]
Johnson, William M. '56 '96 C.101 B.S. L.1119 J.D.
Swiss Re Life & Health America Inc.
Johnson, Tandra S., LLC, (CV) 904 South Calhoun Street
Johnston, Douglas E., (BV) '57 '82 C.210 B.A. L.879 J.D. [Tourkow,C.R.&J.]
Johnston, Mark E. '62 '87 C.347 B.A. L.1119 J.D. UAW-GM Legal Services Plan
Jones, Carolyn B. '43 '79 C&L.608 B.S., J.D. Sr. Coun., Lincoln Natl. Corp.
Jones-Davis, Bettye A. '38 '76 C.992 B.A. L.347 J.D. Sr. Coun., Lincoln Natl. Corp.
Jordan, Denver C., (BV) '53 '80 C.679 B.S.B.A. L.1119 J.D. [Blume,C.J.&S.]
Juba, Mark F. '76 '03 L.602 J.D. [A Baker&D.]
Kabisch, Robert E., (AV) '42 '68 C.679 B.A. L.1119 J.D. [Hunt S.K.]
Kammeyer, W. Randall, (BV) '65 '92 C.679 B.S.I.E. L.347 J.D. [Hawk,H.K.&C.]
Karcher, Richard W., (CV) '65 '99 C.347 B.S. L.1187 J.D. [A Hunt S.K.]
Kast, Michael H., (AV) '28 '52 C.347 B.S. L.1119 LL.B. [Shambaugh,K.B.&W.]
Keaton, R. Mark '63 '91 C.567 B.A. L.347 J.D.
(adm. in IL; not adm. in IN) P.O. Box 11208
Keen, Robert T., Jr., (AV) '57 '82 C&L.602 B.A., J.D. [Carson B.]
Kiefer, Mark Emerson, (BV) '60 '86 C.347 B.A. L.1119 J.D. 202 W. Berry St.
Kilar, Kathleen A., (BV) '62 '87 C&L.477 A.B., J.D. [Hunt S.K.]
Kimbrough, J. Frank, & Associates, (AV) '42 '68
C.210 B.A. L.1119 J.D. 803 South Calhoun Street
Kimbrough, Thomas M., (AV) '54 '80 C.347 B.A. L.345 J.D. [Barrett&M.]
Kimmell, Joseph W., II, (AV) '47 '72 C.228 B.A. L.477 J.D.
[Baker&D.] (⊙Wash., DC)

King, Mark A., Attorney at Law
(See Indianapolis)

Kingdon, V. Scott '50 '76 C.347 A.B. L.273 J.D. Sr. Coun., Lincoln Natl. Corp.
Kiplinger, Roy F., (BV) '65 '91 C&L.477 B.A., J.D. [Beers M.B.&S.]
Kittaka, Mark S., (BV) '— '92 C.347 B.A. L.910 J.D. [Barnes&T.]
Kleven, Yvette Gaff, (BV) '58 '83 C.477 B.A. L.347 J.D. [Skekloff,A.&K.]
Klutz, Zachary E. '78 '05 C.347 B.A. L.345 J.D. [A Barrett&M.]
Knight, John S., (BV) '44 '72 C.679 B.A. L.1119 J.D. [Parrish&K.]
Knight, Thomas J. '54 '80 C.63 B.S. L.345 J.D. [Perry]
Knox, Noel Hollis '51 '83 C.388 B.A. L.1119 J.D.
(adm. in OH; not adm. in IN) Fifth Third Bank
Knox, Rheba J. '51 '84 C&L.329 B.A., J.D. City Atty's Off.
Knuth, Randall J., (BV) '64 '90 C.688 B.S. L.200 J.D. [R.J.Knuth] (Pat.)
Knuth, Randall J., P.C., (BV) 4921 Desoto Dr. (Pat.)
Kobil, Walter '26 '56 C&L.851 B.E., J.D.
(adm. in OH; not adm. in IN) 3425 Bramblewood Ln.
Koday, James, (AV) '51 '76 C.347 A.B. L.1119 J.D. [Bewley&K.]
Kolhoff, David J. '50 '85 C.381 B.A. L.7 J.D.
(adm. in OH; not adm. in IN) Sr. Coun., Lincoln Natl. Corp.
Komisarow, Marvin L. '27 '51 C.347 B.S. L.597 J.D. [Komisarow&B.] ‡
Komisarow & Baach 6734 Mallard Cove Pl.
Kos, Edmund P., (BV) '58 '84 C.1021 B.A. L.982 J.D. [Kos&Assoc.]

Kos & Associate, (BV)
110 West Berry Street Suite 1904, 46802-2374
Telephone: 260-424-2790 Fax: 260-424-1872
Email: ekos@ekoslaw.com URL: http://www.lawyers.com/ekoslaw
Edmund P. Kos. Associate: Steven J. Bradford.
Bankruptcy, Creditors' Rights, Banking Law, Foreclosures, Collections, Commercial Litigation, Commercial Transactions, Corporate Law, Real Estate and Secured Transactions.
See Professional Biographies, FORT WAYNE, INDIANA

Kowalczyk, George, (AV) '11 '36 C&L.966 Ph.B., J.D. [C Schenkel T.&K.]
Kowalczyk, John R., (BV) '46 '72 C&L.602 A.B., J.D. [Schenkel T.&K.]

Krieg DeVault Lundy LLP, (AV)
825 Anthony Wayne Building, 203 East Berry Street, 46802 ⊙
Telephone: 260-422-1534 Fax: 260-423-1590
Email: contact@kdlegal.com URL: http://www.kriegdevault.com
Partner: David A. Lundy.
Acquisitions, Divestitures and Mergers, Antitrust, Appeals, Banking, Bankruptcy, Business and Commercial, Copyright, Corporations, Creditors' Rights, Employee Benefits, Energy, Environmental, ERISA, Estate Planning and Probate, Family/Domestic Relations, Federal and State Taxation, Government Relations, Health Care, Hospital Law, Intellectual Property, Insurance, International, Labor and Employment, Legislative, Litigation, Patent, Public Finance, Public Utilities, Products Liability, Real Estate, Securities Law, Tax-Exempt and Nonprofit Organizations, Technology and E-Commerce, Trademark.
Indianapolis, Indiana Office: Krieg DeVault LLP, One Indiana Square, Suite 2800, 46204. Telephone: 317-636-4341. Fax: 317-636-1507.
Indianapolis Northside Office: 12800 North Meridian Street, Suite 300, Carmel, Indiana 46032. Telephone: 317-566-1110. Fax: 317-636-1507.
Hammond, Indiana Office: Krieg DeVault Galvin LLP, 5231 Hohman Avenue, 46320. Telephone: 219-933-0380. Fax: 219-933-0471.
See Professional Biographies, FORT WAYNE, INDIANA

Krisher, Ralph E., Jr. '38 '66 C.150 M.E. L.273 J.D. 3409 Rosewood Drive (Pat.)
Kruger, Robert C. '72 '01 C.679 B.A. L.1119 J.D. [A Burt,B.D.S.&B.]
Kuchmay, Jason M., (CV) '71 '98 C.475 B.A. L.851 J.D. [Federoff]
Kuker, David J., (BV) '67 '95 C.145 A.B. L.879 J.D. [Baker&D.]
Kus, Susan Hobson, (BV) '64 '89
C.347 B.S. L.1119 J.D. Sr. Coun., North American Van Lines
Kus, Thomas C., (BV) '— '89 C.477 B.A. L.1119 J.D. [A Baker&D.]
Lamp, Sandra G. '50 '76 C.347 B.S. L.345 J.D. Sr. Coun., Lincoln Natl. Corp.
Lange, Brian J., (CV) '59 '89 C.592 B.A. L.1187 J.D. 520 South Calhoun Street
Lanning, Oliver W. '14 '40 C.210 A.B. L.597 J.D. 110 W. Berry St.‡
Larmore, Philip H., (BV) '40 '65 C.347 A.B. L.1119 J.D. 202 West Berry Street
Lauer, Daniel L., (BV) '65 '91 C&L.347 B.S., J.D. 110 W. Berry St.
Lauer, Joletta C. '61 '86 C.128 B.A. L.273 J.D. Coun., Lincoln Natl. Corp.
Lawson, Jack W., (AV) '35 '61 C&L.879 B.A., J.D. [Beckman L.]

Leal, John R., (AV) '29 '61 C&L.879 A.B., J.D.
Metro Building, Suite 710, 202 West Berry Street, 46802
Telephone: 260-424-3104 Fax: 260-426-3360
Probate and Estate Planning, Estate Administration, Trusts, Wills, Elder Law, Real Estate, Guardianships, Corporate Law, Immigration Law.
References: Bankone, NA; National City Bank; Wells Fargo Bank; Tower Bank.
See Professional Biographies, FORT WAYNE, INDIANA

Lebamoff, Ivan A. '32 '57 C.347 B.A. L.1119 J.D. 918 S. Calhoun St.
Lebrato, Gary D. '50 '77 C.347 A.B. L.365 J.D. 6424 Bluffton Rd.
Lee, Judy Jung-Yoon '69 '00 C.645 B.S. L.831 J.D. 11025 Shiregreen Ln.
Lee, Lawrence H. '44 '69 C.347 B.A. L.309 J.D. 13818 Aboite Center Rd.
Lee, William C. '38 '62 C.976 A.B. L.145 J.D. U.S. Dist. J.
Lehman, Michael F. '41 '68 C.347 B.S. L.1119 J.D. 8405 Greenwich Ct.
Leininger, Daniel K., (AV) '51 '76 C.347 A.B. L.1119 J.D. [C Beers M.B.&S.]
Lemert, Martha M., (BV) '67 '93 C.881 A.B. L.930 J.D. [A Baker&D.]

Leonard, Charles F., (AV) ... '42 '73 C.63 B.S. L.602 J.D. [Tremper,B.L.&T.]
Leonard, Deborah M. ... '50 '79 C.170 B.A. L.347 J.D. U.S. Attorney's Off.
Levine, Stanley A. ... '38 '63 C.347 A.B. L.1119 LL.B. Supr. Ct. J.
Lew, Branch R., (AV) ... '57 '82 C.347 B.S. L.1119 J.D. [Hunt S.K.]
Lewis, Marc Evan, (BV) ... '55 '81 C.383 B.S.B.E. L.608 J.D. 1 Summit Square
Lewis, Stephen E., (AV) ... '— '69 C&L.879 B.A., J.D. [Haller&C.]
Lindberg, Jon L. '78 '03 C.970 B.A. L.8 J.D.
(adm. in OH; not adm. in IN) [Baker&D.]
Liston, Grant A. ... '72 '00 C.347 B.S. L.345 J.D. [Carson B.]
Litchin, Kent C., (BV) ... '58 '85 C.347 B.S. L.61 J.D. [Grossman&L.]
Litton, Arthur C., II '44 '68 C&L.383 B.A., J.D.
(adm. in WV; not adm. in IN) General Counsel, Triple Crown Services Company

Locke, Thomas S., (AV) '45 '71 C.602 B.B.A. L.879 J.D.
520 South Calhoun Street, 46802-1290
Telephone: 260-424-1333 Fax: 260-422-5242
Email: tslockeesq@aol.com
Associate: Zachary A. Witte.
Civil Trial Practice in all State Courts. Personal Injury including Wrongful Death, Probate, Estate Planning and Administration, Elder Law, Business, Real Estate Law, Adoption.
Representative Clients: Maysville Regional Sewer District; NCS, Inc., (Health Care).
Reference: NBD Bank, N.A.
See Professional Biographies, FORT WAYNE, INDIANA

Logan, F. L. Dennis, (AV) ... '51 '77 C.210 B.A. L.879 J.D. [Rothberg L.&W.]
Logan, Richard D. ... '28 '53 C.976 A.B. L.1119 J.D. 6941 46th Dr.
Logan, Thomas D., (AV) ... '29 '53 C.602 B.S. L.1119 LL.B. [Rothberg L.&W.]
Logan, Timothy, (BV) ... '59 '84 C.347 B.S. L.345 J.D. [Benson,P.M.J.&L.]
Logan & Stier, (BV) ... 116 E. Berry St. #1525
Longsworth, Jeanne E., (AV) ... '56 '87 C.347 B.S. L.879 J.D. [Baker&D.]
Loomis, J. Michael, (BV) ... '56 '82 C.347 B.A. L.201 J.D. Dep. Pros.
Lowenstein, Solomon L., Jr., (BV) ... '46 '72 C.861 B.A. L.836 J.D. 614 W. Berry St.
Luarde, Frank T. '32 '64 C.930 B.B.A. L.608 J.D.
(adm. in OH; not adm. in IN) 5215 Trier Road, Suite #1200
Lundy, David A., (AV) ... '34 '63 C&L.477 B.S., J.D. [Krieg D.L.] (Pat.)
Lutz, David M., (BV) ... '64 '89 C.347 B.A. L.930 J.D. [D.M.Lutz]
Lutz, David M., LLC, (BV) ... 3344 Mallard Cove Lane
Lyon, J. Barton ... '59 '84 C.5 B.A. L.851 J.D. The Medical Protective Co.
Lyons, John F., (AV) ... '44 '69 C.347 B.S. L.1119 J.D. [Barrett&M.]
Mallers, Peter G., (AV) ... '51 '76 C.894 B.A. L.879 J.D. [Beers M.B.&S.]
Malloy, Jane E., (BV) ... '55 '86 C.201 B.A. L.879 J.D. [Steele,U.&M.]
Mandelbaum, Arthur E., (BV) ... '64 '89 C.347 B.S. L.1119 J.D. [Carson B.]
Manges, Thomas A., (BV) ... '66 '92 C.303 B.A. L.347 J.D. [Roby H.&M.]
Manges, Timothy A., (BV) ... '64 '89 C.309 A.B. L.1119 J.D. City Atty.
Mapes, Christopher L. '62 '89 C.63 B.S. L.851 J.D.
(adm. in MI; not adm. in IN) Dir., Human Res., Essex Grp., Inc.
Markle, Thomas J., (BV) ... '60 '86 C.347 B.S. L.345 J.D. [Barrett&M.]
Martin, George, (BV) ... '45 '71 C.347 A.B. L.145 J.D. 3442 Stellhorn Rd.
Martin, John P., (AV) ... '53 '78 C&L.347 A.B., J.D. [Barrett&M.]
Maser, Laura L., (BV) ... '69 '97 C&L.851 B.A., J.D. [Beers M.B.&S.]
Mattox, Dawn Snow, (BV) ... '66 '92 C.473 B.A. L.347 J.D. [Barrett&M.]
Maxfield, Kenneth W. ... '24 '50 C.424 L.209 J.D. 110 W. Berry St.
McAlister, Dalton C. ... '21 '48 C.821 B.A. L.477 J.D. Ret. Supr. Ct. J.
McCaulay, J. Timothy, (AV) ... '49 '75 C.198 A.B. L.1119 J.D. [Helmke,B.B.&W.]
McEntee, Michael R., (BV) ... '50 '77 C.347 B.S. L.1119 J.D. [Bowman&M.]
McIntosh, Jerry L., Law Office, (CV) '42 '72
C.432 B.S. L.345 J.D. 3601 Hobson Rd., Ste. 208
McLemore, Doyal E., Jr. ... '52 '77 C.347 A.B. L.1119 J.D. [McLemore]

McLemore Firm, The
206 Courtside Building, 803 South Calhoun Street, P.O. Box 15606, 46885-5606
Telephone: 260-426-4451 Fax: 260-422-7469
Email: dmclemore@fortwaynelawyer.com
Doyal E. McLemore, Jr.
General, Trial and Appellate Practice. Federal and State Courts. Business, Commercial, Corporate, Criminal and Personal Injury Law.
See Professional Biographies, FORT WAYNE, INDIANA

McNagny, Charles W., (BV) ... '50 '76 C.309 A.B. L.1119 J.D. 116 East Berry Street
McNagny, William F., (AV) ... '22 '47 C.821 L.1119 LL.B. [Barrett&M.] ‡
McNamara, Daniel G., (BV) ... '62 '91 C.602 B.A. L.347 J.D. [Eilbacher F.]
McNellis, Paul B., (BV) ... '37 '62 C.321 B.S. L.602 LL.B. [Carson B.]
Menzie, John T., (BV) ... '45 '81 C&L.879 B.A., J.D. [Burt,B.D.S.&B.]
Michaels, Patrick G., (AV) ... '46 '73 C.602 B.B.A. L.276 J.D. [Barrett&M.]
Michmerhuizen, Michael H., (BV) ... '73 '99 C.1265 B.B.A. L.477 J.D. [Barrett&M.]
Mileff, John Ward ... '62 '95 C.679 B.S. L.37 J.D. 918 south Calhoun
Miller, Calvert S., (BV) ... '67 '94 C&L.347 B.S., J.D. [Miller M.&M.]
Miller, David H., (AV) ... '41 '73 C.63 B.S. L.477 J.D. Asst. U.S. Atty
Miller, Douglas E., (AV) ... '40 '65 C.350 B.S. L.352 J.D. 200 E. Main St., Ste. 800
Miller, Elizabeth D. '43 '77 C.383 B.S. L.421 J.D.
(adm. in KY; not adm. in IN) Merrill Lynch & Co., Inc.
Miller, Gregory A. ... '69 '97 C.679 B.S. L.1187 J.D. [Miller]
Miller, Mickey M., (AV) '20 '48 C.347 B.S. L.1119 J.D.
110 W. Berry Street, Suite 1800‡
Miller, Milford M., Jr., (AV) ... '— '62 C.197 A.B. L.1119 J.D. [Miller M.&M.]
Miller, P. Michael, (BV) ... '38 '65 C&L.347 A.B., J.D. [Hunt S.K.]
Miller, Roger ... '43 '81 C.679 B.S. L.345 J.D. Navistar Intl. Corp. (Pat.)
Miller, Ted S., (AV) ... '32 '60 C.475 A.B. L.1119 J.D. [Barrett&M.] ‡
Miller, Timothy W., (AV) ... '51 '82 C.145 A.B. L.1119 J.D. 6204 Post Brook Ln.
Miller Law Offices ... 127 West Berry Street

Miller Murphy & Miller, L.L.P., (AV)
110 West Berry Street, Suite 1500, 46802
Telephone: 260-423-1500 Fax: 260-458-8191
Email: info@millermurphymiller.com URL: http://www.millermurphymiller.com
Milford M. Miller, Jr.; Edward L. Murphy, Jr.; Calvert S. Miller; Stephen J. Harants. Associates: Jason A. Scheele; Jonathan R. Huffman; Michael A. Barranda.
Appellate Practice, Alternative Dispute Resolution, Administrative Law, Civil Practice, Civil Rights, Commercial Law, Construction Law, Contracts, Corporate Law, Eminent Domain, Energy, General Practice, Government, Health Care, Insurance Defense, Labor and Employment, Leases and Leasing, Environmental Litigation, Employment Law, Civil Rights Litigation, , Medical, Accountant and Attorney Malpractice Defense, Personal Injury, Premises Liability, Utility Law and Workers Compensation.
See Professional Biographies, FORT WAYNE, INDIANA

Mitchell, Janet E. ... '51 '76 C.238 B.A. L.477 J.D. 10431 Oak Valley Road
Mochamer, Jack A., (BV) ... '31 '60 C.932 B.B.A. L.880 J.D. 202 W. Berry St.
Moellering, Alfred W. ... '26 '53 C.347 B.S. L.1119 LL.B. Sr. J., Supr. Ct.
Moellering, Michael C., (BV) ... '64 '92 C.827 B.A. L.879 J.D. [Burt,B.D.S.&B.]
Moorhead, Thomas M., (AV) ... '21 '50 C.347 A.B. L.362 J.D. 111 E. Wayne St.
More, James M., (BV) ... '46 '74 C.317 B.S. L.347 J.D. [More,M.Y.&T.]

More, Miller, Yates & Tracey, (BV)
116 East Berry Street Suite 610, 46802-2786
Telephone: 260-424-2200 Fax: 260-420-0655
Email: mmyt@centralnet.net URL: http://www.mmytlawfirm.com
Members of Firm: James M. More; Michael T. Yates; J. Brian Tracey. Associate: Angela N. Snyder.
General Practice in all State and Federal Courts. Corporation, Business, Bankruptcy, Reorganization, Collection, Family and Matrimonial Law. Trials.
Representative Clients: NBD Bank NA, General Federal Credit Union. Attorneys Title Group, Inc. (A Title Insurance Agent).
See Professional Biographies, FORT WAYNE, INDIANA

Moreland, Robert D., (BV) ... '62 '88 C.992 B.A. L.1119 J.D. [Baker&D.]
Morgan, Gwendolyn J., (CV) '45 '86
C.679 B.A. L.879 J.D. 110 West Berry Street, Suite 1700
Morris, Jack E., (BV) ... '55 '80 C.63 B.S. L.345 J.D. [Benson,P.M.J.&L.]
Morris, Sandy L. '74 '99 C.823 B.A. L.145 J.D.
(adm. in IL; not adm. in IN) [Dahm&E.] ⊙
Morton, Ramon E. ... '54 '81 C.679 B.S. L.345 J.D. Sr. Coun., Lincoln Natl. Corp.
Moses, Karen T., (BV) ... '60 '85 C.597 B.A. L.1119 J.D. [Baker&D.]
Moss, Kirby G., (BV) ... '54 '79 C.347 B.S. L.345 J.D. [Moss&H.]
Moss, Lindy G., (AV) ... '26 '55 C.347 B.S. L.1119 LL.B. [Moss&H.]
Moss, Parker L., (BV) ... '59 '84 C.347 A.B. L.1119 J.D. [Moss&H.]

Moss & Harris, LLP, (AV)
110 West Berry Street, Suite 1800, P.O. Box 10839, 46854-0839
Telephone: 260-422-1589 Facsimile: 260-422-1594
Email: pmoss@mossharris.com URL: http://www.mossharris.com
Members of Firm: Lindy G. Moss; William E. Harris; Kirby G. Moss; Parker L. Moss.
General Civil Practice in all State and Federal Courts. Personal Injury, Estate Planning, Family, Real Estate and Probate Law, Corporation, Litigation, Collection and Insurance Subrogation Law, Bankruptcy. Trial and Appellate Practice, Social Security Disability.
See Professional Biographies, FORT WAYNE, INDIANA

Mulholland, Shane C., (BV) ... '69 '98 C.63 B.A. L.1187 J.D. [Burt,B.D.S.&B.]
Muller, Henry J., Jr. '30 '55 C.813 A.B. L.309 J.D.
(adm. in DC; not adm. in IN) 5829 Oak Pointe Dr.‡
Murphy, Edward L., Jr., (AV) ... '43 '68 C.347 B.S. L.1119 J.D. [Miller M.&M.]
Murphy, Patrick, (BV) ... '54 '81 C.63 B.A. L.345 J.D. 215 E. Berry
Murphy, Patrick G., (BV) ... '70 '96 C&L.345 B.S., J.D. [Barrett&M.]
Mustard, Michael D., (AV) ... '51 '78 C&L.602 B.A., J.D. [Hunt S.K.]
Myers, Christopher C., & Associates, (BV) '56 '81
C.210 B.A. L.896 J.D. 809 South Calhoun Street, Suite 400
Myers, Harold W. ... '44 '70 C.347 A.B. L.345 J.D. [Wyss&M.]
Myers, Max A., (BV) ... '48 '74 C&L.879 B.A., J.D. [M.Myers]
Myers, Max, (BV) ... 809 S. Calhoun, Ste. 200
Nader, Michael J., (BV) ... '62 '88 C.477 B.A. L.912 J.D. [Baker&D.]
Najdeski, Henry P., (BV) ... '71 '97 C.210 B.A. L.365 J.D. [Barrett&M.]
Najdeski, Orfej Petar, (CV) ... '68 '99 C.679 B.A. L.365 J.D. [Hunt S.K.]
Nakos, Nikos C. ... '59 '85 C.694 B.A. L.365 J.D. [Nakos]
Nakos Law Office ... 126 West Columbia Street On the Landing, Suite 200
Neal, Joshua C. ... '77 '02 C.344 B.A. L.345 J.D. [Barrett&M.]
Neuen, Gary L. '48 '74 C.880 B.A. L.836 J.D.
(adm. in TN; not adm. in IN) Lincoln Natl. Life Ins. Co.
Nicholson, Robert L., (BV) ... '59 '86 C.69 B.A. L.845 J.D. [Beckman L.]
Nickels, Danel Michelle ... '— '02 C.432 B.A. L.345 J.D. [Barnes&T.]
Nieter, Daniel P., (BV) ... '57 '83 C&L.879 B.S., J.D. [Nieter&G.]

Nieter & Goeglein, (BV)
Suite 420 Metro Building, 202 West Berry, 46802
Telephone: 260-426-2244 Fax: 260-424-1774
Email: ng@nietergoeglein.com URL: http://www.lawyers.com/nieter&goeglein
Andrew M. Goeglein; Daniel P. Nieter.
Estate Planning, Estate Administration, Probate, Business Law, Credit Union, Real Estate, Civil Practice, Adoption.
Representative Clients: Lutheran Homes, Inc.; MacDonald Machinery Co., Inc.
See Professional Biographies, FORT WAYNE, INDIANA

Niewyk, Anthony, (AV) ... '41 '73 C.477 B.S. L.273 J.D. [Baker&D.] (See Pat. Sect.)
Niezer, Bernard M. ... '15 '40 C.602 A.B. L.1119 LL.B. 2236 Inverness Lakes Crossing‡
Niezer, Thomas M., (BV) ... '59 '86 C.894 B.A. L.201 J.D. [Barrett&M.]
Noland, Donald F., (BV) '42 '72
C&L.260 B.A., J.D. 2nd V.P. & Sr. Coun., Lincoln Natl. Corp.
Nordmann, Benjamin E. ... '73 '00 C.303 B.A. L.1187 J.D. [Nordmann]
Nordmann Law Offices ... 110 W. Berry St., Ste. 1912
Nuffer, Richard T. ... '46 '75 C.879 B.A. L.69 J.D. 2530 Fox Chase Run‡
Nusbaum, Jonathan H. ... '71 '97 C.855 B.A. L.851 J.D. [Beers M.B.&S.]
O'Connor, James J., Jr. ... '75 '01 C.245 B.A. L.425 J.D. [Barrett&M.]
O'Donnell, Laura C., (CV) '71 '96 C.475 B.A. L.1119 J.D.
[Baker&D.] (⊙Indianapolis)
O'Dowd, Jerome J., (AV) ... '18 '42 C&L.602 Ph.B., J.D. 3530 Stellhorn Rd., Ste. B
Oetting, Dawn M. ... '60 '04 C.347 B.G.S. L.879 J.D. [Shipley&Assoc.]
O'Hara, J. Michael, (AV) ... '28 '53 C.602 A.B. L.477 LL.B. [Barrett&M.] ‡
O'Hara, Michael P., (BV) ... '60 '86 C.602 B.A. L.209 J.D. [Barrett&M.]
Olivero, Mark S., (BV) ... '60 '88 C.801 B.S. L.1187 J.D. [M.Olivero]
Olivero, Mark, P.C., (BV) ... 116 E. Berry St., Ste. 1200
O'Malley, Paul W., Jr., (BV) ... '55 '82 C.597 B.S.E.E. L.879 J.D. [O'Malley&F.] (Pat.)
O'Malley & Firestone, (BV) ... 919 S. Harrison St., Suite 210 (Pat.)
Ormsby, Edward J., (BV) ... '69 '94 C.346 B.S. L.276 J.D. [Beckman L.]

Ouellette, Steven J. '55 '81 C.97 B.S.B.A. L.851 J.D.
Suite 500 2001 Reed Road, 46815
Telephone: 260-420-2091 Fax: 260-422-0882
Email: steven.ouellette@ouellettelaw.com URL: http://www.ouellettelaw.com
Bankruptcy, Creditors Rights, Commercial Litigation, Insolvency, Collections.

Page, Arthur L. '45 '74 C&L.347 B.A., J.D.
V.P. & Dir., Pers., Lincoln Natl. Life Ins. Co.
Palmer, Daniel J., (CV) ... '66 '91 C.108 B.S. L.1119 J.D. [Hunt S.K.]
Palmer, John B., Jr. ... '21 '50 C&L.602 B.S., LL.B. 1413 Chanterelle St.‡
Pantello, Mark S., (BV) ... '53 '80 C.347 B.S. L.345 J.D. [Benson,P.M.J.&L.]
Pape, Timothy M., (BV) ... '68 '95 C.276 B.A. L.347 J.D. [Carson B.]
Pappas, Daniel G., (BV) ... '57 '86 C&L.347 B.S., J.D. (Part-time) Dep. Pub. Def.
Pappas, George, (BV) ... '59 '85 C&L.879 B.S.M.E., J.D. [G.Z.Pappas] (Pat.)
Pappas, George Z., Law Offices of, (BV) ... 919 S. Harrison St. (Pat.)
Parker, Maclyn T., (AV) ... '29 '54 C.210 A.B. L.477 J.D. [Baker&D.]
Parrish, Robert J., (AV) ... '16 '41 C.347 B.A. L.1119 J.D. [Parrish&K.]
Parrish & Knight, (AV) ... 4007 S. Wayne Ave.
Patterson, Craig R., (BV) ... '66 '92 C&L.347 B.A., J.D. [Beckman L.]
Patterson, Emily S. ... '78 '03 C.999 B.S., B.A.A. L.345 J.D. [Burt,B.D.S.&B.]
Paul, Trisha J., (BV) ... '71 '96 C.999 B.S. L.851 J.D. [Barrett&M.]
Payne, Robert Thomas '49 '81 C.870 B.S. L.201 J.D.
(adm. in OH; not adm. in IN; Pat.) Pat. Coun., General Electric Co.

Pearson, Alisa L. .... '79 '05 C.533 B.B.A. L.1205 J.D. [Ⓐ Barrett&M.]
Perry, R. Scott, Jr., (BV) .... '54 '80 C.679 B.A. L.345 J.D. [Perry]

Perry Law Office P.C., (BV)
1010 Memorial Way, Suite 102, 46805
Telephone: 260-483-3110 Fax: 260-483-3220
Email: info@perryoffice.net URL: http://www.perryoffice.net
R. Scott Perry, Jr.; Thomas J. Knight; Johanna J. Campbell.
Collections, Social Security Disability, Creditors Rights.
See Professional Biographies, FORT WAYNE, INDIANA

Peters, David L., (BV) ....'47 '76 C.207 B.A. L.347 J.D. [Peters]
Peters, Sharon Jane, (BV) '47 '85
C.347 B.S. L.345 J.D. Vice President, Tower Bank & Trust Co.
Peters Law Firm, (BV) .... 1700 Lincoln Tower
Picarello, Robert A. '44 '72 C.178 A.B. L.884 J.D.
(adm. in NY; not adm. in IN) V.P. & Chf. Coun., Lincoln Natl. Corp.
Pichon, Emily E. '64 '91 C.170 B.A. L.990 J.D.
(adm. in CA; not adm. in IN) 6207 Constitution Dr.
Pichon, John N., Jr., (AV) '30 '57
C.&L.347 A.B., LL.B. Pres., Olive B. Cole Foundation, Inc.

Plews Shadley Racher & Braun
(See Indianapolis)

Podlaski, Kevin P. .... '60 '90 C.754 B.S. L.997 J.D. [Carson B.]
Polley, Linda A., (BV) .... '59 '85 C.347 B.A. L.201 J.D. [Hunt S.K.]
Posey, James P., (BV) .... '54 '81 C.&L.347 B.A., J.D. [Beers M.B.&S.]
Powell, John B., (BV) .... '57 '82 C.894 B.A. L.347 J.D. [Shambaugh,K.B.&W.]
Powell, Linda Peterson, (BV) '58 '83 C.347 A.B. L.1119 J.D.
Staff Atty., Corp. Counsel for the City of Fort Wayne
Powers, Douglas Dormire, (BV) ....'53 '83 C.604 A.B. L.851 J.D. [Baker&D.]
Prater, Ronald E. ....'50 '75 C.532 B.A. L.608 J.D. Indiana Mich. Elec. Co.
Pratt, Charles F. ....'53 '79 C.347 B.A. L.345 J.D. Supr. Ct. J.
Prendergast, Stephen D. '49 '74 C.602 B.A. L.128 J.D.
(adm. in PA; not adm. in IN) Tax Dept., Lincoln Natl. Corp.
Presley, Susan M. ....'55 '90 C.63 B.S. L.262 J.D. Law Clk., U.S. Dist. Ct.
Prickett, James M., (BV) '46 '71
C.679 B.S. L.145 J.D. 116 E. Berry St, Suite 1225 (⊙Albion)
Probst, Walter F., Jr. ....'15 '37 C.912 A.B. L.477 J.D. 12207 Ill. Rd.
Proctor, Patrick L., (BV) .... '67 '93 C.378 B.A. L.607 J.D. [Eilbacher F.]
Prosser, Raymond L., (AV) '48 '74 C.347 A.B. L.345 J.D.
V.P. & Assoc. Gen. Coun., Lincoln Natl. Corp.
Quirk, Jeremy O., (BV) ....'64 '90 C.&L.347 B.A., J.D. [Blume,C.J.&S.]
Quirk, Thos. E. ....'25 '51 C.&L.352 B.A., LL.B. 110 W. Berry St.‡
Raff, Jeffrey G., (BV) ....'47 '72 C.347 B.S. L.1119 J.D. 229 W. Berry St.
Rahn, Stephen E. '52 '77 C.375 B.S. L.1119 J.D.
2nd V.P. & Dir., State Rel., Lincoln Natl. Life Ins. Co.
Ramos, Carlos R. '66 '91 C.965 B.A. L.801 J.D.
2nd V.P. & Reinsurance Coun., Swiss Re Life & Health America Inc.
Ramsier, Floyd A., (BV) ....'46 '72 C.97 B.A. L.276 J.D. 3505 Lake Ave.
Raskosky, Earl, (BV) ....'48 '76 C.63 B.S. L.345 J.D. [Raskosky]
Raskosky Law Office, (BV) ....6009 Stoney Creek Drive
Rathburn, Charles James, Jr., (CV) .... '61 '91 C.801 B.S. L.1187 J.D. 625 Lincoln Tower
Reed, Shannon K. ....'75 '00 C.965 B.A. L.879 J.D. [Ⓐ Baker&D.]
Regnier, Kingsley G., (BV) ....'54 '89 C.679 B.L.S. L.879 J.D. [K.G.Regnier]
Regnier, Kingsley G., Attorney at Law, P.C., (BV)
4656 West Jefferson Boulevard, Suite 120
Reidy, Jeremy L. ....'76 '04 C.347 B.S. L.200 J.D. [Ⓐ Beckman L.]
Reizian, John L. '51 '86 C.184 B.A. L.1048 J.D.
(adm. in CT; not adm. in IN) 2nd V.P. & Sr. Coun., Lincoln Natl. Corp.
Renbarger, Roberta L. ....'48 '99 C.932 B.A. L.910 J.D. [Renbarger]
Renbarger Law Firm ....202 W. Berry St., Suite 710
Rentschler, Matthew J. ....'69 '95 C.602 L.347 J.D. [Ⓐ Swanson&C.]
Renz, Phillip A., (BV) ....'50 '78 C.999 B.A. L.345 J.D. [Carson B.]
Rhee, Robert E., (CV) ....'54 '97 C.1012 B.B.A. L.347 J.D. [Ⓐ Bonahoom&B.]
Rhodes, Carol Bennett, (BV) ....'45 '94 C.221 B.A. L.347 J.D. [Burt,B.D.S.&B.]
Richards, Karen E., (AV) ....'54 '79 C.597 B.A. L.1119 J.D. 116 E. Berry St.
Richardson, Laurel J. ....'38 '83 C.161 B.S. L.365 J.D. UAW-GM Legal Services Plan
Rickard, Jerry E. '43 '70 C.793 B.S. L.352 J.D.
2nd V.P. & Sr. Coun., Lincoln Natl. Corp.
Riebenack, F. Walter, (BV) ....'39 '65 C.&L.602 B.B.A., LL.B. 110 W. Berry St.
Riecke, Renee L., (BV) ....'59 '85 C.347 B.S. L.1119 J.D. [Ⓐ Barrett&M.]
Rifkin, Martin S. ....'60 '85 C.94 B.S. L.904 J.D. Exec. V.P., Omnisource Corp.
Ritter, Bradley S. '64 '89 C.886 B.A. L.273 J.D.
(adm. in MD; not adm. in IN) Lincoln Natl. Corp.
Roach, Dustin Michael ....'54 '91 C.602 B.A. L.347 J.D. 202 W. Berry St., Ste. 200
Robinson, Richard D., (AV) ....'46 '71 C.347 A.B. L.1119 J.D. [Barrett&M.]
Roby, Daniel A., (AV) ....'41 '66 C.347 B.A. L.1119 J.D. [Roby H.&M.]

Roby Hood & Manges, (AV) BB
200 East Main Street, Suite 520, 46802
Telephone: 260-423-3366 Fax: 260-423-3367
Members of Firm: Daniel A. Roby; G. Stanley Hood; Thomas A. Manges.
Personal Injury, Products Liability, Medical Malpractice, Nursing Home Liability and Trial and Appellate Practice.
References: Wells Fargo Bank; Bank One.
See Professional Biographies, FORT WAYNE, INDIANA

Rocke, Jeffrey A., (AV) ....'49 '78 C.827 B.A. L.930 J.D. 14817 Powderhorn Rd.
Rockwell, Cynthia P., (BV) ....'— '88 C.347 B.A. L.877 J.D. [Haller&C.]
Roebel, Jack E., Law Office of, (BV) ....'50 '78 C.347 B.S. L.345 J.D. 912 S. Calhoun St.
Roebuck, Randolph L., (BV) ....'51 '88 C.679 B.S. L.201 J.D. [Roebuck&Assoc.]

Roebuck & Associates, P.C., (BV)
127 West Berry, Suite 700, 46802
Telephone: 260-426-4444 Fax: 260-424-6006
Email: rroeb@earthlink.net URL: http://www.roebuckassociates.com
Randolph L. Roebuck.
Personal Injury, Automobile Accidents, Boat Accidents, Motorcycle Accidents, Truck Accidents, Slip and Fall, Dog Bites, Medical Malpractice, Head Injuries, Nursing Home Abuse and Neglect, Products Liability, Insurance, Social Security, Social Security Disability, and Wrongful Death.
See Professional Biographies, FORT WAYNE, INDIANA

Roelke, Norman L., (BV) '49 '79 C.679 B.A. L.421 J.D.
Corporate Counsel, Tokheim Corporation (Pat.)
Rogers, F. John, (BV) ....'42 '70 C.784 B.A. L.347 J.D. [Thompson&R.]
Rosemond, Dawn R., (BV) ....'— '96 C.347 B.A. L.339 J.D. [Barnes&T.]
Rosenblatt, Stanley L., (BV) ....'44 '69 C.347 A.B. L.1119 J.D. [Tourkow,C.R.&J.]
Rosenblatt, Warren B., (CV) '44 '69
C.347 B.S. L.1119 J.D. 1310 Anthony Wayne Bk. Bldg.
Rosendahl, David E. .... '49 '77 C.281 A.B. L.851 J.D. The Medical Protective Co.
Rosswurm, Tracey L. ....'67 '00 C.347 B.A. L.1187 J.D. [T.L.Rosswurm]
Rosswurm, Tracey L., LLC, The Law Office of .... 116 E. Berry St., Ste. 1900

Rothberg Logan & Warsco LLP, (AV) BB
2100 National City Center, 110 West Berry Street, P.O. Box 11647, 46859-1647 ⊙
Telephone: 260-422-9454 Telefax: 260-422-1622
Email: law@rlwlawfirm.com URL: http://www.rlwlawfirm.com
Members of Firm: Sol Rothberg (1910-1993); Thomas A. Gallmeyer (1922-1981); George E. Fruechtenicht (1925-1996); F. L. Dennis Logan; Mark A. Warsco; Kathryn A. Brogan; Mark W. Baeverstad; David R. Smelko; Dennis F. Dykhuizen; Anne Carney; Michael T. Deam; J. Rickard Donovan; Theodore T. Storer; Christine M. Stach. Associates: Cindy Ann Wolfer; Susan E. Trent; Peggy A. Carlile; Thomas B. Trent. Of Counsel: Thomas D. Logan; John H. Heiney.
General Civil Litigation in all Courts. Corporate, Banking, Bankruptcy, Commercial, Insurance, Labor and Employment Law, Municipal Law, Municipal Finance, Securities, Real Estate, Construction, Probate and Estate Planning, Transportation, Tax, Creditors' Rights, Agricultural Law, Family/ Domestic Relations, Health Care Law.
Approved Attorneys For: Ameriquest Mortgage Company; Aon Corporation; Avis Industrial Corp.; Bank One, N.A.; Busak + Shamban, Inc.; Cameron Memorial Community Hospital; Construction Management Engineering, Inc.; City of Fort Wayne; Dell Computer Corp.; Farm Credit Services of Mid-America, ASA.
Warsaw, Indiana Office: 212 North Buffalo Street, 46580. Telephone: 574-267-8802. Telefax: 574-267-0605.
See Professional Biographies, FORT WAYNE, INDIANA

Roy, Robert M., Jr. '40 '65 C.755 B.A. L.276
(adm. in IA; not adm. in IN) 4904 Charlotte Ave.‡
Royer, Gary L., (BV) '50 '84
C.63 B.A. L.61 J.D. Mng. Atty., UAW-GM Legal Services Plan
Ruiz, Fernando A. '57 '89 C.871 B.S. L.1048 J.D.
Coun., Motors & Controls, Sourcing, General Electric Company
Runyan, Harley L. ....'32 '69 L.1127 J.D. 3324 S. Anthony Blvd.‡
Rutz, Suzan L., (BV) ....'62 '87 C.347 B.A. L.879 J.D. [Burt,B.D.S.&B.]
Ryan, Thomas L. ....'41 '68 C.347 A.B. L.1119 J.D. Cir. J.
Sachs, Jeremy '43 '69 C.446 B.A. L.273 J.D.
Asst. V.P. & Sr. Coun., Lincoln Natl. Corp.
Samek, Richard P., (AV) ....'51 '76 C.347 B.S. L.345 J.D. [Carson B.]
Sandler, Howard B., (AV) ....'45 '72 C.347 B.S. L.1119 J.D. [Beckman L.]
Sauerteig, Paul J. ....'17 '43 C.&L.178 A.B., LL.B. Ste 1310, 203 E Berry St
Sauerteig, Paul O., (BV) ....'53 '80 C.347 B.A. L.879 J.D. [Snow&S.]
Scheele, Jason A. ....'76 '01 C.265 B.A. L.347 J.D. [Ⓐ Miller M.&M.]
Scheer, Michael A. ....'— '79 C.347 A.B. L.345 J.D. [Barnes&T.]
Scheibenberger, Kenneth R. ....'49 '76 C.347 A.B. L.345 J.D. Supr. Ct. J.
Scheiderer, Patrick A. ....'74 '00 C.679 B.S. L.345 J.D. [Ⓐ Baker&D.]
Schendel, N. Jean, (BV) ....'56 '95 C.679 B.S. L.879 J.D. [Hunt S.K.]
Schenkel, Norbert J., Jr., (BV) ....'46 '71 C.602 B.B.A. L.1119 J.D. [Schenkel T.&K.]
Schenkel Tirpak & Kowalczyk, (BV) ....520 S. Calhoun St.
Schlagenhauf, Ann M. ....'— '93 C.929 B.A. L.347 J.D. 203 W. Wayne St.
Schmidt, Kenneth P. '54 '80
C.594 B.A. L.629 J.D. Fin. Consultant, Financial Planning Servs.
Schmitt, Jennifer A. '66 '91 C.475 B.A. L.851 J.D.
(adm. in MI; not adm. in IN) Indus. Relations Mgr., Essex Grp., Inc.
Schmoll, Robert J., Jr. ....'46 '72 C.201 B.S. L.1119 J.D. Family Ct. Ref.
Schneider, Brandon J. '70 '97 C.846 B.A. L.802 J.D.
(adm. in OH; not adm. in IN) SLE Worldwide Inc.
Schwartz, Michael D. ....'72 '98 C.475 B.S. L.347 J.D. [Ⓐ Baker&D.]
Schweller, Andrew J. ....'72 '97 C.473 B.A. L.201 J.D. Co. Pros. Atty.
Scott, David A., (AV) ....'47 '72 C.473 A.B. L.1119 J.D. [Baker&D.]
Scott, Eve S., (BV) ....'63 '88 C.&L.879 B.A., J.D. Coun., Lincoln Natl. Corp.
Scott, M. Bruce, (BV) ....'62 '88 C.894 B.A. L.879 J.D. [Tourkow,C.R.&J.]
Scrogham, Kenneth L., (BV) ....'37 '65 C.347 A.B. L.345 J.D. [Snyder&S.]
Scudder, Mark D. ....'— '02 C.347 B.A. L.1119 J.D. [Ⓐ Barnes&T.]
Seeger, Richard T. ....'26 '54 C.&L.477 B.S.E.E., LL.B. 1067 Delaware Ave. (Pat.)
Seifert, Martin E., (BV) ....'— '92 C.&L.602 B.A., J.D. [Haller&C.]
Senk, Jeremy V. ....'74 '01 C.679 B.S. L.347 J.D. [Carson B.]
Serrano, Cathy T. ....'56 '03 C.347 B.A. L.1187 J.D. [Ⓐ Skekloff,A.&K.]
Shambaugh, Stephen H. ....'45 '70 C.597 A.B. L.1119 J.D. 5521 Autumn Woods Trail‡
Shambaugh, Kast, Beck & Williams, (AV) ....229 W. Berry St., Ste. 400
Shea, James J., Sr., (AV) ....'59 '84 C.1113 B.A. L.879 J.D. [Hunt S.K.]
Sheets, Ralph E. ....'32 '56 C.347 B.S. L.1119 LL.B. 11228 Creekwood Dr.‡
Sheldon, Vern E., (AV) ....'30 '56 C.265 A.B. L.1119 J.D. Sr. J., Supm. Ct.
Shelton, Cheryl L. ...'62 '89 C.1109 B.A. L.1137 J.D. Gen. Coun., Global Van Lines, Inc.
Sherr, Mitchell A. ....'44 '73 C.446 B.A. L.326 J.D. 130 W. Main St.

Shilts, Perry D., (AV) '53 '78 C.&L.345 B.A., J.D. BB
10311 Dawson's Creek Boulevard, Suite C, 46825
Telephone: 206-489-0700 Fax: 260-497-8954
Email: perry@shiltslaw.com
Domestic Relations, Divorce, Family Law, Personal Injury and Commercial Litigation.
See Professional Biographies, FORT WAYNE, INDIANA

Shine, Lawrence E., (AV) ....'47 '73 C.347 A.B. L.1119 J.D. [Baker&D.]
Shine, Steven R., (BV) ....'52 '78 C.347 B.A. L.607 J.D. [Shine&H.]
Shine & Hardin, (BV) ....2810 Beaver Ave.
Shipley, Grant F., (AV) .... '45 '75 C.103 A.B. L.1119 J.D. [Shipley&Assoc.]

Shipley & Associates, (AV) BB
233 West Baker Street, 46802-3413
Telephone: 260-422-2700 Fax: 260-424-2960 URL: http://www.gshipley.com
URL: http://www.lawyers.com/shipleylaw
Grant F. Shipley. Associate: Dawn M. Oetting.
Bankruptcy other than consumer bankruptcy, Commercial Law, Commercial Litigation.
Representative Clients: Bank One, Indiana, N.A.; Tower Bank & Trust Co.; Fleet Capital Corp.; Comerica Bank; Creditors Committee, Fibrex, Inc. Bankruptcy; Fort Financial Federal Credit Union; Petroleum Traders Corp.; C & M Fine Pack, Inc.; Neff Engineering, Inc.; Shelby County Bank; Grant County State Bank.
See Professional Biographies, FORT WAYNE, INDIANA

Shipman, Matthew R. .... '72 '98 C.&L.347 B.A., J.D. [Ⓐ Dahm&E.]
Shoaff, Thomas M., (AV) ....'41 '68 C.951 B.A. L.880 LL.B. [Baker&D.]
Shrader, Cathleen M., (BV) ....'69 '94 C.347 B.S. L.228 J.D. [Barrett&M.]
Shull, Joseph W., (BV) ....'52 '77 C.347 B.A. L.345 J.D. 2200 Lake Ave.
Shumlas, Stephen J. ....'78 '04 C.475 B.A. L.345 J.D. [Ⓐ Burt,B.D.S.&B.]
Shurtz, Alfred M. '47 '74 C.679 B.S. L.345 J.D.
V.P. & Gen. Coun., Asphalt Equipment Co., Inc.
Silliman, N. Reed, (AV) ....'46 '73 C.303 B.A. L.421 J.D. [Baker&D.]
Simerman, Anne E., (BV) ....'61 '95 C.347 B.S. L.421 J.D. [Ⓐ Barrett&M.]
Simpson, Brian M., (CV) ....'71 '97 C.&L.347 B.S., J.D. [Shambaugh,K.B.&W.]
Sims, Stephen M. ....'46 '73 C.347 B.A. L.345 J.D. 715 S. Calhoun St., Rm. 208
Sistevaris, George, (BV) ....'— '87 C.347 B.S. L.1119 J.D. [Haller&C.]
Skaggs, Matthew B. ....'— '05 C.347 B.A. L.1119 J.D. [Ⓐ Baker&D.]
Skekloff, Daniel J., (AV) ....'53 '79 C.347 B.A. L.1119 J.D. [Skekloff,A.&K.]
Skekloff, Scot T., (BV) ....'66 '91 C.&L.347 J.D. [Skekloff,A.&K.]

Skekloff, Adelsperger & Kleven, LLP, (AV)
927 South Harrison Street, 46802
Telephone: 260-407-7000 Fax: 260-407-7137 URL: http://www.sak-law.com
Email: firm@adelspergerkleven.com URL: http://www.lawyers.com/adelspergerkleven
Daniel J. Skekloff; Douglas R. Adelsperger; Yvette Gaff Kleven; Scot T. Skekloff. Associate: Cathy T. Serrano.
Bankruptcy, Creditors' Rights, Insolvency, and related Commercial Litigation and Transactions.
See Professional Biographies, FORT WAYNE, INDIANA

Skowronski, Thomas E. '52 '79 C.178 A.B. L.436 J.D.
(adm. in WI; not adm. in IN) Coun., Lincoln Natl. Corp.
Smelko, David R., (AV) .... '56 '82 C.347 B.A. L.879 J.D. [Rothberg L.&W.]
Smith, Edward N. .... '30 '62 C.344 B.A. L.345 LL.B. 3622 S. Calhoun St.
Smith, Jeffrey P., (BV) .... '69 '95 C.679 B.A. L.347 J.D. [⊠ Hawk,H.K.&C.]
Smith, Mark Paul, (BV) .... '50 '82 C.210 B.S. L.879 J.D. [M.P.Smith&Assoc.]
Smith, Maxwell P., (BV) .... '24 '50 C&L.879 J.D. [M.P.Smith&Assoc.]
Smith, M. P., & Assocs., P.C., (BV) .... 622 S. Calhoun St.
Snouffer, Eric E., (BV) .... '63 '89 C.347 B.S. L.345 J.D. 110 West Berry Street
Snouffer, Richard I., (AV) .... '28 '54 C.347 B.S. L.1119 J.D. 110 W. Berry St.
Snow, Duane J. .... '— '00 C.347 B.A. L.345 J.D. [⊠ Haller&C.]
Snow, Norman S., (BV) .... '43 '69 C.347 B.A. L.1119 J.D. [Snow&S.]
Snow & Sauerteig, LLP, (BV) .... 1310 Anthony Wayne Building
Snyder, Angela N. .... '72 '98 C&L.838 B.A., J.D. [⊠ More,M.Y.&T.]
Snyder, Bruce R. .... '37 '63 C.347 B.S. L.1119 J.D. [Snyder&S.]

Snyder Birch Cornwell & Morgan LLP, (AV)
904 South Calhoun Street, 46802 ⊙
Telephone: 260-407-0915 Fax: 260-407-7005
URL: http://www.sbcmlaw.com
David D. Cornwell.
Business Litigation, Business Law, Zoning, Planning and Land Use, Real Estate, Civil Litigation, Estate Planning, Trust, Probate, Guardianship, Elder Law, Tax, Banking Law, Employee Benefits, ERISA.
Syracuse, Indiana Office: 200 West Main Street, 46567. Telephone: 574-457-5727. Fax: 574-457-2056.
See Professional Biographies, FORT WAYNE, INDIANA

Snyder & Scrogham, (BV) .... 202 W. Berry St.
Somers, Stacy K. .... '69 '04 C.303 B.A. L.1119 J.D. [⊠ Beers M.B.&S.]
Spencer, M. Randall, (BV) .... '61 '91 C.63 B.A. L.602 J.D. [Carson B.]

Spielman, Kim M., (BV) '53 '87 C.347 B.S. L.607 J.D.
P.O. Box 15175, 46885
Telephone: 260-414-6303; Toll Free: 1-800-866-6303 Fax: 260-486-1426
Email: kspielman@comcast.net
Personal Injury, Litigation, Real Estate Law, Commercial Law, Collections, Criminal Law, Felonies.
See Professional Biographies, FORT WAYNE, INDIANA

Spoltman, Stephen J. .... '51 '77 C.347 B.A. L.345 J.D. 6714 Pointe Inverness Way
Springer, James E. .... '41 '68 C&L.879 B.A., J.D. [J.E.Springer]
Springer, Karen A., (BV) .... '57 '96 C.347 B.A. L.1119 J.D. [⊠ J.F.Kimbrough&Assoc.]
Springer, James E., PC, Elder Law Office of .... 7111 Old Trail
Springmann, Theresa Lazar .... '56 '80 C.347 B.A. L.602 J.D. Dist. J.
Sprinkle, Janell M. .... '72 '01 C.840 B.S. L.347 J.D. [⊠ Barrett&M.]
Stach, Christine M., (BV) .... '70 '95 C.63 B.S. L.879 J.D. [Rothberg L.&W.]
Stallings, C. G. '06 '32 L.146 LL.B.
(adm. in IL; not adm. in IN) 1925 Niagara Dr.‡
Stam, Yvonne K. .... '50 '75 C.518 A.B. L.1119 J.D. Admin. Law J., Soc. Sec. Admn.
Stauffer, Terry A., (BV) .... '57 '82 C.288 B.A. L.1119 J.D. [⊠ Wyss&M.]
Steele, Ulmschneider & Malloy, (BV) .... 127 West Berry Street, Suite 1111
Steere, Allen C. .... '08 '31 L.846 LL.B. 1321 Illsey Pl.‡
Steiner, David R., (BV) .... '63 '89 C.827 B.S. L.1119 J.D. [Barrett&M.]
Steiner, Mark H. '52 '79
C.827 B.A. L.1119 J.D. V.P. & Treasurer, Brotherhood Mut. Ins. Co.
Steininger, Donald B. .... '42 '73 C.8 B.S. L.347 J.D. 5620 Coventry Ln.
Steinkamp, John L. '43 '69 C.347 A.B. L.1119 J.D.
V.P. & Assoc. Gen. Coun., Lincoln Natl. Corp.
Steury, Wesley N., (BV) .... '50 '79 C.827 A.B. L.477 J.D. [Burt,B.D.S.&B.]
Stevens, Wade C. '35 '63 C.475 B.A. L.477 J.D.
(adm. in MI; not adm. in IN) The Medical Protective Co.
Stewart, David A., (AV) .... '43 '68 C.893 B.A. L.1119 J.D. [Hunt S.K.]
Stier, Brian E., (BV) .... '59 '85 C.347 B.S. L.1187 J.D. [Logan&S.]
Stier, Bruce N., (BV) .... '50 '77 C.347 B.A. L.365 J.D. [Logan&S.]
Stineburg, Jeffrey A. .... '72 '99 C.347 B.A. L.1119 J.D. Deputy Prosecutor
Stites, Anthony M., (BV) .... '63 '88 C.851 B.B.A. L.602 J.D. [Barrett&M.]
Storer, Theodore T., (BV) .... '68 '93 C.347 B.A. L.607 J.D. [Rothberg L.&W.]
Storey, David D. .... '— '02 C&L.347 B.S., J.D. [⊠ Baker&D.]
Story, Michael D. .... '— '02 C.97 B.A. L.879 J.D. [⊠ Beckman L.]
Streit, James D., (BV) .... '51 '77 C.347 A.B. L.770 J.D. P.O. Box 11061
Strunk, T. Russell, Jr., (BV) '55 '83 C.347 B.A. L.1119 J.D.
Sr. Coun., Lincoln Natl. Corp.
Stucky, Thomas L., (BV) .... '56 '81 C.347 B.S. L.607 J.D. [Blume,C.J.&S.]
Stucky, Timothy E., (BV) .... '56 '82 C.347 B.S. L.607 J.D. [Blume,C.J.&S.]
Sturm, Paul R., (BV) .... '65 '94 C.347 B.S. L.200 J.D. [Shambaugh,K.B.&W.]
Summers, Roger C. .... '48 '73 C.347 A.B. L.345 J.D. Pres., Summers Fin. Planning Inc.
Surbeck, John F., Jr. .... '46 '71 C.347 B.S. L.1119 J.D. Supr. Ct. J.
Surguine, Arthur G., Jr., (AV) .... '44 '73 C.347 A.B. L.1119 J.D. [Hunt S.K.]
Sutton, Carolyn R., (CV) .... '52 '80 C.231 B.A. L.345 J.D. Atty. Advisor
Sutton, Dennis D., (AV) .... '47 '74 C.347 B.A. L.1119 J.D. [Burt,B.D.S.&B.]
Swanson, Donald C., Jr., (AV) .... '46 '73 C.27 B.A. L.602 J.D. [Swanson&C.]
Swanson & Campbell, (AV) .... 127 W. Berry St.
Sweeney, Charles A., Jr., (AV) .... '38 '64 C.201 B.S. L.602 J.D. [Sweeney]

Sweeney Law Firm, (AV)
8109 Lima Road, Suite B, 46818
Telephone: 260-420-3137 Fax: 260-969-0321 Toll Free: 866-793-6339 URL: http://www.sweeneylawfirm.com
Email: dlf@sweeneylawfirm.com URL: http://www.lawyers.com/sweeneylawfirm
Members of Firm: Charles A. Sweeney, Jr.; David L. Farnbauch.
Personal Injury, Wrongful Death, Automobile Accidents, Trucking Accidents, Products Liability, Toxic Torts, Construction Site Injuries, Unfair Insurance Practices, Premises Liability, Nursing Home Negligence, Medical Malpractice.
See Professional Biographies, FORT WAYNE, INDIANA

Sweet, William L., Jr., (AV) .... '47 '72 C.894 A.B. L.477 J.D. [⊠ Beckman L.]
Swift, William D., (AV) .... '36 '64 C.347 B.S. L.1119 J.D. [Swift&F.]

Swift & Finlayson, (AV)
116 E. Berry Street Suite 590, 46802-2486
Telephone: 260-423-4422 Fax: 260-423-4427
Email: mail@swift-finlayson.com
Members of Firm: William D. Swift; Craig R. Finlayson. Associates: Charles D. Bash; E. Franklin Hill, Jr.; Charles E. Davis.

(This Listing Continued)

Swift & Finlayson (Continued)
Real Estate Law, Corporate, Business Law, Trade Secrets, Business Torts, Zoning Law, Commercial Litigation, Estate Planning, Probate, Banking Law, Mediation, Litigation, Computer Law, International Law, Commercial Transactions.
Affiliated Firm: Leeuw Oberlies & Campbell P.C. 320 N. Meridian Street, Suite 1006, Indianapolis, IN 46204. Telephone: 317-684-6960. Fax: 317-684-6961.
See Professional Biographies, FORT WAYNE, INDIANA

Swihart, Thomas A., (BV) .... '40 '67 C.347 B.S. L.1119 J.D. 710 Lincoln Twr.
Swihart, Thomas D., (BV) ... '49 '76 C.347 B.A. L.345 J.D. 202 W. Berry Street, Suite 10
Talarico, Samuel J., Jr., (BV) .... '68 '96 C.108 B.S. L.347 J.D. [Barrett&M.]
Taylor, Fred H., (CV) .... '23 '54 C.347 L.879 LL.B. 2827 Getz Rd.
Terrill, Jeffrey P., (CV) .... '69 '97 C.347 B.A. L.879 J.D. [⊠ Tremper,B.L.&T.]
Terrill, Philip R., (BV) .... '39 '65 C.347 B.S. L.1119 J.D. [Tremper,B.L.&T.]
Theisen, John C., (AV) .... '— '77 C.477 B.A. L.734 J.D. [Theisen&Assoc.]
Theisen & Associates, (AV) .... 803 South Calhoun, Suite 200
Thieme, Philip R. .... '35 '66 C.347 B.S. L.472 J.D. Ret. Supr. Ct. J.‡
Thoma, Mark A., (BV) .... '58 '83 C.347 A.B. L.1119 J.D. [Tremper,B.L.&T.]
Thompson, Robert L., Jr., (AV) .... '42 '67 C.118 B.A. L.145 J.D. [Thompson&R.]
Thompson & Rogers, (AV) .... 444 East Main St.
Thonert, Richard J., Attorney at Law '49 '74
C.347 B.S. L.345 J.D. 1012 Woodland Plz. Run
Tirpak, Ronald J., (BV) .... '53 '78 C.608 B.S. L.201 J.D. [Schenkel T.&K.]
T'Kindt, Brian J., Attorney at Law, (BV) '52 '82
C.347 B.A. L.879 J.D. 919 S. Harrison St., Ste. 331
Tonn, Colleen E., (BV) .... '60 '85 C.827 B.A. L.345 J.D. Coun., Lincoln Natl. Corp.
Toth, Robert J., Jr. .... '55 '83 C.477 B.A. L.912 J.D. Sr. Coun., Lincoln Natl. Corp.
Tourkow, Frederick R., (AV) .... '18 '39 C.201 L.276 J.D. [Tourkow,C.R.&J.]
Tourkow, Joshua I., (BV) .... '47 '73 C.679 B.S. L.345 J.D. [Tourkow,C.R.&J.]
Tourkow, Crell, Rosenblatt & Johnston, (AV) .... 203 E. Berry Street, Suite 814
Tracey, J. Brian .... '55 '91 C.347 B.S. L.1119 J.D. [More,M.Y.&T.]
Tremper, Bechert, Leonard & Terrill, Professional Corporation, (AV)
800 South Calhoun Street
Trent, Susan E., (BV) .... '72 '98 C.345 B.A. L.575 J.D. [⊠ Rothberg L.&W.]
Trent, Thomas B. .... '76 '01 C.347 B.S. L.861 J.D. [⊠ Rothberg L.&W.]
Trexler, Stephen H., (BV) '49 '74 C.63 B.S. L.1119 J.D.
Sr. V.P. & Gen. Coun., K & K Ins. Grp., Inc.
Trier, Carolyn M., (BV) .... '64 '90 C.880 B.A. L.879 J.D. [Hunt S.K.]
Trotter, Stephen D., (BV) .... '44 '69 C.347 B.A. L.1119 J.D. [Trotter]

Trotter Law Office, (BV)
6079 Stoney Creek Drive, 46825
Telephone: 260-496-8500 Fax: 260-496-8300
Email: TLO8500@aol.com
Member of Firm: Stephen D. Trotter.
Family Law, Bankruptcy, Personal Injury, Traffic Violations, Misdemeanors, Child Custody.
See Professional Biographies, FORT WAYNE, INDIANA

Troyer, Phillip J. '64 '95 C.210 B.S. L.1119 J.D.
Assoc. Gen. Coun., The Medical Protective Co.
Troyer, Ronald L. .... '63 '97 C.63 B.S. L.345 J.D. 6400 Brotherhood Way
Troyer, Tracy L., (BV) .... '69 '94 C&L.347 B.S., J.D. [Boeglin,T.&G.]
Trzynka, Ann M., (BV) .... '67 '93 C&L.347 B.A., J.D. [Avery&V.]
Tubergen, Dane L. .... '45 '70 C.679 B.A. L.1119 J.D. [Hunt S.K.]
Turpin, Kathleen J. '68 '97 C.291 B.A. L.345 J.D.
Assoc. Corp. Coun., Brotherhood Mut. Ins. Co.
Tutwiler, William J., (CV) '58 '90 C.894 B.A. L.851 J.D.
Asst. V.P. & Trust Officer, Natl. City Bank of Indiana
Ulmschneider, Mark D., (BV) .... '52 '78 C.210 B.A. L.910 J.D. [Steele,U.&M.]
Ummel, Jerry L. .... '53 '83 C.63 B.A. L.345 J.D. Small Claims Ref., Supr. Ct.
Urberg, Konrad M. L., (BV) .... '71 '97 C.427 B.A. L.1119 J.D. [⊠ Christoff&C.]
Van Gilder, David C., (BV) .... '58 '83 C.96 B.S. L.904 J.D. [Avery&V.]
Vass, Robert R. .... '— '04 C.894 B.A. L.345 J.D. [⊠ Barnes&T.]
Veracco, Karl J., (BV) .... '66 '92 C.679 B.A. L.347 J.D. [Carson B.]
VerPlanck, Alan, (AV) .... '50 '78 C.475 B.A. L.477 J.D. [Eilbacher F.]
Vian, Brent C. '63 '92 C.347 B.S. L.1187 J.D.
(adm. in CA; not adm. in IN) [⊠ Steele,U.&M.]
Vilutis, V. Anthony, (BV) .... '52 '77 C.347 B.S. L.1119 J.D. 809 S. Calhoun, Ste. 303
Vincent, Deborah W., (BV) '57 '90 C.477 A.B. L.347 J.D.
Legal Coun. & Corp. Coun., Parkview Health System, Inc.
Wagner, Robert A., (AV) .... '39 '65 C.879 B.A. L.1119 LL.B. [Helmke,B.B.&W.]
Walker, Ralph B., (BV) .... '27 '51 C&L.608 B.S., J.D. 1104 W. Jefferson Blvd.
Walters, Robert S., (AV) .... '41 '66 C.477 A.B. L.309 LL.B. [Barrett&M.]
Walther, Donald E. '68 '94 C.228 B.A. L.145 J.D.
(adm. in IL; not adm. in IN) Assoc. Gen. Coun., ITT Industries, Inc.
(⊙White Plains, NY)
Wangberg, David L. .... '40 '71 C.352 B.B.A. L.347 J.D. 3701 Kirkfield Dr.
Warsco, Mark A., (AV) .... '55 '80 C.347 B.A. L.1119 J.D. [Rothberg L.&W.]
Wartenbe, Robert S., (BV) '48 '77
C.347 B.S. L.345 J.D. V.P. & Coun., Three Rivers Title Co., Inc.
Webber, Beth A., (BV) .... '69 '95 C.610 B.A. L.347 J.D. 327 E. Wayne Street
Weber, Marcie J. .... '66 '91 C.475 B.A. L.813 J.D. Coun., Lincoln Natl. Corp.
Webster, Frank A., (CV) .... '30 '61 C.679 B.S. L.345 J.D. 4911 Illinois Rd.
Wehrwein, Frederick .... '45 '77 C.476 B.S. L.1137 J.D. 110 W. Berry St.
Weingartner, Arthur M., (BV) .... '56 '82 C.602 B.A. L.1119 J.D. [Cornelius&W.]
Weinraub, Charles J., (BV) ... '43 '70 C.367 A.B. L.1119 J.D. 4204 West Ferguson Road‡
Weissert, Martin A., (AV) .... '33 '59 C.347 B.S. L.1119 LL.B. 111 E. Wayne St.
Welborn, Andrew J. .... '71 '98 C.894 Phil. L.347 J.D. [⊠ Baker&D.]
Weldy, S. Daniel, III, (BV) .... '46 '74 C.347 A.B. L.1119 J.D. 116 E. Berry St.
Welling, Arthur R., Jr. .... '53 '78 C.973 B.A. L.345 J.D. [A.R.Welling Jr.]
Welling, Marian Clare .... '54 '94 C.74 B.S. L.734 J.D. 3304 Fairfield Avenue
Welling, Arthur R., Jr., Professional Association .... 201 Lexington Avenue
Werling, Mark A., (BV) .... '70 '97 C&L.347 B.S., J.D. [⊠ Baker&D.]
Wernet, John J., (BV) .... '50 '75 C.347 B.S. L.365 J.D. [Carson B.]
White, Keith E., (AV) .... '— '83 C.303 B.A. L.1119 J.D. [Baker&D.]
Whitmore, John M., Jr., (BV) .... '43 '68 C.347 B.S. L.1119 J.D. 116 E. Berry St.
Wiener, Leonard .... '34 '89 C.563 B.E.E. L.1040 J.D. 14210 Sugar Creek Road
Wilkins, Michael D. '47 '74 C.347 B.S. L.345 J.D.
V.P. & Assoc. Gen. Coun., Lincoln Natl. Corp.
Williams, Andrew S. .... '— '02 C.63 B.S. L.69 J.D. [⊠ Hunt S.K.]
Williams, John E., Jr., (BV) .... '36 '67 C.347 B.S. L.345 J.D. 323 W. Berry St.
Williams, Nathan S. J. .... '— '00 C.49 B.A. L.8 J.D. [Shambaugh,K.B.&W.]
Williams, Stephen J., (AV) .... '40 '65 C.347 B.S. L.1119 LL.B. [Shambaugh,K.B.&W.]
Witmer, Mark E., (BV) .... '— '92 C&L.347 B.A., J.D. [Beckman L.]
Witmer, Wayne L., (BV) .... '44 '72 C.347 A.B. L.1119 J.D. The Medical Protective Co.
Witte, Zachary A. .... '— '03 C.347 B.A. L.365 J.D. [⊠ T.S.Locke]
Woenker, Jeffrey M. .... '70 '00 C&L.347 B.S., J.D. [⊠ Barrett&M.]

Anderson, Tracey A. (Continued)

Taxation, Tax Planning, Tax Audits, Wills and Probate, Trusts and Estates, Estate Planning, Asset Protection, Guardianships, Employment Law, Employee Benefits, Business Law, Business Planning, Contracts, Business Litigation, Business Enterprises, Corporate, Small Business Law, Partnerships, Limited Liability Companies, Buying and Selling of Businesses, Business Start-Ups.

See Professional Biographies, GRANGER, INDIANA

Badger, Robert E. '38 '69 C.1070 B.S. L.425 J.D.
(adm. in LA; not adm. in IN) 15275 Quail Hollow Court
Dvorak, Kathleen B. .... '— '97 C.112 B.A. L.602 J.D. 51815 Lake Knoll Court
Hart, Henry R. .... '46 '73 C&L.879 B.A., J.D. 10135 Shadow Wood Dr.
Helling, Joseph T., (AV) .... '24 '54 C.229 A.B. L.602 J.D. 17344 Fergus Dr.
Lopata, Marvin, Law Office of, (CV) '52 '78 C.347 A.B. L.345 J.D.
16021 Cleveland Rd.
Murray, Thomas L., (AV) .... '24 '51 C.999 L.602 J.D. Pres., Woodfield Downs, Inc.
Ramming, John B. .... '31 '68 C.628 B.S. L.347 J.D. Ind. Toll Rd. Comm.
Sanders, Thomas J., Law Office of, (BV) '57 '82
C&L.879 B.A., J.D. 51670 Trail Ridge Dr.
Schnarr, Kristine Elmlund '50 '81 C.339 B.S. L.424 J.D.
(adm. in IL; not adm. in IN) 50770 Waldon Park Lane‡
Trant, John T. .... '38 '69 C.665 B.B.A. L.229 J.D. 17022 Woodshire Ct.
Vance, Susan Mahone .... '49 '77 C.454 B.A. L.1187 J.D. 15777 Lake Forest Ct.
Yeagley, Earl W. .... '22 '49 C.63 L.602 J.D. 51553 Hendon Hall Ct.‡

GREENCASTLE, * 9,880, *Putnam Co.*

Brewer, Delbert H., (BV) .... '42 '74 C.835 B.S. L.345 J.D. 110 W. Walnut St.
Danberry, Cheryl A., (CV) .... '57 '82 C.210 B.A. L.345 J.D. 3 E. Franklin St.
Durham, J. Frank, (AV) .... '15 '41 C.210 B.A. L.347 LL.B. 11 E. Walnut St.
Felling, Darrell E., (CV) .... '47 '72 C.210 B.A. L.347 J.D. P.O. Box 612
Gunn, Helen L. '56 '84 C&L.339 A.B., J.D.
(adm. in IL; not adm. in IN) 144 Hilltop Lane‡
Headley, Matthew L. .... '63 '90 C&L.500 B.A., J.D. Pros. Atty. Off.
Houck, James M., (BV) .... '21 '62 C.210 A.B. L.345 J.D. 11 1/2 S. Indiana St.

Hunt, Hassler & Lorenz LLP
(See Terre Haute)

McGlone, Edward, Law Office
(See Terre Haute)

Phipps, James Wm. .... '43 '88 C.210 B.A. L.1119 J.D. 3447 S. US Highway 231‡
Priest, C. Reid, (BV) .... '23 '79 C.679 B.S.M.E. L.345 J.D. 112 Longcastle Dr., Unit 2
Robertson, Laurie J. .... '64 '89 C.347 B.A. L.1119 J.D. 23 W. Franklin St.
Selvia, Trudy L. .... '69 '95 C.739 B.A. L.347 J.D. 22-1/2 West Washington St.
Sutherlin and Zeiner, (BV) .... 105 East Washington Street
Wilson, Larry J., (BV) .... '51 '76 C.894 A.B. L.1119 J.D. 188 N. Indiana St.
Young, James Harvey, (BV) .... '47 '78 C.210 B.A. L.1119 J.D. 22 1/2 W. Washington St.
Zeiner, John R., (BV) .... '34 '79 C.679 B.S. L.345 J.D. [Sutherlin&Z.]

GREENFIELD, * 14,600, *Hancock Co.*

Allen, Eric N., (AV) .... '52 '78 C.679 B.S. L.345 J.D. [Allen W.M.]

Allen • Wellman • McNew, (AV)
Five Courthouse Plaza, P.O. Box 455, 46140
Telephone: 317-462-3455 Fax: 317-467-6109
Email: mail@awmlaw.com URL: http://www.awmlaw.com
Waldo C. Ging (1892-1971); James L. Brand (1938-1996). Members of Firm: Eric N. Allen; Dawn E. Wellman; James W. McNew; George A. Lohmeier; Kevin G. Harvey. Associates: Jonathan M. Brown; Andrew E. Clark; Andria A. Kerney; Janet L. Manship; Jason A. Childers; Daniel J. Layden; Amy K. Noe.
General Civil and Criminal Practice in all Courts. Trials, Personal Injury, Medical Malpractice, Family/Domestic Relations, Real Estate, Business Association, Trusts, Probate and Estate Planning, Commercial, Litigation, Business Law, Personal and Corporate Bankruptcy, Appeals, Zoning, Mediation.

See Professional Biographies, GREENFIELD, INDIANA

Amick, Larry G., (BV) .... '47 '74 C.347 B.A. L.1119 J.D. 27 American Legion Place
Apple, John A., (BV) .... '67 '94 C.679 B.S. L.1119 J.D. 8 W. Main St.
Billings, C. Thomas, (BV) .... '42 '68 C.265 B.A. L.345 J.D. [Williams,C.&B.]
Blue, Karin L., (BV) .... '57 '88 C.347 B.A. L.345 J.D. [Ⓐ Pritzke&D.]
Bogigian, Robert G., (BV) .... '50 '74 C.894 B.A. L.345 J.D. 17 N. Pennsylvania St.
Boyle, Kevin M. .... '65 '91 C.347 B.A. L.879 J.D. [Ⓐ Overhauser]
Brown, Jonathan M., (CV) .... '71 '98 C.37 B.A. L.345 J.D. [Ⓐ Allen W.M.]
Burrow, Michael R., (BV) .... '62 '88 C.63 B.S. L.347 J.D. [Wolf]
Carlock, Steve .... '55 '81 C.1119 L.345 J.D. 5999 W. Memory Lane
Childers, Jason A. .... '74 '99 C.679 B.A. L.880 J.D. [Ⓐ Allen W.M.]
Clark, Andrew E. .... '72 '00 C.265 B.A. L.345 J.D. [Ⓐ Allen W.M.]
Clark, Laura L., (CV) .... '73 '98 C.679 B.A. L.347 J.D. Dep. Pros. Atty.
Cone, C. Thomas, (AV) .... '38 '62 C.347 A.B. L.1119 LL.B. [Williams,C.&B.]
Culver, Richard D. .... '58 '83 C.265 B.A. L.345 J.D. Supr. Ct. J.
Davis, George B., (AV) .... '14 '38 C.210 L.345 LL.B. 321 N. State St.

Davis, James E., Attorney at Law, (BV) '49 '75 C.210 B.A. L.345 J.D.
321 N. State Street, P.O. Box 950, 46140
Telephone: 317-462-7759 Toll Free: 1-800-570-2928
Email: jimdavislaw@hrtc.net URL: http://www.lawyers.com/jimdavislaw
Personal Injury, Social Security Disability, Wrongful Death, Medical Malpractice, Wills and Probate Law, Automobile Accidents and Injuries, Head Injury, Spinal Injury, Slip and Fall, Trucking Accidents, Construction Accidents, Railroad Accidents, Nursing Home and Abuse and Neglect.

See Professional Biographies, GREENFIELD, INDIANA

Davis, John L., (AV) .... '48 '73 C.602 A.B. L.345 J.D. [Pritzke&D.]
Dobbins, C. Dean, (BV) .... '47 '72 C.679 B.S. L.345 J.D. [D.Dobbins]
Dobbins, Dean, (BV) .... 19 West Main Street
Eicher, Jeffrey K., Law Office .... '61 '92 C.802 B.B.A. L.345 J.D. 3836 N. Forest Ln.
Gottschalk, Ronald L. .... '38 '69 C&L.347 B.S., J.D. Cir. J.
Hamilton, Jeanne M. .... '66 '91 C.973 B.A. L.347 J.D. Supr. Ct. J.
Harvey, Kevin G., (BV) .... '66 '94 C.57 B.A. L.1119 J.D. [Allen W.M.]
Kerney, Andria A. .... '71 '99 C.347 B.S. L.1119 J.D. [Ⓐ Allen W.M.]
Layden, Daniel J. .... '75 '00 C.973 B.A. L.734 J.D. [Ⓐ Allen W.M.]
Lindman, Constance R. .... '63 '89 C&L.347 B.S., J.D. [Ⓒ Overhauser]
Lohmeier, George A., (BV) .... '48 '78 C.259 B.S. L.345 J.D. [Allen W.M.]
Lyons, Holly L. .... '59 '85 C.679 B.A. L.838 J.D. 19 W. Main St.
Manship, Janet L. .... '71 '95 C.999 B.A. L.836 J.D. [Ⓐ Allen W.M.]
McNew, James W., (BV) .... '49 '76 C.383 B.A. L.345 J.D. [Allen W.M.]
Murphy, David P., (BV) .... '47 '72 C&L.347 A.B., J.D. 504 W. Main St.
Nettles, Gaylon .... '47 '97 C.1228 B.S. L.345 J.D. [G.J.Nettles]
Nettles, Gaylon James, P.C. .... 761 N. Raven Field Ct.
Noe, Amy K. .... '72 '00 C.231 B.A. L.345 J.D. [Ⓐ Allen W.M.]
O'Neal, Lyn W., (BV) .... '52 '84 C.346 B.S. L.345 J.D. 206 E. Main St.
Osborne, D. Chris .... '46 '86 C.679 B.S. L.347 J.D. 1207 Sherwood Drive
Overhauser, Paul B., (AV) .... '57 '83 C.679 B.S.B.A. L.347 J.D. [Overhauser] (Pat.)
Overhauser Law Offices, LLC, (AV) .... 737 W. Green Meadows Drive, Suite 300 (Pat.)
Payne, Richard T. .... '44 '69 C.347 A.B. L.1119 J.D. Supr. Ct. J.
Pritzke, Ronald R., (AV) .... '47 '73 C.347 B.S. L.345 J.D. [Pritzke&D.]
Pritzke & Davis, (AV) .... 728 N. State St.
Reason, Roger D., (BV) .... '47 '72 C.346 B.S. L.345 J.D. 17 N. Pennsylvania St.
Richardson, Ray .... '37 '62 C.679 B.S. L.347 LL.B. 202 N. State
Shelby, Glenna Dudley .... '44 '79 C.347 A.B. L.345 J.D. SDS Group Limited
Smith, Christopher T., (BV) .... '68 '93 C&L.347 B.A., J.D. 728 N. State St.
Strahl, Dan L., (BV) .... '47 '87 C.679 B.S. L.345 J.D. 8 W. Main St.
Tosick, Michael J., (BV) .... '44 '71 C.347 A.B. L.345 J.D. Three Courthouse Plaza
Watson, Melville E. .... '13 '40 C.347 B.S. L.1119 J.D. 12 Walnut St.‡
Wellman, Dawn E., (AV) .... '49 '76 C&L.879 B.A., J.D. [Allen W.M.]

Williams, Cone & Billings, (AV)
222 North State Street, P.O. Box 8, 46140
Telephone: 317-462-5577 Fax: 317-462-0084 Email: tbillings@wcblaw.org
Email: tcone@wcblaw.org
Members of Firm: Glenn T. Williams (1906-1970); C. Thomas Cone; C. Thomas Billings.
General Civil and Criminal Practice, Driving While Intoxicates, Drug Crimes, Juvenile Law, all State and Federal Courts. Trials. Wills & Probate, Trusts & Estates, Estate Planning. Insurance, Municipal, Banking and Real Estate Law. Family, Domestic Relations, Adoption Law, Child Custody, Child Support, Divorce, Visitation Rights, Business Law, Contracts, Business Litigation, Business Planning, Business Enterprises, Corporate, Limited Liability Companies, Partnerships, Small Business, Buying and Selling a Business, Business Start-Ups.
Attorneys for: Greenfield Banking Co.; Hancock Memorial Hospital; Community School Corporation of Southern Hancock County.
Local Counsel for: Indiana Insurance Co.; American States Insurance Co.
Reference: Greenfield Banking Co., Greenfield, Indiana.

See Professional Biographies, GREENFIELD, INDIANA

Wolf, Sarah M., (CV) .... '52 '78 C.174 B.A. L.345 J.D. [Wolf]
Wolf, William H., (BV) .... '20 '50 C.231 A.B. L.345 J.D. [Wolf]
Wolf Law Firm, (BV) .... 6 East Main St.
Wooten, Bonnie K., (BV) .... '50 '92 C.347 B.S. L.345 J.D. 728 North State Street
Zelin, Nicole A., (BV) .... '67 '92 C&L.347 B.A., J.D. 515 N. State St., Ste. B

GREENSBURG, * 10,260, *Decatur Co.*

Bass, Kenneth R., (BV) .... '51 '76 C.63 B.S. L.345 J.D. 111 E. Main St.
Beard, Ronald, (BV) .... '18 '41 C&L.347 B.S., LL.B. 111 E. Main St.
Fitch, John W. .... '22 '50 C.347 B.S. L.1119 LL.B. 114 N. Franklin St.‡
Goddard, John W. .... '07 '32 C.108 A.B. L.345 LL.B. 432 E. Walnut‡
Hamilton, Frank I., Jr., (BV) .... '49 '76 C.347 B.S. L.345 J.D. 117 S. Broadway St.
Millis, Benton R. .... '27 '67 C.679 B.S. L.345 J.D. 603 N. Bway.‡
Polanski, Margaret A., (BV) .... '54 '78 C.207 B.A. L.608 J.D. 125 W. Washington
Robbins, William H., (AV) .... '41 '68 C.894 A.B. L.1119 J.D. [Rolfes,G.W.&R.]
Rolfes, Garvey, Walker & Robbins, (AV) .... 132 East Washington Street
Scholl, Melissa S., (BV) .... '67 '94 C.303 B.A. L.1340 J.D. [Taylor&S.]
Smith, G. Daryl .... '49 '75 C.674 B.A. L.345 J.D. 105 S. Broadway St.‡
Smith, William O., (AV) .... '46 '73 C.427 B.A. L.345 J.D. Chief Pros.
Taylor, Stephen T., (BV) .... '48 '79 C.303 B.S. L.1340 J.D. [Taylor&S.]
Taylor & Scholl, Law Office of, (BV) .... 114 North Franklin Street
Tebbe, Christopher Michael .... '73 '00 C.973 B.A.S. L.74 J.D. 117 S. Broadway St.
Walker, Karl F., (AV) .... '34 '60 C.303 A.B. L.345 J.D. [Rolfes,G.W.&R.]
Westhafer, John A. .... '40 '66 C.679 B.A. L.273 J.D. Cir. J.
Wickens, Don H., (AV) .... '36 '61 C.208 B.A. L.345 J.D. 230 N. Franklin St.
Wilke, Warren Michael, (BV) .... '43 '69 C.108 B.A. L.345 J.D. 150 Courthouse Sq.

GREENWOOD, 36,037, *Johnson Co.*

Bailey, Jack L., (CV) .... '53 '84 C.347 A.B. L.345 J.D. Corp. Coun., IDC-USA Corp.
Barrett, William Wallace, (BV) .... '62 '89 C.473 B.A. L.347 J.D. [Williams H.B.&W.]
Barton, Kevin M., (BV) .... '56 '80 C.880 B.A. L.345 J.D. 171 N. Madison Ave., Ste. 263
Bekes, Gregory E. .... '50 '88 C.1116 B.A. L.421 J.D. [Grotke&B.]
Belovic, George '23 '53 C.930 B.B.A. L.1003 LL.B.
(adm. in OH; not adm. in IN) 1081 W. Elm St.‡
Brown, Dennis K., (BV) .... '50 '77 C.347 B.S. L.345 J.D. 374 S. Madison Ave.
Butler, John S. '50 '78 C&L.280 B.A., J.D.
(adm. in GA; not adm. in IN) 720 Executive Park Dr.
Cecere, M. Carolyn, (CV) .... '33 '90 C.456 B.S. L.347 J.D. [Wilson,G.&C.]
Clark, Marla K. '71 '95 C.324 B.B.A. L.347 J.D.
(adm. in TX; not adm. in IN) 1965 Fox Moor Ter.
Clements, Janine M. .... '71 '97 C.347 B.A. L.345 J.D. Dep. Atty.Gen.
Doyle, Rick D., (BV) .... '62 '91 C&L.347 B.S., J.D. 399 North Madison Avenue
Drury, Ronald E., (BV) .... '47 '75 C.346 B.S. L.345 J.D. P.O. Box 67
Dunn, James E., (BV) .... '51 '91 C.347 B.S. L.345 J.D. 3400 S. Morgantown Rd.

Eckert, Stephen P., Law Offices of
(See Indianapolis)

Elrod & Mascher, P.C.
(See Indianapolis)

Erwin, Roger D., (AV) .... '52 '80 C.679 B.S. L.345 J.D. 1183 Vicksburg South Dr.
Fewell, Terry G. .... '40 '65 C.894 A.B. L.1119 J.D. 420 Austin Ln
Flanigan, James T. .... '58 '92 C.679 B.S. L.347 J.D. [Ⓐ McClure M.D.&H.]
Fujawa, Ellen K., Law Office of .... '53 '85 C.347 B.A. L.879 J.D. P.O. Box 526
Green, James R., (CV) .... '48 '74 C.303 B.A. L.345 J.D. [Wilson,G.&C.]
Gregory, Lewis J., (BV) .... '52 '88 C.063 B.S. L.347 J.D. 724 Winding Trail
Griffin, Marc L., (CV) .... '56 '93 C.435 B.S. L.347 J.D. [Griffin,H.&H.]
Griffin, Hicks & Hicks, (BV) .... 821 N. Madison Ave.
Grotke, Allen E. .... '41 '73 C.879 B.A. L.1003 J.D. [Grotke&B.]

Grotke & Bekes, P.C.
720 Fry Road, Suite A, 46142
Telephone: 317-888-1000 Fax: 317-888-1021
Email: gbpc@att.net URL: http://www.grotkebekespc.com
Allen E. Grotke; Gregory E. Bekes. Of Counsel: John R. Panico.
Employment and Labor Defense, Labor Relations.

See Professional Biographies, GREENWOOD, INDIANA

Hall, William D., (BV) .... '24 '59 C.347 A.B. L.345 J.D. 1200 Tanglewood Dr.‡
Henn, David M. .... '68 '94 C.347 B.S. L.421 J.D. [McClure M.D.&H.]
Hewitt, Brian C., (AV) .... '58 '83 C.679 B.A. L.345 J.D. [Williams H.B.&W.]
Hicks, Brian E. .... '69 '95 C&L.347 B.S., J.D. [Griffin,H.&H.]
Hicks, Thomas H., (BV) .... '59 '84 C.108 B.S. L.945 J.D. [Griffin,H.&H.]
Hoover, Kevin A., (AV) .... '58 '84 C.63 B.S. L.345 J.D. [Otten R.&H.]
Kennedy, Steven L. .... '53 '79 C.63 B.A. L.345 J.D. 1343 Flintlock Drive
Lekse, David J. .... '69 '02 C.344 B.S. L.74 J.D. [Ⓐ Williams H.B.&W.]
McClure McClure Davis & Henn, (BV)
225 South Emerson Avenue, Suite F (⊙Indianapolis)
McGovern, Philip R. .... '43 '68 C&L.347 A.B., J.D. 339 Highland Dr.
Meier, Linda K., (BV) .... '50 '87 C.339 B.A. L.345 J.D. [Sargent&M.]
Meiners, Michael J., (AV) .... '51 '80 C.602 B.S. L.345 J.D. 375 N. Madison Ave.
Nies, Joyce A. .... '49 '97 C&L.347 B.S., J.D. [Ⓐ Van Valer]

Otten, Mark F., (BV) '49 '78 C.347 A.B. L.345 J.D. [Otten R.&H.]
Otten Reames & Hoover, A Professional Association, (AV) 1090 South Street Road 135, Suite B
Panico, John R. '52 '90 C.1044 B.A. L.1225 J.D. [Ⓑ Grotke&B.]
Paul, Daniel J. '72 '98 C.265 B.A. L.345 J.D. [Ⓐ Williams H.B.&W.]
Pinnow, John A. '59 '85 C&L.347 B.A., J.D. [J.Pinnow]
Pinnow, John 430 N. Madison Ave., Ste. 2
Pitcher, Joseph R., (BV) '55 '88 C.63 B.S. L.345 J.D. P.O. Box 1501
Prime, Eric W., (BV) '66 '91 C&L.347 B.A., J.D. [Ⓑ Van Valer]
Reames, John M. '53 '84 C.63 B.S. L.345 J.D. [Otten R.&H.]

Reiber Law Office
(See Indianapolis)

Robbins, J. Lee, (BV) '60 '86 C.894 B.A. L.347 J.D. [Williams H.B.&W.]
Rosko, Emily S. '67 '93 C.679 B.A. L.1119 J.D. Conceptioneering, Inc.
Runnels, Charles W., (BV) '28 '65 C.499 B.S. L.345 J.D. 3858 Keyway Dr.

Ruppert & Schaefer, P.C.
(See Indianapolis)

Rybolt, John L. '30 '63 C.893 B.A. L.345 LL.B. P.O. Box 306
Sargent, James F. T., Jr., (AV) '36 '61 C.303 A.B. L.1119 J.D. [Sargent&M.]
Sargent & Meier, (AV) 200 S. Madison Ave.
Schaberg, Terry H. '47 '76 C.172 B.A. L.845 J.D. OMS Intl. Inc.
Schoettle, Amy L. '— '03 C.347 B.A. L.1119 J.D. [Ⓐ Williams H.B.&W.]
Schoettle, Raymond J. '64 '91 C.63 B.S. L.345 J.D. [Ⓐ Williams H.B.&W.]
Sears, Mark W. '42 '69 C.347 A.B. L.345 J.D. 315 U.S. 31 S.
Sharp, Wm. T. '20 '51 C.108 M.A. L.347 J.D. Ret. Cir. J.
Smart, John M., III, (AV) '43 '74 C.347 B.S. L.345 J.D. 1648 Fry Road, Suite A
Smith, Gerald Floyd '42 '87 C.421 L.345 J.D. 1848 Lanarkshire Dr.
Tanner, Scott A., (BV) '64 '90 C.265 B.A. L.74 J.D. 435 E. Main St., Ste. M-1
Torres, Lori A., (BV) '61 '86 C.347 B.A. L.345 J.D. 1648 Fry Rd., Ste. A
Vander Luitgaren, Thomas W. '69 '97 C.1119 B.A. L.347 J.D. [Ⓐ Van Valer]
VanderVeen, Jennifer L. '74 '99 C.20 B.A. L.477 J.D. [Ⓐ Williams H.B.&W.]
Van Valer, Joe N., (AV) '35 '63 C.265 A.B. L.345 LL.B. [Van Valer]
Van Valer Law Firm, (AV) 299 West Main Street
Watson, Stephen K. '65 '92 C.624 B.A. L.347 J.D. [Ⓐ Williams H.B.&W.]
White, John M., (BV) '58 '87 C.346 B.S. L.347 J.D. [Ⓐ Williams H.B.&W.]
Wicker, Robert J., (AV) '36 '66 C.973 B.S. L.345 J.D. 384 N. Madison Ave.
Wilkowski, John P. '66 '94 C.143 B.S. L.347 J.D. [Williams H.B.&W.]
Williams, Jon E., (AV) '43 '76 C.999 B.A. L.345 J.D. [Williams H.B.&W.]

Williams Hewitt Barrett & Wilkowski, (AV)
600 N. Emerson Avenue, 46143
Telephone: 317-888-1121 Fax: 317-887-4069
Partners: Jon E. Williams; Brian C. Hewitt; J. Lee Robbins; William Wallace Barrett; John P. Wilkowski. Associates: John M. White; Stephen K. Watson; Raymond J. Schoettle; Daniel J. Paul; David J. Lekse; Jennifer L. VanderVeen; Amy L. Schoettle.
General Civil and Trial Practice, Probate, Banking, Corporate, Real Estate, Zoning, Commercial Law, Health Care, Elder Law, School Law, Municipal Law, Labor and Employment and Mediation.
See Professional Biographies, GREENWOOD, INDIANA

Wilson, John P., (BV) '47 '74 C.249 B.A. L.345 J.D. [Wilson,G.&C.]
Wilson, Green & Cecere, (BV) 637 South State Road 135, Suite I
Wright, Jan D. '47 '73 C&L.793 B.S.B.A., J.D. Midwest Title Corp.
Yoon, Susan J. '70 '97 C&L.347 B.S., J.D. 4294 Country Ln.

GRIFFITH, 17,334, *Lake Co.*

Breclaw, John D., (BV) '41 '66 C&L.339 B.A, J.D. [Breclaw,H.&T.]
Breclaw, Harris & Taylor, A Professional Corporation, (BV) 200 West Glen Park Avenue

Breclaw - Teeling, Marge E., Law Office of '— '98 C.679 B.S. L.879 J.D.
735 West Glen Park Avenue, 46319
Telephone: 219-934-9344 Fax: 219-934-9346
URL: http://www.lawyers.com/breclaw-teelinglaw
Family Law, Adoption Law, Divorce, Child Custody, Child Support, Premarital Agreements, Paternity, Driving While Intoxicated, Traffic Violations, Wills, Trusts, Probate, Mediation.
See Professional Biographies, GRIFFITH, INDIANA

Bullock, Bryan K., Law Offices of '66 '01 C.999 B.A. L.879 J.D. P.O. Box 701
Cahillane, Thomas E. '25 '63 C&L.209 B.A., J.D. Hyatt Legal Servs.
Harris, Mark Randal '51 '80 C.1172 B.A. L.879 J.D. [Breclaw,H.&T.]
Leal, Victor L., (CV) '39 '81 C.347 B.S. L.365 J.D. 1412 N. Dwiggins St.
Malkowski, Lynn Morrow, (CV) '47 '92 C.739 B.A. L.879 J.D. 417 W. Ave. D
Molnar-Boncela, Catherine L., (BV) '57 '81 C&L.879 B.A., J.D. 842 S. Indiana St.
Ostrowski, Leo A., (CV) '31 '56 C.477 A.B. L.597 J.D. 749 N. Oakwood St.
Taylor, Robert L., (CV) '47 '81 C.347 B.S. L.365 J.D. [Breclaw,H.&T.]
Valtierra, Jose Guadalupe '56 '86 C.679 B.A. L.1119 J.D. 630 S. Cline Ave.
Villalpando, Jesse M., (CV) '59 '85 C&L.347 A.B., J.D. 956 North Griffith Blvd.

HAGERSTOWN, 1,835, *Wayne Co.*

Cox, Matthew Ryan '75 '00 C.63 B.S. L.744 J.D. P.O. Box 144
Federico, David A. '43 '68 C.347 B.S. L.309 J.D. 20 W. Walnut St.‡
Federico, Richard E., (BV) '46 '75 C.347 B.S. L.879 J.D. 20 W. Walnut St.
Justice, Rebecca L., (CV) '62 '91 C&L.347 B.A., J.D. 4910 N. State Rd. 1
Lafuze, Ralph O., (BV) '32 '56 C.679 B.S. L.1119 LL.B. Box 144

HAMMOND, 83,048, *Lake Co.*

Abrahamson, Harold, (AV) '34 '58 C.347 L.209 LL.B. [Abrahamson&R.]

Abrahamson & Reed, (AV)
200 Russell Street, 46320
Telephone: 219-937-1500 Fax: 219-937-3174
Members of Firm: Harold Abrahamson; Kenneth D. Reed. Associates: Scott R. Bilse; John P. Reed.
General Civil Practice in all State and Federal Courts. Trials and Appeals.
References: Calumet National Bank, Hammond; Mercantile National Bank, Hammond.
See Professional Biographies, HAMMOND, INDIANA

Allegretti, Joseph P. '46 '73 C.436 B.A. L.365 J.D. [Sherman&A.]
Allen, David Paul '50 '75 C.108 B.A. L.1119 J.D. 5231 Hohman Ave.
Anderson, Robert A., (CV) '63 '90 C.347 B.S. L.602 J.D. [Krieg D.G.]
Babcock, Michael D. '68 '96 C.347 B.S. L.879 J.D. [Sachs&H.]
Banasiak, Joseph, (CV) '61 '86 C&L.879 B.S., J.D. 7150 Indianapolis Blvd.
Bannwart, Stephen Duane, (CV) '54 '93 C.347 B.A. L.879 J.D. [Ⓐ J.Stalmack&Assoc.]
Beach, David J., (CV) '— '95 C&L.802 B.A., J.D. [Eichhorn&E.]

Beckman, Kelly & Smith, (AV) Ⓑ
5920 Hohman Avenue, 46320
Telephone: 219-933-6200 Fax: 219-933-6201
Email: firm@bkslegal.com URL: http://www.bkslegal.com
(This Listing Continued)

Beckman, Kelly & Smith (Continued)
Members of Firm: John F. Beckman, Jr. (1916-1996); Daniel F. Kelly (1914-1978); J. B. Smith (1944-2004); Andrew J. Fetsch; Randall J. Nye; Daniel W. Glavin; Eric L. Kirschner; Julie R. Murzyn. Of Counsel: Melanie Morgan Dunajeski. Associates: Stephen J. Sullivan; Robin G. Remley; Leeanne C. Foster; Alissa F. Resop.
General Practice, Commercial, Corporation, Transportation and Trucking, Products and Professional Liability Defense, Elder Law, Estate and Trust Planning and Administration, Franchising, Real Estate, Employment, Taxation and Environmental Law, Trials and Appeals in all Courts, Medical Malpractice Defense and Workers Compensation Defense.
Representative Clients: C.R. England; Ericsson, Inc.; Waste Management, Inc.; Northwest Indiana Public Broadcasting, Inc.; Heartland Express; Allen Bradley Company, Inc.; Bombardier Recreational Products, Inc.
See Professional Biographies, HAMMOND, INDIANA

Bellamy, Calvin E. '42 '68 C.347 A.B. L.477 J.D. Chair & CEO, Bank Calumet
Bilse, Scott R., (CV) '61 '87 C&L.602 B.B.A., J.D. [Ⓐ Abrahamson&R.]
Bloom, George E., (BV) '44 '69 C.108 A.B. L.1119 J.D. 6435 Forest Ave.
Bosch, Michael W., (BV) '48 '78 C.1024 B.A. L.146 J.D. 7150 Indianapolis Blvd.

Burke Costanza & Cuppy LLP
(See Merrillville, Munster and Valparaiso)

Cherry, Paul R. '51 '78 C.333 B.A. L.607 J.D. Mag. J.
Chevigny, John E., (BV) '34 '60 C.750 B.A. L.1119 LL.B. [Krieg D.G.]
Clements, Thomas A., (BV) '54 '78 C&L.347 B.A., J.D. [Ruman,C.&H.]
Connor, Kerry Clementine '62 '88 C.347 B.A. L.1119 J.D. Northern Dist. of IN
Conover, Todd M. '50 '82 C.108 B.A. L.1137 J.D. [McHie&M.]
Corliss, Kerry A. '— '01 C.209 B.A. L.221 J.D. [Ruman,C.&H.]
Cox, Shawn D. '72 '97 C.894 B.A. L.1119 J.D. [Ⓐ Krieg D.G.]
Crisman, Gregory A. '63 '92 C&L.347 B.S., J.D. [Eichhorn&E.]
Cuttino, Lieu A. '67 '98 C.530 B.A. L.879 J.D. Co. Pros. Off.
Dabertin, David M. '62 '96 C&L.1119 B.A., J.D. 5246 Hohman Ave.
Demange, Julie A., (CV) '68 '95 C.352 B.B.A. L.879 J.D. [Sachs&H.]
Donahue, Beth E. '73 '97 C.475 B.A. L.146 J.D. (adm. in IL; not adm. in IN) Law Clk., U.S. Dist. Ct.
Downes, W. Patrick, (BV) '47 '72 C&L.602 B.A., J.D. [Krieg D.G.]
Dragus, George H., (CV) '23 '55 C.347 L.879 LL.B. 6210 Hohman Ave.
Dunajeski, Melanie Morgan, (BV) '57 '84 C.210 B.A. L.347 J.D. [Ⓑ Beckman,K.&S.]
Efron, Morton L. '38 '62 C&L.477 B.A., J.D. [Efron&E.]
Efron & Efron, A Professional Corporation 5246 Hohman Ave.
Eichhorn, Frederick F., Jr., (AV) '— '57 C.347 B.S. L.1119 J.D. [Eichhorn&E.] ‡
Eichhorn, William H., (AV) '32 '61 C.347 B.S. L.1119 J.D. [Eichhorn&E.] ‡

Eichhorn & Eichhorn, (AV)
200 Russell Street, P.O. Box 6328, 46325 ⊙
Telephone: 219-931-0560 Fax: 219-931-5370
URL: http://www.eichhornlaw.com
Partners of Firm: Frederick F. Eichhorn, Jr. (Retired); William H. Eichhorn (Retired); David C. Jensen; Paul A. Rake; John M. McCrum; Robert J. Feldt; Gregory A. Crisman; Alyssa Stamatakos; David J. Beach; Louis W. Voelker, III; John P. Twohy.
General Practice, Litigation in State and Federal Courts. Public Utility, Banking, Corporation, Health Care, Insurance, Commercial Transactions, Labor and Employment Law, Real Estate, Professional Liability and Tort Law. Mediation.
Carmel, Indiana Office: 9640 North Augusta Drive, Suite 412, 46032. Telephone: 317-228-9670. Telecopier: 317-228-9569.
See Professional Biographies, HAMMOND, INDIANA

Enslen, Lowell E., (AV) '27 '52 C&L.879 LL.B. [Enslen,E.&M.]
Enslen, William T., (BV) '45 '69 C.221 B.A. L.879 J.D. [Enslen,E.&M.]

Enslen, Charles E.
(See Merrillville)

Enslen, Enslen & Matthews, (AV) 142 Rimbach
Faulkner, Alan R., (BV) '53 '79 C.309 A.B. L.608 J.D. 15 Lawndale St.

Feingold, Eugene M., Law Offices of
(See Munster)

Feldt, Robert J., (CV) '60 '86 C.597 B.S. L.146 J.D. [Eichhorn&E.]
Fernandez, Carmen A., (BV) '52 '77 C.347 B.A. L.1119 J.D. 7207 Indianapolis Blvd.
Fetsch, Andrew J., (BV) '45 '75 C.679 B.S. L.208 J.D. [Beckman,K.&S.]
Fife, James H., III, (CV) '57 '87 C.879 B.S. L.424 J.D. 7207 Indianapolis Blvd.
Foster, James E., (BV) '44 '70 C.347 B.A. L.1119 J.D. [Funk&F.]
Foster, Leeanne C. '77 '02 C.347 B.S. L.1119 J.D. [Ⓐ Beckman,K.&S.]
Funk, R. Cordell, (BV) '41 '66 C.339 B.A. L.145 J.D. [Funk&F.]
Funk & Foster, (BV) 5253 Hohman Ave.
Galvin, Margaret Royce, (CV) '44 '70 C.430 B.A. L.365 J.D. 5253 Hohman Ave.
Galvin, Patrick J., (AV) '39 '64 C.602 B.A. L.276 J.S. [Krieg D.G.]
Glavin, Daniel W., (AV) '54 '80 C.679 B.A. L.1119 J.D. [Beckman,K.&S.]
Glendening, George J., (CV) '41 '66 C.145 A.B. L.477 J.D. 49 Meunich Ct
Goldman, Dolores, (CV) '30 '59 C.679 B.S. L.209 LL.B. 142 Rimbach St.

Green & Kuchel, P.C., (BV)
5930 Hohman Avenue, Suite 102, 46320
Telephone: 219-852-6000 Fax: 219-852-6813
Email: firm@greenkuchel.com URL: http://www.greenkuchellaw.com
Carol M. Green-Fraley; Glenn W. Kuchel.
Commercial Litigation, Negligence, Business, Business Planning, Contracts, Law Suits, Corporate, Real Estate, Wills and Probate, Trusts and Estates, Estate Planning, Estate Administration, Guardianships, Asset Protection, Personal Injury, Automobile Accidents, Slip and Fall, Wrongful Death, Taxation, Municipal Law, Employment Law, Wrongful Termination, Sexual Harassment, Discrimination, Disability Accommodation, Employee Benefits, Social Security Disability, Workers Compensation, Civil Rights, Family Medical Leave Act, ADEA, Litigation.
See Professional Biographies, HAMMOND, INDIANA

Green-Fraley, Carol M., (BV) '46 '87 C.339 B.A. L.365 J.D. [Green&K.]
Gryzbek, Thomas J., (CV) '52 '83 C.339 B.S. L.209 J.D. Chf. Operat. Offic., St. Margaret Mercy Healthcare Ctrs., Inc.
Harkin, Jeffrey A. '51 '95 C.602 B.A. L.365 J.D. Jus.
Hayden, Sheilia Virag, (CV) '42 '83 C.347 B.A. L.879 J.D. Sr. V.P. & Sr. Tr. Offr., Bank Calumet
Hess, Robert M., (AV) '39 '66 C.347 B.S. L.597 J.D. [Sachs&H.]
Hill, Kristen D. '66 '92 C.145 B.A. L.879 J.D. 6920 Hohman Ave.

Hodges & Davis, P.C.
(See Merrillville)

Hoeppner Wagner & Evans LLP
(See Valparaiso)

Jackson, Carol D. '60 '83 C&L.336 B.S., J.D. (adm. in OH; not adm. in IN) 7331 Forest Ave.‡
Jensen, David C., (AV) '46 '71 C.210 B.A. L.477 J.D. [Eichhorn&E.]

Johnson & Rappa, LLC
(See Merrillville)

Jung, Wojciech F. '78 '03 C.724 B.S. L.823 J.D.
(adm. in NJ; not adm. in IN) Law Clk.
Katic, Peter .... '54 '77 C.347 A.B. L.209 J.D. 7150 Indianapolis Boulevard
Katz, J. Michael, (BV) .... '43 '68 C.347 B.S. L.1119 J.D. 5920 Hohman Avenue

Kelly, Timothy F., and Associates
(See Dyer)

Kessler, Fred H. .... '22 '64 C.46 B.S.M.E. L.597 J.D. Pres., Fred H. Kessler, Inc.
Kirsch, Thomas L., II .... '74 '99 C.347 B.A. L.309 J.D. U.S. Attorney's Office
Kirschner, Eric L., (BV) .... '46 '73 C&L.347 B.S., J.D. [Beckman,K.&S.]
Klingeberger, J. Philip .... '50 '75 C.293 B.A. L.1119 J.D. U.S. Bkrptcy. J.
Knish, Andrea, (CV) .... '47 '78 C.679 B.A. L.879 J.D. 7237 Alexander Ave.
Kompier, Nels A., (BV) .... '51 '85 C.679 B.S. L.365 J.D. [Ⓐ Funk&F.]
Kopaczewski, Kristy M. .... '76 '03 C&L.879 B.A., J.D. [Ⓐ J.Stalmack&Assoc.]

Krieg DeVault Galvin LLP, (AV)
5231 Hohman Avenue, 46320 ⊙
Telephone: 219-933-0380 Fax: 219-933-0471
Email: contact@kdlegal.com URL: http://www.kriegdevault.com
Partners: John E. Chevigny; Patrick J. Galvin; W. Patrick Downes; Robert A. Anderson. Associates: Julie A. Rosenwinkel; Shawn D. Cox; Jeffrey M. Monberg.
Acquisitions, Divestitures and Mergers, Antitrust, Appeals, Banking, Bankruptcy, Business and Commercial, Copyright, Corporations, Creditors' Rights, Employee Benefits, Energy, Environmental, ERISA, Estate Planning and Probate, Family/Domestic Relations, Federal and State Taxation, Government Relations, Health Care, Hospital Law, Intellectual Property, Insurance, International, Labor and Employment, Legislative, Litigation, Patent, Public Finance, Public Utilities, Products Liability, Real Estate, Securities Law, Tax-Exempt and Nonprofit Organizations, Technology and E-Commerce, Trademark.
Indianapolis, Indiana Office: Krieg DeVault LLP, One Indiana Square, Suite 2800, 46204. Telephone: 317-636-4341. Fax: 317-636-1507.
Indianapolis Northside Office: 12800 North Meridian Street, Suite 300, Carmel, Indiana 46032. Telephone: 317-566-1110. Fax: 317-636-1507.
Fort Wayne, Indiana Office: Krieg DeVault Lundy LLP, 825 Anthony Wayne Building, 203 East Berry Street, 46802. Telephone: 260-422-1534. Fax: 260-423-1590.
See Professional Biographies, HAMMOND, INDIANA

Kuchel, Glenn W. .... '61 '86 C&L.879 B.S., J.D. [Green&K.]
Kutak, Anne E. .... '37 '62 C.597 B.A. L.145 J.D. 22 Glendale Pk.‡
Lambert, Timothy J., (BVⓉ) '68 '93 C.340 B.S. L.339 J.D.
V.P., Legal Affs., Horseshoe Gaming Holding Corp.
Layer, Ronald F., (AV) .... '43 '72 C.870 B.S. L.1119 J.D. [Sachs&H.] ⊙
Link, Frederick H., (AV) .... '24 '50 C.33 B.A. L.1119 LL.B. 5253 Hohman Ave.
Loitz, Margaret M. .... '68 '95 C.1049 B.A. L.879 J.D. Mercantile Natl. Bk. of Indiana
Lozano, Rudy .... '42 '66 C.347 B.S. L.1119 LL.B. U.S. Dist. J.

Lucas, Holcomb & Medrea LLP
(See Merrillville)

Maish, Stephen M., (CV) .... '53 '80 C.188 B.A. L.879 J.D. [Maish&M.]
Maish & Mysliwy, (CV) .... Suite 200, 5248 Hohman Ave.
Marlowe, Charles F. .... '47 '73 C.347 B.S. L.879 J.D. 6936 Indianapolis Blvd.
Marshall, Kevin W., (CV) .... '61 '86 C.827 B.A. L.602 J.D. [Smith&M.]
Matthews, Gary K., (AV) .... '49 '75 C&L.879 B.S., J.D. [Enslen,E.&M.]
McCrum, John M., (BV) .... '55 '81 C.108 B.A. L.345 J.D. [Eichhorn&E.]
McHie, G. Edward, (AV) .... '20 '48 C.597 B.S.L. L.477 J.D. [McHie&M.]
McHie, James E., (BV) .... '46 '72 C.477 A.B. L.1119 J.D. [McHie&M.]
McHie & McHie, (AV) .... 53 Muenich Court
Monberg, Jeffrey M. .... '74 '99 C.602 B.B.A. L.1119 J.D. [Ⓐ Krieg D.G.]
Moody, James T. .... '38 '63 C&L.347 A.B., LL.B. U.S. Dist. J.
Morrow, Joseph T., (AV) '30 '58 C.347 B.S. L.1119 LL.B.
Chmn. Emeritus of the Bd., Mercantile Natl. Bk. of Indiana
Murphy, J. Justin, (CV) ...... '58 '89 C.425 B.B.A. L.879 J.D. 6949 Kennedy Ave., Ste. E
Murzyn, Julie R. .... '72 '97 C.338 B.S. L.347 J.D. [Beckman,K.&S.]
Mysliwy, Patrick, (CV) .... '56 '81 C.477 B.S. L.345 J.D. [Maish&M.]
Neary, Robert C. .... '70 '99 C.347 B.A. L.345 J.D. Dep. Pros. Atty.
Nye, Randall J., (BV) .... '48 '76 C.473 B.A. L.1119 J.D. [Beckman,K.&S.]
O'Connor, Joseph, (BV) .... '52 '78 C.602 B.A. L.990 J.D. [J.O'Connor&Assoc.]
O'Connor, Joseph, & Associates, (BV) .... 5272 Hohman Ave.
O'Malley, Cortney C. .... '77 '03 C.136 B.S. L.879 J.D. [Ⓐ Ruman,C.&H.]
Oosterhof, Gail .... '48 '75 C.347 B.A. L.1119 J.D. Tr. Offr., Bank Calumet
Opfel, Gregory L. ...... '56 '85 C.894 B.A. L.602 J.D. Law Clerk, Hon. James T. Moody
Ormes, Timothy J. .... '61 '87 C.679 B.S. L.1119 J.D. 7127 Indianapolis Boulevard
Overmyer, Jenifer K., (CV) .... '66 '91 C.63 B.S. L.879 J.D. 5261 Hohman Ave.
Pagano, Michael Neil .... '70 '96 C.210 B.A. L.564 J.D. [Ⓐ Funk&F.]
Pete, Robert A., (BV) .... '52 '77 C.602 B.A. L.1119 J.D. 232 Russell St.

Pinkerton and Friedman, Professional Corporation
(See Munster)

Polen, Michael E., Jr. .... '69 '04 C.999 B.S. L.879 J.D. [Ⓐ Ruman,C.&H.]
Quinn, Terrence M. '49 '75
C.679 B.S. L.602 J.D. Sr. V.P. & Sr. Invest. Offr., Bank Calumet
Rake, Paul A., (AV) .... '48 '75 C&L.347 A.B., J.D. [Eichhorn&E.]
Ratcliffe, Thomas S. .... '71 '97 C.880 B.A. L.597 J.D. Asst. U.S. Atty.
Reed, John P. .... '70 '97 C.347 B.A. L.209 J.D. [Ⓐ Abrahamson&R.]
Reed, Kenneth D., (BV) .... '37 '61 C&L.221 B.S.B.A., LL.B. [Abrahamson&R.]
Remley, Robin G. .... '70 '00 C.679 B.A. L.146 J.D. [Ⓐ Beckman,K.&S.]
Resop, Alissa F. .... '74 '00 C.958 B.S. L.879 J.D. [Ⓐ Beckman,K.&S.]
Rodovich, Andrew P. .... '48 '73 C&L.879 B.A., J.D. U.S. Mag.
Rodriguez, Edgar S. .... '— '99 C.347 B.S.B.A. L.1119 J.D. P.O. Box 2342
Rosenwinkel, Julie A., (CV) .... '70 '95 C.347 B.A. L.1119 J.D. [Ⓐ Krieg D.G.]
Royer, Martell B. .... '40 '69 C.932 B.B.A. L.1119 J.D. Pub. Def.
Rucinski, Thomas E., (BV) .... '49 '74 C.347 B.S. L.879 J.D. [Sachs&H.]
Ruman, Saul I., (AV) .... '25 '52 L.1119 J.D. [Ruman,C.&H.]
Ruman, Clements & Holub, P.C., (AV) .... 5261 Hohman Avenue
Ryan, Mark A. '74 '04 C.339 B.S. L.1119 J.D.
(adm. in NY; not adm. in IN) Law Clk.
Rybicki, Laura L. .... '73 '99 C.347 B.A. L.597 J.D. [Ruman,C.&H.]

Sachs & Hess, P.C., (AV)
5832 Hohman Avenue, 46320 ⊙
Telephone: 219-932-6070 Fax: 219-932-1103
URL: http://www.lawyers.com/sachs&hess
Robert M. Hess; Ronald F. Layer; Thomas E. Rucinski; Andrew R. Tanzillo; Larry D. Stassin; Michael D. Babcock; Julie A. Demange.
Family Law, Adoptions, Child Custody, Child Support, Divorce, Visitations, Personal Injury, Criminal Law, Medical Malpractice, Products Liability, Wills, Probate, Trusts and Estates, Estate Planning, Real Estate, Bankruptcy, Corporations and Business Law.
Schererville, Indiana Office: 141 W. Lincoln Highway, 2nd Floor, Peoples Bank 46375. Telephone: 219-932-6070. Fax: 219-322-1290.
See Professional Biographies, HAMMOND, INDIANA

Schumacher, Richard M., (AV) '48 '73 C.118 B.A. L.477 J.D.
Sr. V.P. & Exec. Tr. Offr., Mercantile Natl. Bk. of Indiana
Sherman, Barry D., (BV) .... '37 '62 C.221 A.B. L.209 J.D. [Sherman&A.]
Sherman & Allegretti, (BV) .... 6920 Hohman Ave.
Smiddy, Harry F., Jr. '24 '51 C.347 B.S. L.1119 LL.B.
Sr. V.P. & Tr. Offr., Mercantile Natl. Bk. of Indiana
Smith, C. Jerome, (BV) .... '31 '57 C.602 B.A. L.472 J.D. [Smith&M.]
Smith & Marshall, Law Office of, (BV) .... 5253 Hohman Avenue
Sorge, Robert H., (CV) .... '58 '89 C.679 B.A. L.345 J.D. 6243 Hohman Ave.

Spangler, Jennings & Dougherty, P.C.
(See Merrillville)

Stalmack, Joseph, (AV) .... '49 '74 C.162 B.A. L.424 J.D. [J.Stalmack&Assoc.]

Stalmack, Joseph, & Associates, P.C., (AV) BB
5253 Hohman Avenue, 46320
Telephone: 219-937-3700 Toll Free: 800-552-6860 Telecopier: 219-931-1677
Email: stalmack@jsalegal.com URL: http://www.jsa.legal.com
Joseph Stalmack;—Stephen Duane Bannwart; Kristy M. Kopaczewski.
General Practice. Trials and Appeals. Insurance, Products Liability, Probate and Estate Planning, Transportation, Asbestos Litigation, Automobile, Common Carrier, Complex and Multi-District Litigation, Computer, Construction, Environmental and Industrial Disease, Environmental, Fire Insurance, Hazardous Materials, Legal Malpractice, Medical Malpractice, Mediation Services, Professional Malpractice, Subrogation, Toxic Substances and Toxic Torts Law, Personal Injury.
Representative Clients: General Electric Co.; General Motors Corporation; Liberty Mutual Insurance Group; Mack Trucks; BP-Amoco Corporation; GMAC Insurance; Hertz Claims Management; Consolidated Electrical Distributors; MIC Property & Casualty; Wausau Insurance Companies.
See Professional Biographies, HAMMOND, INDIANA

Stamatakos, Alyssa .... '67 '92 C.861 B.A. L.347 J.D. [Eichhorn&E.]
Stanish, John R., (BV) .... '45 '70 C.209 A.B. L.597 J.D. 5231 Hohman Ave.
Stassin, Larry D., (CV) .... '65 '90 C&L.347 B.A., J.D. [Sachs&H.]
Stephens, Julie A. .... '70 '98 C.63 B.S. L.365 J.D. [Ⓐ Efron&E.]
Sullivan, Stephen J. .... '70 '00 C.679 B.S. L.1119 J.D. [Ⓐ Beckman,K.&S.]
Tanasijevich, Rudolph, (BV) .... '28 '53 C.347 A.B. L.477 J.D. 5231 Hohman Ave.
Tanzillo, Andrew R., (BV) .... '55 '80 C&L.879 B.A., J.D. [Sachs&H.]
Twohy, John P. .... '67 '96 C.145 B.A. L.347 J.D. [Eichhorn&E.]
Vater, Thomas A., (CV) .... '56 '81 C.679 B.A. L.879 J.D. 7814 Belmont Ave.
Villarreal, Peter, (BV) .... '63 '89 C&L.347 B.A., J.D. 5920 Hohman Avenue
Voelker, Louis W., III .... '69 '95 C.679 B.A. L.347 J.D. [Eichhorn&E.]
Wartman, Edward J. .... '70 '95 C.597 B.A. L.365 J.D. [Ⓐ McHie&M.]
Whitaker, James K., & Associates, (AV) '33 '59
C&L.339 B.S., LL.B. 5231 Hohman Avenue‡
Willis, Karen P. Pulliam, (CV) .... '52 '81 C.66 A.B. L.347 J.D. Pros. Atty.
Yahne, Scott E., (CV) .... '66 '92 C&L.347 B.A., J.D. [Ⓐ Efron&E.]

HARTFORD CITY, * 6,960, *Blackford Co.*

Bade, Bruce C. .... '42 '68 C.108 B.S. L.345 J.D. Cir. J.
Barry, Robert J., (BV) .... '36 '64 C.347 A.B. L.1119 LL.B. [Barry&B.]
Barry & Basey, (BV) .... 211 N. High St.
Basey, Kevin N., (CV) .... '66 '93 [Barry&B.]

Blackburn & Green
(See Fort Wayne)

Brown, Thomas A. .... '31 '60 C.347 B.S. L.245 J.D. 215 W. Water St.
Forbes, Robert G., (BV) .... '52 '77 C.347 A.B. L.1119 J.D. [Forcum&F.]
Forcum, James S., (AV) .... '47 '73 C.679 B.S.M.E. L.930 J.D. [Forcum&F.]
Forcum, John W. .... '49 '78 C.679 B.S. L.345 J.D. Co. Ct. J.
Forcum and Forbes, (AV) .... 300 S. Jefferson Street
Ford, David C. .... '49 '76 C.347 B.A. L.345 J.D. [D.C.Ford]
Ford, David C., Law Office .... 210 W. Main St.
Maddox, John R., Jr. .... '52 '81 C.63 B.S. L.362 J.D. Chmn., Pacesetter Bank
Mattson, Allen C. .... '46 '76 C.63 B.S. L.345 J.D. [Mattson]
Mattson Law Office .... 209 S. High
Wilson, David D., (BV) .... '32 '57 C&L.602 B.S.E., J.D. 116 S. High St.

HEBRON, 3,596, *Porter Co.*

Fitzgerald, Theodore A., (BV) .... '38 '62 C&L.602 B.B.A., LL.B. 107 N. Main St.
Kasich, Gojko, (CV) .... '59 '84 C.347 B.A. L.345 J.D. P.O. Box 428
Less, Brian E. .... '63 '00 C.801 B.S. L.879 J.D. 107 North Main Street

HENRYVILLE, 1,545, *Clark Co.*

Carver, Betty Hogue, (BV) .... '48 '76 C.347 B.S. L.421 J.D. Bank Bldg.
Hurley, William P., Jr., (AVⓉ) '42 '68 C.401 B.S. L.421 J.D.
(adm. in KY; not adm. in IN) 19324 Pixley Knob Rd.

HIGHLAND, 4,107, *Lake Co.*

Alpert, Jonathan, Law Office of .... '44 '69 C.696 A.B. L.421 J.D. 9105 Indianapolis Blvd.
Anderson, Kenneth L. .... '47 '78 C.347 B.A. L.879 J.D. 9105 Indianapolis Blvd., Ste. D
Ball, Frederick J., (BV) .... '44 '73 C&L.347 A.B., J.D. 9013 Indianapolis Blvd.
Berger, Robert G. .... '41 '66 C&L.339 A.B., J.D. 3912 Highway Ave.
Best, Jeffrey D. .... '68 '95 C.339 B.A. L.879 J.D. 9719 Prairie Ave.
Blackmun, Gilbert F., (AV) .... '37 '62 C&L.966 B.B.A., LL.B. [Blackmun,B.&M.]
Blackmun, Bomberger & Moran, (AV) .... 9006 Indianapolis Boulevard
Bomberger, Peter C., (AV) .... '39 '65 C.188 A.B. L.477 J.D. [Blackmun,B.&M.]
Cappas, Samuel L., (BV) .... '61 '86 C.347 B.A. L.879 J.D. [Cappas&J.]
Cappas & Jones, (BV) .... 2546 W. 45th Street
Casbon, Beth A., (CV) .... '70 '95 C.679 B.S. L.879 J.D. [Ⓐ Komyatte&Assoc.]
Cuevas, Philip F. .... '70 '00 C.338 B.S. L.365 J.D. [Ⓐ Dowd&D.] (⊙Chgo., IL)
Cunningham, William J., (BV) .... '51 '76 C.602 B.A. L.425 J.D. [Hilbrich C.S.D.&V.]
Dal Santo, James S., (CV) .... '62 '87 C.679 B.A. L.879 J.D. [J.DalSanto]
Dal Santo, James, (CV) .... 2251 45th St.
Dobosz, Michael D., (BV) .... '63 '89 C.835 B.S. L.347 J.D. [Hilbrich C.S.D.&V.]
Dowd & Dowd, Ltd., (AV) .... 9721 Prairie Avenue (⊙Chgo., IL; Fontana, WI)
Droster, Jill M. .... '65 '92 C.966 B.A. L.879 J.D. 2637 45th St.
Dubovich, Debra Lynch, (CV) .... '55 '87 C.347 B.S. L.879 J.D. [Levy&D.]
Etzler, Steven W. .... '71 '97 C.63 B.S. L.879 J.D. 9635 Saric Court
Feldman, Edward H., (BV) .... '50 '75 C.477 B.A. L.1119 J.D. 2833 Lincoln St.
Fine, William I., (BV) .... '51 '76 C.347 A.B. L.1119 J.D. 2833 Lincoln St.
Freeland, Daniel L., (AV) .... '47 '71 C&L.879 B.A., J.D. [D.L.Freeland&Assoc.]

Freeland, Daniel L., & Associates, P.C., (AV)
Porte de L'eau Plaza, 2136 45th Avenue, 46322
Telephone: 219-922-0800 Facsimile: 219-922-1261
Email: dlf9601@aol.com URL: http://www.lawyers.com/dfreeland
Daniel L. Freeland;—Sheila A. Ramacci.
Bankruptcy Reorganization, Workouts, Commercial and Consumer Bankruptcy, Debtor, Creditor, Trustee and Committee representation in Business and Consumer Bankruptcy cases, Workouts and Receiverships.
See Professional Biographies, HIGHLAND, INDIANA

Gladish, David Stephen, (CV) .... '69 '95 C.999 B.A. L.879 J.D. 9696 Gordon Drive
Goldman, Norman H. .... '39 '65 C.347 B.S. L.345 LL.B [Goldman&P.]
Goldman & Piersma, P.C., (BV) .... 2833 Lincoln St.

Goldsmith, Marshall J., (AVⓉ) '40 '65 C.347 B.A. L.1119 J.D.
2546 45th Street, 46322 ⊙
Telephone: 219-924-4101 Fax: 219-924-4104 URL: http://www.mjgoldsmithlaw.lawoffice.com
Email: goldsmithlaw@aol.com URL: http://www.lawyers.com/goldsmithlaw
Corporations, Tax, Real Estate, Estate Planning, Wills, Trusts and Probate Law, Commercial Real Estate, Elder Law, Asset Protection.
Chicago, Illinois Office: 77 West Wacker Drive, Suite 3200, 60601-1634. Telephone: 312-346-6622. Toll Free: 877-346-6622. Fax: 312-346-1566.

See Professional Biographies, HIGHLAND, INDIANA

Goodman, Samuel J., Law Offices of, (AV) '42 '67
C.679 B.A. L.477 J.D. 9013 Indianapolis Blvd.

Green & Kuchel, P.C.
(See Hammond)

Halcarz, John J., (BV) .... '47 '72 C.1157 B.A. L.879 J.D. 9013 Indianapolis Blvd.
Hand, Albert C., (BV) .... '29 '59 C.645 A.B. L.1017 J.D. 3235 45th St.
Hand, Karl E. .... '67 '93 C.473 B.S. L.1187 J.D. 3235 45th. St.
Hearn, Edward W., (CV) .... '69 '95 C.679 B.S. L.879 J.D. [Johnson&B.] (⊙Chgo., IL)
Hilbrich Cunningham Schwerd Dobosz & Vinovich, LLP, (BV) .... 2637 - 45th Street

Johnson & Bell, Ltd., (AVⓉ)
9000 Indianapolis Boulevard Suite A, 46322 ⊙
Telephone: 219-923-5250 Facsimile: 219-923-6170
Email: mcviskw@jbltd.com URL: http://www.johnsonandbell.com
Shareholders: Edward W. Hearn; William K. McVisk. Associates: Kurt E. Keagle; Daniel J. Zlatic.
Trial practice in state and federal courts, including national coordinating counsel. Appellate Law, Aviation Litigation, Benefits, Business Litigation and Practice, Complex/Class Litigation, Construction Litigation, Corporate Health Care, Criminal Litigation, Employment Law, ERISA, Environmental Law, Financial (White Collar) Crime, Financial Institution Representation, General Negligence and Premises Liability, Gun Litigation, Hospital Law and Medical Liability, Insurance Coverage, Intellectual Property, Medical Device Liability, Mold Litigation, Municipal Liability, National Coordinating Counsel, Pharmaceutical Liability, Premises Liability, Probate, Product Liability, Professional Liability, Railroad Litigation, Retirement Housing and Long Term Care, Title Insurance, Toxic Tort and Trucking and Transportation.
Chicago, Illinois Office: Suite 4100, 55 East Monroe Street, 60603-5896. Telephone: 312-372-0770. Facsimile: 312-372-9818.
Waukegan, Illinois Office: 325 Washington Street, Suite 200, 60085. Telephone: 847-662- 7458. Facsimile: 847-662-7366.

See Professional Biographies, HIGHLAND, INDIANA

Jones, Wanda E., (BV) .... '55 '86 C.910 B.A. L.879 J.D. [Cappas&J.]
Keagle, Kurt E. .... '64 '96 C.679 B.A. L.1119 J.D. [Ⓐ Johnson&B.] (⊙Chgo., IL)
Komyatte, Richard P., (AV) .... '37 '62 C.602 B.A. L.145 J.D. [Komyatte&Assoc.]
Komyatte & Associates, A Professional Corporation, (AV) .... 9650 Gordon Dr.
Kutansky, Rudy C., & Associates, Law Offices of, (BV) '39 '65
C&L.879 B.A., J.D. 9105 Indianapolis Blvd.
Levy, Judith A. .... '40 '76 C.347 B.S. L.879 J.D. [Levy&D.]
Levy & Dubovich, (CV) .... 2850 45th Ave., Ste. A

Maksimovich, John, (BV) '53 '80 C.894 B.A. L.345 J.D.
3145 45th Avenue, Suite G, 46322
Telephone: 219-922-1441 Fax: 219-922-1492 URL: http://www.johnmaksimovich.com
Email: jm@johnmaksimovich.com URL: http://www.lawyers.com/jmaksimovich
Criminal Law in State and Federal Courts. Driving While Intoxicated, Drug Crimes, Felonies, Homicide, Juvenile Law, Misdemeanors, Parole and Probation, Sexual Assault, Traffic Violations, White Collar Crime, Federal and State Criminal Appeals, Family Law, Divorce, Adoption, Child Custody, Child Support, Domestic Violence, Bankruptcy, Personal Injury, Automobile Accidents, Railroad Accidents, Slip and Fall, Wrongful Death.

See Professional Biographies, HIGHLAND, INDIANA

Malloy, Timothy O., (BV) .... '53 '81 C.436 B.A. L.589 J.D. [Schreiner&M.]
Marrie, Kirk E. .... '64 '95 C.679 B.A. L.1187 J.D. 9105 Indianapolis Blvd.
Martinez, Frank R., III, (CV) .... '59 '84 C.347 B.A. L.1119 J.D. 9105 Indianapolis Blvd.
Matuga, Jos. B. .... '32 '57 C.894 A.B. L.1119 LL.B. Probate Comm.‡
McVisk, William K., (AVⓉ) '53 '77 C.339 B.A. L.597 J.D.
[Johnson&B.] (⊙Chgo., IL)
Mears, David E., (CV) .... '42 '70 C.641 B.A. L.879 J.D. 3527 Ridge Rd.
Misner-Skozen, Lisa K., (CV) .... '66 '91 C.679 B.A. L.897 J.D. [Tweedle&S.]
Moody, Keane Joseph, (BV) .... '59 '84 C.347 B.A. L.365 J.D. 3450 Franklin St.
Muenich, Michael L., (BV) .... '46 '71 C&L.879 B.S.B.A., J.D. 3235 45th St.
O'Donnell, Thomas C., Law Offices of '62 '87 C.1119 B.A. L.365 J.D.
9729 Prairie Ave.
Piersma, John M., (BV) .... '50 '76 C.114 B.A. L.879 J.D. [Goldman&P.]
Pierson, Joyce J. .... '52 '89 C.679 B.A. L.879 J.D. [Pierson&R.]
Pierson & Rotz .... 2631 45th Street

Pinkerton and Friedman, Professional Corporation
(See Munster)

Polick, Steven P. .... '54 '81 C.173 B.A. L.365 J.D. [S.P.Polick&Assoc.] ⊙
Polick, Steven P., & Associates, P.C. .... 3235 45th Street, Suite 202 (⊙Chgo., IL)
Ramacci, Sheila A. .... '70 '96 C.177 B.S. L.879 J.D. [Ⓐ D.L.Freeland&Assoc.]
Reardon, Melissa Ann .... '63 '00 C.741 B.S. L.879 J.D. Mirich Medical Corp.
Regenovich, Dean '58 '83 C.347 B.S. L.365 J.D.
(adm. in IL; not adm. in IN) 8308 Kennedy Ave.‡
Rotz, Brenda J. .... '52 '88 C.347 B.A. L.146 J.D. [Pierson&R.]
Sandoval, Walter F. .... '73 '02 C.679 B.A. L.424 J.D. [Ⓐ Hilbrich C.S.D.&V.]
Sangster, Carol .... '76 '03 C&L.879 B.A., J.D. 9635 Saric Court
Sawyier, Michael T., Law Offices of, (AVⓉ) '48 '72 C.309 A.B. L.145 J.D.
2646 Highway Avenue Suite 201 (⊙Chgo., IL)
Scheele, Stephen E. .... '71 '97 C.208 B.A. L.347 J.D. 9013 Indianapolis Blvd.
Schreiner, James E., (AV) .... '37 '62 C&L.602 B.A., J.D. [Schreiner&M.]
Schreiner & Malloy, P.C., (AV) .... 9635 Saric Court
Schwerd, Robert M., (BV) .... '47 '74 C.1108 B.S. L.879 J.D. [Hilbrich C.S.D.&V.]
Sedia, John M., Attorney at Law, (BV) '54 '79
C.347 A.B. L.1119 J.D. 2646 Highway Ave.
Shaver, Barbara M., (CV) .... '52 '84 C.347 L.879 J.D. 9013 Indianapolis Blvd.
Skozen, Joseph M., (BV) .... '50 '77 C.894 B.A. L.347 J.D. [Tweedle&S.]
Skrentny, Stanley T. .... '32 '59 C.347 B.S. L.1119 J.D. 3248 Garfield St.
Smith, Thomas L., (BV) .... '25 '51 C.475 L.602 J.D. 2637 45th St.
Stepanovich, Donald, (BV) .... '46 '79 C.174 B.A. L.678 J.D. 9717 Prairie Ave.
Stevens, David S., (BV) .... '36 '61 C.197 A.B. L.1119 LL.B. 9717 Prairie Ave.
Surowiec, John T. .... '48 '75 C.46 B.S. L.879 J.D. 9225 Southmoor
Tweedle, John F., (BV) .... '42 '67 C.894 A.B. L.1119 J.D. [Tweedle&S.]
Tweedle, Robert Frederick .... '72 '97 C.347 B.A. L.209 J.D. 2834 - 45th St., Ste. B
Tweedle & Skozen, LLP, (BV) .... 2834 45th St., Ste. B
Tyler, Stephen A., (BV) .... '55 '80 C.347 A.B. L.1119 J.D. [Blackmun,B.&M.]
Vass, Michael S., (BV) .... '57 '82 C.346 B.S. L.1119 J.D. 2850 45th St., Ste. A
Vinovich, Daniel Blake, (BV) .... '65 '90 C.679 B.A. L.347 J.D. [Hilbrich C.S.D.&V.]
Walker, Douglas K. .... '70 '97 C&L.879 B.S., J.D. [Ⓐ Blackmun,B.&M.]
Wilk, Kenneth M., (BV) .... '48 '74 C.347 A.B. L.1119 J.D. 3235 45th St.
Zajac, Daniel R. .... '59 '84 C.894 A.B. L.879 J.D. P.O. Box 9263
Zandstra, Charles L., (CV) .... '33 '58 C.114 B.A. L.879 J.D. 9616 Indianapolis Blvd.
Zlatic, Daniel J. .... '71 '97 C.894 B.A. L.879 J.D. [Ⓐ Johnson&B.] (⊙Chgo., IL)

HILLSBORO, 561, *Fountain Co.*

McGrady, Mark E., (CV) .... '59 '84 C.894 A.B. L.228 J.D. P.O. Box 6

HOBART, 25,363, *Lake Co.*

Cefali, Anthony J., (BV) .... '26 '56 C.894 B.A. L.879 LL.B. [Ⓒ Cefali&C.]
Cefali, Jeffrey V., (BV) .... '50 '76 C&L.879 B.A., J.D. [Cefali&C.]
Cefali & Cefali, P.A., (BV) .... 17 Main
Deppe, Michael L. .... '55 '00 C.347 B.S. L.1187 J.D. [Deppe&M.]
Deppe & Mullen, Law Offices of, (CV) .... 8792 E. Ridge Road, Suite C
Ezell, Jerome L., (BV) .... '46 '80 C.347 B.A. L.879 J.D. 759 W. 350 N.
Hallett, Denise M., (CV) .... '55 '80 C.679 B.S. L.1119 J.D. [Hallett]
Hallett, Thomas P. .... '55 '80 C.602 A.B. L.1119 J.D. 651 E. 3rd St.
Hallett Law Office, P.C., (CV) .... 651 E. 3rd St.
Kneifel, Harry R., (BV) .... '27 '53 C.145 L.879 LL.B. 651 E. 3rd St.
Longer, William J. .... '51 '77 C&L.879 B.A., J.D. City Ct. J.
Mullen, Lloyd P., (CV) .... '61 '89 C.679 B.S.C.E. L.209 J.D. [Deppe&M.]
Peddicord, Jarvis R., (BV) .... '19 '49 C.699 B.A. L.597 J.D. 111 W. 10th St.
Rees, Patricia A., (BV) .... '56 '83 C&L.190 B.A., J.D. P.O. Box 488
Scharbach, Linda K. .... '52 '78 C.63 B.A. L.879 J.D. 51 N. Wisconsin
Stanton, Judith Haller, (BV) '39 '80
C.741 B.A. L.879 J.D. IN. First Judicial Dist., Pro Bono Comm.

HUNTINGBURG, 5,598, *Dubois Co.*

Lett, William S., (AV) .... '44 '69 C.210 B.A. L.1119 J.D. 503 Fourth Street
Schneider, Philip C., (AV) .... '51 '76 C.347 B.A. L.345 J.D. 427 East Fourth Street

HUNTINGTON, * 17,450, *Huntington Co.*

Bendall, Theodore L., (AV) .... '39 '64 C.20 A.B. L.477 J.D. [Bendall D.H.M.&R.] ⊙

Bendall DeLaney Hartburg McNeely & Roth LLP, (AV)
533 Warren Street, P.O. Box 269, 46750-0269 ⊙
Telephone: 260-356-4100 Telecopier: 260-359-1000
URL: http://www.bdhmr.com
Members of Firm: Theodore L. Bendall; Richard DeLaney; Michael Hartburg; Dennis L. McNeely; Mathew J. Roth; William S. Gordon, Jr. Associate: Lisa M. Hughes.
General Civil Practice. Business, Government, Probate and Estate Planning. Trials. Personal Injury, Title Insurance, Real Estate, Family Law, Corporate, Elder Law.
Representative Clients: Church of the United Brethren in Christ (International Headquarters); City of Huntington; First Federal Savings Bank; Huntington College; Huntington Schools Federal Credit Union; Shuttleworth, Inc.; United Methodist Memorial Home; Wabash Magnetics.
Approved Attorneys For: National Attorneys' Title Assurance Fund, Inc.
Warren, Indiana Office: 223A North Wayne Street. Telephone: 260-375-2311.
Roanoke, Indiana Office: National City Bank Building. Telephone: 260-672-2992.

See Professional Biographies, HUNTINGTON, INDIANA

Blackburn & Green
(See Fort Wayne)

Bowers, Lee M., II, (BV) .... '62 '88 C.207 B.A. L.902 J.D. [Bowers,B.G.&W.] ⊙

Bowers, Brewer, Garrett & Wiley, (AV)
301 Warren Street, 46750-2854 ⊙
Telephone: 260-356-4800 Facsimile: 260-356-5196
Email: info@bbgw.com URL: http://www.BBGW.com
Fred H. Bowers (1870-1937); Milo N. Feightner (1873-1945); Lee M. Bowers (1896-1964); Arthur J. Palmer (1906-1989); James W. Bowers (1926-2003). Members of Firm: David L. Brewer; Robert S. Garrett; Joseph K. Wiley; Lee M. Bowers II. Associate: Matthew G. Grantham.
General Practice. Corporation and Business Law, Probate and Estate Planning, Litigation, Family/ Domestic Relations, Real Estate, Taxation, Criminal Law.
Counsel for: Norfolk & Southern Railway Co.; Bippus State Bank; MagneTek.
Warren, Indiana Office: 121 North Wayne Street, 46792. Telephone: 260-375-2622.

See Professional Biographies, HUNTINGTON, INDIANA

Brewer, David L., (AV) .... '36 '63 C.347 B.S. L.1119 J.D. [Bowers,B.G.&W.] ⊙
Caruso, George R. .... '36 '64 C.679 B.S.Ch.E. L.424 LL.B. 251 E. Washington St.‡
Clark, Jeremy A. .... '73 '98 C.333 B.A. L.347 J.D. [Garwood&C.]
DeLaney, Richard, (BV) '53 '78
C.347 A.B. L.1119 J.D. [Bendall D.H.M.&R.] (⊙Warren)
Denman, Jill M., (CV) .... '71 '96 C.98 B.A. L.1119 J.D. [Matheny,M.H.&D.]
Garrett, Robert S., (BV) .... '47 '74 C.347 B.S. L.838 J.D. [Bowers,B.G.&W.] ⊙
Garwood, Max .... '52 '97 C.679 B.S.E.E. L.345 J.D. [Garwood&C.]
Garwood & Clark, P.C. .... 450 N. Jefferson Street
Goff, Christopher M. .... '72 '97 C.63 B.A. L.347 J.D. [Mills,N.&G.]
Gordon, Daniel R., (AV) .... '51 '76 C.63 B.A. L.309 J.D. [Gordon&Assoc.] ⊙
Gordon, William S., Jr., (BV) '42 '73
C.63 B.S. L.345 J.D. [Bendall D.H.M.&R.] (⊙Warren)
Gordon & Associates, Professional Corporation, (AV)
2859 Northpark Avenue (⊙Bluffton)
Grantham, Matthew G. .... '78 '05 C.1105 B.A. L.602 J.D. [Ⓐ Bowers,B.G.&W.]
Hahn, Wilford A., (BV) .... '44 '73 C.679 B.S. L.208 J.D. [Matheny,M.H.&D.]
Hartburg, Michael .... '65 '96 C.665 B.A. L.347 J.D. [Bendall D.H.M.&R.]
Harter, Scott A., (CV) .... '57 '82 C.303 B.A. L.345 J.D. [Rollo&H.]
Heffelfinger, Jeffrey R. .... '54 '80 C.333 B.A. L.1119 J.D. Supr. Ct. J.
Hughes, Lisa M. .... '80 '04 C.679 B.S. L.879 J.D. [Ⓐ Bendall D.H.M.&R.] ⊙
Matheny, Stanley H., (AV) .... '34 '59 C.894 A.B. L.1119 J.D. [Ⓒ Matheny,M.H.&D.]

Matheny, Michael, Hahn & Denman, L.L.P., (BV)
45 West Market Street, P.O. Box 191, 46750-0191
Telephone: 260-356-7030 Fax: 260-356-7033
Email: mail@mmhdlaw.com URL: http://www.lawyers.com/mmhblaw
Members of Firm: Stephen J. Michael; Wilford A. Hahn; Jill M. Denman. Associate: Jeremy K. Nix. Of Counsel: Stanley H. Matheny.
General Practice, Civil Litigation, Criminal Defense, Family Law, Federal Income Tax, Corporate Law, Personal Injury, Real Estate, Trusts and Estates, Probate, Elder Law, Workers Compensation, Social Security Disability, Medical Malpractice.
References: Community State Bank in Huntington; The First National Bank in Huntington; Huntington College.

See Professional Biographies, HUNTINGTON, INDIANA

McIntosh, Mark A. .... '33 '64 C.475 B.S. L.1119 J.D. Cir. J.
McNeely, Dennis L., (BV) '51 '76
C.1064 B.A. L.1119 J.D. [Bendall D.H.M.&R.] (⊙Warren)
Michael, Stephen J., (BV) .... '41 '67 C.108 A.B. L.345 J.D. [Matheny,M.H.&D.]
Mills, William N., (BV) .... '32 '66 C.172 B.S.E.E. L.1119 J.D. [Mills,N.&G.]
Mills, Northrop & Goff, LLP, (BV) .... 53 W. State St.
Nix, Jeremy K. .... '77 '03 C.347 B.S. L.424 J.D. [Ⓐ Matheny,M.H.&D.]
Northrop, Joseph S., (BV) .... '49 '74 C.210 B.A. L.1119 J.D. [Mills,N.&G.]
Poling, Stefan J. .... '72 '97 C.347 B.A. L.1119 J.D. [Ⓐ Rollo&H.]

Rickert, Roger M., (BV) .... '36 '68 C.63 B.S. L.30 J.D. P.O. Box 774 (Pat.)

Roebuck & Associates, P.C.
(See Ft.Wayne)

Rollo, Herbert D., (CV) ....'38 '66 C.679 B.S.C.E. L.345 J.D. [Rollo&H.]
Rollo & Harter, (CV) .... 532 Warren Street
Roth, Mathew J. .... '74 '99 C.827 B.A L.347 J.D. [Bendall D.H.M.&R.]
Roush, J. Edward ....'20 '49 C.333 B.A. L.1119 J.D. 45 West Market Street‡
Sees, John T. '52 '80 C.63 B.S. L.345 J.D.
Secy. & Treas., Sees Equip. & Supply Co., Inc.
Wiley, Joseph K., (BV) ....'53 '79 C.679 B.S. L.1119 J.D. [Bowers,B.G.&W.] ⊙

INDIANAPOLIS, * 791,926, *Marion Co.*

Aaron, Anthony .... '— '02 C.870 B.S. L.345 J.D. [Ⓐ Ice M.]
Abbott, Tony H., (BV) .... '51 '76 C.347 B.A. L.345 J.D. [Ⓖ Foley&P.]
Abel, Arend J., (AV) ....'60 '86 C.63 B.A. L.1119 J.D. [Cohen&M.]
Abels, Jon B., (AV) ....'44 '70 C.108 B.A. L.345 J.D. [Dann P.N.&K.]
Abernathy, Jon C., (AV) ....'57 '83 C.275 B.A. L.879 J.D. [Goodin A.&M.]
Abraham, Erin D. ....'— '05 C.347 B.S. L.345 J.D. [Ⓐ Hall,R.K.H.&L.]
Abrams, Jeffrey A., (AV) ....'56 '81 C.473 B.S. L.345 J.D. [Dann P.N.&K.]
Adamczyk, Irene T., (AV) ....'49 '82 C.347 A.B. L.345 J.D. [Baker&D.] ‡
Adams, Cynthia Matson .... '55 '83 C.384 B.A. L.345 J.D. Ind. Univ. School of Law
Adams, David A. ....'76 '01 C.879 B.A. L.347 J.D. [Ⓐ Bingham M.]
Adams, Edward S. .... '63 '88 C.346 B.S. L.345 J.D. 5757 Lowell Ave.
Adams, Jay B. ....'— '02 C.894 B.A. L.345 J.D. [Ⓐ Ice M.]
Adams, Wayne O., III, (AV) ....'49 '74 C.894 B.A. L.345 J.D. [Ice M.]
Addison, Bradford G. ....'— '93 C.346 B.S. L.150 J.D. [Barnes&T.] (See Pat. Sect.)
Adinamis, Carol M., (AV) ....'65 '92 C&L.347 B.S., J.D. [Adinamis,M.&S.]
Adinamis, George P., (AV) ....'33 '63 C.597 B.S. L.365 J.D. [Adinamis&A.]

Adinamis & Adinamis, P.C., (AV) BR
8710 North Meridian Street, 46260
Telephone: 317-580-9000 Fax: 317-587-0288
URL: http://www.lawyers.com/adinamislaw
George P. Adinamis.
Taxation, Estate Planning and Business Administration, Business Planning, Employee Benefits, and Business Law.
See Professional Biographies, INDIANAPOLIS, INDIANA

Adinamis, Michael & Saunders P.C., (AV)
500 E. 96th Street, Suite 360, 46240
Telephone: 317-218-2600 Fax: 317-218-2601
URL: http://www.ams-law.com
Carol M. Adinamis; Susan Adinamis Michael; Jeffrey A. Saunders.
Business Law, Estate Planning, Estate Administration, Trusts and Estates, Charitable Planning, Taxation.
See Professional Biographies, INDIANAPOLIS, INDIANA

Adkins, Christa Klopfenstein '70 '99
C.679 B.S. L.347 J.D. Corp. Coun., Roche Diagnostics Corp.
Adler, Lisa M. ....'— '04 C&L.347 B.S., J.D. [Ⓐ Starkey]
Adler, Michael J. .... '76 '01 C&L.347 B.S., J.D. [Ⓐ Bingham M.]
Adley, Michael C., (BV) ....'51 '79 C.347 B.A. L.345 J.D. [Ⓐ Cohen&M.]
Adolay, Amy J. ....'76 '01 C.473 B.A. L.1119 J.D. [Ⓐ Krieg D.]
Agard, Deborah M., Law Office of '64 '00
C.347 B.A. L.345 J.D. 156 E. Market Street, Suite 200
Agness, Kent E., (AV) ....'— '75 C.347 B.A. L.893 J.D. [Barnes&T.]
Ahlgrim, Robert F., Jr., (AV) '67 '92 C.347 B.S. L.345 J.D.
Lit. Coun., State Farm Claims
Aikman, Richard E., Jr., (AV) .... '— '73 C.210 B.A. L.345 J.D. [Stewart&I.]
Akins, James H., Jr. '46 '77 C.314 B.S.E. L.1243 J.D.
(adm. in AR; not adm. in IN) V.P., Amer. United Life Ins. Co.
Albaugh, Matthew T. ....'— '01 C.347 B.A. L.1119 J.D. [Ⓐ Baker&D.]
Alberts, Joseph R., (AV) ....'69 '94 C.303 B.A. L.347 J.D. 9330 Zionsville Road
Albright, Alan D. ....'56 '82 C&L.347 B.S., J.D. Coun., Anthem, Inc.
Albright, Deborah E., (BV) ....'51 '76 C&L.74 B.A., J.D. [Monday R.J.&A.]
Albright, John A. '58 '85 C&L.546 B.S., J.D.
(adm. in NE; not adm. in IN) Sr. Atty., Simon Property Group
Albright, Terrill D., (AV) ....'38 '65 C.347 A.B. L.1119 J.D. [Baker&D.]
Alden, John T., Jr., (BV) ....'45 '75 C.228 B.A. L.345 J.D. 110 N. Delaware St.
Alden, Robert F., (BV) ....'46 '72 C.210 B.A. L.345 J.D. [Alden&C.]
Alden & Clem, (BV) ....110 N. Delaware
Alder, Catherine A. ....'58 '83 C.303 B.A. L.880 J.D. 7254 N. Grand Ave.
Alderfer, Mark S., (AV) ....'58 '83 C.347 B.A. L.345 J.D. [Hackman H.&C.]
Alerding, Kevin M., (BV) ....'69 '95 C.63 B.S. L.347 J.D. [Ⓐ Ice M.]
Alerding, Michael J. ....'70 '97 C.347 B.A. L.345 J.D. [Bingham M.]
Alexander, Nelson D., (BV) ....'68 '93 C.894 B.A. L.145 J.D. [Locke R.]
Alexander, Scott R., (BV) ....'— '92 C.894 B.A. L.345 J.D. [Sommer B.]
Alexander, Stacy L. ....'69 '96 C.347 B.A. L.734 J.D. [Ⓐ Roberts&B.]
Algase, Benji J. ....'40 '91 C.1036 B.A. L.128 J.D. [O'Koon H.]
Allen, Adrian ....'73 '01 C.347 B.A. L.1119 J.D. [Ⓐ Bose M.&E.]
Allen, David B. ....'62 '95 C.347 B.S.C.J. L.345 J.D. [Findling G.G.&P.]
Allen, David J., (AV) ....'35 '65 C.347 B.S. L.345 J.D. [Hagemier,A.&S.]
Allen, Michael E. ....'56 '81 C&L.879 B.A., J.D. 9000 Keystone Xing
Allen, Niquelle ....'77 '02 C.832 B.S. L.880 J.D. [Ⓐ Ice M.]
Allen, Robert E. ....'53 '83 C.346 B.S. L.345 J.D. Sr. Coun., Guidant Corp.

Allen • Wellman • McNew
(See Greenfield)

Allenza, Francis Horace ....'38 '61 C.696 B.S. L.982 J.D. 6665 Rockville Rd‡
Allie, John H. .... '60 '93 C.1213 B.S.M.E. L.347 J.D. [Krieg D.] (Pat.)
Allington, Thomas B. '42 '66 C&L.546 B.S., J.D.
Prof. and Assoc. Dean, Indiana Univ. Sch. of Law
Allman, Joseph E., (BV) ....'54 '93 C.347 B.A. L.1119 J.D. [Ⓐ Macey S.&A.]
Alpert, Harry A. ....'13 '36 C.108 B.S. L.1119 J.D. Secy., J. Solotken & Co., Inc.‡
Altice, Kristin L., (AV) '62 '89
C.473 A.B. L.986 J.D. Attorney, Shiel Sexton Company, Inc.
Altice, Robert R., Jr. ....'60 '87 C.473 B.A. L.502 J.D. Crim. Ct. J.
Alvarado, Bruce J., (BV) ....'60 '90 C.679 B.S.,B.A. L.347 J.D. [Orfanos&A.]
Alvey, Jennifer M. ....'— '04 C.347 B.S. L.345 J.D. [Ⓐ Ice M.]
Americanos, Peter C., (BV) ....'41 '73 C.999 B.A. L.345 J.D. Dep. Atty. Gen.
Ammeen, James J., Jr., (AV) ....'63 '95 C.478 A.B. L.345 J.D. [Lewis&K.]
Ancel, Jerald I., (AV) ....'— '68 C.347 B.S. L.345 J.D. [Sommer B.]
Ancel, Sorelle J., (AV) ....'39 '79 C.347 B.S. L.345 J.D. [Ancel&D.]
Ancel, Steven H., (AV) ....'— '60 C.347 A.B. L.119 J.D. [Ⓖ Sommer B.]
Ancel & Dunlap, LLP, (AV) ....1 Indiana Square

Anderson, Aline F., (AV) '43 '70 C.679 B.A. L.345 LL.B.
7104 U.S. Highway 31 South
Anderson, Arlene G., (AV) ....'44 '82 C.323 A.B. L.345 J.D. [Ⓖ Price W.R.&D.]
Anderson, Arvie J. ....'70 '98 C.475 B.S. L.477 J.D. Staff Pat. Atty., Eli Lilly & Co. (Pat.)
Anderson, Christi R. ....'60 '03 C&L.347 B.S., J.D. [Ⓐ Lewis W.]
Anderson, David A., (BV) ....'55 '80 C.602 B.A. L.174 J.D. [Anderson&Assoc.]
Anderson, Greg N. ....'60 '94 C.992 B.A. L.345 J.D. IN Supm. Ct., Disciplinary Comm.
Anderson, Knight S., (AV) ....'68 '93 C.602 B.A. L.347 J.D. [Hill,F.M.F.&M.]
Anderson, Kristin L. ....'50 '81 C.347 A.B. L.345 J.D. 4167 Broadway
Anderson, Vicki L., (AV) ....'48 '85 C.347 B.A. L.345 J.D. [Hackman H.&C.]
Anderson & Associates, P.C., (BV) ....3802 West 96th Street
Andres, Jennifer A. ....'— '03 C.74 B.S. L.345 J.D. [Ⓐ Ice M.]
Andrews, Julia M. ....'77 '03 C.347 B.A. L.345 J.D. [Ⓐ Bleecker,B.&A.]
Andrews, Julie M. .... '67 '02 C.347 B.S. L.345 J.D. [Ⓐ Cohen&M.]
Andrews, Michael E. '55 '81
C.347 B.A. L.345 J.D. V.P. & Assoc. Coun., Nat. City Corporation
Andrews, Stephen K., (BV) ....'48 '75 C.347 A.B. L.365 J.D. [Bleecker,B.&A.]
Anweiler, Rick L. ....'48 '92 C&L.347 B.S., J.D. 5523 Carrollton Ave.
Anzinger, F. William '38 '67
C&L.608 A.B., J.D. Tr. Dept.Head, First Natl. Bk. of Huntington
Arany, Lawrence C., (BV) .... '47 '72 C.347 A.B. L.734 J.D. 6525 E. 82nd St.
Arbogast, Donald C. '34 '64 C.260 B.S. L.1045 LL.B.
(adm. in TN; not adm. in IN) Eli Lilly and Company (Law Division)
Arceneaux, Adam, (AV) ....'66 '93 C&L.345 B.S., J.D. [Ice M.]
Archer, Edward P. .... '36 '62 C.688 B.M.E. L.999 LL.B. Prof., Ind. Univ. Law Sch.
Ardery, Charles W., Jr. '31 '57 C.970 B.A. L.477 LL.B.
Admin. Law J., Soc. Sec. Admn.
Arena, Samuel J. .... '76 '01 C&L.347 B.A., J.D. [Ⓐ Wallack S.&H.]
Arland, Karen L. ....'57 '82 C.108 B.A. L.1119 J.D. [Ⓖ Ice M.]
Armitage, Robert A., (AVⓉ) '48 '74 C.20 B.A. L.477 J.D.
Senior V.P. & Gen. Counsel, Eli Lilly & Co. (Pat.)
Armstrong, Anthony T. '62 '91
C&L.347 B.S., J.D. Advanced Research & Technology Institute
Armstrong, Brenda L., (BV) '61 '87
C&L.623 B.B.A., J.D. Assoc. Gen. Coun., Symons Intl. Group, Inc.
Armstrong, Phyllis S. ....'63 '90 C.231 B.A. L.1119 J.D. Pub. Def.
Arnett, Andrew B. ....'62 '87 C.1111 B.A. L.383 J.D. 3545 N. Washington Boulevard
Arnett, Charles W. ....'77 '02 C.701 B.S. L.345 J.D. [Ⓐ Baker&D.] (See Pat. Sect.)
Arnett, Maxine H. .... '30 '63 C.331 A.B. L.564 J.D. 133 Buckingham Dr.‡
Arney, Tracy A. ....'69 '95 C.323 B.A. L.879 J.D. Golden Rule Insurance Co.
Arnold, Bruce G. ....'59 '99 C.1210 B.S. L.1119 J.D. [Ⓐ Feiwell&H.]
Arnold, Ian D. ....'— '01 C.303 B.A. L.1119 J.D. [Ⓐ Sommer B.]
Arrensen, David A., (BV) ....'58 '88 C.347 A.B. L.1119 J.D. [Ⓐ Baker&D.]
Arrowsmith, Lynne E. ....'51 '98 C.63 B.S. L.74 J.D. Family & Soc. Services Admin.
Arthur, Stephen E., (AV) ....'55 '79 C.344 B.A. L.345 J.D. [Harrison&M.]
Arwood, Lindy B. ....'— '05 C.143 B.S. L.879 J.D. [Ⓐ Sommer B.]
Aschleman, James A., (AV) ....'44 '69 C.432 B.A. L.309 J.D. [Baker&D.]
Aspy, Michael A., (BV) '54 '80
C.347 B.A. L.1119 J.D. Sr. Staff Atty., American Family Insurance
Atherton, Thomas M., (AV) ....'44 '72 C.218 B.A. L.339 J.D. [Bose M.&E.]
Atkins, Howard B. ....'47 '88 C.112 B.A. L.1059 J.D. [Buehler&Assoc.]
Atkinson, John K. ....'72 '02 C.303 B.A.B.A. L.345 J.D. [Ⓐ Osborn H.&L.]
Atlas, James, (BV) ....'40 '74 C.435 B.A. L.345 J.D. 1 Virginia Ave.
Atz, Thomas E., (BV) ....'48 '73 C.347 A.B. L.1119 J.D. 155 E. Market St.
Auberry, Brent A. ....'72 '98 C.999 B.A. L.345 J.D. [Ⓐ Baker&D.]
Auberry, Natalie E. ....'69 '98 C.347 A.B. L.345 J.D. Law Clerk, IN Ct. of Appls.
Aust, Ronald K. ....'56 '92 C.346 B.S.E.E.T. L.345 J.D. [Taylor&A.] (Pat.)
Austgen, Peter J. .. '48 '77 C.679 B.S. L.1119 J.D. Eli Lilly and Company (Law Division)
Avery, James W., (BVⓉ) ....'57 '82 C.59 B.A. L.208 J.D. [Avery] ⊙
Avery, Melissa J., (BV) ....'69 '94 C.610 B.S. L.179 J.D. [Avery&C.]

Avery & Cheerva, LLP, (AV) BR
Indiana Bar Center, 230 East Ohio, Sixth Floor, 46204-2149
Telephone: 317-637-7575 Fax: 317-685-1106
URL: http://www.averycheerva.com
Members of Firm: Melissa J. Avery (Board Certified, Family Law Specialist, Indiana State Bar Association, Family Law Certification Board); Michael Cheerva. Associate: Christopher J. Barrows (Board Certified, Family Law Specialist, Indiana State Bar Association, Family Law Certification Board).
Family Law, Dissolution of Marriage, Custody, Paternity, Prenuptial Agreements, Domestic Appellate Practice, Mediation, and Arbitration.
See Professional Biographies, INDIANAPOLIS, INDIANA

Avery Law Firm, (BVⓉ) ....450 E. 96th St., Suite 500 (⊙Denver, CO; Muncie, IN)
Avery-Seagrave, Bobby J. ....'76 '02 C.346 B.S. L.345 J.D. [Ⓐ Zeigler C.&K.]
Ayers, Cynthia J. ....'47 '83 C.347 B.A. L.345 J.D. Supr. Ct. J.
Ayres, William S., (BV) ....'— '76 C.63 B.S. L.347 J.D. [Ayres C.&S.]

Ayres Carr & Sullivan, P.C., (AV)
(Formerly Steers Sullivan Professional Corporation; Steers, Sullivan, McNamar & Rogers; Steers, Klee, Jay & Sullivan and Fenton, Steers, Beasley & Klee)
251 East Ohio Street, Suite 500, 46204 ⊙
Telephone: 317-636-3471 Fax: 317-636-6575
Aquilla Q. Jones (1852-1926); Edwin M. S. Steers (1881-1977); (Mr.) C. Severin Buschmann (1896-1980); Arthur J. Sullivan (1909-1999); Edwin K. Steers (1915-1992); John R. Carr, Jr. (Retired 1919-2004). Attorneys: William S. Ayres; John R. Carr, III; Bret S. Clement; Michael R. Franceschini; Robert W. Loser, II; Ruth E. Myer; Patrick M. O'Brien; Christopher D. Seigel; Charles N. Doberneck. Of Counsel: Raymond M. Adler (Resident, Noblesville Office); Alexander L. Rogers.
General Civil and Criminal Practice in all State and Federal Courts, including Trial and Appellate Practice. Administrative, Bankruptcy Reorganization, Consumer Bankruptcy, Collection and Subrogation, Commercial Law, Construction, Corporation and Business Organizations, Insurance, Legislation and Government Relations, Mediation and Dispute Resolution, Personal Injury, Pension, Profit Sharing and Employee Benefits, Probate, Estate and Succession Planning, Real Estate, Taxation, Transportation and Motor Carrier, and Workers Compensation Law.
Noblesville, Indiana Office: 136 South Ninth Street. Telephone: 317-773-0882. Fax: 317-773-0943.
See Professional Biographies, INDIANAPOLIS, INDIANA

Babb, Bryan H. ....'65 '99 C.870 B.S. L.1119 J.D. [Ⓐ Bose M.&E.]
Babbitt, Robin L., (AV) ....'54 '80 C.249 B.S. L.345 J.D. [Bingham M.]

Babcock, James Dorr, (AV) .... '46 '71 C.347 B.S. L.345 J.D. [J.D.Babcock]

Babcock, James Dorr, P.C., (AV)
500 Barrister Building, 155 East Market Street, 46204
Telephone: 317-634-0229 FAX: 317-637-1901
James Dorr Babcock; Steven L. Yount.
Probate, Wills, Trusts and Estates, Estate Planning, Guardianships, Commercial Law, Commercial and Consumer Collections, Bankruptcy Law, Family Law, Child Custody, Child Support, Business and Corporate Law, Real Estate, Foreclosures, Banking, Finance.
See Professional Biographies, INDIANAPOLIS, INDIANA

Babione, John C. .... '72 '01 C.347 B.S. L.345 J.D. [Ⓐ Mitchell H.J.&D.]
Bach, Robt. L. .... '16 '50 C.755 A.B. L.1119 J.D. 437 Braeside Dr. N.‡
Bachmann, Fred J. .... '— '87 C.63 B.S. L.347 J.D. [Hall,R.K.H.&L.]
Back, Vernon C., (BV) ..... '59 '94 C.679 B.S. L.347 J.D. Gen. Coun., Lauth Group, Inc.
Backer, Stephen A., (AV) .... '46 '71 C.347 B.S. L.1119 J.D. [Backer&B.]

Backer & Backer, A Professional Corporation, (AV) BR
8710 North Meridian Street, 46260
Telephone: 317-571-0500 Telecopier: 317-571-0700
Email: sabacker@backerlaw.com
Herbert J. Backer (1914-1995); Stephen A. Backer.
Real Estate, Construction Law, Business Law and Commercial Law.
Reference: Bank One, Indianapolis.
See Professional Biographies, INDIANAPOLIS, INDIANA

Bade, Abdullah A. .... '35 '75 C&L.999 B.A., LL.B. 5176 E. 75th St.
Badger, David H., (AV) '31 '64
C.701 B.S.E.E. L.345 J.D. [Ⓒ Brinks H.G.&L.] (See Pat. Sect.)
Badger, Robert W., (BV) .... '31 '82 C.870 B.S. L.345 J.D. 342 Massachusetts Av.
Badger, Steven M., (AV) .... '64 '92 C.894 B.A. L.347 J.D. [McTurnan&T.]
Bahret, William F., (BV) .... '51 '82 C&L.150 B.S.E.E., J.D. [Bahret&Assoc.] (Pat.)
Bahret & Associates Co., L.P.A., (BV) .... 320 North Meridan Street, Suite 512 (Pat.)
Baibieri, Suzanne '69 '95 C&L.347 B.A., J.D.
V.P. & Assoc. Cnsl., Nat. City Corporation
Bailey, Brian .... '— '03 C.894 B.A. L.1119 J.D. [Ⓐ Ice M.]
Bailey, James Francis '39 '65 C&L.477 B.A., J.D.
(adm. in MI; not adm. in IN) Prof. of Law, Indiana Univ. Sch. of Law
Bailey, Jeffrey B., (AV) .... '46 '78 C.347 B.S. L.345 J.D. [Bose M.&E.]
Bailey, Jon M., (AV) .... '48 '75 C.63 B.S. L.345 J.D. [Bose M.&E.]
Bailey, Kevin D. .... '— '94 C.472 B.S.M.E. L.910 J.D. [Ⓐ Barnes&T.] (See Pat. Sect.)
Bailey, Mark A. .... '55 '86 C.992 B.A. L.345 J.D. [Stark D.&S.]
Bailey, Patricia Seasor, (BV) .... '56 '81 C.992 B.A. L.345 J.D. [Stark D.&S.]
Bailey, Victoria L. .... '75 '03 C.347 B.A. L.1119 J.D. 902 E. 66th St.
Bainbridge, Phillip E., (AV) .... '42 '68 C.347 B.S. L.345 J.D. [Baker&D.]

Baird, Barbara J., Law Office of, (BV) '50 '77 C.25 B.A. L.1119 J.D.
445 N. Pennsylvania Street, Suite 401, 46204
Telephone: 317-637-2345 Fax: 317-637-2369
Email: bjbaird@bjbairdlaw.com
Estate Planning, Adoption Law, Business Start-Ups, Labor Law, Employment Law.
See Professional Biographies, INDIANAPOLIS, INDIANA

Baird, Martha M. K. .... '67 '92 C.108 B.S. L.851 J.D. 5550 N. Keystone Avenue
Baker, Christopher E., (AV) .... '52 '81 C.894 B.A. L.345 J.D. [Hostetler&K.]
Baker, Hugh G., Jr., (AV) .... '46 '73 333 E. Ohio St.
Baker, John G. .... '46 '71 C.347 A.B. L.1119 J.D. Ct. App. J.
Baker, Nathan A. .... '— '97 C.894 B.A. L.339 J.D. [Ⓐ Barnes&T.]
Baker, Robert M., III, (AV) .... '50 '76 C.473 B.S. L.345 J.D. [Hoover H.B.&H.]
Baker, Ronald L., (BV) .... '27 '59 C.347 B.S.B.A. L.1119 J.D. 144 N. Delaware St.
Baker, Taylor L., Jr. .... '35 '63 C.511 A.B. L.345 J.D. Supr. Ct. J.
Baker, Thomas W. .... '— '98 C.602 B.S.Ch.E. L.339 J.D. [Ⓐ Hatchett&H.]
Baker, Tim A., (AV) .... '62 '89 C.347 B.A. L.879 J.D. Mag. J.

Baker & Daniels LLP, (AV) BR
300 North Meridian Street, Suite 2700, 46204 ⊙
Telephone: 317-237-0300 Fax: 317-237-1000
URL: http://www.bakerdaniels.com
Members of Firm: Irene T. Adamczyk; Terrill D. Albright; James A. Aschleman; Phillip E. Bainbridge; Lewis D. Beckwith; Ben W. Blanton; Ellen E. Boshkoff; Brian K. Burke; H. Patrick Callahan; James M. Carr; Amie Peele Carter; R. Trevor Carter; A. Scott Chinn; Elizabeth Kelley Cierzniak; Stephen A. Claffey; James W. Clark; Mary Beth Claus; Shaun Healy Clifford; Gregory N. Dale; Miriam Smulevitz Dant; Francina A. Dlouhy; Kevin R. Erdman; Theodore J. Esping; Richard T. Freije, Jr.; Thomas C. Froehle Jr.; Chip Garver; Ronald D. Gifford; David A. Given; G. Frederick Glass; Kevin P. Griffith; Eric J. Groen; Paul Lowell Haines; James H. Ham, III; David R. Hamer; Peter L. Hatton; David K. Herzog; Scott D. Himsel; Edward E. Hollis, III; John S. Keeler; Tibor D. Klopfer; Amy E. Kosnoff; Scott M. Kosnoff; Thomas A. Ladd; Jon B. Laramore; Mary Katherine Lisher; Ji-Qing Liu; Christine Graffis Long; Heather L. MacDougall (Not admitted in IN); Michael J. MacLean; Mitzi Harris Martin; Byron K. Mason; Alan L. McLaughlin; David W. Miller; Joseph E. Miller, Jr.; Mark S. Moore; John T. Neighbours; Timothy E. Niednagel; Todd M. Nierman; Robert D. Null; Shaun Healy O'Brien; Laura C. O'Donnell (Also at Fort Wayne Office); J. Daniel Ogren; Stephen H. Paul; Carl R. Pebworth; Hudnall A. Pfeiffer; Thomas A. Pitman; John W. Purcell; Roberta Sabin Recker; Rebecca A. Richardson; Andrea Roberts; Mark J. Romaniuk; Norman P. Rowe; Christopher G. Scanlon; John R. Schaibley, III; Fred E. Schlegel; Gayle L. Skolnik; Andrew Z. Soshnick (Board Certified, Family Law Specialist, Indiana State Bar Association, Family Law Certification Board); Robert K. Stanley; Thomas G. Stayton; John B. Swarbrick, Jr.; John Joseph Tanner; Brent D. Taylor; Nancy G. Tinsley; Kevin M. Toner; Gregory J. Utken; Thomas A. Vogtner; Mark A. Voigtmann; David C. Worrell; Joseph H. Yeager, Jr. Counsel: Virgil L. Beeler; Henry B. Blackwell, II; Marline R. Breece; Joseph B. Carney; Daniel F. Evans; Debra L. Hinshaw; Steven L. Householder; Michael J. Huston; J. B. King; Sandra D. Leek; Madonna Frances McGrath; Vickie L. Norman; Larry R. Prible; Mark C. Sausser; Joseph L. Smith, Jr.; Merrill S. Thompson; Douglas A. Yerkeson. Of Counsel: Suzette Bewley; David Lawther Johnson; Michael R. Maine; Christopher J. Weber. Associates: Matthew T. Albaugh; Charles W. Arnett; David A. Arrensen; Brent A. Auberry; Ryan C. Barker; Maxwell N. Barnes; Jeffrey S. Beck; Gabriel Bender; James S. Birge; Amanda R. Blystone; Craig M. Borowski; C. John Brown; Kristiana M. Brugger; Adrienne F. Busby; Stuart R. Buttrick; Andrew L. Campbell; Carol Warren Collins; Kelley Bertoux Creveling; Jane A. Dall; Cedric A. D'Hue; Shawna M. Eikenberry; Meg A. Gallmeyer; Caryn M. Glawe; Kellye M. Gordon; Philip J. Gutwein, II; Nathan J. Hagerman; Terry E. Hall; Derek C. Hamilton (Not admitted in IN); Norman J. Hedges; John K. Henning, IV; Jennett M. Hill; Kareem A. Howell; Ryan M. Hurley; Sarah M. Jabbari; Brandon S. Judkins; Jason D. Kimpel; Susan W. Kline; Shaune Hawkins Langston; Daniel M. Lechleiter; Matthew C. Lesher; Suzann Weber Lupton; Katherine E. McCanna; Jerome P. McCluskey; Nicole L. McDonald; Catherine A. Meeker; William S. Meyers; M. Sue Michael; Clayton C. Miller; Jeffrey C. Nelson; Shiv Ghuman O'Neill; April L. Opper (Not admitted in IN); Kathy L. Osborn; Scott E. Peck; Louis Thomas Perry; Joseph C. Pettygrove; Sara Manske Powell; Stacy L. Prall; Chad S. Priest; Michael N. Red; Anne K. Ricchiuto; Daniel Roy; Jason M. Schiesser; Randee Sibul-Gelbert; Cynthia K. Springer; Dustin D. Stohler; Keith J. Swedo; Janelle Tranquillo; Christine A. Werner; Paul A. Wolfla; Tareen Zafrullah. Indianapolis - 96th Street, Indiana OfficeMembers of Firm: David W. Barrett; Donald P. Bennett; Daniel L. Boeglin; J. Jeffrey Brown; M. Angella Castille; Patrick S. Cross; Robert W. Elzer; Brian S. Fennerty; David A. Foster; Brant O. Gardner; John A. Gardner; Jay Jaffe; Jerry R. Jenkins; Ji-Qing Liu; Kent A. Rollison; Joseph M. Scimia; Bradley Merrill Thompson; Mark E. Wright; Robert S. Wynne. Counsel: Daniel P. Carmichael; John D. Cochran; Ralph F. Hall; Leah Schlesinger. Associates: Trevor Jon Belden; Jennifer L. Dill-McGill; Troy D. Farmer; John F. W. Fleming; Virginia E. Ho; Leah R. Kendall; Jennifer L. Kremp; Dennis P. Lager; Wataru Matsuyasu; April J. Risk; Kathryn E. Wiley. Fort Wayne Office Members of Firm: J. Stephen Bennett (Not admitted in IN); Jon A. Bomberger; John R. Burns, III; Timothy J. Haffner; Steven H. Hazelrigg; John F. Hoffman; David P. Irmscher; Steven L. Jackson; Michael L. James; Joseph W. Kimmell, II; David J. Kuker; Jeanne E. Longsworth; Robert D. Moreland; Michael J. Nader; Anthony Niewyk; Maclyn T. Parker; Douglas Dormire Powers; David A. Scott; Lawrence E.

(This Listing Continued)

Baker & Daniels LLP (Continued)

Shine; Thomas M. Shoaff; N. Reed Silliman. Counsel: Karen T. Moses. Resident Associates: Thomas R. Biehl, Jr. (Not admitted in IN); Betsy M. Brooks; Michael S. Burns; Scott C. Burns (Not admitted in IN); Abigail Marie Butler; Cynthia M. Cormany; Adam F. Cox; David P. Durm; Brian Thomas Geisler; Jeffrey V. Gery; M. Kristin Glazner; Jeffrey A. Goeglein; Shellie L. Goetz; Damian Gosheff; Jerome Byron Hayes; Julie Annette Hoffman; Jason A. Houser; Mark F. Juba; Thomas C. Kus; Martha M. Lemert; Jon L. Lindberg; Shannon K. Reed; Patrick A. Scheiderer; Michael D. Schwartz; Matthew B. Skaggs; David D. Storey; Andrew J. Welborn; Mark A. Werling. South Bend, Indiana Office Members of Firm: Thomas J. Brunner, Jr.; Gerard T. Gallagher; Carl A. Greci; Eric J. Groen; M. Patricia Hackett; Richard L. Hill; James M. Matthews; Randolph R. Rompola; Edward A. Sullivan, III; Peter G. Trybula. Counsel: D. Lucetta Pope; Robert A. Wade. Associates: Cara R. Brook; Alison G. Fox; Peter J. Gillin (Not admitted in IN); Jeff R. Heck; RaeLee C. Hudson; Jennifer Bickley Hull; Thomas J. Mauch; Shawn E. Peterson; David R. Pruitt; Amy M. Steketee; Daniel Tychonievich. Elkhart, Indiana Office Members of Firm: James R. Brotherson; Glenn E. Killoren; Kennard R. Weaver; Robert C. Whippo. Of Counsel: Robert A. Pfaff. Associates: Jennifer Elaine Greene; Jeremy D. Pfister; Christopher J. Spataro; Krista J. Zimmerman. Washington, D.C. Office Members of Firm: Scott D. Balderston; Thomas A. Jensen; Herbert V. Kerner; Joseph W. Kimmell, II; Charles T. Richardson; Frank S. Swain; Mark W. Weller; David R. Zook. Counsel: Robert J. Kabel; Ted R. Mannen. Of Counsel: Carolyn M. Coleman; Kerry Owens. Associates: David H. Milligan. Qingdao, China Office Members of Firm: Ji-Qing Liu; Brian S. Fennerty; Thomas A. Jensen; Joseph W. Kimmell, II; Frank S. Swain. Of Counsel: Michael R. Maine. Counsel: Andy Wei. Resident Consultant: David M. T. Wang. Beijing, China Office Member of Firm: Ji-Qing Liu.
Antitrust, Business Planning, Commercial, Financial and Bankruptcy, Corporate Finance, Education, Employee Benefits, Environment, Family Business, Federal, State and Local Tax, Food and Drug Law, Government Affairs, Health Care, Individual/Family, Estate and Probate, Insurance and Financial Services, Intellectual Property, International, Labor and Employment, Life Sciences, Litigation, Medical Technology Regulation, Municipal Law/Tax-Exempt Finance, Nonprofit, Product Liability, Real Estate/Land Use, Transportation, and Utilities.
Fort Wayne, Indiana Office: 111 East Wayne Street, Suite 800, 46802. Telephone: 260-424-8000. Fax: 260-460-1700.
South Bend, Indiana Office: First Bank Building, 205 West Jefferson Boulevard, Suite 250, 46601. Telephone: 574-234-4149. Fax: 574-239-1900.
Elkhart, Indiana Office: 317 West Franklin Street, P.O. Box 507, 46515-0507. Telephone: 574-296-6000. Fax: 574-296-6001.
Indianapolis-96th Street, Indiana Office: Parkwood Six, 600 East 96th Street, Suite 600, 46240. Telephone: 317-569-9600. Fax: 317-569-4800.
Washington, D.C. Office: 805 15th Street, N.W., Suite 700, 20005. Telephone: 202-312-7440. Fax: 202-312-7460.
Qingdao, China Office: 4/F, Office Tower, Crowne Plaza Qingdao, No. 76 Hong Kong Middle Road, 266071. Telephone: +011-86-532-575-1051. Fax: +011-86-532-575-1055.
Beijing, China Office: Room 1919, Tower 2, China World Trade Center, No. 1 JianGuoMenWai Avenue, 100004. Telephone: +86-10-6505-7733. Fax: +86-10-6505-8730.
See Professional Biographies, INDIANAPOLIS, INDIANA

Baker, Orbison & Bales, A Professional Association, (AV) .... 8852 El Rico Dr.
Baldwin, Charles B., (AV) .... '58 '83 C.879 B.S. L.201 J.D. [Ogletree,D.N.S.&S.]
Baldwin, Frank A., (BV) .... '54 '79 C.210 B.A. L.1119 J.D. Dep. Atty. Gen.
Baldwin, Jeffrey A., (BV) .... '62 '87 C.894 B.A. L.345 J.D. [Baldwin&D.]
Baldwin, John H., (BV) .... '09 '37 C.108 B.S. L.347 LL.B. 734 Peoples Bk. Bldg.

Baldwin & Dakich, (BV)
151 North Delaware Street, Suite 1510, 46204
Telephone: 317-636-4529 Fax: 317-635-5370
Email: jbaldwin@iquest.net URL: http://www.lawyers.com/baldwin&dakich
Jeffrey A. Baldwin; Thomas P. Dakich. Associate: Ginny Maxwell.
Criminal Defense, Sports Law, Telecommunications Law.
See Professional Biographies, INDIANAPOLIS, INDIANA

Bales, Inezellen .... '17 '52 L.345 LL.B. [Baker,O.&B.] ‡
Balhon, Jennifer L. .... '74 '99 C.249 B.S. L.1119 J.D. 6500 Westfield Blvd.
Ball, Cynthia L., (BV) .... '68 '95 C.108 B.A. L.347 J.D. [Ⓐ Landman&B.]
Ball, Rebecca L. .... '— '99 C.839 B.S. L.326 J.D. [Ⓐ Barnes&T.] (See Pat. Sect.)
Balmaseda, Philip B. .... '78 '05 C.347 B.A. L.884 J.D. Dep. Atty. Gen.
Bamberger, Foreman, Oswald and Hahn, LLP, (AV)
10 W. Market St. (⊙Evansville, Poseyville, Princeton)
Banta, Arthur W., (AV) .... '29 '56 C.210 A.B. L.309 LL.B. 1 Indiana Sq.‡
Banta, Donald G. .... '70 '96 C.679 B.S. L.607 J.D. [Banta]
Banta, Holiday W. '70 '94 C.347 B.A. L.880 J.D.
[Woodard,E.M.M.&H.] (See Pat. Sect.)
Banta Law Office .... 156 East Market Street, Suite 300
Baratz, Arnold P., (AV) .... '43 '69 C&L.345 B.S., J.D. 151 N. Deleware St.
Barber, Keith D. .... '— '95 C.839 B.S. L.326 J.D. [Hall,R.K.H.&L.]
Bardes, Paul M. '29 '59 C&L.861 B.B.A., J.D.
(adm. in LA; not adm. in IN) Gen. Coun. & Secy., Amer. States Ins. Co.
Barger, Sandra K. .... '74 '00 C.739 B.A. L.1119 J.D. Off of the Public Access Coun.
Barkdull, Denise Y. .... '71 '98 C.1193 B.B.A. L.1119 J.D. [Ⓐ Ice M.]
Barker, Charles E., (AV) .... '24 '50 C.347 L.345 LL.B. 9417 Spring Forest Dr.‡
Barker, Ryan C. .... '76 '01 C.228 B.S.E. L.345 J.D. [Ⓐ Baker&D.] (See Pat. Sect.)
Barker, Sarah Evans .... '43 '69 C.347 B.S. L.30 J.D. Chf. J., U.S. Dist. Ct.
Barkley, James M. .... '51 '77 C.347 B.S. L.345 J.D. Gen. Coun., Simon Property Group
Barnard, Thomas A., (AV) .... '— '82 C.679 B.S. L.1119 J.D. [Sommer B.]
Barnes, Barry T. .... '69 '96 C.347 B.A. L.615 J.D. [Feiwell&H.]
Barnes, Mark B., (AV) .... '53 '77 C.1208 B.A. L.608 J.D. [Ice M.]
Barnes, Maxwell N. .... '71 '97 C.477 B.A. L.880 J.D. [Ⓐ Baker&D.]
Barnes, Melissa Stapleton, (AV) ..... '68 '92 C.679 B.A. L.309 J.D. Atty., Eli Lilly & Co.
Barnes, Michael P. .... '— '73 C.707 B.A. L.602 J.D. Ct. App. J.
Barnes, Patricia G. .... '50 '92 C.184 B.A. L.923 J.D. 10027 Leeward Blvd.,
Barnes, Todd C. '74 '99 C.475 B.A. L.602 J.D.
156 East Market Square Street, Suite 600

Barnes & Thornburg LLP, (AV) BR
11 South Meridian Street, 46204 ⊙
Telephone: 317-236-1313 FAX: 317-231-7433
URL: http://www.btlaw.com
Partners: Stephen J. Dutton; Richard L. Johnson; Michael R. Fruehwald; Harold R. Bickham; Donald E. Knebel; Wayne C. Kreuscher; Kristin G. Fruehwald; Daniel W. McGill; Kent E. Agness; Michael R. Conner; Claudia V. Swhier; Catherine L. Bridge; Richard D. Conard; Larry J. Stroble; Michael Rosiello; Peter J. Rusthoven; Larry A. Mackey; John W. Boyd; Stephen W. Lee; Stanley C. Fickle; William M. Pope; Michael P. Lucas; John M. Kyle III; Michael K. McCrory (Certified in Business Bankruptcy Law by the American Board of Certification); Marcus B. Chandler; David B. Millard; Anne N. DePrez; Robert D. MacGill; Robert T. Grand; Mark D. Stuaan; Lawrence E. Lawhead; D. William Moreau, Jr.; Alan A. Levin; Kenneth H. Inskeep; Alan K. Mills; Douglas J. Heckler; Timothy J. Riffle; Steven W. Thornton; Howard E. Kochell; Kenneth J. Yerkes; Neal W. Steinbart; R. Anthony Prather; Richard A. Rezek; Lynn C. Tyler; Bruce D. Donaldson; Eric R. Moy; Jan M. Carroll; Michael G. Paton; Anne C. McGown; James M. Gutting; Richard C. Starkey; Dennis A. Johnson; John R. Maley; Teresa E. Morton; Benjamin A. Pecar; Michael J. Kaye; Dean T. Barnhard; Dwight D. Lueck; J. Michael Grubbs; Anthony C. Sullivan; Joseph C. Chapelle; Joseph E. Loftus; Andrew J. Detherage; Paul B. Hunt; Terry W. Dawson; Nicholas K. Kile; Joseph G. Eaton; Jeffery J. Qualkinbush; Donald E. Williams; Mariana Richmond; Richard J. Hall; Bart A. Karwath; Jeffrey A. Michael; Peter A. Morse, Jr.; Bradford G. Addison; Curt W. Hidde; Edward Sean Griggs; Thomas M. Maxwell; Charles P. Edwards; Bradley J. Dougherty; Elaine Waterhouse Wilson; William E. Padgett; Brian L. Burdick; Mark J. Dinsmore; Thomas F. Shea; Todd G. Vare; Michael H. Gottschlich; Patricia L. Ogden; Susan M. Zoeller; Michael D. Moon, Jr.; James R. Sweeney II; Thomas H. Engle; Shawn D. Bauer; Ronald S. Henderson. Of Counsel: Edward A. Keirn; Guinn P. Doyle; Linda K. Todd; Dilip Kulkarni; Barbara J. Meier; Kirk E. Grable; David R. Warshauer; Bryan G. Tabler; Lynne M. McMahan; Claudia Earls; Elizabeth Haber Lacy; Robert V. Kixmiller; Janet D. Neuenschwander; Kevin L. McLaren; Jack L. Stark, Jr.; Samuel D. Hodson; James T. Burns.

(This Listing Continued)

Barnes & Thornburg LLP (Continued)

Associates: Michael T. Scanlon; Wendy D. Brewer; Jeffrey A. Hopper; Randal J. Kaltenmark; Nathan A. Baker; Julie A. Russell; John P. Fischer, Jr.; Julia Spoor Gard; Christian P. Jones; John B. Baxter; Jonathan D. Mattingly; Terri L. Bruksch; Dennis P. Stolle; Andrew B. Dzeguze; Kevin D. Bailey; Richard P. Winegardner; Karoline E. Jackson; Rebecca L. Ball; Christopher P. Felts; P. Jason Stephenson; William A. Hahn II; John T. L. Koenig; T. Joseph Wendt; Ann S. Grayson; Kepten D. Carmichael; Kimberly Williams Blanchet; Jerimi J. Ullom; Andrea D. Bontrager Unzicker; Mary Jane Frisby; Jeffrey L. Papa; Jeff M. Barron (Not admitted in IN); Martin W. Zivitz; Kendall Millard (Not admitted in IN); Mark J. Crandley; Melanie D. Price; Michelle L. Kossmann; Erin Roth-Bohannon; Stephanie A.H. Blackman; Carli E. Stewart; Michael J. Hulka; Dennis S. Schell; Jason C. Farmer; Joshua B. Fleming (Not admitted in IN); David P. Hooper (Not admitted in IN); Angela K. Imel; Preston B. Ray, IV; Kitisri Sukhapinda; Paul L. Jefferson; Jimmie L. McMillian; Joshua P. Hollingsworth; Kristin S. Shedlock (Not admitted in IN); Hongsun Yoon; Shannon M. Shaw; Yolanda D. Edwards; Scott C. Hollingsworth; Randy L. Campbell, Jr.; Angela M. (Little) Berg; Monica R. Brownewell Smith; David R. Nijhawan; Anika M. Calloway; Hiroaki Nishikawara; Hillary Spike Fordice; Spencer P. Goodson; Scott M. Simmonds; Cheryl A. Gonzalez; Aarika D. Mack-Brown; Anthony H. Green; David M. Heger; Keith R. Donnelly; Asina C. Gant; David A. W. Wong; Glen M. Kellett; Aaron M. Staser. Staff Attorneys: Helen K. Geib; Sharlee C. Little (Not admitted in IN); Ziaddin Mollabashy; Kelly B. Smith; Katherine J. Stotler; Alejandro Valle.

Acquisitions and Divestitures, Ad Valorem Tax, Administrative Tax, Affirmative Action, Agriculture Law, Americans with Disabilities Act, Antidumping, Antitrust, Antitrust and Trade Regulation, Appellate Practice, Attorney Grievances, Automotive Warranty Law, Aviation and Aerospace, Aviation Law, Banking Law, Banking Regulations, Bankruptcy, Bankruptcy Reorganization, Banks and Banking, Biochemical Patents, Biomedical Products Liability, Biomedical Technology, Biotechnology Patent Prosecution, Bond Law, Brain Injury, Breach of Warranty, Brown Fields Redevelopment, Business Immigration, Business Law, Business Litigation, Business Planning, Business Regulatory and Administrative, Business Start-ups, Business Succession Planning, Business Taxation, Business Torts, Business Transactions, Business Transfers, Buying and Selling of Businesses, Cable TV, Cargo Claims, Charitable Trusts and Foundations, Chemical Intellectual Property, Chemical Patent Prosecution, Chemical Patents, Chemical Products Liability, Civil Appeals, Civil Litigation, Civil Practice, Civil RICO, Class Action Defense, Clean Air Act, Clean Water Act, Closely Held Business Estate Planning, Closely Held Businesses, Closely Held Business Law, Closely Held Corporations, Collective Bargaining, Commercial Bankruptcy, Commercial Finance Law, Commercial Law, Commercial Leasing and Financing, Commercial Litigation, Commercial Conveyancing, Commercial Real Estate, Commercial Real Estate Acquisition, Commercial Real Estate Development, Commercial Real Estate Finance, Commercial Transactions, Commodities Fraud, Communications and Media, Complex Commercial Litigation, Complex Litigation, Computer and Software Patents, Computer Law, Computers and Software, Conflicts of Interest, Construction Labor Law, Construction Law, Consumer Credit, Contract Litigation, Cooperatives, Copyrights, Corporate Finance, Corporate Formation, Corporate Law, Corporate Taxation, Corporate Tax Planning, Countervailing Duties, Covenants Not To Compete, Creditors Rights, Creditors Rights in Bankruptcy, Criminal Defense, Criminal Law, Criminal Tax Audits, Customs Law, Dealer and Distributor Termination, Debt and Equity Finance, Decedents Estates, Defense Litigation, Design Patents, Disability Insurance Defense, Discrimination, Distribution, Drug and Medical Device Defense, Economic Development, Education Law, Elder Law, Election, Campaign and Political Law, Electric Power, Electric Utilities, Electrical Intellectual Property, Electrical Patents, Electro-mechanical Patents, Electronic Commerce, Electronic Patents, Eminent Domain, Employee Benefits, Employee Stock Ownership Plans, Employment Defense, Employment Discrimination, Employment Law, Employment Litigation, Energy, Energy Contracts, Energy Regulation, Environmental Administrative Law, Environmental Cleanup, Environmental Compliance, Environmental Criminal Defense, Environmental Law, Environmental Litigation, Environmental Permitting, Environmental Real Estate, Environmental Regulation, Environmental Risk Management, Equal Employment Opportunity Law, ERISA Litigation, Estate Administration, Estate and Gift Taxation, Estate Planning, Estate Planning and Taxation, Estate Planning and Administration, Estate Planning and Probate, Estate Planning for Parents of Handicapped Children, Estate Planning for Unmarried Individuals, Executive Compensation, Executive Severance Contracts, Export Regulation, Fair Employment Practices, Family and Medical Leave Act, Family Business Successions, Family Wealth Transfer, Federal and State Administrative Regulatory Practice, Federal and State Legislative Practice, Federal Civil Litigation, Federal Civil Practice, Federal Criminal Law, Federal Estate and Gift Taxation, Federal Litigation, Federal Tax Controversies, Federal Taxation, Fiduciary Income Tax, Finance, Financial Transactions, First Party Insurance, Foreign Investment in the United States, Freight Claims, Freight Loss and Damage, Gaming Law, Gaming Licensing, Gas Utilities, General Litigation, Government, Government Affairs, Government Agency Practice, Government Contracts, Government Investigations, Government Relations, Groundwater Contamination, Hazardous Materials and Substances, Hazardous Waste, Hazardous Waste Liability, Head Injury, Health Care, Health Care Corporate Law, Health Care Contracts, Health Care Fraud, Health Care Licensing, Health Care Litigation, Health Care Mergers and Acquisitions, Health Care Regulation, Health Care Reimbursement, Health Law, Heavy Equipment Products Liability, Immigration Law, Industrial Revenue Bond Law, Inheritance Tax, Initial Public Offerings, Insurance, Insurance Bad Faith, Insurance Coverage, Insurance Litigation, Insurance Regulation, Integrated Health Care Delivery Systems, Intellectual Property, Intellectual Property General Prosecution, Intellectual Property Infringement, Intellectual Property Licensing, Intellectual Property Litigation, Intellectual Property Procurement, Intellectual Property Protection, Intellectual Property Rights, International Business Law, International Intellectual Property, International Law, International Patents, International Trade, International Transportation Law, Internet Law, Internet Trademark Law, Joint Ventures, Labor and Employment, Labor Arbitration, Labor Law, Labor Relations, Land Use, Lease Law, Leasing, Legal Ethics and Professional Responsibility, Legal Malpractice Defense, Legislative Practice, Licensing, Life Insurance Defense, Limited Liability Company Law, Limited Partnerships, Liquor Licensing, Litigation, Loans, Lobbying, Local Government Law, Logistics, Long Term Care, Managed Care, Managed Care Contracts, Management Employment Law, Management Labor Law, Manufacturers Liability, Maritime Regulations, Mechanical Intellectual Property, Mechanical Patents, Media Law, Mediation, Medical Antitrust, Medical Intellectual Property, Medical Patents, Mental Health Law, Mergers, Acquisitions and Divestitures, Mergers and Acquisitions, Mineral Taxation, Molecular Biology Patents, Motor Carrier Law, Motor Carrier Regulation, Multi-Employer Pensions, Municipal Bonds, Municipal Bonds Taxation, Municipal Finance, Municipal Law, Municipal Leasing, Municipal Redevelopment, Municipal Securities, Municipal Taxation, National Labor Relations Act, Neurolaw, Nonprofit and Charitable Organizations, Nonprofit Organizations Law, North American Free Trade Agreement, Occupational Safety and Health, OSHA, Partnership Law, Partnership Taxation, Patent Infringement, Patent Interference Practice, Patent Litigation, Patent Prosecution, Patents, PCT Legal Export, Personal Injury, Personal Injury Defense, Pesticide Litigation, Pharmaceutical Intellectual Property, Pharmaceutical Patents, Physician Contracts, Physician Practices, Planning and Land Use, Power Line Contact Injury, Probate, Probate Litigation, Products Liability, Products Liability Defense, Professional Liability, Property Law, Property Tax, Property Tax Abatement, Property Tax Appeals, Psychological Injury, Public Finance, Public Sector Labor Relations, Public Utility Law, Railroad Law, Real Estate, Real Estate Acquisitions, Real Estate Contracts, Real Estate Development, Real Estate Finance, Real Estate Licensing, Real Estate Secured Lending, Real Estate Title Insurance, Real Property, Real Property Acquisitions, Real Property Finance, Reorganizations, Resource Conservation and Recovery Act (RCRA), Retirement Benefit Plans, School Law, Securities, Securities Litigation, Securitization, Semiconductor Technology, Sexual Harassment, Small Business Corporations, State Government Law, State Tax Controversies, State Taxation, Structured Finance, Succession Planning, Superfund, Tax Controversies, Tax Exempt Finance, Tax Exempt Organizations, Tax Increment Finance, Tax Law, Tax Litigation, Taxation, Technology and Science, Technology Law, Technology Licensing, Technology Transfers, Telecommunications Competition, Telecommunications Law, Theft of Trade Secrets, Title VII Discrimination, Title IX Discrimination, Tort Defense, Toxic Exposure, Toxic Tort Class Actions, Toxic Torts, Toxic Tort Defense, Trade Dress, Trade Secrets, Trademark Litigation, Trademarks, Trademark Prosecution, Trademark Protection, Trademark Registration, Transportation, Transportation Safety, Trial Practice, Trusts and Estates, Unfair Competition, Unfair Trade, Uniform Commercial Codes, Union Contract Negotiations, Union Elections, Utilities, Utility Law, Wage and Hour Law, WARN Act, Water Pollution, Water Quality, Water Utilities, Wetland Regulation, White Collar Crime, White Collar Criminal Defense, Wills, Workers Compensation, Workouts, World Trade Organization, Wrongful Death, Wrongful Termination, Wrongful Termination Defense, Zoning, Planning and Land Use.

Representative Clients: DePuy Orthopaedics, Inc.; Dow AgroSciences; Eli Lilly and Company; Finish Line, Inc.; Hillenbrand Industries; The Lincoln National Life Insurance Company; Roche Diagnostics Corporation; Toyota Motor Corporation; Whirlpool Corporation.

Fort Wayne, Indiana Office: 600 One Summit Square, 46802. Telephone: 260-423-9440. FAX: 260-424-8316.

South Bend, Indiana Office: 600 1st Source Bank Center, 100 North Michigan, 46601-1632. Telephone: 574-233-1171. FAX: 574-237-1125.

Elkhart, Indiana Office: 121 West Franklin Street, Suite 200, 46516. Telephone: 574-293-0681. FAX: 574-296-2535.

Chicago, Illinois Office: One North Wacker Drive, Suite 4400, 60606-2809. Telephone: 312-357-1313. FAX: 312-759-5646.

(This Listing Continued)

Barnes & Thornburg LLP (Continued)

Washington, D.C. Office: 750 17th Street, N.W., Suite 900. 20006. Telephone: 202-289-1313. FAX: 202-289-1330.

Grand Rapids, Michigan Office: 300 Ottawa Avenue, N.W., Suite 500, 49503. Telephone: 616-742-3930. FAX: 616-742-3999.

See Professional Biographies, INDIANAPOLIS, INDIANA

Barnett, John V., Jr. . . . . . '43 '68 C.210 B.A. L.1119 J.D. [Ⓒ Bose M.&E.]
Barney, John R., Jr. . . . . . '34 '62 C.611 B.A. L.1119 J.D. Supr. Ct. J.
Barnhard, Dean T., (AV) . . . . . '— '83 C.472 B.M. L.345 J.D. [Barnes&T.]
Baron, Arthur G., (CV) . . . . . '24 '74 C&L.347 LL.B. 1321 N. Mitchner Ave.
Barrett, Brian P. . . . . . '63 '94 C.347 B.A. L.1119 J.D. Pat. Atty., Eli Lilly & Co. (Pat.)
Barrett, Daria Anne . . . . . '76 '02 C.925 B.S.B.A. L.879 J.D. 2882 Spring Meadow Ct.
Barrett, David W. . . . . . '71 '96 C.894 B.A. L.347 J.D. [Baker&D.]
Barron, Jeff M. '— '99 C.347 B.A. L.424 J.D.
(adm. in IL; not adm. in IN) [Ⓐ Barnes&T.]
Barrow, Frances . . . . . '55 '90 C.393 B.A. L.896 J.D. Dep. Atty. Gen.
Barrows, Christopher J. . . . . . '72 '99 C.288 B.A. L.345 J.D. [Ⓐ Avery&C.]
Bartlett, Cynthia '63 '89 C.1062 B.A. L.665 J.D.
(adm. in PA; not adm. in IN) Atty., Simon Debartolo Grp.
Bartlett, Rodney J. '49 '74 C.784 B.A. L.383 J.D.
(adm. in IA; not adm. in IN) I.R.S.
Bartol, Michael C. . . . . . '62 '97 C.645 B.S. L.347 J.D. [Bose M.&E.] (Pat.)
Bash, James F. . . . . . '25 '49 C.108 A.B. L.1119 J.D. 8461 Quail Hollow Rd.‡
Basile, Raymond A. . . . . . '74 '99 C.347 B.S. L.345 J.D. [Ⓐ Harrison&M.]
Bassett, M. Scott . . . . . '61 '86 C.347 B.S. L.1119 J.D. One Indiana Sq.‡
Bates, Michael T., (BV) '63 '89
C.701 B.S.Chem.E. L.345 J.D. Pat. Coun., Eli Lilly & Co. (Pat.)
Batesky, Richard P., Jr., (BV) . . . . . '63 '90 C.894 B.A. L.347 J.D. [R.Batesky,Jr.]
Batesky, Richard, Jr., Law Office of, (BV) . . . . . 22 E. Washington St., Ste. 610
Bator, John E., (BV) . . . . . '54 '81 C.347 A.B. L.345 J.D. [Bator R.B.S.&L.]
Bator Redman Bruner Shive & Ludwig, P.C., (AV)
151 North Delaware Street, Suite 1106
Batt, Michael T. . . . . . '— '99 C.249 B.A. L.345 J.D. [Ⓐ Hall,R.K.H.&L.]
Batties, Lilaberdia . . . . . '48 '96 C&L.347 B.S., J.D. 155 E. Market St., Ste. 865
Bauer, Jennifer A., (CV) . . . . . '65 '91 C.210 B.A. L.347 J.D. 115 W. Washington St.
Bauer, Shawn D. . . . . . '— '95 C.679 B.S.E. L.347 J.D. [Barnes&T.] (See Pat. Sect.)
Baumgartner, Frederick L. . . . . . '49 '74 C.347 A.B. L.345 J.D. 8994 E. 10th St.
Baxter, Arthur R., Jr., (BV) . . . . . '61 '86 C.881 A.B. L.345 J.D. [Baxter,J.&R.]
Baxter, John B., (AV) . . . . . '— '97 C.473 B.A. L.347 J.D. [Ⓐ Barnes&T.]
Baxter, James & Rose, (BV) . . . . . 6602 East 75th Street, Suite 115

Bays, Donna J., (AV) '58 '85 C.63 B.S. L.345 J.D.
One North Pennsylvania Street, Suite 905, 46204
Telephone: 317-630-3175 Fax: 317-630-3174
URL: http://www.donnabays.com
(Board Certified, Family Law Specialist, Indiana State Bar Association, Family Law Certification Board).
Family Law, Divorce, Child Custody, Paternity, Premarital Agreements.
See Professional Biographies, INDIANAPOLIS, INDIANA

Bays, Thomas B. . . . . . '64 '90 C.347 B.A. L.1119 J.D. [Ⓐ Goodin A.&M.]
Bayt, David J. . . . . . '— '01 C.347 B.A. L.1119 J.D. [Ⓐ Sommer B.]
Bayt, Phillip L., (AV) . . . . . '52 '80 C.429 B.A. L.1119 J.D. [Ice M.]
Bayt, Robert L. . . . . . '40 '72 C.108 A.B. L.345 J.D. U.S. Bkrptcy. J.‡
Bazley, Frederick A. '29 '62 C.94 A.B. L.818 LL.B.
(adm. in MA; not adm. in IN) V.P., Resch. & Develop., Amer. States Ins. Co.
Beall, Keith . . . . . '61 '87 C.347 B.S. L.201 J.D. [Ⓒ Harrison&M.]
Bearby, Scott A., (BV) . . . . . '65 '92 C.602 B.A. L.347 J.D. Asst. Gen. Coun., NCAA
Beason, Michael A., (BV) . . . . . '63 '90 C.894 B.A. L.347 J.D. [Christopher&T.]
Beattey, James L., (AV) . . . . . '08 '40 C&L.347 1401 E. 81st St.‡
Beattie, Alyssa . . . . . '— '04 C.347 B.A. L.1119 J.D. [Ⓐ Ice M.]
Beatty, James F., (AV) . . . . . '59 '84 C.347 B.S. L.1119 J.D. [Landman&B.]
Beatty, James W., (AV) . . . . . '31 '55 C&L.477 B.A., J.D. [Landman&B.]
Becht, Stephen M. '56 '86 C&L.201 B.S.C.E., J.D.
(adm. in OH; not adm. in IN) Pres., Becht Cos., Inc.
Beck, Jeffrey S. . . . . . '— '04 C.346 B.S. L.1119 J.D. [Ⓐ Baker&D.]
Beck, Michael D. '56 '86 C.1229 B.S.M.E. L.1370 J.D.
[Maginot M.&B.] (See Pat. Sect.)
Becker, Alan W., (AV) . . . . . '56 '81 C.347 B.S. L.1119 J.D. [Bose M.&E.]
Becker, Anne E., (BV) . . . . . '61 '88 C.741 B.A. L.602 J.D. [Stewart&I.]
Becker, Carl J. . . . . . '66 '91 C&L.339 B.S., J.D. [Newton B.B.]
Becker, Jonathan '73 '00 C.992 B.A. L.345 J.D.
Asst. Gen. Coun., American United Life Insurance Co.
Becker, Mark D. '61 '94
C.679 B.S.M.E. L.347 J.D. Coun., Emerson Appliance Solutions (Pat.)
Beckerich, Donald L., (AV) '29 '55 C.108 B.A. L.345 J.D.
151 N. Delaware St., Ste. 2000
Beckwith, Lewis D., (AV) . . . . . '48 '73 C.894 B.A. L.880 J.D. [Baker&D.]
Becsey, David, (AV) . . . . . '53 '91 C.228 B.H.S. L.347 J.D. [Zeigler C.&K.]
Becsey, Tara L. . . . . . '61 '91 C.679 B.A. L.347 J.D. 613 Greenlee Drive
Bedrick, Cynthia A. . . . . . '74 '99 C.108 B.A. L.1119 J.D. [Ⓐ DeLaney&D.]
Bedsole, Thomas F., (AV) . . . . . '64 '91 C.347 B.S. L.608 J.D. [Locke R.]
Beeler, Brian K., (CV) . . . . . '73 '98 C.679 B.S. L.345 J.D. [Ⓐ Krieg D.]
Beeler, Virgil L., (AV) . . . . . '31 '59 C.347 A.B. L.1119 J.D. [Ⓒ Baker&D.]
Beeman, John S., (AV) . . . . '45 '74 C.63 B.S. L.345 J.D. [Ⓒ Leeuw O.&C.] (⊙Tampa, FL)
Been, Jeffrey A. . . . . '59 '84 C.894 A.B. L.345 J.D. Dir., HIV/AIDS Legal Project of Ind.
Beering, Peter S., (BV) '60 '86 C.347 B.A. L.345 J.D.
Dep. Gen. Coun.& Dir., US Filter Indianapolis Water LLC
Beering, Shokrina Radpour, (BV) . . . . . '59 '86 C.679 B.A. L.345 J.D. [Cohen&M.]
Beesley, Brian Keith . . . . . '55 '84 C.249 B.S. L.345 J.D. Atty., State Personnel Dept.
Beesley, Sue A., (AV) . . . . . '55 '80 C.210 B.A. L.347 J.D. [Bingham M.]
Belanger, Todd H., (BV) . . . . . '67 '92 C&L.347 B.A., J.D. [Wood T.G.M.&H.]
Belden, Trevor Jon . . . . . '75 '00 C.679 B.A. L.477 J.D. [Ⓐ Baker&D.]
Beldin, Barry E., (BV) . . . '47 '82 C.347 B.S. L.345 J.D. One American Square, Box 82008
Bell, James J. . . . . . '73 '99 C.210 B.A. L.345 J.D. [Ⓐ Kiefer&M.]
Bell, M. Walter . . . . . '18 '51 C&L.347 B.S., J.D. 136 N. Delaware St.
Bell, Richard N. . . . . . '47 '75 C.347 B.S. L.345 J.D. [Cohen&M.]
Belle, Manuel . . . . . '18 '46 C.108 L.345 155 E Market St.
Beltz, Laurie L., (AV) . . . . . '52 '79 C.992 B.A. L.345 J.D. Pros., Alcoholic Bev. Comm.
Bemenderfer, T. Neil, (AV) . . . . . '56 '82 C.679 B.A. L.345 J.D. The Mediation Group
Bemis, M. Elizabeth . . . . . '66 '92 C.265 B.A. L.345 J.D. [Ruckelshaus,R.K.B.&H.]
Bench, Stuart T., (BV) . . . . . '51 '77 C.932 B.S. L.345 J.D. [Bench]
Bench Law Office, (BV) . . . . . 5202 Madison Ave.
Bender, Gabriel . . . . . '— '00 C.597 B.A. L.1119 J.D. [Ⓐ Baker&D.]
Bender, Timothy J., (AV) . . . . . '59 '84 C.679 B.S. L.345 J.D. [Bingham M.]
Benedict, Anthony M. . . . . . '39 '70 C.435 B.A. L.1119 J.D. [Curran&B.]

Benefield, Michael A. '73 '04
C.701 B.S. L.1119 J.D. [A Woodard,E.M.M.&H.] (See Pat. Sect.)
Benjamin, Jay D., (BV) ....'63 '88 C&L.347 B.S., J.D. P.O. Box 40857
Benjamin, Roger S. ....'38 '66 C.96 B.S. L.161 J.D. Pat. Coun., Eli Lilly & Co. (Pat.)
Benkie, Scott A., (AV) ....'60 '85 C.303 B.A. L.345 J.D. [Benkie&C.]
Benkie & Crawford, (AV) .... 47 South Meridian Street, Suite 305
Bennett, Bryce H., Jr., (AV) ....'53 '78 C.347 B.S. L.345 J.D. [Riley B.&E.]
Bennett, Donald P., (AV) ....'47 '73 C.894 A.B. L.477 J.D. [Baker&D.]
Bennett, Donna D., (AV) ....'61 '86 C.347 B.A. L.1119 J.D. Chief Coun., Dept. of Ins.
Bennett, H. Kennard, (BV) ....'57 '82 C.894 B.A. L.345 J.D. [Severns&B.]
Bennett, Jackie M., Jr., (AV) ....'— '83 C.303 B.A. L.345 J.D. [Sommer B.]
Bennett, Jeffrey T., (AV) ....'63 '89 C.210 B.A. L.1119 J.D. [Bingham M.]
Bennett, Maxine T., (BV) ....'38 '77 C.384 A.B. L.345 J.D. 302 North Alabama Street
Bennett, Patrick J., (BV) ....'33 '70 L.345 LL.B. [Bennett&S.]
Bennett, Rex E., (AV) ....'53 '81 C.291 B.A. L.802 J.D. [Locke R.]
Bennett, Robert B., Jr., (AV) ....'55 '80 C.198 A.B. L.280 J.D. 4600 Sunset Avenue
Bennett & Sheff, (AV) ....3711 E. Southport Rd.
Benton, Richard F. ....'57 '00 C.347 B.S. L.345 J.D. 4911 East 56th Street
Benz, David H. ....'— '96 C.679 B.S. L.345 J.D. [Sommer B.]
Benz, Steven C. '62 '94 C.383 B.A. L.893 J.D.
(adm. in OH; not adm. in IN) Staff Atty., Eli Lilly & Co.
Beougher, Caryn M. ....'78 '03 C.679 B.S. L.345 J.D. [A Feiwell&H.]
Beougher, Craig E. ....'77 '04 C.679 B.S. L.345 J.D. [A Feiwell&H.]
Bepko, Gerald L. ....'40 '65 C.589 B.S. L.146 J.D. V.P., Ind. Univ.
Bereveskos, Spiro, (AV) '56 '81
C.679 B.S. L.1119 J.D. [Woodard,E.M.M.&H.] (See Pat. Sect.)
Berg, Angela M. (Little) ....'— '03 C.741 B.A. L.602 [A Barnes&T.]
Berg, Jan Barteau ....'59 '86 C.347 A.B. L.345 J.D. Law Clk., Ct. of App.
Berg, Jeffrey A., (BV) ....'51 '77 C.347 B.A. L.425 J.D. Co. J.
Berg, Peyton ....'— '02 C.174 B.A. L.602 J.D. [A Bose M.&E.]
Bergin, Michael A., (AV) ....'44 '69 C&L.477 B.A., J.D. [Locke R.]
Berish, William M. ....'70 '96 C.210 B.A. L.1119 J.D. [Meils,T.D.&B.]
Berkebile, Lyn K. ....'58 '88 C.827 B.A. L.345 J.D. 1 American Sq.
Bernhardt, Mark T. ....'77 '05 C.346 B.S. L.1187 J.D. [A Starkey]
Bernstein, Howard N. ....'46 '76 C.347 A.B. L.345 J.D. 7 N. Meridan St., Ste. 210
Berry, David M., (AV) ....'59 '88 C.208 B.A. L.345 J.D. [Bose M.&E.]
Berry, Gil I., Jr., (BV) ....'37 '63 C.347 B.S. L.345 J.D. 302 N. Alabama Street
Betner, Brian C. ....'— '04 C.347 B.A. L.345 J.D. [A Hall,R.K.H.&L.]
Betz, Holly Hapak, (BV) ....'65 '90 C.347 B.S. L.94 J.D. [Wooden&M.]
Betz, Kevin W., (BV) ....'59 '88 C.347 B.A. L.1119 J.D. [Betz&Assoc.]
Betz, Kimberly S. ....'68 '99 C&L.347 B.G.S., J.D. USA Track & Field, Inc.
Betz, Tracy N. ....'— '04 C&L.347 B.A., J.D. [A Sommer B.]
Betz & Associates, (BV) ....One Indiana Square, Suite 1660
Bewley, Suzette ....'68 '98 C.679 B.S. L.1119 J.D. [C Baker&D.]
Beyler, Clifford A., (AV) ....'— '84 C.679 B.A. L.347 J.D. [Hall,R.K.H.&L.]
Bezy, Vicki ....'49 '88 C&L.347 B.S.N., J.D. Dir. & Sr. Coun., Anthem, Inc.
Bibbs, P. Lynn ....'57 '84 C&L.347 A.B., J.D. [O'Koon H.]
Bice, Keith A. ....'72 '98 C.108 B.A. L.602 J.D. [Bingham M.]
Bick, Jeffrey R. ....'62 '92 C.346 B.S. L.347 J.D. Sr. Staff Atty., Amer. Fam. Ins. Grp.
Bickel, Sandra K., (BV) ....'47 '82 C.347 B.S. L.345 J.D. [C Ice M.]
Bickham, Harold R. ....'— '73 C.679 B.A. L.347 J.D. [Barnes&T.]
Biddinger, F. James ....'35 '63 C.347 B.S. L.1119 LL.B. Pres., Ind. Gas Assn., Inc.
Biddle, James H. '47 '75 C.117 B.A. L.1340 J.D.
(adm. in OH; not adm. in IN) Second V.P. & Trust Offr., N. B. D., Indiana
Bielski, Edward G. ....'65 '94 C.602 B.A. L.347 J.D. [Stewart&I.]
Bier, Sylvia A. ....'73 '05 C.170 B.A. L.1119 J.D. [A Locke R.]
Biesecker, Fred R., (AV) ....'53 '80 C.347 B.A. L.976 J.D. [Ice M.]
Bigelow, Michael P., (AV) '67 '92
C.201 B.A. L.880 J.D. Atty., Pharm. Opers., Eli Lilly & Co.
Biggs, Donald C., (AV) ....'— '79 C.347 B.S. L.1119 J.D. [Sommer B.]
Bikoff, David, (BV) ....'43 '71 C.347 B.S. L.345 J.D. 151 North Delaware Street
Biloon, Etta M. ....'58 '83 C.860 B.A. L.818 J.D. 12122 Kingfisher Cir.
Bindner, Michael T., (AV) ....'52 '79 C.602 B.B.A. L.345 J.D. [Locke R.]

Bingham McHale LLP, (AV)
2700 Market Tower Building, 10 West Market Street, 46204-4900 ⊙
Telephone: 317-635-8900 Telecopier: 317-236-9907
Email: firm@binghammchale.com URL: http://www.binghammchale.com
Members of Firm: Michael J. Alerding; Robin L. Babbitt; Sue A. Beesley; Timothy J. Bender; Jeffrey T. Bennett; Keith A. Bice; David G. Blachly; Daniel L. Boots; S. Andrew Bowman; William M. Braman; C. John Brannon; Daniel P. Byron; David C. Campbell; Dennis F. Cantrell; Grantland M. Clapacs; Bryan J. Collins; Paul J. Corsaro; Steven G. Cracraft; Alan J. Dansker; Duane R. Denton; Julia E. Dimick; Michael L. Eckerle; Patrick A. Elward; Daniel R. Fagan; Phillip J. Fowler; Donald J. Graham; Gerard L. Gregerson; Michael Ryan Hartman; Robert B. Hebert; Kandi K. Hidde; James M. Hinshaw; Joseph H. Hogsett; Martha Schmidt Hollingsworth; Dwayne C. Isaacs; Phil L. Isenbarger; William J. Kaiser, Jr.; Larry J. Kane; Jan Kepley Keefer; Gary L. Klotz; Scott R. Leisz; Jeffery M. Mallamad; W. Tobin McClamroch; David T. McGimpsey; Brett J. Miller; Karl L. Mulvaney; Michael W. Padgett; David R. Prechtel; Matthew M. Price; Nana Quay-Smith; James A. Reed; Matthew R. Schantz; Thomas C. Scherer; Randolph L. Seger; Katherine L. Shelby; Laura Moenning Smith; Mary Elizabeth Solada; Hans W. Steck; Amy L. Stewart; James P. Strenski; Robert L. Taggart; John E. Taylor; Jennifer K. Thompson; David O. Tittle; Matthew T. Troyer; Mary Hamilton Watts; D. Bryan Weese; Brian W. Welch. Associates: David A. Adams; Michael J. Adler; Denise W. Chavis; Polly J. Dobbs; Stephen L. Due; Greg J. Duncan; Kelly R. Eskew; Kenan L. Farrell; Melissa J. Ford; Daniel J. Gerritzen; Liane Groth; Andrew W. Gruber; Bradley David Hasler; Joseph Hawkins; Richard J. Hayes; Jeremy E. Hill; Patricia A. Hughel; Bonnie B. Jagoditz; Whitney J. Johnson; Deron S. Kintner; Tonya L. Lengar; Susan J. Long; Brad R. Maurer; Jonna L. McGinley; Whitney L. Mosby; Anna Muehling Mallon; Kevin S. Price; C.W. Raines, III; Julie D. Reed; Candace L. Sage; Rafael A. Sanchez; Jason Ty Sibbitt; Tara J. Stapleton; Michael O. Weems; Isaac Willett; Brad A. Wilt; Christopher M. York. Of Counsel: Joseph L. Champion; John S. Chappell; Lanae M. Harden; Barbara A. Jones; Linda Nichols Kenny; Michael R. Kohlhaas; Dennis P. Lee; Gerald L. Moss; John G. Shubat; A. David Stippler; William F. Welch.
General Civil Practice including: Administrative Law; Agricultural Law; Alternative Dispute Resolution; Antitrust and Trade Regulation; Appeals; Appellate; Architects and Engineers Liability Defense; Banks and Banking; Bankruptcy and Reorganization; Business Law; Business Litigation; Cable Telecommunications Law; Collective Bargaining; Commercial Transactions; Construction Law; Contract Negotiation; Copyright; Corporate Finance; Complex Litigation; Class Actions; Corporate Law; Creditors' Rights; Drug and Medical Device Law; Election, Campaign Finance and Political Law; Employee Benefits; Environmental Law; Estate Planning and Administration; Family Law; Finance; Franchising and Licensing; Gaming Law; Governmental Services; Health Care; Hospital Law; Insurance; Intellectual Property; Labor and Employment; Leases and Leasing; Legal Malpractice, Discipline and Licensing; Libel, Slander and Defamation; Litigation; Lobbying; Matrimonial and Family Law; Media Law; Medicare and Medicaid Reimbursement, Medical and Dental Liability Defense and Disciplines and Licensing; Mergers and Acquisitions; Natural Resources Law; Occupational Safety and Health; Patent; Probate; Product Liability; Professional Liability Defense; Public Finance; Public Utility Law; Real Estate; Securities Law; Tax-Exempt Finance, Taxation (Controversies, Corporate Planning, Income, Gift and Estate, Individual, Partnership, Property, Nonprofit Organizations), Toxic Torts Law; Trademark; White Collar Criminal Defense; Zoning, Planning and Land Use.
Representative Clients: Barth Electric Co., Inc.; Community Bankers Association of Indiana; Indiana State Teachers Assn.; The Medical Protective Co.; St. Paul Insurance Co.
Jasper, Indiana Office: Bingham McHale LLP, 212 West Sixth Street. Telephone: 812-482- 5500. Fax: 812-482-2017.

(This Listing Continued)

Bingham McHale LLP (Continued)
Noblesville, Indiana Office: Bingham McHale LLP, 970 Logan Street. Telephone: 317-776-8668. Fax: 317-776-8651.
Vincennes, Indiana Office: Bingham Mchale LLP, 112 North 7th Street. Telephone: 812-886-9970. Fax: 812-886-0776.
See Professional Biographies, INDIANAPOLIS, INDIANA

Bippus, Gary W., (AV) ....'50 '82 C.346 B.S. L.345 J.D. [Ricos,B.&P.]
Bird, Kenneth L. ....'60 '86 C.145 A.B. L.477 J.D. Dep. Pub. Def.
Birge, James S. ....'— '99 C.309 B.A. L.477 J.D. [A Baker&D.]
Bisbecos, Peter A. '61 '87 C.894 B.A. L.1119 J.D.
National Association of Mutual Insurance Companies
Bishop, MaryEllen K., (AV) ....'57 '83 C.347 B.S. L.345 J.D. [Drewry S.V.]
Bishop, Michael P., (AV) ....'53 '80 C.1201 B.A. L.345 J.D. [Drewry S.V.]
Bishop, Reginald B., (BV) ....'51 '77 C.94 B.S. L.345 J.D. [Roberts&B.]
Bizzell, Susan D. ....'— '96 C.999 B.A. L.347 J.D. [Hall,R.K.H.&L.]
Blachly, David G., (BV) ....'58 '86 C.884 B.S. L.345 J.D. [Bingham M.]
Black, Jamie A. ....'53 '96 C.853 B.A. L.347 J.D. 8686 Madison Ave.
Black, Timothy L., (BV) ....'50 '76 C.879 B.A. L.365 J.D. [A Feiwell&H.]
Blackburn, Thomas L., (BV) ....'58 '84 C.347 B.A. L.345 J.D. [Cohen&M.]
Blackman, Stephanie A.H. ....'— '01 C.339 B.S. L.880 J.D. [A Barnes&T.]
Blackwelder, Charles B., (BV) ....'44 '78 C.992 A.B. L.347 J.D. [Blackwelder,C.&L.]
Blackwelder, Campbell & Leavitt, P.C., (BV) .... 151 North Delaware St.
Blackwell, Henry B., II, (AV) ....'28 '56 C.339 B.S. L.345 J.D. [C Baker&D.]
Blackwell, Joan Ligocki ....'61 '86 C&L.347 B.A., J.D. Staff Coun., U.S. Dist. Ct.
Blackwell, Leo T., (BV) ....'50 '85 C.347 B.S. L.345 J.D. [Ruckelshaus,R.K.B.&H.]
Blackwell, Thomas B., (AV) ....'60 '85 C.880 B.A. L.345 J.D. [Hopper B.]
Blaiklock, A. Richard M., (BV) ....'68 '97 C.303 B.A. L.347 J.D. [Lewis W.]
Blake, Stephen D. ....'75 '01 C&L.347 B.S., J.D. Atty., Indiana Dept. of Revenue
Blanchet, Kimberly Williams ....'— '98 C&L.347 B.S., J.D. [A Barnes&T.]
Blanford, Theodore J., (AV) ....'49 '84 C.347 B.S. L.345 J.D. [Hume S.G.G.&S.]
Blankenship, G. Thomas, (BV) ....'46 '71 C&L.347 B.S., J.D. [Blankenship]
Blankenship Law Office, (BV) ....7050 Madison Ave.
Blanton, Ben W., (AV) ....'56 '82 C.836 B.A. L.880 J.D. [Baker&D.]
Blaufuss, James R. ....'69 '05 C.878 B.S. L.345 J.D. [A Woodard,E.M.M.&H.]
Blazek, Keith G. ....'69 '98 C&L.347 B.S., J.D. [A Eckert C.]
Blazi, Geoffrey L., (CV) ....'65 '93 C&L.602 B.A., J.D. [Stuart&B.]
Blechl, James J. '35 '59 C.960 B.A. L.966 LL.B.
(adm. in WI; not adm. in IN) Amer. States Ins. Co.

Bleecker, Brodey & Andrews, (AV)
An Association - Not in Partnership
9247 North Meridian Street, Suite 200, 46260
Telephone: 317-574-0700 Telecopier: 317-574-0770
Email: info@bbanda.com URL: http://www.bbanda.com
Marc A. Bleecker (1940-1989); Ronald B. Brodey (P.C.); Stephen K. Andrews. Associate: Julia M. Andrews.
Personal Injury Litigation. General Civil, Collection, Creditor's Rights, Corporate, Real Estate, Commercial Law, Probate and Mediation.
See Professional Biographies, INDIANAPOLIS, INDIANA

Bleeke, James F., (AV) ....'60 '85 C.347 B.A. L.1119 J.D. [Tyra&C.]
Blessing, Thomas W., (AV) ....'65 '91 C.210 B.A. L.347 J.D. [Stewart&I.]
Blickman, Michael A., (AV) ....'53 '78 C.473 B.A. L.93 J.D. [Ice M.]
Bloch, Andrew R. ....'78 '03 C.973 B.S. L.74 J.D. [A Zeigler C.&K.]
Bloom, Elias ....'23 '76 C.375 B.S. L.345 J.D. 911 E. 86th St.
Blough, Robert E. '46 '71 C.347 B.S. L.1119 J.D.
Area Coun., Lawyers Title Insurance Corporation
Blue, Janet Roberts, (AV) ......'33 '57 C.347 A.B. L.1119 J.D. Comr., Ct. of App. of Ind.
Blystone, Amanda R. ....'75 '01 C.108 B.A. L.861 J.D. [A Baker&D.]
Blythe, James D., II, (AV) ....'40 '66 C.108 A.B. L.345 J.D. [Blythe&O.]
Blythe & Ost, (AV) ....10585 North Meridian
Boberschmidt, Philip F., (AV) ....'36 '67 C.686 B.S. L.345 J.D. 111 Monument Cir.
Bobilya, Daniel D. ....'74 '01 C.347 B.A. L.345 J.D. [A Locke R.]
Bock, William, III, (BV) ....'62 '89 C.1288 B.A. L.477 J.D. [Kroger,G.&R.]
Bodle, David J., (AV) ....'52 '78 C.436 B.A. L.896 J.D. [Hackman H.&C.]
Boeglin, Daniel L., (AV) ....'59 '85 C.347 B.S. L.893 J.D. [Baker&D.]
Boehm, Theodore R., (AV) ....'38 '64 C.103 A.B. L.309 J.D. Ind. Supreme Ct.
Boese, J. Lynn, (BV) ....'40 '72 C.303 A.B. L.345 J.D. 7321 Royal Oakland Dr.
Bogard, Donald P. ....'41 '71 C.63 B.S. L.1119 J.D. [C Plews S.R.&B.]
Bogard, Shannon D. ....'75 '01 C.108 B.A. L.345 J.D. [A Huffer&W.]
Bogdanowicz, Mark A. '73 '00 C.309 A.B. L.880 J.D.
(adm. in TN; not adm. in IN) [A Ice M.]
Bohrer, James F., (BV) ....'57 '82 C.347 B.s. L.1119 J.D. [Mallor C.G.&B.] ⊙
Boivin, Nicholas M. '— '03 C.597 B.A. L.893 J.D.
(adm. in IL; not adm. in IN; See Pat. Sect.) [A Brinks H.G.&L.]
Bolden, Clarence D. ....'24 '53 C.108 A.B. L.345 J.D. Sr. J., Supm. Ct.‡
Boldt, Jeffrey M. ....'— '01 C.859 B.A. L.188 J.D. [A Locke R.]
Boldt, Michael H., (AV) ....'50 '75 C.912 B.A. L.477 J.D. [Ice M.]
Bolen, James S. ....'— '00 C.1119 B.S. L.200 J.D. [A Laudig G.R.&S.]
Bolenbaugh, Gary E. '61 '97 C.347 B.S. L.1339 J.D.
V.P., Opers. & Corp. Coun., Independent Welding Distributors Cooperative, Inc.
Bolling, Julie C. ....'72 '97 C.344 B.S. L.345 J.D. [A Krieg D.]
Bond, Tonya J. ....'— '04 C.347 B.A. L.1119 J.D. [A Ice M.]
Boodt, David B., (AV) '59 '90
C.701 B.S. L.347 J.D. V.P. & Assoc. Gen. Coun., USA Group, Inc.
Bootcheck, Carrie Wagner ....'— '97 C.472 B.A. L.1119 J.D. [Bose M.&E.]
Booth, Cynthia K. ....'56 '92 C.63 B.S. L.345 J.D. Child Advocates, Inc.
Boothe, Kenneth M. ....'67 '97 C.999 B.S.B.A. L.347 J.D. Amer. United Life Ins. Co.
Boots, Daniel L., (AV) ....'61 '87 C.679 B.S.I.M. L.345 J.D. [Bingham M.] (Pat.)
Boots, Valerie Kent ....'58 '87 C&L.347 B.A., J.D. 5215 E. 72nd. St.
Bordone, Saundria Kay ....'45 '98 C.623 B.A. L.347 J.D. 9951 Southwind Circle
Borek, Rosemary L. ....'71 '97 C.472 B.A. L.347 J.D. [A Stephenson M.&S.]
Borgman, Adam W. '— '05
C.701 B.S. L.345 J.D. [A Woodard,E.M.M.&H.] (See Pat. Sect.)
Borgmann, Louis H. ....'48 '74 C.973 B.S. L.347 J.D. 431 E. Hanna Ave.
Borkowski, Catherine ....'63 '91 C&L.347 B.A., J.D. 7118 N. Shadeland Ave.
Borland, Andrew J. ....'72 '98 C&L.347 B.A., J.D. [Borland&G.]
Borland & Gaerte ....3545 N. Washington Boulevard
Born, S. R., (AV) ....'45 '70 C.784 B.A. L.347 J.D. [Ice M.]
Borowski, Craig M. ....'73 '00 C&L.347 B.S., J.D. [A Baker&D.]
Borschel, Michael Charles .....'46 '00 C.1494 B.A. L.345 J.D. 156 E. Market St., Ste. 200
Borucki, Andrea T. '62 '87
C.347 B.A.Chem. L.879 J.D. Gen. Pat. Coun., Dow AgroSciences (Pat.)
Boruta, Matt ....'51 '78 C&L.213 B.A., J.D. [A M.Norris]

Bose McKinney & Evans LLP, (AV) BR
2700 First Indiana Plaza, 135 North Pennsylvania Street, 46204 ⊙
Telephone: 317-684-5000 Facsimile: 317-684-5173
URL: http://www.boselaw.com
Members of Firm: Lewis C. Bose (1917-2001); William M. Evans (1923-1991); Robert H. McKinney (Retired); Thomas M. Atherton; Jeffrey B. Bailey; Jon M. Bailey; Michael C. Bartol; Alan W. Becker; David M. Berry; Carrie Wagner Bootcheck; David A. Butcher; James E. Carlberg; Gary L. Chapman; Robert B. Clemens; James A. Coles; Kendall C. Crook; Amy L. Cueller; Christopher C. Earle; Ronald E. Elberger; Cathy Elliott; Daniel C. Emerson; Jeffrey R. Gaither; Lisa McKinney Goldner; Steven D. Groth; Kathleen I. Hart; Roberts E. Inveiss; J. Christopher Janak; David J. Jurkiewicz; Robert P. Kassing; Bernie Too Keller; V. Samuel Laurin III; L. Robert Lowe, Jr.; Kathleen G. Lucas; Paul S. Mannweiler; R. J. McConnell; Daniel P. McInerny; Andrew M. McNeil; Donald M. Meyer; Margaret Bannon Miller; John A. Millspaugh; Theodore J. Nowacki; Timothy J. O'Hara; Dennis H. Otten; Craig Pinkus; L. Parvin Price; George E. Purdy; Sarah Steele Riordan; Philip J. Ripani; Charles R. Rubright; C. Joseph Russell; Michael J. Schneider; Daniel B. Seitz; Melinda Shapiro; J. Gregory Shelley; Nikki G. Shoultz; G. Pearson Smith, Jr.; Ronald M. Soskin; Natalie J. Stucky; Karl R. Sturbaum; David A. Suess; David L. Swider; Scott E. Tarter; Harry F. Todd; Alan S. Townsend; Susan E. Traynor; Michael A. Trentadue; Richard S. VanRheenen; John D. Walda; David L. Wills; Bryan B. Woodruff; Judy L. Woods; Karen Ball Woods; Brantley H. Wright; C. Daniel Yates. Of Counsel: John V. Barnett, Jr.; Michael O. Chenoweth; Stephen E. DeVoe; Anthony P. Filomena; Thomas E. Fruechtenicht; Rodger K. Hendershot; Eugene L. Henderson; Jeannette Eisan Hinshaw; Daniel J. Krieger; Carl D. Overman; Karen Glasser Sharp; A.J. Usher IV; Robert T. Wildman. Associates: Adrian Allen; Bryan H. Babb; Peyton Berg; Lea Ann Breeden; Rhonda Yoder Breman; Jennifer L. Day; Carina M. de la Torre; Christopher A. Evens; W. James Hamilton; Stephanie Franco Holtzlander; Alex C. Intermill; Buren E. Jones; Jeffrey J. Kirk, II; Matthew R. Macaluso; Katherine Mayberry; Megan M. Mulford; Susan Oliver; Christine E. M. Orich; Sandra Perry; Beth L. Riga; Theresa M. Ringle; Michael D. Rogers; Brion G. St.Amour; Marisol Sanchez; Kelly M. Scanlan; H. Antonio Setzer; Katherine E. Taylor; Joel W. Thorp; Stephen C. Unger; Paul D. Vink; Ryan O. White (Not admitted in IN); Mark J. Wuellner.
General Civil Practice in all Courts including Agricultural Law, Antitrust, Appellate Practice, Capital Strategies, Civil Rights, Commercial Law, Communications and Media, Constitutional Law, Corporate Law, Creditors Rights, Creditors Rights in Bankruptcy, Debtor Bankruptcy, Education Law, Employee Benefits, Entertainment and the Arts, Entrepreneurial Services, Environmental Law, Finance, Financial Institutions Law, Government Contracts, Government Relations, High Technology, Insurance, Intellectual Property, International Law, Labor and Employment, Legislative Practice, Litigation, Mergers and Acquisitions, Municipal Finance, Municipal Law, Planning and Land Use, Probate, Real Estate, Regulated Industries, Regulatory Agency Practice, Securities, Taxation, Trusts and Estates, Utility Law, Wills and Zoning.
Representative Clients: Duke Realty Corp.; Emmis Communications Corp.; First Indiana Bank; Indianapolis Colts, Inc.; Hillenbrand Industries, Inc.; Indiana Bankers Assn.; Kenra, Inc.; Metropolitan Life Insurance Co.; Thomson, Inc.; US Steel Corp.; Wal-Mart Stores, Inc.
Washington, D.C. Office: 700 North One Lafayette Centre, 1120 20th Street, N.W., 20036. Telephone: 202-973-1229. Fax: 202-973-1212.
Crown Point, Indiana Office: 3577 West Lakeshore Drive, 46307. Telephone: 219-663-2968. Fax: 219-663-2969.
Chesterton, Indiana Office: P.O. Box 957, 46304. Telephone: 219-983-1552. Fax: 219-983-1741.
Other Indianapolis, Indiana Office: 600 East 96th Street, Suite 500. Telephone: 317-684-5300. Fax: 317-684-5316.
West Lafayette, Indiana Office: 3000 Kent Avenue. Telephone: 765-464-3200. Fax: 765-464-3225.
See Professional Biographies, INDIANAPOLIS, INDIANA

Bose McKinney & Evans LLP, (AV)
600 East 96th Street, Suite 500, 46240 ⊙
Telephone: 317-684-5300 Facsimile: 317-684-5316
URL: http://www.boselaw.com
Joseph D. Calderon; James C. Carlino; Tammy K. Haney; Philip A. Nicely. Associates: Andrew J. Held; Angela E. Tempel.
General Civil Practice in all Courts including Agricultural Law, Antitrust, Appellate Practice, Capital Strategies, Civil Rights, Commercial Law, Communications and Media, Constitutional Law, Corporate Law, Creditors Rights, Creditors Rights in Bankruptcy, Debtor Bankruptcy, Education Law, Employee Benefits, Entertainment and the Arts, Entrepreneurial Services, Environmental Law, Finance, Financial Institutions Law, Government Contracts, Government Relations, High Technology, Insurance, Intellectual Property, International Law, Labor and Employment, Legislative Practice, Litigation, Mergers and Acquisitions, Municipal Finance, Municipal Law, Planning and Land Use, Probate, Real Estate, Regulated Industries, Regulatory Agency Practice, Securities, Taxation, Trusts and Estates, Utility Law, Wills and Zoning.
Indianapolis, Indiana Office: 2700 First Indiana Plaza, 135 North Pennsylvania Street, 46204. Telephone: 317-684-5000. Facsimile: 317-684-5173.
Washington, D.C. Office: 700 North One Lafayette Centre, 1120 20th Street, N.W., 20036. Telephone: 202-973-1229. Fax: 202-973-1212.
Crown Point, Indiana Office: 3577 West Lakeshore Drive, 46307. Telephone: 219-663-2968. Fax: 219-663-2969.
Chesterton, Indiana Office: P.O. Box 957, 46304. Telephone: 219-983-1552. Fax: 219-983-1741.
West Lafayette, Indiana Office: 3000 Kent Avenue. Telephone: 765-464-3200. Fax: 765-464-3225.
See Professional Biographies, INDIANAPOLIS, INDIANA

Boshkoff, Ellen E., (AV) .... '60 '92 C.821 B.A. L.347 J.D. [Baker&D.]
Bosma, Brian C., (AV) .... '57 '84 C.679 B.S.E. L.345 J.D. [Kroger,G.&R.]
Bostwick, David E. .... '68 '02 C.347 B.A. L.345 J.D. [🄰 Easter&C.]
Bouaichi, Kristine J. .... '67 '98 C.347 B.A. L.362 J.D. [🄰 Ice M.]
Boudreaux, William R. ...... '65 '92 C&L.420 B.S., J.D. Pat. Coun., Eli Lilly & Co. (Pat.)
Boulton, Matthew C., (CV) ...... '71 '96 C.347 B.A. L.221 J.D. 2850 N. Meridian Street
Bouwkamp, Alan A., (AV) .... '62 '91 C&L.347 B.A., J.D. [Newton B.B.]
Bowers, Howard E. .... '51 '02 C.63 B.A. L.1119 J.D. 216 E. Summer Avenue
Bowes, Gregory P., (BV) .... '59 '85 C.347 B.S. L.345 J.D. [Bowes&Assoc.]
Bowes & Associates, P.C., (BV) .... 6202 N. College Ave.
Bowman, D. Michael, (BV) '47 '74 C&L.347 B.S., J.D.
136 East Market Street Suite 700
Bowman, Felson, (BV) .... '39 '69 C.108 B.S. L.345 J.D. [🄲 Lewis W.]
Bowman, Forrest, III, (AV) .... '66 '92 C.347 B.A. L.1119 J.D. [Bowman,C.&B.]
Bowman, Forrest B., Jr., (AV) .... '34 '62 C.347 B.S. L.345 LL.B. [Bowman,C.&B.]
Bowman, Frank O., III, (AV Ⓣ) '55 '79
C.170 B.A. L.309 J.D. Prof. of Law, Indiana Univ. School of Law
Bowman, Glenn D., (BV) .... '58 '83 C&L.345 B.A., J.D. [Stewart&I.]
Bowman, J. Michael .... '63 '04 C.145 B.A. L.345 J.D. [🄰 Plews S.R.&B.]
Bowman, Joseph C. .... '69 '98 C.347 B.S. L.345 J.D. [🄰 Krieg D.]
Bowman, S. Andrew, (AV) .... '56 '82 C.679 B.S. L.347 J.D. [Bingham M.]
Bowman, Cosby & Bowman, (AV) .... 1 North Penn
Bowman, Heintz, Boscia & Vician, A Professional Corporation, (BV)
251 East Ohio Street, Suite 860 (⊙Chgo., IL; Merrillville, IN)
Bowron-White, Susan C. '51 '77 C.679 B.A. L.347 J.D.
Assoc. Gen. Coun. & Asst. Corp. Secy., Meridian Ins. Cos.
Boyd, Hollie ...... '50 '80 C.347 A.B. L.345 J.D. Dept. of Housing & Urban Development
Boyd, Jack L., (AV) '43 '87
C.63 B.S. L.345 J.D. Asst. Gen. Coun., Simon Property Group
Boyd, John W., (AV) .... '— '76 C.597 B.A. L.347 J.D. [Barnes&T.]
Boyers, James M. .... '72 '98 C.303 B.A. L.347 J.D. [🄰 Wooden&M.]
Boyko, Ihor N. ...... '51 '75 C.347 A.B. L.1119 J.D. Ind. Dept. of Environmental Mgmt.
Boyle, Bernard J. .... '20 '50 C.972 L.209 7320 Hawthorne Ln.‡
Brackemyre, Jayne F. '49 '83 C.63 B.S. L.74 J.D.
Sr. Staff Atty., Simon Property Group‡
Brackenridge, Dean R. .... '68 '95 C.602 B.A. L.608 J.D. [Locke R.]
Bradbury, Sara R. .... '76 '04 C.231 B.A. L.1119 J.D. [🄰 Lewis&K.]
Bradford, Chad J. .... '76 '02 C&L.1119 B.A., J.D. [🄰 Stewart&I.]
Bradford, Daniel Walker ...... '47 '88 C.208 B.S.B.A. L.345 J.D. 4911 East 56th Street
Bradford, Kimberly A. ...... '60 '86 C.347 B.A. L.1119 J.D. Adm., Supm. Ct. Admr's. Off.
Bradley, Larry E., (BV) '58 '82
C.265 B.A. L.345 J.D. Probate Ct. Comr., Marion Co. Probate Cct.
Bradshaw, Henry E., (AV) .... '31 '56 C.347 B.S. L.345 J.D. 9320 Oak Run Circle
Bradshaw, John M. '72 '99
C.602 B.S. L.1119 J.D. [🄰 Woodard,E.M.M.&H.] (See Pat. Sect.)
Bradway, Norma .... '44 '75 C.63 B.A. L.345 J.D. State Gen. Counsels Off.
Braitman, Mary Beth, (AV) .... '50 '81 C.347 B.S. L.345 J.D. [Ice M.]
Braman, William M., (AV) .... '65 '90 C.210 B.A. L.1119 J.D. [Bingham M.]
Brandes, Andrea Lynn '72 '99 C.947 B.A. L.345 J.D.
Asst. Gen. Coun., Indiana Utility Regulatory Commission
Brandt, Robert C. .... '72 '02 C.1266 B.A. L.1119 J.D. [🄰 Riley B.&E.]
Branic, Matthew C. .... '79 '05 C.473 B.S. L.201 J.D. [🄰 Krieg D.]
Brannon, C. John .... '61 '97 C.502 B.S. L.146 J.D. [Bingham M.]
Brant, Kyle S. .... '57 '88 C.1229 B.E.E. L.345 J.D. 5441 Fenmore Rd. (Pat.)
Brashear, Andrea D. .... '77 '02 C.210 B.A. L.345 J.D. [🄰 Krieg D.]
Bratch, Ralph J. .... '65 '90 C.63 B.S. L.879 J.D. [🄲 Doehrman C.]
Brattain, Bruce D., (AV) .... '50 '79 C.63 B.S. L.345 J.D. [Brattain&M.]

Brattain & Minnix, (AV) BR
An Association of Lawyers
151 North Delaware Street Suite 760, 46204
Telephone: 317-231-1750 Facsimile: 317-231-1760
Bruce D. Brattain; Larry A. Minnix; Mario Garcia.
Civil and Criminal Trial Practice in all Courts, Business, Corporate, Commercial, Bankruptcy, Personal Injury, Medical Malpractice, Family/Domestic Relations, Custody, Support.
See Professional Biographies, INDIANAPOLIS, INDIANA

Brauer, James W., (AV) .... '49 '76 C.347 B.S. L.345 J.D. [Stewart&I.]
Braun, Charles N., II, Attorney at Law '52 '77
C.347 B.A. L.345 J.D. 11935 Glen Cove Ct.
Braun, Christopher J., (AV) .... '59 '84 C.894 B.A. L.802 J.D. [Plews S.R.&B.]
Bravard, Walter E., Jr., (BV) .... '36 '69 C.347 B.S. L.345 J.D. 55 Monument Circle
Bray, Michelle Kaiser .... '— '95 C.973 B.A. L.365 J.D. [Sommer B.]
Brazill, Timothy P. .... '56 '82 C.894 A.B. L.345 J.D. [O'Bryan B.&D.]
Bredensteiner, Gregg R. .... '56 '91 C.346 B.S. L.347 J.D. 420 Ottawa Dr.
Breece, Marline R. .... '57 '92 C.679 B.S. L.345 J.D. [🄲 Baker&D.]
Breeden, Lea Ann .... '— '03 C.138 B.A. L.4210 J.D. [🄰 Bose M.&E.]
Breman, Rhonda Yoder .... '— '02 C.347 B.A. L.1119 J.D. [🄰 Bose M.&E.]
Bremer, Frederick S., (BV) .... '50 '75 C.347 A.B. L.345 J.D. 8126 Penway E.
Brennan, Norman E. .... '18 '42 C&L.347 LL.B. 156 E. Market St.
Brennan, Timothy L., (BV) .... '48 '77 C.238 B.A. L.616 J.D. 156 E. Market St.
Breunig, Preston, (BV) .... '42 '67 C.347 A.B. L.1119 J.D. 302 N. Alabama Street
Brewer, Wendy D. .... '— '95 C&L.259 B.A., J.D. [🄰 Barnes&T.]
Brewis, Jesse A. '25 '54 C&L.912 B.A., LL.B.
(adm. in MI; not adm. in IN) 2955 N. Meridian St.‡
Bria, Jason K. .... '— '01 C.63 B.S. L.345 J.D. Asst. Gen. Coun., Lauth Group, Inc.
Bridge, Catherine L., (AV) .... '— '76 C.262 A.B. L.178 J.D. [Barnes&T.]
Bridge, John B., (AV) .... '50 '76 C.894 B.A. L.178 J.D. [Plews S.R.&B.]
Bridwell, Robert V. .... '23 '51 C.347 A.B. L.345 J.D. 5204 Crittenden Ave.‡

Brinks Hofer Gilson & Lione, A Professional Corporation, (AV)
One Indiana Square, Suite 1600, 46204-2001 ⊙
Telephone: 317-636-0886 Facsimile: 317-634-6701
Email: iplaw@usebrinks.com URL: http://www.usebrinks.com
Shareholder: A. James Richardson (Managing Attorney, Indianapolis Office). Counsel: Lawrence A. Steward. Of Counsel: David H. Badger. Associates: Sanders N. Hillis; Nicholas M. Boivin (Not admitted in IN); Michael E. Wever (Not admitted in IN).
Patent, Trademark, Copyright, Trade Secret and Internet Work, Unfair Competition, Technology and Licensing Agreements, Intellectual Asset Management and Intellectual Property Litigation.
Chicago, Illinois Office: NBC Tower, Suite 3600, 455 North Cityfront Plaza Drive. Telephone: 312-321-4200. Facsimile: 312-321-4299. Email: iplaw@usebrinks.com.
Ann Arbor, Michigan Office: 524 South Main Street, Suite 200. Telephone: 734-302-6000. Fax: 734-994-6331.
Arlington, Virginia Office: 2001 Jefferson Davis Highway, Suite 208. Telephone: 703-415-0303. Facsimile: 703-415-0304.
See Professional Biographies, INDIANAPOLIS, INDIANA

Brissenden, Reynolds B. .... '72 '97 C.323 B.A. L.879 J.D. [🄰 Kroger,G.&R.]
Broach, Kent M. .... '60 '85 C.679 B.A. L.345 J.D. [Wooden&M.]
Brodey, Jay Michael, (AV) .... '43 '68 C.347 A.B. L.345 J.D. 9038 Dewsberry Ct.‡
Brodey, Ronald B., (P.C.), (AV) .... '45 '70 C.347 B.S. L.1119 J.D. [Bleecker,B.&A.]
Brodnik, Thomas A. .... '59 '89 C.435 B.S. L.345 J.D. [Stark D.&S.]
Broecker, Edwin J., (AV) .... '— '91 C.894 B.A. L.347 J.D. [Sommer B.]
Brogden, Annette T., (AV) '60 '91
C.628 B.A. L.347 J.D. 8440 Woodfield Crossing, Suite 288
Bromund, David C., (BV) .... '— '88 C.894 A.B. L.880 J.D. [Sommer B.]
Bronicki, Vickie L. .... '62 '94 C&L.347 B.S., J.D. The Hartford
Brook, Sanford M. .... '49 '74 C.347 A.B. L.1119 J.D. Appl. Ct. J.
Brooke, Susan Rogers, (AV) .... '51 '78 C.205 B.A. L.345 J.D. [🄲 Ice M.]
Brookens, Kalynne .... '62 '87 C.477 B.A. L.879 J.D. P.O. Box 29424
Brookie, Terrence L., (AV) .... '55 '81 C.207 B.A. L.345 J.D. [Locke R.]
Brooks, David M., (BV) .... '55 '82 C.894 B.A. L.846 J.D. [Brooks,K.&S.]
Brooks, Mark S. .... '55 '86 C.1081 B.S. L.345 J.D. 1923 N. Glenridge Dr.★
Brooks, Koch & Sorg, (BV) .... 615 Russell Ave.
Brossart, John W. .... '35 '61 C.347 A.B. L.345 LL.B. 1015 W. 73rd St.‡
Brothers, Robert A., (AV) '42 '72 C.531 B.S. L.345 J.D.
151 N. Delaware St., Ste. 1400
Brown, Alan S., (AV) .... '52 '78 C.347 A.B. L.345 J.D. [Locke R.]
Brown, C. John .... '— '05 C.446 B.S. L.1119 J.D. [🄰 Baker&D.]
Brown, Christopher A. .... '67 '96 C.894 A.B. L.1119 J.D. [Woodard,E.M.M.&H.]
Brown, Douglas R., (AV) .... '59 '85 C.880 B.A. L.345 J.D. [Stewart&I.]
Brown, Earl, Jr. .... '49 '74 C.344 B.S. L.345 J.D. 576 Ransom St.
Brown, J. Jeffrey, (AV) .... '60 '88 C.347 B.A. L.893 J.D. [Baker&D.]
Brown, Jack C., (AV) .... '19 '42 C.347 A.B. L.178 LL.B. 320 N. Meridian‡
Brown, James Glenn, (AV) '52 '77
C.347 B.A. L.345 J.D. V.P. & Sr. Attu, Nati. City Corporation
Brown, James J. '60 '88 C.347 B.A. L.893 J.D.
(adm. in NY; not adm. in IN) 707 Massachusetts‡
Brown, Jenifer M. .... '72 '99 C.63 B.A. L.345 J.D. [🄲 Ice M.]
Brown, Jill .... '60 '87 C.105 B.A. L.273 J.D. N.L.R.B.
Brown, Lorie A. .... '61 '91 C&L.347 B.S.N., J.D. 718 Timber Mill Lane
Brown, Mary M. .... '55 '85 C.347 B.A. L.345 J.D. Circle Tower Suite 1328
Brown, Michael E., (AV) .... '52 '78 C.347 B.A. L.1119 J.D. [Kightlinger&G.]
Brown, Michele E. .... '78 '03 C.347 B.S. L.1119 J.D. [🄰 DeLaney&D.]
Brown, Richard L., Jr., (BV) .... '57 '83 C.347 B.S. L.345 J.D. 323 North Delaware
Brown, Ronald, (BV) .... '64 '95 C.800 L.347 J.D. Atty., Eli Lilly & Co.
Brown, Ted R. .... '55 '81 C&L.347 A.B., J.D. Dir. & Coun., Anthem, Inc.
Brown, William R. .... '39 '70 C.265 B.A. L.345 J.D. 251 East Ohio Street‡
Brown, William R. .... '39 '70 C.265 A.B. L.345 J.D. [Stewart&I.]
Browne, James R. .... '69 '94 C.210 B.A. L.347 J.D. [Goodin A.&M.]

Brownewell Smith, Monica R. .... '— '03 C.210 B.A. L.879 J.D. [🄰 Barnes&T.]
Browning, Clifford W., (AV) '50 '78
C.679 B.S.Ch.E. L.345 J.D. [Woodard,E.M.M.&H.] (See Pat. Sect.)
Browning, Rebecca K. .... '65 '92 C.473 B.Phil. L.345 J.D. [🄰 Due,D.F.&M.]
Browning, Robert L., (AV) .... '62 '88 C.679 B.S. L.345 J.D. [Scopelitis,G.L.&H.]
Brownlee, Gary S. .... '49 '79 C.679 B.S. L.345 J.D. Farm Bureau Ins. Cos.
Brown-Niehaus, Robin L. ......'56 '82 C.260 B.A. L.345 J.D. 136 E. Market St., Ste. 800
Brubaker, Gregory C., (CV) .... '71 '98 C.210 B.A. L.1119 J.D. [🄰 Hoover H.B.&H.]
Bruess, Charles E., (AV) ....'38 '63 C.494 A.B. L.1119 J.D. 11 S. Meridian St.
Brugger, Kristiana M. .... '— '04 C.347 B.S. L.893 J.D. [🄰 Baker&D.]
Bruksch, Terri L. .... '— '98 C.210 B.A. L.347 J.D. [🄰 Barnes&T.]
Brundage, Cory, (AV) ....'47 '73 C.347 B.S. L.1119 J.D. [C.Brundage]

Brundage, Cory, LLC, (AV)
1700 One American Square, P.O. Box 82053, 46282-0003
Telephone: 317-639-4875 Fax: 317-639-4882
Email: cb@brundagelaw.com URL: http://www.corybrundagelaw.com
Cory Brundage.
Civil Litigation, Trial and Appellate Practice, Commercial Litigation and Arbitration, Personal Injury and Wrongful Death, Products Liability, Risk Management and Litigation Avoidance, College and University Law, Legal Malpractice and Disciplinary Defense.
See Professional Biographies, INDIANAPOLIS, INDIANA

Brune, Edward I. '37 '62 C&L.150 A.B., LL.B.
(adm. in OH; not adm. in IN) Indpls. Racquet Club
Bruner, Omar S., Jr. .... '25 '50 C.108 A.B. L.477 LL.B. 3901 N. Meridian‡
Bruner, Robert C., (AV) ....'46 '71 C.347 B.S. L.345 J.D. [Bator R.B.S.&L.]
Bruness, Wayne C., (CV) .... '— '70 C.46 B.S. L.345 J.D. 7913 Southeastern Ave.‡
Brunner, Robert H., (BV) .... '32 '81 C.679 B.S. L.345 J.D. [Ross&B.]
Bryant, Sandy Leviticus, (AV) ..... '53 '77 C.347 B.A. L.345 J.D. 244 N. College Avenue
Buchanan, Paul H., Jr. .... '18 '48 C.821 B.A. L.208 LL.B. Ret. Ct. of App. J.‡
Buchanan, Walter W. .... '41 '78 C.347 B.A. L.345 J.D. 799 W. Mich.
Bucheri, Richard C. ....'71 '96 C&L.347 B.S., J.D. [Poynter&B.]
Buchmeier, Ronald W., (AV) .... '52 '79 C.432 B.S. L.345 J.D. [Hopper B.]
Buck, James A., (AV) .... '29 '59 C.108 B.S. L.345 J.D. P.O. Box 44947
Buckley, Gregory D., (BV) ...... '39 '64 C.705 A.B. L.1119 J.D. 9000 Keystone Crossing
Buckley, Lee C. ....'53 '79 C.72 B.A. L.500 J.D. 8944 E. 42nd St., Ste. 210
Buckley, Timothy L., (BV) '49 '74
C.679 B.S. L.345 J.D. 151 North Delaware Street, Suite 2050
Buckley, William R. '58 '83 C.347 A.B. L.1119 J.D.
Sales & Mktg. Admr., The Benjamin Franklin Literary & Medical Soc.‡
Buddenbaum, James A. L., (BV) .... '60 '89 C.347 B.A. L.345 J.D. [Parr R.O.&M.]
Buehler, James C. (J.C.), (AV) .... '55 '80 C&L.347 B.A., J.D. [Buehler&Assoc.]
Buehler Associates, (AV) .... P.O. Box 40924
Buis, Pequita Jay, (BV) .... '50 '85 C.679 B.A. L.345 J.D. 4415 Cherry Lane
Buker, Michael .... '56 '98 C.347 B.S. L.464 J.D. [🄰 Ice M.]
Bulen, L. Keith, (AV) ....'26 '52 C.347 A.B. L.345 J.D. 7872 Clearwater Pkwy‡
Bullington, Michael G., (BV) .... '51 '76 C.108 B.A. L.1119 J.D. [M.Bullington]
Bullington, Michael, (BV) .... 6125 U.S. 31 S.
Bulloff, Steven M. .... '54 '79 C.347 A.B. L.150 J.D. Coun., Gardner & White Corp.
Bumgarner, Jonathan C. ....'— '02 C.894 B.A. L.74 J.D. [🄰 Hall,R.K.H.&L.]
Bunny, Edwin J. .... '22 '51 C.1062 A.B. L.1119 J.D. 6130 Kingsley Dr.
Bunton, Amanda Dickman ....'74 '00 C.347 B.A. L.345 J.D. Clk., U.S. Supm. Ct.
Burdge, Richard W. ....'42 '69 C.108 B.A. L.345 J.D. 534 Sudbury Ct.
Burdick, Brian L., (BV) ....'— '95 C.894 A.B. L.347 J.D. [Barnes&T.]
Burgan, Blake J. ....'— '95 C.347 B.S. L.421 J.D. [Sommer B.]
Burke, Brian K., (AV) ....'48 '73 C&L.880 B.A., J.D. [Baker&D.]
Burke, Craig C. .... '66 '94 C.347 B.S. L.1119 J.D. [🄲 Ice M.]
Burke, Daniel K. .... '72 '99 C.347 B.S. L.802 J.D. [🄰 Ice M.]
Burke, Jason R. ....'68 '94 C.280 A.B. L.902 J.D. [Hopper B.]
Burke, Susan D., (AV) ....'46 '86 C.347 B.A. L.345 J.D. Ind. Pub. Def. Council
Burks, Jessica L. ....'77 '04 C&L.347 B.A., J.D. [🄰 Conour]
Burns, James T. ....'— '75 C.347 B.A. L.345 J.D. [🄲 Barnes&T.]
Burns, Patrick J., (AV) ....'50 '78 C.347 B.S. L.345 J.D. P.O. Box 40857
Burns, Stephen F., (AV) .... '43 '68 C.207 A.B. L.1119 J.D. 8010 Castleton Road
Burns, Timothy J., (BV) .... '46 '73 C.353 B.A. L.345 J.D. 7245 Huntington Rd.
Burr, Alice M. .... '50 '01 C.97 B.A. L.347 J.D. Staff Atty.
Burris, Cathy J. .... '54 '80 C.432 B.S. L.345 J.D. Veteran's Admn.
Burroughs, Philip D., (AV) ....'47 '72 C.210 B.A. L.1119 J.D. [Cremer B.&C.]
Burroughs, Thomas G. .... '58 '90 C.347 B.S. L.345 J.D. [🄲 Sommer B.]
Burton, Dennis E. '47 '77 C&L.560 B.S., J.D.
(adm. in CA; not adm. in IN) U.S. Bankrptcy Clk.‡
Burton, Gerry L., (BV) .... '46 '76 C.679 B.A. L.345 J.D. 7027 W. Lake Rd.
Burton, Jerry M., (AV) '32 '63 C.347 B.S. L.345 J.D.
8425 Keystone Crossing, Suite 180
Busby, Adrienne F. .... '76 '01 C&L.602 B.A., J.D. [🄰 Baker&D.]
Buschmann, Stephen R., (AV) '48 '74
C.679 B.S. L.345 J.D. 151 N. Delaware St., Ste. 1900
Bush, Robert B., (AV) '53 '83 C.871 B.S. L.1119 J.D.
Assoc. Gen. Coun., Community Hospitals of Indiana Inc.
Butcher, David A., (AV) ....'41 '66 C.210 A.B. L.1119 J.D. [Bose M.&E.]
Butiste-Jones, Mary L. ....'65 '90 C.679 B.A. L.347 J.D. Legal Serv(s) Org.
Butler, Duge, (AV) ....'28 '55 C.347 L.345 LL.B. 155 E. Market St.
Butler, Patrick H., (AV) .... '33 '61 C.170 B.A. L.174 J.D. 858 W. 56th St.
Butt, P. Lawrence '41 '68 C.150 B.B.A. L.345 J.D.
Sr. V.P., Coun. & Secy., Marsh Supermarkets, Inc.
Button, Paige T. ....'67 '95 C&L.228 A.B., J.D. [Button]
Button, Timothy H. .... '66 '04 C.299 A.B. L.345 J.D. [🄰 Riley B.&E.]
Button Law Office, P.C. ....500 E. 96th St., Ste. 110
Buttrey, Donald W., (AV) .... '35 '61 C.346 B.S. L.1119 J.D. [🄲 Wooden&M.]
Buttrick, Hilary ....'— '02 C.210 B.A. L.345 J.D. [🄰 Ice M.]
Buttrick, Stuart R. .... '75 '00 C.210 B.A. L.347 J.D. [🄰 Baker&D.]
Butz, Timothy W. ....'46 '76 C.347 A.B. L.345 J.D. 111 Monument Circle, Ste. 782
Byrd, Warren W. '62 '89 C.130 B.A. L.602 J.D.
Corporate Counsel, ADESA Corporation
Byron, Daniel P., (AV) ....'37 '62 C.347 A.B. L.1119 J.D. [Bingham M.]
Byron, Michael S. ....'— '00 C.347 B.A. L.879 J.D. [🄰 Sommer B.]
Byrum, Douglas S. ....'68 '95 C.317 B.A. L.879 J.D. [Hall G.]
Byrum, William K., (AV) ....'33 '59 C.108 A.B. L.345 J.D. 50 S. Meridian, Suite 600
Cable, Randall L. ....'46 '74 C.265 A.B. L.345 J.D. 5954 North College Avenue
Cacioppo, Jayna M. ....'— '05 C.276 B.S. L.345 J.D. [🄰 Sommer B.]
Cade, Joseph W., (BVⓉ) ....'— '92 C&L.16 B.S., J.D. [🄲 Sommer B.]
Cadena, Jose S., Jr. '64 '91 C.744 B.B.A. L.309 J.D.
(adm. in TX; not adm. in IN) Tax Coun., Eli Lilly & Co.
Cafouros, Carl, (CV) '55 '88
C.679 B.A. L.347 J.D. Inhouse Atty., St. Paul Travelers Ins. Co.
Cafouros, Gregory P., (AV) ....'50 '78 C.602 B.S. L.345 J.D. [Kroger,G.&R.]

Calderon, Joseph D., (BV) .... '60 '90 C&L.347 B.S., J.D. [Bose M.&E.]
Calderon, Michele Johnson, (AV) '60 '90 C&L.347 B.S., J.D.
Assoc. Gen. Coun., Clarian Health Partners, Inc.
Calkins, James H., Jr. '53 '81 C.1028 B.S. L.1209 J.D.
(adm. in FL; not adm. in IN) 10527 Indian Lake Blvd S
Calkins, R. Ronald, (AV) ....'31 '56 C&L.347 B.S., J.D. 151 N. Delaware St.
Callahan, H. Patrick, (AV) ....'47 '72 C.347 B.A. L.477 J.D. [Baker&D.]
Calloway, Anika M. ....'— '02 C.811 B.A. L.861 J.D. [🄰 Barnes&T.]
Caltrider, Steven P. '65 '94 C.679 B.S.Ch.E. L.347 J.D.
Assoc. Gen. Pat. Coun., Eli Lilly & Co. (Pat.)
Cambridge, Teresa P. ....'54 '90 C.347 B.S. L.345 J.D. [T.P.Cambridge]
Cambridge, Teresa P., P.C. ....6825 Parkdale Pl.
Campbell, Andrew L. ....'— '05 C.508 B.A. L.1119 J.D. [🄰 Baker&D.]
Campbell, Craig C., (BV) '50 '80
C.894 B.A. L.347 J.D. Pres., Old Hickory Furniture Co., Inc.
Campbell, David C., (AV) ....'49 '74 C.346 B.S. L.345 J.D. [Bingham M.]
Campbell, Jan N., (BV) .... '61 '88 C.929 B.A. L.347 J.D. [Leeuw O.&C.]
Campbell, John W., (BV) ....'42 '82 C.679 B.S.I.M. L.345 J.D. [Blackwelder,C.&L.]
Campbell, Randy L., Jr. ....'— '03 C.679 B.S.E.E. L.345 J.D. [🄰 Barnes&T.]
Campbell, Steven L. ....'70 '97 C.894 B.A. L.345 J.D. Gov. Off., Dir. of Communications
Campbell, Thomas J., (AV) ....'48 '75 C.967 B.A. L.345 J.D. [Locke R.]

Campbell Kyle Proffitt LLP
(See Noblesville)

Campo, Anthony M., & Associates, (BV) '47 '75
C.690 B.A. L.597 J.D. 110 S. Downey Ave.
Canada, Mark P., (AV) .... '58 '83 C.333 B.S. L.1068 J.D. [Krieg D.]
Cannon, Mark D. .... '63 '94 C.347 B.S. L.421 J.D. [Cannon]
Cannon Law Offices LLC ....6235 Carrollton Ave., Ste. B
Cantor, Linda E., (AV) ....'54 '79 C.347 A.B. L.345 J.D. [🄲 Dann P.N.&K.]
Cantrell, Dennis F., (AV) ....'60 '86 C.894 A.B. L.345 J.D. [Bingham M.]
Cantrell, Paul R. ....'57 '94 C.679 B.S. L.347 J.D. Pat. Coun., Eli Lilly & Co. (Pat.)
Cantrell, Pfenne P., (CV) ....'70 '95 C.894 A.B. L.347 J.D. [Kightlinger&G.]
Cantrell, Quentin G. '67 '00
C.679 B.S. L.1119 J.D. [🄰 Woodard,E.M.M.&H.] (See Pat. Sect.)
Cantwell, Camille M. ....'58 '93 C.965 B.A. L.1339 J.D. 1526 Sandi Dr.
Capen, Timothy J. ....'79 '04 C.347 B.A. L.345 J.D. [🄰 Ice M.]
Caplin, Stephen B., (BVⓉ) ....'41 '67 C.347 B.S. L.345 J.D. [S.B.Caplin]
Caplin, Stephen B., PC, (BVⓉ) .... 135 N. Pennsylvania St., Ste. 1150
Cardoza, Edward R. ....'53 '97 C.347 B.A. L.345 J.D. [🄰 Rubin&L.]
Cardoza, Paula F. ....'51 '82 C.999 B.A. L.1119 J.D. Staff Atty.
Cardwell, Richard W., (AV) ....'33 '58 C.347 B.A. L.1119 J.D. [🄲 Voyles,Z.P.H.&M.]
Caress, John H., (BV) ....'36 '61 C.347 B.S. L.345 J.D. 323 N Delaware St.
Caress, Timothy C., (AV) ....'69 '94 C.347 B.A. L.1119 J.D. [Cline F.C.L.&C.]
Carlberg, James E., (AV) ....'50 '74 C.347 B.S. L.1119 J.D. [Bose M.&E.]
Carlino, James C., (AV) ....'60 '85 C.210 B.A. L.1119 J.D. [Bose M.&E.]
Carlisle, Sheila A. .... '63 '88 C&L.347 B.S., J.D. Chf. Trial Dep.
Carlock, Charles ....'67 '93 C&L.347 B.S., J.D. 9000 Keystone Xing
Carmichael, Daniel P. .... '42 '68 C&L.150 B.S., J.D. [🄲 Baker&D.]
Carmichael, Kepten D. ....'— '96 C.210 B.A. L.1119 J.D. [🄰 Barnes&T.]
Carney, Joseph B., (AV) .... '28 '53 C.210 A.B. L.309 LL.B. [🄲 Baker&D.]
Carpenter, H. Paul .... '27 '67 C.112 B.S. L.347 J.D. 3232 Melbourne Rd. S., Dr.‡
Carpenter, Julia A., (AV) .... '63 '88 C.108 B.S. L.345 J.D. [Krieg D.]
Carpenter, Susan K., (AV) ....'51 '76 C.788 B.A. L.1119 J.D. Pub. Def.
Carpentier, Christopher B. ....'74 '00 C&L.345 B.S., J.D. [🄰 Huffer&W.]
Carr, David J., (AV) ....'58 '84 C.210 B.A. L.276 J.D. [Ice M.]
Carr, James M., (AV) ....'50 '75 C.347 B.A. L.1119 J.D. [Baker&D.]
Carr, John L. '53 '78 C.679 B.A. L.880 J.D.
Chf. of Historic Structures, IN Dept. of Nat. Resource
Carr, John R., III, (AV) .... '— '74 C.478 A.B. L.1119 J.D. [Ayres C.&S.]
Carr, John R., Jr., (AV) .... '— '48 C.37 A.B. L.309 J.D. [Ayres C.&S.] ‡
Carr, Matthew S. ....'71 '00 C.347 B.S. L.345 J.D. [🄰 Krieg D.]
Carroll, Bart E. ....'71 '01 C.63 B.S. L.345 J.D. 3750 Kentucky Avenue

Carroll, Daniel R., (BV) '51 '83 C.696 B.M. L.345 J.D.
6500 E. Westfield Boulevard, 46220-1110
Telephone: 317-259-4259 Fax: 317-475-4516
Email: dancarroll51@yahoo.com URL: http://www.lawyers.com/dcarroll
Business Law, Contracts, Litigation, Insurance, Debtor and Creditor, Collections, Business Enterprises, Corporate Law, Partnerships, Real Estate, Commercial Litigation, Commercial Leasing, Buy-Sell Agreements, Employment Law, Noncompete Litigation, Wrongful Termination, Trade Secrets, Personal Injury, Automobile Accidents, Slip and Fall, Wrongful Death, Bankruptcy, Arbitration, Mediation.
See Professional Biographies, INDIANAPOLIS, INDIANA

Carroll, Jan M., (AV) ....'— '84 C.802 B.F.A. L.345 J.D. [Barnes&T.]
Carroll, Kristen M. ....'73 '01 C.327 B.S. L.1119 J.D. [🄰 Kightlinger&G.]
Carroll, Thomas J. '41 '68 C.347 B.S. L.345 J.D.
Supr. Ct. J., Marion Co. Supr. Ct., Civil Div. #6
Carter, Amie Peele ....'70 '96 C.484 B.A. L.245 J.D. [Baker&D.]
Carter, Angelica Theodessa '74 '00 C.347 B.S.C.J. L.345 J.D.
Marion Co. Prosecutors Off.
Carter, Arthur M. ....'68 '93 C.309 A.B. L.602 J.D. [Siegel C.&D.]
Carter, Michael L., (BV) '54 '85
C.347 B.A. L.345 J.D. [🄰 Spangler,J.&D.] (⊙Merrillville)
Carter, R. Trevor .... '68 '95 C.679 B.S.M.E. L.347 J.D. [Baker&D.] (See Pat. Sect.)
Carter, Robert B., II, (BV) '39 '66
C.249 B.A. L.345 J.D. 8720 Castlecreek Parkway East Dr.
Carter, Stephen ....'54 '84 C.309 A.B. L.1119 J.D. P.O. Box 501962
Carter, Yvonne Marie ....'— '99 C.329 B.A. L.1119 J.D. Atty. Gen. Off.
Carusillo, Thomas M., (BV) '54 '79
C.602 B.B.A. L.347 J.D. Staff Atty., Div. of State Ct. Admn.
Caruso, Deborah J., (AV) .... '56 '81 C&L.347 A.B., J.D. [Dale&E.]
Caruso, Ralph A., II ....'— '94 C.1031 B.S. L.602 J.D. [Sommer B.]
Casady, Timothy T. ...... '57 '83 C.210 B.A. L.309 J.D. Dep. Gen. Coun., Eli Lilly & Co.
Case, Michael J. .... '68 '95 C.63 B.S. L.1035 J.D. Coun., Baldwin & Lyons, Inc.
Casey, Ronald D., (BV) .... '52 '84 C.347 B.A. L.345 J.D. 144 N. Delaware Street
Cash, Angela S. .... '66 '95 C.198 B.S. L.347 J.D. [Scopelitis,G.L.&H.]
Cassman, Stephanie L. ....'74 '00 C.347 B.A. L.345 J.D. [🄰 Lewis W.]
Castaldo, Edward A.B. ....'72 '98 C.44 B.C. L.45 J.D. [🄰 Morgan&P.]
Castille, M. Angella ....'56 '89 C.808 B.A. L.602 J.D. [Baker&D.]
Castor, David A. ....'74 '02 C.679 B.S. L.345 J.D. 251 E. Ohio St.
Caudill, Burnett, (BV) ....'44 '70 C.346 A.B. L.345 J.D. Master Comr., Supr. Ct.
Caudill, Virginia Wright, (BV) ....'66 '92 C&L.665 B.A., J.D. [🄲 Gilliland&C.]
Caughey, Ben T. ....'75 '01 C.339 B.S. L.347 J.D. [🄰 Ice M.]
Cavanaugh, James P., III, (BV) ....'59 '85 C.63 B.S. L.345 J.D. [Gaston,C.&G.]
Caviness, Philip James ....'71 '97 C&L.347 B.A., J.D. [🄰 Smith,F.M.&H.]

Cavosie, J. Michael, (BV) ....'58 '92 C.108 B.A. L.347 J.D. [Easter&C.]
Cella, Abigail ....'— '04 C.645 B.S. L.1119 J.D. [Ⓐ Ice M.]
Ceryak, David V., (BV) .... '66 '91 C.473 B.S. L.345 J.D. Coun., Eli Lilly & Co.
Chamberlain, Daniel S., (BV) .... '66 '92 C.63 B.S. L.1119 J.D. [Doehrman C.]
Chambers, Barry A. .... '— '70 C.63 B.S. L.74 J.D. 4619 Blvd. Chambers
Chambers, Michael D. .... '— '97 C.602 B.S. L.145 J.D. [Sommer B.]
Champion, Joseph L. ....'66 '91 C.347 B.S. L.201 J.D. [Ⓒ Bingham M.]
Champion, Larry R., (BV) .... '44 '70 C.347 B.A. L.345 J.D. [Ⓒ Stewart&I.]
Chandler, Alicia Mitchell ....'75 '02 C&L.150 B.S., J.D. [Ⓐ Krieg D.]
Chandler, Madelynne K. '34 '82
C.350 B.S. L.345 J.D. Dept. of Revenue, Crim. Investigation Div.
Chandler, Marcus B., (AV) .... '— '79 C.210 B.A. L.145 J.D. [Barnes&T.]
Chandler, Mary Titsworth, (AV) ...... '60 '86 C.473 A.B. L.1119 J.D. 6457 N. Illinois St.
Chaney, Elaine Marie .... '62 '87 C.347 B.S. L.345 J.D. Law Clk., U.S. Dist. J.
Chapelle, Joseph C., (AV) .... '— '86 C.477 A.B. L.602 J.D. [Barnes&T.]
Chapman, Gary L., (BV) ....'59 '89 C.679 B.S. L.345 J.D. [Bose M.&E.]
Chapman, James B., II ....'68 '96 C.92 B.A. L.801 J.D. [Ⓐ Dann P.N.&K.]
Chappell, John S., (AV) ...... '47 '72 C.347 B.S. L.1119 J.D. [Ⓒ Bingham M.] (⊙Jasper)
Charnstrom, Andrew C., (AV) ....'54 '79 C.347 B.A. L.1119 J.D. [Wooden&M.]
Chastain, Patrick N. .... '64 '97 C&L.347 B.A., J.D. Miller-EADS Co., Inc.
Chavis, Denise W., (CV) ....'67 '98 C.597 B.S. L.1119 J.D. [Ⓐ Bingham M.]
Chavis, John M.T., II ....'64 '93 C.410 B.A. L.259 J.D. [Ⓐ Locke R.]
Chavis, Natalie N. ....'70 '04 C.679 B.S. L.347 J.D. 1 N. Pennsylvania St., Ste. 900
Chavis, Patrick E., IV, (BV) ...... '65 '90 C.511 B.A. L.347 J.D. One North Pennsylvania
Cheek, Barbara J., (BV) ....'57 '89 C.344 B.S. L.345 J.D. 36 S. Pennsylvania St., Ste. 630
Cheerva, Michael, (AV) ....'60 '85 C.894 B.A. L.345 J.D. [Avery&C.]
Chelovitz, Eric Jacob .... '64 '93 C.97 B.S. L.117 J.D. 3077 E. 98th St.
Chen, Sonia S. ....'75 '01 C.880 B.A. L.1119 J.D. [Ⓐ Stewart&I.]
Chenoweth, Jan R. .... '50 '87 C.894 B.A. L.345 J.D. 7399 Shadeland Ave.
Chenoweth, Michael O., (BV) ....'43 '86 C.31 B.A. L.347 J.D. [Ⓒ Bose M.&E.]
Chezem, Linda L. '46 '71 C.346 B.S. L.347 J.D.
Indiana University School of Medicine, 635 Barnhill Drive, MS 1021
Chilcote, Randall L., (BV) ....'49 '75 L.345 7119 U.S. Hwy. 31 S.
Chinn, A. Scott ....'68 '94 C.74 B.A. L.345 J.D. [Baker&D.]
Chinn, Anthony Scott, (AV) ....'68 '94 C.347 B.A. L.345 J.D. Atty. Gen. Off.
Choplin, John M., II, (AV) ....'45 '74 C.221 B.A. L.477 J.D. [Norris C.&S.]
Christ, John C., (BV) .... '27 '50 C.108 B.S. L.345 J.D. 151 N. Delaware St.
Christen, William D. ....'23 '48 C&L.150 LL.B. 6326 Colebrook Dr.‡
Christie, Lee C., (AV) ....'55 '82 C.347 B.S. L.345 J.D. [Cline F.C.L.&C.]
Christopher, Richard L., (BV) ..... '33 '73 C.210 B.A. L.345 J.D. [Ⓒ Christopher&T.] ⊙

Christopher & Taylor, (AV) BV
1219 North Delaware Street, P.O. Box 2850, 46206-2850 ⊙
Telephone: 317-635-9000 Telecopier: 317-686-2200
Rodney V. Taylor; Michael C. Peek; David J. Theising; Randall D. Smith; John D. Connor; Michael A. Beason. Of Counsel: Richard L. Christopher (Resident, Fowler Office).
General Civil Practice. Trial and Appellate Litigation in all Courts. Administrative, Antitrust, Aviation, Bankruptcy, Business and Commercial, Class Actions, Construction, Corporate, Creditor Rights, Fidelity and Surety, Government Contracts, Insurance, Personal Injury and Property Damage, Products Liability, Professional Liability, School, Real Estate and Development, Zoning and Land Use, Trusts and Estates, Wills and Probate Law.
Fowler Office: 306 East Fifth Street, P.O. Box 72. Telephone: 317-884-0810.
See Professional Biographies, INDIANAPOLIS, INDIANA

Chulos, Nicholas J., (BV) .... '59 '85 C.238 B.S. L.910 J.D. [Krieg D.]
Chumlea, Kevin L. '64 '92 C.210 B.A. L.1187 J.D.
(adm. in OH; not adm. in IN) Simon Property Group
Chung, Hong-Sik ....'— '01 C.999 B.A. L.1119 J.D. [Ⓐ Starkey]

Church, Church, Hittle & Antrim
(See Noblesville)

Cierzniak, Elizabeth Kelley .... '57 '95 C.108 B.S. L.347 J.D. [Baker&D.]
Cistrelli, Lawrence ....'45 '84 C.705 B.A. L.345 J.D. Assoc. Coun., The Associated Group
Ciyou, Bryan Lee, (BV) ....'67 '94 C&L.347 B.A., J.D. 320 N. Meridian St., Ste. 311
Claffey, Stephen A., (AV) ....'45 '71 C.894 A.B. L.910 J.D. [Baker&D.]
Claflin, Jeffrey D. ....'58 '90 C.992 B.A. L.345 J.D. [Plews S.R.&B.]
Clancy, Erin A. ....'73 '98 C.679 B.S. L.345 J.D. [Kightlinger&G.]
Clapacs, Grantland M., (BV) ....'69 '95 C.188 B.A. L.228 J.D. [Bingham M.]

Clapp, Sean M., LLC
(See Fishers)

Clark, Christopher E. ....'68 '95 C.37 B.A. L.347 J.D. [Goodin A.&M.]
Clark, J. Murray, (AV) ....'57 '82 C.385 B.A. L.345 J.D. [Clark,Q.M.S.&G.]
Clark, James C., (AV) ....'29 '56 C.894 B.A. L.1119 J.D. [Ⓒ Clark,Q.M.S.&G.]
Clark, James W., (AV) ....'59 '86 C.347 B.A. L.477 J.D. [Baker&D.]
Clark, Lawson J., II, (AV) ... '43 '68 C.347 B.S. L.1119 J.D. 45 North Pennsylvania Street
Clark, Legrand L. ....'54 '92 C.923 B.A. L.74 J.D. Dep. Atty. Gen.
Clark, Matthew R., (BV) ....'58 '85 C.972 B.S. L.345 J.D. [Clark,Q.M.S.&G.]
Clark, Melissa A., (BV) .... '65 '93 C.378 B.S. L.37 J.D. Clk.
Clark, Richard A. ....'58 '83 C.894 B.A. L.1119 J.D. [Ⓒ Scopelitis,G.L.&H.]
Clark, Robert R., (AV) ....'— '79 C&L.879 B.A., J.D. [Sommer B.]
Clark, Timothy V., (BV) ... '54 '82 C.429 B.A. L.347 J.D. 151 N. Delaware St., Ste. 1635

Clark, Quinn, Moses, Scott & Grahn, LLP, (AV)
One Indiana Square, Suite 2200, 46204-2011
Telephone: 317-637-1321 Fax: 317-687-2344
Email: lawyers@clarkquinnlaw.com URL: http://www.clarkquinnlaw.com
Members of Firm: Joseph M. Howard (—1964); Thomas M. Quinn, Sr. (1909-1973); Peter A. Pappas (1922-1986); Alex M. Clark (1916-1991); Thomas Michael Quinn; John M. Moses; J. Murray Clark; Matthew R. Clark; Robert B. Scott; Charles R. Grahn. Associates: Robert V. Clutter; Frank D. Otte; Ralph W. Staples, Jr.; John B. ("Bart") Herriman; David Patrick Coyne; Jeffrey L. Stayte. Of Counsel: James C. Clark; Raymond J. Grahn.
General Practice and Litigation in State and Federal Courts, Real Estate, Land Use and Zoning, Corporate, Mergers and Acquisitions, Probate and Estate Planning, Public Utility, Family/Domestic Relations, Employment, Juvenile and Criminal Defense Law.
Representative Clients: Albertson's/OSCO; CVS; Home Depot U.S.A., Inc.; Indianapolis Colts; Kite Development Corp.; Kroger; Meijer's; Target Corporation; Verizon Wireless; Walmart.
See Professional Biographies, INDIANAPOLIS, INDIANA

Clarke, Russell T., Jr., (AV) ....'54 '79 C.477 B.A. L.880 J.D. [Emswiller,W.N.&C.]
Clase, David A. ....'43 '74 C.679 B.S. L.347 J.D. 129 East Market Street, Suite 1100
Claus, Mary Beth, (AV) ....'60 '86 C.150 B.A. L.345 J.D. [Baker&D.]
Clay, Carolyn A. ....'— '03 C.611 B.A. L.345 J.D. [Ⓐ Price W.R.&D.]
Claycombe, John R., (AV) ....'26 '52 C.210 A.B. L.345 J.D. 7519 Hoover Rd.
Claycombe, Robert A., (AV) ....'23 '50 C.108 L.345 LL.B. [Ⓒ Kortepeter M.H.F.&M.]
Claypool, Joseph L., (BV) ....'50 '78 C.347 B.S. L.345 J.D. 27 E. Westfield Boulevard
Clayton, Laura Lee '45 '77 C.108 B.A. L.345 J.D.
Hearings Comr., State Dept. of Nat. Resources
Clayton, Thomas M. '53 '80 C.25 B.A. L.1003 J.D.
Vice President, Secretary & General Counsel, New Millennium Roofing, Inc.
Claytor, Michael A. ....'52 '84 C.63 B.S. L.345 J.D. Crowe, Chizek & Co.

Cleary, John ....'— '95 C.347 B.S. L.365 J.D. Dir. of Operations, Dynaloy, Inc.
Clem, Richard A., (BV) ....'47 '73 C.347 B.S. L.345 J.D. [Alden&C.]
Clemens, Robert B., (AV) ....'47 '82 C.823 A.B. L.602 J.D. [Bose M.&E.]
Clement, Bret S., (AV) ....'— '79 C.602 B.B.A. L.477 J.D. [Ayres C.&S.]
Clements, Barbara Webb ....'— '88 C&L.347 B.A., J.D. 251 East Ohio Street
Clendening, Gary J., (AV) ....'44 '68 C&L.347 A.B., J.D. [Mallor C.G.&B.] ⊙
Cleveland, Peter D., (AV) ....'55 '81 C.575 B.A. L.1119 J.D. [Cleveland&H.]

Cleveland & Harvey, (AV)
an association of attorneys
6910 N. Shadeland Avenue Suite 200, 46220
Telephone: 317-890-2460; Mobile 317-590-7815 Fax: 317-890-1731 URL: http://www.tharpinvest.com
Email: pcleveland@tharpinvest.com URL: http://www.lawyers.com/petercleveland
Peter D. Cleveland; Eric A. Harvey.
Real Estate Development and Transactions, Zoning, Planning and Land Use and Real Estate Litigation.
See Professional Biographies, INDIANAPOLIS, INDIANA

Clifford, Shaun Healy ....'60 '85 C.201 B.S. L.345 J.D. [Baker&D.]
Cline, Lance D., (AV) ....'51 '80 C.347 B.A. L.345 J.D. [Cline F.C.L.&C.]
Cline, Susan E., (BV) ....'61 '90 C.344 B.S. L.347 J.D. [Locke R.]
Cline Farrell Christie Lee & Caress, (AV) ....951 North Delaware Street
Clingerman, Katrina M. ....'72 '99 C.210 B.A. L.347 J.D. [Ⓐ Ice M.]
Clossin, J. David, (AV) '46 '73
C.347 B.S. L.1119 J.D. Assoc. Reg. Coun., Chicago Title Ins. Co.
Cloyd, Casey D., (CV) '58 '84 C.63 B.S. L.1119 J.D.
136 East Market Street, Suite 1119
Clutter, Robert V., (BV) .... '61 '88 C.679 B.S. L.347 J.D. [Ⓐ Clark,Q.M.S.&G.]
Cobb, A. Thomas, (AV) ....'39 '69 C.347 B.S. L.345 J.D. Sr. Admin. J.
Cochran, John D., (AV) ....'17 '42 C.665 A.B. L.309 J.D. [Ⓒ Baker&D.]
Cochran, John D., Jr., (BV) ....'45 '71 C.894 B.A. L.421 J.D. [Hackman H.&C.]
Coffey, Daniel J., (BV) ....'53 '81 C.347 A.B. L.345 J.D. 6532 Cornell Ave.
Cohen, Alan H. ....'47 '73 C.347 B.S. L.345 J.D. Finish Line, Inc.
Cohen, Andrea L. ....'62 '90 C.347 B.A. L.1119 J.D. [Ⓒ Rubin&L.]
Cohen, Bradley H., (BV) ....'66 '91 C.347 B.A. L.94 J.D. [Cohen G.&G.]
Cohen, Charles A., (AV) ....'41 '67 C.347 B.S. L.1119 J.D. [Cohen G.&G.]
Cohen, Charles E. '47 '93 C.102 B.S. L.1209 J.D.
(adm. in VA; not adm. in IN; Pat.) Patent Atty., Eli Lilly & Co.
Cohen, Gary D., (BV) '52 '78
C.347 B.A. L.1340 J.D. Exec. V.P. & Gen. Coun, Finish Line, Inc.
Cohen, Howard R., (AV) ....'53 '78 C.347 A.B. L.1119 J.D. [Locke R.]
Cohen, Ralph A., (AV) ....'38 '64 C.347 B.S. L.1119 J.D. [Ice M.]
Cohen, Shannon M. ....'76 '02 C.347 B.S. L.1119 J.D. [Ⓐ Scopelitis,G.L.&H.]
Cohen, Steven J., (AV) ....'52 '80 C.597 B.S. L.345 J.D. [Zeigler C.&K.]

Cohen Garelick & Glazier, A Professional Corporation, (AV)
Suite 800, Keystone Crossing Plaza, 8888 Keystone Crossing Boulevard, 46240
Telephone: 317-573-8888 Telecopier: 317-574-3855
Email: ccohen@cgglawfirm.com URL: http://www.cgglawfirm.com
Charles A. Cohen; Robert A. Garelick; Steven J. Glazier; Steven M. Crell; Edward F. Schrager; Russell L. Jones; Sandra Latarus Rothbaum; Bradley H. Cohen; Jill E. Goldenberg (Board Certified, Family Law Specialist, Indiana State Bar Association, Family Law Certification Board); Bryan S. Redding;—Heather S. Wysong Zaiger. Of Counsel: Joseph J. Reiswerg; Richard L. Darst; Samuel J. Mantel (1893-1978); Thomas D. Mantel (Retired).
General Civil Trial Practice in all State and Federal Courts. Business Law, Litigation, Corporate Law, Partnership Law, Commercial Law, Taxation, Divorce, Family Law, Personal Injury, Criminal Law, Creditors Rights, Bankruptcy, Probate, Wills, Trusts and Estates, Estate Planning, Real Estate, Construction Law, Civil Rights, Labor and Employment, Employee Benefits, Medical Malpractice, Patents, Trademarks, Intellectual Property, Alternative Dispute Resolution, Collections, Nonprofit and Charitable Organizations.
Reference: NBD Bank.
See Professional Biographies, INDIANAPOLIS, INDIANA

Cohen & Malad, LLP, (AV) BV
One Indiana Square Suite 1400, 46204
Telephone: 317-636-6481 Fax: 317-636-2593
URL: http://www.cohenandmalad.com
Louis F. Cohen (1936-1992); Richard M. Malad; Irwin B. Levin; Richard N. Bell; David J. Cutshaw; Richard E. Shevitz; Gregory L. Laker; Thomas L. Blackburn; Donald D. Levenhagen; Arend J. Abel; Shokrina Radpour Beering; Brian K. Zoeller;—Michael C. Adley; Laura C. Jeffs; Scott D. Gilchrist; Eric S. Pavlack; Jeffrey S. Gibson; Julie M. Andrews; Elizabeth J. Doepken; Philip Sever; Katherine A. Harmon.
General Civil Practice, State and Federal Courts. Commercial, Class Actions, Insurance, Probate and Estate Planning, Real Estate, Personal Injury, Securities Litigation and Family/Domestic Relations Law, Foreclosure and Creditor's Rights.
Reference: First Indiana, Indianapolis, N.A.
See Professional Biographies, INDIANAPOLIS, INDIANA

Colasessano, Gary L. '66 '92 C.347 B.A. L.879 J.D.
1915 Broad Ripple Avenue, 46220
Telephone: 317-253-9150 Fax: 317-251-1941
Email: colasessanoesq@aol.com URL: http://www.colasessanolaw.com
Criminal Law, Driving While Intoxicated, DUI, Drug Crimes, Homicide, Sex Crimes, Probation and Parole, Traffic Violations, White Collar Crime.
See Professional Biographies, INDIANAPOLIS, INDIANA

Cole, Daniel H. '58 '87 C.605 A.B. L.1051 J.D.
(adm. in NM; not adm. in IN) Assoc. Prof., Indiana Univ. Sch. of Law
Cole, Elsa Kircher ....'49 '74 C.813 A.B. L.94 J.D. Gen. Coun., NCAA
Cole, Troy J. ... '63 '94 C.98 B.S.E.E. L.802 J.D. [Woodard,E.M.M.&H.] (See Pat. Sect.)
Coleman, Charles S., II ....'71 '96 C.602 B.B.A. L.16 J.D. [Krieg D.] (⊙Carmel)
Coleman, David A. ....'56 '82 C&L.347 B.S., J.D. 10401 N. Meridian St.
Coleman, Earl B. ....'44 '75 C.679 B.S. L.345 J.D. 1310 Munsee Circle
Coleman, Jesse L. ....'38 '74 C.347 B.S. L.345 J.D. 136 E. Market St.
Coleman, John L. ....'07 '33 L.345 LL.B. 6640 Spring Mill Rd.‡
Coles, James A., (AV) ....'47 '74 C.701 B.S.E.E. L.734 J.D. [Bose M.&E.] (Pat.)
Colgan, Mark ....'23 '49 C.98 B.S. L.597 J.D. Amer. States Ins. Co.
Collesano, Stanley F. ....'68 '95 C.116 B.S. L.1187 J.D. [Tyra&C.]
Collet, Charles J. ....'40 '71 C.602 A.B. L.1119 J.D. 6100 North Keystone Avenue
Collier, Douglas A. ....'68 '98 C.701 B.S. L.345 J.D. [Krieg D.] (Pat.)
Collier, Thomas C., Jr., (AV) ....'24 '53 C.679 B.S. L.345 J.D. 7351 Shadeland Sta.
Collier-Magar, P.C., Law Offices of ....151 North Delaware Street
Collier-Magar, Kenneth ....'48 '73 C.757 B.A. L.665 J.D. [Collier-Magar]
Collignon, Thomas D. ....'61 '94 C.679 B.S.I.M. L.1119 J.D. 127 E. Michigan St.
Collins, Bryan J., (AV) ....'59 '85 C.347 B.S. L.345 J.D. [Bingham M.]
Collins, Carol Warren, (AV) ....'53 '83 C.63 B.S. L.345 J.D. [Ⓐ Baker&D.]
Collins, W. Thomas '27 '56 C.679 B.S. L.705 LL.B.
(adm. in DC; not adm. in IN; Pat.) V.P., RCA Consumer Electronics
Collyge, Sean C., (CVⓉ) '65 '93
C&L.1243 B.A., J.D. Leg. Dev. Att., Simon Property Group
Colton, Gregory S. .... '57 '86 C.118 B.A. L.1119 J.D. Staff. Atty., Ind. Securities Div.
Colucci, Mark ....'65 '95 C.1044 B.A. L.1119 J.D. [Kroger,G.&R.]

Commons, James W. '27 '61 C.436 B.S. L.345 J.D. 4310 E. 10th St.‡
Commons, Mark D. '49 '90 C&L.347 A.B.,M.B.A., J.D. 4310 E. 10th St.
Conard, Richard D., (AV) '— '75 C.701 B.S.E.E. L.345 J.D. [Barnes&T.]
Conditt, Phyllis A. '57 '97 C.1142 B.A. L.802 J.D. [Ⓐ Roberge&R.]
Coney, Janet M. '50 '78 C.248 B.S. L.345 J.D. Legal Servs. Organ.
Conley, Judith H. '54 '78 C.823 B.A. L.879 J.D. Admin. Law J.
Conlon, John '47 '74 C&L.347 B.S., J.D.
Managing Attorney-Eastern Regions, SAFECO Insurance Companies
Connelly, Francis S. Michael, (AV) '35 '63 C.601 B.S. L.209 J.D. [Krieg D.] ‡
Conner, Matthew W. '67 '93 C.63 B.S. L.347 J.D. [Tabbert H.E.&W.]
Conner, Michael R., (AV) '— '75 C.602 B.A. L.1119 J.D. [Barnes&T.]
Connor, John D., (AV) '53 '78 C.1119 B.A. L.345 J.D. [Christopher&T.]
Conour, William F., (AV) '47 '74 C.347 B.A. L.345 J.D. [Conour]

Conour Law Firm, LLC, (AV)
Four Parkwood Crossing, 500 East 96th Street, Suite 150, 46240-3765
Telephone: 317-846-5550 Fax: 317-846-5552 URL:http://www.conour.com
URL: http://www.conourlaw.com
Member: William F. Conour. Associates: Jessica L. Burks; John P. Daly, Jr.
Plaintiff's Civil Trial and Appellate Practice in all State and Federal Courts. Construction Site Injury Litigation, Personal Injury Law, Products Liability Law, Traumatic Brain Injury, Nursing Home Liability, Auto/Trucking Collisions; Sports/Amusement Park Injury; Swimming/Boating Accidents.
See Professional Biographies, INDIANAPOLIS, INDIANA

Conover, William G. '25 '51 C&L.879 B.A., LL.B. Ct. of App. J.
Conrad, Julie M., (CV) '68 '93 C.477 B.A. L.347 J.D. [Ⓒ Ice M.]
Conrad, Matthew E. '78 '03 C.827 B.S. L.1119 J.D. [Ⓐ Krieg D.] (ⓒCarmel)
Conrad, Robert Allen '52 '85
C.1159 B.S. L.345 J.D. Asst. Gen. Pat. Coun., Eli Lilly & Co. (Pat.)
Conrad, Shelby R. '56 '85 C&L.383 B.A., J.D.
(adm. in KY; not adm. in IN) Assoc. Coun.
Conway, Michael T., (BV) '48 '73 C.210 B.A. L.345 J.D. 151 N. Delaware St.
Cook, Michael C., (AV) '44 '70 C.108 B.S. L.345 J.D. [Wooden&M.]
Cook, Rhonda L. '— '04 C.347 B.A. L.345 J.D. [Ⓐ Ice M.]
Cook, Richard A., (AV) '56 '82 C.679 B.S. L.879 J.D. 150 E. Market St.
Cook, Sally A., (AV) '44 '72 C.145 B.A. L.477 J.D. Educ. Consultant
Cooley, Linda J. '52 '92 C.827 B.S. L.345 J.D. [Krieg D.]
Cooney, Robert J. '21 '74 C.701 B.S.C.E. L.345 J.D. 615 Russell Ave.‡
Coons, Stephen M., (AV) '41 '71 C.894 A.B. L.345 J.D.
Exec. V.P. & Gen. Coun., Standard Mgt. Corp.
Cooper, Jeffrey O. '64 '92 C.309 A.B. L.659 J.D.
(adm. in PA; not adm. in IN) Assistant Prof., Indiana Univ. Sch. of Law‡
Cooper, Neal A. '— '98 C.357 B.S. L.365 J.D. [Ⓐ Hall,R.K.H.&L.]

Coots, Henke & Wheeler, Professional Corporation
(See Carmel)

Cope, Barry C. '62 '88 C.894 A.B. L.345 J.D.
Envir. Claims Supvr., American States Ins. Co.
Coraz, Gerald A., (BV) '52 '79 C.347 B.A. L.365 J.D. Asst. U.S. Atty.
Corbitt, David E. '71 '97 C.829 B.S. L.1119 J.D. [Ⓐ Krieg D.]
Cord, Kathleen '52 '78 C.347 B.S. L.421 J.D. Sr. Staff Atty., Legislative Servs. Agency
Cordingley, Bruce A., (AV) '46 '71 C.679 B.S.I.M. L.309 J.D.
Pres., Pedcor Investments‡
Corey, David E. '69 '00 C.323 B.A. L.345 J.D.
(adm. in MI; not adm. in IN) [Ⓐ Ice M.]
Corey, Richard Jay '56 '89 C&L.347 B.S., J.D. OUCC
Corneglio, Donald L., Jr. '55 '83 C.339 B.S. L.8 J.D.
Assoc. Gen. Pat. Coun., Eli Lilly & Co. (Pat.)
Cornell, Lila J., (BV) '39 '70 C.597 B.A. L.345 J.D. 4720 Dandy Trail
Corsaro, Daniel S., (AV) '63 '90 C.602 B.B.A. L.1119 J.D. 1 American Sq.
Corsaro, Gregory P. '65 '91 C.346 B.S. L.347 J.D. Indpls. Fruit Co., Inc.
Corsaro, Paul J., (AV) '43 '69 C.1024 B.S. L.345 J.D. [Bingham M.]
Corson, Rodney E., (BV) '47 '81 C.679 B.S. L.347 J.D. [Ⓒ Locke R.]
Cortopassi, Santiago J., III, (AVⓉ) '50 '78 C.502 B.S. L.734 J.D.
(adm. in MO; not adm. in IN) Corp. Coun., Dow Agrosciences LLC
Cosby, F. Pen '43 '68 C.347 B.S. L.1119 J.D. [Bowman,C.&B.]
Cosby, Fielding Pentecost, (AV) '43 '68
C&L.347 B.S., J.D. Suite 630, 1 N. Pennsylvania St.
Cossell, Marcia J. '47 '91 C&L.347 B.A., J.D. [Lee B.C.&K.]
Costakis, Thomas J., (AV) '60 '85 C.679 B.S. L.345 J.D. [Krieg D.]
Cotterill, Sarah Dansker '78 '03 C.893 B.A. L.1119 J.D. [Ⓐ Ice M.]
Cottrell, George A., (BV) '34 '72 C.108 B.S. L.345 J.D.
1810 Broad Ripple Ave., Ste. 12
Coughlin, Colleen '62 '89 C.915 B.A. L.347 J.D. Indianapolis Pub. Housing Div.
Courter, Leja D. '55 '88 C.63 B.S. L.200 J.D. IN Utility Consumer Counselor Off.
Courtney, Clifford R. '50 '86 C&L.347 B.A., J.D. 225 N. Delaware St.
Cowan, Gerald L., Law Offices of, (AV) '41 '68
C.347 B.S. L.345 J.D. 3815 River Crossing Parkway, Suite 100
Cowgur, Anne L. '70 '99 C&L.339 B.A., J.D. [Ⓐ McTurnan&T.]
Cox, Barbara F. '59 '94 C.216 B.A. L.345 J.D.
Coun. & Asst. Sec., National Conference of Ins. Guaranty Funds
Cox, C. Russell, (AV) '57 '86 C.679 B.S. L.145 J.D. [Cox&S.]
Cox, Cherry '65 '90 C.329 B.A. L.893 J.D. Assoc. Gen. Coun., Sallie Mae, Inc.
Cox, Dina M. '69 '95 C.63 B.G.S. L.347 J.D. [Lewis W.]
Cox, Paul N. '49 '74 C.877 B.S. L.878 J.D.
(adm. in UT; not adm. in IN) Prof., Indiana Univ. School of Law
Cox & Sargeant, P.C., (AV) 8440 Woodfield Crossing Boulevard, Suite 450
Coy, Gregory B. '70 '96 C.894 B.A. L.1119 J.D. [Krieg D.]
Coyle, William C. '48 '73 C.347 B.S. L.345 J.D. Alcoholic Bev. Comm.
Coyne, David Patrick '73 '00 C.63 B.A. L.345 J.D. [Ⓐ Clark,Q.M.S.&G.]
Cracraft, Michael B., (AV) '45 '73 C.473 B.A. L.345 J.D. [Hackman H.&C.]
Cracraft, Steven G., (AV) '46 '73 C.945 A.B. L.347 J.D. [Bingham M.]
Craig, Darren A. '73 '05 C.679 B.A. L.1119 J.D. [Ⓐ Locke R.]
Crandley, Mark J. '— '00 C&L.347 B.A., J.D. [Ⓐ Barnes&T.]
Craven, R. Daniel '60 '87 C.105 B.S. L.607 J.D. [Eckert C.]
Craven, Robert F. '18 '55 C.108 B.S. L.744 LL.B. P.O. Box 50734
Craver, Ty Michael '72 '98 C&L.347 B.S., J.D. [Ⓐ Hill,F.M.F.&M.]
Crawford, Douglas A., (BV) '60 '86 C.347 B.A. L.879 J.D. [Benkie&C.]
Crawford, James T., Jr., (AV) '47 '73 C.679 B.S. L.345 J.D. [Krieg D.]
Crawford, Stefanie R. '71 '99 C.108 B.S. L.345 J.D. [Ⓐ Lewis W.]
Crawford, William P. '53 '81 C.755 B.A. L.900 J.D.
(adm. in KS; not adm. in IN) V.P., Peripheral Dev., Simon Property Group
Creager, Lisa M. '64 '89 C&L.347 B.A., J.D.
Pension Compl. Consultant, Amer. United Life Ins. Co.
Creason, Stephen Richard '75 '00 C.894 A.B. L.345 J.D.
Indiana Gov Ctr South Fl 5, 302 W Washington St
Creedon, Richard O. '28 '56 C.347 A.B. L.1119 LL.B. 4245 N. Washington Blvd.‡

Cregor, Douglas E., (BV) '48 '74 C.347 A.B. L.1119 J.D. 7949 High Drive
Crell, Steven M., (BV) '63 '88 C.63 B.S. L.345 J.D. [Cohen G.&G.]
Cremer, John A., (AV) '62 '89 C.679 B.A. L.347 J.D. [Cremer B.&C.]

Cremer Burroughs & Cremer, (AV)
An Association Not in Partnership
Two Market Square Center, Suite 915, 251 East Ohio Street, 46204-2133
Telephone: 317-636-8182; Toll-free: 877-636-8182 Fax: 317-636-8199
Email: CMB@INDYLAW.COM URL: http://www.indylaw.com
Charles F. Cremer, Jr. (1933-2000); Edward P. Madinger (1922-1997); Philip D. Burroughs; John A. Cremer; Jonathan E. Palmer; Timothy W. Withers. Associates: Suzanne E. Katt; Melissa A. Lindley. Of Counsel: Diane L. Liptack.
Estate and Trust Litigation in all State and Federal Trial and Appellate Courts. Estate Planning, Wills, Probate and Administration, Business Litigation, Business Formation, Family Law, Real Estate.
See Professional Biographies, INDIANAPOLIS, INDIANA

Creveling, Kelley Bertoux '— '96 C.347 B.A. L.345 J.D. [Ⓐ Baker&D.]
Crews, Kenneth D. '55 '80 C.597 B.A. L.910 J.D.
(adm. in CA; not adm. in IN) Assoc. Prof., Indiana Univ. Sch. of Law
Crider, Donald W., (BV) '24 '62 C.347 A.B. L.1119 J.D. 2915 N. High School Rd.‡
Crist, Brian C., (BV) '71 '97 C.502 B.A. L.880 J.D. [Ⓐ Ice M.]
Crockett, Clyde H. '40 '65 C&L.846 B.A., LL.B.
(adm. in TX; not adm. in IN) Prof., Ind. Univ. Sch. of Law
Crockett, Eric S. '72 '00 C.63 B.S. L.345 J.D. 424 East Wabash Street
Croftchik, Todd A. '76 '02 C.477 B.S. L.475 J.D. [Ⓐ Locke R.]
Cromer, Jeffrey M. '76 '03 C.894 B.A. L.345 J.D. [Ⓐ Dann P.N.&K.]
Cromer, John R., (AV) '46 '71 C.303 A.B. L.345 J.D. [Krieg D.]
Crone, Terry A. '51 '77 C.210 B.A. L.602 J.D. Appl. Ct. J.
Cronin, John M., Attorney at Law, (BV) '44 '69
C.210 B.S. L.345 J.D. 156 E. Market St., Ste. 1300
Crook, Kendall C., (AV) '45 '72 C.309 A.B. L.976 J.D. [Bose M.&E.]
Crosley, Stanley W. '62 '94 C.317 B.S. L.347 J.D. Atty., Eli Lilly & Co.
Cross, Nancy L., (AV) '54 '79 C.932 B.S. L.546 J.D. [Miroff,C.&W.]
Cross, Patrick S., (BV) '63 '93 C&L.347 B.A., J.D. [Baker&D.]
Crouch, Suzanne S. '54 '94 C.347 B.S. L.345 J.D. Golden Rule Insurance Co.
Crow, Frederick W., (AV) '54 '79 C.347 B.A. L.345 J.D. [Young&Y.]
Crow, Patricia Renner '52 '89 C&L.347 B.A., J.D. [Young&Y.]
Crowe, Julia F., (BV) '59 '84 C.347 A.B. L.208 J.D. [Ⓒ Locke R.]
Crowley, Laura R. '59 '00 C.1044 B.S.N. L.345 J.D. 151 N. Delaware St., Ste. 2025
Cruz, Israel Nunez '66 '95 C.436 L.607 Marion Supr. Ct.
Cruz-Burke, Diane, (AV) '65 '91 C.347 B.S. L.309 J.D. Coun., Eli Lilly & Co.
Cueller, Amy L., (BV) '63 '90 C.347 B.S. L.344 J.D. [Bose M.&E.]
Cueller, Daniel, (BV) '61 '86 C.894 B.A. L.1119 J.D. [Schreckengast,H.&C.]
Culp, Charles W., (AV) '31 '58 C.976 B.A. L.309 J.D. [C.W.Culp]
Culp, Charles W., Professional Corporation, (AV) 320 North Meridian Street, Suite 515
Cummer, Jas. W. '29 '59 C.937 A.B. L.345 J.D. Gen. Coun., Best Lock Corp.
Cunning, James S., (AV) '52 '77 C.210 B.A. L.477 J.D. [Ice M.]
Cunningham, Norris, (CV) '— '96 C.58 B.A. L.347 J.D. [Hall,R.K.H.&L.]
Cunningham, Thomas E., (BV) '30 '70
C.894 A.B. L.345 J.D. 5699 East 71st Street, Suite 1-A
Curran, John J. '37 '65 C.999 B.A. L.345 LL.B. [Curran&B.]
Curran & Benedict 146 E. Washington St.
Curry, Davina L. '68 '03 C.679 B.A. L.345 J.D. [Ⓐ Hackman H.&C.]
Curry, Michael J. '52 '81
C.347 B.A. L.345 J.D. Pres., Enterprise Title Services of Ind., Inc.
Curtis, James W., Jr., Law Office of, (BV) '44 '71
C.347 B.S. L.1119 J.D. 8777 Purdue Rd., Ste. 124
Cutshaw, David J., (AV) '56 '82 C.344 B.A. L.345 J.D. [Cohen&M.]
Cutts, Sierra L. '71 '96 C.344 B.A. L.347 J.D. Dep. Atty. Gen.
Czajka, Terri Ann, (AV) '58 '83 C.190 B.A. L.494 J.D. [Ice M.]
Daerr, John H., (AV) '64 '89 C.210 B.A. L.879 J.D. [Locke R.]

Dahm & Elvin, LLP
(See Fort Wayne)

Dailey, Frank W. '19 '48 C&L.228 A.B., LL.B. 7101 Buick Dr.‡
Dakich, Thomas P., (BV) '60 '85 C.894 B.A. L.1119 J.D. [Baldwin&D.]
Dale, Gregory N., (BV) '60 '86 C&L.347 B.S., J.D. [Baker&D.]
Dale, William J., Jr., (AV) '42 '71 C.623 B.B.A. L.345 J.D. [Dale&E.]

Dale & Eke, Professional Corporation, (AV)
9100 Keystone Crossing, Suite 400, 46240-2100
Telephone: 317-844-7400 Fax: 317-574-9426 Computer Fax: 317-581-7436
Email: daleeke@daleeke.com URL: http://www.daleeke.com
William J. Dale, Jr.; Joseph W. Eke; Deborah J. Caruso; Geffrey D. Rainbolt;—Erick P. Knoblock; David D. Deeter; Gregg S. Gordon.
Corporate, Corporate Finance, Commercial, Taxation, Health Care, Probate and Estate Planning, Trust Law, Bankruptcy, Real Estate, Family/Domestic Relations, and Civil Litigation.
See Professional Biographies, INDIANAPOLIS, INDIANA

Dall, Jane A. '78 '03 C.303 B.A. L.602 J.D. [Ⓐ Baker&D.]
Dall, Mark E. '53 '78 C.347 B.A. L.1119 J.D. Sr. Staff Atty., Simon Property Group
Dallmann, Peggy D. '53 '95 C.63 B.S. L.347 J.D. 200 E. Washington Street
Dalrymple, Michael '— '02 C.231 B.A. L.345 J.D. [Ⓐ Ice M.]
Dalrymple, Robert K., (AV) '23 '65 C.870 B.S. L.345 J.D. 320 N. Meridian St.‡
Daly, John P., Jr., (BV) '59 '87 C&L.347 B.A., J.D. [Ⓐ Conour]
Dameron, Jamie B. '69 '04 C.347 B.S. L.1119 J.D. [Ⓐ Plews S.R.&B.]
Danforth, Kimberly H., (BV) '60 '86 C&L.347 B.A., J.D. [Mitchell H.J.&D.]
Daniel, Melvin R., (AV) '42 '72 C.346 B.S. L.345 J.D. [Dann P.N.&K.]
Daniels, Deborah J. '51 '77 C.210 B.A. L.345 J.D. [Krieg D.]
Daniels, Robert S. '70 '96 C.210 B.A. L.1119 J.D. [Tabbert H.E.&W.]
Danielson, Gloria J. '54 '01 C&L.344 B.S., J.D. [Ladendorf&L.]
Daniluck, John V. '52 '95
C.679 B.S.M.E. L.347 J.D. [Woodard,E.M.M.&H.] (See Pat. Sect.)
Dankert, Gary J., (AV) '52 '77 C.347 B.A. L.345 J.D. [Ice M.]
Dann, Dixon B., (AV) '43 '67 C.473 B.S. L.477 J.D. [Ⓒ Rubin&L.]

Dann Pecar Newman & Kleiman, Professional Corporation, (AV)
Suite 2300, One American Square, 46282
Telephone: 317-632-3232; Indiana: 800-622-4799 Fax: 317-632-2962
Email: info@dannpecar.com URL: http://www.dannpecar.com
Theodore R. Dann (1907-1993); Philip D. Pecar (1930-2000); Joel Yonover (1932-1995); Robert A. Rose (1931-2001); Norman R. Newman; David H. Kleiman; Jon B. Abels; Melvin R. Daniel; Lawrence F. Dorocke; Jeffrey A. Abrams; James H. Schwarz; Walter E. Wolf, Jr.; James P. Moloy; Andrew A. Kleiman; Richard O. Kissel, II; Mark R. Waterfill; William L. O'Connor; Peter A. Silver; Neil R. Rafferty; Karin L. Veatch; Jonathan G. Polak; Patrick F. Mastrian III; Andrielle M. Metzel; Eric M. Hylton. Of Counsel: Linda E. Cantor; Richard J. Darko; Steven M. Pecar; Charles R. Rolph, III. Associates: James B. Chapman II; Cynthia M. Kirk; David E. Kress; Amy L. Wright; Laura J. Peters; Jeffrey M. Cromer; Heidi K. Hughes; Jared A. Simmons.
General Federal and Indiana Civil, Trial and Appellate Practice. Administrative, Bankruptcy, Commercial, Commercial Lending, Construction, Corporate, Creditors' Rights, Economic Development Incentives, Employment, Environmental, Franchising, Gaming, Intellectual Property, Land Use,

(This Listing Continued)

Dann Pecar Newman & Kleiman, Professional Corporation (Continued)

Mergers and Acquisitions, Municipal Law and Finance, Privatization, Probate and Estate Planning, Real Estate, Reorganization, Securities, Shopping Center, Sports, Taxation, Trademark and Zoning Law.

Attorneys for: Indianapolis Machinery Co., Inc.; Melvin Simon & Associates, Inc.; Pacers Basketball Corp.; Universal Fire & Casualty Co., Inc.; Bank One, Indianapolis, NA; INB National Bank; Nachi Technology, Inc.; Pharmaceutical Corporation of America; Logo 7, Inc.

See Professional Biographies, INDIANAPOLIS, INDIANA

Dansker, Alan J., (AV) .... '52 '77 C.347 B.S. L.345 J.D. [Bingham M.]
Dant, Miriam Smulevitz, (AV) .... '62 '87 C.347 B.S. L.339 J.D. [Baker&D.]
Danz, Kristine Camron .... '71 '97 C.475 B.A. L.477 J.D. [Ice M.]
Darden, Carr L. .. '37 '70 C&L.347 B.S., J.D. 200 W Washington St Ste 425, State House
Darko, Richard J., (AV) ....'43 '68 C.602 B.A. L.1119 J.D. [Ⓒ Dann P.N.&K.]
Darst, Richard L., (AV) ....'44 '69 C.347 A.B. L.1119 J.D. [Ⓒ Cohen G.&G.]
Darst, Sandy .... '— '93 C&L.347 B.S.N., J.D. Practice Mgmt., Inc.
Das, Sonia C. .... '75 '00 C&L.347 B.A., J.D. [Ⓐ Lewis W.]
Dassow, Robert T., (BV) ....'65 '90 C.72 B.A. L.879 J.D. [Hovde,D.&D.]
Daugherty, Charles C. .... '22 '53 C.108 B.A. L.345 J.D. 6100 N. Keystone Ave.‡
David, Andrew M. ....'70 '95 C.473 B.A. L.879 J.D. [Ⓐ Doyle&F.]
Davidson, Thomas N. .... '52 '98 C.999 B.S. L.347 J.D. Teachers' Retirement Fund
Davies, Robert N., (AV) ... '35 '61 C.210 A.B. L.228 LL.B. Dir., Corp. Fin., SerVaas, Inc.
Davis, Donald D. .... '22 '50 C.375 B.S. L.477 J.D. 452 W. 83rd St.‡
Davis, Geoffrey P. .... '63 '89 C.894 B.A. L.345 J.D. Supm. Ct. Staff Atty.
Davis, Glenn E., Jr., (AV) ..... '49 '76 C.347 B.S. L.345 J.D. 3850 Priority Way, S. Drive
Davis, Glenn E., Sr., (AV) ...... '25 '63 C.108 L.345 LL.B. 3850 Priority Way South Dr.
Davis, Grover B., (BV) .... '44 '74 C.347 B.S. L.345 J.D. [McClure M.D.&H.]
Davis, Heather L. '— '00
C.347 B.S. L.201 J.D. Estate & Guardianship Admr., 5th 3rd Bk.
Davis, John M., (AV) ....'51 '81 C.347 B.S. L.345 J.D. Gen. Coun.
Davis, Michael K. ....'58 '87 C.347 B.S. L.1119 J.D. Exec. Dir., Assoc, of Ind. Counties‡
Davis, Neil A. ....'71 '96 C.651 B.S. L.347 J.D. [Meils,T.D.&B.]
Davis, O. Wayne, (AV) .... '44 '74 C.346 B.S. L.345 J.D. [Henderson D.W.&D.]
Davis, Philip Adam ....'76 '02 C.347 B.A. L.1119 J.D. [Davis&S.]
d'Avis, Ronald .... '50 '87 C.35 B.A. L.345 J.D. [Frank&K.]
Davis, Ronald C. .... '43 '69 C&L.347 B.S.Bus., J.D. Golden Rule Insurance Co.
Davis, Stacey M., Law Office of '— '95
C.197 B.A. L.1194 J.D. 120 E. Market Street, Suite 717
Davis, Steven R. ....'79 '04 C.992 B.A. L.1119 J.D. [Ⓐ Ice M.]
Davis, Thomas L., (BV) ....'22 '50 C.108 B.S. L.345 J.D. 3850 Priority Way S. Drive
Davis, Thomas L., (AV) ....'50 '75 C.347 A.B. L.1119 J.D. [Locke R.]
Davis Dow, Angela .... '68 '95 C.210 B.S. L.347 J.D. 235 North Delaware

Davis, James E., Attorney at Law
(See Greenfield)

Davis & Sarbinoff, LLP ....9765 Randall Dr., Ste. F
Daw, Jack C. .... '24 '51 C.768 B.A. L.345 J.D. 5862 Watson Ct.‡
Dawson, Donald L., (AV) ....'44 '70 C.347 B.A. L.345 J.D. [Kightlinger&G.]
Dawson, James R.A. ....'— '97 C&L.347 B.A., J.D. [Ⓐ Sommer B.]
Dawson, Terry W., (AV) ....'— '90 C.346 B.S. L.801 J.D. [Barnes&T.]
Day, Jennifer L. .... '72 '98 C.265 B.A. L.345 J.D. [Ⓐ Bose M.&E.]

Deal, David E. '76 '01 C.679 B.S. L.1119 J.D.
255 North Alabama Street, 46204
Telephone: 317-916-0000 Fax: 317-955-2570
URL: http://www.daviddeallawfirm.com
Family Law, Creditors Rights, Civil Practice.
See Professional Biographies, INDIANAPOLIS, INDIANA

Dean, Cynthia L. ....'64 '90 C.679 B.A. L.347 J.D. State Gaming Comm.
Dean, Kara J. '70 '02 C.347 B.A. L.345 J.D.
Staff Atty. & Asst. Secy., Best Access Systems (Legal Department)
Dean, Margaret G. ....'48 '84 C.104 A.B. L.347 J.D. 5435 N. New Jersey St.
Dean-Webster, Deanna A., (BV) ...... '59 '85 C.347 B.S. L.425 J.D. [Dean-Webster&W.]
Dean-Webster & Wright, LLP, (BV) .... 50 South Meridian Street, Suite 500
Deardorff, Robert C. ....'11 '32 L.999 LL.B. 4548 Lincoln Rd.‡

Dearing, David E. '— '78 C.976 B.A. L.188 J.D.
6100 North Keystone Avenue Suite 657, 46220
Telephone: 317-920-0824 Fax: 317-920-1865
URL: http://www.dearinglawfirm.com
Environmental Law, Zoning, Civil Appellate, Administrative and General Litigation.
See Professional Biographies, INDIANAPOLIS, INDIANA

Dearing, Teresa E., (BV) ....'53 '79 C.347 B.A. L.345 J.D. 155 E. Market St., Ste. 605
DeBone, Donald W. .... '68 '94 C.436 B.A. L.347 J.D. 9795 Crosspoint Blvd., Ste. 175
DeBrota, Amy Ficklin, (BV) .... '65 '93 C&L.347 B.A., J.D. [Price W.R.&D.]
DeBruler, Roger .... '34 '60 C.347 A.B. L.1119 LL.B. Supm. Ct. Jus.
Deckard, John G., (AV) '55 '82 C.347 B.S. L.309 J.D.
111 Monument Circle, Suite 3310
Deer, Thomas E. ....'69 '94 C.976 B.A. L.347 J.D. [Locke R.]
Deeter, David D., (BV) .... '54 '80 C.602 B.A. L.347 J.D. [Ⓐ Dale&E.]
Deeter, Ellen M. .... '54 '82 C.602 B.A. L.345 J.D. The National Bank of Indianapolis
Deets, Nicholas C., (BV) .... '66 '93 C.679 B.S.I.M. L.347 J.D. [Hovde,D.&D.]
DeFord, Jody .... '72 '02 C.347 B.A. L.345 J.D. [Ⓐ Ice M.]
DeGroff, Joseph E., (AV) .... '53 '79 C.303 B.A. L.345 J.D. [Ice M.]
De Groff, Melissa J. ....'65 '92 C.959 B.A. L.966 J.D. [Ⓒ Locke R.]
De Groff, Todd Stacy .... '55 '86 C.347 A.B. L.1119 J.D. Indiana State Pub. Def.
De Haan, Karen L. ....'— '98 C.587 B.S. L.421 J.D. [Ⓐ Sommer B.]
Deignan, Paul T., (AV) ....'— '80 C.999 B.A. L.1119 J.D. [Sommer B.]
Dein, Henry Y., (BV) .... '39 '66 C.1150 A.B. L.345 LL.B. 748 Bates St., Ste. 205
Deiter, Charles J. .... '37 '65 C.435 B.A. L.1119 LL.B. Supr. Ct. J.
DeLaney, Ann M., (BV) ....'45 '77 C.1349 B.A. L.1119 J.D. [DeLaney&D.]
DeLaney, Edward O., (AV) ....'43 '73 C.1349 B.A. L.309 J.D. [DeLaney&D.]
DeLaney, Kathleen A., (BV) ....'68 '95 C.276 B.S.F.S. L.1119 J.D. [DeLaney&D.]

DeLaney & DeLaney LLC, (AV)
3640 Washington Boulevard, 46205
Telephone: 317-920-0400 Fax: 317-920-0404
Email: kathleen@delaneylaw.net URL: http://www.delaneylaw.net
Members of Firm: Kathleen A. DeLaney; Ann M. DeLaney; Edward O. DeLaney. Associates: Cynthia A. Bedrick; Michele E. Brown.
Language: Russian.
Employment Litigation, Litigation, Products Liability, International Law, Media Law, Election Law, Business Law, Fraud, Breach of Contract, Securities, Estate Administration, First Amendment Law.
See Professional Biographies, INDIANAPOLIS, INDIANA

DeLaruelle, Matthew G. ....'74 '03 C.679 B.A. L.910 J.D. [Ⓐ Ice M.]
de la Torre, Carina M. ....'79 '04 C.472 B.H.S. L.1119 J.D. [Ⓐ Bose M.&E.]
Delehanty, Michael J., (BV) .... '57 '83 C.347 B.A. L.426 J.D. 6393 Monitor Dr.
Delk, Jason R. ....'79 '04 C.63 B.S. L.345 J.D. [Ⓐ Ice M.]

Demeter, John C. '51 '80 C.932 B.S. L.213 J.D.
Assoc. Gen. Pat. Coun., Eli Lilly & Co. (Pat.)
Demos, Anastasia K. ....'74 '99 C.108 B.A. L.345 J.D. [Demos&R.]
Demos & Reyome .... 5954 North College Avenue
DeMoss, David A., & Associates, (BV) '54 '87
C.679 B.S. L.345 J.D. Mng. Atty., State Farm Ins. Co.
Dempsey, Kevin P., (BV) '59 '84 C.57 A.B. L.339 J.D.
Asst. U.S. Trustee, Dept. of Just.
Dennerline, Frederick W., III, (AV) '49 '74 C.228 B.A. L.345 J.D.
[Fillenwarth,D.G.&T.]
Densborn, Donald K., (AV) .... '— '76 C.347 B.S. L.345 J.D. [Sommer B.]
Denton, Barbara Besore, (BV) .....'63 '88 C.347 B.S. L.345 J.D. 9200 Keystone Crossing
Denton, Duane R., (AV) .... '63 '88 C.108 B.S. L.345 J.D. [Bingham M.]
Deppert, Gael S. ....'54 '92 C.347 B.A. L.1119 J.D. 9112 Behner Brook Dr.‡
DePrez, Anne N., (AV) .... '55 '81 C.788 B.A. L.1119 J.D. [Barnes&T.]
Desai, Manisha A. ....'66 '99 C.228 B.A. L.1119 J.D. Staff Atty., Eli Lilly & Co.
Detherage, Andrew J., (AV) ....'— '90 C.347 B.A. L.1119 J.D. [Barnes&T.]
DeTrude, Howard J., (AV) '29 '60 C.108 A.B. L.345 J.D.
Chm., Precedent Fidelity Corp.
Deveau, Frank J., (AV) ....'— '80 C.347 B.A. L.345 J.D. [Sommer B.]
Devenney, Sean T., (CV) ....'73 '98 C.645 B.S. L.1119 J.D. [Ⓐ Drewry S.V.]
Devine, Lynn M. ....'60 '87 C.347 B.A. L.345 J.D. Sup. Ct. Adm. Off.
DeVoe, S. Curtis, (AV) ....'60 '88 C.674 A.B. L.1066 J.D. [Plews S.R.&B.]
DeVoe, Stephen E., (AV) .... '35 '65 C.674 B.S. L.345 J.D. [Ⓒ Bose M.&E.]
DeVoe, Thomas R., (AV) ....'— '92 C.674 A.B. L.347 J.D. [Sommer B.]
DeWester, Franklin N., Attorney at Law '46 '83
C.679 B.A. L.345 J.D. 4040 S. Meridian St.
D'Hue, Cedric A. ....'— '05 C.860 B.S. L.1119 J.D. [Ⓐ Baker&D.]
Dible, Jeffrey S., (AV) .... '55 '79 C.679 B.S. L.1119 J.D. [Locke R.]
Dick, Richard J., (AV) .... '48 '76 C.249 B.A. L.345 J.D. [Mitchell H.J.&D.]
Dick, Steven K. .... '53 '81 C.608 B.S.C.E. L.150 J.D. [W.J.Tucker&Assoc.]
Dickey, Thomas A. ....'67 '94 C&L.347 B.S., J.D. Duke Realty Corporation
Dickson, Brent E. ....'41 '68 C.679 A.B. L.345 J.D. Supm. Ct. J.
Diehl, William F., (BV) ....'42 '72 C.894 A.B. L.345 J.D. [Gagnon&D.]
Diener, William P. ....'41 '68 C.894 B.A. L.345 J.D. [Ⓒ Ice M.]
Dietrick, Patrick J. ....'63 '94 C.679 B.A. L.365 J.D. 310 N. Alabama, Ste. 250
Dietz, Joseph M., (AV) .... '51 '76 C.108 B.A. L.345 J.D. [Meils,T.D.&B.]
Dilk, Gary L., (BV) ....'55 '83 C.347 B.S. L.345 J.D. 606 E. Market Street
Dill McCarty, Virginia ....'— '50 C.347 B.A. L.345 J.D. 151 N. Delaware St.
Dillin, S. Hugh .... '14 '38 C.347 B.A. L.1119 LL.B. U.S. Sr. Dist. J.
Dillinger, Sarah .... '72 '03 C.347 B.S.W. L.74 J.D. [Ⓐ Yarling&R.]
Dillman, Lisa M. .... '69 '95 C.339 B.A. L.1119 J.D. [Ⓒ Lewis W.]
Dill-McGill, Jennifer L. ....'72 '98 C.63 B.A. L.345 J.D. [Ⓐ Baker&D.]
Dillon, Lisa M. ....'76 '01 C.967 B.A. L.1119 J.D. [Ⓐ Due,D.F.&M.]
Dillon, Stephen W., Law Office of '49 '75
C.679 B.A. L.1119 J.D. 3601 N. Pennsylvania St.
Dimick, Julia E., (BV) .... '63 '90 C.63 B.S. L.276 J.D. [Bingham M.]
Dimitri, James D. ....'67 '93 C.347 B.S. L.879 J.D. Indiana Univ., School of Law
Dimos, James, (AV) .... '61 '86 C.894 A.B. L.910 J.D. [Locke R.] (See Pat. Sect.)
Dinsmore, Mark J., (AV) ....'— '94 C.894 B.A. L.851 J.D. [Barnes&T.]
Dinwiddie, Thomas W., (AV) .... '47 '73 C.210 A.B. L.345 J.D. [Wooden&M.]
Disque, Charles R. .... '46 '72 C.894 B.A. L.477 J.D. 8318 Woodall Dr.
Divine, William G., (BV) ....'49 '75 C.435 B.A. L.345 J.D. 6616 Cherbourg Cir.
Dixon, Aaron J. .... '74 '99 C&L.352 B.A., J.D. [Ⓐ Ice M.]
Dixon, Julie C. ....'71 '98 C.347 B.S. L.345 J.D. [Gannon&C.]
Dlouhy, Francina A., (AV) ....'52 '77 C.318 B.A. L.1119 J.D. [Baker&D.]
Dobbs, Polly J. ....'77 '04 C.63 B.S. L.345 J.D. [Ⓐ Bingham M.]
Doberneck, Charles N. .... '— '81 C.602 B.A. L.345 J.D. [Ayres C.&S.]
Dobson, James H., (AV) '50 '77 C.259 B.A. L.477 J.D.
V.P. & Gen. Coun., Community Hospitals of Indiana Inc.
Dodd, Bette J., (AV) ....'52 '83 C.347 B.A. L.345 J.D. [Lewis&K.]
Doehrman, Thomas C., (AV) .... '51 '76 C.347 B.A. L.345 J.D. [Doehrman C.]

Doehrman • Chamberlain, (AV) BB
Three Meridian Plaza, Suite 100, 10333 N. Meridian Street, 46290
Telephone: 317-844-9999 Fax: 317-844-9977 Toll Free: 800-269-3443 URL: http://www.dclawfirm.com URL: http://www.uslaws.com
Email: tcd@tbilawyer.com URL: http://www.tortslaw.com
Members of Firm: Thomas C. Doehrman; Daniel S. Chamberlain. Associate: Ronald S. Todd. Of Counsel: Ralph J. Bratch.
Plaintiff's Civil Trial and Appellate Practice in State and Federal Courts. Personal Injury, Automobile Accidents and Injuries, Wrongful Death, Slip and Fall, Unsafe Products, Product Liability, Construction Site Injury and Safety. Traumatic Brain Injury, Medical Malpractice, Nursing Home Abuse and Neglect, Trucking Accidents and Injuries.
See Professional Biographies, INDIANAPOLIS, INDIANA

Doehrmann, Carrie G. ....'65 '92 C.210 B.A. L.345 J.D. [Ⓒ Locke R.]
Doepken, Elizabeth J. ....'— '01 C.231 B.A. L.74 J.D. [Ⓐ Cohen&M.] (Pat.)
Doerr, Monica S. ....'76 '03 C.679 B.A. L.347 J.D. [Ⓐ Parr R.O.&M.]
Dogan, Kevin W. .... '54 '81 C.347 B.S. L.1119 J.D. 4911 East 56th Street
Doherty, Mary T., (BV) ....'— '92 C.201 B.A. L.347 J.D. [Sommer B.]
Dolack, Robert F. ....'69 '96 C.248 B.A. L.365 J.D. Law Offces of St. Paul Travelers
Dollens, Lucy R. ....'76 '02 C.108 B.A. L.74 J.D. [Ⓐ Locke R.]
Donahoe, Peter H., (AV) .... '55 '84 C.347 B.S. L.345 J.D. [Hill,F.M.F.&M.]
Donaldson, Bruce D., (AV) ....'— '84 C.210 B.A. L.1119 J.D. [Barnes&T.]
Doninger, Clarence H., (AV) .... '35 '60 C.347 B.S. L.1119 J.D. [Ⓒ Stark D.&S.]
Donnelly, Keith R. ....'— '04 C.870 B.S. L.345 J.D. [Ⓐ Barnes&T.]
Donnelly-Miller, Kristin M. ....'67 '97 C.901 B.A. L.209 J.D. Spec. Master
Donnelson, Dean A. ....'50 '77 C.63 B.A. L.345 J.D. 8110 Dean Rd.
Dorelli, Michael A. .... '71 '98 C&L.347 B.S., J.D. [Ⓐ Hoover H.B.&H.]
Dorocke, Lawrence F., (AV) ....'46 '73 C.679 B.S. L.345 J.D. [Dann P.N.&K.]
D'Orso, Jennifer L. .... '— '95 C.679 B.Ch.E. L.347 J.D. [Ⓐ Jensen&Assoc.]
Dorson, Patricia Freeman '56 '81
C.347 B.A. L.345 J.D. V. P. & Gen. Coun., VASA Brougher, Inc.
Dostie, Linda T. ....'49 '88 C.188 A.B. L.424 J.D. U.S. Soc. Sec. Admin.
Doucette, Nancy '69 '96 C&L.108 B.A., J.D.
Corporate Counsel, Communications Products, Inc.
Dougherty, Bradley J. .... '— '82 C.347 B.S. L.1119 J.D. [Barnes&T.]
Douglas, Charles C., (BV) ....'71 '96 C.347 B.S. L.879 J.D. [Riley B.&E.]
Douglas, Christine, (BV) ....'68 '97 C.679 B.A. L.879 J.D. [Douglas]
Douglas, John Hilton, (AV) .... '36 '65 C.347 B.S. L.345 J.D. [Williams&D.]

Douglas Law Offices, P.C., (BV)
225 North Delaware Street, 46204
Telephone: 317-269-3422 Facsimile: 317-269-3419
Email: douglaslaw@dslindiana.net URL: http://www.lawyers.com/douglaslawoffices
Christine Douglas.

(This Listing Continued)

Douglas Law Offices, P.C. (Continued)

Family Law, Divorce, Child Custody, Child Support, Visitation Rights, Adoption, Third-Party Custody, Guardianships, Juvenile Delinquency, Paternity.

See Professional Biographies, INDIANAPOLIS, INDIANA

Douglass, Donald D., Jr. '50 '76 C.473 B.A. L.215 J.D. Mng. Atty., SAFECO Prop. & Cas. Ins. Co.
Dowd, John E., (BV) .... '46 '72 C.347 A.B. L.345 J.D. Asst. U.S. Atty.
Dowling, James E., (AV) ....'34 '61 C.276 B.S. L.1119 J.D. [Ⓒ Due,D.F.&M.]
Dowling, Ralph E., (BV) .... '57 '94 C.173 B.A. L.347 J.D. [Ⓐ Norris C.&S.]
Downer, John D. ....'36 '64 C.347 B.S. L.345 J.D. Supr. Ct. J.
Downs, Thomas K., (AV) ....'49 '80 C.347 B.A. L.1119 J.D. [Ice M.]
Doyle, Craig D., (BV) ....'51 '83 C.347 B.A. L.345 J.D. [Doyle&F.]
Doyle, Guinn P., (AV) ....'— '92 C&L.347 B.A., J.D. [Ⓒ Barnes&T.]
Doyle, Robert J., (AV) .... '59 '85 C.210 B.A. L.345 J.D. [Due,D.F.&M.]

Doyle & Friedmeyer, P.C., (BV)
First Indiana Plaza, Suite 2000, 135 North Pennsylvania Street, 46204-2456
Telephone: 317-264-5000 Telecopier: 317-264-5400 317-264-5420
Email: LPBD@iquest.net
Craig D. Doyle; Joanne B. Friedmeyer. Associates: Mark S. Gray; James L. Shoemaker; Andrew M. David.
General Civil and Appellate Practice in all Courts. Corporate, Real Estate, Probate and Estate Planning, Bankruptcy, Creditors' Rights, Commercial Law, Insurance Law.

Dremonas, George A. .... '— '89 C.347 B.A. L.345 J.D. Coun., Thomson Inc.
Drewes, Mark A. .... '66 '93 C&L.347 B.S., J.D. Frontier Financial Counsultants, Inc.
Drewry, Daniel M. ....'78 '03 C.679 B.A. L.150 J.D. [Ⓐ Drewry S.V.]
Drewry, Michael F., (AV) ....'52 '79 C.679 B.A. L.345 J.D. [Drewry S.V.]
Drewry, Patrick A. ....'76 '01 C.679 B.A. L.345 J.D. [Ⓐ Drewry S.V.]

Drewry Simmons Vornehm, LLP, (AV) BR
8888 Keystone Crossing, Suite 1200, 46240
Telephone: 317-580-4848 Telecopier: 317-580-4855
Email: info@drewrysimmons.com URL: http://www.drewrysimmons.com
Michael F. Drewry; David L. Simmons; David B. Vornehm; Joseph M. Leone; Michael P. Bishop; Robert J. Milford; Maryellen K. Bishop; Paul G. Reis; David A. Temple; Thomas J. Grau;—Patrick A. Drewry; Tammy S. Koch; Matthew J. Schafer; Brian M. Falcon; Sean T. Devenney; Sean M. Mayberry; Patrick M. Miller; Robert J. Orelup; William E. Kelley, Jr.; Daniel M. Drewry. Of Counsel: S. Douglas Trolson (1942-2002).
Business, Construction, Government Contracts, Surety, Commercial and related Arbitration and Litigation, Securities, Estate Planning, Trusts, Taxation, Construction and Public Contracts law, Surety, Civil Litigation, Mediation and Arbitration, Corporations, Business and Securities Law, Estate Planning and Administration, Commercial Real Estate Transactions, Land Use Planning and Zoning, Labor and Employment Law, Adoption.

See Professional Biographies, INDIANAPOLIS, INDIANA

Dreyer, David J. ....'55 '80 C&L.602 B.A., J.D. Supr. Ct. J.
Drics, John Thomas ....'63 '91 C.679 B.A. L.190 J.D. [O'Bryan B.&D.]
Drummond, Mark A., (BV) ....'63 '90 C.347 B.A. L.345 J.D. [Ⓐ Hoover H.B.&H.]
Drummy, John B., (AV) ....'60 '85 C.190 B.S.B.A. L.345 J.D. [Kightlinger&G.]
DuBois, Dustin S. ....'70 '00 C.701 B.S. L.345 J.D. [Ⓐ Ice M.] (See Pat. Sect.)
Duchon, Darryn L., (BV) .... '64 '89 C&L.347 B.S., J.D. 302 N. Ala. St.
Duclos, Catherine Fitzgerald, (AV) '— '88 C.347 B.S. L.1119 J.D. Dep. Gen. Coun., Thomson Inc.
Dudley, Richard O. '33 '63 C.679 B.S. L.472 J.D. V.P. & Tr. Offr., National City Bk., Indiana
Due, Danford R., (AV) .... '48 '73 C.880 B.A. L.345 J.D. [Due,D.F.&M.]
Due, Stephen L. .... '77 '02 C&L.347 B.S., J.D. [Ⓐ Bingham M.]

Due, Doyle, Fanning & Metzger, LLP, (AV)
900 Circle Tower Building, 55 Monument Circle, 46204-5900
Telephone: 317-635-7700 Fax: 317-636-2408
Email: duedoyle@duedoyle.com URL: http://www.duedoyle.com
Members of Firm: Danford R. Due; Robert J. Doyle; Robert A. Fanning; Mark A. Metzger; Michael S. Huntine; Kristen K. Rollison. Associates: Mary A. Schopper; Daniel G. Foote; Cynthia E. Music; Lisa M. Dillon; Daniel L. Quigley; Rebecca K. Browning. Of Counsel: James E. Dowling.
Insurance Defense, Coverage, Corporate Litigation, Personal Injury, Workers Compensation, Products Liability, Toxic Torts, Asbestos, Alternative Dispute Resolution.

See Professional Biographies, INDIANAPOLIS, INDIANA

Duff, Gregory A. ....'— '99 C.679 B.S.Ph. L.893 J.D. [Ⓐ Ice M.] (See Pat. Sect.)
Duff, Robert E. .... '67 '92 C.679 B.A. L.1119 J.D. [Ⓐ Schuckit&Assoc.]
Duffin, Ryan G., (BV) ....'66 '91 C&L.347 B.S., J.D. [Duffin&H.]
Duffin & Hash, LLP, (BV) ....9200 Keystone Crossing
Duga, Terry G., (AV) .... '50 '76 C.347 A.B. L.345 J.D. Dep. Atty. Gen.
Dugan, Michael P., (BV) .... '62 '88 C.435 B.S. L.345 J.D. [Dugan V.&M.]
Dugan Voland & Meagher, LLP, (BV) ....3388 Founders Rd., Ste. A
DuMond, David ....'47 '74 C.432 B.A. L.345 J.D. 2478 S. Delaware St
Dunbar, Danny R. ....'54 '82 C.347 B.S. L.345 J.D. Anacomp, Inc.
Duncan, David J. ....'78 '04 C.347 B.S. L.345 J.D. [Ⓐ Tabbert H.E.&W.]
Duncan, Greg J. ....'73 '99 C.679 B.S. L.1119 J.D. [Ⓐ Bingham M.]
Duncan, Robert A., (BV) '45 '72 C.303 B.A. L.345 J.D. VP & General Counsel, BAA Indianapolis LLC
Dunn, Gregory Scott ....'55 '89 C&L.347 B.A., J.D. Sr. Atty., Allison Engine Co., Inc.
Dunne, Paul J., (AV) .... '55 '80 C.602 B.B.A. L.345 J.D. [Krieg D.]
Durham, Lisa A. .... '58 '05 C.339 B.A. L.345 J.D. [Ⓐ Krieg D.]
Durlacher, James M., (AV) '46 '76 C.679 B.S.M.E. L.345 J.D. [Woodard,E.M.M.&H.] (See Pat. Sect.)
Durnil, Gordon K. .... '36 '65 C.347 B.S. L.345 J.D. P.O. Box 90106
DuSold, Elizabeth L., (CV) '61 '90 C.205 B.A. L.347 J.D. Coun., Envir. Law Dept., Eli Lilly & Co.
Dutcher, Daniel T. '59 '85 C.602 B.A. L.378 J.D. (adm. in ME; not adm. in IN) Chf. of Staff, NCAA
Dutcher, Karen A., (BV) ....'60 '85 C&L.378 B.S., J.D. [Ⓒ Ice M.] (⊙Lawrence, KS)
Dutton, C. Ben, (AV) ....'17 '40 C.347 B.S. L.1119 J.D. 1402 W. 52nd Street
Dutton, Mark C. .... '73 '01 C.347 B.A. L.1119 J.D. [Dutton&Assoc.]
Dutton, Stephen J., (AV) ....'— '69 C.46 B.S. L.345 J.D. [Barnes&T.]

Dutton & Associates, L.L.C.
921 E. 86th Street, Suite 130, 46240
Telephone: 317-254-9000 Fax: 317-254-9010 URL: http://www.duttonandassociates.com
Email: mdutton@duttonandassociates.com URL: http://www.duttonlawfirm.com
Mark C. Dutton.
Bankruptcy Law.

See Professional Biographies, INDIANAPOLIS, INDIANA

Duvall, Lesa C. .... '62 '92 C.63 B.S. L.347 J.D. [Mishkin&D.]
Duvall, Leslie, (AV) ....'24 '49 C.108 A.B. L.347 J.D. [Ⓒ Lewis&K.]
Dwyer, Robert E. .... '46 '72 C.93 A.B. L.818 J.D. Firstmark Fin. Corp.
Dyar, Richard W., (BV) ....'55 '81 C.347 B.A. L.345 J.D. [Stark D.&S.]
Dyer, Ronald L., (BV) .... '44 '72 C.347 B.S. L.345 J.D. 10377 Courageous Drive
Dykstra, Gregg A. '56 '83 C.347 B.A. L.1119 J.D. National Association of Mutual Insurance Companies

Dzeguze, Andrew B., (BV) ....'— '99 C.112 B.A. L.1065 J.D. [Ⓐ Barnes&T.]
Eades, Christopher C. ....'— '97 C&L.347 B.A., J.D. [Ⓐ Hall,R.K.H.&L.]
Eads, Terence L., (AV) .... '39 '64 C.373 B.A. L.477 LL.B. [Eads,M.&P.]
Eads, Murray & Pugh, P.C., (AV) ....7321 Shadeland Station, Suite 250
Eagle, Brian A. ....'64 '90 C.347 B.S. L.1019 J.D. 8500 Keystone Crossing, Ste. 555
Eagle, Sidney '35 '63 C.1138 B.B.A. L.569 LL.B. (adm. in NY; not adm. in IN) [Eagle&F.]
Eagle & Fein .... 8500 Keystone Crossing, Ste. 555
Eaglesfield, R. Davy, III, (AV) ....'41 '71 C.347 A.B. L.345 J.D. [Ⓒ Harrison&M.]
Earle, Christopher C., (BV) ....'58 '86 C.880 B.A. L.345 J.D. [Bose M.&E.]
Earls, Claudia .... '— '84 C.347 B.A. L.345 J.D. [Ⓒ Barnes&T.]
Earnest, Lante K., (AV) .... '46 '73 C.347 B.S. L.345 J.D. [Tabbert H.E.&W.]
Earnhart, Tami A. .... '69 '99 C.249 B.S. L.347 J.D. [Ⓐ Ice M.]
Easter, J. Greg, (BV) ....'59 '84 C.108 B.S. L.1119 J.D. [Easter&C.]

Easter & Cavosie, (AV)
8555 River Road, Suite 400, 46240
Telephone: 317-574-0828 Facsimile: 317-574-0969
URL: http://www.ec-lawfirm.com
J. Greg Easter; J. Michael Cavosie; David A. Tucker. Associates: Theresa L. Silver; David E. Bostwick; Leslie A. Sinnott.
Construction Law.

See Professional Biographies, INDIANAPOLIS, INDIANA

Easterday, Debra S., (AV) ....'56 '81 C.317 B.A. L.345 J.D. [Ⓐ Krieg D.]
Eaton, Joseph G., (BV) .... '— '91 C.108 B.S. L.1119 J.D. [Barnes&T.]
Ebbinghouse, Tom S., (BV) .... '55 '80 C.210 B.A. L.1119 J.D. 320 N. Meridian St.
Ebbs, Robert Henry, (BV) ....'62 '90 C&L.347 B.S., J.D. 129 E. Market St.
Ebert, Kim F., (AV) ....'50 '76 C.894 B.A. L.1119 J.D. [Ogletree,D.N.S.&S.]
Eckard, Margo E. ....'45 '88 C.347 B.A. L.345 J.D. Golden Rule Insurance Co.
Eckerle, Michael L., (AV) ....'52 '77 C.894 B.A. L.228 J.D. [Bingham M.]
Eckerle, Thomas N., (AV) ....'46 '72 C.602 A.B. L.1119 J.D. P.O. Box 80155
Eckert, Philip C., (BV) .... '55 '83 C.347 B.A. L.607 J.D. [Eckert C.]

Eckert, Stephen P., Law Offices of, (BV) '55 '81 C.347 B.A. L.345 J.D.
P.O. Box 17526, 46217
Telephone: 317-885-9600 Fax: 317-885-9200
Personal Injury, Automobile Accidents, Slip and Fall, Wrongful Death, Products Liability.

See Professional Biographies, INDIANAPOLIS, INDIANA

Eckert Craven, P.C., (BV) ....7550 South Meridian Street, Suite C
Ecklund & Frutkin, LLC, (BV) .... 6050 East Tenth Street
Edler, Robert William, Jr. ...... '49 '99 C.347 A.B. L.345 J.D. 151 North Delaware Street
Edminster, Jodie L. ....'70 '99 C.1046 B.A. L.347 J.D. [Ⓐ Wallack S.&H.]
Edwards, Charles P., (BV) .... '— '93 C&L.347 B.A., J.D. [Barnes&T.]
Edwards, Elisabeth M. ....'76 '03 C.303 B.A. L.345 J.D. [Ⓐ Mitchell&Assoc.]
Edwards, Yolanda D. ....'— '03 C.780 B.A. L.1119 J.D. [Ⓐ Barnes&T.]
Effland, Matthew S. ....'— '99 C.187 B.S.S. L.845 J.D. [Ⓐ Ogletree,D.N.S.&S.]
Efroymson, Henry A., (AV) .... '57 '82 C.347 B.A. L.345 J.D. [Ice M.]
Efroymson, Jeremy D. .... '68 '95 C.477 B.A. L.1119 J.D. 5241 N. Illinois St.
Egloff, John L., (AV) ....'53 '78 C.475 B.A. L.1119 J.D. [Riley B.&E.]
Ehresman, May S. ....'57 '85 C.347 B.G.S. L.345 J.D. 8711 Warrington Dr.
Eichholtz, Steven R., (BV) ....'55 '80 C.679 B.S. L.347 J.D. [Ⓒ Locke R.]

Eichhorn & Eichhorn
(See Carmel)

Eikenberry, Dale W., (AV) ....'53 '78 C.602 B.A. L.597 J.D. [Wooden&M.]
Eikenberry, Shawna M. ....'74 '99 C.108 B.A. L.1119 J.D. [Ⓐ Baker&D.]
Einterz, Michael L., (AV) ....'61 '87 C.894 B.A. L.345 J.D. 5455 W. 86th St.
Eisan, Jeannette A. ....'57 '82 C.210 B.A. L.1119 J.D. U.S. Bankrptcy. Ct.
Eisele, Michelle .... '59 '85 C.347 B.A. L.1119 J.D. Supvr. Trial Atty.
Eisenman, Brian Michael ......'73 '99 C.347 B.A. L.608 J.D. Pub. Def., IN Pub. Def. Off.
Eiteljorg, Roger, (BV) ....'48 '74 C.894 B.A. L.861 J.D. [Ⓒ Salyers&E.]
Eke, Joseph W., (AV) ....'40 '73 C.347 B.S. L.345 J.D. [Dale&E.]
Elberger, Ronald E., (AV) ....'45 '69 C.273 A.B. L.30 J.D. [Bose M.&E.]
Eleftheri, Anthony M., (BV) ....'71 '96 C&L.347 B.A., J.D. [Lewis W.]
Eley, Derrick D., Law Office of '66 '97 C.679 B.A. L.347 J.D. 129 E. Market St., Ste. 1100
Elias, Kathryn A. ....'— '97 C.347 B.S. L.602 J.D. [Ⓐ Hall,R.K.H.&L.]
Elkins, Ronald D. ....'50 '83 C&L.347 B.S., J.D. [Ⓒ Buehler&Assoc.]
Ellery, Richard M. '71 '97 C.679 B.A. L.347 J.D. Asst. Gen. Coun., American United Life Insurance Co.
Elliott, Cathy, (BV) .... '— '89 C.445 B.S. L.362 J.D. [Bose M.&E.]
Elliott, Randy A. ....'62 '90 C.1119 B.A. L.345 J.D. Dep. Pub. Def.
Elmore, Rebecca Biller ....'78 '04 C.477 B.A. L.1119 J.D. [Ⓐ Krieg D.]
Elrod, Jonathan R. ....'77 '02 C.973 B.A. L.347 J.D. [Ⓐ Elrod&M.]
Elrod, Robert G., (AV) ....'40 '65 C.210 A.B. L.309 LL.B. [Elrod&M.]

Elrod & Mascher, P.C., (AV)
5329 S. Emerson Avenue, Suite C, 46237
Telephone: 317-786-4929 Fax: 317-786-7899
URL: http://www.eandmlaw.com
French M. Elrod (1906-1985); Robert G. Elrod; Gilbert E. Mascher;—Jonathan R. Elrod.
Probate, Trusts and Estates, Wills, Estate Planning, Family Law, Business Law, Corporate Law, General Practice, Guardianships and Conservatorships, Non-Profit and Charitable Organizations, Partnership Law, Personal Injury, Real Estate.
Reference: National City Bank.

See Professional Biographies, INDIANAPOLIS, INDIANA

Elward, Patrick A., (AV) ....'56 '81 C.63 B.S. L.345 J.D. [Bingham M.]
Elzer, Robert W., (AV) ....'51 '76 C.347 B.A. L.309 J.D. [Baker&D.]
Emanuele, John J., Jr. '56 '02 C.959 B.S. L.966 J.D. [Ⓐ Woodard,E.M.M.&H.] (See Pat. Sect.)
Emenhiser, Jonathan P. ....'75 '00 C.432 B.S. L.1119 J.D. [Ⓐ Plews S.R.&B.]
Emerick, R. David '72 '98 C.679 B.A. L.347 J.D. 500 Century Building, 36 S. Pennsylvania Blvd.
Emerson, Andrew C. .... '29 '53 C.679 B.S. L.1119 LL.B. 5671 Central‡
Emerson, Daniel C., (AV) ....'54 '79 C.429 B.A. L.1119 J.D. [Bose M.&E.]
Emery, Alison ....'— '03 C.992 B.A. L.879 J.D. [Ⓐ Ice M.]
Emhardt, C. David, (AV) '31 '55 C.679 B.S. L.309 LL.B. [Woodard,E.M.M.&H.] (See Pat. Sect.)
Emhardt, Frederick D., (AV) .... '60 '85 C.894 B.A. L.174 J.D. [Plews S.R.&B.]
Emison, Lucy A., (AV) .... '50 '85 C.209 B.A. L.345 J.D. [Ice M.]
Emmerson, Robert D. .... '71 '99 C.339 B.A. L.74 J.D. [Ⓐ Stewart&I.]
Emswiller, Kent, (AV) .... '53 '78 C.347 B.S. L.345 J.D. [Emswiller,W.N.&C.]
Emswiller, Williams, Noland & Clarke, (AV) ....8500 Keystone Crossing
Endris, Lori Kyle, (BV) ....'61 '88 C.63 B.S. L.345 J.D. Co. Small Claims Ct.
Endsley, J. Patrick .... '28 '56 C.347 B.S. L.345 J.D. U.S. Mag. J.‡
Endsley, Nancy G., (BV) .... '47 '88 C&L.347 B.A., J.D. [Ⓒ Landman&B.]
Engelking, Lara D., RN ....'— '97 C&L.347 B.S.N., J.D. [Ⓐ Hall,R.K.H.&L.]

Engelmann, John H. '44 '75 C.959 B.S. L.339 J.D.
(adm. in CT; not adm. in IN; Pat.) Pat. Coun., Eli Lilly & Co.
Engels, Erin Michelle ....'73 '99 C.339 B.A. L.345 J.D. 3830 Southport Rd., Suite 500
England, Brian L., (BV) .... '66 '92 C&L.347 B.A., J.D. [Hunt S.K.]
Engle, Thomas H. ....'— '96 C.63 B.S. L.1119 J.D. [Barnes&T.]
Enright, J. Scott, (AV) '63 '91 C.747 B.A. L.347 J.D.
V.P. & Assoc. Gen. Coun., Emmis Communications
Epstein, Carl L. ....'50 '81 C.415 B.A. L.1000 J.D. 156 E. Market St., Ste. 900
Erdman, Kevin R., (AV) ......'63 '87 C.347 B.S. L.659 J.D. [Baker&D.] (See Pat. Sect.)
Eskenazi, Sidney D. ....'30 '53 C.347 B.S. L.1119 LL.B. 2220 N. Meridian St.
Eskew, Kelly R. ....'64 '01 C.999 B.A. L.345 J.D. [Ⓐ Bingham M.]
Esping, Theodore J., (AV) ....'49 '75 C.260 B.S. L.228 J.D. [Baker&D.]
Etling, Gretchen Holland ....'62 '88 C.999 B.A. L.345 J.D. [Ⓒ Holland&H.]
Evans, Daniel F., (AV) ....'49 '76 C.347 B.A. L.345 J.D. [Ⓒ Baker&D.]
Evens, Christopher A. ....'73 '00 C.347 B.A. L.345 J.D. [Ⓐ Bose M.&E.]
Everitt, Robert H., (AV) '39 '65
C.347 B.S. L.345 J.D. FirstTrust Indiana, First Indiana Bank
Ewbank, Thomas P., (AV) .... '43 '69 C.347 B.A. L.345 J.D. [Krieg D.]
Ewing, Colin W. '54 '80 C.951 B.A. L.178 J.D.
Assoc. Gen. Coun., Litig. Dept., Eli Lilly & Co.
Ewing, Richard S., (AV) ....'— '67 C.210 A.B. L.1119 J.D. 10566 Full Creek Rd.‡
Eyler, Danica L. ....'79 '04 C.347 B.S. L.345 J.D. [Ⓐ Stark D.&S.]
Eyster, Randy C. ....'60 '98 C.679 B.S. L.345 J.D. [Ⓐ Feiwell&H.]
Fabina-Abney, Sherry A., (AV) ....'63 '88 C.679 B.A. L.1119 J.D. [Ice M.]
Fagan, Daniel R., (AV) ....'52 '77 C.347 B.A. L.345 J.D. [Bingham M.]
Fahey, Sean J. ....'— '93 C.696 B.A. L.930 J.D. [Ⓒ Sommer B.]
Fairchild, Richard L., (AV) ....'40 '65 C.210 A.B. L.477 LL.B. [Stewart&I.]
Faires, C. Dickson, Jr., (AV) ....'36 '64 C.347 B.S. L.1119 LL.B. 1 Indiana Sq.
Falcon, Brian M. ....'76 '03 C.63 B.S. L.345 J.D. [Ⓐ Drewry S.V.]
Falk, Andrew R. ....'74 '03 C&L.347 B.S., J.D. [Ⓐ Kroger,G.&R.]
Falk, Kenneth J. ....'54 '77 C&L.178 B.A., J.D. 1031 East Washington Street
Falk, Scott K. ....'66 '91 C&L.347 B.A., J.D. Asst. Chf. Couns.
Fanning, Robert A., (AV) ....'51 '76 C.347 B.S. L.345 J.D. [Due,D.F.&M.]
Fanzini, Sarah Stites ....'71 '99 C.679 B.A. L.347 J.D. [Ⓐ Hoover H.B.&H.]
Fara, Thomas A., (AV) ....'53 '79 C.347 B.A. L.345 J.D. 230 East Ohio, Sixth Floor‡
Farlow, Thomas W., (AV) ....'54 '79 C.347 B.A. L.345 J.D. [Locke R.]
Farmer, Jason C. ....'— '01 C.668 B.A. L.421 J.D. [Ⓐ Barnes&T.]
Farmer, Troy D. ....'62 '98 C.63 B.S. L.1119 J.D. [Ⓐ Baker&D.]
Farnsworth, Jo Ann '59 '83 C.346 B.A. L.345 J.D.
Sr. Trial Atty., Equal Employment Opportunity Comm.
Farrar, John Milton ....'72 '00 C.108 B.S. L.1119 J.D. 8040 Upland Court
Farrell, Kenan L. ....'78 '03 C.347 B.S. L.345 J.D. [Ⓐ Bingham M.]
Farrell, Kevin P., (AV) ....'47 '74 C.435 B.A. L.345 J.D. [Cline F.C.L.&C.]
Farrell, Thomas E., (AV) ...'50 '86 C.347 B.A. L.1119 J.D. [Scopelitis,G.L.&H.]
Fatout, William R., (AV) ....'— '76 C.347 A.B. L.1119 J.D. [Stewart&I.]
Faucett, Homer W., III ....'— '03 C.74 B.S. L.345 J.D. [Ⓐ Ice M.]
Faught, Renee A. '62 '94
C.999 B.S. L.801 J.D. Reg. Legal Sr. Staff Atty., American Family
Faulconer, Thomas J., IV '63 '88 C.108 B.S. L.347 J.D.
Dir., Training, Farm Bureau Ins. Co. of Indiana
Faulconer, Thos. J., III ....'23 '49 C.108 A.B. L.879 LL.B. Ret. U.S. Mag.
Faultless, Scott A. ....'— '91 5845 Lawton Loop E. Dr.
Faust, Raymond L., (BV) ....'50 '76 C.347 B.A. L.1119 J.D. [Norris C.&S.]
Fauth, Douglas R. ....'62 '87 C.855 B.A. L.477 J.D. V.P. & Coun., Anthem, Inc.
Fearnow, Randall R., (BV) ....'55 '81 C.344 B.A. L.345 J.D. [Krieg D.]
Feary, Gregory M., (AV) ....'57 '88 C.234 B.A. L.345 J.D. [Scopelitis,G.L.&H.]
Featherstun, Jeffrey D. ....'67 '93 C.347 B.A. L.477 J.D. [Plews S.R.&B.]
Fecht, Jeffrey B. ....'73 '98 C&L.880 B.A., J.D. [Ⓐ Riley B.&E.]
Fechtman, Matthew ....'— '03 C.893 B.A. L.339 J.D. [Ⓐ Ice M.]
Fedij, Peter ....'53 '79 C.589 B.S. L.365 J.D. Mng. Atty., Amer. Fam. Ins. Grp.
Feeney, Francis J., Jr., (AV) ....'29 '59 C.602 B.S. L.345 J.D. 6100 N. Keystone Ave.
Feeney, Joanne Longo .....'— '92 C.184 B.S. L.575 J.D. Pat. Atty., Eli Lilly & Co. (Pat.)
Fehribach, Gregory S., (BV) ....'58 '86 C.63 B.S. L.607 J.D. [Ⓒ Stark D.&S.]
Feiwell, Michael J., (AV) ....'69 '95 C&L.477 B.A., J.D. [Feiwell&H.]
Feiwell, Murray J., (AV) ....'37 '63 C&L.477 B.A., J.D. [Feiwell&H.]

Feiwell & Hannoy, P.C., (AV) BB
251 North Illinois Street, Suite 1700, P.O. Box 44141, 46244-0141
Telephone: 317-237-2727 Facsimile: 317-237-2722
Email: f&h@feiwellhannoy.com URL: http://www.feiwellhannoy.com
Murray J. Feiwell; Douglas J. Hannoy; Michael J. Feiwell; Matthew S. Love; Barry T. Barnes;—Susan M. Woolley; Jerlyn S. Southwick; Jeffrey S. Wilson; Bruce G. Arnold; Randy C. Eyster; Bryan K. Redmond; Leanne S. Titus; Timothy L. Black; Amy S. Thurmond; Jeffrey D. Wolfe; Michael Ghosh; Caryn M. Beougher; Rose K. Felten; Alan W. McEwan; Andrew P. Seiwert; Craig E. Beougher; Stephanie Reinhart.
General Civil Practice. Bankruptcy and Creditors' Rights, Real Estate and Foreclosure, Family/ Domestic Relations, Administrative, General Business and Commercial Law.
See Professional Biographies, INDIANAPOLIS, INDIANA

Feldhake, Mary Margaret Ruth, (AV) ....'58 '89 C&L.347 B.S., J.D. [Locke R.]
Fels, James A., (AV) ....'44 '74 C.108 B.S. L.345 J.D. The Mediation Group, LLC
Felten, Rose K. ....'72 '02 C.679 B.S. L.345 J.D. [Ⓐ Feiwell&H.]
Felts, Christopher P. ....'— '99 C.210 B.A. L.347 J.D. [Ⓐ Barnes&T.]
Fennell, Monica A. '65 '93
C.951 B.A. L.276 J.D. Exec. Dir., Indiana Pro Bono Commission
Fennerty, Brian S., (AV) .... '61 '89 C&L.347 B.S., J.D. [Baker&D.]
Fennerty, Larry L., (BV) ....'30 '72 2611 E. 55th Place
Ferguson, Maureen H. '57 '87 C&L.347 B.S., J.D.
Indiana Statwide Assn. of Rural Electric Co-Ops.
Ferguson, Robert E., (AV) '57 '84 C.347 B.A. L.345 J.D.
Dep. Gen. Coun., American United Life Insurance Co.
Fernandez, John R. ....'— '93 C.347 B.S. L.1119 J.D. [Ⓒ Krieg D.]
Ferree, John R. ....'64 '00 C.344 B.A. L.345 J.D. Chubb Group of Insurance Cos.
Ferree, Marcia Jo ....'69 '98 C.679 B.A. L.879 J.D. [Ⓐ Laudig G.R.&S.]
Ferrucci, Stephen E. ....'65 '90 C&L.93 B.A., J.D. State Farm Lit. Coun.
Fickle, Stanley C., (AV) ....'— '74 C.347 A.B. L.1119 J.D. [Barnes&T.]
Fields, Christine S. '52 '81 C.265 B.A. L.347 J.D.
Asst. Gen. Coun., Eli Lilly Intl. Corp.
Fierek, Natalie M. ....'76 '04 C.63 B.S. L.345 J.D. [Ⓒ Ice M.]
Fife, Eugene M., III, (BV) ....'47 '73 C.347 B.A. L.345 J.D. 1 Pennsylvania Ave.
Figg, Leigh Ann '58 '85
C.347 B.A. L.345 J.D. Atty. Legl. Leasing, Simon Property Group
Filipow, Elizabeth G. ....'58 '83 C.108 B.A. L.347 J.D. 8730 N. Washington, W.
Fillenwarth, Edward J., Jr., (AV) '39 '63 C&L.602 B.B.A., LL.B.
[Fillenwarth,D.G.&T.]
Fillenwarth, Dennerline, Groth & Towe, (AV) ....1213 N. Arlington Ave.
Filomena, Anthony P. ....'58 '98 C.910 B.S. L.347 J.D. [Ⓒ Bose M.&E.] (Pat.)

Finchum, Cheryl D. ....'73 '01 C.63 B.S. L.345 J.D. [Ⓐ Riley B.&E.]
Findling, Mary Arlien, (AV) ....'50 '86 C.679 B.A. L.345 J.D. [Findling G.G.&P.]

Findling Garau Germano & Pennington, P.C., (AV) BB
151 N. Delaware Street, Suite 1515, 46204
Telephone: 317-822-9530 Telecopier: 317-822-9531
Email: fggplaw@iquest.net URL: http://www.lawyers.com/fggplaw
Mary Arlien Findling; Jerry A. Garau; Barbara J. Germano; Deborah K. Pennington; Jennifer Stephens Love; Marshall S. Hanley; David B. Allen.
General Civil Trial and Appellate Practice. Medical Malpractice, Personal Injury, Commercial Litigation, Employment Discrimination.
See Professional Biographies, INDIANAPOLIS, INDIANA

Fink, Irving L., (AV) ....'20 '48 C.597 B.S. L.477 J.D. 3500 W. Depauw Blvd.
Finklea, A. Jack ....'67 '00 C.347 B.A. L.345 J.D. [Ⓐ Scopelitis,G.L.&H.]
Finnell, Clarissa A. ....'— '97 C&L.347 B.A., J.D. Indianapolis Legal Aid Soc.
Fischer, Alfred ....'17 '41 C.563 L.724 LL.B. 9274 Grinnell St.
Fischer, John P., Jr. ....'— '97 C.602 B.A. L.347 J.D. [Ⓐ Barnes&T.]
Fisher, Amy Kathleen ....'76 '01 C.602 B.A. L.345 J.D. [Ⓐ Ice M.]
Fisher, Donna H., (AV) ....'47 '84 C.820 B.A. L.345 J.D. [Smith,F.M.&H.]
Fisher, James R., (AV) ....'47 '72 C.347 A.B. L.1119 J.D. [Ice M.]
Fisher, Patrick J., (AV) ....'14 '37 C&L.602 A.B., J.D. 5435 Emerson Way
Fisher, Thomas G. ....'40 '65 C.231 A.B. L.1119 LL.B. Tax Ct. J.
Fisher, William L. ....'63 '90 C.347 B.S. L.1187 J.D. [Ⓐ Ortiz&Assoc.]
Fitzgerald, Edward A. ....'58 '97 C&L.347 B.A., J.D. Prof., IN Univ. East
Fitzwater, Jennifer R. ....'74 '01 C.74 B.A. L.1119 J.D. [Ⓐ Wood T.G.M.&H.]
Flaniken, Laure V. ....'66 '90 C.198 B.A. L.245 J.D. 9918 Southwind Circle
Flatt, John B. ....'71 '98 C.679 B.S. L.365 J.D. 3021 East 98th St.
Fleitz, Brett R., (AV) ....'65 '90 C&L.347 B.A., J.D. [Kroger,G.&R.]
Fleming, John F. W. ....'— '03 C.894 A.B. L.577 J.D. [Ⓐ Baker&D.]
Fleming, Joshua B. '— '00 C&L.436 B.S., J.D.
(adm. in WI; not adm. in IN) [Ⓐ Barnes&T.]
Fleming, Mary Kay ....'60 '90 C.346 B.S. L.347 J.D. [Ice M.]
Fleming, Michael E. ...'39 '68 C.347 B.S. L.345 J.D. V.P., Fin. Consultant, Smith Barney
Floreancig, John A. ....'62 '89 C.74 B.S. L.345 J.D. Legal Aid Soc.
Foley, Donald F., (BV) ....'41 '67 C.210 A.B. L.347 J.D. [Foley&P.]
Foley & Pool, LLP, (BV) ....342 Massachusetts Avenue
Foos, Robert R. ....'70 '97 C.347 B.A. L.1000 J.D. [Lewis W.]
Foote, Daniel G., (CV) ....'69 '97 C&L.347 B.A., J.D. [Ⓐ Due,D.F.&M.]
Foote, Heidi H. ....'53 '82 C.347 B.S. L.345 J.D. Amer. Underwriters Grp., Inc.
Forbes, David L., (CV) ....'58 '83 C&L.879 B.A., J.D. Merchants Trust Co.
Forbes, John G., (BV) ....'43 '68 C.347 A.B. L.1119 J.D. 131 East Ohio St.
Forbus, Sharon A. ....'52 '81 C.347 B.S. L.861 J.D. 5802 W. 62nd St.★
Ford, John Charles ....'51 '87 C&L.347 A.B., J.D. 380 Main St.
Ford, Mark W., (AV) ....'49 '74 C.210 L.347 J.D. [Ice M.]
Ford, Melissa J. ....'65 '98 C.347 B.S. L.345 J.D. [Ⓐ Bingham M.]
Forman, Alexander D. ....'75 '01 C.347 B.B.A. L.345 J.D. [Ⓐ Ice M.] (See Pat. Sect.)
Forsythe, Reno H., Jr. ....'17 '46 C&L.966 Ph.B., LL.B. 3635 Delmar Rd.
Foster, David A., (AV) ....'64 '90 C.477 B.A. L.347 J.D. [Baker&D.]
Foster, Kennard P. ....'44 '70 C.63 B.S. L.345 J.D. U.S. Mag.
Foulks, Curtis J. ....'60 '97 C.63 B.S. L.345 J.D. Pros. Atty. Off.
Foust, Cleon H., Jr. ....'07 '33 C.894 A.B. L.37 J.D. 7278 Harbour Isle‡
Foutty, David L., (BV) ....'41 '68 C.346 B.S. L.345 J.D. [Hartman&F.]
Fowler, Phillip J. ....'71 '97 C.347 B.S. L.880 J.D. [Bingham M.] (Pat.)
Fowler, Russell E., II '70 '96
C.679 B.S.E.E. L.345 J.D. [Ⓐ Maginot M.&B.] (See Pat. Sect.)
Fox, Michael R. ....'69 '95 C&L.347 B.S., J.D. 7160 Zionsville Road
Fox, Steven R., (BV) ....'59 '85 C.347 B.S. L.345 J.D. [Gray,R.R.&F.]
Foxworthy, Randolph L., (AV) '44 '70
C.108 B.A. L.345 J.D. Exec. V.P., Simon Property Group
Frahm, Jennifer Bartels ....'73 '03 C.679 B.S. L.345 J.D. [Ⓐ Ice M.]
Frame, Sherri C. ....'69 '98 C.741 B.A. L.1048 J.D. Jud. Clk., Tax Ct.
Franceschini, Michael R., (AV) ....'— '75 C&L.347 B.S., J.D. [Ayres C.&S.]
Francis, Crystal L. ....'57 '82 C.63 B.A. L.36 J.D. Legal Servs. Organization of IN, Inc.
Frank, Lillian L. ....'77 '04 C.108 B.A. L.325 J.D. [Ⓐ Gresk&S.]
Frank, Marvin J., (AV) ....'39 '66 C.347 B.S. L.345 J.D. [Frank&K.]
Frank, Sarah M. ....'37 '77 C.679 B.S. L.345 J.D. [Kortepeter M.H.F.&M.]
Frank, Steven H., (BV) ....'44 '71 C.347 B.A. L.345 J.D. 200 E. Washington St.

Frank & Kraft, A Professional Corporation, (AV)
First Indiana Plaza, Suite 1100, 135 North Pennsylvania Street, 46204-2400
Telephone: 317-684-1100 Telefax: 317-684-6111
Email: info@frankkraft.com URL: http://www.frankkraft.com
Marvin J. Frank; Paul A. Kraft; Ronald d'Avis; Robert M. Hamlett; Rebecca W. Geyer.
Estate Planning, Business, Corporate, Real Estate, Federal and State Taxation, Probate, Estate Administration, Employee Benefits, Mergers and Acquisitions, Medicaid Planning.
See Professional Biographies, INDIANAPOLIS, INDIANA

Frankenstein, Marc C., (AV) '54 '79
C.347 B.A. L.145 J.D. Development Atty., Simon Property Group
Fraser, Shelley S. ....'— '04 C.347 B.A. L.345 J.D. [Ⓐ Sommer B.]
Frazier, Charise R. ....'— '01 C.879 B.S. L.347 J.D. [Ⓐ Hall,R.K.H.&L.]
Frazier, Ronald W., (BV) ....'59 '88 C.63 B.S. L.879 J.D. [Frazier&Assoc.]
Frazier & Associates, (BV) ....612 E. Market St.
Fredland, Valita M. '65 '92 C.518 B.A. L.188 J.D.
Assoc. Gen. Coun., Clarian Health Partners, Inc.
Free, Edwin W., III '55 '89 C.347 B.S. L.345 J.D.
Inv. Broker, A.G. Edwards & Sons, Inc.
Freedman, Jack M., (BV) ....'58 '84 C&L.94 B.S., J.D. [Freedman&Assoc.]
Freedman & Associates, (BV) ....156 E. Market St., Ste. 1C
Freeland, Charles M. ....'— '93 C.477 M.B.A. L.1119 J.D. Sr. Coun., Thomson Inc.
Freeman, Timothy D., (BV) ....'68 '94 C.210 B.A. L.862 J.D. [Freeman]
Freeman Law Firm, The, P.C., (BV) ....310 N. Alabama St., Ste. 100
Freese, Michael Hunter, (BV) ....'55 '83 C&L.347 B.A., J.D. Simon Property Group
Freiberger, Philip W., (BV) ....'28 '56 C.976 B.A. L.1119 LL.B. 9401 Spring Mill Rd.
Freihofer, William A., (AV) ...'31 '58 C.477 B.B.A. L.1119 J.D. [Kortepeter M.H.F.&M.]
Freije, Richard T., Jr., (AV) ....'58 '84 C.679 B.S.E. L.1119 J.D. [Baker&D.]
Freitag, Elizabeth Paige .....'72 '98 C.249 B.S. L.1119 J.D. Indiana Civil Liberties Union
French, Peter S. ....'66 '92 C.945 A.B L.861 J.D. [Lewis&K.]
Frick, Dennis K. '54 '79 C.679 B.S. L.145 J.D.
Staff Atty., Sr. Law Proj. Legal Servs. Organization of Ind., Inc.
Friedlander, Ezra H. ....'41 '65 C.347 A.B. L.1119 LL.B. Ct. of App. J.
Friedman, RiséA. '52 '83 C.665 B.A. L.229 J.D.
(adm. in PA; not adm. in IN) Sr. Atty., Simon Property Group
Friedmeyer, Joanne B., (BV) ....'52 '86 C.741 B.A. L.345 J.D. [Doyle&F.]
Frisby, Mary Jane ....'— '00 C&L.347 B.A., J.D. [Ⓐ Barnes&T.]
Frische, Michael C. ....'53 '76 C&L.879 B.A., J.D. Law Clk., U.S. Dist J.
Frisk, R. Randall, (AV) '59 '85
C.679 B.S.M.E. L.345 J.D. [Woodard,E.M.M.&H.] (See Pat. Sect.)

Fritts, Brian C. ... '73 '99 C.679 B.S. L.345 J.D. [Ⓐ Krieg D.]
Fritz, Charles E., (BV) ... '26 '53 C.108 A.B. L.1119 J.D. 55 Monument Cir.
Froehle, Thomas C., Jr., (AV) ... '63 '88 C.347 B.A. L.477 J.D. [Baker&D.]
Frosch, Frederick J., Sr. ... '19 '51 C&L.912 A.B., J.D. 342 Massachusetts Ave.‡
Frudden, Sarah A. '60 '86 C&L.966 B.A., J.D.
(adm. in WI; not adm. in IN) NHP Mgmt. Co.
Fruechtenicht, Thomas E., (BV) ... '40 '65 C.347 B.S. L.1119 J.D. [Ⓒ Bose M.&E.]
Fruehwald, Kristin G., (AV) ... '— '75 C.546 B.S. L.345 J.D. [Barnes&T.]
Fruehwald, Michael R., (AV) ... '— '73 C.347 A.B. L.1119 J.D. [Barnes&T.]
Frutkin, Lawrence D., (BV) ... '41 '67 C.608 L.469 LL.B. 6050 E. 10th St.
Frutkin, Reynold F., (BV) ... '38 '83 C.973 A.B. L.345 J.D. [Ecklund&F.]
Frye, Anne M., (BVⓉ) '66 '92 C.63 B.A. L.347 J.D.
Gen. Coun., Reilly Industries, Inc. (Legal Department)
Frye, Diane M. ... '54 '81 C.347 B.S. L.1119 J.D. Assoc. Atty., Atty. Gen. Off.
Frye, Robert M. ... '66 '94 C&L.344 B.S., J.D. [Ⓐ Foley&P.]
Fulford, Wade D. ... '68 '96 C.347 B.S. L.1119 J.D. [Ⓐ Locke R.]
Fulk, Jason L. ... '76 '04 C.347 B.S. L.1119 J.D. [Ⓐ Hoover H.B.&H.]
Fulkerson, Paul T. ... '69 '94 C.679 B.S. L.602 J.D. 150 E. Market St., Ste. 200
Funk, David A. '27 '51 C.970 A.B. L.930 J.D.
(adm. in OH; not adm. in IN) Prof. Emeritus of Law, Ind. Univ. Sch. of Law‡
Funk, Norman T., (AV) ... '45 '71 C.347 B.S. L.345 J.D. [Hill,F.M.F.&M.]
Funke, Sarah K. ... '69 '94 C.347 B.A. L.1119 J.D. [Ice M.]
Furnas, Larry D., (BV) ... '40 '76 C.346 B.S. L.345 J.D. [Furnas&Assoc.]
Furnas & Associates, P.C., (BV) ... 3891 Eagle Creek Pkwy., Ste. B
Gabovitch, Ellen S. ... '57 '82 C.347 B.S. L.1119 J.D. Law Clk. to Supm. Ct. J.
Gabovitch, Michael J., (AV) ... '60 '86 C.347 B.A. L.345 J.D. [Katz&K.]
Gabriel, Charleyne L. ... '47 '73 C.665 B.A. L.347 J.D. [Lewis&K.]
Gaddy, Charles P., (BV) ... '48 '85 L.345 LL.B. [Gaddy&G.]
Gaddy, Maureen E., (BV) ... '55 '79 C.63 B.S. L.345 J.D. [Gaddy&G.]
Gaddy & Gaddy, (BV) ... 1010 N. High School Rd.
Gaerte, K. Michael ... '75 '01 C.974 B.A. L.896 J.D. [Borland&G.]
Gagel, Lynn M. ... '69 '95 C.97 B.S. L.150 J.D. Corp. Coun., Roche Diagnostics Corp.
Gagnon, Edwin L., (AV) ... '43 '68 C.679 B.A. L.1119 J.D. [Gagnon&D.]
Gagnon & Diehl, (AV) ... 55 Monument Circle
Gaidoo, Suzanne R. ... '77 '02 C.346 B.S. L.150 J.D. [Ⓐ Lewis&K.]
Gainey, Susan G. ... '73 '99 C.347 B.S. L.879 J.D. [Ⓐ Kightlinger&G.]
Gaither, Jeffrey R., (AV) ... '58 '83 C.347 B.S. L.345 J.D. [Bose M.&E.]
Galanti, Paul J. '38 '63 C.95 A.B. L.145 J.D.
(adm. in IL; not adm. in IN) Prof., Indiana Univ. Sch.of Law
Gallagher, Douglas G. ... '— '03 C.174 B.A. L.1119 J.D. [Ⓐ Woodard,E.M.M.&H.]
Gallivan, Bonnie L., (AV) ... '50 '83 C.347 A.B. L.345 J.D. [Ice M.]
Gallmeyer, Meg A. ... '72 '98 C.347 B.A. L.880 J.D. [Ⓐ Baker&D.]
Gambill, Mark G. '55 '80 C.472 B.A. L.117 J.D.
(adm. in OH; not adm. in IN) Dir. of Development, Simon Property Group
Gammon, Robert F., (BV) ... '27 '54 C.347 B.S. L.345 J.D. Co. J.
Gandy, Kenneth A. '62 '88 C.347 B.S. L.345 J.D.
[Woodard,E.M.M.&H.] (See Pat. Sect.)
Gannon, John Russell, (CV) ... '68 '94 C&L.347 B.S., J.D. [Gannon&C.]
Gannon, Thomas P. ... '61 '90 C.347 B.A. L.345 J.D. Assoc. Univ. Coun., IN Univ.
Gannon & Ciyou, P.C., (CV) ... 11252 Blackwalnut Point
Gant, Asina C. ... '— '04 C.1142 B.A. L.329 J.D. [Ⓐ Barnes&T.]
Garau, Jerry A., (AV) ... '60 '86 C.265 B.A. L.345 J.D. [Findling G.G.&P.]
Garcia, Joel G. '66 '93 C&L.347 B.S., J.D.
Legal Counsel, Automotive Finance Corporation
Garcia, Luther T. ... '62 '94 C.108 B.A. L.345 J.D. 136 E. Market St., Ste. 800
Garcia, Mario ... '73 '99 C.63 B.S. L.347 J.D. [Brattain&M.]
Gard, Julia Spoor ... '— '97 C.63 B.S. L.879 J.D. [Ⓐ Barnes&T.]
Gardner, Brant O. ... '63 '88 C.937 B.A. L.893 J.D. [Baker&D.]
Gardner, John A., (AV) ... '61 '86 C.347 B.S. L.345 J.D. [Baker&D.]
Gardner, Ryan K. ... '78 '04 C.347 B.A. L.345 J.D. [Ⓐ Lewis W.]
Garelick, Robert A., (AV) ... '41 '66 C.347 A.B. L.1119 J.D. [Cohen G.&G.]
Garfield, Helen '25 '67 C.597 B.S.J. L.174 J.D.
(adm. in CO; not adm. in IN) Prof. of Law, Ind. Univ. Law Sch.
Gargula, Mark C., (AV) ... '56 '81 C&L.602 B.B.A., J.D. 5838 Carrollton Ave.
Garrard, William I. ... '32 '59 C.894 A.B. L.1119 J.D. Ct. of App. J.
Garrett, Trent L. ... '66 '97 C.992 B.A. L.1119 J.D. Staff Attys., Simon Property Group
Garrettson, James M. ... '47 '74 C.207 B.A. L.1119 J.D. 5733 Gilford Ave.
Garrison, Christopher L., (BV) ... '57 '83 C.347 B.S. L.345 J.D. [Garrison&K.]
Garrison, J. Gregory, (AV) ... '48 '73 C.347 B.S. L.345 J.D. [Garrison&K.]
Garrison & Kiefer, P.C., (AV) ... 8720 Castle Creek Parkway Suite 200
Garver, Chip ... '68 '93 C.473 B.S. L.851 J.D. [Baker&D.]
Garver, Fred W. ... '— '64 C.347 B.S. L.1119 J.D. [Ⓒ Stewart&I.]
Garvey, William J. '39 '64 C&L.734 B.S., LL.B.
(adm. in MO; not adm. in IN) Ex. V.P., Simon Property Group
Garvin, Norman R., (AV) ... '48 '73 C.346 B.A. L.345 J.D. [Scopelitis,G.L.&H.]
Gaskin, John R., (AV) '61 '87 C.347 B.A. L.345 J.D.
Sr. V.P., Dep. Gen. Coun. & Secy., Duke-Weeks Realty Corp.
Gaston, Keith A., (AV) ... '53 '79 C.357 B.A. L.345 J.D. [Stewart&I.]
Gaston, Lawrence W., Jr., (AV) ... '40 '66 C.178 A.B. L.345 LL.B. [Gaston,C.&G.]
Gaston, Cavanaugh & Giesel, (AV) ... 7168 Graham Rd., Ste. 160
Gath, Neil E., (BV) ... '59 '84 C.30 B.A. L.150 J.D. 1213 N. Arlington Ave.
Gaughan, Mary C. ... '— '87 C.679 B.A. L.345 J.D. [Hall,R.K.H.&L.]
Gaunt, Thomas J. ... '58 '96 C.679 B.S. L.851 B.S. 5525 South Meridian Street
Gauss, Robert L. ... '68 '93 C.210 B.A. L.347 J.D. [Ice M.]
Gavin, Brad S. ... '60 '95 C.679 B.S. L.1194 J.D. 302 W. Washington St., Rm. E208
Gavit, George B., (AV) ... '28 '53 C.894 A.B. L.1119 J.D. 1 Amer. Sq.
Gaylo, Paul J. '61 '91 C.45 B.S. L.910 J.D.
Assoc.Gen. Patent Coun., Eli Lilly & Co. (Pat.)
Geddes, Robert W., (AV) ... '29 '62 C.347 B.S. L.345 J.D. [Hume S.G.G.&S.]
Geib, Helen K. ... '— '00 C.222 B.A. L.365 J.D. [Ⓢ Barnes&T.] (See Pat. Sect.)
Gelinas, Julia Blackwell, (AV) ... '53 '78 C.741 B.A. L.345 J.D. [Locke R.]
Genetos, Philip C., (AV) ... '52 '77 C.188 A.B. L.1119 J.D. [Ice M.]
Gentry, Kristen L. ... '76 '02 C.347 B.S. L.345 J.D. [Ⓐ Krieg D.]
George, Linda S. ... '46 '91 C.1121 B.S. L.347 J.D. [Laudig G.R.&S.]
Gerber, Matthew A. ... '73 '00 C&L.347 B.A., J.D. Pub. Def. Agency
Gerhardt, Paul K., Attorney at Law, (BV) '57 '82
C.879 B.A. L.345 J.D. 3077 E. 98th St., Ste. 260
***Germano, Barbara J.**, (AV) ... '56 '89 C&L.347 B.A., J.D. [Findling G.G.&P.]*
Gerritzen, Daniel J. ... '69 '97 C.347 B.S. L.1119 J.D. [Ⓐ Bingham M.]
Gerth, Mark D., (AV) ... '52 '77 C.347 A.B. L.1119 J.D. [Kightlinger&G.]
Getty, Michael G., (AV) ... '62 '87 C.477 B.A. L.801 J.D. [Hill,F.M.F.&M.]
Gewirtz, Michael I. '46 '72 C.446 B.A. L.273 J.D.
Admn. Law J., U.S. Soc. Sec. Admn.
Geyer, Rebecca W. ... '74 '99 C&L.347 B.A., J.D. [Frank&K.]

Gfell, Kevin J. ... '— '04 C.347 B.S. L.345 J.D. [Ⓐ Hall,R.K.H.&L.]
Ghosh, Michael ... '73 '99 C.210 B.A. L.345 J.D. [Ⓐ Feiwell&H.]
Giacone, Gina M. ... '70 '95 C.801 B.S. L.880 J.D. [Ice M.]
Gibbons, Philip J., Jr. ... '67 '96 C.602 B.A. L.347 J.D. [Haskin L.&L.]
Gibson, Jeffrey S. ... '— '00 C.347 B.A. L.1119 J.D. [Ⓐ Cohen&M.]
Giesel, Richard M. ... '62 '95 C.150 B.A. L.421 J.D. [Gaston,C.&G.]
Gifford, Keith E. ... '65 '94 C&L.347 B.A., J.D. [Ⓐ M.Norris]
Gifford, Patricia J. ... '38 '68 C.945 A.B. L.347 J.D. Supr. Ct. J.
Gifford, Ronald D., (AV) ... '58 '85 C.477 B.A. L.276 J.D. [Baker&D.]
Gigowski, William J., Jr. ... '57 '94 C.688 B.S. L.347 J.D. Allison Engine Co., Inc.
Gilchrist, Scott D. ... '66 '92 C.347 B.A. L.345 J.D. [Ⓐ Cohen&M.]
Gilday, James K., (BV) ... '56 '86 C.973 A.B. L.345 J.D. [Gilday&Assoc.]

Gilday & Associates, P.C., (BV)
Bank One Center Tower, 111 Monument Circle, Suite 3300, 46204-5176
Telephone: 317-624-0033 Fax: 317-638-0300
Email: lawyer@gildaylegal.com URL: http://www.lawyers.com/gildaylegal
James K. Gilday.
Tax Law, Taxation, Tax Controversies, Real Estate Tax, Real Estate, Business Law, Business Planning, Contracts, Business Litigation, Business Enterprises, Corporate Law, Partnership Law, Limited Liability Company Law, Small Businesses, Business Formations, Starting a Business, Buying and Selling a Business, Wills, Probate, Trusts and Estates, Asset Protection, Estate Planning, Non-profit Charitable Organizations.
See Professional Biographies, INDIANAPOLIS, INDIANA

Giles, Cassandra A. ... '78 '04 C.347 B.S. L.345 J.D. [Ⓐ Ice M.]
Gilliland, John C., II, (AVⓉ) ... '45 '79 C.645 B.A. L.276 J.D. [Gilliland&C.]

Gilliland & Caudill, (AVⓉ) BR
3905 Vincennes Road, Suite 204, 46268
Telephone: 317-704-2400 Fax: 317-704-2410URL: URL: http://www.gilliland.com
Email: thefirm@gilliland.com URL: http://www.lawyers.com/gilliland
John C. Gilliland, II. Associates: Robert W. Markette, Jr.; Jennifer S. Milligan. Of Counsel: Virginia Wright Caudill.
Health Law, Labor and Employment Law, Administrative Law, Civil Litigation, Corporate Law, Privacy Law.
See Professional Biographies, INDIANAPOLIS, INDIANA

Gilliom, Richard L., (AV) ... '21 '50 C.108 A.B. L.345 LL.B. 231 E. Ohio St.‡
Gilman, David E. ... '41 '70 C.347 A.B. L.1119 J.D. 4271 N. High School Rd.‡
Gilpin, Kimberly M. W. '65 '90 C.265 B.A. L.300 J.D.
V.P., Asst. Gen. Cnsl, Lease Adm, Finish Line, Inc.
Gimple, Ronald S. '40 '70 C.251 B.B.A. L.1003 J.D.
(adm. in OH; not adm. in IN) V.P., Develop., Simon Debartolo Grp.
Girk, Robert R., (AV) ... '14 '42 C.494 L.347 LL.B. [Ⓒ Robinson W.&Y.]
Givan, Richard M. ... '21 '52 C.347 L.345 LL.B. Ret. Chief Jus.‡
Given, David A., (BV) ... '62 '87 C&L.339 A.B., J.D. [Baker&D.]
Givens, David W., (AV) ... '32 '60 C.894 A.B. L.345 J.D. 1 Indiana Sq.
Glass, G. Frederick, (AV) ... '59 '84 C.347 B.A. L.345 J.D. [Baker&D.]
Glawe, Caryn M. ... '79 '04 C.108 B.A. L.597 J.D. [Ⓐ Baker&D.]
Glazier, Mark A., (AV) ... '68 '93 C.347 B.A. L.94 J.D. [Miroff,C.&W.]
Glazier, Steven J., (BV) ... '56 '80 C.347 B.S. L.345 J.D. [Cohen G.&G.]
Glazner, M. Kristin ... '77 '02 C.108 B.A. L.347 J.D. [Ⓐ Baker&D.]
Gleason, Charles T., (AV) ... '27 '52 C.347 A.B. L.345 LL.B. [Wood T.G.M.&H.] ‡
Gleason, Charles Thomas '50 '79 C.347 B.S. L.365 J.D.
Gen. Coun. & V.P. of Opers., Dallman Industrial Corp.
Gleaves, A. Frank, III, (BV) ... '38 '71 C.108 B.S. L.345 J.D. Dep. Pros. Atty.
Glenn, Lisa M. ... '63 '00 C.344 B.S. L.347 J.D. [Ⓐ Krieg D.]
Glesing, Charles R., Jr. ... '55 '90 C.999 B.A. L.347 J.D. [Ⓒ Buehler&Assoc.]
Goble, Willis R., Jr., (BV) ... '54 '82 C.347 B.A. L.345 J.D. 8127 Lieber Rd.
Goddard, Philip ... '45 '72 C.347 B.S. L.345 J.D. Chf. Coun.
Godich, John Paul ... '44 '69 C.674 A.B. L.976 LL.B. U.S. Mag. J.
Goebel, Edward L., Jr., (BV) ... '31 '65 C.249 B.S. L.345 LL.B. 120 E. Market St.
Gohman, L. Richard, (AV) ... '— '71 C&L.347 A.B., J.D. [Hall,R.K.H.&L.]
Goldenberg, Jill E., (BV) ... '68 '93 C.347 B.S. L.94 J.D. [Cohen G.&G.]
Goldman, Rori Lisa, (BV) ... '70 '96 C.347 B.A. L.1019 J.D. [Hill,F.M.F.&M.]
Goldner, Lisa McKinney ... '66 '92 C.802 B.A. L.347 J.D. [Bose M.&E.]
Goldstein, Alan H., (AV) ... '44 '69 C.347 A.B. L.345 J.D. [Ice M.]
Goldstein, Jame S. ... '57 '93 C.347 B.S.N. L.345 J.D. 135 N. Pennsylvania
Gole, Richard A., and Associates '45 '70
C.347 B.S. L.1119 J.D. 7002 Graham Road, Suite 200.
Golson-Dunlap, Jenice ... '51 '77 C&L.329 B.A., J.D. 1 Virginia Avenue

Gonon, Richard B., (BV) '55 '84 C.690 B.A. L.398 J.D.
9465 Counselors Row, Suite 200, 46240
Telephone: 317-805-4816 Fax: 317-805-4817
Email: rgonon@aol.com URL: http://www.rbgononlaw.com
Collection Agency Representation, Collections, Commercial Law, Creditor's Rights in Bankruptcy, Fair Debt Collection Practices Act Defense Litigation, Subrogation.
See Professional Biographies, INDIANAPOLIS, INDIANA

Gonzalez, Cheryl A. ... '— '04 C.210 B.A. L.494 J.D. [Ⓐ Barnes&T.]

Gonzalez, Saggio & Harlan, L.L.P., (CV)
201 North Illinois Street, Suite 1900, 46204 ⊙
Telephone: 317-686-9800 Fax: 317-686-9821
Email: main@gshllp.com URL: http://www.gshllp.com
Miriam A. Rich.
Business and Corporate Law, Civil Litigation, Insurance Defense Law, Equal Opportunities and Employment, School Law, Municipal Finance, Business and Commercial Litigation, Real Estate, Construction, Condemnation Law, Environmental, Taxation, Utilities Law, Trials and Appeals, Government Relations.
Representative Clients: Accenture; Alliant Energy; Bear, Stears & Co.; Chubb Insurance Company; City of Milwaukee; CNH Global N.V.; Darden Restaurants, Inc.; Denny's; Eastman Kodak Company; E.I. du Pont de Nemours and Company.
West Des Moines, Iowa Office: 1501 42nd Street, Suite 465, 50266. Telephone: 515-453-8509. Fax: 515-267-1408.
Cincinnati, Ohio Office: Carew Tower, 441 Vine Street, Suite 3615, 45202. Telephone: 513-651-3456. Fax: 513-651-3446.
Milwaukee, Wisconsin Office: 225 East Michigan, 4th Floor, 53202. Telephone: 414-277-8500. Fax: 414-277-8521.
Chicago, Illinois Office: 208 LaSalle Street, Suite 1460, 60604. Telephone: 312-236-0475. Facsimile: 312-236-1750.
See Professional Biographies, INDIANAPOLIS, INDIANA

Good, Raymond, (AV) ... '29 '61 C.107 B.S.M.E. L.347 J.D. [Ⓒ Locke R.]
Good, Richard P., Jr. ... '32 '59 C&L.347 B.S., J.D. Sup. Ct. J.
Gooden, Alicia A. ... '70 '96 C&L.347 B.A., J.D. Master Comr.
Gooden, William W., (AV) ... '68 '96 C.63 B.S. L.1119 J.D. [Pastore&G.]
Goodin, Gary P., (BV) ... '63 '90 C&L.347 B.S., J.D. [Goodin,O.&B.]
Goodin, James A., (AV) ... '47 '73 C.436 B.A. L.345 J.D. [Goodin A.&M.]

Goodin Abernathy & Miller, L.L.P., (AV)
Keystone at the Crossing, 8900 Keystone Crossing Suite 1100, 46240
Telephone: 317-843-2606 Fax: 317-574-3095
URL: http://www.gamlawyers.com

(This Listing Continued)

Goodin Abernathy & Miller, L.L.P. (Continued)

James A. Goodin; Jon C. Abernathy; Patrick L. Miller; Karl G. Popowics; Christopher E. Clark; James R. Browne. Associates: Thomas B. Bays; Christie A. Seifert; Bradley J. Schulz; Lia R. Lukaart. Of Counsel: Joseph P. Murdock (1928-2003); Wilson S. Stober; R.D. Zink; Amy White Sevier; Robert C. Lee.
Civil Litigation, Corporate, Business, Real Estate, Insurance Defense, Employment and ERISA Litigation, Aviation and Transportation Law, Probate and Estate Planning, Estate Administration, Family/Domestic Relations, Mediation and Alternative Dispute Resolution.
Representative Clients: Allstate Insurance Companies; American National Property and Casualty Co.; Builder's Square; Continental Loss Adjusting Service; Construction Associates, Inc.; Continental Western Insurance Company; Economy Fire & Casualty; General Casualty Companies.
See Professional Biographies, INDIANAPOLIS, INDIANA

Goodin, Orzeske & Blackwell, P.C., (BV) .... 9102 N. Meridian Street, Suite 400
Goodman, Evan Dee .... '41 '69 C.346 A.B. L.862 J.D. Supr. Ct. J.
Goodson, Spencer P. ....'— '04 C.303 B.A. L.477 J.D. [⊠ Barnes&T.] (See Pat. Sect.)
Gordon, Gregg S. ....'59 '96 C.347 B.S. L.345 J.D. [⊠ Dale&E.]
Gordon, Kellye M. .... '69 '03 C.347 B.S. L.345 J.D. [⊠ Baker&D.]
Gordon, Richard S. '57 '83
C.696 B.A. L.893 J.D. Dir. of Policy & Planning, Off. of the Gov.
Gosnell, Paul C. .... '60 '94 C.886 B.S.M.E. L.345 J.D. 5542 Milhouse Rd.
Gottschlich, Michael H. .... '— '91 C&L.347 B.A., J.D. [Barnes&T.]
Gotwald, Gregory M. ....'77 '04 C.701 B.S. L.1194 J.D. [⊠ Plews S.R.&B.]
Gotway, Patricia H. .... '53 '82 C.98 B.A. L.345 J.D. 5225 N. New Jersey St.
Goudy, Diane M. ....'65 '93 C.63 B.S. L.347 J.D. 155 East Market Street Suite 400
Gould, Jeffrey S. ....'54 '84 C.347 B.S. L.345 J.D. Kosene & Kosene Develop. Co.
Grabb, Laurence W. '40 '66 C.234 B.S. L.339 LL.B.
(adm. in IL; not adm. in IN) General Counsel, eGIX, Inc.
Grable, Kirk E. .... '— '88 C&L.347 B.A., J.D. [© Barnes&T.]
Graham, Donald J., (AV) .... '55 '80 C.679 B.S. L.345 J.D. [Bingham M.]
Graham, Jeffrey J. ....'— '98 C.602 B.A. L.879 J.D. [⊠ Sommer B.]

Graham, Jennifer L., (BV) '47 '83 C.1260 B.B.A. L.345 J.D.
1111 E. 54th Street, Suite 138, 46220
Telephone: 317-257-7640 Fax: 317-257-7642
Commercial Litigation, Plaintiffs Personal Injury, Bankruptcy Litigation, Contract Litigation.
See Professional Biographies, INDIANAPOLIS, INDIANA

Grahn, Charles R., (BV) .... '52 '77 C.347 A.B. L.345 J.D. [Clark,Q.M.S.&G.]
Grahn, Raymond J., (AV) .... '21 '45 C.108 B.A. L.345 LL.B. [© Clark,Q.M.S.&G.]
Gramelspacher, Mark B. '64 '90 C.602 B.B.A. L.1119 J.D.
Pres. & CEO, EverGreen Capital Management Co.
Grand, Robert T., (AV) .... '— '83 C.894 A.B. L.345 J.D. [Barnes&T.]
Grandy, Charles A. ....'64 '93 C&L.228 B.S.E.E., J.D. Atty., Eli Lilly & Co.
Grant, Carolyn Small, (BV) ....'49 '76 C.347 A.B. L.879 J.D. [Grant&G.]
Grant, Mark D. .... '59 '84 C.679 B.S. L.326 J.D. [© Ice M.]
Grant, Robert G., (BV) .... '47 '74 C.347 B.S. L.345 J.D. [Grant&G.]
Grant & Grant, (BV) ....6419 N. Carrollton Ave.
Grau, Thomas J., (AV) ....'50 '83 C.63 B.S. L.345 J.D. [Drewry S.V.]
Graub, John W., II, (AV) ....'48 '75 C.347 B.S. L.345 J.D. [Hostetler&K.]
Gray, David W., (AV) ....'50 '75 C.347 B.S. L.345 J.D. [Lewis&K.]
Gray, George Clyde, (AV) .... '44 '69 C.602 A.B. L.276 J.D. [Gray,R.R.&F.]
Gray, Mark S., (AV) ....'55 '82 C.347 B.A. L.345 J.D. [⊠ Doyle&F.]
Gray, Mark William, (AV) .... '16 '40 C.347 B.S. L.1119 LL.B. [© Kightlinger&G.]
Gray, Maxwell, (AV) ....'38 '64 C.347 B.S. L.1119 J.D. [Lowe G.S.&D.]
Gray, Stephen Gerald, (BV) ....'49 '82 C.679 B.S. L.345 J.D. 55 Monument Cir.
Gray, Wallace T. '51 '76 C.347 A.B. L.421 J.D.
Vice President & General Counsel, Key Benefit Administrators, Inc.
Gray, Robinson, Ryan & Fox, P.C., (AV) ....8122 South Meridian Street
Grayson, Ann S. ....'— '95 C.473 B.A. L.494 J.D. [⊠ Barnes&T.]
Green, Anthony H. ....'— '04 C.1070 B.S. L.345 J.D. [⊠ Barnes&T.]
Green, Barbara McCarthy .... '54 '85 C.821 B.A. L.345 J.D. 1311 Fox Hill Dr.‡
Green, John C., (AV) ....'42 '69 C.347 B.S. L.345 J.D. [Hume S.G.G.&S.]
Green, Kelly J. ....'69 '04 C.63 B.S. L.345 J.D. [⊠ Krieg D.] (⊙Carmel)
Green, William J. ....'66 '92 C&L.339 36 S. Pennsylvania Street, Suite 600
Greenberg, Harold '38 '63
C.831 B.A. L.659 J.D. Prof. of Law, Indiana Univ., Sch. of Law
Greenlee, Kevin .... '71 '01 C&L.347 B.A., J.D. 2134 Pamela Drive
Greer, Charles E., (AV) .... '45 '76 C.347 B.S. L.1119 J.D. 5581 Sunset Lane‡
Greer, Douglas E. '59 '87 C.347 B.S. L.345 J.D.
V.P., Dep. Gen. Coun. & Asst. Sec., Duke Realty Corporation
Greer, Marie Troendle ....'71 '98 C.1216 B.A. L.801 J.D. [⊠ Cline F.C.L.&C.]
Gregerson, Gerard L., (AV) ....'63 '89 C&L.1119 B.A., J.D. [Bingham M.]
Gregory, Danielle L. ....'70 '97 C.63 B.A. L.345 J.D. Dep. Pub. Def.
Greising, Robert A., (AV) ....'53 '79 C.210 B.A. L.345 J.D. [Krieg D.]
Gresham, David A. ....'58 '89 C.63 B.M. L.1119 J.D. Amer. United Life Ins. Co.
Gresk, Paul D., (AV) ....'51 '79 C.347 B.S. L.345 J.D. [Gresk&S.]
Gresk & Singleton, (AV) ....950 N. Meridian St.
Gretencord, Laura S. '65 '91 C&L.347 B.S., J.D.
Assoc. Coun.& Asst. Secy., Marsh Supermarkets, Inc.
Grider, Christopher W. ....'67 '93 C.210 B.A. L.879 J.D. P.O. Box 441474
Gridley, Doreen J. ....'55 '95 C.657 B.S. L.347 J.D. [Ice M.] (See Pat. Sect.)
Griesemer, Steven W. ....'68 '96 C.347 B.S. L.1117 J.D. [⊠ Lewis&K.]
Griffin, Gerald A., M.D. .... '52 '96 C&L.347 J.D. [⊠ Wilson,K.&W.]
Griffin, Jane E. ....'40 '75 C.347 A.B. L.345 J.D. [O'Koon H.]
Griffin, Maureen O'Brien, (AV) ......'— '83 C.679 B.S.N. L.347 J.D. [Hall,R.K.H.&L.]
Griffin, Michael L. .... '73 '98 C.679 B.S. L.1119 J.D. [⊠ Krieg D.]
Griffin, Steven D. ....'55 '90 C&L.347 B.A., J.D. Ind. Chamber of Com.
Griffith, Carlene J. ....'56 '93 C.018 B.A. L.900 J.D. 115 W. Washington St.
Griffith, Kevin P., (AV) .... '61 '90 C.679 B.S.E.E. L.347 J.D. [Baker&D.]
Griffith, Matthew A., (BV) ....'67 '92 C.894 B.S. L.221 J.D. [Thrasher G.&V.]
Griggs, Edward Sean, (BV) .... '— '94 C.701 B.S.Ch.E. L.345 J.D. [Barnes&T.]
Grills, Nelson G., (AV) .... '12 '37 C.347 B.S. L.1119 J.D. 55 Monument Circle
Griman, Amy M. ....'70 '95 C.265 B.A. L.201 J.D. Bank One Wealth Mgmt.
Grisham, Michael J. '56 '82 C.347 B.S. L.345 J.D.
Global Coml. Coun., Compl. Leader, Dow AgroSciences
Grodner, Geoffrey M., (BV) ....'50 '75 C.347 A.B. L.1119 J.D. [Mallor C.G.&B.] ⊙
Groen, Eric J. ....'56 '85 C.679 B.S.M.E. L.117 J.D. [Baker&D.] (See Pat. Sect.)
Gron, Gary M., (AV) '38 '66
C.124 B.S.M.E. L.1003 J.D. [© Woodard,E.M.M.&H.] (See Pat. Sect.)
Gross, Janet M. ....'43 '78 C&L.347 A.B., J.D. Reg. Dir., Bank One Trust Co.
Grosser, Randall B. ....'50 '94 C.347 D.V.M. L.375 J.D. Post Pet Hospital, Inc.
Grossman, Audrey K., (AV) .... '33 '77 C.910 A.B. L.345 J.D. [© Miroff,C.&W.]
Groth, Liane ....'79 '05 C.347 B.A. L.1119 J.D. [⊠ Bingham M.]
Groth, Steven D., (BV) ....'62 '87 C.339 B.S. L.910 J.D. [Bose M.&E.]
Groth, William R., (AV) .... '50 '75 C.108 B.A. L.345 J.D. [Fillenwarth,D.G.&T.]
Grove, Jeffrey W. '43 '69 C.372 B.A. L.273 J.D.
(adm. in DC; not adm. in IN) Prof., Ind. Univ. Sch. of Law
Grove, Kathleen S. ....'48 '79 C.597 B.S. L.345 J.D. ABA
Grubbs, J. Michael, (AV) .... '— '88 C.210 B.A. L.345 J.D. [Barnes&T.]
Gruber, Andrew W. ....'73 '99 C.608 B.A. L.851 J.D. [⊠ Bingham M.]
Gullick, Robert H., (AV) .... '40 '71 C.347 A.B. L.1119 J.D. 6514 RTalston Ave.
Gustafson, Constance J., (AV) ....'51 '77 C.347 B.A. L.345 J.D. [© Hill,F.M.F.&M.]
Gutman, Gretchen K., (BV) ....'— '97 C.347 A.B. L.345 J.D. [© Sommer B.]
Gutting, James M., (AV) ....'— '86 C.346 B.S. L.345 J.D. [Barnes&T.]
Gutwein, Philip J., II ....'73 '01 C.894 B.A. L.1119 J.D. [⊠ Baker&D.]
Guy, Joseph R., (BV) ....'54 '81 C.347 B.S. L.117 J.D. [Guy]
Guy Law Offices, (BV) ....3850 West 86th Street
Gwitt, Brian D. ....'72 '99 C.999 B.A. L.107 J.D. [Ice M.]
Haas, Karl P., (AV) ....'60 '85 C.347 B.S. L.345 J.D. [Wallack S.&H.]
Habegger, Benjamin M. ....'— '99 C.303 B.A. L.345 J.D. [⊠ Ice M.]
Habig, Eric K. ....'71 '99 C.210 B.A. L.345 J.D. [⊠ Scopelitis,G.L.&H.]
Hackman, Marvin L., (AV) ....'34 '59 C.1024 A.B. L.1119 J.D. [Hackman H.&C.]
Hackman, Stephen J., (AV) .... '59 '84 C.347 B.S. L.1119 J.D. [Ice M.]

Hackman Hulett & Cracraft, LLP, (AV) ⊞
One Indiana Square, Suite 2400, 46204-2030
Telephone: 317-636-5401 Facsimile: 317-686-3288
URL: http://www.hhclaw.com
Members of Firm: Marvin L. Hackman; Robert S. Hulett; Michael B. Cracraft; Timothy K. Ryan; Philip B. McKiernan; Vicki L. Anderson; John D. Cochran, Jr.; Mark S. Alderfer; David J. Bodle;—Steven W. Krohne; Ellen Morrison Townsend; Joseph M. Hendel; Anthony S. Ridolfo, Jr.; Davina L. Curry.
General Civil Practice. Corporate, Acquisitions and Mergers, Real Estate, Public Utility, Administrative, Municipal Finance, Environmental, Litigation in Federal and State Courts, Commercial, State and Local Taxation, Probate and Estate Planning.
Representative Clients: Citizens Gas & Coke Utility; F.C. Tucker Company, Inc.; Texas Eastern Products Pipeline Co.; Indiana Municipal Power Agency; Indiana Municipal Electric Association, Inc.; St. Paul Fire and Marine Insurance Co.; State Farm Mutual Automobile Insurance Co.; Allstate Insurance Co.; Walker Information, Inc.; I.V.C. Industrial Coatings, Inc.
See Professional Biographies, INDIANAPOLIS, INDIANA

Hadler, Joseph W., (BV) .... '24 '51 C.108 A.B. L.345 J.D. 151 N. Delaware St.
Hadler, Patrick J., (BV) .... '25 '49 C.108 A.B. L.345 J.D. 151 N. Delaware St.
Hagedorn, Jeffrey W. ....'70 '97 C.929 B.A. L.345 J.D Dep. Gen. Atty.
Hagemier, Robert C., (AV) .... '44 '70 C.210 B.A. L.345 J.D. [Hagemier,A.&S.]
Hagemier, Allen & Smith, (AV) .... 10 West Market Street
Hagenow, Christopher C., (BV) ....'67 '92 C.602 B.A. L.902 J.D. [Hopper B.]
Hagerman, Nathan J. .... '70 '96 C.679 B.A. L.477 J.D. [⊠ Baker&D.] ‡
Haggard, Brandi A. '71 '99 C.63 B.S. L.345 J.D.
36 South Pennsylvania Street, Suite 290
Haggerty, Jay B., (AV) ....'26 '55 C.108 L.345 LL.B. 3045 S. Meridian St.
Haggerty, Jay J., (AV) .... '56 '89 C&L.347 B.A., J.D. [Haggerty,H.&M.]
Haggerty, Jon F., (BV) .... '68 '94 C&L.347 B.A., J.D. [Haggerty,H.&M.]
Haggerty, Judson F., (AV) ....'25 '51 C.108 L.345 LL.B. 3045 S. Meridian St.
Haggerty, Haggerty and Maschmeyer, (AV) ....3045 South Meridian Street
Hague, Joshua D. ....'72 '98 C.347 B.A. L.345 J.D. [⊠ Krieg D.]
Hahn, Andrew ....'67 '95 C.1024 B.S. L.209 J.D. 320 N. Meridian St., Ste. 1006
Hahn, Gregory F., (BV) .... '49 '74 C.249 B.S. L.345 J.D. [Tabbert H.E.&W.]
Hahn, Richard F., (BV) .... '32 '62 C.108 A.B. L.345 J.D. 155 E. Market St.
Hahn, William A., II .... '— '00 C.894 B.A. L.602 J.D. [⊠ Barnes&T.]
Hailey, Richard D., (AV) ....'49 '74 C.108 B.A. L.347 J.D. [Ramey&H.]
Haines, Paul Lowell, (BV) ....'53 '90 C.827 B.A. L.347 J.D. [Baker&D.]
Haith, Aaron E., (BV) .... '51 '78 C.1378 B.S. L.345 J.D. 151 N. Delaware, Rm. 740
Halbrook, Kari H. .... '73 '00 C.679 B.A. L.345 J.D. [© Ice M.]
Hale, Stephanie A. ....'— '99 C.1150 B.A. L.602 J.D. [⊠ Sommer B.]
Hall, Bowman N., (BV) ....'13 '59 C.476 B.S. L.345 J.D. 2001 Remington Pl.‡
Hall, Everett I. ....'08 '35 C.347 A.B. L.345 J.D. 2142 W. 44th St.‡
Hall, Jean A. '23 '81 C.054 B.A. L.285 J.D.
(adm. in WA; not adm. in IN) 6908 Chrysler St.‡
Hall, Ralph F. ....'52 '77 C.347 A.B. L.477 J.D. [© Baker&D.]
Hall, Richard J., (AV) .... '— '92 C.63 B.S. L.597 J.D. [Barnes&T.]
Hall, Richard M., (AV) ....'55 '81 C.347 B.S. L.345 J.D. [Hall G.]
Hall, Steven R., (AV) ....'46 '74 C.63 B.S. L.345 J.D. [Miller,W.M.&H.]
Hall, Terry E. ....'54 '00 C.846 B.A. L.1119 J.D. [⊠ Baker&D.]
Hall Griffin, P.C., (AV) ....9000 Keystone Crossing, Suite 230

Hall, Render, Killian, Heath & Lyman, P.S.C., (AV) ⊞
Suite 2000, One American Square Box 82064, 46282 ⊙
Telephone: 317-633-4884 Fax: 317-633-4878
Email: info@hallrender.com URL: http://www.HallRender.com
John C. Render; R. Terry Heath; Stephen W. Lyman; L. Richard Gohman; Jeffrey Peek; Clifford A. Beyler; Timothy C. Lawson; Douglas P. Long; William H. Thompson; Timothy W. Kennedy; Steven H. Pratt; N. Kent Smith; Mary C. Gaughan; Fred J. Bachmann; Maureen O'Brien Griffin; Robert A. Hicks; Kevin P. Speer; Gregory W. Moore (Resident, Troy, Michigan Office); Donald R. Russell; Jeffrey W. Short; Clifton E. Johnson; Gerald L. Stovall (Resident, Louisville, Kentucky Office); Jon F. Spadorcia; John C. Meade; Gregg M. Wallander; Samuel H. DeShazer (Resident, Louisville, Kentucky Office); Todd J. Selby; James B. Hogan; Christopher L. Riegler; William D. Roberts (Resident, Louisville, Kentucky Office); A. Courtney Guild, Jr. (Resident, Louisville, Kentucky Office); René Remek Savarise (Resident, Louisville, Kentucky Office); James R. Willey, Jr.; Keith D. Barber; Susan D. Bizzell; Douglas M. Kinser; Kimberly Jo Commins (Resident, Troy, Michigan Office); Arthur F. deVaux (Not admitted in IN; Resident, Troy, Michigan Office); Norris Cunningham; Juli K. Shields; John P. Ryan; Angela M. Smith; David B. Honig; Stephan C. Masoncup; Lawrence K. Coon (Resident, Milwaukee, Wisconsin Office); Scott J. Geboy (Resident, Milwaukee, Wisconsin Office); Linda S. McPike (Resident, Milwaukee, Wisconsin Office); Paul W. Seidenstricker (Resident, Milwaukee, Wisconsin Office); David H. Snow (Resident, Milwaukee, Wisconsin Office); Thomas R. Streifender (Resident, Milwaukee, Wisconsin Office); Scott W. Taebel (Resident, Milwaukee, Wisconsin Office); Lori A. Wink (Resident, Milwaukee, Wisconsin Office);—Kirk R. Jocham; Craig M. Williams; Adam J. Richter; Erin D. Abraham; Mary Liatti Hill; Monica C. Hocum (Resident, Milwaukee, Wisconsin Office); David C. Lind, II; Todd A. Nova (Resident, Milwaukee, Wisconsin Office); Edward L. Schoenbaechler (Resident, Louisville, Kentucky Office); Timothy A. McGeath; Barbara A. Killian; Thomas A. Jenkins; Jay P. Turner (Resident, Louisville, Kentucky Office); Charise R. Frazier; Michael J. Philbrick (Resident, Troy, Michigan Office); Laura M. Napiewocki (Resident, Troy, Michigan Office); Christopher J. Allman (Resident, Troy, Michigan Office); James M. Shafer; Douglas J. Kochell; Regan E. Tankersley; Jonathan C. Bumgarner; Charles P. Sukurs; Kevin A. Stella; Neal A. Cooper; Michael L. Kim; Christopher C. Eades; Jennifer Fouts Skeels; Elizabeth Callahan-Morris (Resident, Troy, Michigan Office); John F. Williams, III; Kristine S. Pyzyna; Lara D. Engelking, RN; Thomas D. Shrack; Joan L. Lowes (Resident, Troy, Michigan Office); Melissa L. Markey (Not admitted in IN); Adele Merenstein; Kathryn A. Elias; Karen D. Bolton (Resident, Troy, Michigan Office); Anjali M. Herke; Michael T. Batt; Dana E. Stutzman; Heather H. Macek; Brian C. Betner; Kevin J. Gfell; Robbin S. Craddock (Resident, Louisville, Kentucky Office). Counsel: G. Weldon Johnson; Colleen McKinley (Resident, Louisville, Kentucky Office). Of Counsel: Mark R. Adams (Resident, Troy, Michigan Office).
Health Law, Managed Care Law, Medical Malpractice Defense, Antitrust, Corporations, Labor and Employment, Mediation, Environmental, Employee Benefits, Securities, Probate and Estate Planning, Real Estate and Taxation Law. Litigation and Appeals, Public Finance, Medicare and Medicaid Reimbursement, Computer Law, Construction and Engineering Law, Intellectual Property.
Indianapolis North Office: Suite 820, 8402 Harcourt Road, 46260. Telephone: 317-871-6222. Fax: 317-338-3946.
Louisville, Kentucky Office: 614 West Main Street, Suite 4000, 40202. Telephone: 502-568-1890. Fax: 502-568-4878.
Troy, Michigan Office: Hall, Render, Killian, Heath & Lyman, PLLC, Columbia Center, Suite 315, 201 West Big Beaver Road, 48084. Telephone: 248-740-7505. Fax: 248-740-7501.

(This Listing Continued)

Hall, Render, Killian, Heath & Lyman, P.S.C. (Continued)

Milwaukee, Wisconsin Office: 411 East Wisconsin Avenue, Suite 900, 53202. Telephone: 414-721-0442. Fax: 414-721-0491.

See Professional Biographies, INDIANAPOLIS, INDIANA

Hallal, Jowdat "Joe" ... '39 '77 C.679 B.S. L.345 J.D. 1545 North Post Road
Ham, David J. ... '49 '79 C.1201 B.A. L.972 J.D. 1010 Fox Hill Drive
Ham, James H., III, (AV) ... '50 '75 C.679 B.S. L.597 J.D. [Baker&D.]
Hamer, David R., (AV) ... '45 '71 C.347 A.B. L.345 J.D. [Baker&D.]
Hamill, Thomas R., (BV) ... '51 '76 C.347 B.S. L.345 J.D. Dep. Atty. Gen.
Hamilton, Amy E. '59 '90
C.347 B.S. L.345 J.D. Asst. Gen. Pat. Coun., Eli Lilly & Co. (Pat.)
Hamilton, Anne M. ... '— '92 C.938 B.A. L.345 J.D. [🄲 Sommer B.]
Hamilton, Christopher P., (CV) ... '62 '89 C.210 B.A. L.910 J.D. [🄰 Yarling&R.]
Hamilton, David F. ... '57 '84 C.311 B.A. L.976 J.D. U.S. Dist. J.
Hamilton, David W., (BV) ... '59 '84 C.347 B.S. L.345 J.D. [Rowe&H.]
Hamilton, Derek C. '— '03 C.63 B.A. L.813 J.D.
(adm. in IL; not adm. in IN) [🄰 Baker&D.]
Hamilton, John M. ... '59 '87 C.309 A.B. L.1119 J.D. Lt. Gov. Off.
Hamilton, John W. ... '63 '93 C.198 B.A. L.902 J.D. [Wooden&M.]
Hamilton, W. James ... '72 '97 C.188 B.A. L.347 J.D. [🄰 Bose M.&E.]
Hamlett, Robert M., (BVⓉ) ... '43 '70 C.375 B.S.Che. L.734 J.D. [Frank&K.]
Hamm, Angela L. ... '74 '99 C.347 B.A. L.345 J.D. [🄰 Krieg D.] (⊙Carmel)
Hammel, Linda Y., (AV) ... '45 '75 C.347 B.M.E. L.345 J.D. [Yarling&R.]
Hammerle, Robert W., (AV) ... '46 '73 C.1216 B.A. L.347 J.D. 501 Indiana Ave., Ste. 200
Hammes, Joseph W., (BV) ... '46 '72 C.602 A.B. L.1119 J.D. [🄲 Tabbert H.E.&W.]
Hammond, Jarrell B., (AV) ... '55 '82 C.210 B.A. L.345 J.D. [Lewis W.]
Hammond, Jeffrey A. ... '73 '99 C.679 L.1119 J.D. [🄰 Wooden&M.]
Hammond, John R. ... '26 '58 C.210 A.B. L.345 LL.B. 5727 Madison Ave.
Hammond, John R., III, (AV) ... '54 '91 C.210 B.A. L.347 J.D. [Ice M.]
Hampton, M. Michele ... '57 '82 C.1024 B.S. L.607 J.D. 4318 E. 10th St.
Hanahan, Thomas M., (AV) ... '61 '86 C.602 B.A. L.345 J.D. [Wooden&M.]
Hancock, Morris W. ... '39 '66 C.344 A.B. L.345 J.D. Dept. of Vet. Affairs
Hancock, William J., (BV) ... '57 '82 C.347 B.S. L.345 J.D. [🄲 Harrison&M.]
Hand, John C. '30 '73 C.679 L.345 LL.B.
Sr. V.P., Gen. Coun. & Secy., Farm Bureau Ins. Cos.
Hanefeld, Stacy L., (CV) ... '71 '96 C&L.347 B.A., J.D. [Riley B.&E.]
Haney, Tammy K., (AV) ... '64 '90 C.63 B.A. L.1119 J.D. [Bose M.&E.]
Hanger, JauNae M. '59 '91 C.347 B.A. L.1119 J.D.
Exec. Asst., Ind. Dept. of Envir. Mgt.
Hankey, Charles D. ... '48 '73 C.894 B.A. L.1119 J.D. 434 E. New York St.
Hanley, J. Frank, II, (BV) ... '43 '70 C.302 L.574 LL.B. 4277 Lafayette Road
Hanley, John F. ... '55 '82 C.602 A.B. L.345 J.D. Supr. Ct. J.
Hanley, Marshall S., (AV) ... '52 '77 C.597 B.S. L.345 J.D. [Findling G.G.&P.]
Hanley, Michael L., (BV) ... '60 '85 C.221 B.S. L.345 J.D. 2124 E. Hanna Ave.
Hanley, Ruth Ann ... '34 '89 C.523 A.B. L.347 J.D. 8211 River Bay Dr., E.
Hannah, T. Jeffrey, (BV) ... '57 '82 C.347 A.B. L.345 J.D. Dir. & Coun., Anthem, Inc.
Hannon, Edward R., (AV) ... '53 '81 C.347 B.S.W. L.345 J.D. [Hannon H.&Assoc.]
Hannon Hutton & Associates, P.C., (AV) ... 320 North Meridian Street, Suite 600
Hannoy, Ann Bartlett, (BV) ... '58 '84 C.347 A.B. L.345 J.D. Alcholic Bev. Comm.
Hannoy, Douglas J., (BV) ... '60 '88 C.347 B.S. L.345 J.D. [Feiwell&H.]
Hanson, James H., (AV) ... '56 '81 C.243 B.A. L.345 J.D. [Scopelitis,G.L.&H.]
Hanson, Robert E. '48 '73 C&L.339 B.S., J.D.
(adm. in IL; not adm. in IN) Adm. Law J., Soc. Sec. Admn.
Hardamon, Donald L., (BV) ... '37 '66 C.347 B.S. L.345 J.D. 407 N. Fulton St., #100
Harden, Lanae M. ... '68 '95 C.846 B.A. L.1119 J.D. [🄲 Bingham M.]
Harden, Timothy M., (AV) ... '46 '75 C.679 B.A. L.345 J.D. [Krieg D.]
Hardin, Irene C. ... '10 '33 C.108 L.74 LL.B. 1337 Ridgeview Dr.
Hardy, Brandt N., (BV) '55 '81 C.347 B.A. L.345 J.D.
V.P. & Assoc. Coun., National City Bank, Indiana
Hardy, Frances Watson ... '55 '80 C.63 B.S. L.347 J.D. Prof., IN Univ. Sch. of Law
Hardy, William N., (BV) '50 '76 C.210 A.B. L.345 J.D.
V.P. & Gen. Coun., Em-Roe Sporting Goods Co., Inc.‡
Harkins, Melissa A. ... '73 '03 C.741 B.S. L.347 J.D. [🄲 Ice M.]
Harkness, Scott A., (BV) ... '67 '92 C.210 B.A. L.1119 J.D. [🄰 Norris C.&S.]
Harmon, Katherine A. ... '76 '01 C.347 B.A. L.1119 J.D. [🄰 Cohen&M.]
Harney, Edward F., Jr., (BV) ... '67 '93 C.679 B.A. L.879 J.D. [Hume S.G.G.&S.]
Harnish, J. Matt ... '67 '04 C.679 B.S. L.74 J.D. [🄰 Locke R.]
Harp, Jay Andrew, (BV) ... '59 '85 C.347 B.S. L.345 J.D. 4911 E. 56th St.
Harper, Gordon L. ... '46 '71 C&L.347 A.B., J.D. [G.L.Harper]
Harper, Thomas R. ... '65 '92 C.477 B.A. L.347 J.D. 150 E. Market St., Ste. 200
Harper, Gordon L., P.C. ... 4628 North Franklin Road
Harpring, Michael R. ... '65 '92 C.347 B.S. L.128 J.D. [Henderson D.W.&D.]
Harrell, Terry L. ... '64 '89 C.210 B.S. L.1119 J.D. Clk. Ind. Ct. of Appls.
Harrington, Michael J. '62 '88
C.20 B.A. L.178 J.D. Assoc. Gen. Coun., Eli Lilly Intl. Corp.
Harris, Brent A. '67 '95 C&L.347 B.S., J.D.
Dep. Chf. IP Coun., Boehringer Mannheim Corp. (Pat.)
Harris, Charles W. ... '46 '73 C.63 B.S. L.345 J.D. V.P., Ind. Voc. Tech. College
Harris, Edward W., III, (AV) ... '— '68 C.31 B.A. L.477 J.D. [Sommer B.]
Harris, Kevin D. '56 '86 C.346 B.S. L.209 J.D.
V.P., Sec. & Gen. Coun., National Conference of Ins. Guaranty Funds
Harris, Mark L. ... '55 '82 C&L.477 B.B.A., J.D. V.P., Society National Bank
Harris, Melanie E. ... '— '01 C.210 B.A. L.1541 J.D. [🄰 Ice M.]
Harrison, James D., (AV) ... '14 '37 L.347 J.D. [🄲 Harrison&M.]
Harrison, Lisa Erb, (BV) ... '67 '92 C.108 B.A. L.347 J.D. [🄲 Ice M.]

Harrison & Moberly, LLP, (AV)
135 North Pennsylvania Street, Suite 2100, 46204 ⊙
Telephone: 317-639-4511 Fax: 317-639-9565; 1-800-425-4511
Email: attorneys@h-mlaw.com URL: http://www.harrisonmoberly.com
Partners: Stephen E. Arthur; Timothy J. Hulett; Patricia Polis McCrory; Richard L. McOmber; Janet A. McSharar; Rory O'Bryan; Jeffrey W. Scripture; A. Donald Wiles, II; Paul (Rick) Rauch, III; Paul C. Sweeney; David Williams Russell. Counsel: R. Davy Eaglesfield, III; William J. Hancock (Resident, Carmel Office). Senior Counsel: Keith Beall; Robert J. Hoffman (Resident, Carmel Office). Special Counsel: James J. McGrath. Associates: Thaddeus R. Ailes (Resident, Carmel Office); Raymond A. Basile; Stephen D. LePage; Mark William Pfeiffer; Anderson R. White; A. Barclay Wong. Of Counsel: James D. Harrison.
Acquisitions and Mergers, Complex and Multi-District Litigation, Administrative Law, Antitrust and Trade Regulation. Appellate Practice (State and Federal), Arson and Fraud, Business Litigation, *Collections, Construction Law, Contracts, Corporate Law, Business Transactions*, Labor and Employment, Environmental Law, Environmental Compliance, Trusts and Estates, Financial Institutions, Health Care, Insurance Defense (First Party and Third Party) and Policyholder Law, Intellectual Property, Labor Law, Litigation, Medical Malpractice, Probate Litigation, Products Liability, Product Safety, Real Estate, Taxation (State, Federal, Estate and Gift), Toxic Torts, Trademarks, Copyrights, Warranty, Workers Compensation and Zoning, Planning and Land Use.
Marion Office: 315 South Adams Street, 3rd Floor, Marion, Indiana, 46952. Telephone: 765-673-6499.

See Professional Biographies, INDIANAPOLIS, INDIANA

Hart, Kathleen I., (BV) ... '66 '95 C&L.347 B.A., J.D. [Bose M.&E.]
Hartley, Robert L., (AV) ... '48 '75 C&L.347 B.A., J.D. [🄲 Locke R.]
Hartman, Michael Ryan, (AV) ... '55 '80 C&L.345 A.B., J.D. [Bingham M.]
Hartman, Richd. J., (BV) ... '30 '55 C.347 B.S. L.1119 LL.B. [Hartman&F.]
Hartman & Foutty, (BV) ... 155 E. Market St.
Harts, Jared A. ... '79 '05 C.114 B.S. L.345 J.D. [🄰 Locke R.]
Harvey, Eric A. ... '68 '04 C.999 L.344 J.D. [Cleveland&H.]
Harvey, William F. ... '32 '59 C.502 A.B. L.276 J.D. Prof., Ind. Univ. Law School
Hasbrook, Daniel T. ... '45 '75 C.210 B.A. L.345 J.D. V.P., AON
Hasbrook, William A., (AV) ... '48 '74 C.602 B.A. L.345 J.D. [Ruckelshaus,R.K.B.&H.]
Hash, Robert W., (BV) ... '65 '92 C&L.347 B.S., J.D. [Duffin&H.]
Haskett, David M., (AV) ... '44 '69 C.347 A.B. L.1119 J.D. [Locke R.]
Haskin, John H., (BV) ... '47 '77 C&L.347 B.S., J.D. [Haskin L.&L.]
Haskin Lauter & LaRue, P.C., (AV) ... 255 North Alabama Street
Hasler, Bradley David ... '75 '00 C.210 B.A. L.61 J.D. [🄰 Bingham M.]
Hassett, Robert F. ... '25 '51 C&L.424 A.B., J.D. Dep. Atty. Gen.
Hastings, Thomas E., (BV) ... '57 '83 C.894 B.A. L.345 J.D. 323 N. Delaware Street
Hatchett, David L. ... '71 '96 C&L.347 B.S., J.D. [Hatchett&H.]
Hatchett & Hauck LLP ... 111 Monument Cir., Ste. 301
Hatfield, Ben F., Jr. ... '18 '47 C.347 L.1119 LL.B. 1 Indiana Sq.‡
Hatfield, Beth E. ... '— '04 C.347 B.S. L.345 J.D. [🄰 Ice M.]
Hatfield Bell, Tanya R. ... '— '00 C.346 B.A. L.345 J.D. [🄰 Ogletree,D.N.S.&S.]
Hatton, Peter L., (AV) ... '48 '74 C.894 B.A. L.1119 J.D. [Baker&D.]
Hauber, John M. ... '68 '93 C.894 B.A. L.345 J.D. [🄰 M.Norris]
Hauck, James M. ... '— '98 C.589 B.S. L.347 J.D. [Hatchett&H.]
Haughan, Peter P. ... '60 '87 C.347 B.A. L.345 J.D. Supvr. Atty.
Havel, Linda H. ... '66 '94 C.880 B.A. L.421 J.D. [🄰 Tabbert H.E.&W.]
Hawk Kazmierczak, Michelle ... '76 '01 C&L.347 B.S., J.D. [🄰 Kightlinger&G.]
Hawkins, Gabriel A. ... '— '02 C.801 B.A. L.345 J.D. [🄰 Price W.R.&D.]
Hawkins, Jeffrey D. ... '71 '96 C.347 B.A. L.365 J.D. [Kightlinger&G.]
Hawkins, Joseph ... '78 '05 C.902 B.A. L.345 J.D. [🄰 Bingham M.]
Hawley-Conley, Judith A., (BV) '54 '79
C.823 B.A. L.879 J.D. Gen. Coun., Indiana Civil Rights Comm.
Haworth, Brett M. ... '78 '03 C.265 B.A. L.1119 J.D. [🄰 McClure M.D.&H.]
Hayden, Colleen M. ... '67 '92 C.999 B.S. L.201 J.D. Coun., Anthem, Inc.
Hayes, Carl A. ... '66 '02 C.63 B.S. L.345 J.D. [🄰 McTurnan&T.]
Hayes, Lisa R. ... '57 '82 C.346 B.S. L.861 J.D. Spec. Coun. for Consumer Policy
Hayes, Richard J. ... '76 '02 C.347 B.S. L.597 J.D. [🄰 Bingham M.]
Hays, Thomas C., (AV) ... '51 '77 C.347 A.B. L.969 J.D. [Lewis W.]
Hearn, Sharon B., (AV) ... '56 '84 C.346 B.S. L.345 J.D. [Krieg D.]
Heath, G. Ronald, (AV) ... '38 '65 C.347 A.B. L.1119 LL.B. [Hoover H.B.&H.]
Heath, R. Terry, (AV) ... '— '78 C.679 B.S. L.347 J.D. [Hall,R.K.H.&L.]
Heaton, David R., (AV) ... '08 '33 C.951 A.B. L.309 LL.B. 3706 Candy Cane Dr.‡
Hebenstreit, Michael J., (AV) ... '52 '77 C.973 B.A. L.345 J.D. 151 N. Delaware Street
Hebenstreit, Patricia A. ... '61 '86 C.436 B.A. L.345 J.D. State Alcoholic Beverage Comm.
Hebert, Robert B., (AV) ... '48 '73 C.347 B.S. L.345 J.D. [Bingham M.]
Heck, Jeffrey D. ... '68 '94 C.910 A.B. L.347 J.D. [Heck]
Heck Law Offices, PC ... 310 N. Alabama St., Ste. 320
Heckler, Douglas J., (AV) ... '— '82 C.879 B.A. L.345 J.D. [Barnes&T.]
Hedges, Norman J. ... '71 '98 C.679 B.S.M.E. L.347 J.D. [🄰 Baker&D.] (See Pat. Sect.)
Heerens, Joseph R. ... '62 '87 C.210 B.A. L.1119 J.D. Ind. Ct. of Appls.
Heeter, John M., (BV) ... '18 '48 C.679 B.S. L.345 J.D. [J.M.Heeter]
Heeter, John M., Professional Corporation, (BV) ... Ste 1300, 156 E Market St
Heger, David M. ... '— '04 C.276 B.A. L.910 J.D. [🄰 Barnes&T.]
Hehner, James W., (AV) ... '58 '83 C.347 B.S. L.345 J.D. [Sipe,P.H.R.&H.]
Heidorn, Robert E. ... '63 '88 C.473 B.A. L.966 J.D. Indiana Energy, Inc.
Heins, George V. ... '37 '68 C.494 B.A. L.345 J.D. 110 S. Downey Avenue‡
Heinz, Joan M., (AV) '40 '86 C.473 B.A. L.1119 J.D.
Assoc.Gen.Coun.Envir. Health & Safety, Eli Lilly & Co.
Heinzmann, Jeffrey M., (BV) '68 '93
C.597 B.A. L.345 J.D. Dep. State Editor, The State Editor's Off.
Helbert, Jan E., (BV) ... '39 '72 C.347 B.S. L.345 J.D. 2417 E. 65th St.
Held, Andrew J. ... '76 '03 C&L.347 B.A., J.D. [🄰 Bose M.&E.]
Helm, John R., (AV) ... '59 '84 C.894 A.B. L.1119 J.D. [Schreckengast,H.&C.]
Helmen, Randall C., (BV) ... '56 '82 C.347 B.A. L.1119 J.D. [Hume S.G.G.&S.]
Helmreich, Craig J. ... '75 '00 C.108 B.A. L.347 J.D. [🄰 Scopelitis,G.L.&H.]
Hendel, Joseph M. ... '72 '97 C.347 B.A. L.345 J.D. [🄰 Hackman H.&C.]
Hendershot, Rodger K., (AV) ... '50 '75 C.108 B.A. L.345 J.D. [🄲 Bose M.&E.]
Henderson, Eugene L., (AV) ... '25 '53 C.265 A.B. L.309 J.D. [🄲 Bose M.&E.]
Henderson, Marcus ... '78 '03 C.347 B.A. L.1119 J.D. [🄰 Hunt S.K.]
Henderson, Peter S. '71 '98 C.597 B.A. L.245 J.D.
Corp. Coun., Roche Diagnostics Corp.
Henderson, Ronald S. ... '— '96 C.679 B.S.M.E. L.345 J.D. [Barnes&T.] (See Pat. Sect.)
Henderson Daily Withrow & DeVoe, (AV) ... One Indiana Square Suite 2600
Hendren, Robert H., (BV) ... '45 '74 C.894 B.A. L.259 J.D. 302 N. E. St., Ste. 100
Hendrickson, Debra B. ... '56 '83 C.679 B.A. L.345 J.D. State Family & Social Servs.
Hendrickson, Richard E., (AV) '57 '83
C.210 B.A. L.345 J.D. State Coun., First Amer. Title Ins. Co.
Hendrickson, Thomas A., (AV) ... '27 '52 C.976 A.B. L.1119 J.D. 7979 Lantern Rd.
Henkel, Beth H. ... '52 '82 C.347 B.A. L.345 J.D. [🄲 Ice M.]
Henn, Eugene E. ... '31 '60 C.108 B.S. L.345 J.D. [🄲 Wood T.G.M.&H.]
Hennig, Arthur W. ... '46 '71 C&L.879 B.S., J.D. Internal Rev. Serv.
Henning, John K., IV ... '74 '01 C.840 B.A. L.893 J.D. [🄰 Baker&D.]
Henry, Brett J. ... '71 '03 C.880 B.A. L.345 J.D. [🄰 Krieg D.]
Henry, Geo. A., Jr., (BV) ... '19 '42 C.103 L.345 LL.B. 872 Virginia Ave.
Henry, Thomas Q., (AV) '52 '75
C.679 B.S. L.345 J.D. [Woodard,E.M.M.&H.] (See Pat. Sect.)
Hensel, David J., (AV) ... '— '86 C.894 B.A. L.1119 J.D. [Sommer B.]
Hepler, Deborah K., (BV) ... '52 '94 C.347 B.A. L.345 J.D. [🄰 Locke R.]
Herbst, Hilary F. '67 '92 C.575 B.A. L.347 J.D.
Atty., Envir. Law Dept., Eli Lilly & Co.
Herbst, Scott E. ... '66 '92 C&L.347 B.S., J.D. Sr. V.P., RealMed Corporation
Herke, Anjali M. ... '— '96 C.347 B.A. L.345 J.D. [🄰 Hall,R.K.H.&L.]
Hermer, Andrea L., (CV) ... '65 '90 C.347 B.A. L.1119 J.D. [Stewart&I.]
Hernandez, James Harold '59 '85
C.879 B.S. L.345 J.D. 3925 River Crossing Pkwy., Ste, 200
Herndon, Jane Neuhauser, (AV) ... '64 '89 C.210 B.A. L.273 J.D. [Ice M.]
Herriman, John B. ("Bart") ... '69 '96 C.347 B.S. L.999 J.D. [🄰 Clark,Q.M.S.&G.]
Herrin, John Q., (AV) ... '44 '72 C.894 A.B. L.345 J.D. [🄲 Wood T.G.M.&H.]
Herrmann, Jennifer M. ... '78 '03 C.210 B.A. L.1119 J.D. [🄰 Kightlinger&G.]
Herzog, David K., (AV) ... '55 '80 C.894 A.B. L.880 J.D. [Baker&D.]
Hesselgrave, T. Reginald, (BV) ... '43 '80 C.347 B.A. L.345 J.D. [Palguta&H.]
Hessler, Charles A., (AV) '46 '74
C.347 A.B. L.1119 J.D. Sr. Coun., McCready and Keene, Inc.

Hessler, Jane Titus '43 '74 C.228 B.A. L.1119 J.D. Coun., Pharm. Opers., Eli Lilly & Co.
Hester, Jeffrey Michael, (BV) '73 '99 C.1119 B.A L.345 J.D. [W.J.Tucker&Assoc.]
Hester, Judy Gale '58 '86 C.234 B.S. L.424 J.D. 9465 Counselors Row
Hetzner, Marc A., (AV) '53 '83 C.347 A.B. L.345 J.D. [Krieg D.]
Hibbler, Veronica '— '95 C.679 B.S. L.74 J.D. Defense Finance & Accounting Service
Hickey, Christine Hayes, (AV) '66 '93 C.679 B.A L.347 J.D. [Rubin&L.]
Hicks, Robert A., (AV) '— '88 C.303 B.A. L.1119 J.D. [Hall,R.K.H.&L.]
Hicks, Robert J. '— '87 C.108 B.S. L.945 J.D. [Sommer B.]
Hiday, Lisa A. '64 '95 C.679 B.S.A.A.E. L.347 J.D. [Woodard,E.M.M.&H.] (See Pat. Sect.)
Hidde, Curt W., (BV) '— '93 C.347 B.A. L.201 J.D. [Barnes&T.]
Hidde, Kandi K., (BV) '67 '93 C.746 B.S. L.201 J.D. [Bingham M.]
Higgins, John M. '33 '65 C.973 B.S. L.345 J.D. Hearing Offr., U.S. Dept. of Vet. Affs.
Hightower, Timothy J. '66 '01 C.347 B.A. L.1119 J.D. [[A] Wooden&M.]
Hiland, Douglas E., (BV) '51 '78 C.205 B.A. L.345 J.D. [O'Koon H.]
Hile, Michael W., (AV) '60 '85 C.243 B.A. L.345 J.D. [Katz&K.]
Hill, Douglas J., (AV) '33 '60 C&L.477 B.B.A., LL.B. [Hill,F.M.F.&M.]
Hill, Jennett M. '63 '98 C.210 B.A. L.344 J.D. [[A] Baker&D.]
Hill, Jeremy E. '75 '99 C&L.347 B.S., J.D. [[A] Bingham M.]
Hill, Mary Liatti '— '96 C.150 B.S.N. L.347 J.D. [[A] Hall,R.K.H.&L.]
Hill, R. Martin, Attorney at Law, (AV) '52 '82 C.602 B.A. L.345 J.D. 4954 E. 56th St., Ste. 8

Hill, Fulwider, McDowell, Funk & Matthews, Professional Corporation, (AV)
Suite 2000, One Indiana Square, 46204-2031
Telephone: 317-488-2000 FAX: 317-630-2768
URL: http://www.hillfulwider.com
Douglas J. Hill; Richard R. McDowell; Norman T. Funk; James F. Matthews; Keith A. Kinney; Michael G. Getty; Peter H. Donahoe; Knight S. Anderson; Elizabeth H. Knotts; Alan J. Irvin; Rori Lisa Goldman;—Ty Michael Craver; Emily D. Smith. Of Counsel: Constance J. Gustafson.
General Practice. Litigation. Corporation, Hospital, Federal and State Taxation, Aviation Law. Suretyship. Trusts and Estate Planning Law. General Business Law and Business Enterprises, Wills, Probate, Medical Malpractice, Insurance Defense.
Representative Clients: Aetna Casualty & Surety Co.; Associated Electric & Gas Insurance Services Ltd. (AEGIS); Chubb & Son, Inc.; Great American Insurance Group; Maryland Casualty Insurance Co.; Methodist Hospital of Indiana, Inc.; Sears, Roebuck and Co.; Wausau Insurance Cos.
See Professional Biographies, INDIANAPOLIS, INDIANA

Hillery, David W. '54 '81 C.347 B.S. L.345 J.D. 1 Indiana Sq.‡
Hillery, James L. '69 '98 C.347 B.A. L.1119 J.D. 7119 U.S. Hwy. 31 S.
Hillis, Sanders N. '64 '99 C.610 B.S.E.E. L.347 J.D. [[A] Brinks H.G.&L.] (See Pat. Sect.)
Hillman, George A., (BV) '41 '66 C.976 A.B. L.228 LL.B. 110 N. Delaware
Hillman, Peggy A., (AVⓉ) '43 '68 C.477 B.A. L.145 J.D. 445 N. Pennsylvania
Hiltunen, Charles T., III, (BV) '62 '90 C&L.347 B.S., J.D. 5686 N. Wash. Blvd.
Himsel, Jane Ann, (AV) '64 '90 C.880 B.A. L.597 J.D. [Wooden&M.]
Himsel, Scott D., (AV) '62 '88 C.894 A.B. L.597 J.D. [Baker&D.]
Hiner, Leslie Davis '57 '85 C.970 B.A. L.8 J.D. 8523 Twin Pointe Circle
Hinkle, Donald E. '52 '76 C.347 B.S. L.1119 J.D. V.P. & Controller, Bank One Indianapolis, N.A.

Hinkle & Gibbs
(See Danville)

Hinshaw, Debra L. '54 '84 C.249 B.S. L.345 J.D. [[C] Baker&D.]
Hinshaw, James M., (AV) '67 '92 C.209 B.A. L.347 J.D. [Bingham M.]
Hinshaw, Jeannette Eisan '57 '82 C.210 B.A. L.1119 J.D. [[C] Bose M.&E.]
Hintermeister, Jeffrey P. '57 '85 C&L.420 B.S., J.D. [O'Koon H.] ⊙
Hinton, Jacki D. '56 '85 C.679 B.S. L.145 J.D. 9330 Zionville Rd.
Hirsch, Stan B., (BV) '51 '82 C.347 B.A. L.221 J.D. 151 N. Delaware St., Suite 740
Hittinger, Stewart T. '55 '80 C.347 B.S. L.345 J.D. I.R.S.
Hittle, Max W., Jr., (AV) '44 '69 C.210 B.A. L.1119 J.D. [Krieg D.]
Hitz-Bradley, Chris '57 '93 C.431 B.A. L.1218 J.D. 1 N. Capitol, Suite 800
Ho, Angelin '73 '01 C.347 B.A. L.94 J.D. Neighborhood Christian Legal Clinic
Ho, Virginia E. '74 '01 C.347 B.A. L.1565 J.D. [[A] Baker&D.]
Hoard, John C., (AV) '55 '80 C.597 B.S. L.345 J.D. [Rubin&L.]
Hoberty, Charles L. '28 '64 C.967 B.A. L.345 J.D. 4024 Melbourne Circle‡
Hocker, Janet Davis '65 '93 C.63 B.S. L.879 J.D. [Hocker&Assoc.]

Hocker & Associates
7202 North Shadeland Avenue, Suite 207, 46250-2086
Telephone: 317-578-1630 Fax: 317-849-1892 URL: http://www.hockerlaw.com
Email: janethocker@aol.com URL: http://www.hockerlawfirm.com
Janet Davis Hocker.
Business Litigation, Business Planning, Business Enterprises, Corporate, Small Business, Partnerships, Limited Liability Companies, Business Law, Real Estate, Estate Planning, Trusts and Estates, Wills and Probate, Bankruptcy and Corporate Formation (Sub S, C Corp. and LLC), Starting a Business, Buying and Selling a Business).
See Professional Biographies, INDIANAPOLIS, INDIANA

Hodes, W. William '43 '69 C.309 B.A. L.705 J.D. (adm. in LA; not adm. in IN) 7321 Shadeland Sta. Way., Ste. 230
Hodowal, John R. '45 '71 C.679 B.S.I.E. L.345 J.D. CEO, Indianapolis Power & Light Co.
Hodson, Samuel D., (AV) '— '86 C.347 B.A. L.345 J.D. [[C] Barnes&T.]
Hoeing, Wayne T. '64 '93 C.435 B.S. L.344 J.D. 111 Monument Circle
Hofer, Michael F. '45 '78 C.347 B.S. L.345 J.D. 18 N Sheridan Ave
Hofer, Steven R., (BV) '61 '87 C.679 B.S. L.345 J.D. 6818 Hollingsworth Drive
Hoffman, Geo. B., Jr. '24 '51 C&L.879 J.D. Ret. Sr. App. Ct. J.‡
Hogan, Frank W., (BV) '38 '68 C.1216 B.A. L.345 J.D. [Voyles,Z.P.H.&M.]
Hogan, James B. '— '94 C&L.347 M.B.A., J.D. [Hall,R.K.H.&L.]
Hogsett, Joseph H., (AV) '56 '81 C.347 A.B. L.1119 J.D. [Bingham M.]
Hokanson, Jeffrey A., (AV) '— '89 C.347 B.S. L.345 J.D. [Ice M.]
Hokanson, Maynard '11 '36 C.210 L.345 J.D. Chmn. of the Bd., Hokanson Cos., Inc.‡
Holaday, Ted J., (BV) '51 '77 C.210 B.A. L.345 J.D. Dep. Atty. Gen.
Holland, C. Warren, (AV) '28 '52 C&L.602 A.B., LL.B. [Holland&H.]
Holland, James G. '47 '76 C.150 B.B.A. L.345 J.D. Exec. V.P., K.P. Meiring Construction, Inc.
Holland, Michael W., (AV) '57 '82 C.602 B.A. L.477 J.D. [Holland&H.]

Holland & Holland, (AV) BR
8888 Keystone Crossing, Suite 848, 46240
Telephone: 317-581-4400 Fax: 317-705-3644
Email: hhlaw@sbcglobal.net
C. Warren Holland; Michael W. Holland. Of Counsel: Gretchen Holland Etling; Charles G. Reeder.
Civil Trial Practice. Negligence, Medical Malpractice, Products Liability, Railroad Crossing Accidents and Air Crash Litigation, Wrongful Death.
See Professional Biographies, INDIANAPOLIS, INDIANA

Hollander, Eugene C., (BV) '48 '73 C.347 B.A. L.345 J.D. 156 East Market Street, Suite 300
Hollenberg, Krista '50 '86 C.432 B.A. L.1119 J.D. Assr. Prof., Ivy Tech Comm. Coll.
Hollett, Byron P., (AV) '14 '39 C.894 B.A. L.309 J.D. 300 N. Meridian St.
Hollingsworth, J. David, (BV) '46 '73 C.265 B.A. L.345 J.D. [Hollingsworth,M.M.&M.]
Hollingsworth, Joshua P. '— '00 C.473 B.A. L.347 J.D. [[A] Barnes&T.]
Hollingsworth, Kenneth M. '66 '92 C.347 B.S. L.345 J.D. Marion County Prosecutor's Office
Hollingsworth, Martha Schmidt, (AV) '44 '72 C.347 A.B. L.345 J.D. [Bingham M.]
Hollingsworth, Scott C. '— '03 C.709 B.A. L.329 J.D. [[A] Barnes&T.]
Hollingsworth, Meek, Miller and Minglin, P.C., (BV) 9202 N. Meridian St.
Hollis, Edward E., III '72 '96 C.827 B.A. L.347 J.D. [Baker&D.]
Holloway, Mark A. '58 '92 C&L.347 B.S., J.D. [[A] Stephenson M.&S.]
Holmes, Jack F. '20 '71 C.309 M.B.A. L.345 J.D. 3703 Washington Blvd.
Holt, John M., (AV) '25 '56 C.210 A.B. L.345 J.D. 3421 Bay Road, North Drive‡
Holt, Randolph G. '57 '98 C.63 B.S. L.345 J.D. [Parr R.O.&M.]
Holtzlander, Stephanie Franco, (AV) '68 '93 C.347 B.A. L.221 J.D. [[A] Bose M.&E.]
Holzer, Steven L. '53 '78 C.347 B.A. L.345 J.D. Allied Fidelity Ins. Co.
Homma, Michiharu '50 '96 C.999 B.A. L.150 J.D. [Ogletree,D.N.S.&S.]
Honig, David B., (BVⓉ) '— '87 C.910 B.A. L.260 J.D. [Hall,R.K.H.&L.]
Hook, Sara Anne '56 '94 C.477 B.A. L.1119 J.D. Assoc. Dean, Faculties & Prof. of Dental Informatics
Hooper, David P. '— '01 C.273 B.A. L.879 J.D. (adm. in IL; not adm. in IN) [[A] Barnes&T.]
Hoover, E. Ralph '70 '96 C.1024 B.S. L.347 J.D. [[A] Eckert C.]
Hoover, John David, (AV) '51 '80 C.880 B.A. L.345 J.D. [Hoover H.B.&H.]

Hoover Hull Baker & Heath LLP, (AV)
111 Monument Circle, Suite 4400, P.O. Box 44989, 46244-0989
Telephone: 317-822-4400 Fax: 317-822-0234
URL: http://www.hooverhull.com
John David Hoover; Andrew W. Hull; Robert M. Baker III; G. Ronald Heath; Alice McKenzie Morical;—Sean T. White; Sarah Stites Fanzini; Mark A. Drummond; Michael A. Dorelli; Gregory C. Brubaker; William Joseph Spalding; Jason L. Fulk.
Civil Trial and Appellate Practice in all Federal and State Courts. Practice before Administrative Agencies and Alternative Dispute Resolution Proceedings. Art Law Litigation, Business & Commercial Litigation, Class Action Proceedings, Constitutional Law, Construction Disputes and Litigation, Education Law and School Litigation, Election Campaign and Political Law Litigation, Employee Benefits and Employment Litigation, Tort and Product Liability Litigation, Insurance Litigation, Professional Liability Litigation, Sports Law Litigation.
See Professional Biographies, INDIANAPOLIS, INDIANA

Hoppel, James C. '51 '79 C.932 B.A. L.1119 J.D. [[A] Schneider]
Hopper, Angela M. '— '00 C.347 B.S. L.345 J.D. [[A] Sommer B.]
Hopper, Edward B., II, (AV) '— '64 C&L.880 B.A., LL.B. [Stewart&I.]
Hopper, George W., (AV) '57 '82 C&L.880 B.A., J.D. [Hopper B.]
Hopper, Jeffrey A. '— '97 C.347 B.S. L.209 J.D. [[A] Barnes&T.]

Hopper Blackwell, P.C., (AV) BR
Bank One Center/Circle, 111 Monument Circle, Suite 452, 46204-5170
Telephone: 317-635-5005 Facsimile: 317-634-2501
URL: http://www.hopperblackwelllaw.com
George W. Hopper; Thomas B. Blackwell; Jeffrey E. Ramsey; Ronald W. Buchmeier; Jason R. Burke; Christopher C. Hagenow; Niccole R. Sadowski.
Bankruptcy, Banks and Banking, Collections, Commercial Law, Corporate Law, Debtor and Creditor, Litigation, Commercial Litigation, Civil Litigation, Trial Practice, Mergers, Acquisitions and Divestitures.
Representative Clients: Bank One Corporation; Key Bank; National City Bank; Union Federal Bank; Collision Team of America; Indiana Fiber Network; M.D. Logistics; New Sesco, Inc.; Party Time Rentals; Symons International Group, Inc.
See Professional Biographies, INDIANAPOLIS, INDIANA

Horn, Brenda S., (AV) '49 '81 C.347 A.B. L.345 J.D. [Ice M.]
Horn, Kirk A., (BV) '63 '90 C.303 B.A. L.345 J.D. 8900 Keystone Crossing, Ste. 950
Hosmer, Donald M. '22 '73 C.477 A.B. L.345 J.D. 5130 Boardwalk Pl.‡
Hostetler, Donald '— '03 C.608 B.A. L.339 J.D. [[A] Ice M.]
Hostetler, Gary Lynn, (AV) '53 '79 C.347 B.S. L.345 J.D. [Hostetler&K.]

Hostetler & Kowalik, P.C., (AV) BR
101 West Ohio Street Suite 2100, 46204
Telephone: 317-262-1001 Fax: 317-262-1010
URL: http://www.lawyers.com/hostetler&kowalik
Gary Lynn Hostetler; James S. Kowalik; David R. Krebs; J. Bradley Schooley; John W. Graub, II; Christopher E. Baker.
Commercial, Bankruptcy, Debtors and Creditors Rights Law.
See Professional Biographies, INDIANAPOLIS, INDIANA

Hosty, Thomas C. '63 '89 C.1182 B.A. L.900 J.D. (adm. in KS; not adm. in IN) Natl. Collegiate Athletic Assn.
Houck, David J. '47 '72 C.357 B.A. L.345 J.D. Asst. V.P. & Tr. Offr., Merchants Natl. Bk. & Tr. Co.
Hounshel, Carla R. '71 '96 C.880 B.A. L.347 J.D. [[C] Scopelitis,G.L.&H.]
Householder, Steven L., (AV) '53 '78 C.108 B.A. L.1565 J.D. [[C] Baker&D.]
Hovde, F. Boyd, (AV) '34 '59 C.674 B.A. L.477 J.D. [Hovde,D.&D.]
Hovde, Frederick R., (AV) '55 '80 C.347 B.B.A. L.802 J.D. [Hovde,D.&D.]

Hovde, Dassow & Deets LLC, (AV)
10585 North Meridian Street, Suite 205, P.O. Box 40849, 46240-0849
Telephone: 317-818-3100 Fax: 317-818-3111
Email: firm@hovdelaw.com URL: http://www.hovdelaw.com
F. Boyd Hovde; Frederick R. Hovde; Robert T. Dassow; Nicholas C. Deets.
Aviation, Personal Injury, Automobile Accidents, Head and Spinal Injuries, Nursing Home Abuse, Slip and Fall, Wrongful Death, Trucking Accidents, Drugs and Medical Devices, Medical Malpractice, Construction, Product Liability, Insurance, Securities Fraud and Consumer Fraud.
See Professional Biographies, INDIANAPOLIS, INDIANA

Howard, Kimberly E. '66 '91 C&L.347 B.A., J.D. [Smith,F.M.&H.]
Howard, Robert A., (BV) '37 '70 C.679 B.S. L.345 J.D. 6100 Keystone Ave.
Howe, Howard '— '86 C.347 B.S. L.345 J.D. 50 S. Meridian St.
Howell, Kareem A. '75 '02 C.1286 B.S. L.347 J.D. [[A] Baker&D.] (See Pat. Sect.)
Hoy, Jason J. '71 '98 C&L.347 B.A., J.D. [[A] Kightlinger&G.]
Huber, Brent W., (BV) '65 '91 C.679 B.S. L.345 J.D. [Ice M.]

Huddleston, Stephen Lee
(See Franklin)

Huey, William R., Jr. '30 '59 C.478 A.B. L.477 J.D. (adm. in PA; not adm. in IN) 8900 Keystone Crossing‡
Huff, Bernard '37 '64 C.922 B.A. L.345 J.D. 5335 N. Tacoma Ave.
Huffer, Steven K., (AV) '58 '84 C.118 B.A. L.345 J.D. [Huffer&W.]

Huffer & Weathers, P.C., (AV) BR
1850 Market Square Center, 151 North Delaware Street, 46204-2522
Telephone: 317-822-8010 Toll Free: 888-822-8010 Fax: 317-822-8088
Email: info@hufferandweathers.com URL: http://www.hufferandweathers.com
Steven K. Huffer; Scott A. Weathers;—Christopher B. Carpentier; Shannon D. Bogard.
Alternative Dispute Resolution, Annuities, Arbitration, Appellate Practice, Bank Foreclosures, Business Litigation, Civil Practice, Class Actions, Commercial Law, Commercial Arbitration, Commercial

(This Listing Continued)

Huffer & Weathers, P.C. (Continued)

Litigation, Contracts, Contract Litigation, Corporate Litigation, ERISA, Health Benefits, Fraud and Deceit, General Practice, Health Care, Home Health Care, Long Term Care, Nursing Home Litigation, Nursing Home Negligence, Insurance, Disability Insurance, Excess and Reinsurance, Extra Contractual Insurance Claims, Insurance Agents and Brokers Defense Insurance Agents and Brokers Errors and Omissions, Insurance Bad Faith, Insurance Coverage, Insurance Fraud, Life and Health Insurance, Reinsurance Arbitration, Insurance Coverage Defense, Legal Ethics and Professional Negligence, Federal Litigation, Premises Liability Defense, Professional Liability Insurance Coverage.
Representative Clients: Available upon request.

See Professional Biographies, INDIANAPOLIS, INDIANA

Huffman, Rosemary Adams, (BV) ....'39 '62 C.347 A.B. L.1119 J.D. 6630 E. 56th St.
Hughel, Patricia A. ....'74 '03 C.679 B.A. L.1560 J.D. [A Bingham M.]
Hughes, Dewayne A. ....'66 '00 C.249 B.S. L.345 J.D. [A Ice M.] (See Pat. Sect.)
Hughes, Elizabeth Ann .... '59 '94 C.347 B.A. L.1119 J.D. [A Bowman,H.B.&V.]
Hughes, Heidi K. ....'74 '04 C.597 B.S. L.345 J.D. [A Dann P.N.&K.]
Hughs, Valerie L. ....'73 '00 C.923 B.S. L.345 J.D. [A Lewis W.]
Hugon, Bruce A., (AV) ....'54 '79 C.679 B.A. L.1119 J.D. [Stuart&B.]
Hulbert, Kathy Carr ....'77 '02 C.138 B.A. L.345 J.D. Dep. Atty. Gen. Prof. Lic.
Hulett, Robert S., (AV) ....'44 '69 C.210 B.A. L.1119 J.D. [Hackman H.&C.]
Hulett, Timothy J., (AV) ....'57 '82 C.894 A.B. L.345 J.D. [Harrison&M.]
Hulka, Michael J. ....'— '01 C.347 B.A. L.1119 J.D. [A Barnes&T.]
Hull, Andrew W., (AV) ....'57 '86 C.477 B.G.S. L.1119 J.D. [Hoover H.B.&H.]
Hults, Pauline Jayne ....'58 '84 C.347 B.S. L.345 J.D. 1 Indiana Sq.‡
Hume, John T., III, (AV) .... '33 '58 C.347 B.S. L.1119 J.D. [Hume S.G.G.&S.]
Hume Smith Geddes Green & Simmons, LLP, (AV) ....54 Monument Cir., 4th Fl.
Humke, Steven, (AV) ....'60 '85 C.228 A.B. L.145 J.D. [Ice M.]
Humphrey, John R., (BV) ....'— '99 C.347 B.S. L.345 J.D. [A Sommer B.]
Hunt, Brian T., (AV) '59 '84 C.201 B.S. L.345 J.D.
Vice President & General Counsel, American Trans Air, Inc.
Hunt, Jeffrey A. .... '68 '04 C.63 B.S. L.1370 J.D. [A McCrosson&Assoc.]
Hunt, Kimberly D. '68 '93 C.475 B.A. L.602 J.D.
Corp. Coun., Roche Diagnostics Corp.
Hunt, Paul B., (BV) ....'— '90 C&L.339 B.S.M.E., J.D. [Barnes&T.] (See Pat. Sect.)
Hunt McWilliams, Monique ....'64 '93 C&L.347 B.A., J.D. FDI Pharmaceutical

Hunt Suedhoff Kalamaros LLP, (AV)
6323 S. East Street, 46227 ⊙
Telephone: 317-784-4966 Fax: 317-784-5566
URL: http://www.hsk-law.com
Member of Firm: Brian L. England. Associates: Kevin R. Leslie; Marcus Henderson; Elizabeth Joseph.
General Civil Trial and Appellate Practice. Insurance Defense Litigation. Commercial Real Estate Financing and Transactions. Corporate and Commercial Law. Probate and Estate Planning.
South Bend, Indiana Office: 120 West LaSalle Avenue, Twelfth Floor, P.O. Box 4156, 46634-4156. Telephone: 574-232-4801. Fax: 574-232-9736.
Fort Wayne, Indiana Office: 803 South Calhoun Street, Ninth Floor, P.O. Box 11489, 46858-1489. Telephone: 260-423-1311. Fax: 260-424-5396.
St. Joseph, Michigan Office: 608 S. Pleasant Street, P.O. Box 46, 49085-0046. Telephone: 269-983-4405. Fax: 269-983-5645.

See Professional Biographies, INDIANAPOLIS, INDIANA

Hunter, Charles W., (BV) ....'22 '50 C.347 A.B. L.345 J.D. 7 N. Meridian St.
Hunter, Frederick D. '40 '75 C.665 B.S. L.446 J.D.
(adm. in DC; not adm. in IN; Pat.) Asst. Gen. Pat. Coun., Eli Lilly & Cop.
Hunter, Marilynn L. '44 '81 C.347 B.S. L.345 J.D.
CEO, Professional Assessment of Indiana, Inc.
Huntine, Michael S., (BV) ....'62 '87 C.347 B.S. L.345 J.D. [Due,D.F.&M.]
Huppert, Charles B., (AV) ..... '42 '71 C.701 B.S.E.E. L.345 J.D. 6508 E. Westfield Blvd.
Huppert, Lynda F. ....'44 '72 C.346 B.A. L.345 J.D. Co. Small Claims Ct. J.
Hurley, Ryan M. ....'77 '03 C.347 B.A. L.1119 J.D. [A Baker&D.]
Hursh, Terry N. ....'56 '81 C.347 B.A. L.607 J.D. Co. Small Claims Ct. J.
Hurst, William W., (AV) ....'38 '66 C.347 B.A. L.1119 J.D. [Mitchell H.J.&D.]
Hurwitz, Lainie A. ....'73 '98 C.347 B.S. L.201 J.D. [A Ruppert&S.]
Huse, Stacey A. '— '98 C.210 B.A. L.4210 J.D.
(adm. in KY; not adm. in IN) [A Sommer B.]
Huser, Richard A., (AV) '54 '80 C.210 B.A. L.345 J.D.
Assoc. Gen. Coun., Thomson Inc.
Huston, Michael J., (AV) ....'42 '72 C.870 B.S. L.1119 J.D. [C Baker&D.]
Huston, Richd. H. ....'26 '51 C&L.345 LL.B. J. Mun. Ct.
Hutchens, William V., (AV) ....'33 '63 C.347 B.S. L.1119 LL.B. [C Locke R.]
Hutchinson, Thomas N. ....'70 '96 C.210 B.A. L.345 J.D. [Krieg D.]
Hutton, James J. ....'67 '94 C&L.347 B.A., J.D. [Hannon H.&Assoc.]
Hux, Alan M. ....'— '72 C.210 B.A. L.910 J.D. [C Sommer B.]
Hyatt, Stephen J., (BV) ....'45 '73 C.347 B.S. L.477 J.D. [Hyatt&R.]
Hyatt & Rosenbaum, P.A., (BV) ....6100 N. Keystone Avenue
Hylton, Eric M. ....'71 '97 C&L.347 B.S., J.D. [Dann P.N.&K.]

Ice Miller, (AV) BB
One American Square Box 82001, 46282-0002 ⊙
Telephone: 317-236-2100 Fax: 317-236-2219
Email: info@icemiller.com URL: http://www.icemiller.com
Partners: Wayne O. Adams, III; Adam Arceneaux; Mark B. Barnes; Phillip L. Bayt; Fred R. Biesecker; Michael A. Blickman; Michael H. Boldt; S. R. Born; Mary Beth Braitman; David J. Carr; Ralph A. Cohen; James S. Cunning; Terri Ann Czajka; Gary J. Dankert; Kristine Camron Danz; Joseph E. DeGroff; James V. Donadio; Thomas K. Downs; Henry A. Efroymson; Lucy A. Emison; Sherry A. Fabina-Abney; James R. Fisher; Mary Kay Fleming; Mark W. Ford; Sarah K. Funke; Bonnie L. Gallivan; Robert L. Gauss; Philip C. Genetos; Gina M. Giacone; Alan H. Goldstein; Doreen J. Gridley; Brian D. Gwitt; Stephen J. Hackman; John R. Hammond, III; Jane Neuhauser Herndon; Jeffrey A. Hokanson; Brenda S. Horn; Brent W. Huber; Steven Humke; Harry T. Ice; Lacy M. Johnson; G. Daniel Kelley, Jr.; James D. Kemper; Martin J. Klaper; Kevin R. Knight; Gareth W. Kuhl; Mary Nold Larimore; Lisa A. Lee; Michael J. Lewinski; Jeffrey O. Lewis; David J. Mallon, Jr.; David M. Mattingly; Curtis W. McCauley; Debra Hanley Miller; Merle H. Miller; Michael E. Millikan; Thomas E. Mixdorf; Michelle M. Molin; Byron L. Myers; Timothy E. Ochs; Judy Starobin Okenfuss; E. Van Olson; Richard E. Parker; Gregory L. Pemberton; James L. Petersen; Thomas W. Peterson; Todd W. Ponder; John F. Prescott, Jr.; Melissa Proffitt Reese; Mark J. Richards; Susan Barnhizer Rivas; George P. Ryan; Phillip R. Scaletta, III; Thomas F. Schnellenberger; Marc W. Sciscoe; Rebecca J. Seamands; Christopher S. Sears; Myra C. Selby; James A. Shanahan; Paul H. Sinclair; Richard A. Smikle; Thomas C. Smith; Donald M. Snemis; Jack R. Snyder; Barton T. Sprunger; Dale E. Stackhouse; Lisa A. Stone; Michael A. Swift; Jay G. Taylor; John J. Thar; John R. Thornburgh; Richard J. Thrapp; Michael L. Tooley; Thomas A. Walsh; Zeff A. Weiss; L. Alan Whaley; Philip A. Whistler; Janice C. Wilken; Michael A. Wilkins; Gordon D. Wishard; Kevin C. Woodhouse; Michael A. Wukmer; Patricia A. Zelmer. Senior Counsel: Craig C. Burke; William P. Diener; Mark D. Grant; Kathleen S. Kiefer; Peggy J. Naile; Gregory D. Nichols; Randle B. Pollard; Cynthia Pearson Purvis; Linda R. Rowings; Marilee J. Springer; Tara Schulstad Sciscoe; Stephanie Alden Smithey; Timothy W. Sullivan; Bradley L. Williams. Of Counsel: Karen L. Arland; Sandra K. Bickel; Susan Rogers Brooke; Jenifer M. Brown; Julie M. Conrad; Karen A. Dutcher; Natalie M. Fierek; Kari H. Halbrook; Melissa A. Harkins; Lisa Erb Harrison; Beth H. Henkel; Steven L. Jones; Jeffrey M. Lozer; John T. Murphy; Heather K. Olinger; Kelly Bauman Pitcher; Jill Tabor Powlick; Scott James Preston; Susan Bender Price; William C. Reynolds; Nancy Menard Riddle; Jane H. Ruemmele; Kathleen K. Shortridge; Gary L. Stage; Edward P. Steegmann; Margaret D. Wielenberg; Germaine W. Willett. Senior Associate: Kristine J. Bouaichi. Associates: Anthony Aaron; Jay B. Adams; Kevin M. Alerding; Niquelle Allen; Jennifer M. Alvey; Jennifer A. Andres; Brian Bailey; Denise Y. Barkdull; Alyssa Beattie; Mark A. Bogdanowicz (Not admitted in IN); Tonya J. Bond; Michael Buker; Daniel K. Burke; Hilary Buttrick; Timothy J. Capen; Ben T. Caughey; Abigail Cella;

(This Listing Continued)

Ice Miller (Continued)

Katrina M. Clingerman; Rhonda L. Cook; David E. Corey (Not admitted in IN); Sarah Dansker Cotterill; Brian C. Crist; Michael Dalrymple; Steven R. Davis; Jody DeFord; Matthew G. DeLaruelle; Jason R. Delk; Aaron J. Dixon; Dustin S. DuBois; Gregory A. Duff; Tami A. Earnhart; Alison Emery; Homer W. Faucett, III; Matthew Fechtman; Amy Kathleen Fisher; Alexander D. Forman; Jennifer Bartels Frahm; Cassandra A. Giles; Benjamin M. Habegger; Melanie E. Harris; Beth E. Hatfield; Donald Hostetler; Dewayne A. Hughes; Paul M. Jones, Jr.; Stacy S. Killian; Dorothy Koontz; Angela Pease Krahulik; Scott D. Matthews; William Maynie, IV; Michael McNally; Kimberly C. Metzger; Drew Miroff; Thomas B. Mulhern (Not admitted in IN); Brian J. Paul; Steven F. Pockrass; Ryan M. Poor; April Sparks Pyatt; Elizabeth Townsend Laughlin Raymond; Susan B. Reed; Mark C. Reichel; Jennifer L. Rhodes; Matthew R. St. Louis; Rachel St. Peter; Samuel Schmutte; Eric C. Scroggins; Tiffany A. Sharpley; Mark I. Shublak; Cheryl L. Silverthorne; Jack Skinner; Rabeh M. A. Soofi; Michael C. Steele; Eric Swank; Jennifer A. Thomas; Ann L. Thrasher Papa; Kristina M. Tridico; Nathaniel M. Uhl; Andrew N. Vento; Katherine A. Winchester.
Administrative Law, Antitrust, Appellate Practice, Architectural Malpractice Law, Banking, Bankruptcy, Broadcasting and Communications, Cable TV, Cable TV Franchising, Civil and Criminal Litigation, Civil Rights, Coal Law, College and University Law, Commercial and Business Litigation, Complex Litigation, Computer Law, Contracting and Litigation, Construction Law, Corporate Law, Corporate Finance, Creditors Rights Law, Drug and Medical Device Litigation, Economic Development and Incentives, Education Law, Employee Benefits Law, Entrepreneurial Services, Environmental Law, Estate Development and Finance, Franchise Law, Gaming Law, Gift and Estate Tax, Governmental Affairs, Governmental Relations, Governmental Services and Lobbying, Government Law, Government (Public) Contract Law, Government Procurement, Guardianship, Health Care Law, Immigration Law, Insurance Law, Intellectual Property and Licensing, International Law, Labor and Employment Law (including Equal Employment Litigation, ERISA Practice and Occupational Safety and Health Matters), Liability Risk Management, Licensing, Management Labor Relations Law, Mergers and Acquisitions, Minerals and Mining, Municipal Finance (Bond) Law, Municipal Finance (Bond), Dispute Resolution and Litigation, Municipal Litigation, Municipal Solid Waste Resource Recovery, Municipal Utility Regulation, Occupational Hazards Law (Black Lung, Asbestosis, etc.), Patent, Trademark and Copyright, Plaintiff's Trial Practice, Probate Law, Product Liability Law, Public Agency, Public Authority Financing Law, Public Contract Law, Public Employment Relations, Public Entity Law, Public Finance, Public Health Law, Public Housing Law, Public Schools, Public Sector Collective Bargaining, Public Utility Law, Public Works, Professional Malpractice Law, Real Estate Law (including Sales, Development and Financing, Mortgage Banking, Secured Transactions, Sale/Leasebacks, Condominiums and Zoning), Regulation, Risk and Claims Management, Securities Regulation Law, Sports Law, Taxation (Federal, State and Local), Tax Exempt Organizations, Tort Law, Toxic Torts, Transportation Law, Utility Law, Venture Capital, Venture Finance Services, Workers' Compensation.
Counsel for: American United Life Insurance Co.; Chrysler Corp.; Ford Motor Company; General Electric Company; Indiana Bankers Assn.
Chicago, Illinois Office: 200 West Madison, Suite 3500. Telephone: 312-726-1567. Fax: 312-726-7102. Internet Email: info@icemiller.com. Web Site Address: http://www.icemiller.com.
Washington, D.C. Office: 1090 Vermont Avenue, N.W., Suite 920. Telephone: 202-824-8600. Fax: 202-824-8601. Email: info@icemiller.com.Web Site Address: http://www.icemiller.com
Reviser of the Indiana Law Digest for this Directory.

See Professional Biographies, INDIANAPOLIS, INDIANA

Imel, Angela K. .... '— '02 C.347 B.A. L.345 J.D. [A Barnes&T.]
Indiano, E. Victor, (AV) .... '55 '82 C.347 A.B. L.345 J.D. [Indiano&V.&Assoc.] (Pat.)
Indiano & Vaughan, A Professional Association, (AV)
One North Pennsylvania Street, Suite 850 (Pat.)
Inselberg, Robert F. ....'79 '04 C.347 B.S. L.345 J.D. [A Wooden&M.]
Inskeep, Kenneth H., (AV) ....'— '82 C.265 B.A. L.1119 J.D. [Barnes&T.]
Intermill, Alex C. ....'73 '05 C.679 B.A. L.345 J.D. [A Bose M.&E.]
Inveiss, Roberts E. ....'61 '86 C.966 B.A. L.477 J.D. [Bose M.&E.]
Iosue, Laura B. '67 '92 C.339 B.A. L.209 J.D.
Staff Atty., Disciplinary Comm. of the Supm. Ct.
Irvin, Alan J. ....'66 '92 C&L.347 B.A., J.D. [Hill,F.M.F.&M.]
Irvin, Wendy S. ....'— '92 C.347 B.A. L.1119 J.D. 101 W. Ohio, Suite 1100
Irwin, Michael K., (AV) ....'47 '72 C.210 B.A. L.345 J.D. [Stewart&I.]
Isaac, Ronald G., (BV) ....'42 '71 C.347 A.B. L.345 J.D. [Klapper,I.&P.]
Isaacs, Dwayne C. ....'60 '89 C.1119 B.S. L.345 J.D. [Bingham M.]
Isaacs, Joan .... '57 '94 C.679 B.S. L.347 J.D. [A Tabbert H.E.&W.]
Isenbarger, Phil L., (AV) ....'59 '84 C.347 B.S. L.1119 J.D. [Bingham M.]
Isley, Kenneth D. '62 '88 C.350 B.S. L.352 J.D.
(adm. in IL; not adm. in IN) 9330 Zionville Rd.
Ittenbach, John F., (AV) ....'44 '73 C.63 B.S. L.345 J.D. [Ittenbach J.T.&K.]
Ittenbach Johnson Trettin & Koeller, (AV) .... 6350 N. Shadeland Ave., Ste. 4
Ivers, William N., (AV) ....'61 '87 C.679 B.A. L.879 J.D. [Stewart&I.]
Iverson, L. Peter ....'47 '74 C.679 B.A. L.345 J.D. Allied Fidelity Ins. Co.
Iza, Angela D. ....'74 '04 C.347 B.S. L.345 J.D. [A Lewis&K.]
Jabbari, Sarah M. ....'71 '00 C.679 B.S. L.345 J.D. [A Baker&D.] (See Pat. Sect.)
Jackson, Benjamin S. ....'65 '90 C.894 B.A. L.879 J.D. Hoosier Gasket Corp.
Jackson, Karoline E. ....'— '98 C.63 B.A. L.1119 J.D. [A Barnes&T.]
Jackson, Kimberly ....'— '86 C.347 B.A. L.74 J.D. [A Jensen&Assoc.]
Jackson, Lynn E., (AV) .... '44 '73 C.347 B.S. L.345 J.D. 431 E. Hanna Ave.
Jackson, Thomas E. '44 '90 C.691 B.A. L.1338 J.D.
(adm. in PA; not adm. in IN; Pat.) Pat. Coun., Eli Lilly & Co.
Jacobs, Andrew, Jr. '32 '58 C.347 B.S. L.345 LL.B.
Congressman to U.S. House of Rep.
Jacobs, Samuel L., (AV) ....'49 '76 C.347 B.A. L.345 J.D. [Mitchell H.J.&D.]
Jacobs, Steven R., (AV) ....'49 '74 C.210 B.A. L.345 J.D. 151 N. Delaware
Jacobson, Christine K., (BV) ....'60 '92 C.347 B.S. L.276 J.D. [A Wooden&M.]
Jaffe, Jay, (AV) ....'57 '82 C.347 B.A. L.1119 J.D. [Baker&D.]
Jagoditz, Bonnie B. ....'76 '03 C.347 B.A. L.345 J.D. [A Bingham M.]
Jaimet, Michael G. '49 '74 C&L.347 B.A., J.D.
Dep. Gen. Coun., Clarian Health Partners, Inc.
James, Robert G., (BV) ....'32 '71 C.346 B.S. L.345 J.D. [R.G.James]
James, Robert Garrett, Jr., (BV) .... '63 '92 C.210 B.A. L.345 J.D. [Baxter,J.&R.]
James, Robert G., P.C., (BV) .... 7212 North Shadeland Avenue, Suite 150
Janak, J. Christopher ....'66 '95 C.894 B.A. L.347 J.D. [Bose M.&E.]
Jansen, Margaret Lois ....'48 '95 C.999 B.A. L.345 J.D. 4911 E. 56th Street
Janzen, Todd J. ....'73 '00 C.83 B.A. L.345 J.D. [A Plews S.R.&B.]
Jarzyniecki, Thomas J., Jr., (AV) ....'59 '85 C.107 B.A. L.879 J.D. [Kightlinger&G.]
Jasper, Paul G. ....'08 '32 L.1119 LL.B. 6464 Illinois St.‡
Jebens, Susan Cecelia ....'60 '85 C.347 B.S. L.345 J.D. Tax Mgr., Coopers & Lybrand
Jefferson, Bruce A. ....'58 '83 C.347 B.A. L.209 J.D. 100 N. Senate Ave., Ste. N103
Jefferson, Paul L. ....'— '03 C.894 A.B. L.345 J.D. [A Barnes&T.]
Jeffrey, George B., (AV) ....'22 '50 C.893 L.345 LL.B. 510 W. 63rd St.‡
Jeffs, Laura C., (CV) ....'65 '90 C.347 B.A. L.345 J.D. [A Cohen&M.]
Jegen, Lawrence A., III ....'34 '59 C.72 A.B. L.477 J.D. Prof. of Law, Ind. Univ.
Jenkins, Jerry R., (AV) ....'44 '69 C.798 A.B. L.228 J.D. [Baker&D.]
Jenkins, Sheila F. '— '99
C.999 B.B.S. L.345 J.D. Executive Director, Comm. Dev. Law Center
Jenkins, Thomas A., (AV) ....'— '68 C.679 B.A. L.1119 J.D. [A Hall,R.K.H.&L.]
Jensen, Herbert A., (BV) ....'— '75 C.249 B.A. L.345 J.D. [Jensen&Assoc.]
Jensen, Travis N. ....'— '99 C.679 B.A. L.1119 J.D. [A Tabor]

Jensen & Associates, (BV)
7440 North Shadeland Suite 202, 46250
Telephone: 317-849-5834 Fax: 317-849-5974 URL: http://www.jensenlaw.com
Email: jensen@iquest.net URL: http://www.jensenlaw-firm.com

(This Listing Continued)

Jensen & Associates (Continued)

Herbert A. Jensen. Associates: Arthur E. Johnson; Kimberly Jackson; Jennifer L. D'Orso; Karen H. Young. Of Counsel: Jeanne Lee McMains.
Family Law, Adoptions, Child Custody, Child Support, Divorce, Visitation Rights, Business Law, Business Planning, Contracts, Insurance Business, Business Enterprises, Corporate, Closely Held Business, Limited Liability Companies, Partnerships, Small Business, Business Litigation, Buying and Selling a Business, Starting a Business, Civil Litigation, Wills and Probate, Trusts and Estates, Asset Protection, Guardianships, Estate Planning, Family and Civil Mediation.
See Professional Biographies, INDIANAPOLIS, INDIANA

Jeselskis, Kimberly D. ... '73 '01 C.63 B.S. L.879 J.D. [Ⓐ Macey S.&A.]
Jewell, George B. '44 '71 C.72 B.A. L.910 J.D.
(adm. in IL; not adm. in IN) Vice Pres., Renaissance Inc.
Jocham, Kirk R. ... '— '01 C.999 B.A. L.345 J.D. [Ⓐ Hall,R.K.H.&L.]
Jodka, Eric C., (AV) ... '46 '74 C.249 B.S. L.345 J.D. 6500 E. Westfield Blvd.
Joe, Jowdat ... '39 '76 C.679 B.S. L.345 J.D. 1545 N. Post Rd.
Johanningsmeier, Ryan D. ... '75 '00 C.679 B.S. L.347 J.D. 151 N. Delaware St.
Johnson, Aaron D. '71 '98 C&L.347 B.S., J.D.
Assoc. Coun., Citizens Gas & Coke Utility
Johnson, Amy Stewart, (BV) '64 '92
C.228 B.A. L.347 J.D. Atty., SAFECO Prop. & Cas. Ins. Co.
Johnson, Arthur E., (BV) ... '— '95 C.63 B.S. L.345 J.D. [Ⓐ Jensen&Assoc.]
Johnson, Clifton E., (AV) ... '— '80 C.607 B.A. L.823 J.D. [Hall,R.K.H.&L.]
Johnson, David Lawther, (AV) ... '52 '80 C&L.309 A.B., J.D. [ⓒ Baker&D.]
Johnson, Dennis A., (AV) ... '— '85 C.347 B.S. L.345 J.D. [Barnes&T.]
Johnson, Eric D., (AV) ... '68 '93 C&L.347 B.S., J.D. [Kightlinger&G.]
Johnson, Eric R., (AV) ... '— '75 C.347 B.A. L.813 J.D. [Sommer B.]
Johnson, Erik C. ... '79 '04 C.209 B.S. L.145 J.D. [Ⓐ McTurnan&T.]
Johnson, F. Bradford, (AV) ... '49 '77 C.894 A.B. L.345 J.D. [Ittenbach J.T.&K.]
Johnson, G. Weldon, (AV) ... '— '57 C.347 B.S. L.1119 J.D. [ⓒ Hall,R.K.H.&L.]
Johnson, Herbert W., Jr., (BV) ... '38 '69 C.108 B.S. L.345 J.D. [White&J.]
Johnson, Jeremy B. ... '77 '02 C.265 B.A. L.345 J.D. [Ⓐ Wooden&M.]
Johnson, Kenneth H. ... '44 '72 C.303 A.B. L.345 J.D. Supr. Ct. J.
Johnson, Lacy M., (AV) ... '52 '81 C.679 B.A. L.347 J.D. [Ice M.]
Johnson, Lesa Lux, (BV) ... '55 '82 C.347 B.A. L.345 J.D. P.O. Box 20406
Johnson, Lonnie ... '— '03 C&L.221 B.S., J.D. [Ⓐ Sommer B.]
Johnson, Molly C. ... '74 '02 C.679 B.A. L.424 [Ⓐ C.E.Shirley]
Johnson, Richard L., (AV) ... '— '72 C.585 B.A. L.1065 J.D. [Barnes&T.]
Johnson, Robert W., (BV) ... '68 '93 C.472 B.A. L.1119 J.D. [Ⓐ Tabor]
Johnson, Ruth A. ... '59 '91 C.347 B.S. L.1119 J.D. Dep. Pub. Def.
Johnson, Whitney J. ... '70 '02 C.999 B.A. L.74 J.D. [Ⓐ Bingham M.]

Johnson Lawhead Buth & Pope, P.C.
(See Barnes & Thornburg)

Johnsonbaugh, Steven H., (BV) ... '49 '84 C.63 B.S. L.345 J.D. 302 N.E. St.
Johnston, Harold R., II ... '56 '83 C.347 B.A. L.345 J.D. Adm. Law J.
Jones, Amy M. ... '74 '01 C.679 B.A. L.1187 J.D. [Ⓐ Threlkeld R.]
Jones, Barbara A. ... '— '90 C&L.347 B.A., J.D. [ⓒ Bingham M.]
Jones, Bruce L. ... '51 '83 C.347 B.S. L.345 J.D. [Severns&B.]
Jones, Buren E. ... '62 '00 C.249 B.S. L.345 J.D. [Ⓐ Bose M.&E.]
Jones, Christian P. ... '— '00 C.347 B.A. L.94 J.D. [Ⓐ Barnes&T.]
Jones, David E., (BV) ... '39 '72 C.347 B.A. L.345 J.D. 8855 Southeastern Ave.
Jones, Fred L. ... '47 '77 C.679 B.A. L.345 J.D. Pres., Old Republic Title Co. of Ind., Inc.
Jones, Harold W., (AV) ... '03 '33 C.347 A.B. L.1119 J.D. 54 Monument Cir.
Jones, Jennifer Elaine, (BV) '62 '90
C.679 B.S.I.M. L.347 J.D. Royal Title Servs. - Statewide
Jones, Jerry W., (BV) ... '32 '59 C.347 A.B. L.345 LL.B. 717 S. East St.
Jones, John Paul, Jr., (BV) ... '30 '56 C.894 A.B. L.345 LL.B. 210 S. Audubon Rd.
Jones, Kurt N. ... '61 '92 C.701 B.S. L.347 J.D. [Woodard,E.M.M.&H.] (See Pat. Sect.)
Jones, Kyle A., (BV) ... '63 '88 C.347 B.A. L.345 J.D. [Norris C.&S.]
Jones, Mark A. '55 '80 C.347 B.S. L.345 J.D.
400 Barrister Bldg., 155 East Market Street
Jones, Patricia A. ... '42 '90 C.628 B.S. L.74 J.D. [Monday R.J.&A.]
Jones, Paul M., Jr. ... '75 '02 C.347 B.S. L.345 J.D. [ⓒ Ice M.]
Jones, Russell L. ... '58 '85 C.235 B.S. L.345 J.D. [Cohen G.&G.]
Jones, Steven L. ... '71 '98 C.679 B.S. L.345 J.D. [ⓒ Ice M.]
Jones, Susanne B., (AV) ... '37 '76 C.679 B.S. L.345 J.D. [ⓒ Miroff,C.&W.]
Jordan, Anne Gilmore ... '56 '91 C&L.347 B.A., J.D. 115 W. Washington St., Jud. Ct
Jordan, John E. ... '54 '85 C.701 B.S.C.E. L.345 J.D. Ind. Dept. of Trans.
Jordan, Michael A. ... '49 '74 C.347 A.B. L.1119 J.D. 7650 Central Ave.★
Jordan, R. Brock, (BV) ... '66 '93 C.350 B.S. L.352 J.D. [Rubin&L.]
Jordan, Ronald T. '53 '83 C&L.150 B.B.A., J.D.
(adm. in OH; not adm. in IN) I.R.S.
Jose, David Elliott, (AV) ... '53 '81 C.231 B.A. L.93 J.D. [Krieg D.]
Joseph, Elizabeth ... '78 '04 C.347 B.S. L.1119 J.D. [Ⓐ Hunt S.K.]
Joseph, Rex M., Jr., Law Office of, (BV) '45 '70
C.347 B.S. L.1119 J.D. 5150 E. Stop 11 Rd., Ste. 12
Jost, Anthony R., (BV) ... '67 '93 C.210 B.A. L.1119 J.D. [Riley B.&E.]
Judd, Lisa F., (BV) ... '53 '90 C.344 B.A. L.347 J.D. Pros. Atty.
Judge-Prein, Amy B., (AV) '67 '92
C.207 B.A. L.477 J.D. Atty., Law Div., Eli Lilly & Co.
Judkins, Brandon S. ... '— '03 C.108 B.A. L.1119 J.D. [Ⓐ Baker&D.]
Judson, Lilia G. ... '49 '75 C.347 B.A. L.345 J.D. Dir., Div. of State Ct. Admn.
Juergensen, Randall L., (BVⓉ) ... '54 '81 C.477 B.A. L.912 J.D. 2850 N. Meridian St.
Jurkiewicz, David J., (BV) ... '67 '94 C.912 B.S. L.1119 J.D. [Bose M.&E.]
Justak, Martine H., (Mrs.), (BV) ... '26 '49 C&L.597 LL.B. V.P., Blade-Tech, Inc.
Justak, Raymond J., (BV) '25 '50 C&L.597 B.S., J.D.
Chmn., Ind. Parole Bd., State of Ind.
Kahlenbeck, Douglas H. ... '66 '93 C.659 B.S. L.347 J.D. Corp. Coun., Renaissance Inc.
Kahlenbeck, Howard, Jr., (AV) ... '29 '57 C.347 B.S. L.477 J.D. [Krieg D.] ‡
Kaiser, Douglas ... '50 '98 C&L.347 B.A., J.D. IRS
Kaiser, George T. ... '44 '74 C.347 B.S. L.1119 J.D. 6129 W. 32nd Pl.‡
Kaiser, Todd J., (AV) ... '61 '86 C.210 B.A. L.345 J.D. [Ogletree,D.N.S.&S.]
Kaiser, William J., Jr., (BV) ... '65 '90 C.894 B.A. L.347 J.D. [Bingham M.] (⊙Jasper)
Kalsi, Swadesh S. ... '43 '77 C.054 B.S. L.273 LL.M. [Krieg D.]
Kaltenmark, Randal J. ... '— '96 C.879 B.A. L.347 J.D. [Ⓐ Barnes&T.]
Kamish, Mark Edward ... '60 '00 C.870 B.S. L.345 J.D. 8900 Keystone Crossing, Ste. 400
Kammen, Richard, (AV) ... '46 '71 C.694 A.B. L.569 J.D. 1 Indiana Sq Ste 150
Kamplain, Bruce L., (BV) ... '50 '77 C.303 B.A. L.345 J.D. [Norris C.&S.]
Kane, Larry J. ... '45 '75 C.679 B.S.E.E. L.1119 J.D. [Bingham M.]
Kanne, Roger K., (BV) ... '57 '83 C.347 B.A. L.1049 J.D. [Zeigler C.&K.]
Kappes, Philip S., (AV) ... '25 '48 C.108 B.A. L.477 J.D. [Lewis&K.]
Kappes, Timothy W. '61 '87
C.347 B.A. L.589 J.D. Assoc. Coun., Union Acceptance Corp.
Karlson, Henry C. '43 '68 C&L.339 A.B., J.D.
(adm. in IL; not adm. in IN) Prof. of Law, Indiana Uni. Sch. of Law‡
Karozos, Amy E. ... '60 '89 C&L.347 B.A., J.D. State Pub. Def.
Karpinski, Stacey Herman '67 '93 C.37 B.F.A. L.259 J.D.
(adm. in FL; not adm. in IN) Natl. Collegiate Athletic Assn.
Karwath, Bart A., (AV) ... '— '91 C.347 B.S. L.1119 J.D. [Barnes&T.]
Kashani, Hamid R. ... '55 '86 C.679 B.S.E.E. L.345 J.D. 445 N. Pennsylvania St.
Kasper, David T., (AV) ... '44 '69 C.867 B.A. L.1119 J.D. [Locke R.]
Kassing, Robert P., (AV) ... '37 '64 C.347 B.S. L.1119 J.D. [Bose M.&E.]
Katt, Suzanne E. ... '47 '83 C.999 B.A. L.1119 J.D. [Ⓐ Cremer B.&C.]
Katz, Judith T., (BV) '46 '74 C.347 B.S. L.345 J.D.
Secy., Asst. Treas. & Coun., Max Katz Bag Co., Inc.
Katz, Ronald M., (AV) ... '58 '83 C.347 B.S. L.345 J.D. [Katz&K.]

Katz & Korin, PC, (AV) BB
334 North Senate Avenue, 46204-1708
Telephone: 317-464-1100 Fax: 317-464-1111
URL: http://www.katzkorin.com
Ronald M. Katz; Offer Korin; Sally Franklin Zweig; Michael W. Hile; Michael J. Gabovitch; Michael J. Kerschner; Cathleen L. Nevin;—Ronald G. Sentman; Linda L. Vitone; Brian S. Kenworthy; Robert B. Kirsh; Kristopher N. Kazmierczak. Of Counsel: Bernard Pylitt.
Appellate Practice, Art Law, Business Law, Bankruptcy, Charitable Planning, Collections, Commercial Lending, Contracts, Entertainment Law, Estate Planning and Administration, Health Care Law, Housing and Community Development Law, Intellectual Property Rights, High Technology Law, Labor and Employee Relations Law, Litigation, Mediation Services, Personal Injury, Product Defense, Real Estate Law and Tax Law.
See Professional Biographies, INDIANAPOLIS, INDIANA

Katzin, Michael F. '38 '64 C.145 B.A. L.597 J.D.
(adm. in IL; not adm. in IN) 7602 Woodland Dr.‡
Katzman, Alvin J., (AV) ... '49 '76 C.347 B.S. L.345 J.D. [Katzman&K.]
Katzman, Mariellen, (AV) ... '51 '78 C.347 B.S. L.345 J.D. [Katzman&K.]
Katzman & Katzman, P.C., (AV) ... 3905 Vincennes Road
Kaufman, Barton L. ... '41 '65 C.347 B.S. L.1119 J.D. CEO, Kaufman Fin. Corp.
Kaufman, Hannah ... '79 '04 C.347 B.A. L.345 J.D. [Ⓐ Lewis&K.]
Kaufman, Richard B., (AV) ... '58 '83 C.210 B.A. L.1119 J.D. [Ⓐ Stark D.&S.]
Kautzman, John F., (AV) ... '59 '85 C.347 A.B. L.345 J.D. [Ruckelshaus,R.K.B.&H.]
Kaye, Michael J., (AV) ... '— '87 C.475 B.A. L.345 J.D. [Barnes&T.]
Kazmierczak, Kristopher N. ... '— '96 C.347 B.A. L.1119 J.D. [Ⓐ Katz&K.]
Kear, Fergus M. ... '43 '71 C.63 B.S. L.345 J.D. 1 Virginia Avenue
Kear, Russell H., Jr. ... '38 '67 C&L.608 B.M.E., J.D. Int. Rev. Serv., Appeals Offc.
Keefer, Jan Kepley, (AV) ... '57 '91 C&L.347 B.A., J.D. [Bingham M.]
Keele, Michael D., (BV) ... '56 '82 C.894 B.A. L.345 J.D. Supr. Ct. J.
Keeler, John S., (AV) ... '49 '77 C.37 B.S. L.345 J.D. [Baker&D.]
Keene, Kenneth C. '44 '70 C.303 B.A. L.345 J.D.
Vice Chmn. of the Bd., McCready & Keene, Inc.
Keene, Robert B., (AV) ... '34 '66 C.347 B.S. L.273 J.D. 4713 Sheehan Pl.
Keeven, Richard D. '51 '76
C.701 B.S. L.345 J.D. Boehringer Mannheim Corp. (DePuy Div.)
Kehoe, D. Bruce, (AV) ... '50 '80 C.347 B.S. L.345 J.D. [Wilson,K.&W.] (⊙Richmond)
Keiffner, John D., III., (BV) ... '70 '95 C.853 B.A. L.347 J.D. Dep. Prosecutor
Keirn, Edward A., (AV) ... '— '83 C.999 B.S. L.345 J.D. [ⓒ Barnes&T.]
Keith, Priscilla D. ... '60 '96 C.811 B.S. L.345 J.D. Dep. Couns.
Kelaghan, Catherine I. ... '61 '90 C.201 B.S. L.150 J.D. Coun., Anthem, Inc.
Kellen, Thomas J. '47 '77 C.63 B.S. L.862 J.D.
(adm. in OK; not adm. in IN) P.O. Box 781015
Keller, Bernie Too ... '73 '98 C&L.602 B.A., J.D. [Bose M.&E.]
Keller, George S., (AVⓉ) ... '11 '36 C.477 B.A. L.602 LL.B. [Keller&K.]
Keller, Kelli R. ... '69 '95 C.912 B.S. L.347 J.D. Staff Atty., Simon Property Group
Keller & Keller, (AVⓉ) ... 2850 North Meridian (⊙St. Joseph, MI)
Kellett, Glen M. ... '— '05 C.679 B.S.E.E.T. L.345 J.D. [Ⓐ Barnes&T.]
Kelley, G. Daniel, Jr., (AV) ... '40 '68 C.303 A.B. L.345 J.D. [Ice M.]
Kelley, James J. ... '51 '96 C.477 B.S. L.347 J.D. Pat. Coun., Eli Lilly & Co. (Pat.)
Kelley, Stacy L. ... '69 '96 C.347 B.A. L.734 J.D. [Lee B.C.&K.]
Kelley, William E., Jr ... '78 '03 C.303 B.A. L.345 J.D. [Ⓐ Drewry S.V.]
Kelly, Edward F. ... '— '63 C.602 A.B. L.966 LL.B. 23 E. 39th St.
Kelly, Jerome P., (AV) '53 '86 C.477 B.S. L.215 J.D.
Asst. Gen. Coun., Clarian Health Partners, Inc.
Kelly, Robin L. ... '70 '95 C.945 B.A. L.345 J.D. [Ⓐ Mitchell&Assoc.]
Kelso, M. Jane ... '28 '53 C.339 A.B. L.347 J.D. Orchard Country Day School
Kelso, Robert M., (AV) ... '55 '81 C.347 B.S. L.345 J.D. [Kightlinger&G.]
Keltner, Kristin B. ... '70 '98 C.879 B.A. L.347 J.D. [Ⓐ Ogletree,D.N.S.&S.]
Kemper, James D., (AV) ... '47 '71 C.347 B.S. L.1119 J.D. [Ice M.]
Kempf, Richard A., (AV) ... '— '87 C.347 B.S. L.345 J.D. [Sommer B.]
Kendall, Leah R. ... '77 '02 C.108 B.S. L.1119 J.D. [Ⓐ Baker&D.]
Kendall, Rebecca O., (AV) '48 '75 C.347 B.S. L.345 J.D.
Sen. V.P. & Gen. Coun., Law Div., Eli Lilly & Co.

Kendall, Wood, Lowry & Kessinger
(See Danville)

Kenemore, Max J. '41 '68 C.613 B.S. L.616 J.D.
(adm. in OK; not adm. in IN; Pat.) 9115 Hague Rd.
Kenley, Stephen P. ... '53 '95 C&L.502 B.S., J.D. [Ⓐ Mitchell H.J.&D.]

Kennedy, Diane Hubbard, (AV) '50 '79 C.63 B.S. L.345 J.D.
4911 East 56th Street, 46220-5719
Telephone: 317-254-1443 Fax: 317-254-1449
Email: d_kennedy@iquest.net URL: http://www.dhkennedylaw.com
Estate Planning, Wills and Probate, Trusts and Estates, Estate and Gift Taxation Law.
See Professional Biographies, INDIANAPOLIS, INDIANA

Kennedy, Jay P., (AV) ... '56 '82 C.1365 B.A. L.345 J.D. [Kroger,G.&R.]
Kennedy, Sheila S. '41 '75 C.347 B.S. L.345 J.D.
Indiana Univ. Purdue Univ. Indianpolis
Kennedy, Timothy J., (AV) ... '49 '75 C.347 A.B. L.904 J.D. [Miller M.M.&K.]
Kennedy, Timothy W., (AV) ... '— '83 C.894 B.A. L.345 J.D. [Hall,R.K.H.&L.]
Kenny, Douglas Grant ... '58 '83 C.607 B.A. L.345 J.D. Co. Off. of Fam. & Child.
Kenny, Linda Nichols, (AV) ... '59 '84 C.879 B.S. L.345 J.D. [ⓒ Bingham M.]
Kenworthy, Brian S. ... '72 '02 C.347 B.A. L.345 J.D. [Ⓐ Katz&K.]
Kenworthy, Cindy L., (BV) ... '55 '85 C.347 B.S. L.201 J.D. [C.L.Kenworthy]
Kenworthy, Cindy L., PC, (BV) ... 3891 Eagle Creek Pkwy., Ste. B
Kerkhof, Jerry L., (BV) ... '34 '75 C.178 B.A. L.345 J.D. 3448 W. 16th St.
Kern, Christina L. Benson '59 '83 C.612 B.S. L.623 J.D.
(adm. in OK; not adm. in IN) 12190 Bridgewater Rd.
Kern, Kenneth C. '33 '65 C.150 B.A. L.151 J.D.
5407 East Pleasant Run Parkway South Drive
Kern, Owen S., (BV) ... '25 '51 C.347 B.S. L.1119 J.D. 4701 N. Franklin Rd.
Kerner, Jeffrey K. ... '71 '02 C.894 B.A. L.344 J.D. Indiana State Dept. of Health
Kerr, William A. ... '34 '57 C&L.923 A.B., J.D. Contract Atty., Pub. Def. Agcy‡
Kerschner, Michael J. ... '66 '92 C.339 B.S. L.146 J.D. [Katz&K.]
Ketcham, John M., (BV) ... '55 '88 C.347 B.A. L.477 J.D. [Plews S.R.&B.]

Key, Stephen A. ... '55 '94 C.108 B.S. L.74 J.D. Hoosier State Press Assn.
Key, Walter R. ... '42 '70 6362 Minlo Dr.‡
Kias, Michael J., (AV) ... '38 '62 C.801 B.S. L.345 J.D. 3045 S. Meridian St.
Kibbe, Guy G., (BV) ... '53 '86 C.347 B.S. L.345 J.D. 7119 U.S. Hwy. 31, S.
Kidd, Charles Martin, (AV) ... '57 '88 C.108 B.S. L.345 J.D. Staff Atty.
Kiefer, J. Richard, (AV) ... '48 '75 C.679 B.A. L.1119 J.D. [Kiefer&M.]
Kiefer, Kathleen S. ... '65 '91 C.880 B.A. L.188 J.D. [Ⓒ Ice M.]
Kiefer, Michael A., (BV) ... '47 '73 C.602 B.A. L.345 J.D. [Garrison&K.]

Kiefer and McGoff, (AV) BR
8900 Keystone Crossing, Suite 400, 46240-2146
Telephone: 317-848-2300 Fax: 317-574-3000 URL: http://www.kmlawyers.com
URL: http://www.lawyers.com/kiefer&mcgoff
J. Richard Kiefer; Kevin P. McGoff. Associates: Whitney D. Mauk; James J. Bell; Darlene R. Seymour.
Criminal Trials and Appeals, State and Federal Courts, Health Care Law, Attorney Legal Ethics and Professional Responsibility, Family Law, Civil Litigation.
See Professional Biographies, INDIANAPOLIS, INDIANA

Kiefner, Elizabeth E. ... '75 '03 C.347 B.A. L.74 J.D. Dep. Atty. Gen.
Kielty, Ellen ... '42 '83 C.555 B.A. L.345 J.D. Sr. Staff Atty., Simon Property Group
Kight, Andrew T. ... '— '98 C.299 B.A. L.1119 J.D. [Ⓐ Sommer B.]
Kight, Paula Thrun ... '48 '73 C.108 B.A. L.347 J.D. 156 E. Market St.‡

Kightlinger & Gray, LLP, (AV)
Market Square Center, Suite 600, 151 North Delaware Street, 46204 ⊙
Telephone: 317-638-4521 Telecopier: 317-636-5917
Email: info@k-glaw.com URL: http://www.k-glaw.com
Partners: Donald L. Dawson; Peter G. Tamulonis; Richard A. Young; Michael E. Brown; Mark D. Gerth; Steven E. Springer; Richard T. Mullineaux (Resident, New Albany Office); Robert M. Kelso; Brent R. Weil (Resident, Evansville Office); John B. Drummy; James W. Roehrdanz; Peter A. Velde; Thomas J. Jarzyniecki, Jr.; Van T. Willis (Resident, New Albany Office); Mary Jo Wetzel (Resident, New Albany Office); Steven K. Palmquist (Resident, New Albany Office); William E. Smith, III (Resident, New Albany Office); Eric D. Johnson; D. Bryce Zoeller; Erin A. Clancy; Richard O. Hawley, Jr. (Resident, Evansville Office); R. Jeffrey Lowe (Resident, New Albany Office); Pfenne P. Cantrell; Ginny L. Peterson; Jeffrey D. Hawkins; Marcia A. Mahony. Of Counsel: Mark William Gray. Associates: J. Todd Spurgeon (Resident, New Albany Office); Susan G. Gainey; Libby S. Valos Moss; D. Keith Pulliam (Resident, New Albany Office); Elliott Pinkie; James C. Wade (Resident, New Albany Office); Kristen M. Carroll; Michelle Hawk Kazmierczak; Jason J. Hoy; Adam F. Packer; Jennifer M. Herrmann; Nicholas W. Levi; Aubrey G. Kuchar; Eric E. Lamb; Marie L. Van Dam; Michael Wroblewski; Donna J. Jenkins (Resident, New Albany Office); Sacha L. Armstrong (Resident, Evansville Office); Curtis D. Condict (Resident, Evansville Office); Chad M. Smith (Resident, Evansville Office); Valerie D. Kessler (Resident, New Albany Office).
Civil Litigation, Commercial and Business Litigation, Drug and Medical Device Litigation, Environmental and Toxic Tort Litigation, Casualty, Surety and Life Insurance Law, General Litigation, Malpractice Litigation (Pharmacy, Medical, Legal, Architects and Engineers, Accountants, Insurance Agents, Real Estate Agents and School Boards), Products Liability Law, Trucking Defense Litigation, Construction Law, ICC Regulatory Law, Appeals (State and Federal), Worker's Compensation, Maritime Law, Civil Rights and Wrongful Discharge Law, all areas of Government Liability, including Law Enforcement Liability Litigation, Class Actions, Labor Law, Securities Litigation.
Evansville, Indiana Office: 7311 Eagle Crest Blvd., 47715. Telephone: 812-474-4400. Telecopier: 812-474-4414.
New Albany, Indiana Office: One Commerce Square, 4106 Charlestown Road, 47150. Telephone: 812-949-2300. Telecopier: 812-949-8556.
See Professional Biographies, INDIANAPOLIS, INDIANA

Kile, Nicholas K., (BV) ... '— '90 C.108 B.S. L.1119 J.D. [Barnes&T.]
Killian, Barbara A. ... '— '99 C.147 B.A. L.347 J.D. [Ⓐ Hall,R.K.H.&L.]
Killian, Stacy S. ... '74 '00 C.999 B.A. L.602 J.D. [Ⓐ Ice M.]
Kilpatrick, Stephen L., (BV) ... '39 '66 C.347 B.A. L.1119 J.D. 151 N. Delaware St.
Kim, Marguerite Y. ... '60 '96 C.999 B.A. L.345 J.D. 9155 Woodacre Blvd. N. Dr.
Kim, Michael L. ... '— '96 C.910 B.A. L.862 J.D. [Ⓐ Hall,R.K.H.&L.]
Kimery Looney, Kristyn E. ... '73 '99 C&L.347 B.S.W., J.D. Asst. Chf. Coun.
Kimpel, Jason D. ... '73 '99 C.210 B.A. L.347 J.D. [Ⓐ Baker&D.]
King, Daniel P. ... '76 '01 C.210 B.A. L.1119 J.D. [Ⓐ Locke R.]
King, Douglas B., (AV) ... '51 '76 C.108 B.S. L.345 J.D. [Wooden&M.]
King, Frederick M., (AV) ... '— '64 C.347 B.S. L.1119 J.D. [Sommer B.]
King, J. B., (AV) ... '30 '54 C&L.347 A.B., LL.B. [Ⓒ Baker&D.]

King, Mark A., Attorney at Law '70 '98 C.347 B.A. L.345 J.D.
155 E. Market Street, Suite 450, 46204
Telephone: 317-634-5544 Fax: 317-630-4824
URL: http://www.makinglaw.com
Criminal Law, Driving Under Influence, Felonies, Homicide, Family Law, Child Custody, Child Support, Business Law, Social Security, Social Security Disability, Personal Injury.
See Professional Biographies, INDIANAPOLIS, INDIANA

King, Matthew R. ... '77 '03 C.970 B.A. L.74 J.D. [Ⓐ Locke R.]
King, Maxine E. ... '— '94 C.347 B.A. L.345 J.D. 3833 North Meridian Street, Suite 260

King, Robert D., Law Office of '70 '98 C.93 B.A. L.347 J.D.
152 East Washington Street, 46204-3680
Telephone: 317-916-0000 Fax: 317-633-7680
Email: rking@robertkinglaw.com URL: http://www.lawyers.com/robking
Personal Injury, Automobile Accidents, Dog Bites, Railroad Accidents, Slip and Fall, Wrongful Death, Toxic Mold, Police Brutality, Construction Accidents, Products Liability, Medical Malpractice, Criminal Law, Driving While Intoxicated, Drug Crimes, Felonies, Homicide, Juvenile Law, Misdemeanors, Parole and Probation, Traffic Violations, Sex Offenses, Domestic Battery.
See Professional Biographies, INDIANAPOLIS, INDIANA

Kinnard, Terrance L. ... '68 '00 C.638 B.A. L.345 J.D. [Kinnard]
Kinnard Law Office ... 155 E. Market, Ste. 711
Kinney, Eleanor D. '47 '73 C&L.228 A.B., J.D.
(adm. in OH; not adm. in IN)
Prof. of Law & Co-Dir., Ind. Univ. Sch. of Law, Ctr. Law & Health
Kinney, Keith A., (AV) ... '58 '83 C.210 B.A. L.345 J.D. [Hill,F.M.F.&M.]
Kinser, Douglas M. ... '— '97 C.347 B.A. L.345 J.D. [Hall,R.K.H.&L.]
Kinsey, Madalyn S., (BV) ... '53 '79 C.347 B.S. L.1119 J.D. [Kroger,G.&R.]
Kintner, Deron S. ... '76 '01 C&L.347 B.S., J.D. [Ⓐ Bingham M.]
Kinzie, Jan J., (BV) ... '— '85 C.210 B.A. L.74 J.D. [Ⓒ Ogletree,D.N.S.&S.]
Kipka, Ross Albin '30 '57 C.976 B.A. L.477 J.D.
(adm. in OH; not adm. in IN) 6161 N. Meridian-West Dr.‡
Kiplinger, Victor A., (BV) ... '46 '78 C.265 B.A. L.345 J.D. 302 N. East St.
Kirages, Christopher, (AV) '30 '56
C.894 A.B. L.1119 J.D. 3815 River Crossing Parkway, Suite 100
Kirby, Terrence P., Law Office '59 '85
C.347 B.S. L.201 J.D. 4216 N. College Ave., Ste. 4
Kirk, Carol McQuilkin ... '37 '89 C.339 B.S. L.347 J.D. Staff Atty.
Kirk, Cynthia M. ... '71 '97 C.63 B.S. L.345 J.D. [Ⓐ Dann P.N.&K.]
Kirk, Jeffrey J., II ... '73 '03 C.473 B.S. L.345 J.D. [Ⓐ Bose M.&E.]
Kirkwood, John R., (AV) ... '54 '79 C.347 B.S. L.1119 J.D. [Krieg D.]
Kirsch, James S. ... '46 '74 C.108 B.A. L.345 J.D. Ct. App. J.
Kirsh, Joel D., (AV) ... '59 '84 C.347 B.S. L.345 J.D. [Kirsh&K.]
Kirsh, Robert B. ... '69 '95 C.347 B.A. L.862 J.D. [Ⓐ Katz&K.]
Kirsh, Steven M., (AV) ... '54 '79 C.197 A.B. L.345 J.D. [Kirsh&K.]

Kirsh & Kirsh, P.C., (AV)
2930 East 96th Street (Hamilton County), 46240-3716
Telephone: 317-575-5555 Fax: 317-575-5631 URL: http://www.IndianaAdoption.com
Email: skirsh@kirsh.com URL: http://www.kirshlawfirm.com
Steven M. Kirsh; Joel D. Kirsh.
Adoption Law and Agency Adoptions.
Reference: National Bank of Indianapolis.
See Professional Biographies, INDIANAPOLIS, INDIANA

Kirtley, David E., (AV) '66 '91
C.894 A.B. L.880 J.D. Coun., Trademark Dept., Eli Lilly & Co.
Kissel, Richard O., II, (AV) ... '58 '85 C.347 B.S. L.1119 J.D. [Dann P.N.&K.]
Kitchen, John M., (AV) ... '12 '36 C.894 A.B. L.309 LL.B. 10 W. Market St.
Kittle, Jim, Jr. ... '43 '69 C.347 B.S. L.345 J.D. Chmn., Kittle's Home Furnishings Ctr.
Kitzinger, Kirk R., Law Offices, (AV) '58 '83
C.210 B.A. L.345 J.D. 9465 Counselors Row, Ste. 200
Kivett, Joseph L., (BV) ... '31 '59 C.108 A.B. L.345 LL.B. Admin. Law J.
Kixmiller, Robert V. ... '— '67 C.679 B.S. L.1119 J.D. [Ⓒ Barnes&T.]
Klaper, Martin J., (AV) ... '47 '71 C.347 B.S. L.1119 J.D. [Ice M.]
Klapper, Morris L., (AV) ... '41 '69 C.347 A.B. L.345 J.D. [Klapper,I.&P.]
Klapper, Isaac & Parish, (AV) ... 2506 Willowbrook Pkwy.
Kleiman, Andrew A., (BV) ... '61 '86 C.679 B.S. L.345 J.D. [Dann P.N.&K.]
Kleiman, David H., (AV) ... '34 '59 C.679 B.S. L.597 J.D. [Dann P.N.&K.]
Kleiman, Mary M., (AV) '59 '85 C.435 B.A. L.347 J.D.
V.P. & Assoc. Gen. Coun., Federal Home Loan Bank
Klein, Andrew R. '63 '88 C.966 B.A. L.245 J.D.
(adm. in IL; not adm. in IN) 530 W. New York Street‡
Kleinschmidt, Bruce L. '52 '79 C.269 B.A. L.421 J.D.
Community Organizations Legal Assistance Proj.
Klene, Therese McCullough '46 '86
C.347 B.A. L.209 J.D. Admin. Law J., Utility Regulatory Comm.
Klimek, James A., (BV) ... '67 '93 C.164 B.A. L.347 J.D. [Lewis&K.]
Kline, Casey J. ... '73 '98 C.347 B.S. L.339 J.D. Staff Atty.
Kline, Susan W. ... '— '00 C.108 B.S. L.345 J.D. [Ⓐ Baker&D.]
Klineman, Alan I., (AV) ... '31 '56 C.347 B.S. L.345 J.D. 77 S. Girls School Rd.
Klineman, James M., (AV) ... '37 '61 C.347 B.S. L.1119 J.D. [Ⓒ Miroff,C.&W.]
Klinestiver, David S. ... '59 '85 C&L.347 B.A., J.D. [Lewis&K.]
Klinestiver, John W. ... '26 '66 C&L.347 B.S., LL.B. 5156 E. 74th Pl.‡
Kling, Catherine A. ... '60 '89 C.645 B.S. L.347 J.D. [Ⓐ Miller M.M.&K.]
Klingerman, Trenten D. ... '71 '01 C.679 B.S. L.1119 J.D. [Ⓐ Stuart&B.] ⊙
Klopfer, Tibor D., (AV) ... '54 '79 C.347 B.A. L.145 J.D. [Baker&D.]
Klotz, Gary L., (AV) ... '52 '78 C.210 B.A. L.345 J.D. [Bingham M.]
Knapp, Brian F., (AV) '59 '85 C.347 B.S. L.602 J.D.
Real Estate Coun. & Develop. Mgr., Simon Property Group
Knapp, Paul J., (AV) '57 '82 C.347 B.S. L.602 J.D.
Pres., Young & Laramore Advertising
Knauer, James A., (AV) ... '— '71 C.347 B.S. L.345 J.D. [Kroger,G.&R.]
Knauer, Richard T. '63 '90
C.679 B.S. L.345 J.D. Pat. Atty., Roche Diagnostics Corp. (Pat.)
Knebel, Donald E., (AV) ... '— '74 C.679 B.S. L.309 J.D. [Barnes&T.]
Kniess, October Smith ... '55 '82 C&L.347 B.A., J.D. P.O. Box 44416
Knight, Kevin R., (AV) ... '60 '90 C.999 B.A. L.347 J.D. [Ice M.]
Knight, Teresa E. '72 '04
C.940 B.A. L.345 J.D. [Ⓐ Woodard,E.M.M.&H.] (See Pat. Sect.)
Knoblock, Erick P., (BV) ... '66 '95 C&L.347 B.A., J.D. [Ⓐ Dale&E.]
Knoll, Kirk A. ... '60 '86 C.347 B.S. L.345 J.D. Dep. Atty. Gen.
Knotts, Elizabeth H., (BV) ... '64 '91 C&L.347 B.A., J.D. [Hill,F.M.F.&M.]
Knotts, H. Spencer '56 '84 C.347 B.A. L.345 J.D.
Sr. Staff Atty., Simon Property Group

Knowles & Associates, LLC
(See Carmel)

Koch, Edna M., (BV) ... '51 '80 C.346 B.S. L.345 J.D. [Zeigler C.&K.]
Koch, L. Michael, (BV) ... '64 '90 C.894 B.A. L.345 J.D. [Brooks,K.&S.]
Koch, Tammy S. ... '73 '98 C.679 B.A. L.345 J.D. [Ⓐ Drewry S.V.]
Kochell, Douglas J. ... '— '89 C.1119 B.S. L.345 J.D. [Ⓐ Hall,R.K.H.&L.]
Kochell, Howard E., (AV) ... '— '83 C.347 B.S. L.1119 J.D. [Barnes&T.]
Koehler, Pamela K. ... '72 '97 C.967 B.A. L.347 J.D. [Hall G.]
Koehlinger, Jeffrey S. ... '— '90 C.317 A.B. L.1119 J.D. 9330 Zionsville Road
Koenig, John T. L. ... '— '98 C.347 B.A. L.74 J.D. [Ⓐ Barnes&T.]
Koepper, Paul N. ... '41 '69 C.679 B.S.C.E. L.345 J.D. Atty, I.R.S.
Koers, Stephen M. ... '67 '92 C.597 B.A. L.347 J.D. [Ⓐ Wood T.G.M.&H.]
Kofodimos, Teresa E. ... '63 '88 C.108 B.S. L.345 J.D. Farm Bur. Ins. Cos.
Kohart, Kevin M., (BV) ... '69 '95 C.145 B.A. L.339 J.D. BMW Constructors, Inc.
Kohlhaas, Ian B. ... '67 '97 C.178 B.A. L.990 J.D. [Ⓐ Bowman,H.B.&V.]
Kohlhaas, Michael R. ... '73 '98 C.347 B.A. L.1119 J.D. [Ⓒ Bingham M.]
Koivuniemi, Paul J. '50 '83
C.475 B.A. L.477 J.D. Eli Lilly and Company (Law Division) (Pat.)
Kolas, John E., (AV) ... '56 '83 C.679 B.A. L.424 J.D. 1040 E. 86th St., Ste. 42-A
Kolb, Alan F., (BV) '44 '72
C.475 B.A. L.347 J.D. Coml. Closing Offr., Chicago Title Ins. Co.
Komsiski, Peter O. '54 '81 C.894 B.A. L.347 J.D.
Pension Coun., Gardner & White Corp.
Konnersman, David, (BV) ... '40 '73 C.347 B.A. L.851 J.D. [Lewis W.]
Konomos, Jennifer C. ... '68 '95 C.205 B.A. L.608 J.D. Meridian Ins. Cos.
Koons, Gina Skelton ... '58 '83 C&L.347 B.S., J.D. Meridian Insurance Group, Inc.
Koons, Karl M., III, (BV) ... '60 '85 C.597 B.A. L.1119 J.D. [Locke R.]
Koontz, Dorothy ... '— '03 C.879 B.A. L.339 J.D. [Ⓐ Ice M.]
Kopka, Pinkus, Dolin & Eads, (AV)
10333 N. Meridian Street Suite 475 (⊙Buffalo Grove, Chgo., IL; Crown Point, South Bend, IN; Farmington Hills, MI)
Korin, Offer, (AV) ... '64 '88 C.347 B.A. L.1119 J.D. [Katz&K.]
Kortepeter, Paul F., (AV) ... '— '56 C.309 A.B. L.228 LL.B. [Ⓒ Sommer B.]
Kortepeter McPherson Hux Freihofer & Minton, A Legal Professional Association, (AV)
320 North Meridian Street Suite 500

Kortepeter McPherson Hux & Minton, A Legal Professional Association
(See Sommer Barnard Attorneys, PC)

Koslow, Christopher G. '55 '81
C.602 B.A. L.345 J.D. Sr. Staff Atty., Simon Property Group
Kosnoff, Amy E., (AV) ... '65 '91 C.20 B.A. L.477 J.D. [Baker&D.]
Kosnoff, Scott M., (AV) ... '63 '88 C.347 B.S. L.477 J.D. [Baker&D.]
Kossmann, Michelle L. ... '— '01 C.384 B.A. L.345 J.D. [Ⓐ Barnes&T.]
Kostas, Angelo A. '42 '68 C.347 A.B. L.345 J.D.
Assoc. Gen. Coun., American United Life Insurance Co.
Kostek, Meredith W. ... '75 '00 C.210 B.A. L.851 J.D. IN Dept. of Envir. Mgmt.
Kotzan, Bruce A. ... '44 '69 C&L.347 B.S., J.D. State Ct. Admr.

Kourany, Edgar, Jr. ....'70 '97 C.679 B.S.I.E. L.345 J.D. Andersen Consulting
Kovacs, Peter S., (BV) .... '62 '92 C.184 B.A. L.347 J.D. [Stewart&I.]
Kowalik, James S., (AV) ....'50 '78 C.679 B.A. L.1119 J.D. [Hostetler&K.]
Kraege, Richard C., (AV) ....'47 '73 C.210 B.A. L.910 J.D. The Mediation Grp.
Kraft, Paul A., (AV) .... '61 '86 C.347 B.S. L.345 J.D. [Frank&K.]
Krahulik, Angela Pease ....'74 '01 C&L.347 B.A., J.D. [[A] Ice M.]
Krahulik, David C., (AV) ....'66 '93 C&L.347 B.A., J.D. 5455 W. 86th St., Ste. 215
Krahulik, Jon D. ....'44 '69 C.347 A.B. L.345 J.D. [Yosha K.&L.]
Krahulik, Sam D. ....'74 '01 C.347 B.S. L.345 J.D. 3500 Depauw Blvd., Ste. 1040
Kramer, Beth R. ....'64 '90 C.473 B.S. L.347 J.D. Atty., U.S. Dept. of Jus.
Kramer, Thomas W. ....'71 '98 C.201 B.A. L.347 J.D. [[A] Threlkeld R.]
Krause, John C. ....'68 '97 C.347 B.A. L.345 J.D. [[A] Lewis W.]
Krauss, John L. ....'48 '77 C.170 B.A. L.345 J.D. 815 W. 96th. St.
Krebs, David R., (AV) ....'56 '83 C.210 B.A. L.345 J.D. [Hostetler&K.]
Kreider, Scott A. ....'96 '01 C.346 B.A. L.345 J.D. [[A] Hannon H.&Assoc.]
Kremp, E. Joseph ....'65 '94 C.228 A.B. L.1119 J.D. [Wooden&M.]
Kremp, Jennifer L. ....'64 '94 C.63 B.S. L.347 J.D. [[A] Baker&D.]
Kress, David E. ....'68 '00 C&L.347 B.A., J.D. [[A] Dann P.N.&K.]
Kreuscher, Wayne C., (AV) ....'— '74 C&L.546 B.A., J.D. [Barnes&T.]

Krieg DeVault LLP, (AV)
One Indiana Square, Suite 2800, 46204-2079 ⊙
Telephone: 317-636-4341 Fax: 317-636-1507
Email: contact@kdlegal.com URL: http://www.kriegdevault.com
William H. Krieg (1907-1998); Paul J. DeVault (1908-1993); John A. Alexander (1911-1998); H. Earl Capehart, Jr. (1922-1996). Partners: Anthony W. Mommer; Max W. Hittle, Jr.; William R. Neale; Paul F. Lindemann; Timothy M. Harden; Robert A. Greising; John W. Tanselle; Marc A. Hetzner; Stephen D. Smith; Mark J. R. Merkle; Michael E. Williams; Thomas R. Neal; Leah S. Mannweiler; Nicholas J. Chulos; Thomas J. Costakis; Swadesh S. Kalsi; Mark P. Canada; Elizabeth G. Russell; Thomas P. Ewbank; C. Daniel Motsinger; Paul J. Dunne; Sharon B. Hearn; Lawrence W. Schmits; Mark R. Wenzel; Julia A. Carpenter; Deborah J. Daniels; Kipper V. Tew; Randall R. Fearnow; Michael J. Messaglia; John R. Kirkwood; James T. Crawford, Jr.; Steven M. Sherman; Linda J. Cooley; David Elliott Jose; Alastair J. Warr; Thomas N. Hutchinson; Martha R. Lehman; Scott S. Morrisson; John R. Cromer; Charles S. Coleman, II; Christopher D. Long; L. Scott Paynter; Gregory B. Coy; Douglas A. Collier; Brad A. Schepers; John H. Allie. Of Counsel: James G. McIntire; John R. Fernandez. Senior Attorneys: Debra S. Easterday; Deborah C. McNear; Vicki J. Wright. Associates: Marc T. Quigley; Julie C. Bolling; Brian C. Fritts; David E. Corbitt; Brian K. Beeler; Matthew S. Carr; Joshua D. Hague; Larry C. Tomlin; Greg A. Small; Lisa M. Glenn; Alicia Mitchell Chandler; Andrea D. Brashear; Kristen L. Gentry; Michael L. Griffin; Amy J. Adolay; Matthew E. Conrad; Alexander C. O'Neill; Lesley A. Nearpass; Brett J. Henry; Joseph C. Bowman; Aaron R. Raff; Stacy Walton Long; Kelly J. Green; Rebecca Biller Elmore; Alexander L. Mounts; Angela L. Hamm; Lisa A. Durham; Heath E. Uppencamp; Matthew C. Branic; Jason A. Penninger; Nigel J. Riggins. Retired Partners: Howard Kahlenbeck, Jr.; Francis S. Michael Connelly; Malcolm Carroll Mallette; Richard D. Wagner.
Acquisitions, Divestitures and Mergers, Antitrust, Appeals, Banking, Bankruptcy, Business and Commercial, Copyright, Corporations, Creditors' Rights, Employee Benefits, Energy, Environmental, ERISA, Estate Planning and Probate, Family/Domestic Relations, Federal and State Taxation, Government Relations, Health Care, Hospital Law, Intellectual Property, Insurance, International, Labor and Employment, Legislative, Litigation, Patent, Public Finance, Public Utilities, Products Liability, Real Estate, Securities Law, Tax-Exempt and Nonprofit Organizations, Technology and E-Commerce, Trademark.
Indianapolis Northside Office: 12800 North Meridian Street, Suite 300, Carmel, Indiana 46032. Telephone: 317-566-1110. Fax: 317-636-1507.
Fort Wayne, Indiana Office: Krieg DeVault Lundy LLP, 825 Anthony Wayne Building, 203 East Berry Street, 46802. Telephone: 260-422-1534. Fax: 260-423-1590.
Hammond, Indiana Office: Krieg DeVault Galvin LLP, 5231 Hohman Avenue, 46320. Telephone: 219-933-0380. Fax: 219-933-0471.
See Professional Biographies, INDIANAPOLIS, INDIANA

Krieger, Daniel J. ....'54 '88 C.679 B.S.E.E. L.1119 J.D. [[C] Bose M.&E.] (Pat.)
Krieger, Walter W., Jr. '37 '62
C.1150 B.A. L.421 J.D. Assoc. Prof., Indiana Univ. Sch. of Law
Krise, Thomas H., (AV) ....'19 '49 C.347 B.S. L.1119 J.D. 9098 Pickwick Dr.‡
Kristel, Randolph B. ....'60 '94 C.679 B.S. L.1048 J.D. 5018 S. Madison Avenue
Krizmanich, Mildred F. ....'— '04 C.839 B.S. L.602 J.D. [[A] Sommer B.]

Kroger, Gardis & Regas, (AV)
111 Monument Circle, Suite 900, 46204-5125
Telephone: 317-692-9000 Telecopier: 317-264-6832
URL: http://www.kgrlaw.com
Partners: James A. Knauer; John J. Petr; James G. Lauck; Brian C. Bosma; Jay P. Kennedy; William Bock, III; Gregory P. Cafouros; Madalyn S. Kinsey; Mark Colucci; Brett R. Fleitz. Associates: Marcia E. Roan; Tricia A. Leminger; Reynolds B. Brissenden; Kurtis A. Marshall; Jeffrey L. Logston; Andrew R. Falk; Harley K. Means. Senior Counsel: Sydney L. Steele; David E. Wright. Of Counsel: William J. Regas (Retired); Gary A. Schiffli. Founders: R. McDonald Kroger (1912-2002); John E. Gardis (1909-2002).
General Civil Practice, Bankruptcy and Commercial Litigation, Business Transactions and Litigation, Civil Litigation and Appeals, Collections, Corporate Representation, Environmental Law and Litigation, Municipal Representation, Real Estate and Lending Transactions.
Representative Clients: American Bankers Insurance Company; Auburn Foundry, Inc.; Bank One, Indianapolis, NA; Beneficial Management Corporation of America; Beneficial Finance Company of America; Citicorp Mortgage, Inc.; City of Indianapolis; Environmental Audits, Inc.; First of America Bank; First Financial Bank, FSB.
See Professional Biographies, INDIANAPOLIS, INDIANA

Kroh, Stanley E. ....'59 '87 C.347 B.A. L.879 J.D. 200 East Washington Street
Krohn, Karol H., (BV) '59 '84 C.477 B.B.A. L.1119 J.D.
State Asst. Consumer Counselor
Krohne, Steven W. ....'71 '98 C.347 B.S. L.345 J.D. [[A] Hackman H.&C.]
Krotoszynski, Ronald J., Jr. '67 '91 C.1365 B.A. L.228 J.D.
(adm. in GA; not adm. in IN) Asst. Prof. of Law, Indiana Univ. School of Law
Kuchar, Aubrey G. ....'79 '04 C.138 B.A. L.879 J.D. [[A] Kightlinger&G.]
Kuehn, Kathryn ....'67 '99 C.344 B.S. L.345 J.D. [Lee B.C.&K.]
Kuhl, Gareth W. ....'69 '94 C&L.477 B.B.A., J.D. [Ice M.]
Kuhns, Everett G. ....'43 '68 C.347 A.B. L.1119 J.D. Chicago Title Ins. Co.
Kulkarni, Dilip ....'— '75 C.999 B.S.E. L.347 J.D. [[C] Barnes&T.] (See Pat. Sect.)
Kult, Gregory P. ....'— '94 C.347 B.A. L.966 J.D. [Kult]

Kult Law Office, LLC
9465 Counselors Row, Suite 200, 46240
Telephone: 317-805-4770 Fax: 800-852-3369
Email: gkult@kultlaw.com URL: http://www.kultlaw.com
Member of Firm: Gregory P. Kult.
Employment Law Counsel and Advocacy for Employers.
See Professional Biographies, INDIANAPOLIS, INDIANA

Kunz, Halbert W., (BV) .... '23 '51 C.347 A.B. L.345 J.D. 151 N. Delaware St., Ste. 2000
Kunz, Kathryn, (AV) ....'51 '83 C.787 B.A. L.365 J.D. [Lewis&K.]
Kunz, Willis K., (AV) ......'19 '43 C.347 A.B. L.1119 J.D. 151 N. Delaware St., Ste. 2000
Kurnik, William W., (AV(T)) '46 '75
C.46 B.S. L.365 J.D. [[C] Stephenson M.&S.] (⊙Des Plaines, IL)
Kury, Bernard E., (AV(T)) '38 '64 C.674 A.B. L.659 LL.B.
(adm. in NY; not adm. in IN) V.P. & Gen. Coun., Guidant Corp.
Kuzma, Abigail L. '56 '81
C.966 B.A. L.1119 J.D. Exec. Dir., Neighborhood Christian Clinic
Kyle, John M., III, (AV) ....'— '79 C.347 A.B. L.1119 J.D. [Barnes&T.]

LaCava, Frederick William ....'45 '79 C.1365 B.A. L.1119 J.D. 5146 E. 75th St.
Lacy, Elizabeth Haber ....'— '91 C.228 A.B. L.930 J.D. [[C] Barnes&T.]
Lacy, Jessica Sanders ......'75 '01 C.303 B.A. L.790 J.D. 9135 N. Meridian St., Ste. A-1
Ladd, D. Alan, (AV) ....'52 '81 C.347 A.B. L.345 J.D. [Ladd&Y.]
Ladd, Thomas A. ....'47 '74 C.477 B.S.Eng. L.215 J.D. [Baker&D.] (See Pat. Sect.)
Ladd & Yackey, (AV) ....320 N. Meridian Street
Lade, Jeffrey R. '67 '94 C&L.347 B.S., J.D.
Commercial Title Atty., Commonwealth Land Title Ins. Co.
Ladendorf, Daniel Allen, (AV) ....'61 '87 C.347 B.S. L.345 J.D. [Ladendorf&L.]
Ladendorf, Mark C., (AV) ....'55 '80 C.347 B.A. L.345 J.D. [Ladendorf&L.]

Ladendorf & Ladendorf, (AV) [BB]
7310 North Shadeland Avenue, 46250
Telephone: 317-842-5800 Toll Free: 1-888-925-3700 Facsimile: 317-842-5858 URL: http://www.ladendorf.com
Email: mark@ladendorf.com URL: http://www.ladendorflaw.com
Mark C. Ladendorf; Daniel Allen Ladendorf; Gloria J. Danielson;—Amy Van Ostrand.
Personal Injury, Medical Malpractice, Products Liability, Wrongful Death, Trials and Appeals.
See Professional Biographies, INDIANAPOLIS, INDIANA

Lady, Shirley S. ....'50 '83 C.63 B.S. L.345 J.D. Exec. Dir., The Prudential
Lafuse, Christopher L. '66 '92 C.966 B.S. L.879 J.D.
Staff Atty., American Family Insurance Group (⊙Madison, WI)
Lager, Dennis P. ....'61 '96 C.427 B.A. L.1119 J.D. [[A] Baker&D.]
Lahn, Seth M. ....'57 '84 C&L.976 B.A., J.d. [[C] Yarling&R.]
Laker, Gregory L., (AV) ....'59 '84 C&L.347 B.S., J.D. [Cohen&M.]
Lamb, Edgar H., (BV) ....'34 '64 C.347 B.S. L.345 J.D. 302 N. Alabama St.
Lamb, Eric E. ....'78 '04 C.347 B.S. L.345 J.D. [[A] Kightlinger&G.]
Lambert, Geoffrey C. ....'74 '02 C.347 B.S. L.1119 J.D. [[A] Stewart&I.]
Lambert, Sherry J. '56 '81 C.608 B.A. L.930 J.D.
(adm. in OH; not adm. in IN) 10438 Snapper Ct.‡
LaMere, Phillip A., (BV) ....'55 '80 C.177 B.A. L.879 J.D. [Bowman,H.B.&V.]
Land, Janet L. ....'42 '77 C.63 B.S. L.345 J.D. Intl. Harvester
Landau, Gary R., (AV) ....'37 '64 C.608 A.B. L.345 J.D. 302 North Alabama Street
Landers, Margaret M. ....'64 '91 C.679 B.A. L.347 J.D. Electronic Data Systems (EDS)

Landman & Beatty, (AV)
1150 Market Square Center, 151 North Delaware Street, 46204-2518
Mailing Address: P.O. Box 44953, Indianapolis, IN 46244-0953
Telephone: 317-236-1040 Fax: 317-236-1049
Email: info@landlaw.ws
Members of Firm: Bernard Landman, Jr. (1928-1991); James W. Beatty; Virginia Dill McCarty; James F. Beatty. Counsel: Stephen M. Terrell; Nancy G. Endsley. Associates: J. Chris Reininga; Cynthia L. Ball.
Real Estate, Real Estate Tax, Financing and Corporate Business Transactions, Wills and Probate, Probate and Estates, Personal Injury, Automobile Accidents, Wrongful Death, Libel and Defamation, Media, Municipal and Zoning, Employment and Housing Discrimination, Governmental, Tort Law, Civil Litigation, Bankruptcy and Appellate Practice.
See Professional Biographies, INDIANAPOLIS, INDIANA

Landreth, Shannon D. ....'77 '02 C.798 B.S. L.339 J.D. [[A] McTurnan&T.]
Landwer, Michael ....'54 '83 C.347 B.A. L.345 J.D. [[A] Ricos,B.&P.]
Landwerlen, Thomas L. ....'55 '80 C.344 A.B. L.1119 J.D. [Landwerlen&R.]

Landwerlen & Rothkopf L.L.P.
244 North College Avenue, 46202
Telephone: 317-639-3315 Fax: 317-639-3318
URL: http://www.landrothlaw.com
Thomas L. Landwerlen (Resident, Indianapolis Office); Robert C. Rothkopf (Resident, Indianapolis Office).
Business Law, Business Planning, Contracts, Lawsuits, Insurance, Business Enterprises, Limited Liability Companies, Franchises, Partnerships, Small Business, Closely Held Business, Buying and Selling Business, Debt Credit, Corporate Law, Contracts, Real Estate, Commercial Litigation, Family Law, Adoptions, Divorce, Child Custody, Child Support, Domestic Violence, Visitation Rights, Criminal Law, Felonies, Misdemeanors, Homicide, Driving While Intoxicated, Traffic Violations, Personal Injury, Automobile Accidents, Medical Malpractice, Employment Law, Wills and Probate, Trusts and Estates, Estate Planning, Guardianships, Elder Law.
See Professional Biographies, INDIANAPOLIS, INDIANA

Lane, Christopher T. ....'71 '99 C.602 B.A. L.345 J.D. [[A] Schuckit&Assoc.]
Lange, Mark R. '63 '89 C.910 A.B. L.309 J.D.
Coun., Envir. Law Dept., Eli Lilly & Co.
Lange, Robert D. ....'49 '74 C.347 B.S. L.345 J.D. Admn. Law J., Civil Rights Comm.
Langford, Michael B. ....'69 '94 C.894 B.A. L.347 J.D. [Scopelitis,G.L.&H.]
Langston, Shaune Hawkins ....'— '03 C.577 B.A L.597 J.D. [[A] Baker&D.]
Lanham, Kyle E., (AV) ....'56 '82 C.210 B.A. L.477 J.D. Pres., Senex Servs. Corp.
Lansberry, Kyle A., (CV) ....'72 '98 C.63 B.S. L.347 J.D. [[A] Lewis W.]
Lanzer, David E. '— '98
C.679 B.A. L.1119 J.D. V.P. & Dep. Gen. Coun., Lauth Group, Inc.
Laramore, Jon B., (AV) ....'57 '84 C.674 A.B. L.1565 J.D. [Baker&D.]
Larimore, Mary Nold, (AV) ....'56 '80 C.347 A.B. L.1119 J.D. [Ice M.]
Lark, Matthew D. ....'65 '90 C.347 B.S. L.879 J.D. 55 Monument Cir., Ste. 800
La Rosa, Anthony C. ....'63 '91 C.347 B.S. L.1119 J.D. La Rosa & Co.
LaRue, Denise K., (AV) ....'58 '89 C&L.347 B.S., J.D. [Haskin L.&L.]
Lashbrook, John B. '44 '73 C.339 B.A. L.597 J.D.
(adm. in IL; not adm. in IN) 7540 Washington Blvd.‡
Lathrop, Rick E. ....'58 '92 C.1126 B.B.A. L.347 J.D. 5959 N. Olney St.
Lauck, James G., (AV) ....'53 '79 C.602 B.B.A. L.345 J.D. [Kroger,G.&R.]
Laudig, Stephen ....'52 '77 C.347 B.A. L.1049 J.D. [[C] Laudig G.R.&S.]
Laudig George Rutherford & Sipes, (BV) ....156 East Market Street, Suite 600
Laurin, V. Samuel, III, (AV) ....'60 '87 C.197 A.B. L.1119 J.D. [Bose M.&E.]
Lausch, Eugene W. ....'38 '66 C.344 B.S. L.477 J.D. City Mgr., Regulatory Affs.
Lauter, Kenneth E., (BV) ....'57 '82 C.347 B.S. L.1119 J.D. [Haskin L.&L.]
Law, Nicholas B. ....'63 '91 C&L.347 B.A., J.D. 3226 Falcon Dr.
Law Group, The, LLP, (AV) ....136 E. Market St., 2nd Fl.
Lawhead, Lawrence E., (AV) ....'— '81 C.347 B.S. L.345 J.D. [Barnes&T.]
Lawlis, Gerald L., (AV) ....'38 '66 C.679 B.S. L.477 J.D. [[C] Wilson,K.&W.]
Lawlor, Richard J. ....'42 '79 L.345 J.D. Ind. Univ. School of Med.
Lawrence, Fredric ....'71 '97 C.347 B.A. L.209 J.D. Dept. of Transp.
Lawrence, George J. '— '84 C.602 B.A. L.273 J.D.
(adm. in MA; not adm. in IN) V.P. & Gen. Coun., Thomson Inc.
Lawrence, William T. ....'47 '73 C.347 B.S. L.345 J.D. Mag. J.
Lawson, James Eric ....'51 '82 C&L.347 B.S., J.D. I.R.S.
Lawson, John W. ....'26 '62 C.836 B.B.A. L.345 LL.B. 8102 Oak Hill Dr.
Lawson, Timothy C., (AV) ....'— '86 C.602 B.B.A. L.421 J.D. [Hall,R.K.H.&L.]
Leahy, John E. ....'46 '77 C.894 B.A. L.345 J.D. Assoc. Gen. Coun., Lilly Corp. Center
Leary, Heather A. '73 '99 C.347 B.A. L.1119 J.D.
Legal Services Organizaton of Indiana
Leavitt, Julia M. ....'65 '90 C&L.347 B.A., J.D. 151 North Delaware Street
Leblanc, J. Kirk ....'75 '01 C.130 B.A. L.1119 J.D. [[A] Norris C.&S.]
Lechleiter, Daniel M. ....'— '05 C.201 B.S. L.365 J.D. [[A] Baker&D.]
Lee, Dennis P. ....'53 '86 C.347 B.A. L.851 J.D. [[C] Bingham M.]

Lee, Kathy Ann, (AV) .... '57 '87 C.1216 B.S. L.345 J.D. [Cline F.C.L.&C.]
Lee, Lisa A. .... '63 '97 C.63 B.S. L.345 J.D. [Ice M.]
Lee, Mickey J. .... '— '00 C&L.347 B.S., J.D. [Schuckit&Assoc.]
Lee, Nathaniel, (BV) .... '55 '82 C.510 B.A. L.280 J.D. [Lee B.C.&K.]
Lee, Robert C. .... '69 '95 C.347 B.A. L.880 J.D. [Goodin A.&M.]
Lee, Robert E., Jr. '44 '76 C.884 B.S. L.831 J.D.
(adm. in PA; not adm. in IN; Pat.) Asst. Gen. Pat. Coun., Law Div., Eli Lilly & Co.
Lee, Stephen W., (AV) .... '— '77 C.63 B.S. L.1119 J.D. [Barnes&T.]
Lee Burns Cossell & Kuehn, LLP, (BV) .... 127 E. Michigan St.
Leeds, James P. '59 '92 C&L.347 B.S., J.D.
Assoc. Gen. Pat. Coun., Law Div., Eli Lilly & Co. (Pat.)
Leek, Sandra D. .... '54 '79 C.860 B.A. L.1119 J.D. [Baker&D.]
Leerkamp, Randolph A., (BV) '47 '73
C.347 B.S. L.345 J.D. Pres., Leerkamp Legal Servs., P.C.
Leeuw, Gene R., (AV) .... '44 '69 C.347 A.B. L.345 J.D. [Leeuw O.&C.]
Leeuw Oberlies & Campbell, (AV) .... 320 N. Meridian Street
Lefstein, Norman '37 '61 C.56 L.339 LL.B.
(adm. in IL; not adm. in IN) Dean & Prof., Ind. Univ. Sch. of Law
Lehman, Martha R., (AV) .... '62 '87 C.201 B.A. L.880 J.D. [Krieg D.]
Lehman, Robert E. .... '50 '77 C&L.347 B.A., J.D. [Lehman P.]
Lehman • Payton, P.A. .... 3801 North Meridian Street, Suite 102
Leib, Susan J. .... '63 '89 C.879 B.A. L.347 J.D. Div. of Personnel, State of IN
Leibman, Jordan H. .... '30 '79 C.145 B.A. L.345 J.D. Prof. of Bus. Law, Ind. Univ.
Leisz, Scott R., (AV) .... '59 '86 C.347 B.S. L.1119 J.D. [Bingham M.]
Leitch, Ryan L., (BV) .... '62 '87 C.347 B.S. L.345 J.D. [Riley B.&E.]
Leminger, Tricia A. .... '71 '96 C.679 B.A. L.347 J.D. [Kroger,G.&R.]
Lengar, Tonya L. .... '77 '03 C.679 B.A. L.1119 J.D. [Bingham M.]
Lennington, Lana L. .... '71 '98 C.63 B.A. L.879 J.D. [Newton B.B.]
Lentz, Nelsen L. '60 '95 C.679 B.S. L.151 J.D.
(adm. in OH; not adm. in IN; Pat.) Pat. Atty., Eli Lilly & Co.
Leone, Joseph A., (BV) .... '42 '68 C.999 A.B. L.345 J.D. 872 Virginia Ave.
Leone, Joseph M. .... '66 '95 C.679 B.S. L.347 J.D. [Drewry S.V.]
LePage, Stephen D. .... '63 '90 C.475 B.A. L.209 J.D. [Harrison&M.]
Lerch, Keith W. '46 '72 C.309 A.B. L.976 J.D.
Chief Coun., U.S. Dept. of Housing & Urban Develop.
Lesher, Matthew C. .... '— '05 C.347 B.S. L.1119 J.D. [Baker&D.]
Leslie, Kevin R. .... '— '01 C.679 B.A. L.345 J.D. [Hunt S.K.]
Leslie, Thomas N., (BV) '46 '72
C.679 B.S. L.1119 J.D. 151 North Delaware Street, Suite 1810
Levandoski, Christopher C. .... '60 '89 C.63 B.A. L.345 J.D. Pros. Off.
Levenhagen, Donald D., (AV) .... '59 '84 C.190 B.S.B.A. L.1119 J.D. [Cohen&M.]
Leverton, Justin W. .... '79 '05 C.340 B.A. L.1119 J.D. [Stewart&I.]
Levi, Nicholas W. .... '78 '03 C.347 B.A. L.1119 J.D. [Kightlinger&G.]
Levin, Alan A., (AV) .... '— '82 C.470 B.A. L.1119 J.D. [Barnes&T.]
Levin, Elia A. .... '56 '84 C.347 B.A. L.365 J.D. Gold Seal
Levin, Elliott D., (AV) .... '41 '66 C.347 B.S. L.1119 J.D. [Rubin&L.]
Levin, Irwin B., (AV) .... '53 '78 C.347 B.A. L.345 J.D. [Cohen&M.]
Levy, William, (BV) .... '30 '66 C.108 B.S. L.345 J.D. [Yosha K.&L.]
Lewinski, Michael J., (AV) .... '60 '85 C.894 A.B. L.1119 J.D. [Ice M.]
Lewis, Claire E., (BV) .... '52 '83 C.838 B.S. L.345 J.D. 115 North Girls School Road
Lewis, Dale K., (AV) .... '37 '62 C.352 B.A. L.174 J.D. 9330 Zionville Rd.‡
Lewis, David E., (AV) .... '61 '90
Lewis, David P., (AV) '59 '84
C.894 B.A. L.1119 J.D. Eli Lilly and Company (Law Division)
Lewis, Donna M. .... '86 '99 C.912 L.1187 J.D. Staff Atty.
Lewis, Jeffrey O., (AV) .... '52 '79 C.210 B.A. L.339 J.D. [Ice M.]
Lewis, Jodi J. '65 '98 C.63 B.S. L.347 J.D.
Estate & Gift Tax Atty., Internal Revenue Serv.
Lewis, Lisa Marie .... '76 '01 C.679 B.A. L.345 J.D. [Threlkeld R.]
Lewis, Margaret W. .... '25 '85 C.339 A.B. L.345 J.D. 22 E. Washington St.
Lewis, Robert C. .. '29 '57 C&L.347 B.S., LL.B. Sr. Legal Analyst, Lexis Law Publishing
Lewis, Stephen R., (BV) '47 '75
C.347 B.S. L.345 J.D. 151 North Delaware Street, Suite 1960

Lewis & Kappes, Professional Corporation, (AV)
One America Tower, One American Square, Suite 1700, 46282
Telephone: 317-639-1210 Telecopier: 317-639-4882
Email: Office@Lewis-Kappes.com URL: http://www.Lewis-Kappes.com
Ted B. Lewis (1919-1991); Philip S. Kappes; David W. Gray; John F. Wickes, Jr.; Gary P. Price; Steven L. Tuchman; Thomas R. Ruge; C. Duane O'Neal; Todd A. Richardson; Bette J. Dodd; Peter S. French; Brian Andrew Statz; Timothy L. Stewart; James J. Ammeen, Jr.; Kathryn Kunz; Christopher Poling; Charleyne L. Gabriel; James E. Zoccola; James A. Klimek; David S. Klinestiver; Jennifer Wheeler Terry; Thomas H. Ristine;—Christopher R. Taylor; Suzanne R. Gaidoo; Marco A. Moreno; Paula L. Zelman-Finch; Steven W. Griesemer; Angela D. Iza; Sara R. Bradbury; Hannah Kaufman. Of Counsel: Leslie Duvall; Scott D. Yonover.
General Civil Practice. Appellate, Corporate, Family/Domestic Relations, Real Estate, Municipal, Zoning, Mergers and Acquisitions, Labor and Employment, Copyright, Probate and Estate Planning, Administrative, Environmental, Litigation, State and Federal Taxation, Regulatory, Energy and Utility, Legislative, Immigration and Nationality, Medical Malpractice, Intellectual Properties, Securities, Bankruptcy, Creditor's Rights, Business and Transactional and Intellectual Properties.
See Professional Biographies, INDIANAPOLIS, INDIANA

Lewis Wagner, LLP, (AV)
500 Place, 501 Indiana Avenue, Suite 200, 46202-3199
Telephone: 317-237-0500 Fax: 317-630-2790
Email: lewiswagner@aol.com URL: http://www.lewiswagner.com
Judith Trevor Kirtland (1947-1990); Edward D. Lewis (1922-1996); Mark E. Walker (1969-2000); Robert F. Wagner; David Konnersman; Thomas C. Hays; John C. Trimble; Kenneth P. Reese; Sharon Funcheon Murphy; Jarrell B. Hammond; Theodore L. Nicholas; Mary Foley Panszi; Susan E. Mehringer; Tammy J. Meyer; Daun A. Weliever; Richard K. Shoultz; Dina M. Cox; Anthony M. Eleftheri; A. Richard M. Blaiklock; Robert R. Foos. Associates: John C. Krause; Kyle A. Lansberry; Stefanie R. Crawford; Stephanie L. Cassman; Sonia C. Das; Valerie L. Hughs; Christi R. Anderson; Ryan K. Gardner; Shannon L. Logsdon. Of Counsel: Lisa M. Dillman; Felson Bowman.
General Civil Trial Practice. Administrative Law, Appellate Practice, Business Law, Commercial Law, Construction Law, Contracts, Corporate Law, Drug and Medical Device, Elder Law, Election, Campaign and Political, Environmental Law, Family Law, Finance, Guardianships, Government, Insurance, Labor and Employment, Legal Malpractice, Litigation, Medical Malpractice, Products Liability, Real Estate, Securities, Taxation, Toxic Torts, Trucking and Transportation Law, Trusts and Estates, Wills and Probate, Workers' Compensation.
See Professional Biographies, INDIANAPOLIS, INDIANA

Ley, Paul S. .... '42 '70 C.679 B.S. L.345 J.D. Atty., I.R.S.
Lidke, Lynne D., (AV) .... '57 '82 C.679 B.A. L.345 J.D. [Scopelitis,G.L.&H.]
Lieber, Ronald S., (BV) .... '29 '57 C.347 B.S. L.477 J.D. 129 E. Market St.
Life, Robert L., (AV) .... '23 '50 L.345 LL.B. 7855 S. Emerson Ave.
Light, Andrew K., (AV) .... '54 '80 C.347 B.A. L.345 J.D. [Scopelitis,G.L.&H.]
Lilienkamp, Christopher Arthur .... '62 '97 C.347 B.A. L.1292 J.D. 2520 East 57th Street
Limrick, Michael R. .... '76 '01 C.434 B.A. L.851 J.D. [McTurnan&T.]
Lind, David C., II .... '— '97 C.347 B.S. L.597 J.D. [Hall,R.K.H.&L.]
Lindemann, Paul F., (AV) .... '48 '76 C.879 B.A. L.345 J.D. [Krieg D.]
Linder, Charles W., Jr., (AV) .... '37 '62 C.178 A.B. L.1119 J.D. [Linder&H.]

Linder & Hollowell, P.C., (AV)
728 South Meridian Street, P.O. Box 845, 46206-0845
Mailing Address: P.O. Box 845, Indianapolis, IN 46206-0845
Telephone: 317-637-3170 Fax: Available Upon Request
Robert Hollowell (1899-1980); Charles W. Linder, Jr.;—Sharon L. Wright.
Insurance Defense, General Practice.
See Professional Biographies, INDIANAPOLIS, INDIANA

Lindley, Melissa A. .... '78 '04 C.999 B.S. L.345 J.D. [Cremer B.&C.]
Lingelbach Young, Caroline '64 '92 C.882 B.A. L.893 J.D.
Assoc. Gen. Coun., Hammond Kennedy Whitney & Co., Inc.
Lipshaw, Jeffrey M., (AV) '54 '79 C.477 A.B. L.813 J.D.
(adm. in MI; not adm. in IN) Great Lakes Chemical Corp.
Liptack, Diane L., (AV) .... '— '76 C.381 B.A. L.880 J.D. [Cremer B.&C.]
Lisher, John L., (AV) .... '50 '75 C.347 A.B. L.1119 J.D. [Osborn H.&L.]
Lisher, Mary Katherine, (AV) .... '50 '75 C.880 B.A. L.1119 J.D. [Baker&D.]
Lis-Milam, Julianne S., (AV) '51 '85 C.912 B.A. L.345 J.D.
Part. & Gen. Coun., Hammond Kennedy Whitney & Company, Inc.
Little, Peggy K. .... '56 '02 C.344 B.S. L.345 J.D. [Tyra&C.]
Little, Sharlee C. '— '93 C&L.802 B.S., J.D.
(adm. in TX; not adm. in IN) [Barnes&T.]
Liu, Ji-Qing .... '56 '92 C.999 B.A. L.347 J.D. [Baker&D.] (Beijing, China)
Locke, Cynthia M., (BV) .... '49 '85 C.108 B.A. L.345 J.D. [Stewart&I.]

Locke Reynolds LLP, (AV)
201 North Illinois, Suite 1000, P.O. Box 44961, 46244-0961
Telephone: 317-237-3800 Fax: 317-237-3900
URL: http://www.locke.com
Partners: Nelson D. Alexander; Thomas F. Bedsole; Rex E. Bennett; Michael A. Bergin; Michael T. Bindner; Dean R. Brackenridge; Terrence L. Brookie; Alan S. Brown; Thomas J. Campbell; Susan E. Cline; Howard R. Cohen; John H. Daerr; Thomas L. Davis; Thomas E. Deer; Jeffrey S. Dible; James Dimos; Thomas W. Farlow; Mary Margaret Ruth Feldhake; Julia Blackwell Gelinas; David M. Haskett; David T. Kasper; Karl M. Koons, III; James D. Masur II; John K. McDavid; Michael D. Moriarty; Jeffrey J. Mortier; Kevin Charles Murray; Nicholas C. Pappas; Eric A. Riegner; Randall R. Riggs; Mark J. Roberts; Kevin C. Schiferl; Steven J. Strawbridge; Joel E. Tragesser; Thomas E. Wheeler II. Associates: Sylvia A. Bier; Daniel D. Bobilya; Jeffrey M. Boldt; John M.T. Chavis, II; Darren A. Craig; Todd A. Croftchik; Lucy R. Dollens; Wade D. Fulford; J. Matt Harnish; Jared A. Harts; Deborah K. Hepler; Daniel P. King; Matthew R. King; Daniel M. Long; Andrew A. Manna; Melanie D. Margolin; Leslie B. Morse; Angie L. Ordway; April R. Schilling; Ian L. Stewart; Robert B. Thornburg; Jennifer L. VanLandingham; Matthew P. Voors; Dirk E. Wallsmith; Karen M. R. Weber; Amy S. Wilson; Heather L. Wilson. Senior Counsel: Rodney E. Corson; Julia F. Crowe; Melissa J. De Groff; Carrie G. Doehrmann; Steven R. Eichholtz; Raymond Good; Robert L. Hartley; William V. Hutchens; Lloyd H. Milliken, Jr.; Anthony W. Overholt; Hugh E. Reynolds, Jr.; Thomas E. Satrom; B. Keith Shake; Maggie L. Smith; Gregory G. Taylor; Thomas A. Withrow. Of Counsel: Robert C. Riddell; William H. Vobach. Retired: Emerson Boyd (1914-1986); Theodore L. Locke (1891-1981); Hugh E. Reynolds (1900-1968); William B. Weisell.
Business Services, Construction and Real Estate Services, Financial Institutions, Government and Regulatory Services, Healthcare, Individual Services, Litigation, Products and Manufacturing, Tort Litigation and Insurance Services.
See Professional Biographies, INDIANAPOLIS, INDIANA

Lockman, David M. '55 '89 C.880 B.E.E.E. L.989 J.D.
[Maginot M.&B.] (See Pat. Sect.)
Loftus, John T. '55 '91 C.238 B.S. L.146 J.D.
(adm. in IL; not adm. in IN) [Stewart&I.]
Loftus, Joseph E., (AV) .... '— '83 C.205 B.A. L.347 J.D. [Barnes&T.]
Logsdon, Arthur L. .... '53 '88 C.108 B.S. L.374 J.D. IN Health Care Assn.
Logsdon, Shannon L. .... '71 '05 C.446 B.A. L.345 J.D. [Lewis W.]
Logston, Jeffrey L. .... '73 '04 C&L.347 B.S., J.D. [Kroger,G.&R.]
Lohman, Geoffrey S. .... '70 '97 C.347 B.S. L.345 J.D. Law Clk., Ct. App.
Lohrstorfer, Timothy A. '59 '88 C.357 B.S. L.339 J.D.
(adm. in IL; not adm. in IN) I.R.S.
Lonberger, James E., (BV) .... '29 '65 C.347 B.S. L.345 LL.B. 4912 E. 70th
Long, Christine Graffis .... '70 '95 C.910 B.A. L.1119 J.D. [Baker&D.]
Long, Christopher D., (AV) .... '58 '83 C.473 B.S. L.345 J.D. [Krieg D.]
Long, Dana L. .... '52 '80 C&L.1119 B.S., J.D. Legal Coun., State Dept. of Edu.
Long, Daniel M. .... '70 '96 C&L.347 B.A., J.D. [Locke R.]
Long, Douglas P., (AV) .... '— '79 C.347 B.S. L.309 J.D. [Hall,R.K.H.&L.]
Long, Jim R. '47 '76 C&L.347 B.S., J.D.
Assoc. Gen. Coun., American United Life Insurance Company, a One America Financial Partner
Long, Stacy Walton .... '79 '04 C&L.339 B.A., J.D. [Krieg D.]
Long, Susan J. .... '71 '98 C.699 B.A. L.1119 J.D. [Bingham M.]
Long-Sharp, Rhonda, (AV) .... '59 '84 C.347 B.A. L.734 J.D. 501 Indiana Ave.
Longworth, Nancy Covault .... '54 '85 C.1059 B.S. L.345 J.D. 1126 N. Recter
Lootens, James B., (AV) '56 '81 C.347 B.A. L.880 J.D.
Asst. Secy. & Assoc. Gen. Coun., Eli Lilly & Co.
Lopossa, Paula E. '44 '73 C.357 B.A. L.345 J.D.
Ctr. Township of Marion Co. Small Claims Ct.
Lorenz, Vernon E., Jr .... '58 '94 C.36 B.A. L.879 J.D. [V.E.Lorenz]
Lorenz, Vernon E., P.C. .... 320 North Meridian St.
Loser, Randy D., (AV) '55 '80
C.108 B.S. L.145 J.D. Asst. Gen. Coun., Eli Lilly & Company
Loser, Robert W., II, (AV) .... '— '69 C.347 B.S. L.1119 J.D. [Ayres C.&S.]
Lottes, Paul F., (BV) .... '57 '83 C.347 B.S. L.345 J.D. 1639 North Auburn Street
Love, Jennifer Stephens .... '71 '96 C&L.347 B.A., J.D. [Findling G.G.&P.]
Love, Matthew S. .... '70 '95 C&L.347 B.S., J.D. [Feiwell&H.]
Lovelace, Clifton E. .... '69 '00 C.1070 B.S. L.1338 J.D. Suite 157, 1111 East 54th Street
Lovern, Steven S., (BV) .... '60 '85 C.63 B.S. L.117 J.D. [S.Lovern]
Lovern, Steven, Law Office of, (BV) .... 7255 W. 10th St.
Lowe, L. Robert, Jr., (AV) .... '37 '67 C.679 B.S.C.E. L.345 J.D. [Bose M.&E.]
Lowe Gray Steele & Darko, LLP, (AV) .... 111 Monument Circle, Suite 4600
Lowry, Wilburn G. .... '39 '74 C.347 B.A. L.345 J.D. 9348 E. Southport Rd.
Lozano, Katharine M. .... '68 '98 C.560 B.A. L.602 J.D. Archdiocese of Indianapolis
Lozer, Jeffrey M. .... '— '94 C.198 B.A. L.345 J.D. [Ice M.]
Lucas, Kathleen G., (AV) .... '50 '78 C.347 B.S. L.345 J.D. [Bose M.&E.]
Lucas, Michael P., (AV) .... '— '78 C.966 B.A. L.345 J.D. [Barnes&T.]
Lucas, Stephen L. .... '48 '74 Dir. & Chf. Admin. Law J., Nat. Res. Comm.
Ludlow, James F. .... '59 '87 C.346 B.S. L.345 J.D. 9520 East Washington Street
Ludwig, Paul D., (BV) .... '— '81 C.344 B.A. L.345 J.D. [Bator R.B.S.&L.]
Lueck, Dwight D., (BV) .... '— '88 C.118 B.A. L.494 J.D. [Barnes&T.]
Lueckenhoff, Edward H. '54 '79 C.502 B.A. L.880 J.D.
(adm. in TN; not adm. in IN) F.B.I.
Lueders, Daniel J., (AV) '60 '86
C.597 B.S.C.E. L.1119 J.D. [Woodard,E.M.M.&H.] (See Pat. Sect.)
Lueking, Jason P., (CV) .... '68 '93 C.701 B.S.C.E. L.347 J.D. [Bamberger,F.O.&H.]
Lukaart, Christopher J. .... '74 '00 C.114 B.S. L.879 J.D. [Henderson D.W.&D.]
Lukaart, Lia R. .... '75 '00 C.679 B.S. L.879 J.D. [Goodin A.&M.]
Lukens, William E. '68 '95
C.679 B.S. L.347 J.D. Sr. Staff Atty., American Family Insurance

Lundberg, Donald R. '49 '76 C.288 B.A. L.1119 J.D.
Staff Atty. & Exec. Secy., Supm. Ct. Disciplinary Comm.
Lunn, Lawrence M., (BV) .... '36 '76 C.679 B.S.E.E. L.345 J.D. [Lunn&Assoc.]
Lunn & Associates, Attorneys at Law, P.C., (BV) .... 6125 U.S. Highway 31 South
Lunsford, Thomas .... '77 '02 C.347 B.S. L.1119 J.D. 800 E. 96th Street, Suite 500
Lupton, Suzann Weber .... '66 '91 C.210 B.A. L.345 J.D. [A Baker&D.]
Luthra, Susan W. .... '52 '84 C.347 B.A. L.345 J.D. 14 David Ln.
Lyman, Stephen W., (AV) .... '— '74 C&L.347 B.S., J.D. [Hall,R.K.H.&L.]
Lynch, Debra McVicker, (AV) .... '— '86 C.472 B.A. L.345 J.D. [B Sommer B.]
Lynch, Sheryl L. .... '67 '98 C.347 B.A. L.345 J.D. 155 E. Market St., Ste. 714
Lyons, David C. .... '53 '84 C.679 B.S. L.345 J.D. Ind. Budget Agcy.
Lytle, L. Ben .... '46 '80 C.233 B.S. L.345 J.D. The Associated Group
Maas, Rebecca J., (AV) .... '61 '88 C.827 B.A. L.345 J.D. [Smith,F.M.&H.]
Maas, Robert D., (BV) .... '52 '82 C.347 A.B. L.345 J.D. [B Stark D.&S.]
Macaluso, Matthew R. .... '73 '01 C.679 B.S. L.879 J.D. [A Bose M.&E.]
MacAnally, Melinda Hoover, (AV) '58 '83 C.880 B.A. L.347 J.D.
V.P. & Assoc. Coun., National City Bank, Indiana
MacDougall, Heather L. '69 '94 C.966 B.A. L.436 J.D.
(adm. in WI; not adm. in IN) [Baker&D.]
Macek, Heather H. .... '— '04 C.347 B.A. L.345 J.D. [A Hall,R.K.H.&L.]
Macey, Barry A., (AV) .... '47 '75 C.918 B.A. L.1119 J.D. [Macey S.&A.]
Macey, Nora L., (AV) .... '49 '75 C.856 A.B. L.1119 J.D. [Macey S.&A.]
Macey Swanson and Allman, (AV) .... 445 N. Pennsylvania St., Ste. 401
MacGill, Robert D., (AV) .... '— '81 C.347 B.S. L.345 J.D. [Barnes&T.]
MacGill, Sue Tuohy, (AV) .... '57 '83 C.347 B.S. L.345 J.D. [B Wood T.G.M.&H.]
Mack, R. Gayle, (BV) .... '54 '80 C.347 B.A. L.345 J.D. 136 East Market Street, Suite 800
Mack-Brown, Aarika D. .... '— '04 C.254 B.A. L.276 J.D. [A Barnes&T.]
Mackey, Ann Carr, (AV) .... '— '74 C.675 B.A. L.910 J.D. [Sommer B.]
Mackey, Larry A., (AV) .... '— '76 C.249 B.A. L.1119 J.D. [Barnes&T.]
Mackey, Shannon M. .... '73 '98 C.63 B.A. L.74 J.D. [A Laudig G.R.&S.]
MacLean, Michael J., (BV) .... '65 '90 C.679 B.S. L.345 J.D. [Baker&D.]
Madden, Charles E. .... '26 '56 C.436 B.S. L.345 J.D. 511 N. Illinois Street
Madden, Matthew F. '74 '02 C.602 B.A. L.339 J.D.
(adm. in IL; not adm. in IN) Jud. Law Clerk

Maddox Hargett & Caruso, P.C.
(See Fishers)

Mages, Daniel J. '66 '91 C.190 B.A. L.436 J.D.
Soc. Sec. Admin., Hearings & App. Off.
Magid, Terren B. '64 '90 C.861 B.S.M. L.569 J.D.
(adm. in OH; not adm. in IN) Eli Lilly and Company (Law Division)
Maginot, Paul J., (AV) '61 '89 C.679 B.S. L.347 J.D.
[Maginot M.&B.] (See Pat. Sect.)

Maginot Moore & Beck, (AV)
Bank One Center/Tower, 111 Monument Circle Suite 3000, 46204-5115
Telephone: 317-638-2922 Facsimile: 317-638-2139
URL: http://www.maginot.com
Paul J. Maginot; Harold C. Moore; Michael D. Beck; David M. Lockman. Associates: James D. Wood; Russell E. Fowler, II; David R. Moorman; Gerald W. Roberts.
Patent, Trademark, Copyright, Intellectual Property, Licensing, Counseling and Litigation.
See Professional Biographies, INDIANAPOLIS, INDIANA

Magnant, Suzanne L., (AV) '46 '77
C.347 A.B. L.345 J.D. Comr., Ind. Dept. of Pub. Welfare
Magnus-Stinson, Jane E. .... '58 '83 C.108 B.A. L.1119 J.D. Crim. Ct. J.
Maguire, James F., (AV) '47 '73
C.679 B.S. L.345 J.D. Invest. Coun., McDonald & Co. Secs., Inc.
Maguire, Joseph P., (AV) .... '55 '83 C.347 B.S. L.345 J.D. [A Norris C.&S.]
Maher, Kenneth W. .... '46 '76 C.679 B.S. L.345 J.D. 8888 Keystone Crossing, Suite 1300
Mahony, Marcia A., (BV) .... '59 '95 C.629 B.S. L.1119 J.D. [Kightlinger&G.]
Maier, Brian C. .... '63 '88 C.347 B.S. L.345 J.D. [Schnorr,S.&M.]
Maine, Michael R., (AV) .... '40 '64 C.210 A.B. L.477 J.D. [B Baker&D.]
Mains, Chas. H. .... '15 '50 C.347 L.345 LL.B. 523 Castle Manor Ct.‡
Malad, Richard M., (BV) .... '46 '73 C.435 B.S. L.345 J.D. [Cohen&M.]
Maley, John R., (AV) .... '— '88 C.602 B.A. L.1119 J.D. [Barnes&T.]
Mallamad, Jeffery M., (AV) .... '53 '79 C.851 B.A. L.930 J.D. [Bingham M.]
Mallett, Janet Brown .... '65 '91 C.108 B.A. L.347 J.D. Jud. Law Clk., Ind. Ct. of App.
Mallette, Malcolm Carroll, (AV) .... '41 '67 C.679 B.S. L.1119 J.D. [Krieg D.] ‡
Mallon, Anna Muehling .... '74 '02 C.473 B.A. L.345 J.D. [A Bingham M.]
Mallon, David J., Jr., (AV) .... '46 '75 C.188 B.A. L.1119 J.D. [Ice M.]
Mallor, Andrew C., (AV) .... '49 '74 C.347 B.A. L.1119 J.D. [Mallor C.G.&B.] ⊙
Mallor Clendening Grodner & Bohrer LLP, (AV)
151 N. Delaware Street (⊙Bloomington)
Mandel, Derek L. .... '62 '87 C.705 B.A. L.945 J.D. 8900 Keystone Xing., Ste. 950
Mangan, Pamela Rae .... '46 '79 C.72 B.A. L.347 J.D. 4376 N. Central
Mann, Richard A., (BV) .... '54 '80 C.347 B.S.B.A. L.345 J.D. [R.A.Mann]
Mann, Susan M. .... '53 '82 C.347 B.A. L.345 J.D. Corp. Coun., M.H. Healthcare, Inc.

Mann Law Firm
(See Terre Haute)

Mann, Richard A., P.C., (BV) .... 3750 Kentucky Ave.
Manna, Andrew A. .... '74 '04 C.234 B.A. L.345 J.D. [A Locke R.]
Manns, Bradley .... '69 '94 C.347 B.A. L.1119 J.D. Consolidated Products, Inc.
Mannweiler, Leah S., (AV) .... '50 '76 C.210 B.A. L.345 J.D. [Krieg D.]
Mannweiler, Paul S., (AV) .... '49 '76 C.347 A.B. L.345 J.D. [Bose M.&E.]
Manson, Keith A. .... '62 '91 C.689 B.A. L.1187 J.D. 1509 E. 106th St.★
Mantel, Richard M., (BV) .... '39 '67 C.347 A.B. L.345 J.D. 230 E. Ohio Street, 6th fl.
Mantel, Thomas D., (AV) .... '25 '53 C&L.347 A.B., LL.B. [B Cohen G.&G.] ‡
Mantlo, Bronwen L. .... '— '96 C.118 B.A. L.705 J.D. Attorney, Eli Lilly & Co.
Maple, Stephen M. .... '44 '69 C.344 B.A. L.345 J.D. Univ. of Indpls.

Marcus Law Firm, The
(See Fishers)

Margerum, David K., (BV) .... '44 '73 C.346 B.S. L.345 J.D. 302 N. East St.
Margolin, Melanie D. .... '71 '97 C.339 B.A. L.209 J.D. [A Locke R.]
Markette, Robert W., Jr. .... '72 '98 C.303 B.A. L.1119 J.D. [A Gilliland&C.]
Markey, Melissa L. '— '91 C&L.734 B.A., J.D.
(adm. in TX; not adm. in IN) [A Hall,R.K.H.&L.]
Marksberry, Gary J. .... '73 '03 C.999 B.S. L.213 J.D. [A Stephenson M.&S.]
Marple, Barbara J. .... '48 '76 C.347 B.S. L.345 J.D. 5581 Broadmoor Plaza
Marron, Donna C. .... '55 '94 C.860 B.S. L.347 J.D. [Plews S.R.&B.]
Marsh, Andrea K. .... '— '00 C.347 B.A. L.910 J.D. [A Sommer B.]
Marsh, Mary Y., (Mrs.), (AV) '48 '74 C.108 B.A. L.345 J.D.
Sr. V.P. & Tr. Coun., National City Bk., Indiana
Marsh, Tanya D. .... '72 '01 C.347 B.A. L.309 J.D. Real Estate Coun., Kite Realty Grp.
Marsh, William E. .... '41 '68 C&L.546 B.S., J.D. Prof., Ind. Univ. School of Law
Marshall, Cassandra L., (AV⑦) .... '48 '78 C.150 B.A. L.678 J.D. [Miroff,C.&W.]
Marshall, Kurtis A. .... '72 '02 C&L.347 B.A., J.D. [A Kroger,G.&R.]
Marshall, Patricia L., (BV) .... '58 '83 C&L.879 B.A., J.D. Staff Coun., U.S. Bkrptcy. Ct.
Marshall, Sheila A.
(See Carmel)

Martenet, David L., (BV) .... '40 '67 C.347 B.S. L.345 LL.B. 9423 Lafayette Rd.
Martin, Amberly A. '70 '03 C.1322 B.A. L.74 J.D.
Gen. Coun., Risk Mgr., & Privacy Offr., Redcats USA (F/K/A Brylane)
Martin, Bonnie L. .... '— '97 C.992 B.A. L.896 J.D. [A Ogletree,D.N.S.&S.]
Martin, C. Wendell, (AV) .... '17 '42 C.210 A.B. L.178 J.D. 2600 1 Indiana Sq.
Martin, Catherine M. .... '67 '98 C.837 B.B.A. L.1045 J.D. Coun., Simon Property Group
Martin, Duane C. .... '49 '87 C.346 B.S. L.345 J.D. [Miller,W.M.&H.]
Martin, Joyce Marie .... '48 '89 C.436 B.A. L.494 J.D. 206 Statehouse
Martin, Mac J. .... '44 '93 C.347 B.S. L.1119 J.D. 4000 E. 96th St.
Martin, Mitzi Harris, (AV) .... '47 '85 C.10 B.S. L.345 J.D. [Baker&D.]
Martz, George E., (AV) .... '26 '58 C.347 B.S. L.345 J.D. 6139 Autumn Ln.
Marx, William F. '40 '67 C.197 A.B. L.477 LL.B.
(adm. in DC; not adm. in IN) 10330 N. Meridan St.‡
Marxer, Joseph H. .... '62 '87 C.477 A.B. L.1119 J.D. Assoc. Gen. Coun., Eli Lilly & Co.
Marz, Matthew P. .... '63 '91 C.679 B.A. L.1187 J.D. [Moore&Assoc.]
Mascher, Gilbert E., (BV) .... '45 '73 C.347 B.S. L.345 J.D. [Elrod&M.]
Maschmeyer, William A., (AV) .... '60 '85 C.679 B.A. L.345 J.D. [Haggerty,H.&M.]
Mason, Byron K., (AV) .... '56 '82 C.347 B.A. L.352 J.D. [Baker&D.]
Masoncup, Stephan C. .... '— '94 C.801 B.S. L.365 J.D. [Hall,R.K.H.&L.]
Massa, Mark S. .... '61 '90 C&L.347 B.A., J.D. Ind. Repub. State Comm.
Massey, Marsha C. .... '63 '92 C.896 B.A. L.362 J.D. Asst. U.S. Atty.
Massey, Mel John, Jr. '28 '52 C&L.930 A.B., J.D.
(adm. in OH; not adm. in IN) Advanced Underwriting Consult.
Mastrian, Debra A., (AV) .... '69 '94 C.265 B.A. L.879 J.D. 12073 Old Stone Drive
Mastrian, Patrick F., III, (AV) .... '68 '94 C.665 B.A. L.879 J.D. [Dann P.N.&K.]
Masur, James D., II, (BV⑦) .... '59 '84 C.473 B.A. L.893 J.D. [Locke R.]
Matheny, Marc, (BV) .... '56 '80 C.347 B.A. L.345 J.D. 244 N. College Ave.
Mathias, Paul D. .... '53 '79 C.309 A.B. L.347 J.D. Ct. of Appeals J.
Mathies, David A. .... '— '89 C.347 B.S. L.879 J.D. 225 North Delaware Street
Matsuyasu, Wataru .... '71 '00 C.976 B.A. L.276 J.D. [A Baker&D.]
Matters, Maria .... '59 '98 C.679 B.S. L.347 J.D. 9520 E. Washington St.
Matthews, Dana Elise .... '72 '00 C.1208 B.A. L.345 J.D. Staff Atty., IN Supm. Ct.
Matthews, James D. .... '19 '51 C.707 B.S. L.602 LL.B. [B Norris C.&S.]
Matthews, James F., (AV) .... '33 '63 C.347 B.S. L.345 J.D. [Hill,F.M.F.&M.]
Matthews, Scott D. .... '70 '98 C.347 B.A. L.345 J.D. [A Ice M.]
Mattingly, David M., (AV) .... '46 '71 C.347 B.S. L.477 J.D. [Ice M.]
Mattingly, Jonathan D. .... '— '98 C.602 B.S. L.347 J.D. [A Barnes&T.]
Mauk, Whitney D. .... '74 '99 C&L.347 B.A., J.D. [A Kiefer&M.]
Maurer, Brad R. .... '73 '99 C.679 B.A. L.347 J.D. [A Bingham M.]
Maurer, Michael S. .... '42 '68 C.174 B.S. L.1119 J.D. 10585 N. Meridan‡
Maurer, Todd J. .... '70 '97 C.846 B.A. L.347 J.D. Gershman Brown & Assocs., Inc.

Maurer Rifkin & Hill, P.C.
(See Carmel)

Maxwell, Ginny .... '66 '00 C.610 B.A. L.345 J.D. [A Baldwin&D.]
Maxwell, Mark S. .... '47 '73 C.347 B.S. L.1119 J.D. P.O. Box 501039
Maxwell, Thomas M. .... '— '87 C&L.347 B.A., J.D. [Barnes&T.]
Maxwell-Frieden, Lisa .... '70 '95 C&L.347 B.A., J.D. [O'Koon H.]
May, Susan B. .... '51 '83 C.234 B.A. L.589 J.D. Dir., Methodist Hosp. of Ind., Inc.
Mayberry, Katherine .... '— '01 C.347 B.A. L.477 J.D. [A Bose M.&E.]
Mayberry, Sean M. .... '74 '99 C.347 B.A. L.1119 J.D. [A Drewry S.V.]
Mayer, Gerald Warren .... '50 '87 C.347 A.B. L.345 J.D. [G.W.Mayer]
Mayer, Gerald W., PC .... 4911 E. 56th St.
Mayeux, Kevin Michael, Law Offices of '69 '96 C&L.260 B.A., J.D.
8645 Founders Road
Maynie, William, IV .... '— '04 C&L.339 B.S., J.D. [A Ice M.]
Mayo, Douglas Petty '68 '93 C.679 B.A. L.896 J.D.
(adm. in NC; not adm. in IN) Asst. to the Pres., Commercial Plating Co., Inc.
McAdam, Barbara R. '35 '82 C.1216 B.S. L.1119 J.D.
Supvr. Atty. Advsr., Off. of Hearing & Appl-SSA
McAllister, Brian '66 '94 C.25 B.S. L.1017 J.D.
(adm. in PA; not adm. in IN) Staff Atty., Simon Property Group
McAnlis, Joanne C. .... '69 '94 C.970 B.A. L.347 J.D. Duke Realty Investments, Inc.
McAvoy, David Robert '62 '88
C.602 B.A. L.1119 J.D. Coun., Pharm. Opers., Eli Lilly & Co.
McCall, Laurie H. .... '61 '86 C.839 B.A. L.845 J.D. Ind. State Ethics Comm.
McCann, John F., Jr., (AV) .... '29 '54 C.1024 B.S. L.345 J.D. 4219 E. Mich. St.
McCanna, Katherine E. .... '— '03 C.303 B.A. L.345 J.D. [A Baker&D.]
McCart, Donald K., Jr., (BV) .... '30 '56 C.347 B.S. L.345 LL.B. 6346 N. College Ave.
McCarty, Patrick L., (AV) '48 '74 C.63 B.S. L.345 J.D.
200 E. Washington St., Rm. W406
McCarty, Virginia Dill, (AV) .... '24 '50 C.347 B.A. L.345 LL.B. [Landman&B.]
McCaulay, P. Michael, (BV⑦) '50 '76
C.303 B.A. L.1119 J.D. 135 N. Pennsylvania, Ste. 1375
McCauley, Curtis W. .... '60 '92 C.309 A.B. L.477 J.D. [Ice M.]
McCauley, John F. .... '63 '98 C.321 B.A. L.345 J.D. [McTurnan&T.]
McClain, Janet Treichel .... '64 '91 C&L.966 B.S., J.D. Pat. Coun., Eli Lilly & Co. (Pat.)
McClamroch, W. Tobin, (AV) .... '55 '80 C.210 B.A. L.345 J.D. [Bingham M.]
McClane, Clarence J. '32 '62
C.347 B.S. L.345 J.D. Asst. Reg. Coun., Dept. of Veterans Affairs
McClellan-Leavitt, Julia, (BV) .... '65 '90 C&L.347 B.A., J.D. [Blackwelder,C.&L.]
McClure, David E., (BV) .... '38 '65 C.347 A.B. L.345 LL.B. [McClure M.D.&H.]
McClure, Rebecca S., (AV) '48 '82
C.108 B.S. L.345 J.D. Asst. Dir., State's Pros. Attys. Council

McClure McClure Davis & Henn, (BV)
235 North Delaware, 46204 ⊙
Telephone: 317-221-0800 Facsimile: 317-221-0900
URL: http://www.lawyers.com/mcclure-law
Members of Firm: David E. McClure; Grover B. Davis; David M. Henn (Resident, Greenwood Office). Associates: Christopher Steinmetz; Brett M. Haworth; James T. Flanigan (Resident, Greenwood Office).
General Civil, Insurance Defense, Employment Law, Family/Domestic Relations, Adoption Law, Child Custody, Child Support, Divorce, Visitation Rights, Personal Injury, Automobile Accidents and Injuries, Slip and Fall, Dog Bites, Wrongful Death, Estate Planning, Wills, Probate, Trusts and Estates, Guardianship, Asset Protection, Corporate Law, Business Litigation, Business Law, Business Planning, Business Enterprises, and Real Estate. Trials and Appellate Practice before all Courts.
Reference: NBD.
Greenwood Office: 225 South Emerson Avenue, Suite F, 46143-1959. Telephone: 317-885-0041. Facsimile: 317-885-0506.
See Professional Biographies, INDIANAPOLIS, INDIANA

McCluskey, Jerome P. .... '— '02 C.309 B.A. L.813 J.D. [A Baker&D.]
McColley, John C., (AV) .... '49 '83 C.347 B.A. L.345 J.D. [Whitham,M.&R.]

McConnell, Dean E. ....'— '97 C.679 B.S. L.831 J.D. [Sommer B.] (Pat.)
McConnell, R. J., (AV) ....'60 '85 C.679 B.S. L.1119 J.D. [Bose M.&E.]
McCool, Philip L., (AV) ....'53 '78 C.477 B.A. L.1119 J.D. [Sommer B.]
McCoy, Dionne Carroll '69 '95
C.679 B.A. L.879 J.D. Anthem Blue Cross and Blue Shield
McCoy, Monica M. ....'41 '83 C.739 B.A. L.345 J.D. 135 N. Pennsylvania
McCrory, Jill L., (AV) ....'60 '88 C.346 B.S. L.345 J.D. [Stewart&I.]
McCrory, Michael K., (AV) ....'— '79 C.346 B.S. L.345 J.D. [Barnes&T.]
McCrory, Patricia Polis, (AV) ....'54 '80 C.344 B.S. L.345 J.D. [Harrison&M.]
McCrosson, Dennis F., (BV) ....'52 '83 C.884 B.A. L.345 J.D. [McCrosson&Assoc.]
McCrosson & Associates, P.C., (BV) .... 6125 U.S. Highway 31 South
McDavid, John K., (BV) ....'63 '89 C.602 B.A. L.347 J.D. [Locke R.]
McDermott, Brian L., (BV) ....'66 '92 C.177 B.A. L.352 J.D. [Ogletree,D.N.S.&S.]
McDermott, Martha Mondou, (AV) ....'70 '95 C.352 B.A. L.347 J.D. [Garrison&K.]
McDonald, Harvey E., (BV) ....'40 '69 C.347 A.B. L.1119 J.D. [H.E.McDonald]
McDonald, Nicole L. ....'— '05 C.999 B.S. L.345 J.D. [Baker&D.]
McDonald, Harvey E., P.C., (BV) ....9465 Counselors Row
McDonnell, Amy Elizabeth ....'72 '99 C.679 B.S. L.879 J.D. Atty. Gen. Off.
McDowell, Kevin C. ....'50 '81 C.108 B.S. L.345 J.D. Coun., State Dept. of Educ.
McDowell, Lynn '49 '76 C.347 B.S. L.1119 J.D.
Assoc. Clinical Prof., Indiana Univ. Sch. of Law
McDowell, Richard R., (AV) ....'37 '65 C&L.880 B.E., LL.B. [Hill,F.M.F.&M.]
McDowell, Robert L. ......'47 '80 C.63 B.S. L.345 J.D. Sr. Atty., Allison Engine Co., Inc.
McEwan, Alan W. ....'76 '03 C.894 A.B. L.345 J.D. [Feiwell&H.]
McGeath, Timothy A. ....'— '99 C.303 B.A. L.347 J.D. [Hall,R.K.H.&L.]
McGill, Daniel W., (AV) ....'— '75 C&L.477 B.A., J.D. [Barnes&T.]
McGimpsey, David T. ....'70 '98 C.894 B.A. L.347 J.D. [Bingham M.]
McGinley, Jonna L. ....'78 '03 C.210 B.A. L.1119 J.D. [Bingham M.]
McGoff, Kevin P., (AV) ....'53 '80 C.347 B.A. L.345 J.D. [Kiefer&M.]
McGoff, Sharon L., (AV) ....'63 '91 C&L.347 B.S., J.D. 7323 Tuxedo St.
McGonigal, Joseph F. ....'53 '92 C.884 B.A. L.1119 J.D. U.S. Trustees Off.
McGown, Anne C., (AV) ....'— '87 C&L.347 B.S., J.D. [Barnes&T.]
McGrath, James J., (AV) ....'42 '67 C.397 A.B. L.884 J.D. [Harrison&M.]
McGrath, Madonna Frances, (BV) ......'46 '89 C.1291 A.B. L.1119 J.D. [Baker&D.]
McGrath, R. Christopher ....'68 '99 C.436 B.S. L.284 J.D. 8900 Keystone Crossing
McGregor, Deborah B. '— '83 C.249 B.A. L.276 J.D.
(adm. in VA; not adm. in IN) Ind. Univ. School of Law
McHaffie, Melissa A. ....'57 '89 C.473 B.A. L.345 J.D. 220 Virginia Avenue
McHugh, John T. '16 '48 C.150 L.1340 LL.B.
(adm. in OH; not adm. in IN) 1123 Ivy Lane‡
McInerny, Daniel P., (AV) ....'58 '84 C.602 B.A. L.596 J.D. [Bose M.&E.]
McIntire, Beth W. ....'62 '87 C.63 B.S. L.347 J.D. 107 N. Pennsylvania St., Ste. 500
McIntire, James G., (AV) ....'49 '74 C.347 A.B. L.345 J.D. [Krieg D.]
McKay, William T. ....'69 '97 C.299 B.A. L.1119 J.D. Dep. Pub. Def.
McKean, Jeffrey L., (AV) ....'63 '90 C.679 B.S.I.M. L.345 J.D. [Wooden&M.]
McKenna, William A. ....'80 '05 C.701 B.S. L.1119 J.D. [Woodard,E.M.M.&H.]
McKeon, Thomas J., (AV) '55 '79
C.347 A.B. L.345 J.D. Sr. Staff Atty., Amer. Fam. Ins. Grp.
McKiernan, Holiday Hart, (AV) '58 '83 C.210 B.A. L.1119 J.D.
Exec. Dir. & Coun., Alpha Chi Omega Fraternity, Inc.
McKiernan, Philip B., (AV) ....'52 '83 C.602 B.A. L.1119 J.D. [Hackman H.&C.]
McKinney, Dennis K., (AV) ....'52 '77 C.63 B.S. L.146 J.D. Staff Atty.
McKinney, Larry J. ....'44 '70 C.430 B.A. L.347 J.D. Chf. U.S. Dist. J.
McKinney, Margaret M. ....'53 '78 C.347 B.A. L.345 J.D. P.O. Box 1230‡
McKinney, Rebecca Graham '58 '84
C.679 B.A. L.345 J.D. Associate General Counsel, USA Group, Inc.
McKinney, Robert H. ....'25 '51 C.871 B.S. L.1119 J.D. [Bose M.&E.] ‡
McKinnon, Patricia L., (BV) '61 '94 C.57 B.A. L.602 J.D.
333 East Ohio Street, Suite 200, 46204
Telephone: 317-686-1900 Fax: 317-686-5760 URL: http://www.indianafamilylawyer.com
Email: pmckinnon@indianafamilylawyer.com URL: http://www.divorceindianalaw.com
Family Law, Adoption, Child Custody, Child Support, Divorce, Visitation Rights, Paternity, CHINS, Guardianship.
See Professional Biographies, INDIANAPOLIS, INDIANA
McKinzie, J. Mark, (BVⓉ) ....'53 '79 C.339 B.S. L.1119 J.D. [Riley B.&E.]
McLaren, Kevin L. ....'— '04 C.1167 B.S. L.345 J.D. [Barnes&T.] (See Pat. Sect.)
McLaughlin, Alan L., (AV) ....'57 '83 C.894 A.B. L.880 J.D. [Baker&D.]
McLaughlin, Robert L., (AV) ....'36 '61 C.347 A.B. L.477 J.D. [Wooden&M.]
McLean, Ronald G., (AV) ....'55 '80 C.624 A.B. L.117 J.D. 225 N. Delaware St., Ste. 2
McLin, William C., (BV) ....'40 '69 C.108 B.S. L.345 J.D. 1408 N. Pennsylvania St.
McMahan, Lynne M. ....'— '81 C.97 B.S. L.345 J.D. [Barnes&T.]
McMahon, Michael J. ....'48 '80 C.293 B.A. L.345 J.D. Dir. of Res., IN Jud. Ctr.
McMains, Jeanne Lee ....'— '95 C.679 B.A. L.347 J.D. [Jensen&Assoc.]
McMains, Michael B., (BV) ....'57 '93 C.679 B.S. L.347 J.D. [Goodin,O.&B.]
Mcmath, Patricia C. ....'61 '88 C.347 B.S. L.1119 J.D. 5255 E. 73rd. Ct.
McMillian, Jimmie L. ....'— '02 C.347 B.A. L.345 J.D. [Barnes&T.]
McMinn, Richard W. ....'61 '87 C.344 B.S. L.851 J.D. [Threlkeld R.]
McNair, Jennifer D. ....'73 '98 C.477 B.A. L.831 J.D. [Wood T.G.M.&H.]
McNally, Michael ....'— '02 C.347 B.A. L.345 J.D. [Ice M.]
McNamar, David F., (AV) ....'40 '68 C.679 B.S. L.1119 J.D. [McNamar&Assoc.]
McNamar & Associates, (AV)
111 Monument Circle, Suite 3350, P.O. Box 1883, 46206-1883
Telephone: 317-632-3350 Fax: 317-632-3353
Email: dfmcnamar@mcnamarlaw.com URL: http://www.mcnamarlaw.com
David F. McNamar.
Health Care Regulatory, Administrative Law, Business Organization, Joint Ventures, Mergers, Acquisitions and Divestitures, Shareholder Rights, Business Successions, Estate Planning, Wills, Probate, Trusts and Estates, Insurance Law, Real Estate, State Government Law, Municipal Law.
See Professional Biographies, INDIANAPOLIS, INDIANA
McNeal, James ....'49 '84 C.346 B.A. L.345 J.D. 7743 Wellesley Rd. S.
McNear, Deborah C. ....'52 '90 C.347 B.A. L.345 J.D. [Krieg D.]
McNeil, Andrew M. ....'69 '96 C.827 B.A. L.477 J.D. [Bose M.&E.]
McNelis, Michael T., (AV) ....'62 '88 C.338 B.S. L.345 J.D. [Mitchell H.J.&D.]
McNett, John C., (AV) '44 '70
C.679 B.S. L.273 J.D. [Woodard,E.M.M.&H.] (See Pat. Sect.)
McNevin, Robert W., (AV) ....'28 '57 C.231 A.B. L.345 J.D. [McNevin&M.] ‡
McNevin & McNevin, (AV) .... 748 Bates Street, Suite 205
McOmber, Kori L. ....'76 '01 C.473 B.A. L.345 J.D. [Tyra&C.]
McOmber, Richard L., (AV) ....'46 '83 C.108 B.A. L.345 J.D. [Harrison&M.]
McPherson, Heather, (AV) ....'— '76 *C.914 B.A. L.345 J.D. [Sommer B.]*
McPike, Joseph D., II ....'66 '93 C.10 B.S. L.347 J.D. [Zeigler C.&K.]
McQueen, Erin Marie ....'60 '86 C.347 B.S. L.879 J.D. Civil Rights Comm.
McShane, Kevin, (AV) ....'52 '80 C.686 B.A. L.345 J.D. 1050 N. College Ave.
McSharar, Janet A., (AV) ....'56 '84 C.347 B.A. L.345 J.D. [Harrison&M.]
McTurnan, Lee B., (AV) ....'37 '65 C.309 A.B. L.145 J.D. [McTurnan&T.]
McTurnan & Turner, (AV)
2400 Market Tower, 10 West Market Street, 46204
Telephone: 317-464-8181 Telecopier: 317-464-8131
URL: http://www.mtlitig.com
Lee B. McTurnan; Wayne C. Turner; Steven M. Badger; John F. McCauley. Associates: Jacqueline Bowman Ponder; Anne L. Cowgur; Gregory A. Neibarger; Kenneth J. Munson; Carl A. Hayes; Michael R. Limrick; Shannon D. Landreth; Julianna M. Plawecki; Erik C. Johnson.
Business Litigation in all State and Federal Trial and Appellate Courts, including Antitrust, Contracts, Securities Fraud, Corporate Governance, Public Utility, Accountants' Liability, Legal Professional Liability Law, Class Action Defense, Discrimination, Employment, Noncompetition Agreements, Product Liability, Lender Liability, Uniform Commercial Code, Commercial Fraud, Business Torts, Unfair Competition, Administrative, Tax Litigation, Media and First Amendment.
See Professional Biographies, INDIANAPOLIS, INDIANA
McWilliams, Monique Hunt '64 '93
C&L.347 B.A., J.D. Eli Lilly and Company (Law Division)
Mead, John Michael, (BV) '67 '94 C.838 B.S. L.347 J.D.
320 N. Meridian St., Ste. 1006
Mead, Susanah M. '47 '76 C.788 B.A. L.347 J.D.
Prof. of Law, Indiana Univ. Sch. of Law
Meade, John C., (AV) ....'— '74 C.347 A.B. L.477 J.D. [Hall,R.K.H.&L.]
Meagher, Douglas W. ....'57 '97 C.346 B.S. L.74 J.D. [Dugan V.&M.]
Means, Harley K. ....'75 '01 C.679 B.S. L.347 J.D. [Kroger,G.&R.]
Means, William P. ....'71 '01 C.679 B.A. L.345 J.D. [Riley B.&E.]
Mears, Stephen D., (AV) ....'48 '74 C.347 B.S. L.345 J.D. 8395 Keystone Xing
Meek, Danny E., (BV) ....'48 '74 C.63 B.A. L.345 J.D. [Hollingsworth,M.M.&M.]
Meeker, Catherine A. ....'74 '99 C.63 B.A. L.145 J.D. [Baker&D.]
Meeker, Kenneth C. '44 '68 C.801 L.879 LL.B.
(adm. in IL; not adm. in IN) U.S. Trustee, Dept. of Jus.
Mehringer, Susan E. ....'59 '89 C.347 B.A. L.345 J.D. [Lewis W.]
Meier, Barbara J., (AV) ....'— '91 C.378 B.S.Ed. L.347 J.D. [Barnes&T.]
Meilaender, Ellen Hope ....'74 '00 C.967 B.A. L.347 J.D. Atty. Gen. Off.
Meili, Robert Nelson ....'50 '89 C.108 B.A. L.347 J.D. 9310 Friar Court
Meils, Hannah L. ....'— '03 C.347 B.A. L.74 J.D. [Sommer B.]
Meils, Rick D., (AV) ....'50 '75 C.347 A.B. L.345 J.D. [Meils,T.D.&B.]
Meils, Thompson, Dietz & Berish, (AV)
Two Market Square Center, Suite 830, 251 East Ohio Street, 46204
Telephone: 317-637-1383 Fax: 317-264-2573 Email: joedietz@worldnet.att.net
Email: rmeils@home.com
Members of Firm: Rick D. Meils; Robert C. Thompson, Jr.; Joseph M. Dietz; William M. Berish; Neil A. Davis. Associate: John W. Mervilde.
General Civil and Trial Practice. Insurance Litigation. Probate and Estate Planning, Real Estate. References: Merchants National Bank; Indiana National Bank.
See Professional Biographies, INDIANAPOLIS, INDIANA
Melchiorre, Victor A., Jr. '54 '81
C.894 B.A. L.192 J.D. V.P. & Tr. Off., Bank One Trust Co., N.A.
Mellowitz, James A., (BV) ....'56 '88 C.347 B.A. L.345 J.D. [R.W.York&Assoc.]
Melton, Matthew Walton ....'73 '00 C.679 B.A. L.345 J.D. [Norris C.&S.]
Mendelson, Tilden, (AV) ....'42 '69 C.659 B.S. L.1119 J.D. [Miller M.M.&K.]
Mercer, Charles R., Jr., (BV) ....'42 '68 C.347 B.S. L.345 J.D. [Stewart&I.]
Mercer, John L., (AV) ....'32 '59 C.108 B.S. L.347 J.D. [Wood T.G.M.&H.]
Mercer, John S. (Jay), (AV) ....'60 '86 C.347 B.S. L.345 J.D. [Wood T.G.M.&H.]
Merenstein, Adele ....'— '93 C.107 B.S. L.124 J.D. [Hall,R.K.H.&L.]
Merkle, Mark J. R., (AV) ....'58 '83 C.894 A.B. L.345 J.D. [Krieg D.]
Merrill, Jane B. ....'43 '75 C.679 B.S. L.345 J.D. 3021 East 98th Street, Suite 220
Merrill, William H., Jr. '42 '67
C.108 B.S. L.345 J.D. Gen. Coun., Northwest Developement Corp.
Merriman, Sharon R., (BV) ....'— '75 C.33 B.A. L.345 J.D. [Voyles,Z.P.H.&M.]
Merriman, Vicki J. ....'— '96 C.688 B.S. L.347 J.D. [O'Koon H.]
Mertz, Jennifer Horton '71 '98
C.347 B.A. L.345 J.D. 5329 South Emerson Avenue, Suite C
Mervilde, John W. ....'74 '99 C.74 B.A. L.602 J.D. [Meils,T.D.&B.]
Messaglia, Michael J. ....'67 '93 C&L.602 B.A., J.D. [Krieg D.]
Metz, Anthony J., III ....'47 '72 C.347 B.S. L.1119 J.D. U.S. Bkrptcy. J.
Metzel, Andrielle M. ....'69 '96 C.265 B.A. L.345 J.D. [Dann P.N.&K.]
Metzger, Kimberly C. ....'66 '97 C.602 B.A. L.851 J.D. [Ice M.]
Metzger, Mark A., (AV) ....'62 '89 C.347 B.S. L.345 J.D. [Due,D.F.&M.]
Metzger, Norman P. '39 '64 C.432 A.B. L.477 J.D.
Exec. Dir., Legal Servs. Organization
Metzger, W. Todd ....'71 '97 C.679 B.S. L.347 J.D. [Scopelitis,G.L.&H.]
Meulbroek, Thomas ....'62 '95 C.210 B.A. L.347 J.D. Allison Advanced Develop. Corp.
Meunier, Jeffrey O., (AV) ....'59 '84 C.347 B.S. L.345 J.D. 8900 Keystone Xing, Ste. 400
Meyer, Charles J. '70 '95 C.210 B.A. L.347 J.D.
[Woodard,E.M.M.&H.] (See Pat. Sect.)
Meyer, Donald M., (AV) ....'58 '83 C.249 B.S. L.345 J.D. [Bose M.&E.]
Meyer, Gracia-Jean "G-J", (BV) ....'— '98 C.303 B.A. L.1119 J.D. [Meyer]
Meyer, Jaime L. ....'76 '02 C.108 B.A. L.1119 J.D. [Riley B.&E.]
Meyer, Sue Figert, (AV) ....'55 '81 C.108 B.A. L.347 J.D. [Rubin&L.]
Meyer, Tammy J., (AV) ....'64 '89 C.999 B.S. L.345 J.D. [Lewis W.]
Meyer Law Office, (BV)
10811 Lexington Drive, 46280
Telephone: 317-407-4571
URL: http://www.gjmeyerlaw.com
Gracia-Jean "G-J" Meyer.
Wills, Trusts and Estates, Probate Law, Charitable Giving, Non-profit Organizations, Small Business, Business Law, Real Estate, Income Tax, Estate and Gift Taxation and Wealth Preservation Law.
See Professional Biographies, INDIANAPOLIS, INDIANA
Meyers, William S. ....'— '02 C.701 B.S. L.1119 J.D. [Baker&D.] (See Pat. Sect.)
Michael, Jeffrey A. ....'— '93 C.912 B.S.E.E. L.347 J.D. [Barnes&T.] (See Pat. Sect.)
Michael, M. Sue, (AV) ....'54 '83 C.679 B.A. L.347 J.D. [Baker&D.]
Michael, Rod L. ....'— '02 C.347 B.S. L.345 J.D. [Sommer B.]
Michael, Susan Adinamis, (BV) ....'67 '93 C.347 B.A. L.1119 J.D. [Adinamis,M.&S.]
Michelsen, Jan, (AV) ....'— '94 C.98 B.S. L.347 J.D. [Ogletree,D.N.S.&S.]
Miedema, Lawrence R. ....'46 '88 C.234 B.A. L.347 J.D. Atty. Gen. Off.
Milam, John L.L. ......'52 '78 C.679 B.S.E. L.347 J.D. Mng. Atty., Simon Property Group
Milford, Robert J., (BV) ....'55 '83 C.108 B.S. L.345 J.D. [Drewry S.V.]
Millard, David B., (AV) ....'— '79 C.347 B.S. L.1119 J.D. [Barnes&T.]
Millard, Kendall '— '99 C.513 B.A. L.347 J.D.
(adm. in DC; not adm. in IN) [Barnes&T.]
Millen, David L., (BV) ....'30 '55 C.249 B.S. L.345 LL.B. Dep. Pros. Atty.
Miller, Brett J., (BV) ....'58 '83 C.1213 B.S. L.879 J.D. [Bingham M.]
Miller, C. Joe '56 '85 C.607 B.S.M.E. L.602 J.D.
Bldg. 308 1B, 9330 Zionsville Rd (Pat.)
Miller, Charles F., Jr., (AV) '53 '79 C.894 A.B. L.345 J.D.
151 N. Delaware St., Ste. 1990
Miller, Clayton C. ....'65 '93 C.309 A.B. L.347 J.D. [Baker&D.]

Miller, Danelle R, '— '97 C.862 B.S. L.575 J.D.
Regul. Coun., Roche Diagnostics Corp.
Miller, Daniel R. ....'63 '89 C.210 B.A. L.347 J.D. Jud. Clk., Indiana Ct. of App.
Miller, David A., (BV) ....'46 '73 C.347 B.S. L.345 J.D. 7550 S. Meridian St., Ste. A
Miller, David W., (AV) ....'50 '77 C.347 A.B. L.345 J.D. [Baker&D.]
Miller, Debra Hanley, (AV) ....'60 '84 C.346 B.S. L.345 J.D. [Ice M.]
Miller, Eric I., (BV) ....'50 '80 C&L.347 B.S., J.D. [Miller,W.M.&H.]
Miller, Eugene C., Jr., (AV) ....'29 '53 C.918 A.B. L.309 LL.B. 320 N. Meridian St.‡
Miller, G. William '41 '66
C.344 A.B. L.345 J.D. Asst. Gen. Coun., Law Div., Eli Lilly & Co.
Miller, Gary L., (AV) ....'56 '80 C.347 A.B. L.345 J.D. Alliance Insurance
Miller, Jacob S. ....'05 '30 L.74 9202 N. Meridian St.
Miller, Joseph E., Jr. ....'68 '95 C.827 B.A. L.208 J.D. [Baker&D.]
Miller, Kimberley Sue '62 '99 C.347 B.S.B.A. L.1119 J.D.
B 240, 7915 S Emerson Ave
Miller, Lester C. ....'51 '78 C.170 B.A. L.347 J.D. Exec. Asst. to the Gov.
Miller, M. Kathryn '60 '94
C.788 B.A. L.347 J.D. South Tower, 115 West Washington Street
Miller, Margaret Bannon, (AV) ....'44 '75 C.519 B.A. L.345 J.D. [Bose M.&E.]
Miller, Melissa Ferverda ....'62 '89 C&L.347 B.A., J.D. Amer. United Life Ins. Co.
Miller, Michael S., (AV) ....'46 '75 C.303 B.A. L.345 J.D. [Miller M.M.&K.]
Miller, Patrick L., (AV) ....'65 '90 C.249 B.S. L.1119 J.D. [Goodin A.&M.]
Miller, Patrick M. ....'76 '02 C.966 B.A. L.436 J.D. [A Drewry S.V.]
Miller, Peter D., (P.C.), (BV) ....'47 '82 C.63 B.S. L.345 J.D. 4801 Industrial Pky.
Miller, Ray ....'24 '50 C.436 L.345 LL.B. 5462 Vin Rose Ln.‡
Miller, Sandra H., (BV) '49 '83
C.347 A.B.,M.A. L.345 J.D. V.P., Health-Life Oper., Anthem, Inc.
Miller, Stephen P. ....'61 '87 C.347 B.A. L.201 J.D. Dept. of Admin.
Miller, Troy Michael ....'71 '99 C.63 B.S. L.200 J.D. [Pastore&G.]
Miller Muller Mendelson & Kennedy, (AV) .... 8900 Keystone Crossing Suite 1250
Miller, Waters, Martin & Hall, (AV) ....101 West Ohio Street Suite 660
Miller-Nierste, Sherri K. '66 '97 C&L.347 B.S., J.D.
Asst. Gen. Coun., Indianapolis Motor Speedway, LLC
Milligan, Jennifer S. ....'72 '99 C.346 B.S. L.879 J.D. [A Gilliland&C.]
Millikan, Michael E. ....'71 '98 C.884 B.A. L.347 J.D. [Ice M.]
Milliken, Lloyd H., Jr., (AV) ....'35 '60 C.347 B.S. L.1119 J.D. [C Locke R.]
Mills, Alan K., (AV) ....'— '82 C.123 B.A. L.345 J.D. [Barnes&T.]
Mills, Bruce F. ....'46 '98 C.346 B.S. L.966 J.D. [A Wessels&P.]
Mills, Jeffrey D. '73 '00 C.347 B.S. L.1119 J.D.
Asst. V.P. & Assoc. Coun., Old National Bancorp
Mills, Thomas M. '57 '01
C.347 B.S. L.345 J.D. Ast. Gen. Coun., McCready and Keene, Inc.
Millspaugh, John A., (AV) ....'70 '96 C.63 B.A. L.477 J.D. [Bose M.&E.]
Milne, David C. ....'67 '94 C.894 B.A. L.347 J.D. 500 Century Bldg, 36 S. Penn. St.
Milne, Meagan K. ....'69 '94 C.339 B.S. L.347 J.D. Law Clk.
Miner, R. Michael '46 '75 C.347 B.A. L.345 J.D.
Sr. V.P. & Sr. Tr. Offr., National City Bk., Indiana
Minglin, Michael Alan ....'51 '81 C&L.347 B.A., J.D. 7550 S. Meridian St., Ste. A
Minnix, Larry A., (BV) ....'51 '78 C.347 B.A. L.990 J.D. [Brattain&M.]
Minott, Debra F., (BV) .....'56 '80 C&L.477 B.A., J.D. 111 Monument Circle, 29th Floor
Minton, Phillip H., (AV) ....'— '57 C.210 A.B. L.1119 J.D. [C Sommer B.]
Miroff, Drew ....'73 '99 C.477 B.A. L.597 J.D. [A Ice M.]
Miroff, Franklin I., (AV) ....'37 '65 C.347 A.B. L.345 J.D. [Miroff,C.&W.]
Miroff, Cross & Woolsey, P.C., (AV) ....500 E 96th St., Ste. 100
Mishkin, Sidney, (AV) ....'37 '64 C.952 A.B. L.1119 J.D. [Mishkin&D.]

Mishkin & Duvall, (AV)
Suite 525 200 South Meridian, 46225
Telephone: 317-634-9100 Fax: 317-634-9103
Email: mishkin-duvall@sbcglobal.net
Sidney Mishkin; Lesa C. Duvall.
General Civil Practice in all State and Federal Courts. Litigation. Construction Law. Real Estate and Commercial Law, Documentation of Business Transactions, Employment Law.
See Professional Biographies, INDIANAPOLIS, INDIANA

Mitchell, Gloria K., (AV) ....'61 '88 C.473 B.A. L.347 J.D. [Mitchell&Assoc.]
Mitchell, Jeffrey R., (BV) '64 '90 C.976 B.A. L.1119 J.D.
Reg. Legal Sr. Staff Atty., Amer. Fam. Ins. Co.
Mitchell, Marvin H., (AV) ....'37 '63 C.608 B.S. L.345 J.D. [Mitchell H.J.&D.]
Mitchell, Mary Harter .....'53 '78 C.108 B.A. L.188 J.D. Prof., Indiana Univ. Sch. of Law

Mitchell & Associates, (AV)
3925 River Crossing Parkway, Suite 270, 46240-2279
Telephone: 317-815-5900 Fax: 317-472-0966
Email: info@mitchell-law.net URL: http://www.gmitchelllawfirm.com
Gloria K. Mitchell. Associates: Robin L. Kelly; Elisabeth M. Edwards.
Mitchell & Associates is an association of attorneys who offer services in all areas of family law, including but not limited to divorce and post-divorce modification; domestic litigation; family mediation; qualified domestic relations orders (QDROS); antenuptial agreements; child custody and support; visitation rights; paternity; adoption; domestic violence; guardianships; grandparent's visitation rights; simple wills and trusts and other related matters.
See Professional Biographies, INDIANAPOLIS, INDIANA

Mitchell Hurst Jacobs & Dick, (AV) BB
152 East Washington Street, 46204
Telephone: 317-636-0808 1-800-636-0808 Fax: 317-633-7680 URL: http://www.mhjdlaw.com
URL: http://www.mhjd.com
Members of Firm: Marvin H. Mitchell; William W. Hurst; Samuel L. Jacobs; Richard J. Dick; Kimberly H. Danforth; Michael T. McNelis. Associates: Stephen P. Kenley; John C. Babione.
Civil Litigation, Corporate, Business Litigation, Business Planning, Contracts, Real Estate, Commercial Leasing, Commercial Real Estate, Personal Injury Law, Automobile Accidents, Dog Bites, Slip and Fall, Wrongful Death, Medical Malpractice, Foreclosure, Products Liability, Construction, Lien.
General Counsel for: Premium Optical Co.; Calderon Bros. Vending Machines, Inc.; Grocers Supply Co., Inc.; Power Train Services, Inc.; Frank E. Irish, Inc.; Bedding Liquidators; Galyan's Trading Co.; Harcourt Management Co., Inc.; Kosene & Kosene Mgt. & Dev. Co., Inc.; Hasten Bancorp.
See Professional Biographies, INDIANAPOLIS, INDIANA

Mitlak, Stefany L. '58 '84 C.938 B.S. L.1048 J.D.
Sr. Staff Atty., Simon Property Group
Mixdorf, Thomas E. ....'62 '92 C.351 B.A. L.347 J.D. [Ice M.]
Mize, Dane A. ....'— '01 C.679 B.A. L.347 J.D. [A Ogletree,D.N.S.&S.]
Moberly, Robyn L. ....'53 '78 C.347 B.A. L.345 J.D. Supr. Ct. J.
Moffatt, Michael A., (AV) ....'— '89 C.210 B.A. L.345 J.D. [Ogletree,D.N.S.&S.]
Molin, Michelle M. ....'65 '99 C.679 B.A. L.345 J.D. [Ice M.]
Mollabashy, Ziaaddin ....'— '03 C.347 B.A. L.1541 J.D. [S Barnes&T.]
Molnar, Lawrence V. ....'63 '00 C&L.347 B.A., J.D. CMG Worldwide, Inc.
Moloy, James P., (AV) ....'59 '84 C.347 B.S. L.345 J.D. [Dann P.N.&K.]
Mommer, Anthony W., (AV) ....'44 '68 C.347 A.B. L.1119 J.D. [Krieg D.]
Monday, Terry L., (BV) ....'57 '84 C.347 B.A. L.345 J.D. [Monday R.J.&A.]
Monday Rodeheffer Jones & Albright, (BV) ....1915 Broad Ripple Ave.
Monk, James R. ...'47 '78 C.347 A.B. L.260 J.D. Chmn., Ind. Utility Regulatory Comm.‡

Monroe, Mark T. ....'71 '03 C.63 B.S. L.74 J.D. [A Wooden&M.]
Montgomery, Donita F. ....'56 '84 C.679 B.S. L.339 J.D. Dep. Co. Pros.
Montgomery, Scott W. ....'68 '95 C.63 B.S. L.347 J.D. P.O. Box 33105
Montgomery, Susan G., (BV) '54 '84
C.347 B.A. L.345 J.D. Staff Atty., Legis. Servs. Agency
Montross, W. Scott, (AV) ....'47 '71 C.477 B.B.A. L.345 J.D. [Townsend&M.]
Moon, Michael D., Jr., (BV) ....'— '96 C&L.347 B.A., J.D. [Barnes&T.]
Moore, Daniel L. ....'64 '90 C.63 B.S. L.879 J.D. [Moore&Assoc.]
Moore, Donna L. ....'69 '96 C&L.347 B.A., J.D. Staff Atty., Simon Property Group
Moore, Harold C. ...'66 '93 C.401 B.S.E.E. L.705 J.D. [Maginot M.&B.] (See Pat. Sect.)
Moore, John J. ....'72 '98 C.347 B.S. L.494 J.D. [A Stark D.&S.]
Moore, Mark S., (AV) ....'57 '82 C.894 A.B. L.1119 J.D. [Baker&D.]
Moore, R. Bruce '48 '83 C.604 B.A. L.1003 J.D.
(adm. in OH; not adm. in IN) Div. Couns., Simon Property Group
Moore, Ronald J. ...'69 '95 C.1214 B.A. L.1119 J.D. Mng. Atty., UAW Legal Servs. Plan
Moore, Thomas C., II ....'46 '86 C.152 B.A. L.1119 J.D. [Moore&Assoc.]
Moore, William C., (AV) '40 '65 C.679 B.S. L.345 J.D.
9465 Counselors Row, Suite 200
Moore, Yolanda L., (BV) '49 '77 C.822 A.B. L.1119 J.D.
Assoc. Gen. Coun., McCready and Keene, Inc.
Moore & Associates ....One North Pennsylvania, Suite 880
Moores, Merrill, (AV) ....'27 '53 C.347 A.B. L.345 LL.B. 244 N. College Ave.
Moorman, David R. ....'70 '05 C.347 B.S. L.345 J.D. [A Maginot M.&B.]
Moreau, D. William, Jr., (AV) ....'— '81 C.679 B.S. L.276 J.D. [Barnes&T.]
Morelock, Ronald J. ....'63 '93 [A Scopelitis,G.L.&H.]
Moreno, Marco A. ....'73 '03 C.854 B.A. L.1119 J.D. [A Lewis&K.]
Morfas, Craig C. '59 '85 C.347 B.A. L.345 J.D.
(adm. in OH; not adm. in IN) Gen. Coun., Baldwin & Lyons, Inc.
Morford, Bruce A. ....'51 '00 C.345 B.A. L.1158 J.D. 9292 North Meridian, Suite 308
Morgan, Robert D., (AV) ....'16 '41 C.210 A.B. L.309 J.D. 577 Dillingham Dr.‡
Morgan, Roderick H., (AV) ....'— '79 C.870 B.S. L.276 J.D. [Stewart&I.]

Morgan & Pottinger, P.S.C., (AV)
9801 Fall Creek Road #333, 46256-4802 ⊙
Telephone: 317-287-3961 Telecopier: 317-536-3687
URL: http://www.morganandpottinger.com
—Edward A.B. Castaldo.
Banking, Bankruptcy, Business, Collections, Commercial, Corporate, Consumer Credit.
Louisville, Kentucky Office: 601 West Main Street. Telephone: 502-589-2780. Telecopier: 502-585-3498.
Lexington, Kentucky Office: 133 West Short Street. Telephone: 859-253-1900. Telecopier: 859-255-2038.
Nashville, Tennessee Office: 5543 Edmondson Pike #25. Telephone: 615-831-9554. Telecopier: 615-831-9557.
See Professional Biographies, INDIANAPOLIS, INDIANA

Moriarty, John D., (BV) ....'67 '96 C.347 B.S. L.345 J.D. [A Plews S.R.&B.]
Moriarty, John V., (AV) '40 '69
C.602 B.S.A.E. L.345 J.D. [Woodard,E.M.M.&H.] (See Pat. Sect.)
Moriarty, Michael D., (AV) ....'50 '78 C.347 B.S. L.345 J.D. [Locke R.]
Morical, Alice McKenzie ....'69 '95 C.473 B.A. L.347 J.D. [Hoover H.B.&H.]
Morical, Gregory J. '68 '95 C.210 B.A. L.347 J.D.
Asst. Gen. Coun. & Asst. Secy., Buzzi Unicem USA, Inc.
Morog, Tamie Jo ....'58 '95 C.63 B.S. L.107 J.D. [A Parr R.O.&M.]
Morow, Jewell J. ....'48 '78 C.187 B.A. L.879 J.D. 1225 Frederick S.
Morow, Michael R., (BV) ....'51 '77 C.63 B.A. L.879 J.D. [Stephenson M.&S.]
Morrison, Timothy M., (AV) '49 '74 C.347 A.B. L.1119 J.D.
10 W. Market St., Ste. 2100
Morrisson, Scott S., (AV) ....'62 '87 C.303 B.A. L.345 J.D. [Krieg D.]
Morse, Leslie B. ....'79 '05 C.679 B.A. L.345 J.D. [A Locke R.]
Morse, Peter A., Jr. ....'— '93 C.210 B.A. L.880 J.D. [Barnes&T.]
Mortell, Rebecca Walker '50 '75 C.346 A.B. L.1119 J.D.
Dep. Dir., Legislative Servs. Agcy., Office of Code Revision
Mortier, Jeffrey J., (BV) ....'65 '91 C.597 B.A. L.879 J.D. [Locke R.]
Morton, Don F., (BV) ....'39 '66 C.375 B.S. L.345 J.D. [Parr R.O.&M.]
Morton, Frank W., (BV) ....'12 '36 L.981 LL.B. 5051 E. 71st St.‡
Morton, Teresa E., (AV) ....'— '88 C.108 B.S. L.345 J.D. [Barnes&T.]
Mosby, Timmy D., (AV) ....'49 '77 C.347 B.S. L.345 J.D. Co. Pros.
Mosby, Whitney L. ....'77 '02 C&L.347 B.A., J.D. [A Bingham M.]
Moses, John M., (AV) ....'50 '80 C.174 B.A. L.345 J.D. [Clark,Q.M.S.&G.]
Moss, Gerald L., (AV) ....'36 '62 C.347 B.S. L.1119 LL.B. [C Bingham M.]
Moss, John O., Jr. ....'38 '62 C.217 B.A. L.345 J.D. 1 Virginia Ave.
Moss, Marc J.M. ....'73 '00 C.302 B.A. L.880 J.D. [Moss L.]
Moss Law, LLC ....450 E. 96th St., Ste. 500
Moster, James M. '47 '75 C.63 B.S. L.30 J.D.
(adm. in DC; not adm. in IN) Asst. Chief Coun., U.S. Customs Serv., Treas. Dept.
Motsinger, C. Daniel, (AV) ....'56 '82 C.317 A.B. L.477 J.D. [Krieg D.]
Mounts, Alexander L. ....'79 '04 C.827 B.A. L.345 J.D. [A Krieg D.]
Mowery, Nathan R. '55 '84 C.47 B.A. L.345 J.D.
9000 Keystone Crossing Blvd., Ste. 200
Moy, Eric R. ....'— '85 C.231 B.A. L.178 J.D. [Barnes&T.]
Mueller, Frank A. ....'10 '35 L.74 LL.B. 820 W. Ralston Rd.
Mulder, R. Troy, (AV) ....'67 '92 C.114 B.A. L.345 J.D. [Riley B.&E.]
Mulford, Megan M. ....'79 '05 C.210 B.S. L.345 J.D. [A Bose M.&E.]
Mulhern, Thomas B. '73 '03 C.311 B.A. L.228 J.D.
(adm. in NY; not adm. in IN) [A Ice M.]
Mullen, Patrick W., (BV) ....'34 '63 C.215 B.S. L.345 LL.B. 1222 N. Downey Ave.
Muller, David P. ....'54 '79 C.347 A.B. L.345 J.D. 7068 Central Ave.
Muller, John, (AV) ....'47 '73 C.602 B.A. L.273 J.D. [Miller M.M.&K.]
Muller, Michael J. ...'66 '92 C.210 B.A. L.276 J.D. Coun., Pharm. Opers., Eli Lilly & Co.
Mullett, Michael A., (AV) ....'45 '82 C.477 B.A. L.345 J.D. 309 W. Washinton St.
Mullin, Owen M., (AV) ....'18 '50 C.108 L.345 LL.B. 116 N. Delaware St.‡
Mullins, Lon E. ....'18 '56 C.347 L.1119 6458 N. Olney
Mulvaney, Karl L., (AV) ....'49 '77 C.608 B.S. L.345 J.D. [Bingham M.]
Mundt, James D. ......'45 '74 C.303 A.B. L.345 J.D. Dir., Off. of Fiscal & Mgt. Analysis
Munson, Joseph P. ....'64 '90 C.679 B.S. L.344 J.D. 6840 Eagle Highlands Way
Munson, Kenneth J. ....'70 '01 C&L.74 B.S., J.D. [A McTurnan&T.]
Murphy, C. Abraham ....'72 '02 C.347 B.S. L.345 J.D. [A W.J.Tucker&Assoc.]
Murphy, Jeremiah E., Jr., (BV) ....'34 '63 C.602 A.B. L.345 J.D. 4604 W. 47 St.
Murphy, John T., (AV) ....'56 '83 C.602 B.B.A. L.477 J.D. [C Ice M.]
Murphy, Mark W. ...'36 '65 C.432 B.S. L.309 J.D. 151 North Delaware Street, Suite 1825
Murphy, Mary Judith ....'30 '85 C.347 B.S. L.345 J.D. 1421 Trillium Ct. N.‡
Murphy, Patrick James '69 '98 C.58 B.S. L.213 J.D.
Litigation Coun., State Farm Ins. Co.
Murphy, Sharon Funcheon, (BV) ....'54 '82 C.1105 B.A. L.347 J.D. [Lewis W.]
Murray, Katherine M. ....'61 '00 C.1248 B.A. L.1294 J.D. 2 N. Meridian St.
Murray, Kevin Charles, (AV) ....'53 '79 C.346 B.S. L.345 J.D. [Locke R.]

Murray, Lisa Hays, (AV) ....'56 '85 C&L.347 B.S., J.D. 10 W. Market Street
Murray, P. Thomas, Jr. ....'61 '86 C.347 B.S. L.879 J.D. [Eads,M.&P.]
Musall, Anna K. ....'71 '98 C.36 B.A. L.347 J.D. IN Dept. of Workforce Dev.
Muse, Cynthia A. ....'55 '00 C.30 B.A. L.345 J.D. State Farm Ins. Co.
Musgrave, Kathleen A. ....'72 '97 C.347 B.A. L.879 J.D. [Ⓐ Laudig G.R.&S.]
Music, Cynthia E. ....'70 '98 C.63 B.S. L.1119 J.D. [Ⓐ Due,D.F.&M.]
Musser, Jeffrey A. ....'59 '96 C.150 B.A. L.345 J.D. [Ⓐ Rocap W.]
Mutz, J. Mark ....'60 '87 C.597 B.A. L.976 J.D. Principal, Mosaic Consulting, LLC
Myer, Ruth E., (BV) ....'— '70 C.108 A.B. L.347 J.D. [Ayres C.&S.]
Myers, Byron L., (AV) ....'46 '77 C.701 B.S.M.E. L.1119 J.D. [Ice M.]
Myers, Jos. N. ....'15 '40 C.976 B.A. L.893 J.D. Ret. Mun. Ct. J.‡
Nagy, Sarah L. ....'64 '92 C.108 B.A. L.347 J.D. [S.Nagy]
Nagy, Sarah ....4181 E. 96th St., Ste. 250
Naile, Peggy J., (AV) ....'48 '89 C.881 B.A. L.1119 J.D. [Ⓒ Ice M.]
Najam, Edward W., Jr. ....'47 '72 C.347 B.A. L.309 J.D. Ct. of App. J.
Najjar, Ameen R., (BV) ....'62 '91 C.475 B.A. L.345 J.D. [Miller,W.M.&H.]
Napariu, Olivia A., (AV) ....'62 '89 C.347 B.S. L.345 J.D. [Emswiller,W.N.&C.]
Naughton, Ann E. ....'— '94 C&L.347 B.S.N., J.D. IN Leg. Srvcs. Agency
Naughton, Joseph A., Jr., (AV) '30 '60
C.602 B.S. L.345 LL.B. [Ⓒ Woodard,E.M.M.&H.] (See Pat. Sect.)
Nave, James M. ....'45 '75 C.63 B.S. L.345 J.D. 3947 Rue Renoir St.‡
Neal, Edward Squier, (AV) '44 '69 C.894 A.B. L.1119 J.D.
Sr. Trial Coun., Law Offs. Safeco Property & Casualty Cos.
Neal, Thomas R., (AV) ....'45 '72 C.347 A.B. L.345 J.D. [Krieg D.]
Neale, William R., (AV) ....'48 '73 C.347 B.S. L.74 J.D. [Krieg D.]
Nearpass, Lesley A. ....'77 '03 C.108 B.A. L.345 J.D. [Ⓐ Krieg D.]
Neddo, Leon M., Jr. '48 '75 C.347 B.A. L.345 J.D.
Assoc. Gen. Coun., Meridian Ins. Cos.
Neeb, Randall J. ....'65 '93 C.63 L.1187 J.D. P.O. Box 19365
Neff, Virginia M. ....'53 '94 C.679 B.S. L.347 J.D. [V.Neff]
Neff, Virginia, Attorney at Law ....3890 E. 79th St.
Nehf, James P. '57 '84 C.388 B.A. L.575 J.D.
Atty. & Law Prof., Indiana Univ. School of Law
Nehf, Laura C. '58 '83 C&L.280 B.A., J.D.
Atty. & Law Prof. (Adjunct), Indiana Univ. School of Law
Nehrig, Brian L., (BV) ....'66 '91 C.894 B.A. L.879 J.D. [Yarling&R.]
Neibarger, Gregory A. ....'73 '00 C.502 B.S. L.345 J.D. [Ⓐ McTurnan&T.]
Neighbours, John T., (AV) ....'49 '74 C.210 B.A. L.345 J.D. [Baker&D.]
Neiswinger, Karen B. .... '49 '82 C.347 B.S.N. L.345 J.D. 6100 N. Keystone Ave.
Nell, John D., (AV) ....'46 '74 C.108 B.S. L.345 J.D. [Wooden&M.]
Nelson, Brett E. ....'73 '00 C.347 B.S. L.1119 J.D. [Plews S.R.&B.] (Pat.)
Nelson, Jeffrey C. ....'— '04 C&L.339 B.S., J.D. [Ⓐ Baker&D.]
Nelson, Mark R. ....'— '93 C&L.347 B.S., J.D. [Stewart&I.]
Nelson, Michael O. ....'68 '96 C.112 B.A. L.1065 J.D. [Ⓐ Resolution]
Nelson, Reid ....'52 '89 C&L.347 B.A., J.D. 54 Monument Circle
Nemecek, Sarah H. ....'52 '86 C&L.347 B.A., J.D. Dir. & Sr. Coun., Anthem, Inc.
Nemeroff, Wendy D. '55 '85 C.1044 B.A. L.1065 J.D.
(adm. in CA; not adm. in IN) Canal Plus Technologies
Nemeth, Carol A. ....'69 '94 C&L.347 B.A., J.D. [Price W.R.&D.]
Nerz, C. Warren ....'55 '91 C.433 B.S. L.347 J.D. [Nerz&Assoc.]
Nerz & Associates, P.C. ....5144 E. Stop 11 Road, Suite 20
Nettles, Nelson A. ....'67 '92 C&L.347 B.A., J.D. [Norris C.&S.]
Neuenschwander, Janet D. ....'— '83 C.112 B.A. L.597 J.D. [Ⓒ Barnes&T.]
Neulibbv, Jessica Beth ....'72 '97 C.679 B.A. L.146 J.D. 107 N. Pennsylvania #1002
Nevin, Cathleen L., (BVⓉ) ....'52 '84 C.112 B.A. L.769 J.D. [Katz&K.]
Newby, Thomas R. '50 '87 C&L.347 A.B., J.D.
Prof. of Law, Indiana Univ. Sch. of Law
Newcomb, Thomas E. ....'15 '42 C.424 L.345 LL.B. 920 Kimlough Circle‡
Newman, Jerry W., (BV) ....'34 '59 C.347 B.S. L.1119 J.D. 7729 Cassidy St.
Newman, Lawrence T. ....'54 '81 C.608 B.S. L.930 J.D. [Ⓐ R.W.York&Assoc.]
Newman, Norman R., (AV) ....'34 '60 C.347 A.B. L.345 LL.B. [Dann P.N.&K.]
Newman-Worrell, Terri ...'61 '87 C.231 B.A. L.345 J.D. Exec. Dir., Ind. Comm. for CLE
Newton, Judith Vale ....'46 '79 C.347 B.S. L.1119 J.D. [Newton B.B.]
Newton, M. Kent, (AV) ....'46 '73 C&L.347 B.S., J.D. [Newton B.B.]

Newton Becker Bouwkamp, (AV)
3755 East 82nd Street, Suite 220, 46240
Telephone: 317-598-4529 Fax: 317-598-4530
Email: nbblaw@nbblaw.com URL: http://www.nbblaw.com
Members of the Firm: M. Kent Newton; Carl J. Becker; Alan A. Bouwkamp; Judith Vale Newton. Associate: Lana L. Lennington.
General Practice. Business Law, Estate Planning, Family Law, Insurance Coverage Law, Litigation, Manufactured Housing and Recreational Vehicles Law, Mediation and Arbitration, Not-for-Profit Law and Real Estate Law.
See Professional Biographies, INDIANAPOLIS, INDIANA

Niblack, Kari L. ....'68 '00 C.74 B.S. L.1206 J.D. American United Life Ins. Co.
Nice, Robert J., (AV) ....'59 '85 C.679 B.S. L.884 J.D. [Nice]
Nice Law Firm, The, (AV) ....One North Pennsylvania Street Suite 200
Nicely, Philip A., (AV) ....'42 '67 C.597 A.B. L.477 J.D. [Bose M.&E.]
Nicholas, Theodore L., (BV) ....'58 '86 C&L.347 B.A., J.D. [Lewis W.]
Nichols, Gregory D. ....'55 '81 C.30 B.A. L.345 J.D. [Ⓒ Ice M.]
Nickels, James R., (BV) ....'33 '65 C.347 A.B. L.1119 LL.B. 600 N. Alabama
Nicodemus, Camille R. ....'— '97 C.331 B.A. L.569 J.D. [Ⓐ Schuckit&Assoc.]
Niederhauser, J. Brian, (AV) '48 '75 C.347 A.B. L.345 J.D.
320 N. Meridian St., Ste. 615
Niednagel, Timothy E. .....'63 '89 C.679 B.S.E.E. L.347 J.D. [Baker&D.] (See Pat. Sect.)
Nierman, Todd M., (AV) ....'61 '86 C.477 B.B.A. L.880 J.D. [Baker&D.]
Niermeyer, John H. ....'19 '43 C.108 B.S. L.345 LL.B. 10679 Highland Dr.‡
Nijhawan, David R. ....'— '04 C.679 B.S. L.880 J.D. [Ⓐ Barnes&T.]
Nisenbaum, Nathan, (AV) ....'22 '46 C.347 B.A. L.1119 J.D. 8290 Forest Ln.‡
Nishikawara, Hiroaki ....'— '04 C.937 B.A. L.365 J.D. [Ⓐ Barnes&T.]
Nizamoff, Nicholas C., (AV) ....'42 '69 C.894 A.B. L.345 J.D. [Ⓒ Stuart&B.]
Nobles, Anne, (AV) ....'56 '84 C.309 A.B. L.276 J.D. Eli Lilly and Co.
Noland, Gregory L., (AV) ....'52 '79 C.347 B.S. L.345 J.D. [Emswiller,W.N.&C.]
Norman, Douglas K. '59 '89 C&L.347 B.S., J.D.
Dep. Gen. Patent Coun., Eli Lilly & Co. (Pat.)
Norman, Mary Jane ....'40 '85 C.108 B.A. L.347 J.D. 4911 E. 56th St.
Norman, Vickie L. ....'54 '89 C.63 B.S. L.365 J.D. [Ⓒ Baker&D.]
Norris, Edwin S. ....'75 '00 C.347 B.S. L.1119 J.D. [Ⓐ Norris C.&S.]
Norris, Mike, Law Offices '51 '78
C&L.215 B.A., J.D. 22 East Washington Street, Suite 114
Norris, Richard L., (AV) ....'45 '71 C.108 B.S. L.345 J.D. [Norris C.&S.]

Norris Choplin & Schroeder, LLP, (AV)
Ninth Floor, 101 West Ohio Street, 46204-4213
Telephone: 317-269-9330 Fax: 317-269-9338
Email: ncs@ncs-law.com

(This Listing Continued)

Norris Choplin & Schroeder, LLP (Continued)
Members of Firm: Richard L. Norris; John M. Choplin, II; Peter A. Schroeder; Bruce L. Kamplain; Raymond L. Faust; Kyle A. Jones; Nelson A. Nettles. Associates: Matthew Walton Melton; Ralph E. Dowling; Joseph P. Maguire; Scott A. Harkness; J. Kirk Leblanc; Edwin S. Norris. Of Counsel: Mary Jo Wedding; James D. Matthews.
Civil Litigation and Dispute Resolution.
Reference: National Bank of Indianapolis.
See Professional Biographies, INDIANAPOLIS, INDIANA

Northrup, Arthur H. ....'20 '49 C.309 B.A. L.477 J.D. 7341 Lions Head Dr.‡
Nottingham, Wm. P., (AV) ....'11 '33 C.1365 L.893 LL.B. 7177 Williams Creek Dr.‡
Nowacki, Theodore J., (AV) ....'46 '72 C.602 B.A. L.477 J.D. [Bose M.&E.]
Nowak, David A. ....'54 '81 C.63 B.A. L.1187 J.D. Dep. Atty. Gen.
Nugent, Peter Douglas, (BV) ....'62 '87 C.347 B.S. L.365 J.D. Dep. Pros.
Null, Robert D. ....'65 '95 C.854 B.S.E.E. L.879 J.D. [Baker&D.] (See Pat. Sect.)
Nyhart, Eldon H. ....'27,'52 C.674 A.B. L.1119 J.D. 7468 D Lions Head Dr.‡
Oakes, Hilary Bowe ....'61 '86 C&L.347 B.A., J.D. 148 E. Market St.
Oakes, Timothy W. ....'64 '92 C.894 A.B. L.347 J.D. 3545 N. Washington Blvd.
Ober, John ....'29 '52 C.347 B.S. L.345 LL.B. 101 S. Pennsylvania St.‡
Oberlies, Jeffrey R., (BV) ....'61 '86 C.894 A.B. L.345 J.D. [Leeuw O.&C.]
Obiora, Leslye '63 '89 C.999 LL.B. L.813 J.D.
(adm. in CT; not adm. in IN) Indiana Univ. Sch. of Law
Obremskey, Peter L., (AV) ....'36 '61 C.347 B.S. L.1119 J.D. [Parr R.O.&M.] ⊙
O'Brien, Patrick M. ....'— '86 C.472 B.B.A. L.345 J.D. [Ayres C.&S.]
O'Brien, Shaun Healy, (BV) ....'60 '85 C.201 B.S. L.345 J.D. [Baker&D.]
O'Bryan, Berton W., (AV) ....'33 '67 C.1216 B.A. L.345 J.D. [O'Bryan B.&D.]
O'Bryan, Rory, (AV) ....'47 '72 C.347 A.B. L.1119 J.D. [Harrison&M.] ⊙
O'Bryan, Sheila M., (BV) ....'60 '85 C.201 B.S. L.589 J.D. Asst. Corp. Coun.
O'Bryan Brazill & Drics, LLP, (AV) ....111 Monument Circle, Suite 312
Ochs, Timothy E., (BV) ....'67 '92 C.679 B.S.C.E. L.347 J.D. [Ice M.]
O'Connell, Helen M. W. '44 '83
C.555 B.A. L.345 J.D. Gen. Coun., McCready and Keene, Inc.
O'Connell, Timothy J. ....'44 '71 C.354 B.S. L.188 J.D. UAW Legal Servs. Plan
O'Connor, Ellen M., (BV) ....'58 '87 C.276 B.S.F.S. L.345 J.D. Co. Pros.
O'Connor, William L., (AV) ....'64 '89 C.602 B.A. L.1119 J.D. [Dann P.N.&K.]
Oddi, Marcia J., (AV) ....'41 '69 C.347 B.A. L.345 J.D. 1319 N. Alabama St.
O'Dell, Lara B. '71 '01 C.347 B.A. L.1410 J.D.
(adm. in CO; not adm. in IN) 8821 Stirrup Ct.
O'Dell, Robert S., (AV) ....'62 '87 C.894 A.B. L.1119 J.D. [Ⓐ Osborn H.&L.]
O'Donnell, Laura C., (CV) '71 '96 C.1369 B.A. L.1119 J.D.
[Baker&D.] (⊙Fort Wayne)
O'Gara, Thomas F., (BV) ....'— '96 C.210 B.A. L.347 J.D. [Sommer B.]
Ogden, Patricia L. ....'— '96 C.63 B.S.N. L.347 J.D. [Barnes&T.]

Ogletree, Deakins, Nash, Smoak & Stewart, P.C., (AV) BB
Suite 4600, 111 Monument Circle, 46204 ⊙
Telephone: 317-916-1300 Facsimile: 317-916-9076
Email: clientservices@ogletreedeakins.com URL: http://www.ogletreedeakins.com
Kim F. Ebert; Michiharu Homma; Charles B. Baldwin; Todd J. Kaiser; Brian L. McDermott; Kenneth B. Siepman; Michael A. Moffatt; Jan Michelsen;—Kristin B. Keltner; Brandom M. Shelton; Matthew S. Effland; Bonnie L. Martin; Craig W. Wiley; Dane A. Mize; Robert F. Seidler (Not admitted in IN); Tanya R. Hatfield Bell. Of Counsel: Steven V. Shoup; Candace S. Walker; Jan J. Kinzie; Katy H.H. Yang-Page.
Labor Relations, Employment Litigation, Workers' Compensation. Civil Litigation in all State and Federal Courts and Administrative Agencies.
Atlanta, Georgia Office: 600 Peachtree Street, N.E., Suite 2100. Telephone: 404-881-1300.
Austin, Texas Office: 301 Congress Avenue, Suite 1250. Telephone: 512-344-4700.
Birmingham, Alabama Office: One Federal Place, Suite 1000, 1819 Fifth Avenue North. Telephone: 205-328-1900.
Charleston, South Carolina Office: 134 Meeting Street, Suite 160, P.O. Box 1808. Telephone: 843-853-1300.
Charlotte, North Carolina Office: 400 West Trade Street. Telephone: 704-342-2588.
Chicago, Illinois Office: Twenty-Fifth Floor, Two First National Plaza, 20 South Clark Street. Telephone: 312-558-1220.
Columbia, South Carolina Office: 1320 Main Street, Suite 600. Telephone: 803-252-1300.
Dallas, Texas Office: 700 Preston Commons, 8117 Preston Road. Telephone: 214-987-3800.
Greensboro, North Carolina Office: 2725 Horse Pen Creek Road, Suite 101. Telephone: 336-375-9737.
Greenville, South Carolina Office: The Ogletree Building, 300 North Main Street, P.O. Box 2757. Telephone: 864-271-1300.
Houston, Texas Office: One Allen Center, 500 Dallas Street, Suite 3000. Telephone: 713-655-0855.
Kansas City, Missouri Office: 4717 Grand Avenue, Suite 300. Telephone: 816-471-1301.
Los Angeles, California Office: 633 West Fifth Street, Suite 5300. Telephone: 213-239-9800.
Miami, Florida Office: 80 S.W. 8th Street, Suite 1830. Telephone: 305-374-0506.
Morristown, New Jersey Office: 10 Madison Avenue, Suite 402. Telephone: 973-656-1600.
Nashville, Tennessee Office: SunTrust Center, Suite 800, 424 Church Street. Telephone: 615-254-1900.
Phoenix, Arizona Office: 2415 East Camelback Road, Suite 800. Telephone: 602-778-3700.
Raleigh, North Carolina Office: 2301 Sugar Bush Road, Suite 600, P.O. Box 31608. Telephone: 919-787-9700.
San Antonio, Texas Office: 2600 Weston Centre, 112 East Pecan Street. Telephone: 210-354-1300.
St. Thomas, U.S. Virgin Islands Office: The Tunick Building, 1336 Beltjen Road, Suite 202. Telephone: 340-714-1235.
Tampa, Florida Office: 100 North Tampa Street, Suite 3600. Telephone: 813-289-1247.
Washington, D.C. Office: Fifth Floor, 2400 N Street, N.W. Telephone: 202-887-0855.
See Professional Biographies, INDIANAPOLIS, INDIANA

Ogren, J. Daniel, (AV) ....'52 '78 C.604 A.B. L.145 J.D. [Baker&D.]
O'Hara, Timothy J., (AV) ....'49 '74 C.363 A.B. L.500 J.D. [Bose M.&E.]
O'Keefe, Charles R., Jr. ....'— '94 C.72 B.A. L.345 J.D. [Ⓒ Sommer B.]
Okenfuss, Judy Starobin, (AV) ....'62 '91 C&L.910 B.S.Ch.E., J.D. [Ice M.]
O'Koon, Marvin R., (AVⓉ) '45 '72 C&L.421 B.S.C., J.D.
(adm. in KY; not adm. in IN) [O'Koon H.] ⊙

O'Koon Hintermeister, PLLC, (AVⓉ)
101 West Ohio Street, Suite 1401, 46204 ⊙
Telephone: 317-951-1401 Fax: 317-951-8470
URL: http://www.okoonlaw.com
Marvin R. O'Koon (Not admitted in IN; Resident, Louisville, Kentucky Office); Jeffrey P. Hintermeister.
Benji J. Algase; P. Lynn Bibbs; Jane E. Griffin; Douglas E. Hiland; Lisa Maxwell-Frieden; Dennis V. Panarisi; H. Andrew Sonneborn; Adina A. Teska; Julia R. Wilder; Mark K. Zunk; Katherine D. Zuran; Vicki J. Merriman.
General Civil Practice, Litigation, Personal Injury, Medical Malpractice, Automobile Negligence, Wrongful Death, Commercial Litigation, Employment Law, Bankruptcy, Corporations, Business, Limited Liability Companies, Family Law.
Louisville, Kentucky Office: PNC Plaza, Suite 1100, 500 West Jefferson, 40202. Telephone: 502-581-1630. Fax: 502-581-1821.
See Professional Biographies, INDIANAPOLIS, INDIANA

Oldham, June D. ....'53 '80 C.104 A.B. L.659 J.D. Dep. Pros. Atty.
Oldham, Mary Ann G., (AV) ....'57 '82 C&L.347 B.A., J.D. Supr. Ct. Master Comr.
Oldham, Steve A. '51 '76 C.347 B.A. L.309 J.D.
V.P., Gen. Coun. & Secy., Boehringer Mannheim Corp.
Olinger, Heather K. ....'67 '92 C.108 B.S. L.345 J.D. [Ⓒ Ice M.]
Oliphant, Jeff D. ....'67 '95 C&L.347 B.A., J.D. [Yosha K.&L.]
Oliver, Susan ....'70 '99 C.347 B.S. L.879 J.D. [Ⓐ Bose M.&E.]

Olson, E. Van, (AV) .... '50 '80 C.347 B.S. L.345 J.D. [Ice M.]
Olvey, Thomas N., (AV) .... '47 '72 C.303 B.A. L.893 J.D. 144 N. Delaware St.
Onderdonk, Philip B., Jr. '42 '69
C.367 B.A. L.446 J.D. National Judge Advocate, American Legion
O'Neal, C. Duane .... '50 '85 C.347 B.A. L.345 J.D. [Lewis&K.]
O'Neil, Michael P., (AV) .... '— '86 C.436 B.A. L.477 J.D. [Sommer B.]
O'Neill, Alexander C. .... '75 '03 C.679 B.S. L.1119 J.D. [Ⓐ Krieg D.]
O'Neill, Shiv Ghuman .... '73 '01 C.424 B.S. L.1119 J.D. [Ⓐ Baker&D.]
Opper, April L. '76 '04 C.477 B.A. L.608 J.D.
(adm. in OH; not adm. in IN) [Ⓐ Baker&D.]
Orbison, Carol Jane, (BV) .... '40 '84 C.207 B.A. L.345 J.D. Marion Sup. Ct., Juven. Div.
Orbison, Robert H., (AV) .... '08 '32 C.108 B.A. L.273 LL.B. [Baker,O.&B.] ‡
Ordway, Angie L. .... '77 '04 C.178 B.A. L.569 J.D. [Ⓐ Locke R.]
Orelup, Robert J. .... '73 '99 C.347 B.A. L.1119 J.D. [Ⓐ Drewry S.V.]
Orentlicher, David '55 '87 C.1036 A.B. L.309 J.D.
(adm. in DC; not adm. in IN) Indiana Univ. Sch. of Law
Orfanos, Konstantine G., (CV) .... '53 '81 C.347 B.A. L.1119 J.D. [Orfanos&A.]
Orfanos & Alvarado, LLC, (BV) .... 129 East Market Street, Suite 1100
Orich, Christine E. M. .... '68 '98 C.910 B.S. L.347 J.D. [Ⓐ Bose M.&E.] (Pat.)
Orr, Jeffrey K. .... '42 '74 C.347 A.B. L.345 J.D. 251 E. Ohio
Orr, Joanne .... '55 '86 C.346 B.S. L.67 J.D. IN Univ. Sch. of Law
Orr, Richard M., (BV) .... '27 '51 C.108 L.345 LL.B. 7720 Dean Rd.‡
Ortiz, A. Luis .... '47 '83 C.1282 B.A. L.969 J.D. [Ortiz&Assoc.]
Ortiz & Associates .... 2902 Maywood Rd.
Orzeske, Donald G., (BV) .... '55 '84 C.1183 B.A. L.801 J.D. [Goodin,O.&B.]
Orzeske, Julia Lauderdale, (AV) '60 '85 C.531 B.S. L.801 J.D.
Ind. Commission for Cle
Osborn, Kathy L. .... '63 '00 C&L.347 B.S., B.A., J.D. [Ⓐ Baker&D.]
Osborn, William M., (AV) .... '28 '52 C.108 B.S. L.447 J.D. [Ⓒ Osborn H.&L.]

Osborn Hiner & Lisher, P.C., (AV)
8500 Keystone Crossing, Suite 480, 46240-2456
Telephone: 317-257-2400 Fax: 317-722-4840
URL: http://www.lawyers.com/ohllaw
John R. Hiner (1920-1986); John L. Lisher. Of Counsel: William M. Osborn; Edward A. Straith-Miller;—Robert S. O'Dell; John K. Atkinson; Rhonda Hanna Veen.
General Civil Trial Litigation. Personal Injury, Insurance Defense Law, Probate and Estate, Wills and Trusts Planning, Workers Compensation, Products Liability. Appellate Law, Arson and Fraud.
See Professional Biographies, INDIANAPOLIS, INDIANA

Ost, Barton B., (AV) .... '54 '79 C.303 B.A. L.221 J.D. [Blythe&O.]
Ostendorf, Gregory A., (AVⓉ) .... '55 '80 C.929 B.S. L.345 J.D. [Ⓒ Scopelitis,G.L.&H.]
Oswald, Charles E., Jr., (AV) '22 '48
C.347 B.S. L.1119 J.D. [Ⓒ Bamberger,F.O.&H.] (ⓒEvansville)
Otero, Lettice Margarita .... '52 '78 C.679 B.A. L.1119 J.D. Indiana Dept. of Rev.
Otte, Frank D., (AV) .... '70 '97 C&L.347 B.S., J.D. [Ⓐ Clark,Q.M.S.&G.]
Otte, Frank J. .... '38 '66 C.347 B.S. L.1119 J.D. U.S. Bkrptcy. J.
Otten, Dennis H. .... '72 '98 C.347 B.A. L.345 J.D. [Bose M.&E.]
Overdorf, Scot W., Law Office of ...... '60 '87 C.63 B.S. L.345 J.D. 5913 Camelback Ct.
Overholt, Anthony W. .... '65 '92 C&L.347 B.A., J.D. [Ⓒ Locke R.]
Overman, Carl D., (AV) .... '25 '52 C.347 B.S. L.1119 J.D. [Ⓒ Bose M.&E.]
Overturf, Judith E., (BV) .... '45 '78 C.679 B.S. L.345 J.D. 10585 North Meridian
Owen, James C. .... '60 '00 C.63 B.S. L.345 J.D. Staff Atty., Simon Property Group
Owen, Maureen T. .... '56 '85 C.347 B.A. L.201 J.D. Atty. Gen.'s Off.
Owens, Darrow A., (BV) .... '31 '61 C.347 B.S. L.345 J.D. 302 N. East St.
Owens, Dennis N., (BV) '51 '76
C.347 A.B. L.345 J.D. Sr. Staff Atty., Am. Fam. Ins. Grp.
Pace, Julian D. .... '13 '37 C&L.347 LL.B. 1102 S. Franklin Rd.‡
Packer, Adam F. .... '78 '03 C.894 A.B. L.902 J.D. [Ⓐ Kightlinger&G.]

Pactor, Jon R., (AV) '48 '76 C.894 A.B. L.345 J.D.
Suite 2410, One Indiana Square, 46204
Telephone: 317-636-0686 Fax: 317-636-8094
Email: pactorlaw@iquest.net URL: http://www.lawyers.com/pactorlaw
Legal Malpractice, Libel and Slander, General Practice.
See Professional Biographies, INDIANAPOLIS, INDIANA

Padgett, Gregory L., (AV) .... '59 '84 C.210 B.A. L.597 J.D. [Padgett L.]
Padgett, Michael W. .... '62 '91 C.679 B.S. L.347 J.D. [Bingham M.]
Padgett, William E. .... '— '95 C.894 A.B. L.347 J.D. [Barnes&T.]

Padgett Law, (AV) BB
9000 Keystone Crossing, Suite 230, 46240-2148
Telephone: 317-218-0316 Fax: 317-580-4960
Email: GP@IndianaEstateLaw.com URL: http://www.IndianaEstateLaw.com
Gregory L. Padgett.
Will Contests, Trust Contests, Estate Litigation, Trust Litigation, Contested Wills, Contested Trusts, Probate Disputes, Probate Administration, Probate Litigation, Inheritance, Estate Claims, Estate Administration, Fiduciary Litigation, Contested Guardianships, Trial Practice, Complex Litigation.
See Professional Biographies, INDIANAPOLIS, INDIANA

Paetzmann, David A. .... '57 '82 C.346 B.S. L.347 J.D. Atty. Gen. Off.
Paganelli, F. Anthony .... '— '95 C.602 B.A. L.1119 J.D. [Sommer B.]
Page, Max F. .... '34 '63 C.347 B.S. L.345 LL.B. Mun. Ct. J.
Page, Paul J., (BV) .... '64 '90 C.108 B.A. L.347 J.D. 333 E. Ohio St.
Paige, Pamela A., (BV) .... '61 '89 C.1109 B.A. L.1040 J.D. [Stewart&I.]
Palguta, J. Paul, (BV) .... '49 '75 C&L.347 B.S., J.D. [Palguta&H.]
Palguta & Hesselgrave, (BV) .... 3750 Kentucky Ave.
Pallman, Bruce G. .... '52 '78 C.347 B.S. L.345 J.D. 255 S. Meridian
Palmberg, Arleen .... '46 '94 C.119 B.S. L.347 J.D. Pat. Coun., Eli Lilly & Co. (Pat.)
Palmer, Jonathan E., (BV) .... '53 '81 C.108 B.S. L.345 J.D. [Cremer B.&C.]
Palmer, Mark A., (BV) .... '— '77 C.384 B.A. L.469 J.D. [Sommer B.]
Panarisi, Dennis V., (BV) .... '46 '77 C.347 A.B. L.1119 J.D. [O'Koon H.]
Pankow, Scott D., (AV) .... '56 '82 C.347 B.S. L.345 J.D. [Sipe,P.H.R.&H.]
Panszi, Mary Foley, (BV) .... '47 '88 C.665 B.A. L.347 J.D. [Lewis W.]
Papa, Jeffrey L. .... '— '00 C.701 B.S. L.345 J.D. [Ⓐ Barnes&T.]
Papageorge, John D., (BV) .... '— '92 C.347 B.A. L.879 J.D. [Sommer B.]
Pappas, Nicholas C., (BV) .... '66 '91 C.602 B.A. L.1119 J.D. [Locke R.]
Pardo, David G. .... '64 '92 C&L.347 B.A., J.D. Civil Rights Comm.
Parish, G. R., Jr., (BV) .... '44 '73 C.347 B.S. L.345 J.D. [Klapper,I.&P.]
Park, Terry Kaiser, (BV) '55 '82 C.210 B.A. L.345 J.D.
135 N. Pennsylvania St., Ste. 1150
Parker, Richard E., (AV) .... '47 '72 C.679 B.S. L.309 J.D. [Ice M.]
Parr, Robert .... '26 '51 C&L.347 A.B., J.D. 7711 River Rd.

Parr Richey Obremskey & Morton, (AV)
201 N. Illinois Street, Suite 300, 46204 ⓒ
Telephone: 317-269-2500 FAX: 317-269-2514
Email: indianapolis@parrlaw.com URL: http://www.parrlaw.com
(This Listing Continued)

Parr Richey Obremskey & Morton (Continued)
Partners of Firm: David S. Richey; Peter L. Obremskey; Don F. Morton; Kent M. Frandsen; Charles W. Ritz, III; Paul S. Kruse; Carol Sparks Drake; Larry J. Wallace; James A. L. Buddenbaum; Anthony W. Patterson; Randolph G. Holt. Associates: Tamie Jo Morog; Monica S. Doerr; Randall D. Rogers, Jr.
Personal Injury, Products Liability, Insurance Defense, Business Litigation, Alternative Dispute Resolution, Appellate Practice, School, Business Transactions, Real Estate, Zoning, Utility Regulation and Finance, Estate Planning, Trusts and Estates, Wills and Probate.
Lebanon, Indiana Office: Parr Building. 225 West Main Street. P.O. Box 668. Telephone: 765-482-0110; 317-269-2509. FAX: 765-483-3444.
See Professional Biographies, INDIANAPOLIS, INDIANA

Pastore, Thomas A., (AV) .... '64 '90 C.679 B.S. L.345 J.D. [Pastore&G.]

Pastore & Gooden P.C., (AV)
302 North Alabama Street, P.O. Box 44947, 46244-0947
Telephone: 317-638-3333 Fax: 317-687-9707
Thomas A. Pastore; William W. Gooden; Troy Michael Miller.
Construction Law and Litigation, Business Law, Lawsuits, Contracts Law; Business Disputes, Business Enterprises, Partnerships, Limited Liability Companies, Corporate Law and General Civil Litigation.
See Professional Biographies, INDIANAPOLIS, INDIANA

Patchel, Kathleen '56 '81 C.332 A.B. L.575 J.D.
(adm. in GA; not adm. in IN) Assoc. Prof., Indiana Univ. Sch. of Law
Pate, Rickey Ray .... '47 '75 C.347 B.S. L.345 J.D. Lilly Corp. Ctr.
Paton, Michael G., (AV) .... '— '85 C.602 B.B.A. L.1119 J.D. [Barnes&T.]
Patterson, Mark E. .... '64 '90 C&L.347 B.S., J.D. Sr. Tax Mgr., Duke Realty Corp.
Patterson, Richard M. .... '34 '64 C.344 B.A. L.345 J.D. 8714 Green Braes Dr., N.‡
Paul, Brian J. .... '72 '00 C.679 B.S. L.880 J.D. [Ⓐ Ice M.]
Paul, J. J., III, (AV) .... '48 '76 C.894 B.A. L.345 J.D. [Voyles,Z.P.H.&M.]
Paul, Stephen H., (AV) .... '47 '72 C.347 B.A. L.1119 J.D. [Baker&D.]
Paul, Timothy B. '76 '04
C.421 B.S. L.1119 J.D. [Ⓐ Woodard,E.M.M.&H.] (See Pat. Sect.)
Paunicka, Lisa M. .... '57 '82 C.741 B.A. L.879 J.D. Coun., Anthem, Inc.
Pavlack, Eric S. .... '73 '99 C.1119 B.S. L.345 J.D. [Ⓐ Cohen&M.]
Payne, Frederick D. .... '71 '99 C.1177 B.A. L.1119 J.D. [Ⓐ Wessels&P.]
Payne, James W. .... '46 '72 C.210 B.A. L.345 J.D. Supr. Ct. J.
Payne, Mark A. .... '61 '87 C.894 B.A. L.347 J.D. Staff Atty., Simon Property Group
Paynter, L. Scott .... '62 '94 C.383 B.S. L.345 J.D. [Krieg D.] (Pat.)
Peacock, Andrew S. .... '64 '91 C.602 B.A. L.1119 J.D. [Ⓐ Goodin,O.&B.]
Peak, Terrence F. .... '57 '84 C.701 B.S. L.345 J.D. Sr. V.P., ProLiance Energy, LLC
Pearson, Maureen D. '— '93 C.347 B.A. L.209 J.D.
(adm. in IL; not adm. in IN) Sr. Coun., Thomson Inc.
Pebworth, Carl R., (AV) .... '64 '91 C.95 A.B. L.477 J.D. [Baker&D.]
Pecar, Benjamin A., (BV) .... '— '87 C.597 B.A. L.1119 J.D. [Barnes&T.]
Pecar, Steven M., (AV) .... '59 '86 C&L.347 B.S., J.D. [Ⓒ Dann P.N.&K.]
Peck, Scott E. .... '72 '99 L.347 J.D. [Ⓐ Baker&D.]
Peek, Jeffrey, (AV) .... '— '83 C.108 B.S. L.347 J.D. [Hall,R.K.H.&L.]
Peek, Michael C., (AV) .... '52 '79 C.679 B.A. L.345 J.D. [Christopher&T.]
Pemberton, Gregory L., (AV) .... '52 '81 C.504 B.A. L.339 J.D. [Ice M.]
Pence, Linda L., (AV) .... '— '74 C.347 B.A. L.345 J.D. [Sommer B.]
Pendygraft, George W., (AV) '46 '76
C.265 A.B. L.178 J.D. [G.W.Pendygraft] & [Ⓒ Stewart&I.]

Pendygraft, George W., P.C., (AV)
Building 1, 6770 Spirit Lake, Suite 201, 46220
Telephone: 317-590-3398 Fax: 317-254-0448
Email: EcoLawyer@aol.com URL: http://www.lawyers.com/ecolaw
George W. Pendygraft (Of Counsel, Stewart & Irwin).
National and International Environmental Matters, Toxic Tort Disputes, Environmental Insurance Coverage, Environmental Due Diligence, Utilities Regulations, and Patent, Trademark, and Copyright.
See Professional Biographies, INDIANAPOLIS, INDIANA

Penninger, Jason A. .... '80 '05 C.932 L.213 J.D. [Ⓐ Krieg D.]
Pennington, Deborah K., (AV) .... '52 '81 C.679 B.A. L.912 J.D. [Findling G.G.&P.]
Perkins, Joseph M., Jr., (BV) .... '64 '89 C.674 A.B. L.893 J.D. Sr. Coun., Cummins Inc.
Perrin, John A., (BV) .... '31 '64 C.347 B.S. L.345 LL.B. 302 N. Alabama St.
Perry, Louis Thomas .... '— '05 C&L.602 B.A., J.D. [Ⓐ Baker&D.]
Perry, Sandra .... '62 '00 C.836 B.A. L.1119 J.D. [Ⓐ Bose M.&E.]
Peters, Carl L., (BV) .... '38 '65 C.108 B.A. L.345 J.D. 8902 Otis Ave.
Peters, Laura J. .... '74 '03 C.249 B.S. L.345 J.D. [Ⓐ Dann P.N.&K.]
Peters, Stephen J., (AV) .... '— '81 C.31 B.A. L.1119 J.D. [Stewart&I.]
Petersen, James L., (AV) .... '47 '76 C.338 B.A. L.347 J.D. [Ice M.]
Peterson, Barton R., (AV) .... '58 '83 C.679 B.A. L.477 J.D. Chf. of Staff to Gov.‡
Peterson, Ginny L., (BV) .... '56 '97 C.679 B.A. L.345 J.D. [Kightlinger&G.]
Peterson, Thomas W., (AV) .... '60 '86 C&L.228 A.B., J.D. [Ice M.]
Peterson, Warren R. .... '52 '79 C.610 B.A. L.569 J.D. Coun., Law Div., Eli Lilly & Co.
Petr, John J., (AV) .... '52 '77 C.339 B.S. L.345 J.D. [Kroger,G.&R.]

Petri, Vernon J., & Associates '35 '66 C.347 B.S. L.1119 J.D.
2124 East Hanna Avenue, 46227
Telephone: 317-780-6610 Fax: 317-780-6620
Bodily Injury, Products Liability, Medical Malpractice, Pharmaceutical Litigation, Toxic Tort.
See Professional Biographies, INDIANAPOLIS, INDIANA

Petticrew, Paul S. '54 '79 C.679 B.S. L.345 J.D.
V.P., Corp. Affs., Curtis Publishing Co.
Pettigrew, C. Keith .... '20 '48 L.345 LL.B. 3622 N. Olney
Pettygrove, Joseph C. .... '— '05 C.63 B.S. L.1119 J.D. [Ⓐ Baker&D.]
Pfeiffer, Hudnall A., (AV) .... '53 '83 C.347 B.S. L.345 J.D. [Baker&D.]
Pfeiffer, Mark William .... '58 '95 C&L.347 B.S., J.D. [Ⓐ Harrison&M.]
Pfenninger, P. Frederick, (BV) .... '49 '74 C.347 B.A. L.477 J.D. 9247 N. Meridian St.
Phelps, Michael W. .... '— '97 C.347 B.A. L.117 J.D. [Ⓐ Kopka,P.D.&E.]
Phillips, Andrea L. '68 '93
C.604 B.A. L.309 J.D. Legal Coun., Rolls-Royce, North America
Phillips, Bryan K. '71 '00 C.378 B.S.M.E. L.494 J.D.
(adm. in MN; not adm. in IN) Pat. Coun., Guidant Corp.
Philpot, Dorene Jackson .... '64 '00 C.265 B.A. L.345 J.D. [Philpot]
Philpot Law Office .... 47 S. Pennsylvania St., Ste. 701
Pierce, Matthew S. .... '61 '87 C&L.347 B.A., J.D. House Minority Atty.
Pierson-Treacy, Rebekah F. .... '56 '88 C.679 B.A. L.347 J.D. Master Comr., Supr. Ct.
Pieters, Joseph F., (AV) .... '67 '92 C.894 A.B. L.347 J.D. Assoc. Coun., Anthem, Inc.
Piety, Margaret E., (BV) .... '51 '84 C.347 A.B. L.345 J.D. Chf. Coun.
Pilgrim, Jill '58 '85 C.674 B.A. L.178 J.D.
(adm. in NY; not adm. in IN) USA Track & Field
Pinkerton, Russell D. .... '49 '75 C.347 B.S.Ed. L.879 J.D. I.R.S.
Pinkie, Elliott .... '73 '00 C.63 B.S. L.607 J.D. [Ⓐ Kightlinger&G.]
Pinkus, Craig, (AV) .... '43 '68 C.108 A.B. L.309 LL.B. [Bose M.&E.]
Pinkus, I. Marshall, (AV) .... '47 '73 C.108 B.S. L.345 J.D. 4911 East 56th St.

Pinxie, Elliott I. ... '73 '00 C.63 B.S. L.607 J.D. 151 North Delaware Street
Pippen, David L. ... '69 '95 C.894 A.B. L.347 J.D. [A Plews S.R.&B.]
Pippin, Bradley D. ... '66 '93 Atty., SAFECO Prop & Cas Insurance
Pippin, Mitchell E. ... '69 '96 C.63 B.A. L.879 J.D. 129 East Market St., Ste. 1100
Pitcher, Kelly Bauman, (AV) ... '56 '88 C.347 B.S. L.345 J.D. [C Ice M.]
Pitman, Thomas A., (AV) ... '59 '85 C.976 B.A. L.309 J.D. [Baker&D.]
Pitt, Jerome O., (BV) ... '50 '77 C.367 B.A. L.345 J.D. Chf. Coun., Hasten Bancorp.
Pittenger, Gordon L., (AV) ... '— '77 C.210 A.B. L.345 J.D. [Sommer B.]
Pittman, Paul M. ... '65 '91 C.602 B.B.A. L.347 J.D. 333 E. Ohio St., Ste. 200
Pitts, Richard S., (AV) '61 '86 C.894 A.B. L.345 J.D.
V.P. & Gen. Coun., Arlington/Roe & Co., Inc.
Pivarnik, Alfred J. ... '25 '51 C&L.879 B.A., LL.B. Assoc. Jus., Supm. Ct.
Pizur, Mark J. ... '73 '99 C.1024 B.S. L.146 J.D. [A Tabbert H.E.&W.]
Plager, Martha Helveston ... '63 '88 C.108 B.A. L.1119 J.D. 6010 Old Orchard Rd.
Planck, Cheryl A. ... '66 '91 C.243 B.A. L.347 J.D. [C.A.Planck]
Planck, Cheryl A., P.C. ... 5525 South Meridian Street
Plant, Thomas G. '60 '93 C&L.347 B.S., J.D.
Assoc. Gen. Pat. Coun., Eli Lilly & Co. (Pat.)
Plath, Richard R. ... '42 '74 C.234 B.S. L.347 J.D. Marion County Prosecutor's Office
Plawecki, Julianna M. ... '77 '03 C.679 B.A. L.345 J.D. [A McTurnan&T.]
Pleasants, Edith E. ... '49 '90 C.999 B.A. L.1119 J.D. Jud. Law Clk., Ct. of App. J.
Pleasants, Larry, (P.C.), (BV) ... '43 '72 C.905 B.S. L.345 J.D. 7508 Madison Ave.
Pletcher, Steven A., (AV) ... '58 '91 C.347 B.S. L.879 J.D. [Scopelitis,G.L.&H.]
Plews, Christine C. H., (AV) ... '51 '79 C.674 A.B. L.309 J.D. [C Plews S.R.&B.]
Plews, George M., (AV) ... '52 '79 C.674 A.B. L.309 J.D. [Plews S.R.&B.]

Plews Shadley Racher & Braun, (AV) BR
1346 North Delaware Street, 46202-2415 ⊙
Telephone: 317-637-0700 Telecopier: 317-637-0710
Email: indy@psrb.com URL: http://www.psrb.com
Members of Firm: George M. Plews; Sue A. Shadley; Peter M. Racher; Christopher J. Braun; Jeffrey D. Claflin; Frederick D. Emhardt; Leonardo D. Robinson; S. Curtis DeVoe; John B. Bridge; Stephen A. Studer (Resident, South Bend Office); Jeffrey A. Townsend; Jeffrey D. Featherstun; Donna C. Marron; John H. Lloyd, IV (Resident, South Bend Office); John M. Ketcham; Alexandra S. Sylvia; Brett E. Nelson. Associates: David L. Pippen; John D. Moriarty; Tina M. Richards; Karen B. Scheidler; Amy W. Romig; Jonathan P. Emenhiser; Todd J. Janzen; Jamie B. Dameron; Gregory M. Gotwald; Thao T. Nguyen (Resident, South Bend Office); J. Michael Bowman; Ruth M. Rivera. Of Counsel: Christine C. H. Plews; Mary Ann Fuchs Saggese; F. Ronalds Walker; Donald P. Bogard; P. Kevin Thompson.
Environmental Litigation, Environmental Insurance Coverage, Environmental Cost Recovery, Complex Commercial Litigation, Environmental Corporate and Transaction Law, Environmental Administrative Law, Environmental Permitting, Superfund, Solid and Hazardous Waste, Underground Storage Tanks, Clean Air Act, Clean Water Act, Environmental Business Law, Intellectual Property, Commercial Real Estate and Land Use, Surface Coal Mining and Reclamation Act.
South Bend, Indiana Office: 53232 Generations Drive, 46635-1539. Telephone: 574-273-1010. Fax: 574-271-2050.

See Professional Biographies, INDIANAPOLIS, INDIANA

Plopper, Stephen E., & Associates, (AV) '43 '72
C.108 B.A. L.345 J.D. 111 Monument Circle
Plotinsky, Melvin L. '33 '59 C.385 A.B. L.569 LL.B.
(adm. in NY; not adm. in IN) Indiana University Dept. of English
Pockrass, Steven F. ... '65 '95 C.902 B.A. L.893 J.D. [A Ice M.]
Pogue, Mary Elizabeth '46 '80
C.1216 B.A. L.347 J.D. 22 East Washington Street, Suite 316
Poindexter, Brian G. ... '62 '90 C.63 B.S. L.347 J.D. Co. Pros. Off.
Polak, Jonathan G. ... '68 '94 C&L.802 B.S., J.D. [Dann P.N.&K.]
Polansky, William D. ... '55 '90 C.705 B.A. L.1119 J.D. 1 N. Capitol, Suite 800
Poling, Christopher, (BV) ... '61 '87 C.679 B.S. L.117 J.D. [Lewis&K.]
Pollack, Caren L., (BV) ... '61 '87 C.910 B.A. L.575 J.D. 8900 Keystone Crossing
Pollard, Randle B. ... '63 '89 C.302 B.S. L.276 J.D. [C Ice M.]
Ponader, David W. ... '— '97 C&L.347 B.A., J.D. Simon Property Group
Ponader, Erick D., (AV) ... '— '85 C&L.347 B.A., J.D. [Sommer B.]
Ponder, Jacqueline Bowman, (AV) ... '64 '90 C.802 B.A. L.347 J.D. [A McTurnan&T.]
Ponder, Todd W., (AV) ... '59 '84 C.210 B.A. L.145 J.D. [Ice M.]
Pool, Douglas W., (BV) ... '45 '80 C.679 B.S. L.345 J.D. [Foley&P.]
Poor, Ryan M. ... '73 '98 C.894 A.B. L.347 J.D. [A Ice M.]
Poore, Marvin A., (BV) ... '22 '52 C.108 L.345 LL.B. 1101 Peoples Bk. Bldg.
Poore, Steven G., Law Office of, (BV) '57 '84
C.347 B.S. L.345 J.D. 1 Virginia Ave., Ste. 500
Pope, Allen K. ... '54 '79 C.435 A.B. L.345 J.D. Atty. Gen.'s Off.
Pope, William M., (AV) ... '— '77 C.347 B.A. L.1119 J.D. [Barnes&T.]
Popowics, Karl G., (BV) ... '69 '96 C.210 B.A. L.347 J.D. [Goodin A.&M.]
Porter, Susan R., (BV) '40 '73
C.911 B.A. L.345 J.D. Mng. Lit. Coun., Farm Bureau Ins. Cos.
Posey, Kimberly Ann '63 '89
C.608 B.S.B.A. L.846 J.D. Legal Servs. Organization of Ind., Inc.
Pote, Mitchell M. ... '57 '97 C.205 B.A. L.345 J.D. [A Hume S.G.G.&S.]
Potter, S. Brent, (BV) ... '54 '86 C.347 B.S.P.A. L.345 J.D. [A Rubin&L.]
Potters, Bobby A. ... '49 '81 C.355 B.A. L.345 J.D. Ind. Civil Rights Comm.
Powell, Sara Manske ... '— '02 C.879 B.A. L.145 J.D. [A Baker&D.]
Powers, Brian V. ... '— '05 C.823 B.S. L.345 J.D. [A Sommer B.]
Powers, William B., (AV) ... '29 '68 C.108 B.A. L.345 J.D. 111 Monument Cir., Ste. 4560
Powlick, Jill Tabor ... '— '95 C.119 B.S. L.345 J.D. [C Ice M.] (See Pat. Sect.)
Poy, John T. ... '— '91 54 Monument Circle, 4th Fl.
Poynter, Donald L. ... '70 '96 C.347 B.A. L.345 J.D. [Poynter&B.]
Poynter & Bucheri ... 2601 S. Shelby Street, Suite 2
Prall, Stacy L. ... '67 '96 C&L.347 B.S., J.D. [A Baker&D.]
Prather, R. Anthony, (AV) ... '— '83 C.347 B.A. L.1119 J.D. [Barnes&T.]
Pratt, Steven H., (BV) ... '— '83 C.210 B.A. L.345 J.D. [Hall,R.K.H.&L.]
Prechtel, David R., (AV) ... '59 '85 C.679 B.S. L.345 J.D. [Bingham M.]
Prentice, Dixon W., (AV) ... '19 '41 C.347 L.345 LL.B. 8516 Bent Tree Ct.
Prescott, John F., Jr., (AV) '50 '79 C.1229 B.S.M.E. L.345 J.D.
[Ice M.] (See Pat. Sect.)
Prescott, Victoria M. ... '63 '90 C.347 B.S. L.802 J.D. Licensoft, Inc.
Preston, Ann '53 '79 C.207 B.A. L.446 J.D.
(adm. in MI; not adm. in IN) Dir. of Tax Tech., Ernst & YoungLL.P.
Preston, Scott James ... '66 '97 C.546 B.S. L.190 J.D. [C Ice M.]
Prettyman, Peter J. ... '74 '04 C.800 B.A. L.345 J.D. [A Sommer B.]
Pribila, Louis W. '38 '75 C.171 B.Sc. L.208 J.D.
V.P., General Counsel & Secretary, DowElanco
Prible, Larry R. ... '— '76 C.347 B.A. L.1119 J.D. [C Baker&D.]
Price, Frank J., (AV) ... '27 '62 C.265 A.B. L.345 LL.B. [Ricos,B.&P.]
Price, Gary P., (AV) ... '50 '78 C.959 B.A.G. L.345 J.D. [Lewis&K.]
Price, Henry J., (AV) ... '37 '62 C.967 A.B. L.477 J.D. [Price W.R.&D.]
Price, John L. ... '37 '68 C.63 B.S. L.345 J.D. Supr. Ct. J.
Price, John R., (BV) ... '41 '68 C.894 A.B. L.345 J.D. 9000 Keystone Crossing
Price, Kevin S. ... '76 '03 C.347 B.S. L.345 J.D. [A Bingham M.]

Price, L. Parvin, (AV) ... '52 '77 C.249 B.A. L.421 J.D. [Bose M.&E.]
Price, Lisa Cross ... '— '99 C.63 B.S. L.345 J.D. [A Stewart&I.]
Price, Matthew M., (AV) ... '68 '93 C.894 B.A. L.347 J.D. [Bingham M.]
Price, Melanie D. ... '— '99 C.347 B.A. L.345 J.D. [A Barnes&T.]

Price, Phillip V., (AV) '— '75 C.966 B.A. L.345 J.D.
4249 Lafayette Road, 46254
Telephone: 317-290-1800 Fax: 317-290-1863
Email: phillip@pvprice.net URL: http://www.indianadisabilitylawyer.com
Social Security, Social Security, Disability, Wills, Probate, Trusts and Estates, Guardianship, Estate Planning.

See Professional Biographies, INDIANAPOLIS, INDIANA

Price, Randall E. ... '48 '76 C.347 B.A. L.345 J.D. Vet. Admn.
Price, Susan Bender ... '76 '02 C.210 B.A. L.150 J.D. [C Ice M.]

Price Waicukauski Riley & DeBrota, LLC, (AV)
The Hammond Block Building, 301 Massachusetts Avenue, 46204
Telephone: 317-633-8787 Fax: 317-633-8797
Email: pricelaw@price-law.com URL: http://www.price-law.com
Henry J. Price; Ronald J. Waicukauski; William N. Riley; Amy Ficklin DeBrota; Jana K. Strain; Carol A. Nemeth. Senior Counsel: Arlene G. Anderson;—Gabriel A. Hawkins; Carolyn A. Clay; Jamie R. Sweeney.
Class Actions, Business Litigation, Personal Injury, Products Liability, Medical Malpractice, Legal Malpractice, Employment, Housing, Environmental Litigation, Actions Against Banks, Civil Trials, and Civil Appeals.

See Professional Biographies, INDIANAPOLIS, INDIANA

Priest, Chad S. ... '— '05 C.347 B.S.N. L.273 J.D. [A Baker&D.]
Protogere, Francine ... '57 '82 C.597 B.A. L.345 J.D. Dis. Coun., Small Bus. Admin.
Pruden, Seth Thomas, (BV) ... '57 '84 C.63 B.S. L.1119 J.D. IN Disciplinary Comm.
Pryor, Linda K. ... '52 '90 C&L.347 B.A., J.D. Dept. of Educ.
Puckett, Marta L. ... '77 '03 C.679 B.S.C.E. L.345 J.D. [A Woodard,E.M.M.&H.]
Pugh, Larry S., (AV) ... '44 '70 C.303 B.A. L.345 J.D. [Eads,M.&P.]
Purcell, John W., (AV) ... '48 '76 C.346 B.S. L.1119 J.D. [Baker&D.]
Purdy, George E., (AV) ... '55 '80 C.63 B.A. L.345 J.D. [Bose M.&E.]
Purvis, Cynthia Pearson ... '61 '89 C.108 B.S. L.345 J.D. [C Ice M.]
Purvis, Gregory A. ... '51 '77 C.63 B.S. L.345 J.D. [A Spangler,J.&D.]
Pyatt, April Sparks ... '71 '98 C.63 B.S. L.607 J.D. [A Ice M.]
Pylitt, Bernard ... '48 '75 C.347 B.A. L.345 J.D. [C Katz&K.]
Pyrz, Thomas A. ... '49 '80 C.870 B.S. L.1119 J.D. IN State Bar Assn.
Pytynia, Thomas L. '47 '73 C.347 A.B. L.1119 J.D.
Asst. Gen. Coun., Pharm. Opers., Eli Lilly & Co.
Pyzyna, Kristine S. ... '— '85 C.1106 B.S. L.209 J.D. [A Hall,R.K.H.&L.]
Qualkinbush, Jeffery J., (AV) ... '— '91 C.894 A.B. L.477 J.D. [Barnes&T.]
Quay-Smith, Nana, (AV) ... '62 '87 C.108 B.S. L.345 J.D. [Bingham M.]
Quigley, Daniel L. ... '77 '03 C.269 B.A. L.1119 J.D. [A Due,D.F.&M.]
Quigley, Fran ... '62 '88 C.303 B.A. L.347 J.D. Prof., Indiana Univ. Sch. of Law
Quigley, Marc T. ... '71 '98 C.347 B.A. L.1119 J.D. [A Krieg D.]
Quigley, Thomas D. ... '51 '79 C.679 B.A. L.1119 J.D. Dep. Atty. Gen.
Quill, Adrienne M. ... '66 '97 C.602 B.B.A. L.345 J.D. Law Clk. to Ct. of App. J.
Quinn, Kevin M. ... '77 '03 C&L.347 B.S.P.A., J.D. [A Tabbert H.E.&W.]
Quinn, Thomas F., (BV) ... '11 '37 C.108 L.345 LL.B. 880 Virginia Ave.
Quinn, Thomas Michael, (AV) ... '37 '63 C.347 B.S. L.178 J.D. [Clark,Q.M.S.&G.]
Rabinowitch, Michael, (AV) ... '68 '94 C.210 B.A. L.345 J.D. [Wooden&M.]
Racher, Peter M., (AV) ... '56 '86 C.604 B.A. L.347 J.D. [Plews S.R.&B.]
Rader, Carolyn W., (AV) ... '53 '81 C.347 B.A. L.345 J.D. 1050 N College Ave.
Rafalco, Roy D. ... '55 '84 C.347 B.S. L.345 J.D. G.E. Consumer Electronics
Raff, Aaron R. ... '77 '02 C.347 B.A. L.1119 J.D. [A Krieg D.]
Rafferty, Neil R., (BV⑦) ... '65 '91 C.339 B.A. L.347 J.D. [Dann P.N.&K.]
Rainbolt, Geffrey D., (BV) ... '68 '94 C.249 B.S. L.345 J.D. [Dale&E.]
Raines, C.W., III ... '74 '04 C.249 B.S. L.345 J.D. [A Bingham M.]
Ramage, Gary R. ... '51 '82 C.291 B.A. L.1137 J.D. 11510 Capistrano Ct.
Ramey, Mary Beth, (AV) ... '42 '72 C.347 B.S. L.345 J.D. [Ramey&H.]
Ramey & Hailey, (AV) ... 3815 River Crossing Parkway, Suite 340
Ramsey, Jeffrey E., (AV) ... '58 '85 C&L.879 B.A., J.D. [Hopper B.]
Ransberger, Victoria M. ... '55 '87 C.679 B.A. L.345 J.D. Supr. Ct.
Rasley, Jeffrey S., (BV) ... '53 '79 C.145 B.A. L.345 J.D. 47 S. Pennsylvania St.
Ratliff, Anthony B. ... '69 '94 C.510 B.A. L.347 J.D. [A Stark D.&S.]
Rauch, Paul (Rick), III, (CV) ... '64 '94 C.894 A.B. L.345 J.D. [Harrison&M.]
Ray, G. Westley ... '59 '98 C.910 B.S. L.345 J.D. [C Guy]
Ray, Preston B., IV ... '— '02 C.347 B.S. L.345 J.D. [A Barnes&T.]
Ray, Ryan P. ... '78 '03 C.303 B.A. L.602 J.D. 1800 N Meridian St
Raymond, Elizabeth Townsend Laughlin ... '— '02 C.210 B.A. L.477 J.D. [A Ice M.]
Reahard, Carol M. ... '44 '90 C&L.347 B.S., J.D. State Dept. of Rev.
Ream, Donald M., Jr., (BV) ... '33 '62 C.894 A.B. L.345 LL.B. [D.Ream,Jr.]
Ream, Donald, Jr., (BV) ... 9128 N. Tacoma Ave.
Recker, David H., (AV) ... '43 '75 C.967 B.A. L.831 J.D. Sr. V.P., Inland Container Corp.
Recker, James R. ... '45 '00 C.679 B.S. L.347 J.D. 6104 Carvel Avenue
Recker, James R., II ... '68 '96 C.63 B.S. L.347 J.D. [Recker&Assoc.]
Recker, Roberta Sabin, (AV) ... '43 '74 C.935 B.A. L.1017 J.D. [Baker&D.]
Recker & Associates ... 55 Monument Circle
Red, Michael N. ... '— '04 C.347 B.S. L.345 J.D. [A Baker&D.]
Reddick, Marci A., (BV) ... '— '85 C.347 B.A. L.345 J.D. [C Sommer B.]
Redding, Bryan S. ... '67 '94 C.679 B.S.M.E. L.347 J.D. [Cohen G.&G.]
Redman, Eric C., (BV) ... '52 '80 C.63 B.S. L.345 J.D. [Bator R.B.S.&L.]
Redmond, Bryan K. ... '71 '00 C.880 B.A. L.910 J.D. [A Feiwell&H.]
Redstone, Marion O., (BV) ... '40 '73 C.378 A.B. L.345 J.D. 1512 N. Delaware St.
Reed, Grant E. '61 '99 C.679 B.S. L.273 J.D.
Eli Lilly and Company (Law Division) (Pat.)
Reed, James A., (AV) ... '56 '83 C.347 A.B. L.1119 J.D. [Bingham M.]
Reed, Julie D. ... '75 '04 C.303 B.S. L.345 J.D. [A Bingham M.]
Reed, Laura S., (BV) ... '62 '87 C.118 B.A. L.345 J.D. [Riley B.&E.]
Reed, Susan B. ... '72 '02 C.679 B.A. L.345 J.D. [A Ice M.]
Reeder, Charles G., (AV) ... '39 '65 C.473 B.S. L.345 J.D. [C Holland&H.]
Reeder, Mary K., (AV) ... '57 '83 C.347 B.S. L.345 J.D. [Riley B.&E.]
Reeder, Michael J. ... '73 '99 C.347 B.A. L.345 J.D. [A Hatchett&H.]
Rees, David F., (BV) ... '40 '65 C.967 A.B. L.477 J.D. 9120 Otis Ave.
Reese, Catherine R., (AV) ... '— '89 C.679 B.S. L.477 J.D. [C Sommer B.]
Reese, Kenneth P., (AV) ... '48 '77 C.679 A.B. L.345 J.D. [Lewis W.]
Reese, Melissa Proffitt, (AV) ... '60 '85 C.347 B.A. L.345 J.D. [Ice M.]
Reeves, Charles R., (AV) '51 '77
C.679 B.S. L.345 J.D. [Woodard,E.M.M.&H.] (See Pat. Sect.)
Regas, William J., (AV) ... '18 '42 C.347 B.S. L.1119 LL.B. [C Kroger,G.&R.]
Reiber, Antolin J. ... '71 '98 C&L.347 B.S., J.D. [Reiber]

Reiber Law Office
6745 Gray Road, Suite G, 46237
Telephone: 317-888-5097 Fax: 317-783-7599
Email: indylaw2000@yahoo.com

(This Listing Continued)

Reiber Law Office (Continued)

Antolin J. Reiber.

Family Law, Adoptions, Child Custody, Child Support, Divorce, Domestic Violence, Visitation Rights, Criminal Law, Driving While Intoxicated, Drug Crimes, Juvenile Crimes, Parole and Probation, Traffic Violations, Discrimination, Sexual Harassment, Insurance Defense, Personal Injury, Automobile Accidents, Slip and Fall, Wrongful Death, Dog Bites, Real Estate, Business Law, Contracts, Business Litigation, Limited Liability Companies, Partnerships, Small Business Law, Collections, Debt and Credit.

See Professional Biographies, INDIANAPOLIS, INDIANA

Reich, Marlene, (AV) '— '83 C.347 A.B. L.345 J.D. [Sommer B.]
Reichard, Ruth D., (BV) '60 '85 C.63 B.S. L.345 J.D. Mun. J.
Reichel, Mark C. '74 '02 C.1505 B.S. L.345 J.D. [[A] Ice M.] (See Pat. Sect.)
Reid, Allan W., (BV) '52 '94 C.930 B.S. L.347 J.D. [A.W.Reid]
Reid, S.K. '46 '88 C.679 B.A. L.347 J.D. Supr. Ct. J.
Reid, Allan W., P.C., (BV) 155 East Market Street
Reindl, Gayle A., (AV) '— '87 C.188 B.S.N. L.345 J.D. [Sommer B.]
Reinert, Cynthia '57 '97 C.347 B.A. L.345 J.D. 973 North Shadeland, PMB #154
Reinhart, Stephanie '77 '04 C.1260 B.A. L.8 J.D. [[A] Feiwell&H.]
Reininga, J. Chris '66 '96 C.679 B.S. L.345 J.D. [[A] Landman&B.]
Reis, Paul G., (AV) '54 '80 C.602 B.S. L.345 J.D. [Drewry S.V.]
Reiswerg, Joseph J., (BV) '48 '74 C.347 B.S. L.345 J.D. [[C] Cohen G.&G.]
Relford, Guy A., (AV) '57 '83
C.210 B.A. L.345 J.D. Global Litig. Coun., Dow AgroSciences
Remondini, David Joseph '58 '97 C.694 B.A. L.345 J.D. Sump. Ct.
Rempert, Susan W., (AV) '45 '84 C.683 A.B. L.345 J.D. [[A] Tabor]
Render, John C., (AV) '— '71 C.108 B.S. L.347 J.D. [Hall,R.K.H.&L.]

Resolution Law Group, P.C.
1 North Pennsylvania Street, Suite 530, 46204 ⊙
Telephone: 317-633-6780 Fax: 317-633-6725
Email: firm@resolutionlawgroup.com URL: http://www.resolutionlawgroup.com
Michael O. Nelson.
Civil Litigation, Insurance Coverage, Insurance Bad Faith Litigation, Environmental Law, Environmental Litigation, Toxic Torts Litigation, Securities Litigation and Arbitration.
Lafayette, California Office: 3717 Mt. Diablo Boulevard, Suite 200, 94549. Telephone: 925-284-0840. Facsimile: 925-284-0870. Email: firm@resolutionlawgroup.com. URL: http://www.resolutionlawgroup.com
Washington, D.C., Office: 5335 Wisconsin Avenue, N.W., Suite 305, 20015. Telephone: 202-686-4844. Fax: 202-686-4843. Email: firm@resolutionlawgroup.com. URL: http://www.resolutionlawgroup.com
Woodland Hills, California Office: 21800 Oxnard Street, Suite 780, 91367. Telephone: 323-878-0969. Fax: 323-878-0913. Email: firm@resolutionlawgroup.com URL: http://www.resolutionlawgroup.com

See Professional Biographies, INDIANAPOLIS, INDIANA

Retherford, David A., Law Office of, (BV) '59 '84 C.679 B.S. L.345 J.D.
3416 S. Post Rd.
Rettig, G. Max, (BV) '55 '81 C.347 B.S. L.345 J.D. [G.M.Rettig]
Rettig, G. Max, P.C., (BV) 4622 W. 72nd St., Ste. C
Reuben, Lawrence M., Law Offices of, (AV) '48 '73
C.347 B.S. L.345 J.D. 1 Virginia Ave., Ste. 600
Reynolds, Hugh E., Jr., (AV) '29 '53 C.602 B.S. L.477 J.D. [[C] Locke R.]
Reynolds, Jeffrey L. '58 '90 C.347 B.S. L.345 J.D. Sr. Coun., Golden Rule Ins. Co.
Reynolds, Stephen E., Law Office of '54 '97 C.679 B.S. L.879 J.D.
225 N. Delaware St.
Reynolds, Thomas Todd, (BV) '54 '81 C&L.347 B.S., J.D. [Threlkeld R.]
Reynolds, William C. '42 '68 C.347 A.B. L.1119 J.D. [[C] Ice M.]
Reyome, Jason G. '73 '00 C.623 B.B.A. L.345 J.D. [Demos&R.]
Rezek, Richard A., (AV) '— '84 C.679 B.S.M.E. L.345 J.D.
[Barnes&T.] (See Pat. Sect.)
Rhoades, Kimberley Kelley, (CV) '59 '83 C.210 B.A. L.1119 J.D. 2835 Cahokia Ct.
Rhodes, Jennifer L. '74 '99 C.347 B.S. L.345 J.D. [[A] Ice M.]
Ricchiuto, Anne K. '— '05 C.597 B.S. L.1119 J.D. [[A] Baker&D.]
Rich, Miriam A., (CV) '62 '93 C.347 B.S. L.345 J.D. [Gonzalez,S.&H.]
Richards, Debra G. '56 '99 C.446 A.A. L.1119 LL.B. [[A] Hume S.G.G.&S.]
Richards, Mark J., (AV) '60 '85 C.347 B.S. L.345 J.D. [Ice M.]
Richards, Tina M. '73 '98 C.679 B.S. L.585 J.D. [[A] Plews S.R.&B.]
Richards, William R., (AV) '35 '62 C.108 A.B. L.345 J.D. [W.R.Richards]
Richards, William R., P.C., (AV) 3830 East Southport Road, Suite 500
Richardson, A. James, (AV) '43 '74
C.173 A.B. L.273 J.D. [Brinks H.G.&L.] (See Pat. Sect.)
Richardson, Jane A. '53 '80 C.347 A.B. L.345 J.D. Corp. Coun., Solution Tech., Inc.
Richardson, Rebecca A., (AV) '54 '82 C.347 B.A. L.345 J.D. [Baker&D.]
Richardson, Rodney C., (BV) '48 '76 C.313 B.A. L.1119 J.D. 7 N. Meridian St.
Richardson, Scott '64 '92 C.347 B.S. L.7 J.D. 1050 N. College Avenue
Richardson, Todd A. '61 '86 C.309 B.A. L.477 J.D. [Lewis&K.]
Richey, Darrell S., (AV) '49 '78 C.63 B.S. L.464 J.D.
Senior Vice President & General Counsel, Golden Rule Insurance Company
Richey, David S., (AV) '32 '60 C.108 B.S. L.345 J.D. [Parr R.O.&M.]
Richey, Rand D., (BV) '62 '91
C.210 B.A. L.1202 J.D. Litig. Coun., Citizens Insurance Co.
Richmond, Mariana, (BV) '— '92 C.999 B.A. L.345 J.D. [Barnes&T.]
Richmond, Richard C., III, (AV) '58 '83 C.265 B.A. L.345 J.D. [Sommer B.]
Richter, Adam J. '— '05 C&L.347 B.A., J.D. [[A] Hall,R.K.H.&L.]
Ricos, Nicholas G., (AV) '26 '53 C.108 A.B. L.345 J.D. [Ricos,B.&P.]
Ricos, Bippus and Price, (AV) Suite 205, 1213 N. Arlington Ave.
Riddell, Robert C., (AV) '32 '57 C.108 B.A. L.347 J.D. [[C] Locke R.]
Riddle, Nancy Menard '50 '76 C.589 B.S.Ed. L.339 J.D. [[C] Ice M.]
Rider, Brian A. '56 '81 C.347 B.S. L.1119 J.D. 3091 E. 98th St., Ste. 150
Rider, William (Tim) '43 '86
C.1131 B.S. L.345 J.D. Admin. Law J., Natural Resources Comm.
Ridolfo, Anthony S., Jr. '70 '95 C.894 A.B. L.950 J.D. [[A] Hackman H.&C.]
Riegler, Christopher L., (BV) '— '84 C.999 B.A. L.912 J.D. [Hall,R.K.H.&L.]
Riegner, Eric A., (AV) '63 '88 C&L.347 B.A., J.D. [Locke R.]
Riegner, Richard H., (AV) '36 '65 C.347 B.S. L.345 J.D. [Stewart&I.]
Riesner, Christine M. '— '02 C.347 B.A. L.365 J.D. [[A] Threlkeld R.]
Riffle, Timothy J., (AV) '— '83 C.347 B.A. L.1119 J.D. [Barnes&T.]
Riga, Beth L. '70 '02 C.63 B.A. L.602 J.D. [[A] Bose M.&E.]
Riggins, Kenneth '62 '99 C.679 B.S. L.325 J.D. 111 Monument Circle, Suite 3300
Riggins, Nigel J. '78 '05 C.210 B.A. L.345 J.D. [[A] Krieg D.] (⊙Carmel)
Riggs, Jack A. '54 '85 C.346 B.S. L.345 J.D. Admin. Law J., Ind. Dept. Transp.
Riggs, Randall R., (AV) '52 '77 C.347 A.B. L.1119 J.D. [Locke R.]
Riley, James W., Jr., (AV) '47 '72 C.679 B.S. L.477 J.D. [[C] Riley B.&E.]
Riley, Jennifer E. '76 '01 C.383 B.A. L.345 J.D. [[A] Rubin&L.]
Riley, William N., (AV) '63 '89 C.347 B.A. L.1119 J.D. [Price W.R.&D.]

Riley Bennett & Egloff, LLP, (AV)
141 East Washington Street, Fourth Floor, 46204
Telephone: 317-636-8000 Fax: 317-636-8027
Email: info@rbelaw.com URL: http://www.rbelaw.com
Members of Firm: Bryce H. Bennett, Jr.; John L. Egloff; Donald S. Smith; Mary K. Reeder; Laura S. Reed; Ryan L. Leitch; Raymond T. Seach; R. Troy Mulder; Anthony R. Jost; J. Mark McKinzie; Charles C. Douglas; Stacy L. Hanefeld. Of Counsel: James W. Riley, Jr.; Blair R. Vandivier. Associates: Melinda J. Schwer; Kevin N. Tharp; Jaime L. Meyer; Jeffrey D. Roberts; Steven L. Zakrocki; Laura K. Taylor; William P. Means; Cheryl D. Finchum; Jeffrey B. Fecht; Robert C. Brandt; Austin A. Shadle; Timothy H. Button.
Litigation, Labor and Employment (Management), Employee Benefits, Insurance Defence, Corporation, Real Estate, Commercial, Governmental Relations, Workers Compensation Defense, Environmental, Trusts and Estates, Asset Protection, Guardianships, Estate Planning, Probate and Toxic Torts, Asbestos Litigation.

See Professional Biographies, INDIANAPOLIS, INDIANA

Rimstidt, David L. '49 '74 C.347 B.S. L.345 J.D. 111 Monument Cir., Ste. 302
Ringle, Theresa M. '70 '00 C.63 B.Arch. L.347 J.D. [[A] Bose M.&E.]
Riordan, Sarah Steele, (BV(T)) '68 '93 C.477 B.A. L.347 J.D. [Bose M.&E.]
Ripani, Philip J., (AV) '51 '76 C.347 B.S. L.345 J.D. [Bose M.&E.]
Ripley, Judith G., (AV) '43 '81 C.150 L.345 LL.B.
Comr., State Utility Regulatory Comm.

Risinger, Jeffery B., P.C.
(See Fishers)

Risk, April J. '— '02 C&L.347 B.A., J.D. [[A] Baker&D.]
Risk, Eric L. '62 '89 C.347 B.A. L.801 J.D. [E.L.Risk]
Risk, Eric L., P.C. 4040 S. Meridian Street
Ristine, Thomas H., (AV) '50 '75 C.894 A.B. L.228 J.D. [Lewis&K.]
Ritz, Charles W., III, (BV) '49 '74 C.108 B.S. L.345 J.D. [Parr R.O.&M.]
Rivas, Susan Barnhizer, (AV) '52 '84 C.679 B.A. L.345 J.D. [Ice M.]
Rivera, Ruth M. '— '05 C.677 B.S. L.1119 J.D. [[A] Plews S.R.&B.]
Rivero, Jose M. '75 '01 C.1119 B.A. L.345 J.D. Staff Atty., IN Legal Services
Roach, Neal R., Jr. '62 '87 C.122 B.A. L.976 J.D.
V.P. Ethics & Compliance, Roche Diagnostics Corp.
Roache, Robert D., II '48 '74 C.347 B.S. L.345 J.D. 8144 Bowline Ct.
Roan, Marcia E., (BV) '58 '85 C.679 B.S. L.345 J.D. [[A] Kroger,G.&R.]
Roath, Mark A. '65 '94 C.679 B.S. L.345 J.D. Peoples Bank & Trust
Robb, Margret G. '48 '78 C.679 B.S. L.345 J.D. Ct. of App. J.
Robbin, Thomas G., Law Office of '48 '95
C&L.347 B.A., J.D. 151 N. Delaware St., Ste. 1610
Roberge, Christopher S., (BV) '56 '82 C.347 B.A. L.1119 J.D. [Roberge&R.]
Roberge, Elizabeth A., (CV) '62 '93 C.347 B.A. L.1119 J.D. [Roberge&R.]
Roberge & Roberge, (BV) 9190 Priority Way West Drive, Suite 220
Roberts, Andrea, (AV) '69 '95 C.376 B.A. L.602 J.D. [Baker&D.]
Roberts, Gerald W., (BV) '64 '96 C.701 B.S.E.E. L.345 J.D. [[A] Maginot M.&B.]
Roberts, Jeffrey D. '76 '02 C.347 B.S. L.1119 J.D. [[A] Riley B.&E.]
Roberts, Kenneth T., (BV) '41 '73 C.382 B.A. L.345 J.D. [Roberts&B.]
Roberts, Mark J., (AV) '52 '77 C.347 A.B. L.1119 J.D. [Locke R.]
Roberts, Patricia S., (BV) '53 '78
C.347 B.A. L.1119 J.D. Sr. Corp. Coun., Farm Bureau Ins. Cos.
Roberts & Bishop, (BV) 118 N. Delaware St.
Robertson, Jonathan J. '32 '61 C.347 B.S. L.880 J.D. Ret. Ct. of App. J.‡
Robertson, William L. '38 '65 C.347 B.S. L.345 J.D. Ernst & Young
Robinette, W. Theodore, (BV) '35 '63 C.265 B.A. L.345 LL.B. 247 Narcissus Dr.
Robinson, Angela M. '78 '03 C.347 B.S. L.74 J.D. Atty., Lauth Group, Inc.
Robinson, Charles F., Jr., (AV) '40 '66 C.435 B.A. L.345 J.D. [Yarling&R.]
Robinson, Daniel L., (BV) '55 '81 C.347 B.S. L.345 J.D. [Gray,R.R.&F.]
Robinson, David D., (AV) '65 '91 C.210 B.A. L.347 J.D. [Scopelitis,G.L.&H.]
Robinson, Fredk. B., (BV) '21 '53 C.347 A.B. L.421 LL.B. 5555 N. Tacoma
Robinson, Jay D., Jr. '59 '88 C.802 B.A. L.345 J.D. [Scopelitis,G.L.&H.]
Robinson, Leonardo D. '54 '86 C.118 B.A. L.1162 J.D. [Plews S.R.&B.]
Robinson, Matthew C., (BV) '66 '91 C.894 B.A. L.879 J.D. [Yarling&R.]
Robinson, Robert E. '24 '56 C.352 B.S. L.477 J.D. 7087 Washington Blvd.
Robinson, Steven C., (AV) '51 '79 C.172 B.A. L.174 J.D. [Robinson W.&Y.]
Robinson Wolenty & Young, LLP, (AV) 8888 Keystone Crossing Suite 710
Robles, James S. '51 '76 C.560 B.U.S. L.602 J.D. N.L.R.B.
Rocap, James E., Jr., (AV) '17 '41 C.602 A.B. L.347 LL.B. [Rocap W.]
Rocap, Richard A., (AV) '55 '80 C.602 B.B.A. L.345 J.D. [Rocap W.]

Rocap Witchger LLP, (AV) [BB]
6666 East 75th Street, Suite 410, 46250
Telephone: 317-577-5380 Fax: 317-577-5385
Email: rocap@rocap-witchger.com URL: http://www.lawyers.com/rocapwitchger
James E. Rocap, Sr. (1881-1969); John T. Rocap (1909-1980); Keith C. Reese (1920-1993); James E. Rocap, Jr. (Retired). Members of Firm: James D. Witchger; Richard A. Rocap. Associate: Jeffrey A. Musser.
General Practice. Litigation and Insurance Defense, Motor Carrier Law, Wills and Probate, Trusts and Estates, Estate Planning, Estate Administration, Real Estate, Banking, Commercial, Tax and Corporate Law, Mediation Services, Business Law, Contracts, Business Planning, Business Enterprises, Family Law, Child Custody, Child Support, Divorce, Visitation Rights, Employment Law, Discrimination, Sexual Harassment, Wrongful Death.

See Professional Biographies, INDIANAPOLIS, INDIANA

Rochlin, Arlene, (BV) '56 '88 C&L.347 B A., J.D. 151 N. Delaware St.
Rodeheffer, Brenda Franklin, (BV) '50 '79 C.347 B.A. L.345 J.D. [Monday R.J.&A.]
Rodgers, Ryan M. '76 '01 C.679 B.A. L.347 J.D. [[A] Grant&G.]
Rodriguez, Jorge, Law Offices of '61 '92 7399 N. Shadeland Avenue
Rody, Richard C., (BV(T)) '53 '79 C.611 B.A. L.980 J.D.
(adm. in OH; not adm. in IN) Sr. Atty., Simon Property Group
Roe, Diane Withem, (BV) '56 '81 C.347 B.S. L.339 J.D. [[C] Rubin&L.]
Roehrdanz, James W., (AV) '53 '78 C.347 B.S. L.879 J.D. [Kightlinger&G.]
Roesler, Mark A. '55 '91 C.210 B.A. L.347 J.D. CMG Worldwide, Inc.
Roetter, Frederick A., (AV) '61 '86
C.894 A.B. L.1051 J.D. Asst. Corp. Coun., City of Indianapolis
Rogers, Alexander L., (AV) '43 '68 C.210 A.B. L.1119 J.D. [[C] Ayres C.&S.]
Rogers, Douglas E., (BV) '52 '84
C.63 B.S. L.345 J.D. Sr. Staff Atty., American Family Insurance
Rogers, Douglas E. '58 '84 C.894 A.B. L.879 J.D. 9247 N. Meridian St., Ste. 108
Rogers, John M. '51 '80 C.597 B.A. L.1119 J.D. [[C] Rubin&L.]
Rogers, Joyce Quanita Williamson '56 '97
C.346 B.S. L.1119 J.D. Dep. Dir., Ind. Family & Soc. Servs. Admn.
Rogers, Michael D. '80 '05 C.511 B.S. L.602 J.D. [[A] Bose M.&E.]
Rogers, Randall D., Jr. '72 '00 C.207 B.A. L.347 J.D. [[A] Parr R.O.&M.]
Roland, Paul G., P.C., (AV) '34 '64 C.659 B.S. L.345 J.D. [Ruckelshaus,R.K.B.&H.]
Rollison, Kent A. '67 '93 C.108 B.A. L.1119 J.D. [Baker&D.]
Rollison, Kristen K., (BV) '61 '86 C.347 B.A. L.1049 J.D. [Due,D.F.&M.]
Rolph, Charles R., III '50 '77 C.627 B.G.S. L.546 J.D. [[C] Dann P.N.&K.]
Romaniuk, Mark J., (AV) '66 '90 C.347 B.S. L.1119 J.D. [Baker&D.]
Romig, Amy W. '73 '00 C.421 B.S. L.1119 J.D. [[A] Plews S.R.&B.]

Roney, Kenneth J. ... '57 '01 C&L.347 B.S., J.D. Leg. Atty.
Rose, Cynthia S., (BV) ... '51 '89 C.627 B.S.N. L.344 J.D. [Baxter,J.&R.]
Rose, Merle B., (BV) ... '45 '72 C.210 B.A. L.345 J.D. 156 E. Market St., Ste 1300
Rosenbaum, William T., (BV) ... '52 '77 C.347 B.A. L.117 J.D. [Hyatt&R.]
Rosenberg, Louis ... '45 '69 C.276 B.S. L.145 J.D. Mag.
Rosiello, Michael, (AV) ... '— '77 C.178 A.B. L.813 J.D. [Barnes&T.]
Ross, John M., (AV) ... '47 '74 C.679 B.S. L.345 J.D. [Whitham,M.&R.]
Ross, Mark E. ... '62 '88 C&L.347 B.S., J.D. 1016 Country Club Road
Ross, Roberta L. ... '— '82 [Ross&B.]
Ross & Brunner, (BV) ... 6434 N. College Ave. Ste F
Rossow, James E., Jr. ... '72 '98 C.347 B.A. L.345 J.D. [Ⓐ Rubin&L.]
Rosta, Thomas E. ... '— '95 C.602 B.A. L.347 J.D. [Kopka,P.D.&E.]
Rothbaum, Sandra Lazarus, (AV) ... '44 '84 C.681 A.B. L.345 J.D. [Cohen G.&G.]
Roth-Bohannon, Erin ... '— '01 C.108 B.S. L.276 J.D. [Ⓐ Barnes&T.]
Rothkopf, Robert C. ... '55 '80 C.347 B.S. L.1119 J.D. [Landwerlen&R.]
Rowe, Norman P., (AV) ... '38 '63 C.894 A.B. L.477 LL.B. [Baker&D.]
Rowe, Timothy, (BV) ... '57 '84 C.246 B.A. L.345 J.D. [Rowe&H.]
Rowe & Hamilton, (BV) ... 22 E. Wash. St.
Rowings, Linda R. ... '53 '78 C.893 B.A. L.1119 J.D. [Ⓒ Ice M.]
Rowley, Richard L. ... '— '90 C.347 B.S. L.345 J.D. [Ⓒ Sommer B.]
Roy, Daniel ... '73 '99 C.210 B.A. L.347 J.D. [Ⓐ Baker&D.]
Roy, John T. ... '65 '91 C.494 B.A. L.347 J.D. [Ⓐ Hume S.G.G.&S.]
Rubick, Wade D. ... '21 '49 C.640 B.A. L.502 LL.B. 130 E. Washington‡
Rubin, David I. ... '— '00 C&L.1119 B.S., J.D. [Ⓐ Stewart&I.]
Rubin, George A., (AV) ... '32 '59 C.347 B.S. L.597 J.D. [Rubin&L.]

Rubin & Levin, P.C., (AV)
500 Marott Center, 342 Massachusetts Avenue, 46204-2161
Telephone: 317-634-0300 Toll Free: 800-860-0500 Telecopier: 317-263-9411
Email: law@rubin-levin.net URL: http://www.rubin-levin.com
George A. Rubin; Elliott D. Levin; Sue Figert Meyer; Christine Hayes Hickey; R. Brock Jordan; John C. Hoard;—James T. Young; Gene A. Wheeler; James E. Rossow, Jr.; Jennifer E. Riley; S. Brent Potter; Tamara L. Weisfeld; Edward R. Cardoza. Of Counsel: Diane Withem Roe; Dixon B. Dann; Jennifer Levin Sinder; John M. Rogers; Andrea L. Cohen.
Creditors' Rights, Insolvency Reorganization, Commercial Collections, Bankruptcy, Banking, Corporate, Real Estate, Foreclosure, Federal and State, Civil Trial and Appellate Practice.
Representative Clients: Associates Housing Finance; National Bank of Indianapolis; General Electric Capital Corp.; Goodwill Industries of Central Indiana, Inc.; ITT Commercial Finance, Inc.; American Credit Association of Indiana; Inland Paperboard & Packaging, Inc.; Graybar Electric; GMAC Mortgage Corp.; Kimball International.
See Professional Biographies, INDIANAPOLIS, INDIANA

Rubright, Charles R., (AV) ... '47 '74 C.346 B.S. L.1119 J.D. [Bose M.&E.]
Ruckelshaus, John C., (AV) ... '30 '57 C.602 A.B. L.345 J.D. [Ruckelshaus,R.K.B.&H.]

Ruckelshaus, Roland, Kautzman, Blackwell & Hasbrook, (AV)
Suite 900, 107 North Pennsylvania Street, 46204
Telephone: 317-634-4356 Fax: 317-634-8635
Email: rucklaw@rucklaw.com URL: http://www.rucklaw.com
Members of Firm: John C. Ruckelshaus; William A. Hasbrook; John F. Kautzman; Leo T. Blackwell; M. Elizabeth Bemis; Paul G. Roland, P.C.
General Practice. Civil and Criminal Litigation. Trials and Appeals, Personal Injury, Labor, Administrative, Business Transactions, Family/Domestic Relations, Probate and Estate Planning, Health and Hospital, Corporate Law, Zoning and Planning Law, Law Enforcement Defense, Legislative Representation.
Representative Clients: State Lodge Fraternal Order of Police; Fraternal Order of Police Lodge #86; FOP Labor Council, Inc.; Professional Firefighters Union of Indiana AFL-CIO; Indianapolis Yellow Cab, Inc.; St. Vincent Hospital; Arkanoff Painting, Inc.; Mitchell Masonry, Inc.; Just Marketing, Inc.; Axis Architecture and Interiors.

Rucker, Molly P., (AV) ... '41 '70 C.383 B.B.A. L.345 J.D. 501 Indiana Avenue
Rucker, Robert D. ... '47 '77 C.347 A.B. L.879 J.D. Suprm. Ct. J.
Rudolph, Robert J. ... '53 '82 C.679 B.S. L.345 J.D. Dep. Dir., Legis. Servs. Agcy.
Ruemmele, Jane H., (BV) ... '59 '84 C.421 B.S. L.1119 J.D. [Ⓒ Ice M.]
Ruge, Thomas R., (AV) ... '49 '76 C.347 B.S. L.879 J.D. [Lewis&K.]
Rugg, William F. ... '42 '71 C.902 B.S. L.345 J.D. 8445 Olde Mill Circle W. Dr.
Rumely, William J., (BV) ... '53 '87 C.347 B.A./B.S. L.345 J.D. [Sipe,P.H.R.&H.]
Rupp, Robert C., (BV) ... '36 '63 C.347 B.A. L.345 J.D. 225 N. Delaware St.
Ruppert, Joseph W. ... '51 '79 C.679 B.A. L.744 J.D. [Ⓐ Ruppert&S.]
Ruppert, Michael G., (BV) ... '52 '78 C.347 B.A. L.1003 J.D. [Ruppert&S.]

Ruppert & Schaefer, P.C., (BV)
2910 E. 96th Street Suite D, 46240
Telephone: 317-580-9295 Facsimile: 317-580-9298
Email: law@netdirect.net URL: http://www.ruppertandschaefer.com
Michael G. Ruppert (Board Certified, Family Law Specialist, Indiana State Bar Association, Family Law Certification Board); Paula J. Schaefer;—Lainie A. Hurwitz; Joseph W. Ruppert.
Family Law, Divorce, Pre-marital Agreements, Child Custody, Child Support, Paternity, Visitation Rights, Step Parent Adoptions.
See Professional Biographies, INDIANAPOLIS, INDIANA

Rusnak, Michael J., (AV) ... '— '77 C.346 B.S. L.192 J.D. [Ⓒ Stewart&I.]
Russell, C. Joseph, (AV) ... '50 '80 C.929 B.A. L.347 J.D. [Bose M.&E.]
Russell, David Williams, (AV) ... '45 '76 C.197 A.B. L.597 J.D. [Harrison&M.]
Russell, Donald R., (AV) ... '— '83 C.347 B.A. L.345 J.D. [Hall,R.K.H.&L.]
Russell, Elizabeth G., (AV) ... '57 '83 C.210 A.B. L.345 J.D. [Krieg D.]
Russell, Julie A. ... '— '97 C.108 B.A. L.228 J.D. [Ⓐ Barnes&T.]
Russell, Kathleen, (BV) '59 '93 C.679 B.S. L.345 J.D.
Asst. Gen. Coun., American United Life Insurance Company, a One America Financial Partner
Rusthoven, Peter J., (AV) ... '— '76 C&L.309 A.B., J.D. [Barnes&T.]
Ruthenberg, Joan ... '— '80 C.498 B.A. L.1110 J.D. Indiana Univ. Sch. of Law
Rutherford, Mark W., (BV) ... '59 '86 C.894 B.A. L.879 J.D. [Laudig G.R.&S.]
Ryan, David J., (AV) ... '47 '77 C.602 B.A. L.93 J.D. [Steckler&R.]
Ryan, Douglas N., (BV) ... '55 '81 C.432 B.S. L.345 J.D. [Gray,R.R.&F.]
Ryan, John M. ... '20 '48 C.602 A.B. L.1119 J.D. 221 Olde Mill Cove
Ryan, John P., (AV) ... '46 '72 C.347 B.A. L.345 J.D. 1 America Square
Ryan, John P., (BV) ... '— '98 C&L.347 B.A., J.D. [Hall,R.K.H.&L.]
Ryan, Karl T., (BV) ... '51 '80 C.675 B.A. L.345 J.D. [K.Ryan]
Ryan, Timothy K., (AV) ... '55 '80 C.699 B.A. L.345 J.D. [Hackman H.&C.]
Ryan, Karl, (BV) ... 6502 E. Westfield Blvd.
Ryden, Todd R. ... '71 '97 C.679 B.A. L.345 J.D. ViaStar Energy, Inc.
Rynearson, Max D. ... '— '66 C&L.347 B.S., J.D. 2611 E. 55th Place
Sadowski, Niccole R. ... '74 '99 C.973 B.A. L.201 J.D. [Hopper B.]
Safewright, Deniece Rogers ... '60 '87 C.929 B.A. L.345 J.D. 3611 Fletcher Ave.
Safrin, Franklin A., (BV) ... '41 '67 C.347 B.S. L.345 J.D. [Safrin&Assoc.]
Safrin, Ronald A. ... '67 '95 C.347 B.S. L.1187 J.D. [Ⓐ Safrin&Assoc.]
Safrin & Associates, (BV) ... 9229 Delegates Row, Ste. 490
Sage, Candace L., (BV) ... '45 '95 C&L.347 A.B., J.D. [Ⓐ Bingham M.]
Sage, John C. ... '53 '00 C.421 B.A. L.345 J.D. 56 N. Irvington Ave.
Sage, Justin L. '72 '99 C.602 B.S. L.910 J.D.
Pat. Atty., Roche Diagnostics Corp. (Pat.)
Saggese, Mary Ann Fuchs ... '60 '89 C.679 B.S.C.E. L.273 J.D. [Ⓒ Plews S.R.&B.]

Sahota, Angela '62 '95 C.025 B.A. L.019 LL.B.
(adm. in ON; not adm. in IN) Staff Atty., Simon Property Group
St.Amour, Brion G. ... '78 '04 C.679 B.S. L.345 J.D. [Ⓐ Bose M.&E.] (Pat.)
St. Clair, Talmage H., (BV) ... '33 '65 C.344 B.S. L.345 LL.B. 1349 Sunday Dr.‡
St. Louis, Matthew R. ... '— '04 C.477 B.A. L.1119 J.D. [Ⓐ Ice M.]
St. Peter, Rachel ... '74 '99 C.108 B.S. L.347 J.D. [Ⓐ Ice M.] (See Pat. Sect.)
Salatich, Emily M. ... '76 '04 C.575 B.A. L.1119 J.D. JPMorgan
Salatich, Ronald G., (AV) ... '45 '71 C.108 B.A. L.345 J.D. [Wooden&M.]
Salb, Richard M., (BV) ... '23 '50 C.108 B.S. L.345 LL.B. 151 N. Delaware St.
Sales, James J. ... '62 '89 C.701 B.S.Ch.E. L.347 J.D. Dep. Dir., Eli Lilly & Co. (Pat.)
Salin, William N. ... '31 '59 C.347 B.S. L.1119 J.D. 8455 Keystone Crossing‡
Sallee, Gary D., (AV) ... '52 '81 C.346 B.S. L.221 J.D. 212 W. 10th St.
Salwowski, Brian D. ... '58 '84 C.265 B.A. L.345 J.D. 110 S. Downey Ave.
Salyers, Robert J., (AV) ... '46 '73 C.679 B.S. L.345 J.D. [Salyers&E.]
Salyers & Eiteljorg, (AV) ... 55 Monument Circle
Samper, Fred, (BV) ... '40 '70 C.344 B.S. L.345 J.D. 155 E. Market Street

Sams, Steven '54 '98 C.910 B.S. L.347 J.D.
8720 Castle Creek Parkway, Suite 323, 46250
Telephone: 317-577-1620 Fax: 317-577-1619
Email: steven.sams@stevensamslaw.com URL: http://www.stevensamslaw.com
Employment Law, Wrongful Termination, Disability Accomodation, Employee Benefits, Sexual Harassment, Workers Compensation, Civil Rights, Discrimination, Sexual Harassment, Family Law, Adoptions, Divorce, Child Custody, Child Support, Visitation Rights, Wills, Probate, Trusts and Estates, Estate Planning, Guardianship, Personal Injury, Automobile Accidents, Medical Malpractice, Business Law, Contracts, Commercial Leasing, Business Enterprise, Business Formation, Buying and Selling of Businesses, Mold Litigation, State, Federal and Appellate Courts.
See Professional Biographies, INDIANAPOLIS, INDIANA

Sanchez, Marisol ... '— '02 C.677 B.A. L.1119 J.D. [Ⓐ Bose M.&E.]
Sanchez, Rafael A. ... '74 '02 C.677 B.A. L.1119 J.D. [Ⓐ Bingham M.]
Sandifer, James E., (AV) ... '33 '61 C.347 A.B. L.345 LL.B. [Sandifer&S.]
Sandifer & Sandifer, P.C., (AV) ... Suite 201, 7351 Shadeland Station
Sarbinoff, James G. ... '76 '02 C.347 B.A. L.1119 J.D. [Davis&S.]
Sargeant, Diane R., (AV) ... '50 '87 C.347 B.S. L.345 J.D. [Cox&S.]
Satrom, Thomas E. ... '53 '83 C.951 A.B. L.347 J.D. [Ⓒ Locke R.]
Satz, Mark D. ... '60 '85 C.473 B.S. L.345 J.D. Murrays Development Co.
Sauer, J. Michael ... '55 '80 C.63 B.S. L.36 J.D. Dep. Pub. Def.
Saunders, Jeffrey A., (AV) ... '63 '92 C.63 B.S. L.346 J.D. [Adinamis,M.&S.]
Sausser, Mark C. ... '59 '85 C.894 A.B. L.945 J.D. [Ⓒ Baker&D.]
Savitsky, Jeffrey C. ... '45 '81 C.880 Ph.D. L.345 J.D. Inst. for Public Safety Personnel
Sayles, Michael J. ... '50 '83 C.476 B.S. L.818 J.D. Pat. Coun., Eli Lilly & Co. (Pat.)
Saylor, Jaime K. ... '— '04 C.172 B.S. L.629 J.D. [Ⓐ Hatchett&H.]
Scahill, James N., (AV) ... '54 '84 C.701 B.S. L.345 J.D. [Schnorr,S.&M.]
Scaletta, Phillip R., III, (AV) ... '49 '75 C.679 B.S.I.M. L.1119 J.D. [Ice M.]
Scanlan, Kelly M. ... '74 '05 C.347 B.S.N. L.345 J.D. [Ⓐ Bose M.&E.]
Scanlon, Christopher G., (AV) ... '45 '80 C.347 B.S. L.1119 J.D. [Baker&D.]
Scanlon, Karen D., (AV) ... '50 '83 C.347 A.B. L.345 J.D. 7595 Central Ave.
Scanlon, Michael T., (BV) ... '— '96 C.63 B.S. L.347 J.D. [Ⓐ Barnes&T.]
Schabel, Donald A., (AV) ... '27 '52 C.347 A.B. L.309 J.D. 4455 Bway.‡
Schabler, William M., (BV) ... '50 '80 C.347 B.S. L.345 J.D. P.O. Box 55272
Schaefer, Michael, (BV) ... '45 '71 C.602 A.B. L.1119 J.D. Dep. Atty. Gen.
Schaefer, Paula J. ... '69 '94 C.63 B.S. L.347 J.D. [Ruppert&S.]
Schafer, Kaisa A. ... '61 '02 C.347 B.G.S. L.74 J.D. Dep. Pub. Def.
Schafer, Matthew J. ... '75 '01 C.679 B.S. L.345 J.D. [Ⓐ Drewry S.V.]
Schaibley, John R., III, (AV) ... '53 '82 C.679 B.A. L.1119 J.D. [Baker&D.]
Schantz, Matthew R. ... '69 '95 C.679 B.S. L.145 J.D. [Bingham M.] (Pat.)
Scharf, David P. ... '67 '94 C.347 B.S. L.145 J.D. Assoc. Gen. Coun., Guidant Corp.
Scheidler, Karen B. ... '49 '99 C.347 B.A. L.345 J.D. [Ⓐ Plews S.R.&B.]
Schell, Dennis S. ... '— '01 C.679 B.S.E.E. L.1119 J.D. [Ⓐ Barnes&T.] (See Pat. Sect.)
Schembs, Robert A. ... '52 '77 C.879 B.S. L.1119 J.D. 155 E. Market St.
Schemmel, William T. ... '68 '95 C.347 B.A. L.900 J.D. Golden Rule Insurance Co.
Schenck, Jack M. ... '29 '55 C.894 A.B. L.345 J.D. 3015 River Bay Dr. N.‡
Schepers, Brad A. ... '67 '98 C.999 B.S. L.345 J.D. [Krieg D.] (Pat.)
Scherer, Mark A. ... '51 '78 C&L.347 B.A., J.D. Gen. Coun., IN Health Care Assn.
Scherer, Thomas C., (AV) ... '51 '77 C.608 B.A. L.1119 J.D. [Bingham M.]
Schierholz, Orval P. ... '47 '02 C.870 B.S. L.74 J.D. [Schierholz]
Schierholz Legal Services, LLC ... 4954 E. 56th St., Ste. 14
Schiesser, Jason M. ... '76 '01 C.347 B.S. L.345 J.D. [Ⓐ Baker&D.]
Schiferl, Kevin C., (AV) ... '63 '88 C.679 B.A. L.1119 J.D. [Locke R.]
Schiff, Joel, (BV) ... '53 '78 C.347 B.S. L.345 J.D. Dep. Atty. Gen.
Schiff, John D., (AV) ... '51 '77 C.894 B.A. L.345 J.D. [J.Schiff]
Schiff, John, (AV) ... 748 E. Bates St., Rm. 105
Schiffli, Gary A., (BV) ... '54 '80 C.347 B.S. L.345 J.D. [Ⓒ Kroger,G.&R.]
Schiller, Matthew ... '73 '02 C&L.74 B.A., J.D. [Schiller&S.]
Schiller & Swedarsky, L.L.C. ... 4321 East 82nd St.
Schilling, April R. ... '74 '98 C.347 B.S. L.345 J.D. [Ⓐ Locke R.]
Schlegel, Fred E., (AV) ... '41 '66 C.597 B.A. L.477 J.D. [Baker&D.]
Schlesinger, Leah ... '— '93 C&L.145 A.B., J.D. [Ⓒ Baker&D.]
Schlosser, Chalmer R., (AV) ... '16 '39 C.210 L.345 LL.B. [Schlosser&S.] ‡
Schlosser, William L., (BV) ... '46 '71 C.575 A.B. L.477 J.D. [Schlosser&S.]
Schlosser & Schlosser, (BV) ... 225 North Delaware St.
Schmal, Charles P. '69 '00
C.679 B.S.I.E. L.1209 J.D. [Woodard,E.M.M.&H.] (See Pat. Sect.)
Schmelzer, Roger H. ... '57 '91 C.346 B.S. L.347 J.D. 3601 Vincennes Road
Schmid, Mary F. ... '63 '93 C.347 B.A. L.1119 J.D. [Stewart&I.]
Schmidt, James A. '45 '70 C.347 B.S. L.1119 J.D.
Asst. Ge. Coun., Simon Property Group
Schmidt, James F., (BV) ... '53 '78 C.679 B.A. L.879 J.D. State Atty. Gen. Off.
Schmith, Gregory P., (BV) ... '56 '82 C.346 B.S. L.345 J.D. 3043 S. Keystone Ave.
Schmits, Lawrence W., (AV) ... '48 '76 C.894 B.S. L.345 J.D. [Krieg D.]
Schmitt, Julie Zellers, (BV) ... '56 '81 C.210 B.A. L.345 J.D. 131 E. Ohio St.
Schmutte, Samuel ... '— '04 C.1216 B.S. L.1119 J.D. [Ⓐ Ice M.]
Schneider, James J. ... '47 '76 C.347 B.S. L.345 J.D. [Schneider]
Schneider, Michael J., (AV) ... '52 '77 C.347 B.S. L.1119 J.D. [Bose M.&E.]
Schneider & Company, Inc. ... 10321 North Pennsylvania St.
Schnellenberger, Thomas F., (AV) ... '54 '79 C.602 B.B.A. L.347 J.D. [Ice M.]
Schnorr, David E., (AV) ... '25 '58 C.201 B.S. L.345 J.D. [Schnorr,S.&M.]
Schnorr, Scahill & Maier, (AV) ... 144 N. Delaware St.
Schooley, J. Bradley, (BV) ... '45 '78 C.207 B.A. L.347 J.D. [Hostetler&K.]
Schopper, Mary A., (BV) ... '60 '91 C&L.347 B.A., J.D. [Ⓐ Due,D.F.&M.]
Schrager, Edward F., (AV) ... '53 '80 C.347 B.A. L.1119 J.D. [Cohen G.&G.]
Schreckengast, William O., (AV) ... '26 '56 C.347 L.345 LL.B. [Ⓒ Schreckengast,H.&C.]
Schreckengast, Helm & Cueller, (AV) ... 8007 South Meridian Street
Schroeder, Peter A., (AV) ... '54 '80 C.347 B.A. L.1119 J.D. [Norris C.&S.]
Schubert, R. L. ... '13 '36 C.108 L.345 LL.B. 6030 E. 9th St.‡
Schuckit, Robert J. ... '57 '82 C.1036 B.A. L.966 J.D. [Schuckit&Assoc.]

Schuckit & Associates, P.C.
30th Floor Market Tower, 10 West Market Street Suite 3000, 46204
Telephone: 317-363-2400 Fax: 317-363-2257
URL: http://www.schuckitlaw.com
Robert J. Schuckit. Associates: Christopher T. Lane; Robert E. Duff; Mickey J. Lee; Camille R. Nicodemus.
Business Litigation in State and Federal Trial and Appellate Courts, Property Tax Appeals and Business Transactions.
See Professional Biographies, INDIANAPOLIS, INDIANA

Schug, Richard W. ... '64 '94 C.679 B.S.E.E. L.347 J.D. P.O. Box 1595
Schultheis, Richard L., (BV) ... '34 '67 C.210 A.B. L.1119 LL.B. [R.L.Schultheis]
Schultheis, Richard L., P.C., (BV) ... 6704 Sunny Lane
Schultz, Michael L. ... '69 '97 C.793 B.S. L.345 J.D. [A Laudig G.R.&S.]

Schultz & Pogue, LLP
(See Carmel)

Schulz, Bradley J., (CV) ... '71 '99 C.108 B.A. L.345 J.D. [A Goodin A.&M.]
Schwab, Fred, (BV) ... '50 '75 C.273 B.A. L.1119 J.D. 155 E. Market St.
Schwab, Steven C. ... '46 '74 C.1216 B.A. L.345 J.D. 7218 E. Payne Rd.‡
Schwab, Susan R. ... '51 '83 C&L.347 B.S., J.D. Coun., Anthem, Inc.
Schwarz, James H., (AV) ... '54 '80 C.347 B.S. L.345 J.D. [Dann P.N.&K.]
Schwebel, Paul R. M. ... '38 '83 C.178 B.S. L.1095 J.D. 5657 Rundle Ct.
Schwer, Bradley W. ... '— '00 C.63 B.S. L.345 J.D. [A Sommer B.]
Schwer, Melinda J. ... '71 '96 C&L.347 B.A., J.D. [A Riley B.&E.]
Scimia, Joseph M., (AV) ... '59 '85 C.347 B.S. L.1119 J.D. [Baker&D.]
Sciscoe, Marc W., (AV) ... '54 '80 C.103 A.B. L.309 J.D. [Ice M.]
Sciscoe, Tara Schulstad, (AV) ... '69 '94 C.228 A.B. L.477 J.D. [C Ice M.]
Scodro, Greta Morris ... '57 '82 C.210 B.A. L.345 J.D. IN Suprm. Ct., Admin. Off.
Scopelitis, Alki E., (AV) ... '37 '64 C.976 B.A. L.276 LL.B. [C Scopelitis,G.L.&H.]

Scopelitis, Garvin, Light & Hanson, P.C., (AV) BB
10 West Market Street, Suite 1500, 46204-2968 ⊙
Telephone: 317-637-1777 FAX: 317-687-2414
Email: indianapolis@scopelitis.com URL: http://www.scopelitis.com
Norman R. Garvin; Andrew K. Light; James H. Hanson; Lynne D. Lidke; Thomas E. Farrell; Gregory M. Feary; Robert L. Browning; Steven A. Pletcher; Timothy W. Wiseman; Jay D. Robinson, Jr.; Michael B. Langford; Angela S. Cash; Jeffrey S. Toole; David D. Robinson;—W. Todd Metzger; Christopher R. Whitten; Craig J. Helmreich; A. Jack Finklea; Rebecca S. Smith; Shannon M. Cohen; Eric K. Habig; Allison Owen Smith; Ronald J. Morelock; R. Jay Taylor, Jr. Of Counsel: Alki E. Scopelitis; Carla R. Hounshel; Richard A. Clark; Gregory A. Ostendorf.
General Civil Practice. Litigation in all State and Federal Courts, including Appellate Practice, Transportation, Motor Carrier, Trucking Law, International Trade, Corporate, Mergers & Acquisitions, Administrative, Antitrust and Trade Regulation, Business, Insurance, Insurance Defense, Negligence, Labor and Employment, Employee Benefits, Immigration, Environmental, Workers Compensation, Probate and Estate Planning and Public Utility Law.
Representative Clients: FedEx; J.B. Hunt Transport, Inc.; Landstar System, Inc.; Penske System. Inc.; Schneider National Inc.
Chicago, Illinois Office: 30 West Monroe Street, Suite 600, 60603-2427. Telephone: 312-422-1200. Fax: 312-422-1224.
Washington, D.C. Office: 1850 M Street, N.W., Suite 280, 20036-5804. Telephone: 202-783-9222. Fax: 202-783-9230.
Kansas City, Missouri Office: Two Pershing Square, 2300 Main Street, Suite 900, 64108. Telephone: 816-279-9835. Fax: 816-279-1973.
Pasadena, California Office: 790 East Colorado Boulevard, 9th Floor, 91101. Telephone: 626-795-4700. Fax: 626-795-4790.
See Professional Biographies, INDIANAPOLIS, INDIANA

Scott, Fred D., (AV) ... '43 '72 C.347 B.A. L.345 J.D. 55 Monument Circle, Suite 814
Scott, Robert B., (AV) ... '61 '88 C.347 B.S. L.879 J.D. [Clark,Q.M.S.&G.]
Scott-Mitchell, Renee L. ... '62 '97 C.679 B.S. L.345 J.D. State Farm Litig. Coun.
Scripture, Jeffrey W., (AV) ... '62 '87 C.894 B.A. L.345 J.D. [Harrison&M.] ⊙
Scroggins, Eric C. ... '— '02 C.63 B.S. L.345 J.D. [A Ice M.]
Seach, Raymond T., (BV) ... '64 '93 C.602 B.B.A. L.1119 J.D. [Riley B.&E.]
Seamands, Rebecca J. ... '65 '92 C.339 B.S. L.345 J.D. [Ice M.]
Searcy, Edgar B. ... '40 '91 C.801 B.S. L.347 J.D. P.O. Box 531037
Sears, Christopher S. ... '68 '94 C.347 B.A. L.1119 J.D. [Ice M.]
Secrest, James M., (BV) ... '35 '62 C.108 B.S. L.345 J.D. P.O. Box 68666
Secttor, Jerome M. ... '47 '99 C.231 B.A. L.1119 J.D. State of IN, Dept. of Rev.
Sedwick, Marc S., Law Office of ... '74 '02 C.347 B.A. L.1119 J.D. 9520 E. Washington
Seger, Randolph L., (AV) ... '48 '72 C.347 B.S. L.1119 J.D. [Bingham M.]
Seidler, Robert F. '— '01 C.108 B.A. L.602 J.D.
(adm. in OH; not adm. in IN) [A Ogletree,D.N.S.&S.]
Seifert, Christie A. ... '68 '98 C.347 B.A. L.365 J.D. [A Goodin A.&M.]
Seigel, Christopher D., (AV) ... '— '79 C.63 B.S. L.345 J.D. [Ayres C.&S.]
Seigel, Jane Ann, (AV) ... '54 '79 C.210 B.A. L.345 J.D. Dep. Corp. Coun.
Seiter, David M. ... '70 '98 C.932 B.S. L.347 J.D. 384 Buck Creek Rd.
Seitz, Daniel B., (AV) ... '43 '69 C.347 A.B. L.1119 J.D. [Bose M.&E.]
Seiwert, Andrew P., (BV) ... '59 '86 C.679 B.A. L.347 J.D. [A Feiwell&H.]
Selby, Myra C., (AV) ... '55 '80 C.373 B.A. L.477 J.D. [Ice M.]
Selby, Todd J. ... '— '90 C&L.347 B.S., J.D. [Hall,R.K.H.&L.]
Selig, Gary M. ... '72 '98 C.597 B.A. L.879 J.D. [G.M.Selig]
Selig, Gary M., P.C. ... 8425 Keystone Xing., Ste. 180
Semler, Ronald J. ... '52 '78 C.63 B.S. L.345 J.D. [Stephenson M.&S.]
Sentman, Ronald G., (BV) ... '51 '84 C.347 A.B. L.1119 J.D. [A Katz&K.]
Setzer, H. Antonio ... '— '01 C&L.347 B.A., J.D. [A Bose M.&E.]
Sevenish, Randall R., (BV) ... '50 '85 C.344 B.S. L.345 J.D. [Sevenish]
Sevenish Law Firm, P.C., (BV) ... 255 N. Alabama Street
Sever, Philip ... '70 '95 C.347 B.A. L.8 J.D. [A Cohen&M.]
Severns, Scott R., (AV) ... '50 '79 C.347 B.A. L.345 J.D. [Severns&B.]
Severns & Bennett, P.C., (AV) ... 41 East Washington Street, Suite 300
Sevier, Amy White, (BV) ... '63 '88 C.347 B.S. L.1119 J.D. [C Goodin A.&M.]
Seymour, Darlene R. ... '75 '01 C&L.347 B.S., J.D. [A Kiefer&M.]
Shadle, Austin A. ... '77 '04 C.679 B.S. L.345 J.D. [A Riley B.&E.]
Shadley, Sue A., (AV) ... '52 '77 C.679 B.S. L.1119 J.D. [Plews S.R.&B.]
Shady, Ronald F., Jr., (BV) ... '52 '82 C.347 B.S. L.345 J.D. 3755 E. 82nd Street
Shafer, James M. ... '— '98 C.679 B.A. L.347 J.D. [A Hall,R.K.H.&L.]
Shah, Jatin D. ... '52 '79 C&L.999 B.A., LL.B. 55 Monument Cir., Ste. 814
Shaheed, David A. ... '47 '85 C.249 B.S. L.347 J.D. Supr. Ct. J.
Shake, B. Keith, (AV) ... '58 '83 C&L.347 A.B., J.D. [C Locke R.]
Shanahan, James A., (AV) ... '51 '77 C.602 B.B.A. L.1119 J.D. [Ice M.] (⊙Chgo., IL)
Shanahan, James P. '33 '63 C.973 B.S.B.A. L.1340 J.D.
(adm. in OH; not adm. in IN) Amer. United Life Ins. Co.
Shanahan, Rebecca M., (AV) '53 '77 C.347 A.B. L.1119 J.D.
Pres., Practice Mgmt., Inc.
Shane, David N., (AV) '48 '75 C.894 B.A. L.228 J.D.
Executive Vice President, LDI, Ltd.
Shapiro, Melinda, (BV) ... '67 '94 C.347 B.A. L.201 J.D. [Bose M.&E.]
Sharkey, William B. ... '59 '84 C.210 B.A. L.345 J.D. Coopers & Lybrand
Sharp, Karen Glasser, (BV) ... '62 '89 C.344 B.A. L.345 J.D. [C Bose M.&E.]
Sharpe, John H., (AV) ... '— '81 C.347 B.A. L.345 J.D. [Sommer B.]
Sharpley, Tiffany A. ... '73 '01 C&L.347 B.S., J.D. [A Ice M.]
Sharpnack, John T. ... '33 '60 C&L.150 B.A., LL.B. Chf. J., Ct. of App.
Sharrow, Regina M. ... '— '91 C.477 B.A. L.112 J.D. [Sommer B.]
Shartzer, Jason A. ... '74 '03 C.425 B.A. L.1370 J.D. 1 N Pennsylvania St, Ste 200
Shaw, Shannon M. ... '— '03 C.347 B.A. L.345 J.D. [A Barnes&T.]
Shea, Thomas F. ... '— '94 C.679 B.A. L.347 J.D. [Barnes&T.]
Shedlock, Kristin S. '— '00 C.741 B.A. L.904 J.D.
(adm. in IL; not adm. in IN) [A Barnes&T.]
Sheedy, Stacy Hamilton '61 '96 C.25 B.A. L.347 J.D.
8395 Keystone Crossing, Ste. 201
Sheeks, Charles Reed, (AV) ... '41 '73 C.347 B.S. L.345 J.D. [Ittenbach J.T.&K.]
Sheff, Andrew, (AV) ... '54 '79 C.108 B.A. L.345 J.D. [Bennett&S.]
Shelby, Katherine L., (AV) ... '54 '80 C.347 B.A. L.1119 J.D. [Bingham M.]
Shelley, J. Gregory, (AV) ... '60 '85 C&L.347 B.A., J.D. [Bose M.&E.]
Shelton, Brandon M. ... '— '98 C.801 B.S. L.339 J.D. [A Ogletree,D.N.S.&S.]
Shelton, David A., (BV) ... '64 '89 C.108 B.S. L.345 J.D. [Tabbert H.E.&W.]
Shepard, Clifford W. ... '61 '93 C&L.1119 B.A., J.D. 2325 West Washington Street
Shepard, Randall T. ... '46 '72 C.674 B.A. L.976 J.D. Chief Jus., Supm. Ct.
Shepherd, Kevin D. ... '67 '96 C.347 B.A. L.345 J.D. [Rowe&H.]
Sheridan, John K., II ... '48 '75 C.575 B.S. L.345 J.D. 5243 N. Meridian Street
Sherman, Steven M. ... '49 '74 C.851 B.A. L.836 J.D. [Krieg D.]
Sherwood, Pamela H., (BV) ... '69 '93 C.679 B.A. L.200 J.D. 4625 W. 86th St., Ste. 500
Shevitz, Richard E., (AV) ... '60 '85 C.347 B.A. L.608 J.D. [Cohen&M.]
Shields, Juli K. ... '— '87 C.265 B.A. L.347 J.D. [Hall,R.K.H.&L.]
Shields, V. Sue ... '39 '61 C.63 B.A. L.1119 LL.B. U.S. Mag. J.
Shikany, Joseph F., (BV) ... '49 '75 C.201 B.S. L.345 J.D. 244 N. College Ave.

Shipley & Associates
(See Fort Wayne)

Shircliff, David A. ... '65 '90 C.303 B.A. L.347 J.D. 3143 Meoford Ave.‡

Shirley, Curtis E., (AV) '60 '91 C.249 B.M.E. L.1119 J.D. BB
156 East Market Street, Suite 600, 46204
Telephone: 317-685-6512 Toll Free: 877-953-4900 Facsimile: 317-685-6505 URL: http://www.curtisshirleylaw.com
Email: curtis@shirleylaw.net URL: http://www.shirleylaw.net
Associate: Molly C. Johnson.
Wills and Probate, Guardianships, Contested Wills, Contested Trusts and Estates, Estate Litigation, Trust Litigation, Probate Litigation, Probate Taxation, Probate Administration, Estate Administration, Business Litigation, Complex Business Litigation, Fraud, Securities Fraud, Breach of Contract, Criminal Tax Defense.
See Professional Biographies, INDIANAPOLIS, INDIANA

Shisler, Janna J. ... '60 '88 C.347 B.A. L.345 J.D. Gen. Coun., Hoosier Lottery
Shive, Robert E. ... '65 '95 C.347 B.A. L.74 J.D. [Bator R.B.S.&L.]
Shockley, Steven C., (AV) ... '— '84 C.347 B.A. L.345 J.D. [Sommer B.]
Shoemaker, James L. ... '67 '96 C.608 B.S. L.345 J.D. [A Doyle&F.]
Shook, Robert C., (CV) '49 '75
C.265 B.A. L.345 J.D. Staff Atty., Supm. Ct. Disciplinary Comm.
Short, Jeffrey W., (BV) ... '— '91 C.894 B.A. L.347 J.D. [Hall,R.K.H.&L.]
Shortridge, Kathleen K., (AV) ... '44 '84 C.813 A.B. L.421 J.D. [C Ice M.]
Shoultz, Nikki G. ... '67 '92 C.108 B.A. L.345 J.D. [Bose M.&E.]
Shoultz, Richard K., (AV) ... '65 '90 C.303 B.A. L.345 J.D. [Lewis W.]
Shoup, Jennifer R. ... '67 '96 C.108 B.S. L.347 J.D. [Wallack S.&H.]
Shoup, Steven V., (AV) ... '46 '74 C.347 B.S. L.345 J.D. [C Ogletree,D.N.S.&S.]
Shrack, Thomas D. ... '— '03 C.473 B.A. L.345 J.D. [A Hall,R.K.H.&L.]
Shroyer, Lowell Allen, (AV) '51 '87 C.344 B.S. L.345 J.D.
3850 S. Emerson Ave., Ste. E
Shubat, John G., (AV) ... '58 '88 C.347 B.S. L.345 J.D. [C Bingham M.]
Shublak, Mark I. ... '70 '01 C.63 B.A. L.345 J.D. [A Ice M.]
Shula, Robert J., (AV) '36 '61
C.347 B.A. L.1119 J.D. 3815 River Crossing Pkwy., Ste. 340
Shuster, Elizabeth A. '70 '03
C.339 B.S. L.1119 J.D. [A Woodard,E.M.M.&H.] (See Pat. Sect.)
Siakotos, Ellen C. ... '56 '86 C.679 B.S. L.345 J.D. 9110 Crestview Dr.
Sibbitt, Jason Ty, (CV) ... '68 '98 C.108 B.S. L.345 J.D. [A Bingham M.]
Sibul-Gelbert, Randee ... '53 '83 C.339 B.A. L.146 J.D. [A Baker&D.]
Siegel, Max L., (BV) ... '64 '92 C&L.602 B.A., J.D. [Siegel C.&D.]
Siegel Carter & Dassow, LLP, (BV) ... 133 W. Market St.
Siepman, Kenneth B., (BV) ... '64 '90 C.894 A.B. L.880 J.D. [Ogletree,D.N.S.&S.]
Sifferlen, Sandra Cha ... '67 '92 C&L.597 B.A., J.D. Eli Lilly & Co.
Silas, Don E. ... '49 '97 C&L.347 B.S., J.D. 127 E. Michigan St., Ste. 500
Silva, Jussara ... '78 '04 C.472 B.A. L.345 J.D. [A Starkey]
Silver, Gregory K., (BV) ... '46 '72 C.473 B.A. L.1119 J.D. 342 Massachusetts Ave.
Silver, Peter A., (AV) ... '55 '83 C.347 B.A. L.1119 J.D. [Dann P.N.&K.]
Silver, Theresa L. ... '74 '01 C.679 B.S.C.E. L.879 J.D. [A Easter&C.]
Silverthorne, Cheryl L. ... '71 '03 C.679 B.S. L.345 J.D. [A Ice M.]
Simcox, Edwin J., (AV) '45 '71 C.347 A.B. L.345 LL.B.
22 E. Washington St., Ste. 316
Simmonds, Scott M. ... '69 '04 C.701 B.S.M.E. L.345 J.D. [A Barnes&T.] (See Pat. Sect.)
Simmons, Barbara J. '55 '90
C.739 B.S. L.345 J.D. Staff Coun., Indiana Assn. of Realtors, Inc.
Simmons, Dale R. ... '57 '83 C.347 B.S. L.1119 J.D. 1601 City County Bldg
Simmons, David L., (AV) ... '53 '80 C.347 B.A. L.345 J.D. [Drewry S.V.]
Simmons, Jacqueline A., (AV) '55 '79
C.602 B.A. L.1119 J.D. General Counsel, Reilly Industries, Inc.
Simmons, Jared A. ... '75 '04 C.347 B.S. L.345 J.D. [A Dann P.N.&K.]
Simmons, Michael E., (AV) ... '54 '79 C.347 B.S. L.345 J.D. [Hume S.G.G.&S.]
Simon, Richard J. '46 '71 C&L.352 B.A., J.D.
(adm. in IA; not adm. in IN) N.L.R.B.
Simpson, Charles J., (CV) ... '43 '76 C.679 B.S.C.E. L.345 J.D. Simpson Engineering
Simpson, George Arthur ... '62 '89 C&L.347 B.A., J.D. P.O. Box 36992
Sinclair, Paul H. ... '66 '93 C.101 B.A. L.801 J.D. [Ice M.]
Sinder, Jennifer Levin, (BV) ... '68 '94 C.37 B.S. L.347 J.D. [C Rubin&L.]
Singleton, Julie C. ... '64 '88 C.679 B.A. L.347 J.D. Law Clk., Ct. of App.
Sinnott, Leslie A. ... '51 '86 C&L.059 M.A., LL.B. [A Easter&C.]
Sinnott, Timothy S. '52 '82 C.28 B.A. L.623 J.D.
(adm. in OK; not adm. in IN) I.R.S.★
Sipe, Frederic C., (BV) ... '48 '74 C.36 B.A. L.345 J.D. [Sipe,P.H.R.&H.]
Sipe, Pankow, Han, Rumely & Hehner, A Professional Association, (AV)
225 North Delaware St.
Sipes, W. Russell ... '52 '93 C&L.347 B.S., J.D. [Laudig G.R.&S.]
Skeels, Jennifer Fouts ... '— '91 C.679 B.S. L.424 J.D. [A Hall,R.K.H.&L.]

Skekloff, Adelsperger & Kleven, LLP
(See Fort Wayne)

Skiles, Richard R., (AV) ... '56 '83 C.63 B.S. L.345 J.D. 150 E. Market St.
Skinner, Jack ... '— '03 C.98 B.S. L.339 J.D. [A Ice M.]

Skolnik, Bradley W., (BV) .... '55 '81 C.475 B.A. L.1119 J.D. [Stewart&I.]
Skolnik, Gayle L., (AV) .... '56 '82 C.347 A.B. L.1119 J.D. [Baker&D.]
Skwarcan, Shelly M. .... '65 '91 C.679 B.A. L.1119 J.D. 110 N. Delaware St.
Slaughter, Geoffrey G., (AV) .... '— '89 C&L.347 B.A., J.D. [Sommer B.]
Slaughter, Jeffrey R., (AV) ....'47 '76 C.1229 B.S.M.E. L.345 J.D. 1010 E. 86th St.
Slavens, Julie M. ....'60 '86 C.679 B.S.I.M. L.836 J.D. Staff Atty., Ind. Sch. Bd. Assn.
Small, Arthur M. ....'46 '74 C&L.347 B.S., J.D. Sr. Staff Atty., Amer. Fam. Ins. Grp.
Small, Bobby J., (AV) ....'42 '74 C.894 B.A. L.345 J.D. Exec. Asst. to the Govt.
Small, Greg A. .... '74 '01 C.659 B.A. L.1119 J.D. [Ⓐ Krieg D.]

Small, Mark '55 '89 C.210 B.A. L.347 J.D.
6434 North College Avenue, Suite B, 46220-2426
Telephone: 317-252-4800; 317-253-7476 Fax: 317-475-9578
Email: marksmall2001@yahoo.com URL: http://www.smalllaw.com
Appeals, Criminal, Drug Crimes, Driving While Intoxicated, Death Penalty Cases, Personal Injury.
See Professional Biographies, INDIANAPOLIS, INDIANA

Smeltzer, John K., (AV) ....'— '80 C.347 B.A. L.345 J.D. [Ⓒ Sommer B.]
Smikle, Richard A., (AV) .... '55 '80 C.373 B.A. L.221 J.D. [Ice M.]
Smiler, Brian L. '74 '01 C.475 B.S. L.213 J.D.
(adm. in OH; not adm. in IN; Pat.) Pat. Atty., Roche Diagnostics Corp.
Smith, Allison Owen ....'65 '96 C.174 B.A. L.345 J.D. [Ⓐ Scopelitis,G.L.&H.]
Smith, Angela M., (BV) ....'— '94 C&L.347 B.S., J.D. [Hall,R.K.H.&L.]
Smith, Anne K. '58 '87 C.210 B.M. L.345 J.D.
Divisional Leasing Coun., Simon Property Group
Smith, Bruce E., (AV) ....'47 '72 C.347 A.B. L.477 J.D. [Stark D.&S.]
Smith, C. Roscoe .... '15 '40 C.344 B.A. L.477 J.D. 2839 Maywood Rd.‡
Smith, Christopher A., (AV) ....'46 '74 C.679 B.A. L.345 J.D. [Hagemier,A.&S.]
Smith, Donald J. ....'73 '03 C.347 B.A. L.161 J.D. [Ⓐ Stark D.&S.]
Smith, Donald S., (AV) ....'55 '81 C.210 B.A. L.345 J.D. [Riley B.&E.]
Smith, Elizabeth A., (AV) ....'56 '85 C&L.339 A.B., J.D. Dir. of Philanthropy
Smith, Emily D. ....'79 '03 C.421 B.A. L.347 J.D. [Ⓐ Hill,F.M.F.&M.]
Smith, Everet F. ....'13 '50 C.576 B.S. L.424 J.D. 11 S. Meridian St. (Pat.)
Smith, G. Pearson, Jr., (AV) .... '39 '64 C&L.976 B.A., LL.B. [Bose M.&E.]
Smith, Gordon R., (AV) .... '33 '59 C.894 A.B. L.345 J.D. [Hume S.G.G.&S.]
Smith, Harold S., II '50 '79 C&L.260 B.A., J.D.
(adm. in FL; not adm. in IN) 5405 Greenwillow Rd.‡
Smith, Jacob D. ....'40 '72 C.347 B.S. L.345 J.D. 5835 Oak Ave.

Smith, Janice E., Attorney at Law '41 '92 C.679 B.A. L.345 J.D.
617 E. Michigan Street, Suite A, 46202
Telephone: 317-624-4220 Fax: 317-624-4224 URL: http://www.jansmithlaw.com
Email: jsmithlawofc@indy.rr.com URL: http://www.jsmithlawofc.com
Criminal, Family and Education Law.
See Professional Biographies, INDIANAPOLIS, INDIANA

Smith, Jess M., III .... '67 '93 C.894 B.A. L.1119 J.D. 22 E. Washington St., Ste. 114
Smith, Joseph L., Jr. ....'— '95 C.210 B.A. L.347 J.D. [Ⓒ Baker&D.]
Smith, K. Clay ....'37 '64 C.602 B.B.A. L.276 J.D. Underwood Machinery Transport, Inc.
Smith, Kelly B. ....'— '02 C.679 B.A. L.347 J.D. [Ⓒ Barnes&T.] (See Pat. Sect.)
Smith, Laura Moenning, (BV) ....'66 '91 C.347 B.A. L.273 J.D. [Bingham M.]
Smith, Maggie L., (AV) .... '68 '96 C&L.37 B.A., J.D. [Ⓒ Locke R.]
Smith, Mark R., (AV) ....'59 '84 C.303 B.A. L.345 J.D. [Smith,F.M.&H.]
Smith, Michael R. '56 '94 C.880 B.E. L.347 J.D.
Coun., Env. Law Dept., Eli Lilly & Co.
Smith, N. Kent, (AV) ....'— '81 C.879 B.S. L.347 J.D. [Hall,R.K.H.&L.]
Smith, Randall D. ....'46 '76 C.188 B.A. L.347 J.D. [Christopher&T.]
Smith, Rebecca S. .... '75 '02 C&L.879 B.S., J.D. [Ⓐ Scopelitis,G.L.&H.]
Smith, Ronald C., (AV) ....'43 '68 C.347 B.S. L.345 J.D. [Stewart&I.]
Smith, Stanley H., (BV) ....'21 '56 C.108 B.S. L.421 LL.B. 76 N. Layman Ave.
Smith, Stephen D., (AV) ....'49 '75 C.347 A.B. L.345 J.D. [Krieg D.]
Smith, Stephen Lee, (AV) '53 '79 C.303 B.A. L.345 J.D.
V.P. & Sr. Atty., National City Bank, Indiana
Smith, Thomas C., (AV) .... '61 '88 C.347 B.A. L.1119 J.D. [Ice M.] (ⓞChgo., IL)
Smith, Fisher, Maas & Howard, (AV) .... 7209 North Shadeland Avenue

Smith, Theodore F., Jr.
(See Anderson)

Smithey, Stephanie Alden ....'66 '91 C.602 B.A. L.424 J.D. [Ⓒ Ice M.]
Smulyan, Jeffrey H. ....'47 '76 C&L.800 A.B., J.D. Emmis Communications
Snemis, Donald M., (AV) .... '63 '88 C.63 B.A. L.602 J.D. [Ice M.]
Snethen, John .... '62 '01 C.986 B.A. L.1119 J.D. Indiana Tax Ct.
Snyder, Clark L., (AV) ....'47 '72 C.347 A.B. L.345 J.D. [Ⓒ Henderson D.W.&D.]
Snyder, David M. '60 '85
C.303 B.A. L.1119 J.D. V.P. & Sr. Tr. Offr., Bloomington Nat. Bk.
Snyder, Jack R., (AV) ....'40 '65 C.103 A.B. L.477 LL.B. [Ice M.]
Snyder, Mary .... '66 '99 C.347 B.S. L.345 J.D. Amer. United Life Ins. Co.
Solada, Mary Elizabeth, (AV) ....'57 '82 C.347 B.S. L.345 J.D. [Bingham M.]
Solberg, Kirsten K. ....'— '96 C.311 B.A. L.477 J.D. 11 S. Meridian St.
Solida, Cary J. .... '74 '05 C.265 B.A. L.345 J.D. [Ⓐ Hannon H.&Assoc.]
Solomon, Andrew '— '90 C.477 B.A. L.94 J.D.
(adm. in NY; not adm. in IN) Indiana Univ. Sch. of Law
Somers, George W., (AV) .... '47 '79 C.747 B.A. L.145 J.D. [Wallack S.&H.]
Sommer, James K., (AV) ....'— '59 C.976 B.A. L.309 LL.B. [Ⓒ Sommer B.]
Sommer, John Stewart ....'64 '90 C.597 B.A. L.259 J.D. [Sommer&B.]

Sommer Barnard Attorneys, PC, (AV) [BR]
One Indiana Square, Suite 3500, 46204
Telephone: 317-713-3500 Fax: 317-713-3699
Email: mail@sommerbarnard.com URL: http://www.sommerbarnard.com
Edward W. Harris, III; Frederick M. King; Jerald I. Ancel; James A. Strain; Linda L. Pence; Eric R. Johnson; Robert D. Swhier, Jr.; Donald K. Densborn; Gordon L. Pittenger; Mark A. Palmer; Frank J. Deveau; Robert R. Clark; Michael C. Terrell; Thomas A. Barnard; Marlene Reich; Richard C. Richmond, III; Steven C. Shockley; John H. Sharpe; Erick D. Ponader; Robert J. Hicks; Lawrence A. Vanore; Donald C. Biggs; Gayle A. Reindl; Michael P. O'Neil; David C. Bromund; Geoffrey G. Slaughter; Philip L. McCool; Ann Carr Mackey; Edwin J. Broecker; Thomas R. DeVoe; Mary T. Doherty; Scott R. Alexander; Regina M. Sharrow; Ralph A. Caruso II; Paul T. Deignan; Richard A. Kempf; William C. Wagner; F. Anthony Paganelli; David J. Hensel; Jackie M. Bennett, Jr.; John D. Papageorge; Michelle Kaiser Bray; Blake J. Burgan; David H. Benz; Thomas F. O'Gara; Michael D. Chambers;—James R.A. Dawson; Stacey A. Huse (Not admitted in IN); Karen L. De Haan; Jeffrey J. Graham; Bradley R. Sugarman; Alexa L. Woods; Andrew T. Kight; Stephanie A. Hale; John R. Humphrey; Bradley W. Schwer; Angela M. Hopper; Andrea K. Marsh; Rod L. Michael; David J. Bayt; Ian D. Arnold; Lonnie Johnson; Hannah L. Meils; Mildred F. Krizmanich; Peter J. Prettyman; Shelley S. Fraser; Tracy N. Betz; Brian V. Powers; Jayna M. Cacioppo; Lindy B. Arwood; Michael S. Byron. Of Counsel: James K. Sommer; Dan G. Sterner; Steven H. Ancel; Jerry Williams; W. William Weeks; John K. Smeltzer; Marci A. Reddick; *Debra McVicker Lynch; Catherine R. Reese;* Richard L. Rowley; Thomas G. Burroughs; Anne M. Hamilton; Joseph W. Cade; Sean J. Fahey; Charles R. O'Keefe, Jr.; David J. Tipton; Gretchen K. Gutman; Dean E. McConnell; Stanley Talesnick; Heather McPherson; Alan M. Hux; Paul F. Kortepeter; Phillip H. Minton.
Antitrust and Trade Regulation, Banking, Bankruptcy and Debtors' and Creditors' Rights. Business and Corporate Transactions, Mergers and Acquisitions, Civil Trial and Appellate Litigation, Computer Law, Environmental Litigation and Regulatory Consultation, Debt and Equity Financing,

(This Listing Continued)

Sommer Barnard Attorneys, PC (Continued)

Probate and Estate Planning, Administration, Federal and State Income Tax Planning, Consultation and Litigation, Federal and State Securities Regulation, Telecommunications; Utility Regulatory Law, Franchising and Licensing, Insurance Regulation and Insolvencies, International Law, Labor and Employment, ERISA Law and Litigation, Collective Bargaining and Arbitration, Employment Discrimination Law, Real Estate, Technology Based Transactions, Intellectual Property, Public Finance, Plaintiff Litigation, International, Agricultural Law.
Representative Clients: Comerica Bank; Federal Express; Kimball International; Monsanto; TRW, Inc.
North Office: 8888 Keystone Crossing, Suite 1400, Indianapolis, Indiana, 46240-4609. Telephone: 317-844-4744. Fax: 317-844-4780.
See Professional Biographies, INDIANAPOLIS, INDIANA

Sommer & Benedetto LLC ....3801 N. Meridian St.
Sommers, Sandra J., (AV) '55 '80
C.108 A.B. L.345 J.D. Assoc.Gen.Coun., Eli Lilly & Co.
Sonneborn, H. Andrew, (BV) ....'48 '72 C.602 B.B.A. L.1119 J.D. [O'Koon H.]
Soofi, Rabeh M. A. ....'— '04 C.477 B.A. L.602 J.D. [Ⓐ Ice M.]
Sorg, Terrence J., (BV) ....'61 '97 C.63 B.Arch.B.S. L.347 J.D. [Brooks,K.&S.]
Soshnick, Andrew Z., (AV) .... '62 '88 C&L.597 B.A., J.D. [Baker&D.]
Sosin, Theodore M., (BV) ....'43 '69 L.345 J.D. 200 E. Washington St., Ste. W506
Soskin, Ronald M., (AV) .... '48 '74 C&L.659 B.S., J.D. [Bose M.&E.]
Southwick, Jerlyn S. .... '50 '91 C.347 B.A.B.S. L.1119 J.D. [Ⓐ Feiwell&H.]
Sowers, Edward E. '42 '91
C.894 A.B. L.1119 J.D. [Ⓒ Woodard,E.M.M.&H.] (See Pat. Sect.)
Spadorcia, Jon F., (AV) ....'— '75 C.106 B.S. L.347 J.D. [Hall,R.K.H.&L.]
Spalding, Rosemary G., (AV) '50 '85 C.679 B.S. L.846 J.D.
Dep. Comr. & Gen. Coun., Dept. Envirl. Mgmt.
Spalding, William Joseph ....'76 '03 C&L.347 B.A., J.D. [Ⓐ Hoover H.B.&H.]

Spangler, Jennings & Dougherty, P.C., (AV)
9200 Keystone Crossing Suite 410, 46240 ⊙
Telephone: 317-571-7690 Facsimile: 317-571-7686
Email: sjd.indy@gte.net URL: http://www.sjdlaw.com
—Michael L. Carter.
Gregory A. Purvis.
General Trial and Appellate Practice. Administrative, Banking, Bankruptcy, Business Reorganizations, Business Transactions, Civil Rights, Commercial, Construction, Corporate, Creditors' Rights, Criminal Litigation, Family/Domestic Relations, Drug and Device, Eminent Domain, Environmental, ERISA and Employee Benefits, Probate and Estate Planning and Administration, Fire/Arson, Guardianships, Health Care, Insurance, Labor and Employment, Municipal and Zoning, Personal Injury, Product Liability, Professional Liability, Medical Malpractice Defense, Real Estate, School, Federal, State and Local Taxation, Toxic Torts, Transportation, Workers Compensation, Land Development.
Merrillville, Indiana Office: 8396 Mississippi Street, 46410-6398. Telephone: 219-769-2323. Facsimile: 219-769-5007.
Valparaiso, Indiana Office: 150 Lincolnway, Suite 3001. Telephone: 219-462-6151. FAX: 219-477-4935.
See Professional Biographies, INDIANAPOLIS, INDIANA

Sparrenberger, William H., (AV) ....'22 '50 C.347 L.345 LL.B. 320 N. Meridian St.
Sparrow, Calvin N. .... '22 '60 C.215 B.S. L.424 J.D. 10804 Preston Dr.‡
Spear, Robert S., (BV) .... '47 '72 C.894 A.B. L.145 J.D. Chf. Coun., Ind. Atty. Gen. Off.
Spears, Timothy Paul '54 '90 C.846 B.A. L.150 J.D.
(adm. in OH; not adm. in IN) Dir., Lit., Anthem, Inc.
Spector, Jennifer M. '71 '98
C.973 B.A. L.347 J.D. Marion County Health & Hospital Corp.
Speer, Kevin P., (BV) ....'— '89 C.679 B.A. L.879 J.D. [Hall,R.K.H.&L.]
Spike Fordice, Hillary ....'— '03 C.1375 B.A. L.477 J.D. [Ⓐ Barnes&T.]
Spinrad, Ruben .... '54 '83 C.112 B.A. L.809 J.D. 9330 Zionville Rd.
Spisak, Susanne M. ....'70 '96 C.108 B.A. L.602 J.D. Staff Atty., Eli Lilly & Co.
Spitko, E. Gary '65 '92 C.188 A.B. L.228 J.D.
(adm. in PA; not adm. in IN) Asst. Prof. of Law, Indiana Univ.
Sporleder, Dale E. .... '40 '67 C.593 A.B. L.502 J.D. [Ⓒ Tabbert H.E.&W.]
Springer, Cynthia K., (AV) ....'57 '97 C&L.347 B.M.E., J.D. [Ⓐ Baker&D.]
Springer, Marilee J. ....'— '96 C.679 B.A. L.345 J.D. [Ⓒ Ice M.]
Springer, Ross E. .... '40 '66 C.347 B.S. L.345 J.D. Dist. Coun., I.R.S.
Springer, Steven E., (AV) .... '48 '79 C.679 B.S. L.345 J.D. [Kightlinger&G.]
Sprunger, Barton T., (AV) .... '46 '75 C.679 B.S. L.477 J.D. [Ice M.]
Spurlock, Ben L., Jr. ....'24 '85 C.347 B.S. L.345 J.D. 320 N. Meridian St.
Squier, Robert M., Jr. ....'67 '92 C&L.347 B.S., J.D. Corp. Coun., Anthem, Inc.
Stackhouse, Dale E., (AV) .... '62 '88 C.210 B.A. L.309 J.D. [Ice M.]
Stage, Gary L., (AVⓉ) ....'49 '76 C.945 A.B. L.383 J.D. [Ⓒ Ice M.]
Stall, R. Niven .... '08 '31 C&L.477 B.A., LL.B. 1802 E. 54th St.‡
Stallwood, Patricia Rose ....'70 '00 C.323 B.A. L.345 J.D. [Stallwood]
Stallwood, Robert K., (BV) ....'33 '68 C.679 B.S. L.345 J.D. 6435 Castleway W. Dr.
Stallwood Law Office .... 6435 Castleway West Drive
Stanley, Robert K., (AV) ....'56 '81 C.63 A.B. L.1119 J.D. [Baker&D.]
Staples, Ralph W., Jr. ....'62 '87 C.293 B.A. L.1119 J.D. [Ⓐ Clark,Q.M.S.&G.]
Stapleton, Tara J. ....'74 '00 C.1119 B.S. L.345 J.D. [Ⓐ Bingham M.]
Stark, Gregg J. .... '65 '91 C.347 B.A. L.209 J.D. [Stark]
Stark, Jack L., Jr. ....'— '93 C&L.347 B.A., J.D. [Ⓒ Barnes&T.]
Stark, John C., (AV) ....'35 '64 C.210 B.A. L.345 J.D. [Ⓒ Stark D.&S.]
Stark, Paul ....'29 '77 C.696 Ph.D. L.345 J.D. Pres. & CEO, Intl. Clinical Resch. Corp.

Stark Doninger & Smith, (AV)
Suite 700, 50 South Meridian Street, 46204
Telephone: 317-638-2400 Fax: 317-633-6618; 633-6619
Members of Firm: Bruce E. Smith; John W. Van Buskirk; Richard W. Dyar; Patricia Seasor Bailey; Brian J. Tuohy; Mark A. Bailey; Lewis E. Willis, Jr.; Thomas A. Brodnik. Associates: Richard B. Kaufman; Anthony B. Ratliff; John J. Moore; Dennis R. Tyler; Donald J. Smith; Danica L. Eyler. Senior Counsel: John C. Stark. Counsel: William K. Byrum; Clarence H. Doninger; Gregory S. Fehribach; Robert D. Maas.
General Civil and Business Litigation, Acquisitions and Mergers, Corporate and Business Transactions, Real Estate, Estate Planning and Administration, Commercial Lending, Family, Employment, Americans with Disabilities Act Compliance, Environmental, Health Care, Employee Benefits, Zoning and Land Use and Creditors' Rights and Bankruptcy Law.
Reference: National Bank of Indianapolis.
See Professional Biographies, INDIANAPOLIS, INDIANA

Stark Law Offices, P.C. ....450 E. 96th St., Ste. 500
Starkey, Martha T., (AV) ....'— '81 C.249 B.S. L.345 J.D. [Starkey]
Starkey, Richard C., (AV) ....'— '85 C.150 B.A. L.1119 J.D. [Barnes&T.]

Starkey Law Group, PC, (AV) [BR]
30 South Meridian Street Suite 850, 46204
Telephone: 317-705-8888 Facsimile: 317-705-8884
Email: mts@starkey-law.com URL: http://www.starkey-law.com
Martha T. Starkey;—Hong-Sik Chung; Lisa M. Adler; Jussara Silva; Mark T. Bernhardt.
Estate Planning, Wills and Probate, Trusts and Estates, Estate and Trust Administration, Probate and Fiduciary Litigation, Business and International Law, Real Estate.
See Professional Biographies, INDIANAPOLIS, INDIANA

Staser, Aaron M. ....'— '04 C&L.347 B.S., J.D. [Ⓐ Barnes&T.]

Staton, Robert H. ....'25 '55 C.347 A.B. L.345 J.D. Ct. App. J.
Statz, Brian Andrew ....'69 '94 C.347 B.A. L.477 J.D. [Lewis&K.]
Stautz, Jane Ann Siggelkow ....'62 '89 C.350 B.S. L.477 J.D. 9330 Zionville Rd.
Stayte, Jeffrey L. .... '72 '02 C.108 B.S. L.345 J.D. [Ⓐ Clark,Q.M.S.&G.]
Stayton, Thomas G., (AV) .... '48 '73 C.473 B.S. L.477 J.D. [Baker&D.]
Stearsman, Michael '65 '90 C.679 B.A. L.1059 J.D.
Suite #100, 333 N. Pennsylvania St.
Steck, Hans W., (AV) ....'51 '76 C.894 B.A. L.910 J.D. [Bingham M.]

Steckler & Ryan, (AV)
An Association, Not A Partnership
Chamber of Commerce Building, 320 North Meridian Street, Suite 901, 46204
Telephone: 317-264-1000 Fax: 317-264-1004
URL: http://www.stecklerryan.com
W. Rudolph Steckler (1941-2000); David J. Ryan.
General Practice. Civil and Criminal Trials and Appeals, Tax, Business, Real Estate, Probate and Estate Planning.
See Professional Biographies, INDIANAPOLIS, INDIANA

Steegmann, Edward P., (BV) ....'64 '88 C.347 B.A. L.1119 J.D. [Ⓒ Ice M.]
Steele, Michael C. ....'78 '03 C.63 B.S. L.472 J.D. [Ⓐ Ice M.]
Steele, Sydney L., (AV) .... '39 '64 C.679 B.S.M.E. L.1119 J.D. [Ⓒ Kroger,G.&R.]
Steele, Walter ....'47 '73 NLRB
Stefanovich, Melissa A. ....'69 '95 C.63 B.A. L.879 J.D. Simon Property Group
Stein, Jay David ....'64 '90 C&L.37 B.S., J.D. Sandor Develop. Co.
Steinbart, Neal W., (AV) .... '— '82 C.747 B.A. L.597 J.D. [Barnes&T.]
Steiner, David L., (AV) ....'50 '76 C.347 A.B. L.1119 J.D. 219 State House
Steinkamp, Brian G., (AV) '65 '90 C.221 B.S.B.A. L.352 J.D.
Gen. Coun. & Corp. Secy., Contour Hardening, Inc.
Steinke, Thomas V. ....'62 '97 C.1060 B.A. L.602 J.D. [Steinke]
Steinke Law Office ....7505 North Michigan Road
Steinmetz, Christopher ....'60 '03 C.74 B.S. L.345 J.D. [Ⓐ McClure M.D.&H.]
Steinmetz, Harry J. ....'26 '52 C.108 B.S. L.472 J.D. 2441 Weslynn Dr.‡
Stella, Kevin A. ....'— '02 C.1119 B.A. L.602 J.D. [Ⓐ Hall,R.K.H.&L.]
Stemerick, David M. ....'54 '97 C.150 B.S. L.1161 J.D. Lilly Corp. Ctr. (Pat.)
Stephen, Christopher C. .... '76 '01 C.210 B.A. L.345 J.D. [Ⓐ Hannon H.&Assoc.]

Stephens, A. Douglas, (BV) '59 '88 C.347 B.A. L.345 J.D.
9211 Crawfordsville Road, 46234
Telephone: 317-299-5297 Fax: 317-299-5005
Email: indylaws@aol.com URL: http://www.indylawfirms.com
Criminal Law, Driving While Intoxicated, Drug Crimes, Traffic Violations, Felonies Misdemeanors, Real Estate, Collections, Debtor and Creditor, Bankruptcy, Family Law, Child Support, Adoptions, Wills and Probate, Trusts and Estates, Business Law.
See Professional Biographies, INDIANAPOLIS, INDIANA

Stephenson, James S., (AV) ....'53 '79 C.597 B.A. L.930 J.D. [Stephenson M.&S.]
Stephenson, Mark T. .... '— '05 C.679 B.S. L.1218 J.D. [Ⓐ Woodard,E.M.M.&H.]
Stephenson, P. Jason .... '— '99 C.827 B.A. L.345 J.D. [Ⓐ Barnes&T.]

Stephenson Morow & Semler, P.C., (AV)
8710 North Meridian Street Suite 200, 46260-5307
Telephone: 317-844-3830 Fax: 317-573-4194
URL: http://www.stephlaw.com
James S. Stephenson; Michael R. Morow; Ronald J. Semler;—Tonya M. Aretz (1959-1999); G. Richard Potter (1946-2001); Mark A. Holloway; Rosemary L. Borek; Wayne E. Uhl; Gary J. Marksberry. Of Counsel: William W. Kurnik.
Governmental and Insurance Defense Law.
See Professional Biographies, INDIANAPOLIS, INDIANA

Stern, John H. ....'26 '53 C.347 L.345 LL.B. 1076 W. Southport Rd.
Sterner, Dan G., (AV) ....'— '62 C.597 B.A. L.1119 J.D. [Ⓒ Sommer B.]
Stevenot, James W. '62 '93 C.108 B.S. L.347 J.D.
Assistant General Counsel, Rolls Royce Allison
Stevens, Scott J., (BV) '52 '77
C.475 B.S.E.E. L.705 J.D. [Woodard,E.M.M.&H.] (See Pat. Sect.)
Stevens, Tamatha A. ....'68 '93 C.63 B.S. L.347 J.D. [Stevens&Assoc.]
Stevens & Associates, P.C. ....3755 East 82nd Street, Suite 200
Stevenson, Christopher G. ....'74 '04 [Ⓐ Wilson,K.&W.]
Steward, Lawrence A. ...'50 '79 C&L.851 B.S., J.D. [Ⓒ Brinks H.G.&L.] (See Pat. Sect.)
Stewart, Amy L. ....'63 '99 C.347 B.S. L.357 J.D. [Bingham M.]
Stewart, Carli E. ....'— '01 C.679 B.S.M.E. L.345 J.D. [Ⓐ Barnes&T.] (See Pat. Sect.)
Stewart, Ian L. ....'75 '01 C.210 B.A. L.74 J.D. [Ⓐ Locke R.]
Stewart, John L., (BV) ....'56 '84 C.347 B.S. L.345 J.D. 144 North Delaware Street
Stewart, Judith A., (AV) ....'57 '82 C.108 B.A. L.345 J.D. U.S. Atty.
Stewart, Kent O., (AV) ....'38 '64 C.108 B.S. L.345 J.D. The Mediation Group, LLC
Stewart, Mark J. ....'63 '99 C.108 B.S. L.345 J.D. Patent Atty., Eli Lilly & Co.
Stewart, Peter B., (AV) .... '41 '66 C.108 A.B. L.1119 LL.B. [Stewart&I.]
Stewart, Timothy L., (CV) ....'51 '84 C.347 B.A. L.345 J.D. [Lewis&K.]

Stewart & Irwin, Professional Corporation, (AV)
Two Market Square Center, Suite 1100, 251 East Ohio Street, 46204-2147
Telephone: 317-639-5454 Fax: 317-632-1319
Email: hr@stewart-irwin.com URL: http://www.silegal.com
Richard E. Aikman, Jr.; Stephen W. Sutherlin; Ronald C. Smith; Donn H. Wray; James W. Brauer; Douglas R. Brown; Keith A. Gaston; Anne E. Becker; Edward G. Bielski; Thomas W. Blessing; Glenn D. Bowman; Chad J. Bradford; William R. Brown; Larry R. Champion; Sonia S. Chen; Robert D. Emmerson; Richard L. Fairchild; William R. Fatout; Fred W. Garver; Andrea L. Hermer; Edward B. Hopper, II; Michael K. Irwin; William N. Ivers; Peter S. Kovacs; Geoffrey C. Lambert; Justin W. Leverton; Cynthia M. Locke; John T. Loftus (Not admitted in IN); Jill L. McCrory; Charles R. Mercer, Jr.; Roderick H. Morgan; Mark R. Nelson; Pamela A. Paige; Stephen J. Peters; Lisa Cross Price; Richard H. Riegner; David I. Rubin; Michael J. Rusnak; Mary F. Schmid; Bradley W. Skolnik; Peter B. Stewart; Philip R. Thompson; William A. Wick; Mark E. Wirey.
General Civil Practice. Insurance, Administrative, Business, Taxation, Corporate, Probate, Estate Planning. Environmental, Trial and Appellate Practice, Bankruptcy and Creditor's Rights. International Law and Gaming Law, Transactions, Mergers and Acquisitions, Employment, Labor Law, Real Estate, Medical Malpractice Defense, Automotive Retail, Municipal Finance, Bond and Securities, Banking and Lending, Telecommunications and Utility, Transportation, Insurance Coverage.
See Professional Biographies, INDIANAPOLIS, INDIANA

Stikeleather, Michael H. ....'54 '85 C.1128 B.S. L.347 J.D. Banc One Indiana Corp.
Stilwell, James W., (AV) .... '34 '62 C.108 L.345 LL.B. 3815 River Crossing Parkway
Stimson, Judith N., (AV) '42 '82 C.739 B.S. L.345 J.D.
111 Monument Circle, Suite 3300
Stippler, A. David, (AV) ....'46 '73 C.999 A.B. L.347 J.D. [Ⓒ Bingham M.]
Stober, Wilson S., (AV) ....'40 '65 C.755 B.A. L.912 J.D. [Ⓒ Goodin A.&M.]
Stoehr, Sam A., (BV) .... '44 '70 C.347 B.A. L.345 J.D. 6100 N. Keystone Ave., Ste. 325
Stoffregen, Phillip J., (AV) '58 '84
C.347 B.S. L.1119 J.D. Exec. V.P., Pedcor Investments, L.L.C.
Stohler, Dustin D. ....'77 '03 C.894 B.A. L.345 J.D. [Ⓐ Baker&D.]
Stolle, Dennis P. ....'— '97 C.734 B.S. L.546 J.D. [Ⓐ Barnes&T.]
Stone, Lisa A., (AV) .... '54 '80 C.347 B.A. L.345 J.D. [Ice M.]
Stoner, Ralph V., Jr. '53 '81 C.932 B.B.A. L.1187 J.D.
(adm. in SC; not adm. in IN) Stokely-Van Camp, Inc.

Stotler, Katherine J. ....'— '02 C.347 B.A. L.1119 J.D. [Ⓑ Barnes&T.]
Stowell, Jon K. .... '62 '93 C.265 B.A. L.347 J.D. Staff Coun., Safeco Insurance
Stowers, Gregory A. .... '61 '87 C.329 B.S. L.345 J.D. Suite #400, One Virginia Avenue
Stowers, Scott B. .... '66 '98 C.63 B.S. L.347 J.D. Dep. Pros., Marion Co. Pros. Off.
Strain, James A., (AV) ....'— '69 C.347 A.B. L.1119 J.D. [Sommer B.]
Strain, Jana K. .... '65 '98 C.346 B.A. L.345 J.D. [Price W.R.&D.]
Straith-Miller, Edward A. .... '10 '37 C.210 A.B. L.1119 LL.B. [Ⓒ Osborn H.&L.]
Strawbridge, Steven J., (AV) .... '48 '73 C.347 B.S. L.345 J.D. [Locke R.]
Strenski, James P., (AV) .... '67 '94 C.276 B.S.F.S. L.1119 J.D. [Bingham M.]
Strickland-Padgett, Jennifer A. ....'76 '01 C.597 B.A. L.1119 J.D. [Ⓐ Zeigler C.&K.]
Stroble, Larry J., (AV) ....'— '76 C.347 A.B. L.1119 J.D. [Barnes&T.]
Strodtman, Lawrence E. .... '48 '93 C&L.347 B.A., J.D. 384 Buck Creek Rd.
Strohmeyer, Robert W., Jr., Attorney at Law, (AV) '58 '85
C.871 B.S.M.E. L.345 J.D. 3815 River Crossing Pkwy., Ste. 100
Stroud, Kenneth M. ....'35 '61 C.347 A.B. L.1119 LL.B. Prof., Ind. Univ. School of Law
Stuaan, Mark D., (BV) .... '— '81 C.900 A.B. L.801 J.D. [Barnes&T.]

Stuart & Branigin LLP, (AV)
Suite 640, 8888 Keystone Crossing, 46240 ⊙
Telephone: 317-574-7245 Fax: 317-574-7050
Email: sb@stuartlaw.com URL: http://www.stuartlaw.com
Members of Firm: John M. Stuckey; Bruce A. Hugon; Geoffrey L. Blazi. Of Counsel: Nicholas C. Nizamoff. Associate: Trenten D. Klingerman.
General Practice. Trials and Appeals. Administrative, Banking, Commercial, Computer, Construction, Copyright and Trademark, Corporation, Creditors' Rights, Environmental, Estate Planning, Hospital and Health Care, Insurance, Labor and Employment, Pension, Probate, Railroad, Real Estate, Securities, Taxation, Utility and Zoning Law.
Lafayette, Indiana Office: 300 Main Street, Suite 900, P.O. Box 1010. Telephone: 765-423-1561. Fax: 765-742-8175.
See Professional Biographies, INDIANAPOLIS, INDIANA

Stuckey, Erin S. Bailey ....'68 '99 C&L.347 B.A., J.D. Corp. Atty., USA Group, Inc.
Stuckey, John M., (BV) .... '64 '89 C.679 B.A. L.945 J.D. [Stuart&B.] ⊙
Stucky, Natalie J., (BV) ....'62 '89 C.347 B.A. L.1119 J.D. [Bose M.&E.]
Stump, Yasmin L. ....'— '89 C&L.347 B.A., J.D. 10401 North Meridian Street
Sturbaum, Karl R., (BV) ....'51 '86 C.303 B.A. L.1119 J.D. [Bose M.&E.]
Stutzman, Dana E. ....'— '02 C.347 B.A. L.345 J.D. [Ⓐ Hall,R.K.H.&L.]
Subramaniam, Sujatha '— '00 C.999 B.S. L.602 LL.M.
(adm. in MI; not adm. in IN; Pat.) Roche Diagnostics Corp.
Suess, David A. ....'68 '97 C.145 B.A. L.347 J.D. [Bose M.&E.]
Suess, William E., (BV) ....'30 '59 C.108 B.A. L.345 LL.B. 7202 N. Shadeland Ave.
Sugarman, Bradley R. ....'— '98 C.893 B.A. L.1194 J.D. [Ⓐ Sommer B.]
Sukhapinda, Kitisri ....'— '02 C.576 B.S. L.1119 J.D. [Ⓐ Barnes&T.] (See Pat. Sect.)
Sukurs, Charles P. ....'— '02 C.1119 B.S./B.A. L.880 J.D. [Ⓐ Hall,R.K.H.&L.]
Sullivan, Anthony C., (BV) .... '— '89 C.679 B.S. L.1119 J.D. [Barnes&T.]
Sullivan, Edward W. '22 '50 C.999 L.446 LL.B.
(adm. in MD; not adm. in IN) 500 N. Meridian St.‡
Sullivan, Frank, Jr. ....'50 '82 C.197 A.B. L.1119 J.D. Assoc. Supm. Ct. Jus.

Sullivan, John J., (AV) '51 '76 C.321 A.B. L.1119 J.D.
8900 Keystone Crossing Suite 1250, 46240
Telephone: 317-574-4500 Fax: 317-574-4501
Email: jsullivan@millermuller.com URL: http://www.johnsullivanlaw.com
General Civil Litigation in all State and Federal Courts. Bankruptcy, Government Relations, Health Care, Medical Malpractice, Personal Injury, Automobile Accidents, Wrongful Death, Products Liability, Wills and Probate, Estate Planning, Trusts and Estates, Guardianship, Asset Protection, Insurance, General Negligence and Trials and Appeals.
Representative Client: Crawford and Co.
See Professional Biographies, INDIANAPOLIS, INDIANA

Sullivan, Mark K., (AV) .... '52 '79 C.730 B.S. L.421 J.D. [Ⓒ Tabbert H.E.&W.]
Sullivan, Patrick D. ....'32 '58 C&L.902 B.A., LL.B. Ct. of App. J.
Sullivan, Richard C. ....'59 '85 C.602 B.A. L.345 J.D. Golden Rule Insurance Co.
Sullivan, Timothy W. ....'48 '73 C.894 B.A. L.345 J.D. [Ⓒ Ice M.]
Sundquist, Mark D. ....'71 '02 C.347 B.S. L.569 J.D. 608 E. Market St.
Sutherlin, Michael K., (AV) ....'44 '74 C.846 B.B.A. L.345 J.D. P.O. Box 441095
Sutherlin, Stephen W., (BV) ....'37 '65 C.210 B.A. L.345 J.D. [Stewart&I.]
Sutton, Ann M. ....'63 '91 C.346 B.S. L.347 J.D. Pub. Def. Agcy., Marion Co.
Swank, Eric ....'73 '99 C.747 B.A. L.477 J.D. [Ⓐ Ice M.]
Swanson, Richard J., (AV) ....'51 '80 C.676 B.A. L.597 J.D. [Macey S.&A.]
Swarbrick, John B., Jr., (AV) ....'54 '80 C.602 B.A. L.813 J.D. [Baker&D.]
Sward, Robert E. .... '26 '68 C.108 B.S. L.345 J.D. 9249 W. McCarty St.‡
Swathwood, Jason Michael .... '70 '97 C.347 B.A. L.345 J.D. Coun., Irwin Mtge. Corp.
Swedarsky, Mitchell A. ....'76 '02 C&L.74 B.S., J.D. [Schiller&S.]
Swedo, Keith J. ....'63 '95 C.679 B.S. L.345 J.D. [Ⓐ Baker&D.] (See Pat. Sect.)
Sweeney, James R., II, (CV) '— '96 C.871 B.S. L.602 J.D.
[Barnes&T.] (See Pat. Sect.)
Sweeney, Jamie R. ....'— '04 C.63 B.S. L.345 J.D. [Ⓐ Price W.R.&D.]
Sweeney, Marguerite M., (AV) .... '58 '83 C.679 B.A. L.345 J.D. Asst. Corp. Coun.
Sweeney, Paul C. ....'72 '97 C.347 B.A. L.345 J.D. [Harrison&M.]
Sweet, Nancy D. .... '66 '91 C.108 B.S. L.1119 J.D. Indianapolis Life
Sweetin, Doris L. ....'63 '95 C.942 B.A. L.150 J.D. [Tyra&C.]
Swenson, Houston L. ....'30 '54 C.679 B.S. L.1119 LL.B. 7327 Harbour Pt. (Pat.)
Swhear, John C. '61 '94 C.63 B.A. L.347 J.D.
Asst. Gen. Coun., American United Life Insurance Co.
Swhier, Claudia V., (AV) .... '— '75 C.976 B.A. L.309 J.D. [Barnes&T.]
Swhier, Robert D., Jr., (AV) .... '— '75 C.679 B.S. L.309 J.D. [Sommer B.]
Swider, David L., (AV) ....'53 '78 C.347 B.S. L.345 J.D. [Bose M.&E.]
Swift, Michael A. ....'57 '94 C.854 B.S. L.345 J.D. [Ice M.] (See Pat. Sect.)
Switzer, Dayna L. ....'— '01 C.234 B.S. L.734 J.D. [Ⓐ Wooden&M.]
Sylvia, Alexandra S. ....'71 '97 C&L.347 B.A., J.D. [Plews S.R.&B.]
Symmes, Charles W., (AV) .... '17 '41 C.108 B.A. L.178 LL.B. [Voyles,Z.P.H.&M.]
Szostak, John F. ....'49 '75 C.276 B.S/B.A. L.1019 J.D. 7800 Shelby St.
Tabbert, Don A., (AV) .... '28 '53 C.347 A.B. L.1119 LL.B. [Ⓒ Tabbert H.E.&W.]

Tabbert Hahn Earnest & Weddle LLP, (AV)
Suite 1900, One Indiana Square, 46204-2032
Telephone: 317-639-5444 Fax: 317-639-5232
Email: thew@tabberthahn.com URL: http://www.tabberthahn.com
Gregory F. Hahn; Lante K. Earnest; Robert G. Weddle; Judy M. Tyrrell; E. Scott Treadway; David A. Shelton; Matthew W. Conner; Robert S. Daniels;—Mark J. Pizur; Joan Isaacs; Linda H. Havel; Charles R. Whybrew; Chad T. Walker; Kevin M. Quinn; David J. Duncan. Of Counsel: Don A. Tabbert; Joseph W. Hammes; Mark K. Sullivan; Dale E. Sporleder; Darla Y. Williams.
Civil and Criminal Litigation (Complex), Medical Malpractice Defense, Drug Liability, Product Liability, Legal Malpractice, Healthcare Law, Estate Planning, Estate Administration, Gaming Industry Law, Environmental Law, Family Law, Business Law, Housing Law, Real Estate Law, Corporate Law, Commercial Litigation, International Business, Eminent Domain, Outdoor Advertising.
See Professional Biographies, INDIANAPOLIS, INDIANA

Tabler, Bryan G., (AV) .... '— '72 C.674 A.B. L.976 J.D. [Ⓒ Barnes&T.]

Tabler, Norman G., Jr., (AV) '44 '71
C.674 B.A. L.178 J.D. Sr. V.P., Clarian Health Partners, Inc.
Tabor, Gordon E., (AV) ... '44 '70 C.108 B.S. L.345 J.D. [Tabor]
Tabor, Jeffrey S., (BV) ... '63 '90 C.347 B.A. L.345 J.D. [A Tabor]
Tabor, Roy T., (AV) ... '52 '79 C.880 B.A. L.345 J.D. [Tabor]
Tabor Law Firm, (AV) ... Suite 1990, 151 North Delaware Street
Taggart, Robert L., (AV) ... '57 '85 C.1024 B.S. L.345 J.D. [Bingham M.]
Talbot, Monika Prekopa ... '63 '93 C.705 B.A. L.347 J.D. Atty. Gen. Off.
Talesnick, Stanley, (AV) ... '— '50 C.347 A.B. L.1119 J.D. [C Sommer B.]
Tambasco, Ralph L. ... '52 '84 C.999 B.A. L.1370 J.D. [Tambasco&Assoc.]
Tambasco & Associates, PC ... 1 N. Pennsylvania St., Ste. 500
Tamulonis, Peter G., (AV) ... '50 '75 C.108 B.A. L.880 J.D. [Kightlinger&G.]
Tankersley, Regan E. ... '— '02 C.339 B.S. L.74 J.D. [A Hall,R.K.H.&L.]
Tanner, Jill Harris, (BV) '60 '85 C.347 B.S. L.345 J.D.
Exec. Dir., IN Health Facility Financing Auth.
Tanner, John Joseph, (AV) ... '61 '87 C.473 B.A. L.345 J.D. [Baker&D.]
Tanselle, John W., (AV) ... '56 '81 C.347 B.A. L.345 J.D. [Krieg D.]
Tarter, Scott E., (AV) ... '62 '88 C.210 B.A. L.1119 J.D. [Bose M.&E.]
Taylor, Brent D., (AV) ... '57 '82 C.108 B.A. L.309 J.D. [Baker&D.]
Taylor, Christopher R. ... '74 '02 C.210 B.A. L.879 J.D. [A Lewis&K.]
Taylor, David Robert '66 '95 C.957 B.A. L.374 J.D.
(adm. in FL; not adm. in IN) 11403 Cherry Lake Cir.
Taylor, Gregory G. ... '70 '97 C.347 B.A. L.345 J.D. [C Locke R.]
Taylor, Jay G., (AV) ... '40 '67 C.150 B.S.M.E. L.1119 J.D. [Ice M.] (See Pat. Sect.)
Taylor, John E., (AV) ... '54 '80 C.63 B.S. L.345 J.D. [Bingham M.]
Taylor, Katherine E. ... '74 '02 C.992 B.A. L.802 J.D. [A Bose M.&E.]
Taylor, Laura K. ... '64 '90 C.108 B.S. L.345 J.D. [A Riley B.&E.]
Taylor, R. Jay, Jr. ... '70 '96 C&L.692 B.A., J.D. [A Scopelitis,G.L.&H.]
Taylor, Rodney V., (AV) ... '47 '73 C.339 A.B. L.345 J.D. [Christopher&T.]
Taylor, Walter C., Jr., (AV) ... '21 '48 C.790 A.B. L.178 LL.B. Lilly Corp. Ctr.
Taylor & Aust, P.C. ... 12029 E. Washington Street (Pat.)
Tempel, Angela E. ... '71 '98 C&L.347 B.S., J.D. [A Bose M.&E.]
Tempel, Jonathan T. ... '72 '98 C.347 B.A. L.339 J.D. Assoc. Gen. Coun., Thomson Inc.
Temple, David A., (BV) ... '69 '94 C&L.347 B.S., J.D. [Drewry S.V.]
Temple, Victoria J. Schneider ... '69 '96 C.602 B.A. L.607 J.D. The Schneider Corp.
Tenenbaum, David N. ... '54 '83 C.1111 B.A. L.809 J.D. American United Life Ins. Co.
Terrell, Michael C., (AV) ... '— '84 C.347 B.S. L.345 J.D. [Sommer B.]
Terrell, Stephen M., (AV) ... '52 '80 C.63 B.A. L.345 J.D. [C Landman&B.]
Terry, Jennifer Wheeler ... '69 '98 C.679 B.S. L.347 J.D. [Lewis&K.]
Terry, Stephen W., Jr., (AV) ... '22 '54 C.722 B.A. L.976 LL.B. 300 N. Meridian St.
Terzo, Carol Lynn, (AV) ... '53 '82 C.347 B.S. L.345 J.D. 200 E. Washington St.
Teska, Adina A. ... '65 '96 C.388 B.A. L.1119 J.D. [O'Koon H.]
Tesmer, Stephen K. ... '64 '91 C&L.347 B.A., J.D. Dep. Pros. Atty.
Tew, Kipper V., (BV) ... '61 '89 C.347 B.S. L.345 J.D. [Krieg D.]
Thar, John J., (AV) ... '48 '75 C.932 B.A. L.345 J.D. [Ice M.]
Tharp, Kevin N. ... '75 '00 C.347 B.S. L.345 J.D. [A Riley B.&E.]
Theising, David J., (AV) ... '54 '80 C.347 A.B. L.1119 J.D. [Christopher&T.]
Thiemrodt, Linda M. ... '61 '91 C.679 B.A. L.347 J.D. P.O. Box 30337
Thomas, Dennis L., Jr., (BV) '50 '77 C.347 B.A. L.1209 J.D.
151 North Delaware Street
Thomas, Jennifer A. ... '74 '99 C.92 B.A. L.1119 J.D. [A Ice M.]
Thomas, Joseph A., (BV) ... '29 '63 C.679 B.S.M.E. L.345 J.D. [Thomas]
Thomas, Robert P., (BV) ... '52 '77 C.347 B.S. L.345 J.D. [Thomas]
Thomas, Ross G. ... '69 '95 C.861 B.A. L.345 J.D. 3601 N. Pennsylvania
Thomas, Timothy N. '54 '90
C.679 B.S. L.347 J.D. [Woodard,E.M.M.&H.] (See Pat. Sect.)
Thomas Law Office, (BV) ... 7800 Shelby St.
Thompson, Bradley Merrill, (AV) ... '61 '86 C.339 B.A. L.477 J.D. [Baker&D.]
Thompson, Gayla ... '58 '90 C.265 N.S. L.347 J.D. Jud. Clk. to App. Ct.
Thompson, Jennifer K. ... '68 '94 C.347 B.A. L.201 J.D. [Bingham M.]
Thompson, Merrill S., (AV) ... '30 '57 C&L.339 A.B., J.D. [C Baker&D.]
Thompson, Milton O., (BV) ... '54 '79 C.967 B.A. L.1119 J.D. 7160 Zionsville Road
Thompson, P. Kevin ... '49 '83 C.347 A.B. L.345 J.D. [C Plews S.R.&B.]
Thompson, Philip R. ... '55 '84 C.347 B.A. L.345 J.D. [A Stewart&I.]
Thompson, Robert C., Jr., (AV) ... '48 '74 C.347 B.S. L.345 J.D. [Meils,T.D.&B.]
Thompson, William F., (BV) '40 '67
C.894 A.B. L.1119 J.D. 3500 DePauw Boulevard, Suite 1074
Thompson, William H., (AV) ... '— '87 C&L.347 B.S., J.D. [Hall,R.K.H.&L.]
Thoms, William F., Jr., (BV) ... '37 '63 L.345 LL.B. 120 E. Market St., Ste. 700
Thornburg, Robert B., (BV) ... '70 '96 C.63 B.S. L.347 J.D. [A Locke R.]
Thornburgh, John R., (AV) ... '55 '80 C.210 B.A. L.339 J.D. [Ice M.]
Thornton, Lucy A. ... '59 '02 C.347 B.S.N. L.201 J.D. [A Miller M.M.&K.]
Thornton, Steven W., (AV) ... '— '83 C.473 B.S. L.608 J.D. [Barnes&T.]
Thorp, Joel W. ... '79 '04 C.938 B.A. L.880 J.D. [A Bose M.&E.]
Thorpe, Straley M., (CV) ... '52 '82 C.347 B.S. L.1119 J.D. [Bator R.B.S.&L.]
Thrapp, Richard J., (AV) ... '58 '83 C.210 B.A. L.1119 J.D. [Ice M.]
Thrasher, Philip C., (BV) ... '41 '78 C.347 B.S. L.345 J.D. [Thrasher G.&V.]
Thrasher Griffith & Voelkel, P.C., (BV) ... 151 North Delaware Street, Suite 1900
Thrasher Papa, Ann L. ... '71 '02 C.74 B.A. L.345 J.D. [S Ice M.]
Threlkeld, W. Brent, (AV) ... '46 '72 C.346 B.S. L.345 J.D. [Threlkeld R.]

Threlkeld Reynolds, LLP, (AV)
Century Building, Suite 720, 36 South Pennsylvania Street, 46204
Telephone: 317-655-5200 Telefax: 317-655-3150
Email: tr@threlkeld-reynolds.com URL: http://www.lawyers.com/threlkeld-reynolds
Partners: W. Brent Threlkeld; Thomas Todd Reynolds. Associates: Richard W. McMinn; Thomas W. Kramer; Lisa Marie Lewis; Amy M. Jones; Christine M. Riesner.
General Practice, Litigation and Insurance Defense, Motor Carrier Law, Probate and Estate Planning, Estate Administration, Real Estate, Banking, Commercial, Tax and Corporate Law, Mediation Services.
See Professional Biographies, INDIANAPOLIS, INDIANA

Thurmond, Amy S. ... '71 '97 C.347 B.S. L.345 J.D. [A Feiwell&H.]
Tidwell, Ponce D., Jr. ... '68 '95 C.1378 B.S. L.329 J.D. Eli Lilly & Co.
Tillema, Nick A. ... '47 '88 C.36 M.B.A. L.1119 J.D. 9247 N. Meridian St.
Tillett, William J. ... '21 '53 C.265 A.B. L.345 J.D. 5447 Younkin Drive
Tillman, Douglas L. '48 '77 C.265 A.B. L.345 J.D.
Assoc. Gen. Coun., Litig. Dept., Eli Lilly & Co.
Timmons, Ronald S. ... '34 '66 C.347 B.S. L.345 LL.B. 715 West Ralston Road‡
Tinder, John D. ... '50 '75 C.347 B.S. L.1119 J.D. U.S. Dist. J.
Tinkham, Richard P., Jr., (BV) ... '32 '57 C.210 A.B. L.477 LL.B. [R.P.Tinkham,Jr.]
Tinkham, Richard P., Jr., P.C., (BV) ... 857 W. 96th St.
Tinsley, Nancy G., (AV) ... '61 '90 C.679 B.S. L.347 J.D. [Baker&D.] (See Pat. Sect.)
Tipton, David J., (BVⓉ) ... '— '84 C.347 B.A. L.345 J.D. [C Sommer B.]
Titlow, Robert A. ... '42 '84 C&L.347 B.A., J.D. Sr. Atty., Allison Engine Co., Inc.
Tittle, David O., (AV) ... '42 '67 C.347 B.S. L.1119 J.D. [Bingham M.]
Titus, Leanne S. ... '75 '00 C.36 B.S. L.345 J.D. [A Feiwell&H.]

Tobin, Thomas E., (BV) ... '33 '59 C.679 B.S. L.345 J.D. 10401 N. Meridian St.‡
Todd, Harry F., (AV) ... '58 '84 C.108 B.A. L.345 J.D. [Bose M.&E.]
Todd, Linda K. ... '— '84 C.477 B.A. L.1119 J.D. [C Barnes&T.]
Todd, Ronald S., (CV) ... '64 '95 C.473 B.A. L.602 J.D. [A Doehrman C.]
Todd, Teresa L., (AV) ... '55 '80 C.347 B.A. L.1119 J.D. 136 E. Market St., Ste. 700
Tolliver, Terry W. ... '74 '00 C.74 B.A. L.345 J.D. Dep. Atty. Gen., Atty. Gen. Off.
Tolton, Rebecca S. ... '54 '84 C.347 B.A. L.796 J.D. Corp. Coun., Irwin Mtge. Corp.
Tomlin, Larry C. ... '68 '01 C.347 B.S. L.1119 J.D. [A Krieg D.]
Tomson, Daniel C. ... '70 '02 C.132 B.A. L.879 J.D. [A Wood T.G.M.&H.]
Toner, Kevin M., (AV) ... '61 '86 C.347 A.B. L.309 J.D. [Baker&D.]
Toole, Jeffrey S. ... '67 '97 C&L.347 B.S., J.D. [Scopelitis,G.L.&H.]
Tooley, Michael L., (AV) ... '66 '91 C.880 B.A. L.228 J.D. [Ice M.]
Tooman, Lee D. ... '53 '97 C.608 B.S.B.A. L.347 J.D. Golden Rule Insurance Co.
Torke, James W. '41 '68 C&L.966 B.S., J.D.
(adm. in WI; not adm. in IN) Prof. of Law, Ind. Sch. of Law
Tousley, John W., (AV) ... '51 '76 C.347 B.A. L.345 J.D. [Tousley]
Tousley Law Office, The, (AV) ... 156 E. Market Street, Suite 900
Tow, Wilson L. ... '31 '59 C.347 B.S. L.1119 J.D. 647 Fenster Ct.
Towe, Fred O., (AV) ... '48 '75 C.347 B.A. L.1119 J.D. [Fillenwarth,D.G.&T.]
Townsend, Alan S., (AV) ... '63 '92 C.679 B.S. L.347 J.D. [Bose M.&E.]
Townsend, Earl C., III, (BV) ... '57 '84 C.477 B.A. L.912 J.D. [Townsend&T.]
Townsend, Earl C., Jr., (AV) ... '— '39 C&L.477 A.B., J.D. [C Townsend&T.]
Townsend, Ellen Morrison, (BV) ... '71 '97 C.210 B.A. L.1119 J.D. [A Hackman H.&C.]
Townsend, Jeffrey A., (BV) ... '57 '88 C.347 B.A. L.345 J.D. [Plews S.R.&B.]
Townsend, John F., III, (BV) ... '71 '96 C.477 B.A. L.347 J.D. [Townsend&M.]
Townsend, John F., Jr., (AV) ... '42 '67 C.477 B.A. L.309 J.D. [Townsend&M.]

Townsend & Montross, (AV) BB
230 East Ohio Street, 46244-0902
Telephone: 317-264-4444 Fax: 317-264-2080
Email: townsendmontross@aol.com URL: http://www.townsendmontross.com
John F. Townsend (1916-2001); John F. Townsend, Jr.; W. Scott Montross; John F. Townsend, III.
General Civil Trial Practice in all State and Federal Courts. Personal Injury, Products Liability, Malpractice and Aviation Law. Trials and Appeals.
Reference: Bank One.
See Professional Biographies, INDIANAPOLIS, INDIANA

Townsend & Townsend, (BV) ... 148 East Market Street, Suite 902
Trachtman, Daniel D., (AV) ... '53 '78 C.299 B.A. L.1119 J.D. [Wooden&M.]
Tracy, William L. ... '37 '74 C.347 B.S. L.345 J.D. Sr. Tax Atty., Dept. of Rev.
Tragesser, Joel E. ... '73 '97 C.894 A.B. L.880 J.D. [Locke R.] (See Pat. Sect.)
Traina, James, Jr. ... '25 '55 C.108 A.B. L.209 J.D. 7875 Sand Shoal Ct.
Tranquillo, Janelle ... '76 '01 C.63 B.S. L.602 J.D. [A Baker&D.]
Trathen, Barbara J., (AV) ... '49 '77 C.63 B.S. L.345 J.D. Co. Pros.
Travis, Curtis S., (AV) ... '30 '62 C.309 L.345 LL.B. 144 N. Delaware St.
Traylor, Charles V., (AV) ... '51 '76 C.679 B.S. L.345 J.D. [Kortepeter M.H.F.&M.]
Traynor, Michael J. ... '41 '72 C.363 A.B. L.597 J.D. 4433 Edinburgh Pt.
Traynor, Susan E. ... '61 '90 C&L.347 B.S., J.D. [Bose M.&E.]
Treacy, James W., (AV) ... '27 '55 C.597 B.S. L.345 J.D. 251 E. Ohio St.
Treadway, E. Scott, (BV) ... '62 '89 C.63 B.S. L.345 J.D. [Tabbert H.E.&W.]
Treen, Catherine Mannweiler ... '66 '91 C.347 B.S. L.589 J.D. 1001 W 10th St.
Trentadue, Michael A., (AV) ... '60 '85 C.602 B.S.M.E. L.339 J.D. [Bose M.&E.]
Trettin, Richard T. ... '45 '70 C.473 B.S. L.607 J.D. [Ittenbach J.T.&K.]
Tridico, Kristina M. ... '74 '99 C.610 B.S. L.629 J.D. [A Ice M.]
Trimble, John C., (AV) ... '55 '81 C.152 B.A. L.345 J.D. [Lewis W.]
Troll, John R. ... '47 '81 C.33 B.A. L.107 J.D. [C Woodard,E.M.M.&H.]
Troyer, Matthew T. ... '70 '97 C.473 B.S. L.347 J.D. [Bingham M.]
Trummel, David P. ... '65 '92 C.492 B.S. L.494 J.D. Atty., Law Div., Eli Lilly & Co.
Tsang, Alfred K. B. ... '24 '73 C.158 B.M.P. L.345 J.D. 6450 Miarmar Ct.‡
Tucher, Francis E. ... '24 '56 C.108 B.S. L.347 J.D. 4312 E. 10th St.‡
Tuchman, Steven L., (AV) ... '46 '71 C.347 B.A. L.345 J.D. [Lewis&K.]
Tucker, David A., (AV) ... '63 '89 C.210 B.A. L.347 J.D. [Easter&C.]
Tucker, Frederick C., III ... '46 '73 C.210 B.A. L.345 J.D. Pres., F. C. Tucker Co., Inc.
Tucker, R. Craig ... '59 '98 C.894 B.A. L.345 J.D. Eli Lilly and Company (Pat.)
Tucker, Ronald M. ... '57 '86 C.63 B.S. L.347 J.D. Simon Property Group
Tucker, William J., (AV) ... '49 '75 C.346 B.S. L.1340 J.D. [W.J.Tucker&Assoc.]

Tucker, William J., & Associates, LLC, (AV)
429 North Pennsylvania Street, Suite 400, 46204-1816
Telephone: 317-833-3030 Facsimile: 317-833-3031
Email: wtucker@wjtucker.com URL: http://www.wjtucker.com
Members: William J. Tucker; Steven K. Dick; Jeffrey Michael Hester. Associate: C. Abraham Murphy.
Business Law, Bankruptcy, Commercial Law, Debtor and Creditor Rights, Corporate Law, Collections, Taxes.
See Professional Biographies, INDIANAPOLIS, INDIANA

Tumminello, Lee Mosier ... '62 '87 C.347 B.S. L.477 J.D. Coun., Eli Lilly & Co.
Tuohy, Brian J., (AV) ... '55 '84 C.347 B.S. L.345 J.D. [Stark D.&S.]
Tuohy, James L., (AV) ... '28 '52 C.108 A.B. L.345 J.D. [Wood T.G.M.&H.]
Turner, L. Craig, Attorney at Law, (BV) '47 '74
C.929 B.S. L.500 J.D. 342 Massachusetts Ave., Ste. 300
Turner, Michael F. ... '72 '00 C.1119 B.A. L.345 J.D. 156 East Market Street, Suite 200
Turner, Michelle R. T. ... '55 '89 C.63 B.S. L.345 J.D. 128 N. Delaware St.
Turner, Robert B. ... '51 '85 C.347 B.A. L.345 J.D. 525 W. 65th St.
Turner, Timothy L. ... '65 '98 C.347 B.S. L.1119 J.D. 5556 S. Meckes Lane
Turner, Wayne C., (AV) ... '60 '85 C.679 B.S. L.345 J.D. [McTurnan&T.]
Tushan, Michael F. ... '72 '98 C.910 B.A. L.1119 J.D. Anthem, Inc.
Tuttle, Jodi Len '62 '87 C.63 B.A. L.345 J.D.
Gen. Coun., Indiana Assn. of Realtors, Inc.
Tuytschaeyers, Lisa Michelle '75 '00
C.347 B.A. L.1194 J.D. 135 North Pennsylvania Street, Suite 2100
Tyler, Dennis R. ... '64 '98 C.63 B.S. L.345 J.D. [A Stark D.&S.]
Tyler, Lynn C., (AV) ... '— '84 C.602 B.A. L.188 J.D. [Barnes&T.]
Tyra, Kevin C., (BV) ... '56 '81 C.679 B.A. L.880 J.D. [Tyra&C.]

Tyra & Collesano, P.C., (AV)
8470 Allison Pointe Boulevard, Suite 420 (Castleton), 46250-4364
Telephone: 317-567-2222 Fax: 317-567-2220
Email: kevin.tyra@tycolaw.com URL: http://www.tycolaw.com
James F. Bleeke; Stanley F. Collesano; Doris L. Sweetin; Kevin C. Tyra;—Kori L. McOmber; Peggy K. Little.
Trial and Appellate Practice. Insurance Defense, including Medical Malpractice, Nursing Home Cases, Workers Compensation, Insurance Coverage, Insurance Fraud Investigation. Wills and Probate, Trusts and Estates, Estate Planning, Business, Corporate, Construction Law, Contracts and Employment Law. General Civil Litigation. Arbitration and Mediation.
See Professional Biographies, INDIANAPOLIS, INDIANA

Tyrrell, Judy M., (BV) ... '49 '91 C.347 A.B. L.1209 J.D. [Tabbert H.E.&W.]
Tzeng, Oliver C. S. ... '39 '97 L.345 J.D. 3019 Lehigh Ct.
Ucchino, Jeffrey M. ... '64 '89 C.363 B.A. L.190 J.D. [A Eads,M.&P.]

Uhl, Nathaniel M. ... '— '04 C.303 B.A. L.1119 J.D. [A Ice M.]
Uhl, Susan E. ... '58 '88 C.679 B.S. L.345 J.D. Golden Rule Insurance Co.
Uhl, Wayne E., (AV) ... '56 '81 C.25 B.A. L.880 J.D. [A Stephenson M.&S.]
Uhrig, Harold E. '14 '42 L.128 LL.B.
(adm. in MD; not adm. in IN) 615 Russell Ave.‡
Ulen, E. Clay, (AV) ... '20 '49 C.347 A.B. L.1119 J.D. 300 N. Meridian St.
Ulery, Jeffrey J. ... '66 '91 C.63 B.S. L.1119 J.D. State Farm Ins. Cos.
Ullom, Jerimi J. ... '— '00 C.210 B.A. L.209 J.D. [A Barnes&T.]
Ullrich, Stephen P. ... '51 '91 C&L.347 B.S., J.D. [S.Ullrich]
Ullrich, Stephen, P.C. ... 3901 West 86th Street, Suite 330
Umstead, Raymond L. ... '53 '80 C.1208 B.S. L.150 J.D. Gen. Coun., Anthem, Inc.
Ungar, Kenneth T. ... '63 '88 C.347 B.A. L.178 J.D. Indianapolis Motor Speedway Corp.
Unger, Stephen C. ... '— '05 C.108 B.A. L.345 J.D. [A Bose M.&E.]
Unzicker, Andrea D. Bontrager ... '— '00 C.288 B.A. L.1119 J.D. [A Barnes&T.]
Uppencamp, Heath E. ... '79 '05 C.679 B.A. L.339 J.D. [A Krieg D.]
Ursulskis, Victoria, (BV) ... '47 '74 C.700 B.A. L.345 J.D. 10401 N. Meridian St.
Usher, A.J., IV ... '70 '97 C.701 B.S. L.347 J.D. [C Bose M.&E.] (Pat.)
Utken, Gregory J., (AV) ... '49 '74 C.347 A.B. L.345 J.D. [Baker&D.]
Uva, Anthony N. '59 '85 C.321 B.A. L.262 J.D.
(adm. in NJ; not adm. in IN) Staff. Coun., Simon Property Group
Vaiana, Frederick ... '62 '92 C.879 B.S. L.989 J.D. [Voyles,Z.P.H.&M.]
Vaidik, Nancy H. ... '55 '80 C&L.879 B.A., J.D. Ct. App. J.,
Valadez, Stephanie L. '66 '92 C.249 B.S. L.1119 J.D.
Dir., Compl., American United Life Insurance Co.
Valle, Alejandro ... '— '01 C.893 B.A. L.1119 J.D. [S Barnes&T.]
Valos Moss, Libby S. ... '73 '99 C.63 B.A. L.345 J.D. [A Kightlinger&G.]
Van Antwerp, Mary K. '61 '88
C.679 B.A. L.339 J.D. Wkrs. Comp. Supvr., Wausau Ins. Cos.
Van Buskirk, John W., (AV) ... '52 '78 C.347 B.A. L.345 J.D. [Stark D.&S.]
Van Dam, Marie L. ... '78 '03 C.475 B.A. L.424 J.D. [A Kightlinger&G.]
Vandivier, Blair R., (AV) ... '55 '81 C.108 B.S. L.345 J.D. [C Riley B.&E.]
Vandivier, Richard W. ... '32 '67 C.265 B.A. L.345 J.D. U.S. Bkrptcy. J.
Van Domelen, Harold E. ... '15 '41 C.323 A.B. L.477 LL.B. 8429 Olde Mill Cir.‡
VanLandingham, Jennifer L. ... '73 '03 C.347 B.S. L.74 J.D. [A Locke R.]
Vanore, Lawrence A., (AV) ... '— '86 C.1019 B.A. L.1119 J.D. [Sommer B.]
Van Ostrand, Amy ... '74 '99 C.154 B.A. L.339 J.D. [A Ladendorf&L.]
VanRheenen, Richard S. ... '55 '85 C.303 B.A. L.345 J.D. [Bose M.&E.]
Vare, Todd G. ... '— '95 C.473 B.A. L.345 J.D. [Barnes&T.]
Vaughan, Stephen L., (BV) ... '58 '85 C.679 B.S.E. L.345 J.D. [Indiano&V.&Assoc.]
Veatch, Karin L. ... '69 '94 C.347 B.A. L.851 J.D. [Dann P.N.&K.]
Veen, Rhonda Hanna ... '69 '96 C.603 B.S. L.1119 J.D. [A Osborn H.&L.]
Velde, Peter A., (AV) ... '49 '76 C.679 B.A. L.982 J.D. [Kightlinger&G.]
Vento, Andrew N. ... '74 '00 C&L.347 B.A., J.D. [A Ice M.]
Vertesch, Michael F., (BV) ... '61 '86 C.303 B.A. L.345 J.D. 4040 S. Meridian St.
Vink, Paul D. ... '75 '02 C.1348 B.A. L.345 J.D. [A Bose M.&E.]
Vitello, Ronald J. ... '35 '63 C.150 B.B.A. L.151 J.D. Admn. Law J., HEW
Vitone, Linda L. ... '68 '02 C.509 B.S. L.345 J.D. [A Katz&K.]
Vivo, Tiffany U. ... '74 '01 C&L.879 B.A., J.D. 156 East Market Street, Suite 1110
Vobach, William H., (AV) ... '29 '54 C.604 A.B. L.477 J.D. [C Locke R.]
Voelkel, Dennis ... '65 '93 C&L.347 B.S., J.D. [Thrasher G.&V.]
Vogtner, Thomas A., (AV) ... '49 '76 C.812 B.A. L.893 J.D. [Baker&D.]
Voigtmann, Mark A., (AV) ... '56 '91 C.502 B.J. L.345 J.D. [Baker&D.]
Voland, Sally A. ... '50 '92 C&L.347 B.S., J.D. [Dugan V.&M.]
Voland, Samuel J., (BV) ... '46 '72 C.63 B.S. L.345 J.D. 4040 S. Meridian St.
von Ruhtenberg, Joan Rutencrantz '37 '80
C.498 B.A. L.347 J.D. Ind. Univ. School of Law
Voors, Matthew P. ... '74 '03 C.347 B.S. L.74 J.D. [A Locke R.]
Vornehm, David B. ... '49 '93 C&L.347 B.A., J.D. [Drewry S.V.]
Voyles, James H., (AV) ... '43 '68 C.337 B.S. L.345 J.D. [Voyles,Z.P.H.&M.]
Voyles, Zahn, Paul, Hogan & Merriman, (AV) ... One Virginia Avenue, Suite 700
Wackowski, Bruce ... '47 '72 C.347 A.B. L.1119 J.D. State Civil Rights Comm.
Waddick, William A., (AV) ... '31 '61 C.602 B.S. L.345 J.D. [Waddick]

Waddick Law Firm, The, P.C., (AV)
9000 Keystone Crossing, Suite 1000, 46240
Telephone: 317-843-3980 FAX: 317-573-5280
Email: wwaddick@inct.net URL: http://www.lawyers.com/williamwaddick
William A. Waddick.
Personal Injury, Commercial, Corporate.
See Professional Biographies, INDIANAPOLIS, INDIANA

Wade, Angela K., (BV) '59 '91
C.108 B.A. L.347 J.D. Atty., Pharm. Opers., Eli Lilly & Co.
Wade, Timothy L., (AV) ... '47 '76 C.347 B.S. L.345 J.D. 1 Indiana Sq.
Waggoner, Jeffrey W., Law Office of '60 '98
C.801 B.S. L.345 J.D. 2415 Shelby St., Apt. 14
Wagner, Jay H. '— '92 C.608 B.A. L.150 J.D.
(adm. in OH; not adm. in IN) V.P. & Gen. Coun., Thomson Inc.
Wagner, Richard D., (AV) ... '33 '60 C.347 B.S. L.1119 LL.B. [Krieg D.] ‡
Wagner, Robert F., (AV) ... '35 '67 C.184 B.S. L.345 J.D. [Lewis W.]
Wagner, Timothy J., (BV) ... '51 '78 C.201 B.A. L.345 J.D. 5317 E. 16th St., Ste. 10
Wagner, Vincent O., (AV) '51 '76
C.602 B.S. L.1119 J.D. [Woodard,E.M.M.&H.] (See Pat. Sect.)
Wagner, William C., (AV) ... '— '92 C&L.879 B.A., J.D. [Sommer B.]
Wagoner, Linda M. '51 '76
C.347 A.B. L.345 J.D. Indiana Federal Community Defenders, Inc.
Wahl, Christopher Norman ... '78 '03 C.55 B.A. L.345 J.D. 320 N. Meridian St., Ste. 1006
Waicukauski, Ronald J., (AV) ... '48 '73 C.597 B.S. L.309 J.D. [Price W.R.&D.]
Wain, Norman '70 '96 C.112 B.A. L.990 J.D.
(adm. in CA; not adm. in IN) Asst. Cnsl., Finish Line, Inc.
Waite, Kenneth J. '— '96
C.303 B.A. L.347 J.D. Pat. Atty., Roche Diagnostics Corp. (Pat.)
Walburn, Lynn A. '50 '75 C.602 B.A. L.345 J.D.
Asst. Gen. Coun., American United Life Insurance Company, a One America Financial Partner
Wald, William G. '27 '55 C.502 A.B. L.276 J.D.
V.P., Gen. Coun. & Corp. Secy., Consolidated Products, Inc.
Walda, John D., (AV) ... '50 '75 C&L.347 A.B., J.D. [Bose M.&E.]
Waldschmidt, William E. ... '47 '80 C.894 A.B. L.1119 J.D. Chicago Title Ins. Co.‡
Wales, William W. '49 '79 C.215 B.S.M.E. L.213 J.D.
VP., Secy. & Gen. Coun., Dow AgroSciences
Walker, Bruce A., (AV) ... '51 '76 C.339 B.A. L.345 J.D. 6500 East Westfield Boulevard
Walker, Candace S., (BV) ... '— '81 C.611 B.A. L.345 J.D. [C Ogletree,D.N.S.&S.]
Walker, Chad T. ... '— '01 C.249 B.S. L.345 J.D. [A Tabbert H.E.&W.]
Walker, Charles D. ... '15 '53 C.63 A.B. L.345 J.D. 5215 Will Scarlet Lane‡
Walker, F. Ronalds ... '46 '76 C.976 B.A. L.477 J.D. [C Plews S.R.&B.]
Walker, Rebecca E. ... '65 '97 C.347 B.A. L.339 J.D. Staff Atty.
Walker, Ross P., (BV) ... '34 '60 C.231 A.B. L.145 J.D. 315 Cir. Twr. Bldg.
Wallace, Larry J. ... '37 '63 C.347 A.B. L.345 LL.B. [Parr R.O.&M.]
Wallack, Barry Z., (AV) ... '41 '65 C&L.966 B.S., J.D. [Wallack S.&H.]
Wallack, Michael S., (BV) ... '65 '92 C.597 B.A. L.347 J.D. [Wallack S.&H.]

Wallack Somers & Haas, P.C., (AV) BB
One Indiana Square, Suite 1500, 46204
Telephone: 317-231-9000 FAX: 317-231-9900
URL: http://www.wshlaw.com
Barry Z. Wallack; Michael S. Wallack; George W. Somers; Karl P. Haas; Jennifer R. Shoup;—Jodie L. Edminster; Samuel J. Arena.
Real Estate, Finance, Investment, Development, Construction, Leasing, Corporate, Business, Mediation.
See Professional Biographies, INDIANAPOLIS, INDIANA

Wallander, Gregg M., (BV) ... '— '93 C&L.347 B.S., J.D. [Hall,R.K.H.&L.]
Waller, John D., (BV) ... '68 '93 C.209 B.A. L.347 J.D. [Wooden&M.]
Wallsmith, Dirk E. ... '54 '87 C.63 B.S. L.345 J.D. [A Locke R.]
Walsh, Thomas A. ... '64 '95 C.679 B.S.I.E. L.347 J.D. [Ice M.] (See Pat. Sect.)
Walters, Etta Lachmann ... '74 '99 C&L.74 B.S., J.D. Corp. Coun., The Hunt Corp.
Walters, Wendy Anne '70 '95 C.696 B.A. L.424 J.D.
(adm. in IL; not adm. in IN) P.O. Box 6222
Walton-Pratt, Tanya, (BV) ... '59 '84 C.811 B.A. L.329 J.D. 155 E. Market St.
Waltz, Debora Jo, (AV) '58 '83
C.63 B.S. L.345 J.D. Sr. Corp. Coun., Inland Container Corp.
Wampler, Lloyd C., (AV) ... '20 '47 C.347 A.B. L.1119 J.D. 4000 N. Meridian St.‡
Wampler, Robert J., (AV) ... '36 '63 C.976 B.A. L.345 J.D. 5939 Cape Cod Ct.
Ward, Charles P., (AV) ... '63 '89 C.108 B.A. L.347 J.D. [Ward&W.]
Ward, Donald W., (AV) ... '28 '54 C.303 A.B. L.602 J.D. [Ward&W.]
Ward, Maureen E. ... '53 '93 C.347 B.A. L.421 J.D. [A Wooden&M.]
Ward, Paul S. ... '59 '90 C.383 B.S. L.259 J.D. [P.S.Ward]
Ward, Paul S., P.C. ... 8425 Woodfield Crossing, Suite 100

Ward & Ward, (AV)
1014 Circle Tower Building, 55 Monument Circle, 46204
Telephone: 317-639-9501
Email: cpw@wardlawfirm.com
Members of Firm: Donald W. Ward; Charles P. Ward.
Personal Injury, Products Liability, Wrongful Death, Aviation, Automobile Accidents, Medical Malpractice, Federal Employers Liability Act, Civil Trial, Wills, Probate, Trusts and Estates, Guardianships, Asset Protection, Estate Planning.
See Professional Biographies, INDIANAPOLIS, INDIANA

Warner, David W. '32 '64 C&L.800 B.S., J.D.
(adm. in CA; not adm. in IN) 7811 Holly Creek Lane‡
Warner, Timothy R., (BV) '54 '89 C.679 B.S. L.616 J.D.
Coun., Lawyers Title Ins. Corp.
Warnke, Adam M. ... '72 '00 C.894 A.B. L.1119 J.D. Dept. Dir. & Chf. Coun.
Warr, Alastair J., (AV) ... '65 '91 C.347 B.S. L.345 J.D. [Krieg D.] (Pat.)
Warren, Bradford L., (BV) ... '48 '73 C.347 A.B. L.345 J.D. 926 E. 52nd St.
Warren, Claude M., Jr., (AV) ... '44 '71 C.347 B.S. L.345 J.D. 6508 E. Westfield Blvd.
Warshauer, David R., (AV) ... '— '84 C.910 B.A. L.347 J.D. [C Barnes&T.]
Waterfill, Mark R., (BV) ... '61 '86 C.303 B.A. L.1119 J.D. [Dann P.N.&K.]
Waters, James E. ... '46 '85 C&L.347 B.S., J.D. [Miller,W.M.&H.]
Watson, Harry J., III, (BV) ... '47 '74 C.602 B.A. L.345 J.D. 3141 W 33rd St
Watson, Hugh, (AV) ... '27 '53 C&L.477 A.B., J.D. 4925 N. Meridan St.‡
Watson, Kathryn A. '57 '82
C.347 B.A. L.1119 J.D. Dir. of Enforce., State Dept. of Envir. Mgt.
Watson, Stephen L. ... '45 '74 C.346 B.S. L.345 J.D. Reg. V.P., CSX Transp., Inc.‡
Watson-Duvall, Derelle ... '51 '78 C.210 B.A. L.345 J.D. 5172 East 65th Street
Watts, Mary Hamilton, (AV) ... '50 '84 C.347 B.S. L.345 J.D. [Bingham M.]
Weathers, Scott A., (BV) ... '60 '86 C.285 B.A. L.904 J.D. [Huffer&W.]
Webb, Mark Charles, (BV) ... '61 '88 C.347 B.A. L.1119 J.D. [C Voyles,Z.P.H.&M.]
Webber, Kurt A. ... '66 '93 C.347 B.S. L.339 J.D. [K.A.Webber]
Webber, Larry E. ... '38 '75 C.72 B.A. L.345 J.D. 10705 E. US Hwy. 136
Webber, Kurt A., P.C. ... 104 Granby Drive, Suite G
Weber, Christopher J., (AV) ... '44 '71 C.1216 B.A. L.345 J.D. [C Baker&D.]
Weber, Karen M. R. ... '71 '97 C.679 B.S. L.201 J.D. [A Locke R.]
Webster, Thomas D. ... '50 '94 C.112 B.S. L.1119 J.D. Pat. Atty., Eli Lilly & Co. (Pat.)
Wedding, David S. ... '34 '62 C.303 A.B. L.1119 LL.B. 5539 Senour Rd.
Wedding, Mary Jo, (BV) ... '62 '88 C.210 B.A. L.345 J.D. [C Norris C.&S.]
Weddle, Megan M., (BV) ... '63 '89 C&L.339 B.S., J.D. Suite #400, One Virginia Avenue
Weddle, Robert G., (AV) ... '43 '72 C.679 B.S. L.345 J.D. [Tabbert H.E.&W.]
Weeks, W. William ... '— '79 C.347 B.A. L.1119 J.D. [C Sommer B.]
Weems, Michael O. ... '69 '05 C.469 B.A. L.352 J.D. [A Bingham M.]
Weese, D. Bryan, (BV) ... '65 '90 C.347 B.A. L.893 J.D. [Bingham M.]
Weglarz, Julie M. ... '— '96 C.347 B.A. L.879 J.D. IN Ct. of Appls.
Wegner, C. Dennis ... '42 '74 C.346 B.S. L.347 J.D. 251 E. Ohio St.
Weinheimer, Anne H., (AV) ... '52 '82 C.945 A.B. L.345 J.D. 120 Monument Circle
Weinland, Thomas M. ... '61 '88 C.347 B.S. L.345 J.D. [A Frazier&Assoc.]
Weisell, William B., (AV) ... '12 '40 C&L.178 A.B., LL.B. [C Locke R.] ‡
Weisfeld, Tamara L., (AV) ... '61 '86 C.347 B.S. L.345 J.D. [A Rubin&L.]
Weiss, Brian E. ... '62 '87 C.92 B.A. L.1119 J.D. 8395 Keystone Crossing
Weiss, Zeff A., (AV) ... '57 '83 C.347 B.S. L.1119 J.D. [Ice M.]
Welch, Brian W., (AV) ... '51 '78 C.210 B.A. L.345 J.D. [Bingham M.]
Welch, Lawrence T., (AV(T)) ... '54 '79 C&L.215 B.S., J.D. Eli Lilly Co. (Pat.)
Welch, Richard T. ... '64 '98 C&L.228 A.B., J.D. Ernst & Young, LLP
Welch, William F., (AV) ... '18 '48 C.210 A.B. L.477 J.D. [C Bingham M.]
Weliever, Daun A., (BV) ... '64 '90 C.347 B.S. L.1119 J.D. [Lewis W.]
Wells, Paul T. ... '14 '53 L.345 LL.B. 6042 Hollister Dr.‡
Welsh, Gary R. ... '62 '93 C.234 B.A. L.345 J.D. [G.R.Welsh]

Welsh, Gary R., Attorney at Law, P.C.
320 N. Meridian, Suite 615, 46204
Telephone: 317-684-0099 Fax: 317-634-1754
Email: gwelsh@ameritech.net URL: http://www.welshatlaw.com
Gary R. Welsh.
Business, Real Estate, Immigration, Family Law.
See Professional Biographies, INDIANAPOLIS, INDIANA

Welton, Colin D. '60 '86 C&L.966 B.B.A., J.D.
(adm. in WI; not adm. in IN) Key Asset Mgmt.
Wendt, T. Joseph ... '— '96 C.894 B.A. L.347 J.D. [A Barnes&T.] (©Indianapolis)
Wenning, Steven R. ... '61 '87 C.894 B.A. L.117 J.D. Legislative Servs. Agcy.
Wentworth, Martha B. ... '48 '90 C&L.347 B.S., J.D. 111 Monument Cir.
Wenzel, Mark R., (AV) ... '56 '81 C.679 B.A. L.345 J.D. [Krieg D.]
Werner, Christine A. ... '72 '99 C.473 B.A. L.930 J.D. [A Baker&D.]
Werner, Thomas J., (BV) ... '44 '72 C.249 B.A. L.345 J.D. 6430 Green Leaves Rd.

Wessels & Pautsch, P.C.
Market Tower, 10 West Market Street, Suite 1770, 46204 ⊙
Telephone: 317-656-8800 Fax: 317-656-8855
Email: wessels@stch.w-p.com URL: http://www.w-p.com
—Frederick D. Payne; Bruce F. Mills.
Representing Employers in Labor and Employment Law Matters. NLRA, RLA, all Federal and State Employment Discrimination Laws, Federal and State Disability Laws, Wrongful Discharge, Employment Contracts, Collective Bargaining Negotiations and Arbitrations, Employee Substance Abuse, Safety and Health, Unemployment Insurance, Benefits Law, Wage and Hour, and Employment-Based Immigration Matters. Litigation before all Federal and State Courts and Agencies, Trial and Appellate Practice.
Milwaukee, Wisconsin Office: Two Plaza East, 330 East Kilbourn Avenue, Suite 1475. Telephone: 414-291-0600. Fax: 414-291-0200.
Chicago, Illinois Office: Chicago Bar Association Building, 321 South Plymouth Court, Suite 900. Telephone: 312-461-0500. Fax: 312-461-0595.
Davenport, Iowa Office: Northwest Bank Building, 101 W. Second Street, Suite 307. Telephone: 563-333-9102. Fax: 563-333-9105.
Minneapolis, Minnesota Office: MoneyGram Tower, 1550 Utica Avenue South, Suite 450. Telephone: 952-746-1700. Fax: 952-746-1704.

See Professional Biographies, INDIANAPOLIS, INDIANA

West, Jonathan R., (BV) '57 '83 C.347 B.A. L.345 J.D. Gen. Coun., Sr. V.P. & Corp. Secy., Federal Home Loan Bk. of Indianapolis
West, Judson H. . . . '08 '36 L.345 LL.B. 5825 Oak Ave.‡
West, Lu Carole, (AV) '56 '84 C.210 B.A. L.345 J.D. Assoc. Gen. Coun., Eli Lilly & Co.
Wever, Michael E. '72 '97 C.701 B.S. L.790 J.D. (adm. in SC; not adm. in IN; See Pat. Sect.) [[A] Brinks H.G.&L.]
Whaley, L. Alan, (AV) . . . '54 '81 C.347 B.S. L.1119 J.D. [Ice M.]
Wharton, Charles Rayburn '57 '82 C.880 B.A. L.150 J.D. (adm. in OH; not adm. in IN) U.S. Trustee's Off.
Wheeler, Christopher . . . '62 '91 C.317 B.A. L.347 J.D. Clk., Ct. of App. J.
Wheeler, Gene A. . . . '64 '99 C.63 B.A. L.347 J.D. [[A] Rubin&L.]
Wheeler, Kristina Kern '73 '98 C&L.347 B.S., J.D. Gen. Coun., IN Utility Regulatory Comm.
Wheeler, Leroy M., (BV) . . . '47 '75 C.347 A.B. L.345 J.D. 136 E. Market St., Ste. 1119
Wheeler, Thomas E., II, (AV) . . . '62 '87 C.347 B.S. L.1119 J.D. [Locke R.]
Whelden, George T., Jr. '22 '74 C.347 B.S. L.345 J.D. Admin. Law J., Ind. Dept. of Rev.
Wherry, Michael S. '68 '03 C.701 B.S. L.1119 J.D. [[A] Woodard,E.M.M.&H.] (See Pat. Sect.)
Whistler, Philip A., (AV) . . . '52 '78 C.813 B.A. L.309 J.D. [Ice M.]
Whitaker, John R. '54 '82 C.63 B.S. L.347 J.D. Sr. V.P., Legal & Corp. Affs., Citizens Gas & Coke Utility
White, Anderson R. . . . '66 '99 C&L.347 B.A., J.D. [[A] Harrison&M.]
White, Elizabeth L., (BV) . . . '65 '90 C.347 B.A. L.276 J.D. Co. Pros.
White, Gordon E., Jr., (BV) '52 '77 C.339 B.A. L.345 J.D. Dep. Atty. Gen., IN Atty. Gen Off.
White, James P. . . . '31 '56 C&L.352 B.A., J.D. Prof. of Law, Ind. Univ.
White, James W., (BV) . . . '42 '68 C.339 B.S. L.345 J.D. 6125 U.S. Hwy. 31 S.
White, John F., (BV) . . . '34 '59 L.345 J.D. [White&J.]
White, Ryan O. '73 '00 C.63 B.S. L.201 J.D. (adm. in OH; not adm. in IN; Pat.) [[A] Bose M.&E.]
White, Sean T. . . . '68 '97 C&L.347 B.S., J.D. [[A] Hoover H.B.&H.]
White & Johnson, (BV) . . . 302 North East St.
Whitehill, Charles A. . . . '52 '79 C.435 B.A. L.345 J.D. 521 N. Emerson Ave.
Whitham, Larry F., (AV) . . . '49 '74 C.210 B.A. L.345 J.D. [Whitham,M.&R.]
Whitham, McColley & Ross, P.C., (AV) . . . 151 N. Delaware Street
Whitinger, John L. . . . '20 '49 C.347 A.B. L.345 LL.B. 2535 E. Banta Rd.‡
Whitmer, Lloyd, (CV) . . . '12 '55 C.249 A.B. L.345 LL.B. Dep. Atty. Gen.
Whitney, Larry G. . . . '46 '72 C.63 B.S. L.345 J.D. 970 Fort Wayne Ave., Ste. E
Whitten, Christopher R. . . . '71 '97 C.112 B.A. L.879 J.D. [[A] Scopelitis,G.L.&H.]
Whybrew, Charles R. . . . '72 '98 C.894 B.A. L.347 J.D. [[A] Tabbert H.E.&W.]
Wick, William A., (AV) . . . '18 '48 C.976 B.A. L.309 LL.B. [[C] Stewart&I.]
Wickes, John F., Jr., (AV) . . . '47 '75 C.347 B.A. L.345 J.D. [Lewis&K.]
Wielenberg, Margaret D. . . . '70 '95 [[C] Ice M.]
Wilcox, Sylvia E. . . . '62 '92 C.679 B.S. L.8 J.D. Natl. Res. Comm.
Wild, Kevin C.C. . . . '70 '95 C.894 B.A. L.347 J.D. State Fam. & Soc. Servs. Admn.
Wilder, Julia R. . . . '52 '85 C.1375 B.A. L.347 J.D. [O'Koon H.]
Wildman, Robert T., (AV) . . . '47 '72 C.347 A.B. L.1119 J.D. [[C] Bose M.&E.]
Wiles, A. Donald, II, (AV) . . . '38 '66 C.674 A.B. L.178 LL.B. [Harrison&M.]
Wiles, Charles A. . . . '34 '62 C.1024 B.S. L.345 LL.B. Supr. Ct. J.
Wiley, Craig W., (BV) . . . '— '98 C&L.347 B.S., J.D. [[A] Ogletree,D.N.S.&S.]
Wiley, Kathryn E. . . . '78 '04 C.679 B.A. L.1119 J.D. [[A] Baker&D.]
Wilken, Janice C. . . . '72 '98 C.108 B.A. L.347 J.D. [Ice M.]
Wilkins, David G. . . . '52 '77 C.340 B.A. L.339 J.D. 9330 Zionville Rd.
Wilkins, Gene E., (AV) . . . '32 '57 C.347 A.B. L.1119 J.D. 5001 N. Meridian
Wilkins, Lawrence P. '45 '73 C.608 B.A. L.117 J.D. (adm. in OH; not adm. in IN) Indiana Univ. School of Law
Wilkins, Michael A., (AV) . . . '63 '88 C&L.602 B.A., J.D. [Ice M.]
Wilkinson, Daniel R. . . . '72 '99 C.347 B.S. L.1119 J.D. Ind. Gov Center N-248
Willett, Germaine W. . . . '72 '98 C.210 B.A. L.347 J.D. [[C] Ice M.]
Willett, Isaac . . . '78 '05 C.347 B.A. L.345 J.D. [[A] Bingham M.]
Willey, James R., Jr. . . . '— '95 C.303 B.A. L.347 J.D. [Hall,R.K.H.&L.]
Williams, Bradley L., (AV) . . . '50 '75 C.347 A.B. L.1119 J.D. [[C] Ice M.]
Williams, Cassandra Ann . . . '52 '87 C.329 B.S. L.345 J.D. 3602 Marcella Ln.
Williams, Craig M. . . . '— '97 C.894 A.B. L.345 J.D. [[A] Hall,R.K.H.&L.]
Williams, Darla Y. . . . '63 '01 C.679 B.S. L.862 J.D. [[C] Tabbert H.E.&W.]
Williams, Donald E., (AV) . . . '— '91 C.347 B.S. L.597 J.D. [Barnes&T.]
Williams, Fay H., (BV) . . . '33 '71 C.325 B.A. L.345 J.D. 5 E. Market St.
Williams, Jay B. '66 '92 C.999 B.A. L.1187 J.D. Asst. Gen. Coun., American United Life Insurance Co.
Williams, Jerry, (AV) . . . '— '68 C.108 B.A. L.345 J.D. [[C] Sommer B.]
Williams, John F., III . . . '— '03 C.1333 B.S. L.1209 J.D. [[A] Hall,R.K.H.&L.]
Williams, Kenneth E. . . . '45 '78 C.150 B.S.M.E. L.345 J.D. 5858 Decatur Blvd.
Williams, Lora N. Reed . . . '71 '96 C.679 B.A. L.823 J.D. [Williams]
Williams, Marshall E. . . . '28 '57 C.108 B.A. L.1119 LL.B. Adm. Law J., H.E.W.‡
Williams, Michael E., (AV) . . . '56 '82 C.63 B.S. L.345 J.D. [Krieg D.]
Williams, Pamela C. . . . '— '92 C.608 B.A. L.201 J.D. Litig. Coun., Anthem, Inc.
Williams, Stephen E., (BV) . . . '51 '83 C.347 A.B. L.345 J.D. [Emswiller,W.N.&C.]
Williams, Susan Lysle . . . '46 '99 C.63 B.S. L.345 J.D. American United Life Ins. Co.
Williams, Teresa C., (AV) '56 '84 C.63 B.S. L.345 J.D. Corporate Counsel, Basic American Industries, Inc.
Williams, William O., II, (AV) '64 '93 C.679 B.S. L.201 J.D. Sr. Compl. Coun., Golden Rule Insurance Co.
Williams & Douglas, (AV) . . . 342 Massachusetts Ave., Suite 303
Williams Law Office, P.C. . . . P.O. Box 47502

Willis, Lewis E., Jr. . . . '62 '87 C.347 B.A. L.879 J.D. [Stark D.&S.]
Wills, David L., (AV) . . . '46 '75 C.291 B.S. L.309 J.D. [Bose M.&E.]
Willsey, Donald R., (BV) . . . '29 '54 C.347 A.B. L.345 J.D. 4040 S. Meridian St.
Willsey, Filmore W., (BV) . . . '36 '62 C.347 B.S. L.345 J.D. 4042 S. Meridian St.‡

Willsey, Steven E., (AV) '57 '83 C&L.347 B.A., J.D.
4040 South Meridian Street, 46217
Telephone: 317-783-2500 1-888-783-2500 Fax: 317-782-2994
Email: swillsey01@sbcglobal.net URL: http://www.lawyers.com/stevenwillseylaw
Personal Injury, Automobile Accidents and Injuries, Wrongful Death, Construction Site Accidents, Medical Malpractice, Motorcycle Accidents.

See Professional Biographies, INDIANAPOLIS, INDIANA

Wilson, Amy S. . . . '78 '03 C.303 B.S. L.345 J.D. [[A] Locke R.]
Wilson, David B. . . . '56 '80 C.894 B.A. L.347 J.D. 4040 South Meridian Street
Wilson, Elaine Waterhouse . . . '— '94 C&L.94 B.A., J.D. [Barnes&T.]
Wilson, Heather L. . . . '69 '97 C&L.347 B.A., J.D. [[A] Locke R.]
Wilson, Jeffrey S., (CV) . . . '63 '90 C.894 A.B. L.347 J.D. [[A] Feiwell&H.]
Wilson, K. B. . . . '32 '61 C.475 A.B. L.345 J.D. Pres., Coun., Gardner & White Corp.
Wilson, Kenyon J. . . . '48 '74 C.347 B.A. L.345 J.D. Dir., Indiana State Welfare Dept.
Wilson, Stephen L., (BV) '52 '79 C.679 B.A. L.345 J.D. V.P. & Assoc. Coun., National City Corp.

Wilson, Kehoe & Winingham, (AV) [BR]
2859 North Meridian, 46208 ⊙
Telephone: 317-920-6400 Fax: 317-920-6405
Email: mailbox@wkw.com URL: http://www.wkw.com
Members of Firm: Harry A. Wilson, Jr. (1930-2004); D. Bruce Kehoe; William E. Winingham, Jr. Associates: Gerald A. Griffin, M.D.; Christopher G. Stevenson. Of Counsel: Gerald L. Lawlis.
Civil Trial Practice in State and Federal Courts. Aviation, Medical Legal, Personal Injury, Product Liability, Medical Malpractice, Wrongful Death, Insurance.
Reference: Fifth Third Bank.
Richmond, Indiana Office: 2901 East Main Street, 47374. Telephone: 765-962-9113.
Muncie, Indiana Office: 3620 N. Everbrook Lane, Suite A, 47304. Telephone: 765-284-2474. Fax: 765-288-8655.

See Professional Biographies, INDIANAPOLIS, INDIANA

Wilt, Brad A. . . . '70 '98 C.150 B.S. L.1119 J.D. [[A] Bingham M.]
Wimmer, Basil L., (BV) . . . '20 '51 C.108 B.S. L.345 LL.B. House Call Legal Serv.
Winberg, Bonnie . . . '63 '89 C.97 B.A. L.629 J.D. Co. Off. of Fam. & Child.
Winchester, Katherine A. . . . '68 '97 C.108 B.A. L.1119 J.D. [[A] Ice M.]
Winegardner, Richard P. . . . '— '93 C.63 B.S. L.893 J.D. [[A] Barnes&T.]
Wingerter, Robert B., Jr. . . . '54 '83 C.344 B.S. L.345 J.D. Arthur & Young
Winingham, William E., Jr., (AV) '52 '79 C.347 B.A. L.345 J.D. [Wilson,K.&W.] (⊙Muncie)
Wirey, Mark E. . . . '54 '90 C&L.347 B.S., J.D. [Stewart&I.]
Wirick, Andrew P., (AV) . . . '61 '86 C.210 B.A. L.347 J.D. [Hume S.G.G.&S.]
Wise, William M. . . . '38 '75 L.74 LL.B. P.O. Box 7045
Wiseman, Timothy W. . . . '66 '93 C&L.347 LL.B. [Scopelitis,G.L.&H.]
Wishard, Gordon D., (AV) . . . '45 '69 C.951 B.A. L.1119 J.D. [Ice M.]
Witchger, James D., (AV) . . . '49 '74 C.602 A.B. L.345 J.D. [Rocap W.]
Withers, Timothy W. . . . '68 '98 C.679 B.S. L.879 J.D. [Cremer B.&C.]
Withrow, Thomas A., (AV) . . . '42 '69 C.477 B.A. L.347 J.D. [[C] Locke R.]
Wittler, Brian Eugene . . . '66 '97 C.999 B.S.I.E. L.347 J.D. Genl. Motors Corp.

Woddell, Judith J., (AV) '40 '69 C.108 B.S. L.345 J.D.
Suite 1420, 151 North Delaware Street, 46204
Telephone: 317-269-6262 Fax: 317-269-0016
Probate and Estate Planning, Estate Administration, Taxation Law, Corporate Law.

See Professional Biographies, INDIANAPOLIS, INDIANA

Wojihoski, Lisa L. . . . '58 '86 C.879 B.A. L.345 J.D. 4238 Madison Ave.
Wolenty, Barbara A., (AV) . . . '56 '82 C.679 B.A. L.345 J.D. [Robinson W.&Y.]
Wolf, Mary Therese . . . '46 '74 C.999 B.A. L.352 J.D. Indiana Univ. School of Law
Wolf, Walter E., Jr., (AV) . . . '31 '55 C&L.309 A.B., LL.B. [Dann P.N.&K.]
Wolfard, Mary L., (BV) . . . '15 '38 C&L.347 LL.B. 5875 N. New Jersey St.
Wolfe, Jeffrey D. . . . '75 '02 C.63 B.A. L.345 J.D. [[A] Feiwell&H.]
Wolfla, Paul A. . . . '70 '98 C.347 B.A. L.608 J.D. [[A] Baker&D.]
Womble, Stephen R. '52 '88 C.347 B.A. L.1119 J.D. Soc. Sec. Admin., Hearings & App. Off.
Womer, David W. . . . '49 '75 L.345 J.D. 251 East Ohio Street‡
Wonderlin, Lance W., (BV) . . . '64 '89 C.894 A.B. L.1119 J.D. [L.W.Wonderlin]
Wonderlin, Lance W., P.C., (BV) . . . 8710 North Meridian Street
Wong, A. Barclay . . . '75 '01 C.604 B.A. L.1522 J.D. [[A] Harrison&M.]
Wong, David A. W. . . . '— '04 C.346 B.A. L.347 J.D. [[A] Barnes&T.]
Wood, Clarence E. . . . '13 '35 L.345 LL.B. 5456 N. Park Dr.‡
Wood, David M. . . . '57 '95 C.347 B.S. L.74 J.D. 47 S. Pennsylvania St., Ste. 400
Wood, James D. . . . '60 '98 C.871 B.S. L.273 J.D. [[A] Maginot M.&B.] (See Pat. Sect.)
Wood, John, (AV) . . . '30 '57 C.918 A.B. L.309 LL.B. Ms 27, 402 W. Washington, W-451
Wood, William J., (AV) . . . '28 '52 C.347 A.B. L.1119 J.D. [Wood T.G.M.&H.]
Wood Tuohy Gleason Mercer & Herrin, Professional Corporation, (AV) 111 Monument Circle, Suite 3400
Woodard, John W. . . . '28 '52 C.309 A.B. L.477 LL.B. 6140 N. Meridian St.‡
Woodard, S. Michael, (AV) '50 '83 C.701 B.S.M.E. L.345 J.D. Sr. Coun., Indianapolis Power & Light Company

Woodard, Emhardt, Moriarty, McNett & Henry LLP, (AV) [BR]
Bank One Center/Tower, 111 Monument Circle, Suite 3700, 46204-5137
Telephone: 317-634-3456 Telecopier: 317-637-7561
URL: http://www.uspatent.com
Members of Firm: C. David Emhardt; John V. Moriarty; John C. McNett; Thomas Q. Henry; James M. Durlacher; Charles R. Reeves; Vincent O. Wagner; Stephen E. Zlatos; Spiro Bereveskos; Clifford W. Browning; R. Randall Frisk; Daniel J. Lueders; Kenneth A. Gandy; Timothy N. Thomas; Kurt N. Jones; Holiday W. Banta; Troy J. Cole; Charles J. Meyer; Lisa A. Hiday; John V. Daniluck; Christopher A. Brown; Scott J. Stevens; Charles P. Schmal. Associates: John M. Bradshaw; Quentin G. Cantrell; John J. Emanuele, Jr.; Michael S. Wherry; Douglas G. Gallagher; Marta L. Puckett; Elizabeth A. Shuster; Michael A. Benefield; Timothy B. Paul; Teresa E. Knight; Adam W. Borgman; William A. McKenna; Mark T. Stephenson; James R. Blaufuss. Of Counsel: Joseph A. Naughton, Jr.; Edward E. Sowers; Gary M. Gron; John R. Troll.
Patent, Trademark, Copyright, Unfair Competition, Computer, Franchise and related Antitrust Law. Trials and Appeals.

See Professional Biographies, INDIANAPOLIS, INDIANA

Wooden, William P., (AV) . . . '33 '58 C.210 A.B. L.477 J.D. [[C] Wooden&M.]

Wooden & McLaughlin LLP, (AV) [BR]
One Indiana Square, Suite 1800, 46204-4208
Telephone: 317-639-6151 Fax: 317-639-6444
URL: http://www.woodmaclaw.com
Members of Firm: Michael C. Cook; Ronald G. Salatich; Thomas W. Dinwiddie; John D. Nell; Douglas B. King; Dale W. Eikenberry; Andrew C. Charnstrom; Daniel D. Trachtman; Thomas M. Hanahan; Kent M. Broach; Jeffrey L. McKean; Holly Hapak Betz; Michael Rabinowitch; John W. Hamilton; Jane Ann Himsel; John D. Waller; E. Joseph Kremp. Associates: James M. Boyers; Christine K. Jacobson; Maureen E. Ward; Jeremy B. Johnson; Dayna L. Switzer; Jeffrey A. Hammond; Mark T. Monroe; Robert F. Inselberg; Timothy J. Hightower. Of Counsel: William P. Wooden; Robert L. McLaughlin; Donald W. Buttrey.

(This Listing Continued)

Wooden & McLaughlin LLP (Continued)

General Civil Practice. Litigation, Banking, Corporate and Business, Real Estate, Commercial, Tax, Probate and Estate Planning, Labor and Employment Law, Environmental Law, Medical Malpractice, Wrongful Death, Airplane and Helicopter Crash Litigation, Railroad Accidents, Drug and Medical Device Litigation, Eminent Domain and Administrative Law.
Representative Clients: AIG Aviation, Inc; AT&T; BP Products North America, Inc.; CB Richard Ellis; Columbia/HCA; Huntington National Bank; Lauth Properties; Metropolitan Life Insurance Co.; U.S. Bank.

See Professional Biographies, INDIANAPOLIS, INDIANA

Woodhouse, Kevin C., (BV) ... '64 '89 C.347 B.A. L.477 J.D. [Ice M.]
Woodruff, Bryan B. ... '71 '98 C.679 B.A. L.347 J.D. [Bose M.&E.]
Woods, Alexa L. ... '— '99 C.679 B.A. L.345 J.D. [Ⓐ Sommer B.]
Woods, Jennifer Hays '71 '99
C.178 B.A. L.276 J.D. Staff Atty., IN Protec. & Advocacy Servs.
Woods, John P., (AV) ... '59 '84 C.210 B.A. L.345 J.D. P.O. Box 39147
Woods, Joseph R., (AV) ... '29 '64 C.347 B.S. L.345 J.D. P.O. Box 39147
Woods, Judy L., (AV) ... '52 '87 C.429 B.A. L.345 J.D. [Bose M.&E.]
Woods, Karen Ball, (BV) ... '68 '95 C.477 B.A. L.1119 J.D. [Bose M.&E.]
Woody, Michael J. ... '67 '99 C.63 B.S. L.345 J.D. 2124 E. Hanna Ave.
Woolley, Susan M., (BV) ... '64 '89 C.347 B.A. L.879 J.D. [Ⓐ Feiwell&H.]
Woolsey, Monty K., (AV) ... '58 '84 C.894 B.A. L.345 J.D. [Miroff,C.&W.]
Worland, Diane L. ... '50 '77 C&L.421 B.S., J.D. I.R.S.

Wormser, Peter L., (BV) '43 '68 C.347 B.S. L.1119 J.D.
156 East Market Street, Suite 1300, 46204
Telephone: 317-624-6700 Fax: 317-624-6701
Email: schleppers@aol.com URL: http://www.lawyers.com/peterwormser
Family Law, Divorce, Child Custody, Child Support, Guardianship, Adoption Law, Visitation Rights, Social Security Disability, Consumer Law, Bankruptcy.

See Professional Biographies, INDIANAPOLIS, INDIANA

Worrell, David C., (AV) ... '51 '76 C.894 A.B. L.145 J.D. [Baker&D.]
Wray, Donn H., (AV) ... '55 '80 C&L.879 B.A., J.D. [Stewart&I.]
Wright, Amy L. ... '73 '00 C.1024 B.S. L.345 J.D. [Ⓐ Dann P.N.&K.]
Wright, Brantley H. ... '65 '92 C.347 B.S. L.1119 J.D. [Bose M.&E.]
Wright, David E., (AV) ... '51 '77 C.347 B.S. L.345 J.D. [Ⓒ Kroger,G.&R.]
Wright, G. Robert, (BV) ... '39 '70 C.63 A.B. L.347 J.D. 232 N. College Avenue
Wright, Gerald R. ... '57 '83 C.63 B.S. L.345 J.D. Coun., Farm Bureau Ins. Cos.
Wright, Mark E., (AV) ... '60 '89 C.347 B.A. L.1119 J.D. [Baker&D.]
Wright, Robert W., (BV) ... '64 '90 C.894 B.A. L.395 J.D. [Dean-Webster&W.]
Wright, Ronald A., (BV) ... '44 '77 C.347 L.879 J.D. 9292 N. Meridian St.
Wright, Sharon L. ... '42 '75 C.679 B.S. L.1065 J.D. [Ⓐ Linder&H.]
Wright, Vicki J. ... '59 '99 C.347 B.A. L.345 J.D. [Ⓐ Krieg D.]
Wroblewski, Michael ... '77 '02 C.651 B.A. L.879 J.D. [Ⓐ Kightlinger&G.]
Wu, Lawrence ... '57 '00 C.339 A.B. L.1119 J.D. 100 N. Senae Ave.
Wuellner, Mark J. ... '80 '05 C.108 B.S. L.1556 J.D. [Ⓐ Bose M.&E.]
Wukmer, Michael A., (AV) ... '57 '84 C&L.150 B.A., J.D. [Ice M.]
Wunder, David Hart, (BV) ... '25 '63 C.894 A.B. L.146 J.D. [Wunder&W.] ‡
Wunder, Mary Ann, (BV) ... '48 '79 C.679 B.A. L.347 J.D. [Wunder&W.]
Wunder and Wunder, (BV) ... 4949 S. Carson Ave.
Wurster, William F., (AV) ... '34 '62 C.108 B.S. L.345 LL.B. Peoples Bk. Bldg.
Wykes, Walter F. '25 '59 C&L.912 LL.B.
(adm. in MI; not adm. in IN) Amer. States Ins. Co.
Wynne, Robert S., (AV) ... '57 '85 C.210 B.A. L.1119 J.D. [Baker&D.]
Yackey, Allan L., (BV) ... '45 '80 C.910 B.S. L.345 J.D. [Ladd&Y.]
Yang-Page, Katy H.H. ... '— '95 C.597 B.A. L.569 J.D. [Ⓒ Ogletree,D.N.S.&S.]
Yarling, Richard W., (AV) ... '21 '49 C.347 A.B. L.345 J.D. [Ⓒ Yarling&R.]

Yarling & Robinson, (AV)
151 North Delaware, Suite 1535, P.O. Box 44128, 46204
Telephone: 317-262-8800 Fax: 317-262-3046
Email: yrhl@yarling.com URL: http://www.yarling.com
Members of Firm: Charles F. Robinson, Jr.; Linda Y. Hammel; Matthew C. Robinson; Brian L. Nehrig. Associates: Sarah Dillinger; Christopher P. Hamilton. Of Counsel: Seth M. Lahn; Richard W. Yarling.
General and Appellate Practice. Negligence, Insurance, Commercial, Bankruptcy, Corporation, Products Liability and Probate and Estate Planning. Trials and Appeals.
Representative Clients: Allstate Insurance Co.; American Family Mutual Insurance Company; Chrysler Credit Corporation; Fleet Financenter; General Motors Acceptance Corporation; Household Finance Corporation; Monroe Guaranty Insurance Company; Northbrook Property & Casualty Company; Pafco General Insurance Company; Security Pacific Finance Corporation.

See Professional Biographies, INDIANAPOLIS, INDIANA

Yaser, Vickie ... '52 '84 C.347 B.A. L.345 J.D. Master Comr., Mun. Ct.
Yates, C. Daniel, (AV) ... '47 '73 C.347 A.B. L.1119 J.D. [Bose M.&E.]
Yates, Lynn M. ... '61 '94 C.679 B.A. L.345 J.D. 6330 E. 75th St., Ste. 102
Yates, Michael E. '54 '89 C.932 B.A. L.424 J.D.
(adm. in IL; not adm. in IN; Pat.) Eli Lilly & Co.
Yeager, Joseph H., Jr., (AV) ... '57 '83 C.309 B.A. L.1119 J.D. [Baker&D.]
Yerkes, Kenneth J., (AV) ... '— '83 C.231 B.A. L.1119 J.D. [Barnes&T.]
Yerkes, Wendy V., (AV) ... '60 '86 C.914 B.A. L.424 J.D. 1 Monument Circle
Yerkeson, Douglas A. ... '67 '94 C&L.150 B.S.M.E., J.D. [Ⓒ Baker&D.] (See Pat. Sect.)
Yolles, Jeffrey S. ... '75 '03 C.347 B.S. L.910 J.D. [Ⓐ Henderson D.W.&D.]
Yonover, Scott D. ... '64 '89 C.347 B.A. L.1119 J.D. [Ⓒ Lewis&K.]
Yoon, Hongsun ... '— '02 C.347 B.S. L.1119 J.D. [Ⓐ Barnes&T.] (See Pat. Sect.)
York, Christopher M. ... '63 '99 C&L.347 B.S., J.D. [Ⓐ Bingham M.]
York, Kevin M. '58 '86 C.724 B.S. L.836 J.D.
(adm. in NY; not adm. in IN) Sr. Staff Atty., Simon Property Group
York, Robert W., (AV) ... '44 '73 C&L.347 B.S., J.D. [R.W.York&Assoc.]

York, Robert W., & Associates, (AV) BR
7212 North Shadeland Avenue Suite 150, 46250-2030
Telephone: 317-842-8000 Fax: 317-577-7321
Email: rwyork@york-law.com URL: http://www.yorklaw-firm.com
Member of Firm: Robert W. York;—Lawrence T. Newman. Of Counsel: James A. Mellowitz.
Personal Injury, Automobile Accidents, Wrongful Death, Insurance Disputes, Insurance Bad Faith, Unsafe Products, Family Law, Divorce, Child Support, Child Custody, Trial Practice, Insurance Law, Business Law, Business Planning, Contracts, Lawsuits, Business Enterprises, Corporate, Partnerships, Limited Liability Companies, Small Business, Starting a Business, Buying and Selling a Business, Strategic Alliances, Products Liability, Wills and Probate, Trusts and Estates, Estate Planning, Guardianships, Asset Protection, Estate Disputes.

See Professional Biographies, INDIANAPOLIS, INDIANA

Yosha, Louis Buddy, (AV) ... '37 '63 C.347 B.A. L.1119 J.D. [Yosha K.&L.]
Yosha Krahulik & Levy, (AV) ... 3500 West DePauw Boulevard, Suite 2015
Young, D. Michael '52 '88 C.679 B.S. L.347 J.D.
Chf. Pat. Coun., Roche Diagnostics Corp. (Pat.)
Young, Denise K., (BV) '57 '83
C.475 B.A. L.1187 J.D. 3815 River Crossing Parkway (⊙Aspen, CO)
Young, Elizabeth Theobald, (AV) ... '57 '83 C.347 A.B. L.345 J.D. [Robinson W.&Y.]
Young, Howard S., Jr., (AV) ... '13 '36 C.145 A.B. L.1119 LL.B. [Young&Y.]

Young, J. David, Law Offices of, (BV) '50 '77 C.347 B.A. L.1230 J.D.
3850 Priority Way S. Drive Suite 100, 46240
Telephone: 317-580-2582 Facsimile: 317-571-0177
Email: jdyjd@aol.com URL: http://www.jdyounglawfirm.com
Creditor Rights, Product Liability Defense, Insurance Defense, Business Law, Contracts, Business Litigation, Business Enterprises, Corporate, Partnerships, Limited Liability Companies, Small Business, Buying and Selling a Business, Starting a Business, Debt and Credit, Collections, Business Planning, Entertainment & Sports Law, Real Estate, Commercial Litigation, Wills and Probate, Contested Wills Litigation, Art Law, Intellectual Property, Insurance Law, Environmental Law, Construction Law, Family Law, Divorce, Child Custody, Adoption Law, Employment Law, Personal Injury, Automobile Accidents, Wrongful Death.

See Professional Biographies, INDIANAPOLIS, INDIANA

Young, James H., (AV) ... '56 '81 C.347 A.B. L.345 J.D. [Young&Y.]
Young, James T., (BV) ... '61 '87 C.347 B.S. L.1119 J.D. [Ⓐ Rubin&L.]
Young, John A., (AV) ... '28 '59 C.963 B.E. L.345 J.D. 36 S. Penn St.
Young, John P., (AV) ... '62 '88 C.347 B.A. L.345 J.D. [Young&Y.]
Young, Joseph B., (BV) ... '61 '89 C.347 B.S. L.426 J.D. [Young&Y.]
Young, Karen H. ... '— '05 C.130 L.1119 J.D. [Ⓐ Jensen&Assoc.]
Young, Marilyn A. ... '60 '89 C.679 B.S. L.347 J.D. [Ⓐ Zeigler C.&K.]
Young, Mary McNulty, (BV) ... '25 '51 C.435 A.B. L.345 LL.B. [Young&Y.]
Young, Richard A., (AV) ... '50 '76 C.63 B.S. L.345 J.D. [Kightlinger&G.]
Young, Richard A. "Drew", (AV) ... '45 '71 C.597 A.B. L.345 J.D. [Young&Y.]
Young, Susan D. ... '65 '91 C.108 B.A. L.347 J.D. Law Clk., Assoc. Supm. Ct. Jus.
Young & Young, (AV) ... 128 North Delaware Street
Youngcourt, Lorinda M. ... '63 '88 C&L.347 B.A., J.D. 6202 N. College Ave.
Yount, Steven L., (AV) ... '56 '83 C.210 B.A. L.345 J.D. [J.D.Babcock]
Zaban, Robert A. ... '37 '69 C.679 B.S. L.345 J.D. 5525 S. Meridian St.
Zafrullah, Tareen ... '— '05 C.910 B.S.B.A. L.273 J.D. [Ⓐ Baker&D.]
Zahn, Dennis E., (AV) ... '41 '68 C.1216 B.A. L.345 J.D. [Voyles,Z.P.H.&M.]
Zaiger, Heather S. Wysong ... '74 '02 C&L.347 B.A., J.D. [Ⓐ Cohen G.&G.]
Zakrocki, Steven L. ... '71 '01 C.347 B.S. L.1119 J.D. [Ⓐ Riley B.&E.]
Zappia, Joseph F. ... '25 '71 C.108 B.S. L.347 J.D. 118 N. Gibson Ave.
Zeigler, Robert G., (AV) ... '50 '80 C.337 B.A. L.339 J.D. [Zeigler C.&K.]

Zeigler Cohen & Koch, (AV) BR
9465 Counselors Row, Suite 104, 46240
Telephone: 317-844-5200 Facsimile: 317-844-7200
Robert G. Zeigler; Steven J. Cohen; Edna M. Koch; David Becsey; Roger K. Kanne. Associates: Marilyn A. Young; Joseph D. McPike, II; Jennifer A. Strickland-Padgett; Andrew R. Bloch; Bobby J. Avery-Seagrave.
Health Care and Hospital Law, Medical Malpractice Defense. Civil Trial and Appellate Practice. Insurance Defense, Products Liability Law.

See Professional Biographies, INDIANAPOLIS, INDIANA

Zelman-Finch, Paula L. ... '71 '03 C.679 B.A. L.345 J.D. [Ⓐ Lewis&K.]
Zelmer, Patricia A., (AV) ... '60 '86 C.347 B.S. L.602 J.D. [Ice M.]
Zimmer, Bradley A. '62 '89 C.346 B.S. L.1119 J.D.
Sr. Tax Mgr., Deloitte & Touche LLP
Zimmermann, Albert W., (AV) ... '33 '61 C&L.879 B.A., J.D. 7351 Shadeland Sta.
Zink, R.D., (AV) ... '48 '78 C.701 B.S.M.E. L.345 J.D. [Ⓒ Goodin A.&M.]
Zinkan, Stephen P., (AV) ... '50 '75 C.93 B.S. L.345 J.D. 5332 N. Temple Ave.‡
Zivitz, Martin W. ... '— '00 C.347 B.A. L.345 J.D. [Ⓐ Barnes&T.]
Zlatos, Elizabeth Ann ... '55 '87 C.347 B.S.W. L.345 J.D. Envir. Air Prog. Coun.
Zlatos, Stephen E., (AV) '51 '77
C.679 B.S.E. L.345 J.D. [Woodard,E.M.M.&H.] (See Pat. Sect.)
Zoba, C. David ... '51 '81 C.309 A.B. L.930 J.D. Gen. Coun., Galyans Trading Co.
Zoccola, James E., (BV) ... '66 '91 C.347 B.S. L.345 J.D. [Lewis&K.]
Zoeller, Brian K., (BV) ... '70 '96 C.344 B.A.B.S. L.74 J.D. [Cohen&M.]
Zoeller, Christopher C., (BV) ... '49 '74 C&L.347 A.B., J.D. 543 East Market Street
Zoeller, D. Bryce, (AV) ... '69 '95 C&L.347 B.A., J.D. [Kightlinger&G.]
Zoeller, Gregory F., (AV) ... '55 '82 C.347 B.A. L.1119 J.D. 4808 North Park Avenue
Zoeller, Susan M., (BV) ... '— '95 C.63 B.A. L.1119 J.D. [Barnes&T.]
Zook, Kerry E. ... '69 '96 C.999 B.S. L.893 J.D. Staff Atty., Eli Lilly & Co.
Zore, Gerald S. ... '41 '68 C.1216 A.B. L.345 J.D. Supr. Ct. J.
Zubek, S. Gregory, (AV) ... '51 '76 C.347 B.S. L.365 J.D. 151 N. Delaware St., Ste. 2000
Zuckerberg, Mark S., (AV) ... '61 '87 C.347 B.A. L.117 J.D. [M.S.Zuckerberg]
Zuckerberg, Mark S., P.C., (AV) ... 333 North Pennsylvania Street, Suite 100
Zunk, Mark K. ... '58 '83 C.679 B.A. L.345 J.D. [O'Koon H.]
Zuran, Katherine D. ... '63 '89 C.347 B.A. L.1119 J.D. [Ⓐ O'Koon H.]
Zurek, Thomas M., (AVⓣ) '48 '74 C&L.221 B.S., J.D.
Gen. Coun. & Secy., American United Life Insurance Co.
Zusy, F. Jonathan, (BV) '53 '84
C.174 B.S. L.464 J.D. V.P. & Gen. Coun., Intl. Medical Group, Inc.
Zweig, Sally Franklin, (AV) ... '50 '86 C.910 B.A. L.345 J.D. [Katz&K.]

JASPER, * 12,100, *Dubois Co.*

Bingham McHale LLP, (AV)
212 West Sixth Street, 47546 ⊙
Telephone: 812-482-5500 Fax: 812-482-2017
Email: firm@binghammchale.com URL: http://www.binghammchale.com
John S. Chappell; William J. Kaiser, Jr.
General Civil Practice, Business Law, Business Litigation, Environmental Law, Estate Planning and Administration, Governmental Services, Intellectual Property, Labor and Employment, Patent, Public Finance, Public Utility Law, Real Estate, Zoning, Planning and Land Use.
Indianapolis, Indiana Office: Bingham McHale LLP, 2700 Market Tower, 10 West Market Street. Telephone: 317-635-8900. Fax: 317-236-9907.
Noblesville, Indiana Office: Bingham McHale LLP, 970 Logan Street, Telephone: 317-776-8668. Fax: 317-776-8651.
Vincennes, Indiana Office: Bingham Mchale LLP, 112 North 7th Street. Telephone: 812-886-9970. Fax: 812-886-0776.

See Professional Biographies, JASPER, INDIANA

Birk, John E., (CV) ... '59 '89 C.870 B.S. L.345 J.D. [Birk&B.]
Birk, Thomas H., (BV) ... '56 '81 C.679 B.S.M.E. L.880 J.D. [Birk&B.]

Birk & Birk, Attorneys At Law, P.C., (BV)
520 Main Street, Suite 1, P.O. Box 1024, 47547-1024
Telephone: 812-482-2093 Fax: 812-482-7218 URL: http://www.lawyers.com/birklaw
URL: http://www.birklawfirm.com
John E. Birk; Thomas H. Birk.
Banking, Civil Litigation, Commercial Collections, Construction Law, Creditors Rights and Bankruptcy, Environmental, General Business and Commercial Practice, Government, Municipal, and Administrative, Insurance Defense, Health Care Law, Real Estate, Probate and Estate Planning, Healthcare Planning, Insurance Subrogation, Employment Law & Labor Relations, Intellectual Property Law.
References: Dubois County Bank, Jasper, Indiana; The German American Bank, Jasper, Indiana; Citizens Bank of Jasper, Jasper, Indiana.

See Professional Biographies, JASPER, INDIANA

Blazey, Scott A., (BV) ... '67 '92 C.249 B.S. L.201 J.D. [Ⓐ Ripstra]
Bradley, Steven C., (BV) ... '54 '79 C&L.383 B.A., J.D. [Bradley]
Bradley Law Firm, (BV) ... 4201 N. Mannheim Rd.

Brown, Roger W., (BV) .....'30 '58 C.249 B.A. L.1119 LL.B. Dep. Pros. Atty.; City Atty.
Chappell, John S., (AV) '47 '72 C.347 B.S. L.1119 J.D.
[Bingham M.] (⊙Indianapolis)
Crouse, Kevin D., (BV) .... '62 '91 C&L.347 B.S., J.D. [Nordhoff,C.&S.]
DeMotte, James R., (BV) .... '51 '78 C.346 B.S. L.1119 J.D. [Thom&D.]
Fischer, Gerald L., (CV) ....'49 '77 C.347 B.S. L.1119 J.D. [Fischer,F.&R.]
Fischer, Fritch & Rasche, (BV) .... 302 Main St.
Fritch, David P., (BV) ....'55 '81 C.347 B.S. L.345 J.D. [Fischer,F.&R.]
Fritch, Michael A., (BV) .... '59 '91 C.894 B.A. L.678 J.D. Pros. Atty. Off.
Hedinger, Keith G., (BV) '58 '84
C.602 B.B.A. L.1119 J.D. Hedinger Beverage Distributiing Co.,Inc.
Heitz, Julia E., (BV) .... '65 '91 C.383 B.A. L.347 J.D. Sr. Corp. Coun., Kimball Intl.
Hoffman, John R., Law Offices of '39 '64 C.277 B.I.E. L.1119 J.D.
(adm. in IL; not adm. in IN) P.O. Box 191
Kahle, John H., (BV) '57 '83 C.347 B.S. L.1119 J.D.
Exec. VP, General Counsel & Secretary, Kimball Intl.

Kahn, Dees, Donovan & Kahn, LLP
(See Evansville)

Kaiser, William J., Jr., (BV) '65 '90
C.894 B.A. L.347 J.D. [Bingham M.] (⊙Indianapolis)
Krodel, Karen L., (BV) .... '53 '80 C.679 B.S. L.879 J.D. [Krodel]
Krodel Law Office, P.C., (BV) ....3306 Newton St.
Lytton, Howard B., Jr., (BV) ....'38 '66 C.603 B.S. L.1119 J.D. Supr. Ct. J.
McConnell, Mark R., (BV) ....'59 '85 C.210 B.A. L.345 J.D. [McConnell]
McConnell Law Office, (BV) ....502 Jackson St.
Nordhoff, Arthur C., Jr., (AV) ....'40 '65 C.602 B.B.A. L.347 J.D. [Nordhoff,C.&S.]
Nordhoff, Crouse & Smith, (AV) .... 710 Main Street
Phillips, Ray Chappell '67 '94 C&L.575 B.A., J.D.
(adm. in NC; not adm. in IN) Assoc. Corp. Cnsl., Kimball International
Poag, Jesse R. ....'77 '02 C.999 B.S. L.801 J.D. [Ripstra]
Quinn, Anthony Dean, (BV) ....'72 '98 C.347 B.A. L.879 J.D. [Ripstra]
Rasche, Sandra K., (CV) ....'68 '94 C&L.347 B.A., J.D. [Fischer,F.&R.]
Ripstra, Steven E., (BV) ....'49 '78 C.63 B.S. L.192 J.D. [Ripstra]
Ripstra Law Office, (BV) .... 418 Main St.
Shaneyfelt, William L., (BV) ....'52 '77 C.346 B.S. L.213 J.D. 716 Clay St.
Smith, Debra K., (BV) ....'67 '94 C.249 B.S. L.801 J.D. [Nordhoff,C.&S.]
Smith, Debra Kaye, (BV) ....'58 '83 C.108 B.A. L.345 J.D. 710 Main St.
Songer, Hugo C. ....'31 '60 C.347 B.S. L.1119 LL.B. Cir. J.‡
Thom, Gerald R., (BV) ....'44 '73 C.597 B.S. L.345 J.D. [Thom&D.]
Thom & DeMotte, (BV) .... 714 Main St.
Weikert, William E., (BV) ....'45 '70 C.347 A.B. L.1119 J.D. Pros. Atty.

JEFFERSONVILLE, * 27,362, *Clark Co.*

Abbott, Kenneth R., (BV) .... '55 '85 C.347 B.S. L.421 J.D. P.O. Box 148
Adams, Andrew ....'71 '01 C.347 B.A. L.345 J.D. [Adams]
Adams Law Office ....430 Watt Street
Applegate, Alan M., (BV) .... '61 '87 C&L.260 B.S., J.D. [A.Applegate]
Applegate, Alan, (BV) .... 131 E. Court Ave.
Ballard, Frank E., Jr., (CV) .... '49 '81 C.347 B.A. L.421 J.D. [Ballard]
Ballard Law Office, (CV) .... 425 E. 7th St.
Barker, E. Gerry, (BV) ....'29 '55 C.902 B.A. L.421 LL.B. 220 E. Court Ave
Barthold, Clementine B. ....'21 '80 C&L.347 B.G.S., J.D. [Barthold&D.]
Barthold & DeSimone Law Office, (BV) ....635 East 8th Street
Bartlett, Rick E., (BV) ....'56 '81 C.347 B.S. L.1119 J.D. [Smith,B.H.C.T.&F.]
Bates, Douglas B., (BV) ....'65 '92 C&L.347 B.A., J.D. [Stites&H.]
Bertrand, Jennifer A., (CV) ....'66 '93 C.93 B.A. L.1036 J.D. [Mosley,B.J.&M.]
Blanton, Paul Matthew ....'74 '00 C.383 B.A. L.356 J.D. 530 E. Court Ave.
Blau, Cecile Anne ....'45 '75 C.589 B.S.E. L.421 J.D. Supr. Ct. J.
Bolin, Richard G., (BV) .... '44 '73 C.347 B.A. L.1119 J.D. 1907 Blackiston Mill Rd.
Bradshaw, Samuel A. ....'41 '71 C.347 B.A. L.1119 J.D. P.O. Box 761
Branstetter, Jeffrey Keith ....'63 '00 C.347 B.G.S. L.1036 J.D. 530 E. Court Ave.
Brubeck, David H., Law Office of ....'42 '68 C.347 A.B. L.1119 J.D. 317 E. Riverside Dr.
Byrne, Maurice A., Jr., (BV) '43 '74
C&L.128 B.A., J.D. 432 E. Ct. Ave. (⊙Louisville, KY)
Carmichael, Vicki L., (BV) ....'62 '87 C.347 B.A. L.421 J.D. Asst. Pub. Def.
Carpenter, Cheryl A., (BV) .... '52 '80 C.879 B.A. L.421 J.D. [Smith,B.H.C.T.&F.]
Clary, William M., Jr., (BV) .... '47 '73 C.346 B.S. L.421 J.D. 607 Watt St.
Coleman, Carlo B. ....'44 '71 C.1129 B.S. L.421 J.D. 516 E. Court Ave.

Colomb, Bart, Law Office of
(See New Albany)

Cosby, Dwight A., (CV) ....'64 '93 C&L.383 B.A., J.D. [Cosby]
Cosby Law Office L.L.C., (CV) ....611 Watt Street
Cummins, Rachele Leigh ....'74 '00 [Ⓐ Smith,B.H.C.T.&F.]
DeSimone, Judith A., (BV) ....'44 '81 C.822 B.A. L.1243 J.D. [Barthold&D.]
Doehrman, John W., (BV) ....'44 '71 C.347 A.B. L.1119 J.D. 425 Watt St.
Donahue, Daniel F. ....'40 '64 C.363 A.B. L.421 J.D. Jus.
Fifer, Ronald R., (AV) ..... '31 '58 C.347 B.S. L.421 LL.B. 131 East Court Avenue, #101

Fifer, Vogt & Lanum
(See Stites & Harbison, PLLC)

Fleece, Steven M. ....'50 '82 C.347 B.A. L.421 J.D. Supr. Ct. J.
Fleming, Lisa L. ....'61 '85 C.303 B.A. L.421 J.D. Amer. Coml. Lines LLC
Fondrisi, Mary E., (BV) ....'50 '93 C.1150 B.S. L.421 J.D. [Smith,B.H.C.T.&F.]
Forsee, Michael T., (BV) ....'48 '76 C.347 B.S. L.421 J.D. 408 E. Court St.
Fowler, Anne B., (BV) ....'48 '78 C.347 B.S. L.1119 J.D. 324 E. Court Ave.
Frazier, Carl C., (BV) ....'51 '85 C.275 B.A. L.421 J.D. Deputy Pros.
Fresh, Douglas, (BV) ....'38 '71 C.347 A.B. L.188 J.D. P.O. Box 1476
Gabhart, Charles M., (BV) ....'26 '63 C&L.421 A.B., J.D. 525 E. 7th St.
Gabhart, Charles Paige, (BV) .... '48 '89 C.421 B.M. L.347 J.D. [Gabhart]
Gabhart Law Offices, PC, (BV) .... 525 E. 7th St.
Galligan, Anne Marie, (BV) ....'55 '80 C.347 B.S. L.345 J.D. City Atty.
Gillenwater, Michael A., (BV) ....'58 '85 C.347 B.A. L.421 J.D. 411 Watt St.
Grannan, John L. ....'75 '02 C.894 A.B. L.74 J.D. [Ⓐ Vissing&G.]
Grayson, Joni L., (BV) ....'57 '93 C.346 B.S. L.421 J.D. [Vissing&G.]
Green, Samuel T., (BV) ....'44 '78 C.347 B.S. L.421 J.D. 3307 Holman Ln.
Guilfoyle, J. Charles, (BV) .... '49 '83 431 East Court Avenue
Harlan, Mitchele James, (CV) ....'60 '85 C.27 B.A. L.421 J.D. 1021 Springdale Dr.
Harmon, J. Spencer, (AV) '42 '73
C.378 B.S. L.345 J.D. [Ⓒ Stites&H.] (⊙Louisville, KY)
Harris, Ronald D., (CV) ....'55 '81 C&L.421 B.A., J.D. 3008 Middle Rd.
Heeke, Sandra L., (BV) ....'55 '81 C.347 B.S. L.1119 J.D. [Smith,B.H.C.T.&F.]
Heinrichs, Steven S. '68 '94 C.893 B.A. L.861 J.D.
(adm. in TN; not adm. in IN) Assoc. Gen. Coun. & Asst. Secy., Amer. Coml. Lines LLC
Heinz, A. Joseph ....'61 '96 C.347 B.A. L.421 J.D. 326 E. Court Avenue

Henderson, Joan B., (BV) .... '— '79 C.129 B.A. L.421 J.D. [Henderson]
Henderson Law Office, The, (BV) .... 521 E. 7th St.
Hess, Carroll E., (BV) ....'32 '56 C&L.421 A.B., LL.B. [C.E.Hess]
Hess, Carroll E., Law Office, (BV) ....431 E. Ct. Ave.
Hoehn, Elmer L., (AV) .... '15 '40 C.135 B.S. L.421 J.D. Admr., U.S. Oil Admn.‡
Jacobi, Jerome F., (CV) ....'55 '79 C.347 A.B. L.201 J.D. Co. Pros.
Jacobs, Bradley B. ....'72 '99 [Ⓐ Mosley,B.J.&M.]
Jacobs, George A. ....'46 '75 C.347 B.S. L.421 J.D. 332 Spring St.
Jacobs, Matthew S., (CV) ....'70 '96 [Mosley,B.J.&M.]
Lang, James A., (BV) ....'39 '66 C.1150 A.B. L.1119 J.D. 412 E. Court Ave.
Lanum, Robert W., (AV) ....'36 '68 C.347 B.S. L.421 J.D. [Ⓒ Stites&H.]
Lewis, David A., (BV) ....'51 '76 C.347 B.A. L.421 J.D. 425 Watt St.
Lewis, Sandra Winnett, (BV) '50 '90
C.347 B.A. L.421 J.D. Gen. Coun., Greater Clark Cty. School Corp.
Lindsey, Roger L. ....'52 '77 C.347 B.S. L.421 J.D. 408 E. Court Ave.‡

Lynch, Cox, Gilman & Mahan, P.S.C.
(See Louisville, Kentucky)

Maddox, Cynthia Buss, (BVⓉ) '62 '88 C.597 B.A. L.228 J.D.
(adm. in KY; not adm. in IN) Corp. Coun., American Commercial Lines, LLC
Maschmeyer, Michael M., (BV) .... '56 '81 C.347 B.S. L.345 J.D. 426 E. Court Ave.

Mattox Mattox & Wilson
(See New Albany)

McCall, William P., III, (CV) ....'61 '88 C.235 B.A. L.421 J.D. [Mosley,B.J.&M.]
Merkley, Leslie D., (CV) .... '69 '97 C.347 B.A. L.1187 J.D. [Merkley]

Merkley Law Office, (CV)
538 E. Court Avenue, 47130
Telephone: 812-285-9787 Fax: 812-288-0811
Email: lmerkley@sbcglobal.net URL: http://www.merkleylaw.net
Leslie D. Merkley.
Family Law, Criminal Law, Estates and Wills, Personal Injury, Municipal Law.
See Professional Biographies, JEFFERSONVILLE, INDIANA

Middleton Reutlinger, P.S.C., (AV) ....530 E. Court Ave. (⊙Louisville, KY)
Miller, Gary D. ....'60 '85 C.603 B.S. L.1119 J.D. 412 E. Court Ave.
Montgomery, John G., (BV) ....'45 '72 C.679 B.A. L.421 J.D. 417 E. Court Ave.
Moore, Daniel E., (BV) ....'52 '81 C.265 B.A. L.365 J.D. 411 Watt St.
Morris, Allen L., (BV) ....'48 '78 C&L.421 A.B., J.D. [Stites&H.]
Mosley, David E., (BV) ....'58 '86 C&L.421 B.A., J.D. [Mosley,B.J.&M.]
Mosley, Bertrand, Jacobs & McCall, (BV) ....332 Spring St.
Mull, Jeremy Todd ....'73 '98 C.347 B.A. L.1119 J.D. 2307 Arthur Street
Mull, Keith D., (CV) .... '60 '93 C.235 B.A. L.345 J.D. 131 E. Court Ave., Ste. 101

Murphy, Charles R.
(See New Albany)

Nachand, David D., (BV) ....'47 '73 C.346 B.S. L.421 LL.B. [Nachand&N.]
Nachand, Henry ....'20 '48 [Nachand&N.] ‡
Nachand & Nachand, (BV) .... 426 E. Court Ave.
Paynter, Harry S. ....'26 '64 C.347 A.B. L.421 J.D. 408 E. Court Ave.
Petzinger, Stephen R. ....'57 '87 C.1150 B.A. L.421 J.D. [S.Petzinger]
Petzinger, Stephen ....3310-4 Suite 43, Highway 62
Plumley, Laura C. '60 '85 C.264 B.A. L.1019 J.D.
Sr. V.P. & Gen. Coun., Presbyterian Church (U.S.A.) Foundation
Read, Charles Gregory, (BV) ....'48 '77 C&L.383 B.S., J.D. 432 E. Ct. Ave.
Schell, Kathleen Kearney, (CV) ....'50 '86 C.1150 B.S.N. L.421 J.D. 422 E. 7th St.

Sedwick, Edwin S., Law Office of, (AV) '46 '72 C.347 B.S. L.421 J.D. BB
417 East Court Avenue, 47130
Telephone: 812-282-7200 Facsimile: 812-282-7393
Email: edwinsedwick@sbcglobal.net URL: http://www.edwinsedwick.com
General Personal Injury, Wrongful Death, Insurance Claims, Trials and Appeals, Family Law.
See Professional Biographies, JEFFERSONVILLE, INDIANA

Sewell and Associates
(See Louisville, Kentucky)

Shaw, Amber C., (CV) ....'72 '97 C.881 B.A. L.421 J.D. [Ⓐ Mosley,B.J.&M.]
Silletto, Gary L., Law Office Of, (BV) ... '46 '76 C.593 B.S. L.502 J.D. 424 E. Court Ave.
Smith, Ernest W., (AV) ....'37 '65 C.347 A.B. L.1119 J.D. [Smith,B.H.C.T.&F.]
Smith, Bartlett, Heeke, Carpenter, Thompson & Fondrisi, (AV) .... 209 E. Chestnut St.
Stevens, Andrea K. R. ....'71 '96 C.63 B.A. L.421 J.D. Dep. Pros. Atty.
Stewart, Steven D., (BV) ....'53 '80 C.347 B.A. L.421 J.D. Pros. Atty., Clark Co.

Stites & Harbison, PLLC, (BV)
Formerly Fifer, Vogt & Lanum
323 East Court Avenue, 47130 ⊙
Telephone: 812-282-7566 Fax: 812-284-5519
Email: general@stites.com URL: http://www.stites.com
Members: Allen L. Morris; Douglas B. Bates. Counsel: J. Spencer Harmon. Of Counsel: Robert W. Lanum.
General Civil Practice in all State and Federal Courts. Acquisitions, Divestitures and Mergers, Administrative Hearings and Appeals, Admiralty, Antitrust, Appellate Practice, Aviation, Banking, Bankruptcy, Charitable Trusts and Foundations, Commercial, Complex Litigation, Construction, Corporation, Defense of Legal and Medical Malpractice and Personal Injury, Dissolution of Marriage, Employment, Environmental, Equine, Estate Planning and Probate Administration, Health Care, Insurance Defense, Labor Legislative Practice, Litigation, Mineral, Planning and Zoning, Public Finance, Products Liability Litigation, Real Estate, Securities, Social Security Disability, Taxation (Local, State, Federal Income, Estate and Gift), Toxic Torts Litigation, Trust(s) and Utilities. Intellectual Property, including Patents (Mechanical, Biochemical, Chemical, Computer, Medical, Metallurgical, Pharmaceutical, Electromechanical), Trademarks, Copyrights, and Trade Secrets, Franchising and Licensing Law, and Litigation Related to Intellectual Property Matters, including Infringement, Unfair Competition, and Deceptive Trade Practices.
Atlanta, Georgia Office: 303 Peachtree Street, N.E., 2800 SunTrust Plaza, 30308. Telephone: 404-739-8800. Fax: 404-739-8870.
Frankfort, Kentucky Office: 421 West Main Street, 40601-0634. Telephone: 502-223-3477. Fax: 502-223-4124.
Lexington, Kentucky Office: 250 West Main Street, Suite 2300, 40507-1758. Telephone: 859-226-2300. Fax: 859-253-9144.
Louisville, Kentucky Office: 400 West Market Street, Suite 1800, 40202-3352. Telephone: 502-587-3400. Fax: 502-587-6391.
Nashville, Tennessee Office: 424 Church Street, Suite 1800, 37219-2376. Telephone: 615-244-5200. Fax: 615-782-2371.
Washington, D.C. Office: 1200 G Street, N.W., Suite 800, 20005. Telephone: 202-682-4700. Fax: 703-938-0143.
Alexandria, Virginia Office: 1199 North Fairfax Street, Suite 900, 22314. Telephone: 703-739-4900. Fax: 703-739-9577.
Reviser of the Kentucky Law Digest for this Directory.
See Professional Biographies, JEFFERSONVILLE, INDIANA

Thomas, Thomas R., (BV) ....'46 '72 C&L.383 B.A., J.D. 431 E. Court Ave.
Thompson, Pamela K., (BV) ....'61 '91 C.347 B.S. L.421 J.D. [Smith,B.H.C.T.&F.]
Truman, Karl N., (BV) ....'61 '87 C.383 B.B.A. L.421 J.D. [K.Truman]
Truman, Karl, Law Office, LLC, (BV) ....131 East Court Avenue, Suite 300

Vissing, John R., (BV) .... '48 '76 C.210 B.A. L.421 J.D. [Vissing&G.]
Vissing & Grayson, LLP, (BV) .... 432 East Court Avenue
Voelker, Stephen W., (BVⓉ) .... '44 '74 C&L.421 B.S., J.D. [Voelker]
Voelker Law Office, (BVⓉ) .... 420 Wall St.
Waiz, Michael D. .... '50 '80 C.303 B.S. L.421 J.D. Union Planters Bank
Wathen, Richard B. .... '17 '42 C.674 A.B. L.1119 J.D. State Rep.
Webb, Charles D., Jr., (BVⓉ) '68 '92 C.437 B.B.A. L.383 J.D.
(adm. in KY; not adm. in IN) Assoc. Gen. Coun., American Commercial Lines, LLC

Weber & Rose, Professional Service Corporation
(See Louisville, Kentucky)

Webster, Mark C., (BVⓉ) .... '52 '85 C.602 B.A. L.421 J.D. [K.Truman]
Wilcox, Sandra K. .... '— '97 C.421 B.A. L.1339 J.D. Co. Pros. Off.
Wilder, Darren G. .... '71 '99 C.265 B.A. L.356 J.D. 530 E. Court Ave.
Williams, James N., Jr., (AV) .... '43 '67 C.347 A.B. L.145 J.D. [Middleton R.] ⊙

KENDALLVILLE, 9,616, *Noble Co.*

Abbs, James, (BV) .... '59 '85 C.962 B.S. L.900 J.D. [🄰 Emerick&D.]
Atz, Douglas J., (BV) .... '52 '77 C.347 B.S. L.345 J.D. 202 S. Main St.

Blackburn & Green
(See Fort Wayne)

Diggins, Daniel F., (AV) .... '44 '72 C.347 B.S. L.345 J.D. [Emerick&D.]
Diggins, Merritt W., (AV) .... '13 '36 C.347 L.1119 LL.B. 218 S. Main St.
Emerick, R. Stan, (AV) .... '21 '49 C.894 A.B. L.477 LL.B. [Emerick&D.]
Emerick & Diggins, P.C., (AV) .... 218 South Main Street
Hanson, Howard F., (BV) .... '53 '81 C&L.607 B.S., J.D. [🄰 Emerick&D.]
Hossinger, Hal C., Attorney at Law, (CV) '57 '82 C.347 A.B. L.345 J.D.
729 E. North St.
Mowery, James B., (BV) .... '72 '97 C.679 B.A. L.879 J.D. [Yoder&M.]
Owen, Jon C., (CV) .... '51 '76 C.347 B.S. L.345 J.D. 127 E. Williams St.

Roebuck & Associates, P.C.
(See Ft. Wayne)

Shostak, Denise S. .... '60 '85 C&L.665 B.A., J.D. 610 Timberlane Drive

Stout, Wheeler & Zabona
(See Angola)

Thrapp, John C., (BV) .... '34 '61 C.894 B.A. L.421 LL.B. 116 W. Mitchell St.
Yoder, Michael M., (AV) .... '47 '71 C.63 B.S. L.602 J.D. [Yoder&M.]

Yoder & Mowery, PC, (AV)
515 Professional Way, P.O. Box 633, 46755
Telephone: 260-347-9400 Fax: 260-347-0692 Email: mike.ym@mchsi.com Email: jim.ym@mchsi.com
Email: myoder@yoderlawoffice.com
Michael M. Yoder; James B. Mowery.
General Trial Practice. Probate and Estate Planning, Elder Law, Medicaid Planning, Personal Injury, Corporate, Real Estate and Family/Domestic Relations and Criminal Law.
See Professional Biographies, KENDALLVILLE, INDIANA

KENTLAND, * 1,798, *Newton Co.*

Ballard, Richard, Attorney at Law
(See Knox)

Barce, Ed .... '58 '86 C&L.347 B.S., J.D. 301 East Graham Street
Barce, J. Edward, (BV) .... '58 '86 C&L.347 B.S., J.D. Pros. Atty., Newton Co.
Falk, Harry J., (BV) .... '60 '85 C.347 B.A. L.879 J.D. 202 N. 3rd St.
Molter, Daniel J. .... '51 '78 C.346 B.S. L.1151 J.D. Supr. Ct. J.
Molter, Samuel E., (BV) .... '20 '49 C&L.602 A.B., J.D. 113 N. 3rd St.
Ryan, R. Steven, (AV) .... '42 '68 C&L.347 B.S., J.D. 301 E. Graham St.
Sammons, George M., (BV) .... '28 '54 C.210 B.A. L.1119 J.D. 116 N. Third St.

Tonner, Ned, Attorney at Law
(See Rensselaer)

KNIGHTSTOWN, 2,048, *Henry Co.*

Avery, Willard M., (BV) .... '07 '33 C.210 B.A. L.477 J.D. 120 E. Main St., Suite 1
Dunsmore, E. Edward, (AV) .... '47 '72 C.63 B.S. L.345 J.D. [E.Dunsmore]
Dunsmore, E., (AV) .... 18 N. Jefferson St.
Goodspeed, Patricia E. J. .... '44 '76 C.679 B.A. L.345 J.D. [P.Goodspeed]
Goodspeed, Pat, Attorney at Law .... 119 S. Washington St.

KNOX, * 3,705, *Starke Co.*

Ballard, Richard, Attorney at Law, (BV) '46 '85 C.347 L.879 J.D.
52 E. Washington Street, 46534
Telephone: 571-772-0455 Fax: 571-772-0455
URL: http://www.richardballardlaw.com
Criminal Law, DUI, Drug Crimes, Juvenile Crimes, Traffic Violations, White Collar Crimes, Family Law, Adoptions, Child Custody, Child Support, Divorce, Visitation Rights, Personal Injury, Medical Malpractice, Auto Accidents, Wrongful Death, Slip and Fall, Real Estate.
See Professional Biographies, KNOX, INDIANA

Bartholomew, Krista M. .... '73 '00 C.221 B.A. L.879 J.D. [🄰 Nichols,W.&W.]
Bedrock, Martin, (CV) .... '42 '83 C.347 B.S. L.362 J.D. 53 W. Lake St.
Boczar, James J., (P.A.) .... '47 '72 C.1086 B.S. L.472 J.D. P.O. Box 457‡
Dodge, Steven A., (BV) .... '44 '76 C.679 B.S. L.1119 J.D. [Dodge]
Dodge Law Group P.C., (BV) .... 13 N. Pearl St.
Geisler, David M. .... '49 '78 C&L.879 B.A., J.D. 10 E. Washington St.
Gudeman, Leroy D., (BV) .... '26 '54 C.347 A.B. L.345 J.D. 14 E. Washington St.
Hall, Kim .... '55 '82 C.63 B.A. L.879 J.D. Co. Pros.
Hine, Cassandra .... '67 '03 C.679 B.L.S. L.879 J.D. [🄰 Dodge]

LaTulip, Matthew D., Attorney at Law
(See Schererville)

Morris & Ruiz, P.C.
(See Plymouth)

Nichols, Orville W., Jr., (AV) .... '19 '48 C.347 B.S. L.1119 J.D. [🄲 Nichols,W.&W.]

Nichols, Wallsmith & Weaver, (AV)
54 East Washington Street, 46534-1193
Telephone: 574-772-2900 Fax: 574-772-7036
James W. Nichols (1889-1903); William C. Pentecost (1900-1914); Orville W. Nichols (1914-1970); David J. Wallsmith; Charles W. Weaver. Associate: Krista M. Bartholomew. Of Counsel: Orville W. Nichols, Jr.
Trial and Appellate Practice, Probate and Estate Planning, Real Estate and Personal Injury Law.
Representative Clients: Starke Memorial Hospital; Starke County Airport Authority; Richard H. Gumz Farms; Knox Fertilizer Co.; Westfield Insurance Cos.; City of Knox; Town of Hamlet; Hajek Farms; Starke County Library; Starke County Development Foundation, Inc.

Pease, Lizbeth W., (BV) .... '58 '83 C.1044 B.A. L.879 J.D. [🄰 Dodge]

Tonner, Ned, Attorney at Law
(See Rensselaer)

Wallsmith, David J., (AV) .... '41 '68 C.679 B.S. L.1119 J.D. [Nichols,W.&W.]
Weaver, Charles W., (BV) .... '47 '72 C.679 B.A. L.1119 J.D. [Nichols,W.&W.]

KOKOMO, * 46,113, *Howard Co.*

Alter, Justin M. .... '73 '99 C&L.347 B.A., J.D. [Butcher,B.L.&A.]
Andrews, Kenneth L., (BV) .... '42 '68 C.347 A.B. L.345 J.D. Dep. Pros.
Baird, David T. .... '64 '89 C&L.345 B.A., J.D. Staff Atty., UAW Legal Servs. Plan
Bayliff, Edgar W., (AV) .... '27 '54 C.347 A.B. L.345 J.D. [Bayliff,H.C.&M.] ‡

Bayliff, Harrigan, Cord & Maugans, P.C., (AV)
The Security Building, 123 North Buckeye, P.O. Box 2249, 46904-2249
Telephone: 765-459-3941 Fax: 765-459-3974
URL: http://www.bhcmlaw.com
Edgar W. Bayliff; Daniel J. Harrigan; C. Michael Cord; J. Conrad Maugans;—David A. Cox.
Personal Injury Litigation, Real Estate, Probate and Estate Planning, Estate Administration, Corporations and Family/Domestic Relations, Product Liability, Medical Malpractice, Wrongful Death Law.
Reference: National City Bank, Kokomo, Indiana.
See Professional Biographies, KOKOMO, INDIANA

Beck, William E., II, (AV) '50 '76 C.347 B.S. L.345 J.D.
401 West Walnut, P.O. Box 868, 46903-0868
Telephone: 765-456-1318 FAX: 765-456-1323
Email: bbecklaw@aol.com
Civil Trial, Personal Injury, Wrongful Death, Workman's Compensation.
See Professional Biographies, KOKOMO, INDIANA

Bolinger, Donald J. .... '24 '47 C.347 B.S. L.1119 LL.B. 125 N. Buckeye St.
Bolinger, Donald J., II .... '58 '83 C.347 B.A. L.1119 J.D. [D.J.Bolinger]
Bolinger, Michael O., (BV) .... '51 '77 C.937 B.S. L.345 J.D. 215 N. Wash. St.
Bolinger, Donald J., Law Office of .... 125 N. Buckeye St.
Butcher, James R., (BV) .... '33 '58 C.967 B.A. L.879 LL.B. [Butcher,B.L.&A.]
Butcher, Ball, Lowry & Alter, (BV) .... 201 N. Buckeye St.
Button, Don P., (BV) .... '31 '56 C.347 A.B. L.1119 J.D. 515 W. Sycamore St.

Button, McGarvey, Trauring, Wilson & Oaks, Association of Independent Attorneys, (AV)
515 West Sycamore Street, P.O. Box 958, 46903-0958
Telephone: 765-457-9321 Telecopier: 765-452-0882
Email: lawkokomo@aol.com
Attorneys: Thomas J. Trauring; Alan D. Wilson; Brian L. Oaks.
General Civil Practice. Litigation, Real Estate, Corporate Law, Business Organizations, Insurance, Estate Planning and Estate Administration.
Representative Clients: Cellular One of Kokomo, Inc.; First National Bank, Kokomo; Haynes International, Inc.; Hospital Authority of the City of Kokomo; Kokomo City Hall Building Corp.; Syndicate Sales, Inc.; Star Building Supply, Inc.; Mervis Industries, Inc.; Big R Stores.
See Professional Biographies, KOKOMO, INDIANA

Calhoun, Gary L. '52 '84
C.346 B.S. L.879 J.D. Supervising Atty., UAW Legal Servs. Plan
Cantrell, Richard L. '44 '73 C.862 B.A. L.796 J.D.
(adm. in TX; not adm. in IN) 1819 Dee Ann Dr.
Champagne, Joan E. .... '68 '98 C.347 B.S. L.74 J.D. Staff Atty., UAW Legal Servs. Plan
Chuck, Charles R. Huston .... '60 '86 C.347 B.S. L.1119 J.D. 206 N. Main St.
Cord, C. Michael, (AV) .... '35 '62 C.347 B.S. L.1119 J.D. [Bayliff,H.C.&M.]
Cox, David A. .... '55 '82 C.432 B.S. L.345 J.D. [🄰 Bayliff,H.C.&M.]
Dabrowski, Mark A., Law Offices of, (BV) '57 '82
C.347 A.B. L.879 J.D. 123 W. Sycamore St.
Davis, Joseph H., Jr., (AV) .... '33 '66 C.870 B.S. L.879 J.D. [Davis,M.&T.]
Davis, Murrell & Tate Law Firm, A Professional Corporation, (AV)
119 North Buckeye Street
Dechert, Brent R. .... '72 '97 C.347 B.A. L.208 J.D. [Dechert]
Dechert Law Office .... 217 N. Main St.
Donaldson, Jody E. '69 '95 C.473 B.E.D. L.347 J.D.
United Auto Wkrs. legal Servs. Plans
Doran, Stephanie C. .... '68 '93 C.739 B.A. L.879 J.D. 109 W. Sycamore St.
Elkin, Matthew J. .... '67 '92 C.679 B.A. L.347 J.D. 1118 N. Indiana Ave.
Ellis, G. Richard, (AV) .... '19 '47 C.347 B.S. L.1119 LL.B. [Ellis&G.]
Ellis & Gamble, (AV) .... 119 North Buckeye Street
Fell, John E., Jr., (AV) .... '33 '57 C.347 B.S. L.1119 LL.B. [🄲 Russell,M.H.&W.]
Ferries, Kenneth J., (CV) .... '48 '73 C.347 B.A. L.345 J.D. City Atty.
Fleming, James R., (AV) .... '44 '70 C.347 B.S. L.790 J.D. [Simmons&F.]
Gamble, Daniel J. .... '31 '62 C.347 B.S. L.345 LL.B. [Ellis&G.] ‡
Golitko, Matthew Marion .... '75 '00 C.390 B.A. L.1206 J.D. 125 N. Buckeye St.
Harrigan, Daniel J., (AV) .... '37 '63 C.347 B.S. L.345 J.D. [Bayliff,H.C.&M.]
Harris, Lee G. .... '32 '72 C.347 B.S.B.A. L.345 J.D. 4885E 50 N.‡
Heisey, Geoffrey C. .... '— '98 C&L.347 B.A., J.D. Staff Atty., UAW Legal Servs. Plan
Helms, Ralph L., (BV) .... '21 '48 C.347 B.S. L.1119 J.D. 116 N. Main St.
Hilligoss, Thomas J., Jr., (BV) .... '47 '79 C.347 A.B. L.1119 J.D. [Russell,M.H.&W.]
Hinkle-Briggs, Kelli J. .... '71 '98 C&L.347 B.A., J.D. Staff Atty., UAW Legal Servs. Plan
Hopkins, George A., (BV) .... '41 '66 C.347 A.B. L.1119 J.D. 105 E. Sycamore
Humphrey, Monica L., (BV) .... '66 '92 C.473 B.S. L.347 J.D. [Martin&H.]
Hurt, Mark A., Attorney at Law '62 '98 C.827 B.S. L.213 J.D.
522 Belvedere Dr., Ste. 105
Huston, Charles R., (BV) .... '60 '86 C.347 B.S. L.1119 J.D. 206 N. Main St.
Jessup, Stephen M. .... '44 '69 C.303 B.A. L.345 J.D. Supr. Ct. J.
Kincaid, Steven W. '65 '92 C&L.347 B.S., J.D.
(adm. in PA; not adm. in IN) 201 N. Buckeye St.‡
King, Corbin K., (BV) .... '64 '89 C.347 B.A. L.345 J.D. [King,M.&S.]
King, McCann & Scott, (BV) .... 122 North Main Street
Kuntz, Mark E., (CV) .... '63 '92 C.346 B.S. L.836 J.D. 215 N. Washington St.
Lacey, LeRoy M., (AV) .... '22 '49 C.210 A.B. L.1119 J.D. [🄲 King,M.&S.]
Lachenmaier, Frank D. '42 '01
C.679 B.S.M.E. L.345 J.D. 116 North Main Street, Suite 200 (Pat.)
Linne, R. Steven .... '43 '80 C.679 B.S. L.969 J.D. Haynes Intl., Inc. (Pat.)
Lorentson, Leonard E. .... '43 '70 C.679 B.S. L.345 J.D. P.O. Box 932‡
Lowry, Jeffrey A., (BV) .... '54 '79 C.347 B.A. L.201 J.D. [Butcher,B.L.&A.]
Mahoney, Edward S., (BV) .... '28 '56 C.108 L.345 J.D. [🄲 King,M.&S.]
Martin, James R., (AV) .... '33 '59 C.347 B.S. L.1119 LL.B. [Martin&H.]
Martin & Humphrey, (AV) .... 1517 Rockford Court
Maugans, J. Conrad, (AV) .... '38 '62 C.432 A.B. L.1119 J.D. [Bayliff,H.C.&M.]
May, Dan J. .... '47 '73 C.74 B.A. L.345 J.D. 431 E. Lincoln Road
May, Erik J. .... '76 '04 C.347 B.A. L.345 J.D. [May]
May Law Office .... 421 East Lincoln Road
McCann, Mark A., (BV) .... '64 '90 C.347 B.A. L.879 J.D. [King,M.&S.]
McGarvey, Eugene J., Jr., (AV) .... '36 '61 C.347 B.S. L.1119 J.D. 515 W. Sycamore St.
McIntyre, James B., (BV) .... '44 '70 C.210 A.B. L.345 J.D. [Russell,M.H.&W.]
Menges, William C., Jr., (BV) .... '51 '77 C.390 A.B. L.862 J.D. 208 N. Main St.
Miller, Jeffrey M. .... '47 '72 C.475 B.A. L.477 J.D. 101 N. Washington
Murray, Lynn .... '56 '81 C.679 B.A. L.1292 J.D. Co. J.
Murrell, Lawrence R., (BV) .... '39 '64 C.210 B.A. L.1119 J.D. [Davis,M.&T.]

Myers, Charles J., (BV) .... '43 '70 C.265 A.B. L.347 J.D. 507 W. Walnut St.
Noel, Joseph P., (BV) .... '38 '65 C.210 A.B. L.1119 LL.B. 101 N. Washington St.
Oaks, Brian L., (BV) .... '64 '90 C.894 B.A. L.347 J.D. [Button,M.T.W.&O.]
O'Mahoney, William P., (AV) .... '25 '52 C.108 A.B. L.276 J.D. [King,M.&S.]
Osborn, Fred G., (BV) .... '36 '60 C&L.347 A.B., LL.B. [F.G.Osborn]
Osborn, Fred G., P.C., (BV) .... 216 E. Walnut
Otterman, Merril W., (BV) .... '26 '50 C.363 L.421 LL.B. P.O. Box 507
Parry, Brant J. .... '74 '99 C.473 B.A. L.1410 J.D. [Parry]
Parry, Dennis H. .... '41 '69 C.63 B.S. L.879 J.D. Supr. Ct. J.
Parry Law Office .... 210 N. Main Street
Peelle, Jeremy A .... '73 '99 C.210 B.A. L.345 J.D. [King,M.&S.]
Raquet, Steven K., (BV) .... '50 '83 C.344 L.879 J.D. [Raquet&V.]
Raquet & Vandenbosch, (BV) .... 421 West Sycamore Street
Rosselot, David E., (CV) .... '51 '79 C.347 A.B. L.345 J.D. [D.E.Rosselot]
Rosselot, David E., (P.C.), (CV) .... 123 N. Buckeye
Rush, Annette .... '46 '81 C&L.347 J.D. Mng. Atty., UAW Legal Servs. Plan
Russell, Richard L., (AV) .... '46 '75 C.679 B.A. L.345 J.D. [Russell,M.H.&W.]

Russell, McIntyre, Hilligoss & Welke, (AV)
116 North Main Street, P.O. Box 1047, 46903-1047
Telephone: 765-456-3827 Telecopier: 765-456-3839
Email: rrussell@kokomolaw.com URL: http://www.kokomolawfirm.com
Members of Firm: Richard L. Russell; James B. McIntyre; Thomas J. Hilligoss, Jr.; Curtis C. Welke; Rebecca R. Vent. Of Counsel: John E. Fell, Jr.
General Trial and Appellate Practice in State and Federal Courts. Banking, Bankruptcy, Business and Corporate, Collections and Creditor's Rights, Criminal Defense, Employment, Family/Domestic Relations, Health, Mediation, Medical Malpractice, Personal Injury, Probate and Estate Planning, Real Estate and School Law and Product Liability, Intellectual Property Law.
See Professional Biographies, KOKOMO, INDIANA

Schmidt, Daniel W. .... '73 '00 C.347 B.A. L.345 J.D. [Schmidt]
Schmidt Law Office, P.C. .... 2713 Rockford Lane
Scionti, Joseph J. .... '22 '55 C&L.879 B.A., LL.B. 3109 Susan Dr.‡
Scott, Mark A., (BV) .... '66 '93 C.894 A.B. L.347 J.D. [King,M.&S.]
Scruggs, Charles H., (BV) .... '39 '65 C.347 B.S. L.1119 LL.B. 109 W. Sycamore St.
Shrock, Rodney V., (BV) .... '56 '81 C.346 B.S. L.345 J.D. 2705 S. Berkley Rd.
Simmons, Thomas J., (AV) .... '38 '66 C.108 B.A. L.345 J.D. [Simmons&F.]
Simmons & Fleming, (AV) .... 215 East Sycamore Street
Smith, Theodore F., Jr.
(See Anderson)

Stanley, Merton .... '17 '38 L.347 LL.B. 5711 Princeton Pl.‡
Stein, Eleanor B. .... '24 '50 C.178 B.S. L.569 LL.B. Ret. Co. Ct. J.
Tate, Douglas A., (CV) .... '66 '92 C&L.347 B.A., J.D. [Davis,M.&T.]
Trauring, Thomas J., (AV) .... '45 '72 C.347 B.S. L.1119 J.D. [Button,M.T.W.&O.]
Vandenbosch, Andrew J., (CV) .... '65 '92 C.421 B.S. L.607 J.D. [Raquet&V.]
VanDorn, Carl E. .... '33 '58 L.1119 J.D. Supr. Ct. J.
Vent, Rebecca R. (CV) .... '66 '96 C.260 B.A. L.607 J.D. [Russell,M.H.&W.]
Welke, Curtis C., (BV) .... '46 '73 C.679 B.S.I.M. L.990 J.D. [Russell,M.H.&W.]
Wilson, Alan D., (BV) .... '61 '86 C.679 B.A. L.1119 J.D. [Button,M.T.W.&O.]
Wood, John C. .... '43 '71 C.63 B.S. L.421 J.D. Supr. Ct. J.
Young, Christopher S. '53 '80 C.112 B.A. L.809 J.D.
Staff Atty., UAW Legal Servs. Plan
Young, Kathleen A. .... '48 '74 C.1291 B.A. L.734 J.D. 503 W. Sycamore St.

LAFAYETTE, * 56,397, *Tippecanoe Co.*

Amstutz, Harold E., Attorney at Law, (BV) '54 '79
C.679 B.A. L.345 J.D. 1511 Kossuth St.
Antalis, John S., (BV) .... '50 '76 C.347 B.A. L.1119 J.D. P.O. Box 591
Babcock, Stanton, (AV) .... '19 '49 C&L.477 A.B., J.D. 3508 Mulberry Dr.‡

Ball Eggleston, PC, (AV)
810 Bank One Building, P.O. Box 1535, 47902-1535
Telephone: 765-742-9046 Fax: 765-742-1966
Email: info@ball-law.com URL: http://www.ball-law.com
Cable G. Ball (1904-1981); Owen Crook (1908-1977); Warren N. Eggleston (1923-1991); Joseph T. Bumbleburg; John K. McBride; Jack L. Walkey; Michael J. Stapleton; Jeffrey J. Newell; Brian Wade Walker; Cheryl M. Knodle; Randy J. Williams; Steven P. Meyer; Brenda Mithoefer Clapper; Matthew G. McQueen.
Personal Injury and Wrongful Death, Product Liability, Medical Malpractice, Professional Malpractice, Probate and Estate Planning, Trusts and Estates, Wills, Guardianships, Asset Protection, Corporation and Business Organizations, Business Enterprises, Corporate, Partnerships, Limited Liability Companies, Contracts, Business Law, Business Planning, Family Law, Real Estate, Zoning and Land Use, Municipal Law, Administrative Law, Mediation, Commercial Collections, Insurance, Workers Compensation, General Practice.
General Counsel for: The Lafayette Union Railway Co.
Representative Clients: City of Lafayette Board of Park and Recreation Commissioners; Equitable Life Assurance Society; West Lafayette Community Library (Trustees); Lafayette Regional Association of Realtors; Greater Lafayette Public Transportation Company; Indiana Farmers Insurance Group; American Family Insurance Company; Town of Dayton, Indiana; Lend-Lease Agri-Business; Town of Battle Ground, Indiana.
See Professional Biographies, LAFAYETTE, INDIANA

Bartholomew, Richard L. .... '56 '81 C&L.347 B.S., J.D. 316 Main St.
Bartlett, Joseph D., (CV) .... '43 '78 C.679 B.S. L.421 J.D. [Bartlett&S.]
Bartlett & Sabol, (CV) .... 710 Brown St.
Bauman, Robert L., (BV) .... '50 '75 C.679 B.A. L.347 J.D. [Gambs,M.&B.]
Bean, Jerry, (BV) .... '54 '79 C.894 B.A. L.1119 J.D. Tippecanoe Co. Pros. Atty.
Bennett, Jason W. .... '76 '01 C.894 A.B. L.1119 J.D. 415 Columbia St., Ste. 1000
Bennett, Roger Wm., (BV) .... '48 '82 C.98 B.S. L.1119 J.D. [Bennett,B.&C.]
Bennett, Boehning & Clary, (AV) .... 415 Columbia Street
Benton, Anthony S., (AV) .... '49 '76 C.339 B.A. L.345 J.D. [Stuart&B.]
Boehning, Richard A., (AV) .... '37 '61 C.347 B.S. L.1119 J.D. [Bennett,B.&C.]
Boehning, Stuart P., (CV) .... '69 '95 C.347 B.S. L.900 J.D. [Bennett,B.&C.]
Bonsignore, William .... '58 '83 C.1044 B.S. L.982 J.D. [Reiling,T.&S.]
Bovey, Richard O. ...... '45 '71 C.872 B.A. L.602 J.D. Ste. 673, Union Prof. Park Bldg. III
Bowker, Laura L., (BV) .... '57 '86 C.347 A.B. L.345 J.D. 136 N. Third Street
Broden, Timothy P. .... '59 '84 C.347 B.A. L.602 J.D. Life Bldg., Ste. 416
Brooks, Thomas L., (AV) .... '32 '59 C.347 B.S. L.421 J.D. [Mayfield&B.]
Brooks, Thomas L., Jr., (BV) .... '55 '92 C.973 B.S. L.879 J.D. [Mayfield&B.]
Buckley, Alfred W., (BV) ... '54 '81 C.679 B.S. L.1119 J.D. 1851 Summertime Trl., Ste. 1
Bumbleburg, Joseph T., (AV) .... '37 '61 C.602 A.B. L.1119 J.D. [Ball E.]
Bundy, Melinda Hanzler .... '72 '98 C.347 B.A. L.1119 J.D. 639 Columbia St.

Burgett, John Michael, (AV) '36 '63 C.347 A.B. L.345 J.D.
510 Main Street, 47901-1447
Telephone: 765-742-6006 FAX: 765-429-7368
Practice limited to Real Estate, Estates, Estate Planning, Trusts, Wills, Guardianships, Adoptions, Agricultural and Business Law and Litigation.
Representative Clients will be furnished upon request.
References: Lafayette Bank and Trust Company; Bank One Trust Company, N.A.;Union Planters Bank; Salin Bank.
See Professional Biographies, LAFAYETTE, INDIANA

Burns, Eric H., (BV) .... '57 '82 C.894 B.A. L.902 J.D. [Withered,C.&B.]
Burns, William C., (BV) .... '33 '57 C.347 B.S. L.1119 J.D. [Holder]
Busch, Kelly Vaughan, (CV) .... '59 '87 C.679 B.S.I.E. L.345 J.D. [Vaughan&V.]
Busch, Thomas H. .... '47 '79 C.145 A.B. L.569 J.D. Supr. Ct. J.
Chosnek, Edward, (AV) .... '47 '72 C.679 B.A. L.1119 J.D. [Pearlman,C.M.&H.]
Clapper, Brenda Mithoefer .... '72 '97 C.679 B.A. L.1119 J.D. [Ball E.]
Clary, Brent E., (BV) .... '48 '74 C.347 A.B. L.1119 J.D. [Bennett,B.&C.]
Collins-Cutter, Janet '56 '81
C.932 B.A. L.608 J.D. V.P. & Sr. Tr. Offr., Bank One Tr. Grp.
Cooke, J. Aaron .... '70 '97 C.347 B.A. L.879 J.D. [Cooke]
Cooke, Jeffrey A., (AV) .... '45 '70 C.679 B.A. L.184 J.D. [Cooke]
Cooke Law Office, The, (AV) .... 331 Columbia Street
Corrigan, Christopher D., (BV) .... '63 '88 C.679 B.S. L.345 J.D. [Withered,C.&B.]
Cuculic, Lawrence M., (CV) '56 '84
C.870 B.S. L.602 J.D. Corp. Coun., Wabash National Corp.
Davis, Ann G., Law Office of, (BV) '39 '79
C.881 A.B. L.345 J.D. 216 North 4th Street, Suite 210
Davis, Mark, (CV) .... '53 '79 L.345 J.D. 839 Main St.
Dean, Jonathan R. '56 '00 C.347 B.A. L.345 J.D.
Deputy Pros. Atty., Tippecanoe Co. Pros. Off.
Deible, Charles R. .... '45 '74 C.679 B.A. L.879 J.D. [Gambs,M.&B.]
DeSanctis, Christine A. .... '57 '83 C.318 B.A. L.607 J.D. 415 Columbia, Ste. 1000
DeYoung, Mark E., (BV) .... '56 '83 C.347 B.A. L.345 J.D. [Stuart&B.]
Donat, Gregory J. .... '47 '73 C.63 B.S. L.345 J.D. Supr. Ct. J., Tippecanoe Supr. Ct. 4
Dowell, Anthony E. .... '66 '94 C.679 I.D.E. L.602 J.D. [Dowell B.] (Pat.)

Dowell Baker
1001 Main Street, 47901
Telephone: 765-429-4004 Fax: 765-429-4114
URL: http://www.dowellbaker.com
Member of Firm: Anthony E. Dowell.
General Practice.
Oak Park, Illinois Office: 229 Randolph Street, 60302. Telephone: 708-660-1413. Fax: 312-873-4466.
See Professional Biographies, LAFAYETTE, INDIANA

Dowler, Michael H., (BV) .... '69 '94 C.679 B.S. L.665 J.D. Dep. Pros. Atty.
Doyle, Ellie A. .... '— '96 C.1365 B.A. L.893 J.D. ., Landis & Gyr, Inc.
Duckett, Michael H., (BV) .... '51 '79 C.347 B.A. L.36 J.D. Chief Pub. Def.
Duffey, John C., (AV) .... '56 '82 C.265 B.A. L.276 J.D. [Stuart&B.]
Easterday, Thomas V., (BV) '56 '81 C.347 B.S. L.345 J.D.
VP, Human Resources & Corp. Aff. & General Counsel, Subaru-Isuzu Automotive Inc.
Eicher-Miller, Kirk G. .... '74 '03 C.288 B.A. L.831 J.D. [Holder]
Emerick, William E., (AV) .... '50 '77 C.339 B.A. L.1095 J.D. [Stuart&B.]
Ewan, Paul D., (AV) .... '13 '37 C.347 A.B. L.1119 J.D. 73 Lafayette Bk. & Tr. Bldg.
Ewing, Thomas D. '40 '69 C.579 B.S. L.585 J.D.
(adm. in ND; not adm. in IN) P.O. Box 572‡
Fafarman, Keith R., (CV) .... '54 '91 C.565 B.S. L.347 J.D. [Gambs,M.&B.]
Fisher, Larry R., (AV) .... '39 '68 C.347 B.S. L.1119 J.D. [Stuart&B.]
Forbes, Rodney E., (CV) .... '64 '90 C.347 B.A. L.345 J.D. [Seeger,H.&F.]
Fountain, C. Wayne, (BV) .... '51 '78 C.347 A.B. L.398 J.D. Mag. Judge
Gambs, John R., (BV) .... '44 '69 C.602 B.B.A. L.347 J.D. [Gambs,M.&B.]
Gambs, Mucker & Bauman, (BV) .... 10 North Fourth Street
Garwood, Cynthia L., (BV) .... '57 '86 C.679 B.A. L.910 J.D. 100 Saw Mill Rd., Ste. 1200
Gerde, Cy .... '46 '71 C.679 B.A. L.1119 J.D. [Hanna,G.&R.]
Gilbert, Kimberly A. .... '71 '97 C.1024 B.S. L.879 J.D. [K.A.Gilbert]
Gilbert, Kimberly A., Attorney at Law, P.C. .... 200 Ferry Street, Suite H
Gothard, James A., (BV) .... '43 '69 C.347 B.S. L.345 J.D. [Bennett,B.&C.]
Graham, Bruce W., (BV) .... '51 '79 C.679 B.S. L.345 J.D. [Trueblood&G.]
Grama, Joanna L. .... '74 '00 C.494 B.A. L.339 J.D. [Grama&N.]
Grama & Norton, P.C. .... 200 Ferry Street, Ste. E
Greives, James W., (BV) .... '49 '76 C.347 A.B. L.345 J.D. [Rosenthal,G.&O.]
Gutwein, Andrew S., (CV) .... '70 '95 C.679 B.S. L.273 J.D. [Bennett,B.&C.]
Hagen, Charles W. .... '66 '00 C.74 B.S. L.345 J.D. Co. Pros. Off.
Hamilton, Bradley D., (CV) .... '59 '84 C.63 B.S. L.1119 J.D. P.O. Box 1496
Hammel, H Hanly, Jr., (BV) .... '20 '47 C.347 B.S. L.1119 LL.B. 118 1/2 N. 3rd St.
Hand, Margaret J. .... '51 '79 C.679 B.A. L.345 J.D. Supr. Ct. J.
Hanna, George L., (AV) .... '27 '53 C.679 B.S. L.1119 J.D. [Hanna,G.&R.]
Hanna, Gerde & Russell, (AV) .... Fifth Floor Bank & Trust Building
Harrington, Patrick K., Law Office of, (CV) '58 '83
C.679 B.A. L.879 J.D. 300 Main Street, Suite 101
Hart, Russell H., (AV) .... '28 '56 C.210 A.B. L.1119 J.D. [Stuart&B.]
Heide, Richard T., (BV) .... '31 '61 C.679 B.S. L.345 LL.B. [Heide&S.]
Heide & Sandy, (AV) .... 410 Main St.
Helmerick, Jeffery L., (BV) .... '52 '77 C.679 B.A. L.421 J.D. [Helmerick&S.]
Helmerick & Smith, (BV) .... Suite J, 200 Ferry St.
Hermes, Pamela J., (BV) .... '56 '82 C&L.585 B.S., J.D. [Gambs,M.&B.]

Herr, Thomas J., (BV) '55 '83 C.347 B.A. L.1119 J.D.
324 Main Street, Suite D, P.O. Box 710, 47902-0710
Telephone: 765-420-0230
Email: therr@tjherrlaw.com
Civil Litigation, Personal Injury, Collections, Family Law, Divorce, General Civil Practice, Wills and Probate, Trusts and Estates.
See Professional Biographies, LAFAYETTE, INDIANA

Hodson, James T., (BV) .... '54 '82 C.679 B.S. L.879 J.D. [Seeger,H.&F.]

Hoffman, Luhman & Masson, P.C., (AV)
201 Main Street, P.O. Box 99, 47902-0099
Telephone: 765-423-5404 Fax: 765-742-6448
Email: hlb@hlblaw.com URL: http://www.hlblaw.com
David W. Luhman; Douglas J. Masson.
Commercial Law. General Civil Practice. Personal Injury, Insurance, Probate, Estate Planning, Banking, Appellate Practice, Bankruptcy, Federal Civil Practice, Collections, County Government Law, Insurance Defense, Negligence Defense, Trusts and Estates.
Representative Clients: Farm Bureau Mutual Insurance Co.; Bank of Wolcott; Bright National Bank; American States Insurance Co.; Haywood Publishing Co., Inc.; American Yorkshire Club.
References: Lafayette Bank & Trust Co., Lafayette, Indiana; Farmers & Merchants Bank, Rochester, Indiana; Lafayette Savings Bank, Lafayette, Indiana.
See Professional Biographies, LAFAYETTE, INDIANA

Holder, Carolyn S., (BV) .... '47 '73 C.679 B.A. L.347 J.D. [Holder]

Holder Law Office, (BV)
12 North Third Street, P.O. Box 757, 47902-0757
Telephone: 765-742-1124 Fax: 765-742-5140
Email: all@hdslaw.com
Member of Firm: Carolyn S. Holder;—Kirk G. Eicher-Miller. Of Counsel: William C. Burns.
Family Law, General Civil and Trial Practice, Probate and Estate Planning, Real Estate, Corporate, Guardianships and Adoption.
References: Salin Bank; Bank One, Lafayette.
See Professional Biographies, LAFAYETTE, INDIANA

Hoppes, Ronald L., (CV) '53 '79
C.63 B.S. L.1119 J.D. Legal Servs. Program, Northern Indiana, Inc.
Hopson, Christopher Paul, (CV) ....'64 '89 C&L.801 B.A., J.D. [Pearlman,C.M.&H.]
Houtz, Linda K. '63 '87 C.98 B.A. L.309 J.D.
(adm. in MA; not adm. in IN) 3705 W. 200 St.‡

Hurtt, Diane Rae, Law Office of '53 '96 C.679 B.A. L.1119 J.D.
136 North 3rd Street, 47901
Telephone: 765-429-5333 Fax: 765-428-8660
Email: dhurtt@drhlawoffice.com URL: http://www.drhurttlaw.com
Immigration Law, Family Law, Business Transactions, Corporate Law, Collections.
See Professional Biographies, LAFAYETTE, INDIANA

Kanne, Michael S. ....'38 '68 C.347 B.S. L.1119 J.D. U.S. Ct. App. J.
Katz, Marcel, (BV) ....'47 '72 C.347 B.A. L.1119 J.D. 200 Ferry St.
Kealey, William P., (AV) ....'63 '89 C.309 B.A. L.813 J.D. [Stuart&B.]
Kennedy, William F., Jr. ..... '61 '87 C.894 A.B. L.1119 J.D. Tr. Dept., NBD Bank, N.A.
Kern, Timothy L., (BV) ....'56 '81 C&L.879 B.A., J.D. Dep. Pros. Atty.
Kirkpatrick, Nina B., (BV) ....'42 '75 C.679 B.S. L.966 J.D. [Stuart&B.]
Klausen, Ellen Reesman, (CV) ....'59 '88 C.502 B.S.W. L.986 J.D. [Gambs,M.&B.]
Klingerman, Trenten D. ....'71 '01 C.679 B.S. L.1119 J.D. [A Stuart&B.] ⊙
Klinghammer, Suzanne C. ....'32 '75 C.145 A.B. L.345 J.D. 201 Main St.‡
Klumpp, Michael J. ....'41 '74 C.679 B.A. L.345 J.D. 625 S. Earl Ave.
Knecht, Steven, (BV) ....'58 '83 C.602 B.A. L.347 J.D. 22 N. Second St.
Knight, Ladona E. ....'73 '97 C.94 B.A. L.345 J.D. [A E.McCoy]
Knodle, Cheryl M., (BV) ....'46 '87 C.339 B.A. L.345 J.D. [Ball E.]
Konowitch, Gilbert D. ....'30 '59 C.705 B.S. L.209 J.D. P.O. Box 7007‡
Kozicki, Julia Church ....'69 '94 C.347 B.A. L.424 J.D. Law Clk.
Kretz, Cynthia J. ....'68 '97 C.347 B.A. L.365 J.D. Gen. Coun., Wabash National
Lane, Daniel A. ....'54 '79 C.347 B.A. L.879 J.D. V.P. & Tr. Offr., NBD Bank, N.A.
Laszynski, Robert S., (BV) ....'53 '78 C.602 B.S. L.345 J.D. [Laszynski&M.]

Laszynski & Moore, (AV)
P.O. Box 848, 47902-0848
Telephone: 765-423-5626 Fax: 765-429-5776
URL: http://www.laszynskimoorelaw.com
Robert S. Laszynski; E. Kent Moore. Associate: Daniel J. Moore.
Civil and Criminal Trial Litigation in all Courts, Business Law, Real Estate, Probate and Estate Planning, Family Law, Domestic Relations and School Law.
See Professional Biographies, LAFAYETTE, INDIANA

Layden, Charles Max, (AV) ....'41 '67 C.679 B.A. L.1119 J.D. [Layden&L.]
Layden, Lynn M. ....'41 '67 C.118 B.A. L.1119 J.D. [Layden&L.]

Layden & Layden, (AV)
Suite 712, Bank One Building, 201 Main Street, P.O. Box 909, 47902-0909
Telephone: 765-742-7646 Fax: 765-742-0983
Email: cmlayden@iquest.net URL: http://www.laydenlawfirm.com
Members of Firm: Charles Max Layden; Lynn M. Layden.
General Civil Practice. Wills and Probate, Trusts and Estates, Guardianships, Asset Protection, Estate Planning, Real Estate, Business, Business Enterprises, Personal Injury, Automobile Accidents, Wrongful Death, Insurance and Products Liability, Civil Trials.
See Professional Biographies, LAFAYETTE, INDIANA

Lillianfeld, Mark, (AV) ....'49 '74 C.1044 B.A. L.1119 J.D. [Stuart&B.]
Locke, David A., (AV) ....'57 '95 C.108 B.A. L.347 J.D. [Stuart&B.]
Loftus, Barry L. ....'63 '98 C.436 B.A. L.345 J.D. [Stuart&B.]
Lohorn, James M., (CV) ....'54 '92 C.894 A.B. L.347 J.D. 338 Main St.
Luhman, David W., (AV) ....'50 '77 C.679 B.S. L.345 J.D. [Hoffman,L.&M.]
Lybolt, Robin Marie ....'65 '98 C.112 B.A. L.347 J.D. State Dept. of Nat. Res.
Main, Stuart L. ....'22 '49 C&L.477 A.B., J.D. V.P. & Tr. Offr., NBD Bank, N.A.‡
Marion, Wesley S. '68 '98
C.679 B.A. L.1119 J.D. Paralegal Prog. Chmn., Ivy Tech State Coll.
Masson, Douglas J., (CV) ....'71 '96 C.473 B.A. L.1119 J.D. [Hoffman,L.&M.]

Mayfield & Brooks LLC, (AV)
8 North Third Street, Suite 405, P.O. Box 650, 47902
Telephone: 765-423-5454 Fax: 765-420-8114
Email: info@mayfieldbrooks.com URL: http://www.mayfieldbrooks.com
Thomas L. Brooks; Thomas L. Brooks, Jr. Of Counsel: Phillip J. Scaletta, Jr.
Wills, Revocable Living Trusts, Irrevocable Trusts, Heath Care Documents, Living Wills, Life Insurance Trusts, Durable Powers of Attorney, Estate Planning, Probate, Estate and Trust Settlement, Real Estate, Small Business and Corporate Formation, Bankruptcy, Personal Injury, Collections.
Representative Clients: DeFouw Chevrolet, Inc.; National Attorneys' Title Insurance Fund, Inc.
References: Lafayette Bank & Trust Co.; NBD Bank, N.A.
See Professional Biographies, LAFAYETTE, INDIANA

McBride, John K., (AV) ....'43 '68 C.207 A.B. L.150 J.D. [Ball E.]
McClure, Alfred E. ....'44 '69 C.705 B.A. L.776 J.D. 991 S. Creasy Lane

McCoy, Earl, Law Office of, (CV) '69 '96 C.679 B.S. L.347 J.D.
424 Columbia Street, 47901
Telephone: 765-742-4394 Fax: 765-420-0407
Email: earl.mccoy@verizon.net URL: http://earlmccoylawfirm.com
Associates: Ladona E. Knight; Tricia L. Thompson.
Family Law, Criminal Defense, Personal Injury.
See Professional Biographies, LAFAYETTE, INDIANA

McCully, Thomas R., (AV) ....'41 '66 C.894 A.B. L.1119 J.D. [Stuart&B.]
McGlone, James V., (AV) ....'32 '64 C.679 B.S. L.1119 J.D. [C Stuart&B.]
McQueen, Matthew G. ....'72 '97 C.347 B.A. L.477 J.D. [Ball E.]
McSpadden, Bruce, (AV) ....'51 '82 C.336 B.S. L.347 J.D. [Stuart&B.]
Meade, Les A., (BV) ....'52 '77 C.63 B.S. L.1119 J.D. [L.A.Meade]
Meade, Lesley A., (BV) ....Suite 40, Lafayette Bank and Trust Building
Meessen, Frederick S. ....'40 '67 C.347 A.B. L.1119 J.D. 412 Main Street
Melichar, Ronald E. ....'37 '63 C.602 B.A. L.347 LL.B. Cir. J.
Meyer, Douglas R. '62 '87 C.347 B.S. L.1119 J.D.
Senior Counsel, Subaru-Isuzu Automotive Inc.
Meyer, Kimberly, (BV) '59 '84 C&L.347 B.A., J.D.
Asst. Gen. Coun., The Lafayette Life Insurance Co.
Meyer, Steven P., (BV) ....'59 '84 C.1024 B.S. L.345 J.D. [Ball E.]
Meyer, W. Christian, (CV) ....'54 '87 C.679 B.S. L.345 J.D. P.O. Box 4422
Middleton, Shannon A. ....'75 '02 C.679 B.S. L.345 J.D. [A Stuart&B.]
Miller, Stanley N. ....'45 '69 C.679 B.S. L.1119 J.D. Life Building, Suite 416
Moore, Daniel J. ....'77 '02 C&L.347 B.A., J.D. [A Laszynski&M.]
Moore, E. Kent, (AV) ....'43 '68 C.894 A.B. L.347 J.D. [Laszynski&M.]
Morrissey, Michael A., (CV) ......'54 '85 C.679 B.S.I.M. L.345 J.D. [Pearlman,C.M.&H.]
Mucker, Robert A., (BV) ....'25 '50 C.894 A.B. L.347 J.D. [Gambs,M.&B.]
Newell, Jeffrey J., (BV) ....'55 '80 C.679 B.S.B.A. L.1119 J.D. [Ball E.]
Nicoson, Kevin D., (BV) ....'63 '88 C.347 B.A. L.1119 J.D. [Stuart&B.]
Norton, Faith A. ....'69 '98 C.435 B.A. L.345 J.D. [Grama&N.]
O'Brien, Thomas J., (BV) ....'55 '82 C.472 B.A. L.879 J.D. P.O. Box 5
O'Bryan, John R. (Jack), (BV) ....'48 '73 C.347 B.S. L.345 J.D. [Rosenthal,G.&O.]
O'Reilly, Kevin R. ....'72 '97 C.894 A.B. L.347 J.D. 200 Ferry St.
O'Reilly, Michael J., (CV) ....'46 '76 C.602 B.A. L.724 J.D. 200 Ferry St.
Orr, Karen R., (AV) ....'63 '89 C.347 B.A. L.345 J.D. [Stuart&B.]
Osmon, Charles E. ....'60 '92 C.927 B.S. L.356 J.D. Pros.
Otterbacher, Christine A., (CV) '67 '92 C.679 B.A. L.879 J.D.
Dep. Pros., Tippecanoe Co.
Owen, Marianne Mitten, (BV) ....'64 '91 C.914 B.A. L.347 J.D. [Stuart&B.]
Parent, Thomas B., (BV) ....'60 '86 C.679 B.S. L.1119 J.D. [Stuart&B.]
Pearlman, Chosnek, Morrissey & Hopson, P.C., (AV) ....316 Ferry Street
Pennell, Stephen R., (AV) ....'52 '76 C.347 A.B. L.1119 J.D. [Stuart&B.]
Persin, Sean M. ....'73 '01 C.679 B.S. L.972 J.D. [A Withered,C.&B.]
Poelstra, David A. ....'49 '76 C.63 B.S. L.345 J.D. 15 S. 3rd St.‡
Poynter, Robert E., (BV) ....'39 '66 C&L.347 B.A., J.D. 423 N. 3rd St.
Ray, Rod A., (BV) ....'53 '80 C.679 B.S. L.990 J.D. [Truitt&R.]
Reiling, Robert C., Jr., (AV) ....'47 '72 C.679 B.S. L.273 J.D. [Reiling,T.&S.]

Reiling, Teder & Schrier, LLC, (AV)
415 Columbia Street Suite 3000, P.O. Box 280, 47902-0280
Telephone: 765-423-5333 Fax: 765-423-4564
Email: info@reilingtederschrier.com URL: http://www.reilingtederschrier.com
Members of Firm: Robert C. Reiling, Jr.; Daniel A. Teder; James R. Schrier. Associates: Wayne T. Szulkowski; Kevin J. Riley. Of Counsel: William Bonsignore.
General Business, Contracts, Business Planning, Business Enterprises, Buying and Selling Businesses, Commercial and Business Litigation, Corporations, Banking Law, Business Transactions and Acquisitions, Creditor Representation, Commercial Law, Real Estate, Agriculture Law, Zoning, Wills, Trusts & Estates, Probate and Employment Law.
See Professional Biographies, LAFAYETTE, INDIANA

Renner, Dianne M. ....'50 '84 C.679 B.A. L.347 J.D. 8304 Timber Ln.‡
Riley, Kevin J. ....'74 '02 C.679 B.A. L.1205 J.D. [A Reiling,T.&S.]
Roberts, Susan K., (BV) ....'59 '86 C.347 B.S. L.1119 J.D. [Stuart&B.]
Robinson, Ralph L. ....'36 '70 C.347 B.S. L.345 J.D. 300 Main St., Suite 217
Rosenthal, David A., (AV) ....'46 '71 C.475 B.A. L.597 J.D. [Rosenthal,G.&O.]
Rosenthal, Greives & O'Bryan, (AV) ....210 N. 3rd St.
Roth, James F., (CV) ......'43 '77 C.1216 B.A. L.345 J.D. 2200 Elmwood Ave., Ste. A10
Russell, Mary A., (CV) ....'58 '86 C.679 B.S. L.365 J.D. [Hanna,G.&R.]
Ryan, Thomas L., (AV) ....'29 '58 C.347 B.S. L.1119 J.D. [C Stuart&B.]
Sabol, Lori Stein, (CV) ....'57 '82 C.347 B.A. L.345 J.D. [Bartlett&S.]
Sandy, Carl J., (AV) ....'35 '66 C.108 B.S. L.345 LL.B. [Heide&S.]
Sandy, Mathew S., (BV) ....'64 '89 C.679 B.A. L.347 J.D. [Sandy]
Sandy Law Firm, (BV) ....315 Columbia St.
Sarver, Thomas D. ....— '04 C.894 B.A. L.221 J.D. [A Truitt&R.]
Scaletta, Phillip J., Jr. ....'25 '50 C.513 B.S. L.352 J.D. [C Mayfield&B.]
Schrier, James R., (BV) ....'52 '88 C.679 B.S. L.345 J.D. [Reiling,T.&S.]
Seeger, Jay T., (BV) ....'52 '78 C.679 B.S. L.345 J.D. [Seeger,H.&F.]

Seeger, Hodson & Forbes, (BV)
106 North 9th Street, P.O. Box 878, 47902
Telephone: 765-742-4529 Fax: 765-742-6445 URL: http://www.shf-law.net
URL: http://www.lawyers.com/seeger-forbes
Jay T. Seeger; James T. Hodson; Rodney E. Forbes.
Estates, Estate Planning, Trusts, Trust Planning, Trust Administration, Living Trusts, Wills, Living Wills, Guardianship, Medicaid Planning, Probate Administration, Business Law, Limited Liability Partnerships, Corporations, Business Transactions, Collections, Creditors Rights, Real Estate, Contracts, Civil Litigation, Trial Practice, Tort Liability, Personal Injury, Automobile Accidents, Medical Malpractice, Elder Law, Health Care Law, Wrongful Death, Federal Litigation, Corporate Litigation, Commercial Litigation.
See Professional Biographies, LAFAYETTE, INDIANA

Sharvelle, Sybil ....'48 '84 C.483 B.A. L.345 J.D. Lafayette Eye Ctr.
Smith, Christine B. ....'70 '95 C&L.347 B.A., J.D. Pros. Atty., Tippecanoe Co.
Smith, Cynthia Phillips, (BV) ....'63 '89 C.679 B.A. L.879 J.D. 128 N. 3rd Street
Smith, Donald R., (BV) ....'24 '50 C.347 B.S. L.1119 J.D. 427 N. 6th St.‡
Smith, G. Mark ......'55 '81 C.243 B.S. L.365 J.D. V.P. & Gen. Coun., Smith Enterprises
Smith, Perry S. ....'56 '81 C.347 B.S. L.846 J.D. Heritage Bank & Tr. Co.
Smith, Phillip R., (CV) ....'48 '78 C.679 B.A. L.1137 J.D. [Helmerick&S.]
Snoeberger, Sarah N. ....'77 '02 C.679 B.S. L.345 J.D. [A Stuart&B.]
Snyder, Mark J. '59 '89 C.476 B.S. L.477 J.D.
(adm. in CO; not adm. in IN) Asst. Gen. Coun., The Lafayette Life Insurance Co.
Sorensen, John M., (BV) ....'46 '75 C.347 B.S. L.345 J.D. 100 North Third Street
Spigle, John E. ....'50 '76 C.347 A.B. L.910 J.D. Stallard & Schuh, Inc.
Spykman, Erik D., (BV) ....'54 '80 C.114 B.A. L.602 J.D. [Stuart&B.]
Stachowicz, Edward W., (BV) ....'52 '78 C.347 B.A. L.734 J.D. IN Legal Servs.
Stapleton, Michael J., (AV) ....'47 '72 C&L.383 A.B., J.D. [Ball E.]
Starkweather, David A., (BV) ....'67 '92 C.937 B.A. L.347 J.D. [Stuart&B.]

Stuart & Branigin LLP, (AV)
The Life Building, 300 Main Street, Suite 900, P.O. Box 1010, 47902-1010 ⊙
Telephone: 765-423-1561 Telecopier: 765-742-8175
Email: sb@stuartlaw.com URL: http://www.stuartlaw.com
Members of Firm: Allison Ellsworth Stuart (1886-1950); Roger D. Branigin (1902-1975); Thomas R. McCully; Larry R. Fisher; Nina B. Kirkpatrick; Mark Lillianfeld; Stephen R. Pennell; Anthony S. Benton; Erik D. Spykman; William E. Emerick; John C. Duffey; Bruce McSpadden; Mark E. DeYoung; Thomas B. Parent; Kevin D. Nicoson; Susan K. Roberts; John M. Stuckey; Deborah B. Trice; William P. Kealey; David A. Starkweather; Marianne Mitten Owen; Karen R. Orr; David A. Locke; Barry L. Loftus. Senior Counsel: Russell H. Hart. Counsel: James V. McGlone; Thomas L. Ryan. Associates: Trenten D. Klingerman; Shannon A. Middleton; K. Campbell White; Sarah N. Snoeberger; Margarett A. Wyatt.
General Practice. Trials and Appeals. Administrative, Banking, Commercial, Computer, Construction, Copyright and Trademark, Corporation, Creditors' Rights, Education, Environmental, Hospital and Health Care, Insurance, Labor and Employment, Pension, Mergers, Acquisitions and Divestitures, Wills and Probate, Trusts and Estates, Estate Planning, Products Liability, Railroad, Real Estate, Securities, Taxation, Utility and Zoning Law.
General Counsel for: The Lafayette Life Insurance Co.; INB National Bank, N.W.; Lafayette Home Hospital, Inc.
State Counsel for: Norfolk & Western Railway Co.
Mr. Ryan is Counsel to: The Trustees of Purdue University.
Representative Clients: Aluminum Company of America; Liberty Mutual Insurance Group.
Indianapolis, Indiana Office: Suite 640, 8888 Keystone Crossing, 46240. Telephone: 317-574-7245. Fax: 317-574-7050.
See Professional Biographies, LAFAYETTE, INDIANA

Stuckey, John M., (BV) ....'64 '89 C.679 B.A. L.945 J.D. [Stuart&B.] ⊙

Sum, Michael E., (CV) '55 '81 C.679 B.A. L.1119 J.D.
510 Main Street, 47901
Telephone: 765-742-5909 Fax: 765-429-7368
Email: michaelesum@hotmail.com
General and Civil Trial Practice including Estates, Trusts, Estate Planning, Real Estate, Domestic Relations, Adoptions, Custody, Guardianship, Child Support, Divorce, Family, Bankruptcy and Criminal Law.
Reference: Lafayette Community Bank.

Szulkowski, Wayne T. ....'69 '97 C.679 B.S. L.365 J.D. [A Reiling,T.&S.]
Szumski, David T. ....'73 '98 C.347 B.A. L.879 J.D. Pros. Atty. Off.

Tavitas, Anthony F., Attorneys at Law, A Professional Corporation
(See Munster)

Teder, Daniel A., (AV) ....'46 '72 C.679 B.S. L.345 J.D. [Reiling,T.&S.]
Theobald, Gregg Stuart ....'69 '99 C.894 B.A. L.1187 J.D. 410 Main Street
Thompson, Tricia L. ....'69 '94 C.679 B.A. L.882 J.D. [Ⓐ E.McCoy]
Thompson, Warren B. ....'21 '49 C.347 A.B. L.1119 LL.B. Ret. Cir. J.
Trice, Deborah B., (BV) ....'63 '90 C.679 B.A. L.345 J.D. [Stuart&B.]
Trice, Rakuya K. '77 '02 C.679 B.A. L.1119 J.D.
Staff Atty., Indiana Legal Services, Inc.
Trueblood, J. Michael, (BV) ....'49 '78 C.679 B.A. L.345 J.D. [Trueblood&G.]
Trueblood & Graham, (BV) .... 424 Columbia St.
Truitt, Patricia Peyton, (BV) ....'39 '79 C.228 B.A. L.345 J.D. [Truitt&R.]

Truitt & Ray LLP, (BV)
324 Main Street, Suite C, P.O. Box 711, 47902
Telephone: 765-742-7040 Facsimile: 765-429-5591 URL: http://www.truittraylaw.com
URL: http://www.truittraylawfirm.com
Partners of Firm: Patricia Peyton Truitt; Rod A. Ray;—Thomas D. Sarver.
Civil Litigation in all State and Federal Courts, Trials and Appeals, Wills, Trusts and Estates, Probate and Estate Planning, Corporation and Business Law, Personal Injury, Automobile Accidents, Wrongful Death, Collections, Family Law, Adoptions, Divorce, Child Custody, Child Support, Real Estate.
See Professional Biographies, LAFAYETTE, INDIANA

Vargo, Deborah J. '57 '83 C.8 B.A. L.7 J.D.
V.P., Gen. Coun. & Secy., The Lafayette Life Insurance Co.
Vaughan, Charles R., (AV) ....'29 '57 C.347 A.B. L.879 J.D. [Vaughan&V.]
Vaughan, Charles V., (BV) ....'55 '85 C.1086 B.B.A. L.879 J.D. [Vaughan&V.]
Vaughan and Vaughan, (AV) .... 909 Bank One Building
Vonderheide, Randall L., (BV) ....'54 '80 C.63 B.S. L.345 J.D. 22 N. 2nd St.
Walker, Brian Wade, (BV) ....'57 '84 C.679 B.A. L.345 J.D. [Ball E.]
Walkey, Jack L., (AV) ....'46 '71 C.608 B.S. L.1119 J.D. [Ball E.]
Wallis, Edward B. ....'38 '63 C.347 B.S. L.1119 J.D. P.O. Box 7007‡
White, K. Campbell ....'77 '03 C.679 B.S.B.A. L.345 J.D. [Ⓐ Stuart&B.]
Williams, Randy J., (BV) ....'56 '82 C.299 B.A. L.982 J.D. [Ball E.]
Withered, Jerome L., (AV) ....'51 '80 C.679 B.S. L.345 J.D. [Withered,C.&B.]

Withered, Corrigan & Burns, LLP, (AV) BB
8 North Third Street, Suite 401, P.O. Box 499, 47902-0499
Telephone: 765-742-1988 Fax: 765-742-8774
Email: info@witheredlaw.com URL: http://www.witheredlaw.com
Jerome L. Withered; Christopher D. Corrigan; Eric H. Burns;—Sean M. Persin.
Civil Litigation and Appellate Practice, Personal Injury, Medical Malpractice, Workers Compensation, Family Law, Adoptions, Wills, Trusts and Estates.
See Professional Biographies, LAFAYETTE, INDIANA

Wood, Richard D. ....'53 '79 C.347 B.S. L.345 J.D. Supr., Tippecanoe Sch. Corp.
Wyatt, Margarett A. ....'74 '05 C.768 B.A. L.861 J.D. [Ⓐ Stuart&B.]
Zeman, Laura Weiss ....'57 '87 C.679 B.A. L.345 J.D. Supr. Ct. 5

LaGRANGE, * 2,919, *LaGrange Co.*

Bachman, Kurt Russell, (BV) ....'64 '89 C.432 B.S. L.1119 J.D. [Beers M.B.&S.] ⊙

Beers Mallers Backs & Salin, LLP, (AV)
108 West Michigan Street, 46761 ⊙
Telephone: 260-463-4949 FAX: 260-463-4905
URL: http://www.beersmallers.com
Members of Firm: Kurt Russell Bachman; Kevin P. Bruns. Associate: Lisa M. Bowen-Slaven.
General Trial and Appellate Practice in all State and Federal Courts. Administrative Law, Bankruptcy, Banks and Banking, Business Law, Civil Rights, Collections, Commercial Law, Computers and Software, Construction Law, Contracts, Copyrights, Corporate Law, Debtor and Creditor, Elder Law, Environmental Law, Estate Planning and Administration, Franchising and Licensing, Government, Health Care Insurance, Litigation, Mergers, Acquisitions and Divestitures, Municipal Law, Personal Injury, Probate, Products Liability, Public and Private Sector Labor and Employment (Management), Public Finance, Real Estate, Securities, Trademarks, Trusts and Estates, Zoning, Planning and Land Use.
Representative Client: Farmers Mutual Insurance Co. of Noble County.
Fort Wayne, Indiana Office: 110 West Berry Street, Suite 1100. Telephone: 260-426-9706.
See Professional Biographies, LAGRANGE, INDIANA

Blackburn & Green
(See Fort Wayne)

Bowen-Slaven, Lisa M., (CV) ....'67 '93 C.679 B.S. L.879 J.D. [Ⓐ Beers M.B.&S.] ⊙
Brown, George E. ....'47 '74 C.63 B.S. L.209 J.D. Supr. Ct. J.
Bruns, Kevin P., (CV) ....'66 '93 C.347 B.A. L.1003 J.D. [Beers M.B.&S.] ⊙
Cain, Tim J. ....'58 '84 C.347 A.B. L.879 J.D. Pros. Atty.
Donahue, Duane '52 '79 C.894 B.A. L.365 J.D.
(adm. in IL; not adm. in IN) 3455 S.1095 E

Dresser, Dresser, Haas & Caywood, P.C.
(See Sturgis, Michigan)

Dunten, Jack P., (AV) ....'17 '41 C.347 B.A. L.477 J.D. 115 S. Detroit St.‡
Glick, C. Susan, (BV) '50 '78 C.347 A.B. L.345 J.D.
113 West Spring Street, 46761
Telephone: 260-463-7414 Fax: 260-463-3063
Email: sueglick@ligtel.com
General Civil and Criminal Trial Litigation Practice. Family/Domestic Relations, Probate and Estate Planning, Real Estate, Divorce, Child Custody, Wills & Trusts.
Reference: Farmers State Bank.

Hartz, Frederick J., (BV) ....'49 '75 C.346 B.S. L.1119 J.D. 207 W. Michigan
James, Jeffrey A., (CV) ....'61 '87 C.679 B.S. L.879 J.D. 115 W. Spring St.
Muntz, Richard K., (BV) ....'51 '75 C.679 B.S. L.879 J.D. [R.K.Muntz]
Muntz, Richard K., PC, (BV) ....................P.O. Box 39
Petersen, Howard E. ....'32 '58 C.57 A.B. L.597 J.D. Courthouse
Robinson, Denise A. (CV) ....'61 '87 C.347 B.A. L.494 J.D. Chief Dep. Pros. Atty.
Stoelting, Paul A., (BV)Ⓣ ....'50 '80 C.347 A.B. L.744 J.D. Dep. Pros. Atty.

Stout, Wheeler & Zabona
(See Angola)

VanDerbeck, James Scott, (CV) ....'53 '84 C.475 B.S. L.879 J.D. Cir.J.
Wible, Jeffrey W. '62 '91 C.679 B.S. L.1187 J.D.
(adm. in PA; not adm. in IN) 212 S Detroit St.

LAKE STATION, 13,899, *Lake Co.*

Blatz, Robert F. ....'26 '53 C.347 L.879 J.D. 2860 Grand Blvd.
Crandall, Jas. J., (BV) ....'24 '52 C&L.209 B.S., LL.B. 3799 Central Ave.
Hovanec, John A. ....'25 '53 C&L.221 B.S., LL.B. 2606 Central Ave.
Psomadelis, Paul, The Law Office of, (CV) '58 '85
C.879 B.A. L.616 J.D. 3530 Fairview Ave., Ste. F/G

LA PORTE, * 21,621, *La Porte Co.*

Adamsky, Bradley J. ....'77 '03 C&L.602 B.A., J.D. [Ⓐ Newby,L.K.&J.]
Ambers, David Joseph ....'62 '89 C.679 B.S. L.347 J.D. 105 J Street
Anderton, John M., (BV) ....'22 '49 C&L.602 J.D. 800 Lincoln Hwy.
Baldoni, Paul J. ....'44 '70 C.347 B.A. L.1119 J.D. Supr. Ct. J.

Ballard, Richard, Attorney at Law
(See Knox)

Bamberth, Hugo A., Law Offices, (BV) '48 '74
C.123 B.A. L.879 J.D. 809 Jefferson Avenue
Baugher, Donald E., Jr., (BV) ....'44 '73 C.1081 B.S. L.1119 J.D. [Osborn,B.R.&J.]
Bernacchi, Roger W. ....'48 '74 C.346 B.S. L.1119 J.D. Admin. Law J.
Bianco, Michael A. ....'63 '96 C.1027 B.S. L.424 J.D. [Ⓐ Newby,L.K.&J.]
Bom, Robert S. ....'50 '82 C.243 B.A. L.879 J.D. 628 Boston St.

Crump, R. Tracy
(See New Carlisle)

Curry, Daniel L. '44 '73 C.602 A.B. L.215 J.D.
(adm. in MI; not adm. in IN) Sr. V.P. & Tr. Offr., First of Amer. Bk.-La Porte, N.A.
Daley, John P., (BV) ....'14 '39 C&L.602 B.S.C., LL.B. 1st of America Bk.
Davis, Gary D., (CV) ....'57 '82 C.347 B.S. L.879 J.D. [Schoof,S.&D.]
Drayton, V. Michael, (BV) ....'53 '80 C&L.879 B.A., J.D. [Sallwasser&M.]
Elliott, William A., (BV) ....'51 '76 C.20 B.A. L.477 J.D. [Sallwasser&M.]
Forker, W. Jonathan, (BV) ....'52 '80 C&L.879 B.A., J.D. 609 Michigan Ave.
Friedman, Shaw R., (BV) ....'59 '84 C.165 B.A. L.602 J.D. [Friedman&Assoc.]
Friedman & Associates, P.C., (BV) .... 705 Lincolnway
Gettinger, Robert S. ....'18 '47 C.303 A.B. L.1119 J.D. Sr. J., Supm. Ct.‡
Greenup, George I. '06 '38 C.383 L.421 LL.B.
(adm. in KY; not adm. in IN) 519 W. 650 N.‡
Hagenow, Matthew J. ....'— '00 C&L.602 B.S., J.D. [Ⓐ Newby,L.K.&J.]
Hedge, William E., (CV) ....'47 '73 C.347 B.S. L.1119 J.D. 1033 Indiana Avenue
Hofer, Gregory H., Law Office of, (BV) '56 '81 C.43 B.A. L.201 J.D.
609 Michigan Ave.
Howes, Ralph F., (BV) ....'49 '73 C.347 B.S. L.879 J.D. 1003 Indiana Ave.
Jacobucci, Kristina J. ....'79 '04 C.741 B.A. L.879 J.D. [Ⓐ Newby,L.K.&J.]
Johnson, Kathryn Troy, (CV) ....'56 '86 C.679 B.A. L.879 J.D. [Ⓐ Osborn,B.R.&J.]
Jones, David P., (BV) ....'64 '93 C.347 B.S. L.879 J.D. [Newby,L.K.&J.]
Jones, Gene M., (AV) ....'39 '63 C.347 B.A. L.1119 LL.B. [Newby,L.K.&J.]
Kaminski, James W., (BV) ....'61 '86 C.436 B.S. L.190 J.D. [Newby,L.K.&J.]
Kaminski, Leon R., (AV) ....'24 '50 C.347 A.B. L.345 J.D. [Ⓒ Newby,L.K.&J.]
Kaminski, William S., (BV) ....'65 '92 C&L.190 B.S., J.D. [Newby,L.K.&J.]
Kus, Martin W., (AV) ....'51 '78 C.347 B.S. L.221 J.D. [Newby,L.K.&J.]
Lang, Kathleen B. ....'56 '86 C.589 B.M. L.146 J.D. Mag., La Porte Cir. Ct.

LaTulip, Matthew D., Attorney at Law
(See Schererville)

Lewis, Daniel E., Jr., (AV) ....'35 '61 C.210 A.B. L.477 J.D. [Newby,L.K.&J.]
Lienhoop, Mark A., (AV) ....'56 '81 C&L.879 B.A., J.D. [Newby,L.K.&J.]
Massaro, Jason M., (BV) ....'71 '96 C.679 B.S. L.879 J.D. [Ⓐ Newby,L.K.&J.]
Mazur, Lawrence J., (BV) ....'48 '79 C.347 B.S. L.365 J.D. 609 Michigan Ave.
McCain, David H., (AV) ....'33 '58 C.231 A.B. L.879 LL.B. [Sallwasser&M.]
Mikula, Timothy M., (CV) ....'47 '75 C.1213 B.S. L.365 J.D. [Mikula&S.]
Mikula & Stephan, P.C., (CV) .... 401 State St.
Newby, John W., (AV) ....'42 '67 C.210 B.A. L.1119 J.D. 916 Lincoln Way‡

Newby, Lewis, Kaminski & Jones, LLP, (AV) BB
916 Lincolnway, 46350
Mailing Address: P.O. Box 1816, La Porte, IN 46352-1816
Telephone: 219-362-1577 Direct Line Michigan City: 219-879-6300 Fax: 219-362-2106
Email: nlkj@nlkj.com URL: http://www.nlkj.com
Members of Firm: Daniel E. Lewis (1910-1997); Daniel E. Lewis, Jr.; Gene M. Jones; Edward L. Volk; Mark L. Phillips; Martin W. Kus; Mark A. Lienhoop; James W. Kaminski; William S. Kaminski; David P. Jones. Associates: Matthew J. Hagenow; Michael A. Bianco; Bradley J. Adamsky; Kristina J. Jacobucci; Jason M. Massaro. Senior Counsel: Leon R. Kaminski.
Civil Practice, Corporate Law, Real Estate, Appellate Practice, Personal Injury, Automobile Accidents, Wrongful Death, Wills and Probate, Trusts and Estates, Estate Planning, Civil Rights, Insurance Defense, Labor and Employment Law, Environmental Law, Education Law, Criminal Law, Driving While Intoxicated, Drug Crimes, Bankruptcy Law, Family Law, Adoptions, Divorce, Child Custody, Child Support, Visitation Rights, Medical Malpractice Defense, Mediation Services, Zoning Law.
Counsel for: State Farm Insurance Co.; West Bend Mutual Insurance Co.; Sullair Corp.; United Farm Bureau Mutual Insurance Co.; St. Paul Insurance Co.; Cincinnati Insurance Co.; Medical Protective Co.; LaPorte Regional Health System; American International Group (AIG).
See Professional Biographies, LA PORTE, INDIANA

Osborn, David D., (AV) ....'26 '50 C&L.477 A.B., LL.B. [Osborn,B.R.&J.]
Osborn, Baugher, Roule & Johnson, (AV) .... 800 Lincoln Way
Phillips, Mark L., (AV) ....'50 '76 C.679 B.S.I.M. L.345 J.D. [Newby,L.K.&J.]
Porter, Donald L. ....'35 '60 C.679 B.S. L.1119 J.D. Ind. Abstract Co.
Roule, Arthur L., Jr., (AV) ....'35 '61 C&L.602 B.S., J.D. [Osborn,B.R.&J.]
Sallwasser, Thomas D., (AV) ....'25 '51 C.347 B.S. L.1119 J.D. [Ⓒ Sallwasser&M.]
Sallwasser and McCain, (AV) ....820 Jefferson Ave.
Sauers, C. Brian ....'60 '86 C&L.347 B.S., J.D. Silcone Color Technology, Inc.
Schoof, Gary J., (BV) ....'49 '75 C.347 B.S. L.1119 J.D. [Schoof,S.&D.]
Schoof, Szilagyi & Davis, (BV) .... 3340 Monroe St., Ste. 1
Shoffner, Cory A. ....'74 '01 C&L.879 B.A., J.D. [C.Shoffner]
Shoffner, Cory, Attorney at Law ....3340 Monroe St.
Sirinek, Alan J. ....'54 '98 C.502 B.S.W. L.879 J.D. 705 Lincolnway
Sirugo, David A., (CV) ....'57 '86 C.259 B.A. L.879 J.D. [Sallwasser&M.]
Smith, J. Patrick, (BV) ....'31 '55 C&L.602 A.B., LL.B. 1021 W. 10th St.
Stephan, Cheryl B., (CV) ....'50 '77 C.1174 B.A. L.365 J.D. [Mikula&S.]
Stump, Perry F., Jr., (AV) ....'32 '59 C.344 A.B. L.345 LL.B. 244 Orchard Avenue

Sweeney, Dabagia, Thorne, Janes & Pagos, L.L.P.
(See Michigan City)

Szilagyi, Robert C., (BV) ....'48 '78 C.347 B.S. L.879 J.D. [Schoof,S.&D.]

Tavitas, Anthony F., Attorneys at Law, A Professional Corporation
(See Munster)

Volk, Edward L., (AV) ....'44 '71 C.424 B.S. L.1119 J.D. [Newby,L.K.&J.]
Ware, Jeffery G. '63 '88 C.1101 B.A. L.45 J.D.
(adm. in AR; not adm. in IN) 208 Miller St.‡
Wineholt, Thomas G., Law Office Of '51 '81
C.97 B.A. L.851 J.D. 3772 South U.S. Highway 35

Winski, O. Jerrold
(See Michigan City)

LAWRENCEBURG, * 4,685, *Dearborn Co.*

Blondell, Thomas R. ....'60 '88 C.357 B.A. L.365 J.D. [Ⓐ Wood&L.]
Butler, Richard A., Law Office of, (BV) '66 '92
C.150 B.B.A. L.1119 J.D. 310 W. High St.
Cardis, Francis J. ....'67 '97 C.894 A.B. L.345 J.D. 318 Walnut St.
Coghill, Patricia J., (BV) ....'57 '83 C.347 B.S. L.345 J.D. [Ⓐ Ewbank,K.&D.]
Dornette, John J., (BV) ....'45 '74 C.502 B.S.B.A. L.1340 J.D. [Ewbank,K.&D.]
Ewan, William K., (BV) ....'43 '67 C&L.347 B.S., J.D. 210 W. High St.
Ewbank, Robert J., (BV) ....'48 '78 C.347 B.S. L.345 J.D. [Ewbank,K.&D.]
Ewbank, Kramer & Dornette, (AV) .... 114 West High Street

Fentress, Michelle L. ....'72 '00 C.1161 B.A. L.1340 J.D. 230 West High Street
French-Fentress, Michelle Lynn .... '72 '00 C.1161 B.A. L.999 J.D. 230 W. High St.
Hollenbeck, Michael James, Attorney at Law, (BV) '61 '94
C.347 B.A. L.1340 J.D. 119 Walnut St.
Humphrey, James D. ....'58 '83 C&L.347 A.B., J.D. Dearborn Co. Courthouse
King, David M. .... '72 '97 C.383 B.A. L.945 J.D. [Ⓐ Ewbank,K.&D.]
Kramer, Frank G., (AV) .... '41 '68 C.347 B.S. L.1119 J.D. [Ewbank,K.&D.]
Lehner, Charles W., Law Office of, (BV) '37 '65 C.347 B.S. L.1119 J.D.
208 Walnut St.
Lehner, Lisa deHart, (BVⓉ) .... '66 '93 C.473 B.A. L.29 J.D. [Wood&L.] ⊙
Leininger, George A., Jr., (BV) .... '44 '68 C.108 B.A. L.309 J.D. [Ewbank,K.&D.]
Pfister, William R., Sr., (BV) ....'27 '51 C.303 L.150 LL.B. 119 Walnut St.‡

Rendigs, Fry, Kiely & Dennis, L.L.P.
(See Cincinnati, Ohio)

Sorge, Gary W., (CV) ....'52 '77 C.347 A.B. L.345 J.D. 17 Mary St.
Stroup, John F., (BV) ....'45 '74 C.347 B.A. L.345 J.D. 131 Elm St.
Turner, William H. ....'24 '51 C.347 B.S. L.1119 J.D. 128 W. High St.
Votaw, Joseph W., III, (BV) ....'40 '68 C.347 B.S. L.1340 J.D. 230 High St.
Votaw, Leslie Louise ....'72 '00 C.347 B.A. L.999 J.D. 230 West High St.

Waite, Schneider, Bayless & Chesley Co., L.P.A.
(See Cincinnati, Ohio)

Weissmann, Leanna K., (BV) .... '69 '94 C&L.347 B.A., J.D. P.O. Box 3704
Witte, G. Michael ....'57 '82 C&L.347 B.A., J.D. Co. Ct. J.

Wood & Lamping, L.L.P., (BVⓉ)
208 Walnut Street, 47025 ⊙
Telephone: 812-537-2375 Fax: 812-537-2368
Member of Firm: Lisa deHart Lehner. Associate: Thomas R. Blondell.
Civil and Commercial Litigation, Corporate and Business, including Mergers and Acquisitions, Tax, Labor and Employment, Workers Compensation, Real Estate, Municipal and Administrative, Admiralty, Products Liability Defense, Insurance Defense, Securities, Bankruptcy, Estate Planning, Probate, Family Law, Land Use and Zoning, Employee Benefits, Health and Hospital Law.
Cincinnati, Ohio Office: Wood & Lamping, L.L.P., 600 Vine Street, Suite 2500, 45202-2491. Telephone: 513-852-6000. Fax: 513-852-6087.
See Professional Biographies, LAWRENCEBURG, INDIANA

Zerbe, David L., (BV) ....'56 '86 C.150 B.A. L.1340 J.D. [Zerbe]
Zerbe, Matthew, (BV) .... '60 '93 C.973 A.B. L.151 J.D. 15 W. Center St.
Zerbe Law Office, (BV) ....15 W. Center St.

LEBANON, * 14,222, *Boone Co.*

Andreoli, Michael J., (BV) ....'48 '74 C.347 B.S. L.345 J.D. [Donaldson&A.]
David, Steven H. ....'57 '82 C.531 B.S. L.345 J.D. Cir.J.
Detamore, James R. ....'38 '83 C.347 B.S. L.345 J.D. Supr. Ct. J.
Donaldson, John W., (BV) .... '26 '54 C.210 A.B. L.1119 J.D. State Rep. [Donaldson&A.]
Donaldson & Andreoli, (BV) ....129 North Meridian
Drake, Carol Sparks, (BV) ....'53 '78 C.347 B.A. L.1119 J.D. [Parr R.O.&M.]
Edens, J. Jeffrey, (BV) ....'58 '84 C.347 B.A. L.345 J.D. [Shelby&E.]
Frandsen, Kent M., (AV) ....'50 '75 C.347 B.S. L.345 J.D. [Parr R.O.&M.]
Geeslin, Joseph D., Jr., (AV) ....'37 '70 C.152 B.S. L.345 J.D. [Geeslin&Assoc.]
Geeslin and Associates, (AV) ....127 W. Main Street, Suite 500
Giddings, Lawrence D., (BV) ....'43 '74 C.871 B.S. L.345 J.D. [Giddings,W.&M.]
Giddings, Whitsitt & McClure, P.C., (BV) ....121 North Meridian Street
Gross, Michael D., (BV) .... '50 '79 C.679 B.A. L.345 J.D. 121 N. Meridian St.
Kincaid, Ora A., III ....'44 '69 C.260 B.A. L.1119 J.D. Supr. Ct. J.
Kruse, Paul S., (AV) ....'55 '81 C.347 B.A. L.345 J.D. [Parr R.O.&M.]
Martin, Hollis Roy, (BV) ....'31 '61 C.108 B.S. L.345 LL.B. 107 E. Main St.
McClure, J. David, (BV) ....'43 '76 C.347 A.B. L.345 J.D. [Giddings,W.&M.]
Obremskey, Peter L., (AV) ....'36 '61 C.347 B.S. L.1119 J.D. [Parr R.O.&M.] ⊙

Parr Richey Obremskey & Morton, (AV)
Parr Building, 225 West Main Street, P.O. Box 668, 46052 ⊙
Telephone: 765-482-0110; 317-269-2509 FAX: 765-483-3444
Email: lebanon@parrlaw.com URL: http://www.parrlaw.com
Partners of Firm: Peter L. Obremskey; Carol Sparks Drake; Kent M. Frandsen; Paul S. Kruse; Anthony W. Patterson.
Personal Injury, Products Liability, Insurance Defense, Business Litigation, Alternative Dispute Resolution, Appellate Practice, School, Business Transactions, Real Estate, Zoning, Utility Regulation and Finance, Estate Planning, Trusts and Estates, Wills and Probate.
Indianapolis, Indiana Office: 201 N. Illinois Street, Suite 300, 46204. Telephone: 317-269-2500. FAX: 317-269-2514.
See Professional Biographies, LEBANON, INDIANA

Patterson, Anthony W., (BV) .... '67 '93 C.802 B.A. L.347 J.D. [Parr R.O.&M.]
Porter, Richard B., (BV) ....'49 '75 C.945 A.B. L.938 J.D. City Ct. J.
Ritchie, Morris, Jr. ....'18 '77 C.347 B.S. L.345 J.D. 2017 Elizaville Rd.‡
Shelby, Chris L., (BV) ....'51 '76 C.679 B.S. L.345 J.D. [Shelby&E.]
Shelby & Edens, P.C., (BV) ....116 N.W. Street
Spolyar, Robert J. ....'37 '72 C.871 B.S. L.74 J.D. 310 N. Lebanon St.
Wann, Diana L., (AV) ....'48 '90 C.679 B.S. L.347 J.D. 127 W. Main St.
Whitsitt, Christine S., (CV) ....'47 '84 C.347 B.A. L.345 J.D. Step Ahead Coun.Coord.
Whitsitt, Thomas A., (BV) ....'45 '74 C.347 B.S. L.345 J.D. [Giddings,W.&M.]
Williams, Dennis A. ....'51 '97 C&L.347 B.S., J.D. [Ⓢ Giddings,W.&M.]

LEWIS, 175, *Vigo Co.*

Smith, Brian W. .... '42 '72 C.1060 B.A. L.879 J.D. 7919 E. County Rd., Ste. 1100

LIBERTY, * 2,051, *Union Co.*

Douglass, Michael A., (BV) ....'43 '69 C.228 A.B. L.1119 J.D. [Toney&D.]
Jordan, Ronald L., (BV) ....'44 '73 C.679 B.S. L.879 J.D. Union Co. Pros. Off.
Kolger, Kathy Steffey, (BV) '59 '84
C&L.347 B.A., J.D. Chf. Dep. Pros. Atty., Union Co. Pros. Off.
McCarty, Gary K. ....'41 '68 C.347 A.B. L.345 J.D. Ret. Sr. J.‡

Thompson Law Office
(See Connersville)

Toney & Douglass, (BV)
Seven East Union Street, 47353
Telephone: 765-458-7411 Fax: 765-458-6517
Email: mike@toneyanddouglass.com URL: http://www.toneyanddouglass.com
Michael A. Douglass.
General Practice. Probate, Trusts, Wills, Real Estate and Personal Injury.
Reference: United National Bank Subsidiary.

Williams, Ronald E., (BV) ....'42 '73 C.347 B.S. L.345 J.D. 21 East Union St.

LIGONIER, 4,357, *Noble Co.*

Heckner, Howard G., (BV) ....'32 '60 C&L.879 B.A., J.D. 206 S. Main St.
Kirsch, Robert E., (BV) ....'53 '78 C.63 B.S. L.345 J.D. 206 S. Main St.

Newman, Everett, III, (BV) '50 '81 C.902 B.A. L.345 J.D.
Dep. Pros. Atty. [Wigent&N.]
Wigent, Thomas O., (CV) ....'42 '69 C.679 B.S. L.345 J.D. [Wigent&N.]
Wigent & Newman, (BV) ....321 S. Cavin St.

LINTON, 5,814, *Greene Co.*

Abshire, Marvin R., Law Office of, (CV) '59 '84
C.992 B.A. L.1119 J.D. No. 5 North Main Street
Allen, Erik "Chip" ....'73 '99 C.347 B.S. L.74 J.D. [Rowe&A.]
Baughman, Alan K., (CV) ....'56 '86 C.346 B.S. L.1119 J.D. Pub. Def.
Deckard, Rhonda J. ....'58 '99 C.346 B.S. L.347 J.D. 1359 A St NE
Rowe, John, (AV) ....'48 '74 C.679 B.S. L.345 J.D. [Rowe&A.]
Rowe & Allen, LLC, (AV) ....1000 W. Road
Shonk, Timothy ....'— '02 C.346 B.A. L.1187 J.D. [Shonk]
Shonk Law Office ....P.O. Box 162

LOGANSPORT, * 19,684, *Cass Co.*

Austen, James H., (AV) ....'53 '81 C.63 B.S. L.345 J.D. [Starr A.T.M.&M.]
Baker, Michael W. '50 '81 C.77 B.A. L.37 J.D.
(adm. in AZ; not adm. in IN) 1314 Wright St.‡
Becker, Nelson J., (BV) ....'40 '64 C&L.861 B.B.A., J.D. 208 4th St.

Blackburn & Green
(See Fort Wayne)

Boonstra, Michael E. ....'47 '72 C.210 A.B. L.1119 J.D. 601 E. Market St.
Brown, Mark Y. ....'41 '66 C.597 B.S. L.1119 LL.B. 627 E. Market St.
Brugh, Jim, (BV) ....'46 '83 C.477 B.A. L.347 J.D. 204 4th St.
Burns, Leo T., (BV) ....'52 '86 C.679 B.A. L.879 J.D. Chf. Dep. Pros.
Cassidy, Richard W., Jr. '43 '69 C.894 A.B. L.94 J.D.
Chmn. of the Bd. & Pres., Security Fed. Svgs. Bk.
Cox, Douglas A., (BV) ....'54 '79 C.602 A.B. L.1119 J.D. 208 4th St.
Damm, John S., (BV) ....'62 '88 C&L.347 B.A., J.D. [Miller,T.M.M.G.&D.]
Enyeart, Kevin S., (BV) ....'68 '94 C.894 B.A. L.347 J.D. Co Pros. Off.
Groff, R. Tod, (BV) ....'58 '85 C.373 B.A. L.1119 J.D. [Miller,T.M.M.G.&D.]
Hanna, Frederick B., (AV) ....'13 '38 C.347 B.A. L.1119 J.D. 208 4th St.‡
Hillis, John R., (BV) ....'42 '67 C.473 B.S. L.1119 J.D. [Hillis&H.]
Hillis & Hillis, (BV) ....200 Fourth Street
Hinds, Lawrence H., (AV) ....'10 '37 C&L.347 LL.B. 2522 North St.‡
Hirschauer, Jay T. ....'47 '72 C.210 B.A. L.94 J.D. [Hirschauer&H.]
Hirschauer, Tom F. ....'19 '43 C.602 A.B. L.477 LL.B. [Hirschauer&H.]
Hirschauer & Hirschauer, A Professional Association ....220 4th St.
Hooley, Kevin P. ....'17 '45 C.347 B.S. L.345 LL.B. 1010 E. Bway.‡
Justice, Courtney B. ....'41 '66 C.894 A.B. L.273 LL.B. 627 E. Market St. (⊙Delphi)
Justice, Robert L. ....'44 '71 C&L.309 B.A., J.D. 405 Seventh St.
Knight, James T., (CV) ....'64 '96 C.679 B.A. L.365 J.D. [Knight]
Knight Law Office, (CV) ....220 South 6th Street
Leeman, Wm. Kelly, (BV) ....'49 '74 C.347 B.S. L.345 J.D. 412 E. Broadway
Maughmer, Richard A., (BV) ....'53 '80 C.627 B.S. L.546 J.D. Pros., Jud. Cir. Ct.
McNarny, Patrick E. '36 '67 C.500 M.B.A. L.345 J.D.
Area Pres. & Reg. Exec., Natl. City Bk., Indiana
Miller, Andrew B., (BV) ....'68 '95 C.894 A.B. L.734 J.D. [Starr A.T.M.&M.]
Miller, Tolbert, Muehlhausen, Muehlhausen, Groff & Damm, P.C., (AV)
216 Fourth St., Caller Box: 7010
Molique, Richard A., (AV) ....'12 '36 C&L.602 A.B., LL.B. 212 4th St.
Muehlhausen, James K., (BV) ....'54 '79 C.347 B.B.A. L.345 J.D. [Miller,T.M.M.G.&D.]
Muehlhausen, John C., (BV) ......'52 '77 C.602 B.B.A. L.347 J.D. [Miller,T.M.M.G.&D.]
Murray, Robert Lee, (BV) ....'53 '79 C.210 B.A. L.345 J.D. 208 4th St.
Myers, Jon M., (BV) ....'59 '89 C.894 A.B. L.345 J.D. [Starr A.T.M.&M.]
O'Brien, Linda D. '58 '87 C.347 B.S. L.494 J.D.
(adm. in WI; not adm. in IN) 2413 High St.‡
Perrone, Thomas C. .... '48 '77 C.679 B.S.I.M. L.64 J.D. Dir. of Admin., Off. of Gov.
Ridlen, Julian L. ....'40 '67 C.992 A.B. L.273 J.D. Cir.J.
Stanton, Jeffrey D., (CV) ....'65 '91 C.624 B.A. L.347 J.D. [J.D.Stanton]
Stanton, Jeffrey D., PA, (CV) ....712 E. Broadway
Starr, Scott L., (AV) ....'55 '80 C.63 B.S. L.345 J.D. [Starr A.T.M.&M.]

Starr Austen Tribbett Myers & Miller, (AV)
201 South Third Street, 46947
Telephone: 574-722-6676 Telefax: 574-753-3299
URL: http://www.satmlaw.com
Members of Firm: Scott L. Starr; James H. Austen; Donald J. Tribbett; Jon M. Myers; Andrew B. Miller.
General Civil Practice in State and Federal Courts. Personal Injury Litigation, Securities Fraud Arbitration and Litigation, Insurance, Class Action Litigation, Banking, Corporation, Wills and Probate, Trusts and Estates; Estate Planning, Environmental and Toxic Tort Law, Real Estate Law, Family/Domestic Relations, Appellate Practice.
Representative Clients: Logansport Clinic for Women, Inc.; Maiben's Inc.; Cincinnati Insurance Co.
See Professional Biographies, LOGANSPORT, INDIANA

Stephenson, George W., (BV) ....'53 '78 C.679 B.S. L.1119 J.D. 214 4th St.
Tolbert, Frank E., (AV) ....'28 '55 C.347 A.B. L.1119 LL.B. [Miller,T.M.M.G.&D.]
Tribbett, Donald J., (BV) ....'50 '75 C.108 B.A. L.345 J.D. [Starr A.T.M.&M.]

LOOGOOTEE, 2,741, *Martin Co.*

Jones, Mark J., (BV) ....'51 '76 C.347 B.A. L.988 J.D. [Lett&J.]
Lett, John David, (BV) ....'52 '79 C.265 A.B. L.1187 J.D. [Ⓐ Lett&J.]
Lett, Michael B., (BV) ....'44 '69 C.210 B.A. L.421 J.D. [Lett&J.]
Lett and Jones, (BV) ....103 N. St.

LOWELL, 7,505, *Lake Co.*

Brown, Gregory W., (BV) ....'62 '87 C&L.879 B.S., J.D. [Brown&B.] ⊙
Brown & Brown, Attorneys at Law, P.C., (BV) ..... 771 West Commercial (⊙Merrillville)
O'Dell, Donald R. ....'24 '53 C&L.879 A.B., LL.B. 707 Commercial Ave.
Van Nada, Charles E. ....'17 '48 C.597 B.S. L.602 LL.B. 313 E. Commercial Ave.‡
Zunica, Richard A., (CV) ....'51 '76 C.750 B.A. L.45 J.D. 162 Washington St.

MADISON, * 12,006, *Jefferson Co.*

Ahlbrand, Tracy Ames ....'56 '85 C.1322 B.A. L.502 J.D. P.O. Box 448‡
Alcorn, Merritt K., (BV) ....'49 '75 C.210 B.A. L.421 J.D. [Eckert A.G.&S.]
Auxier, Darrell M., (BV) ....'56 '83 C.63 B.S. L.1119 J.D. [Jenner,A.&J.]
Barlow, Robert L., II, (BV) ....'49 '80 C.63 B.S. L.469 J.D. [Barlow]

Barlow Law Office, (BV)
201 East Main Street, 47250-3493
Telephone: 812-273-4440 FAX: 812-273-2329
Member of Firm: Robert L. Barlow, II;—Mary B. McCuskey; Kristen D. VandeWater.
General Civil and Criminal Practice, Probate, Personal Injury and Domestic Relations Law, Real Estate, Banking, Corporation, Municipal, Probate and Estate Planning, Collections.
Representative Clients: Indiana Gas Co.; Madison Bank & Trust Co.; Farmers Bank of Milton; United Farm Bureau Mutual Ins. Co.; Hanover College; Hartford Insurance.
See Professional Biographies, MADISON, INDIANA

Bordwell, Michelle S. ....'72 '98 C.1204 B.S. L.836 J.D. 1 W. Sixth St.
Brady, Mary E., (CV) ....'66 '91 C.347 B.S. L.1119 J.D. Exec. Dep. Pros.
Castor, Anthony J., (BV) ....'47 '73 C.303 B.A. L.345 J.D. 320 Walnut St.
Collins, Lonnie D., (BV) ....'48 '75 C.347 A.B. L.345 J.D. [Kemper,C.&H.]
Colussi, Joseph A., (BV) ....'56 '81 C.303 B.A. L.1119 J.D. [Colussi]

Colussi Law Office, (BV)
427 East Main, 47250
Telephone: 812-265-4455 Fax: 812-265-4461
Email: colussilaw@msn.com
Member of Firm: Joseph A. Colussi.
Civil and Criminal Trials, Appellate and Federal Practice, Insurance, Corporate, Personal Injury, Real Estate, Commercial, Probate, Estate Planning, Trusts, Domestic Relations, and Bankruptcy.
See Professional Biographies, MADISON, INDIANA

Cox, Joe E. ....'17 '53 C.303 A.B. L.421 J.D. 201 East Main Street‡
Dattilo, Thomas M., (BV) ....'43 '68 C.1150 B.A. L.421 J.D. 311 E. Main St.
Eckert, John C. ....'49 '75 C.347 B.S. L.861 J.D. [Eckert A.G.&S.]
Eckert Alcorn Goering & Sage, (BV) ....One West Sixth Street
Frazier, Alison T. ....'62 '89 C.210 B.A. L.347 J.D. [▣ Eckert A.G.&S.]
George, Sam ....'53 '83 C.303 B.A. L.421 J.D. Madison Chemical Co.
Goering, Wilmer E., II ....'52 '76 C.942 B.A. L.893 J.D. [Eckert A.G.&S.]
Hensley, Jos. L. ....'26 '55 C.347 A.B. L.1119 LL.B. 426 E. Main St.
Hensley, Michael J., (BV) ....'55 '80 C.347 B.S. L.1119 J.D. [Kemper,C.&H.]
Hicks, Michelle K. ....'— '01 C.347 B.S. L.508 J.D. [▣ Jenner,A.&J.]
Hobbs, Daniel H., (CV) ....'50 '81 C.347 B.S. L.345 J.D. 3149 N. Graham Rd.
Hoying, Fred H. ....'— '72 C.1024 B.A. L.421 J.D. Supr. Ct. J.
Jacobs, Nancy C. ....'62 '87 C&L.347 B.A., J.D. [Jenner,A.&J.]
Jenner, William Edward, (AV) ....'42 '66 C.347 A.B. L.1119 LL.B. [Jenner,A.&J.]

Jenner, Auxier & Jacobs, LLP, (AV)
508 East Main Street, 47250
Telephone: 812-265-5132; Toll Free: 888-695-5696 Fax: 812-265-5691
Email: wejenner@jennerauxierjacobs.com
Members of Firm: William Edward Jenner; Darrell M. Auxier; Nancy C. Jacobs; Jason J. Pattison. Of Counsel: Michelle K. Hicks.
Civil and Criminal Practice in all State and Federal Courts. Probate and Estate Planning, Bankruptcy, Personal Injury, Family/Domestic Relations, Corporation Law and Social Security Disability. Trials. General Practice.
Representative Clients: Madison Consolidated School Corp.; Ohio Valley Opportunities, Inc.; Royer Corporation; Vectren Corporation; Meridian Mutual Insurance/State Automobile Mutual Insurance Company; Bulk Truck & Transport Service; Scott Lynch Realty; Community Foundation of Madison & Jefferson County, Inc.; Midwest Tube Mills, Inc.
Reference: Madison Bank and Trust Co.

Joas, Jennifer A. ....'70 '97 C.112 B.A. L.345 J.D. 309 Jefferson St.
Kemper, Gary K., (AV) ....'41 '69 C.303 B.A. L.1119 J.D. [Kemper,C.&H.]
Kemper, Collins & Hensley, A Professional Corporation, (AV) ....307 Jefferson Street
Kendall-Sage, Heidi, (CV) ....'69 '94 C.303 B.A. L.1119 J.D. [Eckert A.G.&S.]
Lewis, Chad T. ....'76 '02 C.929 B.S. L.1119 J.D. [▣ Eckert A.G.&S.]
Mason, Jonathan A., (AVⓉ) '47 '73 C&L.150 B.A., J.D.
(adm. in KY; not adm. in IN) [Mason,S.&M.] ⊙

Mason, Schilling & Mason Co., L.P.A., (AVⓉ)
201 East Main Street, 47250 ⊙
Telephone: 513-489-0829 800-840-3514 Fax: 513-489-0834
Email: msm@mason-law.com URL: http://www.mason-law.com
Jonathan A. Mason (Not admitted in IN).
Commercial, Creditors Rights, Bankruptcy, Collection, Banking and Financial Institution Law, Civil Litigation, Federal Consumer Law Litigation, Foreclosures, Automobile Deficiencies, Credit Cards, Medical Debts, Bad Checks, Business Loans/Commercial Debt, Vehicle and Property Repossessions, Landlord Representation/Evictions/Lease Litigation, Equipment Leasing.
Representative Clients: Fifth Third Bank and its affiliates; Citicorp and Citibank; Contel Credit Corp.; Borg Warner Acceptance Corp.; Park National Bank; U.S. Bancorp; Arcadia Health Services; Firstar Bank; Provident Bank; Information Leasing Corp.
Cincinnati, Ohio Office: 11340 Montgomery Road, Suite 210. Telephone: 513-489-0829; 800-840-3514. Fax: 513-489-0834.
Covington, Kentucky Office: Heritage International, Suite 203, P.O. Box 2158. Telephone: 513-489-0829. Fax: 513-489-0834.
Columbus Office: 460 E. Main Street. Telephone: 513-489-0829. Fax: 513-489-0834.
Dayton, Ohio Office: 319 Liberty Tower. Telephone: 513-489-0829. Fax: 513-489-0834.
Lima, Ohio Office: P.O. Box 937. Telephone: 513-489-0829. Fax: 513-489-0834.
See Professional Biographies, MADISON, INDIANA

Mattox Mattox & Wilson
(See New Albany)

May, Greg ....'66 '93 C.894 A.B. L.221 J.D. 508 E. Main St.
McCuskey, Mary B. ....'51 '75 C.378 B.A. L.900 J.D. [▣ Barlow]
Pattison, Jason J., (CV) ....'70 '97 C.347 B.S. L.345 J.D. [Jenner,A.&J.]
Prime, William, (BV) ....'37 '65 C.303 A.B. L.345 LL.B. 112 E. 3rd St.
Ritchie-Imel, Carla ....'70 '01 C.108 B.A. L.362 J.D. [▣ Kemper,C.&H.]
Schwartz, Ann E. ....'75 '02 C.174 B.A. L.629 J.D. [▣ Eckert A.G.&S.]
Stotts, Mary J. ....'68 '97 C.303 B.A. L.607 J.D. 309 Jefferson St.
Todd, Ted R. ....'39 '64 C.894 A.B. L.228 LL.B. Cir. J.
Townsend, Guy Mannering ....'43 '87 C.1125 B.A. L.1340 J.D. Pros. Atty.
VandeWater, Kristen D. .....'76 '02 C.347 D.Psych. L.421 J.D. [▣ Barlow] (ⓒCin., OH)
Walro, Michael J., (BV) ....'47 '76 C.1024 B.A. L.345 J.D. 426 E. Main St.

MARION, * 31,320, *Grant Co.*

Beal, Shane E. ....'71 '96 C.63 B.A. L.879 J.D. 141 S. Adams St.
Beaman, James T., (BV) ....'42 '70 C.679 B.S. L.345 J.D. [Johnson,B.&T.]
Bolinger, Georgianne Fackelman, (BV) ....'54 '87 C.679 B.A. L.1119 J.D. [▣ Bosley&S.]
Bosley, Wade R., (AV) ....'45 '71 C.385 B.A. L.1119 J.D. [Bosley&S.]
Bosley & Schatz, (AV) .... 1320 Johnson St.
Burke, Deborah S., (BV) ....'62 '88 C.347 B.A. L.1068 J.D. 301 S. Adams St., Ste. 105
Campbell, John W., (BV) ....'45 '71 C.63 B.S. L.345 J.D. Dep. Pros. and City Atty.
Certain, Harry J., (BV) ....'44 '69 C.177 B.A. L.347 J.D. [Kiley,K.H.M.&C.]
Conn, Natalie R. ....'67 '93 C.347 B.S. L.990 J.D. Supr. Ct. J.; Grant Co. Supr. Ct. 3
Conner, Michael D., (BV) ....'60 '88 C.610 B.A. L.345 J.D. [Spitzer H.S.H.M.&C.]
Dawalt, P. Robert ....'49 '77 C.435 A.B. L.7 J.D. 109 E. 3rd St.
Finch, Lloyd L. ....'16 '39 L.407 LL.B. Grant Co. Abstract
Foust, Robert A. ....'23 '48 C.108 B.S. L.37 LL.B. 120 E. 4th St.‡
Gallaway, Larry D. ....'70 '99 C.999 B.S. L.1339 J.D. Dep. Pros., Grant Co. Pros. Off.
Glancy, Lisa L., (BV) ....'65 '91 C.63 B.S. L.347 J.D. Dep. Pros.
Glickfield, David, (CV) ....'64 '89 C.679 B.S. L.200 J.D. 605 S. Washington St.
Glickfield, David ....'25 '51 C.835 L.228 LL.B. 605 S. Washington St.
Grogg, Thomas A. ....'39 '74 C.894 B.A. L.345 J.D. 203 N. Nebraska‡
Haas, Warren, (AV) ....'48 '76 C.347 B.A. L.345 J.D. 514 South Washington St.
Hamill, Robert P. '56 '86 C.1040 B.B.A. L.1194 J.D.
(adm. in NY; not adm. in IN) Brescia Coll.‡
Harker, Albert C., (BV) ....'36 '62 C.347 B.A. L.893 LL.B. [Kiley,K.H.M.&C.]
Harker, Martin A. ....'75 '00 C.150 B.A. L.7 J.D. [▣ Kiley,K.H.M.&C.]
Heck, Bill, (BV) ....'49 '91 C.482 B.A. L.345 J.D. Dep. Pros. Atty.
Herriman, Charles E., (AV) ....'41 '66 C.265 A.B. L.1119 LL.B. [Spitzer H.S.H.M.&C.]
Holderead, Jerome T., (BV) ....'48 '77 C.432 B.S. L.345 J.D. [Spitzer H.S.H.M.&C.]
Hopper, LeAnn ....'74 '04 C.347 B.A. L.345 J.D. [▣ Spitzer H.S.H.M.&C.]
Howell, Joshua M., (CV) ....'67 '97 C.475 B.A. L.345 J.D. [▣ Kiley,K.H.M.&C.]
Hunt, Thomas R. ....'48 '73 C.347 B.S. L.345 J.D. Cir. J.
Johnson, Gene R., (AV) ....'28 '52 C.679 B.S. L.1119 J.D. [Johnson,B.&T.]
Johnson, Randall L., (BV) ....'49 '75 C.63 B.S. L.421 J.D. 101 E. 4th St.
Johnson, Stephen, (BV) ....'37 '62 C.231 A.B. L.1119 LL.B. Pros. Atty.
Johnson, Beaman & Todd, P.C., (AV) ....141 South Adams Street
Kelsay, Morris A., (CV) ....'61 '92 C.679 B.S. L.879 J.D. 514 South Adams Street
Kennedy, Christopher L. '57 '84 C.602 B.B.A. L.851 J.D.
V.P., Hartson-Kennedy Cabinet Top Co., Inc.
Kiley, David L., Sr., (AV) ....'28 '53 C&L.276 B.S., J.D. [▣ Kiley,K.H.M.&C.]
Kiley, Michael J., (AV) ....'34 '59 C.602 A.B. L.276 J.D. [Kiley,K.H.M.&C.]

Kiley, Kiley, Harker, Michael & Certain, (AV)
300 West Third Street, P.O. Box 899, 46952-0899
Telephone: 765-664-9041 Fax: 765-664-8119
Members of Firm: Robert Ralph Batton (1890-1963); Albert L. Harker (1904-1965); Albert Bonner Brown (1911-1981); Thomas W. Michael (1944-2002); Michael J. Kiley; Albert C. Harker; Harry J. Certain. Associates: Joshua M. Howell; Teri A. Pollett; Martin A. Harker. Of Counsel: David L. Kiley, Sr.; Jules Scott Walker.
General Civil Practice. Corporation, Insurance, Trusts and Estates, Personal Injury, Family Law, Guardianships, Zoning and Real Estate Law. Trials. Appeals.
Counsel for: Bank One, Indiana, N.A.; Liniger Co., Inc.; Atlas Foundry Co.
Local Counsel for: GenCorp.; CPC Group; General Motors; Indiana Michigan Power Co./AEP; Indiana Bell Telephone Co.; Foster-Forbes, Division of American National Can Corp.
See Professional Biographies, MARION, INDIANA

Kocher, James F., (BV) ....'53 '80 C&L.1119 109 N. Nebraska St.
Lake, Paul Martin, (BV) ....'39 '73 C.679 B.S. L.345 J.D. 402 S. Washington
Leslie, Donald H., (CV) ....'44 '71 C.347 B.S. L.345 J.D. 208 W. 4th St.
Luttrull, James D., Jr., (AV) ....'56 '81 C.999 B.A. L.345 J.D. 101 E. 4th St.
Martz, Douglas D., (CV) ....'69 '95 C.63 B.S. L.879 J.D. [Schreiber]
McKown, James A., Jr., (BV) ....'53 '79 C.103 A.B. L.879 J.D. 1320 Johnson St.
McLane, Bruce E., (BV) ....'56 '82 [McLane&M.]
McLane, Frank O., (BV) ....'31 '60 C.210 B.A. L.345 LL.B. [McLane&M.]
McLane & McLane, (BV) .... 314 S. Boots St.
Milford, John B., (BV) ....'46 '72 C.317 A.B. L.345 J.D. [J.Milford]
Milford, Robt. Lindley ....'22 '48 C&L.602 B.S., LL.B. 605 S. Washington St.
Milford, John, (BV) ....402 S. Washington, Ste. 701
Musser, Josef D., (BV) ....'51 '80 C.347 A.B. L.1119 J.D. [Spitzer H.S.H.M.&C.]
Osborn, George P., (AV) ....'28 '56 C.347 L.893 LL.B. 402 South Washington Street
Payne, David M., (BV) ....'47 '76 C.446 B.S. L.796 J.D. 112 S. Boots St.
Persinger, Craig R., (CV) ....'63 '96 C&L.347 B.A., J.D. 215 S. Adams Street
Persinger, Kyle C. ....'68 '99 C.344 B.S. L.347 J.D. [Spitzer H.S.H.M.&C.]
Pollett, Teri A. ....'60 '00 C.817 B.S. L.345 J.D. [▣ Kiley,K.H.M.&C.]
Rhetts, Peter Scott '52 '82 C.347 B.A. L.345 J.D.
Mission Coun., World Gospel Mission
Rogers, George Robb, (CV) ....'68 '94 C.473 B.A. L.347 J.D. [▣ Rogers&R.]
Rogers, Kim A., (AV) ....'39 '64 C.347 B.S. L.1119 LL.B. [Rogers&R.]

Rogers & Rogers, P.C., (AV)
525 South Washington Street, P.O. Box 925, 46952
Telephone: 765-664-0003 Fax: 765-664-0373
Email: Rogers1law@aol.com
Kim A. Rogers. Of Counsel: George Robb Rogers.
General Civil Practice. Banking, Probate, Business and Commercial Litigation.
See Professional Biographies, MARION, INDIANA

Ryan, Matthew P., (CV) ....'68 '95 C.347 B.A. L.1187 J.D. [Ryan&R.]
Ryan, Patrick N., (BV) ....'30 '58 C.108 B.A. L.1119 J.D. [Ryan&R.]
Ryan & Ryan, (BV) .... 112 S. Boots St.
Schatz, Robert W., (BV) ....'47 '72 C.347 B.A. L.345 J.D. [Bosley&S.]
Schreiber, Jeffrey A., (AVⓉ) '57 '82 C.95 A.B. L.823 J.D.
(adm. in MA; not adm. in IN) [Schreiber] ⊙
Schreiber Law Firm, The, LLC, (AVⓉ) .... 702 S. Adams St.
Spitzer, Herbert A., Jr., (AV) .....'40 '66 C.435 A.B. L.345 J.D. [Spitzer H.S.H.M.&C.]
Spitzer, Mark E., (BV) ....'65 '90 C.602 B.A. L.347 J.D. [Spitzer H.S.H.M.&C.]

Spitzer Herriman Stephenson Holderead Musser & Conner, LLP, (AV)
One Twenty Two East Fourth Street, P.O. Box 927, 46952-0927
Telephone: 765-664-7307 Fax: 765-662-0574
Email: bsh@nxco.com
Members of Firm: Herbert A. Spitzer, Jr.; Charles E. Herriman; Phillip E. Stephenson; Jerome T. Holderead; Josef D. Musser; Michael D. Conner; Mark E. Spitzer; Kyle C. Persinger;—LeAnn Hopper.
General Practice in State and Federal Courts. Corporate, Insurance, Probate and Estate Planning, Real Estate and Trial Practice. Municipal and Zoning, Personal Injury, Medical, Appeals.
Representative Clients: State Farm Mutual Insurance Company; United Farm Bureau Mutual Insurance Company; Star Financial Group; Ford Motor Company; Tulox Plastics Corp.
See Professional Biographies, MARION, INDIANA

Stephenson, Phillip E., (BV) ....'47 '73 C.63 B.S. L.1119 J.D. [Spitzer H.S.H.M.&C.]
Thompson, Gary L. ....'45 '72 C.1229 B.S.I.E. L.345 J.D. Supr. Ct. J.
Todd, Jeffrey D., (BV) ....'61 '89 C.63 B.S. L.345 J.D. [Johnson,B.&T.]
Walker, Jules Scott, (BV) ....'31 '69 C.894 B.A. L.1119 J.D. [▣ Kiley,K.H.M.&C.]
White, Beau J., (BV) ....'71 '97 C.63 B.S. L.910 J.D. 141 S. Adams St.
Wolfe, Stephen P. ....'54 '80 C.999 B.S. L.345 J.S.D. Human Rel. Comm. Atty.
Wright, Thomas G. ....'35 '65 C.347 B.S. L.1119 LL.B. Supr. Ct. J.
Zobrosky, Ann E., (CV) ....'61 '87 C.970 B.A. L.544 J.D. P.O. Box 473

MARKLE, 1,102, *Huntington & Wells Cos.*

Schrodi, Walter J., Jr. '32 '59 L.212 LL.B.
(adm. in MI; not adm. in IN) P.O. Box 428

MARTINSVILLE, * 11,677, *Morgan Co.*

Baldwin, Brian Buckner ....'53 '87 C.347 A.B. L.1119 J.D. 489 E. Morgan St.
Banfield, Karey A. ....'68 '99 C.347 B.S.B.A. L.345 J.D. Co. Pros. Off.
Barker, Joseph B., (BV) ....'42 '67 C&L.347 B.S., J.D. Courthouse Sq.
Boren, John D., (AV) ....'48 '77 C.63 B.A. L.345 J.D. [Boren&O.]
Boren & Oliver, (AV) .... 59 N. Jefferson St.
Bray, Richard D., (BV) ....'34 '59 C.347 A.B. L.1119 LL.B. [Bray,B.&B.]
Bray, Rodric D. ....'69 '94 C.347 B.A. L.879 J.D. [Bray,B.&B.]
Bray, Bray & Bray, (BV) .... 210 E. Morgan St.
Bredle, James A., Jr. '43 '72
C.347 B.S. L.345 J.D. Sr. Fin. Analyst, Eli Lilly and Company
Coffey, Dale S., (BV) ....'67 '95 C.265 B.A. L.1187 J.D. [▣ Boren&O.]
Coffin, Patricia A., (BV) ....'48 '90 C&L.347 B.S., LL.D. 289 South Ohio Street
Coffin, Roger T., (BV) ....'45 '74 C.347 A.B. L.345 J.D. 289 S. Main St.
Craney, Jane S. ....'54 '79 C.303 B.A. L.345 J.D. Supr. Ct. J., Morgan Supr. Ct. 3
Donovan, R. Stephen ....'42 '74 C.347 B.S. L.345 J.D. Courthouse

Foley, Peter R., (BV) .... '— '97 C.347 B.A. L.345 J.D. [Foley,F.&P.]
Foley, Ralph M., (AV) .... '40 '65 C.347 A.B. L.1119 J.D. [Foley,F.&P.]

Foley, Foley & Peden, (AV)
60 East Morgan Street, P.O. Box 1435, 46151
Telephone: 765-342-8474 Fax: 765-342-0902
Members of Firm: Charles H. Foley (1905-1980); Ralph M. Foley; Mark Peden; Peter R. Foley.
General Civil Practice. Trials and Appeals. Probate, Real Estate Law, Criminal Law, Banking, Zoning, Family Law, Personal Injury and Collection.
Attorneys for: Lincoln Bank; Morgan Hospital & Medical Center; Morgan County Public Library; General Shale Corp.; Morgan County Commissioners.
Reference: First National Bank and Trust.

Gray, G. Thomas .... '48 '73 C.210 B.S. L.345 J.D. Supr. Ct. J.
Griggs, E. Allen .... '42 '01 C.885 B.A. L.347 J.D. 2209 Old State Road, 37 S.
Hagee, Robert Joseph, (BV) '56 '83
C.112 B.A. L.1137 J.D. Dep. Pros. Atty., Morgan Co. Pros.
Ice, Michael C., (BV) .... '59 '84 C.992 B.A. L.345 J.D. 62 East Morgan Street
Lauer, Gregory T., (AV) .... '55 '81 C.602 B.B.A. L.1119 J.D. 489 E. Pike
Lybrook, Robert E., (BV) .... '41 '73 C.347 B.S. L.345 J.D. P.O. Box 1556

Mallor Clendening Grodner & Bohrer LLP
(See Bloomington)

Marvel, John G. .... '37 '70 C&L.347 B.S., J.D. 56 N. Main St.
Oliver, Stephen A., (AV) .... '51 '79 C.347 A.B. L.345 J.D. [Boren&O.]
Peden, Mark, (AV) .... '42 '67 C&L.347 B.A., J.D. [Foley,F.&P.]

Ruppert & Schaefer, P.C.
(See Indianapolis)

St. Clair, Robert D., (BV) .... '26 '55 C.347 A.B. L.1119 J.D. 603 Morgan St.
Smith, Phillip R., (AV) .... '42 '69 C.347 B.S. L.1119 J.D. [P.R.Smith&Assoc.]

Smith, P.R., and Associates, P.C., (AV)
1589 Burton Lane, P.O. Box 1452, 46151-1548
Telephone: 765-342-7148 Fax: 765-342-0739
Phillip R. Smith.
General Practice. Real Estate, Wills and Probate, Trusts and Estates, Estate Planning, Family, Domestic, Civil Litigation, Personal Injury, Trials.
See Professional Biographies, MARTINSVILLE, INDIANA

Sonnega, Steven P., (BV) .... '58 '84 C.475 B.A. L.1119 J.D. Dep. Pros. Atty.
Van Der Pol, William, Jr., (BV) .... '59 '84 C.347 B.A. L.345 J.D. 239 N. Jefferson St.
Wehrle, William H., (AV) .... '30 '57 C.136 B.S. L.1119 LL.B. 89 Woodcrest Drive
Williams, Brian H., (BV) .... '69 '94 C.265 B.A. L.347 J.D. 38 N. Main

MARYSVILLE, —, *Clark Co.*

Geer, Bruce R. '37 '90 C.299 B.A. L.245 J.D.
(adm. in GA; not adm. in IN) 11712 New Market Rd.‡

McCORDSVILLE, 1,134, *Hancock Co.*

Bennett, James A. '40 '67 C.265 A.B. L.1340 J.D.
(adm. in OH; not adm. in IN) 8575 N. Ricks Drive‡
Caldwell, Carolyn Bielefeld, (CV) '64 '89
C.347 B.S. L.345 J.D. 10314 Middlebrook Court
Spencer, Lloyd '06 '31 C.763 L.61
(adm. in CA; not adm. in IN) 9873 Highland Springs Dr. N.‡

MEMPHIS, 400, *Clark Co.*

Hosmer, Charles F. .... '37 '63 C&L.309 A.B., LL.B. 1508 Ebenezer Church Rd.

MERRILLVILLE, 30,560, *Lake Co.*

Abel, David L., II, (BV) .... '50 '76 C.210 B.A. L.345 J.D. [Spangler,J.&D.]
Allen, Dale E. .... '54 '80 C.879 B.A. L.365 J.D. 5655 Broadway
Anderson, Richard E., (BV) .... '48 '73 C.347 B.S. L.1119 J.D. [Anderson&W.]

Anderson & Ward, P.C., (BV)
Barrister Court, 9211 Broadway, 46410
Telephone: 219-769-1892 Facsimile: 219-769-1107 URL: http://www.andersonward.com
Email: law@andersonward.com URL: http://www.andersonwardlaw.com
Richard E. Anderson; Megan L. Ward.
Real Estate, Zoning and Land Use Law, Business Law, Corporate Law, Contracts, Law Suits, Business Enterprises, Partnerships, Limited Liability Companies, Wills and Probate, Trusts and Estates, Estate Planning, Guardianships, Banking Law, Family Law, Adoptions, Divorce, Child Custody, Child Support, Visitation Rights, Bankruptcy, Debtor and Creditor Law, Collections, Taxation.
See Professional Biographies, MERRILLVILLE, INDIANA

Andrews, Doyll H., III .... '72 '97 C.337 B.A. L.879 J.D. 101 E. 90th Dr.
Arshad, Sophia J. .... '75 '03 C.145 B.A. L.879 J.D. [Arshad,P.&W.]

Arshad, Pangere & Warring, LLP
7899 Taft Street, 46410
Telephone: 219-736-6500 Fax: 219-736-6591
URL: http://www.apwlaw.net
Sophia J. Arshad; Vasilia M. Pangere; Matthew J. Warring.
Estate Planning, Trusts and Estates, Wills and Probate, Guardianship, Asset Protection, Elder Law, Business Law, Business Planning, Contracts, Business Litigation, Business Enterprises, Corporate, Starting a Business, Buying and Selling a Business, Personal Injury, Automobile Accidents, Slip and Fall, Wrongful Death, Medical Malpractice, Family Law, Adoptions, Child Custody, Child Support, Divorce, Domestic Violence, Immigration, Municipal, Criminal Law, Driving While Intoxicated, Drug Crimes, Parole and Probation, Juvenile Law.
See Professional Biographies, MERRILLVILLE, INDIANA

Balanoff, Rebecca L. '56 '80 C.145 B.A. L.273 J.D.
Marshall Sq., 2600 W. Lincoln Hwy.
Ballou, Benjamin T. .... '73 '99 C.145 B.A. L.879 J.D. [Hodges&D.] ⊙
Bayless, Rodney H. .... '25 '55 C.894 A.B. L.879 LL.B. 8315 Virginia St.
Bengs, Tina M. .... '67 '97 C.347 B.S. L.1187 J.D. [Hoeppner W.&E.]
Berger, Brian C. .... '68 '97 C.347 B.A. L.879 J.D. 8050 Cleveland Place
Berkman, Bruce J., Law Office of '49 '82
C.679 B.S. L.146 J.D. 1000 E. 80th Pl. N., Ste. 415
Biel, Joseph A. .... '60 '87 C&L.879 B.S., J.D. [🄰 Bowman,H.B.&V.]
Bishop, Gerald M., (BV) .... '50 '76 C.679 B.S. L.345 J.D. [Greco,B.&K.]
Blaskovich, David M. .... '70 '96 C.347 B.A. L.365 J.D. [Casale,W.&B.]
Board, April Lee .... '66 '93 C.999 B.A. L.879 J.D. 300 E. 90th Dr., Ste. A
Bolen, Amy R. .... '71 '98 C.347 B.A. L.879 J.D. 9111 Broadfield Center
Boscia, James D., (BV) .... '48 '75 C.347 A.B. L.1119 J.D. [Bowman,H.B.&V.]
Bower, Stephen C., (AV) .... '39 '63 C&L.602 B.A., J.D. [🄰 Cohen&T.]
Bowman, Gerald E., (BV) .... '50 '74 C.894 B.A. L.879 J.D. [Bowman,H.B.&V.]
Bowman, Heintz, Boscia & Vician, A Professional Corporation, (BV)
8605 Broadway (⊙Chgo., IL; Indpls., IN)
Bradley, Galen A. .... '— '95 C.234 B.S. L.879 J.D. [Querrey&H.] (⊙Chgo., IL)
Brandewie, David J., (BV) .... '53 '79 C&L.602 B.A., J.D. 105 E. 61 St.
Brasovan, George S., (CV) .... '63 '88 C.347 B.A. L.879 J.D. 9219 Broadway
Brenman, Irving I. '12 '35 C.347 L.1119 LL.B.
7895 Broadway, Chapel Plaza, North Complex‡
Brenman, Stephen M., (AV) .... '45 '70 C.473 B.S. L.879 J.D. [S.M.Brenman]
Brenman, Stephen M., P.C., (AV) .... 107 West 79th Avenue
Brown, Edwin T., Jr., (BV) .... '27 '52 C&L.879 LL.B. 7448 Broadway
Brown, Gregory W., (BV) .... '62 '87 C&L.879 B.S., J.D. [Brown&B.] ⊙
Brown, Jim B. .... '47 '76 C.172 B.S. L.879 J.D. 370 W. 80th Pl.
Brown, Robert D., (AV) .... '58 '86 C.338 B.S. L.879 J.D. [Spangler,J.&D.]

Brown & Brown, Attorneys At Law, P.C., (BV)
7448 Broadway, 46410 ⊙
Telephone: 219-769-4230 Fax: 219-769-4237
Email: gwblaw@aol.com URL: http://www.lawyers.com/gwblaw
Gregory W. Brown.
Civil Litigation, Personal Injury, Criminal Law, Trusts and Estates, Probate, Real Estate.
Lowell, Indiana Office: 771 West Commercial, 46356. Telephone: 219-696-8009.
See Professional Biographies, MERRILLVILLE, INDIANA

Buitendorp, Seth R. .... '74 '01 C.477 B.A. L.879 J.D. [🄰 Kopko G.&R.]
Buls, David A., (CV) .... '63 '94 C.347 B.S. L.7 J.D. [Casale,W.&B.]
Buoscio, Angelo A., (AV) .... '38 '63 C.1016 B.A. L.879 LL.B. [Buoscio,P.K.&N.]
Buoscio, Pera, Kramer & Nowak, (AV) .... 1000 E. 80th Pl.
Burchett, Michelle P. .... '61 '87 C.945 B.A. L.893 J.D. [🄰 Spangler,J.&D.]
Burke, Edward L., (AV) .... '30 '54 C&L.602 B.S., LL.B. [🄲 Burke C.&C.]

Burke Costanza & Cuppy LLP, (AV) 🄱🄱
9191 Broadway, 46410-7064 ⊙
Telephone: 219-769-1313 Fax: 219-769-6806
URL: http://www.bcclegal.com
Partners: Joseph E. Costanza; George W. Carberry; David K. Ranich; Robert F. Parker; Kathryn D. Schmidt; Paul A. Leonard, Jr.; Paula E. Neff; Todd A. Etzler; Kevin E. Steele; Victor H. Prasco; Natalie V. Shrader. Associates: Andrew L. Kraemer; Jon A. Schmaltz; Chad J. Melchi; Joseph A. Samreta; Barry W. Pruett. Of Counsel: Edward L. Burke; Frederick M. Cuppy; Gregory R. Lyman; John G. Donner.
General Civil Practice in State and Federal Courts, Trials, Appeals, Civil Mediation, Administrative, Business Law, Business Planning, Contracts, Business Litigation, Business Enterprises, LLC's, Partnerships, Small Business, Corporate, Real Estate, Employee Benefits/ERISA, Banking, Commercial, Insurance Defense, Personal Injury, Automobile Accidents, Wrongful Death, Wills and Probate, Trusts and Estates, Estate Planning, Medical Malpractice, Legal Malpractice, Family Law, Adoptions, Child Custody, Child Support, Divorce, Visitation Rights, Municipal and Zoning, Environmental.
Representative Clients: Lehigh Portland Cement Company; Continental Machine & Engineering Co., Inc.; Gary Steel Products Corp.; Superior Construction Co., Inc.; Federal National Mortgage Association; St. Catherine Hospital of East Chicago, Indiana; Simon DeBartolo Property Group; The Travelers Insurance Companies (Panel Counsel); Guide One Insurance Companies; The City of East Chicago (Contract Counsel).
Munster, Indiana Office: 900 Ridge Road, Suite L. Telephone: 219-513-1000. Fax: 219-513-1001.
Valparaiso, Indiana Office: 57 Franklin Street, Suite 203. Telephone: 219-531-0134. Fax: 219-531-0507.
See Professional Biographies, MERRILLVILLE, INDIANA

Burris, Thomas A., (CV) .... '60 '85 C&L.879 B.A., J.D. [Bowman,H.B.&V.]

Bushemi, John P., & Associates, (BV) '48 '74 C.347 A.B. L.1119 J.D.
8959 Broadway, 46410
Telephone: 219-769-8100 Facsimile: 219-769-8170 URL: http://www.bushemilawfirm.com
Email: jbushatt@netnitco.net URL: http://www.bushemilaw.com
Associate: Kevin E. Werner.
Civil Trial Practice in State and Federal Courts, Collections, Corporate, Domestic Relations, Adoption, Divorce, Child Custody, Child Support, Employment, Wills and Probate, Trusts and Estates, Guardianship, Estate Planning, Medical Malpractice, Municipal, Personal Injury, Product Liability, Public Utilities, Real Estate, State Agencies, Workers Compensation and Zoning.
See Professional Biographies, MERRILLVILLE, INDIANA

Butkovsky, Anna M. '73 '99 C.347 B.A. L.879 J.D.
Atty., State Farm Litigation Counsel
Carberry, George W., (AV) '52 '77 C.602 A.B. L.879 J.D.
[Burke C.&C.] (⊙Valparaiso)
Carmouche, Hamilton L., (BV) .... '43 '71 C&L.546 A.B., J.D. 5425 Bway.
Carpenter, Frederick L. .... '70 '05 C.679 B.A. L.879 J.D. [🄰 Spangler,J.&D.]
Carriveau, John .... '58 '00 C.136 B.S. L.1187 J.D. [🄰 M.P.Whalley&Assoc.]
Cartella, David T. '70 '00 C.854 B.S. L.146 J.D.
(adm. in IL; not adm. in IN) 801 E. 86th Ave.
Carter, Michael L., (BV) '54 '85
C.347 B.A. L.345 J.D. [🄰 Spangler,J.&D.] (⊙Indianapolis)
Casale, Louis M. .... '48 '73 C&L.879 B.A., J.D. [Casale,W.&B.]
Casale, Woodward & Buls, (BV) .... 9223 Broadway
Casey, Mary Linda, (AV) .... '45 '70 C.347 B.A. L.1119 J.D. [Lucas,H.&M.]
Casey, Stephanie S. .... '69 '99 C.249 B.A. L.879 J.D. 300 E. 90th. Drive
Chael, Paul R., (BV) .... '55 '81 C&L.879 B.A., J.D. 401 W. 84th Dr.
Clement, James L., Jr., (BV) .... '62 '91 C.92 B.A. L.879 J.D. [Lucas,H.&M.]
Clymer, Jeffrey W. .... '— '92 C.373 B.A. L.879 J.D. [Querrey&H.]
Cohan, Sheldon H. .... '34 '57 C.145 B.A. L.976 LL.B. 8585 Broadway
Cohen, Max, (AV) .... '26 '51 C.347 A.B. L.1119 J.D. [Cohen&T.] ‡
Cohen & Thiros, P.C., (AV) .... 200 E. 90th Dr.
Coleman, Bonnie C., (BV) .... '60 '84 C.694 A.B. L.879 J.D. [Hodges&D.] ⊙
Compton, Clyde D., (AV) .... '40 '65 C.210 B.A. L.1119 LL.B. [Hodges&D.] ⊙
Coulis, Karen M., (BV) .... '50 '76 C.201 B.A. L.879 J.D. 9120 Connecticut Dr., Ste. G
Cuppy, Frederick M., (AV) .... '41 '66 C.347 B.S. L.345 J.D. [🄲 Burke C.&C.]
Dakich, Roy .... '31 '59 C.1032 B.S. L.879 J.D. 100 E. 90th Dr.‡
Daugherty, James E., Law Office of .... '48 '75 C.477 B.G.S. L.879 J.D. 8550 Broadway
Davis, William B., (AV) .... '41 '67 C.347 B.S. L.1119 J.D. [Hodges&D.] ‡
Dignam, Robert J., (BV) .... '60 '86 C.720 B.A. L.879 J.D. [Spangler,J.&D.]
Donner, John G. .... '51 '77 C.347 A.B. L.1119 J.D. [🄲 Burke C.&C.]
Drenth, Marian C. .... '70 '95 C.424 B.A. L.879 J.D. [🄰 Spangler,J.&D.]
Ellison, Paul H., (BV) .... '54 '79 C.347 A.B. L.345 J.D. [Bowman,H.B.&V.]
Emery, C. Donald, III .... '58 '85 C.645 B.B.A. L.879 J.D. [Lucas,H.&M.]

Enslen, Charles E., (BV) '52 '77 C.347 A.B. L.879 J.D.
500 East 86th Avenue, 46410
Telephone: 219-791-4000 Fax: 219-769-1302
Email: charlesenslen@aol.com URL: http://www.enslenlaw.com
Commercial Law, Personal Injury, Automobile Accidents, Slip and Fall, Wrongful Death, Negligence, Bankruptcy, Business Law, Contracts, Litigation, Business Planning, Business Enterprises, Corporate, Small Business, Partnerships, Limited Liability Company Law, Real Estate, Family Law, Divorce, Child Custody, Child Support, Adoption Law, Visitation Rights, Mediation.
See Professional Biographies, MERRILLVILLE, INDIANA

Etzler, Todd A., (BV) .... '66 '91 C.679 B.S. L.347 J.D. [Burke C.&C.] (⊙Valparaiso)
Evans, Larry G., (AV) .... '39 '62 C&L.879 A.B., J.D. [Hoeppner W.&E.]
Fisher, Lori D. .... '69 '94 C.347 B.A. L.421 J.D. 370 W. 80th Pl.
Fletcher, R. Timothy .... '71 '03 C.346 B.S. L.879 J.D. [🄰 Hodges&D.] ⊙
Foley, Arlington J. .... '46 '76 C.347 B.S. L.209 J.D. 8300 Mississippi St., Ste. 2-B
Frost, Laura B., (CV) .... '65 '91 C.340 B.A. L.879 J.D. [Hodges&D.] ⊙
Galanos, Gus J. .... '31 '57 C&L.879 LL.B 5655 Bway.

Geairn, Cintra D.B. '70 '98 C.696 B.A. L.146 J.D.
(adm. in IL; not adm. in IN) [⊠ Hoeppner W.&E.] ⊙
Genetos, Lambert C., (BV) .... '45 '70 C.347 A.B. L.1119 J.D. [Kopko G.&R.]
Gilyan, David N., (BV) .... '40 '64 C.221 B.S. L.879 LL.B. 5544 Broadway
Gioia, Daniel A., (AV) .... '50 '75 C.276 A.B. L.904 J.D. [Spangler,J.&D.]
Gland, Mark A., (CV) .... '54 '91 C.1119 B.A. L.879 J.D. 1000 E. 80th Place
Glover, Voyle A., (BV) .... '42 '84 C.679 B.A. L.879 J.D. 101 W. 75th Pl.

Gonzalez, Marce, Jr., (AV) '54 '83 C.345 B.S. L.1119 J.D. [BB]
Twin Towers Building, 1000 E. 80th Place, 502 North, 46410
Telephone: 219-769-3030 FAX: 219-769-3031
Email: marceglaw@netnitco.net
Criminal Defense, Drug Crimes, Driving While Intoxicated, Juvenile Law, Felonies and Misdemeanors, Appellate, Traffic Violations, Personal Injury, Automobile Accidents, Slip and Fall, Dog Bites, Wrongful Death. Attorney Discipline Defense.
See Professional Biographies, MERRILLVILLE, INDIANA

Gordon, April M. .... '74 '99 C.1024 B.S. L.209 J.D. Centier Bank Retirement Services
Gouveia, Gordon E., (AV) .... '41 '70 C.347 B.S. L.879 J.D. 433 West 84th Drive
Greco, James A., (BV) .... '40 '68 C.347 B.A. L.879 J.D. [Greco,B.&K.]
Greco, Bishop & Kuechenberg, (BV) .... 2115 West Lincoln Hwy.
Greenberg, Thomas M., (AV) .... '48 '73 C.347 B.A. L.597 J.D. [T.M.Greenberg]

Greenberg, Thomas M., P.C., (AV)
99 East 86th Avenue, Suite E-2, 46410-6267
Telephone: 219-769-2600 Fax: 219-769-2688
Email: tmg@jorsm.com
Thomas M. Greenberg.
General Practice, Trusts and Estates, Estate Planning, Probate, Real Estate, Real Estate Transactions, Employment Law, Employee Benefits, Business Law, Business Formation, Business Enterprises, Limited Liability Company Law, Commercial Law, Professional Practices, Tax Exempt Organizations, Health Law, Mental Health Law, Local Government Law, General Civil Litigation.
See Professional Biographies, MERRILLVILLE, INDIANA

Hall, Edward R. .... '55 '00 C.999 B.S. L.879 J.D. 7520 Broadway
Hall, Hilary R. .... '70 '95 C.103 A.B. L.309 J.D. 370 W. 80th Pl.
Hall, Ricardo A. .... '64 '96 C.892 B.A. L.347 J.D. [Spangler,J.&D.]
Halpin, Michael E., (CV) .... '51 '86 C.347 B.S. L.365 J.D. 5590 Broadway
Halstead, John H. .... '— '02 C.101 B.A. L.1119 J.D. [⊠ Querrey&H.]
Hammond, Lynn, (CV) .... '45 '88 C.966 B.A. L.879 J.D. [L.Hammond]
Hammond, Lynn, Law Office, (CV) .... 7895 Bway.
Hawk, Robert D., (BV) .... '38 '67 C.347 B.S. L.1119 J.D. [Spangler,J.&D.]
Hawk, Robert D., Jr., (BV) .... '68 '95 C.388 B.A. L.221 J.D. [Spangler,J.&D.]
Hedges, Christopher C. .... '70 '96 C.347 B.A. L.879 J.D. [⊠ Bowman,H.B.&V.]
Heintz, George W., (BV) '46 '72 C.894 B.A. L.339 J.D.
[Bowman,H.B.&V.] (⊙Chgo., IL)
Hites, Earle F., (AV) .... '47 '72 C.347 B.S. L.879 J.D. [Hodges&D.] ⊙
Hittinger, J. Brian, (CV) .... '60 '90 C.347 B.S. L.879 J.D. [Hoeppner W.&E.]

Hodges & Davis, P.C., (AV)
8700 Broadway, 46410 ⊙
Telephone: 219-641-8700 Fax: 219-641-8710
URL: http://www.hodgesdavis.com
William F. Hodges (1877-1954); Claude V. Ridgely (1881-1963); Thomas M. Hodges (1906-1969); Herschel B. Davis (1901-1990); Gilbert Gruenberg (1902-1989); Bruce E. Sayers (1939-1990); William B. Davis (Retired); Clyde D. Compton; Earle F. Hites; R. Lawrence Steele; Gregory A. Sobkowski; Bonnie C. Coleman; Laura B. Frost; Benjamin T. Ballou; David H. Kreider; R. Timothy Fletcher; Rebecca C. Hopkins. Of Counsel: Edward J. Hussey.
General Civil Practice in all State and Federal Courts, Trials and Appeals, Insurance Defense, Corporation, Health and Hospital, Municipal and Zoning Law, Criminal, Driving While Intoxicated, Financing, Tax and Administrative Law. EEOC, Negligence, Products Liability, Environmental, Wills and Probate, Trusts and Estates, Estate Planning, Real Estate and Foreclosure Law. Consumer and Commercial Collections, Business Law, Business Planning, Business Litigation, Business Enterprises, Corporate, Partnerships, Small Business, Buying and Selling a Business, Business Start-Ups.
Representative Clients: The Methodist Hospitals, Inc.; City of Portage, Indiana; Portage Township Schools; Indiana-American Water Co.; Gary Steelheads; Vector Pipe Line Co.
Portage, Indiana Office: 6082 Lute Road. P.O. Box 1037. Telephone: 219-762-7129. Fax: 219-762-2826.
See Professional Biographies, MERRILLVILLE, INDIANA

Hoeppner Wagner & Evans LLP, (AV) [BB]
Twin Towers, Suite 606 South, 1000 East 80th Place, P.O. Box 10627, 46410-0627 ⊙
Telephone: 219-769-6552; 800-263-1466 (IN, IL) Fax: 219-738-2349
Email: hwe@hwelaw.com URL: http://www.hwelaw.com
Resident Members: Larry G. Evans; John E. Hughes; F. Joseph Jaskowiak; J. Brian Hittinger; Jack A. Kramer; Jay S. Patheja; Tina M. Bengs. Resident Associates: Michael Eugene Tolbert; Eric P. Mathisen; Gerold L. Stout; Cintra D.B. Geairn (Not admitted in IN); Sean E. Kenyon; Lucretia A. Thornton; Lee I. Lane.
General Practice. Trials and Appeals in State, Federal and Tax Courts. Bankruptcy, Commercial and Banking, Corporate, Creditors' Rights, Probate, Estate Planning, Estate Administration, Financial Resources Planning, Insurance Defense, Municipal Bonds, Municipal Law, Personal Injury, Product Liability, Professional Malpractice, Real Estate, Taxation, Workers Compensation, Zoning Law, Labor and Employment Law. Mediation, OSHA, Employee Benefits Law.
Valparaiso, Indiana Office: 103 East Lincolnway, P.O. Box 2357, 46384-2357. Telephone: 219-464-4961; 800-879-2246 (IN, IL). Fax: 219-465-0603. Email: hwe@hwelaw.com
See Professional Biographies, MERRILLVILLE, INDIANA

Holcomb, James A., (AV) .... '34 '61 C&L.477 B.A., J.D. [Lucas,H.&M.]
Holub, David W., (BV) .... '— '82 C.625 B.A. L.879 J.D. [D.W.Holub]

Holub, David W., Law Offices of, APC, (BV)
8913 Broadway, 46410
Telephone: 219-736-9700 Fax: 219-736-9704
Email: d.holub@verizon.net URL: http://www.davidholublaw.com
David W. Holub.
Personal Injury, Medical Malpractice and Wrongful Death Litigation.
See Professional Biographies, MERRILLVILLE, INDIANA

Hopkins, Rebecca C. .... '54 '03 C.679 B.S. L.879 J.D. [⊠ Hodges&D.] ⊙
Hough, James L. .... '71 '98 C.999 B.A. L.879 J.D. [⊠ Spangler,J.&D.]
Hughes, John E., (AV) .... '46 '71 C.117 B.A. L.879 J.D. [Hoeppner W.&E.]
Hussey, Edward J., (BV) .... '47 '75 C.602 B.B.A. L.1119 J.D. [⊠ Hodges&D.]
Irak, Joseph S., (BV) .... '55 '82 C&L.879 B.A., J.D. Asst. Atty.
Ivancevich, George S., (CV) .... '55 '84 C.347 B.A. L.365 J.D. [⊠ Johnson&R.]
Ivanovich, Roseann P. .... '59 '01 C&L.879 B.A., J.D. 8585 Broadway, Suite 695
Jaskowiak, F. Joseph, (BV) .... '54 '79 C.340 B.A. L.879 J.D. [Hoeppner W.&E.]
Jennings, Harry J., (AV) .... '23 '49 C.352 L.146 LL.B. [⊠ Spangler,J.&D.]
Johnson, Caleb S. .... '77 '03 C.679 B.S. L.879 J.D. [⊠ Spangler,J.&D.]
Johnson, Steven A., (BV) .... '49 '75 C.425 B.B.A. L.472 J.D. [Johnson&R.]

Johnson & Rappa, LLC, (BV)
(Formerly Spangler, Johnson & Associates)
250 East 90th Drive, 46410-8102
Telephone: 219-769-0087 Fax: 219-769-0092 URL: http://www.JohnsonRappa.com
URL: http://www.johnsonrappalaw.com
Steven A. Johnson; Michael J. Rappa; George S. Ivancevich.
Trial, Appellate, Personal Injury, Automobile Accidents, Slip and Fall, Wrongful Death, and Defense Practice in State and Federal Courts. Insurance, Civil Rights, Labor and Employment, Wrongful

(This Listing Continued)

Johnson & Rappa, LLC (Continued)
Termination, Employment Contracts, Mediation and Arbitration, Class Actions, Construction, Administrative, Products Liability and Transportation Law.
See Professional Biographies, MERRILLVILLE, INDIANA

Kalina, Lawrence A., (BV) .... '51 '77 C.884 B.A. L.472 J.D. [Spangler,J.&D.]
Kappos, John, (BV) .... '28 '53 C.347 B.S. L.1119 J.D. 5800 Broadway‡
Kenyon, Sean E., (BV) .... '— '91 C.712 B.B.A. L.347 J.D. [⊠ Hoeppner W.&E.]
Kinney, Richard G., (AV) ... '39 '64 C.339 B.S.E.E. L.145 J.D. 8300 Mississippi St. (Pat.)
Koch, William M. .... '60 '88 C.555 B.A. L.879 J.D. [⊠ Spangler,J.&D.]
Kopko, Andrew J., (BV) .... '39 '64 C&L.602 B.B.A., J.D. [Kopko G.&R.]

Kopko Genetos & Retson LLP, (AV)
8585 Broadway Suite 480, 46410
Telephone: 219-755-0400 Fax: 219-755-0410
URL: http://www.kgr-law.com
Members of Firm: Andrew J. Kopko; Lambert C. Genetos; Demetri J. Retson; Stacia L. Yoon; Marco A. Molina. Associate: Seth R. Buitendorp. Of Counsel: Richard L. Mostak; Lily M. Schaefer.
Bankruptcy, Debtor and Creditor, Landlord and Tenant Law, Foreclosure, Affordable Housing, Multi-Family Housing, Real Estate, Banks and Banking, Commercial Law, Consumer Law, Taxation, Estate Planning, Business Law and Litigation.
See Professional Biographies, MERRILLVILLE, INDIANA

Kopreina, Frank J. .... '58 '89 C.346 B.S. L.1000 J.D. 105 E. 61st Avenue
Kraemer, Andrew L., (BV) .... '64 '89 C.57 A.B. L.879 J.D. [⊠ Burke C.&C.]
Kramer, Jack A., (CV) .... '70 '95 C.63 B.S. L.879 J.D. [Hoeppner W.&E.]
Kramer, Thomas W., (BV) .... '50 '76 C.347 B.A. L.1119 J.D. [Buoscio,P.K.&N.]
Kreider, David H., (BV) .... '41 '70 C.347 A.B. L.345 J.D. [Hodges&D.] ⊙
Krevitz, Arnold, (BV) .... '29 '54 C.347 B.S. L.1119 LL.B. 500 E. 86th Ave.
Kruse, Gary A. .... '59 '84 C.201 B.A. L.893 J.D. NiSource Corporate Services Co.
Kruszynski, Robert S. .... '64 '90 C&L.347 B.S., J.D. 8050 Cleveland Pl.
Kuechenberg, Cheryl A., (CV) .... '— '92 C.347 B.S. L.879 J.D. [Greco,B.&K.]
Kuzman, Daniel C. .... '31 '59 C.347 B.S. L.1119 LL.B. 5800 Bwy.

Lambert, Michael '69 '00 C.347 B.A. L.365 J.D.
500 West Lincoln Highway, Suite Q, 46410
Telephone: 219-769-6171 Fax: 219-769-6172
URL: http://www.lambertlawfirm.com
Criminal Law, Drug Crimes, Driving While Intoxicated, Parole and Probation, Juvenile Crimes, Traffic Violations, Family Law, Adoption, Divorce, Child Custody, Child Support, Domestic Violence, Visitation Rights, Employment Law, Wrongful Termination, Sexual Harassment, Civil Rights, Discrimination, Personal Injury, Automobile Accidents, Slip and Fall, Wrongful Death, Bankruptcy, Wills and Probate, Guardianships, Business Law, Contracts, Lawsuits, Business Enterprises.
See Professional Biographies, MERRILLVILLE, INDIANA

Lane, Lee I. .... '— '05 C.208 B.A. L.879 J.D. [⊠ Hoeppner W.&E.]
Lasser, Herbert S., (BV) .... '28 '53 C&L.879 B.A., J.D. [H.S.Lasser&Assoc.]

Lasser, Herbert S., & Associates, P.C., (BV)
3700 East U.S. 30, 46410
Telephone: 219-942-3710 Fax: 219-942-0064
URL: http://www.lawyers.com/lasserlaw
Herbert S. Lasser;—Robert A. Plantz.
Personal Injury, Wrongful Death, Automobile and All Accidents, Construction Law, Family Law, Divorce, Child Custody, Child Support, Domestic Violence, Visitation Rights, Work Accidents, Trials and Appeals, Business Law, Business Planning, Contracts, Law Suits, Insurance, Business Enterprises, Closely Held Business, Corporate, Limited Liability Companies, Partnerships, Small Business, Franchises, Buying and Selling A Business, Debt and Credit, Collections, Creditors Rights, Banking and Finance, Venture Capital, Employee Benefits, Employment Contracts, Human Resources, Discrimination, Sexual Harassment, Workers Compensation, Wrongful Termination, Real Estate, Buying or Selling, Commercial Leasing, Environmental, Landlord and Tenant, Zoning and Land Use, Starting a Business, Strategic Alliances, Joint Ventures, Mergers, Civil Rights, Consumer Law, Consumer Fraud, Unsafe Products, Criminal Law, Drunk Driving, Misdemeanors, Drug Crimes, Juvenile Crimes, Parole and Probation, Traffic Violations, Medical Malpractice, Legal Malpractice, Products Liability, Slip and Fall, Wills and Probate, Trusts and Estates, Asset Protection, Estate Planning, General Civil and Criminal Practice, General Practice, Trademark Patent Litigation.
See Professional Biographies, MERRILLVILLE, INDIANA

Laszlo, John B., (BV) .... '57 '82 C&L.879 B.S.B.A., J.D. 200 E. 80th Pl.
Leonard, Paul A., Jr., (AV) .... '53 '82 C.321 B.A. L.879 J.D. [Burke C.&C.]
Levinson, Donald P., (BV) .... '45 '70 C.347 B.A. L.1119 J.D. [Levinson&L.]
Levinson, Rosalie B. .... '48 '73 C.347 B.A.,M.A. L.879 J.D. 122 W. 79th Ave.
Levinson, Shana D. .... '73 '99 C.347 B.A. L.879 J.D. [Levinson&L.]
Levinson & Levinson, (BV) .... 122 W. 79th Avenue
Leyden, Jay S. '55 '85 C.602 B.A. L.424 J.D.
(adm. in IL; not adm. in IN) White Lodging Servs.
Lopez, Alexander .... '63 '88 C.679 B.A. L.347 J.D. 101 E. 90th Dr.
Lucas, Mark S., (BV) .... '55 '80 C.602 B.A. L.345 J.D. [Lucas,H.&M.]

Lucas, Holcomb & Medrea LLP, (AV)
300 East 90th Drive, 46410
Telephone: 219-769-3561 Fax: 219-756-7409
Email: lhm@lhmlaw.com
Members of Firm: Robert A. Lucas (1922-1999); James A. Holcomb; John O. Stiles; Daniel A. Medrea; Robert F. Peters; Stephen R. Place; Mary Linda Casey; Glenn R. Patterson; Mark S. Lucas; C. Donald Emery, III; James L. Clement, Jr. Associate: Brooke Shreve.
General Practice, State and Federal Courts. Trials and Appeals. Corporate, Business, Business Litigation, Contracts, Business Planning, Business Enterprises, Commercial, Employment, Wrongful Termination, Banking, Tax, Wills and Probate, Trusts and Estates and Estate Planning, Insurance, Bankruptcy, Personal Injury, Automobile Accidents, Wrongful Death, Products Liability, Family/Domestic Relations, Adoptions, Child Custody, Child Support, Divorce, Visitation Rights, Hospital, Real Estate, Municipal and Zoning Law, Consumer and Commercial Collection Law, Construction Litigation.
Representative Clients: Bank One, Merrillville, N.A.; Indiana University; Munster Medical Research Foundation, Inc. (Operating "The Community Hospital"); St. Cathering Hospital, Inc.; WPM Construction LLC; Coldwell Banker Residential Brokage; Bank Calumet Trust Department; Mercantile National Bank of Hammond Trust Department.
See Professional Biographies, MERRILLVILLE, INDIANA

Lyman, Gregory R., (BV) .... '52 '77 C.475 B.S. L.879 J.D. [⊠ Burke C.&C.]
Maicher, Kathleen M., (BV) .... '49 '83 C.347 B.A. L.426 J.D. [Spangler,J.&D.]
Martin, James W., (AV) .... '61 '86 C.347 B.S. L.879 J.D. [Martin&M.]
Martin, William F., (AV) .... '25 '54 C&L.879 B.A., J.D. [Martin&M.] ‡
Martin and Martin, (AV) .... 8585 Broadway, Ste. 660
Mason, Derrick A. .... '80 '05 C&L.347 B.S., J.D. [⊠ Spangler,J.&D.]
Mathisen, Eric P., (BV) .... '70 '96 C.123 B.A. L.879 J.D. [⊠ Hoeppner W.&E.]
Mayer, Richard A., (AV) .... '34 '61 C.347 B.S. L.1119 J.D. [Spangler,J.&D.]
Mayer, Richard L., (BV) .... '50 '75 C.347 A.B. L.221 J.D. 1205 W. Lincoln Hwy.
McAlpin, America L., (BV) .... '50 '85 C.347 B.A. L.365 J.D. 9111 Broadway
McCafferty, James, (AV⊤) .... '35 '75 C.477 B.S.E. L.1137 J.D. 6 W. 73rd Avenue‡
McDowell, Dock, Jr., (BV) .... '50 '76 C.894 B.A. L.879 J.D. [McDowell]
McDowell Law Firm, The, (BV) .... 7895 Broadway, Ste. C
McFarland, Patrick Arthur .... '50 '75 C&L.339 B.A., J.D. 101 E. 90th Dr.
McQuillan, James D., (BV) .... '50 '75 C.894 B.A. L.352 J.D. [Spangler,J.&D.]
McQuillan, John P., (AV) .... '40 '65 C&L.602 B.B.A., LL.B. [Spangler,J.&D.]
Medrea, Daniel A., (AV) .... '44 '69 C.602 A.B. L.1119 J.D. [Lucas,H.&M.]

Melchi, Chad J. .... '72 '01 C.347 B.S. L.1119 J.D. [Ⓐ Burke C.&C.]
Miller, Richard A., (BV) .... '45 '74 C.347 B.S. L.879 J.D. 370 W. 80th Pl.
Minor, Cynthia A., (BV) .... '57 '83 C.347 B.A. L.325 J.D. [Ⓐ McDowell]
Mirkov, Robert M., (CV) .... '56 '81 C.347 A.B. L.345 J.D. 8550 Bway.
Molina, Marco A. .... '73 '99 C&L.347 B.S., J.D. [Kopko G.&R.]
Mostak, Richard L., (BV) .... '49 '75 C.347 B.S. L.345 J.D. [Ⓒ Kopko G.&R.]
Mulshine, Suzanne Welsh .... '64 '93 C.741 B.B.A. L.602 J.D. Welsh, Inc.
Neff, Paula E., (BV) .... '53 '82 C.347 B.S. L.365 J.D. [Burke C.&C.]
Novak, David R. .... '72 '00 C.679 B.A. L.879 J.D. [Ⓐ Schlyer&Assoc.]
Nowak, Kenneth E., (BV) .... '47 '76 C.221 B.A. L.879 J.D. [Buoscio,P.K.&N.]
Oates, James R. .... '58 '83 C.679 B.S. L.879 J.D. 101 W. 75th Place
O'Connor, Alan E. .... '45 '68 C.724 B.A. L.1119 J.D. Amer. Intl. Fidelity
Oliveira, F. Jeffrey .... '49 '74 C.347 B.S.B.A. L.879 J.D. [J.Oliveira&Assoc.]
Oliveira, Jeffrey, & Associates .... 101 E. 90th Dr.
Olson, Perry T. .... '74 '00 C.123 B.S. L.585 J.D. 2624 West Lincoln Highway
Page, T. Edward .... '54 '78 C.339 A.B. L.347 J.D. [Ⓐ Cohen&T.]
Pangere, Kerry A. .... '68 '99 C.679 B.A. L.879 J.D. 9205 Broadway, Ste. B
Pangere, Vasilia M. .... '78 '03 C&L.879 B.A., J.D. [Arshad,P.&W.]
Parker, Robert F., (AV) .... '51 '77 C.602 B.A. L.347 J.D. [Burke C.&C.]
Patheja, Jay S. .... '69 '94 C.347 B.A. L.424 J.D. [Hoeppner W.&E.]
Patterson, Glenn R., (BV) .... '51 '76 C.347 B.A. L.1119 J.D. [Lucas,H.&M.]
Peek, Kathleen E. .... '67 '97 C.679 B.S. L.879 J.D. 3893 E. U.S. Highway 30
Pera, David W., (BV) .... '48 '76 C.503 B.A. L.879 J.D. [Buoscio,P.K.&N.]
Peters, Mitchell A., (CV) .... '57 '84 C&L.879 B.S., J.D. 370 W. 80th Pl.
Peters, Robert F., (BV) .... '46 '71 C&L.879 B.A., J.D. [Lucas,H.&M.]

Pinkerton and Friedman, Professional Corporation
(See Munster)

Place, Stephen R., (BV) .... '46 '72 C.228 A.B. L.1119 J.D. [Lucas,H.&M.]
Plantz, Robert A. .... '73 '00 C.679 B.A. L.879 J.D. [Ⓐ H.S.Lasser&Assoc.]
Popp, Brian P., (CV) .... '59 '84 C&L.879 B.A., J.D. 200 E. 80th Pl.
Poracky, Paul B., (BV) .... '53 '84 C.679 B.S. L.365 J.D. [Spangler,J.&D.]
Portelli, James M., (BV) .... '68 '93 C.477 B.A. L.347 J.D. [Spangler,J.&D.]
Prasco, Victor H., (CV) .... '65 '93 C.347 B.S. L.879 J.D. [Burke C.&C.]
Pressler, Robert L. .... '37 '68 C.347 B.S. L.879 J.D. 8450 Bway.‡
Pruett, Barry W. .... '70 '05 C.473 B.S. L.879 J.D. [Ⓐ Burke C.&C.]
Psimos, Harry A. .... '24 '54 C.347 B.S. L.879 LL.B. [Psimos&P.]
Psimos, Mark A., (BV) .... '54 '83 C.347 B.S. L.365 J.D. [Psimos&P.]
Psimos & Psimos, (BV) .... 9219 Broadway

Querrey & Harrow, Ltd.
8585 Broadway, Suite 510, 46410 ⊙
Telephone: 219-738-1820 Fax: 219-738-1821
Email: jclymer@querrey.com URL: http://www.querrey.com
Members of Firm: Galen A. Bradley (Also at Chicago, Illinois Office); Jeffrey W. Clymer (Resident);—John H. Halstead (Resident).
General Practice and Trial Practice.
Chicago, Illinois Office: 175 West Jackson Boulevard, Suite 1600. Telephone: 312-540-7000. Fax: 312-540-0578.
Crystal Lake, Illinois Office: 651 West Terra Cotta Avenue, Suite 221. Telephone: 815-479-1929. Fax: 815-479-1978.
Wheaton, Illinois Office: 310 South County Farm Road, Third Floor. Telephone: 630-653-2600. Fax: 630-653-0178.
Waukegan, Illinois Office: 415 West Washington Street, Suite 205. Telephone: 847-249-4440. Fax: 847-249-4932.
Joliet, Illinois Office: 2 Rialto Square, Suite 401, 116 North Chicago Street. Telephone: 815-726-1600. Fax: 815-726-1674.
New York, N.Y. Office: 120 Broadway, Suite 2800. Telephone: 212-233-0130. Fax: 212-233-0172.
London, England Office: 141-142 Fenchurch Street, Fifth Floor. Telephone: 207-929-6670. Fax: 207-929-6671.

See Professional Biographies, MERRILLVILLE, INDIANA

Ranich, David K., (AV) .... '51 '77 C.347 B.S. L.1292 J.D. [Burke C.&C.] (⊙Munster)
Rappa, Michael J., (CV) .... '63 '93 C.966 B.A. L.879 J.D. [Johnson&R.]
Repay, Bridgett Jo .... '71 '97 C.679 B.A. L.879 J.D. State Farm Litigation Counsel
Retson, Demetri J., (AV) .... '52 '77 C.597 B.A. L.309 J.D. [Kopko G.&R.]
Rochau, Alvin A. G. .... '21 '50 C&L.879 LL.B. 7103 Broadway
Roman, Frank V. .... '24 '53 C.894 A.B. L.1119 LL.B. 3700 E. U.S. Hwy. 30
Rooth, Barry D., (BV) .... '57 '82 C.347 B.A. L.879 J.D. 8750 Broadway, Ste. A
Rossi, Paul A. .... '69 '97 C.234 B.S. L.879 J.D. [Ⓐ Cohen&T.]
Samreta, Joseph A. .... '73 '99 C.894 A.B. L.347 J.D. [Ⓐ Burke C.&C.]
Schaefer, Lily M., (BV) .... '53 '79 C&L.879 B.A., J.D. [Ⓒ Kopko G.&R.]
Schafer, Francis J. .... '49 '77 C.347 B.A. L.879 J.D. 3820 E. US 30
Schlyer, Donald E. .... '49 '85 C.339 B.S. L.879 J.D. [Schlyer&Assoc.]
Schlyer & Associates, P.C. .... 200 W. 80th Place
Schmidt, Kathryn D., (BV) .... '47 '80 C.347 B.S. L.879 J.D. [Burke C.&C.]
Schmoll, Jon F., (AV) .... '41 '67 C.347 A.B. L.345 J.D. [Spangler,J.&D.]
Schroer, Edmund A., (AV) .... '28 '52 C.879 A.B. L.597 J.D. 801 E. 86th Ave.‡
Serafini-Smith, Beth A. .... '69 '97 C.679 B.A. L.879 J.D. [Ⓐ Bowman,H.B.&V.]
Shaps, Herbert I. .... '49 '75 C.823 B.A. L.421 J.D. 1205 W. Lincoln Hwy., Ste. D
Shreve, Brooke .... '75 '01 C.679 B.S. L.879 J.D. [Ⓐ Lucas,H.&M.]
Sims, Janis G. .... '48 '04 C.347 B.A. L.345 J.D. [Ⓐ Spangler,J.&D.]
Sircar, Ketaki .... '71 '96 C.477 B.A. L.347 J.D. [Ⓐ Spangler,J.&D.]
Sobkowski, Gregory A., (BV) .... '57 '82 C&L.602 B.A., J.D. [Hodges&D.] ⊙
Spangler, Ronald T., (AV) .... '22 '50 C&L.190 B.S., J.D. 8396 Mississppi St.

Spangler, Jennings & Dougherty, P.C., (AV) BR
8396 Mississippi Street, 46410-6398 ⊙
Telephone: 219-769-2323 Facsimile: 219-769-5007
Email: spangler@sjdlaw.com URL: http://www.sjdlaw.com
Richard A. Mayer; John P. McQuillan; Samuel J. Bernardi, Jr. (Resident, Valparaiso Office); Jon F. Schmoll; Robert D. Hawk; Daniel A. Gioia; James D. McQuillan; David L. Abel, II; Lawrence A. Kalina; Robert P. Stoner; Gregory J. Tonner; Kathleen M. Maicher; Paul B. Poracky; Robert D. Brown; Robert J. Dignam; James M. Portelli; Robert D. Hawk, Jr.; Ricardo A. Hall; Sharon L. Stanzione; Christopher Grabarek (Resident, Valparaiso Office). Associates: James L. Hough; Ketaki Sircar; Gregory A. Purvis (Resident, Indianapolis Office); Jon S. Diston (Resident, Valparaiso Office); Marian C. Drenth; Michelle P. Burchett; Melissa J. Wray; Caleb S. Johnson; Michael L. Carter; William M. Koch; Janis G. Sims; Derrick A. Mason; Frederick L. Carpenter; Ann Marie Wolwine. Of Counsel: Harry J. Jennings; Patrick J. Dougherty (Resident, Valparaiso Office).
General Trial and Appellate Practice. Administrative, Banking, Bankruptcy, Business Reorganizations, Business Transactions, Civil Rights, Commercial, Construction, Corporate, Creditors' Rights, Criminal Litigation, Family/Domestic Relations, Drug and Device, Eminent Domain, Environmental, ERISA and Employee Benefits, Probate and Estate Planning and Administration, Fire/Arson, Guardianships, Health Care, Insurance, Labor and Employment, Municipal and Zoning, Personal Injury, Product Liability, Professional Liability, Medical Malpractice Defense, Real Estate, School, Federal, State and Local Taxation, Toxic Torts, Transportation, Workers Compensation, Land Development.
Representative Clients: Allstate Insurance Company; Farmers Insurance Group; Ford Motor Credit Co.; School Town of Munster; St. Paul Insurance Cos.; State Farm Cos.
Valparaiso, Indiana Office: 150 Lincolnway, Suite 3001. Telephone: 219-462-6151. FAX: 219-477-4935.

(This Listing Continued)

Spangler, Jennings & Dougherty, P.C. (Continued)
Indianapolis, Indiana Office: 9200 Keystone Crossing, Suite 410. Telephone: 317-571-7690. Facsimile: 317-571-7686.

See Professional Biographies, MERRILLVILLE, INDIANA

Stankiewicz, James J. .... '43 '73 C.97 B.A. L.879 J.D. [J.J.Stankiewicz&Assoc.]
Stankiewicz, J.J., & Associates .... 7870 Broadway
Stanzione, Sharon L. .... '71 '97 C.679 B.A. L.347 J.D. [Spangler,J.&D.]
Steele, Kevin E., (BV) .... '67 '93 C.602 B.A. L.347 J.D. [Burke C.&C.]
Steele, R. Lawrence, (AV) .... '47 '74 C.347 B.S. L.345 J.D. [Hodges&D.] ⊙
Stiles, John O., (BV) .... '32 '58 C.347 A.B. L.309 LL.B. [Lucas,H.&M.]
Stoner, Robert P., (BV) .... '53 '78 C.838 B.A. L.345 J.D. [Spangler,J.&D.]
Stout, Gerold L. .... '55 '02 C.679 B.A. L.879 J.D. [Ⓐ Hoeppner W.&E.]
Stracci, Paul G. .... '68 '97 C.424 B.A. L.879 J.D. [Ⓐ Cohen&T.]

Tauber, Westland & Jasaitis, P.C.
(See Schererville)

Tavitas, Adam, (CV) .... '69 '95 C.894 B.A. L.345 J.D. 9120 Connecticut Dr.
Theodoros, Perry W., (BV) .... '58 '83 C.221 B.S. L.879 J.D. 8750 Bway., Ste. A
Theodoros, William, (BV) .... '31 '59 C.347 B.S. L.1119 J.D. 8750 Broadway
Thiros, James N., (CV) .... '61 '88 C.347 B.A. L.879 J.D. [Ⓐ Cohen&T.]
Thiros, Mark A., (CV) .... '62 '87 C.347 B.S. L.345 J.D. [Ⓐ Cohen&T.]
Thiros, Nick J., (AV) .... '32 '57 C.347 B.S. L.879 LL.B. [Cohen&T.]
Thornton, Lucretia A. .... '— '82 C.679 B.S. L.879 J.D. [Ⓐ Hoeppner W.&E.] ⊙
Tiller, Emerson H. .... '63 '87 C.347 B.A. L.1119 J.D. 9111 Bway.
Tiller, Nancy Moore .... '— '81 C.347 B.A. L.879 J.D. 9111 Broadway, Ste. Ff
Tolbert, Michael Eugene .... '75 '00 C&L.879 B.A., J.D. [Ⓐ Hoeppner W.&E.]
Tonner, Gregory J., (BV) .... '57 '82 C.347 B.S. L.862 J.D. [Spangler,J.&D.]
Touchette, William L. .... '55 '81 C.347 B.A. L.1119 J.D. 7414 Iddings Ct.
Trapane, Anthony P. .... '48 '79 C.347 A.B. L.146 J.D. 8719 Jackson St.
Trapane, Terence G., Law Offices of '54 '93
C.347 B.S.B.A. L.879 J.D. 8101 Polo Club Drive
Troumouliaris, Michael J. .... '41 '68 C.679 B.S.M.E. L.209 J.D. 1000 E. 80th Pl.
Tsarnas, Lorie D., (CV) .... '66 '94 C.347 B.S. L.879 J.D. [Ⓐ Bowman,H.B.&V.]
Unterberg, Kenneth W., (AV) .... '55 '80 C.424 B.A. L.209 J.D. [Unterberg&Assoc.]

Unterberg & Associates P.C., (AV)
8050 Cleveland Place, 46410
Telephone: 219-736-5579 Fax: 219-756-1810
Kenneth W. Unterberg.
Mortgage Banking Foreclosures/Bankruptcies and Related Litigation, Real Estate and Title Insurance Law.
Representative Clients: Available upon request.

See Professional Biographies, MERRILLVILLE, INDIANA

Van Der Molen, Mark, (BV) .... '59 '85 C.114 B.A. L.879 J.D. 1000 E. 80th Pl., Ste. 519
Vann, Robert G., (BV) .... '64 '91 C.347 B.S. L.879 J.D. 500 E. 86th Ave.
Vawter, Richard E., (BV) .... '52 '83 C.63 B.S. L.146 J.D. 1000 E. 80th Pl.
Vazanellis, Samuel G. .... '80 '04 C.1119 B.S. L.879 J.D. 200 E. 90th Drive
Vegter, J. Robert, (BV) .... '45 '70 C.932 B.S. L.879 J.D. 100 E. 90th Dr.
Velazco, Eugene M., Jr., (CV) '50 '77 C.347 B.S. L.1119 J.D.
Staff Coun., Lake Co. offc. of Family & Children
Vician, Glenn S., (BV) .... '53 '78 C&L.879 B.A., J.D. [Bowman,H.B.&V.]

Wai, Minh C., Law Offices of '74 '99 C.293 B.A. L.436 J.D.
1000 E. 80th Place, Suite 502N, 46410
Telephone: 219-793-9000 Fax: 219-793-9211
Email: minh_wai@sbcglobal.net URL: http://www.wailaw.com
General Practice, Personal Injury, Auto and Railroad Accidents, Construction Accidents, Property Damage, Slip and Fall, Unsafe Products, Wrongful Death, Bankruptcy, Insurance Defense and Coverage, Corporate Law, Contracts, Landlord-Tenant, Business Defense, Personal Injury Defense, Subrogation, Immigration Law.

See Professional Biographies, MERRILLVILLE, INDIANA

Walker, James T., (AV) .... '47 '72 C&L.602 B.A., J.D. [J.T.Walker]
Walker, James T., Professional Corporation, (AV) .... 99 East 86th Avenue, Suite E
Ward, Megan L. .... '76 '01 C.347 B.S. L.1119 J.D. [Anderson&W.]
Warring, Matthew J. .... '— '03 C.1119 B.S. L.879 J.D. [Arshad,P.&W.]
Weiss, Garry A., Law Office Of, (BV) '54 '80 C.347 B.S. L.365 J.D.
6 West 73rd Avenue
Werner, Kevin E. .... '72 '01 C.679 B.A. L.801 J.D. [Ⓐ J.P.Bushemi&Assoc.]
Whalley, Marshall P. .... '57 '83 C.477 B.S. L.879 J.D. [M.P.Whalley&Assoc.]
Whalley, Marshall P., & Associates, P.C., Law Offices of .... 8915 Broadway
Whitted, Charles K., (AV) .... '22 '50 C.313 LL.B. 1000 E. 80th Pl.
Willard, Jack .... '27 '56 C.347 B.S. L.1119 J.D. 8585 Bway.
Wilson, Kent S., (CV) .... '55 '81 C&L.201 B.S., J.D. 1000 E. 80th Pl.
Woloshansky, I. Alexander, (BV) .... '47 '73 C.347 B.A. L.1119 J.D. 9219 Broadway
Wolter, Richard C., (BV) .... '51 '77 C&L.879 B.A., J.D. 9120 Connecticut Dr., Ste. G
Wolwine, Ann Marie .... '79 '05 C.347 B.A. L.879 J.D. [Ⓐ Spangler,J.&D.]
Woodward, David E., (CV) .... '64 '90 C.894 A.B. L.879 J.D. [Casale,W.&B.]
Woodward, R. Brian, (BV) .... '60 '85 C&L.879 B.S., J.D. [Casale,W.&B.]
Wray, Melissa J. .... '67 '02 C.1193 B.S. L.879 J.D. [Ⓐ Spangler,J.&D.]
Yoon, Stacia L., (BV) .... '63 '92 C.108 B.A. L.347 J.D. [Kopko G.&R.]
Zahorsky, Timothy .... '63 '88 C.894 B.A. L.879 J.D. [Ⓐ Bowman,H.B.&V.]

MICHIANA SHORES, 378, *La Porte Co.*

Palfi, Alfred M. '28 '52 C&L.145 B.A., J.D.
(adm. in IL; not adm. in IN) 100 El Portal St.‡

MICHIGAN CITY, 32,900, *La Porte Co.*

Arness, Lawrence W., (BV) .... '54 '79 C.347 B.A. L.345 J.D. 450 St. John Rd.
Bachman, David .... '75 '03 C&L.879 B.A., J.D. [Ⓐ Huelat&M.]

Beckman, Kelly & Smith
(See Hammond)

Boklund, William J., (BV) .... '51 '77 C.679 B.A. L.879 J.D. Supr. Ct. #4
Braje, Craig V., (AV) .... '49 '74 C.927 B.A. L.879 J.D. [Braje&N.] ⊙

Braje & Nelson, LLP, (AV)
126 West Fourth Street, P.O. Box 1006, 46361-8206 ⊙
Telephone: 219-872-2100 Fax: 219-873-9163
URL: http://www.braje-nelson.com
Members of Firm: Craig V. Braje; William J. Nelson, Jr.; Kurt R. Earnst; Elizabeth Ann Flynn;—Christopher L. Willoughby; Carri N. Crider. Retired: C. T. Kitowski.
Language: English.
General Civil and Criminal Trial Practice. Commercial, Real Estate, Family, Domestic Relations, Personal Injury Law, Estate Planning, Probate and Bankruptcy.
Representative Clients: Northern Indiana Education Foundation.
Reference: NBD Bank, N.A.

See Professional Biographies, MICHIGAN CITY, INDIANA

Chapala, Walter P. .... '42 '70 C.347 B.S. L.879 J.D. Supr. Ct. J.

Chubb, Deborah L. .... '62 '93 C.347 B.G.S. L.879 J.D. 1200 E. Coolspring Avenue
Crider, Carri N. .... '74 '99 C.347 B.A. L.879 J.D. [Ⓐ Braje&N.] ⊙
Dabagia, Lee W., (AV) .... '37 '62 C.72 B.A. L.1119 J.D. [Ⓒ Sweeney,D.T.J.&P.] ‡
Donoghue, Patrick E., (BV) .... '44 '69 C.602 B.A. L.1119 J.D. 709 Franklin Square
DuVal, Benjamin S., Jr. '36 '63 C.893 B.A. L.976 LL.B.
(adm. in NY; not adm. in IN) 220 W. 10th St.‡
Earnst, Kurt R., (CV) .... '70 '96 C.679 B.A. L.879 J.D. [Braje&N.] ⊙
Espar, John M., (CVⓉ) .... '61 '87 C.347 B.A. L.800 J.D. 1310 Franklin Street
Fenton, Steven L., (CV) .... '44 '72 C.347 B.S. L.879 J.D. [Fenton]
Fenton Law Office, (CV) .... 1817 E. Michigan Blvd.
Flynn, Elizabeth Ann .... '70 '95 C.249 B.A. L.879 J.D. [Braje&N.] ⊙
Fox, Mary L., (BV) .... '48 '75 C.679 B.A. L.879 J.D. 2811 E. Michigan Blvd.
Gilmore, Robert W., Jr. .... '44 '71 C.197 B.A. L.1119 J.D. Cir. J.
Hale, Steven A., (BV) .... '44 '76 C.276 B.S. L.879 J.D. 801 Washington St.
Hedge, Cynthia A. .... '52 '78 C.347 A.B. L.879 J.D. 801 Washington St.
Herrbach, William F., Law Offices of '46 '74 C.347 B.S. L.879 J.D.
401 Washington St.
Hoover, R. Dennis .... '44 '69 C.602 L.879 J.D. Dep. Pros. Atty.
Huelat, Jerry E., (AV) .... '53 '81 C.645 B.A. L.589 J.D. [Huelat&M.]

Huelat & Mack, (AV)
Marquette Mall Office Building, 450 St. John Road, Suite 204, 46360
Telephone: 219-879-3253 Fax: 219-879-3090
URL: http://www.huelatandmack.com
Jerry E. Huelat; Beverly J. Mack. Associates: Michael Kreppein; Jaime M. Oss; David Bachman.
Civil Trials and Appeals in State and Federal Courts, Insurance Defense, Insurance Coverage, Personal Injury, Automobile Accidents, Slip and Fall, Sexual Abuse, Wrongful Death, Products Liability, Libel and Slander, Fraud, Insurance, Legal Malpractice, Civil Rights, Discrimination, Consumer Law, Consumer Fraud, Unsafe Products, Warranties, Employment Law, Sexual Harassment, Wrongful Termination, Construction.
§§.

See Professional Biographies, MICHIGAN CITY, INDIANA

Janes, William, (BV) .... '53 '78 C.63 B.S. L.1151 J.D. [Sweeney,D.T.J.&P.]
Katz, Jeffrey B. .... '54 '82 C&L.910 A.B., J.D. 831 Washington St.
Keating, Virginia M. .... '41 '91 C.679 B.A. L.879 J.D. 119 W. 7th Street
Keppen, Arthur A. .... '23 '52 C&L.879 LL.B. Ret. Supr. Ct. J.
King, Steven E. .... '50 '78 C.63 B.S. L.879 J.D. Supr. Ct. J., LaPort Superior Courthouse
Kitowski, C. T. .... '25 '52 C&L.879 LL.B. [Ⓒ Braje&N.] ⊙‡
Kreppein, Michael .... '71 '00 C.339 B.A. L.879 J.D. [Ⓐ Huelat&M.]
Lake, John F., (BV) .... '66 '91 C&L.602 B.A., J.D. [Lake&L.]
Lake & Lake, (BV) .... 2601 E. Michigan Blvd.
Lund, Nancy E. '59 '90 C.477 B.S.N. L.912 J.D.
(adm. in MI; not adm. in IN) St. Anthony Memorial Health Ctrs.
Mack, Beverly J., (CV) .... '61 '89 C.234 B.A. L.339 J.D. [Huelat&M.]
Martin, Donald D. .... '26 '55 C.879 A.B. L.1119 LL.B. Ret. Supr. Ct. J.
Mcgrath, Kevin B. .... '45 '74 C&L.347 B.S., J.D. 401 Washington
Meyer, Marcellus B., (BV) .... '21 '49 C.894 A.B. L.1119 LL.B. 601 Franklin Sq.
Nelson, William J., Jr., (BV) .... '65 '92 C.827 B.A. L.879 J.D. [Braje&N.] ⊙

Newby, Lewis, Kaminski & Jones, LLP
(See La Porte)

Oss, Jaime M. .... '78 '03 C.679 B.A. L.879 J.D. [Ⓐ Huelat&M.]
Pagos, Donald W., (AV) .... '56 '81 C.63 B.S. L.879 J.D. [Sweeney,D.T.J.&P.]
Palmer, Victor D. .... '36 '62 C.1024 B.S. L.879 LL.B. 601 Franklin Sq.
Pedulla Lake, Mary, (CV) .... '66 '92 C.262 B.A. L.602 J.D. [Lake&L.]
Price, Atley C., (BV) .... '54 '83 C.679 B.A. L.1137 J.D. Chf. Dep. Pros. Atty.
Riley, Michael V. .... '43 '68 C.347 B.A. L.879 J.D. 2510 Oriole Trail
Rosenthal, Ruby Leppo '53 '79 C.696 B.A. L.365 J.D.
(adm. in NY; not adm. in IN) Sullair Corp.
Rutkowski, Thomas J. .... '43 '72 C.966 B.S. L.879 J.D. 2710 Franklin St.
Schaaf, Bonita A. '49 '91 C.347 B.G.S. L.879 J.D.
Sentencing Consultant, Pub. Def. Coun.
Stalbrink, Richard R., Jr., (CV) .... '68 '94 C.63 B.S. L.879 J.D. 801 Washington St.
Sweeney, John H., (AV) .... '30 '59 C.347 B.S. L.1119 LL.B. [Sweeney,D.T.J.&P.] ‡

Sweeney, Dabagia, Thorne, Janes & Pagos, L.L.P., (AV) BR
An Indiana Registered Limited Liability Partnership
709 Franklin Square, P.O. Box 769, 46361-0769
Telephone: 219-879-5321 Fax: 219-879-2942
Email: dwp@sdtjp.com
Members of Firm: Clarence T. Sweeney (1899-1980); John H. Sweeney (Retired); Lee W. Dabagia (Retired); Jeffrey L. Thorne; William Janes; Donald W. Pagos. Associate: Aimee M. Talian.
General Civil and Trial Practice in State and Federal Courts. Municipal, Personal Injury, Mediation, Probate and Estate Planning, Corporate, Banking and Creditors Rights, Real Estate, Family Law, Appeals and Criminal Law, Bankruptcy.
Reference: Horizon Bank, N.A.

See Professional Biographies, MICHIGAN CITY, INDIANA

Talian, Aimee M. .... '75 '01 C.63 B.S. L.879 J.D. [Ⓐ Sweeney,D.T.J.&P.]
Thorne, Jeffrey L., (BV) .... '52 '78 C.347 A.B. L.879 J.D. [Sweeney,D.T.J.&P.]
Transki, Donald E. .... '27 '57 C.879 A.B. L.345 J.D. 902 Pine St.
Ulferts, Martin .... '68 '96 C.932 B.S. L.879 J.D. 531 Franklin Sq.
Willoughby, Christopher L. .... '70 '02 C.578 B.A. L.879 J.D. [Ⓐ Braje&N.] ⊙

Winski, O. Jerrold, (AVⓉ) '37 '62 C&L.477 B.B.A., LL.B.
601 Franklin Street, Suite 200, Drawer K, 46361
Telephone: 219-874-4276 Fax: 219-874-9699
Email: oscarwins@comcast.net URL: http://www.lawyers.com/winskilaw
Business Law, Commercial Real Estate, Residential Real Estate, Labor and Employment, Leases and Leasing, Civil Litigation, Business Acquisitions, Business Divestitures, Personal Injury, Mediation, Trusts and Estates, Wills and Probate, Estate Planning, Zoning, Planning and Land Use.

See Professional Biographies, MICHIGAN CITY, INDIANA

Wiseman, Joan F. .... '52 '93 C.679 B.L.S. L.879 J.D. 405 Hendricks St.
Wojcik, John M., (BV) .... '53 '79 C.347 B.S. L.589 J.D. [J.M.Wojcik]
Wojcik, John M., P.C., Law Offices of, (BV) .... 450 Saint John Road

MIDDLEBURY, 2,956, *Elkhart Co.*

Cappelletti, Teresa L., (CV) .... '66 '98 C.741 L.1187 J.D. P.O. Box 58
Cataldo, Theresa L. .... '66 '98 C.741 B.A. L.1187 J.D. 114 South Main Street
Graber, Theora E. .... '41 '90 C.647 B.S. L.1187 J.D. [Ⓒ Graber]
Graber Law Firm, P.C. .... P.O. Box 58
Rogers, Richard W., (CV) .... '55 '80 C.123 B.A. L.365 J.D. 203 W. Warren St.
Schwartz, Fay, (CV) .... '— '91 C.347 B.S. L.879 J.D. 103 N. Brown St.

MIDDLETOWN, 2,488, *Henry Co.*

Wisehart, Robt. F., (AV) .... '26 '54 C.210 A.B. L.345 J.D. 580 Locust St.
Wisehart Phillips, Mary K., (BV) .... '67 '94 C.840 B.S. L.345 LL.D. 580 Locust St.

MILAN, 1,816, *Ripley Co.*

Arkenberg, Franklin W., III, (BV) .... '43 '71 C.679 B.A. L.345 J.D. Pros. Atty.

MISHAWAKA, 46,557, *St. Joseph Co.*

Allsop, Gaylen W., (BV) .... '39 '68 C&L.347 A.B., J.D. 435 Park Place Circle, #200
Arndt, Randall K. .... '56 '89 C.679 B.L.S. L.879 J.D. [Arndt]
Arndt Law Office .... 2201 Division St.
Arnold, Michael W. .... '78 '03 C.894 A.B. L.879 J.D. [Ⓐ May O.L.]
Beamer, George N. .... '35 '60 C&L.347 B.S., J.D. Supr. Ct. J.
Bennett, Jane F., (BV) .... '52 '77 C.347 B.A. L.602 J.D. [May O.L.]
Bent, David V., (BV) .... '51 '76 C&L.602 A.B., J.D. [D.V.Bent]
Bent, David V., P.C, (BV) .... 400 Lincoln Way E.
Beutter, Robert C., (BV) .... '35 '60 C.347 B.S. L.1119 J.D. 437 Lincoln Way, E.
Bingham & Loughlin, P.C., (BV) .... 400 Lincoln Way E.
Bonewitz, Richard D., (AV) '29 '53
C.347 A.B. L.1119 LL.B. 520 Park Place Court, Suite 200
Bowers, Richard S., Jr. .... '46 '71 C.309 B.A. L.93 J.D. [R.S.Bowers]
Bowers, Richard S. .... 55636 Buckeye Road
Burke, James E., (BV) .... '43 '70 C.347 B.S. L.1119 J.D. 549 Lincoln Way, W.
Campiti, Vincent M. ..... '69 '97 C.679 B.A. L.879 J.D. 310 W. McKinley Ave., Ste. 350
Cergnul, John J. .... '54 '80 C.602 B.B.A. L.836 J.D. Bus. Mngr., Radiology, Inc.
Chestovich, Milan J., (BV) '42 '72 C&L.879 B.A., J.D.
Senior Counsel, Natl. Steel Corp.
Cook, Harold J., (AV) .... '18 '49 C.210 A.B. L.602 J.D. 434 Manchester Dr.
Currey, Richard C., (BV) .... '54 '79 C.894 B.A. L.345 J.D. [Currey&C.]
Currey, Robt. S., (BV) .... '23 '49 C.347 B.S. L.1119 LL.B. [Currey&C.]
Currey & Currey, (BV) .... 122 S. Mill St.
Dees, Patricia Brown .... '48 '97 C.1047 B.A. L.879 J.D. Staff Atty., CIBER, Inc.
Delany, Michael James, Jr. '60 '86 C.602 B.A. L.339 J.D.
(adm. in IL; not adm. in IN) 5812 Iroquois Ln., Apt. 1A
Elliott, R. McKinley, (BV) .... '55 '82 C.879 B.S. L.602 J.D. 400 Lincoln Way E.
Filippello, George V., (BV) .... '52 '77 C&L.602 A.B., J.D. 305 E. 3rd. St.
Fountain, Ryan M., (BV) .... '56 '82 C.401 B.S. L.276 J.D. 420 Lincoln Way W. (Pat.)
Gautier, John H., (BV) .... '51 '76 C.602 B.A. L.362 J.D. [Ⓒ Bingham&L.]
Gourley, John P., (BV) .... '37 '62 C.347 B.S. L.1119 J.D. 437 Lincoln Way E.
Herzberg, Audrey .... '52 '78 C.347 A.B. L.602 J.D. 1210 North Willow Street
Hillaert, Diane Shields, (BV) .... '43 '85 C.734 B.S. L.602 J.D. [D.S.Hillaert]
Hillaert, Diane Shields, P.C., (BV) .... 515 Lincoln Way W.
Hinkle, Patrick J., (BV) .... '53 '83 C.347 A.B. L.345 J.D. 3120 Hickory Road
Hostetler, Steven L., (AV) .... '58 '83 C.624 B.S. L.1119 J.D. [Thorne G.]
Johnson, Jeffery A., (AV) .... '55 '80 C.347 B.S. L.602 J.D. [May O.L.]
Knoblich, Marvin M. .... '20 '47 C&L.339 B.S., LL.B. Asst. Secy., Dodge Mfg. Corp.

Lauer, Jay
(See South Bend)

Lorber, John J., (AV) .... '37 '62 C.347 A.B. L.1119 J.D. [Ⓒ May O.L.]
Loughlin, Thomas P., (AV) .... '19 '48 C.436 B.S. L.477 LL.B. [Ⓒ Bingham&L.]
Marnocha, Benedict (Ben) F., (CV) .... '44 '75 C.347 A.B. L.846 J.D. [Marnocha&Assoc.]
Marnocha & Associates, (CV) .... 310 W. McKinley

May Oberfell Lorber, (AV)
4100 Edison Lakes Parkway, 46545-3422 ⊙
Telephone: 574-243-4100 Facsimile: 574-232-9789
URL: http://www.maylorber.com
Members of Firm: John H. Peddycord; E. Spencer Walton, Jr.; Jeffery A. Johnson; Robert J. Palmer; Wendell W. Walsh; Patricia E. Primmer; W. Todd Woelfer; Bradley L. Varner; D. Andrew Spalding; Jane F. Bennett; Richard F. Nugent, Jr.; Christopher R. Putt. Of Counsel: John J. Lorber. Associates: Georgianne M. Walker; Michael W. Arnold.
Corporate and Commercial Transactions, Litigation, Environmental Law, Real Estate, Labor and Employment, Banking and Bank Related Matters, Estate Planning, Municipal and Administration Law, Products Liability, Alternative Dispute Resolution, Health Care, Medical Malpractice Defense, Insurance Litigation, Trademark and Copyright, Tax, Plaintiff's Litigation, General Civil and Appellate Practice in State and Federal Courts.
Representative Clients: Society National Bank, Indiana; Tyler Refrigeration Corporation; Heller Financial, Inc.; Big C Lumber Co., Inc.; Penn Central Corporation; Orbitron Industries, Inc.; Envirocorp Services Technology, Inc.; ITT Hartford; ASA Corporation.
South Bend, Indiana Office: 300 North Michigan Street, Suite 414, 46601. Telephone: 574-232-2031. Fax: 574-232-9789.

See Professional Biographies, MISHAWAKA, INDIANA

Mayette, Anastasia M., (CV) .... '62 '95 C.347 B.A. L.879 J.D. 543 Lincolnway W.
Mayette, Wilfred J., (BV) .... '34 '63 C.745 A.B. L.602 J.D. 543 Lincolnway W.
Melchiorre, Victor A., (BV) .... '21 '50 C&L.602 A.B., LL.B. 1826 Linden Ave.‡
Meyer, James B. .... '50 '75 C&L.436 A.B., J.D. 4220 Edison Lakes Pkwy.
Meyer, James R., Jr. .... '62 '91 C.347 B.S. L.345 J.D. Sr. Atty., Quality Dining, Inc.
Mick, R. Wyatt, Jr., (BV) .... '29 '54 C&L.477 B.B.A., J.D. [Bingham&L.]
Noell, H. Theodore, Law Office of, (BV) '36 '61
C.347 B.S. L.1119 J.D. 206 E. Mishawaka Ave.
Nugent, Richard F., Jr. .... '55 '80 C.602 B.A. L.879 J.D. [May O.L.]
Olson, James J., (AV) .... '42 '67 C.190 B.S.B.A. L.602 J.D. [Schindler&O.]
Palmer, Robert J., (AV) .... '54 '80 C.602 B.A. L.879 J.D. [May O.L.]
Peddycord, John H., (AV) .... '44 '71 C.63 A.B. L.602 J.D. [May O.L.] ⊙
Preisch, James W. '48 '00 C.999 D.D.S. L.117 J.D.
(adm. in OH; not adm. in IN) [J.Preisch]
Preisch, James .... 1210 Aster Ct.
Primmer, Patricia E., (BV) .... '50 '84 C.347 B.A. L.879 J.D. [May O.L.]
Putt, Christopher R. .... '72 '98 C&L.602 B.A., J.D. [May O.L.]
Ready, David T., (AV) .... '37 '71 C.589 B.S. L.345 J.D. Mag., Cir. Ct.
Roggeman, John J., (BV) .... '61 '86 C.347 B.S. L.1119 J.D. 400 Lincoln Way E.
Rosenberg, Irving M. .... '39 '92 C.347 B.S. L.1119 J.D. 420 Lincoln Way West
Schindler, John W., Jr., (AV) .... '22 '48 C.602 A.B. L.145 J.D. [Ⓒ Schindler&O.]
Schindler and Olson, (AV) .... 122 South Mill Street
Scott, Deborah M. .... '56 '82 C.475 B.A. L.209 J.D. 3900 Edison Lakes Pkwy.‡
Spalding, D. Andrew, (BV) .... '61 '86 C.473 A.B. L.879 J.D. [May O.L.]

Stutsman, Mulvaney & DeBoer
(See Elkhart)

Taylor, Susan Marie .... '59 '84 C.347 B.S. L.879 J.D. 824 Calhoun St.‡

Thorne • Grodnik, LLP, (AV)
420 Lincoln Way West, P.O. Box 1210, 46544 ⊙
Telephone: 574-256-5660 FAX: 574-674-6835
Email: firm@tglaw.us URL: http://www.tglaw.us
Members of Firm: Steven L. Hostetler; Michael A. Trippel (Resident). Associate: Jamie C. Woods.
Commercial and Civil Litigation, Creditors Rights, Bankruptcy, Banking and Bank Related Matters, Corporate and Commercial Transactions, Insurance Defense, Personal Injury, Automobile Accidents, Slip and Fall, Wrongful Death, Real Estate and Zoning, Wills and Probate, Trusts and Estates, Estate Planning, School Law and Family Law, Adoptions, Divorce, Child Custody, Child Support, Visitation Rights, Mediation.
Elkhart, Indiana Office: 228 West High Street. Telephone: 574-294-7473. FAX: 574-294-5390.

See Professional Biographies, MISHAWAKA, INDIANA

Trippel, Michael A., (BV) .... '63 '92 C.345 B.S. L.879 J.D. [Thorne G.]
Varner, Bradley L., (BV) .... '60 '86 C.679 B.A. L.879 J.D. [May O.L.]

Verheye, Julie P. '58 '83 C.347 B.A. L.1119 J.D. 216 S. Race St.
Walker, Georgianne M. '75 '01 C.347 B.S. L.879 J.D. [A May O.L.]
Walsh, Wendell W., (AV) '55 '80 C&L.602 B.A., J.D. [May O.L.]
Walton, E. Spencer '13 '36 C&L.602 B.A., LL.B. 346 Park Ave.
Walton, E. Spencer, Jr., (AV) '52 '79 C.347 B.S. L.345 J.D. [May O.L.]
Weisman, David B., (AV) '35 '60 C.611 B.A. L.477 J.D. [Weisman]

Weisman Associates, Professional Corporation, (AV)
400 Lincolnway East, P.O. Box 683, 46544
Telephone: 574-254-1151 Fax: 574-254-9388
Email: DBW294@MSN.COM
David B. Weisman.
General Civil and Criminal Trial Practice. Drug Crimes, Driving While Intoxicated, Parole and Probation, Traffic Violations, Negligence, Real Estate, Business Law, Contracts, Partnership Law, Corporate, Wills and Probate, Trusts and Estates, Estate Planning, Commercial Law, Real Estate, Commercial Leasing, Family Law, Adoption Law, Child Custody, Child Support, Divorce, Visitation Rights.
See Professional Biographies, MISHAWAKA, INDIANA

Werhnyak, Ronald J., (AVⓉ) '45 '75 C.119 B.S. L.477 J.D.
Sr. V.P., Gen. Cou. & Secy., Natl. Steel Corp.
Woelfer, W. Todd, (BV) '67 '93 C&L.879 B.S., J.D. [May O.L.]
Woods, Jamie C. '74 '99 C.432 B.S. L.347 J.D. [A Thorne G.]
Young, John A., Jr. '45 '87 C.390 B.S. L.602 J.D. Pres., Stone Real Estate Grp. Ltd.‡

MITCHELL, 4,567, *Lawrence Co.*

Mullis, William H., (BV) '57 '85 C.347 B.A. L.69 J.D. [W.H.Mullis]

Mullis, William H., P.C., (BV)
112 South Seventh Street, P.O. Box 35, 47446
Telephone: 812-849-9087 Facsimile: 812-849-6938
Email: WHM@mullislaw.com URL: http://www.mullislaw.com
William H. Mullis.
General Civil Trial and Appellate Practice in State and Federal Courts. Insurance Defense, Insurance Coverage, Products Liability, Probate and Estate Planning, Business Law and Estates.
See Professional Biographies, MITCHELL, INDIANA

MONROEVILLE, 1,232, *Allen Co.*

Fogel, Sam, (AV) '26 '48 C.347 A.B. L.1119 J.D. 109 Main St. (⊙Fort Wayne, Grabill)

MONROVIA, 628, *Morgan Co.*

Litz, Steven C., (BV) '59 '84 C.893 B.A. L.1119 J.D. P.O. Box 216

MONTICELLO, * 5,723, *White Co.*

Altman, Jerry D. '42 '69 C.679 B.S. L.1119 J.D. 116 Constitution Plz.
Blair, Donald K., (BV) '42 '67 C.825 B.A. L.421 J.D. 101 North Main Street
Christopher, Robert B., (BV) '42 '69 C.347 B.S. L.1119 J.D. [Guy,C.L.&P.]
Dellinger, L. Dowal, (CV) '71 '96 C.894 B.A. L.345 J.D. [Dellinger,D.&S.]
Dellinger, Lewis D., Jr., (BV) '38 '66 C.347 B.S. L.345 LL.B. [Dellinger,D.&S.]
Dellinger, Dellinger & Smith, (BV) 114 Constitution Plaza
Griffith, Lee '56 '83 C.432 B.S. L.347 J.D. P.O. Box 80
Guy, John M., (BV) '29 '62 C.108 B.S. L.345 J.D. [Guy,C.L.&P.]
Guy, Robert J., (BV) '59 '84 C.679 B.S. L.879 J.D. 124 N. Main St.
Guy, Christopher, Loy & Pherson, (BV) P.O. Box 925
Loy, George W., (BV) '53 '78 C.679 B.S. L.345 J.D. [Guy,C.L.&P.]
Million, John T., (BV) '42 '68 C.373 A.B. L.1119 J.D. 105 E. Bwy.
Mrzlack, Robert B. '57 '82 C.347 A.B. L.345 J.D. Supr. J.
Overbeck, Karl '19 '47 C.347 B.S. L.345 J.D. Ret. Cir. J.
Pherson, Sheryl M., (CV) '56 '94 C.679 B.S. L.347 J.D. [Guy,C.L.&P.]
Roth, Robert W. '29 '58 C.679 B.S. L.1119 J.D. Sr. J., White Co. Courthouse
Simmons, Max E. '42 '72 C.347 B.S. L.421 J.D.
(adm. in KY; not adm. in IN) P.O. Box 13
Smith, Terry L., (BV) '51 '77 C.894 B.A. L.345 J.D. [Dellinger,D.&S.]
Thacker, Robert W. '48 '73 C.597 B.A. L.1119 J.D. Cir. J.

Tonner, Ned, Attorney at Law
(See Rensselaer)

Uttermohlen, Lucille P., Law Office Of '54 '82 C.347 B.A. L.1119 J.D. P.O. Box 278

MONTPELIER, 1,880, *Blackford Co.*

Kyle, Joe E. '39 '70 C.63 B.A. L.802 J.D. 523 W. Oil St.

MOORESVILLE, 9,273, *Morgan Co.*

Currens, Timothy C., (AV) '47 '72 C.347 B.S. L.345 J.D. [Harris&C.]
Goshert, Max E. '29 '60 C.347 B.S. L.345 LL.B. 2159 Country Club Rd.
Harris, James E. '36 '70 C.347 L.345 LL.B. Ret. Sr. J.‡
Harris, Steven L., (AV) '46 '72 C.347 B.S. L.345 J.D. [Harris&C.]
Harris & Currens, Professional Corporation, (AV) 9 W. Main St.
Kough, Thomas J. '48 '78 C.346 B.S. L.345 J.D. State Police
Neely, Susan J. '63 '89 C.879 B.A. L.347 J.D. 545 N. Indiana St.
O'Dell, Melinda '68 '94 C.347 B.S. L.74 J.D. 124 South Indiana Street
Tavel, R. J., (CV) '52 '78 C.264 B.A. L.1187 J.D. 474 Roberson Blvd.

MORGANTOWN, 978, *Morgan Co.*

Barker, Kenneth R., (AV) '43 '68 C.347 A.B. L.309 J.D. 8929 S. 700 W.‡
Butler, Steven E. '57 '87 C.347 B.A. L.1119 J.D. R.R. 1★

MOROCCO, 1,044, *Newton Co.*

Reed, James Robert, (BV) '60 '89 C.679 B.S. L.347 J.D. 110 East State Street

MT. VERNON, * 7,478, *Posey Co.*

Allyn & Givens, (AV)
204 Main Street, 47620
Telephone: 812-838-4476 Fax: 812-838-4491
Email: agblaw@aol.com
***Otis B. Allyn (1912-1985);* David O. Givens.**
General Civil and Criminal Practice in all State and Federal Courts. Probate, Trusts, Real Estate and Natural Resources Law.
See Professional Biographies, MT. VERNON, INDIANA

Anderson, James P. '43 '70 C&L.352 B.S., J.D.
(adm. in IA; not adm. in IN) Edward D. Jones & Co.
Bach, Steve C., (BV) '21 '48 C.347 A.B. L.1119 J.D. 512 Walnut St.
Baier, Donald E. '50 '79 C.679 B.A. L.347 J.D. 128 W. Third St.
Baier, Elizabeth D., Law Office of, (BV) '54 '79 C.347 A.B. L.1119 J.D.
128 W. 3rd St.

Bamberger, Foreman, Oswald and Hahn, LLP, (AV)
309 Main Street, 47620 ⊙
Telephone: 812-838-4495
Member of the Firm: Jerry D. Stilwell (Resident).
(This Listing Continued)

Bamberger, Foreman, Oswald and Hahn, LLP (Continued)
Administrative Law, Antitrust Law, Appellate Practice, Arbitration, Banking Law, Bankruptcy Law, Business Law, Civil Rights, Civil Trial Practice, Commercial Law, Commercial Litigation, Communications Law, Construction Law, Corporate Law, Creditors' Rights, Elder Law, Energy Law, Environmental Law, Health Care Law, Insurance Defense, Intellectual Property Law, Labor and Employment Law, Land Use Law, Medical Malpractice, Mergers and Acquisitions, Product Liability Law, Public Utilities Law, Real Estate Law, Trademark, Copyright and Unfair Competition, Trusts and Estates, Wills and Probate.
Representative Clients: Aetna Life and Casualty Group; AT&T; CNB Bancshares Inc.; Dow Chemical Co.; Medical Protective Insurance Co.; Southern Indiana Gas and Electric Co.; St. Mary's Medical Center of Evansville, Inc.; State Farm Mutual Automobile Insurance Co.; Travelers Insurance Co.; Welborn Clinic/HMO.
Evansville, Indiana Office: 20 NW Fourth Street, Suite 708, P.O. Box 657, 47708. Telephone: 812-425-1591. Fax: 812-421-4936.
Indianapolis, Indiana Office: Market Tower, Suite 2950, 10 West Market Street, 46204. Telephone: 317-464-1591. Fax: 317-464-1592. Toll Free: 888-994-7976.
Poseyville, Indiana Office: 178 South Lockwood, 47633. Telephone: 812-874-3365. Fax: 812-874-3366.
Princeton, Indiana Office: 302 N. Prince Street, 47670. Telephone: 812-386-6482. Fax: 812-386-6480.
See Professional Biographies, MT. VERNON, INDIANA

Fink, Kelli E., (BV) '65 '90 C.249 B.S. L.347 J.D. Chf. Dep. Pros.
Folz, Beth Ann, (BV) '62 '89 C.999 B.S. L.347 J.D. 227 Main Street
Funkhouser, Scott '69 '01 C.929 B.A. L.801 J.D. 409 Main St.
Givens, David O., (AV) '43 '71 C.347 B.S. L.345 J.D. [Allyn&G.]
Gooden, William W., (BV) '48 '73 C.347 A.B. L.1119 J.D. 307 Main Street

Goodridge, John Andrew, Law Office
(See Evansville)

Hadley, Jean Erickson, (CV) '49 '89 C.249 B.S. L.347 J.D. 533 E. 4th St.
Higgins, Beth McFadin, (BV) '62 '87 C.249 B.S. L.345 J.D. 206 Main Street

Kahn, Dees, Donovan & Kahn, LLP
(See Evansville)

McClellan, Thomas G., (BV) '43 '74 C.249 B.A. L.421 J.D. P.O. Box 664
McMahon, Alphonse, (AVⓉ) '53 '85
C.734 B.A. L.910 J.D. Coun., EHS Programs, GE Capital Corp.

Olsen, White & Hambidge, LLP
(See Evansville)

Redwine, James M. '43 '70 C&L.347 A.B., J.D. Cir. J.

Rudolph, Fine, Porter & Johnson LLP
(See Evansville)

Stilwell, Jerry D., (AV) '44 '72
C.603 A.B. L.345 J.D. [Bamberger,F.O.&H.] (⊙Princeton)

Terrell, Baugh, Salmon & Born, LLP
(See Evansville)

Uebelhack, Jodi L. '65 '90 C.346 B.A. L.347 J.D. Pros.

Ziemer, Stayman, Weitzel & Shoulders, LLP
(See Evansville)

MUNCIE, * 67,430, *Delaware Co.*

Abbs, Jan P., (BV) '53 '80 C.63 B.A. L.477 J.D.
Gen. Coun. & Corp. Secy., Ontario Corp.
Abrell, Jennifer J., (CV) '61 '87 C.623 B.S. L.1119 J.D. 324 W. Jackson St.
Abrell, Mark L., (CV) '62 '87 C.63 B.S. L.1119 J.D. [Dennis,W.&A.]
Alexander, Chip, (BV) '55 '80 C.103 A.B. L.1119 J.D. [Bales&A.]
Alexander, Michael J., (BV) '46 '74 C.63 B.S. L.347 J.D. 201 N. High St.
Altland, Steven R., (CV) '54 '88 C.375 B.S. L.1137 J.D. UAW-GM Legal Servs. Plan
Arnold, Jeffrey L., (BV) '52 '85 C.63 B.S. L.345 J.D. [McClellan,M.&A.]
Avery, James W., (BVⓉ) '57 '82 C.59 B.A. L.208 J.D. [Avery] ⊙
Avery Law Firm, (BVⓉ) 7104 West Cheyenne (⊙Denver, CO; Indpls., IN)
Bahlmann, David W. '39 '65 C.317 A.B. L.879 J.D. Pres., Ball St. Univ. Found.‡
Baker, Amy Beth '73 '99 C.249 B.A. L.425 J.D. 215 W. Main Street
Bales, William H., Jr., (AV) '27 '52 C.210 A.B. L.477 LL.B. [Bales&A.]

Bales and Alexander, (AV)
116 North Walnut Street, 47305
Telephone: 765-289-2268 FAX: 765-289-2270
Email: calexander@balesandalexander.com
Members of Firm: William H. Bales (1895-1975); William H. Bales, Jr.; Chip Alexander.
Collection Law, Probate and Estate Planning and Administration and Real Estate.
See Professional Biographies, MUNCIE, INDIANA

Barnet, Robert L. '46 '71 C.63 B.S. L.345 J.D. Supr. Ct. J.

Beasley & Gilkison LLP, (AV)
Mutual Federal Building, 110 East Charles Street, P.O. Box 1648, 47308
Telephone: 765-289-0661 Facsimile: 765-282-4966
Email: email@beasleylaw.com URL: http://www.beasleylaw.com
Members of Firm: William F. White (1871-1946); William T. Haymond (1880-1964); Walter D. White (1900-1981); George W. Pierce (1908-1975); John B. Beasley (1917-2003); Charles R. Clark; William V. Hughes; J. Philip Updike; Mark A. Ervin; Sara E. Shade. Associates: M. Edward Krause; Timothy R. Hollems. Of Counsel: Frank E. Gilkison; Charles V. Retherford; Jack E. Buckles.
General Practice. Civil Litigation and Personal Injury Law, Commercial Law, Corporate Law, Business Law, Probate, Wills, Banking Law, Real Estate, Labor and Employment, Creditors Rights, Bankruptcy, Municipal Law, Zoning Law, School Law, Elder Law, Environmental Law, Family Law, Adoptions Law.
Counsel for: Mutual Federal Savings Bank; Maxon Corp.; Indiana-American Water Co., Inc.; N. G. Gilbert Corp.; Muncie Community Schools; Indiana Michigan Power Co.
See Professional Biographies, MUNCIE, INDIANA

Becker, Rita McGuire, (CV) '21 '48 C.347 A.B. L.345 LL.B. 116 E. Wash. St.
Beebe, Waldo F. '26 '51 C.893 A.B. L.1119 J.D. Beebe & Smith Title Co., Inc.
Beymer, Robert O. '56 '84 C.63 B.A. L.345 J.D. 121 N. High Street

Blackburn & Green
(See Fort Wayne)

Borgmann, James P., (BV) '62 '87 C.679 B.S. L.345 J.D. [DeFur V.]

Boston, Bever, Klinge, Cross & Chidester
(See Richmond)

Brassart, Raymond A., (BV) ....'38 '71 C.347 B.S. L.345 J.D. Co. Atty.
Brock, David R. .... '46 '02 C.267 B.A. L.201 J.D. [🄰 DeFur V.]
Brooke, John H., (BV) ....'59 '84 C.63 B.S. L.345 J.D. [Brooke&M.]

Brooke & Mawhorr, (BV)
112 East Gilbert Street, 47305
Telephone: 765-741-1375; 1-800-481-0900 Fax: 765-288-7763
Members of Firm: John H. Brooke; Douglas K. Mawhorr.
Civil Trial and Appeals, Insurance Defense, Family, Custody and Business Law.

See Professional Biographies, MUNCIE, INDIANA

Bruce, Rebecca S. ....'70 '98 C.63 B.S. L.345 J.D. 106 E. Washington St.
Bruce, Steven James .... '70 '98 C.63 B.S. L.345 J.D. [Bruce]
Bruce Law Office .... 5106 E. Washington St.
Brumfield, R. Carlton, (CV) ....'61 '87 C.999 B.S. L.345 J.D. 112 E. Wash. St.
Bruns, William G., (AV) .... '36 '61 C.313 A.B. L.1119 J.D. [Cannon&B.]
Bryan, Kelly N., (BV) .... '56 '82 C.63 B.S. L.345 J.D. 318 N. Walnut St.
Buckles, Jack E., (AV) .... '27 '53 C.347 B.S. L.345 J.D. [🄲 Beasley&G.]
Campbell, Donna G. '52 '83 C.63 B.S. L.345 J.D.
Gen. Coun., Indiana Futura Grp., LLC
Cannon, Thomas A., (AV) ....'08 '33 C&L.602 A.B., J.D. [Cannon&B.]
Cannon, Thomas A., Jr., (BV) ....'48 '74 C.347 B.S. L.345 J.D. [Cannon&B.]
Cannon & Bruns, (AV) ....119 N. High St.
Chlappetta, Donald D. ....'36 '62 C.347 B.S. L.1119 LL.B. 2810 W. Ethel Ave.
Clark, Charles R., (AV) .... '34 '62 C.210 A.B. L.1119 LL.B. [Beasley&G.]
Cole, Betty Shelton .... '26 '69 C.347 L.345 LL.B. Ret. Sr. State J.‡
Cooper, Michelle L. ....'73 '99 C.63 B.S. L.74 J.D. [🄰 DeFur V.] ⊙
Costello, Elizabeth, (CV) '56 '80
C.1024 B.A. L.345 J.D. Staff Atty., UAW-GM Legal Servs. Plan

Cross, P. Gregory, (AV) '52 '77 C.679 B.S.E. L.477 J.D.
315 East Charles Street, 47305
Telephone: 765-747-1953 Fax: 765-747-1991
Email: pgcross@thecrosslawfirm.com
Civil Litigation, Products Liability, Personal Injury Law, Wrongful Death, Commercial Litigation.

See Professional Biographies, MUNCIE, INDIANA

Cross, Marshall, Schuck & DeWeese, Professional Corporation, (AV)
200 East Washington Street, P.O. Box 3229, 47307-3229
Telephone: 765-289-6151 Fax: 765-289-6158
URL: http://www.crossmarshall.com
J. Richard Marshall; Kenneth P. Schuck; Thomas L. DeWeese.
General Practice, Negligence, Probate and Estate Planning, Corporations, Family/Domestic Relations, Elder Law, Social Security Law, Bankruptcy.

See Professional Biographies, MUNCIE, INDIANA

Daane, Diane M. '53 '80 C.612 B.S. L.502 J.D.
(adm. in MO; not adm. in IN) Prof. of Law, Ball State Univ.
Dague, Mary, (CV) '70 '95 C.347 B.A. L.1119 J.D.
1100 South Martin Luther King Jr. Boulevard, Suite 2
Dailey, Richard A. .... '42 '68 C.63 A.B. L.1119 J.D. Supr. Ct. J.
Davis, Jos. B. ....'18 '43 C&L.347 110 E. Washington St.

DeFur Voran LLP, (AV)
Suite 400, 201 East Jackson Street, 47305-2847 ⊙
Telephone: 765-288-3651 Telecopier: 765-288-7068
Email: atty's first initial, last name"@defur.com URL: http://www.defur.com
Members of Firm: Earl G. DeFur (1903-1986); Marshall E. Hanley (1920-1981); Reed D. Voran (1913-1994); William F. Radcliff (1922-2002); Jon H. Moll; Gregory A. Huffman; Steven D. Murphy; Scott E. Shockley; James P. Borgmann; James R. Williams; William H. Lutz. Associates: Michelle L. Cooper; David R. Brock; Shawn Anne Neal; Brian M. Pierce; Sarah L. Pierce. Of Counsel: Richard D. Hughes.
General Civil Practice. Business Organizations, Personal Planning, Education, Health, Personnel and Employment, Banking, Real Estate, Taxation, Employee Benefit/Retirement Plans, Creditor's Rights, Civil Litigation, Mediation, Intellectual Property, Family.
General Counsel for: Ball State University; Ball Memorial Hospital, Inc.; American National Bank and Trust Company; First Merchants Bank, N.A.; Community Care Centers, Inc.; Mount Pleasant Township Community School; Muncie Housing Authority; Agbest Co-op.
Fishers, Indiana Office: 8409 Fishers Centre Drive, 46038. Telephone: 317-585-8085. Telecopier: 317-585-8858.

See Professional Biographies, MUNCIE, INDIANA

Denney, Louis W., (CV) ....'47 '74 C.1229 B.S.I.E. L.1119 J.D. Dep. Pros.
Dennis, Ralph E., Jr., (AV) .... '25 '50 C.197 A.B. L.1119 J.D. [Dennis,W.&A.]
Dennis, Wenger & Abrell, Prof. Corp., Law Offices of, (AV) .... 324 W. Jackson St.
DeWeese, Thomas L., (BV) ....'43 '75 C.63 B.S. L.345 J.D. [Cross,M.S.&D.]
Dowling, Kimberly S., (BV) '59 '85
C.208 B.A. L.174 J.D. 3620 N. Everbrook Ln., Suite A
Doyle, Gordon P., (BV) ....'48 '72 C.347 A.B. L.1119 J.D. [Rowland&D.]
Ervin, Mark A., (CV) ....'59 '93 C.63 B.S. L.347 J.D. [Beasley&G.]
Freund, Bernard W. ....'12 '36 C&L.477 A.B., J.D. 4308 W. Beechwood Ave.‡
Gilkison, Frank E., (AV) ....'26 '50 C.347 A.B. L.1119 J.D. [🄲 Beasley&G.]

Gonzalez, Jill A., Attorney At Law '60 '00 C.63 B.S. L.1187 J.D.
114 E. Washington Street, 47305
Telephone: 765-282-2246 Fax: 765-282-2256
URL: http://www.jillgonzalez.com
Family Law, Personal Injury, Criminal Law, Divorce.

See Professional Biographies, MUNCIE, INDIANA

Harkness, Richard M., (BV) ....'47 '75 C.63 B.S. L.1119 J.D. 215 W. Main St.
Helms, Larry R. '40 '66 C.108 A.B. L.345 J.D.
Sr. V.P. & Gen. Coun., First Merchants Corp.
Hines, Barbara Gasper ....'45 '82 C.655 B.S. L.345 J.D. City Coun. Atty.
Hiser, Wray C. ....'47 '73 C.679 B.A. L.1119 J.D. Saint-Gobain Corp.
Hollems, Timothy R. .... '65 '97 C.72 B.A. L.966 J.D. [🄰 Beasley&G.]
Huffman, Gregory A., (BV) .... '47 '72 C.347 A.B. L.477 J.D. [DeFur V.]
Hughes, Richard D., (BV) .... '42 '69 C.894 B.A. L.345 J.D. [🄲 DeFur V.]
Hughes, William V., (AV) .... '47 '72 C.367 A.B. L.228 J.D. [Beasley&G.]
Hunt, Dale E. ....'46 '73 C.347 A.B. L.1119 J.D. 114 S. Walnut Plaza
Jordan, James J. ....'32 '60 C.446 A.B. L.1119 J.D. Supr. Ct. J.
Karnes, David Jonathan ....'74 '01 C.92 B.A. L.1119 J.D. 324 West Jackson Street
Knight, David W. '59 '89 C.886 B.S. L.424 J.D.
Assoc. Gen. Coun., Saint-Gobain Corp.
Koenker, Susan J. '44 '88 C.473 B.S. L.424 J.D.
(adm. in IL; not adm. in IN) 3200 W. Beechwood Ave.
Koor, Robert S., (BV) ....'38 '65 C.178 A.B. L.1119 J.D. 215 W. Main St.
Krause, M. Edward ....'76 '04 C.347 B.A. L.1119 J.D. [🄰 Beasley&G.]
Lutz, William H., (BV) ....'59 '91 C.879 B.S.W. L.734 J.D. [DeFur V.] ⊙
Marsh, Loren ....'21 '48 C.145 A.B. L.1119 J.D. 108 E. Washington St.
Marshall, J. Richard, (AV) .... '37 '62 C.679 B.S. L.477 J.D. [Cross,M.S.&D.]
Mawhorr, Douglas K., (CV) .... '65 '98 C.894 B.A. L.345 J.D. [Brooke&M.]

McClellan, Donald K., (BV) .... '55 '81 C.347 A.B. L.1119 J.D. [McClellan,M.&A.]
McClellan, McClellan & Arnold, (BV) .... 400 N. High St.St.
McShurley, Ronald E. .... '48 '76 C.63 B.S. L.607 J.D. 1901 N. Forest Ave.‡
Moll, Jon H., (AV) ....'42 '67 C.347 A.B. L.1119 J.D. [DeFur V.]
Munson, Bruce N., (BV) ....'52 '85 C.63 B.S. L.345 J.D. State Rep.
Murphy, Steven D., (AV) .... '51 '76 C.894 B.A. L.228 J.D. [DeFur V.]
Neal, Shawn Anne ....'71 '00 C.63 B.S. L.345 J.D. [🄰 DeFur V.]
Orlosky, Jon L., (BV) ....'56 '81 C.1111 B.A. L.345 J.D. 116 N. Walnut St.
Painter, Michael M., (BV) ....'45 '72 C.347 A.B. L.1119 J.D. [Painter&S.]
Painter & Schafer, (BV) ....400 N. High St.
Peckinpaugh, Darrel K., (BV) .... '41 '66 C.679 B.S. L.1119 J.D. [D.K.Peckinpaugh]
Peckinpaugh, D. K., (BV) .... 320 W. Adams St.
Pierce, Brian M. .... '76 '03 C.63 B.A. L.1119 J.D. [🄰 DeFur V.]
Pierce, Sarah L. ....'77 '04 C.63 B.S. L.1119 J.D. [🄰 DeFur V.]
Quirk, Jack A., (BV) ....'41 '71 C.63 B.S. L.345 J.D. [Quirk&R.]
Quirk & Rivers, (BV) ....117 E. Main St.
Raisor, Thomas L., (AV) ....'35 '62 C.477 A.B. L.1119 J.D. 322 N. Walnut St.
Rankin, Joseph W., (CV) ....'41 '70 C.344 A.B. L.345 J.D. 500 S. Hawthorne Road
Reed, Richard W., (BV) .... '44 '74 C.63 B.S. L.345 J.D. Pros. Atty.
Retherford, Andrew R., (BV) '58 '83
C.597 B.A. L.94 J.D. Supvr. Atty., UAW-GM Legal Servs. Plan
Retherford, Charles V., (AV) .... '27 '52 C&L.309 A.B., J.D. [🄲 Beasley&G.]
Rivers, Geoffrey A., (BV) .... '42 '71 C.63 B.S. L.345 J.D. Pub. Def. [Quirk&R.]
Roesner, David B. ....'65 '91 C.303 B.A. L.347 J.D. 207 N. High St.‡
Rowland, L. Ross, (BV) ....'45 '74 C.303 B.A. L.1119 J.D. [Rowland&D.]
Rowland & Doyle, (BV) .... 107 S. Mulberry St.
Rufatto, Anthony D. .... '74 '01 C.679 B.S.B.A. L.345 J.D. 309 W. Charles St.
Schafer, James A., (BV) .... '48 '76 C.347 B.S. L.1340 J.D. [Painter&S.]
Schuck, Kenneth P., (BV) .... '44 '69 C.63 A.B. L.339 J.D. [Cross,M.S.&D.]
Segebarth, Stephen A. '46 '76 C.351 B.A. L.352 J.D.
Sr.V.P., Gen. Coun. & Secy., Saint-Gobain Containers, Inc.
Shade, Sara E. ....'76 '01 C.210 B.A. L.1119 J.D. [Beasley&G.]
Shirey, Wayne A., (AV) .... '30 '56 C.347 A.B. L.1119 J.D. [🄲 Cannon&B.]
Shockley, Scott E., (BV) .... '51 '78 C.976 B.A. L.208 J.D. [DeFur V.]
Slagle, Jack A., (BV) ....'25 '58 C.679 B.S. L.345 J.D. P.O. Box 177
Smith, Gregory B. ....'46 '71 C.347 A.B. L.1119 J.D. 119 S. Liberty St.
Smith, James W. .... '61 '86 C.63 B.S. L.347 J.D. Pres., Beebe & Smith Title Co., Inc.
Smith, Van P. .... '28 '55 C.165 A.B. L.276 LL.B. Chmn. of the Bd., Ontario Corp.
Smith, Victor P. .... '68 '96 C.165 B.A. L.128 J.D. V.P. & Gen. Mgr., Ontario Corp.

Smith, Theodore F., Jr.
(See Anderson)

Speece, Joseph M., Jr., (BV) .... '42 '68 C.679 B.S. L.1119 J.D. Master Comr.
Stanley, Kelly N., (BV) ....'43 '68 C.473 B.S. L.1119 J.D. Pres., Ontario Corp.
Steele, Brad D., Law Offices of, (CV) '69 '94
C.1356 B.A. L.623 J.D. 1161/2 N. Walnut St.
Trulock, James W. .... '60 '85 C.894 B.A. L.1119 J.D. Indiana Title Insurance Co., LLC
Updike, J. Philip, (BV) ....'50 '75 C.210 B.A. L.1119 J.D. [Beasley&G.]
Vorhees, Marianne Lafferty ....'58 '83 C.63 B.A. L.602 J.D. Cir.J.
Wallace, David S., (BV) ....'45 '72 C.347 A.B. L.345 J.D. 400 East Jackson Street
Wilkinson, William R. ....'52 '83 C.679 B.S. L.347 J.D. UAW-GM Legal Servs. Plan
Williams, James R., (CV) .... '66 '91 C.894 A.B. L.1119 J.D. [DeFur V.]

Wilson, Kehoe & Winingham, (AV)
3620 N. Everbrook Lane, Suite A, 47304 ⊙
Telephone: 765-284-2474 Fax: 765-288-8655
Email: mailbox@wkw.com URL: http://www.wkw.com
William E. Winingham, Jr.
Civil Trial Practice in State and Federal Courts. Aviation, Medical Legal, Personal Injury, Product Liability, Medical Malpractice, Wrongful Death.
Reference: The Indiana National Bank.
Richmond, Indiana Office: 2901 East Main Street, 47374. Telephone: 765-962-9113.
Indianapolis, Indiana Office: 2859 North Meridian, 46208. Telephone: 317-920-6400.

See Professional Biographies, MUNCIE, INDIANA

Winingham, William E., Jr., (AV) '52 '79
C.347 B.A. L.345 J.D. [Wilson,K.&W.] (⊙Indianapolis)
Wyrick, Stan G., (BV) ....'47 '74 C.63 B.S. L.345 J.D. 318 N. Walnut

MUNSTER, 21,511, *Lake Co.*

Amber, Douglas G. ....'56 '85 C.347 B.A. L.472 J.D. 9250 Columbia Avenue
Austgen, Terence M., (BV) .... '53 '78 C.347 B.S. L.1119 J.D. [Singleton,C.A.&S.]
Bezak, Elizabeth M., (CV) ....'67 '92 C.339 A.B. L.879 J.D. [Singleton,C.A.&S.]
Brauer, Hugh D., (BV) .... '29 '57 C.347 B.A. L.1119 LL.B. Ret. Pres., Town Coun.
Bullaro & Carton, P.C., (AVⓉ) ....8231 Hohman Avenue, Suite 200 (⊙Chgo., IL)
Burke, Scot L., (CV) .... '58 '84 C&L.879 B.A., J.D. 1630 45th Ave., Ste. 103

Burke Costanza & Cuppy LLP, (AV)
900 Ridge Road, Suite L, 46321 ⊙
Telephone: 219-513-1000 Fax: 219-513-1001
URL: http://www.bcclegal.com
Partners: Joseph E. Costanza; David K. Ranich; Natalie V. Shrader.
General Civil Practice in State and Federal Courts, Trials, Appeals, Civil Mediation, Administrative, Business Law, Business Planning, Contracts, Business Litigation, Business Enterprises, LLC's, Partnerships, Small Business, Corporate, Real Estate, Employee Benefits/ERISA, Banking, Commercial, Insurance Defense, Personal Injury, Automobile Accidents, Wrongful Death, Wills and Probate, Trusts and Estates, Estate Planning, Medical Malpractice, Legal Malpractice, Family Law, Adoptions, Child Custody, Child Support, Divorce, Visitation Rights, Municipal and Zoning, Environmental.
Representative Clients: NBD Bank, N.A.; The Post Tribune (Knight Ridder Publications); Continental Machine & Engineering Co., Inc.; Portland Lehigh Cement Company; Gary Steel Products Corp.; Superior Construction Co., Inc.; Federal National Mortgage Association; Morrison Construction Co.; St. Catherine Hospital of East Chicago, Indiana; Travelers/Aetna Casualty Corporation (Regional Consultants for Commercial and Personal Lines).
Merrillville, Indiana Office: 9191 Broadway. Telephone: 219-769-1313. Fax: 219-769-6806.
Valparaiso, Indiana Office: 57 Franklin Street, Suite 203. Telephone: 219-531-0134. Fax: 219-531-0507.

See Professional Biographies, MUNSTER, INDIANA

Bush, Lucinda A., (BVⓉ) .... '47 '77 C.294 B.A. L.665 J.D. 8637 Jefferson Ave.
Carton, Thomas A., (AVⓉ) .... '53 '78 C.57 B.A. L.46 J.D. [Bullaro&C.] ⊙
Clark, Bruce P., & Associates, (AV) ....'55 '80 C.63 B.S. L.345 J.D. 419 Ridge Rd.
Cohen, Stephen B., (AVⓉ) ....'39 '65 C.309 A.B. L.880 J.D. [Cohen,K.O.D.&R.] ⊙

Cohen, Kelly, Olson, DeHaan & Richter, L.L.C., (AVⓉ)
9337 Calumet Avenue, Suite A-1, 46321 ⊙
Telephone: 219-836-1171 Facsimile: 312-836-2003
Member of Firm: Stephen B. Cohen.
Estate Planning, Probate, Banking Litigation, Transactions, Finance, Construction Law, Creditors Rights, General Civil Practice, Personal Injury Law, Mechanics Lien Litigation, Corporate Law, Mediation and Arbitration, Family Law, Divorce.
Chicago, Illinois Office: Kelly, Olson, Michod, DeHaan & Richter, L.L.C., 30 South Wacker Drive, Suite, 2300, 60606. Telephone: 312-236-6700. Facsimile: 312-236-6706.

See Professional Biographies, MUNSTER, INDIANA

Colwell, Joy L., (CV) .... '57 '84 C.347 B.A. L.1119 J.D. 8329 Linden Ave.
Costanza, Joseph E., (AV) .... '36 '61 C.894 A.B. L.597 J.D. [Burke C.&C.]
Crist, Steven R., (AV) .... '43 '68 C.894 A.B. L.1119 J.D. [Singleton,C.A.&S.]
Dasari, Veda Praveen .... '— '02 C.679 B.S. L.879 J.D. [A T.J.Scully,III]
Dittrich, William E., (CV) .... '67 '93 C.93 B.A. L.602 J.D. 131 Ridge Road
Doherty & Progar LLC, (BVⓉ) .... 9245 Calumet Avenue, Suite 202 (⊙Chgo., IL)
Dugan, Julie A. .... '— '01 C.303 B.A. L.150 J.D. [A A.F.Tavitas]

Feingold, Eugene M., Law Offices of, (AV) '29 '53 C.665 B.S. L.309 J.D.
625 Ridge Road, Suite A, 46321-1611
Telephone: 219-836-8800 Fax: 219-836-8944
Email: emfeingoldlaw@aol.com URL: http://www.feingoldlawfirm.com
Associate: Steven P. Kennedy.
General Civil Trial Practice in all State and Federal Courts. Real Estate, Insurance, Corporation, Municipal and Zoning Law, Wills and Probate, Trusts and Estates, Estate Planning Law.
See Professional Biographies, MUNSTER, INDIANA

Friedman, Stuart J., (BV) ....'52 '78 C.994 B.A. L.472 J.D. [Pinkerton&F.]
Froehlich, Cheryl A. .... '63 '97 C.966 B.B.A. L.879 J.D. [A Singleton,C.A.&S.]
Goins, Brian L., (CV) '60 '85
C.347 B.A. L.1119 J.D. V.P., Corp. Coun., CFS Bancorp, Inc.
Granack, Thomas C., (BV) .... '36 '61 C.597 B.S. L.879 J.D. 9337 Calumet Ave.
Gunning, Jeffrey F., (CV) .... '55 '88 C.894 B.A. L.879 J.D. [A Pinkerton&F.]
Harris, James A., (BV) ....'47 '77 C.347 B.S. L.365 J.D. 9337 Calumet Avenue
Hlinka, Craig L. ....'48 '74 C.347 A.B. L.1119 J.D. 1806 Fairway Ave.
Hofstetter, Richard R., (BV) ....'56 '82 C.347 B.A. L.228 J.D. 9250 Columbia Avenue
Holscher, Marilyn R., (CV) ....'48 '91 C.741 B.A. L.879 J.D. [C Singleton,C.A.&S.]
Holtan, Mark H. ....'43 '68 C.182 B.A. L.879 J.D. 8541 Elmwood Drive
Jonelis, William M., (BV) ....'54 '81 C.1024 B.S. L.345 J.D. 9337 Calumet Ave.
Kennedy, Steven P., (BV) ....'49 '74 C.894 A.B. L.880 J.D. [A E.M.Feingold]
Kirsch, Thomas L., (BV) ....'50 '74 C&L.209 B.A., J.D. 131 Ridge Rd.
Knapp, Clement B., Jr. ......'42 '69 C.276 A.B. L.345 J.D. Pres., Amer. Svgs. Bk., F.S.B.
Kohl, George H. ....'24 '51 C.347 B.S. L.1119 J.D. [C Raskosky&K.] ‡
Maronto, Dale A. ....'52 '84 C.1016 B.A. L.879 J.D. 8231 Hohman Ave., Ste. 200
McDevitt, Richard F., Jr., (CV) '54 '86
C.347 B.A. L.1119 J.D. Pres., McDevitt Agency Corp.
McEuen, Patrick B., (BV) .... '67 '93 C.894 B.A. L.347 J.D. [Singleton,C.A.&S.]
Miller, Samuel T., (BV) .... '55 '79 C.347 A.B. L.1119 J.D. 9335 Calumet Avenue
Nagy, James J., (BV) ....'39 '64 C&L.347 B.S., J.D. P.O. Box 3010

Padove, Burton A. '56 '81 C.424 B.A. L.146 J.D.
533 Ridge Road, Suite C, 46321
Telephone: 219-836-2200 Fax: Available Upon Request
Email: BurtonAP@aol.com URL: http://www.lawyers.com/burtonpadove
Personal Injury, Products Liability, Medical Malpractice, Family Law, Divorce, Adoptions, Criminal Law, Wills and Probate, Trusts and Estates, Real Estate, Business Law.
See Professional Biographies, MUNSTER, INDIANA

Pellicciotti, Joseph M., (BV) .... '50 '76 C.24 B.A. L.285 J.D. 8544 Elmwood Dr.
Pinkerton, Kirk A., (AV) .... '49 '75 C&L.347 A.B., J.D. [Pinkerton&F.]

Pinkerton and Friedman, Professional Corporation, (AV)
The Fairmont, 9245 Calumet Avenue Suite 201, 46321
Telephone: 219-836-3050 Fax: 219-836-2955
URL: http://www.pflawoffice.com
Milton Roth (1925-1996); Kirk A. Pinkerton; Stuart J. Friedman; Jeffrey F. Gunning; Richard N. Shapiro; Keith Wolak.
Federal Income and State Taxation, Probate and Estate Planning, Estate Administration, Trusts, Wills, Real Estate, Partnership, Business and Corporate Law. Municipal and Zoning Law, Employee Benefits, Business Litigation, Real Estate, Health Care Law.
Reference Clients Available on Request.
See Professional Biographies, MUNSTER, INDIANA

Progar, Michael J., (BVⓉ) ....'53 '81 C.602 B.A. L.209 J.D. [Doherty&P.] ⊙
Ranich, David K., (AV) ... '51 '77 C.347 B.S. L.1292 J.D. [Burke C.&C.] (⊙Merrillville)
Raskosky, Edward J., (BV) .... '22 '49 C.347 L.1119 LL.B. [Raskosky&K.]
Raskosky and Kohl, (BV) ....9250 Columbia Ave., Suite 2A
Reppa, Jerome J. .... '25 '53 C.347 L.472 LL.B. 8210 Monroe Ave.‡
Rosen, Jeffrey L., & Associates .... '41 '66 C.347 B.S. L.597 J.D. 900 Ridge Road, Ste. C
Schneider, David R. .... '46 '71 C.473 B.A. L.150 J.D. P.O. Box 3597
Scully, Thomas J., III, (BV) '45 '73 C.831 B.A. L.1292 J.D.
506 Ridge Road (⊙Chgo., IL; Chesterton, IN)
Sears, Michael D., (BV) ....'57 '84 C.347 B.S. L.879 J.D. [Singleton,C.A.&S.]
Shapiro, Jerry I., Law Office of, (BV) ...... '47 '76 C.347 B.A. L.365 J.D. 506 Ridge Rd.
Shapiro, Richard N., (CV) ....'55 '94 C.894 B.A. L.879 J.D. [A Pinkerton&F.]
Shrader, Natalie V. .... '67 '94 C.679 B.S. L.879 J.D. [Burke C.&C.]
Singleton, Palmer C., Jr., (AV) .... '21 '49 C.347 A.B. L.477 LL.B. [C Singleton,C.A.&S.]
Singleton, Crist, Austgen & Sears, (AV) ....9245 Calumet Avenue, Suite 200
Tavitas, Anthony F., (BV) ....'63 '89 C.347 B.S. L.599 J.D. [A.F.Tavitas]

Tavitas, Anthony F., Attorneys at Law, A Professional Corporation, (BV)
900 Ridge Road, Suite T, 46321
Telephone: 219-836-0900 Fax: 219-836-1931
Email: AnthonyFTavitas@aftlawoffice.com URL: http://www.aftlawfirm.com
Anthony F. Tavitas. Associate: Julie A. Dugan.
Insurance Defense, Trial Practice, Personal Injury, Insurance Coverage, Workers Compensation.
See Professional Biographies, MUNSTER, INDIANA

Van Bokkelen, Joseph S., (AV) .... '43 '69 C.347 B.A. L.1119 J.D. U.S. Atty.
Wickland, David E., (BV) .... '50 '75 C.347 A.B. L.345 J.D. [D.E.Wickland]

Wickland, David E., Professional Corporation, (BV)
8146 Calumet Avenue, 46321
Telephone: 219-836-8766 Fax: 219-836-8826
Email: dewickland@aol.com
David E. Wickland.
General Civil Trial Practice in all State and Federal Courts, Personal Injury, Family/Domestic Relations, Commercial Litigation, Real Estate, Corporations, Probate and Wills, Collections.

Wolak, Keith .... '69 '98 C&L.347 B.S., J.D. [A Pinkerton&F.]

NAPPANEE, 6,710, *Elkhart & Kosciusko Cos.*

Brinker, Kenneth Chris '53 '83 C.238 B.A. L.209 J.D.
(adm. in IL; not adm. in IN) Secy. & Coun., Fairmont Homes, Inc.
Hoffer, Brian L., (BV) .... '54 '80 C.347 B.A. L.602 J.D. [Kindig&S.]
Holmes & Walter, LLP, (BV) .... 111 N. Main St. (⊙Bremen, Plymouth)
Kindig & Sloat, (BV) ....102 Heritage Pkwy.
Shea, James F., Jr. '27 '53 C&L.215 LL.B.
(adm. in MI; not adm. in IN) P.O. Box 27‡
Sloat, Loren R., (BV) ....'46 '73 C.679 B.S. L.345 J.D. [Kindig&S.]
Spitaels, Randy J., (BV) ....'62 '88 C.432 B.S. L.345 J.D. [A Kindig&S.]
Walter, Christopher G., (BV) ....'67 '93 C.347 B.S. L.879 J.D. [Holmes&W.]

NASHVILLE, * 873, *Brown Co.*

Barr, Thomas M., and Associates, (BV) ...... '51 '77 C.63 B.S. L.1119 J.D. P.O. Box 756

Bunger & Robertson
(See Bloomington)

Gray, Raymond W., (AV) .... '23 '51 C.249 B.S. L.1119 LL.B. 22 Artist Dr.
Grupenhoff, David C. .... '74 '00 C.679 B.S. L.1119 J.D. P.O. Box 756
Lusher, Robert W. .... '23 '52 C.347 B.S. L.1119 J.D. 22 Artist Dr.‡
Mollo, Heather M. ....'55 '83 C.265 B.A. L.1119 J.D. Cir. J.
Reichert, James P. ....'46 '74 C.347 B.A. L.879 J.D. P. O. 809
Reuter, Loren D., (CV) ....'54 '85 C.347 B.A. L.1119 J.D. 3750 State Rd., 135 N.
Roberts, James T. ....'41 '68 C.347 B.A. L.1119 J.D. 57 N. Jefferson St.
Rosen, Samuel R. ....'10 '34 C.178 B.A. L.309 LL.B. Sr. Cir. J.
Stogsdill, Jennifer Saalwaechter .... '64 '91 C.347 B.S. L.846 J.D. Dep. Pros. Atty.
Szakaly, Andrew A., Jr., (BV) .... '47 '75 C.1100 A.B. L.347 J.D. P.O. Box 874
Van Winkle, Douglas E. .... '47 '72 C.347 A.B. L.1119 J.D. Mag., The Browns Cir. Ct.
Wilson, John B., Jr. .... '35 '61 C.347 B.S. L.1119 LL.B. Honeysuckle Lane
Young, Kurt A. .... '49 '79 C&L.347 B.A., J.D. P.O. Box 1549

NEW ALBANY, * 37,603, *Floyd Co.*

Abram, Suzanne L. .... '63 '00 C.347 Ph.D. L.421 J.D. Lexis Nexis
Allen, William L., III ....'43 '68 C.990 A.B. L.421 J.D. 221 E. Main Street
Audry, Debra S. .... '61 '04 C.347 B.S.N. L.1119 J.D. [A Mattox M.&W.]
Beardsley, Stephen J. .... '46 '71 C.303 B.A. L.94 J.D. 227 Pearl St.
Betteau, Bart M., (BV) ....'67 '92 C.894 A.B. L.347 J.D. [Betteau]
Betteau Law Office, (BV) ....1212 State St.
Bierly, Richard A., (BV) ....'46 '76 C.347 B.A. L.1119 J.D. [Wyatt,T.&C.]
Bird, Thomas J. ....'48 '85 C.1287 B.B.A. L.421 J.D. [Bird&S.a.]
Bird, Thomas J., Jr. .... '43 '70 C.150 B.S. L.276 J.D. 400 Pearl Street, Ste. 100 (Pat.)
Bird & Sturgeon Attorneys at Law P.C. ....141 East Spring Street
Bitzegaio, Barry N., (AV) ....'52 '80 C.894 A.B. L.1119 J.D. 506 State St.

Boehl Stopher & Graves, LLP, (BV)
Elsby East, Suite 204, 400 Pearl Street, 47150 ⊙
Telephone: 812-948-5053 Fax: 812-948-9233
URL: http://www.bsg-law.com
Resident Partners: James L. Fischer, Jr.; Jeffrey L. Hansford; Matthew Hunter Jones. Resident Associates: Elizabeth A. Schott; Frederick M. Reinecke; Curtis P. Moutardier.
General Civil Practice.
Louisville, Kentucky Office: Suite 2300, AEGON Center, 400 West Market Street. Telephone: 502-589-5980. Fax: 502-561-9400.
Lexington, Kentucky Office: 444 West Second Street. Telephone: 859-252-6721. Fax: 859-253-1445.
Paducah, Kentucky Office: 410 Broadway. Telephone: 270-442-4369. Fax: 270-442-4689.
Pikeville, Kentucky Office: 137 Main Street, Suite 200. Telephone: 606-432-9670. Fax: 606-432-9680.
See Professional Biographies, NEW ALBANY, INDIANA

Bourne, James E., (AV) ....'40 '65 C.347 B.A. L.1119 J.D. [Scott,F.&B.]
Brengle, John E., (BV) ....'53 '79 Indiana Legal Svcs.

Brown, Todd & Heyburn PLLC
(See Frost Brown Todd LLC)

Buchanan, Lee E., (BV) ....'37 '72 C.679 B.S. L.421 J.D. 810 E. Market St.
Burke, Daniel B., Jr., (BV) ....'37 '62 C.1150 A.B. L.421 LL.B. Mag.
Church, Larry R., (BV) ....'66 '91 C.381 B.A. L.150 J.D. [C Wyatt,T.&C.]
Cody, J. Terrence, (BV) ....'49 '74 C.973 A.B. L.345 J.D. J.

Colomb, Bart, Law Office of '60 '86 C.138 B.A. L.421 J.D.
400 Pearl Street, Suite 100, 47150
Telephone: 812-945-0282 Fax: 812-945-1051
URL: http://www.lawyers.com/colomb
Social Security, Workers Compensation and Family Law.
See Professional Biographies, NEW ALBANY, INDIANA

Conrad, Keith R., (CV) ....'72 '97 C&L.347 B.A., J.D. [A Frost B.T.]
Conrad, Marianne J. ....'71 '96 C&L.347 B.A., J.D. Legal Servs Org. of Ind., Inc.
Coryell, Kathryn Lynne ....'59 '85 C.602 B.A. L.1119 J.D. P.O. Box 6771
Cotner, K. Lee, (BV) .... '61 '87 C.347 B.A. L.879 J.D. 1108 Eastridge Drive
Cunningham, Jean R., (CV) .... '45 '91 C&L.862 B.S.Ed., J.D. 227 Pearl St.
Didat, Louisa Jackson '56 '87 C&L.421 B.A., J.D.
(adm. in KY; not adm. in IN) Cash Tyme
Doane, Kenneth G., Jr., (CV) .... '69 '96 C.158 B.S. L.1017 J.D. [Ward,T.&S.]
Eastridge, William A., Attorney at Law '59 '89 C.894 B.A. L.201 J.D.
3727 Klerner Lane
Elston, Dawn R., (CV) .... '58 '84 C.347 B.A. L.421 J.D. 120 W. Spring St.

Faith, Stanley O., (BV) '— '82 C.347 B.S. L.1119 J.D.
412 E. Main Street, 47150
Telephone: 812-542-0048 Fax: 812-941-4026
Email: staff@stanfaith.com URL: http://www.lawyers.com/stanleydfaith
Corporate Law, Family Law, Criminal Law, Labor Law, Civil Rights.
See Professional Biographies, NEW ALBANY, INDIANA

Faurest, Henry S., Jr. .... '37 '79 C.138 B.A. L.421 J.D. V.P., Floyd Co. Bk.
Fifer, James E. (Jef), (BV) .... '60 '86 C.347 B.S. L.421 J.D. [Fifer]
Fifer Law Office, (BV) ....220 E. Main St.
Fischer, James L., Jr., (BV) ....'63 '89 C.347 B.A. L.421 J.D. [Boehl S.&G.]
Forrest, Donald R., (AV) ....'40 '66 C.347 A.B. L.345 LL.B. [Scott,F.&B.]
Forsythe, Matthew W. '63 '97 C.679 B.A. L.1161 J.D.
(adm. in KY; not adm. in IN) [A Schad&P.]
Fox, Richard R., (BV) ....'55 '87 C.347 A.B. L.879 J.D. [Fox,R.R.]
Fox, Richard R., LLC, (BV) .... 409 Bank Street

Frost Brown Todd LLC, (BV)
120 West Spring Street, Suite 400, 47150-3655 ⊙
Telephone: 812-948-2800 Telecopier: 812-948-7994
Email: info@fbtlaw.com URL: http://www.frostbrowntodd.com
Member: Gene F. Price. Senior Associate: Steven P. Langdon. Associates: Keith R. Conrad; Kristen L. Reese; Joshua T. Rose.
Alternative Dispute Resolution, Bankruptcy and Reorganization, Business Acquisitions, Business and Corporate, Commercial Finance, Commercial Litigation, Commercial/Real Estate, Construction, Copyright, Corporate Responsibility and Defense, Employee Benefits, Energy and Natural Resources, Entrepreneurial, Environmental, Equine, Estate Planning and Administration, Financial Institutions, Fire and Explosion, Health Care, Immigration, International, Intellectual Property, International Business, Internet and Electronic Commerce, Labor and Employment Law, Litigation, Media, Mold and Water Intrusion, Multi-District Litigation, Patent Litigation, Personal Planning and Family Business, Privacy and Information Security, Product Liability, Public Finance, Securities, Tax, Tort & Insurance Law, Trademark, Venture Capital, General Trial Practice in all State and Federal Courts.
Cincinnati, Ohio Office: 2200 PNC Center, 201 East Fifth Street, 45202-4182. Telephone: 513-651-6800. Telecopier: 513-651-6981.
Columbus, Ohio Office: One Columbus, 10 West Broad Street, 43215-3467. Telephone: 614-464-1211. Telecopier: 614-464-1737.
Middletown, Ohio Office: 300 North Main Street, Suite 200, 45042-1919. Telephone: 513-422-2001. Telecopier: 513-422-3010.

(This Listing Continued)

Frost Brown Todd LLC (Continued)

Lexington, Kentucky Office: 250 West Main Street, Suite 2700, 40507-1742. Telephone: 859-231-0000. Telecopier: 859-231-0011.
Louisville, Kentucky Office: 400 West Market Street, 32nd Floor, 40202-3363. Telephone: 502-589-5400. Telecopier: 502-581-1087.
Nashville, Tennessee Office: 424 Church Street, Suite 1600, 37219-2308. Telephone: 615-251-5550. Telecopier: 615-251-5551.

See Professional Biographies, NEW ALBANY, INDIANA

Garry, John R., Jr., (BV) ....'32 '62 C.1150 A.B. L.421 J.D. The Elsby Bldg.
Gesenhues, George W., Jr., (BV) .... '52 '78 C&L.421 B.S., J.D. [Lorch&N.]
Gettelfinger, Dale L. ....'51 '77 C.347 B.S. L.1119 J.D. Monroe Shine & Co.
Gibson, Shane L. ....'61 '89 C.879 B.A. L.421 J.D. Pros. Atty.
Goldberg, Bruce J., (CV) ....'51 '76 C.347 B.A. L.477 J.D. 623 E. Spring St.
Goodwell, Karen R. ....'59 '85 C.210 B.A. L.345 J.D. [🄰 Mattox M.&W.]
Granger, Maria D. .... '69 '94 C.347 B.S. L.345 J.D. 249 City-County Building
Gray, Timothy L. ....'64 '92 C.347 B.A. L.421 J.D. [Gray&S.]
Gray & Stiller, LLC ....3007 Charlestown Crossing Way, Suite B101
Gustafson, Steven A., (CV) ....'59 '83 C.63 B.A. L.1119 J.D. [Fox,R.R.]
Haines, Sarah Criss .... '47 '94 C.346 B.A. L.347 J.D. 3107 Blackiston Mill Rd.
Hamilton, Robert P., (BV) ....'59 '84 C.347 B.S. L.345 J.D. [Lorch&N.]
Hancock, Glenn G., (BV) ....'52 '82 C.347 B.S. L.421 J.D. 421 West 1st Street
Hancock, James B., (BV) ....'52 '79 C.679 B.A. L.365 J.D. 413 W. 1st
Hansford, Jeffrey L., (BV) ....'53 '87 C.347 B.G.S. L.421 J.D. [Boehl S.&G.]
Hay, G. Kenneth, (AV) ....'22 '48 C&L.421 J.D. 318 Pearl Street
Hoffer, C. Allan, (BV) ....'57 '89 C&L.347 B.S., J.D. Suite 27, 3602 Northgate Court
Hollander, William H., (AVⓣ) '53 '84
C.309 A.B. L.1119 J.D. [Wyatt,T.&C.] (⊙Louisville, KY)
Hublar, Robert T. ....'45 '74 C.1150 B.S. L.421 J.D. Co. Ct. J.
Hurst, Cary J., (CV) ....'66 '97 C.1288 B.A. L.421 J.D. [🄰 Lorch&N.]
Jenkins, Donna J. ....'61 '87 C.347 B.A. L.421 J.D. [🄰 Kightlinger&G.]
Johnson, Mark D., (CV) ....'62 '90 C.894 A.B. L.1119 J.D. 3316 Green Valley Road
Jones, Matthew Hunter, (BV) .... '61 '87 C.347 B.A. L.421 J.D. [Boehl S.&G.]
Joyce, Willie M. '46 '92 C.33 B.A. L.1292 J.D.
V.P., Legal & Regul. Affrs., Park Place Entertainment Corp.
Kelso, Robert A., (BV) ....'31 '54 C.347 L.145 J.D. P.O. Box 788‡
Kessler, Valerie D. ....'71 '03 C.275 B.A. L.383 J.D. [🄰 Kightlinger&G.]

Kightlinger & Gray, LLP, (AV)
One Commerce Square, 4106 Charlestown Road, 47150 ⊙
Telephone: 812-949-2300 Telecopier: 812-949-8556
Email: info@k-glaw.com URL: http://www.k-glaw.com
Senior Partner: Samuel A. Day (1952-2003). Resident Partners: Richard T. Mullineaux; Van T. Willis; Mary Jo Wetzel; Steven K. Palmquist; William E. Smith, III; R. Jeffrey Lowe. Resident Associates: J. Todd Spurgeon; D. Keith Pulliam; James C. Wade; Donna J. Jenkins; Valerie D. Kessler.
Civil Litigation, Commercial and Business Litigation, Drug and Medical Device Litigation, Environmental and Toxic Tort Litigation, Casualty, Surety and Life Insurance Law, General Litigation, Malpractice Litigation (Pharmacy, Medical, Legal, Architects and Engineers, Accountants, Insurance Agents, Real Estate Agents and School Boards), Products Liability Law, Trucking Defense Litigation, Construction Law, ICC Regulatory Law, Appeals (State and Federal), Worker's Compensation, Maritime Law, Civil Rights and Wrongful Discharge Law, All areas of Government Liability, including Law Enforcement Liability Litigation, Class Actions, Labor Law, Securities Litigation.
Indianapolis, Indiana Office: Market Square Center, Suite 600, 151 North Delaware Street, 46204. Telephone: 317-638-4521. Telecopier: 317-636-5917.
Evansville, Indiana Office: 7311 Eagle Crest Blvd., 47715. Telephone: 812-474-4400. Telecopier: 812-474-4414.

See Professional Biographies, NEW ALBANY, INDIANA

King, Christopher L. ....'— '00 C.347 B.G.S. L.4210 J.D. [King]
King Law Office .... 1801 E. Spring Street
Koehler, Lloyd E., (BV) ....'37 '61 C&L.421 B.S., LL.B. [Koehler]
Koehler Law Offices, (BV) ....400 Pearl Street, Suite 200
Kruger, Schwartz & Morreau, (BVⓣ) .... 810 E. Market St. (⊙Louisville, KY)
Langdon, Steven P. ....'72 '97 C.347 B.A. L.345 J.D. [🄰 Frost B.T.]
Leist, Henry N. ....'29 '53 C.347 A.B. L.1119 J.D. Cir. J.‡
Lohmeyer, Steven S., (BV) ....'56 '82 C.347 B.A. L.421 J.D. [Lohmeyer]
Lohmeyer Law Office, The, (BV) ....430 West First Street
Lorch, Basil H., III ....'49 '74 C.347 A.B. L.1119 J.D. U.S Bkrptcy. Judge
Lorch, Linda B., (BV) ....'52 '79 C.347 A.B. L.1119 J.D. [Lorch&N.]
Lorch & Naville, LLC, (AV) .... 506 State St.
Lowe, R. Jeffrey ....'72 '98 C.575 B.A. L.4210 J.D. [Kightlinger&G.]
MacGregor, Charles E., (AV) ....'30 '54 C.347 B.A. L.421 J.D. [Wyatt,T.&C.]
Mattox, Linda A., (BV) ....'56 '89 C.679 B.S. L.421 J.D. P.O. Box 1203
Mattox, Richard L., (AV) ....'34 '62 C.347 B.S. L.345 J.D. [Mattox M.&W.]
Mattox, S. Frank, (BV) ....'56 '81 C.894 B.A. L.345 J.D. [Mattox M.&W.]

Mattox Mattox & Wilson, (AV)
Suite 420 Elsby Building, P.O. Box 1203, 47151-1203
Telephone: 812-944-8005 Facsimile: 812-944-2255
Email: mmlaw@win.net
Members of Firm: Richard L. Mattox (Board Certified, Family Law Specialist, Indiana State Bar Association, Family Law Certification Board); S. Frank Mattox (Board Certified, Family Law Specialist, Indiana State Bar Association, Family Law Certification Board); Derrick H. Wilson. Associates: Karen R. Goodwell; Debra S. Audry.
Civil Trial Litigation. Personal Injury and Wrongful Death, Products Liability, Medical Malpractice, Insurance Law, Corporate Law, Business Torts, Family Law, Aviation Law, Labor and Employment Law, Health Care Regulations.
Representative Clients: AAOMS National Insurance; Cablelink, Inc.; Floyd Memorial Hospital; John Deere Co.; Kimball International, Inc.; The Medical Protective Co.; Papa Johns Intl., Inc.; PHICO Insurance Co.; Physicians Group, Inc.; Robinson Nugent, Inc.

See Professional Biographies, NEW ALBANY, INDIANA

McCullum, Jerry L. ....'52 '90 C.347 B.S. L.421 J.D. [McCullum]
McCullum Law Offices .... 1811 State Street
McDaniel, Michael J., (AV) .... '43 '68 C.973 B.S. L.421 J.D. 420 E. Main St.

Merkley Law Office
(See Jeffersonville)

Morgan & Pottinger, P.S.C.
(See Louisville, KY)

Moutardier, Curtis P. .... '74 '02 C.347 B.A. L.74 J.D. [🄰 Boehl S.&G.]
Moyer, William C., (BV) ....'47 '73 C.347 B.S. L.421 J.D. [Lorch&N.]
Mullineaux, Richard T., (AV) ....'52 '78 C.347 B.S. L.1209 J.D. [Kightlinger&G.]

Murphy, Charles R., (BV) '55 '81 C.347 B.S. L.345 J.D.
3707 Charlestown Road, Suite D, 47150-0254
Telephone: 812-944-0515 Fax: 812-944-2996
Email: terrax@win.net URL: http://www.lawyers.com/charlesrmurphy
Real Estate, Elder Law, Business Law, Buying or Selling a Home, Eminent Domain, Landlord and Tenant Law, Zoning and Land Use, Tax Deferred Exchanges, Business Start-Ups, Buying or Selling a Business, Business Enterprises, Limited Liability Company Law, Corporations, Partnerships, Small Business Law.

See Professional Biographies, NEW ALBANY, INDIANA

Nader, John M., & Associates
(See Louisville, Kentucky)

Naville, Herbert F., (BV) ....'19 '50 C.347 L.421 J.D. [🄲 Lorch&N.]
Naville, Michael G., (AV) ....'51 '76 C.347 B.A. L.421 J.D. [Lorch&N.]
Naville, Timothy J., (BV) ....'54 '90 C.871 B.S. L.421 J.D. [Lorch&N.]
Neely, R. Gregory, (BV) ....'49 '74 C.421 A.B. L.245 J.D. 318 Pearl St.
Nord, Mary M. ....'63 '88 C.249 B.S. L.1119 J.D. 4106 Charlestown Rd.
Oakley, Victoria D. '52 '96 C.240 B.A. L.1340 J.D.
(adm. in KY; not adm. in IN) Integra Title Company

O'Bryan, Brown & Toner, PLLC
(See Louisville, Kentucky)

Ollis, David C., Law Office of, (BV) .... '54 '81 C.347 A.B. L.1119 J.D. 201 W. Main St.
Orth, Susan L. ....'58 '85 C.346 B.S. L.1340 J.D. Supr. Ct. J.
Palmer, Peter D., (BVⓣ) ....'70 '95 C.532 B.A. L.421 J.D. [Schad&P.]
Palmquist, Steven K., (BV) ....'54 '79 C.187 B.A. L.150 J.D. [Kightlinger&G.]
Park, Andrew Joseph '11 '36 C&L.424 J.D.
(adm. in IL; not adm. in IN) 80 Lochwood Ct.‡
Platt, Allen C., III ....'68 '95 C.347 B.A. L.879 J.D. [🄲 Wyatt,T.&C.]
Prestigiacomo, MaryAnn, (CV) ....'66 '94 C.347 B.S. L.421 J.D. 200 Elsby Bldg.
Price, Gene F., (BV) ....'56 '89 C&L.421 B.A., J.D. [Frost B.T.]
Pulliam, D. Keith ....'75 '00 C&L.347 B.A., J.D. [🄰 Kightlinger&G.]
Reese, Kristen L. ....'75 '01 C.347 B.A. L.383 J.D. [🄰 Frost B.T.]
Reger, Gregory M., (BV) ....'69 '94 C&L.347 B.S., J.D. [🄰 Lorch&N.]
Reger, Lisa Garcia, (BV) ....'68 '94 C.347 B.S. L.345 J.D. [🄰 Lorch&N.]
Reidinger, Tim, (BV) ....'57 '82 C.347 B.A. L.345 J.D. P.O. Box 6745
Reinecke, Frederick M. ....'68 '99 C.383 B.A. L.421 J.D. [🄰 Boehl S.&G.]
Renfro, Karen Yvonna ....'57 '89 C.999 B.A. L.836 J.D. Dep. Pros. Atty.
Robinson, J. Mark, (BV) ....'47 '74 C.679 B.S.C.E. L.421 J.D. IN Legal Servs.
Robison, Stanley Edwin, Jr. ....'— '83 C.347 B.S. L.421 J.D. 204 Pearl Street, Suite 200
Rose, Joshua T. ....'77 '03 C.383 B.A. L.4210 J.D. [🄰 Frost B.T.]
Rush, Charles R., (CV) ....'65 '96 C.347 B.A. L.421 J.D. 421 W. 1st St.
Sanders, J. Bradley, (CV) ....'64 '93 C.838 B.S. L.421 J.S. 117 E. Spring St.
Schad, Larry J., (BV) ....'41 '67 C.383 B.A. L.421 J.D. [Schad&P.]
Schad, Matthew J., (BV) ....'68 '94 C.347 B.A. L.259 J.D. [Schad&P.]

Schad & Palmer, (BV)
157 East Main Street, 47150-5856
Telephone: 812-945-4555; 800-730-4555 Fax: 812-945-5335
Email: mschad@schadlaw.com URL: http://www.schadlaw.com
Larry J. Schad; Matthew J. Schad; Peter D. Palmer. Associate: Matthew W. Forsythe (Not admitted in IN).
Language: English.
General Practice concentrating in Personal Injury, Medicaid Planning, Social Security Disability and Medical Malpractice.

Schott, Elizabeth A., (CV) ....'69 '96 C&L.421 B.A., J.D. [🄰 Boehl S.&G.]
Schwartz, Richard A., (BVⓣ) ....'58 '83 C.880 B.A. L.608 J.D. [Kruger,S.&M.] ⊙
Scott, David V., (AV) ....'42 '70 C.60 B.A. L.421 J.D. [Scott,F.&B.]
Scott, Rodney L., (BV) ....'65 '89 C.92 B.A. L.345 J.D. [Ward,T.&S.]
Scott, Russell Charles ....'— '77 L.421 J.D. P.O. Box 229

Scott, Forrest & Bourne, (AV)
821 Mount Tabor Road, Suite 302, 47150
Telephone: 812-945-9151 Fax: 812-945-6131
Email: sfb@sfb-law.com URL: http://www.sfb-law.com
David V. Scott; Donald R. Forrest; James E. Bourne.
Wrongful Death, Products Liability and Medical Malpractice Law.

See Professional Biographies, NEW ALBANY, INDIANA

Scrivner, Regina Marie ....'59 '84 C&L.347 B.S., J.D. 5726 Grantline Rd.
Seay, George L., Jr., (BVⓣ) '48 '73
C.303 B.A. L.421 J.D. [Wyatt,T.&C.] (⊙Lexington, KY)
Shickles, Pamela J. ....'63 '98 C&L.347 B.S., J.D 1947 E. Spring St.
Sinex, Thomas W., (AV) .... '40 '65 C.894 A.B. L.309 J.D. [Wyatt,T.&C.]
Smith, William E., III, (BV) ....'53 '79 C.265 B.A. L.201 J.D. [Kightlinger&G.]
Spurgeon, J. Todd, (CV) ....'74 '99 C.894 B.A. L.345 J.D. [🄰 Kightlinger&G.]
Stein, Nicholas, Law Office of, (BV) '49 '78
C.347 B.S.Ed. L.421 J.D. 810 E. Market Street
Stiller, Carrie K. ....'71 '99 C.347 B.A. L.4210 J.D. [Gray&S.]
Sturgeon, Chris ....'63 '88 C&L.421 B.A., J.D. [Bird&S.a.]
Tackett, Dennis R., (BV) ....'54 '79 C.347 B.A. L.421 J.D. 201 W. Main St.
Taurman, Kenneth R., Jr., (BV) ....'54 '79 C.347 B.S. L.421 J.D. 201 W. Main St.
Thomas, Sally Ann, (BV) ....'47 '84 C.739 B.A. L.588 J.D. [Lorch&N.]
Tyler, Scott L., (BV) ....'66 '91 C&L.347 B.A., J.D. [Ward,T.&S.]
Ulrich, Jerry L., (BV) ....'49 '74 C.347 B.A. L.1119 J.D. 430 W. 1st St.
Victor, Karl N., Jr. ....'33 '58 C.477 B.A. L.421 LL.B. P.O. Box 81 (⊙Louisville, KY)
Wade, James C. ....'71 '98 C.1150 B.A. L.421 J.D. [🄰 Kightlinger&G.]
Wallace, Jeffrey E., (AVⓣ) '62 '87
C.679 B.A. L.879 J.D. [Wyatt,T.&C.] (⊙Louisville, KY)
Wallingford, Anthony J., Law Office of '69 '95 C.63 B.S. L.347 J.D.
430 West First Street
Ward, Michael F., (BV) ....'48 '73 C.1024 B.A. L.1119 J.D. [Ward,T.&S.]
Ward, Tyler & Scott, (BV) .... 1947 East Spring Street
Waters, J. Scott, IV ....'54 '80 C.679 B.S. L.345 J.D. 1947 E. Spring St.
West, James R. ....'45 '80 C.347 B.S. L.496 J.D. 227 Pearl St.‡
Wetzel, Mary Jo, (AVⓣ) ....'49 '75 C.347 B.A. L.421 J.D. [Kightlinger&G.]
Willis, Van T., (BV) ....'59 '88 C&L.421 B.A., J.D. [Kightlinger&G.]
Wilson, Derrick H., (BV) ....'66 '91 C&L.421 B.A., J.D. [Mattox M.&W.]
Womack, Jack W. '29 '57 C.437 B.S. L.383 LL.B.
(adm. in KY; not adm. in IN) Coons & Horton, Inc.
Woodard, John W., Jr., (BV) '61 '91
C&L.347 B.A., J.D. [Wyatt,T.&C.] (⊙Louisville, KY)

Wyatt, Tarrant & Combs, LLP, (AV)
(Formerly Orbison, O'Connor, MacGregor & Mattox)
The Community Bank Building, 101 West Spring Street, Suite 500, 47150-3440 ⊙
Telephone: 812-945-3561 Telecopier: 812-949-2524
URL: http://www.wyattfirm.com
Partners: Telford B. Orbison (1901-1990); Charles E. MacGregor; Thomas W. Sinex; Richard A. Bierly; George L. Seay, Jr.; Cynthia W. Young; William H. Hollander; Jeffrey E. Wallace; John W. Woodard, Jr. Counsel: Larry R. Church; Allen C. Platt III (Resident, New Albany, Indiana Office).
Administrative Law, Alternative Dispute Resolution, Antitrust and Trade Regulation, Appellate Practice, Bankruptcy, Banks and Banking, Commercial Law, Commercial Real Estate, Communications and Media, Construction Law, Copyrights, Corporate Law, Debtor and Creditor, Education Law, Employee Benefits, Energy Law, Equine, Environmental Law, Franchises and Franchising, Government, Health Care, Hospital Law, Immigration and Naturalization, Insurance, Insurance Defense, Intellectual Property, International Law, International Trade, Labor and Employment, Leases and Leasing, Legal Ethics and Professional Responsibility, Litigation, Medicare and Medicaid, Merger Acquisitions and Divestitures, Mortgages, Municipal Law, Natural Resources, Nonprofit and Charitable Organizations, Occupational Safety and Health, Partnership Law, Probate, Public Finance, Securities, Taxation, Technology and Science, Trade Secrets, Trademarks, Trusts and Estates, Utility Law, Wills, Workers Compensation, Zoning Planning and Land Use.

(This Listing Continued)

Wyatt, Tarrant & Combs, LLP (Continued)

Representative Clients: Allstate Insurance Co.; Amoco Oil Co.; Ford Motor Credit Corp.; Green Banner Publications, Inc.; Gettelfinger Popcorn Co., Inc.; Joe Huber Farms, Inc.; Indiana Bell Telephone Co.; Province of Our Lady of Consolation, Inc.; Public Service Indiana; United Farm Bureau Mutual Insurance Co.
Louisville, Kentucky Office: 500 West Jefferson Street. Telephone: 502-589-5235. Telecopier: 502-589-0309.
Lexington, Kentucky Office: 250 West Main Street, Suite 1600. Telephone: 859-233-2012. Telecopier: 859-259-0649.
Bowling Green, Kentucky Office: 918 State Street. Telephone: 270-842-1050. Telecopier: 270-842-4720.
Nashville, Tennessee Office: 2525 West End Avenue, Suite 1500. Telephone: 615-244-0020. Telecopier: 615-256-1726.
Memphis, Tennessee Office: The Renaissance Center, 1715 Aaron Brenner Drive, Suite 800. Telephone: 901-537-1000. Telecopier: 901-537-1010.

See Professional Biographies, NEW ALBANY, INDIANA

Young, Cynthia W., (AVⓉ) '55 '82
C.999 B.A. L.421 J.D. [Wyatt,T.&C.] (⊙Louisville, KY)

NEWBURGH, 3,088, *Warrick Co.*

Brinkerhoff Riley LLC
(See Evansville)

Chapman, Angela D., (CV) .... '58 '83 C.249 B.A. L.345 J.D. 315 State St.
Dewey, Dennis J., (BV) .... '38 '66 C.249 B.S. L.1119 LL.B. 107 State St.
Feulner, Melvin J. .... '48 '73 C.347 A.B. L.345 J.D. 107 State St.‡
Gosnell, Ruth A., (CVⓉ) .... '42 '76 C.249 B.A. L.45 J.D. 8077 Cobblestone Ct.‡
Hutson, Jed. W., (CV) .... '59 '86 C.249 B.S. L.345 J.D. P.O. Box 624
Woodburn, Jill L. .... '— '94 C&L.347 B.S., J.D. 6633 Old Stonehouse Dr. (Pat.)

NEW CARLISLE, 1,446, *St. Joseph Co.*

Crump, R. Tracy '65 '92 C.108 B.S. L.879 J.D.
P.O. Box 604, 46552
Telephone: 574-654-8222 Fax: 574-654-8577
Email: rtc@rtclaw.com URL: http://www.rtclaw.com
Intellectual Property, Copyrights, Licensing Agreements, Patents, Trade Secrets, Trademarks.

See Professional Biographies, NEW CARLISLE, INDIANA

McDonagh, John J. .... '26 '55 C.602 A.B. L.421 LL.B 511 W. Michigan St.
Zakrzewski, Daniel M., (CV) .... '51 '83 C.347 M.S. L.1137 J.D. 113 E. Michigan St.

NEW CASTLE, * 17,753, *Henry Co.*

Baker, William G., (BV) .... '42 '71 C.231 A.B. L.345 J.D. 1722 S. Memorial Dr.
Brown, Arthur C., (BV) .... '53 '86 C.63 B.S. L.1187 J.D. [Brown&B.]
Brown, Chas. S., Jr., (BV) .... '25 '54 C&L.347 A.B., LL.B. [Brown&B.]
Brown, Nancy S., (BV) .... '49 '74 C.63 B.A. L.345 J.D. Co. Atty. [Brown&B.]
Brown & Brown, (BV) .... 116 N. Main St.
Buschmann, C. Severin, Jr., (AV) .... '21 '46 C.347 A.B. L.800 LL.B. [Ⓒ Millikan] ‡
Copenhaver, David L., (BV) .... '50 '76 C.879 B.A. L.345 J.D. [Hayes C.C.]
Crane, Kit C. Dean, (BV) .... '57 '89 C.63 B.S. L.345 J.D. Pros. Atty.
Crider, Gregory L., (BV) .... '50 '81 C.347 A.B. L.1119 J.D. [Hayes C.C.]

Davis, James E., Attorney at Law
(See Greenfield)

Dennison, Randall G. .... '25 '65 C.421 L.345 LL.B. 533 S. Main St.
Galyen, Jeffrey D., (AV) .... '57 '82 C.63 B.S. L.879 J.D. [J.D.Galyen]
Galyen, Jeffrey D., Law Office, (AV) .... 595 New York Ave.
Harvey, Joel E. .... '76 '02 C.894 B.A. L.201 J.D. [Ⓐ Hayes C.C.]
Hayes, R. Scott, (AV) .... '46 '72 C.679 B.S. L.345 J.D. [Hayes C.C.]

Hayes Copenhaver Crider, (AV) BB
214 South Main Street, 47362-4286
Telephone: 765-529-2100 Fax: 765-529-3532
Email: attorneys@hcclaw.com URL: http://www.hcclaw.com
Members of Firm: E. G. Scotten (1877-1957); J. R. Hinshaw (1883-1970); James R. Stanley (1910-1980); George W. Hand (1919-1995); R. Scott Hayes; David L. Copenhaver; Gregory L. Crider. Associate: Joel E. Harvey.
Civil Litigation, Trial Practice, Probate Administration, Estate Planning, Medicaid Planning, Bodily Injury, Zoning Law, Banking Law, Divorce, Municipal Law, Real Property.
General Counsel For: Ameriana Bank and Trust.
Representative Clients: Town of Knightstown, Henry County Memorial Hospital; Blue River Valley School Corporation; Town of Middletown; Eastern Indiana Federal Credit Union; Perfect Circle Credit Union; City of New Castle.

See Professional Biographies, NEW CASTLE, INDIANA

Hodson, Gerald K., (BV) .... '25 '51 C.347 B.S. L.1119 J.D. 112 S. Main St.
Hunter, Robt. S., Jr. .... '09 '31 C.347 L.469 LL.B. 1116 Broad St.
Kellam, John L. .... '42 '70 C.347 B.S. L.345 J.D. Cir. J.
Lansinger, John R., (BV) .... '48 '74 C.303 B.A. L.421 J.D. [Whitton&L.]
McNichols, Thomas R. II .... '45 '74 C.347 B.S. L.345 J.D. Supr. Ct. J.
Miller, Jerry W., (BV) .... '44 '73 C.63 B.S. L.879 J.D. 1811 Bundy Ave.
Millikan, James E., (BV) .... '49 '75 C.967 A.B. L.345 J.D. [Millikan]
Millikan Law Office, P.C., (BV) .... 1315 Broad Street
Neal, Wm. David .... '45 '71 C.150 B.A. L.1119 J.D. 1923 S. 18th St.
Peyton, Michael D. .... '43 '68 C.210 A.B. L.1119 J.D. Supr. Ct. J.
Scott, David J. .... '67 '93 C.651 B.A. L.879 J.D. 1815 Bundy Ave.
Shields, Martin R., (BV) .... '54 '79 C.347 A.B. L.1119 J.D. [Yergin&Y.]
Stamper, Mark C., (BV) .... '49 '75 C.347 A.B. L.345 J.D. 1215 Race St., Ste. 170
Taylor, J. Alton, (CV) .... '34 '74 C.63 B.S. L.345 J.D. 241 S. Denny Dr.
Whitton, David W., (BV) .... '44 '70 C.63 B.S. L.345 J.D. [Whitton&L.]
Whitton & Lansinger, (BV) .... 1217 Indiana Ave.
Willis, Mary G. .... '66 '91 C.63 B.S. L.347 J.D. Cir. J.
Witham, Bob A., (BV) .... '66 '92 C.265 B.A. L.347 J.D. [Ⓐ Yergin&Y.]
Yergin, Alan E., (BV) .... '29 '58 C.894 B.A. L.1119 J.D. [Yergin&Y.]
Yergin & Yergin, (BV) .... 1222 Broad Street

NEW HARMONY, 846, *Posey Co.*

Eimer, Ronald W. '49 '85 C.339 B.Arch. L.945 J.D.
(adm. in VA; not adm. in IN) P.O. Box 309

NEW HAVEN, 12,406, *Allen Co.*

Cowen, Bruce S. .... '28 '63 C.347 B.S. L.345 J.D. 8815 Old Orchard Trail‡
Miller, Carl M., (BV) .... '50 '76 C.347 A.B. L.345 J.D. 618 Professional Park Drive
Miller, Jeanne S., (AV) .... '25 '48 C.347 A.B. L.1119 J.D. P.O. Box 286‡
Runyan, Douglas K., (BV) .... '63 '88 C.347 A.B. L.1119 J.D. 1220 Lincoln Hwy. E

NEW PALESTINE, 1,264, *Hancock Co.*

Carlock, Mahlon W., II .... '55 '81 C&L.347 A.B., J.D. 1344 S. Broken Arrow Dr.
Ford, Richard L., (AV) .... '52 '79 C.63 B.A. L.345 J.D. 4320 S. Woodbridge Ln.
Holiday, James E., (BV) .... '53 '79 C.1109 B.A. L.990 J.D. 47 E. Main St.
Merlau, John S., (BV) .... '49 '74 C.679 B.S. L.365 J.D. 31 E. Main St.
Niemier, William T. .... '64 '90 C.894 A.B. L.345 J.D. 21 East Main Street

NEWPORT, * 627, *Vermillion Co.*

Alexander, Nina J., (BV) .... '44 '84 C&L.347 B.S., J.D. Co. Pros. Off.
Aukerman, Malcolm H., Law Office of, (AV) ... '24 '52 C.201 L.150 LL.B. 350 Poplar St.
Carter, Gregory S., (BV) .... '47 '72 C.347 A.B. L.1119 J.D. Chf. Dep. Pros.
Greenwell, Mark A., (BV) ...... '51 '77 C.346 B.S. L.345 J.D. Pros. Atty., Vermillion Co.
Stengel, Bruce V. .... '51 '76 C.347 A.B. L.345 J.D. Cir. J.

NEW WHITELAND, 4,579, *Johnson Co.*

Bergdoll, John C., (BV) .... '51 '80 C.347 B.S. L.496 J.D. 180 North US 31
Dils, Jimmy B., (BV) .... '34 '66 C.347 B.S. L.345 LL.B. 539 Sweetbriar Dr.
Smith, Deana Mcintire .... '65 '90 C.1216 B.A. L.345 J.D. P.O. Box 36

NOBLESVILLE, * 28,590, *Hamilton Co.*

Adams, David M. .... '45 '71 C.347 B.S. L.345 J.D. 40 S. 9th St.
Adler, Raymond M. .... '49 '75 C.679 B.S. L.345 J.D. [Ⓒ Ayres C.&S.]
Antrim, J. Michael, (AV) .... '50 '75 C&L.347 B.S., J.D. [Church,C.H.&A.]

Ayres Carr & Sullivan, P.C., (AV)
136 South Ninth Street, 46060-2619 ⊙
Telephone: 317-773-0882 Fax: 317-773-0943
Of Counsel: Raymond M. Adler (Resident).
General Civil and Criminal Practice in all State and Federal Courts. Administrative, Corporation, Insurance and Probate and Estate Planning, Real Estate, Taxation, Transportation, Trial and Appellate Practice.
Indianapolis, Indiana Office: 251 East Ohio Street, Suite 500. Telephone: 317-636-3471. Fax: 317-636-6575.

See Professional Biographies, NOBLESVILLE, INDIANA

Barker, Andrew M., (BV) .... '60 '89 C.347 B.S. L.345 J.D. [Campbell K.P.]
Becker, Robert C., (BV) .... '62 '89 C.347 B.S. L.345 J.D. 1312 Maple Ave.
Beerbower, Gary D., (AV) .... '34 '64 C.608 B.S. L.345 J.D. 938 Conner St.
Berish, Sally E. .... '69 '96 C.249 B.S. L.345 J.D. Co. Pros. Atty.

Bingham McHale LLP, (AV)
970 Logan Street, 46060 ⊙
Telephone: 317-776-8668 Telecopier: 317-776-8651
URL: http://www.binghammchale.com
Member of Firm: Steven D. Hardin.
General Civil Practice, Architects and Engineers, Business Law, Business Litigation, Commercial Transactions, Construction Law, Corporate Finance, Estate Planning and Administration, Governmental Services, Matrimonial and Family Law, Public Finance, Public Utility Law, Real Estate, Zoning, Planning and Land Use.
Indianapolis, Indiana Office: Bingham McHale LLP, 2700 Market Tower, 10 West Market Street. Telephone: 317-635-8900. Fax: 317-236-9907.
Jasper, Indiana Office: Bingham McHale LLP, 212 West Sixth Street. Telephone: 812-482-5500. Fax: 812-482-2017.
Vincennes, Indiana Office: Bingham Mchale LLP, 112 North 7th Street. Telephone: 812-886-9970. Fax: 812-886-0776.

See Professional Biographies, NOBLESVILLE, INDIANA

Bittner, Bruce M., (BV) .... '54 '81 C.347 B.S. L.36 J.D. [Church,C.H.&A.]
Blumenthal, Shawn D. .... '71 '01 C.347 B.A. L.862 J.D. 829 Conner St.
Boje, Bruce A., (BV) .... '51 '77 C.679 B.S. L.345 J.D. 1312 Maple Avenue
Brant, Anne E. .... '78 '04 C&L.347 B.S., J.D. [Ⓐ Campbell K.P.]
Caldwell, Gregory L., (BV) .... '42 '68 C.347 A.B. L.345 J.D. 453 S. 9th St.

Campbell Kyle Proffitt LLP, (AV) BB
198 South Ninth Street, P.O. Box 2020, 46061-2020 ⊙
Telephone: 317-773-2090 Fax: 317-776-5051
Email: ckplaw@ckplaw.com URL: http://www.ckplaw.com
Members of Firm: Frank S. Campbell (1880-1964); Frank W. Campbell (1916-1991); Robert F. Campbell (1946-2004); John M. Kyle; John D. Proffitt (Resident, Carmel Office); Jeffrey S. Nickloy; Deborah L. Farmer (Resident, Carmel Office); William E. Wendling, Jr. (Resident, Carmel Office); Anne Hensley Poindexter (Resident, Carmel Office); Andrew M. Barker; Michael A. Casati (Resident, Carmel Office); Rodney T. Sarkovics (Resident, Carmel Office); John S. Terry. Associates: Scott P. Wyatt (Resident, Carmel Office); Amy E. Higdon (Resident, Carmel Office); Stephenie K. Gookins; N. Scott Smith (Resident, Carmel Office); Anne E. Brant.
Civil Practice. State and Federal Courts and Administrative Agencies, Domestic Relations, Family Law, Divorce, Adoptions, Personal Injury, Corporation, Business Law, Utility Law, Insurance, Wills and Probate, Trusts and Estates, Estate Planning and Elder Law, Real Estate, Zoning, Employment Law, Criminal Law. Contracts, Taxation, Real Estate, Commercial Litigation.
Representative Clients: PSI Energy, Inc.; Mobil Oil Corp.; Minnesota Mining & Manufacturing Co.; Buck Creek Utilities; Conseco Insurance Companies.
Carmel Office: 11595 N. Meridian, Suite 701. Telephone: 317-846-6514. Fax: 317-843-8097.

See Professional Biographies, NOBLESVILLE, INDIANA

Church, Douglas D., (AV) .... '44 '70 C.347 A.B. L.345 J.D. [Church,C.H.&A.]
Church, Jordan D. .... '70 '97 C.894 A.B. L.347 J.D. [Church,C.H.&A.]
Church, Manson E., (AV) .... '25 '52 C.108 A.B. L.345 J.D. [Ⓒ Church,C.H.&A.]

Church, Church, Hittle & Antrim, (AV) BB
938 Conner Street, P.O. Box 10, 46061-0010
Telephone: 317-773-2190 Telecopier: 317-773-5320
Email: dchurch@cchalaw.com URL: http://www.cchalaw.com
Members of Firm: Douglas D. Church; Jack G. Hittle; J. Michael Antrim; Martin E. Risacher; David R. Day; Bruce M. Bittner; Leslie Craig Henderzahs; Jordan D. Church; Amber D. Sullivan; Eric M. Douthit. Associates: Samuel R. Robinson; Ann M. O'Hara. Of Counsel: Manson E. Church.
General Civil Trial Practice in all State and Federal Courts. Appellate and Federal Practice, Personal Injury, Automobile Accidents, Wrongful Death, Family Law, Adoption Law, Child Custody, Child Support, Divorce, Visitation Rights, Municipal and Governmental Regulations, Real Estate, Zoning Law, Land Use, Commercial Leasing, Wills, Probate, Trusts and Estates, Estate Planning, Asset Protection, Guardianship Law, Estate Administration and Litigation, Tax Planning, Tax Controversies, Business Law, Contracts, Litigation, Business Enterprises, Business Transactions, Corporate Formation, Corporate Litigation, School Law, Commercial Litigation, Professional License Defense, Medical Malpractice, Bankruptcy, Criminal Law, Driving While Intoxicated, Drug Crimes, Felonies, Misdemeanors, Mediation.
Representative Clients: Noblesville Schools; Westfield-Washington Schools; Zionsville School Corp.; Community Bank; Metrobank; Towns of Westfield and Fishers; Reynolds Farm Equipment Co.; Weihe Engineering; Historic Railroad Multijurisdictional Port Authority.

See Professional Biographies, NOBLESVILLE, INDIANA

Cook, S. Matthew .... '68 '94 C&L.347 B.S., J.D. 955 Logan St.
Culp, John F. .... '43 '72 C.303 B.A. L.345 J.D. Gen. Coun., Shorewood Corp.
Day, David R., (AV) .... '52 '77 C.63 B.S. L.309 J.D. [Church,C.H.&A.]
Douthit, Eric M. .... '72 '97 C.880 B.S. L.1119 J.D. [Church,C.H.&A.]
Ellis, Janet S. .... '53 '81 C.339 B.A. L.345 J.D. 401 Regents Park Ln.
Feigenbaum, Edward D. .... '58 '83 C&L.347 B.A., J.D. P.O. Box 383
Fineberg, David A. .... '75 '00 C.207 B.A. L.1119 J.D. Co. Pros. Off.
Fleck, K. Sean, (BV) .... '56 '81 C.679 B.S. L.1119 J.D. [Holt,F.&R.]
Floyd, Douglas B., (BV) .... '48 '73 C.63 B.S. L.345 J.D. Land Rush Develop. Servs., Inc.
Foland, Arvin R., (CV) .... '40 '68 C.679 B.S. L.345 J.D. 813 Conner St.
Foland, Robert C. .... '65 '93 C.679 B.S. L.347 J.D. 813 Conner St.
Forsgren, Steven E. '47 '78 C.399 B.A. L.365 J.D.
(adm. in IL; not adm. in IN) 804 Harbourtown Ct., Apt. D‡
Gascho, Martha B., (CV) .... '36 '73 C.108 A.B. L.345 J.D. 841 Conner St.
Glier, Christl P. .... '79 '04 C.347 B.A. L.345 J.D. [Ⓐ Holt,F.&R.]
Gookins, Stephenie K. .... '72 '98 C&L.347 B.S., J.D. [Ⓐ Campbell K.P.]

Gordon, Sylvia A. '66 '93 C.347 B.A. L.421 J.D. Gordon Mktg., LLC
Hadley, Karl E., (BV) '56 '83 C.63 B.S. L.345 J.D. 813 Conner St.
Hardin, Steven D., (AV) '63 '92 C&L.347 B.S., J.D. [Bingham M.]
Haymaker, Shelley Hiles '67 '94 C&L.1119 B.A., J.D. 124 North 10th St
Henderzahs, Leslie Craig, (BV) '64 '90 C&L.347 B.A., J.D. [Church,C.H.&A.]
Henry, Jolie B. '73 '00 C.473 B.A. L.150 J.D. 198 South Ninth Street
Hittle, Jack G., (AV) '48 '73 C.108 B.A. L.345 J.D. [Church,C.H.&A.]
Hofmann, Richard P. '68 '99 C.473 B.S. L.923 J.D. P.O. Box 1724
Holt, Steven A., (BV) '48 '73 C.210 A.B. L.345 J.D. [Holt,F.&R.]

Holt, Fleck & Romine, (BV)
83 South 9th Street, 46060
Telephone: 317-773-5997 Facsimile: 317-773-5960
Email: hfr@hfrlaw.com URL: http://www.hfrlaw.com
Steven A. Holt; K. Sean Fleck. Of Counsel: Carol Jean Romine. Associate: Christi P. Glier.
Civil and Criminal Trials in all Courts, Criminal Law, Drug Crimes, Driving While Intoxicated, Parole and Probation, Traffic Violations, Wills and Probate, Trusts and Estate, Guardianships, Asset Protection, Estate Planning, Business, Contracts, Business Planning, Lawsuits, Business Enterprises, Closely Held Business, Corporate, Partnerships, Limited Liability Companies, Small Business, Real Estate, Buying and Selling Real Estate, Commercial Leasing, Family Law, Adoptions, Child Custody, Child Support, Divorce, Visitations Rights, Domestic Violence, Domestic Relation, Personal Injury, Automobile Accidents, Slip and Fall, Wrongful Death, Medical Malpractice, Unsafe Products, Bankruptcy, Elder Law.
See Professional Biographies, NOBLESVILLE, INDIANA

Horlander, Joseph C. '45 '73 C&L.421 B.S.C., J.D.
(adm. in KY; not adm. in IN) Buehler Corp.
Howard, Michael A., (BV) '49 '74 C.347 B.S. L.1119 J.D. 694 Logan St.
Hughes, William J. '55 '80 C.249 B.S. L.345 J.D. Supr. Ct. J.
Kenley, Howard A. '45 '72 C.473 A.B. L.309 J.D. Cambridge Investment, Inc.
Kyle, John M., (AV) '27 '54 C.347 B.S. L.1119 J.D. [Campbell K.P.]
Lamey, Gary C., (BV) '48 '73 C.347 A.B. L.345 J.D. Dep. Pros. Atty.
Leach, F. Keith '25 '60 C.108 B.S. L.345 J.D. 17105 Cherry Tree Rd.
Leerkamp, Sonia J., (BV) '47 '75 C.347 A.B. L.345 J.D. Pros. Atty.
Lytle, Shirley A., (BV⊕) '45 '84 C.608 B.S. L.607 J.D.
(adm. in OH; not adm. in IN) 206 Amhurst Cirle

Marcus Law Firm, The
(See Fishers)

Markovich, Carl A. '72 '99 C.679 B.S. L.345 J.D. 1312 Maple Avenue
McIntire, Gerald L. '61 '88 C.679 B.S. L.345 J.D. P.O. Box 1908
Nation, Steven R. '50 '75 C.347 A.B. L.345 J.D. Supr. Ct. J.
Nichols, Wade R., (BV) '50 '84 C.210 B.A. L.879 J.D. Morgan & Assocs.
Nickloy, Jeffrey S., (AV) '48 '73 C.894 B.A. L.228 J.D. [Campbell K.P.]
O'Hara, Ann M. '63 '90 C.1024 B.S. L.347 J.D. [Church,C.H.&A.]
Patrick, William B. '23 '50 C.675 A.B. L.309 LL.B. 8647 Kensington Drive
Pearce, John S. '40 '66 C.347 B.S. L.345 LL.B. P.O. Box 4
Pfleging, Daniel J. '47 '74 C.347 B.S. L.345 J.D. Supr. Ct. J., Hamilton Supr. Ct. # 2
Pickering, James H., Jr., (BV) '54 '79 C.679 B.A. L.345 J.D. 1312 Maple Avenue
Poynter, Richard L., (P.C.), (BV) '41 '69 C.679 B.A. L.345 J.D. 6757 E. 171st Street
Proffitt, Judith S. '42 '71 C.108 B.S. L.345 J.D. Cir. J.
Purcell, Philip M. '58 '86 C.894 A.B. L.1119 J.D. 111 Stony Creek Overlook
Risacher, Martin E., (AV) '47 '75 C.346 B.A. L.1119 J.D. [Church,C.H.&A.]
Roberts, Joseph G., (BV) '32 '56 C.231 A.B. L.1119 J.D. 1154 E. Conner St.
Robinson, Samuel R. '73 '00 C.47 B.A. L.347 J.D. [Church,C.H.&A.]
Romine, Carol Jean, (BV) '42 '96 C&L.347 B.A., J.D [Holt,F.&R.]

Smith, Janice E., Attorney at Law
(See Indianapolis)

Sturtevant, Wayne A., (BV) '51 '77 C.108 B.A. L.345 J.D. Supr. Ct. J.
Sullivan, Amber D. '74 '00 C.210 B.A. L.1119 J.D. [Church,C.H.&A.]
Terry, John S. '72 '98 C.894 A.B. L.347 J.D. [Campbell K.P.]
Tudor, David, (CV) '48 '80 C.347 B.S. L.345 J.D. 1047 Maple Avenue
Webster, Louis I. '12 '54 C.347 L.345 LL.B. 14807 N. Gary Rd.‡
Wright, Frank E. '14 '49 C&L.215 LL.B.
(adm. in MI; not adm. in IN) 499 S. 9th St.

NORTH JUDSON, 1,582, *Starke Co.*

Lucas, Martin R., (CV) '55 '80 C.347 A.B. L.1119 J.D. 307 Lane St.
McLaughlin, Marvin D. '29 '56 C.108 A.B. L.345 LL.B. Cir. J.

NORTH LIBERTY, 1,366, *St. Joseph Co.*

Brown, Deborah Sullivan '56 '82 C.63 B.A. L.602 J.D. 304 N. Main St.
Sullivan Brown, Deborah, (BV) '56 '82 C.63 B.A. L.602 J.D. 304 N. Main St.

NORTH MANCHESTER, 6,260, *Wabash Co.*

Daggett, Schlitt & Stoops, A Professional Corporation, (BV) 204 West Main Street
Downs, Stephen H., (AV) '48 '73 C.347 B.S. L.345 J.D. [Tiede,M.D.L.&S.] ⊙
Hammer, Steven G., (BV) '55 '81 C.432 B.S. L.879 J.D. Tr. Offr., Ind. Lawrence Bk.
Lynn, Kristina L., (BV) '66 '92 C.432 B.S. L.347 J.D. [Tiede,M.D.L.&S.] ⊙
Metz, Donald R., (AV) '33 '62 C.265 B.A. L.1119 J.D. [Tiede,M.D.L.&S.] ⊙
Schlitt, Albert J., (BV) '37 '66 C.801 B.S. L.345 LL.B. [Tiede,M.D.L.&S.] ⊙
Stein, Joel K. '61 '88 C.436 B.A. L.74 J.D. [Tiede,M.D.L.&S.] ⊙
Stoops, Elden E., Jr., (BV) '53 '82 C.63 B.S. L.879 J.D. [Daggett,S.&S.]
Tiede, Charles R., (AV) '29 '56 C.63 B.S. L.1119 J.D. [Tiede,M.D.L.&S.] ⊙
Tiede, Metz, Downs, Lynn & Schlitt, P.C., (AV) 222 East Main St. (⊙Wabash)

NORTH VERNON, 6,515, *Jennings Co.*

Brown, Robert J. '32 '62 C.679 L.421 J.D. 159 E. Walnut St.
Dove, Mark J., (BV) '55 '81 C.679 B.S. L.201 J.D. [Rogers&D.]
Finnerty, Corinne R., (AV) '56 '81 C.347 A.B. L.1119 J.D. [McConnell&F.]
Gay, John D., (BV) '51 '77 C.679 B.S. L.383 J.D. 130 North State Street
McConnell, Harold H., (AV) '18 '48 C.347 L.345 LL.B. [McConnell&F.]

McConnell and Finnerty, (AV)
38 North 5th Street, P.O. Box 90, 47265
Telephone: 812-346-5201 FAX: 812-346-8470
Email: lawyers@mcconnelllaw.net
Members of Firm: Ira B. Hamilton (1899-1982); Harold H. McConnell; Corinne R. Finnerty. Associate: Charles R. Waggoner.
Probate and Estate Planning, Personal Injury and Commercial Law, Family/Domestic Relations. Civil Litigation. Trials, Appeals and Banking.
Representative Clients: Heritage Community Bank; First Financial Bank; Home Federal Savings Bank; Rose Acre Farms, Inc.; CPX, Inc.; North Vernon Industry Corp.; NAC, Inc.; Decatur Plastics, Inc.; National Loan Investors, L.P.
See Professional Biographies, NORTH VERNON, INDIANA

Rogers, Michael L., (BV) '43 '71 C.347 B.S. L.1119 J.D. [Rogers&D.]
Rogers & Dove, (BV) 16 Main St.
Waggoner, Charles R., (CV) '50 '89 C.679 B.S. L.347 J.D. [McConnell&F.]
Webster, Harold W. '30 '70 C.347 B.S. L.421 J.D. 524 N. State St.‡

NOTRE DAME, —, *St. Joseph Co.*

Barrett, Matthew J. '60 '85 C&L.602 B.B.A., J.D.
(adm. in OH; not adm. in IN) Assoc. Prof., Notre Dame Law School
Beauchamp, E. William '42 '75 C.215 B.S. L.602 J.D.
(adm. in MI; not adm. in IN) Exec. V.P., Univ. of Notre Dame
Blakey, Elizabeth E. '61 '88 C.602 B.A. L.426 J.D.
(adm. in CA; not adm. in IN) Univ. of Notre Dame
Blakey, G. Robert '36 '60 C&L.602 A.B., J.D.
(adm. in DC; not adm. in IN) Univ. of Notre Dame
Booker, Frank E. '29 '54 C.798 L.228 LL.B.
(adm. in MO; not adm. in IN) Prof., Notre Dame Law School
Carlin, J. Christopher '48 '80 C.475 B.S. L.602 J.D.
(adm. in MI; not adm. in IN) Dir., Admin. Servs., Univ. of Notre Dame
Conboy, Melissa L., (BV) '60 '85 C.602 B.A. L.378 J.D.
(adm. in KS; not adm. in IN) Joyce Ctr., Room C 109
Doran, Eileen M. '59 '86 C.229 B.S. L.602 J.D. Notre Dame Law School
Dutile, Fernand '40 '65 C.1107 A.B. L.602 J.D.
(adm. in ME; not adm. in IN) Prof. of Law, Notre Dame Law Sch.
Gasperetti, Barbara Szweda '53 '80 C.399 B.A. L.990 J.D. Notre Dame Law School
Gunn, Alan '40 '70 C.688 B.S. L.188 J.D.
(adm. in DC; not adm. in IN) Notre Dame Law School
Jackson, Lois C. '68 '98 C.602 B.A. L.734 J.D.
Asst. V.P. & Coun., Univ. of Notre Dame, Gen. Coun. Off.
Jacobs, Roger F. '37 '70 C&L.215 A.B., J.D.
(adm. in MI; not adm. in IN) Assoc. Dean, Libr. & Info. Servs., Notre Dame Law Sch.‡
Kaesebier, Carol C. '49 '83 C.339 B.S. L.879 J.D. Univ. of Notre Dame
Kirk, William W. '62 '91 C&L.602 B.B.A., J.D. Asst. V.P., University of Notre Dame
Lewis, Alexandria '69 '00 C.1193 B.A. L.336 J.D.
(adm. in CA; not adm. in IN) Univ. of Notre Dame Law School
Link, David T. '36 '61 C&L.602 B.S., LL.B. Dean, Notre Dame Law Sch.
Marc, Rodriguez S. '68 '01 C&L.959 B.A., J.D.
(adm. in WI; not adm. in IN) Asst. Prof. of Law and History, Univ. of Notre Dame
O'Hara, Patricia A. '49 '74 C.770 B.A. L.602 J.D.
(adm. in CA; not adm. in IN)
The Joseph A. Matson Dean and Prof. of Law, Univ. of Notre Dame
Payne, Lucy Salsbury '52 '88
C.243 B.Mus. L.602 J.D. Resch. Libr., Notre Dame Law Sch.
Pearson, John H. '45 '86 C.602 A.B. L.1066 J.D.
(adm. in CA; not adm. in IN) Notre Dame Law Sch.
Peshel, Gail G. '— '00 C&L.879 B.S., J.D. Univ. of Notre Dame
Robinson, John H. '43 '80 C.1149 B.A. L.112 J.D.
(adm. in RI; not adm. in IN) Law Prof., University of Notre Dame
Rodes, Robert E., Jr. '27 '53
C.103 A.B. L.309 J.D. Prof. of Law, Notre Dame Law School
Shaffer, Thomas L. '34 '61 C.1143 B.A. L.602 J.D. Prof. of Law, Univ. of Notre Dame
Smithburn, J. Eric '44 '74 C.347 B.S. L.1119 J.D. Prof., Notre Dame Law School
Thornton, Peter W. '18 '41 C.102 A.B. L.1009 LL.B.
(adm. in NY; not adm. in IN) Prof., Notre Dame Law Sch.
Tidmarsh, Jay '57 '82 C.602 B.A. L.309 J.D.
(adm. in WI; not adm. in IN) Assoc. Prof. of Law, Notre Dame Law School

OAKLAND CITY, 2,588, *Gibson Co.*

Kinkade, Kevin Scott, (BV) '60 '94 C.249 B.S. L.421 J.D. [O'Leary&Assoc.]
McGregor, Loren G., (AV) '16 '42 C.603 A.B. L.1119 J.D. 820 N. Main Dr.‡
O'Leary, Virginia M., (AV) '34 '71 C&L.421 B.A., J.D. [O'Leary&Assoc.]
O'Leary and Associates, (AV) 251 North Main Street
Robinson, Darlene, (CV) '60 '85 C.231 B.A. L.421 J.D. 522 W. College St.

ODON, 1,475, *Daviess Co.*

Murrie, Holli Overton '— '00 C.347 B.S.N. L.502 J.D. RR 2‡

ORLAND, 361, *Steuben Co.*

Lewis, Neal R., (BV) '62 '91 C&L.347 B.A., J.D. 9487 W. State Rd. 120

OSCEOLA, 1,859, *St. Joseph Co.*

Wandling, Michael Keith '68 '95 C.249 B.S. L.616 J.D. 1415 Lincolnway West, Suite J

OSGOOD, 1,688, *Ripley Co.*

Comer, Neil R., (BV) '46 '72 C.347 B.S. L.345 J.D. [N.R.Comer]
Comer, Neil R., A Prof. Corp., Law Offices of, (BV) 115 W. Ripley St.

OSSIAN, 2,943, *Wells Co.*

Gallivan, Hamilton, Seese & Patterson, (BV) 115 S. Jefferson St. (⊙Bluffton)
Seese, William D., (BV) '31 '59 C.303 B.A. L.1119 J.D. [Gallivan,H.S.&P.] ⊙

OWENSVILLE, 1,322, *Gibson Co.*

Dike, Tom '40 '73 C.347 B.A. L.421 J.D. 112 W. Brummitt St.
Singleton, E. Dean, (CV) '61 '86 C&L.347 B.A., J.D. 208 S. Main St.

PAOLI, * 3,844, *Orange Co.*

Apple, Max W. '38 '70 C.347 A.B. L.345 J.D. P.O. Box 329‡
Blanton, Larry R. '44 '89 C.999 B.S. L.421 J.D. Cir. J., Orange Cir. Ct.
Dillard, Arthur L., (BV) '38 '65 C.210 A.B. L.421 J.D. 340 North Court Street
Owen, Steven L., (BV) '59 '84 C.347 B.S. L.260 J.D. Chf. Dep. Pros. Atty.
Rhodes, Rhys D. '26 '53 C.265 A.B. L.421 LL.B. Co. Ct. J.
Theirbah, Thomas C. '38 '74 C.966 B.S. L.285 J.D.
(adm. in WA; not adm. in IN) 188 S. Court St.
Tucker, James C., (AV) '46 '71 C.108 B.A. L.345 J.D. [Tucker&T.]
Tucker, Jennifer A., (CV) '71 '97 C.679 B.A. L.1119 J.D. [Tucker&T.]
Tucker and Tucker, P.C., (AV) 188 South Court Street
Umpleby, David M. '73 '98 C&L.347 B.A., J.D. [Umpleby&U.]
Umpleby, Susan E. '72 '98 C.344 B.A. L.347 J.D. [Umpleby&U.]
Umpleby & Umpleby, PC 102 W. Main St.

PENDLETON, 3,873, *Madison Co.*

Kilmer, Joseph R., (BV) '45 '75 C.63 B.S. L.345 J.D. [J.R.Kilmer]
Kilmer, Joseph R., Law Office, (BV) 100 E. High St.
Ogden, Timothy A. '63 '96 C.432 B.A. L.1119 J.D. 1034 Chipmunk Lane
Owens, Bryce D., (CV) '59 '85 C.880 B.A. L.347 J.D. 119 N. Pendleton Ave.
Owens, G. Douglass, (BV) '33 '59 C&L.347 B.S., J.D. 119 N. Pendleton Ave.
Reasoner, Deborah Dodge '62 '88 C.346 B.A. L.347 J.D. 9364 Fall Creek Drive

PERU, * 12,994, *Miami Co.*

Banina, Daniel C. '57 '83 C.1024 B.S. L.879 J.D. Miami Supr. Ct. J.
Berkshire, James A., (AV) '36 '63 C.347 B.S. L.1119 J.D. [Berkshire]

Berkshire, William F., (BV) ....'67 '95 C.347 B.S. L.1187 J.D. [Berkshire]
Berkshire Law Firm, (AV) ....16 East 5th Street

Blackburn & Green
(See Fort Wayne)

Caravelli, Robert A. ....'45 '81 C.397 B.A. L.1095 J.D. 409 East 2nd Street
Cole, James O. ....'12 '39 C.273 A.B. L.276 J.D. 1 1/2 S. Bway.‡
Cook, Gary A. '55 '88 C.33 B.A. L.1162 J.D.
(adm. in PA; not adm. in IN) [Sands,M.&C.]
Davis, Brent A., (BV) ....'50 '97 C.63 B.S. L.1187 J.D. 11 South Broadway
Embrey, Bruce C., Law Office of ....'43 '76 C.347 B.S. L.345 J.D. 135 W. 3rd. St.
Fern, Donald G., (AV) ....'44 '70 C.63 B.S. L.879 J.D. [Fern,G.&G.]
Fern, Grund & Grund, (AV) ....2 1/2 North Broadway, Suite 200
Grund, J. David, (BV) ....'70 '97 C&L.347 B.A., J.D. [Fern,G.&G.]
Keith, Thomas A., (AV) '43 '68 C.846 B.A. L.1119 J.D.
2 1/2 North Broadway, Suite 210
Loy, William A. ....'29 '58 C&L.602 A.B., J.D. 1 1/2 S. Bway.
Michaud, Bryan J., (BV) ....'64 '89 C.712 B.A. L.201 J.D. [Sands,M.&C.]
Palmer, Garrett W. ....'31 '55 C&L.69 B.B.A., LL.B. Supr. Ct. J.
Price, Elizabeth G. ....'73 '99 C.20 B.A. L.345 J.D. 15 South Wabash
Price, Jeffry G., (BV) ....'48 '73 C.894 A.B. L.345 J.D. 15 S. Wabash St.
Roberts, Patrick J., (BV) ....'41 '69 C.347 B.S. L.1119 J.D. [Roberts]
Roberts Law Firm, P.C., (BV) ....11 S. Broadway
Sands, Christian E., (BV) ....'63 '89 C.63 B.S. L.879 J.D. [Sands,M.&C.]
Sands, Michaud & Cook, (BV) ....25 Court St.
Sinkovics, Jeffrey K., (BV) ....'68 '93 C&L.347 B.A., J.D. [A Roberts]
Spahr, Robert A., (BV) ....'46 '74 C.347 B.A. L.345 J.D. 55 S. Bway.
Spahr, Timothy P., (CV) ....'73 '97 C.347 B.S. L.1119 J.D. [Spahr]
Spahr Law Offices ....55 S. Broadway
Stanley, K. L., (CV) ....'53 '81 C.578 B.A. L.365 J.D. 16 E. 5th St.

PETERSBURG, * 2,570, *Pike Co.*

Baker, Lee F. ....'64 '96 C&L.347 B.S., J.D. Cir. J.
Baker, Lincoln A., (BV) ....'49 '81 C.347 A.B. L.345 J.D. 818 Main St.
Biesterveld, Jeffrey L., (BV) ....'57 '82 C.746 B.A. L.1137 J.D. [Gray,F.&B.]
Chappell, John K. ....'17 '42 C.303 A.B. L.1119 LL.B. P.O. Box 312‡
Chestnut, Michael D. ....'62 '98 C.346 B.S. L.879 J.D. Co. J., Pike Co. Ct.
Fleig, Val J., (BV) ....'47 '73 C.347 B.A. L.345 J.D. [Gray,F.&B.]

Goodridge, John Andrew, Law Office
(See Evansville)

Gray, Fleig and Biesterveld, (BV) ....105 N. 9th St.
Mahoney, Brian K., (CV) ....'62 '88 C.347 B.A. L.1119 J.D. [A Mahoney]
Mahoney, Russell E., (BV) ....'37 '73 C.347 B.S. L.1119 J.D. [Mahoney]
Mahoney Law Office, (BV) ....822 Main St.
Rauch, W. Wyatt ....'39 '68 C.210 B.A. L.1119 J.D. Ref., Pike Co. Cir. Ct.
Stratton, Marvin D. ....'35 '64 C.679 B.S. L.345 J.D. Cir. J.

PLAINFIELD, 18,396, *Hendricks Co.*

Black, Gregory W., (BV) ....'46 '75 C.532 B.A. L.117 J.D. [Black]
Black Law Office, The, (BV) ....1647A East Main
Bock, Tracy Heslin ... '64 '89 C.210 B.A. L.880 J.D. Contract Specialist, PSI Energy, Inc.
Bryant, Buffy M., Law Offices of '69 '98 C.210 B.A. L.347 J.D.
2312 Shadowbrook Drive
Burton, Robbyn E. '52 '81 C.679 B.A. L.472 J.D.
Sr. Atty., Colorado Interstate Gas Co.
Campbell, Chas. W. ....'15 '40 C&L.477 A.B., J.D. 625 Buchanan St.‡
Carpenter, Craig M. '68 '95 C&L.347 B.S., J.D.
Assoc. Gen. Coun. & Asst. Secy., Brightpoint, Inc.
Cavanaugh, Eric M., (AV) '54 '80 C.894 B.A. L.1187 J.D.
Sr. Coun., Cinergy Servs., Inc.
Gifford, Page E., (AV) ....'46 '75 C&L.347 A.B., J.D. Sr. Coun., Cinergy Corp.
Hardin, Paul T. ....'46 '72 C.347 B.S. L.1119 J.D. [Hardin]
Hardin Law Firm, (BV) ....10 S. East Street
Havens, Nancy G. ....'56 '88 C.679 B.S. L.345 J.D. Terry L. Dillon & Co., Inc.
Hesson, Larry R. ....'42 '78 C.347 A.B. L.345 J.D. Co. Councilman
Karn, Kelley ....'71 '00 C.602 B.A. L.345 J.D. Cinergy Servs., Inc.
Meyer, Douglas W., Law Offices of, (BV) '48 '74 C&L.347 A.B., J.D.
2312 East Main St.
Noland, Jon D., (AV) '38 '64 C.347 A.B. L.309 LL.B.
Exec. V.P. & Chf. Admin. Offr., PSI Energy, Inc.
Palmer, M. Dale, (BV) ....'32 '61 C.347 B.S. L.345 J.D. 201 W. Main St.‡
Pashos, Kay E. ....'59 '84 C.209 B.A. L.597 J.D. Sr. Coun., Cinergy Servs., Inc.
Pope, James R. ...... '48 '73 C.894 A.B. L.347 J.D. Cinergy Servs. Coun., Cinergy Servs.
Rosemary, Ralph, (BV) ....'24 '52 C.135 L.345 LL.B. 1203 E. Main St.
Scheidler, John B. ....'54 '79 C.63 B.S. L.345 J.D. Sr. Coun., Cinergy Servs., Inc.
Smith, Mark A. ....'67 '92 C&L.347 B.A., J.D. P.O. Box 445
Spence, Lori A. ....'63 '92 C&L.347 B.S.P.A., J.D. Sr. Coun., Cinergy Servs., Inc.
Valentine, Gail M. ....'65 '91 C.347 B.A. L.1119 J.D. [Valentine]
Valentine Law Office ..................P.O. Box 397

PLYMOUTH, * 9,840, *Marshall Co.*

Ballard, Richard, Attorney at Law
(See Knox)

Black, Tom A., Law Office of, (BV) ...... '54 '79 C&L.347 B.S., J.D. 110 W. Adams St.

Blackburn & Green
(See Fort Wayne)

Bowen, Robert O. ....'52 '77 C.347 B.S. L.879 J.D. Supr. Ct. J.
Bules, June E., (CV) ....'71 '98 C.879 B.A. L.347 J.D. 110 W. Adams St.
Burbrink, Roy D., (BV) ....'48 '76 C.347 A.B. L.477 J.D. 310 N. Michigan St.
Chipman, E. Nelson, Jr., (BV) ....'54 '81 C.347 B.S. L.879 J.D. City Atty. [Chipman]
Chipman, Eugene N. ....'27 '59 C.871 B.S. L.1119 J.D. Ret. Supr. Ct. J.
Chipman Law Offices, (BV) ..................P.O. Box 455
Clarke, R. Alexis ....'26 '51 L.500 LL.B. Ret. Supr. Ct. J.
Clevenger, James N., (BV) ....'52 '78 C.303 B.A. L.345 J.D. [Kizer&N.]
Colvin, Dean A. ....'52 '83 C.347 B.S. L.879 J.D. Supr. Ct. J.
Connolly, Mary Lou, (CV) ....'39 '91 C.630 B.A. L.879 J.D. [Shorter-Pifer&C.]
Cook, Michael D. ....'51 '78 C.347 B.S. L.879 J.D. Cir. J.
Derucki, Michael A. ....'63 '88 C.98 B.S. L.146 J.D. [© Stevens,T.F.&L.]

Doran • Blackmond LLP
(See South Bend)

Easterday, James E., (BV) ....'48 '73 C.347 B.S. L.1119 J.D. [Easterday&U.] ⊙
Easterday & Ummel, (BV) ....300 E. Jefferson St. (⊙Culver)
Fortin, William L., (AV) ....'38 '65 C.1024 B.A. L.424 J.D. [Stevens,T.F.&L.]
Gifford, Ronald D., (BV) ....'51 '76 C.20 B.A. L.245 J.D. [Kizer&N.]
Hite, Douglas N., (BV) ....'44 '72 C.347 B.S. L.345 J.D. 211 W. Jefferson St.
Holmes, David R., (BV) ....'43 '67 C.679 B.A. L.602 J.D. [Holmes&W.] (⊙Bremen)
Holmes & Walter, LLP, (BV) ....519 North Walnut Street (⊙Bremen, Nappanee)
Huff, Ralph R., (BV) ....'44 '78 C.347 A.B. L.879 J.D. [Jones H.&J.]
Humphrey, Jere L., (AV) ....'44 '72 C.63 B.S. L.347 J.D. [Kizer&N.]
Jones, Derek R., (CV) ....'71 '97 C.347 B.A. L.879 J.D. [Jones H.&J.]
Jones, Fred R., (AV) ....'42 '70 C.347 B.S. L.345 J.D. [Jones H.&J.]
Jones Huff & Jones, (AV) ....550 East Jefferson Street
Joyce, Richard F., (AV) ....'31 '61 C.347 B.S. L.345 J.D. [Kizer&N.] ‡

Kizer & Neu, LLP, (AV)
319 West Jefferson Street, P.O. Box 158, 46563 ⊙
Telephone: 574-936-2169 FAX: 574-936-2642
URL: http://www.kizerneu.com
Members of Firm: Marshall F. Kizer (1907-1988); James H. Neu (1917-1991); Richard F. Joyce (Retired); Harold L. Wyland; Jere L. Humphrey; Mark E. Wagner (Resident at Bremen); Ronald D. Gifford; James N. Clevenger; Anthony J. Wagner.
General Practice. Litigation and Trials in all Courts. Corporate, Labor and Employment, Wills and Probate, Trusts and Estates, Estate Planning, Administrative Law, Bankruptcy Law, Creditor's Rights.
Counsel for: 1st Source Bank; Bremen Castings, Inc.; Bornemann Products, Inc., all of Bremen, Indiana; Farm Credit Services.
Bremen, Indiana Office: 1406 West Plymouth Street, P.O. Box 158. Telephone: 574-546-2626. FAX: 574-546-2608.
See Professional Biographies, PLYMOUTH, INDIANA

LaTulip, Matthew D., Attorney at Law
(See Schererville)

Lukenbill, Kenneth H., (BV) ....'42 '69 C.347 A.B. L.345 J.D. [Stevens,T.F.&L.]
Morris, Joseph R., (BV) ....'65 '96 C.63 B.S. L.879 J.D. [Morris&R.]

Morris & Ruiz, P.C., (BV)
401 N. Center Street, 46563
Telephone: 574-935-9500 Fax: 574-935-9537
URL: http://www.lawyers.com/morrisandruiz
Joseph R. Morris; Edward R. Ruiz.
Business Transactions, Corporate Law, Bankruptcy, Litigation, Personal Injury, Domestic Relations, Criminal Law, Juvenile Law, Automobile Accidents, Driving While Intoxicated, Juvenile Criminal Law, Parole and Probation, Traffic Violations, White Collar Crimes.
See Professional Biographies, PLYMOUTH, INDIANA

Palmer, Curtis D., (BV) ....'59 '84 C.679 B.A. L.1119 J.D. Pros. Atty.
Rockaway, Peter L., (BV) ....'35 '67 C.95 A.B. L.912 J.D. 410 N. Plum St.
Roush, Roy Michael, Law Office of, (BV) '56 '81
C.347 B.S. L.1119 J.D. 315 W. Jefferson St.
Ruiz, Edward R. ....'69 '95 C.108 B.A. L.347 J.D. [Morris&R.]
Shorter-Pifer, Holli D., (CV) ....'57 '88 C.63 B.S. L.1187 J.D. [Shorter-Pifer&C.]
Shorter-Pifer & Connolly, P.C., (CV) ....308 E. Jefferson St.
Simanski, Joseph V., (BV) ....'52 '78 C.659 B.A. L.879 J.D. 211 W. Jefferson St.

Stevens, Travis, Fortin & Lukenbill, (AV)
119 West Garro Street, P.O. Box 517, 46563
Telephone: 574-936-4041 Fax: 574-936-3060
Email: stfl@kconline.com
Members of Firm: William L. Fortin; Kenneth H. Lukenbill. Of Counsel: Michael A. Derucki.
General Civil Practice. Real Estate, Wills and Probate, Trusts and Estates, Guardianships, Asset Protection. Estate Planning, Corporation and Insurance Litigation. Law.
See Professional Biographies, PLYMOUTH, INDIANA

Ummel, T. Edward, (BV) ....'55 '80 C.999 B.A. L.879 J.D. [Easterday&U.] ⊙
Wagner, Anthony J. ....'79 '04 C&L.602 B.A., J.D. [Kizer&N.]
Wyland, Harold L., (AV) ....'46 '73 C.347 B.S. L.345 J.D. [Kizer&N.]

PORTAGE, 33,496, *Porter Co.*

Back, Hollis E., Law Offices of, (CV) ...'39 '86 C.1109 B.A. L.426 J.D. 3437 Airport Rd.
Ballou, Benjamin T. ....'73 '99 C.145 B.A. L.879 J.D. [Hodges&D.] ⊙
Borns, Clarence, (AV) ....'31 '56 C.477 A.B. L.1119 LL.B. [Borns&S.]
Borns & Steele, P.C., Law Offices of, (AV) ....6037 Robbins Road
Coffee, Richard P., Sr. ....'45 '79 C.679 B.S. L.879 J.D. National Steel Corp.
Coleman, Bonnie C., (BV) ....'60 '84 C.694 A.B. L.879 J.D. [Hodges&D.] ⊙
Compton, Clyde D., (AV) ....'40 '65 C.210 B.A. L.1119 LL.B. [Hodges&D.] ⊙
Coons, Arnold A., Jr., (CV) ....'45 '72 C&L.879 B.A., J.D. 6382 Central Ave.
DuBois, David R., (CV) ....'38 '65 C.473 B.S. L.1119 LL.B. 2545 Portage Mall
Elwood, Kenneth B. ....'69 '94 C.347 B.S. L.879 J.D. [Rhame&E.]
Fleming, Randy K. ....'68 '93 C&L.879 B.A., J.D. [Sarkisian&F.]
Fletcher, R. Timothy ....'71 '03 C.346 B.S. L.879 J.D. [A Hodges&D.] ⊙
Frost, Laura B., (CV) ....'65 '91 C.340 B.A. L.879 J.D. [Hodges&D.] ⊙
Germann, Gary S., (AV) ....'48 '73 C.679 B.A. L.879 J.D. 3437 Airport Rd.
Handlon, Michael C., (BV) ....'52 '79 C.210 B.A. L.879 J.D. [Handlon&H.]
Handlon, Steven W., (BV) ....'45 '72 C.339 L.879 J.D. [Handlon&H.]
Handlon & Handlon, (BV) ....3207 Willowcreek Rd.
Hites, Earle F., (AV) ....'47 '72 C.347 B.S. L.879 J.D. [Hodges&D.] ⊙

Hodges & Davis, P.C., (AV)
6082 Lute Road, P.O. Box 1037, 46368 ⊙
Telephone: 219-762-9129 Fax: 219-762-2826
URL: http://www.hodgesdavis.com
Clyde D. Compton; Earle F. Hites; R. Lawrence Steele; Gregory A. Sobkowski; Bonnie C. Coleman; Laura B. Frost; Benjamin T. Ballou; David H. Kreider; R. Timothy Fletcher; Rebecca C. Hopkins.
General Civil Practice in all State and Federal Courts, Trials and Appeals, Insurance Defense, Corporation, Health and Hospital, Municipal and Zoning Law, Criminal, Driving While Intoxicated, Financing, Tax and Administrative Law. EEOC, Negligence, Products Liability, Environmental, Wills and Probate, Trusts and Estates, Estate Planning, Real Estate and Foreclosure Law. Consumer and Commercial Collections, Business Law, Business Planning, Business Litigation, Business Enterprises, Corporate, Partnerships, Small Business, Buying and Selling a Business, Business Start-Ups.
Representative Clients: The Methodist Hospitals, Inc.; City of Portage, Indiana; Portage Township Schools; Indiana-American Water Co.; Gary Steelheads; Vector Pipe Line Co.
Merrillville, Indiana Office: 8700 Broadway. Telephone: 219-641-8700. Fax: 219-641-8710.
See Professional Biographies, PORTAGE, INDIANA

Hopkins, Rebecca C. ....'54 '03 C.679 B.S. L.879 J.D. [A Hodges&D.] ⊙
Jent, Julia M. ....'47 '83 C.347 B.S. L.345 J.D. Supr. Ct. J.
Johnson, Susan Kelly, (CV) ....'58 '84 C.679 B.S. L.879 J.D. 6215 Central Ave.
Kravas, William C. ....'35 '62 C.347 B.S. L.1119 LL.B. 5894 Central Ave.‡
Kreider, David H., (BV) ....'41 '70 C.347 A.B. L.345 J.D. [Hodges&D.] ⊙
McClure, Scott R. ....'75 '01 C.347 B.A. L.209 J.D. [A Rhame&E.]
Mcnabnay, Gina M. Torreano ....'71 '96 C.475 B.A. L.347 J.D. Co. Pros. Off.
Melton, David B. ....'57 '95 [Vouga&M.]
Michael, Floyd D. .....'21 '49 C.265 A.B. L.345 J.D. 20 Sunset Trail, 418 Ogden Dunes‡
Moore, Roger T., Sr., (P.C.), (BV) ....'35 '66 C&L.879 B.A., LL.B. [Peters&M.]
Ostojic, Daniel ....'54 '80 C&L.879 B.A., J.D. 6287 Central Ave.
Peters, John W., (BV) ....'48 '74 C&L.879 B.S., J.D. [Peters&M.]
Peters & Moore, (BV) ....6195 Central Ave.

Rhame, John M., III, (BV) .... '47 '74 C.352 B.B.A. L.879 J.D. [Rhame&E.]
Rhame & Elwood, (BV) .... 2684 Willowcreek Road
Rice, Donald W., Law Offices of, (BV) '46 '72
C.347 B.S.B.A. L.879 J.D. 7108 Lenburg Rd.
Rodin, Carl O. .... '31 '58 C.103 A.B. L.145 J.D. 2664 Willowcreek Rd.
Sampson, Walter W., Jr. .... '36 '61 C.210 A.B. L.597 J.D. Ogden Dunes
Sarkisian, Gregory J. .... '49 '75 C.347 B.S. L.879 J.D. [Sarkisian&F.]
Sarkisian & Fleming .... 6165 Central Avenue
Shanahan, John P., (BV) .... '55 '85 C.347 B.A. L.879 J.D. [Rhame&E.]
Sobkowski, Gregory A., (BV) .... '57 '82 C&L.602 B.A., J.D. [Hodges&D.] ⊙
Steele, J. Brian, (CV) .... '69 '94 C.679 B.A. L.61 J.D. [Borns&S.]
Steele, R. Lawrence, (AV) .... '47 '74 C.347 B.S. L.345 J.D. [Hodges&D.] ⊙
Steere, Kimberly Sue .... '71 '97 C&L.879 B.S., J.D. Dep. Pros. Atty.
Studtmann, Earl I., (CV) .... '32 '75 C&L.879 J.D. 6289 Central Ave.
Suarez, William S., (BV) .... '35 '58 2588 Portage Mall
Sullivan, Timothy F., Jr. '40 '74 C.209 B.A. L.365 J.D.
(adm. in IL; not adm. in IN) 5335 Tulip‡
Thode, Jeffrey L. .... '60 '85 C&L.879 B.A., J.D. 3560 Willowcreek Road
Thomas, Joseph N., (AV) .... '29 '54 C.347 B.S. L.309 LL.B. 2999 McCool Rd.‡
Vega, Robert .... '40 '78 C.347 B.S. L.879 J.D. 6195 Central Ave.‡
Vouga, John M. .... '63 '87 C.294 B.A. L.879 J.D. [Vouga&M.]
Vouga & Melton .... 3363 Willowcreek Road
Williford, Margaret A. .... '52 '78 C.249 B.A. L.1119 J.D. [Handlon&H.]
Willis, Russell A., (AV) .... '22 '48 C.347 B.A. L.1119 LL.B. 2576 Portage Mall

Zemaitis, Aimee C. '76 '02 C.679 B.A. L.879 J.D.
3437 Airport Road, 46368
Telephone: 219-764-7172 Fax: 219-763-0519
Email: aczlaw@hotmail.com
Personal Injury, Family Law, Wills, Trusts and Estates, Business Law, Traffic Violations.
See Professional Biographies, PORTAGE, INDIANA

PORTER, 4,972, *Porter Co.*

Iatarola, Nancy S. .... '58 '94 C.350 B.S. L.352 J.D. 371 Spring View Ct.
Martin, James P. '26 '59 C.602 A.B. L.424 J.D.
(adm. in IL; not adm. in IN) 2915 Dudley Dr.‡
Tilden, Cynthia A., (CV) .... '65 '91 C&L.879 B.A., J.D. 130 Lincoln St., Ste. 3

PORTLAND, * 6,483, *Jay Co.*

BDMP Wealth Management .... 100 Middle Street

Blackburn & Green
(See Fort Wayne)

Bright, William D. .... '55 '80 C.63 B.S. L.345 J.D. [Ludy&B.] ‡
Burkett, Bradley K., (CV) .... '55 '84 C.63 B.S. L.345 J.D. 120 N. Commerce St.
Clamme, Robert A., (BV) .... '45 '73 C.63 B.S. L.345 J.D. [Hinkle,R.L.&C.]
Coldren, John E., (BV) .... '44 '69 C.432 B.S. L.1119 J.D. [Coldren&F.]
Coldren & Frantz, (AV) .... 112 1/2 N. Meridian St.
Diller, Tom D. '45 '81 C.347 B.S.B.A. L.1119 J.D.
(adm. in OH; not adm. in IN) Cir. Ct. J.
Frantz, Philip A., (AV) .... '44 '69 C.432 B.A. L.1119 J.D. [Coldren&F.]

Gonzalez, Jill A., Attorney At Law
(See Muncie)

Hinkle, William W., (BV) .... '46 '71 C.347 B.S. L.1119 J.D. [Hinkle,R.L.&C.]

Hinkle, Racster, Lopez & Clamme, Professional Corporation, (AV)
121 West High Street, 47371
Telephone: 260-726-8104 Fax: 260-726-9113
Email: hrl@jayco.net
Wayne W. Hinkle (1906-2000); Lon R. Racster; William W. Hinkle; George O. Lopez; Robert A. Clamme.
General Civil Practice. Corporation, Probate and Estate Planning, Personal Injury and Real Estate Law. Trial and Appellate Practice, Family/Domestic Relations, Collections. Mediation.
Counsel for: The First National Bank of Portland; American States Insurance Co.; Westfield Insurance Co.; Hartford Accident & Indemnity Co.; Indiana Glass Co.; Kerr Glass Manufacturing Corp.; Teledyne-Portland Forge; City of Dunkirk.
See Professional Biographies, PORTLAND, INDIANA

Hutchison, Brian D. .... '62 '95 C.63 B.S. L.345 J.D. Cir.J.
Kohler, Barry L. .... '47 '74 C.659 B.A. L.188 J.D. [BDMP W.M.]
Lopez, George O., (BV) .... '54 '79 C.973 B.S. L.1340 J.D. [Hinkle,R.L.&C.]
Ludy, Max C., Jr., (BV) .... '53 '79 C.827 A.B. L.345 J.D. [Ludy&B.]
Ludy & Bright, (BV) .... 123 North Meridian Street
Meeker, J. Gordon .... '10 '34 C&L.345 1333 S. Meridian‡
Racster, Lon R., (AV) .... '42 '67 C.347 A.B. L.1119 J.D. [Hinkle,R.L.&C.]
Roberts, Joel D. .... '46 '74 C.701 B.S.C.E. L.345 J.D. Supr. Ct. J.

POSEYVILLE, 1,089, *Posey Co.*

Bamberger, Foreman, Oswald and Hahn, LLP, (AV)
178 South Lockwood (⊙Evansville, Indianapolis, Princeton)
Bender, William, (BV) .... '55 '80 C.679 B.S. L.345 J.D. 39 W. Main Street
Broadhead, John P., (AV) '56 '81
C.249 B.S. L.345 J.D. [Bamberger,F.O.&H.] (⊙Evansville)

PRINCETON, * 8,127, *Gibson Co.*

Ankenbrand, George, (BV) .... '42 '68 C.531 B.A. L.1119 J.D. Pros. Atty.
Ballard & Reeves, A Prof. Corp., (BV) .... 116 S. Main

Bamberger, Foreman, Oswald and Hahn, LLP, (AV)
302 N. Prince Street, 47670 ⊙
Telephone: 812-386-6482 Fax: 812-386-6480
Email: info@bamberger.com URL: http://www.bamberger.com
Member of Firm: Jerry D. Stilwell (Resident).
Administrative Law, Antitrust Law, Appellate Practice, Arbitration, Banking Law, Bankruptcy Law, Business Law, Civil Rights, Civil Trial Practice, Commercial Law, Commercial Litigation, Communications Law, Construction Law, Corporate Law, Creditors' Rights, Elder Law, Energy Law, Environmental Law, Health Care Law, Insurance Defense, Intellectual Property Law, Labor and Employment Law, Land Use Law, Medical Malpractice, Mergers and Acquisitions, Product Liability Law, Public Utilities Law, Real Estate Law, Trademark, Copyright and Unfair Competition, Trusts and Estates, Wills and Probate.
Representative Clients: Aetna Life and Casualty Group; AT&T; CNB Bancshares Inc.; Dow Chemical Co.; Medical Protective Insurance Co.; Southern Indiana Gas and Electric Co.; St. Mary's Medical Center of Evansville, Inc.; State Farm Mutual Automobile Insurance Co.; Travelers Insurance Co.; Welborn Clinic/HMO.
Evansville, Indiana Office: 20 NW Fourth Street, Suite 708, 47708. Telephone: 812-425-1591. Fax: 812-421-4936.
Indianapolis, Indiana Office: Market Tower, Suite 2950, 10 West Market Street, 46204. Telephone: 317-464-1591. Fax: 317-464-1592. Toll Free: 888-994-7976.
Mt. Vernon, Indiana Office: 309 Main Street, 47620. Telephone: 812-838-4495. Fax: 812-838-9445.
Poseyville, Indiana Office: 178 South Lockwood, 47633. Telephone: 812-874-3365. Fax: 812-874-3366.
See Professional Biographies, PRINCETON, INDIANA

Clutter, Anna Devoy, (CV) .... '— '96 C.74 B.S. L.879 J.D. Dep.Pros.
Fair, Nixon & Nixon .... 223 West State Street

Hall, Partenheimer & Kinkle, (AV) BR
219 North Hart Street, P.O. Box 13, 47670
Telephone: 812-386-0050 FAX: 812-385-2575
Email: hpk@insightbb.com URL: http://www.hpklawyers.com
Members of Firm: Verner P. Partenheimer; J. Robert Kinkle.
General Civil Practice. Personal Injury, Probate and Estate Planning, Real Estate, Mining, Oil and Gas and Corporate Law, Municipal Law, Trials.
Representative Clients: Interlake Inc.; Fifth Third Bank; Old National Bank; East Gibson School Corporation; Union Planters National Bank; United Federal Savings Bank; Amax Minerals; Wheeler Oil; Gibson County Asbtract and Title Co., Inc.
Approved Attorneys for: Lawyers Title Insurance; National Attorneys Title Fund and Stewart Title.
See Professional Biographies, PRINCETON, INDIANA

Hart Bell LLC
(See Vincennes)

Hicks, John C. .... '38 '71 C.333 B.S. L.347 J.D. 102 N. Main St.
Higginbotham, C. Dean, (BV) .... '47 '83 C.679 B.A. L.1119 J.D. [Higginbotham]

Higginbotham Law Office, (BV)
208 East State Street, 47670
Telephone: 812-386-3040; 812-386-3041 Fax: 812-386-7306
Email: higglaw@gibsoncounty.net URL: http://www.higglaw.com
C. Dean Higginbotham.
Civil and Criminal Litigation, Real Estate, Commercial Law, Probate, Family, Divorce, Custody, Separation Agreements, Personal Injury, Oil and Gas, Collections.
See Professional Biographies, PRINCETON, INDIANA

Kahn, Dees, Donovan & Kahn, LLP
(See Evansville)

Kinkle, J. Robert, (BV) .... '44 '69 C.347 A.B. L.1119 J.D. [Hall,P.&K.]
Krieg, Dale F. .... '51 '00 C.927 B.A. L.345 J.D. R.R. 1
Krieg, Robert D. .... '70 '96 C&L.347 B.A., J.D. 1808 Taylor Ave.
Marshall, William J., (AV) .... '33 '61 C.603 B.S. L.1119 J.D. Chf. Dep. Pros. Atty.
McDonald, James G., III, (BV) .... '60 '87 C.346 B.S. L.879 J.D. [McDonald&M.]
McDonald, James G., Jr., (BV) .... '31 '62 C.894 A.B. L.30 J.D. [McDonald&M.]
McDonald and McDonald, (BV) .... 120 South Main Street
Moody, Lisa A. .... '71 '96 C.999 B.A. L.879 J.D. 102 N. Main Street, Ste. 100
Nixon, L. Matthew .... '72 '99 C.347 B.A. L.879 J.D. [Fair,N.&N.]
Partenheimer, Verner P., (AV) .... '36 '60 C.347 A.B. L.1119 LL.B. [Hall,P.&K.]
Penrod, Earl G. .... '55 '80 C&L.421 A.B., J.D. Supr. Ct. J.
Reeves, Dan L., (BV) .... '42 '73 C.249 B.A. L.345 J.D. [Ballard&R.]
Rehnquist, George R., (BV) .... '42 '69 C.210 B.A. L.347 J.D. 230 W. Bway.

Rudolph, Fine, Porter & Johnson LLP
(See Evansville)

Stilwell, Jerry D., (AV) '44 '72
C.603 A.B. L.345 J.D. [Bamberger,F.O.&H.] (⊙Mt. Vernon)
Stone, Leon C., (BV) .... '42 '71 C.894 B.A. L.345 J.D. 222-224 W. Broadway
Wallace, William R., III, (CV) .... '53 '91 C.999 B.S. L.607 J.D. 630 S. Hall St.
Werne, Sharon H., (BV) .... '54 '93 C.346 B.S. L.347 J.D. Off. of Dep. Pros.
Whitehead, Steven L., (AV) .... '54 '82 C.346 B.S. L.1340 J.D. 111 N. Hart

REMINGTON, 1,247, *Jasper Co.*

Casey, John T.
(See Rensselaer)

O'Neall, Michael D., (BV) .... '44 '69 C.679 B.A. L.1119 J.D. 43 South Ohio

RENSSELAER, * 5,294, *Jasper Co.*

Ballard, Richard, Attorney at Law
(See Knox)

Beaver, James R., (BV) .... '41 '68 C.347 A.B. L.1119 J.D. [Halleck&B.]

Blackburn & Green
(See Fort Wayne)

Blaney, Daniel C. .... '45 '70 217 E. Washington St.

Casey, John T., (BV) '46 '72 C.210 B.A. L.1119 J.D.
217 East Washington Street, 47978
Telephone: 219-866-4656 Fax: 219-866-4219
Civil Litigation, Administrative Law, Probate, Estate Planning, Real Estate.
See Professional Biographies, RENSSELAER, INDIANA

Comingore, Richard F. .... '50 '97 C.679 B.S. L.879 J.D. P.O. Box 223
Daugherty, E. Duane .... '35 '68 C.231 B.A. L.1119 J.D. Cir. J.
Dumas, Edward P., (AV) .... '51 '76 C.686 B.A. L.879 J.D. [Dumas,W.&M.] ⊙

Dumas, Weist & Mahnesmith, (AV)
119 West Harrison Street, 47978 ⊙
Telephone: 219-866-4158 FAX: 219-866-2274
Email: edd@nwiis.com URL: http://www.dumas-moriarty.com
Thomas B. Dumas (1918-1998); William J. Moriarty, Jr. (1939-1993). Members of Firm: Edward P. Dumas; William B. Weist (Resident, Fowler, Indiana Office); Kent E. Mahnesmith.
General Civil and Criminal Trial Practice. Personal Injury, Wills and Probate, Trusts and Estates, Estate Planning, Corporate, Municipal and Zoning Law, Elder Law, Medicaid Planning.
Representative Clients: First of America Bank-Rensselaer; Demotte State Bank; St. Joseph's College; Schumacher Electric Corp.; Jasper County Hospital; Jasper County Public Library; Jasper County Abstract Company; West Central School Corp.; Kankakee Valley School Corp.; Rensselaer Central Schools Corp.
Fowler, Indiana Office: Weist Building, P.O. Box 101, 47944-0101. Telephone: 765-884-1840. Fax: 765-884-8450.
See Professional Biographies, RENSSELAER, INDIANA

Halleck & Beaver P.C., (BV) .... 201 West Washington Street
Lakin, James R., (BV) .... '52 '77 C.63 B.S. L.607 J.D. 119 1/2 N. Cullen St.

Lambert, Michael
(See Crown Point)

LaTulip, Matthew D., Attorney at Law
(See Schererville)

Mahnesmith, Kent E., (BV) .... '66 '93 C.344 B.S. L.879 J.D. [Dumas,W.&M.] ⊙
McGraw, John P. .... '44 '73 C.1024 B.S. L.879 J.D. Supr. Ct. J.
Nesbitt, John R. (Jack) .... '34 '58 C.679 B.S.E.E. L.347 J.D. [Nesbitt] (Pat.)
Nesbitt Law Firm .... 116 North Front Street (Pat.)
O'Brien, Richard M. .... '47 '92 C.174 B.S. L.421 J.D. 122 W. Washington Street
O'Neall, Kathryn B., (BV) .... '48 '75 C.347 B.A. L.345 J.D. Chf. Dep. Pros. Atty.
Potter, John D. .... '69 '96 C.346 B.A. L.1119 J.D. [J.Potter]
Potter, John, Law Office .... 219 W. Harrison St., Ste. 5
Randle, Robert .... '42 '68 C.303 B.A. L.347 J.D. 205 W. Washington St.
Riley, Michael, (BV) .... '39 '65 C.346 A.B. L.345 J.D. 122 W. Washington St.
Riley, Patricia Woodworth, (BV) ... '49 '74 C.347 B.A. L.345 J.D. 122 W. Washington St.

Shelmon, Donald W., (BV) .... '55 '81 C.435 B.S. L.607 J.D. 119 1/2 N. Cullen St.
Tonner, Ned J. .... '60 '86 C.347 B.S. L.862 J.D. [N.Tonner]

Tonner, Ned, Attorney at Law
203 N. Cullen Street, 47978
Telephone: 219-866-8888 Fax: 219-866-0474
Email: ned@tonnerlaw.com URL: http://www.lawyers.com/tonnerlaw
Ned J. Tonner.
Personal Injury, Criminal Law, Estates, Trusts, Real Estate, Divorce, Family Law.
See Professional Biographies, RENSSELAER, INDIANA

Walton, Earl D., (BV) .... '38 '85 C.679 B.S. L.879 J.D. 217 East Washington Street
Weist, William B., (AV) .... '38 '71 C.602 B.B.A. L.421 J.D. [Dumas,W.&M.]

RICHMOND, * 39,124, *Wayne Co.*

Allen • Wellman • McNew
(See Greenfield)

Anderson, Edw. N. .... '27 '53 C.231 A.B. L.347 J.D. Town Atty.
Arnold, Jeffrey T., (CV) .... '61 '93 C.347 B.S. L.879 J.D. 101 1/2 South Fourth Street
Beane, Darrell M. .... '33 '72 C.231 B.A. L.150 J.D. 1401 Chester Boulevard
Bever, Robert L., (BV) .... '53 '78 C.210 B.A. L.345 J.D. [Boston,B.K.C.&C.]
Blair, April .... '77 '03 C.275 B.A. L.1119 J.D. [Ⓐ Gardner,S.&W.]
Boston, Richard E., (BV) .... '46 '71 C.347 B.S. L.1119 J.D. [Boston,B.K.C.&C.]

Boston, Bever, Klinge, Cross & Chidester, (AV)
27 North Eighth Street, 47374-3028
Telephone: 765-962-7527 Fax: 765-966-4597
Email: bbkcc@infocom.com
Members of Firm: John M. Harlan (Retired); Richard E. Boston; Robert L. Bever; Kent G. Klinge; Ronald L. Cross; Walter S. Chidester; Douglas B. Oler. Associate: J. Clayton Miller. Of Counsel: Terry O'Maley.
General Civil, Trial and Appellate Practice, Banking, Business, Commercial, Corporations, Creditors' Rights, Criminal, Family and Domestic Relations, Insurance, Personal Injury, Probate and Estate Planning, Real Estate and Zoning Law.
Representative Clients: City of Richmond; Richmond Community Schools; Northeastern Wayne Schools; Eaton National Bank & Trust Co.; First Bank, Richmond N.A.; Crown Chrysler, Inc.; Fred First Ford, Inc.; PSI Energy (local counsel); Wayne County Health Dept.; Carpenter's Excavating, Inc.
See Professional Biographies, RICHMOND, INDIANA

Bowen, Willard G., (AV) .... '21 '49 C.608 B.S.B.A. L.477 J.D. P.O. Box 818
Brown, Edward E. '42 '76 C&L.347 A.B., J.D.
(adm. in VA; not adm. in IN) Asst. Prof., Criminal Jus., Indiana Univ. E.
Burton, David J., (BV) .... '66 '92 C.477 A.B. L.347 J.D. [Burton&S.]
Burton, Robert G., (AV) .... '37 '63 C.347 A.B. L.477 J.D. [Burton&S.]

Burton and Simkin, (AV)
25 North 7th Street, 47374-3088
Telephone: 765-966-5518 Fax: 765-966-5510
Email: dburton@infocom.com URL: http://www.lawyers.com/burton&simkin
Members of Firm: Robert G. Burton; Donald L. Simkin; David J. Burton.
Personal Injury, Medical Malpractice, Wrongful Death, Civil Trial Practice, Criminal Trial Practice, Real Estate, Family and Domestic Relations, Driving While Intoxicated, Business, Corporate, Employment, Probate and Estate Planning, Bankruptcy, Traffic Violations, Real Estate.
Representative Clients: Furnished Upon Request.
References: Firstar Bank, Richmond; West End Savings Bank, Richmond.
See Professional Biographies, RICHMOND, INDIANA

Cecere, Andrew C., (AV) .... '22 '49 C.207 A.B. L.477 J.D. Kings Row‡
Chidester, Walter S., (BV) .... '46 '78 C.313 A.B. L.221 J.D. [Boston,B.K.C.&C.]
Cross, Ronald L., (AV) .... '47 '76 C.347 B.A. L.345 J.D. [Boston,B.K.C.&C.]

Davis, James E., Attorney at Law
(See Greenfield)

Delaney, Robert J., (CV) .... '41 '67 C.347 A.B. L.1119 LL.B. [Williams,D.&S.]
Dennis & Vertesch, (AV) .... 111 S. 7th St.
Dilworth, Keith, (BV) .... '43 '72 C.63 B.S. L.1119 J.D. P.O. Box 1005
Dolehanty, Darrin, (CV) .... '63 '92 C&L.347 B.S., J.D. Chf. Dep. Pros.
Dyer, Garofalo, Mann & Schultz, A Legal Professional Association, (AV)
3733 National Road East (⊙Bellefontaine, Dayton, Huber Heights, Lima, Middletown, Piqua, Springfield, Troy, Wilmington, Xenia, OH)
English, Jodie Ann, (BV) .... '54 '79 C.674 B.A. L.588 J.D. 117 S. 7th St.
Gardner, Gayle W., (AV) .... '38 '64 C.231 A.B. L.1119 LL.B. [Gardner,S.&W.] ‡

Gardner, Sayre & Weikart, (AV)
Two North Eighth, Third Floor, 47374-3090
Telephone: 765-966-6688 FAX: 765-966-6618
Email: gswinlaw@aol.com
Members of Firm: Alonzo M. Gardner (1886-1941); Wilfred Jessup (1900-1944); Frank K. Chambers (1938-1955); Floyd W. Gardner (1933-1965); John R. Harrington (1907-1999); Clifford M. Haworth (1923-1967); Gayle W. Gardner (Retired); John M. Sayre, III; Kirk A. Weikart;—April Blair.
General Civil and Trial Practice. Corporation, Probate and Estate Planning, Real Estate, Personal Injury and Commercial Transactions.
General Counsel for: First National Bank and Trust; Dunn Mental Health Center, Inc.; Richmond Housing Authority; The Recycling Center, Inc.; Freedom Title Company, Inc.; Milso Industries.
Local Counsel for: Gannett News Service; CIGNA.
See Professional Biographies, RICHMOND, INDIANA

Harlan, John M., (AV) .... '15 '42 C.231 L.347 LL.B. [Boston,B.K.C.&C.] ‡
Hoelscher, William C. .... '51 '77 C.63 B.S. L.200 J.D. Supr. Ct. J.
Horn, Gregory A. .... '54 '80 C.347 A.B. L.345 J.D. Supr. Ct. J.
Hunyadi, Stephen L., Attorney at Law, (BV) '50 '76 C.231 A.B. L.879 J.D.
244 S. 5th St.
Hyde, Charles R., Jr., (BV) .... '55 '82 C.63 B.S. L.201 J.D. 2203 E. Main
Jarecki, Amy A. .... '63 '91 C&L.347 B.S., J.D. 527 W. Main St.
Kehoe, D. Bruce, (AV) ... '50 '80 C.347 B.S. L.345 J.D. [Wilson,K.&W.] (⊙Indianapolis)
Kemp, E. Thomas, (BV) .... '67 '94 C.231 B.A. L.345 J.D. 111 S. 7th St.
Kemper, Kim Ray '55 '81 C.201 B.S. L.150 J.D.
(adm. in OH; not adm. in IN) Star Bk., N.A. East
Kleinknecht, Richard B., (AV) .... '15 '39 C.231 L.893 LL.B. 10 N. 7th St.‡
Klinge, Kent G., (BV) .... '39 '68 C.303 A.B. L.1119 J.D. [Boston,B.K.C.&C.]
Knoll, Kolger, Sowers & Metzger, (BV) .... 111 S. 7th St.
Kolger, Karl J., (BV) .... '24 '57 C.231 A.B. L.345 J.D. [Knoll,K.S.&M.]
Maley, Robert J., (AV) .... '30 '55 C&L.602 B.S., J.D. 43 S. Eighth
Martin, Edward O., Law Office, (CV) ... '68 '94 C.339 B.S. L.879 J.D. 3869 Elizabeth St.
Mendenhall, Paul S., (AV) .... '05 '31 C.210 A.B. L.477 J.D. 10 N. 7th St.‡
Metzger, Bruce D., (BV) .... '55 '81 C.347 B.A. L.345 J.D. [Knoll,K.S.&M.]
Miller, J. Clayton .... '71 '00 C.1119 B.S. L.221 J.D. [Ⓐ Boston,B.K.C.&C.]
Milligan, Thomas S., (BV) .... '34 '59 C.679 B.S. L.976 LL.B. [Reller,P.&M.]
Oler, Douglas B., (BV) .... '40 '65 C.210 A.B. L.477 J.D. [Boston,B.K.C.&C.]
O'Maley, Robert L., (AV) .... '24 '50 C.347 B.A. L.345 J.D. [O'Maley&O.]
O'Maley, Terry, (BV) .... '54 '80 C.347 B.S. L.1119 J.D. [Ⓒ Boston,B.K.C.&C.]
O'Maley & O'Maley, P.C., (AV) .... 34 S. 7th St.
Puckett, James C., (AV) .... '31 '57 C.231 B.A. L.145 J.D. [Reller,P.&M.]
Pyle, Ronald G. .... '41 '79 C.98 B.S. L.339 J.D. F.B.I.
Quigg, James R., Jr. '33 '58
C.473 B.S. L.1119 J.D. Chmn. of the Bd., Richmond Baking Co.
Reinke, Robert L. .... '33 '58 C.894 A.B. L.145 J.D. Supr. Ct. J.‡
Reller, George R., (AV) .... '24 '52 C.231 A.B. L.477 LL.B. [Reller,P.&M.]
Reller, William H., (AV) .... '19 '47 C.821 A.B. L.477 LL.B. 10 N. 7th St.
Reller, Puckett & Milligan, (AV) .... 10 N. 7th St., Ste. 601
Sayre, John M., III, (AV) .... '40 '65 C.210 B.A. L.1119 LL.B. [Gardner,S.&W.]
Seal, Christine M. .... '54 '83 C.63 B.A. L.345 J.D. 245 S. 4th St.
Simkin, Donald L., (BV) .... '49 '74 C&L.347 B.S., J.D. [Burton&S.]
Simkin, Lawrence M., (CV) .... '41 '69 C.347 B.S. L.1119 J.D. [Williams,D.&S.]
Snow, P. Thomas .... '47 '72 C.63 B.S. L.347 J.D. Supr. Ct. J.
Sowers, George M., (BV) .... '44 '69 C.347 A.B. L.893 LL.B. [Knoll,K.S.&M.]

Thompson Law Office
(See Connersville)

Van Middlesworth, Doug .... '42 '76 C.347 B.A. L.345 J.D. Cir. J.
Vertesch, Paul F., (AV) .... '37 '65 C.347 B.S. L.1119 J.D. [Dennis&V.]
Weikart, Kirk A., (BV) .... '62 '87 C.1051 B.S. L.1119 J.D. [Gardner,S.&W.]
Williams, Clyde, Jr., (CV) .... '39 '67 C.369 B.A. L.329 LL.B. [Williams,D.&S.]
Williams, Delaney & Simkin, (CV) .... 48 S. 7th S.

Wilson, Kehoe & Winingham, (AV)
2901 East Main Street, 47374 ⊙
Telephone: 765-962-9113
Email: mailbox@wkw.com URL: http://www.wkw.com
D. Bruce Kehoe.
Civil Trial Practice in State and Federal Courts. Aviation, Medical Legal, Personal Injury, Product Liability, Medical Malpractice, Wrongful Death.
Reference: Fifth Third Bank.
Indianapolis, Indiana Office: 2859 North Meridian, 46208. Telephone: 317-920-6400. Fax: 317-920-6405.
Muncie, Indiana Office: 3620 N. Everbrook Lane, Suite A, 47304. Telephone: 765-284-2474.
See Professional Biographies, RICHMOND, INDIANA

Wissel, Nancy Gardner '53 '78 C.679 B.A. L.347 J.D.
Staff Atty., Primex Plastics Corp.
Wynegar, Jane .... '45 '70 C.231 B.A. L.1119 J.D. 8 South 8th Street, Suite 15
Yim, Edward C. .... '71 '96 C.1494 B.A. L.201 J.D. [Ⓐ Dyer,G.M.&S.] (⊙Dayton, OH)

RISING SUN, * 2,470, *Ohio Co.*

Guidroz, Elaine L. '77 '03 C.575 B.A. L.345 J.D.
In-House Coun., Grand Victoria Casino & Resort
Hemmerle, Mark David '64 '92 C.150 B.A. L.208 J.D.
Asst. Gen. Mgr. & Gen Coun., Grand Victoria Casino & Resort by Hyatt
Holland, Theressa Maria .... '63 '92 C.1161 B.A. L.1340 J.D. P.O. Box 82
Mitchell, John D. .... '37 '69 C.894 A.B. L.345 J.D. Supr. Ct. J.
Sabo, Anthony J., (CV) .... '66 '93 C.347 B.A. L.585 J.D. 108 N. High St.
Siekman, Lane A., (CV) .... '60 '91 C.63 B.S. L.1119 J.D. 110 S. High St.

ROANOKE, 1,495, *Huntington Co.*

Bendall, Theodore L., (AV) .... '39 '64 C.20 A.B. L.477 J.D. [Bendall D.H.M.&R.] ⊙
Bendall DeLaney Hartburg McNeely & Roth LLP, (AV)
Trustcorp Bank Bldg. (⊙Huntington, Warren)
Hughes, Lisa M. .... '80 '04 C.679 B.S. L.879 J.D. [Ⓐ Bendall D.H.M.&R.] ⊙

ROCHESTER, * 6,414, *Fulton Co.*

Blackburn & Green
(See Fort Wayne)

Brown, Lawrence M., (AV) .... '22 '49 C.108 L.1119 LL.B. 227 E. 9th St.
Brown, Richard A., (BV) .... '54 '79 C.879 B.S. L.347 J.D. Pros. Atty.
Burke, Alan D., (BV) .... '48 '73 C&L.602 B.B.A., J.D. 113 E. 10th St.
Delworth, John J., Jr. .... '26 '55 C&L.879 A.B., J.D. Ret. Co. J.
Heller, Gregory L. .... '60 '98 C.347 B.S. L.1119 J.D. 113 E. Tenth St.

Morris & Ruiz, P.C.
(See Plymouth)

Morton, Douglas B. .... '46 '71 C.894 B.A. L.228 J.D. Cir. J.
Perkins, T. Andrew .... '74 '01 C.894 B.A. L.345 J.D. [Ⓐ Peterson&W.]
Peterson, Robert E., (AV) .... '30 '64 C.679 B.S. L.1119 J.D. [Peterson&W.]
Peterson & Waggoner, LLP, (AV) .... 125 East Tenth Street
Rakestraw, Frederick E., (AV) .... '23 '49 C.347 A.B. L.1119 J.D. 227 E. 9th St.‡
Tombaugh, Wendell C. .... '15 '40 C.347 B.S. L.345 J.D. Ret. Cir. Ct. J.‡
Tyler, Keith W. .... '10 '36 C.477 A.B. L.1119 LL.B. 2207 Westside Dr.‡
Waggoner, Ted A., (BV) .... '53 '78 C.346 B.S. L.1119 J.D. [Peterson&W.]
Wells, Christine J. .... '46 '75 C.108 B.A. L.347 J.D. [Wells]
Wells, James O., Jr., (BV) .... '27 '65 C.231 B.A. L.879 J.D. [Wells]
Wells Law Office, P.C., (BV) .... 228 West Ninth Street

ROCKPORT, * 2,160, *Spencer Co.*

Ayer, Eric K., (BV) .... '46 '73 C.500 B.A. L.421 J.D. [Wagoner,A.&H.]
Dartt, Angela L. .... '68 '94 C.1119 B.A. L.345 J.D. Pros. Off.
Dartt, Jon A. .... '66 '91 C&L.347 B.A., J.D. Spencer Co. Pros. Atty. Off.
Hargis, John A., (BV) .... '44 '69 C.347 A.B. L.1119 J.D. [Wagoner,A.&H.]

Kahn, Dees, Donovan & Kahn, LLP
(See Evansville)

Lindsey, Jefferson A., (BV) .... '55 '81 C.347 B.S. L.1119 J.D. [Lindsey&L.]
Lindsey, Sidney R., (BV) .... '24 '53 C.347 B.S. L.421 LL.B. [Lindsey&L.]
Lindsey & Lindsey, (BV) .... 217 Main St.

Robinson, Jack R., (BV) '39 '66 C.347 A.B. L.1119 J.D.
122 South Third Street, P.O. Box 61, 47635
Telephone: 812-649-5011 Fax: 812-649-5012
General Civil Practice, Elder Law, Probate and Estate Planning, Real Estate, Social Security Disability, Bankruptcy and Municipal Law.

Roell, Wayne A. .... '49 '75 C.249 B.A. L.880 J.D. Cir. J.
Wagoner, Ayer & Hargis, (BV) .... 104 S. 3rd St.
Wetherill, Richard A., (BV) .... '46 '70 C.384 A.B. L.192 J.D. 215 Main St.

ROCKVILLE, * 2,706, *Parke Co.*

Asbury, John L., (BV) .... '53 '78 C.894 B.A. L.345 J.D. 114 N. Jefferson
Brown, Ronda R. .... '63 '89 C.346 B.S. L.879 J.D. Cir. J.
Bruner, James A., (CV) .... '56 '82 C.347 B.A. L.345 J.D. 203 1/2 W. High St.
Cvengros, Steve A., (CV) .... '69 '95 C.894 B.A. L.347 J.D. 205 W. High St.
Dowd, Earl M. .... '21 '58 C.894 A.B. L.345 LL.B. Cir. J.
Esteil, Julie A. .... '69 '93 C.739 B.A. L.74 J.D. RR 2 Box 325A
Hanner, Clelland J., (AV) .... '18 '48 C.346 B.S. L.602 J.D. [Hanner,H.&H.]
Hanner, Gary G., (BV) .... '56 '81 C.894 B.A. L.345 J.D. [Hanner,H.&H.]

Hanner, James O., (BV) ....'52 '77 C.894 B.A. L.345 J.D. [Hanner,H.&H.]
Hanner, Hanner and Hanner, (AV) ....Old Parke State Bank Building
Kenley, John R., (BV) ....'31 '71 C&L.347 B.S., J.D. Co. Atty.
Tarvin, Lee T., (BV) ....'44 '78 C.1081 B.S. L.345 J.D. P.O. Box 308

ROLLING PRAIRIE, 550, *La Porte Co.*

Loughnane, John P. ....'43 '91 C.801 B.A. L.879 J.D. 5455 E. 300 N.

ROME CITY, 1,615, *Noble Co.*

Stephens, Jeffrey J. .... '68 '98 C.679 B.A. L.879 J.D. 401 Kerr Island

RUSHVILLE, * 5,995, *Rush Co.*

Ault, Kevin W., Law Office of ....'58 '85 C.347 B.S. L.345 J.D. 127 W. Second St.
Badell, Patrick C. .... '44 '75 C.1070 B.S. L.345 J.D. 110 N. Perkins
Clarkson, C. Jack, (AV) .... '30 '59 C.108 B.A. L.345 J.D. [Clarkson&G.]

Clarkson & Gulde, P.C., (AV)
127 West 2nd Street, P.O. Box 279, 46173
Telephone: 765-932-2227 Fax: 765-932-2197
Email: clarkson@cnz.com
C. Jack Clarkson; Robert G. Gulde.
Accidents and Personal Injury, Family Law, Criminal Law, Probate, General Trial Practice.
See Professional Biographies, RUSHVILLE, INDIANA

Earnest, Foster, Eder & Levi, (AV)
114 West Third Street, P.O. Box 430, 46173
Telephone: 765-932-4118 Fax: 765-932-4486
Email: efel@verizon.net
Kenneth L. Earnest (1916-1995). Of Counsel: James S. Foster. Members of Firm: Robert J. Eder; Richard K. Levi. Associate: Leigh S. Morning.
General Practice. Trials. Personal Injury, Probate and Estate Planning, Real Estate, Commercial and Corporation Law.
Representative Clients: Rush County REMC; First Federal Savings and Loan Association of Rushville; Rush Memorial Hospital; Farm Bureau Insurance Co.; Farmers State Bank; The Sampler, Inc.; Ticor Title Insurance Co.
See Professional Biographies, RUSHVILLE, INDIANA

Eder, Robert J., (AV) ....'27 '55 C.347 B.S. L.1119 J.D. [Earnest,F.E.&L.]
Foster, James S., (AV) ....'27 '52 C.347 B.S. L.1119 J.D. [◎ Earnest,F.E.&L.]
Gulde, Robert G., (BV) ....'65 '91 C&L.347 B.A., J.D. [Clarkson&G.]
Harcourt, Barbara Arnold ....'50 '87 C.231 B.A. L.345 J.D. Cir. J.
Keaton, William B., (AV) ....'45 '71 C.347 B.A. L.345 J.D. [Keaton&K.]

Keaton and Keaton, P.C., (AV)
126 West Second Street, 46173-1874
Telephone: 765-932-3947 Fax: 765-938-2803
Email: keatonlaw@nraonline.com
Walter B. Keaton (1912-1980); William B. Keaton.
General Practice concentrated in Family Law, Probate and Personal Injury.
See Professional Biographies, RUSHVILLE, INDIANA

Levi, Richard K., (AV) ....'45 '71 C.347 B.S. L.345 J.D. [Earnest,F.E.&L.]
Malson, David A., (BV) ....'36 '63 C.347 B.S. L.345 J.D. [Malson]
Malson Law Office, P.C., (BV) ....117 East Third Street
Morning, Leigh S., (CV) ....'71 '96 C&L.347 B.A., J.D. [Ⓐ Earnest,F.E.&L.]
Newhouse, Julie A., (BV) ....'62 '87 C.347 B.A. L.879 J.D. [Newhouse&N.]
Newhouse, Tracy J., (BV) ....'62 '88 C.347 B.A. L.879 J.D. [Newhouse&N.]
Newhouse & Newhouse, (BV) ....301 N. Main St.
Northam, David E. ....'49 '76 C.303 B.A. L.345 J.D. Co. J., West Co. Supr. Ct.
Ribley, Julie L. ....'66 '91 C.679 B.A. L.1119 J.D. 226 N. Main St.

Thompson Law Office
(See Connersville)

Wilson, Ronald L., (BV) .... '45 '74 C.347 B.S. L.345 J.D. 110 N. Perkins St.
Worth, John O., (BV) ....'43 '70 C.347 B.S. L.345 J.D. [Worth]
Worth Law Offices, (BV) ....136 East Second Street

ST. JOHN, 8,382, *Lake Co.*

Babineaux, Margo R. ....'68 '98 C.347 B.A. L.879 J.D. [Meinzer&B.]
Meinzer, Robert L., Jr., (BV) ....'43 '68 C.347 B.A. L.1119 J.D. [Meinzer&B.]
Meinzer & Babineaux, (BV) ....9190 Wicker Avenue

SALEM, * 6,172, *Washington Co.*

Allen, David P., (BV) ....'46 '71 C.347 B.S. L.1119 J.D. [Allen,A.&A.]
Allen, James D., (AV) ....'16 '39 C.347 L.383 LL.B. [Allen,A.&A.]
Allen, Jay D., (BV) ....'42 '66 C.347 A.B. L.1119 J.D. [Allen,A.&A.]
Allen, Allen & Allen, (AV) ....12 Public Sq.
Bartanen, Alice L. ....'76 '02 C.108 B.A. L.1119 J.D. 108 E. Market
Bennett, Robert L. ....'43 '73 C.347 B.S. L.1119 J.D. Cir. J.
Clark, Mark D., (BV) ....'56 '81 C.265 B.A. L.345 J.D. [Mead,M.&C.]

Colomb, Bart, Law Office of
(See New Albany)

Hobbs, Marmaduke A., (AV) ....'11 '41 C.347 B.S. L.904 J.D. 105 N. Shelby St.‡
Leatherbury, Douglas C. ....'41 '68 C.347 A.B. L.1119 J.D. 201 North Main Street

Mattox Mattox & Wilson
(See New Albany)

Maudlin, Lewis E. ....'71 '96 C.347 B.A. L.345 J.D. Co. Pros.
Mead, John W., (AV) ....'45 '70 C&L.347 A.B., J.D. [Mead,M.&C.]
Mead, Mead & Clark, P.C., (AV) ....108 East Market
Medlock, Larry W., (BV) ....'57 '91 C.679 B.S. L.421 J.D. [Ⓐ Allen,A.&A.]

Merkley Law Office
(See Jeffersonville)

Newkirk, Frank E., Jr. ....'57 '81 C.347 A.B. L.1119 J.D. Supr. Ct. J.
Scifres, Thomas E. ....'66 '93 C&L.347 B.S., J.D. 136 East market St.
Thompson, Trent, (BV) ....'51 '77 C.347 B.S. L.345 J.D. [Ⓐ Allen,A.&A.]
Thompson, William L. ....'23 '48 C.347 L.345 LL.B. Supr. Ct. J.
Wright, Andrew, (BV) ....'45 '71 C.347 A.B. L.1119 J.D. [A.Wright]
Wright, Andrew, P.C., (BV) ....31 Public Sq.

SANTA CLAUS, 2,041, *Spencer Co.*

Hohl, Gary D. ....'52 '80 C.679 B.S. L.347 J.D. [G.D.Hohl]
Hohl, Gary D., Law Office ....1 Santa Pl.
Patmore, Kevin R. ....'70 '94 C.152 B.A. L.945 J.D. [Patmore]
Patmore Law Office ....Liberty Building, Suite 201
Price, David E., (BV) ....'45 '70 C&L.383 A.B., J.D. 10 Holly Plaza

SCHERERVILLE, 24,851, *Lake Co.*

Babcock, Michael D. ....'68 '96 C.347 B.S. L.879 J.D. [Sachs&H.]
Bates, Mark A., (BV) ....'56 '82 C&L.879 B.A., J.D. Appl. Pub. Def.
Campagna, Edward A., Attorney at Law '56 '85 C.679 B.S. L.201 J.D.
1843 Burgundy St.
Cockrum, Scott B. ....'69 '98 C.999 B.S. L.602 J.D. [Ⓐ Hinshaw&C.]
Crabtree, William G., II ....'63 '88 C&L.383 B.A., J.D. [W.G.Crabtree II]
Crabtree, William G., II, P.C. ....222 US Highway 41, Ste. 102
Devine, Patrick P. ....'71 '96 C.347 B.S. L.209 J.D. [Ⓐ Hinshaw&C.]
Ellison, Marcus E. ....'76 '01 C.276 B.A. L.602 J.D. [Ⓐ Hinshaw&C.]
Goad, Wendell W., II, (BV) ....'54 '80 C.827 B.A. L.879 J.D. 7803 W. 75th
Hagberg, Harold G., (BV) ....'51 '76 C&L.879 B.S., J.D. 7654 Harvest Drive

Hinshaw & Culbertson LLP, (BV)
Hinshaw & Culbertson LLP is an Illinois registered limited liability partnership that has elected to be governed by the Illinois Uniform Partnership Act (1997)
222 Indianapolis Boulevard Suite 202, 46375 ⊙
Telephone: 219-864-5051 Facsimile: 219-864-5052 Telex: 880248
Email: kfox@hinshawlaw.com URL: http://www.hinshawlaw.com
Partners: Jennifer Kalas; Renee J. Mortimer (Also at Chicago, Illinois Office); Michael E. O'Neill. Associates: Scott B. Cockrum; Patrick P. Devine; Marcus E. Ellison.
Appellate, Banking & Financing, Bankruptcy & Creditors' Rights, Class Action Litigation, Civil Rights Defense, Commercial Litigation, Corporate, Construction Law, Director & Officer Liability, Employee Benefits, Environmental, Fidelity & Surety, General Liability Litigation, Government, Health Care, Insurance Coverage, Insurance and Reinsurance, Labor & Employment, Legal Malpractice, Medical Malpractice, Mergers & Acquisitions, Municipal Liability, Personal Injury Defense, Public Law, Products Liability Litigation, Professional Liability, Regulatory, Real Estate, School Law, Securities, Taxation, Transportation, White Collar Crime and Workers' Compensation Defense.
Other Office Locations: Chicago, Illinois; Appleton, Wisconsin; Belleville, Illinois; Boston, Massachusetts; Champaign, Illinois; Crystal Lake, Illinois; Edwardsville, Illinois; Fort Lauderdale, Florida; Jacksonville, Florida; Joliet, Illinois; Lisle, Illinois; Los Angeles, California; Miami, Florida; Milwaukee, Wisconsin; Minneapolis, Minnesota; New York, New York; Peoria, Illinois; Phoenix, Arizona; Portland, Oregon; Providence, Rhode Island; Rockford, Illinois; St. Louis, Missouri; San Francisco, California; Springfield, Illinois; Tampa, Florida; Waukegan, Illinois.
See Professional Biographies, SCHERERVILLE, INDIANA

Jasaitis, Michael J. ....'74 '00 C&L.879 B.A., J.D. [Tauber,W.&J.]
Kalas, Jennifer, (CV) ....'66 '93 C.249 B.S. L.879 J.D. [Hinshaw&C.]
Kurowski, Steven A., (BV) ....'46 '71 C&L.602 B.A., J.D. 7803 W. 75th Ave.

LaTulip, Matthew D., Attorney at Law '74 '00 C.347 B.S. L.345 J.D.
7654 Harvest Drive, 46375
Telephone: 219-864-9055 Fax: 219-864-9062
Email: mlatulip@hmllaw.net URL: http://www.lawyers.com/latuliplaw
Personal Injury, Medical Malpractice, Auto Accidents, Slip and Fall, Wrongful Death, Criminal, DUI, Traffic Violations, Juvenile Crimes, Employment Discrimination, Sexual Harassment, Nursing Home Abuse, Insurance.
See Professional Biographies, SCHERERVILLE, INDIANA

Layer, Ronald F., (AV) ....'43 '72 C.870 B.S. L.1119 J.D. [Sachs&H.] ⊙
McManama, Patrick J., (CV) '45 '78
C.1103 B.A. L.602 J.D. Gen. Coun., McColly Realtors, Inc.
Mortimer, Renee J., (CV) ....'67 '91 C.347 B.A. L.424 J.D. [Hinshaw&C.] (⊙Chgo., IL)
O'Neill, Michael E., (BV) ....'60 '91 C.424 B.A. L.602 J.D. [Hinshaw&C.]
Reid, Joseph S., (BV) ....'48 '73 C.249 B.S. L.345 J.D. 2315 Normandy Rd.
Sachs & Hess, P.C., (AV)
141 W. Lincoln Highway 2nd Floor, Peoples Bank (⊙Hammond)
Sakoutis, Sophia ....'55 '84 C.339 B.A. L.424 J.D. Prof., Saint Xavier Univ.‡
Sasser, Deanne K. ....'64 '91 C.347 B.A. L.879 J.D. Lit. Coun., State Farm
Spicer, Nicole Bennett .... '73 '98 C.27 B.A. L.879 J.D. [Ⓐ Tauber,W.&J.]
Sterba, Melanie M., (BV) ....'57 '83 C.475 B.A. L.879 J.D. 425 W. US Hwy. 30
Swope, Jill S. ....'70 '95 C&L.879 B.S., J.D. 425 W. Lincoln Hwy.
Tauber, Rhett L., (AV) ....'49 '74 C&L.879 B.A., J.D. [Tauber,W.&J.]

Tauber, Westland & Jasaitis, P.C., (AV)
1415 Eagle Ridge Drive, 46375
Telephone: 219-865-8400 Fax: 219-865-8484 URL: http://www.tauberwestland.com
Email: dww@twjlaw.com URL: http://www.twjlawfirm.com
Rhett L. Tauber; David W. Westland; Michael J. Jasaitis;—Nicole Bennett Spicer.
General Civil and Trial Practice in all State and Federal Courts. Real Estate, Municipal and Zoning, Corporate, Business, Business Planning, Contracts, Lawsuits, Strategic Planning, Banking, Wills and Probate, Trusts and Estates, Asset Protection, Estate Planning, Guardianships, Personal Injury, Automobile Accidents, Negligence Litigation, Wrongful Death, Slip and Fall, Family Law, Adoptions, Child Custody, Child Support, Divorce, Domestic Violence, Visitation Rights, Creditors' Rights and Creditor Bankruptcy, Real Estate, Criminal Law, Driving While Intoxicated, Traffic Violations.
See Professional Biographies, SCHERERVILLE, INDIANA

Tokarski, Steve H., (BV) ....'43 '69 C.679 B.A. L.1119 J.D. 7803 W. 75th Ave.
Tuytschaevers, Thomas L., (CV) ...... '45 '70 C.347 B.S. L.1119 J.D. 7803 W. 75th Ave.
Vasquez, Salvador, (CV) ....'63 '91 C&L.347 B.A., J.D. [Vasquez]
Vasquez Law Firm, PC, (CV) ....226 Lacebark St.
Westland, David W., (BV) ....'70 '95 C.57 B.A. L.879 J.D. [Tauber,W.&J.]
Wieser, James L., (BV) ....'47 '72 C.63 B.A. L.879 J.D. 425 W. Lincoln Highway
Wyllie, Randy H. ....'68 '93 C.347 B.A. L.879 J.D. 425 W. Lincoln Hwy.
Yalowitz, Warren M. ....'29 '68 C.145 B.S. L.365 J.D. 208 St. Andrews Dr.
Zougras, Elizabeth Rizos '— '92 C.347 B.S. L.345 J.D.
222 Indianapolis Blvd., Ste. 105

SCOTTSBURG, * 6,040, *Scott Co.*

Carter, T. Michael .... '47 '72 C.347 B.S. L.1119 J.D. 95 W. Wardell St.

Colomb, Bart, Law Office of
(See New Albany)

Dietrich, John F., (BV) ....'58 '88 C&L.347 B.S., J.D. 63 W. Wardell St.
Dollens, John R., (AV) ....'22 '48 C.347 B.S. L.1119 J.D. 26 1/2 S. Main St.
Duvall, Roger L., (AV) ....'52 '78 C.150 B.A. L.1340 J.D. 1 E. McClain Ave.
Houston, Robert L., III, (BV) ....'46 '74 C.853 B.A. L.421 J.D. [Houston&T.]
Houston & Thompson, P.C., (AV) .... 49 E. Wardell St.
Kearby, Jennings H. ....'26 '48 C&L.383 A.B., LL.B. Gen. Atty., Corps of Engrs.‡
Kleopfer, James D., Jr. ....'42 '68 C.347 B.S. L.421 J.D. Cir. J.
Lewis, Jennifer D. ....'74 '99 C.929 B.S. L.74 J.D. [Ⓐ Houston&T.]

Mattox Mattox & Wilson
(See New Albany)

Merkley Law Office
(See Jeffersonville)

Minton, Kelly C., (BV) ....'62 '90 C.347 B.A. L.37 J.D. Dep. Pros. Atty.
Mount, Jason M. ....'71 '99 C.63 B.S. L.345 J.D. 60 N. Main Street
Randall, Ralph E., Attorney at Law, (BV) .....'47 '74 C.347 B.A. L.345 J.D. 45 N. 1st St.
Thompson, Kerry L., (AV) ....'49 '75 C.347 B.S. L.345 J.D. [Houston&T.]

SELLERSBURG, 6,071, *Clark Co.*

Bolly, Virgil E., Law Office of, (BV) ....'34 '59 C&L.421 B.S., LL.B. 204 E. Utica St.

Colomb, Bart, Law Office of
(See New Albany)

Mackin, Jeffrey L. '61 '86 C.138 B.A. L.201 J.D.
(adm. in KY; not adm. in IN) Gen. Coun., Interlock Industries Inc.
Spiegel, Ted W., (BV) .....'48 '74 C.94 B.S. L.421 J.D. 110 Maple St. (⊙Louisville, KY)

SEYMOUR, 18,101, *Jackson Co.*

Black, Joseph M., Jr., (BV) .... '51 '81 C.347 B.S. L.345 J.D. P.O. Box 846
Brown, Robert R. .... '32 '63 C.265 A.B. L.345 J.D. [Ⓐ Montgomery,E.&P.]
Connell, Denise W. ....'68 '00 C.344 A.S. L.345 LL.B. [Montgomery,E.&P.]
Davis, Karen J. Mellencamp .... '65 '94 C&L.347 B.A., J.D. [Ⓐ Pardieck]
Elsner, Edward P., Jr., (AV) ....'24 '49 C.347 B.S. L.1119 J.D. [Montgomery,E.&P.]
Farrow, Rodney E., (BV) ....'48 '74 C.346 B.S. L.345 J.D. P.O. Box 644
Frey, Donald M., (CV) ....'55 '80 C.879 B.A. L.1119 J.D. Dep. Pros. Atty.
Guthrie, Frank W. ....'47 '73 C.894 B.A. L.347 J.D. Supr. Ct. J.
Hays, Brett M. ....'66 '94 C.303 B.A. L.1187 J.D. Hoosier Media
Hoffar, Taylor, (BV) ....'11 '36 C.347 B.S. L.1008 J.D. 101 1/2 S. Chestnut St.

Jewell, Crump, Angermeier & Prall
(See Columbus)

Kerrigan, George L. .... '17 '42 C.347 B.A. L.1119 LL.B. Ret. Cir. Ct. J.
Lantz, Thomas J., (AV) ....'44 '72 C.347 B.S. L.345 J.D. [Montgomery,E.&P.]
Layton, Kenneth A., (AV) ......'40 '69 C.679 B.S.I.M. L.1119 J.D. [Montgomery,E.&P.]
Lewis, John M. ....'13 '39 C.303 A.B. L.345 LL.B. 300 N. Chestnut St.‡
Lorenzo, Jeffrey J., (BV) ....'53 '82 C.190 B.A. L.1119 J.D. 208 West 2nd Street

Montgomery, Elsner & Pardieck, LLP, (AV)
308 West 2nd Street, P.O. Box 647, 47274
Telephone: 812-522-4109 Fax: 812-522-6473
URL: http://www.meplegal.com
Members of Firm: Richard H. Montgomery (1923-1989); Edward P. Elsner, Jr.; Margarett S. Pardieck; Kenneth A. Layton; Thomas J. Lantz; Steven K. Robison; David W. Paugh; Denise W. Connell; Ryan W. Redmon; Susan E. Sparks. Of Counsel: Robert R. Brown.
General Civil Practice, Estate Planning, Estate Administration, Business and Corporations, Family Law, Banking, Real Estate, Municipal Law, Appeals, Personal Injury and Medical Malpractice, Social Security, Civil and Criminal Trial Practice.
Representative Clients: Jackson County Bank; Seymour Community Schools; Swifty Oil Co., Inc.; Schneck Medical Center; Home Federal Bank; City of Seymour, Indiana; Seymour Economic Development Commission; Jackson County Industrial Development Corp.; Schwarz Pharma Manufacturing, Inc.

Pardieck, Andrew M., (CV) ....'68 '96 C.309 A.B. L.347 J.D. [Ⓐ Pardieck]
Pardieck, Margarett S., (BV) .....'37 '62 C.347 B.S. L.1119 LL.B. [Montgomery,E.&P.]
Pardieck, Roger L., (AV) ....'37 '63 C.347 A.B. L.1119 LL.B. [Pardieck]

Pardieck Law Firm, The, (AV)
100 North Chestnut Street, P.O. Box 608, 47274
Telephone: 812-523-8686 Fax: 812-522-4199
Email: lawyers@pardiecklaw.com
Roger L. Pardieck;—Andrew M. Pardieck; Karen J. Mellencamp Davis.
Personal Injury and Wrongful Death Claims. Products and Professional Liability Law, Commercial Litigation.
Reference: Home Federal Savings Bank, Seymour, Indiana.
See Professional Biographies, SEYMOUR, INDIANA

Paugh, David W., (BV) ....'55 '79 C.63 B.S. L.345 J.D. [Montgomery,E.&P.]
Phillips, Norman W., (BV) ....'46 '72 C.108 A.B. L.345 J.D. [Vance&P.]
Redmon, Ryan W. .... '74 '01 C.344 B.A. L.602 J.D. [Montgomery,E.&P.]
Robertson, Joseph M., (BV) ....'54 '81 C.894 B.A. L.1119 J.D. [Robertson]
Robertson Law Office, (BV) .... 1000 W. 2nd St.
Robison, Steven K., (BV) .... '54 '79 C.210 B.A. L.228 J.D. [Montgomery,E.&P.]
Rothring, John F., (BV) ....'46 '77 C.679 B.S. L.345 J.D. [J.F.Rothring]
Rothring, John F., PC, (BV) ....115 W. Tipton St.
Sparks, Susan E., (CV) ....'56 '98 C.303 B.S. L.421 J.D. [Montgomery,E.&P.]
Vance, William E., (AV) ....'44 '74 C.63 B.S. L.345 J.D. [Vance&P.]
Vance & Phillips, (AV) .... 318 W. Bruce St.

SHELBYVILLE, * 17,951, *Shelby Co.*

Adams, Robert W., (AV) ....'42 '67 C.894 A.B. L.597 J.D. [Adams&C.]

Adams & Cramer, (AV)
33 West Washington Street, P.O. Box 746, 46176
Telephone: 317-398-6626 Fax: 317-392-1962
Ralph Adams (1901-1986); Fred V. Cramer (1907-1998). Members of Firm: Robert W. Adams; N. Gregg Graham.
Trials. General Practice. Real Estate, Insurance, Administrative Law. Wills, Probate, Trusts and Estates, Estate Planning. Banking, Tax and Corporation Law, Elder Law.
See Professional Biographies, SHELBYVILLE, INDIANA

Apsley, R. Kent, (BV) .... '59 '84 C.347 B.A. L.1119 J.D. Shelby Cnty. Prosec.
Arnold, Robert John ....'57 '82 C.347 B.S. L.879 J.D. 21 W. Taylor St.
Asher, Lori Anne ....'74 '00 C.347 B.A. L.1410 J.D. 10 East Taylor Street
Baker, Kyle M. ....'71 '97 C&L.347 B.A., J.D. 30 E. Washington St., Ste. 400
Barrett, Michelle A., (BV) .... '60 '85 C.679 B.S. L.347 J.D. 113 E. Mechanic St.
Bate, Charles T., (AV) ....'32 '62 C.108 A.B. L.345 J.D. [Bate&B.]
Bate, Jeffrey S., (BV) ....'62 '89 C.992 B.A. L.345 J.D. [Bate&B.]
Bate & Bate, Prof. Corp., (AV) ....505 S. Harrison St.
Blackketter, Amanda O., (BV) '68 '94
C.303 B.A. L.1119 J.D. 30 E. Washington St., Ste. 400
Brown, Douglas W., (BV) ....'64 '91 C.894 B.A. L.347 J.D. 416 S. Harrison St.
Brown, Phillip W., (AV) ....'37 '60 C.347 A.B. L.1119 LL.B. [Brown,L.&D.]
Brown, Linder & DePrez, (AV) ....416 S. Harrison St.
DePrez, John C., IV, (BV) ....'62 '87 C.679 B.A. L.345 J.D. P.O. Box 718
DePrez, Peter G., (BV) ....'48 '73 C.855 B.A. L.1119 J.D. [Brown,L.&D.]
Fisk, Jeremy P. ....'75 '01 C.265 B.A. L.345 J.D. 21 West Taylor Street
Graham, N. Gregg ....'46 '72 C.108 B.S. L.345 J.D. [Adams&C.] ‡
Harrold, Dennis E., (AV) ....'47 '72 C.347 B.S. L.345 J.D. [McNeely,S.&T.]
Jones, Robert D. ....'27 '55 C.347 B.A. L.569 LL.B. 563 E. Timber Brook Est.
Linder, Jeffrey M., (AV) ....'50 '75 C.63 B.S. L.345 J.D. [Brown,L.&D.]
Lisher, James R., (BV) .... '47 '75 C.347 A.B. L.345 J.D. 406 S. Harrison Street
Lux, Jerry J., (BV) ....'41 '69 C.347 A.B. L.345 J.D. [Lux&L.]
Lux, John Dale (J.D.), (BV) ....'67 '94 C.265 B.A. L.607 J.D. [Lux&L.]
Lux & Lux, P.A., (BV) ....101 S. Harrison Street, Suite B

Marshall, Robert E., (BV) '31 '56 C.347 B.S. L.1119 J.D.
One Courtside Building, 18 West Polk Street, 46176
Telephone: 317-398-9745 Fax: 317-398-1013
Email: remarshall@lightbound.com URL: http://www.remarshalllaw.com
General and Trial Practice, Personal Injury, Wrongful Death, Automobile Accidents, Slip and Fall, Dog Bites, Products Liability, Medical Negligence, Wills, Trusts and Estates, Estate Planning, Asset

(This Listing Continued)

Marshall, Robert E. (Continued)

Protection, Guardianships, Family Law, Domestic Relations, Adoptions, Child Custody, Child Support, Divorce, Visitation Rights, Business Law, Business Contracts, Business Litigation, Business Planning, Business Enterprises, Partnerships, Small Business, Corporate, Limited Liability Company Law, Buying and Selling a Business, Business Start-Ups, Criminal Law, Drug Crimes, DWI, DUI, Traffic Violations.
Reference: Bank One, Indianapolis, N.A., Shelbyville, Indiana.
See Professional Biographies, SHELBYVILLE, INDIANA

McNeely, J. Lee, (AV) ....'40 '65 C.894 A.B. L.1119 J.D. [McNeely,S.&T.]
McNeely, Mark W., (BV) ....'47 '74 C.265 B.S. L.345 J.D. [McNeely]
McNeely Law Office, (BV) ....30 East Washington Street, Suite 100
McNeely, Stephenson & Thopy, (AV) ....30 E. Washington Street, Suite 400
McQueen, Mary L., (BV) ....'52 '79 C.347 B.A. L.345 J.D. Dep. Pros. Atty.
Meloy, Loretta ....'24 '69 C.347 B.S. L.345 J.D. P.O. Box 454
Meltzer, Kris, (AV) ....'55 '80 C.63 B.S. L.1119 J.D. [Stubbs&M.]
Morgan, Cameron A. ....'70 '95 C.894 A.B. L.950 J.D. [Ⓐ McNeely,S.&T.]
O'Connor, Charles D. ....'46 '72 C.602 A.B. L.345 J.D. Cir. J.
Riggins, David N., (BV) ....'68 '94 C.108 B.A. L.347 J.D. Dep. Pros. Atty.
Robison, James M., (AV) ....'27 '56 C.347 L.345 LL.B. 45 West Washington Street
Schrumpf, Stephen E., (BV) ....'55 '81 C.347 A.B. L.345 J.D. [Ⓐ McNeely,S.&T.]
Speichinger, Susan L. '65 '91 C.210 B.A. L.273 J.D.
(adm. in CO; not adm. in IN) 30 E. Washington St.‡
Stephenson, M. Michael, (AV) ....'57 '82 C.235 B.S. L.347 J.D. [McNeely,S.&T.]
Stubbs, George L., Jr., (AV) ....'39 '65 C.210 A.B. L.1119 J.D. [Stubbs&M.]
Stubbs & Meltzer, (AV) ....220 S. Harrison St.
Tandy, Jack A. ....'57 '82 C.894 B.A. L.345 J.D. Co. Ct. J.
Thopy, Robert T., (AV) ....'44 '74 C.347 B.S. L.345 J.D. [McNeely,S.&T.]
Tolen, George R. ....'21 '48 C.303 L.345 LL.B. Ret. Supr. Ct. J.
Wallace, Wade ....'64 '94 C.679 B.P.E. L.801 J.D. [Ⓐ McNeely,S.&T.]

SHERIDAN, 2,520, *Hamilton Co.*

Connor, Dede K. ....'70 '95 C.249 B.S. L.347 J.D. 10761 East Co. Rd. 200 N
Shields, William E., (BV) ....'33 '63 C.347 B.S. L.345 LL.B. 403 S. Main

SHIRLEY, 817, *Hancock & Henry Cos.*

Porter, David W. ....'52 '83 C.347 B.S. L.345 J.D. 1224 S. State Rd.

SHOALS, * 853, *Martin Co.*

Hart Bell LLC
(See Vincennes)

Howell, R. Joseph ....'63 '88 C.347 B.A. L.1119 J.D. Cir.J., Martin Cir. Ct.
Huebner, Kelley Beckes, (Mrs.) .... '48 '79 C.346 B.S. L.345 J.D. Cir. J.
Pickett, Fremont O., (BV) ....'28 '56 C.347 A.B. L.1119 J.D. 3 Courthouse Dr.
Vogler, Paul J., (CV) ....'46 '73 C.346 B.S. L.345 J.D. Courthouse Dr.

SOUTH BEND, * 107,789, *St. Joseph Co.*

Abeska, Timothy J., (AV) ....'— '82 C.477 B.A. L.602 J.D. [Barnes&T.]
Adey, Mark J., (BV) ....'— '88 C.347 B.A. L.602 J.D. [Barnes&T.]
Agostino, Peter J., (BV) ....'61 '86 C&L.602 B.B.A., J.D. [Anderson A.&K.]
Aigotti, Claire Konopa, (CV) ....'71 '96 C.602 B.A. L.1158 J.D. [Konopa,R.&A.]
Alan, Franklin E. '39 '69 C.679 B.S. L.345 J.D.
Atty., The National Institute of Trial Advocacy
Albert, David W. ....'39 '74 C.723 B.A. L.602 J.D. 514 S. Frances St.
Albright, William H. ....'41 '67 C.119 B.S.M.E. L.602 J.D. Supr. Ct. J.
Aldridge, Linda S., (CV) ....'57 '91 C.84 B.S.N. L.734 J.D. [Gillis&A.]
Amaral, Joseph L., (BV) .... '47 '73 C.347 A.B. L.1119 J.D. [Hammerschmidt,A.&J.]
Ambler, Larry L., (BV) ....'46 '71 C.201 B.S. L.602 J.D. Co. Coun. Atty.
Amor, Roslyn M. ....'63 '89 C.260 B.A. L.362 J.D. Proj. Dir., Farm Coun. of LSPNI
Andersen, William W., Jr. ......'38 '64 C&L.879 B.A., J.D. Sr. Atty. Advsr., Dept. of Jus.
Anderson, D. Michael ....'— '98 C.346 B.S. L.347 J.D. [Ⓐ Barnes&T.]
Anderson, Douglas D. ....'— '94 C&L.602 B.A., J.D. [Barnes&T.]
Anderson, Michael J., (AV) ....'53 '82 C.347 B.S. L.879 J.D. [Anderson A.&K.]
Anderson • Agostino & Keller, P.C., (AV) .... 131 South Taylor Street
Antonis, William N. '28 '53
C.679 B.S. L.602 J.D. Chf. Pat. Coun., AlliedSignal Inc. (Pat.)
Antonovitz, Frank A. '47 '74 C.346 B.S. L.602 J.D.
V.P. & Sr. Coun., Meridian Title Corporation
Asher, Charles A., (AV) ....'52 '77 C.231 B.S. L.1119 J.D. 224 W. Jefferson Blvd.
Baer, Kelly A. ....'69 '02 C.739 B.A. L.1187 J.D. [Cole&B.]
Bagiackas, Peter J., (CV) ....'61 '94 C.602 B.A. L.347 J.D. [Ⓐ Hunt S.K.]

Baker & Daniels LLP, (AV) ▣
First Bank Building, 205 West Jefferson Boulevard, Suite 250, 46601 ⊙
Telephone: 574-234-4149 Fax: 574-239-1900
URL: http://www.bakerdaniels.com
Members of Firm: Thomas J. Brunner, Jr.; Gerard T. Gallagher; Carl A. Greci; M. Patricia Hackett; Richard L. Hill; James M. Matthews; Randolph R. Rompola; Edward A. Sullivan, III; Peter G. Trybula. Counsel: D. Lucetta Pope; Robert A. Wade. Associates: Cara R. Brook; Alison G. Fox; Peter J. Gillin (Not admitted in IN); Jeff R. Heck; RaeLee C. Hudson; Jennifer Bickley Hull; Thomas J. Mauch; Shawn E. Peterson; David R. Pruitt (Not admitted in IN); Amy M. Steketee; Daniel Tychonievich.
Antitrust, Bankruptcy, Business Planning, Commercial, Corporate Finance, Creditors Rights, Employee Benefits, Employment, Environment, Estate and Probate, Family, Financial, Food and Drug, Government Affairs, Health Care, Insurance, Intellectual Property, International, Legislative, Litigation, Medical Technology Regulation, Municipal, Nonprofit, Product Liability, Real Estate, Securities, Sports, Tax, Transportation, Utilities, Year 2000, Zoning and Land Use Law.
Indianapolis, Indiana Office: 300 North Meridian Street, Suite 2700, 46204. Telephone: 317-237-0300. Fax: 317-237-1000.
Fort Wayne, Indiana Office: 111 East Wayne Street, Suite 800, 46802. Telephone: 260-424-8000. Fax: 260-460-1700.
Elkhart, Indiana Office: 317 West Franklin Street, P.O. Box 507, 46515-0507. Telephone: 574-296-6000. Fax: 574-296-6001.
Indianapolis-96th Street, Indiana Office: Parkwood Six, 600 East 96th Street, Suite 600, 46240. Telephone: 317-569-9600. Fax: 317-569-4800.
Washington, D.C. Office: 805 15th Street, N.W., Suite 700, 20005. Telephone: 202-312-7440. Fax: 202-312-7460.
Qingdao, China Office: 4/F, Office Tower, Crowne Plaza Qingdao, No. 76 Hong Kong Middle Road, 266071. Telephone: +011-86-532-575-1051. Fax: +011-86-532-575-1055.
Beijing, China Office: Room 1919, Tower 2, China World Trade Center, No. 1 JianGuoMenWai Avenue, 100004. Telephone: +86-10-6505-7733. Fax: +86-10-6505-8730.
See Professional Biographies, SOUTH BEND, INDIANA

Balko, Timothy E., (BV) ....'61 '89 C&L.879 B.S.W., J.D. [Ⓐ Anderson A.&K.]
Ballard, David E. ....'61 '87 C.473 B.A. L.608 J.D. [Ⓐ Lee&G.]

Barnes & Thornburg LLP, (AV) ▣
600 1st Source Bank Center, 100 North Michigan, 46601-1632 ⊙
Telephone: 574-233-1171 FAX: 574-237-1125
URL: http://www.btlaw.com
Partners: Stephen A. Seall; Nelson J. Vogel, Jr.; Roger W. Benko; Brian J. Lake; Richard L. Mintz; Laurence A. McHugh; Douglas K. Dieterly; Alan B. Feldbaum; Timothy J. Abeska; Gerald F. Lutkus;

(This Listing Continued)

Barnes & Thornburg LLP (Continued)

Nancy L. Ickler; Kathleen K. Brickley; Michael B. Watkins; Seth D. Linfield (Co-chair, Business Technology Practice Group; Chair, Technology Transactions Group); Timothy D. Hernly (Tax Partner); Joseph R. Fullenkamp; Greta Roemer Lewis; Michael D. Hardy; Janilyn Brouwer Daub; Tracy D. Knox; Mark J. Adey; Jeanine M. Gozdecki; Douglas D. Anderson; George E. Horn, Jr.; Jody H. Odell; John C. Smarrella. Of Counsel: Brian E. Casey; Philip J. Faccenda, Jr.; Michael P. Palmer (Not admitted in IN); Timothy J. Maher. Associates: Richard J. Deahl; D. Michael Anderson; James W. Tuesley; Brien P. Crotty; Damon R. Leichty; Michael V. Knight; Andrew P. Heck; Michael J. Hays; Gregory P. Ripple; Laura D. Seng; Kate E. Mueller.

Acquisitions and Divestitures, Ad Valorem Tax, Administrative Law, Affirmative Action, Agriculture Law, Americans with Disabilities Act, Antidumping, Antitrust, Antitrust and Trade Regulation, Appellate Practice, Attorney Grievances, Automotive Warranty Law, Aviation and Aerospace, Aviation Law, Banking Law, Banking Regulations, Bankruptcy, Bankruptcy Reorganization, Banks and Banking, Biochemical Patents, Biomedical Products Liability, Biomedical Technology, Biotechnology Patent Prosecution, Bond Law, Brain Injury, Breach of Warranty, Brown Fields Redevelopment, Business Immigration, Business Law, Business Litigation, Business Planning, Business Regulatory and Administrative, Business Start-ups, Business Succession Planning, Business Taxation, Business Torts, Business Transactions, Business Transfers, Buying and Selling of Businesses, Cable TV, Cargo Claims, Charitable Trusts and Foundations, Chemical Intellectual Property, Chemical Patent Prosecution, Chemical Patents, Chemical Products Liability, Civil Appeals, Civil Litigation, Civil Practice, Civil RICO, Class Action Defense, Clean Air Act, Clean Water Act, Closely Held Business Estate Planning, Closely Held Businesses, Closely Held Business Law, Closely Held Corporations, Collective Bargaining, Commercial Bankruptcy, Commercial Finance Law, Commercial Law, Commercial Leasing and Financing, Commercial Litigation, Commercial Conveyancing, Commercial Real Estate, Commercial Real Estate Acquisition, Commercial Real Estate Development, Commercial Real Estate Finance, Commercial Transactions, Commodities Fraud, Communications and Media, Complex Commercial Litigation, Complex Litigation, Computer and Software Patents, Computer Law, Computers and Software, Conflicts of Interest, Construction Labor Law, Construction Law, Consumer Credit, Contract Litigation, Cooperatives, Copyrights, Corporate Finance, Corporate Formation, Corporate Law, Corporate Taxation, Corporate Tax Planning, Countervailing Duties, Covenants Not To Compete, Creditors Rights, Creditors Rights in Bankruptcy, Criminal Defense, Criminal Law, Criminal Tax Audits, Customs Law, Dealer and Distributor Termination, Debt and Equity Finance, Decedents Estates, Defense Litigation, Design Patents, Disability Insurance Defense, Discrimination, Distribution, Drug and Medical Device Defense, Economic Development, Education Law, Elder Law, Election, Campaign and Political Law, Electric Power, Electric Utilities, Electrical Intellectual Property, Electrical Patents, Electro-mechanical Patents, Electronic Commerce, Electronic Patents, Eminent Domain, Employee Benefits, Employee Stock Ownership Plans, Employment Defense, Employment Discrimination, Employment Law, Employment Litigation, Energy, Energy Contracts, Energy Regulation, Environmental Administrative Law, Environmental Cleanup, Environmental Compliance, Environmental Criminal Defense, Environmental Law, Environmental Litigation, Environmental Permitting, Environmental Real Estate, Environmental Regulation, Environmental Risk Management, Equal Employment Opportunity Law, ERISA Litigation, Estate Administration, Estate and Gift Taxation, Estate Planning, Estate Planning and Taxation, Estate Planning and Administration, Estate Planning and Probate, Estate Planning for Parents of Handicapped Children, Estate Planning for Unmarried Individuals, Executive Compensation, Executive Severance Contracts, Export Regulation, Fair Employment Practices, Family and Medical Leave Act, Family Business Successions, Family Wealth Transfer, Federal and State Administrative Regulatory Practice, Federal and State Legislative Practice, Federal Civil Litigation, Federal Civil Practice, Federal Criminal Law, Federal Estate and Gift Taxation, Federal Litigation, Federal Tax Controversies, Federal Taxation, Fiduciary Income Tax, Finance, Financial Transactions, First Party Insurance, Foreign Investment in the United States, Freight Claims, Freight Loss and Damage, Gaming Law, Gaming Licensing, Gas Utilities, General Litigation, Government, Government Affairs, Government Agency Practice, Government Contracts, Government Investigations, Government Relations, Groundwater Contamination, Hazardous Materials and Substances, Hazardous Waste, Hazardous Waste Liability, Head Injury, Health Care, Health Care Corporate Law, Health Care Contracts, Health Care Fraud, Health Care Licensing, Health Care Litigation, Health Care Mergers and Acquisitions, Health Care Regulation, Health Care Reimbursement, Health Law, Heavy Equipment Products Liability, Immigration Law, Industrial Revenue Bond Law, Inheritance Tax, Initial Public Offerings, Insurance, Insurance Bad Faith, Insurance Coverage, Insurance Litigation, Insurance Regulation, Integrated Health Care Delivery Systems, Intellectual Property, Intellectual Property General Prosecution, Intellectual Property Infringement, Intellectual Property Licensing, Intellectual Property Litigation, Intellectual Property Procurement, Intellectual Property Protection, Intellectual Property Rights, International Business Law, International Intellectual Property, International Law, International Patents, International Trade, International Transportation Law, Internet Law, Internet Trademark Law, Joint Ventures, Labor and Employment, Labor Arbitration, Labor Law, Labor Relations, Land Use, Lease Law, Leasing, Legal Ethics and Professional Responsibility, Legal Malpractice Defense, Legislative Practice, Licensing, Life Insurance Defense, Limited Liability Company Law, Limited Partnerships, Liquor Licensing, Litigation, Loans, Lobbying, Local Government Law, Logistics, Long Term Care, Managed Care, Managed Care Contracts, Management Employment Law, Management Labor Law, Manufacturers Liability, Maritime Regulations, Mechanical Intellectual Property, Mechanical Patents, Media Law, Mediation, Medical Antitrust, Medical Intellectual Property, Medical Patents, Mental Health Law, Mergers, Acquisitions and Divestitures, Mergers and Acquisitions, Mineral Taxation, Molecular Biology Patents, Motor Carrier Law, Motor Carrier Regulation, Multi-Employer Pensions, Municipal Bonds, Municipal Bonds Taxation, Municipal Finance, Municipal Law, Municipal Leasing, Municipal Redevelopment, Municipal Securities, Municipal Taxation, National Labor Relations Act, Neurolaw, Nonprofit and Charitable Organizations, Nonprofit Organizations Law, North American Free Trade Agreement, Occupational Safety and Health, OSHA, Partnership Law, Partnership Taxation, Patent Infringement, Patent Interference Practice, Patent Litigation, Patent Prosecution, Patents, PCT Legal Export, Personal Injury, Personal Injury Defense, Pesticide Litigation, Pharmaceutical Intellectual Property, Pharmaceutical Patents, Physician Contracts, Physician Practices, Planning and Land Use, Power Line Contact Injury, Probate, Probate Litigation, Products Liability, Products Liability Defense, Professional Liability, Property Law, Property Tax, Property Tax Abatement, Property Tax Appeals, Psychological Injury, Public Finance, Public Sector Labor Relations, Public Utility Law, Railroad Law, Real Estate, Real Estate Acquisitions, Real Estate Contracts, Real Estate Development, Real Estate Finance, Real Estate Licensing, Real Estate Secured Lending, Real Estate Title Insurance, Real Property, Real Property Acquisitions, Real Property Finance, Reorganizations, Resource Conservation and Recovery Act (RCRA), Retirement Benefit Plans, School Law, Securities, Securities Litigation, Securitization, Semiconductor Technology, Sexual Harassment, Small Business Corporations, State Government Law, State Tax Controversies, State Taxation, Structured Finance, Succession Planning, Superfund, Tax Controversies, Tax Exempt Finance, Tax Exempt Organizations, Tax Increment Finance, Tax Law, Tax Litigation, Taxation, Technology and Science, Technology Law, Technology Licensing, Technology Transfers, Telecommunications Competition, Telecommunications Law, Theft of Trade Secrets, Title VII Discrimination, Title IX Discrimination, Tort Defense, Toxic Exposure, Toxic Tort Class Actions, Toxic Torts, Toxic Tort Defense, Trade Dress, Trade Secrets, Trademark Litigation, Trademarks, Trademark Prosecution, Trademark Protection, Trademark Registration, Transportation, Transportation Safety, Trial Practice, Trusts and Estates, Unfair Competition, Unfair Trade, Uniform Commercial Codes, Union Contract Negotiations, Union Elections, Utilities, Utility Law, Wage and Hour Law, WARN Act, Water Pollution, Water Quality, Water Utilities, Wetland Regulation, White Collar Crime, White Collar Criminal Defense, Wills, Workers Compensation, Workouts, World Trade Organization, Wrongful Death, Wrongful Termination, Wrongful Termination Defense, Zoning, Planning and Land Use.

Representative Clients: 1st Source Bank; AM General Corp.; Cadence Environmental Energy; Crowe, Chizek and Company LLP; Gast Manufacturing Corporation; Memorial Hospital of South Bend; National Steel Corporation; University of Notre Dame; Whirlpool Corporation; Whiteford, Inc.

Indianapolis, Indiana Office: 11 South Meridian Street, 46204. Telephone: 317-236-1313. FAX: 317-231-7433.

Fort Wayne, Indiana Office: 600 One Summit Square, 46802. Telephone: 260-423-9440. FAX: 260-424-8316.

Elkhart, Indiana Office: 121 West Franklin Street, Suite 200, 46516. Telephone: 574-293-0681. FAX: 574-296-2535.

Chicago, Illinois Office: One North Wacker Drive, Suite 4400, 60606-2833. Telephone: 312-357-1313. FAX: 312-759-5646.

Washington, D.C. Office: 750 17th Street, N.W., Suite 900, 20006. Telephone: 202-289-1313. FAX: 202-289-1330.

Grand Rapids, Michigan Office: 300 Ottawa Avenue, N.W., Suite 500, 49503. Telephone: 616-742-3930. FAX: 616-742-3999.

See Professional Biographies, SOUTH BEND, INDIANA

Bassford, Charles H., IV, (BV) .... '55 '84 C.946 B.S.B.A. L.1015 J.D. [Ⓐ Hunt S.K.]
Beehler, Rae D. .... '62 '01 C.347 B.A. L.879 J.D. [Diamond&D.]
Benchik, Edward P., (BV) '66 '93 C.602 B.A. L.1119 J.D.
218 West Washington Street, Suite 720 (⊙South Bend)

Benchik, Edward P., (BV) '66 '93
C.602 B.A. L.1119 J.D. [Ⓒ Tuesley&H.] (⊙South Bend)
Benko, Roger W., (AV) .... '— '72 C.597 B.B.S. L.879 J.D. [Barnes&T.]
Berger, Donald J., (CV) .... '48 '77 C.679 B.S. L.61 J.D. 110 S. Taylor St.
Berndt, Raymond H., Jr., (CV) '51 '79 C&L.602 B.A., J.D.
Assoc. Prof., Bus. Law, Ind. Univ. South Bend
Blackmond, Don G., (AV) ....'40 '66 C.210 B.A. L.879 J.D. [Doran B.]
Blackmond, Don Gregory, (BV) .... '68 '94 C.475 B.S. L.879 J.D. [Doran B.]
Bodnar, Thomas L., (BV) .... '44 '72 C.276 A.B. L.602 J.D. 1618 E La Salle Ave
BonDurant, Bruce J., (AV) .... '43 '68 C.210 A.B. L.1119 J.D. 1930 Edison Rd.
Botkin, Thomas S., (BV) .... '45 '78 C.347 B.A. L.602 J.D. 105 E. Jefferson Blvd.

Boulac, Mary Ann, (BV) '43 '83 C&L.602 B.A., J.D.
535 Parkovash Avenue, P.O. Box 11654, 46617
Telephone: 574-236-7230 Fax: 574-236-8907
Email: boulac@sbcglobal.net
General Business, Real Estate, Estate Planning, Trusts and Estates, Asset Protection, Guardianships, Elder Law, Medicaid, Wills and Probate.

See Professional Biographies, SOUTH BEND, INDIANA

Boveri, Mark D., (AV) .... '60 '86 C.347 B.S. L.602 J.D. [Boveri M.R.&L.]

Boveri Murphy Rice & LaDue, LLP, (AV)
400 Plaza Building, 210 South Michigan Street, 46601
Telephone: 574-232-0300 Fax: 574-232-0400
URL: http://www.bmrl-law.com
Mark D. Boveri; Patrick D. Murphy; Charles P. Rice; John D. LaDue;—John D. Falvey; R. John Kuehn, III; Timothy M. Curran.
Litigation, State and Federal Trial Practice.

See Professional Biographies, SOUTH BEND, INDIANA

Bradley, Joseph D., (AV) .... '48 '74 C&L.602 B.A., J.D. 105 E. Jefferson Blvd.
Brennan, Dennis M., (BV) ....'49 '75 C.714 B.B.A. L.678 J.D. [Brennan&B.]
Brennan, Michael B. '63 '89 C.602 B.A. L.597 J.D.
(adm. in WI; not adm. in IN) 204 S. Main St.‡
Brennan, Patrick .... '17 '41 C&L.602 B.S., LL.B. 215 W. Marion St.‡
Brennan & Brennan, P.C., (BV) .... 215 W. Marion St. (⊙Milw., WI)
Brickley, Kathleen K. ....'— '82 C.472 B.S. L.602 J.D. [Barnes&T.]
Brobst, Jennifer ....'67 '96 C.999 B.A. L.1049 J.D. Dep. Prosecutor
Broden, John E., (BV) ....'65 '90 C.602 B.A. L.345 J.D. 205 W. Jefferson Blvd., Ste. 605
Brook, Barbara Z. .... '— '87 C.347 B.S. L.602 J.D. U.S. Atty. Off.
Brook, Cara R. ....'— '04 C.347 B.A. L.472 J.D. [Ⓐ Baker&D.]
Brueseke, Harold E., (BV) ....'43 '68 C.238 B.A. L.1119 J.D. Mag.
Brunner, Thomas J., Jr., (AV) .... '— '66 C&L.602 A.B., J.D. [Baker&D.]
Bugh, Claudia J., (CV) .... '61 '95 C.112 L.602 J.D. 205 W. Jefferson Blvd.
Butler, Kevin J., (AV) ....'39 '68 C.602 B.A. L.276 J.D. [Butler&S.]
Butler and Simeri, P.C., (AV) ....520 E. Colfax Avenue
Butt, George F. .... '08 '37 L.345 LL.B. 718 Country Club Lane‡
Byrd, Otis, Jr. '51 '83 C.381 B.A. L.7 J.D.
(adm. in OH; not adm. in IN) AlliedSignal Inc.
Canfield, Robert E., (BV) .... '51 '81 C.347 L.602 J.D. 218 W. Washington St.
Casey, Brian E. .... '— '92 C.691 B.A. L.976 J.D. [Ⓒ Barnes&T.]
Cekanski Farrand, Kathleen E., (BV) '48 '74 C.608 B.S. L.602 J.D.
914 E. Jefferson Blvd.
Cerullo, Deborah Mary .... '53 '80 C.690 B.A. L.94 J.D. 725 Howard St.
Chamblee, R.W., Jr. ....'51 '77 C&L.602 B.A., J.D. Supr. Ct. J.
Chapleau, David C. .... '53 '78 C.602 B.A. L.345 J.D. Cir. Ct. Mag.
Chapleau, Edward A., (AV) ....'40 '68 C.670 B.B.A. L.345 J.D. [Chapleau&K.]

Chapleau & Kuehl, (AV)
419 West Jefferson Boulevard, P.O. Box 928, 46624
Telephone: 574-234-0041; 574-233-5173 Fax: 574-234-6007
Edward A. Chapleau; James R. Kuehl.
General Civil Practice. Probate and Estate Planning, Wills and Trust Law, Real Estate, Family Law, Domestic Relations, Commercial and Personal Injury Law, Medical Malpractice Defense.

Cholis, Alexis T., (AV) ....'17 '42 C&L.602 B.S., J.D. [Cholis&C.]
Cholis, Paul T., (BV) ....'49 '74 C&L.436 A.B., J.D. [Cholis&C.]
Cholis and Cholis, (AV) ....202 South Michigan, Suite 905
Clark, Christine E. .... '71 '99 C&L.347 B.A., J.D. 1003 Hickory Road
Clarke, Sherry L., (BV) ..... '43 '81 C.914 B.A. L.1119 J.D. Dist. 2 Pro Bono Committee
Clarke, Thomas C. '32 '60 C&L.309 A.B., LL.B.
(adm. in MD; not adm. in IN) 100 N. Michigan St.
Clifford, Lawrence J., (CV) .... '50 '75 C.347 B.A. L.879 J.D. 709 E. Washington St.
Cloutier, David L., Jr. .... '70 '96 C&L.602 B.S., J.D. [Ⓐ Gonderman]
Cohen, Thomas F., (BV) ....'53 '78 C.602 A.B. L.345 J.D. [Hunt S.K.]
Cole, Dianna L. ....'— '02 C.63 B.A. L.1187 J.D. [Cole&B.]
Cole & Baer, LLP .... 108 N. Main St., Suite 322
Connell, Michael S., Law Office of '70 '99
C.925 B.S. L.602 J.D. 105 E. Jefferson Boulevard Suite 800
Cotter, Kenneth P., (BV) '62 '90 C&L.602 B.A., J.D.
Chf. Dep. Pros. Atty., St. Joseph Co. Pros. Off.
Cox, Dempsey A., Jr., (AV) ....'25 '51 C.5 L.383 LL.B. 120 W. LaSalle Ave., 9th Fl.
Criss, Jon A., (CV) ....'68 '94 C&L.347 B.A., J.D. [Ⓐ Sweeney,P.M.&S.]
Crotty, Brien P. .... '— '98 C.879 B.A. L.602 J.D. [Ⓐ Barnes&T.]
Crowley, Paul G. .... '51 '95 C.276 B.A. L.602 J.D. 726 E. Washington Ave.

Crump, R. Tracy
(See New Carlisle)

Curran, Timothy M. .... '— '00 C.436 B.A. L.602 J.D. [Ⓐ Boveri M.R.&L.]
Daub, Janilyn Brouwer .... '— '91 C.323 B.A. L.608 J.D. [Barnes&T.]
Deahl, Richard J. ....'— '98 C.347 B.S. L.345 J.D. [Ⓐ Barnes&T.]
Dees, Harry C., Jr. ..... '45 '74 C.210 B.A. L.1119 J.D. U.S. Bkrptcy. J., U.S. Bkrptcy. Ct.

DeRose, Aladean M., (BV) '51 '78 C.276 B.S. L.347 J.D.
105 East Jefferson Boulevard, Suite 512, 46601
Telephone: 574-234-5091 Fax: 574-289-4618
Email: aderose@ci.south-bend.in.us URL: http://www.deroselaw.com
Bankruptcy, Collections, Wills and Probate, Trusts and Estates, Estate Planning, Family/Domestic Relations, Adoptions, Divorce, Child Custody, Child Support, Visitation Rights, Personal Injury, Automobile Accidents, Slip and Fall, Wrongful Death, Social Security Disability, Employment Discrimination, Workers Compensation, Civil Trial Litigation in all State and Federal Courts.

See Professional Biographies, SOUTH BEND, INDIANA

Diamond, Eric L., (AV) .... '58 '83 C&L.602 B.B.A., J.D. [Diamond&D.]

Diamond and Diamond, (AV)
405 West Wayne Street, P.O. Box 1875, 46634-1875
Telephone: 574-232-6918 Fax: 574-233-2267
Email: attydiamond@prodigy.net
Arthur M. Diamond (1925-2000); Eric L. Diamond; Jeffrey M. Jankowski; Rae D. Beehler.
General Civil Practice in all Courts. Corporation, Probate and Estate Planning, Real Estate, Business, Family/Domestic Relations, Labor and Employment, Bankruptcy and Collections Law.
Representative Clients: Creed Excavating Co., Inc.; Eslinger Home Furnishings, Inc.; Ideal Consolidated, Inc.; International Bakers Service, Inc.; Portage Realty Corp.; Radiology, Inc.

(This Listing Continued)

Diamond and Diamond (Continued)

Reference: Wells Fargo Bank, Indiana, N.A., South Bend.

See Professional Biographies, SOUTH BEND, INDIANA

Dieterly, Douglas K., (AV) .... '— '80 C.63 B.A. L.345 J.D. [Barnes&T.]
Doi, Keith C., (BV) .... '63 '90 C&L.1119 B.A., J.D. [Ⓐ Hunt S.K.]
Donnelly, Joseph S., (CV) .... '55 '81 C&L.602 A.B., J.D. [Ⓒ Nemeth,F.&M.]
Doran, John E., (AV) .... '27 '52 C&L.602 B.S., J.D. [Doran B.] ‡

Doran • Blackmond LLP, (AV) BB
City Center, 211 W. Washington Street Suite 1700, 46601
Telephone: 574-288-1800 Fax: 574-236-4265
Email: firm@doranblackmond.com URL: http://www.doranblackmond.com
Members of Firm: M. Edward Doran (1895-1982); John E. Doran (Retired); Don G. Blackmond; Don Gregory Blackmond; Sally P. Norton. Of Counsel: A. Howard Williams.
Civil Trial and Appellate Practice in Federal and State Courts, Insurance Defense and Coverage Questions, Special Investigation, Personal Injury, Product Liability, Architect and Engineer Liability, Legal Malpractice, Worker's Compensation, Construction Law, Commercial, Creditor's Rights, Bankruptcy and Reorganization, Mediation and Arbitration.
Representative Clients: Allstate Insurance Co.; CNA Insurance Co.; Firemans Fund Insurance Co.; Auto Owners Insurance Co.; Horace Mann Insurance Co.; General Casualty Insurance Co.; Royal and Sun Alliance Insurance Co.; Zurich Insurance Co.; Sentry Insurance Co.; Hoosier Insurance Co.

See Professional Biographies, SOUTH BEND, INDIANA

Dowd, Maureen O. .... '46 '85 C.448 B.A. L.602 J.D. Law Clk. to U.S. Dist. J.
Doyle, Richard D., (BV) .... '31 '61 C.602 L.209 LL.B. 720 Park Ave.‡
Drendall, Stephen G., (BV) .... '52 '79 C&L.831 B.Mus., J.D. 218 W. Washington St.
Dutt, Harolyn Hickey, Law Office of ...... '56 '87 C&L.260 B.A., J.D. 108 N. Main Street
Edgar, Alexander L. '48 '73 C.27 B.A. L.602 J.D.
Asst. U.S. Trustee, U.S. Dept. of Jus.‡
Edwards, Bernard E., (CV) .... '57 '85 C.347 B.S. L.602 J.D. [Ⓐ Anderson A.&K.]
Edwards, Robert M., Jr., (AV) .... '50 '76 C.932 B.B.A. L.602 J.D. [Jones O.]
Engel, Michelle LaRock .... '68 '94 C.489 B.A. L.1119 J.D. City Legal Dept.
Erlin, Carrie S. .... '68 '98 C.35 B.S. L.37 J.D. P.O. Box 6872
Eslinger, Stephen L., (CV) .... '51 '80 C.63 B.S. L.345 J.D. 224 West Jefferson Blvd.
Ettl, Joseph G. .... '13 '39 C.347 B.A. L.1119 J.D. 23007 State Rd. 23‡
Ettl, Madeline G. .... '16 '37 C.347 L.1119 LL.B. 23007 State Rd. 23‡
Faccenda, Philip J., Jr., (BV) .... '— '92 C&L.602 B.A., J.D. [Ⓒ Barnes&T.]
Falvey, John D. .... '62 '97 C.347 B.A. L.879 J.D. [Ⓐ Boveri M.R.&L.]
Fedder, Kenneth P., (BV) .... '34 '60 C.1024 B.A. L.1119 LL.B. [Ⓒ Sweeney,P.M.&S.]
Feeney, F. Gerard, (BV) .... '18 '47 C&L.602 B.A., J.D. [Nemeth,F.&M.]
Feldbaum, Alan B., (AV) .... '— '81 C.347 B.A. L.383 J.D. [Barnes&T.]
Finnigan, John E. '20 '48 C&L.602 A.B., LL.B.
(adm. in NE; not adm. in IN) 924 Twyckenham Dr., North‡
Fischer, Rebecca Hoyt, (BV) .... '58 '83 C.347 B.A. L.602 J.D. [Laderer&F.]
Foley, Edmond W., (AV) .... '51 '79 C&L.602 B.B.A., J.D. [Foley&S.]
Foley, Thomas E. .... '14 '48 L.602 LL.B. 1603 Southeast Dr.‡

Foley & Small, (AV)
1002 East Jefferson Boulevard, 46617
Telephone: 574-288-7676; 800-276-2525 Fax: 574-288-4939
Email: info@foleyandsmall.com URL: http://www.foleyandsmall.com
Members of Firm: Edmond W. Foley; Douglas D. Small.
Personal Injury, Premises Liability, Products Liability, Wrongful Death, Automobile Accidents, Insurance Litigation, and General Litigation.
Regional Offices at: Knox, LaPorte, Plymouth and Rochester, Indiana.

See Professional Biographies, SOUTH BEND, INDIANA

Ford, G. Burt, (AV) .... '23 '49 C.679 B.S. L.1119 LL.B. 600 Key Bank Bldg.
Ford, John B., (BV) .... '51 '76 C.611 B.A. L.1119 J.D. [Jones O.]
Fox, Alison G. .... '70 '95 C.339 B.S. L.597 J.D. [Ⓐ Baker&D.]
Fox, Judith L. .... '60 '93 C.1028 B.S. L.601 J.D. Notre Dame Legal Aid
Fox, Kristin R. .... '70 '98 C.347 B.S. L.879 J.D. [Ⓐ Leone,H.&K.]
Frese, Jerome .... '35 '75 C.423 B.A. L.602 J.D. Supr. Ct. J.
Frisk, Arthur W. .... '20 '52 C.347 B.S. L.602 LL.B. 2306 S. Main St.‡
Fullenkamp, Joseph R., (AV) .... '— '88 C&L.352 B.A., J.D. [Barnes&T.]
Gallagher, Gerard T., (BV) ..... '— '92 C&L.602 B.S., J.D. [Baker&D.] (See Pat. Sect.)
Gallagher, James A., Jr. '64 '89 C.188 B.S. L.107 J.D.
(adm. in OH; not adm. in IN) Human Res. Mgr. & Coun., Allied Signal, Inc.
Galos, Ernest P., Attorney at Law, (CV) '64 '89
C.602 B.A. L.1119 J.D. 618 E. Colfax Ave.
Gammage, Andre B. .... '62 '88 C&L.879 B.C.J., J.D. 110 S. Taylor St.
Gardner, Martin J., (AV) .... '61 '87 C.265 B.A. L.345 J.D. [Gardner&R.]
Gardner & Rans, P.C., (AV) .... 112 West Jefferson, Suite 603
Germann, Douglas D., Sr., (BV) ..... '46 '73 C&L.879 B.S.B.A., J.D. [D.D.Germann,Sr.]

Germann, Douglas D., Sr., P.C., (BV)
P.O. Box 2796, 46680-2796
Telephone: 574-291-0022 Fax: 574-291-0024
Email: 76066.515@COMPUSERVE.COM
Douglas D. Germann, Sr.
Estate Planning and Probate Law. Federal, State and Local Taxation Law. Business Acquisitions Law. Corporation Law.
Reference: National City Bank, Mishawaka, Indiana.

Gillin, Peter J. '69 '98 C.602 B.A. L.93 J.D.
(adm. in RI; not adm. in IN) [Ⓐ Baker&D.]
Gillis, Lucinda Kill, (CV) .... '60 '89 C.424 B.S. L.602 J.D. [Gillis&A.]
Gillis & Aldridge, LLP, (CV) .... 17434 State Road 23
Gonderman, Robert F., Jr. .... '59 '85 C.436 B.A. L.602 J.D. [Gonderman]
Gonderman Legal Corporation, P.C. .... 54391 30th Street
Gotsch, Michael G. ..... '57 '87 C&L.602 A.B., J.D. Judge, St. Joseph Cir. Ct. Courthouse
Gozdecki, Jeanine M., (BV) .... '— '92 C&L.602 B.A., J.D. [Barnes&T.]
Grabb, Thomas F., (CV) .... '56 '82 C.347 B.S. L.345 J.D. 108 N. Main Street
Grainger, Brooks J., (CV) .... '70 '96 C&L.879 B.S.B.A., J.D. [Ⓐ Krisor&Assoc.]
Grant, Robert A. .... '05 '30 C&L.602 A.B., J.D. U.S. Sr. Dist. J.‡
Greci, Carl A. .... '62 '93 C&L.347 B.A., J.D. [Baker&D.]
Greene, Cheryl A. .... '51 '97 C.347 B.A. L.602 J.D. City of So. Bend Dept. of Law
Greer, Larry A. ...... '52 '78 C.602 A.B. L.213 J.D. Admin. Servs. Mgr., U.S. Bkrptcy. Ct.
Griffith, John B., (AV Ⓣ) '57 '85 C.910 B.S.B.A. L.188 J.D.
Sr. V.P., Gen. Coun. & Secy., 1st Source Bank
Grimmer, William T., (AV) .... '50 '75 C&L.602 B.A., J.D. Asst. U.S. Atty.
Griner, Gary L. .... '75 '00 C.265 B.A. L.1119 J.D. Dep. Pros. Atty.
Groves, James F., (AV) .... '47 '72 C&L.602 A.B., J.D. [Lee&G.]
Hackett, M. Patricia .... '— '91 C&L.602 B.A., J.D. [Baker&D.]

Hahn, Walz and Knepp, A Professional Association, (BV)
509 West Washington Avenue, 46601-1527
Telephone: 574-234-2118; 574-232-5988 Fax: 574-234-2119
Email: Lawyers@hahnwalz.com URL: http://www.hahnwalz.com/
Charles W. Hahn (1909-1985); Wilford V. Walz (1902-1993); James P. Knepp; Thomas M. Walz;— Andrea Kurek Slagh.

(This Listing Continued)

Hahn, Walz and Knepp, A Professional Association (Continued)

Business and Corporate Law, Elder Law, Estate Planning and Probate, Real Estate, General Civil Litigation (Federal and State Courts), Bankruptcy, Collections, commercial Law, Personal Injury, Labor Law, Wills and Trusts Law, Family Law, Adoptions.

See Professional Biographies, SOUTH BEND, INDIANA

Haines, Gregory J., (CV) .... '65 '91 C.602 B.A. L.347 J.D. [Ⓐ Rowe&R.]
Hains, Fred R., (BV) .... '48 '74 C.967 B.A. L.879 J.D. [Hains]

Hains Law Firm, LLP, (BV)
125 North St. Peter Street, 46617
Telephone: 574-234-7606 Fax: 574-282-1360
URL: http://www.hainslawfirm.com
Members of Firm: Fred R. Hains; Peter M. Yarbro.
General Civil and Criminal Trial Practice in all State and Federal Courts, Appellate Practice, Business Litigation, Domestic Relations, Family Law, Bankruptcy, Real Estate, Intellectual Property, Adoption, Child Custody, Child Support, Divorce, Visitation Rights, Wills and Probate.

See Professional Biographies, SOUTH BEND, INDIANA

Hall, James D., (AV) '36 '61
C.679 B.S.M.E. L.1119 J.D. 105 E. Jefferson Boulevard (Pat.)
Hall, Thomas J., (AV) .... '48 '74 C.347 A.B. L.345 J.D. [Tuesley&H.]
Halpin, Andrea E., (CV) .... '70 '95 C.347 B.S. L.1119 J.D. [Ⓐ Leone,H.&K.]
Hamilton, John C., (AV) .... '40 '68 C.602 B.A. L.309 J.D. [Hamilton]
Hamilton, Thomas R., (BV) .... '55 '83 C.894 A.B. L.879 J.D. [Ⓐ Hunt S.K.]

Hamilton Law Firm, A Professional Corporation, (AV)
300 North Michigan Street Suite 454, 46601
Telephone: 574-289-9987 Fax: 574-289-8138
Email: jch@HamiltonFirm.com
John C. Hamilton.
Civil Trial and Appellate Practice in Federal and State Courts. Commercial, Employment and Environmental Law.

See Professional Biographies, SOUTH BEND, INDIANA

Hammerschmidt, Amaral & Jonas, (BV) .... 137 N. Michigan St.
Hanson, John K., (BV) .... '59 '84 C.347 B.S. L.1119 J.D. [Tuesley&H.]
Hanson, Susan R., (BV) .... '60 '85 C.473 B.A. L.1119 J.D. [Ⓒ Tuesley&H.]
Hardig, Edward W., (AV) .... '36 '61 C&L.602 B.S., J.D. 131 South Taylor Street
Hardig, Edward W., Jr. .... '67 '96 C.201 B.S. L.1187 J.D. Meridian Title Corp.
Hardman, Lyle R., (BV) .... '66 '91 C.210 B.A. L.347 J.D. [Hunt S.K.]
Hardy, Michael D., (BV) .... '— '90 C.1111 B.A. L.1119 J.D. [Barnes&T.]
Havens, Julianne K. ...... '66 '91 C.303 B.A. L.879 J.D. Off. of Pros. Atty., St. Joseph Co.
Hays, Michael J. .... '— '02 C.210 B.A. L.602 J.D. [Ⓐ Barnes&T.]
Heck, Andrew P. .... '— '00 C.894 B.A. L.879 J.D. [Ⓐ Barnes&T.]
Heck, Jeff R. .... '56 '98 C&L.602 B.B.A., J.D. [Ⓐ Baker&D.]
Hegyi, Louis L., (BV) .... '53 '78 C.602 A.B. L.1119 J.D. Pub. Def.
Heppenheimer, Mitchell R., (BV) ... '50 '76 C.347 B.S. L.192 J.D. [Heppenheimer,K.&T.]
Heppenheimer, Korpal & Toth, P.C., (BV) .... 704 W. Washington Ave.
Herendeen, George E., (BV) .... '35 '61 C.435 A.B. L.879 J.D. 205 W. Jefferson Blvd.
Hernly, Timothy D., (AV) .... '— '86 C.347 B.A. L.1119 J.D. [Barnes&T.]
Hilgendorf, Edward C. .... '31 '60 C&L.602 A.B., LL.B. 218 W. Washington Ave.‡
Hilgendorf, Sean P. .... '68 '97 C.602 B.A. L.1003 J.D. [Johnson]
Hill, Dan R. .... '44 '73 C.347 B.A. L.365 J.D. 218 W. Washington St., Ste. 430
Hill, Richard L., (AV) .... '47 '72 C.397 B.A. L.602 J.D. [Baker&D.]
Hiss, Bernard F. .... '17 '41 C&L.602 B.S., J.D. 19090 Summers Ave.‡
Homann, Jacqueline Sells .... '65 '90 C.210 B.A. L.602 J.D. [Jones O.]
Hoogeveen, Angela M. '72 '97
C&L.879 B.A., J.D. Legal Serv(s). Program of N. Indiana, Inc.
Hoover, Henry A. .... '24 '50 C.602 Ph.B. L.309 LL.B. 1439 Argyle Dr.
Horn, George E., Jr., (CV) .... '— '87 C&L.602 B.A., J.D. [Barnes&T.]
Hosinski, William A. .... '19 '44 C&L.602 B.S.C., LL.B. Ret. Supr. Ct. J.‡
Howe, Arvil R. .... '— '80 C&L.879 B.A., J.D. 502 W. Washington
Hudson, RaeLee C. .... '72 '99 C.112 B.A. L.879 J.D. [Ⓐ Baker&D.]
Hughes, John D., (AV) .... '10 '36 C.210 A.B. L.345 LL.B. 1225 S. 26th Street‡
Hughes, John D. .... '46 '89 C&L.63 B.S., J.D. [Hughes&Assoc.]
Hughes Associates .... 1225 S. 26th Street
Hull, Jennifer Bickley .... '— '97 C.475 B.A. L.215 J.D. [Ⓐ Baker&D.]
Hull, L. Kent .... '46 '72 C&L.339 B.A., J.D. 105 E. Jefferson Blvd., #600

Hunt Suedhoff Kalamaros LLP, (AV)
120 West LaSalle Avenue, Twelfth Floor, P.O. Box 4156, 46634-4156 ⊙
Telephone: 574-232-4801 Fax: 574-232-9736
URL: http://www.hsk-law.com
Members of Firm: Thomas F. Cohen; Robert Deane Woods; Kevin W. Kearney; Philip E. Kalamaros; Lynn E. Kalamaros; Carol A. Vogel; Lyle R. Hardman. Associates: Thomas R. Hamilton; Charles H. Bassford, IV; Keith C. Doi; Peter J. Bagiackas; Deanne M. Volheim.
General Civil Trial and Appellate Practice, Insurance Defense Litigation, Commercial Real Estate Financing and Transactions, Corporate and Commercial Law, Probate and Estate Planning.
Fort Wayne, Indiana Office: 803 South Calhoun Street, Ninth Floor, P.O. Box 11489, 46858-1489. Telephone: 260-423-1311. Fax: 260-424-5396.
Indianapolis, Indiana Office: 6323 S. East Street, 46227. Telephone: 317-784-4966. Fax: 317-784-5566.
St. Joseph, Michigan Office: 608 S. Pleasant Street, P.O. Box 46, 49085-0046. Telephone: 269-983-4405. Fax: 269-983-5645.

See Professional Biographies, SOUTH BEND, INDIANA

Ickler, Nancy L., (AV) .... '— '84 C.475 B.A. L.602 J.D. [Barnes&T.]
Inabnit, Brent E., (BV) .... '65 '90 C.63 B.S. L.879 J.D. [Sopko,N.&I.]
Jaicomo, Ronald J., (AV) .... '32 '59 C.98 B.S. L.339 J.D. [Ⓒ Sopko,N.&I.]
Jankowski, Jeffrey M., (BV) .... '62 '88 C&L.602 B.A., J.D. [Diamond&D.]
Johnson, Mark D. '64 '92 C.338 B.A. L.589 J.D.
(adm. in IL; not adm. in IN) [Johnson] ⊙

Johnson Law Group
46601 ⊙
Telephone: 877-333-2889 Fax: 309-827-3991
Email: johnson.law@verizon.net
Mark D. Johnson (Not admitted in IN); Sean P. Hilgendorf (Resident).
Languages: Japanese and Greek.
Felonies, Murder, White Collar Crime, Drugs, Domestic Violence, DWI.
Okemos, Michigan Office: 3474 Alaiedon Parkway, 47764. Telephone: 877-333-2889.
Canton, Ohio Office: 4571 Stephen Circle N.W., 44718. Telephone: 877-333-2889.
Bloomington, Illinois Office: 115 W. Front Street, 61701. Telephone: 309-827-3670.

See Professional Biographies, SOUTH BEND, INDIANA

Jonas, R. William, Jr., (BV) ..... '56 '81 C.347 A.B. L.1119 J.D. [Hammerschmidt,A.&J.]
Jones, Katherine Cobb .... '61 '88 C.851 B.B.A. L.69 J.D. 108 N. main St.
Jones, Margaret M. .... '54 '02 C&L.347 B.S., J.D. P.O. Box 1622
Jones Obenchain, LLP, (AV) .... 202 South Michigan Street
Kaczmarek, Matthew R. .... '68 '96 C.436 B.A. L.879 J.D. [Sopko,N.&I.]
Kalamaros, Lynn E., (BV) .... '68 '93 C&L.602 B.A., J.D. [Hunt S.K.]
Kalamaros, Philip E., (BV) '62 '87 C&L.602 B.B.A., J.D.
[Hunt S.K.] (⊙St. Joseph, MI)
Kalamaros, Timothy E., (BV) .... '71 '96 C.602 B.B.A. L.424 J.D. [T.E.Kalamaros]

Kalamaros, Timothy E., Law Office, P.C., (BV)
328 North Michigan Street, Suite S-2, 46601
Telephone: 574-232-4802 Fax: 574-232-3839
Email: teklaw@sbcglobal.net
Timothy E. Kalamaros.
Wills and Probate, Trusts and Estates, Estate Planning, Elder Law, Business Law, Business Planning, Business Enterprises, Starting a Business, Buying and Selling a Business, Real Estate.
See Professional Biographies, SOUTH BEND, INDIANA

Kamm, Gerald A., (AV) .... '21 '47 C&L.602 A.B., LL.B. 401 E. Colfax Ave., Suite 307‡
Kearney, Kevin W., (BV) .... '61 '86 C.602 B.A. L.776 J.D. [Hunt S.K.]
Keckley, J. David, Attorney at Law, (BV) '48 '73 C.347 B.S. L.345 J.D. 315 N. Main St.
Keefer, Christopher M. .... '74 '99 C.602 B.B.A. L.1119 J.D. [Ⓐ Sopko,N.&I.]
Keller, Scott M., (BV) .... '— '88 C.679 B.S. L.1119 J.D. [Anderson A.&K.]

Keller, Thomas P., (CV) '66 '93 C.1030 B.A. L.602 J.D.
The Tower Building, Suite 720, 218 W. Washington, 46601
Telephone: 574-234-2990 Fax: 574-234-9960
Email: thomas.keller@tkellerlaw.com URL: http://www.tkellerlaw.com
Criminal Law, Felonies, Misdemeanors, Drug Crimes, Traffic Violations, Driving While Intoxicated, White Collar Crime, Personal Injury, Automobile Accidents, Slip and Fall, Wrongful Death, Debt Collection, Debtor and Creditor Law.
See Professional Biographies, SOUTH BEND, INDIANA

Kimmell, Jeff, (CV) .... '64 '95 C&L.347 B.A., J.D. 218 W. Washington Street
Klatch, Louis .... '50 '77 C&L.347 B.A., J.D. York Title & Escrow Co.
Knepp, James P., (BV) .... '47 '75 C.347 B.S. L.1119 J.D. [Hahn,W.&K.]
Knight, Michael V. .... '— '00 C.103 A.B. L.879 J.D. [Ⓐ Barnes&T.]
Knowles, Brenda E. .... '46 '77 C.249 B.A. L.1119 J.D. Prof. of Bus. Law, IN Univ.
Knox, Tracy D., (BV) .... '— '91 C.870 B.S. L.602 J.D. [Barnes&T.]
Kohn, Mary L., (CV) .... '— '91 C.602 B.A. L.347 J.D. 52303 Emmons Rd.
Konopa, Robert J., (AV) .... '41 '67 C&L.602 A.B., LL.B. [Konopa,R.&A.]

Konopa, Reagan & Aigotti, P.C., (AV)
212 East LaSalle Avenue, Suite 200, 46617
Telephone: 574-239-1000 Fax: 574-239-1001
URL: http://www.konopa.com
Directors of Firm: Robert J. Konopa; Margot Fisher Reagan; Claire Konopa Aigotti.
General Civil Practice. Personal Injury, Automobile Accidents, Products Liability, Brain Injury, Truck Accidents, Nursing Home Negligence, Wrongful Death, Insurance (Personal and Commercial Lines), and Commercial Law. Business Law, Contracts, Litigation, Trial and Appellate Practice in all State and Federal Courts. Mediations and Arbitrations.
Reference: Norwest Bank Indiana, N.A.
See Professional Biographies, SOUTH BEND, INDIANA

Konopinski, Robert L. .... '69 '97 C.1265 B.A. L.347 J.D. [Leone,H.&K.]
Kopka, Pinkus, Dolin & Eads, (AVⓉ)
227 South Main Street, Suite 200 (ⓒBuffalo Grove, Chgo., IL; Crown Point, Indpls., IN; Farmington Hills, MI)
Korpal, James F., (BV) .... '52 '78 C.679 B.A. L.192 J.D. [Heppenheimer,K.&T.]
Korzan, Lee, (BV) .... '58 '87 C.870 B.S. L.602 J.D. [Ⓐ Anderson A.&K.]
Kowals, Anthony D., (BV) .... '41 '67 C.259 B.S. L.602 LL.B. 205 W. Jefferson Blvd.
Krisor, John D., Jr., (AV) '47 '72 C.973 B.S.B.A. L.602 J.D. Dep. Pros. Atty. [Krisor&Assoc.]
Krisor & Associates, (AV) .... P.O. Box 6200
Kuehl, James R., (AV) .... '40 '69 C.210 B.A. L.1119 J.D. [Chapleau&K.]
Kuehn, R. John, III .... '75 '00 C&L.602 B.A., J.D. [Ⓐ Boveri M.R.&L.]
Kurek Slagh, Andrea .... '72 '98 C.602 B.A. L.879 J.D. [Ⓐ Hahn,W.&K.]
Laderer, Lewis C., Jr., (AV) .... '43 '68 C.473 B.S. L.602 J.D. [Laderer&F.]
Laderer & Fischer, P.C., (AV) .... 112 West Jefferson Boulevard, Suite 310
LaDue, John D., (BV) .... '62 '90 C.475 B.A. L.602 J.D. [Boveri M.R.&L.]
Lake, Brian J., (AV) .... '— '71 C.602 B.A. L.477 J.D. [Barnes&T.]

Lauer, Jay, (BV) '52 '78 C&L.879 B.A., J.D.
400 Trigon Building, 224 West Jefferson Boulevard, 46601-1824
Telephone: 574-288-5562 Fax: 574-233-9342
URL: http://www.jaylauer.com
General Civil Practice in All State and Federal Courts. Criminal Law, Driving While Intoxicated, Drug Crimes, Juvenile Law, Parole and Probation, Traffic Violations, White Collar Crime, Labor, Employment Discrimination, Sexual Harassment, Wrongful Termination, Medical Malpractice, Personal Injury, Automobile Accidents and Injuries, Slip and Fall, Wrongful Death, Product Liability, Social Security Disability, Workers Compensation, Bankruptcies, Investment Fraud, Municipal Law, Real Estate, Wills, Probate, Trusts and Estates, Estate Planning, Asset Protection, Guardianships, Domestic Relations, Family Law, Adoptions, Child Custody, Child Support, Divorce, Domestic Violence, Visitation Rights.
See Professional Biographies, SOUTH BEND, INDIANA

Lawrence, Stephen A. '43 '70 C.56 B.S. L.838 J.D. (adm. in MN; not adm. in IN) Sr. V.P. & Gen. Coun., Whiteford Systems, Inc.
Lee, Robert D., (AV) .... '39 '66 C.602 B.B.S. L.879 J.D. [Lee&G.]

Lee and Groves, Professional Association, (AV)
Suite 502, 205 West Jefferson Boulevard, 46601-1812
Telephone: 574-232-5923 Fax: 574-232-5942
URL: http://www.leesandgroves.com
Robert D. Lee; James F. Groves;—Clint A. Zalas; David E. Ballard.
Languages: Spanish.
General Civil and Trial Practice in all State and Federal Courts. Personal Injury, Products Liability, Family/Domestic Relations, Insurance, Administrative, Negligence, Corporation and Real Estate Law.
See Professional Biographies, SOUTH BEND, INDIANA

Leichty, Damon R. .... '— '99 C.894 B.A. L.1119 J.D. [Ⓐ Barnes&T.]
Leighton, Judd .... '10 '47 C.46 L.597 J.D. 112 W. Jefferson Blvd.‡
Lenyo, Mark S., (BV) '58 '84 C.602 B.B.A. L.879 J.D. 205 W. Jefferson Blvd., Ste. 606
Leonard-Dent, Marva J., (CV) '57 '83 C.329 B.A. L.1119 J.D. Corp. Staff Atty., Community School Corp.
Leone, Charles S., (BV) .... '47 '75 C.602 B.S. L.273 J.D. [Leone,H.&K.]
Leone, Halpin, & Konopinski, LLP, (BV) .... 205 W. Jefferson Blvd.
Lerman, Gerald F. '41 '65 C.145 B.A. L.976 LL.B. V.P. & Gen. Coun., Steel Warehouse Company, Inc.
Lewis, Greta Roemer, (BV) .... '— '89 C.602 B.A. L.209 J.D. [Barnes&T.]
Lewis, Thomas F., III, (BV) .... '62 '87 C.347 B.S. L.602 J.D. [Jones O.]
Lewis, Thomas F., Jr., (AV) .... '38 '63 C.1024 B.S. L.1119 J.D. [Jones O.]
Linfield, Seth D., (BV) .... '— '84 C.569 B.A. L.813 J.D. [Barnes&T.]
Livingston, John R. .... '— '65 C&L.383 B.S., J.D. 105 East Jefferson Blvd., Suite 400
Lloyd, John H., IV, (CV) .... '67 '92 C.597 B.A. L.602 J.D. [Plews S.R.&B.]
Loeser, Charles M. .... '52 '78 C.475 B.A. L.309 J.D. Gen. Coun., Health Quest Grp.
Loughridge, Gregory D., (BV) .... '48 '73 C.347 A.B. L.602 J.D. [G.D.Loughridge]
Loughridge, Gregory D., P.C., (BV) .... 137 N. Michigan St.
Luber, Anthony V., (BV) .... '41 '67 C.1323 B.A. L.602 J.D. 502 W. Washington St.
Luks-Mcfarland, Georgia C., (CV) .... '43 '76 C.429 B.A. L.602 J.D. 112 W. Jefferson
Lunneen, Thos. E. .... '23 '49 C.999 L.602 LL.B. 120 W. Lasalle
Lutkus, Gerald F., (AV) .... '— '82 C&L.602 B.A., J.D. [Barnes&T.]

Lysohir, Alexander, (AV) .... '18 '53 C.347 B.S. L.602 LL.B. 6171 Darby Ct.‡
Magnuson, Janet A. '64 '91 C.473 B.A. L.347 J.D. (adm. in IL; not adm. in IN) 1148 Ridgedale Rd.‡
Maher, Timothy J., (BV) .... '— '90 C.187 B.S.S. L.602 J.D. [Ⓒ Barnes&T.]
Manier, Jenny Pitts .... '60 '85 C&L.602 B.A., J.D. Supr. Ct.
Manion, Daniel A. .... '42 '73 C.602 B.S. L.345 J.D. Cir. J.
Marnocha, John M., (BV) .... '54 '82 C.347 B.A. L.879 J.D. Supr. Ct. J.

Marshall, Eric '57 '92 C.347 B.S. L.602 J.D.
1318 Mishawaka Avenue, 46615
Telephone: 574-234-9334 Fax: 574-288-1066 URL: http://www.ericmarshall.com
Email: sericmarshall@aol.com URL: http://www.southbendelderlaw.com
Elder Law, Elder Care, Health Care Law, Estate Planning, Trusts and Estates, Wills and Probate, Estate Litigation, Asset Protection, Guardianship and Conservatorship, Charitable Giving, Taxation, Estate and Gift Taxation, Income Tax, Property Tax, Long Term Care, Medicare and Medicaid, Nursing Home Litigation, Real Estate.
See Professional Biographies, SOUTH BEND, INDIANA

Masters, James A., (BV) .... '52 '78 C&L.602 A.B., J.D. [Nemeth,F.&M.]
Matthews, James M., (BV) .... '60 '85 C.894 A.B. L.608 J.D. [Baker&D.]
Mauch, Thomas J. .... '— '01 C.912 B.S. L.602 J.D. [Ⓐ Baker&D.]
May, Arthur A., (AV) .... '22 '47 C.347 L.602 LL.B. 300 N. Michigan St.‡
May, Brian J. .... '43 '70 C.347 B.S. L.1119 J.D. Pub. Def.

May Oberfell Lorber, (AV)
300 North Michigan Street, Suite 414, 46601 ⊙
Telephone: 574-232-2031 Facsimile: 574-232-9789
URL: http://www.maylorber.com
John H. Peddycord.
Corporate and Commercial Transactions, Litigation, Environmental Law, Real Estate, Labor and Employment, Banking and Bank Related Matters, Estate Planning, Municipal and Administration Law, Products Liability, Alternative Dispute Resolution, Health Care, Medical Malpractice Defense, Insurance Litigation, Trademark and Copyright, Tax, Plaintiff's Litigation, General Civil and Appellate Practice in State and Federal Courts.
Representative Clients: Society National Bank, Indiana; Tyler Refrigeration Corporation; Heller Financial, Inc.; Big C Lumber Co., Inc.; Penn Central Corporation; Orbitron Industries, Inc.; Envirocorp Services Technology, Inc.; ITT Hartford; ASA Corporation.
Mishawaka, Indiana Office: 4100 Edison Lakes Parkway, 46545-3422. Telephone: 574-243-4100. Fax: 574-232-9789.
See Professional Biographies, SOUTH BEND, INDIANA

McCormick, Leo H., Jr. '38 '68 C.711 B.S. L.900 J.D. (adm. in KS; not adm. in IN; Pat.) 2112 Mishawaka Ave.
McDonald, Richard J. .... '25 '55 C&L.602 A.B., J.D. 108 N. Main St.
McFadden, Patrick T., (CV) .... '52 '78 C&L.602 B.A., J.D. [McFadden&M.]
McFadden, Victor L., (CV) .... '28 '60 C&L.602 A.B., LL.B. [McFadden&M.]
McFadden & McFadden, (CV) .... 220 S. Taylor St.
McHugh, Laurence A., (AV) .... '— '73 C&L.347 A.B., J.D. [Barnes&T.]
McKinney, David B. '55 '80 C.473 B.S. L.1119 J.D. (adm. in WI; not adm. in IN) 1926 Rockne Dr.‡
McKinney, Ethan C. .... '77 '02 C.679 B.A. L.602 J.D. Dep. Pros. Atty.
McLaughlin, Timothy P., (BV) ..... '44 '70 C.1024 B.A. L.602 J.D. 1017 E. Jeferson Blvd.
McTigue, David M., (BV) ... '51 '80 C&L.602 B.A., J.D. 205 W. Jefferson Blvd., Ste. 606
Means, William T. .... '28 '54 C.800 A.B. L.477 J.D. Supr. Ct. J.
Miller, Debra L. .... '60 '96 C.62 B.A. L.1003 J.D. P.O. Box 11550
Miller, Jane W. .... '50 '78 C.347 A.B. L.602 J.D. 205 W. Jefferson Blvd.‡
Miller, Jos. J., Jr. .... '19 '42 C&L.602 B.S., LL.B. 115 S. Lafayette Blvd.
Miller, Robert L., Jr. .... '50 '75 C.597 B.A. L.345 J.D. U.S. Dist. J.
Miller, Robert L., Sr. .... '20 '47 C&L.602 B.S., J.D. 1609 E. Colfax Ave.‡
Miller, Susan M. .... '53 '80 C.679 B.S.B.A. L.902 J.D. Law Clk., U.S. Dist. Ct.
Milstone, James H., (BV) .... '— '85 C.436 B.A. L.879 J.D. [Kopka,P.D.&E.]
Minczeski, Edward V., (AV) .... '18 '41 C&L.602 B.C.S., J.D. 337 W. N. Shore Dr.‡
Mintz, Richard L., (AV) .... '— '72 C.33 B.A. L.477 J.D. [Barnes&T.]
Mirkin, David L., (BV) .... '56 '81 C.1169 B.A. L.347 J.D. [Mirkin]
Mirkin, Sam, (BV) .... '31 '61 C.347 B.A. L.910 J.D. [Mirkin]
Mirkin Law Offices, P.C., (BV) .... 112 West Jefferson Boulevard
Moerlein, Steven J. .... '53 '81 C&L.879 B.S.B.A., J.D. [Moerlein]
Moerlein Law Offices .... 218 W. Washington St.
Monahan, John E. .... '16 '40 C&L.602 A.B., LL.B. V.P., Abstract & Title Corp.
Montgomery, John W. .... '13 '38 C.388 B.A. L.477 LL.B. Ret. Cir. J.‡
Morgan, Richard W., (AV) .... '46 '73 C.602 B.A. L.345 J.D. [Sweeney,P.M.&S.]
Mueller, Angelika E. '52 '76 C.347 A.B. L.1119 J.D. Mng. Atty., Legal Servs. Program of Northern Ind., Inc.
Mueller, Kate E. .... '— '04 C&L.602 B.A., J.D. [Ⓐ Barnes&T.]
Murphy, Michael C., (BV) .... '53 '79 C&L.602 B.B.A., J.D. [M.C.Murphy]
Murphy, Patrick D., (BV) .... '62 '88 C.602 B.B.A. L.347 J.D. [Boveri M.R.&L.]

Murphy, Michael C., Elder Law P.C., (BV)
Camdon Park on Hickory, 1001 Hickory Road, Suite 7B, 46615
Telephone: 574-235-7950 Fax: 574-235-7954
Email: mike@murphyelderlaw.com URL: http://www.michianaelderlaw.com
Michael C. Murphy.
Elder Law, Estate Planning, Trust and Estates, Wills and Probate, Medicare, Medicaid, Guardianships and Conservatorship, Asset Protection, Health Care.
See Professional Biographies, SOUTH BEND, INDIANA

Mysliwiec, Robert W., (BV) ..... '49 '74 C&L.602 B.B.A., J.D. 150 W. Angela Boulevard
Nafe, James D., (AV) .... '27 '51 C.347 A.B. L.1119 J.D. [Nafe&N.]
Nafe, James D., Jr., (BV) .... '53 '81 C.347 A.B. L.1095 J.D. [Nafe&N.]
Nafe and Nafe, (AV) .... 50817 Indiana State Route 933
Nash, Ann-Carol .... '55 '87 C.328 B.A. L.602 J.D. City Dept. of Law
Nelson, Charles F. .... '47 '83 C&L.602 A.B., J.D. 112 West Jefferson Boulevard
Nemeth, Peter J. .... '41 '66 C.37 B.A. L.178 J.D. Prob. J.
Nemeth, Feeney & Masters, P.C., (BV) .... 215 South St. Joseph Street

Newby, Lewis, Kaminski & Jones, LLP
(See La Porte)

Newman, David W. .... '74 '00 C.679 B.S. L.879 J.D. 133 S. Taylor
Nguyen, Thao T. .... '79 '04 C.604 B.A. L.1119 J.D. [Ⓐ Plews S.R.&B.]
Nickle, Andrew W., (AV) .... '49 '74 C.317 A.B. L.602 J.D. [Nickle&P.]

Nickle & Piasecki, (AV)
205 West Jefferson Boulevard, Suite 600, 46601
Telephone: 574-232-4747 Fax: 574-232-4904
Andrew W. Nickle; Carmen M. Piasecki. Of Counsel: Thomas H. Singer.
Commercial Transactions, Corporate and Business Law, Real Estate, Commercial Collections, Creditors' Rights, Personal Injury Litigation. Practice in all State and Federal Courts.
See Professional Biographies, SOUTH BEND, INDIANA

Norton, Sally P., (BV) .... '64 '91 C&L.347 B.A., J.D. [Doran B.]
Nuechterlein, Christopher A. .... '51 '76 C&L.879 B.A., J.D. Mag. J.‡
Nussbaum, Richard A., II, (AV) .... '52 '77 C&L.602 B.A., J.D. [Sopko,N.&I.]
Obenchain, John R., (AV) .... '42 '70 C.172 B.S. L.879 J.D. [Jones O.]
Oberfell, James W., (AV) .... '27 '50 C&L.602 B.S., J.D. 1361 E. Monroe‡

O'Brien, James A., (BV) '— '93
C&L.602 B.B.A., J.D. 215 S. St. Joseph Street, Room 600
O'Brien, Margot J. '67 '92 C.436 B.S. L.602 J.D.
(adm. in IL; not adm. in IN) 204 S. Main St.‡
Odell, Jody H. .... '— '95 C.937 B.A. L.602 J.D. [Barnes&T.]
Olczak, Edward .... '11 '37 C&L.602 B.A., LL.B. 2517-2521 Western Ave.
Palguta, Larry J. .... '48 '75 C.679 B.S.M.E. L.192 J.D. Sr. Coun., I.P., Honeywell (Pat.)
Palmer, Michael P. '— '97 C.602 B.A. L.424 J.D.
(adm. in IL; not adm. in IN) [🄱 Barnes&T.]
Parish, Julianne R. .... '69 '96 C.345 B.S. L.1187 J.D. [🄰 Anderson A.&K.]
Parker, Robert M., (AV) .... '25 '52 C&L.602 B.S., J.D. 232 Sylvan Glen
Parkman, Steven T., (BV) ... '54 '84 C&L.347 B.A., J.D. 224 W. Jefferson Blvd., Ste. 311
Patton, Geo. T., (BV) .... '22 '53 C&L.602 A.B., LL.B. 115 S. Lafayette
Peddycord, John H., (AV) .... '44 '71 C.63 A.B. L.602 J.D. [May O.L.] ⊙
Perry, Arthur J., (BV) .... '34 '59 C&L.602 B.S.C., J.D. 108 North Main Street
Peterson, Shawn E. .... '— '03 C.347 B.S. L.602 J.D. [🄰 Baker&D.]
Petsche, Frank. J., (CV) .... '33 '60 C&L.851 B.A., LL.B. 17401 Eldorado Ln.
Pfeifer, Daniel H., (BV) .... '54 '79 C.827 B.A. L.602 J.D. [Sweeney,P.M.&S.]
Phillipoff, Mark J., (BV) .... '51 '80 C.602 A.B. L.347 J.D. [Jones O.]
Piasecki, Carmen M., (AV) .... '48 '73 C.739 B.A. L.602 J.D. [Nickle&P.]
Piasecki, Mark J. .... '46 '81 C.602 B.B.A. L.1051 J.D. 511 S. St. Joseph St.
Pieronek, Catherine F. .... '62 '95 C&L.602 B.S.A.E., J.D. [🄱 Shedlak]

Plews Shadley Racher & Braun, (AV)
53732 Generations Drive, 46635-1539 ⊙
Telephone: 574-273-1010 Fax: 574-271-2050
Email: sbend@psrb.com URL: http://www.psrb.com
John H. Lloyd, IV (Resident); Stephen A. Studer. Associate: Thao T. Nguyen.
Environmental Litigation, Environmental Insurance Coverage, Environmental Cost Recovery, Complex Commercial Litigation, Environmental Corporate and Transaction Law, Environmental Administrative Law, Environmental Permitting, Superfund, Solid and Hazardous Waste, Underground Storage Tanks, Clean Air Act, Clean Water Act, Environmental Business Law, Intellectual Property, Commercial Real Estate and Land Use, Surface Coal Mining and Reclamation Act.
Indianapolis, Indiana Office: 1346 North Delaware Street, 46202-2415. Telephone: 317-637-0700. Telecopier: 317-637-0710.
See Professional Biographies, SOUTH BEND, INDIANA

Pope, D. Lucetta .... '62 '88 C.674 B.A. L.813 J.D. [🄱 Baker&D.]
Potts, Christopher C., (BV) .... '57 '82 C.347 B.S. L.879 J.D. 611-17 JMS Bldg.
Potts, Philip C., (AV) .... '30 '59 C.347 B.S. L.1119 J.D. 108 N. Main St.
Pruitt, David R. '70 '99 C&L.602 B.B.A., J.D.
(adm. in VA; not adm. in IN) [🄰 Baker&D.]
Rans, Kristy M. .... '78 '04 C.679 B.A. L.879 J.D. [Gardner&R.]
Reagan, Margot Fisher, (BV) .... '55 '87 C.741 B.B.A. L.602 J.D. [Konopa,R.&A.]
Reilly, Colin J. .... '71 '98 C.705 B.A. L.602 J.D. [🄰 Jones O.]
Reusser, Thomas P. .... '— '92 C.1288 B.A. L.1119 J.D. 1212 High St.
Rhea, Elizabeth M. .... '71 '96 C.502 B.A. L.602 J.D. 1126 E. Irvington Ave.
Rice, Charles E. '31 '56 C.321 A.B. L.93 J.D.
(adm. in NY; not adm. in IN) 210 South Michigan Street
Rice, Charles P., (BV) .... '63 '89 C&L.602 B.A., J.D. [Boveri M.R.&L.]
Rieff, Craig A., (BV) .... '58 '84 C.347 B.A. L.365 J.D. [🄰 Gonderman]
Ripple, Gregory P. .... '— '03 C&L.602 B.A., J.D. [🄰 Barnes&T.]
Ripple, Kenneth F. .... '43 '68 C.262 A.B. L.893 J.D. U.S. Cir. J.
Roberts, Barbara W., (CV) .... '36 '78 C.823 A.B. L.602 J.D. 108 N. Main
Rodibaugh, Robert K. .... '16 '41 C&L.602 B.S.C., J.D. Sr. U.S. Bkrptcy. J.

Roemer & Mintz, LLP
(See Barnes & Thornburg)

Rompola, Randolph R., (BV) .... '62 '91 C.1113 B.A. L.602 J.D. [Baker&D.]
Roper, John J. .... '39 '68 C.178 B.A. L.477 J.D. 414 N. Taylor St.
Rosen, H. Morris, (CV) .... '41 '65 C.347 B.S. L.1119 LL.B. [M.Rosen]
Rosen, Morris, Law Office of, (CV) .... 112 W. Jefferson Blvd.
Rosenfeld, Robert C., (BV) .... '48 '74 C.347 B.S. L.1119 J.D. 110 S. Taylor St.
Rowe, R. Kent, (AV) .... '30 '55 C.714 A.B. L.602 J.D. [Rowe&R.]
Rowe, R. Kent, III, (AV) .... '56 '81 C.347 A.B. L.861 J.D. [Rowe&R.]

Rowe & Rowe, Law Offices, (AV)
1003 North Hickory, 46615
Telephone: 574-233-8200 Fax: 574-234-5987
Email: Rowe.Rowe@attbi.com URL: http://www.roweandrowe.com
R. Kent Rowe; R. Kent Rowe, III. Associate: Gregory J. Haines.
Insurance Defense. Trials and Appeals in State and Federal Courts. Personal Injury, Automobile Accidents, Truck Accidents, Slip and Fall, Traumatic Brain Injury, Wrongful Death, Unsafe Products, Medical Malpractice, Legal Malpractice.
See Professional Biographies, SOUTH BEND, INDIANA

Rubin, Joseph F., (BV) .... '52 '77 C.347 A.B. L.910 J.D. 2740 Miami St.
Russo, Angela E., (CV) .... '48 '79 C.347 B.A. L.602 J.D. 108 North Main Street
Rutkowski, Aric J. .... '71 '97 C.347 B.A. L.345 J.D. [🄰 Zappia Z.&S.]
Ryan, Shawn P., (BV) .... '66 '91 C&L.602 B.A., J.D. 210 South Michigan Street
Sakaguchi, Douglas E. .... '69 '97 C.347 B.A. L.879 J.D. [🄰 Sweeney,P.M.&S.]

Sanders • Pianowski, LLP
(See Elkhart)

Sandler, H. Richard '44 '73 C.588 B.S. L.1202 J.D.
(adm. in MA; not adm. in IN) 701 W. Chippewa Ave.‡
Sanford, W. Russell, Attorney at Law, (CV) '46 '74
C.676 A.B. L.602 J.D. 328 S. Eddy St.
Schlifke, Robert A., (BV) .... '49 '74 C&L.879 B.A., J.D. P.O. Box 11296
Schrager, Allen E. .... '26 '53 C.347 B.S. L.1119 J.D. P.O. Box 1575
Schroeder, Reinhold .... '56 '94 C&L.879 B.S., J.D. [🄱 Nemeth,F.&M.]
Scopelitis, Michael P., (AV) .... '47 '72 C.573 B.A. L.602 J.D. 315 N. Main St.
Seall, Stephen A., (AV) .... '— '66 C.679 B.A. L.602 LL.B. [Barnes&T.]
Seigel, Eric W. .... '70 '99 C.475 B.A. L.602 J.D. [🄰 Tuesley&H.]
Seng, Laura D. .... '— '03 C.249 B.S. L.879 J.D. [🄰 Barnes&T.]
Sharp, Allen .... '32 '57 C.273 A.B. L.1119 J.D. U.S. Dist. J.
Shaughnessy, Daniel C., Jr., (CVⓉ) '45 '71 C.602 A.B. L.823 J.D.
(adm. in NY; not adm. in IN) 3814 Palomino Cir., Apt. 3A
Shedlak, Charles R. .... '64 '91 C.602 B.A. L.188 J.D. [Shedlak]

Shedlak Law Firm, The
402 W. Washington Street, Suite 200, 46601
Telephone: 574-233-7701 Fax: 574-233-7721
URL: http://www.shedlaklaw.com
Member of Firm: Charles R. Shedlak. Of Counsel: Catherine F. Pieronek.
Business Litigation, Real Estate, Land Use, Construction Litigation, Business Torts, Civil Litigation, Commercial Litigation, Condominium Law, Employment Law, Business Transactions, Contracts, Personal Injury, Insurance Law, Business Law, Municipal Law.
See Professional Biographies, SOUTH BEND, INDIANA

Sheetz, Kenneth L. .... '46 '72 C.347 B.S. L.345 J.D. 224 W. Jefferson Blvd.
Shidaker, Gerald L. .... '42 '90 C.347 B.S. L.1187 J.D. 1717 South Bend Avenue

Simeri, Joseph V., (AV) .... '39 '64 C.602 B.A. L.597 J.D. [Butler&S.]
Singer, Katherine E. .... '70 '97 C.323 B.A. L.602 J.D. Co. Pros. Off.
Singer, Thomas H., (AV) .... '34 '60 C&L.477 A.B., LL.B. [🄱 Nickle&P.]
Slattery, Daniel J. '57 '82
C.373 B.A. L.477 J.D. Asst. Legal Coun., York Title & Escrow Co.
Small, Douglas D., (AV) .... '57 '83 C.347 B.A. L.1119 J.D. [Foley&S.]
Smarrella, John C. .... '— '96 C.291 B.A. L.602 J.D. [Barnes&T.]
Snyder, Richard W., (BV) '47 '73
C.5 B.A. L.477 J.D. 105 E. Jefferson Boulevard, Suite 800
Solomon, Mary Louise .... '43 '81 C.683 A.B. L.602 J.D. U.S. Bkrptcy. Ct.
Sopko, Thomas C., (AV) .... '45 '70 C.973 B.S. L.602 J.D. [Sopko,N.&I.]

Sopko, Nussbaum & Inabnit, (AV)
Plaza Building, 5th Floor, 210 South Michigan Street, P.O. Box 300, 46624
Telephone: 574-234-3000 Telecopier: 574-234-4220
Email: SNI@SNI-Law.com URL: http://www.sni-law.com
Members of Firm: Thomas C. Sopko; Richard A. Nussbaum, II; Brent E. Inabnit; Matthew R. Kaczmarek. Associates: Christopher M. Keefer; Joshua A. Visser. Of Counsel: Ronald J. Jaicomo.
General Civil and Trial Practice in State and Federal Courts. Corporate Banking Law, Probate Litigation, Estate Planning, Real Estate, Family/Domestic Relations, Commercial Law, Personal Injury, Franchise Law and Computer Law.
References: 1st Source Bank; Notre Dame Federal Credit Union; Key Corp Bank.
See Professional Biographies, SOUTH BEND, INDIANA

Steinke, Brian W. .... '46 '82 C.932 B.A. L.602 J.D. 101 S. Main Street
Steketee, Amy M. .... '— '04 C.347 B.A. L.1119 J.D. [🄰 Baker&D.]
Stepanek, Michael J., Jr., (BV) '39 '64
C&L.602 B.B.A., J.D. 1908 East Southern View Drive
Stesiak, Jeffrey J., (BV) .... '66 '92 C.347 B.A. L.879 J.D. [Sweeney,P.M.&S.]
Stevens, H. Jay, (AVⓉ) '47 '73 C&L.260 B.S., J.D.
Northern District of Indiana Federal Community Defenders, Inc.
Stipp, Thomas Sean, (BV) .... '70 '96 C.347 B.A. L.602 J.D. [Zappia Z.&S.]
Studer, Stephen A., (BV) .... '51 '76 C.602 A.B. L.424 J.D. [Plews S.R.&B.]

Stutsman, Mulvaney & DeBoer
(See Elkhart)

Sullivan, Edward A., III, (BV) .... '61 '93 C.884 B.A. L.602 J.D. [Baker&D.]
Sullivan, Shawn F. .... '66 '93 C.201 B.A. L.309 J.D. 1717 E. Wayne Street
Sweeney, Pfeifer, Morgan & Stesiak, (AV) .... 53600 North Ironwood Drive
Tamburo, Vincent A. '34 '62 C&L.665 B.S., J.D.
(adm. in PA; not adm. in IN) Sr. V.P., Gen. Coun. & Secy., 1st Source Corp.
Tamke, James K., Law Office Of, (CV) '50 '85
C.602 B.B.A. L.1190 J.D. 52303 Emmons Road
Telloyan, Mark P. .... '63 '99 C.999 B.S. L.602 J.D. 215 South St. Johseph St.
Terlep, Anthony J., Jr. .... '37 '73 C.679 B.S. L.602 J.D. 1330 Cedar Street

Thorne • Grodnik, LLP
(See Elkhart)

Threatt, Judie .... '63 '96 C.776 B.S.N. L.734 J.D. Holy Cross Health Sys. Cop.
Tillemans, Paul J., (BV) '46 '72 C.755 B.A. L.602 J.D.
115 South Lafayette Blvd., Ste 516
Tomas Morgan, Peter L. .... '66 '98 C&L.602 B.A., J.D. 105 E. Jefferson, Ste. 600
Toth, Gregory D., (BV) '56 '86
C.347 B.S. L.192 J.D. 215 South St. Joseph Street, Suite 600
Toth, Susan '65 '94 C.846 B.A. L.602 J.D.
Strategy & Implementation Mgr., Natl. Institute for Trial Advocacy‡
Triebold, Ellen L. '64 '92 C.966 B.S. L.352 J.D.
(adm. in WI; not adm. in IN) Off. of the U.S. Trustee
Truitt, Robert D. .... '44 '73 C.424 B.S. L.879 J.D. 227 S. Main St., Ste. 100
Trybula, Peter G., (BV) .... '55 '83 C.894 B.A. L.309 J.D. [Baker&D.]
Tuesley, James W. .... '— '99 C.347 B.S. L.1119 J.D. [🄰 Barnes&T.]
Tuesley, Malcolm J., (BV) .... '48 '73 C.347 A.B. L.74 J.D. [Tuesley&H.]

Tuesley & Hall, LLP, (AV)
RiverPlace Professional Center, 212 East LaSalle Avenue, Suite 100, 46617
Telephone: 574-232-3538 Facsimile: 574-232-3790
Email: attorneys@tuesley-hall.com URL: http://www.tuesley-hall.com
Members of Firm: Malcolm J. Tuesley; Thomas J. Hall; John K. Hanson. Of Counsel: Susan R. Hanson; Edward P. Benchik. Senior Associate: Eric W. Seigel.
Corporate and Business Law, Business Litigation, Business Formation, Mergers, Buying and Selling a Business, Commercial Transactions, Taxation and Estate Planning, Probate, Commercial Litigation, Real Estate, Land Use, and Construction Law, Personal Injury and Defense Litigation, Automobile Accidents, Wrongful Death, Health Care Law, General Civil and Trial Practice in State and Federal Courts.
See Professional Biographies, SOUTH BEND, INDIANA

Tulchinsky, Maurice M. '12 '37 C&L.602 B.A., LL.B.
120 W. LaSalle Ave., Hazlitt Bldg.
Tychonievich, Daniel '— '96 C.608 B.S.W.E. L.602 J.D.
[🄰 Baker&D.] (See Pat. Sect.)
Urda, Richard B., Jr., (AV) .... '50 '75 C.602 B.A. L.477 J.D. [Urda]

Urda Professional Corporation, (AV)
112 West Jefferson Boulevard, Suite 503, 46601
Telephone: 574-234-2161 Fax: 574-233-6533
Email: rurda@gte.net
Richard B. Urda, Jr.
Pension and Profit Sharing, ERISA, Employee Benefits, Professional Corporations, Wills and Probate, Trusts and Estates, Estate Planning and Taxation Law.
See Professional Biographies, SOUTH BEND, INDIANA

Van Laere, John W., (BV) .... '56 '82 C.679 B.S. L.1119 J.D. [Jones O.]
Veldman, Thomas F. .... '53 '82 C.347 B.S. L.602 J.D. Chmn., The Tire Rack
Vetne, J. Thomas .... '68 '96 C.846 B.A. L.879 J.D. [🄰 Jones O.]
Visser, Joshua A. .... '79 '04 C.477 B.A. L.879 J.D. [🄰 Sopko,N.&I.]
Vogel, Carol A., (BV) .... '50 '94 C&L.347 B.S., J.D. [Hunt S.K.]
Vogel, Nelson J., Jr., (AV) .... '— '71 C.473 B.S. L.602 J.D. [Barnes&T.]
Volheim, Deanne M. .... '74 '01 C&L.879 B.A., J.D. [🄰 Hunt S.K.]
Voltz-Miller, Debra, Law Office of, (CV) '54 '90
C.347 B.G.S. L.602 J.D. 108 North Main Street, Suite 423
Wade, Robert A., (AV) .... '63 '89 C.97 B.A. L.608 J.D. [🄱 Baker&D.]
Walsh, Timothy J., (AV) .... '46 '74 C.347 A.B. L.602 J.D. 131 S. Taylor St.
Walz, Thomas M., (BV) .... '53 '78 C.347 B.S. L.990 J.D. [Hahn,W.&K.]
Washington, Cleo, (CV) .... '— '89 C.894 B.A. L.502 J.D. 520 W. Wayne St.
Watkins, Michael B., (AV) .... '— '86 C.347 B.A. L.345 J.D. [Barnes&T.]
Weaver, Heath O. .... '67 '98 C.347 B.S. L.602 J.D. 1701 East Wayne Street
Weirich, Glen A. .... '55 '80 C.679 B.S.E. L.1119 J.D. P.O. Box 11382
Weisman, Neil L., (CV) .... '46 '90 C&L.347 A.B., J.D. 215 W. Marion St.

Weisman Associates, Professional Corporation
(See Mishawaka)

Wemhoff, David A. .... '57 '88 C.602 B.A. L.464 J.D. 105 E. Jefferson Blvd., Ste. 400

Wertheimer, Donald E., (BV) ..... '44 '69 C.347 A.B. L.1119 J.D. 1017 E. Jefferson Blvd.
Whitman, William C. .... '40 '66 C.228 A.B. L.1119 LL.B. Supr. Ct. J.
Williams, A. Howard, (BV) ....'50 '76 C.347 B.S. L.602 J.D. [Ⓒ Doran B.]
Wilson, William L., (BV) ....'66 '91 C.602 B.A. L.345 J.D. [Ⓐ Anderson A.&K.]
Woods, Robert Deane, (BV) ....'36 '84 C&L.378 B.S., J.D. [Hunt S.K.]
Woods, Timothy W., (AV) ....'43 '68 C.436 B.A. L.602 J.D. [Jones O.]
Wozniak, Terrance F. .... '41 '68 C.679 B.A. L.1119 J.D. 205 W. Jefferson Blvd.
Wright, Timothy C. ...... '41 '68 C.602 B.A. L.665 J.D. 300 N. Michigan Street, Suite 420
Yarbro, Peter M. ....'74 '99 C.367 B.A. L.602 J.D. [Hains]
Yarger, John M. ....'67 '95 C.210 B.A. L.1119 J.D. North American Signs
Zalas, Clint A. ....'74 '01 C.679 B.A. L.879 J.D. [Ⓐ Lee&G.]
Zappia, Anthony M., (AV) ....'49 '76 C.602 L.879 J.D. [Zappia Z.&S.]
Zappia, Mario J., (BV) ....'64 '90 C.597 B.A. L.879 J.D. [Zappia Z.&S.]

Zappia Zappia & Stipp, (AV)
52582 State Road 933 North, 46637
Telephone: 574-277-8720 Fax: 574-272-8167
Email: zappialaw.com URL: http://www.zappialaw.com
Members of Firm: Anthony M. Zappia; Mario J. Zappia; Thomas Sean Stipp. Associate: Aric J. Rutkowski.
Zoning, Planning and Land Use, Business Law, Business Planning, Contracts, Law Suits, Business Enterprises, Corporate Law, Partnerships, Limited Liability Companies, Civil Practice, Criminal Law, Driving While Intoxicated, Drug Crimes, Juvenile Law, Parole and Probation, Traffic Violations, Civil Litigation, Defense Litigation, Trial Practice, Personal Injury, Automobile Accidents, Slip and Fall, Wrongful Death, Bankruptcy, Family Law, Adoptions, Child Custody, Child Support, Divorce, Visitation Rights, Wills, Trusts and Estates, Estate Planning, Real Estate, Worker's Compensation, Family Mediation, Leases, Collections, Grandparents Visitation Rights.
Reference: 1st Source Bank and Trust Company of South Bend, Indiana.
See Professional Biographies, SOUTH BEND, INDIANA

Zawalich, Chet, (BV) '54 '83 C.602 B.A. L.879 J.D.
401 East Colfax Avenue, Suite 307
Zych, Edward A. ....'44 '74 C&L.602 B.A., J.D. 220 West Colfax Avenue Suite 100

SOUTH WHITLEY, 1,782, *Whitley Co.*

Banks, Carl J., (BV) .... '46 '75 C.679 B.A. L.1119 J.D. [Banks&N.]
Banks and Naylor, P.C., (BV) ....P.O. Box 365

SPEEDWAY, 12,881, *Marion Co.*

Barteau, William V., (BV) ....'33 '61 C.423 L.1119 LL.B. 1414 Main St.
Deal, Thomas A., Law Office of, (BV) .... '43 '71 C.1216 B.A. L.345 J.D. 1404 Main St.
Greenwood, Herman E. ....'42 '68 C.347 B.S. L.345 J.D. [H.E.Greenwood]
Greenwood, Herman E., Law Office .... 5135 W. 10th St.
Popcheff, Constance J. Dinn ....'— '90 L.347 J.D. 5023 W. 16th
Popcheff, George T., (BV) ....'22 '56 C&L.208 B.S., LL.B. 5023 W. 16th St.

SPENCER, * 2,508, *Owen Co.*

Andree, Robert G., Jr., (BV) '57 '83
C.98 B.S. L.1119 J.D. Chf. Dep. Pros.Atty., Owen Co. Pros. Off.

Bonnell, Michael K. '54 '86 C.347 B.A. L.1119 J.D.
63 East Market Street, P.O. Box 533, 47460
Telephone: 812-829-2209 URL: http://www.bonnelllawoffice.com
Email: mkbonnell@hotmail.com URL: http://www.bonnelllaw.com
Bankruptcy, Criminal Law, Driving While Intoxicated, Drug Crimes, Juvenile Law, Parole and Probation, Traffic Violations, Employment Law, Wrongful Termination, Discrimination, Family Law, Adoptions, Child Custody, Child Support, Divorce, Visitation Rights, Personal Injury, Wrongful Death, Automobile Accidents, Real Estate, Buying and Selling Real Estate, Commercial Leasing, Construction, Zoning and Land Use, Trusts and Estates, Estate Planning, Wills and Probate, Business Law, Business Planning, Contracts, Litigation, Business Enterprises, Corporate, Small Business, Starting a Business, Buying and Selling a Business.
See Professional Biographies, SPENCER, INDIANA

Chapman & Nelson, P.C.
(See Bloomington)

Childress, Austin B. ....'18 '54 C.347 B.S. L.345 LL.B. P.O. Box 66
Collins, David A., (BV) ....'47 '87 C.347 A.B. L.1119 J.D. P.O. Box AM11
Fountain, Allan L., (AV) ....'45 '71 C.679 B.A. L.879 J.D. Pros. Atty.
Fuhs, John J., (BV) ....'51 '75 C.347 B.S. L.1119 J.D. 59 E. Franklin St.
Hickam, Elliott, (AV) ....'20 '48 C.347 A.B. L.1119 LL.B. 10 S. Main St.
Lorenz, Richard W., (BV) ....'46 '73 C.602 B.S. L.1119 J.D. 10 S. Main St.

Mallor Clendening Grodner & Bohrer LLP
(See Bloomington)

McKay, John R., (BV) ....'58 '85 C.347 B.A. L.276 J.D. 10 S. Main St.
Nardi, Frank M. ....'53 '79 C.347 B.A. L.1119 J.D. Cir. J.
Norman, Richard William ..... '56 '81 C.367 B.A. L.879 J.D. 84 South Washington Street
Quillen, Lori T. ....'64 '89 C.346 B.S. L.347 J.D. Co. Pros. Off.
Spencer, C. Thomas, (BV) ....'47 '71 C&L.347 B.S., J.D. 10 S. Main St.
Watts, Paul J. ....'46 '74 C.347 A.B. L.345 J.D. [Watts]
Watts Law Office ....85 S. Main St.
Williams, MaryAnn O. ....'55 '89 C.546 B.S. L.347 J.D. [Woodruff&W.]
Woodruff, Jack R., (BV) ....'61 '87 C.346 B.S. L.879 J.D. [Woodruff&W.]
Woodruff & Williams, P.C., (BV) ....P.O. Box 46

SULLIVAN, * 4,663, *Sullivan Co.*

Bodine, John D. ....'44 '72 C.347 B.S. L.1119 J.D. 12 North Court Street
Bramer, Richard M., (BV) ....'65 '91 C.894 B.A. L.1119 J.D. P.O. Box 83
Followell, Douglas S., (BV) ....'46 '74 C.346 B.S. L.345 J.D. 104 W. Washington
Hale, J. Carter ....'70 '00 C.347 B.S. L.117 J.D. 112 N. Section St.

Hart Bell LLC
(See Vincennes)

Hawkins, Jeff R., (AV) .... '66 '92 C.347 B.S. L.421 J.D. [Hawkins]
Hawkins, Jennifer J., (BV) ....'65 '92 C.347 B.M.E. L.421 J.D. [Hawkins]

Hawkins Law PC, (AV)
999 North Section Street, P.O. Box 382, 47882-0382
Telephone: 812-268-8777; 812-847-7000 Fax: 812-268-8838
Email: info@hawkinslaw.com URL: http://www.HawkinsLaw.com
Jeff R. Hawkins; Jennifer J. Hawkins.
Estate Planning, Trusts and Estates, Wills and Probate, Estate Planning, Elder Law, Wills and Probate, Business Law, Business Planning, Contracts, Lawsuits, Business Enterprises, Small Business, Corporate, Limited Liability Companies, Adoption Law, Real Estate, Municipal Law.
See Professional Biographies, SULLIVAN, INDIANA

Hunt, Hassler & Lorenz LLP
(See Terre Haute)

Johnson, Thomas E. ....'48 '74 C.347 B.S. L.345 J.D. Supr. Ct. J.
Lowry, Robert G., (AV) ....'25 '61 C.347 B.S. L.1119 J.D. Sullivan St. Bk. Bldg.

McGlone, Edward, Law Office
(See Terre Haute)

Pierson, P. J. .... '50 '83 C.347 B.S. L.61 J.D. Cir. J.

Powell, E. D., (BV) ....'43 '70 C.894 A.B. L.347 J.D. 1 W. Jackson St.
Reed, Mark L., (BV) ....'48 '73 C.347 B.S. L.1119 J.D. 1 W. Jackson St.
Reeves, Tracy Enochs ....'69 '97 C.249 B.S. L.347 J.D. 103 S. Main Street
Sheffler, Julia Johnson ....'51 '83 C.679 B.S. L.1119 J.D. [J.J.Sheffler]
Sheffler, Julia J., Law Office of ....617 S. County Road 700 W
Smith, Ann Kristine ....'71 '97 C.346 B.S. L.347 J.D. 112 N. Section St.
Springer, John Robert ....'70 '00 C.303 B.A. L.801 J.D. 1 West Jackson St.
Springer, Robert E., (BV) ....'45 '73 C.347 B.S. L.345 J.D. Pros.

Wilkinson, Goeller, Modesitt, Wilkinson & Drummy
(See Terre Haute)

SUNMAN, 805, *Ripley Co.*

Watson, John J., (BV) .... '64 '93 C.837 B.S. L.1340 J.D. P.O. Box 430

SYRACUSE, 3,038, *Kosciusko Co.*

Birch, Jack C., (BV) ....'66 '91 C&L.1119 B.A., J.D. [Snyder B.C.&M.]
Cates, David C., (BV) ....'59 '86 C.679 B.S. L.345 J.D. [Green&C.]
Cornwell, David D., (BV) ....'50 '76 C.347 A.B. L.1119 J.D. [Snyder B.C.&M.] ⊙
Girod, Randall K., (CV) ....'59 '84 C.347 B.S. L.345 J.D. 8652 E. Koher Rd. S.
Green, Richard A., (BV) ....'42 '70 C.108 B.S. L.345 J.D. [Green&C.]
Green & Cates, (BV) .... 1416 S. Huntington Street
Grossnickle, Andrew E. ....'73 '99 C.473 B.A. L.879 J.D. [Ⓐ Green&C.]
Hines, Robert L. ....'23 '49 C.347 B.S. L.1119 J.D. Sr. J.
Howard, James R., (CV) ....'44 '76 C.347 B.S. L.345 J.D. 104 E. Main St.
Morgan, Randall L., (CV) ....'68 '94 C&L.347 B.S., J.D. [Snyder B.C.&M.]
Reed, Robert E. ....'33 '62 C.475 A.B. L.345 J.D. 205 W. Main St.
Smith, Robert F., (CV) ....'55 '92 C.173 B.S. L.208 J.D. P.O. Box 219
Snyder, Stephen R., (AV) ....'47 '71 C&L.879 B.A., J.D. [Snyder B.C.&M.]

Snyder Birch Cornwell & Morgan LLP, (AV)
200 West Main Street, 46567 ⊙
Telephone: 574-457-5727 Fax: 574-457-2056
URL: http://www.sbcmlaw.com
Stephen R. Snyder; Jack C. Birch; David D. Cornwell; Randall L. Morgan.
Business Litigation, Business Law, Zoning, Planning and Land Use, Real Estate, Civil Litigation, Estate Planning, Trust, Probate, Guardianship, Elder Law, Tax, Banking Law, Employee Benefits, ERISA.
Fort Wayne, Indiana Office: 904 South Calhoun Street, 46802. Telephone: 260-407-0915. Fax: 260-407-7005.
See Professional Biographies, SYRACUSE, INDIANA

TELL CITY, 7,845, *Perry Co.*

Collins, Robert L. '50 '81 C.591 B.A. L.1187 J.D.
Pros. Atty.; Terry Co. Prosecutors Off.
Evrard, David E. ....'32 '60 C.679 B.S.E.E. L.276 J.D. Cir. J.
Goffinet, Christopher M., (BV) ....'62 '88 C.929 B.S. L.880 J.D. [Huber&G.]
Hagedorn, Michael H. ....'48 '74 C.249 B.S. L.345 J.D. [Hagedorn]
Hagedorn Law Office .... 419 Main St.
Hawk, Donald L. ....'71 '00 C.108 B.A. L.345 J.D. [Ⓐ Huber&G.]
Huber, J. David, (AV) ....'37 '62 C&L.309 A.B., LL.B. [Huber&G.] ‡
Huber & Goffinet, (BV) .... 727 Main Street
McEntarfer, James A., (BV) ....'55 '84 C.249 B.S. L.345 J.D. Cir.J., Perry Cir. Ct.
Ramsey, Mark R., (CV) ....'55 '80 C.602 B.A. L.345 J.D. [Ramsey]
Ramsey Law Office, (CV) ....712 Jefferson St.
Tyler, James G., (BV) ....'49 '76 C.249 B.A. L.365 J.D. [Tyler]
Tyler Law Office, (BV) ....717 Jefferson St.

Waldschmidt & Werner, (AV)
644 12th Street, P.O. Box 547, 47586
Telephone: 812-547-7066 FAX: 812-547-7601
Members of Firm: John R. Werner. Associate: Karen A. Werner.
General Civil Practice, Probate and Estate Planning, Real Estate and Titles, Banking, Corporations, Negligence, and Criminal.
Representative Clients: Old National Bank of Tell City, Indiana; First State Bank; Perry Central Community School Corporation; AND-TRO Rural Water Utility; Perry County Division of Family and Children; Tell City-Troy Township School Corporation; City of Tell City.
Approved Attorneys for: Chicago Title Insurance Company; Farmers Home Administration.

Werner, John R., (AV) ....'44 '69 C.347 B.S. L.1119 J.D. [Waldschmidt&W.]
Werner, Karen A. ....'74 '99 C.347 B.S. L.421 J.D. [Ⓐ Waldschmidt&W.]

TERRE HAUTE, * 59,614, *Vigo Co.*

Abel, Eric M., (BV) ....'49 '75 C.346 B.S. L.862 J.D. 191 Harding Avenue
Adler, Phillip I. ....'46 '71 C.347 B.S. L.1119 J.D. Supr. Ct. J.
Anderson, C. Joseph, (BV) ....'39 '67 C.346 A.B. L.347 J.D. [Anderson&N.]
Anderson & Nichols, (BV) .... 300 Ohio St.
Aukerman, Bruce D., (AV) ....'61 '88 C.347 B.S.Acct. L.801 J.D. [Mann]
Bauer, Frederick T., (AV) ....'35 '59 C.347 A.B. L.1119 LL.B. [Bauer&D.]
Bauer & Duffy, (AV) .... 605 Ohio St.
Beecher, Samuel E., Jr. ....'18 '41 C.346 L.347 LL.B. 229 So. 25th St.
Berry, Todd A. ....'65 '04 C.346 B.A. L.1119 J.D. 1119 E. Southport Drive
Bitzegaio, Harold J. ....'21 '53 C.346 B.S. L.1119 LL.B. 2703 E. Springhill Dr.‡
Bohnet, Eric C. '68 '94 C.879 B.A. L.347 J.D.
(adm. in TX; not adm. in IN) [Ⓐ Bopp,C.&B.]
Bonomo, Donald J. ....'75 '00 C.346 B.S. L.347 J.D. [Cox,Z.G.&S.]
Bopp, James, Jr., (AV) ....'48 '73 C.347 B.A. L.260 J.D. [Bopp,C.&B.]
Bopp, Coleson & Bostrom, (AV) ....1 South Sixth Street
Bostrom, Barry A., (BV) ....'51 '87 C.932 B.A. L.862 J.D. [Bopp,C.&B.]
Boswell, James W., II, (BV) ....'46 '73 C.473 B.S. L.345 J.D. 400 Wabash

Bough, Brad, (BV) '58 '83 C.346 B.S. L.345 J.D.
321 Ohio Street, 47807
Telephone: 812-234-8458 Fax: 812-232-3232
Email: brad@boughlaw.com URL: http://www.bradboughlaw.com
General Civil Litigation, Personal Injury, Automobile Accidents, Slip and Fall, Wrongful Death, Wills and Probate, Trusts and Estates, Insurance Defense, Mediation.
See Professional Biographies, TERRE HAUTE, INDIANA

Boyll, Jeffrey A., (BV) ....'56 '83 C.210 B.A. L.1119 J.D. [Wilkinson,G.M.W.&D.]
Brames, Arnold H., (BV) ....'43 '70 C.346 B.S. L.345 J.D. [Brames&O.]
Brames & Oldham, (BV) .... 191 Harding Avenue
Brattain, George A., (BV) ....'41 '67 C.894 A.B. L.1119 J.D. [Brattain]
Brattain Law Firm, (BV) ....322 S. 6th St.
Brighton, Wm. Curtis, (BV) '54 '81
C.346 B.S. L.221 J.D. V.P. & Gen. Coun., Hulman & Company
Britton, Louis F., (AV) ....'53 '77 C.347 B.A. L.1119 J.D. [Cox,Z.G.&S.]
Campbell, Kristi M. ....'57 '84 C.346 B.A. L.345 J.D. 900 S. 21st St.
Chowning, Thomas J., (CV) ....'47 '89 C.347 B.S. L.851 J.D. 19 S. 6th St.
Coleson, Richard E., (CV) ....'51 '87 C.999 B.A. L.345 J.D. [Bopp,C.&B.]
Cook, William E. ....'24 '52 C.347 A.B. L.1119 J.D. 19 S. 6th St.
Cox, B. Guille, Jr., (AV) ....'46 '71 C.453 B.S. L.309 J.D. [Cox,Z.G.&S.]

Cox, Zwerner, Gambill & Sullivan, LLP, (AV) [BB]
511 Wabash Avenue, P.O. Box 1625, 47808-1625
Telephone: 812-232-6003 Fax: 812-232-6567
Members of Firm: Ernest J. Zwerner (1918-1980); Benjamin G. Cox (1915-1988); Gilbert W. Gambill, Jr. (1921-2001); James E. Sullivan; B. Guille Cox, Jr.; David W. Sullivan; Louis F. Britton; Ronald E. Jumps; Scott Craig; Donald J. Bonomo; Lakshmi Reddy.
General Civil Practice. Trials. Federal and State, Tax, Probate and Estate Planning, Corporate, Real Estate, Banking and Insurance Law, Education/School Law, Mediation, Employment Law.
Counsel for: City of Clinton; First Financial Bank, NA; Farmers Insurance Group; Indiana-American Water Co.; Indiana State University; Old National Bank (Terre Haute); Rose-Hulman Institute of Technology; Tribune-Star Publishing Co., Inc.
See Professional Biographies, TERRE HAUTE, INDIANA

Craig, Scott ... '71 '97 C.894 B.A. L.1119 J.D. [Cox,Z.G.&S.]
Crawford, Frank P., (BV) ... '15 '40 C.346 L.345 LL.B. 1613 S. 6th St.‡
Crawford, James L., (BV) ... '44 '69 C.347 B.S. L.1119 J.D. [Wagner,C.G.&T.]
Creason, Geoffrey G., (CV) ... '48 '74 C.679 B.S. L.345 J.D. 505 Ohio St.
Crossen, Martha J., (CV) ... '50 '79 C.375 B.S. L.608 J.D. [Simbol&C.]
Cuvelier, Steven D., (CV) ... '54 '93 C.346 B.S. L.347 J.D. 825 Indiana Ave.
Dailey, Christopher James ... '63 '89 C.894 B.A. L.345 J.D. 498 Ohio Street
Decker, Donald L., (BV) ... '45 '70 C.165 A.B. L.1119 J.D. Standing Trustee
Drummy, William W., (AV) ... '48 '75 C.347 B.S. L.190 J.D. [Wilkinson,G.M.W.&D.]
Duffy, Patrick L., (BV) ... '48 '73 C.346 A.B. L.1119 J.D. [Bauer&D.]
Earls, William W. ... '68 '96 C.346 B.S. L.1187 J.D. 506 Ohio St., Ste. 4
Effner, Robert O., (BV) ... '46 '75 C.679 B.S. L.345 J.D. [Effner]
Effner Law Firm, (BV) ... 19 S. 6th St., Ste. 1200
Eldred, Michael H. ... '48 '75 C&L.602 B.A., J.D. Supr. Ct. J.
Ellis, Kaleel M. ... '63 '89 [Ellis]
Ellis, Michael Thomas ... '61 '85 C.346 B.S. L.1187 J.D. [Ellis]
Ellis Law Offices, L.L.C. ... 518 Wabash Ave.
Etling, Joseph K., (BV) ... '63 '88 C.894 B.A. L.345 J.D. [Smock&E.]
Everett, Edward S., (AV) ... '07 '34 L.345 LL.B. 18 S. 5th St.
Fears, Timothy E., (BV) ... '65 '90 C.679 B.S. L.345 J.D. [Wright,S.&L.]
Fleschner, G. Steven, (AV) ... '49 '74 C.346 B.S. L.900 J.D. [Fleschner,S.T.&N.]
Fleschner, Stark, Tanoos & Newlin, (AV) ... 201 Ohio Street
Francis, Leroy A., (BV) ... '10 '49 C.347 B.S. L.1119 J.D. 19 S. 6th St.
Francis, Lynn A., (BV) ... '46 '82 C.1243 B.A. L.42 J.D. 118 Arcadia Drive
Frankel, William S., IV ... '78 '04 C.346 B.S. L.345 J.D. [[A] Wilkinson,G.M.W.&D.]
Frey, Eric A., (BV) ... '42 '67 C.347 A.B. L.1119 J.D. [Frey]
Frey Law Firm, (BV) ... 618 Wabash Ave., Ste. 200
Friedrich, David P., (BV) ... '65 '90 C.108 B.S. L.345 J.D. [Wilkinson,G.M.W.&D.]
Gallant, Jeffrey P. '60 '01 C.999 B.A. L.1339 J.D.
(adm. in VA; not adm. in IN) [[A] Bopp,C.&B.]
Gambill, Christopher B., (BV) ... '57 '83 C.347 A.B. L.1119 J.D. [Wagner,C.G.&T.]
Gerdink, Herbert R. ... '24 '55 C.346 B.S. L.1119 J.D. 2820 N. 6 1/2 St.
Goeller, David H., (AV) ... '35 '63 C.347 B.S. L.1119 J.D. [Wilkinson,G.M.W.&D.]
Hassler, Mark D., (AV) ... '56 '81 C.346 B.S. L.347 J.D. [Hunt,H.&L.]
Haynes, David D., (BV) ... '51 '76 C.346 B.A. L.425 J.D. P.O. Box 3124
Hellmann, Robert F., (BV) ... '47 '73 C.346 A.B. L.734 J.D. 30 N. 7th Street
Hepburn, Robert D., (BV) ... '54 '80 C.339 B.A. L.1119 J.D. 605 Ohio Street, Suite 309
Hunt, Robert F., (BV) ... '48 '73 C.347 B.S. L.1119 J.D. [Hunt,H.&L.]

Hunt, Hassler & Lorenz LLP, (AV)
100 Cherry Street, P.O. Box 1527, 47808
Telephone: 812-232-9691 Telecopier: 812-234-2881
URL: http://www.huntlawfirm.net
David E. Rosenfeld (1906-1979); Robert G. Wolfe (1916-1997). Members of Firm: Robert F. Hunt; Mark D. Hassler; Teri M. Lorenz; Robert P. Kondras, Jr.
Insurance Defense, Family/Domestic Relations, Adoptions, Child Custody, Child Support, Divorce, Visitation Rights, Business Law, Business Planning, Contracts, Business Litigation, Business Enterprises, Corporate, Limited Liability Companies, Partnerships, Small Business, Starting a Business, Buying and Selling a Business, Employment Law, Employment Litigation, Wrongful Termination, Commercial, Real Estate, Wills and Probate, Trusts and Estates, Asset Protection, Guardianships, Estate Planning, Insurance Law. Trials and Appeals.
Attorneys for: Liberty Mutual Insurance Co.; The Kemper Group; Royal Globe Insurance Group; Horace Mann Insurance Co.; Empire Fire and Marine Insurance Co; Terre Haute Police Department Merit Commission; Kirkham Hardwoods, Inc.; Advance Waste Management; Dump Trucks, Inc.; Andrews Heating & Air Conditioning, Inc.
See Professional Biographies, TERRE HAUTE, INDIANA

Jackson, Kimberly Antcliff ... '55 '80 C.210 B.A. L.1119 J.D. Co. Pros. Off.
Johnson, Keith L., (AV) ... '55 '80 C&L.879 B.A., J.D. P.O. Box 654
Johnson, R. Steven, (AV) ... '45 '72 C.346 B.S. L.347 J.D. [Sacopulos,J.&S.]
Jones, Kay C. ... '61 '88 [[A] Tofaute&S.]
Jumps, Ronald E., (CV) ... '43 '89 C.679 B.S. L.1119 J.D. [Cox,Z.G.&S.]
Kearns, R. Jerome, (CV) ... '36 '66 C.346 B.S. L.421 LL.B. 215 Wabash
Keller, John E. ... '30 '63 C.347 B.S. L.345 J.D. 74 Heritage Dr.

Kelly, Daniel W., (BV) '61 '88 C.679 B.A. L.879 J.D.
321 Ohio Street, 47808
Telephone: 812-234-1292 Fax: 812-232-3232
Email: danmbk@aol.com URL: http://www.dankellylawfirm.com
Personal Injury, Family Law, Wills, Estate Administration, Bankruptcy.
See Professional Biographies, TERRE HAUTE, INDIANA

Kesler, John A., II ... '54 '79 C.108 B.S. L.607 J.D. [Kesler&K.]
Kesler, John A., Sr. ... '23 '51 C.346 A.B. L.347 J.D. [Kesler&K.]
Kesler and Kesler ... 219 Ohio St.
Kite, John C. ... '39 '69 C.346 B.S. L.345 J.D. 401 Ohio St.
Klotz, John J. ... '78 '04 C.346 B.S. L.879 J.D. [[A] Sacopulos,J.&S.]
Kondras, Robert P., Jr., (CV) ... '67 '94 C.692 B.A. L.347 J.D. [Hunt,H.&L.]
Kuchaes, Delmar P. ... '44 '72 C.347 A.B. L.345 J.D. 648 Walnut Street
Kyrouac, Scott M., (BV) ... '60 '85 C.339 B.S. L.1119 J.D. [Wilkinson,G.M.W.&D.]
Leedy, Stephen R., (BV) ... '45 '73 C.679 B.S. L.1119 J.D. [Leedy&S.]
Leedy & Stagg, (BV) ... 76 Ohio St.
Levin, Kenneth E. ... '24 '51 C.309 A.B. L.597 J.D. 4629 Summerset Dr.‡
Lewellyn, Jeffrey A., (CV) ... '63 '90 C.531 B.S. L.345 J.D. [Wilkinson,G.M.W.&D.]
Lewis, Elizabeth A., (CV) ... '66 '94 C.346 B.S. L.851 J.D. 605 Ohio Street
Lewis, Jordan D. ... '32 '59 C.347 B.S. L.1119 J.D. Part-Time Fed. Mag. Judge‡
Lind, Jeffry A., (AV) ... '63 '88 C.347 B.A. L.209 J.D. 201 Ohio St.
Lorenz, Teri M., (AV) ... '48 '79 C&L.347 B.S., J.D. [Hunt,H.&L.]
Lowery, Norman L., (AV) ... '46 '72 C.346 B.S. L.345 J.D. [[C] Wright,S.&L.]
Lucas, Eric S. ... '62 '89 C.701 B.S. Ch.E. L.347 J.D. Discovision Assocs. (Pat.)

Maher, William J., (BV) '45 '70 C.346 B.S. L.347 J.D.
140 Cherry Street, 47807
Telephone: 812-232-6617 Fax: 812-235-2041
URL: http://www.lawyers.com/wjmaherlaw
General Civil Trial Practice in State and Federal Courts. Personal Injury, Automobile Accidents, Slip and Fall, Dog Bites, Wrongful Death, Product Liability, Wills, Probate, Trusts and Estates,

(This Listing Continued)

Maher, William J. (Continued)
Guardianships, Asset Protection, Estate Planning, Business Law, Contracts, Business Litigation, Business Enterprises, Corporate, Real Estate, Workers Compensation, Social Security Disability, Bankruptcy.
See Professional Biographies, TERRE HAUTE, INDIANA

Majewski, Dennis R. ... '50 '77 C.346 B.S. L.345 J.D. [Majewski]
Majewski Law Offices ... 522 Ohio St.

Mann Law Firm, (AV) [BB]
646 Walnut Street, P.O. Box 1643, 47808-1643
Telephone: 812-232-0107 FAX: 812-232-3414
Email: mannlawfirm.com URL: http://www.mannlawfirm.com
Members of Firm: Hansford C. Mann (1911-1998); Max E. Goodwin (1941-2001); Stephen L. Williams; Bruce D. Aukerman; John T. Roach III;—Chris A. Wrede.
Personal Injury and Business Trial Practice in State and Federal Courts, Condemnation, Eminent Domain, Land Acquisition, Medical Malpractice and Products Liability.
References: Terre Haute First National Bank; Indiana State Bank.
See Professional Biographies, TERRE HAUTE, INDIANA

Martin, Rae E., (CV) ... '69 '94 [[A] Ellis]
Marzen, Thomas J. '46 '78 C.339 B.A. L.146 J.D.
(adm. in IL; not adm. in IN) [[C] Bopp,C.&B.]
McCrory, Charles K. ... '30 '55 C.347 B.S. L.1119 J.D. P.O. Box 942
McDonald, James O., (BV) ... '47 '72 C.346 B.S. L.345 J.D. 648 Walnut St.
McDonald, Misty Y., Attorney at Law '76 '00 C.234 B.A. L.1119 J.D.
506 Ohio St., Ste. 4
McGlone, Daniel J., (CV) ... '63 '88 C.346 B.S. L.345 J.D. [McGlone L.]

McGlone, Edward, Law Office, (CV) '64 '89 C.346 B.S. L.347 J.D.
2022 Wabash Avenue, Suite B, 47807
Telephone: 812-478-3442 Fax: 812-478-3462
Email: edmcglonelaw@aol.com
Personal Injury, Automobile Accidents, Slip and Fall, Dog Bites, Wrongful Death, Criminal Law, Traffic Violations, Driving While Intoxicated, Juvenile Law, Drug Crimes, Felonies, Misdemeanors.
See Professional Biographies, TERRE HAUTE, INDIANA

McGlone, Gerald H., (AV) ... '32 '64 C.701 B.S. L.1119 J.D. [McGlone L.]

McGlone Law, (AV) [BB]
1717 S. Third Street, 47802
Telephone: 812-234-4000 Fax: 812-234-4900 Toll free: 812-234-8400
Email: jerry@2344000.com
Members of Firm: Gerald H. McGlone; Daniel J. McGlone.
Trial Practice in State and Federal Courts. Personal Injury, Workers Compensation, Products Liability, Construction and Probate.
Reference: Regions Bank.
See Professional Biographies, TERRE HAUTE, INDIANA

McKee, Craig M., (BV) ... '58 '83 C.346 B.S. L.345 J.D. [Wilkinson,G.M.W.&D.]
McMahan, Robert D., (BV) '50 '87
C.347 B.A. L.345 J.D. Corporate Sq. 2901 Ohio Blvd. Suite 229
Modesitt, Raymond H., (AV) '43 '68 C.347 A.B. L.1119 J.D.
[Wilkinson,G.M.W.&D.]
Moore, Raeanna S. ... '66 '97 C.412 B.A. L.1119 J.D. [[A] Bopp,C.&B.]
Mullican, Mark W. ... '62 '87 C.346 B.S. L.879 J.D. [Mullican]
Mullican Law Offices ... 505 Ohio St.
Nasser, Woodrow S., (CV) ... '31 '60 C.346 B.S. L.1119 LL.B. 3047 S. 11th. St.
Nattkemper, C. Don, (AV) ... '47 '73 C.347 B.S. L.345 J.D. 2901 Ohio Blvd., Ste. 160
Newlin, Thomas C., (BV) ... '49 '86 C.346 B.S. L.345 J.D. [Fleschner,S.T.&N.]
Newton, Christopher A. ... '60 '89 C.346 B.S. L.101 J.D. Co. J.
Nichols, Geo. O. ... '15 '41 C.659 B.S. L.477 LL.B. Pres., Nichols Investment Corp.
Nichols, John P., (BV) ... '59 '84 C.347 B.S. L.117 J.D. [Anderson&N.]
Olah, William M., (AV) ... '52 '78 C.701 B.S. L.45 J.D. [Wilkinson,G.M.W.&D.]
Oldham, Rhonda D., (BV) ... '53 '82 C.346 B.S. L.347 J.D. [Brames&O.]
Organ, James B., (CV) ... '63 '92 C.347 B.A. L.421 J.D. [Organ]
Organ Law Offices, PC, (CV) ... 19 S. Sixth St., Ste. 1000
Ourand, Richard Charles '53 '78 C&L.45 B.S., J.D.
(adm. in AR; not adm. in IN) U.S. Air Force
Phipps, Lora L. ... '62 '92 L.1153 J.D. 2901 Ohio Blvd., Ste. 246
Pierce, Mary C. ... '70 '97 C.265 B.A. L.1187 J.D. 518 Wabash Ave.
Racop, Scott E. ... '68 '93 C.346 B.A. L.347 J.D. 618 Wabash Ave.
Rader, Michael R., (CV) ... '— '96 C&L.347 M.D., J.D. [[C] Frey]
Ratcliffe, Robert S., (AV) ... '19 '49 C.346 A.B. L.477 J.D. 10190 S. Daniel St.‡
Reddy, Lakshmi ... '70 '97 C.880 B.S. L.74 J.D. [Cox,Z.G.&S.]
Reynolds, Mary Lou ... '47 '72 C.346 B.S. L.1119 J.D. 524 Ohio St.
Rider, Gary V. ... '49 '77 C.347 B.S. L.1119 J.D. Co. Ct. Judge
Roach, John T., III, (CV) ... '61 '88 C&L.801 B.A., J.D. [Mann]
Robertson, Kathryn L., (BV) ... '26 '67 C.112 B.A. L.347 J.D. Dep. Pros.
Roots, Kelvin L., (BV) ... '54 '81 C.210 B.A. L.345 J.D. [Wilkinson,G.M.W.&D.]
Sacopulos, Gus, (AV) ... '35 '60 C.347 L.1119 J.D. [Sacopulos,J.&S.]
Sacopulos, Melony A. ... '62 '88 C.801 B.A. L.345 J.D. Indiana State Univ.
Sacopulos, Michael J., (CV) ... '69 '95 C.309 A.B. L.347 J.D. [Sacopulos,J.&S.]
Sacopulos, Peter J., (BV) ... '63 '88 C.861 B.A. L.345 J.D. [Sacopulos,J.&S.]

Sacopulos, Johnson & Sacopulos, (AV) [BB]
676 Ohio Street, 47807
Telephone: 812-238-2565 FAX: 812-238-1945
Email: office@sacopulos.com
Members of Firm: Gus Sacopulos; R. Steven Johnson; Peter J. Sacopulos; Michael J. Sacopulos. Associate: John J. Klotz.
Civil Litigation, Corporate, Insurance, and Probate and Estate Planning. General Practice, Employment, Medical Malpractice.
Representative Clients: Bituminous Casualty; Auto-Owners Insurance Co.; Beazer-East, Inc.; Victoria Ins. Co.; Physicians & Surgeons Insurance Co.; American Family Insurance Co.; WalMart Stores, Inc.; SAFECO; Progressive Insurance Co.; Motorists Ins. Co.
See Professional Biographies, TERRE HAUTE, INDIANA

Shagley, Richard J., (BV) ... '46 '71 C.346 B.S. L.1119 J.D. [Wright,S.&L.]
Shagley, Richard J., II ... '74 '01 C.265 B.A. L.879 J.D. [Wright,S.&L.]
Shema, Virginia K., (BV) ... '57 '87 C.346 B.S. L.347 J.D. 300 Ohio St.
Simbol, Nellie L., (BV) ... '46 '85 C.346 B.S. L.1119 J.D. [Simbol&C.]
Simbol & Crossen, (BV) ... 76 Ohio Street
Simler, Michael W. ... '67 '94 [Ellis]
Skillman, B. Scott ... '62 '87 C.473 A.B. L.879 J.D. [B.S.Skillman]
Skillman, B. Scott, P.C. ... 30 N. 7th Street, Suite 314
Slagle, Michael A. ... '69 '98 C.63 B.S. L.347 J.D. [[A] Smock&E.]
Smith, Phillip C. ... '56 '99 C.10 B.A. L.345 J.D. 2901 Ohio Boulevard, Suite 160
Smock, William G., (AV) ... '46 '72 C.346 B.S. L.345 J.D. [Smock&E.]

Smock and Etling, (AV)
77 Cherry Street, 47807
Telephone: 812-238-1751 FAX: 812-238-1752
Email: smock.etling@verizon.net URL: http://www.smock-etling.com

(This Listing Continued)

Smock and Etling (Continued)

Members of Firm: William G. Smock; Joseph K. Etling. Associate: Michael A. Slagle.
Criminal, Personal Injury Law, Family Law.

See Professional Biographies, TERRE HAUTE, INDIANA

Spelman, Thomas L., (BV) ... '39 '69 C.531 A.B. L.345 J.D. [Tofaute&S.]
Spurr, Jon Charles ... '68 '98 C.347 B.A. L.1119 J.D. [J.Spurr]
Spurr, Jon, Law Offices ... 2901 Ohio Blvd., Ste. 277
Stagg, R. Paulette, (BV) ... '48 '79 C.346 B.S. L.345 J.D. [Leedy&S.]
Stark, Dennis H., (BV) ... '51 '76 C.346 B.S. L.300 J.D. [Fleschner,S.T.&N.]
Sullivan, David W., (AV) ... '48 '73 C.602 B.B.A. L.1119 J.D. [Cox,Z.G.&S.]
Sullivan, James E., (AV) ... '19 '57 C&L.602 B.S.C., J.D. [Cox,Z.G.&S.]
Tabor, Augustus H., (BV) ... '48 '74 C.346 B.S. L.1119 J.D. 314 Ohio St.
Tanoos, Anthony A., (BV) ... '56 '81 C.346 B.S. L.345 J.D. [Fleschner,S.T.&N.]
Tevlin, Beth A. Ahlemeyer, (CV) '59 '85
C.347 B.S. L.1119 J.D. Exec. Dir., Wabash Valley Comm. Found.
Tofaute, George B., (AV) ... '38 '64 C.477 A.B. L.1119 J.D. [Tofaute&S.]
Tofaute, Phillip G., (BV) ... '61 '91 C.347 B.S. L.1187 J.D. [Ⓐ Tofaute&S.]
Tofaute & Spelman, (AV) ... 20 S. 5th St.
Trout, Joseph D., (BV) ... '56 '83 C.346 B.S. L.345 J.D. [Wagner,C.G.&T.]
Wagner, Larry J., (BV) ... '49 '74 C.347 A.B. L.1119 J.D. [Wagner,C.G.&T.]
Wagner, Crawford, Gambill & Trout, (BV) ... 416 S. 6th St.
Walker, James R., (AV) ... '52 '77 C.346 B.A. L.1119 J.D. Pros. Off.
Wall, John C., (BV) ... '48 '82 C.675 B.A. L.345 J.D. [Wilkinson,G.M.W.&D.]
Weber, Daniel L., (BV) ... '46 '71 C.210 B.A. L.1119 J.D. Pub. Def.
Weber, Tracy M. ... '69 '98 C.339 B.S. L.801 J.D. [Wilkinson,G.M.W.&D.]
West, Murray ... '31 '61 C.910 B.S. L.345 LL.B P.O. Box 7081
Wilkinson, B. Curtis, (AV) ... '47 '72 C.346 A.B. L.1119 J.D. [Wilkinson,G.M.W.&D.]

Wilkinson, Goeller, Modesitt, Wilkinson & Drummy, (AV)
333 Ohio Street, P.O. Box 800, 47808-0800
Telephone: 812-232-4311 Fax: 812-235-5107
Email: BCWilkinson@wilkinsonlaw.com URL: http://www.wilkinsonlaw.com
Members of Firm: David H. Goeller; Raymond H. Modesitt; B. Curtis Wilkinson; William W. Drummy; Kelvin L. Roots; John C. Wall; William M. Olah; Craig M. McKee; Scott M. Kyrouac; Jeffrey A. Boyll; David P. Friedrich; Jeffrey A. Lewellyn; Tracy M. Weber;—William S. Frankel, IV.
General Civil Practice in all Courts. Taxation, Corporation, Trust, Probate, Estate Planning, Insurance Law, Health Law, Municipal Law, Bankruptcy, and Creditors Rights. Insurance Defense, Business Litigation, Mediation and Arbitration.
Representative Corporate Clients: Old National Bank; Old National Trust Company; Old National Bank; CSX, Inc.; MAB Paints; Chicago Title Insurance Co.; Union Hospital; Associated Physicians and Surgeons Clinic, LLC.; PSI Energy, Inc.

See Professional Biographies, TERRE HAUTE, INDIANA

Williams, Stephen L., (AV) ... '49 '74 C.346 B.S. L.345 J.D. [Mann]
Wrede, Chris A. ... '— '00 C.346 B.S. L.345 J.D. [Ⓐ Mann]
Wrede, Jennifer R. ... '73 '00 C.346 B.S. L.345 J.D. [Wright,S.&L.]
Wright, Robert L., (AV) ... '42 '70 C.801 B.S. L.345 J.D. [Wright,S.&L.]
Wright, Shagley & Lowery, (AV) ... 500 Ohio Street

THORNTOWN, 1,506, *Boone Co.*

Cook, J. David, (BV) ... '44 '75 C.210 B.A. L.345 J.D. 206 E. Main St.
Gregg, Isaac D. ... '09 '37 C.999 L.1119 LL.B. 324 S. Market St.‡
Summers, David E. ... '30 '67 C.679 L.345 LL.B. 206 E. Main St.‡

TIPTON, * 5,251, *Tipton Co.*

Bingham, Farrer & Wilson, A Professional Corporation
(See Elwood)

Blackburn & Green
(See Fort Wayne)

Clouser, Laura M. ... '71 '98 C.210 B.A. L.589 J.D. 222 S. Main St.
Curtis, Vance W. ... '49 '76 C.346 B.S. L.192 J.D. Pros. Atty.

Hobbs, Ben B., (BV) '44 '72 C.347 B.S. L.345 J.D.
118 South Independence Street, P.O. Box 219, 46072
Telephone: 765-675-9000 Fax: 765-675-9020
Email: bbhatty@tiptontel.com URL: http://www.lawyers.com/benbhobbslawfirm
Wills, Trusts and Estates, Probate and Estate Planning, Real Estate Transactions, Contracts, Commercial Litigation, Wills, Trust and Estates, Trust and Estate Administration, Business Law, Corporate, Business Entrepreneurs, Small Business, Buying and Selling an Business, Starting a Business, Municipal Law.

See Professional Biographies, TIPTON, INDIANA

Lett, Thomas R., (BV) ... '59 '85 C.303 B.A. L.345 J.D. 222 S. Main St.
Nash, D. P. ... '41 '83 C.679 B.A. L.345 J.D. Cir. J.
Nash, Jane Foley, (BV) ... '40 '82 C.347 B.S. L.345 J.D. P.O. Box 66
Quigley, David B., (AV) ... '47 '74 C.347 B.S. L.345 J.D. [Quigley&Q.]
Quigley, Matthew B. ... '75 '01 C.347 B.A. L.74 J.D. [Quigley&Q.]

Quigley & Quigley, (AV)
117 North Main Street, 46072
Telephone: 765-675-6949+765-675-4675 Fax: 765-675-8835
David B. Quigley; Matthew B. Quigley.
General Civil Practice. Real Estate, Business and Probate Law, Estate Planning, Municipal Law, Utility Law.

See Professional Biographies, TIPTON, INDIANA

Regnier, Mark R., (CV) ... '61 '87 C.999 B.A. L.347 J.D. Dep. Pros.
Regnier, Richard O., (BV) ... '29 '54 C.894 A.B. L.1119 LL.B. 120 S. West St.
Rich, Jay D., (CV) ... '62 '90 C.1093 B.A. L.347 J.D. 222 S. Main St.
Smith, David Langolf, (CV) ... '53 '80 C.63 B.S. L.1119 J.D. 222 S. Main St.
Watson, Joe F. ... '30 '58 C.347 B.S. L.345 J.D. 125 North Main Street

TRAFALGAR, 798, *Johnson Co.*

Stein-Ferguson, Karen L. ... '— '94 C.679 B.S. L.345 J.D. 4487 W. Pitcher Drive

UNION CITY, 3,612, *Randolph Co.*

English, Richard J., (BV) ... '34 '60 C.347 B.S. L.1119 J.D. 309 W. Oak St.
Husmann, Reinert W., (BV) ... '46 '74 C&L.879 B.A., J.D. [Husmann&S.]
Husmann & Stemmer, (BV) ... 218 W. Pearl St.
Stemmer, Linda S. H., (BV) ... '51 '78 C.679 B.S. L.345 J.D. [Husmann&S.]

UNIONVILLE, —, *Monroe Co.*

Franklin, Frederick R. ... '29 '56 C.347 A.B. L.1119 J.D. 7788 N. Lakeview Dr.‡

VALPARAISO, * 27,428, *Porter Co.*

Allen, Kenneth J., & Associates '56 '81 C.879 A.B. L.1119 J.D.
1109 Glendale Boulevard
Alvarido, Brock ... '66 '92 C.347 B.S. L.879 J.D. [Ⓐ K.J.Allen&Assoc.]
Antommaria, Phillip '36 '75 C.665 B.S. L.229 J.D.
(adm. in PA; not adm. in IN) 363 McIntyre Ct.
Appel, David C., Law Office of ... '51 '81 C&L.879 B.A., J.D. 2621 Chicago St., Ste. B
Arnold, Matthew J. ... '65 '96 C.608 B.S.B.A. L.117 J.D. 7 Napoleon St.
Aungst, Ronald V. ... '34 '63 C&L.879 B.S., LL.B. 1 Sheffield Dr.
Back, George William ... '47 '82 C.801 B.S. L.209 J.D. 4213 Oak Grove Dr.
Baechle, Michael S., (BV) ... '45 '77 C.347 A.B. L.1119 J.D. P.O. Box 1758
Banks, Bradley L. ... '74 '00 C.679 B.A. L.879 J.D. [Ⓐ Blachly,T.B.&H.]
Bartelt, Louis F., Jr. '22 '47 C&L.879 A.B., LL.B.
(adm. in WI; not adm. in IN) Prof., Emeritus, Valparaiso Univ. Sch. of Law

Beckman, Kelly & Smith
(See Hammond)

Bengs, David M. ... '67 '92 C.347 B.S. L.607 J.D. 2910 Coachman Trl.
Bernardi, Samuel J., Jr., (AV) ... '41 '66 C.473 B.B.S. L.602 J.D. [Spangler,J.&D.]
Berner, Bruce G. ... '43 '67 C&L.879 B.A., LL.B. Assoc. Prof. of Law, Valparaiso Univ.
Berning, Daniel R. ... '52 '77 C.894 B.A. L.879 J.D. Berning & Berning
Bertig, G. Anthony, (BV) ... '55 '80 C.347 B.S. L.879 J.D. 121 Lincolnway
Billings, Bryce E. ... '25 '52 C&L.879 J.D. Sr. Supr. Ct. J.‡
Blachly, Tabor, Bozik & Hartman, (AV)
56 South Washington Street Suite 401 (⊙Fort Wayne)
Blane, Christine ... '57 '83 C.347 B.A. L.879 J.D. 89 Oak Tree Dr.‡
Boesch, Terry R. ... '65 '92 C.249 B.S. L.879 J.D [Boesch&I.]
Boesch & Istrabadi, P.C., (CV) ... P.O. Box 1985
Boyles, Peter L., (BV) ... '69 '94 C.879 B.A. L.607 J.D. [Martz&B.]
Bozik, James S., (BV) ... '35 '61 C.879 B.A. L.46 LL.B. [Ⓑ Blachly,T.B.&H.]
Bradford, Roger V. ... '45 '73 C.346 A.B. L.879 J.D. Supr. Ct. J., Porter Supr. Ct. No. 1
Bradley, Bryan A. ... '68 '94 C.339 B.A. L.879 J.D. [Ⓐ K.J.Allen&Assoc.]
Brammer, James E. ... '67 '92 C.1260 B.A. L.602 J.D. [Ⓐ K.J.Allen&Assoc.]
Brooks, David A., (BV) ... '56 '85 C.114 B.A. L.879 J.D. [Lyons,S.&B.]

Burke Costanza & Cuppy LLP, (AV)
57 Franklin Street, Suite 203, 46383 ⊙
Telephone: 219-531-0134 Fax: 219-531-0507
URL: http://www.bcclegal.com
Partners: George W. Carberry; Todd A. Etzler. Associate: Jon A. Schmaltz.
General Civil Practice in State and Federal Courts, Trials, Appeals, Civil Mediation, Administrative, Business Law, Business Planning, Contracts, Business Litigation, Business Enterprises, LLC's, Partnerships, Small Business, Corporate, Real Estate, Employee Benefits/ERISA, Banking, Commercial, Insurance Defense, Personal Injury, Automobile Accidents, Wrongful Death, Wills and Probate, Trusts and Estates, Estate Planning, Medical Malpractice, Legal Malpractice, Family Law, Adoptions, Child Custody, Child Support, Divorce, Visitation Rights, Municipal and Zoning, Environmental.
Merrillville, Indiana Office: 9191 Broadway. Telephone: 219-769-1313. Fax: 219-769-6806.
Munster, Indiana Office: 900 Ridge Road, Suite L. Telephone: 219-513-1000. Fax: 219-513-1001.

See Professional Biographies, VALPARAISO, INDIANA

Burow-Flak, David Peter ... '62 '96 C.55 B.A. L.744 J.D. Safeco Prop. & Cas. Ins. Co.
Bush, Steven M., (BV) ... '49 '76 C.346 B.A. L.345 J.D. [Millbranth&B.]
Busse, Richard P. ... '50 '99 C&L.879 B.A., J.D. 7 Napoleon Street
Butterfield, David A., (BV) ... '45 '71 C.347 B.S. L.879 J.D. [Butterfield]
Butterfield Law Offices, (BV) ... 11 Lincolnway
Cagen, Richard M., (CV) ... '53 '80 C.347 B.A. L.879 J.D. [R.Cagen]
Cagen, Richard, Law Office of, (CV) ... 100 East Lincoln Way, Ste. 201
Carberry, George W., (AV) '52 '77
C.602 A.B. L.879 J.D. [Burke C.&C.] (⊙Merrillville)
Carmona, Gale P., (CV) ... '44 '89 C.679 B.A. L.879 J.D. 302 Harrison Blvd.
Carter, Derrick A. '50 '75 C.476 B.S. L.879 J.D.
(adm. in MI; not adm. in IN) Valparaiso University Law School
Catsadimas, Nicholas C. ... '72 '00 C&L.879 B.A., J.D. 2803 Boilermaker Court, Ste. 1-C
Charbonneau, Edward E., & Associates '42 '77
C.894 A.B. L.796 J.D. 2503 Sherwood Drive
Chrzanowski, Thomas L. ... '66 '95 C.347 B.S. L.61 J.D. [Ⓐ Hoeppner W.&E.]
Cichowski, Curtis W. '56 '81
C.121 B.A. L.879 J.D. Assoc. Dean, Valparaiso Univ. Sch. of Law
Clark, Robert L., (BV) ... '65 '90 C.424 B.A. L.790 J.D. [Hoeppner W.&E.]
Clifford, Leo J., (BV) ... '14 '40 C&L.879 A.B., LL.B. 14 Indiana Ave.
Coleman, Mark Warren, Law Offices of, (BV) '57 '83
C.694 B.A. L.1137 J.D. 158 South Napoleon Street, Suite 301
Conison, Jay '53 '81 C.976 B.A. L.494 J.D.
Dean and Prof., Valparaiso Univ. Sch. of Law
Davis, Jennifer E. ... '73 '98 C.347 B.A. L.879 J.D. [Ⓐ Langer&L.]
Davis, Richard M. ... '53 '80 C.879 B.A. L.1119 J.D. [Hoeppner W.&E.]
Diston, Jon S. ... '67 '00 C.1305 B.A. L.879 J.D. [Ⓐ Spangler,J.&D.]
Dougherty, Patrick J., (AV) ... '28 '53 C.1024 L.150 LL.B. [Ⓑ Spangler,J.&D.]
Douglas, Herbert K., (AV) ... '34 '58 C.210 A.B. L.1119 J.D. [Douglas,K.&H.]
Douglas, James H., (BV) ... '44 '68 C.37 L.879 LL.B. Pros. Atty., Porter Co. Pros. Off.

Douglas, Koeppen & Hurley, (AV)
14 Indiana Avenue, P.O. Box 209, 46384-0209
Telephone: 219-462-2126 Fax: 219-477-4408
URL: http://www.dkhlawfirm.com
Members of Firm: Herbert K. Douglas; R. Bradley Koeppen; Brian J. Hurley; Mark A. Hardwick.
General Civil Practice. Corporation, Banking, Personal Injury, Insurance, Probate and Estate Planning, Trial Practice, Municipal and Zoning, Family/Domestic Relations.
Attorneys for: Urschel Laboratories, Inc.; Northern Indiana Public Service Co.; Park District, City of Valparaiso; Emerson Electric; First National Bank, Valparaiso.

See Professional Biographies, VALPARAISO, INDIANA

Eldred, Joanne K. ... '49 '93 C.679 M.S. L.879 J.D. 1158 W. Lincolnway
Etzler, Gordon A., & Associates, (BV) ... '41 '69 C.879 B.A. L.365 J.D. 251 Indiana Ave.
Etzler, Todd A., (BV) ... '66 '91 C.679 B.S. L.347 J.D. [Burke C.&C.] (⊙Merrillville)
Fase, Kent R. '55 '84 C.679 B.S. L.209 J.D.
(adm. in IL; not adm. in IN) 2756 Hearthstone Dr.‡
Ferngren, William A. ... '69 '99 C.679 B.S. L.879 J.D. [Ⓐ Hoeppner W.&E.]
Foelber, David A., (CV) ... '51 '77 C&L.879 B.A., J.D. 504 E. Lincolnway Ave.
Forszt, Robert P., (BV) ... '53 '80 C.103 A.B. L.879 J.D. [Forszt,P.&S.]
Forszt, Pawlowski & Smith, (BV) ... 390 W. U.S. Hwy. 6
Geairn, Cintra D.B. '70 '98 C.696 B.A. L.146 J.D.
(adm. in IL; not adm. in IN) [Ⓐ Hoeppner W.&E.] ⊙
Giannetto, Charles '54 '80 C.494 B.A. L.1035 J.D.
(adm. in MN; not adm. in IN) 2843 Calumet Ave., Ste. 188
Gienapp, Marcia L., (BV) '51 '78
C&L.879 B.A., J.D. Supvr. Atty., Clinical Prof., Valparaiso Univ.
Gingerich, Elizabeth F.R., (CV) ... '59 '86 C.347 B.a. L.345 J.D. [Ⓐ Terrell&T.]
Goldman, Jay A. '48 '74 C.347 A.B. L.1119 J.D.
Exec. V.P. & Chf. Fin. Offr., McDaniel Fire Sys., Inc.
Grabarek, Christopher ... '67 '93 C.602 B.A. L.879 J.D. [Spangler,J.&D.]
Hagan, Gregory, (BV) ... '52 '78 C.347 B.A. L.879 J.D. 304 West U.S. 6
Hardwick, Mark A. ... '68 '93 C.347 B.S. L.879 J.D. [Douglas,K.&H.]
Harper, Harold C. '14 '38 C.862 L.623 LL.B.
(adm. in OK; not adm. in IN) 2503 Sears St.‡
Harper, Harold Thomas ... '66 '97 C.347 B.S. L.879 J.D. 304 W. U.S. Hwy. 6

Harper, Mary Rudasics ... '50 '75 C.173 B.A. L.879 J.D. Co. Ct. J., Porter Co. Courthouse
Harper, Robert P., (BV) .... '41 '68 304 W. U.S. Hwy. 6

Harris, Welsh & Lukmann
(See Chesterton)

Hartman, Domenica N. S. .... '60 '88 C.679 B.S. L.477 J.D. 552 E. 700 N. (Pat.)
Hartman, Duane W., (BV) .... '42 '67 C&L.879 B.S.C.E., J.D. [Blachly,T.B.&H.]
Hartman, Gary M. .... '59 '92 C.854 B.S. L.912 J.D. 552 E. 700 N. (Pat.)
Hires, Jack M. '32 '83 C.347 B.G.S. L.879 J.D.
(adm. in MI; not adm. in IN) Prof. of Law, Valparaiso Univ. College of Business Admn.

Hodges & Davis, P.C.
(See Merrillville)

Hoeppner, Delmar R., (AV) ....'27 '54 C&L.879 A.B., J.D. [Hoeppner W.&E.] ‡

Hoeppner Wagner & Evans LLP, (AV)
103 East Lincolnway, P.O. Box 2357, 46384-2357 ⊙
Telephone: 219-464-4961; 800-879-2246 (IN, IL) Fax: 219-465-0603
Email: hwe@hwelaw.com URL: http://www.hwelaw.com
Retired: Delmar R. Hoeppner (Retired). Of Counsel: William H. Wagner. Members of Firm: Larry G. Evans (Resident, Merrillville Office); William F. Satterlee, III; John E. Hughes (Resident, Merrillville Office); Morris A. Sunkel; James L. Jorgensen; Ronald P. Kuker; F. Joseph Jaskowiak (Resident, Merrillville Office); Richard M. Davis; Mark E. Schmidtke; Todd A. Leeth; J. Brian Hittinger (Resident, Merrillville Office); Lauren K. Kroeger; Robert L. Clark; Jack A. Kramer (Resident, Merrillville Office); Jay S. Patheja (Resident, Merrillville Office); Tina M. Bengs (Resident, Merrillville Office); Kevin G. Kerr. Associates: William A. Ferngren; Michael Eugene Tolbert (Resident, Merrillville Office); Eric P. Mathisen (Resident, Merrillville Office); Gerold L. Stout (Resident, Merrillville Office); Thomas L. Chrzanowski; Cintra D.B. Geairn (Not admitted in IN); Sean E. Kenyon (Resident, Merrillville Office); Lucretia A. Thornton; Lee I. Lane.
General Practice. Trials and Appeals in State, Federal and Tax Courts. Bankruptcy, Commercial and Banking, Corporate, Creditors' Rights, Probate and Estate Planning, Estate Administration, Financial Resources Planning, Insurance Defense, Municipal Bonds, Municipal and Zoning, Personal Injury, Product Liability, Professional Malpractice, Real Estate, Taxation, Workers Compensation, Labor and Employment. Mediation, OSHA, Employee Benefits Law.
Representative Clients: American Family Insurance Group; Bank One; ISG, Inc.; Okaya Electric America, Inc.; State Farm Insurance Cos.; Toys R Us Corp.; Valparaiso University; Whiteco Industries, Inc.; White Lodging Corp.
Merrillville, Indiana Office: Twin Towers, Suite 606 South, 1000 East 80th Place, P.O. Box 10627, 46419-0627. Telephone: 219-769-6552; 800-263-1466 (IN, IL). Fax: 219-738-2349. Email: hwe@hwelaw.com

See Professional Biographies, VALPARAISO, INDIANA

Hoham, Julia M., (BV) ....'60 '88 C.347 B.A. L.1049 J.D. 251 Indiana Ave.
Holiday, Lois Jones ....'54 '81 C.346 B.A. L.1137 J.D. Pros. Off.
Hollenbeck, David L., (AV) ....'47 '74 C&L.879 B.S., J.D. [Blachly,T.B.&H.]
Hurley, Brian J., (BV) ....'58 '84 C.746 B.A. L.879 J.D. [Douglas,K.&H.]
Huss, Rebecca Jean '67 '92 C.351 B.A. L.692 J.D.
(adm. in WA; not adm. in IN) Asst. Prof. of Law, Valparaiso Univ. Sch. of Law
Istrabadi, Feisal A., (CV) .... '62 '88 C.347 B.A. L.1119 J.D. [Boesch&I.]
Johnson, Shelli Wright, (BV) .... '53 '79 C.63 B.S. L.879 J.D. 304 W. U.S. Hwy. 6

Johnson & Rappa, LLC
(See Merrillville)

Jorgensen, James L., (AV) .... '46 '74 C.747 B.A. L.879 J.D. [Hoeppner W.&E.]
Jury, Frank A. ....'74 '98 C.347 B.S. L.879 J.D. 235 West U.S. Highway 30

Kelly, Timothy F., and Associates
(See Dyer)

Kennedy, Robert P., (BV) ..... '40 '65 C.776 B.S.B.A. L.602 J.D. 175 Lincolnway, Ste. F
Kerr, Kevin G. .... '56 '97 C.1101 B.S. L.879 J.D. [Hoeppner W.&E.]
Kickbush, Raymond D. .... '35 '61 C&L.879 B.A., J.D. Cir. J.
Koeppen, R. Bradley, (BV) .... '54 '84 C.63 B.A. L.879 J.D. [Douglas,K.&H.]
Kroeger, Lauren K., (CV) .... '64 '89 C.472 B.S.B.A. L.1017 J.D. [Hoeppner W.&E.]
Kruse, Douglas R. .... '67 '92 C.363 B.A. L.879 J.D. 103 E. Lincolnway
Kuker, Ronald P., (AV) ....'51 '76 C.502 B.S. L.879 J.D. [Hoeppner W.&E.]
Kupsis, Visvaldis P., (CV) ...... '60 '85 C.303 B.A. L.879 J.D. 52 South Valparaiso Street

Lambert, Michael
(See Crown Point)

Lane, Lee I. .... '— '05 C.208 B.A. L.879 J.D. [⊠ Hoeppner W.&E.]
Langer, Michael A., (J.D.), (BV) .... '56 '81 C.347 B.S. L.879 J.D. [Langer&L.]
Langer, Steven L., (J.D.), (BV) .... '54 '80 C.347 B.A. L.879 J.D. [Langer&L.]
Langer & Langer, (BV) .... 15 North Washington Street

Lasser, Herbert S., & Associates, P.C.
(See Merrillville)

Lazarus, William '— '84 C&L.145 B.A., J.D.
(adm. in IL; not adm. in IN) [⊠ K.J.Allen&Assoc.]
Leeth, Todd A., (BV) ....'59 '88 C.347 B.A. L.879 J.D. [Hoeppner W.&E.]
Lerner, Christopher M. ....'69 '05 C.999 B.S. L.879 J.D. 175 W. Lincolnway, Ste. D
Loesche, Marc C. ....'49 '75 C&L.879 B.A., J.D. Pres., Hardwood Interiors Inc.
Lohmeyer, Joanne ....'47 '77 C&L.879 B.A., J.D. 827 E. Lincolnway
Long, Linda L. ....'43 '77 C&L.879 B.A., J.D. Pres., Strategies, Inc.

Lucas, Holcomb & Medrea LLP
(See Merrillville)

Lyons, John M., (BV) ....'33 '58 C&L.879 B.A., J.D. [Lyons,S.&B.]
Lyons, Sullivan & Brooks, (BV) .... 55 S. Franklin St.
Lyp, Patrick A. ....'70 '97 C.128 B.A. L.776 J.D. [⊠ Blachly,T.B.&H.]
Macke, Thomas F., (AV) ....'54 '79 C&L.879 B.A., J.D. [Blachly,T.B.&H.]
Malcom, Stauffer P., Jr. .... '61 '86 C.235 B.A. L.421 J.D. 1300 Winding Ridge Lane★
Martz, Hugo E., (BV) .... '38 '63 C.679 B.S. L.1119 LL.B. [Martz&B.]
Martz & Boyles, P.C., (BV) .... 6 North Michigan Avenue
Massa, Teresa A., (BV) ....'54 '91 C.347 B.A. L.879 J.D. [⊠ Terrell&T.]
Matsey, David Paul ....'44 '69 C.894 B.A. L.879 J.D. [⊠ Millbranth&B.]
McClean, Alicia J., (BV) ....'56 '84 C&L.347 B.A., J.D. 605 Morgan Blvd.
McIlree, Michael P. ....'70 '97 C.347 B.S. L.1339 J.D. McIlree & McIlree
Melion, Walter E., (CV) ....'40 '86 C.1069 B.G.S. L.879 J.D. 205 Jefferson St.
Millbranth, Russell D. ....'44 '74 C.347 B.A. L.945 J.D. [Millbranth&B.]
Millbranth & Bush, (BV) ....2601 Chicago St., Unit B
Miller, Michael B., (CV) ....'57 '94 C.347 B.S. L.879 J.D. [M.B.Miller]

Miller, Michael B., P.C., (CV)
701 East Lincolnway, 46383
Telephone: 219-465-1197 Fax: 219-531-0683
Email: miller.law@gte.net URL: http://www.mmillerlawfirm.com
Michael B. Miller.
Estate Planning, Trusts and Estates, Asset Protection, Living Trusts, Wills and Probate, Retirement Planning, Guardianship, Elder Law, Medicaid, Corporations, Business Law, Contracts, Premarital Agreements, Leases and Leasing, Real Estate, Condemnation, Taxation, Personal Injury, Accidents, Automobile Accidents and Injuries, Slip and Fall, Wrongful Death.

See Professional Biographies, VALPARAISO, INDIANA

Moutaw, Roy G., (CV) ....'41 '77 C.679 B.S. L.879 J.D. 2556 Northbridge St.
Myers, Adam J., III '51 '86 C.645 B.S. L.309 J.D.
(adm. in CA; not adm. in IN) Valparaiso University
Nadzan, Lizabeth R. ....'70 '96 C.475 BS L.879 JD 808 Beech Street
Nelson, Ronald P., (BV) ....'38 '64 C.597 B.S. L.1119 J.D. 205 E. Jefferson St.
Norman, Phillip A., (BV) ....'62 '87 C.275 B.A. L.879 J.D. [P.A.Norman]

Norman, Phillip A., P.C., (BV)
2110 Calumet Avenue, 46383
Telephone: 219-462-5104 Fax: 219-462-9344
Email: phil@normanattorney.com
Phillip A. Norman.
Civil Litigation, Commercial Law, Banking Law, Municipal Law, Zoning Law, Creditor's Rights, Family Law, Mediation.

See Professional Biographies, VALPARAISO, INDIANA

Norris, Bette Ruth '54 '98 C.679 B.A. L.879 J.D.
Memorial Ctr., 1158 West Lincolnway, Ste. 1
Patton, Clay M. ....'72 '99 C.347 B.A. L.345 J.D. 251 Indiana Ave.
Pawlowski, David R., (BV) ....'57 '82 C&L.879 B.A., J.D. [Forszt,P.&S.]
Pelfrey, Vincent E. .... '66 '97 C.347 B.A. L.793 J.D. [V.Pelfrey]
Pelfrey, Vincent, Law Office of .... 205 E. Jefferson St.
Persyn, Mary G. ....'45 '82 C.190 A.B. L.602 J.D. Law Libr., Valparaiso Univ.
Polarek, Cheryl M. ....'70 '97 C.347 B.A. L.190 J.D. Porter Co. Pros. Attys. Off.
Proctor, Lester T., Jr. .... '27 '53 C&L.352 B.S.C., J.D. 4805 Goodrich Road
Rupcich, Richard J., (BV) ....'50 '86 C.734 B.A. L.879 J.D. [Blachly,T.B.&H.]
Satterlee, William F., III, (AV) .... '38 '66 C.434 B.A. L.879 J.D. [Hoeppner W.&E.]
Schmaltz, Jon A. .... '73 '99 C.679 B.S. L.1119 J.D. [⊠ Burke C.&C.]
Schmidtke, Mark E., (AV) .... '56 '81 C&L.879 B.A., J.D. [Hoeppner W.&E.]

Sisson, Jill, (BV) '51 '80 C.1121 B.A. L.879 J.D.
15 North Franklin Street Suite 220, 46383
Telephone: 219-465-3717 Fax: 219-531-0728
Email: mjsisson@verizon.net URL: http://www.lawyers.com/jillsisson
Interstate Adoptions, Private Placement Adoptions, Step Parent Adoptions, Family/Domestic Relations, Divorce, Child Custody, Child Support, Visitation Rights.

See Professional Biographies, VALPARAISO, INDIANA

Smith, Jeffrey H., (BV) ....'50 '88 C.879 B.A. L.365 J.D. [Forszt,P.&S.]
Soliday, Matthew D. .... '67 '92 C.347 B.A. L.879 J.D. 205 Jefferson St.
Sowa, Sharon .... '58 '83 C&L.879 B.A., J.D. 1558 Ransom Rd.

Spangler, Jennings & Dougherty, P.C., (AV) BR
150 Lincolnway, Suite 3001, 46383 ⊙
Telephone: 219-462-6151 Fax: 219-477-4935
Email: spangler@sjdlaw.com URL: http://www.sjdlaw.com
Partners: Samuel J. Bernardi, Jr.; Christopher Grabarek.
Jon S. Diston. Of Counsel: Patrick J. Dougherty.
General Trial and Appellate Practice. Administrative, Banking, Bankruptcy, Business Reorganizations, Business Transactions, Civil Rights, Commercial, Construction, Corporate, Creditors' Rights, Criminal Litigation, Family/Domestic Relations, Drug and Device, Eminent Domain, Environmental, ERISA and Employee Benefits, Probate and Estate Planning and Administration, Fire/Arson, Guardianships, Health Care, Insurance, Labor and Employment, Municipal and Zoning, Personal Injury, Product Liability, Professional Liability, Medical Malpractice Defense, Real Estate, School, Federal, State and Local Taxation, Toxic Torts, Transportation, Workers Compensation, Land Development.
Representative Clients: Ancilla; Allstate Insurance Cos.; American International Group; American National Property and Casualty Company (ANPAC); American States; Associates Financial; Auto Owners; Bank One; Beneficial Finance.
Merrillville, Indiana Office: 8396 Mississippi Street. Telephone: 219-769-2323.
Indianapolis, Indiana Office: 9200 Keystone Crossing, Suite 410. Telephone: 317-571-7690. Facsimile: 317-571-7686.

See Professional Biographies, VALPARAISO, INDIANA

Spores, John M., Law Office of .... '57 '99 C.679 Ph.D. L.879 J.D. P.O. Box 1127
Staley, Ann K., (CV) .... '61 '91 C.679 L.879 J.D. [Lyons,S.&B.]

Stalmack, Joseph, & Associates, P.C.
(See Hammond)

Stan, James L., Law Office Of .... '53 '78 C&L.879 B.S., J.D. 836 Lincolnway
Steele, Albert N., Jr. .... '36 '60 C&L.879 B.A., LL.B. 222 Lincoln Hills Dr.‡

Stutsman, Mulvaney & DeBoer
(See Elkhart)

Sullivan, James L., (BV) .... '36 '61 C&L.879 B.A., LL.B. [Lyons,S.&B.]
Sunkel, Morris A., (BV) ....'48 '74 C.339 B.S. L.879 J.D. [Hoeppner W.&E.]
Svetanoff, Richard E. .... '54 '90 C.347 B.S. L.879 J.D. 404 Fordwick Lane
Tabor, Glenn J., (AV) .... '34 '58 C&L.879 B.A., J.D. [⊡ Blachly,T.B.&H.]
Tapocsi-Lohmeyer, Jo Anne, (CV) ...... '47 '77 C&L.879 B.A., J.D. 827 E. Lincoln Way

Tavitas, Anthony F., Attorneys at Law, A Professional Corporation
(See Munster)

Terrell, George W., Jr., (BV) .... '49 '84 C.645 B.A. L.879 J.D. [Terrell&T.]
Terrell & Thrall, (BV) .... 1158 Lincolnway
Thornton, Lucretia A. .... '— '82 C.679 B.S. L.879 J.D. [⊠ Hoeppner W.&E.] ⊙
Thrall, Larry E., (BV) .... '48 '88 C.347 B.G.S. L.879 J.D. [Terrell&T.]
Truitt, Bryan M. ....'69 '98 C.347 B.S. L.879 J.D. 121 Lincolnway
Tsoutsouris, James V. ....'36 '67 C.347 A.B. L.879 J.D. 121 Lincolnway
Van Schouwen, Craig R., (BV) ....'64 '91 C.347 B.S. L.209 J.D. [Blachly,T.B.&H.]
Vetne, Stephanie A. ... '68 '96 C.431 B.A. L.879 J.D. Asst. Prof. of Law, Valparaiso Univ.
Vincent, G. Craig, (CV) .... '51 '90 C.476 B.B.S. L.146 J.D. 251 Ind. Ave.
Vojslavek, Timothy E., (BV) .... '63 '89 C&L.879 B.A., J.D. [Vojslavek&C.]
Vojslavek & Catsadimas, P.C., (BV) .... 2803 Boilermaker Court, Suite 1-C
Wagner, William H., (BV) .... '33 '58 C&L.879 B.A., J.D. [⊡ Hoeppner W.&E.]
Wagonblast, Scott M. .... '67 '93 C.347 B.M. L.879 J.D. 202 E. Monroe St.
Walter, John A., III ....'52 '77 C.347 A.B. L.1119 J.D. 1109 Glendale Blvd.
Webber, Thomas W., Sr. .... '36 '75 C.679 L.879 J.D. Supr. Ct. J.
Whitton, Linda S. ....'58 '86 C&L.879 B.A., J.D. Valparaiso Law School
Wrage, Jeffrey S., (CV) ....'68 '94 C.1119 B.S. L.879 J.D. [⊠ Blachly,T.B.&H.]
Young, Barbara A., (BV) .... '49 '76 C.174 B.A. L.879 J.D. Partner, Benchmark Ltd.
Yudt, Michael F. .... '24 '52 C.347 L.879 LL.B. 402 Wall St.‡
Yudt, Michael F. II .... '51 '77 C.879 B.S. L.1209 J.D. 402 Wall St.

Zemaitis, Aimee C.
(See Portage)

Zivanovic, Crista '55 '90 C.597 B.A. L.209 J.D.
(adm. in IL; not adm. in IN) Asst. Prof. of Communication, Valparaiso Univ.
Zromkoski, Randall J., (BV) ....'59 '84 C.894 A.B. L.879 J.D. [Blachly,T.B.&H.] ⊙

VEEDERSBURG, 2,299, *Fountain Co.*

Gibson, Donald E., Law Office .... '41 '71 C.597 B.A. L.345 J.D. 108 E. 2nd St.

VERNON, * 370, *Jennings Co.*

Bowman, Ray F., III .... '71 '96 C.473 B.A. L.347 J.D. Co. Pros. Atty.
Funke, James F., Jr. .... '59 '91 C.854 B.A. L.347 J.D. Supr. Ct. J.

Marshall, Alan L., (CV) .... '59 '92 C.679 B.S. L.347 J.D. Co. Comm. Atty. [Marshall]
Marshall Law Office, (CV) .... 28 Perry Street

McConnell and Finnerty
(See North Vernon)

Roche, John T., Jr. .... '49 '83 C.454 B.A. L.818 J.D. P.O. Box 577

VERSAILLES, * 1,791, *Ripley Co.*

Day, Timothy B., (BV) .... '64 '89 C.63 B.S. L.347 J.D. [Eaton&D.]
Eaton, Larry L., (AV) .... '40 '66 C&L.347 A.B., J.D. [Eaton&D.]

Eaton & Day, (AV)
123 South Main Street, P.O. Box 275, 47042-9442
Telephone: 812-689-5111 Fax: 812-689-5165
Email: leaton@seidata.com URL: http://www.lawyers.com/leatonlaw
Members of Firm: Larry L. Eaton; Timothy B. Day.
General Trial and Appellate Practice. Negligence, Corporation, Probate and Estate Planning and Real Estate Law. School Law.
See Professional Biographies, VERSAILLES, INDIANA

Gay, Greeley, (BV) .... '18 '49 C.150 L.383 J.D. 126 Main St.
Gay, Mary Ann, (BV) .... '50 '77 C.383 B.S. L.1119 J.D. [Gay]
Gay Law Office, (BV) .... 126 Main St.
Guenther, Katharine D., (CV) .... '68 '93 C.210 B.A. L.347 J.D. Co. Pros. Off.
McCombs, Steven B., (BV) .... '50 '76 C.150 B.A. L.1119 J.D. Pub. Def. [Gay]
Morris, James Brent .... '48 '87 C.347 B.S. L.345 J.D. Supr. Ct. J., Ripley Supr. Ct.

VEVAY, * 1,735, *Switzerland Co.*

Coy, W. Gregory, (BV) .... '60 '89 C.347 B.A. L.345 J.D. P.O. Box 181
Hensley, Monica L., (CV) .... '69 '95 C.266 B.A. L.1161 J.D. 307 West Main Street
Hickman, David W., Attorney at Law, (BV) '52 '83 C.679 B.S. L.150 J.D.
112 W. Pike St.
Rosenberger, Lisa K., (BV) .... '57 '84 C.265 B.A. L.345 J.D. 307 W. Main Street

VINCENNES, * 18,701, *Knox Co.*

Bell, Donald G., (BV) .... '30 '57 C.347 A.B. L.1119 J.D. 513 Main St.
Biddinger Gregg, Sherry L. .... '60 '86 C.249 B.S. L.1119 J.D. Cir.J.

Bingham McHale LLP, (AV)
112 N. 7th Street, P.O. Box 139, 47591 ⊙
Telephone: 812-886-9970 Telecopier: 812-886-0776
Email: jgregg@binghammchale.com
John R. Gregg.
General Civil Practice including: Administrative Law; Agricultural Law; Alternative Dispute Resolution; Antitrust and Trade Regulation; Appeals; Appellate; Architects and Engineers Liability Defense; Banks and Banking; Bankruptcy and Reorganization; Business Law; Business Litigation; Cable Telecommunications Law; Collective Bargaining; Commercial Transactions; Construction Law; Contract Negotiation; Copyright; Corporate Finance; Complex Litigation; Class Actions; Corporate Law; Creditors' Rights; Drug and Medical Device Law; Election, Campaign Finance and Political Law; Employee Benefits; Environmental Law; Estate Planning and Administration; Family Law; Finance; Franchising and Licensing; Gaming Law; Governmental Services; Health Care; Hospital Law; Insurance; Intellectual Property; Labor and Employment; Leases and Leasing; Legal Malpractice, Discipline and Licensing; Libel, Slander and Defamation; Litigation; Lobbying; Matrimonial and Family Law; Media Law; Medicare and Medicaid Reimbursement, Medical and Dental Liability Defense and Disciplines and Licensing; Mergers and Acquisitions; Natural Resources Law; Occupational Safety and Health; Patent; Probate; Product Liability; Professional Liability Defense; Public Finance; Public Utility Law; Real Estate; Securities Law; Tax-Exempt Finance, Taxation (Controversies, Corporate Planning, Income, Gift and Estate, Individual, Partnership, Property, Nonprofit Organizations), Toxic Torts Law; Trademark; White Collar Criminal Defense; Zoning, Planning and Land Use.
Indianapolis, Indiana Office: Bingham McHale LLP, 2700 Market Tower, 10 West Market Street. Telephone: 317-635-8900. Fax: 317-236-9907.
Jasper, Indiana Office: Bingham McHale LLP, 212 West Sixth Street. Telephone: 812-482- 5500. Fax: 812-482-2017.
Noblesville, Indiana Office: Bingham McHale LLP, 970 Logan Street. Telephone: 317-776-8668. Fax: 317-776-8651.
See Professional Biographies, VINCENNES, INDIANA

Carnahan, J. Dirk, (CV) .... '65 '90 C.679 B.S. L.61 J.D. 1027 Washington Avenue
Crowley, W. Timothy .... '51 '85 C.346 B.S. L.345 J.D. Supr. Ct. J.
Cummings, L. Edward, (BV) .... '46 '73 C.347 A.B. L.1119 J.D. [Hart B.]
Deem, David A., (BV) .... '50 '75 C.265 B.A. L.421 J.D. Assoc. Prof., Vincennes Univ.
Dillon, Shawna Dawn, (CV) ..... '72 '98 C.346 B.S. L.201 J.D. 1027 Washington Avenue
Doolittle, Robert P., (AV) .... '40 '65 C.347 B.S. L.1119 LL.B. [Emison D.K.&R.]
Emison, Rabb, (AV) .... '25 '50 C.210 A.B. L.1119 LL.B. [▣ Emison D.K.&R.] ‡

Emison Doolittle Kolb & Roellgen, (AV) ▣
Eighth & Busseron Streets, P.O. Box 215, 47591
Telephone: 812-882-2280 FAX: 812-885-2308
Email: general@emisonlaw.com
Members of Firm: Robert P. Doolittle; Jeffrey B. Kolb; J. David Roellgen; Yvette Charmaine Kirchoff. Of Counsel: Rabb Emison. Associate: Tonya R. Shaw.
General Practice. Trials, Estate Planning and Administration, Family Law, Bankruptcy, Corporation, Commercial and Insurance Law.
Clients Include: Old National Bank; Sun-Commercial Newspaper; Amoco Pipeline; El Paso Energy; Cincinnati Insurance Co.
See Professional Biographies, VINCENNES, INDIANA

Ewing, Mark, (AV) .... '51 '77 C.823 B.A. L.950 J.D. [Hart B.]
Field, Jason C. .... '70 '00 C.347 B.S. L.879 J.D [Sturm,S.&P.]

Gosnell, Borden, Enloe & Sloss, Ltd.
(See Lawrenceville)

Gregg, John R., (BV) .... '54 '84 C.347 B.A. L.345 J.D. [Bingham M.]

Hall, Partenheimer & Kinkle
(See Princeton)

Hart, Arthur L., (AV) .... '11 '36 C.347 L.1119 LL.B. 206 Massachusetts Pl.

Hart Bell LLC, (AV)
513 Main Street, P.O. Box 979, 47591
Telephone: 812-882-8935 Fax: 812-882-5186; 812-882-9272
Members of Firm: L. Edward Cummings; Mark Ewing; Brent Stuckey; Jeffery S. Neal; Daniel L. Siewers.
General Practice. Litigation, Insurance, Banking, Corporate, Employment, Probate and Estate Planning, State and Federal Tax Law, Real Estate, Construction, Commercial, Business, Elder, Creditors Rights, Personal Injury, Family Law and Criminal Defense.
See Professional Biographies, VINCENNES, INDIANA

Jewel, Bryan A., (CV) .... '64 '90 C.347 B.A. L.201 J.D. 517 Broadway
Kirchoff, Bruce, (BV) .... '48 '74 C.347 A.B. L.345 J.D. 517 Broadway
Kirchoff, Yvette Charmaine, (CV) ..... '62 '98 C.679 B.S. L.776 J.D. [Emison D.K.&R.]
Klueh, James R. .... '52 '77 C.347 A.B. L.1119 J.D. 1324 Bwy.★
Kolb, Jeffrey B., (AV) .... '51 '76 C.347 B.A. L.1119 J.D. [Emison D.K.&R.]
Land, Murphey C. .... '36 '64 C.347 B.S. L.1119 J.D. Ret. Cir. J.‡
Ledford, Paul B., (AV) .... '37 '63 C.347 B.S. L.1119 J.D. [P.B.Ledford]
Ledford, Paul B., Professional Corporation, (AV) .... 707 Busseron Street
Lewis, Robert D., (BV) .... '37 '65 C.347 B.S. L.1119 LL.B. [Lewis&M.]
Lewis & Miller, (BV) .... 4th Fl., Ambank Bldg.
McCormick, Robert S., (BV) .... '20 '48 C.347 B.S. L.1119 J.D. 305 Busseron St.
McGaughey, Jerry J. .... '37 '63 C.347 B.S. L.1119 LL.B. Pros. Atty.
Miller, David L., (BV) .... '39 '68 C&L.347 A.B., J.D. [Lewis&M.]
Murphy, Stephen P., Jr. .... '73 '99 C.346 B.S. L.347 J.D. [Murphy&M.]
Murphy, Suzanne J. .... '73 '99 C.346 B.S. L.1119 J.D. [Murphy&M.]
Murphy & Murphy, LLC .... 521 Main Street
Neal, Jeffery S., (CV) .... '71 '97 C.347 B.A. L.345 J.D. [Hart B.]
Osborne, Jim R. .... '45 '74 C.346 B.S. L.345 J.D. Supr. Ct. J.
Parmenter, Matthew, (BV) .... '55 '85 C.249 B.S. L.1119 J.D. [Sturm,S.&P.]
Roellgen, J. David, (AV) .... '53 '79 C.346 B.S. L.345 J.D. [Emison D.K.&R.]
Rosenberg, Albert .... '18 '41 C.347 B.S. L.1119 LL.B. 318 Main St.‡

Rudolph, Fine, Porter & Johnson LLP
(See Evansville)

Shaw, Tonya R. .... '79 '05 C.346 B.A. L.879 J.D. [▣ Emison D.K.&R.]
Siewers, Daniel L. .... '74 '99 C.265 B.A. L.347 J.D. [Hart B.]
Smith, Bruce A., (AV) .... '52 '76 C.346 B.S. L.345 J.D. [Sturm,S.&P.]
Stuckey, Brent, (BV) .... '53 '78 C.225 B.A. L.1119 J.D. [Hart B.]
Stuckey, H. Brent .... '53 '78 C.225 B.A. L.347 J.D. 513 Main Street
Sturm, Gregory W., (BV) .... '45 '70 C.602 B.B.A. L.1119 J.D. [Sturm,S.&P.]

Sturm, Smith & Parmenter, (AV)
312 Main Street, P.O. Box 393, 47591
Telephone: 812-882-1303 Fax: 812-886-0786 URL: http://www.ssplawfirm.com
URL: http://www.lawyerspages.com/firms/ssp/
Members of Firm: Gregory W. Sturm; Bruce A. Smith; Matthew Parmenter; Jason C. Field.
Litigation, Commercial, Bankruptcy, Business, Collections, Workers Compensation, Social Security, Probate, Estate Planning, Personal Injury, Real Estate, Family.
Representative Clients: Knox County REMC; American National Bank.
See Professional Biographies, VINCENNES, INDIANA

Theobald, Edward C. .... '32 '69 C.347 B.S. L.1119 J.D. Supr. Ct. J.
Webster, Dale P., (BV) .... '48 '73 C.992 B.A. L.1119 J.D. 1027 Washington Ave.

WABASH, * 11,743, *Wabash Co.*

Downs, Stephen H., (AV) .... '48 '73 C.347 B.S. L.345 J.D. [Tiede,M.D.L.&S.] ⊙
Eddingfield, Joseph W., (CV) .... '59 '84 C.679 B.S. L.161 J.D. 23 E. Hill St.
Fisher, Richard P., (AV) .... '47 '73 C.303 B.A. L.345 J.D. [Fisher&I.]
Fisher & Ireland, (AV) .... 65 W. Canal St.
Guenin, Mark C., (BV) .... '52 '78 C.894 A.B. L.1119 J.D. [Guenin]
Guenin Law Office, (BV) .... 574 S. Miami St.
Hartley, William C., Jr., (BV) .... '68 '96 C.347 B.S. L.879 J.D. P.O. Box 403
Johnston, Happi .... '76 '02 1 North Miami St.
Johnston, John R., (BV) .... '37 '68 C.346 B.S. L.345 J.D. [Johnston&L.]
Johnston & Lehman, P.C., (BV) .... 1 N. Miami St.

Kiley, Kiley, Harker, Michael & Certain
(See Marion)

Lehman, Douglas C., (BV) .... '50 '75 C.894 A.B. L.1119 J.D. [Johnston&L.]
Lynn, Kristina L., (BV) .... '66 '92 C.432 B.S. L.347 J.D. [Tiede,M.D.L.&S.] ⊙
Magley, David J., (BV) .... '57 '87 C.999 B.A. L.345 J.D. Chf. Dep. Pros.
Magley, Robert E., (AV) .... '27 '55 C.347 B.S. L.345 J.D. 1452 Inez St.‡
Mattern, Thomas J., Law Office of, (CV) .... '35 '69 C.347 B.S. L.345 J.D. 70 W. Hill St.
McCallen, Robert R. .... '26 '56 C.346 B.S. L.1119 J.D. P.O. Box 924‡
Mccallen, Robert R., III, (BV) ..... '61 '88 C.347 B.S.B.A. L.862 J.D. 40 West Hill Street
Metz, Donald R., (AV) .... '33 '62 C.265 B.A. L.1119 J.D. [▣ Tiede,M.D.L.&S.] ⊙
Plummer, Alfred H., III, Law Office of, (AV) '43 '68
C&L.347 B.S., J.D. 21-27 W. Canal St.
Schlitt, Albert J., (BV) .... '37 '66 C.801 B.S. L.345 LL.B. [Tiede,M.D.L.&S.] ⊙
Smith, Michael Jay .... '63 '90 C.446 B.A. L.1187 J.D. 73 W. Canal St.
Sposeep, Michael L. .... '44 '69 C.347 A.B. L.1119 J.D. Supr. J.
Stein, Joel K. .... '61 '88 C.436 B.A. L.74 J.D. [▣ Tiede,M.D.L.&S.] ⊙
Thrush, Larry C., (BV) .... '48 '73 C.679 B.S. L.1119 J.D. [L.C.Thrush]
Thrush, Larry C., Inc., (BV) .... 1 N. Wabash St.
Tiede, Charles R., (AV) .... '29 '56 C.63 B.S. L.1119 J.D. [▣ Tiede,M.D.L.&S.] ⊙
Tiede, Metz, Downs, Lynn & Schlitt, P.C., (AV) .... 99 W. Canal St. (⊙North Manchester)
Vanderpool, Daniel J. .... '56 '80 C.333 A.B. L.1119 J.D. Cir. J.
Zimmerman, Alan J., (BV) .... '55 '81 C.347 B.A. L.879 J.D. [Zimmerman]
Zimmerman, Randi H., (BV) .... '62 '91 C.347 B.A. L.1187 J.D. [Zimmerman]
Zimmerman Law Offices, P.C., (BV) .... 66 W. Hill St.

WAKARUSA, 1,667, *Elkhart Co.*

Bond, Richard E., (BV) '53 '79 C.347 B.A. L.950 J.D.
Sr. V.P., Chf. Adm. Off. & Gen. Coun., Monaco Coach Corp.
Pangburn, T. Michael, (AV) '60 '86
C.967 B.A. L.879 J.D. Corp. Coun., Monaco Coach Corp.

WARREN, 1,185, *Huntington Co.*

Bendall, Theodore L., (AV) .... '39 '64 C.20 A.B. L.477 J.D. [Bendall D.H.M.&R.] ⊙
Bendall DeLaney Hartburg McNeely & Roth LLP, (AV)
223A North Wayne Street (⊙Huntington, Roanoke)
Bowers, Lee M., II, (BV) .... '62 '88 C.207 B.A. L.902 J.D. [Bowers,B.G.&W.] ⊙
Bowers, Brewer, Garrett & Wiley, (AV) .... 121 North Wayne Street (⊙Huntington)
Brewer, David L., (AV) .... '36 '63 C.347 B.S. L.1119 J.D. [Bowers,B.G.&W.] ⊙
DeLaney, Richard, (BV) '53 '78 C&L.347 A.B., J.D.
[Bendall D.H.M.&R.] (⊙Huntington)
Garrett, Robert S., (BV) .... '47 '74 C.347 B.S. L.838 J.D. [Bowers,B.G.&W.] ⊙
Gordon, William S., Jr., (BV) '42 '73
C.63 B.S. L.345 J.D. [Bendall D.H.M.&R.] (⊙Huntington)
Hughes, Lisa M. .... '80 '04 C.679 B.S. L.879 J.D. [▣ Bendall D.H.M.&R.] ⊙
McNeely, Dennis L., (BV) '51 '76
C.1064 B.A. L.1119 J.D. [Bendall D.H.M.&R.] (⊙Huntington)
Wiley, Joseph K., (BV) .... '53 '79 C.679 B.S. L.1119 J.D. [Bowers,B.G.&W.] ⊙

WARSAW, * 12,415, *Kosciusko Co.*

Ahlersmeyer, David L. '58 '85 C.679 B.S.E.E. L.347 J.D.
Assoc. Gen. Coun. & Dir., Intell. Prop., Biomet, Inc. (Pat.)
Armey, Michael E., (BV) .... '42 '74 C.679 B.S. L.1119 J.D. [Rothberg L.&W.]
Barrett, John D. .... '66 '04 C.560 B.A. L.345 J.D. [▣ D.C.Kolbe]
Bauer, Torrey J. .... '64 '91 C.999 B.S. L.1119 J.D. [Lavender&B.]
Beeson, Larry D., (BV) .... '45 '70 C.347 B.S. L.345 J.D. [Dalton&B.]
Berry, Bryon J. .... '59 '86 C.347 B.A. L.801 J.D. 630 S. Buffalo
Blackford, Amber L., (CV) .... '61 '96 C.432 B.S. L.879 J.D. 216 West Fort Wayne Street
Burner, Charles R. .... '29 '60 C.347 A.B. L.1119 LL.B. Supr. Ct. J.

Butts, James S., (BV) '51 '79 C.347 B.A. L.802 J.D.
119 E. Center Street, Suite B-5, 46580-2852
Telephone: 574-269-9500 Fax: 574-269-2888
Email: jsblawfirm@abanet.org
Civil Litigation, Family Law, Adoptions, Child Custody, Child Support, Divorce, Visitation Rights, Wills, Probate, Trust and Estates, Estate Planning, Personal Injury, Automobile Accidents, Truck Accidents, Wrongful Death.

See Professional Biographies, WARSAW, INDIANA

Condon, Robert C. '41 '66 C.207 B.A. L.339 J.D.
(adm. in IL; not adm. in IN) Lake City Bk.
Dalton, William M., II, (CV) .... '35 '60 C.880 B.A. L.1119 LL.B. [Dalton&B.]
Dalton & Beeson, (BV) .... 211 West Fort Wayne Street, Suite A
Dawson, Todd A., (CV) .... '60 '87 C.679 B.S.E.T. L.879 J.D. Zimmer Inc. (Pat.)
Durgin, Robert E., (BVⓉ) ...... '59 '84 C.602 B.A. L.861 J.D. VP Reg. Aff., Biomet, Inc.
Dvorak, David C. .... '63 '91 C.473 B.S. L.930 J.D. Sr. V.P. & Gen. Coun., Zimmer
Earhart, Thomas W., (BV) .... '48 '74 C.347 B.S. L.345 J.D. [Reed&E.]
Fawley, William S., (CV) .... '56 '93 C.827 B.S. L.879 J.D. [Valentine M.&L.]
Fifelski, Angela M. .... '67 '96 C.1154 B.A. L.213 J.D. Zimmer, Inc. (Pat.)
Fitzsimmons, Laura K., Law Office of ..... '61 '95 C.959 B.S. L.588 J.D. 6 Yarnelle Point
Hall, Robert J. '71 '97 C.347 B.A. L.201 J.D.
(adm. in IL; not adm. in IN) Biomet, Inc.
Hampton, Daniel H., (CV) .... '62 '88 C.63 B.S. L.1187 J.D. [Hampton&V.]
Hampton & Voelz, (CV) .... 301 N. Lake Street
Hann, Daniel P., (BV) '55 '84
C.1109 B.A. L.345 J.D. Sr. V.P. & Gen. Coun., Biomet, Inc.
Harris, Philip J., (AV) .... '26 '50 C.679 B.S. L.1119 J.D. [Harris&H.]
Harris, Stephen P., (BV) .... '57 '88 C.210 B.A. L.345 J.D. [Harris&H.]
Harris & Harris, (AV) .... 222 North Buffalo Street
Hayes, James P., (BV) .... '50 '76 C&L.602 B.A., J.D. 7598 W. Person Rd.
Hearn, R. Steven, (AV) .... '37 '66 C.802 B.B.A. L.345 J.D. [Rothberg L.&W.]
Helm, Richard K., (AV) .... '45 '73 C.894 A.B. L.1119 J.D. [Rockhill P.]
Heyde, Lee L., (BV) .... '— '79 C.347 B.S. L.345 J.D. 1822 E. Center St.
Huffer, Duane, (BV) ...... '48 '74 C.347 A.B. L.362 J.D. Supr. Ct. J., Kosciusko Supr. Ct.
Kehler, Christopher D., (CV) .... '61 '87 C.265 B.A. L.879 J.D. [Rockhill P.]
Keirn, Tammy M. .... '73 '00 C.432 B.A. L.879 J.D. [Walston E.]
Kolbe, David C., (BV) .... '55 '81 C.347 B.A. L.879 J.D. [D.C.Kolbe]

Kolbe, David C., P.C., (BV)
221 North Washington Street, 46580
Telephone: 574-267-5353 Fax: 574-267-0151 URL: http://www.dkolbelawfirm.com
Email: dkolbelaw@kconline.com URL: http://www.dkolbelaw.com
David C. Kolbe;—John D. Barrett.
Languages: Spanish.
Personal Injury, Automobile Accidents, Dig Bites, Head and Spinal Injuries, Nursing Home Abuse, Sexual Abuse, Slip and Fall, Truck Accidents, Products Liability, Drug and Medical Devices, Medical Malpractice, Criminal Law, Drug Crimes, Driving While Intoxicated (DWI), DUI, Juvenile Criminal Law, Parole and Probation, Traffic Violations, White Collar Crime, Family Law, Adoption Law, Child Custody, Child Support, Divorce, Domestic Violence, Visitation Rights, Business Law, Business Planning, Business Litigation, Contract, Commercial Law, Business Enterprises, Small Business Law, Partnership Law, Corporate Law, Limited Liability Company Law (LLC), Buying and Selling a Business, Business Start-Ups, Real Estate, Wills and Probate, Trusts and Estates, Elder Law, Guardianship, Asset Protection, Estate Planning.

See Professional Biographies, WARSAW, INDIANA

Landis, Vern K., (BV) .... '51 '76 C.347 B.S. L.345 J.D. [Rockhill P.]
Lavender, J. L., (CV) .... '49 '82 C.631 B.A. L.117 J.D. [Lavender&B.]

Lavender & Bauer, P.C., (CV)
116 North Buffalo Street, 46580
Telephone: 574-267-4151 Toll Free: 800-567-4151 Fax: 574-267-6263
Email: lavenderlaw@kconline.com
J. L. Lavender; Torrey J. Bauer.
Language: Spanish.
Torts, Criminal Law, Drug Crimes, DWI, DUI, Traffic Violations, Will and Probate, Trusts and Estates, Family Law, Adoptions, Child Custody, Child Support, Divorce, Visitation Rights, Domestic Relations, Probate, Corporate Law, Business Law, Business Planning, Business Contracts, Business Litigation, Business Enterprises, Buying and Selling a Business, Starting a Business.

See Professional Biographies, WARSAW, INDIANA

Lemon, Thomas R., (AV) .... '41 '66 C.347 A.B. L.1119 J.D. [Valentine M.&L.]
Lemon, W. Douglas, (CV) .... '70 '95 C.303 B.A. L.347 J.D. [Valentine M.&L.]
Lennox, Scott J., (CV) .... '68 '96 C.476 B.S. L.347 J.D. [Ⓐ Reed&E.]
Leon, Dana, (CV) .... '73 '98 C.347 B.A. L.345 J.D. [Rockhill P.]
Manich, Stephen J., (AVⓉ) '55 '81 C.679 B.S.E. L.861 J.D.
Pat. Atty., DePuy, Inc. (Pat.)
McCoy, Lisa .... '56 '87 C.347 B.A. L.284 J.D. Dalton Corporation
Miner, Michael L., (BV) .... '48 '76 C.679 B.S. L.345 J.D. [Valentine M.&L.]

Morris & Ruiz, P.C.
(See Plymouth)

Murphy, Warren D., (CV) .... '71 '98 C.346 B.S. L.201 J.D. [Ⓐ Harris&H.]
Ogden, Philip W., (CV) .... '43 '90 C.578 B.A. L.1187 J.D. 301 North Lake Street
Pequignot, Stanley E., (AV) .... '42 '68 C.347 B.S. L.1119 J.D. [Rockhill P.]
Piazza, Mark T. .... '52 '83 C.999 B.A. L.365 J.D. Asst. Gen. Coun., DePuy, Inc.
Plumlee, Millard P., III, (BV) .... '60 '87 C.834 B.S. L.347 J.D. Corp. Coun., Biomet, Inc.
Reed, Max E., (AV) .... '31 '61 C.475 B.A. L.345 J.D. [Ⓒ Reed&E.]
Reed, Michael W., (BV) .... '56 '81 C.602 B.B.A. L.880 J.D. [Reed&E.]
Reed, Rex L. .... '41 '69 C.679 B.S.C.E. L.1119 J.D. Cir. J.
Reed & Earhart, P.C., (BV) .... 318 S. Buffalo St.
Rigdon, Jay A., (BV) .... '60 '84 C.273 B.A. L.1119 J.D. [Rockhill P.]

Rockhill Pinnick LLP, (AV) 🄱🄱
105 East Main Street, 46580-2742
Telephone: 574-267-6116 Telecopier: 574-269-9264
Email: rockhill@rexnet.net URL: http://www.rockhillattorneys.com
Members of Firm: Stanley E. Pequignot; Richard K. Helm; Vern K. Landis; Jay A. Rigdon; Christopher D. Kehler; Dana Leon.
General Civil Trial Practice in all State and Federal Courts. Business Law, Business Planning, Contracts, Business Litigation, Business Enterprises, Partnerships, Corporate, Limited Liability Companies, Small Business, Family Law, Construction Law, Mediation, Wills and Probate, Trusts and Estates, Estate Planning, Asset Protection, Banking, Real Estate, Land Use, Municipal and Zoning, Insurance Law.
Representative Clients: Warsaw Times-Union Newspaper; State Farm Insurance Cos.; Farmers State Bank; C & D Foods, Inc.; Maple Leaf Farms, Inc.; Othy, Inc.; Phend & Brown, Inc.

See Professional Biographies, WARSAW, INDIANA

Rothberg Logan & Warsco LLP, (AV)
(Successor by merger to, Rothberg & Logan and Warsco Brogan)
212 North Buffalo Street, 46580 ⊙
Telephone: 574-267-8802 Telefax: 574-267-0605
Email: law@rlwlawfirm.com URL: http://www.rlwlawfirm.com
Michael E. Armey; R. Steven Hearn.
General Civil Litigation in all Courts. Corporate, Banking, Bankruptcy, Commercial, Insurance, Labor and Employment Law, Municipal Law, Municipal Finance, Securities, Real Estate, Construction, Probate and Estate Planning, Transportation, Tax, Creditors' Rights, Agricultural Law, Family/Domestic Relations, Health Care Law.

(This Listing Continued)

Rothberg Logan & Warsco LLP (Continued)
Approved Attorneys For: Ameriquest Mortgage Company; Aon Corporation; Avis Industrial Corp.; Bank One, N.A.; Busak + Shamban, Inc.; Cameron Memorial Community Hospital; Construction Management Engineering, Inc.; City of Fort Wayne; Dell Computer Corp.; Farm Credit Services of Mid-America, ASA.
Fort Wayne, Indiana Office: 2100 National City Center, 110 West Berry Street, P.O. Box 11647, 46859-1647. Telephone: 260-422-9454. Telefax: 260-422-1622.

See Professional Biographies, WARSAW, INDIANA

Royster, David N. .... '71 '97 C.228 B.A. L.910 J.D. 345 Main St.
Sand, Richard W. .... '29 '60 C.347 B.S. L.1119 LL.B. Sr. Cir. J.
Schoenle, Paul D., (BV) .... '47 '74 C.679 B.S.M.E. L.879 J.D. 345 E. Main St. (Pat.)
Sherer, Mark C., (CV) .... '69 '95 C.303 B.A. L.347 J.D. 210 North Buffalo Street
Smith, Scott A. .... '71 '00 C.999 B.S. L.879 J.D. [Ⓐ Valentine M.&L.]

Stutsman, Mulvaney & DeBoer
(See Elkhart)

Tandy, Bradley J., (BV) '59 '84 C.210 B.A. L.1119 J.D.
V.P., Asst. Gen. Coun. & Corp. Compl. Offr., Biomet, Inc.
Taylor, Patti (Patricia) J., (BVⓉ) .... '66 '95 C.784 B.A. L.221 J.D. [Taylor]
Taylor Law Office, P.C., (BVⓉ) .... 121 N. Washington Street
Valentine Miner & Lemon, LLP, (AV) .... 603 N. Parker St.
Voelz, J. Brad, (CV) .... '65 '92 C.210 B.A. L.1119 J.D. [Hampton&V.]
Wagley, John S. .... '50 '91 C.679 B.S.M.E. L.345 J.D. Pat. Coun., DePuy, Inc.
Waldkoetter, Eric R. '59 '92
C.1300 B.S. L.347 J.D. Biomet, Inc. (Pat.) (⊙Heerlen, Netherlands)
Walmer, James L., (BV) '48 '74 C.63 B.S. L.862 J.D.
827 South Union Street, Suite 220
Walston, W. Wayne .... '42 '71 C.63 B.S. L.1119 J.D. [Walston E.]
Walston Elder Law Office .... 1093 Mariners Drive
Wendt, Timothy M. '45 '70 C.121 B.S. L.966 J.D.
(adm. in WI; not adm. in IN) 345 E. Main St.
Wilson, Sally J., (CV) .... '53 '79 C&L.879 B.A., J.D. 1822 E. Center St.
Yeager, Jerald W. .... '64 '90 C.827 B.S. L.346 J.D. P.O. Box 50

WASHINGTON, * 11,380, *Daviess Co.*

Arthur, Robert L. .... '43 '75 C.346 B.S. L.345 J.D. Cir. J.
Chambers, Blake L., (BV) .... '51 '77 C.929 B.A. L.345 J.D. [Waller,C.&H.]
Dant, Tim J., (BV) .... '55 '88 C&L.347 B.A., J.D. 19 N.E. 3rd St.
Dwyer, J. D., (BV) .... '35 '69 C.347 A.B. L.345 J.D. P.O. Box 650
Dwyer, Judith H. .... '38 '63 C.436 A.B. L.1119 J.D. Supr. Ct. J.

Emison Doolittle Kolb & Roellgen
(See Vincennes)

Hanson, Harry W., (BV) .... '46 '72 C.894 B.A. L.339 J.D. [Waller,C.&H.]

Hart Bell LLC
(See Vincennes)

Havill, James F., (BV) .... '42 '71 C.249 A.B. L.345 J.D. [J.F.Havill]
Havill, James F., Atty. at Law, Prof. Corp., (BV) .... 401 E. South St.
Murrie, Daniel Stephen ...... '74 '00 C.934 B.A. L.1439 J.D. Daviess Co. Prosecutors Off.
Neeriemer, Dean H., (CV) .... '23 '50 C.108 B.S. L.345 LL.B. 1902 Parkdale Dr.
Norris, Jeffrey R., Attorney at Law, (BV) '60 '87 C.347 B.A. L.345 J.D.
105 E. Main St.
Overton, G. Byron, (BV) .... '49 '73 C.347 B.S. L.345 J.D. [Rusk,O.&S.]
Rusk, Richard C., (AV) .... '34 '61 C.347 A.B. L.1119 J.D. [Rusk,O.&S.]
Rusk, Overton & Sobecki, (AV) .... P.O. Box 249
Smith, Bruce A., (BV) .... '48 '76 C.30 B.A. L.1119 J.D. 107 N.E. 2nd St.
Smith, Gregory A., Attorney at Law, (BV) '56 '81
C.346 B.S. L.345 J.D. 401 E. Walnut St.
Smoot, E. Brayton .... '32 '71 C.734 B.S. L.345 J.D. Peoples Bk.
Sobecki, Dean A., (BV) .... '59 '85 C.249 B.S. L.347 J.D. [Rusk,O.&S.]
Waller, David, (BV) .... '42 '67 C.210 B.A. L.345 J.D. [Waller,C.&H.]
Waller, Chambers & Hanson, (BV) .... Suite 206 Peoples Natl. Bank Bldg.

WATERLOO, 2,200, *De Kalb Co.*

Fagan, Charles D. '66 '95 C.352 B.S. L.190 J.D.
(adm. in IA; not adm. in IN) Asst. Pub. Def.
Thomas, Bradley Kim, (BV) .... '50 '75 C.347 B.A. L.365 J.D. 105 West Union Street

WEST COLLEGE CORNER, 686, *Union Co.*

Shoker, Gursaran S., (CV) .... '38 '85 C.91 B.S. L.607 J.D. [Shoker&S.]
Shoker, Lee Ann .... '— '99 C.607 B.A. L.473 J.D. [Shoker&S.]
Shoker & Shoker, (CV) .... 64 Liberty Street

WESTFIELD, 9,293, *Hamilton Co.*

Hittle, Lori A., Law Offices of '— '95
C.347 B.A. L.879 J.D. 17465 Little Eagle Creek Ave.
Lloyd, Steven R. .... '58 '97 C.347 B.S. L.345 J.D. 17767 Sun Park Drive
O'Farrell, Heather M. .... '70 '95 C.20 B.A. L.1119 J.D. 733 East SR 32
O'Farrell, Thomas B. .... '69 '95 C.679 B.A. L.347 J.D. P.O. Box 45
Simmons, Bonnie K. .... '56 '86 C.347 B.S. L.345 J.D. 19845 N. U.S. 31
Stoesz, Jennifer Staton .... '60 '87 C.231 B.A. L.347 J.D. P.O. Box 365
Wendling, Cheryl Judge, (BV) .... '50 '84 C.108 B.A. L.345 J.D. [C.J.Wendling]
Wendling, Cheryl J., (BV) .... 16716 Oak Rd.

WEST HARRISON, 318, *Harrison Co.*

Nienaber, Joseph .... '44 '71 C.602 B.A. L.846 J.D. 3267 Johnson Fork Road

WEST LAFAYETTE, 28,778, *Tippecanoe Co.*

Barash, Eyal H. .... '69 '98 C.347 B.S., B.A. L.597 J.D. [Ⓒ Bose M.&E.] (Pat.)
Benjamin, Mark E. .... '46 '83 C.999 Ph.D. L.345 J.D. Purdue Univ.
Bolognini, Louis T. '56 '81 C.473 B.A. L.851 J.D.
V.P. & Gen. Coun., Great Lakes Chem. Corp.

Bose McKinney & Evans LLP, (AV)
Suite B2-204 3000 Kent Avenue, 47906 ⊙
Telephone: 765-464-3200 Facsimile: 765-464-3225
URL: http://www.boselaw.com
Of Counsel: Eyal H. Barash.
General Civil Practice in all Courts including Agricultural Law, Antitrust, Appellate Practice, Capital Strategies, Civil Rights, Commercial Law, Communications and Media, Constitutional Law, Corporate Law, Creditors Rights, Creditors Rights in Bankruptcy, Debtor Bankruptcy, Education Law, Employee Benefits, Entertainment and the Arts, Entrepreneurial Services, Environmental Law, Finance, Financial Institutions Law, Government Contracts, Government Relations, High Technology, Insurance, Intellectual Property, International Law, Labor and Employment, Legislative Practice, Litigation, Mergers and Acquisitions, Municipal Finance, Municipal Law, Planning and Land Use, Probate, Real Estate, Regulated Industries, Regulatory Agency Practice, Securities, Taxation, Trusts and Estates, Utility Law, Wills and Zoning.
Indianapolis, Indiana Office: 2700 First Indiana Plaza, 135 North Pennsylvania Street, 46204. Telephone: 317-684-5000. Facsimile: 317-684-5173.

(This Listing Continued)

Bose McKinney & Evans LLP (Continued)

Indianapolis, Indiana North Office: 600 East 96th Street, Suite 500 46240. Telephone: 317-684-5300. Facsimile: 317-684-5316.
Washington, D.C. Office: 700 North One Lafayette Centre, 1120 20th Street, N.W., 20036. Telephone: 202-973-1229. Fax: 202-973-1212.
Crown Point, Indiana Office: 3577 West Lakeshore Drive, 46307. Telephone: 219-663-2968. Fax: 219-663-2969.
Chesterton, Indiana Office: P.O. Box 957, 46304. Telephone: 219-983-1552. Fax: 219-983-1741.
See Professional Biographies, WEST LAFAYETTE, INDIANA

Burgett, Jonas Q. '67 '93 C.679 B.S. L.145 J.D.
Pres., CEO & Chf. Legal Coun., Next Generation Care Concepts, Inc.
Chavers, Gordon D. '44 '71 C.679 B.S. L.383 J.D. Purdue Univ.
Duros, Karen Witte, (AVⓉ) '54 '79 C.1182 B.A. L.910 J.D.
(adm. in MO; not adm. in IN) Asst. Gen. Coun., Great Lakes Chemical Corp.
Funk, C. Alan '55 '83 C.679 B.S. L.879 J.D. 352 Pawnee Dr.‡
Gibson, Brett B. '72 '97 C.472 B.B.A. L.347 J.D. 4103 Amesbury Road
Lacci, John V., (BV) '52 '77 C&L.276 B.A., J.D.
V.P. & Gen. Coun., Great Lakes Chem. Corp.
Lazarus, Bruce I. '54 '80 C.645 B.S. L.665 J.D.
(adm. in PA; not adm. in IN) Assoc. Prof., Purdue Univ.
Posthuma, Richard A. '54 '92 C.114 B.A. L.1187 J.D.
(adm. in MI; not adm. in IN) Purdue Univ.
Rollock, Alysa Christmas '59 '85 C.674 A.B. L.976 J.D. Purdue University
Sage, Charles E. '46 '76 C.679 B.A. L.345 J.D. Staff Coun., Purdue Univ.
Westerhaus, Charlotte F. '55 '92 C.610 B.S. L.347 J.D. Purdue Univ.
Wilson, G. Thomas '40 '84 C.679 B.S. L.347 J.D. Purdue Univ.

WESTVILLE, 2,116, *La Porte Co.*

Absalonsen, Vern '34 '64 C.1016 B.S.B.A. L.365 J.D.
(adm. in IL; not adm. in IN) Assoc. Coun., Scot Lad Foods, Inc.
Cochran, Donald E. '39 '72 C.1159 B.S.C.E. L.209 J.D. SuburbanHomes

WHITESTOWN, 476, *Boone Co.*

Baskin, Rae '53 '78 C.823 B.A. L.564 J.D.
(adm. in NY; not adm. in IN) RR 1 Box 289‡
Dazey, William H., Jr., (BV) '52 '78 C.347 A.B. L.345 J.D. 4624 E. 450 S.

WHITING, 5,155, *Lake Co.*

Belshaw, William, (AV) '19 '47 C.210 A.B. L.597 J.D. [⊡ Danko G.&R.]
Bercik, James T. '43 '97 C.1157 B.S. L.879 J.D. 1050-119th St.
Danko, Benedict R., (BV) '24 '51 C.1024 L.602 LL.B. [Danko G.&R.]
Danko Goldsmith & Ritzi, (BV) 1500-119th St.
Goldsmith, Suzanne, (CV) '55 '79 C.347 B.A. L.365 J.D. [Danko G.&R.]
Gray, Donald L., (BV) '30 '56 C&L.879 B.A., J.D. City Atty.
Obermiller, Wm. J. '23 '48 C&L.602 B.N.S., LL.B. City Ct. J.
Paylo, John L. '20 '48 C.1024 L.209 LL.B. 1934 New York Ave.
Ritzi, Joni M., (CV) '66 '91 C.347 B.S. L.879 J.D. [Danko G.&R.]
Tebik, Richard S., (BV) '42 '68 C.347 A.B. L.1119 J.D. 1522 119th St.

WILLIAMSPORT, * 1,935, *Warren Co.*

Hall, Robert M. '44 '69 C.347 B.A. L.1119 J.D. Cir. J.
Larson, John A., (BV) '60 '85 C.894 A.B. L.1119 J.D. 110 N. Monroe St.
Litzenberger, Nancy J., (BV) '42 '66 C.347 A.B. L.1119 LL.B. [Litzenberger&L.]
Litzenberger & Litzenberger, P.C., (BV) 111 E. 2nd St.
McCabe, James E., (BV) '42 '68 C.894 A.B. L.879 J.D. [McCabe's]
McCabe's Law Office, (BV) 112 N. Monroe Street
Rader, John A., (BV) '48 '75 C.347 A.B. L.345 J.D. 33 North Monroe Street

WINAMAC, * 2,418, *Pulaski Co.*

Ballard, Richard, Attorney at Law
(See Knox)

Hizer, Alan F., (CV) '42 '73 C.347 A.B. L.879 J.D. [Hizer]
Hizer Law Office, (CV) 102 West Pearl Street
Johnston, David B. '64 '91 C.63 B.S. L.607 J.D. Gen. Coun., The Braun Corporation
Kocher, John A., (BV) '45 '70 C.260 B.S. L.879 J.D. 115 W. Main St.

LaTulip, Matthew D., Attorney at Law
(See Schererville)

Lloyd, Lisa A., (CV) '63 '89 C.432 B.S. L.347 J.D. 1415 E. 200 S.
Murphy, Daniel P., Law Office of, (BV) '50 '79 C.927 B.S. L.879 J.D. 101 W. Main St.
Murray, Timothy J. '— '89 C.346 B.S. L.879 J.D. [Murray L.]
Murray Law 103 N. Market Street, Suite 102
Shurn, Michael Anthony '49 '75 C.344 B.A. L.345 J.D. Cir. J.
Tankersley, Daniel S., (AV) '40 '65 C.347 B.S. L.1119 LL.B. 115 W. Main St.
Tankersley, Kevin C., (CV) '70 '97 C.347 B.A. L.851 J.D. 115 W. Main St.

Tonner, Ned, Attorney at Law
(See Rensselaer)

Traylor-Wolff, Lisa M., (CV) '60 '86 C.63 B.S. L.879 J.D. 119 W. Main St.

WINCHESTER, * 5,095, *Randolph Co.*

Arnett, Dale W. '49 '87 C.347 A.B. L.607 J.D.
(adm. in OH; not adm. in IN) 207 S. Main St.‡

Blackburn & Green
(See Fort Wayne)

Chalfant, Jan L. '42 '68 C.210 A.B. L.1119 J.D. Cir. J.
Cockerill, Thomas '73 '99 C.210 B.A. L.1119 J.D. 235 S. Meridian St.
Cook, John T., (AV) '27 '54 C.63 L.345 LL.B. [Cook&W.]
Cook, Robert G., (BV) '48 '75 C.801 B.A. L.879 J.D. 235 S. Meridian St.
Cook and Welch, (AV) 111 N. Main St.
Daly, George F. '24 '55 C.63 B.S. L.345 LL.B. 233 W. Franklin St.‡
Haviza, Peter D. '47 '76 C.347 B.A. L.345 J.D. Supr. Ct. J.
Myers, Suzan Dillon '58 '83 C.347 B.A. L.1119 J.D. 223 W. Franklin St.
Oliver, Robert C., Jr., (BV) '48 '77 C.210 B.A. L.345 J.D. Ret. Pros. Atty. [Oliver&O.]
Oliver & Oliver, (BV) 122 S. Meridian St.
Stohler, Zane E. '26 '50 C.347 B.S. L.1119 LL.B. 808 W. Lawn St.‡
Sullivan, Kenneth A. '37 '64 C.347 B.S.B.A L.1119 LL.B. Supr. Ct. J.
Tanner, John E., (BV) '33 '63 C.63 B.S. L.345 LL.B. 214 S. Main St.
Toney, Jay L., (BV) '61 '86 C.894 A.B. L.201 J.D. 114 S. Meridian
Welch, Jason E. '71 '96 C.679 B.S. L.347 J.D. [Cook&W.]
Wickersham, Michael D. '53 '79 C.249 B.A. L.345 J.D. Pres., Wicks Pies, Inc.
Williams, Michael C., (BV) '48 '73 C.303 B.A. L.421 J.D. P.O. Box 247

WOLCOTT, 989, *White Co.*

Dill, Larry L., Attorney At Law, (CV) '48 '85 C.679 B.S. L.1119 J.D.
122 W. Market St.

WOLCOTTVILLE, 879, *LaGrange & Noble Cos.*

Fetters, Jeffrey K. '67 '94 C&L.879 B.A., J.D. 940 E. 670 S.
Rorick, Dennis Lynn, (CV) '48 '87 C.679 B.S. L.1119 J.D. 9105 E. 480 S.

WOLFLAKE, 250, *Noble Co.*

Boyd, Matthew J. '— '00 Corp. Coun., Boyd Machine & Repair Co.
Carson, Jerry L. '42 '72 C.1318 A.B. L.345 J.D. P.O. Box 241

WOODBURN, 1,579, *Allen Co.*

Rochyby, Jack R., (BV) '52 '91 C.927 B.A. L.347 J.D. 4223 Ara Dr.

YORKTOWN, 4,785, *Delaware Co.*

Whitehead, Daniel K. '62 '99 C.63 B.S. L.345 J.D. P.O. Box 487

ZIONSVILLE, 8,775, *Boone Co.*

Atkinson, Christine J. '49 '93 C.112 B.S. L.347 J.D. 67 South Main Street

Bays, Donna J.
(See Indianapolis)

Blackwell, Nancy N. '31 '56 C.339 B.S. L.345 J.D. 3835 W. 116th St.‡
Burrus, Otis C. '24 '52 C&L.879 B.A., J.D. 410 W Oak St.‡
Burrus, Roger L., (BV) '57 '82 C&L.879 B.S., J.D. 410 W. Oak St.
Buskirk, George A., Jr., (AV) '49 '75 C.108 B.S.B.A. L.345 J.D. 2150 South 950 East
Carisch, Christian B., (BV) '43 '75 C.172 B.S. L.345 J.D. 656 Spring Hills Dr.
Carr, Sandra S., (AV) '60 '85 C&L.347 B.S.N., J.D. Town Pros.
Frandsen, Jeffrey H., (BV) '52 '77 C.347 B.A. L.345 J.D. 35 S. Elm St.
Gross, Robert W., (BV) '47 '72 C.210 B.A, L.880 J.D. 7325 Hunt Club Dr.
Hartley, Rebecca S. '— '94 C.197 A.B. L.893 J.D. 905 W. Poplar St.
Huff, Margaret M., (AV) '41 '64 C&L.436 A.B., J.D. 7520 West 92nd Street
Jackson, Price A., Jr., (CV) '52 '77 C.472 B.A. L.345 J.D.
Staff Atty., State Student Assistance Comm. of Ind.
Jacob, Jeffrey S. '71 '97 C.894 L.893 J.D. 1393 W. Oak St.

Knowles & Associates, LLC
(See Carmel)

Lueders, Mary McArdle, (BV) '61 '86 C.207 B.S. L.347 J.D. 4605 S. 975 E.
Mason, Jackie S., (BVⓉ) '47 '80 C.880 B.A. L.208 J.D. 1449 Lancaster Lane
Perry, Samuel Joseph '— '03 C.576 B.A. L.1119 J.D. 3721 Castle Rock Dr.
Starkey, Chris K., (BV) '60 '87 C.894 A.B. L.345 J.D. P.O. Box 288
Stegner, Jean N. '31 '90 C.679 B.S. L.1119 J.D. 205 N. Maple St.‡
Thomas, Robert R. '67 '93 C&L.347 B.A., J.D. Pres., Landquest Title Services, Inc.

IOWA

CAPITAL: DES MOINES

Iowa State Bar Association
521 East Locust Street, Third Floor
Des Moines, Iowa 50309-1939
Telephone: 515-243-3179
Fax: 515-243-2511

Index of Towns and Cities Listed by County

*Indicates County Seat

Adair County
Adair
* Greenfield
Stuart

Adams County
* Corning

Allamakee County
Lansing
Postville
* Waukon

Appanoose County
* Centerville

Audubon County
* Audubon
Exira

Benton County
Belle Plaine
Blairstown
Keystone
Newhall
* Vinton
Walford

Black Hawk County
Cedar Falls
Hudson
La Porte City
* Waterloo

Boone County
* Boone
Madrid
Ogden

Bremer County
Denver
Readlyn
Sumner
Tripoli
* Waverly

Buchanan County
* Independence

Buena Vista County
Albert City
Newell
* Storm Lake

Butler County
* Allison
Aplington
Clarksville
Greene
Parkersburg
Shell Rock

Calhoun County
Lake City
Manson
* Rockwell City

Carroll County
Breda
* Carroll

Carroll Co.—*Continued*
Glidden
Manning

Cass County
Anita
* Atlantic
Griswold

Cedar County
Clarence
Lowden
Mechanicsville
* Tipton

Cerro Gordo County
Clear Lake
* Mason City

Cherokee County
Aurelia
* Cherokee
Marcus
Quimby

Chickasaw County
Lawler
Nashua
* New Hampton

Clarke County
* Osceola

Clay County
* Spencer

Clayton County
* Elkader
Garnavillo
Guttenberg
McGregor
Monona
Postville
Strawberry Point

Clinton County
Camanche
* Clinton
De Witt
Goose Lake

Crawford County
Charter Oak
* Denison

Dallas County
* Adel
Clive
Dallas Center
Perry
Urbandale
Van Meter
Waukee
West Des Moines

Davis County
* Bloomfield

Decatur County
Lamoni
* Leon

Delaware County
Dyersville
* Manchester

Des Moines County
* Burlington
Mediapolis
West Burlington

Dickinson County
Arnolds Park
Milford
Okoboji
* Spirit Lake

Dubuque County
Cascade
* Dubuque
Durango
Dyersville
Epworth
Farley

Emmet County
* Estherville
Ringsted

Fayette County
Elgin
Fayette
Oelwein
* West Union

Floyd County
* Charles City
Rockford

Franklin County
Ackley
* Hampton
Sheffield

Fremont County
* Sidney

Greene County
Grand Junction
* Jefferson

Grundy County
* Grundy Center
Reinbeck

Guthrie County
Adair
* Guthrie Center
Panora
Stuart

Hamilton County
Jewell
* Webster City

Hancock County
Britt
Forest City
* Garner

Hardin County
Ackley
* Eldora
Hubbard
Iowa Falls

Harrison County
* Logan
Missouri Valley
Woodbine

Henry County
* Mt. Pleasant
New London
Salem
Winfield

Howard County
* Cresco

Humboldt County
Dakota City
Gilmore City
Humboldt
Livermore
Renwick

Ida County
Holstein
* Ida Grove

Iowa County
Amana
* Marengo
North English
Victor
Williamsburg

Jackson County
Baldwin
Bellevue
* Maquoketa
Preston

Jasper County
Baxter
Colfax
Mingo
* Newton
Prairie City
Sully

Jefferson County
Batavia
* Fairfield
Libertyville

Johnson County
Coralville
Hills
* Iowa City
Lone Tree
North Liberty
Oakdale
Oxford

Johnson Co.—*Continued*
Solon
Swisher

Jones County
* Anamosa
Cascade
Monticello

Keokuk County
Keota
* Sigourney

Kossuth County
* Algona
Lakota
Swea City
West Bend
Whittemore

Lee County
* Fort Madison
Keokuk
West Point

Linn County
* Cedar Rapids
Center Point
Central City
Ely
Hiawatha
Marion
Mt. Vernon
Springville
Walford

Louisa County
Columbus Junction
Morning Sun
* Wapello

Lucas County
* Chariton

Lyon County
Inwood
Larchwood
* Rock Rapids

Madison County
Earlham
* Winterset

Mahaska County
* Oskaloosa

Marion County
* Knoxville
Pella

Marshall County
* Marshalltown

Mills County
* Glenwood

Mitchell County
* Osage
Saint Ansgar

Monona County
Mapleton
* Onawa

Monroe County
* Albia
Lovilia

Montgomery County
* Red Oak
Villisca

Muscatine County
* Muscatine
West Liberty
Wilton

O'Brien County
Hartley
Paullina
* Primghar
Sanborn
Sheldon
Sutherland

Osceola County
* Sibley

Page County
* Clarinda
Shenandoah

Palo Alto County
* Emmetsburg
West Bend

Plymouth County
Kingsley
* Le Mars
Remsen

Pocahontas County
Gilmore City
Laurens
* Pocahontas
Rolfe

Polk County
Altoona
Ankeny
Bondurant
Clive
* Des Moines
Elkhart
Grimes
Johnston
Mitchellville
Pleasant Hill
Polk City
Urbandale
West Des Moines

Pottawattamie County
Avoca
Carter Lake
* Council Bluffs
Neola
Oakland
Treynor
Walnut

Poweshiek County
Brooklyn
Grinnell
* Montezuma
Victor

Ringgold County
* Mt. Ayr

Sac County
Lake View
Odebolt
* Sac City

Sac Co.—*Continued*
Wall Lake

Scott County
Bettendorf
* Davenport
Eldridge
Le Claire
Riverdale

Shelby County
Earling
Elk Horn
* Harlan
Panama

Sioux County
Alton
Hawarden
Hull
* Orange City
Rock Valley
Sheldon
Sioux Center

Story County
Ames
Huxley
* Nevada
Slater
Story City

Tama County
Dysart
Gladbrook
Tama
* Toledo
Traer

Taylor County
* Bedford
Lenox

Union County
* Creston

Van Buren County
Farmington
* Keosauqua

Wapello County
* Ottumwa

Warren County
Carlisle
Cumming
* Indianola
Norwalk

Washington County
Kalona
* Washington
Wellman

Wayne County
* Corydon
Humeston

Webster County
Dayton
* Fort Dodge
Gowrie
Harcourt

Winnebago County
Buffalo Center
* Forest City
Lake Mills

Winneshiek County
Calmar
* Decorah

Woodbury County
Anthon
Moville
Sergeant Bluff
* Sioux City
Sloan

Worth County
Manly
* Northwood

Wright County
Belmond
* Clarion
Eagle Grove
Goldfield

*Indicates County Seat

ACKLEY, 1,809, *Franklin & Hardin Cos.*

Marshall, Stanley J., (CV) ... '25 '55 C&L.221 B.A., J.D. 714 1st Ave.
Muhlenbruch, Robert H., (BV) ... '43 '69 C&L.352 B.A., J.D. [Muhlenbruch]

Muhlenbruch Law Office, (BV)
621 Main Street, P.O. Box 125, 50601
Telephone: 641-847-2693 Fax: 641-847-3646
Email: mlawo@mchsi.com
Robert H. Muhlenbruch.
General Practice. Trials, Municipal, Probate, Estate Planning, Real Estate and Tax Law. No small collections.
Reference: Ackley State Bank.

ADAIR, 839, *Adair & Guthrie Cos.*

Fisher, John W., (BV) ... '49 '82 C.56 B.A. L.61 J.D. [Fisher,F.&F.]
Fisher, Martin L., (BV) ... '52 '79 C.56 B.A. L.61 J.D. [Fisher,F.&F.]
Fisher, William L., (AV) ... '15 '40 C.707 B.A. L.793 J.D. [Fisher,F.&F.]
Fisher, Fisher & Fisher, P.C., (AV) ... 306 Audubon Street

ADEL, * 3,435, *Dallas Co.*

Bergkamp, James L., Jr., (CV) ... '69 '95 C.221 B.S. L.378 J.D. [Hefner&B.]
Byers, William R., (BV) ... '53 '80 C&L.221 B.S.B.A., J.D. P.O. Box 244
Hefner, Randy V., (AV) ... '53 '78 C.351 B.A. L.221 J.D. [Hefner&B.]
Hefner & Bergkamp, P.C., (AV) ... 218 South 9th Street
Hopkins & Huebner, P.C., (AV) ... 1009 Main Street (⊙Davenport, Des Moines)
Hulse, Gregory A. ... '47 '73 C.352 B.A. L.221 J.D. Dist. J.
Huscher, Paul R., (BV) ... '55 '80 C.612 B.S. L.221 J.D. 801 Court St.
Jennings, Bryan R., (BV) ... '51 '77 C.352 B.B.A. L.190 J.D. [Reich]
Keller, Peter A. ... '38 '63 C.350 L.221 J.D. Dist. J.
Mason, Ronald E., (AV) ... '19 '51 C&L.221 B.A., J.D. 3375 L Ave.‡

McDonald, Brown & Fagen
(See Dallas Center)

Reich, John O., (BV) ... '43 '68 C&L.221 B.A., J.D. [Reich]
Reich Law Firm, (BV) ... 801 Main St.
Reisetter, Wayne M. ... '55 '90 C.999 B.S. L.221 J.D. 207 N. 9th St.
Saluri, Joseph B., (BV) '66 '93 C&L.221 B.S.B.A., J.D. V.P./Gen. Coun., Stine Seed Company
Van Werden, James E., (AV) '39 '64 C.641 B.A. L.352 J.D. [Hopkins&H.] (⊙Des Moines)
Webster, Thomas Franklin ... '74 '00 C.187 B.S.S. L.221 J.D. [Webster]
Webster Law Firm P.L.C. ... P.O. Box 2
Yeager, John J. ... '21 '48 C&L.383 A.B., LL.B. 3364 R Ave.‡

ALBERT CITY, 779, *Buena Vista Co.*

Cornish, Mark T., (BV) ... '52 '78 C.352 B.B.A. L.190 J.D. [Stern,D.C.&J.] ⊙
Diehl, Mary Ann, (AV) ... '23 '50 C.112 L.352 LL.B. [Stern,D.C.&J.] ⊙
Jensen, Nola M., (BV) ... '59 '84 C&L.352 B.B.A., J.D. [Stern,D.C.&J.] ⊙
Stern, Diehl, Cornish & Jensen, (AV) ... 224 Main St. (⊙Storm Lake)

ALBIA, * 3,706, *Monroe Co.*

Albers, Joanna A., (CV) ... '42 '96 C.221 B.A. L.352 J.D. 13 S. Clinton St.
Cash, W. K., (AV) ... '13 '38 C&L.352 B.A., J.D. 108 E. Washington
Colton, Marvin V. ... '30 '58 C.504 L.352 LL.B. 12 Washington Ave., E.
Goodlow, Steven Elza, (BV) ... '66 '92 C.350 B.S. L.190 J.D. 6 Washington Ave. E.
Karpan, Frank J. ... '20 '48 C.112 L.221 LL.B. 520 Benton Ave. W.‡
Pabst, John A., (AV) ... '46 '70 C.197 A.B. L.221 J.D. [Pabst]

Pabst Law Firm, (AV)
212 West Benton, P.O. Box 362, 52531
Telephone: 641-932-5155 Fax: 641-932-2269
Email: pabstlaw@lisco.com
John A. Pabst.
General Civil Trial Practice. Real Estate, Probate and Estate Planning Law.

Scieszinski, Annette J. ... '55 '80 C.353 B.A. L.352 J.D. Dist. J.

Starcevic, Joseph F. '56 '81 C&L.352 B.A., J.D.
13 S. Clinton Street, P.O. Box 576, 52531
Telephone: 641-932-7802 Fax: 641-932-5768
Email: JStarcevic@AlbiaLaw.com URL: http://www.AlbiaLaw.com
General Practice, including but not limited to: Wills, Trusts, Estate Planning and Probate Law; Real Estate Law; Business Law and Corporate Law.
See Professional Biographies, ALBIA, IOWA

ALGONA, * 5,741, *Kossuth Co.*

Allison, Matthew D. '68 '94 C.350 B.A. L.352 J.D. Claims Atty., Pharmacists Mut. Cos.
Andreasen, James H. ... '31 '58 C&L.352 B.S.C., J.D. Sr. J., Supm. Ct.
Bibler, A. David, (AV) ... '52 '78 C&L.352 B.B.A., J.D. [Buchanan,B.B.&G.]
Braunschweig, T. J., (BV) ... '46 '74 C.350 B.S. L.352 J.D. [T.J.Braunschweig]
Braunschweig, Timothy J., (BV) ... 6 E. Call
Buchanan, Gregg A., (BV) ... '47 '74 C.352 B.A. L.221 J.D. [Buchanan,B.B.&G.]
Buchanan, Russell G., (AV) '23 '48 C&L.352 B.A., J.D. [[C] Buchanan,B.B.&G.] (⊙Lakota)
Buchanan, Scott G., (BV) ... '54 '86 C&L.352 B.G.S., J.D. [Buchanan,B.B.&G.]
Buchanan, Todd R., (AV) ... '65 '91 C.352 B.B.A. L.221 J.D. [Buchanan,B.B.&G.]
Buchanan, Bibler, Buchanan and Gabor, (AV) ... 111 N. Dodge St. (⊙Lakota, Swea City)
Buck, John E., (CV) ... '50 '78 C.932 B.S. L.352 J.D. [Fenchel,D.&B.] ⊙
Courtney, Don E., (BV) ... '49 '78 C.490 B.A. L.300 J.D. 120 N. Thorington St.
Doster, Paul R., (BV) ... '54 '79 C.513 B.A. L.352 J.D. [Fenchel,D.&B.] ⊙
Dotson, Robert A., (BV) ... '46 '71 C.350 B.S. L.352 J.D. 101 N. Hall St.
Fenchel, David L., (BV) ... '55 '80 C&L.352 B.A., J.D. [Fenchel,D.&B.] ⊙
Fenchel, Doster & Buck, P.L.C., (BV) ... 107 N. Harlan (⊙Britt)
Gabor, Michael E., (BV) ... '63 '91 C.475 B.S.U.P. L.221 J.D. [Buchanan,B.B.&G.]
Guenther, Sara ... '61 '89 C.351 B.A. L.352 J.D. 715 N. Minnesota St.★
Holmes, Todd M., (CV) ... '67 '97 C.350 B.S. L.1187 J.D. Co. Atty. [Fenchel,D.&B.] ⊙
Laddusaw, Mark J., (CV) ... '64 '92 C.106 B.A. L.190 J.D. [[A] Lynch&L.]
Lage, Scott W. '57 '83 C.350 B.S. L.352 J.D. V.P., Claims Mgmt., Pharmacists Mut. Cos.
Lipps, Thomas W., (AV) ... '54 '79 C&L.546 B.S., J.D. [Peterson&L.]
Lynch, Joseph E., Jr., (AV) ... '22 '49 C&L.352 B.A., J.D. [Lynch&L.]
Lynch, Ryan J., (BV) ... '52 '77 C&L.221 B.S., J.D. [Lynch&L.]
Lynch & Lynch, (AV) ... 215 W. Call St.
MacDonald, Walter B. ... '37 '63 C.473 A.B. L.597 J.D. Assoc. Dist. J.
McMahon, James F., (BV) ... '37 '62 C.602 B.A. L.352 J.D. 120 N. Thorington St.
Morse, Howard E. ... '14 '38 L.211 B.L. 302 E. Oak St.
Nitchals, Louis W. ... '17 '47 L.221 LL.B. 412 W. Kennedy St.‡
Peterson, Martin W., (AV) ... '43 '68 C.221 B.S. L.352 J.D. [Peterson&L.]

Peterson & Lipps, (AV)
6 East State Street, P.O. Box 575, 50511
Telephone: 515-295-9494 Fax: 515-295-9493
Email: info@petelipp.com URL: http://www.petersonlipps.com
Martin W. Peterson; Thomas W. Lipps; David L. Shumway (Retired).
General Practice and Trial Practice. Personal Injury, Workers Compensation, Real Estate, Insurance, Corporation, Tax, Probate, Trusts, Collections, Domestic Relations, Commercial, Estate Planning.
Reference: Iowa State Bank, Algona, Iowa.
See Professional Biographies, ALGONA, IOWA

Shumway, David L. ... '31 '58 C.221 B.S. L.352 LL.B. [Peterson&L.] ‡
Stowater, Todd A., (BV) ... '63 '88 C&L.352 B.B.A., J.D. P.O. Box 514
Straub, Joseph J. ... '30 '56 C&L.602 A.B., J.D. Dist. J.

ALLISON, * 1,000, *Butler Co.*

Gibson, James V., (BV) ... '37 '62 C&L.352 B.A., J.D. 503 N. Main St.
Shepard, Virgil E., (AV) ... '13 '36 C&L.352 B.A., J.D. 519 N. Main St.‡

ALTON, 1,063, *Sioux Co.*

Klay, Veldhuizen, Bindner, De Jong & Pals, (AV) 306-10th St. (⊙Orange City, Paullina)
Mitchell, Edwin L. ... '37 '61 C.513 B.A. L.221 J.D. Dist. J.‡
Veldhuizen, Loren J., (AV) '45 '71 C.114 A.B. L.352 J.D. [Klay,V.B.D.&P.] (⊙Orange City)

ALTOONA, 10,345, *Polk Co.*

Borseth, Eric, (BV) ... '59 '84 C.162 B.A. L.221 J.D. [Borseth]
Borseth Law Office, (BV) ... 111 Second St. S.E.
Daut, Alan M., (BV) ... '60 '86 C.132 B.A. L.221 J.D. 203 1st Ave. S.
David Hance Law Office ... 323 8th St. S.W.
Hance, Elvin D. ... '47 '73 [David H.]
Knox, Larry D., (BV) ... '36 '63 C&L.546 B.S., J.D. P.O. Box 373
Skinner, Ed, (AV) ... '36 '63 C&L.221 B.S., J.D. [Skinner]
Skinner, R. Bradley, (BV) ... '69 '96 C.221 B.A. L.190 J.D. [[A] Skinner]
Skinner Law Offices, P.C., (AV) ... P.O. Box 367
Wieslander, Frank G., (BV) ... '45 '71 C&L.221 J.D. [F.G.Wieslander]
Wieslander, Frank G., P.C., (BV) ... 109 8th St., S.E.
Wilson, Larry G., (BV) ... '51 '78 C.352 B.S. L.221 J.D. 827 17th Ave., S.W.

AMANA, —, *Iowa Co.*

Ritchie, Jeffrey, (CV) ... '72 '98 C.351 B.A. L.352 J.D. [[A] J.C.Wagner] (⊙Marengo)
Wagner, John C. ... '54 '79 C.132 B.A. L.352 J.D. [J.C.Wagner] ⊙
Wagner, John C., Law Offices, P.C. ... 600 39th Avenue (⊙Cedar Rapids, Marengo)

AMES, 50,731, *Story Co.*

Baty, John W., (BV) ... '42 '67 C.350 B.S. L.221 J.D. Iowa Asst. Atty. Gen.

Beattie Law Firm, P.C.
(See Des Moines)

Beckman and Hirsch
(See Burlington)

Benson, David W., (BV) ... '52 '78 C.350 B.S. L.190 J.D. [Nyemaster,G.W.H.&O.]
Bickel, Bruce P., Attorney at Law ... '47 '75 C.350 B.S. L.190 J.D. 616 Burnett Ave.
Brewer, James A., (AV) ... '36 '61 C&L.221 B.S., LL.B. [Newbrough,J.B.M.&H.]
Burger, Julie A. ... '64 '91 C.352 B.B.A. L.221 J.D. Asst. Atty. Gen.
Carabillo, Laura E. '51 '84 C.184 B.A. L.1040 J.D. Gen. Coun., Becker - Underwood, Inc.
Clark, George H., Jr., (BV) ... '30 '59 C&L.352 A.B., J.D. [Clark&H.]
Clark & Hastings, (BV) ... 315 6th St.
Curtis, Larry R., (BV) ... '45 '73 C.350 B.S. L.352 J.D. [Pasley&S.]
Ewald, Robert P., (BV) ... '45 '81 C.879 B.A. L.900 J.D. Dept. of Transp.
Feilmeyer, Franklin J., (CV) ... '66 '90 C&L.352 B.A., J.D. [Sharp J.F.F.&K.]
Feilmeyer, Victoria A., (CV) ... '67 '94 C.350 B.S. L.352 J.D. [Sharp J.F.F.&K.]
Ferree, David A. ... '52 '78 C.350 B.S. L.352 J.D. Spec. Asst. Atty. Gen., Atty. Gen. Off.
Forbes, Carin ... '— '03 C.352 B.A. L.221 J.D. [[A] Sharp J.F.F.&K.]
Formaker, Robin G., (Mr.) ... '54 '79 C.351 B.A. L.352 J.D. Asst. Atty. Gen.
Galyon, Alexander P. ... '59 '94 C.350 B.S L.221 J.D. [Pasley&S.]
Gartin, Timothy L., (CV) ... '67 '96 C.353 B.A. L.351 J.D. [[A] Clark&H.]
Gartner, Michael G. ... '38 '70 C.118 B.A. L.569 J.D. The Daily Tribune
Gelwick-Luecke, Jennifer L. '56 '89 C.1322 B.A. L.1029 J.D. (adm. in PA; not adm. in IA) 1908 Northwestern Ave.‡
Gerlach, Gary G. ... '41 '70 C.352 B.A. L.309 J.D. Pres., Partnership Press, Inc.
Gonnerman, Daniel J. ... '67 '94 C.350 B.B.A. L.221 J.D. [Gonnerman,O.&S.]
Gonnerman, Owen & Stonehocker, LLP, (CV) ... 2515 Elwood Drive, Suite 107 (⊙Boone)
Goodwin, Robert W., (BV) ... '43 '67 C&L.221 B.S., J.D. [Goodwin]
Goodwin Law Office, P.C., (BV) ... 311 Lincoln Way
Gradoville, Steven J. ... '68 '95 C&L.190 B.S.B.A., J.D. Asst. Tr. Offr., First Natl. Bk.
Graham, James E. ... '38 '64 C.177 B.A. L.352 J.D. Iowa Dept. of Transp.
Griffen, Danl. L., Jr. '27 '53 C.350 B.S. L.221 J.D. Iowa State Univ. Research Foundation, Inc.
Grove, Lad E., (CV) ... '48 '73 C.350 B.S. L.221 J.D. [Grove]
Grove Law Office, (CV) ... 218 S.E. 16th, Ste. B
Gunnells, Patty Joan ... '37 '88 C.350 B.S. L.221 J.D. Asst. Co. Atty.
Happel, Jason P. ... '71 '97 C.427 B.A. L.352 J.D. 323 6th St.
Harl, Neil E. ... '33 '61 C.350 B.S. L.352 J.D. Iowa State Univ.
Hastings, Craig R., (BV) ... '49 '74 C.494 B.A. L.477 J.D. [Clark&H.]
Hege, Brent D., (BV) ... '48 '73 C.352 B.S. L.221 J.D. [Terrill&H.]
Heintz, J. Eric ... '45 '71 800 Lincoln Way
Hindt, Noel C., (CV) ... '58 '83 C&L.352 B.A., J.D. Asst. Atty. Gen.
Hippen, Scott L. ... '60 '94 C.44 B.A. L.221 J.D. [Pasley&S.]
Holland, Julie F. ... '55 '82 C.350 B.S. L.221 J.D. Iowa State Univ.
Holm, Stevan A., (AV) ... '41 '66 C&L.352 B.A., J.D. [Pasley&S.]
Howell, Stephen J. ... '56 '97 C.627 B.S. L.221 J.D. [Newbrough,J.B.M.&H.]
Hronek, Thomas R. ... '47 '72 C.177 B.A. L.597 J.D. Assoc. Dist. J.

Huber, Book, Cortese, Happe & Lanz, P.L.C.
(See Des Moines)

Humke, Brian J., (AV) ... '56 '82 C.351 B.A. L.221 J.D. [Nyemaster,G.W.H.&O.] ⊙
Hunacek, Mark, (BV) ... '50 '81 C.102 B.S. L.221 J.D. Asst. Atty. Gen.
Hunziker, Christine A., (BV) ... '57 '82 C.352 B.A. L.221 J.D. [Payer,H.&R.]
Jahn, Lawrence E., (BV) ... '50 '82 C.339 B.S. L.352 J.D. [Sharp J.F.F.&K.]
Johns, Donna E. ... '58 '91 C.350 B.S. L.796 J.D. IA State Univ. Research Found., Inc.
Johnston, Frank B., (AV) ... '34 '61 C&L.352 B.A., J.D. [[C] Newbrough,J.B.M.&H.]
Kaniuk, David J., (CV) ... '51 '91 C.790 B.A. L.221 J.D. 409 S. Duff Ave.
Keenan, Christine ... '74 '00 C.350 B.S. L.221 J.D. [Sharp J.F.F.&K.]
Kellenberger, Gene V. ... '35 '60 C.350 B.S. L.352 J.D. Iowa State Univ.‡
Klaus, John R., (BV) ... '43 '67 C&L.352 B.B.A., J.D. City Atty.

Krauth, Deborah S., (BV) '52 '83 C.351 B.A. L.352 J.D. [Nyemaster,G.W.H.&O.] ⊙
Maddux, Jere C., (AV) '40 '71 C.630 B.A. L.221 J.D. [Newbrough,J.B.M.&H.]
Maffett, Mack D., (BV) '36 '60 C.532 B.A. L.150 LL.B. 621 Main St.
Mahan, Robert E. '46 '73 C.350 B.S. L.352 J.D. 3120 Roxboro Dr.
Martens, John G., (BV) '45 '72 C.350 B.S. L.352 J.D. 511 Duff Ave., Ste. 300
Mathison, Jane Melson, (BV) '52 '77 C.350 B.S. L.352 J.D. [Pasley&S.]
McKean, James Daniel '46 '88 C.339 B.S. L.221 J.D. Iowa State Univ.
McKinney, John L., (BV) '31 '55 C&L.352 B.A., J.D. 315 6th St.
McLaughlin, Steven J. '49 '74 C.352 B.A. L.190 J.D. V.P. & Tr. Offr., First Natl. Bk.
Moothart, Gerald A.L., (CV) '63 '96 C.350 B.S. L.221 J.D. [Moothart]
Moothart Law Office, (CV) 315 6th St., Ste. 300
Mull, Richard E., (BV) '52 '77
C&L.352 B.B.A., J.D. Asst. Atty. Gen., Atty. Gen. Off., Trans. Off.
Nadler, Barry, (AV) '56 '81 C&L.352 B.A., J.D. [Nyemaster,G.W.H.&O.] ⊙
Neal, Walter D. '43 '69 C.293 B.A. L.494 J.D.
(adm. in MN; not adm. in IA) P.O. Box 761‡
Newbrough, D. R., (BV) '28 '53 C&L.352 B.A., LL.B. [Newbrough,J.B.M.&H.]

Newbrough, Johnston, Brewer, Maddux and Howell, L.L.P., (AV)
612 Kellogg Avenue, P.O. Box 847, 50010
Telephone: 515-232-1761 Fax: 515-232-8962
Email: atty@newbroughlaw.com URL: http://www.lawyers.com/newbroughlaw
Members of Firm: D. R. Newbrough; James A. Brewer; Jere C. Maddux; Stephen J. Howell; William T. Talbot. Associates: Angelina M. Thomas; Emil Peterson. Of Counsel: Frank B. Johnston.
General Practice. Trials and Appeals. Estate Planning, Probate, Corporation, Real Estate Law, Personal Injury, Employee Benefits and ERISA.
Local Counsel: Todd & Sargent, Inc.; Ames Daily Tribune-Times, Inc.; American Home Assurance Co.; New Hampshire Insurance Group; Economy Fire & Casualty Co.; The American Home Group.
See Professional Biographies, AMES, IOWA

Norris, John R. '58 '95 C.784 B.A. L.352 J.D. 1605 Roosevelt Avenue
Nutty, John E., (AV) '25 '51 C.350 B.S. L.352 J.D. 618 Douglas‡

Nyemaster, Goode, West, Hansell & O'Brien, A Professional Corporation, (AV)
1416 Buckeye Avenue, 50010 ⊙
Telephone: 515-233-3000 Telecopier: 515-232-3846
URL: http://www.nyemaster.com
David W. Benson (Resident); Brian J. Humke; Deborah S. Krauth; Barry Nadler.
General Civil Practice including Corporate, Securities, Antitrust, Insurance, Banking, Commercial Law, Cooperative Law, Probate, Real Estate, Taxation, Workers Compensation, Municipal, Legislative, Labor, Administrative Law and Trials in all Courts.
Des Moines, Iowa Office: 700 Walnut, Suite 1600, Des Moines, Iowa 50309. Telephone: 515-283-3100. Telecopier: 515-283-3108.
See Professional Biographies, AMES, IOWA

O'Brien, James W., (BV) '63 '92
C.350 B.A. L.221 J.D. Corp. Atty, Unigraphics Solutions, Inc.
Olson, Carolyn J., (BV) '45 '84 C.1085 B.A. L.221 J.D. Asst. Atty. Gen.
Overland, Jody D. '58 '92 C&L.221 B.S.B.A., J.D. Iowa State Univ.
Owen, Stephen A., (CV) '64 '96 C.350 B.S. L.221 J.D. [Gonnerman,O.&S.]
Parks, Judith K., (BV) '58 '84 C&L.221 B.A., J.D. City Legal Dept.
Pasley, Clarke A., (BV) '41 '65 C.350 B.S. L.352 J.D. [Pasley&S.]
Pasley, Robert G., (AV) '15 '39 C&L.352 B.A., J.D. [[B] Pasley&S.] ‡

Pasley and Singer Law Firm, L.L.P., (AV)
323 Sixth Street, P.O. Box 664, 50010
Telephone: 515-232-4732 Fax: 515-232-4756
Email: email@singerlaw.com
C.H. Pasley (1876-1952); Robert G. Pasley (Retired); William A. Singer (Retired). Members of Firm: Clarke A. Pasley; Stevan A. Holm; John L. Timmons; Jane Melson Mathison; Larry R. Curtis; Scott L. Hippen; Alexander P. Galyon.
General Practice. Trials and Appeals in all Courts. Personal Injury and Tort Law, Commercial Litigation, Tax, Corporation, Insurance, Municipal, Adoption Law, Family Law, Probate, Trusts and Estates and Real Estate.
References available upon request.
See Professional Biographies, AMES, IOWA

Pattinson, William J. '49 '77 C.493 B.A. L.352 J.D. Dist. J.
Payer, Donald R., (BV) '28 '54 C.350 L.352 LL.B. [Payer,H.&R.]
Payer, Hunziker & Rhodes, (BV) 535 Main Street
Perkins, Daniel W. '53 '83 C.174 B.A. L.911 J.D. Asst. Atty. Gen.
Peters, Patrick C., (CV) '59 '84 C&L.352 B.S., J.D. [Payer,H.&R.]
Peterson, Emil '46 '78 C.56 B.A. L.146 J.D. [[A] Newbrough,J.B.M.&H.]
Regnolds, Roderick C., (CV) '— '84 126 South Kellogg
Rhodes, Margaret M., (CV) '50 '93 C.352 B.A. L.221 J.D. [Payer,H.&R.]
Rippie, Eloise L. '30 '70 C.383 B.S. L.421 J.D. Assoc. Prof., Iowa State Univ.
Rosenberg, Ralph '49 '74 C.339 B.S. L.221 J.D. State Sen.
Seiser, M. D. '27 '54 C.350 B.S. L.352 J.D. Sr. Dist. J.
Shao, Mary Ann '54 '84 C.477 B.F.A. L.352 J.D. Clk., Ct. of Appeals‡
Sharp, Dale E., (BV) '39 '72 C.350 B.S. L.352 J.D. [Sharp J.F.F.&K.]
Sharp Jahn Feilmeyer Feilmeyer & Keenan, PLC, (BV) 618 Douglas
Singer, William A., (AV) '17 '47 C&L.352 B.A., J.D. [[B] Pasley&S.] ‡
Smith, Donald L., (AV) '31 '62 C.350 B.S. L.273 J.D. 618 Douglas‡
Smith, William Robert '66 '96 C.165 B.S. L.1252 J.D.
(adm. in NY; not adm. in IA) IA State Univ.
Talbot, William T., (CV) '51 '90 C.351 B.A. L.228 J.D. [Newbrough,J.B.M.&H.]
Tanaka, Paul N. '53 '84 C.170 B.A. L.911 J.D.
Dir., Univ. Legal Servs., Iowa State Univ.
Terrill, Stephen M., (BV) '44 '73 C.350 B.S. L.221 J.D. [Terrill&H.]
Terrill & Hege Law Offices, (BV) 511 Duff Ave.
Thomas, Angelina M., (CV) '69 '94 C.350 B.S. L.352 J.D. [[A] Newbrough,J.B.M.&H.]
Timmons, John L., (BV) '46 '75 C.350 B.S. L.352 J.D. [Pasley&S.]
Van Marel, Steven '58 '83 C.350 B.S. L.352 J.D. Dist. Assoc. Ct.
White, B. Joan, (BV) '40 '80 C.350 B.S. L.221 J.D. [White&Z.]
White & Zaffarano, (BV) 621 Main St.
Zaffarano, Dario D., (BV) '48 '80 C.350 B.S. L.300 J.D. [White&Z.]

ANAMOSA, * 5,494, *Jones Co.*

Beckmann, Robert R. '38 '63 C.177 B.A. L.352 J.D. Jud. Mag.
Conmey, Larry J. '40 '65 C.177 B.A. L.734 J.D. 500 Main St.
Eells & Tronvold Law Offices, P.L.C.
(See Cedar Rapids)
Hagge, Marty A., (CV) '65 '90 C&L.352 B.B.A., J.D. 209 E. Main St.
Hruska, Robert A. '52 '97 Asst. Pros.
Knuth, Adrian T., (BV) '50 '76 C.872 B.A. L.352 J.D. 103 N. Davis St.
McKean, Andrew J., Law Office of '49 '80 C.999 B.S. L.352 J.D. 207 W. Main
McQuillen, Matthew G., (BV) '63 '88 C&L.352 B.B.A., J.D. 209 E. Main St.
Remley, Howard M., (AV) '14 '38 C&L.352 B.A., J.D. 306 N. William St.‡
Ricklefs, Connie Sue, (BV) '43 '85 C.352 B.S. L.221 J.D. Co. Atty.
Thomas, James G., (BV) '40 '72 C.350 B.S. L.221 J.D. 102 N. Ford
Voss, Janette S., (CV) '67 '92 C.898 B.A. L.352 J.D. 209 E. Main St.

White & Johnson, P.C.
(See Cedar Rapids)
Willems, Jay A., (AV) '50 '75 C.351 B.A. L.352 J.D. 209 E. Main St.
Yahnke, Gary L. '36 '62 C.352 B.S.C. L.37 J.D. 22962 County Rd., E-34‡

ANITA, 1,068, *Cass Co.*

Jensen, Jerry L. '62 '87 C.106 B.A. L.190 J.D. P.O. Box 126‡
Mailander, James W., (BV) '55 '82 C.352 B.A. L.190 J.D. [Mailander]
Mailander, Karen L., (BV) '57 '83 C&L.190 B.S., J.D. [Mailander]
Mailander Law Office, (BV) 694 Main St.
Mailander Law Office, (BV) 694 Main St.

ANKENY, 27,117, *Polk Co.*

Albaugh, Ryan M. '— '99 C.352 B.B.A. L.284 J.D. [[A] Whitfield&E.]
Barnes, LuAnn L., (BV) '54 '81 C.350 B.S. L.352 J.D. 315 N. Ankeny Blvd.
Beech, Douglas M., (AV) '62 '88 C.352 B.A. L.221 J.D.
Assoc. Legal Coun., Casey's General Stores, Inc.
Block, Craig E., (BV) '57 '82 C&L.221 B.A., J.D. [Handley B.L.Z.&G.]
Gocke, James M., (BV) '54 '89 C.546 B.S. L.221 J.D. [Handley B.L.Z.&G.]
Gray, Mark R., (BV) '— '86 C.587 B.S. L.365 J.D. [Whitfield&E.]
Greaves, E. Michael '48 '73 C.352 B.B.A. L.221 J.D.
Dir., Tax & Corp. Secy., General Growth Cos.
Hall, Robert D., (BV) '31 '65 C.350 B.S. L.221 J.D. 408 S.W. 3rd
Handley, Larry J., (AV) '50 '78 C.350 B.S. L.221 J.D. [Handley B.L.Z.&G.]
Handley Block Lamberti Zinno & Gocke, (AV) 210 NE Delaware Avenue, Suite 200
Jackowski, Julia L., (BV) '66 '92
C.350 B.A. L.221 J.D. Legal Coun., Casey's General Stores, Inc.
Lamberti, Jeffrey M., (AV) '62 '89 C&L.221 B.A., J.D. [Handley B.L.Z.&G.]
Maggert, James R. '32 '59 C&L.352 B.S.C., J.D. 219 S.W. 3rd St.‡
McCann, Michele R., (CV⊙) '68 '93 C.352 B.A. L.546 J.D. [[A] Handley B.L.Z.&G.]
McMurry, Michael S., Law Offices of, (BV) '43 '70
C.1153 B.A. L.221 J.D. 104 E. 1st St., Ste. 210
Michaels, Robert A. '43 '68 C&L.793 B.S., J.D. P.O. Box 498
Nading, Robert A., II, (BV) '52 '81 C&L.221 A.B., J.D. 408 S.W. 3rd
Nelson, David D. '— '79 C.187 B.A. L.221 J.D. [Whitfield&E.]
Pritchard, Charles '66 '95 C.352 B.A. L.221 J.D. 408 S.W. Third St.
Skinner, Gregory A., (BV) '53 '84 C.352 B.B.A. L.221 J.D. 408 S.W. 3rd St.
Waters, James H., (BV) '40 '71 C&L.221 B.A., J.D. 914 N.E. Canterbury Drive
Whitfield & Eddy, P.L.C., (AV)
213 North Ankeny Boulevard, Suite 100 (⊙Des Moines, Mt. Pleasant, West Des Moines)
Wirtz, Eli J., (AV) '43 '69 C&L.352 B.B.A., J.D.
Gen. Coun., Casey's General Stores, Inc.
Wood, Scott M., (BV) '59 '84 C.478 B.A. L.221 J.D. [Wood]
Wood Law Office, (BV) 511 S.W. 3rd St.
Zinno, Deanna L., (AV) '70 '95 C&L.350 B.A., J.D. [Handley B.L.Z.&G.]

ANTHON, 638, *Woodbury Co.*

Gaukel, Nevins & Westergaard, (AV) Main St. (⊙Mapleton, Sloan)
Nevins, Gavin R., (BV) '44 '69 C&L.352 LL.B. [Gaukel,N.&W.] (⊙Mapleton)

APLINGTON, 1,034, *Butler Co.*

Lievens, Gregory M., (BV) '55 '81 C.350 B.S. L.190 J.D. Co. Atty.
Schoeneman, Robt. F. '24 '55 L.221 LL.B. 614 11th St.‡

ARNOLDS PARK, 1,162, *Dickinson Co.*

Martin, Jon M., (BV) '54 '82 C.350 B.S. L.546 J.D. 605 Hwy. 71 S.

ATLANTIC, * 7,257, *Cass Co.*

Barry, James P., (BV) '61 '86 C.225 B.A. L.910 J.D. [Otto,L.&B.]
Cambridge, Feilmeyer, Landsness, Chase & Jones, P.L.C., (AV)
707 Poplar St. (⊙Griswold)
Feilmeyer, Ronald W., (AV) '38 '66 C&L.352 B.A., LL.B. [Cambridge,F.L.C.&J.] ⊙
Friday, Allen G. '58 '84 C&L.352 B.A., J.D.
(adm. in CA; not adm. in IA) 2820 Country Club Dr.‡
Howard, Richard G., (AV) '29 '59 C&L.352 B.A., J.D. [Howard]
Howard Law Office, (AV) 104 East 5th Street
Jones, Lawrence S., (BV) '55 '80 C.999 B.A. L.221 J.D. [Cambridge,F.L.C.&J.]
Knuth, Andrew J. '65 '95 C.351 B.A. L.221 J.D. [Rutherford T.&K.]
Larson, J. R. '12 '37 C.784 L.221 1101 Birch St.
Lorence, Joanne C., (BV) '50 '77 C.132 B.A. L.352 J.D. [Otto,L.&B.]
Miller, Charles E. '23 '62 C&L.221 B.S.B.A., LL.B. 11 Cass Ave.‡
Olson Pellett, Susan J. '65 '92 C.197 A.B. L.1165 J.D. 54880 Fair River Rd.
Otto, John, (BV) '49 '77 C.293 B.A. L.352 J.D. [Otto,L.&B.]
Otto, Lorence and Barry, (BV) 520 Chester St.
Pellett, Susan J. Olson '65 '92 C.197 B.A. L.174 J.D. 54880 Fair River Rd.
Rutherford, Terrance G., (BV) '43 '71 C.352 B.S. L.221 J.D. [Rutherford T.&K.]
Rutherford Trewet & Knuth, (BV) 1407 East 7th Street
Trewet, John M., (BV) '61 '88 C&L.221 B.A., J.D. [Rutherford T.&K.]
Van Ginkel, J. C., (BV) '54 '80 C&L.221 B.S.B.A., J.D. [Van Ginkel]
Van Ginkel, James, (BV) '23 '53 C.352 B.Sc. L.221 J.D. [Van Ginkel]
Van Ginkel Law Offices, (BV) 1908 E. 7th St.

AUDUBON, * 2,382, *Audubon Co.*

Andersen, Brian Paul, (BV) '53 '79 C.194 B.A. L.352 J.D. [Andersen]
Andersen, Francine O'Brien, (BV) '53 '79 C.157 B.A. L.190 J.D. [Andersen]
Andersen Law Offices, (BV) 405 Tracy St.
Groteluschen, William D., (BV) '35 '65 C.173 B.A. L.221 J.D. [Madsen,G.&T.]
Levis, Lance D., (BV) '46 '78 C.293 B.A. L.352 J.D. [Levis&B.]
Levis & Barron, (BV) 417 Tracy Street
Madsen, Leonard K. '15 '38 L.211 [[B] Madsen,G.&T.] ‡
Madsen, Groteluschen & Tinker, (BV) 401 S. Park Pl.
Richardson, James M. '50 '75 C.351 B.A. L.352 J.D. Dist. Ct. J.
Tinker, James M., (BV) '49 '77 C.350 B.S. L.352 J.D. [Madsen,G.&T.]

AURELIA, 1,034, *Cherokee Co.*

Kolpin, Ryan R., (BV) '68 '94 C.162 B.S. L.190 J.D. [Kolpin]
Kolpin Law Firm, PC, (BV) 136 Main St.
Miller, M. Wallace, (BV) '35 '60 C&L.352 B.A., J.D. [Miller,M.M.] ⊙
Miller, Miller, Miller, P.C., (BV) 133 Main St. (⊙Cherokee)

AVOCA, 1,610, *Pottawattamie Co.*

Hanson, Milton L., (AV) '33 '61 C&L.793 LL.B. [Hanson,S.&L.]
Hanson, Sulhoff & Larson, (AV) 165 S. Elm St.
Larson, David J., (BV) '67 '92 C.352 B.S. L.190 J.D. [Hanson,S.&L.]

Peters, Leslie G., (CV) ... '56 '97 C&L.190 B.P.S., J.D. 176 South Elm Street
Sulhoff, James D., (BV) ... '56 '82 C.945 B.A. L.352 J.D. [Hanson,S.&L.]

BALDWIN, 137, *Jackson Co.*

Tabor, Eric J. ... '55 '80 C&L.352 B.A., J.D. 3675 67th St.

BATAVIA, 520, *Jefferson Co.*

Anderson, Arthur John, Jr. ... '44 '70 C.424 B.S. L.45 J.D. 1917 Fruitwood

BAXTER, 1,052, *Jasper Co.*

Billingsley, John E., (BV) ... '55 '82 C.174 B.A. L.221 J.D. [Walker&B.] (⊙Newton)
Walker, Lee M., (BV) ... '50 '75 C.132 B.A. L.221 J.D. [Walker&B.] (⊙Newton)
Walker & Billingsley, (BV) ... 103 E. State St. (⊙Des Moines, Newton)

BEDFORD, * 1,528, *Taylor Co.*

Bonnett, Ronald D., (AV) ... '39 '64 C.641 B.A. L.352 LL.B. [Travis&B.]
Travis, Michael F., (BV) ... '38 '66 C.593 B.S. L.190 J.D. [Travis&B.]
Travis and Bonnett, (AV) ... 402 Main St.

BELLE PLAINE, 2,834, *Benton Co.*

Gocke, Jennifer ... '78 '03 C.350 B.S. L.221 J.D. [Ⓐ Kollmorgen&S.]
Kollmorgen, Walter A., (AV) ... '29 '57 C.350 B.S. L.352 J.D. [Kollmorgen&S.] ‡
Kollmorgen & Schlue, (AV) ... 920 12th St. (⊙Keystone)
Norgaard, Anders J., (BV) ... '44 '76 C&L.352 B.B.A., J.D. [A.J.Norgaard]
Norgaard, Anders J., P.C., (BV) ... 801 12th Street
Schlue, Larry D., (AV) ... '41 '65 C&L.352 B.B.A., J.D. [Kollmorgen&S.] ⊙
Swailes, Harold J. ... '21 '49 C&L.352 B.A., J.D. Dist. Ct. J.

BELLEVUE, 2,350, *Jackson Co.*

Besch, Ronald J., (BV) ... '50 '75 C.177 B.A. L.190 J.D. Mag.
DeVries, Mark W., Law Office, (BV) '60 '89 C.999 B.A. L.502 J.D.
132 N. Riverview Dr.
Wilbers, Michelle H. ... '62 '89 C.187 B.A. L.1206 J.D. 101 Oak St.

BELMOND, 2,500, *Wright Co.*

Berkland, Gary L., (BV) ... '45 '72 C&L.352 LL.B. [Houser&B.]
Houser, James E., (BV) ... '34 '61 C.352 B.S.C. L.221 J.D. [Houser&B.]
Houser, Michael E., (BV) ... '60 '86 C.436 B.A. L.221 J.D. 335 E. Main St.
Houser & Berkland, (BV) ... 335 E. Main St.

BETTENDORF, 31,275, *Scott Co.*

Bernstein, Daniel, (BV) ... '51 '95 C&L.352 B.S., J.D. [Ⓐ W.J.Bribriesco&Assoc.]
Biermann, Sandra Lee ... '60 '95 C.57 B.A. L.352 J.D. 3162 Willowwood Dr.★
Bowlin, Robert H. ... '46 '73 C&L.352 B.A., J.D. 1705 Oak St.‡

Bribriesco, William J., & Associates, (BV) '55 '81 C&L.352 B.B.A., J.D.
2407 18th Street, Suite 200, 52722
Telephone: 563-359-8266 Fax: 563-359-5010
URL: http://www.wjbribriescolaw.com
Associate: Daniel Bernstein.
Personal Injury, Workers Compensation, Products Liability, Business Law.
See Professional Biographies, BETTENDORF, IOWA

Clark, Donald R., (CV) ... '47 '85 C.351 B.A. L.221 J.D. 2240 Hogan Court North
Corsiglia, Thomas ... '48 '83 C.707 B.A. L.589 J.D. 25340 Valley Dr.
Douglas, Joseph H. '37 '66 C.350 B.S. L.262 LL.B.
(adm. in NY; not adm. in IA; Pat.) 11 Estate Ct.
Ellis, Robert G., (BV) ... '59 '84 C.350 B.A. L.352 J.D. Gen. Coun., Alter Co.
Fagan, Burton H., (BV) ... '41 '67 C.1016 B.S. L.146 LL.B. Bankruptcy Trustee
Fritzsche, Thomas C., (BV) '45 '73 C.309 A.B. L.352 J.D.
Spruce Hills Dr. at Middle Rd., N.W. Bk. Twr.

Gallagher, Millage & Gallagher
(See Davenport)

Gellerman, Marc H., (BV) ... '47 '74 C.98 B.S. L.879 J.D. Dep. 1st Asst.
Goedken, Phil L. ... '39 '64 C&L.352 B.A., LL.B. #7 Shaker Ct.‡

Gosma, Tarbox & Associates, P.L.C.
(See Davenport)

Grabow, John M. ... '58 '84 C.177 B.A. L.1035 J.D. 2535 Tech Dr.
Hatch, Matthew D., (CV) ... '65 '90 C&L.352 B.B.A., J.D. [Hatch]
Hatch Law Firm, P.C., (CV) ... 2532 Tech Dr., Ste. 206
Jasper, Dennis D., (BV) ... '49 '74 C.352 B.B.A. L.790 J.D. 2535 Tech Dr., Ste. 200
Little, Peggy S., (CV) ... '59 '91 C.707 B.A. L.352 J.D. 1712 Central Ave.
Munson, Charles J., (BV) ... '23 '49 C.707 B.S. L.597 J.D. [Munson]
Munson Law Offices, P.C., (BV) ... 1630 State Street
Nagle, John E., (AV) ... '21 '45 C.707 B.S. L.352 J.D. 1360 Kimberly Ridge Rd.‡
Peterson, Norman M. ... '24 '49 C&L.352 B.A., J.D. 2825 Hillcrest Ave.‡
Preacher, Thomas H., (BV) ... '50 '80 C.197 A.B. L.352 J.D. 2535 Tech Dr., Ste. 200
Richardson, Robert O. ... '22 '54 C.225 B.S. L.273 J.D. 1445 14th St. (Pat.)‡
Rock, Michael E., (CV) ... '47 '72 C&L.190 B.A., J.D. 2535 Tech Dr.
Roller, Richard M., (BV) ... '51 '89 C&L.352 B.S., J.D. [Roller]
Roller Law Office, (BV) ... 2550 Middle Rd., Ste. 101
Slavens, James E. ... '42 '66 C&L.352 B.B.A., J.D. 2550 Middle Rd.
Stafne, Albert J., Jr. ... '17 '41 L.487 LL.B. 1360 Kimberly Ridge Rd., Unit 105‡
Vesole, Richard I. ... '55 '80 C&L.352 B.A., J.D. 1987 Spruce Hills Dr.

BLAIRSTOWN, 672, *Benton Co.*

Barr, George S., (AVⓉ) '22 '67 L.809 LL.B.
(adm. in CA; not adm. in IA) P.O. Box 238‡

BLOOMFIELD, * 2,580, *Davis Co.*

Ball, Vern M., (BV) ... '36 '62 C.784 B.S. L.221 J.D. [Ball]
Ball Law Offices, (BV) ... 207 South Washington Street
Lynch, Rick L., (BV) ... '60 '92 C.353 B.A. L.352 J.D. P.O. Box 129
Lynch, Susan E., (BV) ... '66 '92 C&L.352 B.A., J.D. 207 S. Washington
Martin, John B., Law Office, (BV) ... '48 '73 C.502 B.A. L.352 J.D. 101 S. Madison
Pettit, Charles K., (AV) ... '45 '72 C&L.352 B.B.A., J.D. [Pettit]
Pettit Law Office, P.C., (AV) ... 111 S. Madison
Richardson, Stephen A., (BV) ... '52 '77 C.352 B.B.A. L.276 J.D. [Richardson]
Richardson Law Office, (BV) ... 201 S. Madison St
Stephens, John A. ... '18 '64 C.353 B.A. L.221 J.D. 101 S. Madison‡
Swaim, Justin K. ... '76 '01 C&L.352 B.B.A., J.D. [Swaim]
Swaim, R. Kurt, (BV) ... '50 '75 C.353 B.A. L.352 J.D. 108 E. Jefferson St.
Swaim Law Firm ... 108 E. Jefferson St.

BONDURANT, 1,846, *Polk Co.*

Ugulini, Susan J., (CV) ... '57 '83 C&L.221 B.S.B.A., J.D. P.O. Box 36

BOONE, * 12,803, *Boone Co.*

Andersen, Mark L. ... '48 '76 C.56 B.A. L.221 J.D. Boone State Bk.
Anderson, Bruce L., (BV) ... '61 '86 C&L.221 B.A., J.D. 809 8th St.
Baltimore, F.D. "Chip", II, (BV) ... '66 '93 C.350 B.B.A. L.494 J.D. 809 Eighth St.
Check, Earl D. ... '32 '65 C&L.352 B.A., LL.B. 1001 W. Mamie Eisenhower
Dakin, Dorothy ... '— '84 L.221 J.D. 712 Arden St.
Danilson, David R. ... '54 '79 C.350 B.S. L.190 J.D. Dist. J.
Doran, Ben T., (BV) ... '55 '80 C&L.352 B.B.A., J.D. 809 8th St.
Doran, William K., (AV) ... '24 '54 C.871 B.S. L.352 J.D. 1603 Kate Shelley‡
Gonnerman, Owen & Stonehocker, LLP, (CV) ... 814 Eighth Street, Suite 201 (⊙Ames)
Hegtvedt, Leo C. ... '26 '58 C.427 A.B. L.352 LL.B. P.O. Box 535‡
Hoekman, Will J. ... '45 '70 C.132 B.A. L.352 J.D. Pres. & CEO, Composite Tech. Corp.
Jordan, C. Ann ... '78 '04 C.898 B.A. L.352 J.D. [Ⓐ K.C.Quinn]
Jordan, John D., (BV) ... '53 '81 C.350 B.S. L.221 J.D. [Jordan,M.J.&Q.] ⊙
Jordan, Richard T., (AV) ... '24 '50 C.190 L.352 LL.B. [Jordan,M.J.&Q.]
Jordan, Mahoney, Jordan & Quinn, P.C., (AV) ... 801 Keeler St. (⊙Madrid)

Kersten Brownlee Hendricks, LLP
(See Fort Dodge)

Mahoney, Michael F., (BV) ... '50 '79 C&L.900 B.B.A., J.D. [Jordan,M.J.&Q.] ⊙
Mahoney, Robert E. ... '23 '48 C&L.352 B.A., J.D. 710 Keeler St.‡
Nalean, Loren A., (BV) ... '50 '79 C.352 B.A. L.345 J.D. [Nalean&N.]
Nalean, Steven K., (BV) ... '54 '81 C&L.352 B.A., J.D. [Nalean&N.]
Nalean & Nalean, (BV) ... 724 Story St.
Quinn, Kirke C., Law Offices of, (AV) '50 '76
C&L.221 B.S., J.D. 615 Story Street, Suite B
Robbins, Jim P., (P.C.), (BV) '49 '74
C&L.221 B.S., J.D. 1001 W. Mamie Eisenhower Ave.
Schroeder, Alan C., (BV) ... '46 '75 C&L.221 B.A., J.D. [Schroeder]
Schroeder Law Office, (BV) ... 72A Story St., Ste. 501
Stonehocker, Adria ... '70 '98 C.350 B.A. L.221 J.D. [Gonnerman,O.&S.]

BREDA, 467, *Carroll Co.*

Polking, William G., (BV) ... '38 '62 C&L.128 A.B., J.D. [Polking] ⊙
Polking Law Office, (BV) ... Lenz Insurance Bldg. (⊙Carroll)

BRITT, 2,133, *Hancock Co.*

Buck, John E., (CV) ... '50 '78 C.932 B.S. L.352 J.D. [Fenchel,D.&B.] ⊙
Doster, Paul R., (BV) ... '54 '79 C.513 B.A. L.352 J.D. [Fenchel,D.&B.] ⊙
Fenchel, David L., (BV) ... '55 '80 C&L.352 B.A., J.D. [Fenchel,D.&B.] ⊙
Fenchel, Doster & Buck, P.L.C., (BV) ... 95 Main Ave. S. (⊙Algona)
Hill, Earl W., (BV) ... '46 '73 C.477 B.A. L.213 J.D. 35 Main Ave., S.
Holmes, Todd M., (CV) ... '67 '97 C.350 B.S. L.1187 J.D. Co. Atty. [Fenchel,D.&B.] ⊙
Jones, Brian D., (CV) ... '63 '90 C.350 B.A. L.352 J.D. 94 Main Ave., N.
Siegrist, David J., (BV) ... '56 '81 C.339 B.S. L.221 J.D. 94 Main Ave., N.

BROOKLYN, 1,439, *Poweshiek Co.*

Gillette, Bert R., (CV) ... '22 '52 C&L.352 B.S.C., LL.B. P.O. Box 15
Schwiebert, James A., (BV) ... '51 '78 C.784 B.A. L.352 J.D. [Schwiebert]
Schwiebert Law Office, (BV) ... 410 Sunset

BUFFALO CENTER, 963, *Winnebago Co.*

Potter, Richard A., (BV) ... '50 '75 C.350 B.S. L.190 J.D. 11 2nd Ave. N.E.

BURLINGTON, * 26,839, *Des Moines Co.*

Adams, James M., (AV) ... '30 '58 C.350 B.S. L.352 J.D. [Hirsch,A.P.C.&R.]
Anderson, H. Eugene, (AV) ... '44 '68 C&L.352 B.B.A., J.D. [Anderson R.&P.]
Anderson Roberts and Porth, (AV) ... Main at Court
Aspelmeier, Kenneth A., (AV) '35 '60
C.641 B.A. L.569 LL.B. [Ⓒ Aspelmeier,F.P.E.&H.] (⊙Mediapolis)

Aspelmeier, Fisch, Power, Engberg & Helling, P.L.C., (AV)
First Federal Savings Bank, 321 North Third Street, P.O. Box 1046, 52601 ⊙
Telephone: 319-754-6587 Fax: 319-754-7514
James F. Fisch; William Scott Power; Robert A. Engberg; Brian J. Helling; William R. Jahn, Jr.; Brent Ruther;—Wyatt P. Peterson. Of Counsel: Kenneth A. Aspelmeier.
Insurance Defense, Estate Planning, Real Estate, Municipal Law, Negligence, Corporate Law, Probate, Taxation, Banking Law, Personal Injury, Workers Compensation, Civil Trial Practice in all State and Federal Courts.
Mediapolis, Iowa Office: 621 Main Street. Telephone: 319-394-3136. Fax: 319-394-3493.
West Point, Iowa Office: 420 Avenue "E". Telephone: 319-837-6614. Fax: 319-837-8813.
See Professional Biographies, BURLINGTON, IOWA

Bauer, William, (AV) ... '35 '61 C.602 B.S. L.276 J.D. 100 Valley‡
Beckman, David D., (BV) ... '50 '76 C.350 B.S.I.E. L.352 J.D. [Beckman&H.]

Beckman and Hirsch, (BV)
314 North Fourth Street, 52601
Telephone: 319-754-8404 Fax: 319-754-6302
URL: http://www.iowalaw.com
Stephen J. Beckman (1873-1950); Richard R. Beckman (1915-1993); David D. Beckman; David A. Hirsch. Associate: Jennifer E. Klever-Kirkman.
Personal Injury, Appeals, Corporation, Taxation, Probate, Insurance, Real Estate, Criminal Defense, Commercial Litigation, Computer Law, Family Law, General Trial Practice in State and Federal Courts.
See Professional Biographies, BURLINGTON, IOWA

Beres, James L., (BV) ... '55 '81 C.879 B.A. L.352 J.D. State Pub. Def. Off.

Bribriesco, William J., & Associates
(See Bettendorf)

Brown, Mary Ann ... '58 '85 C&L.221 B.A., J.D. Dist. Ct. J.
Buffington, Richard ... '69 '99 C.927 B.S. L.607 J.D. 205 Washington St., Ste. 300
Bunger, Darwin, (AV) ... '40 '66 C.351 B.A. L.352 J.D. 320 N. 3rd., Ste. 600
Cahill, Daniel E., (BV) ... '41 '66 C&L.352 B.A., LL.B. [Cahill,D.&S.]
Cahill, William J., (AV) ... '50 '77 C.352 B.A. L.190 J.D. [Hirsch,A.P.C.&R.]
Cahill, William S. ... '24 '51 C&L.352 B.A., J.D. Sr. Dist. J.
Cahill, Dieterich & Schilling, (AV) ... 205 Washington St.
Corson, Barry A. ... '49 '80 C&L.352 B.S., J.D. V.P. & Tr. Offr., Burlington Bk. & Tr.
Cox, Stephanie L. ... '69 '96 C.472 B.A. L.221 J.D. Asst. Co. Atty.
Cray, John D., (AV) ... '33 '57 C&L.352 B.A., J.D. [Cray,G.M.&T.]
Cray, Goddard, Miller & Taylor, LLP, (AV) ... P.O. Box 606
Davis, Timothy F. ... '57 '97 L.352 J.D. Co. Atty
Dieterich, Michael G., (AV) ... '51 '76 C&L.352 B.A., J.D. [Cahill,D.&S.]
Disselhorst, John R. ... '39 '67 C&L.352 B.B.A., J.D. 2804 Garden Circle‡
Dowell, William L. ... '47 '76 C.353 B.A. L.221 J.D. Dist. J.

Ellerhoff, Ronald D., (CV) .... '47 '85 C.353 B.A. L.221 J.D. 200 Jefferson St.
Engberg, Robert A., (AV) .... '46 '73 C&L.352 B.B.A., J.D. [Aspelmeier,F.P.E.&H.]
Fisch, James F., (AV) '40 '65
C.723 B.A. L.352 J.D. [Aspelmeier,F.P.E.&H.] (⊙West Point)
Ford, Merry C., (BV) .... '53 '77 C&L.352 B.S., J.D. [Ford]
Ford, T. K., (AV) .... '23 '57 C.543 L.585 J.D. [Ford] ‡
Ford Law Offices, (AV) .... 205 Hoth Bldg.
Gehrmann, William H. '29 '55 C&L.966 B.B.A., LL.B.
(adm. in WI; not adm. in IA) 2508 Sunnyside Ave.‡
Goddard, Gerald D., (AV) .... '44 '74 C.293 A.B. L.352 J.D. [Cray,G.M.&T.]
Hahn, Steven R. .... '48 '75 C.352 B.B.A. L.190 J.D. 100 Valley
Hansen, Peter W., (CV) .... '55 '83 C&L.352 B.A., J.D. 209 N. Third
Helling, Brian J., (BV) .... '64 '89 C&L.352 B.B.A., J.D. [Aspelmeier,F.P.E.&H.]
Hildreth, William M., (BV) .... '25 '51 C.337 B.A. L.352 J.D. 209 N. 3rd
Hirsch, David A., (BV) .... '47 '73 C.475 B.S. L.352 J.D. [Beckman&H.]
Hirsch, Henry L., (AV) .... '15 '39 C.293 B.A. L.352 J.D. [Hirsch,A.P.C.&R.] ‡

Hirsch, Adams, Putnam, Cahill & Rashid, (AV)
Burlington Bank & Trust Building, Second Floor, 101 Jefferson Street, P.O. Box 1105, 52601
Telephone: 319-754-7545 Fax: 319-753-1037
Email: hirschlaw@mchsi.com
Henry L. Hirsch (Retired). Members of Firm: James M. Adams; Gary L. Putnam; William J. Cahill; Michael J. Rashid. Associate: Shane M. Wiley.
Insurance Defense, Probate, Corporate Law, Taxation, Workers Compensation, Real Estate, Personal Injury, Civil Trial Practice, Appellate Practice, Criminal Defense.

Hoth, Steven S., Law Offices, (BV) ... '41 '66 C.293 A.B. L.352 J.D. 200 Jefferson Street
Jackson, Patrick Charles, (BV) .... '54 '82 L.615 J.D. Des Moines Co. Atty.
Jahn, William R., Jr., (BV) .... '69 '94 C.293 B.A. L.352 J.D. [Cray,G.M.&T.]
Klever-Kirkman, Jennifer E. .... '80 '05 C&L.352 B.A., J.D. [[A] Beckman&H.]
Krekel, Gene R., (AV) .... '41 '66 C&L.352 B.A., J.D. 2720 Lochmoor Lane
Lewis, Kent W., (BV) .... '50 '75 C.898 B.A. L.221 J.D. Asst. Co. Atty.
Linn, John G. .... '51 '76 C&L.352 B.A., J.D. Dist. J.
Loeschen, Terry D., (AV) '38 '65 C&L.352 B.A., J.D.
Suite 300, 218 North Third Street
Loots, Don L. .... '33 '57 C&L.352 B.A., J.D. 2313 West Ave.‡
Metz, William T. .... '26 '53 C&L.352 B.S.E.E., J.D. Suite 300, 218 North Third Street‡
Miller, James W., (BV) .... '57 '82 C.793 B.S. L.352 J.D. [Cray,G.M.&T.]
Miller, John C. .... '42 '75 C&L.352 B.A., J.D. Dist. J.
Monroe, William R. .... '62 '98 C.927 B.A. L.801 J.D. [W.Monroe]
Monroe, William, Law Office of .... 218 N. 3rd, Ste. 300
O'Neill, John F. .... '30 '58 C.602 B.A. L.352 J.D. 2702 Bittersweet Pl.‡
Peterson, Wyatt P. .... '78 '03 C.350 B.S. L.221 J.D. [[A] Aspelmeier,F.P.E.&H.]
Porth, Donald J., (BV) .... '47 '85 C.707 B.A. L.352 J.D. [Anderson R.&P.]
Pothitakis, Nicholas G., (BV) ... '66 '92 C.352 B.B.A. L.846 J.D. 320 North 3rd, Suite 100
Power, William Scott, (AV) .... '45 '71 C&L.352 B.A., J.D. [Aspelmeier,F.P.E.&H.]
Putnam, Gary L., (AV) .... '46 '74 C.927 B.B.A. L.862 J.D. [Hirsch,A.P.C.&R.]
Rashid, Michael J., (BV) .... '64 '93 C.602 B.B.A. L.352 J.D. [Hirsch,A.P.C.&R.]
Robberts, Marlis J., (CV) .... '71 '97 C.351 B.A. L.352 J.D. [Robberts]

Robberts Law Office, (CV)
205 Washington Street, Suite 201, P.O. Box 427, 52601
Telephone: 319-758-9800 Fax: 319-758-9801
Email: rloffice1001@qwest.net URL: http://www.robbertslawoffice.com
Marlis J. Robberts.
Family Law, Divorce, Personal Injury, Appellate Practice, Corporate Law, Litigation, Probate, Insurance, Real Estate, Criminal Law, General Practice.
See Professional Biographies, BURLINGTON, IOWA

Roberts, Timothy D., (BV) .... '57 '83 C&L.352 B.A., J.D. [Anderson R.&P.]
Ruther, Brent, (BV) .... '68 '93 C.352 B.A. L.208 J.D. [Aspelmeier,F.P.E.&H.]
Sapsin, Michelle A. '70 '95 C.597 B.A. L.477 J.D.
(adm. in VA; not adm. in IA) P.O. Box 399
Schilling, Michael J., (AV) .... '51 '76 C&L.352 B.A., J.D. [Cahill,D.&S.]
Schulte, J. Bryan, (BV) .... '42 '67 C&L.352 B.B.A., J.D. 100 Valley
Snyder, Gary J. .... '33 '61 C.350 B.S. L.352 LL.B. Assoc. Dist. J.‡
Swanson, Steven P., (AV) .... '50 '76 C&L.352 B.A., J.D. 100 Valley
Taylor, Mitchell L., (BV) .... '66 '92 C.352 B.B.A. L.221 J.D. [Cray,G.M.&T.]
Wagner, John W. ... '62 '90 C&L.546 B.S., J.D. Tr. Offr., Farmers & Merchants Bk. & Tr.
Walz, John M. .... '54 '79 C&L.352 B.A., J.D. V.P. & Tr. Offr., Burlington Bk. & Tr.
Wiley, Shane M. .... '77 '02 C&L.352 B.A., J.D. [[A] Hirsch,A.P.C.&R.]
Wittkamp, Rodney A., (BV) .... '40 '70 C.927 B.S. L.221 J.D. 1731 N. Roosevelt Ave.

CALMAR, 1,026, *Winneshiek Co.*

Denson, Robert J., P.A., (AVⓉ) '47 '80 C.350 B.S. L.260 J.D.
(adm. in FL; not adm. in IA) Pres., NE Iowa Community College

CAMANCHE, 4,215, *Clinton Co.*

Rasche, Simon W., Jr., (BV) .... '30 '57 C&L.352 B.A., J.D. 305 13th Ave.
Woodin, Mervin D., (CV) .... '42 '68 C&L.793 B.A., J.D. [M.D.Woodin]
Woodin, Mervin D., P.C., (CV) .... 810 7th Ave.

CARLISLE, 3,497, *Warren Co.*

Benton, Robert M., (BV) .... '47 '74 C&L.221 B.A., J.D. [Stuyvesant&B.]
Goodhue, Darrell .... '40 '64 C.784 B.A. L.221 J.D. Dist. J.
Stuyvesant, Robert L., (BV) .... '47 '74 C&L.221 B.A., J.D. [Stuyvesant&B.]
Stuyvesant & Benton, (BV) .... 1005 Hwy. 5

CARROLL, * 10,106, *Carroll Co.*

Bruner, Barry T., (AV) .... '51 '76 C.793 B.S. L.221 J.D. [Bruner&B.]
Bruner, David S., (BV) .... '59 '84 C.351 B.A. L.221 J.D. [Bruner&B.]
Bruner, Robert S., (AV) .... '13 '36 C&L.352 B.A., J.D. [Bruner&B.]
Bruner & Bruner, (AV) .... 225 E. Seventh St.
Carroll, Nicole C. .... '53 '79 C.350 B.S. L.352 J.D. 2226 Ashwood Dr.
Comito, Frank J., (AV) .... '54 '79 C.350 B.S. L.276 J.D. [Neu,M.C.&N.]
Copeland, Vicki R., (BV) .... '59 '86 C.352 B.A. L.221 J.D. [Wilcox,P.G.S.H.&C.] ⊙
Eich, Ronald P. .... '66 '91 C.190 B.A. L.188 J.D. 805 N. Main
Green, Siemann & Greteman, P.L.C., (AV) .... 801 North Adams Street
Halbur, Joseph E., (BV) .... '55 '79 C&L.190 B.S.B.A., J.D. 621 Clark St.
Kolln, Lonny L., II .... '77 '02 C.351 B.A L.352 J.D. [[A] Willson&P.] (⊙Council Bluffs)
Kurth, William D., (AV) .... '38 '62 C&L.352 B.A., J.D. 823 N. Main
Mayhall, Julie Greteman, (CV) .... '71 '96 C.190 B.S.B.A. L.221 J.D. [Green,S.&G.]
McMinimee, Gary L. .... '46 '73 C.352 B.S. L.262 J.D. Dist. J.
Minnich, Jeffrey R., (BV) .... '52 '79 C.352 B.B.A. L.221 J.D. [Neu,M.C.&N.]
Nelson, Michel W., (BV) .... '51 '76 C&L.494 B.A., J.D. 1004 N. Carroll St.
Neu, Arthur A., (AV) .... '33 '58 C&L.597 B.S., J.D. [Neu,M.C.&N.]
Neu, Arthur Eric, (BV) .... '67 '93 C.597 B.A. L.352 J.D. [Neu,M.C.&N.]
Neu, Minnich, Comito & Neu, P.C., (AV) .... 721 North Main Street

Pechacek, Frank W., Jr., (AV) .... '44 '69 C.351 B.A. L.352 J.D. [Willson&P.] ⊙
Peters, Robert W., (BV) .... '45 '70 C&L.352 B.A., J.D. [R.W.Peters]
Peters, Robert W., P.C., (BV) .... 1014 W. 19th St.
Polking, Thomas W., (BV) .... '47 '72 C.352 B.S. L.190 J.D. [Wilcox,P.G.S.H.&C.] ⊙
Polking, William G., (BV) .... '38 '62 C&L.128 A.B., J.D. [Polking] ⊙
Polking Law Office, (BV) .... 225 E. 7th St. (⊙Breda)
Rinn, Andrew J. .... '67 '95 C.480 B.S. L.221 J.D. Asst. Co. Atty.
Schechtman, Ronald H. .... '33 '58 C&L.352 B.S.C., J.D. Chf. Dist. J.
Siemann, Gregory J., (AV) .... '46 '74 C&L.352 B.B.A., J.D. [Green,S.&G.]
Swanson, Joel E. .... '41 '67 C&L.352 LL.B. Dist. J.
Tan Creti, Martin A., (BV) .... '45 '71 C.378 B.S.B.A. L.190 J.D. 1523 N. Carroll St.
Van Dyke, James R., (BV) .... '49 '74 C&L.221 B.A., J.D. [Van Dyke&W.]
Van Dyke & Werden, P.C., (BV) .... 225 East 7th
Werden, John C., Jr., (BV) .... '56 '84 C.293 A.B. L.221 J.D. [Van Dyke&W.]
Wilcox, Polking, Gerken, Schwarzkopf, Hoyt & Copeland, P.C., (AV)
302 E. 7th Street (⊙Jefferson)
Willson & Pechacek, P.L.C., (AV)
110 West 8th Street (⊙Council Bluffs, Harlan, Oakland, Red Oak, Treynor)
Wunschel, Dee Ann, (CV) .... '59 '87 C.352 B.G.S. L.629 J.D. [Wunschel]
Wunschel, Russell S., (AV) .... '27 '52 C.545 L.221 J.D. [Wunschel] ⊙
Wunschel Law Firm, P.C., (AV) .... 805 N. Main St. (⊙Wall Lake)

CARTER LAKE, 3,200, *Pottawattamie Co.*

Meyer, Charles M. '39 '80 C.627 B.S. L.190 J.D.
(adm. in NE; not adm. in IA) 3104 N. 13th St.‡

CASCADE, 1,958, *Dubuque & Jones Cos.*

Hughes, David M., (CV) .... '41 '71 C.177 B.A. L.221 5009 County Road D61
Kurt, Robt. E. .... '22 '50 C.177 L.221 LL.B. Pres., Cascade State Bk.

CEDAR FALLS, 36,145, *Black Hawk Co.*

Beecher, Field, Walker, Morris, Hoffman & Johnson, P.C.
(See Waterloo)

Benson, Judith R., (BV) .... '45 '80 C.293 B.A. L.352 J.D. 411 Main St.
Correll, David H., (AV) .... '44 '70 C.162 B.A. L.352 J.D. [Correll&S.]
Correll & Sheerer, (AV) .... 411 Main St.
Curtis, Russell E. .... '47 '72 C&L.352 B.A., J.D. V.P., Firstar Bk. Iowa, N.A.
DeJoode, Troy M. '71 '97 C.350 B.S.E.E. L.352 J.D.
Gen. Coun. & Dir. of Employee Serv.s, Cedar Falls Utilities
De Mayolo, Miryam Antunez .... '65 '99 C.999 L.352 J.D. [A.DeMayolo]
De Mayolo, Antunez, Law Office .... 325 W. 2nd St.
Demro, Paul W., (BV) .... '60 '89 C.351 B.A. L.352 J.D. 411 Main St.
Dieter, Robert J., (AV) .... '46 '74 C.351 B.A. L.352 J.D. [Redfern,M.D.L.&M.]
Drews, Barbara A. .... '50 '87 C.352 B.A. L.879 J.D. 1603 W. 18th St.

Eells & Tronvold Law Offices, P.L.C.
(See Cedar Rapids)

Engels, Kevin D., (BV) .... '62 '89 C.350 B.A. L.352 J.D. 411 Main St.
Fransdal, Mark W., (BV) .... '60 '85 C&L.352 B.B.A., J.D. [Redfern,M.D.L.&M.]
Galles, Patrick C., (BV) .... '62 '87 C.352 B.B.A. L.190 J.D. 411 Main St.
Gettman, Bruce L., Jr., (BV) .... '59 '85 C.352 B.A. L.45 J.D. [Redfern,M.D.L.&M.]
Gottschalk, Don E. .... '43 '67 C&L.352 B.A., J.D. [Gottschalk&S.]
Gottschalk & Shinkle, (CV) .... 704 Main Street
Hawbaker, Aaron K., (CV) .... '68 '94 C.351 B.A. L.352 J.D. 323 W. 2nd St.
Jacobsen, J. E. .... '25 '52 C.293 B.A. L.352 J.D. [Jacobsen]
Jacobsen Law Office .... 116 West 4th St.
Jones, Gary N. .... '60 '85 C.502 B.S. L.986 J.D. 323 W. 2nd St.
Kardosh, Nabil A. '55 '80 C.747 B.A. L.904 J.D.
(adm. in IL; not adm. in IA) 2517 Royal Dr., #4‡
Larsen, John C., (AV) .... '53 '78 C.898 B.A. L.352 J.D. [Redfern,M.D.L.&M.]
Mason, David H., Jr. .... '72 '98 [[A] Redfern,M.D.L.&M.]
Mason, David R., (AV) .... '44 '69 C&L.352 B.A., J.D. [Redfern,M.D.L.&M.]

McCrindle, C. Kevin, Law Offices of
(See Waterloo)

McGuire Law Firm, P.C.
(See Mason City)

Mellema, Chet A. .... '77 '03 C.221 B.S. L.352 J.D. [[A] Redfern,M.D.L.&M.]
Merner, R. William, (BV) .... '31 '58 C.352 B.A. L.477 J.D. [Merner&S.]
Merner & Sabbath, (BV) .... 209 Franklin St.
Miller, Michael J. .... '76 '02 C&L.352 B.A., J.D. [[A] Redfern,M.D.L.&M.]
Moore, Steven D., (AV) .... '50 '75 C&L.352 B.A., J.D. [Redfern,M.D.L.&M.]
Nardini, Jay A., (BV) .... '47 '73 C&L.352 B.B.A., J.D. [Nardini]
Nardini Law Office, (BV) .... 2712 Orchard Drive, Suite B
Noonan-Day, Heidi L., (CV) .... '66 '92 C&L.352 B.A., J.D. 8227 Buck Ridge
Norby, Steven G., (CV) .... '53 '79 C.350 B.A. L.352 J.D. 1603 W. 18th St.
Podolefsky, Ronnie L., (BV) .... '50 '97 C.1350 B.S. L.352 J.D. [Podolefsky]
Podolefsky Law Office, (BV) .... 215 Franklin Street
Redfern, Donald B., (BV) .... '45 '73 C.118 B.A. L.178 J.D. [Redfern,M.D.L.&M.]
Redfern, LeRoy H., (AV) .... '19 '48 C.544 A.B. L.477 J.D. [Redfern,M.D.L.&M.]

Redfern, Mason, Dieter, Larsen & Moore, P.L.C., (AV)
415 Clay Street, P.O. Box 627, 50613
Telephone: 319-277-6830 Facsimile: 319-277-3531
Email: RMDLM@cflaw.com URL: http://www.cflaw.com
James B. Newman (1870-1958); George F. Newman (1908-1988); William W. McKinley (1926-1981); LeRoy H. Redfern; David R. Mason; Robert J. Dieter; John C. Larsen; Steven D. Moore; Donald B. Redfern; Mark W. Fransdal; Mark S. Rolinger; Bruce L. Gettman, Jr. Associates: Michael J. Miller; Chet A. Mellema; David H. Mason, Jr.
Insurance, Litigation, Medical Malpractice and Product Liability, Wills, Trusts, Estate Planning and Probate Law, Taxation and Tax Returns, Labor Law, Employment Law, Commercial Law, Contracts, Elder Law, Mergers and Acquisitions, Trial Law, Workers' Compensation, Franchise Law, Municipal Law, Real Estate, Business Law, Corporate Law, Family Law, Public Utility Law, Civil Trial Practice in all Courts.
Representative Clients: Wells Fargo Bank Iowa; Community National Bank; Cedar Falls Community School District; University of Northern Iowa Foundation; Fireman's Fund Insurance Companies.
See Professional Biographies, CEDAR FALLS, IOWA

Rolinger, Mark S., (BV) .... '65 '91 C.898 B.A. L.352 J.D. [Redfern,M.D.L.&M.]
Sabbath, John W., (BV) .... '31 '59 C.57 B.A. L.352 J.D. [Merner&S.]
Saunders, Keith '71 '97 C.351 B.A. L.352 J.D.
Asst. Dir. Governmental Rel., Univ. Northern Iowa
Sheerer, R. James, (AV) .... '43 '69 C&L.352 B.A.B.S., J.D. [Correll&S.]
Shinkle, Paul T., (CV) .... '47 '76 C.132 B.A. L.352 J.D. [Gottschalk&S.]
Staudt, Susan Bernau, (BV) .... '68 '92 C&L.352 B.A., J.D. Asst. City Atty.
Truax, Judd E., (BV) .... '34 '62 C&L.352 B.S.C., J.D. City Atty.

CEDAR RAPIDS, * 120,758, *Linn Co.*

Abernathy, Terry J., (AV) .... '47 '73 C.162 B.A. L.352 J.D. [Pickens,B.&A.]
Abou-Assaly, Nicolas, (BV) .... '66 '92 C&L.352 B.B.A., J.D. [Simmons,P.A.&E.]

Ackley, Kopecky & Kingery, (AV) .... 4056 Glass Rd., N.E. (⊙Center Point, Central City)
Adam, Matthew J. ....'76 '02 C.999 B.S. L.352 J.D. [A Moyer&B.]
Adams, Miles N. ....'15 '40 C&L.352 B.A., LL.B. 222 3rd St., S.E.‡
Affeldt, James W., (AV) ....'43 '68 C.602 B.A. L.352 J.D. [Elderkin&P.]
Albrecht, Hugh G., (BV) ....'— '80 C.350 B.S. L.352 J.D. [T.Riley]
Albright, Justin W., (AV) ....'08 '33 C.162 B.Sc. L.352 J.D. 115 3rd Street, S.E.‡
Alt, Connie, (AV) ....'61 '85 C&L.352 B.B.A., J.D. [Shuttleworth&I.]
Andersen, Jill A. H., (CV) '57 '81
C.350 B.S. L.352 J.D. Asst. Gen. Coun., Aegon USA, Inc.
Anderson, Melissa Weets, (BV) ....'62 '87 C.187 B.A. L.352 J.D. [C Bradley&R.]
Anderson, Todd W., (BV) ....'63 '88 C.898 B.A. L.352 J.D. [Elderkin&P.]
Arenson, Michelle L. .... '68 '93 C.393 B.A. L.221 J.D. Atty., Alliant Energy
Baier, Kelly R., (AV) ....'53 '79 C.350 B.A. L.352 J.D. [Bradley&R.]
Barnes, Minor, (AV) ....'30 '61 C&L.352 B.A., J.D. [Pickens,B.&A.] ‡
Beard, Charles P. ....'16 '41 C&L.352 B.A., J.D. P.O. Box 2877‡
Beatty, H. Edward, (AV) ....'34 '61 C.170 B.A. L.352 J.D. [Lynch D.]
Beckelman, Marsha Merrill ....'50 '88 C.338 B.A. L.352 J.D. Co. Ct. J.
Becker, T. Todd, (BV) ....'— '80 C&L.352 B.A., J.D. [T.Riley]
Benischek, LeeAnn M., (BV) '56 '89 C.898 B.A. L.352 J.D.
Sr. Atty., AEGON USA Realty Advisors, Inc.
Bennett, James E., (CV) .... '— '68 C&L.352 LL.B. [T.Riley]
Berg, Jeffrey P., (BV) ..... '44 '69 C.352 B.A. L.221 J.D. 5021 Duffy Drive, NE - Suite B
Bergman, William A., (AV) ....'24 '49 [Moyer&B.] ‡
Bergstrom, Brian D., (AV) ....'62 '89 C&L.309 A.B., J.D. [Shuttleworth&I.]
Bertroche, Joseph G., Jr., (BV) ....'56 '82 C.427 B.A. L.221 J.D. [Bertroche]
Bertroche Law Offices, (AV) ....425 2nd St. S.E., Ste. 940 (⊙Des Moines)
Beyer, Carolyn J., (BV) ....'52 '77 C.546 B.A. L.190 J.D. [C White&J.]
Bickel, John M., (AV) ....'43 '69 C.187 B.A. L.259 J.D. [Shuttleworth&I.]
Bisgard, Jace T. ....'76 '02 C&L.352 B.A., J.D. [A Shuttleworth&I.]
Bishop, John J. ....'66 '92 C&L.352 B.A., J.D. [J.Bishop]
Bishop, John .... 305 2nd St. S.E., Ste. 420
Blackstock, Benjamin W., (BV) ....'38 '68 C&L.352 B.A., J.D. [Blackstock]
Blackstock Law Offices, (BV) ....1000 Collins Road, N.E.
Blades, Charles A., (BV) ....'57 '85 C.197 A.B. L.352 J.D. [Scheldrup]
Blando, Edward M., (AV) ....'38 '68 C.590 B.S. L.793 J.D. [Elderkin&P.]
Blankenship, Kimberly H. ....'75 '01 C&L.352 B.A., J.D. [A Bradley&R.]
Bobenhouse, James E., (CV) .... '45 '70 C.352 B.S. L.221 J.D. 1120 2nd Ave., S.E.
Bogguss, J. Scott, (AV) ....'46 '71 C&L.352 B.B.A., J.D. [Moyer&B.]
Booth, Guy P., (BV) ....'41 '71 C.399 B.A. L.352 J.D. 425 2nd St. S.E.
Boresi, Richard L., (BV) ....'51 '80 C.352 B.A. L.221 J.D. 121 3rd St. S.W.
Borland, Tamara Morrison, (BV) ....'69 '95 C.350 B.A. L.352 J.D. IA Relay
Boyer, Gilda L., (BV) ....'62 '91 C.188 B.S.S. L.352 J.D. [Shuttleworth&I.]
Bradley, F. James, (AV) .... '27 '50 C&L.352 B.A., J.D. [Bradley&R.]

Bradley & Riley PC, (AV)
Attorneys and Counselors
2007 First Avenue SE, P.O. Box 2804, 52406-2804 ⊙
Telephone: 319-363-0101 Fax: 319-363-9824
URL: http://www.bradleyriley.com
F. James Bradley; Byron G. Riley; Michael K. Denney; Patrick M. Courtney; Donald G. Thompson; Kelly R. Baier; Gregory J. Seyfer; Dean A. Spina; Joseph E. Schmall; Bradley G. Hart; William J. Neppl; William T. McCartan; Maureen G. Kenney; Vernon P. Squires; Timothy J. Hill; Paul D. Burns (Resident, Iowa City Office); Michael J. Pugh (Resident, Iowa City Office);—Janice J. Kerkove; Shannon P. Thompson; Kevin C. Papp; Laura C. Mueller; David J. Zylstra; Kimberly H. Blankenship; Sarah E. Swartzendruber (Resident, Iowa City Office); Tyler G. Olson; Joseph W. Younker (Resident, Iowa City Office). Of Counsel: Melissa Weets Anderson.
General Practice. Administrative, Antitrust, Arbitration, Banking, Bankruptcy, Civil Trial and Appellate Practice in all State and Federal Courts, Condominiums, Construction, Copyright, Corporate, E-Commerce, Employee Benefits, Environmental, Estate Planning, General Business, Government, Immigration, Insurance, Intellectual Property Labor and Employment Relations, Land Use, Mergers and Acquisitions, Municipal Bonds, Non-Profit, Pension and Profit Sharing, Personal Injury, Probate, Product Liability, Professional Liability, Real Estate, Securities, Taxation, Trademark and Trust Law. Iowa City, Iowa Office: One South Gilbert Street, 52240-3914. Telephone: 319-466-1511. Fax: 319-358-5560.
See Professional Biographies, CEDAR RAPIDS, IOWA

Brady, Brad J., (AV) ....'52 '78 C.187 B.A. L.352 J.D. [Brady&O.]

Brady & O'Shea, P.C., (AV) BB
2735 First Avenue Southeast, 52402
Telephone: 319-866-9277 Fax: 319-866-9280 URL: http://www.lawyers.com/bradyoshea
Email: bbrady@bradyoshea.com URL: http://www.bradyoshea.com
Brad J. Brady; Robert J. O'Shea; Matthew L. Preston;—Ann E. Brown-Graff.
Personal Injury, Wrongful Death, Business Litigation, Class Actions, Products Liability, Premises Liability, Professional Negligence, Employment Law, Real Estate, Corporate Law, Estate Planning, Probate, Taxation, Appellate Practice, Civil Trial Practice, Worker's Compensation, Accidents, Automobile Accidents and Injuries, Trademark Litigation, Franchise Litigation, Trusts and Estates, Estate Planning, Probate, Wills.
See Professional Biographies, CEDAR RAPIDS, IOWA

Brandes, Matthew J., (AV) ....'53 '81 C.602 B.A. L.1035 J.D. [Simmons,P.A.&E.]
Brooks, Philip D., (AV) ....'50 '77 C.352 B.B.A. L.190 J.D. [Moyer&B.]
Brown-Graff, Ann E. ....'80 '04 C.187 B.A. L.352 J.D. [A Brady&O.]
Broz, John F., (BV) ....'44 '69 C&L.352 B.A., J.D. 222 3rd Ave. S.E., Ste. 504
Bruns, Christopher Lee, (BV) ....'65 '91 C&L.221 B.A., J.D. [Elderkin&P.]★
Bryner, Carrie K. Croft ....'69 '98 C.317 B.A. L.851 J.D. Asst. City Atty.
Burdt, Hugo C. ....'41 '66 C.707 B.A. L.352 J.D. [Burdt]
Burdt Law Office .... 417 First Avenue SE, Suite 101
Burian, Philip A., (CV) .... '68 '96 C.162 B.A. L.352 J.D. [Simmons,P.A.&E.]
Butkowski, Corinne R., (CV) ....'62 '97 C.490 B.S.N. L.352 J.D. [Lynch D.]
Butler, Robert Merrell '52 '81 C.612 B.S. L.623 J.D.
(adm. in OK; not adm. in IA) Asst. U.S. Atty.
Callahan, James J. ....'46 '74 C.350 B.S. L.352 J.D. 1735 4th Ave., S.E.‡
Cardona, Diane M. ....'72 '98 C.107 B.A. L.309 J.D. P.O. Box 5488
Carlson-Wood, Debra ....'60 '85 C.118 B.A. L.910 J.D. V.P., Coe College
Carpenter, John R., (AV) ....'23 '51 C&L.477 B.A., J.D. 115 3rd St.
Carroll, Rosemary F. '35 '83
C.103 A.B. L.352 J.D. Prof. & Chair, Dept. of History, Coe College
Carter, James H. ....'35 '60 C&L.352 B.A., J.D. Supm. Ct. Jus.
Carter, James H., (CV) ....'67 '93 C.350 B.S. L.221 J.D. P.O. Box 1176
Carter, Ryan N. ...... '75 '02 C.352 B.S. L.801 J.D. [A Shuttleworth&I.] (See Pat. Sect.)
Caster, Kevin J., (BV) .... '60 '95 C.351 B.A. L.352 J.D. [Shuttleworth&I.]
Cebuhar, Chas. ....'25 '54 C&L.352 B.A., J.D. Pres., United Security Svgs. Bk.
Charlier, Jennifer N. '71 '01 C.350 B.A. L.221 J.D.
(adm. in CO; not adm. in IA) 2115 29th St. N.W., Apt. 4
Chicchelly, Mary Elizabeth, (CV) ....'67 '92 C&L.352 B.A., J.D. [Seidl&C.]
Childers, Dan, (AV) ....'54 '82 C.929 B.A. L.352 J.D. [Elderkin&P.]
Chipokas, Mark L., (BV) ....'63 '89 C.477 B.A. L.352 J.D. 866 1st Ave., NE
Clark, Craig ....'49 '99 C&L.352 M.D., J.D. 4900 Morelle Rd., N.E.
Clark, Jeffrey L., (BV) ....'53 '86 C&L.352 B.A., J.D. Asst. Co. Atty.
Claussen, Nicole L., (CV) ....'73 '99 C.162 B.A. L.352 J.D. [C Moyer&B.]
Clevenger, Gregory L. ....'70 '03 C&L.352 B.A., J.D. [A Lynch D.]
Collins, Kevin H., (AV) .... '55 '81 C.190 B.A. L.352 J.D. [Shuttleworth&I.]
Collins, Thad J., (BV) ....'64 '90 C.429 B.A. L.352 J.D. [Pickens,B.&A.]
Collins, Thomas M., (AV) ....'27 '52 C&L.352 B.A., J.D. [C Shuttleworth&I.]
Collins, Wayne C., (AV) ....'26 '55 C.350 B.S. L.352 J.D. Firstar Bank Bldg.‡
Colton, Eldon L. ....'27 '55 C&L.352 B.A., J.D. 716 Oakland Rd. N.E.
Combs, Nancy, (CV) .... '60 '91 C&L.339 B.A., J.D. [Glasson,S.M.&C.]
Conn, David R. ....'53 '78 C&L.352 B.A., J.D. V.P.-Law & Reg. Affrs., McLeodUSA Inc.
Connolly, Barbara A. ....'— '96 C.162 B.A. L.221 J.D. [Howes]
Conover, Christine L., (BV) .... '73 '98 C.350 B.A. L.352 J.D. [Simmons,P.A.&E.]
Coppock, Mark L., (AV) ....'47 '75 C.352 B.B.A. L.221 J.D. [Elderkin&P.]
Courtney, Patrick M., (AV) .... '49 '74 C.352 B.B.A. L.190 J.D. [Bradley&R.]
Craig, James P., (BV) ....'56 '83 C&L.352 B.A., J.D. [Moyer&B.]
Craig, Jason M. ....'78 '04 C&L.352 B.A., J.D. [A Lynch D.]
Craig, Laurie J., (BV) ....'61 '87 C.352 B.A. L.900 J.D. Asst. Co. Atty.
Cram, Eva J. ....'44 '79 C&L.352 B.B.A., J.D. IES Industries Inc.

Crawford, Sullivan, Read & Roemerman, P.C., (AV)
1800 1st Avenue NE Second Floor, 52402-5435
Telephone: 319-364-0171 Fax: 319-364-1370
Email: csrr@crawfordsullivan.com URL: http://www.crawfordsullivan.com
James W. Crawford (1911-1988); Gerald T. Sullivan; Thomas B. Read; William H. Roemerman; Robert S. Hatala; James L. Sines; Thomas J. Wilkinson, Jr.;—Peter B. Welch; Sherry L. Schulte.
Insurance Defense, Personal Injury, Products Liability, Workers Compensation, Commercial Litigation and Transactions, Corporate Law, Employment Law, Real Estate, Probate, Family Law, Appellate Practice, Civil Trial Practice in all State and Federal Courts.
Representative Clients: American Home Assurance Co.; Iowa Mutual Insurance Co.; Mutual Fire & Automobile Insurance Co.; Fireman's Fund Insurance Cos.
Names of references on request.
See Professional Biographies, CEDAR RAPIDS, IOWA

Crilley, Christine L., (BV) ....'57 '83 C.351 B.A. L.352 J.D. [Ackley,K.&K.]
Croco, Elizabeth V. .... '74 '00 C.293 B.A. L.352 J.D. [A Simmons,P.A.&E.]
Currell, Dennis .... [Currell]
Currell Law Firm ....222 Edgewood Road, N.W.
Currie, Thomas J., (BV) ....'— '85 C&L.352 B.A., J.D. [T.Riley]
Dake, Matthew D. ....'71 '97 C.351 B.A. L.190 J.D. [A Wertz]
D'Amico, Amanda ....'79 '04 C&L.352 B.B.A., J.D. [A Moyer&B.]
Daufeldt, Susan C. ....'65 '98 C&L.352 B.F.A., J.D. [A Fiegen]
Davis, Theresa C., (BV) ....'67 '95 C.927 B.A. L.352 J.D. [Shuttleworth&I.]
Dawley, Laurie L. ....'73 '98 C.898 B.A. L.352 J.D. [Shuttleworth&I.]
Day, Joseph E., (BV) ....'38 '63 C.602 A.B. L.276 J.D. P.O. Box 2877
DeBoom, Thomas N., (CV) ....'73 '99 C&L.352 B.S., J.D. [Moyer&B.]
Deegan, Peter E., Jr. '70 '95 C.602 B.A. L.912 J.D.
(adm. in MI; not adm. in IA) U.S. Atty.'s Off.
DenBeste, Daniel, (BV) ....'49 '78 C.162 B.A. L.101 J.D. [A Elderkin&P.]
Denney, Michael K., (AV) ....'48 '73 C&L.378 B.S., J.D. [Bradley&R.]
Denton, Harold L., (AV) ....'47 '73 C.838 B.S. L.352 J.D. First Asst. Co. Atty.
Diehl, Susan A., (CV) ....'47 '76 C&L.221 B.S.E., J.D. 4040 1st Ave, N.E.
Dillard, Denver D., (AV) ....'45 '71 C.793 B.A. L.352 J.D. Co. Atty.
Dodge, Don W. .... '14 '41 C&L.352 B.S.C., J.D. 3224 Terry Dr., S.E.‡
Dolezal, Kenneth F. ....'46 '83 C.350 B.S. L.352 J.D. 4920 Johnson Ave., N.W.
Doyle, Melanie, (BV) '67 '94 C.427 B.A. L.352 J.D.
Sr. Atty., AEGON USA Realty Advisors, Inc.
Dufoe, Landon R. ....'71 '04 C.162 B.A. L.352 J.D. [A White&J.]
Eads, William R. ....'27 '57 C&L.352 B.A., J.D. Dist. J.
Eaves-Johnson, James E. ......'77 '03 C.910 B.S.B.A. L.352 J.D. Coun., McLeodUSA Inc.
Edwards, Walter R. '64 '90 C.164 A.B. L.930 J.D.
(adm. in MI; not adm. in IA) 6601 Kent Dr. N.E.
Eells, Lew, (BV) ....'43 '68 C.351 B.A. L.352 J.D. [Eells&T.]

Eells & Tronvold Law Offices, P.L.C., (BV)
1921 51st Street, N.E., 52402
Telephone: 319-393-1020 Fax: 319-393-4000
Email: Jeff@eells-tronvold.com URL: http://www.eells-tronvoldlaw.com
Mr. Lew Eells; Mr. Jeffrey R. Tronvold.
General Practice with emphasis on Personal Injury, Litigation, Probate and Estate Planning, Trusts and Wills, Business Law and Mediation.
See Professional Biographies, CEDAR RAPIDS, IOWA

Egel, Dennis E. '46 '73
C.597 B.S. L.352 J.D. V.P. & Sr. Tr. Offr., Guaranty Bk. & Tr. Co.
Ehrhart, John H., (AV) ....'45 '70 C.215 B.A. L.352 J.D. 425 Second Street SE
Einck, Dean R., (AV) ....'57 '82 C.351 B.A. L.352 J.D. [Shuttleworth&I.]
Elderkin, David A., (AV) ....'41 '66 C&L.352 B.B.A., J.D. [Elderkin&P.]
Elderkin, David M., (AV) .... '13 '37 C&L.352 B.A., J.D. [Elderkin&P.]

Elderkin & Pirnie, P.L.C., (AV) BB
Successor to Barnes and Chamberlain
115 First Avenue, S.E., P.O. Box 1968, 52406
Telephone: 319-362-2137 Fax: 319-362-1640
Thomas H. Pirnie (Deceased); David M. Elderkin; John K. von Lackum; David A. Elderkin; Patrick M. Roby; Mark L. Coppock; Edward M. Blando; James W. Affeldt; Jack C. Paige; Dan Childers; Todd W. Anderson; Christopher Lee Bruns;—Cynthia Hanna; Tamra L. Mitchell; Daniel DenBeste; Robert M. Hogg; Paula L. Roby; Ann M. Klostermann McCrea.
Civil Trial and Appellate Practice in all State and Federal Courts. Construction, Insurance Defense, Professional Liability, Personal Injury, Toxic Torts, Corporation and Business Associations, Health Care and Hospital Law, Estate Planning, Family, Probate, Real Estate, Taxation, Workers Compensation, Bankruptcy.
Representative Clients: Allied Mutual Insurance Company; Allied Property and Casualty Company; Allied-Signal Inc.; The Equitable Life Assurance Society of the United States.
General Counsel For: Mercy Foundation.
See Professional Biographies, CEDAR RAPIDS, IOWA

Ellwood, William P., (AV) ....'09 '33 C&L.352 B.A., J.D. 115 Third St., S.E.
Eneboe-Braithwaite, Tacey '54 '80 C.56 B.A. L.793 J.D.
(adm. in SD; not adm. in IA) Federal Land Bk.
Epping, Gregory J., (BV) ....'55 '80 C.350 B.S. L.352 J.D. [Terpstra,E.&W.]
Erger, Karen ....'64 '90 C&L.145 A.B., J.D. Acct. Exec., Holmes, Murphy & Assocs.
Estlund, Tim A., (BV) ....'50 '76 C&L.352 B.A., J.D. 100 1st Ave. N.E., Ste. 105
Evans, Nancy H. ....'49 '74 C.162 B.A. L.352 J.D. Asst. Prof., Coe College
Faches, William G., (BV) ....'28 '55 C&L.352 B.A., J.D. 318 Paramount Bldg.
Fagan, Brian J. ....'71 '01 C.352 B.B.A. L.221 J.D. [A Moyer&B.]
Fassler, Robert M., (BV) ....'27 '54 C&L.192 LL.B. P.O. Box 11396
Fay, Michael W. ....'42 '66 C&L.972 B.S., J.D. 118 3rd Ave., S.E.
Fiegen, Thomas L., (AV) .... '58 '88 C.375 B.S.B.S. L.352 J.D. [Fiegen]
Fiegen Law Firm, P.C., (AV) .... 316 Eighth Avenue, Southeast
Fleming, Heather L. ....'77 '02 C.351 B.A. L.221 J.D. [A Shuttleworth&I.]
Flitz, James H., (BV) ....'56 '82 C&L.352 B.S., J.D. Asst. City Atty.
Ford, Robert E., (AV) ....'25 '52 C&L.352 B.A., J.D. [Klinger,R.&F.]
Forsythe, Todd P., (CV) ....'66 '92 C.190 B.S.B.A. L.352 J.D. 104 Third Ave. S.W.

Freme, Mark S. '55 '84 C.321 B.A. L.809 J.D.
(adm. in ME; not adm. in IA) 230 Brentwood‡
Fry, Richard S., (AV) .... '46 '74 C.351 B.A. L.352 J.D. [Shuttleworth&I.]
Garberson, C. W., (AV) .... '11 '35 C&L.352 B.A., J.D. 312 Linden Terrace, S.E.‡
Garberson, Richard C., (AV) .... '49 '74 C.352 B.B.A. L.221 J.D. [Shuttleworth&I.]

Gartelos, Wagner & Ament
(See Waterloo)

Gayer, Sarah J. .... '71 '97 C.228 B.A. L.352 J.D. [Shuttleworth&I.]
George, Richard W. .... '55 '80 C&L.352 B.B.A., J.D. McGladrey & Pullen
Gericke, Vernon J. .... '28 '58 C&L.352 B.S.C., J.D. 3908 Nancy Jane Ln.‡
Gerk, James A., (AV) .... '55 '80 C&L.352 B.B.S., J.D. [Simmons,P.A.&E.]
Giddings, Caroline D., (BV) '60 '89 C.707 B.A. L.352 J.D.
V.P. & Gen. Coun., Health Enterprises of Iowa
Gillespie, Thomas, (CV) .... '47 '80 C.350 B.S. L.352 J.D. P.O. Box 1352
Glasson, Matthew A., (BV) .... '53 '81 C&L.352 B.A., J.D. [Glasson,S.M.&C.]
Glasson, Sole, McManus & Combs, P.C., (BV) .... 118 3rd Ave., S.E., Ste. 830
Gloe, H. Nick, (BV) .... '41 '67 C&L.352 B.A., J.D. 318 Paramount Bldg.
Good, David S. .... '46 '72 C.547 B.A. L.352 J.D. Dist. Ct. Judge
Grady, Patrick R. .... '54 '79 C.190 B.A. L.352 J.D. Dist. J.

Gray, Stefani & Mitvalsky, P.L.C., (AV)
200 American Building, 52401
Mailing Address: P.O. Box 456, Cedar Rapids, IA 52406-0456
Telephone: 319-364-1535 FAX: 319-364-1562
URL: http://www.gsmlawyers.com
Raymond R. Stefani; Frank S. Mitvalsky; Raymond R. Stefani, II; Richard A. Stefani; Thomas F. Ochs; Richard F. Mitvalsky.
General Practice. Family Law, Juvenile, Real Estate, Professional Liability, Products Liability, Wills, Trusts and Estates, Estate Planning, Probate, Insurance, Environmental Law, Commercial Law, Corporate Law. Trials and Appeals.
See Professional Biographies, CEDAR RAPIDS, IOWA

Gross, Jay S. .... '29 '58 C&L.597 B.S., J.D. P.O. Box 3013
Grove, Judith A. .... '51 '80 C.490 B.S. L.352 J.D. 301 Cottage Grove Ave.‡
Gruhn, Brian L., (BV) .... '50 '77 C&L.352 B.S., J.D. [Gruhn]
Gruhn Law Firm, (BV) .... 4089 21st Ave. S.W., Ste. 114
Gunning, Gloria G. .... '57 '82 C&L.326 B.A., J.D. United Fire & Casualty Company
Gutz, Larry G., (BV) .... '39 '64 C&L.352 B.A., J.D. [Moyer&B.]
Haas, William A. .....'57 '83 C.350 B.S. L.221 J.D. Assoc. Gen. Coun., McLeodUSA Inc.
Hacker, David A., (AV) .... '44 '82 C.602 B.A. L.352 J.D. [Simmons,P.A.&E.]
Hahn, Laura J., (BV) '47 '77 C&L.352 B.A., J.D.
Assoc. Gen. Coun., McLeod USA Incorporated
Hammond, Jonathan B., (BV) .... '54 '84 C&L.352 B.A., J.D. [Klinger,R.&F.]
Handler, James M. ..... '33 '58 C.659 B.S.E. L.178 LL.B. Pres., Hawkeye Rubber Mfg. Co.
Hanna, Cynthia, (BV) .... '56 '81 C.56 B.A. L.209 J.D. [A Elderkin&P.]
Hanrahan, Mark E. .... '51 '79 C.350 B.A. L.1187 J.D. 4700 N. River Blvd. N.E.
Hanrahan, Renee K., (BV) .... '— '96 C.520 B.S. L.352 J.D. [Willey,O.M.L.&H.]
Hansen, David R. .... '38 '63 C.593 B.A. L.273 J.D. Sr. U.S. Ct. App. J.
Happel, Jana L., (CV) .... '60 '87 C.228 A.B. L.352 J.D. 526 2nd Ave. SE
Hardeman, Kimberly K. .... '70 '96 C.492 B.S. L.221 J.D. [A Moyer&B.]
Harms, Allan L., (BV) .... '45 '74 C.546 B.S.E.E. L.352 J.D. [Wenzel&H.] (Pat.)
Harrington, Lucy E. .... '64 '94 C.162 B.A. L.352 J.D. 3610 Clark Rd. SE
Harris, Joe H., (BV) .. '53 '81 C&L.352 B.A., J.D. Gen. Coun., Sabine Transportation Co.
Harris, Marcia V. '62 '94 C.579 B.S. L.1035 J.D.
(adm. in MN; not adm. in IA) [A Moyer&B.]
Hart, Bradley G., (BV) .... '55 '82 C.350 B.A. L.796 J.D. [Bradley&R.]
Hartman, Lynn Wickham, (BV) .... '62 '87 C&L.352 B.A., J.D. [Simmons,P.A.&E.]
Hatala, Robert S., (BV) .... '52 '83 C.350 B.A. L.352 J.D. [Crawford,S.R.&R.]
Hauser, Ross G., (BV) .... '61 '86 C.106 B.A. L.352 J.D. 210 2nd St. S.E., Ste. 810
Heckel, John M., (BV) .... '48 '73 C&L.352 B.A., J.D. 229 Northland Ct., N.E.
Hedgecoth, John D. .... '69 '88 C.502 B.A. L.352 J.D. 3500 F Avenue NW
Heeren, Lance J., (BV) .... '62 '87 C.350 B.A. L.352 J.D. Asst. Co. Atty.
Heffern, Allison M., (BV) .... '60 '87 C.157 B.A. L.352 J.D. [Simmons,P.A.&E.]
Heiserman, J. E., (AV) .... '05 '32 C&L.352 B.A. 1224 13th St. N.W.‡
Helvey, Larry D., (BV) .... '45 '85 C.629 M.D. L.352 J.D. [◎ Moyer&B.]
Hendrickson, Carl, Jr. .... '27 '54 C&L.352 B.A., J.D. 412 26th St. S.E.‡
Hense, Susan L., (CV) .... '60 '96 C.162 B.A. L.352 J.D. [Lynch D.]
Hershner, Philip A., (BV) .... '59 '84 C&L.352 B.A., J.D. V.P., Firstar Bk. Iowa, N.A.
Herzberger, Mark J., (BV) .... '51 '87 C&L.352 B.B.A., J.D. [A Moyer&B.]
Hess, Russell I., (AV) .... '06 '29 L.352 LL.B. 130 Thompson Drive, S.E.‡
Hickok, Craig W., (CV) .... '38 '84 C.950 B.A. L.352 J.D. 4057 Dalewood Ave., S.E.
Hill, Timothy J., (BV) .... '66 '91 C.352 B.A. L.893 J.D. [Bradley&R.]
Hinz, Stephanie L., (CV) .... '69 '94 C.350 B.A. L.221 J.D. [Pickens,B.&A.]
Hochstetler, William S., (AV) .... '55 '86 C.1124 B.A. L.352 J.D. [Shuttleworth&I.]
Hodges, James D., Jr., (AV) .... '44 '69 C&L.352 LL.B. Clk., U.S. Dist. Ct.
Hoffman-Simanek, Patricia L. .... '76 '01 C.520 B.A. L.602 J.D. [A Shuttleworth&I.]
Hogg, Robert M. .... '67 '95 C.352 B.A. L.494 J.D. [A Elderkin&P.]
Hoke, Robert W., II '51 '77
C.350 B.S., Ch.E. L.352 J.D. [Shuttleworth&I.] (See Pat. Sect.)
Holden, Richard D. .... '28 '52 C&L.352 B.A., LL.B. [Holden&S.] ‡
Holden & Steggall, (BV) .... 1203 Third St., S.E.
Holmes, James C., (BV) .... '60 '88 C.118 B.A. L.300 J.D. [Holmes&H.]
Holmes, James T., (BV) .... '24 '51 C.309 A.B. L.228 J.D. [Holmes&H.]
Holmes and Holmes, (BV) .... 222 Third St., S.E.
Holtman, Stephen J., (AV) .... '45 '72 C&L.352 B.S., J.D. [Simmons,P.A.&E.]
Homsey, Walter, Jr. .... '33 '61 C.162 B.A. L.1035 3213 1st Ave., S.E.‡
Hong, Janet, (BV) .... '49 '90 C&L.352 B.A., J.D. [Lynch D.]
Horan, Thomas M. .... '34 '63 C&L.352 B.S., J.D. Dist. J.
Houghton, Robert D., (AV) .... '46 '71 C&L.352 B.B.A., J.D. [Shuttleworth&I.]
Howes, Steven E., (BV) .... '61 '86 C.162 B.A. L.352 J.D. [Howes]
Howes Law Firm, P.C., (BV) .... 3200 37th Avenue SW
Hughes, David W. .... '66 '98 C.350 B.A. L.352 J.D. U.S. Cellular
Huisinga, Wesley B., (AV) .... '56 '81 C.351 B.A. L.352 J.D. [Shuttleworth&I.]
Jackson, Stephen B., (BV) .... '36 '64 C.162 B.A. L.352 J.D. [Jackson&J.]
Jackson, Stephen B., Jr., (BV) .... '66 '91 C.602 B.A. L.352 J.D. [Jackson&J.]

Jackson & Jackson P.L.C., (BV)
Suite 250 Armstrong Centre, 222 Third Avenue, Southeast, 52401
Telephone: 319-363-2683 Fax: 319-363-3028
Members: Stephen B. Jackson; Stephen B. Jackson, Jr.
Family Law, Adoptions, Child Custody, Child Support, Divorce, Domestic Violence, Visitation Rights, Real Estate, Probate, and Civil Trial Practice, Wills, Trusts, Estates.
Reference: Hills Bank and Trust.
See Professional Biographies, CEDAR RAPIDS, IOWA

Jager, Gregory S., (CV) .... '54 '79 C.191 B.A. L.352 J.D. Asst. City Atty.
Janitzky, K. R. '17 '40 C&L.145 A.B., J.D.
(adm. in IL; not adm. in IA) 1224 13th St.‡

Jarvey, John A. .... '56 '81 C.8 B.S. L.221 J.D. Chief U. S. Mag. J.
Jett, Robert S., III, (CV) '61 '88 C.319 B.A. L.64 J.D.
(adm. in MD; not adm. in IA) Coun., AEGON, USA, Inc.
Jilek, Robert M., (AV) .... '50 '75 C.136 A.B. L.608 J.D. [◎ Simmons,P.A.&E.]
Johnson, Glenn L., (AV) '50 '75
C.173 B.A. L.352 J.D. [Shuttleworth&I.] (See Pat. Sect.)
Johnson, J. Richard, (BV) .... '52 '78 C.434 B.A. L.352 J.D. [White&J.]
Jones, Elmer M., (AV) .... '17 '48 C&L.352 B.S.C., J.D. 4040 1st Ave., N.E.
Junge, Mary B., (CV) .... '57 '90 C&L.352 B.B.A., J.D. 4931 Ellis Rd., N.W.
Kane, Allan D., (CV) .... '41 '66 C&L.352 B.A., J.D. 2055 1st. Ave., S. E.
Kaufman, Kelly J.(Simonsen), (CV) .... '70 '96 C.351 B.A. L.352 J.D. Co. Atty. Off.
Kennedy, Timothy J. '55 '81 C&L.986 B.A., J.D.
(adm. in MO; not adm. in IA) Intermec Tech. Corp.
Kenney, Maureen G., (BV) .... '62 '94 C.742 B.S. L.352 J.D. [Bradley&R.]
Kerkove, Janice J. .... '68 '99 C.999 B.S. L.221 J.D. [A Bradley&R.]
Keyes, Henry M., (CV) .... '32 '61 C&L.352 B.S.C., J.D. P.O. Box 1683
Kilburg, Paul J. .....'45 '74 C.627 B.A. L.900 J.D. U.S. Bkrptcy. J., Bkrptcy Ct. Chambers
Kilpatrick, Amy M. .... '— '90 C.351 B.A. L.352 J.D. Law Clk., U.S. Bkrptcy. Ct.
Kimm, Robert A., Law Offices, (CV) .... '44 '73 C&L.352 B.A., J.D. 1203 3rd St. S.E.
Kingery, Gregory D., (BV) .... '55 '80 C&L.352 B.B.A., J.D. [Ackley,K.&K.]
Kinnamon, Jerald W., (BV) .... '38 '64 C&L.352 B.A., J.D. 330 1st St., S.E. (⊙Iowa City)
Kinnamon, Jon M., (BV) .... '40 '66 330 1st St., S.E. (⊙Iowa City)
Kirkley, Carol J., (CV) .... '63 '87 C.352 B.A. L.221 J.D. [Kirkley]
Kirkley Law Offices, (CV) .... 1921 51st Street, N.E.
Kirsch, Linda M., (BV) .... '59 '84 C.177 B.A. L.352 J.D. [Shuttleworth&I.]
Kleiman, Kathleen A. .... '63 '88 C.352 B.B.A. L.976 J.D. [Simmons,P.A.&E.]
Klinger, Phillip D., (AV) .... '42 '68 C&L.352 B.B.A., J.D. [Klinger,R.&F.]

Klinger, Robinson & Ford, L.L.P., (AV)
401 Old Marion Road, N.E., P.O. Box 10020, 52410-0020
Telephone: 319-395-7400 FAX: 319-395-9041 Cable: TESHUB
Email: Krflaw@mcleodusa.net URL: http://www.krflawoffice.com
Robert E. Ford; Phillip D. Klinger; Gary L. Robinson (1947-1998); Jeffrey P. Taylor; Jonathan B. Hammond; Stephen A. Swift;—Daniel L. Seufferlein.
General Civil Practice. Federal Criminal Defense, Including White Collar Crimes and Drug Crimes, Real Estate, Probate, Environmental, Equal Employment Opportunity, Bankruptcy, Insolvency, Corporate and Commercial Law. Litigation, Family Law, Estate Planning, Drug, Insurance, Municipal Law, Appellate Practice, Mediation, Wills and Probate, Trusts and Estates, DWI, Traffic Violations, Divorce, Juvenile Crimes, Probation.
See Professional Biographies, CEDAR RAPIDS, IOWA

Klopfenstein, Vaughn M., (BV) '62 '88 C.351 B.A. L.352 J.D.
(adm. in MN; not adm. in IA) Rockwell Collins, Inc.
Kloss, John J. '49 '76 C.597 B.A. L.146 J.D.
(adm. in IL; not adm. in IA) Sr. V.P. & Tr. Dept. Mgr., First Tr. & Svgs. Bk.
Knoll, Mona, (AV) .... '48 '80 C.350 B.S. L.352 J.D. [Nazette,M.W.K.&U.]
Knudten, Herbert J., Jr. .... '41 '66 C&L.352 B.B.A., LL.B. 2451 Grande Ave. S.E.‡
Koch, Keith D. .... '25 '53 C.351 B.A. L.221 LL.B. 210 2nd St., S.E.
Koehler, Thomas L. .... '37 '62 C&L.352 B.A., LL.B. Dist. J.
Kokontis, William .... '24 '50 C&L.339 B.S., LL.B. 2101 Linden Dr. S.E.
Konchar, Robert E., (AV) .... '39 '65 C&L.352 B.B.A., J.D. [Moyer&B.]
Kopecky, Eugene J., (AV) .... '42 '66 C.177 B.A. L.734 J.D. [Ackley,K.&K.]
Krigbaum, Matthew J., (CV) .... '— '97 C.629 B.A. L.285 J.D. [Moyer&B.]
Krug, Edward J., (BV) .... '56 '82 C.162 B.A. L.93 J.D. [Krug]

Krug Law Firm, P.L.C., (BV)
The Hach Building, Suite 330, 401 First Street S.E., P.O. Box 186, 52406-0186
Telephone: 319-297-7515 Fax: 319-297-7518
Email: ekrug@kruglawfirm.com URL: http://www.kruglawfirm.com
Edward J. Krug;—Bobbi J. Lammer.
General Civil Trial Practice emphasizing Insurance Defense, Labor and Employment Law (Management), Railroad/Transportation, Workers' Compensation, Mediation and Family Law.
See Professional Biographies, CEDAR RAPIDS, IOWA

Kubicek, David W., (AV) .... '46 '73 C.350 B.S. L.352 J.D. [Simmons,P.A.&E.]
Kubicek, Theodore L., (AV) .... '19 '42 C&L.352 B.A., J.D. 3866 Belden Ct., N.E.‡
Kucera, Gerald J., (BV) .... '— '75 C&L.352 B.A., J.D. [T.Riley]
Kudart, Arthur R., (AV) .... '30 '58 C&L.352 B.A., J.D. [Kudart] ⊙
Kudart Law Offices, (AV) .... 3906 Belden Ct. N.E. (⊙Mechanicsville, Mt. Vernon)
Kudej, Lawrence D., (BV) '49 '74
C.177 B.A. L.352 J.D. Civil Chf. U.S. Atty., Fed. Firm U.S. Atty.
Kutcher, David C. .... '74 '01 C.927 B.S. L.352 J.D. [Simmons,P.A.&E.]
Kutzko, Diane, (AV) .... '46 '81 C.102 B.A. L.352 J.D. [Shuttleworth&I.]
Lahammer, Michael K. .... '59 '93 C.590 B.S. L.352 J.D. [Lahammer]
Lahammer Law Firm, P.C. .... 211 3rd Ave. S.W.
Lam, Eric W., (AV) .... '56 '82 C.429 B.A. L.352 J.D. [Moyer&B.]
Lammer, Bobbi J. .... '77 '04 C&L.352 B.A., J.D. [A Krug]

Lane, John L., (BV) '52 '81 C&L.352 B.A., J.D.
The Law Building, Suite 310, 225 Second Street S.E., 52406-5245
Telephone: 319-363-3839 Fax: 319-363-4851
Email: attyjohnlane@msn.com
Federal Criminal Defense, including White Collar Crimes and Drug Cases.
See Professional Biographies, CEDAR RAPIDS, IOWA

Laverty, Anne M., (CV) .... '— '91 C&L.352 B.A., J.D. [Willey,O.M.L.&H.]
Lederer, Gregory M., (AV) .... '51 '77 C.546 B.A. L.221 J.D. [Simmons,P.A.&E.]
Leehey, Pete, (AV) .... '59 '84 C&L.352 B.A., J.D. [P.Leehey]

Leehey, Pete, Law Firm, P.C., (AV)
6105 Rockwell Drive N.E., P.O. Box 10316, 52410-7490
Telephone: 319-294-4424 Fax: 319-294-4993
Email: pleehey@leeheylaw.com URL: http://www.lawyers.com/leeheylaw
Pete Leehey. Associate: Kent Smith.
Personal Injury, Workers' Compensation, Automobile Accidents, Dog Bites, Sexual Abuse, Slip and Fall, Wrongful Death, Wrongful Termination, Medical Malpractice, Nursing Home Abuse.
See Professional Biographies, CEDAR RAPIDS, IOWA

Legislador, Robert J. .... '72 '00 C.352 B.S. L.221 J.D. [A White&J.]
Leonard, Deborah Lynne, (CV) .... '54 '78 C&L.352 B.A., J.D. P.O. Box 74446
Levin, Deborah J. .... '54 '91 C&L.352 B.S., J.D. Life Investors Ins. Co. of Am.
Lewis, Ted P. .... '17 '43 C&L.352 B.A., J.D. 4610 Aspen Ln., N.E.‡
Liabo, Corenne M. .... '55 '80 C.352 B.A. L.221 J.D. Friend of the Ct.
Liabo, Mark E., (BV) .... '— '79 C.352 B.A. L.221 J.D. [T.Riley]
Liesveld, Barbara H., (BV) .... '55 '87 C&L.352 B.S., J.D. [Thinnes&L.]
Lindeman, Michael .... '62 '89 C.352 B.A. L.351 J.D. 3500 F Avenue, NW, Suite 1
Lipsky, Joan .... '19 '81 C.597 B.S. L.352 J.D. 655 Cottage Grove Ave. S.E.‡
Lobodiak, Nestor, (CV) .... '— '89 C&L.352 B.S., J.D. [T.Riley] ⊙‡
Locher, John F., (BV) .... '46 '72 C.602 B.A. L.352 LL.B. 3518 Heatheridge Dr. N.E.
Luehrsmann, Ronald L., (BV) .... '42 '69 C.177 B.A. L.352 J.D. [◎ White&J.]
Luneckas, Darin H. .... '74 '99 C.162 B.A. L.352 J.D. [Luneckas&N.]
Luneckas & Newhouse, P.C. .... 3717 Center Point Road NE, Suite 100

Lynch Dallas, P.C., (AV) BB
526 Second Avenue SE, P.O. Box 2457, 52406-2457
Telephone: 319-365-9101 Facsimile: 319-365-9512
Email: attorneys@lynchdallas.com URL: http://www.lynchdallas.com
Charles J. Lynch (1905-1983); William M. Dallas (1905-1981); Donald G. Ribble; H. Edward Beatty; Scott E. McLeod; Wilford H. Stone; Sean W. McPartland; Matthew J. Nagle; Janet Hong; Susan L. Hense; Patrick J. O'Connell; Corinne R. Butkowski;—Todd A. Slagter; Amy L. Reasner; Gregory L. Clevenger; Jason M. Craig.
General Civil Practice.
Representative Clients: Alliant Transportation; American States Insurance Co.; CRANDIC Railway; CIGNA Cos.; General Casualty Insurance Companies; Progressive Insurance Companies; Rockwell Collins, Inc.; State Farm Insurance Cos.; The Travelers Insurance Cos.
See Professional Biographies, CEDAR RAPIDS, IOWA

Maher, John M., (CV) .... '41 '75 C&L.352 B.A., J.D. 4201 1st Ave., S.E.
Manor, Thomas G. '52 '77 C.25 B.A. L.880 J.D.
Assistant General Counsel, Rockwell International Corporation
Marner, David L., Jr., (BV) .... '60 '91 C.133 B.A. L.221 J.D. [Nazette,M.W.K.&U.]
Marner, David L., Sr., (AV) .... '33 '58 C.162 B.A. L.350 J.D. [Nazette,M.W.K.&U.]
Martin, Annette F., (CV) .... '61 '92 C.187 B.A. L.352 J.D. 4830 Millbrook Ct. NE
Matias, Robert W. .... '37 '61 C.162 B.A. L.352 LL.B. 210 2nd St., S.E.
Maxwell, Thomas E. .... '72 '00 C.352 B.A. L.1194 J.D. 4089 21st Ave. S.W., Ste. 114
McCartan, William T., (BV) .... '65 '91 C.190 B.A. L.602 J.D. [Bradley&R.]
McCauley, David M. .... '61 '93 C&L.352 B.A., J.D. Staff Atty., GE Capital Corp.
McCool, Janice R., (CV) .... '49 '83 C.162 B.A. L.221 J.D. 222 3rd Ave., S.E.
McCrea, Ann M. Klostermann, (CV) '68 '99 C.352 B.G.S. L.748 J.D.
[A] Elderkin&P.]
McCuskey, Thomas G., (BV) .... '48 '74 C.162 B.A. L.221 J.D. P.O. Box 817
McDermott, Michael O., (AV) .... '38 '63 C&L.352 B.B.A., J.D. [Shuttleworth&I.]
McDonough, Michael, (BV) .... '54 '81 C.352 B.A. L.190 J.D. [Moyer&B.]
McGuire, David F., (AV) .... '29 '52 C.177 B.S. L.352 J.D. City Atty.
McHarg, Jane .... '46 '71 C&L.352 B.B.A., J.D. 10 Clive Drive NW
McLeod, Scott E., (AV) .... '42 '67 C&L.352 B.A., J.D. [Lynch D.]
McManus, David P., (CV) .... '49 '74 C.602 B.A. L.352 J.D. [Glasson,S.M.&C.]
McManus, Edward J. .... '20 '41 C&L.352 B.A., J.D. Sr. U.S. Dist. J.
McMenimen, Dennis J., (AV) .... '53 '78 C.723 B.A. L.352 J.D. [Shuttleworth&I.]
McNamara, Walter L., (CV) .... '32 '61 C&L.352 B.S.C., LL.B. 4403 1st Ave., S.E.
McPartland, Sean W., (BV) .... '58 '84 C&L.352 B.A., J.D. [Lynch D.]
Melloy, Michael J. .... '48 '74 C.177 B.A. L.352 J.D. U.S. Ct. App. J.
Meyer, Douglas C., (BV) '48 '74 C.177 B.A. L.352 J.D.
[Ackley,K.&K.] (⊙Central City)
Meyer, Mark C., (BV) .... '50 '75 C.293 B.A. L.352 J.D. 330 1st St. S.E. (⊙Iowa City)
Miller, Max R. .... '18 '50 C.106 B.A. L.352 J.D. 2043 Grand Ave. S. E.
Mitchell, David D., (CV) .... '35 '63 C&L.352 B.A., J.D. 322 2nd St., S.W.
Mitchell, Tamra L., (BV) .... '60 '89 C.520 B.S.N. L.352 J.D. [A] Elderkin&P.]
Mitvalsky, Frank S., (AV) .... '43 '68 C.597 B.A. L.352 J.D. [Gray,S.&M.]
Mitvalsky, Richard F., (CV) .... '71 '96 C.477 A.B. L.221 J.D. [Gray,S.&M.]
Mollman, Michael L., (CV) .... '50 '76 C&L.352 B.A., J.D. 240 Wiley Blvd., S.W.
Monroe, John C., (BV) .... '47 '72 C&L.352 B.B.A., J.D. 320 8th Ave., S.E.
Monthei, Sasha L. .... '80 '04 C&L.352 B.A., J.D. [A] Moyer&B.]
Moon, Kenneth L., (BV) .... '16 '42 C&L.352 B.A., J.D. 514 Guaranty Bldg.
Moore, Kelly L. .... '57 '83 C.593 B.S. L.352 J.D. Asst. V.P., Firstar Bk. Iowa, N.A.
Morf, Darrel A., (AV) .... '43 '69 C&L.352 B.A., J.D. [Simmons,P.A.&E.]
Morf, Paul P., (BV) .... '72 '98 C.197 A.B. L.976 J.D. [Simmons,P.A.&E.]

Moyer & Bergman, P.L.C., (AV) BB
2720 First Avenue, N.E., P.O. Box 1943, 52406-1943
Telephone: 319-366-7331 Telecopier: 319-366-3668
Email: mb@moyerbergman.com URL: http://www.moyerbergman.com
Retired: William A. Bergman (Retired). Members of Firm: Robert E. Konchar; Stephen C. Nelson; J. Scott Bogguss; Larry G. Gutz; Philip D. Brooks; J. Michael Weston; Kevin J. Visser; Randal J. Scholer; William S. Vernon; James P. Craig; Eric W. Lam; Michael McDonough; Brenda K. Wallrichs; Thomas D. Wolle; Matthew J. Krigbaum; Thomas N. DeBoom. Associates: Mark J. Herzberger; Cynthia Scherrman Sueppel; Marcia V. Harris (Not admitted in IA); Brian J. Fagan; Mark J. Parmenter; Amanda D'Amico; Sasha L. Monthei; Kimberly K. Hardeman; Matthew J. Adam. Of Counsel: Larry D. Helvey; Nicole L. Claussen.
General Practice in all Courts State and Federal. Business and Corporate, Employment and Labor, Real Estate, Insurance Defense, Collection and Bankruptcy, Appellate Practice, Banking and Financial Institutions, Commercial Transactions, Computer Law, Construction Claims, Family Law, Fidelity and Surety Law, Government Contracts, Civil Rights and Discrimination Law, Immigration, Intellectual Property, Interstate Commerce, Motor Carrier Transportation Litigation, Municipal Law, Personal Injury, Professional Malpractice Defense, Wills, Trusts, Probate, Estate Planning, Worker's Compensation and Trademark, Copyright Law, Franchise Law.
Representative Clients: National Oats Co., a division of Curtice-Burns, Inc.; CRST, Inc.; SSangyong (U.S.A.), Inc.; Maquoketa State Bank; Postville State Bank; Ag Services of America, Inc.; American Family Insurance Group.
See Professional Biographies, CEDAR RAPIDS, IOWA

Muchmore, Iris E., (AV) .... '49 '75 C.293 B.A. L.221 J.D. [Simmons,P.A.&E.]
Mueller, Laura C., (CV) .... '72 '98 C.597 B.A. L.352 J.D. [A] Bradley&R.]
Mullin, David E., (BV) .... '— '87 C.339 B.A. L.228 J.D. [Willey,O.M.L.&H.]
Mundy, Richard E. '43 '70 C&L.352 B.A., J.D.
Ste. 465, 150 1st. Ave. N.E. (⊙Iowa City)
Murphy, Richard L., (BV) .... '57 '82 C.723 B.A. L.352 J.D. Asst. U.S. Atty.
Nadler, Charles H., (CV) .... '40 '84 C.178 A.B. L.352 J.D. [Nadler&W.] ⊙
Nadler & Weston, (CV) .... Paramount Bldg. (⊙Iowa City)
Nagle, Matthew J., (BV) .... '61 '87 C.177 B.A. L.352 J.D. [Lynch D.]
Nash, John A. .... '53 '84 C&L.352 B.G.S., J.D. Law Clk., Sr. U.S. Dist. J.
Nazette, Randall A., (AV) .... '50 '75 C.351 B.A. L.221 J.D. [Nazette,M.W.K.&U.]
Nazette, Richard F., (AV) .... '19 '46 C&L.352 B.A., J.D. [Nazette,M.W.K.&U.]
Nazette, Marner, Wendt, Knoll & Usher, LLP, (AV) .... 100 First Street, Southwest
Neff, Robert W., (AV) .... '11 '34 C.162 B.A. L.352 J.D. 2324 Linden Dr. S.E.‡
Nelson, Stephen C., (AV) .... '42 '67 C.350 B.S. L.352 J.D. [Moyer&B.]
Nemmers, James C., (AV) '31 '57
C.350 B.S. L.352 J.D. [C] Shuttleworth&I.] (See Pat. Sect.)
Neppl, William J., (BV) .... '50 '78 C.793 B.S. L.352 J.D. [Bradley&R.]
Neumeyer, Debora Hewitt, (BV) .... '67 '92 C.210 B.A. L.221 J.D. Asst. Atty. Gen.
Neumeyer, Gregory W., (BV) .... '64 '88 C&L.190 B.S.B.A., J.D. P.O. Box 1967
Newhouse, Chad .... '72 '99 C.520 B.A. L.221 J.D. [Luneckas&N.]
Newmeister, Michael J. .... '50 '76 C.352 B.A. L.990 J.D. Courthouse
Neyens, Deborah M., (CV) .... '65 '90 C&L.352 B.A., J.D. Sr. Atty., Alliant Energy
Nicholson, William G., (BV) .... '52 '80 C&L.352 B.A., J.D. [Rush&N.]
Northup, B. V. (Bill) '61 '87 C.132 B.A. L.352 J.D.
V.P. & Mgr., Norwest Bk. Iowa, N.A.
Novak, Matthew G., (AV) .... '56 '82 C.162 B.A. L.734 J.D. [Pickens,B.&A.]

Nyemaster, Goode, West, Hansell & O'Brien, A Professional Corporation
(See Des Moines)

O'Brien, David A., (BV) .... '— '85 C.273 B.A. L.352 J.D. [Willey,O.M.L.&H.]
O'Brien, E. Daniel, (CV) .... '57 '82 C.177 B.A. L.352 J.D. 425 Second Street
O'Brien, Robin Lynn .... '69 '95 C.352 B.B.A. L.607 J.D. Legal Services Corp.
Ochs, Thomas F., (BV) .... '62 '88 C.597 B.A. L.221 J.D. [Gray,S.&M.]
O'Connell, Patrick J. .... '70 '95 C.427 B.A. L.352 J.D. [Lynch D.]
Oelschlaeger, Douglas R., (BV) .... '57 '81 C&L.352 B.A., J.D. [Shuttleworth&I.]
Ogden, Mark H., (AV) .... '47 '77 C.293 B.A. L.221 J.D. [Simmons,P.A.&E.]
Olberg, F. Forbes .... '23 '50 C&L.966 B.B.A., LL.B. 115 3rd St., S.E.‡
Olinger, William F., (CV) .... '38 '64 C&L.352 B.B.A., J.D. 1120 2nd Ave., S.E.
Olson, Tyler G. .... '76 '03 C.154 B.A. L.352 J.D. [A] Bradley&R.]
O'Shea, Robert J., (CV) .... '69 '95 C.162 B.A. L.221 J.D. [Brady&O.]
Pace, Steven J., (AV) .... '52 '77 C.350 B.A. L.352 J.D. [Shuttleworth&I.]
Paige, Jack C., (BV) .... '50 '80 C.351 B.A. L.352 J.D. [Elderkin&P.]
Papenthien, Janet L., (BV) .... '58 '85 C.350 B.S. L.352 J.D. Asst. U.S. Atty.
Papp, Kevin C. .... '73 '98 C.1049 B.S. L.352 J.D. [A] Bradley&R.]
Parmenter, Mark J. .... '63 '03 C.986 B.A. L.221 J.D. [A] Moyer&B.]
Pazdernik, Richard L., Jr. .... '64 '94 C.352 B.A. L.365 J.D. [A] Nazette,M.W.K.&U.]
Pechota, Dominic F. .... '78 '04 C.546 B.A. L.352 J.D. [A] White&J.]
Pedelty, Joshua R. .... '74 '00 C.351 B.A. L.910 J.D. 4333 Edgewood Road
Peffer, Thomas P., (AV) .... '53 '78 C.488 B.A. L.352 J.D. [Shuttleworth&I.]
Peiffer, Joseph A., (BV) .... '56 '82 C.350 B.S. L.352 J.D. P.O. Box 2877
Penner, Nancy J., (AV) .... '58 '94 C.521 B.S. L.352 J.D. [Shuttleworth&I.]
Peters, James M., (AV) .... '55 '80 C&L.352 B.A., J.D. [Simmons,P.A.&E.]
Petrzelka, Matthew J., (BV) .... '58 '85 C&L.352 B.A., J.D. 1000 42nd St. S.E., Ste. A
Petska, Denice Marie .... '56 '82 C.162 B.A. L.352 J.D. 3829 Clark Rd., S.E.

Pickens, Barnes & Abernathy, (AV) BB
Tenth Floor American Building, 101 2nd Street SE, P.O. Box 74170, 52407-4170
Telephone: 319-366-7621 Fax: 319-366-3158
Email: law@pbalawfirm.com URL: http://www.pbalawfirm.com
James F. Pickens (1929-2004). Members of Firm: Terry J. Abernathy; Matthew G. Novak; Thad J. Collins; Stephanie L. Hinz. Retired: Minor Barnes.
Trials and Appeals in all Courts, Civil Litigation, Insurance Defense, Personal Injury, Workers Compensation, Commercial and Construction Litigation, Employment Law, Insurance Coverage, Products Liability, Creditors Remedies and Bankruptcy.
A list of Representative Clients furnished upon request.
See Professional Biographies, CEDAR RAPIDS, IOWA

Piersall, Matthew D. .... '75 '01 C.187 B.A. L.352 J.D/ [Piersall]
Piersall Law Firm, PC .... 3716 First Avenue NE
Pirnie, Thomas H., (AV) .... '12 '48 C.162 A.B. L.352 J.D. [Elderkin&P.] ‡
Powell, Troy M. .... '72 '99 C&L.352 B.A., J.D. [A] Wenzel&H.]
Powers, James M., (BV) .... '42 '67 C&L.352 B.B.A., J.D. 1120 Second Ave., S.E.
Preston, Matthew L., (CV) .... '71 '96 C&L.352 B.B.A., J.D. [Brady&O.]
Prowell, William P., (BV) .... '54 '81 C.855 B.A. L.221 J.D. [Shuttleworth&I.]
Pundt, Richard A., Law Offices, (BV) .... '44 '69 C.352 B.A. L.221 J.D. 330 1st St., S.E.
Quint, Martha Lee, (BV) .... '51 '76 C.352 B.A. L.190 J.D. 305 2nd St. S.E., Ste. 318
Radig, James W., (BV) .... '59 '85 C.585 B.A. L.352 J.D. [White&J.]
Ragsdale, Kent M. '49 '75 C.108 B.A. L.734 J.D.
Mng. Atty. & Asst. Corp. Secy., Alliant Energy
Railsback, Angela M. .... '66 '01 C&L.352 B.A., J.D. [Nazette,M.W.K.&U.]
Rapp, Stephen J., (BV) .... '49 '74 C.309 A.B. L.221 J.D. U.S. Atty.
Read, Thomas B., (AV) .... '49 '75 C.187 B.A. L.221 J.D. [Crawford,S.R.&R.]
Reade, Linda R. .... '48 '80 C&L.221 B.A., J.D. U.S. Dist. Ct. J.
Reasner, Amy L. .... '71 '01 C&L.352 B.A., J.D. [A] Lynch D.]
Reasoner, Carroll J., (AV) .... '51 '76 C&L.352 B.A., J.D. [Shuttleworth&I.]
Reasoner, Janet G., (BV) .... '57 '81 C&L.352 B.S., J.D. Asst. U.S. Trustee
Reilly, Matt J. .... '72 '98 C.352 B.A. L.221 J.D. [A] White&J.]
Reilly-Gruhn, Laurie K. .... '62 '98 C&L.352 B.B.A., J.D. [A] Gruhn]
Reins-Schweer, Lorie E. .... '62 '03 C.351 B.A. L.352 J.D. [A] Simmons,P.A.&E.]
Remley, David M. .... '44 '69 C.399 B.A. L.352 J.D. Dist. J., Linn Co.
Rettig, Mark H., (BV) .... '51 '76 C&L.352 B.A., J.D. P.O. Box 2877
Ribble, Donald G., (AV) .... '30 '55 C.162 B.A. L.352 J.D. [Lynch D.]
Riccolo, John L., (AV) .... '50 '77 C.602 B.A. L.365 J.D. [Riccolo&S.]

Riccolo & Semelroth, P.C., (AV) BB
Suite 1140, APAC Building, 425 Second Street, S.E., 52401
Telephone: 319-365-9200; Toll Free: 1-888-546-6529 Fax: 319-365-1114
Email: rb@riccololaw.com URL: http://www.riccololaw.com
John L. Riccolo; Timothy S. Semelroth.
Trials and Appeals in all State and Federal Courts. Personal Injury, Medical Malpractice, Professional Malpractice, Products Liability, Workers Compensation Law.
See Professional Biographies, CEDAR RAPIDS, IOWA

Richard, Dell A.
(See Coralville)

Richards, Allan M. '54 '90 C.427 B.A. L.940 J.D.
1073 Rockford Road, Suite L (⊙Tama)
Riley, Byron G., (AV) .... '30 '57 C&L.352 B.S., J.D. [Bradley&R.]
Riley, Peter C., (BV) .... '— '80 C&L.352 B.B.A., J.D. [T.Riley]
Riley, Sara, (CV) .... '— '86 C.352 B.B.A. L.221 J.D. [T.Riley]
Riley, Tom, (AV) .... '— '52 C&L.352 B.B.A., J.D. [T.Riley] ⊙

Riley, Tom, Law Firm, P.L.C., (AV) BB
4040 First Avenue N.E., P.O. Box 998, 52406-0998 ⊙
Telephone: 319-363-4040 Fax: 319-363-9789; 319-298-2917 URL: http://www.trlf.com
URL: http://www.tomrileylaw.com
Tom Riley; Peter C. Riley; T. Todd Becker; Mark E. Liabo; Hugh G. Albrecht; Sara Riley; Thomas J. Currie; James E. Bennett; Gerald J. Kucera; Nestor Lobodiak;—James K. Weston, II.
Personal Injury, Medical Malpractice, Products Liability, Civil Litigation, Workers' Compensation and Corporate Litigation.
Iowa City Office: 1210 Highway 6 West. Telephone: 319-351-4996. Fax: 319-351-7063.
See Professional Biographies, CEDAR RAPIDS, IOWA

Rinden, Jennifer E., (CV) .... '67 '97 C.846 B.A. L.221 J.D. [Shuttleworth&I.]
Rings, Randall, (CV) '62 '87
C&L.352 B.S., J.D. Sr. V.P. & Gen. Coun., Ruffalo Cody, LLC
Robbins, Linda Hansen, (CV) '42 '80
C.627 B.S. L.352 J.D. 417 First Avenue SE, Suite 308
Roberts, Jeannine L., (CV) .... '74 '99 C&L.352 B.A., J.D. 121 Third St. S.W.
Roberts, Mark A., (BV) .... '66 '93 C.350 B.A. L.546 J.D. [Simmons,P.A.&E.]
Roby, Patrick M., (AV) .... '47 '72 C.872 B.A. L.352 J.D. [Elderkin&P.]
Roby, Paula L. .... '73 '00 C.351 B.A. L.350 J.D. [A] Elderkin&P.]
Roemerman, William H., (BV) .... '53 '77 C&L.352 B.A., J.D. [Crawford,S.R.&R.]
Rosencrants, Jeffrey K., (BV) .... '62 '88 C.593 B.S. L.221 J.D. Sr. Atty., Alliant Energy
Rosser, Forrest W., (AV) .... '29 '55 C.475 B.A. L.352 J.D. [Terpstra,E.&W.]
Roush, Stanley A., (CV) .... '59 '84 C.784 B.S. L.352 J.D. 866 1st Ave. N.E.
Rush, Robert R., (AV) .... '44 '70 C.597 B.A. L.352 J.D. [Rush&N.]

Rush & Nicholson, PLC, (AV)
100 First Street S.W., 52404
Telephone: 319-363-5209 Fax: 319-363-6664 URL: http://www.rushnicholson.com
Email: info@rushnicholson.com URL: http://www.lawyers.com/rushlawfirm
Mailing Address: P.O. Box 637. Cedar Rapids, Iowa. 52406-0637
Robert R. Rush; William G. Nicholson;—Jeanne M. Steiner.

(This Listing Continued)

Rush & Nicholson, PLC (Continued)

Personal Injury, Product Liability, Professional Liability, Labor and Employment, Workers Compensation.

See Professional Biographies, CEDAR RAPIDS, IOWA

Russell, Douglas S., (BV) ... '48 '78 C.293 B.A. L.352 J.D. J.
Ryan, Richd. J. ... '28 '53 C&L.352 B.A., LL.B. 2442 Bever Ave., S.E.
Sagers, John M. ... '25 '50 C.350 B.S. L.352 J.D. 131 Kyrie, S.E.‡
Sanden, Gerald A. Vander, (BV) ... '56 '83 C.961 B.S. L.352 J.D. Asst. Co. Atty.
Scharmer, Neal R., (BV) ... '56 '81 C.297 B.A. L.494 J.D. 4310 Oak Leaf Ct. N.E.
Scheetz, Raphael M. ... '67 '93 C.427 L.190 J.D. [Scheetz]
Scheetz Law Office ... 1921 51st St. N.E.
Scheldrup, Chris J., (BV) ... '58 '86 C.351 B.A. L.352 J.D. [Scheldrup]

Scheldrup Law Firm, P.C., (BV)
Law Building, 225 Second Street S.E., Suite 200, P.O. Box 36, 52406-0036
Telephone: 319-286-1743 Fax: 319-286-1748
URL: http://www.scheldruplaw.com
Chris J. Scheldrup; Charles A. Blades; David E. Schrock.
General practice in state and federal courts and before administrative agencies, workers' compensation, labor and employment, professional malpractice defense, insurance defense, motor carrier transportation defense, family law.
Representatative Clients: Zurich American Insurance; United Fire & Casualty Group; West Side Transport; Barr-Nunn Transportation, Inc.; Florilli Transportation; TrueNorth Cos.; TMC Trucking; Annett Holdings, Inc.; Risk Administrative Services; EMC Insurance Cos.

See Professional Biographies, CEDAR RAPIDS, IOWA

Schmall, Joseph E., (BV) ... '58 '84 C.177 B.A. L.352 J.D. [Bradley&R.]
Scholer, Randal J., (BV) ... '56 '81 C&L.352 B.B.A., J.D. [Moyer&B.]
Schrock, David E., (BV) ... '67 '92 C&L.352 B.A., J.D. [Scheldrup]
Schulte, Sherry L., (BV) ... '65 '90 C.427 B.A. L.352 J.D. [Ⓐ Crawford,S.R.&R.]
Seeberger, Theresa J. ... '61 '89 C.293 B.A. L.352 J.D. Courthouse, 3rd Ave. Bridge‡
Seger, Rick ... '58 '85 C.999 B.S. L.352 J.D. Sr. V.P., Hawkeye State Bk.
Seidl, Mark J., (CV) ... '59 '84 C&L.190 B.A., J.D. [Seidl&C.]
Seidl, Phillip D., (CV) ... '56 '81 C&L.190 B.A., J.D. [Seidl&C.]
Seidl & Chicchelly, (CV) ... 229 Northland Ct. NE.
Semelroth, Timothy S., (CV) ... '71 '97 C.221 B.A. L.352 J.D. [Riccolo&S.]
Seufferlein, Daniel L. ... '73 '01 C.43 B.A. L.352 J.D. [Ⓐ Klinger,R.&F.]
Severa, Jos. J. ... '17 '48 C.177 B.A. L.190 LL.B. 81 16th Ave., S.W.‡
Seyfer, Gregory J., (AV) ... '54 '79 C&L.221 B.A., J.D. [Bradley&R.]
Shaeffer, Clinton E. ... '09 '31 C&L.221 LL.B. Ret. Dist. J.‡
Shea, Gary J., Law Offices, (BV) '56 '81
C.351 B.A. L.221 J.D. 425 2nd St. S.E., Ste. 1010
Shea, Kevin P., (BV) ... '53 '78 C.350 B.S. L.221 J.D. [Ⓐ Nazette,M.W.K.&U.]
Sheronick, Bedora A. ... '69 '98 C&L.352 B.A., J.D. United Fire & Casualty Company
Sheronick, Mohammad H., (BV) ... '59 '86 C.162 B.A. L.734 J.D. Asst. City Atty.
Shipman, James E., (AV) ... '43 '70 C.1027 B.S. L.424 J.D. [Simmons,P.A.&E.]
Shoemaker, Mary A. ... '52 '77 C.784 B.A. L.221 J.D. 4333 Edgewood Rd. N.E.
Shortley, Rush M., (BV) ... '47 '72 C&L.352 B.A., J.D. 1921 51st Street, NE
Shuttleworth, William R., (AV) ... '26 '53 C.352 B.A. L.976 LL.B. [Ⓒ Shuttleworth&I.]

Shuttleworth & Ingersoll, P.L.C., (AV)
115 Third Street S.E., Suite 500, 52401
Mailing Address: P.O. Box 2107, Cedar Rapids, IA 52406-2107
Telephone: 319-365-9461 Fax: 319-365-8443
URL: http://www.shuttleworthlaw.com
Michael O. McDermott; John M. Bickel; Robert D. Houghton; Richard S. Fry; Richard C. Garberson; Gary J. Streit; Carroll J. Reasoner; Steven J. Pace; Glenn L. Johnson; Robert W. Hoke, II; Thomas P. Peffer; Dennis J. McMenimen; Kevin H. Collins; William P. Prowell; Diane Kutzko; Mark L. Zaiger; Douglas R. Oelschlaeger; Wesley B. Huisinga; Dean R. Einck; Linda M. Kirsch; Connie Alt; William S. Hochstetler; Brian D. Bergstrom; Gilda L. Boyer; Nancy J. Penner; Kevin J. Caster; Theresa C. Davis; Sarah J. Gayer; Laurie L. Dawley; Jennifer E. Rinden;—Patricia L. Hoffman-Simanek; Marty L. Sutcliffe; Jace T. Bisgard; Ryan N. Carter; Heather L. Fleming. Of Counsel: Thomas M. Collins; William R. Shuttleworth; James C. Nemmers. Counsel: Jenna M. Wischmeyer.
Administrative Law, Agricultural Law, Alternative Dispute Resolution, Arbitration, Mediation, Antitrust, Unfair Trade, Bankruptcy, Banks and Banking, Biotechnology, Civil Litigation and Appellate Practice in all State and Federal Courts, Civil Rights, Commercial Law, Commercial Real Estate, Communications and Media, Computers and Software, Constitutional Law, Construction Law, Contracts, Copyrights, Corporate Law, Debtor and Creditor, Disabilities, Education Law, Elder Law, Eminent Domain, Employee Benefits, Employment Law, Energy, Environmental Law, Estate Planning, General Practice, Health Care, Hospital Law, Insurance, Insurance Defense, Intellectual Property, Labor, Land Use, Medical Malpractice, Mergers, Acquisitions, and Divestitures, Municipal Law, Natural Resources, Nonprofit and Charitable Organizations, OSHA, Partnership Law, Patents, Personal Injury, Probate, Products Liability, Professional Liability, Real Estate, Securities, Tax Law, Technology and Science, Trademarks, Trusts and Estates, Utility Law, Wills, Workers Compensation, Zoning Law.
Representative Clients: Amana Society; Archer-Daniels-Midland Co.; Cargill, Inc.; Cryovac, Inc., a Division of W. R. Grace & Co.; General Mills, Inc.; General Motors Corp.; MCI; PMX Industries, Inc.; U.S. Bank, N. A.

See Professional Biographies, CEDAR RAPIDS, IOWA

Siebenmann, John F. ... '29 '57 C.352 A.B. L.221 LL.B. Ret. Assoc. Dist. J.
Siegfried, Daniel L., (CV) '59 '86
C&L.801 B.A., J.D. Sr. Atty. & Asst. Corp. Secy., Alliant Energy
Sieh, Gregory M. ... '47 '73 C&L.352 B.B.A., J.D. 6045 Rockwell Dr., N.E.

Simmons, Perrine, Albright & Ellwood, P.L.C., (AV)
115 Third Street S.E. Suite 1200, 52401 ⊙
Telephone: 319-366-7641 Telecopier: 319-366-1917
URL: http://www.simmonsperrine.com
Members: Darrel A. Morf; James E. Shipman; Stephen J. Holtman; Iris E. Muchmore; Gregory M. Lederer; James A. Gerk; Roger W. Stone; David A. Hacker; David W. Kubicek; Matthew J. Brandes; James M. Peters; Leonard T. Strand; Mark H. Ogden; Webb L. Wassmer; Mark A. Roberts; Chad M. Von Kampen; Gregory G. Williams; Allison M. Heffern; Lynn Wickham Hartman; Kathleen A. Kleiman; Nicolas Abou-Assaly; Paul P. Morf; Philip A. Burian; Christine L. Conover; David C. Kutcher. Associates: Michael F. Williams; Elizabeth V. Croco; Patsy A. Thimmig; Jason M. Steffens; Lorie E. Reins-Schweer; Lance R. Staker. Of Counsel: James R. Snyder; Robert M. Jilek.
General Practice. Trial and Appellate Practice, Commercial, Insurance, Personal Injury, Professional Malpractice, Workers' Compensation, Environmental, Labor, Employment, Banking, Bankruptcy, Antitrust and Unfair Competition, Construction and Products Liability, Corporation Practice, Tax, Probate, Estate Planning, Real Estate, Pension, Profit-Sharing and Employee Benefits, ERISA, Mergers and Acquisitions, International and Domestic Patent and Trademark Law, Domestic Copyright Law, Family Law.
Representative Clients: D.C. Taylor Roofing Co.; Kleiman Construction Co.; Wells Fargo Bank, N.A.; Grain Processing Corp., a division of Varied Investments, Inc.; Crystal Group, Inc.; Diversified Software, Inc.; Amana Company, a Division of Goodman, Inc.; Varied Investments, Inc.; Firstar Bank, N.A., Intermec Technologies Corp.
Iowa City Office: Third Floor Tower Place, 22 South Linn Street, 52240. Telephone: 319-887-1368. Fax: 319-887-1372.

See Professional Biographies, CEDAR RAPIDS, IOWA

Sines, James L., (BV) ... '57 '83 C&L.352 B.A., J.D. [Crawford,S.R.&R.]
Skelton, Deborah M., (CV) ... '53 '96 C.520 B.A. L.352 J.D. [Ⓐ White&J.]
Skinner, L. Michael '43 '77 C.108 B.A. L.1137 J.D.
General Counsel Complex Litigaton Department, Life Investors Insurance Company of America
Slagter, Todd A. ... '75 '01 C.489 B.A. L.208 J.D. [Ⓐ Lynch D.]
Smith, Darin D. ... '65 '93 C.351 B.A. L.352 J.D. Atty., IES Industries Inc.
Smith, DJ, (BV) ... '52 '77 C.162 B.A. L.273 J.D. 121 3rd St. S.W.
Smith, Kent ... '78 '05 C.132 B.A. L.221 J.D. [Ⓐ P.Leehey]
Sneitzer, Renee V., (CV) ... '64 '93 C.350 B.A. L.352 J.D. [Ⓐ White&J.]
Snitker, Gregg R. ... '67 '95 C&L.352 B.B.A., J.D. 4333 Edgewood Rd., N.E.
Snyder, James R., (AV) ... '31 '57 C.755 L.352 LL.B. [Ⓒ Simmons,P.A.&E.]
Sole, Rick L., (BV) ... '53 '78 C&L.352 B.A., J.D. [Glasson,S.M.&C.]
Sorensen, Donna J. '50 '81 C.707 B.A. L.352 J.D.
Exec. V.P. & Tr. Div. Mgr., Firstar Bk. Iowa, N.A.
Sosalla, Robert E. ... '47 '72 Assoc. Dist. J.
Southwick, Stephen W. '46 '75 C&L.221 B.A., J.D.
V.P., Gen. Coun. & Secy., IES Industries Inc. (Pat.)
Sparks, Elizabeth A., (CV) '53 '87 C.188 B.S.S. L.352 J.D.
Gen. Coun., NRG Media, LLC
Spector, Edward M. '20 '50 C&L.659 B.S., LL.B.
(adm. in PA; not adm. in IA) 2666 Rainier Ct. N.E.‡
Spina, Dean A., (BV) ... '52 '81 C&L.352 B.A., J.D. [Bradley&R.]
Squires, Vernon P., (BV) ... '64 '93 C.951 B.A. L.494 J.D. [Bradley&R.]
Staker, Lance R. ... '71 '97 C.162 B.A. L.352 J.D. [Ⓐ Simmons,P.A.&E.]
Stapleton, Keith E., (BV) ... '24 '52 C&L.352 B.A., J.D. 222 3rd Ave. S.E.
Steele, Kelly D., (CV) ... '64 '90 C.949 B.A. L.352 J.D. 425 Second Street SE, Suite 900
Stefani, Raymond R., (AV) ... '29 '55 C&L.221 B.A., J.D. [Gray,S.&M.]
Stefani, Raymond R., II, (AV) ... '53 '79 C&L.221 B.F.A., J.D. [Gray,S.&M.]
Stefani, Richard A., (AV) ... '54 '80 C.352 B.B.A. L.190 J.D. [Gray,S.&M.]
Steffens, Jason M. ... '77 '03 C.898 B.A. L.352 J.D. [Ⓐ Simmons,P.A.&E.]
Steggall, Walter J., Jr., (BV) ... '51 '76 C.187 B.A. L.352 J.D. [Holden&S.]
Steiner, Jeanne M. ... '65 '92 C.491 B.S. L.1035 J.D. [Ⓐ Rush&N.]
Stokke, Leslie E., (BV) ... '49 '75 C.1270 B.A. L.744 J.D. 225 2nd St., SE
Stone, Roger W., (AV) ... '54 '80 C&L.352 B.A., J.D. [Simmons,P.A.&E.]
Stone, Wilford H., (BV) ... '56 '84 C.970 B.A. L.352 J.D. [Lynch D.]
Strand, Leonard T., (BV) ... '65 '90 C&L.352 B.A., J.D. [Simmons,P.A.&E.]
Streit, Gary J., (AV) ... '50 '75 C&L.352 B.S., J.D. [Shuttleworth&I.]
Struthers, Melvin, Jr. ... '28 '56 C&L.273 A.B., LL.B. Pres., MorAmerica Capital Corp.
Sueppel, Cynthia Scherrman, (BV) ... '58 '84 C&L.352 B.A., J.D. [Ⓐ Moyer&B.]
Sullivan, Gerald T., (AV) ... '37 '63 C.352 B.A. L.276 J.D. [Crawford,S.R.&R.]
Sutcliffe, Marty L. ... '78 '01 C&L.352 B.A., J.D. [Ⓐ Shuttleworth&I.]
Swift, Stephen A., (BV) ... '49 '75 C.475 B.A. L.352 J.D. [Klinger,R.&F.]
Taylor, Jeffrey P., (BV) ... '62 '89 C&L.352 B.B.A., J.D. [Klinger,R.&F.]
Taylor, Mary Louise, (CV) ... '53 '83 C&L.352 B.S., J.D. 3809 Tomahawk Trail, S.E.
Taylor, Wallace L., Attorney at Law, (CV) '47 '72
C.350 B.S. L.221 J.D. 118 3rd Ave. S.E., Rm. 326
Terpstra, H. Raymond, II, (AV) ... '56 '81 C.25 B.A. L.221 J.D. [Terpstra,E.&W.]

Terpstra, Epping & Willett, (AV)
An Association of Sole Practitioners
118 Third Avenue, S.E., Suite 500, Higley Building, 52401-1424
Telephone: 319-364-2467 Fax: 319-364-2460
Email: info@tewlaw.net
Harry R. Terpstra (1929-1998); H. Raymond Terpstra, II; Gregory J. Epping; Alfred E. Willett; Forrest W. Rosser.
Creditors Rights, Real Estate, Civil Litigation, Bankruptcy Litigation, Commercial Transactions, Probate.
References: Norwest Bank Cedar Rapids, N.A.; Hawkeye Bank of Cedar Rapids; Palo Savings Bank, Palo, IA.

See Professional Biographies, CEDAR RAPIDS, IOWA

Theobald, Gregory W. '50 '76
C.504 B.A. L.221 J.D. AEGON USA Investment Management, Inc.
Thimmig, Patsy A. ... '66 '99 C.170 B.A. L.734 J.D. [Ⓐ Simmons,P.A.&E.]
Thinnes, David G., (BV) ... '61 '87 C.190 B.A. L.352 J.D. [Thinnes&L.]
Thinnes & Liesveld, L.C., (BV) ... Higley Bldg.
Thomas, William L. ... '45 '73 C.793 B.A. L.352 J.D. Dist. J., Linn Co.
Thompson, Donald G., (AV) ... '49 '76 C&L.546 B.A., J.D. [Bradley&R.] ⊙
Thompson, Shannon P. ... '74 '00 C&L.352 B.A., J.D. [Ⓐ Bradley&R.]
Thorson, Larry J., (BV) ... '51 '76 C&L.352 B.G.S., J.D. [Ackley,K.&K.] (⊙Center Point)
Tilden, Robert C., (P.C.), (AV) ... '28 '51 C&L.352 B.A., J.D. 115 Third At. S.E.

Titler, John M., (AV) '47 '74 C.352 B.A. L.602 J.D.
320 8th Avenue, South East, P.O. Box 1168, 52401-2018
Telephone: 319-363-5563 Fax: 319-363-5678
Email: jmt@t-mlawcr.com URL: http://www.lawyers.com/johnmtitler
Bankruptcy, Real Estate, Business Law, Probate, Wills, Trusts, Estates.

See Professional Biographies, CEDAR RAPIDS, IOWA

Tresnak, Mary Jeanette, (BVⓉ) '60 '84 C.1315 B.S. L.616 J.D.
(adm. in OK; not adm. in IA) Assoc. Gen. Coun., AEGON USA, Inc.
Tripp, Todd D., (BV) ... '51 '78 C&L.352 B.G.S., J.D. Co. Atty. Off., Civil Div.
Tronvold, Jeffrey R. ... '66 '98 C.870 B.S. L.352 J.D. [Eells&T.]
Trueblood, Tralawney S. ... '63 '88 C&L.352 B.B.A., J.D. 4607 Chestnut Ridge Road NE
Turner, Carol A. ... '45 '75 C.529 B.A. L.352 J.D. Asst. Co. Atty.
Turner, Mitchell E., (BV) '54 '79 C.494 B.A. L.352 J.D.
425 Second Street SE, Suite 1010
Tvedt, Daniel C., (BV) ... '61 '87 C&L.352 B.B.A., J.D. Asst. U.S. Atty.
Usher, Crystal L., (BV) ... '56 '81 C.520 B.S.B.A. L.352 J.D. [Nazette,M.W.K.&U.]
Van Allen, Barbara Ann ... '56 '88 C.352 B.A. L.190 J.D. Legal Servs. Corp. of Iowa
Van Es, Amy D. ... '72 '98 C.1348 B.A. L.352 J.D. 302 3rd Ave., S.E.
Vermie, Craig D., (AV) '51 '77
C.350 B.S. L.221 J.D. V.P., Secy. & Gen. Coun., Aegon USA, Inc.
Vernon, William S., (AV) ... '52 '77 C.686 B.S. L.221 J.D. [Moyer&B.]
Visser, Kevin J., (AV) ... '56 '80 C.134 B.S. L.352 J.D. [Moyer&B.]
Volz, Karen A., (BV) ... '58 '83 C&L.352 B.A., J.D. [Ackley,K.&K.]
Von Kampen, Chad M., (BV) ... '67 '92 C.182 B.A. L.546 J.D. [Simmons,P.A.&E.]
von Lackum, John K., (AV) ... '29 '54 C.597 B.S. L.477 J.D. [Elderkin&P.]
Wagner, John C. ... '54 '79 C.132 B.A. L.352 J.D. [J.C.Wagner] ⊙
Wagner, John C., Law Offices, P.C. ... 1000 Collins Road N.E. (⊙Amana, Marengo)
Wallrichs, Brenda K., (CV) ... '70 '95 C.221 B.A. L.352 J.D. [Moyer&B.]
Walseth, James Patrick ... '56 '87 C&L.352 B.A., J.D. Legal Servs. Corp.
Warbasse, Steven K., (BV) ... '47 '76 C&L.352 B.A., J.D. 507 Paramount Bldg.
Wassmer, Webb L., (BV) ... '64 '89 C.910 B.A. L.659 J.D. [Simmons,P.A.&E.]
Watson, C. David '58 '85 C&L.339 B.S., J.D.
(adm. in IL; not adm. in IA) Sr. V.P.-Admin. & Gen. Coun., National Propane Corp.
Way, Daniel C. ... '51 '84 C.173 B.A. L.1035 J.D. Firstar Bk. Iowa, N.A.
Welch, Peter B., (CV) ... '50 '81 C.763 B.S. L.767 J.D. [Ⓐ Crawford,S.R.&R.]
Wendler, Guy H. ... '52 '77 C&L.352 B.B.A., J.D. 615 5th St. S.E.‡
Wendt, Ronald W., (BV) ... '44 '69 C&L.352 B.A., J.D. [Nazette,M.W.K.&U.]
Wenzel, Richard C., (BV) ... '45 '70 C.747 B.A. L.352 J.D. [Wenzel&H.]
Wenzel & Harms, P.C., (BV) ... 2750 First Ave. N.E., Ste. 420 (Pat.)
Wertz, Thomas M., (AV) ... '53 '78 C.352 B.A. L.862 J.D. [Wertz]

Wertz Law Firm, P.C., (AV)
1500 Center Street, N.E., P.O. Box 849, 52406-0849
Mailing Address: P.O. Box 849, Cedar Rapids, IA 52406-0849
Telephone: 319-861-3001 Fax: 319-861-3007
Email: twertz@wertzlaw.com URL: http://www.wertzlaw.com
Thomas M. Wertz;—Matthew D. Dake.
Workers Compensation, Personal Injury.
See Professional Biographies, CEDAR RAPIDS, IOWA

Wessels, John F. .... '14 '37 L.221 LL.B. 3910 Roxbury Dr., N.W.‡
Wessels, Robert J. .... '18 '41 L.221 LL.B. 3910 Roxbury Dr., N.W.‡
Weston, Hanna B., (CV) .... '37 '84 C.604 B.A. L.352 J.D. [Nadler&W.] ⊙
Weston, J. Michael, (AV) .... '55 '80 C&L.352 B.A., J.D. [Moyer&B.]
Weston, James K., II, (CV) .... '— '96 C.352 B.A. L.221 J.D. [T.Riley] ⊙
White, Timothy S., (AV) .... '41 '67 C&L.352 B.A., J.D. [White&J.]

White & Johnson, P.C., (AV)
First Floor American Building, 101 2nd Street, S.E., P.O. Box 5878, 52406-5878
Telephone: 319-364-0900 Facsimile: 319-364-7212
Email: w&j@wjpc.com URL: http://www.wjpc.com
Timothy S. White; J. Richard Johnson; James W. Radig;—Deborah M. Skelton; Matt J. Reilly; Robert J. Legislador; Landon R. Dufoe; Dominic F. Pechota; Renee V. Sneitzer. Independent Counsel: Ronald L. Luehrsmann; Carolyn J. Beyer.
General Practice. Trials, Personal Injury, Insurance, Workers' Compensation, Tax, Corporate, Real Estate, Probate, Domestic Relations.
See Professional Biographies, CEDAR RAPIDS, IOWA

Whittington, Gary '54 '88 C.802 B.A. L.846 J.D.
(adm. in NY; not adm. in IA) Asst. Gen. Coun., AEGON USA Realty Advisors, Inc.
Wilkinson, Thomas J., Jr., (BV) ..... '34 '62 C.162 B.A. L.352 J.D. [Crawford,S.R.&R.]
Willems, Daniel W., (CV) .... '57 '85 C.132 B.A. L.352 J.D. 641 40th St., S.E.
Willett, Alfred E., (BV) .... '58 '84 C&L.546 B.A., J.D. [Terpstra,E.&W.]
Willey, Bruce A., (BV) .... '— '90 C&L.352 B.B.A., J.D. [Willey,O.M.L.&H.]
Willey, Wythe .... '42 '67 C.350 B.S. L.352 J.D. [Willey]
Willey Law Firm .... 101 2nd St. S.E., Ste. 502
Willey, O'Brien, Mullin, Laverty & Hanrahan, L.C., (BV) .... 3519 Center Point Road, NE
Williams, Gregory G., (BV) '59 '85
C&L.352 B.A., J.D. [Simmons,P.A.&E.] (See Pat. Sect.) ⊙
Williams, Michael F. '60 '91
C.898 B.A. L.352 J.D. [Simmons,P.A.&E.] (See Pat. Sect.)
Wilson, Dawn R. .... '66 '04 C.1552 L.352 J.D. 162 Collins Rd. N.E., Ste. 332
Wilson, Robert F., (BV) .... '26 '51 C&L.352 B.A., J.D. 210 2nd St Se Ste 810
Wischmeyer, Jenna M. .... '73 '99 C.350 B.S. L.378 J.D. [Shuttleworth&I.]

Wolff, Karla M., (BV) '61 '90 C.491 B.A. L.352 J.D.
866 First Avenue NE, 52402
Telephone: 319-366-7516 Fax: 319-366-7880
Email: kmwolff2@aol.com URL: http://www.lawyers.com/kmwolff
Family Law, Divorce, Custody, Juvenile Law, Adoption Law.
See Professional Biographies, CEDAR RAPIDS, IOWA

Wolle, Thomas D., (BV) .... '66 '92 C.427 B.A. L.352 J.D. [Moyer&B.]
Wright, Stephanie Johnson, (CV) '— '92
C.502 B.S. L.596 J.D. Asst. U.S. Atty., U.S. Atty. Off.
Yoder, Erica L. .... '67 '00 C.132 B.A. L.352 J.D. United Fire & Casualty Co.
York, Franklin R., (BV) .... '56 '80 C.1257 B.A. L.352 J.D. [Ackley,K.&K.]
Zaiger, Mark L., (AV) .... '53 '80 C.309 A.B. L.352 J.D. [Shuttleworth&I.]
Zbaracki, Andrew J., (BV⊕) ..... '65 '95 C.350 B.S. L.436 J.D. 4333 Edgewood Rd. N.E.
Zimmermann, Richard H., (BV) ..... '44 '77 C.164 B.A. L.352 J.D. 101 2nd St Se Ste 904
Zylstra, David J. .... '72 '98 C.228 A.B. L.352 J.D. [Bradley&R.]

CENTER POINT, 2,007, *Linn Co.*

Ackley, Kopecky & Kingery, (AV) .... Franklin at Iowa St. (⊙Cedar Rapids, Central City)
Thorson, Larry J., (BV) '51 '76 C&L.352 B.G.S., J.D.
[Ackley,K.&K.] (⊙Cedar Rapids)

CENTERVILLE, * 5,936, *Appanoose Co.*

Anders, Thomas L., (BV) .... '45 '73 C&L.352 B.A., J.D. 508 Drake
Craver, James S., (BV) .... '43 '68 C.352 B.B.A. L.221 J.D. Alpine Plaza
Griffing, Meredith R. .... '14 '44 C.351 B.S. L.221 LL.B. 121 N. 13th St.‡
Griffing, Roger M., (BV) .... '37 '80 C.352 B.A. L.221 J.D. [Griffing]
Griffing Law Office, (BV) .... 121 N. 13th St.
Grothe, Bradley M., (BV) .... '67 '94 C.350 B.S. L.221 J.D. [Orsborn,B.M.&G.]
Kreiman, Keith A., (CV) .... '54 '78 C.988 B.A. L.352 J.D. 303 N. 13th St.
Milani, James G., (AV) .... '33 '58 C&L.352 B.A., J.D. [Orsborn,B.M.&G.]

Norris, Verle W.
(See Corydon)

Orsborn, Bauerle, Milani & Grothe, L.L.P., (AV)
105 West Van Buren Street, P.O. Box 518, 52544 ⊙
Telephone: 641-856-3251 Fax: 641-856-5548
Email: obmgc@sirisonline.com URL: http://www.obmglaw.com
James G. Milani (Resident); Bradley M. Grothe; George A. Milani (1900-1992).
General Practice in all Courts. Litigation, Probate and Real Estate.
Representative Clients: Iowa Trust and Savings Bank, Centerville; Farmers Bank of Northern Missouri, N.A.; Centerville, Iowa; Firstar Bank N.A., Centerville; Indian Hills Community College, Centerville; The Continental Holdings Corporation, Centerville; Wells Fargo Bank, Iowa, N.A. .
Ottumwa, Iowa Office: 110 East Third, P. O. Box 878. Telephone: 641-682-5447. Fax: 641-682-6940.
See Professional Biographies, CENTERVILLE, IOWA

Sidles, Sheila D. .... '25 '85 C.350 B.S. L.221 J.D. 110 N. 12th St.‡
Wilson, Daniel P. .... '52 '77 C.352 B.A. L.221 J.D. Dist. J.

CENTRAL CITY, 1,063, *Linn Co.*

Ackley, Kopecky & Kingery, (AV) .... P.O. Box 277 (⊙Cedar Rapids, Center Point)
Meyer, Douglas C., (BV) '48 '74 C.177 B.A. L.352 J.D.
[Ackley,K.&K.] (⊙Cedar Rapids)
Wilkinson, Susan E. '66 '89 C.597 B.A. L.796 J.D.
(adm. in TX; not adm. in IA) 5573 Hills Mill Rd.‡

CHARITON, * 4,616, *Lucas Co.*

Ambelang, Richard L. .... '36 '61 C&L.221 B.S., J.D. [Shelton]
Goldsmith, Paul M., (BV) .... '56 '80 C&L.352 B.B.A., J.D. Co. Atty.
Mefferd, James B., Jr., (BV) .... '43 '72 C.350 B.S. L.900 J.D. [J.B.Mefferd]
Mefferd, James, P.C., (BV) .... 224 N. Main St.
Meyer, Raymond C., (BV) .... '58 '84 C.502 B.A. L.352 J.D. [Meyer]
Meyer Law Office, (BV) .... 106 N. Grand St.
Morr, Richard D. .... '31 '57 C&L.352 B.A., LL.B. Dist. J.
Petersen, R. William, (BV) .... '50 '76 C.352 B.S. L.190 J.D. [Shelton]
Shelton, William L., (AV) .... '38 '62 C.353 B.A. L.352 J.D. [Shelton]
Shelton Law Firm, (AV) .... 1920 Court Ave.

CHARLES CITY, * 7,878, *Floyd Co.*

Antes, Jon W., (BV) .... '44 '70 C&L.221 B.A., J.D. [Elwood,O.S.B.&C.] ⊙
Braun, Joseph Patrick, (CV) .... '68 '95 C.494 B.A. L.1035 J.D. [Elwood,O.S.B.&C.] ⊙
Dettmer, Marilyn J., (BV) .... '46 '92 C.898 B.A. L.221 J.D. Co. Atty.
Eggert, Robert J., (AV) .... '22 '48 C&L.352 B.A., J.D. [Eggert,E.F.&M.]
Eggert, Erb, Frye & Mulcahy, P.L.C., (AV) .... 701 Blunt Parkway
Elwood, Henry L., (AV) .... '34 '59 C.187 B.A. L.221 J.D. [Elwood,O.S.B.&C.] ⊙

Elwood, O'Donohoe, Stochl, Braun & Churbuck, (AV)
116 North Main Street, P.O. Box 307, 50616 ⊙
Telephone: 641-228-8054 Fax: 641-228-8057
Email: elwood@myclearwave.net
Members of Firm: Henry L. Elwood; James E. O'Donohoe (1921-1998); Christopher F. O'Donohoe; Richard D. Stochl; Judith Mack O'Donohoe; Joseph Patrick Braun; Lewis M. Churbuck (1972-2003). Associates: Jeremiah W. White; Todd P. Prichard. Of Counsel: Richard P. TeKippe; Jon W. Antes.
General Practice in State and Federal Courts. Litigation, Insurance Defense, Probate, Estate Planning, Trusts and Wills, Real Estate, Corporate, Banking and Taxation Law. Trials and Appeals.
Representative Clients: Grinnell Mutual Reinsurance Co.; United Fire & Casualty Insurance Co.; Board of Trustees, New Hampton Municipal Light Plant; First Citizens National Bank, New Hampton, Iowa; Alliance Pipeline; Cresco Union Savings Bank, Cresco, Iowa; City of Cresco, Iowa; Featherlite., Inc.; Community First National Bank, Protivin, Iowa.
Cresco, Iowa Office: 217 North Elm Street. P.O. Box 377, 52136. Telephone: 563-547-3321. Fax: 563-547-3189.
New Hampton, Iowa Office: 101 North Locust Avenue, P.O. Box 310, 50659. Telephone: 641-394-5943. Fax: 641-394-5945.
West Union, Iowa Office: 125 N. Vine, P.O. Box 475, 52175. Telephone: 563-422-5631. Fax: 563-422-5632.

Erb, James A., (AV) .... '40 '66 C.352 B.A. L.976 LL.B. [Eggert,E.F.&M.]
Frye, Jack W. .... '21 '48 C.293 B.A. L.352 J.D. Sr. Dist. J.
Frye, William M., (BV) .... '52 '77 C.170 B.A. L.352 J.D. [Eggert,E.F.&M.]

Kennedy and Kennedy
(See New Hampton)

Magee, Gerald W. .... '43 '67 C&L.352 B.A., J.D. Assoc. Juv. J.
Marzen, Jesse .... '78 '05 C.351 B.A. L.1571 J.D. 701 Blunt Parkway
McCartney, Ralph F. .... '24 '50 C.350 B.Sc. L.477 J.D. Sr. J., Ct. of App.
Mulcahy, Rodney Eric, (CV) .... '72 '97 C.350 B.A. L.616 J.D. [Eggert,E.F.&M.]
Noah, Keith S., (AV) .... '20 '48 C&L.352 B.A., J.D. 200 N. Johnson St.‡
Noah, Smith & Schuknecht, P.L.C., (AV) .... 200 N. Johnson St.
O'Donohoe, Christopher F., (AV) '50 '75 C.118 B.A. L.178 J.D.
[Elwood,O.S.B.&C.] ⊙
O'Donohoe, Judith Mack, (BV) '51 '76 C.118 B.A. L.569 J.D.
[Elwood,O.S.B.&C.] ⊙
Pederson, Laurie .... '58 '01 C.106 B.A. L.1035 J.D. 1006 Waller St.
Prichard, Todd P. .... '— '04 C&L.352 B.A., J.D. [Elwood,O.S.B.&C.] ⊙
Schroeder, DeDra, (BV) .... '69 '95 C.352 B.A. L.793 J.D. [Schroeder]
Schroeder, Russell H., Jr., (BV) .... '47 '73 C.352 B.A. L.793 J.D. [Schroeder]
Schroeder Law Office, (BV) .... 507 Clark Street
Schuknecht, Cynthia, (BV) .... '57 '90 C.351 B.A. L.352 J.D. [Noah,S.&S.]
Smith, James F., (AV) .... '23 '50 C.604 B.A. L.352 J.D. 200 N. Johnson St.
Smith, Ralph A., (AV) .... '51 '76 C.118 B.A. L.352 J.D. [Noah,S.&S.]
Stochl, Richard D., (BV) .... '64 '89 C.927 B.S. L.352 J.D. [Elwood,O.S.B.&C.] ⊙
Sutton, Roger L., (BV) .... '44 '69 C.98 B.A. L.221 J.D. [Sutton]
Sutton Law Office, (BV) .... 119 North Jackson
TeKippe, Richard P., (BV) ..... '40 '64 C.177 B.A. L.352 J.D. [Elwood,O.S.B.&C.] ⊙
Troge, Ann M., (BV) .... '63 '92 C.351 B.A. L.221 J.D. 1208 Clark St.
White, Jeremiah W. .... '— '04 C.351 B.A. L.352 J.D. [Elwood,O.S.B.&C.] ⊙

CHARTER OAK, 497, *Crawford Co.*

Boddicker, Joe L., (BV) .... '39 '64 C.177 B.A. L.352 J.D. 50 Main St. (⊙Denison)

CHEROKEE, * 5,369, *Cherokee Co.*

Blair, David J., (AV) .... '42 '68 C.309 B.A. L.352 J.D. [D.J.Blair]

Blair, David J., P.C., Law Office of, (AV)
425 Sumner Street, P.O. Box 458, 51012
Telephone: 712-225-2323 Fax: 712-225-2727
Email: davidblair@blairadr.com URL: http://www.blairadr.com
David J. Blair.
ADR, Mediation, Arbitration.
See Professional Biographies, CHEROKEE, IOWA

Cook, John H., Jr., (BV) .... '49 '74 C.350 B.S. L.221 J.D. [Herrick,A.C.C.C.&C.]
Cook, Richard Ary, (BV) .... '58 '83 C.350 B.S. L.221 J.D. [Herrick,A.C.C.C.&C.]
Cook, William D., (BV) .... '60 '87 C.350 B.S. L.900 J.D. [Herrick,A.C.C.C.&C.]
Cozine, Mark Reed, (BV) .... '56 '84 C.488 B.S. L.793 J.D. [Wibe&C.]
Hankens, Don R. .... '08 '35 L.352 P.O. Box 250‡
Hankens, R. Stephen, (BV) .... '45 '72 C&L.221 B.S.B.A., J.D. 112 N. 2nd St.

Herrick, Ary, Cook, Cook, Cook & Cook, (BV)
209 West Willow Street, P.O. Box 209, 51012
Telephone: 712-225-5175 FAX: 712-225-5178
Members of Firm: William K. Herrick (1878-1944); Lester C. Ary (1893-1962); John Howard Cook (1917-1996); John H. Cook, Jr.; Richard Ary Cook; William D. Cook.
General Practice. Estate Planning, Probate, Corporation, Personal Injury, Commercial Litigation and Taxation Law. Trials.
Attorneys for: Cherokee State Bank; Cherokee Community School District; Lundell Construction Co., Inc.; Tiel Sanford Memorial Fund; Simonsen Mill Inc.; Sioux Valley Memorial Hospital; Obeco Inc.; Christensen Brothers Concrete; Cherokee Community Credit Union; First Trust and Savings Bank of Aurelia.
See Professional Biographies, CHEROKEE, IOWA

Loughlin, John D., (BV) .... '25 '50 C&L.352 B.A. [Loughlin]
Loughlin, John P., (BV) .... '55 '87 C.352 B.B.A. L.300 J.D. [Loughlin]
Loughlin Law Firm, (BV) .... 231 W. Maple Street
Meloy, Daniel A., (CV) .... '58 '95 C.350 B.S. L.190 J.D. [Sayre,W.&M.]
Miller, M. Wallace, (BV) .... '35 '60 C&L.352 B.A., J.D. [Miller,M.M.] ⊙
Miller, Marvin W., (BV) .... '57 '82 C&L.352 B.A., J.D. [Miller,M.M.]
Miller, Miller, Miller, P.C., (BV) .... 216 W. Main St. (⊙Aurelia)
Phillips, Kristal L., (CV) .... '75 '99 C&L.793 B.A., J.D. [Wibe&C.]
Red Deer, Sharon L. .... '53 '02 C.999 B.S. L.793 J.D. [Red D.]
Red Deer Law Office .... 1509 540th St.
Sayre, David L., (AV) .... '19 '42 C&L.352 B.A., J.D. [Sayre,W.&M.] ‡

Sayre, Wittgraf & Meloy, (BV)
223 Pine Street, P.O. Box 535, 51012
Telephone: 712-225-6481 Fax: 712-225-5300
Email: swmlaw@mchsi.com
Lew McDonald (1884-1963); David L. Sayre (Retired). Members of Firm: George W. Wittgraf; Daniel A. Meloy.
General, Trial and Appellate Practice, Probate, Estate Planning, Corporation, Personal Injury, Taxation and Real Estate Law.

(This Listing Continued)

Sayre, Wittgraf & Meloy (Continued)

Representative Clients: Central Trust and Savings Bank; C-M-L Telephone Cooperative Association; Valley Pharmacy Corp.; Schoon Construction, Inc.; Sioux Valley Memorial Hospital; Beck Ranch, Inc.; First Cooperative Association.

See Professional Biographies, CHEROKEE, IOWA

Schaefer, Donavon D. .... '49 '79 C&L.352 B.A., J.D. Dist. Assoc. J.
Wibe, John A., (BV) .... '40 '71 C.350 B.S. L.352 J.D. [Wibe&C.]
Wibe & Cozine, L.L.P., (BV) .... 427 W. Main St.
Wittgraf, George W., (BV) .... '45 '75 C.293 B.A. L.221 J.D. [Sayre,W.&M.]

CLARENCE, 936, *Cedar Co.*

Dircks, Durwood W., (BV) .... '28 '55 C.352 B.A. L.221 J.D. [Dircks,R.&M.]
Dircks, Russell A., (BV) .... '55 '79 C&L.352 B.A., J.D. [Dircks,R.&M.]
Dircks, Ridenour & Macek, (BV) .... P.O. Box 387 (©Davenport)
Freese, Roger D., (BV) .... '44 '68 C.350 B.S. L.352 J.D. Jud. Mag.

CLARINDA, * 5,690, *Page Co.*

Almquist, Anthony J., (BV) ...... '63 '95 C.352 B.A. L.221 J.D. 109 E. Main St., Ste. 478
Anderson, Richard T., (BV) .... '56 '87 C.352 B.A. L.221 J.D. [Millhone&A.]
Bitting, Ronny M., (AV) .... '45 '73 C.351 B.A. L.221 J.D. [Turner,J.&B.]
Cassat, Kenneth L. .... '25 '50 C.641 A.B. L.352 LL.B. 508 N. 15th St.‡
Davidson, Richard G. .... '29 '54 C&L.221 B.A., LL.B. 600 N. 15th St.
Davidson, Richard H., (BV) .... '59 '85 C&L.221 B.A., J.D. [Davidson]
Davidson Law Firm, P.C., (BV) .... 109 E. Main
Jones, Paul W., (AV) .... '37 '62 C.293 B.A. L.477 J.D. [Turner,J.&B.]
Millhone, James N., (AV) .... '37 '61 C.641 A.B. L.477 J.D. [Millhone&A.]
Millhone & Anderson, (AV) .... 101 E. Main St.
Turner, Sanford A., (AV) .... '35 '63 C.593 B.S. L.352 J.D. [Turner,J.&B.]

Turner, Jones & Bitting, (AV)
301 East Main Street, P.O. Box 231, 51632
Telephone: 712-542-2151 Fax: 712-542-2031
Email: tjblaw@clarinda.heartland.net
Members of Firm: Clinton H. Turner (1909-1969); Sanford A. Turner; Paul W. Jones; Ronny M. Bitting.
General Practice. Probate, Real Estate and Banking Law. Trials.
Representative Clients: Citizens State Bank, Clarinda, Iowa; City of Clarinda; Cities of Coin, Braddyville, Shambaugh, Blanchard and Northboro, Iowa; Lisle Corp., Clarinda, Iowa; Page County Federal Savings; Oxley Farms, Inc.
References: Citizens State Bank; Page County State Bank of Clarinda, Iowa.

See Professional Biographies, CLARINDA, IOWA

CLARION, * 2,968, *Wright Co.*

Anderson, Timothy M.
(See Garner)

Bordwell, Richard, (BV) .... '57 '82 C&L.190 B.S.B.A., J.D. [Brinton,B.&J.]
Brinton, Robert W., (BV) .... '47 '72 C.427 B.A. L.352 J.D. [Brinton,B.&J.]
Brinton, Bordwell & Johnson, Law Offices of, (BV) .... 120 Central Ave. W.
Johnson, David R. .... '64 '90 C.351 B.A. L.352 J.D. [Brinton,B.&J.]
Kay, Robert B., (BV) .... '22 '47 C.16 L.221 J.D. 120 Central Ave. W.
Knoshaug, Dewayne A., (BV) .... '37 '63 C.350 B.S. L.221 LL.B. [Knoshaug]
Knoshaug Law Firm, (BV) .... 120 Central Ave. E.

Malloy Law Firm
(See Goldfield)

CLARKSVILLE, 1,382, *Butler Co.*

Ackerman, Ivan J., (BV) ... '39 '63 C&L.352 B.A., J.D. [Engelbrecht,A.&H.] (©Waverly)
Engelbrecht, Ackerman & Hassman, (AV)
101 S. Main St. (©Readlyn, Tripoli, Waverly)
Fokkena, Habbo G., (BV) '47 '75
C.351 B.A. L.352 J.D. Chapter 7 Panel Trustee [Fokkena]
Fokkena Law Office, (BV) .... 109 N. Main St.

CLEAR LAKE, 8,183, *Cerro Gordo Co.*

Berry, Matthew F., (BV) .... '55 '80 C&L.352 B.B.A., J.D. [Berry&C.]
Berry & Casperson, P.L.C., (BV) .... 306 Main Avenue
Biebesheimer, Charles H., (BV) .... '62 '80 C&L.352 B.A., J.D. [Goranson,S.&L.]
Casperson, Timothy A., (CV) .... '68 '96 C.351 B.A. L.352 J.D. [Berry&C.]
Eastman, F. David, (BV) .... '50 '82 C.961 B.S. L.900 J.D. 914 N. 8th Street West
Goranson, Donald L., (AV) .... '26 '49 C&L.352 B.A., J.D. [Goranson,S.&L.]
Goranson, Stone & Lovell, (AV) .... 304 Main Avenue
Grabinski, Douglas R., (CV) .... '47 '74 C.513 B.A. L.352 J.D. [Grabinski]
Grabinski Law Firm, (CV) .... 705 1/2 7th Ave. N.
Isensee, Robt. H. .... '12 '35 C&L.352 B.A., J.D. 3714 Northshore Dr.‡
Kaufman, Karen R., (CV) .... '69 '98 C.106 B.A. L.802 J.D. 314 N. Seventh St.
Krause, Michael J. .... '66 '93 C&L.352 B.B.A., J.D. 22 N. 3rd St.
Lovell, Thomas A., (BV) .... '54 '79 C.221 B.A. L.1051 J.D. [Goranson,S.&L.]
Oltrogge, M. Wayne, (BV) .... '38 '63 C&L.352 B.B.A., LL.B. [Oltrogge]
Oltrogge Law Office, P.C., (BV) .... 314 N. 7th St.
Schoeller, Mark, (BV) .... '51 '76 C&L.221 B.A., J.D. 505 Main Ave.
Schuler, Louis E., (AV) .... '22 '49 C.293 B.A. L.352 J.D. 408 N. Shore Dr.‡
Stone, Phillip J., (BV) .... '50 '76 C&L.352 B.B.A., J.D. [Goranson,S.&L.]
Swanson, Robert S., (BV) .... '44 '69 C.118 B.A. L.802 J.D. 508 Main Avenue
Swift, John L., (BV) .... '34 '60 C&L.352 B.A., LL.B. 1005 N. Shore Dr.

CLINTON, * 27,772, *Clinton Co.*

Bruhn, James D., (BV) .... '55 '80 C.106 B.A. L.352 J.D. [Farwell&B.]
Chambers, J. Drew, (P.C.), (AV) .... '46 '73 C&L.221 B.A., J.D. [Holleran,S.M.&S.]
Current, T. Randy, (BV) .... '56 '82 C&L.352 B.A., J.D. [Frey,H.&C.]
Farwell, Christopher L., (BV) .... '62 '87 C&L.352 B.A., J.D. [🄰 Farwell&B.]
Farwell, Jeffrey L., (BV) .... '62 '91 C.352 B.A. L.589 J.D. [🄰 Farwell&B.]
Farwell, Richard W., P.C., (AV) .... '36 '61 C.350 B.S. L.352 J.D. [Farwell&B.]
Farwell & Bruhn, (AV) .... 343 5th Avenue South
Frey, A. John, Jr., (AV) .... '44 '69 C&L.352 B.A., J.D. [Frey,H.&C.]

Frey, Haufe & Current, P.L.C., (AV)
408 South 2nd Street, P.O. Box 668, 52733-0668
Telephone: 563-242-1832 Fax: 563-242-1845
Email: fhc@cis.net
L. L. Jurgemeyer (1918-1980); A. John Frey, Jr.; Stephen D. Haufe; T. Randy Current.
General Practice. Corporation, Business, Real Estate, Probate, Domestic, Criminal, Administrative Law, Trials and Appeals, Insurance Defense Law, Estate Planning, Personal Injury.

See Professional Biographies, CLINTON, IOWA

Fullerton, Mathew J., (CV) .... '61 '95 C.877 B.S.Econ. L.878 J.D. 230 4th Ave. S.
Haufe, Stephen D., (AV) .... '48 '74 C.118 B.A. L.228 J.D. [Frey,H.&C.]
Helscher, David J. .... '55 '79 C.352 B.A. L.124 J.D. Clinton National Bank
Holleran, Shaw, Murphy & Stoutner, (AV) .... 86 Main Avenue
Johansen, Bruce D., (BV) .... '46 '70 C.350 B.S. L.352 J.D. City Atty.
Kross, Edward J., (BV) .... '49 '74 C.707 B.A. L.352 J.D. [Van Scoy&K.]
Lonergan, Thomas D., (BV) .... '49 '76 C.999 B.A. L.190 J.D. [Lonergan&R.]
Lonergan & Rolfes, (BV) .... 214 Main Ave.

McCarthy, Lammers & Hines
(See Davenport)

McGee, Robert J., (AV) .... '52 '79 C.707 B.A. L.352 J.D. [McGee]
McGee Law Offices, P.C., (AV) .... 1226 N. 2nd St.
Ostergren, Jennifer Lerner, (CV) .... '72 '97 C.293 B.A. L.221 J.D. Asst. Co. Atty.
Pelton, Charles H. .... '40 '66 C&L.352 B.A., J.D. Dist. J.
Pfeffer, Paul E., Law Office, (BV) .... '42 '68 C&L.352 B.B.A., J.D. 511 S. 3rd St.
Pillers, G. Wylie, III, (BV) .... '41 '65 C&L.879 B.A., J.D. [Pillers,P.&P.]
Pillers, James L., (BV) .... '45 '70 C&L.879 B.A., J.D. [Pillers,P.&P.]
Pillers, Pillers & Pillers, P.C., (BV) .... 1127 N. Second St.
Rolfes, Gary J., (BV) .... '47 '76 C.352 B.B.A. L.365 J.D. [Lonergan&R.]
Schoenauer, Kenneth F., (BV) .... '49 '74 C.177 B.A. L.190 J.D. [Schoenauer]
Schoenauer Law Offices, P.C., (BV) .... 230 4th Ave., S.
Schultz, Lawrence H., (CV) .... '59 '84 C.927 B.A. L.221 J.D. Co. Atty.
Searle, Andrew C. .... '55 '80 C&L.352 B.A., J.D. Asst. Co. Atty.
Shaff, David O., (AV) .... '24 '50 C&L.352 B.A., J.D. 408 S. 2nd St.‡
Sivright, David H., Jr. .... '43 '69 C&L.378 B.S., J.D. Dist. Ct. J.
Smith, Lauren Ashley, (CV) .... '24 '57 C&L.494 B.S., J.D. 230 4th Ave., S.
Stoutner, Jeffrey B., (P.C.), (AV) .... '44 '69 C&L.352 B.A., J.D. [Holleran,S.M.&S.]
Van Scoy, Jerry D., (AV) .... '47 '72 C.350 B.S. L.352 J.D. [Van Scoy&K.]

Van Scoy & Kross, P.C., (AV)
410 South Second Street, 52732
Telephone: 563-242-2827 Fax: 563-242-0540
Jerry D. Van Scoy; Edward J. Kross.
General Practice. Probate, Wills, Corporate Law, Real Estate, Personal Injury, Bankruptcy, Trials and Appeals, Family Law, Estate Planning, School Law, Business Law.

See Professional Biographies, CLINTON, IOWA

VanZee, Arlen J. .... '45 '73 C.132 B.A. L.352 J.D. Assoc. Dist. J.
Vilmont, William M., (BV) .... '41 '72 C.177 B.A. L.190 J.D. 519 S. 3rd St.
Watson, Bert M., (BV) .... '49 '76 C.351 B.A. L.352 J.D. Jud. Mag.
Wolfe, John J., Jr., Law Office of, (BV) '39 '66 C&L.276 B.S.F.S., J.D.
337 4th Ave., S.

CLIVE, 12,855, *Dallas & Polk Cos.*

Alphson, John A., Jr. .... '30 '60 C&L.585 Ph.B., LL.B. 1585 N.W. 81 St.
Boecker, Theodore R., (AV) .... '47 '73 C.190 B.A. L.221 J.D. [Petosa,P.&B.]
Boot, Kevin P. .... '— '01 C.352 B.A. L.273 J.D. 1753 N.W. 122nd Ct
Brown, Terrence D., (AV) .... '54 '81 C.502 B.S. L.910 J.D. [Hixson,B.&P.]
Gilyard, Kimberly R. .... '68 '00 C&L.260 B.A., J.D. 1683 NW 100th Place
Goettsch, Cecil L., (AV) .... '43 '68 C&L.352 B.B.A., J.D. 13565 Village Ct.
Goodell, Shelley L. .... '67 '94 C.36 B.S. L.793 J.D. 1400 Country Club Blvd.‡
Hixson, J. Russell, (BV) .... '63 '89 C&L.352 B.B.A., J.D. [Hixson,B.&P.]
Hixson, Brown & Parrish-Sams, P.C., (AV) .... 1360 121st Street, Suite A
Hopkins, Benjamin W., (BV) .... '64 '97 C.252 B.S. L.221 J.D. [Petosa,P.&B.]
Hoyt, Francis C., Jr., (BV) .... '49 '75 C&L.352 B.A., J.D. 10436 Clark St.
Hyland, Thomas P., (AV) .... '30 '59 C&L.221 B.S., LL.B. 13595 Village Ct.
Keating, Anne E. .... '51 '76 C.350 B.S. L.352 J.D. 13703 Lakeshore Drive
Parrish-Sams, R. Saffin .... '71 '98 C&L.352 B.B.A., J.D. [Hixson,B.&P.]
Petosa, Stephen J., (AV) .... '43 '68 C.686 B.S. L.352 J.D. [Petosa,P.&B.]

Petosa, Petosa & Boecker, L.L.P., (AV)
1350 Northwest 138th Street, Suite 100, 50325-8308
Telephone: 515-222-9400 Fax: 515-222-9121
Email: spetosa@petosalaw.com
Members of Firm: Stephen J. Petosa; Theodore R. Boecker; Benjamin W. Hopkins.
General Civil and Trial Practice. Corporation, Real Estate, Foreclosure, Zoning, Municipal, Taxation, Probate, Estate Planning and Bankruptcy Law.
Representative Clients: American Federal Savings Assn.; Hamm's Des Moines Co.; J. C. Service Co.
Reference: Bankers Trust Co.

See Professional Biographies, CLIVE, IOWA

Powell, Mark J. .... '74 '04 C.98 B.A. L.508 J.D. 8554 Alice Ave.
Ramzy, C. Austin, Jr. .... '49 '73 C&L.326 B.B.A., J.D. 1776 N.W. 109th Ct‡
Stone, Irving E., Jr. .... '39 '64 C.350 L.221 J.D. Pres., Peoples Fin. Co.
Welu, Constance, (AV) .... '50 '87 C&L.221 B.S., J.D. 1476 N.W. 75th St.
Wynn, Robert A. .... '41 '66 C&L.221 B.S., J.D. Corp. Coun., MB Investments, Inc.

COLFAX, 2,223, *Jasper Co.*

Bump, Charles M. .... '11 '35 C&L.221 14763 Fame Ave.‡
Luthens, August H., (BV) .... '33 '69 C&L.221 B.S.E., J.D. [Luthens] ©
Luthens, Erik A., (BV) .... '64 '91 C.352 B.S. L.221 J.D. [Luthens] ©
Luthens Law Offices, P.C., (BV) .... Eight West Howard Street (©West Des Moines)

COLUMBUS JUNCTION, 1,900, *Louisa Co.*

Newell, Russell R., (AV) .... '21 '49 C&L.208 B.S., LL.B. [Newell&S.]
Newell & Sents, (AV) .... 213 Main St.
Schweitzer, Jay T., (BV) .... '47 '76 C.352 B.B.A. L.221 J.D. [Schweitzer&W.]
Schweitzer & Wink, (BV) .... 222 Main St.
Sents, Steven A., (BV) .... '59 '84 C.937 B.A. L.352 J.D. [Newell&S.]
Wink, Timothy K., (BV) .... '57 '83 C&L.352 B.B.A., J.D. [Schweitzer&W.]

CORALVILLE, 15,123, *Johnson Co.*

Becker, Janice M., (BV) .... '40 '80 C&L.352 B.A., J.D. [McMurray&B.]
Bowen, Karmell .... '61 '00 C&L.352 B.A., J.D. [Bowen]
Bowen Law Firm, LLC .... 800 Mesquite Dr.
Diehl, Donald L. .... '32 '60 C&L.352 B.A., LL.B. City Atty.

Eells & Tronvold Law Offices, P.L.C.
(See Cedar Rapids)

Fairfield, Clare J. .... '65 '90 C&L.352 B.B.A., J.D. 700 Forest Edge Dr.
Lande, Roger L., (AV) '36 '61
C&L.352 B.A., J.D. [Stanley,L.&H.] (©Davenport, Muscatine)
McAndrew, Paul J., Jr., (BV) .... '57 '83 C&L.352 B.A., J.D. [P.McAndrew]

McAndrew, Paul, Law Firm, (BV)
2590 Holiday Road, Suite 100, 52241
Telephone: 319-887-1690 Fax: 319-887-1693
Email: paulm@paulmcandrew.com URL: http://www.mcandrewlaw.com
Paul J. McAndrew, Jr.
Language: Spanish.
Workers' Compensation, Social Security.

See Professional Biographies, CORALVILLE, IOWA

McMurray, Thomas H., (BV) .... '42 '70 C.293 B.A. L.352 J.D. [McMurray&B.]

McMurray and Becker, (BV) .... 2210 9th St., Ste. 1

Meardon, Sueppel & Downer P.L.C.
(See Iowa City)

Murray, Noelle R., (CVⓉ) ......'67 '93 C.352 B.A. L.496 J.D. 1150 5th Street, Suite 280
Muzzin, Paulina Treiger ......'68 '97 C.477 B.B.A. L.215 J.D. 551 Highland Park Avenue
Nelson, W. Eric ....'63 '99 C&L.352 B.A., J.D. P.O. Box 5554
O'Conner, Timothy R. ....'67 '01 C.351 B.A. L.352 J.D. [T.O'Conner]
O'Conner, Timothy, Attorney at Law .... P.O. Box 5266
Olson, Douglas V., Law Office, (BV) '50 '75 C.350 B.S. L.352 J.D.
1100 5th St., Ste. 210
Olson, Kevin, (CV) ....'72 '99 C.427 B.A. L.1035 J.D. 1400 5th St.

Richard, Dell A., (BV) '49 '75 C.132 B.A. L.352 J.D.
1150 5th Street, Suite 280, 52241
Telephone: 319-354-9592 Facsimile: 319-354-7957
Email: dell@darichardlaw.com URL: http://www.dellarichard.com
Associate: Corey W. Schatz.
Business Law, Commercial Real Estate, Corporate Law, Guardianships and Conservatorships, Leases and Leasing, Partnership Law, Probate, Real Estate Law, Trusts and Estates, Wills.
References: Hills Bank & Trust, Hills, Iowa; Iowa State Bank & Trust Company, Iowa City, Iowa.
Representative Clients: Furnished upon request.

See Professional Biographies, CORALVILLE, IOWA

Schatz, Corey W. ....'— '05 [A] D.A.Richard]
Schultz, Louis W. ....'27 '49 C.132 L.221 LL.B. 1727 Brown Deer Rd.‡

Stanley, Lande & Hunter, A Professional Corporation, (AV)
2201 East Grantview Drive, Suite 200, 52241 ⊙
Telephone: 319-248-9000 Facsimile: 319-248-9001
Email: Contact.us@slhlaw.com URL: http://www.slhlaw.com
Roger L. Lande.
General Civil and Trial Practice. Corporation, Business, Banking, Taxation, Securities, Tax-Exempt Financing, Labor, Employment Discrimination, Administrative, Creditor Bankruptcy and Agricultural Law, Insurance Defense, Personal Injury and Property Damage Law, Pension and Profit-Sharing, Real Estate, Probate, Estate Planning and Charitable Trusts and Foundations Law.
General Counsel for: First National Bank of Muscatine.
Representative Clients: HON Industries, Inc. and its subsidiaries; Milwaukee Mutual Insurance Co.; Stanley Consultants, Inc. and its affiliates.
Davenport, Iowa Office: 900 U.S. Bank Center, 201 West Second Street. Telephone: 563-324-1000. Facsimile: 563-326-6266.
Wilton, Iowa Office: 115 West Fourth, P.O. Box 481. Telephone: 563-732-4000. Facsimile: 563-732-2318.

See Professional Biographies, CORALVILLE, IOWA

Welsh, Allen ....'53 '83 C&L.352 B.A., J.D. 709 10th Ave.

CORNING, * 1,806, *Adams Co.*

Hardisty, Earl E. ....'51 '93 C.106 B.S. L.221 J.D. Pros. Atty.
Millhollin, Jeffrey B., (BV) ....'46 '71 C&L.546 B.S., J.D. [Millhollin]
Millhollin Law Office, (BV) ....625 Benton Ave.
Nielsen, Ann M., (BV) ....'48 '77 C&L.546 B.A., J.D. [Nielsen&N.]
Nielsen, Stuart D., (BV) ....'47 '77 C&L.546 B.A., J.D. Co. Atty. [Nielsen&N.]
Nielsen & Nielsen, P.C., (BV) ....818 Davis Ave.
Stanley, Byron B., (AV) ....'12 '37 C.784 A.B. L.221 1005 Nodaway St.‡

CORYDON, * 1,675, *Wayne Co.*

Birdwell, John W., (BV) ....'44 '71 C.309 A.B. L.178 J.D. 200 S. Franklin St.
Chambers, Roberta A., (BV) ....'45 '92 C&L.221 B.S.B.A., J.D. 405 S. Dekalb
Miles, William H., (BV) ....'26 '52 C&L.352 B.A., LL.B. [Miles]
Miles Law Firm, (BV) ....107 West Jackson

Norris, Verle W., (BV) '63 '90 C.114 B.A. L.221 J.D.
300 West Marion, P.O. Box 256, 50060 ⊙
Telephone: 641-872-1363 Facsimile: 641-872-2468
URL: http://www.vnorris.com
Associate: James G. Rowe.
Humeston, Iowa Office: 125 Broad Street, P.O. Box 117, 50123. Telephone: 641-877-9700. Fax: 641-877-2204.

See Professional Biographies, CORYDON, IOWA

Poston, T. C. ....'25 '52 C&L.221 B.A., LL.B. Jud. Mag.‡
Rowe, James G. ....'75 '05 C.999 B.A. L.1339 J.D. [A] V.W.Norris]
Wilson, Alan M., (BV) ....'58 '83 C&L.221 B.S., J.D. [Miles]

COUNCIL BLUFFS, * 58,268, *Pottawattamie Co.*

Abel, Gordon C. ....'45 '73 C&L.352 B.S., J.D. Dist. J.
Anderson, Gary K. ....'51 '76 C.352 B.A. L.190 J.D. Assoc. Dist. J.
Arch Hunter, Iris ....'48 '00 C.999 B.S. L.190 J.D. [Arch H.]
Arch Hunter Law Firm ....19770 Mynster Springs Rd.
Barntsen, Gregory G., (AV) ....'46 '75 C&L.352 B.B.A., J.D. [Smith P.]
Beckman, Harold T., (AV) ....'21 '48 C.641 B.A. L.597 J.D. [S] Smith P.]
Beckman, Lawrence J., (AV) ....'48 '73 C.388 B.A. L.352 J.D. [Smith P.]
Beno, Robert M. '36 '65 C.602 B.S. L.930 LL.B.
(adm. in FL; not adm. in IA) P.O. Box 1826
Braddy, Thomas M., (BVⓉ) ....'69 '94 C.162 B.A. L.190 J.D. [Locher,C.P.&D.] ⊙

Brumbaugh & Quandahl, P.C., L.L.O.
(See Omaha)

Burgett, Keith E. ....'32 '59 C.221 B.A. L.352 LL.B. Dist. J.
Campbell, James A., (AV) ....'40 '65 C&L.352 B.A., J.D. [Peters]
Caniglia, (BV) ....300 W. Broadway., Ste. 108
Caniglia, Phil R., (BV) ....'49 '76 C&L.190 A.B., J.D. [Caniglia]
Churchman, John P. ....'28 '52 C&L.190 A.B., LL.B. 305 FirsTier Bk. Bldg.‡
Cox, Jamie L. ....'76 '02 C&L.352 B.A., J.D. [A] Willson&P.]
Crotty, Richard D., (BV) ....'49 '75 C.687 B.A. L.190 J.D. 421 West Broadway
Crowl, Richard D., Jr., (BV) .....'59 '85 C.350 B.A. L.352 J.D. [Stuart,T.P.T.H.F.&M.]
Daly, Donald W. '48 '81 C.436 B.A. L.190 J.D.
(adm. in NE; not adm. in IA) 500 W. Bway.‡
DeLorme, Christine, (CV) ....'72 '98 C.585 B.A. L.221 J.D. City Prosecutor
Dippel & McCann, P.C., (AV) ....200 First Bank Building
Ditmars, Lyle W., (AV) ....'51 '77 C.627 B.S. L.190 J.D. [Peters]
Dreismeier, Craig M., (BV) ....'67 '92 C.627 B.S. L.190 J.D. [Reilly,H.&D.]
Ebke, Stephen C., (BV) ....'55 '91 C.999 B.S. L.190 J.D. [Porter,T.&E.]
Eck, Matthew Edmund ....'77 '01 C&L.190 B.A., J.D. [A] Locher,C.P.&D.]
Engel, Keith G., (BV) ....'43 '83 C.999 B.A. L.190 J.D. 227 S. Main St.
Engelhardt, Nicole B. ....'78 '03 C&L.190 B.S.B.A., J.D. [A] Telpner,P.S.R.T.&S.]

Engles, Ketcham, Olson & Keith, P.C.
(See Omaha, Nebraska)

Eppler, Patrick J., (BV) ....'67 '92 C.293 B.A. L.221 J.D. Asst. Pub. Def.
Faust, Gary R., (AV) ....'44 '74 C.351 B.A. L.221 J.D. [Stuart,T.P.T.H.F.&M.]
Finerty • Rosman, P.C., (BV) ....502 S. 7th St.
Fleming, Bruce D. ....'47 '72 C.627 B.A. L.190 J.D. Park Bldg., 500 Willow Ave.
French, John M., (AV) ....'48 '74 C.351 B.S. L.221 J.D. [Peters]
Fretheim, Daniel L., (BV) ....'68 '95 C.351 B.A. L.221 J.D. [Smith P.]

Furlow, Donald G.
(See Omaha, Nebraska)

Galles, Gregory L. ....'71 '98 C.190 B.A. L.352 J.D. [Locher,C.P.&D.] ⊙
Gallner, Michael, (CV) ....'48 '74 C.352 B.B.A. L.190 J.D. 803 3rd Avenue
Gallner, Sheldon M. ....'49 '74 C.30 B.S. L.352 J.D. [Gallner&P.]
Gallner & Pattermann, P.C., (CV) ....300 West Broadway, Suite 145
Gray, Dennis M., (AV) ....'43 '68 C&L.352 B.A., J.D. [Peters]
Green, Bruce B., (BV) ....'68 '93 C&L.352 B.A., J.D. [Willson&P.] (⊙Red Oak)
Greenwood, Patrick E., (AVⓉ) '50 '78 C.602 B.B.A. L.190 J.D.
(adm. in NE; not adm. in IA) 300 West Broadway, Suite 1600
Hammes, Matthew D., (BVⓉ) ....'71 '98 C&L.546 B.S., J.D. [Locher,C.P.&D.] ⊙
Hannan, C. R., (AV) ....'43 '68 C&L.190 A.B., J.D. [Reilly,H.&D.]
Hartje, Keith D. ....'50 '75 C&L.221 B.A., J.D. Midwest Power Systems, Inc.
Heinicke, Martha A., (CV) ....'56 '81 C.513 B.A. L.352 J.D. Asst. Co. Atty.
Heininger, Richard A., (AV) ....'45 '70 C.1101 B.A. L.221 J.D. [Smith P.]
Heisterkamp, Jon E., (BV) ....'64 '90 C&L.221 B.S.B.A., J.D. [Peters]
Heithoff, Curtis J., (BV) ....'51 '78 C.352 B.B.A. L.190 J.D. 508 S. 8th St.
Heithoff, John P., (BV) ....'51 '77 C.350 B.S. L.190 J.D. 222 S. 6th St.
Heithoff, Robert C., (AV) ....'24 '50 C&L.190 J.D. 1525 Madison Ave.‡
Hewett, W. Curtis, (AV) ....'51 '78 C.280 B.A. L.190 J.D. [W.C.Hewett]

Hewett, W. Curtis, P.C., (AV)
227 South Main Street, 51502
Telephone: 712-323-5820 Fax: 712-322-1118
Email: wchpc@qwest.net
W. Curtis Hewett.
Employment Rights, Discrimination, Wrongful Termination, Personal Injury, Products Liability, Workers Compensation and Insurance Defense. Appeals.

Houlihan, John P. '46 '71 C&L.190 B.A., J.D.
(adm. in NE; not adm. in IA) Pres., Zalkin, Inc.
Hrvol, Joseph J., (AV) ....'48 '76 C.339 B.A. L.190 J.D. [J.J.Hrvol]
Hrvol, Joseph J., (P.C.), (AV) .... 541 6th Avenue
Hughes, William R., Jr., (AV) .....'48 '80 C.352 B.S. L.546 J.D. [Stuart,T.P.T.H.F.&M.]
Jennings, Dean T., (BV) ....'51 '76 C.350 B.S. L.190 J.D. [McGinn,M.J.&S.]
Kavanaugh, Tammy J. ....'66 '97 C.546 B.A. L.793 J.D. Pub. Def. Off.
Kieckhafer, Marvin O., (AVⓉ) ....'49 '81 C.310 B.A. L.546 J.D. [A] Smith P.]
Klimesh, Joyce L. ....'61 '86 C.351 B.A. L.352 J.D. 533 S. Main St.
Kolln, Lonny L., II ....'77 '02 C.351 B.A L.352 J.D. [A] Willson&P.] (⊙Carroll)
Krohn, Steven H., (AV) ....'53 '78 C&L.546 B.S., J.D. [Smith P.]
Kwapnioski, John D. ....'72 '98 C.627 B.S. L.546 J.D. [A] Peters]

Lamson, Dugan and Murray, LLP
(See Omaha, Nebraska)

Langdon, Donald A. '21 '50 L.190 J.D.
(adm. in NE; not adm. in IA) 907 Grandview‡
Laubenthal, Robert J., (AV) ....'39 '65 C.351 B.A. L.352 J.D. [Smith P.]
Livingston, Robert ....'70 '00 C.172 B.S. L.221 J.D. [A] Stuart,T.P.T.H.F.&M.]

Locher, Cellilli, Pavelka & Dostal, L.L.C., (AVⓉ)
500 West Broadway, Suite 307, 51503 ⊙
Telephone: 402-898-7000 Fax: 402-898-7130
URL: http://www.lcpdlaw.com
Donald J. Pavelka, Jr.; Matthew D. Hammes; Gregory L. Galles; Thomas M. Braddy;—Matthew Edmund Eck.
General Civil Practice, Trials, General Negligence, Personal Injury, Admiralty and Maritime Law, Banking and Creditor Bankruptcy, Insurance and Commercial Fraud.
Omaha, Nebraska Office: 200 The Omaha Club, 2002 Douglas Street, 68102. Telephone: 402-898-7000. Fax: 402-898-7130.

See Professional Biographies, COUNCIL BLUFFS, IOWA

Long, Kjas T., (CV) ....'51 '75 C&L.352 B.S., J.D. 706 1st Ave.
Madsen, Kristopher K., (AV) .....'63 '89 C.747 B.A. L.221 J.D. [Stuart,T.P.T.H.F.&M.]
Markel, Timothy I., (BV) ....'48 '74 C.593 B.S. L.190 J.D. Asst. Pub. Def.
Martin, Leo P., (BV) ....'53 '82 C.350 B.S. L.494 J.D. [Peters]
McCann, David F., (AV) ....'28 '57 C&L.190 B.S., LL.B. [Dippel&M.]
McCann, David J., (BV) ....'57 '85 C.477 B.A. L.352 J.D. [Dippel&M.]
McDougall, Richard T. '65 '94 C.543 B.S. L.546 J.D.
(adm. in NE; not adm. in IA) Firstar Trust & Investments
McGinn, Edmund A., (BV) ....'28 '52 C&L.190 LL.B. [McGinn,M.J.&S.]
McGinn, Joseph F., (BV) ....'30 '57 C&L.190 B.S., J.D. [McGinn,M.J.&S.]
McGinn, William F., (BV) ....'61 '88 C&L.190 B.A., J.D. [McGinn,M.J.&S.]
McGinn, McGinn, Jennings & Springer, (BV) ....25 Main Pl., Ste. 500
McHale, John M., (BV) ....'57 '82 C.723 B.A. L.546 J.D. [Peters] (⊙Omaha, NE)
Meldrum, Clarence B., Jr., (BV) ....'44 '72 C.106 L.190 J.D. Jud. Mag.
Moser, Thomas L. ....'43 '69 C.641 B.A. L.190 J.D. Omaha Standard, Inc.
Murphy, Michael J., (BV) ....'50 '80 C.546 B.S. L.190 J.D. [Murphy,R.&S.]
Murphy, Rodenburg & Stierman, Law Offices, P.C., (BV) .... P.O. Box 2007
O'Grady, Timothy ....'55 '80 C&L.190 B.A., J.D. Dist. J.
Otte, G. Elizabeth, (BV) ....'45 '70 C.227 B.A. L.190 J.D. 226 S. 6th Street
Over, Oliver O., Jr., (CV) ....'41 '67 C.627 B.S.B.A. L.190 J.D. [Over,O.&O.]
Over, Oscar O., (BV) ....'41 '66 C.627 B.S.B.A. L.352 J.D. [Over,O.&O.]
Over, Over & Over, P.C., (BV) ....604 S. Main St.

Overton, Suellen, (BV) '62 '90 C&L.221 B.A., J.D.
404 Park Building, 500 Willow Avenue, 51503
Telephone: 712-322-6585 Fax: 712-325-6112
Email: soverton@cblaw.omhcoxmail.com URL: http://www.lawyers.com/suellenoverton
General Practice, Family Law, Personal Injury, Child Custody, Child Support, Divorce, Collections, Bankruptcy, Social Security, Wills and Probate Law.

See Professional Biographies, COUNCIL BLUFFS, IOWA

Pattermann, Laura Laubenthal, (CV) ....'67 '94 C.221 B.A L.352 J.D. [Gallner&P.]
Pattermann, T. J., (CV) ....'68 '94 C.221 B.A. L.352 J.D. [Smith P.]
Pavelka, Donald J., Jr., (AVⓉ) ......'57 '84 C.627 B.A. L.190 J.D. [Locher,C.P.&D.] ⊙
Pechacek, Frank W., Jr., (AV) ....'44 '69 C.351 B.A. L.352 J.D. [Willson&P.] ⊙
Peters, Jacob J., (BV) ....'60 '85 C.350 B.S. L.190 J.D. [Peters]
Peters, John M., (AV) ....'23 '49 C&L.546 B.S., J.D. 233 Pearl St.‡
Peters, Scott H., (AV) ....'50 '75 C&L.221 B.A., J.D. [Peters]

Peters Law Firm, P.C., (AV) [BB]
233 Pearl Street, P.O. Box 1078, 51502-1078 ⊙
Telephone: 712-328-3157 FAX: 712-328-9092
Email: peterslawfirm@hotmail.com URL: http://www.peterslawfirm.com
James A. Campbell; Dennis M. Gray; James A. Thomas; Lyle W. Ditmars; Scott H. Peters; John M. McHale; Jacob J. Peters; Leo P. Martin; Scott J. Rogers; Jon E. Heisterkamp; John M. French; Matthew G. Woods;—John C. Rasmussen; John D. Kwapnioski; Jennifer K. Sewell; Justin R. Wyatt.
Personal Injury Litigation and Commercial Litigation. Insurance, Tax, Real Estate, Corporation, Probate and Bankruptcy Law.

(This Listing Continued)

Peters Law Firm, P.C. (Continued)

Representative Clients: Grinnell Mutual Reinsurance Co.; Iowa West Racing Association; Shelter Insurance; State Farm Insurance; Kemper Group; The Cities of Glenwood, Neola, Minden, McClelland, Underwood; MidStates Bank; Ameristar Casino; North Pointe Insurance Co.
Glenwood, Iowa Office: 10 North Walnut. Telephone: 712-527-4877. FAX: 712-527-3418.
Neola, Iowa Office: 401 Front Street, P.O. Box 282. Telephone: 712-485-2265.
South Omaha, Nebraska Office: 4828 South 24th Street, Suite 200, 68107. Telephone: 402-731-1711. Fax: 402-731-3363.

See Professional Biographies, COUNCIL BLUFFS, IOWA

Petersen, Deborah L., (AV) ... '59 '84 C&L.190 B.S.B.A., J.D. 215 S. Main St.
Peterson, Richard W., (AV) ... '25 '51 C&L.352 B.A., J.D. [Telpner,P.S.R.T.&S.]
Pohl, Geoffrey V., (BVⓉ) '50 '81 C.976 B.A. L.190 J.D.
(adm. in NE; not adm. in IA) 300 West Broadway, Suite 1600
Porter, Tauke & Ebke, (AV) ... 500 W. Broadway, Ste. 201
Pratt, James A., (BV) ... '32 '59 C.352 B.A. L.190 J.D. 508 S. 8th St.
Rasmussen, John C., (BV) ... '60 '85 C&L.190 B.S.B.A., J.D. [Ⓐ Peters]

Rasmussen & Mitchell
(See Omaha, Nebraska)

Rater, Mark Joseph, (BV) ... '64 '89 C.352 B.B.A. L.190 J.D. [Sciortino V.&R.]
Reilly, Michael G., (AV) ... '57 '81 C&L.190 B.S., J.D. [Reilly,H.&D.]

Reilly, Hannan & Dreismeier, P.L.C., (AV)
215 South Main Street, P.O. Box 1016, 51502-1016
Telephone: 712-328-1575 Fax: 712-328-1562
C. R. Hannan; Michael G. Reilly; Craig M. Dreismeier.
Personal Injury Litigation. General Practice in all Courts. Probate, Real Estate, Corporation, Domestic Relations, Workers Compensation, Bankruptcy, Construction and Insurance Law. Discrimination and Civil Rights Law. Trials and Appeals. Criminal Law.
Reference: Peoples National Bank of Council Bluffs.

See Professional Biographies, COUNCIL BLUFFS, IOWA

Richter, David E., (AV) ... '44 '68 C.350 L.190 J.D. [D.E.Richter]
Richter, David E., P.C., (AV) ... 222 S. 6th St.
Rodenburg, Aaron, Law Offices of, (CV) '73 '95
C&L.190 B.S.B.A., J.D. 607 South Main Street, Suite 100
Rodenburg, John A., (CV) ... '61 '88 C&L.190 B.S.B.A., J.D. [Rodenburg]
Rodenburg, Robert V., (BV) ... '57 '83 C&L.190 B.A., J.D. [Murphy,R.&S.]
Rodenburg Law Offices, P.C., (CV) ... P.O. Box 2007
Rogers, Scott J., (BV) ... '61 '87 C.194 B.S. L.190 J.D. [Peters] (⊙Neola)
Root, Thomas L. ... '39 '65 C.190 A.B. L.276 J.D. 421 West Broadway, Suite 306‡
Rosman, Stephen L., (BV) ... '54 '79 C&L.190 B.A., J.D. [Finerty R.]
Rubes, Stephen A., (CV) ... '53 '83 C.352 B.S. L.190 J.D. 541 6th Ave.
Ruden, Linda Marie '61 '89 C&L.190 B.S.B.A., J.D.
Tr. Offr., Firstar Bk. Council Bluffs
Ruesch, Jack E., (BV) ... '51 '76 C.350 B.S. L.190 J.D. [Telpner,P.S.R.T.&S.]
Ryan, M. Brett ... '70 '99 C.351 B.A. L.352 J.D. [Willson&P.]
Sacks, Kenneth ... '31 '54 C.546 B.S. L.190 J.D. 215 S. Main St.‡
Sawatzke, Roger L., (AV) ... '50 '80 C.546 B.S. L.190 J.D. [R.Sawatzke]
Sawatzke, Roger, (AV) ... 229 S. Main
Sciortino, Michael A., (AV) ... '49 '76 C&L.190 B.S., J.D. [Sciortino V.&R.]
Sciortino Vannier & Rater, (AV) ... 221 South Main
Sewell, Jennifer K. ... '72 '01 C.791 B.A. L.190 J.D. [Ⓐ Peters]

Sewell, Ryan M. '75 '02 C.546 B.A. L.190 J.D.
215 South Main Street, 51503
Telephone: 712-328-1575 Fax: 712-328-1562
Email: rsewell@cox.net URL: http://www.lawyers.com/sewelllaw
General Practice including, but not limited to, Criminal Law, Personal Injury, Insurance Law, Litigation and Trials.

See Professional Biographies, COUNCIL BLUFFS, IOWA

Shanks, Randall J., (AV) ... '58 '84 C.480 B.A. L.190 J.D. [Shanks]
Shanks Law Firm, (AV) ... 409 West Broadway
Simpson, Shannon Dell'Orfano, (BV) '69 '97
C.35 B.S. L.190 J.D. [Telpner,P.S.R.T.&S.]
Smith, Charles L., (AV) ... '48 '74 C.602 B.A. L.190 LL.B. [Telpner,P.S.R.T.&S.]
Smith, Charles L., III ... '45 '70 C&L.190 J.D. Chf. Dist. J.

Smith Peterson Law Firm, LLP, (AV)
35 Main Place, Suite 300, P.O. Box 249, 51502
Telephone: 712-328-1833 Fax: 712-328-8320 URL: http://www.smithpeterson.com
Email: email@smithpeterson.com URL: http://www.lawyers.com/smithpeterson
Members of Firm: Raymond A. Smith (1892-1977); John LeRoy Peterson (1895-1969). Of Counsel: Harold T. Beckman. Partners: Robert J. Laubenthal; Richard A. Heininger; Lawrence J. Beckman; Gregory G. Barntsen; Steven H. Krohn; Joseph D. Thornton; T. J. Pattermann; Daniel L. Fretheim. Associates: Marvin O. Kieckhafer; Nathan R. Watson.
Litigation, Discrimination and Civil Rights, Workers Compensation, Appeals, Insurance Law, Administrative Law, Corporation and Business Law, Debt and Bankruptcy, Environmental, Municipal, Real Estate, Estates and Probate Law and Banking Law, Commercial Law, Collection, Labor and Employment Law, Mediation, Taxation and Insurance Defense.

See Professional Biographies, COUNCIL BLUFFS, IOWA

Sodoro, Daly & Sodoro, P.C.
(See Omaha, Nebraska)

Sondag, Patrick A., Attorney at Law, (BV) '57 '82
C.352 B.A. L.900 J.D. 421 W. Bway., Ste. 305
Springer, Norman L., Jr., (BV) ... '57 '83 C.350 B.A. L.190 J.D. [McGinn,M.J.&S.]
Steensland, Greg W., (BV) ... '51 '76 C.352 B.A. L.221 J.D. Asst. Pub. Def.
Stierman, Matthew V., (BV) ... '62 '88 C&L.352 B.A., J.D. [Murphy,R.&S.]

Stuart, Tinley, Peters, Thorn, Hughes, Faust & Madsen, (AV)
U.S. West Building, 310 West Kanesville Boulevard, Second Floor, P.O. Box 398, 51502-0398
Telephone: 712-322-4033 Fax: 712-322-6243
Email: lawoffice@stuarttinley.com URL: http://www.stuarttinley.com
Members of Firm: James E. Thorn; William R. Hughes, Jr.; Gary R. Faust; Kristopher K. Madsen; Richard D. Crowl, Jr.; Robert M. Stuart (1914-1986); Jack W. Peters (1931-1993); Emmet Tinley (1916-2002). Associate: Robert Livingston.
Litigation, Trial Law, Products Liability, Discrimination and Civil Rights, Workers' Compensation, Personal Injury, Malpractice, Professional Negligence, Insurance Law, Bankruptcy, Environmental, Real Estate, Wills, Estates and Probate Law, Insurance Defense Litigation, Commercial Litigation, Mediation, Business Law, Family Law, Municipalities, School Law, Divorce, Child Custody.
Representative Clients: Chicago, Burlington Northern Railroad Co.; Firstar Bank Iowa, N.A.; Fireman's Fund-American; Hartford Insurance Group; St. Paul Fire & Marine Group; Liberty Mutual Insurance Company; State Farm Insurance Companies.

See Professional Biographies, COUNCIL BLUFFS, IOWA

Swanson Law Firm
(See Red Oak)

Tauke, A. W. (Tony), (AV) ... '45 '76 C.177 B.A. L.190 J.D. [Porter,T.&E.]
TeKippe, Jeffrey R., (CV) ... '61 '90 C.351 B.A. L.190 J.D. Asst. Co. Atty.
Telpner, Maynard S., (AV) ... '28 '52 C.423 L.190 J.D. [Ⓒ Telpner,P.S.R.T.&S.] ‡

Telpner, Peterson, Smith, Ruesch, Thomas & Simpson, (AV) BR
25 Main Place, Suite 200, P.O. Box 248, 51502-0248
Telephone: 712-325-9000 Fax: 712-328-1946
Email: email@telpnerlaw.com
Members of Firm: Richard W. Peterson; Charles L. Smith; Jack E. Ruesch; Walter P. Thomas; Shannon Dell'Orfano Simpson;—Nicole B. Engelhardt. Retired: Maynard S. Telpner.
Commercial/Banking Law, Corporate Bankruptcy, Real Estate Law, Personal Injury/Workers Compensation, Probate, Estate Planning, Domestic Relations, Environmental, Civil Trial Practice, Unfair Trade Practices, Eminent Domain, Business, Zoning, Debtor and Creditor, Professional Liability and General Practice in State and Federal Courts.
Reference: US Bank, Council Bluffs, Iowa.

See Professional Biographies, COUNCIL BLUFFS, IOWA

Tenny, Peter D. ... '64 '94 C.645 B.S. L.352 J.D. Pub. Def. Off.
Theulen, Jeffrey J., (CV) ... '58 '93 C.625 B.S. L.190 J.D. 2469 Richfield Loop
Thomas, James A., (AV) ... '42 '67 C.513 B.S. L.352 J.D. [Peters] (⊙Glenwood)
Thomas, Walter P., (BV) ... '53 '81 C&L.352 B.B.A., J.D. [Telpner,P.S.R.T.&S.]
Thorn, James E., (AV) ... '35 '63 C.898 B.A. L.352 J.D. [Stuart,T.P.T.H.F.&M.]
Thornton, Joseph D., (BV) ... '59 '84 C&L.352 B.B.A., J.D. [Smith P.]
Tyler, Kenneth E., (BV) ... '46 '73 C.352 B.A. L.190 J.D. Asst. Co. Atty.
Vannier, Marvin L., (BV) ... '47 '75 C.627 B.S. L.1095 J.D. [Sciortino V.&R.]
Watson, Nathan R. ... '78 '04 C.94 B.A. L.221 J.D. [Ⓐ Smith P.]
Weatherhead, Angela, (CV) ... '67 '95 C.627 B.A. L.190 J.D. [Ⓐ Porter,T.&E.]

Welsh & Welsh, P.C., L.L.O.
(See Omaha, Nebraska)

Wheeler, Troyce A., (BV) ... '40 '71 C.393 B.A. L.352 J.D. 31 E. Ridge Dr.
Willson, Philip J., (AV) ... '23 '49 C.641 B.A. L.976 LL.B. [Willson&P.] (⊙Red Oak)

Willson & Pechacek, P.L.C., (AV)
421 West Broadway, Suite 200, P.O. Box 2029, 51502 ⊙
Telephone: 712-322-6000 Fax: 712-322-6200
Email: info@willsonpechacek.com URL: http://www.willsonpechacek.com
Members of Firm: Philip J. Willson; Frank W. Pechacek, Jr.; Bruce B. Green; M. Brett Ryan. Associates: Jamie L. Cox; Lonny L. Kolln II.
Civil and Business Litigation, Insurance, Trial Practice, Product Liability, Malpractice or Professional Negligence, Personal Injury, Workers' Compensation, Employment, Governmental Regulations and Administrative Law, Agriculture, Environmental, Corporations and Limited Liability Companies, Business Transactions, Taxation, Real Estate, Commercial and Retail Collections, Will, Estate, and Probate.
Oakland, Iowa Office: 109 North Main. Telephone: 712-482-6999.
Red Oak, Iowa Office: 608 Second Street, Suite 100. Telephone: 712-623-9623.
Treynor, Iowa Office: 15 East Main Street. Telephone: 712-487-3444.
Harlan Iowa Office: 1121 7th Street. Telephone: 712-755-1111.
Carroll, Iowa Office: 110 West 8th Street. Telephone: 712-792-0001.

See Professional Biographies, COUNCIL BLUFFS, IOWA

Winter, Michael J., (BV) ... '50 '76 C.350 B.S. L.190 J.D. 541 6th Avenue
Woods, Matthew G., (BV) ... '66 '93 C.352 B.B.A. L.190 J.D. [Peters] (⊙Glenwood)
Wyatt, Justin R. ... '75 '03 C&L.190 B.S, J.D. [Ⓐ Peters] (⊙Glenwood)

CRESCO, * 3,905, *Howard Co.*

Anderson, C. J., (AV) ... '24 '50 C&L.352 B.A., J.D. 112 N. Elm St.
Anderson, Mark B., (CV) ... '48 '73 C.747 B.A. L.880 J.D. 126 First Ave., E.
Antes, Jon W., (BV) ... '44 '70 C&L.221 B.A., J.D. [Ⓒ Elwood,O.S.B.&C.] ⊙
Braun, Joseph Patrick, (CV) ... '68 '95 C.494 B.A. L.1035 J.D. [Elwood,O.S.B.&C.] ⊙
Elwood, Frank D., (AV) ... '16 '40 C.872 B.A. L.352 J.D. 217 N. Elm St.‡
Elwood, Henry L., (AV) ... '34 '59 C.187 B.A. L.221 J.D. [Elwood,O.S.B.&C.] ⊙

Elwood, O'Donohoe, Stochl, Braun & Churbuck, (AV) BR
217 North Elm Street, P.O. Box 377, 52136 ⊙
Telephone: 563-547-3321 Fax: 563-547-3189
Email: hlelwood@iowatelecom.net
Members of Firm: Henry L. Elwood; James E. O'Donohoe (1921-1998); Christopher F. O'Donohoe; Richard D. Stochl; Judith Mack O'Donohoe; Joseph Patrick Braun; Lewis M. Churbuck (1972-2003). Associates: Jeremiah W. White; Todd P. Prichard. Of Counsel: Richard P. TeKippe; Jon W. Antes.
General Practice in State and Federal Courts. Litigation, Insurance Defense, Probate, Estate Planning, Trusts and Wills, Real Estate, Corporate, Banking and Taxation Law. Trials and Appeals.
Representative Clients: Grinnell Mutual Reinsurance Co.; United Fire & Casualty Insurance Co.; Board of Trustees, New Hampton Municipal Light Plant; First Citizens National Bank, New Hampton, Iowa; Alliance Pipeline; Cresco Union Savings Bank, Cresco, Iowa; City of Cresco, Iowa; Featherlite, Inc.; Community First National Bank, Protivin, Iowa.
New Hampton, Iowa Office: 101 North Locust Avenue, P.O. Box 310, 50659. Telephone: 641-394-5943. Fax: 641-394-5945.
Charles City, Iowa Office: 116 North Main Street. P.O. Box 307. 50616. Telephone: 641-228-8054. Fax: 641-228-8057.
West Union, Iowa Office: 125 N. Vine, P.O. Box 475, 52175. Telephone: 563-422-5631. Fax: 563-422-5632.

Haskovec, Joseph M., (BV) ... '60 '85 C.351 B.A. L.352 J.D. Co. Atty.
Kowalke, Todd W., (CV) ... '62 '94 C.493 B.S. L.221 J.D. [Kowalke]
Kowalke Law Firm, (CV) ... 712 Second Ave. S.E., Ste. B
Moriarty, James P., (CV) ... '55 '82 C&L.818 A.B., J.D. 110 North Park Place
O'Donohoe, Christopher F., (AV) '50 '75 C.118 B.A. L.178 J.D.
[Elwood,O.S.B.&C.] ⊙
O'Donohoe, Judith Mack, (BV) '51 '76 C.118 B.A. L.569 J.D.
[Elwood,O.S.B.&C.] ⊙
Prichard, Todd P. ... '— '04 C&L.352 B.A., J.D. [Ⓐ Elwood,O.S.B.&C.] ⊙
Schoeberl, Kevin E., (BV) ... '58 '85 C.351 B.A. L.352 J.D. [Story,S.&K.]
Stochl, Richard D., (BV) ... '64 '89 C.927 B.S. L.352 J.D. [Elwood,O.S.B.&C.] ⊙
Story, Robert H., (AV) ... '38 '64 C&L.352 B.B.A., J.D. [Story,S.&K.]
Story, Schoeberl & Kowalke, LLP, (AV) ... 126 North Elm Street
TeKippe, Richard P., (BV) ... '40 '64 C.177 B.A. L.352 J.D. [Ⓒ Elwood,O.S.B.&C.] ⊙
White, Jeremiah W. ... '— '04 C.351 B.A. L.352 J.D. [Ⓐ Elwood,O.S.B.&C.] ⊙

CRESTON, * 7,597, *Union Co.*

Harvey, Edward T., Jr., (AV) ... '30 '58 C&L.190 B.S., J.D. 109 W. Montgomery St.
James, Marion E., (BV) ... '42 '68 C.784 B.A. L.221 J.D. [M.E.James]
James, Marion E., PC, (BV) ... 205 1/2 N. Elm
Kenyon, Arnold O., II, (AV) ... '26 '50 C.293 L.352 LL.B. [A.O.Kenyon,II]
Kenyon, Arnold O., III, (AV) ... '52 '77 C.350 B.S. L.352 J.D. 211 N. Maple
Kenyon, Timothy R., (BV) ... '58 '83 C&L.352 B.S., J.D. Co. Atty.
Kenyon, Arnold O., II, A Prof. Corp., (AV) ... 100 E. Montgomery St.
Mullin, Donald D., (AV) ... '28 '55 C&L.190 B.S.C., J.D. 109 W. Montgomery St.
Nielsen, Todd G., (BV) ... '62 '89 C.88 B.A. L.192 J.D. 211 Maple Ave.

CUMMING, 132, *Warren Co.*

Cass, Harrison E. ... '21 '48 C&L.352 B.A., J.D. 374 Adams St.‡

DAKOTA CITY, 911, *Humboldt Co.*

Schwieger, Derk ... '72 '98 C.221 B.A. L.502 J.D. Co. Attys Off.

DALLAS CENTER, 1,595, *Dallas Co.*

Brown, Ralph R., (AV) ... '44 '69 C&L.221 B.A., J.D. [McDonald,B.&F.] ⊙
Cobb, Virginia ... '56 '82 C&L.221 B.A., J.D. 101 Kellogg St.‡

Fagen, Charles H., (BV) .... '60 '86 C&L.221 B.S., J.D. [McDonald,B.&F.] ⊙
Kimple, Jonathan M., (BV) ....'52 '77 C.226 B.A. L.221 J.D. 1400 Walnut St.
McDonald, John C., (AV) .... '24 '48 C.784 L.221 J.D. [Ⓒ McDonald,B.&F.]

McDonald, Brown & Fagen, (AV)
502-15th Street, P.O. Box 250, 50063-0250 ⊙
Telephone: 515-992-3728 Fax: 515-992-3971
Email: dalctlaw@mindspring.com URL: http://www.dallascenterlawyers.com
Of Counsel: John C. McDonald. Members of Firm: Ralph R. Brown; Charles H. Fagen. Associate: Benjamin L. Rouse.
General Practice, including: Real Estate, Wills, Trusts, Estate Planning, and Probate, Business and Commercial, Taxation Law and Tax Returns, Family Law, Litigation and Appeals, Debtor and Creditor, Municipal and School Law.
Representative Clients: City of Dallas Center; City of Granger; DCI Group, L.L.C.; Dallas Center-Grimes Community School District; Dallas County Care Facility, Inc.; Dallas Mutual Insurance Co.; FYI Messaging, L.L.C.; McK Construction, Inc.; National Alliance for Model State Drug Laws.
Grimes, Iowa Office: 306 South First Street. Telephone: 515-986-9888. Fax: 515-986-9876.
See Professional Biographies, DALLAS CENTER, IOWA

Rouse, Benjamin L. .... '80 '05 C.350 B.S. L.878 J.D. [Ⓐ McDonald,B.&F.] ⊙
White, Jeane Van Voorhis '28 '89 C&L.352 B.G.S., J.D.
(adm. in MN; not adm. in IA) 101 Kellogg‡

DAVENPORT, * 98,359, *Scott Co.*

Alpers, Bobbi M. .... '51 '83 C.226 B.A. L.352 J.D. Dist. J.
Antrim, Glenn H. .... '15 '66 C.784 B.A. L.802 J.D. 4132 Northwest Blvd.‡
Arnold, Marsha J., (CV) ....'49 '78 C.986 B.A. L.352 J.D. 1503 Brady St.
Batcher, Richard M., (AVⓉ) '41 '67 C.350 B.S.M.E. L.352 J.D.
[Bozeman,N.P.&N.] ⊙
Beason, Curtis E., (BV) .... '52 '80 C.210 B.A. L.802 J.D. [Lane&W.]
Beckman, Paul A. .... '21 '53 C.707 B.A. L.215 LL.B. 2810 Jersey Ridge Rd.
Benson, Peter J., (BV) .... '57 '82 C.597 B.A. L.352 J.D. [Lane&W.] ⊙
Berger, A. Fred, (AV) .... '34 '57 C&L.352 B.A., J.D. [Wehr,B.L.&S.] ‡
Berger, Steven A., (BV) ....'60 '85 C&L.352 B.S., J.D. [Wehr,B.L.&S.]

Betty, Neuman & McMahon, (AV)
111 East Third Street, Suite 600, 52801
Telephone: 563-326-4491 Fax: 563-326-4498
Email: bnmcm@bettylawfirm.com URL: http://www.bettylawfirm.com
Members of Firm: H. B. Betty (1874-1953); Frank F. Betty (1880-1974); Thomas F. Daley, Jr. (1930-1979); Henry N. Neuman (1905-1986); Richard M. McMahon (1920-1994); Henry G. Neuman; Steven H. Jacobs; Roger A. Lathrop; Craig A. Levien; Greg A. Egbers; Mark A. Woollums; Deborah A. Dubik; Martha L. Shaff; Jean Dickson Feeney; Peter J. Thill. Associates: Roni N. Halabi; Carrie N. Roseberry; Edward J. Rose; Timothy J. Reichwald.
General Civil Practice in State and Federal Courts, Trials and Appeals, Insurance Defense, Estate Planning, Trusts and Probate, Real Estate, Family, Taxation, Business and Corporation Law.
Counsel for: Oscar Mayer Foods; West Bend Mutual Ins. Co.; The Travelers Insurance Co.; Kemper Insurance Group; The Bituminous Casualty Corp.; Auto Owners Mutual.
See Professional Biographies, DAVENPORT, IOWA

Binegar, G. David, (BV) .... '54 '79 C.350 B.S. L.352 J.D. 1503 Brady St.
Bittner, R. Richard, (P.C.), (AV) .... '28 '57 C.350 B.S. L.352 J.D. [Bittner,L.&W.]

Bittner, Lambert & Werner, (AV)
A Partnership including Professional Corporations
1000 U.S. Bank Center, 201 West 2nd Street, 52801
Telephone: 563-328-3333 Fax: 563-328-3352
John A. Hellstrom (1921-1992); John J. Carlin (Retired, 1993). Members of Firm: R. Richard Bittner (P.C.); Robert D. Lambert (P.C.); Clemens A. Werner, Jr.
All members are admitted and engage in Civil and Trial Practice in Iowa District Courts and in U.S. District Court, Northern and Southern Districts of Iowa, Central District of Illinois and U.S. Court of Appeals. General Practice including but not limited to Wills, Trusts, Estate Planning and Probate Law, Real Estate, Banking Law, Employment Law, Business Law.
See Professional Biographies, DAVENPORT, IOWA

Bowman, John A., (BV) .... '45 '72 C.187 B.A. L.352 J.D. [Bowman&D.]
Bowman & DePree, L.L.C., (BV) ....617 Brady Street

Bozeman, Neighbour, Patton & Noe, LLP, (AVⓉ)
4300 E. 53rd Street, Suite 103, 52807 ⊙
Telephone: 563-449-1037 Fax: 309-764-1371
URL: http://www.bnpn.com
John P. Harris; Gary L. Sissel; Richard M. Batcher; William P. Rector.
General Practice in State and Federal Courts. Trials. Corporation, Taxation, Commercial, Insurance Defense, Insurance Coverage, Product Liability, Medical and Professional Liability, Labor and Employment, Bankruptcy, Probate, Trusts and Estates, Real Estate and Workers Compensation.
Moline, Illinois Office: 1630 5th Avenue, P.O. Box 659, 61266-0659. Telephone: 309-797-0850. Fax: 309-764-1371.
See Professional Biographies, DAVENPORT, IOWA

Breckenfelder, Ted E., (BV) ..... '61 '86 C.339 B.A. L.221 J.D. 220 N. Main St., Ste. 501

Bribriesco, William J., & Associates
(See Bettendorf)

Briggs, Stuart C. .... '25 '53 C&L.352 B.A., J.D. 203 W. 3rd St.
Briles, Margaret S. ....'25 '48 C.578 B.A. L.145 J.D. Sr. Dist. J.‡
Britt, Amy M., (BV) .... '67 '93 C&L.352 B.A., J.D. [Vollertsen&B.]
Britt, Dennis J., (AV) .... '35 '59 C&L.602 B.S.C., LL.B. [Vollertsen&B.]
Broderick, Jack F. .... '26 '51 C&L.352 B.A., LL.B. Ret. Assoc. Dist. Ct. J.
Brooke, Charles W., (AV) .... '43 '68 C.966 B.A. L.352 J.D. 2422 E. River Dr.
Brooke & Halligan, P.L.C., (BV) ....5505 Victoria Ave., Suite. 100
Brooks, Jack L., (AVⓉ) ....'50 '75 C.197 B.A. L.221 J.D. [Brooks&T.]

Brooks & Trinrud, A Professional Corporation, (AVⓉ)
220 Emerson Place, 52801 ⊙
Telephone: 563-326-4900 Fax: 563-326-4944
Email: info@btlawpc.com URL: http://www.BTLawPC.com
Jack L. Brooks;—Milissa K. Hofmann; Henry W. Latham, II.
General Practice, Civil Litigation, Workers Compensation, Bankruptcy, Estate Planning, Trusts and Probate, Business Law (including Corporations, Partnerships), Family Law, Commercial Collections, Real Estate Foreclosure, Real Estate, Commercial Real Estate.
Rock Island, Illinois Office: 3725 Blackhawk Road, P.O. Box 3487, 61204-3487. Telephone: 309-786-4900. Fax: 309-786-4940.
See Professional Biographies, DAVENPORT, IOWA

Bush, Michael K., (AV) .... '52 '77 C.602 B.A. L.879 J.D. [Bush,M.C.H.&K.]
Bush, Roy A. .... '26 '49 C&L.602 LL.B. 2508 E. Garfield St.‡
Bush, William J., (BV) .... '64 '89 C.755 B.A. L.190 J.D. [Bush,M.C.H.&K.]
Bush, Motto, Creen, Hoffman & Koury, P.L.C., (AV) ....5505 Victoria Ave., Ste. 100
Buzzell, Arthur L., (AV) .... '47 '71 C&L.221 B.S.B.A., J.D. 309 W. Kimberly Rd.
Byrne, Michael P., (BV) .... '60 '86 C.352 B.B.A. L.378 J.D. [Lane&W.]

Califf & Harper, P.C.
(See Moline, Illinois)

Carlin, James T., (BV) .... '58 '91 C.707 B.A. L.352 J.D. [Ⓐ Bush,M.C.H.&K.]
Carlin, John J., (AV) .... '32 '59 C.707 B.A. L.352 J.D. [Bittner,L.&W.] ‡
Carlson, Garth Matthew, (CVⓉ) '69 '96 C.352 B.A. L.911 J.D.
(adm. in OR; not adm. in IA) 2322 E. Kimberly Rd.
Carlson, Heather L. '— '99 C.57 B.A. L.734 J.D.
(adm. in KS; not adm. in IA) [Ⓐ McDonald,W.&I.]
Carmody, Edward L. .... '10 '33 C&L.352 B.A., J.D. 203 W. 3rd St.‡
Carroll, Edmund H., Jr., (BV) .... '58 '85 C.276 B.A. L.436 J.D. [Lane&W.]
Carroll, John M., (CV) .... '65 '91 C.436 B.A. L.190 J.D. 310 N. Main St.
Cepican, John E., (BV) ....'48 '74 C.350 B.S. L.221 J.D. [Sturm&F.] (See Pat. Sect.)
Cervantes, Edward J., (BV) .... '58 '88 C.707 B.A. L.221 J.D. [Cervantes&G.]
Cervantes & Gordon, P.L.C., (BV) .... 2208 E. 52nd St., Ste. 3
Christiansen, Clarence H. ....'23 '48 C&L.352 B.A., J.D. 3117 E. Locust St.‡
Clements, James Bryson, (BV) .... '54 '88 C.352 B.A. L.178 J.D. 1503 Brady St.
Coulter, Charles R., (AV) .... '40 '65 C&L.352 B.A., J.D. [Stanley,L.&H.] (⊙Muscatine)
Craig, Dana M., (AV) .... '50 '75 C.350 B.S. L.477 J.D. [Lane&W.] ⊙
Creen, Joseph C., (BV) .... '49 '75 C.602 B.A. L.221 J.D. 5505 Victoria Ave., Ste. 100
Curran, Christopher J. .... '71 '97 C.707 B.A. L.352 J.D. [Lane&W.]
Dane, Harold John, III, (BV) .... '56 '82 C.293 B.A. L.352 J.D. [H.J.Dane]
Dane, H.J., (BV) ....1111 E. River Dr.
Darbyshire, J. Hobart .... '42 '67 C.513 B.A. L.352 J.D. Dist. J.
Davidson, Cameron A., (BV) .... '68 '95 C.746 B.A. L.300 J.D. [Lane&W.]
Davidson, Richard A., (BV) .... '59 '84 C&L.221 B.S.B.A., J.D. [Lane&W.] ⊙
Davidson, William C., (AV) .... '41 '68 C.98 B.A. L.339 J.D. [Lane&W.]
Davis, Taylor S. .... '58 '86 C.1052 B.A. L.796 J.D. Atty., Intercoast Energy Co.
Davis, William E., (AV) .... '41 '70 C&L.221 B.A., J.D. Co. Atty.
DePree, Michael, (BV) .... '58 '84 C.293 B.A. L.352 J.D. [Bowman&D.]
de Silva, Edward B., Jr. .... '31 '58 C.399 B.S. L.352 LL.B. Dist. J.‡
Dettmann, David A., (AV) .... '49 '74 C.427 B.A. L.221 J.D. [Lane&W.]
Dircks, Ridenour & Macek, (BV) .... 111 E. 3rd St. (⊙Clarence)
Dragon, Jean E. ....'61 '95 C.226 B.A. L.352 J.D. [Ⓐ Stanley,L.&H.] (⊙Muscatine)
Driscoll, Patrick W., (BV) .... '45 '78 C.177 B.A. L.424 J.D. [Stanley,L.&H.]
Dubik, Deborah A., (BV) .... '55 '80 C.1062 B.A. L.352 J.D. [Betty,N.&M.]
Duffy, Dennis D., (BV) ..... '55 '89 C&L.352 B.B.A., J.D. 100 E. Kimberly Rd., Ste. 700
Dulceak, Brandy .... '72 '01 C&L.352 B.A., J.D. [Ⓐ Stanley,L.&H.] (⊙Muscatine)
Dusthimer, Jack E., (BV) .... '55 '81 C.589 B.S. L.221 J.D. 1503 Brady St.
Dwyer, Eugene F., (BV) ....'45 '81 C.927 B.A. L.425 J.D. [Dwyer&W.]
Dwyer & Wing, P.C., (BV) .... 1503 Brady St.

Eells & Tronvold Law Offices, P.L.C.
(See Cedar Rapids)

Egbers, Greg A., (AV) .... '54 '79 C.679 B.S. L.221 J.D. [Betty,N.&M.]
Ehlers, Michael G. '51 '77 C.351 B.A. L.352 J.D.
Exec. V.P. & Gen. Coun., General Car & Truck Leasing Sys. Inc.
Ellard, Daniel P., (AV) '55 '80 C.880 B.S. L.280 J.D.
4300 East 53rd Street, Suite 103 (⊙Moline, IL)
Feeney, Jean Dickson, (BV) .... '67 '92 C.427 B.A. L.352 J.D. [Betty,N.&M.]
Filseth, Henry C. .... '36 '63 C.352 B.A. L.221 LL.B. 110 E. Columbia Ave., Apt 2‡
Fleming, Alan R., (CV) ....'53 '80 C.352 B.A. L.221 J.D. 2121 W. 53rd St.
Fowler, Wes A. .... '76 '01 C&L.352 B.A., J.D. [Ⓐ Stanley,L.&H.] (⊙Muscatine)
Franks, David J., (BV) ....'59 '90 C.339 B.S. L.352 J.D. [Franks&R.]
Franks & Roeder PC, (BV) ....5167 Utica Ridge Road
Freeman, Carol A. H., (AV) .... '54 '79 C.375 B.A. L.352 J.D. 220 N. Main St.
Gallagher, Robert H., (AV) .... '44 '69 C&L.352 B.S., J.D. [Gallagher,M.&G.]
Gallagher, Robert S., (BV) .... '69 '94 C.352 B.A. L.436 J.D. [Gallagher,M.&G.]

Gallagher, Millage & Gallagher, (AV)
American Bank Building, 4301 East 53rd Street, Suite 300, 52807
Telephone: 563-388-8417 Fax: 563-388-9240
Email: gmg@gmglawfirm.com URL: http://www.gmglawfirm.com
Robert H. Gallagher; David A. Millage; Robert S. Gallagher. Associates: Matthew A. Ledden; Brian Kennedy; Alicia D. Gieck.
General Civil Practice, including Business, Banking, Real Estate and Corporate Law, Business Transactions, Trusts and Estates, Wills and Probate, and General Litigation.
See Professional Biographies, DAVENPORT, IOWA

Giebelstein, Terry M., (AV) .... '53 '76 C&L.352 B.A., J.D. [Lane&W.]
Gieck, Alicia D. .... '73 '00 C.221 B.A. L.352 J.D. [Ⓐ Gallagher,M.&G.]
Gilmore, Erika L. '77 '05 C.679 B.S. L.352 J.D.
(adm. in IL; not adm. in IA) [Ⓐ Lane&W.]
Goebel, George A., (AV) .... '37 '60 C&L.221 B.S., J.D. 2322 E. Kimberly Rd.
Gordon, Grant Gregory, (CV) .... '61 '93 C.351 B.A. L.365 J.D. [Cervantes&G.]
Gorsline, Michael L., (BV) .... '68 '94 C&L.352 B.B.A., J.D. [Ⓐ Vollertsen&B.]
Gosma, John S., (AV) ....'42 '68 C&L.352 B.A., J.D. [Gosma,T.&Assoc.]

Gosma, Tarbox & Associates, P.L.C., (AV)
American Bank Building, 4301 East 53rd Street, Suite 300, 52807
Telephone: 563-388-8417 Fax: 563-388-9240 URL: http://www.gt-lawfirm.com
Email: jgosma@gt-lawfirm.com URL: http://www.gosma-gallagherplc.com
John S. Gosma; Marie R. Rolling-Tarbox; David A. Mahl; James G. Noth.
General Civil Practice, including Business and Corporate Organization and Transactions, Banking, Real Estate, Estate Planning, Elder Law, Trust and Estate Administration, and Personal Injury, Business and Probate Litigation, Medical Malpractice, Business Enterprises, Slip and Fall, Personal Injury, Automobile Accidents, Wrongful Death, Buying and Selling, Zoning and Land Use, Construction, Asset Protection, Guardianships, Banking and Finance, Closely Held Business, Corporate, Franchise, Limited Liability, Small Business, Partnerships, Buying and Selling of Businesses, Creditors Rights, Contracts, Business Planning, Law Suites, Insurance, Commercial Leasing, Business Start-Ups.
References: American Bank and Trust Company, Davenport and Rock Island; Quad City Bank and Trust Company, Davenport, Iowa.
See Professional Biographies, DAVENPORT, IOWA

Greve, Marlita A., (BV) .... '55 '92 C&L.352 B.S., J.D. [O'Brien&G.]
Grubbs, Kelli R., (BV) ....'65 '90 C&L.352 B.A., J.D. 234 S. Fairmount
Grubisich, Joseph A. ......'47 '72 C.585 B.S. L.352 J.D. 514 E. George Washington Blvd.
Halabi, Roni N. .... '72 '99 C.98 B.A. L.221 J.D. [Ⓐ Betty,N.&M.]
Halligan, Kevin L., (BV) ....'64 '89 C.363 B.A. L.190 J.D. [Brooke&H.]
Hamilton, Jay R. .... '69 '00 C&L.352 B.S.Ch.E., J.D. [J.R.Hamilton] (Pat.)

Hamilton, Jay R., PLC, Law Office of
New Ventures Center, Suite 100, 331 W. 3rd Street, 52801
Telephone: 563-441-0207 Fax: 563-823-4637
Email: jay@qcpatents.com URL: http://www.qcpatents.com
Jay R. Hamilton.
Language: English.
Member: Patent Prosecution and Licensing, Intellectual Property, Trademarks, Copyrights, Trade Secrets, Consumer Fraud.
See Professional Biographies, DAVENPORT, IOWA

Harris, John P., (BVⓉ) ....'55 '80 C&L.352 B.A., J.D. [Bozeman,N.P.&N.] ⊙
Harrison, Andre D. '64 '97 C.927 B.S. L.770 J.D.
(adm. in CA; not adm. in IA) 2810 E. 43rd St.
Hartman, Edward J. ....'24 '50 C&L.352 B.A., J.D. 6401 Utica Ridge Rd.‡
Havercamp, James R. .... '32 '58 C&L.352 LL.B. Chief Dist. J.
Havercamp, Steven J., (CV) .... '65 '98 C.351 B.A. L.221 J.D. [Stanley,L.&H.]
Hawke, Stacey L. ....'76 '03 C.502 B.A. L.352 J.D. [Ⓐ Lane&W.]

Heimer, Robert F., (BV) .... '54 '78 C&L.352 B.A., J.D. HELP Legal Assistance
Heller, Michelle L. .... '77 '02 C&L.352 B.A., J.D. [Ⓐ Nepple L.] ⊙
Heninger, Ralph H., (AV) .... '33 '61 C&L.352 B.A., J.D. [Heninger&H.]
Heninger, Ralph W., (BV) .... '59 '84 C.170 B.A. L.352 J.D. [Heninger&H.]

Heninger and Heninger, Professional Corporation, (AV) BR
Suite 501, 101 West Second Street, 52801
Telephone: 563-324-0418 Fax: 563-324-5808 URL: http://www.heningerlaw.com
URL: http://www.lawyers.com/heningerlaw
Ralph U. Heninger (1908-1993); Ralph H. Heninger; Ralph W. Heninger.
General Practice. Business Law, Probate, Real Estate, Health Care, Labor and Employment, Personal Injury, Estate Planning, Medical Malpractice, Professional Liability, Trial Practice.
See Professional Biographies, DAVENPORT, IOWA

Heriford, Joel K., (BV) .... '57 '85 C.338 B.S. L.209 J.D. [Stanley,L.&H.]
Herrmann, Judith L., (BV) .... '69 '94 C.56 B.A. L.879 J.D. [Lane&W.]
Hines, Michael T., (BV) .... '56 '84 C.755 B.A.Eng. L.734 J.D. [McCarthy,L.&H.]
Hoffman, James D., (BV) .... '47 '73 C&L.352 B.A., J.D. [Bush,M.C.H.&K.]
Hofmann, Milissa K., (BV) .... '68 '93 C.57 B.A. L.221 J.D. [Ⓐ Brooks&T.]
Hollis, Henry A. .... '24 '50 C&L.352 B.A., J.D. 4002 E. 59th St.‡

Hood, James M., (BV) '45 '70 C&L.221 B.A., J.D.
220 Emerson Place, Suite 100, 52801
Telephone: 563-323-5255 Fax: 563-323-7015 URL: http://www.lawyers.com/jhood
Email: james@jameshood.com URL: http://www.jameshood.com
Plaintiffs Trial Practice in all Courts. Personal Injury including Automobile Accidents and Injuries, Workers Compensation.
See Professional Biographies, DAVENPORT, IOWA

Hopkins & Huebner, P.C., (AV)
100 East Kimberly Road., Suite 704, 52806-5944 ⊙
Telephone: 319-445-2264 Fax: 319-445-2267
M. Anne McAtee; Michael C. Walker;—Paul Salabert, Jr.; Nathan M. Sondgeroth.
General Practice. Insurance, Casualty, Workers Compensation, Corporation, Employment, Municipal, Civil Rights, Products Liability, Contracts. Trials in all Courts, Business and Corporation Law, and Real Estate.
Des Moines, Iowa Office: Suite 111, Terrace Center, 2700 Grand Avenue, 50312-5213. Telephone: 515-244-0111. Fax: 515-244-8935.
See Professional Biographies, DAVENPORT, IOWA

Howell, Troy A., (BV) .... '74 '99 C.339 B.A. L.352 J.D. [Lane&W.]
Huizenga, Karen M., (CV) '46 '88
C.1101 B.A. L.589 J.D. Atty., MidAmerican Energy Co.
Hult, Catherine E.E. .... '74 '99 C.793 B.S. L.190 J.D. [Ⓐ Lane&W.]
Humpal, Donna M. .... '63 '91 C.350 B.A. L.352 J.D. Jud. Mag.
Hunter, Steven T., (AV) .... '50 '74 C.707 B.A. L.352 J.D. [Stanley,L.&H.]
Ingham, Bruce A., (BV) '50 '81 C.346 B.A. L.352 J.D.
2322 E. Kimberly Rd., Ste. 120 W.
Ivers, Brian C., (BV) .... '62 '90 C&L.352 B.G.S., J.D. [McDonald,W.&I.]
Jackson, Christopher S., (CV) .... '55 '97 C&L.352 B.M., J.D. 226 W. 4th St.
Jacobs, Steven H., (AV) .... '44 '69 C&L.352 B.B.A., J.D. [Betty,N.&M.]
Jared, Robert P., (CV) .... '53 '79 C.351 B.A. L.352 J.D. MidAmerican Energy Co.
Judge, Joseph C., (CV) .... '70 '98 C.351 B.A. L.352 J.D. [Lane&W.]
Jung, Jay .... '72 '03 C&L.352 B.A., J.D. [Ⓐ Nepple L.] ⊙
Kamp, Thomas N., (AV) .... '38 '65 C.602 B.B.A. L.352 J.D. [Ⓒ Lane&W.]

Katz, Huntoon & Fieweger, P.C.
(See Moline)

Kay-Decker, Courtney M., (CVⓉ) ....'73 '97 C.597 B.A. L.352 J.D. [Lane&W.] ⊙
Kelley, James E. .... '41 '66 C.602 A.B. L.352 J.D. Dist. J.
Kennedy, Brian, (BVⓉ) .... '64 '91 C.350 B.A. L.221 J.D. [Ⓐ Gallagher,M.&G.]
Koury, Michael J., Jr., (BV) .... '47 '74 C.187 B.A. L.352 J.D. [Bush,M.C.H.&K.]
Kuhl, John A., (CV) .... '69 '94 C.436 B.S. L.352 J.D. [Stanley,L.&H.]
Laird, William P., (BVⓉ) .... '49 '75 C&L.221 B.S., J.D. [Ⓐ Pastrnak]
Lambert, Robert D., (P.C.), (AV) .... '51 '77 C.339 B.A. L.221 J.D. [Bittner,L.&W.]
Lammers, Lawrence J., (BV) .... '53 '78 C.602 B.A. L.190 J.D. [McCarthy,L.&H.]
Lande, Robert L., (AV) .... '47 '72 C&L.352 B.S., J.D. [Stanley,L.&H.] (⊙Muscatine)
Lande, Roger L., (AV) '36 '61
C&L.352 B.A., J.D. [Stanley,L.&H.] (⊙Coralville, Muscatine)
Lane, Gary M., (AV) .... '44 '69 C&L.352 B.A., J.D. [Wehr,B.L.&S.]
Lane, Gerda C., (BV) .... '46 '85 C&L.352 B.A., J.D. Off. of Co. Atty.

Lane & Waterman LLP, (AV) BR
220 North Main Street, Suite 600, 52801 ⊙
Telephone: 563-324-3246 Fax: 563-324-1616
URL: http://www.l-wlaw.com
Members of Firm: Joe R. Lane (1902-1931); Charles M. Waterman (1902-1924); William C. Davidson; C. Dana Waterman, III; Charles E. Miller; James A. Mezvinsky; David A. Dettmann; Dana M. Craig; Terry M. Giebelstein; Rand S. Wonio; Curtis E. Beason; Robert V. P. Waterman, Jr.; Peter J. Benson; Michael L. Noyes; R. Scott Van Vooren; Thomas D. Waterman; John D. Telleen; Richard A. Davidson; Michael P. Byrne; Edmund H. Carroll, Jr.; Jeffrey W. Paul; Theodore F. Olt III; Cameron A. Davidson; Judith L. Herrmann; Robert Blake McMonagle; Christopher J. Curran; Joseph C. Judge; Jason J. O'Rourke; Troy D. Venner; Courtney M. Kay-Decker; Troy A. Howell; Diane M. Reinsch. Associates: Catherine E.E. Hult; Mikkie R. Schiltz; Diane E. Puthoff; Stacey L. Hawke; Wendy S. Meyer; Erika L. Gilmore (Not admitted in IA). Of Counsel: Robert A. Van Vooren; Thomas N. Kamp.
General Civil Practice, Corporation, Business, Banking, Taxation, Securities, Labor, Employment Discrimination, Environmental, Health Care, Insurance Defense, Pension and Profit-Sharing, Real Estate, Estate and Probate, Wills and Trusts.
Counsel for: Davenport Community School District; Genesis Health System; Isle of Capri Casinos; Lee Enterprises, Incorporated; MidAmerican Energy Co.; THE National Bank, N.A.; Van Maur, Inc.; Deere & Co.; Employers Mutual Companies; Verizon Wireless.
Rock Island, Illinois Office: 224 18th Street, Suite 500. Telephone: 309-786-1600. Fax: 309-786-1794.
See Professional Biographies, DAVENPORT, IOWA

Latham, Henry W., II .... '64 '91 C.707 B.A. L.352 J.D. [Ⓐ Brooks&T.]
Lathrop, Roger A., (AV) .... '51 '76 C.351 B.A. L.352 J.D. [Betty,N.&M.]
Laverty, Joseph H., (CV) .... '68 '94 C.707 B.A. L.1187 J.D. [Wessels&P.]
Ledden, Matthew A. .... '75 '01 C.352 B.A. L.221 J.D. [Ⓐ Gallagher,M.&G.]
Levien, Craig A., (AV) .... '53 '79 C.93 B.A. L.352 J.D. [Betty,N.&M.]
Liebbe, Michael W., Law Office of, (AV) '46 '71
C&L.352 B.B.A., J.D. 111 E. 3rd St., Ste. 700
Lindburg, Thomas O., (AV) .... '33 '57 C&L.221 B.S., LL.B. [Ⓒ Stanley,L.&H.]
Lovig, Richard G. .... '59 '87 C&L.221 B.S.B.A., J.D. 106 E. 2nd St.
Lussier, Steven C., (CV) .... '54 '80 C.912 B.S. L.190 J.D. City Atty.
Lynch, Michael A. .... '58 '84 C.352 B.B.A. L.1119 J.D. Law Clk., Dist. Ct. J.
Lyness, Janet M. .... '59 '89 C&L.352 B.S., J.D. Law Clk., Dist. Ct.
Macek, Paul L., (BV) .... '48 '73 C&L.352 B.A., J.D. [Dircks,R.&M.]
Machetta, Sally, Law Offices of .... '64 '99 C.707 B.A. L.365 J.D. P.O. Box 2503
Maess, Sheri L., (BV) .... '71 '97 C.57 B.A. L.589 J.D. Lee Enterprises, Inc.
Mahl, David A., (CV) .... '65 '91 C.352 B.B.A. L.734 J.D. [Gosma,T.&Assoc.]
Maness, Barbara E. .... '50 '94 C.208 B.A. L.352 J.D. [Maness,B.]
Maness, Barbara .... 116 E. 6th St.
Martin, John R. .... '47 '72 C&L.352 B.B.A., J.D. Corp. Coun., City of Davenport

McAtee, M. Anne, (BV) .... '61 '89 C.352 B.B.A. L.190 J.D. [Hopkins&H.]
McCarthy, Michael J., (BV) .... '49 '76 C.352 B.A. L.190 J.D. [McCarthy,L.&H.]

McCarthy, Callas, Fuhr & Ellison, P.C.
(See Rock Island, Illinois)

McCarthy, Lammers & Hines, (BV)
701 Kahl Building, 52801
Telephone: 563-324-9117 Fax: 563-324-8367
Email: mjmccarthylwr@aol.com URL: http://www.mccarthylammershines.com
Members of Firm: Martin F. McCarthy (1904-1987); Michael J. McCarthy; Lawrence J. Lammers; Michael T. Hines.
General Civil Practice. Trials, Personal Injury, Workers Compensation, Wills, Trusts, Probate, Criminal Law, Real Estate, Family Law, Divorce, Child Custody, Estate Planning, Bankruptcy, Juvenile.
Reference: Wells Fargo, Davenport, Iowa.
See Professional Biographies, DAVENPORT, IOWA

McCullough, William T., (CV) .... '59 '84 C.352 B.B.A. L.1065 J.D. 220 Emerson Pl.
McDonald, Douglas .... '35 '63 C.174 B.S. L.221 J.D. Assoc. Dist. J.
McDonald, Elliott R., III, (BV) .... '56 '81 C&L.352 B.A., J.D. [McDonald,W.&I.]
McDonald, Elliott R. (Jack), Jr., (AV) .. '29 '52 C&L.352 B.A., J.D. [McDonald,W.&I.]

McDonald, Woodward & Ivers, P.C., (AV)
Jersey Ridge Office Center, 3432 Jersey Ridge Road, P.O. Box 2746, 52809-2746
Telephone: 563-355-6478 Fax: 563-355-1354
URL: http://www.mwilawyers.com
Elliott R. McDonald, III; Patricia Rhodes Cepican (1950-2004); Patrick L. Woodward; Brian C. Ivers; Elliott R. (Jack) McDonald, Jr.;—Heather L. Carlson (Not admitted in IA); Howard Zimmerle II.
Civil Trial Practice and Appeals in State and Federal Courts. Insurance Defense, Workers Compensation, Personal Injury, Real Estate, Professional Negligence, Business Law, Litigation, Probate, Wills, Trusts, Employment Discrimination, Contracts, Corporate Law, Wrongful Death, Medical Malpractice, Commercial Litigation, Construction Litigation.
Representative Clients: CNA Insurance; American Family Insurance; Farm Bureau Insurance; Philadelphia Insurance.
See Professional Biographies, DAVENPORT, IOWA

McKay, William '23 '49 C&L.477 B.A., J.D.
(adm. in MI; not adm. in IA) P.O. Box 2409‡
McKenrick, Gary D., (BV) .... '56 '82 C.187 B.S.S. L.352 J.D. Dist. J.
McMonagle, Robert Blake, (BV) .... '63 '95 C&L.602 B.A., J.D. [Lane&W.]
Meloy, David J., (BV) .... '50 '75 C&L.352 B.A., J.D. [Stanley,L.&H.] (⊙Muscatine)
Meloy, Michael J., (BV) .... '51 '79 C&L.352 B.B.A., J.D. City Atty.
Mestan, Amanda T. .... '78 '03 C.337 B.A. L.221 J.D. 111 E. Third St., Ste. 600
Meyer, Wendy S. .... '72 '03 C&L.352 B.A., J.D. [Ⓐ Lane&W.]
Mezvinsky, James A., (AV) .... '48 '73 C.352 B.B.A. L.802 J.D. [Lane&W.]
Mientus, Sandra J. .... '60 '88 C.350 B.S. L.352 J.D. P.O. Box 4376
Millage, David A., (BV) .... '53 '78 C&L.352 B.B.A., J.D. [Gallagher,M.&G.]
Miller, Charles E., (AV) .... '45 '73 C.597 A.B. L.352 J.D. [Lane&W.] ⊙
Miller, David P. .... '34 '60 C&L.352 B.A., LL.B. [Miller,D.P.]
Miller, David P., PC .... 1707 Washington St.
Moeller, Cynthia A. .... '58 '88 C.966 B.B.A. L.221 J.D. Norwest Bank Iowa, NA

Moeller, John O., (BV) '53 '79 C&L.352 B.G.S., J.D.
601 Brady Street, Suite 303, 52803
Telephone: 563-323-3014 Fax: 563-323-9403
Email: moellerj@muscanet.com URL: http://www.johnmoeller.com
General Practice including but not limited to trial and appellate practice concerning criminal law, personal injury, product liability, real estate, business law, admirality law and maritime law in all State and Federal Courts.
See Professional Biographies, DAVENPORT, IOWA

Molyneaux, John E., (CV) .... '45 '71 C.1107 A.B. L.818 J.D. 230 W. 3rd St.
Motto, Michael J., (BV) .... '53 '82 C.707 B.A. L.285 J.D. [Bush,M.C.H.&K.]
Motto, Vincent J., (BV) .... '47 '72 C.707 B.A. L.734 J.D. [Vander V.&M.]
Nahra, John A. .... '53 '78 C.209 B.A. L.190 J.D. Chf. Dist. J.
Nepple, James A., (AVⓉ) .... '45 '70 C.190 B.A. L.352 J.D. [Nepple L.] ⊙

Nepple Law, P.L.C., (AV)
Wells Fargo Bank Building, 4300 E. 53rd Street, Suite 103, 52807 ⊙
Telephone: 563-355-6841 Telecopier: 563-355-8842 Toll Free: 877-888-0675
Email: tax@nepplelaw.com URL: http://www.nepplelaw.com
James A. Nepple;—Jay Jung; Michelle L. Heller.
Taxation, Estate Planning, Trust and Estate Administration, Wills and Probate Administration, Nonprofit and Charitable Organizations, Businesses and Corporations, Pension and Profit Sharing Plans, Real Estate, Farms and Ranches.
Muscatine, Iowa Office: Hershey Professional Center, 216 Sycamore Street, Suite 500, 52761-3809. Telephone: 563-264-6840. Toll Free: 877-888-0675. Telecopier: 563-264-6844.
Rock Island, Illinois Office: American Bank Building, 1515 Fourth Avenue, Suite 300, 61201. Telephone: 309-732-1230; Toll Free: 877-888-0675. Telecopier: 309-786-0061.

Neuman, Henry G., (AV) .... '48 '74 C.57 B.A. L.174 J.D. [Betty,N.&M.]
Newman, John R., (BV) .... '57 '82 C.57 B.A. L.352 J.D. [Wehr,B.L.&S.]
Newport, Stephen W., (BV) .... '52 '78 C.1281 B.A. L.221 J.D. [Newport&N.]
Newport, Walter .... '17 '48 C.350 B.S. L.352 J.D. 246 W. 3rd St.‡
Newport, Wayne M., (BV) .... '18 '52 C.871 B.S. L.352 J.D. [Newport&N.]
Newport & Newport, (BV) .... 309 W. Kimberly Rd.
Norman, George B., (CV) .... '30 '82 C.352 B.S.C. L.146 J.D. 220 Emerson Pl.
Noth, James G., (AV) .... '20 '48 C.707 B.A. L.276 J.D. [Gosma,T.&Assoc.]
Noyes, Michael L., (AV) .... '46 '71 C&L.352 B.A., J.D. [Lane&W.]

Nyemaster, Goode, West, Hansell & O'Brien, A Professional Corporation
(See Des Moines)

O'Brien, Dorothy A., (AV) .... '49 '84 C.339 B.A. L.352 J.D. [O'Brien&G.]
O'Brien & Greve, P.C., (AV) .... 2322 East Kimberly Rd.
Olt, Theodore F., III, (BV) .... '62 '95 C.871 B.S. L.352 J.D. [Lane&W.]
Oppel, Curt A., (BV) .... '63 '88 C.352 B.B.A. L.221 J.D. [Stanley,L.&H.] (⊙Wilton)
O'Rourke, Jason J., (BVⓉ) .... '73 '98 C&L.190 B.A., J.D. [Lane&W.] ⊙
Ottesen, James L., (BV) .... '43 '68 C&L.352 LL.B. 2717 Fairhaven Rd.
Otto, Kelly W. .... '62 '93 C&L.352 B.A., J.D. Staff Atty., American Family Insurance

Pappas & Schnell, P.C.
(See Rock Island, Illinois)

Pastrnak, Candy K., (BV) .... '58 '83 C&L.221 B.A., J.D. [Pastrnak]
Pastrnak, Thomas J., (BV) .... '59 '84 C.145 B.A. L.221 J.D. [Pastrnak] ⊙

Pastrnak Law Firm, P.C., (BV)
313 West Third Street, 52801 ⊙
Telephone: 563-323-7737 Fax: 563-323-7739
Email: tpastrnak@pastrnak.com
Thomas J. Pastrnak; Candy K. Pastrnak. Of Counsel: Thomas R. Schulz. Associate: William P. Laird.
General Civil and Trial Practice. Corporation, Business, Banking, Tax-Exempt Financing, Labor, Employment Discrimination, Administrative, Creditor Bankruptcy, Personal Injury and Property Damage Law, Real Estate, Probate, Estate Planning and Family Law.
Moline, Illinois Office: 1535-47th Avenue, Suite 3, 61265. Telephone: 309-757-7737. Fax: 309-763-3858.
See Professional Biographies, DAVENPORT, IOWA

Paul, Jeffrey W., (BV) ....'51 '89 C.350 B.S. L.352 J.D. [Lane&W.]
Pauly, Maria K., (CV) .... '70 '97 C.352 B.A. L.793 J.D. [🄰 Wehr,B.L.&S.]
Peart, Charles K., (BV) .... '26 '51 C&L.352 B.A., J.D. [🄲 Wehr,B.L.&S.]
Petruccelli, Don A. .... '13 '40 C.707 B.A. L.793 LL.B. Sr. Dist. Assoc. J.
Phelps, Lauren M., (CV) .... '52 '92 C&L.352 B.L.S., J.D. [Phelps&P.]
Phelps, Robert J., (CV) ....'46 '75 C.352 B.A. L.862 J.D. [Phelps&P.]
Phelps & Phelps, (CV) .... 1622 East Lombard St.
Pries, H. J., (BV) ....'48 '77 C&L.608 B.S., J.D. [Stanley,L.&H.]
Priester, Theodore J., (BV) ....'50 '76 C.674 A.B. L.352 J.D. 601 Brady St.
Puthoff, Diane E. ....'75 '01 C.436 B.A. L.190 J.D. [🄰 Lane&W.]
Raben, Seymore M., (AV) .... '24 '49 C&L.352 B.A., J.D. 121 W. Locust St.
Rector, William P., (BVⓉ) ....'62 '87 C.896 B.A. L.352 J.D. [Bozeman,N.P.&N.] ⊙
Reichwald, Timothy J. .... '78 '04 C.694 B.A. L.221 J.D. [🄰 Betty,N.&M.]
Reier, Angela N. .... '80 '05 C.597 B.S. L.352 J.D. [🄰 Stanley,L.&H.]
Reinsch, Diane M., (BVⓉ) ....'58 '96 C.350 B.A. L.352 J.D. [Lane&W.] ⊙
Reynolds, Brad A., (BV) .... '72 '97 C&L.352 B.A., J.D. [🄰 O'Brien&G.]
Ridenour, Rex J., (BV) .... '45 '69 C.351 B.A. L.352 J.D. [Dircks,R.&M.]
Roeder, Michael L., (BV) ....'40 '67 C&L.352 B.S.I.E., J.D. [Franks&R.]
Roemer, Janice H., (BV) ....'38 '85 C.707 B.A. L.352 J.D. 712 Kahl Bldg.
Rolling-Tarbox, Marie R., (BV) ....'58 '87 C&L.352 B.A., J.D. [Gosma,T.&Assoc.]
Rose, Edward J. .... '76 '02 C.352 B.A. L.972 J.D. [🄰 Betty,N.&M.]
Roseberry, Carrie N. .... '77 '03 C.350 B.A. L.221 J.D. [🄰 Betty,N.&M.]
Salabert, Paul, Jr. ....'70 '96 C.57 B.A. L.597 J.D. [🄰 Hopkins&H.]
Schalk, Stephen L., (BV) ....'47 '72 C.57 B.A. L.352 J.D. 310 Main St.
Schebler, Thomas G., (BV) .... '— '61 C.707 B.A. L.352 J.D. [Schebler,W.&C.]

Schebler, Wine & Collins, (AV)
1414 West Locust Street, 52804
Telephone: 563-324-1387 Fax: 563-324-1389
Email: swclaw@netexpress.net URL: http://www.lawyers.com/scheblerwine
Members of Firm: Thomas G. Schebler; Thomas L. Wine; John J. Collins (1923-2005).
Trusts, Wills, Estate Planning, Probate, Buying/Selling, Real Estate, Elder Law, Mortgage Foreclosure, Landlord/Tenant Law.

See Professional Biographies, DAVENPORT, IOWA

Schermer, Gregory P. '54 '81 C.31 B.A. L.190 J.D.
(adm. in DC; not adm. in IA) Corp. Coun., Lee Enterprises, Inc.
Schiltz, Mikkie R. .... '73 '97 C.1176 B.A. L.339 J.D. [🄰 Lane&W.]
Schmidt, Stephen P. '63 '91 C.999 B.S. L.190 J.D.
(adm. in NE; not adm. in IA) Tr. Offr., Norwest Bk. Iowa, N.A.
Schoenthaler, David E. .... '40 '64 C&L.352 B.A., J.D. Dist. J.
Schroeder, Sara, (CV) ....'62 '95 C.707 B.A. L.352 J.D. 3104 Eads St.
Schulz, Thomas R., (CV) ....'45 '72 C.734 B.S. L.352 J.D. [🄲 Pastrnak]
Shaff, Martha L., (AV) ....'64 '89 C.747 B.A. L.221 J.D. [Betty,N.&M.]
Shaw, Donald H. .... '22 '48 C.309 S.B. L.352 J.D. 246 W. 3rd St.‡
Shaw, Elizabeth O. ....'23 '49 C.221 A.B. L.352 J.D. 29 Hillcrest Ave.‡
Shawver, Bruce A., (BV) .... '33 '60 C&L.221 B.S.B.A., J.D. [🄲 Shawver&S.]
Shawver, Judy A., (BV) ....'55 '80 C.221 B.S. L.209 J.D. [Shawver&S.]
Shawver & Shawver, (BV) ....2805 Eastern Avenue
Shie, Thomas E., Law Offices of, (BV) '66 '91
C.352 B.B.A. L.146 J.D. 601 Brady St., Ste. 220

Simmons, Kent A., (AV) '55 '81 C&L.352 B.A., J.D.
601 Brady Street, Suite 211, 52803
Telephone: 563-322-7784 Fax: 563-323-9309
Email: ttswlaw@bigplanet.com URL: http://www.kentasimmons.com
Criminal Law, Post Conviction and Habeas Corpus, Trial and Appellate Practice, DWI, Drug Crimes, Felonies, Homicide and Sexual Assault.

See Professional Biographies, DAVENPORT, IOWA

Sissel, Gary L., (BVⓉ) ....'48 '73 C&L.352 B.A., J.D. [Bozeman,N.P.&N.] ⊙
Slavens, Joe B., (BV) ...... '64 '88 C&L.352 B.B.A., J.D. Pres., Northwest Bk. & Tr. Co.
Sloane, L. Ted. ....'28 '53 C&L.221 LL.B. 1019 Mound St.‡
Smith, Mark J. .... '49 '75 C.707 B.A. L.734 J.D. Dist. J.

Snyder, Park & Nelson, P.C.
(See Rock Island, Illinois)

Sohr, David J. ....'32 '61 C&L.352 B.S.C., J.D. Dist. J.
Sondgeroth, Nathan M. ....'79 '04 C.57 B.A. L.352 J.D. [🄰 Hopkins&H.]
Soper, Jerry A., (BV) .... '54 '82 C.350 B.S. L.190 J.D. [Soper]
Soper Law Firm PC, (BV) .... 5108 C Jersey Ridge Rd.
Sothmann, James G., (CV) ....'52 '78 C.602 B.A. L.352 J.D. 1503 Brady St.
Souhrada, Penny, (CV) .... '— '93 C.436 B.A. L.352 J.D. 601 Brady Street, Suite 300

Stanley, Lande & Hunter, A Professional Corporation, (AV)
900 U.S. Bank Center, 201 West Second Street, 52801 ⊙
Telephone: 563-324-1000 Facsimile: 563-326-6266
Email: Contact.us@slhlaw.com URL: http://www.slhlaw.com
Roger L. Lande; Charles R. Coulter; Robert L. Lande; Steven T. Hunter; David J. Meloy; Patrick W. Driscoll; Joan U. Axel; Eric J. Thomsen; Curt A. Oppel; John A. Kuhl; Joel K. Heriford; H. J. Pries; Steven J. Havercamp;—Brandy Dulceak; Jean E. Dragon; Wes A. Fowler; Angela N. Reier; Andrew M. Telschow. Of Counsel: Thomas O. Lindburg.
General Civil and Trial Practice. Corporation, Business, Banking, Taxation, Securities, Tax-Exempt Financing, Labor, Employment Discrimination, Administrative, Creditor Bankruptcy and Agricultural Law, Insurance Defense, Personal Injury and Property Damage Law, Pension and Profit-Sharing, Real Estate, Probate, Estate Planning and Charitable Trusts and Foundations Law.
General Counsel for: First National Bank of Muscatine.
Representative Clients: HON Industries, Inc. and its subsidiaries; Milwaukee Mutual Insurance Co.; Stanley Consultants, Inc. and its affiliates.
Muscatine, Iowa Office: 301 Iowa Avenue, Suite 400. Telephone: 563-264-5000. Facsimile: 563-263-8775.
Wilton, Iowa Office: 115 West Fourth, P.O. Box 481. Telephone: 563-732-4000. Facsimile: 563-732-2318.
Coralville, Iowa Office: 2201 East Grantview Drive, Suite 200. Telephone: 319-248-9000. Facsimile: 319-248-9001.

See Professional Biographies, DAVENPORT, IOWA

Steffen, Phillip T., Jr. .... '26 '53 C.707 B.A. L.352 LL.B. Ret. Dist. J.
Stevens, Richard L., (BV) .... '12 '39 C.57 B.A. L.352 J.D. [🄲 Wehr,B.L.&S.]

Sturm & Fix LLP, (AV)
304 Northwest Bank Building-Downtown, 101 West Second Street, 52801-1813 ⊙
Telephone: 563-323-9731 Fax: 563-323-9709
URL: http://www.hsllp.com
Member of Firm: John E. Cepican.
Patent, Trademark, Copyright and Unfair Competition Law, Federal Trial Practice, Intellectual Property.
Des Moines, Iowa Office: 206 Sixth Avenue, Suite 1213, 50309-4076. Telephone: 515-288-9589. Fax: 515-288-4860.

See Professional Biographies, DAVENPORT, IOWA

Suchy, Anton J., (BV) ....'48 '74 C&L.190 B.S., J.D. [Vollertsen&B.]
Tabor, Nancy S. .... '58 '86 C.1174 B.S. L.972 J.D. Dist. J.
Taylor, Cynthia J. Z., (BV) ....'58 '87 C.707 B.A. L.352 J.D. 125 Kirkwood Blvd.
Teel, Katherine Varlas, (CV) .... '57 '89 C.927 B.S. L.352 J.D. 601 Brady
Teitle, Morton A., (BV) ....'40 '65 C&L.352 B.A., LL.B. 326 W. 3rd St.
Telleen, John D., (BV) ....'58 '84 C.57 B.A. L.352 J.D. [Lane&W.] ⊙
Telschow, Andrew M. .... '78 '04 C.705 B.A. L.352 J.D. [🄰 Stanley,L.&H.]
Thill, Peter J., (BV) .... '69 '95 C.340 B.A. L.221 J.D. [Betty,N.&M.]
Thompson, Duane D., (BVⓉ) .... '55 '80 C&L.339 B.A., J.D. P.O. Box 3010
Thomsen, Eric J., (AV) '53 '78
C.350 B.S. L.352 J.D. [Stanley,L.&H.] (⊙Muscatine, Wilton)
Tobey, J. E. "Mike", III, (BV) .... '46 '74 C.607 B.A. L.352 J.D. 601 Brady St.

Treimer, David R., (BV) '54 '92 C.350 B.S. L.352 J.D.
601 Brady Street, Suite 211, 52803
Telephone: 563-323-7889 Fax: 563-323-9309
Email: ttswlaw@bigplanet.com URL: http://www.dtreimer.com
State and Federal Criminal Defense, Felonies, Driving While Intoxicated, White Collar Crime, Drug Crimes, Parole and Probation, Traffic Violations, Juvenile Law.

See Professional Biographies, DAVENPORT, IOWA

Tupper, Timothy J. ....'59 '86 C&L.352 B.B.A., J.D. [Tupper]
Tupper Law Firm .... 5108 Jersey Ridge Rd.
Tyler, M. Leanne, (CV) ....'54 '81 C.593 B.S. L.352 J.D. [Tyler&Assoc.]
Tyler & Associates, (CV) .... 4431 E. 56th St.
Vander Vennet & Motto, P.C., (BV) ....715 Union Arcade Bldg.
Van Driel, Eugene P. .... '36 '63 C.898 B.A. L.352 J.D. 1516 W. 13th Street
Van Vooren, R. Scott, (AV) .... '57 '83 C.190 B.S.B.A. L.352 J.D. [Lane&W.]
Van Vooren, Robert A., (AVⓉ) ....'33 '60 C.436 B.S. L.597 J.D. [🄲 Lane&W.]
Varlas-Teel, Katherine A., (CV) .... '57 '89 C.927 B.S. L.352 J.D. 601 Brady St.
Venner, Troy D., (BV) .... '71 '98 C.958 B.A. L.221 J.D. [Lane&W.]
Vollertsen & Britt, P.C., (AV) ....101 W. Third St.
Volz, Marlin M., Jr. '43 '68 C&L.228 B.A., J.D.
Sr. V.P. & Tr. Coun., Norwest Bk. Iowa, N.A.
Walker, Carol J., (CV) ....'61 '92 C.132 B.A. L.352 J.D. 1503 Brady St.
Walker, Michael C., (BV) ....'65 '92 C.350 B.A. L.352 J.D. [Hopkins&H.]
Wallace, Ted James, (BV) '62 '91
C.351 B.S. L.352 J.D. Sr. Staff Atty., Amer. Fam. Ins. Grp.
Walters, Scott H., (BV) .... '54 '80 C.350 B.S. L.352 J.D. 1503 Brady St.
Walton, Julie A., (BV) ....'64 '91 C.755 B.A. L.352 J.D. Asst. Co. Atty.
Walton, Michael J., (BV) .... '60 '87 C.493 B.S. L.300 J.D. [Walton&W.]
Walton, Raymond T., (BV) .... '21 '56 C.707 B.A. L.221 J.D. [Walton&W.]
Walton & Walton, (BV) ....601 Brady St.
Warhank, Rodney D. ....'59 '88 C.800 B.S. L.900 J.D. 4210 Forest Rd.
Warner, Thomas D., (BV) ....'64 '91 C&L.352 B.B.A., J.D. 600 Davenport Bk. Bldg.
Waterman, C. Dana, III, (AV) .... '46 '71 C.197 A.B. L.352 J.D. [Lane&W.]
Waterman, Robert V. P., Jr., (AV) ....'55 '81 C.597 B.A. L.352 J.D. [Lane&W.] ⊙
Waterman, Thomas D., (AV) .... '59 '84 C.197 B.A. L.352 J.D. [Lane&W.]
Waterman, Wm. B. .... '08 '34 C.197 A.B. L.309 LL.B. 220 N. Main St.‡
Wehr, Edward N., (AV) .... '27 '51 C.707 L.352 LL.B. [Wehr,B.L.&S.]
Wehr, Berger, Lane & Stevens, (AV) ....326 West Third Street
Weinberg, Robert E., (BV) ....'43 '77 C.597 B.A. L.107 J.D. 2348 Hickory Grove Rd.
Weindruch, Linda S., (AV) .... '56 '84 C.707 B.A. L.221 J.D. [L.S.Weindruch]
Weindruch, Linda S., P.C., (AV) .... 6612 Somerset Road
Werner, Clemens A., Jr., (BV) ....'47 '74 C.478 B.A. L.352 J.D. [Bittner,L.&W.]
Wessels, Richard H., (AVⓉ) '39 '67
C.388 B.A. L.209 J.D. [Wessels&P.] (⊙St. Charles, IL)

Wessels & Pautsch, P.C., (AVⓉ)
Northwest Bank Building, 101 West Second Street, Suite 307, 52801 ⊙
Telephone: 563-333-9102 Fax: 563-333-9105
Email: wessels@stch.w-p.com URL: http://www.w-p.com
Richard H. Wessels; Joseph H. Laverty.
Representing Employers in Labor and Employment Law Matters. NLRA, RLA, all Federal and State Employment Discrimination Laws, Federal and State Disability Laws, Wrongful Discharge, Employment Contracts, Collective Bargaining Negotiations and Arbitrations, Employee Substance Abuse, Safety and Health, Unemployment Insurance, Benefits Law, Wage and Hour, and Employment-Based Immigration Matters. Litigation before all Federal and State Courts and Agencies, Trial and Appellate Practice.
St. Charles, Illinois Office: Dunham Center, 2035 Foxfield Drive. Telephone: 630-377-1554. Fax: 630-377-1653.
Milwaukee, Wisconsin Office: Two Plaza East, 330 East Kilbourn Avenue, Suite 1475. Telephone: 414-291-0600. FAX: 414-291-0200.
Chicago, Illinois Office: Chicago Bar Association Building, 321 South Plymouth Court, Suite 900. Telephone: 312-461-0500. Fax: 312-461-0595.
Minneapolis, Minnesota Office: MoneyGram Tower, 1550 Utica Avenue South, Suite 450. Telephone: 952-746-1700. Fax: 952-746-1704.
Indianapolis, Indiana Office: Market Tower, 10 West Market Street, Suite 1770. Telephone: 317-656-8800. Fax: 317-656-8855.

See Professional Biographies, DAVENPORT, IOWA

Williams, Sandra L. N. '49 '81 C.707 B.A. L.352 J.D.
Davenport Human Relations Comm.
Williamson, Kyle D., (BV) ....'67 '93 C.352 B.A. L.190 J.D. [Williamson]
Williamson Law Office, LC, (BV) ....710 E. Kimberly Road, Suite 5
Wine, Thomas L., (AV) ....'— '61 C&L.352 B.S.C., J.D. [Schebler,W.&C.]
Wing, Stephen P., (BV) ....'56 '80 C.694 A.B. L.352 J.D. [Dwyer&W.]

Winstein, Kavensky & Wallace
(See Rock Island, Illinois)

Wonio, Rand S., (AV) .... '50 '77 C.707 B.A. L.733 J.D. [Lane&W.]
Woods, Michael A., (BV) ....'51 '76 C&L.352 B.A., J.D. 125 E. Kirkwood Blvd.
Woodward, Patrick L., (BV) ....'57 '83 C.707 B.S. L.352 J.D. [McDonald,W.&I.]
Woollums, Cathy Schumann, (BV) '60 '87 C.493 B.A. L.221 J.D.
V.P., Envir. & Chf. Envir. Coun., MidAmerican Energy Holdings Co.
Woollums, Mark A., (BV) .... '61 '86 C.350 B.A. L.221 J.D. [Betty,N.&M.]
Yeggy, Thomas J., (BV) ....'50 '76 C.898 B.A. L.352 J.D. 1503 Brady St.
Zamora, Patricia, (BV) ....'39 '86 C.707 B.A. L.352 J.D. 125 Kirkwood Blvd.
Zimmerle, Howard, II .... '81 '05 C.351 B.A. L.352 J.D. [🄰 McDonald,W.&I.]

DAYTON, 818, *Webster Co.*

Ferguson, Keith, (CV) ....'32 '58 C&L.221 J.D. 35 S. Main St.
Holland, Leonard R., (BV) .... '42 '71 C.221 B.A. L.1137 J.D. 307 1st St. N.W.

DECORAH, * 8,172, *Winneshiek Co.*

Anderson, Calvin R., (AV) .... '40 '69 C.350 B.S. L.352 J.D. [Anderson&V.M.]
Anderson & Van Der Maaten, (AV) ....212 Winnebago
Beatty, Marion L., (AV) ....'53 '77 C.427 B.A. L.352 J.D. [Miller,P.G.B.B.&C.]
Belay, Stephen J., (CV) ....'58 '83 C&L.352 B.A., J.D. [Anderson&V.M.]
Burns, James, (BV) ....'48 '74 C.187 B.A. L.352 J.D. [Miller,P.G.B.B.&C.]
Cowie, Robert J., Jr., (AV) ....'55 '80 C.589 B.A. L.352 J.D. [Miller,P.G.B.B.&C.]
Frana, Christy A., (CV) ....'64 '91 C&L.352 B.A., J.D. 312 W. Main St.
Gloe, Donald H., (AV) ....'35 '61 C&L.352 B.A., J.D. [🄲 Miller,P.G.B.B.&C.]
Keefe, Joseph C. ....'26 '52 C&L.352 B.A., J.D. Ret. Dist. Ct. J.‡
Knudson, Karl G. .... '50 '79 C.747 B.A. L.352 J.D. Co. Atty.

Larson, Dennis G., (BV) ... ’47 ’75 C.352 B.A. L.300 J.D. [Larson]

Larson Law Office, (BV) ... 312 W. Main St.

Lickiss, Stephen J. ... ’67 ’95 C&L.352 B.A., J.D. 312 W. Main St.

Lingreen, Margaret L. ... ’52 ’77 C&L.221 B.S., J.D. Dist. J.

Lorentzen, Lance P., (BV) ... ’46 ’74 C.57 B.A. L.879 J.D. [Meyer&L.]

Lynch, Timothy C., (BV) ... ’50 ’75 C&L.352 B.B.A., J.D. [Lynch]

Lynch Law Office, (BV) ... 206 W. Main St.

Maki, Laura J. Parrish ... ’78 ’04 C.187 B.A. L.352 J.D. [🄰 Miller,P.G.B.B.&C.]

Meyer, Isadore, (AV) ... ’15 ’40 C&L.352 B.A., J.D. [Meyer&L.] ‡

Meyer & Lorentzen, (BV) ... P.O. Box 126 101 1/2 East Water Street

Miller, Pearson, Gloe, Burns, Beatty & Cowie, P.L.C., (AV)
301 West Broadway, 52101
Telephone: 563-382-4226 Fax: 563-382-3783
Email: millerlaw@dybb.com
Frank R. Miller (1915-1977); James Burns; Marion L. Beatty; Robert J. Cowie, Jr.;—Laura J. Parrish Maki. Of Counsel: Floyd S. Pearson; Donald H. Gloe.
General Practice, all Courts. Insurance Law, Estate Planning, Personal Injury, Family Law, Taxation and Probate.
Counsel for: Luther College; Decorah Community School District; Winneshiek County Memorial Hospital; Community First National Bank.
Local Counsel for: Iowa Mutual Insurance Cos.; Employers Mutual Liability Insurance Co. of Wisconsin; Continental Casualty Co.; Employers Mutual Casualty Co.; Grinnell Mutual Insurance Co.; Allied Mutual Insurance Co.

See Professional Biographies, DECORAH, IOWA

Nichols, Sherry Raduenz, (BV) ... ’48 ’73 C&L.494 B.A., J.D. [🄰 Larson]

Pearson, Floyd S., (AV) ... ’18 ’48 C&L.352 B.A., J.D. [🄲 Miller,P.G.B.B.&C.]

Petersburg, Paula J. Larson ’54 ’79 C.427 B.A. L.352 J.D. V.P. & Tr. Offr., Community First National Bk.

Putnam, Dale Lee, (CV) ... ’57 ’83 C.350 B.A. L.221 J.D. 518 Montgomery St.

Riker, Christopher R. ’67 ’93 C.352 B.A. L.208 J.D. (adm. in CO; not adm. in IA) [Strand&R.]

Schrader, Steven C., (CV) ... ’48 ’73 C&L.352 B.B.A., J.D. Judicial Mag.

Strand, David L., (BV) ... ’59 ’84 C.350 B.S. L.221 J.D. [Strand&R.]

Strand & Riker, (BV) ... 209 East Water Street

Van Der Maaten, Andrew F., (BV) ’60 ’85 C.595 B.A. L.221 J.D. Co. Atty. [Anderson&V.M.]

Wilmarth, Lee E., (BV) ... ’55 ’80 C&L.352 B.B.A., J.D. 212 Winnebago

Zahasky, Richard D., (BV) ’47 ’73 C.177 B.S. L.190 J.D.
309 West Water Street, P.O. Box 257, 52101
Telephone: 563-382-8409 Fax: 563-382-8400
General, Civil and Trial Practice. Personal Injury, Probate, Real Estate, Insurance, Corporate and Municipal Law. Collective Bargaining Negotiations.

See Professional Biographies, DECORAH, IOWA

DENISON, * 7,339, *Crawford Co.*

Boddicker, Joe L., (BV) ... ’39 ’64 C.177 B.A. L.352 J.D. Mag. (☉Charter Oak)

Brannen, Stephan A., (BV) ... ’55 ’79 C&L.190 B.S.B.A., J.D. [🄰 Gustafson]

Brink, Robert L., (BV) ... ’42 ’72 C.1050 B.A. L.352 J.D. [Eller,B.&S.]

Crandall, Richard H., (BV) ... ’25 ’52 C&L.352 B.A., LL.B. [🄲 Eller,B.&S.] ‡

Eller, Thomas R., (AV) ... ’42 ’67 C.118 A.B. L.352 J.D. [Eller,B.&S.]

Eller, Brink & Sextro, L.L.P., (AV) ... 40 N. Main Street

Franck, D. R., (AV) ... ’48 ’73 C.1070 B.S. L.352 J.D. [Mundt,F.&S.]

Gustafson, Thomas E., (BV) ... ’49 ’76 C.351 B.A. L.352 J.D. Co. Atty. [Gustafson]

Gustafson Law Firm, (BV) ... 27 South Main (☉Bay City, MI)

Lohman, James D., (AV) ... ’46 ’76 C.351 B.A. L.190 J.D. [Reimer,L.&R.]

Mundt, Michael R., (AV) ... ’40 ’69 C.352 B.A. L.190 J.D. [Mundt,F.&S.]

Mundt, Franck & Schumacher, (AV) ... 1231 Broadway, Suite 300

Nelson, Bradley J., (BV) ... ’60 ’88 C.350 B.S. L.221 J.D. [Norelius&N.]

Norelius, Wm. Q., (AV) ... ’28 ’52 C&L.352 A.B., J.D. [Norelius&N.]

Norelius & Nelson, (AV) ... 23 N. 14th St.

Reimer, Robert C., (AV) ... ’27 ’50 C&L.352 B.A., J.D. [Reimer,L.&R.]

Reimer, Lohman & Reitz, (AV) ... 25 S. Main

Reitz, Reed H., (BV) ... ’57 ’83 C&L.546 B.S., J.D. [Reimer,L.&R.]

Schumacher, Julie A., (BV) ... ’67 ’93 C.793 B.A. L.190 J.D. [Mundt,F.&S.]

Sextro, Gregory J., (BV) ... ’60 ’85 C&L.352 B.B.A., J.D. [Eller,B.&S.]

Vipond, Richard J. ... ’38 ’63 C&L.273 A.B., J.D. Dist. J.

DENVER, 1,600, *Bremer Co.*

Baldwin, Timothy M., (BV) ... ’57 ’84 C.351 B.A. L.190 J.D. 171 E. Main

Stumme, Lawrence A., Jr., (BV) ... ’38 ’77 C.898 B.D. L.117 J.D. Co. Atty. [Stumme]

Stumme Law Office, (BV) ... 171 E. Main

DES MOINES, * 198,682, *Polk Co.*

Abbas, Cory D. ... ’73 ’04 C&L.221 B.S.B.A., J.D. [🄰 Patterson,L.D.T.I.B.&O.]

Abbott, Allison R. ... ’73 ’99 C.36 B.A. L.221 J.D. [🄰 Elverson,V.&P.]

Abels, Marcus F., (BV) ... ’58 ’83 C.352 B.B.A. L.221 J.D. [Dreher,S.&J.]

Adams, David A., (BV) ... ’49 ’77 C&L.352 B.A., J.D. 1919 34th St.

Adams, Garth D., (AV) ... ’63 ’90 C.221 B.A. L.178 J.D. [Belin L.M.Z.F.]

Adams, Helen C., (AV) ... ’59 ’88 C&L.352 B.S., J.D. [Dickinson,M.T.&H.]

Adams, James Albert ... ’42 ’67 C&L.228 A.B., J.D. Drake Univ. Law School

Adams, John I. ... ’26 ’52 C&L.352 B.A., LL.B. 406 S.E. Gray St.‡

Adams, Ronald R., (AV) ... ’— ’77 C.1201 B.A. L.902 J.D. [🄲 Whitfield&E.]

Aden, Susan Jacobs, (AV) ’54 ’80 C&L.352 B.B.A., J.D. Assoc. Gen. Coun., Meredith Corp.

Adler, Morton S., (AV) ... ’12 ’35 C&L.352 B.A., J.D. 8450 Hickman Rd. (Pat.)

Ahlers, J. Paul ... ’41 ’66 C.118 B.A. L.352 LL.B. Wells Fargo Bank Iowa, N.A.

Ahlers & Cooney, P.C., (AV) [BR]
100 Court Avenue, Suite 600, 50309-2231
Telephone: 515-243-7611 Fax: 515-243-2149
URL: http://www.ahlerslaw.com
Paul F. Ahlers (1913-2002); James Evans Cooney (1917-1998); Philip J. Dorweiler (Retired); John F. McKinney, Jr.; Richard G. Santi; Edgar H. Bittle; Lance A. Coppock; David H. Luginbill; Mark W. Beerman; Edward W. Remsburg; Randall H. Stefani; Elizabeth Gregg Kennedy; Wade R. Hauser III; William J. Noth; Linda L. Kniep; John D. Hintze; Peter L. J. Pashler; Ivan T. Webber; Jane B. McAllister; James C. Hanks; R. Mark Cory; Ronald L. Peeler; Andrew J. Bracken; Steven L. Serck; Steven Michael Nadel; Elizabeth A. Grob; Jennifer A. Clendenin; Nathan J. Overberg; John H. Bunz; Danielle Jess Haindfield. Of Counsel: Kenneth H. Haynie; Robert G. Allbee; H. Richard Smith; Ronald L. Sutphin; Douglas R. Smith; Jane A.B. Eppink;—Patricia A. Westemeyer; James R. Wainwright; J. Eric Boehlert; Andrew T. Tice; Colin J. Witt; Michael M. Galloway; Gordon D. Greta.
General Practice. Litigation, Municipal Bonds, Public Finance, Government, Administrative, Business Law, Corporate, Banking, Environmental, Taxation, Securities, Antitrust, Education, Municipal, Workers Compensation, Pension, Profit Sharing, Employee Benefits, Real Estate, Labor and Employment, Insurance, Utility, Estate Planning and Probate Law. Practice before *State and Federal Courts, Administrative and Regulatory Agencies.*

See Professional Biographies, DES MOINES, IOWA

Ahlers, Cooney, Dorweiler, Haynie, Smith & Allbee, P.C.
(See Ahlers & Cooney, P.C.)

Ahmann, Matthew C. ... ’72 ’98 C.999 B.A. L.945 J.D. Asst. Gen. Coun., Amerus Group

Akrad, Lila A.T. ... ’71 ’03 C.378 B.S. L.1194 J.D. [🄰 McKee,V.&S.] (See Pat. Sect.)

Albers, Everett H., (AV) ... ’35 ’60 C&L.221 B.A., LL.B. [Denman&A.]

Albert, James A., (AV) ... ’47 ’76 C.221 B.F.A. L.602 J.D. [🄲 Galligan,D.&R.]

Aljets, Mark D., (AV) ... ’56 ’83 C.350 B.S. L.221 J.D. [Nyemaster,G.W.H.&O.]

Allbee, Robert G., (AV) ... ’— ’55 C.170 A.B. L.221 J.D. [🄲 Ahlers&C.]

Allen, A. Patricia ... ’52 ’78 C.732 B.A. L.1187 J.D. Iowa Dept. of Environ. Quality

Allen, Larry H. ... ’51 ’76 C.350 B.A. L.365 J.D. Claims Coun., Allied Insurance

Alt, Jerry P., (AV) ... ’40 ’68 C.352 B.A. L.221 J.D. [Finley,A.S.S.C.H.&G.]

Althoff Wolfe, Megan ... ’75 ’00 C&L.352 B.B.A., J.D. [🄰 Bradshaw,F.P.&F.]

Anania, Louis A. ... ’24 ’49 L.221 LL.B. Ret. Dist. Assoc. J.

Anderson, Andrew R., (BV) ... ’64 ’93 C.427 B.A. L.221 J.D. [🄲 Faegre&B.]

Anderson, Chad R. ... ’— ’99 C&L.352 B.A., J.D. [🄰 Faegre&B.]

Anderson, Daniel S. ’46 ’76 C.429 B.A. L.352 J.D. Admin. Law J., Dept. of Employ. Servs.

Anderson, Debora A. ’56 ’83 C.793 B.A. L.221 J.D. Dist. Coun., U.S. Small Bus. Admn.

Anderson, Jay A., (BV) ... ’60 ’92 C.801 B.S. L.221 J.D. 666 Walnut, Ste. 1450

Anderson, Jerry L. ’59 ’84 C.378 B.S. L.813 J.D. Prof. of Law, Drake Univ. Law School

Anderson, Kermit B., (AV) ... ’50 ’75 C&L.352 B.B.A., J.D. [Finley,A.S.S.C.H.&G.]

Anderson, Kristian, (BV) ... ’58 ’85 C.011 B.S. L.602 J.D. 711 High St.

Anderson, Martin R., (BV) ... ’46 ’76 C.932 B.A. L.221 J.D. [🄲 LaMarca&L.]

Anderson, Roberta M., (AV) ... ’54 ’81 C&L.352 B.A., J.D. [Schroeder&A.] ☉

Anderson, William D. ... ’49 ’74 C.893 B.A. L.276 J.D. Dept. of Environmental Quality

Anderson & Tully, A Professional Corporation
(See West Des Moines)

Andeweg, Robert D., (AV) ’62 ’87 C.132 B.A. L.221 J.D. [Brown,W.G.G.B.&S.] (☉West Des Moines)

Andreasen, Jon A. ... ’63 ’89 C&L.352 B.A., J.D. MidAmerican Energy Holdings Co.

Antenucci, Megan M., (AV) ... ’— ’85 C.350 B.A. L.221 J.D. [Whitfield&E.]

Appel, Brent R., (AV) ... ’50 ’78 C.813 B.A. L.1066 J.D. [Wandro,B.A.&C.]

Appleby, George W., (BV) ... ’47 ’79 C.350 B.S. L.352 J.D. [Carney,A.N.&S.]

Armentrout, Randall D., (BV) ... ’65 ’91 C.352 B.S. L.221 J.D. [Nyemaster,G.W.H.&O.]

Augspurger, Steven M., (BV) ... ’61 ’87 C&L.352 B.B.A., J.D. [Bradshaw,F.P.&F.]

Augustine, Jill M., (BV) ’63 ’90 C.357 B.A. L.221 J.D. Asst. Subrogation Atty., EMC Insurance Cos.

Austin, Bradford L., (AV) ... ’48 ’76 C.494 B.S.B. L.221 J.D. [Nyemaster,G.W.H.&O.]

Austin, James R., Jr., (AV) ... ’46 ’73 C.597 B.S. L.352 J.D. 4216 Greenwood Drive

Autry, Richard R., (BV) ... ’60 ’86 C.293 B.A. L.221 J.D. Off. of Atty. Gen.

Avgerinos, Nick James, (AVⓉ) ’56 ’81 C.378 B.A. L.221 J.D. [🄲 LaMarca&L.] (☉Chgo., IL)

Babich, Leslie, (AV) ... ’49 ’74 C.784 B.A. L.221 J.D. [Babich,G.C.&R.]

Babich, Todd E., (BV) ... ’63 ’88 C&L.221 B.A., J.D. [Babich,G.C.&R.]

Babich, Goldman, Cashatt & Renzo, P.C., (AV)
100 Court Avenue, Suite 403, 50309-2200
Telephone: 515-244-4300 Fax: 515-244-2650
Leslie Babich; Todd E. Babich; Michael J. Carroll; Brent A. Cashatt; David H. Goldman; Kodi A. Peterson; Joseph A. Renzo; Alexander R. Rhoads; Stacey N. Warren.
Family Law, Domestic Relations, Personal Injury, Employment Law, Discrimination, Civil Rights, Constitutional Law, Criminal Law, Juvenile Law, Trials and Appeals and Mediation Services.
Reference: Wells Fargo Bank Iowa, N.A.

See Professional Biographies, DES MOINES, IOWA

Baer, Kimberley K., (BV) ... ’63 ’89 C.352 B.A. L.30 J.D. [🄰 Wandro,B.A.&C.]

Bainbridge, Kirk W. ... ’75 ’02 C&L.352 B.A., J.D. [🄰 Duncan,G.B.&L.]

Bair, Erik D. ... ’— ’01 L.221 J.D. [🄰 Walker&B.] (☉Newton)

Baker, Bruce W., (AV) ... ’57 ’82 C.352 B.B.A. L.1049 J.D. [Nyemaster,G.W.H.&O.]

Baker, David A. ... ’40 ’75 C.912 Ph.B. L.608 J.D. Gen. Coun., ARAG Ins. Co.

Baker, Jeffrey A., (AV) ... ’60 ’89 C.493 B.S. L.221 J.D. [Patterson,L.D.T.I.B.&O.]

Baker, John R., (BV) ... ’47 ’88 C&L.221 B.S., J.D. 4044 S.E., 14th St.

Baker, William D., (BV) ... ’39 ’67 C.351 B.A. L.221 J.D. 315 E. 5th St.

Ballard, Dennis D., (BV) ’49 ’81 C.106 B.A. L.352 J.D. Coun., Principal Mut. Life Ins. Co.

Bandstra, Scott L., (BV) ... ’61 ’93 C&L.221 B.A., J.D. [Bandstra]

Bandstra, Valerie D., (CV) ... ’75 ’00 C.350 B.S. L.352 J.D. [Brown,W.G.G.B.&S.]

Bandstra Law Firm, The, P.C., (BV) ... 505 5th Ave., Ste. 810

Bannister, T. Scott, and Associates, (BV) ’49 ’74 C.352 B.A. L.221 J.D. 1300 Des Moines Building

Barber, Nathan J. ... ’75 ’03 C.352 B.A. L.1375 J.D. [🄰 Hogan]

Barchman, Virginia D., (BV) ... ’46 ’79 C.707 B.A. L.352 J.D. Asst. Atty. Gen.

Barnett, James R. ’47 ’72 C&L.352 B.B.A., J.D. Mng. Sr. Atty., MidAmerican Energy Co.

Barnhill & Associates, P.C.
(See West Des Moines)

Barron, Joseph M., (BV) ... ’63 ’88 C&L.352 B.A., J.D. [Peddicord,W.S.&H.]

Barry, Patricia A., (BV) ... ’55 ’87 C.350 B.S. L.221 J.D. Coun., Principal Financial Group

Bartine, William D., (AV) ... ’52 ’77 C.350 B.A. L.352 J.D. [Belin L.M.Z.F.]

Bartlett, James S. ... ’56 ’86 C.375 B.S. L.221 J.D. State Div. of Labor

Baskerville, Richard W., (AV) ’35 ’59 C&L.352 B.S., LL.B. [Brown,W.G.G.B.&S.] (Pat.)

Bastemeyer, Norman G. ... ’31 ’60 C.173 A.B. L.793 J.D. Ethics Adm., Iowa Supm. Ct.

Baudino, Robert J., Jr., (BV) ... ’53 ’78 C.1100 B.A. L.221 J.D. [Baudino]

Baudino Law Firm, P.C., (BV) ... 1200 Liberty Building

Baustian, Teresa M., (BV) ... ’52 ’79 C.293 B.A. L.352 J.D. Asst. Atty. Gen.

Beamer, John E. ... ’39 ’65 C.187 B.A. L.352 LL.B. Asst. U.S. Atty.

Beary, Donna Ruth, (CV) ... ’50 ’74 C&L.352 B.A., J.D. [Beary’s]

Beary’s Law Office, (CV) ... 1339 19th St.

Beasley, Steven C. ... ’48 ’75 C.352 B.A. L.221 J.D. Iowa Employment Sec. Comm.

Beattie, Amy S., (BV) ... ’58 ’83 C.999 B.A. L.221 J.D. [Brick,G.B.S.S.S.&L.]

Beattie, Donald G., (AV) ... ’47 ’77 C.784 B.A. L.221 J.D. [Beattie]

Beattie, Scott J. ... ’66 ’92 C.130 B.A L.221 J.D. [🄰 Peddicord,W.S.&H.]

Beattie Law Firm, P.C., (AV)
4300 Grand Avenue, 50312
Telephone: 515-263-1000 Fax: 515-263-1411
Email: beattielaw@beattielawfirm.com URL: http://www.donbeattielaw.com
Donald G. Beattie.
Civil Litigation, Personal Injury, Product Liability, Workers Compensation, Wrongful Death, Dog Bites, Legal Malpractice, Business Litigation, Automobile Accidents.

See Professional Biographies, DES MOINES, IOWA

Beatty, Richd. H. ... ’16 ’43 C.350 B.S. L.221 J.D. 5000 Pleasant St.‡

Beaver, Fred E. ... ’49 ’75 C&L.352 B.B.A., J.D. [Hanson,B.&R.]

Becker, Charles F., (AV) ... ’54 ’79 C&L.352 B.B.A., J.D. [Belin L.M.Z.F.]

Beckman and Hirsch
(See Burlington)

Beerman, Mark W., (AV) ... ’— ’73 C&L.879 B.A., J.D. [Ahlers&C.]

Begleiter, Martin D. '45 '71 C.696 B.A. L.188 J.D.
(adm. in NY; not adm. in IA) Prof. of Law, Drake Univ. Law School
Begleiter, Ronni F., (AV) ... '48 '83 C.188 B.A. L.221 J.D. [Brown,W.G.G.B.&S.]

Belin Lamson McCormick Zumbach Flynn, A Professional Corporation, (AV) [BR]
The Financial Center, 666 Walnut Street, Suite 2000, 50309-3989
Telephone: 515-243-7100 Fax: 515-558-0715
URL: http://www.belinlaw.com
David W. Belin (1928-1999); Roger T. Stetson (1953-2004); Jeffrey E. Lamson; Mark McCormick; Steven E. Zumbach; Thomas L. Flynn; Jon L. Staudt; James L. Krambeck; Richard W. Lozier, Jr.; James V. Sarcone, Jr.; James R. Swanger; Jeremy C. Sharpe; Sue Luettjohann Seitz; John T. Seitz; Robert A. Mullen; Patricia A. Shoff; William D. Bartine; Quentin R. Boyken; Charles F. Becker; Sheila K. Tipton; Mark E. Weinhardt; Dennis P. Ogden; Edward M. Mansfield; Stephen R. Eckley; David Swinton; Margaret C. Callahan; Robert D. Sharp; Garth D. Adams; Michael R. Reck; Wayne E. Reames;—S. Christian Nelson; Holly M. Logan; Laura E. Hamady; Lance W. Lange; Silvia J. Hansell; Tricia A. Johnston; Matthew C. McDermott. Of Counsel: Danielle M. Shelton.
General Practice. Civil and Criminal Trials and Appeals, Taxation, Labor and Employment, Probate, Trusts and Estates, Banks and Banking, Bankruptcy, Corporate Law, Real Estate, Antitrust, Environmental Law, Legislative, Education Law.

See Professional Biographies, DES MOINES, IOWA

Benda, James B., (BV) ... '51 '76 C&L.221 B.A., J.D. V.P., Bank of America, N.A.
Beneventi, Robert L. ... '28 '52 C.190 A.B. L.221 J.D. 603 41st St.‡
Benhart, Kenneth D., (BV) ... '46 '73 C.352 B.B.A. L.221 J.D. [Benhart]
Benhart Law Office, (BV) ... 300 Walnut, Ste. 270
Benton, Timothy D., (AV) '51 '77 C.132 B.A. L.352 J.D.
Asst. Atty. Gen., Dept. of Jus., Atty. Gen. Off.
Benzoni, James Arthur, (BV) ... '55 '91 C.999 B.A. L.221 J.D. [Benzoni]
Benzoni Law Office, P.L.C., (BV) ... 2912 Beaver Ave.
Berg, Thomas J., (BV) ... '66 '91 C&L.352 B.B.A., J.D. [Berg,R.S.&S.]
Berg, Rouse, Spaulding & Schmidt, P.L.C., (AV) ... 2423 Ingersoll Ave.
Berglund, Richard W., (AV) ... '27 '50 C&L.221 B.A., J.D. 601 Locust St.
Bergman, Bruce E., (BV) ... '48 '73 C.784 B.A. L.326 J.D. City Atty.
Bergman, Jonathan D. ... '77 '04 C&L.352 B.A., J.D. [Ⓐ Hanson,B.&R.]
Bergstrom, Randy L. '55 '80 C.1106 B.A. L.365 J.D.
Coun., Principal Mut. Life Ins. Co.
Bernard, Aaron D. ... '— '03 C.1335 B.A. L.602 J.D. [Ⓐ Whitfield&E.]
Bertelli, Monty R. ... '48 '75 C&L.221 B.S.B.A., J.D. Dep. Secy. of State
Bertogli, Joseph G., Attorney at Law, (BV) '54 '79
C.350 B.S. L.221 J.D. 300 Walnut, Ste. 270
Bertroche, J. Michael, (BV) ... '58 '83 C&L.221 B.A., J.D. [Ⓒ Bertroche]
Bertroche, Joseph G., Sr., (AV) ... '34 '63 C.351 B.A. L.221 J.D. [Bertroche]
Bertroche Law Offices, (AV) ... 4044 S.E. 14th Street (⊙Cedar Rapids)
Beving, Donald L., (AV) ... '17 '40 C&L.352 B.A., J.D. [Beving,S.&F.] ‡
Beving, Swanson & Forrest, P.C., (AV) ... 321 East Walnut Street
Biederman, Melissa A. ... '68 '97 C.112 B.A. L.352 J.D. Asst. Atty. Gen.
Birkenholtz, Laura K. '— '96 C.421 B.G.S. L.221 J.D.
Coun., Principal Financial Group
Biscoglia, James ... '69 '95 C&L.221 B.S., J.D. [Ⓐ LaMarca&L.]
Bisignano, Christine A., (BV) ... '59 '91 C.1111 B.A. L.221 J.D. [C.A.Bisignano]
Bisignano, Christine A., P.C., Law Office of, (BV) ... P.O. Box 25024
Bittle, Edgar H., (AV) ... '— '67 C.188 B.A. L.477 J.D. [Ahlers&C.]
Bittner, Joel W., (BV) ... '47 '77 C&L.221 B.A., J.D. 1111 E. University
Bjork, Alan H., (AV) ... '49 '76 C.187 B.A. L.221 J.D. [Hanson,B.&R.]
Bjork, Amy ... '78 '03 C.352 B.A. L.221 J.D. [Ⓐ Dorsey&W.]
Blackburn, James S., (BV) ... '54 '80 C.174 B.S. L.221 J.D. [Williams,B.H.&M.]
Blane, Richard G., II ... '49 '73 C&L.221 B.A., J.D. Dist. J.
Blaser, Michael R., (AV) '60 '85
C&L.352 B.B.A., J.D. [Brown,W.G.G.B.&S.] (⊙West Des Moines)
Blink, Robert J., (AV) ... '50 '75 C.578 B.A. L.221 J.D. Dist. J., Dist. Ct. of IA
Blonigan, Cynthia L. '— '95 C.784 B.A. L.221 J.D.
Assoc. Gen. Coun., Wells Fargo Home Mtge., Inc.
Blumberg, Larry M., (BV) ... '46 '71 C.494 B.A. L.221 J.D. [Roehrick,H.B.K.&K.]
Boatwright, William A., (AV) ... '63 '89 C.221 B.A. L.352 J.D. [Davis,B.K.S.&R.]
Boe, Susan M. ... '49 '86 C.350 B.S. L.352 J.D. [Faegre&B.]
Boehlert, J. Eric, (BV) ... '— '99 C&L.221 B.A., J.D. [Ⓐ Ahlers&C.]
Boehlert, Jeffrey A., (AV) ... '53 '78 C.823 B.S. L.221 J.D. [Patterson,L.D.T.I.B.&O.]
Boes, Judith R. "Lynn" ... '56 '96 C.352 B.S.N. L.221 J.D. [Davis,B.K.S.&R.] ⊙
Boesen, Martha E., (BV) ... '66 '91 C.741 B.A. L.602 J.D. Asst. Atty. Gen.
Bogart, Daniel B. '60 '86 C&L.228 B.A., J.D.
(adm. in GA; not adm. in IA) Assoc. Prof. of Law, Drake Univ. Law School
Bohlken, Donald Walter '52 '86
C.352 B.A. L.221 J.D. Admin. Law J., Dept. of Inspections & App.
Boka, Wendy D ... '80 '05 C.784 B.A. L.221 J.D. [Ⓐ Hopkins&H.]
Bolender, Shawn '64 '89 C.610 B.B.A. L.436 J.D.
(adm. in WI; not adm. in IA) Tr. Offr., Firstar Bk. Iowa, N.A.
Boles, Matthew, (BV) ... '66 '93 C.350 B.A. L.221 J.D. 2910 Grand Ave.
Bolin, Randy Doran '61 '87 C.187 B.A. L.352 J.D.
2nd V.P. & Coun., Principal Mut. Life Ins. Co.
Book, Richard G., (AV) ... '54 '79 C.597 B.A. L.352 J.D. [Huber,B.C.H.&L.]
Borg, Joseph M. ... '77 '03 C.132 B.A. L.221 J.D. [Ⓐ Smith,S.S.&S.]
Bosscher, Mark A. ... '75 '01 C.132 B.A. L.221 J.D. [Ⓐ Peddicord,W.S.&H.]
Bouslog, John M., (BV) ... '58 '85 C.927 B.B. L.221 J.D. [Dreher,S.&J.]
Bowe, Sara Jane, (AV) '57 '82
C&L.352 B.A., J.D. 2nd V.P. & Coun., Principal Financial Group
Bowen, William T., Attorney at Law, (BV) '53 '92
C.350 B.S. L.221 J.D. 300 Walnut, Ste. 270
Bowerman, Ronald A. ... '44 '74 C.862 B.A. L.221 J.D. Vet. Admin.
Bowers, James R., (BV) ... '49 '74 C&L.352 B.A., J.D. [Brick,G.B.S.S.S.&L.]
Boyd, Nancy Shimanek, (BV) ... '47 '73 C.157 B.A. L.352 J.D. [Brown,W.G.G.B.&S.]
Boyd, Willard L., III, (AV) ... '59 '84 C.477 A.B. L.352 J.D. [Nyemaster,G.W.H.&O.]
Boyken, Quentin R., (AV) ... '54 '82 C.350 B.S. L.477 J.D. [Belin L.M.Z.F.]
Bracken, Andrew J., (AV) ... '— '88 C.352 B.S. L.221 J.D. [Ahlers&C.]
Bradshaw, Perry D., (AV) '49 '75
C.587 B.A. L.352 J.D. Assoc. Gen. Coun., Meredith Corp.

Bradshaw, Fowler, Proctor & Fairgrave, P.C., (AV)
801 Grand Avenue, Suite 3700, 50309-2727
Telephone: 515-243-4191 Fax: 515-246-5808
URL: http://www.bradshawlaw.com
Charles S. Bradshaw (1871-1953); Rex H. Fowler (1893-1972); W. Z. Proctor (1902-1995); D. J. Fairgrave (1906-1990); Howard A. Steele (1909-1973); Harris M. Coggeshall (1907-1993); Robert E. Drey (1931-1997); Dan Stamatelos (1934-2001); Homer E. Bradshaw (1914-2005); John V. Synhorst (Retired); Kent M. Forney; Michael H. Figenshaw; John C. Cortesio, Jr.; Edward E. Johnson; Larry D. Spaulding; William F. Fanter; David J. W. Proctor; James M. Holcomb; Denny M. Dennis; Donald F. Neiman; Mark L. Tripp; David L. Jenkins; Steven M. Augspurger; Gregory A. Witke; Kenneth R. Munro; D. Brian Scieszinski; Gregory L. Kenyon; Kelly L. McCarty; Karl Tage Olson; Elizabeth A. Nigut; Cynthia A. Hurley; Michael L. Mock; Jeffrey D. Goetz; Douglas A. Fulton; Iris J. Post; Gordon R. Fischer; Ann C. Spellman; Sean M. O'Brien; Todd A. Strother; Patrick D. Smith; Jason T. Madden; Lori A. Brandau; David N. May; Jason C. Palmer; Patrick T. Burk; Matthew J. Haindfield;—Lori

(This Listing Continued)

Bradshaw, Fowler, Proctor & Fairgrave, P.C. (Continued)
E. Cole; Matthew M. Carver; Megan Althoff Wolfe; Thomas D. Leahy; Stacie M. Codr; Brian R. Kohlwes; Andrew C. Johnson; William J. Miller; Karin A. Stramel; Catherine M. Drexler; Anne R. Chu. Of Counsel: J. Edward Power.
General Civil Practice, including Litigation, Insurance, Corporation, Commercial, Probate, Taxation, Real Estate, Antitrust, Bankruptcy and Reorganization, Public Utility, Workers' Compensation, Motor Carrier and Administrative Law.
General Counsel for: IMT Insurance Company (Mutual); Iowa Insurance Guaranty Association.
Representative Clients: Midwest Resources, Inc.; Allied Group; The Prudential Insurance Company of America; The Medical Protective Co.

See Professional Biographies, DES MOINES, IOWA

Brandau, Lori A., (BV) ... '71 '97 C.898 B.A. L.352 J.D. [Bradshaw,F.P.&F.]
Branstad, Christine E., (BV) '68 '95
C.352 B.S. L.221 J.D. Litig. Atty., EMC Insurance Cos.
Branstad, Terry E. ... '46 '74 C.352 B.A. L.221 J.D. Gov.
Brauch, William L., (BV) ... '56 '87 C.959 B.A. L.352 J.D. Asst. Atty. Gen.
Bremer, Celeste F. ... '53 '77 C.707 B.A. L.352 J.D. U.S. Mag. J.
Brenden, Ann E., (AV) ... '56 '81 C.351 B.A. L.221 J.D. Asst. Atty. Gen.
Brennan, Denise Peters '57 '83 C.31 B.A. L.215 J.D.
(adm. in MI; not adm. in IA) Managing Coun., Wells Fargo Home Mtge., Inc.
Brennan, Robert W. ... '23 '50 C.352 L.221 J.D. 4711 SW 19th St.‡
Brennan, Scott M., (BV) ... '62 '94 C.293 B.A. L.352 J.D. [Davis,B.K.S.&R.]
Brick, Angela C. ... '65 '93 C.352 B.B.A. L.221 J.D. V.P., Bankers Tr. Co.
Brick, Ann Marie, (AV) ... '49 '80 C.424 B.S. L.221 J.D. Asst. Atty. Gen.
Brick, David E., (BV) ... '71 '98 C.93 B.A. L.352 J.D. [Brick,G.B.S.S.S.&L.]
Brick, James E., (AV) ... '39 '70 C.446 B.A. L.221 J.D. [Brick,G.B.S.S.S.&L.]
Brick, Joseph S., (AV) ... '37 '62 C.707 B.A. L.221 J.D. [Brick,G.B.S.S.S.&L.]
Brick, Matthew S. ... '72 '01 C&L.352 B.S., J.D. [Ⓐ Brick,G.B.S.S.S.&L.]
Brick, Steven P., (BV) ... '67 '93 C.190 B.A. L.221 J.D. [Brick,G.B.S.S.S.&L.]

Brick, Gentry, Bowers, Swartz, Stoltze, Schuling & Levis, P.C., (AV)
Suite 200, 550 Thirty-Ninth Street, 39th and Ingersoll, 50312
Telephone: 515-274-1450 Telecopier: 515-274-1488
URL: http://www.brickgentrylaw.com
Joseph S. Brick; James E. Brick; Nolden Gentry; James R. Bowers; Clifford S. Swartz; Bruce H. Stoltze; Mark R. Schuling; Thomas J. Levis; Amy S. Beattie; Kenneth L. Butters; Steven P. Brick; Thomas P. Schlapkohl; James E. Nervig; Paul A. Drey; Stephanie L. Brick Drey; David E. Brick; Nolden Brian Gentry; Matthew T. Cronin;—Matthew S. Brick; Billy J. Mallory.
General and Civil Practice and Trials in all Courts. Administrative Law, Public Utility, Telecommunications, Energy, Banking, Corporate, Labor, Municipal, Real Estate, Personal Injury, Federal and State Taxation, Legislative, School, Estate Planning, Health Care, Agricultural Cooperatives and Workers' Compensation Law.

See Professional Biographies, DES MOINES, IOWA

Bridges, Robert G., (AV) ... '— '61 C.966 B.A. L.352 J.D. [Whitfield&E.]
Brinkman, Richard J. ... '30 '54 C&L.352 B.S.C., J.D. 206 8th St., 10th Fl.
Britson, Dennis N. '56 '81 C&L.221 B.B.A., J.D.
Dir., State of IA Ins. Div., Regulated Industries Unit
Brommel, Rebecca A., (CV) ... '76 '01 C&L.221 B.A., J.D. [Ⓐ Brown,W.G.G.B.&S.]
Broughton-Romain, Angela ... '67 '94 C&L.347 B.A., J.D. [Lewis,W.V.&K.]
Brown, Anne Graff, (BV) '55 '81 C.190 B.S. L.910 J.D.
2nd V.P. & Coun., Principal Mut. Life Ins. Co.
Brown, Benjamin W. ... '24 '50 C&L.352 B.A., J.D. 5832 Grand Ave.‡
Brown, David L., (AV) ... '47 '76 C.399 B.A. L.221 J.D. [Hansen,M.&R.]
Brown, Donald J., (AV) ... '34 '58 C&L.352 B.A., J.D. [Ⓒ Davis,B.K.S.&R.]
Brown, F. Montgomery, (BV) ... '60 '86 C.106 B.A. L.221 J.D. [Cook,B.&S.]
Brown, Gregory R., (AV) ... '53 '78 C&L.352 B.A., J.D. [Duncan,G.B.&L.]
Brown, Jo Ann ... '27 '66 C&L.221 J.D. Legis. Serv. Bur., Iowa Code Div.
Brown, Paul E. ... '15 '41 C&L.352 B.A., J.D. 5804 Harwood Dr.
Brown, Roger K., (AV) '57 '84 C.350 B.S. L.378 J.D.
Asst. City Atty., City Legal Dept.
Brown, Scott Edmondson '59 '86
C&L.352 B.B.A., J.D. Exec. Dir., Iowa Trial Lawyers Assn.

Brown, W. Kendall, (AV) '43 '68 C.111 B.S. L.174 J.D.
558 28th Street, 50312
Telephone: 515-282-7702 Fax: 515-282-7706
Email: Kendall@DPS8.com
General Civil Practice. Taxation, Corporate, Probate and Estate Planning, Employee Benefits, Banking and Administrative Law.

See Professional Biographies, DES MOINES, IOWA

Brown, William C., (AV) ... '53 '77 C&L.352 B.A., J.D. [Brown,W.G.G.B.&S.]

Brown, Winick, Graves, Gross, Baskerville and Schoenebaum, P.L.C., (AV) [BR]
666 Grand Avenue, Suite 2000, 50309-2510 ⊙
Telephone: 515-242-2400 Fax: 515-283-0231
Email: bwg@ialawyers.com URL: http://www.ialawyers.com
Walter R. Brown (1921-2000); Richard W. Baskerville; Bruce Graves; Steven C. Schoenebaum; Harold N. Schneebeck; Paul D. Hietbrink; William C. Brown; Richard K. Updegraff; Paul E. Carey; Douglas E. Gross; John D. Hunter; James H. Gilliam; Robert D. Andeweg; Alice Eastman Helle; Michael R. Blaser; Thomas D. Johnson; Christopher R. Sackett; Sean P. Moore; Nancy Shimanek Boyd; James L. Pray; Brenton D. Soderstrum; Michael D. Treinen; Scott L. Long; Ronni F. Begleiter; Miranda L. Hughes; Kelly D. Hamborg; William E. Hanigan; Mary A. Ericson; Barbara Brooker Burnett; G. Brian Pingel; Michael J. Green; Michael A. Dee; Camille L. Urban; Danielle Dixon Smid; Brian P. Rickert; Valerie D. Bandstra; Ann Holden Kendell;—Alexander M. Johnson; James S. Niblock; Rebecca A. Brommel; Mark E. Roth; Tina R. Thompson; Brian M. Green; Dustin D. Smith; Adam W. Jones; Catherine E. Cownie; Erick D. Prohs; Laura N. Martino; Amy R. Piepmeier; Elizabeth A. Coonan; Britney L. Schnathorst; Sara L. Keenan; Rebecca A. Reisinger.
General Civil Practice, including but not limited to, Administrative Law, Adoption Law, Agricultural Law, Alternate Dispute Resolution, Antitrust and Trade Regulation, Appellate Practice, Banking Law, Bankruptcy, Business Law, Civil Rights and Discrimination, Commercial Law, Construction Law, Contracts, Corporate Law, Debtor and Creditor, Election, Campaign and Political, Eminent Domain, Employee Benefits, Employment Law, Energy, Entertainment and Sports, Environmental Law, Estate Planning, Family Law, Finance, Franchise Law, Government, Health Care, Insurance, Intellectual Property, International Law, International Trade, Labor Law, Litigation, Medical Malpractice, Mergers and Acquisitions, Occupational Safety and Health, Pension and Profit Sharing Law, Personal Injury, Product Liability, Professional Liability, Public Utility Law, Real Estate, Securities, Taxation, Toxic Torts, Trademarks and Copyright Law, Transportation, Trial Law, Trusts and Estates, Wills and Probate, Workers' Compensation, Zoning, Planning and Land Use. Litigation in all Courts.
Pella, Iowa Office: 616 Franklin Place, 50219. Telephone: 641-628-4513. Fax: 641-628-8494.
West Des Moines, Iowa Office: Regency West 5, 4500 Westown Parkway, Suite 277, 50266-6717. Telephone: 515-242-2400. Fax: 515-242-2448.

See Professional Biographies, DES MOINES, IOWA

Bruntz, John E., (AV) ... '56 '81 C.793 B.S. L.352 J.D. Pres., CEO, The Wittern Grp.
Bryant, Larry J. '40 '65 C&L.352 B.A., LL.B.
Chf. Admin. Law J., Dept. of Inspection & App.
Buck, Keith A. '63 '91 C.352 B.S.G. L.221 J.D.
Advanced Mktg. Specialist, EMC Ins. Co.
Buckingham, Ben C., (AV) ... '13 '38 C&L.352 B.A., J.D. 3524 Grand Ave.‡
Bumbary-Langston, Inga, (BV) ... '56 '85 C&L.893 B.A., J.D. 3301 Kingman Blvd.
Bunz, John H., (AV) ... '— '90 C.427 B.A. L.221 J.D. [Ahlers&C.]

Burge, Warren '44 '84 C&L.221 B.A., J.D.
2428 S.W. 9th Street, Suite 3, 50315
Telephone: 515-285-2600
Email: WrnBrg@aol.com URL: http://www.warrenburge.com
Bankruptcy, Divorce and Criminal Defense.
See Professional Biographies, DES MOINES, IOWA

Burger, Michael F., (BV) .... '48 '74 C.145 B.A. L.378 J.D. [Dreher,S.&J.]
Burk, Patrick T., (BV) .... '65 '92 C.351 B.A. L.221 J.D. [Bradshaw,F.P.&F.]
Burke, Erin K. .... '66 '93 C.741 B.A. L.352 J.D. Spec. Asst. U.S. Atty.
Burke, Thomas H., (AV) .... '— '80 C&L.352 B.A., J.D. [Whitfield&E.]
Burkey, Max, (BV) .... '47 '78 C.351 B.A. L.221 J.D. 100 Court Ave., Ste. 121
Burlage, David A., (AVⓉ) .... '53 '78 C.309 B.A. L.208 J.D. 1515 Linden St.
Burmeister, Eric W., (AV) .... '56 '81 C.879 B.A. L.221 J.D. [Ⓐ Beving,S.&F.]
Burnett, Barbara Brooker, (BV) ...... '56 '84 C&L.221 B.A., J.D. [Brown,W.G.G.B.&S.]
Burnett, Robert A., Jr., Law Offices of, (AV) '50 '75
C.293 B.A. L.352 J.D. 300 Walnut St., Ste. 270
Burnette, Frank L., II, (AV) .... '40 '65 C&L.221 B.A., J.D. [F.L.Burnette]
Burnette, Frank L., Law Office of, (AV) .... 505 Fifth Avenue
Burns, Laura Lea Goecke, (BV) .... '57 '82 C&L.221 B.A., J.D. 14608 Woodcrest Dr.
Butters, Kenneth L., (AV) .... '45 '71 C&L.352 B.B.A., J.D. [Brick,G.B.S.S.S.&L.]
Byler, Kathleen M. '70 '95 C.352 B.B.A. L.221 J.D.
Asst. Gen. Coun., Wells Fargo Financial, Inc.
Bylund, Jacob D. .... '78 '03 C.350 B.A. L.352 J.D. [Ⓐ Faegre&B.]
Cable, Ronald G., (BV) .... '41 '73 C&L.221 B.S., J.D. 414 E. Grand
Cacciatore, Joseph A., (BV) .... '65 '93 C.351 B.A. L.221 J.D. [Dickinson,M.T.&H.]
Cady, Mark S. .... '53 '78 C&L.221 B.A., J.D. Supm Ct. Jus.
Cain, Hugh J., (BV) .... '55 '83 C.190 B.A. L.911 J.D. [Hopkins&H.]

Calkins, Richard M. '31 '59 C.197 B.A. L.597 J.D.
801 Grand, Suite 3140, 50309-3200
Telephone: 515-283-0331 Fax: 515-283-0702
Email: amta@dwx.com
Mediation and Arbitration.

Callahan, Margaret C., (BV) .... '57 '84 C.221 B.A. L.228 J.D. [Belin L.M.Z.F.]
Calloway, Rory E. .... '60 '96 C.1281 B.A. L.221 J.D. 739 37th St.
Cameron, Streetar, (AV) .... '57 '83 C.352 B.A. L.221 J.D. [Connolly,O.L.H.&O.]
Campbell, Brian L., (AV) .... '49 '77 C.351 B.A. L.190 J.D. [Ⓖ Faegre&B.]
Campbell, Bruce I., (AV) .... '47 '73 C.872 B.A. L.309 J.D. [Davis,B.K.S.&R.]
Campbell, Heather .... '73 '01 C.999 B.S. L.221 J.D. [Ⓐ Dorsey&W.]
Cannon, Peter S., (BV) .... '58 '83 C.602 B.B.A. L.221 J.D. [Cannon]
Cannon Law Offices, (BV) .... 7025 Hickman Rd., Ste. 7
Carey, Paul E., (AV) .... '54 '82 C&L.221 B.S., J.D. [Brown,W.G.G.B.&S.]
Carey, Richard W. .... '28 '55 C.933 B.A. L.352 J.D. 1414 Germania Dr.‡
Carle, Henry M. '27 '59 C.90 L.213 LL.B.
(adm. in MI; not adm. in IA) Amoco Oil Co.
Carlson, Wendy L., (AV) .... '— '85 C.221 B.S.B.A. L.602 J.D. [Ⓖ Whitfield&E.]
Carmoney, Michael A., (BV) .... '66 '99 C.967 B.A. L.221 J.D. [Ⓐ Grefe&S.]
Carney, James W., (AV) .... '48 '75 C.352 B.A. L.221 J.D. [Carney,A.N.&S.]

Carney, Appleby, Nielsen & Skinner, P.L.C., (AV)
400 Homestead Building, 303 Locust Street, 50309
Telephone: 515-282-6803 Fax: 515-282-4700 URL: http://www.carneylawfirmiowa.net
Email: recept@carneylawfirmiowa.com URL: http://www.lawyers.com/carneylaw
James W. Carney; George W. Appleby; Stephen V. Nielsen; Troy A. Skinner;—Diane L. Dornburg; Jennifer Ann Tyler.
General Practice. Legislative Law, Business Law, Torts, Real Estate, Family Law, Administrative Law, Insurance Law, Criminal Law, Family Law, Wills and Trusts, Probate, Bankruptcy, Malpractice. Trials and Appeals in Federal and State Courts.
Reference: Hawkeye Bank.
See Professional Biographies, DES MOINES, IOWA

Carpenter, Robert E. .... '50 '77 C&L.352 B.A., J.D. 5801 Thornton Ave.
Carpenter, Thomas W., (AV) .... '32 '60 C.293 B.A. L.352 J.D. [Grefe&S.]
Carroll, Frank J., (AV) .... '47 '73 C.734 B.S. L.338 J.D. [Davis,B.K.S.&R.]
Carroll, Michael J., (AV) .... '64 '89 C.352 B.A. L.221 J.D. [Babich,G.C.&R.]
Carver, Matthew M. .... '72 '01 C.602 B.A. L.352 J.D. [Ⓐ Bradshaw,F.P.&F.]
Cashatt, Brent A., (BV) .... '62 '89 C.999 B.A. L.221 J.D. [Babich,G.C.&R.]
Casini, Jason M., (BV) .... '— '93 C&L.352 B.A., J.D. [Whitfield&E.]
Casper, Michelle M., (BV) .... '70 '97 C&L.352 B.A., J.D. [Ⓐ Wandro,B.A.&C.]
Cavanaugh, Patrick D. .... '47 '76 C.293 B.A. L.352 J.D. Drake Univ.
Chambers, Bridget A., (BV) .... '59 '85 C&L.352 B.A., J.D. Asst. Atty. Gen.
Chaplinsky, Margaret M., (BV) .... '58 '83 C.884 B.A. L.1338 J.D. [Kalinoski&C.L.]
Charles, David L., (AV) '50 '75 C.641 B.A. L.352 J.D.
666 Walnut Street (⊙Billings, MT)
Charlow, Andrea S. '52 '79 C.881 A.B. L.982 J.D.
(adm. in NY; not adm. in IA) Assoc. Dean & Prof. of Law, Drake Univ. Law School
Chegwidden, Irene Boyd, (AV) .... '37 '88 4111 Ingersoll Ave., Apt. 218
Chesser, Lori Torgerson, (AV) ..... '62 '87 C.927 B.B.A. L.280 J.D. [Davis,B.K.S.&R.]
Christensen, Amy Laurel '52 '81
C.350 B.S. L.221 J.D. Admin. Law J., State Dept. of Educ.
Christensen, Mike, (BV) .... '42 '72 L.221 J.D. 974 73rd St.
Christenson, Jim, (BV) .... '57 '90 C&L.352 B.S., J.D. Asst. Atty. Gen.
Christianson, Bryce T., (AV) .... '20 '50 C.494 B.S.L. L.221 J.D. 1000 73rd St.‡
Chu, Anne R. .... '79 '04 C.352 B.B.A. L.378 J.D. [Ⓐ Bradshaw,F.P.&F.]
Clark, Anne L., (BV) .... '60 '86 C&L.221 B.A., J.D. [Hopkins&H.]
Clark, Beverly, (BV) '44 '80 C.1109 B.A. L.352 J.D.
Corporate Counsel, Pioneer Hi-Bred International, Inc.
Clark, Hunter R. '55 '80 C&L.309 A.B., J.D.
(adm. in DC; not adm. in IA) Drake Univ. Law School
Clark, Jodie L. .... '79 '04 C.350 B.A. L.37 J.D. [Ⓐ Davis,B.K.S.&R.]
Clark, Ryan M. .... '73 '99 C.36 B.A. L.221 J.D. [Patterson,L.D.T.I.B.&O.]
Clark, William R., Jr., (AV) .... '51 '76 C&L.221 B.A., J.D. [Herrick,L.&L.]
Clarke, Thomas J., (BV) .... '43 '68 C.352 B.A. L.228 J.D. 2130 Grand Ave.
Claton, Denise R. .... '70 '96 C.221 B.A. L.352 J.D. [Ⓐ Davis,B.K.S.&R.]
Claypool, David L., (AV) .... '46 '75 C.337 B.A. L.352 J.D. [Dorsey&W.]
Claypool, Megan A., (BV) ..... '72 '97 C&L.352 B.A., J.D. 611 Fifth Avenue, Dept. A-28
Cleavenger, John D., (AV) .... '56 '83 C.976 B.A. L.221 J.D. 711 High St.
Clendenin, Jennifer A., (BV) .... '— '97 C.602 B.A. L.221 J.D. [Ahlers&C.]
Clendenin, John T., (BV) .... '72 '98 C.339 B.A. L.221 J.D. [Nyemaster,G.W.H.&O.]
Clingan-Fischer, Deanna G., (AV) '61 '90 C&L.221 B.A., J.D.
200 Tenth Street, 3rd Floor
Codr, Stacie M. .... '76 '02 C&L.352 B.A., J.D. [Ⓐ Bradshaw,F.P.&F.]
Cohan, Richard C. '66 '94 C.659 B.S. L.145 J.D.
Sr. V.P. & Gen. Coun., AmerUs Group Co., AmerUs Life Ins. Co.
Colacino, Antonio, (AV) ...... '49 '74 C&L.602 B.A., J.D. [Nyemaster,G.W.H.&O.]
Cole, Lori E., (CV) .... '70 '99 C.351 B.A. L.221 J.D. [Ⓐ Bradshaw,F.P.&F.]
Collins, Kathy L. .... '50 '85 C.378 B.S.Ed. L.221 J.D. Sch. Admr. of IA
Colloton, Steven M. .... '63 '88 C.674 A.B. L.976 J.D. U.S. Ct. App. J.

Combs, Terri L., (AV) .... '57 '83 C.804 B.S. L.276 J.D. [Faegre&B.]
Comfort, Frank B., (AV) .... '24 '51 C&L.352 B.A., J.D. [Ⓖ Nyemaster,G.W.H.&O.]
Comito, Frank A., (AV) .... '39 '63 C&L.221 B.A., LL.B. [Gaudineer,C.&G.]
Conley, Robert E., (AV) .... '22 '49 C.190 L.221 J.D. 300 Walnut St.‡
Conlin, Roxanne B., (AV) .... '44 '66 C&L.221 B.A., J.D. [R.B.Conlin&Assoc.]

Conlin, Roxanne B., and Associates, P.C., (AV)
319 7th Street, Suite 600, 50309-3826
Telephone: 515-283-1111 Fax: 515-282-0477
Email: rconlin@roxanneconlinlaw.com URL: http://www.roxanneconlinlaw.com
Roxanne B. Conlin.
Trial and Appellate Practice. Personal Injury, Medical Malpractice, Products Liability, Employment Discrimination Law.
See Professional Biographies, DES MOINES, IOWA

Conn, Blythe C. .... '08 '33 C&L.352 B.S., J.D. 3920 Grand Ave.‡
Conn, Susan Vawter .... '59 '89 C.30 B.A. L.221 J.D. Staff Atty., Youth Law Ctr.

Connolly, O'Malley, Lillis, Hansen & Olson, L.L.P., (AV)
Bank of America Building, 317 6th Avenue, Suite 300, 50309-4127
Telephone: 515-243-8157 Fax: 515-243-3919
Email: colho@connollylawfirm.com URL: http://www.connollylawfirm.com
Members of Firm: William J. Lillis; Russell J. Hansen; Michael W. O'Malley; Eugene E. Olson; Streetar Cameron; Daniel L. Manning; Christopher R. Pose; Adam C. Van Dike.
General Trial Practice, State and Federal Courts. Probate, Real Estate, Zoning, Municipal, Corporation, Workers Compensation, Personal Injury, Administrative, Family, Bankruptcy, Environmental Law and Hospital Law.
A list of Representative Clients will be furnished upon request.
References will be furnished upon request.
See Professional Biographies, DES MOINES, IOWA

Cook, Bruce L., (AV) .... '49 '75 C.106 B.A. L.221 J.D. [Cook,B.&S.]
Cook, Guy R., (AV) .... '56 '82 C.352 B.A. L.221 J.D. [Grefe&S.]
Cook, Brown & Scott, P.L.C., (AV) .... 8554 Alice Avenue, Suite A
Coonan, Elizabeth A. .... '77 '02 C.473 B.A. L.221 J.D. [Ⓐ Brown,W.G.G.B.&S.]
Cooper, Nicholas O. .... '— '04 C.352 B.B.A. L.221 J.D. [Ⓐ Whitfield&E.]
Cooperrider, Ruth H., (BV) .... '— '81 C.597 B.Mus. L.352 J.D. 1112 E. Grand Ave.
Coppock, Lance A., (AV) .... '— '72 C&L.221 B.S., J.D. [Ahlers&C.]
Coppola, Carol L., (AV) .... '51 '80 C.190 B.A. L.221 J.D. 1689 N.W. 102nd St.
Coppola, Jos. M. .... '15 '47 C&L.221 LL.B. 111 3rd St.‡
Correll, Merlen E. .... '16 '38 C&L.221 B.A., J.D. 1716 Merle Hay Rd.‡
Corsello, T. Dominic .... '51 '79 C.352 B.A. L.221 J.D. [Prine&C.]
Cortese, Joseph S., II, (BV) .... '55 '81 C.347 A.B. L.221 J.D. [Huber,B.C.H.&L.]
Cortesio, John C., Jr., (AV) .... '38 '62 C.602 B.A. L.352 J.D. [Bradshaw,F.P.&F.]
Cory, R. Mark, (BV) .... '— '86 C.351 B.A. L.221 J.D. [Ahlers&C.]
Courter, Jeffrey William, (AV) '61 '87 C.350 B.S. L.352 J.D.
[Nyemaster,G.W.H.&O.]
Cownie, Catherine E. .... '75 '99 C.1069 B.A. L.352 J.D. [Ⓐ Brown,W.G.G.B.&S.]
Crabb, Thomas G., (BV) ...... '50 '92 C.190 B.S. L.221 J.D. 505 Fifth Avenue, Suite 630
Craig, David C., (AV) .... '47 '75 C.686 B.S. L.352 J.D. [Finley,A.S.S.C.H.&G.]
Crail, Elizabeth F. .... '— '95 C.340 B.A. L.221 J.D. 1327 24th St., #3★
Cramer, Susan P. .... '36 '72 C.681 A.B. L.221 J.D. Firstar Bk. Iowa, N.A.
Crawford, Gerald W. (Jerry), (AV) .... '49 '75 C.429 B.A. L.352 J.D. [Crawford]

Crawford Law Firm, (AV)
1701 Ruan Center, 666 Grand Avenue, 50309
Telephone: 515-245-5420 Fax: 515-245-5421
Email: crawford@crawfordlawfirm.com
Gerald W. (Jerry) Crawford; James R. Quilty.
Civil Litigation, National and International Government Relations Strategies, Plaintiff's Personal Injury, Administrative Law, Racing and Gaming / Sports Law.
See Professional Biographies, DES MOINES, IOWA

Creighton, Christine M., (BV) ..... '67 '92 C&L.436 B.A., J.D. [Spellman,S.S.S.K.&S.] ⊙
Crispin, Wm. Jeffrey, (BV) .... '51 '77 C.350 B.S. L.190 J.D. 108 3rd Street, Suite 309
Crist, Martha .... '61 '86 C.350 B.A. L.221 J.D. Gov. Alliance on Substance Abuse
Critelli, Lylea Dodson, (BV) .... '56 '81 C.340 B.A. L.221 J.D. [N.Critelli]
Critelli, Mark A., (AV) .... '57 '83 C.352 B.A. L.221 J.D. [Critelli&C.]
Critelli, N. Tré, (BV) .... '66 '96 C.177 B.A. L.221 J.D. [N.Critelli]
Critelli, Nick, Jr., (AV) .... '44 '67 C&L.221 B.A., J.D. [N.Critelli] ⊙
Critelli & Critelli, (AV) .... 4717 Grand Avenue

Critelli, Nicholas, P.C., Law Chambers of, (AV)
Suite 950, 317 Sixth Avenue, 50309-4128 ⊙
Telephone: 515-243-3122 Toll Free: 1-877-243-3122 Telecopier: (Fax) 515-243-2932
Email: critelli@critellilaw.com URL: http://www.CritelliLaw.com
Nick Critelli, Jr.; Lylea Dodson Critelli; N. Tré Critelli.
Practice limited to acting as local Counsel and trial counsel to members of the Bar in matters concerning Commercial Litigation, International, Insurance, Intellectual Property, Trademark, Copyright, Unfair Competition, Business Crime, Mediation and Arbitration.
Reference: Iowa State Bar Association.
London, England Office: 9 Stone Buildings, Lincoln's Inn. Telephone: 011-44-171-404-5055. Fax: 011-44-171-405-1551.
See Professional Biographies, DES MOINES, IOWA

Cronin, Matthew T., (BV) .... '75 '00 C.502 B.A. L.352 J.D. [Brick,G.B.S.S.S.&L.]
Cross, Dustan J., (AVⓉ) '69 '94
C.602 B.A. L.352 J.D. [Gislason&H.] (⊙New Ulm, MN)
Crouch, Jewell C. '23 '50 C&L.208 A.B., J.D.
(adm. in CO; not adm. in IA) 3512 Valdez Dr.‡
Cubbage, Jerome K. .... '23 '52 C.293 L.597 J.D. 5122 Ingersoll Ave.
Culp, Michael J., (BV) .... '61 '87 C.966 B.A. L.221 J.D. 300 Walnut Street, Suite 125
Culp, Doran, Seidlin & Genest, PLC, (AV) .... 300 Walnut Street
Culver, Mariclare Thinnes, (AV) .... '64 '90 C&L.352 B.A., J.D. [Duncan,G.B.&L.]
Cumings, Michael W., (BV) '51 '85
C.351 B.A. L.352 J.D. Coun., Principal Mut. Life Ins. Co.
Cummings, E Jacob .... '76 '04 C.351 B.A. L.221 J.D. [Ⓐ Grefe&S.]
Cunningham, Thomas M., (AV) ... '59 '84 C&L.352 B.A., J.D. [Nyemaster,G.W.H.&O.]

Cutler Law Firm, P.C.
(See West Des Moines)

Dagitz, Mark A., (BV) '63 '89 C.221 B.S.B.A. L.352 J.D.
Assoc. Gen. Coun., Wells Fargo Home Mtge.
Dahl, Harry W., (AV) .... '58 '84 C&L.221 B.A., J.D. [H.W.Dahl]
Dahl, Pamela Greenman, (BV) .... '59 '84 C&L.221 B.A., J.D. [Ⓐ H.W.Dahl]

Dahl, Harry W., P.C., (AV)
974 73rd Street #16, 50312
Telephone: 515-224-1070 Fax: 515-224-4620
Email: harrywdahl@msn.com
Harry W. Dahl (1927-1996); Harry W. Dahl;—Pamela Greenman Dahl.
Workers Compensation Law.
Reference: Norwest Bank, Iowa, N.A.
See Professional Biographies, DES MOINES, IOWA

Danos, John .... '69 '02 C.293 B.A. L.221 J.D. [Ⓐ Dorsey&W.]

Darrah, C. Rex .... '28 '56 C&L.221 B.S., LL.B. 550 39th St.
Darrell, David J., (AV) .... '57 '82 C.108 B.A. L.597 J.D. 2501 Grand Avenue, Suite E
Davis, John F., (AV) ....'18 '48 C.352 B.A. L.309 J.D. 315 E. 5th St.‡

Davis, Brown, Koehn, Shors & Roberts, P.C., (AV) BB
The Financial Center, 666 Walnut Street, Suite 2500, 50309-3993 ⊙
Telephone: 515-288-2500 Cable: Davis Law Facsimile: 515-243-0654
Email: info@lawiowa.com URL: http://www.lawiowa.com
John D. Shors; Stephen W. Roberts; William R. King; Robert F. Holz, Jr.; Robert A. Gamble; Michael G. Kulik; Thomas E. Salsbery; Frank J. Carroll; Bruce I. Campbell; Jonathan C. Wilson; Steven L. Nelson; David B. VanSickel; Gene R. La Suer; Deborah M. Tharnish; Kent A. Herink; Robert J. Douglas, Jr.; Mark D. Walz; Gary M. Myers; Stanley J. Thompson; David A. Tank; David M. Erickson; Lori Torgerson Chesser; Jo Ellen Whitney; Becky S. Knutson; Julie Johnson McLean; Beverly Evans; M. Daniel Waters; Christopher P. Jannes; Sharon K. Malheiro; Kris Holub Tilley; William A. Boatwright; Thomas J. Houser; Kendall R. Watkins; Scott M. Brennan; Debra Rectenbaugh Pettit; Matthew E. Laughlin; Judith R. "Lynn" Boes; Daniel A. Rosenberg; William P. Kelly; Susan J. Freed; William J. Koehn. Associates: Denise R. Claton; Behnaz Soulati; Heather L. Palmer; Jason M. Stone; Amy M. Landwehr; Joseph M. Pawlosky; John C. Pietila; Jason M. Ross; Emily E. Harris; Jodie L. Clark; Denise M. Hill; Tara L. Zager. Of Counsel: Donald J. Brown; David W. Dunn; C. Carleton Frederici; A. J. Greffenius; Dennis D. Jerde; Richard E. Ramsay; Neal E. Smith; William D. Thomas.
Administrative, Agricultural, Alternative Dispute Resolution, Antitrust and Trade Regulation, Appellate Practice, Bankruptcy, Banks and Banking, Biotechnology, Business Law, Civil, Class Actions, Commercial, Commercial Real Estate, Communications and Media, Complex and Multi-District Litigation, Computers and Software, Constitutional, Construction, Consumer, Contracts, Copyrights, Corporate, Debtor and Creditor, Education, Employee Benefits, Energy, Environmental, Equipment Finance and Leasing, Family, Finance, Franchises and Franchising, Government, Government Contracts, Guardianship and Conservatorship, Health Care, Hospital Law, Human and Civil Rights, Immigration and Naturalization, Insurance, Insurance Defense, Intellectual Property, International Law, International Trade, Labor and Employment, Leases and Leasing, Legal Ethics and Professional Responsibility, Libel, Slander and Defamation, Litigation, Media Law, Medical Malpractice, Mergers, Acquisitions and Divestitures, Municipal Law, Natural Resources, Nonprofit and Charitable Organizations, Partnership, Patents, Personal Injury, Probate. Products Liability, Professional Liability, Property, Public Finance, Real Estate, Regulatory, Securities, Taxation, Technology and Science, Torts, Trade and Professional Associations, Trade Secrets, Trademarks, Transportation, Trusts and Estates, Utilities, Wills, Workers Compensation, Zoning, Planning and Land Use.
West Des Moines, Iowa Office: 4201 Westown Parkway, Suite 300, 50266. Telephone: 515-288-2500. Fax: 515-246-7997.

See Professional Biographies, DES MOINES, IOWA

Davoren, Charles J., (AV) ...... '44 '77 C&L.221 B.S., J.D. 3209 Ingersoll Ave., Ste. 207
Dawe, William L., (AV) ....'45 '76 C.446 B.S. L.221 J.D. [Hopkins&H.]
Deats, Philip S. ....'47 '75 C&L.546 B.S., J.D. State Dept. of Rev. & Fin.
Dee, Michael A., (AV) .... '62 '88 C.350 B.S. L.352 J.D. [Brown,W.G.G.B.&S.]
De Lange, Apryl M., (BV) ....'74 '00 C.351 B.A. L.221 J.D. [Ⓐ Hopkins&H.]
Denman & Albers, (AV) .... 218 Sixth Ave.
Dennis, Denny M., (AV) ....'46 '70 C&L.221 B.A., J.D. [Bradshaw,F.P.&F.]
Denny, Ralph K. ....'18 '47 C&L.221 B.S., LL.B. 951 58th St.‡
De Sio, Thomas A., (BV) .... '51 '85 C.784 B.A. L.221 J.D. Asst. City Atty.
Devine, Michael B. ....'53 '80 C.747 B.A. L.221 J.D. 2611 40th Street
Dhar, Anita L. ....'77 '02 C&L.352 B.S., J.D. [Ⓐ Grefe&S.]
Dickinson, Greg A. '51 '78 C.351 B.A. L.190 J.D.
(adm. in NE; not adm. in IA) Pres., Shield Transp. Corp.
Dickinson, Mark C., (AV) ....'55 '81 C.293 B.A. L.352 J.D. [Nyemaster,G.W.H.&O.]

Dickinson, Mackaman, Tyler & Hagen, P.C., (AV) BB
1600 Hub Tower, 699 Walnut Street, 50309-3986 ⊙
Telephone: 515-244-2600 Fax: 515-246-4550
Email: info@dickinsonlaw.com URL: http://www.dickinsonlaw.com
L. J. Dickinson (1873-1968); L. Call Dickinson (1905-1974); Helen C. Adams; Joseph A. Cacciatore; Bret A. Dublinske; Rebecca Boyd Dublinske; Gregory G.T. Ervanian; Joan M. Fletcher; Howard O. Hagen; Paul E. Horvath; Jeffrey A. Krausman; F. Richard Lyford; Richard A. Malm; Arthur F. Owens; Mollie M. Pawlosky; David M. Repp; Russell L. Samson; Philip E. Stoffregen; Jon P. Sullivan; Paul R. Tyler; John K. Vernon; J. Marc Ward. Associates: Jennifer L. Hodge; Jill R. Jensen-Welch; Bridget R. Penick; Charles M. Schneider; Krista K. Tanner; Kristi A. Traynor. Of Counsel: Janet G. Huston; John R. Mackaman. Washington, D.C. Of Counsel: Gene C. Lange; John W. Thomas.
Administrative, Antitrust, Banking, Casualty Insurance and Workers Compensation, Commercial Litigation, Corporate, Energy, Environmental, Family Law, Fidelity and Surety Law, General Practice, Immigration, Intellectual Property, Labor and Employment Law, Probate, Public Utility, Real Estate, School Law, Telecommunications, Trials and Appeals.
Washington, D.C. Office: 1660 L Street, NW, Suite 506, 20036-5603. Telephone: 202-463-6330. Fax: 202-463-6328.

See Professional Biographies, DES MOINES, IOWA

Diekema, Connie L., (AV) .... '61 '88 C.513 B.S. L.221 J.D. [Finley,A.S.S.C.H.&G.]
Dierenfeld, Paula S., (BV) ....'54 '85 C.351 B.A. L.221 J.D. [Nyemaster,G.W.H.&O.]
Dietz-Kilen, Catherine C. .... '58 '93 C.350 B.A. L.221 J.D. 435 E. Grand Ave.
Ding, Chengfei '73 '03 C.999 B.A. L.221 J.D.
(adm. in NY; not adm. in IA) Atty., Principal Financial Group
Dinkla, Dwight, (BV) .... '51 '77 C.513 B.A. L.221 J.D. 521 E. Locust St., 3rd Fl.
Di Paglia, Raymond .... '29 '92 C&L.221 B.G.S., J.D. 4500 Merle Hay Rd.
Dixon, Jennifer S. '64 '88 C.351 B.A. L.352 J.D.
Assoc. Coun., Pub. Emplyees Ret. Sys.
Dixon, Virgil F. .... '16 '48 C&L.221 LL.B. 1109 14th St.‡
Doan, D.T. ....'32 '60 C&L.352 B.S., J.D. 699 Walnut
Donahue, Thomas M. .... '43 '75 C.791 B.S. L.221 J.D. Asst. Atty. Gen.
Donelson, James H., (P.C.), (BV) ....'46 '72 C&L.221 B.S.B.A., J.D. I.R.S.
Donner, Lynette A.F. '59 '84 C.350 B.A. L.221 J.D.
Coun., State Ethics & Campaign Disclosure Bd.
Doohen, Stephen E., (BV) .... '— '96 C.513 B.S. L.546 J.D. [Whitfield&E.]
Dopf, Robert C., (BV) .... '48 '73 C&L.221 B.A., J.D. Asst. U.S. Atty.
Doran, John D., (BV) .... '61 '87 C&L.352 B.B.A., J.D. [Culp,D.S.&G.]
Doré, Laurie Kratky '58 '84 C.190 B.A. L.802 J.D.
(adm. in TX; not adm. in IA) Asst. Prof. of Law, Drake Univ. Law Sch.
Dore, Matthew G. '58 '84 C.691 B.A. L.846 J.D.
(adm. in TX; not adm. in IA) Prof. of Law, Drake Univ. Law School
Dorff, David L., (BV) .... '57 '82 C&L.221 B.A., J.D. Asst. Atty. Gen., Dept. of Jus.
Dorff, Philip H., Jr., (AV) ....'49 '82 C.170 B.A. L.221 J.D. [Hopkins&H.]
Dornburg, Diane L. .... '51 '76 C.297 B.A. L.477 J.D. [Carney,A.N.&S.]

Dorsey & Whitney LLP, (AV)
801 Grand, Suite 3900, 50309 ⊙
Telephone: 515-283-1000 Fax: 515-283-1060
URL: http://www.dorsey.com
Members of Firm: David L. Claypool; David D. Grossklaus; Dennis W. Johnson (Board Certified Civil Trial Specialist, National Board of Trial Advocacy); Robert E. Josten; Brian J. Laurenzo; Edwin N. McIntosh. Associates: Amy Bjork; Heather Campbell; John Danos; Angela Dralle; Darla M. Giese; Jason M. Hunt; Cristina Kuhn. Attorney: Michael C. Gilchrist.
Banking and Commercial, Corporate Finance, Employee Benefits, Environmental, Estate Planning and Administration, Foreign Trade, Health Law, Government and Regulatory Affairs, Intellectual Property, International, Labor and Employment Law, Litigation, Real Estate, Tax, and Municipal and Public Authority Financing. Indian and Gaming Law and Venture Capital.
Minneapolis, Minnesota Office: Suite 1500, 50 South Sixth Street, 55402-1498. Telephone: 612-340-2600.
Seattle, Washington Office: U.S. Bank Centre, 1420 Fifth Avenue, Suite 3400, 98101. Telephone: 206-903-8800.
New York, New York Office: 250 Park Avenue, 10177. Telephone: 212-415-9200.

(This Listing Continued)

Dorsey & Whitney LLP (Continued)
Washington, D.C. Office: 1001 Pennsylvania Avenue, N.W., Suite 400 South, 20004. Telephone: 202-442-3000.
Denver, Colorado Office: 370 Seventeenth Street, Republic Plaza Building, Suite 4700, 80202-5647. Telephone: 303-629-3400.
London, England Office: 21 Wilson Street, EC2M 2TD. Telephone: 011-44-207-588-0800.
Hong Kong Office: Suite 3008, One Pacific Place, 88 Queensway. Hong Kong. Telephone: 011-852-252-65000. Fax: 011-852-252-43000.
Shanghai, China Office: Suite 6211-12, Plaza 66, No. 1266 Nanjing Xi Lu, Shanghai, 200040. Telephone: 86-21-6288-2323. Fax: 86-21-6288-3222.
Toronto, Ontario Office: BCE Place, 161 Bay Street, Suite 4310, P.O. Box 512, M5J 2S1. Telephone: 416-367-7370. Fax: 416-367-7371.
Vancouver, British Columbia Office: 666 Burrard Street, Suite 500, V6C 3P6. Telephone: 604-687-5151.
Anchorage, Alaska Office: 1031 West 4th Avenue, Suite 600, 99501-5907. Telephone: 907-276-4557.
Salt Lake City, Utah Office: Wells Fargo Plaza, 170 South Main Street, Suite 900, 84101. Telephone: 801-933-7360.
Southern California Office: 38 Technology Drive, Irvine, 92618-5310. Telephone: 949-932-3600.
Fargo, North Dakota Office: 51 North Broadway, Suite 402, P.O. Box 1344, 58107-1344. Telephone: 701-235-6000.
Great Falls, Montana Office: 507 Davidson Building, 8 Third Street North, P.O. Box 1566, 59401. Telephone: 406-727-3632.
Missoula, Montana Office: 125 Bank Street, Suite 600, 59802-4407. Telephone: 406-721-6025. Fax: 406-543-0863.
Paramus, New Jersey Office: 95 Route 17 South, Suite 203, 07652. Telephone: 201-291-8904. Fax: 201-712-9444.
Palo Alto, California Office: 1717 Embarcadero Road, 94303. Telephone: 650-857-1717.
San Francisco, California Office: 555 California Street, Suite 1000, 94104-1513. Telephone: 415-781-1989.

See Professional Biographies, DES MOINES, IOWA

Dorweiler, Philip J., (AV) .... '— '50 C&L.221 J.D. [Ahlers&C.] ‡
Douglas, Robert J., Jr., (AV) .... '57 '82 C.723 B.S. L.352 J.D. [Davis,B.K.S.&R.] ⊙
Doyle, Richard H., (AV) .... '49 '76 C&L.221 B.A., J.D. [Galligan,D.&R.]
Drake, Denny, (AV) ....'51 '77 C&L.221 B.A., J.D. Iowa Health System
Dralle, Angela ....'76 '01 C.132 B.A. L.352 J.D. [Ⓐ Dorsey&W.]
Drape, Dana L., (BV) '59 '84 C.350 B.S. L.352 J.D.
2nd V.P. & Coun., Principal Mut. Life Ins. Co.
Draper, Hayward L., (AV) ......'49 '77 C.976 B.A. L.309 J.D. [Nyemaster,G.W.H.&O.]
Drees, Douglas A. .... '71 '96 C.352 B.A. L.221 J.D. Coun., Principal Financial Group
Drees, Nicholas T., (AV) ....'62 '89 C.309 A.B. L.145 J.D. Asst. Pub. Def.
Dreher, Robert E., (AV) ....'15 '42 C&L.221 J.D. [Ⓑ Dreher,S.&J.]

Dreher, Simpson & Jensen, P.C., (AV)
The Equitable Building, 604 Locust Street, Suite 222, 50309-3723
Telephone: 515-288-5000 Telecopier: 515-288-7718
Email: LSimpson@dreherlaw.com URL: http://www.dreherlaw.com
Gregory Brunk (1894-1965); Peter W. Janss (1904-1969); Marvin R. Adams (1930-1982); Robert E. Dreher; Walter T. Hart; Albert L. Harvey; Lyle L. Simpson; Dick L. Jensen; Marcus F. Abels; Gary R. Fischer; Michael F. Burger; D. Scott Simpson; John M. Bouslog;—Joel D. Huston.
General Civil Practice. Corporation, Insurance, Probate, Administrative, Labor, Employment, Personal Injury, Workers Compensation, Real Estate and Business Law, Trials and Appeals, Estate Planning. Tax and Tax Litigation.
Counsel for: J. C. White Companies; Iowa Association of Tobacco Distributors; Little Giant Crane & Shovel, Inc.

See Professional Biographies, DES MOINES, IOWA

Drew, Tom L., (AV) ....'61 '88 C.352 B.B.A. L.221 J.D. [Drew]
Drew Law Firm, P.C., (AV) ....554 28th St.
Drexler, Catherine M. ....'76 '04 C.350 B.S. L.221 J.D. [Ⓐ Bradshaw,F.P.&F.]
Drey, Paul A., (BV) ....'66 '92 C&L.602 B.A., J.D. [Brick,G.B.S.S.S.&L.]
Drey, Stephanie L. Brick, (BV) .... '66 '92 C.602 B.A. L.352 J.D. [Brick,G.B.S.S.S.&L.]
Driscoll, Kevin J., (AV) ....'60 '88 C.177 B.A. L.221 J.D. [Finley,A.S.S.C.H.&G.]
Druker, Michele A., (AV) '55 '82 C.918 B.A. L.352 J.D.
Assoc. Gen. Coun., Wellmark Blue Cross & Blue Shield of Iowa
Dublinske, Bret A., (AV) ....'65 '94 C.350 B.A.B.S. L.352 J.D. [Dickinson,M.T.&H.]
Dublinske, Rebecca Boyd, (BV) '59 '86
C&L.352 B.A., J.D. [Dickinson,M.T.&H.] (⊙Des Moines)
Du Bray, F. Joseph, (AV) '44 '73 C.118 B.A. L.260 J.D.
Sr. V.P., Gen. Coun. & Bd. Secy., Wellmark Blue Cross & Blue Shield of Iowa
Dudley, Danny L. .... '47 '73 C.587 B.S.E. L.37 J.D. 300 Walnut St.
Dugan, Shelley A. ....'63 '88 C.784 B.A. L.190 J.D. Wetland Restoration
Dunahoo, Kermit L., (BV) ....'41 '71 C.350 B.S. L.221 J.D. 6305 S.W. 9th
Duncan, Bette Wolf ....'30 '74 C.86 B.S. L.221 J.D. Dept. of Agriculture
Duncan, H. R., (AV) ....'05 '31 C.999 A.B. L.273 LL.B. 400 Locust St.
Duncan, Hearst R. (Randy), Jr., (AV) '37 '63 C.352 B.A. L.221 J.D.
[Duncan,G.B.&L.]
Duncan, Randolph Mathieson (Matt), (AV) '62 '88
C.352 B.A. L.221 J.D. [Duncan,G.B.&L.]

Duncan, Green, Brown & Langeness, A Professional Corporation, (AV) BB
400 Locust Street, Suite 380, 50309-2363
Telephone: 515-288-6440 Fax: 515-288-6448
URL: http://www.duncangreenlaw.com
Hearst R. (Randy) Duncan, Jr.; Brent B. (Chris) Green; Gregory R. Brown; James B. Langeness; Randolph Mathieson (Matt) Duncan; Mariclare Thinnes Culver; Bradley C. Obermeier; Martin J. Kenworthy;—Christine B. Long; Michele M. Ramsey; Kirk W. Bainbridge; Lynn M. Gaumer. Of Counsel: Timothy S. Eckley.
General Civil Practice, Trials and Appeals State and U.S. Courts, Corporate and Business, Taxation, Real Estate, Estate Planning and Probate, Banking, Trade Regulation, Employment, Products Liability, Legal and Medical Malpractice, Antitrust, Personal Injury, Commercial Litigation, Education, Health, Administrative, Insurance Defense, Coverage and Regulation.
Representative Clients: American Republic Insurance Co.; Charles Gabus Ford, Inc.; Bridgestone/Firestone, Inc.; The Goodyear Co.; City of Des Moines; Federated Rural Electric Insurance Cooperative; Heller Financial, Inc.; Coca Cola Corp.; MidAmerican Energy; Meredith Corp.

See Professional Biographies, DES MOINES, IOWA

Dunlap, Paul D. ....'30 '56 C&L.546 B.S., J.D. 604 Locust St.
Dunn, Andrew J., (BV) ....'64 '89 C.427 B.A. L.221 J.D. [Parrish,K.M.D.&C.]
Dunn, David W., (AV) ... '54 '80 C.221 B.A. L.904 J.D. [Ⓑ Davis,B.K.S.&R.] (⊙Eldora)
Durick, Steven T., (AV) ....'70 '95 C.338 B.S. L.221 J.D. [Peddicord,W.S.&H.]
Dwyer, John F. .... '45 '69 C&L.352 LL.B. 701 55th St.
Eaton, Jay, (AV) ....'46 '71 C&L.352 B.B.S., J.D. [Nyemaster,G.W.H.&O.]
Eckley, Stephen R., (AV) ....'57 '81 C.221 B.A. L.309 J.D. [Belin L.M.Z.F.]
Eckley, Timothy S., (BV) ....'62 '87 C&L.352 B.A., J.D. [Ⓑ Duncan,G.B.&L.]
Eddy, John C., (AV) ....'— '49 C.197 B.A. L.893 LL.B. [Whitfield&E.] ‡
Edgington, Jolene K. '65 '97 C.569 B.A. L.208 J.D.
Asst. Gen. Coun., Wells Fargo Financial, Inc.
Edwards, John D. '53 '78 C.798 B.A. L.986 J.D.
(adm. in MO; not adm. in IA) Prof. of Law, Drake Univ. Law Sch.
Eick, Tina M., (BV) ....'67 '93 C.350 B.A. L.221 J.D. [Hopkins&H.]
Eisenhauer, Larry J. ....'46 '75 C.376 B.S.E. L.221 J.D. Appeals Ct. J.
Ekstrom, Susan L., (BV) ....'50 '76 C&L.221 B.A., J.D. [Ekstrom]
Ekstrom Law Office, (BV) .... 100 Court Ave., Ste. 121

Elcock, Marc A. '74 '04 C.350 B.S. L.221 J.D.
Asst. & Coun., Iowa House of Representatives‡
Elcock, Tara M. ... '75 '03 C.350 B.S. L.221 J.D. [Elcock]
Elcock Law Firm, P.L.C. ... P.O. Box 13438
Elkin, David R., (BV) ... '60 '86 C.350 B.S. L.221 J.D. 315 E. 5th
Elverson, Todd A., (BV) ... '56 '81 C&L.221 B.F.A., J.D. [Elverson,V.&P.]

Elverson, Vasey & Peterson, L.L.P., (AV) [BR]
100 Court Avenue, Suite 405, 50309
Telephone: 515-243-1914 Fax: 515-243-2235
URL: http://www.evpllp.com
Members of Firm: Todd A. Elverson; Jon A. Vasey; Gregory W. Peterson. Associates: Allison R. Abbott; Jennifer L. Oetker.
General Practice, Insurance Defense, Business Law, Corporation Law, Bankruptcy, Divorce, Family Law, Child Custody, Personal Injury, Automobile Accidents, Social Security, Real Estate, Wills, Probate, Trusts and Estates, Criminal Law, Medical Malpractice.
Representative Clients: State Farm Mutual Automobile Insurance Co.; Farmers Casualty Co. Mutual; CIGNA Cos.; Pella Window Co.; Eastman Kodak Co.; Peerless Supply; City of Stratford.
Reference: Bankers Trust.

See Professional Biographies, DES MOINES, IOWA

Emery, Kent, (AV) ... '07 '35 C&L.546 J.D. 3131 Fleur Dr., Apt. 904‡
Emrich, Linny C., (BV) ... '59 '85 C.427 B.A. L.352 J.D. Asst. Atty. Gen.
Engel, Rick, (BV) ... '50 '77 C.350 B.S. L.352 J.D. 6969 University Ave.
Ensign, Kristin Wright, (BV) ... '59 '84 C.350 B.A. L.221 J.D. Asst. Atty. Gen.
Ensley, Michael D., (BV) ... '72 '98 C.350 B.A. L.352 J.D. [Hanson,B.&R.]
Epp, Debra K. ... '63 '95 C&L.352 B.A., J.D. Corp. Coun., Principal Financial Group
Epperly, Brad C., (BV) ... '68 '93 C&L.352 B.B.A, J.D. [Ⓐ Nyemaster,G.W.H.&O.]
Eppink, Jane A.B. ... '— '89 C.347 B.A. L.345 J.D. [Ⓒ Ahlers&C.]
Erbe, Harley Christopher, (BV) ... '74 '99 C.959 B.A. L.221 J.D. [Nelson&E.]
Erickson, David M., (AV) ... '53 '79 C&L.221 B.A., J.D. [Davis,B.K.S.&R.]
Ericson, Mary A. ... '42 '79 C.966 B.A. L.221 J.D. [Brown,W.G.G.B.&S.]
Ervanian, Gregory G.T., (BV) ... '62 '90 C.352 B.G.S. L.190 J.D. [Dickinson,M.T.&H.]
Evans, Beverly, (AV) ... '49 '79 C.190 B.A. L.546 J.D. [Davis,B.K.S.&R.]
Evans, Thomas A., Jr. ... '51 '77 C.550 B.A. L.221 J.D. Polk Co. Labor Rel. Mgr.
Everett, Nora M. '59 '84 C.350 B.S. L.945 J.D.
Sr. V.P. & Dep. Gen. Coun., Principal Financial Group
Everhart, Brian P. '65 '99 C.36 B.S. L.208 J.D.
(adm. in AZ; not adm. in IA) 711 High St.
Ewoldt, Jeffrey D. ... '— '00 C.350 B.S. L.221 J.D. [Ⓐ Whitfield&E.]
Fabritz, Henry L. '26 '52 C.707 B.S. L.221 J.D.
V.P., Ruan Transp. Mgmt. Systems, Inc.

Faegre & Benson LLP, (AV)
801 Grand Avenue, Suite 3100, 50309-8002 ⊙
Telephone: 515-248-9000 Facsimile: 515-248-9010
Email: info@faegre.com URL: http://www.faegre.com
Resident Members: Michael A. Giudicessi; Kimberly J. Walker; Terri L. Combs; Susan M. Boe; Ross W. Johnson. Special Counsel: Brian L. Campbell; Thomas L. Slaughter; Andrew R. Anderson. Resident Associates: William J. Hunnicutt; Chad R. Anderson; Angela J. Morales; Christopher L. McDonald; Brian S. McCormac; Jesse Linebaugh; Jacob D. Bylund; Jennifer Peterson.
General Practice including Agribusiness, Corporate, Banking, E-Commerce, Employment, Insurance, Media and Communications, Products Liability, Real Estate, Antitrust and Commercial Litigation.
Minneapolis, Minnesota: 2200 Wells Fargo Center, 90 South Seventh Street. Telephone: 612-766-7000. Facsimile: 612-766-1600.
Denver, Colorado: 3200 Wells Fargo Center, 1700 Lincoln Street. Telephone: 303-607-3500. Facsimile: 303-607-3600.
London, England: 7 Pilgrim Street, EC4V 6LB. Telephone: 44-20-7450-4500. Facsimile: 44-20-7450-4545.
Frankfurt, Germany: Theodor-Heuss-Allee 108, 60486 Frankfurt am Main. Telephone: 011-49-69-631-561-0. Facsimile: 011-49-69-631-561-11.
Shanghai, China: Shanghai Centre, Suite 425, 1376 Nanjiing Road West, Shanghai, 200040 China. Telephone: 011-86-21-6279-8988. Facsimile: 011-86-21-6279-8968.
Reviser of the Minnesota Law Digest for this Directory.

See Professional Biographies, DES MOINES, IOWA

Fagg, George G. ... '34 '58 C&L.221 B.S., J.D. U.S. Sr. Cir. J.
Fairbank, William L., (AV) ... '— '66 C&L.221 B.A., J.D. [Whitfield&E.]
Fanter, Robert L., (AV) ... '— '69 C&L.352 B.B.A., J.D. [Whitfield&E.]
Fanter, William F., (AV) ... '44 '69 C&L.352 B.B.A., J.D. [Bradshaw,F.P.&F.]
Farmer, Barry D. ... '55 '81 C.351 B.A. L.352 J.D. Wells Fargo Bank Iowa, N.A.
Fasano, Kristine M. ... '51 '78 C&L.221 J.D. Secy. & Treas., National Properties
Fatino, John F., (BV) ... '— '91 C.182 B.A. L.228 J.D. [Whitfield&E.]
Fay, Daniel J. ... '40 '65 C.707 B.A. L.352 J.D. Asst. Atty. Gen.
Feldmann, Mark C., (AV) ... '55 '81 C.597 B.A. L.352 J.D. [Beving,S.&F.]
Feller, William H. ... '61 '90 C.352 B.B.A. L.208 J.D. 665 Locust St.

Fernandez Law Firm
(See Urbandale)

Ferris, Roger L., (AV) ... '43 '69 C.293 B.A. L.352 J.D. [Ⓒ Nyemaster,G.W.H.&O.]
Feuerhelm, Gerald B., (BV) ... '52 '79 C.177 B.A. L.221 J.D. [Feuerhelm,G.B.]
Feuerhelm, Gerald B., P.C., (BV) ... 3231 East Euclid, Suite 300
Fickes, Clyde R. ... '18 '54 C&L.221 B.A., LL.B. 3300 Eula Dr.‡
Fifield, James C., (AV) ... '56 '81 C.350 B.S. L.352 J.D. Coun., Principal Financial Group
Figenshaw, Michael H., (AV) ... '40 '64 C&L.352 B.A., J.D. [Bradshaw,F.P.&F.]
Finley, Kerry A., (BV) ... '65 '93 C.197 B.A. L.352 J.D. [Ⓒ Finley,A.S.S.C.H.&G.]
Finley, Thomas A., (AV) ... '40 '66 C&L.352 B.A., LL.B. [Finley,A.S.S.C.H.&G.]

Finley, Alt, Smith, Scharnberg, Craig, Hilmes & Gaffney, P.C., (AV) [BR]
699 Walnut Street, Suite 1900, 50309
Telephone: 515-288-0145 Telecopier: 515-288-2724
Thomas A. Finley; Jerry P. Alt; Glenn L. Smith; Steven K. Scharnberg; David C. Craig; John D. (Jack) Hilmes; R. Todd Gaffney; Kermit B. Anderson; Kevin J. Driscoll; Connie L. Diekema; Frederick T. Harris;—Brian L. Stowe; Thomas J. Joensen; Kami M. Lang; Eric G. Hoch. Of Counsel: Kerry A. Finley.
General Civil Practice, Litigation and Appeals in all Courts. Banking, Civil Trial, Commercial, Communication, Corporate, Education, ERISA, Employment Law, Estate Planning, Health Care, Insurance, Personal Injury, Product Liability, Professional Malpractice, Probate, Real Estate, Taxation, Transportation, Trust and Workers Compensation.
Representative Clients: ALAS; American Society of Composers, Authors and Publishers; Equitable Life Assurance Society of the U.S.; Meredith Corp.
Iowa Attorneys for: Midwest Medical Insurance Co.
District Attorneys for: Norfolk & Southern Railroad; Soo Line Railroad Company.
Reviser of the Iowa Law Digest for this Directory.

See Professional Biographies, DES MOINES, IOWA

Fischer, Drennan L. ... '73 '01 C.352 B.A. L.61 J.D. [Ⓐ P.Watson]
Fischer, Gary R., (BV) ... '64 '90 C.132 B.A. L.221 J.D. [Dreher,S.&J.]
Fischer, Gordon R., (AV) ... '64 '94 C.352 B.A. L.801 J.D. [Bradshaw,F.P.&F.]
Fisher, Bart A. ... '70 '04 *C.375 B.S. L.900 J.D.* [Ⓐ McKee,V.&S.] (See Pat. Sect.)
Fisher, David J. ... '36 '62 C.293 B.S. Pres. & CEO, Onthank Co.
Fisher, Jeffrey P. ... '77 '03 C.350 B.A. L.300 J.D. [Ⓐ Grefe&S.]
Fisher, Thomas G. ... '31 '59 C&L.30 B.S., J.D. Legal Aid‡
Fitzgerald, Michael C., (BV) '56 '82
C&L.352 B.A., J.D. Gen. Coun., Amer. Repub. Ins. Co.

Fix, Richard L., (AV) ... '43 '76 C.352 B.S. L.221 J.D. [Sturm&F.] (See Pat. Sect.)
Flagg, George E. ... '25 '49 C&L.352 B.A., LL.B. 2716 Grand Ave.‡
Flagg, Jeffrey G., (BV) ... '51 '77 C.352 B.A. L.221 J.D. [Flagg]
Flagg Law Firm, (BV) ... 2716 Grand Ave.
Flaherty, Daniel L., (BV) ... '55 '82 C.593 B.A. L.796 J.D. Asst. Co. Atty.
Fletcher, Joan M., (AV) ... '52 '89 C.352 B.S. L.375 J.D. [Dickinson,M.T.&H.]
Flynn, Thomas L., (AV) ... '46 '72 C.513 B.A. L.221 J.D. [Belin L.M.Z.F.]
Foley, Thomas W., (AV) ... '59 '85 C&L.352 B.B.A., J.D. [Nyemaster,G.W.H.&O.]
Forney, Kent M., (AV) ... '32 '58 C&L.352 B.A., J.D. [Bradshaw,F.P.&F.]
Forrest, F. H. (Mike) ... '23 '53 C.602 B.A. L.221 LL.B. [Beving,S.&F.] ‡
Forsyth, Julie ... '58 '00 C&L.221 B.S., J.D. 6305 S.W. 9th St., Ste. 1
Fox, Terry R., (BV) '54 '80
C&L.793 B.S.B.A., J.D. Mng. Sr. Atty., MidAmerican Energy Co.
Foxhoven, Jerry R., (AV) ... '52 '77 C.513 B.S. L.221 J.D. 321 E. 12th Street
Fraizer, Patrick C., (BV) '59 '85 C&L.352 B.B.A., J.D.
V.P. & Sr. Intl. Coun., Principal Financial Grp.
Frampton, George H., (AV) ... '— '76 C&L.221 B.S.B.A., J.D. [Ⓒ Whitfield&E.]
Frank, Sally Belinkoff '59 '83 C.674 A.B. L.569 J.D.
Assoc. Prof., Drake Univ. Law Sch.
Frederici, C. Carleton, (AV) ... '38 '65 C&L.352 B.A., J.D. [Ⓒ Davis,B.K.S.&R.]
Freed, Susan J. ... '73 '99 C.352 B.S. L.209 J.D. [Davis,B.K.S.&R.]
Freeman, Claude H., (AV) ... '27 '61 C.499 B.S. L.221 LL.B. 2222 Grand Avenue‡
Frohock, Joan W., (Mrs.) '39 '64
C.966 B.A. L.221 J.D. Pres., Standard Bearings Co. of Des Moines
Frost, James W. ... '33 '60 C&L.352 B.A., J.D. 666 Walnut St.‡
Frye, Kristine Corcoran, (BV) ... '58 '83 C.436 B.A. L.221 J.D. 520 - 35th Street
Fulton, Douglas A., (BV) ... '57 '86 C.351 B.A. L.221 J.D. [Bradshaw,F.P.&F.]
Funaro, Charles D., (BV) ... '21 '51 C&L.221 LL.B. 2307 Hubbell Ave.
Funaro, Patricia A. ... '62 '92 C.350 B.A. L.352 J.D. Sr. Legal Coun.
Funk, Mary E., (BV) ... '69 '95 C.221 B.A. L.352 J.D. [Nyemaster,G.W.H.&O.]
Fuson, Charles Steven ... '52 '82 C.293 B.A. L.378 J.D. The Youth Law Printer
Gaffney, R. Todd, (AV) ... '53 '79 C&L.221 B.S.B.A., J.D. [Finley,A.S.S.C.H.&G.]
Gaines, Kerry A. ... '77 '03 C&L.972 B.S., J.D. [Ⓐ Huber,B.C.H.&L.]
Galbraith, Robert C., (AV) '47 '75
C.792 B.S. L.494 J.D. Div. Admin., IA Dept. of Inspection & App.,
Galenbeck, Scott M., (BV) ... '48 '74 C.293 B.A. L.352 J.D. Asst. Atty. Gen.
Galligan, Brian P. ... '74 '00 C.170 B.A. L.352 J.D. [Ⓐ Galligan,D.&R.]
Galligan, Joseph Michael ... '69 '02 C.187 B.S.S. L.221 J.D. [Ⓐ Galligan,D.&R.]
Galligan, Michael J., (AV) ... '42 '67 C.221 B.A. L.1066 J.D. [Galligan,D.&R.]

Galligan, Doyle & Reid, P.C., (AV) [BR]
Suite 5 The Plaza, 300 Walnut, 50309-2292
Telephone: 515-282-3333; 1-800-217-9312 Fax: 515-282-0318
Email: lawyers@galliganlaw.com URL: http://www.galliganlaw.com
Michael J. Galligan; Richard H. Doyle; Timm W. Reid;—Brian P. Galligan; Joseph Michael Galligan. Of Counsel: James A. Albert.
Litigation, Medical Malpractice, Products Liability and Personal Injury.
Reference: US Bank.

See Professional Biographies, DES MOINES, IOWA

Galloway, Joseph M. ... '57 '79 C&L.221 B.A., J.D. 3622 Davidson Rd.
Galloway, Michael M. ... '— '97 C.350 B.B.A. L.221 J.D. [Ⓐ Ahlers&C.]
Galvin, John D. ... '23 '49 C&L.221 LL.B. 1125 High St.
Gamble, Arthur E. ... '52 '78 C&L.352 B.A., J.D. Dist. Ct. J., 5th Cir.
Gamble, Robert A., (AV) ... '38 '62 C&L.352 B.A., LL.B. [Davis,B.K.S.&R.]
Gannon, Mary T. ... '59 '91 C.351 B.A. L.352 J.D. Iowa Assn. of School Bds.
Garbis Nolan, Nicole C., (CV) ... '67 '93 C.98 B.A. L.221 J.D. 218 6th Ave., Ste. 706
Garmer, Richard D., & Associates, Law Firm of '55 '91
C.500 B.A. L.862 J.D. 510 Glenview Drive
Garrett, Julian B., (BV) ... '40 '67 C.132 A.B. L.352 J.D. [Ⓐ Riemenschneider,R.&S.]
Garroutte, Jay, (CVⓉ) '60 '91 C.543 B.S. L.546 J.D.
(adm. in NE; not adm. in IA) Chief Invest., Pros. Off.
Garten, William B., (AV) ... '28 '52 C&L.352 B.A., J.D. 3000 Grand Ave.‡
Garten & Wanek, (AV) ... 835 Insurance Exchange Bldg.
Gastelo, Elias Sergio, Jr. ... '72 '99 C.843 B.S. L.221 J.D. [Ⓐ Benzoni]
Gately, Gary, (AV) ... '— '61 C&L.352 B.S.C., J.D. [Whitfield&E.]
Gaudineer, Lee H., Jr., (AV) ... '32 '58 C.293 B.A. L.221 J.D. [Gaudineer,C.&G.]

Gaudineer, Comito & George, L.L.P., (AV)
P.O. Box 4628, 50306
Telephone: 515-327-1750 Fax: 515-327-1250
Email: gaudineercomito@qwest.net URL: http://www.gaudineercomitogeorge.com
Members of Firm: Lee H. Gaudineer, Jr.; Frank A. Comito; Tom W. George; Carlton G. Salmons; Jon K. Swanson; Patrick J. Hopkins; William W. Schwarz; Kent A. Gummert.
General Civil, Trial and Appellate Practice in State and Federal Courts. Corporation, Insurance, Labor, Municipal, Administrative, Workers' Compensation, Employment, Civil Rights, Probate, Real Estate, Taxation, Personal Injury, Product Liability and Criminal.

See Professional Biographies, DES MOINES, IOWA

Gaumer, Lynn M., (CVⓉ) ... '68 '94 C.352 B.A. L.793 J.D. [Ⓐ Duncan,G.B.&L.]
Genest, Ryan A., (BV) ... '66 '92 C.801 B.A. L.221 J.D. [Culp,D.S.&G.]
Gentry, Nolden, (AV) ... '37 '64 C&L.352 B.S., J.D. [Brick,G.B.S.S.S.&L.]
Gentry, Nolden Brian ... '70 '96 C.393 B.S. L.352 J.D. [Brick,G.B.S.S.S.&L.]
Gentsch, Drew J. ... '— '00 C&L.221 B.A., J.D. [Ⓐ Whitfield&E.]
George, Emmit J., Jr., (CV) ... '49 '75 C.132 B.A. L.352 J.D. [Ⓒ Parrish,K.M.D.&C.]
George, Tom W., (AV) ... '40 '65 C.352 B.B.A. L.221 J.D. [Gaudineer,C.&G.]
German, Judith M. ... '44 '74 C.350 B.S. L.221 J.D. Research Atty. Iowa Supm. Ct.
Gerrish-Lampe, Jennifer, (BV) ... '72 '97 C&L.221 B.A., J.D. [James]
Gibson, Jan D. ... '60 '86 C.352 B.B.A. L.221 J.D. Coverage Coun., EMC Ins Cos.
Giese, Darla M., (BV) ... '62 '97 C.353 B.A. L.221 J.D. [Ⓐ Dorsey&W.]
Gilchrist, Guy G. ... '18 '48 C.350 B.S. L.276 J.D. 1640 66th St.‡
Gilchrist, Michael C., (AV) ... '68 '95 C&L.352 B.S.E., J.D. [Dorsey&W.] (Pat.)
Giles, James A., (AV) '47 '77 C&L.221 B.A., J.D.
V.P. & Sr. Insur. Coun., Principal Mut. Life Ins. Co.
Giles, Jason L. ... '76 '03 C.877 B.A. L.221 J.D. [Ⓐ Nyemaster,G.W.H.&O.]
Gilliam, James H., (AV) ... '55 '80 C&L.352 B.A., J.D. [Brown,W.G.G.B.&S.]
Gillotti, Frank R. ... '20 '42 C&L.352 A.B., J.D. Polk Construction Co.
Gilson, Ilene L. Rootberg '67 '92
C.352 B.A. L.221 J.D. Enforcement Atty., Iowa Insurance Div.
Gilson, Zachary T. ... '63 '93 C.352 B.G.S. L.221 J.D. 909 Locust St.
Giovannetti, E. J., (AV) ... '41 '66 C.109 B.A. L.190 J.D. [Hopkins&H.]

Gislason & Hunter LLP, (AVⓉ)
Liberty Building, 418 Sixth Avenue, Suite 1210, 50309 ⊙
Telephone: 515-244-6199 Facsimile: 515-244-6493.
URL: http://www.gislason.com
Members of Firm: Barry G. Vermeer; Gary W. Koch; Roger H. Gross; Reed H. Glawe; Wade R. Wacholz; Laura L. Myslis; Andrew A. Willaert; Dustan J. Cross; Loree A. Nelson;—James R. Gowling; Peter M. Sand.
General Practice including Agricultural Law, Alternate Dispute Resolution, Banking Law, Bankruptcy, Commercial Law, Corporate Law, Environmental Law, Estate Planning, Family Law, Health

(This Listing Continued)

Gislason & Hunter LLP (Continued)

Law, Insurance, Labor Law, Medical Malpractice, Personal Injury, Wills and Probate, Product Liability, Real Estate, Trial Law, Workers' Compensation.
New Ulm, Minnesota Office: 2700 South Broadway, P.O. Box 458. Telephone: 507-354-3111. Facsimile: 507-354-8447.
Minneapolis, Minnesota Office: Suite 215E, 9900 Bren Road East, P.O. Box 5297. Telephone: 952-933-9900. Facsimile: 952-933-0242.
Mankato, Minnesota Office: Landkamer Building, Suite 200, 124 East Walnut Street, P.O. Box 4157. Telephone: 507-387-1115. Facsimile: 507-387-4413.
See Professional Biographies, DES MOINES, IOWA

Giudicessi, Michael A., (AV) ....'53 '79 C.502 B.J. L.352 J.D. [Faegre&B.]
Glanton, W. Stevenson ....'22 '53 C.832 B.S. L.1014 LL.B. 2200 Chatauqua Pkwy.‡
Glawe, Reed H., (BVⓉ) '61 '86 C.350 B.S. L.352 J.D. [Gislason&H.] (⊙New Ulm, MN)
Godwin, Mark, (AV) ....'51 '85 C.9 B.A. L.221 J.D. Dep. City Atty.
Goettsch, Craig A. ....'50 '75 C&L.352 B.A., J.D. Supt., State Secs. Bur.
Goetz, Jeffrey D. ....'56 '92 C.112 B.A. L.61 J.D. [Bradshaw,F.P.&F.]
Goldman, David H., (AV) ....'42 '77 C.1036 B.A. L.352 J.D. [Babich,G.C.&R.]
Goldsmith, Philip James, Law Offices of '58 '85 C&L.352 B.B.A., J.D. 4415 Greenwood Drive‡
Gonlubol, Ahmet S. ....'58 '86 C&L.190 B.S.B.A., J.D. Asst. Appl. Def.
Goodhue, John D. ......'74 '00 C.701 B.S. L.221 J.D. [A McKee,V.&S.] (See Pat. Sect.)
Goodman, Jeffrey L., (AV) ....'59 '85 C.352 B.A. L.221 J.D. [Goodman&Assoc.] ⊙

Goodman & Associates, P.C., (AV) BB
P.O. Box 12091, 50312 ⊙
Telephone: 515-267-8600 Facsimile: 515-224-2075
Email: jeff@gdmnlaw.com URL: http://www.goodmanandassoc.com
Jeffrey L. Goodman;—Marcy A. O'Brien; Gretchen R. Jensen.
Civil Trial Practice, Products Liability, Design Defect Litigation, Construction Law, Employment Law, Commercial Law, State, County and Municipal Law, Professional Liability, Insurance Defense, Wrongful Death, Personal Injury.
West Des Moines Office: 1501 42nd Street, Suite 300, 50266. Telephone: 515-267-8600. Fax: 515-224-2075.
See Professional Biographies, DES MOINES, IOWA

Gorham, David S., (BV) ....'67 '93 C.350 B.S. L.221 J.D. [Hopkins&H.]
Gorsche, David V., (BV) '62 '91 C.352 B.B.A. L.221 J.D. V.P. & Managing Coun., Wells Fargo Home Mtge., Inc.
Gorsche, Krista M. ......'67 '93 C.350 B.A. L.221 J.D. Coun., Principal Financial Group
Goudelock, Gary D. ....'— '05 C.612 B.A. L.221 J.D. [A Whitfield&E.]
Gowling, James R., (AVⓉ) '42 '69 C.429 B.A. L.1035 J.D. [A Gislason&H.] (⊙Mpls., MN)
Grace, David J., (AV) '46 '72 C.177 B.A. L.352 J.D. Ethics Coun., Iowa State Bar Assn.
Grady, Catherine W. ....'59 '84 C&L.352 B.B.A., J.D. Claims Coun., Allied Insurance
Graham, Bruce '38 '64 C.749 B.S. L.262 LL.B. Admin. Law J., Dept. of Employ. Servs.
Graham, William W., (AV) ....'52 '77 C.659 B.A. L.93 J.D. [Graham]

Graham Law Firm, The, A Professional Corporation, (AV)
630 Equitable Building, 604 Locust Street, 50309
Telephone: 515-282-0230 Fax: 515-282-4235
Email: wwg@grahamlawiowa.com URL: http://www.wgrahamlaw.com
William W. Graham.
General Civil Practice. Trials and Appeals in all Courts. Business and Commercial Litigation. Corporate, Business, Employment, Products Liability and Construction Law.
See Professional Biographies, DES MOINES, IOWA

Grate, Theron B., Jr. ....'22 '49 C&L.221 A.B., LL.B. 4313 Fleur Dr.
Graves, Bruce, (AV) ....'39 '64 C.627 B.S. L.546 J.D. [Brown,W.G.G.B.&S.]
Green, Brent B. (Chris), (AV) ....'41 '65 C&L.352 B.A., J.D. [Duncan,G.B.&L.]
Green, Brian M. ....'69 '96 C.378 B.S. L.221 J.D. [A Brown,W.G.G.B.&S.]
Green, Joyce J., (CV) ....'41 '80 C&L.221 B.M.E., J.D. Asst. City Atty.
Green, Michael J., (AV) '48 '76 C.177 B.A. L.221 J.D. [Brown,W.G.G.B.&S.] (⊙West Des Moines)
Green, Scott K., (BV) '58 '97 C&L.221 B.A., J.D. Assoc. Staff Atty., American Family Insurance Group

Grefe & Sidney, P.L.C., (AV) BB
2222 Grand Avenue, P.O. Box 10434, 50306 ⊙
Telephone: 515-245-4300 Fax: 515-245-4452
Email: grandfirm@grefesidney.com URL: http://www.grefesidney.com
Thomas W. Carpenter; Henry A. Harmon; Stephen D. Hardy; Robert C. Thomson; Craig S. Shannon; Patrick J. McNulty; Mark W. Thomas; Guy R. Cook; Andrew D. Hall; Donna R. Miller;—Michael A. Carmoney; Clark I. Mitchell; Lisa Renee Lemons Perdue; Nicholas J. Mauro; Anita L. Dhar; Jeffrey P. Fisher; Samantha S. Willets; Amy E. H. Miller; E Jacob Cummings; Arthur Krimsky; Julia L. Roose;—John Werner; Rolland E. Grefe (1920-2004).
General Civil and Trial Practice in all State and Federal Courts. Appellate Practice, Product Liability, Insurance, Negligence, Environmental, Toxic Torts, Professional Liability, Employment, Discrimination, Personal Injury, Workers Compensation, Real Estate, Probate and Estate Planning, Corporate Practice, Family Law, Commercial Litigation and Elder Law.
Representative Clients: Adventurelands of America; Caseys General Stores, Inc.; Cincinnati Insurance Companies; Liberty Mutual Insurance Co.; Otis Elevator; State Farm Insurance Company; The St. Paul Companies; State Industries.
Pella, Iowa Office: 810 Washington Street, 50219. Telephone: 641-628-4300.
See Professional Biographies, DES MOINES, IOWA

Greffenius, A. J., (AV) ....'24 '50 C.583 B.A. L.477 LL.B. [C Davis,B.K.S.&R.]
Grell, William H. ....'72 '97 C.1267 B.A. L.352 J.D. [Huber,B.C.H.&L.]
Grenard, Frank M., (BVⓉ) ....'— '77 C.1077 B.A. L.597 J.D. [Whitfield&E.]
Greta, Carol J., (BV) ....'55 '81 C&L.352 B.A., J.D. State Dept. of Educ.
Greta, Gordon D., (CV) ....'— '74 C&L.352 B.S., J.D. [A Ahlers&C.]
Gribble, Charles E., (AV) ....'46 '75 C.755 B.A. L.221 J.D. [C Parrish,K.M.D.&C.]
Griebel, Pamela D., (AV) ....'53 '78 C&L.352 B.A., J.D. Asst. Atty. Gen.
Griffin, Daniel P. ....'44 '68 C&L.352 B.B.A., J.D. 302 28th St.
Griffin, Janet, (AV) '52 '77 C.645 B.A. L.352 J.D. V.P., Pub. Pol. & Govt. Relations, Wellmark Blue Cross & Blue Shield of Iowa
Griffin, Jon T., (BV) ....'45 '70 C&L.221 B.A., J.D. 1217 Army Post Rd.
Griger, Harry M., (AV) ....'41 '66 C&L.352 B.A., J.D. Spec. Asst. Atty. Gen.
Grissom, John A., Jr. '65 '91 C.612 B.S. L.623 J.D. (adm. in XX; not adm. in IA) Asst. Gen. Coun., Wells Fargo Financial, Inc.
Gritton, James H. ....'29 '53 C&L.221 B.S.C., J.D. 4117 Boyd St.
Gritzner, James E. ....'47 '79 C.193 B.A. L.221 J.D. U.S. Dist. J.
Grob, Elizabeth A., (BV) ....'— '96 C.500 B.A. L.221 J.D. [Ahlers&C.]
Groenenboom, Dennis L. ....'53 '78 C.132 B.A. L.352 J.D. Exec. Dir., IA Legal Aid
Gross, Douglas E., (AV) ....'54 '86 C.353 B.A. L.221 J.D. [Brown,W.G.G.B.&S.]
Gross, Roger H., (AVⓉ) '50 '84 C.494 B.S. L.1035 J.D. [Gislason&H.] (⊙Mpls., MN)
Grossklaus, David D., (BV) ....'68 '94 C.351 B.A. L.221 J.D. [Dorsey&W.]
Grotnes, Matthew A., (AV) ....'63 '89 C.427 B.A. L.221 J.D. [Hopkins&H.]
Gummert, Kent A., (BV) ....'66 '93 C.350 B.S. L.221 J.D. [Gaudineer,C.&G.]
Gunderson, Joseph R., (AV) ....'59 '85 C.350 B.S. L.477 J.D. [Gunderson,S.&W.]
Gunderson, Sharp & Walke, LLP, (AV) 317 Sixth Avenue, Suite 600 (⊙Prairie Village, KS)
Guns, RaeAnn M., (CV) ....'57 '86 C.351 B.A. L.352 J.D. [A Hogan]
Haag, Douglas A., (AV) ....'52 '79 C.490 B.S. L.221 J.D. [Patterson,L.D.T.I.B.&O.]
Hadenfeldt, Jerry L., (AV) '47 '74 C.351 B.A. L.221 J.D. Dir., Government Relations, Meredith Corp.
Haesemeyer, Richard E., (AV) ....'28 '58 C.339 B.S. L.309 J.D. 120 30th St.
Hagemeier, Jami J. ....'77 '03 C.350 B.S. L.221 J.D. [A Williams,B.H.&M.]
Hagen, Ann ....'66 '91 C.221 B.A. L.352 J.D. Coun., Principal Financial Group
Hagen, Christopher D., (AV) ....'43 '68 C&L.352 B.A., J.D. U.S. Atty.
Hagen, Dale B. ....'41 '73 C.590 B.A. L.221 J.D. Dist. J.
Hagen, Howard O., (AV) ....'48 '73 C.293 B.A. L.145 J.D. [Dickinson,M.T.&H.]
Haggerty, Joseph K. ....'46 '73 C.1115 A.B. L.665 J.D. [Nyemaster,G.W.H.&O.]
Haindfield, Danielle Jess ....'— '99 C&L.221 B.A., J.D. [Ahlers&C.]
Haindfield, Matthew J., (BV) ....'71 '99 C.350 B.S. L.221 J.D. [Bradshaw,F.P.&F.]
Haley, James D. ....'46 '73 C&L.221 B.A., J.D. Supervisory Atty., U.S. Treasury
Hall, Andrew D., (BV) ....'64 '90 C.813 B.A. L.352 J.D. [Grefe&S.]
Hall, Bryan H. ....'44 '68 C.162 B.A. L.352 J.D. 665 Locust St.
Hall, Sharon K. ....'57 '93 C.475 B.A. L.221 J.D. Iowa Dept. of Justice
Halleck, Roger R. ....'41 '66 C.593 B.A. L.1119 J.D. State Civil Rights Comm.
Halligan-Brown, Julie A., (BV) ....'62 '87 C.350 B.S. L.352 J.D. Asst. Atty. Gen.
Hamady, Laura E. ....'75 '02 C.976 B.A. L.1375 J.D. [A Belin L.M.Z.F.]
Hamborg, Kelly D., (BV) '55 '85 C.352 B.B.A. L.221 J.D. [Brown,W.G.G.B.&S.] (⊙West Des Moines)
Hamilton, Neil D. ....'54 '79 C.350 B.S. L.352 J.D. Drake Univ. Law School
Hancock, R. William, Jr. ....'— '04 C.953 B.A. L.221 J.D. [A Whitfield&E.]
Hancock, Terry C., (AV) ....'46 '74 C.546 B.A. L.221 J.D. [Nyemaster,G.W.H.&O.]
Hancock, William J. ....'13 '40 L.211 LL.B. 7205 Bellaire Ave.‡
Hanes, O. W., (BV) ....'16 '42 C&L.221 B.C.S., LL.B. 915 Ashworth Rd.
Haney, Matthew G. '61 '89 C.880 B.A. L.602 J.D. (adm. in MO; not adm. in IA) Gen. Coun., Amerus Group
Hanigan, William E. ....'67 '93 C&L.190 B.S.B.A., J.D. [Brown,W.G.G.B.&S.]
Hanks, James C., (AV) ....'— '75 C&L.352 B.A., J.D. [Ahlers&C.]
Hanrahan, Vincent M. ....'24 '50 C&L.221 B.S., LL.B. Dist. Assoc. J.
Hansell, Edgar F., (AV) ....'37 '61 C&L.352 B.B.A., J.D. [Nyemaster,G.W.H.&O.]
Hansell, Jordan B. ....'70 '01 C.228 A.B. L.477 J.D. [Nyemaster,G.W.H.&O.]
Hansell, Silvia J. ....'70 '04 C.228 A.B. L.477 J.D. [A Belin L.M.Z.F.]
Hansen, Christina Flores ....'51 '87 C.436 B.A. L.221 J.D. Asst. Atty. Gen .
Hansen, James L. ....'30 '55 C&L.585 Ph.B., LL.B. 6600 Univ. Ave.
Hansen, Russell J., (BV) ....'45 '70 C.350 B.S. L.221 J.D. [Connolly,O.L.H.&O.]

Hansen, McClintock & Riley, (AV) BB
Fleming Building, 8th Floor, 218 Sixth Avenue, 50309-4092
Telephone: 515-244-2141 Fax: 515-244-2931
Email: info@hmrlawfirm.com URL: http://www.hmrlawfirm.com
Members of Firm: Haemer Wheatcraft (1904-1983); J. Rudolph Hansen (1904-1995); Ronald A. Riley (Retired); John A. McClintock; Chester C. Woodburn, III; William D. Scherle; David L. Brown; John E. Swanson; Aaron T. Oliver. Associate: Alexander Wonio.
General Civil Trial Practice in all Courts. Professional Negligence, Workers' Compensation, Corporation and Real Estate Law, Credit Union, Insurance, Administrative Law, Appellate Practice and Products Liability.
Representative Clients: The St. Paul Companies; Bituminous Insurance Companies; Northwestern National Insurance Co.; The Travelers Insurance Companies; American International Companies; Iowa Credit Union League; British American Tobacco Company, Ltd.; Podiatry Insurance (PICA); American International Group.
See Professional Biographies, DES MOINES, IOWA

Hansing, Mark D., (AV) '56 '81 C.427 B.A. L.352 J.D. [McKee,V.&S.] (See Pat. Sect.)
Hanson, Mark V., (BV) ....'— '86 C.350 B.S. L.352 J.D. [Whitfield&E.]
Hanson, Stephen J. '65 '92 C.130 B.A. L.221 J.D. Assoc. Gen. Coun., Wells Fargo Home Mtge.
Hanson, Thomas D., (AV) ....'44 '70 C.352 B.A. L.145 J.D. [Hanson,B.&R.]

Hanson, Bjork & Russell, L.L.P., (AV)
405 6th Avenue, Suite 1300, 50309
Telephone: 515-244-0177 Fax: 515-244-8258
URL: http://www.hbr-law.com
Members of Firm: Thomas D. Hanson; Alan H. Bjork; Barry A. Russell; Lu Ann White; Dale A. Knoshaug; Fred E. Beaver; Clark G. McDermott; Michael D. Ensley. Associates: Jonathan D. Bergman; Kara L. Peterson.
General Practice, Probate and Estate Planning, Trials and Appellate Practice, Insurance Law, Employment Law, Personal Injury Law, Health Care Law, Workers Compensation, Products Liability, Commercial Litigation, Business Planning, Business Formation, Real Estate Law, White Collar Crime, Tax.
Representative Clients: Aetna Life and Casualty; Case Corporation; Central Iowa Lutheran Homes; Columbia Insurance Group; Executive Fund Life Insurance Company; Farm Bureau Life Insurance Co.; Farm Bureau Mutual Insurance Co.; Massachusetts Indemnity and Life Insurance Co.
See Professional Biographies, DES MOINES, IOWA

Hanssen, Dennis L., (AV) ....'43 '68 C.293 B.A. L.221 J.D. [Hopkins&H.]
Happe, Elizabeth Bandoli, (AV) ....'58 '83 C.502 B.S.B.A. L.986 J.D. 711 High St.
Happe, Joseph A., (AV) ....'60 '85 C&L.190 B.A., J.D. [Huber,B.C.H.&L.]
Harding, John S., (BV) ....'51 '89 C.352 B.A. L.221 J.D. [Harding]
Harding, Marc S., (AV) ....'47 '73 C&L.352 B.S., J.D. [Harding]
Harding Law Office, (AV) .... 1217 Army Post Rd.
Hardy, Lucille M. ....'47 '86 C.351 B.S. L.352 J.D. Asst. Atty. Gen.
Hardy, Stephen D., (AV) ....'49 '74 C&L.352 B.A., J.D. [Grefe&S.]
Harmon, Henry A., (AV) ....'40 '65 C.221 B.A. L.494 J.D. [Grefe&S.]
Harms, Wendell J., (BV) ....'50 '76 C.221 B.A. L.352 J.D. 111 3rd St.
Harris, Charles E., (AV) ....'22 '49 C&L.352 B.S.C., J.D. 5141 Robertson Dr.‡
Harris, Cory R. ....'71 '00 C.352 B.B.A. L.221 J.D. [A Nyemaster,G.W.H.&O.]
Harris, Emily E. ....'76 '03 C.293 B.A. L.352 J.D. [A Davis,B.K.S.&R.]
Harris, Frederick T., (AVⓉ) .....'64 '94 C.177 B.A. L.190 J.D. [Finley,A.S.S.C.H.&G.]
Harrison, Frank T., (AV) ....'41 '67 C.221 B.A. L.190 J.D. [Hopkins&H.]
Harrison, Harvey L., (BV) ....'44 '69 C.351 B.A. L.352 J.D. 435 E. Grand Ave.
Hart, Daniel W. ....'57 '83 C.187 B.A. L.352 J.D. Asst. Atty. Gen.
Hart, Walter T., (AV) ....'22 '49 C&L.352 B.A., J.D. [C Dreher,S.&J.]
Hartung, Kirk M., (AV) '55 '82 C.350 B.S. L.352 J.D. [McKee,V.&S.] (See Pat. Sect.)
Harty, Frank B., (AV) ....'59 '84 C.352 B.B.A. L.221 J.D. [Nyemaster,G.W.H.&O.]
Harty, Jeffrey D., (BV) ....'68 '95 C.350 B.S. L.352 J.D. [McKee,V.&S.] (See Pat. Sect.)
Harvey, Albert L., (AV) ....'27 '69 C&L.221 B.A., J.D. [C Dreher,S.&J.]
Haskins, Frederick M., (AV) ....'47 '72 C&L.352 B.B.A., J.D. [Patterson,L.D.T.I.B.&O.]
Haskins, Richard E. ....'27 '51 C&L.221 J.D. Consultant, EMC Ins. Cos.‡
Hauser, Wade R., III, (AV) ....'— '81 C.350 B.S. L.352 J.D. [Ahlers&C.]
Hawkins, Lex, (AV) ....'25 '51 C&L.221 B.A., J.D. [Hawkins&N.]

Hawkins & Norris, PC, (AV)
2501 Grand Avenue, Suite C, 50312-5399
Telephone: 515-288-6532 Fax: 515-288-9733

(This Listing Continued)

Hawkins & Norris, PC (Continued)

Members of Firm: Lex Hawkins; Glenn L. Norris.
General Civil Trial, Trials and Appeals, Contract and Tort Litigation, Personal Injury, Antitrust and Business Litigation.
Reference: West Des Moines State Bank.

See Professional Biographies, DES MOINES, IOWA

Hayden, Maynard J.V. ....'30 '59 C&L.221 B.S.B.A., J.D. Ret. Ct. of Appls. J.
Hayes, Edward R. ....'20 '48 C&L.352 B.S.C., J.D. 1715 Northwest Dr.‡
Hayes, R. Michael ....'49 '76 C.352 B.A. L.309 J.D. City Solr.
Hayne, Philip G. ....'49 '79 C.36 B.S. L.221 J.D. Principal Life Insurance Co.
Haynie, Kenneth H., (AV) .... '— '57 C.210 B.A. L.477 J.D. [Ahlers&C.]
Hayward, Gary L., (BV) ....'51 '76 C&L.352 B.A., J.D. Asst. U.S. Atty.
Heady, Barbara Jean ....'49 '93 C.597 B.S. L.352 J.D. Wells Fargo Bank Iowa, N.A.
Hearn, John R., (AV) ....'46 '70 C&L.221 B.A., J.D. 1300 Locust Street
Hedberg, Arthur C., Jr., (AV) ....'28 '54 C&L.352 B.A., LL.B. [Hedberg,O.&V.]
Hedberg, Mark, (BV) ....'57 '83 C.352 B.A. L.190 J.D. 840 5th Ave.
Hedberg, Owens & Vonderhaar, P.C., (AV) .... 840 5th Ave.
Heinrich, Donald J., (BV) '56 '81
C.742 B.A. L.221 J.D. Claims Legal Offr., Allied Insurance
Heiny, Jon C., (BV) .....'57 '83 C.427 B.A. L.352 J.D. Coun., Principal Mut. Life Ins. Co.
Heitland, Jon E., (BV) ....'52 '77 C.351 B.A. L.352 J.D. Chf. Dep. Indus. Comr.
Heitzman, Walter ....'21 '55 C.352 B.A. L.221 J.D. 907-45th St.‡
Helle, Alice Eastman, (AV) .... '51 '88 C.350 B.S. L.221 J.D. [Brown,W.G.G.B.&S.]
Hellweg, Mary G. ....'26 '74 C.999 B.S.E. L.221 J.D. Asst. City Atty.
Helton, J. Campbell, (BV) ....'— '95 C.878 B.S. L.221 J.D. [Whitfield&E.]
Hemminger, John T. ....'54 '81 C.352 B.G.S. L.221 J.D. 2454 S.W. 9th‡
Hemphill, Patricia, (BV) ....'53 '82 C.627 B.S. L.221 J.D. Asst. Atty. Gen.
Henderson, Christopher J. '64 '89
C&L.352 B.S., J.D. 2nd V.P. & Coun., Principal Financial Group
Henderson, Thomas, (AV) ....'— '80 C&L.221 B.A., J.D. [Whitfield&E.]
Henscheid, James Ray ....'59 '94 C.546 B.A. L.734 J.D. 2171 NW 138th St.
Hering, Barbara A., (AV) ....'56 '86 C.132 B.A. L.221 J.D. [Hopkins&H.]
Herink, Kent A., (AV) '55 '82 C.162 B.A. L.352 J.D.
[Davis,B.K.S.&R.] (See Pat. Sect.)
Hermann, Robin L., (AV) ....'43 '68 C&L.352 LL.B. [Patterson,L.D.T.I.B.&O.]

Herrick, Langdon & Langdon, (AV)
1550 Financial Center, Seventh and Walnut, 50309-3972
Telephone: 515-282-8150 Telecopier: 515-282-8226
Members of Firm: Allan A. Herrick (1896-1989); Herschel G. Langdon (1905-2002); Richard G. Langdon; William R. Clark, Jr.; Richard N. Winders.
General Civil Practice. Litigation and Appeals in Federal and State Courts. Insurance, Corporate and Business, Employment, Products Liability, Dram Shop, Personal Injury, Malpractice, Class Actions, Antitrust, Trade Regulation, Taxation, Real Estate, Estate Planning and Probate and Administrative Law.
Representative Clients: Norwest Bank Iowa, N.A.; MAPCO Inc.; CENEX, Inc.; Mercedes Benz of North America.

See Professional Biographies, DES MOINES, IOWA

Herring, Victoria L., (BV) '47 '76 C.72 B.A. L.221 J.D.
4331 Greenwood Drive, Suite 100
Hesselink, Ann P. '54 '81
C.323 A.B. L.724 J.D. 2nd V.P. & Coun., Principal Financial Group
Hibbard, David W., (AV) ....'49 '77 C&L.352 B.A., J.D. Asst. Co. Atty.
Hickey, Leslie E. W. ....'58 '83 C&L.293 J.D. Legis. Serv. Bur., Iowa Code Div.
Hietbrink, Paul D., (AV) ....'52 '77 C&L.546 B.A., J.D. [Brown,W.G.G.B.&S.] (⊙Pella)
Hill, Denise M. ....'69 '96 C.898 B.A. L.221 J.D. [Davis,B.K.S.&R.]
Hill, Leah C. ....'70 '97 C.898 B.A. L.221 J.D. Jud. Law Clk., Dept. of State
Hill, Luther L., Jr., (AV) .... '22 '51 C.951 B.A. L.309 LL.B. [Nyemaster,G.W.H.&O.]
Hill, Mark L., (AV) '53 '82 L.352 J.D.
Compliance Dir. & Asst. Coun., Equitable of Iowa Cos.
Hill, Russell J. ....'31 '59 C.747 B.A. L.352 J.D. U.S. Bkrptcy. J.
Hilmes, John D. (Jack), (AV) .....'54 '79 C.173 B.A. L.221 J.D. [Finley,A.S.S.C.H.&G.]
Hintze, John D., (AV) ....'— '73 C&L.352 B.B.A., J.D. [Ahlers&C.]
Hjelmaas, Joel S., (AV) ....'59 '89 C.587 B.S. L.352 J.D. 711 High St.
Hoch, Eric G. ....'74 '04 C&L.352 B.A., J.D. [Finley,A.S.S.C.H.&G.]
Hockett, Harlan M., (BV) ....'34 '60 C&L.221 B.A., LL.B. 300 Walnut St.
Hodge, Jennifer L. ....'77 '02 C&L.352 B.B.A., JD. [Dickinson,M.T.&H.]
Hodgson, Robert A. ....'77 '03 C&L.352 B.A., J.D. [McKee,V.&S.] (See Pat. Sect.)
Hoffman, Janet L. ....'65 '90 C.106 B.A. L.352 J.D. 5200 SW 32nd Street
Hoffman, Joyce N. '52 '77 C&L.221 B.A., J.D.
Sr. V.P. & Corp. Secy., Principal Financial Group
Hoffmann, Amy M. ....'70 '01 C.352 B.S. L.221 J.D. [Hoffmann]
Hoffmann, Brandi ....'75 '01 C.350 B.S. L.221 J.D. Atty.
Hoffmann, Jon K., (BV) ....'— '88 C&L.221 B.S.B.A., J.D. [Whitfield&E.]
Hoffmann, Josef Louis ....'78 '03 C.98 B.S.E.P. L.221 J.D. [Zarley] (Pat.)
Hoffmann, Michael R., (AV) ....'47 '72 C.352 B.S. L.221 J.D. [Hoffmann] (Pat.)

Hoffmann Law Firm, P.C., (AV)
3708 75th Street, 50322
Telephone: 515-270-8899 Fax: 515-270-0115
Email: hlf@hoffmannlawfirm.com URL: http://www.iowaworkcomp.com
Michael R. Hoffmann;—Amy M. Hoffmann.
Workers' Compensation Law.
Representative Clients: Crawford & Company; Sedgwick Claims Management Services, Inc.; Lumbermen's Underwriting Alliance; Ryder Services Corporation; Federated Rural Electric Insurance Corporation; Constitution State Service Company; Accident Fund Company.
Reference: West Des Moines State Bank.

See Professional Biographies, DES MOINES, IOWA

Hogan, Timothy C., (AV) ....'59 '85 C&L.352 B.A., J.D. [Hogan]
Hogan Law Office, (AV) ....3101 Ingersoll Ave.
Holcomb, James M., (AV) ....'43 '71 C.350 B.S. L.352 J.D. [Bradshaw,F.P.&F.]
Hollebrands, Curtis B. ....'52 '77 C&L.352 B.S., J.D. 711 High St.
Holmes, Gale H. ....'23 '53 L.221 LL.B. 3920 Franklin Ave.
Holz, Robert F., Jr., (AV) ....'42 '67 C.177 B.A. L.352 J.D. [Davis,B.K.S.&R.]
Holz, Shannon G., (AV) '63 '88
C.747 B.A. L.221 J.D. Gen. Coun., Terrus Real Estate Group
Holzworth, Michael P., (BV) ....'57 '85 C&L.190 B.S.B.A., J.D. [Holzworth]
Holzworth Law Firm, (BV) ....5835 Grand Ave., Ste. 104
Hook, Lee P., (BV) ....'56 '81 C.352 Pol.Sci.Econ. L.221 J.D. [Peddicord,W.S.&H.]
Hopkins, Patrick J., (AV) ....'50 '75 C.352 B.A. L.190 J.D. [Gaudineer,C.&G.]
Hopkins, Terrence A., (AV) ....'29 '54 C&L.221 LL.B. [Hopkins&H.]

Hopkins & Huebner, P.C., (AV)
Suite 111, Terrace Center, 2700 Grand Avenue, 50312-5213 ⊙
Telephone: 515-244-0111 Fax: 515-244-8935
URL: http://www.hopkinsandhuebner.com
Fred D. Huebner (1919-1996); Marvin E. Duckworth (1942-2003); Terrence A. Hopkins; Frank T. Harrison; E. J. Giovannetti; Jeff H. Jeffries; R. Ronald Pogge; Thomas J. Logan; Dennis L. Hanssen;

(This Listing Continued)

Hopkins & Huebner, P.C. (Continued)

Lorraine J. May; James E. Van Werden; William L. Dawe; Philip H. Dorff, Jr.; E. J. Kelly; John E. Orrell, Jr.; Robert C. Landess; Gregory T. Racette; Valerie A. Landis; Jeff M. Margolin; Anne L. Clark; Matthew A. Grotnes; M. Anne McAtee (Resident, Davenport Office); Jane V. Lorentzen; Hugh J. Cain; Tina M. Eick; Mark D. Lowe; Barbara A. Hering; David S. Gorham; Michael C. Walker (Resident, Davenport Office);—Erin Q. Pals; Apryl M. De Lange; Thomas P. Murphy; B. J. Miller; Paul Salabert, Jr. (Resident, Davenport Office); Randall P. Schueller; Sarah M. Kouri; B.J. Terrones; Nathan M. Sondgeroth (Resident, Davenport Office); Wendy D Boka.
General Practice, Insurance, Casualty, Workers Compensation, Corporation, Employment, Municipal, Civil Rights, Products Liability, Contracts, Trials in all Courts, Business and Corporation Law, and Real Estate.
Representative Clients: Allstate Insurance Co.; Auto-Owners Insurance Co.; Wausau Insurance Companies; General Casualty Company; Safeco Insurance Companies; United Services Automobile Assn.; Firemen's Fund American Insurance Co.
Reference: Norwest Bank, Des Moines.
Davenport, Iowa Office: 100 East Kimberly Road, Suite 704, 52806-5944. Telephone: 319-445-2264. Fax: 319-445-2267.
Adel, Iowa Office: 1009 Main Street, P.O. Box 99, 50003-1454. Telephone: 515-993-4545. Fax: 515-993-5214.

See Professional Biographies, DES MOINES, IOWA

Horstmann, Randall G., (AV) ...'48 '76 C.352 B.A. L.221 J.D. [Nyemaster,G.W.H.&O.]
Horvat, Nan M., (AV) ....'56 '83 C.736 B.A. L.228 J.D. Co. Atty. Off.
Horvath, Paul E., (AV) ....'47 '76 C.610 B.A. L.910 J.D. [Dickinson,M.T.&H.]
Houser, Thomas J., (AV) ....'64 '89 C.755 B.A. L.352 J.D. [Davis,B.K.S.&R.] ⊙
Howard, Marty R. '63 '89 C&L.352 B.A., J.D.
(adm. in WI; not adm. in IA) V.P. & Gen. Coun., Jacobson Cos.

Howe, Cunningham & Lowe, P.L.C.
(See Urbandale)

Huber, James C., (AV) ....'45 '70 C.118 B.A. L.910 J.D. [Huber,B.C.H.&L.]

Huber, Book, Cortese, Happe & Lanz, P.L.C., (AV)
2700 Westown Parkway, Suite 170, 50266-1411
Telephone: 515-243-4148 Fax: 515-243-5481
Email: huber@desmoineslaw.com URL: http://www.desmoineslaw.com
Members of Firm: James C. Huber; Richard G. Book; Joseph S. Cortese II; Joseph A. Happe; Jeffrey W. Lanz; William H. Grell; Nathan R. McConkey. Associates: Kerry A. Gaines; Katherine J. Pronk.
Civil Trial and Appellate Practice. Insurance Defense, Workers' Compensation, Insurance, Products Liability, Professional Malpractice Defense and Administrative Law. Commercial, Business and Insurance Litigation.
Representative Clients: Atlantic Mutual Cos.; CNA Insurance Cos.; Fireman's Fund American Insurance Companies; Liberty Mutual Insurance Co.; Prudential Property and Casualty Insurance Co.
Reference: Bank of America.

See Professional Biographies, DES MOINES, IOWA

Hudson, John D., (AV) ....'48 '73 C&L.352 B.A., J.D. [Williams,B.H.&M.]
Hughes, John N. ....'10 '33 C&L.145 Ph.B., J.D. Sr. Dist. Ct. J.‡
Hughes, Miranda L., (AV) ....'67 '92 C&L.352 B.A., J.D. [Brown,W.G.G.B.&S.]
Hulett, Debra L., (BV) ....'67 '97 C&L.352 B.A., J.D. [Nyemaster,G.W.H.&O.]
Hulting, Patricia Mullen, (BV) ....'48 '75 C&L.352 B.A., J.D. [Roehrick,H.B.K.&K.]
Humke, Brian J., (AV) ....'56 '82 C.351 B.A. L.221 J.D. [Nyemaster,G.W.H.&O.] ⊙
Humphrey, Mark A., (AV) ....'53 '79 C.132 B.A. L.221 J.D. 2203 Grand Ave.
Hunnicutt, William J., (BV) ....'71 '96 C.602 B.A. L.221 J.D. [Faegre&B.]
Hunt, Jason M. ....'74 '01 C.347 B.S. L.221 J.D. [Dorsey&W.]
Hunter, Edwin Rhodes, Jr. ....'55 '86 C.575 B.A. L.350 J.D. 1000 Walnut St.
Hunter, John D. '60 '86 C&L.546 B.S., J.D.
[Brown,W.G.G.B.&S.] (⊙West Des Moines)
Hunter, Michael T. ....'62 '90 C.352 B.A. L.221 J.D. Asst. Co. Atty.
Hunter, Robert C. '40 '67 C.665 B.A. L.228 J.D.
(adm. in OH; not adm. in IA) Prof. of Law, Drake Univ. Law School
Hupfer, Justin D. ....'72 '97 C.293 B.A. L.221 J.D. Resch. Analyst, Hse. Rep.
Huppert, Michael D., (AV) ....'57 '82 C&L.221 B.A., J.D. Dist. J.
Hurley, Cynthia A., (AV) ....'68 '94 C.352 B.A. L.221 J.D. [Bradshaw,F.P.&F.]
Hurley, Francis P. ....'64 '95 C.350 B.S. L.190 J.D. 6305 S.W. 9th St., Ste. 1
Huscher, Paul E., (BV) ....'29 '57 C.352 B.A. L.623 LL.B. 8350 Hickman Rd.
Huston, Janet G., (BV) ....'50 '83 C.55 B.A. L.221 J.D. [Dickinson,M.T.&H.]
Huston, Joel D. ....'75 '04 C&L.221 B.A., J.D. [Dreher,S.&J.]
Hutchison, Robert A. ....'49 '74 C.309 B.A. L.352 J.D. Dist. J.
Hutchison, Theodore M., (AV) ....'32 '56 C&L.352 B.A., J.D. 711 High St.
Hyatt, June Lorraine ....'37 '64 C.986 B.A. L.378 LL.B. Mag.
Hyde, Alice J. ....'51 '78 C.696 B.A. L.352 J.D. Dept. of Jus.
Ilic, Zorica ....'73 '98 C.187 B.A. L.221 J.D. 108 3rd Street, Suite 322
Ingber, Stanley '46 '73 C.102 B.A. L.976 J.D.
(adm. in NY; not adm. in IA) Drake Univ. Law School
Ingrassia, Jean ....'36 '78 C.724 B.A. L.128 J.D. Dept. of Indus. Servs.
Irish, Roy M., (AV) ....'39 '64 C&L.221 B.S., J.D. [Patterson,L.D.T.I.B.&O.]
Irvine, Thomas B. ....'10 '39 C&L.627 B.S., LL.B. 4525 Kingman Blvd.
Isaacson, Irving M. ....'58 '86 C.813 A.B. L.352 J.D. Mgr., Firstar Bk. Iowa, N.A.
Iverson, Marvin A. ....'24 '50 C&L.352 B.A., J.D. 1367 Penn. Ave.‡
Jackson, Karen S. '— '87 C.879 1978 L.213 J.D.
Assoc. Gen. Coun., Wells Fargo Home Mtge.
Jackson, Lloyd G. ....'26 '55 C&L.352 B.A., J.D. 1100 Fleming Bldg.
Jackson, Reginald L., (BV) '60 '91 C.784 B.A. L.352 J.D.
Assoc. Gen. Coun., Wells Fargo Home Mtge., Inc.
Jackwig, Lee Margaret ....'50 '76 C.424 B.A. L.209 J.D. U.S. Bkptcy. J.
Jacobs, Louise M., (BV) '49 '81 C.494 B.S. L.221 J.D.
Legal Dept., City of Des Moines
Jacobs, Norene D., (AV) ....'42 '78 C.263 A.B. L.378 J.D. [Kutak R.]
James, Dwight W., (AV) ....'34 '61 C.842 B.B.A. L.221 LL.B. [James]
James, Frederick W., (AV) ....'59 '88 C.352 B.A. L.221 J.D. [James]
James, Paul G., Jr. ....'27 '52 C.221 L.352 LL.B. 6115 Windsor Dr.‡

James Law Firm, The, P.C., (AV)
630 Equitable Building, 604 Locust Street, 50309
Telephone: 515-246-8484 Fax: 515-246-8767
URL: http://www.jameslawfirm.com
Dwight W. James; Frederick W. James; Jennifer Gerrish-Lampe.
Personal Injury, Wrongful Death, Medical Malpractice, Product Liability, Business and Tort Litigation.
Reference: Liberty Bank.

See Professional Biographies, DES MOINES, IOWA

Jankins, Michael L., (BV) ....'57 '82 C.959 B.A. L.221 J.D. [Murray&J.]
Jannes, Christopher P., (BV) ....'63 '89 C.57 B.A. L.352 J.D. [Davis,B.K.S.&R.]
Janssen, Dallas J., (BV) ....'54 '79 C&L.221 B.A., J.D. [Janssen]
Janssen Law Office, (BV) ....701 E. Court Ave., Ste. A
Jayne, Steven C., (BV) '50 '79 C.560 B.A. L.221 J.D.
5835 Grand Avenue Suite 201, 50312
Telephone: 515-255-2945 Fax: 515-255-5997
Social Security, Workers Compensation, Personal Injury, Trials.

See Professional Biographies, DES MOINES, IOWA

Jeffries, Jeff H., (AV) ....'45 '70 C.513 B.A. L.221 J.D. [Hopkins&H.]
Jenkins, David L., (AV) ....'51 '76 C&L.221 B.S., J.D. [Bradshaw,F.P.&F.]
Jensen, Dick L., (AV) ....'30 '54 C&L.352 LL.B. [Dreher,S.&J.]
Jensen, Gretchen R., (BV) ....'73 '98 C.352 B.A. L.221 J.D. [[A] Goodman&Assoc.] ⊙
Jensen-Welch, Jill R. ....'61 '03 C&L.221 B.A., J.D. [[A] Dickinson,M.T.&H.]
Jerde, Dennis D., (AV) ....'42 '67 C&L.352 B.A., J.D. [[C] Davis,B.K.S.&R.]
Jesse, Norman G., (BV) ....'37 '64 C.350 B.S. L.221 LL.B. Co. Mgr.
Jessen, Lloyd K. ....'53 '85 C.791 B.S. L.221 J.D. Resch. Atty., State Supm Ct.
Joensen, Thomas J. ....'72 '03 C.350 B.A. L.352 J.D. [[A] Finley,A.S.S.C.H.&G.]
Johnsen, Kenneth A., Attorney at Law, (BV) '51 '77
C.350 B.S. L.352 J.D. 3209 Ingersoll Ave., Ste. 207
Johnson, Alexander M., (BV) ....'73 '99 C.350 B.A. L.221 J.D. [[A] Brown,W.G.G.B.&S.]
Johnson, Andrew C. ....'78 '03 C.350 B.A. L.352 J.D. [[A] Bradshaw,F.P.&F.]
Johnson, Denise L., (BV) '68 '93 C.106 B.S. L.221 J.D.
Asst. Subrogation Atty., EMC Insurance Cos.
Johnson, Dennis W., (AV) ....'49 '75 C&L.352 B.A., J.D. [Dorsey&W.]
Johnson, Edward E., (AV) ....'43 '68 C.293 B.A. L.352 J.D. [Bradshaw,F.P.&F.]
Johnson, Harold W., (AV) .....'25 '77 C.350 B.S.E.E. L.221 J.D. 3000 Southern Hills Dr.
Johnson, Nancy C. ....'53 '78 C.328 B.A. L.845 J.D. Staff Atty., Dept. of Vet. Affs.
Johnson, R. Scott ....'73 '00 C.350 B.S. L.221 J.D. [McKee,V.&S.] (See Pat. Sect.)
Johnson, Raymond ....'52 '86 C.351 B.A. L.352 J.D. Asst. Atty. Gen.
Johnson, Richard L. '51 '77
C.187 B.A. L.352 J.D. Dep. Dir. & Leg. Coun. Leg. Serv. Bureau
Johnson, Ross W., (BV) ....'70 '97 C.36 B.A. L.352 J.D. [Faegre&B.]
Johnson, Thomas D., (AV) ....'62 '90 C&L.352 B.B.A., J.D. [Brown,W.G.G.B.&S.]
Johnson, Walter H. ....'47 '72 C.352 B.B.A. L.221 J.D. Dept. of Employ. Servs.
Johnston, Tricia A. ....'64 '93 C&L.352 B.A., J.D. [[A] Belin L.M.Z.F.]
Jones, Adam W. '74 '03 C.696 B.A. L.221 J.D.
[[A] Brown,W.G.G.B.&S.] (Pat.) (⊙West Des Moines)
Jones, Michael S., (BV) ......'62 '95 C.352 B.B.A. L.221 J.D. [Patterson,L.D.T.I.B.&O.]
Jones, Oscar E. ....'21 '52 C.352 B.A. L.221 J.D. 2307 Hubbell Ave.
Joneson, Alyssa ....'76 '00 C.351 B.A. L.221 J.D. Legal Aid Society
Josten, Robert E., (AV) ....'42 '71 C.513 B.A. L.273 J.D. [Dorsey&W.]
Joyce, Joseph B., (BV) ....'32 '56 C&L.602 B.A., J.D. Asst. Cty. J.
Kahl, Andrew H. '— '89 C.945 B.A. L.569 J.D.
(adm. in NJ; not adm. in IA) U.S. Atty. Off.

Kalinoski & Chaplinsky Attorneys at Law, (BV)
100 Court Avenue, Suite 205, 50309
Telephone: 515-246-8800 Fax: 515-246-1920
URL: http://www.kclawoffice.net
Members of Firm: Charles J. Kalinoski (1948-2003); Margaret M. Chaplinsky.
General Practice.

See Professional Biographies, DES MOINES, IOWA

Kane, James J. ....'29 '58 C.177 B.A. L.221 LL.B. 2005 75th St.
Kauffman, Ralph M. ....'18 '43 C&L.352 B.A., J.D. 2880 Grand Ave.
Kaut, Norbert W., (BV) ....'62 '91 C&L.352 B.A., J.D. Asst. Coun., Meredith Corp.
Kayser, Ronald M. ....'42 '67 C.177 B.A. L.734 J.D. Asst. U.S. Atty.
Kealhofer, G. Michael, (AV) .....'50 '76 C.506 B.S. L.190 J.D. [Spellman,S.S.S.K.&S.] ⊙
Keenan, David Michael ....'57 '83 C.352 B.B.A. L.221 J.D. [Kuntz,K.&L.] ‡
Keenan, Sara L. ....'73 '05 C.560 B.A. L.190 J.D. [[A] Brown,W.G.G.B.&S.]
Kelinson, Craig A. ....'51 '76 C.350 B.S. L.352 J.D. Spec. Asst. Atty. Gen.
Keller, Michael J. ....'45 '74 C&L.793 B.S., J.D. Dial Financial Corp.
Kelley, Bruce G. '54 '79
C.197 A.B. L.352 J.D. Pres. CEO, Employers Mutual Casualty Co.

Kelley, Dorothy L., (BV) '44 '74 C&L.221 B.A., J.D.
808 Insurance Exchange Building, 505 Fifth Avenue, 50309-2317
Telephone: 515-243-5207 Fax: 515-243-5212
Litigation, Workers Compensation Law.

See Professional Biographies, DES MOINES, IOWA

Kelly, E. J., (AV) ....'47 '73 C.755 B.A. L.190 J.D. [Hopkins&H.]
Kelly, William P., (BV) ....'67 '99 C.103 B.A. L.221 J.D. [Davis,B.K.S.&R.]
Kemming, Richard L. ......'41 '67 C.898 B.A. L.879 J.D. Iowa Bur. of Crim. Investigation
Kempkes, Bruce L., (AV) ....'55 '80 C.132 B.A. L.352 J.D. Asst. Atty. Gen.
Kempkes, Jas. D. ....'24 '49 C.132 A.B. L.221 LL.B. 4242 Woodlawn Dr.‡
Kendell, Ann Holden, (BV) ....'73 '98 C.350 B.S. L.221 J.D. [Brown,W.G.G.B.&S.]
Kendell, Gary W., (BV) ....'71 '96 C&L.221 B.A., J.D. 300 Walnut St.
Kennedy, Elizabeth Gregg, (AV) ....'— '81 C&L.221 B.A., J.D. [Ahlers&C.]
Kennedy, Victor N. ....'31 '58 C&L.597 B.M., J.D. Dept. of Nat. Res.
Kenworthy, Martin J. ....'58 '89 C.98 B.S. L.1340 J.D. [Duncan,G.B.&L.]
Kenyon, Gregory L., (AV) ....'54 '78 C.106 B.A. L.352 J.D. [Bradshaw,F.P.&F.]
Kessler, Kenneth L. '43 '69
C&L.221 B.A., J.D. Dir. of Legal Serv.s, Ruan Leasing Company
Ketelaar, A. Brooke '64 '90
C.861 B.A. L.190 J.D. Asst. Gen. Coun., Equitable of Iowa Cos.
Kiener, Mary E., (BV) ......'60 '88 C.352 B.G.S. L.221 J.D. Principal Life Insurance Co.
King, Carlton T., (AV) ....'44 '69 C.934 B.A. L.623 J.D. [Nyemaster,G.W.H.&O.]
King, Debra D., (BV) ....'69 '95 C&L.352 B.B.A., J.D. Iowa Health System
King, Mark A. ....'73 '01 C.190 B.S. L.221 J.D. [[A] Patterson,L.D.T.I.B.&O.]
King, William R., (AV) ....'39 '66 C&L.352 B.A., J.D. [Davis,B.K.S.&R.]
Kinley, Raymond J., (BV) ....'48 '76 C&L.221 B.A., J.D. Asst. Co. Atty.
Kinney, Cassie N. ....'69 '97 C.352 B.A. L.221 J.D. Employers Mutual Ins.
Kirchner, Patrick A., (BV) '60 '87
C.350 B.B.A. L.221 J.D. Coun., Principal Financial Group
Kirlin, Kevin M., (BV) ....'50 '84 C.350 B.S. L.352 J.D. [Roehrick,H.B.K.&K.]
Kirschman, Richard J., (BV) ....'— '91 C.587 B.S. L.352 J.D. [Whitfield&E.]
Klotz, Ruth B. ....'22 '55 C&L.221 B.S., J.D. Assoc. Prob. J.
Knapp, Chad ....'— '02 C.350 B.A. L.221 J.D. [[A] LaMarca&L.]
Kniep, Linda L., (AV) ....'— '81 C.221 B.A. L.352 J.D. [Ahlers&C.]
Knipfer, Shellie L., (BV) '62 '91
C.187 B.A. L.352 J.D. Asst. Appalette Def., The State of IA
Knoploh, Greg H., (AV) ....'53 '78 C.350 B.A. L.352 J.D. Asst. Atty. Gen.
Knoshaug, Dale A., (AV) ....'61 '87 C.350 B.S. L.221 J.D. [Hanson,B.&R.]
Knoshaug, Kimberly P., (AV) ....'63 '90 C.352 B.A. L.146 J.D. [Lewis,W.V.&K.]
Knutson, Becky S., (AV) ....'57 '81 C&L.352 B.A., J.D. [Davis,B.K.S.&R.]
Koch, Gary W., (AV⊕) ...'54 '79 C&L.352 B.A., J.D. [Gislason&H.] (⊙New Ulm, MN)
Koehler, Donald J., II '60 '91 C.846 B.B.A. L.221 J.D.
Coun., Principal Financial Group
Koehn, William J., (AV) ....'36 '63 C&L.352 B.A., J.D. [Davis,B.K.S.&R.]
Koenig, Guy D. '73 '98 C&L.221 B.S.B.A., J.D.
Sr. Compl. Specialist, Princor Fin. Servs. Corp.
Koenig, Tiffany, (BV) ....'73 '98 C.350 B.A. L.221 J.D. 505 Fifth Avenue
Kohlwes, Brian R. ....'78 '03 C.350 B.S. L.221 J.D. [[A] Bradshaw,F.P.&F.]
Kolks, Carolyn F. '62 '96 C.502 B.A. L.45 J.D.
(adm. in KS; not adm. in IA) Coun., Principal Financial Group

Kouri, Sarah M. ....'78 '03 C.352 B.B.A. L.221 J.D. [[A] Hopkins&H.]
Kraemer, Gretchen Witte ....'— '99 C.692 B.A. L.884 J.D. [[A] Whitfield&E.]
Kragnes, Christopher, Sr., (BV) ....'70 '98 C.60 B.B.A. L.221 J.D. [C.A.Kragnes Sr.]
Kragnes, Christopher A., Sr., P.C., Law Offices of, (BV) .... 505 5th Avenue
Krambeck, James L., (AV) ....'39 '64 C.352 B.A. L.477 J.D. [Belin L.M.Z.F.]
Kramer, Jan Mohrfeld, (BV) ....'66 '91 C&L.221 B.S., J.D. [Smith,S.S.&S.]
Kramer, Jonathan E. ....'— '02 C.350 B.S. L.221 J.D. [[A] Whitfield&E.]
Kramer, Yale ....'44 '69 C&L.221 B.S., J.D. Pres., Reiss Corp.
Krapfl, Terrance J. '64 '96 C.784 B.A. L.352 J.D.
Assoc. Gen. Coun., Wells Fargo Financial, Inc.
Kraus, Paul F. ....'78 '05 C.221 B.A. L.352 J.D. Asst. Atty. Gen.
Krause, Curtis S. ....'54 '79 C.598 B.A. L.1017 J.D. Coun., Principal Financial Group
Krausman, Jeffrey A., (AV) ....'49 '75 C&L.221 B.A., J.D. [Dickinson,M.T.&H.]
Krauth, Deborah S., (BV) ....'52 '83 C.351 B.A. L.352 J.D. [Nyemaster,G.W.H.&O.] ⊙
Kreamer, Robert M., (AV) ....'41 '66 C&L.352 B.A., J.D. 5835 Grand Ave.
Krimsky, Arthur ....'78 '04 C.898 B.A. L.221 J.D. [[A] Grefe&S.]
Kruidenier, Elizabeth, (BV) ....'26 '74 C.183 B.A. L.221 J.D. [Parrish,K.M.D.&C.]
Krull, Curtis J., (BV) ....'52 '85 C.999 B.A. L.221 J.D. [Roehrick,H.B.K.&K.]
Kruse, Kevin J., (BV) ....'60 '86 C.56 B.A. L.221 J.D. Diversified Mgmt. Serv.
Kubat, Rod, (AV) ....'51 '76 C.352 B.B.A. L.378 J.D. [Nyemaster,G.W.H.&O.]
Kuehn, Gerald A. ....'38 '67 C.352 B.B.A. L.221 J.D. Asst. Atty. Gen.
Kuehn, Michael A. ....'59 '88 C.350 B.S. L.352 J.D. Legis. Serv. Bur.
Kuhn, Cristina ....'68 '94 L.221 J.D. [[A] Dorsey&W.]
Kulik, Michael G., (AV) ....'45 '70 C&L.352 B.B.A., J.D. [Davis,B.K.S.&R.]
Kunert, Mitchell R. ....'79 '05 C.36 B.S. L.221 J.D. [[A] Nyemaster,G.W.H.&O.]
Kuntz, Ronald W., (BV) ....'37 '63 C.499 B.S. L.221 LL.B. [Kuntz,K.&L.]
Kuntz, Keenan & Laughlin, (BV) .... 405 6th Ave.

Kutak Rock LLP, (AV)
Suite 124, Highland Building, 4201 Westown Parkway, 50266-6720 ⊙
Telephone: 515-224-1266 Fax: 515-457-7669
URL: http://www.kutakrock.com
Partner: Norene D. Jacobs.
Civil Litigation and Bankruptcy, Public Finance, Corporate and Structured Finance, Banking and Commercial Lending, Real Estate Law, Taxation Law, Health Care and Hospital Law.
Atlanta, Georgia Office: Suite 2100, 225 Peachtree Street, NE, 30303-1731. Telephone: 404-222-4600. Facsimile: 404-222-4654.
Denver, Colorado Office: Suite 3100, 1801 California Street, 80202-2658. Telephone: 303-297-2400. Facsimile: 303-292-7799.
Kansas City, Missouri Office: Valencia Place, Suite 200, 444 West 47th Street, 64112-1914. Telephone: 816-960-0090. Telefax: 816-960-0041.
Fayetteville, Arkansas Office: The Three Sisters Building, 214 West Dickson Street, 72701-5221. Telephone: 501-973-4200. Facsimile: 501-973-0007.
Little Rock, Arkansas Office: Suite 1100, 425 West Capitol Avenue, 72201-3409. Telephone: 501-975-3000. Facsimile: 501-975-3001.
Los Angeles, California Office: Suite 3000, 555 West Fifth Street, 90013-1010. Telephone: 213-996-8478. Facsimile: 213-996-8479.
Oklahoma City, Oklahoma Office: Suite 475, 6305 Waterford Boulevard, 73118-1116. Telephone: 405-848-2475. Facsimile: 405-842-5748.
Omaha, Nebraska Office: The Omaha Building, 1650 Farnam Street, 68102-2186. Telephone: 402-346-6000. Facsimile: 402-346-1148.
Scottsdale, Arizona Office: Suite 300, 8601 N. Scottsdale Road, 85253-2742. Telephone: 480-429-5000. Facsimile: 480-429-5001.
Washington, D.C. Office: Suite 1000, 1101 Connecticut Avenue, NW, 20036-4374. Telephone: 202-828-2400. Facsimile: 202-828-2488.
Irvine, California Office: Suite 1100, 18201 Von Karman Avenue, 92612-1077. Telephone: 949-417-0999. Facsimile: 949-417-5394.
Pasadena, California Office: Suite 308, 201 South Lake Avenue, 91101-3004. Telephone: 626-432-1630. Facsimile: 626-432-1614.
Richmond, Virginia Office: Bank of America Center, Suite 800, 1111 East Main Street, 23219-3103. Telephone: 804-644-0313. Facsimile: 804-783-6192.
Chicago, Illinois Office: One South Wacker Drive, 60606-4614. Telephone: 312-602-4100. Facsimile: 312-602-4101.
Wichita, Kansas Office: Suite 370, 8301 East 21st Street North, 67206-2935. Telephone: 316-609-7900. Facsimile: 316-630-8021.

See Professional Biographies, DES MOINES, IOWA

Kutmus, William L., (AV) ....'38 '65 C&L.352 LL.B. [Kutmus&P.]
Kutmus & Pennington, P.C., (AV) .... 218 6th Ave.
Lacey, Michael F., Jr., (AV) ....'43 '76 C.350 B.S. L.221 J.D. [Patterson,L.D.T.I.B.&O.]
Laden, Robert H., (AV) ....'44 '70 C.589 B.S. L.221 J.D. [Laden&P.]
Laden & Pearson, P.C., (AV) ....3231 East Euclid, Suite 300
Lagomarcino, Mark S., (AV) '56 '80
C.350 B.S. L.221 J.D. Coun., Principal Financial Group
LaMarca, George A., (AV) '45 '70
C.801 B.A. L.221 J.D. [LaMarca&L.] (⊙Sarasota, FL)

LaMarca & Landry, P.C., (AV)
1820 NW 118th Street, Suite 200, 50325
Telephone: 515-225-2600 Fax: 515-225-8581
URL: http://www.lamarcaandlandry.com
George A. LaMarca; Gregory W. Landry;—Gary G. Mattson; Justin E. LaVan; Roman Vald; Chad Knapp; Sara A. Lamme; James Biscoglia. Of Counsel: Martin R. Anderson; Nick James Avgerinos.
Trial Practice in State and Federal Courts. Aviation Law, Commercial Litigation, Personal Injury, Wrongful Death, Medical Malpractice, Legal Malpractice, Workers Compensation, Products Liability.

See Professional Biographies, DES MOINES, IOWA

LaMarche, Margaret G. ....'55 '80 C.966 B.A. L.494 J.D. Admin. Law J.
Lamme, Sara A. ....'77 '03 C.999 B.A. L.190 J.D. [[A] LaMarca&L.]
Lamson, Jeffrey E., (AV) ....'41 '66 C.352 B.A. L.309 J.D. [Belin L.M.Z.F.]
Landess, Robert C., (AV) ....'35 '62 C.352 B.A. L.221 J.D. [Hopkins&H.]
Landis, Valerie A., (AV) ....'60 '87 C.502 B.E.S. L.221 J.D. [Hopkins&H.]
Landry, Gregory W., (AV) ....'57 '83 C.174 B.A. L.221 J.D. [LaMarca&L.]
Landwehr, Amy M. ....'74 '01 C.1175 B.A. L.4210 J.D. [[A] Davis,B.K.S.&R.]
Lang, Kami M. ....'76 '02 C.177 B.A. L.221 J.D. [[A] Finley,A.S.S.C.H.&G.]
Langdon, Richard G., (AV) ....'36 '61 C&L.309 A.B., J.D. [Herrick,L.&L.]
Lange, Lance W. ....'72 '01 C.813 A.B. L.178 J.D. [[A] Belin L.M.Z.F.]
Langeness, James B., (AV) ....'54 '80 C.659 B.S. L.221 J.D. [Duncan,G.B.&L.]
Lann, Lisa M. ....'69 '98 C.350 B.S. L.221 J.D. 340 Maple St.
Lanz, Jeffrey W., (BV) ....'68 '95 C.350 B.A. L.221 J.D. [Huber,B.C.H.&L.]
Larsen, Steven P. ....'56 '81 C.350 B.A. L.352 J.D. V.P., Claims, Allied Insurance
Larson, Charles W. .....'35 '66 C.375 B.S. L.352 J.D. Gov. Alliance on Substance Abuse
Larson, J. L. ....'36 '60 C&L.352 B.A., J.D. Supm. Ct. Jus.
Lasich, A. Robert, Jr. .....'59 '91 C.347 B.A. L.150 J.D. Atty., MidAmerican Energy Co.
La Suer, Gene R., (AV) ....'53 '79 C.350 B.S. L.352 J.D. [Davis,B.K.S.&R.]
Laughlin, Matthew E., (BV) ....'69 '96 C.784 B.A. L.546 J.D. [Davis,B.K.S.&R.]
Laughlin, Michael J. ....'44 '69 C&L.221 B.S., J.D. [Kuntz,K.&L.]
Laurenzo, Brian J., (AV) ....'61 '88 C.350 B.S. L.209 J.D. [Dorsey&W.] (Pat.)
LaVan, Justin E., (BV) ....'72 '98 C.490 B.S. L.221 J.D. [[A] LaMarca&L.]
Lavorato, Charles S., (BV) ....'49 '75 C&L.221 B.A., J.D. Asst. Atty. Gen.
Law, Kathleen K. ....'61 '05 C.949 B.A. L.221 J.D. [[A] Nyemaster,G.W.H.&O.]

Lawyer, Steven Verne, (BV) '65 '91
C.350 B.S. L.221 J.D. [Firm of S.V.Lawyer&Assoc.]
Lawyer, Vivian Jury .... '32 '68 C.350 B.S. L.221 J.D. 5831 N. Waterbury Rd.‡

Lawyer, Steven V., & Associates, P.L.C., Law Firm of, (BV)
Fourth Floor Fleming Building, 218 Sixth Avenue, 50309-4011
Telephone: 515-282-2080 Fax: 515-282-1980; Toll Free: 1-877-282-2080
Email: Info@LawyerLawFirm.com URL: http://www.lawyerlawfirm.com
Steven Verne Lawyer.
Traumatic Brain Injury, Wrongful Death, Automobile Accidents and Injuries, Products Liability, Roadway Design Liability, Aircraft Accidents, Employment Law.
See Professional Biographies, DES MOINES, IOWA

Leahy, Thomas D. .... '67 '02 C&L.221 B.S.B.A., J.D. [Ⓐ Bradshaw,F.P.&F.]
Lebrón-Dykeman, Christine .... '69 '96 C.788 A.B. L.352 J.D. [McKee,V.&S.]
Lehman Bell, Janáe ..... '71 '04 C.627 B.S. L.352 J.D. [Ⓐ McKee,V.&S.] (See Pat. Sect.)
Lemons Perdue, Lisa Renee .... '75 '00 C.351 B.A. L.221 J.D. [Ⓐ Grefe&S.]
Leo, Flory J., Jr. .... '51 '79 C.221 B.A. L.300 J.D. 711 High St.
Lerner, Dean A., (AV) '52 '82
C.293 B.A. L.221 J.D. Dep. Dir., Dept. of Inspection & App.
Leto, Patricia L. .... '61 '87 C&L.352 B.A., J.D. EMC Insurance Cos.
Levin, Jack D. .... '38 '62 C&L.221 B.S.B.A., LL.B. Dist. J.‡
Levine, Sidney C. .... '16 '42 C&L.221 B.A., LL.B. 4313 Fleur Dr.
Levis, Thomas J., (AV) .... '53 '77 C&L.221 B.A., J.D. [Brick,G.B.S.S.S.&L.]
Lewis, R. Jeffrey, (AV) .... '47 '72 C.378 B.A. L.494 J.D. [Lewis,W.V.&K.]

Lewis, Webster, Van Winkle & Knoshaug, L.L.P., (AV) BB
620 Liberty Building, 418 Sixth Avenue, 50309
Telephone: 515-243-1000 Fax: 515-288-7000
Email: attorneys@lewislaw-ia.com
R. Jeffrey Lewis; Kimberly P. Knoshaug; Jason B. Wittgraf; Angela Broughton-Romain; Bennett A. Webster (1923-2002). Counsel: Joseph G. Van Winkle.
Litigation in all Courts. Insurance, Negligence, Personal Injury, Workers' Compensation, Products Liability, Transportation Litigation, Commercial, Agency Law and Appeals.
See Professional Biographies, DES MOINES, IOWA

Lierely, Patrice, (CV) .... '54 '83 C&L.221 B.A., J.D. 2815 Druid Hill Rd.
Lillis, William J., (AV) .... '43 '68 C.221 B.A. L.190 J.D. [Connolly,O.L.H.&O.]
Lindebak, Layne M., (AV) .... '53 '79 C&L.352 B.A., J.D. Asst. Atty. Gen.
Lindh, Jason F. .... '73 '05 C.909 B.S. L.285 J.D. [Ⓐ McKee,V.&S.]
Linebaugh, Jesse .... '76 '02 C.352 B.B.A. L.228 J.D. [Ⓐ Faegre&B.]
Lipman, Andi S. .... '63 '87 C&L.352 B.S., J.D. Asst. App. Def.
Loftsgard, Rick, (CV) '65 '92 C.597 B.A. L.352 J.D.
Asst. Gen. Coun., Wells Fargo Financial, Inc.
Loftus, Thomas J. '53 '87 C.1200 A.B. L.276 J.D.
(adm. in MA; not adm. in IA) Coun., Principal Financial Group
Logan, Holly M. .... '76 '01 C.201 B.S. L.352 J.D. [Ⓐ Belin L.M.Z.F.]
Logan, Thomas J., (AV) .... '51 '76 C&L.221 B.A., J.D. [Hopkins&H.]
Loney, Eric .... '— '01 L.221 J.D. [Ⓐ Walker&B.] (ⒸNewton)
Long, Christine B., (AV) .... '65 '91 C.321 B.A. L.352 J.D. [Ⓐ Duncan,G.B.&L.]
Long, James J. .... '47 '71 C&L.966 J.D. [Beving,S.&F.]
Long, Scott L., (AV) .... '62 '87 C.352 B.B.A. L.477 J.D. [Brown,W.G.G.B.&S.]
Longnecker, Anthony A., (AV) '55 '80 C.350 B.S. L.352 J.D.
[Nyemaster,G.W.H.&O.]
Longstaff, Ronald E. .... '41 '65 C.375 B.A. L.352 J.D. U.S. Dist. Ct. Chief J.
Lorentzen, Jane V., (AV) .... '63 '91 C.352 B.S.N. L.221 J.D. [Hopkins&H.]
Lorentzen, John F., (AV) .... '57 '82 C.747 B.A. L.221 J.D. [Nyemaster,G.W.H.&O.]
Lovell, Russell E., II '44 '69 C.602 B.B.A. L.546 J.D.
Prof. of Law, Drake Univ. Law Sch.
Low, Susan A. .... '46 '72 C.787 B.A. L.273 J.D. Asst. City Atty.
Lowe, Mark D., (AV) .... '66 '93 C.350 B.S. L.221 J.D. [Hopkins&H.]
Lozier, Richard W., Jr., (AV) .... '44 '69 C&L.352 B.A., J.D. [Belin L.M.Z.F.]
Luchtel, Keith E., (AV) .... '41 '73 C.1070 B.S. L.221 J.D. [Nyemaster,G.W.H.&O.]
Luedeman, Robert W. .... '48 '96 C.1042 B.A. L.221 J.D. 1315 Randall Place
Luginbill, David H., (AV) .... '— '76 C.352 B.A. L.221 J.D. [Ahlers&C.]
Luxa, Mary Clare, (AV) .... '60 '85 C.208 B.A. L.190 J.D. Asst. U.S. Atty.
Lyford, F. Richard, (AV) .... '44 '72 C.145 B.A. L.352 J.D. [Dickinson,M.T.&H.]
Lyman, Chester J. .... '19 '48 C&L.352 B.S.C., J.D. 612 Locust‡
Lynch, David J., (AV) .... '58 '83 C.976 B.A. L.352 J.D. State Util. Bd.
Lynch, Richard B. .... '51 '76 C&L.378 B.S., J.D. [Shinkle&L.]
Lyons, David J. .... '58 '83 C.177 B.A. L.352 J.D. Dir., Econ. Develop.
Lytle, Steven H., (AV) .... '45 '76 C&L.221 B.S.B.A., J.D. [Nyemaster,G.W.H.&O.]
Mack, William F. '50 '78 C.347 A.B. L.1066 J.D.
V.P. & Assoc. Gen Coun., Wells Fargo Financial, Inc.
Mackaman, John R., (AV) .... '29 '56 C&L.221 B.A., J.D. [Ⓒ Dickinson,M.T.&H.]
Macro, Venessa .... '66 '91 C.351 B.A. L.221 J.D. Dir. Human Res., Drake Univ.
Madden, Jason T., (BV) .... '72 '97 C.898 B.A. L.221 J.D. [Bradshaw,F.P.&F.]
Maddox, O. Gene, (BV) .... '38 '63 C&L.597 B.S.S., J.D. 2024 N.W. 92nd Ct.
Maharry, Rodney K., (BV) .... '68 '94 C.350 B.B.A. L.221 J.D. [Williams,B.H.&M.]
Mahoney, Mark B. ..... '51 '76 C.352 B.B.A. L.221 J.D. Pres., Sioux City Brick & Tile Co.
Malheiro, Sharon K., (AV) .... '56 '89 C&L.221 B.A., J.D. [Davis,B.K.S.&R.]
Mallory, Billy J. .... '73 '01 C.352 B.S. L.221 J.D. [Ⓐ Brick,G.B.S.S.S.&L.]
Malm, Richard A., (AV) .... '49 '74 C.350 B.S. L.221 J.D. [Dickinson,M.T.&H.]
Manatt, Adam C. '— '04 C.350 B.A. L.352 J.D.
[Ⓐ Whitfield&E.] (ⒸWest Des Moines)
Manders, John M. .... '33 '61 C.177 B.S. L.602 J.D. 2901 Douglas Ave.
Mannheimer, Robert E., (AV) .... '19 '41 C.293 A.B. L.352 J.D. 699 Walnut St.‡
Manning, Daniel L., (BV) .... '58 '83 C&L.190 B.A., J.D. [Connolly,O.L.H.&O.]
Mansfield, Edward M., (AV) .... '57 '83 C.309 A.B. L.976 J.D. [Belin L.M.Z.F.]
Marberry, Douglas S. .... '56 '90 C.352 B.S. L.221 J.D. [Marberry]
Marberry Law Firm, P.C. .... 5835 Grand Ave., Ste. 202

Marcucci & Conger, P.L.C.
(See West Des Moines)

Marek, Douglas R., (AV) .... '54 '84 C.170 B.A. L.221 J.D. Asst. Atty. Gen.
Marett, Stephanie L., (BV) ...... '73 '99 C.427 B.A. L.221 J.D. [Nyemaster,G.W.H.&O.]
Margolin, Jeff M., (AV) .... '55 '81 C.352 B.A. L.365 J.D. [Hopkins&H.]
Marks, Joseph L., (BV) .... '45 '69 C.352 B.B.A. L.221 J.D. [Marks]
Marks Law Firm, (BV) .... 4225 University Ave.
Marquett, Gary L. .... '53 '78 C.350 B.S. L.352 J.D. Enforce. Dir., Iowa Secs. Bur.
Marsh, Wendy K., (BV) ..... '67 '94 C&L.221 B.S., J.D. [McKee,V.&S.] (See Pat. Sect.)
Marshall, Dan .... '50 '76 C.293 B.A. L.309 J.D. Staff Atty. Supm. Ct.
Marso, Stephen D. '— '99 C.323 B.A. L.352 J.D.
[Ⓐ Whitfield&E.] (ⒸWest Des Moines)
Martin, Robert L. .... '26 '51 C.350 L.221 LL.B. 1000 E. Grand Ave.
Martin, Steven M. .... '57 '84 C.187 B.S.S. L.221 J.D. 665 Locust St.
Martino, Laura N. .... '78 '03 C.177 B.A. L.352 J.D. [Ⓐ Brown,W.G.G.B.&S.]
Mason, Heidi L. '65 '90 C.350 B.S. L.276 J.D.
Assoc. Gen. Coun., Wells Fargo Home Mtge., Inc.

Mason, Marcia, (BV) .... '54 '82 C.350 B.S. L.352 J.D. Asst. Atty. Gen.
Masterpole, Kathleen, (BV) .... '43 '67 C&L.352 B.A., J.D. Pub. Def. Off.
Mattson, Gary G., (AV) .... '62 '89 C.427 B.A. L.221 J.D. [Ⓐ LaMarca&L.]
Mauro, Nicholas J. .... '76 '02 C&L.352 B.A., J.D. [Ⓐ Grefe&S.]
May, David N., (BV) .... '71 '98 C.502 B.A. L.221 J.D. [Bradshaw,F.P.&F.]
May, Lorraine J., (AV) .... '52 '76 C&L.221 B.A., J.D. [Hopkins&H.]
Mayer, J. Michael, (BV) .... '51 '76 C&L.352 B.A., J.D. 300 Walnut, Ste. 270
Mayes, Thomas A., (CV) .... '70 '96 C.69 B.A. L.352 J.D. Staff Atty, Iowa Ct. of Appeals
Mazie, Marvin E. .... '30 '55 C&L.309 A.B., LL.B. 206 8th St., 10th Fl.
McAfee, Eldon L., (AV) .... '55 '91 C.352 B.S. L.221 J.D. [Beving,S.&F.]
McAllister, Jane B., (AV) .... '— '74 C.378 B.S. L.900 J.D. [Ahlers&C.]
McCarthy, Timothy, (BV) .... '29 '54 C.436 B.S. L.352 J.D. 505 5th Ave.

McCarthy & Hamrock, P.C.
(See West Des Moines)

McCarty, Kelly L., (BV) .... '57 '82 C&L.352 B.B.A., J.D. [Bradshaw,F.P.&F.]
McClintock, John A., (AV) .... '31 '58 C.293 A.B. L.352 J.D. [Hansen,M.&R.]
McCollough, Jason E. .... '79 '04 C.612 B.S. L.221 J.D. [Ⓐ Wandro,B.A.&C.]
McConkey, Emily A. '70 '95
C.350 B.A. L.221 J.D. Asst. Gen. Coun., Amer. Repub. Ins. Co.
McConkey, Nathan R., (BV) .... '68 '95 C.352 B.B.A. L.221 J.D. [Huber,B.C.H.&L.]
McCord, David '53 '78 C.340 B.A. L.309 J.D.
(adm. in AZ; not adm. in IA) Drake Univ. Law School‡
McCormac, Brian S. .... '74 '00 C.162 B.A. L.352 J.D. [Ⓐ Faegre&B.]
McCormick, Curtis G., (BV) .... '51 '76 C&L.221 B.F.A., J.D. [Neiman,S.&M.]
McCormick, Mark, (AV) .... '33 '60 C.884 A.B. L.276 LL.B. [Belin L.M.Z.F.]
McDermott, Clark G., (BV) .... '65 '91 C.221 B.A. L.494 J.D. [Hanson,B.&R.]
McDermott, Matthew C. .... '77 '03 C.352 B.A. L.1375 J.D. [Ⓐ Belin L.M.Z.F.]
McDonald, Christopher L. .... '74 '01 C.999 B.A. L.352 J.D. [Ⓐ Faegre&B.]
McDonough, T. James, (BV) .... '35 '63 C&L.352 A.B., J.D. 3355 S.W. 24th St.
McDowell, Lawrence R., (AV) .... '59 '84 C&L.352 B.A., J.D. Dep. City Atty.

McEnroe, Gotsdiner, Brewer, Burdette & Steinbach, P.C.
(See West Des Moines)

McFarland, Patricia J., (AV) '54 '79 C&L.352 B.B.A., J.D.
Sr. V.P., Gen. Coun. & Secy., Wells Fargo Financial, Inc.
McGhee, Odell Gene, (BV) '52 '79 C.187 B.A. L.221 J.D.
Dept. of Environmental Quality
McGiverin, Arthur A. .... '28 '56 C&L.352 B.S.C., J.D. Chf. Jus., Supm. Ct.
McGovern, Michelle A., (AV) ..... '50 '80 C.350 B.S. L.221 J.D. Div. of Workers Comp.
McGrory, Matthew, (BVⓉ) '65 '91 C&L.352 B.A., J.D.
Asst. Gen. Coun., Wells Fargo Financial, Inc.

McGuire Law Firm, P.C.
(See Mason City)

McIntosh, Edwin N., (AV) .... '50 '76 C&L.352 B.A., J.D. [Dorsey&W.]
McKee, Bruce W., (AV) '34 '59 C.350 B.S.E. L.904 J.D.
[McKee,V.&S.] (See Pat. Sect.)

McKee, Voorhees & Sease, P.L.C., (AV) BB
801 Grand, Suite 3200, 50309-2721
Telephone: 515-288-3667 Facsimile: 515-288-1338
Email: patatty@ipmvs.com URL: http://www.ipmvs.com
Members of Firm: Bruce W. McKee; Michael G. Voorhees; Edmund J. Sease; Mark D. Hansing; Kirk M. Hartung; Heidi Sease Nebel; Wendy K. Marsh; Jeffrey D. Harty; Christine Lebrón-Dykeman; R. Scott Johnson. Associates: John D. Goodhue; Lila A.T. Akrad; Steven P. Smith; Robert A. Hodgson; Bart A. Fisher; Janáe Lehman Bell; Jason F. Lindh; Kurt Van Thomme; Janet E. Phipps-Burkhead.
Intellectual Property and Technology Law, including Patent, Trademark, Copyright, Trade Secret, Licensing, Antitrust. State and Federal Trial Practice.
Reference: Bank of America (Des Moines, Iowa).
See Professional Biographies, DES MOINES, IOWA

McKinney, John F., Jr., (AV) .... '— '65 C&L.221 B.A., J.D. [Ahlers&C.]
McLaughlin, Donn C. .... '43 '68 C.293 B.A. L.352 J.D. First Fed. State Bk.
McLaughlin, Joseph P., (AV) .... '56 '85 C.351 B.A. L.221 J.D. [Wiedenfeld&M.]
McLean, Julie Johnson, (BV) .... '56 '81 C.162 B.A. L.352 J.D. [Davis,B.K.S.&R.]
McLeish, Daria .... '74 '02 C.351 B.M. L.221 J.D. [McLeish]

McLeish Law Office
6165 NW 86th Street, 50131
Telephone: 515-252-2528 Cell: 515-224-1651 Fax: 515-252-2529
Email: mcleishlaw@iowabar.org URL: http://www.mcleishlaw.com
Member: Daria McLeish.
Bankruptcy, Commercial Litigation, Wills and Trusts, and Divorce.
See Professional Biographies, DES MOINES, IOWA

McManus, Walter R., Jr. .... '28 '52 C&L.190 J.D. Dep. Worker's Comp. Comm
McNulty, Patrick J., (AV) .... '51 '77 C&L.352 B.A., J.D. [Grefe&S.]
Mead, Rosanne M., (BV) .... '57 '86 C.958 B.S. L.221 J.D. 2001 44th Street
Meade, Victoria L., (BV) .... '55 '81 C.784 B.S. L.221 J.D. Pub. Def. Off.
Mendt, Denise M. .... '60 '86 C.351 B.A. L.352 J.D. [Nyemaster,G.W.H.&O.]
Mercer, Forrest C. .... '18 '42 C&L.352 B.A., J.D. 5621 Kingman Ave.‡
Mercer, Naomi S. .... '— '68 C&L.221 B.A., J.D. 2880 Grand Ave.‡
Mickle, Nelda Barrow .... '39 '77 C.43 B.A. L.221 J.D. City Solr.
Middleton, Lyle D. '37 '64 C&L.221 B.A., LL.B.
Pres. & Gen. Coun., Atlas Products Inc.
Miglani, Shabnam B. .... '61 '89 C.999 B.Sc. L.976 LL.M. Principal Financial Group
Miller, Amy E. H. .... '76 '04 C.132 B.A. L.221 J.D. [Ⓐ Grefe&S.]
Miller, Andrew G. '63 '92 C&L.352 B.A., J.D.
VP and Asst. Gen. Coun., Amerus Group
Miller, B. J. .... '75 '02 C.351 B.A. L.221 J.D. [Ⓐ Hopkins&H.]
Miller, Donna R., (BV) .... '71 '95 C.587 B.S. L.352 J.D. [Grefe&S.]
Miller, James D., (AV) .... '51 '77 C.793 B.S. L.221 J.D. Asst. Atty. Gen.
Miller, Keith C. '51 '76 C&L.986 B.A., J.D.
(adm. in MO; not adm. in IA) Drake Univ. Law School‡
Miller, Michael J. .... '43 '68 C.293 A.B. L.910 J.D. 300 Walnut
Miller, Thomas H., (AV) .... '50 '75 C&L.352 B.A., J.D. Asst. Atty. Gen., Atty. Gen. Off.
Miller, W. Kent '50 '76 C&L.208 B.A., J.D.
(adm. in CO; not adm. in IA) Wells Fargo Bank Iowa, N.A.
Miller, William J. .... '77 '02 C.1267 B.A. L.221 J.D. [Ⓐ Bradshaw,F.P.&F.]
Miller-Todd, Kathrine S. .... '48 '74 C&L.896 B.A., J.D. Asst. Atty. Gen.
Mills, Amy J., (AV) '58 '84
C.350 B.A. L.352 J.D. V.P. & Coun., Principal Mut. Life Ins. Co.
Minear, Barry N., (BV) .... '28 '54 C&L.352 A.B., LL.B. 6600 Univ. Ave.‡
Mitchell, Clark I., (BV) .... '68 '00 C&L.221 B.A., J.D. [Ⓐ Grefe&S.]
Mock, Michael L., (AV) .... '69 '95 C&L.221 B.A., J.D. [Bradshaw,F.P.&F.]
Moeller, Joanne Lee, (BV) .... '59 '84 C.221 B.A. L.352 J.D. Asst. Atty. Gen.
Mohr, Onita .... '55 '87 C.350 B.A. L.352 J.D. Law Clk. to Dist. Ct.
Moisan, Cynthia M. .... '57 '83 C.927 B.A. L.221 J.D. Assoc. Dist. J.
Moline, Stephen H. .... '60 '86 C.350 B.S. L.352 J.D. Atty's Gen. Off.

Monaghan, Sean C. ...... '71 '99 C.790 B.A. L.245 J.D. Asst. Gen. Coun., Amerus Group
Monson, Terry L., (AV) .... '47 '72 C.579 B.A. L.597 J.D. [Nyemaster,G.W.H.&O.]
Montag, Guy R. .... '62 '87 C.293 B.A. L.221 J.D. Coun., Principal Financial Group
Montgomery, Charles R., (AV) '54 '80
C&L.352 B.A., J.D. Sr. Atty., MidAmerican Energy Co.
Mooney, William H. .... '70 '95 C.012 B.A. L.352 J.D. [Ⓐ Murray&J.]
Moore, David B. .... '43 '68 C.593 B.S. L.262 LL.B. 3116 Leadd Ave.‡
Moore, Sean P., (AV) .... '62 '91 C&L.352 B.B.A., J.D. [Brown,W.G.G.B.&S.]
Moore, Virgil, (BV) .... '31 '57 C&L.221 B.A., J.D. [V.Moore]
Moore, Virgil, P.C., (BV) .... 1815 Park Avenue

Morain & Pugh, P.L.C.
(See West Des Moines)

Morales, Angela J. .... '76 '01 C&L.221 B.A., J.D. [Ⓐ Faegre&B.]
Morel, Janeen C. '38 '83 C.933 B.A. L.425 J.D.
(adm. in LA; not adm. in IA) 4130 Ashby Ave.‡
Morgan, Candy, (BV) .... '48 '73 C.1281 B.A. L.352 J.D. P.O. Box 7270
Morse, David A., (BV) .... '64 '89 C.162 B.A. L.221 J.D. [Rosenberg,S.&M.]
Moss, Maggi .... '52 '76 C.383 B.G.S. L.221 J.D. [Parrish,K.M.D.&C.]
Mossman, Burns, (AV) .... '43 '68 C&L.352 B.S., J.D. [Nyemaster,G.W.H.&O.]
Mountsier, Ronald L., (AV) .... '57 '82 C&L.221 B.S.B.A., J.D. [Smith,S.S.&S.]
Mullen, Robert A., (AV) .... '49 '78 C.350 B.S. L.221 J.D. [Belin L.M.Z.F.]
Mullins, Darrel, (BV) .... '68 '97 C.293 B.A. L.208 J.D. Iowa Department of Justice
Munro, Kenneth R., (AV) .... '63 '88 C.602 B.A. L.352 J.D. [Bradshaw,F.P.&F.]
Munro, Maureen A. .... '64 '89 C.190 B.A. L.352 J.D. Trust Officer, Norwest Bank
Murphy, Michael P. .... '45 '74 C&L.352 B.A., J.D. State Dept. of Nat. Resources
Murphy, Thomas P., (BV) .... '63 '92 C.436 B.A. L.221 J.D. [Ⓐ Hopkins&H.]
Murray, W. Michael, (BV) .... '47 '73 C&L.352 B.A., J.D. [Murray&J.]
Murray & Jankins, (BV) .... 2903 Ingersoll Ave.
Musgrave, Edgar, (AV) .... '08 '32 C&L.221 B.A., LL.B. 3721 Grand Ave.‡
Myers, Gary M., (BV) .... '61 '86 C.350 B.A. L.352 J.D. [Davis,B.K.S.&R.]
Myers, Lawrence E., (AV) ...... '30 '56 C.352 B.A. L.221 J.D. [Nyemaster,G.W.H.&O.]
Myslis, Laura L. .... '56 '85 C.597 B.A. L.1035 J.D. [Gislason&H.] (☉Mpls., MN)
Naanep, Yvonne C., (BV) .... '71 '97 C.352 B.A. L.221 J.D. [Y.Naanep]
Naanep, Yvonne, (BV) .... P.O. Box 12026
Nadel, Steven Michael, (BV) .... '— '92 C.352 B.B.A. L.188 J.D. [Ahlers&C.]
Nadler, Barry, (AV) .... '56 '81 C&L.352 B.A., J.D. [Nyemaster,G.W.H.&O.] ☉
Nagel, Dennis J. .... '49 '84 C&L.352 B.A., J.D. State Utilities Bd.
Naylor, Greg A., (AV) '— '78
C.352 B.A. L.221 J.D. [Whitfield&E.] (☉West Des Moines)
Nebel, Heidi Sease, (AV) '67 '92 C.352 B.S. L.221 J.D.
[McKee,V.&S.] (See Pat. Sect.)
Needles, Gene L. .... '29 '57 C&L.221 LL.B. Dist. J.
Neiderbach, Jonathan .... '56 '83 C.293 B.A. L.629 J.D. State Leg. Fiscal Bur.
Neifert, Jason D., (BV) ..... '70 '95 C.351 B.A. L.221 J.D. 6611 University Ave., Ste. 200
Neiman, Donald F., (AV) .... '44 '69 C.352 B.B.A. L.221 J.D. [Bradshaw,F.P.&F.]
Neiman, Stone & McCormick, P.C., (BV) .... 7405 University Avenue
Nelson, Brian, (BV) .... '73 '99 C.784 B.A. L.221 J.D. [Nelson&E.]
Nelson, Jeffrey W. '60 '87 C.162 B.A. L.352 J.D.
Coun., Wellmark Blue Cross & Blue Shield of Iowa
Nelson, Loree A., (BV) .... '57 '94 C.1085 B.S. L.221 J.D. [Gislason&H.]
Nelson, Richard S. .... '57 '83 C&L.221 B.A., J.D. 711 High St.
Nelson, S. Christian .... '75 '01 C.350 B.B.A. L.477 J.D. [Ⓐ Belin L.M.Z.F.]
Nelson, Steven L., (AV) .... '52 '76 C&L.352 B.B.A., J.D. [Davis,B.K.S.&R.]
Nelson & Erbe, PLC, (BV) .... 604 Locust Street, Suite 512
Nervig, James E., (AV) .... '50 '76 C.132 B.A. L.352 J.D. [Brick,G.B.S.S.S.&L.]
Netolicky, Sara R. ... '70 '95 C.352 B.B.A. L.221 J.D. Coun., Principal Life Insurance Co.
Neumann, G. R., (AV) .... '50 '76 C.174 B.A. L.221 J.D. [Nyemaster,G.W.H.&O.]
Newbrough, Gerald J., (AV) .... '47 '73 C&L.221 B.A., J.D. [Nyemaster,G.W.H.&O.]
Niblock, James S., (BV) .... '59 '96 C&L.352 B.B.A., J.D. [Ⓐ Brown,W.G.G.B.&S.]
Nielsen, Stephen V., (AV) .... '63 '91 C.352 B.A. L.1187 J.D. [Carney,A.N.&S.]
Nigut, Elizabeth A., (BV) .... '69 '94 C.784 B.A. L.221 J.D. [Bradshaw,F.P.&F.]
Noon, Hillis W. .... '13 '34 C.351 L.352 2909 Woodland Ave.‡
Noonan, Thomas E., (BV) .... '56 '82 C.520 B.S.B.A. L.352 J.D. Asst. Atty. Gen.
Norris, Glenn L., (AV) .... '46 '71 C.784 B.A. L.352 J.D. [Hawkins&N.]
Norton, Gary A., (AV) .... '— '84 C.350 B.S. L.900 J.D. [Whitfield&E.]
Noth, William J., (AV) .... '— '82 C.723 B.A. L.352 J.D. [Ahlers&C.]
Novak, Joel D. .... '40 '65 C&L.352 B.A., J.D. Dist. J.
Nussbaum-Bell, Mindy .... '64 '91 C&L.352 B.A., J.D. V.P. & Tr. Offr., Bankers Tr. Co.

Nyemaster, Goode, West, Hansell & O'Brien, A Professional Corporation, (AV) BB
700 Walnut, Suite 1600, 50309 ☉
Telephone: 515-283-3100 Telecopier: 515-283-3108
Email: info@nyemaster.com URL: http://www.nyemaster.com
James B. West; Edgar F. Hansell; R. Craig Shives; Lawrence E. Myers; Keith E. Luchtel; Gerald J. Newbrough; Robert A. VanOrsdel; Richard J. Sapp; G. R. Neumann; Carlton T. King; Gregory P. Page; Randall G. Horstmann; Jay Eaton; Burns Mossman; Bradford L. Austin; Sara J. Sersland; Hayward L. Draper; Michael W. Thrall; Mark C. Dickinson; Gregory B. Wilcox; John F. Lorentzen; Rod Kubat; Steven J. Roy; Frank B. Harty; James C. Wine; Bruce W. Baker; Thomas W. Foley; Steven H. Lytle; Terry C. Hancock; Anthony A. Longnecker; Joseph A. Quinn; Wade H. Schut; Mark D. Aljets; G. Thomas Sullivan; Thomas H. Walton; Willard L. Boyd III; Jeffrey William Courter; Hallie E. Still-Caris; Joseph K. Haggerty, Senior Vice President and General Counsel; Terry L. Monson; Barry Nadler; David W. Benson (Resident, Ames Office); Brian J. Humke; Deborah S. Krauth; Paula S. Dierenfeld; Coreen K. Sweeney; Antonio Colacino; Jill M. Stevenson; Angel A. West; Angela L. Watson Cook; Mary E. Funk; Randall D. Armentrout; Thomas M. Cunningham; Denise M. Mendt; Debra L. Hulett; Mark A. Schultheis; John T. Clendenin; Neal K. Westin; Stephanie L. Marett; Jordan B. Hansell;—L. W. "Bill" Rosebrook; Cory R. Harris; Patrick B. White; Stephanie G. Techau; Brad C. Epperly; Scott A. Sundstrom; Benjamin P. Roach; Allison M. Steuterman; Hannah M. Rogers; Kathleen K. Law; Jason L. Giles; Mitchell R. Kunert. Of Counsel: Samuel G. O'Brien; LeRoy R. Voigts; Drew R. Tillotson; Frank B. Comfort; Russell E. Schrage; Roger L. Ferris; Luther L. Hill, Jr.
General Civil Practice including Corporate, Securities, Antitrust, Insurance, Banking, Commercial Law, Cooperative Law, Probate, Real Estate, Taxation, Workers Compensation, Municipal, Legislative, Labor, Administrative Law and Trials in all Courts.
Representative Clients: The Burlington Northern and Santa Fe Railway Company; BP Amoco Co.; General Electric Co.; Deere & Co.; Eli Lilly and Co.; Monsanto Agricultural Co.; The Hertz Corp.; Aventis; 3M Corp.; HON Industries.
Ames, Iowa Office: 1416 Buckeye Avenue, Ames, Iowa 50010. Telephone: 515-233-3000. Telecopier: 515-232-3846.

See Professional Biographies, DES MOINES, IOWA

Oberbillig, Robert C., (BV) .... '34 '58 C&L.221 B.A., LL.B. Dir., Legal Aid Soc.
Obermeier, Bradley C., (AV) .... '70 '97 C&L.352 B.B.A., J.D. [Duncan,G.B.&L.]
O'Brien, Marcy A., (BV) .... '70 '95 C.350 B.A. L.352 J.D. [Ⓐ Goodman&Assoc.] ☉
O'Brien, Samuel G., (AV) .... '20 '47 C&L.352 B.A., J.D. [Ⓒ Nyemaster,G.W.H.&O.]
O'Brien, Sean M., (BV) .... '69 '95 C.293 B.A. L.352 J.D. [Bradshaw,F.P.&F.]
Oetker, Jennifer L. .... '73 '99 C.350 B.A. L.221 J.D. [Ⓐ Elverson,V.&P.]
Ogden, Dennis P., (AV) .... '57 '82 C.350 B.A. L.352 J.D. [Belin L.M.Z.F.]
O'Hara, Kimerlee Petrik '54 '78 C.339 A.B. L.801 J.D.
Chf. Admin. Offr., Bening Financial Organization, Inc.
O'Keefe, Michael J. .... '45 '72 C.475 B.A. L.309 J.D. Asst. Co. Atty.
Oliver, Aaron T., (BV) .... '71 '96 C.375 B.S. L.221 J.D. [Hansen,M.&R.]
Oliver, Arvid D., (BV) .... '33 '71 C.352 B.B.A. L.221 J.D. 2635 Hubbell Ave.
Olson, Alan O., (AV) .... '67 '93 C&L.221 B.A., J.D. [Olson]
Olson, Eugene E., (AV) .... '43 '68 C&L.352 B.A., J.D. [Connolly,O.L.H.&O.]
Olson, Karl Tage, (BV) .... '58 '92 C.945 B.A. L.221 J.D. [Bradshaw,F.P.&F.]
Olson, Rick L., (AV) .... '51 '76 C&L.221 B.A., J.D. 2635 Hubbell Ave.

Olson Law Office, P.C., (AV) BB
3116 Ingersoll Avenue, 50312-3910
Telephone: 515-271-9100 Fax: 515-271-8100
Email: lem@olson-law.net
Alan O. Olson.

See Professional Biographies, DES MOINES, IOWA

O'Malley, Bernard J., (BV) .... '37 '61 C&L.190 A.B., J.D. Wkrs. Comp. J.
O'Malley, Michael W., (BV) .... '49 '74 C&L.190 A.B., J.D. [Connolly,O.L.H.&O.]
O'Meara, Michael B., (BV) .... '51 '92 C.177 B.A. L.221 J.D. Asst. Co. Atty.
O'Meara, Stephen Patrick, (AV) .... '49 '74 C&L.190 A.B., J.D. Asst. U.S. Atty.
Ordway, Gary D., (AV) .... '42 '66 C&L.221 B.S., J.D. [Patterson,L.D.T.I.B.&O.]
Ormiston, Tammie B. .... '48 '74 C.337 L.352 Asst. Atty. Gen.
Orrell, John E., Jr., (AV) .... '57 '82 C.585 B.S. L.221 J.D. [Hopkins&H.]
Orton, Byron K. .... '50 '75 C.793 B.A. L.546 J.D. State Labor Comr.
Outka, Ann E., (BV) .... '55 '83 C.350 B.A. L.352 J.D. 711 High St.
Overberg, Nathan J., (BV) .... '— '97 C.132 B.A. L.352 J.D. [Ahlers&C.]
Ovrom, Eliza J., (AV) .... '53 '79 C.162 B.A. L.352 J.D. Asst. Atty. Gen.
Owens, Arthur F., (AV) .... '48 '73 C.784 B.A. L.221 J.D. [Dickinson,M.T.&H.]
Owens, Roger P., (BV) .... '43 '70 C&L.221 B.A., J.D. [Hedberg,O.&V.]
Oxberger, Leo E. .... '30 '57 C&L.221 B.A., LL.B. Chief J., Ct. of App.
Ozga, Martin J. .... '52 '78 C.276 A.B. L.273 J.D. Legal Servs. Corp. of Iowa
Pace, William R. .... '43 '69 C.546 B.S. L.190 J.D. U.S. Treasury Dept.
Paff, Lester, (AV) .... '45 '73 Asst. Dist. Atty.
Page, Gregory P., (AV) .... '52 '77 C&L.352 B.A., J.D. [Nyemaster,G.W.H.&O.]
Pallesen, Reginald A. .... '51 '78 C.350 B.S. L.352 J.D. Iowa Supm. Ct.
Palmer, Heather L., (BV) .... '70 '99 C.352 B.A. L.221 J.D. [Ⓐ Davis,B.K.S.&R.]
Palmer, Jason C., (BV) .... '70 '97 C.352 B.S. L.221 J.D. [Bradshaw,F.P.&F.]
Pals, Erin Q. .... '75 '00 C.132 B.A. L.221 J.D. [Ⓐ Hopkins&H.]
Parker, Addison M., (AV) .... '16 '40 C.197 A.B. L.309 J.D. 699 Walnut St.‡
Parks, Nicole A. .... '76 '02 C.602 B.A. L.190 J.D. Clerk, Iowa Court of Appeals
Parmeter, John M., (BV) .... '50 '83 C.351 B.A. L.221 J.D. Asst. Atty. Gen.
Parrish, Alfredo G., (AV) .... '47 '71 C.226 B.A. L.352 J.D. 2910 Grand Avenue
Parrish, Stephen B. '52 '78 C.747 B.A. L.1035 J.D.
(adm. in MN; not adm. in IA) Mktg. Servs. V.P., American Mutual Life Ins. Co.
Parrish, Kruidenier, Moss, Dunn & Cook, L.L.P., (BV) .... 2910 Grand Ave.
Parrott, Rebecca Boyd, (BV) '59 '86
C&L.352 B.A., J.D. 699 Walnut Street (☉Des Moines)
Parsons, Robert M., (AVⓉ) '45 '72 C&L.608 B.A., J.D.
V.P. & Assoc. Gen. Coun., Allied Insurance, A Nationwide Ins. Co.
Parwani, Rinky S. '73 '98 C.221 B.S. L.494 J.D.
Wells Fargo Financial, Inc. (Legal Department)
Pashler, Peter L. J., (BV) .... '— '86 C.210 B.A. L.221 J.D. [Ahlers&C.]
Pasternak, I. Joel .... '20 '48 C&L.352 B.A., J.D. 3801 Grand Ave.

Patterson, Lorentzen, Duffield, Timmons, Irish, Becker & Ordway, L.L.P., (AV) BB
505 Fifth Avenue, Suite 729, 50309-2390
Telephone: 515-283-2147 Fax: 515-283-1002
URL: http://www.pattersonfirm.com
Members of Firm: Roy M. Irish; Gary D. Ordway; Robin L. Hermann; Harry Perkins, III; Michael F. Lacey, Jr.; Gregory J. Wilson; Jeffrey A. Boehlert; Douglas A. Haag; Jeffrey A. Baker; Janice M. Thomas; Patrick V. Waldron; Martin C. Sprock; William A. Wickett; Frederick M. Haskins; Michael S. Jones; Ryan M. Clark;—Mark A. King; Cory D. Abbas.
General Civil Practice. Litigation and Appeals in State and Federal Courts. Insurance, Casualty and Workers Compensation Law. Corporation, Probate and Estate Planning Law.
General Counsel for: Iowa Insurance Institute.
Representative Clients: Allied Mutual Insurance Company/Nationwide; CNA Insurance Company; Chubb Insurance Group; Continental Western Insurance Co.; Farmers Insurance Group; Farmland Insurance Company; Grinnell Mutual Reinsurance Company; CGU/Hawkeye Security Insurance Company; St. Paul Travelers Insurance Company.

See Professional Biographies, DES MOINES, IOWA

Paulsen, Donna L. .... '48 '75 C&L.352 B.A., J.D. Dist. J.
Pawlosky, Joseph M. .... '59 '96 C.923 M.B.A. L.209 J.D. [Ⓢ Davis,B.K.S.&R.]
Pawlosky, Mollie M. .... '70 '96 C.293 B.A. L.209 J.D. [Dickinson,M.T.&H.]
Payton, Patrick H., (CV) .... '45 '71 C&L.221 B.A., J.D. [P.H.Payton&Assoc.]
Payton, Patrick H., & Associates P.C., (CV) .... 513 E. 6th St., Ste. A
Pearce, William R., (BV) .... '45 '78 C.318 B.A. L.221 J.D. 3000 Grand Ave.
Pearson, Timothy G., (AV) .... '50 '75 C.187 B.A. L.221 J.D. [Laden&P.]

Pearson Van Houten PLC
(See West Des Moines)

Pearston, Karen A., (BV) '56 '82 C.350 B.A. L.352 J.D.
2nd V.P. & Coun., Principal Mut. Life Ins. Co.
Peddicord, Roland D., (AV) ... '36 '62 C&L.221 B.S. in B.A., J.D. [Peddicord,W.S.&H.]

Peddicord, Wharton, Spencer and Hook, LLP, (AV) BB
700 Des Moines Building, 405 Sixth Avenue, P.O. Box 9130, 50306
Telephone: 515-243-2100 Fax: 515-243-2132 1-800-383-2100
URL: http://www.peddicordwharton.com
Roland D. Peddicord; John M. Wharton; Stephen W. Spencer; Lee P. Hook; Joseph M. Barron; Timothy W. Wegman; Michael S. Roling; Steven T. Durick;—Scott J. Beattie; Anne Updegraff; Mark A. Bosscher.
Litigation—all Courts. Aviation, Insurance, Negligence, Personal Injury, Workers Compensation, Product Liability, Medical Malpractice, Professional Liability, Bankruptcy, Real Estate, Corporation and Employment Law, Medical Malpractice.

See Professional Biographies, DES MOINES, IOWA

Pederson, Merle T., (AV) '56 '81
C&L.585 B.A., J.D. Asst. Coun., Principal Mut. Life Ins. Co.
Peeler, Ronald L., (AV) .... '— '87 C.350 B.S. L.221 J.D. [Ahlers&C.]
Penick, Bridget R. .... '73 '98 C.132 B.A. L.352 J.D. [Ⓐ Dickinson,M.T.&H.]
Pennington, Mark S., (AV) .... '50 '75 C&L.352 B.A., J.D. 604 Locust St.
Pennycooke, Colin '71 '97 C.228 A.B. L.309 J.D.
(adm. in NY; not adm. in IA) Coun., Principal Financial Group
Percival, Peter C., (AV) .... '53 '81 C.436 B.A. L.678 J.D. V.P., Norwest Bk. Iowa, N.A.‡
Perkins, Harry, III, (AV) '47 '73 C.190 B.S.B.A. L.221 J.D.
[Patterson,L.D.T.I.B.&O.]
Perkins, Harry, Jr. .... '23 '50 C&L.221 LL.B. 9941 Sunset Terr.‡
Perkins, John R., (AV) .... '43 '68 C&L.352 B.A., J.D. Atty. Gen., Iowa
Perkins, Michael K. '58 '86 C.101 B.A. L.878 J.D.
(adm. in NM; not adm. in IA) Drake University
Peters, Amy L., (BV) .... '71 '96 C.352 B.A. L.221 J.D. 218-6th Ave., Ste. 706

Peters, David L., (BV) '59 '91 C.350 B.S. L.221 J.D.
Assoc. Gen. Coun., Wells Fargo Home Mtge., Inc.
Petersen, Becky J. '78 '03 C.351 B.A. L.190 J.D. [P.Watson]
Petersen, Jack M., (AV) '56 '81
C.351 B.A. L.221 J.D. V.P., Govt. Rel., Principal Mut. Life Ins. Co.
Peterson, Gregory W., (AV) '53 '79 C.187 B.A. L.221 J.D. [Elverson,V.&P.]
Peterson, Jennifer '74 '03 C&L.352 B.A., J.D. [Faegre&B.]
Peterson, Kara L. '80 '05 C.350 B.A. L.352 J.D. [Hanson,B.&R.]
Peterson, Kodi A. '79 '05 C.784 B.A. L.221 J.D. [Babich,G.C.&R.]
Peterson, Kurt S., (BV) '63 '94 C.999 L.986 J.D. [M.R.Rudoff]
Peterson, Scott C. '53 '86 C.871 B.S. L.352 J.D. Off. of Ombudsman; State of Iowa
Peterzalek, Jeffrey C., (BV) '59 '89
C&L.352 B.B.A., J.D. Hoover State Office Building, 2nd Floor
Petosa, Joseph J., (AV) '10 '34 L.221 J.D. 4400 Westown Pkwy. (W. Des Moines)‡
Petosa, Petosa & Boecker, L.L.P.
(See Clive)
Pettit, Debra Rectenbaugh, (BV) '69 '94 C.221 B.A. L.597 J.D. [Davis,B.K.S.&R.] ⊙
Philiph, Douglas P., (BV) '60 '86 C.350 B.S. L.221 J.D. Asst. City Atty.
Phillips, Charles K., (BV) '57 '83 C.293 B.A. L.178 J.D. Atty. Gen. Off.
Phipps, David L., (AV) '— '69 C&L.221 B.A., J.D. [Whitfield&E.]
Phipps, J. Blaine, (BV) '22 '51 C&L.221 J.D. 7409 Benton Dr.
Phipps-Burkhead, Janet E. '54 '05 C.350 B.S. L.221 J.D. [McKee,V.&S.]
Piepmeier, Amy R. '79 '04 C.502 B.S. L.352 J.D. [Brown,W.G.G.B.&S.]
Pierick, Jeffrey M. '62 '88
C.106 B.A. L.352 J.D. Counsel, Principal Residential Mortgage, Inc.
Pietila, John C. '74 '02 C.791 B.A. L.352 J.D [Davis,B.K.S.&R.]
Pietz, Nancy L., (BV) '67 '94 C&L.793 B.A., J.D. [N.Pietz]
Pietz, Nancy, (BV) 1602 47th St.
Pille, Glenn E. '47 '73 C.177 B.A. L.221 J.D. Dist. J.
Pingel, G. Brian, (AV) '40 '70 C.352 B.S.E.E. L.546 J.D.
[Brown,W.G.G.B.&S.] (Pat.) (⊙West Des Moines)
Pitts, Sarah J., (AV) '45 '87 C.289 B.A. L.221 J.D. Coun., Principal Mut. Life Ins. Co.
Placzek, Sandra B. '61 '93 C.546 B.A. L.190 J.D.
(adm. in NE; not adm. in IA) Drak Univ. Law School
Ploeger, Gregory Lewis '59 '85
C.350 B.B.A. L.1288 J.D. V.P. & Coun., Consol. Supply Co.
Plummer, Amy D. '76 '02 C.494 B.S. L.1117 J.D. [Smith,S.S.&S.]
Poetting, Gary M. '50 '75 C.1182 B.S. L.352 J.D.
Asst. Gen. Coun., Wells Fargo Financial, Inc.
Pogge, R. Ronald, (AV) '51 '76 C.602 B.A. L.221 J.D. [Hopkins&H.]
Polden, Donald J. '48 '76
C.273 B.B.A. L.345 J.D. Asst. Dean & Prof. of Law, Drake Univ.
Polle, Ronald C. '54 '79 C.927 B.A. L.221 J.D. Off. of Consumer Advocate
Pope, Lawrence E., (AV) '40 '67
C&L.221 B.A., J.D. Prof. of Law, Drake Univ. Law School
Porter, Robert K. '75 '01 C.218 B.A. L.352 J.D. Asst. Atty. Gen.
Pose, Christopher R., (AV) '63 '89 C.352 B.A. L.221 J.D. [Connolly,O.L.H.&O.]
Pospisil, Thomas R. '59 '89 C.352 B.A. L.221 J.D. Coun., Principal Financial Group
Post, Iris J., (AV) '56 '81 C&L.352 B.A., J.D. [Bradshaw,F.P.&F.]
Potter-Hall, Traevena '71 '98 C&L.352 B.A., J.D.
Dir., Iowa Comm. on the Status of African-Americans
Pottorff, Julie F., (BV) '52 '78 C.350 B.A. L.352 J.D. Dep. Atty. Gen.
Poulsen, Edward C."Ted", (BV) '64 '95 C&L.352 B.B.A., J.D. Amerus Group
Powell Law Firm, The, P.C.
(See Norwalk)
Power, Daniel L. '34 '60 C&L.734 B.S., J.D.
Prof. of Law and Dir., Drake Univ. Law School
Power, J. Edward, (AV) '38 '64 C&L.352 B.A., J.D. [Bradshaw,F.P.&F.]
Powers, Robert W., (BV) '50 '76 C.351 B.A. L.221 J.D. Pub. Def.
Pratt, Robert W. '47 '72 C.177 B.A. L.190 J.D. U.S. Dist. J.
Pray, James L., (BV) '59 '85 C.627 B.S. L.352 J.D. [Brown,W.G.G.B.&S.]
Prickett, R. C. '18 '49 L.986 LL.B. Int. Rev. Ser.
Prine, Ted E., (BV) '51 '77 C&L.221 B.S.B.A., J.D. [Prine&C.]
Prine & Corsello, (BV) 213 4th St.
Proctor, David J. W., (AV) '46 '71 C&L.352 B.A., J.D. [Bradshaw,F.P.&F.]
Prohs, Erick D. '73 '02 C.172 B.S.B.A. L.352 J.D. [Brown,W.G.G.B.&S.]
Pronk, Katherine J. '79 '04 C&L.221 B.A., J.D. [Huber,B.C.H.&L.]
Puntenney, Keith deT. '46 '74 C.350 B.S. L.352 J.D. I.R.S.
Quilty, James R., (BV) '68 '93 C.707 B.A. L.339 J.D. [Crawford]
Quinn, Joseph A., (AV) '61 '87 C&L.221 B.S., J.D. [Nyemaster,G.W.H.&O.]
Rabe, Richd. F. '19 '52 C.352 D.D.S. L.221 J.D. 5709 N. Waterbury Rd.‡
Racette, Gregory T., (AV) '50 '79 C.477 B.A. L.1187 J.D. [Hopkins&H.]
Ramsay, Reed '65 '90 C.221 B.A.S. L.896 J.D.
Asst. Gen. Coun., Wells Fargo Financial, Inc.
Ramsay, Richard E., (AV) '37 '61 C&L.221 B.A., J.D. [Davis,B.K.S.&R.]
Ramsey, Michele M., (BV) '71 '97 C.132 B.A. L.352 J.D. [Duncan,G.B.&L.]
Rasmussen, Lynette Skow, (AV) '65 '92
C.57 B.A. L.221 J.D. Gen. Coun., The Rasmussen Group, Inc.
Ray, Robert D. '28 '54 C&L.221 B.S., LL.B.
Pres. & CEO, Wellmark Blue Cross & Blue Shield of Iowa
Reames, Wayne E. '75 '00 C.427 B.A. L.477 J.D. [Belin L.M.Z.F.]
Reavely, Sally A., (BV) '— '88 C.352 B.S.N. L.221 J.D. [Whitfield&E.]
Reavely, Thomas S., (AV) '— '71 C&L.945 B.A., J.D. [Whitfield&E.]
Reck, Michael R., (BV) '65 '91 C.352 A.B. L.309 J.D. [Belin L.M.Z.F.]
Reid, Timm W., (BV) '63 '89 C.92 B.A. L.221 J.D. [Galligan,D.&R.]
Reilly, Thomas J. '43 '70 C.72 B.A. L.221 J.D. 4900 University
Reis, Artis I. Van Roekel '47 '76 C&L.352 B.S., J.D. Dist. Ct. J.
Reisinger, Rebecca A. '74 '05 C.351 B.A. L.1209 J.D. [Brown,W.G.G.B.&S.]
Remsburg, Edward W., (AV) '— '73 C&L.352 B.A., J.D. [Ahlers&C.]
Renda, Thomas A. '37 '63 C.177 B.A. L.221 B.L. Assoc. Dist. J.
Reno, Stephen E., (AV) '49 '81 C.352 B.A. L.221 J.D. Asst. Atty. Gen.
Renzo, Joseph A., (BV) '49 '92 C.560 B.A. L.221 J.D. [Babich,G.C.&R.]
Repp, David M., (BV) '61 '90 C&L.352 B.B.A., J.D. [Dickinson,M.T.&H.]
Reynolds, Kevin M., (AV) '— '81 C.350 B.A. L.352 J.D. [Whitfield&E.]
Reznicek, Rebecca Colton '55 '84
C.560 B.U.S. L.221 J.D. Adm. Asst. Iowa State Supr. Ct.
Rhoads, Alexander R. '65 '96 C.293 B.A. L.221 J.D. [Babich,G.C.&R.]
Rice, Ann M. '70 '97 C.544 B.S. L.190 J.D. Corp. Coun., ARAG Insurance Co.
Rice, G. Mark, (BV) '— '83 C.793 B.A. L.190 J.D. [Whitfield&E.]
Richards, Richard L., (AV) '52 '77 C.56 B.A. L.221 J.D. Asst. U.S. Atty.
Ricker, Ronald R., (AV) '44 '72 C.350 B.S. L.352 J.D. 604 Locust St.
Rickert, Brian P., (BV) '72 '98 C.352 B.B.A. L.221 J.D. [Brown,W.G.G.B.&S.]
Riemenschneider, Scott S., (BV) '68 '93 C.162 B.A. L.221 J.D.
[Riemenschneider,R.&S.]
Riemenschneider, Rydell & Smalley, (AV) 309 Court Ave., Ste. 231
Riepe, Milton O., (AV) '09 '34 C.352 A.B. L.813 J.D. 699 Walnut St.
Ries, Roscoe A., Jr., (CV) '— '94 C&L.221 B.S.B.A., J.D. [Whitfield&E.]
Rigg, J. Keith, (AV) '58 '82 C.338 B.S. L.221 J.D.
Suite 409, 100 Court Avenue, 50309
Telephone: 515-284-7930 Facsimile: 515-284-7928 URL: http://www.keithrigg.com
Email: jkrigg@dwx.com URL: http://www.lawyers.com/jkeithrigg
Criminal Trial Practice in Federal and State Courts. Civil Litigation.
See Professional Biographies, DES MOINES, IOWA
Rigg, Robert R. '54 '78 C&L.221 B.A., J.D. Drake Univ. Law Sch.
Riley, Philip T., (AV) '26 '59 C.871 B.S. L.93 J.D. 650 Harwood Dr.‡
Riley, Ronald A., (AV) '36 '65 C&L.221 B.A., J.D. [Hansen,M.&R.] ‡
Ritchie, Corwin, (BV) '45 '75 C.350 B.S. L.352 J.D. Exec. Dir., Iowa Cty. Atty. Assn.
Rittgers, Kenneth W., (BV) '42 '67 C.350 B.S. L.221 J.D. 8350 Hickman Rd.
Roach, Benjamin P. '76 '03 C.351 B.A. L.352 J.D. [Nyemaster,G.W.H.&O.]
Robak, William E. '67 '95 C.793 B.S. L.352 J.D. [Robak]
Robak Law Firm, P.L.C. 3705 Grand Avenue
Robbins, Rocky J. '77 '04 C.351 B.A. L.221 J.D. [P.Watson]
Roberts, Charles L., (CV) '28 '55 C&L.221 J.D. 206 6th Ave.
Roberts, Stephen W., (AV) '39 '64 C.674 B.A. L.477 J.D. [Davis,B.K.S.&R.]
Robinson, Stephen C., (BV) '35 '62 C.352 B.A. L.221 J.D. Asst. Atty. Gen.
Rockwell, Ted. W., (CV) '30 '53 C&L.221 J.D. 2329 Reynolds Lane
Roehrick, John P., (AV) '43 '66 C&L.221 B.A., J.D. [Roehrick,H.B.K.&K.]
Roehrick, Hulting, Blumberg, Kirlin & Krull, P.C., (AV) 505 5th Avenue
Rogers, Craig S. '59 '88 C&L.221 B.A., J.D.
Asst. Dir., Community Invest. Fed. Home Loan Bk.
Rogers, Hannah M. '75 '04 C&L.221 B.A., J.D. [Nyemaster,G.W.H.&O.]
Rogers, Jack A. '45 '71 C.679 B.S. L.209 J.D. 665 Locust St.
Rolands, Diana L., (BV) '67 '94
C.1310 B.S. L.502 J.D. Staff Atty., Travelers Property Casualty
Roling, Michael S., (BV) '66 '94 C.985 B.A. L.221 J.D. [Peddicord,W.S.&H.]
Romano, Karen Ann, (BV) '61 '87 C.190 B.A. L.352 J.D. Assoc. Dist. J.
Roose, Julia L. '76 '01 C.351 B.A. L.221 J.D. [Grefe&S.]
Rosebrook, L. W. "Bill", (AV) '44 '69 C&L.352 B.A., J.D.
[Nyemaster,G.W.H.&O.]
Rosenbaum, James R. '39 '72 C.352 B.B.A. L.221 J.D. Clk., U.S. Dist. Ct.
Rosenberg, Brent D., (AV) '49 '80 C.352 B.G.S. L.221 J.D. [Rosenberg,S.&M.]
Rosenberg, Daniel A., (BV) '56 '97
C.350 B.S. L.221 J.D. [Davis,B.K.S.&R.] (See Pat. Sect.)
Rosenberg, Paul H., (AV) '51 '78 C&L.221 B.A., J.D. [P.Rosenberg&Assoc.]
Rosenberg, Raymond, (AV) '21 '48 C&L.352 B.A., J.D. 505 Fifth Avenue‡
Rosenberg, Paul, & Associates, P.C., (AV) 666 Grand Avenue, Suite 1837
Rosenberg, Stowers & Morse, (AV) BB
1010 Insurance Exchange Building, 505 Fifth Avenue, 50309
Telephone: 515-243-7600; 515-243-0583 URL: http://www.rosenbergstowersmorse.com
URL: http://www.lawyers.com/rosenbergstowersmorse
Members of Firm: Dean A. Stowers; Brent D. Rosenberg; David A. Morse.
General Practice, Civil, Criminal Trial and Appellate practice in Federal and State Courts. Criminal Law, Personal Injury, Family Law, Business Litigation, Bankruptcy, White Collar Crimes, Criminal Appeals, Securities Litigation and Arbitration.
Reference: Firstar Bank, Des Moines, Iowa.
See Professional Biographies, DES MOINES, IOWA
Ross, Jason M. '73 '99 C.339 B.A. L.352 J.D. [Davis,B.K.S.&R.]
Ross, Thomas G., Law Office, (BV) '53 '85 C.350 B.S. L.352 J.D.
4507 Wakonda Pkwy.
Roth, Mark E. '54 '02 C.602 B.S. L.221 J.D. [Brown,W.G.G.B.&S.]
Roughton, Michael D., (AV) '51 '84 C.94 A.B. L.221 J.D.
V.P. & Sr. Securities Coun., Principal Mut. Life Ins. Co.
Rouse, Ward A., (AV) '65 '90 C.187 B.S.S. L.221 J.D. [Berg,R.S.&S.]
Roy, Margaret A., (BV) '60 '89 C.475 B.A. L.494 J.D. Atty., MidAmerican Energy Co.
Roy, Steven J., (AV) '59 '83 C&L.221 B.S.B.A., J.D. [Nyemaster,G.W.H.&O.]
Royal, Lewis A. '19 '47 C.604 B.A. L.597 J.D. 600 E. 5th. St.
Rudoff, Mark R., The Law Offices of '54 '80
C.934 B.A. L.502 J.D. 701 5th Avenue, 1st Floor
Ruhtenberg, Maria L., (BV) '— '95 C.347 B.A. L.221 J.D. [Whitfield&E.]
Russell, Barry A., (AV) '49 '76 C.187 B.A. L.352 J.D. [Hanson,B.&R.]
Ryan, Rodney J. '34 '60 C.352 B.A. L.221 LL.B. [R.J.Ryan]
Ryan, Rodney J., P.C. 309 Court Ave.
Rydell, Robert R., (AV) '29 '53 C.999 L.221 LL.B. [Riemenschneider,R.&S.]
Ryman, Arthur E., Jr. '29 '56 C&L.208 B.S., LL.B. Prof., Drake Univ. Law Sch.
Rypma, Jacqueline Stetson, (BV) '46 '90 C.1174 B.A. L.221 J.D. [J.S.Rypma]
Rypma, Jacqueline Stetson, PC, (BV) 2404 Forest Dr.
Sackett, Christopher R., (AV) '67 '93 C.132 B.A. L.352 J.D. [Brown,W.G.G.B.&S.]
Saf, Ronald V. '23 '51 C&L.221 B.S.E., LL.B. 6510 Allison St.‡
St. Pierre, Joni '61 '01 C.999 B.A. L.221 J.D. Exec. Dir., IA Paralyzed Vet. of Amer
Salmons, Carlton G., (AV) '47 '76 C.338 B.S. L.221 J.D. [Gaudineer,C.&G.]
Salsbery, Thomas E., (AV) '46 '72 C&L.352 B.A., J.D. [Davis,B.K.S.&R.] ⊙
Samson, Russell L., (AV) '48 '75 C.350 B.S. L.276 J.D. [Dickinson,M.T.&H.]
Samuelson, Jaki K., (AV) '— '80 C.98 B.A. L.352 J.D. [Whitfield&E.]
Sand, Peter M., (BV) '66 '93 C.707 B.A. L.190 J.D. [Gislason&H.]
Sanders, Margaret D. '48 '75 C.221 B.A. L.339 J.D. [Beving,S.&F.]
Sanders, Mary McDermott '53 '78 C.350 B.A. L.352 J.D. 4222 Sheridan Ave.‡
Sandler, Robt. G. '18 '42 C&L.352 A.B., J.D. 4004 Grand Ave.‡
Santi, Richard G., (AV) '— '69 C.350 B.S. L.352 J.D. [Ahlers&C.]
Sap, Richard J., (AV) '50 '76 C&L.221 B.A., J.D. [Nyemaster,G.W.H.&O.]
Sarcone, James V., Jr., (AV) '44 '69 C.698 B.A. L.276 J.D. [Belin L.M.Z.F.]
Sarcone, James V., Sr. '15 '48 C.698 B.S. L.276 J.D. 2000 Financial Ctr.
Sarcone, Stephanie G. '57 '89 C.132 B.A. L.221 J.D. V.P., Norwest Bk. Iowa, N.A.
Saunders, Ruth C. '72 '97 C&L.221 B.A., J.D.
(adm. in MO; not adm. in IA) Asst. Gen. Coun., Wells Fargo Financial, Inc.
Scase, Christie, (AV) '59 '85 C.513 B.S. L.221 J.D. Asst. Atty. Gen.
Schachterle, John C., (BV) '58 '84 C.350 B.S. L.221 J.D. [Williams,B.H.&M.]
Schaphorst, William K., (AV) '32 '60 C.791 B.S.E.E. L.569 J.D. 909 High St.
Scharnberg, Steven K., (AV) '49 '74 C&L.352 B.A., J.D. [Finley,A.S.S.C.H.&G.]
Scheidler, Sam F., (AV) '47 '72
C.351 B.A. L.352 J.D. Exec. V.P., Corn States Hybrid Servs., Inc.
Schemmel, Carla Tolbert, (AV) '48 '85 C.465 B.S. L.221 J.D. J., Polk Co. Courthouse
Scherle, William D., (AV) '50 '75 C.839 B.A. L.190 J.D. [Hansen,M.&R.]
Schira, Jacques D., (BV) '55 '84 C.958 B.S. L.221 J.D. [J.D.Schira]
Schira, Jacques D., P.C., (BV) 13250 N.E. 14th Street
Schlapkohl, Thomas P., (AV) '51 '81 C.187 B.A. L.221 J.D. [Brick,G.B.S.S.S.&L.]
Schmidt, John D., (AV) '53 '78 C.350 B.A. L.352 J.D.
V.P. & Sr. Tax Coun., Principal Financial Group
Schmidt, Richard R., (BV) '68 '94 C.350 B.A. L.221 J.D. [Berg,R.S.&S.]
Schnathorst, Britney L. '81 '05 C&L.221 B.A., J.D. [Brown,W.G.G.B.&S.]

Schneebeck, Harold N., (AV) .... '42 '76 L.352 J.D. [Brown,W.G.G.B.&S.]
Schneider, Charles M. .... '73 '02 C.190 B.A. L.352 J.D. [🄰 Dickinson,M.T.&H.]
Schneider, Fred R. .... '43 '67 C&L.221 B.A., J.D. [Smith,S.S.&S.]
Schoenebaum, Steven C., (BV) ....'46 '70 C.352 B.A. L.221 J.D. [Brown,W.G.G.B.&S.]
Schott, Max James, (AV) ... '43 '87 C.723 B.A. L.221 J.D. 6611 University Ave., Ste. 200
Schrader, Craig V. ....'53 '78 C.350 B.S. L.352 J.D. Wells Fargo Bank Iowa, N.A.
Schrage, Russell E., (AV) ... '38 '63 C&L.352 B.B.A., LL.B. [🄲 Nyemaster,G.W.H.&O.]
Schreiber, Jack R. '36 '66
C.784 B.S.B.A. L.221 J.D. Exec. V.P. & Sr. Tr. Offr., Iowa State Bk.
Schroeder & Anderson, (AV) .... 699 Walnut St. (⊙Mason City)
Schueller, Randall P. ....'75 '03 C.351 B.A. L.221 J.D. [🄰 Hopkins&H.]
Schuling, Mark R., (AV) ....'55 '80 C&L.221 B.A., J.D. [Brick,G.B.S.S.S.&L.]
Schultheis, Mark A., (AV) .... '65 '93 C&L.352 B.A., J.D. [Nyemaster,G.W.H.&O.]
Schut, Wade H., (BV) ....'62 '87 C.1348 B.A. L.352 J.D. [Nyemaster,G.W.H.&O.]
Schwager, Greg L. '62 '88 C&L.352 B.A., J.D.
Assoc. Gen. Coun., Wells Fargo Home Mtge., Inc.
Schwarz, William W., (BV) .... '48 '79 C&L.221 B.S., J.D. [Gaudineer,C.&G.]
Schweiker, Wm. A. .... '13 '42 C.221 4124 Forest Avenue‡
Scieszinski, D. Brian, (BV) .... '62 '87 C&L.352 B.S., J.D. [Bradshaw,F.P.&F.]
Scieszinski, John J., (BV) .... '53 '78 C.352 B.A. L.190 J.D. [Scieszinski]
Scieszinski Law Office, (BV) .... 637 41st St., Ste. A
Scott, Paul D., (BV) .... '62 '87 C&L.221 B.A., J.D. [🄰 Cook,B.&S.]
Sease, Edmund J., (AV) ..... '42 '67 C&L.221 B.A., J.D. [McKee,V.&S.] (See Pat. Sect.)
Seidlin, Joseph W., (AV) ....'60 '85 C&L.221 B.A., J.D. [Culp,D.S.&G.]
Seitz, John T., (AV) ....'49 '76 C.813 B.A. L.352 J.D. [Belin L.M.Z.F.]
Seitz, Sue Luettjohann, (AV) ....'52 '76 C&L.352 B.A., J.D. [Belin L.M.Z.F.]
Senneff, Donald G., (AV) .... '39 '67 C&L.352 B.A., J.D. Asst. Atty. Gen.
Serangeli, William B., (AV) .... '49 '75 C.338 B.S. L.221 J.D. [Smith,S.S.&S.]
Serck, Steven L., (AV) .... '— '89 C.351 B.A. L.352 J.D. [Ahlers&C.]
Sersland, Sara J., (AV) ....'48 '79 C.427 B.A. L.221 J.D. [Nyemaster,G.W.H.&O.]
Shaff, Karen E., (AV) '54 '79 C.597 B.A. L.221 J.D.
Gen. Coun. & Exec. V.P., Principal Mut. Life Ins. Co.
Shank, Warren, (AV) .... '40 '68 C&L.352 B.A., J.D. 711 High St.
Shannon, Craig S., (AV) ....'53 '78 C.1304 A.B. L.221 J.D. [Grefe&S.] ⊙
Sharp, Richard D., (AV) .... '54 '87 C.351 B.A. L.221 J.D. [Belin L.M.Z.F.]
Sharpe, Jeremy C., (AV) ....'50 '75 C&L.178 B.A., J.D. [Belin L.M.Z.F.]
Shearer, Leon R., (AV) '43 '67 C.106 B.A. L.352 J.D.
Vice President & General Counsel, Pioneer Hi-Bred International, Inc.
Sheehy, Richard E. '61 '87 C.276 B.A. L.472 J.D.
(adm. in FL; not adm. in IA) 100 Market St.
Sheeley, John E. '62 '92 C.188 B.S. L.477 J.D.
(adm. in DC; not adm. in IA) General Counsel & Secretary, IGF Insurance Company
Sheih, Gene .....'69 '95 C.339 B.S. L.8 J.D. Asst. Gen. Coun., Wells Fargo Financial, Inc.
Shelton, Danielle M. .... '70 '95 C.57 B.A. L.309 J.D. [🄲 Belin L.M.Z.F.]
Sheridan, David R., (AV) .... '53 '78 C.351 B.A. L.352 J.D. Off. of Atty. Gen.
Sheridan-Lucht, Gail A. .... '60 '86 C.352 B.A. L.221 J.D. State Div. of Labor
Shinkle, David C., (AV) ....'50 '75 C.378 B.A. L.221 J.D. [Shinkle&L.]
Shinkle & Lynch, (AV) .... 5835 Grand Ave.
Shives, R. Craig, (AV) .... '45 '70 C.187 B.A. L.352 J.D. [Nyemaster,G.W.H.&O.]
Shodeen, Anita L., (AV) ....'58 '85 C.494 B.A. L.221 J.D. [Beving,S.&F.]
Shoff, Patricia A., (AV) ....'48 '73 C&L.352 B.A., J.D. [Belin L.M.Z.F.]
Shors, John D., (AV) ....'37 '64 C.350 B.S. L.352 J.D. [Davis,B.K.S.&R.]
Shriver, Christina .... '71 '99 C.846 B.A. L.221 J.D. [Murray&J.]
Shutts, Anjela A., (BV) ....'— '96 C.427 B.A. L.221 J.D. [Whitfield&E.]
Siddens, Robert N., (BV) .... '51 '78 C&L.221 B.A., J.D. [Siddens]
Siddens Law Office, (BV) ....650 42nd Street
Sidney, Ross H., (AV) ....'23 '48 C&L.352 B.S., J.D. 2222 Grand Avenue‡
Simms, Theodore C., II ....'— '01 C.446 B.A. L.221 J.D. [🄰 Whitfield&E.]
Simpson, D. Scott, (BV) ....'66 '93 C&L.221 B.A., J.D. [Dreher,S.&J.]
Simpson, Lou Ann '43 '68 C&L.221 B.S.B.A., J.D.
Assoc. Dean, Drake Univ., Coll. of Bus. & Pub. Admn.
Simpson, Lyle L., (AV) ....'37 '63 C&L.221 B.A., J.D. [Dreher,S.&J.]
Sinnard, Kara M. .... '— '02 C.352 B.A. L.221 J.D [🄰 Whitfield&E.]
Sisk, Gregory C. ....'60 '85 C.506 B.A. L.911 J.D. Drake Univ. Law School
Skinner, Ira, Jr. .... '28 '55 C&L.221 B.A., J.D. 9102 Summit Dr.
Skinner, Troy A., (BV) ....'69 '96 C.352 B.B.A. L.190 J.D. [Carney,A.N.&S.]
Skrivanek, Stephen G. '56 '81 C.627 B.S. L.352 J.D.
Coun., Principal Mut. Life Ins. Co.
Slaughter, Thomas L. .... '54 '79 C.467 B.A. L.352 J.D. [🄲 Faegre&B.] ‡
Smallenberger, James A., Jr., (AV) '42 '68 C.473 A.B. L.188 J.D.
Sr. V.P. & Corp. Secy., AmerUs Life Holdings, Inc.
Smalley, Douglas R., (BV) ...... '46 '71 C.352 B.A. L.221 J.D. [Riemenschneider,R.&S.]
Smeader, Gerry W. ....'55 '83 C.1044 B.S. L.862 J.D. The Medical Protective Co.
Smid, Danielle Dixon, (BV) ....'72 '98 C.350 B.S. L.221 J.D. [Brown,W.G.G.B.&S.]
Smith, Brian Lester, (BV) '61 '87 C.966 B.S. L.352 J.D.
Coun., Wellmark Blue Cross & Blue Shield of Iowa
Smith, Dan W. .... '31 '55 C&L.221 B.S., J.D. 555 Walnut St.
Smith, Douglas R., (AV) ....'— '70 C.350 B.S. L.352 J.D. [🄲 Ahlers&C.]
Smith, Dustin D. '70 '97 C.352 B.A. L.221 J.D.
[🄰 Brown,W.G.G.B.&S.] (⊙West Des Moines)
Smith, Frank Murray, (BV) ....'51 '76 C&L.221 B.A., J.D. 4215 Hubbell Ave.
Smith, Glenn L., (AV) .... '44 '68 C&L.221 B.A., J.D. [Finley,A.S.S.C.H.&G.]
Smith, H. Richard, (AV) ....'— '58 C.784 B.S. L.221 J.D. [🄲 Ahlers&C.]
Smith, Joe E. ....'43 '89 C.174 B.S. L.221 J.D. Employ. App. Bd.
Smith, Michael H., (BV) ....'44 '84 C&L.352 B.A., J.D. Asst. Atty. Gen.
Smith, Michael L. ....'— '95 C.351 B.A. L.352 J.D. 3917 Twana Dr.
Smith, Neal E. ....'20 '50 C.502 L.221 J.D. [🄲 Davis,B.K.S.&R.]
Smith, Patrick D., (BV) .... '67 '93 C.221 B.A. L.352 J.D. [Bradshaw,F.P.&F.]
Smith, Steven P. .... '74 '01 C.351 B.A. L.1119 J.D. [🄰 McKee,V.&S.]
Smith, William H., Jr. '44 '72 C.976 B.A. L.188 J.D.
(adm. in DC; not adm. in IA) Chf., Bur. of Rate & Safety Evaluation
Smith, William S., (AV) .... '44 '68 C&L.352 B.B.A., J.D. [Smith,S.S.&S.]

Smith, Schneider, Stiles & Serangeli, P.C., (AV) BB
The Equitable Building, 604 Locust, Suite 1000, 50309
Telephone: 515-245-6789 Fax: 515-244-1328
Email: stelford@smithlawiowa.com
Jan Mohrfeld Kramer; Ronald L. Mountsier; Fred R. Schneider; William B. Serangeli; William S. Smith; William R. Stiles; CeCelia Ibson Wagner;—Joseph M. Borg; Amy D. Plummer.
General Civil Trial, Civil, Criminal, Commercial and Tax Litigation and Appellate Practice in all Courts. Commercial, Corporation, Workers Compensation, Real Estate, Taxation, Personal Injury, Probate and Administrative Law, Business Transactions.
See Professional Biographies, DES MOINES, IOWA

Snell, Bruce M., Jr. .... '29 '56 C.293 A.B. L.352 J.D. Supm. Ct. Jus.
Snyder, James L. '59 '85 C.267 B.S. L.464 J.D.
(adm. in CA; not adm. in IA) U.S. Trustees Off.
Snyder, Robert R. ....'33 '59 C&L.221 B.S., J.D. 3911 Muskogee‡
Soderstrum, Brenton D., (BV) .....'63 '89 C.427 B.A. L.352 J.D. [Brown,W.G.G.B.&S.]
Soulati, Behnaz ....'69 '99 C&L.352 B.A., J.D. [🄰 Davis,B.K.S.&R.]
Spaeth, Bernard L. "Jerry", Jr., (AV) ...'— '74 C.1158 B.A. L.352 J.D. [Whitfield&E.]
Spaulding, Christopher D., (BV) .... '65 '92 C.352 B.S. L.221 J.D. [Berg,R.S.&S.]
Spaulding, Larry D., (AV) .... '41 '70 C.351 B.A. L.221 J.D. [Bradshaw,F.P.&F.]
Spellman, Ann C., (BV) .... '69 '94 C.352 B.A. L.221 J.D. [Bradshaw,F.P.&F.]
Spellman, Daniel J., (AV) ....'43 '68 C&L.190 B.A., J.D. [Spellman,S.S.S.K.&S.] ⊙
Spellman, Daniel Jay, (AV) ..... '69 '95 C.352 B.A. L.190 J.D. [Spellman,S.S.S.K.&S.] ⊙
Spellman, Edward M. (Ted), (BV) '74 '99
C.190 B.A. L.221 J.D. [Spellman,S.S.S.K.&S.] ⊙
Spellman, James L., (BV) .... '33 '57 C&L.190 B.S., LL.B. 1300 Locust St.
Spellman, Mark E., (BV) .... '68 '94 C.436 B.A. L.221 J.D. [Spellman,S.S.S.K.&S.] ⊙
Spellman, Martin E., (AV) ....'44 '67 C&L.190 B.A., J.D. [Spellman,S.S.S.K.&S.] ⊙
Spellman, Patrick J., (AV) ....'51 '74 C.221 L.190 J.D. [Spellman,S.S.S.K.&S.] ⊙
Spellman, Thomas L., (AV) ... '58 '85 C.221 B.A. L.1187 J.D. [Spellman,S.S.S.K.&S.] ⊙
Spellman, Spellman, Spellman, Spellman, Kealhofer & Spellman, (AV)
666 Grand Ave., 18th Fl. (⊙Perry)
Spellman Walsh, Mary .... '63 '89 C&L.190 B.A., J.D. 11201 Douglas Ave.
Spencer, Katherine, (BV) ....'69 '96 C.293 B.A. L.93 J.D. 2415 Ingersoll Ave.
Spencer, Stephen W., (AV) .... '55 '80 C&L.221 B.A., J.D. [Peddicord,W.S.&H.]
Sporer, Theodore F. .... '59 '85 C.352 B.L.A. L.221 J.D. [Sporer]
Sporer Law Firm, P.C. ....108 Third St.
Sprock, Martin C., (AV) .... '52 '77 C&L.221 B.A., J.D. [Patterson,L.D.T.I.B.&O.]
Sprole, John ....'48 '76 C.432 B.A. L.352 J.D. P.O. Box 12084
Stanfield, B. Macpaul "Mac" ....'— '02 C.454 B.A. L.221 J.D. [🄰 Whitfield&E.]
Starr, Donald F. .... '34 '61 C&L.221 J.D. 3911 Ingersoll
Staskal, Douglas F. ....'54 '79 C&L.352 B.S., J.D. Assoc. Dist. J.
Staudt, Jon L., (AV) ....'49 '76 C&L.352 B.A., J.D. [Belin L.M.Z.F.]
Stead, Ben ....'50 '74 C.352 B.A. L.378 J.D. Off. of Consumer Advocate
Stefani, Randall H., (AV) ....'— '81 C&L.352 B.B.A., J.D. [Ahlers&C.]
Steffe, Shirley A., (BV) .... '47 '79 C&L.352 B.A., J.D. Asst. Atty. Gen.
Steger, Merlin A. .... '28 '56 C.177 A.B. L.276 J.D. 5100 Welker
Steinger, Charles S. .... '44 '82 C.174 B.A. L.221 J.D. 7301 Benton Dr.
Steinmetz, Charles E. .... '28 '58 C.350 B.S. L.221 J.D. 2803 47th St.
Steuterman, Allison M. .... '78 '04 C.587 B.A. L.221 J.D. [🄰 Nyemaster,G.W.H.&O.]
Stevenson, Jill M., (AV) .... '57 '95 C.350 B.S. L.221 J.D. [Nyemaster,G.W.H.&O.]
Steward, David S., (BV) ....'69 '94 C.352 B.S. L.221 J.D. Asst. Atty. Gen.
Stewart, Gary D. .... '46 '74 C&L.352 B.B.A., J.D. Off. of Consumer Advocate
Stiles, William R., (AV) .... '46 '73 C&L.221 B.A., J.D. [Smith,S.S.&S.]
Still-Caris, Hallie E., (AV) ...... '61 '86 C.350 B.S. L.352 J.D. [Nyemaster,G.W.H.&O.]
Stoffregen, Philip E., (AV) .... '47 '77 C&L.352 B.A., J.D. [Dickinson,M.T.&H.]
Stokes, William S. ....'71 '97 C.351 B.S. L.221 J.D. Amerus Life Holdings, Inc.
Stoltze, Bruce H., (BV) ....'53 '77 C&L.352 B.S., J.D. [Brick,G.B.S.S.S.&L.]
Stone, Jason M. ....'73 '00 C.352 B.S. L.900 J.D. [🄰 Davis,B.K.S.&R.]
Stone, R. Ben ...'63 '95 C.350 B.S. L.221 J.D. Executive Dir., Iowa Civil Liberties Union
Stork, Frank J., (AV) '52 '77 C.177 B.A. L.352 J.D.
Assoc. Gen. Coun., Wellmark Blue Cross & Blue Shield of Iowa
Stovall, J. Philip ....'33 '68 C&L.221 B.S., J.D. Int. Rev. Serv.
Stover, Melissa A. '72 '97 C.352 B.A. L.221 J.D.
Asst. VP & Trust Off., Bankers Tr. Co.
Stowe, Brian L., (BV) ....'72 '00 C.898 B.A. L.221 J.D. [🄰 Finley,A.S.S.C.H.&G.]
Stowers, Dean A., (AV) .... '64 '89 C.966 B.S. L.221 J.D. [Rosenberg,S.&M.]
Stramel, Karin A. .... '79 '04 C.427 B.A. L.221 J.D. [🄰 Bradshaw,F.P.&F.]
Strassberg, Maura Irene '56 '85 C.821 B.A. L.178 J.D.
(adm. in MA; not adm. in IA) Asst. Prof., Drake Univ. Law School
Strater, Donald B. '49 '75 C.339 B.S. L.221 J.D.
Exec. V.P. & Gen. Coun., Roberts & Dybdahl Inc.
Streit, Michael J. .... '50 '75 C.352 B.A. L.1049 J.D. Supm. Ct.
Strother, Todd A., (BV) ....'68 '95 C&L.352 B.B.A., J.D. [Bradshaw,F.P.&F.]
Strutt, Charles F. .... '52 '78 C&L.221 B.A., J.D. Hearing Offr., Dept. of Rev.
Strutt, David S., (AV) '53 '79
C.221 B.S. L.352 J.D. General Counsel, Weitz Company, LLC
Struve, Kevin B., (BV) .... '54 '79 C.350 B.S. L.352 J.D. Asst. Atty. Gen.
Stuart, William C. ....'20 '42 C&L.352 A.B., J.D. Sr. U.S. Dist. J.
Stuchel, Beth E. '60 '87 C.121 B.A. L.221 J.D.
Asst. Gen. Coun., Wells Fargo Financial, Inc.
Stump, Gary D., (AV) ....'54 '78 C&L.221 B.A., J.D. Dep. Gen. Coun.
Stumpff, Timothy E. .... '63 '91 C.502 B.S. L.309 J.D. Principal Financial Group
Sturm, Michael O., (AV) .....'43 '73 C.350 B.S. L.1128 J.D. [Sturm&F.] (See Pat. Sect.)

Sturm & Fix LLP, (AV) BB
206 Sixth Avenue, Suite 1213, 50309-4076 ⊙
Telephone: 515-288-9589 Fax: 515-288-4860
Email: sturm@hsllp.com URL: http://www.hsllp.com
Members of Firm: Michael O. Sturm; John E. Cepican; Richard L. Fix.
Patent, Trademark, Copyright and Unfair Competition Law, Federal Trial Practice, Intellectual Property.
Reference: Wells Fargo Bank Iowa, N.A.
Davenport, Iowa Office: 304 Northwest Bank Building-Downtown, 101 West Second Street, 52801-1813. Telephone: 563-323-9731. Fax: 563-323-9709.
See Professional Biographies, DES MOINES, IOWA

Sullivan, G. Thomas, (AV) ...... '58 '85 C.350 B.S. L.221 J.D. [Nyemaster,G.W.H.&O.]
Sullivan, J. M., (BV) .... '45 '73 C.178 B.A. L.221 J.D. P.O. Box 694
Sullivan, Jon P., (AV) ....'54 '79 C.351 B.A. L.352 J.D. [Dickinson,M.T.&H.]
Sundstrom, Scott A. .... '72 '00 C.118 B.A. L.569 J.D. [🄰 Nyemaster,G.W.H.&O.]
Sutphin, Ronald L., (AV) ....'— '64 C&L.221 B.A., J.D. [🄲 Ahlers&C.]
Sutton, Earl W., (AV) ....'30 '59 C&L.221 B.S.Ed., J.D. 800 W. Euclid‡
Swanger, James R., (AV) ....'46 '71 C&L.221 B.A., J.D. [Belin L.M.Z.F.]
Swanson, Elizabeth D. ... '64 '90 C.221 B.A. L.597 J.D. Coun., Principal Financial Group
Swanson, John E., (AV) .... '56 '82 C.898 B.A. L.221 J.D. [Hansen,M.&R.]
Swanson, Jon K., (AV) ....'54 '79 C.793 B.S. L.352 J.D. [Gaudineer,C.&G.]
Swanson, Terrance E. .... '41 '74 C.162 B.A. L.273 J.D. [Swanson]
Swanson Law Office ....520 35th St.
Swartwood, Thomas M. '56 '83 C.197 B.A. L.276 J.D.
(adm. in NY; not adm. in IA) Mng. Dir., Swartwood Hesse Inc.
Swartz, Clifford S., (AV) .... '42 '79 C.999 B.A. L.221 J.D. [Brick,G.B.S.S.S.&L.]
Sweeney, Coreen K., (AV) .....'65 '91 C.352 B.B.A. L.221 J.D. [Nyemaster,G.W.H.&O.]
Swinton, David, (AV) .... '56 '81 C.352 B.A. L.228 J.D. [Belin L.M.Z.F.]
Synhorst, John V., (AV) ....'23 '49 C&L.352 B.A., J.D. [Bradshaw,F.P.&F.] ‡
Takes, Nicole M. ....'79 '04 [Takes]
Takes Law Office .... 701 E. Court Ave., Ste. A
Tank, David A., (AV) .... '59 '84 C.165 B.A. L.352 J.D. [Davis,B.K.S.&R.]
Tanner, Krista K. ....'74 '00 C.351 B.A. L.221 J.D. [🄰 Dickinson,M.T.&H.]

Tapscott, Leo J., (AV) .... '20 '49 C.602 L.221 J.D. 3520 Grand Ave.
Tarbox, Thomas T., Law Office of, (BV) '54 '79
C.190 B.A. L.352 J.D. 309 Court Ave., Ste. 240
Tarvin, Charles B. '54 '81
C.350 B.A. L.352 J.D. Admin. Law J., Dept. Of Inspections & App.
Tassell-Getman, Terri L. .... '56 '82 C.945 B.A. L.221 J.D. 711 High St.
Tauber, Thomas S., (AV) .... '47 '89 C.352 B.A. L.221 J.D. Asst. Atty. Gen.
Taylor, Karen A., (BV) .... '69 '95 C.949 B.A. L.221 J.D. [Taylor]
Taylor Law Offices, (BV) .... 5001 S.W. 9th Street
Techau, Stephanie G., (AV) ..... '66 '92 C&L.352 B.A., J.D. [[A] Nyemaster,G.W.H.&O.]
Tempero, Richard M. .... '37 '62 C&L.546 B.S.Ed., J.D. 700 55th St.‡
Ternus, Marsha K. .... '51 '77 C.352 B.A. L.221 J.D. Supm. Ct. Jus.
Terrones, B.J. .... '77 '04 C.352 B.A. L.221 J.D. [[A] Hopkins&H.]
Tharnish, Deborah M., (AV) .... '55 '80 C.350 B.A. L.352 J.D. [Davis,B.K.S.&R.]
Thielking, Paul M., (BV) .... '47 '73 C&L.221 B.S.B.A., J.D. [P.M.Thielking]
Thielking, Paul M., PC, (BV) .... 8230 Hickman Rd.
Thomas, Janice M., (BV) ..... '64 '89 C.352 B.B.A. L.221 J.D. [Patterson,L.D.T.I.B.&O.]
Thomas, Mark W., (AV) .... '55 '81 C.221 B.A. L.190 J.D. [Grefe&S.]
Thomas, William D., (BV) '45 '73
C&L.352 B.S., J.D. [[B] Davis,B.K.S.&R.] (⊙Pocahontas)
Thompson, Nancy L., (BV) .... '59 '84 C.350 B.A. L.352 J.D. [Thompson]
Thompson, Stanley J., (AV) .... '60 '85 C.350 B.A. L.273 J.D. [Davis,B.K.S.&R.]
Thompson, Tina R. .... '74 '03 C.898 B.A. L.352 J.D. [[A] Brown,W.G.G.B.&S.]
Thompson Law Office, (BV) .... 309 Court Avenue, Suite 217
Thoms, Allan T. .... '38 '65 C.641 B.A. L.352 LL.B. Exec. Asst. to The Gov.
Thomson, Robert C., (AV) .... '48 '73 C.352 B.B.A. L.221 J.D. [Grefe&S.]
Thrall, Michael W., (AV) .... '55 '80 C.350 B.S. L.352 J.D. [Nyemaster,G.W.H.&O.]
Throckmorton, Robert B., (AV) .... '15 '38 C&L.221 A.B., LL.B. 699 Walnut St.‡
Tice, Andrew T. .... '— '01 C.350 B.A. L.339 J.D. [[A] Ahlers&C.]
Tichenor, James G. .... '34 '66 C.378 A.B. L.502 J.D. 4044 S.E. 14th St.‡
Tidrick, Don L. .... '09 '33 C&L.221 B.A., LL.B. Ret. Dist. J.
Tiernan, Nan .... '42 '95 C.221 B.S. L.352 J.D. [N.Tiernan]

Tiernan, Nan, The, Law Firm, P.L.C.
P.O. Box 12034, 50312
Telephone: 515-277-7136; 1-866-977-7136 Cell: 515-988-3540
Email: nantiernan@yahoo.com URL: http://www.lawyers.com/nantiernan
Nan Tiernan.
Family Law, Adoptions, Interstate Adoptions, Step Parent Adoption, Child Custody, Child Support, Divorce, Parental Rights, Domestic Violence, Visitation Rights, Alimony, Grandparent Rights, General Practice, Wills and Probate, Bankruptcy, Guardianships, Appellate Practice, Post Divorce Modification, Surrogacy Law, Assisted Reproduction Technology, Termination of Parental Rights, Grandparent Adoption, Premarital Agreements, Mental Health and Developmental Disabilities, Incompetence Proceedings, Paternity, Spousal Support, Modification of Custody.
See Professional Biographies, DES MOINES, IOWA

Tilley, Kris Holub, (BV) .... '65 '90 C.520 B.A. L.352 J.D. [Davis,B.K.S.&R.]
Tillotson, Drew R., (AV) .... '30 '55 C&L.221 B.S., J.D. [[B] Nyemaster,G.W.H.&O.]
Tingle, Bryan, (BV) .... '65 '99 L.221 J.D. 418 6th Ave., Ste. 200
Tipton, Sheila K., (AV) .... '51 '80 C.610 B.S. L.221 J.D. [Belin L.M.Z.F.]
Tobin, Maureen Roach, (AV) '— '87
C.352 B.A. L.221 J.D. [Whitfield&E.] (⊙West Des Moines)
Tofflemire, Cynthia .... '— '91 C.933 B.S. L.221 J.D. 4119 Allison Avenue‡
Tonini, Melio A., (BV) .... '13 '36 C&L.221 LL.B. Midland Financial Bldg.
Traynor, Kristi A. .... '72 '98 C.132 B.A. L.352 J.D. [[A] Dickinson,M.T.&H.]
Traynor, Steven P. '55 '81 C.942 B.A. L.45 J.D.
(adm. in AR; not adm. in IA) Coun., Principal Financial Group
Treinen, Michael D., (AV) .... '41 '72 C.190 B.A. L.352 J.D. [Brown,W.G.G.B.&S.]
Trier, Michael G., (AV) .... '47 '74 C.350 B.S. L.221 J.D. Dep. Indus. Comr.

Tripp, P.C.
(See Pella)

Tripp, Mark L., (AV) .... '52 '81 C.350 B.S. L.221 J.D. [Bradshaw,F.P.&F.]
Trout, Brett J., (AV) .... '66 '92 C.293 B.A. L.352 J.D. [B.J.Trout] (Pat.)
Trout, William J., (BV) .... '37 '62 C.436 L.221 LL.B. 111 3rd St.

Trout, Brett J., P.C., The Law Offices of, (AV)
516 Walnut Street, 50309
Telephone: 515-280-1939 Fax: 515-280-7114 URL: http://www.bretttrout.com
Email: trout@bretttrout.com URL: http://www.brettjtrout.com
Brett J. Trout (Resident).
Patent, Trademark and Copyright Law, E-Commerce, Software Licensing, Intellectual Property, Information Technology, Trade Secrets.
See Professional Biographies, DES MOINES, IOWA

Truesdell, Mark E., (BV) .... '51 '76 C&L.352 B.A., J.D. [Beving,S.&F.]
Tucker, Robert E., (BV) .... '55 '91 L.221 J.D. [Tucker]
Tucker Law Office, (BV) .... 7109 Hickman Rd.
Tuel, Larry L. .... '51 '81 C.490 B.S. L.221 J.D. 21 56th St.

Turner Law Offices
(See West Des Moines)

Tyler, Jennifer Ann, (BV) .... '59 '88 C&L.352 B.A., J.D. [Carney,A.N.&S.]
Tyler, Paul R., (AV) .... '42 '67 C&L.352 B.A., J.D. [Dickinson,M.T.&H.]
Uehling, Kathleen K. '58 '88 C&L.352 B.A., J.D.
(adm. in MD; not adm. in IA) 1000 E. Grand Ave.‡
Uhl, Keith E., (BV) .... '46 '72 C.793 B.A. L.273 J.D. 3101 Elmwood Dr.
Ullem, Benjamin B., (AV) .... '— '69 C&L.221 B.A., J.D. [Whitfield&E.]
Updegraff, Anne, (CV) .... '71 '96 C.352 B.A. L.221 J.D. [[A] Peddicord,W.S.&H.]
Updegraff, Richard K., (AV) .... '51 '76 C&L.352 B.A., J.D. [Brown,W.G.G.B.&S.]
Urban, Camille L. '64 '98
C.350 B.A. L.352 J.D. [Brown,W.G.G.B.&S.] (⊙West Des Moines)
Vald, Roman, (BV) .... '70 '95 C&L.352 B.A., J.D. [[A] LaMarca&L.]
Valentine, Leanne M. '62 '88 C&L.352 B.A., J.D.
(adm. in IL; not adm. in IA) 2nd V.P. & Coun., Principal Financial Group
Van Dike, Adam C. .... '75 '01 C.352 B.A. L.190 J.D. [Connolly,O.L.H.&O.]
Van Dyke, Kevin D., (AV) '57 '84 C.793 B.S. L.352 J.D.
Asst. Gen. Coun., Wellmark Blue Cross & Blue Shield of Iowa
Van Ekeren, Jacklyn K. .... '64 '89 C.350 B.A. L.352 J.D. AmerUs Fin.
Van Heuvelen, Wayne F., (AV) .... '52 '86 C.1348 B.A. L.221 J.D. 665 Locust St.
VanOrsdel, Robert A., (AV) '44 '75 C.352 B.B.A. L.221 J.D.
[Nyemaster,G.W.H.&O.]
VanSickel, David B., (BV) .... '53 '77 C.351 B.A. L.352 J.D. [Davis,B.K.S.&R.]
Van Thomme, Kurt .... '76 '05 C&L.221 B.A., J.D. [[A] McKee,V.&S.]
Van Voorhis, Harold L. .... '36 '60 C&L.221 B.S.B.A., J.D. 4902 University Ave.
Van Werden, James E., (AV) ..... '39 '64 C.641 B.A. L.352 J.D. [Hopkins&H.] (⊙Adel)
Van Winkle, Joseph G., (AV) .... '53 '78 C.350 B.S. L.352 J.D. [[B] Lewis,W.V.&K.]
Vasey, Jon A., (AV) .... '57 '83 C.352 B.B.A. L.221 J.D. [Elverson,V.&P.]
Vasquez, Rose A., (BV) .... '54 '85 C.352 B.A. L.221 J.D. Asst. Atty. Gen.
Vavroch, Mary W., (BV) .... '46 '82 C&L.352 B.S.N., J.D. Asst. Co. Atty.

Velazquez-Dussias, Amanda .... '73 '00 C.502 B.A. L.221 J.D. 811 Hickman Road
Vermeer, Barry G., (AVⓉ) '55 '80 C.352 B.A. L.494 J.D.
[Gislason&H.] (⊙Mpls., MN)
Vernon, John K., (AV) .... '46 '75 C.711 B.A. L.678 J.D. [Dickinson,M.T.&H.]
Vestal, David D., (BV) .... '57 '83 C.170 B.A. L.352 J.D. 1585 NW 122nd St.
Vietor, Harold D. .... '31 '58 C&L.352 B.A., J.D. 123 E. Walnut St.
Vogel, Gayle N. .... '49 '83 C.697 B.A. L.221 J.D. J., Ct. of App.
Voigts, LeRoy R., (AV) .... '27 '55 C.898 B.A. L.221 J.D. [[B] Nyemaster,G.W.H.&O.]
Vonderhaar, Phillip, (AV) .... '51 '77 C&L.352 B.B.A., J.D. [Hedberg,O.&V.]
Voorhees, Michael G., (AV) '41 '68
C.350 B.S. L.221 J.D. [McKee,V.&S.] (See Pat. Sect.)
Vukelich, Milo Michael ..... '62 '87 C&L.972 B.S., J.D. Coun., Principal Financial Group
Wacholz, Wade R., (AVⓉ) '60 '87 C.182 B.A. L.494 J.D.
[Gislason&H.] (⊙Mpls., MN)
Wagner, CeCelia Ibson, (BV) .... '63 '89 C.350 B.A. L.910 J.D. [Smith,S.S.&S.]
Wagner, Steve R. '52 '77 C.932 B.S. L.347 J.D.
Sr. Asst. Gen. Coun., Wells Fargo Financial, Inc.
Wainwright, James R. .... '— '99 C.93 B.A. L.221 J.D. [[A] Ahlers&C.]
Walding, Lynn M., (BV) .... '55 '81 C&L.352 B.A., J.D. Asst. Atty. Gen.
Waldron, Patrick V., (AV) ..... '69 '95 C.707 B.A. L.221 J.D. [Patterson,L.D.T.I.B.&O.]
Walke, Jason D., (BV) .... '71 '96 C.351 B.A. L.352 J.D. [Gunderson,S.&W.]
Walker, Corey J. L., (BV) .... '— '97 C.132 B.S. L.221 J.D. [Walker&B.] (⊙Newton)
Walker, David S. '44 '70 C.976 B.A. L.893 LL.B.
(adm. in OH; not adm. in IA)
Dwight D. Opperman Prof. of Law, Drake Univ. Law School
Walker, E. Ralph, (AV) ...... '42 '72 C.309 B.A. L.659 J.D. 2501 Grand Avenue, Suite E
Walker, Kimberly J., (AV) .... '54 '79 C&L.352 B.S., J.D. [Faegre&B.]
Walker, Timothy J., (AV) .... '— '65 C&L.221 B.A., J.D. [Whitfield&E.] ‡
Walker & Billingsley, (BV) .... 1000 73rd St., Suite 24 (⊙Baxter, Newton)
Walleser, Helenjean, (BV) '49 '80 C.999 B.A. L.352 J.D.
Dep. Indus. Comr., State Div. of Indus. Servs.
Walsh, Joseph L., (BV) .... '70 '96 C&L.221 B.A., J.D. 840 Fifth Ave.
Walter, James B. .... '45 '75 C&L.352 B.A., J.D. Iowa Bur. of Crim. Investigation
Walters, Ross A. .... '49 '77 C.645 B.A. L.352 J.D. U.S. Mag. J.
Walton, Thomas H., (AV) .... '63 '89 C.351 B.A. L.352 J.D. [Nyemaster,G.W.H.&O.]
Walz, Mark D., (AV) .... '58 '83 C&L.352 B.A., J.D. [Davis,B.K.S.&R.] ⊙
Wandro, Steven P., (AV) .... '57 '84 C&L.352 B.A., J.D. [Wandro,B.A.&C.]

Wandro, Baer, Appel and Casper, P.C., (AV) [BV]
2501 Grand Avenue, Suite B, 50312
Telephone: 515-281-1475 Fax: 515-281-1474
Email: scarter@2501grand.com URL: http://www.wandrolaw.com
Steven P. Wandro; Kimberley K. Baer; Brent R. Appel; Michelle M. Casper;—Jason E. McCollough.
General Civil and Trial Practice in all Courts, Commercial Litigation, Administrative Law, Personal Injury, Bankruptcy, Products Liability, Medical Malpractice and Business Law.
See Professional Biographies, DES MOINES, IOWA

Wanek, Jerrold, (AV) .... '58 '83 C.352 B.A. L.221 J.D. [Garten&W.]
Ward, J. Marc, (AV) .... '58 '84 C.350 B.S. L.221 J.D. [Dickinson,M.T.&H.]
Ward, James Patrick, (BV) .... '60 '87 C.352 B.A. L.190 J.D. Asst. Co. Atty.
Ward, John R., (BV) .... '35 '59 C&L.221 LL.B. 840 5th Ave.
Ward, Rhonda B. .... '67 '97 C.966 B.A. L.818 J.D. Coun., Amer. Repub. Ins. Co.
Warner, Marilyn Sue .... '52 '78 C&L.221 B.A., J.D. State Pub. Employ. Rel. Bd.
Warren, Norma .... '20 '48 C&L.221 LL.B. 1121 3rd St.
Warren, Stacey N., (BV) .... '69 '94 C&L.378 B.A., J.D. [Babich,G.C.&R.]
Waters, John E. .... '53 '78 C.352 B.S. L.350 J.D. Off. of U.S. Trustee
Waters, M. Daniel, (AV) .... '64 '89 C&L.352 B.B.A., J.D. [Davis,B.K.S.&R.]
Watkins, Kendall R., (BV) .... '60 '85 C.388 B.A. L.221 J.D. [Davis,B.K.S.&R.]
Watson, Frank, Jr., (BV) ... '29 '59 C&L.221 B.A., LL.B. 900 2 Ruan Ctr., 601 Locust St.
Watson, Phil, (AV) .... '41 '67 C.784 B.A. L.221 J.D. [P.Watson]
Watson Cook, Angela L. .... '70 '96 C.221 B.S.B.A. L.352 J.D. [Nyemaster,G.W.H.&O.]

Watson, Phil, P.C., (AV)
535 East Army Post Road, 50315
Telephone: 515-287-7000 Fax: 515-287-0875; URL: http://philwatson.com
Email: firm@watsonpc.com URL: http://www.watsonpc.com
Phil Watson;—Drennan L. Fischer; Becky J. Petersen; Rocky J. Robbins.
Commercial and Retail Collections, Corporate and Commercial Law, Bankruptcy Law, Estate Planning, Probate, Real Estate and Business Litigation.
Representative Clients: Wells Fargo Card Services; Greyhound Lines, Inc.; John Deere Credit; Daimler Chrysler Financial Corp.
Reference: Community State Bank, Indianola, Iowa.
See Professional Biographies, DES MOINES, IOWA

Watts, Harry T., (AV) .... '27 '51 C.352 B.A. L.477 J.D. 699 Walnut St.
Watts, JoEllen J., (BV) .... '58 '83 C&L.221 B.S., J.D. Coun., Principal Mut. Life Ins. Co.
Webber, Ivan T., (AV) .... '— '73 C&L.352 B.A., J.D. [Ahlers&C.]
Webster, Cassandra .... '71 '98 C.221 B.A. L.352 J.D. 2507 Maryland Pike
Weeg, Theresa O'Connell, (AV) .... '57 '81 C.1169 B.A. L.352 J.D. Asst. Atty. Gen.
Wegman, Timothy W., (AV) .... '64 '89 C.352 B.A. L.221 J.D. [Peddicord,W.S.&H.]
Wegman, William L., (BV) .... '38 '64 C&L.352 B.A., J.D. Chf. State Pub. Def.
Weiland, Kenneth J., Jr. .... '69 '94 C.351 B.A. L.221 J.D. 1502 30th St., Ste. 2
Weinhardt, Mark E., (AV) .... '60 '85 C.197 A.B. L.477 J.D. [Belin L.M.Z.F.]
Weiss, Steven R. '54 '82
C.293 B.A. L.352 J.D. Sr. Gen. Couns., MidAmerican Energy Co.
Weist, Mary Margaret '64 '90 C.734 B.S. L.190 J.D.
(adm. in NE; not adm. in IA) Coverage Coun., EMC Ins. Co.
Welu, David J., (BV) .... '48 '73 C.177 B.S. L.221 J.D. 5711 Kingman Ave.
Werner, John, (AV) .... '48 '73 C.221 B.A. L.352 J.D. [[B] Grefe&S.]
Wessels, Jana S. Rhatigan .... '52 '79 C&L.352 B.A., J.D. State Dept. of Bking
West, Angel A., (BV) .... '71 '97 C.352 B.A. L.221 J.D. [Nyemaster,G.W.H.&O.]
West, Debra K., (BV) .... '56 '91 C.351 B.A. L.221 J.D. Asst. Atty. Gen.
West, James B., (AV) .... '33 '60 C&L.221 B.A., J.D. [Nyemaster,G.W.H.&O.]
West, Mitchell L., (CV) .... '55 '85 C.427 B.A. L.221 J.D. 4044 S.E. 14th St.
Westemeyer, Patricia A., (BV) .... '— '98 C.350 B.A. L.352 J.D. [[A] Ahlers&C.]
Westin, Neal K. .... '74 '99 C.352 B.A. L.846 J.D. [Nyemaster,G.W.H.&O.]
Wethington-Smith, September, (AV) '61 '87 C.350 B.A. L.352 J.D.
Assoc. Gen. Coun., Wells Fargo Home Mtge., Inc.
Wetsch, David L., (AV) .... '54 '79 C.352 B.B.A. L.221 J.D. 974 73rd St., Ste. 20
Wharton, John M., (AV) .... '44 '70 C.350 B.S. L.221 J.D. [Peddicord,W.S.&H.]
Wheatcraft, William G., (BV) .... '36 '60 C&L.221 B.A., J.D. 7630 Hickman Rd.
Wheeler, Mark W. .... '49 '80 3911 10th St.
White, Lu Ann, (BV) .... '56 '81 C.187 B.A. L.352 J.D. [Hanson,B.&R.]
White, Patrick B. .... '73 '02 C&L.221 B.S.B.A., J.D. [[A] Nyemaster,G.W.H.&O.]
White, Thomas L. '29 '59 C.378 B.S. L.986 LL.B.
(adm. in KS; not adm. in IA) Amoco Oil Co.
Whitfield, Harley A., (AV) .... '— '56 C.350 B.S. L.221 J.D. [[B] Whitfield&E.]

Whitfield & Eddy, P.L.C., (AV)
317 6th Avenue, Suite 1200, 50309-4195 ⊙
Telephone: 515-288-6041 Fax: 515-246-1474
Email: info@whitfieldlaw.com URL: http://www.whitfieldlaw.com
Megan M. Antenucci; Robert G. Bridges; Thomas H. Burke; Jason M. Casini; Danny L. Cornell (Resident, Mt. Pleasant Office); Stephen E. Doohen; William L. Fairbank; Robert L. Fanter; John F. Fatino; Gary Gately; Mark R. Gray (Resident, Ankeny Office); Frank M. Grenard; Mark V. Hanson; J. Campbell Helton; Thomas Henderson; Richard J. Kirschman; Philip D. McCormick (Resident, Mt. Pleasant Office); Greg A. Naylor (Resident, West Des Moines Office); David D. Nelson (Resident, Ankeny Office); Gary A. Norton; David L. Phipps; Sally A. Reavely; Thomas S. Reavely; Kevin M. Reynolds; G. Mark Rice; Roscoe A. Ries, Jr.; Jaki K. Samuelson; Anjela A. Shutts; Bernard L. "Jerry" Spaeth Jr.; Jeffrey D. Stone (Resident, West Des Moines Office); John A. Templer, Jr. (Resident, West Des Moines Office); Maureen Roach Tobin; Benjamin B. Ullem;—Ryan M. Albaugh (Resident, Ankeny Office); Aaron D. Bernard; Nicholas O. Cooper; Jeffrey D. Ewoldt; Erik S. Fisk (Resident, West Des Moines Office); Drew J. Gentsch; Gary D. Goudelock; R. William Hancock, Jr.; Jon K. Hoffmann; Gretchen Witte Kraemer; Jonathan E. Kramer; Adam C. Manatt; Stephen D. Marso; Maria L. Ruhtenberg; Theodore C. Simms, II; Kara M. Sinnard; B. Macpaul "Mac" Stanfield. Of Counsel: Ronald R. Adams; Wendy L. Carlson; Alanson K. Elgar (Resident, Mt. Pleasant Office); George H. Frampton; Harley A. Whitfield. Retired: John C. Eddy; Timothy J. Walker; A. Roger Witke.
General Practice including Trial and Appellate Practice and Business and Banking. Alternative Dispute Resolution, Antitrust and Trade Regulation, Arbitration, Bankruptcy, Banks and Banking, Business, Civil Rights, Commercial, Construction, Corporate, Criminal, Environmental, Family, Fidelity and Surety, Foreclosures, Health Care, Immigration and Naturalization, Insurance, Insurance Defense, Intellectual Property, Labor and Employment, Mediation, Municipal, Personal Injury, Probate, Products Liability, Professional Liability, Real Estate, Securities, Taxation, Transportation, Trust and Estates, Utility, Wills, Workers Compensation.
General Counsel for: Hawkeye-Security Insurance Co.; Iowa Funeral Directors Assn.; Tom Fairweather Trust Farms; Townsend Engineering Co.; United Security Insurance Co.
Representative Clients: Brenton Bank; Crum & Forster Commercial Insurance; Decker Truck Line, Inc.; General Motors Co.
Mt. Pleasant, Iowa Office: 110 North Jefferson, Suite 101, 52641-2016 Telephone: 319-385-9522. Fax: 319-385-3633. Email: info@whitfieldlaw.com. URL: http://www.whitfieldlaw.com.
Ankeny, Iowa Office: 213 North Ankeny Boulevard, Suite 100, 50023-1749. Telephone: 515-964-3633. Fax: 515-964-3692. Email: info@whitfieldlaw.com. URL: http://www.whitfieldlaw.com.
West Des Moines, Iowa Office: 3737 Woodland Avenue, Suite 400, 50266. Telephone: 515-558-0111. Fax: 515-222-0318. Email: info@whitfieldlaw.com. URL: http://www.whitfieldlaw.com.
See Professional Biographies, DES MOINES, IOWA

Whitney, Jo Ellen, (BV) ... '63 '88 C&L.228 B.A., J.D. [Davis,B.K.S.&R.]
Wickett, William A., (AV) ... '45 '81 C.747 B.A. L.221 J.D. [Patterson,L.D.T.I.B.&O.]
Wieck, Paul H., II, (AV) ... '— '82 C.350 B.S. L.221 J.D. Exec. Dir. & Asst. Ct. Admr.
Wiedenfeld, Mark J., (AV) ... '50 '78 C.793 B.S. L.352 J.D. [Wiedenfeld&M.]
Wiedenfeld & McLaughlin, L.L.P., (AV) ... 8400 Hickman Road
Wilcox, Gregory B., (AV) ... '54 '82 C.352 B.B.A. L.221 J.D. [Nyemaster,G.W.H.&O.]
Willaert, Andrew A., (BVⓣ) '58 '83
C.723 B.S. L.1035 J.D. [Gislason&H.] (⊙Mankato, MN)
Willets, Samantha S. ... '78 '03 C.352 B.B.A. L.221 J.D. [Ⓐ Grefe&S.]
Williams, Brian P. ... '38 '62 C&L.221 B.A., J.D. 2600 Grand Ave.‡
Williams, Richard A. ... '41 '71 C&L.352 B.A., J.D. Asst. Atty. Gen.
Williams, Timothy R., (AV) ... '47 '73 C.352 B.A. L.221 J.D. [Williams,B.H.&M.]

Williams, Blackburn, Hudson & Maharry, P.L.C., (AV)
740 Bank of America Building, 317 6th Avenue, 50309
Telephone: 515-280-3300 Fax: 515-280-3322
URL: http://www.desmoineslawfirm.com
Timothy R. Williams; James S. Blackburn; John D. Hudson; Rodney K. Maharry;—Jami J. Hagemeier. Of Counsel: John C. Schachterle.
General Civil and Legislative Practice. Securities Litigation and Arbitration, Real Estate Law, Insurance Regulation, Personal Injury.
See Professional Biographies, DES MOINES, IOWA

Wilson, George A., Jr., (AV) ... '24 '51 C.273 L.221 LL.B. 317 Sixth Avenue
Wilson, Gregory J., (AV) ... '50 '77 C.352 B.A. L.221 J.D. [Patterson,L.D.T.I.B.&O.]
Wilson, Janet L. ... '33 '68 C.784 B.A. L.208 J.D. Iowa Legis-Serv. Bureau
Wilson, Jonathan C., (AV) ... '45 '71 C.513 B.A. L.352 J.D. [Davis,B.K.S.&R.]
Wilson, Randall C. '49 '74 C.337 B.A. L.221 J.D.
Legal Dir., Iowa Civil Liberties Union
Wilson, Robert D. ... '51 '81 C.870 B.S. L.352 J.D. Dist. J.
Wilson, Rosemary F. '51 '97 C.999 A.A. L.1001 J.D.
(adm. in CA; not adm. in IA) 2003 E. Maish Ave.
Wilson, Valorie Kay ... '59 '85 C.878 B.S. L.221 J.D. Off. Pub. Def.
Winders, Richard N., (AV) ... '45 '70 C&L.221 B.A., J.D. [Herrick,L.&L.]
Wine, James C., (AV) ... '57 '82 C.674 A.B. L.352 J.D. [Nyemaster,G.W.H.&O.]
Winick, Alfred Z. '41 '66 C&L.352 B.A., J.D.
Pres., Norwest Financial Info. Servs. Grp., Inc.
Winters, Barbara Kay ... '47 '86 C.338 B.S. L.221 J.D. Principal Mutal Life Ins. Co.
Wirt, Brian L., (AV) ... '53 '79 C&L.793 B.A., J.D. Assoc. Gen. Coun., Meredith Corp.
Wisby, James S. ... '42 '68 C.351 B.B.A. L.352 J.D. Asst. Atty. Gen.
Witke, A. Roger, (AV) ... '— '59 C.784 B.A. L.477 J.D. [Whitfield&E.] ‡
Witke, Gregory A., (AV) ... '61 '87 C.350 B.S. L.352 J.D. [Bradshaw,F.P.&F.]
Witt, Colin J. ... '— '99 C&L.352 B.A., J.D. [Ⓐ Ahlers&C.]
Witt, Michael J. ... '55 '82 C.188 B.A. L.705 J.D. 800 Walnut St.
Wittgraf, Jason B. ... '75 '01 C.694 B.A. L.352 J.D. [Ⓐ Lewis,W.V.&K.]
Wodtke, Griff ... '44 '78 C.118 B.A. L.221 J.D. Staff Atty., U.S. Dist. Ct.
Wolle, Charles R. ... '35 '61 C.309 A.B. L.352 J.D. U.S. Dist. Ct. J.
Wonio, Alexander ... '79 '04 C.177 B.A. L.221 J.D. [Ⓐ Hansen,M.&R.]
Wood, Heather L. ... '79 '03 C&L.221 B.A., J.D. 418 6th Ave.
Woodburn, Chester C., III, (AV) ... '48 '75 C.352 B.A. L.221 J.D. [Hansen,M.&R.]
Woods, Marne E. ... '54 '91 C.502 B.H.S. L.221 J.D. Asst. Atty Gen.
Woodward, Edna M. ... '10 '40 L.221 LL.B. 2725 Des Moines St.
Wright, Brian C. ... '60 '85 C&L.352 B.A., J.D. Wells Fargo Bank Iowa, N.A.
Wright, Robert A., Jr. ... '48 '81 C.352 B.A. L.221 J.D. [Wright]
Wright, Robert A., Sr. ... '25 '54 C.352 B.A. L.221 LL.B. 3869 Merle Hay Rd.‡
Wright, Terry, (BV) ... '39 '68 C.170 B.A. L.221 J.D. 666 Grand Avenue
Wright Law Offices ... 400 Locust Street, Suite 358
Wunn, Michael A. ... '68 '01 C&L.221 B.A., J.D. [Ⓐ Beving,S.&F.]
Young, Harold A., (BV) ... '40 '67 C&L.221 B.S., J.D. Spec. Asst. Atty. Gen.
Young, Joe D. ... '30 '54 C&L.352 B.S.C., LL.B. 314 Equitable Bldg.
Young, John J. ... '16 '42 C&L.352 B.A., J.D. 3824 Sherman Blvd.‡
Zacherle, Hedo M., (AV) ... '10 '32 C&L.221 B.A., J.D. Spec. Ethics Coun., Supr. Ct.‡
Zager, Tara L. ... '80 '05 C.352 B.A. L.221 J.D. [Ⓐ Davis,B.K.S.&R.]
Zarley, Timothy J., (AV) ... '60 '98 C&L.221 B.S., J.D. [Zarley] (Pat.)

Zarley Law Firm, P.L.C., (AV)
Capital Square, 400 Locust Street, Suite 200, 50309-2350
Telephone: 515-558-0200 Fax: 515-558-7790
Email: tzarley@zarleylaw.com URL: http://www.zarleylaw.com
Timothy J. Zarley;—Josef Louis Hoffmann.
Patents, Trademarks, Copyrights, Intellectual Property Litigation, Trade Secrets and Unfair Competition.
See Professional Biographies, DES MOINES, IOWA

Zenk, Sandra M., (AV) ... '54 '79 C&L.352 B.A., J.D. 711 High St.
Zieser, John S. '59 '86 C.352 B.B.A. L.188 J.D.
(adm. in GA; not adm. in IA) V.P., Gen. Coun. & Secy., Meredith Corp.
Zimmer, Van D. ... '47 '72 C&L.352 B.A., J.D. Ct. of App. J.
Zimmerman, Brent R., Law Offices of, (BV) '60 '89
C.352 B.S. L.221 J.D. 8350 Hickman Rd., Ste. 14
Zohn, Jack, (BV) ... '30 '59 C.851 B.B.A. L.221 J.D. 300 Walnut St.
Zoss, Paul A., (AV) ... '47 '72 C.347 B.S. L.846 J.D. Fed. Pub. Def.
Zumbach, Steven E., (AV) ... '50 '75 C.350 B.S. L.352 J.D. [Belin L.M.Z.F.]

DE WITT, 5,049, *Clinton Co.*

Condon, Daniel J., (AV) ... '40 '65 C&L.352 B.A., J.D. 610 9th St
Pillers, David M., (CV) ... '68 '98 C&L.879 B.A., J.D. 615 10th St.
Richmond, James P., Law Office of, (BV) .. '38 '67 C.177 B.B.A. L.352 J.D. 624 11th St.

Van Scoy & Kross, P.C.
(See Clinton)

DUBUQUE, * 57,686, *Dubuque Co.*

Ackley, Monica L. ... '64 '92 C&L.1049 B.A., J.D. Dist. J.
Arenz, A. John, (AV) ... '52 '78 C.436 A.B. L.276 J.D. [O'Connor&T.]
Arling, Peter D. ... '77 '03 C.177 B.A. L.190 J.D. [Ⓐ O'Connor&T.]
Bauer, David C. ... '46 '72 C&L.352 B.B.A., J.D. 4050 Westmark Drive
Becker, John R., (CV) ... '50 '75 C&L.352 B.A., J.D. 1890 Kennedy Rd.
Bitter, Joseph J. ... '37 '64 C.177 B.S. L.352 J.D. [Bitter]
Bitter Law Office ... 5th & Locust
Blair, Jennifer ... '71 '97 C.484 B.A. L.910 J.D. Staff Atty., Legal Servs. Corp. of Iowa
Blum, William G., (BV) ... '43 '68 C.226 B.S. L.352 J.D. 300 Main Street

Bribriesco, William J., & Associates
(See Bettendorf)

Carew, Allan J., (AV) ... '33 '60 C&L.352 B.S., J.D. [Fuerste,C.C.J.&S.]
Clemens, David L., (BV) ... '40 '65 C&L.352 B.B.A., J.D. [Reynolds&K.]
Clemens, Jennifer A., (BV) ... '67 '92 C.351 B.A. L.352 J.D. [Reynolds&K.]
Collins, Thomas S. ... '61 '98 C&L.352 B.B.A., J.D. [Ⓐ O'Connor&T.]
Conzett, William A. ... '36 '62 C.177 B.A. L.352 J.D. [Conzett&O.]
Conzett & O'Brien, (BV) ... 491 W. 4th St.
Cox, Chadwyn D., (BV) ... '54 '79 C.300 B.A. L.352 J.D. [Reynolds&K.]
Coyle, Michael J., (AV) ... '45 '70 C&L.352 B.B.A., J.D. [Fuerste,C.C.J.&S.]
Curnan, Robert J. ... '38 '64 C.162 B.A. L.494 LL.B. Dist. J.
Curtiss, Davin C., (BV) ... '70 '95 C.436 B.A. L.352 J.D. [O'Connor&T.]
Day, Robert L., Jr., (BV) ... '49 '74 C.429 B.A. L.352 J.D. 1141 Main St.
Deeny, Kevin T. ... '76 '01 C.427 B.A. L.350 J.D. [Kane,N.&R.]
Dipietro-Wilson, Diane '59 '90
C.1111 B.A. L.362 J.D. Mng. Atty., Legal Servs. Corp. of Iowa
Drake, D. Flint, (CV) ... '66 '91 C.351 B.A. L.352 J.D. [Kane,N.&R.]

Eells & Tronvold Law Offices, P.L.C.
(See Cedar Rapids)

Ernst, Daniel P., (AV) ... '31 '56 C.197 B.A. L.477 J.D. 899 Mount Carmel St.‡
Even, Chris M., (CV) '63 '93 C.1201 B.A. L.546 J.D.
2nd V.P. & Tr. Offr., American Trust & Savings Bank
Faber, Denis D., Jr., (CV) ... '59 '84 C.177 B.A. L.352 J.D. 1660 Embassy West Drive
Fautsch, Lawrence H. ... '49 '74 C.602 B.A. L.221 J.D. Dist. J.
Fitzsimmons, Paul J., (BV) ... '42 '66 C&L.352 B.A., LL.B. 850 White Street
Fleming, MaryBeth Pfeiler, (CV) ... '67 '95 C.720 B.A. L.352 J.D. [Kane,N.&R.]
Freund, John D. ... '78 '04 C.177 B.A. L.352 J.D. [Kane,N.&R.]
Fuerste, William C., (AV) ... '23 '47 C&L.352 B.A., J.D. [Fuerste,C.C.J.&S.]

Fuerste, Carew, Coyle, Juergens & Sudmeier, P.C., (AV)
200 Security Building, 151 West 8th Street, 52001
Telephone: 563-556-4011 Telecopier: 563-556-7134
Email: mail@fccjs.com URL: http://www.fccjs.com
William C. Fuerste; Allan J. Carew; Michael J. Coyle; Stephen J. Juergens; Robert L. Sudmeier; Douglas M. Henry; Mark J. Willging; Michael J. Shubatt; A. Theodore Huinker; Norman J. Wangberg; Danita L. Grant; John F. Hodges.
General Practice, including Construction Law, Corporate and Commercial, Discrimination, Education Law, Employment and Labor, Estate Planning, Trusts and Wills, Probate, Family Law, Insurance, Litigation, Personal Injury, Products Liability, Workers Compensation and Wrongful Death.
Representative Clients: State Farm Mutual Automobile Insurance Co.; Farm Bureau Mutual Insurance Co.; Medical Protective Co.; Dubuque Community School District; Continental Insurance Cos.; Northwestern National Insurance Group; Continental Western Insurance Co.
See Professional Biographies, DUBUQUE, IOWA

Gallagher, Timothy J., (CV) ... '51 '77 L.190 J.D. Asst. Co. Atty.
Galliart, Lyle R., (CV) ... '52 '77 C.177 B.A. L.352 J.D. Asst. Co. Atty.
Gilloon, Arthur F., (BV) ... '53 '78 C.602 A.B. L.352 J.D. [Norman,G.W.&H.]
Gilloon, Frank D., Jr. ... '18 '47 C.177 A.B. L.352 J.D. Ret. Sr. Assoc. Dist. J.
Goen, Timothy G. ... '64 '90 C.352 B.A. L.190 J.D. 412 Loras Boulevard
Goodman, James E., Jr., (BV) ... '63 '88 C.338 B.S. L.352 J.D. [O'Connor&T.]
Goodman, Thomas J., (CV) ... '58 '82 C.177 B.A. L.352 J.D. Pub. Def.
Grant, Danita L. ... '75 '00 C.966 B.A. L.221 J.D. [Fuerste,C.C.J.&S.]
Gustoff, William R. ... '68 '95 C.273 B.A. L.352 J.D. 2148 Graham Circle
Hamel, Dirk J., (BV) ... '59 '86 C.177 B.A. L.352 J.D. [Norman,G.W.&H.]
Hammer, David L., (AV) ... '29 '56 C.293 B.A. L.352 J.D. [Hammer,S.&J.] ⊙

Hammer, Simon & Jensen, (AV)
770 Main Street, 52001-6820 ⊙
Telephone: 563-583-4010 Fax: 563-583-3402
Email: hsjlaw@hammerlawoffices.com
David L. Hammer; Angela C. Simon; Philip F. Jensen; Paul T. Jensen.
General Trial and Appellate Practice. Litigation, Wills, Estate and Trusts, Corporate and Business, Real Estate, Domestic Relations and Workers Compensation.
Galena, Illinois Office: 303 North Bench. Telephone: 815-777-1101. Fax: 815-777-9241.
See Professional Biographies, DUBUQUE, IOWA

Harmon, Darin S., (BV) ... '64 '89 C&L.352 B.A., J.D. [Kintzinger]
Heckmann, James M. ... '53 '82 C.154 B.A. L.352 J.D. 1660 Embassy West Dr.
Hefel, Kristy L. ... '65 '90 C&L.352 B.A., J.D. Asst. Pub. Def.
Henry, Douglas M., (BV) ... '52 '77 C&L.352 B.A., J.D. [Fuerste,C.C.J.&S.]
Herrig, James W., (CV) '50 '76
C.177 B.A. L.352 J.D. Exec. V.P., Harvest Financial Servs., Inc.
Heying, Brad J., (CV) ... '66 '92 C.351 B.A. L.352 J.D. [Kane,N.&R.]
Hodge, Steven J., (CV) ... '53 '79 C&L.352 B.A., J.D. 1st Asst. Pub. Def.
Hodges, John F. ... '80 '05 C.132 B.A. L.221 J.D. [Ⓐ Fuerste,C.C.J.&S.]
Hoover, Stuart G., (CV) ... '61 '87 C&L.352 B.A., J.D. 850 White St.
Hughes, Alfred E., (AV) ... '29 '56 C.177 B.A. L.352 J.D. [Hughes&T.]
Hughes & Trannel, P.C., (AV) ... 1154 Iowa St.
Huinker, A. Theodore ... '73 '98 C.177 B.A. L.352 J.D. [Ⓐ Fuerste,C.C.J.&S.]
Jacobs, William J., (CV) ... '54 '92 C.494 B.A. L.1178 J.D. 280 Nesler Ctr.
Jensen, Paul T., (CV) ... '50 '97 C.999 B.A. L.352 J.D. [Hammer,S.&J.] ⊙
Jensen, Philip F., (BV) ... '59 '84 C.338 B.S. L.546 J.D. [Hammer,S.&J.] ⊙

Juergens, Stephen J., (AV) ...'47 '73 C.177 B.A. L.352 J.D. [Fuerste,C.C.J.&S.]
Kane, Brian J., (AV) ...'57 '82 C.177 B.A. L.352 J.D. [Kane,N.&R.]

Kane, Norby & Reddick, P.C., (AV)
2100 Asbury Road, Suite 2, 52001
Telephone: 563-582-7980 Fax: 563-582-5312
Brian J. Kane; Gary K. Norby; Les V. Reddick; D. Flint Drake; Brad J. Heying; Todd L. Stevenson; MaryBeth Pfeiler Fleming; Kevin T. Deeny; John D. Freund. Of Counsel: Louis P. Pfeiler.
General Practice. Corporate/Commercial (including Litigation), Probate, Estate Planning, Trusts and Wills, Real Estate, Taxation and Contested Wills, Employee Benefits, Litigation, Workers' Compensation.

See Professional Biographies, DUBUQUE, IOWA

Kapler, David J. ...'64 '97 C.177 B.A. L.705 J.D. Heartland Financial USA, Inc.
Kaufman, Paul J., (BV) ...'51 '76 C.177 B.A. L.352 J.D. Chief Pub. Def.
Kelley, Mary C., (BV) ...'50 '81 C&L.352 B.G.S., J.D. Asst. Pub. Def.
Keuter, Kim J. ...'53 '78 C.177 B.A. L.190 J.D. US Bank
Kienast, Karen Brandstetter ...'58 '88 C.589 B.S. L.966 J.D. 280 Nesler Ctr.
Kintzinger, David N. ...'20 '48 C.177 A.B. L.352 J.D. 1076 Mt. Loretta‡
Kintzinger Law Firm, P.L.C., (AV) ...100 West 12th Street
Klapatauskas, Todd N. ...'73 '98 C.177 B.A. L.190 J.D. [Reynolds&K.]
Klauer, Robert D., (BV) ...'42 '69 C.226 B.S. L.221 J.D. 1043 Main St.
Klearman, Gail R. ...'59 '84 C.910 B.A. L.494 J.D. 799 Main St.
Klemesrud, Normand C., (BV) '47 '76 C.351 B.A. L.300 J.D.
Legal Servs. Corp. of Iowa
Konrardy, Dean J., (AV) ...'61 '87 C&L.352 B.B.A., J.D. [Kintzinger]
Kordell, Kathryn Conway ...'68 '94 C.177 B.A. L.190 J.D. 1761 Plymouth Court
Krumpe, Stephen C., (BV) ...'54 '85 C.779 B.A. L.352 J.D. [O'Connor&T.]
Lange, Francis J., (CV) ...'50 '76 C.177 B.A. L.352 J.D. Jud. Mag.
Larson, Kelly ...'66 '91 C&L.352 B.S., J.D. Exec. Dir.
Leifker, David W., (BV) ...'40 '66 C.177 B.A. L.436 J.D. 700 Locust St., Ste. 701
Leitch, Chad C., (BV) ...'52 '80 C.350 B.S. L.352 J.D. [O'Connor&T.]
Lemanski, David A. ...'51 '79 C.966 B.A. L.221 J.D. 701 Bluff St.
Liedtke, Kerrie L. ...'76 '01 C.898 B.A. L.352 J.D. [A O'Connor&T.]
Lindahl, Barry A., (AV) ...'46 '73 C&L.352 B.A., J.D. 300 Main Street, Suite 330
Maiers, William J., (BV) ...'54 '79 C.723 B.A. L.352 J.D. [Reynolds&K.]
McCarthy, Leo A., (AV) ...'36 '63 C&L.190 B.S.B.A., J.D. [© Reynolds&K.] ‡
McCauley, Michael S., (CV) ... '36 '62 C.177 B.A. L.352 LL.B. 648 S. Grandview Ave.
McCaw, Fred H., (BV) ...'45 '73 C&L.352 B.A., J.D. Co. Atty.
McKay, Thomas W., (BV) ...'33 '58 C&L.352 B.S.C., J.D. 1485 Oeth Ct.
Meier, Leo J., (BV) '37 '62 C&L.966 B.S., LL.B.
Exec. V.P., Secy. & Dir., Amer. Tr. & Svgs. Bk.
Murphy, Thad J. ...'74 '00 C.293 B.A. L.352 J.D. [Murphy&S.]
Murphy & Silich, LLP, Law Offices of ...1890 John F. Kennedy Road
Mylrea, Jane C. ...'55 '79 C.747 B.A. L.494 J.D. Juv. J.
Nelson, Scott J., (BV) ...'58 '91 C.106 B.A. L.352 J.D. 412 Loras Boulevard
Nemmers, John T., (CV) ...'67 '95 C.352 B.A. L.146 J.D. [Reynolds&K.]
Neuhaus, Mary Lynn, (BV) ...'53 '80 C.177 B.A. L.190 J.D. Loras Coll.
Neuwoehner, Russel A. ...'47 '72 C.177 B.A. L.352 J.D. 698 Central Ave.
Nigg, Randal J. ...'49 '74 C.177 B.A. L.1049 J.D. Dist. Assoc. J.
Norby, Gary K., (AV) ...'41 '67 C&L.352 B.A., J.D. [Kane,N.&R.]
Norman, Wayne A., Jr., (BV) ...'46 '71 C.174 B.A. L.352 J.D. [Norman,G.W.&H.]
Norman, Gilloon, Wright & Hamel, P.C., (BV) ...800 Main Street
O'Brien, James A., (BV) ...'46 '72 C.025 B.A. L.477 J.D. [Conzett&O.]
O'Connor, John C., (AV) ...'49 '74 C.425 B.B.A. L.190 J.D. [O'Connor&T.]

O'Connor & Thomas, P.C., (AV) BB
Dubuque Building, 700 Locust Street, Suite 200, P.O. Box 599, 52004-0599
Mailing Address: P.O. Box 599, Dubuque, IA 52004-0599
Telephone: 563-557-8400 Facsimile: 563-556-1867
URL: http://www.octhomaslaw.com
John C. O'Connor; Brendan T. Quann; A. John Arenz; Chad C. Leitch; Richard K. Whitty; Stephen C. Krumpe; James E. Goodman, Jr.; Davin C. Curtiss; Paul J. Sigwarth;—Kerrie L. Liedtke; Peter D. Arling; Joshua P. Weidemann; Christopher Fry; Emily E. Reiners. Of Counsel: Thomas S. Collins.
General Practice, Banking, Commercial, Corporate, Estate Planning, Family Law, Litigation, Personal Injury, Workers' Compensation, Probate, Product Liability, Real Estate and Taxation.
Representative Clients: American Trust & Savings Bank; Dubuque Bank & Trust Company; Firstar Bank; The Archdiocese of Dubuque; A.Y. McDonald Industries, Inc.

See Professional Biographies, DUBUQUE, IOWA

Paar, Christopher R., (BV) ...'71 '97 C&L.352 B.S., J.D. [A Norman,G.W.&H.]
Pearce, Douglas C., (BV) ...'32 '63 C.226 B.S.B.A. L.966 J.D. [Kintzinger]
Pearson, Alan L. ...'46 '71 C.350 B.S. L.352 J.D. Chf. Dist. J.
Peckosh, Paul J. ...'45 '70 C.177 B.A. L.436 J.D. Sr. V.P., Dubuque Bk. & Tr. Co.
Peters, Brian W., (CV) ...'58 '84 C.350 B.A. L.352 J.D. [A Kintzinger]
Pfeiler, Louis P., (AV) ...'35 '64 C.177 B.A. L.602 J.D. [© Kane,N.&R.]
Potter, Ralph R., (BV) ...'53 '78 C.177 B.A. L.352 J.D. 1st Asst. Co. Atty.
Quann, Brendan T., (AV) ...'41 '73 C.870 B.S. L.352 J.D. [O'Connor&T.]
Quinn, Anthony J., (CV) ...'66 '91 C.339 B.A. L.1119 J.D. [Hughes&T.]
Reddick, Les V., (AV) ...'48 '77 C&L.352 B.A., J.D. [Kane,N.&R.]
Rehmke, Bruce C. '53 '79 C&L.352 B.B.A., J.D.
V.P. & Tr. Offr., Dubuque Bk. & Tr. Co.
Reiners, Emily E. ...'79 '05 C.351 B.A. L.221 J.D. [A O'Connor&T.]
Reisen, Patricia M., (BV) ...'66 '97 C.350 B.S. L.352 J.D. [A Kintzinger]
Reynolds & Kenline, L.L.P., (BV) ...Suite 222 Fischer Building
Roddick, Kim ...'50 '83 C.383 B.G.S. L.589 J.D. [Reynolds&K.]
Roth, James J., (BV) ...'51 '75 C.177 B.A. L.352 J.D. 1400 University Ave.
Sabers, Robert E., (CV) ...'61 '91 C.177 B.A. L.352 J.D. 3003 Asbury Rd.
Schilling, James G., (BV) ...'45 '70 C.177 B.A. L.352 J.D. 1890 J.F.K. Rd.
Scott, Stephen W., (BV) ...'48 '73 C&L.352 B.A., J.D. [Kintzinger]
Seligman, Marcia S. ...'51 '77 C.94 B.A. L.300 J.D. 400 East 3rd Street
Setter, David F., (BV) ...'40 '64 C.177 B.A. L.352 J.D. [Kintzinger]
Shubatt, Michael J., (BV) ...'65 '90 C&L.352 B.A., J.D. [Fuerste,C.C.J.&S.]

Shuttleworth & Ingersoll, P.L.C.
(See Cedar Rapids)

Sigwarth, Paul J., (BV) ...'72 '97 C&L.352 B.A., J.D. [O'Connor&T.]
Silich, Paul A. ...'72 '97 C.350 B.S. L.589 J.D. [Murphy&S.]
Simon, Angela C., (AV) ...'49 '85 C.177 B.A. L.352 J.D. [Hammer,S.&J.] ⊙
Singsank, Richard C. ...'52 '77 C.602 B.B.A. L.190 J.D. 3460 Starlite Dr.‡
Smith, Donna L. ...'41 '98 C.177 B.A. L.352 J.D. 1827/Keyway Dr.
Soppe, Christopher M. ...'73 '99 C.351 B.A. L.300 J.D. 850 White St.
Stenlund, Paula M. ...'47 '83 C.494 B.A. L.1035 J.D. P.O. Box 239‡
Stevenson, Todd L., (CV) ...'65 '90 C.106 B.A. L.352 J.D. [Kane,N.&R.]
Straka, Thomas J., (CV) ...'68 '95 C.351 B.A. L.190 J.D. 1141 Main St.
Sudmeier, Robert L., (AV) ...'48 '73 C&L.352 B.B.A., J.D. [Fuerste,C.C.J.&S.]
Sullivan, Mark J., (BV) ...'53 '80 C.177 B.A. L.190 J.D. [Reynolds&K.]
Thein, Cory R. ...'75 '01 C.520 B.A. L.221 J.D. [A Kintzinger]
Trannel, James A., (BV) ...'47 '75 C.177 B.A. L.221 J.D. [Hughes&T.]
Trannel, Jeffrey A., (BV) ...'58 '83 C.177 B.A. L.352 J.D. [Hughes&T.]

Vandenburgh, Edward C., (AV⑦) ...'15 '40 C.350 B.S. L.228 LL.B. 1065 Clara Ct.‡
Van Etten, Arnold J., (BV) ...'30 '60 C.98 B.S. L.352 J.D. [Kintzinger]
Walters, Jeffrey L., (BV) ...'60 '87 C.352 B.S. L.809 J.D. [Reynolds&K.]
Wangberg, Norman J., (BV) ...'48 '76 C.899 B.A. L.352 J.D. [Fuerste,C.C.J.&S.]
Whalen, Michael J., (CV) ...'57 '85 C.177 B.A. L.190 J.D. Asst. Co. Atty.
Whitty, Richard K., (BV) ...'55 '80 C.221 B.A. L.352 J.D. [O'Connor&T.]
Willging, Mark J., (BV) ...'53 '78 C.177 B.A. L.352 J.D. [Fuerste,C.C.J.&S.]
Wright, E. David, (BV) ...'53 '78 C.309 A.B. L.352 J.D. [Norman,G.W.&H.]
Zwack, Joseph P., (BV) ...'39 '64 C.177 B.A. L.352 J.D. 1890 John F. Kennedy Rd.

DURANGO, 34, *Dubuque Co.*

Hellmer, Werner ...'47 '76 C.226 B.A. L.352 J.D. Rte. 1 Box 855★

DYERSVILLE, 4,035, *Delaware & Dubuque Cos.*

Casey, Marc W., (BV) ...'48 '74 C&L.352 B.A., J.D. [Moss,H.&C.]
Goen, John J., (BV) ...'30 '57 C.177 L.352 LL.B. [Jenk&G.]
Heims, Louis F., (BV) ...'33 '65 C.177 B.A. L.352 J.D. [Moss,H.&C.]
Jenk, Thomas H., (BV) ...'30 '55 C.352 L.221 LL.B. [Jenk&G.]
Jenk & Goen, (BV) ...320 1st Ave., E.
Moss, Kenneth L., (BV) ...'35 '61 C.723 B.S. L.352 J.D. [Moss,H.&C.]
Moss, Heims & Casey, (BV) ...129 1st Ave., E.

DYSART, 1,230, *Tama Co.*

Griffin, Gordon H. '28 '55 C.352 B.A. L.221 J.D.
Sr. V.P. & Chmn. of the Bd., Dysart State Bk.
Irvine, David H., II ...'39 '67 C&L.352 LL.B. P.O. Box 237
Rathjen, Daniel Y., (BV) ...'50 '75 C&L.352 B.S.B.A., J.D. [Willett&R.] ⊙
Willett, John J., (BV) ...'40 '66 C&L.352 B.A., LL.B. [Willett&R.] ⊙
Willett & Rathjen, P.L.C., (BV) ...511 Main St. (⊙Tama)

EAGLE GROVE, 3,671, *Wright Co.*

Ivers, Larry E., (BV) ... '36 '72 C.626 B.G.E. L.352 J.D. 221 W. Broadway (⊙Renwick)
Long, William A., (BV) ...'43 '71 C.221 B.S.B.A. L.793 J.D. [McGrath&L.]
McGrath, Don L., (BV) ...'26 '51 L.221 LL.B. [McGrath&L.]
McGrath & Long Law Office, P.C., (BV) ...P.O. Box 145
Wright, George, (AV) ...'08 '33 C.177 A.B. L.209 J.D. 119 N. Washington St.‡

EARLHAM, 1,298, *Madison Co.*

Braland, Samuel H., (AV) ...'52 '78 C&L.352 B.B.A., J.D. [Peer,N.&B.]
Le Tourneau, Lawrence F., (BV) ...'37 '64 C.912 B.A. L.221 LL.B. 3487 Jewell Circle
Nelson, Dean R., (BV) ...'40 '69 C&L.221 B.S.Phar., J.D. [Peer,N.&B.]
Peer, Nelson & Braland, (AV) ...115 E. First Street
Ramsey, Martin S. ...'59 '96 C.350 B.S. L.221 J.D. Pros. Atty [A Peer,N.&B.]

EARLING, 466, *Shelby Co.*

Deren, Patrick T., (AV) '47 '75
C.801 B.A. L.838 J.D. [Salvo,D.S.&L.] (⊙Harlan, Panama)
Salvo, Deren, Schenck & Lauterbach, P.C., (AV) ... 122 Main (⊙Harlan, Panama, Walnut)

ELDORA, * 3,038, *Hardin Co.*

Craig, Patrick J., (AV) ...'48 '73 C.350 B.S. L.494 J.D. [Craig&S.] ⊙

Craig & Smith L.L.P., (AV) BB
1305 Twelfth Street, P.O. Box 431, 50627-0431 ⊙
Telephone: 641-939-5475 Fax: 641-939-3157
Email: cslaw2@netins.net
Patrick J. Craig; Michael A. Smith;—Lawrence B. Cutler; Carrie S. Jones.
Civil Litigation, Tax, Probate, Commercial, Domestic Relations, Real Estate, Personal Injury, Estate Planning, Corporate and School Law.
Representative Clients: Hardin County Savings Bank, Eldora, Iowa; Security State Bank, Hubbard, Iowa; Harold H. Luiken & Sons, Inc., Steamboat Rock, Iowa; Dodger Industries, Inc., Eldora, Iowa; Whink Products Co., Eldora, Iowa; Heart of Iowa Telecommunications Cooperative, Union, Iowa; BCLUW School District, Conrad, Iowa; Praire Land Cooperative, Hubbard, Iowa; Cities of New Providence, Steamboat Rock, Union and Whitten, Iowa.
Hubbard, Iowa Office: 213 East Maple. Telephone: 641-864-3338. Tuesday A.M. only.

Cutler, Lawrence B. ...'— '02 C.170 B.A. L.352 J.D. [A Craig&S.]
Dunn, David W., (AV) ...'54 '80 C.221 B.A. L.904 J.D. [D.W.Dunn] (⊙Des Moines)
Dunn, Jean McNeil, (BV) ...'54 '81 C.352 B.S. L.339 J.D. [D.W.Dunn]
Dunn, Richard N., (BV) ...'61 '87 C&L.221 B.A., J.D. [Dunn&D.]
Dunn, David W., Law Firm PLC, (AV) ...1250 Washington Street
Dunn & Dunn, P.C., (BV) ...1123 Edgington Avenue
Haywood, Harry L., (CV) ...'48 '89 C.36 L.221 J.D. 25043 X Ave.
Jones, Carrie S. ...'— '02 C.1342 B.A. L.352 J.D. [A Craig&S.]
Lundy & Butler, P.C. ...1301 Twelfth Street
Smith, Michael A., (AV) ...'58 '84 C.351 B.A. L.352 J.D. [Craig&S.]
Sween, Jim R., (BV) ...'43 '69 C&L.352 B.A., J.D. [Sween&T.]

Sween & Tilton, P.C., (BV)
1209 14th Avenue, P.O. Box 516, 50627-0516
Telephone: 641-939-5461 Fax: 641-939-2539
Jim R. Sween; Randall J. Tilton.
General Trial Practice in State and Federal Courts. Civil Litigation, Probate and Tax, Real Estate, Domestic Relations and Criminal Law.

Tilton, Randall J., (CV) ...'60 '85 C&L.352 B.A., J.D. [Sween&T.]

ELDRIDGE, 4,159, *Scott Co.*

Fairfield, Tricia Spratt ...'69 '94 C&L.352 B.S., J.D. 115 N. 6th Street Ct.

ELGIN, 637, *Fayette Co.*

Katsumes, T. David, (BV) ...'46 '77 C&L.221 B.A., J.D. 221 Center St.

ELKADER, * 1,510, *Clayton Co.*

Clefisch & Saunders, (BV) ...205 A S. Main (⊙Garnavillo)
Ehrhardt, L. J., (AV) ...'08 '32 C&L.352 B.A., J.D. 103 E. Bridge‡
Gnagy, John D., (BV) ...'46 '72 C.429 B.A. L.352 J.D. P.O. Box 306
McCorkindale, J. Steven, (BV) ...'56 '81 C.310 B.A. L.209 J.D. 103 E. Bridge St.
Saunders, Stephen D., (BV) '47 '75
C.966 B.A. L.190 J.D. Asst. Co. Atty. [Clefisch&S.] ⊙

ELKHART, 388, *Polk Co.*

Hudson, Frederick M. ...'23 '51 C.352 B.A. L.208 LL.B. 219 Main St.

ELK HORN, 672, *Shelby Co.*

Childs, Michael P., (BV) ...'45 '72 C&L.352 B.A., J.D. [Larson,C.H.&C.] ⊙
Larson, Childs, Hall & Christensen, P.C., (BV) ... Elk Horn Realty Bldg. (⊙Harlan)

ELY, 1,149, *Linn Co.*

Tjelmeland, Kurt Thomas ...'62 '88 C.162 B.A. L.1051 J.D. 1215 State St.

EMMETSBURG, * 3,940, *Palo Alto Co.*

Berkland, Roger A., (AV) ...'38 '68 C&L.352 B.B.A., J.D. [Berkland&B.]

Berkland & Brown, (AV)
2112 Main Street, 50536
Telephone: 712-852-4215 Fax: 712-852-3405
Email: berkbrow@ncn.net
Members of Firm: Roger A. Berkland; John D. Brown.
General Practice. Probate, Real Estate, Corporation and Banking Law. Trials.
Representative Clients: Iowa Trust and Savings Bank, Emmetsburg, Iowa and Cylinder, Iowa; Cities of Ayrshire and Graettinger; Farm Credit Services; Bank Plus Graettinger, Iowa.

Bormann, Donald J., (BV) ... '42 '66 C&L.793 B.A., J.D. Mun. J.
Brown, John D., (AV) ... '48 '73 C&L.352 B.A., J.D. [Berkland&B.]
Brown, Michael L., (BV) ... '49 '75 C.112 B.A. L.1049 J.D. 905 Broadway
Doran, John F., (BV) ... '35 '62 C&L.352 B.S.C., J.D. P.O. Box 552
Hanson, Joseph L., (BV) ... '26 '51 C&L.352 B.A., J.D. 1010 Bway. St.
Magee, Thomas M., (BV) ... '58 '94 C.845 B.A. L.793 J.D. 3131 W. Main St.
Perkins, Fred Blake, (CV) ... '69 '97 C.352 B.A. L.793 J.D. 905 Broadway

EPWORTH, 1,428, *Dubuque Co.*

Moonen, Donald F., (CV) ... '49 '76 C.340 B.A. L.339 J.D. 204 S. Center St.

ESTHERVILLE, * 6,720, *Emmet Co.*

Bauermeister, Scot, (CV) ... '66 '91 C.350 B.B.A. L.352 J.D. [Fitzgibbons]
Fillenwarth, Julie A., (BV) ... '53 '79 C.352 B.S. L.190 J.D. [Ⓐ Fillenwarth&F.]
Fillenwarth, Kenneth K. ... '24 '50 C&L.352 B.A., LL.B. [Fillenwarth&F.]
Fillenwarth, Lynn Kay, (BV) ... '51 '76 C.352 B.A. L.190 J.D. [Ⓐ Fillenwarth&F.]
Fillenwarth, Ruth H., (AV) ... '25 '49 C&L.352 B.A., J.D. [Fillenwarth&F.]

Fillenwarth & Fillenwarth, (AV)
104 North Seventh Street, 51334-2233
Telephone: 712-362-7701 Fax: 712-362-7703
Kenneth K. Fillenwarth; Ruth H. Fillenwarth. Associates: Lynn Kay Fillenwarth; Julie A. Fillenwarth; Richard Meyer.
General Practice. Probate, Real Estate, Estate Planning, Personal Injury and Domestic Relations Law.
Reference: Emmet County State Bank.

Fitzgibbons, Joseph L., (AV) ... '54 '79 C.861 B.A. L.352 J.D. [Fitzgibbons]

Fitzgibbons Law Firm, (AV) BB
A Partnership including a Professional Corporation
108 North Seventh Street, P.O. Box 496, 51334
Telephone: 712-362-7215 Fax: 712-362-3526
Email: jfitz@fitzgibbonslawfirm.com
Members of Firm: Leo E. Fitzgibbons (1915-2005); Francis Fitzgibbons (1924-2004); Joseph L. Fitzgibbons; Harold W. White (P.C.); Ned A. Stockdale; Scot Bauermeister; Kevin R. Sander.
General Practice in all Courts. Trials and Appeals, Personal Injury, Litigation, Insurance, Banking, Corporation, Real Estate, Probate and School Law.
See Professional Biographies, ESTHERVILLE, IOWA

Forsyth, David D., (BV) ... '57 '90 C.490 B.S. L.221 J.D. [Forsyth]
Forsyth, Gordon J., (AV) ... '28 '54 C&L.352 B.S.C., J.D. 121 North Sixth Street‡

Forsyth Law Office, (BV)
121 North Sixth Street, 51334
Telephone: 712-362-2637 Fax: 712-362-2638
Email: forlaw@rconnect.com
David D. Forsyth.
General Practice. Probate, Real Estate, Taxation, Personal Injury, Litigation and Municipal Law.
See Professional Biographies, ESTHERVILLE, IOWA

Hart, James D., (BV) ... '39 '63 C&L.221 B.S., LL.B. [Pelzer&H.]
Kauer, John A., (CV) ... '49 '95 C&L.793 B.A., J.D. 826 N. 7th St.
Lester, David A. ... '56 '91 C.56 B.A. L.352 J.D. Dist. J.
Meyer, Richard, (BV) ... '49 '76 C.793 B.A. L.352 J.D. [Ⓐ Fillenwarth&F.]
Pelzer, Max O., (BV) ... '31 '60 C&L.352 B.A., J.D. [Pelzer&H.] ⊙
Pelzer & Hart, (BV) ... 113 N. 6th St. (⊙Ringsted)
Ridout, William B., (BV) ... '38 '67 C.513 B.S. L.352 J.D. [Sanderson,R.&M.]
Sander, Kevin R. ... '75 '00 C&L.352 B.A., J.D. [Fitzgibbons]
Sanderson, William J., (BV) ... '46 '72 C.490 B.S. L.190 J.D. [Sanderson,R.&M.]
Sanderson, Ridout & Martens, (BV) ... 703 1st Ave., S.
Shadle, George H. ... '38 '62 C&L.352 B.A., J.D. V.P., North Star Bank & Agency‡
Stockdale, Ned A., (AV) ... '46 '75 C.350 B.S. L.221 J.D. [Fitzgibbons]
White, Harold W., (P.C.), (AV) ... '46 '74 C.834 B.S. L.352 J.D. [Fitzgibbons]

EXIRA, 810, *Audubon Co.*

Nelson, Robert D., (AV) ... '37 '66 C.352 B.A. L.569 J.D. [Rasmussen&N.]
Rasmussen & Nelson, (AV) ... 117 West Washington Street

FAIRFIELD, * 9,509, *Jefferson Co.*

Brown, Michael R., (BV) ... '53 '79 C.927 B.A. L.221 J.D. [Morrissey&B.]
Cameron, Gary L., (AV) ... '33 '58 C.999 B.A. L.352 J.D. [Ⓐ Foss,K.G.&C.]
Civera-Tomaselli, Caterina '64 '97 C.569 B.A. L.564 J.D.
(adm. in NY; not adm. in IA) Maharishi Univ. of Management
Cochran, Sarah W., (BV) ... '60 '85 C&L.352 B.A., J.D. [Foss,K.G.&C.]
Courtade, John, (AV) ... '49 '76 C&L.846 B.A., J.D. 504 N. 4th St., Ste. 105
Denbaum, Lewis H. '54 '83 C.415 B.S. L.352 J.D.
(adm. in DC; not adm. in IA) 1830 Prairie Rose Cir.‡
Dille, Timothy W., (BV) ... '66 '92 C.162 B.A. L.221 J.D. Co. Atty.
Foss, Craig R., (AV) ... '49 '75 C.350 B.S. L.352 J.D. [Foss,K.G.&C.]
Foss, Kuiken, Gookin & Cochran, P.C., (AV) ... First National Bank Building
Goldstein, William P. ... '50 '78 C.164 B.A. L.1049 J.D. 1811 Granville Ave.
Gookin, Myron L., (BV) ... '58 '83 C.350 B.S. L.221 J.D. [Foss,K.G.&C.]

Harrison, Moreland & Webber, P.C.
(See Ottumwa)

Johanson, Charles E. '40 '65 C&L.846 B.A., J.D.
(adm. in TX; not adm. in IA) Corp. Coun., Telegroup, Inc.
Kreglow, Alan F., Jr. '45 '76 C.273 A.B. L.128 J.D.
(adm. in DC; not adm. in IA) 1001 Oakwood Blvd.‡
Kuiken, Timothy B., (BV) ... '51 '76 C.194 B.A. L.352 J.D. [Foss,K.G.&C.]
Louden, Thomas A. ... '19 '42 C&L.352 B.A., J.D. 905 E. Adams St.‡
Makeig, Thomas H., (BV) ... '53 '82 C.999 B.A. L.569 J.D. [T.H.Makeig]
Makeig, Thomas H., P.C., (BV) ... 500 N. 3rd St., Ste. 213
Mallard, John E. ... '55 '81 C.309 A.B. L.880 J.D. 1603 Pleasant Plain Rd.
Marcus, Jay B., (AV) ... '42 '66 C.705 B.A. L.893 LL.B. 504 N. 4th St.
Miller, David P., (BV) ... '46 '74 C.208 B.A. L.352 J.D. 119 N. Court
Morrissey, John A., (BV) ... '46 '71 C.351 B.A. L.352 J.D. [Morrissey&B.]
Morrissey & Brown, (BV) ... 109 N. Court St.
Nelson, Brandon B. ... '53 '80 C&L.546 B.A., J.D. [B.Nelson]
Nelson, Brandon, P.C. ... 60 W. Burlington
Noyes, Edward F. ... '55 '85 C.546 B.S. L.352 J.D. 104 1/2 N. Main
Pearson, James D., (BV) ... '44 '74 C.352 B.A. L.45 J.D. 506 N. 4th
Rutt, Robert G., (BV) ... '54 '79 C.282 B.A. L.818 J.D. 504 N. 4th St.

Small, Stephan H., Law Office of, (BV) ... '51 '84 C.112 B.A. L.1067 J.D. P.O. Box 422
Steinberg, Robert E. '54 '80 C&L.910 B.A., J.D.
(adm. in DC; not adm. in IA) 3000 W. Gear Ave.‡
Waggpmer, Benny B. ... '45 '70 C&L.880 B.A., J.D. 2280 W. Tyler
Watkins, Nancy L. ... '44 '76 C.788 B.A. L.273 J.D. P.O. Box 155

FARLEY, 1,354, *Dubuque Co.*

Ankeny, Gary ... '42 '69 C&L.352 B.A., J.D. 104 1st St., N.W.
Davis, George A. ... '62 '93 C&L.546 B.S.B.A., J.D. P.O. Box 7
Healy, Timothy J. ... '47 '73 C.988 B.A. L.285 J.D. 207 2nd Ave., S.W.
Locher, John M., (BV) '37 '62 C.177 B.A. L.352 LL.B.
2022ndAVENUENW, POBOX7
Locher, Todd J. ... '66 '91 C&L.352 B.S., J.D. 202 2nd Ave. N.W.

FARMINGTON, 756, *Van Buren Co.*

Westercamp, Steven J., (CV) ... '67 '95 C.350 B.S. L.221 J.D. [Westercamp]
Westercamp Law Firm, (CV) ... 107 Elm St.

FAYETTE, 1,317, *Fayette Co.*

Hanson, David J., (CV) ... '61 '88 C.351 B.A. L.221 J.D. [Hofmeyer,H.&H.]
Hofmeyer, John W. D., (BV) ... '22 '53 C.350 B.S. L.352 J.D. [Hofmeyer,H.&H.]
Hofmeyer, Hurley & Hanson, P.C., (BV) ... 231 S. Main
Hurley, Charles D., (CV) ... '58 '83 C.375 B.S. L.378 J.D. [Hofmeyer,H.&H.]

FOREST CITY, 4,362, *Hancock & Winnebago Cos.*

Anderson, Timothy M.
(See Garner)

Bakke, Steven R., (BV) ... '48 '74 C.351 B.A. L.221 J.D. [Bakke&R.]
Bakke & Reiter Law Office, (BV) ... 150 North Clark
Beebe, Raymond M., (BV) '42 '67 C.350 B.S. L.352 J.D.
V.P., Gen. Coun. & Secy., Winnebago Industries, Inc.
Cooper, Elliott E., (CV) ... '24 '51 C&L.221 B.A., J.D. 145 S. Clark St.
Cooper, Michael R. ... '72 '98 C&L.221 B.S.B.A., J.D. [Cooper]
Cooper, Robert P., (BV) ... '48 '74 C&L.221 B.A., J.D. 145 S. Clark St.
Cooper Law Firm ... 145 S. Clark St.
Hagen, Terry E. '56 '94
C.898 B.A. L.793 J.D. Asst. Gen. Coun., Winnebago Industries, Inc.
Hansen, Ronald L. ... '37 '64 C&L.352 LL.B. Manufacturers Bk. & Tr. Co. Bldg.‡
Johanson, Steven L., (BV) ... '48 '73 C.350 B.S. L.352 J.D. 141 E. "K" St.
Newman, Mark A., (CV) ... '— '94 C.351 B.A. L.221 J.D. 215 S. 4th St.
Reiter, W. Alex ... '65 '99 L.1059 J.D. [Bakke&R.]
Wolters, Lynn A. ... '69 '95 C.351 B.B.A. L.300 J.D. 206 E. Park St.

FORT DODGE, * 25,136, *Webster Co.*

Bennett, Herbert R., (AV) ... '21 '48 C&L.352 B.A., J.D. [Bennett,C.&O.]
Bennett, Crimmins & Ostrander, (AV) ... 704 Central Avenue
Bice, Thomas J., (AV) ... '47 '72 C.352 B.A. L.221 J.D. [Johnson,E.B.K.G.&M.]
Breen, Fredrick E. ... '38 '64 C.821 B.A. L.145 J.D. Assoc. Dist. J.
Breen, Maurice C., (BV) ... '45 '70 C.711 B.A. L.585 J.D. Snell Bldg.
Brownlee, Mark S., (BV) ... '54 '79 C.350 B.A. L.352 J.D. [Kersten B.H.]
Cochrane, Stuart J., (BV) ... '59 '85 C.351 B.A. L.352 J.D. [Johnson,E.B.K.G.&M.]
Coleman, C. Joseph, III ... '73 '00 C.602 B.A. L.273 J.D. [Coleman&E.]
Coleman, C. Joseph, Jr. ... '46 '72 [Coleman&E.]
Coleman and Enke ... 822 Central Ave.
Cornell, Bruce E. ... '42 '67 C&L.190 B.S.B.A., J.D. 704 Central Ave.
Crimmins, Mark R., (BV) ... '61 '85 C&L.190 B.S., J.D. [Bennett,C.&O.]
Crumley, David D., (AV) ... '31 '60 C&L.352 B.S.C., J.D. [Crumley&J.]
Crumley & Jacobs, (AV) ... 805 Central Avenue
Driscoll, Darren D. ... '76 '03 C&L.352 B.B.A., J.D. [Ⓐ Johnson,E.B.K.G.&M.]
Eide, Eric J., (BV) ... '63 '88 C.350 B.S. L.352 J.D. [Johnson,E.B.K.G.&M.]
Enke, William G., (BV) ... '47 '75 C&L.352 B.B.A., J.D. [Enke]
Enke Law Office, (BV) ... 822 Central Ave., Ste. 340
Estes, Jerry C., (BV) ... '42 '66 C.106 L.352 LL.B. [Estes]
Estes Law Offices, (BV) ... Suite 400, Boston Centre
Fisher, Monty L., (BV) ... '49 '74 C.1270 B.A. L.744 J.D. 200 Snell Bldg.
Fitchett, Rhonda, (BV) ... '60 '85 C.106 B.A. L.352 J.D. Asst. Co. Atty.
Fitzgerald, James E., (BV) '58 '84 C.177 B.A. L.190 J.D.
805 Central Avenue, Suite 403
Gailey, John W. ... '34 '62 C.106 A.B. L.352 J.D. 704 Central Ave.
Good, William J., (AV) ... '50 '77 C.350 B.S. L.352 J.D. [Johnson,E.B.K.G.&M.]
Goode, Allan L. ... '41 '66 C&L.352 B.A., J.D. Dist. J.
Guinan, Terry W. ... '36 '62 C&L.352 B.A., J.D. 12 N. 7th St.‡
Habhab, Albert L. ... '25 '52 C&L.352 B.A., LL.B. App. Ct. J.‡
Habhab, William H., (BV) ... '55 '80 C.352 B.A. L.221 J.D. 1216-A Central Ave.
Hamilton, Howard D., (BV) ... '25 '52 C&L.352 B.A., J.D. 805 Central Ave.
Hanson, Rebecca J. ... '57 '95 C.958 L.221 J.D. 811 N. 14th St.
Hendricks, Steven W., (AV) ... '57 '82 C.352 B.A. L.221 J.D. [Kersten B.H.]
Jacobs, Rolland B., (BV) ... '39 '66 C.350 B.S. L.813 J.D. [Crumley&J.]
Johnson, Arthur H., (AV) ... '21 '48 C&L.352 A.B., J.D. [Ⓒ Johnson,E.B.K.G.&M.]

Johnson, Erb, Bice, Kramer, Good & Mulholland, P.C., (AV)
600 Boston Centre, 809 Central Avenue, P.O. Box 1396, 50501-1396 ⊙
Telephone: 515-573-2181 Fax: 515-573-2548
URL: http://www.lawyers.com/jebkgmlawfirm
Dean P. Erb (Gowrie Office); Thomas J. Bice; James L. Kramer; William J. Good; Neven J. Mulholland; Stuart J. Cochrane; Eric J. Eide. Associate: Darren D. Driscoll. Of Counsel: Arthur H. Johnson.
General Practice Before all State and Federal Courts. Personal Injury, Corporation, Utility, Labor, Insurance, Real Estate and Probate Law. Trials and Appeals.
Representative Clients: Cigna Property & Casualty Co.; Farmland Mutual Insurance Co. New Cooperative, Inc.; Trinity Regional Hospital; First American Bank Group, Ltd.; First Federal Savings Bank; Iowa Commodities, Ltd.; Trimark Physicians Group.
Gowrie, Iowa Office: 1103 Market Street. Telephone: 515-352-3111. Fax: 515-352-3113.
See Professional Biographies, FORT DODGE, IOWA

Kelley, Thos. X. ... '23 '50 C&L.276 A.B., J.D. 1312 13th Ave., N.‡
Kersten, Ernest '57 '85 C.221 B.B.A. L.352 J.D.
(adm. in TX; not adm. in IA) 805 Central Ave., Ste. 403
Kersten, Stephen G., (AV) ... '53 '80 C.276 B.S. L.221 J.D. [Kersten B.H.]

Kersten Brownlee Hendricks, LLP, (AV)
Snell Building, 805 Central Avenue, Seventh Floor, P.O. Box 957, 50501
Telephone: 515-576-4127 Fax: 515-576-6340
Email: brownlee@frontiernet.net URL: http://www.kerstenbrownleehendricks.com
Members of Firm: Don N. Kersten (1925-1998); Stephen G. Kersten; Mark S. Brownlee; Steven W. Hendricks.
General Practice. Personal Injury Law, Corporation, Insurance Defense, Workers Compensation, Bankruptcy, Banking, Probate and Estate Planning and Taxation Law. Trials.

(This Listing Continued)

Kersten Brownlee Hendricks, LLP (Continued)

Representative Clients: Employers Mutual Cos.; Allied Insurance Co.; Mutual Fire & Auto; Kemper Group; Farm Bureau Mutual Insurance Company; CNA; Auto-Owners Insurance Co.; Heritage Insurance Company; American Family Insurance; Norwest Bank.

See Professional Biographies, FORT DODGE, IOWA

Koll, James J., (BV) ....'54 '79 C.350 B.A. L.221 J.D. Chief Local Pub. Def.
Kramer, James L., (BV) ....'48 '73 C.813 B.A. L.494 J.D. [Johnson,E.B.K.G.&M.]
Larson, Ann A. ....'35 '89 C.350 B.S. L.190 J.D. 2706 4th Ave., N.
Lose, Thomas J., (BV) ....'27 '53 C&L.436 B.S., LL.B. 617 1st Ave., N.
Martin, Robert A. '11 '37 C&L.352 B.A., J.D.
(adm. in MN; not adm. in IA) 2510 19th Ave. N.‡
McCarthy, James W., (CV) ....'50 '82 C.477 A.B. L.221 J.D. [McCarthy]
McCarthy Law Office, (CV) ....306 Snell Bldg.
McCarville, Joseph B., (CV) ....'62 '89 C.350 B.S. L.352 J.D. 1039 N. 19th St.
McGrevey, Dan T., (BV) .... '45 '73 C.352 B.B.A. L.190 J.D. [McGrevey]
McGrevey Law Office, (BV) ....142 N. 9th St.
Mulholland, Neven J., (BV) ......'53 '79 C.793 B.S. L.190 J.D. [Johnson,E.B.K.G.&M.]
Osborn-Williamson, Ricki L. ....'72 '98 C.352 B.A. L.190 J.D. Off. of Co. Atty.
Ostrander, Angela J., (CV) ....'60 '84 C&L.190 B.S.B.A., J.D. [Bennett,C.&O.]
Parker, Blake, Law Office of, (BV) '49 '78
C.352 B.A. L.365 J.D. 809 Central Ave., Ste. 350
Pearson, Jeane W., (CV) ....'— '82 C.350 B.A. L.502 J.D. [Price&P.]
Perkins, John M., (BV) ....'49 '75 C.424 B.A. L.221 J.D. [Perkins]
Perkins Law Office, (BV) ....300 Norwest Ctr.
Peters, John M. ....'27 '51 C&L.352 B.A., J.D. 1236 11th Ave. N.‡
Peters, Merrell M., (CV) ....'50 '84 C.293 B.A. L.221 J.D. P.O. Box 336
Pittner, Kurt T., (BV) ....'50 '76 C.627 B.A. L.190 J.D. 805 Central Ave., Ste. 503
Price, R. Thomas, (BV) ....'37 '63 C.351 B.A. L.352 J.D. [Price&P.]
Price & Pearson, (BV) ....805 Central Avenue

Schnurr, Jerry L., III, (BV) '60 '86 C&L.352 B.B.A., J.D.
403 Snell Building, 805 Central Avenue, P.O. Box 953, 50501-0953
Telephone: 515-576-3977 Fax: 515-576-0941
Email: schnurlw@frontiernet.net URL: http://www.iowainjurylawfirm.com
General Trial Practice in all State and Federal Courts, Personal Injury, Workers Compensation, Insurance, Probate and Real Estate Law.

Sergeant, David A., (AV) ....'45 '70 C.747 B.A. L.221 J.D. [D.A.Sergeant]
Sergeant, David A., P.C., (AV) ....1728 Central Avenue, Suite 3
Thatcher, William J., (BV) ....'48 '72 C.350 B.S. L.352 J.D. 136 N. 9th St.
Thomas, Reynolds B., (AV) ....'15 '39 C.118 A.B. L.352 J.D. P.O. Box 1256‡
Thompson, Lisa M. ....'55 '80 C&L.221 B.A., J.D. 804 Wraywood Dr.
Trevino, Tito W., (AV) ....'47 '74 C.602 B.A. L.221 J.D. Suite 801, Carver Bldg.
Valentine, Janece M., (BV) ....'67 '92 C.221 B.A. L.352 J.D. [Valentine]
Valentine Law Office, (BV) ....809 Central Avenue
Walker, Charles A. ....'46 '84 C.350 B.S. L.221 J.D. [Walker]
Walker, Robert E., (CV) ....'48 '86 C.106 B.A. L.221 J.D. [Walker]
Walker Law Office, P.C., (CV) ....M-38 Warden Pl.
Wilke, Kurt L. ....'49 '74 C.494 B.A. L.585 J.D. Dist. J.

FORT MADISON, * 10,715, *Lee Co.*

Beckman and Hirsch
(See Burlington)

Eschman, Elaine Fehseke, (BV) ....'72 '98 C.880 B.A. L.464 J.D. [Fehseke&E.]
Fahey, R. David ....'49 '75 C&L.602 B.A., J.D. Dist. J.
Fehseke, R. L., Jr., (AV) ....'44 '68 C&L.352 B.A., J.D. [Fehseke&E.]
Fehseke, Richard L., III, (BV) ....'68 '94 C.880 B.A. L.352 J.D. [Fehseke&E.]

Fehseke & Eschman Law Offices, (AV)
1023 Avenue G, 52627
Telephone: 319-372-7181 FAX: 319-372-7185
Email: info@fehsekelaw.com URL: http://www.fehsekelaw.com
Members of Firm: R. L. Fehseke (1918-1985); R. L. Fehseke, Jr.; Richard L. Fehseke, III; Elaine Fehseke Eschman.
General Civil Practice including Trials and Appeals, Personal Injury, Probate, Real Estate, Workers Compensation Law, Maritime Law, Medical Malpractice, Products Liability, Trusts and Estates, Estate Planning, and Elder Law.

See Professional Biographies, FORT MADISON, IOWA

Glaser, Robert J., (CV) ....'49 '78 C.985 B.A. L.190 J.D. IA State Penetentiary
Gordon, Toby J., (BV) ....'69 '98 C.351 B.A. L.221 J.D. [Ⓐ G.Hoyer]
Hoyer, Gary L., (BV) ....'58 '83 C.602 B.B.A. L.352 J.D. [G.Hoyer]
Hoyer, Gary, Law Firm, P.L.C., (BV) ....619 10th Street
Humphrey, Gregory J., (CV) ....'52 '77 C.350 B.S. L.190 J.D. [Saunders,H.&J.]
Johnson, Gregory A., (BV) ....'51 '77 C.742 B.A. L.221 J.D. [Johnson&S.]
Johnson, Robert N., III, (CV) ....'43 '71 C.686 A.B. L.221 J.D. [Saunders,H.&J.]
Johnson & Skewes, Law Offices of, (BV) ....516 7th St.
Kamp, Joel J. ....'44 '70 C.352 B.A. L.500 J.D. Assoc. Dist. J.
Napier, Douglas H., (BV) ....'63 '90 C&L.352 B.B.A., J.D. [Napier,W.&N.]
Napier, William H., (AV) ....'36 '59 C&L.352 B.A., J.D. [Napier,W.&N.]
Napier, Wolf & Napier, (AV) ....607 Eighth Street, Suite 1
Popejoy, Christy L., (CV) ....'51 '98 C.927 B.A. L.352 J.D. [Napier,W.&N.]
Sallen, David U., (CV) ....'52 '77 C.707 B.A. L.352 J.D. Chf. Pub. Def.
Saunders, Carl A., (BV) ....'40 '67 C&L.352 B.B.A., J.D. [Saunders,H.&J.]
Saunders, Humphrey & Johnson, LLP, (BV) ....627 Ave. G
Skewes, Thomas T., (BV) ....'44 '73 C.352 B.A. L.221 J.D. [Johnson&S.]
Werner, Kathleen M., (CV) ....'70 '95 C.352 B.B.A. L.221 J.D. 619 10th St.
Wolf, Lloyd H., (BV) ....'37 '71 C.587 B.S. L.352 J.D. [Napier,W.&N.]
Wright, George E., (AV) ....'34 '60 C&L.352 B.A., J.D. [Wright]
Wright, John M., (BV) ....'64 '90 C.352 B.A. L.221 J.D. [Wright]
Wright Law Firm, (AV) ....532 Avenue F

GARNAVILLO, 727, *Clayton Co.*

Clefisch, Kevin H., (BV) ....'49 '74 C.898 B.A. L.352 J.D. [Clefisch&S.]
Clefisch & Saunders, (BV) ....108 South Main Street (⊙Elkader)
Saunders, Stephen D., (BV) '47 '75
C.966 B.A. L.190 J.D. Asst. Co. Atty. [Clefisch&S.] ⊙

GARNER, * 2,916, *Hancock Co.*

Anderson, Timothy M., (BV) '58 '84 C&L.352 B.A., J.D.
165 East 4th Street, 50438
Telephone: 641-923-2769 Fax: 641-923-0016
General Practice, Agricultural Law, Premarital Agreements, Long Term Care, Medicare and Medicaid, Probate, Real Estate, Commercial Real Estate, Condominium Law, Landlord and Tenant Law

(This Listing Continued)

Anderson, Timothy M. (Continued)

and Mortgages, Taxation, Estate and Gift Taxation and Income Tax, Wills, Trusts and Estates, Asset Protection, Charitable Giving, Estate Planning, Guardianship, Trusts and Estates and Wills.
Reference: Liberty Bank.

Berge, B. C., (AV) ....'13 '36 C.427 750 W. Lyon St.‡
Garland, Philip L., (BV) ....'45 '73 C&L.190 B.A., J.D. 200 State St. (⊙Mason City)
Hovda, Theodore J. ....'51 '77 C.350 B.S. L.352 J.D. Co. Atty. [Hovda]
Hovda Law Office ....395 State St.
Pronk, Thomas F., (BV) ....'47 '75 C&L.221 B.A., J.D. 190 East Fifth Street
Templeton, G. W., (AV) ....'18 '42 C.352 L.221 LL.B. 190 E. 5th St.‡
Wetterling, James A. ....'63 '98 C.350 B.S. L.221 J.D. [Wetterling]
Wetterling Law Office ....275 State St.

GILMORE CITY, 560, *Humboldt & Pocahontas Cos.*

Stoebe, Gregory H., (BV) ....'50 '76 C.352 B.A. L.300 J.D. [Stoebe] ⊙
Stoebe Law Office, (BV) ....407 S. Gilmore St. (⊙Livermore)

GLADBROOK, 1,015, *Tama Co.*

Livingston, John S., (BV) ....'43 '68 C.350 B.S. L.352 J.D. 710 King St.

GLENWOOD, * 5,358, *Mills Co.*

Beattie, Brian F. ....'61 '86 C.350 B.S. L.190 J.D. 211 N. Locust★
Bird-Sell, DeShawne L. ....'69 '00 C.627 B.A. L.190 J.D. [D.L.Bird-Sell]
Bird-Sell, DeShawne L., P.C. ....21386 Howley Rd.
Dean, John C. ....'25 '54 C&L.546 B.S., J.D. Pres., Glenwood State Bk.

Eaton, Edward E. (Gene)
(See Sidney)

McGee, Glen M. ....'27 '55 C.351 B.A. L.352 J.D. Dist. J.

Peters Law Firm, P.C., (AV)
10 North Walnut, 51534 ⊙
Telephone: 712-527-4877 FAX: 712-527-3418
URL: http://www.peterslawfirm.com
James A. Thomas; Matthew G. Woods;—Justin R. Wyatt.
Personal Injury Litigation and Commercial Litigation. Insurance, Tax, Real Estate, Corporation, Probate and Bankruptcy Law.
Representative Clients: Bluffs Run Casino; Grinnell Mutual Reinsurance Co.; Iowa West Racing Association; Rockwell International; Shelter Insurance; State Farm Insurance; Kemper Group; The Pillsbury Co.; The Cities of Crescent, Glenwood, Treynor, McClelland, Underwood.
Council Bluffs, Iowa Office: 233 Pearl Street. P.O. Box 1078. Telephone: 712-328-3157. FAX: 712-328-9092.
Neola, Iowa Office: 401 Front Street, P.O. Box 282. Telephone: 712-485-2265.
South Omaha, Nebraska Office: 4828 South 24th Street, Suite 200, 68107. Telephone: 402-731-1711. Fax: 402-731-3363.

See Professional Biographies, GLENWOOD, IOWA

Swenson, Richard C., (BV) ....'47 '78 C.546 L.190 J.D. [Swenson&W.]
Swenson & Whitacre, (BV) ....26 North Walnut St.
Thomas, James A., (AV) ....'42 '67 C.513 B.S. L.352 J.D. [Peters] (⊙Council Bluffs)
Webering, James C., (BV) ....'52 '79 C.352 B.A. L.861 J.D. P.O. Box 28
Whitacre, C. Kenneth, (CV) ....'50 '77 C.350 B.A. L.352 J.D. [Swenson&W.]
Woods, Matthew G., (BV) ... '66 '93 C.352 B.B.A. L.190 J.D. [Peters] (⊙Council Bluffs)
Wyatt, Justin R. ....'75 '03 C&L.190 B.S, J.D. [Ⓐ Peters] (⊙Council Bluffs)

GLIDDEN, 1,253, *Carroll Co.*

Beltz, John A. ....'51 '77 C.350 B.S. L.352 J.D. P.O. Box 467‡
Hall, Patrick W., (CV) ....'56 '83 C.190 B.S.B.A. L.352 J.D. [Hall]
Hall Law Office, (CV) ....118 Idaho Street
Snook, Raymond O., (BV) ....'40 '72 C.1060 B.A. L.221 J.D. Hwy. 30., W.

GOLDFIELD, 710, *Wright Co.*

Malloy, Robert P., (BV) ....'48 '74 C.352 B.A. L.221 J.D. [Malloy] ⊙

Malloy Law Firm, (BV)
Professional Services Building, 503 Main Street, P.O. Box 128, 50542 ⊙
Telephone: 515-825-3181 Fax: 515-825-3898
Email: malloy@goldfieldaccess.net
Robert P. Malloy. Associate: Lynn Collins Seaba.
General Trial and Appellate Practice Before State and Federal Courts and Administrative Agencies, Agricultural, Corporate, Insurance, Personal Injury, Real Estate, Probate, Estate Planning Law.
Representative Clients: Security Savings Bank; Gold-Eagle Coop; Goldfield Telephone Co.; Grinnell Mutual Insurance Co.; Oakridge Farms, Inc.; Murphy of Iowa, Inc.; Poky Feeders, Inc.; Hoffman-Rettig Foods, Inc.; Stratford Telephone Co.; Ennis Corporation.
West Des Moines, Iowa Office: 6935 Vista Drive, 50266. Telephone: 515-457-8501.

See Professional Biographies, GOLDFIELD, IOWA

Seaba, Lynn Collins ....'69 '96 C.280 B.S.A. L.221 J.D. [Ⓐ Malloy]

GOOSE LAKE, 274, *Clinton Co.*

Farrell, Brian R., Attorney at Law, (BV) ......'72 '98 C.707 B.A. L.352 J.D. P.O. Box 56

GOWRIE, 1,028, *Webster Co.*

Erb, Dean P., (BV) ....'40 '65 C&L.352 B.B.A., LL.B. [Johnson,E.B.K.G.&M.]
Johnson, Erb, Bice, Kramer, Good & Mulholland, P.C., (AV)
1103 Market St. (⊙Fort Dodge)

GRAND JUNCTION, 964, *Greene Co.*

Eichhorn, George S., (AV) ....'54 '80 C&L.221 B.A., J.D. Rueter's Red Power, Inc.

GREENE, 1,142, *Butler Co.*

Vickers, Patrick G., (BV) ....'53 '89 C.352 B.A. L.1035 J.D. [Vickers]
Vickers, Richard, (BV) ....'45 '74 C&L.352 B.B.A., J.D. [Vickers]
Vickers Law Office, (BV) ....118 First St., S.

GREENFIELD, * 2,074, *Adair Co.*

Emerson, Karen K., (BV) ....'51 '91 C.999 B.A. L.221 J.D. 113 W. Iowa St.
Hight, Clint, (BV) ....'58 '83 C.352 B.S. L.221 J.D. [C.Hight]
Hight, Clint, P.C., (BV) ....164 Public Square
Howe, Jay E., (AV) ....'40 '66 C&L.352 B.A., J.D. [Howe&O.]
Howe & Olesen, (AV) ....230 Public Square
Hughbanks, Amy ....'75 '03 C.350 B.S. L.190 J.D. 113 W. Iowa St.
Jensen, Steven A., (BV) ....'49 '74 C.352 B.B.A. L.190 J.D. 110 Public Sq.
Maynes, Michael ....'64 '00 C.106 B.S. L.190 J.D. 110 Public Sq.
Olesen, Willard W., (AV) ....'47 '76 C&L.352 B.B.A., J.D. [Howe&O.]
Wietzke, John E., (BV) '37 '72
C.350 B.S.M.S. L.352 J.D. Gen. Coun., Farmers Elec. Coop.

GRIMES, 5,098, *Polk Co.*

Brown, Ralph R., (AV) ....'44 '69 C&L.221 B.A., J.D. [McDonald,B.&F.] ⊙
Fagen, Charles H., (BV) ....'60 '86 C&L.221 B.S., J.D. [McDonald,B.&F.] ⊙

McDonald, Brown & Fagen, (AV) .... 306 S. 1st St. (⊙Dallas Center)
Noble, Gregory Scott, (BV) .... '61 '88 C&L.190 B.A., J.D. P.O. Box 145
Raisch, William F., (AV) ....'49 '74 C&L.221 B.S., J.D. Gen. Coun., Ryko Mfg. Co.
Rouse, Benjamin L. .... '80 '05 C.350 B.S. L.878 J.D. [🄰 McDonald,B.&F.] ⊙

GRINNELL, 9,105, *Poweshiek Co.*

Bierman, John F. (Rick), III, (AV) ....'44 '69 C.293 B.A. L.352 J.D. [Bierman&B.]
Bierman & Bierman, P.C., (AV) .... 920 Main Street
Boliver, Gail E., (BVⓉ) ....'49 '79 C.350 B.S. L.190 J.D. [Boliver] ⊙
Boliver Law Firm, (BVⓉ).............717 5th Avenue (⊙Marshalltown, IA; Omaha, NE)
Booker, Trisha L. '76 '02 C.1119 B.A. L.838 J.D.
(adm. in GA; not adm. in IA) [🄰 Brierly C.] (⊙Newton)
Borchert, Kristin L. ....'67 '95 C&L.352 B.A., J.D. Coun., Grinnell Mut. Reins. Co.
Brierly Charnetski L.L.P., (AV) .... 1022 Broad Street (⊙Newton, Sully)
Chalupa, Dennis F., (AV) ....'44 '70 C.641 B.A. L.352 J.D. [Brierly C.] ⊙
Charnetski, Donald J., (BV) ....'47 '75 C.966 B.A. L.352 J.D. [Brierly C.] (⊙Newton)
Clower, Robert P., III ....'60 '96 C.103 A.B. L.93 J.D. [🄰 Brierly C.] (⊙Newton)
Day, Dennis G. .... '49 '76 C&L.221 B.S.E., J.D. Gen. Coun., Grinnell Mut. Reins. Co.
Kendrick, John A. .... '56 '81 C&L.339 B.A., J.D. Sr. Coun., Grinnell Mut. Reins. Co.
Lacina, Thomas A., (BV) ....'56 '83 C.942 B.A. L.352 J.D. [🄲 Brierly C.] (⊙Newton)
Lahn, Peter D. .... '63 '94 C.339 B.A. L.64 J.D. Coun., Grinnell Mut. Reins. Co.
Lamb, Dale A., (CV) ....'55 '81 C.293 A.B. L.221 J.D. 717 5th Ave.
Manly, C. M., (AV) ....'28 '51 C&L.221 J.D. City Atty. [Manly]
Manly, Charles M., III, (AV) .... '50 '76 C.784 B.A. L.300 J.D. [Manly]
Manly Law Firm, (AV) ....720 4th Ave.
McCall, Bradley, (BV) ....'54 '79 C.352 B.S. L.221 J.D. [Brierly C.] ⊙
McElderry, Stanley R. ..... '62 '88 C.1281 B.A. L.352 J.D. Admin. Law J., Dept. of Corrs.
McKinney, John, III '72 '97
C.132 B.A. L.221 J.D. Coun, Grinnell Mutual Reinsurance Co.
Michaels, Eric M. ..... '47 '76 C.415 B.A. L.851 J.D. Sr. Coun., Grinnell Mut. Reins. Co.
Munyon, Wendy N. '49 '75 C.914 B.A. L.245 J.D.
(adm. in GA; not adm. in IA) Assoc. Gen. Coun., Grinnell Mut. Reins. Co.
Olson, William D., (BV) ....'47 '81 C&L.352 B.A., J.D. [Brierly C.] (⊙Newton)
Otto, Mark A., (BV) ....'56 '82 C.800 B.A. L.221 J.D. [Brierly C.] ⊙
Pinder, Peggy ....'53 '80 C.187 B.A. L.976 J.D. Iowa Assn. For The Blind
Schild, Donald L., (BV) .... '44 '69 C&L.352 B.A., J.D. 833 Broad St.
Stewart, Michael R. .... '44 '73 C.293 B.A. L.846 J.D. Assoc. Dist. J.
Terpstra, John H., (BV) ....'59 '92 C.350 B.S. L.352 J.D. [Brierly C.] ⊙
Vroom, Lois J., (CV) ....'68 '94 C.132 B.A. L.352 J.D. [🄰 Brierly C.] (⊙Newton)

GRISWOLD, 1,049, *Cass Co.*

Cambridge, Feilmeyer, Landsness, Chase & Jones, P.L.C., (AV)
206 Montgomery St. (⊙Atlantic)
Feilmeyer, Ronald W., (AV) ......'38 '66 C&L.352 B.A., LL.B. [Cambridge,F.L.C.&J.] ⊙

GRUNDY CENTER, * 2,596, *Grundy Co.*

Goodman, Charles I. ....'23 '50 C.352 L.221 J.D. 627 G Ave.
Harris, Bradley J., (BV) ....'55 '81 C.177 B.S. L.352 J.D. [Kliebenstein,H.S.&H.]
Heronimus, Thomas J., (AV) ..... '37 '62 C.352 B.A. L.221 J.D. [Kliebenstein,H.S.&H.]
Kliebenstein, Don, (AV) ....'36 '61 C&L.352 B.A., J.D. [Kliebenstein,H.S.&H.]

Kliebenstein, Heronimus, Schmidt & Harris, (AV)
630 G Avenue, Box 365, 50638
Telephone: 319-824-6951 Fax: 319-824-6953
Email: khshlaw@gcmuni.net
Don Kliebenstein; Thomas J. Heronimus; Kirby D. Schmidt; Bradley J. Harris.
General and Trial Practice, Probate, Real Estate, Family Law, Insurance, Corporation, Banking, Taxation, Personal Injury, Agricultural and Commercial Law.
Counsel for: Grundy National Bank, Grundy Center; City of Grundy Center; Grundy Center Community Schools; Kruger Seed Co.
Local Counsel for: NCM Ltd Partnership; First State Bank, Conrad, Iowa; Peoples Savings Bank, Wellsburg, Iowa.

Monk, Gerald R., (BV) ....'42 '72 C&L.352 B.A., J.D. [Monk]
Monk Law Office, (BV) .... 308 E. G Ave., Suite 2
Schmidt, Kirby D., (BV) ....'46 '73 C.350 B.S. L.352 J.D. [Kliebenstein,H.S.&H.]

GUTHRIE CENTER, * 1,614, *Guthrie Co.*

Baxter, Joel ....'72 '03 C.350 B.S. L.221 J.D. [🄰 B.Wild]
Cramer, Valerie ....'48 '03 C.145 B.A. L.589 J.D. [🄰 Taylor&F.]
Feilmeyer, Robert E., (AV) ....'38 '63 C&L.352 B.A., LL.B. [Taylor&F.]
Hasbrouck, Richard L. .... '24 '53 C.352 B.A. L.221 LL.B. 701 North St.
Sand, Christine L. ....'71 '03 C.513 B.A. L.221 J.D. [🄰 B.Wild]
Taylor & Feilmeyer, P.L.C., (AV) .... 207 N. 5th Street
Wild, Beverly, (BV) ....'43 '87 C&L.221 B.S., J.D. [B.Wild]

Wild, Beverly, Law Office, P.C., (BV)
105 South Fourth Street, 50115
Telephone: 641-332-2900 Toll Free 888-554-3214 Fax: 641-332-2903
Email: wildlaw@netins.net URL: http://www.lawyers.com/wild
Beverly Wild;—Joel Baxter; Christine L. Sand.
Family, Divorce, Guardianships, Juvenile, Real Estate, Probate and Estate Planning and Criminal Law.
See Professional Biographies, GUTHRIE CENTER, IOWA

GUTTENBERG, 1,987, *Clayton Co.*

Degnan, L. John ....'14 '41 C&L.352 B.A., J.D. Sr. Dist. J.
Mick, Gary L., (BV) ....'51 '76 C.187 B.A. L.190 J.D. [Schuster&M.]
Schuster, Michael J., (BV) ....'48 '74 C.177 B.A. L.190 J.D. [Schuster&M.]
Schuster & Mick, (BV) .... 318 S. River Pk. Dr.

HAMPTON, * 4,133, *Franklin Co.*

Allbee, Richard A., (BV) ....'44 '69 C&L.221 B.A., J.D. ABCN Corp.
Blum, Lee B., (BV) ....'17 '48 C&L.352 B.S., J.D. 116 First Ave., N.W.‡
Cady, G. A., III, (AV) ....'52 '77 C&L.221 B.A., J.D. [Hobson,C.&C.]
Cady, G. Arthur, (AV) ....'26 '52 C.352 B.A. L.221 J.D. [Hobson,C.&C.]
Carroll, Stephen P. .... '46 '77 C.293 B.A. L.221 J.D. Co. J.
Coonley, James E. ....'10 '34 City Atty.
Coonley, John E., (BV) ....'57 '82 C&L.36 B.S., J.D. 121 First Ave., N.W.
Cross, Michael J., (BV) ....'43 '73 C.350 B.S. L.352 J.D. 117 1st Ave. N.W.
Drew, Raymond P., (AV) .... '30 '60 C&L.352 B.S., J.D. [Drew&M.]
Drew & Miller, P.C., (AV) ....320 Central Ave. E.

Hobson, Cady & Cady, (AV)
9 First Street S.W., P.O. Box 456, 50441
Telephone: 641-456-2555 Fax: 641-456-3315
Email: cadyart@rconnect.com
Members of Firm: A. J. Hobson (1903-1972); G. Arthur Cady; G. A. Cady, III.
General Practice in State and Federal Courts. Trials and Appeals. Insurance and Probate Law.
General Counsel for: Ag Services of America, Inc.
A list of Representative Clients will be furnished upon request.

(This Listing Continued)

Hobson, Cady & Cady (Continued)
References: First National Bank of Hampton; Commercial Federal.
See Professional Biographies, HAMPTON, IOWA

Miller, Brian D., (CV) ....'71 '96 C&L.352 B.A., J.D. [Drew&M.]
Swenson, Stephen James ....'67 '93 C.351 B.A. L.221 J.D. P.O. Box 397
Wiechmann, Daniel F., Jr., (CV) ....'49 '74 C.350 B.S. L.221 J.D. P.O. Box 513

HARCOURT, 306, *Webster Co.*

Fors, Kevin A., (CV) ....'56 '86 C.106 B.S. L.221 J.D. P.O. Box 366

HARLAN, * 5,282, *Shelby Co.*

Childs, Michael P., (BV) ....'45 '72 C&L.352 B.A., J.D. [Larson,C.&H.] ⊙
Christensen-Mores, Donna '56 '85 C.350 B.S. L.190 J.D.
Dir., Human Res., Myrtue Memorial Hospital
Deren, Patrick T., (AV) '47 '75
C.801 B.A. L.838 J.D. [Salvo,D.S.&L.] (⊙Earling, Panama)
Hall, Robert W., (BV) ....'51 '76 C.352 B.B.S. L.190 J.D. [Larson,C.&H.]
Larson, Jeffrey L., (BV) ....'60 '85 C.793 B.S. L.352 J.D. [Larson,C.&H.]
Larson, Childs & Hall, P.C., (BV) .... 1005 7th St. (⊙Elk Horn)
Lauterbach, Joseph C., (BV) ....'53 '80 C.187 B.S.S. L.352 J.D. [Salvo,D.S.&L.] ⊙
Lewis, William O., (AV) ....'21 '48 C.597 B.S. L.352 J.D. 711 Court St.‡
Louis, Fred, Jr., (AV) ....'10 '34 C.378 B.S. L.352 J.D. 602 Market St. Bldg.‡
Louis, John C., (BV) ....'40 '78 C.31 B.A. L.184 J.D. 602 Market St.
Pechacek, Frank W., Jr., (AV) ....'44 '69 C.351 B.A. L.352 J.D. [Willson&P.] ⊙
Salvo, J. C., (AV) .... '47 '72 C&L.190 J.D. [Salvo,D.S.&L.]

Salvo, Deren, Schenck & Lauterbach, P.C., (AV)
711 Court Street, P.O. Box 509, 51537 ⊙
Telephone: 712-755-3141 Fax: 712-755-3144
URL: http://www.sdslaw.com
J. C. Salvo; Patrick T. Deren; Richard C. Schenck; Joseph C. Lauterbach;—Bryan D. Swain.
General Practice. Commercial, Family, Negligence, Corporation, Real Estate, Tax and Probate Law. Trials, Civil and Criminal.
Earling, Iowa Office: 122 Main. Telephone: 712-747-6191.
Panama, Iowa Office: 100 Main. Telephone: 712-489-2424.
Walnut, Iowa Office: 301 Antique City Drive. Telephone: 712-784-3907.
Woodbine, Iowa Office: 414 Walker. Telephone: 712-647-3269.
See Professional Biographies, HARLAN, IOWA

Schenck, Richard C., (BV) ..... '53 '78 C&L.352 B.A., J.D. [Salvo,D.S.&L.] (⊙Walnut)
Sojka, Kenneth W., (BV) ....'37 '69 C&L.352 B.B.A., J.D. 1121 7th St.
Swain, Bryan D. ....'75 '00 C.999 B.A. L.352 J.D. [🄰 Salvo,D.S.&L.]
Willson & Pechacek, P.L.C., (AV)
1121 7th Street (⊙Carroll, Council Bluffs, Oakland, Red Oak, Treynor)

HARTLEY, 1,733, *O'Brien Co.*

Cmelik, Dennis, (BV) ....'51 '76 C.513 B.A. L.221 J.D. Asst. Co. Atty.
Sease, Randall G., (BV) ....'54 '85 C.350 B.S. L.221 J.D. 147 S. Central

HAWARDEN, 2,439, *Sioux Co.*

Gubbrud, John D., (BVⓉ) .... '41 '66 C&L.793 B.S., J.D. [Gubbrud&H.] (⊙Alcester, SD)
Gubbrud & Haugland, (BV) .... 800 Central Ave.
Haugland, Charles B., (BV) '50 '75 C.56 B.A. L.793 J.D.
[Gubbrud&H.] (⊙Alcester, SD)
Pickner, James H., (BV) ....'52 '95 C&L.793 B.S., J.D. [Pickner]
Pickner Law Office, P.C., (BV) ....P.O. Box 113
Slife, E. V., Jr., (AV) '21 '50 C&L.793 B.A., J.D.
V.P. & Trust Offr., Farmers State Bk.

HIAWATHA, 6,480, *Linn Co.*

Eells & Tronvold Law Offices, P.L.C.
(See Cedar Rapids)

Peterson, Clifford E. ....'21 '51 C&L.352 B.A., J.D. Farm Bur. Ins.

HILLS, 662, *Johnson Co.*

Cilek, Thomas J. ....'46 '72 C&L.352 B.B.A., J.D. Sr. V.P., Hills Bk. & Tr. Co.
Honohan, Jay H., (BV) '30 '60 C.350 B.S. L.352 J.D.
[🄲 Honohan,E.B.&B.] (⊙Iowa City)
Honohan, Epley, Braddock & Brenneman, (BV)
Main St. (⊙Iowa City, Kalona, Lone Tree)

HOLSTEIN, 1,449, *Ida Co.*

Cosgrove, Thaddeus E., (AV) '59 '84 C.352 B.A. L.190 J.D.
102 North Main, P.O. Box 50, 51025-0050 ⊙
Telephone: 712-368-2616 Fax: 712-368-2389
Email: cosgrovelaw@netllc.net
General Civil Trial Practice. Probate, Personal Injury, Insurance Defense and Corporate Law.
Ida Grove, Iowa Office: 607 W Second Street, 51445. Telephone: 712-364-4138. Fax: 712-364-4445.
Email: tcosgroveig@yahoo.com.
See Professional Biographies, HOLSTEIN, IOWA

Forristal, Matthew J., (BV) ....'60 '85 C&L.190 B.S.B.A., J.D. [Forristal&H.]

Forristal & Henderson, (BV)
103 North Hamburg Street, P.O. Box 160, 51025
Telephone: 712-368-2646 Fax: 712-368-4588
Email: idaca@pionet.net URL: http://www.forristallaw.com
Members of Firm: Matthew J. Forristal; Karla J. Henderson.
Real Estate, Contracts, Family Law, Divorce, Estate Planning, Tax and Personal Injury Law.
See Professional Biographies, HOLSTEIN, IOWA

Henderson, Karla J., (BV) ....'52 '87 C.784 B.A. L.352 J.D. [Forristal&H.]

HUBBARD, 814, *Hardin Co.*

Craig, Patrick J., (AV) ....'48 '73 C.350 B.S. L.494 J.D. [Craig&S.] ⊙
Craig & Smith, L.L.P., (AV) ....213 E. Maple (⊙Eldora)

HUDSON, 2,037, *Black Hawk Co.*

Coonrad, Douglas V., (BV) ....'45 '75 C.197 B.A. L.1202 J.D. [Coonrad]
Coonrad Law Firm, (BV) ....315 5th St.
Hoffey, Matthew W., (CV) ....'65 '92 C.352 B.S. L.221 J.D. 315 5th St.
McCrindle, C. Kevin, Law Offices of, (AV) '50 '75
C.747 B.A. L.424 J.D. 326 4th St. (⊙Waterloo)
Reed, Mark, (CV) ....'60 '85 C.187 B.A. L.352 J.D. 315 5th St.

HULL, 1,960, *Sioux Co.*

DeKoster, John G., (AV) ....'50 '75 C.350 B.S. L.174 J.D. [DeKoster&D.]

DeKoster & DeKoster, (AV)
1102 Main Street, P.O. Box 801, 51239-0801
Telephone: 712-439-2511 FAX: 712-439-2519
Lucas J. DeKoster (1918-2000); John G. DeKoster.

(This Listing Continued)

DeKoster & DeKoster (Continued)
General Practice.
Represent: City of Hull; Boyden-Hull Community School District; City of Boyden.

HUMBOLDT, 4,438, *Humboldt Co.*

Arends, Marc D., (BV) ... '48 '74 C.187 B.A. L.221 J.D. 520 Sumner Ave.
Baker, Robert H., (AV) ... '34 '59 C&L.352 B.A., J.D. [Baker,J.&S.] ‡
Baker, Johnsen & Sandblom, (AV) ... 30 North 8th Street
Johnsen, Brian R., (AV) ... '47 '72 C.350 B.S. L.352 J.D. [Baker,J.&S.]
Lee, Robert E., (BV) ... '48 '75 C.352 B.A. L.900 J.D. P.O. Box 644
Parsons, C. D. ... '18 '47 C&L.352 B.A., J.D. 612 6th St. N.‡
Sandblom, Steven K., (BV) ... '51 '76 C&L.221 B.A., J.D. [Baker,J.&S.]

HUMESTON, 543, *Wayne Co.*

Franklin, Monty W., (BV) ... '53 '78 C.350 B.A. L.352 J.D. [M.Franklin]
Franklin, Monty, (BV) ... 205 Broad St.
Norris, Verle W., (BV) ... '63 '90 C.114 B.A. L.221 J.D. 125 Broad Street (☉Corydon)

HUXLEY, 2,316, *Story Co.*

Parmenter, Dennis W., (BV) ... '50 '77 C.350 B.S. L.221 J.D. State Rep. [Parmenter]
Parmenter Law Office, (BV) ... 204 N. Hwy. 69

IDA GROVE, * 2,357, *Ida Co.*

Boerner & Goldsmith Law Firm, P.C., (BV) ... 500 Second Street

Cosgrove, Thaddeus E., (AV) '59 '84 C.352 B.A. L.190 J.D.
607 West Second Street, 51445-1011 ☉
Telephone: 712-364-4138 Fax: 712-364-4445
Email: tcosgroveig@yahoo.com
General Civil Trial Practice. Probate, Personal Injury, Insurance Defense and Corporate Law.
Holstein, Iowa Office: 102 North Main, P.O. Box 50, 51025-0050. Telephone: 712-368-2616. Fax: 712-368-2389. Email: cosgrovelaw@netllc.net.

Forristal & Henderson
(See Holstein)

Goldsmith, Peter A., (BV) ... '54 '80 C&L.352 B.S., J.D. [Boerner&G.]
Jacobson, Edward A., (AV) ... '48 '74 C.513 B.S. L.793 J.D. [Jacobson]
Jacobson Law Firm, The, P.C., (AV) ... 607 West Second Street

INDEPENDENCE, * 5,972, *Buchanan Co.*

Dryer, Andrea Jordan, (BV) ... '67 '92 C&L.352 B.A., J.D. Asst. Co. Atty.
Flickinger, A. J. (Lans), (BV) ... '52 '79 C.352 B.A. L.190 J.D. 316 1st St., E.
Harden, Shawn M. ... '77 '03 C.1552 B.A. L.221 J.D. P.O. Box 133
Hoeger, Donald L., (BV) ... '37 '65 C.177 B.A. L.352 J.D. [Hoeger&M.]
Hoeger & McClintock, (BV) ... 317 1st St., E.
Klotzbach, William G. ... '25 '53 C.118 B.A. L.352 J.D. Dist. J.
McClintock, Gary F., (BV) ... '39 '65 C.177 B.A. L.352 LL.B. [Hoeger&M.]
Peters, James T., (CV) ... '58 '83 C.427 B.A. L.352 J.D. 309 1st St. E.
Roberts, Daryl E., (BV) ... '37 '62 C.350 B.S. L.352 J.D. 110 3rd Ave. S.W.
Sauer, Franklin W. ... '41 '66 C&L.352 B.A., J.D. Jud. Mag.
Vander Hart, Allan W., (BV) ... '45 '74 C&L.352 B.A., J.D. Co. Atty.
Wilson, Denny R., (BV) ... '43 '76 C.350 B.S. L.221 J.D. 316 1st St., E.

INDIANOLA, * 12,998, *Warren Co.*

Bennett, Candice L. ... '54 '78 C.350 B.A. L.221 J.D. Juv. Ct. Servs.
Clogg, Richard B., (AV) ... '49 '74 C.784 B.A. L.221 J.D. P.O. Box 379
Criswell, John W., (BV) ... '49 '74 C.352 B.A. L.221 J.D. 208 W. Ashland St.
Crouch, John P. ... '32 '69 C&L.221 B.A., J.D. Assoc. Dist. J.
Dryer, David M., (CV) ... '48 '74 C.352 B.A. L.221 J.D. [Dryer]
Dryer Law Firm, (CV) ... 124 W. Ashland
Elgin, P. F., (AV) ... '26 '48 C.784 B.A. L.352 J.D. [▣ Elgin,P.&P.]
Elgin, Patin and Parker, (AV) ... P.O. Box 215
Fowler, James F., (AV) ... '39 '65 C&L.352 B.A., LL.B. [Wilson,F.&F.]
Fusco, Louis M., (BV) ... '49 '75 C.784 B.A. L.724 J.D. [Wilson,F.&F.]
Haddox, Kimberly G., (AV) ... '64 '99 C.112 B.A. L.221 J.D. 106 E. Salem
Hall, Stephen A., (AV) ... '40 '68 C.231 B.A. L.221 J.D. [Hall&S.]
Hall and Schlenker, (AV) ... 115 South Howard Street
Herrick, M. C. ... '12 '37 C&L.352 A.B., J.D. Sr. Dist. J.
Hoyman, John R., Attorney at Law, (BV) ... '57 '84 C&L.352 B.A., J.D. 205 N. Buxton
Johnson, Joanna L. '66 '91 C.388 B.A. L.589 J.D.
(adm. in IL; not adm. in IA) P.O. Box 432‡
May, Michael R., (AV) ... '47 '74 C.72 B.A. L.221 J.D. 1216 E. Franklin Avenue
Ouderkirk, Mason G., (BV) ... '23 '51 C&L.221 B.A., J.D. [▣ Ouderkirk] ‡
Ouderkirk, Mason J., (AV) ... '53 '78 C&L.221 B.A., J.D. [Ouderkirk]

Ouderkirk Law Firm, (AV) ▣
108 South Howard Street, P.O. Box 156, 50125-0156
Telephone: 515-961-5315 Fax: 515-961-0304
Email: ouderkirklaw@aol.com URL: http://www.lawyers.com/ouderkirk
Mason J. Ouderkirk. Of Counsel: Mason G. Ouderkirk.
Personal Injury, Family and Domestic Law, Probate, Workers Compensation, Real Estate.
See Professional Biographies, INDIANOLA, IOWA

Parker, Kevin, (AV) ... '55 '80 C.1062 B.A. L.221 J.D. 106 E. Salem
Patin, Claire B., (BV) ... '53 '78 C.350 B.S. L.221 J.D. [Elgin,P.&P.]

Rigg, J. Keith
(See Des Moines)

Ryan, Roxann M., (AV) ... '55 '80 C.350 B.A. L.352 J.D. Simpson Coll., Wallace 306
Schlenker, Mark F., (BV) ... '54 '78 C.350 B.S. L.190 J.D. [Hall&S.]

Wilson, Fowler & Fusco, (AV)
209 North Howard Street, P.O. Box 197, 50125
Telephone: 515-961-5377 FAX: 515-961-2658
Email: wilsonfowler@yahoo.com URL: http://www.lawyers.com/wilsonfowler
Members of Firm: J. Berkley Wilson (1909-1993); James F. Fowler; Louis M. Fusco.
General Practice, Probate, Estate Planning, Real Estate, Tax, Criminal Law and Family Law.
References: List Furnished upon request.
See Professional Biographies, INDIANOLA, IOWA

Winjum, Stephen J., (CV) ... '63 '89 C.190 B.S.B.A. L.602 J.D. P.O. Box 519

INWOOD, 824, *Lyon Co.*

Honrath, Francis A., (CV) ... '53 '81 C.491 B.A. L.190 J.D. [Honrath]
Honrath Law Office, (CV) ... *318 Main St.*

IOWA CITY, * 62,220, *Johnson Co.*

Addink, Sylvan ... '42 '94 C.628 B.S. L.352 P.O. Box 1457
Akins, Brenda Lee '63 '92
C.234 B.S. L.352 J.D. Asst. Dir., Sponsored Prog., Univ. of Iowa
Albul, Iulia ... '76 '03 C.999 B.A. L.352 J.D. [Ⓐ Hayes L.]
Anderson, Lars G., (BV) ... '70 '95 C.427 B.A. L.352 J.D. 123 N. Linn St.
Anderson, Steven C., (CV) ... '64 '90 C&L.352 B.A., J.D. [Kennedy,C.F.&B.]
Baker, Thomas R. ... '59 '85 C&L.352 B.A., J.D. Univ. of Iowa
Ballard, Steven E., (BV) ... '62 '90 C.221 B.A. L.352 J.D. [Leff]
Balmer, James W. ... '51 '76 C.36 B.B.A. L.352 J.D. Pres., Plumbers Supply Co.
Bartlett, Larry D. ... '42 '74 C.351 B.A. L.546 J.D. Assoc. Prof., Univ. of Iowa
Bartley, Jean, (AV) ... '27 '61 C&L.352 B.A., J.D. [▣ Meardon,S.&D.]
Bauer, Patrick B. ... '50 '75 C.918 B.A. L.145 J.D. Prof., Univ. of Iowa Coll. of Law
Beasley, John E., (BV) ... '61 '90 C&L.352 B.A., J.D. [Phelan,T.M.W.T.&G.]
Behr, Mitchel T., (BV) ... '67 '93 C&L.352 B.A., J.D. [Ⓐ Lynch,G.&M.]
Bergan, Marsha A., (BV) ... '51 '77 C.427 B.A. L.352 J.D. Jud. Mag. [Bergan&W.]
Bergan & Weyer, (BV) ... P.O. Box 3188
Bezanson, Randall P. '46 '71
C.597 B.S. L.352 J.D. Prof. of Law, Univ. of Iowa Coll. of Law
Bonfield, Arthur E. ... '36 '61 C.102 B.A. L.976 J.D. Prof. of Law, Univ. of Iowa
Boyer, Christine ... '68 '95 C.477 A.B. L.352 J.D. 531 Center St.
Boyle, Daniel W., (BV) ... '33 '60 C&L.352 B.S.C., J.D. [Ⓐ Phelan,T.M.W.T.&G.]
Braddock, Maurine A., (BV) '53 '82
C.788 B.A. L.352 J.D. [Honohan,E.B.&B.] (☉Lone Tree)

Bradley & Riley PC, (AV)
Attorneys and Counselors
Tower Place, One South Gilbert Street, 52240-3914 ☉
Telephone: 319-466-1511 Telecopier: 319-358-5560
URL: http://www.bradleyriley.com
Donald G. Thompson; Paul D. Burns; Michael J. Pugh;—Sarah E. Swartzendruber; Joseph W. Younker; Aimee H. Rhodes.
General Practice. Administrative, Antitrust, Arbitration, Banking, Bankruptcy, Civil Trial and Appellate Practice in all State and Federal Courts, Condominiums, Construction, Copyright, Corporate, E-Commerce, Employee Benefits, Environmental, Estate Planning, General Business, Government, Immigration, Insurance, Intellectual Property Labor and Employment Relations, Land Use, Mergers and Acquisitions, Municipal Bonds, Non-Profit, Pension and Profit Sharing, Personal Injury, Probate, Product Liability, Professional Liability, Real Estate, Securities, Taxation, Trademark and Trust Law.
Cedar Rapids, Iowa Office: 2007 First Avenue SE, 52406-2804. Telephone: 319-363-0101. Telecopier: 319-363-9824.
See Professional Biographies, IOWA CITY, IOWA

Bray, Daniel L., (BV) ... '47 '73 C&L.352 B.A., J.D. [Bray&K.]

Bray & Klockau, P.L.C., (BV)
402 South Linn Street, 52240
Telephone: 319-338-7968 Fax: 319-354-4871
Email: brayklockau@bkfamilylaw.com URL: http://www.lawyers.com/bray&klockau
Daniel L. Bray; Lori L. Klockau. Associates: Chad A. Kepros; Kimberly M. Murphy.
Practice Limited to Domestic Relations, Family Law and Adoption Law.
See Professional Biographies, IOWA CITY, IOWA

Brenneman, Michael J., (BV) '53 '88
C.288 B.A. L.352 J.D. [Honohan,E.B.&B.] (☉Kalona)
Briscoe, Kandie K., (CV) ... '63 '96 C&L.352 B.A., J.D. [Ⓐ Kennedy,C.F.&B.]
Brown, David E., (BV) ... '49 '80 C&L.352 B.A., J.D. [Hayek,H.B.M.&H.]
Burbidge, David, (CV) ... '— '94 C.723 B.A. L.494 J.D. [Johnston&N.]
Burger, William H. ... '38 '63 C.641 B.A. L.352 J.D. Mercantile Trust Co., NA
Burns, Paul D., (BV) ... '67 '93 C.351 B.A. L.352 J.D. [Bradley&R.]
Cain, Patricia Ann '45 '74 C.881 B.A. L.280 J.D.
(adm. in AL; not adm. in IA) Prof. of Law, Univ. of Iowa
Carlson, Jonathan C., (BV) ... '54 '81 C.012 B.A. L.145 J.D. Prof. of Law, Univ. of Iowa
Carrington, Dean D., (BV) ... '58 '93 C&L.352 B.B.A., J.D. [Phelan,T.M.W.T.&G.]
Chapman, Ansel J. ... '15 '39 C.352 B.A. L.976 LL.B. Sr. Dist. Ct. J.‡
Corcoran, Kathleen ... '47 '91 C&L.352 B.A., J.D. State Supm. Ct. Comm. on Planning
Cox, Lois K. ... '49 '78 C.691 B.A. L.94 J.D. Clinical Prof. of Law, Univ. of Iowa‡
Cruise, John D., (BV) ... '48 '76 C&L.352 B.B.A., J.D. [Kennedy,C.F.&B.]
Danielson, Mark C., (BV) ... '64 '89 C.350 B.S. L.352 J.D. [Leff]
David, Marcella '64 '93 C.688 B.S. L.477 J.D.
(adm. in NY; not adm. in IA) Univ. of Iowa Coll. of Law
Davidson, Charles W. '18 '49 C&L.608 B.S., J.D.
Prof. Emeritus, Univ. of Iowa Law Sch.
Davis, Lillian Lyons ... '— '98 L.352 J.D. [Ⓐ Kennedy,C.F.&B.]
Diaz, Martin A., (AV) ... '58 '83 C&L.190 B.S.B.A., J.D. [M.Diaz]

Diaz, Martin, Law Firm, (AV)
528 South Clinton Street, 52240
Telephone: 319-339-4350 Fax: 319-339-4426
URL: http://www.lawyers.com/diazlaw
Martin A. Diaz.
Plaintiffs Personal Injury, Automobile Accidents and Injuries, Medical Malpractice, Civil Rights.
See Professional Biographies, IOWA CITY, IOWA

Downer, Robert N., (AV) ... '39 '63 C&L.352 B.A., J.D. [Meardon,S.&D.]

Eells & Tronvold Law Offices, P.L.C.
(See Cedar Rapids)

Eicher, Thomas E. '43 '81 C&L.352 B.A., J.D.
Sr. Refer. Libr., Univ. of Iowa Law Libr.
Eitel, Douglas R. '57 '87 C.732 B.S. L.893 J.D.
(adm. in PA; not adm. in IA) 630 Ronalds St.‡
Epley, Lloyd A., (BV) '25 '55 C.933 B.A. L.352 J.D.
[▣ Honohan,E.B.&B.] (☉Kalona)‡
Estin, Ann Laquer, (AVⓉ) '56 '83 C.197 A.B. L.659 J.D.
(adm. in CO; not adm. in IA) Univ. Of Iowa
Fields, Jeffrey ... '68 '97 C.293 B.A. L.352 J.D. P.O. Box 680
Flynn, Scott D. ... '71 '00 C.350 B.S. L.352 J.D. 119 Wright St.
Ford, Patrick J. ... '68 '04 C&L.352 B.A., J.D. [Ⓐ Leff]

Foster, Davis L., (BV) '56 '81 C&L.352 B.A., J.D.
703 South Clinton, P.O. Box 720, 52244
Telephone: 319-339-7727 Fax: 319-339-7712
Email: dfoster@fosterlaw.com URL: http://www.davisfoster.com
Trials and Appeals in State and Federal Courts, Civil Litigation, Criminal Litigation, Personal Injury and Medical Malpractice Law.
See Professional Biographies, IOWA CITY, IOWA

Frey, Kirsten H., (BV) ... '68 '95 C&L.352 B.B.A., J.D. [Kennedy,C.F.&B.]
Frye, Susan J., (CV) ... '51 '89 C&L.352 B.S., J.D. [Phelan,T.M.W.T.&G.]

Gartelos, Wagner & Ament
(See Waterloo)

Gelman, Thomas H., (AV) ... '53 '78 C.309 B.A. L.352 J.D. [Phelan,T.M.W.T.&G.]
Gerard, Stephen C., II ... '50 '75 C.221 B.B.A. L.352 J.D. Assoc. Dist. Ct. J., State of IA
Gilmere, Julie A. ... '58 '84 C.352 B.A. L.300 J.D. 36 Ealing Dr.
Greenleaf, Stephen N., (BV) ... '53 '79 C&L.352 B.A., J.D. [Lynch,G.&M.]
Griffee-Ross, Jill R. '62 '87 C&L.352 B.A., J.D.
(adm. in NE; not adm. in IA) 1511 W. Benton St.‡

Gwilliam, Dai .... '59 '99 C.857 B.A. L.352 J.D. [Ⓐ Lynch,G.&M.]
Hagle, Timothy M. '56 '82 C.475 B.S. L.1187 J.D.
(adm. in MI; not adm. in IA) Univ. of Iowa
Hamer, Mark T., (BV) .... '47 '72 C&L.352 B.A., J.D. [Meardon,S.&D.]
Haupert, R. Bruce, (AV) .... '39 '68 C&L.352 B.S., J.D. [Leff]
Hauserman, Nancy R. .... '48 '76 C.689 B.A. L.352 J.D. Prof., Univ. of Iowa
Hayek, C. Peter, (BV) .... '44 '73 C.813 B.A. L.352 J.D. [Ⓒ Hayek,H.B.M.&H.]
Hayek, John W., (AV) .... '41 '66 C&L.309 B.A., J.D. [Hayek,H.B.M.&H.]
Hayek, Matthew J. .... '69 '97 C&L.477 B.A., J.D. [Hayek,H.B.M.&H.]

Hayek, Hayek, Brown, Moreland & Hayek, L.L.P., (AV)
120 1/2 East Washington Street, 52240-3976
Telephone: 319-337-9606 Fax: 319-338-7376 URL: http://www.hhbmlaw.com
URL: http://www.lawyers.com/hhbm
Members of the Firm: Will J. Hayek (1896-1982); John W. Hayek; David E. Brown; Joseph T. Moreland; Matthew J. Hayek. Associate: Alison W. Smith. Of Counsel: C. Peter Hayek.
General Practice, Real Estate, Municipal, Probate, Family Law, Trusts and Estates, Insurance, Criminal, Banking Law, Bankruptcy Law, Business and Corporate Law. Trials and Appeals in all Courts.
Reference: First National Bank, Iowa City, Iowa.
See Professional Biographies, IOWA CITY, IOWA

Hayes, James P., (AV) .... '38 '64 C.177 B.A. L.352 J.D. [Hayes L.]

Hayes Lorenzen Lawyers, PLC, (AV) BB
Plaza Centre One, Suite 580, 125 Dubuque Street, 52244
Telephone: 319-887-3688 Fax: 319-887-3687
URL: http://www.lawyers.com/lorenzenlaw
James P. Hayes; Karen A. Lorenzen;—Iulia Albul.
Medical Malpractice.
See Professional Biographies, IOWA CITY, IOWA

Haymond, Gary L. .... '49 '78 C&L.352 B.A., J.D. Tr. Offr., Hills Bk. & Tr. Co.
Hernandez, Eugenia M. .... '71 '00 C.604 B.A. L.352 J.D. 220 Lafayette
Hibbs, Kristin Lucas .... '48 '77 C.351 B.A. L.352 J.D. Dist. J.
Hines, N. William, Jr. ... '36 '61 C.60 A.B. L.378 LL.B. Dean, Univ. of Iowa Coll. of Law
Hobart, Thomas D., (AV) .... '47 '74 C&L.352 B.A., LL.B. [Meardon,S.&D.]
Hoefer, Mary K., (CV) .... '56 '81 C&L.352 B.A., J.D. 209 E. Washington
Holland, C. Joseph, (AV) .... '49 '77 C&L.352 B.A., J.D. 123 N. Linn St., Ste. 300
Honohan, Jay H., (BV) .... '30 '60 C.350 B.S. L.352 J.D. [Ⓒ Honohan,E.B.&B.] (⊙Hills)‡
Honohan, Epley, Braddock & Brenneman, (BV)
330 E. Court St. (⊙Hills, Kalona, Lone Tree)
Houghton, James D., (BV) .... '55 '80 C&L.352 B.A., J.D. 216 Stevens Dr.

Jackson & Jackson P.L.C.
(See Cedar Rapids)

Johnson, Creola '— '94 C.1098 B.S. L.923 J.D.
(adm. in PA; not adm. in IA) Asst. Prof., Univ. of Iowa College of Law
Johnston, Joseph C., (AV) .... '— '68 C&L.352 B.B.A., J.D. [Johnston&N.]

Johnston & Nathanson, P.L.C., (AV)
1902 Broadway, P.O. Box 3400, 52244
Telephone: 319-354-1712 Fax: 319-354-7265 URL: http://www.jpnlaw.com
Email: jpnlaw@jpnlaw.com URL: http://www.lawyers.com/johnstonnathanson
Joseph C. Johnston; Jon R. Pearce; David Burbidge; Constance Peschang Stannard; Steven G. Klesner; Jacob R. Koller.
Personal Injury, Property Damage, Trial Practice, Corporation and Business, Debt and Bankruptcy, Estate Planning, Tax, Real Estate, Criminal, Domestic Relations, Workers Compensation, Business Litigation.
Cedar Rapids Office: 129 First Avenue, S.W., P.O. Box 74210. Telephone: 319-366-1000. Fax: 319-366-6973.
See Professional Biographies, IOWA CITY, IOWA

Keifer, Eugene V. .... '24 '49 C&L.352 B.A., J.D. 2802 Brookside Dr.
Kennedy, Michael W., (BV) .... '52 '77 C.593 B.A. L.352 J.D. [Kennedy,C.F.&B.]
Kennedy, Cruise, Frey & Briscoe LLP, (BV) .... 920 S. Dubuque St.
Kepros, Chad A., (CV) .... '71 '96 C.162 B.A. L.352 J.D. [Ⓐ Bray&K.]
Kinnamon, Jerald W., (BV) '38 '64
C&L.352 B.A., J.D. 615 Iowa State Bank Bldg. (⊙Cedar Rapids)
Kinnamon, Jon M., (BV) .... '40 '66 615 Iowa State Bank Bldg. (⊙Cedar Rapids)
Kittle, Bruce A. .... '59 '89 C&L.352 B.A., J.D. 2625 Highway 1 S.W.
Klesner, Steven G., (CV) .... '— '91 C.132 B.A. L.352 J.D. [Johnston&N.]
Klockau, Lori L., (BV) .... '53 '91 C&L.352 B.S., J.D. [Bray&K.]
Koller, Jacob R. .... '— '03 C.927 B.A. L.352 J.D. [Johnston&N.]
Koontz, Richard F. .... '55 '89 C.1307 B.A. L.1202 J.D. Univ. of IA Sch. of Law
Krapf Greenhoe, Gerhild, (BV) '55 '86
C&L.352 B.M., J.D. Coun., Univ. of Iowa Hospitals & Clinics
Kringlen, James .... '62 '88 C&L.350 B.S., J.D. 430 Iowa Ave.
Kron, Theodore L., (BV) .... '50 '76 C&L.352 B.A., J.D. Tr. Offr., Firstar

Krug Law Firm, P.L.C.
(See Cedar Rapids)

Krumm, Timothy J., (BV) .... '60 '86 C.747 B.A. L.352 J.D. [Meardon,S.&D.]
Kurtz, Sheldon F. .... '43 '67 C&L.823 A.B., LL.B. Prof., Univ. of Iowa Law Sch.
Lahey, Ann, (CV) .... '49 '77 C.157 B.A. L.190 J.D. Asst. Co. Atty.
Lainson, Margaret T., (BV) .... '39 '76 C&L.352 B.A., J.D. [Meardon,S.&D.] ‡
Lanning, Lynne D. .... '55 '84 C.228 B.S.N. L.325 J.D. 11 Cherry Ln.
Larew, James C., (BV) .... '54 '85 C.309 B.A. L.352 J.D. [Larew]
Larew Law Office, (BV) .... 504 East Bloomington Street
Larson, Randy, (CV) .... '55 '83 C.350 B.A. L.352 J.D. 335 S. Clinton St.
Leff, Alan R., (AV) .... '36 '63 C&L.352 B.S.E.E., J.D. 311 E. Wash St.‡
Leff, Philip A., (AV) .... '32 '59 C&L.352 B.A., J.D. [Leff]

Leff Law Firm, LLP, (AV)
222 South Linn Street, P.O. Box 2447, 52244-2447
Telephone: 319-338-7551 FAX: 319-338-6902
Email: lhtw@qwest.net URL: http://www.lawyers.com/lhts
Members of Firm: Arthur O. Leff (1906-1989); Philip A. Leff; R. Bruce Haupert; Charles T. Traw; Randall B. Willman; Steven E. Ballard; Mark C. Danielson. Associates: Patrick J. Ford; Jennifer K. Wendtgeisler.
General Practice. Real Estate, Corporate Law, Banks and Banking, Commercial Law, Insurance, Tax, Probate, Civil Litigation, Workers Compensation, Family Law and Trusts and Estates, Employment Law, Mediation, Arbitration, Divorce, Child Custody, Support and Adoptions.
Representative Clients: The Proctor & Gamble Manufacturing Co.; Farm Bureau Insurance Co.; University of Iowa; City of University Heights, Iowa.
See Professional Biographies, IOWA CITY, IOWA

Levey, Linda M., (CV) .... '41 '93 C.705 B.A. L.352 J.D. [Levey]
Levey Law Office, (CV) .... 118 South Clinton Street, Suite 250
Lew, Elizabeth G. '70 '97 C.198 B.A. L.352 J.D.
Gen. Coun., Univ. of Iowa Hospitals & Clinics
Lewis, Sylvia A. .... '48 '74 C.162 B.A. L.352 J.D. Juv. Ct. Srvs.
Lobodiak, Nestor, (CV) .... '— '89 C&L.352 B.S., J.D. [T.Riley] ⊙‡
Lorenzen, Karen A., (BV) .... '66 '93 C&L.352 B.S., J.D. [Hayes L.]

Luzzie, Christine M., (AV) '51 '75
C&L.145 B.A., J.D. Dep. Dir., Litig., Legal Servs. Corp. of Iowa
Lynch, Lawrence L., (BV) .... '45 '71 C&L.352 B.S., J.D. [Lynch,G.&M.]
Lynch, Greenleaf & Michael, LLP, (BV) .... 1402 Willow Creek Court
Martin, Richard C. .... '21 '58 C.352 B.A. L.276 J.D. 306 Ridgeview Ave.‡
Martinek, James H., (BV) .... '51 '78 C&L.352 B.A., J.D. [Neely&M.]
Maurer, Vincent L. .... '28 '62 C&L.352 B.A., J.D. Sr. V.P. & Tr. Offr., First Natl. Bk.

McAndrew, Paul, Law Firm
(See Coralville)

McCarragher, James D., (BV) .... '46 '71 C&L.352 B.B.A., J.D. [Meardon,S.&D.]
McDonald, James L. .... '25 '51 C&L.352 B.A., J.D. Dist. J.
Meardon, Charles A., (BV) .... '62 '89 C&L.352 B.A., J.D. [Meardon,S.&D.]

Meardon, Sueppel & Downer P.L.C., (AV) BB
122 South Linn Street, 52240
Telephone: 319-338-9222 Fax: 319-338-7250
URL: http://www.meardonlaw.com
William L. Meardon (1919-1997); Robert N. Downer; James D. McCarragher; Mark T. Hamer; Thomas D. Hobart; Margaret T. Lainson (Retired); Douglas D. Ruppert; Timothy J. Krumm; William J. Sueppel; Charles A. Meardon;—Dennis J. Mitchell. Of Counsel: William F. Sueppel; Jean Bartley.
General Practice.
Representative Clients: United Technologies-Automotive; Perpetual Savings Bank; Economy Advertising Company; Metro Pavers, Inc.; League of Iowa Municipalities; Hills Bank and Trust Co.; J.M. Swank Co.; City of Muscatine; McComas-Lacina Construction Co., Inc.; Diamond Dave's Taco Company, Inc.
See Professional Biographies, IOWA CITY, IOWA

Mears, Julia, (BV) .... '48 '80 C.293 B.A. L.352 J.D. 209 E. Washington St.
Mears, Philip B., (BV) .... '49 '77 C.293 B.A. L.352 J.D. 209 E. Washington St.
Mellon, Sharon A., (AV) .... '46 '74 C&L.352 B.A., J.D. [Mellon&S.]

Mellon & Spies, (AV)
102 S. Clinton Street, Suite 411, 52240
Telephone: 319-337-4193 Fax: 319-337-2396
Members of Firm: Sharon A. Mellon; Leon F. Spies.
Family Law and Domestic Relations, State and Federal Criminal and Civil Trial and Appellate Practice.
Reference: Iowa State Bank & Trust Co.
See Professional Biographies, IOWA CITY, IOWA

Meyer, Mark C., (BV) '50 '75
C.293 B.A. L.352 J.D. 615 Iowa State Bank Bldg. (⊙Cedar Rapids)
Michael, Robert S., (BV) .... '62 '87 C&L.352 B.S., J.D. [Lynch,G.&M.]
Miller, Paul D., (BV) .... '51 '76 C.351 B.A. L.352 J.D. 150 E. Court St., Ste. 101
Mitchell, Dennis J., (CV) .... '68 '95 C&L.221 B.A., J.D. [Ⓐ Meardon,S.&D.]
Moen, Marc B., (AV) .... '53 '79 C.350 B.A. L.352 J.D. 123 North Linn Street
Moreland, Joseph T., (CV) .... '70 '95 C.602 B.A. L.352 J.D. [Hayek,H.B.M.&H.]
Mundy, Richard E. ...... '43 '70 C&L.352 B.A., J.D. 335 S. Clinton St. (⊙Cedar Rapids)
Murphy, Kimberly M. .... '77 '04 C.350 B.A. L.352 J.D. [Ⓐ Bray&K.]
Nadler, Charles H., (CV) .... '40 '84 C.178 A.B. L.352 J.D. [Nadler&W.] ⊙
Nadler & Weston, (CV) .... 715 River St. (⊙Cedar Rapids)
Nagl, Susan .... '— '81 P.O. Box 3188‡
Naides, Perrie H. .... '52 '89 C.112 A.B. L.352 J.D. Law Clk., Supm. Ct.
Neely, Marion R., (BV) .... '24 '59 C&L.352 B.S., J.D. [Neely&M.]
Neely and Martinek, (BV) .... 510 Iowa State Bank Building
Neuzil, Ralph L., (BV) .... '30 '57 C&L.352 B.A., LL.B. [Neuzil&S.]
Neuzil & Sanderson, (BV) .... 119 Wright St.
Nolan, Elizabeth A. .... '28 '55 C.741 B.S. L.352 J.D. 513 S. Summit‡
Nolan, John T., (AV) .... '36 '62 C.436 B.S. L.352 J.D. [J.T.Nolan]
Nolan, John T., (AV) .... 22 East Court Street
Orr, Charles W. .... '50 '75 C&L.352 B.B.A., J.D. 2141 Slagle Cir.‡
Otto, Robert M. .... '42 '71 C.352 B.B.A L.221 J.D. 733 W. Benton St.
Park, Richard C. .... '22 '47 C&L.352 B.S.C., J.D. 80 Ealing Dr.‡
Parsons, Cynthia E., Law Offices of, (BV) '51 '76
C&L.352 B.S., J.D. 123 N. Linn St., Ste. 300
Pearce, Jon R., (AV) .... '— '66 C.490 B.A. L.221 J.D. [Johnston&N.]
Peck, Sally H. .... '— '79 C.1044 B.A. L.345 J.D. [Peck]

Peck Law Office
403 Iowa State Bank Building, 102 South Clinton Street, 52240
Telephone: 319-351-2332 Fax: 319-358-8873
Email: sallipeck@aol.com URL: http://www.pecklawoffice.com
Sally H. Peck.
Criminal Defense, Felonies, Sexual Abuse, Child Endangerment, Assault, Forgery, Theft, Misdemeanors, Drunk Driving, Family Law, Divorce, Custody, Support, Adoptions, Juvenile Law
See Professional Biographies, IOWA CITY, IOWA

Pence, Susan M. '51 '87 C&L.352 B.A., J.D.
Second V.P. & Trust Officer, Iowa State Bk. & Tr. Co.
Petsche, Randy .... '59 '94 C.351 B.A. L.190 J.D. 1st V.P. & Tr. Offr., First Natl. Bk.
Phelan, William V., (AV) .... '22 '49 C&L.602 J.D. [Phelan,T.M.W.T.&G.]

Phelan, Tucker, Mullen, Walker, Tucker & Gelman, L.L.P., (AV)
321 East Market, P.O. Box 2150, 52244
Telephone: 319-354-1104 Fax: 319-354-6962
URL: http://www.ptmlaw.com
Members of Firm: Louis Shulman (1908-1982); William M. Tucker (1922-2003); Charles A. Mullen (1937-2001); Bruce L. Walker; Richard M. Tucker; Thomas H. Gelman; Gary J. Schmit; Margaret P. Winegarden; John E. Beasley; Dean D. Carrington; Susan J. Frye; William V. Phelan. Associates: Daniel W. Boyle; Pope S. Yamada.
General Civil Practice in State and Federal Courts. Trials, Appeals, Banking, Business Transactions, Contracts, Corporations and Business Entities, Probate and Estate Administration, Wills, Trusts and Estate Planning, Zoning, Land Use and Development, Criminal, Environmental, Exempt Organizations, Hospital and Health Care, Real Estate, Negligence, Workers Compensation, Defense, Tax Planning and Tax Return Preparation and Family Law.
Representative Clients: Iowa State Bank & Trust Co.; Mercy Hospital, Iowa City; University of Iowa Foundation.
See Professional Biographies, IOWA CITY, IOWA

Pincus, Mary C. P. .... '49 '79 C.665 B.S.N. L.734 J.D. 72 Penfro Dr.‡
Pitton, Michael J., (AVⓉ) .... '53 '77 C.190 B.A. L.352 J.D. [Pitton]
Pitton Law Offices, P.A., (AVⓉ) .... 102 South Clinton Street
Pugh, Catherine A., (BV) .... '66 '91 C.339 B.S. L.347 J.D. [Stein&P.]
Pugh, Michael J., (BV) .... '65 '91 C.352 B.A. L.347 J.D. [Bradley&R.]
Quigley-Rick, Mary H. .... '50 '87 C&L.352 B.A., J.D. University of Iowa
Radig, Eugene L., (CV) .... '24 '56 C&L.352 B.S.C., J.D. 310 E. Burlington St.
Rate, Edward F., (AV) .... '— '21 C&L.352 B.A., LL.B. 22 E. Court St.‡
Reisetter, Philip M., (CV) .... '44 '70 C&L.352 B.A., J.D. 321 E. Market St., Ste. 102
Reitz, John C. .... '48 '75 C.309 B.A. L.477 J.D. Prof., Univ. of Iowa Coll. of Law
Rhodes, Aimee H. .... '73 '99 C.94 B.A. L.734 J.D. [Ⓐ Bradley&R.]
Rhodes, Ann Marie ...... '54 '82 C.753 B.S. L.352 J.D. Univ. of Iowa Hospitals & Clinics

Richard, Dell A.
(See Coralville)

Riley, Tom, (AV) .... '— '52 C&L.352 B.B.A., J.D. [T.Riley] ⊙

Riley, Tom, Law Firm, P.L.C., (AV)
1210 Highway 6 West, 52246 ⊙
Telephone: 319-351-4996 Fax: 319-351-7063
URL: http://www.tomrileylaw.com
Tom Riley; Nestor Lobodiak;—James K. Weston, II.
Personal Injury, Medical Malpractice, Products Liability, Civil Litigation and corporate Litigation.
Cedar Rapids Office: 4040 First Avenue, N.E., P.O. Box 998. Telephone: 319-363-4040. Fax: 319-363-9789.

See Professional Biographies, IOWA CITY, IOWA

Robinson, L. Vern ... '43 '68 C.293 B.A. L.352 J.D. Dist. J.
Roemig, Martin ... '23 '47 C&L.352 B.A., J.D. 2514 Bluffwood Circle‡
Ross, Robert E. '48 '80 C.352 B.A. L.213 J.D.
V.P. & Tr. Offr., Iowa State Bk. & Tr. Co.
Ruppert, Douglas D., (BV) ... '57 '82 C&L.352 B.A., J.D. [Meardon,S.&D.]
Rush & Nicholson, PLC
(See Cedar Rapids)
Rutledge, Janice E., (BV) ... '50 '82 C.182 B.A. L.352 J.D. IA Legal Aid
Sale, Hillary A. '61 '94 C.94 B.A.M.A. L.309 J.D.
(adm. in MA; not adm. in IA) Assoc. Prof. of law, Univ. of Iowa
Sanderson, Dale E., (BV) ... '50 '75 C.350 B.S. L.352 J.D. [Neuzil&S.]
Schmeiser, A. Russell ... '49 '81 C&L.352 B.B.A., J.D. First Natl. Bk.
Schmit, Gary J., (CV) ... '63 '88 C.1233 B.A. L.352 J.D. [Phelan,T.M.W.T.&G.]
Semel, Theresa M. ... '42 '81 C.851 B.A. L.352 J.D. 331 S. Summit St.
Senneff, Thomas C. ... '31 '58 C.177 L.352 LL.B. Asst. Dean of Law, Univ. of Iowa
Shanks, Krista Lyn ... '69 '94 C&L.502 B.S., J.D. Univ. of Iowa
Shields, Dennis J. ... '55 '84 C.1281 B.A. L.352 J.D. Univ. of Iowa College of Law
Shupe, Caryl E. ... '16 '51 C.351 B.A. L.352 J.D. 5 Heather Circle‡
Shuttleworth & Ingersoll, P.L.C.
(See Cedar Rapids)
Siegel, Martha S. '48 '80 C.119 B.A. L.744 J.D.
(adm. in TN; not adm. in IA) 30 Brookfield Dr.‡
Sigafoose, Jay W., (CV) ... '69 '95 C.132 B.A. L.352 J.D. [🄰 Neuzil&S.]

Simmons, Perrine, Albright & Ellwood, P.L.C., (AV)
Third Floor Tower Place, 22 South Linn Street, 52240 ⊙
Telephone: 319-887-1368 Fax: 319-887-1372
URL: http://www.simmonsperrine.com
Gregory G. Williams.
General Practice. Trial and Appellate Practice, Commercial, Insurance, Personal Injury, Professional Malpractice, Workers' Compensation, Environmental, Labor, Employment, Banking, Bankruptcy, Antitrust and Unfair Competition, Construction and Products Liability, Corporation Practice, Tax, Probate, Estate Planning, Real Estate, Pension, Profit-Sharing and Employee Benefits, ERISA, Mergers and Acquisitions, International and Domestic Patent and Trademark Law and Domestic Copyright Law.
Representative Clients: D.C. Taylor Roofing Co.; Kleiman Construction Co.; Wells Fargo Bank, N.A.; Grain Processing Corp., a division of Varied Investments, Inc.; Crystal Group, Inc.; Diversified Software, Inc.; Amana Company, a Division of Goodman, Inc.; Varied Investments, Inc.; Firstar Bank, N.A., Intermec Technologies Corp.
Cedar Rapids Office: 115 Third Street S.E., Suite 1200, 52401. Telephone: 319-366-7641. Telecopier: 319-366-1917.

See Professional Biographies, IOWA CITY, IOWA

Sladek, John R. ... '43 '70 C&L.352 B.S., J.D. Ret. Assoc. Dist. J.‡
Smith, Alison W. ... '74 '99 C&L.352 B.A., J.D. [🄰 Hayek,H.B.M.&H.]
Sokol, Howard N. ... '12 '67 C.350 B.S. L.352 J.D. P.O. Box 1460‡
Spies, Leon F., (AV) ... '50 '75 C&L.352 B.B.A., J.D. [Mellon&S.]
Stannard, Constance Peschang ... '— '85 C.430 B.A. L.352 J.D. [Johnston&N.]
Stein, L. Jay, (BV) ... '46 '77 C&L.352 B.A., J.D. [Stein&P.]
Stein & Pugh, LLP, (BV) ... 518 S. Clinton St.
Stier, Serena D. ... '39 '81 C.813 B.A. L.352 J.D. 3691 Forest Gate Dr. N.E.‡
Strayer, Hilary, (CV) ... '57 '84 C.766 B.A. L.352 J.D. [Strayer]
Strayer Law Office, (CV) ... 321 East Market Street, Suite 102
Sueppel, William F., (AV) ... '29 '58 C.707 B.A. L.352 J.D. [🄱 Meardon,S.&D.]
Sueppel, William J., (BV) ... '59 '85 C.707 B.A. L.300 J.D. [Meardon,S.&D.]
Summerwill, Suzanne '54 '83 C&L.352 B.A., J.D.
Sr. V.P. & Tr. Offr., Iowa State Bk. & Tr. Co.
Swartzendruber, Sarah E. ... '76 '01 C&L.352 B.A., J.D. [🄰 Bradley&R.]
Sylvan, Addink ... '42 '94 C.628 B.S. L.352 P.O. Box 1457
Terpstra, Epping & Willett
(See Cedar Rapids)
Thomas, Randall S. '55 '87 C.311 B.A. L.477 J.D.
(adm. in DE; not adm. in IA) Prof. of Law, Univ. of Iowa
Thompson, Donald G., (AV) ... '49 '76 C&L.546 B.A., J.D. [Bradley&R.] ⊙
Thompson, Mark D. ... '77 '04 [Thompson]
Thompson Law Office ... 332 S. Linn St., Ste. 15
Tiffany, David V., (BV) ... '46 '82 C.351 B.A. L.352 J.D. Asst. Co. Atty.
Traw, Charles T., (AV) ... '41 '67 C&L.352 B.A., J.D. [Leff]
Trca, Randy E., (CV) ... '57 '81 C.593 B.S. L.352 J.D. [R.Trca]

Trca, Randy, Law Firm, (CV)
1232 East Burlington Street, 52240-3212
Telephone: 319-354-8440 Fax: 319-354-8441
Email: RTLAWFIRM@prodigy.net URL: http://www.randytrcalawoffice.com
Member of Firm: Randy E. Trca.
Family Law, Personal Injury, Bankruptcy Law.

See Professional Biographies, IOWA CITY, IOWA

Trease, H. William ... '23 '49 C.197 B.A. L.352 J.D. Univ. of Iowa
Tucker, Bradley L. ... '69 '95 C&L.352 B.A., J.D. [🄰 Neuzil&S.]
Tucker, Richard M., (AV) ... '49 '75 C.813 B.A. L.352 J.D. [Phelan,T.M.W.T.&G.]
Walker, Bruce L., (AV) ... '46 '72 C&L.352 B.A., J.D. [Phelan,T.M.W.T.&G.]
Walsh, Shannon ... '— '00 C.162 B.A. L.352 J.D. P.O. Box 1455
Ward, Larry D., (AV) ... '44 '70 C&L.378 B.S., J.D. Prof. of Law, Univ. of Iowa
Warren, Chad T. ... '— '99 C.101 B.A. L.352 J.D. [🄰 Kennedy,C.F.&B.]
Webster, H. Richard ... '62 '97 C&L.352 B.A., J.D. [Webster]
Webster Law Office, PLC ... 212 S. Johnson St.
Weiner, Merle H. '63 '91 C.197 B.A. L.309 J.D.
(adm. in MD; not adm. in IA) Assoc. Prof., Univ. of Iowa of Law
Wendtgeisler, Jennifer K. ... '75 '02 C&L.352 B.A., J.D. [🄰 Leff]
Wenger, Howard B., (AV) ... '22 '48 C&L.352 B.S., J.D. 805 Eastmoor Dr.‡
Weston, Hanna B., (CV) ... '37 '84 C.604 B.A. L.352 J.D. [Nadler&W.] ⊙
Weston, James K., II, (CV) ... '— '96 C.352 B.A. L.221 J.D. [🄰 T.Riley] ⊙
Weyer, Sally A., (BV) ... '50 '81 C&L.352 B.A., J.D. [Bergan&W.]
Whiston, John B., (BVⓉ) '47 '84
C.976 B.A. L.508 J.D. College of Law, 280 Boyd Law Bldg
White, J. Patrick, (BV) ... '40 '65 C&L.352 B.B.A., J.D. Co. Atty.
Williams, Gregory G., (BV) ... '59 '85 C&L.352 B.A., J.D. [Simmons,P.A.&E.] (Pat.) ⊙
Willis, Craig N., (BV) ... '49 '75 [Willis&W.]
Willis, Nancy B., (BV) ... '49 '80 C&L.352 B.A., J.D. [Willis&W.]
Willis & Willis, (BV) ... 150 E. Court (⊙Chico, CA; North Andover, MA; El Campo, TX)
Willman, Randall B., (BV) ... '57 '83 C&L.352 B.A., J.D. [Leff]
Winegarden, Margaret P., (BV) ... '60 '87 C&L.352 B.B.A., J.D. [Phelan,T.M.W.T.&G.]
Woito, Linda Newman, (BV) ... '40 '78 C.112 B.A. L.352 J.D. City Atty.
Wolfe, Mary Lynn, (BV) ... '63 '92 C&L.352 B.A., J.D. [Wolfe]

Wolfe Law Office, (BV)
337 E. College Street, 52240
Telephone: 319-338-6529 Fax: 319-338-6531
Email: wolfelaw@aol.com URL: http://www.lawyers.com/wolfejustice
Member of Firm: Mary Lynn Wolfe.
Criminal Law, Family Law, Bankruptcy

See Professional Biographies, IOWA CITY, IOWA

Yamada, Pope S. ... '— '03 C.918 B.A. L.352 J.D. [🄰 Phelan,T.M.W.T.&G.]
Yanecek, Ted O. ... '56 '81 C&L.352 B.A., J.D. Univ. of Iowa
Younker, Joseph W. ... '78 '05 C.190 B.A. L.350 [🄰 Bradley&R.]
Zuber, Bradford C. '56 '81 C&L.352 B.B.A., J.D.
V.P. & Sr. Tr. Offr., Hills Bk. & Tr. Co.

IOWA FALLS, 5,193, *Hardin Co.*

Barker, Don W., (AV) ... '12 '41 C.351 B.A. L.352 J.D. 400 Jason‡
Bowden, Mona M., (BV) ... '62 '91 C.350 B.B.A. L.352 J.D. P.O. Box 786
Hamilton, Jay W. ... '42 '68 C&L.352 B.A., J.D. 1108 70th St.‡
Holt, Michael D., (BV) ... '51 '76 C&L.352 B.B.A., J.D. The Barker Bldg.
Johnson, Larry W., (BV) ... '46 '83 C.593 B.S. L.221 J.D. [Walters&J.]
McNeal, Clark E., (AV) ... '42 '67 C.187 A.B. L.352 J.D. The Barker Bldg.
Stockdale, Daniel L., (BV) ... '61 '90 C.350 B.S. L.352 J.D. P.O. Box 786
Walters, James P., (BV) ... '43 '70 C&L.352 B.A., J.D. [Walters&J.]
Walters & Johnson, (BV) ... 222 Oak St.
Whitesell, John P., (AV) ... '28 '52 C&L.352 B.A., LL.B. [Whitesell&B.]
Whitesell & Bicknese, (AV) ... P.O. Box 786
Wiese, Lynn J., (BV) ... '51 '76 C.351 B.A. L.352 J.D. 615 Railroad

JEFFERSON, * 4,626, *Greene Co.*

Copeland, Vicki R., (BV) ... '59 '86 C.352 B.A. L.221 J.D. [Wilcox,P.G.S.&C.] ⊙
Cudahy, Francis L. ... '09 '35 L.190 J.D. 206 N. Olive‡
Doll, Adam ... '77 '05 C.784 B.A. L.221 J.D. 115 E. Lincolnway, Ste. 200
Gerken, John A., (AV) ... '49 '75 C&L.352 B.S., J.D. [Wilcox,P.G.S.&C.]
Handley, Randall, (AV) ... '36 '60 C&L.221 B.A., J.D. [Mumma,P.&H.]
Harris, K. David ... '27 '51 C&L.352 B.A., J.D. Sr. Supm. Ct. J.‡
Hoyt, David A., (BV) ... '56 '82 C.162 B.A. L.352 J.D. [Hoyt]
Hoyt Law Firm PC, (BV) ... 101 N. Grimmell
Ladd, Dennis W., (BV) ... '42 '69 C&L.221 B.S., J.D. 1407 Southfield Dr.
Martino, Nicola J., (Mr.), (BV) ... '51 '76 C.177 B.A. L.221 J.D. Co. Atty.
Mumma, Michael F., (AV) ... '46 '75 C.966 B.S. L.221 J.D. [Mumma,P.&H.]
Mumma, Pedersen & Handley, LLP, (AV) ... 114 South Wilson Avenue
Ostlund, William C., (AV) ... '47 '73 C.352 B.A. L.972 J.D. Jud. Mag.
Pauley, James L., Jr., (AV) ... '16 '40 C&L.352 B.A., J.D. [🄱 Mumma,P.&H.]
Pedersen, Rita Harmening, (BV) ... '58 '84 C&L.221 B.A., J.D. [Mumma,P.&H.]
Polking, Thomas W., (BV) ... '47 '72 C.352 B.S. L.190 J.D. [Wilcox,P.G.S.&C.] ⊙
Rasmussen, Mark J., (BV) ... '56 '82 C.872 B.A. L.190 J.D. P.O. Box 70
Schwarzkopf, Robert A., (BV) ... '48 '76 C.352 B.S. L.190 J.D. [Wilcox,P.G.S.&C.]
Wilcox, Polking, Gerken, Schwarzkopf & Copeland, P.C., (AV)
115 East Lincolnway, Suite 200 (⊙Carroll)

JEWELL, 1,239, *Hamilton Co.*

Brekken, Deppe, Wynia & Cook, P.C., (BV) ... 614 B Main Street (⊙Story City)
Deppe, Charles D., (BV) ... '42 '68 C.351 B.A. L.221 J.D. [Brekken,D.W.&C.] ⊙
Henry, Ellen, (BV) ... '38 '86 C.352 B.A. L.221 J.D. [🄰 Henry]
Henry, Russell R., (AV) ... '37 '62 C&L.352 B.Sc., J.D. [Henry]
Henry Law Firm, (AV) ... 600 Edwards St.

JOHNSTON, 8,649, *Polk Co.*

Arrington, Ronald K. ... '55 '82 C&L.1335 B.S., J.D. Asst. Chf. Coun., John Deere Credit
Billings, Jos. A., (AV) ... '21 '49 C.350 L.221 LL.B. 5125 N.W. 62nd Ave.
Blair, Debra L. '— '99 C&L.221 B.S., J.D.
Sr. Intell. Prop. Coun., Pioneer Hi-Bred Int'l., Inc.
Brown, John L., (BV) '55 '80 C.597 B.A. L.352 J.D.
Asst. Chf. Coun., John Deere Credit
Bruce, Karen Moon '59 '03 C.318 B.S. L.221 J.D.
Corp. Intell. Prop. Coun., Pioneer Hi-Bred, Intl. (Pat.)
Bunz, Susan K. '64 '90 C.352 B.A. L.221 J.D.
Corp. Coun., Pioneer Hi-Bred Int'l., Inc.
Callistein, Steven J. '66 '91 C.339 B.S. L.597 J.D.
Intell. Prop. Coun., Pioneer Hi-Bred Int'l., Inc.
Cornelison, Daniel, (AV) '56 '82 C.784 B.A. L.221 J.D.
V.P., Secy., & Gen. Coun., Optimum Quality Grains, L.L.C.
Cosgrove, Daniel J., (BV) '66 '92 C.350 B.S.I.E. L.221 J.D.
Corp. Coun., Pioneer Hi-Bred Int'l., Inc. (Pat.)
Cox, Garry M., (BV) ... '53 '78 C.347 B.A. L.221 J.D. 6165 NW 86th Street
Critelli, Cheryl M., (BV) '60 '85
C.352 B.B.A. L.221 J.D. Asst. Chf. Coun., John Deere Credit
Davenport, Michael Joseph, (CV) '71 '96 C.627 B.S. L.352 J.D.
V.P. & Gen. Coun., Rain and Hail Insurance Service Inc.
Fiedler, Paige E., (BV) ... '65 '94 C.784 B.A. L.221 J.D. 5501 N.W. 86th St.
Foutch, Louise A. '59 '92 C.475 B.S. L.1218 J.D.
(adm. in NY; not adm. in IA; Pat.) Sr. Intell. Prop. Coun., Pioneer Hi-Bred Int'l., Inc.
Gibson, Terry L. ... '61 '86 C.427 B.A. L.352 J.D. Asst. Chf. Coun., John Deere Credit
Gorsche, James F., Jr., (BV) '64 '92
C.784 B.A. L.221 J.D. Corp. Coun., Pioneer Hi-Bred Int'l., Inc.
Haight, Timothy V., (AVⓉ) '53 '81
C&L.352 B.A., J.D. V.P. & Chf. Coun., John Deere Credit
Hartwig, Robert '65 '97 C.350 B.S. L.221 J.D.
Staff Atty. & Gov't Rel. Mngr., Iowa Bankers Assoc.
Hupfer, A. Michael, (BV) '46 '85
C.587 B.A. L.1340 J.D. House Coun., Heartland Education Agcy.
Jacobi, Daniel E., (BV) '54 '86
C&L.221 B.A., J.D. Gen. Coun., Pioneer Hi-Bred Int'l., Inc.
Jenkins, Richard S., (AV) '48 '88 C.350 B.S. L.352 J.D.
Corp. Coun. & Sr. V.P., ITS, Inc.
Kaiser, Steven C., (BV) ... '53 '78 C.350 A.B. L.221 J.D. [S.C.Kaiser]
Kaiser, Steven C., P.C., (BV) ... 6165 N.W. 86th St.
Liljedahl, Lori A. ... '56 '86 C.351 B.A. L.990 J.D. 8935 Lyndhurst Dr.
Michel, Marianne H. '— '92 C.350 B.S. L.352 J.D.
(adm. in OK; not adm. in IA; Pat.) Intell. Prop. Grp. Leader, Pioneer Hi-Bred Int'l., Inc.

Mohr, Dean C. '55 '86
C.350 B.A. L.352 J.D. Asst. Gen. Coun., Pioneer Hi-Bred Int'l., Inc.
Rowe, Jeffrey D. '73 '02 C.350 B.S. L.221 J.D.
Corp. Coun., Pioneer Hi-Bred International, Inc.
Shepard, Gene W. ....'39 '65 C&L.352 B.A., LL.B. Dir., Iowa Law Enforce. Academy
Smith, Christy M. '70 '96 C.378 B.A. L.221 J.D.
V.P. for Staff/Corp. Coun., ChildServe

KALONA, 2,293, *Washington Co.*

Anderson, Tracy E., (BV) .... '38 '72 C.351 B.A. L.352 J.D. [T.Anderson]
Anderson, Tracy, (BV) ....201 5th St.
Brenneman, Michael J., (BV) '53 '88
C.288 B.A. L.352 J.D. [Honohan,E.B.&B.] (⊙Iowa City)
Buffer, Pete F., & Associates ....'44 '73 C&L.352 B.A., J.D. 208 5th St.
Epley, Lloyd A., (BV) ...'25 '55 C.933 B.A. L.352 J.D. [Honohan,E.B.&B.] (⊙Iowa City)
Honohan, Epley, Braddock & Brenneman, (BV)
P.O. Box 66 (⊙Hills, Iowa City, Lone Tree)

KEOKUK, 11,427, *Lee Co.*

Abfalter, Kendra M. '72 '97 C&L.201 B.S., J.D.
(adm. in MS; not adm. in IA) Pub. Def.
Anderson, Barry M., (BV) ....'43 '68 C.293 B.A. L.352 J.D. P.O. Box 248
Boddicker, Clinton R., (BV) ....'70 '96 C.351 B.A. L.352 J.D. [Smith,K.&B.]
Concannon, Joseph A., (BV) ....'10 '34 C&L.352 B.A., J.D. 1415 Grand Ave.
Dickey, Robert B., (AV) ....'28 '52 C&L.352 B.A., J.D. [Smith,K.&B.] ‡
Frazier, Charles O., (BV) ....'24 '56 C&L.352 B.A., J.D. 206 N. 7th St.
Hendrickson, David B. ....'37 '63 C&L.352 B.A., J.D. Dist. J.

Hoffman, James P., Law Offices of, (AV) '43 '67 C.351 B.A. L.352 J.D.
3550 270th Avenue, P.O. Box 1087, 52632-1087
Telephone: 319-524-4441 Fax: 319-524-1638
Email: jameshoffman@aol.com
Personal Injury, Workers' Compensation Law and Corporate Law.
See Professional Biographies, KEOKUK, IOWA

Kultala, John E., (BV) ....'49 '75 C.350 B.S. L.352 J.D. [Smith,K.&B.]
Logan, William Tyler, (CV) .... '57 '83 C.813 B.A. L.352 J.D. Pres., State Central Bk.
Marion, Thomas D., (BV) ....'48 '78 C.784 B.A. L.1194 J.D. [Marion]
Marion Law Office, (BV) ....421 Main St.
McDonald, Bruce C., (BV) ....'52 '78 C&L.352 B.A., J.D. [McDonald]
McDonald Law Office, (BV) ....607 Main St.
McMurray, M. Carl, (AV) ....'39 '68 L.352 LL.B. 18 North Fifth Street
Noneman, Gary R. ....'55 '80 C.350 B.A. L.352 J.D. Assoc. Dist. J.
Norman, George L., (AV) ....'26 '59 C.871 B.S. L.352 J.D. 30 N. 4th St.
Smith, John H., (AV) ....'42 '66 C&L.352 B.A., J.D. [Smith,K.&B.]

Smith, Kultala and Boddicker, L.L.P., (AV)
511 Blondeau Street, P.O. Box 520, 52632
Telephone: 319-524-3723 Fax: 319-524-3730 Email: jkultala@keokuklaw.com; Email: cboddicker@keokuklaw.com
Email: jsmith@keokuklaw.com
Members of Firm: Ralph B. Smith (1883-1967); R. Buell Smith (1913-1974); Robert B. Dickey (Retired); John H. Smith; John E. Kultala; Clinton R. Boddicker.
General Civil and Trial Practice in all Courts; Corporation and Business Law; Real Estate; Will, Estate and Probate Law; Family Law and Domestic Relations; Criminal Defense Law; Juvenile Law; Workers' Compensation; Personal Injury.
Representative Clients: Roquette America, Inc.; Griffin Wheel Co.; First Community Bank FSB; Employers Mutual Insurance Co.; AXA Global; Risk U.S. Insurance; Farm Bureau Insurance; Safeco Insurance Company.

Swan, Steven J., (CV) ....'63 '90 C&L.352 B.B.A., J.D. 1013 Concert St.
Winnike, Jean Doyle, (CV) '51 '88
C.429 B.A. L.879 J.D. Sr. V.P. & Coun., State Central Bk.

KEOSAUQUA, * 1,020, *Van Buren Co.*

Cronk, Crystal S., (BV) ....'66 '96 C.587 B.A. L.502 J.D. [Dorothy,L.C.&M.]
Dorothy, James A., (AV) ....'31 '59 C&L.352 B.S.C., LL.B. [Dorothy,L.C.&M.] ‡

Dorothy, Lytle, Cronk & Miller, (AV)
903 Fourth Street, P.O. Box 496, 52565
Telephone: 319-293-3755 Fax: 319-293-6250
James A. Dorothy (Retired); Richard H. Lytle (Retired); Crystal S. Cronk; H. Craig Miller.
General Practice, Income Tax, Probate and Real Estate Law.
Representative Clients: Community First Bank, Keosauqua and Cantril; Farmers and Traders Savings Bank, Douds; Van Buren Community School District; Harmony Community School District; Van Buren Telephone: Company Inc.; Van Buren Mutual Insurance Company; Municipalities of Keosauqua.

Lytle, Richard H. ....'45 '74 C.221 B.S. L.352 J.D. [Dorothy,L.C.&M.] ‡
McGrath, James W., (AV) ....'17 '41 C&L.352 B.A., J.D. 4th & Dodge Sts.‡
McGrath, James Wm., (AV) ....'44 '71 C.162 B.A. L.221 J.D. [McGrath&M.]
McGrath & McGrath, P.C., (AV) ....4th & Dodge Sts.
Miller, H. Craig, (BV) ....'62 '88 C.587 B.S. L.352 J.D. [Dorothy,L.C.&M.]
Ovrom, Arthur P. ....'26 '51 L.352 J.D. P.O. Box 130
Watkins, Ronald K., (BV) ....'50 '79 C.587 B.A. L.285 J.D. 402 4th St.

KEOTA, 1,000, *Keokuk Co.*

Railsback, D. Scott, (BV) ....'45 '71 C.293 A.B. L.145 J.D. 207 E. Bway.

KEYSTONE, 687, *Benton Co.*

Kollmorgen & Schlue, (AV) ....103 Main St. (⊙Belle Plaine)
Schlue, Larry D., (AV) ....'41 '65 C&L.352 B.B.A., J.D. [Kollmorgen&S.] ⊙

KINGSLEY, 1,245, *Plymouth Co.*

Creasey, Wm. C. ....'16 '40 C&L.352 B.A., J.D. 411 Dover St.‡
Ehrich, Neal B., (CV) ....'47 '72 C&L.352 B.A., J.D. P.O. Box 250
Metcalf, Glenn A., (BV) ....'50 '86 C.352 B.A. L.793 J.D. [Metcalf,T.&P.] (⊙Moville)
Metcalf, Thompson & Phipps, (BV) ....4 East Second Street (⊙Moville, Remsen)
Thompson, Barry S., (BV) ....'47 '73 C&L.793 B.A., J.D. [Metcalf,T.&P.]
Thompson, Chad C. ....'74 '00 C.793 B.S.B.A. L.190 J.D. [Metcalf,T.&P.]

KNOXVILLE, * 7,731, *Marion Co.*

Barbour, Alex V., (AV) ....'41 '65 C&L.352 B.A., J.D. 113 W. Montgomery St.
Conrad, Robert W., (BV) ....'55 '81 C.352 B.S. L.190 J.D. 218 S. 2nd St.
Griffith, Barry L., (BV) ....'48 '88 C.352 B.B.A. L.221 J.D. [Johnston,H.G.&G.]
Guiter, Steven Wayne, (BV) ....'56 '82 C.350 B.S. L.221 J.D. [Johnston,H.G.&G.]
Hardin, William W., (BV) ....'20 '48 C.132 B.A. L.352 J.D. 210 S. 1st St.
Hicks, James V., (BV) ....'48 '73 C.784 B.A. L.221 J.D. [Johnston,H.G.&G.]
Johnson, Carroll, (AV) ....'13 '36 C&L.145 A.B., J.D. 113 E. Marion St.‡
Johnson, David A., (AV) ....'49 '74 C.187 B.A. L.352 J.D. [Johnson&L.]

Johnson & Lane, (AV)
113 East Marion Street, P.O. Box 111, 50138-0111
Telephone: 641-828-7373 Fax: 641-828-7376 Email: dajjllaw@lisco.com
Email: jllaw@lisco.com

(This Listing Continued)

Johnson & Lane (Continued)
Members of Firm: Michael J. Lane; David A. Johnson.
General Practice. Personal Injury, Taxation, Corporation, Estate Planning, Wills and Trusts. Family and Related Family Matters.
Representative Clients: City of Melcher-Dallas, Iowa; Marion County Rural Water District; State Bank of Bussey; Knoxville Chamber of Commerce.

Johnston, Hicks, Guiter & Griffith, (BV) ....109 N. 3rd St.
Jordan, Jerrold W. ....'34 '61 C&L.221 B.S.B.A., LL.B. Dist. J.
Lane, Michael J., (BV) ....'37 '62 C.177 B.A. L.352 J.D. [Johnson&L.]
Mertz, Martha L., (BV) ....'53 '82 C.587 B.S.E. L.221 J.D. [Mick&M.]
Mick, E. Raymond ....'15 '38 C&L.352 B.A., J.D. [Mick&M.]
Mick & Mertz, (BV) ....401 E. Robinson
Walker, Ronald F., (BV) ....'56 '86 C.353 B.A. L.862 J.D. 210 S. 1st St.

LAKE CITY, 1,841, *Calhoun Co.*

Jacobs, Frank, (AV) ....'17 '48 C.106 A.B. L.352 J.D. 116 N. Roy St.‡
Willis, David L., (BV) ....'43 '68 C.293 B.A. L.352 J.D. 107 W. Main St.

LAKE MILLS, 2,143, *Winnebago Co.*

Schwarm, Richard P., (BV) ....'48 '74 C.513 B.A. L.221 J.D. 110 W. Main St.

LAKE VIEW, 1,303, *Sac Co.*

McCullough, Colin J. ....'48 '72 C&L.190 B.S.B.A., J.D. P.O. Box 305 (⊙Sac City)
McCullough, Erin Elizabeth, (CV) ....'58 '87 C&L.190 B.S., J.D. [E.McCullough]
McCullough, Erin, Law Offices of, (CV) ....326 4th St.

LAKOTA, 281, *Kossuth Co.*

Buchanan, Russell G., (AV) '23 '48
C&L.352 B.A., J.D. [Buchanan,B.B.B.&H.] (⊙Algona)
Buchanan, Buchanan, Bibler, Buchanan & Handsaker, (AV)
Farmers Tr. & Svgs. Bk. Bldg. (⊙Algona, Swea City)

LAMONI, 2,444, *Decatur Co.*

Greenwood, Patrick W., (BV) ....'70 '98 C.350 B.S. L.221 J.D. 117 South Linden
Jones, George B., (BV) ....'59 '86 C.1281 B.S. L.208 J.D. 117 S. Linden Street
Phipps, Sherman W., (BV) ....'43 '73 C.1281 B.A. L.221 J.D. [Phipps&R.]
Phipps & Rolfe, (BV) ....619 South State
Rolfe, Robert A., (BV) ....'43 '73 C.1281 B.A. L.221 J.D. [Phipps&R.]
Strand, Howard E. ....'13 '60 C&L.352 B.A., J.D. 115 S. Linden‡

LANSING, 1,007, *Allamakee Co.*

Mueller, Barry S., (BV) ....'54 '80 C.340 B.A. L.221 J.D. 298 Main St. (⊙Postville)

LA PORTE CITY, 2,275, *Black Hawk Co.*

Lubben, Rick R., Attorney at Law, (CV) ......'59 '83 C.352 B.A. L.221 J.D. 304 Main St.
Robertson, James L., (BV) ....'36 '59 C.351 L.352 LL.B. 211 Main St.

LARCHWOOD, 739, *Lyon Co.*

Bonander, Lachlan M., (BV) ....'50 '76 C.508 B.A. L.972 J.D. [L.M.Bonander]
Bonander, Rodney B. ....'51 '77 C.793 B.S. L.972 J.D. Security Svgs. Bk. Bldg.‡
Bonander, Lachlan M., P.C., (BV) ....Security Svgs. Bk. Bldg.
Trott, Emil, Jr., (AV) ....'45 '72 C.494 B.A. L.352 J.D. P.O. Box 342‡

LAURENS, 1,550, *Pocahontas Co.*

Alexander, William M., (BV) ....'42 '72 C&L.190 B.A., J.D. 101 N. 3rd St.
Beneke, Ann E., (BV) ....'48 '78 C.352 B.A. L.365 J.D. Co. Atty.
Winkler, Donald M., (BV) ....'49 '74 C.350 B.S. L.221 J.D. Jud. Mag.

LAWLER, 534, *Chickasaw Co.*

Kennedy, Michael K., (AV) ....'39 '68 C.602 B.A. L.352 J.D. [Kennedy&K.] ⊙
Kennedy and Kennedy, (AV) ....411 E. Grove (⊙New Hampton)

LE CLAIRE, 2,847, *Scott Co.*

Neuman, Linda K. ....'48 '74 C&L.174 B.A., J.D. 28218 218th Street

LE MARS, * 9,237, *Plymouth Co.*

Bauerly, Craig R., (BV) ....'64 '89 C&L.793 B.S., J.D. [Bauerly,T.&B.]
Bauerly, Richard A., (AV) ....'42 '70 C&L.793 B.S., J.D. [Bauerly,T.&B.]
Bauerly, Trotzig & Bauerly, P.L.C., (AV) ....104 Central Avenue, N.E.
Beekman, John C., (BV) ....'32 '57 C.513 B.S. L.352 J.D. Co. Atty.

Berenstein, Moore, Berenstein, Heffernan & Moeller, L.L.P.
(See Sioux City)

Bixenman, Scott L., (BV) ....'69 '96 C.350 B.A. L.221 J.D. [Murphy,C.&B.]
Collins, W. E. (Gene), (BV) ....'59 '93 C.351 B.S. L.546 J.D. [Murphy,C.&B.]
Dull, Robert J. ....'47 '73 C.976 B.A. L.221 J.D. Assoc. Dist. J.
Flannery, Joseph W., (BV) ....'55 '92 C&L.793 B.S., J.D. [Flannery&O.]
Flannery & O'Connor, (BV) ....11 Central Avenue N.W.
George, James L., (BV) ....'47 '74 C.352 B.A. L.190 J.D. 17 1st. Ave., N.E.
Hoffman, Thomas J., (CV) ....'43 '70 C&L.352 B.A., J.D. 19 First Ave., N.W.
Murphy, Michael P. ....'79 '05 C.350 B.S. L.221 J.D. [Murphy,C.&B.]
Murphy, Patrick N., (AV) ....'46 '73 C.546 A.B. L.190 J.D. [Murphy,C.&B.]

Murphy, Collins & Bixenman, P.L.C., (AV)
38 First Avenue, Northwest, P.O. Box 526, 51031-0526
Telephone: 712-546-8844 Telecopier: 712-546-8847
Email: murphlaw@lemarscomm.net
Patrick N. Murphy; W. E. (Gene) Collins; Scott L. Bixenman; Michael P. Murphy.
General Practice, Civil and Criminal Trials and Appeals, Personal Injury and Worker's Compensation, Products Liability, Commercial and Banking Law, Probate, Estate Planning, Real Estate, Family Law, Corporations, Agricultural and Municipal Law, School Law.
Reference: Le Mars Bank & Trust Co., Le Mars, Iowa.
See Professional Biographies, LE MARS, IOWA

O'Connor, Carrie, (CV) ....'72 '97 C.177 B.A. L.221 J.D. [Flannery&O.]
Oetken, Amy K., (CV) ....'70 '97 C&L.352 B.B.A., J.D. Asst. Co. Atty.

Rawlings, Nieland, Probasco, Killinger, Ellwanger, Jacobs & Mohrhauser
(See Sioux City)

Sturges, William S., (AV) ....'27 '53 C&L.546 B.S., J.D. [Sturges]
Sturges Law Offices, (AV) ....16 Second St., S.E.
Trotzig, Marten A., (BV) ....'53 '79 C&L.793 B.S., J.D. [Bauerly,T.&B.]

LENOX, 1,303, *Taylor Co.*

Christensen, David L. ....'42 '73 C&L.352 B.B.A., J.D. 1311 Tomahawk Trail
Hughes, Jas. E. ....'12 '37 C&L.352 B.A., J.D. Ret. Dist. J.
Wilson, Richard L., (AV) ....'38 '64 C.350 B.S. L.352 J.D. [R.L.Wilson]

Wilson, Richard L., P.C., A Professional Corporation, (AV)
103 South Main Street, 50851-1299
Telephone: 641-333-2283 Fax: 641-333-2706
Email: lawoffice@frontiernet.net

(This Listing Continued)

Wilson, Richard L., P.C., A Professional Corporation (Continued)

Richard L. Wilson.
Trial Practice. Probate, Taxation, Domestic Relations, Real Estate and School Law.
Representative Clients: Union Bank, Lenox, Iowa; U.S. Bank of Mt. Ayr, Iowa; Great Western Bank; Area Education Agency #14, Creston, Iowa.
Approved Attorneys for: Farm Service Agency (FSA).
References: Union Bank, Lenox, Iowa.; U.S. Bank of Mt. Ayr, Iowa.
Mt. Ayr, Iowa Office: 111 South Fillmore, 50854. Telephone: 641-464-3901. Fax: 641-464-3185. Email: wilsonlaw@iowatelecom.net.

LEON, * 2,047, *Decatur Co.*

Elson, Charles L. .... '21 '47 C&L.221 LL.B. [Elson&F.]
Elson and Fulton, (BV) .... 203 N.E. Idaho
Fulton, Robert L., (BV) .... '35 '60 C&L.352 B.A., J.D. [Elson&F.]
Hill, Angela .... '73 '01 C&L.221 B.A., J.D. 203 N.E. Idaho
Hoffman, G. F., II, (AV) .... '25 '50 C.784 B.A. L.352 J.D. [Hoffman]
Hoffman, G. F., III, (BV) .... '56 '81 C.352 B.B.A. L.221 J.D. [Hoffman]
Hoffman Law Firm, (AV) .... 906 W. First St.

LIBERTYVILLE, 264, *Jefferson Co.*

Kauffman, Robert K. .... '39 '68 C.353 B.A. L.352 J.D. Law Editor, Estate Planning Dept.

LIVERMORE, 436, *Humboldt Co.*

Stoebe, Gregory H., (BV) ...... '50 '76 C.352 B.A. L.300 J.D. Asst. Co. Atty. [Stoebe] ⊙
Stoebe, Kurt John, (BV) .... '56 '80 C.793 B.A. L.352 J.D. Co. Atty. & City Atty. [Stoebe]
Stoebe Law Office, (BV) .... 416 4th Ave. (⊙Gilmore City)

LOGAN, * 1,545, *Harrison Co.*

Altwegg, Gary J., (AV) .... '38 '64 C.351 B.A. L.221 J.D. [Altwegg&A.]
Altwegg & Anderson, (AV) .... 110 N. 2nd Ave.
Anderson, Alan J., (AV) .... '49 '74 C.350 B.S. L.352 J.D. [Altwegg&A.]
Foland-Sieck, Jacqueline G. '51 '89 C.627 B.S. L.190 J.D.
(adm. in NE; not adm. in IA) P.O. Box 93
Frisk, Judson L., (BV) .... '51 '76 C&L.352 B.A., J.D. [J.Frisk]
Frisk, Judson, (BV) .... 207 E. 7th St.

Salvo, Deren, Schenck & Lauterbach, P.C.
(See Harlan)

Scott, Howard B. .... '04 '27 L.352 J.D. 302 E. 7th St.

LONE TREE, 1,151, *Johnson Co.*

Braddock, Maurine A., (BV) '53 '82
C.788 B.A. L.352 J.D. [Honohan,E.B.&B.] (⊙Iowa City)
Honohan, Epley, Braddock & Brenneman, (BV)
104 Jayne St. (⊙Hills, Iowa City, Kalona)

LOVILIA, 551, *Monroe Co.*

McCoy, Hugh B., (AV) .... '18 '41 C&L.352 B.A., J.D. P.O. Box 111‡

LOWDEN, 726, *Cedar Co.*

Norton, Bradley L., (BV) .... '54 '82 C.350 B.A. L.221 J.D. [Norton&N.]
Norton, William B., (BV) .... '27 '53 C&L.221 B.A., J.D. [Norton&N.]
Norton & Norton, P.C., (BV) .... P.O. Box 100

MADRID, 2,264, *Boone Co.*

Jordan, John D., (BV) .... '53 '81 C.350 B.S. L.221 J.D. [Jordan,M.J.&Q.] ⊙
Jordan, Mahoney, Jordan & Quinn, P.C., (AV) .... 210 State St. (⊙Boone)
Mahoney, Michael F., (BV) .... '50 '79 C&L.900 B.B.A., J.D. [Jordan,M.J.&Q.] ⊙

MANCHESTER, * 5,257, *Delaware Co.*

Bernau, John W., (BV) .... '62 '91 C.132 B.A. L.352 J.D. Co. Atty.
Carr, John, (CV) .... '72 '97 C.898 B.A. L.352 J.D. 117 S. Franklin St.
Carr, Steven .... '75 '01 C.898 B.A. L.221 J.D. P.O. Box 333
Feeney, Richard M., II .... '54 '79 C&L.352 B.S., J.D. Dist. Atty., Del Cty. Office
Hanson, Thomas J., (BV) .... '52 '79 C.177 B.A. L.190 J.D. [Hanson&W.]
Hanson & Werger, (BV) .... 401 E. Main St.
Roeder, Mark A., (BV) .... '57 '84 C.352 B.B.A. L.259 J.D. 119 E. Main St.
Swift, Daniel H., (CV) .... '54 '80 C.898 B.A. L.190 J.D. [Swift&S.]
Swift, John Q., (AV) .... '22 '49 C.350 L.190 J.D. [Swift&S.]
Swift and Swift, (AV) .... 108 N. Madison St.
Tracey, David C., (BV) .... '34 '62 C&L.477 A.B., LL.B. [Tracey&T.]
Tracey, Mary Lou, (BV) .... '33 '68 C.118 B.A. L.352 J.D. [Tracey&T.]
Tracey & Tracey, (BV) .... 105 North Franklin Street
Werger, William D. .... '57 '83 C.546 B.A. L.352 J.D. [Hanson&W.]

White & Johnson, P.C.
(See Cedar Rapids)

MANLY, 1,349, *Worth Co.*

Cook, Dave J. .... '41 '65 C&L.352 B.A., LL.B. P.O. Box 280‡
Heiny, James R., (AV) .... '28 '53 C.293 B.A. L.352 J.D. 213 S. Bdwy (⊙Mason City)
Marolf, Robert J. .... '27 '52 L.221 LL.B. 213 S. Bway.

MANNING, 1,484, *Carroll Co.*

Hansen, Erwin H. .... '07 '32 C&L.546 A.B., LL.B. 206 Main St.‡
Ranniger, William W. .... '50 '76 C.985 B.A. L.190 J.D. 517 East St.

MANSON, 1,844, *Calhoun Co.*

Madson, Gordon L., (AV) '27 '57 C&L.221 B.A., J.D.
931 Main Street, P.O. Box 788, 50563-0788
Telephone: 712-469-3325 FAX: 712-469-3305
General Practice. Probate and Real Estate Law. Trials.
Representative Clients: Security Savings Bank, Gowrie, Iowa; Manson State Bank, Manson, Iowa; Pro-Cooperative Elevator Co., Manson, Iowa.
References: Manson State Bank, Manson, Iowa; Security Savings Bank, Gowrie, Iowa.

MAPLETON, 1,416, *Monona Co.*

Gaukel, James F., (AV) .... '36 '62 C.755 B.S. L.793 LL.B. [Gaukel,N.&W.]

Gaukel, Nevins & Westergaard, (AV)
515 Main Street, 51034 ⊙
Telephone: 712-881-2321 Fax: 712-882-2323
Members of Firm: James F. Gaukel; Gavin R. Nevins; James R. Westergaard.
General Practice. Probate, Real Estate, Personal Injury, Corporation, Estate Planning and Taxation Law. Trials and Appeals.
Representative Clients: First State Bank of Mapleton; Mac's Chevrolet-Pontiac, Inc.; City of Mapleton; Valley Bank and Trust, Mapleton, Iowa; Heritage Bank, Anthon, Iowa; Soldier Valley Savings Bank, Soldier, Iowa.
References: First State Bank of Mapleton, Mapleton, Iowa; Mapleton Trust & Savings Bank; Heritage Bank, Anthon, Iowa; Soldier Valley Savings Bank, Soldier, Iowa.

(This Listing Continued)

Gaukel, Nevins & Westergaard (Continued)

Anthon, Iowa Office: Main Street. Telephone: 712-373-5294.
Sloan, Iowa Office: Murray Insurance Building. Telephone: 712-428-3861.
See Professional Biographies, MAPLETON, IOWA

Mohrhauser, Thomas R., Law Office, (BV) .... '47 '77 C.513 B.A. L.190 J.D. 314 Main St.
Nevins, Gavin R., (BV) .... '44 '69 C&L.352 LL.B. [Gaukel,N.&W.] (⊙Anthon)
Westergaard, James R., (AV) '52 '78 C.513 B.S. L.221 J.D.
[Gaukel,N.&W.] (⊙Sloan)

MAQUOKETA, * 6,111, *Jackson Co.*

Bartelt, Glenn, (BV) .... '50 '75 C.350 B.S. L.352 J.D. [Schoenthaler,R.B.&K.]
Baty, Corliss C., (BV) .... '45 '76 C.350 B.S. L.221 J.D. 126 W. Platt St.
Breuch, Thomas F., (BV) .... '41 '71 C.966 B.S. L.352 J.D. 231 S. Main St.

Fuerste, Carew, Coyle, Juergens & Sudmeier, P.C.
(See Dubuque)

Goodenow, J. E., (AV) .... '15 '39 C&L.352 B.A., J.D. 115 S. 2nd St.‡
Kahler, Steven J., (AV) .... '59 '86 C.351 B.A. L.221 J.D. [Schoenthaler,R.B.&K.]
Lawson, Mark R., (BV) .... '54 '79 C.707 B.A. L.221 J.D. [M.R.Lawson]
Lawson, Mark R., P.C., (BV) .... 114 W. Platt St.
Peckosh, Thomas F., (BV) .... '41 '67 C.177 B.S. L.352 J.D. 201 S. Main St.
Roberg, LaVerne M., (AV) .... '34 '62 C&L.352 B.A., J.D. [Schoenthaler,R.B.&K.] ‡

Schoenthaler, Roberg, Bartelt & Kahler, (AV)
123 North Main Street, 52060
Telephone: 563-652-4963 Fax: 563-652-4965
Members of Firm: E. L. Schoenthaler (1900-1989); LaVerne M. Roberg (Retired); Glenn Bartelt; Steven J. Kahler.
Probate, Real Estate, Corporate Law, Insurance, Estate Planning, Insurance Defense, Business Law, Appellate Practice, General Trial Practice.
Representative Clients: Maquoketa State Bank; Preston Mutual Insurance Assn.; Woodform, Inc.; Knake Farms, Inc.; Jackson County Public Hospital; Wendling Quarries, Inc.

Schroeder, Asher E. .... '25 '50 C&L.352 B.A., J.D. 810 Niles St.‡
Tabor, Phillip J., (BV) .... '58 '84 C.352 B.A. L.972 J.D. 126 W. Platt St.
Wright, Kenneth E., (BV) .... '41 '68 C&L.352 B.A., J.D. 116 South 2nd Street

MARCUS, 1,171, *Cherokee Co.*

Brady, Dennis A., (BV) .... '59 '85 C&L.352 B.A., J.D. [Knudson&B.] ⊙
Knudson, Charles F., (BV) ..... '32 '57 C&L.352 B.S.C., J.D. City Atty. [Knudson&B.] ⊙
Knudson & Brady, (BV) .... 400 North Main Street (⊙Remsen)

MARENGO, * 2,535, *Iowa Co.*

Buchanan, Thomas M., (BV) '49 '74
C.734 A.B. L.352 J.D. Co. Jud. Mag. [Elwood,E.B.&L.] ⊙
Elwood, Michael J., (BV) .... '42 '67 C.707 B.A. L.585 J.D. [Elwood,E.B.&L.] ⊙
Elwood, Richard H., (BV) .... '35 '64 C.707 B.A. L.585 J.D. [Elwood,E.B.&L.] ⊙
Elwood, Elwood, Buchanan & Leinen, (BV)
246 E. Washington St. (⊙North English, Williamsburg)
Harned & McMeen, (AV) .... 888 Court Avenue
Leinen, Robert J., (BV) '57 '82 C.350 B.S. L.352 J.D.
Co. Jud. Mag. [Elwood,E.B.&L.] ⊙
Martens, Kenneth R., (BV) .... '46 '74 C&L.838 B.S., J.D. [Martens]
Martens Law Office, (BV) .... 1017 Court Ave. (⊙Victor)
Mathahs, Dennis .... '61 '01 C&L.352 B.A., J.D. 246 E. Washington
McMeen, L. C., (AV) .... '42 '67 C.793 L.352 LL.B. [Harned&M.]
McMeen, Tim D., (BV) .... '71 '96 C.352 B.B.A. L.221 J.D. [Harned&M.]
Ritchie, Jeffrey, (CV) .... '72 '98 C.351 B.A. L.352 J.D. [⊠ J.C.Wagner] (⊙Amana)
Smolik, Kandyce .... '78 '04 C.352 B.A. L.1194 J.D. [⊠ Elwood,E.B.&L.]
Wagner, John C. .... '54 '79 C.132 B.A. L.352 J.D. [J.C.Wagner] ⊙
Wagner, John C., Law Offices, P.C. .... 1049 Court Avenue (⊙Amana, Cedar Rapids)

MARION, 26,294, *Linn Co.*

Aasgaard, Janice A., (BV) .... '50 '80 C.351 B.A. L.352 J.D. [White,S.A.&L.]
Allen, Morris L., (BV) .... '26 '55 C&L.352 B.A., J.D. [Allen&V.]
Allen & Vernon, P.L.C., (BV) .... 1175 Eighth Ave.
Beatty, Dennis E. .... '39 '66 C.162 B.A. L.352 J.D. Tr. Offr., Farmers State Bk.
Butz, Melody .... '63 '00 C&L.352 B.S., J.D. [Allen&V.]

Eells & Tronvold Law Offices, P.L.C.
(See Cedar Rapids)

Gibson, Gordon R., (CV) .... '36 '67 C&L.352 LL.B. [Allen&V.]
Harstad, Brent G. .... '43 '69 C&L.352 B.A., J.D. 151 Marion Blvd.
Hoover, Judith Jennings, (CV) .... '55 '89 C.520 B.A. L.352 J.D. 766 13th St.
Hoskins, Anne E. H., (BV) .... '62 '92 C.961 B.S. L.352 J.D. 766 Thirteenth St.
Hoskins, Donald C., (BV) .... '45 '70 C&L.352 B.A., J.D. City Atty.
Kenyon, Lisa M., (BV) .... '54 '84 C.477 B.S.N. L.352 J.D. 2915 Midway Rd.
Lawrence, Jean C., (BV) .... '55 '81 C.475 B.A. L.352 J.D. [White,S.A.&L.]
Naughton, Dennis J., (CV) .... '46 '71 C&L.190 A.B., J.D. [Naughton]
Naughton Law Firm, (CV) .... 1175 8th Ave.
Robison, Jeffrey K., (BV) .... '61 '86 C&L.352 B.B.A., J.D. [Allen&V.]
Rodriguez, B. Vincent .... '57 '86 C.912 B.A. L.597 J.D. 3795 Windemere Way‡
Schuettpelz, Carl .... '52 '77 C.352 B.B.A. L.585 J.D. 655 Marion Blvd.
Seidl, Gerald D. .... '33 '55 C&L.190 B.S.C., J.D. 776-13th St.
Smith, Leslie D., (BV) ... '47 '80 C.353 B.A. L.201 J.D. Gen. Coun., Berthel Fisher & Co.
Stone, Robert J., (AV) .... '30 '57 C.162 B.A. L.352 J.D. [⊠ White,S.A.&L.] ‡
Vernon, John G., (BV) .... '29 '56 C&L.352 B.A., J.D. [Allen&V.]
White, Stone, Aasgaard & Lawrence, P.L.C., (BV) .... 1080 Ninth Avenue
Wilson, Anne K. .... '— '02 C.123 B.A. L.69 J.D. 766 13th St.

MARSHALLTOWN, * 26,009, *Marshall Co.*

Adams, E. W., (AV) .... '18 '42 C&L.477 B.A., J.D. [Adams,A.&A.]
Adams, Adams & Adams, (AV) .... 23 South Center St.
Allbee, Donald G., (CV) .... '23 '49 C.162 B.A. L.352 LL.B. 402 W. Main St.
Baker, Carl D. .... '46 '71 C&L.352 B.A., J.D. Dist. J.
Barten, JoAnn L., (CV) .... '— '98 C.350 B.S. L.734 J.D. [⊠ Boliver]
Bartine, Edwin W., II, (BV) .... '42 '67 C.350 B.S. L.352 J.D. 106 N. Center St.
Beach, Gene L. .... '41 '81 C.543 B.A. L.221 J.D. [Grimes,B.S.B.&H.] ‡
Beals, Douglas W., (BV) .... '61 '87 C.106 B.A. L.190 J.D. [Moore,M.G.L.&E.]
Bloom, Michael W. .... '48 '73 C&L.352 B.A., J.D. 11 N. 1st Ave.
Boliver, Gail E., (BVⓉ) .... '49 '79 C.350 B.S. L.190 J.D. [Boliver] ⊙
Boliver Law Firm, (BVⓉ) .... 2414 S. 2nd St. (⊙Grinnell, IA; Omaha, NE)
Brennecke, Allen E., (AV) .... '37 '61 C&L.352 B.B.A., J.D. [⊠ Moore,M.G.L.&E.]
Brooks, Patrick W., (BV) .... '43 '71 C.350 B.A. L.352 J.D. 6 W. Main St.
Buck, Max H., (AV) .... '37 '61 C.350 B.S. in I.E. L.352 J.D. [Grimes,B.S.B.&H.]
Carter, Joseph T. '62 '93 C.350 B.S. L.45 J.D.
(adm. in MO; not adm. in IA) Pres., Marshalltown Trowel Co.‡

Carter, Macauley, Jr. .... '41 '66 C.674 A.B. L.309 LL.B. 2119 Three Bridges Rd‡

Cartwright, Druker & Ryden, (AV) BB
112 West Church Street, P.O. Box 496, 50158
Telephone: 641-752-5467 Fax: 641-752-4370
Members of Firm: H. G. Cartwright (1902-1982); Harry Druker (1907-2004); Rex J. Ryden; John B. Grier; John F. Veldey; Joel T. S. Greer; Sharon Soorholtz Greer. Associate: Merrill C. Swartz.
Insurance Defense and Insurance Law, Trials and Appeals. Corporation, Banking, Taxation, Labor, Real Estate and Probate Law, Personal Injury, Workers Compensation, Estate Planning and General Practice.
Representative Clients: Marshalltown Company; State Farm Mutual Insurance Co., Bloomington, Ill.; Farm Bureau Mutual Insurance Co.; Allied Group; IMT Insurance Co.; Marshalltown Medical & Surgical Center; Marshalltown Community School District; Merged Area VI Community College District; Members First Community Credit Union.
See Professional Biographies, MARSHALLTOWN, IOWA

Clausen, Christopher, (CV) .... '66 '93 C.350 B.A. L.352 J.D. [A Boliver]
Crawford, Paul G., (BV) .... '59 '84 C.190 B.A. L.352 J.D. Asst. Co. Atty.
Danielson, Brian L., (BV) .... '59 '84 C.898 B.A. L.352 J.D. 103 W. State St.
Ellefson, James C., (AV) .... '51 '77 C.898 B.A. L.221 J.D. [Moore,M.G.L.&E.]
Fairall, Charles F., (AV) .... '37 '62 C&L.352 B.Sc., J.D. 34 S. First Ave.‡
Fairall, Loyal S. .... '09 '40 C.352 B.A. L.221 LL.B. 34 S. First Ave.
Geffe, Kent L., (CV) .... '57 '81 C.187 B.A. L.352 J.D. [Welp&G.]
Gervich, Sam .... '17 '46 C&L.352 B.A., J.D. M. Gervich & Sons, Inc.
Giannetto, Randal J., (BV) .... '56 '88 C&L.352 B.A., J.D. 25 N. Center St.
Goins, Cynthia L. .... '61 '86 C.350 B.S. L.221 J.D. Jud. Clk., 2nd Jud. Dist.
Goodman, James L., (AV) .... '50 '81 C.350 B.S. L.221 J.D. [Moore,M.G.L.&E.]
Greer, Joel T. S., (AV) .... '53 '78 C&L.352 B.A., J.D. [Cartwright,D.&R.]
Greer, Sharon Soorholtz, (AV) .... '55 '82 C.350 B.S. L.352 J.D. [Cartwright,D.&R.]
Grier, John B., (AV) .... '38 '63 C&L.352 B.S.C., J.D. [Cartwright,D.&R.]
Grimes, Leonard L., (AV) .... '25 '49 C.197 A.B. L.309 LL.B. [C Grimes,B.S.B.&H.]

Grimes, Buck, Schoell, Beach & Hitchins, (AV)
102 East Church Street, P.O. Box 776, 50158-0776
Telephone: 641-752-4507 Fax: 641-752-5179
Email: mxb@thewebunwired.com
Max H. Buck; Roger R. Schoell; Kevin R. Hitchins; Gene L. Beach (Retired). Of Counsel: Leonard L. Grimes. Associate: Jennifer L. Steffens.
General Practice in State and Federal Courts. Corporation, Real Estate, Tax, Probate, Estate Planning, Domestic Relations, Bankruptcy and Personal Injury Law. Civil and Criminal Trials and Appeals.
Reference: Wells Fargo Bank, Marshalltown, Iowa.

Haney, John J., (BV) .... '60 '96 C.293 B.A. L.352 J.D. 103 W. State Street
Harrison, Roger E., (AV) .... '32 '58 C&L.352 B.S.C., J.D. [C Moore,M.G.L.&E.]
Heitmann, Sean K. .... '79 '03 C.999 B.A. L.352 J.D. [A Moore,M.G.L.&E.]
Hinshaw, George W., (BV) .... '26 '51 C&L.494 B.S.L., J.D. [Pattie,H.D.&K.]
Hitchins, Kevin R., (CV) .... '65 '91 C&L.352 B.B.A., J.D. [Grimes,B.S.B.&H.]
Hoglan, Theodore R., (BV) .... '56 '83 C.352 B.A. L.221 J.D. 2648 Reed Ave.
Horn, Michael R., (CV) .... '66 '92 C.352 B.A. L.221 J.D. [Moore,M.G.L.&E.]
Irvine, Stephen R., (BV) .... '43 '72 C.162 B.A. L.352 J.D. 25 N. Center St.

Johnson, Sudenga, Latham, Peglow & O'Hare, P.L.C., (AV) BB
118 East Main Street, P.O. Box 1180, 50158-1180
Telephone: 641-752-8800 Voice mail: 641-752-9965 Telecopier: 641-752-8095
Email: jslpo@jslpo-law.com URL: http://www.jslpolaw.com
Members of Firm: Craig L. Johnson (1931-1997); George W. Sudenga; W. J. Latham, Jr.; Paul C. Peglow; Kevin M. O'Hare; Reyne L. See.
General Practice, Corporation, Employment Law, Insurance Defense, Personal Injury, Banking, Real Estate, Probate, Criminal, Estate Planning and Taxation.

Kemler, R. W., (AV) .... '14 '39 C&L.352 B.A., J.D. 106 N. Center St.‡
Kilbride, Robert J. .... '15 '41 L.494 LL.B. 30 W. Main St.
Klaessy, Susan S., (BV) .... '44 '83 C.352 B.A. L.221 J.D. Asst. Co. Atty.
Kloberdanz, Steven A., (BV) .... '53 '79 C.352 B.B.A. L.190 J.D. [Pattie,H.D.&K.]
Latham, W. J., Jr., (BV) .... '40 '75 C.293 B.A. L.221 J.D. [Johnson,S.L.P.&O.]
Lorenz, William J., (AV) .... '52 '80 C.351 B.A. L.221 J.D. [Moore,M.G.L.&E.]
Lovig, Paul .... '42 '67 C&L.352 B.A., J.D. 2358 Sand Rd.‡
McKibben, Larry E., (BV) .... '47 '73 C.351 B.A. L.352 J.D. [Moore,M.G.L.&E.]
Meade, Norma J., (CV) .... '66 '97 C.350 B.A. L.221 J.D. [Moore,M.G.L.&E.]
Moon, Michael J. .... '45 '74 C.352 B.A. L.221 J.D. Dist. Ct. J.
Moore, James R., (AV) .... '40 '66 C.350 B.S. L.221 J.D. [Moore,M.G.L.&E.]

Moore, McKibben, Goodman, Lorenz & Ellefson, LLP, (AV) BB
302 Masonic Temple Building, P.O. Box 618, 50158
Telephone: 641-752-4271 Fax: 641-752-5266
Email: MWW@MTNIA.COM
Members of Firm: G. A. Mote (1874-1965); Arley J. Wilson (1913-1982); William L. Welp (1920-1997); Leslie E. Smaha (1943-2003); James R. Moore; Larry E. McKibben; James L. Goodman; William J. Lorenz; James C. Ellefson; Douglas W. Beals; Michael R. Horn; Norma J. Meade;—Sean K. Heitmann. Of Counsel: Roger E. Harrison; Allen E. Brennecke.
General Practice. Trials in all State and Federal Courts. Banking, Corporation, Taxation, Probate, Real Estate, Personal Injury, Family Law, Bankruptcy and Commercial Law, Criminal.
Representatve Clients: Furnished Upon Request.
See Professional Biographies, MARSHALLTOWN, IOWA

Noonan, Honorah .... '27 '52 C&L.352 B.A., J.D. 412 N. 8th St.‡
O'Hare, Kevin M., (BV) .... '55 '82 C.187 B.A. L.352 J.D. [Johnson,S.L.P.&O.]
Pattie, J. Warren, (AV) .... '07 '30 C&L.352 B.A., J.D. 103 W. State St.
Pattie, Hinshaw, Danielson & Kloberdanz, P.C., (BV) .... 103 W. State St.
Peglow, Paul C., (AV) .... '51 '76 C.502 B.A. L.221 J.D. [Johnson,S.L.P.&O.]
Peterson, Carl E. .... '33 '57 C&L.221 B.A., J.D. Dist. J.
Rutherford, Bradley J., (BV) .... '52 '77 C.352 B.A. L.607 J.D. [Rutherford]
Rutherford Law Office, (BV) .... 106 S. 1st Ave.
Ryden, Rex J., (AV) .... '30 '57 C&L.352 B.S., J.D. [Cartwright,D.&R.]
Schoell, Roger R., (BV) .... '42 '70 C&L.352 B.A., J.D. [Grimes,B.S.B.&H.]
See, Reyne L. .... '74 '00 C.293 B.A. L.221 J.D. [Johnson,S.L.P.&O.]
Springer, William L., (CV) .... '24 '51 C&L.352 B.A., J.D. 204-208 E. Linn St.
Steffens, Jennifer L. .... '76 '02 C.351 B.A. L.221 J.D. [A Grimes,B.S.B.&H.]
Sudenga, George W., (AV) .... '38 '64 C&L.352 B.B.A., J.D. [Johnson,S.L.P.&O.]
Swain, John B., (CV) .... '47 '80 C&L.589 B.A., J.D. Pub. Def. Off.
Swartz, Merrill C., (CV) .... '70 '95 C.513 B.A. L.352 J.D. [A Cartwright,D.&R.]
Tank, William M. .... '28 '77 C.299 A.B. L.221 J.D. 414 N. 8th St.‡
Veldey, John F., (AV) .... '42 '67 C&L.352 B.A., J.D. [Cartwright,D.&R.]
Vogel, Blair D. .... '53 '80 C.999 B.A. L.190 J.D. Diamond-Vogel Products Co.
Ward, Curtis A., (BV) .... '50 '75 C.350 B.S. L.352 J.D. 6 W. Main St.
Weiss, Robert J., (BV) .... '52 '78 C.350 B.A. L.464 J.D. 106 S. 1st Ave.
Welp, William A., (CV) .... '49 '74 C.755 B.A, L.793 J.D. [Welp&G.]
Welp & Geffe, (CV) .... 110 W. Southridge Rd.
Wilson, Patrick L. .... '53 '82 C&L.221 B.S., J.D. 26 S. 1st Ave.

MASON CITY, * 29,172, *Cerro Gordo Co.*

Anderson, J. Mathew, (BV) .... '56 '81 C.221 B.A. L.352 J.D. [Heiny,M.D.S.&A.]
Anderson, Roberta M., (AV) .... '54 '81 C&L.352 B.A., J.D. [Schroeder&A.] ⊙
Armstrong, Jackie D., (CV) .... '53 '78 C&L.477 B.A., J.D. [A Brown,K.F.&L.]
Aronsen, Rolf V., (BV) .... '51 '78 C.56 B.S. L.990 J.D. [R.Aronsen]
Aronsen, Rolf, (BV) .... 122 W. State St.
Arthur, Jacquelyn K., (CV) .... '70 '95 C.350 B.A. L.352 J.D. [Heiny,M.D.S.&A.]
Arzberger, Kristy B. .... '60 '86 C&L.221 B.A., J.D. 1531 S. Monroe Avenue
Boomhower, Leslie L. .... '20 '44 C.999 L.352 LL.B. Ret. Dist. Assoc. J.
Bovard, Gilbert K. .... '27 '52 C.668 B.A. L.352 J.D. Dist. J.
Brown, James R., (AV) .... '19 '42 C&L.352 B.A., J.D. 603 S. Grant‡
Brown, Scott D., (AV) .... '56 '82 C.352 B.A. L.221 J.D. [Brown,K.F.&L.]

Brown, Kinsey, Funkhouser & Lander, P.L.C., (AV) BB
214 North Adams, P.O. Box 679, 50402-0679
Telephone: 641-423-6223 Fax: 641-423-9995
URL: http://www.lawyers.com/brownkinseyfunkhouser
Members of Firm: David E. Funkhouser; Robert S. Kinsey, III; Scott D. Brown; John P. Lander. Associates: Jackie D. Armstrong; Kim R. Snitker.
General Practice. Trials and Appeals. Corporation, Insurance, Workers' Compensation, Probate, Real Estate and Employment Law, Criminal Law, Personal Injury, Social Security Disability.
Representative Clients: The St. Paul Companies; Continental Western Ins. Co.; Home Ins. Co.; American Family Ins. Co.
See Professional Biographies, MASON CITY, IOWA

Byrne, Michael G., (BV) .... '54 '79 C&L.352 B.A., J.D. [Winston&B.]
Byrne, Patrick B., (CV) .... '59 '84 C.351 B.A. L.221 J.D. 119 Second Street, N.W.
Cherry, John R., (CV) .... '45 '70 C.162 B.A. L.259 J.D. Jud. Mag.
Conway, Jacqueline R., (BV) .... '64 '91 C.177 B.A. L.352 J.D. [Heiny,M.D.S.&A.]
Davenport, Rustin T., (BV) .... '59 '85 C.221 B.A. L.352 J.D. [De Vries,P.&D.]
De Vries, Warren L., (AV) .... '25 '49 L.221 LL.B. [De Vries,P.&D.] ‡

De Vries, Price & Davenport, A Professional Corporation, (AV)
30 Fourth Street, N.W., P.O. Box 1953, 50401
Telephone: 641-423-1173 Fax: 641-423-1731
Email: info@devrieslawfirm.com
Warren L. De Vries (Retired); C. Bradley Price; Rustin T. Davenport.
General Practice. Trials and Appeals. Insurance Defense and Workers' Compensation.
Representative Clients: Allstate Insurance Co.; Auto Owners Insurance Co.; Farm Bureau Mutual Insurance Co.; Federated Mutual Insurance Co.; General Casualty Insurance Co. of Wisconsin; Integrity Mutual Insurance Co.; Iowa Mutual Insurance Co.; Northwestern National Insurance Group; Scottsdale Insurance; Travelers Insurance Group.
See Professional Biographies, MASON CITY, IOWA

Duffy, John L., (AV) .... '47 '73 C.177 B.A. L.352 J.D. [Heiny,M.D.S.&A.]
Dunn, B. Michael, (AV) .... '34 '61 C.723 B.A. L.221 J.D. 23 3rd Street N.W.
Eide, Larry S., (AV) .... '51 '77 C&L.352 B.B.A., J.D. [Pappajohn,S.E.&N.]
Esser, Donald E., (BV) .... '60 '85 C&L.352 B.B.A., J.D. [Finley,T.&E.]
Finley, Teas and Esser, (AV) .... 23 Third St., N.W., Ste 200
Fitzsimmons, James T., (BV) .... '66 '92 C&L.190 B.A., J.D. [Fitzsimmons&V.]

Fitzsimmons & Vervaecke, Law Firm, PLC, (BV)
5 North Federal Avenue, Suite 200, P.O. Box 1661, 50402-1661
Telephone: 641-422-0066 Toll Free: 1-877-476-9365 Fax: 641-422-0086
URL: http://www.fvinjurylaw.com
James T. Fitzsimmons; Mindi M. Vervaecke;—Colin C. Murphy.
Trials and Appeals. Personal Injury and Workers Compensation Law.
Reference: First Citizens National Bank.
See Professional Biographies, MASON CITY, IOWA

Flander, Susan R., (BV) .... '54 '82 C.352 B.A. L.221 J.D. Pub. Def.
Folkers, H. P., (BV) .... '42 '67 L.352 LL.B. [Folkers&K.]
Folkers & Keen, (BV) .... 23 3rd N.W.
Funkhouser, David E., (AV) .... '41 '67 C&L.352 B.A., J.D. [Brown,K.F.&L.]
Garland, Philip L., (BV) .... '45 '73 C&L.190 B.A., J.D. 114 4th St. NW (⊙Garner)
Grooters, David A. .... '73 '99 C&L.352 B.B.A., J.D. 103 E. State Street, Suite 800
Grupp, Carlynn D. .... '44 '78 C.350 B.S. L.352 J.D. Assoc. Dist. J.
Heiny, James R., (AV) ...... '28 '53 C.293 B.A. L.352 J.D. [Heiny,M.D.S.&A.] (⊙Manly)
Heiny, McManigal, Duffy, Stambaugh & Anderson, P.L.C., (AV) ... 11 Fourth Street N.E.

Hobson, Cady & Cady
(See Hampton)

Isaacson, Darrell J., (AV) .... '55 '81 C.106 B.A. L.352 J.D. [Yunek I.]
Jolas, Thomas E. .... '31 '58 C&L.352 B.A., J.D. [T.E.Jolas]
Jolas, Thomas E., P.C. .... 208 1st, N.W.
Jones, Joaquin Ann, (CV) .... '60 '85 C.872 B.A. L.352 J.D. Asst. Co. Atty.
Jorgensen, J. Vance .... '58 '88 C.106 B.A. L.221 J.D. [V.Jorgensen]
Jorgensen, Vance, Law Firm .... P.O. Box 1664
Keen, William J., (BV) .... '46 '73 C&L.352 B.A., J.D. [Folkers&K.]
King, Charles H. .... '25 '53 C&L.221 LL.B. Jud. Mag.
Kinsey, Robert S., III, (AV) .... '44 '73 C.293 B.A. L.352 J.D. [Brown,K.F.&L.]
Lander, John P., (CV) .... '69 '95 C.339 B.A. L.221 J.D. [Brown,K.F.&L.]
Lapointe, Joseph R., (CV) .... '52 '78 C&L.352 B.A., J.D. [Lapointe&L.]
Lapointe, Timothy, (CV) .... '65 '90 C.351 B.A. L.352 J.D. [Lapointe&L.]
Lapointe & Lapointe, P.C., (CV) .... 810 12th Street, N.W.
Levad, Charles H., (BV) .... '40 '71 C.589 B.A. L.146 J.D. 30 2nd St., N.E.
Locher, James J., (AV) .... '46 '74 C.602 B.A. L.228 J.D. [Locher&M.]

Locher & Morrison, (AV)
103 E. State Street Suite 721, 50401
Telephone: 641-423-2432 Fax: 641-423-2433
Members of Firm: Hugh H. Shepard (1876-1970); Robert H. Shepard (1919-1989); James J. Locher; William T. Morrison.
General Practice. Corporation, Probate and Real Estate Law.
General Counsel for: Indianhead Farms, Inc.; MacNider & Co.; Mason City Hotel Corp.; Mid-State Distributing Co.; Mason City Airport Commission.
References: Mid-State Distributing Co.; Boatmen's Bank Iowa, N.A.
See Professional Biographies, MASON CITY, IOWA

Mackey, John S. .... '57 '83 C.352 B.A. L.623 J.D. Dist. J.
Martin, Paul L., (BV) .... '53 '78 C.352 B.A. L.190 J.D. Co. Atty.
McGuire, James P., (AV) .... '42 '68 C&L.190 B.S., J.D. [McGuire]

McGuire Law Firm, P.C., (AV)
101 South Delaware Avenue, 50401
Telephone: 641-424-1614 Fax: 641-424-1568
Email: jpmcguire@mcguirelawfirm.com URL: http://www.mcguirelawfirm.com
James P. McGuire.
Personal Injury Law, Medical Malpractice, Severe Burns, Water Heater Flammable Vapor Litigation, Products Liability, Railroad Litigation, Trial Practice.
See Professional Biographies, MASON CITY, IOWA

McManigal, Charles W., (AV) .... '39 '63 C&L.352 B.A., J.D. [C Heiny,M.D.S.&A.]
Morrison, William T., (CV) .... '63 '89 C&L.352 B.B.A., J.D. [Locher&M.]
Murphy, Colin C., (CV) .... '69 '97 C.293 B.A. L.221 J.D. [A Fitzsimmons&V.]
Nelsen, David M., (BV) .... '38 '66 C.490 B.A. L.221 J.D. 956 E. State St.
Nicholas, Gregory C., (BV) .... '55 '80 C.747 B.A. L.352 J.D. [Pappajohn,S.E.&N.]
Nielsen, Randall E., (BV) .... '56 '82 C.350 B.S.E. L.352 J.D. [Pappajohn,S.E.&N.]

Ocheltree, Evelyn M., (BV) '58 '84 C.785 B.A. L.352 J.D.
600 1st. Street NW, Suite 103
Ollenburg, Kristen N., (CV) '72 '97 C&L.352 B.B.A., J.D.
103 E. State Street, Suite 800
Pappajohn, Socrates G., (AV) ... '33 '58 C&L.352 B.A., J.D. [Pappajohn,S.E.&N.]
Pappajohn, Shriver, Eide & Nicholas P.C., (AV) ... 103 E. State Street, Suite 800
Price, C. Bradley, (AV) ... '50 '82 C&L.352 B.B.A., J.D. [De Vries,P.&D.]
Reuber, John H., (BV) ... '31 '58 C.350 B.S. L.221 J.D. 23 3rd Street, N.W.
Rosenbladt, Gregg R., (BV) ... '62 '87 C.898 B.A. L.352 J.D. Asst. Co. Atty.
Schickel, Candila Coutts, (CV) ... '54 '84 C&L.352 B.S.N., J.D. 1443 E. State St.
Schroeder, Walter C., (AV) ... '31 '57 C&L.352 B.A., J.D. [🄲 Schroeder&A.]

Schroeder & Anderson, (AV)
119 Second Street N.W., 50401 ⊙
Telephone: 641-423-4935 Fax: 641-424-4154
Email: rma@netconx.net
Member of Firm: Roberta M. Anderson. Of Counsel: Walter C. Schroeder.
Health Care Law, Medical Malpractice Defense, General Practice, Probate, Real Estate and Family Law.
Affiliated with, Finley, Alt, Smith, Scharnberg, Craig, Hilmes & Gaffney, P.C.: 699 Walnut Street, 1900 Hubb Tower, Des Moines, Iowa, 50309. Telephone: 515-288-0145.

See Professional Biographies, MASON CITY, IOWA

Scoles, Jon Stuart ... '51 '79 C.351 B.A. L.352 J.D. Dist. J.
Shriver, Jay M., (AV) ... '43 '68 C&L.352 B.B.A., J.D. [Pappajohn,S.E.&N.]
Snitker, Kim R. ... '70 '03 C.999 B.A. L.352 J.D. [🄰 Brown,K.F.&L.]
Stambaugh, Gerald M., (AV) ... '51 '77 C.350 B.S. L.352 J.D. [Heiny,M.D.S.&A.]
Teas, Thomas C., (AV) ... '17 '46 C&L.352 B.A., J.D. [Finley,T.&E.]
Thomsen, Sarah J. ... '78 '04 C.898 B.A. L.352 J.D. [🄰 Heiny,M.D.S.&A.]
Tynan, Steven D., (BV) ... '61 '87 C.597 B.A. L.221 J.D. Asst. Co. Atty.
Vervaecke, Michael S., (CV) ... '69 '96 C&L.352 B.B.A., J.D. [Heiny,M.D.S.&A.]
Vervaecke, Mindi M., (BV) ... '71 '96 C&L.352 B.S., J.D. [Fitzsimmons&V.]
Waddell, Darren L. ... '65 '92 C.352 B.S. L.300 J.D. State Farm Fire & Cas. Co.
Wagenaar, Ronald James, (BV) '58 '84
C.999 B.A. L.911 J.D. Managing Atty., Legal Servs. Corp. of Iowa
Williams, ConGarry D. ... '66 '00 C.563 B.B.A L.221 J.D. 600 First St. NW, Ste. 103
Winga, Richard R., (AV) ... '39 '63 C&L.352 B.A., J.D. [🄲 Heiny,M.D.S.&A.]
Winston, Harold R., (AV) ... '32 '58 C&L.352 B.A., J.D. [Winston&B.]

Winston & Byrne, Lawyers, A Professional Corporation, (AV)
119 Second Street, N.W., 50401
Telephone: 641-423-1913 Fax: 641-423-8998
Email: hwinston@netins.net URL: http://www.winstonbyrne.com
Harold R. Winston; Michael G. Byrne.
General Practice. Trials and Appeals. Corporation Law. Civil Litigation, Real Estate, Probate, Estate Planning, Trusts, Wills, Family Law.
Representative Clients: Woodharbor Molding & Millworks, Inc.; Winkleman Farms, Inc.; Sparboe Iowa Corporation; Schmidt Family Farms, Inc.; First Citizen's National Bank of Mason City; Norwest Bank Iowa, N.A.

See Professional Biographies, MASON CITY, IOWA

Wornson, Clayton L. ... '14 '40 C.273 L.30 LL.B. 406 Brick & Tile Bldg.‡
Young, Mark A., (BV) ... '58 '85 C.351 B.A. L.221 J.D. [Young]
Young Law Office, (BV) ... 114 4th Street Northwest
Yunek, Joel J., (BV) ... '54 '80 C&L.352 B.A., J.D. [Yunek I.]
Yunek Isaacson, PLC, (AV) ... 10 N. Washington, Suite 204

McGREGOR, 797, *Clayton Co.*

Coon, Robert E. ... '15 '38 C.352 B.A. L.309 LL.B. 214 Main St.

MECHANICSVILLE, 1,173, *Cedar Co.*

Kudart, Arthur R., (AV) ... '30 '58 C&L.352 B.A., J.D. [Kudart] ⊙
Kudart Law Offices, (AV) ... 203 E. First St. (⊙Cedar Rapids, Mt. Vernon)
Kuehnle, John L., (BV) ... '30 '54 C.177 L.352 LL.B. 222 E. 1st St.
Sebesta, Walter E. ... '13 '36 C.707 L.221 LL.B. 222 E. 1st St.‡

MEDIAPOLIS, 1,685, *Des Moines Co.*

Aspelmeier, Kenneth A., (AV) '35 '60
C.641 B.A. L.569 LL.B. [Aspelmeier,F.P.E.&H.] (⊙Burlington)
Aspelmeier, Fisch, Power, Engberg & Helling, P.L.C., (AV)
621 Main St. (⊙Burlington, West Point)

MILFORD, 2,474, *Dickinson Co.*

Carmichael, William H., (AV) ... '36 '61 C&L.352 B.S.C., J.D. 2122 Lakeside Ave.
Roseberry, Robert H., (AV) ... '21 '48 C.933 B.A. L.352 J.D. 2704 Breezy Hts. Dr.‡
Sackett, Robert W., (BV) ... '33 '60 C.350 B.S. L.221 LL.B. Lakeland Square, Unit 3
Stein, David J., Sr., (BV) ... '41 '67 C.106 B.A. L.221 J.D. [Stein]
Stein, David John, Jr., (BV) ... '69 '95 C&L.221 B.S.B.A., J.D. [🄰 Stein]

Stein Law Office, LLP, (BV)
926 Okoboji Avenue, P.O. Box 537, 51351
Telephone: 712-338-2431 Fax: 712-338-2432 Email: davidjr@steinlawoffice.com
Email: davidjr@steinlawoffice.com
David J. Stein, Sr. Associate: David John Stein, Jr.
General Practice.
Representative Clients: City of Milford; Milford Utilities; United Community Bank; City of Terril.
Reference: United Community Bank, Milford, Iowa.

MINGO, 252, *Jasper Co.*

Phelps, Richard E. H., II, (BV) ... '46 '78 C.802 B.A. L.862 J.D. 201 S. Station

MISSOURI VALLEY, 2,992, *Harrison Co.*

Kellogg, John W., (BV) ... '44 '74 C.627 L.190 J.D. [Kellogg]
Kellogg Law Firm, P.C., (BV) ... P.O. Box 335
Mumm, Noel K., (BV) ... '43 '68 C&L.352 B.A., J.D. 507 E. Erie St.
Niebaum, Joel T., (CV) ... '53 '98 [Kellogg]

MITCHELLVILLE, 1,670, *Polk Co.*

Vos, Paul E., (BV) ... '44 '71 C.1304 B.A. L.221 J.D. 115 Center Ave., N. (⊙Prairie City)

MONONA, 1,520, *Clayton Co.*

Kramer, Eugene F., (CV) ... '33 '84 C.999 B.A. L.152 J.D. 105 W. Center St.
Pattison, Richard G., (BV) ... '35 '66 C.352 B.A. L.221 J.D. City Atty.
Schiller, Gregory J., (BV) ... '59 '84 C&L.352 B.A., J.D. 105 W. Center St.

MONTEZUMA, * 1,440, *Poweshiek Co.*

Johnson, Rachelle L. K., (CV) ... '69 '95 C.898 B.A. L.352 J.D. [R.L.K.Johnson]
Johnson, Vincent E., (AV) ... '17 '47 C.352 B.S.C. L.477 J.D. 107 S. 4th St.
Johnson, Rachelle L.K., P.C., (CV) ... 204 East Liberty Street
Karlak, Laura C. '61 '87 C.500 B.A. L.356 J.D.
(adm. in MS; not adm. in IA) P.O. Box 151

Kivi, James, (AV) ... '45 '75 C.429 B.A. L.352 J.D. Asst. Atty. Gen.
Mahaffey, Michael W., (AV) ... '48 '75 C.352 B.A. L.378 J.D. Co. Atty. [Mahaffey]
Mahaffey Law Office, (AV) ... 107 S. 4th St.
Sunleaf, Roger W., (AV) ... '38 '63 C&L.352 B.A., J.D. 105 N. 4th St.
Vogel, Richard J. ... '40 '65 C.707 B.A. L.352 LL.B. Dist. J.

MONTICELLO, 3,522, *Jones Co.*

Bowman, Michael A., (BV) ... '52 '78 C.162 B.A. L.902 J.D. 114 S. Cedar
Erdahl, H. Elvin, (BV) ... '28 '53 C&L.221 B.S.B.A., J.D. 808 W. 1st St.
Herman, Douglas D. ... '67 '94 C.427 L.300 J.D. [Herman]
Herman Law Office ... 206 S. Cedar St.
Matthiessen, C. J., (CV) ... '26 '72 C.870 B.S. L.352 J.D. 203 W. 1st St.
Shimanek, Robert F., (BV) ... '43 '68 C.177 B.A. L.352 J.D. 114 S. Cedar
Strittmatter, A. N., (BV) ... '19 '42 C.999 L.221 J.D. 123 E. 1st St.
Strittmatter, Nicholas L., (BV) ... '52 '78 C.602 B.A. L.352 J.D. 123 E. 1st St.

MORNING SUN, 841, *Louisa Co.*

Moore, Kenneth R. ... '14 '39 C.187 L.221 LL.B. P.O. Box 159‡
Moore, Steven C., (BV) ... '46 '73 C&L.221 B.S., J.D. P.O. Box 159

MT. AYR, * 1,796, *Ringgold Co.*

Pedersen, James L., (BV) ... '48 '85 C.172 B.S. L.221 J.D. [J.L.Pedersen]
Pedersen, James L., P.C., (BV) ... 105 E. Madison St.

MT. PLEASANT, * 8,751, *Henry Co.*

Bainter, Seleta, (BV) ... '59 '83 C&L.352 B.A., J.D. [Bainter&T.]
Bainter and Thomas, (BV) ... 100 E. Clay
Becker, James M., Jr., (BV) ... '49 '79 C&L.190 B.A., J.D. [Becker]
Becker Law Office, (BV) ... 201 South Main Street

Beckman and Hirsch
(See Burlington)

Bell, Richard J., (BV) ... '56 '82 C.694 B.A. L.221 J.D. [Bell]
Bell Law Office, (BV) ... 111 East Washington Street
Cornell, Danny L., (CV) ... '— '95 C.999 B.A. L.352 J.D. [Whitfield&E.]
Danielson, Cynthia H., (BV) ... '50 '76 C&L.352 B.A., J.D. Jud. Hosp.Ref. [Danielson]
Danielson Law Office, P.C., (BV) ... 1007 E. Linden Dr.
Elgar, Alanson K., (AV) ... '— '51 C.353 B.A. L.221 J.D. [🄲 Whitfield&E.]
Griffith, James E. ... '24 '55 C.351 B.A. L.352 LL.B. 306 W. State St.‡
McAllister, Rande A., (BV) ... '45 '71 C.353 B.A. L.900 J.D. [McAllister]

McAllister Law Office, (BV)
300 South Jefferson Street, P.O. Box 618, 52641
Telephone: 319-385-9524 Fax: 319-385-8921
Email: maclaw@iowatelecom.net
Rande A. McAllister.
Real Estate, Probate, Estate Planning, Trusts and Wills, Corporate, Commercial Law and Abstract of Title and Escrow Services.
References: Pilot Grove Savings Bank, Pilot Grove, Iowa; Henry County Bank, Mt. Pleasure, Iwoa.

See Professional Biographies, MT. PLEASANT, IOWA

McCoid, David L., (BV) ... '40 '68 C.352 B.A. L.502 J.D. 202 N. Jefferson St.
McCormick, Philip D., (BV) ... '— '84 C.352 B.B.A. L.221 J.D. [Whitfield&E.]
Riepe, Michael A., (BV) ... '45 '74 C.378 B.A. L.352 J.D. Courthouse
Slater, Darin, (CV) ... '71 '97 C.339 B.S. L.589 J.D. [🄰 Becker]
Thomas, Jeffrey D., (BV) ... '58 '91 C.350 B.S. L.352 J.D. [Bainter&T.]
Thomson, W. Kent, (BV) ... '45 '72 C.293 B.A. L.352 J.D. P.O. Box 622
Vance, Michael C., (BV) ... '51 '76 C&L.352 B.A., J.D. [Vance]
Vance Law Office, (BV) ... 101 N. Jefferson St.

Whitfield & Eddy, P.L.C., (AV)
110 N. Jefferson, Suite 101, 52641-2016 ⊙
Telephone: 319-385-9522 Fax: 319-385-3633
Email: info@whitfieldlaw.com URL: http://www.whitfieldlaw.com
Philip D. McCormick; Danny L. Cornell. Of Counsel: Alanson K. Elgar.
General Practice including Trial and Appellate Practice and Business and Banking. Alternative Dispute Resolution, Antitrust and Trade Regulation, Arbitration, Bankruptcy, Banks and Banking, Business, Civil Rights, Commercial, Construction, Corporate, Criminal, Environmental, Family, Fidelity and Surety, Foreclosures, Health Care, Immigration and Naturalization, Insurance, Insurance Defense, Intellectual Property, Labor and Employment, Mediation, Municipal, Personal Injury, Probate, Products Liability, Professional Liability, Real Estate, Securities, Taxation, Transportation, Trust and Estates, Utility, Wills, Workers Compensation.
For a complete list of Representative Clients, see Des Moines.
Des Moines, Iowa Office: 317 6th Avenue, Suite 1200, 50309-4195. Telephone: 515-288-6041. Fax: 515-246-1474. Email: info@whitfieldlaw.com. URL: http://www.whitfieldlaw.com.
Ankeny, Iowa Office: 213 North Ankeny Boulevard, Suite 100, 50021-1749. Telephone: 515-964-3633. Fax: 515-964-3692. Email: info@whitfieldlaw.com. URL: http://www.whitfieldlaw.com.
West Des Moines, Iowa Office: 3737 Woodland Avenue, Suite 400, 50266. Telephone: 515-558-0111. Fax: 515-222-0318. Email: info@whitfieldlaw.com. URL: http://www.whitfieldlaw.com.

See Professional Biographies, MT. PLEASANT, IOWA

Wiegel, Gary L., (AV) ... '37 '65 C.504 B.A. L.221 J.D. 114 E. Monroe St., Suite 102

MT. VERNON, 3,390, *Linn Co.*

Johansen, Kay M., (BV) ... '50 '91 C&L.352 B.A., J.D. 318 Second Ave. N.
Kudart, Arthur R., (AV) ... '30 '58 C&L.352 B.A., J.D. [Kudart] ⊙
Kudart Law Offices, (AV) ... 122 1st St., West (⊙Cedar Rapids, Mechanicsville)
Wolfe, Douglas D., (CV) ... '50 '76 C.187 B.A. L.221 J.D. [Wolfe]
Wolfe, R. B. ... '06 '30 C.187 B.A. L.352 J.D. [Wolfe] ‡
Wolfe Law Offices, (CV) ... 202 W. First St.

MOVILLE, 1,583, *Woodbury Co.*

Metcalf, Glenn A., (BV) ... '50 '86 C.352 B.A. L.793 J.D. [Metcalf,T.&P.] (⊙Kingsley)
Metcalf, Thompson & Phipps, (BV) ... 232 Main St. (⊙Kingsley, Remsen)
Phipps, Patrick J., (BV) ... '57 '82 C.1348 B.A. L.190 J.D. [Metcalf,T.&P.]

MUSCATINE, * 22,697, *Muscatine Co.*

Allbee, Harvey G., Jr., (AV) '34 '58
C&L.352 B.A., J.D. [Allbee,B.A.D.&O.] (⊙West Liberty)

Allbee, Barclay, Allison, Denning & Oppel, A Professional Corporation, (AV)
115 East Second Street, P.O. Box 8127, 52761 ⊙
Telephone: 563-263-1960 Fax: 563-263-1976
Email: lawyers@albeelaw.com
Gus Allbee (1879-1947); Robert Brooke (1879-1961); Robert H. Wilson (1921-1981); Robert F. Barclay (1917-1997); Harvey G. Allbee (1907-2000); Harvey G. Allbee, Jr.; Gary R. Allison; Gerald F. Denning; Linda L. Allison; R Craig Oppel.
General Practice. Corporate, Banking, Bankruptcy, Real Estate, Trust, Probate, Estate Planning, Domestic Relations, Personal Injury, Wrongful Death and Negligence Law, Trials and Appeals, Municipal Law.
Representative Clients: Central State Bank; Cities of Muscatine, Wilton, Durant, Atalissa, Conesville and Fruitland; Wilton Savings Bank; West Liberty State Bank; First National Bank of Muscatine; Alcoa Employees and Community Credit Union.

(This Listing Continued)

Allbee, Barclay, Allison, Denning & Oppel, A Professional Corporation (Continued)

Local Counsel For: Wells Fargo Home Mortgage; Principal Residential Mortgage, Inc.; Wilton Savings Bank; US Bank; Countrywide Home Mortgage.
Wilton, Iowa Office: 603 W. Fifth Street, Sunel, 52778-0004. Telephone: 563-732-2666. Fax: 563-732-2667.
West Liberty, Iowa Office: 110 East Third Street, 52776-0346. Telephone: 319-627-2713. Fax: 319-627-6826.

Allison, Gary R., (BV) '46 '71 C&L.352 B.B.A., J.D. [Allbee,B.A.D.&O.] (⊙West Liberty)
Allison, Linda L., (BV) '47 '85 C&L.352 B.S.N., J.D. [Allbee,B.A.D.&O.] (⊙West Liberty)
Axel, Joan U., (BV) .... '43 '82 C.350 B.S. L.352 J.D. [Stanley,L.&H.] (⊙Wilton)
Baker, Neva Rettig, (CV) .... '61 '87 C&L.352 B.A., J.D. Muscatine Legal Servs.
Bloom, Elmer E. .... '20 '47 C&L.352 B.A., J.D. 2707 Bidwell Rd.‡
Bonady, Mark S. .... '44 '73 C&L.966 B.B.A., J.D. V.P., HNI Co., Inc.
Bouska, Paul C., (BV) .... '68 '96 C&L.352 B.A., J.D. 610 Cedar St.

Bribriesco, William J., & Associates
(See Bettendorf)

Burns, Jack L. .... '32 '65 C&L.352 B.A., J.D. Dist. J.
Caldwell, Roland M., (CV) .... '56 '93 L.352 J.D. 210 E. Second St.
Clifton, Michael T. .... '73 '02 C.351 B.A. L.352 J.D. Staff Atty., Bandag, Inc.
Conlon, Walter J., (BV) .... '47 '75 C.177 B.A. L.352 J.D. [Metcalf,C.&S.]
Cottrell, Kristin A. .... '67 '93 C.339 B.S. L.352 J.D. 301 Iowa Ave.
Coulter, Charles R., (AV) .... '40 '65 C&L.352 B.A., J.D. [Stanley,L.&H.] (⊙Davenport)
Creasey, William F., (BV) .... '47 '80 C.293 B.A. L.352 J.D. [Goedken&C.]
Dekock, Robert H. .... '47 '73 C&L.352 B.B.A., J.D. [Dekock]
Dekock Law Office .... 227 Mulberry Ave.
Denning, Gerald F., (BV) .... '50 '76 C&L.352 B.A., J.D. [Allbee,B.A.D.&O.] ⊙
Dragon, Jean E. .... '61 '95 C.226 B.A. L.352 J.D. [Ⓐ Stanley,L.&H.] (⊙Davenport)
Dulceak, Brandy .... '72 '01 C&L.352 B.A., J.D. [Ⓐ Stanley,L.&H.] (⊙Davenport)
Eichelberger, John R., (BV) .... '57 '83 C&L.352 B.B.A., J.D. [J.R.Eichelberger]
Eichelberger, Rosalinda A. .... '70 '02 C&L.352 B.B.A., J.D. [Ⓐ J.R.Eichelberger]
Eichelberger, John R., P.C., (BV) .... 208 West 2nd Street, Suite 201
Fishburn, John C., (BV) .... '18 '47 C&L.352 A.B., J.D. 2807 Cedar St.
Fowler, Wes A. .... '76 '01 C&L.352 B.A., J.D. [Ⓐ Stanley,L.&H.] (⊙Davenport)
Goedken, Duane J., (BV) .... '38 '63 C&L.352 B.A., J.D. [Goedken&C.]
Goedken and Creasey, (BV) .... 319 East Second Street, Suite 301

Gosma, Tarbox & Associates, P.L.C.
(See Davenport)

Hargrafen, William J., (BV) .... '51 '77 C&L.352 B.B.A., J.D. 1102 Park Ave.
Heller, Michelle L. .... '77 '02 C&L.352 B.A., J.D. [Ⓐ Nepple L.] ⊙
Hill, Frank B., (BV) .... '34 '64 C.475 B.S. L.912 LL.B. 2905 N. Hwy. 61 (Pat.)
Hintermeister, John L., (BV) ... '38 '66 C&L.352 B.A., J.D. 300 East 2nd Street, Suite 301
Huff, Jay S., (CV) '53 '80 C.352 B.A. L.966 J.D. Secy. & Asst. Gen. Coun., Varied Investments, Inc.
Johnson, James I. '48 '76 C.494 B.S. L.1035 J.D. (adm. in MN; not adm. in IA) V. P., Gen. Coun. & Secy., HNI Corporation
Johnson, Jeffrey M., (BV) .... '56 '81 C.187 B.A. L.352 J.D. 109 Canon Ave.
Johnston, Douglas E., (BV) .... '48 '74 C.705 B.S. L.221 J.D. 323 E. 2nd St.
Johnston, Gregory A., (CV) .... '47 '77 C.513 B.S. L.221 J.D. 323 E. 2nd St.
Jung, Jay .... '72 '03 C&L.352 B.A., J.D. [Ⓐ Nepple L.] ⊙
Knoernschild, Eric M., (AV) .... '48 '73 C.350 B.S. L.352 J.D. 300 E. 2nd St., Ste. 301
Lande, Robert L., (AV) .... '47 '72 C&L.352 B.S., J.D. [Stanley,L.&H.] (⊙Davenport)
Lande, Roger L., (AV) '36 '61 C&L.352 B.A., J.D. [Stanley,L.&H.] (⊙Coralville, Davenport)
Lorenger, Jeffrey D. '65 '91 C&L.352 B.B.A., J.D. (adm. in MN; not adm. in IA) V.P., Gen. Coun. & Secy., HNI Corporation
Madden, Patrick Jefferson .... '41 '77 C.813 B.A. L.352 J.D. Dist. J.
Marquard, Henry F. '54 '79 C&L.209 B.A., J.D. Corp. Counsel, Stanley Consultants, Inc.

McCarthy, Lammers & Hines
(See Davenport)

McGuire, Richard P. .... '71 '97 C.367 B.A. L.884 J.D. HNI Corporation
Mealy, Terrence L., (BV) .... '30 '57 C.177 B.A. L.276 J.D. 301 E. Second St.
Meloy, David J., (BV) .... '50 '75 C&L.352 B.A., J.D. [Stanley,L.&H.] (⊙Davenport)
Metcalf, J. Michael, (BV) .... '50 '76 C&L.352 B.A., J.D. [Metcalf,C.&S.]
Metcalf, Conlon & Siering, P.L.C., (BV) .... 126 W. Second St.
Nelson, Kenza B. .... '79 '05 C.898 B.A. L.352 J.D. [Ⓐ Stanley,L.&H.]
Nepple, James A., (AV) .... '45 '70 C.190 B.A. L.352 J.D. [Nepple L.] ⊙

Nepple Law, P.L.C., (AV)
Hershey Professional Center, 216 Sycamore Street, Suite 500, 52761-3809 ⊙
Telephone: 563-264-6840 Telecopier: 563-264-6844 Toll Free: 877-888-0675
Email: tax@nepplelaw.com URL: http://www.nepplelaw.com
James A. Nepple;—Jay Jung; Michelle L. Heller.
Taxation, Estate Planning, Trust and Estate Administration, Wills and Probate Administration, Nonprofit and Charitable Organizations, Businesses and Corporations, Pension and Profit Sharing Plans, Real Estate, and Farms.
Rock Island, Illinois Office: American Bank Building, 1515 Fourth Avenue, Suite 300, 61201. Telephone: 309-732-1230; Toll Free: 877-888-0675. Telecopier: 309-786-0061.
Davenport, Iowa Office: Wells Fargo Bank Building, 4300 E. 53rd Street, Suite 103, 52807. Telephone: 563-355-6841. Toll Free: 877-888-0675. Telecopier: 563-355-6842.

Newell, David W., (BV) .... '39 '66 C.641 B.A. L.352 J.D. 323 East 2nd St.
Oppel, R Craig, (CV) '67 '95 C.112 B.A. L.221 J.D. [Allbee,B.A.D.&O.] (⊙West Liberty)
Ostergren, Alan R., (BV) .... '72 '97 C.293 B.A. L.221 J.D. Asst. Co. Atty.
Phillips, Richard R., (BV) .... '53 '80 C.350 B.A. L.221 J.D. Co. Atty.
Reidel, Thomas G., (BV) .... '67 '92 C.350 B.A. L.352 J.D. 300 E. 2nd St., Ste. 301
Schmidt, Rebecca L., (BV) .... '69 '94 C.427 B.A. L.352 J.D. Coun., HNI Corporation
Schoenig, Rachel R. Watkins '68 '94 C.707 B.A. L.221 J.D. Dir. Legal Serv., Bandag Incorporated
Sharar, Darrell L. .... '29 '57 C&L.352 B.A., J.D. 509 Centre Dr.
Siering, Michael, (CV) .... '56 '82 C.934 B.A. L.352 J.D. [Metcalf,C.&S.]

Stanley, Lande & Hunter, A Professional Corporation, (AV)
301 Iowa Avenue, Suite 400, 52761 ⊙
Telephone: 563-264-5000 Facsimile: 563-263-8775
Email: Contact.us@slhlaw.com URL: http://www.slhlaw.com
Roger L. Lande; Charles R. Coulter; Robert L. Lande; David J. Meloy; Joan U. Axel; Eric J. Thomsen;—Brandy Dulceak; Jean E. Dragon; Wes A. Fowler; Kenza B. Nelson.
General Civil and Trial Practice. Corporation, Business, Banking, Taxation, Securities, Tax-Exempt Financing, Labor, Employment Discrimination, Administrative, Creditor Bankruptcy and Agricultural Law, Insurance Defense, Personal Injury and Property Damage Law, Pension and Profit-Sharing, Real Estate, Probate, Estate Planning and Charitable Trusts and Foundations Law.
General Counsel for: First National Bank of Muscatine.

(This Listing Continued)

Stanley, Lande & Hunter, A Professional Corporation (Continued)

Representative Clients: HON Industries, Inc. and its subsidiaries; Milwaukee Mutual Insurance Co.; Stanley Consultants, Inc. and its affiliates.
Davenport, Iowa Office: 900 U.S. Bank Center, 201 West Second Street. Telephone: 563-324-1000. Facsimile: 563-326-6266.
Wilton, Iowa Office: 115 West Fourth, P.O. Box 481. Telephone: 563-732-4000. Facsimile: 563-732-2318.
Coralville, Iowa Office: 2201 East Grantview Drive, Suite 200. Telephone: 319-248-9000. Facsimile: 319-248-9001.

See Professional Biographies, MUSCATINE, IOWA

Stohr, R. K. .... '13 '37 C&L.352 B.A., J.D. Sr. Dist. J.‡
Thomsen, Eric J., (AV) '53 '78 C.350 B.S. L.352 J.D. [Stanley,L.&H.] (⊙Davenport, Wilton)
Timm, Donald A. .... '41 '73 C.350 B.S. L.352 J.D. 3004 Lucas St.★
Trent, William B., Jr., (AV) '47 '72 C.1108 B.A. L.276 J.D. Sr. V.P. & Gen. Coun., Varied Investments, Inc.
Weaver, James A. .... '53 '79 C.57 B.A. L.352 J.D. Assoc. Dist. J.
Wunder, John, (BV) .... '55 '82 C.898 B.A. L.352 J.D. [Wunder]
Wunder Law Office, (BV) .... 610 Cedar St.

NASHUA, 1,618, *Chickasaw Co.*

Cronin, Skilton & Skilton .... 205 Brasher St.
Demro, James M., (BV) .... '20 '50 C.910 L.734 J.D. 12 Woodbridge St.
Skilton, Christine Bishop .... '59 '84 C&L.221 B.S.B.A., J.D. Jud. Mag. [Cronin,S.&S.]
Skilton, David H. .... '58 '83 C.966 B.A. L.221 J.D. [Cronin,S.&S.]

NEOLA, 894, *Pottawattamie Co.*

Peters Law Firm, P.C., (AV)
401 Front Street, P.O. Box 282, 51559 ⊙
Telephone: 712-485-2265
URL: http://www.peterslawfirm.com
Scott J. Rogers.
Personal Injury Litigation and Commercial Litigation. Insurance, Tax, Real Estate, Corporation, Probate and Bankruptcy Law.
Representative Clients: Bluffs Run Casino; Grinnell Mutual Reinsurance Co.; Iowa West Racing Association; Rockwell International; Shelter Insurance; State Farm Insurance; Kemper Group; The Pillsbury Co.; The Cities of Crescent, Glenwood, Treynor, McClelland, Underwood.
Council Bluffs, Iowa Office: 233 Pearl Street. P.O. Box 1078. Telephone: 712-328-3157. FAX: 712-328-9092.
Glenwood, Iowa Office: 10 North Walnut. Telephone: 712-527-4877. FAX: 712-527-3418.
South Omaha, Nebraska Office: 4828 South 24th Street, Suite 200, 68107. Telephone: 402-731-1711. Fax: 402-731-3363.

See Professional Biographies, NEOLA, IOWA

Rogers, Scott J., (BV) .... '61 '87 C.194 B.S. L.190 J.D. [Peters] (⊙Council Bluffs)

NEVADA, * 6,658, *Story Co.*

Bappe, Daniel E., (BV) .... '50 '81 C.870 B.S. L.352 J.D. 511 J Ave.
Bender, Bradley M. '75 '01 C.477 B.A. L.221 J.D. Asst. Pub. Def., Off. of the State Pub. Def.
Cahill, Joseph R., (AV) .... '51 '76 C&L.352 B.A., J.D. [Cahill]
Cahill, Thomas J., (AV) .... '44 '69 C&L.352 B.A., J.D. [Cahill]

Cahill Law Offices, (AV)
1015 Fifth Street, 50201
Telephone: 515-382-6571 Fax: 515-382-4338
URL: http://www.lawyers.com/cahilllawoffice
Members of Firm: Donald L. Nelson (1922-1984); Thomas J. Cahill; Joseph R. Cahill.
General Trial Practice. Probate, Corporation, Municipal, Negligence, Real Estate and Insurance Law. Estate Planning, Trusts, Wills, Estates and Probate.
General Counsel for: Community Bank.
Representative Clients: Colo Telephone Co.; Allied Group; Iowa Mutual Insurance Co.

See Professional Biographies, NEVADA, IOWA

Countryman, Dayton W., (BV) .... '18 '48 C.350 B.S. L.352 J.D. [D. Countryman]
Dayton Countryman Law Offices, P.C., (BV) .... 1001 5th St.
Finn, Timothy J. .... '48 '74 C.352 B.A. L.221 J.D. Dist. J.
Holmes, Russell E. .... '54 '89 C.351 B.A. L.221 J.D. Legal Aid Soc.
Holmes, Stephen H., (BV) .... '53 '89 C.352 B.G.S. L.221 J.D. Asst. Co. Atty.
Jordening, Steven D., (CV) .... '48 '91 C.350 B.S. L.221 J.D. [Jordening]
Jordening Law Office, P.C., (CV) .... 517 J Avenue
Juhl, Donald G., (CV) .... '38 '74 C.243 B.S. L.352 J.D. 616 J Ave.
LoRang, Gerald A. .... '47 '75 C.352 B.B.A. L.879 J.D. [Ⓒ Jordening]
Miller, John B., (AV) .... '17 '46 C.350 B.S. L.352 J.D. [Ⓒ Jordening]
Olberding, Mark J., (CV) .... '61 '86 C&L.190 B.A., J.D. [Olberding]
Olberding Law Office, (CV) .... 1129 5th Street
Parker, Richard O., (BV) .... '47 '74 C&L.352 B.B.A., J.D. [Parker]

Parker Law Firm, (BV)
1009 Sixth Street, P.O. Box 553, 50201
Telephone: 515-382-5431 Fax: 515-382-5433
Richard O. Parker.
General Practice in all Courts. Negligence, Real Estate, Banking and Probate. Trials and Appeals.
Representative Client: State Bank & Trust Co.

Rigg, J. Keith
(See Des Moines)

Ryman, Kathy Pett, (CV) '45 '89 C.30 B.A. L.221 J.D. Exec. Dir., Legal Aid Soc. of Story Co.
West, Kim Marlow, (Mr.), (CV) .... '53 '83 C&L.352 B.S., J.D. Asst. Pub. Def.

NEWELL, 887, *Buena Vista Co.*

Gailey, James W., (BV) .... '37 '64 C.106 B.A. L.352 LL.B. Jud. Mag.

NEWHALL, 854, *Benton Co.*

Weichman, David E., (BV) .... '21 '48 C&L.352 B.A., J.D. 218 1st St. E.

NEW HAMPTON, * 3,660, *Chickasaw Co.*

Antes, Jon W., (BV) .... '44 '70 C&L.221 B.A., J.D. [Ⓒ Elwood,O.S.B.&C.] ⊙
Bottum, Mary P. '39 '80 C.1265 B.S. L.1162 J.D. (adm. in DC; not adm. in IA) 2055 Newell Ave.‡
Braun, Joseph P., (CV) .... '68 '95 C.494 B.A. L.1035 J.D. [Elwood,O.S.B.&C.] ⊙
Elwood, Henry L., (AV) .... '34 '59 C.187 B.A. L.221 J.D. [Elwood,O.S.B.&C.] ⊙

Elwood, O'Donohoe, Stochl, Braun & Churbuck, (AV)
101 North Locust Avenue, P.O. Box 310, 50659 ⊙
Telephone: 641-394-5943 Fax: 641-394-5945
Email: elwood@myclearwave.net
Members of Firm: Henry L. Elwood; James E. O'Donohoe (1921-1998); Christopher F. O'Donohoe; Richard D. Stochl; Judith Mack O'Donohoe; Joseph P. Braun; Lewis M. Churbuck (1972-2003).
Associates: Jeremiah W. White; Todd P. Prichard. Of Counsel: Richard P. TeKippe; Jon W. Antes.
General Practice in State and Federal Courts. Litigation, Insurance Defense, Probate, Estate Planning, Trusts and Wills, Real Estate, Corporate, Banking and Taxation Law. Trials and Appeals.

(This Listing Continued)

Elwood, O'Donohoe, Stochl, Braun & Churbuck (Continued)

Representative Clients: Grinnell Mutual Reinsurance Co.; United Fire & Casualty Insurance Co.; Board of Trustees, New Hampton Municipal Light Plant; First Citizens National Bank, New Hampton, Iowa; Alliance Pipeline; Cresco Union Savings Bank, Cresco, Iowa; Featherlite, Inc.; Community First National Bank, Protivin, Iowa; City of Cresco, Iowa.
Cresco, Iowa Office: 217 North Elm Street. P.O. Box 377, 52136. Telephone: 563-547-3321. Fax: 563-547-3189.
Charles City, Iowa Office: 116 North Main Street. P.O. Box 307. 50616. Telephone: 641-228-8054. Fax: 641-228-8057.
West Union, Iowa Office: 125 N. Vine, P.O. Box 475, 52175. Telephone: 563-422-5631. Fax: 563-422-5632.

Kennedy, Kevin J., (BV) .... '48 '74 C.602 A.B. L.352 J.D. [Kennedy&K.]
Kennedy, Michael K., (AV) ....'39 '68 C.602 B.A. L.352 J.D. [Kennedy&K.] ⊙

Kennedy and Kennedy, (AV)
Kennedy Law Building, 12 East Main Street, P.O. Box 406, 50659 ⊙
Telephone: 641-394-3113 FAX: 641-394-5173
Email: kenndlaw@rconnect.com URL: http://www.lawyers.com/kenndlaw
Members of Firm: William J. Kennedy (1935-1979); Michael K. Kennedy; Kevin J. Kennedy.
Probate, Real Estate, Criminal Law, Trial Practice.
Lawler, Iowa Office: 411 East Grove. Telephone: 563-238-8761.
See Professional Biographies, NEW HAMPTON, IOWA

O'Connor, James D., (AV) .... '33 '59 C&L.352 LL.B. 101 N. Locust Ave.‡
O'Donohoe, Christopher F., (AV) '50 '75 C.118 B.A. L.178 J.D. [Elwood,O.S.B.&C.] ⊙
O'Donohoe, Judith Mack, (BV) '51 '76 C.118 B.A. L.569 J.D. [Elwood,O.S.B.&C.] ⊙
Prichard, Todd P. .... '— '04 C&L.352 B.A., J.D. [▣ Elwood,O.S.B.&C.] ⊙
Schwickerath, Mark W., (CV) ....'45 '75 C.351 B.A. L.352 J.D. [M.W.Schwickerath]
Schwickerath, Mark W., P.C., (CV) ....2069 170th St.
Stochl, Richard D., (BV) ....'64 '89 C.927 B.S. L.352 J.D. [Elwood,O.S.B.&C.] ⊙
TeKippe, Richard P., (BV) ..... '40 '64 C.177 B.A. L.352 J.D. [▣ Elwood,O.S.B.&C.] ⊙
White, Jeremiah W. .... '— '04 C.351 B.A. L.352 J.D. [▣ Elwood,O.S.B.&C.] ⊙

NEW LONDON, 1,992, *Henry Co.*

Bell, Donald J., (AV) ....'13 '37 C.352 L.597 LL.B. [Bell&O.]
Bell & Ort, P.C., (AV) ....121 W. Main St.
Hansen, Robert L. .... '26 '52 C.106 B.A. L.221 J.D. 200 W. Main St.‡
Ort, Steven E., (BV) .... '54 '79 C.353 B.A. L.352 J.D. [Bell&O.]

NEWTON, * 15,579, *Jasper Co.*

Bair, Erik D. ....'— '01 L.221 J.D. [▣ Walker&B.] (⊙Des Moines)
Basler, David K. '69 '94 C.999 B.A. L.228 J.D. Assoc. Gen. Cnsl., Maytag Corporation (Legal Department)
Bennett, E. James, (AV) '41 '66 C&L.352 B.A., J.D. Secretary & Assistant General Counsel, Maytag Corporation
Billingsley, John E., (BV) ....'— '82 L.221 J.D. [Walker&B.] (⊙Baxter)
Brierly Charnetski L.L.P., (AV) ....211 First Avenue West (⊙Grinnell, Sully)
Brown, Thomas R. .... '38 '74 C.339 B.S. L.352 J.D. Sr. J.
Caldwell, Gilbert R., III, (AV) ....'52 '78 C&L.862 B.A., J.D. [Caldwell,C.&C.]
Caldwell, Randal B., (AV) ....'55 '79 C.132 B.A. L.352 J.D. [Caldwell,C.&C.]

Caldwell, Caldwell & Caldwell, P.L.C., (AV)
102 First Street North, P.O. Box 187, 50208
Telephone: 641-792-7235 Toll Free: 1-888-323-0654 Fax: 641-792-1721 URL: http://www.lawyeriowa.com
Email: caldwell1@iowatelecom.net URL: http://www.lawyers.com/caldwell
Gilbert R. Caldwell (1921-1998); Gilbert R. Caldwell, III; Randal B. Caldwell.
General Practice in all Courts. Probate, Real Estate, Bankruptcy, Business Law, Employment, Special Education, Corporation and Taxation Law. Trials and Appeals. Family and Juvenile Law, Municipal.
See Professional Biographies, NEWTON, IOWA

Campbell, Tim J., Jr., (AV) ....'17 '42 C.504 A.B. L.352 J.D. [Matthias,C.T.&R.]
Chalupa, Dennis F., (AV) ....'44 '70 C.641 B.A. L.352 J.D. [Brierly C.] ⊙
Charnetski, Donald J., (BV) ....'47 '75 C.966 B.A. L.352 J.D. [Brierly C.] (⊙Grinnell)
Clayton, Benjamin C., (AV) ....'29 '53 C&L.352 B.A., J.D. [Selby,U.S.&H.]
Cleverley, James W., Jr., (BV) '55 '82 C.132 B.S. L.221 J.D. Asst. Co. Atty. [Johnson&C.]
Clower, Robert P., III ....'60 '96 C.103 A.B. L.93 J.D. [▣ Brierly C.] (⊙Grinnell)
Foust, William R. '42 '71 C.47 B.A. L.192 J.D. (adm. in AL; not adm. in IA) Maytag Corp.
Goodwin, Kirk '68 '99 C.352 B.S.E. L.221 J.D. Sr. Patent Atty, Maytag Corporation (Legal Department) (Pat.)
Gran, James M. '55 '80 C.350 B.S. L.352 J.D. N. Amer. Dist. Proj. Leader, Maytag Corp.
Greear, Trisha L. .... '76 '02 C.1119 B.A. L.838 J.D. [▣ Brierly C.] (⊙Grinnell)
Hamilton, Darrin T., (CV) ....'65 '90 C.352 B.S. L.221 J.D. City Atty.
Holwerda, Steven J., (BV) .... '57 '83 C.1304 B.A. L.879 J.D. [Selby,U.S.&H.]
Jacobsen, Michael K., (BV) ....'67 '93 C.791 B.S. L.221 J.D. Co. Atty.'s Off.
Johnson, R. Steven .... '47 '74 C.172 B.S. L.221 J.D. Co. Atty. [Johnson&C.]
Johnson & Cleverley, (BV) .... 118 1st St. N.
Lacina, Thomas A., (BV) ....'56 '83 C.942 B.A. L.352 J.D. [▣ Brierly C.] (⊙Grinnell)
Loney, Eric ....'— '01 L.221 J.D. [▣ Walker&B.] (⊙Des Moines)
Martin, Patricia J., (AV) '53 '81 C.375 B.S. L.352 J.D. Secretary & Dep. Gen Cnsl, Maytag Corp.
Matthias, Frederic, (AV) ....'15 '39 C&L.352 B.A., J.D. [▣ Matthias,C.T.&R.]
Matthias, Campbell, Tyler & Rickers, (AV) .... 112 N. 2nd Ave. E. (⊙Sully)
McCall, Bradley, (BV) ....'54 '79 C.352 B.S. L.221 J.D. [Brierly C.] ⊙
Mott, Thomas W. ....'45 '75 C&L.352 B.A., J.D. Assoc. Dist. J.
Nicholson, Scott W., (CV) .... '69 '96 C.352 B.A. L.221 J.D. Off. of Co. Atty.
Odland, Jane ....'55 '04 C.350 B.S. L.352 J.D. [▣ Walker&B.]
Olson, William D., (BV) ....'47 '81 C&L.352 B.A., J.D. [Brierly C.] (⊙Grinnell)
Otto, Mark A., (BV) ....'56 '82 C.800 B.A. L.221 J.D. [Brierly C.] ⊙
Rickers, Terry R., (BV) ....'60 '86 C.350 B.A. L.546 J.D. [Matthias,C.T.&R.]

Rigg, J. Keith
(See Des Moines)

Schnack, Ronald L., (BV) '42 '84 C.187 B.A. L.352 J.D. Sr. Corp. Cnsl., Maytag Corporation (Legal Department)
Scholten, Roger K. '55 '79 C.1348 B.A. L.352 J.D. Sr. V.P. & Gen. Cnsl., Maytag Corporation (Legal Department)
Selby, Herbert Spencer, (AV) ....'25 '49 C&L.352 B.A., J.D. [Selby,U.S.&H.]
Selby, Updegraff, Smith & Holwerda, (AV) ....101 First Avenue West
Smith, Ken J., (BV) ....'45 '73 C&L.352 B.S., J.D. [Selby,U.S.&H.]
Sorenson, David G., (BV) ....'41 '66 C&L.352 B.B.A., LL.B. [D.G.Sorenson]
Sorenson, David G., P.C., (BV) ....107 W. 2nd St., S.
Stonner, Dean F., (BV) ....'60 '86 C.804 B.S. L.221 J.D. Gen. Cnsl., Maytag Corp.
Terpstra, John H., (BV) ....'59 '92 C.350 B.S. L.352 J.D. [Brierly C.] ⊙
Tyler, James L., (AV) ....'27 '54 C&L.221 J.D. [Matthias,C.T.&R.] ⊙

Vroom, Lois J., (CV) ....'68 '94 C.132 B.A. L.352 J.D. [▣ Brierly C.] (⊙Grinnell)
Walker, Corey J. L., (BV) ... '— '97 C.132 B.S. L.221 J.D. [Walker&B.] (⊙Des Moines)
Walker, Kathryn "Beth" E., (BV) ....'— '00 L.221 J.D. [▣ Walker&B.]
Walker, Lee M., (BV) ....'— '75 L.221 J.D. [Walker&B.] (⊙Baxter)

Walker & Billingsley, (BV)
208 North Second Avenue West, P.O. Box 157, 50208 ⊙
Telephone: 641-792-3595 Fax: 641-792-0289 URL: http://www.walklaw.com
Email: corey@walklaw.com URL: http://www.lawyers.com/wkblaw
Members of Firm: Lee M. Walker; John E. Billingsley; Corey J. L. Walker. Associates: Kathryn "Beth" E. Walker; Erik D. Bair; Eric Loney; Jane Odland.
General Practice, Personal Injury and Wrongful Death, Family Law and Domestic Relations (Divorce), Real Estate, Wills, Trusts, Estate Planning and Probate Law, Criminal Law, Taxation and Tax Returns, Litigation and Trial Law, Product Liability, Employment Law, Medical Malpractice, Workers' Compensation.
Des Moines, Iowa Office: 1000 73rd Street, Suite 24. Telephone: 515-440-2852. Fax: 515-440-6077.
Baxter, Iowa Office: 103 East State. Telephone: 641-227-3800.
See Professional Biographies, NEWTON, IOWA

Watson, Bruce P. '65 '94 C.823 B.S.M.E. L.1218 J.D. Sr. Corp. Intellectual Prop. Cnsl., Maytag Corporation (Legal Department) (Pat.)
Wendel, Clifford D., Jr., (BV) ....'53 '85 C.872 B.A. L.221 J.D. 820 S. 6th Ave. West

NORTH ENGLISH, 944, *Iowa Co.*

Buchanan, Thomas M., (BV) '49 '74 C.734 A.B. L.352 J.D. Co. Jud. Mag. [Elwood,E.B.&L.] ⊙
Elwood, Michael J., (BV) .... '42 '67 C.707 B.A. L.585 J.D. [Elwood,E.B.&L.] ⊙
Elwood, Richard H., (BV) .... '35 '64 C.707 B.A. L.585 J.D. [Elwood,E.B.&L.] ⊙
Elwood, Elwood, Buchanan & Leinen, (BV) .....102 E. Clark (⊙Marengo, Williamsburg)
Leinen, Robert J., (BV) '57 '82 C.350 B.S. L.352 J.D. Co. Jud. Mag. [Elwood,E.B.&L.] ⊙

NORTH LIBERTY, 5,367, *Johnson Co.*

Brydon, Deb ....'68 '97 C&L.352 B.A., J.D. Univ. of Iowa
Leggott, L. Kirk '60 '86 C&L.1165 B.S.B.A., J.D. (adm. in CO; not adm. in IA) 15 Pinehurst Court

NORTHWOOD, * 2,050, *Worth Co.*

Ensign, Craig G., (BV) ....'42 '67 C.187 B.A. L.352 J.D. Mag.
Greve, John H., (BV) ....'39 '63 C.82 L.352 LL.B. 736 Central Ave.
Krull, Douglas A., (BV) ....'58 '85 C.872 B.A. L.352 J.D. [Krull]
Krull Law Office, (BV) .... 840 Central Ave.
Norland, Phillip N., (BV) ....'26 '59 C.352 B.A. L.767 J.D. 88 8th St., N.

NORWALK, 6,884, *Warren Co.*

Beery, James J., (CV) ....'54 '80 C&L.221 B.S., J.D. [Beery]
Beery Law Firm, P.C., (CV) .... 1329 Sunset Dr.
Daman, Katherine ....'77 '04 L.221 J.D. [▣ Powell]
DeVolder, Steven P., (AV) ....'59 '85 C.350 B.a. L.352 J.D. [DeVolder]
DeVolder Law Firm, The, (AV) .... 1228 Sunset Dr., Ste. C
Powell, Rod, (BV) ....'47 '73 C&L.352 B.A., J.D. [Powell]

Powell Law Firm, The, P.C., (BV)
1424 Sunset Drive, P.O. Box 189, 50211
Mailing Address: P.O. Box 189, Norwalk, Iowa 50211
Telephone: 515-981-9150 Fax: 515-981-9220
Email: powelaw@aol.com URL: http://www.lawyers.com/powelllawfirmpc
Rod Powell;—Katherine Daman.
Business Law, Construction Law, Family Law, Personal Injury, Real Estate, Administrative Law, Appellate Practice, Commercial Law, Consumer Law, Contracts, Federal Practice, Government Contracts, Guardianship and Conservatorship, Litigation, Probate, Trusts and Estates, Wills, Elder Law, Child Custody, Child Support, Divorce, Criminal Defense, Automobile Accidents and Injuries, Commercial Real Estate, Residential Real Estate Sales, Zoning Planning and Land Use, Corporate Law, Franchise Law, Small Business Law, Business Organization.
See Professional Biographies, NORWALK, IOWA

Schmidt, Katherine E. '58 '85 C.784 B.A. L.221 J.D. Associate Corporate Counsel, Allied Group Companies
Waltz, James F. ....'40 '70 C.350 B.S. L.221 J.D. 616 Jackson St.
Welp, Arthur, Jr. ....'47 '74 C&L.352 B.B.A., J.D. I.R.S.

OAKDALE, —, *Johnson Co.*

Wennerholm, Robert W. .... '39 '73 C.927 B.A. L.339 J.D. P.O. Box 161

OAKLAND, 1,496, *Pottawattamie Co.*

Hogzett, Donald D., (AV) ....'20 '48 C.194 A.B. L.221 J.D. 100 Linden St.
Pechacek, Frank W., Jr., (AV) ....'44 '69 C.351 B.A. L.352 J.D. [Willson&P.] ⊙
Willson & Pechacek, P.L.C., (AV) 105 N. Main (⊙Carroll, Council Bluffs, Harlan, Red Oak, Treynor)

ODEBOLT, 1,158, *Sac Co.*

Dresselhuis, George W., (AV) .... '10 '34 C&L.221 J.D. [Dresselhuis&H.]
Dresselhuis and Heidenreich, (AV) .... 100 Main St.
Heidenreich, Joseph J., (BV) ....'54 '79 C.350 B.S. L.190 J.D. [Dresselhuis&H.]

OELWEIN, 6,692, *Fayette Co.*

Hofmeyer, John W., III, (CV) ....'53 '78 C.872 B.S. L.221 J.D. 8 E. Charles St.
Johnson, J. G. ....'34 '59 C.309 B.A. L.221 J.D. Assoc. Dist. J.
Saur, W. Wayne, (BV) ....'53 '78 C&L.352 B.A., J.D. [Saur&S.]
Saur, Walter L., (BV) ....'27 '59 C.162 A.B. L.221 J.D. [Saur&S.]
Saur and Saur, (BV) ....120 E. Charles
Van Veldhuizen, Ron L., (BV) .... '53 '78 C.350 B.S. L.1049 J.D. 19 E. Charles St.
Woods, Larry F., (CV) .... '50 '77 C.872 B.A. L.221 J.D. 24 N. Frederick Ave.

OGDEN, 2,023, *Boone Co.*

Johnson, Lee R., (BV) .... '50 '75 C.293 B.A. L.352 J.D. [Johnson&M.]
Johnson & Malloy, P.C., (BV) ....214 W. Walnut
Malloy, James B., (BV) ....'54 '84 C.350 B.S. L.546 J.D. [Johnson&M.]
Oeth, Steven J., (BV) ....'55 '82 C&L.221 B.A., J.D. 1246 Javelin Place

OKOBOJI, 775, *Dickinson Co.*

Hamilton, Tom .... '32 '57 C&L.352 B.A., J.D. Dist. J.
Sackett, Rosemary Shaw .... '40 '63 C.106 B.A. L.221 LL.B. Appl. Ct. J.

ONAWA, * 3,091, *Monona Co.*

Gaukel, Nevins & Westergaard
(See Mapleton)

Jensen, Michael Paul, (BV) .... '51 '77 C.793 B.S. L.221 J.D. 710 Iowa Ave.
Taylor, Gary G., (BV) ....'42 '69 C&L.352 B.S., J.D 1019 9th St.
Underhill, James R. ....'34 '58 C&L.352 B.A., J.D. P.O. Box 135‡

ORANGE CITY, * 5,582, *Sioux Co.*

Bindner, Roger D., (BV) ......'39 '66 C&L.221 B.A., J.D. [Klay,V.B.D.&J.] (⊙Paullina)
De Jong, Bradley K., (BV) .... '56 '83 C.1348 B.A. L.190 J.D. [Klay,V.B.D.&J.]
Huibregtse, Robert R., (BV) .... '34 '63 C.352 B.S.C. L.221 LL.B. Asst. Atty. Gen.
Huitink, Terry L. .... '51 '77 C.352 B.A. L.221 J.D. Dist. J.
Jacobsma, Michael J., (CV) ....'69 '97 C.1348 B.A. L.190 J.D. [Klay,V.B.D.&J.]
Karssen, Paul M., (AV) .... '56 '81 C.1109 B.A. L.800 J.D. 612 8th St. S.E.

Klay, Veldhuizen, Bindner, De Jong & Jacobsma, P.L.C., (AV)
121 Albany Avenue, N.E., P.O. Box 405, 51041 ⊙
Telephone: 712-737-4851 Fax: 712-737-4853
Loren J. Veldhuizen; Roger D. Bindner; Bradley K. De Jong; Michael J. Jacobsma.
General Practice. Probate, Trusts and Estates, Real Estate, Taxation, Agricultural, Municipal, Corporate and Negligence Law. Trials and Appeals.
Alton, Iowa Office: Mitchell Building, 306-10th Street, P.O. Box H, 51003-0908. Telephone: 712-756-4141, Fax: 712-756-4646.
Paullina, Iowa Office: 111 South Main Street, P.O. Box 617, 51046-0617. Telephone: 712-949-2142. Fax: 712-949-2140.

See Professional Biographies, ORANGE CITY, IOWA

Pluim, Dan W., (BV) .... '54 '79 C.1304 B.A. L.352 J.D. [Rensink,P.&V.]
Rens, Gerrit L., (AV) .... '12 '36 L.793 LL.B. 108 Central Ave., N.E.‡
Rensink, John L., (BV) .... '37 '65 C.793 B.A. L.221 J.D. [Rensink,P.&V.]
Rensink, Pluim & Vogel, (BV) .... 108 Central Ave., N.W.
Veldhuizen, Loren J., (AV) ... '45 '71 C.114 A.B. L.352 J.D. [Klay,V.B.D.&J.] (⊙Alton)
Vogel, Patricia L., (BV) .... '68 '92 C&L.221 B.A., J.D. [Rensink,P.&V.]

OSAGE, * 3,439, *Mitchell Co.*

Dunkelberg, A. G., (AV) .... '22 '52 C&L.221 J.D. 804 Poplar St.‡
Dunkelberg, McKinley, Folkers & Walk, (AV) .... 515 State Street
Folkers, Jerry H., (AV) '38 '63 C.898 B.A. L.352 LL.B.
Co. Atty. [Dunkelberg,M.F.&W.]
Gaffney, Robert T. .... '54 '95 C.350 B.S. L.352 J.D. 515 State St.
Gross, Richard H., (BV) .... '52 '77 C.352 B.B.A. L.190 J.D. [Gross&M.]
Gross & McPhail, (BV) .... 631 Main St.
Kloberdanz, Murray A., (BV) ....'49 '76 C.602 B.A. L.352 J.D. [A Kratchmer&K.]
Kratchmer, Vernon E., (AV) ....'35 '62 C&L.352 B.A., J.D. [Kratchmer&K.]
Kratchmer & Kloberdanz, (AV) .... 500 Main Street
McKinley, Bryan H. ....'51 '76 C.352 B.B.A. L.221 J.D. Dist. J.
McKinley, Keith A., (AV) ....'33 '60 C.966 B.S. L.221 J.D. [Dunkelberg,M.F.&W.]
McPhail, Brian R., (BV) ....'56 '83 C.351 B.A. L.623 J.D. [Gross&M.]
Murphy, Aaron R., (CV) ....'69 '97 C.352 B.A. L.221 J.D. 515 State St.
Walk, Mark L., (BV) ....'56 '90 C.106 B.A. L.352 J.D. [Dunkelberg,M.F.&W.]

OSCEOLA, * 4,614, *Clarke Co.*

Booth, Unes J., (BV) ....'46 '77 C.339 B.S. L.192 J.D. [Booth]
Booth Law Firm, (BV) .... 122 W. Jefferson St.
Brown, James W. ....'30 '59 C.293 B.A. L.221 J.D. Dist. J.
Kimes, Gary G. ....'45 '74 C.350 B.S. L.221 J.D. Dist. J.
Mueller, Helmut ....'26 '51 C.339 L.365 J.D. Rt. 5
Murphy, Richard J., (BV) ....'39 '64 C.177 B.A. L.352 LL.B. 116 W. Jefferson St.
Murphy, Thomas Richard, (CV) ....'66 '95 C.352 B.B.A. L.190 J.D. 116 W. Jefferson
Reynoldson, Elisabeth S., (BV) .....'67 '92 C.350 B.B.A. L.352 J.D. [Reynoldson,V.&R.]
Reynoldson, Robert W., (AV) ....'48 '74 C&L.352 B.A., J.D. [Reynoldson,V.&R.]
Reynoldson, W. Ward, (AV) ....'20 '48 C.545 B.A. L.352 J.D. [C Reynoldson,V.&R.]
Reynoldson, Van Werden & Reynoldson, L.L.P., (AV) ....200 West Jefferson Street
Van Werden, Lawrence Philip, (AV) '37 '66 C.350 B.S. L.221 J.D.
[Reynoldson,V.&R.]

OSKALOOSA, * 10,938, *Mahaska Co.*

Anderson, Allen A., (BV) ....'48 '77 C&L.221 B.A., J.D. [Spayde,W.&A.]
Blomgren, James Q., (AV) ....'47 '73 C.352 B.A. L.893 J.D. Dist. Ct. J.
Brice, Michael P. ....'46 '74 C.350 B.S. L.352 J.D. [M.P.Brice]
Brice, Michael P., P.C. ....115 1st Ave., W., Suite 1
Broerman, Michael W., (BV) ....'55 '80 C&L.352 B.B.A., J.D. 216 S. 1st St.
Clements, Robert K., (BV) ....'49 '74 C&L.190 J.D. [Clements,P.S.&Y.]
Clements, Pothoven, Stravers & Yates, (AV) ....110 N. Market St.
Crookham, Joe P. ....'39 '68 C.352 B.A. L.221 J.D. V.P., Mycro Grp. Co.
DeGeest, Randy S., (BV) ....'53 '78 C&L.221 B.A., J.D. 219 First Avenue East
Faulkner, Hugh V., (AV) ....'28 '57 C&L.352 B.S.C., J.D. 216 S. 1st St.
Fisher, Julie Bond, (BV) ....'68 '96 C.132 B.A. L.352 J.D. Musco Corporation
Hansen, James M., (BV) '58 '86
C.293 B.A. L.352 J.D. General Counsel, Musco Corporation
Life, Greg A., (BV) ....'48 '74 C.587 B.S. L.221 J.D. 102 First Ave. E.
Lind, George L. ....'40 '72 C.1029 B.S. L.602 J.D. 241 Terrace Dr.‡
Moore, Matthew B., (BV) ....'63 '91 C&L.352 B.A., J.D. 118 N. Market St.

Orsborn, Bauerle, Milani & Grothe, L.L.P.
(See Ottumwa)

Palmer, Eric Jonathon, (CV) ....'60 '87 C.949 B.A. L.221 J.D. 114 1st Ave., E.
Rielly, James P. ....'31 '58 C.933 B.A. L.352 J.D. Dist. J.
Spayde, White & Anderson, (BV) ....115 North Market Street
Stravers, Randall C., (AV) ....'51 '83 C.114 B.A. L.879 J.D. [Clements,P.S.&Y.]
Stream, Charles A., (BV) ....'41 '67 C.949 B.A. L.352 J.D. Co. Atty.
White, Bob O. ....'40 '71 C&L.352 B.A., J.D. [Spayde,W.&A.]
Yates, Joel D., (BV) ....'63 '95 C.520 B.A. L.221 J.D. [Clements,P.S.&Y.]

OTTUMWA, * 24,998, *Wapello Co.*

Appel, William H., (BV) ....'47 '85 C&L.352 B.A., J.D. 114 N. Market Street
Barnes, W. T., (AV) ....'18 '42 C&L.352 B.A., J.D. 424 Bryan Rd.‡
Bauerle, Richard C., (AV) ....'31 '56 C.350 B.S. L.352 J.D. [Orsborn,B.M.&G.]
Beaver, Jerome M., (AV) ....'40 '67 C.226 B.A. L.352 J.D. [C Kiple,D.B.G.&Z.]
Box, Herbert F., (BV) ....'08 '35 C.293 B.A. L.352 J.D. [Box&B.]
Box, James M., (BV) ....'46 '73 C.784 B.A. L.221 J.D. [Box&B.]
Box and Box, (BV) ....304 N. Court St.
Breckenridge, Robert E., II, (BV) .....'57 '82 C.352 B.A. L.546 J.D. [Breckenridge&D.]

Breckenridge & Duker, PC, (BV)
226 West Main Street, Suite 408, P.O. Box 616, 52501-0616
Telephone: 641-684-6097 Fax: 641-684-0209
Email: bdpc@ottumwalaw.net URL: http://www.ottumwalaw.net
Members of Firm: Robert E. Breckenridge, II; Kenneth A. Duker.
General Practice, Civil and Criminal Trials and Appeals in all Courts, Corporation, Domestic Relations, Labor and Employment Relations, Insurance Defense, Products Liability, Probate, Personal Injury, Real Estate, Administrative, Government and School Law.

See Professional Biographies, OTTUMWA, IOWA

Collett, Phillip R. ....'35 '61 C&L.221 B.S., J.D. Chf. Dist. J.‡
Daily, Kirk A. ....'59 '84 C&L.352 B.A., J.D. Assoc. Ct. J.
Denefe, J. Terrence, (AV) ....'47 '73 C&L.221 B.S.B.A., J.D. [Kiple,D.B.G.&Z.]
Detlie, H. Edwin, (BV) ....'50 '76 C.784 B.A. L.273 J.D. 303 E. 2nd. St.
Duker, Kenneth A., (BV) ....'67 '93 C.698 B.A. L.352 J.D. [Breckenridge&D.]
Elliott, James F., (BV) ....'53 '79 C.1156 B.A. L.1218 J.D. Legal Servs. Corp. of Iowa
Emanuel, Dennis W., (BV) ....'46 '73 C.602 B.S. L.190 J.D. [Webber,G.E.&D.]
Erhardt, Samuel K., (BV) ....'51 '77 C&L.352 B.A., J.D. 111 E. Court St.
Ferren, Philip K., (CV) ....'42 '68 C&L.352 B.A., J.D. [Ferren]
Ferren Law Office, (CV) ....2942 Oak Meadow Dr.
Gagnon, Tammi L. '68 '95 C.513 B.S. L.793 J.D.
(adm. in SD; not adm. in IA) Firstar Bank
Gardner, Steven, (AV) ....'59 '84 C.352 B.B.A. L.221 J.D. [Kiple,D.B.G.&Z.]
Gaumer, Richard J., (BV) ....'47 '74 C.933 B.A. L.352 J.D. [Webber,G.E.&D.]
Glenn, Gene W. ....'28 '60 C.352 B.A. L.273 LL.B. Juv. Ref.
Gourley, Mary Linn Ketron .....'70 '96 C.352 B.A. L.585 J.D. Legal Servs. Corp. of Iowa
Harrison, Gayla R., (BV) ....'60 '86 C&L.221 B.F.A., J.D. [Harrison,M.&W.]

Harrison, Moreland & Webber, P.C., (AV)
129 West Fourth Street, P.O. Box 250, 52501
Telephone: 641-682-8326 Fax: 641-682-8329
Email: hmmw@hmmw.com
John R. Webber, III; Michael J. Moreland; Gayla R. Harrison;—Shannon J. Woods. Of Counsel: John N. Moreland.
General Practice. Probate, Corporate, Real Estate, Health and Hospital, Labor and Employment and Insurance Law. Trials and Appeals.
Representative Clients: Insurance Company of North America; Allied Group; State Farm Insurance Co.

See Professional Biographies, OTTUMWA, IOWA

Hester, David J., (AV) ....'40 '66 C&L.352 B.A., J.D. 111 West Second Street
James, Timothy W., (CV) ....'56 '85 C.587 B.S. L.352 J.D. 515 Church St.
Johnson, Walter F., (AV) ....'25 '52 C&L.352 B.A., J.D. 111 West Second Street‡
Juvan, Frank T. .....'46 '72 C&L.352 B.A., J.D. Sr. V.P. & Tr. Offr., Firstar Bk. Ottumwa
Keith, Joni, (BV) ....'56 '80 C&L.221 B.A.J., J.D. [Keith]
Keith, Kenneth L., (AV) ....'26 '52 C&L.352 B.S.C., J.D. [Keith]
Keith, Lloyd E., (BV) ....'54 '80 C&L.221 B.A., J.D. [Keith]

Keith Law Firm, (AV)
1313 North Court, 52501
Telephone: 641-682-4377 Toll Free: 800-903-4377 Fax: 641-683-3472
Kenneth L. Keith; Joni Keith; Lloyd E. Keith.
General, Civil and Trial Practice in all Courts, Appellate Practice, Corporation, Insurance, Real Estate, Estate Planning and Probate, Personal Injury and Employment Discrimination Litigation.

See Professional Biographies, OTTUMWA, IOWA

Kiple, Charles M., (AV) ....'39 '68 C&L.352 B.B.A., J.D. 20 Woodshire Dr.‡

Kiple, Denefe, Beaver, Gardner & Zingg, L.L.P., (AV) BB
104 South Court Street, P.O. Box 493, 52501
Telephone: 641-683-1626 Fax: 641-683-3597
Email: KIPLELAW@LISCO.COM
Members of Firm: J. Terrence Denefe; Steven Gardner; Paul Zingg. Of Counsel: Jerome M. Beaver.
General Practice. Civil and Criminal Trials and Appeals, Probate, Real Estate, Labor, Insurance, Corporate, Personal Injury, Commercial, Workers Compensation, Municipal Law, Employment and Civil Rights Law.
General Counsel for: Winger Contracting Co.; Wapello Rural Water Association, Inc.; Norris Asphalt Paving Co; J.D. Carpenter Companies, Inc.; Elliott Oil, Inc.
Representative Clients: Farm Bureau Mutual Insurance Co.

See Professional Biographies, OTTUMWA, IOWA

Klein, Jon ....'70 '99 C.293 B.S. L.352 J.D. Law Clk., Dist. Ct.
Krafka, Mary Baird, (CV) '42 '93
C.949 B.A. L.352 J.D. 101 South Market Street, Suite 203
Logan, Jeffrey R., (CV) ....'69 '95 C.182 B.A. L.190 J.D. P.O. Box 936
Meadows, E. Richard, Jr. ....'47 '86 C.1369 B.S. L.221 J.D. Dist. J.
Milani, Gregory G., (BV) ....'60 '87 C&L.221 B.S., J.D. [Orsborn,B.M.&G.]
Mitchell, Ryan J. ....'78 '03 C.898 B.S. L.221 J.D. [A Orsborn,B.M.&G.]
Moreland, John N., (AV) ....'36 '61 C&L.602 B.A., J.D. [C Harrison,M.&W.]
Moreland, Michael J., (AV) ....'62 '91 C.190 B.S. L.352 J.D. [Harrison,M.&W.]
Orsborn, Allan C., (AV) ....'51 '77 C&L.352 B.S., J.D. [Orsborn,B.M.&G.]

Orsborn, Bauerle, Milani & Grothe, L.L.P., (AV)
110 East Third, P.O. Box 878, 52501 ⊙
Telephone: 641-682-5447 Fax: 641-682-6940
Email: obmglaw@pcsia.net URL: http://www.obmglaw.com
Members of Firm: Richard C. Bauerle; Allan C. Orsborn; Gregory G. Milani; Wilbur R. Dull (1914-1994). Associate: Ryan J. Mitchell.
General Civil and Trial Practice in All Courts. Real Estate, Estate Planning and Probate Law, Personal Injury, Employment Litigation, Family Law, Products Liability and Insurance Defense.
Representative Clients: Answer Plus, Inc.; Grinnell Mutual ReInsurance Co.; Edward D. Jones & Co.; George A. Hormel & Co.; MICO Inc.; Purina Mills Inc.; Employers Mutual Cos.
Centerville, Iowa Office: 105 West Van Buren, P. O. Box 518. Telephone: 641-856-3251. Fax: 641-856-5548.

See Professional Biographies, OTTUMWA, IOWA

Owens, William S. ....'59 '84 C.378 B.A. L.221 J.D. Assoc. Juv. J.
Pepper, William ....'71 '97 C&L.352 B.A., J.D. Legal Services Corp.
Schlegel, Dick R. ....'22 '50 C&L.352 B.A., J.D. Sr. Ct. App. J.
Schlegel, Richard R., II, (BV) ....'45 '75 C.352 B.S. L.426 J.D. 335 E. 4th St.
Webber, John R., III, (BV) ....'56 '82 C.112 B.A. L.221 J.D. [Harrison,M.&W.]
Webber, Gaumer, Emanuel & Daily, P.C., (BV) ....112 N. Court St.
Woods, Shannon J. ....'78 '03 C.106 B.A. L.221 .D [A Harrison,M.&W.]
Wynes, Timothy '55 '86 C.187 B.S.S. L.734 J.D.
(adm. in MO; not adm. in IA) 21 Woodshire Dr.‡
Zingg, Paul, (BV) ....'62 '88 C&L.352 B.A., J.D. [Kiple,D.B.G.&Z.]

OXFORD, 663, *Johnson Co.*

Klein, L. G. ....'24 '54 C&L.352 B.A., J.D. 4148 Cosgrove Rd. S.W.
Maiers, Sarah S., (BV) ....'52 '92 C&L.352 B.A., J.D. 4010 Will Ct. SW

PANAMA, 229, *Shelby Co.*

Deren, Patrick T., (AV) '47 '75 C.801 B.A. L.838 J.D.
[Salvo,D.S.&L.] (⊙Earling, Harlan)
Salvo, Deren, Schenck & Lauterbach, P.C., (AV) ....100 Main (⊙Earling, Harlan, Walnut)

PANORA, 1,100, *Guthrie Co.*

Bump, Jeffrey, (BV) ....'61 '89 C.350 B.S. L.221 J.D. [Bump&B.] ⊙
Bump, William E., (BV) ....'58 '84 C&L.221 B.A., J.D. [Bump&B.] ⊙
Bump and Bump, (BV) .... 7011 E. Lake Panorama, Hwy. 4 N. (⊙Stuart)
Ferree, Donald R. ....'23 '51 L.352 LL.B. 111 N. 1st St.‡
Perkins, Mary Ellen, (BV) ....'58 '88 C&L.221 B.A., J.D. P.O. Box 355

PARKERSBURG, 1,804, *Butler Co.*

Hansmann, Dale L., (BV) ....'52 '77 C&L.352 B.A., J.D. [Klinkenborg,H.&M.]
Klinkenborg, C. E., (BV) ....'32 '64 C&L.352 B.A., J.D. [C Klinkenborg,H.&M.]

Klinkenborg, Hansmann & Mansheim, (BV) .... 1201 Hwy. 20
Lawler, Thomas A., (AV) .... '46 '72 C.707 B.A. L.128 J.D. [Lawler&S.]
Lawler & Swanson, PLC, (AV) .... 601 Coates St.
Mansheim, David, (BV) .... '45 '77 C.352 B.A. L.1035 J.D. [Klinkenborg,H.&M.]
Papenheim, Gary R., (BV) .... '54 '79 C.352 B.A. L.190 J.D. [Papenheim]
Papenheim Law Office, (BV) .... 234 3rd St.
Pepples, Ronald J., (BV) .... '47 '73 C.351 B.A. L.352 J.D. 206 4th St.
Petersen, Martin M., (BV) '66 '92
C.350 B.S. L.221 J.D. Asst. Co. Atty. [Ⓐ Klinkenborg,H.&M.]
Swanson, Amy K., (CV) .... '68 '94 C.352 B.A. L.221 J.D. [Lawler&S.]

PAULLINA, 1,134, *O'Brien Co.*

Bindner, Roger D., (BV) '39 '66 C&L.221 B.A., J.D.
[Klay,V.B.D.&P.] (⊙Orange City)
Klay, Veldhuizen, Bindner, De Jong & Pals, P.L.C., (AV)
111 S. Main St. (⊙Alton, Orange City)

PELLA, 9,832, *Marion Co.*

Boehlje, Boyd W., (AV) .... '39 '67 C.350 B.S. L.352 J.D. [Gaass,K.&B.]
Boehlje, Chad A. .... '69 '95 C.352 B.A. L.208 J.D. [Ⓐ Gaass,K.&B.]

Brown, Winick, Graves, Gross, Baskerville and Schoenebaum, P.L.C., (AV)
616 Franklin Place, 50219 ⊙
Telephone: 641-628-4513 Fax: 641-628-8494
Email: bwg@ialawyers.com URL: http://www.ialawyers.com
Paul D. Hietbrink.
Des Moines, Iowa Office: 666 Grand Avenue, Suite 2000, 50309-2510.
West Des Moines, Iowa Office: Regency West 5, 4500 Westown Parkway, Suite 277, 50266-6717. Telephone: 515-242-2400. Fax: 515-242-2448.

See Professional Biographies, PELLA, IOWA

Chaplin, Wesley A., (CV) .... '73 '98 C.132 B.S. L.352 J.D. 700 Main St., Ste. 201
DeMeulenaere, William J. ... '65 '91 C.351 B.A. L.352 J.D. Gen. Coun., Pella Corporation
Dorman, Joel H., (BV) '61 '88 C.352 B.S. L.221 J.D.
Associate General Counsel, Pella Corporation
Gaass, Peter G., (AV) .... '17 '41 C.132 B.S. L.352 729 Main St.‡
Gaass, Klyn & Boehlje, (AV) .... 729 Main St.

Grefe & Sidney, P.L.C., (AV)
810 Washington Street, 50219 ⊙
Telephone: 641-628-4300 Fax: 515-245-4452
Email: grandfirm@grefesidney.com URL: http://www.grefesidney.com
Craig S. Shannon.
General Civil and Trial Practice in all State and Federal Courts. Appellate Practice, Product Liability, Insurance, Negligence, Environmental, Toxic Torts, Professional Liability, Employment, Discrimination, Personal Injury, Workers Compensation, Real Estate, Probate and Estate Planning, Corporate Practice, Family Law, Commercial Litigation and Elder Law.
Des Moines, Iowa Office: 2222 Grand Avenue, P.O. Box 10434, 50306. Telephone: 515-245-4300. Telecopier: 515-245-4452.

See Professional Biographies, PELLA, IOWA

Heerema, M. Timothy, (BV) .... '65 '92 C.36 B.S. L.352 J.D. 810 Main St.
Hietbrink, Paul D., (AV) '52 '77
C&L.546 B.A., J.D. [Brown,W.G.G.B.&S.] (⊙Des Moines)
Klyn, Andrew Wm., (AV) .... '14 '39 C.132 B.A. L.352 J.D. 729 Main St.‡
Klyn, Vincent S., (BV) .... '50 '75 C.208 B.S.B.A. L.190 J.D. [Gaass,K.&B.]
Kreykes, Fred J., (AV) .... '51 '79 C.1304 A.B. L.221 J.D. 700 Main St., Ste. 201
Meyer, Dwaine F. .... '29 '57 C.350 B.S. L.221 LL.B. 810 Main St.‡
Shannon, Craig S., (AV) .... '53 '78 C.1304 A.B. L.221 J.D. [Grefe&S.] ⊙
Shepperd, Chris D., (BV) '— '87 C.352 B.A. L.221 J.D.
Corp. Coun., Vermeer Manufacturing Company
Smith, Robert R., (AV) '58 '83 C.210 B.A. L.221 J.D.
V.P. and Gen. Coun., Vermeer Manufacturing Company

Tripp, P.C., (BV)
810 Washington Street, 50219-1525
Telephone: 641-628-9343 Toll Free: 800-368-1423 515-267-0110 Fax: 641-628-7252 URL: http://www.triplawfirm.com
URL: http://www.tripplaw.us
Timothy N. Tripp.
Social Security Law, General Practice.

See Professional Biographies, PELLA, IOWA

Tripp, Timothy N., (BV) .... '61 '90 C.966 B.A. L.1009 J.D. [Tripp]
Vander Ploeg, Charles L. .... '28 '55 C.132 B.A. L.221 J.D. V.P., Pella Natl. Bk.
Worthington, Julie S. .... '58 '00 C.523 B.A. L.1340 J.D. 414 Liberty Street

PERRY, 7,633, *Dallas Co.*

Creighton, Christine M., (BV) .... '67 '92 C&L.436 B.A., J.D. [Spellman,S.S.S.K.&S.] ⊙
Dalen, DuWayne J., (BV) .... '69 '94 C.898 B.A. L.352 J.D. [Willis,S.&D.]
Finneseth, C. Scott, (BV) .... '62 '91 C&L.190 B.A., J.D. [Shirley,P.&F.]
Joy, William H. .... '43 '68 C&L.352 B.A., J.D. Dist. J.
Joy, Poffenberger & Poffenberger, (BV) .... 1220 Second Street
Kealhofer, G. Michael, (AV) .... '50 '76 C.506 B.S. L.190 J.D. [Spellman,S.S.S.K.&S.] ⊙
Poffenberger, Richard L., (BV) .... '35 '58 C&L.221 B.S., LL.B. [Joy,P.&P.]
Poffenberger, Virginia Joy, (BV) .... '34 '78 C.352 B.S. L.221 J.D. [Joy,P.&P.]
Powell, John C., (AV) .... '44 '74 C.351 B.B.A. L.221 J.D. [Shirley,P.&F.]
Sackett, G. Robert, (AV) .... '32 '60 C.293 A.B. L.221 J.D. [Willis,S.&D.]
Scott, Todd A. .... '69 '96 C.352 B.S. L.221 J.D. [Ⓐ Joy,P.&P.]
Shirley, Alan, (AV) .... '37 '63 C.352 L.221 LL.B. [Shirley,P.&F.]
Shirley, Powell & Finneseth, (AV) .... P.O. Box 487
Spellman, Daniel J., (AV) .... '43 '68 C&L.190 B.A., J.D. [Spellman,S.S.S.K.&S.] ⊙
Spellman, Daniel Jay, (AV) ..... '69 '95 C.352 B.A. L.190 J.D. [Spellman,S.S.S.K.&S.] ⊙
Spellman, Edward M. (Ted), (BV) '74 '99
C.190 B.A. L.221 J.D. [Spellman,S.S.S.K.&S.] ⊙
Spellman, Mark E., (BV) .... '68 '94 C.436 B.A. L.221 J.D. [Spellman,S.S.S.K.&S.] ⊙
Spellman, Martin E., (AV) .... '44 '67 C&L.190 B.A., J.D. [Spellman,S.S.S.K.&S.] ⊙
Spellman, Patrick J., (AV) .... '51 '74 C.221 L.190 J.D. [Spellman,S.S.S.K.&S.] ⊙
Spellman, Thomas L., (AV) ... '58 '85 C.221 B.A. L.1187 J.D. [Spellman,S.S.S.K.&S.] ⊙
Spellman Law Firm .... 1024 Second St.
Spellman, Spellman, Spellman, Spellman, Kealhofer & Spellman, (AV)
1024 Second St. (⊙Des Moines)
Spellman-Mcdevitt, Anne Marie .... '76 '01 C.352 B.A. L.190 J.D. [Spellman]
Willis, Sackett & Dalen, (AV) .... 1212 Second Street

PLEASANT HILL, 5,070, *Polk Co.*

Krell, LeAnne, (BV) .... '— '99 P.O. Box 57002

POCAHONTAS, * 1,970, *Pocahontas Co.*

Beneke, Donald A., (BV) .... '44 '69 C&L.352 LL.B. 309 N. Main
Fitzgerald, Dennis P., (BV) .... '45 '72 C.350 B.S. L.190 J.D. 221 N. Main St.
Hudson, James W., (AV) .... '25 '50 C&L.352 B.A., LL.B. [Hudson]
Hudson Law Firm, (AV) .... 321 N. Main
Thomas, William D., (BV) ... '45 '73 C&L.352 B.S., J.D. 216 N. Main St. (⊙Des Moines)

POLK CITY, 2,344, *Polk Co.*

Anderson, Alan A., (BV) .... '42 '70 C&L.221 B.A., J.D. 212 Van Dorn

POSTVILLE, 2,273, *Allamakee & Clayton Cos.*

Erickson, Matthew J., (BV) .... '50 '77 C.350 B.S. L.221 J.D. [Erickson]
Erickson Law Office, (BV) .... 127 S. Lawler St.
Kelly, Charles .... '51 '76 C.352 B.G.S. L.221 J.D. [C.Kelly]
Kelly, Charles, Law Office, P.C. .... P.O. Box 550
Mueller, Barry S., (BV) ..... '54 '80 C.340 B.A. L.221 J.D. 125 S. Lawler St. (⊙Lansing)

PRAIRIE CITY, 1,360, *Jasper Co.*

Vos, Paul E., (BV) .... '44 '71 C.1304 B.A. L.221 J.D. P.O. Box 177 (⊙Mitchellville)

PRESTON, 1,025, *Jackson Co.*

Kunau, Richard D. .... '45 '72 C.747 B.A. L.352 J.D. 343 N. Main St.‡

PRIMGHAR, * 950, *O'Brien Co.*

Green, Bruce A., (BV) .... '48 '75 C.351 B.A. L.221 J.D. Co. Atty.
Klinker, William K., (BV) .... '59 '83 C.57 B.A. L.352 J.D. [Smith,G.S.&K.] ⊙
Shea, Ronald J., (AV) .... '48 '73 C&L.190 B.A., J.D. [Smith,G.S.&K.] ⊙

Smith, Grigg, Shea & Klinker, A Professional Corporation, (AV)
120 South Hayes, P.O. Box 98, 51245 ⊙
Telephone: 712-957-5465 Fax: 712-957-0121
Email: sgsk@tcaexpress.net
Richard T. Smith (1921-1990); Harold R. Grigg (1919-1997); Ronald J. Shea; William K. Klinker.
General Practice. Estate Planning, Probate, Personal Injury, Torts, Taxation and Mediation, Arbitration, Litigation and Real Estate, Family Law. Practice before State and Federal District and Appellate Courts and Administrative and Regulatory Agencies.
Representative Clients: First National Bank, Primghar, Iowa; Security State Bank, Sutherland, Iowa; State Farm Mutual Automobile Insurance Co.; Farmland Mutual Insurance Co.; Sheldon Livestock Sales, Inc.; Grinnell Mutual Reinsurance Co.; American Family Insurance Group; Mutual Fire and Auto Insurance Co.
Sutherland, Iowa Office: Professional Building, 105 West Second Street, 51058. Telephone: 712-446-3650.

See Professional Biographies, PRIMGHAR, IOWA

QUIMBY, 334, *Cherokee Co.*

Simonsen, Richard D. ...... '49 '76 C.221 B.A. L.37 J.D. Coun., Simonsen Industries, Inc.

READLYN, 858, *Bremer Co.*

Engelbrecht, Wm. H., (AV) '27 '51
C.898 L.221 J.D. [Engelbrecht,A.&H.] (⊙Tripoli, Waverly)
Engelbrecht, Ackerman & Hassman, (AV)
307 Main St. (⊙Clarksville, Tripoli, Waverly)

RED OAK, * 6,264, *Montgomery Co.*

Billings, LaVon E., (BV) .... '30 '57 C&L.546 B.S., J.D. 111 Reed St.
Bloom, Dennis D. .... '48 '73 C&L.546 B.S., J.D. 801 Propect St.‡
Green, Bruce B., (BV) ...... '68 '93 C&L.352 B.A., J.D. [Willson&P.] (⊙Council Bluffs)
Mensen, Brian Steven .... '76 '02 C.351 L.221 J.D. P.O. Box 76
Neal, Dana K., (CV) .... '56 '84 C&L.546 B.S., J.D. 706 W. 2nd St.
Pechacek, Frank W., Jr., (AV) .... '44 '69 C.351 B.A. L.352 J.D. [Willson&P.] ⊙
Richards, Charles Emery, (CV) ...... '46 '79 C.351 B.A. L.221 J.D. Jud. Mag. [Richards]
Richards Law Office, (CV) .... First Natl. Bank Bldg., 501 3rd St.
Stamets, Thomas E., (BV) .... '47 '75 C.707 B.A. L.190 J.D. [Stamets&W.]
Stamets & Wearin, P.C., (BV) .... 508 Fourth Street
Swanson, Bruce E., (BV) .... '57 '83 C.352 B.S. L.190 J.D. [Swanson]
Swanson, Mark D., (BV) .... '51 '78 C.976 B.A. L.94 J.D. [Swanson]
Swanson, R. John, (AV) .... '20 '48 C&L.352 B.A., J.D. [Swanson] ⊙

Swanson Law Firm, (AV)
209 East Coolbaugh Street, P.O. Box 78, 51566 ⊙
Telephone: 712-623-2554 Fax: 712-623-3193
Email: swanlaw@heartland.net
Members of Firm: Ralph J. Swanson (1889-1968); R. John Swanson; Mark D. Swanson; Bruce E. Swanson.
General Civil and Trial Practice in all Courts, Personal Injury and Negligence Litigation, Probate, Domestic Relations, Taxation, Real Estate.
Local Counsel for: Farm Credit Service; Safetrans.
References: Houghton State Bank, Red Oak, Iowa; US Bank, Red Oak, Iowa.
Villisca, Iowa Office: Bickford Building. Telephone: 712-826-9562.

See Professional Biographies, RED OAK, IOWA

Wearin, Josiah C., (BV) .... '54 '79 C.813 B.A. L.966 J.D. [Stamets&W.]
Willson, Philip J., (AV) '23 '49 C.641 B.A. L.976 LL.B.
[Willson&P.] (⊙Council Bluffs)
Willson & Pechacek, P.L.C., (AV)
608 2nd St., Ste. 100 (⊙Carroll, Council Bluffs, Harlan, Oakland, Treynor)

REINBECK, 1,751, *Grundy Co.*

Beard, Robert L., (BV) .... '37 '64 C.898 B.A. L.879 LL.B. [Beard&S.]
Beard & Sweet, P.L.C., (BV) .... 305 Main St.
Leistikow, Kurt R., (CV) .... '71 '96 C.352 B.B.A. L.221 J.D. [Ⓐ Rickert]
Rickert, Michael W., (BV) .... '43 '69 C.513 B.S. L.352 J.D. [Rickert]
Rickert Law Office, P.C., (BV) .... 115 Broad Street
Sweet, Timothy M., (BV) .... '50 '76 C.898 B.A. L.352 J.D. City Atty. [Beard&S.]
Thompson, Robert W. .... '47 '72 C.350 B.S. L.221 J.D. [Thompson]
Thompson Law Office, P.C. .... 117 Broad Street

REMSEN, 1,762, *Plymouth Co.*

Brady, Dennis A., (BV) .... '59 '85 C&L.352 B.A., J.D. [Knudson&B.] ⊙
Hames, Orville A. .... '22 '50 C&L.748 B.S., J.D. P.O. Box 447‡
Knudson, Charles F., (BV) .... '32 '57 C&L.352 B.S.C., J.D. [Knudson&B.] ⊙
Knudson & Brady, (BV) .... 224 South Washington (⊙Marcus)
Kuchel, Jeff, (CV) .... '71 '96 C&L.793 B.S., J.D. [Metcalf,T.&P.]
Metcalf, Thompson & Phipps, (BV) ... 216 South Washington Street (⊙Kingsley, Moville)

RENWICK, 287, *Humboldt Co.*

Ivers, Larry E., (BV) '36 '72 C.626 B.G.E. L.352 J.D.
Hawkeye Bank of Humboldt Co. Bldg. (⊙Eagle Grove)

RINGSTED, 481, *Emmet Co.*

Pelzer, Max O., (BV) .... '31 '60 C&L.352 B.A., J.D. [Pelzer&H.] ⊙
Pelzer & Hart, (BV) .... Telephone Bldg. (⊙Estherville)

RIVERDALE, 656, *Scott Co.*

Bawden, Caroline K., (CV) .... '61 '92 C.802 B.A. L.352 J.D. 5004 State St.

ROCKFORD, 863, *Floyd Co.*

Allison, M. D., (AV) ... '40 '64 C&L.352 B.A., J.D. 114 Main St.

ROCK RAPIDS, * 2,601, *Lyon Co.*

Austin, Michael R., (BV) ... '45 '71 C&L.793 B.S., J.D. [Austin,H.&K.]
Austin, Haberkorn & Kippley, (BV) ... 110 N. Marshall
Casjens, David W. ... '39 '70 C&L.352 B.B.A., J.D. P.O. Box 390‡
Haberkorn, James E., (BV) ... '52 '77 C.338 B.S. L.221 J.D. [Austin,H.&K.]
Kippley, Paul, (BV) ... '58 '84 C.791 B.S. L.546 J.D. [Austin,H.&K.]
Kramer, Timothy J., (CV) ... '67 '93 C.1304 B.A. L.793 J.D. [Waagmeester&K.] ⊙
Petersen, Carl J., (CV) ... '67 '93 C.352 B.S. L.300 J.D. Co. Atty.
Roorda, Hessel R., (BV) ... '56 '81 C.513 B.A. L.190 J.D. [A Waagmeester&K.] ⊙
Waagmeester, Randy L., (BV) ... '53 '78 C.106 B.A. L.221 J.D. [Waagmeester&K.] ⊙

Waagmeester & Kramer, P.L.C., (BV)
104 South Marshall Street, P.O. Box 630, 51246-0630 ⊙
Telephone: 712-472-3777 Fax: 712-472-3778
Email: waaglaw@rockrapids.net URL: http://www.lawyers.com/waagmeester
Simon Fisher (1861-1954); Earl H. Fisher (1908-1990); Don DeWaay (1916-1992). Members of Firm: Randy L. Waagmeester; Timothy J. Kramer;—Hessel R. Roorda.
General Practice including but not limited to Trial Law, Appellate Practice, Wills, Trusts, Estate Planning and Probate Law, Criminal Law, Family Law, Real Estate, Personal Injury, Worker's Compensation, Business Law and Contracts.
Sioux Center, Iowa Office: 235 First Avenue N.E., 51250. Telephone: 712-722-3499. Facsimile: 712-722-2199.

See Professional Biographies, ROCK RAPIDS, IOWA

White, Paul L., (CV) ... '63 '91 C.352 B.A. L.190 J.D. Co. Atty.

ROCK VALLEY, 2,702, *Sioux Co.*

Klein, Donald F. ... '14 '39 C.132 L.221 LL.B. [C Klein&K.] ‡
Klein, Donald R., (BV) ... '52 '78 C.513 B.A. L.190 J.D. [Klein&K.]
Klein & Klein, (BV) ... 1433 Main St.
McGill, Maureen E., (BV) ... '69 '94 C.352 B.A. L.190 J.D. [A McGill&M.]
McGill, Michele M., (BV) ... '52 '83 C.352 B.S. L.190 J.D. [McGill&M.]
McGill, T.N., (AV) ... '29 '52 C&L.352 B.A., J.D. [C McGill&M.]
McGill & McGill, (BV) ... 1403 Main St.
O'Rourke, Melissa R., (CV Ⓣ) ... '— '94 C.338 B.S. L.793 J.D. Pros., Sioux Co.
Scott, James D. ... '52 '76 C&L.793 B.S., J.D. Dist. J.

ROCKWELL CITY, * 2,264, *Calhoun Co.*

Gidel, David D., (BV) ... '48 '76 C.352 B.B.A. L.190 J.D. Jud. Mag. [Gray&G.]
Gray, Jack R., (AV) ... '27 '52 C&L.352 B.A., LL.B. [Gray&G.]
Gray & Gidel, (AV) ... 423 Court St.

Hendricks, Lewis S., (AV) '19 '42 C&L.352 B.A., J.D.
408 Fifth Street, P.O. Box 111, 50579
Telephone: 712-297-7567 Fax: 712-297-5407
Probate, Trust and Estate Planning.
Reference: United Bank of Iowa, Rockwell City, Iowa, formerly Alliance Bank and National Bank of Rockwell City.

See Professional Biographies, ROCKWELL CITY, IOWA

Meth-Farrington, Tina ... '62 '88 C.352 B.A. L.221 J.D. Co. Atty. Off.

ROLFE, 721, *Pocahontas Co.*

Gunderson, Charles A., (CV) ... '43 '69 C.350 B.S. L.352 J.D. 315 Garfield St.

SAC CITY, * 2,368, *Sac Co.*

Becker, Bruce E., (AV) ... '53 '78 C.350 B.A. L.221 J.D. P.O. Box 38
Graven, Jim K., (BV) ... '40 '64 C.898 B.A. L.352 J.D. [Schulte&G.]
McCullough, Colin J. ... '48 '72 C&L.190 B.S.B.A., J.D. 701 W Main St (⊙Lake View)
McCullough, Thomas L. ... '24 '48 C.273 L.190 J.D. 701 W. Main St.‡
Murray, Kevin, (BV) ... '57 '82 C.898 B.A. L.221 J.D. Main & State St.
Schulte, Charles A., (BV) ... '46 '73 C.436 B.A. L.221 J.D. [Schulte&G.]
Schulte, John A., (AV) ... '10 '33 C&L.221 B.A., LL.B. [Schulte&G.]
Schulte and Graven Law Firm, P.C., (AV) ... 421 Main Street

SAINT ANSGAR, 1,063, *Mitchell Co.*

Rourick, Patrick J., (BV) ... '51 '79 C.350 B.S. L.352 J.D. P.O. Box 505

SALEM, 464, *Henry Co.*

Bainter, Harlan W., (AV) ... '30 '58 C&L.352 B.A., J.D. 1870 335th St.

SANBORN, 1,345, *O'Brien Co.*

Comstock, John T. ... '21 '49 C&L.352 B.A., J.D. 214 Main St.‡
Queck, Jeffrey P., (BV) ... '58 '83 C.57 B.A. L.352 J.D. Mag. [Queck]
Queck Law Office, (BV) ... P.O. Box 459
Schultz, Hubert H., (BV) ... '14 '37 C&L.352 B.A., J.D. 411 W. 5th St.

SERGEANT BLUFF, 3,321, *Woodbury Co.*

Kaiser, Stacy K. ... '63 '90 1395 220th St.‡

Lundberg Law Firm, P.L.C.
(See Sioux City)

SHEFFIELD, 930, *Franklin Co.*

DeMoss, Philip F., (CV) ... '46 '75 C.352 B.A. L.221 J.D. 214 Gilman St.
Johansen, Randy D., (CV) ... '49 '75 C&L.352 B.A., J.D. [Johansen]
Johansen Law Firm, (CV) ... 1562 200th Street

SHELDON, 4,914, *O'Brien & Sioux Cos.*

De Hoogh, John F., (BV) ... '44 '73 C.907 B.A. L.500 J.D. [Wolff,W.D.&S.]
Merrill, Freeman G. ... '19 '43 L.16 LL.B. 824 3rd Ave.‡
Murray, G. H. ... '23 '50 C&L.352 B.A., LL.B. P.O. Box 328‡
Postma, Larry, (BV) ... '53 '78 C.1304 B.A. L.352 J.D. 917 3rd Ave.
Schreurs, Micah John ... '74 '00 C.1304 B.A. L.352 J.D. [Wolff,W.D.&S.]
Whorley, Thomas J., (AV) ... '47 '72 C&L.793 B.A., J.D. [Wolff,W.D.&S.]

Wolff, Whorley, De Hoogh & Schreurs, (AV) BB
Security Professional Plaza, 934 Third Avenue, Suite 200, P.O. Box 309, 51201
Telephone: 712-324-4385 FAX: 712-324-5106
URL: http://www.sheldon-law.com
Members of Firm: Paul Wolff (1909-1987); Thomas J. Whorley; John F. De Hoogh; Micah John Schreurs.
General Practice, Personal Injury, Probate, Estate Planning, Real Estate, Corporate and Business Law, School, Banking and Taxation Law, Family, Workers' Compensation, Social Security Disability Claims, Municipal and Zoning, Trials and Appeals.
References: Citizens State Bank, Sheldon, Iowa; Security State Bank, Sheldon, Iowa.

See Professional Biographies, SHELDON, IOWA

SHELL ROCK, 1,385, *Butler Co.*

Holley, John H. ... '23 '50 C.162 B.A. L.352 J.D. 219 E. Railroad St.‡
Nelson, Karl A., (BV) ... '49 '74 C.427 B.A. L.221 J.D. 209 S. Cherry St.
Toenjes, Bruce J., (BV) ... '58 '84 C.351 B.A. L.352 J.D. 209 Cherry St.

SHENANDOAH, 5,572, *Page Co.*

Eaton, Edward E. (Gene)
(See Sidney)

Falk, William E. ... '26 '53 C&L.352 B.A., J.D. 301 Maple St.‡
Foley, James J. ... '35 '61 C.350 B.S. L.221 J.D. Corp. Coun., Shenandoah Computer LC
Gee, Gary T., (BV) ... '52 '78 C.352 B.A. L.221 J.D. 112 S. Elm St.
Irvin, J. C. ... '41 '67 C.352 B.A. L.378 J.D. Dist. J.
Lindburg, Fred, (BV) ... '16 '38 C.352 L.190 J.D. 711 W. Sheridan Ave.
Norris, Robert E., (BV) ... '38 '68 C.784 B.S.B.A. L.221 J.D. 301 Maple Street
Perry, George H. ... '46 '74 C.352 B.A. L.221 J.D. Chmn. of the Bd., City Natl. Bk.
Ross, Robert S. ... '15 '39 C&L.352 B.A., J.D. Chmn. of the Bd., City Natl. Bk.
Stevens, G. Rawson, Attorney at Law, (BV) '46 '72
C.546 B.B.A. L.208 J.D. 723 W. Thomas Ave.

SIBLEY, * 2,815, *Osceola Co.*

Dawson, Harold D., (BV) ... '55 '84 C.36 B.S. L.352 J.D. [DeKoter,T.&D.]
DeKoter, Daniel E., (BV) ... '55 '80 C.114 B.A. L.352 J.D. [DeKoter,T.&D.]

DeKoter, Thole & Dawson, P.L.C., (BV)
315 Ninth Street, P.O. Box 253, 51249
Telephone: 712-754-4601 Fax: 712-754-2301
URL: http://www.lawyers.com/sibleylaw
Louis L. Corcoran (1912-1992); Donald E. Skiver (1923-1989); Richard D. Zito (1944-1994); Daniel E. DeKoter; Michael E. Thole; Harold D. Dawson. Associate: Nicole M. Jensen-Harris.
General Practice, Trials, Insurance Defense, Products Liability, Personal Injury Litigation/Workers Compensation, Estate Planning, Probate and Real Estate, Family Law, Corporate Business Law.
Representative Clients: Sibley State Bank; City of Harris; City of Ocheyedan; The First National Bank of Sibley, Sibley, Iowa; Ocheyedan Savings Bank, Ocheyedan, Iowa; Melvin Savings Bank, Melvin, Iowa; The Continental Insurance Co.; Marine Office of America Corp.; American Marine Underwriters, Inc.; Commercial Union Insurance Cos.

See Professional Biographies, SIBLEY, IOWA

Feller, Joseph M., (BV) ... '53 '78 C.177 B.A. L.190 J.D. [Kennedy&F.]
Jensen-Harris, Nicole M. ... '76 '01 C.791 B.S. L.793 J.D. [A DeKoter,T.&D.]
Kennedy, Frank E., (BV) ... '35 '62 C.273 L.221 J.D. [Kennedy&F.]
Kennedy & Feller, (BV) ... 823 3rd Ave.
Philiph, E. H., (BV) ... '29 '55 C&L.879 J.D. 231 9th St.
Thole, Michael E., (BV) ... '52 '79 C.352 B.B.A. L.190 J.D. [DeKoter,T.&D.]

SIDNEY, * 1,253, *Fremont Co.*

Danley, Vicki R., (BV) ... '48 '76 C&L.352 B.A., J.D. 806 Illinois St.

Eaton, Edward E. (Gene), (AV) '37 '62 C&L.352 B.A., J.D.
416 Clay Street, P.O. Box 429, 51652-0429
Telephone: 712-374-2641 Fax: 712-374-2642
Email: eatonlaw@iowatelecom.net
Edward E. Eaton (1903-1978).
General Practice including but not limited to Commercial Law, Contracts, Corporate Law, Elder Law, Real Estate, Wills, Trusts, Estate Planning and Probate Law, Trial Law.
Representative Clients: First State Bank, Tabor, Iowa; Missouri Valley Drainage District; Benton-Washington Levee District; Nishna Insurance Agency; Walnut Creek Drainage District; Mickelwaite Drainage District.

See Professional Biographies, SIDNEY, IOWA

Falk-Goss, Lori L., (CV) ... '71 '96 C&L.190 B.S.B.A., J.D. Asst. Co. Atty.
Johnson, Jon H., (BV) ... '42 '77 C.932 B.A. L.190 J.D. [Johnson&G.]
Johnson & Graeser, P.C., (BV) ... 811 Indiana St.
Leonard, Robert F., (AV) ... '30 '66 C.784 B.A. L.221 J.D. 710 Illinois St.

SIGOURNEY, * 2,111, *Keokuk Co.*

Conrad, Edward M., (CV) ... '63 '89 C&L.352 B.B.A., J.D. 117 S. Jefferson
Morrison, Dan F. ... '47 '76 C.351 B.A. L.221 J.D. Dist. J.
Schroeder, John E., (BV) ... '51 '76 C&L.352 B.A., J.D. Co. Atty.
Wehr, John N., (BV) ... '52 '77 C.352 B.A. L.190 J.D. 116 E. Washington

SIOUX CENTER, 6,002, *Sioux Co.*

Bierma, Lloyd W., (BV) ... '42 '74 C.114 B.A. L.879 J.D. [Oostra&B.]
Evans, Roger W. ... '43 '74 C.352 B.A. L.221 J.D. [Evans]
Evans Law Office ... 20 3rd St. N.E.
Kramer, Timothy J., (CV) ... '67 '93 C.1304 B.A. L.793 J.D. [Waagmeester&K.] ⊙
Oostra, Ronald J., (BV) ... '47 '74 C.1304 A.B. L.793 J.D. [Oostra&B.]
Oostra & Bierma, P.L.C., (BV) ... 32 Sixth St. N.W.
Puetz, Curtis R., (BV) ... '70 '95 C&L.793 B.S., J.D. [Puetz]
Puetz Law Office, P.C., (BV) ... 235 1st Ave., N.E.
Roorda, Hessel R., (BV) ... '56 '81 C.513 B.A. L.190 J.D. [A Waagmeester&K.] ⊙
Toering, Myron D., (BV) ... '48 '79 C.352 B.B.A. L.862 J.D. [M.D.Toering]
Toering, Myron D., PC, (BV) ... 40 3rd St. N.W.
Van Engen, Brian K., (BV) ... '70 '95 C.1304 B.A. L.352 J.D. [A Oostra&B.]
Waagmeester, Randy L., (BV) ... '53 '78 C.106 B.A. L.221 J.D. [Waagmeester&K.] ⊙
Waagmeester & Kramer, P.L.C., (BV) ... 235 First Avenue N.E. (⊙Rock Rapids)

SIOUX CITY, * 85,013, *Woodbury Co.*

Abshier, James L., (BV) ... '41 '68 C&L.352 B.B.A., J.D. City Atty.
Ackerman, John D., (BV) ... '57 '82 C.513 B.S. L.352 J.D. 620 Douglas St.
Adams, William E. ... '32 '58 C&L.352 LL.B. Ret. Assoc. Dist. J.
Anderson, John B., (AV) ... '36 '60 C&L.352 B.A., J.D. [Corbett,A.C.P.&V.]
Andreasen, Steven J., (BV) ... '66 '92 C&L.352 B.A., J.D. [Willia,S.&A.]
Arneson, Bryan J., (BV) ... '53 '78 C.793 B.S. L.352 J.D. [Bikakis,A.K.&H.]
Baker, John C. ... '44 '71 C&L.546 B.S., J.D. Asst. Co. Atty. (⊙South Sioux City, NE)
Barlow, Ross J. ... '65 '91 C.351 B.A. L.352 J.D. Woodbury Co. Courthouse
Baron, A. Frank, (AV) ... '45 '71 C&L.352 B.A., J.D. [Baron,S.G.G.&L.]

Baron, Sar, Goodwin, Gill & Lohr, (AV) BB
750 Pierce Street, P.O. Box 717, 51102
Telephone: 712-277-1015 FAX: 712-277-3067
Members of Firm: A. Frank Baron; Jeffrey A. Sar; F. Lee Goodwin; David L. Gill; Gregory N. Lohr.
General Civil and Trial Practice in all Courts. Business, Commercial, Bankruptcy, Insurance, Workers Compensation, Banking, Corporation, Adoption, Labor Relations, Real Property, Probate Law, Administrative, Criminal and Domestic Relations Law.

See Professional Biographies, SIOUX CITY, IOWA

Beebe, Richard W. ... '16 '41 C&L.352 B.S.C., J.D. 3237 Viking Dr.‡
Bennett, Mark W. ... '50 '75 C.297 B.A. L.221 J.D. Chf. U.S. Dist. J.
Berenstein, Craig S., (BV) ... '— '85 C&L.352 B.A., J.D. [Berenstein,M.B.H.&M.]
Berenstein, Marvin S., (AV) ... '— '61 C&L.352 J.D. [Berenstein,M.B.H.&M.]

Berenstein, Moore, Berenstein, Heffernan & Moeller, L.L.P., (AV) BB
U.S. Bank Building, 501 Pierce Street, Suite 300, P.O. Box 3207, 51102
Telephone: 712-252-0020 Fax: 712-252-0656
Email: BMBHM@berensteinlawfirm.com

(This Listing Continued)

Berenstein, Moore, Berenstein, Heffernan & Moeller, L.L.P. (Continued)

Members of Firm: Marvin S. Berenstein; Dan A. Moore; Craig S. Berenstein; Maureen Brown Heffernan; Richard H. Moeller; Jeffrey A. Johnson; Robert F. Meis; Mitchell A. Herigstad; Dawn E. Mastalir; Kimberly K. Wolff. Associate: Kelly K. Salker.
General Civil and Trial Practice. Banking, Probate, Taxation, ERISA, Education Law, Employment Law, Trusts and Estates, Creditor's Rights, Real Estate, Corporation, Health and Hospital Law.
Representative Clients: Aalfs Mfg., Inc.; Beef Products, Inc.; Briar Cliff College; Canal Capital Corporation - Sioux City Stockyards; Dakota Dunes Development Co.; First American Bank; Firstar Bank Iowa, N.A.; Mercy Medical Center - Sioux City; Sioux City Community School District; Wells Dairy & Blue Bunny Ice Cream.

See Professional Biographies, SIOUX CITY, IOWA

Bertsch, Robert M., Jr. '64 '89 C.352 B.B.A. L.190 J.D.
Tr. Offr., Norwest Bk. Iowa, N.A.
Bikakis, Emmanuel S., (AV) ....'36 '63 C.513 B.S. L.793 J.D. [Bikakis,A.K.&H.]

Bikakis, Arneson, Karpuk & Hindman, (AV)
701 Pierce Street, Suite 300, P.O. Box 1678, 51102-1678
Telephone: 712-277-1434 Fax: 712-255-8049
URL: http://www.bikakislaw.com
Members of Firm: Emmanuel S. Bikakis; Bryan J. Arneson; Theodore E. Karpuk; Scott A. Hindman. Associate: Timothy A. Scherle.
General Civil Trial Practice. Insurance, Personal Injury, Workers Compensation, Corporations, Probate, Real Estate, Employment, Estate Planning and Bankruptcy Law. Appeals.

See Professional Biographies, SIOUX CITY, IOWA

Blair, David J., P.C., Law Office of
(See Cherokee)

Blum, Jonathan J. ....'78 '04 C.513 B.S. L.352 J.D. [Crary,H.I.S.R.H.&S.]
Boden, Suzan E., (BV) ....'55 '87 C.350 B.S. L.793 J.D. [Vriezelaar,T.E.B.B.&R.]
Bossman, William H. '50 '75 C.480 B.A. L.616 J.D.
(adm. in OK; not adm. in IA) 5600 Windsor Avenue
Bottaro, Timothy S., (BV) .... '58 '83 C.190 B.A. L.352 J.D. [Vriezelaar,T.E.B.B.&R.]
Brawner, Darron L. ....'73 '99 C.929 B.S. L.221 J.D. 701 Pierce Street, Suite 200
Buckmeier, Brian E., (BV) ....'62 '88 C&L.793 B.S., J.D. [Buckmeier&D.]
Buckmeier & Daane, (BV) .... 700 Pierce Street
Buell, Willis A., (AV).... '37 '65 C.793 B.A. L.352 J.D. Asst. U.S. Atty.
Campbell, Mark A., (BV) ....'57 '83 C&L.352 B.B.A., J.D. Woodbury Co. Atty. Off.
Carlin, James M., (CV) ....'62 '92 C.454 B.A. L.436 J.D. 3108 South Lakeport Street
Clausen, Timothy A., (BV) ....'64 '90 C&L.793 B.A., J.D. [Klass,S.M.V.P.O.C.&L.]
Clem, Robert C. .... '35 '60 C.293 B.A. L.352 J.D. Dist. J.
Corbett, Cecelia L. .... '11 '34 C&L.145 Ph.B., J.D. 4016 Hiawatha, W.‡
Corbett, Charles L., (AV) ....'47 '72 C.293 B.A. L.352 J.D. [Corbett,A.C.P.&V.]

Corbett, Anderson, Corbett, Poulson & Vellinga, (AV)
400 Security Building, 423 Sixth Street, P.O. Box 3527, 51102-3527
Telephone: 712-277-1261 Fax: 712-277-6631
Email: caclawfirm@corbettanderson.com URL: http://www.corbettanderson.com
Members of Firm: Edward M. Corbett (1868-1940); Edward V. Corbett (1904-1973); Carlton M. Corbett (1901-1976); Stanley M. Corbett (1909-2004); John B. Anderson; Charles L. Corbett; Jeffrey L. Poulson; Rodney D. Vellinga. Associates: Delaine C. Peterson; Michele M. Lewon.
General Civil and Trial Practice in all Courts. Real Estate, Probate, Estate Planning, Corporation and Business, Banking, Bankruptcy and Commercial, Agricultural, Adoption, Health, Personal Injury, Workers Compensation, Social Security, Criminal, Employment, and Family Law.
Attorneys For: American Popcorn Co.; First Federal Savings Bank of Siouxland; St. Lukes Regional Medical Center of Sioux City; Palmer Enterprises; Charlie Zook Motors, Inc.; Standard Ready Mix Concrete Co.;
Local Attorneys For: Commerical Federal Savings & Loan Assn.; PHH-Homequity; Carl I. Brown & Co.; First Union Mortgage Corp.

See Professional Biographies, SIOUX CITY, IOWA

Cosgrove, Frank, (CV) .... '52 '78 C.985 B.A. L.190 J.D. 705 Douglas St., Ste. 623
Cosgrove, James M., (AV) ....'29 '55 C&L.190 LL.B. 505 5th St.
Crary, David R., (AV) ....'31 '55 C&L.793 LL.B. 614 Pierce Street‡

Crary, Huff, Inkster, Sheehan, Ringgenberg, Hartnett & Storm, P.C., (AV)
614 Pierce Street, P.O. Box 27, 51102-0027 ⊙
Telephone: 712-277-4561 Fax: 712-277-4605
Email: shuff@craryhuff.com URL: http://www.craryhuff.com
S. D. Crary (1875-1969); Wallace W. Huff (1910-1973); Ralph W. Crary (1898-1992); Bruce A. Crary (1927-2001); Robert J. Crary (1917-2001); Stewart A. Huff; Sandra K. Inkster Ehrich (Resident, South Sioux City, Nebraska Office); Rosemary F. Sheehan; Dennis R. Ringgenberg; Daniel L. Hartnett; Larry A. Storm; Michael P. Schmiedt (Resident, South Sioux City, Nebraska Office); Darrell A. Jesse (Resident, Dakota Dunes, South Dakota Office); Cody M. McCullough; Laura D. Schmitt; Marci L. Iseminger;—Ryan W. Snell; Jonathan J. Blum; Sabrina L. LaFleur-Sayler (Resident, Dakota Dunes, South Dakota Office).
General Practice, Agricultural, Banking, Bankruptcy, Business Formation, Business Transactions, Civil and Appellate Trial Practice, Civil Rights, Commercial, Commercial Collections, Construction, Contracts, Corporate, Criminal Law, Domestic, Education, Employer/Employee Relations, Employment Discrimination, Estate Planning, Family, Insurance, Insurance Defense Litigation, Medical Malpractice, Negligence, Personal Injury, Probate, Product Liability, Real Property, Reorganization, Taxation, Title, Workers Compensation, Wrongful Termination, Zoning, Planning and Land Use.
General Counsel for: Interstates Electric and Engineering Co. Inc.; Phillips Kiln Services, Ltd.; Schaller Telephone; Nutra-Flo Co.; Iowa-Nebraska State Bank.
South Sioux City, Nebraska Office: 1419 Dakota Avenue, 68776. Telephone: 402-494-2052.
Dakota Dunes, South Dakota Office: 600 Stevens Port Drive, Suite 300, 57049. Telephone: 605-232-3340.

See Professional Biographies, SIOUX CITY, IOWA

Daane, James N., (BV) ....'60 '85 C&L.793 B.S., J.D. [Buckmeier&D.]
Dandos, Phillip S. .... '29 '54 C&L.352 B.A., J.D. Dist. J.
Daniels, John D., (BV) '49 '76
C.350 B.S. L.352 J.D. Sr. V.P., St. Luke's Health System, Inc.
Deck, Paul W., Jr., (BV) ....'46 '71 C&L.546 A.B., J.D. [Deck&D.]
Deck, Paul W., Sr. ....'15 '41 C&L.546 A.B., J.D. [Deck&D.]
Deck, Robert B., (BV) ....'47 '73 C.513 B.S. L.793 J.D. 505 5th St.
Deck, William G., (BV) ....'54 '79 C&L.546 B.A., J.D. [Deck&D.]
Deck & Deck, L.L.P., (BV) .... 505 5th St., Ste. 635
Denne, Jay E., (BV) .... '70 '95 C.350 B.A. L.352 J.D. [Munger,R.&D.]
Denton, Missy J. ....'70 '99 C.112 B.A. L.793 J.D. [Mayne&M.]
Doyle, Donald V. ....'25 '53 C.513 B.S. L.793 J.D. State Sen.‡
Dykstra, Daniel D., (AV) .... '55 '80 C.1304 B.A. L.352 J.D. [Heidman,R.F.P.P.D.&P.]
Early, Matthew T. E., (CV) .... '66 '96 C.350 B.A. L.352 J.D. [Rawlings,N.P.K.E.J.&M.]
Eckert, Denis R., (BV) ... '47 '72 C&L.793 B.A., LL.B. 705 Douglas St. (⊙Elk Point, SD)
Edgington, Ray H., (BV) .... '55 '81 C.513 B.A. L.352 J.D. [Vriezelaar,T.E.B.B.&R.]
Edmonds, William L. .... '44 '78 C.502 B.A. L.352 J.D. U.S. Bkrptcy. J.
Ehmcke, Lance D., (BV) .... '50 '80 C.350 B.S. L.221 J.D. [Heidman,R.F.P.P.D.&P.]
Eidsmoe, Robert R., (AV) '31 '55 C.513 B.A. L.569 J.D.
[Heidman,R.F.P.P.D.&P.] ‡
Ellis, Amy L. ....'77 '02 C.793 L.190 J.D. Asst. Co. Atty.
Ellwanger, Cyril A. .... '25 '52 C.177 L.352 LL.B. 614 Surrey Lane‡
Ellwanger, Michael W., (AV) '50 '75 C.513 B.A. L.352 J.D.
[Rawlings,N.P.K.E.J.&M.]
Fachman, John M. ....'27 '50 C.513 L.793 LL.B. Sr. J.
Fagg, Martha A., (BV) .... '57 '85 C.350 B.A. L.221 J.D. U.S. Atty. Off.

Faith, Jack A., (BV) ....'51 '80 C.352 B.B.A. L.221 J.D. [J.A.Faith]
Faith, Jack A., P.C., (BV) .... 505 6th St.
Fent, Tomme J., (BV⊕) .... '54 '91 C&L.623 B.A., J.D. P.O. Box 201
Ford, Alvin J., (BV) ....'34 '74 C.546 B.S. L.793 J.D. [A.J.Ford]
Ford, Alvin J., P.C., (BV) .... 1306 Pierce St.
Forker, Wil L., (BV) '54 '79 C.221 B.S. L.352 J.D.
705 Douglas Street, Suite 303, 51101
Telephone: 712-252-1395 Fax: 712-252-4858
Email: forkerlaw@aol.com
Bankruptcy.

See Professional Biographies, SIOUX CITY, IOWA

Forsyth, Priscilla E., (CV) .... '61 '86 C&L.352 B.A., J.D. 3412 Dearborn Boulevard
Fredregill, Alan E., (P.C.), (AV) '48 '75
C.352 B.B.A. L.221 J.D. [Heidman,R.F.P.P.D.&P.]
Frey, Michael J., (CV) .... '65 '90 C.933 B.A. L.221 J.D. [Hellige,F.&R.]
Furlong and Pierson, Law Offices, P.C., (BV) ....520 Nebraska Street, Suite 400-401
Galvin, Daniel C., (AV) ....'24 '51 C&L.190 LL.B. 922 Douglas St.
Gates, Wm. W. ....'28 '51 C.513 L.221 J.D. 1612 120th St.‡
Gaul, Dewie J. ....'28 '55 C.177 A.B. L.276 J.D. Dist. J.
Gerhart, Steven G. ....'48 '73 C&L.352 B.A., J.D. Sioux City Brick & Tile Co.
Gildemeister, G. Daniel, (AV) ....'43 '68 C&L.352 B.B.A., J.D. [Gildemeister&K.]

Gildemeister & Keane, L.L.P., (AV)
Suite 702 Terra Centre, 600 Fourth Street, P.O. Box 1379, 51101
Telephone: 712-234-3088 Fax: 712-234-3077
G. Daniel Gildemeister; Edward J. Keane.
General Practice. Insurance Defense, Personal Injury, Workers' Compensation, Real Estate, Corporate, Commercial Transactions and Family Law.

See Professional Biographies, SIOUX CITY, IOWA

Giles, Gregory Gifford ....'61 '88 C.103 A.B. L.793 J.D. [Giles] ‡
Giles, W. Jefferson, III, (AV) .... '36 '61 C.112 B.S. L.793 LL.B. [Giles] ⊙
Giles Law Office, (AV) .... P.O. Box 147 (⊙Crofton, NE)
Gill, David L., (BV) .... '51 '76 C.190 B.S.B.A. L.352 J.D. [Baron,S.G.G.&L.]
Goodwin, F. Lee, (BV) ....'49 '74 C&L.546 B.S.B.A., J.D. [Baron,S.G.G.&L.]
Goosmann, Jeana L. .... '77 '02 C.546 B.S. L.190 J.D. [Heidman,R.F.P.P.D.&P.]
Gray, John C., (AV) .... '55 '81 C&L.352 B.A., J.D. [Heidman,R.F.P.P.D.&P.]
Grimm, Rita C., (BV) .... '60 '85 C.218 B.A. L.546 J.D. [Heidman,R.F.P.P.D.&P.]
Hagberg, Marilyn Joyce .... '49 '98 C.513 B.A. L.793 J.D. Security National Bank
Hamilton, Mary C., (CV) ....'56 '97 C.106 B.A. L.190 J.D. [Hamilton] ⊙
Hamilton, Steven D., (BV) .... '47 '72 C.602 B.A. L.37 J.D. [Hamilton] ⊙
Hamilton, Willis J., (AV) .... '49 '74 C&L.190 B.A., J.D. [Hamilton] ⊙
Hamilton Law Firm, P.C., (AV) ....1119 Historic Fourth Street, Suite 202 (⊙Storm Lake)
Harper, Duncan M., (AV) .... '22 '48 C.513 A.B. L.352 J.D. 2829 Mulberry Ct.‡
Harris, Robert L. '46 '79 C.791 B.S. L.793 J.D.
V.P., Sioux City Chamber of Commerce
Hartnett, Daniel L., (AV) ....'56 '81 C&L.546 B.A., J.D. [Crary,H.I.S.R.H.&S.]
Heeger, D. Maurine Holland .... '24 '53 C&L.352 B.A., J.D. Asst. Co. Atty.
Heffernan, Maureen Brown, (BV) '— '85
C&L.352 B.B.S., J.D. [Berenstein,M.B.H.&M.]
Heidman, Marvin F., (AV) ... '38 '62 C.350 B.S. L.221 J.D. [Heidman,R.F.P.P.D.&P.]

Heidman, Redmond, Fredregill, Patterson, Plaza, Dykstra & Prahl, L.L.P., (AV)
A Registered Limited Liability Partnership including Professional Corporations
701 Pierce Street, Suite 200, P.O. Box 3086, 51102
Telephone: 712-255-8838 Fax: 712-258-6714
Email: mail@heidmanlaw.com URL: http://www.heidmanlaw.com
Members of Firm: James W. Redmond; Alan E. Fredregill (P.C.); Thomas M. Plaza; Daniel D. Dykstra; Lance D. Ehmcke; Cynthia C. Moser; John C. Gray; Daniel B. Shuck; Rita C. Grimm; Patrick L. Sealey; Jeff W. Wright. Associates: Sarah Kuehl Kleber; Rosalynd J. Koob; Joel D. Vos; Jeana L. Goosmann; Lisa A. Peterson. Of Counsel: Marvin F. Heidman; John W. Gleysteen (1911-2000); Robert R. Eidsmoe (Retired); Jacob C. Gleysteen (1883-1943); H. Clifford Harper (1891-1959); Charles T. Patterson; Margaret M. Prahl.
General Practice, Litigation and Transactional Law.
Representative Clients: Mercy Medical Center; Allied Insurance Group; Irving F. Jensen, Co.; Terra Industries, Inc.; PIC USA, Inc., P.L.C.; Grinnell Mutual Reinsurance Co.; Travelers Insurance Co.; United Fire & Casualty; American Family Insurance.

See Professional Biographies, SIOUX CITY, IOWA

Hellige, Michael R., (AV) ....'46 '71 C&L.352 B.A., J.D. [Hellige,F.&R.]

Hellige, Frey & Roe, R.L.L.P., (AV)
700 Frances Building, 505 Fifth Street, P.O. Box 1828, 51102
Telephone: 712-255-4444 Telecopier: 712-255-4465
Email: helligelaw@helligelaw.com
Members of Firm: Michael R. Hellige; Michael J. Frey; Kathleen C. Roe;—E. A. Charlie Nichols.
General and Trial Practice in Iowa, South Dakota and Nebraska State and Federal Courts.
Representative Clients: American Family Insurance Group; The Cincinnati Companies; Diocese of Sioux City; Employers Mutual Cos.; Ford Motor Co.; ITT Hartford; Liberty Mutual Group; Prince Manufacturing Corp.; Sioux City Journal; The Travelers Group.

See Professional Biographies, SIOUX CITY, IOWA

Herigstad, Mitchell A., (CV) ....'— '94 C.755 B.A. L.221 J.D. [Berenstein,M.B.H.&M.]
Hindman, Scott A., (BV) .... '61 '86 C.985 B.A. L.352 J.D. [Bikakis,A.K.&H.]
Hobart, Michael M., (BV) .... '46 '78 C.352 B.B.A. L.793 J.D. Asst. U.S. Atty.
Horak, Shelley A., (BV) .... '57 '90 C.513 B.S. L.793 J.D. [Horak&Assoc.]
Horak and Associates, P.C., (BV) .... 505 5th St., Ste. 500
Horneber, Alice Schumacher, (BV) ....'52 '82 C.590 B.S. L.793 J.D. [Horneber]
Horneber, William F., (BV⊕) .... '50 '78 C.590 B.S. L.793 J.D. [Horneber]
Horneber Law Firm, (BV) .... 401 Douglas Street, Suite 500B
Hruska, Karrie R. .... '74 '99 C.793 B.A. L.352 J.D. [Rawlings,N.P.K.E.J.&M.]
Huff, Stewart A., (AV) ....'40 '65 C&L.352 B.A., LL.B. [Crary,H.I.S.R.H.&S.]
Irgens, Todd A. ....'71 '03 C.513 B.A. L.352 J.D. [Rawlings,N.P.K.E.J.&M.]
Iseminger, Marci L., (CV) .... '63 '92 C.350 B.B.A. L.208 J.D. [Crary,H.I.S.R.H.&S.]
Jacobs, Michael P., (BV) ....'54 '79 C&L.793 B.S., J.D. [Rawlings,N.P.K.E.J.&M.]
Jarman, Timothy T. .... '55 '81 C.177 B.A. L.352 J.D. Dist. Assoc. J.
Johansen, Gary L. .... '37 '66 C.513 B.A. L.793 J.D. 1824 S. Lemon St.‡
Johansen, Raymond B. .... '27 '51 C.513 B.S. L.793 LL.B. 2928 S. Olive St.‡
Johnson, Gary E. ....'41 '66 C.513 B.A. L.793 J.D. Sr. Atty., Midwest Gas
Johnson, Hilary E. ....'72 '97 C.513 B.A. L.352 J.D. 400 Security Building
Johnson, Jeffrey A., (BV) ....'— '91 C.350 B.B.A. L.502 J.D. [Berenstein,M.B.H.&M.]
Jones, Gregory E., (BV) ....'51 '77 C&L.221 B.A., J.D. Pub. Def. Off.
Kalafut, Mark A., (BV) '53 '78 C&L.477 B.A., J.D.
V.P. Gen. Counsel & Corp. Sec., Terra Industries Inc.
Kaplan, Daniel F. '61 '85 C.861 B.A. L.145 J.D.
(adm. in IL; not adm. in IA) Cloverleaf Cold Storage
Karpuk, Theodore E., (BV) .... '56 '81 C.985 B.A. L.352 J.D. [Bikakis,A.K.&H.]
Katcher, James J., (CV) ....'63 '88 C.351 B.A. L.352 J.D. Asst. Co. Atty.
Keane, Edward J., (AV) ....'54 '79 C&L.190 B.S.B.A., J.D. [Gildemeister&K.]
Killinger, Sam S., (BV) ....'40 '63 C&L.352 B.A., LL.B. [Rawlings,N.P.K.E.J.&M.]
Kittredge, Paul E., Jr., (BV) ....'57 '91 C.37 B.S.E.E. L.221 J.D. Asst. Co. Atty.

Klass, Stoik, Mugan, Villone, Phillips, Orzechowski, Clausen & Lapierre, L.L.P., (AV)
627 4th Street, Suite 300
Kleber, Sarah Kuehl ....'72 '98 C.221 B.A. L.902 J.D [Ⓐ Heidman,R.F.P.P.D.&P.]
Knoepfler, Jas. C. ....'20 '48 C.197 B.A. L.352 J.D. 320 Mapel Place‡
Kohl, Steven C., (CV) ....'56 '83 C.118 B.A. L.352 J.D. 520 Pierce St., #383
Kollars, Bradford F., (BV) ....'49 '75 C.546 B.S. L.846 J.D. 705 Douglas St., Ste. 402
Koob, Rosalynd J. ....'75 '01 C.985 B.A. L.190 J.D. [Ⓐ Heidman,R.F.P.P.D.&P.]
Lane, Craig H., (CV) ....'54 '81 C.627 B.S. L.190 J.D. [C.H.Lane]
Lane, William J., III ....'46 '79 C.627 B.S. L.190 J.D. [Lane]
Lane, Craig H., PC, (CV) ....505 5th St., Ste. 702
Lane Law Offices ....2831 Hamilton Blvd., Suite 188
Lapierre, René Charles ....'57 '85 C&L.793 B.S., J.D. [Klass,S.M.V.P.O.C.&L.]
Lessmann, Colby M. ....'73 '00 C&L.793 B.S.B.A., J.D. [Ⓐ Munger,R.&D.]
Lessmann, Marlin M. ....'44 '69 C&L.793 B.S.B.A., J.D. R. R. 1, Box 144
Lewon, Michele M. ....'— '02 C&L.546 B.S., J.D. [Ⓐ Corbett,A.C.P.&V.]
Loftus, Marleen J., (BV) ....'44 '87 C.513 B.A. L.793 J.D. 1600 Rebecca St.
Lohr, Gregory N., (BV) ....'52 '80 C.985 B.A. L.190 J.D. [Baron,S.G.G.&L.]
Lundberg, Paul D., (AV) ....'51 '81 C.627 B.S. L.352 J.D. [Lundberg]

Lundberg Law Firm, P.L.C., (AV)
906 Terra Centre, 600 4th Street, 51101
Telephone: 712-234-3030 Fax: 712-234-3034
Email: paull@terracentre.net URL: http://www.lundberglawfirm.com
Paul D. Lundberg.
Languages: English.
General Practice including Personal Injury, Employment Law, Professional Liability and Commercial Law.
Representative Clients: The Cincinnati Companies; Mobren Biological; Siouxland Orthopedics; Jones Eye Clinic; Safeco Insurance.
See Professional Biographies, SIOUX CITY, IOWA

Madsen, George F., (AV) ....'33 '60 C.747 B.A. L.309 LL.B. [Mayne&M.] ‡

Mahr, Dennis J., (BV) '50 '77 C&L.352 B.G.S., J.D.
Commerce Building, Suite 334, 520 Nebraska Street, 51101-1316
Telephone: 712-233-1623 Toll Free: 1-800-621-0783 Fax: 712-233-1625
Email: mahrlaw@cableone.net
Workers Compensation, Personal Injury and Social Security Disability Law for Plaintiffs and Claimants only.
See Professional Biographies, SIOUX CITY, IOWA

Mastalir, Dawn E., (CV) ....'— '92 C.546 B.A. L.352 J.D. [Berenstein,M.B.H.&M.]
Mayne, John D., (AV) ....'47 '76 C.309 B.A. L.221 J.D. [Mayne&M.]
Mayne, Wiley, (AV) ....'17 '41 C.309 S.B. L.352 J.D. [Mayne&M.] ‡

Mayne & Madsen, (AV) BR
Suite 405 Pioneer Bank Building, 701 Pierce Street, P.O. Box 1347, 51102-1347
Telephone: 712-252-3220 Fax: 712-252-1535
Email: jmayne@iowabar.org URL: http://www.lawyers.com/maynemarks
Members of Firm: Wiley Mayne (Retired); George F. Madsen (Retired); John D. Mayne; Missy J. Denton.
Civil Trials and Appeals in all State and Federal Courts. Insurance, Commercial, Tort, Corporation, Estate Planning, Probate, Medical and Legal Malpractice.
Representative Clients: American Telephone & Telegraph Co.; Amoco Oil Company; Central United Life Insurance Company; Century 21-Marketplace; Credit Bureau of Sioux City; Ford Motor Credit Company; Intensive Medical Services of Siouxland, P.C.; Metz Baking Company; Shell Chemical Company; U.S. West Communications Company.
See Professional Biographies, SIOUX CITY, IOWA

McCormick, Patrick C. ....'40 '66 C.513 B.A. L.352 LL.B. Assoc. Dist. J.
McCullough, Cody M., (CV) ....'70 '96 C&L.352 B.A., J.D. [Crary,H.I.S.R.H.&S.]
McDermott, Lesa A. ....'67 '94 C.755 B.S. L.546 J.D. McDermott & Grace, LLC
McElwain, Dennis M., (BV) ....'56 '83 C&L.352 B.G.S., J.D. [Smith&M.]
McGarry, Joseph B. '64 '90 C&L.602 B.B.A., J.D.
Corporate Counsel, Williams TV & Appliance Company
Meis, Robert F., (BV) ....'58 '83 C&L.352 B.B.A., J.D. [Berenstein,M.B.H.&M.]
Michaelson, Brian L. ....'52 '78 C.933 B.A. L.352 J.D. Assoc. Juv. J.
Mishne, Robert D., (AV) ....'25 '49 C.436 B.N.S. L.178 LL.B. P.O. Box 3316‡
Moeller, John S., (BV) ....'58 '85 C.350 B.S. L.190 J.D. 705 Douglas St., Ste. 214
Moeller, Richard H., (BV) ....'— '85 C.350 B.S. L.352 J.D. [Berenstein,M.B.H.&M.]
Mohrhauser, Jeffrey R., (AV) '55 '81 C.351 B.A. L.793 J.D.
[Rawlings,N.P.K.E.J.&M.]
Molstad, Donald H., (BV) ....'49 '75 C.793 B.S. L.190 J.D. [Molstad]
Molstad Law Firm, (BV) ....505 6th St., Ste. 308
Monzel, Peter M. ....'67 '01 C.491 B.A. L.793 J.D. [Ⓐ Horak&Assoc.]
Moore, Dan A., (AV) ....'— '77 C&L.221 B.A., J.D. [Berenstein,M.B.H.&M.]
Moser, Cynthia C., (AV) ....'52 '77 C.999 B.A. L.352 J.D. [Heidman,R.F.P.P.D.&P.]
Mugan, John R., (AV) ....'49 '73 C&L.190 J.D. [Klass,S.M.V.P.O.C.&L.]
Mullin, Thomas S., (BV) ....'48 '78 C.985 B.A. L.190 J.D. Co. Atty.
Munger, Stanley E., (AV) ....'48 '74 C.350 B.S. L.36 J.D. [Munger,R.&D.]
Munger, Reinschmidt & Denne, L.L.P., (AV) ....600 4th St., Ste. 303
Myers, Jeffrey T., (CV) ....'47 '74 C.793 B.S. L.190 J.D. 705 Douglas St., Ste. 402
Nelson, John C., (BV) ....'65 '90 C&L.352 B.A., J.D. 705 Douglas St., Ste. 509
Nelson, Rebecca A., (BV) ....'53 '95 C.513 B.S. L.793 J.D. [Rawlings,N.P.K.E.J.&M.]
Nichols, E. A. Charlie ....'79 '05 C.511 B.A. L.352 J.D. [Ⓐ Hellige,F.&R.]
Nieland, Maurice B., (AV) ....'46 '70 C&L.352 B.A., J.D. [Rawlings,N.P.K.E.J.&M.]
Nyberg, David C. ....'40 '65 C.977 B.A. L.145 J.D. 424 Buckwalter Drive
O'Brien, Donald E. ....'23 '48 C.857 L.190 LL.B. Sr. U.S. Dist. J.
O'Brien, Michael J., (CV) ....'54 '83 C&L.793 B.L.S., J.D. 520 Nebraska St., Ste. 300
O'Connell, Robert E. '45 '77 C.755 B.A. L.300 J.D.
V.P., Blue Cross & Blue Shield of Ia. & Blue Cross of S. Dak.
Orzechowski, Barbara F., (AV) '47 '80 C.221 B.F.A. L.793 J.D.
[Klass,S.M.V.P.O.C.&L.]
Patterson, Charles T., (AV) .. '50 '75 C.801 B.S. L.221 J.D. [Ⓒ Heidman,R.F.P.P.D.&P.]
Pendleton, Donald M. ....'14 '37 C&L.352 B.A., J.D. 627 Francis Bldg.
Peterson, Delaine C. ....'36 '66 C&L.352 B.B.A., J.D. [Ⓐ Corbett,A.C.P.&V.]
Peterson, Lisa A. ....'77 '04 C.134 B.A. L.221 J.D. [Ⓐ Heidman,R.F.P.P.D.&P.]
Phillips, Douglas L., (BV) ....'54 '80 C.350 B.S. L.990 J.D. [Klass,S.M.V.P.O.C.&L.]
Pierson, Robert J., (BV) ....'48 '82 C.545 B.A.E. L.546 J.D. [Furlong&P.]
Pirog, John F., (BV) ....'25 '52 C.513 B.S. L.221 J.D. 401 Davidson Bldg.
Plaza, Thomas M., (BV) ....'54 '79 C.351 B.A. L.352 J.D. [Heidman,R.F.P.P.D.&P.]
Polifka, John C., (BV) ....'50 '88 C.791 B.S. L.793 J.D. 520 Nebraska St., Ste. 300
Poulson, Jeffrey L., (BV) ....'51 '77 C.972 B.A. L.221 J.D. [Corbett,A.C.P.&V.]
Prahl, Margaret M., (BV) .... '38 '81 C.546 B.A. L.793 J.D. [Ⓒ Heidman,R.F.P.P.D.&P.]
Rawe, C. Maurice, (BV) ....'47 '71 C.793 L.546 J.D. Chf. Dep. City Atty.

Rawlings, Nieland, Probasco, Killinger, Ellwanger, Jacobs & Mohrhauser, (AV) BR
522 Fourth Street, Suite 300, 51101
Telephone: 712-277-2373 FAX: 712-277-3304
Email: rawlingsnieland.com

(This Listing Continued)

Rawlings, Nieland, Probasco, Killinger, Ellwanger, Jacobs & Mohrhauser (Continued)

James W. Kindig (1879-1950); Lowell C. Kindig (1913-1992); Robert E. Beebe (1913-1988); Gene A. Probasco (1931-1999). Members of Firm: Maurice B. Nieland; Sam S. Killinger; Michael W. Ellwanger; Michael P. Jacobs; Jeffrey R. Mohrhauser; Rebecca A. Nelson; Matthew T. E. Early. Associates: Karrie R. Hruska; Todd A. Irgens.
General Civil Practice. Appeals, Bankruptcy, Commercial Law and Litigation, Corporation, Creditors Rights, Employment, Estate Planning, Insurance, Medical-Legal, Personal Injury, Probate, Real Estate, Taxation, Trial Practice and Worker's Compensation.
Representative Clients: Chesterman Co.; CNA Insurance Co. Mutual; Farmers Savings Bank, Remsen, Iowa; Farm Bureau Insurance Co.; Minnesota Mutual Insurance Co.; Premium Waters, Inc.; Sabre Communications Corp.; St. Paul Fire and Marine Insurance Co.; Wells Fargo Bank, N.A.; Wells Fargo Equipment Finance, Inc.
See Professional Biographies, SIOUX CITY, IOWA

Redmond, James W., (AV) ..... '47 '73 C.985 B.A. L.436 J.D. [Heidman,R.F.P.P.D.&P.]
Rehan, Robert J. ....'59 '84 C&L.352 B.A., J.D. 700 4th St, #504
Reinschmidt, David L., (BV) .... '60 '87 C.793 B.A. L.893 J.D. [Munger,R.&D.]
Rhinehart, Richard S., (BV) ....'27 '54 C.793 B.A. L.352 J.D. Suite 310
Ringgenberg, Dennis R., (BV) ..... '52 '80 C.351 B.A. L.546 J.D. [Crary,H.I.S.R.H.&S.]
Rocklin, James M. ....'42 '67 C&L.352 B.B.A., J.D. 627 Frances Bldg., 505 5th St.
Roe, Kathleen C., (BV) ....'71 '99 C.513 B.A. L.190 J.D. [Hellige,F.&R.]

Rosenbaum, Elizabeth A., (BV) '61 '89 C&L.793 B.S., J.D.
Suite 903, Terra Centre, 600 4th Street, 51101
Telephone: 712-233-3632 Fax: 712-233-6101
Domestic Relations, Family Law, Adoptions, and Indian Child Welfare Act.
See Professional Biographies, SIOUX CITY, IOWA

Ross, Ryan C., (CV) .... '70 '95 C.218 B.A. L.950 J.D. [Vriezelaar,T.E.B.B.&R.]
Row, Elizabeth A., (BV) ....'66 '91 C.985 B.A. L.352 J.D. [E.A.Row]
Row, Elizabeth A., P.C., (BV) ....719 Nebraska St.
Rowse, Delbert D., Attorney at Law ....'40 '73 C.427 B.A. L.1035 J.D. [Rowse L.]
Rowse Law, P.C. ....705 Douglas Street, Suite 315
Runge, Ronald E. ....'31 '58 C&L.793 B.B.S., LL.B. P.O. Box 2007
Rusch, John S., (CV) ....'70 '97 C.490 B.A. L.793 J.D. Asst. Co. Atty.
Rye, Michael David ....'67 '95 C.427 B.A. L.352 J.D. Jud. Law Clk., Dist. Ct.
Salker, Kelly K., (CV) .... '71 '97 C.513 B.S. L.352 J.D. [Ⓐ Berenstein,M.B.H.&M.]
Saltzman, Kathleen D., (CV) ....'66 '91 C.352 B.A. L.546 J.D. 906 Pebble Beach Dr.
Samore, Edward F., (AV) ....'13 '42 C&L.352 B.A., J.D. 505 6th St.‡
Sar, Jeffrey A., (BV) ....'49 '75 C.350 B.S. L.793 J.D. [Baron,S.G.G.&L.]
Schaeffer, Stephen L. '42 '68 C.475 B.A. L.477 J.D.
(adm. in MI; not adm. in IA) 4000 Country Club Blvd.‡
Scherle, Timothy A., (BV) ....'58 '83 C&L.352 B.A., J.D. [Ⓐ Bikakis,A.K.&H.]
Schmiedt, Michael P., (BV) '63 '91 C.912 B.S. L.546 J.D.
[Crary,H.I.S.R.H.&S.] (ⓒSouth Sioux City, NE)
Schmitt, Laura D. .... '67 '94 C.513 B.A. L.793 J.D. [Crary,H.I.S.R.H.&S.]

Schrunk, Irene A., (BV) '49 '78 C.190 B.S.N. L.352 J.D.
Terra Centre, Suite 308, 600 Fourth Street, 51101
Telephone: 712-233-3625 Fax: 712-233-3675
Domestic Relations, Family Law, Divorce, Domestic Violence and Juvenile Law.
See Professional Biographies, SIOUX CITY, IOWA

Sealey, Patrick L., (BV) .... '70 '95 C.546 B.A. L.352 J.D. [Heidman,R.F.P.P.D.&P.]
Seff, Robert M. ....'46 '71 C&L.793 B.A., J.D. 2400 Pierce St.
Sheehan, Rosemary F., (AV) ...... '38 '77 C.157 B.A. L.793 J.D. [Crary,H.I.S.R.H.&S.]
Shuck, Daniel B., (AV) .... '60 '85 C.190 B.A. L.221 J.D. [Heidman,R.F.P.P.D.&P.]
Sloan, Dewey P. ....'43 '88 C.513 B.S. L.352 J.D. Off. of Co. Atty.
Small, Peter A., (CV) ....'62 '93 C.293 B.A. L.352 J.D. Legal Servs. Corp. of Iowa
Smith, Jay M. .... '78 '04 C.602 B.A. L.352 J.D. [Ⓐ Smith&M.]
Smith, MacDonald, (AV) ....'48 '73 C.602 A.B. L.352 J.D. [Smith&M.]

Smith & McElwain, (AV) BR
505 Fifth, Suite 530, P.O. Box 1194, 51102
Telephone: 712-255-8094 Fax: 712-255-3825
Email: smitmcel@aol.com URL: http://www.smitmcel.com
Members of Firm: MacDonald Smith; Dennis M. McElwain; Harry H. Smith (1916-1999). Associate: Jay M. Smith.
Labor and Employment Law, Workers' Compensation Law.
Representative Clients: Iowa Federation of Labor; Iowa State Building & Construction Trades Council.
Reference: Wells Fargo Bank, N.A.
See Professional Biographies, SIOUX CITY, IOWA

Snell, Ryan W. .... '68 '03 C.350 B.A. L.793 J.D. [Ⓐ Crary,H.I.S.R.H.&S.]
Sokolovske, Mary Jane ....'52 '77 C.687 B.A. L.190 J.D. Pub. Def. Off.
Stahle, Robert J., (BV) ....'60 '86 C.352 B.A. L.546 J.D. [Willia,S.&A.]
Stenander, Robert L. ....'45 '70 C.353 B.A. L.221 J.D. 505 Fifth St.
Stewart, Suzan M., (AV) '51 '80
C&L.352 B.A., J.D. Mng. Sr. Atty., MidAmerican Energy Co.
Stoik, Anthony J., (AV) ....'48 '73 C&L.352 B.A., J.D. [Klass,S.M.V.P.O.C.&L.]
Storm, Larry A., (AV) .... '48 '76 C.747 B.A. L.1035 J.D. [Crary,H.I.S.R.H.&S.]
Stroud, Stephen D. '53 '79 C.352 B.S. L.190 J.D.
V.P. & Tr. Offr., Northwestern Natl. Bk.
Sturgeon, Al, Law Offices of '56 '90 C.513 B.S. L.352 J.D.
507 Seventh Street, Suite 540
Sylvester, Donald W. ....'36 '60 C.177 L.190 LL.B. 321 Badgerow Bldg.
Taylor, Donald H. ....'46 '80 C&L.326 B.S., J.D. 2207 Hardy St.
Tenuta, Frank Cal, (BV) ....'59 '85 C.966 B.A. L.494 J.D. Iowa Legal Aid
Thoman, Charles N., (BV) ....'52 '76 C.985 B.A. L.190 J.D. Asst. Atty. Gen.
Thomas, Bruce G., (BV) .... '51 '76 C.659 B.A. L.352 J.D. 705 Douglas St., Ste. 509
Tiefenthaler, Bob ....'69 '94 C&L.793 B.S., J.D. [Tiefenthaler]

Tiefenthaler Law Office, P.C.
518 8th Street, Suite D, 51101
Telephone: 712-252-5080 Fax: 712-252-5087
Email: btief@hotmail.com URL: http://www.tieflaw.com
Bob Tiefenthaler.
Personal Injury, Workers' Compensation, Criminal Defense.
See Professional Biographies, SIOUX CITY, IOWA

Tigges, Dale C., (AV) ....'53 '80 C.793 B.S. L.221 J.D. [Vriezelaar,T.E.B.B.&R.]
Timmins, Terrence L. ....'48 '73 C.985 B.A. L.352 J.D. Asst. City Atty.
Tinkle, Lloyd L. ....'10 '48 C&L.793 M.A., LL.B. 1903 Rebecca St.‡
Tott, Patrick H., (CV) ....'67 '91 C&L.190 B.S.B.A., J.D. 705 Douglas St., Ste. 509
Turek, Ernest ....'26 '51 C.513 L.221 LL.B. 2109 Grandview Blvd.‡
Twidwell, Joseph '50 '75 C&L.190 B.A., J.D.
Sr. V.P. & Trust Off., Security Nat'l Bank
Updegraff, David L. ....'50 '75 C&L.352 B.A., J.D. [D.L.Updegraff]
Updegraff, David L., P.C. ....505 Fifth St.
Vakulskas, Thomas A., (BV) ....'48 '73 C.352 B.A. L.190 J.D. 1721 Jackson St.
Vellinga, Rodney D., (BV) ....'44 '72 C&L.352 B.A., J.D. [Corbett,A.C.P.&V.]

Villone, James R., (BV) .... '46 '82 C.793 A.B. L.352 J.D. [Klass,S.M.V.P.O.C.&L.]
Vondrak, E. Phil. .... '35 '62 C&L.190 B.S., J.D. Sioux Pointe, Inc.
Vos, Joel D. .... '77 '02 C.1304 B.A. L.352 J.D. [Ⓐ Heidman,R.F.P.P.D.&P.]
Vriezelaar, Kent, (AV) .... '51 '76 C&L.352 B.B.A., J.D. [Vriezelaar,T.E.B.B.&R.]

Vriezelaar, Tigges, Edgington, Bottaro, Boden & Ross, L.L.P., (AV)
421 Nebraska Street, 51101
Mailing Address: P.O. Box 1557, Sioux City, IA 51102
Telephone: 712-252-3226 Fax: 712-252-4873
Email: vterbblaw@siouxcitylawyers.com URL: http://www.siouxcitylawyers.net
Members of Firm: Kent Vriezelaar; Dale C. Tigges; Ray H. Edgington; Timothy S. Bottaro; Suzan E. Boden; Ryan C. Ross.
General Civil and Trial Practice in all Courts, ERISA, Corporate and Estate Planning, Probate, Taxation, Real Estate, Banking, Creditor's Rights, Employment, Personal Injury and Negligence Litigation (Plaintiff and Defense) and Workers' Compensation Law.
See Professional Biographies, SIOUX CITY, IOWA

Walsh, Michael S. .... '41 '69 C&L.793 B.S., J.D. Dist. J.
Washburn, Brenda K. .... '55 '83 C.513 B.S. L.793 J.D. 617 S. Lewis
Wenell, Gary E. .... '46 '70 C.793 B.A. L.352 J.D. Dist. J.
Wichser, Robert A., (AVⓉ) .... '49 '74 C.513 B.A. L.793 J.D. 12 38th St.
Widdison, Harold Kearl .... '62 '95 C.35 B.S. L.793 J.D. 505 5th St.
Willia, N. Richard, Jr., (AV) .... '48 '74 C.490 B.S. L.793 J.D. [Willia,S.&A.]
Willia, Stahle & Andreasen, L.L.P., (AV) .... 501 Pierce
Wilson, Theresa .... '73 '98 C.350 B/A/ L.221 J.D. Law Clk., Dist. Ct.
Wolff, Kimberly K., (CV) .... '— '94 C&L.793 B.A., J.D. [Berenstein,M.B.H.&M.]
Wright, Jeff W. .... '73 '98 C.595 B.A. L.352 J.D. [Heidman,R.F.P.P.D.&P.]
Yung, Brian L., (BV) .... '64 '89 C.350 B.S. L.352 J.D. [Klass,S.M.V.P.O.C.&L.]
Zirbel Olson, Kendra .... '— '88 C.293 B.A. L.352 J.D. 505 6th St., Ste. 520

SLATER, 1,268, *Story Co.*

Bower, Byard B. .... '49 '75 C.352 B.A. L.192 J.D. 703 Park Circle★
Rewoldt, Dana .... '61 '87 C.352 B.A. L.221 J.D. Coun., Zeneca Inc. (Pat.)
Strobl, Edward J., Jr. .... '45 '71 C.276 A.B. L.823 J.D. Coun., Garst Seed Co.★

SLOAN, 938, *Woodbury Co.*

Gaukel, Nevins & Westergaard, (AV) .... Murray Insurance Bldg. (⊙Anthon, Mapleton)
Smith, Dale B. .... '48 '72 C&L.546 B.S., J.D. Sloan State Bk.
Westergaard, James R., (AV) '52 '78 C.513 B.S. L.221 J.D.
[Gaukel,N.&W.] (⊙Mapleton)

SOLON, 1,177, *Johnson Co.*

Malenda, Irene A. .... '51 '85 C.645 B.S. L.678 J.D. 305 Pleasantview Dr. NE‡
McLaughlin, Sandra J. '54 '90 C.352 B.L.S. L.744 J.D.
(adm. in TX; not adm. in IA) 415 Pleasant View Dr. N.E.

SPENCER, * 11,317, *Clay Co.*

Alderman, Robert L. .... '28 '53 C&L.585 LL.B. 812 W. 11th St.‡
Avery, Stephen F., (AV) .... '42 '66 C&L.352 B.A., J.D. [Cornwall,A.B.&S.]
Barry, Richard J., (AV) .... '44 '69 C&L.352 B.B.A., J.D. [Montgomery,B.&B.]
Berg, Redge O., (BV) .... '39 '64 C&L.352 B.A., J.D. [Berg&H.]
Berg & Howe, (BV) .... 110 W. 4th St.
Bjornstad, Christopher A., (AV) .... '48 '74 C&L.352 B.A., J.D. [Cornwall,A.B.&S.]
Borth, Charles K., (BV) .... '69 '95 C.490 B.A. L.221 J.D. [Zenor,H.&B.]
Bovee, Michael R., (AV) .... '51 '76 C.350 B.S. L.352 J.D. [Montgomery,B.&B.]
Carr, Patrick M. .... '50 '75 C.352 B.A. L.221 J.D. Dist. Ct. J.
Cornwall, Tom W., (BV) .... '27 '53 C.197 B.A. L.352 J.D. [Cornwall,A.B.&S.]

Cornwall, Avery, Bjornstad & Scott, (AV)
407 Grand Avenue, P.O. Box 999, 51301
Telephone: 712-262-1630 Fax: 712-262-1211
URL: http://www.cabslaw.com
Members of Firm: Tom W. Cornwall; Stephen F. Avery; Christopher A. Bjornstad; David A. Scott.
General Practice in all Courts. Corporation, Banking, Taxation, Probate and Insurance Law. Trials and Appeals.
Attorneys for: Hawkeye Bank of Clay County, Spencer, Iowa; Farmers Trust & Savings Bank; Northwest Federal Savings Bank.
Representative Clients: The Hartford Insurance Co.; Minnesota Mutual Fire and Casualty; Milwaukee Insurance; Continental Casualty Co.; Travelers Insurance Co.; American Surety Co.; Liberty Mutual Insurance Co.
See Professional Biographies, SPENCER, IOWA

Greer, John J., (AV) .... '20 '43 C&L.352 B.A., J.D. 13 W. 4th St.‡
Greer, John P., (CV) .... '57 '84 C.352 B.B.A. L.190 J.D. [Greer]
Greer Law Office, (CV) .... 13 W. Fourth St.
Houchins, Michael James, (BV) .... '59 '87 C.351 B.A. L.221 J.D. [Zenor,H.&B.]
Howe, Bradley B., (BV) .... '49 '75 C.352 B.A. L.378 J.D. [Berg&H.]
Montgomery, Dick H., (AV) .... '43 '69 C&L.352 B.B.A., J.D. [Montgomery,B.&B.]
Montgomery, Barry & Bovee, (AV) .... 316 11th Street, S.W. Plaza
Nelson, Frank B. .... '32 '59 C.350 B.S. L.352 J.D. Dist. J.
Scott, David A., (BV) .... '47 '72 C.793 B.A. L.352 J.D. [Cornwall,A.B.&S.]
Underwood, Murray S. .... '21 '48 C&L.352 B.A., J.D. Sr. Dist. J.
Whittenburg, Nancy L., (BV) .... '57 '88 C&L.221 B.A., J.D. 12 E. 4th St.
Zenor, Michael L., (AV) .... '49 '75 C.352 B.A. L.221 J.D. [Zenor,H.&B.]

Zenor, Houchins & Borth, (AV)
2000 Highway Boulevard, P.O. Box 317, 51301
Telephone: 712-262-1187 Fax: 712-262-1189
Email: zenorlaw@ncn.net
Members of Firm: Michael L. Zenor; Michael James Houchins; Charles K. Borth.
General Trial and Appellate Practice including Personal Injury, Insurance, Labor, Tort, Probate, Corporate and Commercial Law.
Reference: Farmers Trust & Savings Bank, Spencer, Iowa.
See Professional Biographies, SPENCER, IOWA

SPIRIT LAKE, * 4,261, *Dickinson Co.*

Barlow, Charles H. .... '31 '58 C&L.221 B.A., J.D. Dist. J.
Bedell, Jack H., (AV) .... '23 '50 C&L.352 LL.B. 24750 140th St.‡
Benz, James L., (BV) .... '50 '76 C&L.352 B.A., J.D. [Benz]
Benz Law Office, (BV) .... 15357 212th Ave.
Bjornstad, Edward Wallace, (BV) .... '54 '82 C.723 B.A. L.190 J.D. [Bjornstad]
Bjornstad, Jack, (CV) .... '74 '99 C.723 B.A. L.352 J.D. [Bjornstad]
Bjornstad, John M., (BV) .... '52 '87 C.376 B.S. L.190 J.D. [Bjornstad]
Bjornstad Law Office, (BV) .... 832 Lake Street
Blankers, Beth S. .... '75 '03 C.221 B.S.B.A. L.494 J.D. [Ⓐ Ladegaard,M.&O.]
Brands, Bethany J., (CV) .... '69 '94 C.1304 B.A. L.352 J.D. 703 Lake Street
Chozen, Michael J., (BV) .... '52 '78 C&L.190 B.S.B.A., J.D. [Chozen&S.]
Chozen & Saunders, (BV) .... 2304 30th St.

Clarity, James A., III, (AV) '50 '76 C.350 B.S. L.190 J.D.
1601 Keokuk, P.O. Box 469, 51360
Telephone: 712-336-4611 Facsimile: 712-336-5072 Email: jaciii@rconnect.com
Email: jclarity@rconnect.com URL: http://www.lawyers.com/jamesclarity

(This Listing Continued)

Clarity, James A., III (Continued)
Civil Litigation and Criminal Defense in State and Federal Courts.
See Professional Biographies, SPIRIT LAKE, IOWA

Hess, Raymond A. .... '18 '47 C.597 B.S.C. L.352 LL.B. 20650 Nautica Dr.‡
Johnson, Michael H. .... '57 '82 C&L.221 B.A., J.D. [Stoller&J.]
Ladegaard, James C., (AV) .... '42 '68 C.352 B.S. L.494 J.D. [Ladegaard,M.&O.]

Ladegaard, Maahs & Owens, (AV)
708 Lake Street, P.O. Box AK, 51360
Telephone: 712-336-1292 Fax: 712-336-1317
Members of Firm: James C. Ladegaard; Earl H. Maahs; Gregg L. Owens. Associates: Beth S. Blankers; Abby L. Walleck.
General Practice, Trials, Appeals, Probate, Real Estate, Corporation and Taxation, Estate Planning, Wills and Trusts.
Representative Clients: Iowa Great Lakes Sanitary District; Arco Dehydrating, Co.; Spirit Lake Community School; Iowa Lakes Orthopedics, P.C.; Nodland Realty; Bank Midwest, Okoboji; City of Spirit Lake, Iowa; Dickinson County Mutual; Grinnell Mutual Reinsurance Company.

Larson, David C., (BV) .... '55 '81 C.350 B.S. L.190 J.D. Assoc. Dist. J.
Maahs, Earl H., (BV) .... '43 '74 C.350 B.S. L.793 J.D. [Ladegaard,M.&O.]
McDonald, William B. .... '29 '55 C&L.352 B.A., J.D. P.O. Box 121
McMahon-Boies, Carole, (BVⓉ) '55 '82 C.627 B.S.W. L.546 J.D.
(adm. in NE; not adm. in IA) [Pepperl&M.-B.]
Narey, Peter B., (AV) .... '20 '47 C.162 B.A. L.352 J.D. P.O. Box 255‡
Olson, Rosalise, (CVⓉ) .... '57 '86 C.1025 B.A. L.560 J.D. Asst. Co. Atty.
Owens, Gregg L., (BV) .... '59 '86 C&L.352 B.B.A., J.D. [Ladegaard,M.&O.]
Pepperl, Donald J., (BVⓉ) '50 '75 C&L.546 B.A., J.D.
(adm. in NE; not adm. in IA) [Pepperl&M.-B.]
Pepperl & McMahon-Boies, Law Offices, P.C., (BV) .... 15667 250th Ave.
Sandy, Shannon L., (BV) .... '55 '84 C.352 B.A. L.221 J.D. [Sandy]
Sandy Law Firm, (BV) .... 304 18th St.
Saunders, Lonnie B., (BV) .... '60 '85 C.106 B.A. L.352 J.D. [Chozen&S.]
Stoller, Larry A., (BV) .... '56 '80 C.36 B.A. L.190 J.D. [Stoller&J.]
Stoller & Johnson, (BV) .... 1305 18th Street
Thomas, Michael J. '— '71 C.352 B.A. L.477 J.D.
(adm. in NY; not adm. in IA) 1748 310th Ave.
Walleck, Abby L. .... '79 '04 C&L.190 B.A., J.D. [Ⓐ Ladegaard,M.&O.]
Welch, Edward J. .... '29 '53 C&L.190 LL.B. 15548 Percival Dr.‡
Wilcke, Ernest W., (BV) .... '25 '53 C.898 B.A. L.221 LL.B. P.O. Box 455
Wingert, Pamela A., (CV) .... '60 '96 C.985 B.A. L.793 J.D. [Wingert]
Wingert Law Office, (CV) .... 1510 Hill Avenue

SPRINGVILLE, 1,068, *Linn Co.*

Buresh, Ernest J. '26 '57 C.350 B.S. L.352 LL.B.
Chmn. of the Bd. & Pres., The Exchange State Bk.

STORM LAKE, * 10,076, *Buena Vista Co.*

Armstrong, Gary W., (BV) .... '51 '76 C.427 B.A. L.352 J.D. [Mack,H.G.A.&B.]
Bridge, Alan L. .... '43 '75 C.352 B.A. L.221 J.D. 208 Ontario St.‡
Brown, W. Ted, (BV) .... '53 '78 C&L.352 B.A., J.D. [Mack,H.G.A.&B.]
Connell, Dan, (BV) .... '37 '64 C.106 B.A. L.221 LL.B. [D.Connell]
Connell, Dan, P.C., (BV) .... 205 E. 6th St.
Cornish, Mark T., (BV) .... '52 '78 C.352 B.B.A. L.190 J.D. [Stern,D.C.&J.] ⊙
Crippin, Byron M., Jr. '28 '52 C&L.494 B.S.L., J.D.
(adm. in MN; not adm. in IA)
Dir., Stewardship Ministries, Minn.-Iowa Christian Broadcasting‡
Diehl, Mary Ann, (AV) .... '23 '50 C.112 L.352 LL.B. [Ⓢ Stern,D.C.&J.] ⊙
Duffy, John P., (BV) .... '40 '65 C.106 B.A. L.221 J.D. Dist. J.
Emerson, Emery H., Jr., (BV) .... '27 '54 C&L.793 B.S., LL.B. 519 Cayuga St.
Gadd, Stephen R., (AV) .... '41 '66 C&L.352 B.A., J.D. [Ⓢ Mack,H.G.A.&B.]
Hamilton, Mary C., (CV) .... '56 '97 C.106 B.A. L.190 J.D. [Ⓐ Hamilton] ⊙
Hamilton, Steven D., (BV) .... '47 '72 C.602 B.A. L.37 J.D. [Hamilton] ⊙
Hamilton, Willis J., (AV) .... '49 '74 C&L.190 B.A., J.D. [Hamilton] ⊙
Hamilton Law Firm, P.C., (AV) .... 606 Ontario Street (⊙Sioux City)
Hansen, Douglas W., (AV) .... '29 '58 C.293 A.B. L.352 J.D. 316 East Sixth Street‡
Havens, Paul D., (BV) .... '42 '73 C.871 B.S. L.352 J.D. City Atty. [Havens&H.]
Havens, Philip E., (BV) .... '53 '78 C&L.352 B.A., J.D. Co. Atty. [Havens&H.]
Havens and Havens, (BV) .... 716 Lake Ave.
Jennett, David P., (BV) .... '53 '79 C.350 B.A. L.221 J.D. 205 E. 6th
Jensen, Nola M., (BV) .... '59 '84 C&L.352 B.B.A., J.D. [Stern,D.C.&J.] ⊙
Kimble, Rick C., (CV) .... '70 '95 C.350 B.B.A. L.352 J.D. Asst. Co. Atty.
Lochray, Paul J. ...'52 '79 C&L.190 B.A., J.D. Sr. Legal Tr. Offr., Citizens First Natl. Bk.
Mack, Hansen, Gadd, Armstrong & Brown, P.C., (BV) .... 316 East Sixth Street
McCollum, Mary Lynn, (BV) .... '56 '83 C&L.152 B.A., J.D. Juv. Ref.
Moore, Frederick V. '56 '89 C&L.575 B.A., J.D.
(adm. in NC; not adm. in IA) Pres., Buena Vista Univ.
Murray, Edean, (BV) .... '66 '92 C.352 B.B.A. L.221 J.D. [Murray&M.]
Murray, John M., (BV) .... '64 '95 C&L.190 B.S., J.D. [Murray&M.]
Murray & Murray, P.L.C., (BV) .... 530 Erie St.
Patton, David Wm., (BV) .... '53 '79 C.350 B.S. L.221 J.D. 606 Geneseo St.
Perry, Hugh J., (BV) .... '46 '73 C.350 B.A. L.352 J.D. [Perry&P.]
Perry, William B. .... '08 '33 C.293 A.B. L.352 J.D. [Perry&P.] ‡
Perry & Perry, (BV) .... 116 E. 5th (⊙Wash., DC)
Prichard, James M., (AV) .... '26 '50 C&L.352 B.A., J.D. 109 West 5th Street
Redenbaugh, Phil C., (AV) .... '41 '70 C.106 B.A. L.221 J.D. [P.C.Redenbaugh]

Redenbaugh, Phil C., P.C., (AV)
111 West 6th Street, P.O. Box 1284, 50588
Telephone: 712-732-1873 Fax: 712-732-4274
Phil C. Redenbaugh.
General Civil and Trial Practice. Personal Injury, Workers' Compensation and Real Estate, Insurance, Bad Faith.
Representative Clients: Employers Mutual Casualty Co.; Rasmussen Ford Inc.; Farmers Casualty Mutual; IMT Insurance Co.; Hartford Insurance Co.; Great West Casualty Co.
Reference: Citizens First National Bank.
See Professional Biographies, STORM LAKE, IOWA

Roth, Steven T., (BV) .... '47 '72 C.793 B.S. L.221 J.D. [Roth]

Roth Law Office, (BV)
608 Seneca Street, P.O. Box 1126, 50588
Telephone: 712-732-4373 Fax: 712-732-4712
Email: rothlaw@iw.net URL: http://www.lawyers.com/rothlaw
Steven T. Roth.
General Practice, Personal Injury, Social Security Disability, Trusts and Estates, Business Law, Wills, Probate.
References: Citizens First National Bank; Security Trust and Savings Bank.
See Professional Biographies, STORM LAKE, IOWA

Schall, James A., (BV) .... '42 '67 C.707 B.A. L.221 J.D. 505 Erie St.
Smith, Andrew J. .... '73 '98 C.587 B.A. L.352 J.D. [Ⓐ Mack,H.G.A.&B.]

Stern, Diehl, Cornish & Jensen, (AV)
Fritcher Building, 533 Erie Street, 50588 ⊙
Telephone: 712-732-1624 Fax: 712-732-1686
Email: sternlaw@iw.net
Members of Firm: Ellis R. Stern (1900-1982); Robert H. Diehl (1923-1967); Mark T. Cornish; Nola M. Jensen. Of Counsel: Mary Ann Diehl.
General and Trial Practice. Estate Planning, Probate, Taxation, Real Estate and Corporate Law.
References: Citizens First National Bank; Commerical Trust & Savings Bank; Security Trust and Savings Bank, Storm Lake; Community State Bank, Albert City, Iowa.
Albert City, Iowa Office: 224 Main Street. Telephone: 712-843-2255. Fax: 712-843-2256.

STORY CITY, 3,228, *Story Co.*

Brekken, Judean C., (BV) .... '19 '48 C.747 B.A. L.352 J.D. [Brekken,D.W.&C.]
Brekken, Deppe, Wynia & Cook, P.C., (BV) ....523 Broad Street (⊙Jewell)
Buchanan, Joseph H., (CV) .... '13 '37 C.352 B.S. L.145 J.D. Rte. #2
Deppe, Charles D., (BV) ....'42 '68 C.351 B.A. L.221 J.D. [Brekken,D.W.&C.] ⊙
Huffer, Robert L., (BV) .... '45 '70 C.350 B.S. L.352 J.D. [Huffer]
Huffer Law Office, (BV) .... 622 Broad St.
Larson, Fred A., (BV) ....'53 '78 C.351 B.A. L.221 J.D. [Larson]
Larson Law Office, (BV) .... 607 Broad St.
Wynia, Thomas C., (BV) ....'51 '78 C.793 B.S. L.352 J.D. [Brekken,D.W.&C.]

STRAWBERRY POINT, 1,357, *Clayton Co.*

Compton, John C., (BV) .... '56 '81 C.121 B.A. L.221 J.D. [J.C.Compton]
Compton, John C., PC, (BV) ....116 1/2 W. Mission St.
Martin, Linzy E., (CV) .... '45 '76 C.872 B.A. L.221 J.D. 103 Elkader St.
Schloss, Timothy T., (BV) ....'51 '77 C.352 B.A. L.1340 J.D. 118 W. Mission St.

STUART, 1,712, *Adair & Guthrie Cos.*

Bump, Jeffrey, (BV) ....'61 '89 C.350 B.S. L.221 J.D. [Bump&B.] ⊙
Bump, William E., (BV) ....'58 '84 C&L.221 B.A., J.D. [Bump&B.] ⊙
Bump and Bump, (BV) .... 1311 N. 2nd St. (⊙Panora)
Hartman, Leonard, (BV) .... '48 '74 C&L.352 B.B.A., J.D. 1312 N. 2nd St.
Varley, Warren A., (BV) ....'60 '88 C.350 B.S. L.188 J.D. City Atty.

SULLY, 841, *Jasper Co.*

Brierly Law Office, L.L.P., (AV) .... 618 4th St. (⊙Grinnell, Newton)
Chalupa, Dennis F., (AV) .... '44 '70 C.641 B.A. L.352 J.D. [Brierly] ⊙
Matthias, Campbell, Tyler, Nuzum, Greta & Rickers, (AV) ....613 4th St. (⊙Newton)
McCall, Bradley, (BV) ....'54 '79 C.352 B.S. L.221 J.D. [Brierly] ⊙
Otto, Mark A., (BV) .... '56 '82 C.800 B.A. L.221 J.D. [Brierly] ⊙
Terpstra, John H., (BV) ....'59 '92 C.350 B.S. L.352 J.D. [Brierly] ⊙
Tyler, James L., (AV) ....'27 '54 C&L.221 J.D. [Matthias,C.T.N.G.&R.] ⊙

SUMNER, 2,078, *Bremer Co.*

Fosselman, Earl E. .... '25 '53 C.351 B.A. L.602 LL.B. 507 N. Walnut St.‡
Murphy, Thomas E., (BV) .... '21 '48 C&L.477 B.A., J.D. 119 N. Carpenter St.
Teeter, Tim R. ....'72 '98 C.350 B.S. L.190 J.D. 108 W. 1st St.
Tremaine, John S., (BV) .... '49 '75 C.352 B.A. L.190 J.D. [Tremaine]
Tremaine Law Office, (BV) ....110 E. 1st

SUTHERLAND, 714, *O'Brien Co.*

Klinker, William K., (BV) ....'59 '83 C.57 B.A. L.352 J.D. [Smith,G.S.&K.] ⊙
Shea, Ronald J., (AV) ....'48 '73 C&L.190 B.A., J.D. [Smith,G.S.&K.] ⊙
Smith, Grigg, Shea & Klinker, A Professional Corporation, (AV)
Professional Bldg. (⊙Primghar)

SWEA CITY, 634, *Kossuth Co.*

Buchanan, Buchanan, Bibler, Buchanan & Handsaker, (AV)
Swea City State Bk. Bldg. (⊙Algona, Lakota)
Handsaker, Jerrold L., (BV) ....'50 '76 C.352 B.S. L.221 J.D. [Buchanan,B.B.B.&H.]

SWISHER, 813, *Johnson Co.*

O'Flaherty, Anna Wirt, (BV) .... '54 '87 C.928 B.A. L.352 J.D. [O'Flaherty]
O'Flaherty, Thomas J., (BV) ....'50 '83 C&L.221 B.S.Ed., J.D. [O'Flaherty]
O'Flaherty Law Firm, (BV) ....P.O. Box 520

TAMA, 2,697, *Tama Co.*

Anderson, Gary F. ....'42 '67 C.351 B.A. L.352 J.D. 202 W. 14th St.
Rathjen, Daniel Y., (BV) .... '50 '75 C&L.352 B.B.A, J.D. [Willett&R.] ⊙
Richards, Allan M. '54 '90
C.427 B.A. L.940 J.D. 116 West Fourth Street (⊙Cedar Rapids)
Willett, John J., (BV) ....'40 '66 C&L.352 B.A., LL.B. [Willett&R.] ⊙
Willett, Walter J., (AV) ....'11 '34 C&L.352 215 W. 3rd St.‡
Willett & Rathjen, P.L.C., (BV) ....215 W. 3rd St. (⊙Dysart)

TIPTON, * 3,155, *Cedar Co.*

Beine, Lee W., (BV) .... '49 '75 C.350 B.S. L.352 J.D. Co. Atty. [Beine&B.]
Beine & Benz, (BV) ....419 Cedar St.
Benz, Sterling, (BV) .... '50 '75 C&L.352 B.A., J.D. [Beine&B.]
Casterline, James F., (AV) ....'17 '41 C&L.352 A.B., J.D. [Casterline&D.] ‡
Casterline & Dendinger, (BV) ....409 Cedar St.
Dendinger, Lowell E., (BV) .... '44 '72 C.545 A.B. L.352 J.D. [Casterline&D.]
Hamiel, Norman J. ....'26 '51 C&L.352 B.A., J.D. 500 East St.‡
Leff, Edward J., (BV) ....'59 '86 C&L.352 B.A., J.D. 525 E. 4th St.
Singleton, Norman D. ....'56 '94 C.898 B.A. L.966 J.D. 319 Cedar St.
Werling, Max R. ....'23 '50 C&L.352 B.A., J.D. Sr. Dist. J.
Werling, Stuart P., (CV) ....'56 '81 C.352 B.A. L.45 J.D. Mag.
Zearley, L. Jeffrey, (CV) .... '48 '75 C.350 B.S. L.352 J.D. 323 Cedar St.

TOLEDO, * 2,539, *Tama Co.*

Appelgate, Dennis D., (BV) .... '52 '77 C&L.221 B.F.A., J.D. [Appelgate&K.]
Appelgate & Kenkel, (BV) ....120 E. High St.
Burk, Nancy L., (BV) ....'50 '90 C.784 B.A. L.352 J.D. 219 W. High St.
Heeren, Brent D., (BV) ....'57 '82 C.350 B.S. L.221 J.D. Co. Atty.
Kenkel, Stephen A., (BV) ....'55 '83 C.350 B.S. L.352 J.D. [Appelgate&K.]
Pingenot, David J. ....'47 '80 C&L.352 B.A., J.D. Dept. of Corrections
Roan, James E., (AV) ....'32 '57 C.190 B.A. L.352 LL.B. 120 E. High St.

TRAER, 1,552, *Tama Co.*

Bauch, Jared O., (AV) ....'41 '65 C&L.352 B.A., J.D. [Bauch]
Bauch, John S., (AV) ....'29 '54 C&L.352 B.A., J.D. [Bauch]
Bauch Law Office, (AV) ....P.O. Box 57
Powell, Marc, (BV) ....'48 '75 C&L.221 B.S., J.D. [Roan&P.]
Powell, Robert, (AV) ....'14 '36 C&L.352 B.S., J.D. 517 2nd St.‡
Reinders, Bruce E. ....'63 '92 C.1348 L.546 J.D. 517 2nd St.
Roan, John T., (BV) ....'36 '61 C&L.352 LL.B. [Roan&P.]
Roan & Powell, (BV) .... 517 2nd St.

TREYNOR, 897, *Pottawattamie Co.*

Pechacek, Frank W., Jr., (AV) ....'44 '69 C.351 B.A. L.352 J.D. [Willson&P.] ⊙
Willson & Pechacek, P.L.C., (AV)
15 E. Main St. (⊙Carroll, Council Bluffs, Harlan, Oakland, Red Oak)

TRIPOLI, 1,310, *Bremer Co.*

Engelbrecht, Wm. H., (AV) '27 '51
C.898 L.221 LL.B. [Engelbrecht,A.&H.] (⊙Readlyn, Waverly)
Engelbrecht, Ackerman & Hassman, (AV)
207 S. Main St. (⊙Clarksville, Readlyn, Waverly)

URBANDALE, 29,072, *Dallas & Polk Cos.*

Abendroth, Mark U., (AV) .... '53 '79 C&L.221 B.S., J.D. [Abendroth&R.]
Abendroth and Russell, P.C., (AV) ....2536 73rd Street
Barnett, Ross F., (BV) ....'69 '95 C.293 B.A. L.221 J.D. [[A] Abendroth&R.]
Chapman, Joseph '71 '01 C.473 B.S. L.36 J.D.
(adm. in AZ; not adm. in IA) 2815 149th St.
Christy, Cynthia Ullem '69 '97 C.210 B.A. L.221 J.D.
(adm. in CO; not adm. in IA) 12815 Wilden Dr
Cullen, Mark J., (BV) '59 '86 C.351 B.A. L.221 J.D.
Asst. V.P. & Subrogation Mgr., EMC Ins. Cos.
Cunningham, Michael J., (BV) ....'51 '76 C&L.190 B.A., J.D. [Howe,C.&L.]
Dewey, Blair H. ....'15 '38 C.352 L.221 J.D. State Dept. of Job Serv.
Dolezal, Wayne Elliott '64 '88 C.544 B.S. L.546 J.D.
Dir. of Bus. and Legal Aff., Multi-State Lottery Assn.
Duncan, David C., (BV) ....'64 '90 C&L.352 B.B.A., J.D. 2987 100th Street
Erbe, Norman A. .... '19 '47 C&L.352 B.A., J.D. 8126 Rocklyn Dr.‡
Fernandez, Joseph W., (BV) ....'— '94 C.999 B.A. L.352 J.D. [Fernandez]

Fernandez Law Firm, (BV)
2759 86th Street, Suite 102, 50322
Mailing Address: P.O. Box 65344, West Des Moines, IA 50265
Telephone: 515-254-1881 Fax: 515-254-1881
URL: http://www.fernandezlawiowa.com
Joseph W. Fernandez.
Family Law, Bankruptcy, Personal Injury, Divorce, General Practice.
See Professional Biographies, URBANDALE, IOWA

Gajdel, John J., (BV) ....'52 '77 C.424 B.A. L.221 J.D. 7109 Hickman Road
Grodt, Paul O. ....'26 '50 C&L.221 B.C.S., J.D. 10627 Sharon Circle
Guyer, Steven C. '59 '88 C.351 B.A. L.352 J.D.
Dir. Environ. & Environmental Coun., MidAmerican Energy Co.
Hoffmann, Linda L. '47 '74 C.112 B.A. L.1068 J.D.
Asst. Secy. & Bong Claims Mgr., EMC Insurance Companies (Legal Department)
Hoffmann, Richard W., (AV) '53 '79
C.197 A.B. L.174 J.D. V.P. & Gen. Coun., EMC Insurance Cos.
Howe, Richard D., (AV) .... '47 '73 C&L.221 B.S., J.D. [Howe,C.&L.]

Howe, Cunningham & Lowe, P.L.C., (AV)
2824 104th Street, 50322
Telephone: 515-278-4200 Fax: 515-278-4655
Richard D. Howe; Michael J. Cunningham; Chip Lowe; Jeffrey A. Kelso.
General Practice including Trial and Appellate Practice in State and Federal Courts. Corporate, Transportation, Administrative, Insurance, Family, Divorce, Personal Injury, Estate Planning, Wills, Probate, Real Estate, and Creditor Law.
References: Norwest Bank Iowa, N.A.; Firstar Bank Des Moines, N.A.
See Professional Biographies, URBANDALE, IOWA

Hrubetz, Matthew F., (BV) ....'63 '92 C&L.221 B.A., J.D. 2536 73rd Street
Johnson, Kristi K., (BV) '62 '89 C&L.221 B.A., J.D.
Asst. V.P. & Assoc. Gen. Coun., EMC Insurance Cos.
Kelso, Jeffrey A. .... '72 '97 C.132 B.A. L.221 J.D. [Howe,C.&L.]
Low, Christopher L. ....'— '01 C.352 B.A. L.221 J.D. [[A] Abendroth&R.]
Lowe, Chip, (BV) ....'53 '79 C.546 B.A. L.793 J.D. [Howe,C.&L.]
May, Clint J. ....'70 '97 C.784 B.A. L.221 J.D. 14220 Mapple Dr.
Mercer-Klimowski, Jenifer L., (BV) '53 '79
C.914 B.A. L.221 J.D. V.P. & Corp. Coun., EMC National Life Co.
Minkler, Debra J. '59 '90 C.132 B.A. L.836 J.D.
(adm. in TN; not adm. in IA) 2824 Eula Dr.‡
Narigon, David O., (AV) '52 '81
C.72 B.A. L.352 J.D. S.V.P. - Claims, EMC Insurance Co.
Pelletier, Sean A., (BV) '72 '97 C.350 B.S. L.221 J.D.
Assoc. Staff Atty., EMC Insurance Companies (Legal Department)
Root, John H., (BVⓉ) '55 '83 C.103 A.B. L.569 J.D.
(adm. in MA; not adm. in IA) 15012 Wilden Dr.
Russell, David B., (BV) ....'51 '80 C&L.221 B.A., J.D. [Abendroth&R.]
Schneider, Harvey E. '41 '73 C.932 B.A. L.383 J.D.
(adm. in KY; not adm. in IA) 3904 Patricia Drive
Shostrom, Earl R., (AV) ....'21 '47 C&L.352 B.A., J.D. 6855 Oliver Smith Dr.‡
Simonetta, Lisa A., (AV) '59 '85 C.321 B.A. L.1049 J.D.
(adm. in CA; not adm. in IA)
V.P. & Litig. Specialist, Home Off. Claims, EMC Ins. Cos.
Sullivan, T. Sue ....'65 '92 C.502 B.A. L.986 J.D. 4305 101st Street‡
Wright, Charles K. .... '41 '78 C.798 B.S. L.734 J.D. IA Bd. of Regents

VAN METER, 866, *Dallas Co.*

Westfall, Edith Ann, (CV) ....'49 '78 C.627 B.S.B.A. L.190 J.D. 2825 S. 13th St.

VICTOR, 966, *Iowa & Poweshiek Cos.*

Bloethe, Orville W., (AV) ....'19 '47 C&L.352 B.S.C., J.D. 702 3rd St.
Stiefel, Fred, (BV) ....'56 '81 C&L.352 B.A., J.D. [Stiefel]
Stiefel Law Office, (BV) ....216 Washington Street (⊙Marengo)

VILLISCA, 1,332, *Montgomery Co.*

Swanson, R. John, (AV) ....'20 '48 C&L.352 B.A., J.D. [Swanson] ⊙
Swanson Law Firm, (AV) .... Bickford Bldg. (⊙Red Oak)

VINTON, * 5,103, *Benton Co.*

Duncan, Karen ....'60 '88 C&L.494 B.A., J.D. Asst. Co. Atty.
Fischer, Bennett M., (AV) ....'24 '60 C&L.352 B.S., J.D. [Fischer]
Fischer, John K., (BV) ....'50 '79 C.399 B.A. L.352 J.D. City Atty. [Fischer]
Fischer, Karl W., (AV) ....'22 '50 C.871 B.S. L.352 J.D. [[C] Fischer]
Fischer, Robert B., (BV) ....'54 '85 C.352 B.B.A. L.221 J.D. [Fischer]
Fischer Law Firm, (AV) ....110 E. 4th. St.
Fraker, J.C., (BV) ....'53 '83 C&L.352 B.A., J.D. [Fraker]
Fraker Law Office, (BV) ....209 W. 4th St.
Happel, David E., (CV) ....'39 '64 C&L.879 B.A., LL.B. 201 E. 4th St.

Kerdus, Richard H. .... '47 '74 C.350 B.S. L.352 J.D. P.O. Box 640‡
Lough, Patricia, (CV) ....'63 '90 C.221 B.S.E. L.880 J.D. 100 W. Fourth St.
Lough, Ray, (BV) ....'61 '86 C.352 B.A. L.221 J.D. 306 E. 13th St.
Milroy, Boyd J., (BV) ....'18 '51 C&L.352 B.A., LL.B. 408 B Ave.
Mossman, John ....'76 '03 C.352 B.A. L.221 J.D. 122 E. 4th St.
Mossman, Keith D., (AV) ....'21 '48 C.337 A.B. L.339 LL.B. [Mossman&M.]
Mossman, Mark E., (AV) ....'50 '75 C.352 B.A. L.221 J.D. [Mossman&M.]
Mossman & Mossman, L.L.P., (AV) ....122 East Fourth Street
Thompson, David C., (CV) ....'64 '91 C.352 B.A. L.221 J.D. Co. Atty.

White & Johnson, P.C.
(See Cedar Rapids)

WALFORD, 1,224, *Benton & Linn Cos.*

Enusha, Bruce A. ....'55 '83 C.878 B.A. L.36 J.D. P.O. Box 131
Happe, Daniel G., Law Office of ....'73 '99 C.351 B.A. L.1018 J.D. 445 G Avenue

WALL LAKE, 875, *Sac Co.*

Bush, Warren L., (BV) ....'48 '73 C.352 B.B.A. L.36 J.D. [Bush]
Bush Law Office, (BV) .... 101 Boyer St.
Wunschel, Russell S., P.C., (AV) ....'27 '52 C.545 L.221 J.D. [Wunschel] ⊙
Wunschel Law Firm, P.C., (AV) .... P.O. Box 129 (⊙Carroll)

WALNUT, 857, *Pottawattamie Co.*

Salvo, Deren, Schenck & Lauterbach, P.C., (AV)
301 Antique City Drive (⊙Earling, Harlan, Panama)
Schenck, Richard C., (BV) ....'53 '78 C&L.352 B.A., J.D. [Salvo,D.S.&L.] (⊙Harlan)

WAPELLO, * 2,124, *Louisa Co.*

Darby, Kenneth V. ....'31 '66 C&L.352 B.S.C., LL.B. 219 S. 2nd St.
Hicklin, E. A., (AV) ....'22 '48 C&L.352 B.A., J.D. [⊠ Hicklin&M.]
Hicklin & Matthews, (AV) ....Hicklin Bldg.
Huddle, Roger A., (BV) ....'54 '79 C&L.221 B.A., J.D. 327 N. 2nd St.
Matthews, David L., (CV) ....'58 '86 C.353 B.A. L.221 J.D. [Hicklin&M.]
Matthews, William L., (AV) ....'30 '59 C.353 B.A. L.352 J.D. [Hicklin&M.]
Moore, Robert D. ....'42 '73 C.187 B.A. L.221 J.D. Jud. Mag.

WASHINGTON, * 7,074, *Washington Co.*

Arbuckle, Craig, (BV) '47 '73 C.350 B.S. L.352 J.D.
315 South Iowa Avenue, 52353
Telephone: 319-653-6693 Fax: 319-653-6695
Probate, Real Estate, Tax, Estate Planning, Civil Litigation and Municipal Law.
Reference: Mercantile Bank.

Baldrige, John E., (BV) ....'27 '60 C.350 B.S. L.352 J.D. [⊠ Tindal,E.G.&N.]
Bates, Robert ....'31 '58 C&L.352 B.A., J.D. Dist. J.
Bordwell, Richard S., (BV) ....'46 '72 C.350 B.S. L.352 J.D. [Bordwell]
Bordwell Law Office, (BV) ....206 W. Main St.
Davis, Craig A., (P.C.), (BV) ....'61 '86 C&L.793 B.S., J.D. [Morrison,L.M.D.&G.]
Day, Robert, (AV) ....'19 '42 C&L.352 B.A., J.D. [Day M.L.&S.] ‡

Day Meeker Lamping & Schlegel, (AV)
112 South Avenue B, P.O. Box 929, 52353-0929
Telephone: 319-653-2147 Fax: 319-653-5181
Members of Firm: Schuyler W. Livingston (1872-1959); Louis J. Kehoe (1896-1969); Robert Day (Retired); Everett Meeker; Leslie D. Lamping; Robert G. Schlegel. Associate: Patricia J. Lipski.
General Practice. Insurance, Probate, Corporation and Tax Law. Trials and Appeals. No Small Collections.
Reference: Washington State Bank.
See Professional Biographies, WASHINGTON, IOWA

Edmondson, Barbara A., (BV) ....'59 '84 C.350 B.A. L.352 J.D. Asst. Co. Atty.
Erdahl, Clemens A., II, (BV) ....'47 '80 C&L.352 B.G.S., J.D. [Tindal,E.G.&N.]
Goddard, Bruce D., (BV) ....'45 '80 C&L.352 B.A., J.D. [Tindal,E.G.&N.]
Goers, Eric R., (CV) ....'71 '97 C.427 B.A. L.352 J.D. Asst. Co. Atty.

Kiesey, D. Bradley, (BV) '45 '71 C&L.352 B.A., J.D.
315 South Iowa Avenue, 52353
Telephone: 319-653-6693 FAX: 319-653-6695
Email: bkiesey@iowatelecom.net
General Practice. Commercial, Real Estate, Trusts and Estates and Family Law. Trials and Appeals.
References: U.S. Bank; Washington State Bank; Federation Bank.

Kitchen, Daniel P., (BV) ....'70 '95 C&L.352 B.A., J.D. 305 W. Main St., Ste. A
Lamping, Leslie D., (BV) ....'53 '81 C.339 B.A. L.365 J.D. [Day M.L.&S.]
Lipski, Patricia J. ....'75 '01 C.177 B.A. L.352 J.D. [⊠ Day M.L.&S.]
Lloyd, James E., (P.C.), (AV) ....'33 '61 C&L.352 B.S.C., J.D. [Morrison,L.M.D.&G.]
McConnell, Joseph L., (P.C.), (BV) ....'46 '77 C&L.352 B.S., J.D. [Morrison,L.M.D.&G.]
Meeker, Everett, (AV) ....'25 '53 C&L.352 B.S.C., J.D. [Day M.L.&S.]
Morrison, G. Gifford, (BV) ....'19 '42 C&L.352 B.A., J.D. [⊠ Tindal,E.G.&N.]
Morrison, Lloyd, McConnell, Davis & Gorham, LLP, (AV)
211 West Washington Street
Nestor, Bruce D., (BV) ....'65 '92 C&L.352 B.A., J.D. [Tindal,E.G.&N.]
Partridge, Gerald N., (BV) ....'48 '79 C.338 B.S. L.352 J.D. Co. Atty.
Schlegel, Robert G., (BV) ....'53 '88 C.352 B.F.A. L.464 J.D. [Day M.L.&S.]
Tindal, Douglas L., (BV) ....'45 '74 C&L.352 B.A., J.D. [Tindal,E.G.&N.]
Tindal, Erdahl, Goddard & Nestor, PLC, (BV) ....305 W. Main St., Suite A

WATERLOO, * 68,747, *Black Hawk Co.*

Abbott, Andrew C. ....'75 '02 C.351 B.S. L.352 J.D [⊠ Dunakey&K.]
Abebe, Yeshimebet ....'— '02 C.188 B.S. L.472 J.D. [Abebe]
Abebe Law Office ....501 Sycamore Street
Ahrenholz, Kevin D., (CV) ....'68 '93 C.937 B.A. L.436 J.D. [Beecher,F.W.M.H.&J.]
Albright, Sue, (CV) ....'51 '77 C.351 B.A. L.352 J.D. Off. of Pub. Def.
Ament, Timothy D., (BV) ....'62 '88 C.351 B.A. L.352 J.D. [Gartelos,W.&A.]
Anderson, Samuel C., (BV) ....'59 '84 C.352 B .A. L.221 J.D. [Swisher&C.]
Andres, Robert C., (BV) ....'51 '77 C.351 B.A. L.352 J.D. [Fulton,M.&A.]
Augustine, Charles P., (BV) ....'70 '96 C&L.352 B.A., J.D. [⊠ Dunakey&K.]
Ball, William C., (AV) ....'28 '56 C&L.352 B.S.C., J.D. [Ball,K.&H.] ‡

Ball, Kirk & Holm, P.C., (AV)
3324 Kimball Avenue, P.O. Box 2696, 50704
Telephone: 319-234-2638 Fax: 319-234-2237
Email: bkh@ballkirkholm.com URL: http://www.ballkirkholm.com
William C. Ball (Retired); Max E. Kirk; H. Daniel Holm, Jr.; David W. Stamp; Michael W. Buckner;—Obie Saddler, Jr.; Jen Bries.
General Civil Trial Practice in all courts. Personal Injury, Product Liability, Professional Negligence, Medical Malpractice, Corporate Law, Workers Compensation, Probate and Estate Planning, Real Estate and Tax Law, Family Law and General Practice.
See Professional Biographies, WATERLOO, IOWA

Banning, Tammy L., (CV) ....'71 '97 C.351 B.A. L.221 J.D. [T.L.Banning]
Banning, Tammy L., PLC, (CV) .... P.O. Box 1586
Bauch, James C. ....'45 '69 C&L.352 B.A., J.D. 316 E. 5th Street★
Beatty, Samuel T. ....'22 '51 C.351 L.352 LL.B. 3151 Brockway Rd.‡
Beecher, W. Louis, (AV) ....'21 '47 C&L.352 B.A., J.D. [Beecher,F.W.M.H.&J.]

Beecher, Field, Walker, Morris, Hoffman & Johnson, P.C., (AV)
Suite 300 Court Square Building, 620 Lafayette Street, P.O. Box 178, 50704
Telephone: 319-234-1766 Telecopier: 319-234-1225
URL: http://www.beecherlaw.com
W. L. Beecher (1891-1976); John W. Rathert (Retired); W. Louis Beecher; Hugh M. Field; John R. Walker, Jr.; Richard R. Morris; Theresa E. Hoffman; Eric W. Johnson; Kevin D. Ahrenholz;—D. Raymond Walton; John J. Wood; Adnan Mahmutagic; Heather A. Prendergast; Elizabeth Leyttze Lounsberry.
General Practice. Taxation, Real Estate, Probate, Estate Planning, Trust and Corporation Law, Bankruptcy, Personal Injury, Family Law, Banking, Environmental, Workers Compensation, Health Care, Employment Law, Social Security, Business Litigation, Consumer and Commercial Collections.
General Counsel for: American Black Hawk Broadcasting Co.
Representative Clients: Chubb/Pacific Indemnity Group; The Equitable Life Assurance Society of the United States.
See Professional Biographies, WATERLOO, IOWA

Bevel, Henry J., III, (BV) ....'59 '88 C.382 B.A. L.383 J.D. [Yagla,M.&R.]
Bixby, Aaron R., (CV) ....'69 '95 C.350 B.S. L.352 J.D. [Swisher&C.]
Block, Daniel ....'62 '89 C.352 B.G.S. L.190 J.D. Assoc. Juv. Ct. J.
Boller, Timothy C., (BV) ....'56 '81 C&L.352 B.A., J.D. [Gallagher,L.&G.]
Bower, Thomas N. ....'60 '87 C.338 B.S. L.221 J.D. Dist. J.
Braley, Bruce L., (AV) ....'57 '83 C.350 B.A. L.352 J.D. [Dutton,B.S.&H.]
Braun, Robert W., (AV) ....'38 '63 C&L.352 B.B.A., J.D. [Dutton,B.S.&H.]
Bries, Jen ....'75 '00 C.351 B.A. L.190 J.D. [⊠ Ball,K.&H.]
Briner, Karl D. ....'39 '78 C.898 B.A. L.352 J.D. Dist. J.
Buckner, Michael W., (BV) ....'46 '71 C.98 B.S. L.352 J.D. [Ball,K.&H.]
Burk, Peter W., (BV) ....'38 '65 C.190 A.B. L.352 LL.B. 501 Sycamore, Suite 502
Burris, Natalie Williams, (BV) ....'69 '94 C.351 B.A. L.352 J.D. [Swisher&C.]
Butler, Wallace W., (AV) ....'20 '48 C&L.352 B.S., J.D. [Clark,B.W.&H.] ‡
Chin, Sharon, (CV) ....'72 '99 C.696 B.S. L.770 J.D. U.S. Bank, N.A.

Clark, Butler, Walsh & Hamann, (AV)
315 East 5th Street, P.O. Box 596, 50704
Telephone: 319-234-5701 Fax: 319-232-9579
Email: WLOOLAW@ATTGLOBAL.NET URL: http://www.cbwh-law.com
Members of Firm: Fred G. Clark (1894-1976); Fred G. Clark, Jr. (1922-1984); Wallace W. Butler (Retired); Craig O. Clark (1923-2004); James E. Walsh, Jr.; Timothy W. Hamann; Christy R. Liss; Christopher S. Wendland. Associates: Jared R. Knapp; Matthew Pittenger.
General Practice. Trials and Appeals. Probate, Trust, Corporation, Real Estate, Banking, Surety, Dramshop, Subrogation and Insurance Law, Personal Injury, Workers Compensation.
Local Counsel for: Aetna Life & Casualty Co.; Bankers Life Co.; Equitable Life Assurance Society of the United States; New Hampshire Insurance Group; Reliance Insurance Co.
See Professional Biographies, WATERLOO, IOWA

Clarke, Stephen C. ....'44 '73 C.999 B.A. L.500 J.D. Dist. J.
Cohrt, Larry J., (AV) ....'42 '69 C.747 B.A. L.352 J.D. [L.J.Cohrt]

Cohrt, L.J., Law Firm, (AV)
3356 Kimball Avenue, 50702
Telephone: 319-233-0217 Fax: 319-287-6867
Email: ljcohrt@qwest.net
Larry J. Cohrt.
Civil Litigation, Medical Malpractice, Wills, Trusts and Estates, Probate, Real Estate, Employment Law.
See Professional Biographies, WATERLOO, IOWA

Coil, James D. ....'51 '77 C.784 B.A. L.190 J.D. Dist. Assoc. J.
Conway, Mark F., (BV) ....'60 '91 C.106 B.A. L.793 J.D. [Swisher&C.]
Cook, James H., (AVⓣ) ....'59 '87 C&L.352 B.S., J.D. [Dutton,B.S.&H.]
Daniels, Steven K., (BV) ....'58 '83 C&L.221 B.A., J.D. [Dutton,B.S.&H.]
Dawson, Donal S. ....'09 '33 3720 Village Place, Apt. 5110‡
DeKoster, Jim D., (BV) ....'45 '70 C.350 B.S. L.352 J.D. [Swisher&C.]
Dunakey, David D., (BV) ....'47 '76 C.351 B.A. L.190 J.D. [Dunakey&K.]
Dunakey & Klatt, P.C., (BV) ....531 Commercial, Suite 700
Dunbar, Carol F., (BV) ....'53 '79 C.352 B.A. L.190 J.D. [Dunbar&D.]
Dunbar, Michael C., (BV) ....'52 '77 C&L.352 B.A., J.D. [Dunbar&D.]
Dunbar & Dunbar, (BV) ....738 Chicago Central Bldg.
Dutton, David J., (AV) ....'36 '60 C&L.352 B.A., J.D. [Dutton,B.S.&H.]

Dutton, Braun, Staack & Hellman, P.L.C., (AV) BB
3151 Brockway Road, P.O. Box 810, 50704
Telephone: 319-234-4471 Fax: 319-234-8029
Email: dbsh@wloolaw.com
David J. Dutton; Robert W. Braun; Thomas L. Staack; James R. Hellman; Michael A. McEnroe; Cheryl L. Weber; Steven K. Daniels; Bruce L. Braley; John J. Hines; James F. Kalkhoff; James H. Cook; Carolyn A. Rafferty; Chad A. Swanson; Lynn M. Smith;—Corey R. Lorenzen; Michael R. Young; Erin P. Lyons.
General Trial Practice in all Courts, Insurance, Personal Injury, Products Liability, Malpractice or Professional Negligence, Corporate, Workers Compensation and Labor Employment, Probate and Estate Planning, Real Estate.
Representative Clients: CNA Insurance Cos.; Chubb Group of Insurance Companies; Crossroads Ford, Ltd.; Black Hawk County Solid Waste Management Commission; Allen Memorial Hospital; Tri/Mark, Inc.; John Deere; Heartland Inns of America, L.L.C.; Community National Bank; Ameican Express Proeprty Casualty Companies.
See Professional Biographies, WATERLOO, IOWA

Duven, Dawn R. '52 '78 C&L.546 B.S., J.D.
(adm. in NE; not adm. in IA) 3112 Brockway Rd.‡
Eastman, Forest E. ....'28 '54 C&L.352 B.A., J.D. Sr. Dist. J.

Eells & Tronvold Law Offices, P.L.C.
(See Cedar Rapids)

Engelkes, Carroll E. ....'20 '48 C&L.352 B.A., J.D. Ret. Dist. Ct. J.‡
Fereday, Megan S. ....'74 '00 C.602 B.A. L.436 J.D. [⊠ Swisher&C.]
Ferguson, Thomas J., (AV) ....'56 '80 C&L.190 B.S.B.A., J.D. Co. Atty.
Field, Hugh M., (BV) ....'44 '69 C.597 B.S. L.352 J.D. [Beecher,F.W.M.H.&J.]
Fister, Jon C. ....'43 '71 C&L.352 B.S., J.D. Dist. J.
Frerichs, Clarence A., (AV) ....'30 '59 C.351 L.352 LL.B. Russell Lamson Bldg.
Frost, Michael L. ....'— '04 C.351 B.A. L.221 J.D. 131 Tower Park Dr.
Fulton, Robert D., (AV) ....'29 '58 C&L.352 B.S.C., J.D. [Fulton,M.&A.]
Fulton, Martin & Andres, P.C., (AV) .... Sycamore and East 4th Street
Gallagher, Edward J., III, (BV) ....'49 '74 C.755 B.A. L.276 J.D. [Gallagher,L.&G.]
Gallagher, Edward J., Jr., (AV) ....'25 '50 C.177 B.A. L.276 J.D. [Gallagher,L.&G.]

Gallagher, Langlas & Gallagher, P.C., (AV)
Law Building, 405 East Fifth Street, P.O. Box 2615, 50704
Telephone: 319-233-6163 Fax: 319-233-6435
Edward J. Gallagher, Jr.; Thomas W. Langlas; Edward J. Gallagher, III; George L. Weilein; Timothy C. Boller; Thomas C. Verhulst; David A. Roth; Linda A. Hall;—Laura E. Range.
Personal Injury, Insurance Defense, Corporate Law, Negligence, Professional Malpractice, Real Estate, Municipal Law, Family Law, Labor and Employment Law, Workers Compensation, Probate, General Trial Practice in all Courts.
See Professional Biographies, WATERLOO, IOWA

Gartelos, Peter J., (AV) .... '43 '74 C.57 B.A. L.879 J.D. [Gartelos,W.&A.]

Gartelos, Wagner & Ament, (AV)
3604 Kimball Avenue, 50702
Telephone: 319-234-3500 Fax: 319-234-0837
URL: http://www.gwalawoffice.com
Members of Firm: Peter J. Gartelos; James L. Wagner; Timothy D. Ament.
General Trial Practice and Appeals. Corporation, Family, Insurance, Personal Injury, Real Estate, Probate, Estate Planning, Workers Compensation and Bankruptcy Law.
See Professional Biographies, WATERLOO, IOWA

Geer, Todd A. .... '60 '84 C.221 B.A. L.352 J.D. Dist. J.
Greene, Mitchell Amos, III .... '53 '83 C.511 B.A. L.574 J.D. Asst. Co. Atty.
Greiner, Gregory F. .... '69 '95 C.132 B.A. L.221 J.D. 751 Progress Avenue★
Griffin, Robert C., (BV) .... '51 '76 C&L.352 B.B.A., J.D. [Griffin's]
Griffin's Law Firm, (BV) .... 220 W. Ridgeway, Ste. 107
Griffith, Kimberly A. .... '60 '85 C.504 B.A. L.607 J.D. Asst. Co. Atty.
Guernsey, Dennis M. .... '51 '76 C&L.352 B.A., J.D. [Guernsey]
Guernsey Law Office .... 607 Sycamore St., Ste. 409
Hahn, Kathleen A., (CV) .... '58 '87 C.351 B.A. L.352 J.D. 3633 Cadillac Dr.
Halbach, Steven J., (CV) .... '59 '89 C.352 B.B.A. L.900 J.D. Asst. Co. Atty.
Hall, Linda A., (CV) .... '60 '86 C.694 B.A. L.862 J.D. [Gallagher,L.&G.]
Hamann, Timothy W., (BV) .... '54 '81 C&L.352 B.B.A., J.D. [Clark,B.W.&H.]
Hansen, Beth E., (BV) .... '51 '91 C.352 B.A. L.190 J.D. [Swisher&C.]
Harris, John W., (CV) .... '64 '96 C.350 B.B.A. L.300 J.D. [Ⓐ C.K.McCrindle]
Hauser, Jason T., (CV) .... '71 '97 C.209 B.A. L.1158 J.D. Asst. Pub. Def.
Hellman, James R., (AV) .... '50 '77 C&L.352 B.A., J.D. [Dutton,B.S.&H.]
Hines, John J., (BV) .... '55 '80 C.427 B.A. L.352 J.D. [Dutton,B.S.&H.]
Hoffman, Theresa E., (AV) .... '58 '85 C.177 B.A. L.352 J.D. [Beecher,F.W.M.H.&J.]
Holm, H. Daniel, Jr., (AV) .... '55 '79 C.351 B.A. L.221 J.D. [Ball,K.&H.]
Holmes, John W., (BV) .... '45 '74 C&L.352 B.A., J.D. [Holmes&H.]

Holmes & Holmes, (BV)
531 Commercial Street, Suite 612, 50701
Telephone: 319-234-7506 Fax: 319-234-8277
Email: john@holmeslaw.us URL: http://www.holmeslaw.us
Member of Firm: Wendell A. Holmes (1916-2002); John W. Holmes.
Business Law, Closely Held Business Law, Buying and Selling of Businesses, Lawsuits, Contracts, Business Planning, Professional Liability.
See Professional Biographies, WATERLOO, IOWA

Iversen, Gary D., (BV) .... '53 '77 C.351 B.A. L.352 J.D. 726 West 4th Street
Johnson, Eric W., (BV) .... '65 '91 C&L.352 B.A., J.D. [Beecher,F.W.M.H.&J.]
Kalkhoff, James F., (BV) .... '61 '87 C.350 B.A. L.221 J.D. [Dutton,B.S.&H.]
Kelsen, David S., (BV) .... '38 '62 C&L.221 B.A., J.D. P.O. Box 2158
Kersenbrock, Sara A., (BV) .... '50 '78 C.351 B.A. L.190 J.D. 607 Sycamore Street
Kirk, Max E., (AV) .... '47 '75 C.872 B.A. L.352 J.D. [Ball,K.&H.]
Klatt, Curtis J., (BV) .... '48 '76 C&L.352 B.B.A., J.D. [Dunakey&K.]
Knapp, Jared R. .... '75 '01 C.187 B.A. L.352 J.D. [Ⓐ Clark,B.W.&H.]
Kober, K. L. .... '18 '42 C&L.352 B.A., J.D. [Pickett&K.]
Langlas, Thomas W., (AV) .... '43 '67 C.755 B.A. L.352 J.D. [Gallagher,L.&G.]
Larsen, Diane Ruisch, (CV) .... '50 '75 C&L.352 B.A., J.D. P.O. Box 2352
Lindeman, George, (AV) .... '27 '52 C&L.352 B.A., J.D. 327 E. 4th St., Suite 300‡
Liss, Christy R., (BV) .... '66 '92 C.543 B.A. L.352 J.D. [Clark,B.W.&H.]
Lorenzen, Corey R. .... '77 '02 C.351 B.A. L.352 J.D. [Ⓐ Dutton,B.S.&H.]
Lounsberry, Elizabeth Leyttze, (CV) '68 '93
C.597 B.A. L.352 J.D. [Ⓐ Beecher,F.W.M.H.&J.]
Luce, Timothy J., (BV) .... '51 '77 C&L.190 B.A., J.D. 726 W. 4th St.
Lybbert, L. D. .... '28 '51 C&L.352 B.A., J.D. Sr. Dist. J.
Lyons, Erin P. .... '76 '05 C&L.352 B.A., J.D. [Ⓐ Dutton,B.S.&H.]
Mahmutagic, Adnan .... '76 '03 C.1552 B.B.A. L.221 J.D. [Ⓐ Beecher,F.W.M.H.&J.]
Martin, D. Quinn .... '33 '59 C.707 B.A. L.352 J.D. P.O. Box 2158‡
Martin, Jerald L., (BV) .... '48 '74 C.602 A.B. L.276 J.D. [Fulton,M.&A.]
Mason, David J., (BV) .... '58 '83 C.351 B.A. L.221 J.D. [Mason]
Mason, Robt. D. .... '18 '47 C&L.352 B.A., J.D. 3720 W. 9th St.
Mason Law Office, (BV) .... 3265 W. 4th St.
McCoy, John T., (AV) .... '50 '77 C.602 B.A. L.352 J.D. [Yagla,M.&R.]

McCrindle, C. Kevin, Law Offices of, (AV) '50 '75 C.747 B.A. L.424 J.D.
Suite 500, First National Building 607 Sycamore Street, P.O. Box 928, 50704-0928 ⊙
Telephone: 319-234-0535 Fax: 319-234-0320
Email: lawckm@mchsi.com
Associate: John W. Harris.
Agricultural Law, Business Planning, Real Estate, Probate, Estate Planning, Trusts and Estates, Taxation and Health Care.
Hudson, Iowa Office: 326 4th Street. 50643, Telephone: 319-988-4315.
See Professional Biographies, WATERLOO, IOWA

McEnroe, Michael A., (BV) .... '57 '82 C.350 B.S. L.352 J.D. [Dutton,B.S.&H.]
McGivern, Patricia A., (BV) .... '52 '77 C.350 B.S. L.352 J.D. 10 W. 4th St.

McGuire Law Firm, P.C.
(See Mason City)

McLendon, Sally B. .... '24 '51 C.352 B.A. L.273 LL.B. 907 Meadow Lane‡
Metcalf, James M., (BV) .... '45 '75 C&L.793 B.A., J.D. [J.M.Metcalf]
Metcalf, James M., P.C., (BV) .... 318 E. 4th St.
Meyer Betts, Vivian P., (CV) ... '51 '79 C.966 B.A. L.352 J.D. Legal Servs. Corp. of Iowa
Miller, Eric R., Law Office, (BV) '37 '63
C.674 B.A. L.352 J.D. 607 Sycamore St., Ste. 500
Molinaro-Blonigan, Mary Robin '— '95
C.352 B.A. L.607 J.D. In-House Coun., Warren Transport, Inc.
Moothart, Joseph M. .... '50 '77 C.190 B.A. L.546 J.D. Assoc. Dist. J.
Morris, Richard R., (BV) .... '52 '77 C&L.352 B.A., J.D. [Beecher,F.W.M.H.&J.]

Nagle, David R., (BV) '43 '68 C.351 L.352 LL.B.
Suite 704, 501 Sycamore Street, P.O. Box 792, 50703
Telephone: 319-234-3623 Facsimile: 319-236-2228
Email: davenaglelaw@aol.com
Domestic Relations, Family Law, Personal Injury and Criminal Defense.
See Professional Biographies, WATERLOO, IOWA

Nelson, Kenneth P., (BV) .... '64 '91 C&L.352 B.A., J.D. P.O. Box 1020
Nicholson, Howard C. .... '27 '54 C&L.352 B.S., J.D. Jud. Mag.
Nutting, N. Joseph, (BV) .... '31 '59 C&L.352 B.A., J.D. P.O. Box 2158
Oderkirk, David P., (BV) .... '67 '94 C&L.352 B.A., J.D. [Ⓐ Dunakey&K.]
Olson, Dean S., Jr., (BV) .... '50 '76 C.352 B.A. L.990 J.D. Chf. Pub. Def.
Pedersen, Michael M., (BV) .... '43 '71 C&L.352 B.A., J.D. P.O. Box 2158
Peterson, Roger F. .... '28 '56 C.162 B.A. L.352 J.D. Sr. J.‡
Pickett, Charles J., (AV) .... '11 '37 C.976 B.A. L.352 J.D. [Pickett&K.] ‡
Pickett and Kober, (AV) .... 503 W. 4th St.
Pittenger, Matthew .... '72 '03 C.513 B.S. L.221 J.D. [Ⓐ Clark,B.W.&H.]
Powell, Stephen J., (AV) .... '50 '75 C.173 B.A. L.221 J.D. [Swisher&C.]
Prendergast, Heather A. .... '70 '95 C.339 B.A. L.1048 J.D. [Ⓐ Beecher,F.W.M.H.&J.]
Rafferty, Carolyn A., (CV) .... '63 '88 C.755 B.A. L.346 J.D. [Dutton,B.S.&H.]
Randall, Ross S., (BV) .... '42 '68 C.352 B.A. L.221 J.D. 3112 Brockway Rd.
Range, Laura E. .... '79 '05 C.351 B.A. L.352 J.D. [Ⓐ Gallagher,L.&G.]
Rathert, John W., (AV) .... '32 '59 C&L.352 B.S.C., J.D. [Beecher,F.W.M.H.&J.] ‡
Rausch, John J., (BV) .... '70 '95 C.352 B.A. L.221 J.D. [Rausch]
Rausch, Robert L., (BV) .... '32 '61 C&L.352 B.S.C., LL.B. [Rausch]
Rausch Law Firm, (BV) .... 2022-2024 Bopp Street

Redfern, Mason, Dieter, Larsen & Moore, P.L.C.
(See Cedar Falls)

Riley, David, (AV) .... '54 '79 C&L.352 B.A., J.D. [Yagla,M.&R.]
Roberts, Jay P., (BV) .... '42 '67 C&L.352 B.A., J.D. [Roberts&S.]
Roberts & Stevens, P.L.C., (BV) .... 321 E. 4th St.
Rogers, Kevin R., (BV) .... '58 '87 C.352 B.A. L.221 J.D. [Swisher&C.]
Roth, David A., (BV) .... '63 '91 C.350 B.L.S. L.221 J.D. [Gallagher,L.&G.]
Rothschild, Walter W. .... '32 '57 C&L.352 B.A., J.D. Assoc. Dist. J.

Rush & Nicholson, PLC
(See Cedar Rapids)

Saddler, Obie, Jr., (BV) .... '70 '96 C.352 B.S. L.546 J.D. [Ⓐ Ball,K.&H.]
Sayer, Brian G., (CV) .... '74 '99 C.350 B.S. L.352 J.D. [Ⓐ Dunakey&K.]
Schlicher, Mary A., (BV) .... '49 '82 C.351 B.A. L.352 J.D. Asst. Co. Atty.
Schulte, Duane J. .... '61 '90 C.351 B.A. L.352 J.D. 3151 Brockway Rd.
Shea, Karla J., (BV) .... '65 '91 C.350 B.A. L.221 J.D. [Yagla,M.&R.]

Shuttleworth & Ingersoll, P.L.C.
(See Cedar Rapids)

Smith, D. Berkeley .... '08 '36 C&L.352 B.A., J.D. 414 Terrace Dr.‡
Smith, Kelly, (CV) .... '70 '99 C.352 B.A. L.862 J.D. 209 E. 5th St.
Smith, Lynn M., (CV) .... '71 '97 C.898 B.A. L.221 J.D. [Dutton,B.S.&H.]
Staack, Thomas L., (AV) .... '46 '71 C&L.352 B.A., J.D. [Dutton,B.S.&H.]
Stamp, David W., (BV) .... '61 '86 C.351 B.a. L.352 J.D. [Ball,K.&H.]
Stevens, Carter J., (BV) .... '61 '87 C.427 B.A. L.352 J.D. [Roberts&S.]
Stigler, George L. .... '50 '75 C.351 B.A. L.352 J.D. Dist. J.
Strack, Thomas C. '19 '49 C&L.352 B.A., J.D.
Asst. V.P., Black Hawk Co. Abstract Co.
Swanson, Chad A., (CV) .... '70 '95 C&L.352 B.A., J.D. [Dutton,B.S.&H.]

Swisher & Cohrt, P.L.C., (AV)
528 West 4th Street, P.O. Box 1200, 50704-1200
Telephone: 319-232-6555 FAX: 319-232-4835
Email: office@s-c-law.com URL: http://www.swishercohrt.com
Steven A. Weidner; Stephen J. Powell; Jim D. DeKoster; Samuel C. Anderson; Kevin R. Rogers; Beth E. Hansen; Mark F. Conway; Natalie Williams Burris; Aaron R. Bixby;—Megan S. Fereday.
General Civil, Trial and Appellate Practice in all State and Federal Courts; Insurance; Insurance Defense; Corporation; Banks and Banking; Commercial; Labor and Employment (public and private sector); Workers Compensation; Probate; Wills; Trusts & Estates; Business; Civil Rights; Education; Municipal; Premises Liability; Products Liability Defense; Utility; Employee Benefits; Collections; Debtor-Creditor; Environmental; Leases and Leasing; Professional Liability; Media; Medical Malpractice; Franchise and Franchising; Contracts; Family; Estate Planning; Public Utility; Administrative; Real Estate; and Personal Injury Law; Torts.
See Professional Biographies, WATERLOO, IOWA

Teske, Max R., Jr., (AV) .... '20 '54 C.351 L.221 J.D. 1937 W. 7th St.‡
Thielen, James E., (BV) '53 '79 C.351 B.A. L.221 J.D.
Sr. V.P. & Tr. Offr., Mercantile Bk. of Northern IA
Thomas, Sydney A., (AV) .... '23 '49 C.145 B.S. L.477 J.D. 3151 Brockway Rd.‡
Tyler, W. David, (AV) .... '38 '63 C.132 B.A. L.352 J.D. 531 Commercial St., Ste. 500
Van Metre, Peter .... '26 '53 C.855 B.A. L.352 J.D. Sr. Dist. J.‡
Verhulst, Thomas C., (BV) .... '63 '88 C.56 B.A. L.352 J.D. [Gallagher,L.&G.]
Wagner, James L., (BV) .... '50 '74 C&L.352 B.A., J.D. [Gartelos,W.&A.]
Walker, John R., Jr., (AV) .... '48 '73 C.755 B.A. L.221 J.D. [Beecher,F.W.M.H.&J.]
Walsh, James E., Jr., (AV) .... '49 '75 C.339 B.A. L.424 J.D. [Clark,B.W.&H.]
Walton, D. Raymond, (BV) ..... '55 '82 C.351 B.A. L.352 J.D. [Ⓐ Beecher,F.W.M.H.&J.]
Walz, Brad Paul, (CV) .... '70 '95 C.221 B.A. L.802 J.D. Asst. Co. Atty.
Weber, Cheryl L., (AV) .... '57 '83 C.106 B.A. L.352 J.D. [Dutton,B.S.&H.]
Weems, Vernon E., Jr. .... '48 '77 C.352 B.A. L.472 J.D. 637 Independence Ave.‡
Weidner, Steven A., (AV) .... '40 '65 C&L.602 B.B.A., J.D. [Swisher&C.]
Weilein, George L., (AV) .... '55 '81 C.177 B.A. L.352 J.D. [Gallagher,L.&G.]
Wendland, Christopher S., (CV) .... '65 '95 C.309 A.B. L.352 J.D. [Clark,B.W.&H.]
Wessels, DuWayne J., (BV) .... '22 '48 C.999 L.221 LL.B. 574 Sheridan Rd.
Wessels, Pete M., (AVⓉ) .... '49 '76 C.351 B.A. L.190 J.D. [Wessels,S.&S.] ⊙
Wessels, Stojan & Stephens P.C., (AVⓉ)
Ste. 2, 227 East San Marnan Dr. (⊙Rock Island, IL)
White, Frederick G., (AV) .... '27 '51 C.972 L.145 J.D. 501 Sycamore Street, Suite 706
Wolf, Melvin H., (BV) .... '23 '49 C&L.352 B.A., J.D. E. Fourth and Mulberry
Wood, John J., (CV) .... '68 '99 C.352 B.B.A. L.221 J.D. [Ⓐ Beecher,F.W.M.H.&J.]
Wright, Justin L. '61 '86 C&L.546 B.A., J.D.
(adm. in NE; not adm. in IA) State Farm Ins. Co.
Yagla, Gene R., (AV) .... '46 '74 C.351 B.A. L.352 J.D. [Yagla,M.&R.]

Yagla, McCoy & Riley, P.L.C., (AV)
Lincoln Park Building, 327 East Fourth Street, Suite 300, P.O. Box 960, 50704-0960
Telephone: 319-234-4631 Fax: 319-234-8346
Email: gyagla@ymrlaw.com
Members of Firm: James H. Yagla (1937-1985); Gene R. Yagla; John T. McCoy; David Riley; Karla J. Shea; Henry J. Bevel III.
Insurance Defense, Corporate, Trust, Business and Administrative Law. Personal Injury, Insurance, Real Estate, General Trial Practice..
Representative Clients: Allen Memorial Hospital; Allstate Insurance Co.; Farm Bureau Mutual of Iowa; National Indemnity Co.; Iowa Mutual Insurance Co.; State Farm Mutual Fire & Casualty Insurance Co.; State Farm Mutual Auto Insurance Co.; West Bend Insurance Co.; Tri-State Insurance Co.
See Professional Biographies, WATERLOO, IOWA

Young, Michael R. .... '76 '01 C.840 B.B.A. L.352 J.D. [Ⓐ Dutton,B.S.&H.]
Young, Robert A., Jr. .... '34 '57 C&L.352 B.S., J.D. 135 Pershing Rd.‡
Zager, Bruce B. .... '52 '81 C.352 B.B.A. L.221 J.D. Dist. Ct. J.
Zellhoefer, David R., (BV) .... '53 '80 C.560 B.A. L.352 J.D. [Zellhoefer]
Zellhoefer, Richard G., (AV) .... '18 '42 C&L.352 B.S.C., J.D. [Zellhoefer]
Zellhoefer Law Firm, (AV) .... 615 Grant Street
Zimmerman, Carl B. .... '30 '56 C&L.352 B.A., J.D. 2805 Fairlane Ave

WAUKEE, 5,126, *Dallas Co.*

Coppinger, David J. .... '37 '66 C&L.352 B.A., J.D. 3320 V. Ct.
Downey, J. Michael .... '52 '77 C.350 B.S. L.352 J.D. Pres., Downey Printing, Inc.

McDonald, Brown & Fagen
(See Dallas Center)

McKinney, James V., (BV) .... '59 '85 C&L.221 B.A., J.D. [McKinney]

McKinney, Robert E., (AV) .... '51 '78 C.221 B.A. L.352 J.D. [McKinney]
McKinney, Wayne H., Jr., (BV) .... '50 '76 C.350 B.S. L.352 J.D. [McKinney]
McKinney Law Offices, P.C., (AV) .... P.O. Box 609
Piercy, Rex E. .... '49 '82 C.193 B.A. L.352 J.D. The United Methodist Church

WAUKON, * 4,131, *Allamakee Co.*

Abrams, Jerrald B. '46 '73 C.264 B.A. L.365 J.D.
(adm. in IL; not adm. in IA) 1103 Park Rd.
Bauercamper, John J. .... '48 '73 C.351 B.A. L.494 J.D. Dist. J.
Bristol, James D., (AV) .... '19 '48 C.352 B.A. L.190 J.D. [Jacobson,B.G.&S.]
Garrett, James A., (BV) .... '51 '76 C.293 B.A. L.352 J.D. [Jacobson,B.G.&S.]
Hart, Maurice, (BV) .... '35 '65 C.872 B.A. L.190 J.D. 1001 Iron Mine Dr. N.E.
Hart, William S., (BV) .... '32 '59 C.755 L.352 LL.B. 10 1st Ave.

Jacobson, Bristol, Garrett & Swartz, (AV)
P.O. Box 49, 52172-0049
Telephone: 563-568-3439 Fax: 563-568-3210
Email: bristol@rconnect.com
Members of Firm: Arthur H. Jacobson (1910-1986); James D. Bristol; James A. Garrett; Jeffrey L. Swartz.
General Practice. Civil Litigation. Personal Injury. Insurance Defense. Workers' Compensation. Municipal Law. Commercial Law. Probate. Real Estate. Taxation.
Representative Clients: Farmers & Merchants Savings Bank, Waukon, Iowa; Eitzen State Bank; Kerndt Brothers Savings Bank; City of Waukon; City of Marquette.

Mellick, James U., (AV) '39 '64 C.177 B.A. L.734 J.D.
18 First Avenue N.W., Suite 101
Morrow, Lynn W. .... '16 '41 C.187 B.A. L.352 J.D. 314 1st Ave. S.E.‡
Shafer, John W., (BV) .... '30 '58 C&L.352 B.S.C., LL.B. [Shafer&S.]
Shafer, William J., (BV) .... '64 '90 C&L.352 B.B.A., J.D. [Shafer&S.]
Shafer & Shafer, (BV) .... 23 Allamakee St.
Swartz, Jeffrey L., (CV) .... '61 '86 C.492 B.A. L.352 J.D. [Jacobson,B.G.&S.]
Thomson, James E., (AV) .... '26 '56 C.351 B.A. L.352 J.D. 25 First Ave.‡
White, Mary Jane .... '53 '79 C.685 B.A. L.352 J.D. 402 Allamakee Street

WAVERLY, * 8,968, *Bremer Co.*

Ackerman, Ivan J., (BV) '39 '63 C&L.352 B.A., J.D.
[Engelbrecht,A.&H.] (⊙Clarksville)
Boveia, Gary J., (BV) .... '42 '68 C.898 B.A. L.352 J.D. [Boveia]
Boveia Law Firm, (BV) .... 208 1st Avenue, S.E.
Carney, Gerald B., (BV) .... '47 '74 C.351 B.A. L.221 J.D. City Atty.
Collins, Keith D., (BV) .... '47 '78 C.187 B.A. L.352 J.D. [Leslie,C.&F.]
Drenkow, Rodney D. ...... '53 '80 C.56 B.A. L.352 J.D. Pres., R. D. Drenkow & Co., Inc.
Engelbrecht, David M., (BV) .... '58 '82 C.898 B.A. L.221 J.D. [Engelbrecht,A.&H.]
Engelbrecht, Wm. H., (AV) '27 '51
C.898 L.221 J.D. [Engelbrecht,A.&H.] (⊙Readlyn, Tripoli)

Engelbrecht, Ackerman & Hassman, (AV)
123 First Street, S.E., P.O. Box 59, 50677 ⊙
Telephone: 319-352-1148 FAX: 319-352-5603
Members of Firm: Wm. H. Engelbrecht; Ivan J. Ackerman; Gaylen V. Hassman; David M. Engelbrecht.
General Civil and Trial Practice in State and Federal Courts. Real Estate, Probate, Negligence and Corporation Law. Trials and Appeals. Corporation, Estate Planning, Insurance, Personal Injury, Workers Compensation and Administrative Law.
Clarksville, Iowa Office: 101 South Main Street. Telephone: 319-278-4402.
Tripoli, Iowa Office: 207 South Main Street. Telephone: 319-882-3203.
Readlyn, Iowa Office: 307 Main Street. Telephone: 319-279-3185.
See Professional Biographies, WAVERLY, IOWA

Foy, Christopher C., (CV) .... '61 '87 C.351 B.A. L.352 J.D. [Leslie,C.&F.]
Goeke, Dale E., (BV) .... '50 '79 C.898 B.A. L.352 J.D. 100 E. Bremer Ave.
Goeke, Quintin A., (CV) .... '69 '98 C.898 B.A. L.986 J.D. 100 E. Bremer Ave.
Gohlke, Frances L. .... '39 '85 C.898 B.A. L.352 J.D. 303 1st Ave., N.E.
Hassman, Gaylen V., (BV) .... '45 '74 C.351 B.A. L.352 J.D. [Engelbrecht,A.&H.]
Laird, Ralph E., III, (AV) .... '30 '58 C.388 B.A. L.221 J.D. 114 W. Bremer Ave.
Leslie, Richard V., (AV) .... '26 '52 C&L.602 Ph.B., LL.B. [Leslie,C.&F.]
Leslie, Collins & Foy, (AV) .... 303 1st Ave., N.E.
Reeve, Oliver J. .... '14 '36 100 E. Bremer Ave., Suite 4
Riffel, Paul W. .... '46 '73 C&L.221 B.A., J.D. Dist. J.
Secor, Barbara L. '57 '82 C&L.966 B.S., J.D.
(adm. in WI; not adm. in IA)
Asst. V.P. & Assoc. Gen. Coun., CUNA Mutual Life Ins. Co.
Thalacker, Karen L., (BV) .... '66 '91 C.898 B.A. L.221 J.D. 100 E. Bremer Ave.

WEBSTER CITY, * 8,176, *Hamilton Co.*

Ahlers, Paul B., (BV) .... '69 '94 C.350 B.B.A. L.352 J.D. 913 Seneca St.
Carlson, Duane Arnold .... '51 '99 C.350 B.B.A. L.793 J.D. 1014 Elm Street
Chambers, Patrick B., (BV) .... '44 '71 C.793 B.A. L.352 J.D. 623 2nd St.
Greenley, Joseline L., (BV) .... '57 '81 C.350 B.S. L.221 J.D. 512 2nd St.
Groves, Gary J., (BV) .... '37 '63 C.352 B.A. L.221 LL.B. [Groves&H.]
Groves & Hemmingson, (BV) .... 805 Des Moines Street
Hemingway, Whitley M., (AV) .... '15 '38 C&L.352 A.B., J.D. [Hemingway]
Hemingway Law Office, (AV) .... 741 Second St.
Hemmingson, Mark L., (BV) .... '53 '78 C.793 B.S. L.352 J.D. [Groves&H.]
Karr, Margaret P., (BV) .... '18 '43 [Karr,K.&K.]
Karr, Richard L., (BV) .... '47 '73 C.1306 B.A. L.190 J.D. [Karr,K.&K.]
Karr, Karr & Karr, P.C., (BV) .... 711 2nd St.
Kayser, Lawrence R., Jr., (BV) .... '42 '68 C.221 B.A. L.793 J.D. [Kayser]
Kayser Law Office, (BV) .... 817 Des Moines St.

Kersten Brownlee Hendricks, LLP
(See Fort Dodge)

McGlynn, James A., (CV) .... '50 '75 C.221 B.A. L.190 J.D. J., Juvenile Ct.
Moss, Calvin E. .... '61 '86 C&L.352 B.S., J.D. 1304 Elm St.‡
Rodenborn, Edna S., (CV) .... '24 '46 728 2nd St.

WELLMAN, 1,393, *Washington Co.*

Young, Albion J., (AV) .... '27 '53 C.162 B.A. L.352 J.D. 201 8th Ave.

WEST BEND, 834, *Kossuth & Palo Alto Cos.*

Capotosto, Donald H. .... '48 '73 C&L.221 B.A., J.D. [Capotosto]
Capotosto Law Office .... 211C S. Bway.

WEST BURLINGTON, 3,083, *Des Moines Co.*

Gerard, Timothy F. .... '52 '77 C.350 B.S. L.351 J.D. Southeastern Community Coll.
Hales, James A. .... '59 '91 C.352 B.A. L.61 J.D. Rader Precast Concrete, Inc.
Mandsager, Greggory Jon .... '69 '98 C.350 B.A. L.221 J.D. 122 Broadway St

WEST DES MOINES, 46,403, *Dallas & Polk Cos.*

Adams, Mark R., (AV) .... '52 '77 C.351 B.A. L.221 J.D. [Wasker,D.W.&M.]
Adams, Michael H., Law Office, (BV) .... '64 '90 C&L.221 B.A., J.D. 808 46th St.
Althoff, Angela T., (AV) .... '61 '87 C.352 B.A. L.221 J.D. [Morain&P.]
Anderson, Frederick B., (AV) .... '52 '77 C.489 B.A. L.221 J.D. [Anderson&T.]
Anderson, Ronald L., (AV) .... '50 '77 C.352 B.B.A. L.945 J.D. [Howes&A.]

Anderson & Tully, A Professional Corporation, (AV)
700 West Towers, 1200 Valley West Drive, 50266-1908
Telephone: 515-225-4844 Facsimile: 515-225-7549
Email: lawfirm@andersontullylaw.com URL: http://www.andersontullylaw.com
Frederick B. Anderson; Robert G. Tully.
General Civil and Trial Practice in State and Federal Courts. Corporation, Securities, Estate Planning, Trusts, Probate, Real Estate, Insurance, Personal Injury, Workers Compensation and Administrative Law.
See Professional Biographies, WEST DES MOINES, IOWA

Andeweg, Robert D., (AV) '62 '87
C.132 B.A. L.221 J.D. [Brown,W.G.G.B.&S.] (⊙Des Moines)
Barnes, Susan, (BV) .... '52 '78 C.753 B.A. L.945 J.D. Norwest Corp.
Barnhill, Kathryn Schweiker, (BV) ...... '— '89 C&L.221 B.A., J.D. [Barnhill&Assoc.]

Barnhill & Associates, P.C., (BV)
2100 Westown Parkway, Suite 210, 50265
Telephone: 515-223-7230 Facsimile: 515-223-7234
Email: dalfrey@barnhillpclaw.net URL: http://www.barnhillpc.com
Kathryn Schweiker Barnhill;—Steve R. Newlander; Deborah Lepes.
Construction Law, Government Contracts, Public Construction, Business Law, Contracts, Real Estate, Architectural Copyrights, Corporate Law and Litigation, Eminent Domain, Intellectual Property, Labor and Employment Law, Civil Practice, Class Actions, Construction Litigation, Highways, Commercial Law, Litigation, Trusts and Estates Litigation, Zoning, Planning and Land Use, Unfair Competition, Trade Secrets, Collections, Public Bids and Bidding, Tax Litigation, Business Litigation, Shareholder and Business Valuation Litigation, Trademark and Copyright Litigation.
See Professional Biographies, WEST DES MOINES, IOWA

Barton, C. Christy, (AV⓽) .... '47 '74 C.502 B.A. L.477 J.D. [Barton] ⊙
Barton Law Firm, The, L.L.C., (AV⓽)
400 Mills Civic Parkway Suite 205 (⊙Columbia, MO)
Baum, John P. .... '61 '86 C.352 B.B.A. L.326 J.D. Claims Dir., Allied Grp., Inc.
Beatty, James D., (AV) .... '58 '84 C.350 B.S. L.221 J.D. [Beatty&M.]
Beatty & Miller, P.C., (AV) .... 2829 Westown Pkwy., Ste. 310
Beebout, Kathleen J., (BV) .... '62 '91 C.999 B.S.N. L.221 J.D. [Beebout]
Beebout Law Office, (BV) .... 1025 Ashworth Rd., Ste. 505
Bellis, Scott S., (BV) .... '67 '92 C.352 B.B.A. L.221 J.D. [Bellis,H.&N.]
Bellis, Hook & Nigut, L.L.P., (BV) .... 1001 Office Park Road, Suite 317
Bennett, James L., (BV) .... '20 '49 C&L.221 B.C.S., J.D. 402 Maple St.
Berkson, Edward J. '39 '64 C.352 B.A. L.424 J.D.
(adm. in IL; not adm. in IA) 3420 Briar Ridge Road
Bernabe, Mary S., (AV) .... '61 '89 C&L.221 B.S.E., J.D. 5971 Highland Cir.
Bernau, Thomas R., (BV) ...... '61 '88 C.350 B.B.A. L.221 J.D. 1501 42nd St., Suite 472
Beyer, Teresa A., (BV) .... '48 '91 C.353 B.A. L.221 J.D. 733 20th St.
Blaser, Michael R., (AV) '60 '85
C&L.352 B.B.A., J.D. [Brown,W.G.G.B.&S.] (⊙Des Moines)
Boes, Judith R. "Lynn" .... '56 '96 C.352 B.S.N. L.221 J.D. [Davis,B.K.S.&R.] ⊙
Bolender, Sue Ellen '63 '89 C.963 B.S. L.436 J.D.
(adm. in WI; not adm. in IA) 5143 Coachlight Dr.‡
Bray, Robert L. .... '37 '62 C&L.190 B.S.B.A., LL.B. Asst. Co. Atty.
Brewer, William G., (BV) .... '57 '82 C.352 B.B.A. L.221 J.D. [McEnroe,G.B.B.&S.]
Brown, M. Kathleen, (BV) .... '73 '99 C.741 B.A. L.221 J.D. [Cutler]

Brown, Winick, Graves, Gross, Baskerville and Schoenebaum, P.L.C., (AV)
Regency West 5, 4500 Westown Parkway, Suite 277, 50266-6717 ⊙
Telephone: 515-242-2400 Fax: 515-242-2448
Email: bwg@ialawyers.com URL: http://www.ialawyers.com
Robert D. Andeweg; Michael R. Blaser; Michael J. Green; Kelly D. Hamborg; John D. Hunter; G. Brian Pingel; Camille L. Urban;—Adam W. Jones; Dustin D. Smith.
Des Moines, Iowa Office: 666 Grand Avenue, Suite 2000, 50309-2510.
Pella, Iowa Office: 616 Franklin Place, 50219. Telephone: 641-628-4513. Fax: 641-628-8494.
See Professional Biographies, WEST DES MOINES, IOWA

Bruntz, Julie Kron '56 '81 C&L.352 B.A., J.D.
Soc. Sec. Admn., Off. of Hearings & App.
Bump, Wilbur N., (AV) .... '29 '58 C&L.352 B.S.C., J.D. 1501 42nd St.
Burdette, Michael J., (BV) .... '49 '75 C.350 B.S. L.45 J.D. [McEnroe,G.B.B.&S.]
Burlingame, Thomas E., (AV) .... '45 '75 C&L.352 B.B.A., J.D. [⊡ Morain&P.]
Butz, Joseph T. '63 '89 C.63 B.S. L.209 J.D.
(adm. in IL; not adm. in IA) Central Iowa Health System
Camp, Lawr. D. .... '28 '54 C.177 B.S. L.352 LL.B. Aetna Cas. & Surety Co.
Caspar, Stephen '51 '93 C.645 B.A. L.831 J.D.
(adm. in PA; not adm. in IA) 805 58th St.‡
Catterall, Donald P. .... '20 '52 C&L.221 B.C.S., J.D. 1256 33rd St.‡
Chabot, Richard R., (AV) .... '37 '64 C.436 B.S. L.494 J.D. [Sullivan&W.]
Chaplin, William L., (AV) .... '46 '74 C.351 B.A. L.352 J.D. 5204 Cody Dr.
Chrisman-Terry, Mary Elissa '53 '81 C.834 B.S. L.836 J.D.
(adm. in TN; not adm. in IA) 2600 Westown Pkwy., Ste. 110
Conger, John C., (AV) .... '53 '79 C.352 B.S. L.221 J.D. [Marcucci&C.]
Coppola, Charles A., (BV) .... '46 '72 C&L.221 B.A., J.D. [Coppola,S.M.&C.]
Coppola, Christopher Brian, (BV) .... '74 '99 C.352 B.A. L.221 J.D. [Coppola,S.M.&C.]
Coppola, Sandre, McConville & Carroll, A Professional Corporation, (AV)
2100 Westown Pkwy, Ste. 200
Corry, Jill Mataya, (BV) .... '68 '94 C.221 B.A. L.352 J.D. [⊡ Sullivan&W.]
Cutler, Charles E., (AV) .... '56 '81 C&L.352 B.S., J.D. [Cutler]

Cutler Law Firm, P.C., (AV)
1307 50th Street, 50266
Telephone: 515-223-6600 FAX: 515-223-6787
Email: mkb@cutlerfirm.com URL: http://www.lawyers.com/cutlerfirm
Charles E. Cutler; Bruce E. Johnson; M. Kathleen Brown;—Jack H. Pennington.
See Professional Biographies, WEST DES MOINES, IOWA

Davis, Brown, Koehn, Shors & Roberts, P.C., (AV)
4201 Westown Parkway, Suite 300, 50266 ⊙
Telephone: 515-288-2500 Fax: 515-246-7997
Thomas E. Salsbery; Robert J. Douglas, Jr.; Mark D. Walz; Thomas J. Houser; Judith R. "Lynn" Boes; Debra Rectenbaugh Pettit.
Administrative, Agricultural, Alternative Dispute Resolution, Antitrust and Trade Regulation, Appellate Practice, Bankruptcy, Banks and Banking, Biotechnology, Business Law, Civil, Class Actions, Commercial, Commercial Real Estate, Communications and Media, Complex and Multi-District Litigation, Computers and Software, Constitutional, Construction, Consumer, Contracts, Copyrights, Corporate, Debtor and Creditor, Education, Employee Benefits, Energy, Environmental, Equipment Finance and Leasing, Family, Finance, Franchises and Franchising, Government, Government Contracts, Guardianship and Conservatorship, Health Care, Hospital Law, Human and Civil Rights, Immigration and Naturalization, Insurance, Insurance Defense, Intellectual Property, International Law, International Trade, Labor and Employment, Leases and Leasing, Legal Ethics and Professional Responsibility, Libel, Slander and Defamation, Litigation, Media Law, Medical Malpractice, Mergers, Acquisitions and Divestitures, Municipal Law, Natural Resources, Nonprofit and Charitable Organizations, Partnership, Patents, Personal Injury, Probate. Products Liability, Professional Liability,

(This Listing Continued)

Davis, Brown, Koehn, Shors & Roberts, P.C. (Continued)

Property, Public Finance, Real Estate, Regulatory, Securities, Taxation, Technology and Science, Torts, Trade and Professional Associations, Trade Secrets, Trademarks, Transportation, Trusts and Estates, Utilities, Wills, Workers Compensation, Zoning, Planning and Land Use.
Des Moines, Iowa Office: The Financial Center, 666 Walnut Street, Suite 2500, 50309-3993. Telephone: 515-288-2500. Facsimile: 515-243-0654.

See Professional Biographies, WEST DES MOINES, IOWA

Deege, J. Michael, (AV) . . . . '42 '68 C.337 B.A. L.221 J.D. 1601 22nd Street
Delanoit, Heidi L. . . . . '— '88 C.352 B.B.A. L.221 J.D. Mng. Atty., Amer. Fam. Ins. Grp.
Despotovich, Steven C., (AV) . . . . '58 '83 C&L.221 B.S., J.D. 1601 22nd St., Ste. 300
Donnelly, John V., (AV) . . . . '40 '65 C.309 A.B. L.477 LL.B. [Sullivan&W.]
Dorr, Fred L., (AV) . . . . '47 '76 C.597 B.S. L.221 J.D. [Wasker,D.W.&M.]
Dorsey, Francis P. '23 '48 C&L.734 LL.B.
(adm. in MO; not adm. in IA) Admin. Law J., Off. of Hearing & App.
Dougherty, John P., (BV) . . . . '64 '90 C.352 B.B.A. L.221 J.D. [Lawyer,D.&P.]
Douglas, Robert J., Jr., (AV) . . . . '57 '82 C.723 B.S. L.352 J.D. [Davis,B.K.S.&R.] ⊙
Drake, David D., (AV) . . . . '52 '77 C&L.221 B.A., J.D. [Lawyer,L.D.&D.]
Dutton, Channing L., (AV) . . . . '54 '80 C.547 B.A. L.221 J.D. [Lawyer,L.D.&D.]
Eichhorn, John C. . . . . '20 '48 C&L.352 B.A., J.D. 4925 W. Park Dr.‡
Farr, Thomas C., (AV) '52 '81 C.293 B.A. L.221 J.D.
Sr. V.P., Secy. & Gen. Coun., GuideOne Insurance Grp.
Fenton, Ray A. . . . . '30 '57 C.608 L.221 LL.B. [[C] Hudson,M.&S.]
Fisk, Erik S. . . . . '— '05 C&L.221 B.A., J.D. [[A] Whitfield&E.]
Flansburg, Elizabeth, (BV) . . . . '60 '95 C.352 B.A. L.221 J.D. [[A] Lawyer,D.&P.]
Foster-Smith, Danielle, (BV) . . . . '56 '00 C&L.221 B.A., J.D. [R.J.Kuhle]
Freeman, Jeanine M., (AV) '48 '78
C.985 B.A. L.352 J.D. Sr. V.P. of Legal Affs., Iowa Medical Soc.
Gardner, Matthew D., (BV) . . . . '69 '97 C.350 B.A. L.221 J.D. [Sullivan&W.]
Garretson, William W. . . . . '35 '60 C.353 B.A. L.273 J.D. P.O. Box 27136
Garver, Robert B., (AV) . . . . '53 '80 C&L.352 B.B.A., J.D. [R.B.Garver]
Garver, Robert B., P.C., (AV) . . . . 475 S. 50th St., Ste. 200
Geadelmann, Lori K., (BV) . . . . '65 '93 C.350 B.A. L.221 J.D. [Morain&P.]
Gilbertson, Christine K. . . . . '55 '86 C.352 B.A. L.345 J.D. 805 48th St.‡
Ginkens, Aaron H. . . . . '77 '03 C&L.221 B.A., J.D. [Ginkens]
Ginkens Law Firm, P.L.C. . . . . 4401 Westown Parkway, Suite 307

Gonzalez, Saggio & Harlan, L.L.P., (BV)
1501 42nd Street, Suite 465, 50266 ⊙
Telephone: 515-453-8509 Fax: 515-267-1408
Email: main@gshllp.com URL: http://www.gshllp.com
Kerrie M. Murphy; Lora L. McCollom.
Business and Corporate Law, Civil Litigation, Insurance Defense Law, Equal Opportunities and Employment, School Law, Municipal Finance, Business and Commercial Litigation, Real Estate, Construction, Condemnation Law, Environmental, Taxation, Utilities Law, Trials and Appeals, Government Relations.
Representative Clients: Accenture; Alliant Energy; Bear, Stears & Co.; Chubb Insurance Company; City of Milwaukee; CNH Global N.V.; Darden Restaurants, Inc.; Denny's; Eastman Kodak Company; E.I. du Pont de Nemours and Company.
Milwaukee, Wisconsin Office: 225 East Michigan, 4th Floor, 53202. Telephone: 414-277-8500. Fax: 414-277-8521.
Indianapolis, Indiana Office: 201 North Illinois Street, Suite 1900, 46204. Telephone: 317-686-9800. Fax: 317-686-9821.
Cincinnati, Ohio Office: Carew Tower, 441 Vine Street, Suite 3615, 45202. Telephone: 513-651-3456. Fax: 513-651-3446.
Chicago, Illinois Office: 208 LaSalle Street, Suite 1460, 60604. Telephone: 312-236-0475. Facsimile: 312-236-1750.

See Professional Biographies, WEST DES MOINES, IOWA

Goodman, Jeffrey L., (AV) . . . . '59 '85 C.352 B.A. L.221 J.D. [Goodman&Assoc.] ⊙
Goodman & Associates, P.C., (AV) . . . . 1501 42nd Street (⊙Des Moines)
Goplerud, J. Barton, (BV) . . . . '58 '90 C.352 B.A. L.221 J.D. [Hudson,M.&S.]
Gotsdiner, Murray B., (AV) . . . . '53 '80 C&L.221 B.A., J.D. [McEnroe,G.B.B.&S.]
Green, Michael J., (AV) '48 '76
C.177 B.A. L.221 J.D. [Brown,W.G.G.B.&S.] (⊙Des Moines)
Hamborg, Kelly D., (BV) '55 '85
C.352 B.B.A. L.221 J.D. [Brown,W.G.G.B.&S.] (⊙Des Moines)
Hamrock, Aaron D., (BV) . . . . '70 '95 C.133 B.A. L.221 J.D. [McCarthy&H.]
Hansen, Jill Thompson, (AV) . . . . '— '80 C.597 B.A. L.352 J.D. Gen. Coun., W. Bk.
Haraldson, John O., (BV) . . . . '65 '92 C.494 B.A. L.352 J.D. [R.J.Kuhle]
Harper, Douglas B. . . . . '43 '68 C.477 A.B. L.608 J.D. 300 Ashworth Road
Hays, Johnine R. . . . . '64 '93 C&L.221 B.S.B.A., J.D. 1091 S. 50th Pl.
Heller, Michael B., (BV) . . . . '57 '81 C.221 B.A. L.352 J.D. 1621 S. 50th Pl.
Hellstern, David J. . . . . '78 '05 C.352 B.B.A. L.221 J.D. [[A] Kreamer]
Hendricks, Charles . . . . '72 '99 C.957 B.B.A. L.221 J.D. [[A] Wasker,D.W.&M.]
Henrichsen, Patrick A. . . . . '70 '00 C.350 B.B.A. L.352 J.D. [[A] McEnroe,G.B.B.&S.]
Hervey, Ryan D. . . . . '77 '04 C.784 B.A. L.221 J.D. [[A] Pearson V.P.]
Hobbs, Kevin . . . . '59 '96 C.593 B.S. L.494 J.D. 1200 35th St., Ste. 304-3
Hockenberg, Harlan (Bud), (AV) . . . . '27 '52 C&L.352 B.A., J.D. [Sullivan&W.]
Hockenberg, Louis R., (AV) . . . . '48 '73 C.352 B.A. L.221 J.D. [Sullivan&W.]
Hoffman, John W. '26 '49 C&L.215 J.D.
(adm. in MI; not adm. in IA) U.S. Admin. Law J., Dept. H.& H. S.
Holliday, Robert M., (AV) . . . . '43 '68 C&L.221 B.A., J.D. [Sullivan&W.]
Houser, Thomas J., (AV) . . . . '64 '89 C.755 B.A. L.352 J.D. [Davis,B.K.S.&R.] ⊙
Howes, Richard J., (AV) . . . . '43 '68 C&L.352 B.A., J.D. [Howes&A.]
Howes & Anderson, P.C., (AV) . . . . 1001 Office Park Rd.
Howie, Andrew B., (BV) . . . . '71 '96 C.898 B.A. L.352 J.D. [Hudson,M.&S.]
Hoyne, Michele A., (BV) '68 '93
C.587 B.S. L.221 J.D. Sr. Staff Atty., Amer. Fam. Ins. Grp.
Hudson, R. J., II, (BV) . . . . '66 '93 C.352 B.S. L.221 J.D. [Hudson,M.&S.]
Hudson, Roger J., (AV) . . . . '43 '72 C&L.221 B.A., J.D. [Hudson,M.&S.]

Hudson, Mallaney & Shindler, P.C., (AV)
5015 Grand Ridge Drive, Suite 100, 50265
Telephone: 515-223-4567 Fax: 515-223-8887
Email: lawyers@hudsonlaw.net URL: http://www.hudsonlaw.net
Roger J. Hudson; Michael P. Mallaney; Steven H. Shindler; R. J. Hudson, II; J. Barton Goplerud; Andrew B. Howie;—Ryan Edward Weese; Bryan S. Witherwax. Of Counsel: Ray A. Fenton.
General Civil Trial, Civil, Criminal, Commercial Litigation and Appellate Practice in all Courts, Commercial, Corporation, Family Law, Mediation, Workers Compensation, Real Estate, Taxation, Personal Injury, Bankruptcy, Probate, Administrative Law and Employment Law.

See Professional Biographies, WEST DES MOINES, IOWA

Hunter, John D. . . . . '60 '86 C&L.546 B.S., J.D. [Brown,W.G.G.B.&S.] (⊙Des Moines)
Hurn, Matthew M., (BV) . . . . '69 '98 C.784 B.A. L.221 J.D. [Wasker,D.W.&M.]
Huston, Michael L., (AV) '42 '67 C&L.221 B.A., J.D.
Asst. Gen. Coun., Hawkeye-Security Insurance
Ingle, Michelle F. . . . . '69 '94 C&L.896 B.A., J.D. [Morain&P.]
Janssen, Carmen, (BV) . . . . '52 '87 C&L.221 B.A., J.D. [C.L.Janssen]
Janssen, Carmen L., (BV) . . . . 4090 Westown Pkwy., Ste. A-302
Jaskolka-Brown, Jennifer, (BV) . . . . '73 '99 C.627 [[A] Sullivan&W.]
Jensen, Gretchen R., (BV) . . . . '73 '98 C.352 B.A. L.221 J.D. [[A] Goodman&Assoc.] ⊙
Johnson, Bruce E., (AV) . . . . '47 '73 C&L.352 B.A., J.D. [Cutler]
Johnson, J. Michael . . . . '48 '75 C.469 B.A. L.280 J.D. Hearing Off. Chief
Johnson, James L., (BV) . . . . '61 '87 C&L.352 B.A., J.D. [K.L.Smith]
Johnson, John P. '44 '82 C.900 B.A. L.546 J.D.
(adm. in NE; not adm. in IA) J., Hearings & Appeals Off.
Johnson, Sara K., (AV) '52 '77 C.352 B.A. L.221 J.D.
Vice President, Assoc. Counsel & Asst. Secretary, Kirke-Van Orsdel Inc.
Jones, Adam W. '74 '03 C.696 B.A. L.221 J.D.
[[A] Brown,W.G.G.B.&S.] (Pat.) (⊙Des Moines)
Jones, Nancy K. . . . . '18 '41 C.856 A.B. L.273 J.D. 915 Ashworth Rd.‡
Jongleux, Lynn Brundage '47 '77
C.347 A.B. L.345 J.D. Sr. V.P. & Sec., Farm Bur. Life Ins. Co.
Jorgensen, Thomas P., (AV) '59 '85
C.350 B.S. L.221 J.D. Secy. & Gen. Coun., Hy-Line International
Joynt, Michael P., (AV) . . . . '41 '71 C.352 B.A. L.221 J.D. [Sullivan&W.]
Kading, Linda King, (BV) . . . . '55 '92 C.352 B.A. L.221 J.D. Sr. Coun., Wells Fargo
Kaplan, Elizabeth A., (BV) . . . . '59 '84 C&L.378 B.A., J.D. 1111 Ashworth Road
Karn, Leo H. . . . . '24 '50 L.221 LL.B. 2401 Meadow Lane
Kern, Matthew D., (AV) . . . . '67 '93 C.351 B.A. L.221 J.D. [Wasker,D.W.&M.]
Kozlowski, David P., Law Office of, (BV) '58 '92
C.1154 B.A. L.221 J.D. 2600 Vine St., Ste. 300
Kreamer, Samuel I., C.P.A., (AV) . . . . '56 '81 C.800 B.S. L.221 J.D. [Kreamer]

Kreamer Law Firm, P.C., (AV) [BB]
6600 Westown Parkway, Suite 260, 50266
Telephone: 515-727-0900 Fax: 515-727-0939
Email: sikjdcpa@kreamerlaw.com URL: http://www.kreamerlaw.com
Samuel I. Kreamer, C.P.A;—David J. Hellstern.
Business Law, Corporate, Mergers and Acquisitions, Estate Planning, Wills, Trusts and Estates, Probate.

See Professional Biographies, WEST DES MOINES, IOWA

Krpan, Larry D., (AV) . . . . '50 '75 C.352 B.B.A. L.221 J.D. [L.D.Krpan]
Krpan, Larry D., PC, (AV) . . . . 2700 Westown Pkwy., Ste. 300
Kruidenier, Kyle A. . . . . '71 '04 C.352 B.S. L.221 J.D. [[A] Sullivan&W.]
Kuhle, Roger J., (AV) . . . . '45 '72 C.226 B.A. L.221 J.D. [R.J.Kuhle]
Kuhle, Roger J., P.C., Law Office of, (AV) . . . . 1501 42nd Street
Kukowski, Richard D. . . . . '26 '53 C&L.221 B.A., LL.B. Midwest Mut. Ins. Co.
Laird, Russell H. . . . . '27 '52 C&L.546 B.S., LL.B. [[C] Wasker,D.W.&M.]

LaMarca & Landry, P.C.
(See Des Moines)

Landa, Mark, (AV) . . . . '54 '81 C.755 B.A. L.221 J.D. [Sullivan&W.]
Lawyer, David Mark, (BV) . . . . '62 '89 C.352 B.B.A. L.221 J.D. [Lawyer,D.&P.]
Lawyer, James, (AV) . . . . '25 '50 C&L.221 J.D. [Lawyer,L.D.&D.] ‡
Lawyer, James R. (Jim), (AV) . . . . '54 '79 C.352 B.B.A. L.221 J.D. [Lawyer,L.D.&D.]
Lawyer, Dougherty & Palmer, P.L.C., (BV) . . . . 4090 Westown Pkwy.
Lawyer, Lawyer, Dutton & Drake, L.L.P., (AV) . . . . 1200 Valley West Drive, Suite 500
Leitner, David L., (BV) . . . . '56 '79 C.1044 B.A. L.352 J.D. [Leitner]

Leitner Law Office, (BV)
West Towers, Suite 302 1200 Valley West Drive, 50266
Telephone: 515-252-0777 Fax: 515-252-0798
Email: dleitnerlaw@cs.com URL: http://www.leitnerlawfirm.com
David L. Leitner.
General Civil Trial Practice. Insurance and Personal Injury Law.

See Professional Biographies, WEST DES MOINES, IOWA

Lenihan, Thomas P., (BV) . . . . '52 '77 C.352 B.B.A. L.221 J.D. [Lenihan]
Lenihan Law Office, (BV) . . . . 2600 Vine, Ste. 300
Lepes, Deborah . . . . '73 '01 C.696 B.A. L.93 J.D. [[A] Barnhill&Assoc.]
Levine, Michael A., (AV) . . . . '51 '77 C.352 B.A. L.221 J.D. 213 S. 29th St.
Lombardi, Stephen D., (BV) . . . . '54 '81 C.352 B.S. L.221 J.D. 3737 Woodland Avenue
Luthens, August H., (BV) . . . . '33 '69 C&L.221 B.S.E., J.D. [Luthens] ⊙
Luthens, Erik A., (BV) . . . . '64 '91 C.352 B.S. L.221 J.D. [Luthens] ⊙
Luthens Law Offices, P.C., (BV) . . . . 1200 Valley West Dr., Ste. 206-24 (⊙Colfax)
Mallaney, Michael P., (AV) . . . . '49 '80 C.234 B.S. L.221 J.D. [Hudson,M.&S.]
Malloy, Robert P., (BV) . . . . '48 '74 C.352 B.A. L.221 J.D. [Malloy] ⊙
Malloy Law Firm, (BV) . . . . 6935 Vista Drive (⊙Goldfield)
Manatt, Adam C. . . . . '— '04 C.350 B.A. L.352 J.D. [[A] Whitfield&E.] (⊙Des Moines)
Manno, Michael J., (BV) . . . . '49 '85 C.190 B.A. L.221 J.D. [Manno]
Manno Law Office, (BV) . . . . P.O. Box 27065
Marcouiller, D. Mark, (AV) . . . . '54 '79 C&L.221 B.S.B.A., J.D. [Wasker,D.W.&M.]
Marcucci, Lawrence L., (AV) . . . . '50 '75 C.321 A.B. L.221 J.D. [Marcucci&C.]

Marcucci & Conger, P.L.C., (AV) [BB]
701 West Towers, 1200 Valley West Drive, 50266
Telephone: 515-440-2400 Fax: 515-440-2408
Lawrence L. Marcucci; John C. Conger.
General Civil Trial Practice, Commercial Litigation, Negligence, Personal Injury.

See Professional Biographies, WEST DES MOINES, IOWA

Marso, Stephen D. . . . . '— '99 C.323 B.A. L.352 J.D. [[A] Whitfield&E.] (⊙Des Moines)
Martell, Martha, (BV) '51 '76
C.352 B.A. L.190 J.D. Gen. Coun., Iowa Auto. Dealers Assn.
Maxwell, Michael D., (CV) . . . . '50 '87 C.352 B.S. L.326 J.D. 1001 Office Park Rd.
McCarthy, James E., (BV) . . . . '49 '76 C.602 B.B.A. L.190 J.D. [[C] Morain&P.]
McCarthy, Timothy, II, (AV) . . . . '58 '83 C&L.221 B.A.,B.A., J.D. [McCarthy&H.]

McCarthy & Hamrock, P.C., (AV)
1200 Valley West Drive, Suite 400, 50266
Telephone: 515-279-9700 Fax: 515-279-8355 Email: tim@mccarthyandhamrock.com
Email: aaron@mccarthyhamrock.com URL: http://www.mccarthyhamrock.com
Timothy McCarthy II; Aaron D. Hamrock.
Criminal Law, Personal Injury, Driving While Intoxicated, Drug Crimes, Juvenile Criminal Law, Parole and Probation, Traffic Violations, Automobile Accidents, Slip and Fall, Wrongful Death.

See Professional Biographies, WEST DES MOINES, IOWA

McCollom, Lora L., (BV) . . . . '68 '93 C&L.190 B.A., J.D. [Gonzalez,S.&H.]
McConville, Richard O., (AV) . . . . '48 '73 C&L.190 B.A., J.D. [Coppola,S.M.&C.]
McCormick, David C. . . . . '59 '88 C.177 B.S. L.221 J.D. Soc. Sec. Admn.
McCrary, Toni M. . . . . '52 '79 C.221 B.A. L.61 J.D. 617 45th. St.‡
McElderry, Leslie, (CV) . . . . '17 '42 C&L.211 LL.B. 229 Prospect
McEnroe, Michael L., (AV) . . . . '51 '76 C.177 B.A. L.190 J.D. [McEnroe,G.B.B.&S.]

McEnroe, Gotsdiner, Brewer, Burdette & Steinbach, P.C., (AV) [BB]
Westown Business Center I, 1701 48th Street, Suite 100, 50266-6723
Telephone: 515-267-9000 FAX: 515-267-8100
William G. Brewer; Michael J. Burdette; Murray B. Gotsdiner; Michael L. McEnroe; Frank Steinbach, III;—Patrick A. Henrichsen; William J. Schadle.
General Practice. Corporate, Real Estate, Bankruptcy, Commercial Collection, Personal Injury, Criminal, Probate, Domestic Relations, Transportation and Products Liability Law. Litigation in all Courts.

(This Listing Continued)

McEnroe, Gotsdiner, Brewer, Burdette & Steinbach, P.C. (Continued)
Reference: Bankers Trust Company.
See Professional Biographies, WEST DES MOINES, IOWA

McLaughlin, Paul A. .... '64 '95 C.352 B.A. L.221 J.D. 7126 Dakota Drive
McLellan, Lawrence P., (AV) .... '57 '83 C&L.221 B.A., J.D. [Sullivan&W.]
McNeill, David A., (AV) .... '54 '85 C.784 B.A. L.221 J.D. [Morain&P.]
Meade, James M., Law Offices of, (AV) '44 '70
C.208 A.B. L.309 J.D. 2829 Westown Pkwy., Ste. 310
Michelson, Ann, (AV) .... '59 '84 C.339 B.A. L.221 J.D. GuideOne Insurance Group
Miller, Todd A., Attorney at Law, (BV) '70 '97
C.351 B.A. L.221 J.D. 3737 Woodland Ave., Ste. 130
Miller, Ned P., (AV) .... '36 '64 C.221 B.A. L.352 LL.B. [Beatty&M.]
Miller, Philip F., Law Office of, (BV) ..... '42 '67 C&L.221 B.A., J.D. 808 Ashworth Rd.
Miller, Theo. H. .... '19 '47 C&L.221 J.D. Sr. Dist. J.
Milligan, David R., (BV) '47 '74 C&L.221 B.S., J.D.
V.P. & Sr. Tr. Offr., West Des Moines State Bk.
Moorman, Jennifer S. .... '69 '97 C.350 B.A. L.352 J.D. [Morain&P.]
Morain, Stephen M., (AV) .... '45 '71 C&L.352 B.A., J.D. [Morain&P.]

Morain & Pugh, P.L.C., (AV)
5400 University Avenue, 50266
Telephone: 515-225-5410 Fax: 515-225-4686
Stephen M. Morain; James A. Pugh; Robert A. Simons; David A. McNeill; Angela T. Althoff; Lori K. Geadelmann; Edward G. Parker; Paul S. Swinton; Jennifer S. Moorman; Michelle F. Ingle. Of Counsel: Thomas E. Burlingame; James E. McCarthy.
General Practice, Corporation, Insurance, Administrative, Probate, Real Estate, Litigation and Appeals in Federal and State Courts.
General Counsel for: Iowa Farm Bureau Federation; Farm Bureau Life Insurance Co.; Farm Bureau Mutual Insurance Co.
Representative Client: GROWMARK, Inc.
References: Firstar Bank, Des Moines, Iowa; Bank of America, Des Moines, Iowa.
See Professional Biographies, WEST DES MOINES, IOWA

Moranville, Barry, (AV) .... '32 '60 C.352 B.A. L.221 J.D. 1601 22nd St.
Morris, Larry D. '49 '75 C.976 B.A. L.802 J.D.
(adm. in TX; not adm. in IA) Sr. Vice-Pres., The London Agcy., Inc.
Murphy, Kerrie M., (BV) .... '64 '91 C.352 B.A. L.221 J.D. [Gonzalez,S.&H.]
Naylor, Greg A., (AV) ..... '— '78 C.352 B.A. L.221 J.D. [Whitfield&E.] (⊙Des Moines)
Neugent, Gerard D., (AV) .... '51 '76 C.436 A.B. L.221 J.D. Knapp
Newlander, Steve R. .... '— '04 C.801 B.S. L.221 J.D. [Ⓐ Barnhill&Assoc.]
Nigut, Rush, (BV) .... '58 '94 C.784 B.A. L.221 J.D. [Sullivan&W.]
Nugent, Joseph A., (BV) .... '45 '72 C&L.221 B.A., J.D. 401 Grand Ave.
Nutt, Kathleen L., (AV) .... '56 '85 C.352 B.G.A. L.221 J.D. 4915 Hawthorne Dr.
O'Brien, Marcy A., (BV) .... '70 '95 C.350 B.A. L.352 J.D. [Ⓐ Goodman&Assoc.] ⊙
Owen, Brent H. .... '54 '79 C&L.221 B.A., J.D. Atty., GuideOne Insurance
Palmer, Thomas A., (BV) .... '58 '88 C.352 B.A. L.221 J.D. [Lawyer,D.&P.]
Parker, Edward G., (BV) .... '59 '93 C.351 B.S. L.352 J.D. [Morain&P.]
Paulsen, Donald L. .... '22 '49 C&L.221 B.C.S., J.D. 1111 Ashworth Road
Pearson, Phyllis E., (AV) .... '47 '79 C.350 B.S. L.221 J.D. [Pearson V.P.]

Pearson Van Houten PLC, (AV)
1415 28th Street, Suite 160, 50266
Telephone: 515-327-0101 Fax: 515-327-8514 URL: http://www.pvhlaw.com
URL: http://www.pearsonvanhouten.com
Phyllis E. Pearson; Margaret D. Van Houten; Joan D. Trout;—Ryan D. Hervey.
Business Law, Banking Law, Probate, Estate Planning, Taxation, Trusts and Estates, Wills, Employee Benefits, Real Estate, Elder Law.
See Professional Biographies, WEST DES MOINES, IOWA

Pennington, Jack H. .... '78 '03 C.352 B.A. L.190 J.D. [Ⓐ Cutler]
Pettit, Debra Rectenbaugh, (BV) ... '69 '94 C.221 B.A. L.597 J.D. [Davis,B.K.S.&R.] ⊙
Peyton, Bradley R. '56 '84 C.350 B.S. L.352 J.D.
Pres. & CEO, Premier Capital Grp., Inc.
Pingel, G. Brian, (AV) '40 '70
C.352 B.S.E.E. L.546 J.D. [Brown,W.G.G.B.&S.] (Pat.) (⊙Des Moines)
Plunk, Robert M. '32 '73 C.836 B.A. L.1137 J.D.
(adm. in CA; not adm. in IA) Preferred Risk Financial, Inc.
Poldberg, Mindy Larsen .... '73 '98 C&L.221 B.A., J.D. 5400 University Ave.
Porto, Steven M., (BV) .... '52 '77 C.190 B.A. L.221 J.D. 1200 Valley West Dr.
Puckett, Dennis L., (BV) .... '66 '91 C.378 B.S. L.221 J.D. [Sullivan&W.]
Pugh, James A., (AV) .... '52 '77 C.350 B.S. L.190 J.D. [Morain&P.]
Pulliam, David C., (BV) .... '69 '95 C.350 B.A. L.352 J.D. [Wasker,D.W.&M.]
Rahm, Timothy J., (BV) .... '47 '76 C.885 B.A. L.221 J.D. [Rahm]
Rahm Law Offices, (BV) .... 950 Office Park Rd., Ste. 333
Reed, Steven C., (BV) .... '48 '75 C&L.221 B.S.E., J.D. 1741 Grand Ave.
Roberts, Ted Blake, (AVⓉ) '52 '77 C.352 B.B.A. L.846 J.D.
(adm. in TX; not adm. in IA) 5788 Coachlight Court
Rogers, Jack W., (AV) .... '31 '55 C&L.221 B.A., J.D. 1001 Office Park Rd.
Romar, Barbara, (BV) .... '58 '83 C&L.221 B.S.B.A., J.D. 1441 29th St., Ste. 111
Rossi, I. John .... '29 '62 C.352 B.A. L.1035 LL.B. Admin. Law Judge State of Iowa
Roupe, Rex V., (BV) .... '32 '59 C&L.221 B.S., LL.B. 1100 Grand Ave.
Rouwenhorst, Robert C., (AV) .... '53 '78 C.132 B.A. L.352 J.D. 3408 Woodland Ave.
Salsbery, Thomas E., (AV) .... '46 '72 C&L.352 B.A., J.D. [Davis,B.K.S.&R.] ⊙
Sandre, John R., (AV) .... '47 '73 C.352 B.A. L.221 J.D. [Coppola,S.M.&C.]
Scalise, Lawrence F. .... '33 '58 C&L.352 B.A., LL.B. [Ⓒ Sullivan&W.]
Schadle, William J., (BV) .... '32 '84 C.352 B.A. L.221 J.D. [Ⓐ McEnroe,G.B.B.&S.]
Schindler, Ralph J. .... '14 '38 C&L.352 B.A., J.D. 548 30th St.‡
Schodde, Stephen C. .... '36 '76 C.494 B.S. L.221 J.D. 401 Grand Ave.
Schoenfeld, Craig R. .... '68 '94 C.963 B.A. L.221 J.D. [Wasker,D.W.&M.]
Sellers, Michael M., (BV) .... '43 '67 C&L.352 LL.B. 1501 42nd St., Ste. 380
Shindler, Steven H., (BV) .... '54 '83 C.221 B.A. L.61 J.D. [Hudson,M.&S.]
Simons, Robert A. '47 '72 C.801 B.S. L.424 J.D.
(adm. in IL; not adm. in IA) Sr. Coun., Investments, Farm Bureau Life Ins. Co.
Simons, Robert A., (AV) .... '45 '73 C.56 B.A. L.494 J.D. [Morain&P.]
Sinclair, James A. .... '64 '91 C.352 B.B.A. L.221 J.D. 4940 Pleasant St.
Slater, Thomas S., (BV) .... '54 '79 C.132 B.A. L.221 J.D. 5070 Grand Ridge Dr.
Smith, Dustin D. '70 '97 C.352 B.A. L.221 J.D.
[Ⓐ Brown,W.G.G.B.&S.] (⊙Des Moines)
Smith, Jennifer M. .... '59 '91 C.999 B.S.N. L.221 J.D. 208 S. 30th St.
Smith, Kim L., (AV) .... '55 '80 C.350 B.S. L.352 J.D. [K.L.Smith]
Smith, K. L., P.C., (AV) .... 1012 Grand Ave.
Steffens, John S. '47 '73 C.602 L.802 J.D.
(adm. in PA; not adm. in IA) 3737 Woodland Ave., Ste. 601‡
Stegmaier, Patricia Gray .... '48 '85 C.363 B.A. L.221 J.D. Off. of Hearings & App.
Steinbach, Frank, III, (BV) .... '64 '89 C.350 B.S. L.221 J.D. [McEnroe,G.B.B.&S.]
Stewart, Robert H. .... '52 '77 C.352 B.B.A. L.809 J.D. Iowa Realty Co., Inc.
Stone, Jeffrey D., (BV) .... '— '93 C.350 B.S. L.221 J.D. [Whitfield&E.]
Strasser, Jos. L. .... '14 '38 C.211 P.O. Box 65020‡

Sullivan & Ward, P.C., (AV) [BB]
6601 Westown Parkway, Suite 200, 50266
Telephone: 515-244-3500 Telecopier: 515-244-3599
Email: swpc@sullivan-ward.com URL: http://www.sullivan-ward.com
John T. Ward; Harlan (Bud) Hockenberg; Michael P. Joynt; Louis R. Hockenberg; Richard R. Chabot; Robert M. Holliday; Mark Landa; John V. Donnelly; Dennis L. Puckett; Lawrence P. McLellan; Matthew D. Gardner; Rush Nigut. Of Counsel: Lawrence F. Scalise; Jill Mataya Corry;—Jennifer Jaskolka-Brown; Kyle A. Kruidenier.
General Civil Practice. Corporation, Public Utility, Labor, Environmental, OSHA, Real Estate, Probate, Taxation, Insurance and Administrative Law. Trials in all Courts, Family Law, Mediation and Arbitration.
Representative Clients: National Rural Utilities Cooperative Finance Corp; First Union Mortgage Corporation; Quality Wine Company, Inc.; Greenfield Plaza/Hills of Conventry Sanitary District; Commercial Federal Bank; EarthWeb, Inc.; Meredith Corporation; Federated Rural Electric Insurance Co.; Iowa Wireless Services, L.P.; Iowa Telecommunications Services, Inc.
See Professional Biographies, WEST DES MOINES, IOWA

Swennumson, Glenn R. .... '21 '49 L.221 LL.B. 1111 Ashwood Rd.‡
Swinton, Paul S., (BV) .... '61 '95 C.351 B.A. L.221 J.D. [Morain&P.]
Templer, John A., Jr., (AV) .... '— '75 C&L.352 B.A., J.D. [Whitfield&E.]
Thune, Paul C., (AV) .... '56 '81 C.879 B.A. L.221 J.D. [P.Thune]
Thune, Paul, Law Firm, P.L.C., (AV) .... 1501 42nd Street, Suite 175
Tobin, Maureen Roach, (AV) '— '87
C.352 B.A. L.221 J.D. [Whitfield&E.] (⊙Des Moines)
Trout, Joan D., (BV) .... '67 '92 C&L.352 B.B.A., J.D. [Pearson V.P.]
Tully, Robert G., (AV) .... '55 '81 C.602 B.A. L.221 J.D. [Anderson&T.]
Turner, Eric F., (AV) .... '55 '81 C.221 B.S.B.A. L.352 J.D. [Turner]

Turner Law Offices, (AV)
1200 Grand Avenue, 50265
Telephone: 515-245-9509 Fax: 515-245-9519
Email: attorneys@turnerlaw.com
Eric F. Turner.
General Civil and Trial Practice in all State and Federal Courts. Litigation, Corporate and Business, Insurance, Labor and Employment, Construction, Personal Injury, Real Estate, Wills and Probate, Trusts and Estates.
See Professional Biographies, WEST DES MOINES, IOWA

Urban, Camille L. '64 '98 C.350 B.A. L.352 J.D.
[Brown,W.G.G.B.&S.] (⊙Des Moines)
Van Houten, Margaret D., (AV) .... '53 '79 C.350 B.A. L.352 J.D. [Pearson V.P.]
Veenstra, Henry R., Jr. .... '49 '76 C.350 B.S. L.221 J.D. 801 29th St.
Von Gillern, Jon F. .... '53 '78 C.221 B.S. L.546 J.D. 6085 Colt Dr.‡
Walz, Mark D., (AV) .... '58 '83 C&L.352 B.A., J.D. [Davis,B.K.S.&R.] ⊙
Ward, John T., (AV) .... '40 '64 C&L.221 B.A., J.D. [Sullivan&W.]
Wasker, Charles F., (AV) .... '26 '52 C&L.221 B.A., J.D. [Wasker,D.W.&M.]

Wasker, Dorr, Wimmer & Marcouiller, P.C., (AV)
Three Fountains Office Park, Highland Building 4201 Westown Parkway, Suite 250, 50266-6720
Telephone: 515-283-1801 Facsimile: 515-283-1802
Email: lawfirm@wdwm.net URL: http://www.lawyers.com/waskerdorrwimmermarcouiller
Charles F. Wasker; Fred L. Dorr; William J. Wimmer; D. Mark Marcouiller; Matthew D. Kern; Mark R. Adams; David C. Pulliam; Matthew M. Hurn; Craig R. Schoenfeld;—Charles Hendricks. Retired: Russell H. Laird.
General Civil and Trial Practice, Real Estate, Government Relations, Corporation, Public Utility, Labor, Probate, Estate Planning, Taxation, Insurance and Administrative Law.
See Professional Biographies, WEST DES MOINES, IOWA

Waters, D. Samuel, (AV) ...... '57 '91 C.350 B.S. L.221 J.D. GuideOne Insurance Group
Weese, Ryan Edward .... '76 '01 C&L.221 B.S.A., J.D. [Ⓐ Hudson,M.&S.]
Werner, Thomas M., (AV) .... '54 '80 C&L.221 B.A., J.D. 1441 29th St., Ste. 111
Whitfield & Eddy, P.L.C., (AV)
3737 Woodland Avenue, Suite 400 (⊙Ankeny, Des Moines, Mt. Pleasant)
Williams, Robert D. .... '40 '67 C.170 B.A. L.221 J.D. 1200 35th St.‡
Wilson, Wayne I., (AV) .... '46 '74 C.352 B.B.A. L.221 J.D. 1601 22nd Street
Wimmer, William J., (AV) .... '49 '76 C.593 B.S. L.192 J.D. [Wasker,D.W.&M.]
Winjum, Ken A., (BV) '63 '89
C&L.352 B.B.A., J.D. Sr. Staff Atty., Amer. Fam. Ins. Grp.
Witherwax, Bryan S. .... '71 '04 C.352 B.S. L.221 J.D. [Ⓐ Hudson,M.&S.]
Wood, David C. .... '43 '68 C&L.502 A.B., J.D. 121 S. 32nd St.
Wood, Michael D. .... '70 '96 C.502 B.A. L.1206 J.D. Sr. Coun., Wells Fargo
Young, Donald B. .... '36 '61 C.352 B.A. L.339 J.D. Donald B. Young Law Firm

WEST LIBERTY, 3,332, *Muscatine Co.*

Allbee, Harvey G., Jr., (AV) '34 '58
C&L.352 B.A., J.D. [Allbee,B.A.D.&P.] (⊙Muscatine)
Allbee, Barclay, Allison, Denning & Person, A Professional Corporation, (AV)
110 E. Third St. (⊙Muscatine, Wilton)
Allison, Gary R., (BV) '46 '71 C&L.352 B.B.A., J.D.
[Allbee,B.A.D.&P.] (⊙Muscatine)
Allison, Linda L., (BV) '47 '85 C&L.352 B.S.N., J.D.
[Allbee,B.A.D.&P.] (⊙Muscatine)
Denning, Gerald F., (BV) .... '50 '76 C&L.352 B.A., J.D. [Allbee,B.A.D.&P.] ⊙
Keele, James R., (BV) .... '47 '73 C.187 B.A. L.352 J.D. City Atty. [Keele]
Keele Law Offices, P.C., (BV) .... 101 E. Third St.
Oppel, R Craig, (CV) '67 '95 C.112 B.A. L.221 J.D.
[Ⓐ Allbee,B.A.D.&P.] (⊙Muscatine)

WEST POINT, 980, *Lee Co.*

Aspelmeier, Fisch, Power, Engberg & Helling, P.L.C., (AV)
420 Avenue "E" (⊙Burlington, Mediapolis)
Fisch, James F., (AV) '40 '65
C.723 B.A. L.352 J.D. [Aspelmeier,F.P.E.&H.] (⊙Burlington)

WEST UNION, * 2,490, *Fayette Co.*

Allbee, Alan D. .... '53 '78 C&L.352 B.B.A., J.D. Assoc. Juv. Ct. J.
Antes, C. W. .... '15 '38 C&L.352 B.A., J.D. Ret. Dist. J.
Antes, Jon W., (BV) .... '44 '70 C&L.221 B.A., J.D. [Ⓒ Elwood,O.S.B.&C.] ⊙
Beeghly, James L. .... '41 '74 C.350 B.S. L.352 J.D. Dist. J.
Braun, Joseph P., (CV) .... '68 '95 C.494 B.A. L.1035 J.D. [Elwood,O.S.B.&C.] ⊙
Clements, Jeffrey E., (BV) .... '55 '83 C&L.221 B.A., J.D. 117 1/2 S. Vine St.
Elwood, Henry L., (AV) .... '34 '59 C.187 B.A. L.221 J.D. [Elwood,O.S.B.&C.] ⊙

Elwood, O'Donohoe, Stochl, Braun & Churbuck, (AV) [BB]
125 N. Vine, P.O. Box 475, 52175 ⊙
Telephone: 563-422-5631 Fax: 563-422-5632
Email: elwood@myclearwave.net
Members of Firm: Henry L. Elwood; James E. O'Donohoe (1921-1998); Christopher F. O'Donohoe; Richard D. Stochl; Judith Mack O'Donohoe; Joseph P. Braun; Lewis M. Churbuck (1972-2003). Associates: Jeremiah W. White; Todd P. Prichard. Of Counsel: Richard P. TeKippe; Jon W. Antes.
General Practice in State and Federal Courts. Litigation, Insurance Defense, Probate, Estate Planning, Trusts and Wills, Real Estate, Corporate, Banking and Taxation Law. Trials and Appeals.
(This Listing Continued)

Elwood, O'Donohoe, Stochl, Braun & Churbuck (Continued)

Representative Clients: Grinnell Mutual Reinsurance Co.; United Fire & Casualty Insurance Co.; Board of Trustees, New Hampton Municipal Light Plant; First Citizens National Bank, New Hampton, Iowa; Alliance Pipeline; Cresco Union Savings Bank, Cresco, Iowa; Featherlite, Inc.; Community First National Bank, Protivin, Iowa; City of Cresco, Iowa.
Cresco, Iowa Office: 217 North Elm Street. P.O. Box 377, 52136. Telephone: 563-547-3321. Fax: 563-547-3189.
Charles City, Iowa Office: 116 North Main Street. P.O. Box 307. 50616. Telephone: 641-228-8054. Fax: 641-228-8057.
New Hampton, Iowa Office: 101 North Locust Avenue, P.O. Box 310, 50659. Telephone: 641-394-5943. Fax: 641-394-5945.

Koempel, Alice T., (BV) .... '25 '48 C&L.352 B.A., J.D. 103 N. Vine St.
O'Donohoe, Christopher F., (AV) '50 '75 C.118 B.A. L.178 J.D. [Elwood,O.S.B.&C.] ⊙
O'Donohoe, Judith Mack, (BV) '51 '76 C.118 B.A. L.569 J.D. [Elwood,O.S.B.&C.] ⊙
Prichard, Todd P. .... '— '04 C&L.352 B.A., J.D. [🄰 Elwood,O.S.B.&C.] ⊙
Stochl, Richard D., (BV) .... '64 '89 C.927 B.S. L.352 J.D. [Elwood,O.S.B.&C.] ⊙
TeKippe, Richard P., (BV) .... '40 '64 C.177 B.A. L.352 J.D. [🄲 Elwood,O.S.B.&C.] ⊙
Updegraff, James S., (BV) .... '42 '67 C&L.352 B.A., J.D. 117 1/2 S. Vine St.
Villont, J.D., (BV) .... '52 '77 C&L.352 B.B.A., J.D. Asst. Co. Atty.
White, Jeremiah W. .... '— '04 C.351 B.A. L.352 J.D. [🄰 Elwood,O.S.B.&C.] ⊙

WHITTEMORE, 535, *Kossuth Co.*

Thul, Brian W. .... '69 '94 C&L.190 B.S.B.A., J.D. [Thul]
Thul Law Firm .... 405 Broad St.

WILLIAMSBURG, 2,622, *Iowa Co.*

Buchanan, Thomas M., (BV) .... '49 '74 C.734 A.B. L.352 J.D. [Elwood,E.B.&L.] ⊙
Claypool, James E., (AV) .... '62 '88 C&L.352 B.B.A., J.D. [Claypool&C.]
Claypool, Rebecca L., (BV) .... '58 '83 C&L.352 B.S., J.D. [Claypool&C.]
Claypool, Thomas H., (BV) .... '58 '83 C&L.352 B.A., J.D. [Claypool&C.]
Claypool & Claypool, (AV) .... 505 Court St.
Elwood, Michael J., (BV) .... '42 '67 C.707 B.A. L.585 J.D. [Elwood,E.B.&L.] ⊙
Elwood, Richard H., (BV) .... '35 '64 C.707 B.A. L.585 J.D. [Elwood,E.B.&L.] ⊙
Elwood, Elwood, Buchanan & Leinen, (BV) 305 West State Street (⊙Marengo, North English)
Leinen, Robert J., (BV) '57 '82 C.350 B.S. L.352 J.D. Co. Jud. Mag. [Elwood,E.B.&L.] ⊙
Oliver, Douglas A. .... '63 '95 C.352 B.A. L.221 J.D. 600 Court St.
Saylor, Ronald L., (BV) .... '35 '64 C.350 B.S. L.352 J.D. 600 Court St.
Shafer, William K., (CV) .... '53 '91 C.350 B.S. L.352 J.D. [Shafer]
Shafer Law Office, (CV) .... 204 West State St.
Winborn, Erik L. .... '50 '76 C.1070 B.S. L.352 J.D. 401 Wilson St.★

WILTON, 2,829, *Muscatine Co.*

Allbee, Barclay, Allison, Denning & Person, A Professional Corporation, (AV) 603 W. Fifth Street, Sunel (⊙Muscatine, West Liberty)
Axel, Joan U., (BV) .... '43 '82 C.350 B.S. L.352 J.D. [Stanley,L.&H.] (⊙Muscatine)
Denning, Gerald F., (BV) .... '50 '76 C&L.352 B.A., J.D. [Allbee,B.A.D.&P.] ⊙
Oppel, Curt A., (BV) .... '63 '88 C.352 B.B.A. L.221 J.D. [Stanley,L.&H.] (⊙Davenport)
Scieszinski, David L., (BV) .... '36 '63 C&L.352 B.S.C., J.D. 106 E. 4th St.

Stanley, Lande & Hunter, A Professional Corporation, (AV)
115 West Fourth, P.O. Box 481, 52778 ⊙
Telephone: 563-732-4000 Facsimile: 563-732-2318
Email: Contact.us@slhlaw.com URL: http://www.slhlaw.com
Joan U. Axel; Curt A. Oppel; Eric J. Thomsen.
General Civil and Trial Practice. Corporation, Business, Banking, Taxation, Securities, Tax-Exempt Financing, Labor, Employment Discrimination, Administrative, Creditor Bankruptcy and Agricul-

(This Listing Continued)

Stanley, Lande & Hunter, A Professional Corporation (Continued)

tural Law, Insurance Defense, Personal Injury and Property Damage Law, Pension and Profit-Sharing, Real Estate, Probate, Estate Planning and Charitable Trusts and Foundations Law.
Muscatine, Iowa Office: 301 Iowa Avenue, Suite 400. Telephone: 563-264-5000. Facsimile: 563-263-8775.
Davenport, Iowa Office: 900 U.S. Bank Center, 201 West Second Street. Telephone: 563-324-1000. Facsimile: 563-326-6266.
Coralville, Iowa Office: 2201 East Grantview Drive, Suite 200. Telephone: 319-248-9000. Facsimile: 319-248-9001.

See Professional Biographies, WILTON, IOWA

Thomsen, Eric J., (AV) '53 '78 C.350 B.S. L.352 J.D. [Stanley,L.&H.] (⊙Davenport, Muscatine)

WINFIELD, 1,051, *Henry Co.*

Carty, John W., (BV) .... '23 '52 C.106 B.A. L.221 J.D. Farmers Natl. Bk. Bldg.

WINTERSET, * 4,768, *Madison Co.*

Blessum, A. Zane, (BV) .... '57 '84 C.352 B.S. L.221 J.D. [Blessum]
Blessum Law Firm, (BV) .... 113 N. John Wayne Dr.
Casper, John E., (AV) .... '46 '70 C&L.352 B.A., J.D. [Flander&C.]
Chickering, Chet R., (BV) .... '43 '74 C.350 B.S. L.734 J.D. 621 W. Benton
Darling, Gordon K., (AV) .... '26 '50 C&L.221 J.D. [Darling&D.]
Darling, Gordon K., Jr., (BV) .... '52 '77 C&L.221 B.A., J.D. [Darling&D.]
Darling & Darling, (AV) .... 53 Jefferson St.
Flander, Leonard M., (BV) .... '34 '59 C&L.352 B.A., J.D. [Flander&C.]
Flander and Casper, P.C., (AV) .... 223 E. Court Ave.
Frederick, Robert O. .... '14 '40 C.162 B.A. L.352 J.D. Sr. Dist. J.
Janssen, Susan K., (BV) .... '44 '85 C.194 B.S. L.221 J.D. Mag.
Jordan, Lewis H., (AV) .... '30 '58 C&L.352 B.A., J.D. [Jordan,O.&W.]

Jordan, Oliver & Walters, P.C., (AV)
Farmers & Merchants Bank Building, P.O. Box 230, 50273
Telephone: 515-462-3731 Fax: 515-462-3734
Shirley A. Webster (1909-1989); Lewis H. Jordan; Jerrold B. Oliver; G. Stephen Walters.
Elder Law, General Practice, Personal Injury, Real Estate, Taxation, Trusts and Estates, Wills and Probate, Family Law, Insurance.
Reference: Farmers & Merchants State Bank, Winterset, Iowa.

See Professional Biographies, WINTERSET, IOWA

Libby, Walt '44 '74 C.784 B.A. L.494 J.D. (adm. in MN; not adm. in IA) 317 E. Court Ave.‡
Mills, Philip C. .... '36 '61 C&L.352 B.A., J.D. 622 W. South St.★
Moore, W. Dean, (AV) .... '31 '61 C.950 L.221 LL.B. 2493 Knoll Ridge Trail
Oliver, Jerrold B., (AV) .... '43 '67 C&L.352 B.A., J.D. [Jordan,O.&W.]

Rigg, J. Keith
(See Des Moines)

Schmitt, Kathryn B. .... '52 '80 C.352 B.A. L.221 J.D. 223 E. Court‡
Serrano, Ava West, (BVⓉ) .... '53 '90 C.347 B.A. L.345 J.D. [A.Serrano]
Serrano, Ava Law Offices, (BVⓉ) .... 204 W. Washington St.
Walters, G. Stephen, (AV) .... '48 '73 C.350 B.S. L.352 J.D. [Jordan,O.&W.]

WOODBINE, 1,500, *Harrison Co.*

Lauterbach, Joseph C., (BV) '53 '80 C.187 B.S.S. L.352 J.D. [Salvo,D.S.&L.] (⊙Harlan)
Salvo, Deren, Schenck & Lauterbach, P.C., (AV) 414 Walker (⊙Earling, Harlan, Panama, Walnut)

PATENT AND TRADEMARK PRACTICE PROFILES SECTION

Legal Professionals Practicing

BEFORE THE

UNITED STATES PATENT AND TRADEMARK OFFICE

IDAHO, ILLINOIS
INDIANA, IOWA

The listings in this section are, according to information available to the publisher at press time, for those subscribers who are registered to practice Patent Law and for those who practice Trademark Law before the U.S. Patent and Trademark Office and who devote a considerable portion of their time or duties to Patent, Trademark and other related matters. It should be noted that registration is not necessary to practice Trademark Law before the U.S. Patent and Trademark Office.

Firms are not registered with the U.S. Patent and Trademark Office and the listings of such entities are limited to those whose practice includes Patent or Trademark and related matters.

The symbols shown have the same meaning as when used elsewhere in this directory. See page IX for Explanatory Notes and Symbols.

BOISE, * 185,787, *Ada Co.*

Dykas, Frank J., (AV) .... '46 '75 C.1156 B.S. L.972 J.D. [Dykas,S.&N.]
*PRACTICE AREAS: Patent Law; Trademark Law; Trade Secrets; Litigation; Contracts.

Dykas, Shaver & Nipper, LLP, (AV)
P.O. Box 877, 83701
Telephone: 208-345-1122 Fax: 208-345-8370 Toll Free: 1-877-611-1122
Email: info@dykaslaw.com URL: http://www.dykaslaw.com
Frank J. Dykas; Robert L. Shaver; Stephen M. Nipper;—Derek H. Maughan.
Intellectual Property, Patent, Trademark, including National and International Filing, Copyright, Contracts, Unfair Competition, Trade Secrets, Licensing, Litigation and Related Matters.
See Professional Biographies, BOISE, IDAHO

Maughan, Derek H. .... '71 '01 C.101 B.S. L.336 J.D. [A Dykas,S.&N.]
*PRACTICE AREAS: Trademarks; Copyrights; Trade Secrets; Contracts; Patents.
Nipper, Stephen M., (BV) .... '72 '98 C.999 B.S. L.801 J.D. [Dykas,S.&N.]
*PRACTICE AREAS: Patents; Trademarks; Copyrights; Trade Secrets; Contracts.
Shaver, Robert L., (BV) ....'50 '95 C.1079 B.A. L.336 J.D. [Dykas,S.&N.]
*PRACTICE AREAS: Patent; Trademark; Copyright; Litigation; Contracts.

BARRINGTON, 10,168, *Cook & Lake Cos.*

Meroni, Charles F., Jr., (AV) .... '— '60 C.170 A.B. L.365 J.D. [Meroni&M.]
*PRACTICE AREAS: Intellectual Property; Patents; Trademarks; Copyrights; International Patents.

Meroni & Meroni, P.C., (AV)
5 Bellwood Drive, P.O. Box 309, 60011
Telephone: 847-304-1500 Telefax: 847-382-5478
Email: meronilaw@ameritech.net URL: http://www.meronilaw.com
Charles F. Meroni, Jr.;—Christopher J. Scott.
Patent, Trademark, Copyright, Licensing and Related Intellectual Property Law.
See Professional Biographies, BARRINGTON, ILLINOIS

Scott, Christopher J. .... '— '00 C.1157 B.A. L.209 J.D. [[A] Meroni&M.]
*PRACTICE AREAS: Intellectual Property; Patents; Trademarks; Copyrights; International Patents.

CHICAGO, * 2,896,016, *Cook Co.*

Aaronson, Lawrence H. .... '65 '91 C.477 B.S.E.E. L.339 J.D. [McDonnell B.H.&B.]
Abramic, John L. .... '74 '01 C.46 B.S. L.146 J.D. [[A] McAndrews,H.&M.]
*PRACTICE AREAS: Intellectual Property Law.
Abrell, Matthias .... '— '01 C.763 B.S. L.365 J.D. [[A] Marshall,G.&B.]
*PRACTICE AREAS: Intellectual Property.
Abuel, Christine A. .... '79 '04 C.912 B.A. L.209 J.D. [[A] Fitch,E.T.&F.]
*PRACTICE AREAS: Intellectual Property; Litigation.
Addy, Meredith Martin, (AV) ...... '68 '93 C.691 B.S.E.E. L.280 J.D. [Brinks H.G.&L.]
*PRACTICE AREAS: Intellectual Property Portfolio Management; Intellectual Property Litigation; Intellectual Property Procurement.
Airan, David M. .... '67 '93 C.436 B.S.E.E. L.597 J.D. [Leydig,V.&M.]
Albers, Daniel P., (AV) .... '— '83 C&L.339 B.S., J.D. [Barnes&T.]
*PRACTICE AREAS: Products Liability; Professional Liability; Commercial Litigation; Litigation; Patent Litigation.
Alex, John L., (AV) .... '36 '62 C&L.597 B.S.Ch.E., J.D. [Cook,A.M.M.C.&M.]
*PRACTICE AREAS: Intellectual Property; Patents; Trademarks; Copyrights; Unfair Competition.
Altman, Louis, (AV) .... '— '59 C.188 A.B. L.309 LL.B. [[C] Michael B.&F.]
*PRACTICE AREAS: Patent Law; Trademark Law; Copyright Law; Unfair Competition Law; Litigation.
Anderfuren, Jill, (BV) .... '— '90 C.597 B.S. L.146 J.D. [[A] Marshall,G.&B.]
*PRACTICE AREAS: Trademark and Copyright Prosecution and Litigation.
Anderson, Richard H., (AV) .... '— '73 C.383 B.S.Ch.E. L.273 J.D. [Marshall,G.&B.]
*PRACTICE AREAS: Chemical Patents; Chemical Patent Prosecution.
Anderson, Theodore W., (AV) ..... '26 '53 C.339 B.S.E.E. L.209 J.D. [[C] Leydig,V.&M.]
Arnold, Patrick J., Jr., (AV) .... '66 '90 C.339 B.A. L.424 J.D. [McAndrews,H.&M.]
Augustyn, John M., (AV) .... '59 '87 C.146 B.S. L.424 J.D. [Leydig,V.&M.]
Auten, Stephen R. .... '71 '97 C.339 B.S. L.146 J.D. [[A] Leydig,V.&M.]
Bagley, Mark R. .... '73 '99 C.309 A.B. L.145 J.D. [[A] Olson&H.]
Baim, Stacy A. .... '— '98 C&L.477 B.S.E., J.D. [[A] Jones D.]
Baniak, Michael H., (AV) .... '55 '80 C.201 B.S. L.1119 J.D. [Baniak P.&G.]
*PRACTICE AREAS: Litigation; Intellectual Property; Licensing; Trademark; Copyright.

Baniak Pine & Gannon, (AV) [BB]
150 North Wacker Drive, Suite 1200, 60606
Telephone: 312-673-0360 Fax: 312-673-0361
URL: http://www.bpglaw.com
Members of Firm: Michael H. Baniak; Jeffrey A. Pine; Michael D. Gannon; Christina L. Brown; Charles C. Valauskas; Charles C. Kinne. Associates: Allison Dudley; Christopher E. Haigh (Not admitted in IL); Andrew F. Pratt; Anuj K. Wadhwa; William F. Ward, III. Counsel: Gary E. Hood.
Intellectual Property, Patent, Trademark, Copyright and Trade Secret Law, Litigation, Licensing.
See Professional Biographies, CHICAGO, ILLINOIS

Banner, Mark T., (AV) .... '—'79 C.679 B.A. L.365 J.D. [Banner&W.]
*PRACTICE AREAS: Intellectual Property Law; Patents; Trademarks; Intellectual Property Litigation; Appellate Practice.

Banner & Witcoff, Ltd., (AV)
Established In 1920 - Predecessor Parent
Ten South Wacker Drive, Suite 3000, 60606-7407 ⊙
Telephone: 312-463-5000 Facsimile: 312-463-5001
Email: info@bannerwitcoff.com URL: http://www.bannerwitcoff.com
Mark T. Banner; Matthew P. Becker; Joseph J. Berghammer; Aimee Boss Kolz; Scott A. Burow; James V. Callahan; Marc S. Cooperman; Allen E. Hoover; Timothy C. Meece; Charles Miller; Janice V. Mitrius; Jon O. Nelson; Binal J. Patel; Thomas K. Pratt; Christopher J. Renk; Robert H. Resis; Rebecca P. Rokos; Charles W. Shifley; Jason Shull; Richard Stockton; J. Pieter van Es. Of Counsel: Sheldon W. Witcoff. Associates: William J. Klein; Erik S. Maurer; Phoebe K. Phillips.
Intellectual Property including Procurement of Patents, Trademarks, Copyrights, Trade Secrets, Counseling & Opinions, Unfair Competition, Interferences, Licensing, Antitrust and International Trade Matters. Litigation including Trials and Appeals in Federal and State Courts and International Trade Commission.
Washington, D.C. Office: 1001 G Street, N.W., Suite 1100. Telephone: 202-824-3000. Facsimile: 202-824-3001.
Boston, Massachusetts Office: 28 State Street, 28th Floor. Telephone: 617-720-9600. Fax: 617-720-9601.
Portland, Oregon Office: 601 SW Second Avenue, Suite 1900. Telephone: 503-425-6800. Fax: 503-425-6801.
See Professional Biographies, CHICAGO, ILLINOIS

Barich, Joseph M. .... '72 '98 C.339 B.S.E.E. L.93 J.D. [McAndrews,H.&M.]
*PRACTICE AREAS: Electrical Intellectual Property; Electronic Intellectual Property; Intellectual Property Licensing; International Intellectual Property; International Licensing.
Barkoff, Aaron F. .... '71 '02 C.399 B.A. L.145 J.D. [[A] McDonnell B.H.&B.]

Barnes & Thornburg LLP, (AV) [BB]
One North Wacker Drive, Suite 4400, 60606-2833 ⊙
Telephone: 312-357-1313 FAX: 312-759-5646
URL: http://www.btlaw.com
Partners: Daniel P. Albers; Alice O. Martin; Melissa A. Vallone. Associates: Mark J. Nahsen; Vladimir Khodosh; John P. Wappel.
Acquisitions and Mergers, Antitrust, Chemical Intellectual Property, Copyrights, Electrical Intellectual Property, Electronic Intellectual Property, Franchise Licensing, Intellectual Property Arbitration, Intellectual Property Infringement, Intellectual Property Litigation, Intellectual Property Portfolio Management, Intellectual Property Licensing, International Intellectual Property, Literary Property, Mechanical Intellectual Property, Medical Intellectual Property, Patents, Patent Litigation, Patent Protection, Pharmaceutical Intellectual Property, Proprietary Rights, Protection of Personality, Software Licensing, Taxation of Intellectual Property, Trademarks, Trademark Litigation, Trademark Registration.
Representative Intellectual Property Clients: ARCH Development Corporation; Argonne National Laboratory; Biotechnology Research & Development Corporation; Enteron; Indian Motorcycle Supply, Inc.; Pennsylvania State University; University of Illinois.
Indianapolis, Indiana Office: 11 South Meridian Street, 46204. Telephone: 317-236-1313. FAX: 317-231-7433.
Fort Wayne, Indiana Office: 600 One Summit Square, 46802. Telephone: 260-423-9440. FAX: 260-424-8316.
South Bend, Indiana Office: 600 1st Source Bank Center, 100 North Michigan, 46601-1632. Telephone: 574-233-1171. FAX: 574-237-1125.
Elkhart, Indiana Office: 121 West Franklin Street, Suite 200, 46516. Telephone: 574-293-0681. FAX: 574-296-2535.
Washington, D.C. Office: Suite 900, 750 17th Street, N.W., 20006. Telephone: 202-289-1313. FAX: 202-289-1330.
Grand Rapids, Michigan Office: 300 Ottawa Avenue, N.W., Suite 500, 49503. Telephone: 616-742-3930. FAX: 616-742-3999.
See Professional Biographies, CHICAGO, ILLINOIS

Barthel, Renee C. .... '73 '01 C.260 B.S.ENE L.146 J.D. [[A] Cook,A.M.M.C.&M.]
*PRACTICE AREAS: Intellectual Property; Patents; Trademarks; Copyrights.
Baumann, Timothy R. .... '63 '95 C.350 B.S.E.E. L.339 J.D. [[A] Fitch,E.T.&F.]
*PRACTICE AREAS: Patent Litigation; Patent Prosecution; Electrical Engineering.
Baxendale, Scott E. .... '— '96 C.930 B.S. L.365 J.D. [Marshall,G.&B.]
*PRACTICE AREAS: Mechanical, Electro-Mechanical and Process Control Systems; Patent Prosecution; Computer Software; Intellectual Property Portfolio Management.
Bays, Gregory C. .... '67 '95 C.477 B.S.M.E. L.930 J.D. [Leydig,V.&M.]
Becker, Matthew P. .... '— '98 C.679 B.S. L.597 J.D. [Banner&W.]
*PRACTICE AREAS: Intellectual Property Law; Patents; Trademarks; Intellectual Property Litigation.
Belvis, Glen P., (AV) .... '58 '85 C.602 B.S. L.209 J.D. [Brinks H.G.&L.]
*PRACTICE AREAS: Litigation; Intellectual Property; Antitrust Trade Regulation; Patents; Copyrights.
Benson, Joel W., (AV) .... '49 '78 C.477 B.S.E.E. L.276 J.D. [Brinks H.G.&L.]
*PRACTICE AREAS: Patent Litigation; Patent Prosecution; Trade Secrets; Copyrights.
Berenzweig, Jack C., (AV) .... '42 '68 C.188 B.E.E. L.30 J.D. [Brinks H.G.&L.]
*PRACTICE AREAS: Intellectual Property.
Berghammer, Joseph J. .... '— '95 C.453 B.S. L.976 J.D. [Banner&W.]
*PRACTICE AREAS: Intellectual Property Litigation; Intellectual Property Law; Patents; Trademarks; Copyrights.
Berghoff, Paul H., (AV) .... '56 '81 C.399 B.A. L.477 J.D. [McDonnell B.H.&B.]
Berntsen, Denis A., (AV) .... '47 '72 C&L.339 B.S.E.E., J.D. [[C] McDonnell B.H.&B.]
Bianco, Brian C. .... '77 '03 C&L.339 B.S.E.E., J.D. [[A] McAndrews,H.&M.]
*PRACTICE AREAS: Intellectual Property Litigation; Patent Prosecution.
Blackman, Marc S. .... '— '96 C.477 B.S. L.273 J.D. [[A] Jones D.]
Blackstone, Raiford A., Jr., (AV) '43 '70
C.150 B.S.E.E. L.424 J.D. [Trexler,B.G.B.&M.]
*PRACTICE AREAS: Intellectual Property; Intellectual Property Licensing; Litigation; Trademarks; Copyrights.
Bluestone, David H. .... '74 '99 C.339 B.S.E.E. L.597 J.D. [[A] Brinks H.G.&L.]
*PRACTICE AREAS: Intellectual Property; Litigation; Patent Prosecution; Copyrights; Trademarks.
Bock, Joel H., (AV) .... '52 '77 C.477 B.S. L.1119 J.D. [Cook,A.M.M.C.&M.]
*PRACTICE AREAS: Patent, Trademark and Copyright Law; Unfair Competition Causes.
Boehnen, Daniel A., (AV) .... '50 '76 C.602 B.S.Ch.E. L.188 J.D. [McDonnell B.H.&B.]
Bootzin, Joel H. .... '67 '96 C.999 B.S. L.146 J.D. [[A] Fitch,E.T.&F.]
Borun, Michael F., (AV) .... '— '70 C.145 B.S. L.424 J.D. [Marshall,G.&B.]
*PRACTICE AREAS: International Intellectual Property; Biotechnology Patent Prosecution; Molecular Biology Patents; Patent Interference Practice; Patent Litigation.
Braidwood, George Christopher .... '70 '95 C&L.477 B.S.E.E., J.D. [[A] Marshall,G.&B.]
Brezina, David C., (AV) .... '— '78 C.187 B.S.S. L.146 J.D. [Barnes&T.]
*PRACTICE AREAS: Intellectual Property Law (90%); Patents; Trademarks; Copyrights; Litigation (5%).
Brim, Scott W. .... '76 '02 C.201 B.S.E.E. L.339 J.D. [[A] Brinks H.G.&L.]
*PRACTICE AREAS: Intellectual Property.
Brinks, Henry L., (AV) .... '24 '51 C.937 A.B. L.273 J.D. [Brinks H.G.&L.]
*PRACTICE AREAS: Patent Counseling; Patent Litigation; Patent Prosecution; Interferences.

Brinks Hofer Gilson & Lione, A Professional Corporation, (AV) [BB]
NBC Tower, Suite 3600, 455 North Cityfront Plaza Drive, 60611-5599 ⊙
Telephone: 312-321-4200 Facsimile: 312-321-4299
Email: iplaw@usebrinks.com URL: http://www.usebrinks.com
Languages: Arabic, Croatian, French, German, Greek, Hebrew, Japanese, Korean, Latvian, Macedonian, Polish, Romanian, Russian, Serbian and Spanish.
Henry L. Brinks; Roy E. Hofer; Richard G. Lione; Jack C. Berenzweig; Jerold A. Jacover; Gary M. Ropski; Joel W. Benson; John K. Lucas; Raymond W. Green; James R. Sobieraj; Richard A. Kaplan; Allan J. Sternstein; Steven P. Shurtz; Jeffery M. Duncan; Harold V. Johnson; Rodney A. Daniel; Glen P. Belvis; Thomas J. Filarski; William H. Frankel; Gustavo Siller, Jr.; James P. Naughton; Timothy Q. Delaney; Bradley G. Lane; Ralph J. Gabric; G. Peter Nichols; Michael E. Milz; Dominick P. Zanfardino; Robert S. Mallin; William F. Prendergast; John C. Freeman; Laura Beth Miller; Michael P. Chu; Meredith Martin Addy; Kent E. Genin; Craig A. Summerfield; Marc V. Richards; Andrew D. Stover; K. Shannon Mrksich; Jason C. White; Joseph F. Hetz; John G. Rauch; Tadashi Horie. Counsel: Amir N. Penn; Donald J. Silvert; Jonathan E. Retsky; Jeffrey H. Canfield; Janet A. Pioli; Robert B. Polit. — Vineet Gauri; Carmen Matos Michael; Jasper W. Dockery; Christoper A. Harkins; James A.Collins; James L. Katz; Vincent J. Gnoffo; Richard E. Stanley, Jr.; David H. Bluestone; Charles M. McMahon; David W. Okey; Anastasia Heffner; Justin B. Rand; Timothy P. Lucier; Sean P. Springman; Scott W. Brim; Benjamin B. Cotton; Heidi A. Dare; Robert G. Pluta; Samuel E. Shjehadeh; Joseph A. Yosick; Anthony P. Curtis; Timothy J. Le Duc; John F. Nethery; Rashida MacMurray; Stephnie J. Felicetty; Miyoung Shin; Thomas J. Wrona; Jeffrey A. Marx; Richard D. Watkins. Indianapolis Office: A. James Richardson. Of Counsel: David H. Badger. Counsel: Lawrence A. Steward;— Sanders N. Hillis; Nicholas M. Boivin; Michael E. Wever. Ann Arbor Office: David D. Murray; Steven L. Oberholtzer; Eric J. Sosenko. Counsel: Margaret Dobrowitsky;— Raymond J. Vivacqua; Lawrence G. Almeda; John M. Card; Robert K. Fergan; Jon Beaupre; James K. Cleland.
Patent, Trademark, Copyright and Unfair Competition and Related Antitrust Law. Trials.
Indianapolis, Indiana Office: One Indiana Square, Suite 1600. Telephone: 317-636-0886. Facsimile: 317-634-6701.
Ann Arbor, Michigan Office: 524 South Main Street, Suite 200. Telephone: 734-302-6000. Facsimile: 734-994-6331.
Arlington, Virginia Office: 2001 Jefferson Davis Highway, Suite 208. Telephone: 703-415-0303. Facsimile: 703-415-0304.
See Professional Biographies, CHICAGO, ILLINOIS

Brown, Christina L. .... '65 '91 C.5 B.S. L.851 J.D. [Baniak P.&G.]
*PRACTICE AREAS: Litigation; Intellectual Property; Licensing; Trademarks; Copyrights.
Brown, Paul L., (AV) .... '39 '66 C.504 B.A. L.477 J.D. [Emrich&D.]
*PRACTICE AREAS: Patents; Trademarks; Copyrights.
Buechle, Kurt T. .... '74 '02 C.311 B.S. L.1119 J.D. [[A] Leydig,V.&M.]
Bullwinkel, George E., (AV) .... '36 '64 C.188 B.M.E. L.309 LL.B. [Bullwinkel]
*PRACTICE AREAS: Intellectual Property Law; Trial Practice; Appellate Practice; Computer Law; Aviation Law.

Bullwinkel Partners, Ltd., (AV)
19 South La Salle Street, Suite 1300, 60603-1493
Telephone: 312-201-0777 Fax: 312-201-0737
URL: http://www.bullwinkel.com
George E. Bullwinkel.
General Practice, Litigation, Intellectual Property, Patents, Entrepreneurial Law.
See Professional Biographies, CHICAGO, ILLINOIS

Burgan, Jeffrey B., (AV) .... '55 '90 C.701 B.S.Ch.E. L.425 J.D. [Leydig,V.&M.]
Burkholder, Samuel P. '58 '94 C.288 B.A. L.831 J.D.
(adm. in NJ; not adm. in IL) [Fitch,E.T.&F.]
Burow, Scott A. .... '— '97 C.966 B.S.M.E. L.365 J.D. [Banner&W.]
*PRACTICE AREAS: Intellectual Property Law; Intellectual Property Litigation; Appellate Practice; Patent Prosecution; Patents.
Caliri, Robert R. .... '46 '73 C.188 A.B. L.575 J.D. [Emrich&D.]
*PRACTICE AREAS: Trademarks; Copyrights.
Callahan, James V., (AV) .... '— '59 C.602 B.S.M.E. L.424 J.D. [Banner&W.]
*PRACTICE AREAS: Intellectual Property Law; Patents; Trademarks; Intellectual Property Licensing.
Canfield, Jeffrey H. .... '63 '93 C.474 B.S.E.E. L.365 J.D. [[C] Brinks H.G.&L.]
*PRACTICE AREAS: Intellectual Property.
Carani, Christopher V. .... '73 '99 C.436 B.S.I.E. L.145 J.D. [McAndrews,H.&M.]
*PRACTICE AREAS: Intellectual Property Litigation; Intellectual Property Licensing; Intellectual Property Prosecution.
Carden, S. Richard .... '67 '99 C.861 B.S.E. L.910 J.D. [McDonnell B.H.&B.]
Carnahan, J. Aron .... '71 '97 C&L.339 B.S.M.E., J.D. [Welsh&K.]
*PRACTICE AREAS: Intellectual Property.
Carroll, Christopher R. .... '— '03 C&L.339 B.S., J.D. [[A] McAndrews,H.&M.]
*PRACTICE AREAS: Patent Litigation; Patent Prosecution; Intellectual Property.
Cavan, Christopher M. .... '64 '92 C.597 B.S.M.E. L.424 J.D. [McDonnell B.H.&B.]

Cepuritis, Talivaldis, (AV) . . . . '35 '65 C.477 B.S.E. L.569 J.D. [Olson&H.]
Chael, Mark L. . . . . '59 '01 C.679 B.S. L.365 J.D. [Ⓐ McDonnell B.H.&B.]
Chalfie, Edward J., (AV) . . . . '48 '78 C.453 B.S. L.424 J.D. [Ⓐ Ladas&P.]
*PRACTICE AREAS: Intellectual Property; Patent Prosecution; Trademark Prosecution; Licensing; Patents.
Chang, Y. Kurt . . . . '57 '95 C.966 Ph.D. L.597 J.D. [Leydig,V.&M.]
Cherry, Daniel R., (AV) . . . . '48 '76 C.453 B.S. L.309 J.D. [Welsh&K.]
*PRACTICE AREAS: Intellectual Property.
Cherskov, Michael J., (AV) . . . . '58 '88 C.450 B.A. L.145 J.D. [Cherskov&F.]

Cherskov & Flaynik, (AV)
The Civic Opera Building, 20 North Wacker Drive, Suite 1447, 60606
Telephone: 312-621-1330 Telefax: 312-621-0088
Email: mail@cherskov.com
Members of Firm: Michael J. Cherskov; Donald G. Flaynik, Jr. Of Counsel: Charles Nissim-Sabat. Legal/Technical Support Personnel: Dana P. McDermott, Ph.D.; Albert Y. Tsui; Thomas J. Motzny; Jillian M. Szafranski.
Intellectual Property and Technology Related Law including Patents, Trademarks, Trade Secrets, Copyrights, Unfair Competition, Entertainment and Related Litigation.
See Professional Biographies, CHICAGO, ILLINOIS

Childs, Lisa C. . . . . '— '97 C.691 B.A. L.424 J.D. [Michael B.&F.]
*PRACTICE AREAS: Patents; Trademarks; Copyrights; Unfair Competition; Litigation.
Chinlund, Gregory J. . . . . '— '96 C.350 B.A. L.589 J.D. [Ⓐ Marshall,G.&B.]
*PRACTICE AREAS: Trademarks; Copyrights; Trade Secrets; Design Patents.
Christensen, Jon P. . . . . '48 '89 C.966 B.S.E.E. L.365 J.D. [Welsh&K.]
*PRACTICE AREAS: Intellectual Property.
Christus, Daniel N., (AV) . . . . '51 '80 C&L.966 B.S.Ch.E., J.D. [Wallenstein W.&R.]
*PRACTICE AREAS: Intellectual Property Law.
Chu, Michael P., (AV) . . . . '67 '92 C.339 B.S.M.E. L.945 J.D. [Brinks H.G.&L.]
*PRACTICE AREAS: Intellectual Property.
Churilla, Paul W. '65 '00 C.475 B.S. L.596 J.D.
(adm. in OR; not adm. in IL) [McDonnell B.H.&B.]
Clair, Edward E. . . . . '72 '99 C.436 B.S.E.E. L.46 J.D. [Fitch,E.T.&F.]
*PRACTICE AREAS: Intellectual Property; Patent Prosecution; Electrical Patents; Electronic Patents; Computer and Software Patents.
Clark, Jeffrey L., (AV) . . . . '53 '79 C.679 B.S. L.801 J.D. [Wood,P.K.C.&M.]
*PRACTICE AREAS: Patents; Trademarks; Copyrights.
Clise, Brian Sommer . . . . '72 '99 C.228 B.S.E. L.910 J.D. [Ⓐ Fitch,E.T.&F.]
*PRACTICE AREAS: Patent Prosecution; Patent Litigation; Mechanical Patents; Electrical Patents; Computer and Software Patents.
Cochran, Christine M. . . . . '77 '03 C.145 A.B. L.910 J.D. [Ⓐ Leydig,V.&M.]
Cohen, Eric D. . . . . '55 '93 C.107 B.S.E.E. L.201 J.D. [Welsh&K.]
*PRACTICE AREAS: Intellectual Property.
Collins, James A. . . . . '— '97 C.961 B.S.E.E. L.436 J.D. [Brinks H.G.&L.]
*PRACTICE AREAS: Intellectual Property; Copyrights; Patent Prosecution; Litigation.
Conklin, John B., (AV) . . . . '52 '78 C&L.930 B.S.E.E., J.D. [Leydig,V.&M.]
Conte, James B., (CV) . . . . '— '93 C.339 B.S. L.112 J.D. [Barnes&T.]
*PRACTICE AREAS: Unfair Competition; Patent Litigation; Trademark Litigation; Intellectual Property Portfolio Management.
Cook, Granger, Jr., (AV) . . . . '26 '55 C.597 B.S.E.E. L.477 J.D. [Cook,A.M.M.C.&M.]
*PRACTICE AREAS: Intellectual Property; Patent; Trademarks; Copyrights; Unfair Competition.

Cook, Alex, McFarron, Manzo, Cummings & Mehler, (AV)
200 West Adams, Suite 2850, 60606
Telephone: 312-236-8500 Fax: 312-236-8176
Email: firm@cammcm.com URL: http://www.cammcm.com
Granger Cook, Jr.; John L. Alex; Daniel M. Riess; Eugene M. Cummings; James S. Pristelski; Gary W. McFarron; Raymond M. Mehler; Edward D. Manzo; Joel H. Bock; Stephen B. Heller; David Lesht; Andrew G. Kolomayets; Mark J. Murphy; Michael J. McGee; David Michael Mundt. Associates: Renee C. Barthel; Panasarn Aim Jirut. Of Counsel: Fred S. Lockwood (P.C.); William H. Magidson; Daniel C. McEachran; Edward M. Keating.
Patent, Trademark, Copyright and Unfair Competition Law, Intellectual Property Practice.
See Professional Biographies, CHICAGO, ILLINOIS

Coons, Gordon R., (AV) . . . . '39 '65 C.350 B.S.Ch.E. L.276 J.D. [Leydig,V.&M.]
Cooperman, Marc S., (AV) . . . . '— '89 C&L.339 B.S., J.D. [Banner&W.]
*PRACTICE AREAS: Intellectual Property Law; Patents; Trademarks; Copyrights; Intellectual Property Litigation.
Cotton, Benjamin B. . . . . '76 '02 C.701 B.S.M.E. L.365 J.D. [Ⓐ Brinks H.G.&L.]
*PRACTICE AREAS: Intellectual Property.
Cox, Pamela L. . . . . '— '00 C.347 B.S. L.602 J.D. [Ⓐ Marshall,G.&B.]
*PRACTICE AREAS: Patent Prosecution; Patent Litigation.
Craane, Paul C. . . . . '— '93 C.339 B.S.M.E. L.589 J.D. [Marshall,G.&B.]
*PRACTICE AREAS: Intellectual Property Counseling; Intellectual Property Licensing; Intellectual Property Litigation; Patent Prosecution; Trademark Prosecution.
Crawford, Bradley W. . . . . '66 '03 C.339 B.S. L.146 J.D. [Ⓐ McDonnell B.H.&B.]
Cruz, Michael T. '— '97 C.339 B.S.E.E. L.477 J.D.
(adm. in CA; not adm. in IL) [Ⓐ McAndrews,H.&M.]
*PRACTICE AREAS: Intellectual Property; Patents.
Cummings, Eugene M., (AV) '41 '70 C.597 B.S.E.E. L.424 J.D.
[Cook,A.M.M.C.&M.]
*PRACTICE AREAS: Patent; Trademark; Copyright; Unfair Competition.
Curtis, Anthony P. . . . . '66 '03 C.453 B.S.E.E. L.424 J.D. [Ⓐ Brinks H.G.&L.]
*PRACTICE AREAS: Intellectual Property; Computer Technology; Information Technology; Electrical Intellectual Property; Electrical Patent Prosecution.
Cwik, Joseph E. . . . . '69 '95 C.339 B.S.C.E. L.365 J.D. [Welsh&K.]
*PRACTICE AREAS: Intellectual Property.
Dalal, Mirut P. . . . . '69 '97 C&L.846 B.S., J.D. [McAndrews,H.&M.]
*PRACTICE AREAS: Intellectual Property.
Daniel, Rodney A., (AV) . . . . '54 '85 C.679 B.S. L.339 J.D. [Brinks H.G.&L.]
*PRACTICE AREAS: Intellectual Property.
Dare, Heidi A. . . . . '— '02 C.20 B.A. L.912 J.D. [Ⓐ Brinks H.G.&L.]
*PRACTICE AREAS: Intellectual Property; Patent Prosecution; Biotechnology Patents; Licensing.
Dean, Jeffrey H. . . . . '— '92 C.145 A.B. L.309 J.D. [Marshall,G.&B.]
*PRACTICE AREAS: Litigation; Patent; Copyright; Trade Secrets; Biotechnology.
Delaney, Timothy Q., (AV) . . . . '60 '88 C.339 B.S. L.273 J.D. [Brinks H.G.&L.]
*PRACTICE AREAS: Patents; Intellectual Property; Litigation.
Depke, Robert J. . . . . '62 '92 C.339 B.S.E.E. L.424 J.D. [Trexler,B.G.B.&M.]
Dockrey, J. William . . . . '53 '96 C.793 B.S. L.365 J.D. [Ⓒ Brinks H.G.&L.]
*PRACTICE AREAS: Patent Law.
Docter, Stephen H. . . . . '64 '99 C.424 B.A. L.365 J.D. [McDonnell B.H.&B.]
Donovan, Thomas J. . . . . '— '87 C.339 B.S.M.E. L.146 J.D. [Barnes&T.]
*PRACTICE AREAS: Intellectual Property; Patents; Trademarks; Copyrights; Trade Secrets.
Dossas, Vasilios (Bill) D., (AV) . . . . '52 '82 C.339 B.S. L.424 J.D. [Niro,S.H.&N.]
*PRACTICE AREAS: Intellectual Property; Litigation; Patent and Trademark Prosecution; Counseling.
***Drehkoff, W. Dennis**, (AV) . . . . '46 '72 C.999 B.S. L.502 J.D. [Ⓐ Ladas&P.]*
Drutchas, Grantland G. . . . . '61 '85 C.453 B.S.M.E. L.477 J.D. [McDonnell B.H.&B.]
Dudley, Allison . . . . '— '02 C.339 B.S.M.E. L.146 J.D. [Ⓐ Baniak P.&G.]
*PRACTICE AREAS: Intellectual Property; Litigation; Intellectual Property Licensing; Patent Prosecution.
Duffy, Meggan F. . . . . '73 '98 C.339 B.S. L.424 J.D. [Ⓒ Marshall,G.&B.]
*PRACTICE AREAS: Intellectual Property.
Duk, Jennifer M. . . . . '72 '02 C.1260 B.S. L.424 J.D. [Ⓐ Leydig,V.&M.]

Duncan, Jeffery M., (AV) . . . . '56 '84 C&L.101 B.S., J.D. [Brinks H.G.&L.]
*PRACTICE AREAS: Intellectual Property Licensing; Chemical Intellectual Property; Pharmaceutical Intellectual Property; Biotechnology; Intellectual Property.
Duston, Thomas L., (AV) . . . . '— '87 C.178 B.A. L.1065 J.D. [Marshall,G.&B.]
*PRACTICE AREAS: Intellectual Property Litigation; Patent Litigation; Theft of Trade Secrets; Trademark Litigation.
Elliott, Merle . . . . '78 '03 C.188 B.S. L.276 J.D. [Ⓐ McAndrews,H.&M.]
*PRACTICE AREAS: Intellectual Property; Patent Litigation; Chemical Patents.
Elliott, Thomas C., Jr., (BV) . . . . '55 '81 C.210 B.A. L.146 J.D. [Wallenstein W.&R.]
*PRACTICE AREAS: Intellectual Property Litigation; Intellectual Property Counseling.

Emrich & Dithmar LLC, (AV)
125 South Wacker Drive, Suite 2080, 60606-4401
Telephone: 312-663-9800 FAX: 312-663-9822
URL: http://www.emrichdithmar.com
Members of Firm: Paul L. Brown; James J. Hill; Harry M. Levy; Robert R. Caliri; Thomas E. Hill; Jonathan J. Krit.
Patent, Trademark, Copyright, and Unfair Competition Law. Trials and Appeals before Federal and State Courts and Governmental Agencies.
See Professional Biographies, CHICAGO, ILLINOIS

Engling, Timothy J. . . . . '— '95 C.870 B.S. L.146 J.D. [Barnes&T.]
*PRACTICE AREAS: Intellectual Property Law; Patents; Trademarks; Copyrights; Litigation.
Ertel, Patrick D., (AV) . . . . '— '73 C.602 B.S.A.E. L.597 J.D. [Marshall,G.&B.]
*PRACTICE AREAS: Intellectual Property Licensing; Intellectual Property Litigation; Intellectual Property Counseling; Electro-Mechanical Patents; Mechanical Patents.
Even, Francis A., (AV) . . . . '20 '49 C.339 B.S.M.E. L.273 J.D. [Fitch,E.T.&F.]
*PRACTICE AREAS: Intellectual Property Law; Litigation; Appellate Practice; Mechanical; Electro-Mechanical.
Fairchild, Jeffery N. . . . . '62 '97 C.339 B.S.M.E. L.365 J.D. [Wood,P.K.C.&M.]
*PRACTICE AREAS: Patents; Trademarks; Copyrights.
Fairhall, Thomas A., (AV) . . . . '59 '91 C.174 B.A. L.365 J.D. [McDonnell B.H.&B.]
Favakeh, Stephen S. . . . . '64 '91 C.862 B.S. L.339 J.D. [Fitch,E.T.&F.]
*PRACTICE AREAS: Intellectual Property; Electromechanical; Mechanical; Infringement; Patents.
Feigelson, Aaron R. . . . . '69 '02 C.477 A.B. L.145 J.D. [Ⓐ Leydig,V.&M.]
Feldman, Steven E. . . . . '70 '95 C.597 B.S.M.Sc. L.273 J.D. [Welsh&K.]
*PRACTICE AREAS: Intellectual Property.
Ferguson, Kevin P. . . . . '— '99 C.894 A.B. L.477 J.F. [Ⓐ Jones D.]
Fieseler, Robert W., (AV) . . . . '55 '84 C.688 B.S. L.424 J.D. [McAndrews,H.&M.]
Filarski, Thomas J., (AV) . . . . '56 '86 C.424 B.A. L.209 J.D. [Brinks H.G.&L.]
*PRACTICE AREAS: Intellectual Property; Patents; Chemical; Biotechnology and Pharmaceutical; Internet/E-Commerce.
Fineman, Marc E. . . . . '70 '96 C.705 B.S. L.365 J.D. [Ⓐ Kegan&K.]
*PRACTICE AREAS: Patents; Computer Law; Trademarks; Copyrights; Inventions.
Fink, Karl R., (BV) . . . . '56 '81 C&L.477 B.S.E., J.D. [Fitch,E.T.&F.]
*PRACTICE AREAS: Civil Litigation; Trial Practice; Intellectual Property Litigation; Patent Litigation; Trademark Litigation.
Fitch, Morgan L., Jr., (AV) . . . . '22 '49 C.46 B.S. L.477 J.D. [Fitch,E.T.&F.]
*PRACTICE AREAS: Intellectual Property Law; Technology and Science; Licensing; Patents; Trademarks.

Fitch, Even, Tabin & Flannery, (AV) BB
120 South La Salle, Suite 1600, 60603 ⊙
Telephone: 312-577-7000 Fax: 312-577-7007
Email: email@fitcheven.com URL: http://www.fitcheven.com
Members of Firm: Morgan L. Fitch, Jr.; Francis A. Even; Julius Tabin; John F. Flannery; Robert B. Jones; James J. Schumann (Resident, San Diego, California Office); James J. Hamill; Timothy E. Levstik; Joseph E. Shipley; Kenneth H. Samples; Philip T. Petti; Richard A. Kaba (Not admitted in IL); Karl R. Fink; Mark W. Hetzler; Timothy P. Maloney; James P. Krueger; Stephen S. Favakeh; Richard E. Wawrzyniak (Resident, San Diego, California Office); Steven G. Parmelee (Not admitted in IL; Resident at Omaha, Nebraska Office); Thomas F. Lebens; Kendrew H. Colton (Resident, Washington, D.C. Office); G. Paul Edgell (Resident, Washington, D.C. Office); Michael A. Sanzo, Ph.D. (Resident, Washington, D.C. Office); Scott J. Menghini (Resident, San Diego, California Office); Norman Kunitz (Resident, Washington, D.C. Office); Ramon R. Hoch (Not admitted in IL; Also at Washington, D.C. Office); John D. Bauersfeld (Resident, Woodland Hills, California Office); Gary D. Mann (Resident, Woodland Hills, California Office); Edward E. Clair; Samuel P. Burkholder (Not admitted in IL); David W. Maher, Ph.D. (Not admitted in IL); John J. Gresens. Of Counsel: George H. Spencer (Resident, Washington, D.C. Office);—Brian Sommer Clise; Martin R. Bader (Resident, San Diego, California Office); Timothy R. Baumann; Nicholas T. Peters; Grace Law O'Brien; Christine A. Abuel; Joel H. Bootzin; James M. Wakely.
Intellectual Property and Technology-Related Law including United States and International Patents, Trademarks, Trade Secret, Copyrights and Unfair Competition, Antitrust and International Trade Commission Causes and Related Litigation.
San Diego, California Office: 9276 Scranton Road, Suite 250, 92121. Telephone: 858-552-1311. Telecopier: 858-552-0095.
San Luis Obispo, California Office: 1010 Peach Street, 93406-0031. Telephone: 805-541-2800. Fax: 805-541-2802.
Washington, D.C. Office: Suite 1801 K Street, N.W., Suite 401L, 20006-1201. Telephone: 202-419-7000. Fax: 202-419-7007.
Boulder, Colorado Office: 1942 Broadway, Suite 213, 80302. Telephone: 303-402-6966. Fax: 303-402-6970.
Los Angeles, California Office: Warner Center Towers, Suite 780, 21800 Oxnard Street, Woodland Hills, California, 91367. Telephone: 818-715-7025. Fax: 818-715-7033.
See Professional Biographies, CHICAGO, ILLINOIS

Fitzpatrick, Michael J. . . . . '76 '01 C.339 B.S. L.893 J.D. [Ⓐ McAndrews,H.&M.]
*PRACTICE AREAS: Intellectual Property.
Flachsbart, William W. . . . . '67 '96 C.145 B.S. L.424 J.D. [Niro,S.H.&N.]
*PRACTICE AREAS: Intellectual Property; Intellectual Property Litigation; Technology Law.
Flannery, John F., (AV) . . . . '28 '59 C.339 B.S.E.E. L.424 J.D. [Fitch,E.T.&F.]
*PRACTICE AREAS: Intellectual Property Law; Appellate Practice; Litigation; Technical Litigation; Licensing Law.
Flaynik, Donald G., Jr. . . . . '52 '80 C.339 B.S.E.E. L.146 J.D. [Cherskov&F.]
Flerlage, Joseph W. . . . . '— '00 C.339 B.S.E.E. L.209 J.D. [Ⓐ Brinks H.G.&L.]
*PRACTICE AREAS: Intellectual Property; Patent Prosecution; Copyrights; Litigation; Electrical and Computer.
Flom, Erik B. . . . . '63 '98 C.323 B.S. L.597 J.D. [Welsh&K.]
*PRACTICE AREAS: Intellectual Property.
Flowers, Kevin M. . . . . '— '97 C&L.608 B.S., J.D. [Marshall,G.&B.]
*PRACTICE AREAS: Intellectual Property Litigation; Biotechnology Patents; Patent Litigation.
Foley, James R. . . . . '69 '95 C.339 B.S. L.365 J.D. [Trexler,B.G.B.&M.]
*PRACTICE AREAS: Intellectual Property; Patent, Trademark and Copyright Law; Trade Secrets; Unfair Competition.
Frankel, William H., (AV) . . . . '55 '80 C&L.861 B.S.M.E., J.D. [Brinks H.G.&L.]
*PRACTICE AREAS: Intellectual Property Litigation and Counseling; Patent Litigation; Copyright Litigation; Trademark Litigation; Unfair Competition.
Frantzen, Sandra A. . . . . '74 '99 C.350 B.S. L.145 J.D. [McAndrews,H.&M.]
*PRACTICE AREAS: Intellectual Property.
Freeman, John C., (BV) . . . . '59 '90 C.339 B.S. L.273 J.D. [Brinks H.G.&L.]
*PRACTICE AREAS: Patent Prosecution; Patent Applications; Patent Litigation; Patent Licensing; Computer and Software Patents.
Friedman, Leonard . . . . '48 '79 C.696 B.S.E.E. L.145 J.D. [Welsh&K.]
*PRACTICE AREAS: Intellectual Property.
Frischkorn, David M., (AV) '57 '89 C.112 B.S.Ch.E. L.209 J.D.
[McDonnell B.H.&B.]
Fulton, Brady J. . . . . '70 '96 C.424 B.A. L.146 J.D. [Niro,S.H.&N.]
*PRACTICE AREAS: Commercial Litigation; Intellectual Property.
Gabric, Ralph J., (AV) . . . . '62 '88 C.93 B.S. L.209 J.D. [Brinks H.G.&L.]
*PRACTICE AREAS: Intellectual Property; Litigation; Trials; Copyright; Interference.

Gabrielides, John T., (AV) '63 '88 C.339 B.A. L.209 J.D. [Brinks H.G.&L.]
*PRACTICE AREAS: Intellectual Property Litigation; Intellectual Property Counseling.
Gagala, Bruce M., (AV) '52 '77 C.221 B.A. L.46 J.D. [Leydig,V.&M.]
Gallagher, Priscilla F., (BV) '58 '84 C.578 B.A. L.424 J.D. [McAndrews,H.&M.]
*PRACTICE AREAS: Intellectual Property.
Gamson, Edward P., (AV) '43 '78 C.855 B.S. L.365 J.D. [Welsh&K.]
*PRACTICE AREAS: Intellectual Property.
Gannon, Michael D. '65 '91 C&L.436 B.S.E.E., J.D. [Baniak P.&G.]
*PRACTICE AREAS: Litigation; Intellectual Property; Licensing; Trademarks; Copyrights.
Gasey, Arthur A. '67 '92 C.602 B.S. L.365 J.D. [Niro,S.H.&N.]
*PRACTICE AREAS: Litigation; Intellectual Property Law.
Gass, David A. '— '92 C.477 B.S. L.1066 J.D. [Marshall,G.&B.]
*PRACTICE AREAS: Medical Intellectual Property; Biotechnology Patent Prosecution; Biotechnology Patents; Medical Patents; Molecular Biology Patents.
Gattari, Patrick G. '62 '92 C.477 B.S. L.802 J.D. [McDonnell B.H.&B.]
Gauri, Vineet '— '97 C.477 B.S. L.94 J.D. [Brinks H.G.&L.]
*PRACTICE AREAS: Intellectual Property; Patent Litigation.
Geimer, Stephen D., (AV) '52 '77 C.339 B.S.M.E. L.424 J.D. [Wood,P.K.C.&M.]
*PRACTICE AREAS: Patents.
Genin, Kent E. '66 '93 C.813 B.S.E.E. L.150 J.D. [Brinks H.G.&L.]
*PRACTICE AREAS: Intellectual Property.
George, Christopher N. '— '02 C&L.339 B.S., J.D. [🄰 McAndrews,H.&M.]
*PRACTICE AREAS: Intellectual Property.
Geren, Gerald S., (AV) '— '66 [🄲 Barnes&T.]
*PRACTICE AREAS: Intellectual Property Law; Patents; Trademarks; Copyrights; Litigation.
Gerstein, Allen H., (AV) '— '63 C.339 B.S. L.597 J.D. [🄲 Marshall,G.&B.]
*PRACTICE AREAS: Intellectual Property Infringement; Intellectual Property Litigation; Proprietary Rights; Trademark Licensing; Trademark Litigation.
Gerstein, Robert M., (AV) '— '88 C&L.477 B.S.E., J.D. [Marshall,G.&B.]
*PRACTICE AREAS: Licensing; Intellectual Property Counseling and Opinions; Intellectual Property Litigation; Computer and Software Patents; Electro-Mechanical Patents.
Giangiorgi, Richard A., (AV) '39 '67 C.436 B.S.M.E. L.276 J.D. [Trexler,B.G.B.&M.]
*PRACTICE AREAS: Intellectual Property; Patent, Trademark and Copyright Law; Trade Secrets Law; Unfair Competition Law.
Gibbons, Paul C. '67 '97 C.971 B.S.E.E. L.818 J.D. [Niro,S.H.&N.]
*PRACTICE AREAS: Patent Litigation; Intellectual Property Law.
Gnoffo, Vincent J. '69 '98 C.339 B.S.E.E. L.365 J.D. [🄰 Brinks H.G.&L.]
*PRACTICE AREAS: Intellectual Property; Patent Prosecution; Electrical and Computer; Litigation.
Golant, Joseph H., (AV⑦) '— '66 C.399 B.S. L.145 J.D. [🄲 Jones D.]
Graham, Michael R., (BV) '— '86 C.473 B.S. L.262 J.D. [Marshall,G.&B.]
*PRACTICE AREAS: Internet Law; International Trademarks; Trademark Litigation; Trademark Protection; Trademark Registration.
Gray, Jeffrey R. '— '88 C.146 B.S.C.E. L.365 J.D. [Barnes&T.]
*PRACTICE AREAS: Intellectual Property Law; Patents; Trademarks; Copyrights; Litigation.
Green, Raymond W., (AV) '40 '66 C&L.477 B.S., J.D. [Brinks H.G.&L.]
*PRACTICE AREAS: Patents; Litigation.
Green, Robert F., (AV) '49 '74 C.339 B.S.Chem. L.365 J.D. [Leydig,V.&M.]
Greenfield, Michael S. '60 '92 C.339 B.S. L.813 J.D. [McDonnell B.H.&B.]
Greenspoon, Robert P. '70 '95 C.145 A.B. L.477 J.D. [Niro,S.H.&N.]
*PRACTICE AREAS: Patent Litigation; Patent Prosecution.
Gresens, John J. '59 '86 C.723 B.S. L.300 J.D. [Fitch,E.T.&F.]
Griffith, Christopher T. '59 '88 C.475 B.S.Ch.E. L.326 J.D. [Leydig,V.&M.]
Groetken, Troy A. '70 '97 C&L.221 B.S., J.D. [McAndrews,H.&M.]
*PRACTICE AREAS: Patents; Trademarks; Copyrights; Intellectual Property Litigation.
Grubner, Judith L., (AV) '51 '76 C.604 A.B. L.273 J.D. [Michael B.&F.]
*PRACTICE AREAS: Intellectual Property; Unfair Competition Law; Sweepstakes Law; Litigation; Licensing.
Gryzlo, Matthew J. '69 '97 C.339 B.S.M.E. L.365 J.D, [Wallenstein W.&R.]
*PRACTICE AREAS: Intellectual Property Law.
Gumina, James C., (AV) '59 '87 C.602 B.S. L.365 J.D. [McDonnell B.H.&B.]
Gupta, Rashmi V. '— '01 C&L.494 B.S., J.D. [🄰 Marshall,G.&B.]
*PRACTICE AREAS: Chemical Patent Prosecution; Litigation.
Gurak, Richard J. '65 '97 C.339 B.S. L.365 J.D. [🄰 Welsh&K.]
*PRACTICE AREAS: Intellectual Property.
Gurfinkel, Daniel M., (BV) '61 '87 C.339 B.S.C.E. L.1119 J.D. [🄰 Welsh&K.]
*PRACTICE AREAS: Intellectual Property.
Hackett, Dennis P. '— '02 C.757 B.A. L.209 J.D. [🄰 McAndrews,H.&M.]
*PRACTICE AREAS: Intellectual Property Law; Intellectual Property Litigation; Patent Prosecution.
Hafertepe, James M. '69 '95 C.339 B.S.A.A.E. L.145 J.D. [McAndrews,H.&M.]
Haigh, Christopher E. '— '00 C.679 B.S.E. L.345 J.D.
(adm. in IN; not adm. in IL) [🄰 Baniak P.&G.]
*PRACTICE AREAS: Patent Litigation; Trademark Litigation; Copyright Litigation; Trade Secrets Litigation; Patents Procurement and Analyses.
Haller, Timothy J., (AV) '46 '75 C.158 B.S.M.E. L.276 J.D. [Niro,S.H.&N.]
*PRACTICE AREAS: Patent, Trade Secret, Antitrust, Trademark and Copyright Litigation.
Hamill, James J., (AV) '33 '61 C.277 B.M.E. L.273 LL.B. [Fitch,E.T.&F.]
*PRACTICE AREAS: Intellectual Property Law; Licensing Law; Litigation; Patents; Trademarks.
Hampton, Steven J., (AV) '51 '86 C.339 B.S. L.146 J.D. [McAndrews,H.&M.]
Harding, Joseph F. '69 '00 C.679 B.S.M.E. L.477 J.D. [McAndrews,H.&M.]
*PRACTICE AREAS: Intellectual Property; Patent Litigation; Patent Prosecution.
Harkins, Christopher A. '65 '91 C.338 B.S. L.339 J.D. [🄲 Brinks H.G.&L.]
*PRACTICE AREAS: General Practice; Federal Litigation; Patent Litigation; Trade Secrets.
Harlin, Michael B. '68 '96 C.976 B.S. L.146 J.D. [McAndrews,H.&M.]
*PRACTICE AREAS: Chemical Intellectual Property; Intellectual Property Licensing; Pharmaceutical Intellectual Property; Biotechnology Patents; Chemical Patents.
Harper, David S. '61 '98 C.589 B.A. L.146 J.D. [McDonnell B.H.&B.]
Hart, Herbert D., III, (AV) '52 '77 C.347 B.A. L.1119 J.D. [McAndrews,H.&M.]
*PRACTICE AREAS: Patent Interference Practice; Patent Infringement; Litigation; Licensing; Chemical Patents.
Hartmann, H. Michael, (AV) '48 '76 C.171 B.S. L.209 J.D. [Leydig,V.&M.]
Hartzell, Julianne '— '01 C.228 B.S. L.477 J.D. [🄰 Marshall,G.&B.]
Hasan, Salim A. '67 '93 C&L.347 B.A., J.D. [Leydig,V.&M.]
Hawkins, Brent A. '71 '97 C.477 B.S.E.E. L.339 J.D. [Wallenstein W.&R.]
*PRACTICE AREAS: Intellectual Property Law.
Headrick, David D. '66 '93 C.436 B.S.E.E. L.494 J.D. [McAndrews,H.&M.]
Heffner, Anastasia '69 '00 C.339 B.S. L.209 J.D. [🄰 Brinks H.G.&L.]
*PRACTICE AREAS: Patent Prosecution; Electro-Mechanical Patents; Patent Litigation; Copyright Litigation; Copyright Prosecution.
Hefner, M. Daniel '67 '96 C.340 B.A. L.339 J.D. [Leydig,V.&M.]
Held, John J., (AV) '38 '65 C.679 B.S.M.E. L.276 J.D. [McAndrews,H.&M.]
*PRACTICE AREAS: Patents; Trademarks; Copyrights; Trade Secrets; Unfair Competition.
Heller, Stephen B., (AV) '55 '80 C.350 B.S.Aero E. L.339 J.D. [Cook,A.M.M.C.&M.]
*PRACTICE AREAS: Intellectual Property; Patents; Trademarks; Unfair Competition.
Heppermann, Roger A. '— '92 C.502 B.S. L.597 J.D. [Marshall,G.&B.]
*PRACTICE AREAS: Intellectual Property Licensing; Intellectual Property Litigation; Computer and Software Patents; Electrical Patent Prosecution; Patent Infringement.
Hesterberg, Brett A., (AV) '59 '84 C&L.339 B.S.E.E., J.D. [Leydig,V.&M.]
Hetz, Joseph F. '72 '96 C.597 B.S.E.E. L.477 J.D. [Brinks H.G.&L.]
Hetzler, Mark W., (AV) '66 '93 C.597 B.S.M.E L.424 J.D. [Fitch,E.T.&F.]
*PRACTICE AREAS: Intellectual Property Law; Litigation; Patents; Trademarks; Copyrights.
Hierl, Michael A., (AV) '53 '80 C.801 B.S. L.365 J.D. [Olson&H.]
Hill, James J., (AV) '37 '65 C.436 B.E.E. L.209 J.D. [Emrich&D.]
*PRACTICE AREAS: Patents; Trademarks; Copyrights.
Hill, Thomas E., (AV) '44 '78 C.927 B.S. L.273 J.D. [Emrich&D.]
*PRACTICE AREAS: Patents; Trademarks; Copyrights.
Hillman, Lisa M. W. '— '99 L.260 J.D. [McDonnell B.H.&B.]
Himelhoch, Richard C. '63 '90 C&L.966 B.S., J.D. [Wallenstein W.&R.]
*PRACTICE AREAS: Intellectual Property Law.
Hind, Anthony S. '— '99 C.1059 B.A. L.424 J.D. [🄰 Marshall,G.&B.]
Hirsch, Martin J. '— '85 C&L.339 B.S., J.D. [Marshall,G.&B.]
*PRACTICE AREAS: Internet Law; Electronic Commerce; Computer Software Law; Computer Law; Software Protection.
Hoch, Ramon R. '59 '91 C.378 B.S.Ch.E. L.1209 J.D.
(adm. in VA; not adm. in IL) [Fitch,E.T.&F.] (⊙Wash., DC)
*PRACTICE AREAS: Intellectual Property.
Hofer, Roy E., (AV) '35 '61 C.679 B.Ch.E. L.276 J.D. [Brinks H.G.&L.]
*PRACTICE AREAS: Intellectual Property.
Hoffman, Richard B., (AV) '— '73 C.339 B.S.G.E. L.209 J.D. [Marshall,G.&B.]
*PRACTICE AREAS: Intellectual Property Litigation; Patent Infringement; Patent Prosecution; Mechanical Patents; Licensing.
Hogg, Kevin D., (AV) '— '84 C&L.150 B.S.M.E., J.D. [Marshall,G.&B.]
*PRACTICE AREAS: Intellectual Property Litigation.
Holt, Thomas L. '71 '97 C.502 B.S. L.424 J.D. [Brinks H.G.&L.]
Hood, Gary E. '— '96 C.800 B.S.E.E. L.285 J.D. [🄲 Baniak P.&G.]
*PRACTICE AREAS: Intellectual Property; Litigation; Patents; Copyrights; Trademarks.
Hoover, Allen E., (AV) '— '93 C&L.339 B.S., J.D. [Banner&W.]
Hoover, Allen J., (AV) '40 '65 C.436 B.M.E. L.209 J.D. [Wood,P.K.C.&M.]
*PRACTICE AREAS: Patents; Trademarks; Copyrights.
Horie, Tadashi '— '98 C.688 M.B.A. L.424 J.D. [Brinks H.G.&L.]
*PRACTICE AREAS: Intellectual Property.
Hosteny, Joseph N., III, (AV) '45 '76 C.436 B.S.M.E. L.209 J.D. [Niro,S.H.&N.]
*PRACTICE AREAS: Trade Secrets; Patents; Trademarks; Copyright Litigation.
Hosty, Gretchen M. '— '03 C.339 B.S. L.146 J.D. [🄰 Michael B.&F.]
*PRACTICE AREAS: Intellectual Property.
Hoyle, Patricia M. '— '00 C.054 Ph.D. L.966 J.D.
(adm. in WI; not adm. in IL) [🄰 Ladas&P.]
Hughes, A. Blair '58 '91 C.701 B.S. L.209 J.D. [McDonnell B.H.&B.]
Hulbert, Bradley J., (AV) '52 '77 C&L.494 B.E.E., J.D. [McDonnell B.H.&B.]
Hwang, Sharon A. '68 '93 C.339 B.S. L.93 J.D. [McAndrews,H.&M.]
*PRACTICE AREAS: Patent Litigation; Electrical Patents; Mechanical Patents; Medical Patents; Patent Prosecution.
Irvine, Robert J., III '62 '94 C.339 B.S. L.597 J.D. [McDonnell B.H.&B.]
Izraelewicz, Mark H. '— '01 C.107 B.S. L.145 J.D. [🄰 Marshall,G.&B.]
*PRACTICE AREAS: Patent; Copyright; Trademark.
Jacover, Jerold A., (AV) '45 '72 C.966 B.S.E.E. L.276 J.D. [Brinks H.G.&L.]
Jani, Maitreya P. '74 '99 C.339 B.S.G.E. L.273 J.D. [🄰 Welsh&K.]
*PRACTICE AREAS: Intellectual Property.
Janka, John C., (BV) '50 '87 C.46 B.S. L.145 J.D. [Niro,S.H.&N.]
*PRACTICE AREAS: Trade Secret, Patent, Trademark and Copyright Litigation.
Jarvis, Lawrence M., (AV) '50 '77 C.339 B.S.E.E. L.128 J.D. [McAndrews,H.&M.]
Jirut, Panasarn Aim '78 '04 C.880 B.E. L.209 J.D. [🄰 Cook,A.M.M.C.&M.]
*PRACTICE AREAS: Intellectual Property; Patents; Trademarks; Copyrights; Unfair Competition.
Johnson, Harold V., (AV) '56 '84 C.474 B.S.E.E. L.982 J.D. [Brinks H.G.&L.]
*PRACTICE AREAS: Patent Prosecution and Counseling; Antitrust Litigation.
Jones, Robert B., (AV) '32 '60 C.350 B.S. L.477 J.D. [Fitch,E.T.&F.]
*PRACTICE AREAS: Intellectual Property Law; Intellectual Property Arbitration; Trademark Arbitration; Technology and Science; Chemical Litigation.

Jones Day, (AV)
77 West Wacker, 60601-1692 ⊙
Telephone: 312-782-3939 Telecopier: 312-782-8585
Email: counsel@jonesday.com URL: http://www.jonesday.com
Languages: French, German, Hebrew, Hindi, Korean, Marathi, Russian, Serbo-Croatian, Spanish, and Ukrainian.
Members of Firm in Chicago: Ronald A. Sandler; David L. Witcoff. Of Counsel: Joseph H. Golant; John A. Marlott; James B. Raden. Counsel: Sandra Byster Weiss. Associates: Stacy A. Baim; Marc S. Blackman; Kevin P. Ferguson; Matthew D. Kellam; Brian J. Murray; Krista S. Schwartz.
Patent, Trademark and Copyright Law.
In Atlanta, Georgia: 1420 Peachtree Street, N.E., Suite 800. Telephone: 404-521-3939. Telecopier: 404-581-8330.
In Beijing, China: 3201 China World Tower 1, No. 1 Jianguomenwai Avenue. Telephone: 86-10-5866-1111. Telecopier: 86-10-5866-1122.
In Brussels, Belgium: Boulevard Brand Whitlocklaan 165, 1200 Brussels. Telephone: 32-2-645-14-11. Telecopier: 32-2-645-14-45.
In Cleveland, Ohio: North Point, 901 Lakeside Avenue. Telephone: 216-586-3939. Telecopier: 216-579-0212.
In Columbus, Ohio: 325 John H. McConnell Boulevard, Suite 600. Telephone: 614-469-3939. Telecopier: 614-461-4198.
In Dallas, Texas: 2727 North Harwood Street. Telephone: 214-220-3939. Telecopier: 214-969-5100.
In Frankfurt, Germany: Hochhaus am Park, Grüneburgweg 102, 60323 Frankfurt am Main. Telephone: 49-69-9726-3939. Telecopier: 49-69-9726-3993.
In Hong Kong, China: 31st Floor, Edinburgh Tower, The Landmark, 15 Queen's Road, Central. Telephone: 852-2526-6895. Telecopier: 852-2868-5871.
In Houston, Texas: 717 Texas, Suite 3300. Telephone: 832-239-3939. Telecopier: 832-239-3600.
In Irvine, California: 3 Park Plaza, Suite 1100. Telephone: 949-851-3939. Telecopier: 949-553-7539.
In London, England: 21 Tudor Street. Telephone: 44-20-7039-5959. Telecopier: 44-20-7039-5999.
In Los Angeles, California: 555 South Flower Street, Fiftieth Floor. Telephone: 213-489-3939. Telecopier: 213-243-2539.
In Madrid, Spain: Velázquez 51, 4th Floor. Telephone: 34-91-520-39-39. Telecopier: 34-91-520-39-38.
In Menlo Park, California: 2882 Sand Hill Road, Suite 240. Telephone: 650-739-3939. Telecopier: 650-739-3900.
In Milan, Italy: Via Turati, 16/18. Telephone: 39-02-7645-4001. Telecopier: 39-02-7645-4400.
In Moscow, Russia: Smolenskaya Square 3, 9th Floor, 121099 Moscow. Telephone: 7-095-980-6769. Telecopier: 7-095-980-6765.
In Munich, Germany: Prinzregentenstr. 11, 80538 Munich. Telephone: 089-20 60 42-200. Telecopier: 089-20 60 42-293.
In New York, New York: 222 East 41st Street. Telephone: 212-326-3939. Telecopier: 212-755-7306.
In Paris, France: 120, rue du Faubourg Saint-Honoré. Telephone: 33-1-56-59-39-39. Telecopier: 33-1-56-59-39-38.
In Pittsburgh, Pennsylvania: 500 Grant Street, One Mellon Bank Center, 31st Floor. Telephone: 412-391-3939. Telecopier: 412-394-7959.
In San Diego, California: 12750 High Bluff Drive, Suite 300. Telephone: 858-314-1200. Telecopier: 858-314-1150.
In San Francisco, California: 555 California Street, 26th Floor. Telephone: 415-626-3939. Telecopier: 415-875-5700.
In Shanghai, China: 30th Floor, Shanghai Kerry Centre, 1515 Nanjing Road West. Telephone: 86-21-2201-8000. Telecopier: 86-21-5298-6569.
In Singapore, Singapore: 30 Cecil Street, #29-01 Prudential Tower. Telephone: 65 6 538 3939. Telecopier: 65 6 536 3939.
In Sydney, Australia: Australia Square, Level 38, 264-278 George Street. Telephone: 61-2-8272-0500. Telecopier: 61-2-8272-0599.
In Taipei, Taiwan: 6th Floor, 2 Tun Hwa South Road, Section 2. Telephone: (886-2) 2704-6808 or (886-2) 7712-3399. Telecopier: (886-2) 2704-6791.
In Tokyo, Japan: Shiroyama MT Building, 6th Floor, 1-17 Toranomon 4-chome, Minato-ku, Tokyo 105-0001. Telephone: 81-3-3433-3939. Telecopier: 81-3-5401-2725.
In Washington, D.C.: 51 Louisiana Avenue, N.W. Telephone: 202-879-3939. Telecopier: 202-626-1700.
See Professional Biographies, CHICAGO, ILLINOIS

Joy, Mark, (AV) '65 '90 C.339 B.S. L.477 J.D. [Leydig,V.&M.]

Kaba, Richard A. '47 '89 C.160 B.S. L.477 J.D.
(adm. in MI; not adm. in IL) [Fitch,E.T.&F.]
*PRACTICE AREAS: Biochemical Technology; Biomedical Technology; Biotechnology Licensing; Genetics; Immunology.

Kaplan, Richard A., (AV) ... '57 '82 C.674 B.S.E. L.982 J.D. [Brinks H.G.&L.]
*PRACTICE AREAS: Intellectual Property Litigation; Patents; Trade Secrets.

Katz, A. Sidney, (AV) ... '39 '66 C.46 B.S.E.E. L.273 J.D. [Welsh&K.] ⊙
*PRACTICE AREAS: Intellectual Property.

Katz, James L. ... '68 '98 C.477 B.S.C.E. L.347 J.D. [Brinks H.G.&L.]
*PRACTICE AREAS: Intellectual Property; Patent Prosecution; Patent Opinions; Litigation; Electrical and Computer.

Katz, Martin L. ... '42 '68 C.690 B.S. L.276 J.D. [Wood,P.K.C.&M.] (⊙Arlington, VA)
*PRACTICE AREAS: Patents; Trademarks; Copyrights; Intellectual Property Licensing.

Kawula, Walter J., Jr. ... '63 '94 C.339 B.S.E.E. L.146 J.D. [Welsh&K.]
*PRACTICE AREAS: Intellectual Property.

Keating, Edward M., (AV) ... '30 '60 C.46 B.S. L.209 J.D. [Ⓒ Cook,A.M.M.C.&M.]
*PRACTICE AREAS: Patent, Trademark and Copyright Law; Unfair Competition Causes.

Kegan, Daniel L., (AV) ... '44 '84 C.821 B.S. L.597 J.D. [Kegan&K.]
*PRACTICE AREAS: Computer Law; Intellectual Property; Business; Litigation; Trademarks.

Kegan & Kegan, Ltd., (AV)
79 West Monroe Street, Suite 1320, 60603-4969
Telephone: 312-782-6495 Fax: 312-782-6494
Email: info@KeganLaw.com URL: http://www.KeganLaw.com
Esther O. Kegan (1913-2000); Daniel L. Kegan;—Marc E. Fineman.
U.S. and International Patents, Trademarks, Copyrights, Computers, Internet, Information Technology, Licensing, Unfair Trade Practices, Advertising Matters, Federal Litigation, Counsel to Counsel.

See Professional Biographies, CHICAGO, ILLINOIS

Kellam, Matthew D. ... '— '01 C.602 B.S. L.1119 J.D. [Ⓐ Jones D.]

Kelly, Adam G. ... '— '02 C.347 B.A. L.365 J.D. [Ⓐ Marshall,G.&B.]
*PRACTICE AREAS: Biotechnology; Chemistry; Chemical Engineering; Litigation; Patent Prosecution.

Kenney, Dolores T., (AV) ... '— '84 C.719 B.S. L.146 J.D. [Olson&H.]

Khodosh, Vladimir ... '— '02 C&L.339 B.A., J.D. [Ⓐ Barnes&T.]
*PRACTICE AREAS: Intellectual Property; Computers and Software; Copyrights; Patents; Intellectual Property Licensing.

Kilyk, John, Jr., (AV) ... '59 '83 C.385 B.A.Chem. L.276 J.D. [Leydig,V.&M.]

Kinne, Charles C., (AV) ... '58 '84 C.696 B.S. L.846 J.D. [Baniak P.&G.]
*PRACTICE AREAS: Patent, Trademark, Copyright and Trade Secret Litigation; Patent, Trademark and Copyright Procurement and Analyses.

Kitzinger, Paige A. ... '68 '94 C.436 B.S. L.209 J.D. [Trexler,B.G.B.&M.]
*PRACTICE AREAS: Intellectual Property; Patent, Trademark and Copyright Law.

Klein, William J. ... '— '95 C.645 B.S. L.1292 J.D. [Ⓐ Banner&W.]
*PRACTICE AREAS: Intellectual Property Law; Patents; Trademarks; Copyrights; Electrical Intellectual Property.

Klobuchar, Peter M. ... '72 '96 C.679 B.S.MetE L.146 J.D. [Wallenstein W.&R.]
*PRACTICE AREAS: Intellectual Property Law.

Kolomayets, Andrew G., (BV) ... '61 '88 C.424 B.A. L.339 J.D. [Cook,A.M.M.C.&M.]
*PRACTICE AREAS: Intellectual Property; Patents; Trademarks; Copyrights; Unfair Competition.

Kolz, Aimee Boss ... '— '99 C.277 B.S. L.365 J.D. [Banner&W.]
*PRACTICE AREAS: Intellectual Property Law; Intellectual Property Litigation.

Korniczky, Paul J., (AV) ... '61 '86 C.186 B.E. L.107 J.D. [Leydig,V.&M.]

Kozak, John W., (AV) ... '43 '68 C.602 B.S.E.E. L.276 J.D. [Leydig,V.&M.]

Kramer, William J., (AV) ... '— '92 C.339 B.S. L.597 J.D. [Marshall,G.&B.]
*PRACTICE AREAS: Electrical Patents; Computer and Software Patents; Intellectual Property Litigation; Patent Licensing; Business Method Patents.

Krause, Joseph P. ... '55 '83 C.46 B.S.E.E. L.365 J.D. [Ⓐ Ladas&P.]

Kriegel, Jeremy R. ... '— '95 C.696 B.S.M.E. L.910 J.D. [Marshall,G.&B.]
*PRACTICE AREAS: Intellectual Property; Litigation; Patent and Trademark Prosecution; Counseling.

Krit, Jonathan J., (BV) ... '64 '89 C&L.597 B.S., J.D. [Emrich&D.]
*PRACTICE AREAS: Patents; Trademarks; Copyrights.

Krol, Michael A. ... '65 '04 C&L.477 B.Sc., J.D. [Ⓐ Welsh&K.]
*PRACTICE AREAS: Intellectual Property.

Krueger, James P. ... '58 '93 C.999 B.A. L.46 J.D. [Fitch,E.T.&F.]
*PRACTICE AREAS: Intellectual Property Law; Chemical Intellectual Property; Inorganic Chemistry; Organic Chemistry; Medical Technology.

Kuczma, Linda A. ... '56 '81 C.742 B.A.Biol. L.424 J.D. [Wallenstein W.&R.]
*PRACTICE AREAS: Intellectual Property Law.

Kuelper, Jean Dudek, (AV) ... '54 '80 C.602 B.S.E.E. L.424 J.D. [McAndrews,H.&M.]
*PRACTICE AREAS: Electrical and Electronic Intellectual Property; Intellectual Property Arbitration; Intellectual Property Infringement; Intellectual Property Licensing; Intellectual Property Litigation.

Kuo, Joseph M. ... '68 '93 C.597 B.S. L.861 J.D. [Olson&H.]

LaBarge, Richard M., (AV) ... '— '85 C.339 B.S.C.E. L.896 J.D. [Marshall,G.&B.]
*PRACTICE AREAS: Mechanical Patents; Trademark Protection.

Lacroix, Jennifer E. ... '— '00 C.971 B.S. L.597 J.D. [McAndrews,H.&M.]
*PRACTICE AREAS: Intellectual Property; Patent Law.

Ladas & Parry LLP, (AV)
224 South Michigan Avenue, 60604 ⊙
Telephone: 312-427-1300 Telecopy: 312-427-6663; 312-427-6668
Email: chmail@ladasparry.com URL: http://www.ladas.com
Members of Firm: Richard J. Streit; Frederick W. Meyers. Associates: Edward J. Chalfie; W. Dennis Drehkoff; Patricia M. Hoyle (Not admitted in IL); Joseph P. Krause. Of Counsel: Donald P. Reynolds.
Patent, Trademark, Copyright, Unfair Competition, Licensing, Entertainment and Litigation.
New York, N.Y. Office: 26 West 61st Street. Telephone: 212-708-1800. Telecopy: 212-246-8959; 212-246-8925.
Los Angeles, California Office: 5670 Wilshire Boulevard. Telephone: 323-934-2300. Telecopier: 323-934-0202.
London, England Office: High Holborn House, 52-54 High Holborn, WC1V 6RR. Telephone: 44-71-242-5566. Telex: 262433 MONREF G. Telecopy: 44-207-405-1908.
Munich, Germany Office: Dachauerstrasse 37, 80335 Munich, Germany. Telephone: (089) 269077. Fax: 49-89-269040.

See Professional Biographies, CHICAGO, ILLINOIS

Laff, Charles A., (AV) ... '34 '59 C.679 B.S.Ch.E. L.309 J.D. [Michael B.&F.]
*PRACTICE AREAS: Patent, Trademark, Copyright and Unfair Competition Law; Litigation.

Lane, Bradley G. ... '63 '88 C.339 B.S. L.477 J.D. [Brinks H.G.&L.]
*PRACTICE AREAS: Litigation; Intellectual Property; Patents; Copyrights; Trademarks.

Lawrence, Andrew M. ... '— '99 C.602 B.S. L.174 J.D. [Ⓐ Marshall,G.&B.]
*PRACTICE AREAS: Chemical Intellectual Property; Mechanical Intellectual Property; Patent Prosecution; Pharmaceutical Intellectual Property.

Le Duc, Timothy J. ... '69 '03 C.966 B.S. L.494 J.D. [Ⓐ Brinks H.G.&L.]
*PRACTICE AREAS: Intellectual Property.

Lee, Christopher J., (AV) ... '64 '93 C.339 B.S. L.146 J.D. [Niro,S.H.&N.]
*PRACTICE AREAS: Intellectual Property Litigation.

Lee, George I. ... '64 '94 C.966 B.S.E.E. L.339 J.D. [McDonnell B.H.&B.]

Lee, William M., Jr., (AV) ... '— '75 C.188 B.S. L.273 J.D. [Barnes&T.]
*PRACTICE AREAS: Intellectual Property Law; Patents; Trademarks; Copyrights; Litigation.

Lempia, Bryan J. ... '— *'93 C.645 B.S.M.E. L.215 J.D. [Marshall,G.&B.]*
*PRACTICE AREAS: Patent Prosecution.

Lesht, David, (AV) ... '51 '81 C.339 B.S. L.46 J.D. [Cook,A.M.M.C.&M.]
*PRACTICE AREAS: Patents; Trademarks; Copyrights; Unfair Competition.

Levstik, Timothy E., (AV) ... '45 '70 C.124 B.S. L.494 J.D. [Fitch,E.T.&F.]
*PRACTICE AREAS: Intellectual Property Law; Technology and Science; Chemicals; Inorganic Chemistry; Coatings Technology.

Levy, Harry M., (AV) ... '40 '65 C.679 B.S.Ch.E. L.597 J.D. [Emrich&D.]
*PRACTICE AREAS: Patents; Trademarks; Copyrights.

Leydig, C. Frederick, (AV) ... '25 '50 C.46 B.S.Ch.E. L.209 J.D. [Ⓒ Leydig,V.&M.]

Leydig, Voit & Mayer, Ltd., (AV) BR
Two Prudential Plaza, 180 North Stetson Avenue, Suite 4900, 60601-6780 ⊙
Telephone: 312-616-5600 Telecopier: 312-616-5700
Email: mail@leydig.com URL: http://www.leydig.com
James B. Muskal; Dennis R. Schlemmer; Gordon R. Coons; John E. Rosenquist; John W. Kozak; Charles S. Oslakovic (Resident, Rockford Office); Mark E. Phelps; H. Michael Hartmann; Bruce M. Gagala; Charles H. Mottier; John Kilyk, Jr.; Robert F. Green; John B. Conklin; James D. Zalewa; Mark J. Liss; John M. Belz (Resident, Washington, D.C. Office); Brett A. Hesterberg; Jeffrey A. Wyand (Resident, Washington, D.C. Office); Paul J. Korniczky; Pamela J. Ruschau; Steven P. Petersen; John M. Augustyn; Christopher T. Griffith; Wesley O. Mueller; Jeremy M. Jay (Resident, Washington, D.C. Office); Lynn A. Sullivan; Jeffrey B. Burgan; Eley O. Thompson; Mark Joy; David M. Airan; Thomas A. Belush;— Allen E. Hoover; Xavier Pillai (Resident, Washington, D.C. Office); Y. Kurt Chang; Gregory C. Bays; Carol Larcher; Steven H. Sklar; Ali R. Sharifahmadian; Tamara A. Miller; M. Daniel Hefner; Kenneth P. Spina; Andrea M. Augustine; Andrew J. Heinisch (Resident, Rockford Office); Jeffery J. Makeever (Resident, Rockford Office); Salim A. Hasan; Richard A. Wulff; Phillip M. Pippenger; Anne E. Naffziger; Jamison E. Lynch; Vladan M. Vasiljevic; Lisa D. Graver; Robert M. Gould; Claudia M. Werner; Kevin L. Wingate (Resident, Rockford Office); Michael N. Spink (Resident, Rockford Office); Paul J. Filbin; Leonard S. Smith; John L. Gase; John T. Bretscher; Elizabeth C. Diskin; Robert T. Wittmann; Shannon D. Schemel (Resident, Washington, D.C. Office); Adrian R. Cyhan; Leah C. Oubre (Resident, Washington, D.C. Office); Andrew M. Alul; Amy J. Davison; Matthew O. Brady. Of Counsel: C. Frederick Leydig; Theodore W. Anderson; John P. Bundock, Jr.; Paul L. Ahern; John D. Foster; Noel I. Smith; Berton Scott Sheppard.
Patent, Trademark, Copyright, Unfair Competition, Licensing and Related Antitrust and International Trade Law. Trials and Appeals.
Rockford, Illinois Office: 6815 Weaver Road, Suite 300. Telephone: 815-963-7661. Telecopier: 815-963-7664.
Washington, D.C. Office: Leydig, Voit & Mayer, 700 Thirteenth Street, N.W., Suite 300. Telephone: 202-737-6770. Telecopier: 202-737-6776.
Seattle, Washington Office: 1420 Fifth Avenue, Suite 2200. Telephone: 206-521-5985. Telecopier: 206-224-3557.

See Professional Biographies, CHICAGO, ILLINOIS

Lione, Richard G., (AV) '31 '60
C.966 B.S. L.273 J.D. [Brinks H.G.&L.] (⊙Arlington, VA)

Lockwood, Fred S., (P.C.), (AV) '16 '42
C.823 B.Ch.E. L.365 J.D. [Ⓒ Cook,A.M.M.C.&M.]
*PRACTICE AREAS: Patents; Trademarks; Copyrights; Unfair Competition.

Lucas, John K., (AV) ... '46 '72 C.46 B.S. L.209 J.D. [Brinks H.G.&L.]
*PRACTICE AREAS: Intellectual Property Law.

Lucier, Timothy P. ... '71 '98 C.1229 B.S.M.E. L.424 J.D. [Ⓐ Brinks H.G.&L.]
*PRACTICE AREAS: Intellectual Property.

Lungmus, John B., (AV) ... '— '54 C&L.597 B.S., J.D. [Ⓒ Marshall,G.&B.]
*PRACTICE AREAS: Intellectual Property; Litigation; Patent and Trademark Prosecution; Counseling.

Lyerla, Bradford P., (AV) ... '— '80 C&L.339 A.B., J.D. [Marshall,G.&B.]
*PRACTICE AREAS: Litigation.

Lyons, Kathleen A., (AV) ... '54 '84 C.424 B.S. L.209 J.D. [Wallenstein W.&R.]
*PRACTICE AREAS: Intellectual Property Law.

Ma, Dennis H. ... '76 '01 C.597 B.A. L.1556 J.D./LL.M. [Ⓐ Olson&H.]

Ma, Yufeng ... '74 '02 C.999 B.Sc. L.880 J.D. [Ⓐ McAndrews,H.&M.]
*PRACTICE AREAS: Intellectual Property; International Intellectual Property; Chemical Patents; International Patents; Patent Litigation.

Machonkin, Richard A. ... '68 '96 C.477 B.S. L.309 J.D. [McDonnell B.H.&B.]

Magidson, William H. ... '31 '56 C&L.597 B.S., J.D. [Ⓒ Cook,A.M.M.C.&M.]
*PRACTICE AREAS: Patents.

Maher, David W., Ph.D. '61 '99 C.602 B.S. L.770 J.D.
(adm. in CA; not adm. in IL) [Fitch,E.T.&F.]

Mallin, Robert S. ... '63 '90 C.339 B.S. L.424 J.D. [Brinks H.G.&L.]
*PRACTICE AREAS: Intellectual Property.

Malloy, Timothy J., (AV) ... '44 '69 C&L.602 B.S.E.E., J.D. [McAndrews,H.&M.]
*PRACTICE AREAS: Intellectual Property; Patents; Trademarks; Copyrights; Unfair Competition.

Maloney, Timothy P., (BV) ... '66 '93 C&L.339 B.S.Ch.E., J.D. [Fitch,E.T.&F.]
*PRACTICE AREAS: Intellectual Property; Appellate Practice; Litigation; Patents; Trademarks.

Mansfield, Bruce R., (AV) ... '48 '75 C.46 B.S.E.E. L.365 J.D. [Ⓐ Olson&H.]

Manzo, Edward D., (AV) ... '50 '76 C.667 B.S. L.107 J.D. [Cook,A.M.M.C.&M.]
*PRACTICE AREAS: Intellectual Property; Patents; Trademarks; Copyrights; Unfair Competition.

Marcus, Joseph R., (AV) ... '36 '65 C.119 B.S.Ch.E. L.146 J.D. [Welsh&K.]
*PRACTICE AREAS: Intellectual Property.

Marlott, John A. ... '— '95 C.339 B.S. L.273 J.D. [Jones D.]
*PRACTICE AREAS: Intellectual Property Litigation; Intellectual Property Rights; Intellectual Property Licensing; Computer and Software Patents; Internet Patents.

Marlow, Christopher K. ... '74 '04 C.502 B.S.E.E. L.597 J.D. [Ⓐ Welsh&K.]
*PRACTICE AREAS: Intellectual Property.

Marr, David J. ... '58 '87 C.339 B.S. L.146 J.D. [Trexler,B.G.B.&M.]
*PRACTICE AREAS: Intellectual Property; Patent, Trademark and Copyright Law; Trade Secrets Law; Unfair Competition Law; Licensing.

Marshall, Gerstein & Borun LLP, (AV) BR
Sears Tower 6300, 233 South Wacker Drive, 60606-6357
Telephone: 312-474-6300 Fax: 312-474-0448
Email: info@marshallip.com URL: http://www.marshallip.com
Partners: Richard H. Anderson; Scott E. Baxendale; Michael F. Borun; Paul C. Craane; Jeffrey H. Dean; Thomas L. Duston; Patrick D. Ertel; Kevin M. Flowers; David A. Gass; Robert M. Gerstein; Michael R. Graham; Roger A. Heppermann; Martin J. Hirsch; Richard B. Hoffman; Kevin D. Hogg; William J. Kramer; Jeremy R. Kriegel; Richard M. LaBarge; Bryan J. Lempia; Bradford P. Lyerla; Gregory C. Mayer; William K. Merkel; Carl E. Moore, Jr.; Michael Muczynski; James J. Napoli; Sandip H. Patel; David C. Read; Li-Hsein (Lily) Rin-Laures, M.D.; Thomas I. Ross; Jeffrey S. Sharp; Anthony G. Sitko; Paul B. Stephens; Thomas K. Stine; Michael R. Weiner; Joseph A. Williams, Jr.; James P. Zeller. Of Counsel: Allen H. Gerstein. Special Counsel: Meggan F. Duffy; John B. Lungmus. Associates: Matthias Abrell; Jill Anderfuren; George Christopher Braidwood; Gregory J. Chinlund; Pamela L. Cox; Rashmi V. Gupta; Julianne Hartzell; Anthony S. Hind; Mark H. Izraelewicz; Adam G. Kelly; Andrew M. Lawrence; Nabeela R. McMillian; Matthew C. Nielsen; Oliver T. Ong; Chirag B. Patel; Aaron M. Peters; Russell C. Petersen; Randall G. Rueth; Alisa C. Simmons; Sharon M. Sintich; Gregory E. Stanton.
Patent, Trademark, Copyright Litigation and Prosecution; Intellectual Property, Antitrust Law and Related Litigation.

See Professional Biographies, CHICAGO, ILLINOIS

Martin, Alice O., (AV) ... '— '90 C.1150 B.S. L.424 J.D. [Barnes&T.]
*PRACTICE AREAS: Patent Prosecution; International Patent Prosecution; Litigation; Biotechnology; Medical.

Marx, Jeffrey A. ... '78 '05 C.94 B.S. L.966 J.D. [Ⓐ Brinks H.G.&L.]
*PRACTICE AREAS: Intellectual Property Prosecution; Intellectual Property Litigation; Patents; Copyrights; Trademarks.

Mas, Edward A., II ... '65 '92 C.597 B.S.M.E. L.659 J.D. [McAndrews,H.&M.]

Maurer, Erik S. ... '— '01 C.339 B.S. L.597 J.D. [Ⓐ Banner&W.]
*PRACTICE AREAS: Intellectual Property Law; Intellectual Property Litigation; Trademarks; Appellate Practice.

Mayer, Gregory C. ... '— '93 C.339 B.S.A.A.E. L.145 J.D. [Marshall,G.&B.]
*PRACTICE AREAS: Electro-Mechanical Patents; Mechanical Patents; Patent Licensing; Patent Litigation; Copyright Litigation.

McAndrews, George P., (AV) ... '35 '62 C&L.602 B.S.M.E., J.D. [McAndrews,H.&M.]

McAndrews, Matthew G. ... '66 '95 C.602 B.A. L.365 J.D. [Niro,S.H.&N.]
*PRACTICE AREAS: Patent Litigation; Intellectual Property.

McAndrews, Peter J. ... '68 '95 C.436 B.S.E.E. L.365 J.D. [McAndrews,H.&M.]

McAndrews, Held & Malloy, Ltd., (AV)
34th Floor, 500 West Madison Street, 60661
Telephone: 312-775-8000 Fax: 312-775-8100
URL: http://www.mhmlaw.com
George P. McAndrews; John J. Held; Timothy J. Malloy; William M. Wesley; Lawrence M. Jarvis; Gregory J. Vogler; Jean Dudek Kuelper; Herbert D. Hart III; Robert W. Fieseler; Thomas J. Wimbiscus; Steven J. Hampton; Priscilla F. Gallagher; Stephen F. Sherry; Patrick J. Arnold, Jr.; George F. Wheeler; Janet M. McNicholas; Christopher C. Winslade; Edward A. Mas, II; Gregory C. Schodde; Edward W. Remus; Donald J. Pochopien; Sharon A. Hwang; David D. Headrick; Alejandro Menchaca; Kirk A. VanderLeest; Richard T. McCaulley, Jr.; Peter J. McAndrews; James M. Hafertepe; Jonathan R. Sick; Eligio C. Pimentel; James P. Murphy; Dean A. Pelletier; Michael B. Harlin; James R. Nuttall; Joseph M. Barich; Scott P. McBride; Patricia J. McGrath; Troy A. Groetken; Gerald C. Willis, Jr.; John A. Wiberg; Sandra A. Frantzen; Christopher V. Carani; Mirut P. Dalal; Jennifer E. Lacroix; Joseph F. Harding;—John L. Abramic; Michael J. Fitzpatrick; Michael T. Cruz (Not admitted in IL); Christopher N. George; Yufeng Ma; Dennis P. Hackett; Christopher R. Carroll; Christopher M. Scharff; Peter J. Prommer; Merle Elliott; Brian C. Bianco; Jonathan M. Rushman.
Federal and State Trial, Appellate and Agency Practice, Dispute Resolution and Licensing Involving Patents, Trademarks and Copyrights, Environmental Law, Trade Association, Warranty, Complex Technology and Antitrust Matters.

See Professional Biographies, CHICAGO, ILLINOIS

McBride, Scott P. .... '73 '98 C.966 B.S. L.201 J.D. [McAndrews,H.&M.]
*PRACTICE AREAS: Intellectual Property; Litigation; Patent Litigation; Intellectual Property Arbitration; Trademark Prosecution.
McBride, Thomas K., Jr. .... '67 '04 C.339 B.S. L.424 J.D. [[A] Leydig,V.&M.]
McCarthy, James M. ....'69 '94 C.602 B.S.E.E. L.201 J.D. [McDonnell B.H.&B.]
McCarthy, Timothy M., (AV) ....'54 '81 C.339 B.S. L.326 J.D. [Trexler,B.G.B.&M.]
*PRACTICE AREAS: Intellectual Property Prosecution, Litigation and Counseling.
McCaulley, Richard T., Jr. .... '65 '94 C.855 B.S. L.602 J.D. [McAndrews,H.&M.]
McDonnell, John J., (AV) ....'39 '74 C.589 B.S. L.146 J.D. [McDonnell B.H.&B.]

McDonnell Boehnen Hulbert & Berghoff LLP, (AV) [BR]
300 South Wacker Drive, 60606-6709
Telephone: 312-913-0001 Fax: 312-913-0002
Email: info@mbhb.com URL: http://www.mbhb.com
John J. McDonnell; Daniel A. Boehnen; Bradley J. Hulbert; Paul H. Berghoff; Grantland G. Drutchas; James C. Gumina; David M. Frischkorn; Leif R. Sigmond, Jr.; A. Blair Hughes; Lawrence H. Aaronson; Thomas A. Fairhall; Matthew J. Sampson; Curt J. Whitenack; Michael S. Greenfield; Steven J. Sarussi; Christopher M. Cavan; Kevin E. Noonan; George I. Lee; Joshua R. Rich; James M. McCarthy; Robert J. Irvine, III; Thomas E. Wettermann; Sean M. Sullivan; Richard A. Machonkin; Emily Miao; Patrick G. Gattari; David S. Harper; Marcus J. Thymian; Stephen H. Docter; Lisa M. W. Hillman; Anita J. Terpstra; S. Richard Carden; Jeremy Edward Noe; Paul S. Tully; Anthoula Pomrening; Jeffrey A. Steck; Paul W. Churilla (Not admitted in IL). Of Counsel: Denis A. Berntsen. Associates: Eric R. Moran; Andrew W. Williams; Aaron F. Barkoff; Mark L. Chael; Donald L. Zuhn; Bradley W. Crawford; Raef Shaltout.
Intellectual Property Law, Federal Trial and Appellate Practice in Patent, Trademark, Trade Dress, Trade Secrets, International Trade, Unfair Competition, Copyright and Antitrust Causes before Federal and State Courts and Administrative Agencies; All phases of Prosecution before the United States and Foreign Patent and Trademark Offices.

See Professional Biographies, CHICAGO, ILLINOIS

McEachran, Daniel C., (AV) '32 '59 C.350 B.S.E.E. L.424 J.D.
[[C] Cook,A.M.M.C.&M.]
*PRACTICE AREAS: Patent, Trademark and Copyright Law; Unfair Competition Causes.
McFarron, Gary W., (AV) .... '48 '74 C.679 B.S.M.E. L.597 J.D. [Cook,A.M.M.C.&M.]
*PRACTICE AREAS: Intellectual Property; Patents; Trademarks; Copyrights; Unfair Competition.
McGee, Michael J. ....'70 '97 C.259 B.S.E.E. L.365 J.D. [Cook,A.M.M.C.&M.]
*PRACTICE AREAS: Patent; Trademark; Copyright; Unfair Competition Law.
McGrath, Patricia J. .... '— '98 C.720 B.S. L.146 J.D. [McAndrews,H.&M.]
*PRACTICE AREAS: Intellectual Property Law; Litigation.
McLaughlin, F. William, (AV) .... '56 '85 C.602 B.S.E.E. L.209 J.D. [Wood,P.K.C.&M.]
*PRACTICE AREAS: Patents; Trademarks; Copyrights.
McMahon, Charles M. ....'74 '99 C.602 B.S.E.E. L.273 J.D. [[A] Brinks H.G.&L.]
*PRACTICE AREAS: Intellectual Property.
McMillian, Nabeela R. ....'— '03 [[A] Marshall,G.&B.]
*PRACTICE AREAS: Intellectual Property.
McNicholas, Janet M., (AV) ....'51 '86 C.700 B.A. L.145 J.D. [McAndrews,H.&M.]
*PRACTICE AREAS: Intellectual Property; Biotechnology; Patents.
McWilliams, Dennis M., (AV) .... '— '68 C.602 B.A. L.424 J.D. [Barnes&T.]
*PRACTICE AREAS: Intellectual Property Law; Patents; Trademarks; Litigation.
Meece, Timothy C., (AV) ....'— '95 C.339 B.S.E.E. L.365 J.D. [Banner&W.]
*PRACTICE AREAS: Patent Litigation; Copyright Litigation; Appellate Practice; Computer and Software Patents.
Mehler, Raymond M., (AV) ....'44 '74 C.46 B.S. L.145 J.D. [Cook,A.M.M.C.&M.]
*PRACTICE AREAS: Patents; Trademarks; Copyrights; Unfair Competition.
Menchaca, Alejandro, (AV) ... '63 '89 C.453 B.S.Ch.E. L.424 J.D. [McAndrews,H.&M.]
Merkel, William K. ....'— '94 C.388 Ph.D. L.569 J.D. [Marshall,G.&B.]
*PRACTICE AREAS: Biotechnology Patents; Patent Infringement; Patent Licensing; Patent Litigation; Pharmaceutical Patents.
Meyers, Frederick W., (BV) .... '55 '81 C.45 B.A. L.930 J.D. [Ladas&P.]
Miao, Emily .... '60 '97 C.569 Ph.D. L.146 J.D. [McDonnell B.H.&B.]

Michael Best & Friedrich LLP, (AV) [BR]
401 North Michigan Avenue Suite 1900, 60611 ⊙
Telephone: 312-222-0800 Facsimile: 312-222-0818
Email: info@michaelbest.com URL: http://www.michaelbest.com
Partners: Lisa C. Childs; Judith L. Grubner; Charles A. Laff; Larry L. Saret; Joseph F. Schmidt; Martin L. Stern. Of Counsel: Louis Altman. Associates: Gretchen M. Hosty; Susan D. Reinecke; Stephen C. Smith.
Litigation, Corporate and Commercial Law, Management Labor and Employment, Employee Benefits, Patents, Trademarks, Internet Law, Computer Technology, Intellectual Property, Financial Institutions, Securities and Mergers and Acquisitions, Real Property and Commercial, Industrial and Residential Land Development, Federal and State Taxation, Associations, Antitrust and Unfair Trade Practices, Public and Corporate Finance, Creditors' Rights, Bankruptcy and Insolvency, International Business, Estate and Trust Planning, Business Succession Planning, Health Care, Immigration, Environmental, Government Relations and Administrative, Retail Distribution, Communications, Sports and Entertainment, Trade and Professional, Alternative Dispute Resolution, Venture Capital, Insurance Defense, Law Firm Disputes, Divorce and Family Law, Construction Law.
Milwaukee, Wisconsin Office: 100 East Wisconsin Avenue, 53202-4108. Telephone: 414-271-6560. Telecopier: 414-277-0656.
Madison, Wisconsin Office: One South Pinckney Street, Firstar Plaza, P.O. Box 1806, 53701-1806. Telephone: 608-257-3501. Telecopier: 608-283-2275.
Manitowoc, Wisconsin Office: 1000 Maritime Drive, 54220. Telephone: 920-686-2800. Telecopier: 920-686-2810.
Waukesha, Wisconsin Office: Two Riverwood Place, Suite 200, N19 W24133 Riverwood Drive, 53188-1174. Telephone: 262-956-6560. Telecopier: 262-956-6565.
Center Valley, Pennsylvania Office: Stabler Corporate Center, 3773 Corporate Parkway, 18034. Telephone: 610-798-2170. Telecopier: 610-798-2180.

See Professional Biographies, CHICAGO, ILLINOIS

Miller, Amanda M. .... '77 '02 C.117 B.A. L.608 J.D. [[A] Brinks H.G.&L.]
*PRACTICE AREAS: Patent Prosecution; Patent Litigation; Patent Licensing.
Miller, Charles ....'— '99 C.801 B.A. L.1209 J.D. [Banner&W.]
*PRACTICE AREAS: Intellectual Property Law; Intellectual Property Litigation; Patent Prosecution; Electrical Intellectual Property; Computer Technology.
Miller, Laura Beth, (AV) ....'60 '85 C.893 B.A. L.945 J.D. [Brinks H.G.&L.]
Milz, Michael E. ....'60 '90 C.339 B.S. L.146 J.D. [Brinks H.G.&L.]

Mitrius, Janice V. .... '— '97 C.46 B.S.M.E. L.36 J.D. [Banner&W.]
*PRACTICE AREAS: Intellectual Property Law; Patents; Trademarks; Copyrights; Intellectual Property Licensing.
Monco, Dean A., (AV) ....'50 '79 C.424 B.S. L.209 J.D. [Wood,P.K.C.&M.]
*PRACTICE AREAS: Patents; Trademarks; Copyrights.
Moore, Carl E., Jr., (AV) .... '— '69 C&L.424 B.S., J.D. [Marshall,G.&B.]
*PRACTICE AREAS: Patent Litigation; Patent Prosecution.
Moran, Eric R. ....'71 '01 C.602 B.S. L.146 J.D. [[A] McDonnell B.H.&B.]
Morneault, Monique A. ....'62 '94 C.339 B.S. L.146 J.D. [Wallenstein W.&R.]
*PRACTICE AREAS: Intellectual Property Law.
Mortimer, John S., (AV) ....'54 '80 C.602 B.S.M.E. L.209 J.D. [Wood,P.K.C.&M.]
*PRACTICE AREAS: Patents; Trademarks; Copyrights.
Mottier, Charles H., (AV) .... '55 '81 C&L.339 B.S.G.E., J.D. [Leydig,V.&M.]
Mrksich, K. Shannon ....'66 '97 C.324 B.S. L.276 J.D. [Brinks H.G.&L.]
Muczynski, Michael ....'— '98 C.475 B.S. L.477 J.D. [Marshall,G.&B.]
*PRACTICE AREAS: Intellectual Property.
Mueller, Lisa von Bargen .... '67 '92 C.879 B.S. L.897 J.D. [Wood,P.K.C.&M.]
*PRACTICE AREAS: Patents; Utility and Plant Patents; Trademarks; Intellectual Property; Plant Variety Protection.
Mueller, Wesley O., (AV) .... '61 '88 C.150 B.S.E.E. L.608 J.D. [Leydig,V.&M.]
Mundt, David Michael ......'70 '97 C.352 B.S.B.M.E. L.365 J.D. [Cook,A.M.M.C.&M.]
*PRACTICE AREAS: Intellectual Property; Patent; Trademark; Copyrights; Unfair Competition Law.
Muraff, James P. ....'67 '94 C.339 B.S. [Wallenstein W.&R.]
*PRACTICE AREAS: Intellectual Property Law.
Murphy, James P. .... '65 '92 C.475 B.S. L.209 J.D. [McAndrews,H.&M.]
*PRACTICE AREAS: Intellectual Property; Patent Litigation; Trademark Litigation; Copyright Litigation; Patent Procurement.
Murphy, Mark J. .... '64 '89 C.602 B.S. L.436 J.D. [Cook,A.M.M.C.&M.]
*PRACTICE AREAS: Intellectual Property; Patents; Trademarks; Copyrights; Unfair Competition.
Murray, Brian J. ....'— '00 C&L.602 B.S., J.D. [[A] Jones D.]
Muskal, James B., (AV) ....'38 '63 C.339 B.S.M.E. L.209 J.D. [Leydig,V.&M.]
Myrick, James J., (AV) ....'43 '69 C.339 B.S. L.477 J.D. [[C] Welsh&K.]
*PRACTICE AREAS: Intellectual Property.
Nahnsen, Mark J. ....'— '00 C.679 B.S.C.E. L.365 J.D. [[A] Barnes&T.]
*PRACTICE AREAS: Intellectual Property; Patents; Trademarks; Copyrights; Litigation.
Napoli, James J., (AV) ....'91 C.608 B.S. L.209 J.D. [Marshall,G.&B.]
*PRACTICE AREAS: Chemical Intellectual Property; Pharmaceutical Intellectual Property; Chemical Patent Prosecution; Chemical Patents; Patent Prosecution.
Naughton, James P., (AV) .... '57 '81 C&L.339 B.S.E.E., J.D. [Brinks H.G.&L.]
Nelson, Jon O., (AV) ....'— '66 C.679 B.S. L.339 J.D. [Banner&W.]
*PRACTICE AREAS: Intellectual Property Law; Patents; Trademarks; Copyrights; Intellectual Property Litigation.
Nethery, John F. ....'68 '97 C.350 B.S. L.339 J.D. [[A] Brinks H.G.&L.]
*PRACTICE AREAS: Patents.
Nichols, G. Peter, (AV) ....'58 '89 C.494 B.S.Ch.E. L.209 J.D. [Brinks H.G.&L.]
*PRACTICE AREAS: Chemical Intellectual Property (40%); Mechanical Intellectual Property (25%); International Intellectual Property (25%); Intellectual Property Portfolio Management (10%).
Nichols, Jeffry M. ....'75 '00 C.587 B.S. L.306 J.D. [[A] Brinks H.G.&L.]
*PRACTICE AREAS: Patent Litigation; Patent Prosecution; Trademarks.
Nielsen, Matthew C. ....'— '99 C&L.602 B.S., J.D. [[A] Marshall,G.&B.]
*PRACTICE AREAS: Patent Litigation; Patent Infringement; Biotechnology Patents.
Niro, Dean D., (BV) ....'65 '91 C.174 B.S. L.209 J.D. [Niro,S.H.&N.]
*PRACTICE AREAS: Intellectual Property Law.
Niro, Raymond P., (AV) ....'42 '70 C.665 B.S.Ch.E. L.273 J.D. [Niro,S.H.&N.]
*PRACTICE AREAS: Patent, Trade Secret, Antitrust, Trademark and Copyright Litigation.
Niro, William L. ....'45 '74 C.665 B.S.Ch.E. L.209 J.D. [Niro,S.H.&N.]
*PRACTICE AREAS: Patent; Trademark; Copyright; Trade Secret; Unfair Competition.

Niro, Scavone, Haller & Niro, (AV) [BR]
181 West Madison, Suite 4600, 60602-4515
Telephone: 312-236-0733 Facsimile: 312-236-3137
URL: http://www.niroscavone.com
Members and Associates: Raymond P. Niro; Thomas G. Scavone; Timothy J. Haller; William L. Niro; Joseph N. Hosteny, III; Robert A. Vitale, Jr.; John C. Janka; Dean D. Niro; Arthur A. Gasey; Christopher J. Lee; Vasilios (Bill) D. Dossas; Robert P. Greenspoon; Matthew G. McAndrews; Paul C. Gibbons; William W. Flachsbart; Brady J. Fulton; Kara L. Szpondowski.
Intellectual Property and Technology-Related Law including Patent, Trademark, Trade Secret, Copyright, Licensing, Unfair Competition, Related Antitrust Matters.

See Professional Biographies, CHICAGO, ILLINOIS

Nissim-Sabat, Charles, Ph.D. .... '38 '95 C.178 B.S. L.146 J.D. [[C] Cherskov&F.]
Noe, Jeremy Edward ....'63 '00 C.339 B.S. L.146 J.D. [McDonnell B.H.&B.]
Noonan, Kevin E. ....'54 '93 C.1350 B.S. L.989 J.D. [McDonnell B.H.&B.]
Nuttall, James R. ....'72 '97 C.339 B.S.I.E. L.424 J.D. [McAndrews,H.&M.]
*PRACTICE AREAS: Intellectual Property; Litigation.
O'Brien, Grace Law ....'70 '00 C.1169 B.A. L.146 J.D. [[A] Fitch,E.T.&F.]
*PRACTICE AREAS: Intellectual Property.
Odell, Paul M., (AV) ....'45 '73 C.966 B.S.N.E. L.209 J.D. [Wood,P.K.C.&M.]
*PRACTICE AREAS: Patents; Trademarks; Copyrights.
Ohlson, Glenn W., (AV) ....'— '76 C.339 B.S.C.E. L.365 J.D. [Barnes&T.]
*PRACTICE AREAS: Intellectual Property Law; Patents; Trademarks; Copyrights; Litigation.
Okey, David W. .... '46 '00 C.174 B.A. L.365 J.D. [[A] Brinks H.G.&L.]
*PRACTICE AREAS: Patent Prosecution; Litigation; Licensing; Chemical; Electrical and Computer.
Oliver, Wallace L., (AV) ....'44 '74 C.111 B.S. L.597 J.D. [[C] Welsh&K.]
*PRACTICE AREAS: Intellectual Property.
Olson, Arne M., (AV) ....'55 '80 C.145 A.B. L.209 J.D. [Olson&H.]

Olson & Hierl, Ltd., (AV)
20 North Wacker Drive 36th Floor, 60606-3181
Telephone: 312-580-1180 Telecopier: 312-580-1189
Email: firm@olsonhierl.com URL: http://www.olsonandhierl.com
Michael A. Hierl; Arne M. Olson; Dolores T. Kenney; Talivaldis Cepuritis; Joseph M. Kuo;—Dennis H. Ma; Bruce R. Mansfield; Mark R. Bagley. Of Counsel: Seymour Rothstein.
Intellectual Property and Technology-Related Law including Patents, Trademarks, Trade Secrets, Copyrights and Unfair Competition, Related Licensing and Litigation.

See Professional Biographies, CHICAGO, ILLINOIS

O'Malley, James A. .... '74 '99 C.436 B.S.M.E. L.1000 J.D. [Trexler,B.G.B.&M.]
*PRACTICE AREAS: Intellectual Property; Patent; Trademark; Copyright.
Ong, Oliver T. ....'— '03 C.339 B.S.E.E. L.597 J.D. [[A] Marshall,G.&B.]
Palomar, Linda L. .... '68 '94 C.679 B.S.A.A.E. L.424 J.D. [Trexler,B.G.B.&M.]
*PRACTICE AREAS: Intellectual Property; Patent, Trademark and Copyright Law.
Parmelee, Steven G. '53 '78 C.701 B.S.E.E. L.190 J.D.
(adm. in MN; not adm. in IL) [Fitch,E.T.&F.]
*PRACTICE AREAS: Intellectual Property; Electrical Intellectual Property; Intellectual Property Protection; Intellectual Property Rights; Computer and Software Patents.
Patel, Binal J. ....'— '96 C.339 B.S.E.E. L.597 J.D. [Banner&W.]
*PRACTICE AREAS: Intellectual Property Litigation; Patents; Trademarks; Electrical Intellectual Property; Computer and Software Patents.
Patel, Chirag B. ....'— '02 C.999 B.E. L.276 J.D. [[A] Marshall,G.&B.]
*PRACTICE AREAS: Patent Prosecution; Electrical; Computer Software Law; Computer Hardware Patents.
Patel, Sandip H. ....'— '96 C.475 B.S. L.1119 J.D. [Marshall,G.&B.]
*PRACTICE AREAS: Patent Prosecution; Patent Litigation; Patent Interference Proceedings.

Pelletier, Dean A. . . . . . '69 '95 C.597 B.S. L.910 J.D. [McAndrews,H.&M.]
*PRACTICE AREAS: Intellectual Property; Intellectual Property Litigation; Trademark Litigation; Patent Litigation.
Penn, Amir N. . . . . . '67 '94 C.150 B.S.E.E. L.597 J.D. [🄲 Brinks H.G.&L.]
*PRACTICE AREAS: Intellectual Property Infringement; Intellectual Property Licensing; Intellectual Property Litigation; Electrical Patent Prosecution; Mechanical Patent Prosecution.
Peters, Aaron M. . . . . . '— '00 C.477 B.S.E.E. L.1218 J.D. [🄰 Marshall,G.&B.]
*PRACTICE AREAS: Patent Prosecution.
Peters, Grant H. . . . . . '— '91 C.352 B.S. L.424 J.D. [Barnes&T.]
*PRACTICE AREAS: Intellectual Property; Patent, Trademark and Copyright Law; Design Patents; Trade Secrets; Unfair Competition.
Peters, Nicholas T. . . . . . '76 '03 C.880 B.S. L.424 J.D. [🄰 Fitch,E.T.&F.]
*PRACTICE AREAS: Intellectual Property; Litigation.
Petersen, Russell C. . . . . . '— '01 C.966 B.S. L.273 J.D. [🄰 Marshall,G.&B.]
*PRACTICE AREAS: Intellectual Property.
Petersen, Steven P., (AV) . . . . . '62 '87 C.597 B.S.E.E. L.477 J.D. [Leydig,V.&M.]
Petti, Philip T., (AV) . . . . . '58 '85 C.118 B.S. L.221 J.D. [Fitch,E.T.&F.]
*PRACTICE AREAS: Intellectual Property Infringement; Patent Infringement; Patents; Trademarks; Copyrights.
Phelps, Mark E., (AV) . . . . . '48 '75 C.453 B.S.M.E. L.597 J.D. [Leydig,V.&M.]
Phillips, Phoebe K. . . . . . '— '02 C.893 B.S.S.E. L.339 J.D. [🄰 Banner&W.]
*PRACTICE AREAS: Intellectual Property Law.
Phillips, Richard S., (AV) . . . . . '26 '51 C&L.339 B.S., LL.B. [🄲 Wood,P.K.C.&M.]
*PRACTICE AREAS: Patents; Trademarks; Copyrights.
Pillai, Xavier . . . . . '52 '94 C.930 Ph.D. L.146 J.D. [Leydig,V.&M.]
Pimentel, Eligio C. . . . . . '66 '95 C.813 B.S. L.494 J.D. [McAndrews,H.&M.]
*PRACTICE AREAS: Intellectual Property; Litigation.
Pine, Jeffrey A. . . . . . '62 '91 C.339 B.S.E.E. L.424 J.D. [Baniak P.&G.]
*PRACTICE AREAS: Litigation; Intellectual Property; Licensing; Trademarks; Copyrights.
Pioli, Janet A., (AV) . . . . . '59 '84 C.338 B.S. L.589 J.D. [🄲 Brinks H.G.&L.]
*PRACTICE AREAS: Intellectual Property.
Pippenger, Phillip M. . . . . . '69 '98 C.111 B.S.E.E. L.188 J.D. [🄰 Leydig,V.&M.]
Pluta, Robert G. . . . . . '— '02 C.436 B.S. L.209 J.D. [🄰 Brinks H.G.&L.]
*PRACTICE AREAS: Intellectual Property Litigation; Patent Prosecution; Patent Applications; Antitrust.
Pochopien, Donald J., (BV) . . . . . '46 '88 C.424 B.S. L.365 J.D. [McAndrews,H.&M.]
*PRACTICE AREAS: Chemical Patent Prosecution; Biochemical Patent Prosecution; Pharmaceutical Patent Prosecution; Biotechnology Patent Prosecution; Licensing.
Polit, Robert B., (BV) . . . . . '62 '91 C.339 B.S.E.E. L.365 J.D. [🄲 Brinks H.G.&L.]
*PRACTICE AREAS: Patent Prosecution; Trademarks; Copyrights.
Pomrening, Anthoula . . . . . '67 '99 C.46 B.S.M.E. L.365 J.D. [McDonnell B.H.&B.]
Pratt, Andrew F. . . . . . '70 '98 C.911 B.S. L.831 J.D. [🄰 Baniak P.&G.]
*PRACTICE AREAS: Patent Litigation; Trademark Litigation; Trade Secrets Litigation; Patent Prosecution.
Pratt, Thomas K., (AV) . . . . . '— '92 C&L.378 B.S.E.E., J.D. [Banner&W.]
*PRACTICE AREAS: Patents; Trademarks; Intellectual Property Litigation; Electrical Intellectual Property; Computer and Software Patents.
Prendergast, William F., (AV) . . . . . '65 '90 C.424 B.S. L.339 J.D. [Brinks H.G.&L.]
*PRACTICE AREAS: Intellectual Property.
Pristelski, James S., (AV) . . . . . '43 '73 C.966 B.S.E.E. L.352 J.D. [Cook,A.M.M.C.&M.]
*PRACTICE AREAS: Intellectual Property; Patents; Trademarks; Copyrights; Unfair Competition.
Prommer, Peter J. . . . . . '— '03 C&L.339 B.S.C.E., J.D. [🄰 McAndrews,H.&M.]
*PRACTICE AREAS: Intellectual Property.
Raden, James B. . . . . . '— '66 C.339 B.S. L.145 J.D. [🄲 Jones D.]
Rand, Justin B. . . . . . '75 '00 C.347 B.S. L.94 J.D. [🄰 Brinks H.G.&L.]
*PRACTICE AREAS: Intellectual Property.
Rauch, John G. . . . . . '61 '92 C.679 B.S.E.E. L.46 J.D. [Brinks H.G.&L.]
*PRACTICE AREAS: Patent Prosecution; Patent Counseling; Intellectual Property Licensing.
Read, David C., (AV) . . . . . '— '92 C.679 B.S.C.E. L.879 J.D. [Marshall,G.&B.]
*PRACTICE AREAS: Patent Prosecution; Intellectual Property Litigation; Mechanical Patents; Electro-Mechanical Patents; Patent Infringement.
Reinecke, Susan D. . . . . . '— '99 C.831 B.S. L.107 J.D. [🄰 Michael B.&F.]
*PRACTICE AREAS: Intellectual Property.
Remus, Edward W., (AV) . . . . . '42 '70 C.494 B.Ch.E. L.209 J.D. [McAndrews,H.&M.]
*PRACTICE AREAS: Patent Litigation.
Renk, Christopher J., (AV) . . . . . '— '88 C.350 B.S. L.494 J.D. [Banner&W.]
*PRACTICE AREAS: Intellectual Property Law; Intellectual Property Litigation; Appellate Practice; Intellectual Property Licensing.
Resis, Robert H., (AV) . . . . . '— '86 C.339 B.S.Ch.E. L.597 J.D. [Banner&W.]
*PRACTICE AREAS: Intellectual Property Law; Patents; Intellectual Property Litigation; Patent Prosecution; Chemical Intellectual Property.
Retsky, Jonathan E., (AV) . . . . . '62 '89 C.98 B.S.E.E. L.846 J.D. [Brinks H.G.&L.]
Reynolds, Donald P. . . . . . '29 '61 C&L.188 B.E.E., J.D. [🄲 Ladas&P.]
Rheintgen, Kathleen A. . . . . . '63 '88 C.339 B.S. L.424 J.D. [Welsh&K.]
*PRACTICE AREAS: Intellectual Property.
Rich, Joshua R. . . . . . '69 '94 C.446 B.S.B.A. L.893 J.D. [McDonnell B.H.&B.]
Richards, Marc V. . . . . . '60 '93 C.910 B.S.Ch.E. L.424 J.D. [Brinks H.G.&L.]
*PRACTICE AREAS: Patent Prosecution; Biotechnology and Pharmaceutical; Chemical; International Patents and Trademarks; Internet/E-Commerce.
Riess, Daniel M., (AV) . . . . . '36 '68 C.597 B.S.Ch.E. L.276 J.D. [Cook,A.M.M.C.&M.]
*PRACTICE AREAS: Patent; Trademark; Copyright; Unfair Competition.
Rin-Laures, Li-Hsein (Lily), M.D. . . . . . '— '93 C.367 B.A. L.309 J.D. [Marshall,G.&B.]
*PRACTICE AREAS: Biotechnology; Pharmaceutical; Litigation; Patent Prosecution; Patent Interference Proceedings.
Rivas, Marcos P. '69 '03 C.145 B.A. L.659 J.D.
(adm. in MA; not adm. in IL) [🄰 Leydig,V.&M.]
Rockey, Keith V., (AV) . . . . . '41 '67 C.679 B.S.Ch.E. L.273 J.D. [Wallenstein W.&R.]
*PRACTICE AREAS: Intellectual Property Law.
Rockman, Howard B., (AV) . . . . . '— '63 C.223 B.S.M.E. L.273 J.D. [Barnes&T.]
Rokos, Rebecca P. . . . . . '— '96 C&L.477 B.S.Ch.E., J.D. [Banner&W.]
*PRACTICE AREAS: Patents; Trademarks; Copyrights; Trade Secrets; Intellectual Property Litigation.
Ropski, Gary M., (AV) . . . . . '52 '76 C.119 B.S. L.597 J.D. [Brinks H.G.&L.]
*PRACTICE AREAS: Patent Litigation; Trademark Litigation; Copyright Litigation.
Rosenquist, John E., (AV) . . . . . '40 '68 C.742 B.A.Chem. L.365 J.D. [🄲 Leydig,V.&M.]
Ross, Thomas I., (AV) . . . . . '— '79 C.679 B.S.M.E. L.276 J.D. [Marshall,G.&B.]
*PRACTICE AREAS: Intellectual Property Litigation.
Rothstein, Seymour, (AV) . . . . . '31 '58 C.124 B.S.M.E. L.273 LL.B. [🄲 Olson&H.]
Rueth, Randall G. . . . . . '— '98 C.927 B.S. L.209 J.D. [🄰 Marshall,G.&B.]
*PRACTICE AREAS: Patent Prosecution.
Ruschau, Pamela J. . . . . . '59 '87 C.1229 B.M.E. L.608 J.D. [Leydig,V.&M.]
Rushman, Jonathan M. . . . . . '77 '04 C.477 B.S.E. L.209 J.D. [🄰 McAndrews,H.&M.]
*PRACTICE AREAS: Patent Litigation; Patent Prosecution.
Ryndak, James D., (AV) . . . . . '52 '77 C.679 B.S.Ch.E. L.146 J.D. [Ryndak&S.]
*PRACTICE AREAS: Patents; Trademarks; Copyrights; Unfair Competition Law; Intellectual Property Litigation.

Ryndak & Suri, (AV) 🄱🄱
200 West Madison Street, Suite 2100, 60606
Telephone: 312-214-7770 Fax: 312-214-7715
URL: http://www.ryndaksuri.com
James D. Ryndak; Mark K. Suri; Eric H. Weimers.
Intellectual Property, Patents, Trademarks, Copyrights, Unfair Competition, Litigation, Computer Software.
See Professional Biographies, CHICAGO, ILLINOIS

Salmon, Jeffrey W. . . . . . '66 '93 C.597 B.S. L.347 J.D. [Welsh&K.]
*PRACTICE AREAS: Intellectual Property.
Samples, Kenneth H., (AV) . . . . . '46 '73 C.546 B.S.E.E. L.365 J.D. [Fitch,E.T.&F.]
*PRACTICE AREAS: Intellectual Property; Technology and Science; International Technology and Science; Computer and Software; Electronics.
Sampson, Matthew J., (AV) . . . . '63 '91 C.339 B.S.E.E. L.209 J.D. [McDonnell B.H.&B.]
Sandler, Ronald A., (AV) . . . . . '— '66 C.339 B.S.I.E. L.273 J.D. [Jones D.]
*PRACTICE AREAS: Patent Litigation; Copyright Litigation; Trademarks; Intellectual Property Licensing; Intellectual Property Portfolio Management.
Saret, Larry L., (AV) . . . . . '50 '75 C.188 B.A. L.424 J.D. [Michael B.&F.]
*PRACTICE AREAS: Patent Law; Trademark Law; Copyright Law; Unfair Competition Law; Litigation.
Sarussi, Steven J. . . . . . '60 '92 C.424 A.B. L.365 J.D. [McDonnell B.H.&B.]
Scavone, Thomas G., (AV) . . . . . '46 '73 C.215 B.S.Ch.E. L.912 J.D. [Niro,S.H.&N.]
*PRACTICE AREAS: Patent; Trade Secrets; Trademark Litigation.
Scharff, Christopher M. . . . . . '78 '03 C.597 B.S. L.188 J.D. [🄰 McAndrews,H.&M.]
*PRACTICE AREAS: Intellectual Property Litigation; Patent Prosecution; Trademark Prosecution; Intellectual Property Licensing.
Scheer, James A., (AV) . . . . . '47 '78 C.602 B.S. L.589 J.D. [Welsh&K.]
*PRACTICE AREAS: Intellectual Property.
Schlemmer, Dennis R., (AV) . . . . . '39 '64 C&L.339 B.S., J.D. [Leydig,V.&M.]
Schmidt, Joseph F., (AV) . . . . . '48 '73 C.424 B.A. L.146 J.D. [Michael B.&F.]
*PRACTICE AREAS: Trademark Law; Copyright Law; False Advertising; Unfair Competition Law; Litigation.
Schnayer, Jerold B., (AV) . . . . . '50 '77 C.339 B.S.E.E. L.146 J.D. [Welsh&K.]
*PRACTICE AREAS: Intellectual Property.
Schodde, Gregory C. . . . . . '64 '92 C.659 B.S.E.E. L.221 J.D. [McAndrews,H.&M.]
Schulhof, Scott H. . . . . . '71 '03 C.597 B.A. L.146 J.D. [🄰 Leydig,V.&M.]
Schur, Gerald S., (AV) . . . . . '35 '63 C.679 B.Ch.E. L.365 J.D. [Welsh&K.]
*PRACTICE AREAS: Intellectual Property.
Schwartz, David L. . . . . . '70 '95 C.339 B.S. L.477 J.D. [Wallenstein W.&R.]
*PRACTICE AREAS: Intellectual Property Law.
Schwartz, Krista S. . . . . . '— '96 C.339 B.S. L.146 J.D. [🄰 Jones D.]
Segrest, Philip D., Jr. . . . . . '67 '92 C&L.16 B.S., J.D. [🄲 Welsh&K.] (⊙Tallassee, AL)
*PRACTICE AREAS: Intellectual Property.
Shaltout, Raef . . . . . '69 '04 C.804 B.S. L.146 J.D. [🄰 McDonnell B.H.&B.]
Sharp, Jeffrey S., (AV) . . . . . '— '84 C.674 B.S.E. L.280 J.D. [Marshall,G.&B.]
*PRACTICE AREAS: Biotechnology Patents; Chemical Patents.
Shehadeh, Samuel E. . . . . . '— '02 C.966 B.S. L.273 J.D. [🄰 Brinks H.G.&L.]
*PRACTICE AREAS: Patent Prosecution; Patent Litigation.
Shekleton, Gerald T., (AV) . . . . . '47 '73 C.973 B.S.Chem. L.1003 J.D. [Welsh&K.]
*PRACTICE AREAS: Patents; International Patents; Trademarks; International Trademarks; Copyrights.
Sheppard, Berton Scott, (AV) . . . . '36 '62 C.475 B.S.Engr. L.597 J.D. [🄲 Leydig,V.&M.]
Sherry, Stephen F., (AV) . . . . . '56 '82 C.886 B.S. L.209 J.D. [McAndrews,H.&M.]
*PRACTICE AREAS: Patent Infringement; Intellectual Property Litigation.
Shifley, Charles W., (AV) . . . . . '— '76 C&L.608 B.S.M.E., J.D. [Banner&W.]
*PRACTICE AREAS: Intellectual Property Law; Intellectual Property Litigation; Appellate Practice; Patent Prosecution.
Shin, Miyoung . . . . . '71 '03 C.999 B.S. L.597 J.D. [🄰 Brinks H.G.&L.]
*PRACTICE AREAS: Patents; Intellectual Property.
Shipley, Joseph E., (AV) . . . . . '56 '82 C.597 B.S.M.E. L.339 J.D. [Fitch,E.T.&F.]
*PRACTICE AREAS: Intellectual Property Law; Patents; Trademarks; Copyrights; Litigation.
Shull, Jason . . . . . '— '00 C.475 B.S. L.146 J.D. [Banner&W.]
*PRACTICE AREAS: Intellectual Property Litigation; Patents; Trademarks; Chemical Patents; Mechanical Patents.
Shurtz, Steven P., (BV) . . . . . '56 '83 C&L.878 B.S.Ch.E., J.D. [Brinks H.G.&L.]
*PRACTICE AREAS: Chemical Patents; Design Patents; International Patents; Mechanical Patents; Metallurgical Patents.
Sick, Jonathan R. . . . . . '69 '95 C.339 Ch.E. L.146 J.D. [McAndrews,H.&M.]
Siegel, Joel E., (AV) . . . . . '43 '69 C.679 B.S.I.E. L.904 J.D. [Wood,P.K.C.&M.]
*PRACTICE AREAS: Patents; Trademarks; Copyrights.
Sigmond, Leif R., Jr., (AV) . . . . . '65 '90 C.390 B.S. L.1338 J.D. [McDonnell B.H.&B.]
Siller, Gustavo, Jr., (AV) . . . . . '56 '83 C.597 B.S.M.E. L.209 J.D. [Brinks H.G.&L.]
Silvert, Donald J. . . . . . '53 '92 C.674 A.B. L.569 J.D. [🄲 Brinks H.G.&L.]
*PRACTICE AREAS: Intellectual Property; Biotechnology; Pharmaceutical; Agricultural Law; Chemical.
Simmons, Alisa C. . . . . . '— '99 C.345 B.A. L.597 J.D. [🄰 Marshall,G.&B.]
Sintich, Sharon M. . . . . . '— '04 [🄰 Marshall,G.&B.]
*PRACTICE AREAS: Biotechnology; Genetics.
Sitko, Anthony G., (AV) . . . . . '— '93 C.477 B.S.M.E. L.912 J.D. [Marshall,G.&B.]
*PRACTICE AREAS: Electrical Intellectual Property; Intellectual Property Licensing; Mechanical Intellectual Property; Computer and Software Patents; Trademark Prosecution.
Sklar, Steven H. . . . . . '69 '96 C.910 B.S.Ch.E. L.597 J.D. [Leydig,V.&M.]
Smith, Stephen C. . . . . . '50 '03 C&L.339 B.S., J.D. [🄰 Michael B.&F.]
*PRACTICE AREAS: Intellectual Property; Patent Prosecution.
Sobieraj, James R., (AV) . . . . . '57 '82 C&L.477 B.S.E.E., J.D. [Brinks H.G.&L.]
*PRACTICE AREAS: Litigation; Patents; Trade Secrets; Intellectual Property; Unfair Competition.
Sodikoff, Brian J. . . . . . '77 '03 C.880 B.S. L.209 J.D. [🄰 Welsh&K.]
*PRACTICE AREAS: Intellectual Property.
Spina, Kenneth P. . . . . . '62 '96 C.424 M.S. L.209 J.D. [Leydig,V.&M.]
Stanley, Richard E., Jr. . . . . . '67 '99 C.792 B.S.M.E. L.69 J.D. [🄰 Brinks H.G.&L.]
*PRACTICE AREAS: Intellectual Property; Patent Prosecution; Patent and Trade Secret Litigation; Mechanical; Electrical and Computer.
Stanton, Gregory E. . . . . . '— '99 C.339 B.S.E.E. L.597 J.D. [🄰 Marshall,G.&B.]
Steadman, Lewis T., Sr., (AV) . . . . '26 '52 C.823 B.M.E. L.273 J.D. [Trexler,B.G.B.&M.]
*PRACTICE AREAS: Intellectual Property Law; Patent; Trademark; Copyright; Litigation.
Steck, Jeffrey A. . . . . . '72 '01 C.145 B.A. L.1375 J.D. [McDonnell B.H.&B.]
Stein, Roger H., (AV) . . . . . '58 '84 C&L.339 B.S.G.E., J.D. [Wallenstein W.&R.]
*PRACTICE AREAS: Intellectual Property Law.
Stephens, Paul B. . . . . . '— '98 C&L.477 B.S.E., J.D. [Marshall,G.&B.]
*PRACTICE AREAS: Intellectual Property Law.
Stern, Martin L., (AV) . . . . . '52 '77 C.146 B.S. L.597 J.D. [Michael B.&F.]
*PRACTICE AREAS: Patent Law; Trademark Law; Copyright Law; Unfair Competition Law; Litigation.
Stine, Thomas K., (AV) . . . . . '— '84 C.679 B.S.E.E. L.209 J.D. [Marshall,G.&B.]
*PRACTICE AREAS: Electronics; Computer Software Law; Litigation; Patent Prosecution.
Stockton, Richard . . . . . '— '00 C&L.339 B.S., J.D. [Banner&W.]
*PRACTICE AREAS: Patents; Trademarks; Internet Law; Copyrights; Antitrust and Trade Regulation.
Stover, Andrew D. . . . . . '65 '94 C.910 B.S.M.E. L.597 J.D. [Brinks H.G.&L.]
Streit, Richard J., (AV) . . . . . '35 '65 C.602 B.S.M.E. L.365 LL.B. [Ladas&P.]
Sullivan, Sean M. . . . . . '70 '95 C.339 B.S.M.E. L.424 J.D. [McDonnell B.H.&B.]
Summerfield, Craig A. . . . . . '— '93 C.378 B.S.E.E. L.146 J.D. [Brinks H.G.&L.]
*PRACTICE AREAS: Intellectual Property.
Suri, Mark K., (AV) . . . . . '60 '88 C.427 B.A. L.352 J.D. [Ryndak&S.]
*PRACTICE AREAS: Intellectual Property; Litigation; Licensing; Patents; Trademarks.
Szpondowski, Kara L. . . . . . '74 '04 C.679 B.S.I.E. L.146 J.D. [🄰 Niro,S.H.&N.]
*PRACTICE AREAS: Intellectual Property Litigation; Patents; Trademarks; Copyrights.
Tabin, Julius, (AV) '19 '49 C.145 B.S. L.309 LL.B.
[Fitch,E.T.&F.] (⊙San Diego, CA)
*PRACTICE AREAS: Intellectual Property Law; Technology and Science; Biotechnology; Physics; Litigation.
Terpstra, Anita J. . . . . . '61 '98 C.67 B.A. L.734 J.D. [McDonnell B.H.&B.]
Thompson, Eley O., (AV) . . . . . '64 '90 C.886 B.S.E.E. L.1189 J.D. [Leydig,V.&M.]
Thymian, Marcus J. . . . . . '72 '98 C&L.494 B.S.E.E., J.D. [McDonnell B.H.&B.]

Tolpin, Thomas W., (AV) .... '45 '70 C.339 B.S. L.30 J.D. [Welsh&K.] ⊙
*PRACTICE AREAS: Intellectual Property.

Trexler, Bushnell, Giangiorgi, Blackstone & Marr, Ltd., (AV)
The Clark Adams Building, 105 West Adams Street Suite 3600, 60603-6299
Telephone: 312-704-1890 Fax: 312-704-8023
Email: info@trexlaw.com URL: http://www.trexlaw.com
Richard R. Trexler (1906-1995); Richard A. Giangiorgi; Raiford A. Blackstone, Jr.; David J. Marr; Linda L. Palomar; James R. Foley; James A. O'Malley; Timothy M. McCarthy; Paige A. Kitzinger; Robert J. Depke; Lewis T. Steadman, Sr.
Intellectual Property Law including Patent, Trademark, Trade Secrets, Copyright, Unfair Competition Law, all phases including Prosecution, Licensing and Litigation.
See Professional Biographies, CHICAGO, ILLINOIS

Tully, Paul S. .... '67 '00 C.234 B.S. L.365 J.D. [McDonnell B.H.&B.]
Valauskas, Charles C., (AV) .... '52 '81 C.339 B.S. L.209 J.D. [Baniak P.&G.]
*PRACTICE AREAS: Litigation; Intellectual Property; Licensing; Trademarks; Copyrights.
VanderLeest, Kirk A. .... '64 '94 C.350 B.S.I.E. L.146 J.D. [McAndrews,H.&M.]
van Es, J. Pieter .... '— '92 C&L.339 B.A.Ec., J.D. [Banner&W.]
*PRACTICE AREAS: Intellectual Property Law.
Van Santen, William A., (AV) ... '39 '65 C.46 B.S.C. L.273 J.D. [Ⓒ Wood,P.K.C.&M.] ‡
*PRACTICE AREAS: Patents; Trademarks; Copyrights.
Vargo, Paul M., (AV) .... '41 '77 C.124 B.S.E.E. L.146 J.D. [Welsh&K.]
*PRACTICE AREAS: Intellectual Property.
Vasiljevic, Vladan M. .... '74 '98 C&L.339 B.S.E.E., J.D. [Ⓐ Leydig,V.&M.]
Vigil, Thomas R., (AV) .... '38 '66 C.46 B.S.E.E. L.209 J.D. [Ⓒ Welsh&K.]
*PRACTICE AREAS: Intellectual Property.
Vitale, Robert A., Jr. .... '60 '85 C.105 B.S.C.E. L.229 J.D. [Niro,S.H.&N.]
*PRACTICE AREAS: Intellectual Property Litigation.
Vitellaro, Lizabeth K. .... '75 '00 C.385 A.B. L.1000 J.D. [Ⓐ Brinks H.G.&L.]
*PRACTICE AREAS: Intellectual Property; Patent Prosecution; Patent Litigation.
Vogler, Gregory J., (AV) .... '54 '84 C.679 B.S. L.209 J.D. [McAndrews,H.&M.]
*PRACTICE AREAS: Patent Litigation.
Wadhwa, Anuj K. .... '75 '00 C.999 B.S. L.124 J.D. [Ⓐ Baniak P.&G.]
*PRACTICE AREAS: Intellectual Property; Litigation; Intellectual Property Licensing; Patent Prosecution.
Wagner, Robert E., (AV) .... '30 '61 C.350 B.S.E. L.30 J.D. [Ⓒ Wallenstein W.&R.]
Wakely, James M. .... '75 '00 C.98 B.S.E.E. L.597 J.D. [Ⓐ Fitch,E.T.&F.]
*PRACTICE AREAS: Intellectual Property; Patents.

Wallenstein Wagner & Rockey, Ltd., (AV) BB
Suite 5300 311 South Wacker Drive, 60606-6630
Telephone: 312-554-3300 Facsimile: 312-554-3301
Email: iplaw@wwrfirm.com URL: http://www.wwrfirm.com
Daniel N. Christus; Thomas C. Elliott, Jr.; Matthew J. Gryzlo; Brent A. Hawkins; Richard C. Himelhoch; Peter M. Klobuchar; Linda A. Kuczma; Kathleen A. Lyons; Monique A. Morneault; James P. Muraff; Keith V. Rockey; David L. Schwartz; Roger H. Stein. Of Counsel: Robert E. Wagner.
Intellectual Property and Technology Related Law including Protection and Licensing of United States and International Patent, Trademark, Copyright Trade Secret and Unfair Competition Matters and Related Litigation in the Courts and United States International Trade Commission.
See Professional Biographies, CHICAGO, ILLINOIS

Walsh, Louise T. .... '59 '95 C.602 B.S. L.209 J.D. [Welsh&K.]
*PRACTICE AREAS: Intellectual Property.
Wappel, John P. .... '— '04 C.339 B.S.M.E. L.146 J.D. [Ⓐ Barnes&T.]
*PRACTICE AREAS: Intellectual Property.
Ward, William F., III .... '76 '02 C.436 B.S.C.E. L.365 J.D. [Ⓐ Baniak P.&G.]
*PRACTICE AREAS: Intellectual Property; Litigation; Patent Prosecution; Intellectual Property Licensing.
Watkins, Richard D. '75 '00 C.511 B.S. L.276 J.D.
(adm. in PA; not adm. in IL) [Ⓐ Brinks H.G.&L.]
*PRACTICE AREAS: Intellectual Property; Chemical Intellectual Property; Intellectual Property Litigation; Intellectual Property Prosecution; International Intellectual Property.
Weimers, Eric H., (AV) .... '58 '85 C&L.861 B.S., J.D. [Ryndak&S.]
*PRACTICE AREAS: Intellectual Property; Technology Law.
Weiner, Michael R. .... '— '93 C&L.339 B.S., J.D. [Marshall,G.&B.]
*PRACTICE AREAS: Patent Litigation; Patent Interference Practice; Patent Prosecution; Chemical Patents.
Weinstein, Mitchell J. .... '58 '93 C.1044 B.S.Ch.E. L.365 J.D. [Welsh&K.]
*PRACTICE AREAS: Intellectual Property.
Weiss, Sandra Byster, (AV) .... '— '84 C.339 B.S. L.209 J.D. [Ⓒ Jones D.]

Welsh & Katz, Ltd., (AV) BB
120 South Riverside Plaza 22nd Floor, 60606-3912 ⊙
Telephone: 312-655-1500 Fax: 312-655-1501
URL: http://www.welshkatz.com
A. Sidney Katz; Richard L. Wood; Jerold B. Schnayer; Joseph R. Marcus; Gerald S. Schur; Gerald T. Shekleton; James A. Scheer; Daniel R. Cherry; Edward P. Gamson; Kathleen A. Rheintgen; Thomas W. Tolpin; Mitchell J. Weinstein; Eric D. Cohen; Jon P. Christensen; Walter J. Kawula, Jr.; Leonard Friedman; Steven E. Feldman; Jeffrey W. Salmon; Louise T. Walsh; Paul M. Vargo; Joseph E. Cwik; J. Aron Carnahan; Erik B. Flom;—Richard J. Gurak; Daniel M. Gurfinkel; Brian J. Sodikoff; Michael A. Krol; Christopher K. Marlow; Maitreya P. Jani. Of Counsel: James J. Myrick; Thomas R. Vigil; Philip D. Segrest, Jr.; Wallace L. Oliver.
Technology and Intellectual Property Law including Patent, Trademark, Copyright, Trade Secret, Unfair Competition and Related Antitrust Law, and Trials and Appeals.
Arlington, Virginia Office: Crystal Plaza One, Suite 311, 2001 Jefferson Davis Highway, 22202-3603. Telephone: 703-415-4777.
See Professional Biographies, CHICAGO, ILLINOIS

Wesley, William M., (AV) .... '43 '71 C.436 B.E.E. L.424 J.D. [McAndrews,H.&M.]
Wettermann, Thomas E. .... '64 '95 C.436 B.S.E.E. L.209 J.D. [McDonnell B.H.&B.]
Wheeler, George F., (AV) .... '53 '77 C&L.966 B.S., J.D. [McAndrews,H.&M.]
*PRACTICE AREAS: Chemical Patent Prosecution; Chemical Patents; Design Patents; Mechanical Patent Prosecution; Mechanical Patents.
Whitenack, Curt J. .... '61 '91 C&L.966 B.S., J.D. [McDonnell B.H.&B.]
Wiberg, John A. .... '68 '98 C.959 B.S.E.E. L.146 J.D. [McAndrews,H.&M.]
*PRACTICE AREAS: Patent Prosecution; Electrical Patents; Computer Patents; Trademark Law.
Williams, Andrew W. .... '66 '01 C.352 B.S. L.273 J.D. [Ⓐ McDonnell B.H.&B.]
Williams, Joseph A., Jr. .... '— '00 C.576 B.S. L.209 J.D. [Marshall,G.&B.]
Willis, Gerald C., Jr. .... '68 '96 C.338 B.S. L.365 J.D. [McAndrews,H.&M.]
*PRACTICE AREAS: Patent Litigation; Trademark Litigation; Antitrust Litigation.

Wimbiscus, Thomas J., (AV) .... '60 '85 C&L.339 B.S., J.D. [McAndrews,H.&M.]
Winslade, Christopher C. .... '65 '92 C.602 B.A. L.608 J.D. [McAndrews,H.&M.]
Witcoff, David L., (AV) .... '— '82 C.813 B.S.E.E. L.1066 J.D. [Jones D.]
*PRACTICE AREAS: Intellectual Property Litigation; Intellectual Property Licensing; Intellectual Property Rights.
Witcoff, Sheldon W., (AV) .... '— '53 C.446 B.S.E.E. L.273 J.D. [Ⓒ Banner&W.]
*PRACTICE AREAS: Intellectual Property Law.
Wittmann, Robert T. .... '67 '00 C.436 B.S.E.E. L.209 J.D. [Ⓐ Leydig,V.&M.]
Wood, Richard L., (AV) .... '35 '64 C.477 B.S.M.E. L.273 J.D. [Welsh&K.] ⊙
*PRACTICE AREAS: Intellectual Property.

Wood, Phillips, Katz, Clark & Mortimer, (AV)
Citicorp Center, Suite 3800, 500 West Madison Street, 60661-2511
Telephone: 312-876-1800 Telecopier: 312-876-2020
Email: info@woodphillips.com URL: http://www.woodphillips.com
Members of Firm: Jeffrey L. Clark; Jeffery N. Fairchild; Stephen D. Geimer; Allen J. Hoover; Martin L. Katz; F. William McLaughlin; Dean A. Monco; John S. Mortimer; Lisa von Bargen Mueller; Paul M. Odell; Joel E. Siegel. Of Counsel: Richard S. Phillips; William A. Van Santen (Retired).
Intellectual Property and Unfair Competition Law.
See Professional Biographies, CHICAGO, ILLINOIS

Wrona, Thomas J. .... '— '02 C.339 B.S. L.365 J.D. [Ⓐ Brinks H.G.&L.]
*PRACTICE AREAS: Intellectual Property Law.
Yosick, Joseph A. .... '— '02 C&L.339 B.S.Ch.E., J.D. [Ⓐ Brinks H.G.&L.]
*PRACTICE AREAS: Intellectual Property; Patent Prosecution; Patent Litigation.
Zalewa, James D., (AV) .... '47 '74 C.339 B.S. L.145 J.D. [Leydig,V.&M.]
Zanfardino, Dominic P., (AV) .... '60 '90 C&L.424 B.S., J.D. [Brinks H.G.&L.]
*PRACTICE AREAS: Intellectual Property.
Zeller, James P., (AV) .... '— '76 C.602 B.S.Ch.E. L.1119 J.D. [Marshall,G.&B.]
*PRACTICE AREAS: Biotechnology Patents; Chemical Patents; Mechanical Patents; Patent Prosecution; Trademark Protection.

Zickert, Lloyd L., (AV) '26 '53 C.679 B.S.M.E. L.273 J.D.
79 West Monroe Street, Suite 1100, 60603
Telephone: 312-236-1888 Fax: 312-236-1885
Email: zickert@compuserve.com
Patent, Trademark, Copyright and Unfair Competition Law.
See Professional Biographies, CHICAGO, ILLINOIS

Zuhn, Donald L. .... '62 '02 C.424 B.S. L.365 J.D. [Ⓐ McDonnell B.H.&B.]

PEORIA, * 112,936, *Peoria Co.*

Chambers, David A. .... '— '02 C.98 B.A. L.339 J.D. [Ⓐ Husch&E.]
*PRACTICE AREAS: Intellectual Property.

Husch & Eppenberger, LLC, (AV)
401 Main Street, Suite 1400, 61602-1241 ⊙
Telephone: 309-637-4900 FAX: 309-637-4928
URL: http://www.husch.com
Associates: David A. Chambers.
Administrative Law, Agricultural Law, Alternative Dispute Resolution, Antitrust, Appellate Practice, Asset Protection, Bankruptcy, Banks and Banking, Business Law, Casinos and Gambling, Children, Civil Practice, Class Action, Commercial Law, Commercial Real Estate, Communications and Media, Complex and Multi District Litigation, Computers and Software, Constitutional Law, Construction Law, Consumer Law, Contracts, Copyrights, Corporate Finance, Corporate Law, Debtor and Creditor, Education Law, Election, Campaign and Political Law, Eminent Domain, Employee Benefits, Entertainment Law, Environmental Law, Estate Planning, Family Law, Fidelity and Surety, Finance, Government, Guardianship and Conservatorship, Health Care, Hospital Law, Immigration and Naturalization, Insurance, Insurance Defense, Intellectual Property, International Law, International Trade, Investments, Labor and Employment, Litigation, Medical Malpractice, Mergers, Acquisitions and Divestitures, Municipal Law, Nonprofit and Charitable Organizations, Occupational Safety and Health, Partnership Law, Patents, Probate, Products Liability, Property Law, Real Estate, Securities, Taxation, Technology and Science, Torts, Toxic Torts, Trade Secrets, Trademarks, Trusts and Estates, Wills, Worker's Compensation, Zoning, Planning and Land Use.
Jefferson City, Missouri Office: 235 East High Street, Monroe House, Suite 300, P.O. Box 1251. Telephone: 573-635-9118. FAX: 573-634-7854.
Kansas City, Missouri Office: 1200 Main, Suite 2300. Telephone: 816-421-4800. FAX: 816-421-0596.
St. Louis, Missouri Office: 190 Carondelet Plaza, Suite 600. Telephone: 314-480-1500. FAX: 314-480-1505.
Springfield, Missouri Office: 1949 E. Sunshine Street, Suite 2-300. Telephone: 417-862-6726. FAX: 417-862-6948.
Chattanooga, Tennessee Office: 736 Georgia Avenue, Suite 300. Telephone: 423-266-5500. FAX: 423-266-5499.
Memphis, Tennessee Office: One Memphis Place, 200 Jefferson Avenue, Suite 1450, 38103. Telephone: 901-523-1123. FAX: 901-523-7472.
Nashville, Tennessee Office: 2525 West End Avenue, Suite 1400, 37203. Telephone: 615-963-2200. FAX: 615-963-3611.
See Professional Biographies, PEORIA, ILLINOIS

ROCKFORD, * 150,115, *Winnebago Co.*

Leydig, Voit & Mayer, Ltd., (AV) BB
6815 Weaver Road, Suite 300, 61114-8018 ⊙
Telephone: 815-963-7661 Telecopier: 815-963-7664
Email: mail@leydig.com URL: http://www.leydig.com
Charles S. Oslakovic (Resident);—Andrew J. Heinisch (Resident); Jeffery J. Makeever (Resident); Kevin L. Wingate (Resident); Michael N. Spink (Resident).
Patent, Trademark, Copyright, Unfair Competition and Related Antitrust and International Trade Law. Trials and Appeals.
Chicago, Illinois Office: Two Prudential Plaza, 180 North Stetson Avenue, Suite 4900. Telephone: 312-616-5600. Telecopier: 312-616-5700.
Washington, D.C. Office: Leydig, Voit & Mayer, 700 Thirteenth Street, N.W., Suite 300. Telephone: 202-737-6776. Telecopier: 202-737-6776.
Seattle, Washington Office: 1420 Fifth Avenue, Suite 2200. Telephone: 206-521-5985. Telecopier: 206-224-3557.
See Professional Biographies, ROCKFORD, ILLINOIS

Oslakovic, Charles S., (AV) .... '41 '73 C.46 B.S.E.E. L.209 J.D. [Ⓒ Leydig,V.&M.]

BROWNSBURG, 14,520, *Hendricks Co.*

Tucker, Mary Ann .... '— '73 C.579 B.S. L.345 J.D. [Tucker]
*PRACTICE AREAS: Intellectual Property.

Tucker Law Offices
61 Ridgeway Drive, 46112-1004
Telephone: 317-852-3291 Fax: 317-852-7537
Email: mtuckeresq@aol.com
Mary Ann Tucker.
Intellectual Property, Patent and Trademark Law.
See Professional Biographies, BROWNSBURG, INDIANA

FORT WAYNE, * 205,727, *Allen Co.*

Baker & Daniels LLP, (AV) [BB]
111 East Wayne Street, Suite 800, 46802 ⊙
Telephone: 260-424-8000 Fax: 260-460-1700
URL: http://www.bakerdaniels.com
Members of Firm: John F. Hoffman; Anthony Niewyk. Resident Associates: Adam F. Cox; Brian Thomas Geisler (Not admitted in IN); Jason A. Houser.
Antitrust, Bankruptcy, Business Planning, Commercial, Corporate Finance, Creditors Rights, Employee Benefits, Employment, Environment, Estate and Probate, Family, Financial, Food and Drug, Government Affairs, Health Care, Insurance, Intellectual Property, International, Legislative, Litigation, Medical Technology Regulation, Municipal, Nonprofit, Product Liability, Real Estate, Securities, Sports, Tax, Transportation, Utilities, Year 2000, Zoning and Land Use Law.
Indianapolis, Indiana Office: 300 North Meridian Street, Suite 2700, 46204. Telephone: 317-237-0300. Fax: 317-237-1000.
South Bend, Indiana Office: First Bank Building, 205 West Jefferson Boulevard, Suite 250, 46601. Telephone: 574-234-4149. Fax: 574-239-1900.
Elkhart, Indiana Office: 317 West Franklin Street, Suite 507, P.O. Box 507, 46515-0507. Telephone: 574-296-6000. Fax: 574-296-6001.
Indianapolis-96th Street, Indiana Office: Parkwood Six, 600 East 96th Street, Suite 600, 46240. Telephone: 317-569-9600. Fax: 317-569-4800.
Washington, D.C. Office: 805 15th Street, N.W., Suite 700, 20005. Telephone: 202-312-7440. Fax: 202-312-7460.
Qingdao, China Office: 4/F, Office Tower, Crowne Plaza Qingdao, No. 76 Hong Kong Middle Road, 266071. Telephone: +011-86-532-575-1051. Fax: +011-86-532-575-1055.
Beijing, China Office: Room 1919, Tower 2, China World Trade Center, No. 1 JianGuoMenWai Avenue, 100004. Telephone: +86-10-6505-7733. Fax: +86-10-6505-8730.
See Professional Biographies, FORT WAYNE, INDIANA

Barnes & Thornburg LLP, (AV) [BB]
600 One Summit Square, 46802 ⊙
Telephone: 260-423-9440 FAX: 260-424-8316
URL: http://www.btlaw.com
Partner: Bobby B. Gillenwater. Associate: Gregory S. Cooper.
Acquisitions and Mergers, Antitrust, Chemical Intellectual Property, Copyrights, Electrical Intellectual Property, Electronic Intellectual Property, Franchise Licensing, Intellectual Property Arbitration, Intellectual Property Infringement, Intellectual Property Litigation, Intellectual Property Portfolio Management, Intellectual Property Licensing, International Intellectual Property, Literary Property, Mechanical Intellectual Property, Medical Intellectual Property, Patents, Patent Litigation, Patent Protection, Pharmaceutical Intellectual Property, Proprietary Rights, Protection of Personality, Software Licensing, Taxation of Intellectual Property, Trademarks, Trademark Litigation, Trademark Registration.
Representative Intellectual Property Clients: Deister Machine Company, Inc.; Do it Best Corp.; Karl Schmidt Unisia-Zollner; Lincoln National Corporation; PHD, Inc.; Phelps Dodge Magnet Wire, Inc.; Pyromation, Inc.; Starcraft Corporation; Gast Manufacturing, Inc.; University of Notre Dame.
Indianapolis, Indiana Office: 11 South Meridian Street, 46204. Telephone: 317-236-1313. FAX: 317-231-7433.
South Bend, Indiana Office: 600 1st Source Bank Center, 100 North Michigan, 46601-1632. Telephone: 574-233-1171. FAX: 574-237-1125.
Elkhart, Indiana Office: 121 West Franklin Street, Suite 200, 46516. Telephone: 574-293-0681. FAX: 574-296-2535.
Chicago, Illinois Office: One North Wacker Drive, Suite 4400, 60606-2833. Telephone: 312-357-1313. FAX: 312-759-5646.
Washington, D.C. Office: Suite 900, 750 17th Street, N.W., 20006. Telephone: 202-289-1313. FAX: 202-289-1330.
Grand Rapids, Michigan Office: 300 Ottawa Avenue, N.W., Suite 500, 49503. Telephone: 616-742-3930. FAX: 616-742-3999.
See Professional Biographies, FORT WAYNE, INDIANA

Cooper, Gregory S. .... '— '98 C.679 B.S. L.229 J.D. [A Barnes&T.]
*PRACTICE AREAS: Intellectual Property; Mechanical Patent Prosecution; Technology Protection; Patent Prosecution; Intellectual Property Infringement.
Cox, Adam F. .... '74 '99 C.473 B.S. L.347 J.D. [A Baker&D.]
*PRACTICE AREAS: Intellectual Property.
Geisler, Brian Thomas '— '03 C.980 B.E. L.8 J.D.
(adm. in OH; not adm. in IN) [A Baker&D.]
*PRACTICE AREAS: Intellectual Property.
Gillenwater, Bobby B., (AV) ....'— '83 C.838 B.S.E.E. L.93 J.D. [Barnes&T.]
*PRACTICE AREAS: Intellectual Property; Patents; Trademarks; Copyrights.
Hoffman, John F., (AV) ....'47 '72 C.602 B.S. L.273 J.D. [Baker&D.]
*PRACTICE AREAS: Intellectual Property.
Houser, Jason A. ....'77 '04 C.679 B.S.E.E. L.879 J.D. [A Baker&D.]
*PRACTICE AREAS: Intellectual Property.
Niewyk, Anthony, (AV) ....'41 '73 C.477 B.S. L.273 J.D. [Baker&D.]
*PRACTICE AREAS: Intellectual Property.

INDIANAPOLIS, * 791,926, *Marion Co.*

Addison, Bradford G. ....'— '93 C.346 B.S. L.150 J.D. [Barnes&T.]
*PRACTICE AREAS: Patent Law; Trademark Law; Copyrights.
Arnett, Charles W. ....'77 '02 C.701 B.S. L.345 J.D. [A Baker&D.]
*PRACTICE AREAS: Intellectual Property.
Badger, David H., (AV) ....'31 '64 C.701 B.S.E.E. L.345 J.D. [C Brinks H.G.&L.]
*PRACTICE AREAS: Intellectual Property Law.
Bailey, Kevin D. ....'— '94 C.472 B.S.M.E. L.910 J.D. [A Barnes&T.]
*PRACTICE AREAS: Mechanical Intellectual Property; Intellectual Property Litigation.

Baker & Daniels LLP, (AV) [BB]
300 North Meridian Street, Suite 2700, 46204 ⊙
Telephone: 317-237-0300 Fax: 317-237-1000
URL: http://www.bakerdaniels.com
Members of Firm: R. Trevor Carter; Kevin R. Erdman; Eric J. Groen; Thomas A. Ladd; Timothy E. Niednagel; Robert D. Null; Nancy G. Tinsley. Counsel: Douglas A. Yerkeson. Associates: Charles W. Arnett; Ryan C. Barker; Norman J. Hedges; Kareem A. Howell; Sarah M. Jabbari; William S. Meyers; Keith J. Swedo. Resident Associates: Jason A. Houser. Washington, D.C. Office Members of Firm: Scott D. Balderston; Herbert V. Kerner. Of Counsel: Kerry Owens.
Antitrust, Business Planning, Commercial, Financial and Bankruptcy, Corporate Finance, Education, Employee Benefits, Environment, Family Business, Federal, State and Local Tax, Food and Drug Law, Government Affairs, Health Care, Individual/Family, Estate and Probate, Insurance and Financial Services, Intellectual Property, International, Labor and Employment, Life Sciences, Litigation, Medical Technology Regulation, Municipal Law/Tax-Exempt Finance, Nonprofit, Product Liability, Real Estate/Land Use, Transportation, and Utilities.
Representative Clients: Anthem Insurance Companies, Inc.; AT&T Corp.; Bank One, Indianapolis, N.A.; Bindley Western Industries, Inc.; City of Indianapolis; Conseco, Inc.; Cummins Engine Co., Inc.; Eli Lilly & Co.; Paul Harris Stores, Inc.; United Airlines.
Fort Wayne, Indiana Office: 111 East Wayne Street, Suite 800, 46802. Telephone: 260-424-8000. Fax: 260-460-1700.
South Bend, Indiana Office: First Bank Building, 205 West Jefferson Boulevard, Suite 250, 46601. Telephone: 574-234-4149. Fax: 574-239-1900.

(This Listing Continued)

Baker & Daniels LLP (Continued)
Elkhart, Indiana Office: 317 West Franklin Street, P.O. Box 507, 46515-0507. Telephone: 574-296-6000. Fax: 574-296-6001.
Indianapolis-96th Street, Indiana Office: Parkwood Six, 600 East 96th Street, Suite 600, 46240. Telephone: 317-569-9600. Fax: 317-569-4800.
Washington, D.C. Office: 805 15th Street, N.W., Suite 700, 20005. Telephone: 202-312-7440. Fax: 202-312-7460.
Qingdao, China Office: 4/F, Office Tower, Crowne Plaza Qingdao, No. 76 Hong Kong Middle Road, 266071. Telephone: +011-86-532-575-1051. Fax: +011-86-532-575-1055.
Beijing, China Office: Room 1919, Tower 2, China World Trade Center, No. 1 JianGuoMenWai Avenue, 100004. Telephone: +86-10-6505-7733. Fax: +86-10-6505-8730.
See Professional Biographies, INDIANAPOLIS, INDIANA

Ball, Rebecca L. ....'— '99 C.839 B.S. L.326 J.D. [A Barnes&T.]
*PRACTICE AREAS: Chemical Intellectual Property; Medical Intellectual Property; Pharmaceutical Intellectual Property.
Banta, Holiday W. ....'70 '94 C.347 B.A. L.880 J.D. [Woodard,E.M.M.&H.]
*PRACTICE AREAS: Patents; Trademarks; Copyrights; Intellectual Property Arbitration; Intellectual Property Infringement.
Barker, Ryan C. ....'76 '01 C.228 B.S.E. L.345 J.D. [A Baker&D.]

Barnes & Thornburg LLP, (AV) [BB]
11 South Meridian Street, 46204 ⊙
Telephone: 317-236-1313 FAX: 317-231-7433
URL: http://www.btlaw.com
Intellectual Property Department Partners: Richard D. Conard; Richard A. Rezek; Lynn C. Tyler; Dwight D. Lueck; James R. Sweeney II. Of Counsel: Dilip Kulkarni. Associates: Julia Spoor Gard; Spencer P. Goodson; Kitisri Sukhapinda; Scott M. Simmonds; Dennis S. Schell; Hongsun Yoon.
Acquisitions and Mergers, Antitrust, Chemical Intellectual Property, Copyrights, Electrical Intellectual Property, Electronic Intellectual Property, Franchise Licensing, Intellectual Property Arbitration, Intellectual Property Infringement, Intellectual Property Litigation, Intellectual Property Portfolio Management, Intellectual Property Licensing, International Intellectual Property, Literary Property, Mechanical Intellectual Property, Medical Intellectual Property, Patents, Patent Litigation, Patent Protection, Pharmaceutical Intellectual Property, Proprietary Rights, Protection of Personality, Software Licensing, Taxation of Intellectual Property, Trademarks, Trademark Litigation, Trademark Registration.
Representative Intellectual Property Clients: Arvin Industries, Inc.; Best Access Systems; Cosco, Inc., DePuy Orthopaedics, Inc.; Eli Lilly and Company; Hillenbrand Industries; Illinois Tool Works Incorporated; Purdue Research Foundation; Roche Diagnostics Corporation; Stant Manufacturing, Inc.
Fort Wayne, Indiana Office: 600 One Summit Square, 46802. Telephone: 260-423-9440. FAX: 260-424-8316.
South Bend, Indiana Office: 600 1st Source Bank Center, 100 North Michigan, 46601-1632. Telephone: 574-233-1171. FAX: 574-237-1125.
Elkhart, Indiana Office: 121 West Franklin Street, Suite 200, 46516. Telephone: 574-293-0681. FAX: 574-296-2535.
Chicago, Illinois Office: One North Wacker Drive, Suite 4400, 60606-2809. Telephone: 312-357-1313. FAX: 312-759-5646.
Washington, D.C. Office: 750 17th Street, N.W., Suite 900. 20006. Telephone: 202-289-1313. FAX: 202-289-1330.
Grand Rapids, Michigan Office: 300 Ottawa Avenue, N.W., Suite 500, 49503. Telephone: 616-742-3930. FAX: 616-742-3999.
See Professional Biographies, INDIANAPOLIS, INDIANA

Bauer, Shawn D. ....'— '95 C.679 B.S.E. L.347 J.D. [Barnes&T.]
*PRACTICE AREAS: Intellectual Property; Patent Law; Trademark Law.
Beck, Michael D. .... '56 '86 C.1229 B.S.M.E. L.1370 J.D. [Maginot M.&B.]
*PRACTICE AREAS: Intellectual Property.
Benefield, Michael A. .... '73 '04 C.701 B.S. L.1119 J.D. [A Woodard,E.M.M.&H.]
*PRACTICE AREAS: Patents; Trademarks; Copyrights.
Bereveskos, Spiro, (AV) .... '56 '81 C.679 B.S. L.1119 J.D. [Woodard,E.M.M.&H.]
*PRACTICE AREAS: Patents; Trademarks; Copyrights.
Boivin, Nicholas M. '— '03 C.597 B.A. L.893 J.D.
(adm. in IL; not adm. in IN) [A Brinks H.G.&L.]
*PRACTICE AREAS: Patents; Federal Litigation.
Borgman, Adam W. ....'— '05 C.701 B.S. L.345 J.D. [A Woodard,E.M.M.&H.]
*PRACTICE AREAS: Patents; Trademarks; Copyrights.
Bradshaw, John M. .... '72 '99 C.602 B.S. L.1119 J.D. [A Woodard,E.M.M.&H.]
*PRACTICE AREAS: Copyrights; Patents; Trademarks.

Brinks Hofer Gilson & Lione, A Professional Corporation, (AV)
One Indiana Square, Suite 1600, 46204-2001 ⊙
Telephone: 317-636-0886 Facsimile: 317-634-6701
Email: iplaw@usebrinks.com URL: http://www.usebrinks.com
Shareholder: A. James Richardson (Managing Attorney, Indianapolis Office). Counsel: Lawrence A. Steward. Of Counsel: David H. Badger. Associates: Sanders N. Hillis; Nicholas M. Boivin (Not admitted in IN); Michael E. Wever (Not admitted in IN).
Patent, Trademark, Copyright, Trade Secret and Internet Work, Unfair Competition, Technology and Licensing Agreements, Intellectual Asset Management and Intellectual Property Litigation.
Chicago, Illinois Office: NBC Tower, Suite 3600, 455 North Cityfront Plaza Drive. Telephone: 312-321-4200. Facsimile: 312-321-4299. Email: iplaw@usebrinks.com.
Ann Arbor, Michigan Office: 524 South Main Street, Suite 200. Telephone: 734-302-6000. Fax: 734-994-6331.
Arlington, Virginia Office: 2001 Jefferson Davis Highway, Suite 208. Telephone: 703-415-0303. Facsimile: 703-415-0304.
See Professional Biographies, INDIANAPOLIS, INDIANA

Browning, Clifford W., (AV) '50 '78 C.679 B.S.Ch.E. L.345 J.D.
[Woodard,E.M.M.&H.]
*PRACTICE AREAS: Patents; Trademarks; Copyrights.
Cantrell, Quentin G. .... '67 '00 C.679 B.S. L.1119 J.D. [A Woodard,E.M.M.&H.]
*PRACTICE AREAS: Copyrights; Patents; Trademarks.
Carter, R. Trevor ....'68 '95 C.679 B.S.M.E. L.347 J.D. [Baker&D.]
*PRACTICE AREAS: Intellectual Property.
Cole, Troy J. ....'63 '94 C.98 B.S.E.E. L.802 J.D. [Woodard,E.M.M.&H.]
*PRACTICE AREAS: Patents; Trademarks; Copyrights.
Daniluck, John V. .... '52 '95 C.679 B.S.M.E. L.347 J.D. [Woodard,E.M.M.&H.]
*PRACTICE AREAS: Patents; Trademarks; Copyrights.
Dimos, James, (AV) ....'61 '86 C.894 A.B. L.910 J.D. [Locke R.]
*PRACTICE AREAS: Intellectual Property Litigation; Piracy; Unfair Competition; Trade Secrets; Complex Litigation.
DuBois, Dustin S. ....'70 '00 C.701 B.S. L.345 J.D. [A Ice M.]
*PRACTICE AREAS: Intellectual Property; Patents; Business Transactions; Strategic Alliances; Joint Ventures.
Duff, Gregory A. ....'— '99 C.679 B.S.Ph. L.893 J.D. [A Ice M.]
*PRACTICE AREAS: Intellectual Property; Intellectual Property Litigation.
Durlacher, James M., (AV) '46 '76 C.679 B.S.M.E. L.345 J.D.
[Woodard,E.M.M.&H.]
*PRACTICE AREAS: Patents; Trademarks; Copyrights.
Emanuele, John J., Jr. ....'56 '02 C.959 B.S. L.966 J.D. [A Woodard,E.M.M.&H.]
*PRACTICE AREAS: Patents; Trademarks; Copyrights.
Emhardt, C. David, (AV) ....'31 '55 C.679 B.S. L.309 LL.B. [Woodard,E.M.M.&H.]
*PRACTICE AREAS: Patents; Trademarks; Copyrights.
Erdman, Kevin R., (AV) .... '63 '87 C.347 B.S. L.659 J.D. [Baker&D.]
*PRACTICE AREAS: Intellectual Property; Computer Law; Internet Law.
Forman, Alexander D. ....'75 '01 C.347 B.B.A. L.345 J.D. [A Ice M.]
*PRACTICE AREAS: Intellectual Property.
Fowler, Russell E., II ....'70 '96 C.679 B.S.E.E. L.345 J.D. [A Maginot M.&B.]
*PRACTICE AREAS: Patent Law; Trademark Law; Copyright Law; Intellectual Property Licensing.

Frisk, R. Randall, (AV) ...... '59 '85 C.679 B.S.M.E. L.345 J.D. [Woodard,E.M.M.&H.]
*PRACTICE AREAS: Patents; Trademarks; Copyrights.
Gandy, Kenneth A. ....'62 '88 C.347 B.S. L.345 J.D. [Woodard,E.M.M.&H.]
*PRACTICE AREAS: Patents; Trademarks; Copyrights.
Geib, Helen K. .... '— '00 C.222 B.A. L.365 J.D. [🅂 Barnes&T.]
*PRACTICE AREAS: Intellectual Property Litigation.
Goodson, Spencer P. .... '— '04 C.303 B.A. L.477 J.D. [🄰 Barnes&T.]
*PRACTICE AREAS: Intellectual Property; Litigation.
Gridley, Doreen J. .... '55 '95 C.657 B.S. L.347 J.D. [Ice M.]
*PRACTICE AREAS: Intellectual Property; Technology Law; Computer Law; Contracts; Sports Law.
Groen, Eric J. ....'56 '85 C.679 B.S.M.E. L.117 J.D. [Baker&D.]
*PRACTICE AREAS: Intellectual Property.
Gron, Gary M., (AV) ..... '38 '66 C.124 B.S.M.E. L.1003 J.D. [🄲 Woodard,E.M.M.&H.]
*PRACTICE AREAS: Patent Law; Trademark Law.
Hedges, Norman J. ....'71 '98 C.679 B.S.M.E. L.347 J.D. [🄰 Baker&D.]
Henderson, Ronald S. ....'— '96 C.679 B.S.M.E. L.345 J.D. [Barnes&T.]
*PRACTICE AREAS: Intellectual Property Procurement; Intellectual Property Rights; International Intellectual Property.
Henry, Thomas Q., (AV) ....'52 '75 C.679 B.S. L.345 J.D. [Woodard,E.M.M.&H.]
*PRACTICE AREAS: Patents; Trademarks; Copyrights.
Hiday, Lisa A. .... '64 '95 C.679 B.S.A.A.E. L.347 J.D. [Woodard,E.M.M.&H.]
*PRACTICE AREAS: Patents; Trademarks; Copyrights.
Hillis, Sanders N. ....'64 '99 C.610 B.S.E.E. L.347 J.D. [🄰 Brinks H.G.&L.]
*PRACTICE AREAS: Intellectual Property; Patents; Trademarks; Copyrights; Trade Secrets.
Howell, Kareem A. ....'75 '02 C.1286 B.S. L.347 J.D. [🄰 Baker&D.]
*PRACTICE AREAS: Intellectual Property.
Hughes, Dewayne A. .... '66 '00 C.249 B.S. L.345 J.D. [🄰 Ice M.]
*PRACTICE AREAS: Intellectual Property; Computers and Software; Contracts; Internet Law.
Hunt, Paul B., (BV) .... '— '90 C&L.339 B.S.M.E., J.D. [Barnes&T.]
*PRACTICE AREAS: Intellectual Property Litigation; Intellectual Property Licensing; Intellectual Property Portfolio Management; Theft of Trade Secrets.

Ice Miller, (AV) BB
One American Square Box 82001, 46282-0002 ⊙
Telephone: 317-236-2100 Fax: 317-236-2219
Email: info@icemiller.com URL: http://www.icemiller.com
Partners: Doreen J. Gridley; John F. Prescott, Jr.; Michael A. Swift; Jay G. Taylor; Thomas A. Walsh. Of Counsel: Jill Tabor Powlick. Associates: Gregory A. Duff; Dewayne A. Hughes; Rachel St. Peter.
Trademark, Copyright and Unfair Competition Law.
Representative Clients: Delco Remy America; Thomson Consumer Electronics, Inc.; Tivoli Systems, Inc.; BioAnalytical Systems, Inc.; Reilly Industries, Inc.; Ontario Corp.; Guide Corp.; Tokheim Corp.; Gaska, Tape, Inc.; Made2Manage Systems, Inc.; WaveTek Communications, Inc.; Wilhelm Environmental Technologies, Inc.; Sigma/Micro Corp.
Chicago, Illinois Office: 200 West Madison, Suite 3500. Telephone: 312-726-1567. Fax: 312-726-7102. Internet Email: info@icemiller.com. Web Site Address: http://www.icemiller.com.
Washington, D.C. Office: 1090 Vermont Avenue, N.W., Suite 920. Telephone: 202-824-8600. Fax: 202-824-8601. Email: info@icemiller.com.Web Site Address: http://www.icemiller.com
Reviser of the Indiana Law Digest for this Directory.
See Professional Biographies, INDIANAPOLIS, INDIANA

Jabbari, Sarah M. .... '71 '00 C.679 B.S. L.345 J.D. [🄰 Baker&D.]
Jones, Kurt N. ....'61 '92 C.701 B.S. L.347 J.D. [Woodard,E.M.M.&H.]
*PRACTICE AREAS: Patents; Trademarks; Copyrights.
Knight, Teresa E. .... '72 '04 C.940 B.A. L.345 J.D. [🄰 Woodard,E.M.M.&H.]
*PRACTICE AREAS: Patents; Trademarks; Copyrights.
Kulkarni, Dilip ....'— '75 C.999 B.S.E. L.347 J.D. [🄲 Barnes&T.]
*PRACTICE AREAS: Intellectual Property Licensing; Patent Prosecution; Business Law.
Ladd, Thomas A. ....'47 '74 C.477 B.S.Eng. L.215 J.D. [Baker&D.]
*PRACTICE AREAS: Intellectual Property.

Locke Reynolds LLP, (AV) BB
201 North Illinois, Suite 1000, P.O. Box 44961, 46244-0961
Telephone: 317-237-3800 Fax: 317-237-3900
URL: http://www.locke.com
Partners: James Dimos; Joel E. Tragesser.
Business Services, Construction and Real Estate Services, Financial Institutions, Government and Regulatory Services, Healthcare, Individual Services, Litigation, Products and Manufacturing, Tort Litigation and Insurance Services.
See Professional Biographies, INDIANAPOLIS, INDIANA

Lockman, David M. ....'55 '89 C.880 B.E.E.E. L.989 J.D. [Maginot M.&B.]
*PRACTICE AREAS: Intellectual Property; Computer and Software Patents; Patent Litigation; Trademark Litigation.
Lueders, Daniel J., (AV) .....'60 '86 C.597 B.S.C.E. L.1119 J.D. [Woodard,E.M.M.&H.]
*PRACTICE AREAS: Patents; Trademarks; Copyrights; Trade Secrets.
Maginot, Paul J., (AV) ....'61 '89 C.679 B.S. L.347 J.D. [Maginot M.&B.]
*PRACTICE AREAS: Patent Law; Trademark Law; Copyright Law.

Maginot Moore & Beck, (AV)
Bank One Center/Tower, 111 Monument Circle Suite 3000, 46204-5115
Telephone: 317-638-2922 Facsimile: 317-638-2139
URL: http://www.maginot.com
Paul J. Maginot; Harold C. Moore; Michael D. Beck; David M. Lockman. Associates: James D. Wood; Russell E. Fowler, II.
Patent, Trademark, Copyright, Intellectual Property, Licensing, Counseling and Litigation.
See Professional Biographies, INDIANAPOLIS, INDIANA

McLaren, Kevin L. .... '— '04 C.1167 B.S. L.345 J.D. [🄲 Barnes&T.]
*PRACTICE AREAS: Patents.
McNett, John C., (AV) ....'44 '70 C.679 B.S. L.273 J.D. [Woodard,E.M.M.&H.]
*PRACTICE AREAS: Patents; Trademarks; Copyrights.
Meyer, Charles J. ....'70 '95 C.210 B.A. L.347 J.D. [Woodard,E.M.M.&H.]
*PRACTICE AREAS: Patents; Trademarks; Copyrights.
Meyers, William S. .... '— '02 C.701 B.S. L.1119 J.D. [🄰 Baker&D.]
*PRACTICE AREAS: Intellectual Property.
Michael, Jeffrey A. ....'— '93 C.912 B.S.E.E. L.347 J.D. [Barnes&T.]
*PRACTICE AREAS: Patents; Computer and Software Patents; Electrical Patents; Semiconductor Technology; Mechanical Patents.
Moore, Harold C. ....'66 '93 C.401 B.S.E.E. L.705 J.D. [Maginot M.&B.]
*PRACTICE AREAS: Patent Law; Trademark Law; Licensing; Litigation.
Moriarty, John V., (AV) ......'40 '69 C.602 B.S.A.E. L.345 J.D. [Woodard,E.M.M.&H.]
*PRACTICE AREAS: Patents; Trademarks; Copyrights.
Naughton, Joseph A., Jr., (AV) '30 '60
C.602 B.S. L.345 LL.B. [🄲 Woodard,E.M.M.&H.]
*PRACTICE AREAS: Patents; Trademarks; Copyrights.
Niednagel, Timothy E. .... '63 '89 C.679 B.S.E.E. L.347 J.D. [Baker&D.]
*PRACTICE AREAS: Intellectual Property.
Null, Robert D. .... '65 '95 C.854 B.S.E.E. L.879 J.D. [Baker&D.]
*PRACTICE AREAS: Intellectual Property.
Paul, Timothy B. .... '76 '04 C.421 B.S. L.1119 J.D. [🄰 Woodard,E.M.M.&H.]
*PRACTICE AREAS: Patents; Copyrights; Trademarks.
Powlick, Jill Tabor .... '— '95 C.119 B.S. L.345 J.D. [🄲 Ice M.]
*PRACTICE AREAS: Intellectual Property; Biotechnology Patent Prosecution.
Prescott, John F., Jr., (AV) ....'50 '79 C.1229 B.S.M.E. L.345 J.D. [Ice M.]
*PRACTICE AREAS: Intellectual Property Litigation; Copyrights; Computer Software Litigation; Patent Litigation; Trade Secrets.
Reeves, Charles R., (AV) ....'51 '77 C.679 B.S. L.345 J.D. [Woodard,E.M.M.&H.]
*PRACTICE AREAS: Patents; Trademarks; Copyrights.

Reichel, Mark C. .... '74 '02 C.1505 B.S. L.345 J.D. [🄰 Ice M.]
*PRACTICE AREAS: Intellectual Property; Intellectual Property Prosecution.
Rezek, Richard A., (AV) .... '— '84 C.679 B.S.M.E. L.345 J.D. [Barnes&T.]
*PRACTICE AREAS: Intellectual Property Licensing; Patent Prosecution; International Patents; Mechanical Intellectual Property; Patent Infringement.
Richardson, A. James, (AV) .... '43 '74 C.173 A.B. L.273 J.D. [Brinks H.G.&L.]
*PRACTICE AREAS: International Patent and Trademark; Licensing; Patent Prosecution; Technology Transfer; Mechanical.
St. Peter, Rachel .... '74 '99 C.108 B.S. L.347 J.D. [🄰 Ice M.]
*PRACTICE AREAS: Intellectual Property.
Schell, Dennis S. ....'— '01 C.679 B.S.E.E. L.1119 J.D. [🄰 Barnes&T.]
*PRACTICE AREAS: Electrical Patent Prosecution; Electronic Patent Prosecution; Computer and Software Patent Prosecution; Electro-Mechanical Patent Prosecution; Business Methods Patent Prosecution.
Schmal, Charles P. .... '69 '00 C.679 B.S.I.E. L.1209 J.D. [Woodard,E.M.M.&H.]
*PRACTICE AREAS: Patent; Trademark.
Shuster, Elizabeth A. .... '70 '03 C.339 B.S. L.1119 J.D. [🄰 Woodard,E.M.M.&H.]
*PRACTICE AREAS: Copyrights; Patents; Trademarks.
Simmonds, Scott M. ....'69 '04 C.701 B.S.M.E. L.345 J.D. [🄰 Barnes&T.]
*PRACTICE AREAS: Intellectual Property; Intellectual Property Portfolio Management; Patents; Patent Litigation; Patent Infringement.
Smith, Kelly B. .... '— '02 C.679 B.A. L.347 J.D. [🅂 Barnes&T.]
*PRACTICE AREAS: Patent Litigation.
Sowers, Edward E. .... '42 '91 C.894 A.B. L.1119 J.D. [🄲 Woodard,E.M.M.&H.]
*PRACTICE AREAS: Patents; Trademarks; Copyrights.
Stevens, Scott J., (BV) ....'52 '77 C.475 B.S.E.E. L.705 J.D. [Woodard,E.M.M.&H.]
*PRACTICE AREAS: Patents; Trademarks; Copyrights.
Steward, Lawrence A. .... '50 '79 C&L.851 B.S., J.D. [🄲 Brinks H.G.&L.]
*PRACTICE AREAS: Intellectual Property; Patent Prosecution; Patent Litigation; Biotechnology and Pharmaceuticals; Chemical.
Stewart, Carli E. .... '— '01 C.679 B.S.M.E. L.345 J.D. [🄰 Barnes&T.]
*PRACTICE AREAS: Intellectual Property Law.
Sukhapinda, Kitisri .... '— '02 C.576 B.S. L.1119 J.D. [🄰 Barnes&T.]
*PRACTICE AREAS: Patent Prosecution; Patent Litigation; Patent Licensing.
Swedo, Keith J. .... '63 '95 C.679 B.S. L.345 J.D. [🄰 Baker&D.]
*PRACTICE AREAS: Patents; Intellectual Property; Trademarks.
Sweeney, James R., II, (CV) ....'— '96 C.871 B.S. L.602 J.D. [Barnes&T.]
*PRACTICE AREAS: Intellectual Property; Computers and Software; Business Law.
Swift, Michael A. .... '57 '94 C.854 B.S. L.345 J.D. [Ice M.]
*PRACTICE AREAS: Intellectual Property; Litigation; Information and Privacy; Business Law.
Taylor, Jay G., (AV) ....'40 '67 C.150 B.S.M.E. L.1119 J.D. [Ice M.]
*PRACTICE AREAS: Intellectual Property; Patent; Trademark; Copyright; Trade Secrets Law.
Thomas, Timothy N. ....'54 '90 C.679 B.S. L.347 J.D. [Woodard,E.M.M.&H.]
*PRACTICE AREAS: Patents; Trademarks; Copyrights.
Tinsley, Nancy G., (AV) .... '61 '90 C.679 B.S. L.347 J.D. [Baker&D.]
*PRACTICE AREAS: Litigation; Intellectual Property.
Tragesser, Joel E. ....'73 '97 C.894 A.B. L.880 J.D. [Locke R.]
*PRACTICE AREAS: Business Litigation; Intellectual Property.
Wagner, Vincent O., (AV) ...... '51 '76 C.602 B.S. L.1119 J.D. [Woodard,E.M.M.&H.]
*PRACTICE AREAS: Patents; Trademarks; Copyrights.
Walsh, Thomas A. .... '64 '95 C.679 B.S.I.E. L.347 J.D. [Ice M.]
*PRACTICE AREAS: Patent Law; Computers and Software; Internet Law; Information and Privacy; Trademarks.
Wever, Michael E. '72 '97 C.701 B.S. L.790 J.D.
(adm. in SC; not adm. in IN) [🄰 Brinks H.G.&L.]
*PRACTICE AREAS: Intellectual Property.
Wherry, Michael S. .... '68 '03 C.701 B.S. L.1119 J.D. [🄰 Woodard,E.M.M.&H.]
*PRACTICE AREAS: Copyrights; Patents; Trademarks.
Wood, James D. ....'60 '98 C.871 B.S. L.273 J.D. [🄰 Maginot M.&B.]
*PRACTICE AREAS: Patents; Trademarks; Litigation.

Woodard, Emhardt, Moriarty, McNett & Henry LLP, (AV) BB
Bank One Center/Tower, 111 Monument Circle, Suite 3700, 46204-5137
Telephone: 317-634-3456 Telecopier: 317-637-7561
URL: http://www.uspatent.com
Members of Firm: C. David Emhardt; John V. Moriarty; John C. McNett; Thomas Q. Henry; James M. Durlacher; Charles R. Reeves; Vincent O. Wagner; Stephen E. Zlatos; Spiro Bereveskos; Clifford W. Browning; R. Randall Frisk; Daniel J. Lueders; Kenneth A. Gandy; Timothy N. Thomas; Kurt N. Jones; Holiday W. Banta; Troy J. Cole; Charles J. Meyer; Lisa A. Hiday; John V. Daniluck; Scott J. Stevens; Charles P. Schmal. Associates: John M. Bradshaw; Quentin G. Cantrell; John J. Emanuele, Jr.; Michael S. Wherry; Elizabeth A. Shuster; Michael A. Benefield; Timothy B. Paul; Teresa E. Knight; Adam W. Borgman. Of Counsel: Joseph A. Naughton, Jr.; Edward E. Sowers; Gary M. Gron.
Patent, Trademark, Copyright, Unfair Competition, Computer, Franchise and related Antitrust Law. Trials and Appeals.
See Professional Biographies, INDIANAPOLIS, INDIANA

Yerkeson, Douglas A. .... '67 '94 C&L.150 B.S.M.E., J.D. [🄲 Baker&D.]
*PRACTICE AREAS: Intellectual Property.
Yoon, Hongsun .... '— '02 C.347 B.S. L.1119 J.D. [🄰 Barnes&T.]
*PRACTICE AREAS: Intellectual Property; Intellectual Property Litigation; Intellectual Property Prosecution.
Zlatos, Stephen E., (AV) ....'51 '77 C.679 B.S.E. L.345 J.D. [Woodard,E.M.M.&H.]
*PRACTICE AREAS: Patents; Trademarks; Copyrights.

NEW CARLISLE, 1,446, *St. Joseph Co.*

Crump, R. Tracy '65 '92 C.108 B.S. L.879 J.D.
P.O. Box 604, 46552
Telephone: 574-654-8222 Fax: 574-654-8577
Email: rtc@rtclaw.com URL: http://www.rtclaw.com
***PRACTICE AREAS: Patent; Trademark; Copyright; Intellectual Property.**
Intellectual Property, Copyrights, Licensing Agreements, Patents, Trade Secrets, Trademarks.
See Professional Biographies, NEW CARLISLE, INDIANA

SOUTH BEND, * 107,789, *St. Joseph Co.*

Baker & Daniels LLP, (AV) BB
First Bank Building, 205 West Jefferson Boulevard, Suite 250, 46601 ⊙
Telephone: 574-234-4149 Fax: 574-239-1900
URL: http://www.bakerdaniels.com
Members of Firm: Gerard T. Gallagher. Associates: Daniel Tychonievich.
Antitrust, Bankruptcy, Business Planning, Commercial, Corporate Finance, Creditors Rights, Employee Benefits, Employment, Environment, Estate and Probate, Family, Financial, Food and Drug, Government Affairs, Health Care, Insurance, Intellectual Property, International, Legislative, Litigation, Medical Technology Regulation, Municipal, Nonprofit, Product Liability, Real Estate, Securities, Sports, Tax, Transportation, Utilities, Year 2000, Zoning and Land Use Law.
Indianapolis, Indiana Office: 300 North Meridian Street, Suite 2700, 46204. Telephone: 317-237-0300. Fax: 317-237-1000.
Fort Wayne, Indiana Office: 111 East Wayne Street, Suite 800, 46802. Telephone: 260-424-8000. Fax: 260-460-1700.
Elkhart, Indiana Office: 317 West Franklin Street, P.O. Box 507, 46515-0507. Telephone: 574-296-6000. Fax: 574-296-6001.
Indianapolis-96th Street, Indiana Office: Parkwood Six, 600 East 96th Street, Suite 600, 46240. Telephone: 317-569-9600. Fax: 317-569-4800.
Washington, D.C. Office: 805 15th Street, N.W., Suite 700, 20005. Telephone: 202-312-7440. Fax: 202-312-7460.
Qingdao, China Office: 4/F, Office Tower, Crowne Plaza Qingdao, No. 76 Hong Kong Middle Road, 266071. Telephone: +011-86-532-575-1051. Fax: +011-86-532-575-1055.

(This Listing Continued)

Baker & Daniels LLP (Continued)

Beijing, China Office: Room 1919, Tower 2, China World Trade Center, No. 1 JianGuoMenWai Avenue, 100004. Telephone: +86-10-6505-7733. Fax: +86-10-6505-8730.

See Professional Biographies, SOUTH BEND, INDIANA

Gallagher, Gerard T., (BV) .... '— '92 C&L.602 B.S., J.D. [Baker&D.]
*PRACTICE AREAS: Intellectual Property.

Tychonievich, Daniel ....'— '96 C.608 B.S.W.E. L.602 J.D. [Ⓐ Baker&D.]
*PRACTICE AREAS: Intellectual Property.

CEDAR RAPIDS, * 120,758, *Linn Co.*

Carter, Ryan N. . . . . '75 '02 C.352 B.S. L.801 J.D. [🄰 Shuttleworth&I.]
*PRACTICE AREAS: Patent; Trademark; Intellectual Property; General Practice; Copyrights.

Hoke, Robert W., II . . . .'51 '77 C.350 B.S., Ch.E. L.352 J.D. [Shuttleworth&I.]
*PRACTICE AREAS: Trademarks; Patents; Copyrights; Intellectual Property Licensing; Intellectual Property.

Johnson, Glenn L., (AV) . . . . '50 '75 C.173 B.A. L.352 J.D. [Shuttleworth&I.]
*PRACTICE AREAS: Patents; Trademarks; Civil Litigation; Technology and Science; Employment Law.

Nemmers, James C., (AV) . . . .'31 '57 C.350 B.S. L.352 J.D. [🄲 Shuttleworth&I.]
*PRACTICE AREAS: Patents; Trademarks; Copyrights; Intellectual Property.

Shuttleworth & Ingersoll, P.L.C., (AV)
115 Third Street S.E., Suite 500, 52401
Mailing Address: P.O. Box 2107, Cedar Rapids, IA 52406-2107
Telephone: 319-365-9461 Fax: 319-365-8443
URL: http://www.shuttleworthlaw.com
James C. Nemmers; Glenn L. Johnson.
Representative Clients: Aegon USA; Diamond V Mills; HWH Corporation; PMX Industries; Swiss Valley Farms; Quaker Oats Company; Iowa Precision Industries, Inc.; American Trencher, Inc.; Stamats Communications, Inc.

See Professional Biographies, CEDAR RAPIDS, IOWA

Simmons, Perrine, Albright & Ellwood, P.L.C., (AV)
115 Third Street S.E. Suite 1200, 52401 ⊙
Telephone: 319-366-7641 Telecopier: 319-366-1917
URL: http://www.simmonsperrine.com
Partner: Gregory G. Williams. Associate: Michael F. Williams
Iowa City Office: Third Floor Tower Place, 22 South Linn Street, 52240. Telephone: 319-887-1368. Fax: 319-887-1372.

See Professional Biographies, CEDAR RAPIDS, IOWA

Williams, Gregory G., (BV) . . . . '59 '85 C&L.352 B.A., J.D. [Simmons,P.A.&E.] ⊙
*PRACTICE AREAS: Patents; Trademark and Unfair Competition; Copyrights.

Williams, Michael F. . . . . '60 '91 C.898 B.A. L.352 J.D. [🄰 Simmons,P.A.&E.]
*PRACTICE AREAS: Intellectual Property; Patents; Trademarks.

DAVENPORT, * 98,359, *Scott Co.*

Cepican, John E., (BV) . . . . '48 '74 C.350 B.S. L.221 J.D. [Sturm&F.]

Sturm & Fix LLP, (AV)
304 Northwest Bank Building-Downtown, 101 West Second Street, 52801-1813 ⊙
Telephone: 563-323-9731 Fax: 563-323-9709
URL: http://www.hsllp.com
Member of Firm: John E. Cepican.
Patent, Trademark, Copyright and Unfair Competition Law, Federal Trial Practice, Intellectual Property.
Des Moines, Iowa Office: 206 Sixth Avenue, Suite 1213, 50309-4076. Telephone: 515-288-9589. Fax: 515-288-4860.

See Professional Biographies, DAVENPORT, IOWA

DES MOINES, * 198,682, *Polk Co.*

Akrad, Lila A.T. . . . . '71 '03 C.378 B.S. L.1194 J.D. [🄰 McKee,V.&S.]
*PRACTICE AREAS: Intellectual Property; Patents; Biotechnology Patents; Trademarks; Copyrights.

Davis, Brown, Koehn, Shors & Roberts, P.C., (AV) [BR]
The Financial Center, 666 Walnut Street, Suite 2500, 50309-3993 ⊙
Telephone: 515-288-2500 Cable: Davis Law Facsimile: 515-243-0654
Email: info@lawiowa.com URL: http://www.lawiowa.com
Kent A. Herink;—Daniel A. Rosenberg.
Patent Law.
West Des Moines, Iowa Office: 4201 Westown Parkway, Suite 300, 50266. Telephone: 515-288-2500. Fax: 515-246-7997.

See Professional Biographies, DES MOINES, IOWA

Fisher, Bart A. . . . .'70 '04 C.375 B.S. L.900 J.D. [🄰 McKee,V.&S.]
*PRACTICE AREAS: Intellectual Property; Patents; Trademarks; Copyrights.

Fix, Richard L., (AV) . . . . '43 '76 C.352 B.S. L.221 J.D. [Sturm&F.]

Goodhue, John D. . . . .'74 '00 C.701 B.S. L.221 J.D. [🄰 McKee,V.&S.]
*PRACTICE AREAS: Intellectual Property; Business Method Patents; Software Protection; Domain Names.

Hansing, Mark D., (AV) . . . . '56 '81 C.427 B.A. L.352 J.D. [McKee,V.&S.]
*PRACTICE AREAS: Patents; Trademarks; Copyrights.

Hartung, Kirk M., (AV) . . . .'55 '82 C.350 B.S. L.352 J.D. [McKee,V.&S.]
*PRACTICE AREAS: Patents; Trademarks; Copyright Litigation.

Harty, Jeffrey D., (BV) . . . .'68 '95 C.350 B.S. L.352 J.D. [McKee,V.&S.]
*PRACTICE AREAS: Patents; Trademarks; Copyrights; Litigation.

Herink, Kent A., (AV) . . . . '55 '82 C.162 B.A. L.352 J.D. [Davis,B.K.S.&R.]
*PRACTICE AREAS: Intellectual Property; Trademarks.

Hodgson, Robert A. . . . . '77 '03 C&L.352 B.A., J.D. [🄰 McKee,V.&S.]
*PRACTICE AREAS: Intellectual Property; Patents; Trademarks; Copyrights; Litigation.

Johnson, R. Scott . . . .'73 '00 C.350 B.S. L.221 J.D. [McKee,V.&S.]
*PRACTICE AREAS: Intellectual Property; Patents; Trademarks; Copyrights; Litigation.

Lehman Bell, Janáe . . . .'71 '04 C.627 B.S. L.352 J.D. [🄰 McKee,V.&S.]
*PRACTICE AREAS: Intellectual Property; Patents; Trademarks; Copyrights; Litigation.

Marsh, Wendy K., (BV) . . . .'67 '94 C&L.221 B.S., J.D. [McKee,V.&S.]
*PRACTICE AREAS: Intellectual Property; Chemical Patents; Pharmaceutical Patents; Trademarks; Copyrights.

McKee, Bruce W., (AV) . . . .'34 '59 C.350 B.S.E. L.904 J.D. [McKee,V.&S.]
*PRACTICE AREAS: Patents; Trademarks; Copyrights.

McKee, Voorhees & Sease, P.L.C., (AV) [BR]
801 Grand, Suite 3200, 50309-2721
Telephone: 515-288-3667 Facsimile: 515-288-1338
Email: patatty@ipmvs.com URL: http://www.ipmvs.com
Members of Firm: Bruce W. McKee; Michael G. Voorhees; Edmund J. Sease; Mark D. Hansing; Kirk M. Hartung; Heidi Sease Nebel; Wendy K. Marsh; Jeffrey D. Harty; R. Scott Johnson. Associates: John D. Goodhue; Lila A.T. Akrad; Robert A. Hodgson; Bart A. Fisher; Janáe Lehman Bell.
Intellectual Property and Technology Law, including Patent, Trademark, Copyright, Trade Secret, Licensing, Antitrust. State and Federal Trial Practice.
Reference: Bank of America (Des Moines, Iowa).

See Professional Biographies, DES MOINES, IOWA

Nebel, Heidi Sease, (AV) . . . .'67 '92 C.352 B.S. L.221 J.D. [McKee,V.&S.]
*PRACTICE AREAS: Intellectual Property; Biotechnology Patents.

Rosenberg, Daniel A., (BV) . . . .'56 '97 C.350 B.S. L.221 J.D. [Davis,B.K.S.&R.]
*PRACTICE AREAS: Intellectual Property; Trademarks; Copyrights; Patents.

Sease, Edmund J., (AV) . . . . '42 '67 C&L.221 B.A., J.D. [McKee,V.&S.]
*PRACTICE AREAS: Patents; Trademarks; Copyrights; Litigation.

Sturm, Michael O., (AV) . . . . '43 '73 C.350 B.S. L.1128 J.D. [Sturm&F.]

Sturm & Fix LLP, (AV) [BR]
206 Sixth Avenue, Suite 1213, 50309-4076 ⊙
Telephone: 515-288-9589 Fax: 515-288-4860
Email: sturm@hsllp.com URL: http://www.hsllp.com
Members of Firm: Michael O. Sturm; John E. Cepican; Richard L. Fix.
Patent, Trademark, Copyright and Unfair Competition Law, Federal Trial Practice, Intellectual Property.
Reference: Wells Fargo Bank Iowa, N.A.
Davenport, Iowa Office: 304 Northwest Bank Building-Downtown, 101 West Second Street, 52801-1813. Telephone: 563-323-9731. Fax: 563-323-9709.

See Professional Biographies, DES MOINES, IOWA

Voorhees, Michael G., (AV) . . . .'41 '68 C.350 B.S. L.221 J.D. [McKee,V.&S.]
*PRACTICE AREAS: Patents; Trademarks; Copyrights; Litigation.

PROFESSIONAL BIOGRAPHIES SECTION

IDAHO, ILLINOIS
INDIANA, IOWA

BEARD ST. CLAIR GAFFNEY McNAMARA CALDER PA

BLACKFOOT, IDAHO

(See Idaho Falls)

Agricultural Law, Acquisitions, Americans with Disabilities Act, Antitrust, Arbitration, Asset Protection, Automobile Accidents, Automobile Insurance, Banking Law, Breach of Contract, Business Law, Buying and Selling Businesses, Charitable Giving, Collections, Commercial Insurance, Commercial Law, Commercial Real Estate, Computers and Software, Condominiums, Construction Law, Contested Wills, Contracts, Copyrights, Corporations, Creditors Rights, Crop Damage and Chemical Applications, Debtor and Creditor, Discrimination, Distribution and Distributorships, Divorce with significant assets, Elder Care, Elder Law, Employment Discrimination, Employment Law, Estate Planning, Estate and Gift Taxation, Family Business Law, Family and Medical Leave Act, Farm and Ranch Law, Fire Loss, Food, Drug and Cosmetic Law, Franchises and Franchising, Foreclosures, General Trial and Appellate Practice, Guardianship, Harassment, Health Care, Health Insurance, Income Taxation, Insurance, Insurance Bad Faith, Investments, Landlord and Tenant Law, Leasing, Liens, Life and Health Insurance, Limited Liability Company Law, Litigation, Long-term Care, Mechanics Liens, Mediation, Medical Malpractice and Malpractice Defense, Medicare and Medicaid, Minority Business Law, Mortgages, Multilevel Sales, Nonprofit and Charitable Organizations, Nursing Homes, PACA, Partnerships, Pension and Benefits, Personal Injury, Post Mortem Administration of Trusts and Estates, Products Liabilities, Professional Malpractice, Property Tax, Professional Practices, Property Insurance, Railroad Accidents, Real Estate, Sexual Abuse, Slip and Fall, Small Business Law, Social Security, Social Security Disability, Taxation, Torts, Trademarks, Trade Secrets, Trust and Estates, Valuations, Warranties, Wills and Probate, Workers Compensation, Wrongful Death, Wrongful Termination, Zoning, Planning and Land Use.

MERRILL & MERRILL

CHARTERED

BLACKFOOT, IDAHO

(See Pocatello)

General Civil Practice. Trials and Appeals in all State and Federal Courts. Probate, Real Estate, Insurance Law, Negligence, Corporate, Estate Planning, Education Law, Taxation, Hospital Law, Workers Compensation and Public Utility Law.

ANDERSON, JULIAN & HULL

Established in 1998

C.W. MOORE PLAZA
250 SOUTH 5TH STREET, SUITE 700
P.O. BOX 7426
BOISE, IDAHO 83707-7426
Telephone: 208-344-5800
Fax: 208-344-5510
URL: http://www.andersonjhlaw.com
Email: ajhlaw@ajhlaw.com
URL: http://www.ajhlaw.com

Insurance Defense, Education Law, Worker's Compensation, Complex Commercial Litigation, Construction Law, Real Estate, Professional Liability, Personal Injury Defense, Employment Law, Defense of Governmental Entities, Civil Rights, Insurance Coverage Disputes, Automobile Insurance, Fire Insurance, ERISA Litigation, Products Liability, Commercial Transactions, Trial Practice, Appellate Practice, Alternative Dispute Resolution, Immigration and Naturalization, Environmental Litigation, and Natural Resources Litigation.

FIRM PROFILE: Established August 1, 1998, Anderson, Julian & Hull LLP, has established itself as a respected member of the Idaho legal community. AJH is dedicated to providing skilled and comprehensive legal services to a wide range of clients. We understand the need to provide a carefully planned representation in a cost-sensitive environment. We pledge to work with each client, regardless of size, to carefully develop a budgetary framework for each case, and then execute a well-structured plan for the handling of diverse legal matters. Through the use of technological advances, we will provide our clients with the latest innovations in legal research, billing requirements, and client communication.

MEMBERS OF FIRM

ROBERT A. ANDERSON, born Stillwater, Oklahoma, May 17, 1951; admitted to bar, 1977, Idaho and U.S. District Court, District of Idaho and U.S. Court of Appeals, Ninth Circuit. *Education:* University of Utah (B.S., magna cum laude, 1973); University of Colorado (J.D., 1977). Phi Kappa Phi. Regional Editor: "Covered Events," DRI publication: DRI Construction Law Committee Newsletter. Author: "Construction Arbitration-The Answer or Ambush?" Idaho State Bar Publication, The Advocate, August 1993; "The Cardinal Change Doctrine's Difficult Transition from Federal to State Courts," 1997, Wiley Construction Law Update; "Insurance Law: Third Party Coverage in Idaho," NBI publication, 1996; "Insurance Coverage Law in Idaho," NBI publication, 1997; "Insurance Law: Third-Party Claims in Idaho," NBI Publication, 1998; "Consequential Damages: Do They Really Threaten the Construction Industry and, If So, Is the AIA 'Mutual Waiver' The Cure?" Wiley Construction Law Update, 1999; "Idaho Construction Law: Contracts, Administration and Claim Disputes on Commercial Projects," 2000. Lecturer: American Society of Professional Engineers; American Institute of Architects; Consulting Engineers of Idaho; National Business Institute Seminar, and Idaho Law Foundation. Moderator: Seminar on Insurance Fraud in Idaho. Chairman, Interest on Lawyers' Trust Accounts Committee, 1993—. *Member:* Idaho State Bar (Chairman, Law Foundation Ethics Committee, 1991); Fourth District (President, 1991) and American (Member, Sections on Tort and Insurance) Bar Associations; Defense Research Institute; Idaho Association of Defense Counsel.

(This Listing Continued)

PRACTICE AREAS: Insurance Defense; Construction Litigation; Trial Practice; Professional Malpractice; Commercial Litigation; Insurance Coverage Disputes; Appellate Practice. ***Email:*** raanderson@ajhlaw.com

BRIAN K. JULIAN, born Montpelier, Idaho, June 15, 1954; admitted to bar, 1979, Idaho and U.S. District Court, District of Idaho; 1980, U.S. Court of Appeals, Ninth Circuit; 1987, U.S. Supreme Court; Nez Perce Indian Tribal Court. *Education:* Utah State University (B.S., cum laude, 1976); University of Idaho (J.D., cum laude, 1978). Phi Alpha Delta. Managing Editor, University of Idaho Law Review, 1978-1979. Author: "The Prosecutor's Duty to Disclose Exculpatory Evidence," 14 Idaho Law 223, 1977. Author and Lecturer: "Sexual Harassment Claims," Sixth Annual Education Law Institute, 1997; "The Handling and Documentation of Employment Investigations," Seventh Annual Education Law Institute, 1998; "Evaluations & Their Roles in the Litigation Process," Eighth Annual Education Law Institute, 1999; "Sexual Harassment," Ninth Annual Education Law Institute, 2000; "Avoiding Discrimination Claims in the Hiring Process," Tenth Annual Education Law Institute, 2001. Author and Publisher, "The Law of Education in Idaho," and the "Idaho Uniform Manual of Policies and Procedures for Schools." *Member:* Boise and American (Tort and Insurance Practice Sections) Bar Associations; Idaho State Bar; Defense Research Institute; Idaho Association of Defense Counsel; Boise Adjuster's Association. ***PRACTICE AREAS:*** Trial Practice; Insurance Defense; Education Law; Employment Law; Governmental Entities; Civil Rights; Products Liability; Professional Malpractice; Premises Liability; Appellate Practice. ***Email:*** bjulian@ajhlaw.com

ALAN K. HULL, born Moscow, Idaho, June 30, 1947; admitted to bar, 1973, Idaho. *Education:* University of Idaho (B.S., 1969; J.D., 1973). Editor in Chief, University of Idaho Law Review, 1972-1973. Law Clerk, Justice Charles R. Donaldson, Idaho Supreme Court, 1973-1974. Author: "Idaho's Expanding Security Act," University of Idaho Law Review, 1972. Lecturer: Idaho Industrial Commission Annual Convention; Idaho State Bar Workers Compensation Section, Annual Meetings; Workers Compensation Matters, Continuing Legal Education Seminars. Chief Deputy, Prosecuting Attorney's Office, Civil Division, Ada County. *Member:* Idaho State Bar (Chairman, Insurance Committee, 1981-1983; Member, Board of Advisors, 1981-1983, and Member, Workers Compensation Section); American Bar Association; Defense Research and Trial Lawyers Association; International Association of Industrial Accident Boards and Commissions. ***PRACTICE AREAS:*** Workers' Compensation. ***Email:*** akhull@ajhlaw.com

CHRIS H. HANSEN, born Boise, Idaho, July 22, 1957; admitted to bar, 1983, Idaho and U.S. District Court, District of Idaho. *Education:* Boise State University (B.B.A., 1979); University of Idaho (J.D., 1983). Co-Author: "Evaluations and Their Role in Litigation," Eighth Annual Education Law Institute, 1999; "A Practical Guide to Federal Court Rules and Procedures in Idaho: Ethical Considerations," National Business Institute, 2000. *Member:* Idaho State Bar; American Bar Association; Boise Adjuster's Association. ***PRACTICE AREAS:*** Insurance Defense; Trial Practice; Professional Malpractice; Accountant Malpractice; Legal Malpractice; Real Estate Broker Malpractice; Products Liability; Personal Injury; Employment Law. ***Email:*** chhansen@ajhlaw.com

PHILLIP J. COLLAER, born Blackfoot, Idaho, January 2, 1956; admitted to bar, 1985, Idaho and U.S. District Court, District of Idaho; 1988, U.S. Court of Appeals, Ninth Circuit; 1994, U.S. Supreme Court. *Education:* University of Idaho (B.S., 1979); Gonzaga University (J.D., 1985). Phi Alpha Delta. Author and Lecturer: "Employee Recommendations, Tort of Negligent Hiring and Referral," Sixth Annual Education Law Institute, 1997; "Search and Seizure in the Public Schools," Seventh Annual Education Law Institute, 1998; "Individual Liability of Trustees and Administrations," Eighth Annual Education Law Institute, 1999; "At -Will Employment and the Rights of Classified Employees," Ninth Annual Education Law Institute, 2000; "How to Conduct Investigations, Including Proper Use of a Garrity' Notice," Tenth Annual Education Law Institute, 2001. Prosecuting Attorney, Ada County, 1985-1989. *Member:* Boise Bar Association; Idaho State Bar; Boise Adjuster's Association. ***PRACTICE AREAS:*** Insurance Defense; Real Estate Litigation; Appellate Practice; Education Law; Governmental Entities Defense; Employment Law; Agricultural Claims. ***Email:*** pcollaer@ajhlaw.com

MICHAEL P. STEFANIC II, born Pueblo, Colorado, January 9, 1963; admitted to bar, 1989, Idaho and U.S. District Court, District of Idaho; 1992, Colorado. *Education:* The Colorado College (B.A., 1985); University of Idaho (J.D., 1989). National Moot Court Team. *Member:* Idaho State Bar; Colorado Bar Association; Defense Research Institute; Idaho Association of Defense Counsel; Boise Adjusters Association (President, 2001); Idaho Motor Transportation Association; Conference of Freight Counsel; American Inns of Court, Inn. No. 130. ***PRACTICE AREAS:*** Insurance Defense; Transportation; Trucking Law; Construction Litigation; Commercial Disputes. ***Email:*** mstefanic@ajhlaw.com

AMY G. WHITE, born Pittsburgh, Pennsylvania, August 11, 1967; admitted to bar, 1992, Pennsylvania; 1993, U.S. District Court, Western District of Pennsylvania; 1994, Idaho and U.S. District Court, District of Idaho; 1995, U.S. Court of Appeals, Ninth Circuit. *Education:* Pennsylvania State University (B.S., 1989); McGeorge School of Law, University of the Pacific (J.D., 1992) Dean's List, 1991-1992. Phi Delta Phi. Law Clerk, Honorable Gerald F. Schroeder and Thomas F. Neville, Fourth Judicial District, Idaho, 1994-1995. Co-Author: "Sexual Harassment Claims," Sixth Annual Education Law Institute, 1997; "The Handling and Documentation of Employment Investigations," Seventh Annual Education Law Institute, 1998; "Sexual Harassment," Ninth Annual Education Law Institute, 2000; "Avoiding Discrimination Claims in the Hiring Process," Tenth Annual Education Law Institute, 2001. Contributing Author and Editor, "The Law of Education in Idaho," and the "Idaho Uniform Manual of Polices and Procedures for Schools." *Member:* Pennsylvania and American Bar Associations; Idaho State Bar; Boise Adjuster's Association; Defense Research Institute; American Inns of Court, Inn No. 130. ***PRACTICE AREAS:*** Insurance Defense; Employment Law; Governmental Entity Defense; Education Law; Premises Liability. ***Email:*** agwhite@ajhlaw.com

ASSOCIATES

RANDALL L. SCHMITZ, born West Covina, California, July 30, 1970; admitted to bar, 1999, Oregon; 2000, Idaho. *Education:* Willamette University (B.S., 1993; M.B.A., 1997; J.D., 1997). Phi Delta Phi. *Member:* Idaho State Bar; American Bar Association. ***Email:*** rschmitz@ajhlaw.com

(This Listing Continued)

ANDERSON, JULIAN & HULL, Boise—Continued

JUSTIN P. AYLSWORTH, born Seattle, Washington, February 13, 1971; admitted to bar, 1997, Idaho and U.S. District Court, District of Idaho. *Education:* Boise State University (B.S., 1994); Gonzaga University School of Law (J.D., 1997). Recipient, American Jurisprudence Award in Research and Writing. Law Clerk for U.S. District Court, District of Idaho. *Member:* Idaho State Bar; American Bar Association. ***PRACTICE AREAS:*** Workers Compensation; Insurance Defense. ***Email:*** jaylsworth@ajhlaw.com

PAUL J. STARK, born Bountiful, Utah, January 1, 1970; admitted to bar, 1999, Idaho. *Education:* Boise State University (B.A., 1996); University of Arkansas (J.D., 1998). Honor Society, Boise State University. Member, American Inns of Court, 2002-2003. Member, Editorial Advisory Board, The Advocate, 2001—. Member, Interagency Coordinating Council, 2002—. *Member:* Idaho State Bar. ***LANGUAGES:*** Danish. ***Email:*** pstark@ajhlaw.com

MATTHEW O. PAPPAS, born Moscow, Idaho, May 4, 1975; admitted to bar, 2000, Idaho. *Education:* University of Idaho (B.S., 1997; J.D., 2000). *Member:* Idaho State Bar. ***Email:*** mpappas@ajhlaw.com

BRIAN J. COFFEY, born Washington, D.C., December 15, 1970; admitted to bar, 1996, California; 2003, Idaho. *Education:* University of San Diego (B.A., 1993; J.D., 1996). Formerly with: Ling, Robinson & Walker, Rupert, Idaho; Neil, Dymott, Perkins, Brown & Frank, San Diego, California. *Member:* Idaho State Bar (Member, Water Law Committee); State Bar of California; American Bar Association. ***PRACTICE AREAS:*** Civil Litigation; Business Litigation; Employment Law. ***Email:*** bcoffey@ajhlaw.com

TODD M. JOYNER, born Whittier, California, December 1, 1962; admitted to bar, 1991, Idaho. *Education:* Utah State University (B.S., 1988); Brigham Young University (J.D., 1991). Magistrate, 2003-2004. ***PRACTICE AREAS:*** Education Law; Construction Law; Employment Law; Personal Injury; Products Liability. ***Email:*** tjoyner@ajhlaw.com

GLENDA M. TALBUTT, born Naha, Okinawa, Japan, September 29, 1963; admitted to bar, 1997, Idaho and U.S. District Court, District of Idaho. *Education:* University of South Carolina (B.S., 1984); University of Oregon (J.D., 1997). *Member:* Idaho State Bar; Idaho Women Lawyers. ***PRACTICE AREAS:*** Insurance Defense; Adoption Law; Guardianship; Wills. ***Email:*** gtalbutt@ajhlaw.com

RACHAEL M. O'BAR, born Thomasville, Alabama, November 2, 1967; admitted to bar, 1998, Idaho. *Education:* University of West Florida (B.A., 1994); Cumberland School of Law of Samford University (J.D., 1998). Phi Delta Phi. Recipient, Presidential Scholar; Scholar of Merit. Historian; Editor, Am. Journal of Trial Advocacy. Author: "Contributory Negligence," American Journal of Trial Advocacy, Vol 21:1, 1997. *Member:* Idaho State Bar (Member, Sections on: Intellectual Property and Young Lawyers; Workers Compensation). ***PRACTICE AREAS:*** Workers Compensation; Personal Injury. ***Email:*** robar@ajhlaw.com

OF COUNSEL

KENNETH D. NYMAN, born Seward, Alaska, June 20, 1948; admitted to bar, 1975, Arizona; 1984, Idaho; U.S. District Court, District of Idaho; U.S. Court of Appeals, Ninth and Tenth Circuits. *Education:* University of Idaho (B.A., 1971); Harvard University (J.D., 1975). *Member:* State Bar of Arizona; Idaho State Bar; American Bar Association (Member, Sections on: Litigation and Antitrust). ***PRACTICE AREAS:*** Commercial Litigation; Commercial Transactions. ***Email:*** knyman@ajhlaw.com

BARKER ROSHOLT & SIMPSON LLP

205 NORTH 10TH STREET, SUITE 520
P.O. BOX 2139
BOISE, IDAHO 83701-2139
Telephone: 208-336-0700
Facsimile: 208-344-6034
Email: brs@idahowaters.com
URL: http://www.idaho-waters.com

Twin Falls, Idaho Office: 113 Main Avenue West, Suite 303, 83301. Telephone: 208-733-0700. Facsimile: 208-735-2444.

Natural Resources, Water, Environmental, Construction and Commercial Litigation.

ALBERT P. BARKER, born Fort Jackson, South Carolina, September 6, 1954; admitted to bar, 1981, Virginia; 1982, Idaho. *Education:* Yale University (B.A., 1976); College of William and Mary (J.D., 1981). Order of the Coif. Law Clerk, Hon. Allan G. Shepard, Idaho Supreme Court, 1981-1982. ***PRACTICE AREAS:*** Environmental Law; Natural Resources Law; Construction Law; Trademark Law. ***Email:*** apb@idahowaters.com

JOHN K. SIMPSON, born Moscow, Idaho, May 3, 1957; admitted to bar, 1990, Idaho and U.S. District Court, District of Idaho; 1992, Oregon. *Education:* University of Idaho (B.S., Engineering, 1980); Boise State University (M.B.A., 1987); Lewis & Clark College, Northwestern School of Law (J.D., 1990). *Member:* Idaho State Bar; Oregon State Bar. ***PRACTICE AREAS:*** Natural Resources; Construction; Energy Law. ***Email:*** jks@idahowaters.com

REPRESENTATIVE CLIENTS: Twin Falls Canal Co.; Northside Canal Co.; Boise Project Board of Control; Idawest Energy; Idaho Power Co.; Hecla Mining Co.

BATT & FISHER, LLP

A Limited Liability Partnership
Established in 1997
U.S. BANK PLAZA, SUITE 500
101 SOUTH CAPITOL BOULEVARD
P.O. BOX 1308
BOISE, IDAHO 83701
Telephone: 208-331-1000
Fax: 208-331-2400
URL: http://www.battfisher.com

Business Transactions, Civil Trial and Appellate Practice before State and Federal Courts and Administrative Agencies, Arbitration and Mediation regarding all types of Business and Commercial Disputes, Antitrust, Banking, Lending, Communications, Computers and Software, Construction, Corporations, Partnerships and Other Entities, Estate Planning, Trusts, Health Care, Insurance, Intellectual Property, Legislative and Regulatory, Mergers and Acquisitions, Probate, Guardianships, Conservatorships, Project and Venture Capital Financing, Public Contracts, Public Utilities, Real Estate, Securities, Taxation.

MEMBERS OF FIRM

WILLIAM J. BATT, born Caldwell, Idaho, November 5, 1950; admitted to bar, 1982, Idaho and U.S. District Court, District of Idaho; 1984, U.S. Court of Appeals, Ninth Circuit. *Education:* Oberlin College; Albertson College of Idaho (B.S., magna cum laude, 1974); University of Idaho (J.D., cum laude, 1982). Previous Employment: Counsel, Mountain Bell/U.S. West, 1985-1988. *Member:* Idaho State Bar (Member Governing Council, Business and Corporate Law Section, 1988-1998; Chair, 1994-1995); American Bar Association (Member, Sections on Business; Antitrust; Public Utility; Tort and Insurance Sections); Federal Communications Bar; Idaho Law Foundation; Idaho Association of Commerce and Industry (Chair, Legal Advisory Committee, 2000—). ***SPECIAL AGENCIES:*** Securities and Exchange Commission; Federal Communication Commission; Idaho Department of Finance; Idaho Department of Insurance; Idaho Public Utilities Commission. ***PRACTICE AREAS:*** Business Law; Business Litigation; Corporate Law; Securities; Mergers and Acquisitions; Public Utilities; Telecommunications Law; Insurance Law. ***Email:*** wjb@battfisher.com

MELVILLE W. FISHER, II, born Little Rock, Arkansas, February 16, 1952; admitted to bar, 1977, Idaho; 1984, U.S. Tax Court. *Education:* University of Idaho (B.S., cum laude, 1974); University of Denver (J.D., 1977). Co-Author: "Idaho Probate and Estate Administration Forms," Section of Taxation, Probate and Trust Law, Idaho State Bar, 1992; *Idaho Guardianship and Conservatorship Administration Forms Handbook,* Idaho Law Foundation, 1996. *Member:* Idaho State Bar (Member, Sections On: Taxation, Probate, Trust Law; Chairman, 1994-1995); American (Member, Sections on: Real Property, Probate and Trust Law) Bar Association; Boise Estate Planning Council; Treasure Valley Estate Planning Council (President, 1981-1982). Fellow, The American College of Trust and Estate Counsel. ***PRACTICE AREAS:*** Estate Planning; Will Contests; Trusts and Estates; Guardianship; Conservatorship. ***Email:*** mwf@battfisher.com

DAVID B. LINCOLN, born Twin Falls, Idaho, November 20, 1945; admitted to bar, 1971, Idaho. *Education:* University of Idaho (B.A., 1968); Hastings College of Law, University of California (J.D., 1971). Order of the Coif. Legal Clerk, Securities and Exchange Commission, 1970. Co-Author: *Idaho Real Estate Handbook,* Idaho Law Foundation, 1980, 1988. *Member:* Idaho State Bar (Member: Real Estate, Business and Water Law Sections). Fellow, American College of Mortgage Attorneys. ***PRACTICE AREAS:*** Real Estate Law; Commercial Law; Business Law; Banking Law. ***Email:*** dbl@battfisher.com

JEFFREY W. PUSCH, born Bellevue, Washington, June 1, 1964; admitted to bar, 1992, Idaho and U.S. District Court, District of Idaho; 1993, U.S. Court of Appeals, Ninth Circuit. *Education:* Pomona College (B.A., cum laude, 1987); Boston College (J.D., 1992). Phi Beta Kappa. Business & Articles Editor, Boston College Environmental Affairs Law Review. *Member:* Idaho State Bar (Member: Governing Council Business & Corporate Law Section; Idaho Business Corporation Act Revision Sub-Committee, 1996 and 2003); American Bar Association (Member, Business Law Section; Idaho Liaison, State Regulation of Securities Committee). ***SPECIAL AGENCIES:*** Idaho Department of Finance; Idaho Department of Insurance. ***PRACTICE AREAS:*** Business Planning; Corporate Organization; Securities Offering; Securities Regulation; Mergers and Acquisitions; Insurance Law; Insurance Regulation. ***Email:*** jwpusch@battfisher.com

JOHN R. HAMMOND, JR., born Pusan, South Korea, October 3, 1969; admitted to bar, 1996, Idaho. *Education:* University of Idaho (B.S., 1993; J.D., 1996). *Member:* Young Lawyers of Idaho Bar Association.

JAMES B. ALDERMAN, born Mountain Home, Idaho, August 7, 1974; admitted to bar, 2001, Idaho. *Education:* Albertson College of Idaho (B.A., 1996); University of Idaho (J.D., 2001). Phi Delta Phi. Fall Edition Editor, Idaho Law Review. *Member:* Idaho State Bar (Member, Sections on: Business and Corporate Law; Real Property). ***PRACTICE AREAS:*** Business Law; Corporate Law; Real Estate; Agricultural Law.

REPRESENTATIVE CLIENTS: Boise WestCoast Hotels; Bridge Trading Co.; Charles Schwab & Co.; Citicorp USA; Clearwater Research; D & B Supply Co.; FCC National Bank; Finance America Bancorporation; Ford Motor Credit Co.; Hoj Engineering; Home Style-Industries; Financial; Idaho Life & Health Insurance; Guarantee Assn.; Idaho Motor Transport Assn.; Idaho Office of the Governor; Idaho State Insurance Fund; Idaho Timber; J.R. Simplot Co.; Jordan-Wilcomb Construction; Keybank National Assn.; Life Care Centers of America; Lincoln National Life Insurance Co.; Loewen Group International; Micron Technology; PCL Construction; Prudential Securities; Quest Health Care; Qwest Corp.; Qwest Wireless Communications; Regence Blue Shield of Idaho; Rhone-Poulenc Basic Chemicals; Schindler Elevator Corp.; Sun Valley Co.; Transamerica Financial Services; United Heritage Life Insurance Co.; US Bank National Assn.; Washington Group International, Inc.; Westinghouse Electric.

BAUER & FRENCH

Established in 1992
733 NORTH SEVENTH STREET
P.O. BOX 2730
BOISE, IDAHO 83701-2730
Telephone: 208-383-0090
Fax: 208-383-0412
URL: http://www.bauerandfrench.com

Trial and Appellate Practice. Family Law, Divorce, Interstate Child Custody, Community Property Law. Commercial, Bankruptcy, Real Estate.

MEMBERS OF FIRM

CHARLES B. BAUER, born Kearney, Nebraska, August 23, 1953; admitted to bar, 1979, Idaho, U.S. District Court, District of Idaho and U.S. Federal Court; 1984, U.S. Court of Appeals, 9th Circuit; 1991, Washington. *Education:* The Principia College (B.A., cum laude, 1976); University of Idaho (J.D., 1979). Member, Board of Editors, Idaho Law Review, 1979. Author: "Child Custody and Visitation, including UCCJA and UCCJEA," in Idaho Family Law Handbook, Idaho State Bar, Family Law Section, 1998; "Family Law in Idaho," Legal Education Institute, 1991; "Child Custody Jurisdiction and Practice," Family Law Section, Idaho State Bar Association, 1998; "Relocation of Children After Divorce," Advocate, Idaho State Bar Association, June, 2001; "Relocation of Children -- An Update," Advocate, Idaho State Bar Association, September, 2002. Chair, Editorial Advisory Board, Idaho State Bar Advocate, 1988-1989. Teacher, Idaho Law Foundation: "Representing Clients in Interstate Custody Disputes," 1999; "Ethical Issues for the Family Law Practitioner," 2000; "The UCCJEA and How It Affects Your Practice," 2000. Attorney Representative and Member, Idaho Bench Bar Committee to Protect Children of High Conflict Divorce, 1998-2000. Member, Board of Directors, Hays Shelter Home, 1984-1988 (President, 1986). *Member:* Boise, Washington State and American Bar Associations; Idaho State Bar (Member, 1993 and Chair, 1996, Board of Governors, Family Law Section; President, Family Law Section, 1995-1996). ***SPECIAL AGENCIES:*** Idaho Department of Health and Welfare. ***REPORTED CASES:*** Bondy v. Levy, 119 Idaho 961, 812 P.3d 268 (1991); Iverson v. Iverson, 127 Idaho 631, 903 P.2d 1328 (1995); Dooley v. Dooley, 128 Idaho 703, 918 P.2d 287 (Ct. App. 1996); Idaho ex.rel. Henderson v. Smith, 128 Idaho 444, 915 P.2d 6 (Ct. App. 1996); Howard v. Cornell, 3 P.2d 528 (2000); Brownson v. Allen, 995 P.2d 830 (2000). ***PRACTICE AREAS:*** International Family Law; Community Property Law; Alimony; Post Divorce Modification; Child Support; Child Custody; Visitation Rights; Divorce; Family Law; Adoption Law; Guardianship; Paternity; Spousal Support; Childrens Rights; Premarital Agreements. ***Email:*** cblaw@bauerandfrench.com

RANDAL J. FRENCH, born Omaha, Nebraska, September 12, 1955; admitted to bar, 1983, Idaho and U.S. District Court, District of Idaho; 1990, U.S. Court of Appeals, Ninth Circuit; 1996, U.S. Supreme Court. *Education:* Boise State University (B.B.A., 1980); University of Idaho (J.D., 1982). Law Clerk to: Hon. Jesse R. Walters, Chief Judge, Idaho Court of Appeals, 1983-1984; Hon. Alfred C. Hagan, U.S. Bankruptcy Court, District of Idaho, 1984-1986. Contributing Author: "Idaho Appellate Handbook," Idaho Law Foundation, 1985. *Member:* Boise (Member, Bankruptcy/Commercial Law Section, 1986—) and American Bar Associations; Idaho State Bar. ***REPORTED CASES:*** Rincover v. State, Dept. of Finance, Securities Bureau, 132 Idaho 547,976 P.2d 473 (Idaho, Apr 02, 1999) (NO. 24195); Rincover v. State, Dept. of Finance, Securities Bureau, 128 Idaho 653, 917 P.2d 1293, Blue Sky L. Rep.P 74,103 (Idaho, June 04,1996) (NO.21722); Rincover v. State, Dept. of Finance, Securities Bureau,124 Idaho 920, 866 P.2d 177 (Idaho, Nov 29, 1993) (NO. 20156). ***PRACTICE AREAS:*** Business Reorganization; Commercial Bankruptcy; Commercial Litigation; Real Estate. ***Email:*** rfrench@bauerandfrench.com

BEVIS, CAMERON & JOHNSON, P.A.

Established in 1979
SUITE 220, 960 BROADWAY AVENUE
P.O. BOX 827
BOISE, IDAHO 83706-3667
Telephone: 208-345-1040
Fax: 208-345-0365
Email: mjohnson@bevislaw.com
URL: http://www.bevislaw.com

General Trial and Appellate Practice before State and Federal Courts. Personal Injury, Family Law, Business, Corporation, Real Estate and Military Law.

JAMES A. BEVIS, born Vancouver, British Columbia, Canada, May 6, 1948; admitted to bar, 1974, Idaho and U.S. District Court, District of Idaho; 1977, U.S. Court of Appeals, Ninth Circuit; 1978, U.S. Supreme Court. *Education:* University of Colorado (B.S., 1970); University of Idaho (J.D., 1974). Law Clerk, Judge J. Blaine Anderson, U.S. District Court, District of Idaho, 1975-1976. Assistant United States Attorney, 1976-1978. President, Boise Bar Association, 1982-1983. Member, Idaho Child Support Guideline Committee, 1988—. Member, Criminal Justice Advisory Council, Boise State University, 1982-1983. *Member:* Idaho State Bar. Fellow, American Academy of Matrimonial Lawyers. [Colonel, JAGC, Staff Judge Advocate, Idaho Army National Guard, 1980]. ***PRACTICE AREAS:*** Family Law; Trial Practice; Appellate Practice; Personal Injury. ***Email:*** jbevis@bevislaw.com

MICHAEL R. JOHNSON, born Alameda, California, September 19, 1964; admitted to bar, 1993, Idaho, U.S. District Court, District of Idaho and U.S. Court of Appeals, Ninth Circuit. *Education:* Arizona State University; Boise State University (B.B.A., 1989); University of Idaho (J.D., 1992). Phi Delta Phi (Vice Magister, 1992). Pupil, American Inns of Court, No. 130. *Member:* Idaho State Bar (Member, Family Law Section). ***PRACTICE AREAS:*** Family Law; Credit Union Law; Real Estate; Personal Injury; Business Law; Criminal Law; Collections; Wills; Probate. ***Email:*** mjohnson@bevislaw.com

(This Listing Continued)

KRISTA DAWN THIRY, born Boise, Idaho, October 1, 1975; admitted to bar, 2000, Idaho and U.S. District Court, District of Idaho. *Education:* University of Idaho (B.S., 1997; J.D., 2000). Sigma Tau Delta; University of Idaho Student Alumni Honor Society. Intern: Boise County Prosecutors Office, Idaho City, Idaho, 1998; Debrha Carnahan Law Office, Boise, Idaho, 1999-2000. Extern to Theresa Gardunia. Assistant, Clerk of the Court, District of Idaho, Fourth Judicial District, Idaho City, Idaho. Member: Student Bar Association (Member, Student Division); Student Mentor Program. Associate, Debrha Carnahan Law Office, Boise, Idaho, August 2000-2003. *Member:* Idaho State (Member, Sections on: Family Law; Young Lawyers) and American (Member, Women's Law Caucus) Bar Associations; Association of American Trial Lawyers; Environmental Law Society. ***PRACTICE AREAS:*** Family Law; Personal Injury; Probate; Wills. ***Email:*** kthiry@bevislaw.com

REPRESENTATIVE CLIENTS: State of Idaho Military Division; Idaho Credit Union League; Capital Educators Federal Credit Union; Boise U.S. Employees Federal Credit Union; Idaho Concrete Company.
REFERENCE: U.S. Bank.

BLACKBURN & JONES LLP

1673 W. SHORELINE DRIVE, SUITE 200
P.O. BOX 7808
BOISE, IDAHO 83707-7808
Telephone: 208-489-8989
Fax: 208-489-8988
URL: http://www.blackburnjoneslaw.com

Civil Trial and Appellate Practice, Products Liability, Personal Injury, Transportation, Aviation, Corporate, Labor, Employment, Public Utilities, Administrative Law.

MEMBERS OF THE FIRM

REX BLACKBURN, born Burns, Oregon, March 14, 1955; admitted to bar, 1980, California and U.S. District Court, Northern District of California; 1984, Idaho and U.S. District Court, District of Idaho; 1987, U.S. Court of Appeals, Ninth Circuit; 1999, U.S. Court of Appeals, Fifth Circuit; 2000, U.S. Supreme Court. *Education:* Albertson College of Idaho (B.A., summa cum laude, 1977); Hastings College of the Law, University of California (J.D., 1980). Lawrence Henry Gipson Scholar. Member, Hastings Moot Court Board. National Institute for Trial Advocacy, National Session, 1987. Contributing Editor: "Product Liability Desk Reference, A Fifty-State Compendium," Little Brown and Company, 1994-2001. Barrister, American Inn of Court, No. 130, 1993-1995. *Member:* State Bar of California; Idaho State Bar; American Bar Association (Member, Tort and Insurance Practice Section); National Conference of Commissioners on Uniform State Laws (Commissioner, 1993—); Idaho Association of Defense Counsel. ***PRACTICE AREAS:*** General Litigation; Tort Law; Products Liability Law; Employment Law; Commercial Litigation. ***Email:*** rex@blackburnjoneslaw.com

BRUCE C. JONES, born Boise, Idaho, December 7, 1953; admitted to bar, 1982, California and U.S. District Court, Northern District of California; 1984, Idaho and U.S. District Court, District of Idaho; 1985, U.S. Court of Appeals, Ninth Circuit; U.S. Court of Appeals, Tenth Circuit. *Education:* Albertson College of Idaho (B.A., magna cum laude, 1977); Hastings College of the Law, University of California (J.D., 1982); National Institute for Trial Advocacy, National Session (1987). Lawrence Henry Gipson Scholar. Contributing Editor: "Product Liability Desk Reference, A Fifty-State Compendium," Little Brown & Company, 1994-2001. Barrister, American Inn of Court No. 130, 1994-2001. *Member:* Idaho State Bar; State Bar of California; American Bar Association (Member, Litigation Section). ***PRACTICE AREAS:*** General Litigation; Products Liability Law; Commercial Litigation; Professional Malpractice Law. ***Email:*** bruce@blackburnjoneslaw.com

PATRICK E. MAHONEY, born Spokane, Washington, April 17, 1970; admitted to bar, 1995, Idaho. *Education:* University of Washington (B.A., Political Science, 1992); University of Idaho (J.D., 1995). Recipient, American Jurisprudence Awards in Contracts and Constitutional Law. National Political Science Honor Society, University of Washington, 1991-1992. Executive Board, 1994 Fall Edition Editor, University of Idaho Law Review. Law Clerk to the Honorable D. Duff McKee and the Honorable Alan Schwartzman, Fourth Judicial District, Idaho, 1995-1996. Author, Casenote, "Implied Consent to Motorist Blood Alcohol Testing: Pangburn v. State," 31 Idaho Law Rev 313 (1994). Member, American Inns of Court, No. 130 Barrister. *Member:* Idaho State Bar; American Bar Association (Member, Litigation Section); Idaho Trial Lawyers Association (Member: Publications Committee). ***REPORTED CASES:*** Selkirk Seed Co. v. State Ins. Fund, 135 Idaho 649 22 P.3d IU28 (2000). ***PRACTICE AREAS:*** Civil Litigation; Torts; Personal Injury; Products Liability; Toxic Torts; Commercial Litigation. ***Email:*** patrick@blackburnjoneslaw.com

ERIC B. SWARTZ, born Oklahoma City, Oklahoma, December 30, 1973; admitted to bar, 2001, Idaho and U.S. District Court, District of Idaho and U.S. Court of Appeals, Ninth Circuit. *Education:* Utah State University (B.S., Environmental Studies, 1996); University of Tulsa (J.D., 2001). National Energy-Environment Law and Policy Institute Certificate of Natural Resources, Energy and Environmental Law, 2001. University of Tulsa, College of Law Certificate of Alternative Dispute Resolution, 2001. Executive Articles Editor, Energy Law Review, 1999-2001. Editor, American Bar Association's Year-in-Review, Section on Environment, Energy, Resources Law, 2000-2001. *Member:* Idaho State Bar; American Bar Association. ***PRACTICE AREAS:*** Civil Litigation. ***Email:*** eric@blackburnjoneslaw.com

DANIEL L. GLYNN, born Omaha, Nebraska, December 28, 1969; admitted to bar, 1995, Idaho and U.S. District Court, District of Idaho; 1998, U.S. Court of Appeals, Ninth Circuit. *Education:* Whitman College (B.S., 1992); Gonzaga University (J.D., cum laude, 1994). ***REPORTED CASES:*** Levin, 987 P2d 1028; Roberts, 64 P3d 327; Hayes, 96 P3d 652. ***PRACTICE AREAS:*** Commercial Litigation; Employment Law; Appellate Practice. ***Email:*** daniel@blackburnjoneslaw.com

(This Listing Continued)

BLACKBURN & JONES LLP, Boise—Continued

REPRESENTATIVE CLIENTS: Alaska Airlines, Inc.; The American National Red Cross; American Trucking Associations, Inc.; Attorneys Liability Protection Society (ALPS); Bottlers' Services, Inc. (Coca Cola Bottlers' Association); Braunschweigische Maschinenbauanstalt AG (BMA); Briggs & Stratton Corporation; Countrywide Adjusting Services Inc.; Deere & Co.; Home Depot, The; Horizon Air Industries, Inc.; Idacorp Inc.; Idaho Housing and Finance Association; Idaho Motor Transport Association; Idaho Power Co.; Interstate Brands Corporaion; John Deere Co.; Phillips Petroleum Company; Playtex Family Products, Inc.; Raytheon Company; Showa Denko K.K.; Treasure Valley Transit, Inc.; Western States Equipment Company; Westinghouse Electric Corp.; Weyerhaeuser Co.
INSURANCE CLIENTS: Fireman's Fund Insurance Company; Great West Casualty Co.; John Deere Insurance Co.
REFERENCE: KeyBank of Idaho.

BOSCH, DAW & BALLARD

CHARTERED

Established in 1981

9TH AND IDAHO CENTER
225 NORTH 9TH STREET, SUITE 210
BOISE, IDAHO 83702
Telephone: 208-344-8990
Telecopier: 208-344-9140
Email: dbdb@dbdb.com
URL: http://www.dbdb.com

Commercial and Business Law including Real Estate, Employee Benefit Plans, Estate Planning, Taxation, Litigation, Transportation, Immigration, Bankruptcy and Health, Law and Taxation of Nonprofit Organizations.

ALLAN R. BOSCH, born Rugby, North Dakota, May 20, 1954; admitted to bar, 1979, Nebraska; 1980, Idaho; 1983, U.S. Tax Court. *Education:* University of North Dakota (B.S.B.A., magna cum laude, 1976); Creighton University School of Law (J.D., 1979). Certified Public Accountant, Idaho, 1982. Accredited Pension Administrator. Author: "Cafeteria Plans - Getting Your Cake and Eating it Too," Idaho Advocate Vol. 30, No. 12, Nov. 1987. Co-Author: "Employee Benefits in Idaho," National Business Institute, Inc., 1989. *Member:* Idaho State Bar (Chairman, Taxation, Probate & Trust Section, 1995-1996; Chairman, Annual Advanced Estate Planning Conference, 2002-2005); Nebraska State Bar Association; National Lawyers Association; Idaho Society of Certified Public Accountants; American Institute of Certified Public Accountants; Boise Estate Planning Council (President, 1996-1997); National Institute of Pension Administrators, Idaho Chapter (President, 1998-1999); National Institute of Pension Administrators, Program Committee (22nd & 23rd Annual Conference). ***PRACTICE AREAS:*** Employee Benefits; Qualified Retirements Plans; Tax Exempt Organizations; Estate Planning; Partnership Taxation. ***Email:*** allanb@dbdb.com

C. A. DAW, born Moscow, Idaho, May 14, 1953; admitted to bar, 1979, Idaho; 1988, U.S. Tax Court; 1991, U.S. Court of Appeals, Eighth Circuit; 1992, U.S. Supreme Court; 1998, U.S. Court of Appeals, Ninth Circuit. *Education:* University of Idaho (B.S. Ch.Eng., 1975; J.D., cum laude, 1979). Blue Key; Tau Beta Pi; Phi Alpha Delta. Member, Idaho Law Review, 1978-1979. Author: "Personal Property and Equalization," Proceedings 55th International Conference on Assessment Administration 185 (I.A.A.O. 1989). Co-Author: "Survey of Developments in Idaho Law: 1977-1978," 15 Idaho Law Review 359 (1979). Recipient, Idaho Law Foundation Scholarship, 1979. Deputy Attorney General, Idaho Attorney General's Office, 1982-1988. Member and Legal Section Chair, 1986-2005, National Conference on Unit Valuation States. Technical Standards Subcommittee and Research and Technology Committee, International Association of Assessing Officers, 1992-1993. *Member:* Idaho State Bar. ***REPORTED CASES:*** Florida E. Coast Ry. Co. v. Dept. of Revenue, State of Florida, 620 So.2d 1051 (Fla. App. 1st D.C.A. 1993); Burlington Northern R. Co. v. Bair 957 F.2d 599 (8th Cir. 1992); Central Paving Co., Inc. v. Idaho Tax Comm'n, 126 Idaho 174, 879 P.2d 1107 (1994); Union Pacific R. Co. v. Looney, 111 Idaho 1000, 729 P.2d 1063 (1986); Simmons v. Idaho State Tax Comm. 111 Idaho 343, 723 P.2d 887 (1986). ***PRACTICE AREAS:*** State Taxation; Commercial Litigation. ***Email:*** cadaw@dbdb.com

DAVID G. BALLARD, born Council, Idaho, January, 13, 1953; admitted to bar, 1980, Idaho and U.S. District Court, District of Idaho; 1982, U.S. Court of Appeals, Ninth Circuit. *Education:* Boise State University (B.A., 1976); University of Idaho (J.D., 1980). Member: Association for Transportation Law, Logistics and Policy; Idaho Motor Transport Association. *Member:* Idaho State Bar. ***REPORTED CASES:*** Bell v. Smith 232 BR 461 BK Idaho 1998. ***PRACTICE AREAS:*** Collections; Creditors Rights in Bankruptcy; Real Estate; Outdoor Advertising; Motor Carrier. ***Email:*** dgb@dbdb.com

LES BOCK, born Rolette, North Dakota, March 5, 1949; admitted to bar, 1979, California; 1983, Idaho; 1992, U.S. Tax Court. *Education:* University of California at Davis (B.A., magna cum laude, 1973); University of California, Hastings College of Law (J.D., 1979); New York University. Recipient: Idaho State Bar Award for Outstanding Service, 1995; Idaho State Bar Pro Bono Award, 1991. Author: "An Idaho County Seeks Property Taxes From an Exempt Hospital," 9 Journal of Taxation of Exempt Organizations 164, 1998; "Sales in the Information Age," 27 Idaho Law Review 463, 1994. Editor: "Handbook for Idaho Nonprofit Corporations." Member, Idaho State Commission for Children and Youth, 1988-1990. *Member:* Idaho State Bar (Member, Sections on: Business Law; Taxation, Probate and Trust Law) State Bar of California. Lifetime Fellow: Idaho Law Foundation. ***LANGUAGES:*** *French and Spanish.* ***PRACTICE AREAS:*** *Nonprofit Organizations Law; Nonprofit Tax Law; Tax Appeals; Tax Litigation; Taxation; Immigration Law; Bankruptcy.* ***Email:*** lesbock@dbdb.com

A List of Representative Clients Will be Furnished Upon Request.

BRASSEY, WETHERELL, CRAWFORD & GARRETT, L.L.P.

Established in 1993

203 W. MAIN STREET
P.O. BOX 1009
BOISE, IDAHO 83701-1009
Telephone: 208-344-7300
Facsimile: 208-344-7077
Email: bwcm@brassey.net
URL: http://www.bwcmlaw.com

General Civil and Trial Practice, Appeals, Insurance Defense, Business Defense, Defense of Governmental Entities, Trucking Law, Medical Malpractice, DEF, Environmental, Civil Rights, Commercial, Real Estate, Employment, Personnel, Agriculture, and Products Liability.

ANDREW C. BRASSEY, born Boise, Idaho, January 30, 1952; admitted to bar, 1977, Idaho, U.S. District Court, District of Idaho and U.S. Court of Appeals, Ninth Circuit; 1981, Texas and U.S. District Court, Northern District of Texas; 1982, U.S. District Court, Southern District of Texas; 1983, U.S. District Court, Western District of Texas. *Education:* University of Idaho (B.A., 1974; J.D., 1977). Special Deputy Attorney General, State of Idaho. *Member:* Boise and Tarrant County Bar Associations; Idaho State Bar; State Bar of Texas; Defense Research Institute (Member, Trucking Law Committee); Idaho Association of Defense Counsel; Boise Adjusters Association. ***PRACTICE AREAS:*** Medical Malpractice Defense; Administrative Law; Professional Licensing; Civil Trial Practice; Insurance Defense Litigation; Commercial Litigation; Civil Rights; Trucking Law; Agricultural Tort Claims; Crop Damage. ***Email:*** acb@brassey.net

ROBERT T. WETHERELL, born Mountain Home, Idaho, February 17, 1958; admitted to bar, 1983, Idaho and U.S. District Court, District of Idaho; U.S. Court of Appeals, Ninth Circuit. *Education:* St. John's University (B.A., 1980); University of Salzburg; University of Idaho (J.D., 1982). Law Clerk, U.S. District Court, District of Idaho, 1983-1985. Member, Juvenile Justice Committee, 1975-1977. Lecturer: Insurance Coverage Law in Idaho, 1998; Personnel Law in Idaho, 1996; Boundary Disputes in Idaho, 1995. Special Deputy Attorney General, State of Idaho. General Counsel: Idaho Special Olympics; Linella, Inc. *Member:* Idaho State Bar; American Bar Association; Idaho Association of Defense Counsel; Boise Adjusters Association. ***LANGUAGES:*** German. ***SPECIAL AGENCIES:*** Idaho Dept. of Risk Mng.; Idaho Dept. of Labor. ***REPORTED CASES:*** Hoyle v. Utica Mut. Ins. Co., 137 ID 367, 48 P.3d 1256 (2002); Courtney v. Big O Tires; Cont. Gen. Tire et. al., 139 ID 821, 87 P.3d 930 (2003). ***PRACTICE AREAS:*** Insurance Coverage; Civil Trial Practice; Real Estate; Personnel; Civil Rights; Appellate Practice; Trial Practice. ***Email:*** rtw@brassey.net

J. NICK CRAWFORD, born Buhl, Idaho, May 24, 1958; admitted to bar, 1984, Idaho and U.S. District Court, District of Idaho; 1990, Utah and U.S. District Court, District of Utah; U.S. Court of Appeals, Ninth Circuit. *Education:* University of Idaho (B.S., 1980; J.D., 1984). Recipient, Langroise Scholarship. Lecturer: "Trying the Automobile Injury Case in Idaho: The Defense Perspective," June 1993, "Disputing Damages in Idaho", December 1993, and "Civil Trial Procedures in Idaho," July 1994; "Winning Strategies for Jury Selection in Idaho," May, 1998; National Business, Inc. of Eau Claire, Wisconsin Seminar, Boise, Idaho. Special Deputy Attorney General, State of Idaho. *Member:* Idaho State Bar; Utah State Bar; American (Member, Sections on: Litigation; Tort and Insurance Practice) Bar Association; Idaho Association of Defense Counsel; Defense Research Institute; Federation of Defense and Corporate Counsel; Boise Adjusters Association. ***PRACTICE AREAS:*** Insurance Coverage; Civil Trial Practice; General Insurance Defense Litigation. ***Email:*** jnc@brassey.net

NANCY JO GARRETT, born Twin Falls, Idaho, November 12, 1949; admitted to bar, 1989, Idaho; U.S. District Court, District of Idaho. *Education:* Idaho State University (B.S., Nursing, 1974; M.S., Nursing, 1982); University of Idaho (J.D., 1989). Registered Nurse, Idaho, 1974. *Member:* Boise and Idaho State Bar Associations; Washington State Bar Association; Defense Research Institute; Idaho Association of Defense Counsel; Idaho Association of Healthcare Risk Management. ***PRACTICE AREAS:*** Litigation; Medical Malpractice Law; Administrative Law; Professional Licensing; Insurance Law; Personal Injury. ***Email:*** njg@brassey.net

---

JOHN McEVOY HOWELL, born Edina, Minnesota, June 2, 1974; admitted to bar, 2001, Idaho and U.S. District Court, District of Idaho. *Education:* St. John's University (B.A., 1996); University of Idaho (J.D., 2000). *Idaho State Bar (Member, Young Lawyers Section).* ***SPECIAL AGENCIES:*** State of ID. Dept. of Risk Management. ***PRACTICE AREAS:*** Insurance Defense (50%); Products Liability (20%); Business Law (20%); Medical Malpractice Defense (10%). ***Email:*** jhowell@brassey.net

ELLEN S. ELLIOTT, born Elko, Nevada, September 21, 1975; admitted to bar, 2003, Idaho. *Education:* Oregon State University (M.P.H., 2000); McGeorge School of Law (J.D., 2003). ***PRACTICE AREAS:*** Insurance Defense; Civil Practice; Civil Litigation; Special Education Law. ***Email:*** ese@brassey.net

CHRISTOPHER P. GRAHAM, born Washington, D.C., 1972; admitted to bar, 2000, Idaho; U.S. District Court, District of Idaho. *Education:* Boise State University (B.A., 1995); University of Idaho (J.D., cum laude, 2000). Delta Theta Phi. Editor-in-Chief, Idaho Law Review, 1999-2000. Law Clerk to Justice Jesse Walters, Idaho Supreme Court, 2000-2001. Co-Author: "The Importance of Being Honest:" Exploring the Need for Tribal Court Approval for Search Warrants Executed in Indian Country after State v. Mathews, 38 Idaho L.Rev. 581 (2002) (with Douglas R. Nash); "Cobell v. Norton-Indian Trust Fund Management Takes Center Stage," The Advocate (March 2003) (with Douglas R. Nash). *Member:* Idaho State Bar (Vice President, Young Lawyers Section, 2002-2003); American Bar Association. ***PRACTICE AREAS:*** Civil Litigation (100%). ***Email:*** cpg@brassey.net

CLINTON S. CODDINGTON, born Palo Alto, California, February 28, 1974; admitted to bar, 2000, California and U.S. District Court, Northern District of California; 2002, Idaho and U.S. District Court, District of Idaho. *Education:* Boston College (B.A., cum

(This Listing Continued)

laude, 1996); University of San Diego (J.D., 1999). *Member:* Idaho State Bar; State Bar of California. ***PRACTICE AREAS:*** Civil Practice; Insurance Defense; Criminal Defense. **Email:** csc@brassey.net

REPRESENTATIVE CLIENTS: Accordia Ski Resort Services; Ada County; Albertson's, Inc.; All Nation Insurance Company; American Motorists Insurance Company; American International Group; AMICA; Boise City/Ada County Housing Authority; Bruneel Tire Company; Cigna (Special Investigative Unit); CNA Insurance Companies; Colonial Insurance Company of California; Colonial Penn Insurance Company; Commercial Union Insurance Company; Commonwealth Title; Compass Insurance Company; Continental Insurance Company; Coregis; Firemans Fund Insurance Company (Special Investigative Unit); GAB Business Services, Inc.; Gordon Trucking, Inc.; Homestead Insurance Company; Houston General Insurance Company; Idaho Youth Ranch; Idaho Special Olympics; Idaho Intermountain Claims, Inc.; Industrial Indemnity Company; Insurance Company of North America; Liberty Northwest Insurance Corp.; Marker USA; May Trucking; Medical Insurance Exchange of California; Mill End Fabrics, Inc.; Ohio Casualty Insurance Company; Reliance Insurance Company; Royal Insurance Company; Safeco; Sinclair Oil Corporation; State Farm Fire & Casualty Company; State Farm Insurance Companies (Special Investigative Unit); State Farm Mutual Automobile Insurance Company; State of Idaho, Bureau of Risk Management; Sun Valley Company; The Benchmark, Inc.; Transamerica; Title Insurance; United States Fidelity & Guaranty Company; Willis Shaw Frozen Express.

KIMBERLY D. BROOKS

BOISE, IDAHO

(See Nampa)

Family Law, Divorce, Domestic Relations, Child Custody, Child Support, Adoptions, Guardianship, Visitation Rights, Separation Agreements, Domestic Violence, Alimony.

CAMACHO MENDOZA LAW OFFICE

623 W. HAYS STREET
BOISE, IDAHO 83702
Telephone: 208-342-2960
Fax: 208-345-0050
Email: camacho@cableone.net

Workers' Compensation, Immigration, Indian Law.

MEMBER OF FIRM

NATALIE CAMACHO MENDOZA, born Pocatello, Idaho, September 8, 1963; admitted to bar, 1991, Idaho; 1995, Texas. *Education:* Idaho State University (B.A., Political Science, 1985); Washburn University of Topeka (J.D., 1989). President, Student Radiology Technology Association, 1982-1983 and Member, Bridging the Gap Task Force, 1989-1991, Idaho State University. Student Organizer, Law Student Division of Hispanic National Bar Association, 1988. Co-Chair, Hispanic Issues Training Conference, Boise, Idaho, 1996, 1997, 2005. Vice Chair, Human Relations Advisory Committee, City of Pocatello, 1985-1986. Co-Chair, Project Due Process, 1987-1989. Commissioner, Idaho Commission on Hispanic Affairs, 1989-1992. Board Member, Refugee Aid Program, 1992-1993. Member: Advisory Committee, United Way Success by Six, 1997; Hispanic Advisory Committee to Senator Larry Craig, 2002; Advisory Committee, Put Your Skills to Work Program, University of Idaho; Jalisco Task Force, Idaho Department of Commerce, 2004; Idaho Tribal/Latino Caucus, 2004; Mission Committee, St. Alphonsus Regional Medical Center, 2005— Idaho Hispanic Business Association; Idaho Network for New Americans. Advisor to the Woman of Color Alliance, 1998-2004. Idaho Delegate, National Hispanic Leadership Summit, Washington, D.C., 2002. *Member:* Idaho State Bar (Member, Sections on: Workers' Compensation; Indian Law); State Bar of Texas (Member, Hispanic Issues Section); Hispanic National Bar Association. ***REPORTED CASES:*** Cutsinger v Spears Mfg. Co., Inc. 137 Idaho 464, 50 P3d 479 (2002); Richardson v Payless Shoe Source #0575, 2002 IIC 0168 (March 1, 2002); Denise2003 v Employer, American Home Insurance Company, 2003 IIC 0587 (September 19, 2003); Dale2004 v Employer, Insurance Company of the State of Pennsylvania, 2004 IIC 0041 (January 23, 2004); Stolle v Bennett, IC 04-001592 (June 15, 2005). ***PRACTICE AREAS:*** Workers Compensation; Immigration Law; Indian Law. **Email:** Camacho@Cableone.net

CANTRILL, SKINNER, SULLIVAN & KING, LLP

Established in 1980

1423 TYRELL LANE
P.O. BOX 359
BOISE, IDAHO 83701
Telephone: 208-344-8035
Fax: 208-345-7212
Email: cssklaw@cssklaw.com

Insurance Defense, Workers Compensation, Corporate and Real Estate Law, Criminal Law, Domestic Relations. Trial and Appellate Practice.

MEMBERS OF FIRM

DAVID W. CANTRILL, born Pocatello, Idaho, July 24, 1942; admitted to bar, 1970, Idaho, U.S. District Court, District of Idaho and U.S. Court of Appeals, Ninth Circuit; 1977, U.S. Supreme Court. *Education:* Idaho State University (B.A., 1966); University of Idaho (J.D., 1970). *Member:* Idaho State Bar; American Bar Association; Defense Research Institute. Fellow, American College of Trial Lawyers. ***PRACTICE AREAS:*** Insurance Defense Law; Workers Compensation Law. **Email:** cssklaw@cssklaw.com

GARDNER W. SKINNER, JR., born Boise, Idaho, September 28, 1944; admitted to bar, 1970, Idaho and U.S. District Court, District of Idaho; 1975, U.S. Court of Appeals, Ninth Circuit. *Education:* University of Santa Clara (B.A., 1966); University of Idaho (J.D., 1970). Notes Editor, Idaho Law Review, 1969-1970. *Member:* Idaho State Bar; American Bar Association; Idaho Trial Lawyers Association. ***PRACTICE AREAS:*** Trial and Appellate Practice Law; Workers Compensation Law. **Email:** cssklaw@cssklaw.com

WILLIS E. SULLIVAN, III (1941-2001)

(This Listing Continued)

JOHN L. KING, born Glendale, California, January 22, 1942; admitted to bar, 1967, Idaho, U.S. District Court, District of Idaho and U.S. Court of Appeals, Ninth Circuit. *Education:* University of Oregon (B.A., 1964; J.D., 1967). Law Clerk to Honorable Fred M. Taylor, U.S. District Court, District of Idaho, 1967-1969. Assistant U.S. Attorney for the District of Idaho, 1969-1973. *Member:* Idaho State Bar; Defense Research Institute. ***PRACTICE AREAS:*** Insurance Defense Law; Litigation; Public School Law; Management/Labor Negotiations. **Email:** cssklaw@cssklaw.com

ROBERT D. LEWIS, born Wheatland, Wyoming, December 3, 1953; admitted to bar, 1981, Idaho, U.S. District Court, District of Idaho and U.S. Court of Appeals, Ninth and Tenth Circuits. *Education:* Colorado College; University of Colorado at Boulder (B.A., magna cum laude, 1977); University of Idaho (J.D., 1980). Law Clerk to Honorable Jesse R. Walters, Idaho Court of Appeals. *Member:* Idaho State Bar; American Bar Association; Defense Research Institute. ***REPORTED CASES:*** Miner vs. Farmers Ins. Co., 116 Idaho 656, 778 P.2d 778 (Idaho 1989); Garrett Freight Lines, Inc. vs. Bannock Paving Co., 112 Idaho 722, 755 P.2d 1033 (Idaho 1987). ***PRACTICE AREAS:*** Insurance Defense Law; Insurance Coverage Law; Commercial Transactions. **Email:** cssklaw@cssklaw.com

CLINTON O. CASEY, born Pocatello, Idaho, December 25, 1963; admitted to bar, 1990, California; 1991, Idaho, U.S. District Court, District of Idaho and U.S. Court of Appeals, Ninth Circuit. *Education:* University of Idaho (B.S., 1986); University of San Francisco (J.D., 1990). *Member:* Idaho State Bar; American Bar Association; State Bar of California (inactive); Defense Research Institute; Idaho Association of Defense Counsel. ***PRACTICE AREAS:*** Insurance Defense Law; Subrogation. **Email:** cssklaw@cssklaw.com

DEAN C. SORENSEN, born Boise. Idaho, April 28, 1972; admitted to bar, 1999, Idaho and U.S. District Court, District of Idaho. *Education:* University of Utah (B.S., 1995); University of Idaho (J.D., cum laude, 1998). Member, Fall Edition, Idaho Law Review, 1998. *Member:* American Bar Association; Idaho State Bar. ***PRACTICE AREAS:*** Insurance Defense; Real Estate; Trusts and Estates; Business Law; Zoning; Land Use and Planning; Commercial Litigation; Insurance Coverage Law; Business Transactions. **Email:** cssklaw@cssklaw.com

ASSOCIATE

STEVEN J. MEADE, born Corvallis, Oregon, April 9, 1962; admitted to bar, 2000, Idaho. *Education:* Boise State University (B.S., 1995); University of Idaho (J.D., 2000). Delta Theta Phi. Member, National School Board's Association Council of School Attorneys. *Member:* Idaho State Bar (Member, Family Law Section). [Machinist Mate 2nd Class, Submarines, U.S. Navy, 1988-1992]. ***REPORTED CASES:*** Barnedt v. Wilder, 49 P3d 1265 (June 2002). ***PRACTICE AREAS:*** Education Law; Family Law; Wills; Probate. **Email:** smeade@cssklaw.com

REPRESENTATIVE CLIENTS: Safeco Insurance Company; Safeco Life Insurance Co.; Ram, Inc.; Black Angus Enterprises of Idaho; Prudential Property and Casualty Insurance Co.; Mutual of Enumclaw Insurance Co.; Employers Insurance of Wausau; State Insurance Fund; Liberty Northwest Insurance Co.; Farmers Insurance Co.; Cessna Finance Corp.; Nature Conservancy; Independent School District of Boise City; Hartford Insurance Group; Midvale Telephone Exchange, Inc.; United Fire and Casualty; Cincinnati Insurance, Co.; Continental Insurance Company; Marsing School District; IDA-Tran Freight Systems; J.R. Simplot Co.; Zurich-American Insurance Group; CNA Insurance Companies.
REFERENCE: Key Bank.

ANDREA L. CARDON

355 WEST MYRTLE STREET, SUITE 103
P.O. BOX 2633
BOISE, IDAHO 83701
Telephone: 208-384-0011
Fax: 208-344-7100
Email: cardon5747@aol.com
URL: http://www.andrealcardonlaw.com

Construction Contracts and Social Security Disability.

ANDREA L. CARDON, born Fairfield, California, September 17, 1965; admitted to bar, 1992, Idaho and U.S. District Court, District of Idaho. *Education:* Washington State University (B.S., 1987); University of Idaho (J.D., 1990). Computer Assisted Legal Research Librarian, Idaho State Supreme Court, 1990-1992. Legal Counsel, 1992-2000 and Contract Manager, Power Division, 2000-2001, Washington Group International. Associate, Debra Young Irish and Associates, 2001-2002. Member, National Organization of Social Security Claimants' Representatives. *Member:* Idaho State Bar (Member, IOLTA Fund Committee, 1992-1998); American Bar Association. ***PRACTICE AREAS:*** Construction Contracts; Social Security Disability.

DEBRHA J. CARNAHAN

101 SOUTH CAPITOL BOULEVARD, SUITE 400
P.O. BOX 2125
BOISE, IDAHO 83701
Telephone: 208-338-1420
Facsimile: 208-338-0762
Email: debrha@carnahanlawoffice.com

Family Law, Probate, Child Custody and Domestic Relations.

DEBRHA J. CARNAHAN, born Pullman, Washington, November 22, 1952; admitted to bar, 1978, Idaho. *Education:* University of Idaho (B.S., 1975; J.D., 1978). Deputy Ada County Prosecuting Attorney, 1978-1982. ***PRACTICE AREAS:*** Family Law.

CARTY LAW, P.A.

380 SOUTH 4TH STREET
SUITE 102
BOISE, IDAHO 83702
Telephone: 208-342-3501
Fax: 208-342-3548
URL: http://www.carty-law.com
URL: http://www.cartylaw.us
URL: http://www.cartylaw.net

Personal Injury, Medical Malpractice, Products Liability, Trucking Liability, Mediation, Arbitration, Torts, Insurance Bad Faith, Slip and Fall, Dog Bites, Wrongful Death, Airplane Accidents, Automobile Accidents, Brain Injury, Spinal Injury, Truck Accidents.

STUART W. CARTY, born Cleveland, Ohio, February 6, 1944; admitted to bar, 1974, Idaho. *Education:* University of Tennessee at Knoxville (B.A., 1967; J.D., 1974). Phi Gamma Delta. *Member:* Idaho State Bar; Idaho Trial Lawyers Association. [Capt., U.S.A.F., 1968-1972]. ***PRACTICE AREAS:*** Personal Injury; Medical Malpractice; Insurance; Products Liability.

CHASAN & WALTON, L.L.C.

Established in 1981
1459 TYRELL LANE
P.O. BOX 1069
BOISE, IDAHO 83701
Telephone: 208-345-3760
Fax: 208-345-0288
URL: http://www.chasanwalton.com

Personal Injury, Wrongful Death, Interstate Trucking Litigation, Insurance Bad Faith, Products Liability, Mediation, Medical Malpractice.

FIRM PROFILE: Andy Chasan and Tim Walton have been partners since 1981. Both are active in, and have served as president of, the Idaho Trial Lawyers Association. The firm limits its practice to significant injury cases, and mediation (Mr. Walton). The firm and its staff (some of whom have been employed here for 25 years) have a strong commitment to putting the interests of its clients above all else.

MEMBERS OF FIRM

ANDREW M. CHASAN, born 1950; admitted to bar, 1977, Idaho; U.S. District Court, District of Idaho; U.S. Court of Appeals, Ninth Circuit. *Education:* Ohio Wesleyan University (B.A., 1972); Case Western Reserve University (J.D., 1977). Named Idaho Trial Lawyer of the Year, 2004. *Member:* Idaho Trial Lawyers Association (President, 2002-2003); The Association of Trial Lawyers of America (Officer, Executive Committee, Interstate Trucking Litigation Group). ***PRACTICE AREAS:*** Personal Injury; Truck Accidents; Products Liability; Workers Compensation. ***Email:*** andrew.chasan@chasanwalton.com

TIMOTHY C. WALTON, born 1951; admitted to bar, 1977, Idaho and U.S. District Court, District of Idaho. *Education:* Valparaiso University (B.A., 1973); University of Idaho (J.D., cum laude, 1977). Member, Idaho Law Review. *Member:* Idaho Trial Lawyers Association (President, 1999-2000); Association of Trial Lawyers of America (Member and Delegate, State of Idaho). ***PRACTICE AREAS:*** Personal Injury; Medical Malpractice; Mediation; Products Liability; Workers Compensation; Truck Accidents. ***Email:*** timwalton2000@hotmail.com

RON CHRISTIAN ATTORNEY AT LAW

671 E. RIVERPARK LANE, SUITE 130
BOISE, IDAHO 83706
Telephone: 208-322-6448; 208-424-7985
URL: http://www.ronchristianlaw.com
Email: rchristian@ronchristianlaw.com
URL: http://www.ronchristianlawfirm.com

Family Law, Adoptions, Alimony, Child Support, Custody, Divorce, Domestic Violence, Separation Agreements, Visitation Rights, Grandparents Rights, Restraining Orders, Criminal Law, Drugs Crimes, Drunk Driving, Felonies, Misdemeanors, Business Litigation and Transactions, Corporations, Limited Liability Companies, Employment Litigation, Real Estate Transactions and Litigation.

RON CHRISTIAN, born Spokane, Washington, September 29, 1960; admitted to bar, 1991, Idaho and U.S. District Court, District of Idaho; 1995, U.S. Court of Appeals, 9th Circuit. *Education:* University of California at Irvine (B.S., 1987); Brigham Young University (M.B.A., 1991; J.D., 1991). Lead Articles Editor, BYU Law Review, 1989-1991. *Member:* Idaho State Bar. ***LANGUAGES:*** Spanish.

COMSTOCK & BUSH

199 N. CAPITOL BOULEVARD, SUITE 500
P.O. BOX 2774
BOISE, IDAHO 83701-2774
Telephone: 208-344-7700
Telecopier: 208-344-7721
URL: http://www.comstockandbush.com

Accident and Personal Injury Law, Wrongful Death, Head Injuries, Insurance Bad Faith Law, Medical Malpractice Law, Aviation Law, Employment Law, Product Liability Law.

(This Listing Continued)

FIRM PROFILE: Comstock & Bush, founded in 1991, has its major emphasis in all phases of plaintiff's related litigation. The firm, although small, can effectively administer all types of litigation, be it a modest personal injury suit or a large and complex products liability action. The strength of the firm is premised on the trial experience and commitment of its attorneys and staff for effective and personal representation.

DAVID E. COMSTOCK, born San Francisco, California, January 18, 1954; admitted to bar, 1979, Idaho and U.S. District Court, District of Idaho; 1981, U.S. Court of Appeals, Ninth Circuit. *Education:* University of Idaho (B.S., 1976); Gonzaga University (J.D., 1979). 1988 Plaintiffs' Steering Committee MDL-751 in Re Air Crash Disaster Stapleton International Airport, Denver, CO., Nov. 15, 1987. 1989 Exemplar Trial Counsel MDL-751 In Re Air Crash Disaster at Stapleton International Airport, Denver, CO., Nov. 15, 1987. *Member:* Boise and American (Member, Sections on: Litigation; Tort and Insurance Practice) Bar Associations; Idaho State Bar; International Academy of Trial Lawyers; Association of Trial Lawyers of America; Idaho Trial Lawyers Association; American Board of Trial Advocates (Advocate Member). ***PRACTICE AREAS:*** Product Liability Law; Accident and Personal Injury Law; Medical Malpractice Law; Aviation Law; Insurance Bad Faith Law. ***Email:*** decomstock@rmci.net

JOHN A. BUSH, born Idaho Falls, Idaho, December 23, 1961; admitted to bar, 1988, Idaho, U.S. District Court, District of Idaho and U.S. Court of Appeals, Ninth Circuit. *Education:* University of Idaho (B.S., Business, 1984; J.D., 1988). Law Clerk, Mikel H. Williams, U.S. Magistrate, District of Idaho, 1988-1990. *Member:* Idaho State Bar; American Bar Association (Chair, Young Lawyers Section, 1991-1992); Idaho Trial Lawyers Association; American Inns of Court, #130; American Trial Lawyers Association; Idaho Law Foundation (Board of Directors). ***PRACTICE AREAS:*** Accident and Personal Injury Law; Insurance Bad Faith. ***Email:*** jabush@rmci.net

RICHARD A. CUMMINGS

Established in 1997
999 MAIN STREET
P.O. BOX 1545
BOISE, IDAHO 83701-1545
Telephone: 208-367-0722
Fax: 208-367-0892
Email: cummingsricharda@qwest.net
URL: http://www.racummings.com

Business Law, Commercial Litigation, Real Estate Law, Estate Planning, Tax Planning, Wills, Trusts and Estates, Wills and Probate, Family Trusts, Living Trust, Off-Shore Trusts, Wealth Preservation, Fiduciary Law, Tax Controversies.

RICHARD A. CUMMINGS, born Kearney, Nebraska, August 26, 1948; admitted to bar, 1975, Idaho; 1976, U.S. Tax Court; 1982, U.S. Court of Appeals, Ninth Circuit. *Education:* Northwestern University (B.A., 1970); University of Nebraska (J.D., with distinction, 1975). Order of the Coif. Member, The Order of Barristers. Member: Moot Court National Competition Team; Allen Moot Court Board. Director, National Association of Estate Planners. Director, Estate Law Specialist Board. *Member:* Boise and American Bar Associations; Idaho State Bar; Association of Accredited Estate Planners. ***PRACTICE AREAS:*** Business Law; Commercial Litigation; Real Estate Law; Estate Planning Law; Tax Planning; Tax Controversies; Construction Law.

DAVISON, COPPLE, COPPLE & COX

Established in 1924
199 NORTH CAPITOL BOULEVARD, SUITE 600
P.O. BOX 1583
BOISE, IDAHO 83702
Telephone: 208-342-3658
Fax: 208-386-9428
Email: edcopple@davisoncopple.com
URL: http://www.davisoncopple.com

General Civil and Trial Practice, Litigation, Commercial Banking, Real Estate, Title Insurance, Corporation, Antitrust, Eminent Domain, Condemnation and Inverse Condemnation, Probate, Estate Planning, Family Law, Personal Injury, Products Liability, Insurance Bad Faith, Land Use Planning and Shopping Center Law.

FIRM PROFILE: Davison, Copple, Copple & Cox, one of the oldest law firms in Idaho, is a general practice law firm established in the early 1900's. W. Howard Davison was one of the firm's founders, and was joined in practice by his son, Frank H. Davison in the 1920's; both remained with the firm throughout their lives. In 1945, Robert H. Copple joined the firm; he was joined by his nephews, E. Don Copple in 1966 and Terry C. Copple in 1976. Robert Copple practiced with Davison Copple for his entire career, which spanned 50 years. Jon R. Cox became a partner of the firm in 2002.

The firm's philosophy of providing the highest quality legal services possible in a timely and cost-effective manner has remained constant for nearly a century. Currently, the firm is composed of E. Don Copple, Terry C. Copple, Jon R. Cox and five associates, Heather A. Cunningham, Jay M. Gustavsen, Terri R. Yost, Edward J. Guerricabeitia and Cynthia L. Yee-Wallace.

Davison & Copple is located in the heart of downtown Boise, yet serves corporate and individual clients throughout the state. Since 1945 the firm has served title companies and major financial institutions involved in complex business and real estate transactions; representative clients include Pioneer Title Companies, Washington Federal Savings, Farmers and Merchants State Bank, Maxim Technologies, Inc. and Hewlett-Packard Employee Federal Credit Union. We are also one of the few Idaho firms with an extensive history of representing property own-

(This Listing Continued)

ers involved in eminent domain or inverse condemnation proceedings against governmental agencies, and we regularly represent other clients in litigation involving a wide array of other subjects including personal injury and business litigation.

MEMBERS OF FIRM

W. HOWARD DAVISON (1878-1964)

FRANK H. DAVISON (1907-1984)

ROBERT H. COPPLE (1919-1995)

E. DON COPPLE, born Boise, Idaho, August 19, 1942; admitted to bar, 1966, Idaho, U.S. District Court, District of Idaho and U.S. Court of Appeals, Ninth Circuit; U.S. Supreme Court. *Education:* University of Idaho (B.A., 1964; J.D., 1966). Phi Alpha Delta; Phi Beta Kappa; Phi Kappa Phi; Pi Gamma Mu. Member, Idaho State Legislature, 1968-1974. *Member:* Idaho State Bar; American Bar Association; Idaho Trial Lawyers Association; The Association of Trial Lawyers of America. ***REPORTED CASES:*** Middlekauff, et al v. Lake Cascade, Inc., et al, 654 P.2d 1385 (1982); Ada County Highway District, By & Through Fairbanks, Bass & Silva v. Acarrequi & First Federal Savings & Loan Association of Boise, 673 P.2d 1067 (1983); Emery v. United Pacific Ins. Co., 815 P.2d 442 (1991). ***PRACTICE AREAS:*** Litigation; Eminent Domain; Regulatory Law; Personal Injury; Probate; Real Estate Law; Estate Planning; Shopping Center Law. ***Email:*** edcopple@davisoncopple.com

TERRY C. COPPLE, born Boise, Idaho, January 10, 1952; admitted to bar, 1976, Idaho, U.S. District Court, District of Idaho and U.S. Court of Appeals, Ninth Circuit; 1980, U .S. Tax Court and U.S. Supreme Court. *Education:* University of Idaho (B.A., 1974; J.D., 1976). Phi Beta Kappa; Phi Kappa Phi; Phi Alpha Theta; Phi Alpha Delta. Selective Service Board, Boise Idaho, 1983-1991. *Member:* Idaho State Bar; American Bar Association. ***REPORTED CASES:*** Capps v. Wood, et al., 718 P.2d 1216 (1986); Leppaluoto v. Warm Springs Hollow Homeowners Assoc., Inc., 752 P.2d 605 (1988); Blechmann v. Blaine County, 109 Idaho 181, 701 P.2d 70 (1985); International Engineering Co.; v. Daum Industries, 102 Idaho 363, 630 P.2d 155 (1981); Gibbens v. Weisshaupt, 98 Idaho 633, 570 P.2d 870 (1977). ***PRACTICE AREAS:*** Complex Business Transactions; Commercial Banking Law; Title Insurance Law; Litigation; Estate Planning; Probate; Real Estate; Shopping Center Law. ***Email:*** tccopple@davisoncopple.com

JON R. COX, born Burlingame, California, December 12, 1963; admitted to bar, 1992, Idaho and U.S. District Court, District of Idaho; U.S. Supreme Court. *Education:* Boise State University (B.S., 1987); University of Idaho (J.D., 1991). Delta Theta Phi. Member, American Inn of Court, No. 130, 1996-1997. *Member:* Idaho State Bar; American Bar Association; The Association of Trial Lawyers of America; Idaho Trial Lawyers Association; National Association of Criminal Defense Lawyers; Idaho Association of Criminal Defense Lawyers. ***REPORTED CASES:*** Holmes v. Holmes, 874 P.2d 595 (1994); Cameron v. Neal, Idaho Supreme Court Opinion No. 130 (1997); State of Idaho v. James Eytchison, Idaho Supreme Court Opinion No. 52 (2001). ***PRACTICE AREAS:*** Litigation; Personal Injury; Criminal; Domestic Relations; Medical Malpractice; Real Estate; Probate; Contracts. ***Email:*** cox@davisoncopple.com

ASSOCIATES

HEATHER A. CUNNINGHAM, born Laramie, Wyoming, October 9, 1970; admitted to bar, 1996, Idaho and U.S. District Court, District of Idaho; 2000, Oregon; 2004, U.S. Supreme Court. *Education:* Hillsdale College (B.A., 1993); Pepperdine University (J.D., 1996). Member, American Inn of Court No. 130, 1997-1998. *Member:* Idaho State Bar; Oregon State Bar; American Bar Association; The Association of Trial Lawyers of America; Idaho Trial Lawyers Association; Southwestern Legal Foundation; Affiliate Member of the Appraisal Institute. ***REPORTED CASES:*** State of Idaho v. Jo Grace Jardine et. al. 130 Idaho 318, 940 P.2d 1137 (1997 Amicus); Boel v. Stewart Title Guaranty Company, 137 Idaho 9, 43 P.3d. 768 (2002); KMST v. County of Ada and ACHD, 138 Idaho 577, 67 P.3d. 56 (2003); C&G, Inc. v. Canyon Highway Dist. No. 4, 75 P.3d. 194 (2003). ***PRACTICE AREAS:*** Litigation; Eminent Domain; Inverse Condemnation; Regulatory Law; Contracts; Personal Injury; Real Estate; Constitutional Law; Zoning, Planning and Land Use. ***Email:*** cunningham@davisoncopple.com

JAY M. GUSTAVSEN, born San Juan, Puerto Rico, September 28, 1968; admitted to bar, 1997, Idaho and U.S. District Court of Idaho. *Education:* University of California at Santa Barbara (B.A., 1991); University of Idaho (J.D., 1995). Justice, Phi Alpha Delta. *Member:* American Bar Association; Association of Trial Lawyers of America; American Inns of Court, 1998-1999. ***LANGUAGES:*** Spanish. ***PRACTICE AREAS:*** Litigation; Real Estate; Contracts; Business Transactions; Landlord and Tenant Law; Family Law; Personal Injury; Estate Planning. ***Email:*** gustavsen@davisoncopple.com

EDWARD J. GUERRICABEITIA, born Nampa, Idaho, August 1, 1972; admitted to bar, 2000, Idaho and U.S. District Court, District of Idaho. *Education:* University of Utah (B.S., 1994); University of Idaho College of Law (J.D., 1999). *Member:* Association of Trial Lawyers of America; Idaho Trial Lawyers Association. ***LANGUAGES:*** Spanish, Basque. ***REPORTED CASES:*** BHA Investments, Inc. v. City of Boise, 138 Idaho 356, 63 P.3d 482 (2003). ***PRACTICE AREAS:*** Eminent Domain; Inverse Condemnation; Regulatory Law; Personal Injury; Estate Planning; Real Estate; Probate. ***Email:*** guerricabeitia@davisoncopple.com

CYNTHIA L. YEE-WALLACE, born Boise, Idaho, February 26, 1978; admitted to bar, 2003, Idaho. *Education:* University of Idaho (B.S., Finance, 2000; J.D., 2003). Member, Idaho Law Review, 2001-2003. Mortar Board Honor Society, 1999-2000. Author: Idaho Law Review, "The Anders Brief and the Idaho Rule: It is Time for Idaho to Reevaluate Criminal Appeals after Rejecting the Anders Procedure," 39 Idaho L. Rev. 143 (2002). Civil Litigation Intern, Idaho Attorney General's Office. Criminal Intern, Ada County Prosecutor's Office. *Member:* American Bar Association; Idaho Trial Lawyer's Association; Association of Trial Lawyers of America; Idaho State Bar. ***PRACTICE AREAS:*** Litigation; Employment Law; Complex Litigation; Family Law; Business Law. ***Email:*** wallace@davisoncopple.com

REPRESENTATIVE CLIENTS: Pioneer Title Company of Ada County; Washington Federal Savings; Hewlett-Packard Federal Credit Union; Verex, Farmers & Merchants State Bank; Maxim Technology, Inc.
REFERENCES: Washington Federal Savings; Pioneer Title Company of Ada County.

DOCKSTADER LAW OFFICE

Established in 2005

199 NORTH CAPITOL BOULEVARD
SUITE 302
BOISE, IDAHO 83702
Telephone: 208-338-5000
Fax: 208-336-4980
Email: kdockstader@dockstaderlaw.com
URL: http://www.dockstaderlaw.com

Labor and Employment, Employment Litigation, Civil Litigation.

KIM J. DOCKSTADER, born Rupert, Idaho, August 15, 1964; admitted to bar, 1990, Idaho and U.S. District Court, District of Idaho. *Education:* Utah State University (B.S., magna cum laude, 1987); University of Utah (J.D., 1990). ***PRACTICE AREAS:*** Labor and Employment; Employment Litigation; Civil Litigation. ***Email:*** kdockstader@kdockstaderlaw.com

DROZDA LAW OFFICES, PLLC

Established in 1993

P.O. BOX 6370
BOISE, IDAHO 83707
Telephone: 208-344-9355
Fax: 208-386-9944
Email: drozdarl@drozdalaw.com
URL: http://www.drozdalaw.com

Estate Planning, Taxation, Entity Formation, Operation and Dissolution, Business, Real Estate.

ROBERT L. "BOB" DROZDA, born Omaha, Nebraska, June 19, 1954; admitted to bar, 1980, Nebraska; 1988, California; 1993, Idaho. *Education:* University of Nebraska at Omaha (B.S.B.A.); Creighton University (J.D., 1980); University of the Pacific McGeorge School of Law (LL.M., Taxation, 1992). Omicron Delta Kappa; Phi Alpha Delta. Member, Treasure Valley Estate Planning Council, 1993—. *Member:* State Bar of California (Member, Tax Section, 1987—); Idaho State Bar (Member, Taxation, Probate, Corporate and Security Law Sections, 1993—); Idaho Society of Certified Public Accountants (Member, Federal/State Taxation Committee, 1992—); American Institute of Certified Public Accountants (Member, Tax Section, 1981—). ***PRACTICE AREAS:*** Estate Planning; Taxation; Entity Formation; Business Operations; Business Dissolutions; Business; Real Estate. ***Email:*** drozdarl@drozdalaw.com

DYKAS, SHAVER & NIPPER, LLP

Established in 1985

P.O. BOX 877
BOISE, IDAHO 83701
Telephone: 208-345-1122
Fax: 208-345-8370
Toll Free: 1-877-611-1122
Email: info@dykaslaw.com
URL: http://www.dykaslaw.com

Intellectual Property, Patent, Trademark, including National and International Filing, Copyright, Contracts, Unfair Competition, Trade Secrets, Licensing, Litigation and Related Matters.

FIRM PROFILE: Dykas, Shaver & Nipper, LLP ("the Firm") began in Boise in 1985 as Dykas Law Offices, with the goal of bringing high quality, reasonably priced legal service in the fields of technology and intellectual property law to emerging businesses with the need to protect intellectual property of any type.

The Firm specializes in the preparation and prosecution of patent applications, trademark and copyright applications, as well as related licensing. The Firm also handles litigation involving intellectual property law disputes in state and federal courts and is experienced in alternate forms of dispute resolution.

FRANK J. DYKAS, born Meriden, Connecticut, December 6, 1946; admitted to bar, 1975, Idaho; U.S. District Court, District of Idaho and U.S. Court of Appeals, Ninth and Federal Circuits; registered to practice before U.S. Patent and Trademark Office. *Education:* University of New Haven (B.S., 1968); University of Wyoming (J.D., 1975). Adjunct Professor, University of Idaho. Twin Falls County Prosecutor, 1977-1978. Special Prosecutor, Idaho State Bar, 1985-1986. *Member:* Idaho State Bar; American Intellectual Property Law Association; Inter-Pacific Bar Association. ***PRACTICE AREAS:*** Patent Law; Trademark Law; Trade Secrets; Litigation; Contracts. ***Email:*** frank@dykaslaw.com

ROBERT L. SHAVER, born Wichita, Kansas, June 19, 1950; admitted to bar, 1995, Washington; 1996, Idaho; U.S. Court of Appeals, Ninth Circuit; registered to practice before U.S. Patent and Trademark Office. *Education:* California State, Stanislaus (B.A., 1972); City University (M.B.A., 1988); University of Idaho (J.D., 1995). *Member:* Idaho State Bar; Washington State Bar Association. ***LANGUAGES:*** Spanish. ***PRACTICE AREAS:*** Patent; Trademark; Copyright; Litigation; Contracts. ***Email:*** shaver@dykaslaw.com

STEPHEN M. NIPPER, born Twin Falls, Idaho, January 28, 1972; admitted to bar, 1998, Idaho; U.S. District Court, District of Idaho and U.S. Court of Appeals, Federal Circuit; registered to practice before U.S. Patent and Trademark Office. *Education:* Truman State University (B.S., 1994); Southern Illinois University, Carbondale (J.D., 1998). *Member:* Idaho State Bar. ***PRACTICE AREAS:*** Patents; Trademarks; Copyrights; Trade Secrets; Contracts. ***Email:*** stephen@dykaslaw.com

(This Listing Continued)

DYKAS, SHAVER & NIPPER, LLP, Boise—Continued

DEREK H. MAUGHAN, born Murray, Utah, April 9, 1971; admitted to bar, 2001, Idaho; U.S. District Court, District of Idaho and U.S. Court of Appeals, Federal Circuit; registered to practice before U.S. Patent and Trademark Office. *Education:* Brigham Young University (B.S., 1995); University of Idaho (J.D., 2001). Member, American Society of Clinical Pathologists; MT (ASCP); CLS (NCA) USA. ***LANGUAGES:*** Spanish. ***PRACTICE AREAS:*** Trademarks; Copyrights; Trade Secrets; Contracts; Patents; Unfair Competition; Litigation. ***Email:*** maughan@dykaslaw.com

REPRESENTATIVE CLIENTS: ProTeam, Inc.; Diamond Z Manufacturing, Inc.; Robert Comstock, LLC; Simonds Industries; Dept. of Transportation; State of Idaho; Multiquip Corporation; Whiteman Industries, Inc.; Transit Dynamics; Preco New Products Corporation; DBSI, Inc.; Bon Aire Industries; ConectL, Inc.
REFERENCE: Key Bank of Idaho.

EBERLE, BERLIN, KADING, TURNBOW, McKLVEEN & JONES

CHARTERED

Established in 1903

CAPITOL PARK PLAZA
300 NORTH SIXTH STREET
P.O. BOX 1368
BOISE, IDAHO 83701-1368
Telephone: 208-344-8535
Facsimile: 208-344-8542
Email: jbc@eberle.com
URL: http://www.eberle.com

Personal Injury, Products Liability, Toxic Torts, Professional Liability, Aviation, Construction, Lender Liability, Commercial and Business Litigation, Insurance Bad Faith Defense, Healthcare, Workers Compensation, Corporations and Partnerships, Antitrust, Corporate Finance and Securities, Securities Litigation and Arbitration, Mergers, Acquisitions, Tender Offers, and other Business Transactions, Copyright and Trademark, Banking and Creditor's Rights, Bankruptcy, Real Estate Finance and Development, Land Use, Taxation, Estate Planning and Employee Benefits, Governmental Relations (Administrative, Regulatory, Legislative), Securities and Insurance Regulation, Environment, Energy, Water Rights, Natural Resources and Agriculture Law.

J. LOUIS EBERLE (1890-1964)

T. H. EBERLE (1922-1977)

JAMES L. BERLIN (1926-2000)

R. M. TURNBOW, born Kellogg, Idaho, September 16, 1936; admitted to bar, 1960, Idaho. *Education:* University of Idaho (B.A., 1958; LL.B., 1960). Phi Alpha Delta. *Member:* Boise and American Bar Associations; Idaho State Bar. ***PRACTICE AREAS:*** Antitrust; Mergers and Acquisitions; Corporate Law; Commercial Law. ***Email:*** rturnbow@eberle.com

WILLIAM J. McKLVEEN, born Des Moines, Iowa, November 18, 1943; admitted to bar, 1968, Texas; 1969, Idaho. *Education:* Grinnell College (B.A., 1965); University of Texas (J.D., 1968). Phi Delta Phi. Recipient, Idaho State Bar Professionalism Award, 1998. *Member:* Boise and 4th Judicial District Bar Associations; State Bar of Texas; Idaho State Bar; American College of Real Estate Lawyers; Idaho Association of Defense Counsel. ***PRACTICE AREAS:*** Real Estate Law; Business Law; Corporate Law; Commercial Law; Farm and Ranching Law. ***Email:*** wmcklveen@eberle.com

WARREN EUGENE JONES, born Montpelier, Idaho, October 19, 1943; admitted to bar, 1968, Idaho. *Education:* College of Idaho (B.A., magna cum laude, 1965); University of Chicago (J.D., 1968). Law Clerk for Chief Justice Joseph J. McFadden, Idaho Supreme Court, 1968-1970. *Member:* Boise and American Bar Associations; Idaho State Bar; American Board of Trial Advocates. ***PRACTICE AREAS:*** Civil Litigation; Insurance Law; Intellectual Property Law; Trade Secrets; Products Liability; Commercial Litigation; Professional Malpractice; Construction Law. ***Email:*** wjones@eberle.com

THOMAS R. LINVILLE, born Boise, Idaho, March 23, 1951; admitted to bar, 1976, Idaho. *Education:* University of Idaho (B.S., 1972; J.D., 1976). Author and Lecturer: "Commercial Loan Transactions," Idaho State Bar. Author: "Enforcement of Secured Claims"; "Strategic Administration of Distressed Agricultural Loans"; "How to Protect Creditors' Rights in Bankruptcy". *Member:* Boise Bar Association; Idaho State Bar (Member, Sections on: Commercial Law and Bankruptcy; Corporate and Securities Law). ***PRACTICE AREAS:*** Commercial Law; Foreclosures; Bankruptcy; Banking; Corporate Law; Real Estate Law; Business Litigation and Transactions. ***Email:*** tlinville@eberle.com

JOSEPH H. UBERUAGA, II, born Boise, Idaho, May 29, 1952; admitted to bar, 1978, Washington and Idaho; 1981, U.S. Tax Court. *Education:* Gonzaga University (B.A., 1974; J.D., 1977); University of Florida (LL.M. in Taxation, 1978). Author: Taxation Chapter, Idaho Real Estate Practice Handbook, Idaho Law Foundation, 1988. Co-Author: Idaho Probate & Estate Administration Forms Handbook, Idaho Law Foundation, 1992 and Idaho Guardianship and Conservatorship Administration Forms Handbook, Idaho Law Foundation, 1996. Lecturer: Institute on Partnership Law, Idaho Law Foundation, 1981; Business Law Institute, Idaho Law Foundation, 1984; Idaho Practical Probate, National Business Institute, 1985; Estate Planning and Probate in Idaho, National Business Institute, 1987; Idaho Practical Probate, Professional Education Systems, 1988; Potpourri of Tax, Probate & Trust Issues for the General Practitioner, Idaho Law Foundation, 1990; Estate Planning *Trends & Idaho Probate & Estate Administration Forms, Idaho Law Foundation, 1992;* Washington State Tax Conference, Washington Society of CPAs, 1993; 21st Annual Tax Institute, Gonzaga University School of Law, 1994; 38th Annual Idaho State Tax Institute, 1996. Member: Boise Estate Planning Council; The Idaho State Tax Institute Planning Committee. *Member:* Boise, Washington State and American (Member, Sections of: Taxation; Real Property, Probate and Trust Law) Bar Associations; Idaho State Bar (Chairman, Taxation, Probate and Trust Law Section, 1990-1991). Fellow, American College of Trust and Estate Counsel. ***PRACTICE AREAS:*** Federal and State Taxation; Estate Planning; Trust Law; Probate; General Business. ***Email:*** juberuaga@eberle.com

(This Listing Continued)

NEIL D. McFEELEY, born Orlando, Florida, October 29, 1949; admitted to bar, 1986, Idaho; 1993, U.S. Supreme Court. *Education:* University of Texas (B.A., magna cum laude, 1971; Ph.D., 1975); Duke University (J.D., with high honors, 1985). Phi Beta Kappa; Phi Kappa Phi; Order of the Coif; Latty Scholar. Editor-in-Chief, Duke Law Journal, 1984-1985. Law Clerk to Hon. Robert Boochever, U.S. Court of Appeals, Ninth Circuit, 1985-1986. Author: "Appointment of Judges: The Johnson Presidency," University of Texas Press, 1987; "En Banc Proceedings in the United States Courts of Appeals," Idaho Law Review, 1987-1988. *Member:* Boise and American Bar Associations; Idaho State Bar; American Judicature Society. ***PRACTICE AREAS:*** Commercial Litigation; Employment Law; Workers' Compensation. ***Email:*** nmcfeeley@eberle.com

STANLEY J. THARP, born Pocatello, Idaho, September 18, 1961; admitted to bar, 1988, Idaho. *Education:* Idaho State University (B.A., cum laude, 1985); University of Idaho (J.D., 1988). Editor-in-Chief, Idaho Law Review, 1987. Author: Casenote, "State v. Cutler: Limitation on Indians' Hunting Rights in Idaho," 23 Idaho L. Rev. 327, 1987. Who's Who Among American Law Students, 1988-8th Ed. Law Clerk to the Hon. Marion J. Callister, U.S. District Judge, U.S. District Court for the District of Idaho, 1988-1990. Idaho State Bar Director in ABA/YLD Disaster Legal Assistance, 1991-1998. Chairman, Idaho State Bar, Young Lawyers Section, 1992-1993. *Member:* Boise Bar Association; Idaho State Bar. ***PRACTICE AREAS:*** Civil Litigation; Commercial Litigation; Insurance Law; Employment Law. ***Email:*** stharp@eberle.com

SAMUEL A. DIDDLE, born Peoria, Illinois, May 27, 1965; admitted to bar, 1990, Tennessee; 1994, Idaho. *Education:* Miami University (B.S., 1987); University of North Carolina (J.D., 1990). Member: North Carolina Journal of International Law and Commercial Regulation. *Member:* Boise and Idaho State Bar Associations. ***PRACTICE AREAS:*** Construction Litigation; Health Care; Insurance Coverage Litigation; Insurance Bad Faith Defense; ERISA Litigation; Business Litigation; Foreclosures; Bankruptcy; Commercial Transactions; Mergers and Acquisitions. ***Email:*** sdiddle@eberle.com

---

PETER W. WARE, JR., born Bronxville, New York, July 20, 1966; admitted to bar, 1994, Idaho; 1999, Arizona. *Education:* University of Arizona (B.A., 1989); Willamette University (J.D., 1994). *Member:* Idaho State Bar; State Bar of Arizona. ***PRACTICE AREAS:*** Commercial Transactions; Real Estate Transactions; Real Estate Development; Business Law; Corporate Law. ***Email:*** pware@eberle.com

STEPHEN J. OLSON, born Milwaukee, Wisconsin, September 28, 1961; admitted to bar, 1989, Idaho. *Education:* University of California at Santa Barbara (B.A., Law & Society, 1984); University of Denver (J.D., 1989). *Member:* Idaho State Bar. ***PRACTICE AREAS:*** Commercial Litigation; Civil Litigation; Employment Law; Landlord and Tenant Law; Real Estate Law. ***Email:*** solson@eberle.com

COREY J. RIPPEE, born Fresno, California, August 23, 1977; admitted to bar, 2003, Idaho. *Education:* University of Idaho (B.S., 2000; J.D., magna cum laude, 2003). Editor in Chief, Idaho Law Review, 2002-2003. *Member:* Idaho State Bar (Young Lawyers Section). ***PRACTICE AREAS:*** Commercial Litigation; Business Transactions; General Practice. ***Email:*** crippee@eberle.com

RICHARD W. STOVER, born Boise, Idaho, March 7, 1974; admitted to bar, 2003, Idaho. *Education:* Albertson College of Idaho (B.A., Political and International Relations, 1997); University of Idaho College of Law (J.D., 2003). *Member:* Idaho State Bar. ***PRACTICE AREAS:*** Business Transactions; Commercial Litigation.

OF COUNSEL

R. B. KADING, JR., born Boise, Idaho, March 26, 1930; admitted to bar, 1958, Idaho. *Education:* University of Oregon (B.B.A., 1952); University of Idaho (LL.B., 1958). *Member:* Boise and American Bar Associations; Idaho State Bar; Idaho Association of Defense Counsel; Lawyer-Pilots Bar Association; Association of Insurance Attorneys; American Board of Trial Advocates. Fellow, American College of Trial Lawyers. ***PRACTICE AREAS:*** Civil Litigation; Aviation Law; Professional Malpractice; Products Liability. ***Email:*** rkading@eberle.com

REPRESENTATIVE CLIENTS: Ada County Highway District; Agri Beef Co.; Associated Food Stores, Inc.; Bank United of Texas; Cessna Aircraft Co.; Chase Manhattan Leasing & Co.; C.I.T. Corp.; CIT Group Equipment Financing, Inc.; Citicorp National Services, Inc.; Clark Equipment and Credit Corporation; Deloitte & Touche; First Banks; Employers Resource Management Company; Franklin Building Supply Company; New Holland, North America; Gates Rubber Company; General Electric Co.; Hecla Mining Company; Edward D. Jones & Co.; Key Bank National Association; Key Corp Leasing, Ltd.; McDonnell Douglas Corporation; NationsBank Mortgage Corporation; Phillips Petroleum; Piper Jaffrey, Inc.; Prudential Securities; Robacor; Roebbelen Land Company; Shearson/American Express; U.S. Steel Corp.; Waddell & Reed; Wells Fargo Bank.
REPRESENTATIVE INSURANCE COMPANIES: Aetna Insurance Company; Aetna Casualty and Surety Co.; American Manufacturers Mutual Insurance Company; American Motorists Insurance Company; Associated Aviation Underwriters; Blue Cross of Idaho; Chubb Group of Insurance Companies; CIGNA; Commercial Union Insurance Co.; Colonial Life and Accident Company; Colony Insurance Group; Crown Life Insurance Company; Employers Reinsurance Insurance Co.; Employers Surplus Insurance Co.; Equitable Life Assurance Society of the United States; Farmers Insurance Group; Fred A. Moreton & Co.; Guardian Life Insurance Company; Government Employers Insurance Company (GEICO); John Hancock Mutual Life Insurance Co.; Investor's Diversified Services, Inc.; Investors Property Management; Kendall Insurance Company; Kemper National Companies; Lumbermans Mutual Insurance Company; Metropolitan Property and Casualty Company; Minnesota Mutual Life Insurance Company; Mutual Life Insurance Company of New York; National Indemnity Company; North American Insurance Company of California (NAICC); Petit-Morry Insurance Company; Principal Casualty Insurance Company; Provident Life and Accident Insurance Company; Puritan Insurance Co.; Reliance Surety Company; Risk Enterprise Management Limited; St. Paul Fire & Marine Insurance Company; Standard Insurance Company; State Insurance Fund; The Home Indemnity Company; The Home Insurance Company; The Travelers Insurance Company; Unisource Worldwide, Inc.; UNUM Provident Corporation; Westport Insurance Co.; Zurich-American Insurance Group.

ELAM & BURKE

A PROFESSIONAL ASSOCIATION

Established in 1928

251 E. FRONT STREET, SUITE 300
P.O. BOX 1539
BOISE, IDAHO 83702
Telephone: 208-343-5454
Telecopier: 208-384-5844
Email: eblaw@elamburke.com
URL: http://www.elamburke.com

Administrative Litigation, Appellate Practice, Arbitration, Automobile Insurance Defense, Aviation Defense, Bankruptcy, Banks and Banking, Business Law, Casinos and Gambling, Class Action Defense, Commercial Law, Commercial Transactions, Construction Law, Contracts, Corporate Law, Environmental Litigation, Federal Civil Practice, Fire Insurance Defense, General Liability Defense, Insurance Bad Faith Defense, Intellectual Property; Local Government Law, Mediation, Municipal Law, Products Liability Defense, Real Estate, Self Insured Defense, Ski Area Liability, State Government Law, Torts, Trusts and Estates, Wills.

FIRM PROFILE: ELAM & BURKE was founded in 1928 by Laurel E. Elam and Carl A. Burke, and became a professional corporation in 1992. We are located in Idaho's state capital, in close proximity to both federal and state courts and numerous administrative agencies. Over time, we have developed a wide range of specialized capabilities to meet our clients' needs, although our cornerstone remains our litigation, commercial and business practice. The firm's clients include those in the corporate, business, banking, governmental and insurance fields.

Attorneys in the firm maintain current membership in the American Bar Association, the Idaho State Bar and other professional organizations such as the American College of Trial Lawyers and the Defense Research Institute. Members are also active in many civic organizations and activities. The firm encourages professional development and specialization and education for all of its members and support staff and believes it is important to take an active role in governmental and political activities.

MEMBERS OF FIRM

LAUREL E. ELAM (1888-1974)

CARL A. BURKE (1898-1961)

M. ALLYN DINGEL, JR., born Twin Falls, Idaho, October 10, 1936; admitted to bar, 1961, Idaho. *Education:* University of Idaho (B.A., in Econ., 1958); New York University (LL.B., 1961). Pomroy Scholar, New York University, 1958-1961. Named, Distinguished Lawyer of the Year 2004, Idaho State Bar. Associate Editor, New York University Law Review, 1960-1961. Assistant Attorney General, Idaho, 1964-1966. Deputy Attorney General, Idaho (Counsel for Departments of Insurance and Finance). Chief Criminal Deputy, Attorney General, 1966-1967. Lawyer-representative and Chairperson, Ninth Circuit Conference of the United States Courts, 1985-1988. Commissioner, 1990-1998 and Chairperson, 1996-1998, Idaho State Code Commission. *Member:* American Bar Association (Member, House of Delegates, 1998-2004); Idaho State Bar; Idaho Bar Foundation (Vice-President, 1976-1978); Idaho Association of Defense Counsel (President, 1977-1978). American College of Trial Lawyers; American Bar Association. ***PRACTICE AREAS:*** Litigation; Business Law; Administrative Law; Commercial Law; Insurance Defense. ***Email:*** mad@elamburke.com

JOHN MAGEL, born Twin Falls, Idaho, September 18, 1938; admitted to bar, 1964, California; 1965, Idaho and U.S. District Court, District of Idaho; 1979, U.S. Court of Appeals, Ninth Circuit; 1986, U.S. Tax Court. *Education:* University of Idaho (B.S., 1961); University of California at Berkeley (LL.B., 1964). *Member:* Idaho State Bar; State Bar of California; Idaho Mediation Association; Idaho Trial Lawyers Association; Idaho Association of Defense Counsel. Fellow American College of Trial Lawyers. ***PRACTICE AREAS:*** Mediation; Products Liability; Commercial Law; Alternative Dispute Resolution; Arbitration; Litigation; Medical Malpractice; Legal Malpractice. ***Email:*** jmagel@elamburke.com

JAMES D. LaRUE, born Rupert, Idaho, March 6, 1946; admitted to bar, 1975, Idaho and U.S. District Court, District of Idaho. *Education:* University of Idaho (B.A., 1968; J.D., 1975). Phi Alpha Delta. Member, Order of Barristers. Editor, Idaho Law Review, 1974-1975. *Member:* Idaho State Bar; Idaho Association of Defense Counsel (President, 1993-1994); Defense Research Institute; Federation of Defense and Corporate Counsel. Fellow, American College of Trial Lawyers. ***PRACTICE AREAS:*** Insurance Defense; Products Liability Defense; Professional Errors and Omissions. ***Email:*** jdl@elamburke.com

RYAN P. ARMBRUSTER, born Chicago, Illinois, February 28, 1951; admitted to bar, 1976, Idaho and U.S. District Court, District of Idaho; 1979, U.S. Court of Appeals, Ninth Circuit. *Education:* Bradley University (B.A., 1973); University of Denver (J.D., 1975). Deputy City Attorney, City of Boise, 1976-1979. *Member:* American Bar Association (Member, Local Government Law Section); Idaho State Bar (Member, Workers Compensation Section, President, 1989-1990); Defense Research Institute; Idaho Municipal Attorneys, Inc. (Associate Member). ***SPECIAL AGENCIES:*** Idaho Industrial Commission. ***PRACTICE AREAS:*** Municipal Law; Workers Compensation; Real Estate Development; Public Authority Finance. ***Email:*** rpa@elamburke.com

WILLIAM G. DRYDEN, born Los Angeles, California, January 24, 1953; admitted to bar, 1978, Idaho and U.S. District Court, District of Idaho; 1987, U.S. Court of Appeals, Ninth Circuit. *Education:* Brown University and Stanford University (B.A., with distinction, 1975); Willamette University (J.D., 1978). Law Clerk: Idaho Supreme Court, 1978-1979; U.S. District Court, 1979-1980. *Member:* Idaho State Bar; Defense Research Institute; Federation of Defense and Corporate Counsel; Idaho Association of Defense Counsel; American Inns of Court # 130. ***LANGUAGES:*** Spanish. ***PRACTICE AREAS:*** Litigation; Insurance Defense; Commercial Litigation; Administrative Law (pari-mutuel racing); Alternative Dispute Resolution; Environmental Litigation. ***Email:*** wgd@elamburke.com

JAMES A. FORD, born Bellingham, Washington, July 6, 1960; admitted to bar, 1985, Idaho and U.S. District Court, District of Idaho. *Education:* University of Montana (B.S., 1982); University of Idaho (J.D., 1985). *Member:* Idaho State Bar (Chairperson, Young Lawyers Section, 1989-1990; Member, Sections on: Worker's Compensation; Litigation; Professionalism); Defense Research Institute; Idaho Association of Defense Counsel (President, 2001-2002). American Inns of Court #130 (Secretary/Treasurer, 1991-1997); International Association of Defense Counsel. ***SPECIAL AGENCIES:*** Idaho Industrial Commission. ***PRACTICE AREAS:*** Automobile Negligence; Personal Injury; Professional Malpractice; Workers Compensation. ***Email:*** jaf@elamburke.com

JEFFREY A. THOMSON, born U.S. Air Force Base, Japan, July 7, 1959; admitted to bar, 1985, Idaho and U.S. District Court, District of Idaho; 1987, U.S. Court of Appeals, Ninth Circuit. *Education:* University of Idaho (B.S., 1981; J.D., 1985). Idaho Law Review, 1984-1985. Law Clerk, U.S. Court of Appeals, 9th Circuit, 1985-1987. Member, Rotary. *Member:* Idaho State Bar; Defense Research Institute; Idaho Association of Defense Counsel. ***PRACTICE AREAS:*** Appellate Practice; Litigation; Corporate Law; Insurance Coverage Defense; Insurance Bad Faith Defense; Contracts; Business Law. ***Email:*** jat@elamburke.com

LOREN C. IPSEN, born Soda Springs, Idaho, January 20, 1950; admitted to bar, 1975, Idaho and U.S. District Court, District of Idaho; 1978, U.S. Tax Court. *Education:* Harvard University (B.A., 1972); Hastings College of The Law (J.D., 1975). Formerly with Howard Ellsworth Ipsen Perry and Lopez. *Member:* Idaho State Bar. ***PRACTICE AREAS:*** Estate Planning; Wills; Trust Law; Business Transactions; Real Estate; Banking Law. ***Email:*** lci@elamburke.com

JOSHUA S. EVETT, born Nashville, Tennessee, November 4, 1965; admitted to bar, 1997, Idaho and U.S. District Court, District of Idaho;. *Education:* Macalester College (B.A., cum laude, 1987); Hastings College of the Law (J.D., 1994). Member, American Inns of Court. *Member:* State Bar of California; Idaho State Bar; American Bar Association; Idaho Trial Lawyers Association. ***PRACTICE AREAS:*** Insurance Defense; Insurance Bad Faith Defense; Medical Malpractice; Civil Litigation; Intellectual Property. ***Email:*** jse@elamburke.com

ASSOCIATES

JON M. BAUMAN, born Corvallis, Oregon, October 14, 1953; admitted to bar, 1982, Idaho and U.S. District Court, District of Idaho; 1985, Utah and U.S. District Court, District of Utah; 2003, U.S. Court of Appeals, Ninth Circuit. *Education:* University of Utah (B.A., magna cum laude, 1976; M.A., 1980); University of Idaho (J.D., 1982). Phi Beta Kappa; Phi Eta Sigma; Phi Kappa Phi. Adjunct Professor, Workers Compensation Law, University of Idaho, 1995 — .Referee, Workers Compensation, Idaho Industrial Commission. *Member:* Idaho State Bar (Member, Workers Compensation Section); Utah State Bar; Idaho Association of Defense Counsel. ***PRACTICE AREAS:*** Workers Compensation; Civil Litigation; Insurance Defense; Appellate Practice. ***Email:*** jmb@elamburke.com

MATTHEW L. WALTERS, born Livingston, Montana, January 1, 1975; admitted to bar, 2002, Idaho and U.S. District Court, District of Idaho. *Education:* University of Montana (B.A., cum laude, 1997); University of Idaho (J.D., 2002). Law Clerk, Idaho State District Court. *Member:* Idaho State Bar; Young Lawyers Association (Secretary, 2005-2006); American Inns of Court #130. ***PRACTICE AREAS:*** Litigation; Insurance Defense. ***Email:*** mlw@elamburke.com

W. BEN SLAUGHTER III, born Boise, Idaho, October 1, 1974; admitted to bar, 2000, Idaho, U.S. District Court, District of Idaho. *Education:* University of Utah (B.S., 1996); University of Idaho (J.D., 2000). Member, Boise Metro Chamber of Commerce. *Member:* American Bar Association; Idaho State Bar (Member, Sections on: Commercial Law; Real Property; Bankruptcy). ***PRACTICE AREAS:*** Bankruptcy; Real Estate; Construction Law; Commercial Law. ***Email:*** wbs@elamburke.com

SOO Y. KANG, born Seoul, South Korea, November 14, 1976; admitted to bar, 2003, Idaho and U.S. District Court, District of Idaho. *Education:* Boise State University (B.A., 2000); University of Idaho (J.D., 2003). *Member:* Idaho State Bar; American Inns of Court 130. ***PRACTICE AREAS:*** Litigation; Appellate Practice; Insurance Defense. ***Email:*** syk@elamburke.com

JOSEPH N. PIRTLE, born Boise, Idaho, December 4, 1978; admitted to bar, 2004, Idaho and U.S. District Court, District of Idaho. *Education:* University of Idaho (B.S., 2001; J.D., 2004). *Member:* Idaho State Bar. ***PRACTICE AREAS:*** Litigation; Insurance Defense. ***Email:*** jnp@elamburke.com

OF COUNSEL

R. MICHAEL SOUTHCOMBE, born Spokane, Washington, April 24, 1935; admitted to bar, 1962, Idaho and U.S. District Court, District of Idaho; 1972, U.S. Court of Appeals, Ninth Circuit. *Education:* University of Idaho (B.A., 1957; LL.B., 1962). Chairman, Idaho State Tax Commission, 1993-2000. Chairman, Vice-Chairman and Treasurer, Multi-State Tax Commission, 1996-2000. *Member:* Boise Bar Association; Idaho State Bar (Chairman, Bankruptcy Section, 1986-1987); American Bankruptcy Institute. [U.S. Army, 1957-1959; Army Reserve, 1959-1987, Colonel Retired]. ***PRACTICE AREAS:*** Bankruptcy; Commercial Law; Sales Tax and Nexus; Administrative Law. ***Email:*** rms@elamburke.com

MACK A. REDFORD, born Wendell, Idaho, July 16, 1937; admitted to bar, 1967, Idaho and U.S. District Court, District of Idaho; 1993, U.S. Court of Appeals, Ninth Circuit. *Education:* University of Idaho (B.S., 1961; J.D., 1967). Phi Alpha Delta (President, 1965-1966). Deputy Attorney General, State of Idaho, 1967-1970. Assistant Attorney General (Chief Litigation). General Counsel, Morrison-Knudsen Saudi Arabia Consortium, Saudi Arabia, 1980-1981. Vice President, Secretary and General Counsel, Morrison-Knudsen Engineers, Inc., Morrison-Knudsen International Co., Inc., 1980-1990. University of Idaho Foundation (President, 1981-1994). Counsel & Claims Advisor: Transmanche-Link (Channel Tunnel Contractors), England-France, 1990; World Bank, Nepal Electric Authority, Arun, III Hydro Project, 1991—. Member, AAA Panel of Arbitrators, Commercial Disputes, 1990—. *Member:* Idaho State Bar (Commissioner, 1974-1977; President, 1976-1977); American Bar Association; International Bar Association. [U.S. Army, 1959-1961]. ***PRACTICE AREAS:*** Construction Law; Business Law; Real Estate; Commercial Transactions; Corporate Law. ***Email:*** mar@elamburke.com

COUNSEL FOR: Idaho Falls Redevelopment Agency.

(This Listing Continued)

ELAM & BURKE, A PROFESSIONAL ASSOCIATION, Boise—Continued

REPRESENTATIVE CLIENTS: American Ecology Corporation; Attorneys Liability Protection Society; Berkshire Hatheway Homestate Companies; Blue Lakes Trout Farm, Inc.; Bogus Basin Recreational Association; Capital One; ConAgra Foods, Inc.; Daimler Chrysler Corporation; Employers Reinsurance Corporation; Enterprise Rent-A-Car; Farmers Insurance Company; Ford Motor Credit Company; Jerome Urban Renewal Agency; Les Schwab Tire Centers of Idaho; Marsh & McLennan Companies, Inc.; Meridian Development Corporation; Northwest Physicians Mutual; Ohio Casualty Insurance Company; Philadelphia Insurance Companies; Regence Blue Shield of Idaho; Salvation Army; Sel-Equity Realty; State Farm Insurance Companies; Sublimity Insurance Company; The Hartford; Thomas Development Company; United Heritage Mutual Life Insurance Company.

LAW OFFICE OF MICHAEL J. ELIA

1199 SHORELINE LANE, SUITE 308
BOISE, IDAHO 83702
Telephone: 208-331-9800
Fax: 208-331-9805
Email: melia@mjelawpc.com
URL: http://www.mjelawfirmpc.com

Insurance, Personal Injury, Insurance Defense, Business Litigation, General Practice.

MICHAEL J. ELIA, born Spokane, Washington, July 15, 1962; admitted to bar, 1987, California and U.S. District Court, Southern District of California; 1992, Washington; 1994, Idaho and U.S. District Court, District of Idaho; 1997, U.S. Court of Appeals, Ninth Circuit. *Education:* Gonzaga University (B.A., magna cum laude, 1984); University of Washington (J.D., 1987). Alpha Sigma Nu; Phi Alpha Theta; Phi Alpha Delta. Chevron Merit Scholar. *Member:* State Bar of California; Washington State Bar Association; Idaho State Bar (Litigation Section; Fee Dispute Committee); Defense Research Institute. ***PRACTICE AREAS:*** Insurance (35%); Personal Injury (25%); Insurance Defense (25%); Business Litigation (10%); General Practice (5%).

ELLSWORTH KALLAS & TALBOY, P.L.L.C.

THE GREYHAWK BUILDING
2402 WEST JEFFERSON STREET
BOISE, IDAHO 83702
Telephone: 208-336-1843
Fax: 208-345-8945
Email: rwt@greyhawklaw.com
URL: http://www.greyhawk-law.com

General Civil and Criminal Practice, Trials, Insurance, Business, Real Estate, Collections, Workers Compensation, Probate, Estate Planning and Mediation, Water Law, Wills.

ROBERT W. TALBOY, born Boise, Idaho, September 8, 1959; admitted to bar, 1986, Idaho and U.S. District Court, District of Idaho; 1991, U.S. Claims Court. *Education:* Creighton University; Boise State University (B.A., 1982); University of Idaho (J.D., 1986). Delta Theta Phi. Order of the Barristers. Member: National Moot Court Team. National Moot Court Team Competition; National Finalist. Recipient: American Jurisprudence Award in Constitutional Law. Adjunct Professor, Legal Research and Writing and Westlaw Advanced Research, Legal Assistant Program, Boise State University. *Member:* Boise and Fourth Judicial District (President, 1996-1997) Bar Associations; Idaho State Bar; Idaho Trial Lawyers Association. ***PRACTICE AREAS:*** Workers Compensation; Personal Injury; Insurance Defense; Collections; Water Law; Mediation. ***Email:*** rwt@greyhawklaw.com

REPRESENTATIVE CLIENTS: Great West Casualty; Bonneville Billing and Collections; Boise-Kuwa Irrigation District.

EVANS KEANE LLP

Established in 1984
1405 WEST MAIN STREET
BOISE, IDAHO 83702
Telephone: 208-384-1800
Facsimile: 208-345-3514
Email: firm@evanskeane.com
URL: http://www.evanskeane.com

Kellogg, Idaho Office: 111 Main Street, P.O. Box 659. Telephone: 208-784-1105.

General Trial and Appellate Practice, Products Liability, Personal Injury Law, Corporate, Real Property, Banking, Employment, Labor, Mining, Public Utilities, Legislative and Administrative.

MEMBERS OF FIRM

JED W. MANWARING, born Rexburg, Idaho, April 15, 1954; admitted to bar, 1983, Idaho and U.S. District Court, District of Idaho. *Education:* Brigham Young University (B.A., 1978); University of Idaho (J.D., 1982). Recipient, American Jurisprudence Awards for Civil Procedure and Torts. Clerkship Idaho Supreme Court, Hon. Robert E. Bakes, 1983-1985. Lecture and Instruction: "Collecting Judgments in Idaho", National Business Institute, 1993 and 1994; "Collection Law in Idaho," Lorman Business Institute, 1994 and 1995; "Basic Bankruptcy Considerations for Creditors," NALM, 2000; "Legal Aspects of Credit," National Association of Credit Managers, 2001; "Trustees Avoiding Litigation," Advanced Bankruptcy Class, University of Idaho, 2002. *Member:* Idaho State Bar (Member, Bankruptcy Section); American Bar Association; The Association of Trial Lawyers of America; The Forwarders List of Attorneys. ***REPORTED CASES:*** State Ins. Fund v. Jarolimek, 139 Idaho 173, 75 P.3d 191 (2003); Primary Health Network v. Dept. of Admin., State of Idaho, 137 Idaho 663, 52 P.3d 307 (2002); Hawks v. Epi Products USA, 121 Idaho 281, 923 P.2d 988 (1996); Hawley v. Green, 124 Idaho 385, 860 P.2d 1 (1993); In re Bybee, Sr.; Krommenhoek v. A-Mark Precious Metals, Inc., 945 F.2d 309 (9th Cir. 1991). ***PRACTICE AREAS:*** Commercial Litigation; Collections; Bankruptcy Litigation; Construction Litigation; Crop Loss; Product Liability; Personal Injury. ***Email:*** jmanwaring@evanskeane.com

JAMES D. HOVREN, born Salmon, Idaho, November 18, 1957; admitted to bar, 1985, Idaho and U.S. District Court, District of Idaho; 1987, U.S. Court of Appeals, Ninth Circuit. *Education:* College of Idaho (B.A., summa cum laude, 1980); University of Washington (J.D., M.B.A., 1985). Instructor, Idaho Small Business Development Center. Author: "Business Entities-What's Frequently Used Today," The Messenger (Idaho Small Business Development Center, Winter 2001). Co-Author: "Handbook for Idaho Nonprofit Corporations, first edition," (Idaho State Bar Corporate and Securities Section, 1990); "Basic Corporate Law in Idaho," (National Business Institute, Inc., 1995); "Business Law Developments in Idaho, 1995 - The Legal Year in Review" (CCM, The American Lawyer's Corporate Counsel Magazine, 1995) Business Law Developments in Idaho, USA, 1996 - The Legal Year in Review" (CCM, the American Corporate Counsel Magazine, 1996) "Dissenters Rights Under Part 13 of the New Idaho Business Corporation Act" (The Advocate, April 1997); Idaho Submission—Global Legal Update for Business, 1998. (American Corporate Counsel Association). *Member:* Idaho State Bar (Member: Corporate and Securities Section; Committee to revise the Idaho Corporate Code); American Bar Association (Member, Section on Business Law). ***PRACTICE AREAS:*** Corporate Law; Securities; Business Transactions; Real Property. ***Email:*** jhovren@evanskeane.com

DAVID W. GRATTON, born Emmett, Idaho, January 11, 1960; admitted to bar, 1985, Idaho and U.S. District Court, District of Idaho; 1987, U.S. Court of Appeals, Ninth Circuit. *Education:* Boise State University (B.A., 1982); University of Idaho (J.D., 1985). Author: "Local Rules of the United States District Court for the District of Idaho," The Advocate, May, 1988. Contributing Editor: "Product Liability Desk Reference, A Fifty State Compendium," Aspen Publishers, Inc. Instructor: "Federal Preemption in Product Liability Cases," 1994; "Real Estate Titles and Title Insurance," 1997. Law Clerk to Hon. Harold L. Ryan, U.S. District Court, District of Idaho, 1985-1987. Extern to Hon. J. Blaine Anderson, U.S. Court of Appeals, Ninth Circuit, 1984. *Member:* Idaho State and Fourth District Bar Associations. ***PRACTICE AREAS:*** Product Liability; Litigation; Business Transactions; Real Estate. ***Email:*** dgratton@evanskeane.com

---

DAVID M. SWARTLEY, born San Jose, California, September 7, 1970; admitted to bar, 1998, Idaho. *Education:* University of Puget Sound (B.A., 1992); University of Idaho (J.D., 1995). *Member:* Idaho State Bar. ***PRACTICE AREAS:*** Products Liability; Personal Injury; Real Property; Corporate Litigation; Criminal Litigation; Civil Litigation. ***Email:*** dswartley@evanskeane.com

JEREMY P. PISCA, born Boise, Idaho, June 24, 1973; admitted to bar, 1999, Idaho. *Education:* Boise State University (B.A., cum laude, 1995); University of Idaho (J.D., 1999). Delta Theta Phi. Board of Editors, Idaho Law Review. Author: "Betting on the Future," 34 Idaho Law Review, 651. Staff Assistant, Idaho Office of the Governor, 1995-1998. Member, 1999-2004 and President, 2004, Idaho Legislative Advisors. *Member:* Idaho State Bar (Member, Real Property Section; Chairman, Young Lawyers Sections, 2001). (Resident, Boise Office). ***PRACTICE AREAS:*** Government Relations; Real Estate; Business Law; Construction Law. ***Email:*** jpisca@evanskeane.com

VICTOR S. VILLEGAS, born Manila, Philippines, May 30, 1972; admitted to bar, 1999, Idaho. *Education:* University of Nevada, Las Vegas (B.A., Political Science, 1995); Gonzaga University School of Law (J.D., 1998). ***PRACTICE AREAS:*** Litigation; Products Liability Defense; Business Transactions. ***Email:*** vvillegas@evanskeane.com

JUDY L. GEIER, born Nampa, Idaho, September 28, 1960; admitted to bar, 2002, Idaho. *Education:* American University (M.A., 1988); University of Idaho (J.D., 2002). Formerly with, Foley, Freeman, Boston and Stern. Law Clerk: Idaho Supreme Court, Honorable Daniel T. Eismann (2001-2004); Fourth Judicial District of Idaho, Honorable Daniel T. Eismann (2000). ***PRACTICE AREAS:*** Civil Litigation; Environmental Law; Family Law. ***Email:*** jgeier@evanskeane.com

OF COUNSEL

BLAINE F. EVANS, born St. Anthony, Idaho, December 15, 1923; admitted to bar, 1950, Idaho. *Education:* Reed College and University of Idaho (B.A., 1947); Harvard Law School (LL.B., 1950). Assistant Attorney General of Idaho, 1950-1952. Prosecuting Attorney, Ada County, Idaho, 1952-1956. Senator, Ada County, Idaho, 1957-1959. *Member:* Boise (President, 1968-1969) and American Bar Associations; Idaho State Bar (Chairman: Bar Committee on Recertification of Attorneys, 1974-1978); Rules of Evidence Committee, 1980-1985; American Board of Trial Advocates; Association of Trial Lawyers of American; Idaho Trial Lawyers Association; International Association of Defense Counsel. ***PRACTICE AREAS:*** Antitrust Law; Litigation; Business Law. ***Email:*** bevans@evanskeane.com

KELLOGG OFFICE

JAMES P. KEANE (1925-1988)

CHARLES L. A. COX, born Camp Polk, Louisiana, October 3, 1952; admitted to bar, 1981, Idaho; 1989, U.S. Court of Appeals, Ninth Circuit; 1993, U.S. Court of Federal Claims. *Education:* University of Kent at Canterbury, England; Western State College (B.A., 1975); University of Iowa (J.D., 1981). Phi Alpha Delta. Managing Editor, The Journal of Corporation Law, 1980-1981. *Member:* First Judicial District and American Bar Associations; Idaho State Bar. ***PRACTICE AREAS:*** General Litigation and Appellate; Corporate Law; Environmental Law.

GENERAL COUNSEL FOR: City of Kellogg; Northwest Boise Sewer District; South County Water Co.; West Boise Sewer District.
REPRESENTATIVE CLIENTS: Albertson's., Inc.; The American National Red Cross; AMOCO; Anheuser-Busch, Inc.; Attorneys Liability Protection Society (ALPS); Audi NSU Auto Union Aktiengesellschaft; Bottlers' Services, Inc. (Coca Cola Bottlers' Association); Briggs & Stratton Corporation; CIT Group; Cannondale Corporation; Coeur d'Alene Mines Corp.; Compaq Computer Corp.; Countrywide Adjusting Services Inc.; Richard Crawforth, Bankruptcy Trustee; D. B. Riley, Inc.; debis Financial Services; E.I. Du Pont de Nemours & Company; Ford Motor Co.; GlaxoSmithKline; Hecla Mining Co.; Hoffman-La Roche Inc.; HomeStreet Bank; Horizon Air Industries, Inc.; Hyundai Motor America; Idacorp Inc.; Idaho

(This Listing Continued)

Association of REALTORS; Idaho Building Contractors Association; Idaho State Insurance Fund; State of Idaho; Idaho Power Co.; Idaho Timber Corp.; Intermountain Wood Products Inc.; Interstate Brands Corporation; John Deere Co.; Krommenhoek, John H., Bankruptcy Trustee; Las Vegas Discount Golf & Tennis, Inc.; Leasecomm Corporation; Marsh Advantage America; Larry Miller Group; Murphy, Lois K., Bankruptcy Trustee; Office Value, Inc.; Pfizer Inc.; Pearle Vision Express; Philip Morris, Inc.; Playtex Family Products, Inc.; Rakozy, Bernie R., Bankruptcy Trustee; Raytheon Company; R.J. Reynolds Tobacco Co.; RJR Nabisco, Inc. Seabury & Smith, Inc.; Showa Denko K.K.; Stewart Title Guaranty Co.; Tesoro Petroleum Companies, Inc.; Treasure Valley Transit, Inc.; Vasquez Management Consultants; Viking Freight, Inc.; Volkswagen of America, Inc.; Volkswagenwerk Aktiengesellschaft; Wels Fargo Mortgage; Westinghouse Electric Corp.; Weyerhaeuser Co.; Wyeth.
INSURANCE CLIENTS: Argonaut Insurance Co.
REFERENCE: KeyBank of Idaho.

FENWICK & WEST LLP

Established in 1972

877 WEST MAIN STREET
SUITE 706
BOISE, IDAHO 83702
Telephone: 208-331-0700
Fax: 208-331-7723
URL: http://www.fenwick.com

San Francisco, California Office: 275 Battery Street, Suite 1600. Telephone: 415-875-2300. Fax: 415-281-1350.
Mountain View, California Office: Silicon Valley Center, 801 California Street. Telephone: 650-988-8500. Fax: 650-938-5200.

General Practice. Corporate, Securities, Mergers and Acquisitions, Executive Compensation and Employee Benefits, Intellectual Property, Patent, Trademark and Copyright, Science and Technology Transactions, Life Sciences and High Technology Law, Litigation and Alternative Dispute Resolution, Antitrust and Trade Regulation, Privacy and Security, Trade Secrets, Employment and Labor Law, Domestic and International Taxation, and Venture Capital.

FIRM PROFILE: Established in 1972, Fenwick & West LLP is one of the nation's premier law firms providing comprehensive legal services to national and international high technology and biotechnology clients, particularly in the areas of intellectual property, venture capital and other corporate finance, joint ventures, M&A and strategic relationships, litigation and dispute resolution, antitrust, taxation, and employment and labor law. Fenwick & West's national offices, its diverse clientele, its international correspondent relationships, and its size and breadth of experience enable it to offer both a full-service national and international practice and an entrepreneurial, aggressive approach to counseling and problem solving. The only law firm named to Fortune's 1999-2002 lists of the "100 Best Companies to Work For".

PARTNER

ROBERT A. FREEDMAN, born Boston, Massachusetts, January 31, 1966; admitted to bar, 1993, California; 1997, Idaho. *Education:* Bowdoin College (A.B., summa cum laude, 1987); Stanford University (J.D., with distinction, 1993). (Resident). ***PRACTICE AREAS:*** Private Finance; Mergers and Acquisitions; Public Offerings; Securities. ***Email:*** rfreedman@fenwick.com

ASSOCIATE

ILANA SIMONE RUBEL, admitted to bar, 1997, Illinois; 2001, Idaho. *Education:* Georgetown University (B.A., magna cum laude, 1994); Harvard Law School (J.D., cum laude, 1997). Phi Beta Kappa. (Resident). ***PRACTICE AREAS:*** Litigation; Corporate; Bankruptcy. ***Email:*** irubel@fenwick.com

FINCH & BROADBENT, P.A.

103 WEST IDAHO STREET
BOISE, IDAHO 83702
Telephone: 208-385-0800
Fax: 208-389-2186
Email: fandblaw@finchbroadbent.com
URL: http://www.finchbroadbentlaw.com

Mailing Address: P.O. Box 1296, Boise, ID 83701

Adoption, Child Custody, Corporate Law, Divorce, Elder Law, Family Law, General Practice, Guardianship and Conservatorship, Insurance Bad Faith, Insurance Law, Interstate Trucking Litigation, Mediation, Medical Malpractice, Personal Injury, Probate, Wills, Trusts and Estates, Wrongful Death.

MICHELLE R. FINCH, born Tacoma, Washington, September 14, 1960; admitted to bar, 1985, Idaho and U.S. District Court, District of Idaho; 1987, U.S. Court of Appeals, Ninth Circuit; 1991, U.S. Court of Federal Claims; 1993, Montana. *Education:* Eastern Montana College (B.S.B.A., with honors, 1982); Gonzaga University (J.D., cum laude, 1985). *Member:* Idaho State Bar (Member, Section on Taxation, Probate and Trust; Chairperson, 2003); National Association of Elder Law Attorneys; National Guardianship Association. ***PRACTICE AREAS:*** Elder Law; Guardianship and Conservatorship; Wills; Trusts and Estates; Corporate Law; Business Law; Divorce. ***Email:*** mrf@finchbroadbent.com

REBECCA A. BROADBENT, born Houston, Texas, December 4, 1966; admitted to bar, 1989, Utah; 1991, Idaho. *Education:* Kansai University of Foreign Studies, Osaka, Japan; Boise State University (B.A., 1985); Brigham Young University (J.D., 1988). *Member:* Idaho State Bar (Secretary, Litigation Section; Member, ADR); Idaho Trial Lawyers Association (Council Member, 2001—, Regional Director, 2003-2005); The Association of Trial Lawyers of America. ***LANGUAGES:*** Japanese. ***PRACTICE AREAS:*** Personal Injury; Medical Malpractice; Mediation; Administrative Hearings and Appeals; Employment Law; Insurance; Insurance Bad Faith; Commercial Litigation; Contested Estates; Adoption Law; Family Law; General Litigation. ***Email:*** rab@finchbroadbent.com

(This Listing Continued)

BROOKE A. O'NEIL, born Los Gatos, California, May 21, 1971; admitted to bar, 1997, California; 2001, Idaho. *Education:* University of California at Santa Cruz (B.A., 1994); Santa Clara University (J.D., 1997). *Member:* State Bar of California; Idaho State Bar. ***PRACTICE AREAS:*** Wills and Trusts; Probate; Trust Administration; Guardianship and Conservatorship; Family Law; Business Planning. ***Email:*** bao@finchbroadbent.com

MYRON DAN GABBERT, J.D. P.A.

BOISE, IDAHO
(See McCall)

General and Trial, Banking, Business, Commercial, Corporate, Insurance Defense, Real Estate, Wills, Trusts, Probate and Estate Planning.

JAMES R. GILLESPIE, P.A.

Established in 1966

300 WEST MYRTLE, SUITE 100
BOISE, IDAHO 83702
Telephone: 208-344-8400
Fax: 208-344-7100
URL: http://www.jamesrgillespie.com

General Practice. Business, Commercial Real Estate, Agricultural, Natural Resources Law, Environment and Construction Law, Mediation and Arbitration.

JAMES R. GILLESPIE, born Tooele, Utah, September 12, 1939; admitted to bar, 1964, Utah; 1965, Idaho. *Education:* University of Utah (B.S., 1961; M.S., 1964; J.D., 1964). *Member:* Boise (President, 1978-1979) and American Bar Associations; Utah State Bar; Idaho State Bar; Idaho Trial Lawyers Association; American Judicature Society; The Association of Trial Lawyers of America. ***PRACTICE AREAS:*** General Practice; Business Law; Commercial Real Estate; Agricultural Law; Natural Resources; Environment Law; Construction Law; Mediation; Arbitration.

GIVENS PURSLEY LLP

Established in 1977

601 W. BANNOCK ST.
BOISE, IDAHO 83702
Telephone: 208-388-1200
Fax: 208-388-1300
Email: info@givenspursley.com
URL: http://www.givenspursley.com

Business, Commercial, Mergers and Acquisitions, Communications and Media, Employment, Environmental, Water, Public Lands and Natural Resources, Financial Transactions, Securitization, Structured Finance, Banking, Credit Recovery and Bankruptcy, Public Policy, Health Care and Hospital, Intellectual Property, Real Estate, Real Estate Financing and Land Use, Securities and Bonds, Tax and Estate Planning, Trial and Appellate Litigation, Telecommunications, Energy, Utilities and Regulatory Affairs.

LAW FIRM ALLIANCES/ASSOCIATIONS: ***STATE LAW RESOURCES, INC.:*** *A National Network of Independent Law Firms.*

MEMBERS OF FIRM

KENNETH L. PURSLEY, born Sandpoint, Idaho, April 4, 1940; admitted to bar, 1965, Illinois; 1970, Idaho. *Education:* Deep Springs College and Cornell University (B.A., 1962); University of Chicago (J.D., 1965). Order of the Coif. The Best Lawyers in America. *Member:* Idaho State Bar; American Bar Association; American Judicature Society; American College of Real Estate Lawyers. ***PRACTICE AREAS:*** Real Estate; Finance; Land Use; Commercial Transactions. ***Email:*** klp@givenspursley.com

L. EDWARD MILLER, born Salmon, Idaho, June 3, 1952; admitted to bar, 1977, Idaho. *Education:* College of Idaho (B.A., cum laude, 1974); University of Idaho (J.D., cum laude, 1977). Listed in, The Best Lawyers in America. Member: Urban Land Institute; Boise Smart City Initiative; Boise Metro Economic Development Council; Boise Chamber of Commerce Executive Committee. *Member:* Idaho State Bar. ***PRACTICE AREAS:*** Real Estate; Real Estate Finance; Land Use; Business Law; Commercial Law; Health Care; Hospital Law. ***Email:*** lem@givenspursley.com

CHRISTOPHER J. BEESON, admitted to bar, 1980, Idaho. *Education:* University of Idaho (B.S., Accounting, magna cum laude, 1973; J.D., cum laude, 1980). Faculty Member, Idaho Law Foundation. Seminars: Real Property Law; Retail Leases; Environmental Law Transactional Aspects. Participant, Georgetown University Law Center Advanced Commercial Leasing Institute. Listed in, The Best Lawyers in America, Real Estate Law. *Member:* Idaho State Bar; American College of Real Estate Lawyers; International Council of Shopping Centers (Lawyers Division). ***PRACTICE AREAS:*** Business Law; Commercial Law; Real Estate; Real Estate Finance; Tax Law; Estate Planning. ***Email:*** chrisbeeson@givenspursley.com

KENNETH R. McCLURE, born Ontario, Oregon, December 18, 1954; admitted to bar, 1980, Idaho. *Education:* College of William & Mary (B.A., with high honors, 1977); University of Idaho (J.D., 1980). Deputy Attorney General, Idaho State Tax Commission, 1980-1981. Chief, Legislative and Administrative Affairs Division, 1981-1984. *Member:* Idaho State Bar (Member, Business, Corporate and Health Sections). ***PRACTICE AREAS:*** Public Policy; Health Care; Public Utility Law; Administrative Law; Regulatory Law. ***Email:*** krm@givenspursley.com

JEFFREY C. FEREDAY, born Boise, Idaho, December 27, 1949; admitted to bar, 1980, Washington; 1981, Idaho, Colorado and U.S. District Court, District of Idaho; 1982, U.S. District Court, District of Colorado and U.S. Court of Appeals, Tenth Circuit; 1987, U.S. Court of Appeals, Ninth Circuit; 1999, U.S. Supreme Court. *Education:* Columbia

(This Listing Continued)

GIVENS PURSLEY LLP, Boise—Continued

University (A.B., 1972); Northwestern School of Law of Lewis & Clark College (J.D., 1980). Listed in, The Best Lawyers in America. ***PRACTICE AREAS:*** Environmental Law; Water Law; Public Land Law; Natural Resources. ***Email:*** jefffereday@givenspursley.com

CONLEY E. WARD, born Nampa, Idaho, August 16, 1947; admitted to bar, 1974, Idaho and U.S. District Court, District of Idaho; 1987, U.S. Court of Appeals, Ninth Circuit. *Education:* Columbia University (B.A., 1969); University of Colorado (J.D., 1974). Assistant Attorney General, State of Idaho, 1974-1976. Idaho Public Utilities Commissioner, 1977-1986, Chairman, 1979-1981, 1983-1985. Listed in, The Best Lawyers in America. *Member:* Idaho State Bar; American Bar Association. ***PRACTICE AREAS:*** Telecommunications; Energy; Public Utilities; Regulatory Affairs. ***Email:*** cew@givenspursley.com

PATRICK J. MILLER, born Caldwell, Idaho, March 17, 1959; admitted to bar, 1984, Idaho; 1994, U.S. Court of Appeals, Ninth Circuit. *Education:* University of Idaho (B.A., cum laude, 1981; J.D., cum laude, 1984). Phi Beta Kappa; Phi Kappa Phi. Law Clerk to Hon. Ray McNicholls, U.S. District Judge, District of Idaho, 1984-1985. Adjunct Professor of Law, University of Idaho, Health Law, 2001-2002. *Member:* Idaho State Bar; Health Lawyers Association; American Inns of Court. ***PRACTICE AREAS:*** Health Care; Hospital Law; Trial Practice; Commercial Law. ***Email:*** pjm@givenspursley.com

DAVID R. LOMBARDI, born Bremerton, Washington, March 27, 1949; admitted to bar, 1976, Idaho. *Education:* Stanford University (B.A., 1971); University of Santa Clara (J.D., magna cum laude, 1976). Listed in, The Best Lawyers in America. *Member:* Idaho State Bar; Defense Research Institute; American Health Lawyers; American Inns of Court. (Certified Civil Trial Specialist by Idaho Trial Lawyers Association). ***PRACTICE AREAS:*** Trial Practice; Appellate Practice; Health Care; Hospital Law; Business Law; Commercial Law. ***Email:*** drl@givenspursley.com

CHRISTOPHER H. MEYER, born Springfield, Missouri, September 29, 1952; admitted to bar, 1981, District of Columbia; 1982, U.S. Court of Appeals for the District of Columbia Circuit; 1983, U.S. Court of Appeals, Ninth Circuit; 1985, Colorado and U.S. Court of Appeals, Tenth Circuit; 1995, Idaho and U.S. Court of Appeals, Eighth Circuit; 2004, Oregon. *Education:* University of Michigan (A.B., with high honors, 1977; J.D., cum laude, 1981). Phi Beta Kappa. James B. Angell Scholar. Recipient, Osterweil Prize in Economics. Associate Professor Adjunct, University of Colorado Law School, Boulder, Colorado, 1984-1991. ***PRACTICE AREAS:*** Water Law; Land Use; Environmental Law; Natural Resources; Administrative Law; Constitutional Law; Trial Practice; Appellate Practice. ***Email:*** chrismeyer@givenspursley.com

ROY LEWIS EIGUREN, born Nampa, Idaho, January 10, 1952; admitted to bar, 1978, Idaho and U.S. District Court, District of Idaho; 1986, District of Columbia. *Education:* University of Idaho (B.S., 1974; J.D., 1977); Georgetown University. Special Assistant to the Administrator, Bonneville Power Administration, 1981-1983. Deputy Attorney General and Division Chief, Legislative and Administrative Affairs for Idaho Attorney General, 1979-1981. Deputy Prosecuting Attorney, Ada County, 1978. Listed in, The Best Lawyers in America. ***PRACTICE AREAS:*** Public Policy; Telecommunications Law; Energy; Utility Law; Regulatory Law; Environmental Law; Natural Resources; Health Care; Hospital Law. ***Email:*** rle@givenspursley.com

W. HUGH O'RIORDAN, born Chicago, Illinois, June 3, 1947; admitted to bar, 1978, Idaho. *Education:* University of Arizona (B.A., 1969; J.D., 1972); George Washington University (LL.M., Environmental Law, 1979). Member, National Academy of Sciences Committee on Remediation of Buried and Tank Wastes. Office of the Solicitor, Department of the Interior, 1973-1976. Chief of Natural Resources Division, Office of the Idaho Attorney General, 1978-1980. ***PRACTICE AREAS:*** Environmental Law; Water Law; Public Lands; Natural Resources. ***Email:*** who@givenspursley.com

GARY G. ALLEN, born Pocatello, Idaho, March 30, 1961; admitted to bar, 1987, California; 1991, Idaho. *Education:* Dartmouth College (A.B., magna cum laude, 1983); Stanford University Law School (J.D., 1987). Phi Beta Kappa. McLain-Bowler Scholar. Editor, Stanford Environmental Law Journal, 1987. *Member:* State Bar of California; Idaho State Bar. ***PRACTICE AREAS:*** Environmental Law; Natural Resources; Real Estate; Land Use. ***Email:*** garyallen@givenspursley.com

MICHAEL C. CREAMER, born 1957; admitted to bar, 1989, Idaho. *Education:* Colorado State University (B.S., 1979); University of Colorado at Boulder (J.D., 1989). Certified Wildlife Biologist, 1986. Co-Author, Handbook on Idaho Water Law, 1996. *Member:* Idaho State Bar (Chair, Water Law Section, 1998-2000). ***PRACTICE AREAS:*** Environmental Law; Water Law; Public Lands; Natural Resources; Real Estate; Telecommunications; Energy; Utility Law. ***Email:*** mcc@givenspursley.com

JUDSON B. MONTGOMERY, born Nurnberg, West Germany, May 5, 1967; admitted to bar, 1993, Idaho. *Education:* Duke University (B.A., cum laude, 1989); University of Notre Dame (J.D., 1993). *Member:* Idaho State Bar; American Bar Association. ***PRACTICE AREAS:*** Real Estate; Real Estate Finance; Land Use; Business Law; Health Care. ***Email:*** jbm@givenspursley.com

DEBORA K. KRISTENSEN, born Bellevue, Pennsylvania, August 17, 1965; admitted to bar, 1990, California; 1991, Washington; 1996, Idaho. *Education:* University of California at Berkeley (B.A., 1987); University of Santa Clara (J.D., 1990). Commissioner, Idaho State Bar, Central Division, 2002-2005. Editor-in-Chief, Santa Clara Law Review, 1989-1990. Member: Media Law Resource Center; State Media Courts Committee; Idaho State Broadcasters Association; Idaho Press Club. *Member:* Idaho State Bar (President, 2005); American Bar Association; American Inns of Court. ***PRACTICE AREAS:*** Media Law; Litigation; Employment Law; Public Policy. ***Email:*** dkk@givenspursley.com

KELLY GREENE McCONNELL, admitted to bar, 1989, California; 1994, Idaho; 2003, Oregon. *Education:* California State University, Sacramento (B.S., 1986); McGeorge School of Law (J.D., 1989). Order of the Coif. *Member:* Idaho State Bar (Board Member, Commercial and Bankruptcy Section); American Bar Association; Risk Management Association; American Bankruptcy Institute; PEO. ***PRACTICE AREAS:*** Financial Law; Banking Law; Credit Recovery; Bankruptcy. ***Email:*** kgm@givenspursley.com

ROBERT B. WHITE, born Denver, Colorado, July 3, 1963; admitted to bar, 1992, Idaho and U.S. District Court, District of Idaho; 1994, U.S. Court of Appeals, Ninth Circuit. *Education:* University of Idaho (B.S., 1986; J.D., 1991). Member, Executive Board, University of Idaho Law Review, 1990-1991. Judicial Clerk to Hon. B. Lynn Winmill, Idaho District Court, 1991-1993. Certificate in Civil Mediation, 2003. *Member:* Idaho State Bar. ***PRACTICE AREAS:*** Employment Law; Civil Litigation; Alternative Dispute Resolution. ***Email:*** rbw@givenspursley.com

KARL T. KLEIN, born San Diego, California, August 27, 1967; admitted to bar, 1994, Florida; 1995, Idaho and U.S. District Court, District of Idaho; 1999, U.S. Court of Appeals, Ninth Circuit. *Education:* University of California, Davis (B.A., 1989); University of Florida (J.D., cum laude, 1993). *Member:* Idaho State Bar (Member, Litigation and Employment Law Sections); The Florida Bar; Defense Research Institute (Member, Medical Liability and Health Law Committee); Idaho Association of Defense Counsel. ***PRACTICE AREAS:*** Litigation; Appellate Practice; Employment Law; Medical Malpractice Defense; Products Liability. ***Email:*** ktk@givenspursley.com

THOMAS E. DVORAK, born Spokane, Washington, September 26, 1967; admitted to bar, 1994, Idaho and U.S. District Court, District of Idaho. *Education:* Boise State University (B.A., cum laude, 1991); University of Idaho (J.D., 1994). Law Clerk to Honorable Mikel H. Williams, U.S. Magistrate Judge, District of Idaho, 1994-1996. *Member:* Idaho State Bar (Member, Commercial Law Section). [Sgt., USMCR, 1985-1991]. ***PRACTICE AREAS:*** Trial Practice; Appellate Practice; Litigation; Business Law; Commercial Law; Real Estate; Real Estate Finance; Land Use; Financial; Banking; Credit Recovery; Bankruptcy. ***Email:*** ted@givenspursley.com

STEVEN J. HIPPLER, born Boise, Idaho, July 6, 1966; admitted to bar, 1991, Idaho and U.S. District Court, District of Idaho. *Education:* Boise State University (B.A., cum laude, 1988); University of Utah (J.D., 1991). Order of the Coif. *Member:* Idaho State Bar (Founding Member, Health Law Section; Member, Litigation Section); American Bar Association (Member, Health Law Section; Member, Litigation Section; Tort and Insurance Practice); American Health Lawyers Association; Defense Research Institute (Member, Health Law and Medical Liability Sections). ***PRACTICE AREAS:*** Health Care; Regulatory Law; Business Law; Corporate Law; Medical Malpractice Defense; Commercial Litigation. ***Email:*** sjh@givenspursley.com

WILLIAM C. COLE, born Phoenix, Arizona, July 8, 1964; admitted to bar, 1991, California; 1994, Idaho. *Education:* Northern Arizona University (B.S., summa cum laude, 1986); University of San Diego (J.D., cum laude, 1991). Lead Articles Editor, University of San Diego Law Review, 1990-1991. *Member:* State Bar of California; Idaho State Bar (Member, Business and Corporate Law and Real Estate Sections). ***PRACTICE AREAS:*** Business Law; Commercial Finance; Securities; Securitization; Structured Finance; Real Estate; Credit Law; Commercial Litigation. ***Email:*** wcc@givenspursley.com

KIMBERLY D. MALONEY, born Washington, D.C., December 25, 1969; admitted to bar, 1994, Illinois; 1995, Idaho. *Education:* Indiana University (B.S., with honors, 1991); University of Notre Dame (J.D., magna cum laude, 1994). *Member:* Idaho State Bar (Member, Real Property Section). ***PRACTICE AREAS:*** Real Estate; Real Estate Finance; Business Law; Commercial Law. ***Email:*** kdm@givenspursley.com

ANGELA K. NELSON, born Boise, Idaho, June 10, 1970; admitted to bar, 1995, Idaho and U.S. District Court, District of Idaho. *Education:* Bowdoin College (B.A., 1992); Tulane University (J.D., cum laude, 1995). Recipient: American Jurisprudence Award in Commercial Paper. *Member:* Idaho State Bar. ***PRACTICE AREAS:*** Business Law; Commercial Law; Real Estate; Securities. ***Email:*** akn@givenspursley.com

DEBORAH E. NELSON, born Iowa City, Iowa, May 29, 1972; admitted to bar, 1997, Idaho. *Education:* Rhodes College (B.A., 1994); Northwestern College of Law (J.D., 1997). Recipient: Honors Moot Court Award; Certificate in Environmental and Natural Resources Law; Idaho Business Review's "Accomplished 40 Under 40" Award. President, Idaho Women Lawyers, Inc. *Member:* Idaho State Bar (Member, Environmental and Natural Resources, Water Sections); American Bar Association. ***PRACTICE AREAS:*** Water Law; Environmental Law; Natural Resources; Land Use; Litigation. ***Email:*** den@givenspursley.com

ASSOCIATES

EMILY MacMASTER, born Patterson, New Jersey, April 7, 1959; admitted to bar, 1995, California; 2002, Idaho; U.S. District Court, District of Idaho; U.S. District Court, Eastern, Central and Southern Districts of California; U.S. Court of Appeals, Ninth Circuit. *Education:* California State University, Northridge (B.A., summa cum laude, 1982); University of California, Los Angeles (J.D., 1995). Formerly with, Gray Cary Ware & Freidenrich. Member: Boise Chapter, Western Pension and Benefits Conference; American Inns of Court, 2002-2003. *Member:* State Bar of California; Idaho State Bar (Member, Employment and Litigation Sections; American Bar Association; Human Resources Association of Treasure Valley; Boise Chamber of Commerce (Member, Small Business Council). ***PRACTICE AREAS:*** Labor and Employment; Health Care; Litigation. ***Email:*** emd@givenspursley.com

TIMOTHY P. FEARNSIDE, born Bowling Green, Ohio, October 24, 1967; admitted to bar, 1996, Idaho; 1997, Oregon and U.S. District Court, District of Idaho. *Education:* Bowling Green State University (B.A., 1990); Gonzaga University School of Law (J.D., 1996). *Member:* Idaho State Bar (Member, Litigation and Commercial Law and Bankruptcy Sections); Oregon State Bar (Member, Litigation Section). ***PRACTICE AREAS:*** Commercial Litigation; Civil Litigation; Trial Practice; Appellate Practice; Bankruptcy. ***Email:*** tpf@givenspursley.com

JOHN M. MARSHALL, born Colorado Springs, Colorado, June 14, 1972; admitted to bar, 1997, Idaho. *Education:* University of Colorado (B.A., magna cum laude, 1994; J.D., 1997). *Member:* Idaho State Bar (Member, Water Law Section). ***PRACTICE AREAS:*** Environmental; Water; Public Lands; Natural Resources; Trial Practice; Appellate Practice; Litigation. ***Email:*** jmm@givenspursley.com

CYNTHIA A. MELILLO, born Dubois, Pennsylvania, October 16, 1962; admitted to bar, 1998, Idaho and U.S. District Court, District of Idaho. *Education:* University of Southern California (B.A., magna cum laude, 1984); University of Kent (M.A., 1989); University of Arizona (J.D., summa cum laude, 1998). Order of the Coif. Note Editor, "Arizona Law

(This Listing Continued)

Review," 1997-1998. *Member:* Idaho State Bar. ***PRACTICE AREAS:*** Real Estate; Real Estate Finance; Business Law; Commercial Law; Telecommunications Law. ***Email:*** cam@givenspursley.com

H. BARTON THOMAS, born Princeton, New Jersey, July 10, 1965; admitted to bar, 1998, Oregon; 2000, U.S. Tax Court; 2001, District of Columbia; 2003, Idaho. *Education:* Rollins College (A.B., 1988); Lewis and Clark College (J.D., cum laude, 1998); Georgetown University Law Center (LL.M., with distinction, 2003). Cornelius Honors Society, Lewis & Clark College. Attorney Advisor, U.S. Tax Court, 1998-2000. Attorney Delegate, U.S. Tax Court Judicial Conference, 2001. *Member:* American Bar Association (Member, Tax Section, 1999—). ***PRACTICE AREAS:*** Taxation; Trusts and Estates; Business Law. ***Email:*** hbt@givenspursley.com

FRANKLIN G. LEE, born Pocatello, Idaho, February 3, 1970; admitted to bar, 1999, Idaho. *Education:* University of Nebraska-Lincoln (B.S., 1992); University of Idaho (B.Arch., 1994; J.D., magna cum laude, 1999). Editor, Idaho Law Review, Spring Edition, 1998-1999. Author, "Transferable Development Rights and the Deprivation of All Economically Beneficial Use: Can TDR'S Salvage Regulations That Would Otherwise Constitute A Taking?" 34 Idaho Law Review 679, 1998. Member: American Institute of Architects (Affiliate Member, 1999—). ***PRACTICE AREAS:*** Real Estate; Real Estate Finance; Land Use; Intellectual Property; Business Law; Commercial Law. ***Email:*** fgl@givenspursley.com

BRADLEY V. SNEED, born Oscoda, Michigan, June 27, 1971; admitted to bar, 1999, Oregon; 2000, Idaho. *Education:* Michigan State University (B.S., high honors, 1995); Northwestern School of Law (J.D., cum laude, 1999). Judicial Clerk to Honorable Alan M. Schwartzman, Idaho Court of Appeals, 1999-2001. ***PRACTICE AREAS:*** Environmental Law; Natural Resources; General Litigation; Land Use; Bankruptcy; Employment Law. ***Email:*** bvs@givenspursley.com

D. DAVID LORELLO, JR., born Tacoma, Washington, November 19, 1969; admitted to bar, 2000, Idaho. *Education:* Eastern Washington University (B.A., summa cum laude, 1997); Gonzaga University (J.D., magna cum laude, 2000). Associate Editor, Gonzaga Law Review, 1999-2000. Author: "The Abandoned Shipwreck Act of 1987: Navigating Through the Fog," 35 Gonzaga Law Review 75. *Member:* Idaho State Bar. ***PRACTICE AREAS:*** Real Estate; Real Estate Finance; Land Use; Communications and Media; Business Law. ***Email:*** ddl@givenspursley.com

ANNE C. KUNKEL, born Carrollton, Kentucky, July 15, 1975; admitted to bar, 2001, Idaho. *Education:* University of Kentucky (B.A., Political Science, 1997; B.A., History, cum laude, 1998); Northwestern School of Law (J.D., cum laude, 2001). ***PRACTICE AREAS:*** Commercial Leasing; Real Estate; Business Transactions; Corporate Law. ***Email:*** ack@givenspursley.com

MICHAEL C. ORR, born Watertown, New York, June 20, 1957; admitted to bar, 2001, Oregon; 2003, Idaho. *Education:* Michigan State University (B.S., Forestry, 1980); University of Oregon (J.D., 2001). Order of the Coif. Law Clerk to Judge T.G. Nelson, Ninth Circuit. ***PRACTICE AREAS:*** Civil Litigation; Real Property Law; Land Use; Commercial Law; Business Law; Water Law; Natural Resources Law. ***Email:*** mco@givenspursley.com

KELLY T. BARBOUR, born March 16, 1974; admitted to bar, 2001, Texas (Not admitted in Idaho). *Education:* Albertson College of Idaho (B.A., magna cum laude, 1996); University of Virginia (J.D., 2001). Author: "The Domain Name Debacle: Evidence Mounts Against the Introduction of Additional TLDs," Journal of Internet Law and Business, January, 2002. ***PRACTICE AREAS:*** Real Estate; Business Law; Commercial Law; Financial Law. ***Email:*** kellybarbour@givenspursley.com

JEREMY G. LADLE, born Provo, Utah, December 21, 1976; admitted to bar, 2004, Idaho. *Education:* Albertson College of Idaho (B.A., summa cum laude, 2001); University of Idaho (J.D., summa cum laude, 2004). Author: "Protecting Pedophiles and Valuing Virtual Child Pornography: A Critique of Free Speech Coalition v. Ashcroft," 40 Idaho Law Review 457 (2004). *Member:* Idaho State Bar. ***Email:*** jeremyladle@givenspursley.com

JOHN WILKINSON (WILL) VARIN, born Boise, Idaho, June 6, 1978; admitted to bar, 2004, Idaho. *Education:* George Fox College (B.S., 2001); Hastings College of the Law, University of California (J.D., 2004). *Member:* Idaho State Bar. ***PRACTICE AREAS:*** Litigation. ***Email:*** willvarin@givenspursley.com

OF COUNSEL

RAYMOND D. GIVENS, born Boise, Idaho, May 7, 1917; admitted to bar, 1941, District of Columbia; 1947, Idaho. *Education:* University of Idaho (B.A., 1939); Georgetown University and University of Idaho (J.D., 1946). Special Assistant Attorney General, Idaho, 1947. *Member:* Fourth Judicial District (President, 1956-1957) and American Bar Associations; Idaho State Bar. ***PRACTICE AREAS:*** Water Law; Probate Law.

JAMES A. McCLURE, born Payette, Idaho, December 27, 1924; admitted to bar, 1950, Idaho; 1977, U.S. Supreme Court. *Education:* University of Idaho (J.D., 1950). Payette County Prosecuting Attorney, 1950-1957. Payette City Attorney, 1953-1959, 1963-1966. Member: Idaho State Senate, 1960-1966; U.S. House of Representatives, 1967-1972; U.S. Senate, 1972-1990 (Chairman, 1981-1986 and Ranking Minority Member, 1987-1990, Energy and Natural Resources Committee; Chairman, Republican Conference, 1980-1984).

GJORDING & FOUSER, PLLC

509 WEST HAYS STREET
P.O. BOX 2837
BOISE, IDAHO 83701
Telephone: 208-336-9777
Facsimile: 208-336-9177
Email: jgjording@g-g.com
URL: http://www.g-f-law.com

Insurance Defense, Medical Malpractice Defense, Employment and Commercial Litigation.

(This Listing Continued)

MEMBERS

JACK S. GJORDING, born Boise, Idaho, January 19, 1939; admitted to bar, 1966, Idaho and U.S. District Court, District of Idaho; U.S. Court of Appeals, Ninth Circuit. *Education:* University of Idaho (B.S., 1961; J.D., 1966). *Member:* Boise and Idaho State Bar Associations; American Board of Trial Advocates (President, 1984-1985; 1993-1994); Defense Research Institute; Idaho Association of Defense Counsel. American College of Trial Lawyers. ***PRACTICE AREAS:*** Medical Malpractice Law; Insurance Defense Law; Commercial Litigation. ***Email:*** jgjording@g-g.com

TRUDY HANSON FOUSER, born Malad, Idaho, April 5, 1955; admitted to bar, 1981, Idaho and U.S. District Court, District of Idaho. *Education:* University of Utah; Georgia State University (B.A., magna cum laude, 1977); University of Idaho (J.D., 1981). Law Clerk, Idaho Supreme Court, Chief Justice Donaldson, 1981-1983. Member: U.S. District Local Rules Committee; Member: Idaho State Discovery Rules Committee; District of Idaho Civil Justice Reform Act Advisory Committee. *Member:* Boise and Idaho State Bar Associations; Federal Bar Association (Idaho Chapter; President-elect); Idaho Association of Defense Counsel; Defense Research Institute. American College of Trial Lawyers. ***PRACTICE AREAS:*** Litigation; Employment Law; Medical Malpractice Defense; Insurance Bad Faith Defense. ***Email:*** tfouser@g-g.com

ASSOCIATE

ELAINE HERRICK LEE, born Moscow, Idaho, March 29, 1973; admitted to bar, 2000, Idaho; 2003, U.S. Court of Appeals, Ninth Circuit. *Education:* Yale University (B.A., cum laude, 1995); University of Idaho (J.D., summa cum laude, 2000). Law Clerk to Judge Stephen Trott, Ninth Circuit Court of Appeals, 2000-2001. *Member:* Idaho State Bar; Idaho Association of Defense Counsel. ***PRACTICE AREAS:*** Medical Malpractice Law; Insurance Law; Employment Law. ***Email:*** elee@g-g.com

OF COUNSEL

BOBBI KILLIAN DOMINICK, born Boise, Idaho, December 16, 1955; admitted to bar, 1982, Idaho and U.S. District Court, District of Idaho; 1984, U.S. Court of Appeals, Ninth Circuit; 1986, U.S. Supreme Court. *Education:* Boise State University (B.A., cum laude, 1978); University of Idaho (J.D., cum laude, 1982). Law Clerk, Idaho Supreme Court, 1982-1984; Certified Senior Professional in Human Resources; Idaho Supreme Court Appellate Rules Advisory Committee; Ninth Circuit Court of Appeals Rules Advisory Committee, 1993-1999. *Member:* Idaho State Bar; Human Resources Association of Treasure Valley; Society of Human Resource Management. American Academy of Appellate Lawyers. ***PRACTICE AREAS:*** Wrongful Discharge Law; Employer/Employee Relations Law; Appellate Law. ***Email:*** bkdominick@velocitus.net

GREENER BANDUCCI SHOEMAKER P.A.

Established in 2005

THE CARNEGIE BUILDING
815 WEST WASHINGTON STREET
BOISE, IDAHO 83702
Telephone: 208-319-2600
Fax: 208-319-2601
Email: TBanducci@greenerlaw.com
URL: http://www.greenerlaw.com

General Civil Trial Practice including Commercial Litigation, Securities, Real Estate, Product Liability, Construction, Eminent Domain, Employment, and Personal Injury, Insurance, Intellectual Property. The firm also has substantial expertise in class actions.

FIRM PROFILE: Idaho's only litigation boutique, Greener Banducci Shoemaker P.A. represents both plaintiffs and defendants in its national practice. The Firm is dedicated to client service and effective use of technology for discovery and trial.

Firm attorneys are admitted in Idaho, California, Washington, New Mexico, Nebraska and Oregon. The firm also acts as national trial counsel for a Fortune 100 Company. The firm attorneys maintain memberships in the American College of Trial Lawyers, American Board of Trial Advocates, American Academy of Real Estate Lawyers, International Association of Defense Counsel, Defense Research Institute, Idaho Trial Lawyers Association, and Idaho Association of Defense Counsel. One firm member is president elect to the Idaho State Bar and is a current Idaho State Bar Commissioner. Firm attorneys have been recognized among the "Best Lawyers in America".

RICHARD H. GREENER, born Rugby, North Dakota, September 21, 1942; admitted to bar, 1968, Idaho and Washington. *Education:* University of Washington (B.A., 1965); University of Idaho (J.D., 1968). Phi Alpha Delta. Justice Court Judge, Latah County, 1967-1968. Member, Ada County Planning and Zoning Commission, 1973. Selected, Best Lawyer of America, 1999-2004. *Member:* Washington State and American Bar Associations; Idaho State Bar; American College of Trial Lawyers; American Board of Trial Advocates; American College of Real Estate Lawyers; Defense Research Institute; Idaho Trial Lawyers Association. ***PRACTICE AREAS:*** Civil Litigation; Commercial Litigation; Legal Malpractice; Professional Malpractice; Insurance; Products Liability; Eminent Domain; Intellectual Property; Securities; Construction; Environmental Law; Employment; Patent Infringement; Drug and Medical Device Litigation; Business Law. ***Email:*** rgreener@greenerlaw.com

THOMAS A. BANDUCCI, born San Mateo, California, October 15, 1954; admitted to bar, 1979, Idaho, U.S. District Court, District of Idaho, U.S. Court of Appeals, Ninth Circuit. *Education:* Stanford University (A.B., with honors, 1976); Hastings College of Law, University of California (J.D., 1979). Idaho State Bar Commissioner, 2004-2007. *Member:* Federal Bar Association (Founding Member and Secretary); Idaho State Bar (President-Elect, 2007); International Association of Defense Counsel. ***PRACTICE AREAS:*** Civil

(This Listing Continued)

GREENER BANDUCCI SHOEMAKER P.A., Boise—Continued

Litigation; Complex Litigation; Unfair Competition; Trade Secret Misappropriation; Products Liability; Construction Litigation; Employment Law; Technology Law. ***Email:*** tbanducci@greenerlaw.com

FREDRIC V. SHOEMAKER, born Omaha, Nebraska, October 27, 1948; admitted to bar, 1974, Nebraska and Idaho. *Education:* University of Nebraska at Lincoln (B.S., 1971; J.D., 1974). Phi Delta Phi. Member, Outstanding Lawyers of America. *Member:* Nebraska State Bar Association; Idaho State Bar; Idaho Trial Lawyers Association. [2nd Lt., USAR, 1969-1975]. ***PRACTICE AREAS:*** Business Law; Real Estate; Civil Litigation; Personal Injury; Land Use; Condemnation; Eminent Domain; Municipal Law; Products Liability. ***Email:*** fshoemaker@greenerlaw.com

CHRISTOPHER C. BURKE, born Boise, Idaho, December 16, 1950; admitted to bar, 1977, Idaho. *Education:* Stanford University (B.A., 1973); University of Idaho (J.D., 1977). Member, Legislative Staff, Senator Frank Church, 1973-1974. *Member:* American Bar Association; Idaho State Bar; Defense Research Institute; Idaho Association of Defense Counsel. ***PRACTICE AREAS:*** Civil Litigation; Products Liability; Personal Injury; Insurance; Commercial Law; Business Law; Construction Law; Mass Torts; Toxic Torts; Patents; Class Actions. ***Email:*** cburke@greenerlaw.com

ERIK F. STIDHAM, born Whittier, California, December 25, 1964; admitted to bar, 1991, California and U.S. District Courts, Central, Northern, Southern and Eastern Districts of California; 1993, U.S. Court of Appeals, 9th Circuit; 1994, U.S. District Court, District of Arizona; 1996, Idaho. *Education:* Arizona State University (B.A., summa cum laude, 1987); University of Virginia (J.D., 1991). Phi Beta Kappa. Honors Program Graduate, 1987. *Member:* American Bar Association (Vice-Chair; Member, General Practice Section; Criminal Committee, 1995-1998). ***PRACTICE AREAS:*** Civil Litigation; Products Liability; Business Torts; Business Fraud Litigation; Civil Fraud Litigation; Securities Fraud; False Claims Act Litigation. ***Email:*** estidham@greenerlaw.com

JON T. SIMMONS, born Rexburg, Idaho, May 2, 1968; admitted to bar, 1994, Idaho. *Education:* Idaho State University (B.B.A., Business Management, 1991); University of Idaho (J.D., cum laude, 1994). Member, Idaho Law Review. Law Clerk to Honorable Linda Copple Trout, Idaho Supreme Court, 1994-1996. Author, "A Bridge Over Claim Preclusion: Kawai Farms, Inc. v. Longstreet," 29 Idaho Law Review 491, 1992-1993. *Member:* Idaho State Bar. ***PRACTICE AREAS:*** Civil Litigation; Medical Malpractice; Commercial Real Estate Development; Lender Liability; Insurance Bad Faith. ***Email:*** jsimmons@greenerlaw.com

WADE L. WOODARD, born San Jose, California, August 25, 1970; admitted to bar, 1997, New Mexico; 2001, Idaho, U.S. District Court, District of New Mexico. *Education:* Brigham Young University (B.A., 1994; J.D., magna cum laude, 1997). *Member:* American Bar Association (Member, Litigation Section); Idaho State Bar; Defense Research Institute. ***PRACTICE AREAS:*** Commercial Litigation; Insurance Bad Faith; Construction Liability; Antitrust; Unfair Trade; Securities Fraud; Products Liability; Commercial Law; Employment Law; Banking Law; Natural Resources; Water Rights; Real Estate. ***Email:*** wwoodard@greenerlaw.com

---

CURTIS D. McKENZIE, born Corvallis, Oregon, February 9, 1969; admitted to bar, 1995, Maryland; 1996, District of Columbia; 1997, Idaho and U.S. District Court, District of Maryland, U.S. Court of Appeals, Ninth Circuit. *Education:* Northwest Nazarene College (B.S., magna cum laude, 1992); Georgetown University Law Center (J.D., magna cum laude, 1995). Order of the Coif. *Member:* Idaho State Bar (Senator, 2002—; Joint Finance and Appropriations Committee, Local Government and Taxation Committee). ***PRACTICE AREAS:*** Civil Litigation; Complex Business Litigation. ***Email:*** cmckenzie@greenerlaw.com

LADAWN MARSTERS, born Boise, Idaho, November 14, 1965; admitted to bar, 1997, Idaho; 2003, Washington. *Education:* Boise State University (B.S., magna cum laude, 1994); University of Idaho (J.D., with honors, 1997). Psi Chi; Phi Kappa Phi; Delta Theta Phi. *Member:* Idaho State Bar (Bar Exam Grader; Member: Publications Committee; Fee Arbitration Committee); Idaho Trial Lawyers Association. ***PRACTICE AREAS:*** Civil Litigation; Personal Injury Litigation; Drug and Medical Device Litigation; Products Liability. ***Email:*** lmasturs@greenerlaw.com

DANIEL J. GORDON, born San Francisco, California, November 6, 1973; admitted to bar, 1999, Idaho. *Education:* University of California at Davis (B.S., with honors, 1996); University of California, Davis, School of Law (J.D., 1999). *Member:* American Bar Association (Member, Litigation Section); Idaho State Bar (Member, Litigation and Young Lawyers Sections); Idaho Association of Defense Counsel. ***PRACTICE AREAS:*** Civil Litigation; Commercial Litigation; Complex Business Litigation; Business Torts; Products Liability; Construction and Design Law. ***Email:*** dgordon@greenerlaw.com

G. REY REINHARDT, IV, born Lewiston, Idaho, August 24, 1976; admitted to bar, 2000, Idaho, U.S. District Court, District of Idaho, U.S. Court of Appeals, Ninth Circuit. *Education:* University of Idaho (B.S., summa cum laude, 1998; J.D., 2000). ***PRACTICE AREAS:*** Civil Litigation; Construction Litigation; Complex Business Litigation. ***Email:*** greinhardt@greenerlaw.com

MATTHEW E. HEDBERG, born Boise, Idaho, February 4, 1974; admitted to bar, 2002, Idaho; 2003, California; U.S. District Court, District of Idaho; U.S. District Court, Eastern District of California;. *Education:* University of Idaho (B.S., summa cum laude, 1999); University of Washington School of Law (J.D., 2002). *Member:* Idaho State Bar (Officer, Professionalism and Ethics Section); State Bar of California. [Petty Officer Second Class, U.S. Navy, 1992-1996]. ***PRACTICE AREAS:*** Civil Litigation; Commercial Litigation; Creditors Rights. ***Email:*** mhedberg@greenerlaw.com

SCOTT E. RANDOLPH, born Twin Falls, Idaho, December 9,1977; admitted to bar, 2003, Idaho and U.S. District Court, District of Idaho. *Education:* Oregon State University (B.S., summa cum laude, 2000); University of Texas (J.D., with honors, 2003). Volunteer Attorney, CASA Program. *Member:* Idaho State Bar (Chair, Young Lawyers Section; Member, Litigation Section). ***PRACTICE AREAS:*** Civil Litigation; Commercial Litigation; Commercial Contracts; Business Torts; Employment Litigation; Products Liability; Construction and Design Litigation; Insurance Bad Faith. ***Email:*** srandolph@greenerlaw.com

OF COUNSEL

CARL P. BURKE, born Boise, Idaho, December 30, 1927; admitted to bar, 1950, Idaho, U.S. District Court for the District of Idaho and U.S. Supreme Court. *Education:* Stanford University (B.A., 1947; LL.M., 1950). *Member:* Idaho State Bar; American Bar Associations; International Association of Defense Counsel (Founder and First President). Fellow, American College of Trial Lawyers (3 time Idaho State Chairman). Life Fellow American Bar Foundation. [U.S. Army Infantry WW II, 114th Regiment]. ***PRACTICE AREAS:*** Civil Litigation; Securities Litigation; Products Liability; Employment Law; Appellate Practice. ***Email:*** cpburke@greenerlaw.com

WILLIAM C. THARP, born Peoria, Illinois, April 13, 1948; admitted to bar, 1973, Oregon; 1986, Idaho; U.S. District Court, District of Idaho; U.S. District Court, District of Oregon; U.S. Court of Appeals, Ninth Circuit. *Education:* Willamette University (B.A., 1970; J.D., 1973). *Member:* Oregon State Bar (Member, Board of Bar Examiners, 1985-1988); Idaho State Bar. ***PRACTICE AREAS:*** Civil Litigation; Commercial Law; Professional Malpractice; Legal Malpractice; Medical Malpractice; Insurance Defense; Insurance Bad Faith; Products Liability; Intellectual Property; Construction Litigation; Employment Litigation. ***Email:*** btharp@greenerlaw.com

Firm is a member of American Law Firm Associations.

REPRESENTATIVE CLIENTS: Aceto Agricultural Chemical Corporation; Agrium, Inc.; Albertsons Stores; Alliance Title; Boise Cascade Corporation; Boise Housing Corp.; Circle A Construction, Inc.; Contract Freighters, Inc.; DBSI Companies; Eagle-Picher Industries, Inc.; Electro-Scientific Industries, Inc.; Futura Corporation; Holiday Inns, Inc.; Laidlaw Transportation, Inc.; MCMS, Inc.; Micron Technology, Inc.; MRI Associates; Noikia; Old Dominion Freight Line, Inc.; Prudential Bache; Regence Blue Shield of Idaho; Schindler Elevator Corporation; J.R. Simplot Company; University of Idaho; Weyerhaeuser.
REFERENCES: Syringa Bank; Washington Trust Bank; J.R. Simplot Co.; Micron Technology, Inc.; Farmers & Merchants State Bank, N.A.

JOHN F. GREENFIELD, P.A.

Established in 1975
242 NORTH 8TH STREET, SUITE 220
P.O. BOX 854
BOISE, IDAHO 83701
Telephone: 208-345-0380
Fax: 208-345-0422
URL: http://www.johnfgreenfield.com

Workers' Compensation, Personal Injury, and Labor Law.

JOHN F. GREENFIELD, born Washington, D.C., December 8, 1943; admitted to bar, 1974, Idaho; 1983, U.S. Court of Appeals, Ninth Circuit and U.S. Supreme Court. *Education:* Seattle University (B.A., 1968); University of Idaho (J.D., 1973). Member, Governor's Advisory Committee on Workers Compensation, 1983-1995. Member, 2000— and Chairman, 2005—, Idaho Industrial Commission Advisory Committee. Chairman, 1977-1978 and National Committeeman, 1988-2000, Idaho Democratic Party. *Member:* Boise Bar Association; Idaho State Bar; The Association of Trial Lawyers of America; Idaho Trial Lawyers Association. [U.S. Army, Vietnam, 1968-1970]. ***PRACTICE AREAS:*** Workers Compensation; Personal Injury; Labor Law.

DARIN G. MONROE, admitted to bar, 2001, Idaho. *Education:* Idaho State University (B.S., 1997); University of Idaho College of Law (J.D., 2001); University of Washington School of Law (LL.M., Taxation, 2002). Phi Alpha Delta (Vice Justice, 2000-2001). McNichol's Moot Court Competition, 1999-2000. Student Chapter, Idaho Trial Lawyers Association (Vice President, 2000-2001). *Member:* American Bar Association (Tax Section). ***LANGUAGES:*** Spanish.

REPRESENTATIVE CLIENTS: Idaho State AFL/CIO; Bakery, Confectionery, Tobacco and Grain Millers International Union; United Food & Commercial Workers; Idaho Service Employees International Union; International Brotherhood of Electrical Workers; Operating Engineers International Union.
REFERENCE: Farmers and Merchants State Bank.

GAR HACKNEY, P.L.L.C.

500 W. BANNOCK
BOISE, IDAHO 83702
Telephone: 208-342-7600
Fax: 208-342-6553
Email: hackney@spro.net
URL: http://www.ghackney.com

Criminal Law, Driving Under the Influence, Domestic Violence, Sexual Assault, Drug Crimes, Burglary, Search and Seizure, White Collar Crime, Federal Crimes, State and Felony Misdemeanor, Petty Theft, Personal Injury, Automobile Accidents, Bicycle Accidents, Pedestrian Accidents.

GAR HACKNEY, born Pocatello, Idaho, 1949; admitted to bar, 1976, Idaho; 1980, U.S. District Court, District of Idaho; 1983, U.S. Court of Appeals, Ninth Circuit. *Education:* University of Utah (B.A., 1972); University of Idaho College of Law (J.D., 1976). Member, Criminal Rules Committee, 1996—. *Member:* Idaho Trial Lawyers Association; Idaho Association of Criminal Defense Lawyers. ***PRACTICE AREAS:*** Criminal Law (90%, 250); Personal Injury (10%, 10). ***Email:*** hackney@spro.net

(This Listing Continued)

HALL, FARLEY, OBERRECHT & BLANTON, P.A.

Established in 1988
KEY FINANCIAL CENTER
702 WEST IDAHO STREET, SUITE 700
P.O. BOX 1271
BOISE, IDAHO 83701-1271
Telephone: 208-395-8500
Facsimile: 208-395-8585
Email: contact@hallfarley.com
URL: http://www.hallfarley.com

Litigation, Insurance Defense, Medical Malpractice and Professional Liability, Employment Law, Labor Relations, Products Liability, Construction, Health and Hospital, Corporation, Commercial, Banking, Real Estate, Legislative Counseling, Bankruptcy, Appellate Law, Administrative Agencies, Agricultural, Municipal, Estate Planning and Probate.

FIRM PROFILE: Hall, Farley, Oberrecht & Blanton, P.A. was established December 1988, by six attorneys and has grown rapidly to twenty-three attorneys, eight paralegals and thirty staff. We are a highly experienced firm with extensive trial practice and emphasis on several areas including: Insurance Defense; Medical Malpractice and Professional Liability, Employment (including wrongful discharge discrimination, affirmative action, ERISA and wage and hour law) and Labor Relations, Health Care Law, Products Liability, Construction, Corporation, Intellectual Property, Business Transactions, Banking, Real Estate, Legislative Counseling, Bankruptcy, Appellate Practice, Administrative Agencies, Agricultural, Municipal, Estate Planning and Probate. As our practice continues to grow, our commitment to provide effective legal services on a cost-conscious basis will remain the same.

RICHARD E. HALL, born Boise, Idaho, February 7, 1944; admitted to bar, 1970, Idaho; 1971, U.S. Court of Appeals, Ninth Circuit; 2004, Washington. *Education:* University of Idaho (B.A., cum laude, 1966); Harvard University (J.D., 1969). Phi Beta Kappa; Phi Kappa Phi; Pi Gamma Mu; Phi Eta Sigma. Listed in "Best Lawyers in the United States." Co-Author: "Medical Malpractice Law in Idaho: An Update," 23 Idaho Law Review 173 (1986-1987). Author: "Using Improvements in Medical Technology to Prove Timing of Newborn Brain Injury," FICC Quarterly, Summer, 1991, p. 495. Lecturer: "Legal Malpractice Avoidance," Idaho Law Foundation, 1985; "Medical Malpractice," Idaho Law Foundation, 1986; "Tort Reform," Idaho Hospital Association, 1986; "Brain Damaged Baby Cases," Federation of Insurance and Corporate Counsel, Winter Meeting, February, 1992; "Cross Examination of the Difficult Expert Witness," Federation of Insurance and Corporate Counsel, Summer Meeting, London, 1996. Chairman, Board of Directors, United Heritage Financial Group. Lecturer, 26th Annual Pacific Northwest Review of Obstetrics and Gynecology, Portland, Oregon, 2002. *Member:* Boise and American Bar Associations; Idaho State Bar; Idaho Association of Defense Counsel (President, 1979-1980); Defense Research Institute; Federation of Insurance and Corporate Counsel (Member, Board of Directors, 2001; General Convention Chair, 2001 Winter Meeting, Tucson, Arizona); American Board of Trial Advocates (President, Idaho Chapter, 1987, 1988). Fellow, American College of Trial Lawyers. ***PRACTICE AREAS:*** Medical Malpractice; Professional Liability; Litigation; Business Litigation; Insurance Defense. ***Email:*** reh@hallfarley.com

DONALD J. FARLEY, born June 17, 1948; admitted to bar, 1973, Idaho; 1977, U.S. Court of Appeals, Ninth Circuit; 1978, U.S. Supreme Court. *Education:* University of Idaho (B.A., 1970; J.D., 1973). Law Clerk, U.S. District Court, District of Idaho, 1973-1975. Author and Frequent lecturer on topics related to trial and litigation practice. Representative to the Harmonie Group (a national network of defense attorneys offering services to insurers and self-insured companies). *Member:* Idaho State Bar; American Bar Association; Idaho Association of Defense Counsel; International Association of Defense Counsel; Defense Research Institute. Fellow, American College of Trial Lawyers. ***PRACTICE AREAS:*** Litigation; Insurance; Products Liability; Business Litigation; Business Law; Commercial Litigation; Intellectual Property Litigation. ***Email:*** djf@hallfarley.com

PHILLIP S. OBERRECHT, born Hamilton, Ohio, February 25, 1948; admitted to bar, 1976, Idaho and U.S. District Court, District of Idaho; 1987, U.S. Court of Appeals, Ninth Circuit and U.S. Court of Federal Claims; 1989, U.S. District Court, District of Arizona; 1992, U.S. Court of Appeals for the Federal Circuit. *Education:* Ohio State University (B.A., cum laude, 1970; J.D., summa cum laude, 1976). Phi Beta Kappa. Member, Associated General Contractors Labor Lawyers Council, 1984—. *Member:* Boise and American Bar Associations; Idaho State Bar (Chairman, Client Security Fund Committee, 1988; Chairman, Professional Conduct Board, 1997-2000); American Academy of Healthcare Attorneys; Boise Insurance Adjusters Association; International Association of Defense Counsel. ***PRACTICE AREAS:*** Construction Contracts and Claims; Commercial Law; Litigation; Health Care; Labor and Employment. ***Email:*** pso@hallfarley.com

RAYMOND D. POWERS, born New York, N.Y., July 2, 1956; admitted to bar, 1981, Idaho and U.S. Court of Appeals, Ninth Circuit; 2004, Washington. *Education:* Alfred University (B.A., 1978); Ohio Northern University (J.D., 1981). Lead Articles Editor, Ohio Northern University Law Review, 1979-1980. Member, Board of Directors, University of Washington Family Practice Residency of Idaho, 1988-2000. Member, Board of Directors, Brain Injury Association of Idaho, 1999-2000. *Member:* Boise and American Bar Associations; Idaho State Bar; Idaho Association of Defense Counsel; Boise Insurance Adjusters Association. ***REPORTED CASES:*** Keyser v. Garner, 129 Idaho 112; 922 P.2d 409 (Idaho App. 1996); Pearson v. Parsons, 114 Idaho 334; 757 P.2d 197 (Idaho 1988); Dunlap v. Garner, 127 Idaho 599; 903 P.2d 1296 (Idaho 1994); Bott, Berg & Hoar v. Idaho State Bldg. Authority 122 Id. 471, 835 P.2d 1282 (Idaho 1992); Bott, Berg & Hoar v. Idaho State Bldg. Authority 128 Idaho 580; 917 P.2d 737 (Idaho 1996). ***PRACTICE AREAS:*** Personal Injury; Medical Malpractice Defense; Drug Products Liability Defense; Health Care; Insurance Defense. ***Email:*** rdp@hallfarley.com

CANDY WAGAHOFF DALE, born Boise, Idaho, November 7, 1956; admitted to bar, 1982, Idaho; 1986, U.S. Court of Appeals, Ninth Circuit. *Education:* Warnborough College, Oxford, England; College of Idaho (B.S., cum laude, 1979); University of Idaho (J.D., cum laude, 1982). Editor in Chief, Idaho Law Review, 1981-1982. Author: "Has Casual Day Gone Too Far?" The Employer's Handbook, The Labor Letter, Inc. (1998). Co-Author: "Medical Malpractice Law in Idaho: An Update," 23 Idaho Law Review 173 (1986-1987).

(This Listing Continued)

Author: Casenote, "Procedural Due Process of Idaho Public School Teachers," 17 Idaho Law Review (1981). Ninth Circuit Lawyer Representative, 1996-1999. Trainer, University of Idaho, Trial Advocate Course, 1996. *Member:* Boise and American (Member, Sections on: Litigation; Labor and Employment Law) Bar Associations; Idaho State Bar (Member, Labor and Employment Law Section); Idaho Association of Defense Counsel (Director, 1994-2000; President, 1999-2000); Ninth Circuit Advisory Board (2004—); Federation of Defense and Corporate Counsel (2002—); Defense Research Institute; Idaho Law Foundation (Chairman, CLE Committee, 1989-1990); Human Resources Association of Treasure Valley; American Inns of Court #130 (Bencher, Past President); Federal Defenders of Eastern Washington and Idaho (Board Member); Emeritus Member, Advisory Council, University of Idaho College of Law (1998-2004). ***REPORTED CASES:*** Blake v. Cruz, 698 P.2d 315 (Idaho 1984); Holmes v. Union Oil, 760 P.2d 1189 (Idaho Appl 1988); Paterson v. State of Idaho, 915 P.2d 724 (1996); Parker v. Boise Telco Federal Credit Union, 923 P.2d 493 (Idaho App. 1996); Jeremiah v. Yanke Machine Shop, 131 Idaho 242, 953 p.2d 992 (1998); Zaleha v. Robertson, Rosholt & Tucker, et al., 953 P.2d 1363 (1998); Anderson v. Spaulding, Idaho Supreme Court, Docket #26648, Opinion #91, July 2, 2002. ***PRACTICE AREAS:*** Labor and Employment; Professional Liability Defense; Litigation; Mediation. ***Email:*** cwd@hallfarley.com

J. KEVIN WEST, born Provo, Utah, March 15, 1958; admitted to bar, 1984, Utah; 1985, Idaho; 1986, U.S. Court of Appeals, Ninth Circuit; 2004, Washington. *Education:* Brigham Young University (B.A., cum laude, 1981; J.D., cum laude, 1984). Editor-in-Chief, Brigham Young University Journal of Legal Studies, 1983-1984. Judicial Clerk, U.S. District Court, District of Idaho, Chief Judge Marion J. Callister, 1984-1986. Author: "Utah Products Liability Law," Journal of Legal Studies, 1983; "Medicare Audit Handbook," 1999; "Sound Medicare Charting and Documentation Practices," 2000; "Navigating the Minefield: The Anti-Kickback Statute," 2001; "Stark Reality: the Physician Self-Referral Laws," Footlights, Summer 2001; Medicare Compliance: A Training Program for Podiatrists and Their Staff, multi-media CD-Rom, Data Trace Publishing Co., Summer 2002; APMA HIPAA Privacy Manual, American Podiatric Medical Association, 2002; HIPAA Training, Forms and Policies, multi-media CD-Rom, Data Trace Publishing Co., 2003; "The HIPAA Privacy Rules and Their Impact on Litigation Attorneys," The Advocate, Summer 2003; "Closing or Selling Your Practice - What Are Your Responsibilities With Respect to Client Records?," Idaho Psychological Association, Fall 2003; "Death and Disability - What Are Your Responsibilities With Respect to Client Records?," Idaho Psychological Association, Winter 2004; APMA HIPAA Security Manual, American Podiatric Medical Association 2004. *Member:* Washington State and American (Member, Health Law and Litigation Sections) Bar Associations; Idaho State Bar; Utah State Bar; Idaho Association of Defense Counsel; American Health Lawyers Association. ***LANGUAGES:*** Spanish. ***PRACTICE AREAS:*** Health Care; Employment Law; Commercial Litigation; Professional Liability; Insurance Defense; Insurance Law; Litigation; Adoption Law; Medicare Fraud and Abuse. ***Email:*** jkw@hallfarley.com

BART W. HARWOOD, born American Falls, Idaho, September 27, 1942; admitted to bar, 1966, Idaho. *Education:* University of Idaho (LL.B., 1966). Member, Editorial Staff, University of Idaho Law Review, 1965-1966. *Member:* Boise and American (Member, Sections on: Corporation, Banking and Business Law; Real Property, Probate and Trust Law; Tort and Insurance Practice) Bar Associations; Idaho State Bar; Idaho Association of Defense Counsel; Defense Research Institute; American Inns of Court #130 (President, 1992-1993); National Health Lawyers Association; Boise Estate Planning Council; Corporate Code Revision Committee. ***PRACTICE AREAS:*** Business; Trusts and Estates; Real Estate; Environmental Insurance; Estate Planning; Probate. ***Email:*** bwh@hallfarley.com

JOHN J. BURKE, born Long Beach, California, June 10, 1955; admitted to bar, 1992, Idaho and U.S. District Court, District of Idaho; 1995, U.S. Court of Appeals, Ninth Circuit. *Education:* Weber State College (A.S., 1981; B.S., magna cum laude, 1989); University of Utah (J.D., 1992). William H. Leary Scholar, 1990-1991. Recipient, American Jurisprudence Award in Legal Writing. Registered Nurse, Utah, 1981; Idaho, 1993. *Member:* Idaho State Bar; American Bar Association; Defense Research Institute; Idaho Association of Defense Counsel. ***PRACTICE AREAS:*** Medical Malpractice Defense; Products Liability; Insurance Defense. ***Email:*** jjb@hallfarley.com

KEVIN J. SCANLAN, born Grenada Hills, California, March 28, 1970; admitted to bar, 1996, Idaho and U.S. District Court, District of Idaho; 2001, U.S. Court of Appeals, Ninth Circuit. *Education:* Carroll College (B.B.A., 1992); Seattle University School of Law (J.D., cum laude, 1996). Editor, Seattle University Law Review, 1994-1996. President, 2001 and Member, Executive Committee 1999—, Board of Directors, Ronald McDonald House Charities of Idaho. Member, Board of Directors, Family Practice Residency of Idaho. *Member:* Idaho State Bar; American Bar Association. ***PRACTICE AREAS:*** Civil Litigation; Medical Malpractice Defense; Products Liability; Intellectual Property. ***Email:*** kjs@hallfarley.com

TAMSEN L. LEACHMAN, born Moscow, Idaho, September 14, 1964; admitted to bar, 1993, Washington and U.S. District Court, Western District of Washington; 1997, Idaho, U.S. District Court, Eastern District of Washington and U.S. District Court, District of Idaho; 2004, Oregon. *Education:* Eastern Washington University (B.A., 1990); University of Idaho (J.D., 1993). Delta Theta Phi. Member, Environmental Law Society, 1991-1993. Member, 1991-1993 and Vice President, 1992-1993, Moot Court Honor Board. Recipient, Langroise Academic Scholarship, University of Idaho. Author: "Limitations Upon Employee Hiring Practices Under the Americans With Disabilities Act," The Advocate, Sept. 2000; "Limiting the Scope of the "Direct Threat" Defense Under the ADA," The Advocate, Sept. 2000; "The Employer's Affirmative Defense - The 'Devilish' Three Year Old," The Advocate, Sept. 2001. Member: Pacific Coast Labor and Employment Law Conference Planning Committee, 1994-1996; Washington Women Lawyers, 1996-1997. Recipient, Tribute to Women in Industry (TWIN) Award, sponsored by The Women's and Children's Alliance. *Member:* King County (Member, Labor and Employment Law Section, 1996-1997), Washington State (Member, Labor and Employment Law Section) and American (Member, Labor and Employment Law Section) Bar Associations; Idaho State Bar (Past Chair, Labor and Employment Law Section); Defense Research Institute; Human Resource Association of Treasure Valley; Idaho Association of Defense Counsel; Inns of Court. ***PRACTICE AREAS:*** Labor and Employment. ***Email:*** tll@hallfarley.com

(This Listing Continued)

HALL, FARLEY, OBERRECHT & BLANTON, P.A., Boise—Continued

J. CHARLES BLANTON, born American Falls, Idaho, February 2, 1926; admitted to bar, 1951, Idaho and U.S. District Court, District of Idaho; 1962, U.S. Supreme Court; 1974, U.S. Court of Appeals, Ninth Circuit; 1978, U.S. Tax Court. *Education:* University of Idaho (LL.B., 1951; J.D., 1969). Phi Alpha Delta. Author: "Life Insurance: An Argument for Adoption of the Risk Payment Doctrine in Idaho," Idaho Law Review, 1981. Lecturer, Community Property Law, "The Multiple Marriage Situation: His, Hers and Theirs," Reno, Nevada, 1982. *Member:* Boise (President, 1960-1961) and American Bar Associations; Idaho State Bar (Editor, The Advocate, 1959-1961); Idaho Association of Defense Counsel (President, 1973-1974); American College of Trust and Estate Counsel; Federation of Insurance and Corporate Counsel; The International Academy of Estate and Trust Law; Defense Research Institute; Boise Estate Planning Council (President, 1968-1969). ***PRACTICE AREAS:*** Estate Planning; Probate; Real Estate; Corporate. ***Email:*** jcb@hallfarley.com

KEELY E. DUKE, born Missoula, Montana, March 21, 1974; admitted to bar, 1999, Idaho. *Education:* Carroll College (B.A., Business Administration, 1996; B.A., Political Science, 1996); Willamette University College of Law (J.D., 1999). Order of the Barristers. Form Editor, Willamette Journal of International Law and Dispute Resolution, 1998-1999. *Member:* Idaho State and American Bar Associations. ***PRACTICE AREAS:*** Civil Litigation; Products Liability; Employment Law; Insurance Defense; Medical Malpractice; Commercial Law. ***Email:*** ked@hallfarley.com

JAMES S. THOMSON, II, born Lewiston, New York, March 21, 1968; admitted to bar, 1996, Tennessee; 2000, Idaho. *Education:* University of Florida (B.S., Business Administration, 1990); Cecil C. Humphreys School of Law, University of Memphis (J.D., with honors, 1996). *Member:* Idaho State Bar (Member, Section on: Litigation); American Bar Association; American Inns of Court (Associate). ***PRACTICE AREAS:*** Civil Litigation; Insurance Defense; Construction Law; Civil Rights; Military Law. ***Email:*** jst@hallfarley.com

SCOTT R. LEARNED, born Boise, Idaho, July 11, 1976; admitted to bar, 2001, Idaho. *Education:* Whitman College (B.A., 1998); Georgetown University Law Center (J.D., 2001). ***LANGUAGES:*** French. ***PRACTICE AREAS:*** Civil Litigation. ***Email:*** srl@hallfarley.com

BRYAN A. NICKELS, admitted to bar, 2001, Idaho. *Education:* University of Idaho (B.A., 1995); Boston College (J.D., 2001). Phi Beta Kappa. Author: "Native American Free Passage Rights," 24 BC Int'l & Comp. L.Rev. 313. ***PRACTICE AREAS:*** Insurance Defense. ***Email:*** ban@hallfarley.com

MATTHEW J. RYDEN, born Chapel Hill, North Carolina, November 12, 1968; admitted to bar, 2002, Idaho. *Education:* Santa Clara University (B.S.C., 1991); University of Idaho (J.D., 2002). *Member:* Idaho State Bar (Member, Sections on: Real Property; Employment Law). ***PRACTICE AREAS:*** Civil Litigation; Employment Law; Insurance Defense; Real Estate Litigation. ***Email:*** mjr@hallfarley.com

BRENT T. WILSON, admitted to bar, 2002, Idaho; U.S. District Court, District of Idaho. *Education:* Utah State University (B.S., cum laude, 1997); Willamette University (J.D., 2002). Note & Comment Editor, Willamette Law Review, 2001-2002. Law Clerk to the Honorable Wayne L. Kidwell, Idaho Supreme Court. Author: "Pleading versus Proving Scienter under the Private Securities Litigation Reform Act of 1995 in the Ninth Circuit After In re Silicon Graphics and Howard v. Everex: Meet the Pleading Standard and the Fat Lady Has Already Sung," 38 Willamette Law Review 321 (2002). *Member:* Idaho State Bar (Member, Young Lawyers Section); American Bar Association.

CHRIS D. COMSTOCK, admitted to bar, 2002, Idaho; U.S. District Court, District of Idaho. *Education:* Boise State University (B.A., History, 1998); University of Idaho College of Law (J.D., 2002). Extern for Federal Magistrate Judge, Semester in Practice, University of Idaho College of Law. Law Clerk, U.S. District Court, District of Idaho. *Member:* Idaho State Bar; American Bar Association.

JILL M. TWEDT, admitted to bar, 2003, Idaho; U.S. District Court, District of Idaho. *Education:* Albertson College of Idaho (B.A., Political Science, 2001); University of Idaho College of Law (J.D., 2003). Extern, Legal Department, St. Luke's Regional Medical Center, Semester in Practice Program, University of Idaho College of Law.*Member:* Idaho State Bar (Member, Sections on: Young Lawyers, Health Care, Employment and Labor Law); American Bar Association.

JENNIFER A. SWARTZ, born Tulsa, Oklahoma, July 8, 1975; admitted to bar, 2001, Idaho and U.S. District Court, District of Idaho. *Education:* University of Oklahoma (B.A., 1997); University of Tulsa College of Law (J.D., with honors, 2001). Phi Delta Phi. Production Editor, Tulsa Law Journal, 2000-2001. Member, American Inns of Court, 2001-2002. *Member:* Idaho State Bar (Member, Health Law Section); American Bar Association (Member, Tort Trial and Insurance Practice and Litigation Sections); American Health Lawyers Association.

KARIN DWELLE, born Pocatello, Idaho, 1977; admitted to bar, 2003, Idaho. *Education:* Whitman College (B.A., History, with honors, 2000); University of Idaho (J.D., with honors, 2003). Phi Delta Phi. Editor, Idaho Law Review, 2003. Author, Idaho Adoption Law Article, Idaho Law Review, 2002. *Member:* Idaho State Bar (Member, Young Lawyers Section).

REPRESENTATIVE CLIENTS: Ace USA: AIG Claims Services, Co.; Albertson College of Idaho; Allianz; The Amalgamated Sugar Co., LLC; American Custom Ins. Services, Inc.; American Express Corp.; American Fine Foods; Amwest Surety; Archer Daniels Midland; Armed Forces Insurance Co.; Associated Food Stores, Inc.; Attorneys Liability Protection Society (ALPS); Battelle Energy Alliance, LLC; Bayer; Bench Sewer District; BlueCross of Idaho; Brown and Caldwell; Certain Underwriters of Llyods of London; Chubb Grp. of Insurance; CIGNA; CNA Insurance Companies; CNA Pro; CNA Surety; CRI, The Resource Group; *Columbia HCA; Continental Loss Adj. Svcs.; Continental Western Insurance Co.; Correctional Medical Services; Crawford & Co.;* Darmody Enterprises, d/b/a McDonald's; Dennis Dillon Auto Group; The Doctors' Co.; The ES-O-EN Corp., a Taco Bell franchisee; Farm Bureau Mutual Insurance Company of Idaho; Farmers Insurance Co.; Food Services of America, Inc.; Great American Insurance; Grocers Ins. Group; Hansen-Rice, Inc.; Health Care Indemnity, Inc.; Idaho Associated General Contractors; Idaho Power Company; Idaho Elks Rehabilitation Hospital; Idaho Survey & Rating Bureau; Interstate Insurance Group; Kemper Insurance; Key Corp.; Kingsway Insurance Co. of Canada; Lexington Insurance; Lombard Canada; Medical Insurance Exchange of California; Nationwide Ins. Cos.; Northland Ins. Co.; Northwest Physicians Mutual Ins. Co.; Pfizer Corporation; Physicians Insurance Companies; Pioneer Title Co.; Podiatry Insurance Co. of America; Professional Underwriters Liability Ins. Co.; Republic Western Ins. Co.; Safeco Insurance; Saint Alphonsus Regional Medical Center; The Hartford Co.; The St. Paul Cos.; SmithKline Beecham; Sorrento Lactalis, Inc.; State of Idaho; Stryker Corporation; Travelers Ins. Co.; Trinity Health; Unigard Ins. Group; U.S. Bancorp; U.S. Specialty Insurance; United National Insurance Co.; Western Litigation Specialists; West Valley Medical Center; Zurich.

REFERENCES: Farm Bureau Mutual Insurance Company of Idaho; Medical Insurance Exchange of California; The St. Paul Cos.; Travelers.

HAWLEY TROXELL ENNIS & HAWLEY LLP

877 MAIN STREET, SUITE 1000
P.O. BOX 1617
BOISE, IDAHO 83702
Telephone: 208-344-6000
Facsimile: 208-342-3829
Email: info@hteh.com
URL: http://www.hawleytroxell.com

Ketchum, Idaho Office: 540 Second Avenue North, P.O. Box 297. Telephone: 208-726-1700. Facsimile: 208-726-9743.

Pocatello, Idaho Office: 333 South Main Street, P.O. Box 100. Telephone: 208-233-0845. Facsimile: 208-233-1304.

Reno, Nevada Office: 6490 S. McCarran, Suite 4. Telephone: 775-829-9944. Facsimile: 775-829-2627.

General Civil Trial and Appellate Practice before all State and Federal Courts and Administrative Agencies. Alternative Dispute Resolution, Antitrust, Aviation, Banking, Bankruptcy and Creditor Rights, Communications, Construction, Copyright, Corporate, Education, Employee Benefits, Environmental, ERISA, Trusts and Estates, Finance, Health Care and Hospital, Insurance, Intellectual Property, Labor and Employment, Legislative, Media, Mergers and Acquisitions, Mining, Natural Resources, Probate, Products Liability, Public Contract, Public Finance, Public Utility, Qualified and Nonqualified Deferred Compensation, Real Estate, Securities, Taxation, Technology and Science, Trademark and Workers' Compensation Law.

FIRM PROFILE: Hawley Troxell Ennis & Hawley LLP, one of Idaho's largest law firms with three offices in Idaho and one in Nevada, provides legal services to a base of regional and national clients.

MEMBERS OF FIRM

PAUL B. ENNIS (1916-1982)

ROBERT I. TROXELL (1908-1998)

JOHN T. HAWLEY, (P.A.) (1920-1999)

JESS B. HAWLEY, JR., born Boise, Idaho, July 12, 1914; admitted to bar, 1940, District of Columbia and Idaho. *Education:* University of Notre Dame (A.B., cum laude, 1936); Georgetown University (J.D., 1940). Fellow, American College of Trial Lawyers (Regent, 1982-1986). (Retired). ***Email:*** JBH@HTEH.COM

THOMAS A. MILLER, born Pocatello, Idaho, March 19, 1930; admitted to bar, 1956, Idaho. *Education:* Boise Junior College (A.A., 1950); University of Idaho (B.A., cum laude, 1954; J.D., 1956). ***PRACTICE AREAS:*** Real Estate Law; Water Law; Legislation; Public Utility Law; Natural Resources Law. ***Email:*** TAM@HTEH.COM

CRAIG L. MEADOWS, born American Falls, Idaho, July 24, 1940; admitted to bar, 1966, Idaho. *Education:* Colorado State University (B.S., 1963); University of Idaho (J.D., 1966). Idaho State Bar Commissioner, 1998-2001. President, Idaho State Bar, 2001. Fellow, American College of Trial Lawyers. ***PRACTICE AREAS:*** Litigation; Insurance Law; Professional Malpractice Law; Aviation; Commercial Litigation. ***Email:*** CLM@HTEH.COM

JOSEPH D. McCOLLUM, JR., born Memphis, Tennessee, August 18, 1945; admitted to bar, 1970, Idaho; 1971, California. *Education:* University of Idaho (B.S., cum laude, 1967); Hastings College of Law, University of California (J.D., 1970). Fellow, American College of Trial Lawyers. ***PRACTICE AREAS:*** Hospital Law; Health Law; Medical Malpractice Defense; Professional Rights; Insurance Law; Peer Review Litigation; Workers Compensation. ***Email:*** JDM@HTEH.COM

GARY D. BABBITT, born Wendell, Idaho, January 30, 1946; admitted to bar, 1973, Idaho. *Education:* College of Idaho (B.A., cum laude, 1968); University of Chicago (J.D., 1972). Trustee, Rocky Mountain Mineral Institute. Associate Member, Society of Mining Engineers. ***PRACTICE AREAS:*** Environmental Law; Litigation; Commercial Litigation. ***Email:*** GDB@HTEH.COM

RICHARD F. GOODSON, born Pocatello, Idaho, January 26, 1949; admitted to bar, 1974, Idaho. *Education:* Gonzaga University (B.B.A., 1971; J.D., 1974). ***PRACTICE AREAS:*** Real Estate Law; Banking Law; Finance Law; Creditors' Rights Law; Probate Law. ***Email:*** RFG@HTEH.COM

MERLYN W. CLARK, born Grand Forks, British Columbia, Canada, October 27, 1937; admitted to bar, 1964, Idaho. *Education:* University of Idaho (J.D., 1964). Certified Professional Mediator; Commercial Panel and Employment Panel of Arbitrators and Mediators, American Arbitration Association. Master of the Bench, The American Inns of Court Foundation. Fellow: American College of Trial Lawyers; The American Bar Foundation; American College of Civil Trial Mediators. ***PRACTICE AREAS:*** Commercial Litigation; Alternative Dispute Resolution. ***Email:*** MWC@HTEH.COM

EUGENE A. RITTI, born Philadelphia, Pennsylvania, November 16, 1948; admitted to bar, 1973, Pennsylvania; 1978, Idaho. *Education:* Villanova University (A.B., cum laude, 1970); Duke University (J.D., 1973). ***PRACTICE AREAS:*** Antitrust; Construction Litigation; Tax Litigation; Professional Malpractice Law; Commercial Litigation. ***Email:*** EAR@HTEH.COM

JOHN F. KURTZ, JR., born Glendale, California, January 22, 1951; admitted to bar, 1978, California; 1979, Idaho. *Education:* California State University at Northridge (B.S.,

(This Listing Continued)

1975); Loyola University of Los Angeles (J.D., cum laude, 1978). (Certified in Business Bankruptcy Law by the American Bankruptcy Board of Certification). ***PRACTICE AREAS:*** Commercial Litigation; Creditors; Litigation. ***Email:*** JFK@HTEH.COM

RICHARD G. SMITH, born Eugene, Oregon, April 29, 1952; admitted to bar, 1979, Idaho; 2003, Washington. *Education:* University of Idaho (B.A., 1974; B.S., summa cum laude, 1975); Georgetown University (J.D., cum laude, 1979). Certified Public Accountant, Idaho, 1976. ***PRACTICE AREAS:*** Tax Litigation, including income, property and sales tax; Business Organzation Law; Finance Law; Business and Commercial Litigation. ***Email:*** RGS@HTEH.COM

NICHOLAS G. MILLER, born Caldwell, Idaho, March 13, 1950; admitted to bar, 1977, California and New York; 1983, Idaho. *Education:* Stanford University (A.B., with distinction, 1972; J.D., 1976). *Member:* National Association of Bond Lawyers. ***PRACTICE AREAS:*** Public Finance Law; Securities Law; Venture Capital. ***Email:*** NGM@HTEH.COM

STEVEN W. BERENTER, born Nampa, Idaho, October 5, 1954; admitted to bar, 1980, Idaho. *Education:* Stanford University (B.A., 1976); University of Washington (J.D., with high honors, 1980). Order of the Coif. ***PRACTICE AREAS:*** Employment Law; Litigation. ***Email:*** SWB@HTEH.COM

KENNETH C. HOWELL, born Caldwell, Idaho, June 11, 1960; admitted to bar, 1984, Idaho. *Education:* College of Idaho (B.A., cum laude, 1981); University of Idaho (J.D., 1984). ***PRACTICE AREAS:*** Intellectual Property Law; Trademark Law; Copyright Law; Creditors; Bankruptcy; Banking Law; Real Estate Law. ***Email:*** KCH@HTEH.COM

PATRICK V. COLLINS, born Aberdeen, South Dakota, February 14, 1955; admitted to bar, 1980, Idaho. *Education:* South Dakota State University (B.S., with high honors, 1977); Stanford University (J.D., 1980). Fellow, American College of Mortgage Attorneys. ***PRACTICE AREAS:*** Banking Law; Finance Law; Real Estate Law; Bankruptcy Law; Creditors. ***Email:*** PVC@HTEH.COM

MICHAEL M. STODDARD, born Boise, Idaho, October 10, 1959; admitted to bar, 1985, Idaho. *Education:* Occidental College (A.B., 1982); Vanderbilt University (J.D., 1985). *Member:* National Association of Bond Lawyers. ***PRACTICE AREAS:*** Bond Law; Finance Law; Corporate Law; Mergers & Acquisitions Law. ***Email:*** MMS@HTEH.COM

BRIAN L. BALLARD, born Council, Idaho, July 29, 1950; admitted to bar, 1980, Idaho. *Education:* Boise State University (B.A., 1975); University of Idaho (J.D., 1980). ***PRACTICE AREAS:*** Real Estate Law. ***Email:*** BLB@HTEH.COM

BRAD P. MILLER, born San Diego, California, September 17, 1961; admitted to bar, 1986, Idaho. *Education:* University of Idaho (B.S., cum laude, 1983; J.D., summa cum laude, 1986). ***PRACTICE AREAS:*** Employment Law; Commercial Litigation. ***Email:*** BPM@HTEH.COM

THOMAS B. CHANDLER, born Boise, Idaho, July 2, 1954; admitted to bar, 1979, Illinois; 1981, Idaho; 2003, Washington. *Education:* Stanford University (B.A., with honors, 1976); University of Chicago (J.D., 1979). Co-author: "Idaho Mechanics' Liens," Idaho Construction Law and Mechanics' Liens, 1987. Presentation: "Audit Committees and Evolution of Internal Audits," Deputy Seminar, Conference of State Banking Supervisors, San Francisco, CA 2005; "Bank Audit Committees: Requirements & Functions," Examiner's Forum, Conference of State Banking Supervisors, Phoenix, AZ 2005; "Director Duties and Liabilities," CFO Exchange, American Bankers Association, Chicago, IL 2005; "Board Committees: Requirements, Structure & Function" and "Corporate Governance in Action," Directors Seminar, Conference of State Banking Supervisors, Coeur d'Alene, ID 2005; "Comparison of the Sarbanes-Oxley Act and FDIC Requirements for Banks," Examiner's Forum, Conference of State Banking Supervisors, Lake Tahoe, CA 2004; "FDIC and Sarbanes-Oxley Requirements for Community Banks: Code of Ethics and Audit Committee Charter," Boise, Pocatello and Coeur d'Alene, ID 2003; "Sarbanes-Oxley One Year Later," Idaho Society of Certified Public Accountants, Southwest Chapter, Boise, ID 2003; "Sarbanes-Oxley Update," Idaho Society of Certified Public Accountants, Southwest Idaho Industry, Education and Government Section, Boise, ID 2003. Member, Construction Specifications Institute. Member, Panel of Arbitrators, American Arbitration Association. ***PRACTICE AREAS:*** Business Law; Corporate Governance; Mergers and Acquisitions; Construction Law. ***Email:*** TBC@HTEH.COM

STEPHEN C. HARDESTY, born Philadelphia, Pennsylvania, October 5, 1962; admitted to bar, 1987, California; 1991, Idaho. *Education:* Earlham College (B.A., with honors, 1984); University of California at Davis (J.D., 1987). Current Periodicals Editor, U.C. Davis Law Review, 1986-1987. ***PRACTICE AREAS:*** Business Law; Structured Finance; Real Estate. ***Email:*** SCH@HTEH.COM

KIM C. STANGER, born Burley, Idaho, March 28, 1962; admitted to bar, 1990, Arizona; 1997, Nevada; 1998, Idaho. *Education:* Brigham Young University (B.A., cum laude, 1987; J.D., magna cum laude, 1990). Order of the Coif. ***PRACTICE AREAS:*** Health Law; Insurance Coverage; Insurance Defense. ***Email:*** KCS@HTEH.COM

RICHARD A. RILEY, born New Haven, Connecticut, January 29, 1950; admitted to bar, 1977, Idaho. *Education:* Dartmouth College (B.A., cum laude, 1972); Temple University; University of Denver (J.D., 1977). *Member:* Idaho State Bar (Member: Corporate and Securities Law Section; Committee to Revise Corporate Code; Committee to Revise Securities Act); American Health Lawyers Association. ***PRACTICE AREAS:*** Business Law; Securities; Insurance Regulation; Mergers and Acquisitions; Business Transactions; Business Litigation; Health Law. ***Email:*** RAR@HTEH.COM

SHEILA R. SCHWAGER, born Pocatello, Idaho, March 23, 1969; admitted to bar, 1994, Idaho. *Education:* University of Idaho (B.S., cum laude, 1991; J.D., summa cum laude, 1994). ***PRACTICE AREAS:*** Creditors Rights; Bankruptcy Law; Commercial Litigation; Lender Liability Defense; Banking Law; Collections. ***Email:*** SRS@HTEH.COM

THOMAS J. MORTELL, born Idaho Falls, Idaho, November 25, 1966; admitted to bar, 1994, Utah; 1995, Idaho. *Education:* Brigham Young University (B.S., 1991; J.D., cum laude, 1994). Order of the Barristers. ***PRACTICE AREAS:*** Construction Law; Health Law; Litigation. ***Email:*** TJM@HTEH.COM

STEVEN F. SCHOSSBERGER, born Denver, Colorado, August 20, 1970; admitted to bar, 1995, California; 1996 Idaho; U.S. Court of Appeals, Ninth Circuit; U.S. District Court, Northern District of California. *Education:* Pepperdine University (B.A., cum laude, 1992); University of San Francisco (J.D., 1995). ***PRACTICE AREAS:*** Commercial Litigation; Professional Malpractice Law. ***Email:*** SFS@HTEH.COM

OF COUNSEL

KATE KELLY, born Ayer, Massachusetts, 1957; admitted to bar, 1992, Idaho. *Education:* George Mason University (B.A., 1981); University of Idaho (M.S., 1983); University of Utah (J.D., 1990). *Member:* Utah State Bar; Idaho State Bar. ***PRACTICE AREAS:*** Environmental Law. ***Email:*** kkel@hteh.com

JOHN McGOWN, JR., born Bowling Green, Kentucky, June 15, 1949; admitted to bar, 1975, Colorado (inactive); 1981, U.S. Tax Court; 1982, Idaho. *Education:* University of Kentucky (B.S. Acct., 1971); University of Colorado (J.D., 1974); University of Denver (LL.M. in Taxation, 1981). Certified Public Accountant: Idaho, 1982. Idaho Author, The State and Local Tax Lawyer, 1996—. Idaho Correspondent for State Tax Notes, 1993—. Fellow, American College of Trust and Estate Counsel. Certified as a Qualified Mediator for Multistate Tax Disputes Under the Multistate Tax Commission Alternative Dispute Resolution Program. ***PRACTICE AREAS:*** State Taxation; Sales and Use Tax; Estate Planning; Probate Administration; Mediation; Nonprofit Corporations. ***Email:*** JSM@HTEH.COM

ASSOCIATES

Lynnette M. Davis	***Michelle Burke Points***
Paula Landholm Kluksdal	***Sara C. 'Danielle' Quade***
Timothy W. Tyree	***Aaron C. Charrier***
Geoffrey M. Wardle	***John K. Olson***
Jason D. Scott	***William E. Wardwell***
Janine P. Reynard	***D. John Ashby*** (Not admitted in ID)
Robert F. Thomas	***Kristin E. Bjorkman***
Brian C. Larsen	***Dylan Lawrence***

REPRESENTATIVE CLIENTS: Ada County; Albertson's, Inc.; A-Mark Auction Galleries; American Insurance Assn.; American Microsystems, Inc.; BP Amoco Oil Company; AT&T; Bank of America; Basin Electric Power Cooperative; Blaine County School District; Boise State University; Bridgestone/Firestone, Inc.; Chevron U.S.A., Inc.; Chicago Title Insurance Co.; CIGNA Insurance; City of Sun Valley; Connecticut General Life Insurance Co.; Green Tree Financial Servicing Corp.; GTE Wireless; M.A. Hanna Co.; Hecla Mining Co.; Idaho Health Facilities Authority; Idaho Hospital Assn.; Idaho State Building Authority; Idaho State University; IIB; J.R. Simplot Co.; Jacksons Food Stores; Lumberman's; Medical Insurance Exchange; Meridian School District; Micron Technology, Inc.; MotivePower Industries; Northwest Pipeline Corp.; Novartis Seeds; Post Register; Syringa Bank; The Goodyear Tire and Rubber Co.; Union Pacific Corp.; United Heritage Life Insurance Co.; University of Idaho; U.S. Bank; Washington Mutual Bank; Wells Fargo Bank; Western PCS; Williams Companies, Inc.; WGI; Woodgrain Millwork, Inc.; W.R. Grace & Co.

(For Complete Biographical Data on Other Personnel, see Professional Biographies at Ketchum and Pocatello, Idaho and Reno, Nevada)

HEPWORTH, LEZAMIZ & JANIS

CHARTERED

Established in 1952

537 WEST BANNOCK

P.O. BOX 2582

BOISE, IDAHO 83701-2582

Telephone: 208-343-7510

Fax: 208-342-2927

Email: hlhboise@aol.com

URL: http://www.hljlawyers.com

Twin Falls, Idaho Office: 133 Shoshone Street North, P.O. Box 389. Telephone: 208-734-7510. Fax: 208-734-4115.

General Civil and Trial Practice in State and Federal Courts. Automobile Liability, Personal Injury, Medical Malpractice, Negligence, Products Liability, Business and Commercial Law, Corporations, Real Estate, Banking, Probate and Estate Planning, Appellate Practice.

FIRM PROFILE: Our firm was founded as a solo practice by John C. Hepworth in 1952, and now employs nine lawyers, with offices in both Twin Falls and Boise. We provide a broad range of services on a statewide basis, with emphasis on plaintiff's personal injury, wrongful death and insurance litigation. We are firmly committed to excellence in the practice of law, and take pride in the fact that several recoveries made by our firm are among the largest in Idaho.

J. CHARLES HEPWORTH, born Buhl, Idaho, July 26, 1956; admitted to bar, 1981, California; 1982, Idaho; 1993, U.S. Court of Appeals, Ninth Circuit. *Education:* Stanford University (B.A., 1978); University of California, Hastings College of the Law (J.D., 1981). *Member:* Fourth Judicial District and American Bar Associations; State Bar of California; Idaho State Bar; Idaho Trial Lawyers Association; American Inns of Court (Boise Chapter). (Resident). ***REPORTED CASES:*** Marchand v. Mercy Medical Center, 22 F.3d 933 (9th Cir. 1994); Braley v. Pangburn, 118 Idaho 575, 798 P2d 34 (1990); Bubak v. Evans, 117 Idaho 510, 788 P2d 1333 (Ct. App. 1989) (rev. den.). ***PRACTICE AREAS:*** Personal Injury; Products Liability; Automobile Liability; Medical Malpractice; Commercial Litigation; Civil Trial Practice. ***Email:*** ch@hljlawyers.com

JOHN J. JANIS, born New York, N.Y., November 17, 1953; admitted to bar, 1986, Idaho. *Education:* Kean College of New Jersey (B.S., 1976); University of Idaho (J.D., 1986). Phi Alpha Delta. Executive Editor, Idaho Law Review, 1985-1986. *Member:* Idaho State Bar; American Bar Association; Idaho Trial Lawyers Association; American Inns of Court (Member, Boise Chapter); Association of Ski Defense Attorneys. (Resident). ***REPORTED CASES:*** Cameron v. Minidoka County Hwy. Dist., 125 Idaho 801, 874 P.2d 1108 (1994). ***PRACTICE AREAS:*** Personal Injury; Automobile Liability; Products Liability; Medical Malpractice; Employment Law; Civil Trial Practice. ***Email:*** johnjanis@aol.com

(This Listing Continued)

HEPWORTH, LEZAMIZ & JANIS, CHARTERED, Boise—Continued

JOHN W. KLUKSDAL, born Boise, Idaho, March 10, 1972; admitted to bar, 1997, Idaho; 2000, U.S. Court of Appeals, Ninth Circuit. *Education:* Albertson College (B.A., cum laude, 1994); University of Idaho (J.D., magna cum laude, 1997). Member, Albertson College National Alumni Board. *Member:* Idaho State Bar; Idaho Trial Lawyers Association; American Inns of Court. (Resident). ***PRACTICE AREAS:*** Civil Trial Practice; Personal Injury; Medical Malpractice; Employment Law. ***Email:*** jwk@hljlawyers.com

REFERENCES: Wells Fargo Bank (Main Avenue branch); Magic Valley Bank.

(For complete biographical data on other personnel, see Professional Biographies at Twin Falls, Idaho)

HIMBERGER LAW OFFICES, CHTD.

Established in 1996

575 EAST PARKCENTER BOULEVARD, SUITE 100
BOISE, IDAHO 83706
Telephone: 208-336-8442
Fax: 208-336-1690
Email: info@himbergerlaw.com
URL: http://www.himbergerlaw.com

Commercial Law, Business Litigation, Government Contracts, Lien and Bond Claims, Mediation, Arbitration, Construction Law, Creditors Rights, Bankruptcy, Collections, Foreclosures, Land Use, Commercial Development, Residential Development, Zoning, Real Estate, Alternative Dispute Resolution, Mediation and Arbitration, Eminent Domain, Government Contracts, Mergers, Acquisitions, Real Property, Easements, Lien and Board Claims.

RICHARD D. HIMBERGER, born Seattle, Washington, January 9, 1954; admitted to bar, 1989, Washington; 1990, U.S. District Court, Western District of Washington and U.S. Court of Appeals, Federal Circuit; 1994, Idaho; 1995, U.S. District Court District of Idaho. *Education:* Brigham Young University (B.A., Economics, 1984, M.P.A., 1986); Willamette University (J.D., 1989, Certificate of Alternative Dispute Resolution, 1989); University of Washington (LL.M., 1993). Phi Delta Phi. Law Journal Associate Editor, Willamette University Law Review, 1988-1989. Author: "Unjust Discharge: Why Nonunion Employees Need a Just Cause Statute," 25 Willamette Law Review 135, 1988. Publications: Mr. Himberger has published several articles in the Idaho State Bar Magazine ("The Advocate") and the Idaho State Bar Real Property section newsletter. *Member:* Idaho State Bar (Member, Real Property Section, 1996—, Chairman, 2000-2001; Commercial Law and Bankruptcy Section, 2000—). ***PRACTICE AREAS:*** Construction Contracts; Construction Claims; Real Property; Real Estate; Land Use; Zoning, Planning and Land Use; Commercial Law; Creditors Rights; Bankruptcy; Business Law; Water Law; Arbitration; Mediation; Litigation. ***Email:*** rdh@himbergerlaw.com

ERNEST A. HOIDAL

960 BROADWAY AVENUE, SUITE 220
BOISE, IDAHO 83706
Telephone: 208-342-4647
Facsimile: 208-342-0027
Email: eahoidal@hoidallaw.com
URL: http://www.lawyers.com/hoidal

General Civil and Trial Practice, Immigration and Naturalization Law, Business and Corporate Law, Family, Insurance/Negligence Defense, Personal Injury (Plaintiff's) and Probate Law.

ERNEST A. HOIDAL, born Boise, Idaho, August 26, 1949; admitted to bar, 1974, Idaho and U.S. District Court, District of Idaho; 1976, California. *Education:* Boise State University; University of San Francisco (B.S., 1971); University of Idaho (J.D., 1974). Assistant City Attorney, Boise, Idaho, 1974-1976. Deputy Prosecuting Attorney, Ada County, Idaho, 1977. *Member:* Boise and American Bar Associations; Idaho State Bar; State Bar of California; American Immigration Lawyers Association.

REFERENCE: U.S. Bank.

HOLLAND & HART LLP

Established in 1947

U.S. BANK PLAZA, SUITE 1400
101 SOUTH CAPITOL BOULEVARD
P.O. BOX 2527
BOISE, IDAHO 83701
Telephone: 208-342-5000
Telecopier: 208-343-8869
Email: info@hollandhart.com
URL: http://www.hollandhart.com

Regional Offices:
Denver, Colorado
Denver Tech Center, Greenwood Village, Colorado
Aspen, Colorado
Boulder, Colorado
Colorado Springs, Colorado
Billings, Montana
Salt Lake City, Utah
Cheyenne, Wyoming
Jackson, Wyoming
Santa Fe, New Mexico
Washington, D.C.

Alternative Dispute Resolution, Antitrust, Appellate, Banking and Finance, Bankruptcy, Business Transactions, Class Actions, Commercial Litigation, Construction Law, Contracts, Copyrights, Corporate Law, E-Commerce, Emerging Business, Employee Benefits, Endangered Species, Energy, Environmental, Estate Planning and Administration, Finance, Healthcare and Hospitals, Immigration, Indian Law, Intellectual Property, International, Labor and Employment, Legislative, Litigation, Medical Malpractice, Mergers, Acquisitions and Divestitures, Natural Resources, Oil/Gas and Minerals, Patents, Product Liability, Professional Liability, Public Land, Public Utilities and Energy Regulation, Personal Injury, Real Estate, Securities, Tax, Technology and Trade Regulation, Telecommunications, Torts and Insurance, Toxic Torts, Trade Secrets, Trademarks, Trusts and Estates, Venture Capital, Water, Wealth Transfer, White Collar Crime.

FIRM PROFILE: Holland & Hart LLP is the leading law firm in the Rocky Mountain West. With 12 offices and more than 280 attorneys throughout the six western states of Colorado, Utah, New Mexico, Idaho, Wyoming, Montana and Washington, D.C. Holland & Hart serves clients from emerging growth businesses to many of the Fortune 500. Our attorneys combine legal expertise with specialized industry depth to provide interdisciplinary services to our clients in industries such as agricultural, aerospace, biotechnology, broadband communications, construction, healthcare, hospitality, manufacturing, mining, oil and gas, real estate, retail, recreation and telecommunications. "Best Lawyers in America" lists 42 attorneys from the firm in areas ranging from litigation and employment (management-side) to natural resources and securities law. Chambers USA ranks the firm among the top firms in the states in which we practice. Holland & Hart LLP is ranked among the top firms in America for its use of technology, commitment to Pro Bono work and diversity. Through its in-house service, Persuasion Strategies (www.persuasionstrategies.com), the firm offers trial consulting services such as focus groups, mock trials, jury panel selection analysis as well as state-of-the-art trial graphics including animation, virtual reality exhibits and electronic courtroom presentation services. Through its affiliated service, CaseShare (www.caseshare.com), the firm provides secure and easy-to-use legal and business extranets to help teams manage people, paper and work processes. The Holland & Hart Foundation (www.hhfoundation.org) donates thousands of hours and dollars to hundreds of organizations throughout the Rocky Mountain Region. Holland & Hart is a member of several leading legal networks, including Terralex (www.terralex.com) and The Employment Law Alliance(www.employmentlawalliance.com), which gives our clients access to quality legal representation around the globe.

LAW FIRM ALLIANCES/ASSOCIATIONS: **TERRALEX, THE WORLDWIDE NETWORK OF INDEPENDENT LAW FIRMS**
EMPLOYMENT LAW ALLIANCE

MEMBERS

WALTER H. BITHELL, born Twin Falls, ID, 1942; admitted to bar, 1968, Idaho; U.S. District Court, District of Idaho; 1991, U.S. Court of Federal Claims; 1992, U.S. Court of Appeals, Ninth Circuit; U.S. Supreme Court. *Education:* University of Idaho (B.S., 1965; J.D., 1968). Listed in: The Best Lawyers in America 10 plus years; Chambers USA, Litigation, Band 1. Chief Counsel, Idaho State Tax Commission and Idaho Department of Insurance, Idaho Attorney General's Office, 1968-1971; Member, Governor's Advisory Committee on Products Liability, 1980-1981; Idaho Law Foundation (Board of Governors, 1980-1983); University of Idaho Alumni Association (Recipient, Silver and Gold Award, 2001); Sustaining Member, SCRIBES, The American Society of Writers on Legal Subjects. *Member:* Idaho State Bar (President, 1998-1999); American Bar Association; Idaho Trial Lawyers Association (President, 1981-1982; Board of Governors, 1977-1982, 1992-1995; Board of Directors, 2005-2006); Association of Trial Lawyers of America (State Delegate, 1992; Board of Governors, 1993-1996); American Inn of Court No. 130 (Master of the Bench; President, 2004-2005); American College of Trial Lawyers. ***PRACTICE AREAS:*** Crop Damage; Commercial; Business; Construction; Personal Injury; Product Liability; Professional Negligence; Agricultural Law; Crop Damage; Litigation.

J. FREDERICK MACK, born Boise, ID, 1946; admitted to bar, 1973, Idaho; U.S. District Court, District of Idaho. *Education:* University of Idaho (B.A., 1969; J.D., 1972). Listed in: The Best Lawyers in America (Corporate Law); Chambers USA, Corporate/M & A. President, Boise Estate Planning Council, 1984-1985. Member, University of Idaho Law School Advisory Board (2001—). Chairman of the Board, United Way of Treasure Valley, 1995. Member, Boise Art Museum (Board of Trustees, 1988-1996; President, Board of Trustees, 1993-1994). Deputy Prosecuting Attorney (Ada County, Idaho, 1975). *Member:* Idaho State Bar; American Bar Association (Member, Sections on: Business Law; Family Law; Real Property/Probate/Trust Law; Taxation Law); Idaho Trial Lawyers Association (Member, Board of Governors, 1978); Association of Trial Lawyers of America. ***PRACTICE AREAS:*** Corporate Law; Business Organization Law; Mergers and Acquisitions; Banking Law; Commercial Real Estate; Real Estate Law; Real Estate Finance; Land Use; State Taxation; Local Taxation; Emerging Growth Companies; Venture Capital; Estate Planning. ***Email:*** fmack@hollandhart.com

LARRY E. PRINCE, born Gooding, ID, 1950; admitted to bar, 1975, Idaho; 1978, U.S. Court of Appeals, Ninth Circuit; 2003, Washington. *Education:* Boise State College (B.A., magna cum laude, 1972); University of California, Hastings College of Law (J.D., 1975). Order of the Coif; Member: McAuliffe Law Honor Society; Thurston Society. Listed in: The Best Lawyers in America (Bankruptcy Law and Creditor/Debtor Rights); Chambers USA. Member: District of Idaho Local Bankruptcy Rules Committee, 1990—, Chairman, 1993—. *Member:* Idaho State Bar (Chairman, Commercial Law and Bankruptcy Section, 1982-1983, 1997-1998; Board of Governors, 1982-1984 and 1991-1999); Federal Bar Association (Idaho Chapter, Founding Member and Officer); American Bankruptcy Institute. Fellow, American College of Bankruptcy. ***PRACTICE AREAS:*** Bankruptcy Law; Debtor and Creditor; Banking Law; Commercial Law; Business Law; Commercial Real Estate; Leases and Leasing; Real Estate; Corporate Law. ***Email:*** lprince@hollandhart.com

B. NEWAL SQUYRES, born Phillips, TX, 1946; admitted to bar, 1972, Texas; 1974, Idaho; U.S. District Court, District of Idaho; 1980, U.S. Court of Appeals, Fifth and Ninth Circuits. *Education:* Texas Tech University (B.A., 1968; J.D., with high honors, 1972). Order of the Coif. Editor-in-Chief, Texas Tech Law Review, 1971-1972. Law Clerk, Hon. Joe

(This Listing Continued)

Ingraham, U.S. Court of Appeals, 5th Circuit, 1972-1974. Assistant to the Attorney General of the U.S. Office of Legal Counsel, U.S. Department of Justice, 1977-1979. Member, Department of Energy's Blue Ribbon Panel on Waste Isolation Pilot Plant, 1989-1992. Listed in: The Best Lawyers in America; Chambers USA (Litigation). *Member:* American Bar Association; Idaho Trial Lawyers Association; Association of Trial Lawyers of America. ***PRACTICE AREAS:*** Commercial Litigation and Torts; Employment Litigation; False Claims Act Litigation; Civil Appeals; Complex and Multi-District Litigation; Construction Litigation; Environmental Litigation; Insurance Litigation; Coverage and Bad Faith; Intellectual Property Litigation; Personal Injury; Products Liability; Energy Litigation. ***Email:*** nsquyres@hollandhart.com

STEVEN B. ANDERSEN, born Ogden, UT, 1952; admitted to bar, 1980, Idaho; 1985, U.S. Court of Appeals, Ninth Circuit. *Education:* University of Utah; Brigham Young University (B.A., summa cum laude, 1977); J. Reuben Clark Law School, Brigham Young University (J.D., cum laude, 1980). Listed in: Best Lawyers in America (Personal Injury Litigation); Chambers USA. *Member:* Idaho Trial Lawyers Association (Board of Directors, President 1998-1999). ***PRACTICE AREAS:*** Commercial Litigation; Personal Injury; Products Liability; Professional Liability Law; Crop Damage; Airplane Crash Litigation; Lender Liability; Insurance Bad Faith; Patent Litigation; Trademark Litigation. ***Email:*** sandersen@hollandhart.com

LINDA B. JONES, born Blackfoot, ID, 1950; admitted to bar, 1986, California; 1990, Idaho. *Education:* San Jose State University (B.A., with high distinction, 1981); University of California at Berkeley (M.P.P., 1985); University of California, Boalt Hall School of Law (J.D., 1985). *Member:* Idaho State Bar (Environment and Natural Resources Section, Governing Council, 1995-2001, Chair, 1997-1999; Business and Corporate Law Section, Governing Council, 1999-2004, CLE Chair, 2000). ***PRACTICE AREAS:*** Environmental Law; Natural Resources Law; Water Law; Commercial and Secured Transactions; Commercial Real Estate; Corporate Law. ***Email:*** ljones@hollandhart.com

MURRAY D. FELDMAN, admitted to bar, 1989, California; 1990, Idaho; 1991, Colorado; 1995, U.S. Court of Appeals, Ninth Circuit; 2001, U.S. Court of Appeals, Tenth Circuit; 2002, U.S. Court of Appeals, Fifth Circuit. *Education:* University of California at Berkeley (B.S., with high honors, 1982); University of Idaho (M.S., 1985); University of California, Boalt Hall School of Law (J.D., 1988). Phi Beta Kappa. Listed in The Best Lawyers in America (Environmental Law). Law Clerk, Hon. George E. Lohr, Colorado Supreme Court, 1988-1989. *Member:* Idaho State Bar (Member, Sections on: Environment and Natural Resources; Water Law); American Bar Association (Member, Environment, Energy, and Resources Law Section; Endangered Species Committee). ***PRACTICE AREAS:*** Environmental Law and Litigation; Wildlife and Endangered Species Law; Environmental Mediation; Environmental Permitting; Public Lands and Natural Resources Law; Appellate Practice; Land Use Law; Water Law. ***Email:*** mfeldman@hollandhart.com

ROBERT A. FAUCHER, born Moscow, ID, 1962; admitted to bar, 1988, Massachusetts; 1993, Idaho. *Education:* Yale University (B.A., summa cum laude, 1984); Harvard University (J.D., cum laude, 1988). Phi Beta Kappa. Visiting Professor, University of Idaho School of Law (Bankruptcy), 1997, 2001. *Member:* Idaho State Bar (Member: Commercial Law and Bankruptcy Section, 1988—; Business and Corporate Law Section, 1988—); American Bankruptcy Institute. ***PRACTICE AREAS:*** Bankruptcy and Creditors Rights; Commercial Litigation; Commercial Transactions; Real Estate Litigation; Contracts; Perishable Agricultural Commodities Act (PACA). ***Email:*** rfaucher@hollandhart.com

DANIEL J. GLIVAR, born Denver, CO, 1967; admitted to bar, 1992, Colorado; 2004, Idaho. *Education:* University of Santa Clara (B.S., Finance, 1989); University of Notre Dame (J.D., magna cum laude, 1992). ***PRACTICE AREAS:*** Telecommunications Contracts; Software Copyright; Software Licensing; Piracy; High Technology Contracts; Business Transactions; Cable Communications; Cable TV; Digital Communications; Satellite Communications; Computer Technology; Information Technology Licensing; Software Protection; Breach of Contract; Commercial Contracts; Copyright Infringement; Intellectual Property Licensing; E-Commerce; Web Site Development; Business Acquisitions; Business Divestitures; Mergers and Acquisitions; Easements; Real Estate Contracts; Right of Way Easements; High Technology; Technology Licensing; Technology Transfers. ***Email:*** dglivar@hollandhart.com

STEVEN C. BOWMAN, born Idaho Falls, ID, 1960; admitted to bar, 1991, Idaho and U.S. District Court, District of Idaho. *Education:* Idaho State University (B.A., 1988); University of Idaho (J.D., magna cum laude, 1991). Law Clerk to Hon. Harold L. Ryan, Chief U.S. District Judge, District of Idaho, 1991-1995. ***PRACTICE AREAS:*** Commercial Litigation; Construction Litigation; Real Estate Litigation; Land Use Litigation; Banking Litigation; Personal Injury; Products Liability. ***Email:*** sbowman@hollandhart.com

AMANDA K. BRAILSFORD, born Twin Falls, ID, 1967; admitted to bar, 1993, Idaho and U.S. District Court, District of Idaho; 1995, U.S. Court of Appeals, Ninth Circuit. *Education:* University of Idaho (B.A., cum laude, 1989; J.D., summa cum laude, 1993). Phi Beta Kappa; Phi Kappa Phi. Law Clerk to Hon. Thomas G. Nelson, Ninth Circuit Court of Appeals, 1993-1995. ***PRACTICE AREAS:*** Civil Litigation; Commercial Litigation; Employment Law and Litigation. ***Email:*** abrailsford@hollandhart.com

IRENE F. GALLAGHER, born Chicago, IL, 1971; admitted to bar, 1996, Illinois; 2000, Colorado; 2004, Idaho. *Education:* University of Chicago (B.A., 1992); University of Illinois (J.D., 1996). Member, Western Pension and Benefits Conference, Boise Chapter Board and Denver Chapter Board. (Also at Denver, Colorado). ***PRACTICE AREAS:*** ERISA; Qualified Retirement Plans; Pension and Profit Sharing Plans; Executive Compensation; Equity Compensation; Flexible Benefit Plans; COBRA; Deferred Compensation; Employee Benefit Taxation; Employee Compensation; Employee Stock Ownership Plans; Employee Stock Ownership Trusts; Executive Compensation Taxation; Fringe Benefits; Health Benefits; Non-Qualified Benefits; Pension Fund Investments; Pension Plans; Pension Taxation; Profit Sharing; Public Employee Retirement; Retirement Benefit Plans; 401(k) Plans. ***Email:*** igallagher@hollandhart.com

OF COUNSEL

TED C. MURDOCK, born Pocatello, ID, 1968; admitted to bar, 1996, Idaho; U.S. District Court, District of Idaho. *Education:* Boise State University (B.B.A., cum laude, 1993); University of Idaho (J.D., 1996). Phi Delta Phi. Law Clerk, Honorable Mikel H. Williams, United States Magistrate, District of Idaho, 1996-1998. ***PRACTICE AREAS:*** Civil Litigation; Commercial Litigation; Insurance Insolvency; Insurance Rehabilitational Liquidation; Plaintiffs Personal Injury; Tort Liability. ***Email:*** tmurdock@hollandhart.com

WILLIAM G. MYERS, III, born Roanoke, VA, 1955; admitted to bar, 1981, Colorado; 1982, Wyoming; 1987, District of Columbia; 1997, Idaho. *Education:* College of William and Mary (A.B., 1977); University of Denver (J.D., 1981). Legislative Counsel to U.S. Senator Alan Simpson (WY-Ret.), 1985-1989. Assistant to the Attorney General, U.S. Department of Justice, 1989-1992. Deputy General Counsel for Programs, U.S. Department of Energy, 1992-1993. Solicitor of the Department of the Interior, 2001-2003. ***PRACTICE AREAS:*** Natural Resources; Environmental Law; Appellate Practice; Government. ***Email:*** wmyers@hollandhart.com

WENDY THOMAS WENDROWSKI, born Jeanette, PA, 1963; admitted to bar, 1991, California and U.S. District Court, Central District of California; 1992, U.S. Claims Court; 1993, District of Columbia; 1994, U.S. District Court, Northern District of California; 2003, Idaho and U.S. District Court, District of Idaho. *Education:* College of William & Mary (B.A., 1985); Marshall-Wythe School of Law, College of William & Mary (J.D., 1991). Law Clerk to Hon. Loren A. Smith, Chief Judge, U.S. Claims Court, 1991-1992. Co-Author: Project, "The Impact of Cost-Benefit Analysis on Federal Administrative Law," 42 Admin.L.Rev. 545 (1990); Project, "State Judicial Review of Administrative Action," 43 Admin.L.Rev. 571 (1991). ***PRACTICE AREAS:*** Civil Litigation; Commercial Litigation; Construction Litigation. ***Email:*** wwendrowski@hollandhart.com

MARY V. YORK, born Pocatello, ID, 1968; admitted to bar, 1994, Idaho; U.S. District Court, District of Idaho. *Education:* Gonzaga University (B.A., cum laude, 1990); University of Idaho (J.D., 1994). Law Clerk to Hon. Charles F. McDevitt, Chief Justice, Idaho Supreme Court, 1994-1996. ***PRACTICE AREAS:*** Eminent Domain; Construction Litigation; Property Rights; Zoning Law; Real Estate and Land Use Litigation; Local Government Law. ***Email:*** myork@hollandhart.com

ASSOCIATES

DEAN B. ARNOLD, born Tacoma, WA, 1969; admitted to bar, 2003, Idaho and U.S. District Court, District of Idaho. *Education:* Washington State University (B.A., 1991); University of Idaho (J.D., cum laude, 2003). ***PRACTICE AREAS:*** Commercial Litigation; Civil Litigation. ***Email:*** dbarnold@hollandhart.com

BENSON BARRERA, born Metairie, LA, 1980; admitted to bar, 2005, Idaho. *Education:* University of Utah (B.S., 2002); University of San Diego School of Law (J.D., 2005). Order of the Coif; Phi Delta Phi. San Diego Law Review life member. ***PRACTICE AREAS:*** Business Litigation. ***Email:*** bbarrera@hollandhart.com

JAMES D. BOWEN, born Moses Lake, WA, 1975; admitted to bar, 2003, Idaho; 2005, Nevada. *Education:* Brigham Young University (B.S., Economics, 2000); Gonzaga University School of Law (J.D., magna cum laude, 2003). Phi Theta Kappa; Alpha Sigma Nu. Author: "The Collision of Land Use and Water Law in the Methow River Valley," 38 Gonz. L.Rev. 655. ***PRACTICE AREAS:*** Real Estate; Business Law; Corporate Law; Mergers and Acquisitions. ***Email:*** jdbowen@hollandhart.com

KEVIN C. BRALEY, born Parkston, SD, 1966; admitted to bar, 1998, South Dakota; 1999, Minnesota; U.S. District Court, District of Minnesota; 2004, Idaho, U.S. District Court, District of Idaho. *Education:* South Dakota State University (B.S.E.E., 1988); University of South Dakota (J.D., with honors, 1997). Law Clerk to the Hon. Roger Wollman, U.S. Court of Appeals for the Eighth Circuit, 1997-1998. *Member:* Idaho State Bar. [U.S. Navy, 1989-1994, Lt.]. ***PRACTICE AREAS:*** Business Litigation; ERISA Litigation; Civil Appeals; Civil Litigation; Aviation Litigation. ***Email:*** kbraley@hollandhart.com

TRACY JACK CRANE, born Fullerton, CA, 1974; admitted to bar, 2003, Idaho. *Education:* Idaho State University (B.S., Geology, 1996; M.S. Geology, 2000); University of Idaho (J.D., summa cum laude, 2003). Managing Editor, Idaho Law Review, 2002-2003. Recipient, Faculty Award of Outstanding Academic Achievement, University of Idaho. Author: "Passive Migration of Pollutants and CERCL PRP Liability", (Carson Harbor Village, Ltd. v. Unocal (Corp.) 30 Idaho Law Review 619-648 (2003). ***PRACTICE AREAS:*** Litigation. ***Email:*** tcrane@hollandhart.com

JOHN M. EUSTERMANN, born Modesto, CA, 1965; admitted to bar, 1995, California; 1996, Washington; 1998, Oregon; 2002, Idaho. *Education:* University of Notre Dame (B.A., 1987; M.B.A., Finance, 1989); Seattle University (J.D., 1994). ***PRACTICE AREAS:*** Mergers and Acquisitions; Intellectual Property Licensing; Corporate Commercial Law; Corporate Contracts; Ethanol. ***Email:*** jeustermann@hollandhart.com

BRIAN THOMAS FISCHENICH, born Columbus, OH, 1974; admitted to bar, 2004, Idaho. *Education:* Lehigh University (B.A., 1998); Georgetown University Law Center (J.D., 2004). ***PRACTICE AREAS:*** Litigation; Class Actions; Commercial Litigation; Business Law. ***Email:*** bfischenich@hollandhart.com

BRAD A. GOERGEN, born Salem, OR, 1972; admitted to bar, 2002, Idaho. *Education:* Western Oregon University (B.S., Public Policy, 1999); University of Washington Law School (J.D., 2002). Associate Editor-in-Chief, Washington Law Review. Recipient, ABI Medal of Excellence (Bankruptcy). Author: "The Error of Kim v. Lee and Equitable Subrogation: Why Biforcating Lien Priorities is a Better Remedy," 77 Wash. L.Rev 235 (2002). Member, Local Bankruptcy Rules Committee, District of Idaho, 2002-2005. Member, Board of the Advocate (official publication of the Idaho Bar), 2004—. *Member:* American Bankruptcy Institute. ***PRACTICE AREAS:*** Bankruptcy; Business Law. ***Email:*** bagoergen@hollandhart.com

MATTHEW M. HICKS, born Santa Monica, CA, 1970; admitted to bar, 1996, Illinois; 1997, Idaho. *Education:* Baylor University (B.A., 1992); University of Notre Dame (J.D., 1996). Recipient, American Jurisprudence Award in Evidence. Law Clerk to the Hon. Thomas F. Neville, Fourth District Court of Idaho, 1997-1999. ***PRACTICE AREAS:*** Business Law; Corporate Law; Mergers and Acquisitions; Technology Law; Emerging Growth Companies; Banking Law; Commercial Loans; Loan Workouts; Loan Restructuring; Real Estate Sales; Real Estate Leasing; Real Property Acquisitions; Real Property Development; Real Property Workouts. ***Email:*** mhicks@hollandhart.com

PAMELA SIMMONS HOWLAND, born Boise, ID, 1970; admitted to bar, 2000, Idaho and Washington. *Education:* Montana State University (B.S., 1993); Gonzaga Uni-

(This Listing Continued)

HOLLAND & HART LLP, Boise—Continued

versity (J.D., 2000). Law Clerk to Hon. Wayne Kidwell, Idaho Supreme Court, 2000-2001. ***PRACTICE AREAS:*** Commercial Litigation; Employment Law; Product Liability; Construction Litigation. ***Email:*** phowland@hollandhart.com

TOBI J. MOTT, born Weiser, ID, 1974; admitted to bar, 2002, Idaho. *Education:* Westminster College (B.A., 1996); University of Utah (M.B.A., 1999); University of Colorado (J.D., 2002). ***PRACTICE AREAS:*** Corporate Law; Mergers and Acquisitions; Emerging Growth Companies; Intellectual Property; Trademarks; Technology Licensing. ***Email:*** tmott@hollandhart.com

MAUREEN G. RYAN, born Milwaukee, WI, 1979; admitted to bar, 2004, Washington; 2005, Idaho. *Education:* Gonzaga University (B.A., History, 2001); Gonzaga University School of Law (J.D., summa cum laude, 2004). Notes/Comments Editor, Gonzaga Law Review. ***PRACTICE AREAS:*** Business Law; Business Transactions. ***Email:*** mgryan@hollandhart.com

NICOLE SNYDER, born Rexburg, ID, 1975; admitted to bar, 2001, Washington; 2002, Idaho. *Education:* University of San Diego (B.A., 1997); University of Michigan (J.D., 2001). ***PRACTICE AREAS:*** Corporate; Real Estate; Employment Law; Emerging Growth and Technology; Securities Law; Mergers and Acquisitions; Local Government Law. ***Email:*** nsnyder@hollandhart.com

(For complete biographical data on all personnel, see Professional Biographies at Denver, Colorado)

HOPKINS RODEN CROCKETT HANSEN & HOOPES, PLLC

Established in 1973

802 WEST BANNOCK, SUITE 900
P.O. BOX 2110
BOISE, IDAHO 83701-2110
Telephone: 208-336-7930
Fax: 208-336-9154
Email: BoiseLaw@hrchh.com
URL: http://www.hrchh.com

Idaho Falls, Idaho Office: 428 Park Avenue, P.O. Box 51219, 83405-1219. Telephone: 208-523-4445. Fax: 208-523-4474.

Washington, D.C. Office: 8 East Street, S.E., 20003. Telephone: 202-546-0361. Fax: 202-546-6294.

General Civil, Trial and Appellate Practice before all State and Federal Courts and Administrative Agencies, Administrative Law, Agricultural Law, Alcoholic Beverages, Banking Law, Bankruptcy, Business Law, Civil Rights, Contracts, Construction Law, Corporate Law, Criminal Law, Debtor and Creditor, Election, Campaign and Political Law, Eminent Domain, Employment Law, Family Law, Government, Insurance, Health Care, Hospital Law, Immigration Law, Natural Resources, Negligence, Personal Injury (plaintiffs and defense), Real Estate, Social Security, Taxation, Trusts and Estates, Utility Law, Wills and Probate, Workers' Compensation Law, and Zoning, Planning and Land Use.

RESIDENT PARTNERS

WILLIAM C. RODEN, born Camas, Washington, 1929; admitted to bar, 1953, Idaho; 1964, U.S. Court of Appeals, Ninth Circuit. *Education:* University of Idaho (B.A., 1951; LL.B., 1953). Phi Alpha Delta. Assistant Attorney General, Idaho, 1957-1958. Prosecuting Attorney, Ada County, Idaho, 1959-1960. State Senator, Ada County, Idaho, 1960-1968. Vice-President, American Heart Association, 1978-1979. Member, Board of Directors, American Heart Association, 1976-1979. Legal Advisory Committee, Idaho Association of Commerce & Industry (Chairman, 1995-1996). *Member:* Idaho State Bar. [U.S. Army, Counter-Intelligence Corps, 1954-1956]. ***PRACTICE AREAS:*** Litigation; Public Utility Law; Administrative Law; Legislative Affairs. ***Email:*** bill@hrchh.com

JOHN MICHAEL BRASSEY, born Boise, Idaho, 1946; admitted to bar, 1971, Idaho, U.S. District Court, District of Idaho and U.S. Court of Appeals, Ninth Circuit. *Education:* University of Idaho (B.S., Finance, 1968; J.D., 1971). Phi Alpha Delta. Administrator, Executive Office of the Governor, Division of Financial Management, 1996-1997. Director, State of Idaho Department of Insurance, 1995. Deputy Attorney General, Chief Business Regulation Division, 1979-1981. Deputy Director, State of Idaho Department of Finance, 1974-1979. Member, Executive Committee, National Association of Consumer Credit Administrators, 1973-1975. President, American Conference of Uniform Consumer Credit States, 1973-1974. Deputy Administrator of Securities and the Uniform Consumer Credit Code, State of Idaho Department of Finance, 1973-1974. Deputy Administrator, Uniform Consumer Credit Code, State of Idaho Department of Finance, 1972-1973. Assistant Attorney General, State of Idaho, 1971-1972. Board of Directors, Boise Area Chamber of Commerce. (Resident). ***PRACTICE AREAS:*** Legislative Practice; Corporate Law; Administrative Law; Commercial Law. ***Email:*** mike@hrchh.com

OF COUNSEL

BRUCE L. THOMAS, born Tacoma, Washington, 1948; admitted to bar, 1974, Idaho; 1981, U.S. Tax Court; 1985, U.S. Court of Appeals, Ninth Circuit. *Education:* Whitman College (B.A., 1970); University of Denver (J.D., 1974). Law Clerk to Chief Justice, Joseph J. McFadden, Supreme Court of Idaho, 1974-1976. Member, Panel of Mediators and Panel of Arbitrators, American Arbitration Association. *Member:* Boise and American Bar Associations; Idaho State Bar (Chair: Alternative Dispute Resolution Section; Corporate and Securities Law Sections). ***PRACTICE AREAS:*** Business Law; Mediation and Arbitration; Litigation; Estate Planning and Probate. ***Email:*** bruce@hrchh.com

(For complete biographical data on all personnel, see Professional Biographies at Idaho Falls, Idaho)

HOWARD LOPEZ & KELLY PLLC

702 WEST IDAHO STREET
P.O. BOX 856
BOISE, IDAHO 83701-0856
Telephone: 208-342-4300
Fax: 208-342-4344
URL: http://www.idahodefense.com

Construction Litigation, Commercial Litigation, Environmental Litigation, Insurance Defense, Insurance Coverage, Products Liability, Professional Malpractice Defense and Subrogation Law.

JOHN P. HOWARD, born Boise, Idaho, July 5, 1948; admitted to bar, 1973, Idaho; 1989, U.S. Supreme Court. *Education:* University of Idaho (B.S., 1970); University of Washington (J.D., 1973). Member, Editorial Staff, Washington Law Review, 1972-1973. *Member:* Idaho State Bar; Oregon State Bar; Defense Research Institute.

THOMAS H. LOPEZ, born Coldwater, Michigan, September 28, 1951; admitted to bar, 1986, Idaho and U.S. District Court, District of Idaho; 1989, U.S. Court of Appeals, Ninth Circuit. *Education:* Western Michigan University; University of Michigan (B.S., 1973); University of Idaho (J.D., 1986). Law Clerk to Justice Robert E. Bakes, Idaho Supreme Court, 1986-1988. *Member:* Idaho State Bar; Defense Research Institute.

MICHAEL E. KELLY, born Rockville Centre, New York, May 16, 1958; admitted to bar, 1989, New York; 1992, Idaho and U.S. District Court, District of Idaho; 2002, Oregon and U.S. District Court, District of Oregon. *Education:* Virginia Military Institute (B.A., 1980); Pace University School of Law (J.D., 1989). *Member:* New York State Bar Association; Idaho State Bar; Oregon State Bar; Defense Research Institute; Boise Adjusters Association.

ASSOCIATES

RANDALL CURTIS PROBASCO, born Jerome, Idaho, June 30, 1969; admitted to bar, 2000, Idaho and Washington. *Education:* Boise State University (B.A., 1993); University of Idaho College of Law (J.D., 1999). Vice-President, Christian Legal Society, University of Idaho, 1998-1999. *Member:* Idaho State Bar; Washington State Bar Association.

LOU PICCIONI, born Vineland, New Jersey, October 7, 1966; admitted to bar, 1992, Wyoming; 2000, Idaho. *Education:* Saint Bonaventure University (B.A., 1989); University of Wyoming (J.D., 1992). *Member:* Idaho State Bar; Wyoming State Bar.

PEG M. DOUGHERTY, born Denver, Colorado, August 22, 1958; admitted to bar, 1999, Idaho. *Education:* University of Northern Colorado (B.A., Education, 1982); University of Idaho (J.D., 1999).

KRISTA GRAY, born Chula Vista, California, February 19, 1971; admitted to bar, 1999, Idaho and U.S. District Court, District of Idaho. *Education:* Boise State University (B.A., 1996); University of Idaho (J.D., 1999). Inns of Court, 2003-2004.

REPRESENTATIVE CLIENTS: ABM Insurance Services; Aegon Special Markets Group; American Commerce Insurance Company; American International Group; Assurant Group; Crawford Claims Management Services; Continental Western Group; Employees Reinsurance Corp; General Fire & Casualty Company; General Star Management Company; Hertz Claim Management Corporation; Nova Casualty Company; Oregon Mutual Insurance Company; PFL Life Insurance Company; Physicians Insurance Companies; Safeco Insurance Companies; State of Idaho; Union Security Life Insurance Company; XL Design Professional Insurance Co.; ZC Insurance Company.

JOHNSON & MONTELEONE, LLP

405 SOUTH 8TH STREET, SUITE 250
BOISE, IDAHO 83702
Telephone: 208-331-2100
Fax: 208-947-2424
Email: jason@treasurevalleylawyers.com
URL: http://www.treasurevalleylawyers.com

Personal Injury, Employment Law, Automobile Accidents and Injuries, Head Injury, Dog Bites, Wrongful Termination, Slip and Fall.

SAM JOHNSON, born Clarkston, Washington, January 11, 1966; admitted to bar, 1993, Idaho and U.S. District Court, District of Idaho. *Education:* University of Idaho (B.S., 1989; J.D., 1993). *Member:* Ninth Circuit Court of Appeals, Third District, Fourth District and American Bar Associations.

JASON R.N. MONTELEONE, born Dayton, Ohio, September 26, 1969; admitted to bar, 1998, Idaho. *Education:* Dickinson College (B.A., 1991); Washburn University School of Law (J.D., with honors, 1996). Member: Washburn Law Journal; Moot Court Honor Society. *Member:* American Bar Association (Member, Litigation Section, 1998—); American Inns of Court. ***PRACTICE AREAS:*** Personal Injury; Employment Law.

LEGAL SUPPORT PERSONNEL

CARA RICE, (Paralegal)

GABRIELA SOLUM, (Legal Assistant). ***LANGUAGES:*** (Spanish).

JONES GLEDHILL HESS FUHRMAN & EIDEN, P.A.

225 N. NINTH STREET, SUITE 820
P.O. BOX 1097
BOISE, IDAHO 83701
Telephone: 208-331-1170
Fax: 208-331-1529
Email: jg@idalaw.com
URL: http://www.idalaw.com

Civil and Business Litigation, Employment Law, Family Law, Commercial Litigation and Appeals, Insurance Coverage and Defense, Business and Finance, Construction Law, Real Property, Estate Planning and Tax Law.

(This Listing Continued)

RORY R. JONES, born Cascade, Idaho, April 30, 1955; admitted to bar, 1982, Idaho, U.S. District Court, District of Idaho, U.S. Court of Appeals, Ninth Circuit and U.S. Supreme Court. *Education:* University of Idaho (B.S., cum laude, 1978; LL.B., 1982). Law Clerk, Hon. Ray McNichols, U.S. District Judge, District of Idaho, 1982-1983. Trustee, 1986— and President, 2000—, Boise School Board. *Member:* Boise and American Bar Associations; Idaho State Bar. ***PRACTICE AREAS:*** Employment Law; Commercial Litigation; Business Litigation; Domestic Relations; Trial Practice. ***Email:*** rjones@idalaw.com

STEPHEN J. GLEDHILL, born Pocatello, Idaho, December 10, 1952; admitted to bar, 1979, Idaho, U.S. District Court, District of Idaho and U.S. Court of Appeals, Ninth Circuit. *Education:* College of Idaho (B.A., summa cum laude, 1975); Duke University; University of Idaho (J.D., 1979). D.A.R. Scholar. Gibson Scholar. *Member:* Boise and American Bar Associations; Idaho State Bar; Defense Research Institute. ***PRACTICE AREAS:*** Personal Injury; Business Litigation; Insurance Defense. ***Email:*** sgledhill@idalaw.com

SCOTT D. HESS, born Portland, Oregon, April 12, 1953; admitted to bar, 1978, New Mexico; 1980, U.S. Court of Appeals, Tenth Circuit; 1982, Colorado, Idaho, U.S. District Court, Districts of Idaho, Colorado and New Mexico and U.S. Court of Appeals, Ninth Circuit. *Education:* University of Oregon (B.A., with honors, 1974); University of Kansas (J.D., 1978). Senior Law Clerk, New Mexico Court of Appeals, 1978-1980. Author and Lecturer: "Environmental Law Insurance Coverage Litigation," Idaho State Bar, 1991, 1992. Staff Attorney, U.S. Court of Appeals, Tenth Circuit. Law Clerk to Chief Judge Oliver Seth, 1980-1982. *Member:* Boise, Colorado and American Bar Associations; State Bar of New Mexico; Idaho State Bar; Defense Research Institute; Idaho Association of Defense Counsel; Washington Trial Lawyers Association; American Inns of Court (Charter Member). ***PRACTICE AREAS:*** Environmental Law; Insurance Litigation; Civil Litigation; Business Litigation; Commercial Litigation. ***Email:*** shess@idalaw.com

WILLIAM A. FUHRMAN, born San Diego, California, June 12, 1954; admitted to bar, 1982, Idaho. *Education:* Boise State University (B.A., magna cum laude, 1978); University of Idaho (J.D., with highest honors, 1982). Law Clerk to Honorable J. Blaine Anderson, U.S. Court of Appeals, Ninth Circuit, 1982-1984. *Member:* Boise and American Bar Associations; Idaho State Bar; American Inns of Court; Defense Research Institute; Idaho Association of Defense Counsel. ***PRACTICE AREAS:*** Civil Litigation; Commercial Litigation; Insurance Litigation. ***Email:*** bfuhrman@idalaw.com

DERRICK J. O'NEILL, born Eugene, Oregon, May 20, 1964; admitted to bar, 1989, Idaho. *Education:* University of Idaho (B.S., 1986); University of Utah (J.D., 1989). *Member:* Boise Bar Association; Idaho State Bar. ***PRACTICE AREAS:*** Civil Litigation; Insurance Law; Mortgage Foreclosure. ***Email:*** doneill@idalaw.com

SCOTT A. TSCHIRGI, born Helena, Montana, April 25, 1958; admitted to bar, 1990, Idaho; 1996, Montana. *Education:* Montana State University (B.A., 1982); Willamette University (J.D., 1990); University of Florida (LL.M., Taxation, 1991). Author: "Aiming the Tax Code at Distressed Areas", University of Florida Law Review, Vol. 43:5 Tax Edition. ***PRACTICE AREAS:*** Business; Tax Law; Estate Planning; Mergers and Acquisitions. ***Email:*** stschirgi@idalaw.com

KIMBELL D. GOURLEY, born Walnut Creek, California, July 23, 1959; admitted to bar, 1986, Idaho. *Education:* University of Portland (B.B.A., 1981); University of Idaho (J.D., 1986). Delta Theta Phi. Executive Editor, Idaho Law Review, 1985-1986. *Member:* Idaho State Bar. ***PRACTICE AREAS:*** Financial Institutions Law; Creditors Rights; Bankruptcy; Commercial Law; Commercial Litigation; Real Estate; Construction Law; Eminent Domain. ***Email:*** kgourley@idalaw.com

DAVID M. PENNY, born Durham, North Carolina, April 9, 1960; admitted to bar, 1986, Idaho. *Education:* North Carolina State University; Boise State University (B.B.A., Economics, 1983); Gonzaga University (J.D., magna cum laude, 1986). President of Board of Directors, Family Advocate Program; Volunteer, Idaho State Bar Volunteer Lawyers Program; Rotarian, Boise Sunrise Rotary. *Member:* Boise Bar Association; Idaho State Bar. ***PRACTICE AREAS:*** Business Law; Construction Law; Landlord and Tenant Law; Personal Injury; Litigation. ***Email:*** dpenny@idalaw.com

TERRI R. YOST, born Pocatello, Idaho, July 15, 1972; admitted to bar, 1998, Idaho; U.S. District Court, District of Idaho and U.S. Court of Appeals, Ninth Circuit. *Education:* University of Southern California (B.A., 1994); University of Idaho (J.D., 1998). Phi Delta Phi. *Member:* Idaho State Bar; American Bar Association; Idaho Trial Lawyers Association; The Association of Trial Lawyers of America. ***LANGUAGES:*** Spanish. ***REPORTED CASES:*** Frost v. Agnos, et al., 152 F.3d 1124 (9th Cir. 1998); Ultrawall, Inc. v. Washington Mutual Bank, 25 P.3d 855 (Idaho, 2001); Champion Produce, Inc. v. Ruby Robinson Co., Inc., 342 F.3d 1016 (9th Cir. 2003). ***PRACTICE AREAS:*** Civil Litigation; Complex Litigation; Easements; Commercial Transactions; Title Insurance Defense; Real Estate; Business Formation; Estate Planning; General Practice.

ELLEN N. SMITH, born Boise, Idaho; admitted to bar, 1999, Idaho. *Education:* University of Idaho (B.S., 1996; J.D., 1999). Law Clerk to Honorable J.William Hart, Rupert, U.S. District Court of Idaho, 1999-2000. *Member:* Idaho State Bar; Idaho Association of Defense Counsel; Idaho Women Lawyers; American Inns of Court. ***PRACTICE AREAS:*** Employment Litigation; Civil Litigation; Criminal Defense; Insurance Defense.

VICKY J. ELKIN, born Twin Falls, Idaho, September 29, 1973; admitted to bar, 1999, Idaho. *Education:* University of Idaho (B.A., 1996; J.D., 1999). Sigma Tau Delta; Delta Theta Phi. Law Clerk, Honorable Edward J. Lodge, U.S. District Court, District of Idaho, 1999-2001. *Member:* Boise Bar Association; Idaho State Bar (Member, Young Lawyers Section); American Inns of Court. ***PRACTICE AREAS:*** Civil Litigation; Family Law. ***Email:*** velkin@idalaw.com

OF COUNSEL

MAX A. EIDEN, born Boise, Idaho, November 8, 1942; admitted to bar, 1966, Idaho. *Education:* University of Nevada and University of Idaho; University of Idaho (LL.B., 1966). Assistant Attorney General, State of Idaho, 1966-1968. *Member:* Boise and American Bar Associations; Idaho State Bar; Idaho Association of Defense Counsel; Defense Research Institute. ***PRACTICE AREAS:*** Insurance Defense; Personal Injury; Business. ***Email:*** meiden@idalaw.com

REPRESENTATIVE CLIENTS: Ada County Highway District; Bank of the West; CHUBB Group of Companies; Fireman's Fund Insurance Co.; First American Title Co.; Geico Insurance Co.; Idaho Banking Co.; Idaho Power Co.; J.R. Simplot Co.; Kemper Casualty Insurance Co.; KeyBank National Association; MetLife Auto & Home; Northwest Lineman College; Phoenix Aviation Managers, Inc.; SYSCO, Inc.; Tomlinson & Associates; Zurich North America.

KANE & TOBIASON, LLP

A Limited Liability Partnership

Established in 1995

BLUE HERON BUILDING
1087 WEST RIVER STREET
SUITE 100
BOISE, IDAHO 83702
Telephone: 208-342-4545
Fax: 208-342-2323
Mailing Address: P.O. Box 2865, Boise, ID 83701-2865

Tort Litigation, Insurance Related Issues, Administrative and Governmental Relations.

FIRM PROFILE: Kane & Tobiason are general practice attorneys with expertise in several areas of law, including Government Relations, Tort Litigation, Legislative Lobbying, Probate and Wills. Each partner has experience as Division Chief in the Attorney General's Office, with supervisory responsibilities. While serving as Prosecuting Attorney for Nez Perce County, Steven Tobiason developed a victim's restitution program, a multi-county drug task force and a child abuse protocol agreement. Michael Kane is a Certified Criminal Trial Specialist.

MICHAEL KANE, born New York, N.Y., May 19, 1952; admitted to bar, 1980, Idaho, U.S. District Court, District of Idaho. *Education:* Idaho State University (B.A., 1977); University of Idaho (J.D., 1980). Member, Idaho Law Review. Author, "State v. Guzman Point, Counterpoint," The Advocate, November 1993. Division Chief, Criminal Law Division, Idaho Attorney General's Office, 1988-1994. Chief Deputy Prosecuting Attorney, 1987-1988, Deputy Prosecuting Attorney, 1981-1987, Kootenai County. *Member:* Idaho State Bar (Member, Professional Conduct Board, 1995-2000). (Certified as Criminal Trial Specialist by the Idaho Trial Lawyers Association). ***REPORTED CASES:*** State v. Hoffman, 851 P2d 934; State v. Tolman, 828 P2d 304. ***PRACTICE AREAS:*** Personal Injury; Administrative Law; Legislative Lobbying; Governmental Law. ***Email:*** mkane@ktlaw.net

STEVEN J. TOBIASON, born Denver, Colorado, July 27, 1951; admitted to bar, 1979, Idaho, U.S. District Court, District of Idaho. *Education:* Colorado State University (B.A., 1973); University of Idaho (J.D., 1979). Phi Alpha Theta. Recipient: Victim Services Award for Public Policy Leadership, 1994; MADD Certificate of Special Appreciation. Comments Editor, Idaho Law Review, 1978-1979. Author, "Peculiar Risk: Going or Coming", Vol. 14 N.3, P. 739, Idaho Law Review. Nez Perce County Prosecuting Attorney, 1983-1990. Member: Governor's Children at Risk Task Force, 1988-1994; Idaho Commission on Children and Youth, 1988-1990. Member, 1987-1989, Chairman, 1989, Idaho Peace Officers Standards and Training Council. Division Chief, Legislative and Public Affairs, Idaho Attorney General's Office, 1991-1995. Deputy Prosecuting Attorney, 1980-1982, Prosecuting Attorney, 1983-1990, Nez Perce County. Member, 1980-1994, President, 1989, Idaho Prosecuting Attorneys Association. *Member:* Idaho State Bar (Member, Sections of: Health Law; Taxation, Probate & Trust Law); Idaho Trial Lawyers Association. ***PRACTICE AREAS:*** Personal Injury; Legislative Lobbying; Administrative Law; Probate; Wills & Trusts. ***Email:*** stobiason@ktlaw.net

ASSOCIATE

LAURA A. CHESS, born Kellogg, Idaho, June 29, 1975; admitted to bar, 2000, Idaho and U.S. District Court, District of Idaho. *Education:* Whitworth College (B.A., History and American Studies, 1997); University of Idaho College of Law (J.D., 2000). Laureate Society Whitworth College, 1995-1997. Inns of Court, 1999-2000, 2001-2002. Member, Idaho Law Review, 1998-2000. Author: "Wit and Wisdom from the Masters," The Advocate, March 2002; "Teaching Civility in Law School Point/Counterpoints," The Advocate, May 2001. *Member:* Fourth District Bar Association; Idaho State Bar (CLE Chair, Young Lawyers Section, 2001; Officer, Professional and Ethics Section, 2000-2004). ***PRACTICE AREAS:*** Social Security Disability; Governmental Defense; Administrative Law; Wills; Personal Injury. ***Email:*** lchess@ktlaw.net

REPRESENTATIVE CLIENTS: Idaho Outfitters & Guides Board; State of Idaho Department of Health and Welfare; Intermountain Health Care; State of Idaho Department of Transportation; Idaho Board of Professional Engineers and Land Surveyors; Idaho Sheriff's Association; Idaho Attorney General's Office; Idaho Association of Health Plans; Idaho Counties' Risk Management Program (ICRMP); Idaho Thoroughbred Association; Idaho Board of Veterinary Medicine; Idaho Board of Dentistry; Idaho Health Underwriters; Aladdin Bail Bonds.

LOJEK LAW OFFICES

CHARTERED

Established in 1984

1199 WEST MAIN STREET
P.O. BOX 1712
BOISE, IDAHO 83701
Telephone: 208-343-7733
Facsimile: 208-389-1294
Email: lojeklaw@aol.com

General and Civil Trial Practice, Aviation, Business, Commercial, Corporate, Employment, Healthcare, Insurance, Medical, Products Liability and Transportation.

(This Listing Continued)

LOJEK LAW OFFICES, CHARTERED, Boise—Continued

DONALD W. LOJEK, born Buffalo, New York, November 6, 1940; admitted to bar, 1972, Idaho and Colorado; 1975, U.S. Court of Appeals, Ninth Circuit; 1987, U.S. Supreme Court; 1989, Utah; 1991 U.S. Court of Appeals, Tenth Circuit. *Education:* Canisius College (B.A., 1962); University of North Carolina (M.A., 1969); University of Denver (J.D., 1971). Adjunct Professor: Business Law and Aviation Law, Boise State University, 1978—; Law of Higher Education, University of Idaho, 1995. Adjunct Professor of Law, University of Idaho College of Law. Member and Pilot: AOPA; Legal Services Panel, 1987—. Member: Panel of Arbitrators, American Arbitration Association; Commercial Panel, 1998—; Employment Panel, 1999—. Trustee, Boise Samaritan Village, 1988—. Board Member, BSU Friends of Nursing, 1994—.*Member:* Idaho State Bar (Member, 1974-1977 and Chairman, 1975, Ethics Committee; Bar Examiner, 1975, 1983, 1987, 1989-1993); Utah State Bar; Colorado Bar Association; Idaho Trial Lawyers Association; National Health Lawyers Association; Lawyer-Pilots Bar Association. ***LANGUAGES:*** Spanish. ***PRACTICE AREAS:*** Aviation Law; Appellate Practice; Employment Law; Health and Hospital Law; University Law. ***Email:*** lojeklaw@aol.com

REPRESENTATIVE CLIENTS: Ag-Air Turbines, Inc.; AIA Air, Inc.; Arnold Aviation, Inc.; Aviation Office of America; Aviation Specialties, Inc.; Boise Samaritan Village; Casade Reservoir Association; Chartham Management, Inc.; CSHQA Architects; Design Professionals Insurance Cos.; Design West Architects, P.A.; Idaho Association of Nurse Anesthetists; Idaho State Board of Education; Idaho State University; Nie Consulting, LLC; Security Insurance Company of Hartford; Shore and Shore Aviation, Inc.; Western Air Express; Western Health Care Corp.; West One Aircraft Sales and Services, Inc.; Turbo Air, Inc.; Ranchero Tractors, LLC.; Thomas Helicopters, Inc.; Ponderosa Flying Club, Inc; Silverhawk Aviation, LLC; Montego Bay, Inc.; Hammon Plating, Inc; Parkview Care and Rehabilitation Center, Inc.
REFERENCES: Idaho Independent Bank; U.S. Bank.

LYNCH & ASSOCIATES, P.L.L.C.

1412 WEST IDAHO STREET, SUITE 200
P.O. BOX 739
BOISE, IDAHO 83701
Telephone: 208-331-5088
Fax: 208-331-0088
Email: lynchlaw@qwest.net
URL: http://www.lynch-lawfirm.com

General Civil Trial and Appellate Practice including Negligence, Product Liability and Professional Liability Litigation in the areas of Insurance Coverage, Insurance Defense, Commercial Litigation and Collections, Construction, Employment and Managed Health Care, General Liability Defense, Trusts and Estates, Wills, Probate, Self Insured Law.

FIRM PROFILE: James B. Lynch practiced in the firm of Imhoff and Lynch from 1970 until 1995 with the practice concentrated primarily during those years in insurance defense and insurance coverage cases. In 1995 the firm of Lynch & Associates was formed in order to obtain flexibility in directly representing parties involved in litigation including self-insureds, business enterprises and individuals. The firm members are involved in developing a diversified practice in their areas of interest while continuing to place emphasis on litigation, insurance coverage and health care disputes.

JAMES B. LYNCH, born Denver, Colorado, January 19, 1932; admitted to bar, 1957, Idaho, U.S. Court of Appeals, Ninth Circuit and U.S. Supreme Court. *Education:* Boise Junior College (A.A., 1952); University of Idaho (B.A., 1954; LL.B., 1956). Phi Alpha Delta. Judge Advocate, USAF, 1958-1960. *Member:* Fourth Judicial District (President, 1974-1975) and American (Member, Litigation and Health Sections) Bar Associations; Idaho State Bar (Executive Secretary, 1963-1966; Chairman, State Bar Court Reform Committee, 1968-1970); Idaho Association of Defense Counsel. [Judge Advocate, USAF, 1958-1960]. ***PRACTICE AREAS:*** Negligence; Products Liability; Aviation Law; Insurance Coverage; Health Care; General Practice; Self Insured Law. ***Email:*** jblynch@qwest.net

---

KATHERINE M. LYNCH, born Boise, Idaho, June 9, 1965; admitted to bar, 1995, Idaho; 1996, Oregon. *Education:* University of Idaho (B.S., 1990, J.D., 1995). Recipient, American Jurisprudence Awards: Torts; Administrative Law, 1993. *Member:* Idaho (Member, Sections on: Young Lawyers; Litigation; Tax Law; Probate; Trust Law) State Bar; Oregon State Bar; American Bar Association. ***PRACTICE AREAS:*** Insurance Coverage; Health Care; Trusts and Estates; Wills; Probate; Products Liability; Estate Planning. ***Email:*** kmlynch@qwest.net

REPRESENTATIVE CLIENTS: Admiralty Insurance Co.; AIG American International Companies; Great America Casualty Co.; Professional Risk Management Services, inc.; Western Litigation Specialists, Inc.; Western World Insurance Company; Alfa Laval Agri, Inc.; Blue Cross of Idaho; Carl Warren & Co.; Coleman Co.
REFERENCE: U.S. Bank-Broadway.

MANWEILER, MANWEILER, BREEN & BALL, PLLC

Established in 1998
290 BOBWHITE COURT, SUITE 300
P.O. BOX 937
BOISE, IDAHO 83701-0937
Telephone: 208-424-9100
Facsimile: 208-424-3100
Email: markm@mmbb-law.com
URL: http://www.mmbb-law.com

General Trial and Appellate Practice before State and Federal Courts. Business Law, Criminal Law, Family Law, Insurance, Personal Injury and Workers Compensation.

(This Listing Continued)

MARK H. MANWEILER, born Moscow, Idaho, February 22, 1958; admitted to bar, 1983, Idaho, U.S. District Court, District of Idaho and U.S. Court of Appeals, Ninth Circuit. *Education:* University of Colorado (B.A., with distinction, 1980); University of Idaho (J.D., 1983). Phi Beta Kappa. Barrister, American Inn of Court, No. 130, 1991-1994. Listed, Outstanding Lawyers of America. *Member:* Idaho State Bar; Idaho Trial Lawyers Association (Governmental Relations Chairman, 1989-1990; Judicial Chairman, 1992-1993); National Association of Criminal Defense Lawyers; Idaho Association of Criminal Defense Lawyers. ***REPORTED CASES:*** Sterling v. Bloom, 111 Idaho 211, 723 P.2d 755 (1986). ***PRACTICE AREAS:*** Litigation; Criminal Law; Personal Injury; Business Law; Family Law. ***Email:*** markm@mmbb-law.com

DAVID D. MANWEILER, born Boise, Idaho, May 23, 1961; admitted to bar, 1986, Idaho and U.S. District Court, District of Idaho, U.S. Court of Appeals, Ninth Circuit; U.S. Army Court of Military Review; U.S. Court of Military Appeals and U.S. Supreme Court. *Education:* University of Colorado (B.A., Pol.S., cum laude, 1983); University of Idaho College of Law (J.D., 1986). Barrister, American Inn of Court, No. 130. Member, Moot Court Board; Order of the Barristers. Member: Idaho Juvenile Rules Committee; Children at Risk Evaluation Services (CARES) Advisory Board; Idaho Volunteer Lawyers Program Advisory Board. *Member:* Idaho State Bar; Idaho Trial Lawyers Association (President, 2000-2001); Idaho Association of Criminal Defense Lawyers. [Major (ret.), JAGC, Idaho Army National Guard]. ***PRACTICE AREAS:*** General Trial and Appellate Litigation; Criminal Law; Personal Injury; Juvenile Law. ***Email:*** davidm@mmbb-law.com

M. SEAN BREEN, born Austin, Texas, March 23, 1963; admitted to bar, 1993, Idaho, U.S. District Court, District of Idaho and U.S. Court of Appeals, Ninth Circuit. *Education:* Idaho State University (B.A., with honors, 1986); University of Idaho (J.D., 1992). Barrister, American Inns of Court. *Member:* Idaho State Bar (Member, Sections on: Family Law; Professional Ethics); Idaho Trial Lawyers Association. [Major, JAGC, U.S. Army (retired)]. ***PRACTICE AREAS:*** Civil Litigation; Family Law; Workers Compensation. ***Email:*** msean@mmbb-law.com

JAMES K. BALL, born Sacramento, California, March 2, 1970; admitted to bar, 1997, Idaho; U.S. District Court, District of Idaho; U.S. Court of Appeals, Ninth Circuit. *Education:* Boise State University (B.S., 1993); University of Idaho (J.D., 1996). Private Practice, James K. Ball, P.A., 2000-2002. Deputy Ada County Prosecuting Attorney, 1996-2000. Lobbyist, Idaho Prosecuting Attorney's Association, 1998-2000. *Member:* Fourth District Bar Association; Idaho State Bar; American Inn of Court, No. 130 (Barrister); Idaho Volunteer Lawyers; Idaho Association of Criminal Defense Lawyers; Idaho Trial Lawyers Association. ***REPORTED CASES:*** State v. Lamay, —Idaho—, 103 P.3d 448 (Idaho 2004); Reyes v. Craven, 111 Fed. App., 46 2d (9th Cir. 2004). ***PRACTICE AREAS:*** Criminal Law; Juvenile Law; Personal Injury; Wills; Family Law. ***Email:*** jkball@mmbb-law.com

OF COUNSEL

HOWARD I. MANWEILER (1931-2001)

REPRESENTATIVE CLIENTS: Godfather's Pizza Inc.; Toothman-Orton Engineering Co.; Riedesel Engineering, LLC; All Season's Mental Health, Inc.

MARTENS LAW OFFICE, PLLC

EIGHTH STREET MARKETPLACE
404 S. 8TH STREET, SUITE 300
BOISE, IDAHO 83702
Telephone: 208-322-9488
Fax: 208-322-3360
Email: info@martenslawoffice.com
URL: http://www.martenslawoffices.com

Bankruptcy, Personal Bankruptcy, Commercial Bankruptcy, Criminal Law, DUI, DWI, Drug Crimes, White Collar Crimes, Felonies, Fraud and Deceit, Juvenile Law, Misdemeanors, Family Law, Divorce, Custody and Visitation, Adoption, Alimony, Spousal Support, Children's Rights, Guardianship, Conservatorship, Wills, Trusts, Estate, Probate.

JARED B. MARTENS, born Twin Falls, Idaho, August 13, 1974; admitted to bar, 2001, Idaho, U.S. District Court, District of Idaho and U.S. Court of Appeals, 9th Circuit; 2002, Colorado. *Education:* Boise State University (B.A., Political Science, 1997); University of Denver (J.D., 2001). Member, Ducks Unlimited, 2002-2004; American Kennel Club, 2002-2004. *Member:* Colorado State (Member: Criminal Defense Division; Young Lawyers Division) and American Bar Associations; Idaho State Bar; Boise State Alumni Association; Boise State Athletic Association; Boise Metro Chamber of Commerce. ***PRACTICE AREAS:*** Bankruptcy; Criminal Defense; Family Law. ***Email:*** jmartens@northwest-attorneys.com

MATTHEWS LAW OFFICES

Established in 1965
413 WEST JEFFERSON, SUITE 4
P.O. BOX 1988
BOISE, IDAHO 83701
Telephone: 208-336-1433
Fax: 208-336-9133
Email: matlaw@aol.com
URL: http://www.lawyers.com/matthewslawoffices

General Civil and Criminal Trial Practice. Personal Injury Litigation and Appeals. Federal and State.

ELLISON M. MATTHEWS, born Boise, Idaho, May 26, 1938; admitted to bar, 1965, Idaho. *Education:* Boise Junior College (A.A., 1961); University of Idaho (B.S., 1963); University of Idaho College of Law (LL.B., 1965). Ada County Prosecuting Attorney, 1967-1970. *Member:* Boise and American Bar Associations; Idaho State Bar; The Association of Trial Lawyers of America (Member, Board of Governors, 1978-1979); Idaho Trial Lawyers Association (President, 1977-1978); Idaho Prosecuting Attorney's Association

(This Listing Continued)

(President, 1969-1970); Idaho Attorneys for Criminal Justice (Board Member); National Association of Criminal Defense Lawyers. (Certified as Criminal Trial Specialist by the Idaho Trial Lawyers Association). ***PRACTICE AREAS:*** Drug Crimes; Driving While Intoxicated; Sexual Assault; Parole and Probation Violations; Automobile Accidents; Slip and Fall; Dog Bites.

REFERENCE: Wells Fargo Bank, N.A.

MAUK & BURGOYNE

515 SOUTH 6TH STREET
P.O. BOX 1743
BOISE, IDAHO 83701-1743
Telephone: 208-345-2654
Facsimile: 208-345-3319
Email: maukburgoyne@rmci.net
URL: http://www.lawyers.com/m&b-law

Litigation, Labor and Employment Law, Personal Injury, Commercial Law, Insurance, Health Care, Government Law, Administrative Law.

MEMBERS OF FIRM

WILLIAM L. MAUK, born Pocatello, Idaho, March 15, 1947; admitted to bar, 1975, Idaho; 1979, U.S. Court of Appeals, Ninth Circuit. *Education:* University of Southern California (B.A., 1969); Columbia University (M.A., 1971); Antioch School of Law (J.D., 1975). Member: Order of the Palm; Skull and Dagger. Law Clerk to Justice Allen G. Shepard, Idaho Supreme Court, 1975-1976. Author: "Wrongful Discharge: The Erosion of 100 Years of Privilege," Idaho Law Review, Vol. 21, Summer, 1985. General Counsel, Shoshone-Paiute Tribes, 1981-1989. Manager, Industrial Special Indemnity Fund, State of Idaho, 1987-1989. Member, Governor's Advisory Committee on Worker's Compensation, 1987-1995. Chair, Idaho Democratic Party, 1993-1997. Director, Litigation Support, Trial Lawyers Care, 2002. Distinguished Service Award, Association of Trial Lawyers of America, 2002. *Member:* Idaho State Bar; Western Trial Lawyers Association (Member, Board of Directors, 1988-1992); The Association of Trial Lawyers of America (State Delegate, 1987-1989; Membership Committee, 1987-1988; Chairman, Employment Rights Section, 1989-1991; Board of Governors, 1996—); National College of Advocacy (Co-Chairman, 2001-2003; Faculty, 1985—); Idaho Trial Lawyers Association (Member, Board of Directors, 1985—; President, 1986-1987). ***LANGUAGES:*** Spanish. ***PRACTICE AREAS:*** Employment Law; Personal Injury; Commercial Litigation; Homicide Defense. ***Email:*** maukburgoyne@rmci.net

GRANT T. BURGOYNE, born Ketchikan, Alaska, August 9, 1953; admitted to bar, 1988, Idaho; 1991, U.S. Court of Appeals, Ninth Circuit. *Education:* University of Idaho (B.A., 1975); University of Kansas (J.D., 1988). Co-author: "Idaho Employment Policies Handbook," 1998, Revised 2001. Author, articles: "The Temporary Employee Industry," 1997; "The Current Status of At-Will Employment in Idaho," 1999; "Covenants Not to Compete in Idaho," 2001; "The ADA and Disability Income Claims," 2000. Author, legislation: Senate Bill 1084 (1997) eliminating multiple worker's compensation premiums for staffing service employees; Senate Bill 1036 (1998) defining unemployment insurance benefits for staffing service employees; Senate State Bill 1083 (1999) providing confidentiality and limited liability for employee assistance programs. Adjunct Professor of Human Resource Law, Boise State University. Chair, Ada County Democratic Party, 1991-1994. Chair, Idaho Democratic Party Platform Committee, 1992. Member, Democratic National Committee, July 2004—. *Member:* Idaho State Bar (Member, Sections on: Business and Corporations; Employment and Labor; Health Law); The Association of Trial Lawyers of America; Idaho Trial Lawyers Association; Idaho Association of Commerce and Industry; The Human Resources Association of the Treasure Valley (Member, Board of Directors, 1998-2000); The Idaho State Council for Human Resource Management (Legislative Affairs Representative, 2001). ***PRACTICE AREAS:*** Litigation; Labor and Employment; Commercial Law; Insurance; Health Care; Personal Injury; Government; Administrative Law. ***Email:*** gtb@rmci.net

W. CRAIG JAMES, born Buffalo, New York, October 8, 1944; admitted to bar, 1976, Idaho; 1987, U.S. Court of Appeals, Ninth Circuit; 1989, U.S. Court of Appeals, Federal Circuit. *Education:* Colby College (B.A., 1966); Gonzaga University (J.D., 1976). *Member:* Idaho State Bar; Idaho Trial Lawyers Association. ***PRACTICE AREAS:*** Federal Personnel Practice; Employment Law; Administrative Law. ***Email:*** maukburgoyne@rmci.net

WILLIAM A. McCURDY

702 W. IDAHO, SUITE 1000
BOISE, IDAHO 83702-8911
Telephone: 208-947-7250
Fax: 208-947-5910
Email: wam@mccurdylaw.com

Litigation.

WILLIAM A. McCURDY, born Boise, Idaho, April 25, 1949; admitted to bar, 1974, Idaho, U.S. District Court, District of Idaho and U.S. Court of Appeals, Ninth Circuit. *Education:* University of Idaho (B.A., 1971; J.D., 1974). Law Clerk, Idaho Supreme Court, 1974-1975. Deputy Prosecuting Attorney, Ada County, Idaho, 1975-1976. Idaho Supreme Court Civil Rules Advisory Committee, 1985-1994. Special Deputy Attorney General, State of Idaho. President, American Inn of Court No. 130, 1994. *Member:* Boise and American (Member, Section on Tort and Insurance Practice) Bar Associations; Idaho State Bar (Commissioner, 1987-1990; President, 1990); Defense Research Institute; Idaho Association of Defense Counsel; National Association of Bar Presidents. ***PRACTICE AREAS:*** Litigation.

McDEVITT & MILLER, LLP

Established in 1997
420 WEST BANNOCK STREET
P.O. BOX 2564-83701
BOISE, IDAHO 83702
Telephone: 208-343-7500
Telecopy: 208-336-6912
Email: chas@mcdevitt-miller.com
Email: joe@mcdevitt-miller.com
URL: http://www.mcdevitt-millerlaw.com

Business Law, Public Utility Law, Administrative Law, Litigation, Water Law, Family Law, Franchising.

DEAN J. MILLER, born Caldwell, Idaho, October 26, 1948; admitted to bar, 1976, Idaho and U.S. Court of Appeals, Ninth Circuit. *Education:* University of Santa Clara (B.A., 1971); University of Idaho (J.D., cum laude, 1976). Member: Gigray, Miller, Downen & Weston, Caldwell, Idaho, 1976-1986; Idaho Public Utilities Commission, 1986-1994, President, 1988-1992. Chairman, Communications Committee, National Association of Regulatory Utility Commissioners, 1990-1992. ***PRACTICE AREAS:*** Utility Litigation; Administrative Law; Business Law. ***Email:*** joe@mcdevitt-miller.com

CHAS. F. McDEVITT, born Pocatello, Idaho, January 5, 1932; admitted to bar, 1956, Idaho. *Education:* Idaho State University; University of Idaho (J.D., 1956). Member: Richards, Haga & Eberle, 1956-1962; Idaho State Legislature, 1963-1966. Vice President, Secretary and General Counsel, Boise Cascade Corporation, 1962-1968; Beck Industries; The Singer Co., 1968-1976. Ada County Public Defender, 1976-1978. Founding Partner, Givens, McDevitt, Pursley & Webb (now known as Givens & Pursley), 1978-1989. Justice Idaho Supreme Court, 1989-1993. Chief Justice Idaho Supreme Court, 1993-1997. Idaho Member, Ninth Circuit Grand Jury Reform Committee, 1978-1979. Member, Governor's Blue Ribbon Tax Committee. Director YMCA. Listed in Best Lawyers in America, 1989-1990. Member, Legislative Compensation Select Committee. Director, Girl Scouts Silver Sage Council. *Member:* Idaho State Bar; American Inns of Court (President). ***PRACTICE AREAS:*** Corporate Law; Litigation; Water Law. ***Email:*** chas@mcdevitt-miller.com

JOHN MEIENHOFER

300 WEST MYRTLE STREET, SUITE 200
BOISE, IDAHO 83702
Telephone: 208-343-3600
Fax: 208-344-7100
Email: meienhofer@earthlink.net
URL: http://www.meienhofer.com

Federal and State Drugs and Narcotics, Land Use, Criminal Defense, DUI, Theft, White Collar Crime, Embezzlement, Civil Forfeiture, Personal Injury, Divorce, Child Custody, Domestic Violence Protection Orders, Social Security Disability, Corporate Law, Wills.

JOHN MEIENHOFER, born Aachen, Germany, September 5, 1964; admitted to bar, 1992, Idaho; 1994, Oregon. *Education:* Bowdoin College (B.A., cum laude, 1986); University of Oregon (J.D., 1992). Deputy Prosecutor: Jerome County, ID, 1994-1996; Blaine County, ID, 1996-1997. *Member:* Idaho State Bar; Oregon State Bar; The Idaho Association of Criminal Defense Lawyers. ***LANGUAGES:*** German. ***PRACTICE AREAS:*** Criminal Defense; Domestic Relations; Personal Injury; Corporate Law; Wills.

MEULEMAN MOLLERUP LLP

Established in 1981
UNIVERSITY PLAZA
960 BROADWAY AVENUE, SUITE 500
BOISE, IDAHO 83706
Telephone: 208-342-6066
Fax: 208-336-9712
Email: firm@lawidaho.com
URL: http://www.lawidaho.com

Construction Law, Real Estate Law, Business Law.

FIRM PROFILE: Since its inception in 1981, Meuleman Mollerup LLP has provided legal services to clients in the real estate, business, and construction communities. Our knowledge and experience in these areas avoids the cost and time of a "learning curve" and allows our attorneys to provide effective legal advice from a client's first contact through resolution. Meuleman Mollerup attorneys are committed to becoming fully acquainted with each client's business practices and the industry in which it operates, leading to innovative, cost-effective and results-oriented legal counsel. Our focused approach to business, real estate, and construction matters enables our clients to proper in today's competitive business environment.

MEMBERS OF FIRM

WAYNE V MEULEMAN, born Rupert, Idaho, February 24, 1948; admitted to bar, 1972, Idaho; 1973, U.S. Court of Appeals, Ninth Circuit; 1986, U.S. Claims Court. *Education:* University of Idaho (B.S., cum laude, 1970; J.D., 1972). Phi Kappa Phi. Member, Editorial Board, Idaho Law Review, 1971-1972. Deputy Attorney General, 1972-1975, Idaho. Executive Director, Idaho State Building Authority. Listed in "The Best Lawyers in America," Construction Law. Member and Previous Director, Idaho Association of General Contractors. Member: Education Committee, Idaho Association of Commerce and Industry; Idaho Board of Education; Boise Metro Chamber of Commerce. Past Chairman, Idaho Legislature's Statewide Public School Facilities Needs Assessment Committee. *Member:*

(This Listing Continued)

MEULEMAN MOLLERUP LLP, Boise—Continued

Idaho State Bar. ***SPECIAL AGENCIES:*** Idaho State Building Authority. ***PRACTICE AREAS:*** Business Law; Construction Law; Litigation. ***Email:*** meuleman@lawidaho.com

KIMBAL L. GOWLAND, born Twin Falls, Idaho, August 21, 1959; admitted to bar, 1984, Idaho. *Education:* University of Idaho (B.S., cum laude, 1981; J.D., 1984). Phi Kappa Phi. Certified Public Accountant, Idaho, 1985. Touche Ross & Co., 1984-1987. Member: Tax Policy Committee, Idaho Association of Commerce and Industry; Board of Directors, Construction Financial Management Association. *Member:* Idaho State Bar; Idaho Society of Certified Public Accountants; American Institute of Certified Public Accountants. ***PRACTICE AREAS:*** Real Estate Law; Business Law. ***Email:*** gowland@lawidaho.com

RICHARD W. MOLLERUP, born Caldwell, Idaho, August 30, 1948; admitted to bar, 1993, Idaho. *Education:* Idaho State University; Boise State University (B.B.A., 1989); University of Idaho (J.D., magna cum laude, 1993). Listed in Chambers USA, America's Leading Lawyers for Business, Real Estate, 2005. Editor, University of Idaho Law Review, 1993. Author: "Improvements to Real Property During Marriage," 28 Idaho L. Rev. 1021 (1992); Idaho Chapter, "State by State Guide to Real Estate Leases," updated 2005. Co-Author: with Baxter Dunaway, Idaho Sections, "The Law of Distressed Real Estate," 1993. Chairman, Legislative Committee, Idaho Land Title Association. Graduate, "Leadership Boise" Program, Boise Metro Chamber of Commerce. Founding Member, City Club of Boise. Co-Chair, March of Dimes Real Estate Award Event, 2005. ***PRACTICE AREAS:*** Real Estate; Business Law. ***Email:*** mollerup@lawidaho.com

GEOFFREY J. McCONNELL, born Walnut Creek, California, January 3, 1959; admitted to bar, 1986, California; 1993, Idaho; 2000, Utah. *Education:* Bucknell University (B.A., 1983); McGeorge School of Law (J.D., 1986). Contributing Author: "Fifty State Public Construction Contracting," Wiley Law Publications, 1996; "The Design/Build Process," ABA Publications, 1997; "The Design/Build Deskbook," ABA Publications, 2000. Adjunct Professor, University of Idaho, College of Law. Lecturer: Associated General Contractors of America; National Electrical Contractors Association; Sheet Metal and Air Conditioning Contractors' National Association; ASHRAE; National Association of Women in Construction. Member, Construction Management Association of America. *Member:* State Bar of California; Idaho State Bar; Utah State Bar; American Bar Association (Member, Forum Committee on the Construction Industry, Public Contract Law Section). ***PRACTICE AREAS:*** Construction Law; Government Contracts; Business Law. ***Email:*** mcconnell@lawidaho.com

JEFF R. SYKES, born Billings, Montana, November 9, 1967; admitted to bar, 1994, California and Idaho; 1997, U.S. Court of Appeals, Ninth Circuit. *Education:* California State University, Chico (B.A., 1990); Gonzaga University (J.D., summa cum laude, 1993). Order of Barristers. Member, Jessup Cup International Moot Court Team, 1991-1993. Recipient, Idaho Business Review's "2005 Accomplished Under 40" Award. Update Author, Standards of Appellate Review in State and Federal Court, Idaho Appellate Handbook, 1996. Judicial Clerk to Hon. Justice Linda Copple Trout, Idaho Supreme Court, 1993-1994. Member: Idaho Association of Commerce and Industry; Judiciary Committee, Idaho Land Title Association; Board of Directors, Youth Government Program, Boise Family YMCA. *Member:* State Bar of California; Idaho State Bar; American Bar Association. ***REPORTED CASES:*** Cornerstone Builders v. McReynolds, 136 Idaho 843, 41 P.3d 271 (Ct.App. 2001); Meikle v. Watson, 138 Idaho 680, 69 P.3d 100 (2003). ***PRACTICE AREAS:*** Real Estate Litigation; Construction Litigation; Business Litigation. ***Email:*** sykes@lawidaho.com

ARNOLD L. WAGNER, born Bremerton, Washington, January 5, 1972; admitted to bar, 1997, Idaho. *Education:* Western Washington University (B.A., cum laude, 1994); University of Washington (J.D., 1997). Phi Alpha Delta. Recipient, Idaho Business Review's "2005 Accomplished Under 40" Award. Member, Board of Directors and Co-Chair, Real Estate Awards Event, March of Dimes. Member: Associates Committee, Idaho Association of General Contractors; Local Government Committee, Boise Metro Chamber of Commerce. Frequent Author and Speaker on Construction and Litigation Matters. *Member:* Idaho State Bar; American Bar Association. ***PRACTICE AREAS:*** Construction Litigation; Real Estate Litigation; Business Litigation. ***Email:*** wagner@lawidaho.com

ASSOCIATES

PAUL A. BOICE, born Independence, Missouri, November 7, 1970; admitted to bar, 2001, Idaho. *Education:* University of Utah (B.S., cum laude, 1996); University of Idaho (J.D., cum laude, 2001). Lead Articles Editor, Idaho Law Review, 2000-2001. Judicial Clerk to the Hon. Justice Cathy R. Silak, Idaho Supreme Court, 1999. Member, Boise Metro Chamber of Commerce. *Member:* Idaho State Bar; American Bar Association. [Judge Advocate, Idaho Army National Guard, 2002—; Trial Counsel, Office of the Staff Judge Advocate, U.S. Army's 116th Brigade Combat Team, Kirkuk, Iraq]. ***PRACTICE AREAS:*** Construction Law; Real Estate; Estate Planning; Probate. ***Email:*** boice@lawidaho.com

RICHARD L. STACEY, JR., born Rexburg, Idaho, November 21, 1970; admitted to bar, 2003, Idaho. *Education:* Boise State University (B.A., magna cum laude, 2000); University of Utah College of Law (J.D., 2003). Phi Kappa Phi. Golden Key National Honor Society. Member: Associated General Contractors (2003—); Board of Directors, Idaho Young Constructors Forum (2003—). Judicial Clerk to the Hon. Judge Harvey Sweitzer, Office of Hearings and Appeals, United States Department of the Interior. *Member:* Idaho State Bar; American Bar Association. ***PRACTICE AREAS:*** Construction Law; Litigation; Real Estate; Business Law; Environmental Law; Natural Resources. ***Email:*** stacey@lawidaho.com

JONATHAN R. BAUER, born Stamford, Connecticut, June 2, 1972; admitted to bar, 2002, Massachusetts; 2004, Idaho. *Education:* Washington University (B.A., 1994); Benjamin N. Cardozo School of Law, Yeshiva University (J.D., cum laude, 2001). Alexander Fellow, 2000. Member, Editorial Board, Cardozo Law Review, 1999-2001. Member, Kickstand. Graduate, "Leadership Boise" Program, Boise Metro Chamber of Commerce. *Member:* Massachusetts and American Bar Associations; Idaho State Bar; Treasure Valley Estate Planning Council. ***SPECIAL AGENCIES:*** Idaho State Building Authority. ***PRACTICE AREAS:*** Business Law; Real Estate; Corporate Law; Trusts and Estates. ***Email:*** jbauer@lawidaho.com

(This Listing Continued)

MICHAEL E. BALDNER, born Minot, North Dakota, August 29, 1968; admitted to bar, 1994, Idaho. *Education:* Boise State University (B.A., magna cum laude, 1991); University of Idaho School of Law (J.D., summa cum laude, 1994). Member, Boise State University Alumni Association. *Member:* Idaho State Bar; American Bar Association. [Sgt., U.S. Army National Guard, 1986-1992]. ***PRACTICE AREAS:*** Real Estate Development; Real Estate Transactions; Real Estate Litigation. ***Email:*** baldner@lawidaho.com

LEGAL SUPPORT PERSONNEL

VIVIAN OTERO-EPLEY, (Marketing & Client Services Manager)

REPRESENTATIVE CLIENTS: Albertson's, Inc.; Alliance Title & Escrow Corporation; Boise Centre on the Grove; Bronco Motors, Inc.; Chicago Title Insurance Co.; CM Company, Inc.; Contractors Northwest, Inc.; F&C Corporation; Earthtech, Inc.; Hawkins-Smith Developers; H-K Contractors, Inc.; Idaho Power Company; Interior Systems, Inc.; Kaiser Engineers & Constructors, Inc.; McAlvain Construction, Inc.; Micron Technology, Inc.; Stewart Title Guaranty Company; Ticor Title Insurance Co.; Western Construction, Inc.

MOFFATT THOMAS BARRETT ROCK & FIELDS

CHARTERED

101 SOUTH CAPITOL BOULEVARD, 10TH FLOOR
P.O. BOX 829
BOISE, IDAHO 83701
Telephone: 208-345-2000
FAX: 208-385-5384
URL: http://www.moffatt.com

Idaho Falls, Idaho Office: 420 Memorial Drive, P.O. Box 51505, 83405. Telephone: 208-522-6700. Fax: 208-522-5111.

Pocatello, Idaho Office: 412 West Center, Suite 2000, P.O. Box 817, 83204. Telephone: 208-233-2001. Fax: 208-232-0150.

Twin Falls, Idaho Office: 621 N. College Road, Suite 103, P.O. Box 5483, 83303-5483. Telephone 208-734-7500. Fax: 208-734-7508.

General Civil, Trial and Appellate Practice. Administrative Law, Alternative Dispute Resolution, Antitrust and Trade Regulation, Aviation, Bankruptcy, Banks and Banking, Business Law, Commercial Real Estate, Construction Law, Contracts, Corporate Law, Debtor and Creditor, Disabilities, Employee Benefits, Environmental Law, Finance, Government Relations, Health Care, Hospital Law, Insurance Defense, Intellectual Property, Labor and Employment Law, Leases and Leasing, Litigation, Medical Malpractice, Mergers, Acquisitions and Divestitures, Mortgages, Nonprofit and Charitable Organizations, Partnership Law, Probate, Products Liability, Professional Liability, Public Utility Law, Real Estate, Regulatory Law, Securities, Taxation, Torts, Trusts and Estates, Water Law, Worker's Compensation.

FIRM PROFILE: At Moffatt Thomas we work in partnership with our clients to achieve practical solutions to legal issues. The diverse nature of our practice, coupled with our talented and experienced attorneys and staff, enables the firm to provide comprehensive advice in various fields of practice. We pride ourselves on our ability to balance both the difficult and everyday needs of each client. With four offices located on the Snake River Plain, "We Know Idaho".

WILLIS C. MOFFATT (1907-1980)

JOHN W. BARRETT, born Ellendale, North Dakota, August 23, 1931; admitted to bar, 1959, Idaho; 1985, U.S. Supreme Court. *Education:* Minot State University, Eastern New Mexico University (Service Extension-USAF); and University of Idaho (B.S., 1956; LL.B., 1959). ***PRACTICE AREAS:*** Workers Compensation; Insurance Law; Insurance Coverage.

R. B. ROCK, born Rexburg, Idaho, June 27, 1938; admitted to bar, 1965, Idaho; 1977, U.S. Tax Court; 1978, U.S. Supreme Court; 1981, U.S. Court of Appeals, Ninth Circuit. *Education:* Ricks College (B.A., 1962); University of Idaho (LL.B., 1965). ***PRACTICE AREAS:*** High Technology Law; Environmental Liability Law; Antitrust Law; Products Liability Law; Securities Litigation. ***Email:*** rbr@moffatt.com

RICHARD C. FIELDS, born Waterloo, Iowa, January 10, 1931; admitted to bar, 1964, Colorado; 1965, U.S. Court of Appeals, Tenth Circuit; 1966, Idaho; 1970, U.S. Court of Appeals, Ninth Circuit. *Education:* Harvard University (A.B., 1952); University of Denver (J.D., 1964). Fellow, American College of Trial Lawyers. ***PRACTICE AREAS:*** Labor and Employment Law; Health Care and Hospital Law; Alternative Dispute Resolution. ***Email:*** rcf@moffatt.com

JOHN S. SIMKO, born Chicago, Illinois, February 3, 1939; admitted to bar, 1966, Idaho. *Education:* University of Idaho (B.A., 1961; J.D., 1966). Senior Vice President and General Counsel, 1984-1991, Chairman and Chief Executive Officer, Sunshine Mining and Refining Company, 1991-2001. *Member:* Silver Institute (President, 1996-1998); Association of Publicly Traded Companies (Director, 1998-2001); Idaho Research Foundation (President, 1999—). ***PRACTICE AREAS:*** Corporate Law; Finance; Public Offerings; Private Placements. ***Email:*** jss@moffatt.com

JOHN C. WARD, born Boise, Idaho, December 3, 1941; admitted to bar, 1967, Idaho; 1992, U.S. Court of Appeals, Ninth Circuit. *Education:* Boise Junior College; Idaho State University (B.A., 1964); University of Idaho (J.D., 1967). ***PRACTICE AREAS:*** Commercial Law; Banks and Banking; Business Law; Mergers, Acquisitions and Divestitures. ***Email:*** jcw@moffatt.com

LARRY C. HUNTER, born Ogden, Utah, October 17, 1946; admitted to bar, 1976, Idaho; 1988, U.S. Court of Appeals, Ninth Circuit. *Education:* Harvard College (A.B., cum laude, 1968); Brigham Young University; Northwestern University (J.D., 1976). ***PRACTICE AREAS:*** General Litigation; Commercial Litigation; Products Liability; Agricultural Law; Environmental Law; Arbitration and Mediation. ***Email:*** lch@moffatt.com

RANDALL A. PETERMAN, born Walla Walla, Washington, February 20, 1951; admitted to bar, 1977, Idaho. *Education:* Northwest Nazarene University (B.A., summa cum laude, 1973); University of Washington (J.D., 1976). Fellow, American College of Bankruptcy. ***PRACTICE AREAS:*** Bankruptcy Law; Banking Law; Commercial Litigation. ***Email:*** rap@moffatt.com

(This Listing Continued)

MARK S. PRUSYNSKI, born Milwaukee, Wisconsin, April 11, 1953; admitted to bar, 1978, Iowa and Idaho; 1980, U.S. Court of Appeals, Ninth Circuit. *Education:* Colby Community College; Kansas State University (B.S., 1975); University of Iowa (J.D., 1978). ***PRACTICE AREAS:*** Insurance Defense and Coverage Law; Litigation. ***Email:*** msp@moffatt.com

STEPHEN R. THOMAS, born Boise, Idaho, August 13, 1953; admitted to bar, 1978, Idaho; 1979, New York; 1982, U.S. Court of Appeals, Ninth Circuit; 1983, U.S. Court of Appeals, Second Circuit; 2000, U.S. Supreme Court. *Education:* Yale College (A.B., 1975); Columbia University (J.D., 1978); National Institute of Trial Advocacy (1987); Stanford University Graduate School of Business (Executive Program for Smaller Companies, 1991). ***PRACTICE AREAS:*** Commercial Litigation; Products Liability; Insurance Coverage; Securities and Trade Secrets; Legislative Advocacy. ***Email:*** srt@moffatt.com

GLENNA M. CHRISTENSEN, born Logan, Utah, July 30, 1943; admitted to bar, 1978, Idaho; 1982, U.S. Court of Appeals, Ninth Circuit; 1998, U.S. Supreme Court. *Education:* Utah State University (B.A., 1965); Ohio University (M.A., 1967); Brigham Young University (J.D., 1978). ***PRACTICE AREAS:*** Workers Compensation Law; Employment Law; Adoption Law. ***Email:*** gmc@moffatt.com

GERALD T. HUSCH, born Ft. Monroe, Virginia, November 5, 1951; admitted to bar, 1978, Iowa; 1980, Idaho, U.S. Court of Appeals, Eighth Circuit; 1984, U.S. Court of Appeals, Ninth Circuit. *Education:* Drake University (B.A., 1973; J.D., 1978). ***PRACTICE AREAS:*** Noncompete Litigation; Covenants Not To Compete; Trade Secrets; Employment Litigation; Employment Law; Civil Litigation; Federal Litigation; Commercial Litigation; Insurance Defense; Insurance Coverage; Appellate Practice; Mediation. ***Email:*** gth@moffatt.com

SCOTT L. CAMPBELL, born Boise, Idaho, January 11, 1952; admitted to bar, 1978, Idaho; 1979, U.S. Court of Appeals, Ninth Circuit. *Education:* Heidelberg Universität, Heidelberg, West Germany; Whitman College (B.A., 1974); University of Idaho (J.D., 1978). ***PRACTICE AREAS:*** Water Rights Law; Water Quality Law; Environmental Litigation; Land Development Law. ***Email:*** slc@moffatt.com

ROBERT B. BURNS, born Boise, Idaho, January 25, 1952; admitted to bar, 1982, Texas; 1987, Idaho. *Education:* Boise State University; Stanford Law School (J.D., 1982). . ***PRACTICE AREAS:*** Commercial; Real Estate. ***Email:*** rbb@moffatt.com

MICHAEL E. THOMAS, born Boise, Idaho, June 30, 1952; admitted to bar, 1983, Idaho; 1988, U.S. Tax Court. *Education:* Yale University (B.A., 1974); University of Idaho College of Law (J.D., 1982). ***PRACTICE AREAS:*** Corporate; Nonprofit and Charitable Organizations; Banks and Banking; Mergers, Acquisitions and Divestitures; Finance; Health Care; Insurance; Real Estate. ***Email:*** met@moffatt.com

PATRICIA M. OLSSON, born Chicago, Illinois, December 24, 1954; admitted to bar, 1983, Idaho; 1984, U.S. Court of Appeals, Ninth Circuit. *Education:* New College of The University of South Florida; Illinois Institute of Technology, Chicago-Kent College of Law (J.D., 1983). *Member:* American College of Trial Lawyers. ***PRACTICE AREAS:*** Labor and Employment; Medical Malpractice; Commercial Litigation; General Litigation. ***Email:*** pmo@moffatt.com

JAMES C. DeGLEE, born Jerome, Idaho; admitted to bar, 1984, Idaho; 1990, U.S. Court of Appeals, Ninth Circuit. *Education:* University of Utah (B.S., 1976; J.D., 1984). ***PRACTICE AREAS:*** Health Care and Hospital Law. ***Email:*** jcd@moffatt.com

MICHAEL O. ROE, born Mountain View, California, January 6, 1964; admitted to bar, 1989, Texas; 1992, Idaho. *Education:* University of Idaho (B.A., 1986); Columbia University (J.D., 1989). ***PRACTICE AREAS:*** Corporate; Securities; General Business; Litigation. ***Email:*** mor@moffatt.com

DAVID S. JENSEN, born Colorado Springs, Colorado, January 2, 1962; admitted to bar, 1990, South Dakota and Idaho. *Education:* Carleton College; University of Minnesota (J.D., 1989). ***PRACTICE AREAS:*** Business Law; Corporate Law; Commercial Loans; Consumer Banking; Real Estate. ***Email:*** dvj@moffatt.com

JAMES L. MARTIN, born Douglas, Arizona, June 27, 1964; admitted to bar, 1990, Idaho; 1995, U.S. Court of Appeals, Ninth Circuit. *Education:* Boise State University (B.S., 1987); University of Idaho (J.D., 1990). ***PRACTICE AREAS:*** Commercial Litigation; Environmental Litigation; Insurance Defense. ***Email:*** jlm@moffatt.com

C. CLAYTON GILL, born Louisville, Kentucky, August 11, 1969; admitted to bar, 1994, Idaho. *Education:* Vanderbilt University (B.A., 1991); Tulane Law School (J.D., cum laude, 1994). ***PRACTICE AREAS:*** Litigation; Employment Law; Commercial Litigation; Business Law. ***Email:*** ccg@moffatt.com

ANGELA SCHAER KAUFMANN, born April 17, 1969; admitted to bar, 1996, Idaho. *Education:* Pacific Lutheran University (B.A., 1991); University of Idaho College of Law (J.D., 1996). ***PRACTICE AREAS:*** Water Law; Natural Resources; Environmental Law; Agricultural and Land Use Law. ***Email:*** ads@moffatt.com

MICHAEL W. McGREAHAM, born Los Angeles, California, January 31, 1953; admitted to bar, 1994, Washington; 2002, Idaho. *Education:* Brigham Young University (B.S., 1978); Gonzaga University School of Law (J.D., 1994). ***PRACTICE AREAS:*** Estate Planning; Trust Law; Probate; Business Law. ***Email:*** mwm@moffatt.com

OF COUNSEL

EUGENE C. THOMAS, born Idaho Falls, Idaho, February 8, 1931; admitted to bar, 1954, Idaho; 1958, U.S. Court of Appeals, Ninth Circuit; 1970, U.S. Supreme Court. *Education:* Columbia University (A.B., 1952; J.D., 1954); Awarded LL.D.: University of Idaho, 1986; College of Idaho, 1987. *Member:* American Bar Association (President, 1986-1987; Chairman, House of Delegates, 1980-1981; Board of Governors, 1980-1981, 1985-1986; Board of Governors, Executive Committee, 1980-1982). ***Email:*** ect@moffatt.com

MORGAN W. RICHARDS, JR., born Berwyn, Illinois, March 30, 1947; admitted to bar, 1976, Idaho; 1982, U.S. Court of Appeals, Ninth Circuit. *Education:* Colorado State University (B.A., 1969); University of Idaho (J.D., 1976). ***PRACTICE AREAS:*** Administrative Law; Business Law; Government Regulation; Health Care; Hospital Law; Insurance Regulation; Legislative Lobbying; Public Utility Law; Securities. ***Email:*** mwr@moffatt.com

(This Listing Continued)

ROBERT E. BAKES, born Boise, Idaho, January 11, 1932; admitted to bar, 1956, Idaho; 1961, U.S. District Court, District of Idaho; 1963, U.S. Court of Appeals, Ninth Circuit. *Education:* Boise Junior College (A.A., 1952); University of Idaho (B.A., 1954; J.D., 1956); Awarded LL.D. by Albertson College of Idaho. Justice, Idaho Supreme Court, 1971-1993. Chief Justice, Idaho Supreme Court, 1981-1983, 1989-1993. ***PRACTICE AREAS:*** Alternative Dispute Resolution; Trial and Appellate Practice and Procedure. ***Email:*** reb@moffatt.com

REPRESENTATIVE CLIENTS: American International Group (AIG); AIG Aviation; Allied Insurance Company; AMRESCO; Argonaut Insurance Company; Ashley Manor Care Center; Associated Loggers Exchange; Bayer; Blue Cross of Idaho Health Services; Boy Scouts of America; Building Materials Holding Corporation; Burlington Northern Santa Fe; Capitol One, Inc.; Champion Enterprises; ChevronTexaco Corp.; Chubb Group of Insurance Companies; Cropscience; Darigold, Inc.; DBSI Group of Companies; Everest National Insurance Company; Farm Bureau Mutual Insurance; Fireman''s Fund Insurance Company; General Motors Corporation; Grupo Modelo; Hewlett-Packard, Inc.; Idaho Banking Company; Intermountain Gas Company; Key Bank; Lancer Claims Services; Medical Insurance Exchange; Micron; Mitsubishi Motors; Morgan Stanley; Northwest Nazarene University; NW Physicians Mutual; Public Employee Retirement System of Idaho; RskCo; SAFECO; St. Luke''s Regional Medical Center; Seneca Foods Corporation; St. Paul Companies; Travelers; TJT, Inc.; United Services Automobile Association; Utah Medical Insurance; Washington Casualty Company; Washington Mutual Bank; Wells Fargo Bank; Zurich-American Insurance Company.
REFERENCE: Wells Fargo.

(For complete biographical data on other personnel, see Professional Biographies at Pocatello, Idaho Falls and Twin Falls, Idaho)

MOORE, BASKIN & PARKER

Established in 1995

WASHINGTON FEDERAL PLAZA
1001 WEST IDAHO STREET, SUITE 400
P.O. BOX 6756
BOISE, IDAHO 83707
Telephone: 208-336-6900
Facsimile: 208-336-7031

General Civil Trial and Appellate Practice. Aviation, Insurance, Civil Rights, Governmental Liability, Construction, Employment, Negligence, Product Liability, Professional Liability and Workers Compensation Law.

MEMBERS OF FIRM

MICHAEL W. MOORE, born Moscow, Idaho, June 30, 1951; admitted to bar, 1976, Idaho; U.S. Court of Appeals, Ninth Circuit; U.S. Court of Federal Claims. *Education:* University of Idaho (B.S. and B.A., 1973; J.D., 1976). Phi Beta Kappa; Pi Gamma Mu; Phi Kappa Phi. Member, Idaho Law Review, 1975-1976. *Member:* Fourth Judicial District Bar Association; Idaho State Bar; Idaho Defense Counsel Association; Defense Research Institute. ***PRACTICE AREAS:*** Civil Rights; Governmental Liability; Personal Injury Law; Insurance Law; Aviation Law; Employment Law; Products Liability; Automobile Accidents and Injuries. ***Email:*** mmoore@MBPLAW.com

THOMAS P. BASKIN, III, born Lewiston, Idaho, June 6, 1956; admitted to bar, 1981, Idaho and U.S. Court of Appeals, Ninth Circuit. *Education:* University of Idaho (B.S., 1978; J.D., 1981). Phi Alpha Delta (Marshal, 1980). President, University of Idaho College of Law Student Bar Association, 1980-1981. Law Clerk, Fifth Judicial District, 1981-1983. *Member:* Idaho State Bar; Idaho Association of Defense Counsel; American Inns of Court. ***PRACTICE AREAS:*** Workers Compensation Law; Employment Law; Securities. ***Email:*** tbaskin@MBPLAW.com

PAIGE ALAN PARKER, born Bell, California, August 14, 1947; admitted to bar, 1986, Idaho, U.S. District Court, District of Idaho and U.S. Court of Appeals, Ninth Circuit. *Education:* Washington State University (B.A., 1969); Bowling Green State University (M.A., 1974); University of Florida (Ph.D., 1980); University of Idaho (J.D., magna cum laude, 1986). Member, National Moot Court. Assistant Lead Article Editor, University of Idaho Law Review, 1985-1986. Author: "Fishing from the Bank: Public Recreational Rights Along Idaho's Rivers and Lakes," 21 Idaho Law Review 275, 1985; "Chapter 13 Idaho, in Fifty State Construction Lien and Bond Law," (Cushman ed. 1992). Law Clerk, Fourth Judicial District, 1986-1987. *Member:* Idaho State Bar; Idaho Defense Lawyers Association. ***PRACTICE AREAS:*** Civil Rights; Governmental Liability; Personal Injury Law; Insurance Law; Employment Law; Products Liability; Estate Planning; Small Business Law. ***Email:*** paige@MBPLAW.com

ASSOCIATES

MARTIN C. HENDRICKSON, born Pullman, Washington, March 1, 1971; admitted to bar, 1998, Idaho and U.S. District Court, District of Idaho. *Education:* University of Idaho (B.S., 1994); Texas Tech University (J.D., 1998). Phi Delta Phi; Order of the Coif; Order of the Barristers; Board of Barristers. *Member:* Idaho State Bar. ***PRACTICE AREAS:*** Civil Rights; Governmental Liability; Personal Injury Law; Insurance Law; Aviation Law; Employment Law; Products Liability. ***Email:*** martin@MPBLAW.com

STEVE R. KRAFT, born Boise, Idaho, February 23, 1965; admitted to bar, 1993, Idaho; 2000, U.S.; District Court, District of Idaho. *Education:* Boise State University (B.S., 1990); Seattle University School of Law (J.D., 1993). Phi Alpha Delta. *Member:* Idaho State Bar (Employment and Labor Law Section - Chairperson, 1998-1999). ***PRACTICE AREAS:*** Civil Rights; Governmental Liability; Personal Injury; Insurance Law; Aviation Law; Employment Law; Products Liability. ***Email:*** steve@mbplaw.com

REPRESENTATIVE CLIENTS: St. Paul Travelers Companies; American International Adjusters; United States Automobile Association; Capitol Indemnity Co.; Clarendon Insurance Co.; Crawford and Co.; Empire Fire & Marine Insurance Co.; Fireman's Fund Insurance Cos.; Idaho Counties Risk Management Program; Idaho State Insurance Fund; Insurance Company of the West; Protective Insurance Co.; Scottish York International Insurance Group; Sedgwick James of Idaho, Inc.; GAB Robins North America; Self Insured Management Services, Inc.; Underwriters at LLoyds, Inc.; Unigard Insurance Co.; United States Aviation Underwriters; Willis Corroon Management Co., Inc.; Boise State University ADA County Highway District; City of Boise; State of Idaho; Ada County; Adams County; Boise County; Boundary County; Canyon County; Cassia County; Clearwater County; Idaho County; Kootenai County; Nez Perce County; Payette County; Shoshone County; Twin Falls County; Valley County; Washington County; Champion Enterprises, Inc.; Champion Home Builders

(This Listing Continued)

MOORE, BASKIN & PARKER, Boise—Continued

Co.; FMC Corp.; Fred Meyer, Inc.; Lamb Weston, Inc.; Morrison-Knudsen; Boise Cascade Corporation; Payless Stores Northwest, Inc.; Perini Corp.; Rite Aid; Woodgrain Millwork; Hewlett Packard; Intermountain Claims, Inc.; Quest.

MOORE SMITH BUXTON & TURCKE, CHARTERED

Established in 1993

225 NORTH 9TH, SUITE 420
BOISE, IDAHO 83702
Telephone: 208-331-1800
Fax: 208-331-1202
Email: info@msbtlaw.com
URL: http://www.msbtlaw.com

Nampa, Idaho Office: 17 12th Avenue South, Burns and Fox Building, 83651. Telephone: 208-466-1300.

Business, Employment, Environmental, General Municipal Law, Mining, Municipal Bond, Natural Resource, Public Utility, Land Use, Telecommunications, Water Law, General Civil Trial and Appellate Practice in State and Federal Courts and before Various Federal and State Administrative Tribunals.

SUSAN E. BUXTON, born Long Beach, California, October 4, 1963; admitted to bar, 1989, Idaho and U.S. District Court, District of Idaho; 1991, Oregon and U.S. District Court, District of Oregon; 1992, U.S. Court of Appeals, Ninth Circuit. *Education:* Whitman College (B.A., 1985); University of Idaho (J.D., 1989). Symposium Editor, University of Idaho Law Review, 1988-1989. Law Clerk: Hon. James A. Redden, U.S. District Court, District of Oregon; Hon. Roger Swanstrom, Idaho Court of Appeals. ***PRACTICE AREAS:*** Natural Resources; Public Lands; Municipal; Employment; Land Use. ***Email:*** seb@msbtlaw.com

MICHAEL C. MOORE, born Spokane, Washington, August 26, 1942; admitted to bar, 1968, Idaho; 1984, Washington. *Education:* Dartmouth College (B.A., 1964); University of Idaho (J.D., 1968). Author: "Powers and Authorities of Idaho Cities," 14 Idaho Law Review 143, 1977; "Constitutional Debt Limitations on Local Governments," 17 Idaho Law Review 55, 1980; "The Idaho Constitution and Local Governments", 31 Idaho Law Review 417, 1995. Adjunct Professor of Law, Municipal Corporations Law, Community Property Law, University of Idaho, College of Law, 1974-1986. *Member:* Washington State Bar Association; Idaho State Bar; National Association of Bond Lawyers. ***PRACTICE AREAS:*** Municipal Bond Law; General Municipal Law. ***Email:*** mcm@msbtlaw.com

PAUL A. TURCKE, born Anchorage, Alaska, October 4, 1965; admitted to bar, 1993, Idaho and U.S. District Court, District of Idaho; 1994, South Dakota; 1997, U.S. Court of Appeals, Ninth Circuit; 2000, U.S. Court of Appeals, Tenth Circuit; 2001, U.S. Court of Appeals, Seventh Circuit and U.S. Supreme Court. *Education:* Whitman College (B.A., with honors, 1987); University of Idaho (J.D., cum laude, 1993). Member, Moot Court, 1992-1993. *Member:* Idaho State Bar; State Bar of South Dakota. ***PRACTICE AREAS:*** Natural Resources; Public Land Law; Municipal Law; Litigation. ***Email:*** pat@msbtlaw.com

BRUCE SMITH, born New Orleans, Louisiana, February 23, 1950; admitted to bar, 1985, Idaho, U.S. District Court, District of Idaho and U.S. Court of Appeals, Ninth and Tenth Circuits. *Education:* Auburn University (B.S., Business, 1972; M.S., Wildlife Biology/Forestry 1978); University of Idaho (J.D., 1985). Phi Alpha Delta. Member, University of Idaho Law Review, 1984-1985. Law Clerk to The Honorable Jesse L. Walters, Chief Justice, Idaho Court of Appeals, 1985-1987. Member, Idaho Ground Water Quality Council. *Member:* Idaho State Bar (Member: Natural Resources and Environmental Law Sections, 1995—; Water Law Section, 1987—); American Bar Association (Member: Natural Resources and Environmental Law Sections, 1987—; Real Property Section, 1994—). ***PRACTICE AREAS:*** Natural Resources Law; Environmental; Water Law; Business Law; Administrative Law. ***Email:*** bms@msbtlaw.com

---

CHRISTOPHER E. YORGASON, born Fairfield, California, December 25, 1969; admitted to bar, 1998, Idaho. *Education:* Brigham Young University (B.S., 1995); J. Reuben Clark-Brigham Young University (J.D., 1998). *Member:* Idaho State Bar (Member, Sections on: Real Property, Young Lawyers). ***LANGUAGES:*** Thai. ***PRACTICE AREAS:*** Local Government Law; Municipal Finance; Real Estate. ***Email:*** cey@msbtlaw.com

TAMMY A. ZOKAN, born Jacksonville, Florida, August 23, 1970; admitted to bar, 1996, Idaho; 1998, New Mexico. *Education:* University of Wisconsin-Stevens Point (B.S., 1992); Universitiy of Idaho (J.D., 1996). *Member:* Idaho State Bar; State Bar of New Mexico; American Bar Association. ***PRACTICE AREAS:*** Natural Resources; Water Law; Local Government Law. ***Email:*** taz@msbtlaw.com

RANSOM J. BAILEY, born Rockland, Maine, September 25, 1971; admitted to bar, 2002, Idaho. *Education:* Whitman College (B.A., 1994); University of Idaho College of Law (J.D., 2001). Dean's List. Finalist, Best Oralist. *Member:* Idaho State Bar. ***PRACTICE AREAS:*** Municipal Law; General Practice. ***Email:*** rjb@msbtlaw.com

OF COUNSEL

TODD LAKEY, born Portland, Oregon; admitted to bar, 1993, Idaho. *Education:* Brigham Young University (B.S., International Business); Lewis and Clark Northwestern School of Law (J.D., 1993). Cornelius Honor Society. Member, Moot Court Board. Recipient, Best Oral Advocate. Co-President, International Law Society, 1992-1993. Co-Editor, International Legal Perspectives, 1992-1993. Member, and Member, Board of Directors, 2000-2004; Idaho Association of Counties. Commissioner, Canyon County, 1999-2004. President, Idaho Association of Commissioners and Clerks, 2000-2001. *Member:* Idaho State Bar (Member, Local Government Section, 1996-1999). ***LANGUAGES:*** Spanish. ***PRACTICE AREAS:*** Land Use; Local Government Law; Government Relations; Real Estate; Immigration Law. ***Email:*** tml@msbtlaw.com

(This Listing Continued)

JOHN J. McFADDEN, born Sun Valley, Idaho, September 4, 1957; admitted to bar, 1988, Idaho, Oregon and Washington. *Education:* University of Idaho (B.S. Civil Engineering, 1981); Williamette University (J.D., 1987). Member, 1986-1987 and Managing Editor, 1987, Willamette Law Review. Law Clerk to the Honorable Byron Johnson, Idaho Supreme Court. *Member:* Idaho State Bar; Oregon State Bar; Washington State Bar Association. ***PRACTICE AREAS:*** Energy Law; Environmental Law; Telecommunications Law; Municipal Law; Land Use. ***Email:*** jjm@msbtlaw.com

REPRESENTATIVE CLIENTS: Ada County Highway District; Association of Idaho Cities; Boise Independent School District; Cities of Eagle, Glenns Ferry, Kuna, Star, Hailey, McCall, Moscow, Notus, Orofino, Payette, Middleton, Horseshoe Bend, Fruitland; Counties of Ada, Adams, Bonneville, Canyon, Kootenai, Valley; Federal Land Bank of Spokane; Ridgeview Irrigation District; Farmers Union Ditch Company; Idaho State Treasurer; U.S. Bank of Idaho; Blue Ribbon Coalition; Rouse Bros. Ranch; Boise Cascade, International Forest Association; Idaho Water Users Association; Intermountain Forest Association.

NAYLOR & HALES, P.C.

1199 NORTH SHORELINE LANE, SUITE 200
P.O. BOX 9496
BOISE, IDAHO 83707
Telephone: 208-383-9511
Fax: 208-383-9516

Corporate Law, Banking, Real Estate, Employment, Commercial Litigation, Business Law, Civil Rights, Litigation, Estate Planning, Insurance Defense, Administrative Law, Contract Law, Wills, Trusts, Intellectual Property Law, Technology Licensing, Landlord and Tenant Law, Education Law, Adoptions, Municipality Defense, Construction Law, Finance, Product Liability, Collections, Mergers and Acquisitions, Transactions, Sexual Harassment, Discrimination, Wrongful Termination, Government Law, Law Enforcement, Personal Injury.

KIRTLAN G. NAYLOR, born Salt Lake City, Utah, November 15, 1958; admitted to bar, 1986, Idaho. *Education:* Brigham Young University (B.A., 1983); J. Reuben Clark Law School of Brigham Young University (J.D., 1986). Member: American Inn of Court I, 1985-1986. *Member:* Idaho State Bar; National School Boards Association (Council of School Attorneys, 1990—). ***LANGUAGES:*** Norwegian. ***PRACTICE AREAS:*** Litigation; Civil Rights; Employment Law; Municipality Defense; Education Law; Product Liability. ***Email:*** kgn@naylorhales.com

ROGER J. HALES, born Ogden, Utah, November 20, 1961; admitted to bar, 1987, Idaho. *Education:* University of Idaho (B.S., 1984; J.D., 1987). Law Clerk, District Court Judge, 1987-1989. Deputy Ada County Prosecuting Attorney, 1988-1991. *Member:* Idaho State Bar. ***PRACTICE AREAS:*** Business Law and Litigation; Corporate Law; Transactions; Administrative Law; Real Estate; Adoption Law; Contracts. ***Email:*** rjh@naylorhales.com

---

CARLTON R. ERICSON, born Killeen, Texas, May 1, 1956; admitted to bar, 1987, California and U.S District Court, Eastern District of California; 1989, Utah and U.S. District Court, District of Utah; 1990, U.S. District Court, Northern District of California; 1991, U.S Court of Appeals, Ninth Circuit; 1992, U.S. Court of Appeals, Tenth Circuit; 1998, Idaho and U.S. District Court, District of Idaho; 2002, U.S. Supreme Court. *Education:* Brigham Young University (B.A., 1982); University of Idaho, College of Law (1984); J. Reuben Clark Law School (J.D., cum laude, 1986). Member, Layton City Utah Planning Commission, 1995-1998. *Member:* State Bar of California; Utah State Bar; Idaho State Bar. ***LANGUAGES:*** Spanish. ***PRACTICE AREAS:*** Litigation; Civil Rights; Employment; Estate Planning; Commercial Law. ***Email:*** cre@naylorhales.com

COLLEEN D. ZAHN, born Concord, California; admitted to bar, 2000, Idaho and U.S. District Court, District of Idaho; 2004, U.S. Court of Appeals, Ninth Circuit. *Education:* University of Idaho (B.S., cum laude, 1995; J.D., magna cum laude, 2000). Delta Theta Phi. Law Clerk: Fourth District Court, State of Idaho, 2000-2001; Idaho Court of Appeals, 2001-2002. President, Women's Law Caucus. *Member:* Idaho State Bar (Young Lawyers Section, 2000-2004; Co-Chair, 2003-2004; Public Information Committee, 2001—). ***PRACTICE AREAS:*** Civil Litigation; Municipal Defense; Business Law; Business Litigation; Real Estate. ***Email:*** cdz@naylorhales.com

BRUCE CASTLETON, born Provo, Utah; admitted to bar, 2004, Idaho, U.S. District Court, District of Idaho. *Education:* University of Idaho (B.A., English, cum laude, 1997); Brigham Young University, J. Reuben Clark Law School (J.D., 2003). Phi Delta Phi. Senior Editor, Brigham Young University Law Review, 2001-2003. Law Clerk, Idaho Supreme Court, 2003-2004. *Member:* Idaho State Bar (Member, Young Lawyers Section, 2004-2005; Real Estate Section, 2004-2005). [Lieutenant, U.S. Army, 1997-2000; Captain, Utah Army National Guard, 2000-2003]. ***PRACTICE AREAS:*** Commercial Litigation; Construction Law; Real Estate; Business Law. ***Email:*** bjc@naylorhales.com

OF COUNSEL

ROBERT G. HAMLIN, born 1946; admitted to bar, 1973, Idaho. *Education:* California State University at Sacramento (B.A., 1970); University of the Pacific and University of Idaho (J.D., 1973). Member, University of Idaho Law Review, 1972-1973. Law Clerk, Idaho Supreme Court, 1973-1974. *Member:* Idaho State Bar. [Lt., U.S. Army, 1966-1969]. ***PRACTICE AREAS:*** Corporate; Technology Licensing and Royalties; Real Estate; Employment; Commercial; Business Law and Litigation. ***Email:*** rgh@naylorhales.com

NEAL & UHL, PLLC

1101 WEST RIVER STREET, SUITE 110
P.O. BOX 1926
BOISE, IDAHO 83701
Telephone: 208-343-5931
Fax: 208-343-5807
URL: http://www.IdahoRealEstateLaw.com
Email: info@idahorealestatelaw.com
URL: http://www.nealuhl.com

Business Law, Real Estate, Commercial Law, E-Commerce, Community Association Law, Landlord and Tenant Law, Fair Housing and Bankruptcy.

FIRM PROFILE: The firm's primary practice areas are commercial law, including all facets of real property law, with an emphasis on creditors rights, bankruptcy representation and real estate foreclosures, litigation and transactions.

GARY L. NEAL, born San Diego, California, November 26, 1960; admitted to bar, 1994, Idaho, Oregon, U.S. District Court, District of Idaho and U.S. District Court, District of Oregon; U.S Court of Appeals, Ninth Circuit. *Education:* Augustana College (B.A., Religion, 1983); University of Oregon (J.D., 1993). Co-Author: "Evictions and Landlord/Tenant Law in Idaho," National Business Institute, 2002. *Member:* Idaho State Bar; Oregon State Bar. ***PRACTICE AREAS:*** Fair Housing; Homeowners Association Law; Mobile Home Law; Real Estate Fraud; Real Estate Litigation; Civil Litigation. ***Email:*** gln@idahorealestatelaw.com

HOLGER UHL, born Russelsheim, Germany, June 20, 1963; admitted to bar, 1993, Idaho and U.S. District Court, District of Idaho; 1995, Oregon. *Education:* Albertson College of Idaho (B.A., cum laude, 1989); Willamette University (J.D., 1992). Phi Alpha Delta. Law Clerk to Judge G.F. Schroeder, 4th District, State of Idaho. *Member:* Idaho State Bar; Oregon State Bar; American Bar Association (Member, Sections On: Business Law; International Law ; Science and Technology Law). ***LANGUAGES:*** German. ***PRACTICE AREAS:*** Real Estate; Commercial Leasing; International Business Law; E-Commerce; Foreclosures; Bankruptcy. ***Email:*** holger@idahorealestatelaw.com

---

ROBERT E. RICE, born Boise, Idaho, February 17, 1972; admitted to bar, 1998, Idaho and U.S. District Court, District of Idaho. *Education:* Albertson College of Idaho (B.A., 1994); University of Idaho (J.D., 1998). Law Clerk, Judge Gerald L. Weston, Third Judicial District, Idaho, 1998-1999. *Member:* Idaho State Bar (Member, Young Lawyers Section); American Inn of Court No. 130. ***PRACTICE AREAS:*** Real Estate; Business Law; Litigation; Landlord and Tenant Law; Bankruptcy. ***Email:*** rrice@idahorealestatelaw.com

JAMES W. COLBORN, born Omaha, Nebraska, October 18, 1968; admitted to bar, 1995, Washington; 2000, U.S. District Court, Western District of Washington; 2002, Idaho and U.S. District Court, District of Idaho. *Education:* Washington State University (B.A.,1991); Willamette University (J.D., 1995). Executive Editor, Willamette Bulletin of International Law & Policy, 1994-1995. Law Clerk, Judge Stephen W. Drescher, Third Judicial District, Idaho, 1996-1997. Author, " International Labour Organization Convention No. 169: Celebrate the Differences," Vol. 2, No. 1 Willamette Bulletin of International Law and Policy. *Member:* King County and Washington State Bar Associations; Idaho State Bar. ***PRACTICE AREAS:*** Business Law; Litigation; Wills; Probate; Homeowners Association Law; Landlord and Tenant Law. ***Email:*** jwc@idahorealestatelaw.com

REPRESENTATIVE CLIENTS: Capstead Mortgage; Temple-Inland Mortgage Corp.; Ocwen Federal Bank; Young Electric Sign Company (YESCO); Boise Cascade Employees Credit Union; G.E. Capital Mortgage Services; Colliers International.
REFERENCES: Idaho Association of Realtors; Idaho Apartment Owners Assoc.

NEVIN, BENJAMIN & McKAY, LLP

Established in 1983

303 WEST BANNOCK STREET
P.O. BOX 2772
BOISE, IDAHO 83701
Telephone: 208-343-1000
Fax: 208-345-8274
URL: http://www.nbmlaw.com

Criminal Defense, Personal Injury and Civil Litigation.

MEMBERS OF FIRM

DAVID Z. NEVIN, born Shreveport, Louisiana, April 30, 1949; admitted to bar, 1979, Idaho; 1984, U.S. Court of Appeals, Ninth Circuit and U.S. Supreme Court. *Education:* Colorado State University (B.A., 1974); University of Idaho (J.D., cum laude, 1978). Law Clerk to Hon. Jos. J. McFadden, Justice, Idaho Supreme Court, 1979-1980. Adjunct Professor, Trial Practice, University of Idaho College of Law. Member, Idaho Supreme Court Criminal Rules Committee, 1985-1990, Criminal Jury Instructions Committee, 1991—, Capital Counsel Committee, 1996-1999, Death Penalty Jury Instruction Committee, 2003—. *Member:* Idaho State Bar; Idaho Association of Criminal Defense Lawyers (Founder and Former President). Fellow, American College of Trial Lawyers, 1999—. (Certified as a Criminal Trial Specialist by the Idaho Trial Lawyers Association). ***PRACTICE AREAS:*** Criminal Defense; Personal Injury. ***Email:*** dnevin@nbmlaw.com

DENNIS BENJAMIN

SCOTT McKAY, born Omaha, Nebraska, November 5, 1963; admitted to bar, 1991, Idaho and California; 1996, U.S. Court of Appeals, Ninth Circuit; 1998, U.S. Supreme Court. *Education:* Whitworth College (B.A., cum laude, 1986); Gonzaga University (J.D., magna cum laude, 1990). Thomas More Scholar. Associate Editor, Gonzaga Law Review, 1989-1990. Law Clerk to Hon. Byron J. Johnson, 1990-1991, and Hon. Linda Copple Trout, 1992-1993, Idaho Supreme Court. *Member:* Idaho Association of Criminal Defense Lawyers. ***PRACTICE AREAS:*** Criminal Defense; Civil Litigation. ***Email:*** smckay@nbmlaw.com

(This Listing Continued)

MICHAEL J. BARTLETT, born Boise, Idaho, February 11, 1969; admitted to bar, 1996, Idaho. *Education:* Willamette University (B.S., 1992); University of Idaho (J.D., 1996); National Criminal Defense College (2000). Managing and Lead Articles Editor, Idaho Law Review. Law Clerk to Hon. Karen Lansing, Idaho Court of Appeals, 1996-1998. Author: Idaho Law Review, Volume 31. Adjunct Professor, Criminal Justice, Boise State University, 2002. *Member, Idaho Association of Criminal Defense Lawyers; Idaho Trial Lawyers Association.* ***PRACTICE AREAS:*** Criminal Defense; Personal Injury. ***Email:*** bartlett@nbmlaw.com

---

DEBORAH WHIPPLE

SHERYL L. MUSGROVE, born Spokane, Washington, April 18, 1960; admitted to bar, 1995, Idaho and U.S. District Court, District of Idaho; 1996, U.S. Court of Appeals, Ninth Circuit; 2001, Alaska and U.S. District Court, District of Alaska. *Education:* University of Idaho (B.S., 1989; J.D., 1995). Law Clerk to, Honorable Thomas G. Nelson, U.S. Court of Appeals, Ninth Circuit, 1995-2001; Honorable B. Lynn Winmill, Chief Judge U.S. District Court, District of Idaho, 2002-2003. ***Email:*** smusgrove@nbmlaw.com

---

HAROLD Q. NOACK, JR., P.A.

Established in 1990

733 NORTH 7TH STREET
P.O. BOX 875
BOISE, IDAHO 83702
Telephone: 208-336-9292
Fax: 208-336-6701
Email: pete@noacklaw.com
URL: http://www.noacklaw.com

Creditor and Debtor Bankruptcy, General Civil, Trial and Appellate Practice. Commercial, Corporation, Family Law, Divorce, Alimony, Child Support, Real Estate, Construction Law, Elder Law, Wills and Probate.

FIRM PROFILE: Sole Practitioner.

HAROLD Q. NOACK, JR., admitted to bar, 1960, California; 1969, Idaho. *Education:* University of California at Berkeley (B.A., 1953); Hastings College of the Law, University of California (LL.B., 1959). Phi Delta Phi. Author: "Revocation of Physicians' Licenses for Misconduct Involving Moral Turpitude," Hastings Law Review, 1958. Participating Attorney, AARP Legal Services Network. *Member:* Boise, Alameda County and American (Member, Section on General Practice) Bar Associations; State Bar of California (Assistant Secretary, 1962-1964); Idaho State Bar (Member, Bankruptcy Section). [2nd Lt. Anti-Aircraft, U.S. Army, 1954-1955, Honorable Discharge]. ***SPECIAL AGENCIES:*** Affiliated Attorney for AARP Legal Services. ***PRACTICE AREAS:*** Bankruptcy Law; Commercial Law; Business Law; Family Law; Elder Law; Wills; Probate. ***Email:*** pete@noacklaw.com

LEGAL SUPPORT PERSONNEL

CANDICE CONLIN

REPRESENTATIVE CLIENTS: Rocky Mountain Pizza Huts, Inc.; Pizza Hut of Idaho, Inc.; North Idaho Pizza Huts, Inc.; Northwest Restaurant Group, Inc.; Polk, Scheer & Prober, A Law Corporation.
ATTORNEY FOR: AARP Legal Services.
REFERENCE: Idaho Independent Bank.

NUMBERS LAW OFFICE

Established in 1999

611 WEST HAYES
BOISE, IDAHO 83703
Telephone: 208-424-0800
Fax: 208-343-5791
Email: audreyn@numberslaw.com
URL: http://www.numberslawfirm.com

Family Law, Divorce, Custody, Child Support, Adoption, Guardianship, Conservatorship.

AUDREY NUMBERS, born Greenville, Michigan, January 1, 1953; admitted to bar, 1993, Idaho, Washington and U.S. District Court, District of Idaho. *Education:* St. Mary's College of California (M.A., 1983); University of Idaho (J.D., 1993). *Member:* Washington State, Idaho State and American Bar Associations; Idaho Trial Lawyers Association; Idaho Women Lawyers. ***PRACTICE AREAS:*** Family Law; Divorce; Child Custody; Child Support; Adoption Law; Guardianship; Conservatorship; Domestic Relations; Domestic Violence; Paternity; Premarital Agreements; Postnuptial Agreements; Alimony; Spousal Support; Name Changes; Separation Agreements; Property Law; Qualified Domestic Relations Orders (QDROs). ***Email:*** audreyn@numberslaw.com

---

ORNDORFF LAW OFFICES

Established in 1979

1087 WEST RIVER STREET, SUITE 230
BOISE, IDAHO 83702
Telephone: 208-343-8880
Telecopy: 208-345-0314
Email: orndorfflaw@aol.com

Business Law, Estate Planning and Probate, Real Estate Law, Power Project Development.

(This Listing Continued)

ORNDORFF LAW OFFICES, Boise—Continued

OWEN H. ORNDORFF, born Chicago, Illinois, January 4, 1946; admitted to bar, 1974, Idaho and Illinois; U.S. District Court, District of Idaho and U.S. Supreme Court. *Education:* Michigan State University (B.A., 1968); Harvard University; Northwestern University (J.D., 1973). Phi Beta Kappa; Phi Kappa Phi. Counsel to Boise Cascade Corporation, 1974-1979. *Member:* Illinois State and American Bar Associations; Idaho State Bar; Boise Estate Planning Council. ***PRACTICE AREAS:*** Estate Planning; Utility Law; Corporate Law; Property Rights; Probate Law. ***Email:*** orndorfflaw@aol.com

LORI A. DINGEL, born Lawton, Oklahoma, September 7, 1969; admitted to bar, 1994, Idaho. *Education:* University of Idaho (B.S., 1991; J.D., 1994). Member, University of Idaho Law Review. Law Clerk, Chief Justice McDevitt, Idaho Supreme Court, 1995-1997. Author, "Idaho's Implementation of Section 210 of PURPA," Idaho Law Review, 1994. *Member:* Idaho State Bar; American Inns of Court. ***PRACTICE AREAS:*** Real Property; Corporate Law; Business Law. ***Email:*** orndorfflaw@aol.com

OF COUNSEL

R. LEE ROBERTS, born Juneau, Alaska, December 22, 1941; admitted to bar, 1978, California; 1979, U.S. District Court, Eastern and Central Districts of California; 1987, U.S. Supreme Court (Not admitted in Idaho). *Education:* University of Southern California (B.S., 1973); Western State University (J.D., 1978). *Member:* Los Angeles County and American (Vice Chairman, Alternate Energy Committee, Natural Resources Law Section, 1987-1988) Bar Associations; State Bar of California; Federal Energy Bar Association. ***PRACTICE AREAS:*** Energy Law; Utility Law; Corporate Law; Administrative Law. ***Email:*** viellevigne@aol.com

REPRESENTATIVE CLIENTS: HOMS, Inc.; Vaagen Bros. Lumber Co.; Rosebud Energy Corp.; Colstrip Energy Limited Partnership; Muskegon Generation, Inc.; Jackson Energy, Inc.; Billings Generation, Inc.; F/S Electric, Inc.; Empire Lumber Co.; Stilwell Enterprises; Rosebud Enterprises, Inc.

PENLAND MUNTHER GOODRUM

CHARTERED

Established in 1979

1161 WEST RIVER STREET, SUITE 260
P.O. BOX 199
BOISE, IDAHO 83701
Telephone: 208-344-4566
Fax: 208-344-9836
URL: http://www.PMGAttorneys.com
Email: general@PMGAttorneys.com
URL: http://www.pmea-lawfirm.com

FIRM PROFILE: Penland Munther Goodrum Chartered was founded in 1979. The firm advises and represents clients in a variety of matters including: banking, civil rights, commercial contracts and collections, construction, corporate and business planning, employment law (representing management), general civil litigation, insurance defense, legislative affairs, municipal entity representation, real estate and worker's compensation. Penland Munther Goodrum Chartered serves clients throughout Idaho.

PAUL S. PENLAND, born Dallas, Texas, June 30, 1949; admitted to bar, 1976, Texas and Idaho; 1984, Oregon and U.S. Supreme Court. *Education:* Southern Methodist University (B.A., 1971); Baylor University (J.D., 1975). Member, Board of Editors, Baylor Law Review, 1974-1975. *Member:* Idaho State Bar; Oregon State Bar; Boise Insurance Adjusters Association (President, 1986-1987); American Arbitration Association (Panel of Arbitrators, 1992—). ***LANGUAGES:*** Italian. ***SPECIAL AGENCIES:*** Idaho Industrial Commission. ***PRACTICE AREAS:*** Workers Compensation Law; Civil Litigation. ***Email:*** ppenland@pmgattorneys.com

MERRILY MUNTHER, born Spokane, Washington, June 24, 1946; admitted to bar, 1976, Idaho. *Education:* University of Stockholm, Stockholm, Sweden; University of Washington (B.A., 1968); University of Idaho (J.D., 1976). Editor-in-Chief, Idaho Law Review, 1975-1976. *Member:* Boise (President, 1981-1982) and American Bar Associations; Idaho State Bar. Life Fellow, American Bar Foundation (State Chair, 2003—). ***LANGUAGES:*** Swedish, German, French and Italian. ***SPECIAL AGENCIES:*** EEOC/Idaho Human Rights Commission, DOL, OSHA, MSHA, NLRB, P&Z. ***PRACTICE AREAS:*** Business Law; Labor Law; Employment Law; Construction Law; Real Estate Law; Governmental Affairs. ***Email:*** mmunther@pmgattorneys.com

FORREST R. GOODRUM, admitted to bar, 1971, New Jersey (Not admitted in Idaho). *Education:* University of North Carolina (B.A., 1968); Rutgers University (J.D., 1971). Member, Rutgers University Law Review, 1970-1971. Planning Board Attorney: Morris TP, N.J., 1977-1981; General Counsel, Lincoln Federal Savings & Loan, 1981-1988. *Member:* Idaho State Bar (Member, Commercial Law and Bankruptcy Section; Chairman, Real Property Section, 1996-1997); American Arbitration Association (Commercial Arbitrator, Construction Panel Arbitrator, 1987—). ***REPORTED CASES:*** Idaho Building Contractors Association v. City of Coeur d'Alene, 126 Idaho 740, 890 P.2d 326 (1995); Greenfield Village Apartments, L.P. v. Ada County, 130 Idaho 207, 938 P.2d 1245 (1997); Albee v. Judy, 136 Idaho 236, 31 P.3d 248 (2001). ***PRACTICE AREAS:*** Business Law; Real Estate; Banking; General Civil Litigation; Creditor Bankruptcy. ***Email:*** fgoodrum@pmgattorneys.com

---

THOMAS V. MUNSON, born Ithaca, New York, June 16, 1952; admitted to bar, 1981, Idaho; 1982, U.S. Court of Appeals, Ninth Circuit; 1987, U.S. Supreme Court. *Education:* Boise State University (B.S., 1978); University of Idaho (J.D., 1981). *Member:* Boise and American Bar Associations; Idaho State Bar (Member, Workers' Compensation Section; Chairman, Systems Analysis Committee, 1987-1989); Idaho Trial Lawyers Association

(This Listing Continued)

(Member, Workers Compensation Section); Idaho Association of Workers' Compensation Sureties. ***PRACTICE AREAS:*** Workers Compensation; Personal Injury; General Litigation. ***Email:*** tmunson@pmgattorneys.com

SKIP SPERRY, born Tahoe, Nevada, January 7, 1966; admitted to bar, 1993, Idaho. *Education:* University of Idaho (B.S., 1989); Creighton University (J.D., cum laude, 1993). Phi Alpha Delta. Editor, Creighton Law Review, 1992-1993. *Member:* Idaho State Bar (Charter Member, and Co-Founder, Employment and Labor Section, 1995). ***PRACTICE AREAS:*** Labor and Employment; Business Law; Corporate Law; Construction Law; Real Estate. ***Email:*** ssperry@pmgattorneys.com

REPRESENTATIVE CLIENTS: General Electric Credit Corporation; Hartford Insurance Company; Home Federal Bank; Homestyle Industries; Idaho Building Contractors Assn.; The Insurance Company of the West; McAlvain Construction, Inc.; Royal/Sun Alliance; The Travelers Insurance Co.; Trinity Universal Insurance Co.; U.S. Liability; Washington Group International, Inc.; Wells Fargo Bank.
REFERENCE: Key Bank of Idaho.

PERKINS COIE LLP

251 EAST FRONT STREET, SUITE 400
BOISE, IDAHO 83702-7310
Telephone: 208-343-3434
Facsimile: 208-343-3232
Email: perkins@perkinscoie.com
URL: http://www.perkinscoie.com

REVISER OF THE WASHINGTON LAW DIGEST FOR THIS DIRECTORY.

Other Offices: Anchorage, Alaska; Bellevue, Washington; Chicago, Illinois; Denver, Colorado; Los Angeles, California; Menlo Park, California; Olympia, Washington; Phoenix, Arizona; Portland, Oregon; San Francisco, California; Seattle, Washington; Washington, D.C.

General Civil Trial and Appellate Practice in Federal and State Courts and before various Federal and State Administrative Tribunals. Administrative; Antitrust and Trade Regulation; Aviation and Aerospace; Banks and Banking; Bankruptcy; Biotechnology; Business Law; Corporate Law; Employee Benefits; Energy; Environmental; Estate Planning; Federal Indian Law; Franchising; General Litigation; Government Contracts; Government Relations; Immigration; Intellectual Property; International Trade; International Law; Internet and Electronic Commerce; Labor and Employment; Land Use; Life Sciences; Mergers, Acquisitions and Divestitures; Municipal/Public Finance; Natural Resources; Nonprofit and Charitable Organizations; Probate; Patents; Product Liability; Project Finance; Political Law; Public Utility; Real Estate; School Law; Securities Law and Litigation; Taxation; Technology; Telecommunications; Toxic Torts; Trademarks and Copyrights; Venture Capital and Investment Funds; Water Rights; White-Collar Criminal Representation; Workers' Compensation.

FIRM PROFILE: Perkins Coie LLP is a leading, full-service international law firm. With more than 600 lawyers in 13 offices across the United States, the firm represents clients that range in size from Fortune 100 companies to start-ups, and has historically represented market leaders in traditional and cutting-edge technology industries.

PARTNERS

RICHARD C. BOARDMAN, born Lackawanna, New York, December 6, 1951; admitted to bar, 1982, Idaho; 1987, Washington. *Education:* Idaho State University (B.A., 1978); University of Idaho (J.D., 1982). Member, University of Idaho Law Review. Law Clerk to Justice Stephen Bistline, Idaho Supreme Court, 1982. ***PRACTICE AREAS:*** Civil Litigation; Commercial Law; Construction Law; Environmental Law; Insurance Coverage Law. ***Email:*** boarr@perkinscoie.com

ROBERT A. MAYNARD, born Huntington, West Virginia, July 17, 1953; admitted to bar, 1981, District of Columbia; 1986, Alaska; 1997, Idaho. *Education:* Virginia Polytechnic Institute and State University (B.S., with distinction, 1976); University of Michigan (J.D., magna cum laude, 1979). Law Clerk to Hon. Jay R. Rabinowitz, Chief Justice Alaska Supreme Court, 1979-1980. Assistant Regional Attorney and Senior Counsel, U.S.D.A., 1983-1997. ***PRACTICE AREAS:*** Environmental Law; Natural Resources; Public Land Law; Forest Industry Law; Endangered Species; Mining Law; Water Law. ***Email:*** maynr@perkinscoie.com

OF COUNSEL

JACQUE L. PALMER, admitted to bar, 1986, Arizona; 1988, Washington; 1989, Idaho; 2001, California. *Education:* University of Idaho (B.S., 1982; J.D., 1986). ***PRACTICE AREAS:*** Intellectual Property; Licensing; Mergers and Acquisitions; Emerging Companies. ***Email:*** jpalmer@perkinscoie.com

MELANIE RUBOCKI, admitted to bar, 1997, Illinois; 2000, Idaho. *Education:* University of Pennsylvania (B.S., Economics, 1993; B.A., Psychology, 1993); University of Notre Dame (J.D., 1997). *Member:* Chicago, Illinois State and Idaho State Bar Associations. ***PRACTICE AREAS:*** Business Counseling; Corporate Finance; Corporate Securities; Corporate Governance; Emerging Companies; Technology Licensing; Technology Transfers; Mergers and Acquisitions; Private Equity; Venture Capital; Project Finance; Real Estate. ***Email:*** mrubocki@perkinscoie.com

ASSOCIATES

ERIC AASERUD, admitted to bar, 1992, Washington (Not admitted in Idaho). *Education:* Western Washington University (B.A., 1988); Seattle University (J.D., 1992). ***PRACTICE AREAS:*** Government Contracts. ***Email:*** eaaserud@perkinscoie.com

BROOK B. BOND, born Twin Falls, Idaho; admitted to bar, 1989, California (Not admitted in Idaho). *Education:* University of California at Davis (B.S., 1986); University of San Diego (J.D., 1989). Law Clerk to the Hon. Ronald W. Rose, 1990. ***PRACTICE AREAS:*** Commercial Litigation; Biotechnology; Life Sciences; Environmental Law; Natural Resources. ***Email:*** bbond@perkinscoie.com

ERIC R. BJORKMAN, JR., born Santa Rosa, California, October 6, 1970; admitted to bar, 1997, Idaho; 1999, U.S. Court of Appeals, Ninth Circuit. *Education:* Dartmouth Col-

(This Listing Continued)

lege (A.B., 1993); University of Idaho College of Law (J.D., 1997). ***PRACTICE AREAS:*** Civil Litigation; Commercial Litigation; Construction Law; Products Liability. ***Email:*** ebjorkman@perkinscoie.com

KELLY A. CAMERON, born Fullerton, California, October 26, 1967; admitted to bar, 1995, Maryland; 1998, District of Columbia (Not admitted in Idaho). *Education:* Brigham Young University (B.A., 1992); Washington & Lee University (J.D., 1995). ***PRACTICE AREAS:*** Litigation; Telecommunications Law. ***Email:*** camek@perkinscoie.com

SHELLY COZAKOS, born Santa Rosa, California, 1968; admitted to bar, 1996, Idaho. *Education:* University of Idaho (B.S., 1991; J.D., 1995). Board of Editors, Idaho Law Review. Law Clerk to Judge Ida Leggett and Judge Ron Schilling, State District Court of Idaho, 1995. ***PRACTICE AREAS:*** Commercial Litigation; Civil Litigation; Torts and Insurance Litigation; Products Liability. ***Email:*** cozas@perkinscoie.com

SHAINA JENSEN, (admission pending). *Education:* Miami University (B.A., 2000); University of Michigan (J.D., 2003). ***PRACTICE AREAS:*** Litigation; Corporate Business. ***Email:*** sjensen@perkinscoie.com

CHRISTINE M. SALMI, born Peoria, Illinois, March 10, 1967; admitted to bar, 1997, Idaho. *Education:* Illinois State University (B.A., 1990); University of Idaho (J.D., 1997). Law Clerk to the Hon. Schroeder, Idaho Supreme Court. Articles Editor, Idaho Law Review. ***PRACTICE AREAS:*** Litigation. ***Email:*** csalmi@perkinscoie.com

REVISER OF THE WASHINGTON LAW DIGEST FOR THIS DIRECTORY.

(For biographical data on other Perkins Coie personnel, see Professional Biographies for those offices)

DEREK A. PICA, P.L.L.C.

Established in 1992

199 N. CAPITOL BOULEVARD, SUITE 302

BOISE, IDAHO 83702

Telephone: 208-336-4144
Fax: 208-336-4980
URL: http://www.picalaw.com
Email: derekpica@msn.com
URL: http://www.picalawfirm.com

Divorce, Child Custody, Real Estate, Probate, Contracts, Personal Injury.

FIRM PROFILE: Derek A. Pica is a sole-practitioner with a practice that emphasises family law, including divorce, child custody, guardianships, and conservatorships. Mr Pica also has extensive experience representing clients in probate matters, real estate, business law (including the formation of legal entities) and personal injury. Mr Pica is a bona fide trial attorney who knows what the inside of a courtroom looks like. He is not afraid to go to trial if necessary and will aggressively pursue a client's cause. Mr Pica is very proficient at getting divorce clients through the emotional upheaval of a divorce. He has tried dozens of divorce and child custody cases. He has also gone to trial in numerous personal injury cases.

DEREK A. PICA, born Kalamazoo, Michigan, July 26, 1961; admitted to bar, 1986, Idaho and U.S. District Court, District of Idaho. *Education:* University of Idaho (B.S., cum laude, 1983); University of Utah (J.D., 1986). Phi Kappa Phi; Phi Eta Sigma; Mortar Board. Law Clerk, Idaho Public Utilities Commission, Boise, Idaho, 1985. Author, "The Tender Years Doctrine: Is It Still The Law?," The Advocate, January 1995. *Member:* Idaho State Bar. ***REPORTED CASES:*** Nanney v. Linella, Inc., 130 Idaho 477, 943 P.2d 67 (App. 1997). ***PRACTICE AREAS:*** Divorce; Child Custody; Guardianship; Conservatorship; Wills; Trust Law; Probate; Business Law; Real Estate; Contracts; Personal Injury; Appellate Practice. ***Email:*** derekpica@msn.com

LEGAL SUPPORT PERSONNEL

PENNY BELL

QUANE SMITH LLP

U.S. BANK PLAZA, 16TH FLOOR
P.O. BOX 519

BOISE, IDAHO 83701-0519

Telephone: 208-345-8600
Facsimile: 208-345-8660
Email: info@quanesmith.net
URL: http://www.quanesmith.net

Coeur d'Alene, Idaho Office: 2020 Lakewood Drive, Suite 312, P.O. Box 1758. Telephone: 208-664-9281. Facsimile: 208-664-5380.
Idaho Falls, Idaho Office: 2325 West Broadway, Suite B. Telephone: 208-529-0000. Facsimile: 208-529-0005.

Insurance, Insurance Defense, Litigation, Accountants Liability, Advertising and Marketing, Agents and Brokers Liability, Agricultural Law, Airplane Crashes, Alcoholic Beverages, Alternative Dispute Resolution, Americans with Disabilities Act Defense, Appellate Practice, Architects and Engineers Liability, Arson and Insurance Fraud, Asbestos Defense, Automobile Insurance, Aviation, Brain Injury, Business Law, Casualty Insurance Defense, Catastrophic Injury, Civil Practice, Commercial Insurance, Commercial Law, Complex and Multi-District Litigation, Computers and Software, Construction Accidents, Construction Defects, Construction Law, Contracts, Corporate Law, Design Professionals Liability, Drug and Medical Device Defense, Education Law, Employer Liability, Environmental Law, ERISA Litigation, Extra Contractual Insurance Defense, Federal Practice, Fire Insurance, Firearms Litigation, Food Products Liability, Fraud and Deceit, Government, Hazardous Waste Liability, Head Injury, Health Care, Health Insurance Defense, Insurance Bad Faith Defense, Labor and Employment, Legal Malpractice Defense, Libel, Slander and Defamation, Life Insurance Defense, Manufacturers Liability, Medical Malpractice, Natural Resources, Negligence, Nursing Home Litigation, Personal Injury, Pesticide Litigation, Physicians Licensing, Pollution, Premises Liability, Products Liability, Professional Discipline, Professional Liability, Propane Products Liability, Property Damage Defense, Property Insurance, Real Estate, Recreational Products Liability, School Board Defense, Sexual Harassment Defense, Slip and Fall, Spinal Injury, Subrogation, Torts, Toxic Torts, Transportation, Transportation Law, Workers Compensation, Wrongful Death and Wrongful Termination Defense.

FIRM PROFILE: A regional law firm headquartered in Boise, Idaho with offices located to service several western states. The Boise office manages large litigation actions and coverage analyses throughout the intermountain region. The office in Boise represents clients throughout southwestern Idaho, Oregon and Washington. The Coeur d'Alene office is responsible for cases in northern Idaho and eastern Washington. The Idaho Falls office represents clients in eastern Idaho and western Wyoming.

The firm's major focus is in the representation of insurance companies and their policyholders, governmental entities and self-insured corporations. The firm emphasizes all aspects of civil litigation, alternative dispute resolution and risk management.

MEMBERS OF FIRM

JEREMIAH A. QUANE, admitted to bar, 1962, Idaho. *Education:* University of Idaho (B.A., 1958); University of Washington and University of Idaho (LL.B., 1962). ***PRACTICE AREAS:*** Catastrophic Injury Defense; Health Care; Insurance; Medical Malpractice Defense; Products Liability Defense. ***Email:*** jaquane@quanesmith.net

E.B. SMITH (1896-1975)

BRUCE R. McALLISTER, admitted to bar, 1980, Idaho. *Education:* University of Minnesota (B.A., 1976; J.D., 1979). ***PRACTICE AREAS:*** Dental Malpractice Defense; Insurance Bad Faith Defense; Health Care; Medical Malpractice; Toxic Tort Defense. ***Email:*** brmcallister@quanesmith.net

RANDALL R. ADAMS, admitted to bar, 1983, Idaho; 1995, Washington. *Education:* University of Southern California (B.A., 1979); University of Idaho (J.D., 1983). (Resident, Coeur d'Alene Office). ***PRACTICE AREAS:*** Insurance Defense; Government; Products Liability Defense; Professional Liability Defense; Transportation Liability. ***Email:*** rradams@quanesmith.net

RICHARD L. STUBBS, admitted to bar, 1984, Idaho. *Education:* Carleton College (B.A., 1979); Northwestern School of Law of Lewis and Clark College (J.D., 1984). ***PRACTICE AREAS:*** Health Care; Insurance Defense; Medical Malpractice Defense; Commercial Law; Drug and Medical Device Defense. ***Email:*** rlstubbs@quanesmith.net

DONALD F. CAREY, admitted to bar, 1991, Idaho; 1992, Wyoming. *Education:* Mesa State College (B.A., 1984); University of Wyoming (J.D., 1991). (Resident, Idaho Falls Office). ***PRACTICE AREAS:*** Insurance Defense; Personal Injury Defense; Construction Law; Education Law; Professional Malpractice. ***Email:*** dfcarey@quanesmith.net

DAVID W. KNOTTS, admitted to bar, 1986, Idaho. *Education:* Indiana University (B.A., with honors and highest distinction, 1977); University of North Carolina (M.A., 1982); University of Oregon (J.D., 1985). ***PRACTICE AREAS:*** Personal Injury Defense; Environmental Law; ERISA Litigation; Insurance Bad Faith Defense; Products Liability Defense. ***Email:*** dwknotts@quanesmith.net

DAVID S. PERKINS, admitted to bar, 1991, Idaho. *Education:* University of Utah (B.S., 1988); University of Idaho (J.D., 1991). ***PRACTICE AREAS:*** Business Law; Construction Law; Labor and Employment; Professional Liability Defense; Transportation Liability. ***Email:*** dsperkins@quanesmith.net

MICHAEL L. HAMAN, admitted to bar, 1994, Idaho. *Education:* University of Idaho (B.S., 1990; J.D., 1993). (Resident, Coeur d'Alene Office). ***PRACTICE AREAS:*** Automobile Liability Defense; Insurance Defense; Construction Law; Education Law; Premises Liability. ***Email:*** mlhaman@quanesmith.net

TYRA H. STUBBS, admitted to bar, 1984, Idaho. *Education:* Carleton College (B.A., 1979); Northwestern School of Law of Lewis and Clark College (J.D., 1984). ***PRACTICE AREAS:*** Education Law; Health Care; Labor and Employment; Medical Malpractice Defense; Workers Compensation Defense. ***Email:*** thstubbs@quanesmith.net

TERRENCE S. JONES, admitted to bar, 1998, Idaho. *Education:* Boise State University (B.A., Pol. Science, 1994); University of Idaho (J.D., cum laude, 1998). ***PRACTICE AREAS:*** Medical Malpractice; Insurance Defense; Agricultural Law; Nursing Home Litigation. ***Email:*** tsjones@quanesmith.net

ASSOCIATES

LESLIE S. BROWN, admitted to bar, 1997, Idaho. *Education:* University of Puget Sound (B.A., 1992); McGeorge School of Law (J.D., 1997). ***Email:*** lsbrown@quanesmith.net

ROBERT D. WILLIAMS, admitted to bar, 1994, Idaho; 2001, Wyoming. *Education:* University of Wisconsin-Madison (B.S., 1991); University of Idaho (J.D., 1994). (Resident, Idaho Falls Office). ***Email:*** rdwilliams@quanesmith.net

HANS A. MITCHELL, admitted to bar, 1996, Oregon; 1997, Idaho. *Education:* University of Oregon (B.A., 1991); Willamette University (J.D., 1996). ***LANGUAGES:*** Spanish. ***Email:*** hamitchell@quanesmith.net

MATTHEW F. McCOLL, admitted to bar, 1999, Idaho. *Education:* Albertson College of Idaho (B.A., cum laude, 1995); University of Utah (J.D., 1999). ***Email:*** mfmccoll@quanesmith.net

WILLIAM G. POPE, admitted to bar, 1997, Washington; 2001, Idaho. *Education:* Brigham Young University (B.A., 1994; J.D., 1997). ***Email:*** wgpope@quanesmith.net

DARI M. HUSKEY, admitted to bar, 2002, Idaho. *Education:* Brigham Young University (B.A., 1997); University of Idaho (J.D., 2002). ***Email:*** dmhuskey@quanesmith.net

JENNIFER D. GAFFANEY, admitted to bar, 2002, Washington; 2003, Idaho and U.S. District Court, District of Idaho. *Education:* Gonzaga University (B.A., 1998; J.D., 2002). (Resident, Coeur d'Alene Office). ***Email:*** jdgaffaney@quanesmith.net

(This Listing Continued)

QUANE SMITH LLP, Boise—Continued

CARSTEN A. PETERSON, admitted to bar, 2001, Idaho. *Education:* Utah State University (B.S., Biology, 1998); University of Idaho (J.D., 2001). ***Email:*** capeterson@quanesmith.net

JENNIFER L. GORMAN, admitted to bar, 2003, Idaho. *Education:* Kansas State University (B.S., 2000); Washburn University (J.D., 2003). (Resident, Coeur d'Alene Office). ***Email:*** jlgorman@quanesmith.net

CAROLE I. WESENBERG, admitted to bar, 2000, Idaho. *Education:* Montana State University (B.S., 1994); Southern Illinois University (J.D., 2000). (Resident, Idaho Falls Office). ***Email:*** ciwesenberg@quanesmith.net

BRAD S. RICHARDSON, admitted to bar, 2005, Idaho. *Education:* Brigham Young University (B.A., 1999); University of Idaho (J.D., 2004). ***Email:*** bsrichardson@quanesmith.net

REPRESENTATIVE CLIENTS: American National Property and Casualty Co.; Bristol Myers-Squibb Company; Canadian Indemnity Co.; Chubb Insurance Companies; Cigna Cos.; CNA Insurance; Colonial Penn Insurance Co.; Coregis Group; Crum & Forster Insurance Group; EMC Insurance Cos.; Employers Insurance of Wausau; Farmers Insurance Group; Fireman"s Fund Insurance Cos.; Greyhound Lines, Inc. (self-insured); Hartford Insurance Group; Horace Mann Insurance Group; Industrial Indemnity Co.; Interstate Insurance Group; Jefferson Insurance Group; Kemper National Insurance Cos.; Markel Insurance Co.; Maryland Casualty Co.; Minnesota Mutual Insurance Co.; National Farmers Union Insurance Cos.; Nova Casualty Co.; Ohio Casualty Group; Old Republic Ins. Co.; Oregon Mutual Insurance Co.; Royal-Globe Insurance Cos.; Scottsdale Ins. Co.; Sentry Insurance Cos.; St Paul Travelers; State Farm Insurance Cos.; State of Idaho (self-insured); Sublimity Insurance Co.; Underwriters of Lloyds London; United Services Automobile Association; Unitrin Insurance Companies; Utica Mutual Insurance Co.; Vikings Ins. Co.; Zurich American Insurance Cos.

RACINE OLSON NYE BUDGE & BAILEY

CHARTERED

Established in 1940

101 SOUTH CAPITOL BOULEVARD
U.S. BANK PLAZA, SUITE 208
BOISE, IDAHO 83702
Telephone: 208-395-0011
Fax: 208-433-0167
Email: cja@racinelaw.net
URL: http://www.racinelaw.net

Pocatello, Idaho Office: 201 East Center, P.O. Box 1391, 83201-1391. Telephone: 208-232-6101. Fax: 208-232-6109.

Litigation, Probate, Real Estate, Corporation, Insurance and Utility Law. Creditor's Bankruptcy.

FIRM PROFILE: Founded in 1940, our firm enjoys an excellent reputation throughout the state. Our attorneys focus on specific areas of emphasis and provide prompt, efficient resolution of client needs.

CONRAD J. AIKEN, born Greenville, Ohio, November 3, 1944; admitted to bar, 1969, Ohio; 1971, Kentucky; 1975, Colorado; 1977, Idaho. *Education:* Wittenberg University (A.B., 1966); Duke University (J.D., 1969). *Member:* Idaho State Bar. (Resident). ***PRACTICE AREAS:*** Banking Law; Loans; Creditors Rights; Commercial Law. ***Email:*** cja@racinelaw.net

---

LISA R. TANNER, born Bonners Ferry, Idaho, June 29, 1979; admitted to bar, 2003, California; 2004, Idaho. *Education:* Oak Brook College of Law (J.D., cum laude, 2003). Law Clerk to the Hon. Daniel T. Eismann, Justice, Idaho Supreme Court. *Member:* State Bar of California; Idaho State Bar. (Resident). ***PRACTICE AREAS:*** Insurance Defense; Banking Law. ***Email:*** lrt@racinelaw.net

JOSHUA D. JOHNSON, born Springfield, Illinois, January 4, 1971; admitted to bar, 1997, Illinois; 2004, Idaho. *Education:* Southern Oregon State College (B.S., 1994); John Marshall Law School (J.D., 1997). *Member:* Idaho State Bar. (Resident). ***PRACTICE AREAS:*** Insurance Defense. ***Email:*** jdj@racinelaw.net

REPRESENTATIVE CLIENTS: Anheuser-Busch Cos.; Portneuf Medical Center; Boise Radiology Group; Chubb Pacific Indemnity; Colonial Penn Insurance; Commercial Union Cos.; Cuna Mutual Insurance Group; Continental Western; Deere & Co.; Eastern Idaho Agricultural Credit Assn.; Farm Bureau Insurance Company of Idaho; Farmer's Alliance Mutual Insurance Co.; Farmer's Home Mutual Ins. Co.; Farmers Insurance Group of Cos.; Farmer's Professional Liability Group; Forum Insurance Co.; FMC; General Motors Corp.; Great Western Life; Idaho Banking Company; Idaho Groundwater Assn., Inc.; Idaho Irrigation Pumpers Assn.; Ireland Bank; ITT Hartford; Kemper Ins. Group; Last Chance Canal Co.; Lockheed-Martin; Marsh Valley Hydro-Electric Co.; McCammon Ditch Co.; Medical Imaging Association; Monsanto Co.; North Pacific Insurance Co.; Panhandle State Bank; Pioneer Title Co.; Portneuf-Marsh Valley Canal Co.; Reliance Insurance Co.; Solutia, Inc.; State of Idaho (self-insured); Transamerica Insurance Co.; Transport Indemnity Co.; Underwriters Adjusting Co.; Unigard Insurance Group; Uniroyal Goodrich Tire Co.; U.S.A.A.; U.S. Bank; U.S. West; Viking Insurance Co.; Washington Mutual Bank; Washington Trust Bank.
REFERENCES: U.S. Bank; Wells Fargo Bank.

(For complete biographical data on all personnel see Professional Biographies at Pocatello, Idaho)

RINGERT CLARK

CHARTERED

455 SOUTH THIRD STREET
BOISE, IDAHO 83702
Telephone: 208-342-4591
Fax: 208-342-4657
Email: reception@ringertclark.com
URL: http://www.ringertclark.com

Hammett, Idaho Office: P.O. Box 105, 83627. Telephone: 208-366-7993. Fax: 208-366-7994.

(This Listing Continued)

General and Civil Trial Practice, Administrative, Agricultural, Bankruptcy, Appeals, Condemnation, Corporation, Insurance, Family Law, Insurance Defense, Legislative, Negligence, Personal Injury, Probate, Real Estate, Tort, Water, Environmental and Workers Compensation Law.

FIRM PROFILE: Ringert Clark, originally founded in 1937, has always been known for its work in agricultural law, especially water rights and irrigation matters. The firm has developed specialized capabilities in commercial and business matters; bankruptcy liquidations and reorganizations for both debtors and creditors; real estate sales, financing and foreclosures; estate planning and needs of the elderly; family law and domestic relations; and litigation for plaintiffs and defendants. The firm's clients include national mortgage and financial institutions, irrigation districts and water users, insurance companies, bankruptcy trustees, and businesses.

LAURA E. BURRI, admitted to bar, 1986, Idaho. *Education:* Northwest Nazarene College (B.A., magna cum laude, 1983); University of Idaho (J.D., 1986). *Member:* Idaho State Bar. ***PRACTICE AREAS:*** Bankruptcy Law; Collection Law; Business Law. ***Email:*** lburri@ringertclark.com

JEFFREY R. CHRISTENSON, admitted to bar, 1976, Idaho. *Education:* Ohio University (B.S.J., 1972); Ohio Northern University (J.D., 1976). Member, United States Foreclosure Network (including USFN Commercial Division). *Member:* Boise and American (Family Law Section) Bar Associations; Idaho State Bar Fellow, American Academy of Matrimonial Lawyers. ***PRACTICE AREAS:*** Family Law; Mortgage Banking Law; Commercial Litigation. ***Email:*** jeffc@ringertclark.com

D. BLAIR CLARK, admitted to bar, 1971, Idaho. *Education:* University of Idaho (B.S., 1969; J.D., 1971). *Member:* Idaho State Bar (Chairman, Bankruptcy Section, 2001); American Bankruptcy Institute. ***PRACTICE AREAS:*** Bankruptcy Law; Commercial Litigation; General Practice. ***Email:*** dbc@ringertclark.com

DAVID HAMMERQUIST, admitted to bar, 1983, Idaho. *Education:* Boise State University; University of Idaho (B.S., 1980; J.D., 1983); Pepperdine University. *Member:* Idaho State Bar; Idaho Association of Criminal Defense Lawyers; National Association of Criminal Defense Lawyers. ***PRACTICE AREAS:*** Criminal Defense; Business Law; Family Law; Wills; Trust Law. ***Email:*** dlhammer@ringertclark.com

CHARLES L. HONSINGER, admitted to bar, 1995, Idaho; 1998, Colorado. *Education:* Northern Arizona University (B.S., 1984); Lewis & Clark College (J.D., 1995). *Member:* Idaho State Bar (Member, Water Law Section). ***PRACTICE AREAS:*** Water Rights; Property Law; Natural Resources. ***Email:*** clh@ringertclark.com

JAMES P. KAUFMAN, admitted to bar, 1973, Idaho. *Education:* University of Idaho (B.A., 1968; J.D., 1973). Member, Association of Life Underwriters, 1999 and 2000. *Member:* Idaho State Bar (Member: Legislative Committee, Guardianship Forms Committee, Tax, Probate and Trust Law Section; Chairman, Fiduciary Review Committee); Treasure Valley Estate Planning Council (President, 1988); National Academy of Elder Law Attorneys. ***PRACTICE AREAS:*** Probate Law; Trust Law; Guardianships Law; Estate Planning. ***Email:*** jimkauf@ringertclark.com

JAMES G. REID, admitted to bar, 1971, Idaho. *Education:* University of Idaho (B.S., 1968; J.D., 1971). *Member:* Idaho State Bar; American Bar Association; Idaho Trial Lawyers Association; Idaho Association of Defense Counsel. ***PRACTICE AREAS:*** Corporate; Insurance Defense; Personal Injury. ***Email:*** jgr@ringertclark.com

DANIEL V. STEENSON, admitted to bar, 1991, Idaho. *Education:* St. Olaf College (B.A., 1983); University of Colorado (J.D., 1990). *Member:* Idaho State Bar; American Bar Association. ***PRACTICE AREAS:*** Water Law; Natural Resources Law; Environmental Law. ***Email:*** dvs@ringertclark.com

ASSOCIATES

JENNIFER REID MAHONEY, admitted to bar, 1995, Idaho and U.S. District Court, District of Idaho. *Education:* University of California at San Diego (B.A., 1991); University of Idaho (J.D., 1995). *Member:* Idaho State Bar. ***Email:*** jmahoney@ringertclark.com

S. BRYCE FARRIS, admitted to bar, 1997, Idaho. *Education:* Albertson College (B.A., 1994); University of Idaho College of Law (J.D., 1997). *Member:* Idaho State Bar. ***PRACTICE AREAS:*** Water Law; Property Law; Natural Resources; Business Law. ***Email:*** bryce@ringerclark.com

DAVID P. CLAIBORNE, born Boise, Idaho, January 28, 1978; admitted to bar, 2002, Idaho, U.S. District Court, District of Idaho. *Education:* Boise State University (B.A., 1999); Willamette University (J.D., cum laude, 2002). Member, Willamette University Law Review, 2000-2002. *Member:* Idaho State Bar; American Agricultural Law Association; American Bankruptcy Institute. ***PRACTICE AREAS:*** Family Law; Real Estate; Wills; Trust Law. ***Email:*** dpc@ringertclark.com

JON C. GOULD, admitted to bar, 2004, Idaho and U.S. District Court, District of Idaho. *Education:* California State University (B.S., Physical Science, 1988); University of Nevada (M.S., Hydrogeology, 1992); University of Idaho (J.D., 2002). *Member:* Idaho State Bar. ***PRACTICE AREAS:*** Natural Resources. ***Email:*** jon@ringertclark.com

OF COUNSEL

WILLIAM F. RINGERT, admitted to bar, 1962, Idaho. *Education:* University of Idaho (B.S., 1953); Southern Methodist University (LL.B., 1962). State Senator, 1982-1988. *Member:* Idaho State Bar (Member, Water Law Section). ***PRACTICE AREAS:*** Water Law; Legislative Law; Natural Resources Law; Agricultural Law; Public Land Law. ***Email:*** bringert@yahoo.com

ALLYN L. SWEENEY, admitted to bar, 1980, Idaho. *Education:* Boise State University (B.A., magna cum laude, 1977); University of Idaho (J.D., 1979). *Member:* Boise Bar Association; Idaho State Bar; Defense Research Institute. ***PRACTICE AREAS:*** Insurance Defense; Risk Management; Product Liability; Civil Rights; Federal and State Civil Appeals. ***Email:*** als2@ringertclark.com

REPRESENTATIVE CLIENTS: Ace USA Ins. Co., Alaska Pacific Assurance Co.; ATT Corp.; Auto Owners Ins. Co.; B & A Engineers, Inc.; Boise Town Square Mall; Borden, Inc.; Boston Scientific; Bruneau Cattle Co.; Idaho Bureau of Risk Management; Carteret Mortgage Co.;

(This Listing Continued)

CC & T Land & Cattle Co.; Central National Ins. Co.; Century Indemnity Co.; Chiron Corp.; Citifed Mortgage Co.; Commercial Credit Corp.; Comprehensive Ensurers Market; Continental Insurance Co.; CSB Mortgage Co.; Dairyland Insurance Companies; Dynatronics Corp.; EMC Ins. Cos.; Federated Ins. Cos.; GAB Services, Inc.; General Mills; General Motors Acceptance Corp.; Glenfed Mortgage Co.; Grindstone Butte Project; Harsco Corp. Highlands Ins. Co.; Idaho Power; Indemnity Ins. Company of North America; Ins. Co. of North America; Ins. Co. of the West; International Multifoods; Interstate Industries Electric Supply, Inc.; Invacare Corp.; Kissell Co.; Liberty International Underwriters; Liberty Life Ins.; Little Valley Mutual Irrigation Co.; McDonald's; Medmarc/Hamilton Resources Corp.; Motor Vehicle Casualty Co.; Mountain Home Irrigation Dist.; Mountain View Title, Inc.; Nampa & Meridian Irrigation Dist.; National Service Industries; Pacific Employers Ins. Co.; PNS Stores, Inc.; Price Development Co.; Property Management Services, Inc.; Redlands Insurance Cos.; Riddle Ranches, Inc.; Rim View Trout Co.; Ryder Transportation Resources; Sentry Ins. Cos.; Snake River Irrigation District; State of Idaho; Synthes, Inc.; Sulzer Orthopedics; Teledyne Continental Motors; Travelers Indemnity Co.; United Technologies; USX (US Steel); Veterans Administration; WFS Financial.

RUNFT & STEELE LAW OFFICES, PLLC

1020 WEST MAIN STREET, SUITE 400
BOISE, IDAHO 83702-5745
Telephone: 208-333-8506
Fax: 208-343-3246
URL: http://www.runftlaw.com
Email: jlrunft@runftlaw.com
URL: http://www.lawyers.com/runftlaw.com

General Civil and Trial Practice in all Courts with emphasis on Business, Corporate, Contract, Administrative Law; Business Litigation, Bad Faith Insurance Defense.

JOHN L. RUNFT, born Baker City, Oregon, August 14, 1937; admitted to bar, 1965, Idaho, Idaho Supreme Court and U.S. District Court, District of Idaho; 1970, U.S. Court of Appeals, Ninth Circuit; 1977, U.S. Supreme Court; 1980, U.S. Claims Court; 1983, U.S. Court of Appeals for the Federal Circuit. *Education:* College of Idaho (B.A., 1962); University of Chicago (J.D., 1965). Recipient, Justice Jackson Award in Constitutional Law, University of Chicago Law School, 1965. Member: Idaho Law Foundation, 1965—; Board of Litigation, Mountain States Legal Foundation, 1977—. Civilian Aide, Secretary of the Army of the United States, 1988-1995. Member, Board of Directors of Idaho Community Foundation, 1988-1996. *Member:* Idaho State Bar; American Bar Association. ***LANGUAGES:*** German. ***PRACTICE AREAS:*** Business Law; Corporate Law; Contract Law; Commercial Law; Administrative Law; Civil Litigation; Torts; Contracts; Business Litigation. ***Email:*** jlrunft@runftlaw.com

JON M. STEELE, born Cedar Rapids, Iowa, February 17, 1950; admitted to bar, 1976, Idaho Supreme Court and U.S. District Court, District of Idaho; 1982, U.S. Court of Appeals, Ninth Circuit. *Education:* University of Iowa (B.A., 1973); Drake University (J.D., 1975). National Institute of Trial Advocacy, 1981; Advanced National Institute of Trial Advocacy, 1982. *Member:* Idaho Trial Lawyers (Board of Directors, 1981-1987); Capital Youth Soccer Association (Member, Board of Directors, 1992-2002); Idaho State Bar. ***PRACTICE AREAS:*** Real Estate; Business Law; Corporate Law; Contracts; Commercial Law; Personal Injury; Business Litigation. ***Email:*** jmsteele@runftlaw.com

KARL J. RUNFT, born Boise, Idaho, November 14, 1975; admitted to bar, 2002, Wisconsin; 2003, Idaho and U.S. District Court, District of Idaho. *Education:* University of Chicago (B.A., cum laude, 1998); University of Wisconsin School of Law (J.D., cum laude, 2002). Recipient, Constitutional Law Award, University of Wisconsin Law School, 2002. Law Clerk, Idaho Supreme Court, 2002-2003. *Member:* Idaho State Bar (Member: Young Lawyers Section; Sub Committee on Corporate Law); American Bar Association; Idaho Legal Foundation; Lincoln Day Committee. ***Email:*** kjrunft@runftlaw.com

SASSER & INGLIS, P.C.

3100 SOUTH VISTA AVENUE, SUITE 200
BOISE, IDAHO 83705
Telephone: 208-344-8474
Fax: 208-344-8479
Email: si@sasseringlis.com
URL: http://www.sasseringlis.com

General Civil, Trial and Appellate Practice. Business and Corporate Practice, Civil Rights, Construction, Domestic, Employment, Environmental, Governmental, Insurance, Labor, Negligence, Personal Injury, Products Liability, Professional Liability, Real Estate Law and Transportation.

M. MICHAEL SASSER, born 1948; admitted to bar, 1974, Idaho. *Education:* University of Maryland (B.A., 1970); University of Idaho (J.D., 1974). Member, Idaho Law Review, 1973-1974. Author: "Journalistic Privilege," Idaho Law Review, Spring, 1974. *Member:* Idaho State Bar; Defense Research; Idaho Association of Defense Counsel. ***PRACTICE AREAS:*** Construction; Environmental; Intellectual Property; Insurance; Litigation; Medical; Personal Injury; Products Liability; Transportation. ***Email:*** mms@sasseringlis.com

PATRICK J. INGLIS, born 1960; admitted to bar, 1986, Idaho. *Education:* University of Washington (B.A., 1983); University of Idaho (J.D., 1986). Extern, U.S. Court of Appeals, Ninth Circuit, 1985. Law Clerk, Idaho Supreme Court, 1986-1987. *Member:* Idaho State Bar; American Bar Association; Defense Research Institute; Idaho Association of Defense Counsel. ***PRACTICE AREAS:*** Insurance; Litigation; Personal Injury. ***Email:*** pji@sasseringlis.com

CLAY M. SHOCKLEY, born 1962; admitted to bar, 1993, Idaho. *Education:* Boise State University (B.A., 1989); University of Idaho (J.D., 1993). *Member:* Idaho State Bar. ***Email:*** cms@sasseringlis.com

JASON G. DYKSTRA, born Helena, Montana, October 21, 1969; admitted to bar, 1995, Montana; 1996, U.S. District Court, District of Montana; 2002 Idaho. *Education:* University of Montana (B.S., 1992; J.D., 1995). *Member:* Idaho State Bar.

ANDREW E. SCHEPP, born Columbus, Ohio, May 8, 1971; admitted to bar, 2000, Idaho. *Education:* Western State College of Colorado (B.A., 1994); University of Idaho (J.D., 2000). ***Email:*** aes@sasseringlis.com

REPRESENTATIVE CLIENTS: Alcoa; Allstate Insurance Co.; American Hardware Mutual Insurance Co.; Amex Life Assurance Co.; Attorney Liability Protection Society, Inc.; Baxter Healthcare Corp.; Beneficial Finance Co.; CNA Insurance Cos.; CIGNA Cos.; Colonial Life & Accident Insurance Co.; Commercial Union Insurance Co.; Continental Group, Inc.; Continental Weston Group; Great American Insurance Co.; Gulf Insurance Group; Horace Mann Insurance Co.; INAPRO; Insurance Company of North America; LDS Church; Lanser Insurance Co.; National Casualty Insurance Co.; National Union Fire Insurance Co.; Nobel Insurance Co.; Ohio Casualty Insurance Co.; Orion Auto Group; PIE Nationwide, Inc.; Reliance Insurance Co.; Royal & SunAlliance USA Ins. Group; Ryder System, Inc.; St. Paul Fire and Marine Insurance; State Farm Insurance Cos.; Underwriters at Lloyd's, London; Universal Underwriters.

SCHROEDER & LEZAMIZ LAW OFFICES, L.L.P.

447 WEST MYRTLE
P.O. BOX 267
BOISE, IDAHO 83701
Telephone: 208-384-1627
Fax: 208-384-1833
URL: http://www.schroederlezamiz.com

Public Land Law, Civil Litigation, Family Law, Bankruptcy (Creditors), Probate and Wills, Real Estate, Plaintiff's Personal Injury and Workmens Compensation, Timber Trespass.

MEMBERS OF FIRM

JOHN T. SCHROEDER, born Nyssa, Oregon, July 3, 1956; admitted to bar, 1981, Idaho and U.S. District Court, District of Idaho; 1982, U.S. Court of Appeals, Ninth Circuit. *Education:* Pacific Lutheran University (B.A., 1977); University of Idaho Graduate School-Range Management; University of Idaho (J.D., 1981). *Member:* Idaho State Bar (Family Law Section); Idaho Trial Lawyers Association.

MARGARET M. LEZAMIZ, born Boise, Idaho, December 20, 1956; admitted to bar, 1983, Idaho and U.S. District Court, District of Idaho; 1985, U.S. Court of Appeals, Ninth Circuit. *Education:* College of Idaho (B.A., 1979); University of Idaho (J.D., 1982). *Member:* Idaho State Bar (Wills and Probate Section).

W. ALAN SCHROEDER, born Nyssa, Oregon, May 8, 1961; admitted to bar, 1986, Washington; 1987, U.S. District Court, Western District of Washington; 1990, Idaho, U.S. District Court, District of Idaho and U.S. Court of Appeals, Ninth Circuit; 1992, U.S. Court of Appeals, Tenth Circuit and U.S. Court of Federal Claims; 1994, U.S. Court of Appeals for the Federal Circuit; 1996, U.S. Supreme Court; 2000, U.S. Court of Appeals, Eighth Circuit. *Education:* Pacific Lutheran University (B.B.A., 1983); University of Puget Sound (J.D., 1986). Member: Idaho Cattle Association; National Cattlemen's Beef Association (Charter Member); Association of Rangeland Consultants; Society of Range Management. *Member:* Washington State Bar Association; Idaho State Bar (Member, Environment and Natural Resources Section).

SEINIGER LAW OFFICES

Established in 1980
942 WEST MYRTLE
BOISE, IDAHO 83702
Telephone: 208-345-1000
Fax: 208-345-4700
Email: wbs@seinigerlaw.com
URL: http://www.seinigerlaw.com

Seattle, Washington Office: 601 Union Street, Suite 4200, 98101. Telephone: 208-345-1000. Fax: 208-345-1000.

Personal Injury, Workers Compensation, Employment Discrimination and Harassment, Business Torts, Insurance Disputes.

WILLIAM BRECK SEINIGER, JR., born Richmond, Virginia, October 28, 1947; admitted to bar, 1979, Idaho; 1985, District of Columbia; 2003, Oregon. *Education:* University of Massachusetts (B.A., 1972); University of Idaho College of Law (J.D., 1978). Member, Civil Rules Committee, Idaho Supreme Court. *Member:* Idaho State Bar (Chairman, Solo and Small Firm Section); Idaho Trial Lawyers Association (Member, Board of Directors). ***PRACTICE AREAS:*** Personal Injury; Workers Compensation; Employment Discrimination; Employment Harassment; Business Torts; Insurance Disputes. ***Email:*** wbs@seinigerlaw.com

LAWRENCE G. SIRHALL, JR.

Established in 1994
IMPERIAL PLAZA
200 NORTH 3RD, SUITE 8
BOISE, IDAHO 83702
Telephone: 208-342-2444
Fax: 208-342-2676
Email: sirhalllaw@aol.com
URL: http://www.sirhalllaw.com

Personal Injury, Tax, Criminal Tax Defense, Real Estate, Adoption, Neck and Back Injuries, Slip and Fall, Car Accidents.

LAWRENCE G. SIRHALL, JR., born Boise, Idaho, June 12, 1958; admitted to bar, 1984, Idaho and U.S. Tax Court. *Education:* University of Idaho (B.A., 1980; M.B.A., cum laude, 1981); University of Notre Dame (J.D., 1984). Phi Beta Kappa; Phi Kappa Phi; Phi

(This Listing Continued)

LAWRENCE G. SIRHALL, JR., Boise—Continued

Eta Sigma; Eta Sigma Phi. *Member:* Idaho State Bar; American Bar Association; American Institute of Certified Public Accountants.

SPINK BUTLER, LLP

251 EAST FRONT STREET, SUITE 200
P.O. BOX 639
BOISE, IDAHO 83701
Telephone: 208-388-1000
Fax: 208-388-1001
Email: contact@sb-attorneys.com
URL: http://www.sb-attorneys.com

Commercial Real Estate, Zoning, Planning and Land Use, Business Law, Commercial Litigation.

MICHAEL T. SPINK, born Pontiac, Michigan, March 6, 1950; admitted to bar, 1978, Idaho; 1981, U.S. Supreme Court. *Education:* Denison University; Stanford University (B.A., 1972); University of Denver (J.D., 1977). Notes Editor, Transportation Law Journal, 1977. Faculty, Idaho Law Foundation Seminars: Real Property Law, Boundary Law, Construction Law and Liens. Deputy Attorney General, Idaho State Tax Commission, 1981-1982. *Member:* Idaho State Bar. ***PRACTICE AREAS:*** Real Estate; Business Law; Commercial Litigation; Appellate Practice. ***Email:*** mspink@sb-attorneys.com

JoANN C. BUTLER, born Geneva, New York, July 18, 1951; admitted to bar, 1987, Illinois; 1990, Idaho. *Education:* State University of New York at Buffalo (B.S., 1974); Pennsylvania State University; University of Natal, R.S.A. (M.A., 1980); Chicago-Kent College of Law (J.D., 1987). *Member:* Idaho State Bar; Illinois State and American Bar Associations; American Planning Association; Idaho Planning Association; American Water Works Association. ***PRACTICE AREAS:*** Real Estate; Zoning, Planning and Land Use; Appellate Practice; Environmental Law. ***Email:*** jbutler@sb-attorneys.com

---

LAUREN MAIERS REYNOLDSON, born Bremerton, Washington, December 19, 1971; admitted to bar, 1998, Washington; 1999, Idaho. *Education:* University of Washington (B.A., 1994); Gonzaga University College of Law (J.D., magna cum laude, 1998). Executive Editor, Gonzaga Law Review, 1997-1998. *Member:* Idaho State Bar; Washington State Bar Association. ***PRACTICE AREAS:*** Real Estate; Commercial Transactions. ***Email:*** lreynoldson@sb-attorneys.com

REPRESENTATIVE CLIENTS: Albertson's; Ameritel Inns; Commonwealth Title; Harty & Harty; Idaho Truss & Component Co.; Idaho Properties; John L. Scott BOI; Neighborhood Housing Services; Oaas Laney; Sel-Equity Real Estate; Sperry Van Ness; The Terteling Co.; Transnation Title; United Water Idaho; Wal-Mart Stores.

STOEL RIVES LLP

101 S. CAPITOL BOULEVARD
SUITE 1900
BOISE, IDAHO 83702-5958
Telephone: 208-389-9000
Facsimile: 208-389-9040
URL: http://www.stoel.com

Portland, Oregon Office: Suite 2600, 900 S.W. Fifth Avenue. Telephone: 503-224-3380.
Seattle, Washington Office: Suite 3600, One Union Square, 600 University. Telephone: 206-624-0900.
Vancouver, Washington Office: Suite 725, 805 Broadway. Telephone: 360-699-5900.
Salt Lake City, Utah Office: Suite 1100, One Utah Center, 201 South Main Street. Telephone: 801-328-3131.
San Francisco, California Office: 111 Sutter Street, Suite 700. Telephone: 415-617-8900.
Sacramento, California Office: 770 L Street, Suite 800. Telephone: 916-447-0700.
Tahoe City, California Office: 3000 N. Lake Boulevard, Suite 1, P.O. Box 7336. Telephone: 530-583-2116.
Fresno, California Office: 1233 W. Shaw Avenue, Suite 103. Telephone: 559-228-9900.

General Practice and Litigation in State and Federal Courts; Corporate Transactions; Finance; Securities; Labor and Employment Law; Construction; Products Liability; Real Estate and Development; Environmental; State and Local Taxation; Federal Taxation; Trusts and Estates; Banking; Commercial Law; Bankruptcy and Secured Lending; Legislative Affairs.

FIRM PROFILE: Stoel Rives is a business law firm providing services throughout the western United States. It is regarded as a regional leader in energy, natural resources, environment, corporate and intellectual property law and complex litigation. The firm's 375 lawyers and 500 support staff provide client-focused services to a wide range of businesses and individuals from eight offices in Oregon, Washington, California, Utah and Idaho. For more information, visit www.stoel.com.

RESIDENT MEMBERS

KEVIN J. BEATON, born Englewood, New Jersey, August 30, 1957; admitted to bar, 1984, Idaho; 1986, Massachusetts. *Education:* Boston College (B.A., magna cum laude, 1979); George Washington University (J.D., with honors, 1983). ***PRACTICE AREAS:*** Environmental Law. ***Email:*** kjbeaton@stoel.com

PAUL M. BOYD, born Seattle, Washington, October 1, 1949; admitted to bar, 1982, Washington; 1994, Idaho. *Education:* Stanford University (A.B., with great distinction, 1971); Georgetown University (J.D., magna cum laude, 1982). ***PRACTICE AREAS:*** Corporate Law; Securities; Finance. ***Email:*** pmboyd@stoel.com

MARY S. HOBSON, born The Dalles, Oregon, April 14, 1950; admitted to bar, 1977, Idaho and U.S. District Court, District of Idaho; 1978, U.S. Court of Appeals, Ninth Circuit. *Education:* Washington State University (B.A., 1972; M.A., with high honors, 1974); University of Idaho (J.D., cum laude, 1977). ***PRACTICE AREAS:*** Regulatory Law; Commercial Litigation. ***Email:*** mshobson@stoel.com

QUENTIN M. KNIPE, born Boise, Idaho, February 9, 1964; admitted to bar, 1989, Washington; 1992, Idaho. *Education:* Lewis and Clark College (B.S., 1986); University of Washington Law School (J.D., 1989). ***PRACTICE AREAS:*** Real Estate. ***Email:*** qmknipe@stoel.com

KRISTA K. McINTYRE, born Miami Beach, Florida, November 11, 1964; admitted to bar, 1989, Florida; 1991, District of Columbia; 1993, Idaho. *Education:* Vanderbilt University (B.A., 1986); University of Miami Law School (J.D., 1989). ***PRACTICE AREAS:*** Environmental Law; Environmental Regulatory Compliance. ***Email:*** kkmcintyre@stoel.com

KRIS ORMSETH, born Portland, Oregon, March 9, 1961; admitted to bar, 1992, Idaho. *Education:* Stanford University (B.A., 1983); Boalt Hall School of Law, University of California at Berkeley (J.D., 1991). ***PRACTICE AREAS:*** Corporate Law; Securities; Finance. ***Email:*** kjormseth@stoel.com

J. WALTER SINCLAIR, born Twin Falls; admitted to bar, 1978, Idaho. *Education:* Stanford University (B.A., 1975); University of Idaho (J.D., 1978). Fellow, American College of Trial Lawyers. ***PRACTICE AREAS:*** Commercial Litigation; Business Litigation. ***Email:*** jwsinclair@stoel.com

RESIDENT ASSOCIATES

Bradley J. Dixon — ***Teresa A. Hill***
Nicole C. Hancock — ***Christopher Pooser***
Marla S. Henken — ***Gregory C. Tollefson***
Samia E. McCall (Not admitted in ID)

OF COUNSEL

MARK S. GESTON, born Atlantic City, New Jersey, June 20, 1946; admitted to bar, 1971, Idaho. *Education:* Kenyon College (A.B., cum laude, with high honors, 1968); New York University (J.D., 1971). ***PRACTICE AREAS:*** Litigation; Products Liability Defense; Legal and Professional Malpractice Defense; Negligence. ***Email:*** msgeston@stoel.com

JAMES C. DALE, born Dover, Massachusetts, December 24, 1956; admitted to bar, 1982, Idaho and U.S. District Court, District of Idaho; 1987, U.S. Court of Appeals, Ninth Circuit. *Education:* University of Massachusetts (B.A., 1979); University of Idaho (J.D., 1982). *Member:* Idaho State Bar. ***PRACTICE AREAS:*** Litigation; Labor and Employment. ***Email:*** jcdale@stoel.com

DALE G. HIGER, born Emmett, Idaho, June 23, 1941; admitted to bar, 1966, Idaho and U.S. District Court, District of Idaho; 1970, U.S. Court of Appeals, 9th Circuit; 1971, U.S. Supreme Court. *Education:* University of Washington (B.A., cum laude, 1963); Harvard University (J.D., 1966). ***PRACTICE AREAS:*** Corporate Law; Creditors Rights Law; Bankruptcy; Commercial Law; Real Estate Law; Estate Planning and Probate; Taxation; Legislative Affairs. ***Email:*** dghiger@stoel.com

REPRESENTATIVE CLIENTS: Albertson's, Inc.; Cogentrix Energy, Inc.; Micron Technology, Inc.; Potlatch Corporation; Qwest Corporation; St. Luke's Regional Medical Center; Trus Joist, a Weyerhaeuser Company.

(For complete biographical data on other personnel, see Professional Biographies at Portland, Oregon, Salt Lake City, Utah, Washington, D.C. and Vancouver and Seattle, Washington)

TECHNOLOGY LAW GROUP, LLC

Established in 2003
3355 NORTH FIVE MILE ROAD, SUITE 333
BOISE, IDAHO 83713
Telephone: 208-939-4472
Fax: 208-939-5755
Email: info@technologylawgroup.com
URL: http://www.technologylawgroup.com

Intellectual Property Licensing, International Business Transactions and Trade, Intellectual Property, Internet and E-Commerce.

FIRM PROFILE: Technology Law Group, LLC is an intellectual property law firm serving technology innovators in intellectual property and Internet legal matters and litigation matters; international IP licensing and strategic due diligence are emphasized.

EMILE LOZA, admitted to bar, 2003, Idaho and U.S. District Court, District of Idaho. *Education:* Oklahoma State University (B.S., Science and Technology, 1980); University of Houston (M.B.A., 1993); George Washington University (J.D., 2001). *Member:* Idaho State Bar (Vice Chair, Intellectual Property Law Section); American Bar Association (Co-Chair, International Tech. Transfer Subcommittee); AIPLA; Licensing Executive Society. ***PRACTICE AREAS:*** Intellectual Property; International; Internet Law.

ASSOCIATE

SCOTT R. CLEERE, born 1969; admitted to bar, 2000, Idaho and U.S. District Court, District of Idaho; registered to practice before U.S. Patent and Trademark Office. *Education:* Brigham Young University (B.S., 1996); University of Idaho (J.D., 2000). *Member:* Idaho State Bar (Chair, Professionalism and Ethics Section, 2002-2004; Chair, Intellectual Property Section, 2004-2005). ***PRACTICE AREAS:*** Patent; Trademark; Licensing.

SPECIAL COUNSEL

PAUL D. ROATH, admitted to bar, 2001, Virginia and U.S. Court of Appeals, Fourth Circuit; 2003, District of Columbia and U.S. Court of Appeals, Federal Circuit; 2005, Pennsylvania; registered to practice before U.S. Patent and Trademark Office (Not admitted in Idaho). *Education:* University of New Mexico (B.S., 1979; B.S.M.T., 1980); North Dakota

(This Listing Continued)

State University (Ph.D., 1995); George Washington University (J.D., 2000). Member, American Society for Micro Biology. *Member:* American Bar Association; AIPLA. [With U.S. Army, 1972-1975, SP 4]. ***PRACTICE AREAS:*** Patents; Federal Taxation; Corporate Law.

Languages: Chinese, Korean, Japanese, Spanish, German, French and English.

REPRESENTATIVE CLIENTS: Available Upon Request.

ROBERT A. WALLACE

Established in 1976

815 PARK BOULEVARD, SUITE 130
BOISE, IDAHO 83712
Telephone: 208-342-0100
Fax: 208-343-2069
URL: http://www.rwallacelaw.com
Email: lawyer@idahocrimlaw.com
URL: http://www.idahocrimlaw.com

Criminal Defense, DWI, Drug Crimes, Felonies, Misdemeanors, Traffic Violations, Juvenile, Plaintiffs' Personal Injury, Collections.

ROBERT A. WALLACE, born Los Angeles, California, December 17, 1950; admitted to bar, 1976, Idaho, U.S. District Court, District of Idaho and U.S. Court of Appeals, Ninth Circuit. *Education:* University of California at Berkeley (B.A., 1973); Hastings College of Law, University of California (J.D., 1976). Phi Delta Phi. Lecturer, College of Business, Boise State University, Spring Semester, 1980. Senior Deputy, Boise City Criminal Prosecutor, 1989-1998. Deputy Attorney General, Natural Resources Division, 1977-1979. Secretary, Mayor's Transit Advisory Committee, 1976-1985. Law Clerk to Hon. W. E. Smith, 1976-1977 and Member, Committee on Unauthorized Practice of Law, 1984-1985, Fourth Judicial District. *Member:* Idaho State Bar (Member, Pro Bono Pilot Project Steering Committee, 1982-1984); Idaho Association of Criminal Defense Lawyers (Lifetime Member). ***LANGUAGES:*** Spanish. ***PRACTICE AREAS:*** Criminal Defense; Plaintiffs Personal Injury; Collections.

Languages: Espanol.

WESTBERG, McCABE & COLLINS

CHARTERED
Established in 1989

THE TULLIS BUILDING
516 WEST FRANKLIN STREET, LOWER LEVEL
P.O. BOX 2836
BOISE, IDAHO 83701-2836
Telephone: 208-336-5200
Fax: 208-336-2121
URL: http://www.wmclaw-firm.com

General Practice, Real Estate, Probate, Estate Planning, Federal and State Court Civil Litigation, Criminal Defense, White Collar Crimes, Administrative, Business and Corporate Law, Government Contract, Water Rights and Mining Law.

PAUL L. (LARRY) WESTBERG, born Watertown, New York, January 21, 1943; admitted to bar, 1968, Idaho and U.S. District Court, District of Idaho; 1975, U.S. Court of Appeals, Ninth Circuit; 1976, U.S. District Court, Southern District of Texas; 1977, U.S. Supreme Court. *Education:* University of Idaho (B.S., 1966; J.D., 1968). Listed in, Best Lawyers in America. Law Clerk, U.S. District Court, District of Idaho, 1968-1970. District Counsel, U.S. Small Business Administration, Boise, Idaho, 1970-1973. Assistant U.S. Attorney, District of Idaho, 1973-1977. Special Assistant U.S. Attorney, Southern District of Texas, 1976. U.S. Attorney, District of Idaho, 1977. Ex-officio Member, Idaho Law Enforcement Planning Commission, 1977. Bencher, Boise, American Inns of Court 1991—, Idaho. Coordinator, U.S. District Court, Criminal Justice Act Attorney Panel, 1991. Lawyer Representative, U.S. Court of Appeals, Ninth Circuit, 2001-2003. *Member:* Boise, Federal (President, Idaho Chapter, 2004—) and American Bar Associations; Idaho State Bar; Idaho Trial Lawyers Association; National Association of Criminal Defense Lawyers; American Judicature Society; Idaho Association of Criminal Defense Attorneys (Secretary, 1989-1994). ***PRACTICE AREAS:*** Criminal Defense; Civil Litigation; White Collar Crime. ***Email:*** lwstbrg@attglobal.net

THOMAS J. McCABE, born Philadelphia, Pennsylvania, May 21, 1946; admitted to bar, 1980, Idaho and U.S. District Court, District of Idaho; 1981, U.S. Court of Appeals, Ninth Circuit; 1987, U.S. Supreme Court. *Education:* La Salle College (B.A., cum laude, 1968); University of Oregon; University of Idaho (J.D., 1979); National Criminal Defense College (1989). Listed in, Best Lawyers in America. Co-Author: *Advanced Drinking/Driving Litigation in Idaho,* Professional Education Systems, Inc., Eau Claire, Wisconsin, 1986. Lecturer: DUI and Criminal Defense, 1983—, Continuing Legal Education Program. Law Clerk to: Hon. Ray McNichols, Chief Judge, U.S. District Court for the District of Idaho, 1978-1981; Hon. Fred M. Taylor, Senior U.S. District Judge, District of Idaho, 1981. Member: Idaho Supreme Court's Misdemeanor Rules Advisory Committee, 1984-1988; Evidence Rules Advisory Committee, 1989-1995; Criminal Jury Instructions Committee, 1988—. *Member:* Boise and American Bar Associations; Idaho State Bar; National Association of Criminal Defense Lawyers; Idaho Association of Criminal Defense Lawyers (Founding President, 1989-1994). [Captain, U.S. Army, 1968-1971]. (Certified as Criminal Trial Specialist by the Idaho Trial Lawyer s Association). ***PRACTICE AREAS:*** Criminal Defense; Driving While Intoxicated; Drug Crimes; Parole and Probation; White Collar Crime; Homicide. ***Email:*** tmccabe9@cableone.net

WILLIAM D. COLLINS, born Idaho Falls, Idaho, September 30, 1939; admitted to bar, 1965, Idaho and U.S. District Court, District of Idaho; 1990, U.S. Court of Appeals, Ninth Circuit. *Education:* University of Idaho (B.S. Ch.Eng., 1961; M.S. Chem.E., 1963); Cornell University and University of Idaho (LL.B., 1965). Assistant Attorney General of Idaho, Department of Water Resources, 1965-1970. Boise County Prosecuting Attorney,

(This Listing Continued)

1970-1975. *Member:* Boise Bar Association; Idaho State Bar (Member, Sections on: Taxation; Probate and Trust Law; Environmental and Natural Resources; Water Law; Real Property); Idaho Trial Lawyers Association; Boise Estate Planning Council; Society of Minning Engineers; Rocky Mountain Mineral Law Institute. ***PRACTICE AREAS:*** Real Estate; Probate; Water Rights; Estate Planning; Mining Law. ***Email:*** collinsw@cableone.net

ASSOCIATE

CHRISTIAN D. COLLINS, born Boise, Idaho, November 3, 1968; admitted to bar, 1999, Idaho and U.S. District Court, District of Idaho. *Education:* Boise State University (B.A., Criminal Justice Administration, 1991); University of Idaho (J.D., 1998). Deputy Canyon County Public Defender, Canyon County, Idaho, 2000-2001. Deputy Ada County Public Defender, Ada County, Idaho, 2001-2003. Member, American Inns of Court #130, 2001-2002. *Member:* Idaho State Bar; National Association of Criminal Defense Lawyers; Idaho Association of Criminal Defense Lawyers. ***PRACTICE AREAS:*** Criminal Defense; Driving While Intoxicated; Drug Crimes. ***Email:*** cdcollins@cableone.net

WILSON McCOLL & RASMUSSEN

Established in 1981

420 WASHINGTON STREET
P.O. BOX 1544
BOISE, IDAHO 83701
Telephone: 208-345-9100
FAX: 208-384-0442
Email: jeff@wilsonmccoll.com
URL: http://www.wilsonmccoll.com

General Civil Practice, Bankruptcy, Real Property, Insurance, Commercial Litigation, Agricultural, Farm, Family Law, Personal Injury, Estate, Probate, Commercial Transactions, Collections, Communications and Media Law, Professional Liability, Creditors Rights, Business Law, Trials.

JEFFREY M. WILSON, born Ravenna, Ohio, September 17, 1949; admitted to bar, 1974, Idaho. *Education:* University of Denver (B.S.B.A., 1971); Ohio Northern University College of Law (J.D., 1974). Commissioner, 1992-1995 and President, 1994-1995, Idaho State Bar. Chancellor, Jack Rabbit Bar, 1996-1997. Board Certified Creditors Rights Specialist, Commercial Law League of America. *Member:* Boise Bar Association; Idaho State Bar (Member, Sections on: Bankruptcy; Commercial Law); Commercial Law League of America; American Alliance of Creditors' Attorneys; National Attorney Network; Fidelity Foreclosure Network; National Association of Retail Collection Attorneys (NARCA). ***PRACTICE AREAS:*** Commercial Litigation; Bankruptcy; Trials; Tort Defense; Creditor's Rights. ***Email:*** jeff@wilsonmccoll.com

BRIAN F. McCOLL, born Hamilton, Ontario, April 8, 1947; admitted to bar, 1978, Idaho. *Education:* University of Western Ontario (B.A., with honors, 1969); The Johns Hopkins University; University of Baltimore (J.D., 1977). *Member:* Idaho State Bar (Member, Business and Corporate Law and Real Property Section). ***PRACTICE AREAS:*** Commercial Transactions; Real Property; Commercial Litigation. ***Email:*** brian@wilsonmccoll.com

LISA B. RASMUSSEN, born Rexburg, Idaho, February 18, 1963; admitted to bar, 1994, Idaho. *Education:* Brigham Young University (B.A., 1989; J.D., 1993). *Member:* Idaho State Bar. ***PRACTICE AREAS:*** Commercial Litigation; Personal Injury; Tort Defense; Insurance; Employment Law; Creditors Rights; Bankruptcy.

REPRESENTATIVE CLIENTS: Allied Insurance; American Bureau of Collections, I.C. System, Inc.; American Commerce Insurance; American Family Insurance; American Honda Finance; American Investment Bank; Associates Housing Finance; Attorneys Liability Protection Society (ALPS); Bank of America; Beneficial Finance; Berkeley Federal; Bio Flora NW; Bob Rice Ford; Boise-Winemucca Stages; Caterpillar Financial Corp./John Deere Credit Corp.; Cavalry Investments LLC; Chase Financial; Chase Manhattan Mortgage; Circle Business Credit; Citicapital; Citibank; Colonial Pacific Leasing; Conseco Financial Group; Contemporary Media, Inc.; Credit Acceptance Lease Comm.; Employer Insurance Co of Nevada; Employment Reinsurance Co.; First Merchants Acceptance; Harley Davidson Financial; Higgins and Rutledge Insurance Co., Inc.; Holland Realty, Inc.; Homecoming Financial; Household Finance; Hurley State Bank; Idaho Independent Bank; Idaho Properties, Inc.; Ikon Office; IOS Capital; Kawasaki Motor Corp. USA; LaSalle N.W. Bank; Les Schwab Tires Inc.; MB Financial Bank; MBNA; Mitsubishi Motor Credit; Northwestern Stages; Nuvell Financial Services; Onyx Acceptance Corp.; Peak Medical Corp.; Providian National Bank; Republic Leasing; State of Idaho; State of Idaho Dept of Administration/Office of Insurance Management; State of Idaho - Dept. of Agriculture; State of Idaho - Dept. of Labor & Industrial Services; Sun HealthCare Group; The Hartford; Toyota Motor Credit Co.; Transamerican Commercial Finance Corp.; TranSouth Finance 21st Mortgage; Textron Financial; Vanderbilt Finance; Volvo Commercial Finance; Washington Trust Bank; Information Leasing; Wachovia Bank; Wells Fargo; Western Farm Service; Yamaha Motor Corp. USA.
REFERENCE: Idaho Independent Bank.

LING, ROBINSON & WALKER

BURLEY, IDAHO

(See Rupert)

BAUER & FRENCH

CALDWELL, IDAHO

(See Boise)

Trial and Appellate Practice. Family Law, Divorce, Interstate Child Custody, Community Property Law. Commercial, Bankruptcy, Real Estate.

BEVIS, CAMERON & JOHNSON, P.A.

CALDWELL, IDAHO

(See Boise)

General Trial and Appellate Practice before State and Federal Courts. Personal Injury, Family Law, Business, Corporation, Real Estate and Military Law.

BRASSEY, WETHERELL, CRAWFORD & GARRETT, L.L.P.

CALDWELL, IDAHO

(See Boise)

General Civil and Trial Practice, Appeals, Insurance Defense, Business Defense, Defense of Governmental Entities, Trucking Law, Medical Malpractice, DEF, Environmental, Civil Rights, Commercial, Real Estate, Employment, Personnel, Agriculture, and Products Liability.

ANDREA L. CARDON

CALDWELL, IDAHO

(See Boise)

Construction Contracts and Social Security Disability.

RON CHRISTIAN ATTORNEY AT LAW

CALDWELL, IDAHO

(See Boise)

Family Law, Adoptions, Alimony, Child Support, Custody, Divorce, Domestic Violence, Separation Agreements, Visitation Rights, Grandparents Rights, Restraining Orders, Criminal Law, Drugs Crimes, Drunk Driving, Felonies, Misdemeanors, Business Litigation and Transactions, Corporations, Limited Liability Companies, Employment Litigation, Real Estate Transactions and Litigation.

SANDRA L. CLAPP & ASSOCIATES, P.A.

CALDWELL, IDAHO

(See Eagle)

Trusts and Estates, Business Transactions, Property Law.

EVANS KEANE LLP

CALDWELL, IDAHO

(See Boise)

General Trial and Appellate Practice, Products Liability, Personal Injury Law, Corporate, Real Property, Banking, Employment, Labor, Mining, Public Utilities, Legislative and Administrative.

JAMES R. GILLESPIE, P.A.

CALDWELL, IDAHO

(See Boise)

General Practice. Business, Commercial Real Estate, Agricultural, Natural Resources Law, Environment and Construction Law, Mediation and Arbitration.

GJORDING & FOUSER, PLLC

CALDWELL, IDAHO

(See Boise)

Insurance Defense, Medical Malpractice Defense, Employment and Commercial Litigation.

GAR HACKNEY, P.L.L.C.

CALDWELL, IDAHO

(See Boise)

Criminal Law, Driving Under the Influence, Domestic Violence, Sexual Assault, Drug Crimes, Burglary, Search and Seizure, White Collar Crime, Federal Crimes, State and Felony Misdemeanor, Petty Theft, Personal Injury, Automobile Accidents, Bicycle Accidents, Pedestrian Accidents.

KANE & TOBIASON, LLP

CALDWELL, IDAHO

(See Boise)

Tort Litigation, Insurance Related Issues, Administrative and Governmental Relations.

MANWEILER, MANWEILER, BREEN & BALL, PLLC

CALDWELL, IDAHO

(See Boise)

General Trial and Appellate Practice before State and Federal Courts, Business Law, Criminal Law, Family Law, Insurance, Personal Injury and Workers Compensation.

HAROLD Q. NOACK, JR., P.A.

CALDWELL, IDAHO

(See Boise)

Creditor and Debtor Bankruptcy, General Civil, Trial and Appellate Practice. Commercial, Corporation, Family Law, Divorce, Alimony, Child Support, Real Estate, Construction Law, Elder Law, Wills and Probate.

AMARO LAW OFFICE

Established in 2001

1875 NORTH LAKEWOOD DRIVE, SUITE 102

COEUR D'ALENE, IDAHO 83814

Telephone: 208-667-4002

Facsimile: 208-667-9992

Email: contact@amarolaw.com

URL: http://www.amaro-law.com

General Practice, Mediation.

FIRM PROFILE: General civil litigation firm practicing in all areas of the law except criminal. Also offering mediation service. Solving complex legal problems with extraordinary legal service.

RAMI AMARO, born Austin, Texas, October 14, 1968; admitted to bar, 1996, Ohio; 1998, Idaho; 1999, Washington; 2002, U.S. Court of Appeals, Ninth Circuit. *Education:* The Evergreen State College (B.A., 1992); University of Cincinnati (J.D., 1996). Registered Mediator, Idaho Supreme Court. Pro Tem Judge, DUI Court, First District, Kootenai County, Idaho. Special Deputy Attorney General, Idaho Transportation Department. Administrative Law Judge, Idaho Transportation Department. Board Member, Law Related Education Committee. Chair, National Federation of Independent Business. Chair, Sister Cities Committee, KCRW. *Member:* Kootenai County, Spokane County and Washington State Bar Associations; Idaho State Bar; Idaho Mediation Association; North Idaho Women's Law Group (President). ***Email:*** ramaro@amarolaw.com

ASSOCIATES

JOSHUA LEONARD, born Bountiful, Davis County, Utah, November 19, 1975; admitted to bar, 2005, Idaho. *Education:* George Mason University (B.A. 2002); Gonzaga University School of Law (J.D. 2005). *Member:* Idaho State Bar. ***PRACTICE AREAS:*** Business Transactions; Real Estate; Personal Injury; Wills.

ADAM H. GREEN, born Moscow, Idaho, February 25, 1979; admitted to bar, 2004, Idaho; 2005, Washington. *Education:* University of Idaho (B.A. 2001); University of Idaho College of Law (J.D. 2004). *Member:* Idaho State Bar; Idaho State Bar Foundation. ***PRACTICE AREAS:*** Contracts; Business Law; Family Law; Labor and Employment; Personal Injury.

REPRESENTATIVE CLIENTS: State of Idaho; City of Spokane Valley; Grouse Meadows Home Owners Association; Greenstone Corporation; Adirondack Village Home Owner's Association; Association at the Gardens; Coeur d'Alene Place Home Owner's Association; Lyon's Park Home Owner's Association; Meadowwood Home Owner's Association; Monterose Home Owner's Association; Parkside Home Owner's Association; Ponderosa Ridge Home Owner's Association; River Crossing Home Owner's Association; The Village Home Owner's Association; Country Plaza Partners; J&E Enterprises; Eye Medical Associates; KC Lanes; Sterling Codifiers; Westland Electric; Border Sheet Metal & Heating; Design Associates; Finley enterprises; Evergreen Produce; International Contracting; Accent Landscaping; Highland Homeowners Association; Bonner Physical Therapy; Loan Closers; Northern Rockies Corporation.

WILLIAM F. BOYD

601 SHERMAN AVENUE

SUITE ONE

COEUR D'ALENE, IDAHO 83814

Telephone: 208-665-0666

Fax: 208-665-0864

Email: WBOYD1@GTE.NET

General Practice including Business, Environmental, Employee and Labor Issues, Mining Law, Probate, Civil Litigation and Appeals in all Courts.

WILLIAM F. BOYD, born Omaha, Nebraska, February 22, 1939; admitted to bar, 1965, Idaho; 1975, U.S. Court of Appeals, 9th Circuit; 1976, U.S. Court of Appeals, 10th Circuit; 1977, U.S. Supreme Court; 1981, U.S. Court of Appeals for the District of Columbia Circuit; 1983, U.S. Court of Federal Claims. *Education:* Oregon State University (B.S., 1962); University of Idaho (LL.B., 1965). *Member:* First Judicial District and American Bar Associations; Idaho State Bar. ***PRACTICE AREAS:*** Business Law; Environmental Law; Employee Law; Mining Law; Civil Litigation; Appeals.

REPRESENTATIVE CLIENTS: Coeur d'Alene Mines Corporation; Coeur Silver Valley, Inc.; Forest Capital Partners LLC.

BROWN, JUSTH, & ROMERO, PLLC

Established in 1978

627 GOVERNMENT WAY

P.O. BOX 1148

COEUR D'ALENE, IDAHO 83816-1148

Telephone: 208-664-2191

Fax: 208-664-2193

1-888-302-9101

Email: brnjusth@my180.net

URL: http://www.lawyers.com/cdalawyers

General Civil Practice. Commercial and Residential Real Estate, Estate Planning, Business, Wills, Trusts, Probate. Collections over $1500.

(This Listing Continued)

FIRM PROFILE: Brown, Justh & Romero, PLLC is a general practice small law firm, across from the county courthouse. It has built a reputation for providing its clients with excellent quality legal representation, and handling their clients' business with diligence and attention to detail.

MEMBERS OF FIRM

R. ROMER BROWN, born Kellogg, Idaho, 1942; admitted to bar, 1968, Idaho. *Education:* Oregon State University (B.S., 1965); University of Denver (J.D., 1968). Past President and Member, North Idaho College Foundation. Senior Deputy Prosecuting Attorney, Kootenai County, Idaho, 1971-1976. *Member:* Idaho State Bar (Chairman, Public Relations Committee, 1975-1980; Member, Examination Committee, 1975-1977). [Capt., U.S. Army, 1968-1970]. ***PRACTICE AREAS:*** Real Estate Law; Wills; Collections; Probate; Business Law; Civil Practice; Contracts. ***Email:*** brnjusth@my180.net

CAROLYN JUSTH, born Astoria, Oregon, 1947; admitted to bar, 1976, Idaho. *Education:* Northwest Nazarene College (B.A., 1968); University of Idaho (J.D., 1976). President, Coeur d'Alene Estate Planning Council, 1994-1995. *Member:* First District Bar Association (President, 1983-1984); Idaho State Bar (Member, Sections on: Commercial Law & Bankruptcy; Taxation, Probate and Trust Law). ***PRACTICE AREAS:*** Living Trusts; Wills; Trusts; Estate Planning and Probate; Guardianship and Conservatorship. ***Email:*** brnjusth@my180.net

ROBERT R. ROMERO, JR, admitted to bar, 1996, Idaho; 1997, U.S. Court of Appeals, Ninth Circuit. *Education:* California State University, Chico (B.S., 1990); University of Idaho (J.D., 1995). President, Federalist Society, 1994-1995. Past Member, Board of Zoning Adjustments, City of Moscow. ***PRACTICE AREAS:*** Real Estate; Business Law; Criminal Law; Juvenile Law; Civil Practice. ***Email:*** brnjusth@my180.net

LEGAL SUPPORT PERSONNEL

KAREN GITTEL, (Legal Assistant)
TONYA ARCHER, (Legal Assistant)
KATHY KRAPFL, (Bookkeeper)

REFERENCES: Mountain West Bank, Coeur d'Alene, Idaho.

CALLAHAN & ASSOCIATES, CHTD.

Established in 1998
1103 BEST AVENUE
P.O. BOX 2226
COEUR D'ALENE, IDAHO 83816
Telephone: 208-664-9228
Fax: 208-664-5369
Email: kwc@idahoestatelaw.com
URL: http://www.idahoestatelaw.com

Other Offices: Sandpoint, Idaho Office: Telephone: 208-265-4506.

Living Trusts, Estate Planning, Probate, Elder Law, Guardianship & Conservatorship, Asset Protection Planning, Wills, Estate & Gift Taxation, Generation Skipping Tax, Trusts, Living Wills, Advanced Directives, Charitable Trusts and Foundations.

FIRM PROFILE: Established in 1998, Callahan & Associates Chtd. has earned a solid reputation for providing quality estate planning and elder law services at reasonable rates. Our unique "Unlimited Support," which we provide to your estate planning clients, is just one of many ways our commitment to client service and satisfaction distinguishes us from our peers.

We offer complete estate planning services in Coeur d'Alene, Idaho, Sandpoint, Idaho, and Spokane, Washington. A large portion of our new clients come from existing client referrals and referrals from other professionals. We believe that this is one of the best measures of client satisfaction.

KIMMER W. CALLAHAN, born Lake Tahoe, California, August 17, 1970; admitted to bar, 1995, Idaho; 1996, Colorado and U.S. Tax Court; 2004, Washington. *Education:* University of Idaho (B.S., Accounting, 1992); Gonzaga University (J.D., 1995); University of Denver (LL.M., Taxation, 1996). Previous Employment: Michael J. Shidler & Associates, P.C., 1995-1996; The Prohaska Law Firm, 1996-1998. *Member:* Idaho State Bar (Member, Taxation, Probate and Trust Section); National Academy of Elder Law Attorneys (Member); Idaho Community Foundation; Panhandle Estate Planning Council (President, 1998-1999 and Treasurer, 1997-1998); Sunrise Rotary; Big Brother/Big Sister of North Idaho (Past President and Board Member). ***PRACTICE AREAS:*** Living Trusts; Estate Planning; Probate; Elder Law; Guardianship and Conservatorship; Asset Protection; Wills; Estate and Gift Taxation; Generation Skipping Tax; Trusts; Living Wills; Advance Directives; Charitable Trusts and Foundations. ***Email:*** kwc@idahostatelaw.com

REFERENCES: Pinkerton Retirement Specialists, Coeur d'Alene; Michael Bibin, CPA, Coeur d'Alene, Idaho.

ELSAESSER JARZABEK ANDERSON MARKS ELLIOTT & McHUGH

CHARTERED
1400 NORTHWOOD CENTER COURT, SUITE C
COEUR D'ALENE, IDAHO 83814
Telephone: 208-667-2900
Fax: 208-667-2150

Sandpoint Office: Lake Plaza Building, 123 South Third Street, P.O. Box 1049, Sandpoint, Idaho, 83864. Telephone: 208-263-8517. Facsimile: 208-263-0759.

(This Listing Continued)

General Civil Trial Practice in all Courts and Agencies. Bankruptcy, Commercial, Creditor's Rights, Estate Planning, Labor, Personal Injury, Planning and Zoning, Probate, Public Utility, Real Estate, Social Security, Taxation, Workers Compensation Law and Family Law.

FIRM PROFILE: Elsaesser Jarzabek Anderson Marks Elliott & McHugh was founded in Sandpoint in 1980. The firm now provides a full range of legal services throughout Northern Idaho. The firm has a special emphasis in Chapter 11 proceedings throughout the state and the region.

(For complete biographical data on all personnel, see Professional Biographies at Sandpoint, Idaho)

ESPOSITO, GEORGE & CAMPBELL, PLLC

COEUR D'ALENE, IDAHO

(See Spokane)

General Civil Trial and Appellate Practice in Federal and State Courts. Probate, Corporation, Business, Business Acquisitions, Partnerships, Real Estate, Commercial, Real Estate and Business Litigation, Bankruptcy, Bankruptcy Litigation and Probate Law, Commercial, Bankruptcy and Real Estate Mediation.

EVANS, CRAVEN & LACKIE, P.S.

Established in 1978
1424 SHERMAN AVENUE
EASTLAKE PROFESSIONAL SUITES, #300
COEUR D'ALENE, IDAHO 83814
Telephone: 208-667-8276

Spokane, Washington Office: 818 West Riverside Avenue, Suite 250. Telephone: 509-455-5200. Fax: 509-455-3632.

General Civil Trial and Appellate Practice. Professional Liability, Workman's Compensation, Personal Injury, Insurance Defense, Criminal, Municipal and Governmental, Zoning, Land Use, Environmental and Administrative Law, Wills, Trusts and Probate, Corporate and Personal Tax.

FIRM PROFILE: Evans, Craven & Lackie, P.S., is a Spokane, Washington based, litigation oriented law firm which emphasizes the defense of tort and business claims. The firm has built an excellent reputation providing the very best representation to its clients, which include insurance companies and their insureds, architects, engineers, attorneys and citizens with claims or grievances requiring litigation. These services are provided in the states of Washington and Idaho.

GREGORY M. KANE, born Detroit, Michigan, October 13, 1951; admitted to bar, 1980, Washington; 1982, U.S. District Court, Eastern District of Washington; 2003, Idaho. *Education:* Northern Illinois University (B.A., 1973); Gonzaga University (J.D., 1979). *Member:* Spokane County and Washington State Bar Associations; Washington Self-Insured Employer Association. (Also at Spokane, Washington, Office). ***PRACTICE AREAS:*** Industrial Insurance Defense. ***Email:*** gkane@ecl-law.com

MICHAEL E. McFARLAND JR., born Spokane, Washington, December 9, 1966; admitted to bar, 1993, Washington; 1995, U.S. District Court, Eastern District of Washington; 2004, Idaho. *Education:* University of Washington (B.A., 1989); Gonzaga University (J.D., magna cum laude, 1993). *Member:* Spokane County, Washington State and American Bar Associations. ***PRACTICE AREAS:*** Insurance Defense; Municipal Liability. ***Email:*** mmcfarland@ecl-law.com

AMY C. CLEMMONS, born Glen Cove, New York, October 19, 1966; admitted to bar, 1993, Washington and U.S. District Court, Eastern District of Washington; 1994, Idaho. *Education:* University of Texas; Fort Lewis College (B.A., 1989); Gonzaga University (J.D., 1993). Recipient, Best Brief Award, 1992. *Member:* Spokane County and Washington State Bar Associations; Idaho State Bar. (Also at Spokane, Washington Office). ***PRACTICE AREAS:*** Municipal Law; Civil Litigation; Employment Law. ***Email:*** aclemmons@ecl-law.com

LISETTE F. CARTER, born Great Falls, Montana, December 22, 1967; admitted to bar, 1993, Washington and U.S. District Court, Eastern District of Washington; 1994, Oregon; 2001, Montana; 2002, Idaho. *Education:* University of Montana (B.A., 1990); Willamette University (J.D., 1993). Phi Alpha Delta (President, 1992). *Member:* Spokane County and Washington State Bar Associations; Oregon State Bar; Idaho State Bar; State Bar of Montana; Washington State Trial Lawyers Association; Washington Defense Trial Lawyers; Washington Women Lawyers. ***PRACTICE AREAS:*** General Insurance Defense; Family Law. ***Email:*** lcarter@ecl-law.com

EVERETT B. COULTER, JR., born Spokane, Washington, March 21, 1949; admitted to bar, 1976, Washington and U.S. District Court, Eastern District of Washington; 1978, U.S. District Court, Western District of Washington; 1988, Idaho; Colville Confederated Tribe; Spokane Tribe; Kalispel Tribe; Nez Perce Tribe; Confederated Tribes; Bands of the Yakima Nation; Coeur d'Alene Tribe. *Education:* Lewis and Clark College (B.A., 1971); Gonzaga University (J.D., 1976). *Member:* Spokane County and Washington State Bar Associations; Idaho State Bar; Washington State Trial Lawyers Association; Idaho Trial Lawyers Association; Washington Defense Trial Lawyers. ***PRACTICE AREAS:*** Insurance Defense; Commercial Litigation. ***Email:*** ecoulter@ecl-law.com

JON D. FLOYD, born Spokane, Washington, February 18, 1968; admitted to bar, 1993, Washington; 1994, U.S. District Court, Western District of Washington; 1995, U.S. District Court, Eastern District of Washington; 2003, Idaho and U.S. District Court, District of Idaho. *Education:* Washington State University (B.A., 1990); Gonzaga University (J.D., 1993). Alpha Phi Sigma. Recipient, American Jurisprudence Award. *Member:* Spokane County and Washington State Bar Associations. (Also at Spokane, Washington, Office). ***PRACTICE AREAS:*** Workers Compensation (75%); Labor and Employment (25%). ***Email:*** jfloyd@ecl-law.com

JAMES F. TOPLIFF, born Saginaw, Michigan, March 17, 1952; admitted to bar, 1981, Washington and U.S. Tax Court; 2003, Idaho. *Education:* Alma College; Michigan State

(This Listing Continued)

EVANS, CRAVEN & LACKIE, P.S., Coeur d'Alene—Continued

University (B.A., 1975); Gonzaga University (J.D., magna cum laude, 1980). Certified Public Accountant: Michigan, 1977; Washington, 1978. *Member:* Spokane County, Washington State (Member, Taxation Section, 1981—) and American (Member, Real Estate, Probate and Trust Section, 1981—) Bar Associations; American Institute of Certified Public Accountants. (Also at Spokane, Washington, Office). ***PRACTICE AREAS:*** Estate Planning; Probate; Trust; Corporate; Limited Liability Company Law; Business Acquisitions; Real Estate; Business Valuations. ***Email:*** jtopliff@ecl-law.com

HEATHER C. YAKELY, born Spokane, Washington, September 8, 1971; admitted to bar, 1999, Washington; 2004, Idaho. *Education:* University of Washington (1991); Gonzaga University (B.A., 1993; J.D., 1998). *Member:* Spokane County and Washington State Bar Associations. ***PRACTICE AREAS:*** Municipal Law; Litigation; Employment Law. ***Email:*** hyakely@ecl-law.com

OF COUNSEL

HUGH O. EVANS, born Seattle, Washington, December 15, 1944; admitted to bar, 1975, Washington and U.S. District Court, Eastern District of Washington; 1991, Idaho. *Education:* University of Washington (B.A., 1971); Gonzaga University (J.D., 1974). Member, Gonzaga Law Review, 1973-1974. Lecturer in Law, Litigation Conduct I & II, Gonzaga University, 1978-1985. *Member:* Spokane County, Washington State, Idaho State and American Bar Associations; Washington State Trial Lawyers Association; The Association of Trial Lawyers of America. (Also at Spokane, Washington, Office). ***PRACTICE AREAS:*** Plaintiff's Personal Injury; Professional Liability Defense. ***Email:*** hevans@ecl-law.com

(For complete biographical data on all personnel see Professional Biographies at Spokane, Washington)

HALL, FARLEY, OBERRECHT & BLANTON, P.A.

COEUR D'ALENE, IDAHO

(See Boise)

Litigation, Insurance Defense, Medical Malpractice and Professional Liability, Employment Law, Labor Relations, Products Liability, Construction, Health and Hospital, Corporation, Commercial, Banking, Real Estate, Legislative Counseling, Bankruptcy, Appellate Law, Administrative Agencies, Agricultural, Municipal, Estate Planning and Probate.

KENNETH B. HOWARD, P.A.

Attorney at Law

250 NORTHWEST BOULEVARD, SUITE 107A
P.O. BOX 2528
COEUR D'ALENE, IDAHO 83816-2528
Telephone: 208-676-8890
Fax: 208-676-0981
Email: ken@kbhoward.com
URL: http://www.kbhoward.com

Personal Injury, Product Liability, Insurance, Medical Malpractice, Contracts/Torts, Insurance Bad Faith, Automobile Accidents.

KENNETH B. HOWARD, JR., born Flint, Michigan, September 11, 1943; admitted to bar, 1971, Michigan and U.S. District Court, Eastern District of Michigan; 1976, Idaho and U.S. District Court, District of Idaho; 1984, U.S. Court of Appeals, 9th Circuit; 1987, U.S. Supreme Court; 1988, Washington and U.S. District Court, District of Washington. *Education:* Kettering Institute (B.S.M.E., 1967); Wayne State University (J.D., 1971). Recipient: Professionalism Award, 1997; Pro Bono Award, 2001; Civil Rights Award for 2000 presented by Kootenai County Task Force on Human Relations. Instructor & Lecturer, National College of Advocacy, 1984-1986. Member, 1985-1995 and State Chairman, 1988-1992, Trial Lawyers for Public Justice. Member, Idaho Supreme Court: Civil Rules Committee, 1984-1990 and 2000—; Equality in Courts Committee, 1990—; Special Committee on Discovery Rules, 2001—. *Member:* State Bar of Michigan; Idaho State Bar (President, 1995; Commissioner, 1992-1995; Co-Chair, Legal Education Conclave, 1995; Member: Law Related Education (LRE), 1989-1991; Lawyer Advertising Advisory Committee; Long Range Planning Committee, 1996-2001; Financial Planning Committee, 1997; Bar Counsel Oversight Committee, 1998-2001); Washington State (Member: Professional Conduct Board, 1999-2001; Ethics 2003 Committee, 2003-2004) and American Bar Associations; Idaho Trial Lawyers Association (Member, Board of Directors, 1981-1985; Secretary, 1982-1983; Seminar Chairman, 1983-1984; Vice President/President Elect, 1986-1987; President, 1987-1988); Washington State Trial Lawyers Association; The Association of Trial Lawyers of America (Member: Everyday Law Editorial Board, 1988-1989; Product Liability Advisory Board, 1989-1990; Board of Governors, 1988-1993); American College of Trial Lawyers (Fellow, 1996—; Member, 1997— and Chair, 1999-2002, Idaho State Committee; Member: Legal Ethics Committee, 1997-1998; Professionalism Committee, 1997—; Teaching/Trial and Appellate Advocacy Committee, 1997-1998; Courage in Advocacy Committee, 2002). ***PRACTICE AREAS:*** Personal Injury; Product Liability; Insurance; Medical Malpractice; Contracts/Torts. ***Email:*** ken@kbhoward.com

HUPPIN EWING ANDERSON & PAUL, P.S.

2101 LAKEWOOD DRIVE, SUITE 236
COEUR D'ALENE, IDAHO 83814
Telephone: 208-667-7990
Fax: 509-838-4906
Email: lawyers@huppinlaw.com
URL: http://www.huppinlaw.com

Spokane, Washington Office: 221 North Wall Street, Suite 500. Telephone: 509-838-4261. Fax: 509-838-4906.

(This Listing Continued)

General Civil and Trial Practice. Aviation, Bankruptcy, Business and Commercial, Condemnation, Construction, Corporations, Creditor-Debtor Relations, Employment Law, Environmental Law, Estate Planning, Family Law, Insurance, Insurance Defense, Medical Malpractice Defense, Personal Injury, Probate, Real Property and Land Use, Taxation, and Criminal Law.

IRVING "BUDDY" PAUL, born Tucson, Arizona, April 4, 1947; admitted to bar, 1974, Michigan; 1976, Washington; 1986, Idaho. *Education:* Northwestern University (B.A., 1969); University of Michigan (J.D., 1973). Law Clerk to the Honorable John Feikens, U.S. District Judge, Eastern District of Michigan, 1974-1975. Adjunct Professor, Insurance Law, University of Idaho Law School, 2000—. *Member:* Washington State Bar Association; Idaho State Bar. ***PRACTICE AREAS:*** Product Liability Law; Insurance Law; Commercial Litigation. ***Email:*** bpaul@huppinlaw.com

PATRICK F. DELFINO, born Bakersfield, California, April 2, 1949; admitted to bar, 1986, Idaho; 1988, Washington. *Education:* University of California at Santa Barbara (B.A., 1971); Gonzaga University (J.D., summa cum laude, 1986). Thomas More Scholar. Law Clerk to Judge Phillip J. Thompson, Washington State Court of Appeals, Division III. *Member:* Washington State Bar Association; Idaho State Bar; Washington State Trial Lawyers Association. ***PRACTICE AREAS:*** Civil Litigation; Insurance Law; Personal Injury Law. ***Email:*** pdelfino@huppinlaw.com

DAVID E. EASH, born Spokane, Washington, July 26, 1948; admitted to bar, 1976, Washington; 1994, Idaho. *Education:* University of Washington (B.A., 1971); Gonzaga University School of Law (J.D., 1975). Articles Editor, Gonzaga Law Review, 1974-1975. *Member:* Washington State Bar Association; Idaho State Bar; Federal Bar Association, Eastern District of Washington (Member, Bankruptcy Section); American Bankruptcy Institute. ***REPORTED CASES:*** In Re Koubourlis, 869 F.2d 1319 (9th Circ 1989). ***PRACTICE AREAS:*** Creditors Rights Law; Commercial Law; Bankruptcy Law; Business Law; Cash Flows. ***Email:*** deash@huppinlaw.com

BRAD E. SMITH, born Longview, Washington, January 26, 1960; admitted to bar, 1986, Washington and U.S. District Court, Western District of Washington; 1992, U.S. District Court, Eastern District of Washington; 1997, U.S. Court of Appeals, Ninth Circuit; 1998, Idaho and U.S. District Court, District of Idaho. *Education:* University of Washington (B.A., 1982; J.D., 1986). *Member:* Washington State Bar Association; Idaho State Bar; Washington Defense Trial Lawyers Association; The Defense Research Institute. ***PRACTICE AREAS:*** Civil Litigation; Landlord and Tenant Law; Insurance Coverage; Insurance Defense Law. ***Email:*** bsmith@huppinlaw.com

MARLA S. CAREY, born Anchorage, Alaska, April 5, 1970; admitted to bar, 1997, Washington; 2003, Idaho. *Education:* Arizona State University (B.A., 1992); Gonzaga University (J.D., 1997). *Member:* Washington State Bar Association; Washington Women Lawyers. ***PRACTICE AREAS:*** Family Law; Guardian Ad Litem; Guardianship; Civil Litigation. ***Email:*** mcarey@huppinlaw.com

CONSTANCE H. SHIELDS, born Bloomington, Indiana, August 25, 1956; admitted to bar, 2000, Washington; 2005, Idaho. *Education:* Indiana University (B.S., 1979); Gonzaga University (J.D., cum laude, 2000). *Member:* Washington State Bar Association; Idaho State Bar; Washington Women Lawyers. ***PRACTICE AREAS:*** Family Law; Guardian Ad Litem; Paternity; Adoption Law. ***Email:*** cshields@huppinlaw.com

All Members of Firm are Members of Spokane County and Washington State Bar Associations.

REPRESENTATIVE CLIENTS: Citicapital Commercial Corp.; Citicorp Vendor Finance, Inc.; Citybank; Commercial Equipment Lease Corporation; Commercial Finance Corporation; Crescent Electric Company; Crown Bank; Federal Leasing; Foreclosure Management Co.; GMAC Commercial Mortgage Corp.; Graybar Electric Co.; Greenpoint Credit Corp. Services; HOMEQ Servicing Corp.; Matrix Financial; MCI Telecommunications Corp.; Metropolitan Mortgage and Securities Co.; Mountain West Bank, NA; National Association of Credit Management, Spokane Division; North American Van Lines; North Cascades National Bank; PacifiCorp Credit, Inc.; Pepsi Cola Co.; Purina Mills, Inc.; Safeco Credit Corp.; Settlement Capital Corp.; Summit Securities, Inc.; Thrivent Financial for Lutherans; United Airlines Credit Union; USAA Federal Savings; VW Credit, Inc.; Washington Mutual Savings Bank; Wells Fargo Home Mortgage; Western Bottling Co.; Western States Equipment (Caterpillar); Western United Life Assurance Company; Wilmington Trust.
INSURANCE CLIENTS: Banker's Life Insurance Co.; CSE Insurance Co.; Cascade National Insurance Co.; General Insurance Company of America; Grange Insurance Association; Mutual of Enumclaw Insurance Co.; J.C. Penney Life Ins. Co.; Physicians Insurance Group; Provident Life & Accident Insurance Co.; Reliance Insurance Cos.; Safeco Insurance Company of America; Security Mutual Life; State Farm Fire & Casualty Insurance; Underwriters at Lloyd's of London; USAA.

JOHNSON LAW GROUP

COEUR D'ALENE, IDAHO

(See Spokane, Washington)

General Civil Trial Practice in all Courts, Appellate Practice, Complex and Multi-District Litigation, Contracts, Insurance, Commercial Vehicle Liability, Professional Liability, Torts.

KEEFE, KING & BOWMAN, P.S.

COEUR D'ALENE, IDAHO

(See Spokane, Washington)

General Civil Trial Practice with emphasis on Medical and Dental Malpractice, Insurance Defense, Products Liability, Civil Litigation, Casualty Insurance Law, Pollution Liability, Business Litigation, Drug Liability, Employment Litigation, Government Tort Liability.

LAYMAN, LAYMAN & ROBINSON, PLLP

110 WALLACE AVENUE
COEUR D'ALENE, IDAHO 83814
Telephone: 208-665-7270
Fax: 208-665-7290
URL: http://www.braininjurylaw.net
Email: info@laymanlawfirm.com
URL: http://www.laymanlawfirm.com

Seattle, Washington Office: 316 Occidental Avenue S., Suite 500, 98104. Telephone: 206-340-1314. Fax: 206-292-1790.

Spokane, Washington Office: 601 South Division, 99202. Telephone: 509-455-8883. Fax: 509-624-2902.

General Civil and Trial Practice, Banking, Creditor's Rights, Real Estate, Commercial, Personal Injury, Brain Injury and Aquatic Injury, Products Liability, Insurance, Corporate, Antitrust, Securities Litigation.

JOHN R. LAYMAN, born Spokane, Washington, January 3, 1958; admitted to bar, 1983, Washington; 1984, U.S. District Court, Eastern District of Washington and U.S. Court of Appeals, Ninth Circuit; 2003, Idaho and U.S. District Court, District of Idaho. *Education:* Washington State University (B.A., cum laude, 1980); Gonzaga Law School (J.D., cum laude, 1983). Real Estate License, Washington, 1978. Aquatics Litigation Certification. Member: Chairman, Board of Directors, INHS Foundation and Brain Injury Association of Washington. Director and Vice-Chairman, Farmers & Merchants Bank of Rockford. *Member:* Spokane County, Washington State and American Bar Associations; The Association of Trial Lawyers of America; Washington State Trial Lawyers Association. ***PRACTICE AREAS:*** Personal Injury Law; Corporate Law; Product Liability Law; Aquatic Injuries; Spinal Cord Injury; Brain Injury.

REPRESENTATIVE CLIENTS: Appleway Automotive Group; Boise Family Restaurants, Inc.; Brown Contracting and Development Corporation; Farmers & Merchants Bank (General Counsel); Northwest Hospitality, Inc.; Spokane Computer Inc.; Black Rock Development, Inc.; Spokane County Association of Realtors; Tomlinson Black Realtors; Pacific Ridge Homes; Re/Max of Spokane.

LUKINS & ANNIS, P.S.

SUITE 102 COEUR D'ALENE NORTH
250 NORTHWEST BOULEVARD
COEUR D'ALENE, IDAHO 83814-2971
Telephone: 208-667-0517
Telecopier: 208-664-4125
Email: info@lukins.com
URL: http://www.lukins.com

Spokane, Washington Office: 1600 Washington Trust Financial Center, West 717 Sprague Avenue. Telephone: 509-455-9555. Telecopier: 509-747-2323.

Moses Lake, Washington Office: 1405 South Pioneer Way. Telephone: 509-765-9555. Telecopier: 509-765-4265.

Antitrust, Banking and Bankruptcy, Business and Personal Injury, Litigation, Financing, Federal and State Tax, Commercial, Corporations and Partnerships, Franchise, Labor and Employment Law, Environmental Law, Estate Planning and Probate, Real Property, Insurance, Pension and Profit Sharing, Securities, Hospital and Health Care, Construction Law, Government Contracts, Class Action, Professional Malpractice, and Workers Compensation.

FIRM PROFILE: Lukins & Annis, P.S. was founded in 1972. The firm now serves Washington, Idaho, Oregon, and Montana, and maintains three offices with a work force of approximately 115 - made up of 50 attorneys and 65 staff. Lukins & Annis is a full service law firm emphasizing Business and Tax, Complex Litigation, including Class Action representation, Employment Law, Commercial Law, Real Estate Law, and Probate and Estate Planning.

The Coeur d'Alene office, opened in 1983 by Ed Wroe, now has a complement of 5 attorneys and 3 staff members and is a leading law office in the region.

MISCHELLE R. FULGHAM, admitted to bar, 1992, Washington; 1993, Idaho, U.S. District Court, District of Idaho and U.S. District Court, Eastern District of Washington; 1995, U.S. Supreme Court; 1996, U.S. Court of Appeals, Ninth Circuit. *Education:* University of Montana; University of Massachusetts at Amherst (B.A., cum laude, 1989); Western New England College School of Law (J.D., 1992). *Member:* Kootenai County, Spokane County, First District (Member, Sections on: Litigation; Employment Law) and Washington State Bar Associations; Idaho State Bar(Member, Sections on: Young Lawyers; Litigation; Employment Law). (Also at Spokane, Washington Office). ***PRACTICE AREAS:*** Real Estate Litigation; Land Use; Contract Litigation; Torts; Employment Litigation. ***Email:*** mfulgham@lukins.com

RICHARD WAYNE SWENEY, admitted to bar, 1974, Idaho. *Education:* Drexel University (B.S., 1968); University of Maryland (J.D., 1974). Author, "An Analysis of the Buyer's Security Interest Under UCC Section 2-711(c) and the Secured Party's Remedies...," 97 Comm. L.J. No. 2. *Member:* Idaho State Bar (Chairman, Section on Bankruptcy and Commercial Law, 1985-1986); American Bar Association (Member, Committees on Banking Law and Commercial Litigation). (Resident). ***PRACTICE AREAS:*** Commercial Law; Banking; Litigation; Title Insurance. ***Email:*** rsweney@lukins.com

EDWARD F. WROE, admitted to bar, 1973, California; 1979, Washington; 1984, Idaho. *Education:* Princeton University (B.S., cum laude, 1970); Stanford University (J.D., 1973). *Member:* Spokane County, Kootenai County, Washington State and American Bar Associations; State Bar of California; Idaho State Bar. (Resident). ***PRACTICE AREAS:*** Real Property; Commercial Transactions; Contracts; Municipal Law. ***Email:*** ewroe@lukins.com

ASSOCIATES

MICHAEL G. SCHMIDT, admitted to bar, 2003, Washington; 2004, Idaho and U.S. District Court, District of Idaho. *Education:* Weber State College (B.A., with honors, 2000); University of Idaho (J.D., 2003). Editor, Idaho Law Review, 2002-2003. *Member:* Washington State Bar Association; Idaho State Bar. ***LANGUAGES:*** German. ***PRACTICE AREAS:*** Banks and Banking; Bankruptcy; Commercial Law; Business Law; Real Property; Contracts; Debtor and Creditor; Litigation; Mortgages; Real Estate. ***Email:*** mschmidt@lukins.com

PETER J. SMITH, IV, admitted to bar, 2004, Idaho. *Education:* Walla Walla College (B.B.A., International Business, cum laude, 2001); Pepperdine University School of Law (J.D., 2004). Chair, Moot Court Board. Editor-in-Chief, Pepperdine Dispute Resolution Law Journal, 2003-2004. Author, "Investors Win: How Sam v. Dean Witter Makes Getting to Securities Arbitration Faster, Easier, and Less Expensive," Pepperdine Dispute Resolution Law Journal. *Member:* Idaho State Bar. ***PRACTICE AREAS:*** Commercial Law; Business Law; Litigation. ***Email:*** psmith@lukins.com

REPRESENTATIVE CLIENTS: Beneficial Mortgage Co.; FirstBank Northwest; Knudtsen Chevrolet Co.; Mountain West Bank; Old Republic National Title Insurance; U.S. Bancorp; Wells Fargo Bank.

PAINE, HAMBLEN, COFFIN, BROOKE & MILLER LLP

701 FRONT AVENUE, #101
P.O. BOX E
COEUR D'ALENE, IDAHO 83816-0328
Telephone: 208-664-8115
Facsimile: 208-664-6338
Email: info@painehamblen.com
URL: http://www.painehamblen.com

Spokane, Washington Office: 717 West Sprague Avenue, Suite 1200. Telephone: 509-455-6000.

Spokane Valley, Washington Office: 12209 East Mission Avenue. Telephone: 509-777-1087.

Kennewick, Washington Office: 7025 West Grandridge Boulevard, Suite A. Telephone: 509-735-1542.

General Civil and Trial Practice, Complex Litigation, Insurance Defense, Insurance Coverage, Professional Liability, Product Liability, Negligence Defense, Workers Compensation, Employment Law, Commercial Litigation, Corporate, Real Estate, Zoning, Planning and Land Use, Hospital and Healthcare Law, Railroad Law, Probate, Family Law and Criminal Law.

LAW FIRM ALLIANCES/ASSOCIATIONS: **THE BRIDGE GROUP**

AMERICAN LAW FIRM ASSOCIATION (ALFA)

MEMBERS OF FIRM

E. L. MILLER, born 1922; admitted to bar, 1949, Idaho and U.S. Dist. Court, Dist. of Idaho; 1953, U.S. Court of Appeals, Ninth Circuit; U.S. Supreme Court. *Education:* Univ. of Toledo; Univ. of Idaho (LL.B., 1949). *Member:* Idaho State Bar (President, 1970-1971); Idaho Assoc. of Defense Counsel. Fellow: American College of Trial Lawyers. Fellow, American Academy of Hospital Attorneys. ***PRACTICE AREAS:*** Insurance Defense; Insurance Coverage; Insurance Bad Faith; Products Liability; Negligence Defense; Contract Litigation; Probate; Trial Practice; Appellate Practice; Professional Liability. ***Email:*** eugene.miller@painehamblen.com

PATRICK E. MILLER, born 1950; admitted to bar, 1975, Idaho; 1976, U.S. Court of Military Appeals; 1979, U.S. Dist. Court, Dist. of Idaho; 1985, U.S. Court of Appeals, Ninth Circuit. *Education:* Willamette Univ. (B.A., 1972); Univ. of Idaho (J.D., 1975). Lawyer Representative to Ninth Circuit Judicial Conf. (3 years). *Member:* First Judicial Dist. Bar Assoc.; Idaho State Bar; Defense Research Institute; Idaho Association of Defense Counsel; American Health Lawyers Assoc. ***PRACTICE AREAS:*** Trial Practice; Professional Liability; Tort Defense; Commercial Litigation; Healthcare. ***Email:*** pat.miller@painehamblen.com

AUSEY H. ROBNETT III, born 1953; admitted to bar, 1979, Oregon; 1980, U.S. Dist. Court, Dist. of Oregon; 1984, Idaho; U.S. Supreme Court; U.S. Court of Appeals, Ninth Circuit and U.S. Dist. Court, Dist. of Idaho. *Education:* Univ. of Puget Sound (B.A., 1976); Northwestern School of Law of Lewis & Clark College (J.D., 1979). Cornelius Honor Society. *Member:* Kootenai County and American Bar Assocs.; Idaho State Bar (President, 2001; President, Workers Comp. Section, 1991-1992); Oregon State Bar; National Assoc. of Railroad Trial Counsel. ***PRACTICE AREAS:*** Trial Practice; Employment Litigation; Railroad Litigation; Personal Injury Litigation. ***Email:*** ausey.robnett@painehamblen.com

JANET D. ROBNETT, born 1955; admitted to bar, 1980, Oregon and U.S. Dist. Court, Dist. of Oregon; 1984, Idaho and U.S. Dist. Court, Dist. of Idaho. *Education:* Univ. of Puget Sound (B.A., cum laude, 1977); Univ. of Oregon (J.D., 1980). Past Chairman, Kootenai County Planning and Zoning Commission. Legal Counsel, Coeur d'Alene Area Chamber of Commerce. Board of Directors, Jobs Plus. *Member:* Oregon State Bar; Idaho State Bar; American Bar Assoc. ***PRACTICE AREAS:*** Real Estate; Land Use; Commercial Transactions; Business Law. ***Email:*** janet.robnett@painehamblen.com

PETER C. ERBLAND, born 1952; admitted to bar, 1979, Idaho and U.S. Dist. Court, Dist. of Idaho; 1991, U.S. Court of Appeals, Ninth Circuit and U.S. Supreme Court. *Education:* Saint Bonaventure Univ. (B.A., cum laude, 1975); Gonzaga Univ. (J.D., cum laude, 1978). Deputy Prosecuting Attorney, Kootenai County, 1980-1986. Criminal Law Division Chief, Office of Idaho Attorney General, 1987-1988. *Member:* Idaho State Bar. ***PRACTICE AREAS:*** Trial Practice; Appellate Practice; Commercial and Personal Injury Litigation; Mediation. ***Email:*** peter.erbland@painehamblen.com

MICHAEL B. HAGUE, born 1960; admitted to bar, 1986, Idaho and U.S. Dist. Court, Dist. of Idaho; 1998, U.S. Supreme Court. *Education:* Univ. of Idaho (B.S., 1983; J.D., 1986). *Member:* Kootenai County, First Judicial Dist. and American Bar Assocs.; Idaho State Bar (Former Bd. of Gov., Young Lawyers Div.). ***PRACTICE AREAS:*** Trial Practice; Personal Injury; Debtor and Creditor; Commercial Litigation; Health Care; Insurance. ***Email:*** michael.hague@painehamblen.com

(This Listing Continued)

PAINE, HAMBLEN, COFFIN, BROOKE & MILLER LLP, Coeur d'Alene—Continued

SCOT D. NASS, born 1961; admitted to bar, 1992, Idaho, Supreme Court of Idaho, and U.S. Dist. Court, Dist. of Idaho. *Education:* Willamette Univ. (B.A., B.A., 1983); Univ. of Idaho (J.D., 1992). *Member:* Kootenai County (President, 1992-1994) and American Bar Assocs; Idaho State Bar. ***PRACTICE AREAS:*** Civil Litigation; Domestic Relations; Criminal Defense; Government Tort Liability Defense; Professional Malpractice Defense; Personal Injury Defense. ***Email:*** scot.nass@painehamblen.com

ASSOCIATES

FONDA L. JOVICK, born 1972; admitted to bar, 2004, Washington (Not admitted in Idaho). *Education:* Gonzaga University (B.A., magna cum laude, 2001); Gonzaga University School of Law (J.D., cum laude, 2004). ***PRACTICE AREAS:*** Civil Litigation; Commercial Litigation; Estate Planning. ***Email:*** fonda.jovick@painehamblen.com

TYLER WIRICK, born 1972; admitted to bar, 2005, Idaho. *Education:* Weber State University (B.S., in Microbiology); University of Nebraska (J.D., 2005). *Member:* Idaho State Bar. ***PRACTICE AREAS:*** Civil Litigation; Environmental Law; Environmental Litigation; National Environmental Policy Act (NEPA); Groundwater Contamination; Hazardous Waste Management. ***Email:*** tyler.wirick@painehamblen.com

IDAHO COUNSEL FOR: Hagadone Corp.; Hagadone Hospitality Co.; Hagadone Investment Co.; Coeur d'Alene Press; Pend Oreille Printers, Inc.; Kootenai Medical Center; Burlington Northern Santa Fe Railroad Co.; Federated Rural Electric; Kootenai Hospital District; Avista, Honda of N.A.

REPRESENTATIVE CLIENTS: Union Pacific Railroad Co.; Plum Creek; Sacred Heart Medical Center; Eastern Idaho Railroad; WATCO, Inc. *Insurance:* Aetna Casualty & Surety; Farmers Insurance Group; Truck Insurance Exchange; Fireman's Fund; Foremost Insurance Co.; Hartford Insurance Group; Safeco Insurance Co.; USAA; Electric Mutual Liability; Federated Rural Ins. Co.; Nationwide Insurance Co.; General Insurance Co.; Pettit Morry Co.; Federated Insurance Co.; Attorney's Liability Protection Society; Viking Insurance Co.; Guaranty National Insurance Co.; Great Western Casualty Co.; Empire Fire & Marine Ins. Co.; U.S. Fidelity & Guaranty; Idaho Counties Risk Management.

REFERENCE: U.S. Bank (Coeur d'Alene, Idaho Branch).

PRESTON GATES & ELLIS LLP

1200 IRONWOOD DRIVE, SUITE 315
COEUR D'ALENE, IDAHO 83814
Telephone: 208-677-1839
Facsimile: 208-765-2494
Email: info@prestongates.com
URL: http://www.prestongates.com

Anchorage, Alaska Office: 420 L Street, Suite 400, 99501-1937. Telephone: 907-276-1969. Facsimile: 907-276-1365.

Washington, D.C. Office: Preston Gates Ellis & Rouvelas Meeds LLP, 1735 New York Avenue, N.W., Suite 500, 20006-5209. Telephone: 202-628-1700. Facsimile: 202-331-1024.

Irvine, California Office: 1900 Main Street, Suite 600, 92614-7319. Telephone: 949-253-0900. Facsimile: 949-253-0902.

Portland, Oregon Office: 222 S.W. Columbia Street, 1400 KOIN Tower, 97201-6632. Telephone: 503-228-3200. Facsimile: 503-248-9085.

San Francisco, California Office: 55 Second Street, Suite 1700, 94105. Telephone: 415-882-8200. Facsimile: 415-882-8220.

Seattle, Washington Office: 925 Fourth Avenue, Suite 2900, 98104-1158. Telephone: 206-623-7580. Facsimile: 206-623-7022.

Spokane, Washington Office: 601 West Riverside Drive, Suite 1400, 99201-0636. Telephone: 509-624-2100. Facsimile: 509-456-0146.

Beijing, China Office: Preston Gates & Ellis, Suite 1003, Tower E3, Oriental Plaza, No. 1 East Chang An Avenue. Telephone: +86 10 8518 8528. Facsimile: +86 10 8518 9299.

Hong Kong Office: Preston Gates & Ellis, 35th Floor, Two International Finance Centre, 8 Finance Street, Central, Hong Kong. Telephone: 852-2511-5100. Facsimile: 852-2511-9515.

Taipei, Taiwan Office: Preston Gates & Ellis, 2/F, No. 131, Min Sheng E. Rd., Sec. 3. Telephone:+886 (2) 2717 6657. Facsimile:+886 (2) 2712-8264.

General Practice. Administrative, Affordable Housing, Americans with Disabilities Act, Bankruptcy Litigation, Business Transactions and Business Planning, Business Reorganization and Bankruptcy, Commercial Transactions and Litigation, Construction, Corporate, Corporate Financing, Creditors' Rights, Emerging Business, Employment, Environmental, Forest Products and Timber, Governmental Relations, Insurance, Intellectual Property and Technology Law (domestic and international, includes copyrights, trademarks, trade secrets, licensing and internet/e-commerce); International Business Transactions, Internet/E-Commerce Law, Labor, Land Use, Leasing, Legislative, Litigation, Mergers and Acquisitions, Municipal (general and finance), Natural Resources, Probate, Products Liability, Public Law, Real Estate, Real Estate Financing and Leasing, Securities, Solid Waste, Tax, Telecommunications, Uniform Commercial Code, Utilities and Transportation Law.

PARTNERS

J. CHRISTOPHER LYNCH, born Seattle, Washington, February 2, 1961; admitted to bar, 1987, Washington and U.S. Dist. Court, Eastern Dist. of Washington; 1988, Idaho and U.S. Dist. Court, Dist. of Idaho; 1989, U.S. Dist. Court, Western Dist. of Washington; 1991, U.S. Court of Appeals, Ninth Circuit; 1993, U.S. Court of Appeals, Federal Circuit; registered to practice before the U.S. Patent and Trademark Office. *Education:* University of Washington (B.S.C.E., 1984; J.D., 1987). Chi Epsilon. Adjunct Professor, Gonzaga Univ. School of Law, 1992—; Visiting Professor, Universidad Autónoma de Guadalajara, 1994. *Member:* American Bar Association (Member, Law, Science & Technology and Intellectual Property Sections); American Intellectual Property Law Association. ***PRACTICE AREAS:*** Patent, Trademark and Copyright Law; Commercial Litigation; Computer Law. ***Email:*** jclynch@prestongates.com

(This Listing Continued)

MICHAEL C. ORMSBY, born Spokane, Washington, January 6, 1957; admitted to bar, 1981, Washington; 1990, Idaho. *Education:* Gonzaga University (B.A., 1979; J.D., 1981). Recipient: Harry S. Truman Fellowship, State of Washington, 1977. Member, Board of Directors, Spokane Public Schools, 1975-1983. Member, Board of Trustees, Eastern Washington University, 1985— and Chairman, 1988-1989 and 1994-1995. Member, Board of Directors, Spokane Joint Center for Higher Education. Chairman, State Advisory Committee of the Department of Social and Health Services, 1988-1993. Member, Board of Trustees, Spokane County Bar Association, 1988-1992. President, Spokane County Bar Association, 1991-1992. Member, Board of Directors of United Way of Spokane County, 1989-1992. President, Valley Sunrise Rotary Club, 1995-1996. Member, Board of Directors, Spokane Valley Chamber of Commerce. Member, Board of Directors, Inland Empire Chapter of the Boy Scouts of America. Member, Board of Directors, Momenturm. ***PRACTICE AREAS:*** Municipal Law; Municipal Finance; Commercial Finance Litigation. ***Email:*** mormsby@prestongates.com

TODD REUTER, born Indianapolis, Indiana, June 6, 1965; admitted to bar, 1991, Washington; 1992, U.S. District Court, Eastern and Western Districts of Washington; 2002, Idaho and U.S. Court of Appeals, Ninth Circuit. *Education:* University of Washington (B.A., 1988); Seattle University School of Law (J.D., 1991). (Also at Spokane, Washington Office). ***PRACTICE AREAS:*** Real Property Litigation; Technology Litigation; Environmental Litigation; Civil Litigation; NASD. ***Email:*** treuter@prestongates.com

ASSOCIATES

DAVID K. DAGGETT, born Los Angeles, California, August 28, 1964; admitted to bar, 1998, Washington (Not admitted in Idaho). *Education:* University of California at Los Angeles (B.A., 1987); Gonzaga University (J.D., 1998). Phi Delta Phi. Member, Alpha Sigma Nu Jesuit Honor Society. Recipient: CALI Excellence For The Future Award (formerly AmJur Award), 1995, 1996, 1997 and 1998; Dean's Medal; Member, First Place Team and Best Oralist Overall, Linden Cup Appellate Advocacy Competition, Spring, 1997. Member: National Moot Court Team; Regional First Place Team. (Also at Spokane, Washington Office). ***PRACTICE AREAS:*** Automobile Insurance Defense Law; Casualty Insurance Defense Law; Insurance Defense Law; Intellectual Property Law. ***Email:*** ddaggett@prestongates.com

J. MICHAEL KEYES, born 1971; admitted to bar, 1998, Washington; 2003, Idaho. *Education:* Loyola University (B.M., 1993); Gonzaga University (J.D., magna cum laude, 1998); Columbia University (LL.M., 1999). Harlan Fiske Stone Scholar. Recipient, "Best Oralist" Award, National Moot Court Competition, Northwest Region. 1993-1994, Visiting Piano Student, Tbilisi State Conservatoire, Former Soviet Republic of Georgia. Law Clerk to Associate Justice Gerry L. Alexander, Supreme Court of Washington, 1999-2000. Author: *"State v. Rose: The Re-emergence of Colonial Writs?"* 32 Gonz. L.Rev. 177 (1996); *"Whatever Happens To Works Deferred: Reflections on the Ill-Given Deferments of the Copyright Term Extension Act,"* 26 Sea. L. Rev 97 (2002); *"Musical Musings: The Case For Rethinking Music Copyright Protection,"* 10 Mich. Telecommunications & Tech. L. Rev. 407 (2004). *Member:* Spokane County (Founding Member, Intellectual Property Section, 2004), Washington State (Chair Elect, Intellectual Property Section, 2005) and American Bar Associations. (Also at Spokane, Washington Office). ***PRACTICE AREAS:*** Intellectual Property Litigation (75%); General Litigation (15%); Intellectual Property Counseling (10%). ***Email:*** jmkeyes@prestongates.com

THERESA LYNN KEYES, born Missoula, Montana, April 11, 1969; admitted to bar, 1995, Washington (Not admitted in Idaho). *Education:* University of Washington (B.A., 1991); Gonzaga University (J.D., 1994). Recipient, American Jurisprudence Awards, Research & Writing, Contracts, Criminal Procedure. (Also at Spokane, Washington Office). ***PRACTICE AREAS:*** Intellectual Property; Commercial; Employment; Environmental Litigation. ***Email:*** theresak@prestongates.com

PETER G. SCOTT, admitted to bar, 1999, Washington, Oregon and Idaho; U.S. District Court, Eastern District of Washington; U.S. District Court, District of Idaho. *Education:* University of Massachusetts at Amherst (B.S., Geology, cum laude, 1991); Northwestern School of Law (J.D., 1999). [U.S. Navy, 1980-1986]. ***PRACTICE AREAS:*** Energy; Water Rights; Environmental Law; Land Use; Litigation. ***Email:*** pscott@prestongates.com

Languages: Chinese, French, German, Japanese, Korean, Russian, Spanish and Taiwanese.

REPRESENTATIVE CLIENTS: Allstate Life Insurance Co.; Cabinet Mountains Water District; Chicago Title Insurance Co.; City of Coeur d'Alene; City of Hailey; City of Post Falls; City of Plummer; City of Priest River; Counties of: Beneuah, Latah and Kooteuai; East Shoshone County Water District; Ellisport Bay Sewer District; Louisiana-Pacific Corp.; School Districts of: Kooteuai Joint, Lakeland, Payette Joint NO. 371, Post Falls and West Bonner County; Tidyman's LLC; Van Waters & Rogers Inc.

(For complete Biographical data on all Personnel, see Professional Biographies at Seattle and Spokane, Washington; Anchorage, Alaska; Portland, Oregon; Washington, D.C.; Irvine and San Francisco, California and Hong Kong)

QUANE SMITH LLP

2020 LAKEWOOD DRIVE, SUITE 312
P.O. BOX 1758
COEUR D'ALENE, IDAHO 83816-1758
Telephone: 208-664-9281
Facsimile: 208-664-5380
Email: info@quanesmith.net
URL: http://www.quanesmith.net

Boise, Idaho Office: U.S. Bank Plaza, 16th Floor. P.O. Box 519. Telephone: 208-345-8600. Facsimile: 208-345-8660.

Idaho Falls, Idaho Office: 2325 West Broadway, Suite B. Telephone: 208-529-0000. Facsimile: 208-529-0005.

Insurance, Insurance Defense, Litigation, Accountants Liability, Advertising and Marketing, Agents and Brokers Liability, Agricultural Law, Alcoholic Beverages, Alternative Dispute Resolution, Architects and Engineers Liability, Arson and Insurance Fraud, Asbestos Defense, Brain Injury, Business Law, Casualty Insurance Defense, Catastrophic Injury, Civil Practice, Commercial Law, Complex and Multi-District Litigation, Computers and Software, Construc-

(This Listing Continued)

tion Law, Contracts, Corporate Law, Design Professionals Liability, Drug and Medical Device Defense, Education Law, Employer Liability, Environmental Law, ERISA Litigation, Extra Contractual Insurance Defense, Federal Practice, Fire Insurance, Firearms Litigation, Food Products Liability, Fraud and Deceit, Government, Hazardous Waste Liability, Head Injury, Health Care, Insurance Bad Faith Defense, Labor and Employment, Legal Malpractice Defense, Libel, Slander and Defamation, Life Insurance Defense, Manufacturers Liability, Medical Malpractice, Natural Resources, Negligence, Personal Injury, Pesticide Litigation, Physicians Licensing, Pollution, Premises Liability, Products Liability, Professional Discipline, Professional Liability, Propane Products Liability, Property Damage Defense, Real Estate, Recreational Products Liability, School Board Defense, Slip and Fall, Spinal Injury, Subrogation, Torts, Toxic Torts, Transportation, Workers Compensation and Wrongful Death.

FIRM PROFILE: A regional law firm headquartered in Boise, Idaho with additional offices located in Idaho Falls, Idaho and Coer D'Alene, Idaho. The Coeur d'Alene office is responsible for cases in northern Idaho and eastern Washington. The firm's major focus is in the representation of insurance companies and their policyholders, governmental entities and self-insured corporations. The firm emphasizes all aspects of civil litigation, alternative dispute resolution and risk management.

RANDALL R. ADAMS, admitted to bar, 1983, Idaho; 1995, Washington. *Education:* University of Southern California (B.A., 1979); University of Idaho (J.D., 1983). ***PRACTICE AREAS:*** Insurance Defense; Government; Products Liability Defense; Professional Liability Defense; Transportation Liability. **Email:** rradams@quanesmith.net

MICHAEL L. HAMAN, admitted to bar, 1994, Idaho and U.S. District Court, District of Idaho. *Education:* University of Idaho (B.S., 1990; J.D., 1993). ***PRACTICE AREAS:*** Automobile Liability Defense; Insurance Defense; Construction Law; Education Law; Premises Liability. **Email:** mlhaman@quanesmith.net

---

JENNIFER D. GAFFANEY, admitted to bar, 2002, Washington; 2003, Idaho. *Education:* Gonzaga University (B.A., 1998; J.D., 2002). (Resident). **Email:** jdgaffaney@quanesmith.net

JENNIFER L. GORMAN, admitted to bar, 2003, Idaho. *Education:* Kansas State University (B.S., 2000); Washburn University (J.D., 2003). (Resident). **Email:** jlgorman@quanesmith.net

---

RAMSDEN & LYONS

Established in 1994

618 NORTH 4TH STREET
P.O. BOX 1336
COEUR D'ALENE, IDAHO 83816-1336
Telephone: 208-664-5818
Fax: 208-664-5884
Email: firm@ramsdenlyons.com
URL: http://www.ramsdenlyons.com

General Civil Trial and Appellate Practice. Insurance Defense, Eminent Domain/Condemnation, Arbitration, Mediation, Class Action Defense, Business Formation, Insurance Bad Faith, Land Use, Professional Liability, Product Liability, Negligence, Construction, Real Estate, Environmental, Error and Omission Defense, Governmental Liability, Worker Compensation and Employment Law.

MICHAEL E. RAMSDEN, born Seattle, Washington, April 9, 1952; admitted to bar, 1979, Idaho; 1986, Washington; 1987, U.S. District Court, Eastern District of Washington. *Education:* University of Washington (B.A., 1976); University of Idaho (J.D., 1978). Co-Author: with R. Daniel Bowen, "Worker's Compensation: The Continuing Dilemma of Third-Party Actions," 21 Idaho Law Review 57 (1985). *Member:* Washington State Bar Association; Idaho State Bar; Defense Research Institute; American College of Trial Lawyers; International Association of Defense Counsel; Spokane Adjusters Association. ***PRACTICE AREAS:*** Medical Malpractice; Insurance Defense; Litigation.

MARC A. LYONS, born Coeur D'Alene, Idaho, April 10, 1954; admitted to bar, 1983, Idaho and U.S. District Court, District of Idaho; 1985, U.S. Court of Appeals, Ninth Circuit; 1991, Washington; 1992, U.S. District Court, Eastern District of Washington; 1998, U.S. Supreme Court. *Education:* University of Idaho (B.S., 1977; J.D., 1983). Recipient, American Jurisprudence Award. Certified Public Accountant, Idaho, 1980. *Member:* Kootenai County and Washington State Bar Associations; Idaho State Bar; Idaho Society of Certified Public Accountants; Defense Research Institute. ***PRACTICE AREAS:*** Civil Litigation; Insurance Defense; Governmental Law.

DOUGLAS S. MARFICE, born Lincoln, Nebraska, July 23, 1964; admitted to bar, 1989, Idaho and U.S. District Court, District of Idaho; 1996, Washington; 1997, U.S. District Court, Eastern District of Washington. *Education:* University of Nebraska (B.A., 1986; J.D., 1989). Phi Alpha Delta. Author: "The Mischief of Court-Ordered Mediation," 39 Idaho Law Review 57 (2002). Instructor: Real Estate Law, Idaho Real Estate Education Council, 1994. *Member:* Kootenai County Bar Association; Idaho State Bar; Washington State Bar Association. ***PRACTICE AREAS:*** Insurance Defense; Real Estate; Civil Litigation; Professional Malpractice; Eminent Domain.

ASSOCIATES

MICHAEL A. EALY, born Spokane, Washington, May 26, 1966; admitted to bar, 1997, Idaho and U.S. District Court, District of Idaho; 1999, Washington; 2001, U.S. District Court, Eastern District of Washington. *Education:* University of Idaho (B.S., 1989; J.D., 1997). President, Phi Delta Phi, 1996-1997. Member, Idaho Law Review. *Member:* Idaho State Bar; Kootenai County and Washington State Bar Associations; American Inns of Court. ***PRACTICE AREAS:*** Construction Law; Civil Litigation; Real Estate.

JEDEDIAH J. WHITAKER, born Sheridan, Wyoming, November 17, 1970; admitted to bar, 1999, Idaho and U.S. District Court, District of Idaho. *Education:* Boise State University (B.B.A., 1994); Gonzaga University (J.D., cum laude, 1999). Ben B. Cheney Scholar. *Member:* Idaho State Bar; Kootenai County, Ada County and American Bar Associations. ***PRACTICE AREAS:*** Corporate Law; Insurance Defense; Real Estate; Governmental Defense; Creditors Rights; Civil Litigation; Eminent Domain.

TERRANCE R. HARRIS, born Plattsburg, New York, July 18, 1963; admitted to bar, 1991, Arizona; 1996, Idaho and U.S. District Court, District of Idaho. *Education:* Eastern Washington University (B.A., 1987); Gonzaga University (J.D., summa cum laude, 1991). Associate Editor, Gonzaga Law Review, 1989-1990. *Member:* Idaho State Bar; Kootenai County Bar Association; Spokane Adjusters Association. [Sgt., U.S.A.F., 1983-1990]. ***PRACTICE AREAS:*** Insurance Defense; Medical Malpractice; Corporate Law; Real Estate; Workers Compensation.

REPRESENTATIVE CLIENTS: Allied Group Insurance; Attorneys Liability Protection Society (ALPS); CNA; Coregis; ESIS; Financial Indemnity Company; Grange Insurance Group; Great West Casualty Company; Hanover Insurance Companies; Horace Mann; Liberty Mutual Group; Motorist Insurance Companies; North Idaho College; North Pacific Insurance; Northwest Physicians Mutual Insurance; Old Republic Insurance; OneBeacon Insurance Group; Rice Insurance Services; Safeco; State Farm Fire & Casualty; State Farm Mutual Automobile; State of Idaho; Unitrin; Universal Underwriters Insurance; Wausau Insurance; Zurich American Insurance.

SCOTT W. REED

401 FRONT STREET
P.O. BOX A
COEUR D'ALENE, IDAHO 83816
Telephone: 208-664-2161
Fax: 208-765-5117
Email: scottwreed@imbris.com

General Civil and Trial Practice, Business and Commercial, Land Use and Environmental Law, Local Government Law.

SCOTT W. REED, born Klamath Falls, Oregon, April 26, 1928; admitted to bar, 1955, California and U.S. Court of Appeals, Ninth Circuit; 1956, Idaho and U.S. District Court, District of Idaho; 1965, U.S. Supreme Court; 1986, U.S. Claims Court. *Education:* Princeton University (A.B., 1950); Stanford University (LL.B., 1955). Assistant U.S. Attorney, 1959-1961. *Member:* 1st Judicial District (President, 1966-1967) and American Bar Associations; Idaho State Bar; State Bar of California.

REPRESENTATIVE CLIENTS: Coeur D'Alene Garbage Co.; Resort Aviation, Inc.; Hayden Area Regional Sewer Board; City of Sandpoint.
REFERENCE: Washington Trust Bank.

DAVID K. ROBINSON, JR.

Established in 1980

2005 IRONWOOD PARKWAY, SUITE 140
COEUR D'ALENE, IDAHO 83814
Telephone: 208-664-1414
Telecopier: 208-667-6603
Email: dkrjratty@icehouse.net
URL: http://www.davidkrobinsonjr.com

General Practice. Divorce, Juvenile, Visitation, Support, Paternity, Family, Interstate Child Custody, Adoption, Mediation, Enforcement of Foreign Judgments, Criminal, Personal Injury, Negligence, Auto Accidents, Slip and Fall, General and Child Support Collections over $1,000.

DAVID K. ROBINSON, JR., born Pasadena, California, July 20, 1947; admitted to bar, 1975, Idaho and U.S. District Court, District of Idaho. *Education:* DePauw University; University of California, Berkeley (B.A., 1969); University of Utah (J.D., 1973). Deputy Attorney General, State of Idaho, 1976-1980. Certified Professional Mediator. *Member:* Kootenai County, First District and American (Member, Family Law Section) Bar Associations; Idaho State Bar; Idaho Trial Lawyers Association; Idaho Mediation Association; Association of Family and Conciliation Courts. ***PRACTICE AREAS:*** General Practice; Family Law; Personal Injury; Business Law.

REFERENCE: US Bank.

TRIGG LAW FIRM, P.C.

COEUR D'ALENE, IDAHO

(See Kalispell, Montana)

Personal Injury, Real Estate, Land Use and Zoning, Construction, Family Law, Wills and Probate.

KEVIN J. WAITE, P.C.

Established in 1995

OLD CITY HALL
424 SHERMAN AVENUE, SUITE 106
COEUR D'ALENE, IDAHO 83814
Telephone: 208-667-8553
Fax: 208-667-8630
URL: http://www.waitelaw.com
URL: http://www.waitelawoffice.com
URL: http://www.waite-law.com
URL: http://www.waitelawfirm.com
Email: kevinjwaite@aol.com
URL: http://www.waitelaw.com

Family Law, Divorce, Child Custody, Child Support, Criminal Defense, Driving While Intoxicated, Drug Crimes, Parole and Probation and Civil Litigation.

(This Listing Continued)

KEVIN J. WAITE, P.C., Coeur d'Alene—Continued

KEVIN J. WAITE, born Peoria, Illinois, July 20, 1952; admitted to bar, 1981, Illinois, Wisconsin and U.S. District Court, Western District of Wisconsin; 1983, U.S. District Court, Northern District of Illinois; 1995, Idaho. *Education:* Knox College (B.A., cum laude, 1974); University of Wisconsin (J.D., 1981). Note and Comment Editor, Wisconsin Law Review, 1980-1981. Law Clerk to the Hon. Hubert L. Will, Northern District of Illinois, 1981-1983. *Member:* Idaho State Bar (Member, Sections on: Family Law; Litigation); Idaho Trial Lawyers Association; Idaho Association of Criminal Defense Lawyers. ***LANGUAGES:*** French. ***PRACTICE AREAS:*** Family Law; Divorce; Child Custody; Child Support; Criminal Defense; Driving While Intoxicated; Drug Crimes; Parole and Probation; Civil Litigation.

MARC E. WALLACE & ASSOCIATES, P.A.

2370 N. MERRITT CREEK LOOP, SUITE 1
COEUR D'ALENE, IDAHO 83814
Telephone: 208-667-2264
Fax: 208-667-2419

Trusts and Estates, Probate.

MARC E. WALLACE, born Spokane, Washington, April 22, 1949; admitted to bar, 1977, Washington and 1983, Idaho; U.S. Tax Court; 1981, U.S. District Court, Eastern District of Washington; 1997, U.S. Supreme Court. *Education:* University of Washington (B.A., 1971); Gonzaga University (J.D., 1975); University of Miami (LL.M., Taxation, 1976). Estate Tax Attorney, Internal Revenue Service, 1977-1983. Fellow, The American College of Trust and Estate Counsel. ***PRACTICE AREAS:*** Estate Planning; Trusts and Estates; Probate. ***Email:*** mwallace@mewallace.com

---

MARY W. CUSACK, born Lewiston, Idaho, January 19, 1959; admitted to bar, 1997, Washington; 2003, U.S. District Court, Eastern District of Washington; 2004, Idaho and U.S. District Court, District of Idaho. *Education:* University of Idaho (B.S., Business Mgmt, 1981); Gonzaga University (J.D., 1995); University of Washington (LL.M., Taxation, 1996). Adjunct Professor, University of Washington, Summer 1999. *Member:* Kootenai County Bar Association; Idaho State Bar; Washington State Bar Association. ***PRACTICE AREAS:*** Estate Planning; Probate; Corporate. ***Email:*** mcusack@mewallace.com

WETZEL & WETZEL, P.L.L.C.

Established in 1990

1322 KATHLEEN AVENUE
SUITE 2
COEUR D'ALENE, IDAHO 83815-8339
Telephone: 208-667-3400
Fax: 208-664-6741
Email: wetzel@imbris.com

Commercial Litigation, Civil Litigation, Municipal Law, Real Estate Development, Land Use Regulation, Business Organization, Personal Injury, Probate, Construction Law, Employment Discrimination, Bad Faith, Banking Law, Municipal Bonds and Bankruptcy.

FIRM PROFILE: Wetzel & Wetzel, P.L.L.C. is a full-service firm dedicated to providing our clients with the finest, most innovative legal representation available in Northern Idaho. Wetzel & Wetzel, P.L.L.C. focuses in the area of litigation from both plaintiff and defense perspectives and has been used as local counsel for insurance and Fortune 500 companies. The firm is also extremely active in land use regulation and municipal law and serves as Bond Counsel to many municipal entities.

STEVEN C. WETZEL, born Pocatello, Idaho, July 14, 1951; admitted to bar, 1982, Idaho and the U.S. District Court, District of Idaho. *Education:* Idaho State University (B.A., Government, magna cum laude, 1978); University of Idaho (J.D., 1982). Member: Peace Corps, Guatemala, C.A., 1973-1976; Board, TESH (Transitional Educational Services to Handicapped), 1986-1992, President, 1992. Member, Coeur d'Alene Chamber of Commerce Board, 1994-1996. *Member:* Kootenai County, First Judicial District and American Bar Associations; Urban Land Institute; Idaho Affirmative Action Association; Idaho Trial Lawyers Association; Coeur d'Alene Rotary, 1989—. ***PRACTICE AREAS:*** Personal Injury; Litigation; Real Estate; Land Use Regulation; Employment; General Business. ***Email:*** wetzel@nidlink.com

DANA L. RAYBORN WETZEL, born Hailey, Idaho, January 11, 1951; admitted to bar, 1982, Idaho and U.S. District Court, District of Idaho. *Education:* Idaho State University (B.S., Government, cum laude, 1977; Masters of Public Administration, magna cum laude, 1978); University of Idaho (J.D., 1982). Member, Board of Editors, University of Idaho Law Review, 1979-1981. Coeur d'Alene City Attorney, 1984-1986; City Administrator, 1986-1990. Member: Peace Corp, Guatemala, C.A., 1973-1976; Kootenai County Task Force on Human Relations, Founding member, 1984-1990; United Way of Kootenai County, 1990-1992. *Member:* Kootenai County and First Judicial District Bar Associations; Idaho State Bar; Association of City Attorneys; National Association of Bond Lawyers. ***PRACTICE AREAS:*** Land Use Regulation; Administrative Law; Employment; Education; Municipal Bond Law; Municipal Law; Probate. ***Email:*** wetzel@nidlink.com

REPRESENTATIVE CLIENTS: AIC Construction; City of Coeur d'Alene; Coeur d'Alene Downtown Business Association, Inc.; Coeur d'Alene School District 271; City of Hayden Lake, Idaho; Hallmark Homes Inc.; Interstate Concrete & Asphalt; North Idaho Health Care; City of Post Falls, Idaho; Post Falls Urban Renreal Agency; Prairie Falls Development LLC; City of Sandpoint, Idaho; Sunshine Meadow Homeowners Association Inc.; Tomlinson Black of North Idaho; City of Wallace, Idaho.
REFERENCE: Mountain West Savings Bank.

WINSTON & CASHATT, LAWYERS

A PROFESSIONAL SERVICE CORPORATION

Established in 1972

250 NORTHWEST BOULEVARD, SUITE 107A
COEUR D'ALENE, IDAHO 83814
Telephone: 208-667-2103
Fax: 208-765-2121
Email: info@winstoncashatt.com
URL: http://www.winstoncashatt.com

Spokane, Washington Office: Bank of America Financial Center, 601 W. Riverside, Suite 1900. Telephone: 509-838-6131. Fax: 509-838-1416.
Seattle, Washington Office: 1620 Fourth Avenue, Suite 200. Telephone: 425-486-0170. Fax: 425-486-0431.

General and Trial Practice including Construction, Insurance, Alternative Dispute Resolution, Corporate, Accident and Personal Injury, Municipalities, Banking, Land Use Development, Criminal Defense, Employment and Labor, Environmental, Commercial Litigation, Taxation, Antitrust and Trade Regulation, Public and Governmental Contracts, Worker's Compensation, Immigration and Bankruptcy.

FIRM PROFILE: Successor firms established in Spokane in 1946 and in Coeur d'Alene in 1986, the firm focuses its practice on litigation and alternative dispute resolution (ADR) with an emphasis on early and cost-effective resolution. The members of the firm practice with a strong sense of professional ethics and are experienced advocates before the courts in Washington and Idaho and in utilization of all ADR processes. The firm has considerable expertise in construction law and also represents individuals; sureties and insurers; banks and lenders; municipalities; national corporations and local businesses including manufacturers, retailers and developers; educational institutions; and automotive industry manufacturers, financiers and dealers.

MERIWETHER D. (MIKE) WILLIAMS, born Asheville, North Carolina, July 29, 1949; admitted to bar, 1978, Washington and U.S. District Court, Eastern District of Washington; 1980, U.S. Court of Appeals, Ninth Circuit; 2001, Wyoming; 2002, Idaho. *Education:* University of North Carolina (B.A., 1971); American Graduate School of International Management (M.B.A., International Management, 1972); Gonzaga University (J.D., magna cum laude, 1977). Member, Gonzaga Law Review, 1975-1976. Author: "Blending Mary Carter's Colors: A Tainted Covenant," 12 Gonzaga Law Review 266, 1977; "Commercial Bribery, Antitrust Injury and Section 2(c) of the Robinson-Patman Act," 26 Gonzaga Law Review 167, 1991. *Member:* Washington State Bar Association; Idaho State Bar; Wyoming State Bar. ***REPORTED CASES:*** Kirk et al. v. Ford Motor Company, ___ P.3d ___; 2005 WL 1475405 (Idaho 2005); Eugster v. City of Spokane, ___ Wn. App. ___, 114 P.3d 1200 (2005); 110 Wn. App. 212, 39 P.3d 380 (2002); Hansen v. Transworld Wireless TV-Spokane, Inc., 111 Wn. App. 361, 44 P.3d 929 (2002); Gerken v. Mutual of Enumclaw Ins. Co., 74 Wn. App. 220, 872 P.2d 1108 (1994); Dickinson v. Edwards, 105 Wn.2d 457, 716 P.2d 814 (1986). ***PRACTICE AREAS:*** Accidents; Personal Injury; Commercial Litigation; Products Liability; Civil Rights; Employment Litigation. ***Email:*** mdw@winstoncashatt.com

C. MATTHEW ANDERSEN, born DeKalb, Illinois, March 21, 1949; admitted to bar, 1976, Washington; 1977, U.S. Court of the Armed Forces; 1978, U.S. District Court, Eastern District of Washington and U.S. Court of Federal Claims; 1982, U.S. Court of Appeals, Ninth Circuit and U.S. Supreme Court; 1986, Idaho; 1988, U.S. District Court, District of Idaho. *Education:* Iowa State University (B.S., 1971); Gonzaga University (J.D., cum laude, 1976). Adjunct Professor, Gonzaga University Law School. *Member:* American Bar Association; Idaho State Bar; Washington State Trial Lawyers Association. [Capt., U.S. Army (JAG Corps), 1976-1979]. ***REPORTED CASES:*** Johnson v. Central Valley School District, 97 W.2d 419,645 P.2d (1982); Smith v. Ohio Casualty Ins. Co., 37 W.App. 71,678 P.2d 829 (1984); Havelick v. Chobot, 851 P.2d 1010 Idaho (1993); IPCA v. MacHugh, 61 W.App. 403,810 P.2d 535 (1991); Hoffman v. United States, 178 F.3d 1313 (1999); Flood v. Miller, Fed. Sec. L. Rep. §91, 919 (2002). ***PRACTICE AREAS:*** Commercial Litigation; Employment Law; Construction Law; Contracts; Products Liability. ***Email:*** cma@winstoncashatt.com

JOHN H. GUIN, born Spokane, Washington, May 15, 1972; admitted to bar, 1997, Washington and U.S. District Court, Eastern and Western Districts of Washington; 1998, Idaho and U.S. District Court, District of Idaho; 1999, Montana, U.S. District Court, District of Arizona and U.S. Court of Appeals, Ninth Circuit; 2000, U.S. Court of Appeals, Federal Circuit; 2003, U.S. Court of Federal Claims; 2004, U.S. District Court, District of Montana. *Education:* University of Washington (B.S., 1994); University of Oregon (J.D., 1996). Order of the Coif. Associate Editor, University of Oregon, Law Review, 1996. *Member:* Idaho State Bar. ***PRACTICE AREAS:*** Construction Law; Contracts; Commercial Litigation; AAA Arbitrator. ***Email:*** jhg@winstoncashatt.com

BRIAN T. McGINN, born Spokane, Washington, April 26, 1968; admitted to bar, 1994, Washington; 1996, U.S. District Court, Eastern District of Washington; 1997, U.S. Court of Appeals, Ninth Circuit; 1998, Idaho. *Education:* Gonzaga University (B.A., 1990; J.D., 1994). Recipient, Albert Mann Debate Award. *Member:* Idaho State Bar; Federal Bar Association; Young Lawyers Association; Washington State Trial Lawyers Association. ***PRACTICE AREAS:*** Real Property; Commercial Law; Contracts; Land Use. ***Email:*** btm@winstoncashatt.com

PATRICK J. CRONIN, born Spokane, Washington, November 27, 1958; admitted to bar, 1998, Washington; 1999, Idaho. *Education:* San Diego State University (B.S., Marketing, 1980); Gonzaga University (J.D., magna cum laude, 1998). Articles Editor, Gonzaga Law Review, 1997-1998. Author, "A Call for Legislation for Statutory New Home Warranties," Gonzaga Law Review, Vol. 33, No. 3, 1998. *Member:* Washington State Trial Lawyers Association; Association of Trial Lawyers of America. **REPORTED CASES:** New Hampshire Indemnity Insurance Co., v. Budget Rent-A-Car Systems, 148 Wn. 2d 929, 64 P.3d 1239 (2003). ***PRACTICE AREAS:*** Personal Injury; Medical Malpractice; Dental Malpractice; Insurance Coverage; Insurance Defense; Products Liability. ***Email:*** pjc@winstoncashatt.com

(This Listing Continued)

LAWRENCE H. VANCE, JR., born Corvallis, Oregon, February 1, 1950; admitted to bar, 1976, Washington; 1978, U.S. District Court, Eastern and Western Districts of Washington; 1982, U.S. Court of Federal Claims; 1989, U.S. Court of Appeals, Federal Circuit (Not admitted in Idaho). *Education:* Gonzaga University (B.B.A., 1972; J.D., 1975). Editor, Gonzaga Law Review, 1974-1975. Former Member, State Board of Bar Examiners. *Member:* Washington State (Past Chairman, Construction Law Section) and American Bar Associations; American Arbitration Association (Member, Construction Industry Arbitration Panel). ***PRACTICE AREAS:*** Construction Law; Government Contracts; Construction Insurance; Surety Law. ***Email:*** lhv@winstoncashatt.com

---

TAMARA W. MUROCK, born Butte, Montana; admitted to bar, 1996, Washington; 1998, Idaho. *Education:* Gonzaga University (B.A., cum laude, 1992; J.D., magna cum laude, 1996); University of Washington (LL.M., 1997). Member, Tax Section, Washington State Bar Association. *Member:* Idaho State Bar. ***PRACTICE AREAS:*** Taxation; Business Law; Corporate Law; Estate Planning; Probate; Commercial Litigation; Securities Litigation. ***Email:*** twm@winstoncashatt.com

MICHAEL T. HOWARD, born Royal Oak, Michigan, September 19, 1969; admitted to bar, 1999, Washington; 2000, Idaho. *Education:* University of Idaho (B.S., 1992; J.D., 1999). Delta Theta Phi. ***PRACTICE AREAS:*** Personal Injury; Products Liability; Medical Malpractice; Premises Liability; Insurance Coverage; Construction Law. ***Email:*** mth@winstoncashatt.com

COURTNEY R. BEAUDOIN, born Spokane, Washington, January 8, 1975; admitted to bar, 2000, Washington and U.S. District Court, Eastern District of Washington; 2001, Idaho. *Education:* Santa Clara University (B.A., 1997); Gonzaga University (J.D., cum laude, 2000). *Member:* Washington State Bar Association; Idaho State Bar. ***PRACTICE AREAS:*** Employment Law; Contracts; Commercial Litigation; Real Estate Law. ***Email:*** crb@winstoncashatt.com

REPRESENTATIVE CLIENTS: Albertson, Inc.; Dan Davis Realty; Diversified Machinery Works; Ford Motor Company; General Motors Corporation; General Motors Acceptance Corporation; Keystone Lighting, Inc.; Lennox International, Inc.; Lennox Retail, Inc.; Louisiana-Pacific Corporation; Mazda North American Operations; McFerrin & Marcus Exploration; Navistar International Corp.; Pacific Gas Transmission Co.; R.A. Hanson Co. (RAHCO); Shopko Stores, Inc.; Unicare, Inc.; Washington Waste Systems/Waste Management, Inc.; Western Equipment Co. *Construction Related Clients:* Associated General Contractors; Aztech Electric, Inc.; N.A. Degerstrom, Inc.; Lydig Construction Co.; Max J. Kuney Co.; TML, Inc.; W.A. Botting Plumbing & Heating Co. *Fire Surety & Casualty Companies:* All Nation Insurance Co.; American International Group and Affiliated Companies; Fidelity and Deposit Co. of Maryland (Surety); Royal Insurance Companies; UTICA National Insurance Co. *Banking:* Bank of America, N.A.

(For Complete Biographical Data on all Personnel, see Professional Biographies at Spokane, Washington)

WITHERSPOON, KELLEY, DAVENPORT & TOOLE, P.S.

Established in 1884

THE SPOKESMAN REVIEW BUILDING, SUITE 401
608 NORTHWEST BOULEVARD
COEUR D'ALENE, IDAHO 83814-2146
Telephone: 208-667-4000
Fax: 208-667-8470
Email: info@wkdtlaw.com
URL: http://www.wkdtlaw.com

Spokane, Washington Office: 1100 U.S. Bank Building. 422 West Riverside. Telephone: 509-624-5265. FAX: 509-458-2728.

General Civil and Trial Practice. Antitrust, Banking, Business, Commercial, Construction, Corporate Employment, Environmental, Estate Planning, Government Relations, Health Law, Insurance Defense, Mining, Medical, Personal Injury, Probate, Media, Real Estate Land Use, Securities and Taxation Law.

EDWARD J. ANSON, born Philadelphia, Pennsylvania, January 9, 1951; admitted to bar, 1977, Idaho and U.S. District Court, District of Idaho; 1979, U.S. Court of Appeals, Ninth Circuit. *Education:* Washington College (B.A., 1974); Gonzaga University (J.D., cum laude, 1977). Magistrate Commissioner, First Judicial District of Idaho, 1984-1988. *Member:* Idaho State Bar; American Bar Association; Idaho Trial Lawyers Association; American Inns of Court. (Resident). ***PRACTICE AREAS:*** Trial Practice; Banking; Commercial; Real Estate.

DENNIS M. DAVIS, born Ontario, Oregon, February 28, 1951; admitted to bar, 1977, Idaho and U.S. District Court, District of Idaho. *Education:* University of Idaho (B.S., 1973; J.D., 1977). Member, Coeur d'Alene Planning and Zoning Commission, 1985-1989. Legal Counsel, Coeur D'Alene Area Chamber of Commerce, 1988-1989, 1995-2000. Senator, Idaho State Senate, 1989-1994. Assistant Minority Leader, 1993-1994. Member, Idaho Judicial Council, 1999—. *Member:* Idaho State Bar (Member: Bankruptcy/Commercial Law Section; Board of Governors, Real Property Law Section, 2003—); Fifth District (Secretary/Treasurer, 1978-1979) and American Bar Associations. (Resident). ***PRACTICE AREAS:*** Banking Law; Commercial Law; Corporate Law; Probate Law; Real Estate Law; Employment Law. ***Email:*** dmd@wkdtlaw.com

MARK A. ELLINGSEN, born San Francisco, California, September 16, 1966; admitted to bar, 1992, Washington; 1993, Idaho; 1998, Montana, U.S. District Court, District of Montana, U.S. District Court, District of Idaho, U.S. District Court, Eastern and Western Districts of Washington and U.S. Court of Appeals, Ninth Circuit. *Education:* Whitman College (B.A., 1989); Williamette University (J.D., 1992). *Member:* Washington State Bar Association; Idaho State Bar; State Bar of Montana; American Inns of Court. (Resident). ***PRACTICE AREAS:*** Commercial Law; Civil Litigation; Insurance Defense; Real Estate Litigation; Bankruptcy Law. ***Email:*** mae@wkdtlaw.com

JOEL P. HAZEL, born Yakima, Washington, October 17, 1967; admitted to bar, 1994, Idaho and U.S. District Court, District of Idaho; 1996, Washington and U.S. District Court, Eastern District of Washington. *Education:* Gonzaga University (B.A., 1990); University of Idaho (J.D., 1994). Recipient: American Jurisprudence Award, Criminal Law. Deputy Prosecutor, Kootenai County, 1994-1999. Pro Temp DUI Court Judge. *Member:* Idaho State Bar (Member, Character and Fitness Committee); Washington State Bar Association; American Inns of Court. ***PRACTICE AREAS:*** Trial Practice; Business Litigation; Commercial Litigation; Real Estate Litigation; Employment Law; Eminent Domain. ***Email:*** jph@wkdtlaw.com

(This Listing Continued)

(For Complete Personnel and Biographical Data, see Professional Biographies at Spokane, Washington)

BAUER & FRENCH

EAGLE, IDAHO

(See Boise)

Trial and Appellate Practice. Family Law, Divorce, Interstate Child Custody, Community Property Law. Commercial, Bankruptcy, Real Estate.

ANDREA L. CARDON

EAGLE, IDAHO

(See Boise)

Construction Contracts and Social Security Disability.

SANDRA L. CLAPP & ASSOCIATES, P.A.

1025 S. BRIDGEWAY PLACE, SUITE 180
P.O. BOX 2660
EAGLE, IDAHO 83616
Telephone: 208-938-2660
Fax: 208-938-2674
URL: http://www.clapp-legal.com

Trusts and Estates, Business Transactions, Property Law.

SANDRA L. CLAPP, born Preston, Idaho, September 14, 1966; admitted to bar, 1991, Idaho and U.S. District Court, District of Idaho; 1992, U.S. Court of Appeals, Ninth Circuit. *Education:* University of Idaho (B.A., 1988; J.D., magna cum laude, 1991). Former Law Clerk to the Honorable Stephen S. Trott, U.S. Court of Appeals, Ninth Circuit. *Member:* Idaho State Bar. ***PRACTICE AREAS:*** Trusts and Estates; Business Transactions; Property Law.

HAROLD Q. NOACK, JR., P.A.

EAGLE, IDAHO

(See Boise)

Creditor and Debtor Bankruptcy, General Civil, Trial and Appellate Practice. Commercial, Corporation, Family Law, Divorce, Alimony, Child Support, Real Estate, Construction Law, Elder Law, Wills and Probate.

YTURRI ROSE, LLP

FRUITLAND, IDAHO

(See Ontario, Oregon)

General Civil and Trial Practice. Medical and Legal Malpractice, Insurance Defense, Insurance Law, Personal Injury, Business Litigation, Commercial Law, Corporations, Estate Administration, Estate Planning, Foreclosures, Debtor and Creditor, Zoning and Land Use, Real Estate, Farm and Ranch Law, Labor and Employment Law.

CREASON, MOORE & DOKKEN, PLLC

GRANGEVILLE, IDAHO

(See Lewiston)

General Civil Practice, Insurance Defense, Appeals, Business Organizations, Commercial, Real Property, Probate and Estate Planning, Tax Law, Personal Injury, Criminal Defense, Auto Accident, Head Injury.

BENOIT, ALEXANDER, HARWOOD, HIGH & VALDEZ, L.L.P.

HAILEY, IDAHO

(See Twin Falls)

General Civil Trial Practice. Business Corporation, Partnership, Wills, Estate Planning, Probate, Municipal, Banking, Insurance Defense, Real Estate, Environmental, Agriculture, Real Estate Transactions, Real Estate Litigation, Residential Real Estate and Commercial Real Estate, Product Liability Defense, Professional Liability Defense, Criminal Defense.

LAWSON & LASKI, PLLC

HAILEY, IDAHO

(See Ketchum)

Real Estate, Business Organizations, Civil Litigation, Contracts, Securities, Commercial Law.

ANDREW PARNES

HAILEY, IDAHO

(See Ketchum)

Criminal Trial and Appellate Practice in all State and Federal Courts. Habeas Corpus. DUI, Felonies, Misdemeanors, Homicide, Juvenile, Traffic Violations and Drug Crimes.

BEARD ST. CLAIR GAFFNEY McNAMARA CALDER PA

Established in 1963

2105 CORONADO STREET
IDAHO FALLS, IDAHO 83404-7495
Telephone: 208-523-5171
Fax: 208-529-9732
Email: law@idahofallslaw.com
URL: http://www.lawyers.com/idahofallslaw

Agricultural Law, Acquisitions, Americans with Disabilities Act, Antitrust, Arbitration, Asset Protection, Automobile Accidents, Automobile Insurance, Banking Law, Breach of Contract, Business Law, Buying and Selling Businesses, Charitable Giving, Collections, Commercial Insurance, Commercial Law, Commercial Real Estate, Computers and Software, Condominiums, Construction Law, Contested Wills, Contracts, Copyrights, Corporations, Creditors Rights, Crop Damage and Chemical Applications, Debtor and Creditor, Discrimination, Distribution and Distributorships, Divorce with significant assets, Elder Care, Elder Law, Employment Discrimination, Employment Law, Estate Planning, Estate and Gift Taxation, Family Business Law, Family and Medical Leave Act, Farm and Ranch Law, Fire Loss, Food, Drug and Cosmetic Law, Franchises and Franchising, Foreclosures, General Trial and Appellate Practice, Guardianship, Harassment, Health Care, Health Insurance, Income Taxation, Insurance, Insurance Bad Faith, Investments, Landlord and Tenant Law, Leasing, Liens, Life and Health Insurance, Limited Liability Company Law, Litigation, Long-term Care, Mechanics Liens, Mediation, Medical Malpractice and Malpractice Defense, Medicare and Medicaid, Minority Business Law, Mortgages, Multilevel Sales, Nonprofit and Charitable Organizations, Nursing Homes, PACA, Partnerships, Pension and Benefits, Personal Injury, Post Mortem Administration of Trusts and Estates, Products Liabilities, Professional Malpractice, Property Tax, Professional Practices, Property Insurance, Railroad Accidents, Real Estate, Sexual Abuse, Slip and Fall, Small Business Law, Social Security, Social Security Disability, Taxation, Torts, Trademarks, Trade Secrets, Trust and Estates, Valuations, Warranties, Wills and Probate, Workers Compensation, Wrongful Death, Wrongful Termination, Zoning, Planning and Land Use.

FIRM PROFILE: Beard St. Clair Gaffney McNamara Calder PA has a firm history dating back to the 1960's. Members of the firm have gone on to be a member of the US House of Representatives, an Idaho Supreme Court Justice, a Federal Magistrate and a Senator in the Idaho legislature. The firm has represented major insurance carriers, agribusiness, banks, manufacturers, high-technology companies, and the health care industry. The firm has always maintained a strong estate planning group. Our practice is grouped into three major areas, litigation, business, and estate planning.

WINSTON V. BEARD, born Salt Lake City, Utah, June 1, 1941; admitted to bar, 1967, Idaho; 2003, Washington. *Education:* Brigham Young University; University of Utah (J.D., 1967). Author: Note, "Regulation of Rural Electrical Co-operatives," Utah Law Review, 1967. Assistant Editor, Utah Law Review, 1966-1967. General Counsel, Rogers Foods, Inc., 1975-1980. Chairman of the Board, Westmark Federal Credit Union, 1983-1989. *Member:* Seventh Judicial District (Secretary, 1974) Bar Association; Idaho State Bar (Member, Governing Council and Chairman, Business and Corporate Section, 1996—); American Health Lawyers Association. ***PRACTICE AREAS:*** Business Law; Corporate Law; Taxation Law; Healthcare Law; Business Litigation; Franchise and Multilevel Sales; Anti-Trust; Trade Regulation; Mergers, Acquisitions and Divestitures; Agency and Distributorships; Copyrights; Franchises and Franchising; Intellectual Property; Trademarks; Trade Secrets. ***Email:*** winston@idahofallslaw.com

JOHN G. ST. CLAIR, born Rupert, Idaho, September 21, 1945; admitted to bar, 1970, Idaho; 1971, U.S. Court of Military Appeals; 1996, U.S. Court of Appeals, Ninth Circuit. *Education:* Chapman College (Seven Seas Division); University of Idaho (B.S., 1967; J.D., 1970). Member, Advisory Committee, Idaho State University Tax Institute, 1967-1994, 1999—. Member, Advisory Board, National Network of Estate Planning Attorneys, 2002-2004. Board of Directors: Idaho Community Foundation, 1989-1997; Eastern Idaho Technical College Foundation, 1992-1994; Yo Murphy Foundation, 2002—. Member, Board of Trustees, Idaho Falls Public Library, 1990-2000. United States Golfing Fellowship of Rotarians, President, 1992-1995, Executive Secretary, 1995—. *Member:* Idaho State Bar (Member, Sections on: Tax, Probate and Trust; Real Property); Southeast Idaho Estate Planning Council; Wealth Counsel. [With U.S.A.R., active duty, 1970-1974; Capt., JAGC, 1967]. ***PRACTICE AREAS:*** Alternative Dispute Resolution; Mortgages; Probate; Real Estate; Nonprofit and Charitable Organizations; Estate and Gift Taxation; Trusts and Estates Taxation; Trusts and Estates; Wills; Foreclosure; Charitable Giving; Estate Planning. ***Email:*** john@idahofallslaw.com

MICHAEL D. GAFFNEY, born Waterloo, Iowa, October 26, 1952; admitted to bar, 1986, Idaho and U.S. District Court, District of Idaho; 1988, U.S. Court of Appeals, Ninth Circuit; 1989, Wyoming and U.S. District Court, District of Wyoming; 1995, U.S. Court of Appeals, Tenth Circuit; 1999, U.S. District Court, District of Colorado; 2004, Oregon and U.S. District Court, District of Oregon. *Education:* Regis College (B.S., 1974); University of South Dakota (M.A., 1978); University of Idaho (J.D., 1986). Member, Idaho Law Review, 1985-1986. Special Deputy Attorney General, Idaho Attorney General's Office, 1995—. Federal Mediator Roster, U.S. District Court, District of Idaho. Panel Counsel for Fraternal Order of Police. *Member:* Idaho State Bar (Member, Litigation Section); Idaho Law Foundation; Wyoming Law Foundation; Association of Trial Lawyers of America; Idaho Trial Lawyers Association; Million Dollar Advocates Forum. ***REPORTED CASES:*** Doe v. Glanzer, 232 F.3d 1258 (9th Cir. 2000); Wheeler Elec. v. ABT serv. Corp, 116 F.3d 488 (9th Cir. 1997); Dow v. Louisiana Land & Exploration Co., 77 F.3d 342 (10th Cir. 1996); In re Helmut Co., 1992 Bankr. LEXIS 486 (1992); Perkins v. U.S. Transformer, 132 Idaho 427, 974 P.2d 73 (1999); Valentine v. Perry, 118 Idaho 653, 798 P. 2d 935 (1990); Lehmkuhl v. Bolland, 114 Idaho 503, 757 P.2d 1222 (Ct. App. 1988). ***PRACTICE AREAS:*** Civil Litigation; Complex Business Litigation; Complex Commercial Litigation; Construction Litigation; Agribusiness; Crop Litigation; Trade Secrets; Unfair Competition. ***Email:*** gaffney@idahofallslaw.com

(This Listing Continued)

HARLOW J. McNAMARA, born Idaho Falls, Idaho, February 16, 1942; admitted to bar, 1970, Virginia; 1973, Idaho. *Education:* Ricks College; Brigham Young University (B.S., 1967); George Washington University National Law Center (J.D., 1970). General Counsel, Rogers Brothers Seed Company, 1968-1973. *Member:* Seventh Judicial District Bar Association; Idaho State Bar (Member, Taxation, Probate and Trust Law Sections); Wealth Counsel; Southeast Idaho Estate Planning Council; National Academy of Elder Law Attorneys. ***PRACTICE AREAS:*** Estate Planning; Wills; Probate; Estates; Trust; Elder Law; Elder Rights; Guardianship; Conservatorship; Taxation; Estate and Gift Taxation. ***Email:*** hjm@idahofallslaw.com

GREGORY C. CALDER, born San Francisco, California, August 21,1966; admitted to bar, 1995, Idaho. *Education:* Brigham Young University (B.S., 1992); University of Idaho (J.D., 1995). Author: "Compliance With Idaho's Procedures for Submitting a Proposed Constitutional Amendment: Disingenuous and Underinclusive, or Deliberately Misleading and Intentionally Oblique?" Idaho Law Review 649 (1995). *Member:* Idaho State Bar (Member, Sections on:Business and Corporate Law; Health Law); Wealth Counsel; Southeast Idaho Estate Planning Council (President, 2000-2002). ***LANGUAGES:*** Spanish. ***PRACTICE AREAS:*** Business Law; Buying and Selling of Businesses; Family Business Law; Limited Liability Company Law; Professional Practices; Small Business Law; Private Placement Law; Health Care; Taxation; Estate and Gift Taxation; Income Taxation; Trusts and Estates; Asset Protection; Charitable Giving; Estate Planning; Wills and Probate. ***Email:*** calder@idahofallslaw.com

JARIN O. HAMMER, born Idaho Falls, Idaho, April 1, 1967; admitted to bar, 1997, Idaho. *Education:* Brigham Young University (B.S., Accounting, 1991); University of Idaho (J.D., 1996); University of Florida (LL.M., Taxation, 1997). *Member:* Idaho State Bar (Member, Sections on: Business and Corporate; Real Estate); Idaho Grower Shippers Association. ***PRACTICE AREAS:*** Mergers and Acquisitions; Federal and State Tax Controversies; Income Tax; Estate and Gift Taxation; Trademark; Small Business Law; Limited Liability Company Law; Professional Practices; Real Estate; Agribusiness. ***Email:*** hammer@idahofallslaw.com

JARED W. ALLEN, born Idaho Falls, Idaho, May 3, 1970; admitted to bar, 1998, Idaho. *Education:* Brigham Young University (B.A., 1995); University of Idaho (J.D., 1998). Phi Delta Phi. *Member:* Idaho State Bar (Member, Employment Section). ***LANGUAGES:*** Portuguese. ***REPORTED CASES:*** Zollinger v. Carrol, 137 Idaho 397, 49 P.3d 402(2002). ***PRACTICE AREAS:*** Civil Litigation; Employment; Agribusiness; Complex Business Litigation; Complex Commercial Litigation; Construction Litigation; Trade Secrets; Unfair Competition; Crop Damage. ***Email:*** allen@idahofallslaw.com

---

CHAD A. CAMPOS, born Newport Beach, California, July 7, 1971; admitted to bar, 2000, Idaho. *Education:* Brigham University (B.A., Psychology, 1995); University of Idaho (J.D., cum laude, 2000). Member, University of Idaho Law Review. *Member:* American Bar Association. ***PRACTICE AREAS:*** Litigation; Contract Disputes; Personal Injury; Family Law; Collections. ***Email:*** chad@idahofallslaw.com

KARI MARIE CAMPOS, born Bountiful, Utah, July 17, 1969; admitted to bar, 2000, Idaho. *Education:* Idaho State University (B.S., Accounting, 1991); Brigham Young University (J.D., 1994). Certified Public Accountant. *Member:* Idaho State Bar (Member, Sections on: Business; Real Estate; Bankruptcy); Eastern Idaho Home Builders Association; South East Idaho Estate Planning Council; Idaho Society of CPA's; Inns of Court. ***PRACTICE AREAS:*** Business Law; Business Transactions; Taxation; Bankruptcy; Creditors Rights; Secured Transactions; Construction Law; Adoption. ***Email:*** kari@idahofallslaw.com

JEFFREY D. BRUNSON, born Kennewick, Washington, May 14, 1977; admitted to bar, 2004, Idaho. *Education:* Brigham Young University (B.S., 2000); University of Idaho (J.D., cum laude, 2004). Idaho Law Review. *Member:* Idaho State Bar (Member, Young Lawyers Section). ***LANGUAGES:*** Spanish. ***PRACTICE AREAS:*** Litigation; Business Law; Estate Planning. ***Email:*** jeff@idahofallslaw.com

REPRESENTATIVE CLIENTS: Agribusiness, Inc.; Alpine Counseling, PLLC; American Credit Indemnity; American International Companies; AMX Technologies, Inc.; Bechtel BWXT Idaho, LLC; Doug Andrus Distributing; Arave Construction; Armstrong Electric; A.T.&T. Small Business; Babe's Inc.; Beauty For All Seasons, Inc.; Blackfoot Medical Clinic; Capital Indemnity Corporation; Clark County True Value Hardware; CMR Dental Lab; CNA Insurance Company; Community First National Bank; Community Services; Computer Sales and Service; Control Systems Technology; Digestive Health Center; Eastern Idaho Cardiology Associates PLLC; Environmental Recycling LLC; EPIC Energy, LLC; Fauna Industries; First American Title Company; First Community Industrial Bank; Forde Johnson Insurance Company; Harker Design; High Desert Investment Association; HomeCare Medical; Idaho Alcohols, L.L.C.; Idaho Innovation Center, Inc.; Idaho Physician's Association; Idaho Falls Chiropractic Clinic; Idaho Falls Recovery Center; Idaho Falls Surgical Center; Idaho Heart Institute; Insight Counseling Associates PLLC; International Indemnity Group; Jensen Land Corporation; K&B Food Group; Larsen Farms; Larsen of Idaho; Larsen Processing; Life Care Centers of America; Lockheed Martin Idaho Technologies; Martin Brothers Land & Livestock; Max Ker Lumber; Medical Facilities Company; Medical Mart; Mercury Insurance; Merrill Lynch; MicroServ Telecomputing; Morgan Stanley; Mountain West Farm Bureau; Natural Energy Systems; Neutron Therapies LLC; New Day Property Solutions, LLC; Oral Health Center; Pacific Steel & Recycling; Pacific Hide & Fur; Professional Risk Management Services; Precision Plastics; Pro Power Equipment Company; Russett Valley Farms Inc.; RW Professional Leasing Services Corp.; Security Union Title Insurance; Silver Creek Distillers; Spectrum Corporation; State Farm Insurance Company; State of Idaho; Steele Memorial Hospital; Steiner Elevator; Sun States Insurance Group; Teton Clinical Pharmacy; Teton Radiology; Teton Secured Transport; Teton Medical Specialty Center; Travelers Insurance; United Agencies Realty; US Bank of Idaho; Vernon Recycling; Vernon Steel, Inc.; Wheeler Electric, Inc.; Wood Funeral Home; Woodland Furniture.

COX, OHMAN & BRANDSTETTER

CHARTERED

Established in 1979

510 D STREET

P.O. BOX 51600

IDAHO FALLS, IDAHO 83405

Telephone: 208-522-8606

Fax: 208-522-8618

Email: cobjmo@ida.net

URL: http://www.coblaw.com

General Civil and Criminal Trial, Appellate and Administrative Practice in State and Federal Courts. Social Security, Workmen's Compensation and Corporation. Personal Injury, Insurance, Family Law, Divorce, Child Support, Child Custody, Automobile Accidents and Injuries, Wrongful Death, Head Injury, Criminal Law.

ROGER D. COX, born Idaho Falls, Idaho, May 26, 1938; admitted to bar, 1967, Idaho and U.S. District Court, District of Idaho; 1972, U.S. Supreme Court; 1976, U.S. Court of Appeals, Ninth Circuit; 1977, U.S. Tax Court. *Education:* Brigham Young University (B.S., 1964); George Washington University (J.D., 1967). Chief Deputy Bonneville County Prosecuting Attorney, 1972-1974. Attorney, Office of the General Counsel, Administrative Office of the United States Courts, 1967-1968. *Member:* Seventh District (Chairman, Ethics Committee, 1987—), Federal and American (Member, Sections on: Litigation; Tort and Insurance Practice; Commercial Law; Taxation) Bar Associations; Idaho State Bar; The Association of Trial Lawyers of America; Idaho Trial Lawyers Association (Member, Board of Governors, 1973-1976); American Judicature Society; National Association of Social Security Claimants Representatives. ***PRACTICE AREAS:*** Workers Compensation; Personal Injury; Social Security; Domestic Relations; Trial Practice.

JOHN M. OHMAN, born Anaconda, Montana, December 22, 1948; admitted to bar, 1972, Nebraska and U.S. District Court, District of Nebraska; 1973, Idaho and U.S. District Court, District of Idaho; 1978, U.S. Court of Appeals, Ninth Circuit and U.S. Supreme Court. *Education:* Creighton University (B.S.B.A., 1971; J.D., 1972). Phi Alpha Delta; Omicron Delta Epsilon. Author: Case and Comment, "Federal Judges: The Complexity of Recruitment, Appointment, Tenure and Removal," Vol. 78, No. 4., 1973. Chairman, Idaho Transportation Board, 1986-1990. State Committeeman, 1980-1986. Precinct Committeeman, 1978-1986. *Member:* Seventh Judicial District, Nebraska State and American (Member, Sections on: Litigation; Tort and Insurance Practice; Member, Committee on Divorce Laws and Procedures, Section on Family Law) Bar Associations; Idaho State Bar; Idaho Trial Lawyers Association; The Association of Trial Lawyers of America; Defense Research Institute; Idaho Law Foundation. [Capt., U.S. Army, 1971-1980]. (Certified as Civil Trial Specialist by the Idaho Trial Lawyers Association). ***PRACTICE AREAS:*** Personal Injury; Insurance Defense; Trial Practice; Appellate Practice. ***Email:*** cobjmo@ida.net

DEAN C. BRANDSTETTER, born Idaho Falls, Idaho, February 14, 1957; admitted to bar, 1982, Idaho and U.S. District Court, District of Idaho; 1995, U.S. Court of Appeals, Ninth Circuit. *Education:* University of Idaho (B.S., 1979; J.D., 1982). *Member:* Seventh Judicial District and American Bar Associations; Idaho State Bar; Idaho Trial Lawyers Association; The Association of Trial Lawyers of America. ***PRACTICE AREAS:*** Domestic Relations; Criminal Law; Family Law; Child Custody; Child Support. ***Email:*** cobdcb@ida.net

REPRESENTATIVE CLIENTS: State Farm Insurance; American Hardware Mutual Insurance; Oregon Mutual Insurance; Price Development Co.; Medical and Professional Credit Union; Wester Wholesale, Inc.
REFERENCES: Bank of Commerce; Wells Fargo.

DOCKSTADER LAW OFFICE

IDAHO FALLS, IDAHO

(See Boise)

Labor and Employment, Employment Litigation, Civil Litigation.

EHARDT, SMITH & TORGESEN

2235 EAST 25TH STREET, SUITE 290

IDAHO FALLS, IDAHO 83404

Telephone: 208-542-9292

Fax: 208-552-2518

Business, Corporate, Estate Planning, Wills and Trusts, Real Estate, Taxation, Probate, Bankruptcy, Real Property, Criminal Defense, Family Law, Litigation, Juvenile Law.

GREGORY J. EHARDT, born Idaho Falls, Idaho, April 13, 1970; admitted to bar, 1998, Idaho and Utah. *Education:* Brigham Young University (B.A., 1994); University of Tulsa (J.D., 1997); Georgetown University (LL.M., Taxation and Employee Benefits, 1998). Senior Case Note and Comments Editor, Tulsa International and Comparative Law Journal, 1996-1997. Author: "Proposition 187: A Decision for the Supreme Court," 3 Tulsa J. Comp. & Int'l L. 293. *Member:* Idaho State Bar (Member, Sections on: Real Property; Business and Corporate Law; Commercial Law and Bankruptcy; Taxation, Probate and Trust). ***LANGUAGES:*** Spanish. ***PRACTICE AREAS:*** Corporate; Estate Planning; Real Estate; Tax Law; Probate. ***Email:*** greg@eastidaholaw.com

SAMUEL R. TORGESEN, born Provo, Utah, December 31, 1971; admitted to bar, 2002, Idaho. *Education:* Brigham Young University (B.A., 1997); University of the Pacific, McGeorge School of Law (J.D., 2001) Boston University (LL.M., Taxation, 2002). ***PRACTICE AREAS:*** Business; Corporate; Estate Planning; Bankruptcy; Real Property; Taxation. ***Email:*** sam@eastidaholaw.com

CURTIS REED SMITH, born Idaho Falls, Idaho, December 13, 1965; admitted to bar, 1994, Idaho and U.S. District Court, District of Idaho. *Education:* Idaho State University (B.S., 1990); University of Idaho (J.D., 1993). Board of Student Advocates. Jessup Moot Court Team. *Member:* Idaho State Bar; American Bar Association; Idaho Association of Criminal Defense Lawyers; Idaho Trial Lawyers Association. ***PRACTICE AREAS:*** Criminal Defense; Family Law; Litigation; Juvenile Law.

MARTY R. ANDERSON, born Pocatello, Idaho, February 23, 1970; admitted to bar, 1999, Idaho; U.S. District Court, District of Idaho. *Education:* University of Idaho (B.S., Environmental Science, 1995; J.D., 1998; M.S., Public Lands Policy, 2001). Phi Alpha Delta. Recipient, Board of Student Advocates Outstanding Trial Advocate Award, 1997-1998. *Member:* Idaho State Bar (Member, Environmental Law Section); Idaho Trial Lawyers Association (Member, Young Lawyers Section); Idaho Criminal Defense Lawyers Association. ***PRACTICE AREAS:*** Insurance Defense; Domestic Relations; Criminal Defense; Water Law; Administrative Law; Real Property; Personal Injury; General Practice.

HALL, FARLEY, OBERRECHT & BLANTON, P.A.

IDAHO FALLS, IDAHO

(See Boise)

Litigation, Insurance Defense, Medical Malpractice and Professional Liability, Employment Law, Labor Relations, Products Liability, Construction, Health and Hospital, Corporation, Commercial, Banking, Real Estate, Legislative Counseling, Bankruptcy, Appellate Law, Administrative Agencies, Agricultural, Municipal, Estate Planning and Probate.

HOLDEN, KIDWELL, HAHN & CRAPO, P.L.L.C.

Established in 1902

1000 RIVERWALK DRIVE, SUITE 200

P.O. BOX 50130

IDAHO FALLS, IDAHO 83405

Telephone: 208-523-0620

Telefax: 208-523-9518

Email: hkhc@holdenlegal.com

General and Trial Practice. Banking, Corporation, Taxation, Insurance, Real Estate, Condemnation, Trust and Probate, Bankruptcy, Creditors Rights, Negligence, Products Liability, Water Rights, Labor and Construction, Education, Estate Planning, Local Government, Planning and Zoning, Employee Benefits and Pension.

FIRM PROFILE: HOLDEN, KIDWELL, HAHN & CRAPO, P.L.L.C. is a full service law firm serving Idaho and neighboring states with each attorney trained and focused in the indicated areas of concentration. Our attorneys have served the state and region in a variety of functions for over a century.

MEMBERS OF FIRM AND ASSOCIATES

ARTHUR W. HOLDEN (1877-1967)

ROBERT BONNIFIELD HOLDEN (1911-1971)

TERRY L. CRAPO (1939-1982)

WILLIAM SUTHERLAND HOLDEN (1907-1988)

KENT W. FOSTER, born St. Anthony, Idaho, September 2, 1941; admitted to bar, 1968, Idaho. *Education:* University of Utah (B.A., 1965; J.D., 1968). Delta Theta Phi. Chairman, 1977-1982, Idaho Water Users Association Resolutions Committee. Member, Governors Swan Falls Task Force, 1983. Member, City of Idaho Falls, Special Water Rights Counsel, 1975—. *Member:* Idaho State Bar (Chairman, Water Law Section, 1989-1990); American Bar Association. ***PRACTICE AREAS:*** Water Rights Law; Mining Law; Adoption Law. ***Email:*** kfoster@holdenlegal.com

ROBERT E. FARNAM, born Oakland, California, September 12, 1945; admitted to bar, 1969, Idaho. *Education:* University of Idaho (B.S., summa cum laude, 1966; J.D., cum laude, 1969). Phi Alpha Delta; Phi Kappa Phi. Editor-in-Chief, Idaho Law Review, 1968-1969. *Member:* Seventh Judicial District (President, 1989-1990) and American Bar Associations; American College of Trust and Estate Counsel. ***PRACTICE AREAS:*** Probate Law; Estate Planning Law; Real Estate; Charitable Giving. ***Email:*** rfarnam@holdenlegal.com

WILLIAM D. FALER, born Independence, Kansas, April 1, 1947; admitted to bar, 1972, Idaho. *Education:* University of Kansas (B.A., 1969; J.D., 1972). Phi Delta Phi. Member, University of Kansas Law Review, 1971-1972. *Member:* Idaho State Bar (Member, Evidence Committee); American Bar Association; Defense Research Institute, Inc.; The Association of Trial Lawyers of America. ***PRACTICE AREAS:*** Personal Injury Law; Products Liability Law; Insurance Litigation. ***Email:*** wfaler@holdenlegal.com

CHARLES A. HOMER, born Idaho Falls, Idaho, April 5, 1949; admitted to bar, 1974, Idaho. *Education:* Brigham Young University (B.A., 1971); University of Idaho (J.D., cum laude, 1974). Articles Editor, Idaho Law Review, 1973-1974. *Member:* Idaho State Bar (Member, Sections on: Commercial Law; Bankruptcy; Business; Corporate; Real Property); Idaho Law Foundation (Director, 2001—); American Bar Association. ***PRACTICE AREAS:*** Real Property; Commercial Litigation; Real Estate Law; Creditors Rights Law; Corporate. ***Email:*** chomer@holdenlegal.com

GARY LANE MEIKLE, born Driggs, Idaho, February 1, 1950; admitted to bar, 1977, Idaho. *Education:* Brigham Young University (B.A., magna cum laude, 1974; J.D., magna cum laude, 1977). J. Reuben Clark Scholar. Member, 1975-1976 and Chairman, 1976-1977, Board of Advocates. President, Eastern Idaho Estate Planning Council, 1983-1984. *Member:* Idaho State Bar (Member, Corporate and Securities Law Section Governing Council 1991-1994); Idaho Law Foundation (Member, Continuing Legal Education Committee, 1989-1992, Chairman 1990-1991); American Bar Association. ***LANGUAGES:*** Italian. ***PRACTICE AREAS:*** Estate Planning; Probate; Real Estate; Corporate; Taxation; ERISA. ***Email:*** gmeikle@holdenlegal.com

(This Listing Continued)

HOLDEN, KIDWELL, HAHN & CRAPO, P.L.L.C., Idaho Falls—Continued

DONALD L. HARRIS, born Albany, California, February 26, 1947; admitted to bar, 1976, Idaho and U.S. District Court, District of Idaho; 1979, U.S. Court of Appeals, Ninth Circuit; 1983, U.S. Tax Court. *Education:* Contra Costa College (A.A., 1968); University of California at Berkeley (B.A., 1973); Brigham Young University (J.D., 1976). Deputy Attorney General, State of Idaho, 1976-1979. Assistant United States Attorney, District of Idaho, 1979-1983. Member, Idaho Motor Transport Association, 2004—. *Member:* Idaho State Bar (Member: Bar Examination Preparation Committee, 1979-1982; Fee Arbitrator, 1998—; Seventh District Magistrate Commission, 1990-1993; Litigation Section, Chair 2002— and Alternative Dispute Resolution Section); American Bar Association (Vice Chair, Governmental Law Committee, 2002); Idaho Association of Defense Counsel; Defense Research Institute; Bencher American Inns of Court. ***PRACTICE AREAS:*** Litigation Defense; Public Entity Defense; Commercial Litigation; Business Litigation; Insurance Litigation; Transportation Litigation; Tax Litigation. ***Email:*** dharris@holdenlegal.com

DALE W. STORER, born Idaho Falls, Idaho, September 5, 1950; admitted to bar, 1977, Idaho. *Education:* Brigham Young University (B.S., cum laude, 1974); J. Rueben Clark Law School (J.D., 1977). City Attorney, City of Idaho Falls, City of Idaho, 1982—. *Member:* Idaho State Bar; American Bar Association; Idaho Municipal Attorneys Association (President, 1986-1987; 1991-1992; 2004-2005). ***LANGUAGES:*** Indonesian. ***PRACTICE AREAS:*** Local Government Law; Planning and Zoning; Real Estate; Employment Law; Education Law; Insurance Litigation. ***Email:*** dstorer@holdenlegal.com

MARIE T. TYLER, born Bronx, New York, October 12, 1939; admitted to bar, 1987, Idaho and U.S. District Court, District of Idaho. *Education:* Idaho State University (B.A., with high honors, 1979); University of Idaho (J.D., 1987). Phi Kappa Phi; Phi Alpha Delta. Member, Jessup International Moot Court Team. President, Women's Law Caucus, 1986-1987. Member, Evidence Rules Committee, State of Idaho, 1992—. Member, Idaho Supreme Court Committee, Children and Families in the Courts. *Member:* Idaho State Bar (Member, Family Law Section); American Bar Association (Member, Family Law Section); The Association of Trial Lawyers of America; Idaho Trial Lawyers Association. ***PRACTICE AREAS:*** Family Law. ***Email:*** mttyler@holdenlegal.com

FREDERICK J. HAHN, III, born Idaho Falls, Idaho, November 13, 1963; admitted to bar, 1990, Idaho and U.S. District Court, District of Idaho; 1992, U.S. Court of Appeals, Ninth Circuit; 1999, U.S. Supreme Court; 2003, U.S. Court of Federal Claims. *Education:* University of Idaho (B.A., 1986; J.D., 1990). *Member:* Idaho State Bar; American Bar Association. ***LANGUAGES:*** German. ***PRACTICE AREAS:*** Commercial Litigation; Government Contracts; Construction Litigation. ***Email:*** fjhahnIII@holdenlegal.com

KARL R. DECKER, born Provo, Utah, 1954; admitted to bar, 1985, Idaho. *Education:* Ricks College (A.A., Highest Honors, 1977); Brigham Young University (B.A., cum laude, 1979; J.D., cum laude, 1985). Recipient, Spori Scholar, Ricks College, 1977. Member, 1983-1984 and Note and Comment Editor, 1984-1985, Brigham Young University Law Review. *Member:* Idaho State Bar; Seventh Judicial District Bar Association; American Bankruptcy Institute. ***LANGUAGES:*** German. ***PRACTICE AREAS:*** Litigation; Commercial Law; Fidelity and Surety; Real Estate; Bankruptcy. ***Email:*** kdecker@holdenlegal.com

THEL W. CASPER, born Idaho Falls, Idaho, 1964; admitted to bar, 1993, Arizona and Utah; 1994, Idaho. *Education:* Brigham Young University (B.S., summa cum laude, 1988); Boalt Hall School of Law, University of California, Berkeley (J.D., 1992). Phi Kappa Phi; Beta Gamma Sigma; Pi Delta Phi. *Member:* State Bar of Arizona; Utah State Bar; Idaho State Bar (Member, Sections on: Real Property; Business and Corporate); American Bar Association. ***LANGUAGES:*** French. ***PRACTICE AREAS:*** Real Property; Business; Corporate. ***Email:*** tcasper@holdenlegal.com

SHAN B. PERRY, born Jacksonville, Florida, July 30, 1969; admitted to bar, 1996, Idaho. *Education:* University of Idaho (B.A., summa cum laude, 1993); University of Utah (J.D., 1996). Phi Beta Kappa. Phi Kappa Phi. Recipient, William H. Leary Scholar, University of Utah. Member, Utah Law Review, University of Utah. Assistant City Attorney, City of Idaho Falls. *Member:* Idaho State Bar; American Bar Association. ***PRACTICE AREAS:*** Local Government Law; Civil Litigation; Public Entity Defense Law; Employment Law. ***Email:*** sperry@holdenlegal.com

---

ROBERT MARINUS FOLLETT, born Ogden, Utah, July 22, 1961; admitted to bar, 1988, Idaho. *Education:* University of Utah (B.A., cum laude, 1985; J.D., 1988). Phi Beta Kappa; Phi Kappa Phi. William H. Leary Scholar. Intern to the Hon. Justice I. Daniel Stewart Associate Chief Justice, Utah Supreme Court, 1987. *Member:* Idaho State Bar; American Bar Association. ***LANGUAGES:*** Spanish. ***PRACTICE AREAS:*** Business Law; Real Estate Law; Environmental Law. ***Email:*** rfollett@holdenlegal.com

AMELIA A. SHEETS, born San Diego, California; admitted to bar, 1999, Idaho. *Education:* University of California at San Diego (B.A., 1985); Thomas Jefferson School of Law (J.D., 1998). Lead Articles Editor, Thomas Jefferson School of Law Review, 1997-1998. Author: Note: "The 'Rats' Are Stonewalled: U.S. v. Virginia," TJSL L. Rev. Vol. 19 No. 1, Spring 1997. *Member:* Idaho State Bar (Member, Family Law Section); Association of Trial Lawyers of America. ***PRACTICE AREAS:*** Family Law; Civil Litigation. ***Email:*** asheets@holdenlegal.com

DEANNE CASPERSON, born Preston, Idaho; admitted to bar, 1999, Missouri; 2000, Kansas; 2001, U.S. District Court, Western District of Missouri; 2002, U.S. District Court District of Kansas; 2003, Idaho. *Education:* Utah State University (B.S., 1988); University of Missouri at Kansas City (J.D., with distinction, 1999). Order of the Bench and Robe; Order of Barristers. Member, Law Review. ***PRACTICE AREAS:*** Labor and Employment. ***Email:*** dcasperson@holdenlegal.com

ROBERT L. HARRIS, born Bexburg, Idaho, June 7, 1977; admitted to bar, 2004, Idaho. *Education:* Utah State University (B.S., 2001); University of Idaho (J.D., 2004). ***PRACTICE AREAS:*** Water Law; Real Property. ***Email:*** rharris@holdenlegal.com

(This Listing Continued)

OF COUNSEL

FRED JOSEPH HAHN, born Idaho Falls, Idaho, August 22, 1933; admitted to bar, 1958, Idaho. *Education:* Carroll College (B.A., 1955); Georgetown University (LL.B., 1958; LL.M., 1959). Attorney, National Labor Relations Board, 1958-1959. Member, American Inns of Court. *Member:* Idaho State Bar (Member, Board of Commissioners, 1976-1979; President, 1978-1979); Bar Association of the District of Columbia; Idaho Law Foundation (Director, 1990-1999; President, 1999; Recipient, Idaho State Bar Distinguished Lawyer Award, 2000). Fellow, American Judicature Society. ***PRACTICE AREAS:*** Labor Relations Law; Education Law; Construction Law. ***Email:*** fjhahn@holdenlegal.com

REPRESENTATIVE CLIENTS: The Equitable Life Assurance Society of the United States (Commercial, Farm and City Loans); John Hancock Mutual Life Insurance Co. (Farm Loans and Foreclosures); American Fabrication, Inc.; Ormond Construction Co., Inc.; Industrial Contractors, Inc.; Intermountain Construction Co.; Idaho Growers & Shippers Assn.; School District Nos. 52, 55, 59, 161, 215, 252, 253, 401; Melaleuca, Inc.; Steel West, Inc.; City of Idaho Falls; City of Salmon; City of Iona; Greater Idaho Falls Association of Realtors; GPOD of Idaho; Fred A. Moreton Company; Atlas Mechanical and Industrial, Inc.; Industrial Construction, Inc.; Ormond Builders, Inc.; Commercial General Construction, Inc.; Idaho Steel Products, Inc.; Ovard Construction, Inc.; Snake River Anesthesia, P.A.; Blaine Larsen Farms, Inc.; Frito-Lay; Fireman's Fund Interstate Insurance Group; Gulf Insurance Company; Wilshire Insurance Company; Salmon River Electrical Cooperative; Travelers Ins.; CNA Insurance Co.; National Indemnity Company.

HOPKINS RODEN CROCKETT HANSEN & HOOPES, PLLC

Established in 1973

428 PARK AVENUE
P.O. BOX 51219
IDAHO FALLS, IDAHO 83405-1219
Telephone: 208-523-4445
Fax: 208-523-4474
Email: IFLaw@hrchh.com
URL: http://www.hrchh.com

Boise, Idaho Office: 802 West Bannock, Suite 900, P.O. Box 2110, 83701-2110. Telephone: 208-336-7930. Fax: 208-336-9154. Email: BoiseLaw@hrchh.com.
Washington, D.C. Office: 8 East Street, S.E., 20003. Telephone: 202-546-0361. Fax: 202-546-6294.

General Civil, Trial and Appellate Practice before all State and Federal Courts and Administrative Agencies, Administrative Law, Agricultural Law, Alcoholic Beverages, Banking Law, Bankruptcy, Business Law, Civil Rights, Contracts, Construction Law, Corporate Law, Criminal Law, Debtor and Creditor, Election, Campaign and Political Law, Eminent Domain, Employment Law, Family Law, Government, Insurance, Health Care, Hospital Law, Immigration Law, Natural Resources, Negligence, Personal Injury (plaintiffs and defense), Real Estate, Social Security, Taxation, Trusts and Estates, Utility Law, Wills and Probate, Workers' Compensation Law, and Zoning, Planning and Land Use.

MEMBERS OF FIRM

C. TIMOTHY HOPKINS, born Idaho Falls, Idaho, 1936; admitted to bar, 1964, California; 1965, Idaho; 1969, U.S. Supreme Court. *Education:* Stanford University (A.B., 1960); George Washington University (J.D., with honors, 1963). Order of the Coif. Associate Editor, George Washington Law Review, 1962-1963. *Member:* Idaho State Bar (Commissioner, 1988-1991; President, 1990-1991; Distinguished Lawyer Award, 2003); Idaho Law Foundation (Director, 1983-1988); State Bar of California; American Bar Association (Member, House of Delegates, 1991—; Standing Committee on Federal Judiciary, 2002-2005); Eagle Rock Inns of Court (Bencher and First President). Fellow: American Bar Foundation; American Academy of Appellate Lawyers. ***PRACTICE AREAS:*** Litigation; Appellate Practice; Corporate Law; Real Estate. ***Email:*** tim@hrchh.com

WILLIAM C. RODEN, born Camas, Washington, 1929; admitted to bar, 1953, Idaho; 1964, U.S. Court of Appeals, Ninth Circuit. *Education:* University of Idaho (B.A., 1951; LL.B., 1953). Phi Alpha Delta. Assistant Attorney General, Idaho, 1957-1958. Prosecuting Attorney, Ada County, Idaho, 1959-1960. State Senator, Ada County, Idaho, 1960-1968. Vice-President, American Heart Association, 1978-1979. Member, Board of Directors, American Heart Association, 1976-1979. Legal Advisory Committee, Idaho Association of Commerce & Industry, (Chairman, 1995-1996). *Member:* Idaho State Bar. [U.S. Army, Counter-Intelligence Corps, 1954-1956]. (Resident, Boise Office). ***PRACTICE AREAS:*** Litigation; Public Utility Law; Administrative Law; Legislative Affairs. ***Email:*** bill@hrchh.com

GREGORY L. CROCKETT, born Idaho Falls, Idaho, 1949; admitted to bar, 1974, Idaho; U.S. District Court, District of Idaho and U .S. Court of Appeals, Ninth Circuit. *Education:* University of Idaho (B.S., Finance, 1971; J.D., 1974). *Member:* Idaho State Bar (Member, Commercial Law and Bankruptcy Section). ***PRACTICE AREAS:*** Litigation; Insurance; Negligence; Real Estate; Commercial. ***Email:*** greg@hrchh.com

JOHN D. HANSEN, born Idaho Falls, Idaho, 1933; admitted to bar, 1959, Idaho. *Education:* University of Idaho (B.S., 1956; LL.B., 1959). Senator, Idaho State Legislature, 1986-1998. *Member:* Idaho State Bar; Seventh Judicial District (President, 1971-1972) and American (Member, General Practice Section) Bar Associations; Idaho Trial Lawyers Association. ***PRACTICE AREAS:*** Real Estate; Probate; Estate Planning; Water Law. ***Email:*** john@hrchh.com

D. FREDRICK HOOPES, born Rexburg, Idaho, 1940; admitted to bar, 1973, Idaho; 1973, U. S. District Court, District of Idaho; 1988, U.S. Court of Appeals, Ninth Circuit. *Education:* American University; Brigham Young University (B.S., 1970); Texas Tech University (J.D., 1973). Recipient, Thurgood Marshall Liberty Award, American Civil Liberties Union of Idaho. Member, Idaho Bar Commission 2000-2003 and President of the Idaho State Bar 2002-2003. Adjunct Professor, Trial Practice, University of Idaho College of Law. *Member:* Idaho State and American Bar Associations; Idaho Trial Lawyers Association (Director, Board of Directors, 1980-1996; President, 1988-1989); The Association of Trial

(This Listing Continued)

Lawyers of America (Member, Board of Governors, 1993-1996); National Association of Criminal Defense Lawyers; Idaho Association of Criminal Defense Lawyers (Board of Directors, 1993-2005); American College of Trial Lawyers (Member: Idaho State Committee; Teaching/Trial & Appellate Advocacy Committee). Fellow: American College of Trial Lawyers; American Bar Foundation. (Certified as a Criminal Trial and Civil Trial Specialist by the Idaho Trial Lawyers Association). ***PRACTICE AREAS:*** Litigation; Personal Injury; Product Liability; Professional Liability; Criminal Law. ***Email:*** fred@hrchh.com

JOHN MICHAEL BRASSEY, born Boise, Idaho, 1946; admitted to bar, 1971, Idaho, U.S. District Court, District of Idaho and U.S. Court of Appeals, Ninth Circuit. *Education:* University of Idaho (B.S., Finance, 1968; J.D., 1971). Phi Alpha Delta. Administrator, Executive Office of the Governor, Division of Financial Management, 1996-1997. Director, State of Idaho Department of Insurance, 1995. Deputy Attorney General, Chief Business Regulation Division, 1979-1981. Deputy Director, State of Idaho Department of Finance, 1974-1979. Member, Executive Committee, National Association of Consumer Credit Administrators, 1973-1975. President, American Conference of Uniform Consumer Credit States, 1973-1974. Deputy Administrator of Securities and the Uniform Consumer Credit Code, State of Idaho Department of Finance, 1973-1974. Deputy Administrator, Uniform Consumer Credit Code, State of Idaho Department of Finance, 1972-1973. Assistant Attorney General, State of Idaho, 1971-1972. Board of Directors, Boise Area Chamber of Commerce. (Resident, Boise, Idaho Office). ***PRACTICE AREAS:*** Legislative Practice; Corporate Law; Administrative Law; Commercial Law. ***Email:*** mike@hrchh.com

LARY S. LARSON, born Salt Lake City, Utah, 1953; admitted to bar, 1980, Idaho. *Education:* University of North Carolina (B.A., 1975); Brigham Young University (J.D., cum laude, 1980). *Member:* Idaho State Bar. ***PRACTICE AREAS:*** Estate Planning; Trust Law; Probate; Commercial Law; Civil Rights; Labor and Employment; Real Estate; Litigation. ***Email:*** lary@hrchh.com

PAUL B. RIPPEL, born Borger, Texas, 1952; admitted to bar, 1981, Idaho. *Education:* University of Idaho (B.S., 1976; J.D., 1981); New Mexico State University (M.S., 1978). *Member:* Idaho State Bar (Workers Compensation Section, Board Member, Professionalism and Service Awards); Idaho Association of Defense Counsel. (Certified as a Workers' Compensation Specialist by the Idaho Trial Lawyers Association). ***PRACTICE AREAS:*** Litigation; Real Estate; Divorce; Insurance; Contracts; Business Law; Workers Compensation. ***Email:*** rip@hrchh.com

STEVEN K. BROWN, born Boise, Idaho, January 25, 1955; admitted to bar, 1985, Idaho. *Education:* University of Idaho (B.S., 1981; J.D., cum laude, 1985). *Member:* Idaho State Bar; Idaho Trial Lawyers Association; The Association of Trial Lawyers of America. ***PRACTICE AREAS:*** Litigation; Commercial Law; Intellectual Property; Personal Injury; Criminal Law; Products Liability; Professional Malpractice; Insurance. ***Email:*** steveb@hrchh.com

DAVID H. SHIPMAN, born Springfield, Illinois, January 19, 1960; admitted to bar, 1986, Illinois and U.S. District Court, Northern District of Illinois; 1990, Idaho and U.S. District Court, District of Idaho. *Education:* University of Illinois (B.S., with highest honors, 1983); Northwestern University (J.D., 1986). *Member:* Idaho State Bar. ***PRACTICE AREAS:*** Litigation; Commercial Law. ***Email:*** david@hrchh.com

LANCE J. SCHUSTER, born Fullerton, California, 1967; admitted to bar, 1996, Idaho and U.S. District Court, District of Idaho; 1997, U.S. Court of Federal Claims. *Education:* Brigham Young University (B.A., 1991; M.A., 1996); University of Idaho (J.D., 1996). Magister, Phi Delta Phi, 1995-1996. *Member:* Idaho State Bar; American Bar Association. ***LANGUAGES:*** Spanish. ***PRACTICE AREAS:*** Health Care; Litigation; Business Law; Personal Injury. ***Email:*** lance@hrchh.com

OF COUNSEL

BRUCE L. THOMAS, born Tacoma, Washington, 1948; admitted to bar, 1974, Idaho; 1981, U.S. Tax Court; 1985, U.S. Court of Appeals, Ninth Circuit. *Education:* Whitman College (B.A., 1970); University of Denver (J.D., 1974). Law Clerk to Chief Justice, Joseph J. McFadden, Supreme Court of Idaho, 1974-1976. Member, Panel of Mediators and Panel of Arbitrators, American Arbitration Association. *Member:* Boise and American Bar Associations; Idaho State Bar (Chair: Alternative Dispute Resolution Section; Corporate and Securities Law Sections). (Resident, Boise Office). ***PRACTICE AREAS:*** Business Law; Mediation and Arbitration; Litigation; Estate Planning and Probate. ***Email:*** bruce@hrchh.com

ORVAL HANSEN (Resident, Washington, D.C. Office)

GEORGE L. DENISON (Resident, Washington, D.C. Office)

JUST LAW OFFICE

Established in 1990

381 SHOUP AVENUE, SUITE 211
P.O. BOX 50271
IDAHO FALLS, IDAHO 83405
Telephone: 208-523-9106; Toll Free: 800-923-9106
Fax: 208-523-9146
Email: cjust@justlawidaho.com
URL: http://www.justlawidaho.com

Real Estate, Foreclosures, Bankruptcy, Deeds-in-Lieu, Evictions, Document Preparation, Title Packages, Centralized Statewide Reconveyances, REO Services, REO Closings, Real Estate Litigation.

FIRM PROFILE: Idaho's only Law Firm devoted to the Mortgage Banking Industry.

LAW FIRM ALLIANCES/ASSOCIATIONS: **U.S. FORECLOSURE NETWORK**

CHARLES C. JUST, born Idaho Falls, Idaho, October 28, 1949; admitted to bar, 1976, Idaho and U.S. District Court, District of Idaho. *Education:* University of Idaho (B.A., 1972; J.D., 1975). Phi Alpha Delta; Inns of Court. Author: Idaho Section of "The National Mortgage Servicers Reference Directory." *Member:* Bonneville County Bar Association; Idaho State Bar (Member, Sections on: Real Estate; Solo Practitioner); USFN Idaho Land Title Association; Idaho Mortgage Bankers Association. ***PRACTICE AREAS:*** Real Estate; Bankruptcy; Evictions; Real Estate Titles; Real Estate Litigation. ***Email:*** cjust@justlawidaho.com

LEGAL SUPPORT PERSONNEL

PAULA PETERSON, (Office Manager)

(Firm is a member of Idaho Mortgage Bankers)

Languages: English and Spanish.

REPRESENTATIVE CLIENTS: Associates Financial Services; Aames Home Loans; ABN-AMRO; Ameriquest; Advanta Mortgage Corporation; American Reconveyance Company; BancPlus Mortgage Corporation; BancShares Mortgage Group; Bank of America; Bank of New York; Banker's Trust; Bank United; Beneficial Mortgage Corporation; CIT Group/Consumer Finance; Cendant Mortgage Services; Cenlar Mortgage Corporation; Chase Manhattan Bank; CitiCorp; City Mortgage Corporation; Countrywide Home Loans; Crestar Mortgage; Colonial Savings & Loan; Conseco Financial; Crown Bank; Dime Savings Bank; Dovenmuehle; Emerald Mortgagee Assistance; Empire Mortgage; Equicredit Corporation; ExtraCo Mortgage; Fairbanks Capital Corporation; First American National Default Services; First Horizon; First Union National Bank; FirstPlus Mortgage Corporation; Flagstar Bank; Greenpoint Mortgage; Guild Mortgage Corporation; Household Finance Company; Idaho Independent Bank; Integrated Lenders Services; Indymac, Inc.; Interlink Mortgage Services; James B. Nutter; Liberty Lending; Master Financial Corporation; Matrix Capital; Midfirst Mortgage; Morequity; Nations Credit; NovaStar; Oakwood Homes; Old Kent Mortgage Services; Pacific Guaranty; Provident Consumer Finance; R.W. Utterbeck Construction; Realty Executives; Resource BancShares Mortgage Group; Standard Federal Savings Bank; SunTrust; Transworld Mortgage Corporation; Wells Fargo; U.S. Bank, National Association.

MARTIN & ESKELSON, P.L.L.C.

Established in 1998

425 SOUTH HOLMES AVENUE
P.O. BOX 3189
IDAHO FALLS, IDAHO 83403-3189
Telephone: 208-523-6644
Fax: 208-522-0791
URL: http://www.stephenemartinlaw.com

Estate Planning, Federal Taxation, Real Estate, Probate, Business Law, Estate and Gift Taxation.

STEPHEN E. MARTIN, born Idaho Falls, Idaho, March 4, 1947; admitted to bar, 1972, Utah; 1974, Idaho. *Education:* Northwestern University (B.A., cum laude, 1969; J.D., 1972). Co-Author: "Idaho Estate Planning Desk Book," Idaho Law Foundation, 1982. Faculty Member, Idaho Estate Planning Institute, sponsored by Idaho State Law Foundation, 1982-2003. Chairman, Idaho Law Foundation Continuing Legal Education Committee, 1985-1986. Chair, Estate and Gift Tax Committee, Section of Taxation, 1989-1991 and Chair, Tax Problems of Farmers and Ranchers Committee, Real Property, Probate and Trust Law Section, 1992-1993, American Bar Association. *Member:* Idaho State Bar; Utah State Bar; American Bar Association; American College of Trust and Estate Counsel (Chairman, Estate and Gift Tax Committee, 1998-2001; Regent, 1993-1998). ***PRACTICE AREAS:*** Estate Planning; Federal Taxation; Probate; Business Law; Estate and Gift Taxation; Real Estate. ***Email:*** semartin@onewest.net

SCOTT P. ESKELSON, born Logan, Utah, June 20, 1953; admitted to bar, 1979, Utah; 1980, Arizona; 1983, Idaho. *Education:* Utah State University (B.S., cum laude, 1976); University of Utah (J.D., 1979). Assistant General Counsel, Del E. Webb Development Company, Phoenix, Arizona, 1979-1981. *Member:* Utah State Bar; State Bar of Arizona; Idaho State Bar. ***PRACTICE AREAS:*** Real Estate; Estate Planning; Corporate; Business Law. ***Email:*** seskelson@onewest.net

McGRATH, MEACHAM & SMITH, PLLC

414 SHOUP AVENUE
P.O. BOX 50731
IDAHO FALLS, IDAHO 83405
Telephone: 208-524-0731
Fax: 208-529-4166
Email: info@eidaholaw.com
URL: http://www.lawyers.com/eidaholaw

General Civil Practice, Banking, Insurance Defense, Business, Real Estate, Worker's Compensation, Products Liability, Commercial, Personal Injury, Trusts and Estates, Wills and Probate, Creditor Bankruptcy, Municipal Law.

MEMBERS OF FIRM

STEPHEN J. McGRATH, born Burlington, Iowa, May 26, 1946; admitted to bar, 1973, Idaho. *Education:* University of Stockholm, Stockholm, Sweden and University of Iowa (B.A., in Sociology, 1968); University of Idaho (J.D., 1973). Member, Moot Court Board. Member, Idaho Law Review, 1972-1973. *Member:* Idaho State Bar; American Bar Association; Idaho Trial Lawyers Association; Defense Research Institute. ***PRACTICE AREAS:*** Personal Injury; Business Litigation; Products Liability; Commercial Law; Real Estate; Insurance Defense; Subrogation; Agriculture Law; Banking Law.

GREGORY P. MEACHAM, born Lewiston, Idaho, June 14, 1946; admitted to bar, 1974, Idaho. *Education:* Utah State University (B.S., magna cum laude, 1970); University of California: Davis (M.S., 1971); University of Idaho (J.D., 1974). Phi Kappa Phi. Comments Editor, Idaho Law Review, 1973-1974. Author: Comment, "The Multiple Use-Sustained Yield Act: A Decade of Consideration," Idaho Law Review Vol. 10 No. 1, 1973. *Member:* Idaho State Bar; Seventh Judicial District Bar Association. ***PRACTICE AREAS:*** Business Litigation; Corporations; Employment Law; Real Estate; Trusts and Estates; Probate; Wills. ***Email:*** greg@eidaholaw.com

BRYAN D. SMITH, born Boise, Idaho, May 23, 1962; admitted to bar, 1989, California; 1991, Idaho. *Education:* Brigham Young University (B.A., 1986); McGeorge School of Law, University of the Pacific (J.D., with distinction, 1989). Member, Traynor Honor So-

(This Listing Continued)

McGRATH, MEACHAM & SMITH, PLLC, Idaho Falls—Continued

ciety. Comment Editor, Pacific Law Journal, 1988-1989. Author: 19 Pacific Law Journal 4, 1988. *Member:* Idaho State Bar; State Bar of California. ***LANGUAGES:*** Dutch. ***PRACTICE AREAS:*** Litigation; Commercial Law; ERISA; Insurance Defense.

ASSOCIATE

BUSTER J. DRISCOLL, born Pingree, Idaho, December 2, 1977; admitted to bar, 2004, Idaho. *Education:* Brigham Young University (B.A., magna cum laude, 2001; J.D., 2004). Member: Moot Court and Trial Advocacy Team, 2002-2004; Board of Directors, Moot Court, 2003-2004. Order of Barristers. *Member:* Idaho State Bar. ***LANGUAGES:*** Portuguese. ***PRACTICE AREAS:*** Civil Litigation; Insurance Law; Municipal Law. ***Email:*** bjd@eidaholaw.com

REPRESENTATIVE CLIENTS: United Fire & Casualty Company; United Life Insurance Company; Fireman's Fund Insurance Company; Bombardier Corporation; Idaho Supreme Pototoes, Inc.; Sauer Farms, Inc.; Wells Fargo Bank; R.H. Simpson Properties, Ltd.; Bonneville Blueprint Supply; Broadway Ford, Inc.; Rocky Mountain Toyota-Lincoln-Mercury Daewoo; Farmland Insurance; U.S.A.I.G.; Eastern Idaho Economic Development Corp.; Regence Blue Shield of Idaho; Snake River Plains Pototoes, Inc.; Phenix of Idaho, Inc.; Beco Construction, Inc.; Universal Underwriters Insurance Co.; SGI Insurance; Safeco Insurance Company; City of Shelley.

MERRILL & MERRILL

CHARTERED

IDAHO FALLS, IDAHO

(See Pocatello)

General Civil Practice. Trials and Appeals in all State and Federal Courts. Probate, Real Estate, Insurance Law, Negligence, Corporate, Estate Planning, Education Law, Taxation, Hospital Law, Workers Compensation and Public Utility Law.

MOFFATT THOMAS BARRETT ROCK & FIELDS

CHARTERED

420 MEMORIAL DRIVE
P.O. BOX 51505
IDAHO FALLS, IDAHO 83405
Telephone: 208-522-6700
Fax: 208-522-5111
URL: http://www.moffatt.com

Boise, Idaho Office: 101 South Capitol Boulevard, 10th Floor, P.O. Box 829, 83701. Telephone: 208-345-2000. Fax: 208-385-5384.
Pocatello, Idaho Office: 412 West Center, Suite 2000, P.O. Box 817, 83204. Telephone: 208-233-2001. Fax: 208-232-0150.
Twin Falls, Idaho Office: 621 N. College Road, Suite 103, P.O. Box 5483, 83303-5483. Telephone: 208-734-7500. Fax: 208-734-7508.

General Civil, Trial and Appellate Practice. Administrative Law, Alternative Dispute Resolution, Antitrust and Trade Regulation, Aviation, Bankruptcy, Banks and Banking, Business Law, Commercial Real Estate, Construction Law, Contracts, Corporate Law, Debtor and Creditor, Disabilities, Employee Benefits, Environmental Law, Finance, Government Relations, Health Care, Hospital Law, Insurance Defense, Intellectual Property, Labor and Employment Law, Leases and Leasing, Litigation, Medical Malpractice, Mergers, Acquisitions and Divestitures, Mortgages, Nonprofit and Charitable Organizations, Partnership Law, Probate, Products Liability, Professional Liability, Public Utility Law, Real Estate, Regulatory Law, Securities, Taxation, Torts, Trusts and Estates, Water Law, Worker's Compensation.

BRADLEY J. WILLIAMS, born Blackfoot, Idaho, May 29, 1960; admitted to bar, 1989, Idaho. *Education:* Idaho State University (B.A., 1986); University of Idaho (J.D., 1989). ***PRACTICE AREAS:*** Insurance Defense; Commercial Litigation; Labor and Employment; Medical Malpractice; Legal Malpractice Defense. ***Email:*** bjw@moffatt.com

LEE RADFORD, born Idaho Falls, Idaho, April 8, 1963; admitted to bar, 1989, Illinois; 1997, Idaho. *Education:* Brigham Young University (B.A., cum laude, 1986; J.D., magna cum laude, 1989). ***PRACTICE AREAS:*** Litigation; Toxic Torts. ***Email:*** klr@moffatt.com

(For complete biographical data on other personnel, see Professional Biographies at Boise, Pocatello and Twin Falls, Idaho)

PETERSEN, MOSS & HALL

Established in 1950

485 E STREET
IDAHO FALLS, IDAHO 83401
Telephone: 208-523-4650
FAX: 208-524-3391

General Civil and Trial Practice in all State and Federal Courts and Administrative Agencies. Corporation, Partnership, Business, Personal Injury, Real Estate, Employment, Insurance, Estate Planning, Probate, Taxation and Construction.

MEMBERS OF FIRM

GEORGE C. PETERSEN, JR., born Salt Lake City, Utah, April 23, 1924; admitted to bar, 1950, Idaho. *Education:* University of North Carolina; University of Utah (J.D., 1949). Phi Alpha Delta. Member, City Council, 1953-1961. *Member:* Seventh Judicial District (President, 1963-1964) and American Bar Associations; Idaho State Bar. ***PRACTICE AREAS:*** Estate Planning; Business Law; Personal Injury.

STEPHEN D. HALL, born Maywood, California, October 7, 1952; admitted to bar, 1979, Idaho. *Education:* Brigham Young University (B.A., cum laude, 1976; J.D., magna cum laude, 1979). J. Reuben Clark Scholar. Editorial Associate, Brigham Young University Law Review, 1978-1979. Resident Caribbean Counsel, Church of Jesus Christ of Latter-Day Saints, 1983-1986. *Member:* Seventh Judicial District Bar Association; Idaho State Bar. ***LANGUAGES:*** Spanish. ***PRACTICE AREAS:*** Litigation; Estate Planning; Probate; Business; Personal Injury. ***Email:*** sdhlaw@onewest.net

OF COUNSEL

REED L. MOSS, born Ririe, Idaho, November 21, 1930; admitted to bar, 1960, Idaho. *Education:* Ricks College and Brigham Young University (B.A., with highest honors, 1957); George Washington University (J.D., with honors, 1960).

REPRESENTATIVE CLIENTS: CAL Stores; Church of Jesus Christ of Latter-Day Saints; Custom Land Development Co.; Deseret Mutual Benefit Assn.; Federated Rural Electric Insurance Co.; Interstate Lending Corp.; Monsanto Co.; Mountain Sales Helicopters, Inc.; Pacific Mutual Insurance Co.; Pillsbury Co.; Security Pacific Mortgage Corp.; South Fork Lodge; Teton Crane and Transport, Inc.; United Agencies, Inc.; United Pacific Insurance.

QUANE SMITH LLP

2325 WEST BROADWAY, SUITE B
IDAHO FALLS, IDAHO 83402
Telephone: 208-529-0000
Facsimile: 208-529-0005
Email: info@quanesmith.net
URL: http://www.quanesmith.net

Boise, Idaho Office: U.S. Bank Plaza, 16th Floor, P.O. Box 519. Telephone: 208-345-8600. Facsimile: 208-345-8660.
Coeur d'Alene, Idaho Office: 2020 Lakewood Drive, Suite 312, P.O. Box 1758. Telephone: 208-664-9281. Facsimile: 208-664-5380.

Insurance, Insurance Defense, Litigation, Accountants Liability, Advertising and Marketing, Agents and Brokers Liability, Agricultural Law, Alcoholic Beverages, Alternative Dispute Resolution, Architects and Engineers Liability, Arson and Insurance Fraud, Asbestos Defense, Brain Injury, Business Law, Casualty Insurance Defense, Catastrophic Injury, Civil Practice, Commercial Law, Complex and Multi-District Litigation, Computers and Software, Construction Law, Contracts, Corporate Law, Design Professionals Liability, Drug and Medical Device Defense, Education Law, Employer Liability, Environmental Law, ERISA Litigation, Extra Contractual Insurance Defense, Federal Practice, Fire Insurance, Firearms Litigation, Food Products Liability, Fraud and Deceit, Government, Hazardous Waste Liability, Head Injury, Health Care, Insurance Bad Faith Defense, Labor and Employment, Legal Malpractice Defense, Libel, Slander and Defamation, Life Insurance Defense, Manufacturers Liability, Medical Malpractice, Natural Resources, Negligence, Personal Injury, Pesticide Litigation, Physicians Licensing, Pollution, Premises Liability, Products Liability, Professional Discipline, Professional Liability, Propane Products Liability, Property Damage Defense, Real Estate, Recreational Products Liability, School Board Defense, Slip and Fall, Spinal Injury, Subrogation, Torts, Toxic Torts, Transportation, Workers Compensation and Wrongful Death.

FIRM PROFILE: A regional law firm headquartered in Boise, Idaho with additional offices located in Coeur d'Alene, Idaho and Idaho Falls, Idaho. The Idaho Falls office represents clients in eastern Idaho and western Wyoming. The firm's major focus is in the representation of insurance companies and their policyholders, governmental entities and self-insured corporations. The firm emphasizes all aspects of civil litigation, alternative dispute resolution and risk management.

DONALD F. CAREY, admitted to bar, 1991, Idaho 1992, Wyoming. *Education:* Mesa State College (B.A., 1984); University of Wyoming (J.D., 1991). ***PRACTICE AREAS:*** Insurance Defense; Personal Injury Defense; Construction Law; Education Law; Professional Malpractice. ***Email:*** dfcarey@quanesmith.net

---

ROBERT D. WILLIAMS, admitted to bar, 1994, Idaho; 2001, Wyoming. *Education:* University of Wisconsin-Madison (B.S., 1991); University of Idaho (J.D., 1994). ***Email:*** rdwilliams@quanesmith.net

CAROLE I. WESENBERG, admitted to bar, 2000, Idaho. *Education:* Montana State University (B.S., 1994); Southern Illinois University (J.D., 2000). (Resident). ***Email:*** ciwesenberg@quanesmith.net

EVANS KEANE LLP

111 MAIN STREET
P.O. BOX 659
KELLOGG, IDAHO 83837
Telephone: 208-784-1105
Facsimile: 208-783-7601
Email: ccox@usamedia.tv

Boise, Idaho Office: 1405 W. Main Street, P.O. Box 959. Telephone: 208-384-1800

General Trial and Appellate Practice, Corporation, Mining, Labor, Banking, Real Property, Insurance, Products Liability, Workers Compensation Law, Environmental Law, Personal Injury.

JAMES P. KEANE (1925-1988)

CHARLES L. A. COX, born Camp Polk, Louisiana, October 3, 1952; admitted to bar, 1981, Idaho; 1989, U.S. Court of Appeals, Ninth Circuit; 1993, U.S. Court of Federal Claims. *Education:* University of Kent at Canterbury, England; Western State College (B.A., 1975); University of Iowa (J.D., 1981). Phi Alpha Delta. Managing Editor, The Journal of Corporation Law, 1980-1981. *Member:* First Judicial District and American Bar Associations; Idaho State Bar. ***PRACTICE AREAS:*** General Litigation and Appellate; Corporate Law; Environmental Law.

(This Listing Continued)

REPRESENTATIVE CLIENTS: Beamis Oil Co.; City of Kellogg; City of Wardner; Coeur d'Alene Mines Corp.; Hecla Mining Co.; Coeur Silver Valley, Inc.; Kellogg School District No. 391; Shoshone County; Sidney Resources Corporation; S.V.L. Analytical, Inc.; U.S. Bank; West Shoshone Hospital District No. 1; Silver Mountain Corp.; Eagle Crest.

(For complete biographical data on all personnel, See Professional Biographies at Boise, Idaho)

BENOIT, ALEXANDER, HARWOOD, HIGH & VALDEZ, L.L.P.

Established in 1919

160 SECOND STREET EAST, SUITE 218
P.O. BOX 2246
KETCHUM, IDAHO 83340
Telephone: 208-726-4900
Fax: 208-726-3101
Email: benoitlaw@benoitlaw.com
URL: http://www.benoitlaw.com

Twin Falls, Idaho Office: 126 Second Avenue North. Telephone: 208-733-5463. Fax: 208-734-1438.

General Civil Trial Practice. Business Corporation, Partnership, Wills, Estate Planning, Probate, Municipal, Banking, Insurance Defense, Real Estate, Environmental, Agriculture, Real Estate Transactions, Real Estate Litigation, Residential Real Estate and Commercial Real Estate, Product Liability Defense, Professional Liability Defense, Criminal Defense.

ROBERT M. HARWOOD, born American Falls, Idaho, November 2, 1946; admitted to bar, 1971, Idaho. *Education:* University of Idaho (B.A., magna cum laude, 1969; J.D., cum laude, 1971). Phi Beta Kappa; Phi Kappa Phi; Phi Alpha Delta (President, 1970). Member: Idaho Law Review, 1970-1971; Moot Court Team. *Member:* 5th Judicial District and American Bar Associations; Idaho State Bar; Idaho Association of Defense Counsel; Defense Research Institute. Master, American Inns of Court. ***PRACTICE AREAS:*** Civil Trial Practice; Business; Real Estate; Product Liability; Insurance Defense; Legal Malpractice Defense; Construction Law; Mediation. ***Email:*** harwood@benoitlaw.com

(For complete biographical data on all personnel, see Professional Biographies at Twin Falls, Idaho)

BRIAN E. ELKINS

BITTERROOT SQUARE PROFESSIONAL BUILDING
208 SPRUCE AVENUE NORTH
P.O. BOX 766
KETCHUM, IDAHO 83340
Telephone: 208-726-4338
Facsimile: 208-726-9328
URL: http://www.lawyers.com/elkinslaw

Criminal Defense, DUI, General Litigation and Appellate Practice.

BRIAN E. ELKINS, born Spokane, Washington, December 6, 1955; admitted to bar, 1983, Idaho, and U.S. District Court, District of Idaho; 1994, U.S. Court of Appeals, Ninth Circuit and U.S. Supreme Court. *Education:* University of Idaho (B.S., 1979); University of Idaho College of Law (J.D., 1983). Member: Honor Court, University of Idaho College of Law, 1983. Attorney General, Associated Students of the University of Idaho, 1983. Author: "Idaho's Repeal of The Insanity Defense: What Are We Trying to Prove?" 31 Idaho L.Rev. 151. Law Clerk to the Honorable Douglas D. Kramer, Idaho District Court, 1983-1985. Deputy Prosecuting Attorney, Blaine County, Idaho, 1985. Public Defender, Blaine County, Idaho, 1986-1990. Certified as a Criminal Trial Specialist by the Idaho Trial Lawyers Association. Member, Criminal Justice Act Panel, U.S. District Court, District of Idaho, 1993—. *Member:* Idaho State Bar; Idaho Association of Criminal Defense Lawyers (Member, Board of Directors, 1998-2004); National Association of Criminal Defense Lawyers; American Inns of Court; National College of DUI Defense.

HAWLEY TROXELL ENNIS & HAWLEY LLP

540 SECOND AVENUE NORTH
P.O. BOX 297
KETCHUM, IDAHO 83340
Telephone: 208-726-1700
Facsimile: 208-726-9743
Email: info@hteh.com
URL: http://www.hawleytroxell.com

Boise, Idaho Office: Suite 1000, 877 Main Street. Telephone: 208-344-6000. Facsimile: 208-342-3829.
Pocatello, Idaho Office: 333 South Main Street, P.O. Box 100. Telephone: 208-233-0845. Facsimile: 208-233-1304.
Reno, Nevada Office: 6490 S. McCarran, Suite 4. Telephone: 775-829-9944. Facsimile: 775-829-2627.

General Civil Trial and Appellate Practice before all State and Federal Courts and Administrative Agencies. Alternative Dispute Resolution, Antitrust, Aviation, Banking, Bankruptcy and Creditor Rights, Communications, Construction, Copyright, Corporate, Education, Employee Benefits, Environmental, ERISA, Trusts and Estates, Finance, Health Care and Hospital, Insurance, Intellectual Property, Labor and Employment, Legislative, Media, Mergers and Acquisitions, Mining, Natural Resources, Probate, Products Liability, Public Contract, Public Finance, Public Utility, Qualified and Nonqualified Deferred Compensation, Real Estate, Securities, Taxation, Technology and Science, Trademark and Workers' Compensation Law.

(This Listing Continued)

FIRM PROFILE: Hawley Troxell Ennis & Hawley LLP, one of Idaho's largest law firms with three offices in Idaho and one in Nevada, provides legal services to a base of regional and national clients.

MEMBER OF FIRM

RAND L. PEEBLES, born Phoenix, Arizona, July 3, 1946; admitted to bar, 1973, California; 1980, Idaho. *Education:* University of Hawaii (B.A., 1969); University of San Francisco (J.D., 1973). *Member:* State Bar of California; Idaho State Bar; International Municipal Lawyers Association. ***PRACTICE AREAS:*** Business Organizations; Business Transactions; Municipal Law; Education Law; Construction Law. ***Email:*** RLP@HTEH.COM

ASSOCIATE

ADAM BRUNO KING, born Champaign/Urbana, Illinois, February 23, 1961; admitted to bar, 1989, California; 1997, Idaho; 1998, Hawaii. *Education:* University of California at Berkeley (B.A., magna cum laude, 1984); Hastings College of the Law, University of California (J.D., 1989). Phi Beta Kappa. *Member:* State Bar of California; Idaho State Bar; Hawaii State Bar Association. ***PRACTICE AREAS:*** Business Law; Real Estate; Landlord and Tenant; School Law; Municipal Law; Immigration, Naturalization. ***Email:*** ABK@HTEH.COM

(For biographical data on other personnel, see Professional Biographies at Boise and Pocatello, Idaho and Reno, Nevada)

HIMBERGER LAW OFFICES, CHTD.

KETCHUM, IDAHO

(See Boise)

Commercial Law, Business Litigation, Government Contracts, Lien and Bond Claims, Mediation, Arbitration, Construction Law, Creditors Rights, Bankruptcy, Collections, Foreclosures, Land Use, Commercial Development, Residential Development, Zoning, Real Estate, Alternative Dispute Resolution, Mediation and Arbitration, Eminent Domain, Government Contracts, Mergers, Acquisitions, Real Property, Easements, Lien and Board Claims.

KNEELAND, KORB, COLLIER & LEGG

KNEELAND PROFESSIONAL BUILDING
128 SADDLE ROAD, SUITE 103
P.O. BOX 249
KETCHUM, IDAHO 83340
Telephone: 208-726-9311
Telecopier: 208-726-4515
Email: kneeland@cox-internet.com

General Civil Practice. Trials. Appellate, Condominium, Business and Corporation, Probate and Estate, Zoning, Real Estate, Family and Municipal Law.

MEMBERS OF FIRM

ROBERT KORB, III, born Pueblo, Colorado, February 7, 1944; admitted to bar, 1972, Idaho and Wyoming. *Education:* University of Colorado (B.A., 1968); University of Denver (J.D., 1971). *Member:* Idaho State Bar; Wyoming State Bar. ***PRACTICE AREAS:*** Real Estate Law; Business Law; Condominium and Land Development; General Practice; Estate and Probate. ***Email:*** bkorb@cox-internet.com

BRUCE J. COLLIER, born Boise, Idaho, January 13, 1949; admitted to bar, 1974, Idaho. *Education:* Boise State University (B.A., 1971); University of Utah (J.D., 1974). *Member:* Idaho State Bar (Member, Family Law Section); American Bar Association (Member, Family Law Section); American Inns of Court. ***PRACTICE AREAS:*** Family Law; Municipal Law; General Civil Litigation; Hospital Law. ***Email:*** brucecollier@cox-internet.com

ANN LEGG, born Weiser, Idaho, October 27, 1952; admitted to bar, 1980, Idaho. *Education:* Boise State University (B.A., 1976); University of Idaho (J.D., 1980). *Member:* Idaho State Bar. ***PRACTICE AREAS:*** Business Law; Real Estate and Contract Law; Estate and Probate.

OF COUNSEL

G.R. KNEELAND, born Shelton, Washington, May 28, 1918; admitted to bar, 1949, Washington; 1950, Idaho. *Education:* Central Washington College (B.S., 1940); University of Washington (LL.B., 1949). Delta Theta Phi. Prosecuting Attorney, Blaine County, Idaho, 1952-1954. *Member:* Idaho State Bar; Washington State Bar Association.

REPRESENTATIVE CLIENTS: Sun Valley Title Co.; Centinnel Fire and Security, Inc.
REFERENCE: First Security Bank of Idaho, N.A.

LAWSON & LASKI, PLLC

675 SUN VALLEY ROAD, SUITE A
P.O. BOX 3310
KETCHUM, IDAHO 83340
Telephone: 208-725-0055
Fax: 208-725-0076
URL: http://www.lawyers.com/lawsonlaski

Real Estate, Business Organizations, Civil Litigation, Contracts, Securities, Commercial Law.

EDWARD A. LAWSON, born San Francisco, California, May 8, 1950; admitted to bar, 1975, California; 1979, Idaho. *Education:* University of San Francisco (A.B., 1972); Hastings College of Law, University of California (J.D., 1975). Pi Sigma Alpha. Research Editor, Hastings Constitutional Law Quarterly, 1974-1975. ***REPORTED CASES:*** Loomis Const. vs. Cudaly, 104 Id 106 (1982); Investors Ltd of Sun Valley vs Sun Mountain Con-

(This Listing Continued)

LAWSON & LASKI, PLLC, Ketchum—Continued

dominiums HOA 106 Id. 855 (1984); Evans vs Sautooth Partners, 111 Id. 381 (Id Ct App. 1986); Exposs Publishing v. Ketchum, 114 Id. 114 (1988); Black vs Young, 122 Id 302 (1992); Ketchum v Sinclair Oil Corp. 123 Id 665 (1993); Sun Valley Land & Minerals v Burt 123 Idaho 862 (Ct App. 1993); Enright vs Joanessen, 129 Id 69 (1997); Sun Valley Hot Sp. Ranch v Kelsey 131 Idaho 657 (1998); Karteman v. Janeson, 132 Id 910 (Ct. App. 1999); D.A.R. vs Sheffer, 134 Id 141 (2000); Robbins v Blaine County, 134 Id. 113 (2000); Hawkes, et. al. v Sun Valley Lad & Minerals, 138 Id 543 (2003). ***PRACTICE AREAS:*** Real Estate; Business Organization; Civil Litigation; Contracts; Securities; Commercial Law. ***Email:*** eal@lawsonlaski.com

JAMES R. LASKI, born Buffalo, New York, February 15, 1966; admitted to bar, 1995, Pennsylvania; 1996, Idaho. *Education:* College of the Holy Cross (B.A., 1989); Widener University (J.D., cum laude, 1995). Phi Kappa Phi. Law Clerk, Hon. William F. Moran, Pennsylvania Court of Common Pleas, 1995-1996. ***REPORTED CASES:*** Bakker v. Thunder Spring-Wareham, LLC 141 Idaho 185, 108 P.3d 332 (2005). ***PRACTICE AREAS:*** Real Estate; Business Organization; Civil Litigation; Contracts; Securities; Commercial Law. ***Email:*** jrl@lawsonlaski.com

---

ERIN FARRELL CLARK, born Redondo Beach, California, November 17, 1967; admitted to bar, 1993, California; 2002, Idaho. *Education:* University of Virginia (B.A., 1989); Boalt Hall School of Law (J.D., 1993). Author: "Accepting the Inevitable," California Law Business, Supplement of the Los Angeles Daily Journal and San Francisco Daily Journal (January 1997) (Co-authored with Terrence McMahon, Gary Weiss and Sean Lincoln). *Member:* State Bar of California; Idaho State Bar. ***PRACTICE AREAS:*** Litigation; Intellectual Property; Business Law; Real Estate. ***Email:*** emf@lawsonlaski.com

JILL W. ESHMAN, born Los Angeles, California, October 31, 1961; admitted to bar, 1986, California; 1995, Idaho. *Education:* University of Southern California (B.S., cum laude, 1983); Loyola Law School (J.D., cum laude, 1986). Beta Gamma Sigma. Staff, 1984-1985 and Business Editor, 1985-1986, International and Comparative Law Journal. ***PRACTICE AREAS:*** Real Estate; Business Organization; Estate Planning. ***Email:*** jwe@lawsonlaski.com

---

ANDREW PARNES

160 2ND STREET EAST, SUITE 216
P.O. BOX 5988
KETCHUM, IDAHO 83340
Telephone: 208-726-1010
Facsimile: 208-726-1187
Email: aparnes@mindspring.com

Criminal Trial and Appellate Practice in all State and Federal Courts. Habeas Corpus. DUI, Felonies, Misdemeanors, Homicide, Juvenile, Traffic Violations and Drug Crimes.

ANDREW PARNES, born Brooklyn, New York, January 6, 1946; admitted to bar, 1978, California and U.S. District Court, Northern District of California; 1981, U.S. Court of Appeals, Ninth Circuit; 1982, U.S. Supreme Court; 1990, Idaho; 1996, U.S. Court of Appeals, Tenth Circuit. *Education:* Williams College (B.A., cum laude, 1967); Stanford University (M.A., 1971; Ph.D, 1973); Boalt Hall School of Law, University of California (J.D., 1978). President, Palo Alto Bar Association, 1988-1989. *Member:* State Bar of California; Idaho State Bar; California Attorneys for Criminal Justice; Idaho Association of Criminal Defense Lawyers (Member, Board of Directors; President, 2002-2003); National Association of Criminal Defense Lawyers. ***PRACTICE AREAS:*** Criminal Trial Practice; Appellate Practice.

SPECK & AANESTAD

A PROFESSIONAL CORPORATION
Established in 1975
120 EAST AVENUE
P.O. BOX 987
KETCHUM, IDAHO 83340
Telephone: 208-726-4421
Fax: 208-726-0752
Email: sandalaw@mindspring.com

Business Transactions, Civil Litigation, Real Estate, Estate Planning, Probate, Water and Family Law.

JAMES P. SPECK, born Washington, D.C., February 20, 1945; admitted to bar, 1976, Colorado and U.S. District Court, District of Colorado; 1977, Idaho and U.S. District Court, District of Idaho. *Education:* Dartmouth College (B.A., cum laude, 1967; M.S., 1969); University of Colorado at Boulder (J.D., 1976). Deputy Prosecuting Attorney, Blaine County, Idaho, 1976-1977. *Member:* Colorado and American Bar Associations; Idaho State Bar; Idaho Trial Lawyers Association. ***PRACTICE AREAS:*** Real Estate; Water Law; Municipal Law; Civil Litigation; Business Transactions; Commercial Transactions; Estate Planning. ***Email:*** jimspeck@cox-internet.com

DOUGLAS J. AANESTAD, born Richmond, California, July 6, 1948; admitted to bar, 1974, California and U.S. District Court, Northern District of California; 1976, U.S. Tax Court; 1980, Idaho and U.S. District Court, District of Idaho. *Education:* Stanford University (A.B., 1970); Hastings College of Law, University of California (J.D., 1974). Author: *"Are There Still Advantages To Revocable Trusts After Recent Probate and Tax Law Changes?"* Estate Planning, Vol. 9, July, 1982. *Member:* State Bar of California; Idaho State Bar; Idaho Trial Lawyers Association. ***PRACTICE AREAS:*** Civil Litigation; Estate Planning; Family Law; Probate; Real Estate. ***Email:*** aanestad@cox-internet.com

REPRESENTATIVE CLIENTS AND REFERENCES: Provided upon request.

AHERIN, RICE & ANEGON

A PROFESSIONAL ASSOCIATION
Established in 1974
1212 IDAHO STREET
DRAWER 698
LEWISTON, IDAHO 83501
Telephone: 208-746-3646
Fax: 208-746-3650
Email: araoffice@valley-internet.net
URL: http://www.aralawoffice.com

Personal Injury, Auto Accidents, Wrongful Death, Products Liability, Automobile Negligence, Insurance Bad Faith, Medical and Legal Negligence, Workers Compensation, Criminal Defense, Libel and Slander, Condemnation, General Litigation including Domestic Relations, Contracts and Commercial Law, Probate, Real Property, Estate Planning, Employment and Environmental Law.

FIRM PROFILE: The law firm was established in 1974 by Darrel W. Aherin. In 1975 Stephen C. Rice became a partner and in 1984 Anthony C. Anegon became a member of the firm. We are a highly experienced firm with a support staff and up-to-date systems which allow us to handle many types of cases, including complex personal injury cases, while still maintaining personal contact with our clients.

DARREL W. AHERIN, born Colfax, Washington, July 11, 1946; admitted to bar, 1973, Idaho and U.S. District Court, District of Idaho; 1980, U.S. Court of Appeals, 9th Circuit and U.S. Supreme Court; 1982, U.S. Tax Court; 1983, U.S. Claims Court; 1992, Nez Perce Indian Tribal Court. *Education:* Lewis-Clark State College (B.A., 1969); University of Idaho (J.D., 1973). Member, Idaho Judicial Counsel, 1997-2003. *Member:* Second Judicial District (President, 1977-1979) and American Bar Associations; Idaho State Bar; Idaho Trial Lawyers Association (Treasurer, 1986-1987; State Delegate, 1987-1988, 1989-1990; Seminar Chairman, 1988-1989; Secretary, 1992-1993; President-Elect, 1993-1994; President, 1994-1995; Governor to ATLA 1996—; Member, Board of Governors, 1984—); The Association of Trial Lawyers of America (Member, Board of Governors, 1996—); Washington State Trial Lawyers Association; Western Trial Lawyers Association (Member, Board of Governors, 1996—); American Inns of Court (Bencher/Co-Leader, 1997-1999). ***PRACTICE AREAS:*** Insurance; Personal Injury; Premises Liability; Products Liability; Professional Liability; Medical Malpractice; Legal Malpractice; Commercial Law; Construction Law; Torts. ***Email:*** araoffice@valley-internet.net

STEPHEN C. RICE, born Council, Idaho, October 22, 1945; admitted to bar, 1975, Idaho and U.S. District Court, District of Idaho; 1980, U.S. Court of Appeals, 9th Circuit and U.S. Supreme Court; 1982, U.S. Tax Court; 1983, U.S. Claims Court. *Education:* Lewis-Clark State College; Idaho State University (B.S., 1969); University of Idaho (J.D., 1975). Phi Theta Kappa; Blue Key. *Member:* Second Judicial District and American Bar Associations; Idaho State Bar (Commissioner, 1995-1998; President, 1997-1998); Idaho Trial Lawyers Association (Secretary, 1979-1981; Vice-President, 1982-1983; President, 1983-1984; State Delegate, 1984 -1987; Member, Board of Governors, 2001—); The Association of Trial Lawyers of America; American Inns of Court. [U.S. Army, 1969-1972, Sp-5, Judge Advocate General Corp.]. ***PRACTICE AREAS:*** Business Law; Contracts; Probate; Real Estate; Trusts and Estates; Wills; Estate Planning; Family Law; Corporate Law. ***Email:*** araoffice@valley-internet.net

ANTHONY C. ANEGON, born Saginaw, Michigan, January 22, 1957; admitted to bar, 1982, Idaho, U.S. District Court, District of Idaho and U.S. Tax Court; 1987, U.S. Court of Appeals, 9th Circuit; 1988, U.S. Supreme Court. *Education:* University of Michigan (A.B., with distinction, 1979); University of Idaho (J.D., 1982). *Member:* Second Judicial District Bar Association; Idaho State Bar; Idaho Trial Lawyers Association; The Association of Trial Lawyers of America; American Inns of Court. ***PRACTICE AREAS:*** Criminal Law; Medical Malpractice; Personal Injury; Products Liability; Workers Compensation; Consumer Law; Family Law; Professional Liability. ***Email:*** araoffice@valley-internet.net

Language: English.

REPRESENTATIVE CLIENTS: Central Orchards Sewer District; Twin River National Bank; Boyer Land and Cattle Co.; Snoline Express, Inc.; Northwest Siding Wholesalers, Inc.; Bi-State Siding & Roofing.
REFERENCE: Twin River National Bank.

CLARK AND FEENEY

Established in 1983
THE TRAIN STATION, SUITE 201
13TH AND MAIN
P.O. BOX 285
LEWISTON, IDAHO 83501
Telephone: 208-743-9516; 1-800-865-9516
Fax: 208-746-9160
URL: http://www.clarkandfeeneylaw.com
Email: cflaw@lewiston.com
URL: http://www.clarkandfeeney.com

Trial Practice, Personal Injury, Corporation, Commercial, Construction, Surety, Real Property, Probate, Domestic Relations, General Practice, Criminal Law, Bankruptcy.

PAUL T. CLARK, born Sacramento, California, July 19, 1945; admitted to bar, 1970, Idaho and U.S. District Court, District of Idaho; 1986, U.S. Court of Appeals, Ninth Circuit; U.S. Supreme Court. *Education:* Northwest Nazarene College (B.A., 1967); University of Idaho (J.D., 1970). Member, University of Idaho Law Review, 1969-1970. *Member:* Idaho State Bar; American Bar Association; The Association of Trial Lawyers of America. ***REPORTED CASES:*** Keller v. Inland Metals All Weather Conditioning, 2003 WL 22024243, 76 P.3d 977 (ID. 2003); Steelsmith v. Trout, 2003 WL 21756079, 76 P.3d 960 (ID. 2003); Trees v. Kersey, 56 P.3d 765, 138 Idaho 3 (ID. 2003). ***PRACTICE AREAS:*** Litigation; Personal Injury Law; Divorce Law; Criminal Law. ***Email:*** tclark@clarkandfeeney.com

(This Listing Continued)

THOMAS W. FEENEY, born Lewiston, Idaho, July 31, 1922; admitted to bar, 1950, Idaho. *Education:* University of Idaho (LL.B., 1950). Phi Alpha Delta. General Counsel, Port of Lewiston, 1958—. *Member:* Clearwater Bar Association (President, 1959-1961); Idaho State Bar (Member: Permanent Bar Examination Grading Team, 1971; Executive Committee, 1972-1978).

RON T. BLEWETT, born Clarkston, Washington, June 16, 1957; admitted to bar, 1982, Idaho and U.S. District Court, District of Idaho; 1986, U.S. Court of Appeals, Ninth Circuit and U.S. Claims Court; 1989, U.S. Court of Appeals for the Federal Circuit; U.S. Supreme Court. *Education:* University of Idaho (B.S., with honors, 1979; J.D., with honors, 1982). AAA Arbitrator, 1987—. AAA Mediator, 1997—. *Member:* American (Member, Public Contract Law, Construction Law and Tort/Insurance Practice Law Sections) Bar Association; Idaho State Bar (Member Sections on: Alternative Dispute Resolution and Real Property). ***REPORTED CASES:*** Highland Enterprises, Inc. v. Barker, 133 Idaho 330, 986 P.2d 966 (1999); Polk v. Larrabee, 135 Idaho 303, 17 P.2d 247 (2000); Driver v. SI Corp., 80 P.3d 1024 (2003). ***PRACTICE AREAS:*** Litigation; Construction; Suretyship; Arbitration; Mediation. ***Email:*** rblewett@clarkandfeeney.com

RUBE G. JUNES, born Menahga, Minnesota, August 19, 1944; admitted to bar, 1984, Washington and U.S. District Court, Western District of Washington; 1989, U.S. District Court, Eastern District of Washington and U.S. Claims Court; 2002, Oregon (Not admitted in Idaho). *Education:* University of Idaho (B.S., cum laude, 1967; J.D., 1984). Certified Public Accountant, Idaho, 1971-1994. *Member:* Washington State and American (Member, Sections on: Public Contract Law; Litigation) Bar Associations. ***PRACTICE AREAS:*** Litigation; Construction; Arbitration; Business Law; Personal Injury. ***Email:*** rgjunes@clarkandfeeney.com

DOUGLAS L. MUSHLITZ, born San Jose, California, November 15, 1959; admitted to bar, 1985, Idaho and U.S. District Court, District of Idaho; 1990, U.S. Court of Appeals, Ninth Circuit; 1995, U.S. Supreme Court. *Education:* Idaho State University (B.B.A., with honors, 1982); University of Idaho (J.D., 1985). *Member:* Second Judicial District (President, 1991-1992) Bar Association; Idaho State Bar (Member, Bankruptcy Section); Idaho Trial Lawyers Association; The Association of Trial Lawyers of America. ***REPORTED CASES:*** State v. Wren, 768 P2.d 1351 (1989); State v. Wilson, 780 P.2d 93 (1989); State v. Thompson, 803 p.2d 973 (1990); State v. Crea, 806 P.2d 445 (1991); State v. Ausman, 864 P.2d 1126 (1993); State v. Holcomb, 912 P.2d 664 (1995); State v. Benefiel, 97.61.C.A.R. 275 (March, 1997). ***PRACTICE AREAS:*** Litigation; Personal Injury Law; Bankruptcy Law; Divorce; Family Law; Criminal Law. ***Email:*** dlm@clarkandfeeney.com

CHARLES M. STROSCHEIN, born Lewiston, Idaho, August 27, 1958; admitted to bar, 1983, Idaho and U.S. District Court, District of Idaho. *Education:* Gonzaga University (B.A., 1980); St. Louis University (J.D., 1983). Phi Alpha Delta. Elected Member: Lewiston School District Board of Education, 1993, 1993-1999; Potlatch No. 1 Federal Credit Union Board of Directors, *Member:* Second Judicial District Bar Association (President, 1999-2002); Idaho State Bar; Idaho Trial Lawyers Association; The Association of Trial Lawyers of America; Idaho Attorneys for Criminal Justice; National Association of Criminal Defense Lawyers. ***REPORTED CASES:*** State v. Victor H. Smith, 120 Id 77, 813 P2 888 (1991). ***PRACTICE AREAS:*** Litigation; Personal Injury; Family Law; Criminal Law; General Practice. ***Email:*** charm@clarkandfeeney.com

CONNIE W. TAYLOR, born Hemingford, Nebraska June 7, 1954; admitted to bar, 1993, Idaho; 1994, Washington. *Education:* Lewis Clark State (B.S., summa cum laude, 1988); University of Idaho (J.D., cum laude, 1993). Recipient, American Jurisprudence Awards in Real Estate Finance, Land Use and Local government. *Member:* Idaho State Bar; Washington State Bar; Asotin-Garfield Bar Association (President, 1998); Idaho Trial Lawyers Association; The Association of Trial Lawyers of America. ***REPORTED CASES:*** State of Idaho v Marcus Mathews, 1994. ***PRACTICE AREAS:*** Litigation; Personal Injury; Criminal Law; Real Estate; Estate Planning; Estate Administration; General Practice. ***Email:*** ctaylor@clarkandfeeney.com

SCOTT D. GALLINA, born Ravenna, Ohio, October 31, 1963; admitted to bar, 1990, Idaho and U.S. District Court, District of Idaho; 1991, Washington, 1998, U.S. District Court, District of Eastern Washington. *Education:* Washington State University (B.A., 1985); University of Idaho (J.D., 1990). Recipient, American Jurisprudence Award - Sales. Municipal Judge: Town of Colton, Washington; Town of Unitown, Washington. Standing Court Commissioner, Asotin, Garfield and Columbia Counties, Washington. *Member:* Asotin County (Vice President, 1993) and Washington State Bar Associations; Idaho State Bar. ***PRACTICE AREAS:*** Family Law; Criminal Defense; Personal Injury. ***Email:*** sgallina@clarkandfeeney.com

ASSOCIATES

TINA L. KERNAN, born Lewiston, Idaho, June 26, 1966; admitted to bar, 1993, Washington; 1994, Idaho and U.S. District Court, District of Idaho. *Education:* University of Idaho (B.A., 1988; J.D., 1993). Recipient, Professionalism Award, Asotin/Garfield County Bar Association, 2002. *Member:* Asotin/Garfield County Bar Association; Idaho State Bar. ***PRACTICE AREAS:*** Family Law; Litigation; Personal Injury; General Practice. ***Email:*** tkernan@clarkandfeeney.com

JONATHAN D. HALLY, born Eugene, Oregon, February 21, 1966; admitted to bar, 1994, Idaho and U.S. District Court, District of Idaho. *Education:* Boise State University (B.B.A., 1991); University of Idaho at Moscow (J.D., 1994). *Member:* Second Judicial District (Secretary/Treasurer, 1995-1996) and Idaho State Bar Associations. ***REPORTED CASES:*** Zener v. Velde, 135 Idaho 352 (CT. App. 2000). ***PRACTICE AREAS:*** Litigation; Construction Law; Criminal Law; Personal Injury; General Practice. ***Email:*** jhally@clarkandfeeney.com

WILLIAM J. CARR, born St. Louis, Missouri, February 2, 1975; admitted to bar, 2003, Idaho. *Education:* Northwest Nazarene College (B.S., Biology, 1997); Idaho University (J.D., 2003; M.S., 2003). *Member:* Idaho State Bar (Member, Environmental and Natural Resource Section). ***PRACTICE AREAS:*** General Practice; Property Law; Natural Resources; Environmental Compliance; Personal Injury. ***Email:*** jcarr@clarkandfeeney.com

REPRESENTATIVE CLIENTS: Hall Copeland Ford; Seubert Excavators, Inc.; Militec Defense Systems, Inc.; Highland Enterprises, Inc.; Steelman-Duff, Inc.; Fidelity and Deposit Company of Maryland; Employers Insurance of Wausau. Barnes, Inc.; Poe Asphalt Paving, Inc.; M.A. Deatley Construction; Deatley Crushing Co.; Barnes, Inc.
REFERENCE: Sterling Savings Bank.

CLEMENTS, BROWN & McNICHOLS, P.A.

321 13TH STREET
P.O. BOX 1510
LEWISTON, IDAHO 83501
Telephone: 208-743-6538
FAX: 208-746-0753
URL: http://www.clbrmc.com

Civil Trial and Appellate Practice. Banking, Corporation, Education Law, Health Care Law, Estate Planning, Real Estate, Probate, Products Liability, Insurance Defense, Surety, Workers Compensation Law and Employment Law.

V. R. CLEMENTS (1896-1982)

PHILIP E. PETERSON (1922-2003)

ROBERT P. BROWN, born Hutchinson, Kansas, October 6, 1940; admitted to bar, 1964, Idaho; 1965, U.S. District Court, District of Idaho. *Education:* University of Idaho (B.A., 1962; LL.B., 1964). *Member:* American Bar Association. ***PRACTICE AREAS:*** Banks and Banking; Education Law; Probate; Corporate Law; Health Care; Estate Planning; Civil Litigation. ***Email:*** rbrown@clbrmc.com

MICHAEL E. McNICHOLS, born Lewiston, Idaho, July 1, 1939; admitted to bar, 1963, Idaho; 1964, U.S. District Court, District of Idaho; 1976, U.S. Court of Appeals, Ninth Circuit. *Education:* University of Idaho (B.A., 1960; LL.B., 1963). *Member:* Idaho State Bar (Commissioner, 1979-1980); American Bar Association; Idaho Association of Defense Counsel (President, 1981-1982); International Association of Defense Counsel. Fellow, American College of Trial Lawyers. ***PRACTICE AREAS:*** Civil Litigation; Product Liability; Professional Malpractice; Insurance Law; Labor and Employment. ***Email:*** mmcnichols@clbrmc.com

BENTLEY G. STROMBERG, born Minneapolis, Minnesota, December 8, 1961; admitted to bar, 1987, Idaho and U.S. District Court, District of Idaho; 1988, U.S. Court of Appeals, Ninth Circuit. *Education:* University of Idaho (B.A., 1984; J.D., cum laude, 1987). Phi Beta Kappa. Member, National Moot Court Team. *Member:* American Bar Association; Idaho Association of Defense Counsel. ***PRACTICE AREAS:*** Civil Litigation; Insurance Defense; Civil Rights Defense; Workers Compensation Defense; Labor and Employment. ***Email:*** bstromberg@clbrmc.com

ERIC K. PETERSON, born Moscow, Idaho, February 24, 1955; admitted to bar, 1987, Idaho, Washington and U.S District Court of Idaho. *Education:* University of Idaho (B.S., 1977, M.S., 1979; J.D., 1986); University of Minnesota (Ph.D., 1984). *Member:* Washington State (Member, Real Property, Probate and Trust Section) and American Bar Associations; Idaho State Bar (Commissioner, 2001-2004); Idaho Trial Lawyers Association. ***PRACTICE AREAS:*** Real Estate; Corporate; Commercial Law; Estate Planning; Probate; Civil Litigation. ***Email:*** epeterson@clbrmc.com

SONYALEE R. NUTSCH, born Antioch, California, August 2, 1975; admitted to bar, 2000, Idaho and U.S. District Court, District of Idaho. *Education:* Lewis-Clark State College (B.S.J.S., summa cum laude, 1997); University of Idaho College of Law (J.D., cum laude, 2000). Idaho Law Review. Member, National AMTA Mock Trial Team. *Member:* Idaho State Bar; American Bar Association. ***PRACTICE AREAS:*** Civil Litigation Defense; Civil Rights Defense; Insurance Defense; Medical Malpractice Defense; Workers Compensation. ***Email:*** snutsch@clbrmc.com

REPRESENTATIVE CLIENTS: Blount, Inc.; Cuna Mutual Group; Capitol Indemnity Co.; Farm Bureau Mutual Insurance Co.; FirstBank Northwest; Idaho Beverages, Inc.; Idaho Counties Risk Management Program; Independent School District No. 1; Lewis-Clark State College; Northwest Children's Home, Inc.; Northwest Physicians Mutual Insurance Co.; Potlatch Corporation; Regence BlueShield of Idaho; Safeco Insurance Co.; St. Joseph Regional Medical Center; State of Idaho; State Farm Fire & Casualty Co.; State Farm Mutual Automobile Insurance Co.; University of Idaho; Workers Compensation Exchange.
REFERENCE: FirstBank Northwest.

CREASON, MOORE & DOKKEN, PLLC

Established in 1902
LEWISTON PROFESSIONAL BUILDING
1219 IDAHO STREET
DRAWER 835
LEWISTON, IDAHO 83501
Telephone: 208-743-1516
Fax: 208-746-2231
URL: http://www.cmd-law.com
Email: cmd@cmd-law.com
URL: http://www.creasonmdlaw.com

General Civil Practice, Insurance Defense, Appeals, Business Organizations, Commercial, Real Property, Probate and Estate Planning, Tax Law, Personal Injury, Criminal Defense, Auto Accident, Head Injury.

FIRM PROFILE: Eugene A. Cox established the firm following his admission to practice law in the state of Idaho on October 7, 1902. He was joined by Noel B. Martin in 1921, then by Marcus J. Ware in 1927. Marcus Ware practiced law with the firm from 1927 until his retirement sixty years later in 1987. Daniel O'Connell was admitted to practice law in 1953 and developed a highly respected insurance defense and business law practice prior to his death in 1988. In 1985, Theodore O. Creason became a partner and the firm name was changed to Ware, O'Connell & Creason. In 1992, the firm became Creason, Moore & Dokken following the admission of Christopher J. Moore and David E. Dokken into the partnership.

Creason, Moore & Dokken, PLLC currently has four members, Theodore O. Creason, Christopher J. Moore, David E. Dokken and Tod D. Geidl. The firm's client list includes insurance companies, banking institutions, medical facilities, corporations and individuals. The firm encourages participation in continuing legal education programs, professional development and civic affairs.

(This Listing Continued)

CREASON, MOORE & DOKKEN, PLLC, Lewiston—Continued

MEMBERS OF FIRM

DANIEL W. O'CONNELL (1928-1988)

MARCUS J. WARE (1904-1996)

THEODORE O. CREASON, born American Falls, Idaho, May 28, 1948; admitted to bar, 1973, Idaho and U.S. District Court, District of Idaho; 2002, Washington. *Education:* University of Idaho (B.A., 1970; J.D., 1973). Phi Beta Kappa; Phi Kappa Phi. Deputy Prosecutor, Nez Perce County, 1975-1978. Member, Rupert City Council, 1975. Member, Idaho Commission of Pardons and Parole, 1983-1987. Member, Ninth Circuit Conference Committee, 1998—.Counselor, Ray McNichols Chapter, American Inns of Court. *Member:* Idaho State Bar; Washington State and American Bar Associations; Idaho Association of Defense Counsel; Defense Research Institute; International Association of Defense Counsel; International Society of Barristers; The Fellows of the American Bar Association; Washington Defense Trial Lawyers. ***REPORTED CASES:*** Robert W. Andre, Conservator of the Estate of Beatrice Morrow, Conservatee, v. Kenneth C. Morrow and Billie Jo Morrow, No. 14843, Supreme Court of Idaho, 106 Idaho 455, 680 P.2d 1355 (1984); Potlatch Corporation v. Beloit Corporation, Docket No. 24202, Supreme Court of Idaho, 132 Idaho 712, 979 P.2d 114 (1999), 40 U.C.C. Rep. Serv. 2d (Callaghan) 646; Virginia McIntire, v. Milton D. Orr and Nellie Orr, No. 19513, Supreme Court of Idaho, 122 Idaho 351, 834 P.2d 868 (1992); Larry W. Watson and Sherry Watson, v. Navistar International Transportation Corp. formerly known as International Harvester Co. and Dokken Implement Company. Larry W. Watson and Sherry Watson, v. Navistar International Transportation Corp., and Dokken Implement Company, Nos. 16850, 17032, Supreme Court of Idaho, 121 Idaho 653, 827 P.2d 656 (1992); Rejena Coghlan; Pamela J. Clarke, individually and as parent and guardian ad litem of Thomas Adam Coghlan and Michael J. Clarke, Jr., v. Beta Theta Pi Fraternity, Sigma Alpha Epsilon Fraternity, Phi Kappa Alpha Fraternity, and The University of Idaho, The Idaho State Board of Education and John Does I-X, Docket No. 24318, Supreme Court of Idaho, 133 Idaho 388, 987 P.2d 300 (1999), August 30, 1999, filed; In re Declaration of Death of James Thomas Cole, Sandra L. Thomas, v. John Hancock Mutual Life Insurance Company, No.16555, Court of Appeals of Idaho, 113 Idaho 98, 741 P.2d 734 (1987); Christine A. McGreevy vs. Oregon Mutual Insurance Company, No. 94-35038, United States Court of Appeals for the Ninth Circuit, 1995 U.S. App. 46 F.3d 1142 (9th Cir. 1995). ***PRACTICE AREAS:*** Civil Litigation; Insurance Defense; Commercial; Corporate Law; Probate; Estate Planning; Alternative Dispute Resolution; Product Liability. ***Email:*** tcreason@cmd-law.com

CHRISTOPHER J. MOORE, born Sheridan, Wyoming, March 12, 1952; admitted to bar, 1989, Idaho and U.S. District Court, District of Idaho; 1990, Washington. *Education:* University of Idaho (B.S., 1975; J.D., magna cum laude, 1989). Member, University of Idaho Law Review, 1988-1989. Certified Public Accountant, Idaho, 1976. *Member:* Idaho State, Washington State and American Bar Associations; Idaho Society and American Institute of Certified Public Accountants; Estate Planning Law Specialists. ***PRACTICE AREAS:*** Estate Planning; Business Organizations; Taxation; Probate; Elder Law; Real Property; Corporate Law; Leases and Leasing; Nonprofit and Charitable Organizations; Partnership Law; Trusts; Wills. ***Email:*** cmoore@cmd-law.com

DAVID E. DOKKEN, born Cottonwood, Idaho, September 29, 1954; admitted to bar, 1982, Idaho and U.S. District Court, District of Idaho; 2002, Washington. *Education:* Idaho State University; University of Idaho (B.A., 1978; J.D., 1982). Deputy Prosecutor, Nez Perce County, 1982-1990. Chief Deputy Prosecutor, 1985-1990. *Member:* Second District Bar Association; Idaho State Bar; Idaho Trial Lawyers Association; Washington Defense Trial Lawyers; Idaho Association of Defense Counsel; Ray McNichols American Inns of Court. ***PRACTICE AREAS:*** Criminal Law; Creditor's Rights; Insurance Defense; Personal Injury Litigation; Real Property. ***Email:*** ddokken@cmd-law.com

TOD D. GEIDL, born Juneau, Alaska, March 9, 1973; admitted to bar, 1998, Idaho and U.S. District Court, Central District of Idaho; 1999, Washington. *Education:* University of Idaho (B.S., summa cum laude, 1995; J.D., 1998). *Member:* Idaho State Bar; Washington State and American Bar Associations; Ray McNichols American Inns of Court; Defense Research Institute; Washington Defense Trial Lawyers. ***PRACTICE AREAS:*** Business Organization; Creditors' Rights in Bankruptcy; Real Property; Insurance Defense; Civil Litigation; Collections. ***Email:*** tgeidl@cmd-law.com

REPRESENTATIVE CLIENTS: A.I. Management & Professional Liability (A.I.G.); American West Insurance Co.; Amerisure Insurance; Blue Ribbon Linen Supply, Inc.; Casualty Insurance Co.; Clearwater Medical Center, P.L.L.C.; Community Action Agency, Inc.; Cottonwood Community Credit Union; CUNA Mutual Group; Cutting Edge Federal Credit Union; E. & O. Professionals; First American Title Insurance Company; General Motors Acceptance Corp.; Government Employees Insurance Co.; Great West Casualty; Guaranty National Insurance Co.; Horace Mann Insurance Co.; Kamiah Community Credit Union; Lapwai School District; Latah Federal Credit Union; Lewis Clark Credit Union; Lewis & Clark Orthopaedic Institute, LLC; Masonic Temple Association; National Farmers Union; National Insurance Assn.; Nautilus Insurance Company; Northwest Physicians Mutual; Northwestern National Insurance Group; Oregon Mutual Insurance Co.; Oregon Territory Federal Credit Union; Pathologists' Regional Laboratory; Pine Tree Community Credit Union; Poe Asphalt Paving, Inc.; Potlatch No. 1 Federal Credit Union; Scottsdale Insurance Company; Shriners Hospital for Children; State of Idaho Bureau of Risk Management; Valley Medical Center/Children's Clinic, P.A.; Vassar-Rawls Funeral Home, Inc.; Westco, Inc.; Western Heritage Insurance Company; Zurich North America;

HALL, FARLEY, OBERRECHT & BLANTON, P.A.

LEWISTON, IDAHO

(See Boise)

Litigation, Insurance Defense, Medical Malpractice and Professional Liability, Employment Law, Labor Relations, Products Liability, Construction, Health and Hospital, Corporation, Commercial, Banking, Real Estate, Legislative Counseling, Bankruptcy, Appellate Law, Administrative Agencies, Agricultural, Municipal, Estate Planning and Probate.

KEETON & TAIT

312 MILLER STREET
LEWISTON, IDAHO 83501
Telephone: 208-743-6231
Fax: 208-746-0962
URL: http://www.ktlaw.org
Email: lewlawus@lewiston.com
URL: http://www.keeton-tait.com

General Practice, Workers Compensation, Personal Injury, Criminal Defense, Probate, Real Estate, Family Law, Housing and Employment Discrimination, Indian Law, Appellate Practice.

MEMBERS OF FIRM

PAUL C. KEETON (1913-2005)

JOHN REID TAIT, born Toledo, Ohio, April 7, 1946; admitted to bar, 1974, Idaho, U.S. Court of Appeals, Ninth Circuit, U.S. Supreme Court and Nez Perce Tribal Court. *Education:* Columbia University (B.A., 1968); Vanderbilt University (J.D., 1974). Member: Idaho State Board, Legal Aid Service Inc., 1975-2000; Idaho Housing Agency Commission, 1984-1991. *Member:* Clearwater (Secretary, 1974-1976; President, 1984-1986) and American Bar Associations; Idaho State Bar (Member, Ethics Committee, 1977-1980; Chairman, 1978-1980; Chairman, Workers Compensation Section, 2004—); Idaho Trial Lawyers Association; The Association of Trial Lawyers of America; Consumer Attorneys of California; Worker's Injury Law and Advocacy Group Board, 2002—). [With U.S. Army, 1968-1971; Special Agent, Military Intelligence]. ***PRACTICE AREAS:*** Workers Compensation; Civil Trial; Appellate; Personal Injury; Probate; Real Estate. ***Email:*** lewlawus@lewiston.com

ASSOCIATE

KEN EVERETT NAGY, born Perth Amboy, New Jersey, December 7, 1964; admitted to bar, 2000, Idaho; U.S. District Court, District of Idaho; U.S.Court of Appeals, Ninth Circuit; Nez Perce Tribal Court. *Education:* Rutgers University (B.A., 1989); University of Idaho (J.D., 2000). City Attorney, Genesee, Idaho. Member: Advisory Committee, 2nd Judicial District Court Assistance Office Project, 2000—; Intermountain Fair Housing Council, 1999—. Secretary, City of Moscow Fair and Affordable Housing Commission, 2000—. *Member:* Idaho State Bar; Second Judicial District Bar Association (Secretary, 2002—); Association of Trial Lawyers of America. ***PRACTICE AREAS:*** Fair Housing; Employment Discrimination; Civil Rights; Landlord-Tenant; Criminal Defense; Family Law; Indian Law. ***Email:*** knagy@lewiston.com

A List of Representative Clients will be Furnished upon Request.

LIBEY, ENSLEY, ESSER & NELSON, PLLC

LEWISTON, IDAHO

(See Colfax, Washington)

General Civil and Trial Practice. Probate, Real Estate, Banking, Corporate and Business Tax Law.

RAMSDEN & LYONS

LEWISTON, IDAHO

(See Coeur d'Alene)

General Civil Trial and Appellate Practice. Insurance Defense, Eminent Domain/Condemnation, Arbitration, Mediation, Class Action Defense, Business Formation, Insurance Bad Faith, Land Use, Professional Liability, Product Liability, Negligence, Construction, Real Estate, Environmental, Error and Omission Defense, Governmental Liability, Worker Compensation and Employment Law.

RANDALL, BLAKE & COX, P.A.

Established in 1990
1106 IDAHO STREET
P.O. BOX 446
LEWISTON, IDAHO 83501
Telephone: 208-743-1234
Telefax: 208-743-1266
Email: david@rbcox.com
URL: http://www.rbclaw.com

General Practice, Agricultural Law, Bankruptcy, Business Law, Contracts, Criminal Law, Debtor and Creditor Law. Employment Law, Family Law, Domestic Relations, Personal Injury, Products Liability, Real Estate, Taxation, Trusts and Estates, Estate Planning, Wills, Probate, Workers Compensation, Zoning, Planning and Land Use.

STEVE R. COX, born Lewiston, Idaho, November 25, 1946; admitted to bar, 1973, Idaho; 2002, Washington. *Education:* University of Idaho (B.S., 1970; J.D., 1973). Member, Idaho Law Review, 1972-1973. Certified Public Accountant, Idaho, 1973. *Member:* Clearwater Bar Association; Idaho State Bar. ***PRACTICE AREAS:*** Estate Planning; Real Estate; Business Law; Corporate Law. ***Email:*** steve@rbcox.com

DAVID R. RISLEY, born Spokane, Washington, July 23, 1950; admitted to bar, 1975, Idaho; 2002, Washington. *Education:* North Idaho College (A.A., 1970); Linfield College (B.A., 1972); University of Idaho (J.D., 1975). Phi Alpha Delta. Member, Board of Editors, University of Idaho Law Review, 1974-1975. Author: "Limitations on Personal Injury, Tort Litigation by Married Persons in Community Property States: Interspousal Immunity and the Community Property Classification of Personal Injury Recovery," Idaho Law Review, Spring, 1975. Visiting Professor of Law, Land Use Planning and Municipal Corporations,

(This Listing Continued)

University of Idaho, 1981. Deputy City Attorney, Lewiston, Idaho, 1977-1980. Judge Pro-Tem, Nez Perce Tribal Court, 1997—. *Member:* Clearwater Bar Association (Member, Sections on: Commercial Law; Bankruptcy Law); Idaho State Bar. ***SPECIAL AGENCIES:*** Nez Perce Tribal Court. ***PRACTICE AREAS:*** Business Law; Small Business Law; Contracts; Debtor and Creditor Law; Collections; Bankruptcy; Foreclosure; Family Law; Real Estate; Commercial Law; Landlord and Tenant Law; Wills; Probate; Zoning, Planning and Land Use Law; Indian Law. ***Email:*** david@rbcox.com

KERRY A. WAGNER, born Cottonwood, Idaho, July 7, 1958; admitted to bar, 1983, Idaho; 2002, Washington. *Education:* University of Idaho (B.S., 1980; J.D., 1983). *Member:* Idaho State Bar. ***PRACTICE AREAS:*** Business Law; Corporate Law; Estate Planning; Timber and Logging; Retirement Plans. ***Email:*** kerry@rbcox.com

SCOTT M. CHAPMAN, born Corvallis, Oregon, July 18, 1956; admitted to bar, 1985, Idaho; 2003, Washington. *Education:* Blue Mountain Community College; University of Oregon (B.S., 1979) ; University of Idaho (J.D., 1985). *Member:* Clearwater Bar Association; Idaho State Bar; Idaho Trial Lawyers Association; National Association of Criminal Defense Attorneys. ***SPECIAL AGENCIES:*** Certified lead counsel capital defense licensed to practice in front of the United States Supreme Court. ***PRACTICE AREAS:*** Criminal Law; Personal Injury; Family Law; Appeals. ***Email:*** scott@rbcox.com

---

DERRICK A. ATER, born Newgulf, Texas, July 23, 1948; admitted to bar, 1990, Idaho. *Education:* University of Idaho (B.A., 1986); University of Idaho Law School (J.D., 1990). *Member:* Idaho State Bar; American Bar Association. [With U.S. Navy, 1965-1968]. ***PRACTICE AREAS:*** Family Law; Real Property; Landlord/Tenant. ***Email:*** derrick@rbcox.com

APRIL A. SMITH, born Moscow, Idaho, June 15, 1979; admitted to bar, 2004, Idaho. *Education:* University of Idaho (B.A., 2001; J.D., 2004). *Member:* Idaho State Bar. ***PRACTICE AREAS:*** Civil Litigation; Corporate Law; Business Law; Domestic Relations; Criminal Law; Estate Administration; Wills. ***Email:*** april@rbcox.com

OF COUNSEL

RUSSELL S. RANDALL (1908-2004)

WYNNE M. BLAKE, born Pomeroy, Washington, April 10, 1922; admitted to bar, 1948, Idaho. *Education:* Montana State College and University of Idaho; University of Idaho (LL.B., 1948). *Member:* Clearwater Bar Association; Idaho State Bar. ***PRACTICE AREAS:*** Workers Compensation.

REPRESENTATIVE CLIENTS: Lewis-Clark Terminal, Inc.; Lewiston Orchards Sewer District; Guy Bennett Lumber Co.; Bennett Lumber Products; Farm Credit Services; McGregor Co.; Isothermal Systems Research, Inc.; Primeland Cooperative; Workers Compensation Exchange.

SMITH & CANNON

Established in 1983

508 EIGHTH STREET

LEWISTON, IDAHO 83501

Telephone: 208-743-9428

Fax: 208-746-8421

Email: s-claw@lewiston.com

URL: http://www.smithandcannon.com

General Trial Practice. Personal Injury, Aviation, Automobile Accidents and Injuries, Wrongful Death, Family Law, Divorce, Child Custody, Child Support, Alternative Dispute Resolution, Insurance, Probate Law, Workers Compensation Claims, Arbitration and Mediation.

FIRM PROFILE: The firm was established in 1983 with the forming of a partnership between Jerry V. Smith, who had been a solo practitioner for most of his practice, and Ned A. Cannon, who had clerked for Smith while in law school and remained in the firm following his admission to practice.

The firm is engaged in general practice with emphasis on general litigation in Idaho and Washington in both State and Federal Court, primarily in the fields of personal injury, probate, commercial and family law.

MEMBERS OF FIRM

JERRY V. SMITH, born Boise, Idaho, May 3, 1924; admitted to bar, 1950, Idaho and U.S. District Court, District of Idaho; 1969, U.S. Court of Appeals, Ninth Circuit and U.S. Supreme Court. *Education:* University of Idaho (LL.B., 1950). Phi Alpha Delta. Counselor, American Inns of Court, Ray McNichols Chapter. Arbitrator, American Arbitration Association, 1969—. Member, Western States Bar Conference (President, 1975-1976). Recipient, Distinguished Lawyers Award, Idaho State Bar, 2002. *Member:* Clearwater County (Secretary, 1951; President, 1963-1965) and American (State Bar Delegate, House of Delegates, 1967; Member, Committee on Specialization, 1972-1977; Member, Court Modernization Committee, 1972-1978 and Chairman, Automobile Reparations Committee, 1973-1978; General Practice Section: Member, Committee on Municipal Penal Codes, 1973-1974; Section of Criminal Practice) Bar Associations; Idaho State Bar (Commissioner, 1965-1966; Vice President, 1966-1967; President, 1967-1968; Member, Disciplinary Committee, 1970-1973); American Trial Lawyers Association; American College of Trial Lawyers, 1999; Idaho Association of Defense Counsel; Defense Research Institute. Fellow: American Bar Foundation; Idaho State Bar Foundation (Recipient: Idaho State Bar Professionalism Award, 1992; Member, Alternative Dispute Resolution Section). ***PRACTICE AREAS:*** General Litigation; Personal Injury; Automobile Accidents and Injuries; Wrongful Death; Insurance Law; Probate Law; Family Law; Environmental Law; Health Law; Alternative Dispute Resolution.

NED A. CANNON, born Tonasket, Washington, December 14, 1952; admitted to bar, 1978, Idaho and U.S. Court of Appeals, Ninth Circuit. *Education:* Whitworth College (B.B.A., 1975); University of Idaho (J.D., 1978). *Member:* Clearwater (Vice President, 1981-1982) and American Bar Associations; Idaho State Bar (Member, Public Relations Committee, 1982-1984); Idaho Trial Lawyers Association. ***PRACTICE AREAS:*** General Litigation; Automobile Accidents and Injuries; Wrongful Death; Personal Injury; Workers Compensation; Probate Law; Family Law; Divorce; Child Custody; Child Support; Insurance Coverage and Related Issues.

REPRESENTATIVE CLIENTS: Aetna Casualty & Surety Co.; Firemans Fund; North Central District Health Department. Reference: Banner Bank, Lewiston, Idaho.

(This Listing Continued)

WULLENWABER LAW FIRM

703 8TH STREET

P.O. BOX 452

LEWISTON, IDAHO 83501

Telephone: 208-743-8981

Fax: 208-743-9442

Email: dwlawfirm@cableone.net

Personal Injury Litigation, Insurance Law, Product Liability, Civil Litigation, Workers Compensation, Criminal Law.

DEAN WULLENWABER, born Los Angeles, California, March 14, 1948; admitted to bar, 1979, Idaho and U.S. District Court, District of Idaho; 2002, Washington. *Education:* Occidental College (B.A., 1970); University of Idaho (M.S., 1975; J.D., 1979). Adjunct Professor, University of Idaho Law School. Annual Presenter, Idaho Law Foundation CLEs, 1990-2003. Chair, Tenure Committee, University of Idaho Law School, 1990. Founding Member, Raymond F. McNichols American Inn of Court. *Member:* Idaho State Bar (Commissioner, 1989-1992; President, 1992); Washington State and American Bar Associations; International Association of Defense Counsel; Idaho Association of Defense Counsel. ***REPORTED CASES:*** Painter v. Potlatch Corp., 138 Idaho 309, 63 P.3d 435 (2003); Ball v. Daw Forest Products Co., 136 Idaho 155, 30 P.3d 933 (2002); Peterson v. Romine, 131 Idaho 537, 960 P.2d 1266 (1998); Barber v. State Farm Mut. Auto. Ins. Co., 129 Idaho 677, 931 P.2d 1195 (1997); Berglund v. Potlatch Corp., 129 Idaho 752, 932 P.2d 875 (1996); Beardsley v. Idaho Forest Industries, 127 Idaho 404, 901 P.2d 55 (1995). ***PRACTICE AREAS:*** Personal Injury Litigation; Insurance Law; Product Liability; Civil Litigation; Workers Compensation; Criminal Law.

REPRESENTATIVE CLIENTS: State Farm Mutual Automobile Ins. Co.; State Farm Fire & Casualty Co.; Farm Bureau Mutual Ins. Co. of Idaho; Allstate Insurance Co.; Twin Falls Mutual Ins. Co.; Workers Compensation Exchange; New St. Andrews College; Nez Perce County.

MYRON DAN GABBERT, J.D. P.A.

Established in 1967

YACHT CLUB BUILDING

P.O. BOX 2349

McCALL, IDAHO 83638

Telephone: 208-634-2200

Fax: 208-634-2200

Email: gabbert@frontiernet.net

URL: http://www.lawyers.com/gabbertlaw

Council, Idaho Office: P.O. Box 546, 83612. Telephone: 208-253-6896. Fax: 208-253-4880. Email: gabbert@frontiernet.net.

General and Trial, Banking, Business, Commercial, Corporate, Insurance Defense, Real Estate, Wills, Trusts, Probate and Estate Planning.

FIRM PROFILE: Mr. Gabbert is the elected prosecutor of Adams County, therefore, he cannot handle criminal defense cases.

MYRON DAN GABBERT, born Chicago, Illinois, February 13, 1943; admitted to bar, 1967, Illinois; 1968, Idaho; 1972, U.S. Court of Appeals, Ninth Circuit. *Education:* Bradley University (B.A., 1967); University of Illinois (J.D., 1967). Phi Alpha Delta. Law Clerk, Idaho Supreme Court, 1967-1968. *Member:* Boise Bar Association; Idaho State Bar (Member, Fee Arbitration Committee); Idaho Association of Defense Counsel; Boise Estate Planning Council (President, 1980-1981). (Also at Council, Idaho Office). ***LANGUAGES:*** German and Spanish. ***PRACTICE AREAS:*** Business; Commercial; Estate Planning; Insurance Defense; Real Estate.

Languages: German; Spanish.

REPRESENTATIVE CLIENTS: Amerigas; Argonaut Insurance Co.; Bergen Brunswig Drug Co.; Clark Real Estate; Commonwealth Land Title Ins. Co.; Meadowcreek Property Owners; McCall Veterinary Clinic; Red Lion Inns; Reliance Group; Rogers Electric; South Coast Lumber Co.
REFERENCES: Wells Fargo Bank, Boise; U.S. Bank, McCall.

MALLEA LAW OFFICES

78 S.W. 5TH AVENUE

MERIDIAN, IDAHO 83642-2923

Telephone: 208-888-2790

Fax: 208-888-2789

Email: KLM@MalleaLaw.com

Mailing Address: P.O. Box 857, Meridian, ID 83680-0857

General Practice, Business Law, Wills, Trusts and Probate, Civil Litigation, Workers Compensation Defense, Education Law, Real Estate.

KENNETH L. MALLEA, born Caldwell, Idaho, November 24, 1952; admitted to bar, 1978, Washington, 1979, Idaho and U.S. Dist.Ct., Dist.of Idaho; U.S. Ct. of Appeals, Ninth Cir. *Education:* Gonzaga Univ.(B.A., summa cum laude, 1975); Univ. of Washington (J.D., 1978). Law Clerk, Hon. Joseph J. McFadden, ID Supreme Ct., 1978-1979. Dep. A.G., State of ID, 1979-1980. ***REPORTED CASES:*** Middlekauff v. Lake Cascade, Inc., 719 P.2d 1169, 110 Idaho 909; 654 P.2d 1385, 103 Idaho 832; Combes v. State Industrial Special Indemnity Fund 942 P.2d 554, 130 Idaho 430; 20 P.3d 689, 135 Idaho 505; Jensen v. West-

(This Listing Continued)

MALLEA LAW OFFICES, Meridian—Continued

berg, 707 P.2d 490, 109 Idaho 379; 772 P.2d 228, 115 Idaho 1021; James v. Idaho Dept. of Trans., 876 P.2d 590, 125 Idaho 892; Evans v. Hara's, 840 P.2d 934, 123 Idaho 473; Gardner v. Evans, 719 P.2d 1185, 110 Idaho 925; Smith v. J.B. Parson, 908 P.2d 1244, 127 Idaho 937; Dickerson v. Crutcher, 613 P.2d 934, 101 Idaho 377; Aldape v. Akins, 668 P.2d 130, 105 Idahho 254; Brown v. Iowa Beef Processors, 691 P.2d 1173, 107 Idaho 558; ID State Tax Comm. v. Staker, 663 P.2D 270, 104 Idaho 734; Phinney v. Industrial Special Indemnity Fund, 960 P.2d 1258, 131 Idaho 527; Quincy v. Quincy, 27 P.3d 410. ***PRACTICE AREAS:*** Education Law; Workers Compensation Defense; Litigation; Business Law; Wills; Trust Law; Probate; Real Estate.

REPRESENTATIVE CLIENTS: State of Idaho Industrial Special Indemnity Fund; Idaho Funeral Service Assoc; Idaho High School Activities Assoc.; Idaho Assoc.of School Administrators; Weiser, Kuna and Fruitland School Districts; HealthSouth Treasure Valley Hospital; Idaho Neurological Surgery; CNA Healthpro.

TROUT, WEEKS & NEMEC, PLLC

3067 E. COPPER POINT DRIVE
MERIDIAN, IDAHO 83642
Telephone: 208-376-4461
Fax: 208-376-4481
URL: http://www.trout-law.com
URL: http://www.lawyers.com/twnpllc

Construction, Commercial Litigation, Business Litigation, Business Formation, Real Estate Development, Agribusiness, Buying and Selling of Businesses, Energy/Cogeneration, Bankruptcy and Appeals.

KIM J. TROUT, born Lewiston, Idaho, July 30, 1954; admitted to bar, 1979, Idaho. *Education:* University of Idaho (B.S., Business Management and B.S., Business Marketing, cum laude, 1976; J.D., 1978). Certified Mediator, Business and Construction Mediations, State and Federal Court, Idaho. Author: "Real Estate Litigation in Idaho," National Business Institute, June 1997; "Keys to Success in a Real Estate Transaction in Idaho," National Business Institute, 1996. Deputy Prosecuting Attorney, Nez Perce County, 1979, 1980. Appointed Assistant Deputy Attorney General (Construction Law) 1997. Acting General Counsel (U.S. Operations) for multi-national Bradson Mercantile, Inc. in staffing business. *Member:* Idaho State Bar; American Bar Association; Idaho Trial Lawyers Association. ***REPORTED CASES:*** Brown v. Perkins, 129 Idaho 189, 923 P.2d 434(1996); Idaho Power Co. v. Cogeneration, Inc. 129 Idaho 46, 921 P.2d 746(1996). ***PRACTICE AREAS:*** Construction Law; Business Litigation; Agribusiness; Civil Appeals; Buying and Selling Business; Energy/Cogeneration; Bankruptcy; Commercial Real Property. ***Email:*** kjtrout@trout-law.com

STEVEN R. WEEKS, born Nampa, Idaho, February 3, 1965; admitted to bar, 1993, Idaho. *Education:* University of Arizona (B.A., 1987); University of Idaho (J.D., 1993). Langroise and Idaho Law Foundation Scholar. Editor-in-Chief, Idaho Law Review, 1992-1993. Author: "The Emerging Trend of Corporate Negligence," Idaho Law Review No. 2, 1993. Teaching Assistant, Research and Writing, University of Idaho, 1991-1992. *Member:* Idaho State Bar. ***PRACTICE AREAS:*** Real Estate Law; Corporate Law; Securities Law. ***Email:*** sweeks@trout-law.com

AARON H. NEMEC, born Boise, Idaho, May 5, 1968; admitted to bar, 1994, Idaho. *Education:* University of Idaho (B.S., honors, 1991; J.D., 1994). Member, National Association of Home Builders, 1995-1997. *Member:* Idaho State Bar. ***PRACTICE AREAS:*** Real Estate Law; Construction Law; Construction Litigation; Business Law. ***Email:*** anemec@trout-law.com

---

WILLIAM L. SMITH, born Twin Falls, Idaho, November 16, 1973; admitted to bar, 2000, Idaho. *Education:* University of Idaho (B.S., 1997; J.D., 1999). Member, Idaho Trial Lawyers Association, 1999-2000. Associate Member, Idaho Law Review. Law Clerk to the Hon. J. William Hart, 2000. *Member:* Fifth Judicial District, Idaho State (Member, Sections on: Employment Law; Professionalism & Ethics; Environment & Natural Resource) and American Bar Associations; Defense Research Institute; American Inns of Court (Advocate, Theron Ward Chapter); Idaho Association of Defense Council. ***PRACTICE AREAS:*** Employment Law; Business Transactions; Bankruptcy; Civil Litigation; Estate Planning.

DAVID T. KRUECK, born Madison, Wisconsin, March 28, 1971; admitted to bar, 2000, Idaho, U.S. District Court, District of Idaho, U.S. Court of Appeals, Ninth Circuit. *Education:* San Francisco State University (B.A., 1996); University of Idaho (J.D., 2000). Phi Alpha Delta. *Member:* American Bar Association; Idaho Trial Lawyers Association; Association of Trial Lawyers of America. ***PRACTICE AREAS:*** Commercial Litigation; Construction Law; Real Estate.

ROB H. SHOCKLEY, born Jerome, Idaho, August 29, 1967; admitted to bar, 1993, Idaho and U.S. District Court, District of Idaho. *Education:* Boise State University (B.A., 1990); University of Idaho (J.D., 1993). Phi Kappa Phi; Xi Chi; Pi Sigma Alpha. Boise City Prosecutor, 1995-1997. *Member:* American Inns of Court. ***PRACTICE AREAS:*** Civil Litigation (80%); Criminal Law (20%). ***Email:*** rshockley@trout-law.com

ROBERT M. ADELSON, born Detroit, Michigan, July 15, 1971; admitted to bar, 1997, Georgia; 2003, Idaho. *Education:* Emory University (B.A., 1993); Georgia State University (J.D., 1997). *Member:* Idaho State Bar; State Bar of Georgia. ***PRACTICE AREAS:*** Construction Litigation (90%); Constitutional Law (5%); Entertainment Law (5%). ***Email:*** radelson@trout-law.com

REPRESENTATIVE CLIENTS: Engineered Structures, Inc.; Nelson Construction; McAlvain Construction, Inc.; Western Construction; Turn Key Construction.

AHERIN, RICE & ANEGON

A PROFESSIONAL ASSOCIATION
MOSCOW, IDAHO
(See Lewiston)

Personal Injury, Auto Accidents, Wrongful Death, Products Liability, Automobile Negligence, Insurance Bad Faith, Medical and Legal Negligence, Workers Compensation, Criminal Defense, Libel and Slander, Condemnation, General Litigation including Domestic Relations, Contracts and Commercial Law, Probate, Real Property, Estate Planning, Employment and Environmental Law.

CLARK AND FEENEY

MOSCOW, IDAHO
(See Lewiston)

Trial Practice, Personal Injury, Corporation, Commercial, Construction, Surety, Real Property, Probate, Domestic Relations, General Practice, Criminal Law, Bankruptcy.

CREASON, MOORE & DOKKEN, PLLC

MOSCOW, IDAHO
(See Lewiston)

General Civil Practice, Insurance Defense, Appeals, Business Organizations, Commercial, Real Property, Probate and Estate Planning, Tax Law, Personal Injury, Criminal Defense, Auto Accident, Head Injury.

TIM GRESBACK

312 SOUTH WASHINGTON
P.O. BOX 9696
MOSCOW, IDAHO 83843
Telephone: 208-882-2222
Fax: 208-892-3535
Email: gresslaw@turbonet.com
URL: http://www.gresbacklaw.com

Criminal Defense, Personal Injury, Car Crashes, Wrongful Death, Brain Injury, Civil Rights.

TIM GRESBACK, born St. Paul, Minnesota, August 13, 1960; admitted to bar, 1987, Idaho; 1989, District of Columbia and Minnesota; 1994, U.S. Supreme Court; 2003, Nez Perce Tribal Court. *Education:* St. Olaf College (B.A., 1983); Lancaster University, England, Antioch School of Law (J.D., 1987). Adjunct Professor, Trial Advocacy. *Member:* Idaho State Bar; Idaho Association of Criminal Defense Lawyers (President, 2000-2001); Idaho Trial Lawyers Association (Regional Director, 2002-2004). ***PRACTICE AREAS:*** Criminal Defense; Personal Injury; Wrongful Death; Brain Injury.

KEETON & TAIT

MOSCOW, IDAHO
(See Lewiston)

General Practice, Workers Compensation, Personal Injury, Criminal Defense, Probate, Real Estate, Family Law, Housing and Employment Discrimination, Indian Law, Appellate Practice.

LIBEY, ENSLEY, ESSER & NELSON, PLLC

MOSCOW, IDAHO
(See Colfax, Washington)

General Civil and Trial Practice. Probate, Real Estate, Banking, Corporate and Business Tax Law.

MOSMAN LAW OFFICES

803 SOUTH JEFFERSON STREET
P.O. BOX 8456
MOSCOW, IDAHO 83843
Telephone: 208-882-0588
Fax: 208-882-0589
URL: http://www.mosmanlaw.com

General Practice, Litigation, Personal Injury, Automobile Accidents, Wrongful Death, Criminal Law, Family Law, Divorce, Child Custody, Probate, Wills, Trusts, Estate Planning, Real Estate.

OF COUNSEL

ROY E. MOSMAN, born Boise, Idaho, June 28, 1932; admitted to bar, 1960, Idaho. *Education:* University of Idaho (B.S., 1953); University of Oregon (LL.B., 1959; J.D., 1971). Phi Delta Phi. *Member:* Idaho State Bar; Clearwater Bar Association; National Prosecuting Attorneys Association. ***PRACTICE AREAS:*** Workman's Compensation Law; Domestic Relations Law; Business Law; Employment Law; Personal Injury Law.

MEMBER OF FIRM

WYNN R. MOSMAN, born Lewiston, Idaho, March 3, 1964; admitted to bar, 1992, Idaho and Washington. *Education:* University of Utah (B.A., 1988); University of Idaho (J.D., 1992); Graduate, National Institute of Trial Advocacy, Advocacy Skills Course. *Mem-*

(This Listing Continued)

ber: Second Judicial District and American Bar Associations; Association of Trial Lawyers of America; Washington State Trial Lawyers Association; Idaho Trial Lawyers Association. Raymond McNichols American Inns of Court. ***LANGUAGES:*** Japanese. ***PRACTICE AREAS:*** Personal Injury; Family Law; Litigation; Business Law; Criminal Law; Insurance; Trusts and Estates; Wills; Probate. ***Email:*** wynnmosman@moscow.com

ASSOCIATE

MARK T. MONSON, born Provo, Utah, April 29, 1973; admitted to bar, 2000, Idaho, Washington and U.S. District Court, District of Idaho. *Education:* Arizona State University (B.S., 1997); University of Idaho (J.D., 2000). *Member:* Idaho Trial Lawyers Association; Association of Trial Lawyers of America. The Ray McNichols American Inns of Court. ***LANGUAGES:*** Spanish. ***PRACTICE AREAS:*** Criminal Defense; Family Law; Personal Injury; Wills; Trusts and Estates; Probate. ***Email:*** monson@moscow.com

RANDALL, BLAKE & COX, P.A.

MOSCOW, IDAHO

(See Lewiston)

General Practice, Agricultural Law, Bankruptcy, Business Law, Contracts, Criminal Law, Debtor and Creditor Law. Employment Law, Family Law, Domestic Relations, Personal Injury, Products Liability, Real Estate, Taxation, Trusts and Estates, Estate Planning, Wills, Probate, Workers Compensation, Zoning, Planning and Land Use.

SMITH & CANNON

MOSCOW, IDAHO

(See Lewiston)

General Trial Practice. Personal Injury, Aviation, Automobile Accidents and Injuries, Wrongful Death, Family Law, Divorce, Child Custody, Child Support, Alternative Dispute Resolution, Insurance, Probate Law, Workers Compensation Claims, Arbitration and Mediation.

HALL, FRIEDLY & WARD

Established in 1937

340 EAST SECOND NORTH
MOUNTAIN HOME, IDAHO 83647
Telephone: 208-587-4412
Fax: 208-587-3144
Email: hfwlaw@adelphia.net

General and Trial Practice. Corporate Law, Business Law, Real Estate, Personal Injury, Trucking, Automobile, and Construction Accidents, Wrongful Death, Slip and Fall, Probate, Family Law, Divorce, Domestic Relations, Adoptions, Support, Custody, Bankruptcy, Estate Planning, Agricultural and Appellate Work.

MEMBERS OF FIRM

JAY R. FRIEDLY, born Humboldt, Nebraska, September 1, 1947; admitted to bar, 1972, Idaho and Nebraska; 1988, U.S. Court of Appeals, Ninth Circuit. *Education:* University of Nebraska (B.A., 1969; J.D., 1972). Delta Theta Phi. *Member:* Idaho State Bar; American Bar Association; Idaho Trial Lawyers Association. ***REPORTED CASES:*** Post v. Idaho Farmway, Inc., 135 Idaho 475 (2001); Ladurini v. Hazzord, 130 Idaho 192 (1997); Walburn v. Walburn, 127 Idaho 720 (1995); Suitts v. First Security Bank, 125 Idaho 27 (1993); Walburn v. Walburn, 120 Idaho 494 (1991); Leydet v. City of Mountain Home, 119 Idaho 1041 (1991); Clampitt v. A.M.R. Corp., 109 Idaho 145 (1985). ***PRACTICE AREAS:*** General Practice; Business Law; Family Law; Real Estate (Property) Law; Probate; Trusts and Estates. ***Email:*** jay@hfwlaw.net

ROBERT W. WARD, born Rexburg, Idaho, April 30, 1962; admitted to bar, 1991, Idaho. *Education:* Ricks College (A.A., 1985); Brigham Young University (B.S., 1988); University of Idaho (J.D., 1991). Author, Survey Article on Property and Water Law, Idaho Law Review, Volume 26, Spring Edition. *Member:* Idaho State Bar; American Bar Association; Idaho Trial Lawyers Association. ***LANGUAGES:*** Spanish. ***PRACTICE AREAS:*** General Practice; Domestic Relations; Personal Injury; Bankruptcy; Trial Practice. ***Email:*** hfwlaw@adelphia.net

BRIAN B. PETERSON, born Boise, Idaho, March 25, 1974; admitted to bar, 2005, Idaho and U.S. District Court, District of Idaho. *Education:* Boise State University (B.B.A., magna cum laude, 2002); University of Idaho (J.D., 2005). Phi Delta Phi. *Member:* Idaho State Bar; American Bar Association; The Association of Trial Lawyers of America. ***LANGUAGES:*** Russian. ***PRACTICE AREAS:*** General Practice; Real Estate; Business Law; Trusts and Estates; Probate. ***Email:*** brian@hfwlaw.net

OF COUNSEL

PERCE HALL

KIMBERLY D. BROOKS

Established in 2001

5700 EAST FRANKLIN ROAD, SUITE 250
NAMPA, IDAHO 83687
Telephone: 208-442-7489
Fax: 208-468-4030
URL: http://www.kbrookslaw.com
Email: kim@kbrookslaw.com
URL: http://www.lawyers.com/kimberlydbrooks

Family Law, Divorce, Domestic Relations, Child Custody, Child Support, Adoptions, Guardianship, Visitation Rights, Separation Agreements, Domestic Violence, Alimony.

(This Listing Continued)

KIMBERLY D. BROOKS, born Sacramento, California, April 10, 1971; admitted to bar, 1999, Idaho. *Education:* University of San Francisco (B.A., 1995); Southern Methodist University School of Law (J.D., 1999).

LEGAL SUPPORT PERSONNEL

DENA M. WINFIELD, born Caldwell, Idaho, March 24, 1970; admitted to bar, 1997, Oregon. *Education:* The College of Idaho (B.A., cum laude, 1994); Willamette University College of Law (J.D., 1997). Member, National Scholastic Honor Society. Listed in: Who's Who, College of Idaho Dean's List; Who's Who Among Students in American Colleges and Universities. Formerly with: Kennedy, Watts, Arellano & Ricks; Garrett, Heman, Robertson, P.C. *Member:* Multnomah County, Marion County (Member, Law Day Committee) and American Bar Associations; Oregon State Bar (inactive). (Legal Intern). ***PRACTICE AREAS:*** Family Law (90%); Real Estate (10%). ***Email:*** dena@kbrookslaw.com

ANDREA L. CARDON

NAMPA, IDAHO

(See Boise)

Construction Contracts and Social Security Disability.

LAW OFFICE OF MICHAEL J. ELIA

NAMPA, IDAHO

(See Boise)

Insurance, Personal Injury, Insurance Defense, Business Litigation, General Practice.

JAMES R. GILLESPIE, P.A.

NAMPA, IDAHO

(See Boise)

General Practice. Business, Commercial Real Estate, Agricultural, Natural Resources Law, Environment and Construction Law, Mediation and Arbitration.

GJORDING & FOUSER, PLLC

NAMPA, IDAHO

(See Boise)

Insurance Defense, Medical Malpractice Defense, Employment and Commercial Litigation.

GREENER BANDUCCI SHOEMAKER P.A.

NAMPA, IDAHO

(See Boise)

General Civil Trial Practice including Commercial Litigation, Securities, Real Estate, Product Liability, Construction, Eminent Domain, Employment, and Personal Injury, Insurance, Intellectual Property. The firm also has substantial expertise in class actions.

GAR HACKNEY, P.L.L.C.

NAMPA, IDAHO

(See Boise)

Criminal Law, Driving Under the Influence, Domestic Violence, Sexual Assault, Drug Crimes, Burglary, Search and Seizure, White Collar Crime, Federal Crimes, State and Felony Misdemeanor, Petty Theft, Personal Injury, Automobile Accidents, Bicycle Accidents, Pedestrian Accidents.

JOHNSON & MONTELEONE, LLP

NAMPA, IDAHO

(See Boise)

Personal Injury, Employment Law, Automobile Accidents and Injuries, Head Injury, Dog Bites, Wrongful Termination, Slip and Fall.

McDEVITT & MILLER, LLP

NAMPA, IDAHO

(See Boise)

Business Law, Public Utility Law, Administrative Law, Litigation, Water Law, Family Law, Franchising.

JOHN MEIENHOFER

NAMPA, IDAHO

(See Boise)

Federal and State Drugs and Narcotics, Land Use, Criminal Defense, DUI, Theft, White Collar Crime, Embezzlement, Civil Forfeiture, Personal Injury, Divorce, Child Custody, Domestic Violence Protection Orders, Social Security Disability, Corporate Law, Wills.

HAROLD Q. NOACK, JR., P.A.

NAMPA, IDAHO

(See Boise)

Creditor and Debtor Bankruptcy, General Civil, Trial and Appellate Practice. Commercial, Corporation, Family Law, Divorce, Alimony, Child Support, Real Estate, Construction Law, Elder Law, Wills and Probate.

DEREK A. PICA, P.L.L.C.

NAMPA, IDAHO

(See Boise)

Divorce, Child Custody, Real Estate, Probate, Contracts, Personal Injury.

SEINIGER LAW OFFICES

NAMPA, IDAHO

(See Boise)

Personal Injury, Workers Compensation, Employment Discrimination and Harassment, Business Torts, Insurance Disputes.

LAWRENCE G. SIRHALL

NAMPA, IDAHO

(See Boise)

Personal Injury, Tax, Criminal Tax Defense, Real Estate, Adoption, Neck and Back Injuries, Slip and Fall, Car Accidents.

ROBERT A. WALLACE

NAMPA, IDAHO

(See Boise)

Criminal Defense, DWI, Drug Crimes, Felonies, Misdemeanors, Traffic Violations, Juvenile, Plaintiffs' Personal Injury, Collections.

WHITE PETERSON, P.A.

Established in 1968

5700 EAST FRANKLIN ROAD, SUITE 200
NAMPA, IDAHO 83687-7901
Telephone: 208-466-9272
Facsimile: 208-466-4405
Email: contact@whitepeterson.com
URL: http://www.whitepeterson.com

Trusts and Estates, Wills, Guardianship and Conservatorship, Probate, Business Law, Contracts, Debtor and Creditor, Corporate Law, Taxation, Partnership Law, Labor and Employment, Employee Benefits, Real Estate, Leases and Leasing, Mortgages, Municipal Law, Civil Rights, Zoning, Planning and Land Use, Eminent Domain, Environmental Law, Workers Compensation, Litigation, Personal Injury, Medical Malpractice, Collections, Agricultural Law, Family Law, Torts, Products Liability, Education Law, Nonprofit and Charitable Organizations, Civil Practice, General Practice.

FIRM PROFILE: For over a quarter of a century White Peterson, P.A. has been serving the Treasure Valley and beyond. Community and family conscious, we emphasize practical approaches and effective litigation to help our clients manage their present legal needs and plan for the future.

White Peterson, P.A. was founded in 1968, and is currently comprised of fifteen attorneys. We are the largest firm in Southwest Idaho outside of Boise. Our attorneys and staff assist with a wide range of civil legal issues. All attorneys in the firm are licensed to practice before all courts in Idaho. Some of our attorneys are also licensed in California, Oregon and Washington.

Although the firm practices a wide variety of areas, we have significant expertise in civil litigation and appeals, corporate and business law, real estate and water rights issues, personal injury, malpractice, construction law, estate planning, trust administration, probate, guardianship, conservatorship, municipal law, family law, lien foreclosures, collection and evictions.

TERRENCE R. WHITE, admitted to bar, 1971, Idaho; 1980, U.S. Tax Court; 1988, U.S. Court of Appeals, Ninth Circuit; 1992, Washington. *Education:* University of Idaho (B.A., 1968; J.D., cum laude, 1971). Member, Board of Editors, Idaho Law Review, 1969-1971. Deputy Prosecuting Attorney, Ada County, 1972. President, Southwest Idaho Estate Planning Council, 1978. *Member:* Third District (President, 1979-1980) and American Bar Associations; Idaho State Bar (Commissioner, 2005-2008; Chairman, Bar Exam Preparation Committee, 1991-1992); Southwest Idaho Estate Planning Council. ***PRACTICE AREAS:*** Municipal Labor Law; Zoning, Planning and Land Use; Probate; Real Property; Estate Planning; Litigation. ***Email:*** trw@whitepeterson.com

PHILIP A. PETERSON, admitted to bar, 1979, Idaho and U.S. District Court, District of Idaho; 1980, U.S. Tax Court. *Education:* University of Idaho (B.S., Accounting, cum laude, 1969; J.D., cum laude, 1979). Phi Eta Sigma; Phi Kappa Phi. President, Southwest Idaho Estate Planning Council, 1984. *Member:* Third District Bar Association; Idaho State Bar (Member, Taxation Section); Southwest Idaho Estate Planning Council. [LT, SC, USN, 1969-1976]. ***PRACTICE AREAS:*** Estate Planning; Employee Benefits; Real Estate; Probate; Tax Planning; Business Litigation. ***Email:*** pap@whitepeterson.com

(This Listing Continued)

WILLIAM A. MORROW, admitted to bar, 1979, Idaho and U.S. District Court, District of Idaho; U.S. Court of Appeals, Ninth and Tenth Circuits; U.S Court of Appeals for the District of Columbia Circuit; U.S. Tax Court. *Education:* Kent State University (B.A., cum laude, 1973); University of Idaho (J.D., 1979). Chief Deputy Prosecuting Attorney, Canyon County, 1985-1987. *Member:* Third District (President, 1989-1990) and American (Member, Section on Litigation) Bar Associations; Idaho State Bar; Idaho Trial Lawyers Association (Member, Board of Governors, 1987-1988). ***PRACTICE AREAS:*** Probate; Environmental Law; Business Law; Real Property; Civil Rights Defense; Complex Litigation. ***Email:*** wam@whitepeterson.com

WILLIAM F. GIGRAY III, admitted to bar, 1973, Idaho and U.S. District Court, District of Idaho; 1980, U.S. Supreme Court; U.S. Court of Appeals, Ninth Circuit. *Education:* University of Idaho (B.A., 1969; J.D., 1972). *Member:* Third Judicial District Bar Association (President, 1978-1979); Idaho State Bar; Idaho Trial Lawyers Association (President, 2001-2002; Member, Board of Directors, 1998-2003); The Association of Trial Lawyers of America. ***PRACTICE AREAS:*** Municipal Law; Local Government Law; Personal Injury; Estate Planning; Probate; Corporate Law. ***Email:*** wfg@whitepeterson.com

CHRISTOPHER S. NYE, admitted to bar, 1982, Idaho. *Education:* University of Kansas (B.A., 1979; J.D., 1982). Phi Delta Phi. *Member:* Idaho Trial Lawyers Association; The Association of Trial Lawyers of America. ***PRACTICE AREAS:*** Civil Litigation; Real Property; Family Law. ***Email:*** csn@whitepeterson.com

TODD A. ROSSMAN, admitted to bar, 1989, Idaho and U.S. District Court, District of Idaho; 1990, U.S. Tax Court; U.S. Court of Appeals, Ninth and Tenth Circuits. *Education:* Boise State University (B.B.A., 1986); Gonzaga Law School (J.D., 1989); University of Denver (LL.M., in Taxation, 1990). *Member:* Third District Bar Association (President, 2001-2002); Idaho State Bar (Member, Taxation Division); Southwest Idaho Estate Planning Council (President, 1995); National Academy of Elder Law Attorneys, Inc. ***PRACTICE AREAS:*** Taxation; Estate Planning; Wills; Trust Law; Probate; Elder Law; Real Property; Business Law. ***Email:*** tar@whitepeterson.com

JULIE KLEIN FISCHER, admitted to bar, 1992, Idaho, U.S. District Court, District of Idaho. *Education:* College of Idaho (B.A., magna cum laude, 1989); University of Idaho (J.D., 1992). Gipson Honor Student, College of Idaho. Symposium Editor, Idaho Law Review, 1991-1992. Member, Executive Committee, Student Bar Association, 1991-1992. Author: "Muddy Waters: Rights to Conserved Water in Idaho," 27 Idaho L. Rev. 303 (1991). ***PRACTICE AREAS:*** Employment Law; Water Law; Real Estate; Civil Litigation. ***Email:*** jkf@whitepeterson.com

WILLIAM F. NICHOLS, admitted to bar, 1980, Oregon; 1983, U.S. District Court, District of Oregon; 1984, U.S. Tax Court; 1986, Idaho. *Education:* Linfield College (B.A., magna cum laude, 1977); University of Oregon (J.D., 1980). Phi Delta Phi. *Member:* Oregon State Bar; Idaho State Bar. ***PRACTICE AREAS:*** Municipal Law; Probate; Real Estate; Foreclosures; Creditors Rights. ***Email:*** wfn@whitepeterson.com

KEVIN E. DINIUS, admitted to bar, 1999, Idaho and U.S. District Court, District of Idaho. *Education:* Boise State University (B.S., cum laude, 1996); University of Idaho (J.D., summa cum laude, 1999). Phi Kappa Phi; Delta Theta Phi. Editor in Chief, Idaho Law Review, 1998-1999. [Sgt., U.S. Army, 1987-1991]. ***PRACTICE AREAS:*** Commercial Litigation; Lender Liability; Personal Injury; Construction Litigation. ***Email:*** ked@whitepeterson.com

T. GUY HALLAM, JR., admitted to bar, 1999, Oregon; 2000, Idaho and U.S. District Court, District of Idaho; 2001, U.S. District Court, District of Oregon; 2003, U.S. Court of Appeals, Ninth Circuit. *Education:* University of Tennessee (B.A., 1993); Northwestern School of Law at Lewis & Clark College (J.D., cum laude, 1998). Phi Delta Phi. Co-Author: *Appellate Practice and Procedure,* Idaho State Bar Journal, The Advocate, 1999. *Member:* Third Judicial District Bar Association (Member, Technology Committee, 2003); Idaho Trial Lawyers Association; The Association of Trial Lawyers of America. ***PRACTICE AREAS:*** Business Litigation; Lender Liability; Contracts; Employment Law; Insurance Litigation; Medical Malpractice. ***Email:*** tgh@whitepeterson.com

REPRESENTATIVE CLIENTS: Nampa Radiologists, P.A.; Caldwell Internal Medicine, P.A.; City of Nampa; City of Wilder; Caldwell Rural Fire Protection District; Canyon Highway District; School District No. 132; Crookham Co. (Seed Co.); Gem Fuel Co.; Terry Reilly Health Services; Disaster Kleenup, Inc.; Gale Insulation; Simplot Employees Credit Union; Kuna Rural Fire Protection District; Homedale Rural Fire Protection District; Golden Gate Highway District No.3; Wilder Rural Fire Protection District; Nampa Rural Fire Protection District; Idaho Association of Highway Districts; D&B Supply, Co. Inc.; Garden Valley Recreation District; Wilder Public Library District; City of Homedale.
REFERENCE: Farmers & Merchants State Bank, Idaho.

CREASON, MOORE & DOKKEN, PLLC

OROFINO, IDAHO

(See Lewiston)

General Civil Practice, Insurance Defense, Appeals, Business Organizations, Commercial, Real Property, Probate and Estate Planning, Tax Law, Personal Injury, Criminal Defense, Auto Accident, Head Injury.

BEARD ST. CLAIR GAFFNEY McNAMARA CALDER PA

POCATELLO, IDAHO

(See Idaho Falls)

Agricultural Law, Acquisitions, Americans with Disabilities Act, Antitrust, Arbitration, Asset Protection, Automobile Accidents, Automobile Insurance, Banking Law, Breach of Contract, Business Law, Buying and Selling Businesses, Charitable Giving, Collections, Commercial Insurance, Commercial Law, Commercial Real Estate, Computers and Software, Condominiums, Construction Law, Contested Wills, Contracts, Copyrights, Corporations, Creditors Rights, Crop Damage and Chemical Applications, Debtor and Creditor, Discrimination, Distribution and Distributorships, Divorce with significant assets, Elder Care, Elder Law, Employment Discrimination, Employment Law, Estate Planning, Estate and Gift Taxation, Family Business Law, Family and Medical Leave Act, Farm and Ranch Law, Fire Loss, Food, Drug and

(This Listing Continued)

Cosmetic Law, Franchises and Franchising, Foreclosures, General Trial and Appellate Practice, Guardianship, Harassment, Health Care, Health Insurance, Income Taxation, Insurance, Insurance Bad Faith, Investments, Landlord and Tenant Law, Leasing, Liens, Life and Health Insurance, Limited Liability Company Law, Litigation, Long-term Care, Mechanics Liens, Mediation, Medical Malpractice and Malpractice Defense, Medicare and Medicaid, Minority Business Law, Mortgages, Multilevel Sales, Nonprofit and Charitable Organizations, Nursing Homes, PACA, Partnerships, Pension and Benefits, Personal Injury, Post Mortem Administration of Trusts and Estates, Products Liabilities, Professional Malpractice, Property Tax, Professional Practices, Property Insurance, Railroad Accidents, Real Estate, Sexual Abuse, Slip and Fall, Small Business Law, Social Security, Social Security Disability, Taxation, Torts, Trademarks, Trade Secrets, Trust and Estates, Valuations, Warranties, Wills and Probate, Workers Compensation, Wrongful Death, Wrongful Termination, Zoning, Planning and Land Use.

CRAIG W. CHRISTENSEN

CHARTERED

Established in 1992

414 SOUTH GARFIELD
P.O. BOX 130
POCATELLO, IDAHO 83204-0130
Telephone: 208-234-9353
Fax: 208-234-9357
Email: cwcc@ida.net
URL: http://www.cwc-law.com

Litigation, Banking, Bankruptcy, Personal Bankruptcy, Chapters 7, 11, 12, 13, Commercial, Corporations, Creditor's Rights, Real Estate Law.

CRAIG W. CHRISTENSEN, born Soda Springs, Idaho, July 13, 1951; admitted to bar, 1977, Idaho and U.S. District Court, District of Idaho; 1994, U.S. District Court, District of Arizona; U.S. Court of Appeals, Ninth Circuit; 2005, Utah. *Education:* Idaho State University (B.B.A., 1974); University of Idaho (J.D., 1977). Certified by American Board of Certification in Business Bankruptcy Law, 1996. Co-Author: "How to Protect Creditors' Rights in Bankruptcy in Idaho," NBI, Inc., Eau Claire, 1987. Author: "Creditors' Rights and Protection of Security Interests in Bankruptcy," NBI, Inc., Eau Claire, 1988; "Foreclosure and Repossession," NBI, Inc., Eau Claire, 1987; "Strategies for Unsecured Creditors in Bankruptcy," Idaho Law Foundation, 1990; "An Analysis of Claims from a Debtor's Perspective," Idaho Law Foundation, 1993; "Bankruptcy Issues Related to Real Estate," Idaho Law Foundation, 1995; "Bankruptcy Procedures From a Secured Creditors Perspective," Idaho Law Foundation, 2003; "Bankruptcy Case Update," Idaho Law Foundation, 2004. Ninth Circuit Lawyer Representative, 1995-1998. Member, 1995— and President, 2001-2002, Porteuf Inns of Court. *Member:* Sixth District (President, 1985-1986), Federal and American Bar Associations; Idaho State Bar (Member, Bankruptcy Section; Board of Governors, 1989-1995); Utah State Bar; Idaho Trial Lawyers Association; American Bankruptcy Institute. ***PRACTICE AREAS:*** Litigation; Banking Law; Bankruptcy Law; Commercial Law; Corporate Law; Creditor's Rights; Real Estate.

REPRESENTATIVE CLIENTS: Wells Fargo Bank; J.R. Simplot Company; Citizens Community Bank; Ireland Bank; L.D. Fitzgerald, Bankruptcy Trustee; Farm Credit Leasing; GEM State Distributors, Inc.; R & G Potatoes Inc.; Western Farm Service; Farm Bureau Finance Company; Jack B. Parson Company; Pocatello Simplot Credit Union; Power County; Clark Real Estate; Forrest Hymas, Trustee; Bank of Utah; Inkom Cement Employees Credit Union; Staker & Parsons, Inc.
REFERENCES: Wells Fargo Bank; Ireland Bank.

COOPER & LARSEN

Established in 1998

151 NORTH 3RD AVENUE, SUITE 210
P.O. BOX 4229
POCATELLO, IDAHO 83205-4229
Telephone: 208-235-1145
Fax: 208-235-1182
Email: gary@cooper-larsen.com
URL: http://www.cooper-larsen.com

Trial Practice, Appellate Practice, Personal Injury, Insurance Defense, Federal Employers Liability Act (FELA); Railroad Litigation, Workers Compensation, Agricultural Claims, Products Liability, Commercial Law, Indian Law.

GARY L. COOPER, born Caldwell, Idaho, April 12, 1950; admitted to bar, 1975, Idaho, U.S. Court of Appeals, 9th Circuit and U.S. Supreme Court; Shoshone Bannock Tribal Court. *Education:* University of Idaho (B.S., 1972; J.D., 1975). Recipient, Professionalism Award, Idaho State Bar, 1996. Founding Member, Porteuf Inn of Court (President, 1999-2000). Member, Idaho State Bar Ethics Committee (2003—). *Member:* Idaho State Bar (Member: Federal Court Local Rules Committee, 1998—). ***PRACTICE AREAS:*** Personal Injury; Insurance Defense; Workers Compensation; Civil Appeals. ***Email:*** gary@cooper-larsen.com

REED W. LARSEN, born Burley, Idaho, December 4, 1957; admitted to bar, 1985, Idaho and U.S. Court of Appeals, Ninth Circuit; Shoshone Bannock Tribal Court. *Education:* Brigham Young University (B.A., 1982); University of Idaho (J.D., 1985). Delta Theta Phi. *Member:* Sixth Judicial District Bar Association (President, 2003); Idaho State Bar. ***PRACTICE AREAS:*** Personal Injury; Railroad Law; Civil Rights; Products Liability; Insurance Defense. ***Email:*** reed@cooper-larsen.com

OF COUNSEL

RON KERL, born Spokane, Washington, January 10, 1950; admitted to bar, 1975, Idaho and U.S. District Court, District of Idaho; 1978, U.S. Court of Appeals, Ninth Circuit. *Education:* University of Idaho (B.A., cum laude, 1972; J.D., cum laude, 1975). Phi Beta Kappa. Editor in Chief, Idaho Law Review, 1974-1975. *Member:* Sixth District (President, 1981) and American (Member, Section on Litigation) Bar Associations; Idaho State Bar (President, 1993-1994); Idaho State Bar Commission (1991-1994); Lawyer Representative, Ninth Circuit Court of Appeals, 2003—; Porteuf American Inns of Court (President, 1995-1996). ***PRACTICE AREAS:*** Commercial Litigation; Bankruptcy Law. ***Email:*** ron@cooper-larsen.com

ASSOCIATES

M. ANTHONY SASSER, born Moscow, Idaho, October 9, 1971; admitted to bar, 1999, Idaho. *Education:* Brigham Young University (B.A., 1995); University of Idaho (J.D., 1999). Law Clerk to Hon. N. Randy Smith, Idaho Sixth Judicial District Court, 1999-2000. *Member:* Idaho State Bar. ***PRACTICE AREAS:*** Insurance Defense; Workers Compensation; Commercial Litigation; Personal Injury. ***Email:*** tony@cooper-larsen.com

E.W. "SKIP" CARTER, born Pueblo, Colorado, March 5, 1959; admitted to bar, 1990, Idaho and U.S District Court, District of Idaho. *Education:* Columbia University (B.A., 1981); University of Tulsa (J.D., 1989). Member, Porteuf Inns of Court, 1995-1997. *Member:* Sixth District Bar Association (President, 2000-2001). ***PRACTICE AREAS:*** Personal Injury; Insurance Defense; Criminal Law; Employment Law; Civil Rights. ***Email:*** skip@cooper-larsen.com

JAMES D. RUCHTI, born Pocatello, Idaho, April 2, 1969; admitted to bar, 2001, Idaho and U.S. District Court, District of Idaho. *Education:* United States Military Academy (B.S., 1993); University of Idaho (J.D., 2001). Law Clerk to Honorable B. Lynn Winmill, Chief Judge, U.S. District Court of Idaho, 2001-2002. *Member:* Idaho State Bar. [Capt., U.S. Army, Military Intelligence Branch, 1993-1998]. ***PRACTICE AREAS:*** Insurance Defense; Personal Injury; Employment Law; Commercial Litigation. ***Email:*** james@cooper-larsen.com

MARVIN K. SMITH, born American Fork, Utah, December 29, 1976; admitted to bar, 2004, Idaho, U.S. District Court, District of Idaho. *Education:* Boise State University (B.A., cum laude, 2001); University of Idaho (J.D., 2004). Member, Board of Editors, Idaho Law Review, 2003-2004. *Member:* Idaho State Bar. ***PRACTICE AREAS:*** Insurance Defense; Personal Injury; Commercial Litigation; Employment Law. ***Email:*** marvin@cooper-larsen.com

REPRESENTATIVE CLIENTS: Albertsons; Federated; Farmers; Hartford; State Farm; Orion Auto; Safeco; Northwest Farm Credit Services; Deere & Co.; Zion's National Bank; The Travelers Ins. Co.; Idaho Central Credit Union.

COX, OHMAN & BRANDSTETTER

CHARTERED

POCATELLO, IDAHO

(See Idaho Falls)

General Civil and Criminal Trial, Appellate and Administrative Practice in State and Federal Courts. Social Security, Workmen's Compensation and Corporation. Personal Injury, Insurance, Family Law, Divorce, Child Support, Child Custody, Automobile Accidents and Injuries, Wrongful Death, Head Injury, Criminal Law.

DIAL, MAY & RAMMELL

CHARTERED

Established in 1975

216 W. WHITMAN
P.O. BOX 370
POCATELLO, IDAHO 83204-0370
Telephone: 208-233-0132
Facsimile: 208-234-2961
Email: dmr@dats.com
URL: http://www.dialmayrammell-law.com

General Civil and Criminal Practice. Workers Compensation, Commercial, Corporation, Creditor, Real Estate, Bankruptcy, Immigration, Litigation, Family, Personal Injury, Head Injury, Trucking Accidents, Wrongful Death, and Estate and Probate Law.

THOMAS F. DIAL, born Idaho Falls, Idaho, February 9, 1938; admitted to bar, 1967, Idaho and U.S. District Court, District of Idaho; 1971, U.S. Supreme Court. *Education:* Idaho State University (B.A., 1965); University of Idaho (J.D., 1967). Phi Alpha Delta. Recipient: Idaho State Bar Family Law Section Award of Distinction and Merit, 1996; Idaho State University Professional Achievement Award, 1999. Author: "Constitutional Rights of Unwed Fathers," ABA, Family Advocate, Fall, 1981; "Due Process in Adoption and Termination," Family Law Practice Handbook, 1981; "Jury Selection," Idaho Civil Trial Manual, 1988. Editor, "Idaho Family Law Handbook," 1998—. Criminal Magistrate, 6th District Court, 1971-1974; Idaho Supreme Court Rules of Evidence Committee; Idaho Supreme Court Child Support Guidelines Committee, 1990—. Idaho Bench/Bar Committee on the Family, 1995-2001. Co-Chair, Idaho Supreme Court Committee, Children and Family in the Courts, 2001—. *Member:* Sixth District and American Bar Associations; Idaho State Bar (Chair, Family Law Council, 2000-2001); Idaho Trial Lawyers Association (Past Member, Board of Governors); The Association of Trial Lawyers of America. Fellow, American Academy of Matrimonial Lawyers; Porteuf Inns of Court. ***PRACTICE AREAS:*** Family Law; Personal Injury Law; Probate; Wills. ***Email:*** tfdial@cableone.net

GREGORY C. MAY, born Rockland, Idaho, May 16, 1949; admitted to bar, 1977, Idaho and U.S. District Court, District of Idaho. *Education:* Ricks Junior College; University of Utah (B.S., cum laude, 1973); University of Idaho (J.D., 1976). Member, Magistrate Commission, 1994-1996. CLE Faculty, Family Law. *Member:* Sixth District Bar Association (President, 1988-1989); Idaho State Bar; Idaho Trial Lawyers Association. ***PRACTICE AREAS:*** Workers Compensation Law; Personal Injury Law; Criminal Defense Law; Domestic Relations Law; Adoption; Litigation; Wills. ***Email:*** gcmay@cableone.net

BRON M. RAMMELL, born Provo, Utah, January 20, 1963; admitted to bar, 1992, Idaho and U.S. Court of Appeals, Federal Circuit. *Education:* Ricks Junior College; Brigham Young University (B.A.,1987); Willamette University (J.D., 1991). Recipient, Dis-

(This Listing Continued)

DIAL, MAY & RAMMELL, CHARTERED, Pocatello—Continued

pute Resolution Certificate, 1991. Author: "Pre Nuptial Agreements," National Business Institute Family Law in Idaho, 1991. Pro Tempore Municipal Judge, The Dalles, Oregon, 1990-1991. *Member:* Sixth Judicial District and American (Member: Litigation Section; PreTrial Practice & Discovery Committee) Bar Associations; Idaho State Bar; The Association of Trial Lawyers of America; Idaho Trial Lawyers Association. ***LANGUAGES:*** Japanese. ***PRACTICE AREAS:*** Litigation; Personal Injury; Civil Rights; Criminal Law; Social Security; Business Law; Domestic Relations Law; Health Care Law; Real Estate; Commercial Law. **Email:** rammell@cableone.net

AARON N. THOMPSON, born Alexandria, Indiana, March 17, 1975; admitted to bar, 2000, Idaho; U.S. District Court, District of Idaho; 2001, U.S. Court of Appeals, Federal Circuit. *Education:* Ball State University (B.S., 1997); University of Wyoming (J.D., 2000). *Member:* Sixth District Bar Association; Idaho Trial Lawyers Association ; American Inns of Court. ***PRACTICE AREAS:*** Labor Law; Employment Law; Criminal Defense; Personal Injury; Politics; Family Law; Civil Rights Litigation; Workers Compensation; Lien Law; Appellate Practice. ***Email:*** athompson1@cableone.net

---

BRIAN J. CHENEY, born Caldwell, Idaho, September 10, 1973; admitted to bar, 2004, Idaho and U.S. District Court, District of Idaho. *Education:* Brigham Young University (M.S., Botany, 2002; J.D., 2004). ***LANGUAGES:*** Portuguese. ***PRACTICE AREAS:*** Domestic Relations; Personal Injury; Criminal Defense; Business Law; Wills. ***Email:*** bcheney@cableone.net

REPRESENTATIVE CLIENTS: Idaho Power Company; Idaho Business Systems; Yamaha Motor Corporation; Transamerica Commercial Finance Corp.; Consolidated Electrical Distributors, Inc.; McDonnell Douglas Finance Corp.; The Travelers Insurance Co.; Grubb & Ellis Property Mgt.; Crossland Credit Corp.; Church of Jesus Christ of Latter Day Saints; Ratzlaff Architects, Chtd., Ford's Electric, LLC; Holtsizen Painting; Snake River Realty; Box Elder County Federal Credit Union; D&D Trucking, Inc.; Thiokol Credit Union; JHS Architects, Chtd.; Pine Ridge Mall; Universal Building Contractors; Blaze Sign and Graphics, Inc.; Pocatello PreCast, Inc.; Tri Phase Electric, Inc.; Popcorn Paradise, Inc.; Plastic Surgery Associates, P.A.; Idaho SurgiCenter; Central Christian Church.

EHARDT, SMITH & TORGESEN

POCATELLO, IDAHO

(See Idaho Falls)

Business, Corporate, Estate Planning, Wills and Trusts, Real Estate, Taxation, Probate, Bankruptcy, Real Property, Criminal Defense, Family Law, Litigation, Juvenile Law.

GIVENS PURSLEY LLP

POCATELLO, IDAHO

(See Boise)

Business, Commercial, Mergers and Acquisitions, Communications and Media, Employment, Environmental, Water, Public Lands and Natural Resources, Financial Transactions, Securitization, Structured Finance, Banking, Credit Recovery and Bankruptcy, Public Policy, Health Care and Hospital, Intellectual Property, Real Estate, Real Estate Financing and Land Use, Securities and Bonds, Tax and Estate Planning, Trial and Appellate Litigation, Telecommunications, Energy, Utilities and Regulatory Affairs.

GREENER BANDUCCI SHOEMAKER P.A.

POCATELLO, IDAHO

(See Boise)

General Civil Trial Practice including Commercial Litigation, Securities, Real Estate, Product Liability, Construction, Eminent Domain, Employment, and Personal Injury, Insurance, Intellectual Property. The firm also has substantial expertise in class actions.

HALL, FARLEY, OBERRECHT & BLANTON, P.A.

POCATELLO, IDAHO

(See Boise)

Litigation, Insurance Defense, Medical Malpractice and Professional Liability, Employment Law, Labor Relations, Products Liability, Construction, Health and Hospital, Corporation, Commercial, Banking, Real Estate, Legislative Counseling, Bankruptcy, Appellate Law, Administrative Agencies, Agricultural, Municipal, Estate Planning and Probate.

HAWLEY TROXELL ENNIS & HAWLEY LLP

333 SOUTH MAIN STREET
P.O. BOX 100
POCATELLO, IDAHO 83204
Telephone: 208-233-0845
Facsimile: 208-233-1304
Email: info@hteh.com
URL: http://www.hawleytroxell.com

Boise, Idaho Office: Suite 1000, 877 Main Street. Telephone: 208-344-6000. Facsimile: 208-342-3829.
Ketchum, Idaho Office: 540 Second Avenue North, P.O. Box 297. Telephone: 208-726-1700. Facsimile: 208-726-9743.
Reno, Nevada Office: 6490 S. McCarran, Suite 4. Telephone: 775-829-9944. Facsimile: 775-829-2627.

(This Listing Continued)

General Civil Trial and Appellate Practice before all State and Federal Courts and Administrative Agencies. Alternative Dispute Resolution, Antitrust, Aviation, Banking, Bankruptcy and Creditor Rights, Communications, Construction, Copyright, Corporate, Education, Employee Benefits, Environmental, ERISA, Trusts and Estates, Finance, Health Care and Hospital, Insurance, Intellectual Property, Labor and Employment, Legislative, Media, Mergers and Acquisitions, Mining, Natural Resources, Probate, Products Liability, Public Contract, Public Finance, Public Utility, Qualified and Nonqualified Deferred Compensation, Real Estate, Securities, Taxation, Technology and Science, Trademark and Workers' Compensation Law.

FIRM PROFILE: Hawley Troxell Ennis & Hawley LLP, one of Idaho's largest law firms with three offices in Idaho and one in Nevada, provides legal services to a base of regional and national clients.

MEMBER OF FIRM

HOWARD D. BURNETT, born Pocatello, Idaho, March 18, 1950; admitted to bar, 1977, New York; 1985, Idaho. *Education:* Harvard College (B.A., cum laude, 1972); Oxford University, Trinity College (B.Phil., 1974); University of Pennsylvania (J.D., 1977). ***PRACTICE AREAS:*** Intellectual Property Law; Business Law; Litigation. ***Email:*** HDB@HTEH.COM

(For Biographical Data on Other Personnel, see Professional Biographies at Boise and Ketchum, Idaho and Reno, Nevada)

JONES, CHARTERED

Established in 1976

203 SOUTH GARFIELD
POCATELLO, IDAHO 83204-0967
Telephone: 208-232-5911
Fax: 208-232-5962
URL: http://www.joneschartered law.com
Mailing Address: P.O. Box 967, Pocatello, ID 83204-0967

Banking Law, Business Law, Civil Trial Practice, Commercial Law, Commercial Litigation, Construction Law, Corporate Law, Creditors Rights, General Practice, Healthcare Law, Labor and Employment Law, Nonprofit and Tax Exempt Organizations, Partnership Law, Pension and Profit Sharing, Real Estate Law, Tax Law, Trusts and Estates, Wills and Probate..

LAMONT JONES, born Malad, Idaho, December 8, 1929; admitted to bar, 1958, Idaho and U.S. District Court, District of Idaho; 1962, U.S. Tax Court; 1987, U.S. Court of Appeals, Ninth Circuit. *Education:* Idaho State College (B.S., 1953); University of Idaho (LL.B., 1958). Recipient, Idaho State Bar Professionalism Award, 1992. Chairman, Idaho Housing Agency Commission, 1984-1994. *Member:* Sixth District (President, 1966) and American Bar Associations; Idaho State Bar (Member, Board of Commissioners, 1967-1970; President, 1969-1970); Association of the Bars of the Northwestern Plains and Mountains (Chancellor, 1969-1970). [Capt., USNR, Retired]. ***PRACTICE AREAS:*** Banking Law; Banking Litigation; Commercial Banking; Secured Lending; Lender Liability; Corporate Law; Closely Held Corporations; Nonprofit Corporations; Corporate Finance; Corporate Litigation; Probate; Real Estate; Commercial Real Estate Finance; Residential Real Estate Finance; Trusts and Estates; Estate Administration; Estate Planning; Estate Litigation; Commercial Law; Secured Transactions; Commercial Litigation. ***Email:*** ldavie@joneschartered.com

JACK H. ROBISON, born Idaho, December 5, 1951; admitted to bar, 1977, Idaho and U.S. District Court, District of Idaho; 1983, U.S. Court of Appeals, Ninth and Tenth Circuits and U.S. Court of Appeals for the Federal Circuit. *Education:* Idaho State University (B.B.A., 1974); University of Idaho (J.D., 1977). *Member:* Sixth Judicial District Bar Association (President, 1984); Idaho State Bar. ***PRACTICE AREAS:*** Litigation; Commercial Law; Construction Law; Hospital Law; Real Estate Law; Employment. ***Email:*** jhrobison@joneschartered.com

THOMAS J. HOLMES, born Plainview, Nebraska, January 3, 1950; admitted to bar, 1977, Iowa and Nebraska; 1979, Idaho and U.S. District Court, District of Idaho; 1985, U.S. Tax Court; 1989, U.S. Court of Appeals, Ninth Circuit. *Education:* Nebraska Wesleyan University (B.S., 1972); University of Nebraska at Lincoln (J.D., 1976). Associate Editor, Nebraska Law Review, 1975-1976. Certified Public Accountant, Nebraska, 1974. Chubbuck City Attorney, 1985—. Founding Organizer and Chairman of the Board of Directors, Citizens Community Bank, 1996-1999; Director, 1999—. *Member:* Sixth District (President, 1990-1991) and American (Member, Sections on Taxation and Real Property, Probate, Trust Law) Bar Associations; Idaho State Bar; Pocatello Estate Planning Council; American Institute of Certified Public Accountants. ***PRACTICE AREAS:*** Business Law; Tax Law; Probate; Municipal Law; Estate and Gift Taxation. ***Email:*** tholmes@joneschartered.com

REPRESENTATIVE CLIENTS: Wells Fargo Bank; Ireland Bank; Idaho State University; Idaho Power Co.; Alliance Title and Escrow Corp.; City of Chubbuck; I.H.C. Hospitals, Inc.; Pocatello Board of Realtors; Old Republic National Title Insurance Company.
REFERENCES: Wells Fargo Bank; Ireland Bank; Citizens Community Bank.

MAGUIRE & KRESS, P.C.

Established in 1951

1414 E. CENTER
P.O. BOX 4758
POCATELLO, IDAHO 83205-4758
Telephone: 208-232-5167
Fax: 208-232-5181;
URL: http://www.maguire-kress.com
URL: http://www.maguirekress.com

Business and Commercial Litigation, Personal Injury Claims, Product Liability Claims, Business and Corporation Matters, Insurance Defense, Insurance Coverage Disputes, Construction Claims, Environmental Law, Agricultural Claims, Domestic Relations, Criminal Law, Probate.

(This Listing Continued)

FIRM PROFILE: Since the firm was founded, Maguire & Kress, P.C. is dedicated to serve the people of southeastern Idaho. Based in Pocatello, the firm extends service to all adjacent counties. The practice specializes in the areas of business and commercial litigation and personal injury. The firm is committed to provide quality, cost-effective representation reflecting the highest diligence and integrity.

DAVID H. MAGUIRE, born Pocatello, Idaho, June 11, 1951; admitted to bar, 1977, Idaho; U.S. District Court, District of Idaho; U.S. Court of Appeals, Ninth Circuit. *Education:* University of Idaho (B.A., 1973; J.D., 1977). *Member:* International Association of Defense Counsel; Sixth Judicial District (President, 1986-1987) and American (Member, Litigation Section) Bar Associations; Idaho State Bar (Member, Professional Conduct Board, 1992-1998); Shoshone-Bannock Tribal Bar Association; Idaho Association of Defense Counsel (President, 1986-1987); Idaho Law Foundation (Member, Legal Education Committee, 1985-1986). ***REPORTED CASES:*** North Pacific v. Mai 939 P.2d 570 (1997); Van Velson Corp. v. Westwood Mall, 126 Idaho 401, 884 P.2d 414 (1994); Fairway Development Co. v. Petersen, Moss, Olsen, Meacham and Carr, 124 Idaho 866, 865 P.2d 957 (1993); Jarman v. Hale, 122 Idaho 952, 842 P.2d 288 (1992); Hansen v. White and Bear Lake County, 114 Idaho 907, 762 P.2d 820; Hansen v. White and Bear Lake County, 947 F.2d 1378 (9th Cir, 1991); Universal Underwriters Insurance Co. v. Farmers Insurance Co., 108 Idaho 249, 697 P.2d 1263; Chancellor v. American Hardware Mutual Insurance Co., 107 Idaho 953, 694 P.2d 1301; Wilkins v. Fireman's Fund Insurance American Life Insurance Co., 107 Idaho 1006, 695 P.2d 391; Unigard v. United States Fidelity & Guaranty Co., 111 Idaho 891, 728 P.2d 780; Miller v. United States Fidelity & Guaranty Co., 112 Idaho 955, 738 P.2d 425; Conda Partnership v. M.D. Construction, 115 Idaho 902, 771 P.2d 920; State v. Owsley, 105 Idaho 836, 673 P.2d 436 (1983); Maguire, Ward, Maguire & Eldredge v. Idaho Insurance Guaranty Association, 112 Idaho 166, 730 P.2d 1086 (1986); Bullock v. CIT Co. Federal Credit Union, 106 Idaho 767, 683 P.2d 415 (1984); Taylor v. Choules, 102 Idaho 220, 628 P.2d 1056 (1981); Roberts v. Hollandsworth, 101 Idaho 522, 616 P.2d 1058 (1980). ***PRACTICE AREAS:*** Business and Commercial Litigation; Environmental Law; Insurance Defense; Insurance Coverage Disputes. ***Email:*** maguire@maguire-kress.com

DAVID R. KRESS, born Soda Springs, Idaho, December 30, 1967; admitted to bar, 1994, Idaho and U.S. District Court, District of Idaho. *Education:* Idaho State University (B.S., Political Science, 1991) Pi Sigma Alpha; University of Idaho (J.D., 1994). Executive Lt. Governor, American Bar Association Law Student Division, 1993-1994. Member, Board of Student Advocates, 1993-1994. Program Director/Vice President, Portneuf Inns of Court (2002-2004). *Member:* Sixth District Bar Association (President, 2004-2005); American Bar Association; Idaho State Bar. ***REPORTED CASES:*** Emery v. United Pacific Insurance Company, 120 Idaho 244, 815 P.2d 442 (1991). ***PRACTICE AREAS:*** Trial Practice; Criminal Law; Family Law; Personal Injury; Accidents. ***Email:*** kress@maguire-kress.com

---

DAVID K. PENROD, born Salt Lake City, Utah, June 3, 1973; admitted to bar, 2003, Idaho. *Education:* Idaho State University (B.S., Political Science, 1999); University of Idaho (J.D., 2002). *Member:* Idaho State Bar. ***PRACTICE AREAS:*** Domestic Relations; Criminal; Civil Litigation; Business; Construction. ***Email:*** penrod@maguire-kress.com

REPRESENTATIVE CLIENTS: Hartford Mutual Insurance Co.; Transport Indemnity Co.; Aetna Insurance Co.; Transamerica Insurance Group; American Hardware Mutual Insurance Co.; The Hartford Commercial Union Assurance Cos.; Guaranty National Insurance Co.; Oregon Automotive Insurance Co.; Western Surety Insurance Co.; State Farm Mutual Insurance; Foremost Insurance; Globe Life Assurance Corp.; Diversified Insurance Services, Inc.; MSI Insurance Co.; Idaho Transport, Inc.; DÆ Electric; City of Pocatello; Idaho Wireless Corp.; Mountain Tile Corp.; Allianz Life Insurance Co. of N.A.; West American Insurance Co.; Commercial General Union Group, North Pacific Insurance Co.; Hawkeye; Scottsdale Insurance; Ireland Bank; ReMax Realty, Pocatello; St. Paul Insurance Co.; Steele & Associates; Liberty Northwest Insurance Group; One Beacon Insurance Group.
REFERENCE: Ireland Bank, Pocatello, ID.

MERRILL & MERRILL

CHARTERED

Established in 1913

KEY BANK BUILDING
P.O. BOX 991
POCATELLO, IDAHO 83204
Telephone: 208-232-2286
Fax: 208-232-2499
Email: mmlaw@merrillandmerrill.com

REVISER OF THE IDAHO LAW DIGEST FOR THIS DIRECTORY.

General Civil Practice. Trials and Appeals in all State and Federal Courts. Probate, Real Estate, Insurance Law, Negligence, Corporate, Estate Planning, Education Law, Taxation, Hospital Law, Workers Compensation and Public Utility Law.

FIRM PROFILE: Merrill & Merrill was originally founded by A.L. Merrill, Harvard Law School (1912), in Pocatello, Idaho in 1913. He was joined by a brother, R.D. Merrill, Harvard Law School (1923), and later by a son, Wesley F. Merrill, Harvard Law School (1948). The firm now has nine attorneys and serves clients throughout the State of Idaho in general practice.

Clients consist of a wide variety of insurance companies, major utility, medical and health care organizations, banking interests, locally oriented professional practices, business entities, and interests in water and water resources, farming, etc. All shareholders and associates participate in continuing legal education seminars, frequently as lecturers, professional association activities and civic affairs and are members of the American Bar Association, Idaho Bar Association and the local Sixth District Bar.

A. L. MERRILL (1886-1961)
R. D. MERRILL (1893-1972)
WESLEY F. MERRILL (Retired)

(This Listing Continued)

DAVE R. GALLAFENT, born Pocatello, Idaho, January 27, 1948; admitted to bar, 1975, Idaho. *Education:* Brigham Young University (B.S., cum laude, 1972); George Washington University (J.D., with honors, 1975). Beta Gamma Sigma. *Member:* Sixth Judicial District (President, 1986-1987) and American Bar Associations; Idaho State Bar. ***PRACTICE AREAS:*** Civil Litigation; Banking Law; Real Estate; Probate; Business Law; School Law. ***Email:*** davegallafent@merrillandmerrill.com

STEPHEN S. DUNN, born Twin Falls, Idaho, March 15, 1950; admitted to bar, 1977, Idaho. *Education:* Brigham Young University (B.S., 1972; J.D., magna cum laude, 1977). Member, Brigham Young University Law Review, 1975-1977. Former part-time U.S. Magistrate Judge, 1990-1992. *Member:* Sixth Judicial District and American Bar Associations; Idaho State Bar; Idaho Association of Defense Counsel. ***REPORTED CASES:*** Kunz vs. UP&L, 792 P2d 926, 913 F2d 599; UP&L vs. IPUC, 730 P2d 930; Permann vs. Nationwide Ins. Co., 697 P2d 1206; Schiess vs. Bates, 693 P2d 440. ***PRACTICE AREAS:*** Civil Litigation; Civil Appeals; Public Utility Law; Insurance Law; Products Liability; Workers' Compensation. ***Email:*** steve@merrillandmerrill.com

DAVID C. NYE, born Lynwood, California, October 10, 1958; admitted to bar, 1986, Utah; 1987, Idaho. *Education:* University of Utah; Brigham Young University (B.A., 1982; J.D., 1986). Member, Brigham Young University Journal of Legal Studies, 1985-1986. *Member:* Sixth District and American Bar Associations; Utah State Bar; Idaho State Bar (Member, Committee on Client Security Funds, 1994-1996; Member, Board of Professional Conduct, 1998—); Idaho Association of Defense Counsel. ***REPORTED CASES:*** Krueger v. Bd. of Medicine, 836 P.2d 523; Karlson v. Harris, 2004 WL 1469777 (ID 2004). ***PRACTICE AREAS:*** Civil Litigation; Civil Appeals; Insurance Defense; Products Liability. ***Email:*** dnye@merrillandmerrill.com

KENT L. HAWKINS, born Cody, Wyoming, August 29, 1959; admitted to bar, 1987, Utah; 1988, Idaho; 1995, U.S. Court of Federal Claims. *Education:* Brigham Young University (B.A., 1984; J.D., 1987). Editor, BYU Journal of Public Law, 1986-1987. *Member:* Sixth District and American Bar Associations; Utah State Bar; Idaho State Bar; Idaho Association of Defense Counsel (Member, 6th District Bench Bar Committee). ***PRACTICE AREAS:*** Civil Litigation; Insurance Defense; Insurance Coverage Defense; Insurance Bad Faith Defense. ***Email:*** KLH@merrillandmerrill.com

THOMAS W. CLARK, born Pocatello, Idaho, August 13, 1956; admitted to bar, 1983, Idaho and U.S. District Court, District of Idaho; 1985, U.S. Tax Court; 1995, U.S. Court of Appeals, Ninth Circuit. *Education:* Idaho State University; Brigham Young University (B.S., 1980); University of Idaho (J.D., 1982). Beta Gamma Sigma. Who's Who in Practicing Attorneys, 1990. Outstanding Young Men of America, 1985. Who's Who in American Law, 1998. Public Defender, 1989-1995. *Member:* Sixth Judicial District (President, 1996-1997) and American (Worker's Compensation Section) Bar Associations; Idaho State Bar; Idaho Trial Lawyers Association; National Organization of Social Security Claimants (Representative); Portneuf Inn of Court (President, 2000-2001). ***REPORTED CASES:*** Hofmeister v. Bauer, 719 P.2d 1220 (Ct. App. 1986). ***PRACTICE AREAS:*** Social Security Disability; Bankruptcy; Criminal Defense; Workers Compensation; Collections; Personal Injury. ***Email:*** tomclark@merrillandmerrill.com

THOMAS J. LYONS, born Fontana, California, December 9, 1967; admitted to bar, 1995, Idaho. *Education:* Brigham Young University (J.D., 1995). *Member:* Idaho State Bar; American Bar Association. ***LANGUAGES:*** French. ***PRACTICE AREAS:*** Civil Litigation; Real Estate; Insurance Defense; Collections; Family Law. ***Email:*** toml@merrillandmerrill.com

BRENDON C. TAYLOR, born Pocatello, Idaho, August 23, 1971; admitted to bar, 1999, Idaho; 2000, U.S. District Court, District of Idaho. *Education:* Idaho State University (B.S., 1995); Washburn University School of Law (J.D., with honors, 1999). President, J. Reuben Clark Law Society, Washburn University, 1998. Author: "Kansas Denies Religion-Based Defense to Rastafarians," Washburn L.J., Vol. 38, No. 1 (1998). ***PRACTICE AREAS:*** Civil Litigation; Family Law; Criminal Law; Estate Planning; Administrative; Insurance Defense. ***Email:*** bt@merrillandmerrill.com

KENT A. HIGGINS, born Pocatello, Idaho, August 26, 1952; admitted to bar, 1982, Utah; 1983, Idaho, U.S. District Court, District of Utah and U.S. District Court, District of Idaho; 1991, U.S. Court of Federal Claims and U.S. Tax Court. *Education:* Brigham Young University (B.A., 1979; J.D., 1982). Member: Idaho State Legislature, House of Representatives, 2001-2003; Porteneuf Inns of Court; Brigham Young University Journal of Legal Studies, 1981-1982. Author: "Chapter 3, Incorporation," Summary of Utah Corporate Law, Brigham Young University Journal of Legal Studies, 1982. *Member:* Utah State Bar; Idaho State Bar; American Bar Association (Member, Sections on: Corporation, Banking and Business Law; Taxation); The Association of Trial Lawyers of America. ***LANGUAGES:*** Japanese. ***PRACTICE AREAS:*** Business Law; Taxation; Estate Planning; Probate; Civil Litigation; Commercial Litigation. ***Email:*** khiggins@merrillandmerrill.com

C. EDWARD CATHER, III, born Winchester, Virginia, March 21, 1968; admitted to bar, 1999, Virginia; 2001, Idaho. *Education:* Brigham Young University (B.S.,1994; M. Acc.,1994); University of Virgnia (J.D., 1999). Certified Public Accountant, Idaho. *Member:* Virginia State Bar; Idaho State Bar. ***PRACTICE AREAS:*** Business Law; Taxation; Estate Planning; Civil Litigation. ***Email:*** ecather@merrillandmerrill.com

COUNSEL FOR: Aetna Life and Casualty Co.; Hartford Insurance Group; The Travelers Insurance Co.; MSI Insurance; Equitable Life Assurance Society of the United States; New York Life Insurance Co.; Phillips Petroleum Co.; Utah Power & Light Co. (PacifiCorp); Farm Bureau Mutual Insurance Co. of Idaho; Royal Globe Insurance Cos.; Nationwide Insurance; St. Paul Insurance Cos.; Ranger Insurance Co.; National Fire & Marine Insurance Co.; School District 25, Bannock County, Idaho; Advantage Plus Federal Credit Union; United States Aviation Underwriters; Farmers Alliance Mutual Insurance Co.; Allstate Insurance Co.; National Indemnity Insurance Co.; Shand, Morihan & Co.; Portneuf Medical Center; First American Title Insurance Co.; Allied Van Lines; Western States Equipment Co.; Omaha Property & Casualty; Attorneys Liability and Protection Society, Inc.; Podiatry Insurance Company of America; Transamerica; Colonial Insurance Company of California; Chrysler Corp.; Fibreboard Corporation; Owens-Illinois, Inc.; Pittsburgh Corning Corporation; Keene Corp.; Electric Mutual; J.I. Case Co.; City of Inkom; Allstate Insurance Co.; Lanview Fertilizer Company.
REFERENCES: Key Bank of Idaho; U.S. Bank, Idaho.

REVISER OF THE IDAHO LAW DIGEST FOR THIS DIRECTORY.

MOFFATT THOMAS BARRETT ROCK & FIELDS

CHARTERED
412 WEST CENTER, SUITE 2000
P.O. BOX 817
POCATELLO, IDAHO 83204-0817
Telephone: 208-233-2001
Fax: 208-232-0150
URL: http://www.moffatt.com

Boise, Idaho Office: 101 South Capitol Boulevard, 10th Floor, P.O. Box 829, 83701. Telephone: 208-345-2000. Fax: 208-385-5384.

Idaho Falls, Idaho Office: 420 Memorial Drive, P.O. Box 51505, 83405. Telephone: 208-522-6700. Fax: 208-522-5111.

Twin Falls, Idaho Office: 621 N. College Road, Suite 103, P.O. Box 5483, 83303-5483. Telephone 208-734-7500. Fax: 208-734-7508.

General Civil, Trial and Appellate Practice. Administrative Law, Alternative Dispute Resolution, Antitrust and Trade Regulation, Aviation, Bankruptcy, Banks and Banking, Business Law, Commercial Real Estate, Construction Law, Contracts, Corporate Law, Debtor and Creditor, Disabilities, Employee Benefits, Environmental Law, Finance, Government Relations, Health Care, Hospital Law, Insurance Defense, Intellectual Property, Labor and Employment Law, Leases and Leasing, Litigation, Medical Malpractice, Mergers, Acquisitions and Divestitures, Mortgages, Nonprofit and Charitable Organizations, Partnership Law, Probate, Products Liability, Professional Liability, Public Utility Law, Real Estate, Regulatory Law, Securities, Taxation, Torts, Trusts and Estates, Water Law, Worker's Compensation.

GARY T. DANCE, born Pocatello, Idaho, April 21, 1946; admitted to bar, 1973, Idaho; 1977, U.S. Court of Appeals, Ninth Circuit. *Education:* Boise State College (B.A., 1970); Willamette University (J.D., 1973); Idaho State University (M.S. Hazardous Waste Management, 1994). ***PRACTICE AREAS:*** Insurance Defense Law; Medical Malpractice; Environmental Law; Hazardous Waste Law. ***Email:*** gtd@moffatt.com

D. JAMES MANNING, JR., born Cordova, Alaska, March 30, 1942; admitted to bar, 1967, Idaho. *Education:* University of Idaho (J.D., 1967); University of Denver (LL.M. in Taxation, 1981). ***PRACTICE AREAS:*** Taxation Law; Estate Planning Law; Bankruptcy Law; Creditors Rights Law. ***Email:*** djm@moffatt.com

DAVID P. GARDNER, born Seattle, Washington, October 25, 1967; admitted to bar, 1996, Idaho. *Education:* Brigham Young University (B.S., 1992); Seattle University School of Law (J.D., 1995). ***PRACTICE AREAS:*** Litigation; Insurance Defense; Employment Law; Medical Malpractice Defense; Personal Injury. ***Email:*** dpg@moffatt.com

JULIAN E. GABIOLA, born July 25, 1971; admitted to bar, 1996, Idaho. *Education:* University of Idaho (B.A., summa cum laude, 1993; J.D., 1996). ***PRACTICE AREAS:*** Personal Injury; Medical Malpractice; Bad Faith Insurance Defense; Employment Law; Litigation. ***Email:*** jeg@moffatt.com

(For complete biographical data on other personnel, see Professional Biographies at Boise, Idaho Falls and Twin Falls, Idaho)

NICK L. NIELSON

120 NORTH 12TH AVENUE, SUITE 2
P.O. BOX 6159
POCATELLO, IDAHO 83201
Telephone: 208-232-1735
Fax: 208-232-0048
Email: nielson1199@aol.com
URL: http://www.nicknielsonlaw.com

Insurance Bad Faith, Products Liability, Personal Injury, Automobile Accidents, Business, Employment, Sexual Harassment, Wrongful Termination, Discrimination, Contracts, Family Law, Divorce, Child Custody, Child Support, Adoption, Wills and Probate.

NICK L. NIELSON, born Idaho Falls, Idaho, September 10, 1958; admitted to bar, 1988, Idaho and U.S. District Court, District of Idaho; 1990, Montana; 1992, Shoshone-Bannock Tribal Court. *Education:* Brigham Young University (B.A., 1983; M.P.A., 1987); J. Rueben Clark Law School, Brigham Young University (J.D., 1987). Member, Moot Court. Law Clerk, Judge William Hart, Fifth Judicial District, Minidoka, 1987-1988. *Member:* Idaho State Bar; State Bar of Montana. ***LANGUAGES:*** Thai.

RACINE OLSON NYE BUDGE & BAILEY

CHARTERED
Established in 1940
201 EAST CENTER
P.O. BOX 1391
POCATELLO, IDAHO 83201-1391
Telephone: 208-232-6101
Fax: 208-232-6109
Email: racine@racinelaw.net
URL: http://www.racineolson.com

Boise, Idaho Office: 101 South Capitol Boulevard, U.S. Bank Plaza, Suite 208, 83702. Telephone: 208-395-0011. Fax: 208-433-0167.

Idaho Falls, Idaho Office: 477 Shoup Avenue, Suite 203A, 83402. Telephone: 208-528-6101. Fax: 208-528-6109.

Litigation, Probate, Real Estate, Corporation, Insurance, Banking, Commercial and Utility Law. Creditor's Rights and Creditor's Bankruptcy.

FIRM PROFILE: Founded in 1940, our firm enjoys an excellent reputation throughout the state. Our attorneys focus on areas of emphasis and provide prompt, efficient resolution of client needs.

LOUIS F. RACINE, JR., born Pocatello, Idaho, December 25, 1917; admitted to bar, 1940, Idaho; 1960, U.S. Supreme Court. *Education:* University of Idaho (B.A., 1938; J.D., 1940). Phi Alpha Delta; Delta Sigma Rho. Prosecuting Attorney, Elmore County, Idaho, 1941-1942. Assistant General Counsel for Idaho of Union Pacific R.R., 1946-1948. President, Southeastern Idaho Bar Association, 1946-1948. *Member:* Idaho State Bar (Member, Board of Bar Examiners, 1949-1952; Board of Commissioners, 1952-1955; President, 1954-1955); American Bar Association; American Board of Trial Advocates (Advocate). Fellow: International Academy of Trial Lawyers; American College of Trial Lawyers. ***Email:*** racine@racinelaw.net

WILLIAM D. OLSON, born Mullan, Idaho, April 7, 1933; admitted to bar, 1959, Idaho; 1976, U.S. Court of Appeals, 9th Circuit; 1982, U.S. Court of Appeals, 10th Circuit. *Education:* Idaho State College (B.A., 1956); Washington University (J.D., 1959). Member, Board of Editors, Washington University Law Quarterly, 1958-1959. *Member:* Sixth Judicial District Bar Association (President, 1969-1970); Idaho State Bar (Member: The Examining Committee, 1969-1973; Character and Fitness Committee). Civil Justice Reform Act Committee. ***PRACTICE AREAS:*** Insurance Defense; Products Liability; Personal Injury; Commercial Litigation. ***Email:*** racine@racinelaw.net

W. MARCUS W. NYE, born New York, N.Y., August 3, 1945; admitted to bar, 1974, Idaho. *Education:* Harvard University (A.B., 1967); University of Idaho (J.D., 1974). Member, Board of Editors, Idaho Law Review, 1973-1974. Adjunct Professor, Design Engineering, Idaho State University College of Engineering. Lecturer, Products Liability, University of Idaho, College of Law, 1983-1984. President, Idaho State Insurance Defense Counsel, 1982-1983. *Member:* Sixth Judicial District (President, 1982-1983) and American (Board of Governors, 1997-2000) Bar Associations; Idaho State Bar (President, 1987-1988); American Board of Trial Advocates (Nat'l Board, 2000—); American Bar Foundation (Past State Chairman). Fellow, American College of Trial Lawyers. ***PRACTICE AREAS:*** Commercial Litigation. ***Email:*** nye@racinelaw.net

RANDALL C. BUDGE, born Logan, Utah, May 29, 1951; admitted to bar, 1976, Idaho. *Education:* Utah State University (B.S., 1973); University of Idaho (J.D., 1976). *Member:* Idaho State Bar; Pocatello Estate Planning Council. ***PRACTICE AREAS:*** Business Law; Estate Planning; Probate; Real Estate; Water Law. ***Email:*** rcb@racinelaw.net

JOHN A. BAILEY, JR., born Pocatello, Idaho, January 27, 1954; admitted to bar, 1980, Idaho; 1982, U.S. Court of Appeals, 9th Circuit. *Education:* Idaho State University (B.S., 1977); University of Idaho (J.D., 1980). Phi Kappa Phi; Omicron Delta Epsilon. *Member:* Idaho State Bar (Commissioner, 1997—); American Bar Association. Member, Sixth District Bench Bar Liaison Committee (President, 6th District Bar Association, 1991). ***PRACTICE AREAS:*** Personal Injury; Commercial Litigation; Construction Law; Agricultural Law. ***Email:*** jab@racinelaw.net

JOHN R. GOODELL, born Lansing, Michigan, October 5, 1956; admitted to bar, 1981, Illinois; 1982, Idaho; 1985, U.S. Court of Appeals, 9th Circuit; 1991, Wyoming. *Education:* Georgetown University (B.A., 1977); Southern Illinois University (J.D., 1981). *Member:* Idaho State Bar; Wyoming State Bar; Illinois State and American Bar Associations. ***PRACTICE AREAS:*** Insurance; Business Law; Real Estate; Construction Litigation. ***Email:*** jrg@racinelaw.net

JOHN B. INGELSTROM, born Pocatello, Idaho, November 3, 1953; admitted to bar, 1980, Idaho and U.S. District Court, District of Idaho; 1981, U.S. Court of Appeals, 9th Circuit; 1985, U.S. Court of Federal Claims. *Education:* Idaho State University (B.S., 1977); University of Idaho (J.D., 1980). Law Clerk, Honorable J. Blaine Anderson, U.S. Court of Appeals, Ninth Circuit, 1980-1982. President, Student Bar Association, University of Idaho, 1979-1980. *Member:* Sixth Judicial District Bar Association; Idaho State Bar. ***PRACTICE AREAS:*** Personal Injury; Litigation. ***Email:*** jbi@racinelaw.net

DANIEL C. GREEN, born Ogden, Utah, August 8, 1955; admitted to bar, 1984, Idaho and U.S. District Court, District of Idaho; 1994, U.S. Court of Appeals, Ninth Circuit. *Education:* Weber State College (B.A., magna cum laude, 1980); Brigham Young University (J.D., cum laude, with honors, 1984). Phi Kappa Phi; Phi Delta Phi. Member, Moot Court Board of Advocates, 1983-1984. Author: "Effect of Bankruptcy on Pending State Court Litigation," U.S. Federal Court, 2002; "Revised Article 9 and Bankruptcy, Idaho Law Foundation, 1999; "Continuing Trends in the Trustee's Exercise of Avoiding Powers," Idaho Law Foundation, 1996; "Anatomy of a Small Business Reorganization," Idaho Law Foundation, 1994; "Professionals Eligibility and Fees," NBI, Inc., Eau Claire, WI, 1992; "The Trustee," NBI, Inc., Eau Claire, WI, 1992; "Bankruptcy - Effects on Secured Claims," NBI, Inc., Eau Claire, WI, 1991; "The Legal Issues of Problem Collections in Idaho," NBI, Inc.; Eau Claire, WI, 1990. Co-Author: "Successful Creditors' Strategies in Bankruptcy in Idaho," NBI, Inc., Eau Claire, WI, 1990. Lecturer and Author, bankruptcy related topics: Idaho State Bar; Idaho Law Foundation; Federal District Court; National Business Institute; Idaho State University; University of Idaho. Member, Local Bankruptcy Rules Advisory Committee, District of Idaho. *Member:* Sixth District (Chairman, Bankruptcy Section) and American Bar Associations; Idaho State Bar (Chairman, Commercial Law and Bankruptcy Sections); American Bankruptcy Institute (Member, Legislative, Bankruptcy Rules and Research and Education Committees). Certified in Business Bankruptcy and Creditor's Rights Law by the American Board of Bankruptcy Certification. ***LANGUAGES:*** Japanese. ***PRACTICE AREAS:*** Business Litigation; Commercial Litigation; Banking Law; Bankruptcy Law; Commercial Law; Corporate Law; Creditors Rights. ***Email:*** dcg@racinelaw.net

BRENT O. ROCHE, born Pocatello, Idaho, January 31, 1955; admitted to bar, 1980, Idaho and U.S. District Court, District of Idaho. *Education:* Idaho State University (B.A., with high honors, 1977); University of Washington (J.D., 1980). *Member:* Sixth Judicial District Bar Association; Idaho State Bar; Idaho Trial Lawyers Association; The Association of Trial Lawyers of America. ***PRACTICE AREAS:*** Personal Injury Litigation; Products Liability; Commercial Litigation. ***Email:*** bor@racinelaw.net

KIRK B. HADLEY, born Pocatello, Idaho, January 17, 1960; admitted to bar, 1988, Idaho and U.S. District Court, District of Idaho. *Education:* University of Idaho (B.S., 1982); University of Idaho (J.D., 1985). Delta Theta Phi (Founder and Dean, Idaho Chapter). *Member:* Idaho State Bar (Member, Probate and Trust Sections); American Bar Asso-

(This Listing Continued)

ciation; National Academy of Elder Law Attorneys. ***PRACTICE AREAS:*** Estate Planning; Probate; Elder Law; Business Transactions; Real Estate. ***Email:*** kbh@racinelaw.net

FRED J. LEWIS, born Salt Lake City, Utah, April 1, 1959; admitted to bar, 1988, Idaho and U.S. District Court, District of Idaho. *Education:* University of Utah (B.S., 1985); University of Idaho (J.D., 1988). Member: Board of Student Advocates, 1987-1988; American Bar Association Moot Court Team, 1988. Lead Articles Editor, Idaho Law Review, 1987-1988. Author: "Survey of Idaho Criminal Law and Procedure," Idaho Law Review, Vol. 23, No. 1, 1986. Co-Author: "Basic Real Estate Law in Idaho," NBI, Inc., Eau Claire, WI, 1992. *Member:* Sixth Judicial District Bar Association; Idaho State Bar (Member, Bankruptcy Section). ***PRACTICE AREAS:*** Bankruptcy Law; Commercial Transactions and Litigation; Worker's Compensation Law. ***Email:*** fjl@racinelaw.net

MITCHELL W. BROWN, born Afton, Wyoming, May 16, 1961; admitted to bar, 1990, Idaho and U.S. District Court, District of Idaho. *Education:* University of Wyoming; Utah State University (B.S., 1986); University of Idaho (J.D., 1990). Delta Theta Phi. *Member:* Idaho State Bar; American Bar Association. ***PRACTICE AREAS:*** Commercial Litigation; Insurance Defense. ***Email:*** mwb@racinelaw.net

ERIC L. OLSEN, born Idaho Falls, Idaho, March 31, 1965; admitted to bar, 1993, Idaho. *Education:* Brigham Young University (B.S., 1990); University of Idaho (J.D., 1993); University of Florida College of Law (LL.M., Taxation, 1997). Managing Editor of Annual Review of Community Property Law, University of Idaho Law Review, 1993-1994. Law Clerk, Hon. B. Lynn Winmill, Idaho Sixth Judicial District Court, 1993-1994. *Member:* Idaho State Bar; American Bar Association. ***PRACTICE AREAS:*** Taxation; Business Planning; Estate Planning; Commercial Litigation. ***Email:*** elo@racinelaw.net

---

CONRAD J. AIKEN, born Greenville, Ohio, November 3, 1944; admitted to bar, 1969, Ohio; 1971, Kentucky; 1975, Colorado; 1977, Idaho. *Education:* Wittenberg University (A.B., 1966); Duke University (J.D., 1969). *Member:* Idaho State Bar. (Resident, Boise Office). ***PRACTICE AREAS:*** Banking Law; Loans; Creditors Rights; Commercial Law. ***Email:*** cja@racinelaw.net

RICHARD A. HEARN, born Birmingham, Alabama, May 25, 1948; admitted to bar, 1993, District of Columbia; 1997, Idaho. *Education:* University of Alabama (B.S., 1970); Georgetown Law Center (J.D., magna cum laude, 1991). Order of the Coif. Licensed, M.D., Alabama, 1976. *Member:* 6th District Bar; The District of Columbia Bar; Idaho State Bar; Idaho Medical Association. ***LANGUAGES:*** German. ***PRACTICE AREAS:*** Health Care; Litigation. ***Email:*** rah@racinelaw.net

DAVID E. ALEXANDER, born Tulsa, Oklahoma, June 28, 1961; admitted to bar, 1991, Missouri; 1992, Idaho. *Education:* Trinity University (B.S., 1983); Washington University (J.D., 1990). Clerk to the Hon. Harold L. Satz, Judge, Missouri Court of Appeals, Eastern District, 1990-1991. *Member:* The Missouri Bar; Idaho State Bar. ***PRACTICE AREAS:*** Trademarks; Copyrights; Litigation. ***Email:*** dea@racinelaw.net

LANE V. ERICKSON, born Idaho Falls, Idaho, April 29, 1970; admitted to bar, 1999, Idaho; 2000, Utah. *Education:* Idaho State University (B.A., Business Management, 1996); University of Idaho (J.D., 1999). Member, Board of Editors, Idaho Law Review, 1998-1999. Edited, "Conducting a Lawful Employment Interview". *Member:* Sixth Judicial District and American Bar Associations; Idaho State Bar. ***PRACTICE AREAS:*** Bankruptcy; Creditor Law; Commercial Litigation. ***Email:*** lve@racinelaw.com

LISA M. CHRISTON, born Buffalo, New York, December 8, 1964; admitted to bar, 1992, Illinois; 1996, Idaho. *Education:* State University of New York at Geneseo (B.A., 1987); Ohio Northern University Law School (J.D., cum laude, 1992). Phi Kappa Phi. Editor in Chief, Ohio Northern University Law Review, 1991-1992. Author, "Confrontation Clause: An Escape Hatch for Defendants in Sexual Abuse Cases?," 17 ONVL Rev 693. Instructor, Lawyering Skills III, John Marshall Law School, 1994-1995. *Member:* Idaho State Bar; Illinois State and American Bar Associations. ***PRACTICE AREAS:*** Insurance Defense; Family Law. ***Email:*** lmc@racinelaw.net

PATRICK N. GEORGE, born Anchorage, Alaska, February 8, 1969; admitted to bar, 1999, Idaho. *Education:* Brigham Young University (B.S., 1996); University of Idaho (J.D., cum laude, 1999). *Member:* Idaho State Bar. ***PRACTICE AREAS:*** Litigation. ***Email:*** png@racinelaw.net

SCOTT J. SMITH, born Fort Belvoir, Virginia, September 17, 1969; admitted to bar, 1999, Idaho. *Education:* Brigham Young University (B.S., 1995); University of Idaho (J.D., 1999). Member, Board of Editors, Idaho Law Review, 1998-1999. Recipient, Editor of the Year Award, Idaho Law Review, 1999. *Member:* Idaho State Bar. ***Email:*** sjs@racinelaw.net

LISA A. WOOD, born Logan, Utah, July 7, 1966; admitted to bar, 2001, Idaho. *Education:* Idaho State University (B.S., 1991); Thomas M. Cooley Law School (J.D., 2000). Delta Theta Phi. Member, American Institute of Certified Public Accountants, 1995. *Member:* Idaho State Bar. ***PRACTICE AREAS:*** Estate Planning; Business Law; Taxation. ***Email:*** law@racinelaw.net

STEPHEN J. MUHONEN, born Boise, Idaho, January 18, 1971; admitted to bar, 2003, Idaho. *Education:* Idaho State University (B.A., 1999); University of Idaho (J.D., 2002). Member, Idaho Law Review. ***Email:*** sjm@racinelaw.net

BRENT L. WHITING, born Driggs, Idaho, January 17, 1971; admitted to bar, 2002, Idaho. *Education:* Idaho State University (B.A., 1997); University of Montana (J.D., 2002). Law Clerk to Hon. Stephen S. Trott, Circuit Judge, U.S. Court of Appeals, Ninth Circuit, 2002-2003. *Member:* Idaho State Bar; American Bar Association. ***PRACTICE AREAS:*** Litigation; Commercial Law; Constitutional Law. ***Email:*** blw@racinelaw.net

LISA R. TANNER, born Bonners Ferry, Idaho, June 29, 1979; admitted to bar, 2003, California; 2004, Idaho. *Education:* Oak Brook College of Law (J.D., cum laude, 2003). Law Clerk to the Hon. Daniel T. Eismann, Justice, Idaho Supreme Court. *Member:* State Bar of California; Idaho State Bar. (Resident, Boise Office). ***PRACTICE AREAS:*** Insurance Defense; Banking Law. ***Email:*** lrt@racinelaw.net

(This Listing Continued)

JUSTIN R. ELLIS, born Idaho Falls, Idaho, March 12, 1979; admitted to bar, 2004, Idaho. *Education:* Idaho State University (B.S., 2001); University of Montana (J.D., with honors, 2004). Publication Editor, Public Land and Resources Law Review, 2003-2004. *Member:* Idaho State Bar. (Resident). ***PRACTICE AREAS:*** Business Law; Commercial Law; Land Use; Real Estate; Taxation; Litigation. ***Email:*** jre@racinelaw.net

JOSHUA D. JOHNSON, born Springfield, Illinois, January 4, 1971; admitted to bar, 1997, Illinois; 2004, Idaho. *Education:* Southern Oregon State College (B.S., 1994); John Marshall Law School (J.D., 1997). *Member:* Idaho State Bar. (Resident, Boise Office). ***PRACTICE AREAS:*** Insurance Defense. ***Email:*** jdj@racinelaw.net

JONATHON BYINGTON, born Logan, Utah, 1977; admitted to bar, 2004, Idaho. *Education:* Utah State University (B.S., 2001); University of Idaho (J.D., summa cum laude, 2004). Member, Idaho Law Review, 2003-2004. Law Clerk to Chief Justice Linda Copple Trout, Idaho Supreme Court, 2004-2005. Author: "How to Make Your Appellate Brief More 'Readable,'" The Advocate, official publication of Idaho State Bar, July, 2005. *Member:* Idaho State Bar. ***PRACTICE AREAS:*** Business Law; Commercial Law; Contract Law; Real Estate; Land Use; Bankruptcy; Creditors Rights. ***Email:*** jsb@racinelaw.net

REPRESENTATIVE CLIENTS: Anheuser-Busch Cos.; Portneuf Medical Center; Boise Radiology Group; Chubb Pacific Indemnity; Colonial Penn Insurance; Commercial Union Cos.; Cuna Mutual Insurance Group; Continental Western; Deere & Co.; Eastern Idaho Agricultural Credit Assn.; Farm Bureau Insurance Company of Idaho; Farmer's Alliance Mutual Insurance Co.; Farmer's Home Mutual Ins. Co.; Farmers Insurance Group of Cos.; Farmer's Professional Liability Group; Forum Insurance Co.; FMC; General Motors Corp.; Great Western Life; Idaho Banking Company; Idaho Groundwater Assn., Inc.; Idaho Irrigation Pumpers Assn.; Ireland Bank; ITT Hartford; Kemper Ins. Group; Last Chance Canal Co.; Lockheed-Martin; Marsh Valley Hydro-Electric Co.; McCammon Ditch Co.; Medical Imaging Association; Monsanto Co.; North Pacific Insurance Co.; Panhandle State Bank; Pioneer Title Co.; Portneuf-Marsh Valley Canal Co.; Reliance Insurance Co.; Solutia, Inc.; State of Idaho (self-insured); Transamerica Insurance Co.; Transport Indemnity Co.; Underwriters Adjusting Co.; Unigard Insurance Group; Uniroyal Goodrich Tire Co.; U.S.A.A.; U.S. Bank; U.S. West; Viking Insurance Co.; Washington Mutual Bank; Washington Trust Bank.
REFERENCES: U.S. Bank; Wells Fargo Bank.

BEARD ST. CLAIR GAFFNEY McNAMARA CALDER PA

REXBURG, IDAHO

(See Idaho Falls)

Agricultural Law, Acquisitions, Americans with Disabilities Act, Antitrust, Arbitration, Asset Protection, Automobile Accidents, Automobile Insurance, Banking Law, Breach of Contract, Business Law, Buying and Selling Businesses, Charitable Giving, Collections, Commercial Insurance, Commercial Law, Commercial Real Estate, Computers and Software, Condominiums, Construction Law, Contested Wills, Contracts, Copyrights, Corporations, Creditors Rights, Crop Damage and Chemical Applications, Debtor and Creditor, Discrimination, Distribution and Distributorships, Divorce with significant assets, Elder Care, Elder Law, Employment Discrimination, Employment Law, Estate Planning, Estate and Gift Taxation, Family Business Law, Family and Medical Leave Act, Farm and Ranch Law, Fire Loss, Food, Drug and Cosmetic Law, Franchises and Franchising, Foreclosures, General Trial and Appellate Practice, Guardianship, Harassment, Health Care, Health Insurance, Income Taxation, Insurance, Insurance Bad Faith, Investments, Landlord and Tenant Law, Leasing, Liens, Life and Health Insurance, Limited Liability Company Law, Litigation, Long-term Care, Mechanics Liens, Mediation, Medical Malpractice and Malpractice Defense, Medicare and Medicaid, Minority Business Law, Mortgages, Multilevel Sales, Nonprofit and Charitable Organizations, Nursing Homes, PACA, Partnerships, Pension and Benefits, Personal Injury, Post Mortem Administration of Trusts and Estates, Products Liabilities, Professional Malpractice, Property Tax, Professional Practices, Property Insurance, Railroad Accidents, Real Estate, Sexual Abuse, Slip and Fall, Small Business Law, Social Security, Social Security Disability, Taxation, Torts, Trademarks, Trade Secrets, Trust and Estates, Valuations, Warranties, Wills and Probate, Workers Compensation, Wrongful Death, Wrongful Termination, Zoning, Planning and Land Use.

RIGBY, THATCHER, ANDRUS, RIGBY & MOELLER

CHARTERED

Established in 1950

25 NORTH SECOND EAST
P.O. BOX 250
REXBURG, IDAHO 83440
Telephone: 208-356-3633
Fax: 208-356-0768
Email: rexlaw@rigby-thatcher.com

General Practice, Trials, Negligence, Personal Injury, Probate, Commercial, Real Estate, Workers Compensation, Corporate, Estate Planning, Utility, Water Rights Law and Appeals.

RAY W. RIGBY, born Rexburg, Idaho, April 16, 1923; admitted to bar, 1950, Idaho. *Education:* University of Idaho (B.A., 1948; LL.B., 1950). Phi Alpha Delta. County Attorney, 1950-1964. State Senator, 1965-1973. *Member:* Seventh Judicial District (President, 1978-1979) and American Bar Associations; Idaho State Bar; Idaho Trial Lawyers Association. ***PRACTICE AREAS:*** Water Law; Rural Electrification Cooperative Law; Estate Planning; Probate; Corporations, Partnerships and Business Entities.

GORDON S. THATCHER, born Rexburg, Idaho, November 15, 1931; admitted to bar, 1958, Idaho; 1962, U.S. Court of Appeals, Ninth Circuit; 1981, U.S. Supreme Court and U.S. Tax Court. *Education:* Ricks College (B.S., salutatorian, 1955); George Washington University (J.D., with honors, 1958). Phi Delta Phi (Graduate of Year, Province II); Order of the Coif. *Member:* Seventh Judicial District (President, 1969-1970) and American Bar Associations; Idaho State Bar; Idaho Trial Lawyers Association (President, 1979-

(This Listing Continued)

RIGBY, THATCHER, ANDRUS, RIGBY & MOELLER, CHARTERED, Rexburg—Continued

1980); National Network of Estate Planning Attorneys. ***PRACTICE AREAS:*** Estate and Tax Planning; Probate and Trust Administration; Elder Law; Trusts and Estates Litigation. ***Email:*** gthatcher@rigby-thatcher.com

G. RICH ANDRUS, born Idaho Falls, Idaho, August 17, 1944; admitted to bar, 1971, Idaho. *Education:* Brigham Young University (B.A., 1968); University of Oregon (J.D., with honors, 1971). Order of the Coif. *Member:* Seventh Judicial District and American Bar Associations; Idaho State Bar; Idaho Trial Lawyers Association; The Association of Trial Lawyers of America. ***LANGUAGES:*** Finnish. ***SPECIAL AGENCIES:*** National Transportation Safety Board; Idaho Department of Water Resources; Idaho Industrial Commission; Social Security Administration; Idaho State Tax Commission. ***PRACTICE AREAS:*** Tort Law; Contract Law; Real Estate-Commercial Law; Workers Compensation; Probate.

JERRY R. RIGBY, born Rexburg, Idaho, October 11, 1951; admitted to bar, 1979, Idaho. *Education:* Brigham Young University (B.A., 1976); J. Rueben Clark Law School, Brigham Young University (J.D., 1979). Member, Idaho Water Resource Board. *Member:* Idaho State Bar Association. ***LANGUAGES:*** Mandarin Chinese. ***PRACTICE AREAS:*** Water Law; Estate Planning; Probate; Rural Electrification Cooperative Law; Corporations, Partnerships and Business Entities. ***Email:*** jrigby@rigby-thatcher.com

MICHAEL S. KAM (1954-2001)

GREGORY W. MOELLER, born Norwalk, California, May 1, 1963; admitted to bar, 1990, Idaho. *Education:* Brigham Young University (B.A., magna cum laude, 1987); J. Rueben Clark Law School, Brigham Young University (J.D., 1990). Phi Kappa Phi. *Member:* Idaho State and American Bar Associations. ***LANGUAGES:*** Japanese. ***PRACTICE AREAS:*** Litigation; Trial Practice; Personal Injury; Criminal Defense; Appeals; Intellectual Property Law; Water Law; Family Law; Estate Planning; Probate; Election Law; Adoption Law. ***Email:*** gmoeller@rigby-thatcher.com

REED E. ANDRUS, born Provo, Utah, 1968; admitted to bar, 1994, Idaho, U.S. District Court, District of Idaho; 1999, U.S. Supreme Court; registered to practice before U.S. Patent and Trademark Office. *Education:* Brigham Young University (B.A., cum laude, 1991; J.D., cum laude, 1994). Recipient: Hugh B. Brown Barristers. Executive Editor, Brigham Young University Journal of Public Law, 1993-1994. ***LANGUAGES:*** Cantonese. ***PRACTICE AREAS:*** Patents; Trademarks; Copyrights; Contracts; Patent Licensing; Trade Secrets; Employment Law; Internet Law.

REPRESENTATIVE CLIENTS: North Fork Reservoir Co.; Fremont-Madison School District No. 322; Fall River, Raft River, Lost River Electric Cooperatives; Madison Cooperative Assn., Inc.; Fremont-Madison Irrigation District; The Committee of Nine of Snake River Water District No. 1; Nedrow Farms, Inc.; Taylor Chevrolet Co.; Walters Ready-Mix, Inc.; Sun-Glo of Idaho, Inc.; Summerco, Inc.; Paul Cherry Farms; Hathaway's, Inc.; Harold L. Harris Construction, Inc.; Porter Office Products; Raybold Bros. Farms; Ashton Memorial Hospital, Inc.; New Technicians, Inc.

THOMSON LAW OFFICES, CHARTERED,

A PROFESSIONAL CORPORATION
115 EAST MAIN STREET
P.O. BOX 609
REXBURG, IDAHO 83440
Telephone: 208-356-9000
Fax: 208-356-9336
Email: thomson@nstep.net

Collections, Foreclosures, Creditor Law, Real Estate, Mortgages, Family Law, Business Law, Criminal Law, Wills, Probate.

DALE P. THOMSON, born Rexburg, Idaho, November 3, 1950; admitted to bar, 1980, Idaho. *Education:* Ricks College (A.A., 1974); Brigham Young University (B.A., summa cum laude, 1977; J.D., 1980). County Prosecuting Attorney, 1986-1994. *Member:* Idaho State Bar; American Bar Association; Idaho Trial Lawyers Association. ***PRACTICE AREAS:*** Bankruptcy; Business Law; Criminal Law; Debtor and Creditor Law; Family Law; General Practice; Real Estate; Wills; Probate. ***Email:*** thomson@nstep.net

RIGBY, THATCHER, ANDRUS, RIGBY & MOELLER

CHARTERED
RIGBY, IDAHO
(See Rexburg)

General Practice, Trials, Negligence, Personal Injury, Probate, Commercial, Real Estate, Workers Compensation, Corporate, Estate Planning, Utility, Water Rights Law and Appeals.

LING, ROBINSON & WALKER

615 H STREET
P.O. BOX 396
RUPERT, IDAHO 83350
Telephone: 208-436-4717
Fax: 208-436-6804

General Civil Trial Practice, Bankruptcy Law, Water Rights, Appellate Practice, Agricultural, Family, Negligence, Real Estate Law, Estate Planning, Probate, Personal Injury and Criminal Law.

MEMBERS OF FIRM

BRENT T. ROBINSON, born Idaho Falls, Idaho, August 10, 1949; admitted to bar, 1976, Idaho; 1988, U.S. Court of Appeals, Ninth Circuit. *Education:* Brigham Young University (B.A., Econ., 1973); University of Idaho (J.D., 1976). Phi Alpha Delta. Member, Idaho Law Review, 1975-1976. *Member:* Idaho State Bar; Idaho Trial Lawyers Association. ***PRACTICE AREAS:*** Bankruptcy Law; Estate Planning Law; Probate Law; Trial Practice. ***Email:*** btr@idlawfirm.com

JASON DAVID WALKER, born Burley, Idaho, April 8, 1967; admitted to bar, 1998, Idaho. *Education:* Brigham Young University (B.S., Sports Medicine, 1995); University of Idaho (J.D., 1998). Law Clerk to Judge J. William Hart, Fifth Judicial District, Minidoka County, 1998-1999. Minidoka County Prosecuting Attorney, 2003—. *Member:* Fifth Judicial District Bar Association; Idaho State Bar (Member, Water Law Section); American Bar Association (Member, Environment and Natural Resources Sections). ***PRACTICE AREAS:*** Litigation; Education Law; Personal Injury; Water Law; Business Law; Criminal Law; Local Government Law; Municipal Law. ***Email:*** jdw@idlawfirm.com

ASSOCIATE

KELLY ARTHUR ANTHON, born Burley, Idaho, August 4, 1974; admitted to bar, 2002, Idaho. *Education:* Brigham Young University (B.A., 1998); University of Idaho (J.D., 2002). Bistline Scholar, 2002. Recipient, IOLTA Scholarship, 2002. President, Student Bar Association, 2001-2002. Member, University of Idaho Media Board, 2000-2001. Member, LSADR, 2001-2002. City Attorney, cities of Rupert, Acequia and Minidoka, 2003—. ***LANGUAGES:*** Japanese. ***PRACTICE AREAS:*** Bankruptcy; Family Law; Personal Injury; Estate Planning; Criminal Defense; Real Property; Probate; Municipal Law. ***Email:*** kaa@idlawfirm.com

OF COUNSEL

ROGER D. LING, born Rupert, Idaho, November 5, 1933; admitted to bar, 1964, Idaho; 1969, U.S. Tax Court; 1978, U.S. Court of Appeals, Ninth Circuit; 1984, U.S. Supreme Court. *Education:* Idaho State University (B.S., 1963); Willamette University (LL.B., 1964). Phi Delta Phi. Life Member, National Water Resources Association. *Member:* Fifth Judicial District Bar Association (Secretary, 1970-1971); American Bar Association; Idaho State Bar; Idaho Trial Lawyers Association. ***PRACTICE AREAS:*** Real Estate; Water Law; Probate; Estate Planning; Trial Practice. ***Email:*** rdl@idlawfirm.com

REPRESENTATIVE CLIENTS: A & B Irrigation District; Aberdeen-Springfield Canal Company; Burley Irrigation District; Falls Irrigation District; Minidoka County School District 331; Triple C Concrete; Flat Top Sheep Co.; Idaho Water Users Assoc.; BAN, Inc.; Water Dist. 01.
REFERENCES: Wells Fargo Bank Northwest (Rupert Branch); U.S. Bank (Rupert Branch); D.L. Evans Bank (Rupert Branch).

MORRIS AND WOLFF, P.A.

722 MAIN AVENUE
ST. MARIES, IDAHO 83861
Telephone: 208-245-2523
Fax: 208-245-4392

Commercial and Corporate, Real Estate, Natural Resource and Environmental Law, Probate, Civil Litigation, Business Law.

NANCY A. WOLFF, born Portsmouth, Virginia, January 5, 1952; admitted to bar, 1982, Idaho and U.S. District Court, District of Idaho; U.S. Court of Appeals, 9th Circuit and U.S. Supreme Court. *Education:* University of Denver (B.A., 1973); University of Idaho (J.D., 1982). Instructor, University of Idaho, 1984-1988. Deputy Prosecuting Attorney, 1982-1985, Prosecuting Attorney, 1985-1987, Latah County, Idaho. Prosecuting Attorney, Benewah County, Idaho, 1993-1995. City Attorney, St. Maries, Idaho. Member: Idaho Juvenile Justice Commission, 1985-1998; Idaho Board of Juvenile Corrections, 1998—. *Member:* Idaho State Bar. ***LANGUAGES:*** Spanish.

CALLAHAN & ASSOCIATES, CHTD.

SANDPOINT, IDAHO
(See Coeur d' Alene)

Living Trusts, Estate Planning, Probate, Elder Law, Guardianship & Conservatorship, Asset Protection Planning, Wills, Estate & Gift Taxation, Generation Skipping Tax, Trusts, Living Wills, Advanced Directives, Charitable Trusts and Foundations.

ELSAESSER JARZABEK ANDERSON MARKS ELLIOTT & McHUGH

CHARTERED
Established in 1980
LAKE PLAZA BUILDING
THIRD & LAKE STREETS
P.O. BOX 1049
SANDPOINT, IDAHO 83864
Telephone: 208-263-8517
Fax: 208-263-0759

Coeur d'Alene, Idaho Office: 1400 Northwood Center Court, Suite C, 83814. Telephone: 208-667-2900. Facsimile: 208-667-2150.

General Civil Trial Practice in all Courts and Agencies. Bankruptcy, Commercial, Creditor's Rights, Estate Planning, Labor, Personal Injury, Planning and Zoning, Probate, Public Utility, Real Estate, Social Security, Taxation, Workers Compensation Law and Family Law.

FIRM PROFILE: Elsaesser Jarzabek Anderson Marks Elliott & McHugh was founded in Sandpoint in 1980. The firm now provides a full range of legal services throughout Northern Idaho. The firm has a special emphasis in Chapter 11 proceedings throughout the state and the region.

FORD ELSAESSER, born Cleveland, Ohio, October 29, 1951; admitted to bar, 1978, Idaho and U.S. District Court, District of Idaho; 1992, U.S. Court of Appeals, Ninth Circuit;

(This Listing Continued)

1994, U.S. Supreme Court. *Education:* Goddard College (B.S., 1973); University of Idaho (J.D., 1977). Member: Moot Court Team; Order of the Barristers. *Member:* Idaho State Bar (Recipient, Professionalism Award, 1999; Pro Bono Award, 1990; Fee Arbitration Committee, 1982—; Bankruptcy Law Section, 1982—; Chairman, Bankruptcy Law Section, 1988-1989); American Bankruptcy Institute (Member, Executive Committee, 1992-2002; President, 1999-2000; Chair, 2001-2002). Fellow, American College of Bankruptcy, Sixth Class. ***REPORTED CASES:*** U.S. Bancorp Mortgage Co. v. Bonner Mall Partnership, U.S. Supreme Court No. 93-714 (November 1994). ***TRANSACTIONS:*** General Counsel, Coldwater Creek Inc.; Lifestream Technologies, Inc.; Intermountain Community Bancorp; Federal Receiver for Schweitzer Ski Resort/Pack River Ltd. Co, 1996-2001; lead counsel for Creditors Committee and Chapter 11 bankruptcies of Output, Gulf, Sisco Seeds; Creditor Representation in AgriBioTech; Chapter 11 Trustee and Liquidating Agent for Myers Financial Group; counsel for debtors in bankruptcy of Bonner Mall Partnership, Bunker Hill Mining Co. (U.S.), Riley Creek Lumber Co.; Chapter 7 Panel Trustee-Northern Idaho; Chapter 12 Panel Trustee-Northern Idaho and Eastern Washington. ***PRACTICE AREAS:*** Commercial Law; Bankruptcy Law; Real Estate Litigation. ***Email:*** ford@ejame.com

JOSEPH E. JARZABEK, born Phoenix, Arizona, September 22, 1954; admitted to bar, 1980, Idaho and U.S. District Court, District of Idaho. *Education:* Northern Arizona University (B.S., 1976); University of Idaho (J.D., 1980). *Member:* Idaho State Bar; American Bar Association; Idaho Trial Lawyers Association; Washington State Trial Lawyers Association; The Association of Trial Lawyers of America. ***PRACTICE AREAS:*** Workers Compensation Law; Personal Injury Law.

BRUCE A. ANDERSON, born Spokane, Washington, November 8, 1956; admitted to bar, 1985, Idaho and U.S. District Court, District of Idaho; 1986, U.S. Tax Court; 1988, Colorado and U.S. District Court, District of Colorado; 1997, U.S. Court of Appeals, Ninth Circuit. *Education:* Eastern Washington University (B.A., 1980); University of Idaho (J.D., 1985); University of Denver (LL.M., Taxation, 1987). Certified Public Accountant, Idaho, 1980. Senior Trial Attorney, Office of Chief Counsel, Internal Revenue Service, 1986-1994. Private Civil Litigation Evaluator, Idaho, 2002—. *Member:* Idaho State Bar (Member Sections on: Taxation, Corporate, ADR and Bankruptcy Law); Colorado State Bar Association. ***PRACTICE AREAS:*** Taxation; Probate; Bankruptcy; Estate Planning; Civil Litigation; Real Estate; Mediation; Arbitration. ***Email:*** brucea@ejame.com

DOUG B. MARKS, born Provo, Utah, July 19, 1969; admitted to bar, 1997, Idaho; 1998, Washington. *Education:* Brigham Young University (B.S., 1994; J.D., 1997). Order of the Coif. Member and Lead Articles Editor, Brigham Young University Law Review. Author: "The Practical Lawyer," The American Law Institute, Jan., 1999; Article, "Anything You Can Do, I Can Do Better: Why a Debtor Should File Under Chapter 7 Rather Than Chapter 13."; Norton Bankruptcy Advisor, "Ninth Circuit Bankruptcy Review," 1997-2004. Founding Member and Board of Directors, Panhandle Alliance for Education. Scoutmaster and Committee Chairman, Boy Scouts of America, 1998—. *Member:* Idaho State Bar; Washington State Bar Association. ***LANGUAGES:*** French. ***PRACTICE AREAS:*** Commercial Law; Bankruptcy; Real Estate. ***Email:*** dmarks@ejame.com

CINDY ELLIOTT, born Milwaukee, Wisconsin, January 4, 1949; admitted to bar, 1989, Idaho. *Education:* Eastern Montana College (B.S., 1986); Gonzaga University (J.D., 1989). Member, Sandpoint City Council, 1999—. *Member:* First District Bar Association (President, 1994-1995); Idaho State Bar (Health Law Section). ***PRACTICE AREAS:*** Commercial Law; Probate; Real Estate. ***Email:*** cindy@ejame.com

BARRY McHUGH, born Coeur d'Alene, Idaho, March 10, 1958; admitted to bar, 1987, Idaho and U.S. District Court, District of Idaho; 1991, U.S. Court of Appeals, Ninth Circuit. *Education:* Boise State University (B.S., 1980); University of Idaho (J.D., 1985). Certified Public Accountant, Idaho, 1982. Assistant United States Attorney, District of Idaho, 1991-2002. Member, Board of Directors, Cocur d'Alere Rotary Club, 2002—. *Member:* Idaho State Bar (Real Property Section). ***PRACTICE AREAS:*** Civil Litigation; Bankruptcy; Family Law; Personal Injury Law. ***Email:*** bmchugh@ejame.com

---

TAEYA HOWELL, born Spokane, Washington, August 17, 1978; admitted to bar, 2003, Idaho. *Education:* Washington State University (B.A., magna cum laude, 2000); Brigham Young University (J.D., cum laude, 2003). ***LANGUAGES:*** French. ***PRACTICE AREAS:*** Commercial Law. ***Email:*** thowell@ejame.com

JAMES S. MACDONALD, born Dallas, Texas, September 6, 1969; (admission pending). *Education:* Northern Arizona University (B.A., 1993); University of Idaho (J.D., 2005).

LEGAL SUPPORT PERSONNEL

DONNA LaRUE, born Berkeley, California, October 8, 1947. *Education:* University of Arizona, College of Southern Idaho. Certified Legal Assistant. *Member:* National Association of Legal Assistants; Idaho Association of Paralegals (Past Vice President, Membership). ***LANGUAGES:*** Spanish. ***PRACTICE AREAS:*** Bankruptcy Law; Real Estate; Probate; Collections; Criminal Law. ***Email:*** dlarue@ejame.com

LOIS LA POINTE, born Lewiston, Idaho, December 21, 1954. *Education:* San Joaquin Delta College. PACE Registered Paralegal. *Member:* National Federation of Paralegal Associations, Inc. (Member, 2000—); Idaho Association of Paralegals (Member, 2002—); National Association of Legal Secretaries (Past Member). ***PRACTICE AREAS:*** Bankruptcy; Corporate Commercial Law; Real Estate. ***Email:*** lois@ejame.com

---

RAMSDEN & LYONS

SANDPOINT, IDAHO

(See Coeur d'Alene)

General Civil Trial and Appellate Practice. Insurance Defense, Eminent Domain/Condemnation, Arbitration, Mediation, Class Action Defense, Business Formation, Insurance Bad Faith, Land Use, Professional Liability, Product Liability, Negligence, Construction, Real Estate, Environmental, Error and Omission Defense, Governmental Liability, Worker Compensation and Employment Law.

KEVIN J. WAITE, P.C.

SANDPOINT, IDAHO

(See Coeur d'Alene)

Family Law, Divorce, Child Custody, Child Support, Criminal Defense, Driving While Intoxicated, Drug Crimes, Parole and Probation and Civil Litigation.

MERRILL & MERRILL

CHARTERED

SODA SPRINGS, IDAHO

(See Pocatello)

General Civil Practice. Trials and Appeals in all State and Federal Courts. Probate, Real Estate, Insurance Law, Negligence, Corporate, Estate Planning, Education Law, Taxation, Hospital Law, Workers Compensation and Public Utility Law.

HALL, FARLEY, OBERRECHT & BLANTON, P.A.

SUN VALLEY, IDAHO

(See Boise)

Litigation, Insurance Defense, Medical Malpractice and Professional Liability, Employment Law, Labor Relations, Products Liability, Construction, Health and Hospital, Corporation, Commercial, Banking, Real Estate, Legislative Counseling, Bankruptcy, Appellate Law, Administrative Agencies, Agricultural, Municipal, Estate Planning and Probate.

BARKER ROSHOLT & SIMPSON LLP

113 MAIN AVENUE WEST, SUITE 303

TWIN FALLS, IDAHO 83301

Telephone: 208-733-0700
Facsimile: 208-735-2444
URL: http://www.idaho-waters.com

Boise, Idaho Office: 205 North 10th Street, Suite 520, P.O. Box 2139, 83701-2139. Telephone: 208-336-0700. Facsimile: 208-344-6034.

Natural Resources, Water, Environmental, Construction and Commercial Litigation.

JOHN A. ROSHOLT, born Lewiston, Idaho, December 21, 1937; admitted to bar, 1964, Idaho. *Education:* University of Idaho (B.A., 1959; LL.B., 1964). President, National Water Resources Association, 1975. *Member:* Idaho State Bar; American Bar Association. [Lt., U.S. Army, 1959-1961]. (Resident). ***PRACTICE AREAS:*** Natural Resources-Water; Water Rights; Environmental; Cogeneration; Business and Commercial.

(For complete biographical data on all personnel, see professional Biographies at Boise, Idaho)

BENOIT, ALEXANDER, HARWOOD, HIGH & VALDEZ, L.L.P.

Established in 1919

126 SECOND AVENUE NORTH

P.O. BOX 366

TWIN FALLS, IDAHO 83303-0366

Telephone: 208-733-5463
Fax: 208-734-1438
Email: benoitlaw@benoitlaw.com
URL: http://www.benoitlaw.com

Ketchum, Idaho Office: 160 Second Street East, Suite 218. Telephone: 208-726-4900. Fax: 208-726-3101.

General Civil Trial Practice. Business Corporation, Partnership, Wills, Estate Planning, Probate, Municipal, Banking, Insurance Defense, Real Estate, Environmental, Agriculture, Real Estate Transactions, Real Estate Litigation, Residential Real Estate and Commercial Real Estate, Product Liability Defense, Professional Liability Defense, Criminal Defense.

FIRM PROFILE: Benoit, Alexander, Harwood, High & Valdez, L.L.P. is a full service law firm serving Idaho and neighboring states with offices in Twin Falls and Ketchum. The firm retains a commitment to high quality and service which dates back to its founding in 1919 by Harry Benoit.

MEMBERS OF FIRM

HARRY BENOIT (1893-1966)

EDWARD L. BENOIT (1921-1998)

J. ROBERT ALEXANDER, born Butte, Montana, March 31, 1940; admitted to bar, 1964, Idaho. *Education:* University of Idaho (B.A., 1962; LL.B., 1964). Lawyer Representative, Ninth Circuit Judicial Conference. *Member:* 5th Judicial District and American Bar Associations; Idaho State Bar; Idaho Bar Foundation (Member, Board of Directors, 1977, 1993-1999); Idaho Association of Defense Counsel (President, 1980-1981); American Board of Trial Advocates (President, Idaho Chapter, 1979-1981); American Inns of Court (President, Theron W. Ward Chapter, 1995-1996). Fellow: American College of Trial Lawyers; American Bar Foundation. ***PRACTICE AREAS:*** Civil Litigation; Educational Law; Business and Property; Product Liability; Legal Malpractice Defense; Medical Malpractice Defense; Mediation; Arbitration. ***Email:*** alexander@benoitlaw.com

ROBERT M. HARWOOD, born American Falls, Idaho, November 2, 1946; admitted to bar, 1971, Idaho. *Education:* University of Idaho (B.A., magna cum laude, 1969; J.D., cum laude, 1971). Phi Beta Kappa; Phi Kappa Phi; Phi Alpha Delta (President, 1970).

(This Listing Continued)

BENOIT, ALEXANDER, HARWOOD, HIGH & VALDEZ, L.L.P., Twin Falls—Continued

Member: Idaho Law Review, 1970-1971; Moot Court Team. *Member:* 5th Judicial District and American Bar Associations; Idaho State Bar; Idaho Association of Defense Counsel; Defense Research Institute. Master, American Inns of Court. (Resident, Ketchum Office). ***REPORTED CASES:*** Cox v. Mueller, 125 Idaho 734, 874 P. 2d 545 (Idaho, May 20,1994); Rath v. Managed Health Network, Inc., 123 Idaho 30, 844 P. 2d 12 (Idaho, 1992); Meldco, Inc. v. Hollytex Carpet Mills, Inc., 118 Idaho 265, 796 P. 2d 142, 12 UCC Rep.Serv.2d 1013 (Idaho App.1990); Howes v. Fultz, 115 Idaho 681, 769 P.2d 558 (Idaho, 1989); Hawkes v. Sparks, 108 Idaho 917, 702 P. 2d 1377 (Idaho App., 1985); Pichon v. Benjamin, 108 Idaho 852, 707 P.2d 890 (Idaho App. 1985); Mann v. Safeway Stores, Inc., 95 Idaho 732, 518 P. 2d 1194 (Idaho, 1974); Holland v. Peterson, 95 Idaho 728, 518 P. 2d 1190 (Idaho, 974) (NO. 11306); Weeks v. M-P Publications, Inc., 95 Idaho 634, 516 P. 2d 193 (Idaho, 1973). ***PRACTICE AREAS:*** Civil Trial Practice; Business; Real Estate; Product Liability; Construction Law; Insurance; Employment Law; Legal Malpractice Defense; Mediation. ***Email:*** harwood@benoitlaw.com

THOMAS B. HIGH, P.A., born Twin Falls, Idaho, August 24, 1952; admitted to bar, 1979, Idaho. *Education:* University of Utah (B.S., cum laude, 1973); University of Tennessee; University of Idaho (J.D., 1979). Recipient: DRI Exceptional Performance Citation, 1992; Idaho State Bar Outstanding Service Award, 1996; Idaho State Bar Professionalism Award, 2003. *Member:* 5th Judicial District (President, 1987-1988) and American Bar Associations; Idaho State Bar; Idaho Law Foundation; Idaho Association of Defense Counsel (President, 1991-1992); Defense Research Institute (State Chair, 1991-1995); International Association of Defense Counsel, 1995. Fellow, International Society of Barristers (State Chair, 1999—); Master, Theron Ward Inns of Court. ***REPORTED CASES:*** Hunter v. State, P.3d, Idaho (Sept. 2002); Tuttle v. Wayment Farms, 131 Idaho 105, 952 P.2d 1241 (1998); Boley v. State, 130 Idaho 278, 939 P.2d 854 (1997); State v. Salisbury, 129 Idaho 307, 924 P.2d 208 (1996); Fairway Development Co. v. Petersen, Moss, Olsen, Meacham & Carr, 865 P.2d 957 (Idaho, Dec. 22, 1993) (No. 20292); Fuller v. Wolters, 119 Idaho 415, 807 P.2d 633 (Idaho, Mar. 11, 1991) (No. 18271); Vulk v. Haley, 112 Idaho 855, 736 P.2d 1309 (Idaho, Apr. 9, 1987) (No. 16302); Vannoy v. Uniroyal Tire Co., 111 Idaho 536, 726 P.2d 648, 54 USLW 2331, Prod. Liab. Rep. (CCH)P. 10,889 (Idaho, Nov. 22, 1985) (No. 15529). ***PRACTICE AREAS:*** Insurance Defense Law; Product Liability Litigation; General Business Practice; Estate Planning; Personal Injury Litigation (Defense); Mediation. ***Email:*** high@benoitlaw.com

ANTHONY M. VALDEZ, born Grand Junction, Colorado, May 12, 1968; admitted to bar, 1994, Colorado; 1996, Idaho. *Education:* Fort Lewis College (B.A., 1989); University of Colorado (J.D., 1994). Recipient, Legal Aid Award, Criminal Program, 1993-1994. *Member:* The Colorado Bar Association; Idaho State Bar; American Bar Association; National Association of Criminal Defense Lawyers; Idaho Association of Criminal Defense Lawyers; Idaho Association of Defense Counsel; American Inns of Court; Idaho Supreme Court Capital Defense Counsel Roster. ***PRACTICE AREAS:*** Civil Litigation; Criminal Defense; Insurance Defense. ***Email:*** valdez@benoitlaw.com

ASSOCIATE

NICHOLAS M. STALEY, born Blackfoot, Idaho, September 12, 1976; admitted to bar, 2003, Idaho. *Education:* Idaho State University (B.A., 1999); University of Idaho (J.D., 2003). Member: Idaho Legal Aid Clinic, 2003; Law Related Education Committee. *Member:* Idaho State Bar (Member, Sections on: Professional Ethics; Young Lawyers); American Bar Association; Idaho Association of Defense Counsel; American Inns of Court (Theron Ward Chapter, 2003—). ***PRACTICE AREAS:*** Bodily Injury; Personal Injury Defense; Plaintiffs Personal Injury; Business Law; Trusts and Estates; Probate; Wills; Workers Compensation Defense; Agricultural Law. ***Email:*** staley@benoitlaw.com

PARALEGAL

JUDY S. IMLAY, born Twin Falls, Idaho, May 19, 1949. *Education:* Utah State University (B.S., 1971); National Academy of Paralegal Studies, 1990, Certified with highest honors; Litigation & Trial Practice, 1985; Certified, Legal Research Business Organization Course, 1989. ***PRACTICE AREAS:*** Litigation; Trial Work; Corporate Law; Probate Law. ***Email:*** imlay@benoitlaw.com

COUNSEL FOR: College of Southern Idaho; K & T Steel Co.; State Farm Insurance; Twin Falls Highway District; Independent Meat Co.
LOCAL COUNSEL FOR: All-Nation Insurance Co.; ALPS; American Hardware Mutual Insurance Co.; American International Adjusters; Avemco Insurance Co.; Cargill, Incorporated; Chubb Insurance; Commercial Union Insurance; Zurich Insurance; Farmers Alliance Mutual; Foremost Insurance Co.; Fremont Indemnity Co.; Great American Insurance Co.; Guaranty National Insurance Co.; Idaho Industrial Special Indemnity Fund; I. N. A. Pro; Insurance Company of North America; K-Mart Corp.; Magic Valley Bank; Mastec; Miller Group; Monsanto; MSI Insurance Co.; Mutual of Enumclaw Ins.; National Farmers Union Insurance Co.; Northland Insurance Co.; Ohio Casualty Group; Progressive Casualty Co.; Risk Enterprise Management; St. Paul Insurance; The Goodyear Tire & Rubber Co.; The Hartford; Travelers Insurance Co.; Uniroyal Chemical, Inc.; U.S. Bank; Western Surety Co.; Zurich Insurance.
REFERENCE: First Federal Savings Bank of Twin Falls, Idaho.

BEVIS, CAMERON & JOHNSON, P.A.

TWIN FALLS, IDAHO

(See Boise)

General Trial and Appellate Practice before State and Federal Courts. Personal Injury, Family Law, Business, Corporation, Real Estate and Military Law.

BRASSEY, WETHERELL, CRAWFORD & GARRETT, L.L.P.

TWIN FALLS, IDAHO

(See Boise)

General Civil and Trial Practice, Appeals, Insurance Defense, Business Defense, Defense of Governmental Entities, Trucking Law, Medical Malpractice, DEF, Environmental, Civil Rights, Commercial, Real Estate, Employment, Personnel, Agriculture, and Products Liability.

CARTY LAW, P.A.

TWIN FALLS, IDAHO

(See Boise)

Personal Injury, Medical Malpractice, Products Liability, Trucking Liability, Mediation, Arbitration, Torts, Insurance Bad Faith, Slip and Fall, Dog Bites, Wrongful Death, Airplane Accidents, Automobile Accidents, Brain Injury, Spinal Injury, Truck Accidents.

FINCH & BROADBENT, P.A.

TWIN FALLS, IDAHO

(See Boise)

Adoption, Child Custody, Corporate Law, Divorce, Elder Law, Family Law, General Practice, Guardianship and Conservatorship, Insurance Bad Faith, Insurance Law, Interstate Trucking Litigation, Mediation, Medical Malpractice, Personal Injury, Probate, Wills, Trusts and Estates, Wrongful Death.

GIVENS PURSLEY LLP

TWIN FALLS, IDAHO

(See Boise)

Business, Commercial, Mergers and Acquisitions, Communications and Media, Employment, Environmental, Water, Public Lands and Natural Resources, Financial Transactions, Securitization, Structured Finance, Banking, Credit Recovery and Bankruptcy, Public Policy, Health Care and Hospital, Intellectual Property, Real Estate, Real Estate Financing and Land Use, Securities and Bonds, Tax and Estate Planning, Trial and Appellate Litigation, Telecommunications, Energy, Utilities and Regulatory Affairs.

GREENER BANDUCCI SHOEMAKER P.A.

TWIN FALLS, IDAHO

(See Boise)

General Civil Trial Practice including Commercial Litigation, Securities, Real Estate, Product Liability, Construction, Eminent Domain, Employment, and Personal Injury, Insurance, Intellectual Property. The firm also has substantial expertise in class actions.

HALL, FARLEY, OBERRECHT & BLANTON, P.A.

TWIN FALLS, IDAHO

(See Boise)

Litigation, Insurance Defense, Medical Malpractice and Professional Liability, Employment Law, Labor Relations, Products Liability, Construction, Health and Hospital, Corporation, Commercial, Banking, Real Estate, Legislative Counseling, Bankruptcy, Appellate Law, Administrative Agencies, Agricultural, Municipal, Estate Planning and Probate.

HEPWORTH, LEZAMIZ & JANIS

CHARTERED

Established in 1952

133 SHOSHONE STREET NORTH
P.O. BOX 389
TWIN FALLS, IDAHO 83303-0389
Telephone: 208-734-7510
Fax: 208-734-4115
Email: hepworth@spro.net
URL: http://www.hljlawyers.com

Boise, Idaho Office: 537 West Bannock, P.O. Box 2582. Telephone: 208-343-7510. Fax: 208-342-2927.

General Civil and Trial Practice in State and Federal Courts, Automobile Liability, Personal Injury, Medical Malpractice Probate and Estate Planning, Appellate Practice.

FIRM PROFILE: Our firm was founded as a solo practice by John C. Hepworth in 1952, and now employs nine lawyers, with offices in both Twin Falls and Boise. We provide a broad range of services on a statewide basis, with emphasis on plaintiff's personal injury, wrongful death and insurance litigation. We are firmly committed to excellence in the practice of law, and take pride in the fact that several recoveries made by our firm are among the largest in Idaho.

JOHN C. HEPWORTH, born Salt Lake City, Utah, June 18, 1927; admitted to bar, 1952, Idaho; 1965, U.S. Court of Appeals, Ninth Circuit; 1978, U.S. Supreme Court. *Education:* University of Idaho, Southern Branch and University of Utah (B.S., 1950); University of Idaho (LL.B., 1952). Phi Alpha Delta. Asst. Prosecuting Attorney, 1952-1955. City Attorney, Buhl, 1956—. *Member:* Fifth Judicial District (President, 1962) and American (Member, Tort and Insurance Law Section) Bar Associations; Idaho State Bar; Idaho Trial Lawyers Association; The Inner Circle of Advocates; The Association of Trial Lawyers of

(This Listing Continued)

America. Fellow, American College of Trial Lawyers. Advocate, American Board of Trial Advocates (State Delegate, 1987—); Master of the Bench, Theron Ward Chapter, American Inns of Court. ***REPORTED CASES:*** Shields v. Morton Chem. Co., 95 Idaho 674, 518 P.2d 857 (1974); Meissner v. Smith, 94 Idaho 563, 494 P.2d 567 (1972); Canyon View Irr. Co. v. Twin Falls Canal Co., 101 Idaho 604, 619 P.2d 122 (1980). ***PRACTICE AREAS:*** Personal Injury; Automobile Liability; Medical Malpractice; Civil Trial Practice. ***Email:*** hlj@hljlawyers.com

JOHN T. LEZAMIZ, born Boise, Idaho, September 12, 1952; admitted to bar, 1977, Idaho; 1989, U.S. Court of Appeals, Ninth Circuit. *Education:* College of Idaho (B.A., 1974); University of Idaho (J.D., 1977). Law Clerk to Hon. Joseph J. McFadden, Idaho Supreme Court, 1977-1978. Recipient, International Trial Lawyers Trial Advocacy Award, 1977. Member, Idaho Supreme Court Appellate Rules Committee (1990-1991). *Member:* Fifth Judicial District and American Bar Associations; Idaho State Bar; Idaho Trial Lawyers Association (Regional Director, 1987-1988); The Association of Trial Lawyers of America; American Agricultural Law Association. Advocate, American Board of Trial Advocates; Master of the Bench, Theron Ward Chapter, American Inns of Court. Fellow, American College of Trial Lawyers. ***LANGUAGES:*** Spanish. ***REPORTED CASES:*** In re Wiggins, 273 B.R. 839 (2001); Sanchez v. Galey, 112 Idaho 609, 733 P.2d 1234 (1987); Runcorn v. Shearer Lumber Products, Inc. 107 Idaho 389, 690 P.2d 324 (1984); Hogan v. Hermann, 101 Idaho 893, 623 P.2d 900 (1980). ***PRACTICE AREAS:*** Wrongful Death; Personal Injury; Automobile Liability; Products Liability; Civil Trial Practice. ***Email:*** hepworth@spro.net

J. CHARLES HEPWORTH, born Buhl, Idaho, July 26, 1956; admitted to bar, 1981, California; 1982, Idaho; 1993, U.S. Court of Appeals, Ninth Circuit. *Education:* Stanford University (B.A., 1978); University of California, Hastings College of the Law (J.D., 1981). *Member:* Fourth Judicial District and American Bar Associations; State Bar of California; Idaho State Bar; Idaho Trial Lawyers Association; American Inns of Court (Boise Chapter). (Resident, Boise Office). ***REPORTED CASES:*** Marchand v. Mercy Medical Center, 22 F.3d 933 (9th Cir. 1994); Braley v. Pangburn, 118 Idaho 575, 798 P2d 34 (1990); Bubak v. Evans, 117 Idaho 510, 788 P2d 1333 (Ct. App. 1989) (rev. den.). ***PRACTICE AREAS:*** Personal Injury; Products Liability; Automobile Liability; Medical Malpractice; Commercial Litigation; Civil Trial Practice. ***Email:*** ch@hljlawyers.com

JOHN J. JANIS, born New York, N.Y., November 17, 1953; admitted to bar, 1986, Idaho. *Education:* Kean College of New Jersey (B.S., 1976); University of Idaho (J.D., 1986). Phi Alpha Delta. Executive Editor, Idaho Law Review, 1985-1986. *Member:* Idaho State Bar; American Bar Association; Idaho Trial Lawyers Association; American Inns of Court (Member, Boise Chapter); Association of Ski Defense Attorneys. (Resident, Boise Office). ***REPORTED CASES:*** Cameron v. Minidoka County Hwy. Dist., 125 Idaho 801, 874 P.2d 1108 (1994). ***PRACTICE AREAS:*** Personal Injury; Automobile Liability; Products Liability; Medical Malpractice; Employment Law; Civil Trial Practice. ***Email:*** johnjanis@aol.com

ROBYN MADDOX BRODY, born Wayne, Michigan, February 13, 1970; admitted to bar, 1997, Idaho. *Education:* University of Denver (B.A., cum laude, 1992; J.D., 1997; M.B.A., International Management, 1997); St. Petersburg State University, St. Petersburg, Russia, 1995. Order of St. Ives. Member, University of Denver Law Review, 1994-1997. *Member:* Idaho State Bar; Fifth Judicial District (Past President) and American Bar Associations; Idaho Trial Lawyers Association; The Association of Trial Lawyers of America; American Inns of Court (Member and Past President, Theron Ward Chapter). ***LANGUAGES:*** Russian. ***REPORTED CASES:*** Newcomb v. Standard Ins. Co., 187 F.3d 1004 (9th Cir. 1999); Clear Springs Foods, Inc v. Clear Lakes Trout Co., 130 Idaho 761, 40 P.3d 119 (2002); In re Wiggins, 273 B.R. 839 (2001). ***PRACTICE AREAS:*** Personal Injury; Civil Trial Practice; Automobile Liability; Products Liability. ***Email:*** hlj@hljlawyers.com

BENJAMIN J. CLUFF, born Corvallis, Oregon, November 5, 1969; admitted to bar, 2000, Idaho. *Education:* Brigham Young University (B.S., 1995); University of Idaho (J.D., cum laude, 2000). Managing Editor, Idaho Law Review, 1999-2000. *Member:* Fifth Judicial District and American Bar Associations; Idaho State Bar; Idaho Trial Lawyers Association; American Inns of Court (Member, Theron Ward Chapter); The Association of Trial Lawyers of America. ***LANGUAGES:*** Spanish. ***PRACTICE AREAS:*** Personal Injury; Automobile Liability; Workers Compensation. ***Email:*** bjc@hljlawyers.com

---

JOHN W. KLUKSDAL, born Boise, Idaho, March 10, 1972; admitted to bar, 1997, Idaho; 2000, U.S. Court of Appeals, Ninth Circuit. *Education:* Albertson College (B.A., cum laude, 1994); University of Idaho (J.D., magna cum laude, 1997). Member, Albertson College National Alumni Board. *Member:* Idaho State Bar; Idaho Trial Lawyers Association; American Inns of Court. (Resident, Boise Office). ***PRACTICE AREAS:*** Civil Trial Practice; Personal Injury; Medical Malpractice; Employment Law. ***Email:*** jwk@hljlawyers.com

JOEL A. BECK, born American Falls, Idaho, August 1, 1973; admitted to bar, 2002, Idaho. *Education:* University of Utah (B.A., 1998); University of Idaho (J.D., 2001). *Member:* Fifth Judicial District and American Bar Associations; Idaho State Bar; Idaho Trial Lawyers Association; American Inns of Court (Member, Theron Ward Chapter); The Association of Trial Lawyers of America. ***LANGUAGES:*** Spanish. ***PRACTICE AREAS:*** Civil Litigation; Personal Injury. ***Email:*** hlj@hljlawyers.com

OF COUNSEL

WILLIAM L. NUNGESTER

REFERENCES: Wells Fargo Bank; Magic Valley Bank.

(For complete biographical data on other personnel, see Professional Biographies at Boise, Idaho)

HOLLIFIELD LAW OFFICE

249 THIRD AVENUE EAST
P.O. BOX 66
TWIN FALLS, IDAHO 83303-0066
Telephone: 208-734-5610; 800-296-5610
FAX: 208-734-8077
Email: bill@hollifieldlawoffice.com

Civil and Criminal Trial Practice. Mediation, Bankruptcy (Creditor-Trustee), Commercial, Real Estate, Personal Injury, Automobile Accidents and Injuries, Wrongful Death, Head Injury, and DUI Defense.

WILLIAM R. HOLLIFIELD, born Twin Falls, Idaho, June 6, 1944; admitted to bar, 1969, Idaho, U.S. District Court, District of Idaho and U .S. Court of Appeals, Ninth Circuit. *Education:* University of Idaho (B.A., 1966; J.D., 1969). Attorney, U.S. Department of Justice, Civil Rights Division, 1973-1974. Prosecuting Attorney, Twin Fall County, Idaho, 1975-1976. Representative, Ninth Circuit Lawyers, 1992. Member, Biden Advisory Committee, Federal District Court. *Member:* Fifth Judicial District (President, 1977) and American Bar Associations; Idaho State Bar (Commissioner, 1984-1987; President, 1986-1987); Idaho Trial Lawyers Association; The Association of Trial Lawyers of America. ***PRACTICE AREAS:*** Bankruptcy; Personal Injury; Driving While Intoxicated Defense; Commercial Law; Agricultural Credit; Farm and Ranch Law; Criminal Law; Mediation. ***Email:*** bill@hollifieldlawoffice.com

MOFFATT THOMAS BARRETT ROCK & FIELDS

CHARTERED
621 N. COLLEGE ROAD, SUITE 103
P.O. BOX 5483
TWIN FALLS, IDAHO 83303-5483
Telephone: 208-734-7500
FAX: 208-734-7508
Email: jof@moffatt.com
URL: http://www.moffatt.com

Boise, Idaho Office: 101 South Capitol Boulevard, 10th Floor, P.O. Box 829, 83701. Telephone: 208-345-2000. Fax: 208-385-5384.
Idaho Falls, Idaho Office: 420 Memorial Drive, P.O. Box 51505, 83405. Telephone: 208-522-6700. Fax: 208-522-5111.
Pocatello, Idaho Office: 412 West Center, Suite 2000, P.O. Box 817, 83204. Telephone: 208-233-2001. Fax: 208-232-0150.

General Civil, Trial and Appellate Practice. Administrative Law, Alternative Dispute Resolution, Antitrust and Trade Regulation, Aviation, Bankruptcy, Banks and Banking, Business Law, Commercial Real Estate, Construction Law, Contracts, Corporate Law, Debtor and Creditor, Disabilities, Employee Benefits, Environmental Law, Finance, Government Relations, Health Care, Hospital Law, Insurance Defense, Intellectual Property, Labor and Employment Law, Leases and Leasing, Litigation, Medical Malpractice, Mergers, Acquisitions and Divestitures, Mortgages, Nonprofit and Charitable Organizations, Partnership Law, Probate, Products Liability, Professional Liability, Public Utility Law, Real Estate, Regulatory Law, Securities, Taxation, Torts, Trusts and Estates, Water Law, Worker's Compensation.

JOHN O. FITZGERALD, II, born Moscow, Idaho, April 8, 1963; admitted to bar, 1990, Idaho; U.S. District Court, District of Idaho. *Education:* University of Idaho (B.S., Accounting, 1986; J.D., 1990). ***PRACTICE AREAS:*** Litigation; Business Law; Real Estate; Commercial Law; Agricultural Law; Medical Malpractice; Appellate Practice; Environmental Law.

(For complete biographical data on other personnel, see Professional Biographies at Boise, Pocatello and Idaho Falls, Idaho)

JEFFREY E. ROLIG, P.C.

Established in 1997
139 RIVER VISTA PLACE, SUITE 104
P.O. BOX 5455
TWIN FALLS, IDAHO 83303-5455
Telephone: 208-733-0075
Fax: 208-733-0717
Email: jrolig@roliglaw.com
URL: http://www.jroliglaw.com

Agricultural Creditors Rights, Bankruptcy Collections, Creditor Bankruptcy, Commercial Foreclosure, Business Formation, Business Litigation, Business Transactions, Commercial Collections, Secured Collections, Unsecured Collections, Commercial Transactions, Contract Litigation, Commercial Contracts, Evictions, Real Estate Contracts, Real Estate Foreclosures.

JEFFREY E. ROLIG, born Wadsworth, Ohio, December 7, 1948; admitted to bar, 1977, Idaho. *Education:* Whitman College (B.A., 1971); University of Idaho (J.D., 1977). Member, Planning and Zoning Commission, City of Twin Falls, 1991-1993. *Member:* Fifth Judicial District and American Bar Associations; Idaho State Bar; Idaho Association of Trial Lawyers.

REPRESENTATIVE CLIENTS: AgAmerica, FCB; Archer Daniels Midland Co.; Case Credit Corporation; Financial Pacific Leasing, LLC; O.K. Paving, Inc; PM Ag Products, Inc.; Seneca Foods Corp.; Monroc, Inc.; Guardian Management Corp; United California Bank (Sanwa Bank); Magic Valley Collections & Recovery, Inc.; Genex Cooperative, Inc.

ROY, NIELSON, BARINI-GARCÍA & PLATTS

A Partnership of Professional Corporations

Established in 1986

780 EASTLAND DRIVE, SUITE 1
P.O. BOX 487
TWIN FALLS, IDAHO 83303-0487
Telephone: 208-734-4450
FAX: 208-734-4452

General Civil Trial Practice. Personal Injury, Commercial Banking, Corporation, Family, Insurance, Probate, Real Estate, Workers Compensation, Bankruptcy Law, Criminal Defense Law and Immigration.

MEMBERS OF FIRM

SUSAN P. ROY, (CHRTD), born Quincy, California, November 3, 1948; admitted to bar, 1976, Idaho. *Education:* California State University at Chico (B.A., magna cum laude, 1972); Hastings College of Law, University of California (J.D., 1976). Member, State of Idaho Child Support Guidelines Committee, 1986-2004. ***PRACTICE AREAS:*** Family Law. ***Email:*** roynielson@cableone.net

BRENT H. NIELSON, (CHRTD), born Burley, Idaho, December 8, 1954; admitted to bar, 1981, Idaho. *Education:* Brigham Young University (B.A., magna cum laude, 1978); University of Utah (J.D., 1981). *Member:* American Bar Association; Idaho Trial Lawyers Association; The Association of Trial Lawyers of America. ***LANGUAGES:*** Finnish. ***PRACTICE AREAS:*** Workers Compensation Law; Bankruptcy Law; Business Law; Personal Injury Litigation. ***Email:*** brentn@cableone.net

LISA BARINI-GARCÍA, (CHRTD), born New York, N.Y., September 24, 1960; admitted to bar, 1988, Idaho. *Education:* State University of New York at Stony Brook (B.A., 1982); Antioch School of Law (J.D., 1987). ***LANGUAGES:*** Spanish. ***PRACTICE AREAS:*** Criminal Law; Domestic Relations; Immigration Law. ***Email:*** lisabg@cableone.net

SETH CRAIG PLATTS, born Fort Lewis, Washington, January 14, 1970; admitted to bar, 1996, Idaho. *Education:* University of Idaho (B.A., 1993; J.D., 1996). ***PRACTICE AREAS:*** Family Law; Bankruptcy; Personal Injury. ***Email:*** sethp@cableone.net

ASSOCIATE

BRENT BRADFORD NIELSON, born Salt Lake City, Utah, May 5, 1979; admitted to bar, 2005, Idaho and U.S. District Court, District of Idaho. *Education:* Brigham Young University (B.A. cum laude, 2002); J. Reuben Clark Law School, Brigham Young University (J.D. cum laude, 2005). ***Email:*** brentbn@cableone.net

REPRESENTATIVE CLIENTS: Twin Falls Truck and Equipment; Randy Hansen Chevrolet; Rock Creek Trading, Inc.; Ameripride Linen, Inc.
REFERENCE: Wells Fargo Bank.

TOLMAN LAW OFFICE P.C.

Established in 1994

132 3RD AVENUE EAST
P.O. BOX 1276
TWIN FALLS, IDAHO 83303
Telephone: 208-733-5566
Fax: 208-733-5444
Email: STolman@TolmanLaw.com
URL: http://www.lawyers.com/tolmanlawoffice

General Civil, Trial and Appellate Practice. Medical Malpractice and Professional Liability, Commercial, Real Estate, Employment Law, Insurance Law, Agricultural and Appellate Law.

FIRM PROFILE: Tolman Law Office is almost exclusively a litigation firm with extensive trial experience in many areas with emphasis in medical malpractice.

STEVEN K. TOLMAN, born Pocatello, Idaho, September 16, 1946; admitted to bar, 1975, Idaho; U.S. District Court, District of Idaho and U.S. Court of Appeals, Ninth Circuit. *Education:* Brigham Young University (B.A., 1968); University of Utah (M.B.A., 1972); University of Idaho (J.D., 1975). *Member:* Fifth District Bar Association; Idaho State Bar; International Society of Barristers; Idaho Association of Defense Counsel (Past President); International Association of Defense Counsel; Defense Research Institute (Idaho State Representative, 1998); American Board of Trial Advocates; American College of Trial Lawyers; American Inns of Court. [1st Lt., U.S. Army, 1968-1971]. ***PRACTICE AREAS:*** Civil Practice; Appellate Practice; Medical Malpractice; Employer/Employee Law; Real Estate Law; Insurance Law; Litigation Defense. ***Email:*** STolman@TolmanLaw.com

ASSOCIATES

JENNIFER KAUTH BRIZEE, born Seattle, Washington, July 16, 1966; admitted to bar, 1994, Idaho; U.S. District Court, District of Idaho. *Education:* University of Washington (B.A., Journalism, 1988); University of Idaho (J.D., 1994). Lead Articles Editor, Idaho Law Review, 1993-1994. *Member:* Fifth District Bar Association; Idaho State Bar; American Inns of Court; Defense Research Institute; Idaho Association of Defense Counsel. ***PRACTICE AREAS:*** Civil Practice; Appellate Practice; Employer/Employee Law; Medical Malpractice; Litigation Defense. ***Email:*** jbrizee@tolmanlaw.com

TARA MARTENS, born Twin Falls, Idaho, April 5, 1972; admitted to bar, 1998, Idaho. *Education:* Boise State University (B.B.A., 1994); Tulane University of Louisiana (J.D., 1997). Recipient, Maritime Certificate, Tulane University, 1997. Instructor, Commercial Law, Boise State University, 2001—. Formerly with Taylor & Martens, LLP. *Member:* Fifth District and American Bar Associations; Idaho State Bar; Idaho Association of Defense Counsel. ***PRACTICE AREAS:*** Litigation Defense; Insurance; Health Care; Medical Malpractice; Business Law; Real Estate. ***Email:*** tmartens@tolmanlaw.com

(This Listing Continued)

REPRESENTATIVE CLIENTS: Allied Mutual Insurance Co.; Farmers Insurance Group; MIEC Group; MSI Insurance; Nationwide Insurance Co.; Northwest Physicians; Washington Casualty Insurance Company; Physicians Insurance; St. Paul Fire and Marine Insurance Company (formerly USF&G Co.); The Cincinnati Ins. Co.; Cornhusker Casualty Co.

WEBB, WEBB & GUERRY

Established in 1976

155 SECOND AVENUE NORTH
P.O. BOX 1768
TWIN FALLS, IDAHO 83303-1768
Telephone: 208-734-1616
Fax: 208-734-5769
URL: http://www.curtiswebb.net
Email: crwebb@mindspring.com
URL: http://www.vaccineinjurycompensation.com

General Civil Trial Practice. Vaccine Injury Compensation, Personal Injury, Legal Malpractice, Products Liability, Immigration, Land Use and Family Law..

MEMBERS OF FIRM

LLOYD J. WEBB, (CHARTERED), born Twin Falls, Idaho, October 6, 1931; admitted to bar, 1955, Utah; 1956, Idaho and Alaska. *Education:* Brigham Young University and University of Idaho; University of Utah (LL.B., 1955). Phi Delta Phi. Law Clerk to U.S. District Judge, Alaska, 1956-1957. Eleventh District Judge, 1963-1966. *Member:* Fifth Judicial District (President, 1967), Alaska and American Bar Associations; Idaho State Bar; Utah State Bar; The Association of Trial Lawyers of America; Idaho Trial Lawyers Association (President, 1979-1980). ***PRACTICE AREAS:*** Civil Trial Practice; Personal Injury Law; Appellate Practice.

CURTIS R. WEBB, (CHARTERED), born Twin Falls, Idaho, April 23, 1958; admitted to bar, 1984, Idaho; 1988, U.S. Supreme Court and Court of Federal Claims; 1991, U.S. Court of Appeals, Federal Circuit; 1995, U.S. Court of Appeals, First Circuit. *Education:* University of Utah; Utah State University (B.A., magna cum laude, 1981); Brigham Young University (J.D., magna cum laude, 1984). Order of the Coif. Member, 1982-1983 and Editor, 1983-1984, Brigham Young University Law Review. Member, 1993-1995 and Chairman, 1995, Advisory Commission on Childhood Vaccines. *Member:* Fifth Judicial District Association; Idaho State Bar; The Association of Trial Lawyers of America; Idaho Trial Lawyers Association. ***LANGUAGES:*** Spanish. ***REPORTED CASES:*** Shyface vs. HHS, 165 F3d 1344 (Fed. Cir. 1999); Koston vs. HHS, 974 F2d. 157 (Fed. Cir. 1992); Toner vs. Lederle Laboratories, 828 F.2d 510 (9th Cir. 1988); Sharpnack vs. HHS, 27 Fed. Cl. 457 (1993); Estep vs. HHS, 28 Fed. Cl. 664 (1993). ***PRACTICE AREAS:*** Vaccine Injury Compensation Act; Legal Malpractice; Vaccine Injury. ***Email:*** crwebb@mindspring.com

MARK J. GUERRY, born Twin Falls, Idaho, April 24, 1959; admitted to bar, 1991, Idaho; U.S. Court of Federal Claims. *Education:* Boise State University (Campus in Spain, 1978-1979; B.A., cum laude, 1982); University of Idaho (J.D., 1990). Deputy Criminal Prosecutor, City of Buhl, 1992-1995. Deputy Civil Prosecutor, Ada County, Idaho, 1995-1996. Chief Civil Prosecutor, Twin Falls County, 1997-1999. *Member:* Fifth Judicial District; Idaho State Bar; Idaho Trial Lawyers' Association;. ***LANGUAGES:*** Spanish and Basque. ***PRACTICE AREAS:*** Civil Practice; Trial Practice; Personal Injury; Products Liability; Immigration Law; Land Use; Family Law. ***Email:*** mjguerry@hotmail.com

REPRESENTATIVE CLIENT: National Vaccine Information Center (Dissatisfied Parents Together).
REFERENCE: Wells Fargo Bank N.W.

HULL & BRANSTETTER CHARTERED

Established in 1923

416 RIVER STREET
P.O. BOX 709
WALLACE, IDAHO 83873
Telephone: 208-752-1154
Fax: 208-752-0951

General Civil and Trial Practice. Personal Injury, Corporation, Mining, Probate, Real Estate, Workers Compensation, Municipal, Negligence, Insurance Law and Planning and Zoning.

H.J. HULL (1888-1975)

ALDEN HULL (1919-1984)

PIATT HULL (1914-1992)

MICHAEL K. BRANSTETTER, born Hot Springs, Montana, September 15, 1953; admitted to bar, 1979, Idaho; 1988, U.S. Court of Appeals, Ninth Circuit. *Education:* University of Idaho (B.S., 1976); Gonzaga University (J.D., 1979). *Member:* Shoshone County and First Judicial District Bar Associations; Idaho State Bar; Idaho Association of Defense Counsel; Defense Research Institute. ***PRACTICE AREAS:*** Insurance Defense; Workers Compensation; Probate; Mining; Personal Injury; Municipal Law.

REPRESENTATIVE CLIENTS: ASARCO, Inc.; Zanetti Brothers, Inc.; Mine Owners Association ; National Casualty/Markel Insurance Co.; Scottsdale Insurance Co.; Great American Insurance Company; Scottsdale Insurance Company; City of Osburn; Wallace School District; Mullan School District.
REFERENCES: U.S. Bank-Wallace Branch; Bank of America, Osburn Branch.

GAILAN & NAJERA, P.C.

1690 W. LAKE STREET
ADDISON, ILLINOIS 60101-1833
Telephone: 630-467-0400
Fax: 630-467-0500
Email: gailan@mcleodusa.net
URL: http://www.theodoregailan.com

Criminal Defense, Family Law, Divorce, Child Custody, Adoption, Grandparents Rights, Domestic Violence, Visitation Rights, Child Support, Criminal Law, Driving While Intoxicated, Drug Crimes, Juvenile Crimes, Parole and Probation, Traffic Violations, White Collar Crimes.

THEODORE GAILAN, born Chicago, Illinois, May 27, 1952; admitted to bar, 1983, Illinois. *Education:* Lake Forest College (B.A., 1974); DePaul University (M.B.A., 1977); John Marshall Law School (J.D., 1983). Certified in DUI Detection and Standardized Field Sobriety Testing by the National Highway Traffic Safety Administration. Member, National Criminal Defense College, 1991. DuPage County Public Defender's Office, 1988-1995. Cook County State's Attorney's Office, 198401988. National Bank Examiners, United States Treasury Department, 1978-1980. *Member:* DuPage County and Illinois State Bar Associations. ***PRACTICE AREAS:*** Bankruptcy; Criminal Defense; Family Law; Divorce; Child Custody; Adoption; Grandparents Rights; Domestic Violence; Visitation Rights; Child Support; Criminal Law; Driving While Intoxicated; Drug Crimes; Juvenile Crimes; Parole and Probation; Traffic Violations; White Collar Crime.

MARIA GLORIA NAJERA, born 1952; admitted to bar, 1987, Texas; 1988, Illinois.

JAY M. REESE

286 W. FULLERTON
ADDISON, ILLINOIS 60101-3767
Telephone: 630-628-0773
Fax: 630-628-3652
Email: lawofficeofjmreese@sbcglobal.net
URL: http://www.jayreeselaw.com

Criminal Law, Personal Injury, Family Law, Real Estate, Bankruptcy, Wills, Probate, General Practice.

JAY M. REESE, born 1950; admitted to bar, 1975, Illinois. *Education:* University of Illinois (B.A., 1971; J.D., 1975). ***PRACTICE AREAS:*** Bankruptcy Law; Bankruptcy Chapter 11 and 12 Law; Real Estate Law; Bankruptcy; Criminal Defense.

RHINE, ERNEST & VARGO

ALBION, ILLINOIS
(See Mount Carmel)

Coal, Oil and Gas Law, Real Estate, Corporate, Civil Trial Practice, Wills and Estates, Environmental Law.

FORD LAW FIRM

409 SOUTH MAIN STREET
ALGONQUIN, ILLINOIS 60102
Telephone: 847-854-9800
Fax: 847-854-9809
Email: fordfirm1@comcast.net

Employer Liability, Construction Accidents, Product Liability, School District Liability, Municipal Liability, Dram Shop, Civil Rights Litigation, Premises Liability.

STEPHEN E. FORD, born Rochester, New York, April 12, 1952; admitted to bar, 1977, Illinois and U.S. District Court, Northern District of Illinois; 1981, U.S. Court of Appeals, 7th Circuit; 1991, U.S. Supreme Court. *Education:* State University of New York at Binghamton (B.A., with high honors, 1974); John Marshall Law School (J.D., 1977). Phi Beta Kappa. *Member:* Chicago and Illinois State Bar Associations; Illinois Association of Defense Trial Counsel. ***PRACTICE AREAS:*** Employer Liability; Construction Accidents; Product Liability; School District Liability; Municipal Liability; Dram Shop; Civil Rights Litigation; Premises Liability.

MICHLING HOFMANN VINTON PLAZA & WICK, P.C.

ALGONQUIN, ILLINOIS
(See Woodstock)

Personal Injury, Workers Compensation, Criminal Law, Family Law, Civil Litigation, Corporate Law, Residential Real Estate, Commercial Real Estate, Landlord and Tenant Law, Wills and Trusts, Land Use and Development, Zoning, Appellate Practice.

MATHEW R. P. PERRONE

210 S. MAIN STREET
ALGONQUIN, ILLINOIS 60102-2639
Telephone: 847-658-5140
Fax: 847-658-1088
Email: matperon@mc.net

Patents, Trademarks, Copyrights, Intellectual Property, Real Estate, Wills.

MATHEW R. P. PERRONE, JR., born 1943; admitted to bar, 1970, Maryland; 1971, District of Columbia; 1975, Illinois. *Education:* University of Illinois (B.S., 1965); Catholic University of America (J.D., 1969). ***LANGUAGES:*** German. ***PRACTICE AREAS:*** Patents; Trademarks; Copyrights; Real Estate; Wills.

LAW OFFICES OF RICHARD E. TRAVIS

ALGONQUIN, ILLINOIS
(See Elgin)

General Practice in all Courts. Personal Injury, Wrongful Death, Commercial Litigation, Medical Malpractice, Products Liability and Worker's Compensation Law. Civil Litigation Practice, Automobile Accidents, Dog Bites, Slip and Fall.

JULIE HARPER

612 BELLE STREET, SUITE 101
ALTON, ILLINOIS 62002
Telephone: 618-462-5299
Fax: 618-462-5311
Email: julieharperlaw@cbnstl.com
URL: http://www.julieharperlaw.com

Traffic, DWI, Bankruptcy, Estate Planning, Real Estate, Contracts, Wills, Probate, Trusts, General Practice, Criminal, Buying and Selling Homes, Guardianships, Automobile Accidents, Adoptions.

JULIE HARPER, born Alton, Illinois, December 17, 1966; admitted to bar, 2002, Illinois and Missouri. *Education:* Southern Illinois University (B.A., 1991); St. Louis University (J.D., 2001). Co-Author, with attorney James E. Schrempf, "What constitutes a prevailing party for determining who pays attorney fees? An end to the catalyst theory and fee-shifting in light of the Buckhannon case," Local Government Law Section, Illinois State Bar Association Vol. 39, No.2, September 2002. Seminar Lecturer, "Accumulating, Preserving and Passing Wealth". *Member:* Alton, Wood River, Madison County and Illinois State Bar Associations. ***PRACTICE AREAS:*** Traffic Violations; Driving While Intoxicated; Bankruptcy; Estate Planning; Real Estate; Contracts; Wills; Probate; Trust Law; General Practice; Personal Injury.

HOAGLAND, FITZGERALD, SMITH & PRANAITIS

401 MARKET STREET
P.O. BOX 130
ALTON, ILLINOIS 62002
Telephone: 618-465-7745
Telecopier: 618-465-3744
Email: hfsp@il-mo-lawfirm.com
URL: http://www.il-mo-lawfirm.com

General Practice and Trials in all Federal and State Courts. Insurance, Litigation, Negligence, Product Liability, Malpractice, Employment Discrimination, Corporate, Banking, Probate, Trusts, Estates, Labor Relations, Tax Law, Workers Compensation, Commercial Transactions, Real Estate, Governmental, Bankruptcies and Foreclosures.

MEMBERS OF FIRM

WILLIAM H. HOAGLAND, born Alton, Illinois, September 15, 1940; admitted to bar, 1965, Illinois. *Education:* University of Michigan (B.A., 1962); University of Illinois (LL.B., 1965). Phi Delta Phi. *Member:* Alton-Wood River (Secretary, 1970-1971; Vice President, 1984; President, 1985), Madison County, Illinois State and American Bar Associations; Illinois Association of Defense Trial Counsel. [With U.S. Army, 1966-1969]. ***PRACTICE AREAS:*** Insurance Law; Employment Discrimination Law; Personal Injury Defense Law. ***Email:*** billhoag@il-mo-lawfirm.com

R. EMMETT FITZGERALD, born Alton, Illinois, February 27, 1926; admitted to bar, 1952, Illinois. *Education:* University of Notre Dame (A.B., 1951; J.D., 1952). Law Clerk for Justice Roger Kiley, Appellate Court of Illinois, 1952-1953. *Member:* Alton-Wood River and Illinois State Bar Associations; National Lawyers Association. [With U.S. Navy, 1944-1946]. ***PRACTICE AREAS:*** Corporate Law; Banking Law; Commercial Law; Probate Law; Real Estate Law. ***Email:*** refitz@il-mo-lawfirm.com

DONALD L. SMITH, born Carbondale, Illinois, October 28, 1938; admitted to bar, 1962, Illinois. *Education:* University of Illinois (B.S., 1960; LL.B., 1962). *Member:* Alton-Wood River (President, 1974-1975), Madison County (President, 1981-1982) and Illinois State Bar Associations. [Lieut., U.S. Naval Reserve, 1962-1966]. ***PRACTICE AREAS:*** Personal Injury Law; Products Liability; Governmental Law; Banking Law; Family Law; Bankruptcy. ***Email:*** dsmith@il-mo-lawfirm.com

ALPHONSE J. PRANAITIS, born Granite City, Illinois, July 27, 1948; admitted to bar, 1975, Illinois; 2004, Missouri. *Education:* University of Illinois (B.S., with honors, 1970); St. Louis University (J.D., 1975). Law Clerk for Justice Charles Jones, Appellate Court of Illinois, 1975-1976. Publications: "Monograph: Voir Dire in Civil Jury Trials: Illinois," IDC Quarterly, Vol. 14, No. 1, First Quarter-2004, pp. M-1 to M-11; "Collaring the Collateral Source Rule," IDC Quarterly, Vol. 14, No. 1, First Quarter-2004, pp. 51 to 54; "Removal of Illinois Cases to Federal District Court, Confronting the 'Amount in Controversy' Conundrum and Other Concerns," IDC Quarterly, Vol. 14, No. 3, Third Quarter-2004. *Member:* Alton-Wood River (Vice President, 2000; President, 2002), Madison County (Treasurer, 1979-1980; Secretary, 1984-1985), Illinois State and American Bar Associations; Illinois Association of Defense Trial Counsel; Defense Research Institute; Fellow, American College of Trial Lawyers. ***PRACTICE AREAS:*** Personal Injury Law; Product Liability Law; Insurance Law; Medical Malpractice; Legal Malpractice; Employment Discrimination Law. ***Email:*** alpran@il-mo-lawfirm.com

(This Listing Continued)

HOAGLAND, FITZGERALD, SMITH & PRANAITIS, Alton—Continued

STEPHEN J. MAASSEN, born Clifton Springs, New York, May 2, 1951; admitted to bar, 1977, Indiana; 1978, Illinois; 1999, Missouri. *Education:* Central College (B.A., 1973); Valparaiso University (J.D., 1977). Managing Editor, Valparaiso University Law Review, 1976-1977. Delta Theta Phi. Law Clerk for Justice Dorothy W. Spomer and Justice George W. Kasserman, Appellate Court of Illinois, 1979-1981. *Member:* Alton-Wood River, Madison County, Illinois State, Indiana State and American Bar Associations; The Missouri Bar and the Bar Association of Metropolitan St. Louis; Federal Bar Association of Central and Southern Districts (Member, Legislation Committee); Defense Research Institute; Illinois Association of Defense Trial Counsel; International Association of Defense Counsel-IADC. ***PRACTICE AREAS:*** Personal Injury Law; Employment Law; Construction Litigation; Admiralty Law; Toxic Torts; Product Liability Law; Insurance Law. ***Email:*** maassen@il-mo-lawfirm.com

SCOTT D. BJORSETH, born Columbia, Missouri, December 16, 1964; admitted to bar, 1990, Illinois; 1991, Missouri. *Education:* University of Missouri (B.J., 1987); Southern Illinois University (J.D., cum laude, 1990). *Member:* Madison County, Alton-Wood River and Illinois State Bar Associations; The Missouri Bar; Illinois Association of Defense Trial Counsel; Defense Research Institute. ***PRACTICE AREAS:*** Personal Injury Defense Law; Civil Litigation; Insurance Law. ***Email:*** scottb@il-mo-lawfirm.com

ASSOCIATE

ANNE K. GARCIA, born St. Louis, Missouri, February 8, 1980; admitted to bar, 2005, Illinois. *Education:* University of Notre Dame (B.A., cum laude, 2001); Tulane University Law School (J.D., 2004). Vice President, Student Bar Association, Tulane University Law School. *Member:* Madison County, Alton-Wood River, Illinois State and American Bar Associations. ***PRACTICE AREAS:*** Medical Malpractice; Legal Malpractice; Personal Injury Law; Insurance Law. ***Email:*** agarcia@il-mo-lawfirm.com

OF COUNSEL

KARL K. HOAGLAND, JR., born St. Louis, Missouri, August 21, 1933; admitted to bar, 1958, Illinois. *Education:* University of Pennsylvania (B.A., 1955); University of Illinois (LL.B., 1958). Phi Delta Phi; Beta Gamma Sigma; Order of the Coif. Trustee, The Monticello College Foundation, 1965—. Vice President and General Counsel, Container Corporation of America, 1986-1992 and Jefferson Smurfit Corporation, 1960-1992. *Member:* Alton-Wood River, Madison County and Illinois State Bar Associations. [With U.S. Air Force, 1958-1959]

REPRESENTATIVE CLIENTS: American Family Insurance Group; American International Insurance Group; Carrollton Bank; ConAgra Foods, Inc.; Crown Cork & Seal Co.; Federated Insurance Co.; Fischer Lumber Co.; First Community Bank of Godfrey; ICON Health & Fitness, Inc.; International Truck & Engine Corp.; J.S. Alberici Construction Co.; John Deere Insurance Co.; Kane Mechanical, Inc.; Madison County, Illinois; Midco Industries, Inc.; Millers First Insurance Companies; Mississippi Lime Co.; The Monticello College Foundation; Multimetco, Inc.; North Pointe Insurance Company; OneBeacon Insurance; Oshkosh Truck Corporation; Penske Truck Leasing Co.; Rollins, Inc.; St. Anthony's Health Center; St. Clare's Hospital; Shell Oil Co.; Simon Property Group; Smurfit-Stone Container Corporation; SSM Health Care; The Travelers; U.S. Bank.
REFERENCES: First Community Bank of Godfrey; U.S. Bank.

LAW OFFICES OF THOMAS E. KENNEDY, III, L.C.

2745 EAST BROADWAY, SUITE 101
ALTON, ILLINOIS 62002
Telephone: 618-474-5326
Fax: 618-474-5331
Email: tkennedy@ezl.com

Disability Rights, Civil Rights, Constitutional Law, School Law, Elder Law, Probate, Estate Planning, Trusts and Estates, Wills, Social Security Disability.

THOMAS E. KENNEDY, III, born San Francisco, California, March 14, 1945; admitted to bar, 1971, Illinois; 1995, Missouri. *Education:* Wesleyan University (B.A., 1967); University of Illinois, Urbana-Champaign, School of Law (J.D., 1971). *Member:* St. Clair County and Illinois State Bar Associations; The Missouri Bar. ***PRACTICE AREAS:*** Civil Rights; Americans with Disabilities Act; School Law; Probate. ***Email:*** tkennedy@ezl.com

DEBORAH S. GREIDER, born Newton, Massachusetts, January 3, 1950; admitted to bar, 1979, Illinois, 1984, Missouri. *Education:* State University of New York at Stony Brook (B.A., 1973); University of Illinois, Urbana-Champaign (J.D., 1977). *Member:* Illinois State Bar Association; The Missouri Bar; National Organization of Social Security Claimants Representatives. ***PRACTICE AREAS:*** Civil Rights; Americans with Disabilities Act; Not-For-Profit Corporations; Probate; School Law; Social Security. ***Email:*** dgreider@ezl.com

TALBERT & ASSOCIATES, P.C.

Established in 1974
630 EAST BROADWAY
P.O. BOX 800
ALTON, ILLINOIS 62002
Telephone: 618-465-1000; 1-800-465-1529
Fax: 618-465-1506
Email: talbertlawfirm@charter.net
URL: http://www.talbertlawfirm.com

St. Louis, Missouri Office: 10 Branford Drive, 63132. Telephone: 314-231-5305.

(This Listing Continued)

Practice Limited to Personal Injury for Plaintiff. Maritime, Federal Employers Liability Act (Railroad), Malpractice, Products Liability, all types of Negligence and Workers' Compensation.

HUGH M. TALBERT, born Kennett, Missouri, December 3, 1937; admitted to bar, 1962, Missouri; 1965, Illinois and U.S. District Court, Eastern District of Missouri; 1966, U.S. District Court, Southern District of Illinois; 1971, U.S. Court of Appeals, 7th Circuit; 2001, Kentucky. *Education:* University of Missouri; Washington University (A.B., 1962; LL.B., 1962). Phi Delta Phi. Assistant Adjunct Professor, Trial Advocacy, St. Louis University Law School, 1992—. Lecturer: "Investigation of Maritime Injuries," National Association of Legal Investigators, 1987, Illinois Trial Lawyers Association, 1986; "Civil Practice Evidence," Illinois Institute of Continuing Legal Education, 1984; "Investigation of Medical Malpractice," National Association of Legal Investigators, 1973. *Member:* The Bar Association of Metropolitan St. Louis; Alton-Wood River (Vice President, 1976-1977; President, 1977-1978), Madison County, Illinois State (Member, Sections on: Admiralty Law; Torts) and American (Member, Litigation Section) Bar Associations; The Missouri Bar (Member, Tort Section); Illinois Trial Lawyers Association (Member, Board of Managers, 1981-1987); The Association of Trial Lawyers of America (Member, Sections on: Admiralty Law; Railroad Law); Missouri Association of Trial Attorneys; The Maritime Law Association of the United States; Academy of Rail Labor Attorneys; Kentucky Association of Trial Attorneys. ***PRACTICE AREAS:*** Personal Injury; FELA; Maritime. ***Email:*** hughtalbert@charter.net

LAURA A. COLE, born Granite City, Illinois, August 8, 1969; admitted to bar, 1995, Illinois; 1996, Missouri. *Education:* Southern Illinois University (B.A., 1990); Florida International University (M.A., International Studies, 1992); Washington University (J.D., 1995). Phi Delta Phi. *Member:* Madison County and Illinois State Bar Associations; The Missouri Bar; Illinois Trial Lawyers Association. ***PRACTICE AREAS:*** Personal Injury; Workers Compensation. ***Email:*** lauracole@charter.net

REFERENCE: The Bank of Alton.

LAW OFFICE OF PAUL R. IDLAS

ANTIOCH, ILLINOIS

(See Grayslake)

Bankruptcy, Real Estate, Chapter 7 Bankruptcy, Real Estate Closings.

ADLER LAW OFFICES, LTD.

9 NORTH VALE, SUITE 102
ARLINGTON HEIGHTS, ILLINOIS 60005
Telephone: 847-394-0100
Fax: 847-394-0500
Email: ca@alderltd.com
URL: http://www.adlerltdlaw.com

Personal Injury, Automobile Accidents, Medical Malpractice, Products Liability, Wrongful Death.

CHARLES E. ADLER, born Chicago, Illinois, May 27, 1952; admitted to bar, 1977, Illinois; 1978, U.S. District Court, Northern District of Illinois; 1980, U.S. Court of Appeals, Seventh Circuit. *Education:* University of Illinois (B.A., 1973); John Marshall Law School (J.D., 1977). Co-Author: "Soft Tissue Accident Is No Soft Case" 2004. Lecturer, Senior Law Academy. Sheriff, Cook County, Illinois, 2002-2005. Member: Tort Committee, Chicago Bar Association, 2002-2004; Committee on Legislation, Illinois Trial Lawyers Association. *Member:* Illinois State Bar Association (Member, Committee on Legislation); Northwest Suburban Bar Association; Association of Trial Lawyers of America. ***PRACTICE AREAS:*** Personal Injury; Automobile Accidents and Injuries; Medical Malpractice; Products Liability; Wrongful Death. ***Email:*** ca@adlerltd.com

ANDERSON & ASSOCIATES, P.C.

ARLINGTON HEIGHTS, ILLINOIS

(See Schaumburg)

Family Law, Bankruptcy, Real Estate Litigation and Transactions, Estate Planning and Probate.

BUDIN LAW OFFICES

ARLINGTON HEIGHTS, ILLINOIS

(See Chicago)

Automobile Accidents, Catastrophic Accidents and Injuries, Head Trauma, Spinal Cord Injuries, Construction Site Accidents, Work Related Injuries.

DALEIDEN & TREMAINE, LTD.

Established in 1984
2815 NORTH DOUGLAS AVENUE
ARLINGTON HEIGHTS, ILLINOIS 60004
Telephone: 847-577-7438
Fax: 847-577-7458

General Practice, Corporate, Tax, Employee Benefits, Estate Planning, Probate, Real Estate, Litigation, Elder Law.

(This Listing Continued)

NORBERT A. DALEIDEN, born Evanston, Illinois, September 24, 1942; admitted to bar, 1968, Illinois. *Education:* Northwestern University (B.S., 1964; M.B.A., 1965; J.D., cum laude, 1968). Phi Alpha Delta. *Member:* Illinois State Bar Association. **Email:** ndaleiden@aol.com

ARTHUR J. TREMAINE, born Chicago, Illinois, April 5, 1948; admitted to bar, 1977, Illinois. *Education:* Duke University (B.A., 1971); DePaul University (J.D., 1977). Certified Public Accountant, North Carolina, 1973. *Member:* Illinois State and American Bar Associations. **Email:** arttremaine@aol.com

LAW OFFICES OF CARYL JACOBS GABE & ASSOCIATES, INC.

ARLINGTON HEIGHTS, ILLINOIS

(See South Barrington)

Family, Divorce, Paternity, Mediation, Child Custody, Child Support, Matrimonial Law, Domestic Relations, Orders of Protection, Prenuptial Agreements, Adoptions, and Injunctions.

THE LAW OFFICES OF THOMAS GLASGOW, LTD.

ARLINGTON HEIGHTS, ILLINOIS

(See Schaumburg)

Criminal, Federal, State, Felony, Misdemeanor, DUI, Traffic, Drunk Driving, Revoked and Suspended License, Murder, Drug Offense, Weapons Charge, Civil, Contracts Litigation, Administrative, Divorce, Family Law.

DOUGLAS A. JUDSON

132 WEST NORTHWEST HIGHWAY
ARLINGTON HEIGHTS, ILLINOIS 60004
Telephone: 847-577-5800
Fax: 847-577-5869
Email: lawofc@judson.com
URL: http://www.lawyers.com/judsonlaw

Criminal Defense, Driving While Intoxicated, Divorce.

DOUGLAS A. JUDSON, born Chicago, Illinois, February 7, 1951; admitted to bar, 1976, Illinois; 1977, U.S. District Court, Northern District of Illinois; 1984, Trial Bar; 2002, Illinois Capital Litigation Trial Bar. *Education:* University of Illinois (B.A., 1973); John Marshall Law School (J.D., 1976). Author: "Statutory Summary Suspension: The First Six Months," Northwest Suburban Bar Association Journal, Summer, 1986. Instructor, Continuing Legal Education Program, Northwest Suburban Bar Association, March, 1987. Assistant Public Defender, Cook County, Illinois, 1977-1983. *Member:* Chicago, Northwest Suburban (President, 1995-1996; Member, Board of Governors, 1985-1990; Chairman, Criminal Law Committee, 1986-1987; Member, Judicial Screening Committee, 1983—), Illinois State (Member, Committee on Traffic Laws and Courts, 1981-1987) and American (Criminal Law Section) Bar Associations; National Association of Criminal Defense Lawyers. ***PRACTICE AREAS:*** Criminal Defense; Driving While Intoxicated; Divorce.

KLEST LAW FIRM

ARLINGTON HEIGHTS, ILLINOIS

(See Schaumburg)

Personal Injury, Medical Malpractice, Products Liability, Legal Malpractice, Construction Accidents, Airplane Crash Litigation, Insurance Bad Faith, Automobile Accidents, Motorcycle Accidents, Birth Trauma, Sexual Abuse, Child Abuse and Neglect, Slip and Fall, Wrongful Death, Dog Bites, Railroad Accidents and Injuries, Automobile Products, Liability and Drug and Medical Device Litigation, Trial Practice.

MARAMBA & ASSOCIATES, LLC

121 SOUTH WILKE ROAD, SUITE 101
ARLINGTON HEIGHTS, ILLINOIS 60005
Telephone: 847-255-3222
Fax: 847-255-4119
Email: idm@idmaramba.com
URL: http://www.idmaramba.com

Business Law, Chancery Practice, Corporate Litigation, Civil Litigation, Complex Litigation, Defense Litigation, Federal Litigation, Administrative Litigation, Business Enterprises, Business Litigation, Closely Held Business Law, Real Estate Litigation, Veterans Rights, Military Law, Wills, Commercial Collections, Post Judgment Collections, Closely Held Corporations.

FIRM PROFILE: Maramba & Associates, LLC is a law firm geared to provide efficient, effective and attentive legal services to its clients. Its principal, Ignacio D. Maramba is a seasoned and skilled trial lawyer who has advised and represented individual and corporate clients in all aspects of business law, civil litigation, real estate and estate planning.

A nationally experienced litigation attorney, Mr. Maramba has handled state and federal cases in Illinois, New York, Virginia, Florida, Texas, Arizona, Colorado, Minnesota, Connecticut, Rhode Island, North Carolina, and in military settings, consistently obtaining favorable results for clients. His 12 years of trial experience, motion practice and appellate experience have been documented in various Chicago newspapers, the Chicago Daily Law Bulletin, the Chicago Lawyer, and published in various legal reporters including the Federal Reporter, Federal Rules Decisions, Federal Supplement, and the Illinois Appellate Reports.

(This Listing Continued)

MEMBER OF FIRM

IGNACIO D. MARAMBA, born Chicago, Illinois; admitted to bar, 1993, Illinois, U.S. District Court, Northern (including Trial Bar) and Central Districts of Illinois, and U.S. Court of Appeals, Seventh Circuit; 1998, U.S. District Court, District of Colorado, U.S. District Court, District of Arizona and U.S. Supreme Court; 2005, U.S. Court of Appeals for the Armed Forces. *Education:* Loyola University (B.A., 1990; J.D., 1993); The United States Army Judge Advocate General School (Officer Basic Course, Officer Advanced Course, Legal Assistance Course, Military Justice Manager's Course). Recipient: Loyola School of Law Academic Achievement Award; Loyola Leadership and Service Award. Certified Arbitrator: Circuit Court of Cook County (IL); Circuit Court for the 18th Judicial Circuit (IL). Member: Rotary Club of Park Ridge (Member, Board of Directors); Union League Club of Chicago (Member, Admissions Committee, 2003; Military Affairs, 2005); American Legion; Reserve Officers Association. Finisher, Chicago Marathon 2002. *Member:* Chicago Bar Association (Committee Chair, Tort Litigation Section, 1997-1998; Entertainment Committee); Illinois State Bar Association; American Bar Association; Illinois Trial Lawyers Association, Chicago Council of Lawyers (Judicial Investigator). [Captain, United States Army Reserve, 2003—; Veteran, Operation Enduring Freedom]. ***REPORTED CASES:*** Smith v. Short Term Loans, LLC, 2001 U.S. Dist. LEXIS 1554 (N.D. Ill. 2001); Reed v. Chartwell Fin. Servs., 2000 U.S. Dist. LEXIS 22566 (N.D. Ill 2000); Taylor v. Halsted Financial Services, LLC, 2000, U.S. Dist. LEXIS 384 (N.D. Ill. 2000); Gutierrez v. Devon Fin. Servs., 1999 U.S. Dist. LEXIS 18686 (N.D. Ill. 1999); Garner v. Healy, 184 F.R.D. 598 (N.D. 10, 1999); Krause v. GE Capital Mortg. Servs., 1998 U.S. Dist. LEXIS 18863 (N.D. Ill. 1998); Randle v. GC Servs., L.P., 181 F.R.D. 602 (N.D. Ill. 1998); In re CBC Cos. Collection Letter Litig., 181 F.R.D. 380 (N.D. Ill. 1998); Arango v. GC Servs., L.P., 1998 U.S. Dist. LEXIS 9124 (N.D. Ill. 1998); Peterson v. H & R Block Tax Servs., 174 F.R.D. 78 (N.D. Ill. 1997); Walker v. National Recovery, Inc., 200 F.3d 500 (7th Cir. 1999) ; Newland v. Budget Rent-A-Car Systems, Inc., et al, 378 Ill. App. 3d 453 (1st Dist. 2001); Brandt v. Time Ins. Co., et al, 302 Ill. App. 30 158 (1st Dist. 1998); Hill v. Amoco Oil Co., 1999 U.S. Dist. LEXIS 11233 (N.D. Ill. 1989); Chancellor v. Nationwide Credit, Inc., 1999 U.S. Dist. LEXIS 62 11 (N.D. Ill. 1999); Majchrowski v. Norwest Mortg., 6 F. Supp. 2d 948 (N.D. Ill. 1998). ***PRACTICE AREAS:*** Business Law; Business Litigation; Chancery Practice; Federal Litigation; Employment Law; Federal Employment Law; Closely Held Business Law; Real Estate Litigation; Military Law; Wills; Commercial Collections. **Email:** idm@idmaramba.com

THE LAW FIRM OF WENDY R. MORGAN

1845 EAST RAND ROAD
SUITE 211
ARLINGTON HEIGHTS, ILLINOIS 60004
Telephone: 847-259-5700
1-800-WRMORGAN
Fax: 847-259-6560
URL: http://www.wendymorgan.com
Email: WRM@lawyer.com
URL: http://www.lawyers.com/wendyrmorgan

Family Law, Divorce, Child Custody, Interstate Custody, Adoptions, Child Support, Paternity, Premarital Agreements, Domestic Violence, Visitation Rights, Adoption Law, Domestic Violence, Visitation Rights.

FIRM PROFILE: The Law Firm of Wendy R. Morgan is a full-service practice of law and Court litigation, concentrating in marital and family law since 1981. The firm is also well known in the area of interstate and intrastate custody. Ms. Morgan is the Senior Attorney, President, and Chief Executive Office of the firm.

WENDY R. MORGAN, born Chicago, Illinois, January 17, 1955; admitted to bar, 1981, Illinois. *Education:* Loyola University (B.A., magna cum laude, Philosophy and Political Science, 1977); IIT Chicago-Kent College of Law (J.D., 1981). Phi Alpha Delta. Listed in National and International Who's Who Directories. Member, Board of Directors, Suburban Summer Symphony Orchestra, 1994—. *Member:* Chicago, Northwest Suburban, West Suburban, Du Page County, Illinois State and American Bar Associations; Illinois Trial Lawyers Association; The Association of Trial Lawyers of America. ***PRACTICE AREAS:*** Divorce; Separation Agreements; Child Custody; Interstate Child Custody; Child Support; Paternity; Premarital Agreements; Postnuptial Agreements; Family Law; Adoptions; Domestic Violence; Visitation Rights.

MOSKOVIC & ASSOCIATES

Established in 1993

120 WEST EASTMAN STREET, SUITE 207
ARLINGTON HEIGHTS, ILLINOIS 60004
Telephone: 847-797-1300
Fax: 847-797-1350
URL: http://www.moskoviclaw.com
Email: attorneys@moskoviclaw.com
URL: http://www.lawyers.com/moskovic&assoc

Civil Practice, Litigation, Commercial Law, Contracts, Personal Injury, Medical Malpractice, Divorce, Child Support, Child Custody, Visitation Rights, Family Law, Collections.

FIRM PROFILE: The attorneys at Moskovic & Associates are experienced professionals offering clients the highest quality legal services available. We strive to maintain constant communication with our clients regarding case activity. In addition, we provide our clients with an ongoing cost benefit analysis, allowing our clients to continually monitor their investment in our legal services.

(This Listing Continued)

MOSKOVIC & ASSOCIATES, Arlington Heights—Continued

ALEX MOSKOVIC, born Chicago, Illinois, August 10, 1967; admitted to bar, 1993, Illinois and U.S. District Court, Northern District of Illinois; 1997, U.S. Court of Appeals, Seventh Circuit; 2002, U.S. Supreme Court; Federal Trial Bar. *Education:* Illinois State University (B.S., 1989); Valparaiso University School of Law (J.D., 1992). Board of Directors and Executive Board, Greater O'Hare Association of Industry and Commerce. *Member:* Chicago, Northwest Suburban and Illinois State Bar Associations. ***LANGUAGES:*** Spanish. ***PRACTICE AREAS:*** Personal Injury; Family Law; Divorce; Child Support; Child Custody; Visitation Rights; Commercial Litigation; Contract Litigation; Collections; Medical Malpractice. ***Email:*** amoskovic@moskoviclaw.com

ASSOCIATE

JOANNE S. MOSKOVIC, born Decatur, Illinois, April 16, 1969; admitted to bar, 1994, Illinois and U.S. District Court Northern District of Illinois; 2002, U.S. Supreme Court. *Education:* Augustana College (B.A., 1991); Valparaiso University School of Law (J.D., 1994). *Member:* Chicago and Illinois State Bar Associations. ***PRACTICE AREAS:*** Personal Injury; Medical Malpractice. ***Email:*** jmoskovic@moskoviclaw.com

Language: Spanish.

REPRESENTATIVE CLIENTS: The Film & Tape Works; Chicago Social Magazine; Arlington Acceptance Corporation.
OF COUNSEL: Greater O'Hare Association of Industry and Commerce.

RICHARD A. NELSON & ASSOCIATES, P.C.

A Professional Corporation
11 SOUTH DUNTON AVENUE
ARLINGTON HEIGHTS, ILLINOIS 60005
Telephone: 847-788-0055
Fax: 847-577-3897
Email: ranelson1@earthlink.net
URL: http://www.lawyers.com/ranelsonlaw

Estate Planning Law, Living Trusts, Probate Administration Law, Closely Held Corporations, Business Estate Planning, Commercial Real Estate Sales, Civil Litigation.

FIRM PROFILE: As a result of a survey of over 76,000 lawyers in Illinois conducted in 2002-2003 by Law Bulletin Publishing Company, based on experience, reputation and legal skills, a committee of his peers recommended Dick as a leading lawyer in the area of trusts, wills and estate planning. This distinction was earned by fewer than 5% of all lawyers licensed in the state.

RICHARD A. NELSON, born Cleveland, Ohio, October 22, 1935; admitted to bar, 1962, Illinois; 1963, U.S. District Court, Northern District of Illinois. *Education:* Ripon College (B.A., 1957); Chicago-Kent College of Law, Illinois Institute of Technology (J.D., 1962). Phi Delta Phi. Author: "Public School Segregation: Does the Fourteenth Amendment Require Affirmative Integration," 38 Chicago-Kent Law Review 169, October, 1961. Lecturer, National Business Institute, Inc. *Member:* Northwest Suburban (Member, Board of Governors, 1965-1976; President, 1972-1973; Current Member, Probate and Estate Planning Committee), Chicago (Member, Probate Practice Committee, 1971-1973), Illinois State and American (Member: Committee on Administration and Distribution of Decedent's Estate, Section of Real Property, Probate and Trust Law, 1970-1972; Committee on Public Regulation of Land Use, 1972-1973) Bar Associations; Northwest Suburban Estate Planning Council (President, 1996 and 1997); Fellow, American College of Trust and Estate Counsel. ***PRACTICE AREAS:*** Estate Planning Law; Probate Administration Law; Closely Held Corporations; Business Estate Planning; Commercial Real Estate Sales; Civil Litigation.

NEWLAND, NEWLAND & NEWLAND

121 S. WILKE ROAD, SUITE 101
ARLINGTON HEIGHTS, ILLINOIS 60005
Telephone: 708-797-8000
Fax: 708-797-9090
Email: newlandglaw@aol.com

Real Estate; Personal Injury.

(For complete biographical data on all personnel, see Professional Biographies at Libertyville,Illinois)

THE LAW OFFICES OF BRUCE D. PAYNTER

3345 NORTH ARLINGTON HEIGHTS ROAD, SUITE G
ARLINGTON HEIGHTS, ILLINOIS 60004
Telephone: 847-392-1212
Fax: 847-392-1222
Email: paynterlaw@earthlink.net
URL: http://www.paynterlaw.com

Criminal Law, Felonies, Misdemeanors, Drug Offenses, Driving While Intoxicated, Assaults, Weapons Charges, Drivers License Suspension, Traffic Violations, Sex Offenses, Personal Injury, Automobile Accidents, Motorcycle Accidents, Trucking Accidents, Wrongful Death, Real Estate Transactions, Buying and Selling Real Estate.

BRUCE D. PAYNTER, born Evanston, Illinois, November 9, 1951; admitted to bar, 1976, Illinois; 1977, U.S. District Court, Northern District of Illinois including Trial Bar; 2003, Illinois Capital Litigation Trial Bar. *Education:* Northwestern University (B.A., with honors, 1973; J.D., 1976). Assistant State's Attorney, Cook County, IL, 1976-1997; Felony Trial Supervisor, 1988-1997. Formerly with: Williams, Montgomery & John, Chicago, IL, 1997-2000. Solo Practitioner, Criminal Law, The Law Offices of Bruce D. Paynter, 2000—. *Member:* Chicago, Northwest Suburban, Illinois State and American Bar Associations; State of Illinois Capital Litigation Trial Bar. ***PRACTICE AREAS:*** Criminal Defense; Criminal Law; Felonies; Capital Offenses; Homicide; Sex Crimes; Drugs and Narcotics; Driving While Intoxicated; Misdemeanors; Assault and Battery; Burglary; Search and Seizure; Traffic Violations; Drivers License Suspension; Litigation.

LEONARD F. PERKINS & ASSOCIATES

1139 NORTH RIDGE AVENUE
ARLINGTON HEIGHTS, ILLINOIS 60004
Telephone: 847-577-0757
Fax: 847-577-0754
Email: lenperkins@comcast.net
URL: http://www.lawyers.com/lenperkins

General Business Law, State Taxation, Intellectual Property and Unclaimed Property, Corporations, Business Enterprises; Business Start-Ups, Promotion Law.

LEONARD F. PERKINS, born Wilton, Wisconsin, May 1, 1946; admitted to bar, 1974, Illinois. *Education:* University of Wisconsin-Madison (B.B.A., 1968; M.B.A., 1973); Georgetown University (J.D., 1974). Formerly with A.C. Nielsen Company, 1980-1994. Speaker, on Unclaimed Property and Sales Tax Issues. Chair, Tax Committee, Information Industry Association, 1989-1993. Member, Annual Tax Practitioners Meeting, Illinois Dept. of Revenue, 1996—. *Member:* Illinois State Bar Association (Member: State & Local Taxation Committee, Business Advice & Financial Planning Section; Intellectual Property Section). [U.S. Army, 1969-1971]. ***PRACTICE AREAS:*** Business Law; State Taxation; Intellectual Property; Unclaimed Property; Corporate Law; Promotion Law.

Y. JACQUELINE PERKINS

1655 N. ARLINGTON HEIGHTS ROAD, SUITE 102E
ARLINGTON HEIGHTS, ILLINOIS 60004
Telephone: 847-394-8121
Fax: 847-394-1775

Family Law, Criminal, Murder, Homicide, Drug Crimes, Wrongful Felonies, Misdemeanors, Sex Assault, Police Misconduct, Divorce, Child Support, Domestic Violence.

Y. JACQUELINE PERKINS, born Kingston, Jamaica, October 9, 1946; admitted to bar, 1981, Illinois. *Education:* New York Institute of Technology (R.N., 1972); John Jay College of Criminal Justice of the City University of New York (B.C.J., 1977); New York Law School (J.D., 1980). Former Cook County Prosecutor, 1981-1992. *Member:* Northwest Suburban Bar Association.

DANIEL K. ROBIN, LTD

121 S. WILKE ROAD, SUITE 201
ARLINGTON HEIGHTS, ILLINOIS 60005
Telephone: 847-670-9100
Fax: 847-398-8377
Email: danatlaw@aol.com
URL: http://www.danrobin.com

Bankruptcy, Chapter 7, Chapter 13, Divorce, Family Law, Child Support, Separation, Prenuptial Agreements, Equitable Distribution, Driving While Intoxicated, Traffic Violations, Criminal Law, Wills and Trusts, Estate Planning, Asset Protection.

DANIEL K. ROBIN, born Chicago, Illinois, August 25, 1950; admitted to bar, 1977, Illinois. *Education:* Indiana University (B.A., 1972); Chicago-Kent College of Law (J.D., 1977). *Member:* Northwest Suburban Bar Association.

LAW OFFICES OF ROGER W. STELK

Established in 1995
1500 W. SHURE DRIVE, SUITE 245
ARLINGTON HEIGHTS, ILLINOIS 60004
Telephone: 847-506-7330
Fax: 847-506-7331
URL: http://www.stelklaw.com
Email: rwstelk@aol.com
URL: http://www.stelklawfirm.com

Family Law, Divorce, Real Estate, Buying and Selling a Home, Civil Litigation.

ROGER W. STELK, born Evanston, Illinois, July 7, 1961; admitted to bar, 1987, Illinois and U.S. District Court, Northern District of Illinois. *Education:* University of Illinois, Urbana-Champaign (B.A., 1983); John Marshall Law School (J.D., 1987). *Member:* Illinois State, American and Northwest Suburban Bar Associations. ***PRACTICE AREAS:*** Family Law; Adoption Law; Child Custody; Child Support; Equitable Distribution; Divorce; Domestic Violence; Visitation Rights; Real Estate; Buy-Sell Agreements; Civil Litigation.

STITT, KLEIN, DADAY, ARETOS & GIAMPIETRO, LLC

121 S. WILKE ROAD, SUITE 500
ARLINGTON HEIGHTS, ILLINOIS 60005
Telephone: 847-590-8700
Fax: 847-590-9825
URL: http://www.skdaglaw.com

Chicago, Illinois Office: 300 W. Adams Street, Suite 350, 60602. Telephone: 312-853-3485.

(This Listing Continued)

Litigation, Employment Litigation, Business Litigation, Intellectual Property Litigation, Commercial Litigation, Personal Injury Litigation, Divorce, Family Law, Estate Planning, Foreclosure, Civil Rights Litigation and Real Estate.

MEMBERS OF FIRM

LEMOINE D. STITT, JR. (1926-1997)

JOSEPH J. KLEIN, born Evanston, Illinois, July 27, 1957; admitted to bar, 1983, Illinois; 1984, U.S. District Court, Northern District of Illinois. *Education:* University of Illinois (B.S., 1979; M.Ed., 1983); Illinois Institute of Technology/Chicago-Kent College of Law (J.D., with honors, 1983). Kappa Delta Pi. Member: Illinois High School District 214 Board of Education, 1985-1989; Arlington Heights Housing Commission, 1985. *Member:* Northwest Suburban, Illinois State and American Bar Associations. ***PRACTICE AREAS:*** Family Law; Real Estate; Estate Planning. **Email:** jklein@skdaglaw.com

STEPHEN G. DADAY, born Bucks County, Pennsylvania, February 27, 1955; admitted to bar, 1980, Illinois and U.S. District Court, Northern District of Illinois; 1981, U.S. Court of Appeals, Tenth Circuit; 1982, U.S. District Court, Northern District of Illinois including Trial Bar. *Education:* University of Notre Dame (B.A., 1977); John Marshall Law School (J.D., 1980). Member, Arlington Heights, IL., Centennial Commission, 1985-1987. Special Assistant Attorney General of the State of Illinois, 1987—. *Member:* Chicago, Illinois State and American Bar Associations. ***PRACTICE AREAS:*** Litigation; Personal Injury Law; Commercial Litigation; Banking Law; Foreclosures. **Email:** sdaday@skdaglaw.com

MICHAEL G. ARETOS, born Chicago, Illinois, February 7, 1963; admitted to bar, 1989, Illinois and U.S. District Court, Northern District of Illinois. *Education:* Hillsdale College (B.A., 1985); John Marshall Law School (J.D., 1988). Formerly with Stitt, Klein, Daday & Aretos. *Member:* Illinois State Bar Association. ***PRACTICE AREAS:*** Real Estate; Commercial Real Estate; Residential Real Estate; Real Estate Litigation; Banking Law; Contract Litigation. **Email:** maretos@skdaglaw.com

WAYNE B. GIAMPIETRO, born Chicago, Illinois, January 20, 1942; admitted to bar, 1966, Illinois; 1967, U.S. Court of Appeals, Seventh Circuit; 1971, U.S. Court of the Armed Forces and U.S. Supreme Court; 1977, U.S. Tax Court. *Education:* Purdue University (B.A., 1963); Northwestern University (J.D., 1966). Phi Alpha Delta; Order of the Coif. Author: "The Civil Rights Act—A Federal Remedy for State Torts," 62 Illinois Bar Journal #6, February 1974; "The Constitutional Rules of Defamation," 64 Illinois Bar Journal, Volume 64 #1, September 1975; "Evening the Odds in Defamation—Troman v. Wood," Loyola University of Chicago Law Journal, Volume 7, #3, Summer 1976; "Constitutional Responsibilities of Law Enforcement Officers," Police Law Quarterly, April 1978; "The Countersuit," Vol. 6 #1, Litigation, Fall 1979 (Litigation Section of the American Bar Association). *Member:* Chicago (Chairman, Civil Practice Section, 1983-1984), Illinois State (Council Member, Individual Rights and Responsibilities Section, 1982-1990) and American (Member, Litigation Section) Bar Associations; Chicago Council of Lawyers (Member, Ethics Committee); Illinois Trial Lawyers Association; Illinois Appellate Lawyers Association; First Amendment Lawyers Association (President, 1988); The Association of Trial Lawyers of America. ***PRACTICE AREAS:*** Litigation; Appellate Practice; Intellectual Property; Commercial Litigation. **Email:** wgiampietro@skdaglaw.com

TIMOTHY J. O'DONOGHUE, born January 25, 1965; admitted to bar, 1992, Illinois and U.S. District Court, Northern District of Illinois. *Education:* John Carroll University (B.A., 1987); John Marshall Law School (J.D., 1992). ***PRACTICE AREAS:*** Litigation; Banking Law; Real Estate. **Email:** todonoghue@skdaglaw.com

ASSOCIATES

JONATHAN N. ROGERS, born 1961; admitted to bar, 1997, Illinois; 1998, U.S. District Court, Northern District of Illinois. *Education:* University of Illinois (B.A., 1993); DePaul University (J.D., 1997). *Member:* Chicago, Illinois and American Bar Associations. ***PRACTICE AREAS:*** Bankruptcy; Civil Litigation; Foreclosures. **Email:** jrogers@skdaglaw.com

RICHARD E. BIOSCA, born March 24, 1972; admitted to bar, 2000, Illinois. *Education:* University of Illinois at Chicago (B.A., 1994); DePaul University (J.D., 1998). ***PRACTICE AREAS:*** Foreclosures; Wills; Trusts; Family Law. **Email:** rbiosca@skdaglaw.com

CHRISTOPHER N. ACKERET, born Elk Grove, Illinois, April 1, 1978; admitted to bar, 2003, Illinois. *Education:* Loyola University (B.S., 2000); Chicago-Kent College of Law, Illinois Institute of Technology (J.D., 2003). *Member:* Chicago and Illinois State Bar Associations. ***PRACTICE AREAS:*** Civil Litigation. **Email:** cackeret@skdaglaw.com

SHANNON BARRY RIGBY, born Park Ridge, Illinois, August 29, 1970; admitted to bar, 2001, Illinois. *Education:* United States Military Academy (B.S., 1992); Northern Illinois University (J.D., 2000). Cook County State's Attorney. ***PRACTICE AREAS:*** Real Estate; Appellate Practice.

OF COUNSEL

THOMAS M. KLEIN, born Hammond, Indiana, December 4, 1921; admitted to bar, 1948, Illinois. *Education:* DePaul University (LL.B., 1948). Member, Arlington Heights Housing Commission, 1985. *Member:* Chicago Bar Association. [U.S. Army Air Force, 1943-1945]

NANCY S. SCOTILLO, born 1949; admitted to bar, 1975, Illinois.

MARK D. OLSON, born Brainerd, Minnesota, September 29, 1943; admitted to bar, 1966, Illinois and U.S. Court of Appeals, Seventh Circuit; 1970, U.S. District Court, Northern District of Illinois. *Education:* North Dakota State College (B.A., 1962); Concordia College; Valparaiso University (J.D., 1965). Author: Tax Problems of the Hospital Auxiliary, *The Volunteer Leader,* AHA, 1973; Illinois Malpractice Legislation, *Medicine on the Midway,* U of Chicago, 1975; Hospital Corporate Organization, *Illinois Hospital Law Manual,* ISBA, 1977; The Out of Control ED Patient, *The Hospital Medical Staff,* AHA, 1978; Hospital Corporate Organization and Corporate ByLaws, *Hospital Law,* ISBA, 1980 and 1985; The Case for Self-Insurance, *Trustee,* AHA, May 1981; Nosocomial Infections-Next Target for Malpractice Suits, *The Hospital Medical Staff,* AHA, July, 1981; Organizing a Successful PHO (two parts), *Orthopedics Today,* February and April 1994; Join the IDN Revolution (two parts), *Trustee,* April and September 1996. Assistant Professor, School of Nursing, Northern Illinois University, 1981-1986. Vice Chairman, Committee on Law and Medicine, American Bar Association, 1979-1982. *Member:* National Health Lawyers Association (formerly American Society of Hospital Attorneys) (Secretary, 1971-1974); Catholic Hospital Association (Member, Legal Relations Panel, 1981-1982); American Association of Preferred Providers (Member, Legislative Committee, 1992-1996; Regional Board of Directors, 1992-2001); Children's Memorial Hospital (Member, Ethics Advisory Board). ***PRACTICE AREAS:*** Health Care Law; Litigation.

(This Listing Continued)

ROBERT S. THOMAS

1655 NORTH ARLINGTON HEIGHTS ROAD
SUITE 300 WEST
ARLINGTON HEIGHTS, ILLINOIS 60004
Telephone: 847-392-5893
Fax: 847-392-5894
Email: rstlaw2000@yahoo.com
URL: http://www.arlingtonheightslawyers.com

Bankruptcy, Chapter 7, Personal Bankruptcy, Collections, Residential and Commercial Real Estate, Buying and Selling a Home, Zoning and Land Use, Family Law, Divorce, Adoption, Child Custody, Child Support, Wills and Probate, Trusts and Estates, Estate Planning, Asset Protection, Contracts, Breach of Contract.

ROBERT S. THOMAS, admitted to bar, 1984, Ohio; 1985, Illinois. *Education:* Indiana University (B.A., cum laude, 1979); Cleveland Marshall College of Law (J.D., 1983). Attorney, General Motors (GMH Division), 1985-1988. *Member:* Illinois State and Ohio State Bar Associations; Federal Trial Bar Association.

THOMAS YOUNG LAW FIRM

ARLINGTON HEIGHTS, ILLINOIS

(See Palatine)

ARIANO, HARDY, NYULI, JOHNSON, RICHMOND & GOETTEL, P.C.

AURORA, ILLINOIS

(See Elgin)

General Civil and Criminal Practice in all Courts. Banking, Probate, Real Estate, Corporation, Federal Taxation, Transactional, Employment, Family, Personal Injury, Collections, Creditor Bankruptcy, Foreclosures, Landlord and Tenant Law, Workers Compensation Law, Mediation, Zoning, Planning and Land Use.

LAW OFFICE OF BRUCE A. BROWN

2000 WEST GALENA, SUITE 201
AURORA, ILLINOIS 60506
Telephone: 630-897-2800
Fax: 630-897-2876
Email: bbrown@bablegal.com

Corporate Law, Banks and Banking, Business Law, Construction Law, Commercial Real Estate, Real Estate, Mortgages, Contracts, Contested Estates, Litigation.

BRUCE A. BROWN, born Chicago, Illinois, October 10, 1946; admitted to bar, 1973, Illinois, U.S. District Court, Northern District of Illinois, including Trial Bar and U.S. Court of Appeals, Seventh Circuit. *Education:* University of Illinois (B.A., 1968; J.D., 1973). Phi Alpha Theta. *Member:* Kane County, Illinois State and American Bar Associations. ***REPORTED CASES:*** Foxcroft Townhome Owners Association v. Hoffman Rosner Corp., 96 Ill.2d 150, 449 N.E.2d 125 (1983); In re Semmler, 107 Ill.2d 130, 481 N.E.2d 716 (1985); Desmond Co. v. Jackson National Life Insurance Co., 223 Ill.App.3d 616, 166 Ill.Dec. 98 (1992); Knauf v. Ryan, 338 Ill. App.3d 265, 273 Ill.Dec 214 (2003); Shore Packaging Corp. v. Melchiorre, 341 Ill.App.3d 345, 275 Ill.Dec 164 (2003). ***PRACTICE AREAS:*** Corporate Law; Banks and Banking; Business Law; Construction Law; Commercial Real Estate; Real Estate; Mortgages; Contracts; Contested Estates; Litigation.

OF COUNSEL

CAROL L. ANFINSON, admitted to bar, 1970, Illinois. *Education:* University of Illinois (B.S.; J.D.); John Marshall (LL.M., Taxation). ***PRACTICE AREAS:*** Criminal Law; Real Estate Law; Family Law; Taxation.

STEPHEN A. BRUNDAGE

AURORA, ILLINOIS

(See Wheaton)

Criminal Law, Driving While Intoxicated, Drug Crimes, Felonies, Homicide, Juvenile Law, Misdemeanors, Parole and Probation, Sexual Assault, Traffic Violations, Assault and Battery, Burglary, Criminal Defense, Drivers License Suspension, Forgery, Manslaughter, Search and Seizure, Sex Crimes, Theft, Juvenile Law, Family Law, Divorce, Child Custody, Child Support, Domestic Violence, Premarital Agreements, Spousal Support, Martial Agreements, Marital Property Distribution, Martial Property Law, Marital Property Settlements, Matrimonial Law, Paternity, Post Divorce Modification, Real Estate, Real Estate Sales, Residential Real Estate, Residential Real Estate Sales, Personal Injury, Automobile Accidents and Injuries, Dog Bites, Sexual Abuse, Slip and Fall and Wrongful Death Law.

LAW OFFICES OF SUSAN G. CASTAGNOLI, P.C.

Established in 1991

1444 NORTH FARNSWORTH AVENUE, SUITE 107
AURORA, ILLINOIS 60505
Telephone: 630-717-1594; TT4-630-566-5222
Fax: 630-717-1596
Email: susancastagnoli@scastagnolilaw.com
URL: http://www.castagnolilaw.com

Naperville, Illinois Office: 1119 North Washington Street, 60563. Telephone: 630-717-1594. Fax: 630-717-1596.

Bankruptcy, Commercial Bankruptcy, Consumer Bankruptcy, Foreclosures, Debt Management, Family, Divorce, Divorce Planning, Premarital Agreements, Custody, Adoptions, Child Support, Real Estate, Financial Planning, Wills and Probate, Estate Planning, Trusts and Estates, Equine Law.

FIRM PROFILE: 26 Years of personal attention to the needs of the client are the benchmark of the firm. All clients meet personally with attorney Susan G. Castagnoli.

Languages: Sign Language.

(for complete biographical data on personnel see Professional Biographies at Naperville, Illinois)

DICKSON & HASENBALG

Established in 1924

2000 WEST GALENA BOULEVARD
SUITE 305
AURORA, ILLINOIS 60506-4360
Telephone: 630-859-3300
Fax: 630-859-3375
Email: chasenbalg@d-hlaw.com
URL: http://www.d-hlaw.com

Corporate Law, Business Law, Taxation, Trusts and Estates, Commercial Real Estate, Litigation, General Civil and Trial Practice.

FIRM PROFILE: The firm has roots tracing back to 1924. The firm regularly practices in Kane, Kendall, DuPage, Cook, DeKalb, Will, Lake and McHenry counties and also serves a variety of clients nationwide. Each attorney is encouraged to concentrate his or her practice in a defined area of expertise and to focus his or her continuing education in this area. Lawyers of the firm recognize the importance of professional development and their duty to actively participate in legal training and educational programs, professional activities and civic affairs. The firm is the successor to Goldsmith, Thelin, Dickson & Brown, with the firm name changed to its current name October 1, 2003.

MEMBERS OF FIRM

FREDERICK H. DICKSON, born Aurora, Illinois, March 10, 1938; admitted to bar, 1964, Illinois and U.S. District Court, Northern District of Illinois, including Trial Bar; 1987, U.S. Tax Court. *Education:* University of Illinois (B.S., 1962; LL.B., 1964); Illinois Institute of Technology/Chicago-Kent College of Law (LL.M., with honors in Taxation, 1986). Member, Federal Taxation Section Council of the Illinois State Bar Association, 1988-1996; Secretary, 1992-1993; Vice Chairman, 1993-1994; Chairman, 1994-1995. Editor, Federal Tax Newsletter, 1990-1993; Member, Trust and Estates Council, Illinois State Bar Association, 1995-2004. Fellow, American College of Trust and Estate Counsel. *Member:* Kane County, DuPage County, Illinois State and American Bar Associations. ***REPORTED CASES:*** Crestview Builders, Inc. v. Noggle Family Limited Partnership, 352 Ill. App. 3d 1182 (2004). ***PRACTICE AREAS:*** Taxation; Corporate Law; Trusts and Estates; Probate. ***Email:*** fdickson@d-hlaw.com

CRAIG D. HASENBALG, born Los Angeles, California, March 26, 1968; admitted to bar, 1993, Illinois and U.S. District Court, Northern District of Illinois; 1995, U.S. Tax Court. *Education:* University of California at San Diego (B.A., magna cum laude, 1990); University of California at Berkeley (J.D., 1993); Illinois Institute of Technology/Chicago-Kent College of Law (LL.M., Taxation, 1998). *Member:* Kane County, Illinois State and American Bar Associations. ***REPORTED CASES:*** Crestview Builders, Inc. v. Noggle Family Limited Partnership, 352 Ill. App. 3d 1182 (2004). ***PRACTICE AREAS:*** Taxation; Trusts and Estate Planning; Corporate Law; Real Estate. ***Email:*** chasenbalg@d-hlaw.com

ASSOCIATES

JEAN C. FRANCISSEN, born DesPlaines, Illinois, June 16, 1966; admitted to bar, 1992, California and U.S. District Court, Northern District of California; 1993, Illinois. *Education:* University of Illinois (B.S., 1988); Hastings College of the Law, University of California (J.D., 1992). *Member:* Kane County Bar Association. ***PRACTICE AREAS:*** Trusts and Estates; Commercial Litigation; Appellate Practice. ***Email:*** jfrancissen@d-hlaw.com

ANDREW G. WHITE, born Jacksonville, Illinois, May 3, 1979; admitted to bar, 2004, Illinois; 2005, U.S. District Court, Northern District of Illinois. *Education:* University of Illinois (B.S., 2001); Ohio Northern University (J.D., 2004). *Member:* Chicago, Kane County and Illinois State Bar Associations. ***PRACTICE AREAS:*** Trusts and Estates; Wills; Probate; Real Estate; Tax Law; Appellate Practice; Agricultural Law. ***Email:*** awhite@d-hlaw.com

OF COUNSEL

CALVIN B. THELIN, born Oak Park, Illinois, September 8, 1929; admitted to bar, 1958, Illinois, U.S. District Court, Northern District of Illinois and U.S. Tax Court including Trial Bar. *Education:* Colgate University (A.B., 1951); Northwestern University (J.D., 1957). Assistant Attorney General, 1960-1961. City Attorney, Aurora, 1961-1964. Special Assistant Attorney General, 1970-1982. *Member:* Kane County, Illinois State and American Bar Associations. ***PRACTICE AREAS:*** Business Law; Real Estate; Trusts and Estates; Probate. ***Email:*** cal@farnsworthoffice.com

Language: English.

REPRESENTATIVE CLIENTS: *Banks:* Aurora Earthmovers Credit Union; Old Kent Bank; LaSalle Bank (Lisle). *Corporations:* Aurora Bearing Co.; Cable Plus, Inc.; JKS Tool & Manufacturing Co.; Midway Development Co.; Quantum Data; Universal Equipment Exchange, Inc.; Wadsworth Golf Construction Co.

DOMMERMUTH, BRESTAL, COBINE AND WEST, LTD.

Established in 1983

OLD SECOND NATIONAL BANK BUILDING
111 WEST DOWNER PLACE, SUITE 300
AURORA, ILLINOIS 60506
Telephone: 630-892-5700
Email: PLP@DBCW.com

Naperville, Illinois Office: 123 Water Street. Telephone: 630-355-5800.

General Civil Practice. Personal Injury, Worker's Compensation, Corporate, Banking, Municipal, Zoning and Development, Real Estate, Family and Probate Law, Litigation, Federal and State Taxation, Commercial Collection.

REPRESENTATIVE CLIENTS: DuPage Precision Products, Inc.; North Central College; Naperville Fire Protection District; Macom Corp.; Mid America Federal Savings and Loan Association; Beidelman-Kunsch Funeral Home; Engineering Equipment Co.; Shell Oil Co.; Phillips 66 Co.; Amoco Oil Co.; Mobil Oil Co.; Pulte Home Corp.; Prime Group; Catholic Diocese of Joliet; Our Savior Lutheran Church; Hawthorne Credit Union; Home Builders of Illinois; Wiseman-Hughes Enterprises, Inc.; Lakewood Homes, Inc.; Pep Boys; McDonald's Corp.; Walsh, Higgins & Co.; Crestview Builders, Inc.; Inland Realty; Central DuPage Health System; Edward Hospital; Moser Enterprises; MAF Corporation; Meijer, Inc.; Ocean Atlantic Woodland Corporation; Security Bank of DuPage; DePaul University; Cambridge Homes, Inc.; BFI, Incorporated.

(For Complete Biographical Data of all Personnel, see Professional Biographies at Naperville, Illinois)

DREYER, FOOTE, STREIT, FURGASON AND SLOCUM

A PROFESSIONAL ASSOCIATION

Established in 1963

1999 W. DOWNER PLACE
AURORA, ILLINOIS 60506-4384
Telephone: 630-897-8764
FAX: 630-897-1735
Email: info@dreyerfoote.com
URL: http://www.dreyerfoote.com

Civil and Criminal Trial and Appellate Practice in all State and Federal Courts. Business Planning, Commercial, Corporate, Estate Planning, Wills, Probate, Trusts and Estates, Elder Law, Family Law, Healthcare, Insurance and Insurance Defense, Labor, Municipal, Personal Injury, Probate, Real Estate, State and Federal Taxation, Adoption, Child Support, Child Custody, Divorce, Domestic Violence, DWI, Automobile Accidents, Wrongful Death, Buying and Selling a Home, Landlord/Tenant, Construction, Bankruptcy, Guardianships, Collections, Buying and Selling a Business, Business Enterprises, Franchise, Closely Held Business, Limited Liability, Partnerships, Small Business, Contracts, Lawsuits, Starting a Business, Zoning.

WILLIAM J. FOOTE, born Sandwich, Illinois, May 11, 1932; admitted to bar, 1958, Illinois, U.S. District Court, Northern District of Illinois including Trial Bar, U.S. Court of Appeals, Seventh Circuit and U.S. Tax Court. *Education:* Harvard University (A.B., magna cum laude, 1955; LL.B., 1958). Corporation Counsel, City of Aurora, 1965-1973. Special Assignment Lawyer, City of Aurora, 1973-1977. *Member:* Kane County and Illinois State Bar Associations. ***PRACTICE AREAS:*** Litigation; Family Law; Estate Planning; Commercial Transactions; Real Estate; Zoning Law. ***Email:*** wfoote@dreyerfoote.com

THOMAS J. STREIT, born Aurora, Illinois, August 3, 1940; admitted to bar, 1965, Illinois. *Education:* Marquette University (A.B., 1962); University of Michigan (LL.B., 1965). Phi Delta Phi; Pi Gamma Mu; Phi Alpha Theta. *Member:* Kane County and Illinois State Bar Associations. ***PRACTICE AREAS:*** Real Estate; Zoning Law; Commercial Transactions; Probate. ***Email:*** tstreit@dreyerfoote.com

RICHARD M. FURGASON, born Chicago, Illinois, November 2, 1949; admitted to bar, 1974, Illinois, U.S. District Court, Northern District of Illinois including Trial Bar and U.S. Court of Appeals, Seventh Circuit. *Education:* St. Mary's College and DePaul University (B.A., summa cum laude, 1971); University of Notre Dame (J.D., cum laude, 1974). Notre Dame Law Review, 1973-1974. *Member:* Kane County, Illinois State and American Bar Associations; Illinois Trial Lawyers Association; Association of Trial Lawyers of America. ***PRACTICE AREAS:*** Civil Litigation; Commercial Litigation; Business Planning; Business Transactions; Commercial Transactions; Health Care; Real Estate; Estate Planning; Elder Law; Probate. ***Email:*** rfurgason@dreyerfoote.com

RICHARD C. SLOCUM, born Beloit, Wisconsin, December 29, 1950; admitted to bar, 1976, Illinois and U.S. District Court, Northern District of Illinois. *Education:* Western Illinois University (B.A., magna cum laude, 1973); Drake University (J.D., 1976); The John Marshall Law School (Master of Laws, Taxation, 1984). Phi Kappa Phi. *Member:* Chicago, Kane County and Illinois State Bar Associations; Illinois Trial Lawyers Association; American Arbitration Association. ***PRACTICE AREAS:*** Personal Injury; Family Law; Real Estate; Zoning Law; Business Transactions; Estate Planning. ***Email:*** rcslocum@dreyerfoote.com

PAUL T. PATRICOSKI, born Fort Rucker, Alabama, March 24, 1955; admitted to bar, 1981, Illinois; 1982, U.S. District Court, Northern District of Illinois including Trial

(This Listing Continued)

Bar; 1997, U.S. Court of Appeals, Seventh Circuit. *Education:* St. Vincent College (B.S., 1977); University of Notre Dame (J.D., 1981). *Member:* Kane County, Illinois State and American Bar Associations. **PRACTICE AREAS:** Divorce; Family Law; Child Support; Child Custody; Visitation Rights; Landlord-Tenant; Civil Litigation; Commercial Litigation; Real Estate; Wills; Probate. **Email:** ppatricoski@dreyerfoote.com

ROBERT F. BROUCH, born Aurora, Illinois, August 17, 1961; admitted to bar, 1986, Illinois and U.S. District Court, Northern District of Illinois. *Education:* Illinois State University (B.S., 1983); Northern Illinois University (J.D., 1986). *Member:* Kane County, Illinois State and American Bar Associations. **PRACTICE AREAS:** Personal Injury; Workers Compensation; Real Estate; Civil Litigation; Criminal Defense; Insurance Defense. **Email:** rbrouch@dreyerfoote.com

JONATHAN B. SHANOWER, born Naperville, Illinois, November 24, 1962; admitted to bar, 1989, Illinois and U.S. District Court, Northern District of Illinois; 1997, U.S. Court of Appeals, Seventh Circuit; 1998, Montana. *Education:* North Central College (B.A., 1985); Ohio Northern University College of Law (J.D., 1989). Recipient: American Jurisprudence Awards, Real Estate Transactions and Finance; Jurisprudence. *Member:* Kane County, Illinois State and American Bar Associations; State Bar of Montana. **PRACTICE AREAS:** Civil Litigation; Condominium Law; Collections; Real Estate. **Email:** jshanower@dreyerfoote.com

---

MICHAEL W. HUSEMAN, born Crown Point, Indiana, October 16, 1977; admitted to bar, 2003, Illinois. *Education:* St. Joseph's College (B.A., 2000); Northern Illinois University College of Law (J.D., 2003). **PRACTICE AREAS:** Divorce; Misdemeanors; Post Judgment Collections; Garnishments; Post Divorce Modification; Domestic Violence. **Email:** mhuseman@dreyerfoote.com

JACKIE L. JALLEY, admitted to bar, 2002, Illinois. *Education:* University of Illinois (B.A., cum laude, 1997); Northern Illinois University (J.D., 2002). Phi Alpha Delta (Treasurer, 2000-2001). **PRACTICE AREAS:** Family; Real Estate; Civil Litigation; Criminal. **Email:** jjalley@dreyerfoote.com

OF COUNSEL

JOHN E. DREYER, born Chicago, Illinois, February 22, 1929; admitted to bar, 1953, Illinois, U.S. District Court, Northern District of Illinois including Trial Bar and U.S. Court of Appeals, Seventh Circuit. *Education:* Loyola University (B.S., 1951); DePaul University (J.D., 1953). Phi Alpha Delta. Member, Society of Trial Lawyers. Member, Board of Editors, De Paul Law Review, 1952 and 1953. *Member:* Aurora, Kane County, Illinois State (Member: Executive Council, Junior Bar Section, 1961-1964; Assembly, 1972-1978) and American Bar Associations; American Judicature Society; National Association of Railroad Trial Counsel.

REPRESENTATIVE CLIENTS: Old Second National Bank; Aurora Eye Clinic; Aurora Pediatric Clinic; Rush Copley Medical Center; Industrial Motor Service, Inc.; R.D. Marcley, Inc.; Aurora Fast Freight, Inc.; Mid-States Express, Inc.; United Express System, Inc.; Fox Valley Machining Co., Inc.; National Metalware's, Inc.; Prairie Cleaners; Bockman Brothers Jewelers; Cipher, Ltd.; Feltes Plumbing, Inc.; Vermeer - Illinois Inc.; Valley Cartage, Inc.; Georgetown of Batavia Condominium II Ass'n.; Georgetown of Batavia Condominium Ass'n; Oakhurst Community Association; Millpond Condominium Ass'n.; Woodland Lakes Townhomes Ass'n.; Assisi Homes - Batavia Apartments; White Eagle Homeowner's Ass'n.; Orchard Valley Homeowner's Ass'n.; Aurora Public Library and it's Foundation.
APPROVED ATTORNEYS FOR: Attorneys' Title Guaranty Fund, Inc.; First American Title Ins. Co.; Chicago Title Ins. Co.
REFERENCE: The Old Second National Bank of Aurora.

DYKEMA GOSSETT PLLC

Established in 1926

2 HANKES ROAD
AURORA, ILLINOIS 60506
Telephone: 630-844-2200
Fax: 630-844-2277
URL: http://www.dykema.com

Ann Arbor, Michigan Office: 2723 South State Street, Suite 400, 48104. Telephone: 734-214-7660. Fax: 734-214-7696.
Bloomfield Hills, Michigan Office: 39577 Woodward Avenue, Suite 300, 48304-2820. Telephone: 248-203-0700. Fax: 248-203-0763.
Chicago, Illinois Office: 10 South Wacker Drive, Suite 2300. Telephone: 312-876-1700. Fax: 312-876-1155.
Detroit, Michigan Office: 400 Renaissance Center, 48243-1668. Telephone: 313-568-6800. Fax: 313-568-6545.
Grand Rapids, Michigan Office: Suite 700, 300 Ottawa Avenue, N.W., 49503-2306. Telephone: 616-776-7500. Fax: 616-776-7573.
Joliet, Illinois Office: 111 North Ottawa Street. Telephone: 815-727-4511. Facsimile: 815-727-1586.
Lansing, Michigan Office: 124 W. Allegan Street, Suite 800, 48933-1742. Telephone: 517-374-9100. Fax: 517-374-9191.
Lisle, Illinois Office: 4200 Commerce Court, Suite 300. Telephone: 630-245-0400. Facsimile: 630-245-0140.
Los Angeles, California Office: 333 South Grand Avenue, Suite 2100, 90071. Telephone: 213-457-1800. Fax: 213-457-1850.
Washington, D.C. Office: Franklin Square, Suite 300 West, 1300 I Street, N.W., 20005-3353. Telephone: 202-906-8600. Fax: 202-906-8669.

Antitrust and Trade Regulation, Automotive, Banking and Financial Services, Bankruptcy, Biotechnology and Life Sciences, Casino Gaming, Class Action Defense, Computer and Software Law, Construction, Consumer Financial Services, Corporate Finance, E-Commerce, Emerging Business and Technology, Employee Benefits, Entertainment and Sports, Environmental Law, Family Law, Franchise Law and Regulation, Government Contracts, Government Policy and Practice, HealthCare, Indian Law, Insurance, Intellectual Property, International Law, Labor and Employment, Litigation and Dispute Resolution, Mergers and Acquisitions, Products Liability Defense, Public Finance, Real Estate, Retail Law, Securities, Taxation and Estates, Trade Associations.

FIRM PROFILE: Dykema Gossett PLLC represents the interests of domestic and foreign-based companies and institutions on a broad array of matters. Our diversified practice and Midwest work ethic have long made Dykema the choice of Fortune 100 companies, privately-held businesses, entrepreneurial enterprises and emerging businesses. With offices in Michigan, California, Illinois and Washington, D.C., Dykema has expanded beyond its original Michigan roots to become one of the largest firms in the United States. Our recent merger with Rooks Pitts in Illinois, effective April 1, 2004, is a significant milestone in our continued growth in the Midwest. We are proud to be recognized by area businesses as a corporate leader, and our broad-based litigation practice is routinely chosen by clients and peers alike as one of the best in the nation. Dykema is equally well known for our experienced government relations specialists, whose experience at the national, state and local levels is unrivalled. From manufacturers and automotive suppliers to financial institutions, from patent and trademark disputes to complex class action defense, from startups to large multinational corporations, our clients repeatedly look to Dykema to help them navigate through an ever-increasing stream of complex litigation and changing business environments.

MEMBER OF FIRM

BRUCE L. GOLDSMITH, born Aurora, Illinois, December 21, 1945; admitted to bar, 1971, Illinois and U.S. District Court, Northern District of Illinois; 1975, U.S. Court of Appeals, Seventh Circuit; 1981, U.S. Supreme Court. *Education:* Northwestern University (B.A., summa cum laude, 1968); University of Chicago (J.D., 1971). Phi Beta Kappa. **PRACTICE AREAS:** Commercial Real Estate Law; Corporate Law; Labor and Employment; Commercial Litigation; Zoning, Planning and Land Use. **Email:** bgoldsmith@dykema.com

---

LAW OFFICES OF MICHAEL C. FUNKEY, P.C.

2111 PLUM STREET, SUITE 301
AURORA, ILLINOIS 60506
Telephone: 630-897-4284
FAX: 630-897-4220
URL: http://www.michaelcfunkeypc.com

General Practice, Civil Litigation, Contested Litigation, and Trials and Appeals in all civil matters including Automobile Accidents, Slip and Fall, Dog Bites, Wrongful Death, Products Liability, Divorce, Child Custody, Child Support, Proceedings involving Orders of Protection, Family Law Matters, Personal Injury, Eminent Domain, Real Estate, Juvenile Law, Municipal and Election Law, Wills, Probate, Trusts and Estates, Estate Planning, DUI, Trials and Appeals in Misdemeanor and Criminal Matters.

MICHAEL C. FUNKEY, born Berwyn, Illinois, May 7, 1945; admitted to bar, 1970, Illinois. *Education:* Loyola University in New Orleans (B.A., 1967); Loyola University and DePaul University (J.D., 1970). Adjunct Professor, Northern Illinois University College of Law, 1996—. Chairman, Board of Directors, Harris Bank, Aurora, Illinois, 2001—. Township Attorney, Town of Aurora, 1997—. Member: Illinois Board of Admissions to the Bar, 1994-2003; Fox Metro Water Reclamation District, Trustee, 2005—. *Member:* Kane County, DeKalb County and Illinois State (Secretary, 2001-2002; Vice-Chair, 2002-2003, Chair, 2003-2004, Civil Practice and Procedure Section Council) Bar Associations; Northern Illinois University American Inns of Court. **PRACTICE AREAS:** General Practice; Civil Litigation; Trial Practice; Appellate Practice; Misdemeanors; Criminal Practice; Contested Divorce; Divorce; Child Custody; Child Support; Family Law; Personal Injury; Eminent Domain; Real Estate; Juvenile Law; Municipal Law; Election Law; Wills; Probate; Trusts and Estates; Estate Planning; Driving While Intoxicated.

KINNALLY, KRENTZ, LORAN, HODGE & HERMAN, P.C.

Established in 2000

2114 DEERPATH ROAD
P.O. BOX 5030
AURORA, ILLINOIS 60506
Telephone: 630-907-0909
Fax: 630-907-0913
URL: http://www.kklhhlaw.com
Email: pkinnally@kklhhlaw.com
URL: http://www.lawyers.com/kklhhlaw

General Practice. Civil Trial Practice, Personal Injury, Auto Accidents, Worker's Compensation, Corporate Law, Immigration and Naturalization, Business Law, Estate Planning, Trusts, Estates and Probate, Municipal and Zoning Law, Education Law, Environmental and Eminent Domain.

FIRM PROFILE: Concentrating in civil litigation, the firm has a long and successful record in representing its clients in personal injury cases, workers compensation claims, commercial litigation, injunction trials, probate litigation, immigration law, and condemnation cases.

The firm has attained record verdicts and settlements for its clients and its members are frequent lecturers at continuing legal seminars. Members of the firm also practice in a broad number of areas, including real estate, local government law, school law, estate planning and corporate law.

PATRICK M. KINNALLY, born Aurora, Illinois, March 16, 1950; admitted to bar, 1980, Indiana and Illinois, U.S. District Court Northern and Southern, Districts of Indiana,

(This Listing Continued)

KINNALLY, KRENTZ, LORAN, HODGE & HERMAN, P.C., Aurora—Continued

U.S. District Court, Northern, Central, Southern, Districts of Illinois, U.S. Supreme Court. *Education:* Loyola University (B.A., cum laude, 1972); John Marshall Law School (J.D., 1980). Law Clerk, Illinois Third District Appellate Court, 1981-1982. Adjunct Professor of Law, Northern Illinois University, 1999—. Special Assistant State's Attorney, Kane County; Kendall County. Listed: "Leading Lawyers" Commercial Litigation. *Member:* Kane County and Illinois State Bar Associations; Illinois Trial Lawyers Association; American Immigration Lawyers Association. ***LANGUAGES:*** Spanish. ***PRACTICE AREAS:*** Business Law; Civil Trial Practice; Appellate Practice; Local Government Law; Environmental Law; Immigration and Naturalization. ***Email:*** pkinnally@kklhhlaw.com

PAUL G. KRENTZ, born Aurora, Illinois, November 16, 1958; admitted to bar, 1983, Illinois including Trial Bar and U.S. District Court, Northern District of Illinois. *Education:* Valparaiso University (B.S., 1980; J.D., 1983). Mediator, DuPage County. *Member:* Kane County, DeKalb County, DuPage County, Illinois State and American Bar Associations. Illinois Trial Lawyers Association; The Association of Trial Lawyers of America. ***REPORTED CASES:*** Eichler vs. Plitt Theater, Inc. (2nd. Dist. 1988) 167 Ill. App. 3d 685, 521 N.E. 2d 1196. ***PRACTICE AREAS:*** Civil Trial Practice; Personal Injury; Sexual Abuse; Eminent Domain. ***Email:*** pkrentz@kklhhlaw.com

JOSEPH C. LORAN, born Chicago, Illinois, March 10, 1959; admitted to bar, 1985, Illinois and U.S. District Court, Northern District of Illinois. *Education:* University of Illinois; Brown University (B.A., 1981); Loyola University (J.D., 1985). *Member:* Kane County and Illinois State Bar Associations; Illinois Trial Lawyers Association; The Association of Trial Lawyers of America; Workers' Compensation Lawyers Association. ***PRACTICE AREAS:*** Civil Trial Practice; Personal Injury; Workers Compensation; School Law. ***Email:*** jloran@kklhhlaw.com

GERALD K. HODGE, born Geneva, Illinois, April 13, 1959; admitted to bar, 1984, Illinois. *Education:* Augustana College (B.A., 1981); Valparaiso University (J.D., 1984). Associate Editor, Valparaiso University Law Review, 1983-1984. *Member:* Kane County, Illinois State and American Bar Associations. ***PRACTICE AREAS:*** Corporate Law; Real Estate; Business Law; Trusts and Estates; Wills; Probate. ***Email:*** ghodge@kklhhlaw.com

MATTHEW J. HERMAN, born Rahway, New Jersey, April 12, 1970; admitted to bar, 1996, Illinois and U.S. District Court, Northern District of Illinois. *Education:* University of Delaware (B.S., 1992); John Marshall Law School (J.D., cum laude, 1996). Order of John Marshall. Member, John Marshall Law Review. *Member:* Kane County and Illinois State Bar Associations; Illinois Trial Lawyers Association. ***PRACTICE AREAS:*** Civil Trial Practice; Corporate Law; Appellate Practice. ***Email:*** mherman@kklhhlaw.com

---

DIANA M. LAW, born Aurora, Illinois, June 6, 1978; admitted to bar, 2004, Illinois. *Education:* Goshen College (B.A., 2000); Northern Illinois University (J.D., 2004). ***LANGUAGES:*** Spanish. ***PRACTICE AREAS:*** Civil Litigation; Immigration Law.

OF COUNSEL

WILLIAM C. MURPHY, born Chicago, Illinois, December 5, 1920; admitted to bar, 1949, Illinois. *Education:* Harvard University (S.B., 1942; J.D., 1948). City Attorney, 1948-1952. *Member:* Kane County (President, 1972-1973), Illinois State and American Bar Associations; The Association of Trial Lawyers of America; American Law Institute. Fellow, American College of Trial Lawyers. ***PRACTICE AREAS:*** Civil Litigation; Personal Injury Law; Environmental Defense Law; Asbestos Litigation.

Language: Spanish.

REPRESENTATIVE CLIENTS: Apex Builders, Inc.; Aurora Interfaith Food Pantry; Aurora Tri-State Fire Protection, Inc.; Charlestowne Mall, LLC; Chicago Title Insurance Company; Conco Western Stone Company; Cress Creek Country Club; Dolan & Murphy, Inc.; First Bank Inc.; Fox Valley Park District; Genesee Management, Inc.; Hinsdale Township High School District 86; County of Kane; Kane County Forest Preserve District; County of Kendall; David P. Lauzen & Company; Law Title Insurance Company; Little Rock Township; Lyon Metal Products, LLC; Marmion Academy; Masoncorp, Inc.; Missionaries of the Sacred Heart; The National Bank & Trust Company of Sycamore; The Peter Orum Nurseries; Paris Metal Products, LLC; Superior Beverage Co.; Sycamore Systems, LLC; Wilmorite Inc.

DANIEL F. KLENKE

Established in 1993

563 WEST GALENA BOULEVARD
AURORA, ILLINOIS 60506-3854
Telephone: 630-896-1020
Fax: 630-892-7184
Email: dfklaw@sbcglobal.net
URL: http://www.dfklawfirm.com

Alternative Dispute Resolution, Business, Commercial, Employment, Discrimination, Wrongful Termination, Administrative, Family Law, Divorce, Adoption, Real Estate and Litigation, Buying and Selling, Municipal Law, Child Custody, Child Support, Grandparent Rights, Stepparent.

DANIEL F. KLENKE, born Ft. Wayne, Indiana, July, 1955; admitted to bar, 1981, Illinois and U.S. District Court, Northern District of Illinois. *Education:* University of Illinois (B.A., 1977); Washington University (J.D., 1981). Panelist, Kane County Mandatory Arbitration. Certified Guardian Ad Litem, Kane County. Former Counsel, Aurora University. Administrative Hearing Officer: City of Aurora, 1994-1998; Village of Park Forest, 2000—. *Member:* Kane County and Illinois State Bar Associations. ***PRACTICE AREAS:*** Family Law; Commercial Law; Employment Law; Litigation.

LINDNER, SPEERS & REULAND, P.C.

Established in 1979

54 WEST DOWNER PLACE
P.O. BOX 5055
AURORA, ILLINOIS 60507
Telephone: 630-892-8109
Fax: 630-892-8151
Email: Help@auroralawfirm.com
URL: http://www.auroralawfirm.com

The firm represents persons injured by vehicles, trains, aircraft, doctors, hospitals, and products, as well as victims of sexual harassment, police misconduct, and all forms of employment discrimination. The firm also represents persons and businesses in disputes between business entities and business owners, and litigates will contests and zoning disputes.

GEORGE P. LINDNER, born Sandwich, Illinois, May 22, 1940; admitted to bar, 1965, Illinois. *Education:* University of Colorado (B.A., 1962; LL.B., 1965). Phi Alpha Delta. *Member:* Kane County (Past Chair, Medical Negligence Committee) and Illinois State Bar Associations; The Association of Trial Lawyers of America; Illinois Trial Lawyers Association (Member, Board of Managers). ***PRACTICE AREAS:*** Personal Injury; Medical Negligence; Hospital Negligence; Products Liability; Wrongful Death; Airplane Crash Litigation; Railroad Accidents and Injuries; Automobile Accidents. ***Email:*** GL@auroralawfirm.com

ROBERT L. SPEERS, born Evanston, Illinois, August 10, 1945; admitted to bar, 1972, Illinois. *Education:* Iowa State University (B.S., 1967); University of Illinois (J.D., 1972). *Member:* Kane County (President, 1988-1989) and Illinois State Bar Associations; Illinois Trial Lawyers Association; The Association of Trial Lawyers of America. ***PRACTICE AREAS:*** Litigation; Plaintiff Personal Injury; Wrongful Death; Products Liability; Automobile Accidents; Mediation; Arbitration. ***Email:*** RS@auroralawfirm.com

TIMOTHY J. REULAND, born Aurora, Illinois, August 5, 1948; admitted to bar, 1973, Illinois. *Education:* Loyola University, Chicago (B.A., cum laude, 1970); Northwestern University (J.D., cum laude, 1973). Alpha Sigma Nu; Phi Sigma Tau; Blue Key. Executive Editor, Journal of Criminal Law and Criminology, 1972-1973. *Member:* Kane County, Chicago, Illinois State and American Bar Associations; The Association of Trial Lawyers of America; Illinois Trial Lawyers Association. ***PRACTICE AREAS:*** Plaintiffs Personal Injury; Business Litigation; Automobile Accidents. ***Email:*** TR@auroralawfirm.com

JULIE L. CIBULSKIS, born Aurora, Illinois, May 11, 1973; admitted to bar, 1998, Illinois. *Education:* Creighton University (B.A., summa cum laude, 1995); Seton Hall University, School of Law (J.D., magna cum laude, 1998). *Member:* Chicago, Kane County (Director, 2002—; Chair, Continuing Legal Education Committee, 2004-2005), Illinois State and American Bar Associations; Illinois Trial Lawyers Association. ***PRACTICE AREAS:*** Plaintiffs Personal Injury; Business Litigation; Civil Litigation; Automobile Accidents. ***Email:*** JC@auroralawfirm.com

---

TERRANCE W. HEADY, born Oak Lawn, Illinois, May 17, 1968; admitted to bar, 1996, Illinois; U.S. District Court, Northern District of Illinois; U.S. Court of Appeals, Seventh Circuit. *Education:* University of Central Florida (B.A., 1992); Northern Illinois University, College of Law (J.D., 1996). Trial Bar, United States District Court. *Member:* Kane County, Illinois State and American Bar Associations; Illinois Trial Lawyers Association; The Association of Trial Lawyers of America. ***PRACTICE AREAS:*** Plaintiff Personal Injury; Plaintiff Medical Malpractice; Employment Discrimination and Retaliation. ***Email:*** TH@auroralawfirm.com

JONATHAN G. PFLEEGER, born LaGrange, Illinois, January 28, 1977; admitted to bar, 2003, Illinois. *Education:* Denison University (B.A., summa cum laude, 1999); The Ohio State University (J.D., 2003). Phi Beta Kappa. Associate Editor, The Ohio State University Journal of Law, 2001-2003. *Member:* Chicago, Kane County, Illinois State and American Bar Associations; Illinois Trial Lawyers Association; The Association of Trial Lawyers of America. ***PRACTICE AREAS:*** Personal Injury Litigation; Business Litigation; Civil Litigation. ***Email:*** JP@auroralawfirm.com

LOWE AND STEINMETZ, LTD.

Established in 1958

407 WEST GALENA BOULEVARD
P.O. BOX 1625
AURORA, ILLINOIS 60507-1625
Telephone: 630-897-0900
FAX: 630-897-9500
URL: http://www.lslegal.net

Real Estate Law, Civil Litigation, Corporate Law, Trusts and Estates, Syndications and Tax Law, Wills and Probate, Contracts, Business Law.

FIRM PROFILE: Ralph E. Lowe established a private practice in Aurora, Illinois, in 1958. In 1971 he was joined by Herbert C. Steinmetz, Jr. and the firm of Lowe and Steinmetz, Ltd. was formed in 1974. The firm serves Northern Illinois including Cook, DuPage, Kane and Kendall Counties. Members of the firm are also admitted to practice in the States of Florida (inactive), Georgia and South Carolina. Each member of the firm has expertise in particular areas of practice including civil litigation, corporate law, administrative law and real estate. The firm has been recognized by its peers as having preeminent legal ability and upstanding professional ethics.

RALPH E. LOWE, born Hinsdale, Illinois, November 24, 1931; admitted to bar, 1956, Illinois; 1974, Georgia; 1990, South Carolina. *Education:* DePauw University (B.A., 1953); University of Illinois (LL.B., 1956). Delta Theta Phi. *Member:* State Bar of Georgia;

(This Listing Continued)

South Carolina Bar; Illinois State and American Bar Associations; The Association of Trial Lawyers of America. *PRACTICE AREAS:* Civil Litigation; Administrative Law; Public Utility Law; Alternative Dispute Resolution. *Email:* ralphlowe@lslegal.net

HERBERT C. STEINMETZ, JR., born Chicago, Illinois, December 14, 1942; admitted to bar, 1968, Illinois; 1972, Florida. *Education:* St. Joseph's College (A.B., 1964); University of Illinois (J.D., 1967). Phi Alpha Delta; Delta Epsilon Sigma. *Member:* Kane County (Director, 1984-1986; General Counsel, 1991-1992), Illinois State and American Bar Associations; The Florida Bar. [Lt., JAGC, U.S. Navy, 1968-1971]. *PRACTICE AREAS:* Real Estate; Trusts and Estates; Corporate Law; Zoning, Planning and Land Use. *Email:* hstein@lslegal.net

OF COUNSEL

WADE R. JOYNER, born Atlanta, Georgia, August 18, 1964; admitted to bar, 1988, Illinois. *Education:* Purdue University (B.A., 1985); Syracuse University (M.A., Economics, 1988; J.D. 1988). Recipient, Andrews Scholars Fellowship. *Member:* Chicago and Illinois State Bar Associations. *PRACTICE AREAS:* Zoning Law; Litigation; Employment Law; Appellate Practice. *Email:* ddwoodslaw@yahoo.com

REPRESENTATIVE CLIENTS: Van Der Molen Properties; Attorneys' Title Guaranty Fund, Inc.; Fox Valley Properties, L.L.C.; Dreyer Clinic, Inc.; Advocate Health Care; Aurora Tri-County Association of Realtors John Biris Real Estate Services, Inc.; Waubonsee Community College.

JOSEPH P. McCAFFERY
ATTORNEY AT LAW

2210 SANDBURG DRIVE
AURORA, ILLINOIS 60506
Telephone: 630-801-8691
Fax: 630-896-2638
Email: jpmlaw@covad.net
URL: http://www.josephmccaffery.com

Criminal Litigation, White Collar, Felonies, Misdemeanors, Civil Defense, Legal Malpractice Defense, Insurance Defense, Medical Malpractice, Personal Injury, Divorce, Wills and Trusts, Real Estate Transactions, Banking, Securities, Corporate and Commercial Litigation.

JOSEPH P. McCAFFERY, born Bryn Mawr, Pennsylvania; admitted to bar, 1991, Illinois, U.S. Court of Appeals, Seventh Circuit and U.S. District Court, Northern District of Illinois, including Trial Bar. *Education:* University of Dayton (B.A., 1987); DePaul University (J.D., 1990). Dean's List. Member, Honor Society. Certified Title Examiner, TICOR Title Insurance. *Member:* Chicago, Illinois State and American Bar Associations. *LANGUAGES:* Russian, Greek and Spanish. *PRACTICE AREAS:* Criminal Litigation; Insurance Defense; Personal Injury; White Collar Criminal Defense; Felonies; Misdemeanors; Medical Malpractice; Legal Malpractice Defense; Divorce; Wills; Trusts and Estates; Real Estate; Banks and Banking; Securities; Civil Litigation; Corporate Litigation; Corporate Formation; Corporate Insurance Defense; Incorporation; Commercial Litigation.

MICKEY, WILSON, WEILER, RENZI & ANDERSSON, P.C.

2111 PLUM STREET, 2ND FLOOR
P.O. BOX 787
AURORA, ILLINOIS 60507-0787
Telephone: 630-801-9699
Fax: 630-801-9715
URL: http://www.mickeywilson.com
Email: office@mickeywilson.com
URL: http://www.lawyers.com/mwwr

State and Federal Civil Practice. Trials and Appeals. Personal Injury, Corporation Law, Probate, Estate Planning, Real Estate, Workers Compensation, School Law, Aviation Law and Elder Law.

FIRM PROFILE: Mickey, Wilson, Weiler, Renzi, & Andersson, P.C., which traces its history to the law firm founded in 1946 by William C. O'Brien, serves clients throughout the northern Illinois area, offering a wide range of legal services, including municipal, school, corporate and civil litigation. The firm is also actively involved in, and committed to, community affairs, regularly providing speakers to participate in various legal, educational and community/school based programs.

GARY K. MICKEY, born Hammond, Indiana, June 26, 1939; admitted to bar, 1966, Illinois, U.S. District Court, Northern District of Illinois including Trial Bar and U.S. Court of Appeals, Seventh Circuit. *Education:* Illinois Wesleyan University (A.B., 1961); University of Illinois (LL.B., 1965). Blue Key; Pi Sigma Alpha; Phi Delta Phi. *Member:* Kane County and Illinois State Bar Associations; Illinois Defense Council; Defense Research Institute. *PRACTICE AREAS:* Civil Litigation; General Practice; Personal Injury; School Law; Corporate Law. *Email:* gkm@mickeywilson.com

PETER K. WILSON, JR., born Lamesa, Texas, December 4, 1942; admitted to bar, 1967, Illinois, U.S. District Court, Northern District of Illinois including Trial Bar and U.S. Court of Appeals, Seventh Circuit. *Education:* Miami University; Valparaiso University (B.A., 1965); Valparaiso University (J.D., 1967). Phi Alpha Delta. Articles and Book Review Editor, Valparaiso University Law Review, 1966-1967. Associate Circuit Judge, 1988-1991. Presiding Judge, Family Division, 1991 (faculty member, Illinois Judicial Conference, 1990, 1991). *Member:* Kane County (President, 1994) and Illinois State Bar Associations; National Council of School Attorneys; Illinois Council of School Attorneys. *PRACTICE AREAS:* School Law; Corporate Law; Municipal Law; Aviation Law (COM, ASMEL, INST.); Civil Trials and Appeals. *Email:* pkw@mickeywilson.com

(This Listing Continued)

BERNARD K. WEILER, born Aurora, Illinois, July 31, 1953; admitted to bar, 1978, Illinois, U.S. District Court, Northern District of Illinois including Trial Bar and U.S. Court of Appeals, Seventh Circuit. *Education:* Loyola University (B.A., 1975; J.D., 1978). *Member:* Chicago, Kane County and Illinois State Bar Associations. *PRACTICE AREAS:* Corporate Law; School Law; Municipal Law; Civil Litigation; Civil Appeals. *Email:* bkw@mickeywilson.com

CONSTANCE BURNETT RENZI, born Lockport, Illinois, October 8, 1962; admitted to bar, 1986, Illinois. *Education:* Illinois State University (B.S., magna cum laude, 1983); University of Illinois (J.D., 1986). *Member:* Kane County and Illinois State Bar Associations; Illinois Council of School Attorneys; National Council of School Attorneys; National Academy of Elder Law Attorneys. *PRACTICE AREAS:* Elder Law; School Law. *Email:* cbr@mickeywilson.com

STEVEN A. ANDERSSON, born Midlothian, Illinois, August 15, 1964; admitted to bar, 1992, Illinois and U.S. District Court, Northern District of Illinois. *Education:* Northern Illinois University (B.A., 1986; J.D., magna cum laude, 1992). Recipient, American Jurisprudence Award in Trusts and Estates, 1991. Member, Northern Illinois University Law Review, 1990-1992; National Mock Trial Competition Team Member, 1992. Assistant Student Works Editor, Northern Illinois University Law Review, 1991-1992. *Member:* Kane County (President, 2001-2002) and Illinois State Bar Associations; National Association of Elder Law Attorneys. *LANGUAGES:* Swedish. *PRACTICE AREAS:* Civil Litigation; Municipal Law; Elder Law; Trademarks; Corporate Law; Real Estate. *Email:* saa@mickeywilson.com

DEAN M. FRIEDERS, born Kane, Illinois, January 26, 1979; admitted to bar, 2004, Illinois and U.S. District Court, Northern District of Illinois. *Education:* North Central College (B.A., summa cum laude, 2001); Chicago-Kent College of Law (J.D., with honors, 2004). Dean's List. Member, Chicago-Kent College of Law Moot Court Honor Society. Student Editor, Illinois State Bar Association Alternative Dispute Resolution Section Council ADR Newsletter, 1999-2001. Recipient: Chicago-Kent CALI Award, 2003; Presidential Scholar, North Central College, Naperville, Illinois, 1997-2001; 3 Merit Based Research Grants; Illinois State Bar Association Alternative Dispute Resolution Section Council Pro Bono Recognition Award, 2001. Author: "Mandatory Arbitration Clauses in Employment Contracts," Illinois State Bar Association "In the Alternative" Section on Alternative Dispute Resolution Newsletter, February 2000; "Focus on the Issue: Confidentaility in Mediation," Illinois State Bar Association "In the Alternative" Section of Alternative Dispute Resolution Newsletter, June 2000; "Growing Concerns About Monopolies and Anti-Competitive Behavior in Agriculture," Academy of Legal Studies in Business, presented at 1999 National Conference and printed in "1999 ALSB National Conference Proceedings.". *PRACTICE AREAS:* Civil Litigation; Municipal Law; Personal Injury; Corporate Law; Elder Law. *Email:* dmf@mickeywilson.com

GENERAL COUNSEL FOR: Geneva Construction Co.; West Aurora School District #129; Sandwich School District #430; Williams Building & Land, Inc.; Aurora Animal Hospital, Inc.; Flight Visions, Inc.; Mulligan Masonry, Inc.; Denton Cartage, Inc.; Central Graphics, Inc.; Coffman Truck Sales, Inc.; Winfield Fire Protection District; Marywood Fire Protection District; Village of Montgomery, Illinois; Village of Sugar Grove, Illinois; Dempsey-Ing, Inc.; Hagerty and Sons, Inc.; Slivacor, Inc.; Sky Haven of Aurora, Inc.; Air Supreme, Inc.; Dynamic Flights, Inc.; Numina Systems, Inc.; Board Room, Inc.; Walter E. Deuchler Associates, Inc.
LOCAL COUNSEL FOR: American Family Insurance Co.; Auto-Owners Insurance Co.; Commonwealth Edison Co.; United Fire & Casualty Insurance Co.; Indiana Insurance Co.; Pekin Insurance Co.; Aurora Sanitary District; Copley Memorial Hospital; Community Counseling Center; Goodyear Tire & Rubber Co.; America Insurance Co.

RUDDY, MILROY & KING

FARNSWORTH COMMONS OFFICE CENTER
1700 NORTH FARNSWORTH AVENUE, SUITE 12
AURORA, ILLINOIS 60505-1512
Telephone: 630-820-0333
Fax: 630-820-0594
URL: http://www.ruddyvmlaw.com
Email: rvlawfirm@aol.com
URL: http://www.rvmlawfirm.com

Bankruptcy, Commercial Litigation, Family Law, Import-Export Law, Secured Transactions, Lender Liability.

MEMBERS OF FIRM

C. JOHN RUDDY, born Aurora, Illinois, September 25, 1950; admitted to bar, 1977, Illinois; U.S. District Court, Northern District of Illinois including Trial Bar and U.S. Court of Appeals, Seventh Circuit. *Education:* University of Denver (B.A., 1972); John Marshall Law School (J.D., 1977). Faculty Member, Lorman Education Seminars. *Member:* Kane County and Illinois State Bar Associations. *LANGUAGES:* Spanish. *PRACTICE AREAS:* Bankruptcy; Secured Transactions; Family Law; Commercial Litigation; International Commercial Law; International Litigation; Lender Liability; Bankruptcy Chapter 7; Bankruptcy Chapter 11; Bankruptcy Chapter 13; Bankruptcy Chapter 12; Bankruptcy Collections; Bankruptcy Fraud; Bankruptcy Litigation; Bankruptcy Reorganization; Commercial Bankruptcy; Commercial Insolvency; Commercial Foreclosure; Commercial Recovery; Commercial Workouts; Consumer Bankruptcy; Creditor Bankruptcy; Debtor Bankruptcy; Foreclosures; Fraudulent Conveyance; Insolvency; International Bankruptcy; Liquidations; Personal Bankruptcy; Repossessions; Business Law; Business Associations Law; Business Cooperatives; Business Development; Business Dissolutions; Business Enterprises; Business Formation; Business Fraud; Business Litigation; Business Organization; Business Planning; Business Regulation; Business Reorganization; Business Start-Ups; Business Torts; Business Transactions; Business Transfers; Business Valuation; Buy-Sell Agreements; Buying and Selling of Businesses; Closely Held Business Law; Entrepreneurial Business Law; Family Business Law; Family Business Mediation; Family Business Successions; International Business Law; International Joint Ventures; Joint Ventures; Limited Liability Company Law; Private Business Law; Sole Proprietorships; Small Business Law; Professional Practices; Chancery and Equity; Chancery Practice; Civil Practice; Federal Civil Practice; Commercial Collections; Garnishments; Post Judgment Collec-

(This Listing Continued)

RUDDY, MILROY & KING, Aurora—Continued

tions; Secured Collections; Unsecured Collections; Commercial Law; Commercial Bad Faith; Commercial Fraud; Commercial Liability; Commercial Transactions; Commercial Transfers; Complex Commercial Litigation; Negotiable Instruments; Sale of Goods; Uniform Commercial Code; Consumer Law; Consumer Collections; Consumer Credit; Consumer Credit Compliance; Consumer Finance; Consumer Fraud; Consumer Litigation; Consumer Protection; Consumer Rights; Contracts; Breach of Contract; Commercial Contracts; Contract Fraud; Contract Litigation; International Commercial Contracts; International Contracts; Corporate Law; Closely Held Corporations; Corporate Commercial Law; Corporate Contracts; Corporate Dissolutions; Corporate Fiduciary Law; Corporate Formation; Corporate Governance; Corporate Litigation; Corporate Organization; Corporate Partnerships; Corporate Planning; Corporate Reorganization; Corporate Successions; Corporate Workouts; Family Corporations; Incorporation; International Corporate Law; Nonprofit Corporations; Professional Corporations; Public Corporations; S Corporations; Small Business Corporations; Debtor and Creditor; Creditors Rights; Creditors Rights in Bankruptcy; Debtor and Creditor Collections; Debtor and Creditor Remedies; Debtor and Creditor Reorganization; Debtor and Creditor Rights; Debtor and Creditor Workouts; Debtors Rights; Fair Debt Collection Practices Act; International Creditors Rights; Secured Creditors Rights; Unsecured Creditors Rights; Equipment Finance and Leasing; Alimony; Annulment; Cohabitation Agreements; Collaborative Family Law; Community Property Law; Divorce; Domestic Partnerships; Domestic Relations; Domestic Torts; Domestic Violence; Equitable Distribution; Interstate Support; Marital Agreements; Marital Property Distribution; Marital Property Law; Marital Property Settlements; Matrimonial Bankruptcy Law; Matrimonial Law; Paternity; Post Divorce Modification; Postnuptial Agreements; Premarital Agreements; Qualified Domestic Relations Orders (QDROs); Restraining Orders; Separation Agreements; Spousal Support; Uncontested Divorce; International Law; International Trade; Import and Export Law; International Trade Regulation; Civil Litigation; Defense Litigation; Federal Civil Litigation; Federal Litigation; Mortgages; Commercial Mortgages; Mortgage Banking Law; Mortgage Bankruptcy; Mortgage Finance; Mortgage Foreclosure; Mortgage Insurance; Mortgage Lien Foreclosure; Mortgage Refinancing; Mortgage Securitization; Mortgage Tax; Mortgage Workouts; Secondary Mortgage Market; Negligence; Negligence Defense; Partnership Law; Family Partnerships; Limited Liability Partnerships; Limited Partnerships; Partnership Dissolution; Partnership Formation; Partnership Organization; International Property Law; Civil Liability; Intentional Torts; Trade Secrets; Theft of Trade Secrets; Trade Secret Misappropriation.

JOHN P. MILROY, born Aurora, Illinois, July 21, 1949; admitted to bar, 1977, Illinois; U.S. District Court, Northern District of Illinois, U.S. Court of Appeals, Seventh and Eleventh Circuits and U.S. Supreme Court. *Education:* Northwestern University (B.A., 1971); University of Denver (J.D., 1977). *Member:* National Association of Railroad Trial Counsel; Illinois Appellate Lawyers Association. [With U.S. Army, active 1971-1972, reserve 1972-1977; SP4]. ***PRACTICE AREAS:*** Civil Litigation; Torts; Contracts; Appellate Practice; Discrimination; Labor Law; Railroad Law.

LINCOLN M. KING, born Peoria, Illinois, August 10, 1977; admitted to bar, 2003, Illinois and U.S. District Court, Northern District of Illinois. *Education:* Eastern Illinois University (B.A., 1999); Northern Illinois University (J.D., 2003). *Member:* Kane County and Illinois State Bar Associations. ***PRACTICE AREAS:*** Bankruptcy; Personal Bankruptcy; Debtor Bankruptcy; Consumer Bankruptcy; Creditor Bankruptcy; Creditors Rights in Bankruptcy; Commercial Bankruptcy; Bankruptcy Chapter 7; Bankruptcy Chapter 13; Bankruptcy Chapter 11; Bankruptcy Fraud; Bankruptcy Reorganization; Bankruptcy Litigation; Liquidations; Insolvency; Debtors Rights; Creditors Rights; Secured Creditors Rights; Unsecured Creditors Rights; Debtor and Creditor; Debtor and Creditor Rights; Debtor and Creditor Remedies; Debtor and Creditor Reorganization; Fraudulent Conveyance; Foreclosures; Bank Foreclosures; Mortgage Foreclosure; Mortgage Lien Foreclosure; Commercial Foreclosure; Repossessions; Family Law; Domestic Relations; Divorce; Uncontested Divorce; Marital Agreements; Marital Property Settlements; Marital Property Distribution; Matrimonial Bankruptcy Law; Separation Agreements; Business Formation; Corporate Formation; Chancery Practice; Chancery and Equity; Commercial Law; Contracts; Breach of Contract; Contract Litigation; Consumer Litigation; Consumer Protection; Fair Debt Collection Practices Act; Civil Liability; Paternity; Traffic Violations; Tort Defense.

THOMPSON, LAMONT, FLAHERTY & MASUR

A PROFESSIONAL CORPORATION

Established in 1981

1281 NORTH FARNSWORTH AVENUE
AURORA, ILLINOIS 60505-2011
Telephone: 630-851-6500
Fax: 630-851-6523
Email: info@tlfmlaw.com
URL: http://www.tlfmlaw.com

Practice limited to Personal Injury Litigation, including General Negligence, Automobile Accidents, Medical Malpractice, Product Liability, Wrongful Death and Workers Compensation, Transportation, Negligence, Slip and Fall, Dog Bites, Sexual Abuse. Serving all clients in DuPage, Kane, Kendall, DeKalb, Will and Cook Counties.

FIRM PROFILE: Nila v. Hartford, Ins. Co., 362 Ill. App. 3d 811, 728 N.E. 2d 281 (2nd Dist. 2001); Kus v. Sherman Hospital, 268 Ill. App. 3d 771, 644 N.E.2d 1214, 206 Ill. Dec. 161 (2nd Dist. 1995); Testin v. Dreyer Medical Clinic, 238 Ill. App. 3d 883, 605 N.E.2d 1070, 179 Ill. Dec. 56 (2nd Dist. 1992), vacated on other grounds, 162 Ill. 2d 205, 205 Ill. Dec. 147 (1995); Kresin v. Sears 316 Ill. App. 3d 433, 736 N.E.2d 171 (1st Dist. 2000).

CHARLES F. THOMPSON, JR., born Harvey, Illinois, July 9, 1937; admitted to bar, 1962, Illinois. *Education:* Carleton College (B.A., 1959); University of Chicago (J.D., 1962). *Member:* Kane County (President, 1991-1992), Illinois State Bar Association; The Association of Trial Lawyers of America; Illinois Trial Lawyers Association (Member, Board of Managers); Workers Compensation Lawyers Association. Fellow, Illinois Bar Foundation. ***PRACTICE AREAS:*** General Negligence Law; Medical Malpractice; Product Liability Law; Wrongful Death Law; Workers Compensation Law. ***Email:*** cthompson@tlfmlaw.com

JOHN M. LAMONT, born Chicago, Illinois, November 12, 1940; admitted to bar, 1965, Illinois; 1966, Indiana. *Education:* University of Notre Dame (A.B., 1962; LL.B., 1965). Member of the Staff, 1963-1964 and Book Review Editor, 1964-1965, *Notre Dame Lawyer. Author:* Ch 1, "Evidence, Sources & Preparation," Civil Trial Evidence (IICLE, 1995). Lecturer: Anatomy of a Trial (ISBA Law Ed. Series, Nov. 1994). Life Member, National Registry of Who's Who. Member, Million Dollar Advocate Forum. *Member:* Kane County and Illinois State Bar Associations; The Association of Trial Lawyers of America; Illinois Trial Lawyers Association, (Member, Board of Managers); American Board of Trial Advocates. ***PRACTICE AREAS:*** General Negligence Law; Medical Malpractice; Product Liability Law; Wrongful Death Law. ***Email:*** jlamont@tlfmlaw.com

PATRICK M. FLAHERTY, born Aurora, Illinois, September 20, 1951; admitted to bar, 1978, Illinois. *Education:* DePaul University (B.A., 1975); Northern Illinois University (J.D., 1978). Law Clerk, Illinois Appellate Court, Second District, 1979-1981. *Member:* Kane County and Illinois State Bar Associations; The Association of Trial Lawyers of America; Illinois Trial Lawyers Association. ***PRACTICE AREAS:*** General Negligence Law; Medical Malpractice; Product Liability Law; Wrongful Death Law; Workers Compensation Law. ***Email:*** pflaherty@tlfmlaw.com

WOLODYMYR MARK MASUR, born Pittsburgh, Pennsylvania, March 19, 1964; admitted to bar, 1989, Illinois. *Education:* University of Illinois (B.A., 1986); John Marshall Law School (J.D., with distinction, 1989). *Member:* Kane County, Chicago, Illinois State and American Bar Associations; The Association of Trial Lawyers of America; Illinois Trial Lawyers Association. ***PRACTICE AREAS:*** General Negligence Law; Medical Malpractice; Product Liability Law; Wrongful Death Law; Workers Compensation Law; Personal Injury Law. ***Email:*** mmasur@tlfmlaw.com

LEGAL SUPPORT PERSONNEL

SHAWNTA M. MATEJA, born Naperville, Illinois, April 9, 1971. *Education:* Illinois State University (B.S., 1993); Roosevelt University (Paralegal Certificate, with honors, 1995). Member, Illinois Paralegal Association. Member, National Federation of Paralegal Associations.*Member:* Kane County Bar Association. (Legal Assistant). ***Email:*** smateja@tlfmlaw.com

KATHLEEN VAUGHT, P.C.

AURORA, ILLINOIS

(See Wheaton)

Bankruptcy, Consumer Bankruptcy, Business Bankruptcy, Financial Planning, Litigation, Tort Litigation, Contract Litigation, Real Estate, Divorce, Family, Estate Planning, Probate Law, Arbitration, Mediation, Alternative Dispute Resolution, Debt Relief Agent.

WHITT LAW

Established in 1987

105 EAST GALENA BOULEVARD, 8TH FLOOR
AURORA, ILLINOIS 60505-3338
Telephone: 630-897-8875
Fax: 630-897-1258
URL: http://www.lawyers.com/stuartlwhitt
Email: swhitt@whittlaw.com
URL: http://www.whittlaw.com

Education Law, Municipal Law, Tax Law.

FIRM PROFILE: Whitt Law is one of a small number of firms outside of Chicago that concentrates in school and municipal law. Representing taxing bodies throughout Illinois, Whitt Law has a broad range of experience in all matters which affect school districts and other governmental agencies.

Whitt Law has extensive experience in arbitration and litigation in all courts and before administrative tribunals including the Illinois Property Tax Appeal Board, the Illinois Educational Labor Relations Board, the Illinois Industrial Commission, the Illinois Human Rights Commission and the Equal Employment Opportunity Commission.

The goal of Whitt Law is to provide comprehensive, quality legal services and common sense solutions in today's complex world. We strive to be fully knowledgeable of each client's unique needs and to tailor our services to provide cost-effective counsel and representation.

STUART L. WHITT, born Aurora, Illinois, May 12, 1952; admitted to bar, 1977, Illinois and U.S. District Court, Northern District of Illinois; 1986, U.S. Supreme Court. *Education:* Arizona State University and Aurora College (B.A., with honors, 1974); Loyola University (J.D., 1977). Associate Editor, Loyola University Law Journal, 1976-1977. Member, Illinois General Assembly Electric Utility Property Assessment Task Force, 1998-2000. *Member:* Kane County, Illinois State and American Bar Associations; National Association of School Boards; Illinois Association of School Boards; National Council of School Attorneys; Illinois Council of School Attorneys; Illinois Association of School Administrators; Illinois Association of School Business Officials; The Association of Trial Lawyers of America; Illinois Trial Lawyers Association. ***Email:*** swhitt@whittlaw.com

ASSOCIATES

RICHARD T. PETESCH, born Aurora, Illinois, June 25, 1956; admitted to bar, 1983, Illinois and U.S. District Court, Northern District of Illinois. *Education:* Aurora University (B.A., 1979); John Marshall Law School (J.D., 1983). *Member:* Kane County, Illinois State and American Bar Associations; The Association of Trial Lawyers of America; Illinois Trial Lawyers Association. ***SPECIAL AGENCIES:*** Volunteer Pro Bono Attorney for CASA Kane County, Il. ***REPORTED CASES:*** Reed-Custer School District #255-U v. City of

(This Listing Continued)

Wilmington, 253 Ill. App. 3d 503, 625 N.E. 2d. 381, 192 Ill. Dec. 421. ***PRACTICE AREAS:*** Education Law; Real Estate; Personal Injury; Workers Compensation. ***Email:*** rpetesch@whittlaw.com

JOSHUA S. WHITT, born Aurora, Illinois, December 24, 1977; admitted to bar, 2003, Illinois. *Education:* Eastern Illinois University (B.A., 2000); Capital University (J.D., magna cum laude, 2003). Order of the Curia. Publishing Editor, Capital University Law Review, 2002-2003. *Member:* Kane County, Illinois State and American Bar Associations; National Council of School Attorneys; Illinois Council of School Attorneys. ***PRACTICE AREAS:*** Education Law; Tax Law. ***Email:*** jwhitt@whittlaw.com

GRETCHEN M. HARRIS, born Winfield, Illinois, September 30, 1975; admitted to bar, 2005, Illinois. *Education:* University of Wisconsin, Madison (B.S., 1999); Loyola University School of Law (J.D., 2005). Executive Publication Editor, Annals of Health Law, 2004-2005. *Member:* Kane County Bar Association; Illinois State Bar Association; American Bar Association. ***LANGUAGES:*** Spanish. ***SPECIAL AGENCIES:*** Illinois Council of School Attorneys National; Council of School Attorneys. ***PRACTICE AREAS:*** Education Law; Municipal Law; Taxation. ***Email:*** gharris@whittlaw.com

REPRESENTATIVE CLIENTS: Byron Community Unit School District No. 226; Braceville Elementary School District No. 75; Channahon Elementary School District No. 17; Coal City Community Unit School District No. 1; Crawford County; Erie Community Unit School District No. 1; Fair Assessment Information Resource Committee (FAIRCOM); Gibson City-Melvin-Sibley School District No. 5; Geneva Community Unit School District No. 304; Homer Community Consolidated School District No. 33-C; Indian Prairie Community Unit School District No. 204; Midland Unit School District No. 7; Morris Elementary School District No. 54; Naperville Community Unit School District No. 203; Oswego Community Unit School District No. 308; Reed-Custer Community Unit School District No. 255-U; Robinson Community Unit School District No. 2; Rock Island County; Will County School District No. 92.

CASEY WOODRUFF & ASSOCIATES

MILLENNIUM PARK PLAZA
75 EXECUTIVE DRIVE, SUITE 105
AURORA, ILLINOIS 60504
Telephone: 630-585-2320
Fax: 630-585-2327
Email: cwoodruff@woodrufflawyers.com
URL: http://www.cwoodrufflaw.com

Chicago, Illinois Office: 155 N. Michigan Avenue, Suite 500, 60601. Telephone: 630-585-2320. Toll Free: 1-866-891-9211. Fax: 630-585-2327.

Workers Compensation, Personal Injury, Automobile Accidents, Social Security, Medical Malpractice, Products Liability.

FIRM PROFILE: Casey Woodruff & Associates is a statewide Plaintiff injury law firm. We protect the rights of workers injured on the job, motorists injured in accidents, victims of medical malpractice, and consumers hurt by faulty products. Winning cases is what we do at Casey Woodruff & Associates. Over the years we have recovered millions for our clients with our firm's practice of personal attention from the entire legal team at Casey Woodruff & Associates. Our initial consultation is free with no upfront out-of-pocket expenses to you. Our legal fee is based on what we recover for you. We handle every aspect of your case, from start to finish. Casey Woodruff & Associates is experience and professionalism.

Language: Spanish.

REPRESENTATIVE CLIENTS: Int'l Brotherhood of Teamster; United Auto Workers; Int'l Boilermakers Union; United Food & Commercial Workers; Service Employees Int'l Union (SEIU); Champaign County AFL-CIO; Illinois Education Association; Mexican Consulate; Garment & Leather Workers Union.

(For Complete Personnel and Biographical Data, see Professional Biographies at Chicago, Illinois)

BERGER SCHATZ

A Partnership including Professional Corporations
2333 WAUKEGAN ROAD, SUITE 260
BANNOCKBURN, ILLINOIS 60015
Telephone: 847-405-9500
Fax: 847-405-9563
Email: info@ksbfamilylaw.com
URL: http://www.ksbfamilylaw.com

Chicago, Illinois Office: 161 North Clark Street, Suite 2800. Telephone: 312-782-3456. Fax: 312-782-8463.

Matrimonial, Family, Domestic Relations Law, Trial and Appellate Practice: Including Divorce, Child Custody, Child Support, Paternity, Spousal Support and Visitation Rights.

FIRM PROFILE: Berger Schatz dedicates its practice solely to matrimonial and family law, and is one of the largest firms of its kind in the country.

On both the trial and appellate levels, the Firm's 25 attorneys handle cases involving substantial estates, valuation, tax, custody and issues of paternity. Members of the Firm are also proficient in drafting prenuptial and postnuptial agreements.

The Firm includes Fellows, Board Members and the Past President of the Illinois Chapter of the American Academy of Matrimonial Lawyers as well as three recent chairs of the Illinois State Bar Association Family Law Section Council and the past President of the Lake County Bar Association.

MARY J. CLARK, born Elmhurst, Illinois, December 14, 1954; admitted to bar, 1979, Illinois. *Education:* Barat College (B.A., 1976); Northern Illinois University (J.D., 1979). (Resident). ***PRACTICE AREAS:*** Family Law; Domestic Relations; Matrimonial Law; Divorce. ***Email:*** mclark@bergerschatz.com

DEBBIE K. LERNER, born New York, N.Y.; admitted to bar, 1992, Wisconsin and U.S. District Court, Eastern District of Wisconsin; U.S. District Court, Western District of Wisconsin; 1994, California; 1999, Illinois. *Education:* San Diego State University (B.A. in history, cum laude, 1986); Marquette University (J.D., cum laude, 1992). Phi Alpha Theta. Sutherland Memorial Scholarship. Judge Noel Fox Scholarship. *Member:* State Bar of California, Illinois State and American Bar Associations; State Bar of Wisconsin. (Resident). ***PRACTICE AREAS:*** Family Law; Domestic Relations; Matrimonial Law; Divorce. ***Email:*** dlerner@bergerschatz.com

JASON G. ADESS (Resident, Chicago Office)
AMANDA B. CLAYMAN (Resident, Chicago Office)
P. ANDRÉ KATZ (Resident, Chicago Office)
DAVID H. LEVY, (P.C.) (Resident, Chicago Office)
MICHAEL S. SABATH (Resident, Chicago Office)
TRACEY A. WERTMAN (Resident, Chicago Office)
BARRY A. SCHATZ, (P.C.) (Resident, Chicago Office)
MICHAEL J. BERGER, (P.C.) (Resident, Chicago Office)
ANDREW D. EICHNER (Resident, Chicago Office)
LEON I. FINKEL (Resident, Chicago Office)
NORMAN RUBER (Resident, Chicago Office)

JOSHUA E. HORNADAY, born Soldotna, Alaska, January, 20, 1974; admitted to bar, 2000, Illinois and U.S. District Court, Northern District of Illinois. *Education:* Monmouth College (B.A., 1996); University of Iowa (J.D., 2000). *Member:* Illinois State Bar Association. (Resident). ***PRACTICE AREAS:*** Family Law; Domestic Relations; Matrimonial Law; Divorce.

MARCELLE R. KOTT (Resident, Chicago Office)
MARGARET E. KEANE (Resident, Chicago Office)
SHARON STEINBERG MOBLEY (Resident, Chicago Office)
KRISTINA L. JARVIS (Resident, Chicago Office)
CATHERINE M. DUNN (Resident, Chicago Office)
BRIAN J. BLITZ (Resident, Chicago Office)
LAURENCE B. HIRSCH (Resident, Chicago Office)
KAREN ROSE KREHBIEL (Resident, Chicago Office)
MELINDA C. ROGERS (Resident, Chicago Office)

(For firm profile and complete biographical data on all personnel, see Professional Biographies at Chicago, Illinois)

GALLITANO & O'CONNOR LLP

257 E. MAIN STREET, SUITE 300
BARRINGTON, ILLINOIS 60010
Telephone: 224-633-5000
Fax: 224-633-5006
URL: http://www.gallitanoocconnor.com

Information Technology, Corporate Law, telecommunications Law, Health Care, Technology Law, Technology Licensing, Outsourcing.

FIRM PROFILE: Gallitano & O'Connor LLP is a boutique technology law firm serving technology leaders in multiple industries. For a more complete overview of our attorneys please visit our website.

MEMBERS OF FIRM

DENNIS J. GALLITANO, admitted to bar, 1984, Illinois. *Education:* Northwestern University (B.A., 1978); DePaul University (J.D., with honors, 1984). Articles and Casenote Editor, DePaul Law Review, 1983-1984. Adjunct Professor, Graduate Program in Health Information Management, University of Illinois at Chicago, College of Associated Health Professions. Member, Intellectual Property & Information Technology Advisory Board, DePaul University. Village President, Elk Grove Village, 1993-1997. Village Trustee, 1985-1993. Board Member, Northern Cook County Joint Action Water Agency (1993-1997). Board Member, Solid Waste Agency of Northern Cook County (1993-1997), Executive Committee, Chicago Area Transportation Study (1993-1997). Board Member, Northwest Council of Mayors (1993-1997). Member, Editorial Board, The Journal of College and University Law. *Member:* American Bar Association; American Health Lawyers Association (Member and Past Chair, Health Information and Technology Committee, 1994-1997). Fellow, Healthcare Information Management System Society (FHIMSS). ***PRACTICE AREAS:*** Information Technology (80%); Corporate Law (5%); Telecommunications Law (2%); Health Care (3%); Technology Law (5%); Technology Licensing (5%). ***Email:*** dennis.gallitano@gallitanooconnor.com

KAREN J. O'CONNOR, admitted to bar, 1990, Illinois. *Education:* Western Illinois University (B.B., summa cum laude, 1986); Northwestern University School of Law (J.D., 1990). Phi Kappa Phi; Mortar Board. ***PRACTICE AREAS:*** Technology and Science; Contracts; Technology Law (5%); Technology Licensing (5%); Technology Contracts (90%). ***Email:*** karen.oconnor@gallitanooconnor.com

MARCUS D. LAWLOR, admitted to bar, 1997, Missouri; 1998, Illinois. *Education:* University of Illinois (B.A., 1994); St. Louis University (J.D., 1997). Law Clerk, Hon. Carol E. Jackson, U.S. District Court, Eastern District of Missouri. Author, "Ivory Tower Paternalism and Lawyer Advertising: The Case of Florida Bar v. Went For It, Inc.," 40 St. Louis University Law Review 895, 1996. ***PRACTICE AREAS:*** Information Technology (90%); Corporate (10%). ***Email:*** marc.lawlor@gallitanooconnor.com

HEIDI L. BAUDERS, admitted to bar, 1994, Ohio; 1997, California; 2003 Illinois. *Education:* University of Cincinnati (B.A., magna cum laude, 1991); University of Toledo

(This Listing Continued)

GALLITANO & O'CONNOR LLP, Barrington—Continued

College of Law (J.D., cum laude, 1994). ***PRACTICE AREAS:*** Information Technology (90%); Corporate (10%); Debt Finance. ***Email:*** heidi.bauders@gallitanooconnor.com

LAW OFFICES OF ALEXANDRA M. GODDARD

18-3 EAST DUNDEE ROAD, SUITE 202
BARRINGTON, ILLINOIS 60010
Telephone: 847-382-3995
Fax: 847-382-4038
Email: agodatty@aol.com
URL: http://www.alexandragoddard.com

Family Law, Adoptions, Child Custody, Child Support, Divorce, Domestic Violence, Premarital Agreements, Spousal Support, Visitation Rights, Prenuptial Agreements, Guardianships, Unmarried Couples, Real Estate, Buying or Selling a Home, Estate Planning, Corporate Law.

ALEXANDRA M. GODDARD, born Albany, Georgia, August 4, 1948; admitted to bar, 1973, Illinois and Nebraska. *Education:* Iowa State University (B.S., 1969); University of Nebraska (J.D., 1972). *Member:* Northwest Suburban, Lake County, Illinois State and Nebraska State Bar Associations; The Collaborative Law Institute of Illinois.

HANSON PETERS NYE

1301 SOUTH GROVE AVENUE, SUITE 200
BARRINGTON, ILLINOIS 60010
Telephone: 847-277-9988
Fax: 847-277-7339

Commercial Litigation and Arbitration, Insurance Coverage, Complex Insurance Litigation, Complex Professional Liability Coverage.

FIRM PROFILE: Commercial litigation and counseling, coverage representation of insurers in professional liability, general liability, directors and officers, umbrella, fidelity and surety, employment practices and related fields; defense of corporations and individuals in professional liability and employment practices matters; counseling and advising insurers in product development, regulatory relations and underwriting of insurance products, alternative risk transfer arrangements, breach of contract, construction law, wrongful death, franchise law, professional malpractice and risk management.

MEMBERS OF FIRM

KEITH A. HANSON, born Milwaukee, Wisconsin, March 6, 1953; admitted to bar, 1976, Wisconsin; 1977, Illinois, U.S. District Court, Western District of Wisconsin and U.S. District Court, Northern District of Illinois; 1986, U.S. Court of Appeals, Fifth Circuit. *Education:* University of Wisconsin-Madison (B.S., with honors, 1974; J.D., 1976). ***PRACTICE AREAS:*** Commercial Litigation; Insurance Coverage; Insurance Litigation; Complex Professional Liability. ***Email:*** keithhanson@hpnlaw.com

VICTOR C. PETERS, born Keokuk, Iowa, November 21, 1956; admitted to bar, 1982, Illinois and U.S. District Court, Northern District of Illinois; 2000, U.S. District Court, Central District of Illinois. *Education:* University of Iowa (B.A., 1979; J.D., with distinction, 1982). Member, 1980 and Editor, 1981, University of Iowa Law Review. ***PRACTICE AREAS:*** Insurance Coverage; Insurance Litigation; Complex Professional Liability. ***Email:*** victorpeters@hpnlaw.com

ANASTASIA MARKAKIS NYE, born East Lansing, Michigan, August 26, 1962; admitted to bar, 1987, Illinois. *Education:* University of Michigan (B.A., with distinction, 1984); Ohio State University (J.D., 1987). Member, Professional Liability Underwriting Society. Editor-in-Chief, Ohio State Journal on Dispute Resolution, 1986-1987. ***PRACTICE AREAS:*** Insurance Coverage; Insurance Litigation; Complex Professional Liability. ***Email:*** natashanye@hpnlaw.com

NANCY K. TORDAI, born Chicago, Illinois, April 9, 1957; admitted to bar, 1982, Illinois and U.S. District Court, Northern District of Illinois; 1998, U.S. Court of Appeals, Seventh Circuit; 2000, U.S. District Court, Central District of Illinois. *Education:* University of Chicago (B.A., with honors, 1979); Loyola University (J.D., 1982). Editor, Women's Law Reporter, 1981-1982. *Member:* American Bar Association. ***LANGUAGES:*** Hungarian. ***PRACTICE AREAS:*** Insurance Coverage; Insurance Litigation; Professional Liability Insurance Coverage. ***Email:*** nancytordai@hpnlaw.com

LYNNE REINDERS MILLER, born Janesville, Wisconsin, September 10, 1968; admitted to bar, 1993, Missouri; 1994, Illinois. *Education:* Marquette University (B.A., cum laude, 1990); Washington University (J.D., 1993). Member, 1991-1992 and Executive Notes and Comments Editor, 1992-1993, Journal of Urban and Contemporary Law. ***Email:*** lynnemiller@hpnlaw.com

ELIZABETH J. CAPRINI, born Morristown, New Jersey, February 4, 1955; admitted to bar, 1980, Illinois and U.S. District Court, Northern District of Illinois including Trial Bar. *Education:* University of Kentucky (B.A., 1976); Vanderbilt University (J.D., 1980). Phi Beta Kappa. Jessup International Moot Court Team - Best Oralist, 1979-1980. *Member:* Chicago, Illinois State and American Bar Associations; The Association of Trial Lawyers of America. ***Email:*** elizabethcaprini@hpnlaw.com

ASSOCIATES

JULIANNE PIOTROWSKI NERY, born Buffalo, New York, March 16, 1973; admitted to bar, 1998, Illinois. *Education:* Northwestern University (B.S., 1995); Pace University (J.D., 1998). Phi Alpha Delta (Chapter Justice, 1997); Member, Moot Court Board, 1997-1998. *Member:* Chicago Bar Association. ***Email:*** juliannenery@hpnlaw.com

(This Listing Continued)

JEREMY M. MOEN, born Berwyn, Illinois, April 9, 1975; admitted to bar, 2000, Illinois and U.S. District Court, Northern District of Illinois. *Education:* University of Illinois (B.A., with distinction, 1997); Chicago-Kent College of Law, Illinois Institute of Technology (J.D., with honors, 2000). ***Email:*** jeremymoen@hpnlaw.com

ROBERT B. FISH, born Royal Oak Michigan, April 19, 1970; admitted to bar, 1996, Illinois; 2000, U.S. District Court, Northern District of Illinois including Trial Bar. *Education:* Michigan State University (B.S., with honors, 1992); University of Minnesota (J.D., 1996). Member, Minnesota Journal of Global Trade. ***Email:*** robfish@hpnlaw.com

PAMELA GREENFIELD, born Indianapolis, Indiana, November 28, 1969; admitted to bar, 1996, Massachusetts and New York; 2001, Illinois. *Education:* State University of New York at Albany (B.S., magna cum laude, 1992); State University of New York at Buffalo (J.D., 1995). Beta Gamma Sigma. Golden Key. ***Email:*** pamelagreenfield@hpnlaw.com

RENEE C. ROBAK, born Chicago, Illinois, November 12, 1976; admitted to bar, 2000, Illinois and U.S. District Court, Northern District of Illinois. *Education:* University of Illinois (B.S., 1997); Chicago-Kent College of Law, Illinois Institute of Technology (J.D., 2000). ***LANGUAGES:*** Polish. ***Email:*** reneerobak@hpnlaw.com

JOANNE M. SNOW, born Chicago, Illinois, February 27, 1959; admitted to bar, 1999, Illinois. *Education:* Cardinal Stritch University (B.S., 1996); John Marshall Law School (J.D., 1999). Phi Delta Phi. Recipient, George B. Trubow Award of Academic Excellence in Research and Writing, 1999. Staff Editor, John Marshall Journal of Computer and Information Law, 1997-1998. Author, "CD-Rom Briefs: Must Today's High Tech Lawyers Wait Until the Playing Field is Level," The John Marshall Journal of Computer and Information Law, Vol.17, Issue 2. ***Email:*** joannesnow@hpnlaw.com

ANNE K. LEWIS, born Toledo, Ohio, March 21, 1964; admitted to bar, 1989, Illinois and U.S. District Court, Northern District of Illinois; 1992, District of Columbia. *Education:* Stanford University (B.A., 1986); University of Chicago (J.D., with honors, 1989). Tony Patiño Fellow. ***LANGUAGES:*** French. ***Email:*** annelewis@hpnlaw.com

RICHARD B. WICKA, born Wihona, Minnesota, December 13, 1974; admitted to bar, 2002, Wisconsin and U.S. District Court, Western District of Wisconsin; 2004, Illinois. *Education:* University of Wisconsin-Madison (B.S., 1997; J.D., cum laude, 2002). Order of the Coif. *Member:* American Bar Association. ***Email:*** richardwicka@hpnlaw.com

MIGUEL A. FERNANDEZ, born Miami, Florida, March 11, 1978; admitted to bar, 2003, Illinois and U.S. District Court, Northern District of Illinois. *Education:* University of Florida (B.A., 2000); University of Chicago (J.D., 2003). ***LANGUAGES:*** Spanish. ***Email:*** miguelfernandez@hpnlaw.com

MATTHEW T. HOOVER, born Aurora, Illinois, July 9, 1978; admitted to bar, 2003, Illinois. *Education:* University of Illinois (B.A.S., 2000); University of Illinois College of Law (J.D., 2003). Dean's List. ***PRACTICE AREAS:*** Insurance; Insurance Litigation. ***Email:*** matthewhoover@hpnlaw.com

NATELLE M. WICK, born Oskaloosa, Iowa, June 19, 1978; admitted to bar, 2003, Illinois. *Education:* Loyola University (B.S., magna cum laude, 2000); University of Iowa (J.D., 2003). ***Email:*** natellewick@hpnlaw.com

FARHAN YOUNUS, born Evanston, Illinois, May 23, 1969; admitted to bar, 1995, Illinois; 1996, U.S. District Court, Northern District of Illinois. *Education:* University of Illinois, Urbana-Campaign (B.A., 1991); University of Iowa (J.D., 1995). Member, University of Iowa, Journal of Corporation Law. ***LANGUAGES:*** Urdu.

ALISON K. LANDECK, born Elgin, Illinois, November 3, 1976; admitted to bar, 2001, Illinois and U.S. District Court, Northern District of Illinois. *Education:* University of Illinois, Urbana-Champaign (B.S., 1998); Chicago-Kent College of Law (J.D., 2001). *Member:* Chicago Bar Association. ***PRACTICE AREAS:*** Insurance Coverage; Insurance Litigation. ***Email:*** alisonlandeck@hpnlaw.com

MICHELLE L. STONE, born Des Plaines, Illinois, March 19, 1979; admitted to bar, 2004, Illinois. *Education:* Illinois Wesleyan University (B.A., magna cum laude, 2001); University of Georgia (J.D., 2004). Economic Research Honors. Research Assistant, University of Georgia, 2001 (Fall-Schoenbaum). *Member:* Chicago and American Bar Associations; Student Bar Association (Senator, 2002). ***PRACTICE AREAS:*** Insurance Coverage. ***Email:*** michellestone@hpnlaw.com

ZHANNA RONDEL, born Minsk, Belarus, June 17, 1977; admitted to bar, 2004, Wisconsin and Illinois. *Education:* University of Wisconsin, Milwaukee (B.B.A., magna cum laude, 2000); University of Wisconsin, Madison (J.D., 2004). ***LANGUAGES:*** Russian. ***PRACTICE AREAS:*** Insurance Coverage. ***Email:*** zhannarondel@hpnlaw.com

CHARLES J. MADDEN, III, born Chicago, Illinois, October 18, 1970; admitted to bar, 2004, Illinois. *Education:* University of Illinois, Urbana-Champaign (B.A., 1992); Loyola University Chicago School of Law (J.D., 2004). ***PRACTICE AREAS:*** Insurance Law. ***Email:*** charlesmadden@hpnlaw.com

OF COUNSEL

DAVID A. WILFORD, born Davenport, Iowa, August 26, 1968; admitted to bar, 1993, Illinois; 1994, U.S. District Court, Northern District of Illinois. *Education:* University of Iowa (B.B.A., 1990); Creighton University (J.D., cum laude, 1993). *Member:* Chicago and American Bar Associations. ***Email:*** davidwilford@hpnlaw.com

HUDSON COOK, LLP

Established in 1997
111 NORTH AVENUE, SUITE 11
BARRINGTON, ILLINOIS 60010
Telephone: 847-277-7039
Fax: 847-277-7243
Email: contact@hudco.com
URL: http://www.hudco.com

Linthicum, Maryland Office: 971 Corporate Boulevard, Suite 301, 21090-2232. Telephone: 410-684-3200. Fax: 410-684-2001.

(This Listing Continued)

El Segundo, California Office: 2301 Rosecrans Avenue, Suite 2175, 90245. Telephone: 310-536-9099. Fax: 310-536-7644.
Charlottesville, Virginia Office: 301 E. Market Street, 22902. Telephone: 434-220-9310. Fax: 434-220-9311.
New Haven, Connecticut Office: Building One, Unit 7, Third Floor, 85 Willow Street, 06511. Telephone: 203-776-1911. Fax: 203-776-1922.
Clifton Park, New York Office: 636 Plank Road, Suite 107, 12065. Telephone: 518-383-9440. Fax: 518-383-9401.
Washington, D.C. Office: 1900 M Street NW, Suite 700, 20036. Telephone: 202-223-6930. Fax: 202-223-6935

Consumer Financial Services.

FIRM PROFILE: Hudson Cook, LLP is one of the nation's most highly regarded law firms practicing exclusively in the area of consumer financial services. Led by Thomas B. Hudson and Robert A. Cook, both Fellows of the American College of Consumer Financial Services Lawyers, Hudson Cook, LLP offers a full range of legal services to local, national and international clients.

Hudson Cook, LLP helps clients establish and maintain consumer financial services programs. The firm focuses on a wide array of issues that arise in connection with such programs, including documentation, consumer disclosures, and state licensing.

ELENA A. LOVOY, born Huntsville, Alabama, August 11, 1962; admitted to bar, 1987, Alabama; 1995, Louisiana; 2001, Illinois. *Education:* University of Alabama (B.S., 1984; J.D., 1987; M.B.A., 1992). Co-Author: "Update on Consumer Financial Privacy Legislation and Regulation," The Business Lawyer, May, 2003; "Recent Federal and State Consumer Privacy Developments," The Business Lawyer, May 2002; "Motor Vehicle Financing Via The Internet," The Business Lawyer, May 2001; "The New Regulations Implementing the Community Reinvestment Act," Consumer Finance Law Quarterly Report, Winter 1995. Author: "The New Appraisal Disclosure Requirements under Regulation B," Alabama Banker, December 1993. Associate, McGlinchey Stafford, PLLC, New Orleans, Louisiana, 1994-1999. *Member:* Alabama State Bar; Illinois State and Louisiana State; Chicago Bar Association (Member, Financial Institutions Committee); American Bar Association (Member, Business Law Section, Consumer Financial Services Committee). ***PRACTICE AREAS:*** Consumer Credit; Consumer Financial Services Law; Banking Law. ***Email:*** elovoy@hudco.com

REPRESENTATIVE CLIENTS: Reynolds & Reynolds; Chase Manhattan Bank, N.A.; Wells Fargo Bank; Bank of America, N.A.; World Omni Financial Corp.; Mercedes Benz Credit Corporation; Auto One Acceptance Corp.; Banc One Corporation; Merrill Lynch Credit Corporation; Honda North America, Inc.; Toyota Motor Credit Corporation; Nissan Motor Acceptance Corporation; Transamerica Financial Services; MBNA America Bank; Long Beach Acceptance Corporation; JP Morgan Chase; Goldman, Sachs & Company; Salomon Smith Barney, Inc.; Wachovia Bank, N.A.; AutoNation USA Corporation; American Automotive Leasing Association; American Financial Services Association; National Automotive Finance Association; Harland Financial Solutions; PeopleFirst Finance; DealerTrack.com, Inc; Stoneage.com; CitiFinancial, Inc.

MERONI & MERONI, P.C.

Established in 1984
5 BELLWOOD DRIVE
P.O. BOX 309
BARRINGTON, ILLINOIS 60011
Telephone: 847-304-1500
Telefax: 847-382-5478
Email: meronilaw@ameritech.net
URL: http://www.meronilaw.com

Patent, Trademark, Copyright, Licensing and Related Intellectual Property Law.

CHARLES F. MERONI, SR. (1905-1986)

CHARLES F. MERONI, JR., born Evanston, Illinois; admitted to bar, 1960, Illinois; 1962, U.S. District Court, Northern District of Illinois, including Trial Bar; U.S. Court of Appeals, Seventh Circuit; 1966, U.S. Court of Customs and Patent Appeals; 1967, U.S. District Court, Western and Eastern Districts of Wisconsin; 1974, U.S. Supreme Court; 1982, U.S. District Court, Southern District of Florida and U.S. Court of Appeals, Federal Circuit; registered to practice before the U.S. Patent and Trademark Office. *Education:* Colorado College (A.B., 1952); John Marshall Law School (J.D., 1960). Delta Theta Phi. Member, Judicial Panel on Multi District Litigation, 1982. Policy Partner: Hill, Sherman, Meroni, Gross & Simpson and Successor Firms, Chicago, Illinois, 1960-1984. Senior Partner, Vigil, Meroni & White, Barrington, Illinois, 1984-1986. Founder, Meroni & Meroni, Barrington Hills, Illinois, 1986—. *Member:* American Bar Association; Intellectual Property Law Association of Chicago. ***PRACTICE AREAS:*** Intellectual Property; Patents; Trademarks; Copyrights; International Patents; International Trademarks; Patent Licensing; Trademark Licensing. ***Email:*** meronilaw@ameritech.net

CHRISTOPHER J. SCOTT, born Naperville, Illinois; admitted to bar, 2000, Illinois; registered to practice before the U.S. Patent and Trademark Office. *Education:* St. Joseph College (B.A., 1992); DePaul University (J.D., 2000). *Member:* Chicago and Illinois Bar Associations. ***LANGUAGES:*** German. ***PRACTICE AREAS:*** Intellectual Property; Patents; Trademarks; Copyrights; International Patents; International Trademarks; Patent Licensing; Trademark Licensing. ***Email:*** meronilaw@ameritech.net

OF COUNSEL

JIM XU, born Shanghai, P.R. China; admitted to bar, 1998, Illinois. *Education:* John Marshall Law School (LL.M., 1999); DePaul University (J.D., 1998). ***LANGUAGES:*** Chinese. ***PRACTICE AREAS:*** Patent Law; Tax Law; Immigration Law. ***Email:*** meronilaw@ameritech.net

ANTHONY PERRELLI

BARRINGTON, ILLINOIS

(See Deerfield)

Business Corporate, Small Business, Contracts, Business Planning, Real Estate, Commercial Litigation and Taxation.

SPRINGER, CASEY & DIENSTAG, P.C.

509 WEST OLD NORTHWEST HIGHWAY
BARRINGTON, ILLINOIS 60010
Telephone: 847-382-9797
847-382-4213
Email: SCDCHGO@global.net

Chicago, Illinois Office: 100 West Monroe Street 60603. Telephone: 312-372-0800. Fax: 312-372-0842.

General Practice. Civil Trial and Appellate Litigation in State and Federal Courts. Insurance Defense and Coverage Litigation. Administrative Agencies. Corporation, Estate Planning and Probate, Federal Taxation, Matrimonial, Municipal and Real Estate Law.

FIRM PROFILE: Commercial transactions and dissolution of marriage, insurance disputes and regulation, domestic relations, municipal law, real estate, estate planning.

(For complete biographical data on all personnel, see Professional Biographies at Chicago)

LAW OFFICE OF GREGORY J. MARTUCCI, P.C.

BARTLETT, ILLINOIS

(See Roselle)

Bankruptcy, Criminal Law, Driving While Intoxicated, Juvenile Criminal Law, Traffic Violations, Domestic Violence, Personal Injury, Automobile Accidents and Injuries, Slip and Fall, Workers Compensation.

BENSON, MAIR & GOSSELIN

Established in 1951
133 SOUTH BATAVIA AVENUE
P.O. BOX 129
BATAVIA, ILLINOIS 60510-0129
Telephone: 630-879-1560
Facsimile: 630-879-9473

Real Estate, Estate Planning, Probate, Business, Personal Injury, Civil Litigation, Family Law, Taxation, Collections, Wills and Workers Compensation.

FIRM PROFILE: Founded in 1951 by Emil J. Benson and Thomas A. Mair, the firm of Benson, Mair & Gosselin serve individuals and corporate clients.

MEMBERS OF FIRM

JOHN W. GOSSELIN, born Aurora, Illinois, February 20, 1934; admitted to bar, 1959, Illinois. *Education:* Wabash College and Beloit College (B.A., 1956); University of Chicago (J.D., 1959). City Attorney, Batavia, Illinois, 1964-1976. *Member:* Kane County and Illinois State Bar Associations. ***PRACTICE AREAS:*** Real Estate; Estate Planning; Probate; Business; Personal Injury; Family Law; Taxation; Wills; Workers Compensation.

GABRIELLE A. GOSSELIN, born Chicago, Illinois, December 4, 1958; admitted to bar, 1995, Illinois and U.S. District Court, Northern and Eastern Districts of Illinois. *Education:* George Washington University (B.A., Russian Language and Literature, 1981); Illinois Institute of Technology (M.B.A., Finance, 1990); Chicago-Kent College of Law (J.D., 1995). *Member:* Kane County and Illinois State Bar Associations. ***LANGUAGES:*** French. ***PRACTICE AREAS:*** Civil Litigation; Real Estate; Family Law; Estate Planning; Collections; Probate; Workers Compensation.

THOMAS W. GOSSELIN, born Geneva, Illinois, January 17, 1969; admitted to bar, 2001, Illinois. *Education:* Ripon College (B.A., 1997); John Marshall Law School (J.D., 2001). Member, The Order of John Marshall. ***PRACTICE AREAS:*** Real Estate; Estate Planning; Probate; Family Law; Business Law.

ATTORNEYS FOR: Shumway Foundry, Inc.; Thryselius Machining, Inc.; K & D Sandblasting, Inc.; Frank Saupp Tree Service and Landscaping, Inc.; Hide-A-Way Lakes, Inc.; Rogers Pump Sales & Service, Inc.; McMaster Custom Homes, LLC.

DRENDEL & DRENDEL

A PROFESSIONAL CORPORATION
201 HOUSTON STREET, SUITE 300
BATAVIA, ILLINOIS 60510
Telephone: 630-406-5440
Fax: 630-406-6179
Email: dandd@batavialaw.com
URL: http://www.lawyers.com/drendeltatnall

Family Law, Real Estate Development, Zoning, Sales and Acquisitions, Corporate, Business, Planning Sales and Acquisitions, Estate and Trust Planning and Administration, Commercial and other Civil Litigation, Banking and Collection Law, Trials and Appeals in all State Courts and Mediation Services, Municipal Law and Local Government Law.

(This Listing Continued)

DRENDEL & DRENDEL, A PROFESSIONAL CORPORATION, Batavia—Continued

FIRM PROFILE: Drendel & Drendel concentrates in Family Law and related practice, Municipal, School and Local Governmental Law, in addition to significant experience and practice in the following areas: Real Estate Development, Zoning, Sales and Acquisitions, Corporate, Business Planning and Sales and Acquisitions, Estate and Trust Planning and Administration, Commercial and other Civil Litigation, Banking and Collection Law, Trials and Appeals in State Courts and Mediation Services.

GILBERT X. DRENDEL, JR., born Aurora, Illinois, August 9, 1936; admitted to bar, 1961, Illinois; 1965, U.S. District Court, Northern District of Illinois, U.S. Tax Court and U.S. Court of Appeals, Seventh Circuit. *Education:* Cornell College (A.B., summa cum laude, 1958) Phi Beta Kappa; Harvard University (J.D., 1961). Recipient: Kane County Bar Association Community Service Award; Illinois State Bar Association Community Service Award. Continuing Legal Education Lecturer in Family Law, Pensions and Taxes, 1978—. Village Attorney of North Aurora, 1965-1991. Trained Mediator. *Member:* Kane County (President, 1976-1977; Past Chairperson, Family Law Committee; Past Chairperson, Judicial Evaluation Committee, 1995-1999) and Illinois State Bar Associations. ***PRACTICE AREAS:*** Family Law; Adoption; Pre-Marital Agreements; Municipal Law; Real Estate Law; School Law. ***Email:*** GxD@batavialaw.com

KEVIN G. DRENDEL, born Boston, Massachusetts, December 29, 1959; admitted to bar, 1991, Illinois; 1992, U.S. District Court, Northern District of Illinois. *Education:* Cornell College (B.S.S., cum laude, 1982); Northern Illinois University (J.D., magna cum laude, 1991). Author: "When Self Abuse Becomes Child Abuse: The Need for Coercive Prenatal Government Action in Response to the Cocaine Baby Problem," NIU Law Review 73, 1990. Attorney for Village of North Aurora, 1991—. *Member:* Kane County (Past-Chairman, Membership Committee; Secretary/Treasurer, 2000-2001; 1st Vice President, 2002-2003; President, 2003-2004) and Illinois State (Member, Christian Legal Society; Illinois Council of School Attorneys; Illinois Association of School Administrators) Bar Associations; Illinois Municipal League; Illinois Institute for Local Government Law. ***PRACTICE AREAS:*** Real Estate Development; Zoning Law; Corporate Planning; Business Planning; Estate Administration; Estate Planning; Trust Planning; Commercial Litigation; Civil Litigation; Municipal Law; Local Government Law; School Law; Appellate Practice; Collections. ***Email:*** KGD@batavialaw.com

---

CAROLYN JANSONS, born Columbus, Ohio, September 5, 1974; admitted to bar, 2001, Illinois. *Education:* Northern Illinois University, DeKalb (B.S,. Sociology/Criminology, 1996; J.D., magna cum laude, 2001). Phi Delta Phi. Assistant Editor, Northern Illinois University Law Review, 1999-2001. *Member:* Kane County (Co-Chair, New Lawyers Division, 2003—) and Illinois State Bar Associations. ***PRACTICE AREAS:*** Commercial Litigation; Civil Litigation; Corporate Planning; Business Planning; Collections; Guardianship; Family Law; Municipal Law; Real Estate. ***Email:*** cdj@batavialaw.com

LEGAL SUPPORT PERSONNEL

SHEILA PERSINGER (Legal Assistant)

REPRESENTATIVE CLIENTS: Old Second National Bank of Aurora; Kane County Bank; Cassapa Corporation; Chek Lab, Inc.; Havlicek Builders, Inc.; Millbrook Veterinary Hospital; Prestige Plumbing, Inc.; Batavia School District 101; Village of North Aurora; Campana Properties; Batavia Chamber of Commerce; Walvoil, SPA; Western Engineering, P.C.; Harding Industrial Sales and 302 West; Carlton Healthcare, Corp.

AMELUNG, WULFF & WILLENBROCK, P.C.

Established in 1973

P.O. BOX 368
BELLEVILLE, ILLINOIS 62222
Telephone: 618-233-9765
Email: info@awwstl.com
URL: http://www.awwstl.com

St. Louis, Missouri Office: 11th Floor, 705 Olive Street 63101. Telephone: 314-436-6757. Telecopier: 314-231-7305.

General Trial and Appellate Practice in State and Federal Courts of Missouri and Illinois; Automobile Liability, Contract, Employment Discrimination, Environmental, General Liability, Insurance, Medical Malpractice, Premises Liability, Products Liability, Professional Liability, Errors and Omissions and Workers Compensation Law.

ROBERT J. WULFF
RONALD D. ROBINSON

AMBER LEE KEMPF
PETER M. WESTHOFF
DAVID C. BERWIN (Not admitted in Illinois).

REPRESENTATIVE CLIENTS: Acceptance Insurance Co.; ACE-INA; Allstate Ins. Co.; American Family Insurance Group; Church Mutual Insurance Co.; Continental Western Ins. Co.; COREGIS, Group; Farm Bureau Town & Country Insurance Company of Missouri; Farmers Alliance Mutual Insurance Co.; Federated Mutual Insurance Co.; Great Central Insurance Co.; Holeim (US) Inc.; LaForge Corp.; Lititz Mutual Insurance Co.; Lutheran Benevolence Insurance Co.; Mack Truck Co.; Podiatry Insurance Company of America; Intrelex Insurance; R.L.I. Insurance Co.; Ranger Insurance Cos.; Sinclair Oil Co.; St. Paul Cos.; State Automobile Insurance Co.; State Farm Fire & Casualty Co.; U.S.A.A.

(For Complete Biographical Data on all Personnel, see Professional Biographies at St. Louis, Missouri)

ARMSTRONG TEASDALE LLP

A Partnership including Professional Corporations

23 SOUTH FIRST STREET
BELLEVILLE, ILLINOIS 62220
Telephone: 618-397-4411
Email: armstrongteasdale@armstrongteasdale.com
URL: http://www.armstrongteasdale.com

St. Louis, Missouri Office: One Metropolitan Square, Suite 2600, 63102. Telephone: 314-621-5070. Facsimile: 314-621-5065.
Kansas City, Missouri Office: 2345 Grand Boulevard, Suite 2000, 64108. Telephone: 816-221-3420. Facsimile: 816-221-9786.
Jefferson City, Missouri Office: 3405 West Truman Blvd., Suite 210, 65109-5713. Telephone: 573-636-8394. Facsimile: 573-636-8457.
Springfield, Illinois Office: 3201 Pleasant Run, Suite A, P.O. Box 13317, 62791-3317. Telephone: 217-726-8200. Facsimile: 217-726-8300.
Washington, D.C. Office: 1747 Pennsylvania Avenue, N.W., Suite 300, 20006. Telephone: 202-454-2800. Facsimile: 202-454-2805.
Overland Park, Kansas Office: 7400 West 132nd Street, Suite 200, 66213.
Edwardsville, Illinois Office: 241 North Main Street, 62025. Telephone: 618-650-7087. Facsimile: 618-655-4004.
Henderson, Nevada Office: 701 North Green Valley Parkway, Suite 200, 89074. Telephone: 702-678-5070. Facsimile: 702-990-3003.
Sydney, Australia Office: C/Clayton Utz, Level 31, No. 1 O'Connell Street, Sidney, NSW 2000, Australia. Telephone: 61-29-262-6700. Facsimile: 61-29-262-3263.
New York, New York Office: 230 Park Avenue, Suite 2300, 10169. Telephone: 212-867-9500. Facsimile: 212-599-1759.
Shanghai, China Office: 1376 Nan Jing Xi Lu, Shanghai Center - Suite 718, Shanghai 200040, P.R. China. Telephone: 011-8621-6279-8808. Facsimilie: 011-8621-6279-8866.

General Civil Practice. Administrative Law, Agricultural Law, Alternative Dispute Resolution, Antitrust and Trade Regulation Law, Appellate Practice, Banking and Financial Services, Biotechnology/Life Sciences, Business Law, Civil Rights, Class Actions, Communications Law, Computer, Constitutional Law, Construction Law, Corporate Compliance and Governance, Corporate Law, Corporate Finance, Education Law, Eminent Domain, Employee Benefits, Employment and Labor, Energy, Entertainment & Sports, Environmental Law, Financial Restructuring, Reorganization and Bankruptcy, Distribution and Franchise, Government Contracts, Governmental Relations, Health Care, Immigration and Naturalization, Insurance Coverage/Reinsurance and Extracontractual Liability, International Law, International Trade, Internet Law, Investments, Litigation, Medical Malpractice, Mergers & Acquisitions, Natural Resources, Occupational Safety & Health Administration, Patent, Trademark and Intellectual Property, Pension and Executive Compensation, Personal Injury, Products Liability, Professional Liability, Public Law and Finance, Real Estate, Securities, Taxation, Technology and Science, Toxic Torts, Transportation, Trusts and Estates, White Collar Crime, Workers Compensation and Zoning, Planning & Land Use and Development.

FIRM PROFILE: Armstrong Teasdale LLP conducts a comprehensive nationwide civil law practice from offices in St. Louis, Kansas City and Jefferson City, Missouri; Overland Park, Kansas; Edwardsville, Belleville and Springfield, Illinois; Las Vegas, Nevada; Washington, D.C.; New York, New York; Shanghai, P.R.C.; and Sydney, Australia. The firm is the Missouri member of Lex Mundi, an international association of independent law firms, as well as State Law Resources, Inc. and United States Law Firm Group, both national networks of independent law firms.

(For Biographical Data on other Personnel, see Professional Biographies at St. Louis, Kansas City and Jefferson City, Missouri; Washington, D.C.; Edwardsville and Springfield, Illinois; Henderson, Nevada; and Shanghai, China Offices)

BRAD L. BADGLEY

PROFESSIONAL CORPORATION

Established in 1978

26 PUBLIC SQUARE
BELLEVILLE, ILLINOIS 62220
Telephone: 618-235-1000
Fax: 618-235-1086
URL: http://www.bbadg.wld.com

Negligence, Automobile, Products Liability, Medical Malpractice, Railroad, Marine, Workers Compensation and Labor Law.

FIRM PROFILE: Mr. Badgley has practiced law for over 27 years. The firm is listed in the Bar Register of Preeminent Lawyers.

BRAD L. BADGLEY, born Jacksonville, Florida, August 16, 1952; admitted to bar, 1978, Illinois. *Education:* University of Illinois (B.A., 1974); John Marshall Law School (J.D., 1978). Member: Board of Directors, Leader/Funds, 1997—; Magna Trust Co., 1985-1997; Banc Star One, 1995—; Fairview Heights Community Bank, 1980-1985; Regions Financial Corporation; Bank of O'Fallon. *Member:* Bar Association of Metropolitan St. Louis; East St. Louis, St. Clair County, Illinois State and American Bar Associations; Illinois Trial Lawyers Association (Member, Board of Managers, 1989—; Past Co-Chairman, Products Liability Section); The Association of Trial Lawyers of America; Workers Compensation Lawyers Association Limited; American Board of Trial Advocates (Advocate; Past Chapter President, Missouri and Southern Illinois). ***PRACTICE AREAS:*** Plaintiffs Personal Injury Law; Workers Compensation Law; Products Liability; Medical Malpractice; Railroad Law; Marine Law.

OF COUNSEL

CHRISTIAN E. HEILIGENSTEIN, born St. Louis, Missouri, December 7, 1929; admitted to bar, 1955, Illinois; 1956, U.S. District Court, Southern District of Illinois and U.S. Court of Appeals, Seventh Circuit; 1960, U.S. District Court, Central District of Illinois;

(This Listing Continued)

1978, U.S. Supreme Court. *Education:* University of Illinois (B.S., in Law, 1953; J.D., 1955). Honors: Who's Who in American Law; Who's Who in Society; Who's Who in the World; Who's Who in America; Men of Achievement of International Biographical Center of London, England; International Leaders in Achievement of the International Biographical Center of London, England; Alumni of the Month, December 1979, College of Law, University of Illinois. Member: Board of Directors, Magna Bank; Board of Directors, Magna Group, Inc., 1984—. Member, Union Planters Corporation, 1998—. *Member:* St. Louis, St. Clair County and Illinois State Bar Associations; The Association of Trial Lawyers of America (Board of Governors, 1985-1987); Illinois Trial Lawyers Association (Board of Managers, 1975-1988, President, 1988-1989); Inner Circle of Advocates; American Board of Professional Liability Attorneys, (Gov., 7th Circuit); International Academy of Trial Lawyers (Member, 1984 and Board of Directors, 1991—); American Board of Trial Advocates (President, St. Louis-Southern Chapter, 1992-1993). (Retired). ***PRACTICE AREAS:*** Plaintiffs Personal Injury Law; Workers Compensation Law; Medical Malpractice; Negligence; Products Liability; Marine Law; Railroad Law.

REFERENCE: Union Planters Bank.

BLAKE & ALLEN, P.C.

Established in 1983

RICHLAND EXECUTIVE PLAZA II
SUITE 100, 521 WEST MAIN STREET
BELLEVILLE, ILLINOIS 62220
Telephone: 618-233-7900; 618-398-1000
Fax: 618-233-9490
URL: http://www.BlakeandAllen.com
Email: law@BlakeandAllen.com
URL: http://www.blakeallenpc.com

Estates and Trusts, Family Law, Divorce, Guardianships, Litigation, Real Estate Law, Tax Law, Business Law as well as General Practice.

EDWARD J. BLAKE, JR., born East Saint Louis, Illinois, August 3, 1952; admitted to bar, 1978, Illinois; 1979, U.S. Tax Court. *Education:* St. Louis University (B.S.B.A., 1975; J.D., 1978); Southern Illinois University (M.B.A., 1977); Washington University (LL.M., Taxation, 1982). *Member:* The Bar Association of Metropolitan St. Louis; St. Clair County, Illinois State (Member, Section on: Estate Planning, 1987-1988; Federal Taxation, 1988-1989; Business Advise and Financial Planning, 1995-1996) and American Bar Associations. ***PRACTICE AREAS:*** Trusts and Estates; Family Law; Divorce; Guardianship; Litigation; Real Estate Law; Tax Law; Business Law; General Practice. ***Email:*** EBlake@BlakeandAllen.com

BRADLEY C. ALLEN, born East St. Louis, Illinois, July 4, 1967; admitted to bar, 2001, Illinois; 2003, U.S. District Court, Southern District of Illinois and U.S. Tax Court. *Education:* Illinois State University (BS., Political Science, 1988); Southern Illinois University (M.A., Political Science, 1995); St. Louis University (J.D., 2001). *Member:* St. Clair County, Madison County, Illinois State and American Bar Associations. ***PRACTICE AREAS:*** Trusts and Estates; Family Law; Divorce; Guardianship; Litigation; Real Estate Law; Tax Law; Business Law; General Practice. ***Email:*** BAllen@BlakeandAllen.com

REPRESENTATIVE CLIENT: Union Planters Bank, N.A.

BOGGS, BOGGS & BATES, LLC

23 SOUTH FIRST STREET
BELLEVILLE, ILLINOIS 62220-2029
Telephone: 618-746-9540
Fax: 618-746-9541
Email: bbblawyers.com

St. Louis, Missouri Office: 7912 Bonhomme, Suite 400, 63105-1912. Telephone: 314-726-2310. Fax: 314-726-2360.
Kansas City, Missouri Office: 1300 N.W. Jefferson Court, Kansas City, 64105. Telephone: 816-472-5599. Fax: 816-472-0870.
Collinsville, Illinois Office: 120 East Church Street, 62234. Telephone: 618-343-0031. Fax: 618-343-0177.

Insurance Defense, Workers Compensation Defense. Professional Liability, Employment Law, Environmental, Insurance Coverage, Products Liability, Negligence Defense.

(For Complete Biographical Data on all Personnel, See Professional Biographies at St. Louis, Missouri)

BROWN & ASSOCIATES

Established in 1988

5520 WEST MAIN STREET
BELLEVILLE, ILLINOIS 62226
Telephone: 618-236-2887
Fax: 618-236-2086
Email: terry@tbrownandassociates.com
URL: http://www.lawyers.com/brown&associates

Civil Litigation, Personal Injury, Medical Malpractice, Products Liability, Admiralty Law, Railroad Law and Commercial Law.

FIRM PROFILE: Brown & Associates is a plaintiff's litigation firm. Mr. Brown is a former defense attorney who has been practicing in Belleville since 1974. The firm is located in southwest Illinois, is licensed to practice in Illinois and Missouri, and has represented clients nationwide. The firm handles diverse cases involving maritime and railroad litigation, medical and nursing home malpractice, products liability, automobile liability, construction litigation, and worker's compensation.

(This Listing Continued)

TERRY N. BROWN, born Chester, Illinois, September 7, 1949; admitted to bar, 1974, Illinois; U.S. Court of Appeals, Seventh Circuit; U.S. District Court, Southern District of Illinois; 1994, Missouri and U.S. District Court, Eastern District of Missouri; 2004, U.S. District Court, Northern and Central Districts of Illinois. *Education:* University of Colorado (A.B., 1971); St. Louis University (J.D., 1974). Member of Staff, St. Louis University Law Journal, 1973-1974; Former Adjunct Professor of Law, St. Louis University; Designated Counsel, Transportation Communications Union; Arbitrator and Mediator, Alternative Dispute Resolution; Presenter, Trial Techniques Seminar, Illinois Trial Lawyers Association. *Member:* The Bar Association of Metropolitan St. Louis; St. Clair County, Illinois State and American Bar Associations; Bar Association of the Central and Southern Districts of Illinois; The Missouri Bar; The Association of Trial Lawyers of America; Illinois Trial Lawyers Association (Member, Board of Managers); American Board of Trial Advocates. ***PRACTICE AREAS:*** Personal Injury; Medical Malpractice; Admiralty Law; Products Liability; Railroad Law. ***Email:*** terry@tbrownandassociates.com

ASSOCIATE

KEVIN T. DAWSON, born Mascoutah, Illinois, December 11, 1979; admitted to bar, 2005, Illinois, Missouri, U.S. District Court, Southern District of Illinois and U.S. District Court, Eastern District of Missouri. *Education:* McKendree College (B.A., 2002); Southern Illinois University School of Law (J.D., 2004). Phi Alpha Delta. *Member:* Chicago, St. Clair County, Illinois State and American Bar Associations; Bar Association of the Southern District of Illinois; The Missouri Bar; Bar Association of Metropolitan St. Louis; American Trial Lawyers Association; Illinois Trial Lawyers Association. ***PRACTICE AREAS:*** Personal Injury; Medical Malpractice; Admiralty Law; Products Liability; Railroad Law. ***Email:*** kevin@tbrownandassociates.com

REPRESENTATIVE CLIENT: Transportation Communications Union.

BROWN & JAMES, P.C.

RICHLAND EXECUTIVE PLAZA, SUITE 200
525 WEST MAIN
BELLEVILLE, ILLINOIS 62220-1502
Telephone: 618-235-5590
Facsimile: 618-235-5591
Email: brownjames@bjpc.com
URL: http://www.brownjames.com

St. Louis, Missouri Office: 1010 Market Street, 20th Floor. Telephone 314-421-3400. Facsimile: 314-421-3128.
Kansas City, Missouri Office: City Center Square, 1100 Main Street, Suite 1900. Telephone: 816-472-0800. Facsimile: 816-421-1183.
Springfield, Missouri Office: 300 John Q. Hammons Parkway, Suite 202. Telephone: 417-831-1412. Facsimile: 417-831-6062.

Civil Trials, Appeals and Arbitrations with respect to the following areas: Accountants Liability; Agents and Brokers Liability; Appellate; Arson Fraud Litigation; Business Litigation; Commercial Litigation; Computer Law; Construction Law; Consumer Law; Design Professional Liability; Employment Law; Environmental Law; Fire Subrogation; Health Care Liability; Insurance Law; Intellectual Property; Legal Professional Liability; Medical Malpractice Defense; Premises Liability; Product Liability; Technology Law; Transportation; Worker's Compensation.

JOHN L. McMULLIN, III, born Cape Girardeau, Missouri, September 16, 1946; admitted to bar, 1972, Missouri; 1974, Illinois. *Education:* Washington University (B.S.B.A., 1969); University of Missouri (J.D., 1972). *Member:* St. Clair County and Illinois State Bar Associations; The Missouri Bar; International Association of Defense Counsel; American Board of Trial Advocates. ***PRACTICE AREAS:*** Civil Jury Trials; Products Liability; Construction Accidents; Malpractice (Doctors, Lawyers and Design Professionals). ***Email:*** JMcMullin@bjpc.com

A. J. BRONSKY, born Lafayette, Indiana, December 27, 1956; admitted to bar, 1981, Missouri; 1982, Illinois. *Education:* St. Louis University (B.A., cum laude, 1978); Washington University (J.D., 1981). *Member:* The Missouri Bar; Illinois State Bar Association; Missouri Organization of Defense Lawyers. ***PRACTICE AREAS:*** Environmental; Hazardous Substances; Toxic Tort; Insurance Law; Products Liability; Professional Liability (Architect, Broker, Engineer, Physician and Lawyer. ***Email:*** AJBronsky@bjpc.com

BETH KAMP VEATH, born Elgin, Illinois, August 20, 1957; admitted to bar, 1983, Illinois; 1984, Missouri. *Education:* Phoenix College; University of Illinois (B.S., 1979); Southern Illinois University (J.D., 1983). Recipient, American Jurisprudence Awards for Insurance and for Legal Professional Ethics. *Member:* Illinois State Bar Association; The Missouri Bar. ***PRACTICE AREAS:*** Medical Malpractice Defense; Premises Liability; Transportation. ***Email:*** BVeath@bjpc.com

JOHN P. CUNNINGHAM, born Chicago, Illinois, September 9, 1961; admitted to bar, 1986, Illinois; 1987, Missouri. *Education:* Elmhurst College (B.S., cum laude, 1983); Southern Illinois University (J.D., magna cum laude, 1986). Recipient, American Jurisprudence Awards in: Evidence; Remedies; Constitutional Law. *Member:* Illinois State Bar Association; The Missouri Bar. ***PRACTICE AREAS:*** Insurance Law; Products Liability; Torts; Premises Liability; Subrogation. ***Email:*** JCunningham@bjpc.com

KENNETH M. BURKE, born St. Louis, Missouri, September 2, 1953; admitted to bar, 1991, Missouri; 1992, Illinois; U.S. Court of Appeals, Seventh and Eighth Circuits. *Education:* Webster College (B.A., 1987); St. Louis University (J.D., 1991). *Member:* The Missouri Bar; Illinois State Bar Association; Missouri Organization of Defense Lawyers. ***PRACTICE AREAS:*** Products Liability; Professional Liability; Health Care Liability; Transportation; Employment Law. ***Email:*** KBurke@bjpc.com

EUTHA F. OCHOA, born St. Louis, Missouri, November 26, 1952; admitted to bar, 1999, Missouri; 2000, Illinois. *Education:* Webster University (B.S., 1990); St. Louis University (J.D., 1999). ***Email:*** EOchoa@bjpc.com

(This Listing Continued)

BROWN & JAMES, P.C., Belleville—Continued

DENISE BAKER SEAL, born Alton, Illinois, January 30, 1973; admitted to bar, 1998, Illinois; 1999 Missouri; 2000, U.S. District Court, Eastern District of Missouri and U.S. District Court, Southern District of Illinois. *Education:* Millikin University (B.A., 1995); Northeastern University (J.D., 1998). ***Email:*** dseal@bjpc.com

ERICKA D. McCASKILL, born St. Louis, Missouri, September 29, 1974; admitted to bar, 2001, Illinois. *Education:* Southern Illinois University (B.A., 1996; J.D., 2001). ***Email:*** emccaskill@bjpc.com

TARA L. MORRIS, born Charleston, Mississippi, March 11, 1970; admitted to bar, 1997, Mississippi; 1999, Illinois. *Education:* University of Mississippi (B.A., 1992; J.D., 1997). ***Email:*** tmorris@bjpc.com

LEE J. KARGE, born Peoria, Illinois, March 1, 1971; admitted to bar, 1999, Illinois; 2004, Missouri. *Education:* Washburn University (B.A., 1994); Drake University Law School (J.D., 1997).

DANIEL G. HASENSTAB, born Belleville, Illinois, December 25, 1975; admitted to bar, 2002, Missouri; 2003, Illinois. *Education:* St. Louis University (B.A., 1999; J.D., 2002).

ELIZABETH S. PHIPPS, born Mt. Vernon, Illinois, August 27, 1977; admitted to bar, 2003, North Carolina (Not admitted in Illinois). *Education:* University of Illinois (B.S., 1999); Tulane University Law School (J.D., 2002).

ANTHONY E. DOS SANTOS, born Springfield, Massachusetts, April 26, 1971; admitted to bar, 1998, Illinois; 1999, Missouri. *Education:* Boston University (B.A., 1993); Southern Illinois University (J.D., 1998). ***Email:*** adossantos@bjpc.com

AARON J. BYRAM, born Belleville, Illinois, February 3, 1972; admitted to bar, 1998, Illinois. *Education:* University of Illinois (B.A., 1995); St. Louis University (J.D., 1998). ***Email:*** abyram@bjpc.com

DEANNE R. JOCKISH, born Belleville, Illinois, July 8, 1971; admitted to bar, 2004, Missouri (Not admitted in Illinois). *Education:* Southern Illinois University (B.S.N., 1994); St. Louis University (J.D., 2004). ***Email:*** djockish@bjpc.com

REPRESENTATIVE CLIENTS: *Corporate:* AlliedSignal, Inc.; Bally Total Fitness; Bi-State Development Agency; The Boeing Company; Bridgestone/Firestone, Inc.; Burns & McDonnell Engineering; Burns International Security Services Corp.; Coca-Cola Enterprises; Cooper Tire & Rubber Co.; Dick Simon Trucking, Inc.; Foodmaker, Inc.; Garden Way Incorporated; Global Van Lines; Harsco Corporation; HBE Corporation; Hellmuth Obata & Kassabaum, Inc.; Ingersoll-Rand Company; Jack in the Box, Inc.; Marathon Oil Company; Marten Transport, Ltd.; McDonald's Corporation; PPG Industries, Inc.; Quest Diagnostics Incorporated; Raytheon Company; Saint Louis University; Schnuck Markets, Inc.; Sears Roebuck & Co.; Shoney's Inc.; Slay Industries, Inc.; The Stanley Works; Swift Transportation Co., Inc.; Taco Bell Corp.; U.S. Xpress Enterprises, Inc.; USF Holland, Inc.; Walgreen Company; Wal-Mart Stores, Inc. ; The Washington University; Wells Fargo Alarm Enterprises, Inc.; Werner Co. *Insurance:* Allstate Insurance Co.; Associated Aviation Underwriters; Church Mutual Insurance Company; Cincinnati Insurance Company; CNA Insurance Companies; Crum & Forster Group of Insurance Companies; Design Professionals Insurance Companies; Essex Insurance Company; Fireman's Fund Insurance Company; General Star Management Company; Hanover Insurance Co.; Hartford Insurance Group; Kemper Insurance Companies; Medical Assurance Corporation; Metropolitan Insurance Company; National General Insurance Corp.; Nationwide Mutual Insurance Co.; Safeco Insurance Companies; St. Paul Fire & Marine Insurance Companies; State Farm Insurance Companies; Travelers Insurance Co.; Zurich American Insurance Co.

BURROUGHS, HEPLER, BROOM, MacDONALD, HEBRANK & TRUE, LLP

BELLEVILLE, ILLINOIS

(See Edwardsville)

General Civil Trial and Appellate Practice. Personal Injury, Negligence, Products Liability, Structural Work Act, Admiralty, Professional Malpractice, Insurance, Employment Law, Environmental, Asbestos and Toxic Tort, School, Municipal, Corporate, Tax, Real Estate and Probate Law.

JACK CAREY

Established in 1986

23 SOUTH FIRST STREET
BELLEVILLE, ILLINOIS 62220-2029
Telephone: 618-234-2424
Fax: 618-234-2470
Email: jclaw@compu-type.net

Civil Litigation, Personal Injury, Labor, Criminal Defense.

JACK CAREY, born East St. Louis, Illinois, October 6, 1942; admitted to bar, 1976, Illinois and U.S. District Court, Southern District of Illinois; 1984, Missouri; 1997, Colorado. *Education:* Westminster College (B.A., 1964); Southern Illinois University (M.A., 1967); St. Louis University (J.D., 1974). Alpha Sigma Nu. Editor, St. Louis University Law Review, 1973-1974. Author: "Amnesty—An Act of Grace," St. Louis Law Journal, Vol. 17, No. 4, Summer 1973. President, Signal Hill School Board of Education, 1984-1997. Board of Directors, Signal Hill Fire Protection District, 1975-1986; Incorporator, Signal Hill Education Foundation, Ltd. Member, American Arbitration Association. *Member:* St. Clair County (President, 1986-1987), Madison County, Illinois State (Member: Assembly, 1981-1988; 1990-2000; 2004—; Board of Governors, 2000-2003; Treasurer, 2002-2003; Chair, Unauthorized Practice Law Committee) and American Bar Associations; The Association of Trial Lawyers of America; Illinois Trial Lawyers Association. ***PRACTICE AREAS:*** Plaintiff Litigation; Family Law; Criminal; Labor Law; Arbitration; Driving Under the Influence; Felonies; Misdemeanors; Traffic Violations; Personal Injury; Workers' Compensation.

CATES, KUROWSKI, BAILEY & SHULTZ, LLC

24 BRONZE POINTE (SWANSEA)
BELLEVILLE (SWANSEA), ILLINOIS 62226
Telephone: 618-277-5500
Fax: 618-277-6334
URL: http://www.kbslaw.net
Email: kbs@kbslaw.net
URL: http://www.lawyers.com/kurowskibailey

Civil Litigation Practice. Toxic Tort, Asbestos, Insurance, Bad Faith Claims, Insurance Defense, Employment Law, Family Law.

JUDY L. CATES, born Belleville, Illinois, April 22, 1952; admitted to bar, 1978, Illinois; 1979, Florida; 1984, Missouri; U.S. District Court, Southern District of Illinois; 2002, U.S. Court of Appeals, 7th Circuit; 2003, U.S. Court of Appeals, 11th Circuit. *Education:* Cornell University (B.A., 1973); Washington University (J.D., 1977). Instructor, Business Law, Belleville Area College, 1979-1982. Assistant State's Attorney, St. Clair County, Illinois, 1978-1982. *Member:* St. Clair County and Illinois State Bar Associations; The Florida Bar; The Association of Trial Lawyers of America; Illinois Trial Lawyers Association. (Board Certified Civil Trial Advocacy Specialist by the National Board of Trial Advocacy). ***PRACTICE AREAS:*** Personal Injury; Class Action. ***Email:*** jcates@cateskurowski.com

JOHN J. KUROWSKI, born East St. Louis, Illinois, July 18, 1953; admitted to bar, 1978, Illinois and U.S. District Court, Southern District of Illinois; 1981, U.S. Court of Appeals, Seventh Circuit; 1987, U.S. District Court, Central District of Illinois; 1991, U.S. District Court, Southern District of Indiana; 1993, Missouri and U.S. District Court, Eastern District of Missouri; 1996, Texas. *Education:* Loyola University of Chicago (B.A., cum laude, 1975); St. Louis University (J.D., 1978). Member, St. Louis University Law Journal, 1977-1978. *Publications:* Co-author: "Toxic and Hazardous Substances and Environmental Law: Annual Survey," 28 Tort & Ins., L.J. 445, 1992. Lecturer, Defense Research Institute, 1999-2001; Illinois Institute for Continuing Legal Education, 1986, 1987, 1995, Illinois State Bar Association, 1985-1999. *Member:* St. Clair County (Member: Board of Directors, 1988-1990; Judiciary Committee, 1991-1993; Family Law Committee, 1993), East St. Louis (Member, Board of Directors, 1986-1988; President, 1990-1991), Illinois State (Assembly Member, 1982-1984; Member: Family Law Section Council, 1983-1995; Chair, 1993-1994; Standing Committee on Legislation, 1988-1994) and American (Member, Tort and Insurance Practice Section) Bar Associations; Defense Research Institute. Fellow, American Academy of Matrimonial Lawyers. ***LANGUAGES:*** Italian. ***PRACTICE AREAS:*** Trials; Toxic Tort Law; Insurance Defense; Insurance Bad Faith; Employment; Family Law. ***Email:*** jkurowski@cateskurowski.com

CURTIS R. BAILEY, born Moberly, Missouri, February 24, 1966; admitted to bar, 1991, Missouri; 1992, Illinois, U.S. District Court, Eastern District of Missouri and U.S. District Court, Southern District of Illinois. *Education:* Westminster College (B.A., 1988); University of Missouri-Columbia (J.D., 1991). Phi Alpha Theta; Epsilon Beta Alpha. Recipient, American Jurisprudence Award in Dispute Resolution. *Member:* East St. Louis, St. Clair County and Illinois State Bar Associations; The Missouri Bar. ***PRACTICE AREAS:*** Toxic Tort Defense; Insurance; Family Law; Defense Litigation. ***Email:*** cbailey@cateskurowski.com

WILLIAM D. SHULTZ, JR., born Belleville, Illinois, November 28, 1966; admitted to bar, 1991, Illinois; 1992, Missouri; 1993, U.S. District Court, Southern District of Illinois and U.S. Court of Appeals, Sixth Circuit; 1994, Missouri and U.S. Court of Appeals, Seventh Circuit; 1997, U.S. District Court, Central District of Illinois. *Education:* Benedictine College (B.A., 1988); Creighton University (J.D., 1991). Phi Delta Phi. Co-Author: "Retaliatory Discharge Under the Workers' Compensation Act," Illinois Institute for Continuing Legal Education, 1996. Adjunct Professor, Business Law I and II, McKendree College, Lebanon, Illinois, 1992—. *Member:* St. Clair County, Seventh Circuit, Illinois State and American Bar Associations; Illinois Bankers Association; Appellate Lawyers Association of Illinois; Defense Research Institute. ***REPORTED CASES:*** Manufacturers' Industrial Relations Association and Trustees of Mira-GMP Allied Workers Pension Trust vs. East Akron Casting Company and Howark Wenk, 58 F.3d 204 (6th Cir. 1995); Gloria R. Clark v. Owens-Brockway Glass Container, Inc., 697N.E.2d 743, 232 Ill. Dec. 1 (5th Dist. 1998). ***PRACTICE AREAS:*** Torts; Insurance Defense Litigation; Commercial Litigation; Business Representation; Employment Law; Construction Law; Insurance Bad Faith. ***Email:*** wshultz@cateskurowski.com

---

MELISSA R. BADGETT, born Knoxville, Tennessee, January 6, 1970; admitted to bar, 1999, Illinois and Missouri. *Education:* University of Mississippi (B.P.A., 1991); St. Louis University (J.D., 1999). *Member:* St. Clair County, East St. Louis, Illinois State (Member, Young Lawyers Division) and American Bar Associations. ***PRACTICE AREAS:*** Family Law; Insurance Defense; Litigation; Torts; Insurance Bad Faith. ***Email:*** mbadgett@cateskurowski.com

MICHAEL WADE TACKETT, born Ft. Wayne, Indiana, November 17, 1973; admitted to bar, 2000, Illinois; 2001, Missouri. *Education:* St. Joseph's College (B.S., cum laude, 1996); Washington University (J.D., 2000). *Member:* St. Louis County and East St. Louis, Illinois State and American Bar Associations; Bar Association of Metropolitan Saint Louis. ***PRACTICE AREAS:*** Torts; Insurance Defense Litigation; Commercial Litigation; Insurance Bad Faith; Family Law. ***Email:*** mtackett@cateskurowski.com

LINDSAY A. DIBLER, born St. Louis, Missouri, November 14, 1960; admitted to bar, 1993, Nevada; 1994, Missouri, U.S. District Court, Eastern District of Missouri, Illinois and U.S. District Court, Southern District of Illinois. *Education:* United States Naval Academy (B.S., Aerospace Engineering, 1983); St. Louis University (J.D., 1993). Phi Delta Phi. *Member:* Illinois State and American Bar Associations; The Missouri Bar. [Lieutenant, United States Navy, 1983-1988]. ***PRACTICE AREAS:*** Toxic Tort Defense; Insurance Defense; Commercial Litigation; Insurance Bad Faith; Construction Law. ***Email:*** ldibler@cateskurowski.com

ROBERT C. ANDERSON, born St. Louis, Missouri, November 18, 1953; admitted to bar, 1991, Missouri; 1992, Illinois; U.S. District Court, Eastern District of Missouri. *Education:* Southern Illinois University (B.S., 1982); St. Louis University (J.D., 1991). Certifi-

(This Listing Continued)

cate in Employment Law. *Member:* Bar Association of Metropolitan St. Louis; The Missouri Bar; Illinois State Bar Association; Missouri Organization of Defense Lawyers. ***PRACTICE AREAS:*** Litigation. ***Email:*** randerson@cateskurowski.com

STEVEN A. TREFTS, born St. Louis, Missouri, January 16, 1973; admitted to bar, 1999, Missouri; 2000, Illinois. *Education:* Missouri Baptist College (B.S., 1996); Creighton University (J.D., 1999). ***PRACTICE AREAS:*** Defense Litigation; Medical Malpractice; Personal Injury. ***Email:*** strefts@cateskurowski.com

JEROME S. WARCHOL, JR., born Belleville, Illinois, August 4, 1979; admitted to bar, 2004, Illinois; 2005, Missouri. *Education:* St. Louis University (B.S., 2001; J.D., 2004). ***PRACTICE AREAS:*** Defense Litigation. ***Email:*** jwarchol@cateskurowski.com

TRACY L. BAUM, born Centreville, Illinois, August 20, 1975; admitted to bar, 2000, Illinois. *Education:* Illinois College (B.A., 1997); St. Louis University (J.D., 2000). ***PRACTICE AREAS:*** Medical Malpractice; Personal Injury; Civil Litigation. ***Email:*** tbaum@cateskurowski.com

CANDICE C. KUSMER, born Lawton, Oklahoma, December 14, 1976; admitted to bar, 2005, Illinois. *Education:* University of Oklahoma (B.A., 1999); Washington University (J.D., 2002). ***PRACTICE AREAS:*** Medical Malpractice; Personal Injury. ***Email:*** ckusmer@cateskurowski.com

REPRESENTATIVE CLIENTS: A.W. Chesterton Co.; Liberty Mutual Insurance Co.; Sears, Roebuck & Co; Interstate Fire and Casualty Co.; Interstate Indemnity Co.; Congoleum Corp.; Village of Swansea, Illinois; D.B. Riley, Inc.; Hinz Claim Management Co.; Signal Hill School District; Taylor Morley, Inc.; Warrior Insurance Group; Stookey Township, Illinois; Western Auto Co.; The Riverstone Group; The Traveler's; East St. Louis Board of Election Commissioners, Lincoln General Insurance Co.; Stuart Title Guaranty Co.; Nationwide Indemnity Co.

NEAL A. CONNORS LAW FIRM, P.C.

Established in 2005

422 SOUTH HIGH STREET
BELLEVILLE, ILLINOIS 62220
Telephone: 618-233-2466
Fax: 618-233-8447
Email: nconnors@peaknet.net

Immigration Law, Criminal Law, Business Law, Military and International Law.

FIRM PROFILE: Since 1997, Neal Connors has been engaged in private practice in the State of Illinois and later in the State of Missouri. Originally founding the Law Offices of Grueninger & Connors with his partner, Dan Grueninger, recently Neal opened his own office alongside the original firm so that he could concentrate in immigration law and expand existing office space to the present building. With the assistance of paralegal Shannon Walther since 2002, and Elizabeth Rogers, who recently joined the firm as an office manager and client account manager, Neal hopes to provide assistance to more clients in more ways.

Law Firm Alliance: Burke & Poirier Law Firm; Grueninger & Connors.

NEAL A. CONNORS, born LaGrange, Illinois, December 16, 1962; admitted to bar, 1989, Illinois; 1996, U.S. District Court, Southern District of Illinois; 1999, Missouri. *Education:* University of Illinois (B.A., 1985; J.D., 1989). ***LANGUAGES:*** French, Spanish and Japanese. ***Email:*** nconnors@peaknet.net

Languages: French, Spanish and Japanese.

DIXON & JOHNSTON, P.C.

103 WEST MAIN STREET
BELLEVILLE, ILLINOIS 62220-1501
Telephone: 618-233-1103
1-800-733-2440
Fax: 618-233-9368
Email: johnjohnston@compu-type.net
URL: http://www.dixonandjohnston.com

Family Law, Social Security Disability, Personal Injury, Bankruptcy, Mortgage Foreclosure.

MEMBERS OF FIRM

SCOTT DIXON, born Colorado Springs, Colorado, November 6, 1953; admitted to bar, 1978, Illinois and U.S. District Court, Southern District of Illinois; 1979, Missouri and U.S. District Court, Eastern District of Missouri; 1980, U.S. Court of Appeals, Eighth Circuit. *Education:* University of Illinois (B.A., 1975); John Marshall Law School (J.D., 1978). Phi Delta Phi. Illinois Special Assistant Attorney General, 1987—. *Member:* The Bar Association of Metropolitan St. Louis; St. Clair County, St. Louis County, Illinois State Bar Association; The Association of Trial Lawyers of America; National Organization of Social Security Claimant's Representatives. Fellow, Illinois Bar Foundation. ***PRACTICE AREAS:*** Social Security Disability; Personal Injury. ***Email:*** scottdixon@compu-type.net

JOHN J. JOHNSTON, born East St. Louis, Illinois, January 19, 1954; admitted to bar, 1979, Illinois; 1981. U.S. District Court, Southern District of Illinois; 1983, U.S. Court of Appeals, Seventh Circuit. *Education:* University of Kansas (B.S., 1976); University of Illinois (J.D., 1979). Member, Board of Directors, St. Clair County Children First Foundation. Associate Editor, Illinois State Bar Journal. *Member:* St. Clair County and Illinois State (Member, Section on Family Law; Member, Board of Governors, 1990-1992; Former Chair, Bar Publications Board) Bar Associations; National Association of Consumer Bankruptcy Attorneys; Bankruptcy Association of Southern Illinois. Fellow, Illinois Bar Foundation. ***PRACTICE AREAS:*** Bankruptcy; Family Law; Mortgage Foreclosure. ***Email:*** johnjohnston@compu-type.net

ASSOCIATE

STANLEY R. WELLER, born St. Louis, Missouri, December 11, 1969; admitted to bar, 1998, Illinois and U.S. District Court, Southern District of Illinois. *Education:* University of Wisconsin at Madison (B.S., 1992); Southern Illinois University (J.D., 1998). *Member:* St. Clair, Monroe County and Illinois State Bar Associations; Bankruptcy Association of Southern Illinois; National Association of Consumer Bankruptcy Attorneys. ***PRACTICE AREAS:*** Family Law; Bankruptcy. ***Email:*** stanweller@compu-type.net

(This Listing Continued)

DONOVAN, ROSE, NESTER & JOLEY, P.C.

8 EAST WASHINGTON STREET
BELLEVILLE, ILLINOIS 62220
Telephone: 618-235-2020
Telecopier: 618-235-9632
Email: firm@ilmoattorneys.com

Admiralty and Maritime Law, Alcoholic Beverages, Appellate Practice, Civil Practice, Civil Rights, Environmental Law, Estate Planning, Health Care Law, Hospitals, Insurance, Insurance Defense, Litigation, Medical Malpractice, Legal Malpractice, Negligence, Personal Injury, Premises Liability, Products Liability, Professional Liability, Railroads, Torts.

DENNIS E. ROSE, born East St. Louis, Illinois, April 24, 1947; admitted to bar, 1972, Illinois; 1978, Missouri; U.S. Court of Appeals, Seventh Circuit; U.S. District Court, Southern and Central Districts of Illinois; U.S. District Court, Eastern District of Missouri. *Education:* University of Illinois (B.A., 1969; J.D., 1972). *Member:* St. Clair County and Illinois State (Past Member, Board of Governors) Bar Associations; Illinois Association of Defense Trial Counsel; Defense Research Institute. ***Email:*** drose@ilmoattorneys.com

MICHAEL J. NESTER, born St. Louis, Missouri, April 18, 1948; admitted to bar, 1973, Illinois and U.S. Court of Appeals, Seventh Circuit; U.S. District Court, Southern and Central Districts of Illinois; 1998, Missouri; 2002, U.S. Supreme Court. *Education:* St. Louis University (A.B., cum laude, 1970; J.D., with honors, 1973). Law Clerk for U.S. District Court Judge Omer Poos, Southern District of Illinois, 1973-1974. Assistant U.S. Attorney for the Eastern District of Illinois, 1974-1976. *Member:* East St. Louis (President, 1995-1996), St. Clair County (President, 1993-1994) and Illinois State Bar Associations; The Missouri Bar; American Board of Trial Advocates; American Academy of Healthcare Attorneys; Defense Research Institute; Illinois Association of Healthcare Attorneys. ***Email:*** mnester@ilmoattorneys.com

CHARLES L. JOLEY, born Peoria, Illinois, December 8, 1958; admitted to bar, 1984, Illinois; 1985, Missouri; U.S. District Court, Southern and Central Districts of Illinois; U.S. District Court, Eastern District of Missouri and U.S. Court of Appeals, Seventh and Eighth Circuits. *Education:* University of Illinois (B.A., with highest distinction, 1980; J.D., 1984). *Member:* The Bar Association of Metropolitan St. Louis; St. Clair County and Illinois State Bar Associations; The Missouri Bar; Defense Research Institute; Illinois Defense Counsel. ***Email:*** cjoley@ilmoattorneys.com

ROBERT J. BASSETT, born Belleville, Illinois, April 26, 1961; admitted to bar, 1986, Illinois; 1992, Missouri; U.S. District Court, Southern and Eastern Districts of Illinois and U.S. Court of Appeals, Seventh Circuit. *Education:* Murray State University (B.S., magna cum laude, 1983); Washington University at St. Louis (J.D., 1986). *Member:* St. Clair County (Member, Board of Directors), Illinois State and American Bar Associations; The Missouri Bar; Defense Research Institute; The International Association of Defense Counsel. ***Email:*** rbassett@ilmoattorneys.com

KENNETH M. NUSSBAUMER, born East St. Louis, Illinois, April 17, 1959; admitted to bar, 1988, Illinois and U.S. District Court, Southern District of Illinois; 1999, Missouri. *Education:* Southern Illinois University-Edwardsville (B.A., 1981); Southern Illinois University School of Law (J.D., 1988). *Member:* East St. Louis, St. Clair County and Illinois State Bar Associations; The Missouri Bar. ***Email:*** knussbaumer@ilmoattorneys.com

GEORGIANN OLIVER, born Harrisburg, Illinois, October 1, 1960; admitted to bar, 1986, Missouri and U.S. District Court, Western District of Missouri; 1987, Illinois, U.S. District Court, Southern District of Illinois and U.S. Court of Appeals, Eighth Circuit; 2001, U.S. District Court, Eastern District of Missouri. *Education:* Southeastern Illinois College (A.A., 1979); Southern Illinois University (B.S., with highest honors, 1981); Washington University (J.D., 1986). Associate Editor, Journal of Urban & Contemporary Law, 1985-1986. Law Clerk to Justice Warren D. Welliver, Missouri Supreme Court, 1986-1987. *Member:* Bar Association of Metropolitan St. Louis; St. Clair County and Illinois State Bar Associations; The Missouri Bar. ***Email:*** goliver@ilmoattorneys.com

KRISTINE McGEE MACK, born Springfield, Illinois, January 13, 1966; admitted to bar, 1991, Illinois, U.S. District Court, Southern and Central Districts of Illinois and U.S. Court of Appeals, Seventh Circuit; 1992, Missouri and U.S. District Court, Eastern District of Missouri. *Education:* Southern Illinois University (B.S., 1988; J.D., 1991). *Member:* Bar Association of Metropolitan St. Louis; St. Clair County and Illinois State Bar Associations; The Missouri Bar. ***Email:*** kmack@ilmoattorneys.com

Chi-yong Throckmartin

REPRESENTATIVE CLIENTS: Aetna Life & Casualty Co.; AIG; American Enterprise Surplus Lines; Anheuser Busch Cos., Inc.; Automobile Club of Missouri; Auto Owners Insurance Co.; Axia, Inc.; Capitol Indemnity, Casualty Insurance Co.; Chatlins Group, Inc.; CIGNA Cos.; Clark Oil Refinery; Continental Western Insurance Co.; Country Cos. Insurance Co.; Country Mutual Insurance Co.; Crum & Forster Insurance Co.; Eagle Picher Industries, Inc.; Employer's Mutual Insurance Co.; General Tire, Inc.; Great American Insurance Co.; Government Employees Insurance Co.; HealthLink, Inc.; Home Depot; Liberty Mutual Insurance Co.; Merk & Company; Metropolitan Property and Casualty Insurance Co.; Mutual Fire, Marine & Inland Insurance Co.; National Fire & Marine Insurance Co.; National General Insurance Co.; National Indemnity Co.; National Liability and Fire Insurance Co.; Accidental Fire and Casualty Co. of N.C.; Ohio Insurance Guaranty Association; Papco General Insurance Co.; Progressive Casualty Insurance Co.; Progressive Specialty Insurance; Royal Insurance Co.; St. Elizabeth's Hospital; Sentry Insurance Co.; Standard Mutual Insurance Co.; State Farm & Fire Casualty Co.; State Farm Auto Insurance Co.; Tennessee Farmer's Insurance Co.; The Traveler's Insurance Co.; United States Fire Insurance Co.; United Van Lines, Inc.; Wal-Mart Stores; Western World Insurance Co.; World Wide Underwriters; Yellow Freight Systems; Zurich Insurance Co.

DUNHAM, BOMAN & LESKERA

208 N. HIGH
BELLEVILLE, ILLINOIS 62220
Telephone: 618-235-7222
Telecopier: 618-236-2800
Email: dbl103@mvp.net

Collinsville Office: 300 West Clay Street. Telephone: 618-344-7734. Telecopier: 618-344-3853.

General Civil Trial and Appellate Practice. Negligence and Products Liability, Medical Malpractice, Probate, Insurance, Family, Real Estate, Environmental, School, Criminal and Bankruptcy Law.

M.F. OEHMKE (1887-1963)

WM. C. DUNHAM (1893-1975)

HOWARD BOMAN (1917-1985)

JOHN W. LESKERA, born East Saint Louis, Illinois, June 19, 1931; admitted to bar, 1955, Illinois. *Education:* University of Illinois (A.B., 1953; J.D., 1955). Assistant Attorney General, 1968—. *Member:* Illinois State and American Bar Associations; Illinois Defense Counsel. Fellow, American College of Trial Lawyers. ***PRACTICE AREAS:*** Civil Litigation; Insurance Coverage; Products Liability Defense; Negligence Defense; School Law; Municipal Law; Litigation; Family Law; Matrimonial Law; Probate; Trust Law. ***Email:*** dbl300@wberry.com

WILLIAM L. BERRY, born East Saint Louis, Illinois, July 7, 1948; admitted to bar, 1973, Illinois. *Education:* MacMurray College; Millikin University (B.A., 1970); Washington University (J.D., 1973). *Member:* Illinois State and American Bar Associations. ***PRACTICE AREAS:*** Civil Litigation; Insurance Coverage; Products Liability; Negligence; Family Law; Probate; Trust Law; Criminal Law. ***Email:*** wberry@wberry.com

ERIC C. YOUNG, born Belleville, Illinois, February 27, 1950; admitted to bar, 1975, Illinois; 1980, Missouri. *Education:* St. Benedict's College (B.A., 1972); University of Illinois (J.D., 1975). *Member:* Illinois State Bar Association; The Missouri Bar. ***PRACTICE AREAS:*** Civil Litigation; Insurance Defense; Products Liability Defense; Negligence Defense; Insurance Coverage. ***Email:*** dbl103@mvp.net

JOHN L. BITZER

ASSOCIATES

JASON W. CORRAY, born Urbana, Illinois, May 29, 1973; admitted to bar, 2001, Illinois; 2002, Missouri. *Education:* University of Illinois, Urbana-Champaign (A.B., 1996); Southern Illinois University, Carbondale (J.D., 2000). ***PRACTICE AREAS:*** Corporate Law; Asbestos Litigation; Insurance Coverage Litigation; Subrogation; Plaintiffs Personal Injury. ***Email:*** jcorray@wberry.com

TAMARA R. CHANDLER, born Belleville, Illinois, November 10, 1974; admitted to bar, 2001, Illinois and U.S. District Court, Southern District of Illinois. *Education:* Deaconess College of Nursing (B.S.N., 1996); Southern Illinois University (J.D., 2001). Associate, Brown & James, P.C., 2001; Donovan, Rose, Nester & Joley, P.C., 2001-2003. Registered Professional Nurse, Illinois and Missouri, 1996—. *Member:* Illinois State and American Bar Associations. ***PRACTICE AREAS:*** Products Liability (40%); Automobile Liability (5%); Insurance Defense (50%); Insurance Coverage (5%).

HARVEY TAYLOR, JR., born East St. Louis, Illinois, February 4, 1977; admitted to bar, 2003, Illinois. *Education:* University of Illinois (B.A., 2000; J.D., 2003). *Member:* Illinois State and American Bar Associations. ***PRACTICE AREAS:*** Civil Litigation; Asbestos Litigation; Products Liability; Insurance Coverage. ***Email:*** htaylor@wberry.com

KEVIN J. NEWTON, born St. Louis, Missouri, January 23, 1975; admitted to bar, 2004, Illinois. *Education:* University of Illinois (B.A., 1997); St. Louis University (J.D., 2000).

ATTORNEYS FOR: Collinsville School District #10; Hartford Insurance Group; State Farm Insurance Cos.; The Travelers Indemnity Co.; Wausau Insurance Cos.; Nationwide Insurance Co.; RLI Insurance Group; Beaser East.
REPRESENTATIVE CLIENT: State Farm Mutual Automobile Insurance Company.

ENYART & PEEBLES

12 SOUTH SECOND STREET
BELLEVILLE, ILLINOIS 62220
Telephone: 618-235-8300; 398-4505
Fax: 618-235-8673
Email: mspeebles_2000@yahoo.com
URL: http://www.lawyers.com/enyart&peebles

Social Security Disability, Personal Injury, Military Law, Trial Practice, Administrative Law, Criminal Law, Probate, Municipal Law.

WILLIAM L. ENYART, born Pensacola, Florida, September 22, 1949; admitted to bar, 1979, Illinois and U.S. District Court, Southern and Central Districts of Illinois; 1980, Missouri; U.S. Court of Appeals, Seventh Circuit and U.S. Court of Appeals for the Armed Forces. *Education:* Southern Illinois University (B.A., Journalism and Political Science, 1974; J.D., 1979); U.S. Army War College (M.S., 2000). Certified, Military Trial Lawyer. *Member:* American Trial Lawyers Association; National Organization of Social Security Claimants' Representatives. [Colonel, U.S. Army Reserve]. ***PRACTICE AREAS:*** Administrative Hearings and Appeals; Arbitration; Trial Practice; Military Courts Martial; Accidents; Bodily Injury; Plaintiffs Personal Injury; Social Security Disability; Supplemental Security Income Disability. ***Email:*** enyart@icss.net

MARK S. PEEBLES, born Belleville, Illinois, September 5, 1963; admitted to bar, 1994, Illinois; 1998, U.S. district Court, Southern District of Illinois. *Education:* Brown University (A.B., 1987); Washington University (M.F.A., 1989); St. Louis University (J.D., 1994). Administrative Hearing Officer. Recipient, Alfred H. Joslin Award for Service to the Brown Community. Formerly with: Hotto & Peebles; Mark S. Peebles, Attorney at Law.

(This Listing Continued)

Member: St. Clair County and Illinois State Bar Associations. ***LANGUAGES:*** Spanish. ***PRACTICE AREAS:*** Personal Injury; Criminal Law; Trial Practice; Probate; Municipal Law. ***Email:*** mspeebles_2000@yahoo.com

FOX GALVIN, LLC

Established in 2001

5111 WEST MAIN STREET
BELLEVILLE, ILLINOIS 62226
Telephone: Toll Free: 866-588-7001

St. Louis, Missouri Office: One Memorial Drive, 8th Floor, 63102. Telephone: 314-588-7000; 866-588-7001. Telecopier: 314-588-1965. URL: http://www.foxgalvin.com.

Trial and Appellate Practice in State and Federal Courts. Areas of practice: Admiralty, Product Liability, Class Action, Insurance Coverage, Professional Liability, Employment Law, Commercial Law and Personal Injury.

FIRM PROFILE: Fox Galvin, LLC was founded in April 2001. The firm is proud to represent national, regional and local clients in complex and high exposure litigation. Fox Galvin attorneys are committed to providing the highest quality and most responsive legal service available in the St. Louis area and the midwest. The firm has invested in the most effective personnel and the latest computer technology with which we aggressively respond to the needs of our clients. Fox Galvin attorneys combine knowledge, experience and energy to deliver service and results.

(For Personnel and Biographical Data, see Professional Biographies at St. Louis, Missouri)

GAVIN LAW FIRM

#17 PARK PLACE PROFESSIONAL CENTRE
BELLEVILLE, ILLINOIS 62226
Telephone: 618-236-0100
Toll Free: 888-360-0100
Fax: 618-236-2684
URL: http://www.gavinlaw.com
Email: billg@gavinlaw.com
URL: http://www.lawyers.com/gavinlaw

Civil Trial Practice, consisting primarily of Personal Injury, Federal Employers Liability, Medical Malpractice, Admiralty, Products Liability, Occupational Disease, Environmental, Toxic Tort and Commercial Law in State and Federal Courts.

WILLIAM P. GAVIN, born East St. Louis, Illinois, November 17, 1955; admitted to bar, 1980, Illinois; 1982, Missouri; U.S. Court of Appeals, Seventh and Eighth Circuits; U.S. District Court, Southern and Central Districts of Illinois; U.S. District Court, Eastern District of Missouri. *Education:* St. Louis University (A.B., cum laude, 1977; J.D., cum laude, 1980). Member, Order of Woolsack, St. Louis University. Member of Staff, St. Louis University Law Review, 1979-1980. Author: "A Comparison of the Modified Uniform Products Liability Act and Medical Malpractice Reform Legislation," 24 St. Louis University Law Journal 554, 1980; "Railroad Diesel Exhaust and Lung Cancer," November Trial 1992; "Railroad Welders, Lung Disease and the FELA," February Trial 1993; Review, "Train Accident Reconstruction and FELA & Railroad Litigation," 2nd Edition, November Trial, 1995. Speaker, "Handling a Federal Employers Liability Act Diesel Exhaust Exposure Case," ATLA Convention, 1998. Recipient: Service to Youth Award, 1976, 1986, 1995; YMCA Lowell Linnes Award, 2000. Member, YMCA, Southwest Illinois (Chairman, Board of Directors, 1990-1995; Vice Chairman, Board of Directors, 1995-1999; Chairman, Endowment Committee, 1985-2000— Sustaining Fund Drive, 1985; Membership Drive Committees, 1985). Member, First Baptist Church, Fairview Heights (Discipleship Training Teacher; Chairman, Building Finance Committee; Chairman, Personnel Committee; Chairman, Vision 21 Capital Funds Campaign).*Member:* The Bar Association of Metropolitan St. Louis; St. Clair County (Director, 1984-1985), Illinois State and American Bar Associations; The Missouri Bar; The Association of Trial Lawyers of America; Illinois Trial Lawyers Association; Missouri Association of Trial Attorneys. The Supreme Court of Illinois does not recognize certifications of specialties in the practice of law and board certification is not a requirement to practice law in Illinois. (Board Certified Civil Trial Advocate by the National Board of Trial Advocacy). ***PRACTICE AREAS:*** Personal Injury; Federal Employers Liability Act; Toxic Tort; Products Liability; Admiralty; Environmental Law; Commercial Litigation.

RACHEL MARIE LEWIS, born Benton, Illinois; admitted to bar, 2003, Illinois; 2004. Missouri. *Education:* University of Illinois (B.A., 2000); Southern Illinois University, School of Law, Carbondale (J.D., 2003). *Member:* Illinois State and American Bar Associations; Illinois Trial Lawyers Association; Association of Trial Lawyers of America. ***PRACTICE AREAS:*** Personal Injury; Federal Employers Liability Act (FELA); Toxic Torts; Products Liability; Admiralty Law; Environmental Law; Commercial Litigation.

COUNSEL FOR: RNG Land Development Inc.; R. McMillin Truck Service Inc.; Sonnenberg Asphalt Co., Inc.

GREENSFELDER, HEMKER & GALE, P.C.

12 WOLF CREEK DRIVE
SUITE 100 (SWANSEA)
BELLEVILLE, ILLINOIS 62226
Telephone: 618-257-7308
Telefax: 618-257-7353
Email: ghg@greensfelder.com
URL: http://www.greensfelder.com

St. Louis, Missouri Office: 2000 Equitable Building, 10 South Broadway. Telephone: 314-241-9090. Telefax: 314-241-8624.

(This Listing Continued)

Antitrust, Appellate Practice, Creditors' Rights and Bankruptcy, Communications and Television, Computer and High Technology, Construction, Corporate and Finance, Employee Benefits and Employment, Environmental, Food Processing and Distribution, General Trial Practice in all State and Federal Courts, Health Care, Immigration, Intellectual Property, International Business, Labor, Litigation, Manufacturing and Distribution, Probate and Estate Planning, Real Estate, Securities, Tax Exempt Financing, Taxation, Trade Secret.

EDWARD S. BOTT, JR., born East St. Louis, Illinois, October 26, 1955; admitted to bar, 1980, Illinois; 1981, Missouri, U.S. Supreme Court and U.S. Court of Appeals, Seventh Circuit. *Education:* Duke University (A.B., 1977); Western New England College (J.D., 1980). (Also at St. Louis, Missouri Office). ***PRACTICE AREAS:*** Products Liability; Medical Malpractice; Labor and Employment.

THOMAS F. HENNESSY, III, born East St. Louis, Illinois, July 2, 1950; admitted to bar, 1975, Missouri; 1976, Illinois and U.S. Court of Military Appeals. *Education:* St. Louis University (B.S., magna cum laude, 1972; J.D., cum laude, 1975). [Colonel, United States Air Force Reserve, Active Duty, USAF, 1975-1979]. (Resident). ***PRACTICE AREAS:*** Litigation; Labor and Employment; Tort Defense.

CHERIE K. MACDONALD, born Jacksonville, Illinois, September 23, 1961; admitted to bar, 1990, Missouri; 1991, Illinois, U.S. District Court, Eastern District of Missouri and U.S. District Court, Southern District of Illinois; 1995, U.S. Court of Appeals, Seventh Circuit; 2002, U.S. Court of Appeals, Eight Circuit; 2003, U.S. District Court, Central District of Illinois. *Education:* Illinois College (B.A., magna cum laude, 1983); Western Illinois University (M.B.A., 1985); St. Louis University (J.D., magna cum laude, 1990). (Resident). ***PRACTICE AREAS:*** Commercial Litigation; Bankruptcy; Creditors' Rights; Secured Transactions.

JOSEPH B. McDONNELL, born Salina, Kansas, November 20, 1935; admitted to bar, 1960, Illinois and Missouri. *Education:* St. Louis University (B.S., 1958; LL.B., 1960). (Resident). ***PRACTICE AREAS:*** Legal Malpractice; Commercial Litigation; Probate.

GARRETT C. REUTER, born Springfield, Illinois, December 29, 1947; admitted to bar, 1973, Missouri, Illinois; 1980, California and U.S. Tax Court. *Education:* Southern Illinois University (B.S. in Accounting, 1969); St. Louis University (J.D., cum laude, 1973). (Resident). ***PRACTICE AREAS:*** Employee Benefits; Commercial Transactions; Estate Planning.

WILLIAM A. SCHMITT, admitted to bar, 1976, Illinois. *Education:* Western Illinois University (B.A., magna cum laude, 1973); St. Louis University (J.D., cum laude, 1976). (Resident). ***PRACTICE AREAS:*** Labor and Employment Law; Tort Defense; Commercial Litigation; Appellate Practice.

DONALD K. SCHOEMAKER, born Santa Ana, California, July 14, 1963; admitted to bar, 1988, Illinois; 1989, Missouri and U.S. District Court, Northern, Central and Southern Districts of Illinois. *Education:* University of Illinois (A.B., 1985); Southern Illinois University (J.D., cum laude, 1988). (Resident). ***PRACTICE AREAS:*** Civil Litigation; Trial Practice; Products Liability; Workers' Compensation.

RUSSELL K. SCOTT, born Nashville, Tennessee, August 24, 1949; admitted to bar, 1974, Illinois; 1975, Missouri, U.S. Court of Appeals, Seventh and Eighth Circuits and U.S. Supreme Court. *Education:* Earlham College (B.A., 1971); Washington University (J.D., 1974). (Resident). ***PRACTICE AREAS:*** Civil Litigation; Insurance Defense; Legal Malpractice Defense; Medical Malpractice Defense; Negligence Defense; Products Liability Defense; Insurance Coverage; Mediation; Arbitration.

GEORGE A. UHL, born Belleville, Illinois, August 29, 1954; admitted to bar, 1987, Missouri and Illinois. *Education:* University of Illinois (B.S., with honors, 1976; M.Arch., 1978); University of Edinburgh, Edinburgh, Scotland; Washington University (J.D., 1986). (Also at St. Louis, Missouri Office). ***PRACTICE AREAS:*** Litigation; Commercial Law; Construction Law.

L. KEVIN VICK, born East Saint Louis, Illinois, January 11, 1963; admitted to bar, 1988, Missouri and Illinois. *Education:* Washington University (A.B., cum laude, 1984; J.D., 1987). (Also at St. Louis, Missouri Office). ***PRACTICE AREAS:*** Real Estate; Business Law; Business Transactions; Corporate Law.

DONALD E. WEIHL, born East St. Louis, Illinois, November 9, 1937; admitted to bar, 1961, Illinois. *Education:* University of Illinois (A.B., 1959; J.D., 1961). (Resident). ***PRACTICE AREAS:*** Commercial Litigation; General Corporate; Probate.

DAYNA L. JOHNSON, born Cherokee, Iowa, September 6, 1950; admitted to bar, 1995, Missouri; 1996, Illinois. *Education:* McKendree College (B.S., summa cum laude, 1990); St. Louis University (J.D., cum laude, 1995). (Resident). ***PRACTICE AREAS:*** Litigation.

LINDA M. KNIEPKAMP, born Belleville, Illinois, July 18, 1959; admitted to bar, 1989, Missouri and Illinois. *Education:* Southern Illinois University (B.S., with high honors, 1981); St. Louis University (J.D., 1988). (Resident). ***PRACTICE AREAS:*** Real Estate; Business Law; Probate.

MICHELLE ROUSSEAU, born St. Anne, Illinois, November 11, 1974; admitted to bar, 2001, Illinois; 2002, Missouri. *Education:* University of Memphis (B.A., cum laude, 1997); Southern Illinois University (J.D., magna cum laude, 2001). (Resident). ***PRACTICE AREAS:*** Litigation; Real Estate.

EMILY C. SINGLEY, born Quito, Ecuador, March 18, 1975; admitted to bar, 2000, Illinois. *Education:* Baylor University (B.M., summa cum laude, 1996); University of Illinois, Urbana-Champaign (J.D., 2000). (Resident). ***PRACTICE AREAS:*** Litigation.

DAVID W. YBARRA, born Belleville, Illinois, September 6, 1971; admitted to bar, 2000, Illinois; 2002, Missouri. *Education:* University of North Texas (B.A., 1997); University of Illinois (J.D., magna cum laude, 2000). (Resident). ***PRACTICE AREAS:*** Litigation.

(This Listing Continued)

OF COUNSEL

JOSEPH R. LOWERY, born Belleville, Illinois, May 28, 1924; admitted to bar, 1950, Illinois. *Education:* James Millikin University; University of Illinois (B.S., 1948; J.D., 1950). (Resident). ***PRACTICE AREAS:*** Business Law; Mergers, Acquisitions and Divestitures; Banks and Banking.

KARL D. DEXHEIMER, born St. Louis, Missouri, May 16, 1942; admitted to bar, 1967, Illinois; 1985, Missouri. *Education:* Millikin University (B.A., 1964); Washington University (J.D., 1967). (Resident). ***PRACTICE AREAS:*** Tort Defense; Medical Malpractice; Products Liability.

REPRESENTATIVE CLIENTS: Alberici Group, Inc.; Archdiocese of St. Louis; Ascension Health; Associated Bank; Bemis Co.; BP Products North America Inc.; Brand Services, Inc.; BSI Constructors Inc.; Centene Corporation; Centrue Bank; CRB Builders, Inc.; Community Newspapers Holding, Inc.; Delta Dental; Desco Group; Direct TV; Disabled American Veterans; Drury Industries, Inc.; Edward D. Jones & Co., L.P.; Enterprise Financial Services, Inc.; Express Services Inc.; The Farnsworth Group; Fidelity Communications Co.; Fontbonne University; Forklifts of St. Louis, Inc.; Fru-Con Corp.; Harrah's Entertainment, Inc.; HBD Contracting, Inc.; HBE Corporation; Jacobs Engineering Group, Inc.; J. Henges Enterprises, Inc.; KCI Construction Company; Kelsey Hayes Company; Koplar Communications, Inc.; The Korte Company; Lafarge Corporation; Lange-Stegmann Company; L. E. Sauer Machine Co.; McBride and Son Cos.; McCarthy; Memorial Hospital; MetroMedia Fiber Network Services, Inc.; Missouri Hospital Association; Murphy Co.; Net Lease Holdings, L.L.C.; O'Reilly Automotive, Inc.; Pace Properties Incorporated; Prudential Securities; Raycom Media; R.G. Brinkmann Company; Regions Financial Corporation; Regions Morgan Keegan Trust; Rock Hill Mechanical Corp.; Sachs Electric Co.; Schnuck Markets, Inc.; Sequa Corporation; Shell Oil Co.; Sherwood Services; Shriners Hospital for Children; Site Oil Co.; Southern Commercial Bank; Sprint Spectrum; SSM Cardinal Glennon Children's Hospital; SSM Health Care; State Farm Fire & Casualty; Stifel Nicolaus & Company, Incorporated; St. Paul Travelers; Superfast Ferries S.A.; Telecorp Holding; Tenet HealthSystem; The Travelers Casualty & Surety Company; Tubular Steel, Inc.; Tyco Healthcare Group, LP; UMB Bank of St. Louis NA.; Vatterott Educational Centers, Inc.; Verizon Wireless; Watlow Electric Manufacturing Co.; Westar Aerospace & Defense Group, Inc.; West Pointe Bank and Trust Company.

GUNDLACH, LEE, EGGMANN, BOYLE & ROESSLER LLC

Established in 1882

5000 WEST MAIN STREET
P.O. BOX 23560
BELLEVILLE, ILLINOIS 62223-0560
Telephone: 618-277-9000; East St. Louis: 271-8000
Telecopier: 618-277-4594
Email: info@gundlachlee.com
URL: http://www.gundlachlee.com

St. Louis, Missouri Office: 1010 Market Street, Suite 1640. Telephone: 314-231-2084. Telecopier: 314-231-1960.

General Civil and Trial Litigation Practice, State and Federal Courts, Corporate and Insurance Litigation: Products Liability, Medical Malpractice, Professional Liability, Railroad, Automobile, Aviation, Admiralty, Life, Surety Bond, Cargo, Casualty, Commercial, Toxic Tort, Civil Rights, Fire and Construction.

MEMBERS

NORMAN J. GUNDLACH (1907-1996)

CARL W. LEE, born Streator, Illinois, November 14, 1927; admitted to bar, 1951, Illinois. *Education:* University of Illinois (B.S., 1950; J.D., 1952). Editor, 1966-1967 and Chairman, 1970-1971, Insurance Law Newsletter, Insurance Law Section, Illinois State Bar Association. Member, Rules Committee, Illinois Supreme Court, 1972-1994. *Member:* St. Clair County, Illinois State (Chairman, Insurance Law Section, 1970-1971) Bar Associations; National Association of Railroad Trial Counsel. Fellow: American College of Trial Lawyers; American Bar Foundation. Diplomat, American Board of Trial Advocates. ***PRACTICE AREAS:*** Civil Practice; Medical Malpractice; Legal Malpractice; Products Liability; Commercial Litigation; Toxic Torts; Aviation Litigation. ***Email:*** c.lee@gundlachlee.com

ROBERT E. EGGMANN (1928-1986)

RICHARD E. BOYLE, born Westville, Illinois, March 27, 1937; admitted to bar, 1961, Illinois; 1985, Missouri. *Education:* University of Illinois (A.B., 1959; J.D., 1961). Phi Alpha Delta. Appointee to Advisory Group under the Civil Justice Reform Act of 1990. *Member:* Bar Association of Metropolitan St. Louis; East St. Louis, St. Clair County (President, 1979-1980), Illinois State (Assembly Delegate, 1972-1974) Bar Associations; The Missouri Bar; Missouri Organization of Defense Lawyers; National Association of Railroad Trial Counsel (President, 1991-1992; Executive Committee, 1982—; Central Region Vice-President, 1985-1987); Illinois Association of Defense Trial Counsel; Defense Research Institute. Fellow: American College of Trial Lawyers (Member, National Trial Competition Committee, 1998-2003); American Bar Foundation; American Board of Trial Advocates. ***PRACTICE AREAS:*** Aviation Law; Civil Practice; Class Actions; Commercial Litigation; Legal Malpractice; Premises Liability; Products Liability; Transportation. ***Email:*** r.boyle@gundlachlee.com

RICHARD M. ROESSLER, born St. Louis, Missouri, May 26, 1939; admitted to bar, 1968, Missouri and Illinois. *Education:* Washington University (B.S., 1962); St. Louis University (J.D., 1968). Phi Alpha Delta. *Member:* The Bar Association of Metropolitan St. Louis; St. Clair County, Illinois State and American Bar Associations; The Missouri Bar; National Association of Railroad Trial Counsel; Defense Research Institute; Federation of Insurance and Corporate Counsel; Missouri Organization of Defense Lawyers; Illinois Association of Defense Trial Counsel. Fellow, American College of Trial Lawyers. ***PRACTICE AREAS:*** Civil Practice; Medical Malpractice; Professional Liability; Insurance Defense; Products Liability. ***Email:*** r.roessler@gundlachlee.com

KENNETH L. HALVACHS, born Decatur, Illinois, March 14, 1959; admitted to bar, 1984, Illinois; 1985, Missouri. *Education:* Illinois State University (B.S., highest honors, 1981); University of Illinois (J.D., 1984). *Member:* Bar Association of Metropolitan St. Louis; St. Clair County, Illinois State and American Bar Associations; The Missouri Bar;

(This Listing Continued)

GUNDLACH, LEE, EGGMANN, BOYLE & ROESSLER LLC, Belleville—Continued

Missouri Organization of Defense Lawyers; Illinois Association of Defense Trial Counsel; National Association of Railroad Trial Counsel. ***PRACTICE AREAS:*** Civil Practice; Products Liability; Insurance Defense; Professional Liability. ***Email:*** k.halvachs@gundlachlee.com

THOMAS R. PETERS, born Two Rivers, Wisconsin, July 11, 1960; admitted to bar, 1987, Illinois and Missouri. *Education:* University of Wisconsin-Oshkosh (B.B.A., magna cum laude, 1982); University of Illinois (J.D., cum laude, 1986). *Member:* Bar Association of Metropolitan St. Louis; St. Clair County, Illinois State and American Bar Associations; The Missouri Bar; Missouri Organization of Defense Lawyers; Illinois Association of Defense Trial Counsel; National Association of Railroad Trial Counsel. ***PRACTICE AREAS:*** Civil Practice; Personal Injury; Products Liability; Toxic Torts; Transportation. ***Email:*** t.peters@gundlachlee.com

CHARLES J. SWARTWOUT, born New Orleans, Louisiana, March 3, 1960; admitted to bar, 1985, Illinois; 1989, Missouri. *Education:* Purdue University at Lafayette (B.S., 1982); Southern Illinois University (J.D., 1985). *Member:* St. Clair County (Member, Board of Directors, 1998-2000), Illinois State and American Bar Associations; The Missouri Bar; Missouri Organization of Defense Lawyers; Illinois Association of Defense Trial Counsel; National Association of Railroad Trial Counsel; Defense Research Institute; Illinois Association of Health Care Attorneys. ***PRACTICE AREAS:*** Civil Practice; Medical Malpractice; Railroad Law; Transportation; Nursing Home Litigation; Insurance Defense. ***Email:*** c.swartwout@gundlachlee.com

ROBERT D. ANDREKANIC, born McKeesport, Pennsylvania, December 28, 1954; admitted to bar, 1979, Missouri; 1984, Illinois. *Education:* LaSalle University (B.A., cum laude, 1976); St. Louis University (J.D., 1979; M.A., 1980). *Member:* The Bar Association of Metropolitan St. Louis; The Missouri Bar; Illinois State Bar Association; Missouri Organization of Defense Lawyers. ***PRACTICE AREAS:*** Civil Practice; Environmental Law; Insurance Defense; Insurance; Personal Injury; Products Liability; Toxic Torts; Transportation. ***Email:*** r.andrekanic@gundlachlee.com

CURTIS R. PICOU, born Kaskaskia, Illinois, March 7, 1963; admitted to bar, 1991, Illinois; 1992, Missouri. *Education:* Southern Illinois University (B.A., 1986; J.D., 1991). Phi Alpha Delta; Sigma Tau Delta. Member, National Order of the Barristers. Case Note/Comment Editor, Southern Illinois University Law Journal, 1990-1991. *Member:* Illinois State and American Bar Associations; The Missouri Bar; The Bar Association of Metropolitan St. Louis. ***PRACTICE AREAS:*** Personal Injury; Products Liability; Insurance; Civil Litigation. ***Email:*** c.picou@gundlachlee.com

MARK R. KURZ, born Teaneck, New Jersey, November 3, 1967; admitted to bar, 1992, Illinois and U.S. District Court, Southern District of Illinois; 1993, Missouri. *Education:* Marquette University (B.A., 1989); University of Illinois (J.D., 1992). Phi Alpha Theta; Phi Alpha Delta; Delta Theta Phi (Vice President, 1990-1991). Treasurer/Student Bar Association, University of Illinois. *Member:* Bar Association of Metropolitan, St. Louis; St. Clair, Illinois State and American Bar Associations; The Missouri Bar. ***PRACTICE AREAS:*** Civil Practice; Insurance Defense; Personal Injury; Products Liability; Toxic Torts; Transportation. ***Email:*** m.kurz@gundlachlee.com

ASSOCIATES

BRAD G. PELC, born Belleville, Illinois, September 6, 1969; admitted to bar, 1994, California and U.S. District Court, Southern District of California; 1995, Illinois; 1996, Missouri and U.S. District Court, Southern District of Illinois. *Education:* University of Illinois (B.A., 1991); California Western School of Law (J.D., 1994). *Member:* The Missouri Bar; St. Clair County and Illinois State Bar Associations. ***PRACTICE AREAS:*** Civil Practice; Insurance Defense; Insurance; Personal Injury; Toxic Torts; Appellate Practice; Medical Malpractice. ***Email:*** b.pelc@gundlachlee.com

JAMES R. GARRISON, born Mt. Vernon, Illinois, February 3, 1955; admitted to bar, 1982, Illinois; 1983, U.S. District Court, Southern District of Illinois 1984, Missouri; 1991, U.S. District Court, Eastern District of Missouri; 2003, U.S. Court of Appeals, Eighth Circuit. *Education:* University of Illinois (B.S., 1977; M.B.A., 1982; J.D., 1982). Phi Eta Sigma. Member, Board of Education, Wolf Branch SD113, Nov., 1997-Nov. 2001. *Member:* The Bar Association of Metropolitan St. Louis; St. Clair County, Illinois State and American Bar Associations; The Missouri Bar. ***PRACTICE AREAS:*** Civil Practice; Class Actions; Health Care; Insurance Defense; Personal Injury; Products Liability. ***Email:*** j.garrison@gundlachlee.com

ANDREW C. CORKERY, born Fairfax County, Virginia, October 14, 1973; admitted to bar, 2000, Missouri, U.S. District Court, Eastern District of Missouri and U.S. District Court, Southern District of Illinois; 2001, Illinois. *Education:* St. Louis University (B.A., summa cum laude, 1997; J.D., cum laude, 2000). Executive Articles Editor, St. Louis-Warsaw Transatlantic Law Journal. *Member:* Bar Association of Metropolitan St. Louis; St. Clair County and Illinois State Bar Associations; The Missouri Bar. ***PRACTICE AREAS:*** Civil Practice; Railroad Law; Personal Injury Defense. ***Email:*** a.corkery@gundlachlee.com

TODD R. McFARLAND, born Quincy, Illinois, May 29, 1973; admitted to bar, 2000, Illinois; 2001, Missouri. *Education:* Southern College (B.A., History, 1997); University of Illinois (J.D., 2000). *Member:* St. Clair County and Illinois State Bar Associations; The Missouri Bar. ***PRACTICE AREAS:*** Civil Practice; Insurance Defense; Insurance; Labor and Employment; Personal Injury; Products Liability; Toxic Torts; Trademarks; Copyrights; Unfair Competition. ***Email:*** t.mcfarland@gundlachlee.com

DAVID B. SCHNEIDEWIND, born Pinckneyville, Illinois, January 11, 1975; admitted to bar, 2000, Illinois; 2003, U.S. District Court, Southern District of Illinois. *Education:* Southern Illinois University (B.S., 1997; J.D., 2000). Recipient, CALI Award Land Use Planning. Member, The Southern Illinois American Inn of Court, 1999-2000. *Member:* St. Clair County and Illinois State Bar Associations. ***PRACTICE AREAS:*** Land Use; Medical Malpractice; Personal Injury Defense. ***Email:*** d.schneidewind@gundlachlee.com

DAVID R. BUTZ, II, born Fairfax, Virginia, August, 30, 1977; admitted to bar, 2003, Illinois and U.S. District Court, Southern District of Illinois; 2004, Missouri. *Education:* University of Notre Dame (B.A., Business Management, cum laude, 1999); University of Illinois (J.D., cum laude, 2003). Contract Advisor, Certified National Football League Player's Association, 2001—. *Member:* Illinois State (President, University of Illinois Law School Chapter, 2002-2003) and American Bar Associations; The Missouri Bar. ***PRACTICE AREAS:*** Civil Practice; Personal Injury; Contracts. ***Email:*** d.butz@gundlachlee.com

DAVID H. FRIESS, born Centerville, Illinois, July 16, 1968; admitted to bar, 1999, Illinois and U.S. District Court, Northern and Southern Districts of Illinois; 2002, Missouri. *Education:* Mercer University (B.S., 1996); John Marshall Law School (J.D., 1999). *Member:* Chicago and Illinois State Bar Associations; The Missouri Bar. ***PRACTICE AREAS:*** Civil Rights Defense; Asbestos Defense. ***Email:*** d.friess@gundlachlee.com

SEAN K. BROUSSEAU, born Manchester, New Hampshire, August 7, 1971; admitted to bar, 2004, Missouri; 2005, Illinois. *Education:* Williams College (B.A., 1994); St. Louis University (J.D., 2004). Phi Alpha Delta. Member, St. Louis University Health Law Moot Court Team, 2002. Lead Articles Editor, AHLA Journal of Health Law, 2003. *Member:* The Missouri Bar. ***PRACTICE AREAS:*** Bankruptcy; Health Care; Contracts; Civil defense. ***Email:*** s.brousseau@gundlachlee.com

REPRESENTATIVE CLIENTS: Canadian National/Illinois Central Railroad Company; Minnesota Mining and Manufacturing Company; Division Counsel for Norfolk Southern Railway Company; BNSF Railway Company; National Railroad Passenger Corporation; Terminal Railroad Association of St. Louis; Mack Trucks, Inc.; Raytheon Aircraft Company; Vought Aircraft Company; Liberty Mutual Insurance Company; Volvo Trucks North America, Inc.; Illinois State Medical Insurance Service; AIG; Attorneys' Liability Assurance Society, Inc. (ALAS); Grinnell Mutual Reinsurance Co.; Progressive Insurance Companies; Onyx North American Corp.; A.O. Smith Corporation; Medmarc; Smokeless Tobacco Council Inc.; International Business Machines; NVE Pharmaceuticals; Foster Wheeler LLC; Illinois & Midland Railroad, Inc.; Paducah & Louisville Railway, Inc.; CSX Transportation, Inc.; R.J. Reynolds Tobacco Company; Ford Motor Company; Crum and Forster Insurance Company; Pro Assurance; Guardian and Prudential Life Insurance Companies; Lloyds of London; Zurich American Insurance Company; Crawford & Company; CNA; YMCA; Illinois Insurance Guaranty Fund; St. Paul Travelers; United Fire & Casualty Company; Preferred Physicians Medical; Brokers Risk Placement Service, Inc.

HERZOG CREBS LLP

5111 WEST MAIN STREET
BELLEVILLE, ILLINOIS 62226
Telephone: 618-235-7656

St. Louis, Missouri Office: 515 North Sixth Street, 24th Floor, 63101. Telephone: 314-231-6700. Fax: 314-231-4656. Email: Webmaster@HerzogCrebs.com. Website: http://www.HerzogCrebs.com.

General Civil Practice, including Trial and Appellate Practice in Federal and State Courts. Products Liability, General Corporate and Corporate Litigation, Insurance and Insurance Defense, Asbestos and Toxic Tort Litigation, Estate Planning, Probate and Trust, Real Estate, Construction Law, Taxation, Employment Law, Zoning.

MARY ANN HATCH, born East St. Louis, Illinois, December 11, 1950; admitted to bar, 1978, Illinois; 1992, Missouri. *Education:* St. Louis University (B.S., summa cum laude, 1972; J.D., 1978). Member, Board of Directors, Lawyers Trust Fund of Illinois, 2001—. *Member:* The Bar Association of Metropolitan St. Louis; St. Clair County (President, 1995-1996; Member, Public Relations Committee, 1982-1997), Illinois State (Assembly Delegate, 1994-1996; Member, Tort Law Section Council, 1991-1995) and American Bar Associations; The Missouri Bar; The Illinois Association of Defense Trial Counsel. Fellow, Illinois Bar Foundation (Chair of the Fellows, 1999-2000); The American Board of Trial Advocates. ***Email:*** mah@HerzogCrebs.com

(For Complete Biographical Data on all Personnel, see Professional Biographies at St. Louis, Missouri)

HINSHAW & CULBERTSON LLP

Hinshaw & Culbertson LLP is an Illinois registered limited liability partnership that has elected to be governed by the Illinois Uniform Partnership Act (1997)

Established in 1934

521 WEST MAIN STREET
SUITE 300
P.O. BOX 509
BELLEVILLE, ILLINOIS 62222-0509
Telephone: 618-277-2400
Facsimile: 618-277-1144
Telex: 880248
Email: kfox@hinshawlaw.com
URL: http://www.hinshawlaw.com

Other Office Locations: Chicago, Illinois; Appleton, Wisconsin; Boston, Massachusetts; Champaign, Illinois; Crystal Lake, Illinois; Edwardsville, Illinois; Fort Lauderdale, Florida; Jacksonville, Florida; Joliet, Illinois; Lisle, Illinois; Los Angeles, California; Miami, Florida; Milwaukee, Wisconsin; Minneapolis, Minnesota; New York, New York; Peoria, Illinois; Phoenix, Arizona; Portland, Oregon; Providence, Rhode Island; Rockford, Illinois; St. Louis, Missouri; San Francisco, California; Schererville, Indiana; Springfield, Illinois; Tampa, Florida; Waukegan, Illinois.

Appellate, Banking & Financing, Bankruptcy & Creditors' Rights, Class Action Litigation, Civil Rights Defense, Commercial Litigation, Corporate, Construction Law, Director & Officer Liability, Employee Benefits, Environmental, Fidelity & Surety, General Liability Litigation, Government, Health Care, Insurance Coverage, Insurance and Reinsurance, Labor & Employment, Legal Malpractice, Medical Malpractice, Mergers & Acquisitions, Municipal Liability, Personal Injury Defense, Public Law, Products Liability Litigation, Professional Liability, Regulatory, Real Estate, School Law, Securities, Taxation, Transportation, White Collar Crime and Workers' Compensation Defense.

(This Listing Continued)

FIRM PROFILE: Hinshaw & Culbertson LLP is a national AMLaw 200 firm with 425 lawyers in 27 offices coast-to-coast. The firm offers a full-service practice, with an emphasis in commercial and defense litigation, corporate, environmental, employment and construction law, as well as the representation of professionals in their liability and risk management matters.

Hinshaw provides services to a range of clients in financial services, construction, health care, not-for-profit, insurance, legal, manufacturing, real estate, transportation and other industries. Firm clients also include government agencies, municipalities and schools.

Hinshaw was founded in 1934. The firm is headquartered in Chicago, and maintains offices in 12 states: Arizona, California, Florida, Illinois, Indiana, Massachusetts, Minnesota, Missouri, New York, Oregon, Rhode Island and Wisconsin.

PARTNERS

MARK D. BAUMAN, born St. Louis, Missouri, February 23, 1959; admitted to bar, 1984, Illinois and U.S. District Court, Southern District of Illinois; 1985, Missouri, U.S. District Court, Central District of Illinois and U.S. Court of Appeals, Seventh Circuit. *Education:* St. Louis University (B.A., 1981); Southern Illinois University (J.D., 1984). *Member:* St. Clair County (Member, Membership Committee, 1985-1986) and Illinois State Bar Associations; The Missouri Bar; Defense Research Institute; Association of Defense Trial Attorneys (Member, Executive Council, 1995-1998). (Also at Edwardsville, Illinois Office). ***PRACTICE AREAS:*** Product Liability Litigation; Personal Injury Defense Litigation; Legal Negligence Defense; Medical Negligence Defense; Construction Injury Litigation; Commercial Litigation; Class Action Defense; Insurance; Professional Liability Defense. ***Email:*** mbauman@hinshawlaw.com

JAMES F. CLAYBORNE, JR., born St. Louis, Missouri, December 29, 1963; admitted to bar, 1988, Illinois; 1991, U.S. District Court, Southern District of Illinois; 1994, Missouri and U.S. District Court, Eastern District of Missouri. *Education:* Tennessee State University (B.S., Political Science, 1985); University of Miami (J.D., 1988). State Senator, 1995—. Member, St. Louis Sports Commission. Delegate, American Bar Association House of Delegates. NFL Agent. *Member:* Metro-East and Illinois State (Member, Board of Governors, 1995—) Bar Associations. (Also at Edwardsville, Illinois Office). ***PRACTICE AREAS:*** Products Liability Litigation; Class Action Litigation; Commercial Litigation; Personal Injury Litigation; Municipal Law. ***Email:*** jclayborne@hinshawlaw.com

JOHN L. GILBERT, born Alton, Illinois, November 18, 1950; admitted to bar, 1975, Illinois and U.S. District Court, Southern District of Illinois; 1979, U.S. Supreme Court; 1983, U.S. Court of Appeals, Seventh Circuit; 1987, U.S. District Court, Central District of Illinois; 1990, Missouri. *Education:* University of Illinois (B.A., Phi Beta Kappa, high honors with distinction, 1972); Washington University (J.D., 1975). Phi Eta Sigma; Phi Beta Kappa; Phi Delta Phi. Illinois Civil Service Commissioner, 1978-1991. Adjunct Assistant Professor of Management, Southern Illinois University Edwardsville. Former Chairman, Mercantile Bank, Edwardsville. Assistant State's Attorney, Madison County, Illinois. Member, National Association of College and University Attorneys. Member, Hearing Panel, Illinois Attorney Registration and Disciplinary Commission, Former Member, SIUE School of Business Advisory Committee, Board Member, St. Louis Metropolitan Major Case Squad. Former President and Secretary, Edwardsville, Illinois Rotary Club. *Member:* Madison County and Illinois State Bar Associations. (Also at Edwardsville, Illinois Office). ***PRACTICE AREAS:*** Labor Law; Civil Rights Defense; Class Actions; College and University Law. ***Email:*** jgilbert@hinshawlaw.com

JEFFREY R. GLASS, born Xenia, Ohio, July 7, 1953; admitted to bar, 1978, Illinois; 1980, U.S. District Court, Southern District of Illinois; 1987, Missouri; U.S. District Court, Eastern District of Missouri; U.S. District Court, Central District of Illinois. *Education:* St. Louis University (B.A., magna cum laude, 1974; J.D., 1978). Phi Delta Phi. Assistant State's Attorney, St. Clair County, Illinois, 1978-1982. *Member:* Madison County, St. Clair County and Illinois State Bar Associations; Defense Research Institute; Association of Defense Trial Attorneys; Missouri Organization of Defense Lawyers. (Partner-in-Charge of Hinshaw Offices in Belleville, Illinois and Edwardsville, Illinois. Chairman on Hinshaw's Diversity Committee). ***LANGUAGES:*** French. ***PRACTICE AREAS:*** Professional Liability Litigation; Medical Malpractice; Class Actions; Products Liability Litigation; Personal Injury Litigation. ***Email:*** jglass@hinshawlaw.com

DENNIS J. GRABER, born Manhattan, Kansas, September 23, 1959; admitted to bar, 1984, Illinois; 1986, U.S. District Court, Southern District of Illinois and U.S. Court of Appeals, Seventh Circuit; 1992, Missouri; 1994, U.S. District Court, Central District of Illinois. *Education:* Illinois College (B.A., 1981); Southern Illinois University School of Law (J.D., 1984). Phi Alpha Theta; Phi Alpha Delta. *Member:* Bar Association of Metropolitan St. Louis; St. Clair County and Illinois State Bar Associations; Workers' Compensation Claims Association. (Also at Edwardsville, Illinois Office). ***PRACTICE AREAS:*** Commercial Litigation; Complex and Multi-District Litigation; Insurance Defense; Labor and Employment. ***Email:*** dgraber@hinshawlaw.com

JEFFREY A. KOPIS, born Belleville, Illinois, May 12, 1964; admitted to bar, 1992, Illinois and U.S. District Court, Southern District of Illinois; 1993, Missouri; 1994, U.S. District Court, Eastern District of Missouri; 1997, U.S. Court of Appeals, Seventh Circuit; 1999, U.S. District Court, Central District of Illinois. *Education:* University of Illinois, Champaign-Urbana (B.A., 1986); St. Louis University (J.D., 1992). *Member:* St. Clair County, Madison County and Illinois State Bar Associations; Bar Association of Metropolitan St. Louis; The Missouri Bar. ***PRACTICE AREAS:*** Defense Litigation; Personal Injury Defense; Civil Rights Defense; Municipal Liability; Medical Malpractice Defense. ***Email:*** jkopis@hinshawlaw.com

CHARLES A. PIERCE, born Dunlap, Illinois, March 21, 1966; admitted to bar, 1991, Illinois; 1992, Missouri; 1993, U.S. District Court, Southern District of Illinois; 2001, U.S. District Court, Central District of Illinois; 2002, U.S. Court of Appeals, Seventh Circuit. *Education:* University of Iowa (B.S., 1988); Southern Illinois University School of Law (J.D., magna cum laude, 1991). Order of the Barristers. Law Clerk, Illinois Appellate Court, Third District, 1991-1992. Editor, 1991 and Member, 1990-1991, Survey of Illinois Law, Southern Illinois University Law Review. *Member:* St. Clair County and Illinois State Bar Associations; The Missouri Bar; Defense Research Institute; Illinois Association of Defense Trial Counsel. (Also at Edwardsville, Illinois Office). ***REPORTED CASES:*** Sneed v. Howell, 306 Ill.App.3d 1149, 716 N.E.2d 336, 240 Ill.Dec. 203, (5th Dist. 1999); Burris v. Shaw, 124 Fed.Appx. 431 (7th Cir. 2004); Johnny Vegas, Inc. v. City of Alton, Ill., 2005 WL 578966, (S.D.Ill. 2005). ***PRACTICE AREAS:*** Civil Rights Defense Litigation; Civil Rights Section 1983; Municipal Liability; Products Liability Litigation; Personal Injury Litigation; General Liability Litigation; Insurance Coverage Litigation; Professional Liability Litigation. ***Email:*** cpierce@hinshawlaw.com

JEFFREY T. REEL, born Waukegan, Illinois, September 2, 1963; admitted to bar, 1991, Illinois and U.S. District Court, Southern District of Illinois; 2000, Louisiana and U.S. District Court, Western District of Louisiana (inactive). *Education:* Southern Illinois University (B.S., 1986); Thomas M.Cooley Law School (J.D, 1990). *Member:* St. Clair County, Illinois State and American Bar Associations. ***PRACTICE AREAS:*** Products Liability Litigation; Personal Injury Litigation; Architectural, Engineering and Design Professionals Liability; General Liability Litigation. ***Email:*** jreel@hinshawlaw.com

JOHN E. SABO, born St. Louis, Missouri, January 6, 1957; admitted to bar, 1987, Illinois and U.S. District Court, Southern District of Illinois; 1988, Missouri; 1990, U.S. Court of Appeals, Seventh Circuit. *Education:* McKendree College (B.B.A., 1983); Southern Illinois University (J.D., 1987). Appointed: Administrative Law Judge, Illinois Department of Public Health, 1999-2001; Special Assistant Attorney General by the Illinois Attorney General to represent the Office of the Governor in civil action, 2002; Special Assistant States Attorney for Madison County, Illinois to represent the County in a civil action, 2002. Court Appointed Arbitrator, Circuit Court, St. Clair County, Illinois, 1999—. Voted one of the leading lawyers in Illinois by Illinois attorneys, 2003. *Member:* St. Clair County and Illinois State Bar Associations; The Missouri Bar. (Also at Edwardsville, Illinois Office). ***PRACTICE AREAS:*** Banks and Banking; Class Actions; Commercial Law; Complex and Multi District Litigation; Contracts; Insurance; Litigation; Personal Injury; Products Liability. ***Email:*** jsabo@hinshawlaw.com

DAWN A. SALLERSON, born Terre Haute, Indiana, April 18, 1961; admitted to bar, 1986, Illinois; 1987, Missouri and U.S. District Court, Southern District of Illinois. *Education:* St. Mary-of-the-Woods College (B.A., 1983); St. Louis University School of Law (J.D., cum laude, 1986). Kappa Gamma Pi. U.S. District Court Rules Committee, U.S. District Court Magistrate Selection Panel, 1994. Speaker: "Your Deposition, Preparation and Examination: Defense of Company Procedures," 1995; "Limitations of Actions in Medical Malpractice Claims"; "Illinois Uninsured and Underinsured Motorist Provisions"; "Illinois Tort Reform, The Practical Effects," 1996; "Illinois Code of Civil Procedure, New Provisions, and the Impact Upon Claim Handling"; "Major Provisions and Immunities in the Illinois Tort Immunity Act," 1997; "Jury Instructions, Their Use and Effect, Under the Tort Reform Act"; "Significant Recent Decisions Impacting the Tort Immunity Act"; "Impact of Unconstitutionality of the Tort Reform Act"; "The Future of Tort Reform," 1998; "Municipal Immunities"; "Petrillo Violations," 2000; "Discovery and Investigation in Tort Actions," 2002; "Settlement/Release Protection"; "Pleadings: A Practitioner's View"; "Pleading Issues in Tort Defense," 2004; "Spoliation of Evidence," 2005; "Responsive Pleadings". *Member:* Illinois State Bar Association; American Bar Association; St. Clair County Bar Association. (Also at Edwardsville, Illinois Office). ***PRACTICE AREAS:*** Medical Negligence Defense; Class Actions Defense; Product Liability Litigation; Personal Injury Defense Litigation; Legal Negligence Defense; Municipal Law; Insurance Defense. ***Email:*** dsallerson@hinshawlaw.com

MICHAEL L. WAGNER, born Belleville, Illinois, April 11, 1972; admitted to bar, 1997, Missouri and U.S. District Court, Southern District of Illinois; 1998, Illinois. *Education:* University of Illinois (B.S., 1994); St. Louis University (J.D., 1997). Chief of the Misdemeanor, Domestic and DUI Department, St. Clair County, Illinois State's Attorney Office. Corporation Counsel, City of East St. Louis, Illinois. *Member:* East St. Louis (Member, Board of Directors), St. Clair County, Illinois State and American Bar Associations. ***PRACTICE AREAS:*** Municipal; Environmental; General Liability. ***Email:*** mwagner@hinshawlaw.com

ASSOCIATES

ROBERT D. BAS, born Orange County, California, December 27, 1976; admitted to bar, 2004, Illinois. *Education:* San Diego State University (B.A., Political Science, cum laude, 1998); DePaul University (J.D., 2002). Member, Asian American Association of Greater Chicago. *Member:* Chicago, St. Clair County, Illinois State and American Bar Associations. ***PRACTICE AREAS:*** Personal Injury Defense; Defense Litigation; Medical Malpractice Defense. ***Email:*** rbas@hinshawlaw.com

HEIDI L. ECKERT, born St. Louis, Missouri, April 2, 1971; admitted to bar, 1999, Illinois; 2003, U.S. District Court, Southern District of Illinois and U.S. Court of Appeals, Seventh Circuit. *Education:* University of Missouri (B.A., 1994); Southern Illinois University (J.D., 1999). *Member:* Illinois State Bar. ***PRACTICE AREAS:*** Criminal Law; Civil Law. ***Email:*** heckert@hinshawlaw.com

JULIE CONSTANCE ELLIOT, born Belleville, Illinois, August 25, 1970; admitted to bar, 2000, Illinois; 2001 Missouri and U.S. District Court, Southern District of Illinois. *Education:* DePauw University (B.A., 1992); St. Louis University (J.D., 2000). Recipient, David Grant Student Attorney Award. Moot Court Finalist. Speaker, Saving Time and Money and Improving Quality of Care: A Proactive Approach to Managing Worker's Compensation. *Member:* East St. Louis, St. Clair County, Illinois State and American Bar Associations. ***LANGUAGES:*** Spanish. ***PRACTICE AREAS:*** Professional Liability Litigation; Medical Malpractice; Workers' Compensation Defense. ***Email:*** jelliot@hinshawlaw.com

CHAD A. JENNINGS, born Belleville, Illinois, August 22, 1975; admitted to bar, 2002, Illinois; 2005, U.S. District Court, Southern District of Illinois. *Education:* Southern Illinois University (B.S., Political Science and Sociology, 1998); The John Marshall Law School (J.D., 2002). Participant, Hertzog Moot Court Competition. Representative, Student Bar Association. *Member:* St. Clair County and Illinois State Bar Associations; Hispanic National Bar Association. ***PRACTICE AREAS:*** General Liability Litigation; Municipal Liability; Medical Malpractice; Personal Injury; Workers Compensation Defense. ***Email:*** cjennings@hinshawlaw.com

A. RANDALL KNOPF, born Fort Smith, Arkansas, March 23, 1966; admitted to bar, 1992, Missouri; 2001, Illinois; U.S. District Court, Eastern District of Missouri and Southern District of Illinois. *Education:* Tulane University (B.A., Sociology, 1988); Whittier Col-

(This Listing Continued)

HINSHAW & CULBERTSON LLP, Belleville—Continued

lege School of Law (J.D., 1992). *Member:* Illinois State Bar Association. ***PRACTICE AREAS:*** Medical Malpractice Defense; General Liability Litigation. ***Email:*** arknopf@hinshawlaw.com

MADELYN J. LAMB, born 1956; admitted to bar, 1981, Illinois; 1982, Missouri and U.S. District Court, Southern District of Illinois; 1987, U.S. Supreme Court; 1994, U.S. Court of Appeals, Seventh Circuit. *Education:* University of Illinois, Champaign-Urbana (B.A., 1978); St. Louis University (J.D., cum laude, 1981). *Member:* St. Clair County and Illinois State Bar Associations; The Missouri Bar. ***REPORTED CASES:*** Lowe v. Norfolk and Western Ry. Co., 124 Ill.App.3d 80,463 N.E.2d 792(5th Dist. 1984); Galliher v. Holloway, 130 Ill.App.3d 628, 474 N.E.2d 797(5th Dist. 1985); Yates v. Muir, 112 Ill.2d 205, 492 N.E.2d 1267(1986); Dungey v. U.S. Steel, 148 Ill.App.3d 484, 499 N.E.2d 545(5th Dist. 1986); Stewart v. BF Goodrich Co., 153 Ill.App.3d 1078, 506 N.E.2d 783(5th Dist. 1987); Perkinson v. Manion, 163 Ill.App. 3d 262, 516 N.E.2d 977(5th Dist. 1987); Wilson v. CIPS, 165 Ill.App.3d 533, 519 N.E.2d 44(5th Dist. 1988); Wheeler v. Roselawn Memory Gardens, 188 Ill.App.3d 193, 543 N.E.2d 1328(5th Dist.1989); West v. Granny's Rocker Niteclub, Inc., 268 Ill.App.3d 207, 643 N.E. 2d 850(5th Dist. 1994); Homola v. McNamara, 59 F.3d 647(7th Cir. 1995). ***PRACTICE AREAS:*** Professional Liability Litigation; Medical Malpractice; Insurance Coverage; General Liability Litigation. ***Email:*** mlamb@hinshawlaw.com

---

JOHNSON & JOHNSON

11 SOUTH HIGH
BELLEVILLE, ILLINOIS 62220
Telephone: 618-277-3600
Fax: 618-277-1184
Email: pkjiv@aol.com
Email: pkjlv@aol.com
URL: http://www.lawyers.com/johnson&johnson

General Civil Practice. Family Law and Divorce, Probate, Wills, Trust Law, Estate Planning, Real Estate, Personal Injury, Corporate Law, Banking Law.

P. K. JOHNSON, SR., III (1915-1997)

P. K. JOHNSON, IV, born 1945; admitted to bar, 1971, Illinois. *Education:* University of Illinois (B.A., with honors, 1967); Illinois Institute of Technology, Chicago-Kent College of Law (J.D., with honors, 1971). *Member:* St. Clair County and Illinois State Bar Associations. ***PRACTICE AREAS:*** Family Law; Divorce; Probate; Wills; Trust Law; Estate Planning; Real Estate; Personal Injury; Banking Law; Corporate Law. ***Email:*** pkjiv@aol.com

P. K. JOHNSON, V, born Chicago, Illinois, June 5, 1970; admitted to bar, 1995, Illinois; 1996, Missouri. *Education:* University of Illinois (B.S., with honors, 1992); Chicago-Kent College of Law, Illinois Institute of Technology (J.D., with honors, 1995). *Member:* St. Clair County and Illinois State Bar Associations; The Missouri Bar. ***PRACTICE AREAS:*** Family Law; Divorce; Probate; Wills; Trust Law; Estate Planning; Real Estate; Personal Injury; Banking Law; Corporate Law. ***Email:*** pkjv@aol.com

---

KNAPP, OHL & GREEN

BELLEVILLE, ILLINOIS

(See Edwardsville)

Negligence, Products Liability, Insurance Coverage, Personal Injury, Workers Compensation, School Law, Municipal Law, Admiralty, Consumer Law, Medical Malpractice, Toxic Torts.

KOREIN TILLERY

Established in 1972

10 EXECUTIVE WOODS COURT
BELLEVILLE, ILLINOIS 62226
Telephone: 618-277-1180
Telecopier: 618-222-6939
URL: http://www.koreintillery.com

St. Louis, Missouri Office: 701 Market Street, Suite 300, 63101-1820. Telephone: 314-241-4844. Telecopier: 314-241-3525.

Class Action, Securities Law, Environmental Law, Commercial Litigation, Pension and Profit Sharing, Railroad, Maritime, Medical Malpractice, Product Liability, Toxic Tort, General Negligence, Trial Practice.

FIRM PROFILE: The Firm serves both Missouri and Illinois in a specialized Tort Practice maintaining two staffed offices in St. Louis, Missouri and Belleville, Illinois. Its partners are instructors at both National Seminars and those conducted on State levels in Missouri and Illinois.

The firm is included in the Martindale-Hubbell Bar Register of Preeminent Lawyers.

REFERENCES: Union Bank; First Illinois Bank.

(For complete biographical data on all personnel, see Professional Biographies at St. Louis, Missouri)

T. FRITZ LEVENHAGEN

4495 NORTH ILLINOIS STREET
SUITE E
BELLEVILLE, ILLINOIS 62226
Telephone: 618-235-2562
Toll Free: 877-235-2562
Fax: 618-235-2631
Email: fritz@levenhagen.com
URL: http://www.levenhagen.com

Workers Compensation, , Automobile Accidents and Injuries, Products Liability, Wrongful Death, Personal Injury, Medical Malpractice and Premises Liability.

T. FRITZ LEVENHAGEN, born Meadville, Pennsylvania, 1960; admitted to bar, 1986, Illinois; 1987, Missouri and U.S. District Court, Southern District of Illinois; 1989, U.S. District Court, Eastern District of Missouri. *Education:* Southern Illinois University, Carbondale (B.A., Political Science, 1983); St. Louis University (J.D., 1986). Phi Delta Phi. *Member:* Illinois State Bar Association; The Association of Trial Lawyers of America; Illinois Trial Lawyers Association; The Missouri Association of Trial Attorneys; Workers' Compensation Lawyers Association; St. Clair County Bar Association; Workers Compensation Lawyers Association; Workplace Injury Litigation Group. ***REPORTED CASES:*** Contour Designs Inc. v. The Industrial Commission, 627 N.E.2d 717, 194 Ill.Dec. 380 (Il-l.App.Ct. 1994); Nascote Industries v. The Industrial Commission, 353 Ill. App. 3d 1067, 820 N.E.2d 570 (Ill.App.Ct. 2004). ***PRACTICE AREAS:*** Medical Malpractice; Automobile Accidents and Injuries; Products Liability; Wrongful Death; Personal Injury; Premises Liability; Workers Compensation.

REPRESENTS INJURED WORKERS INCLUDING MEMBERS OF THE FOLLOWING UNIONS:
o	American Federation of State, County and Municipal Employees (AFL-CIO)
o	Glass, Molders, Pottery, Plastics & Allied Workers Intl. Un. AFL-CIO International Association of Machinists
o	Intl Union Untd. Auto, Aero & Agr. Imp. Wkrs. of Am.- UAW No 1766
o	Ironworkers
o	Operating Engineers - Local 520
o	Utd. Auto Aero & Agr. Imp. Wkrs. Of America - UAW
o	United Mine Workers Association.

LEWIS, RICE & FINGERSH

A Limited Liability Company
325 SOUTH HIGH STREET
BELLEVILLE, ILLINOIS 62220
Telephone: 618-234-8636
Telecopier: 618-234-8671
Email: For attorney e-mails use: first initial of first name and last name @lewisrice.com e.g., jsmith@lewisrice.com
URL: http://www.lewisrice.com

Kansas City, Missouri Office: 1010 Walnut, Suite 500. Telephone: 816-421-2500.
St. Louis, Missouri Office: 500 North Broadway, Suite 2000. Telephone: 314-444-7600.
Creve Coeur, Missouri Office: 555 North New Ballas Road, Suite 260. Telephone: 314-569-2262.
Overland Park, Kansas Office: 7015 College Boulevard, Suite 135. Telephone: 913-381-8898.
Washington, Missouri Office: 216 West Main, P.O. Box 1040. Telephone: 636-239-7747.
Jefferson City, Missouri Office: 221 East Capitol Avenue. Telephone: 573-893-7724.

General Civil Trial and Appellate Practice. Administrative, Admiralty, Agricultural Law, Antitrust, Banking, Bankruptcy, Business Law, Commercial, Corporation, Defamation, Divestitures, Employee Benefits, Environmental, Estate Planning, Health Care, High Technology, Insurance, Intellectual Property, Labor and Employment, Limited Liability Company, Media, Mergers and Acquisitions, Municipal, Not-for-Profit Institutions, Probate, Products Liability, Real Estate, Securities, Taxation, Toxic Torts, Zoning.

RESIDENT MEMBER

FREDERICK J. HESS, born Highland, Illinois, September 22, 1941; admitted to bar, 1971, Kansas; 1976, Illinois and District of Columbia. *Education:* St. Louis University (B.S., 1963); Washburn University of Topeka (J.D., 1971).

ASSOCIATE

G. ETHAN SKAGGS, born February 9, 1966; admitted to bar, 1992, Illinois. *Education:* Carroll College (B.A., 1988); Southern Illinois University (J.D., 1992). ***PRACTICE AREAS:*** Litigation.

JEFFREY J. LOWE, P.C.

BELLEVILLE, ILLINOIS

(See St. Louis, Missouri)

Personal Injury, Automobile Accidents, Wrongful Death, Medical Malpractice, Class Actions, Products Liability, Pharmaceutical Drugs, Toxic Torts, Commercial Torts, Intellectual Property Litigation.

MATHIS, MARIFIAN, RICHTER & GRANDY, LTD.

Established in 1984

23 PUBLIC SQUARE, SUITE 300
P.O. BOX 307
BELLEVILLE, ILLINOIS 62220
Telephone: 618-234-9800; 314-421-2325
Fax: 618-234-9786
URL: http://www.mmrg.com

St. Louis, Missouri Office: 7751 Carondelet Avenue, Suite 500, 63105. Telephone: 314-421-2325. Fax: 314-727-3046.

Federal and State Tax Law and Controversy. Banking, Civil and Criminal Trial Practice. Tort and Commercial Litigation, Corporate, Business, ERISA Litigation, Employee Benefits, Real Estate, Probate, Estate Planning, Bankruptcy and Creditors Rights Law, Product Liability, Public Utilities, Medical Malpractice, Class Actions, Personal Injury, Wrongful Death, Employment Discrimination, Wrongful Discharge and Employment Law.

PATRICK B. MATHIS, born Pinckneyville, Illinois, February 1, 1952; admitted to bar, 1978, Missouri; 1979, Illinois. *Education:* St. Louis University (B.A., 1973); Washington University (M.B.A., 1978; J.D., 1978; LL.M. in Taxation, 1979). Author: "Advanced Payments of Proposed Deficiencies Useful in Today's High Interest Rate Climate," 56 Journal of Taxation, June, 1982; "Civil Tax Penalties," Federal Tax Practice and Procedure Handbook, Ill. Inst. for CLE, 1991; "Tax Aspects of Litigation," Civil Procedure Handbook, Illinois Institute for CLE, 1995, 1997 and 2002; "Tortious Interference With Inheritance Expectancies," Illinois Bar Journal, 1996. Director, 1990-1998 and Chairman, 1996-1997, Illinois Institute for Continuing Legal Education. *Member:* Bar Association of Metropolitan St. Louis (Member, Taxation Section); The Missouri Bar (Member, Taxation Committee, 1978-1982); Illinois State (Member, Federal Taxation Section Council, 1981-1984; 1989-1994; Chairman, 1992-1993) and American (Member: Sections on: Taxation; General Practice; Chairman, Taxation Committee, 1989-1991, 1996-1997) Bar Associations; American College of Trust and Estate Counsel. ***PRACTICE AREAS:*** Taxation Law; Corporate Law; Criminal Tax Litigation; Estate Planning Law. ***Email:*** pmathis@mmrg.com

GEORGE E. MARIFIAN, born East St. Louis, Illinois, April 12, 1950; admitted to bar, 1977, Illinois; 1982, U.S. Tax Court; 1990, Missouri; U.S. Court of Appeals, Seventh Circuit; U.S. District Court, Southern and Central Districts of Illinois. *Education:* Washington University (B.S.B.A., 1972); St. Louis University (M.B.A., 1975; J.D., 1976). Phi Alpha Delta. Certified Public Accountant, Missouri and Illinois. Author: "Offers in Compromise: Did the IRS Get the Message?" Journal of Tax Practice and Procedure, June/July 1999; "Representing a Taxpayer Before the IRS," The Complete Lawyer, Jan/Feb 1999; "A Walk-Through of a Detailed Checklist and Initial Ethical Issues and Engagement Letters," Handbook of Illinois Institute for CLE, 1995. *Member:* The Bar Association of Metropolitan St. Louis; St. Clair County, Illinois State (Chair, Special Committee on GATS, 2004-2005; Chair, Federal Taxation Section Council, 1999-2000; Chair, Business Advice and Financial Planning Section, 1992-1993; Estate Planning, Probate and Trust Section Council, 1984-1988; Member, Committee on Professional Conduct, 1999-2005) and American (Chair, Employment Tax Committee, Section of Taxation, 2000-2002; Co-Chair, Business Advice and Financial Planning Committee, General Practice Section, 1990-1991) Bar Associations; The Missouri Bar. ***PRACTICE AREAS:*** Business Law; Tax Law; Estate Planning; Criminal Litigation; Tax Litigation; Business Litigation; Trust Litigation; Probate Litigation. ***Email:*** gmarifian@mmrg.com

KEVIN J. RICHTER, born Belleville, Illinois, July 3, 1958; admitted to bar, 1983, Illinois; 1984, Missouri and U.S. Tax Court. *Education:* Southern Illinois University (B.S., 1980); St. Louis University (J.D., 1983). Certified Public Accountant, Missouri, 1984 and Illinois, 1984. Author: "Evaluation and Division of Retirement Benefits in Dissolution of Marriage," Employee Benefits Handbook, Ill. Inst. for CLE, 1987. *Member:* Bar Association of Metropolitan St. Louis; St. Clair County, Illinois State (Member, 1985, 1996-2002 and Chair, 2001-2002, Employee Benefits Section Council); Sections on: Corporate Tax; Federal Tax) and American (Member, Tax and Corporate Sections) Bar Associations; The Missouri Bar; American Society of Pension Actuaries; Illinois Society of C.P.A.'s (Southern Chapter). ***PRACTICE AREAS:*** Business Law; Business Sales; Business Acquisitions; Estate Planning; Probate; ERISA Litigation; Employment Law; Employee Benefits; Taxation. ***Email:*** krichter@mmrg.com

LAURA KOENEMAN GRANDY, born Chester, Illinois, October 4, 1958; admitted to bar, 1984, Illinois and U.S. District Court, Southern District of Illinois; 1989, Missouri; 1997, U.S. Supreme Court. *Education:* Kansas State University; Eastern Illinois University (B.A., with highest honors, 1980); St. Louis University (J.D., 1984). Recipient, Kniep Moot Court Brief Award. Panel Trustee, United States Bankruptcy Court, Southern District of Illinois. *Member:* St. Clair County, Illinois State and American Bar Associations; The Missouri Bar; Southern Illinois Bankruptcy Institute. ***PRACTICE AREAS:*** Banking Law; Bankruptcy Law; Real Estate Law; Creditors Rights Law; Probate; Corporate Litigation. ***Email:*** lgrandy@mmrg.com

KEVIN J. STINE, born Portsmouth, Virginia, March 31, 1961; admitted to bar, 1987, Illinois, Missouri and U.S. District Court, Central and Southern Districts of Illinois; 1988, U.S. Court of Appeals, Seventh Circuit; 1997, U.S. Supreme Court. *Education:* Southern Illinois University (B.S.B.A., 1983); Washington University (J.D., 1986). Author: "Illinois Courts Require Strict Rule Compliance For Mechanic's Lien," St. Louis Construction News and Review, May, 1989. Panel Arbitrator/Chair of the St. Clair County Arbitration Center. *Member:* Illinois State Bar Association (Member, Commercial, Banking and Bankruptcy Section Council; Editor, 1990-1995; Chairman, 1997-1998); The Missouri Bar. ***PRACTICE AREAS:*** Bankruptcy; Creditors Rights; Commercial Litigation; Banking. ***Email:*** kstine@mmrg.com

MARK J. STEGMAN, born Belleville, Illinois, April 9, 1957; admitted to bar, 1982, Missouri; 1983, Illinois; 1989, U.S. Tax Court. *Education:* MacMurray College; Northern Illinois University (B.S., cum laude, 1979); St. Louis University (J.D., cum laude, 1982). Member, Order of Woolsack. Certified Public Accountant, Illinois, 1979. Co-Author, *Tax Aspects of Litigation,* Illinois Civil Practice, Volume II, Chapter 3, Ill. Inst. for CLE, 1995, 1997, 2003. *Member:* The Bar Association of Metropolitan St. Louis; Illinois State and American (Member, Taxation Section) Bar Associations; The Missouri Bar; American Institute of Certified Public Accountants; Illinois Society of Certified Public Accountants. ***PRACTICE AREAS:*** Taxation; General Corporate; Real Estate; Estate Planning. ***Email:*** mstegman@mmrg.com

T. BRADFORD WALTRIP, born Mattoon, Illinois, February 18, 1955; admitted to bar, 1987, Illinois and U.S. District Court, Southern District of Illinois; 1988, Missouri. *Education:* Eastern Illinois University (B.A., 1984); Southern Illinois University (J.D., cum laude, 1987). Lead Articles Editor, Southern Illinois University Law Journal, 1986-1987. *Member:* St. Clair County and Illinois State Bar Associations. ***PRACTICE AREAS:*** Commercial Litigation; Corporate Law; Probate; Real Estate; Real Estate Taxation. ***Email:*** bwaltrip@mmrg.com

MARK S. SCHUVER, born St. Louis, Missouri, October 23, 1959; admitted to bar, 1987, Missouri; 1988, Illinois. *Education:* University of Missouri at Columbia (B.A., 1983; J.D., 1987). Contributing Author, "Illinois Products Liability," Lawyers Cooperative Publishing. *Member:* The Bar Association of Metropolitan St. Louis; St. Clair County, Illinois State and American Bar Associations; The Missouri Bar. ***PRACTICE AREAS:*** Personal Injury; Commercial Litigation; Employment Discrimination; Medical Malpractice; Products Liability; Class Actions. ***Email:*** mschuver@mmrg.com

KURT S. SCHROEDER, born Carlinville, Illinois, July 1, 1956; admitted to bar, 1985, Illinois. *Education:* Southern Illinois University (B.S., with honors; 1980; M.B.A., 1981); Washington University (J.D., 1984). Beta Gamma Sigma. Author: "Tax Considerations," Basic Real Estate Practice Handbook, Ill. Inst. for CLE. Lecturer, National Business Institute. *Member:* Bar Association of Metropolitan St. Louis; East St. Louis, St. Clair County, Illinois State and American Bar Associations. ***PRACTICE AREAS:*** Corporate Law; Probate; Trust Law; Real Estate; Commercial Litigation. ***Email:*** kschroeder@mmrg.com

WILLIAM J. NIEHOFF, born St. Louis, Missouri, January 1, 1960; admitted to bar, 1986, Illinois; 1987, Missouri; U.S. District Court, Southern District of Illinois; U.S. District Court, Eastern District of Missouri; U.S. Court of Appeals, Seventh Circuit. *Education:* University of Missouri (B.S.B.A., 1982); Washington University (J.D., 1986). *Member:* Bar Association of Metropolitan St. Louis; The Missouri Bar; Illinois State Bar Association (Member, Utilities Committee, 2000—). ***REPORTED CASES:*** Castellano v. Wal-Mart, 373 F301817 (7th Cir. 2004). ***PRACTICE AREAS:*** Litigation; Personal Injury; Commercial Litigation; Class Actions; Utility Law; Administrative Law. ***Email:*** wniehoff@mmrg.com

LORRAINE KAY CAVATAIO, born Belleville, Illinois, July 9, 1969; admitted to bar, 1995, Illinois, U.S. District Court, Southern District of Illinois, U.S. Court of Appeals, Seventh Circuit and U.S. Tax Court; 1996, Missouri. *Education:* University of Kansas (B.S., 1991); Washington University (J.D., 1995). Certified Public Accountant, Illinois, 1994. Author and Lecturer: Illinois Estate Administration Handbook, Ill. Inst. for CLE, 1999; "Estate Planning for Illinois Attorneys," The Basic and Beyond Handbook, Ill. Inst. for CLE, 2001. *Member:* St. Clair County (Secretary, 2003-2004; Board Member, 2004-2006) and Illinois State Bar Associations; The Missouri Bar; American Institute of Certified Public Accountants; Illinois CPA Society. ***PRACTICE AREAS:*** Corporate Law; Probate; Probate Litigation; Trust Law; Estate Planning; Taxation; Real Estate. ***Email:*** lcavataio@mmrg.com

TERESA A. GENEROUS, born Middletown, Connecticut, September 1, 1956; admitted to bar, 1988, Missouri and U.S. District Court, Western and Eastern Districts of Missouri; 1989, Illinois and U.S. District Court, Southern and Central Districts of Illinois; 1997, U.S. Supreme Court. *Education:* St. Lawrence University (B.S., 1979) Omicron Delta Kappa; University of Missouri, Columbia (M.Ed., 1983; J.D., 1988). Associate Editor in Chief, University of Missouri Journal of Dispute Resolution, 1987. Co-Author: Chapter 7, Stays, 1992, 2004 and Chapter 3 Supplement, Property of the Estate, 1995, 1996, Missouri CLE Desk Reference Book on Bankruptcy Practice. NASD Arbitrator. *Member:* Bar Association of Metropolitan St. Louis (Former Chairperson, Local Bankruptcy Rule Committee for Adversary Proceedings; Former Chairperson: Business Law Section; Bankruptcy Committee; Member, Women in Legal Profession Committee); The Missouri Bar (Member, Commercial Law Committee); Women Lawyers Association of Metropolitan St. Louis (Former President); American Bankruptcy Institute; Turnaround Management Association; St. Louis Volunteer Lawyers Association. ***PRACTICE AREAS:*** Asset Protection; Banking Law; Business Law; Commercial Law; Creditors Rights; Workouts; Corporate Reorganization; Insolvency. ***Email:*** tgenerous@mmrg.com

KELLI E. MADIGAN, born Lincoln, Nebraska, October 3, 1970; admitted to bar, 1996, Missouri and U.S. Tax Court; 1997, Illinois. *Education:* St. Louis University (B.A., 1993; J.D., 1996); Washington University, St. Louis (LL.M., 2001). *Member:* Bar Association of Metropolitan St. Louis; The Missouri Bar; Women's Lawyers Association of Greater St. Louis; Illinois State Bar Association (Chair, Federal Taxation Section Council, 2004-2005). ***PRACTICE AREAS:*** Taxation; Estate Planning; Corporate. ***Email:*** kmadigan@mmrg.com

BRADLEY W. SMALL, born Centralia, Illinois, May 23, 1955; admitted to bar, 1979, Illinois and U.S. District Court, Southern District of Illinois; 1988, U.S. District Court, Central District of Illinois. *Education:* Southern Illinois University (B.A., 1976); St. Louis University (J.D., 1979). Director, St. Louis Federal Reserve Bank, 2000-2004. Partner, Hoht, House, DeMoss & Johnson, Nashville, IL, 1979-1990. President and General Counsel, Farmers & Merchants National Bank, 1990-2004. ***PRACTICE AREAS:*** Banking Law; Corporate Law; Bankruptcy; Probate; Real Estate. ***Email:*** bsmall@mmrg.com

---

MARY E. LOPINOT, born Belleville, Illinois, September 30, 1962; admitted to bar, 1998, Illinois; 1999, Missouri and U.S. District Court, Southern District of Illinois. *Education:* Southern Illinois University (B.S.A., 1995); St. Louis University, School of Law (J.D., 1998). Certified Public Accountant, 1996. *Member:* Bar Association of Metropolitan St. Louis; Illinois State and American Bar Associations; The Missouri Bar. ***PRACTICE AREAS:*** Taxation; Bankruptcy. ***Email:*** mlopinot@mmrg.com

DEANNA L. LITZENBURG, born Centralia, Illinois, January 21, 1974; admitted to bar, 1999, Illinois; 2000, Missouri; 2001, U.S. District Court, Southern District of Illinois; 2004, U.S. District Court, Eastern District of Missouri. *Education:* Southeast Missouri State University (B.A., 1995); Southern Illinois University School of Law (J.D., 1999). Phi

(This Listing Continued)

MATHIS, MARIFIAN, RICHTER & GRANDY, LTD., Belleville—Continued

Alpha Delta (Chapter Clerk, 1998-1999). *Member:* Bar Association of Metropolitan St. Louis; Illinois State, Missouri and American Bar Associations. ***PRACTICE AREAS:*** Civil Litigation; Workers Compensation; Commercial Litigation; Class Actions. ***Email:*** dlitzenburg@mmrg.com

JOSEPH P. O'KEEFE, born St. Louis, Missouri, April 1, 1971; admitted to bar, 1996, Missouri; 1997, Illinois. *Education:* St. Louis University (B.A., magna cum laude, 1993; J.D., cum laude, 1996). *Member:* Bar Association of Metropolitan St. Louis; The Missouri Bar (Member, Probate and Trust Committee); Illinois State and American Bar Associations. ***PRACTICE AREAS:*** Estate Planning; Estate and Gift Taxation; Probate; Trust Administration; Corporate Law; Business Law. ***Email:*** jokeefe@mmrg.com

PHILIP D. SPEICHER, born Kansas City, Missouri, July 22, 1978; admitted to bar, 2004, Missouri (Not admitted in Illinois). *Education:* Mid-America Nazarene College (B.A., 2001); Washington University (J.D., 2004). ***PRACTICE AREAS:*** Taxation; Estate Planning; Corporate Law; Business Law. ***Email:*** pspeicher@mmrg.com

REPRESENTATIVE CLIENTS: Empire Comfort Systems; Chelar Tool and Die Co.; Casper Stolle Quarry and Contracting Co.; E. T. Simonds Construction Co.; Fulford Construction Co.; Moto Inc.; Illinois Development Finance Authority; American Bank; Gateway Petroleum Co.; Crown Therapeutics, Inc.; American Bancshares, Inc.; Robert "Chick" Fritz, Inc.; Laclede Gas; The Maschhoffs, Inc.

McGLYNN & McGLYNN

Established in 1896

116 SOUTH CHARLES STREET
BELLEVILLE, ILLINOIS 62220
Telephone: 618-234-8800; 314-381-5112
Telecopier: 618-234-8813
Email: mcglaw@htctech.net
URL: http://www.lawyers.com/mcglynn&mcglynn

General Civil and Trial Practice in Illinois, Missouri and the Federal Courts in the following areas: Torts, Admiralty (Jones Act), FELA, Medical Malpractice, Products Liability, and Workers Compensation. Also Election, Campaign and Political Law, Transportation Law and Transactions, Commercial Transactions, VCG & Warranty Litigation and Contracts, Government Law, Civil Rights.

FIRM PROFILE: McGlynn & McGlynn was founded in 1896. Since then, four generations of McGlynns have practiced law in Illinois, Missouri and the Federal Courts. The firm is currently made up of three litigators offering expertise in complex tort, and commercial litigation. The size of the firm insures personal attention to each file and to the needs of their clients. A significant percentage of the firm's business comes from referrals from other attorneys in the St. Louis Metropolitan area and from attorneys around the country. The McGlynns represent both plaintiffs and defendants.

MEMBERS OF FIRM

ROBERT E. McGLYNN, born East St. Louis, Illinois, September 6, 1926; admitted to bar, 1951, Illinois. *Education:* University of Notre Dame (A.B., 1950; LL.B., 1951). Assistant Attorney General, 1953-1960; Special Assistant Attorney General, 1958-1961; 1969-1978, State of Illinois. *Member:* East St. Louis (President, 1968), St. Clair County and Illinois State Bar Associations. [With U.S. Navy, 1944-1946]. ***SPECIAL AGENCIES:*** Commissioner, Bi-State Development Agency. ***REPORTED CASES:*** Phillips v. Graham, 86 Ill. 2d 274, 427 N.E.2d 550, 56 Ill. Dec 355 (Ill. 1981). ***PRACTICE AREAS:*** Banking; Commercial Transactions; Commercial Litigation. ***Email:*** mcglaw@htctech.net

JAMES McGLYNN (Retired)

MICHAEL L. McGLYNN, born Belleville, Illinois, August 10, 1959; admitted to bar, 1984, Illinois; 1985, Missouri, U.S. District Court, Central and Southern Districts of Illinois and Eastern District of Missouri and U.S. Court of Appeals, Seventh Circuit. *Education:* University of Notre Dame (B.A., 1981); St. Louis University (J.D., 1984). *Member:* Bar Association of Metropolitan St. Louis; East St. Louis, St. Clair County and Illinois State Bar Associations; The Missouri Bar; The Association of Trial Lawyers of America. ***PRACTICE AREAS:*** Products Liability; Tort; Medical Malpractice; Admiralty; Jones Act; Catastrophic Injuries. ***Email:*** mcglaw@htctech.net

STEPHEN P. McGLYNN, born East St. Louis, Illinois, May 23, 1962; admitted to bar, 1987, Illinois, U.S. District Court, Southern District of Illinois and U.S. Court of Appeals, Eighth Circuit; 1988, Missouri and U.S. District Court, Eastern District of Illinois; 1994, U.S. Supreme Court, U.S. District Court, Central District of Illinois. *Education:* University of Dayton (B.A., 1983); St. Louis University (J.D., 1987). Recipient, American Jurisprudence Award in Advanced Commercial Transactions. *Member:* St. Clair County and Illinois State Bar Associations; The Missouri Bar; National Transportation Safety Board Bar Association. ***SPECIAL AGENCIES:*** Special Assistant Attorney General, 1996—; Co-Chairman, Illinois Republican Party, 2002—. ***REPORTED CASES:*** Snelling vs. Chrysler Motor Corp., 859 S.W. 2d 755 (Mo. App. 1993). ***PRACTICE AREAS:*** Commercial Litigation; Government Law; Aviation Law; Transportation Law; Civil Rights. ***Email:*** mcglaw@htctech.net

REPRESENTATIVE CLIENTS: Available upon request.

McMAHON, BERGER, HANNA, LINIHAN, CODY & McCARTHY

A PROFESSIONAL CORPORATION

BELLEVILLE, ILLINOIS

(See Collinsville)

Labor Relations, Civil Rights and Administrative Law, Employment Litigation in all Courts.

NEVILLE, RICHARDS & WULLER

Established in 1994

5 PARK PLACE
BELLEVILLE, ILLINOIS 62226
Telephone: 618-277-0900
Facsimile: 618-277-0970
URL: http://www.nrw-law.com

General Civil Trial and Appellate Practice, Personal Injury, Negligence, Products Liability, Premises Liability, Admiralty, Railroad, Medical and Legal Malpractice, Professional Negligence, Construction, Insurance Defense, Employment Law, Environmental, Municipal, Corporate, Real Estate and Probate Law.

MEMBERS OF FIRM

JAMES E. NEVILLE, born East St. Louis, Illinois, January 1, 1955; admitted to bar, 1980, Illinois; 1982, Missouri and U.S. District Court, Eastern District of Missouri. *Education:* St. Louis University (B.S., 1977; J.D., 1980). Co-Author: "The Bystander's Right Under Strict Liability Does Exist: A Call For Reform of The Restatement," 25 St. Louis University Law Journal, 543 (1981); "1991 Evidence Update," 12th Annual Seminar, September 1991, and "1997 Evidence Update," 18th Annual Seminar, September 1997, Illinois Association of Defense Trial Counsel. Contributing Editor: "Illinois Supreme Court Limits Application of Medical Malpractice Statute of Repose," Illinois Defense Counsel Quarterly, 2nd Quarter, 1993. *Member:* The Bar Association of Metropolitan St. Louis; St. Clair County, Illinois State and American Bar Associations; The Missouri Bar; Illinois Association of Defense Trial Counsel; Missouri Organization of Defense Trial Counsel; Maritime Law Association; Southeastern Admiralty Law Institute; Defense Research Institute; American Board of Trial Advocates; Adjusters Association of Central Illinois; Leading Lawyers Network; Leading Lawyers Advisory Board. ***PRACTICE AREAS:*** Professional Negligence; Personal Injury; Insurance Defense. ***Email:*** jneville@nrw-law.com

TIMOTHY S. RICHARDS, born Peoria, Illinois, August 7, 1956; admitted to bar, 1982, Illinois; 1983, Missouri and U.S. District Court, Eastern District of Missouri. *Education:* Augustana College (A.B., 1978); Southern Illinois University (J.D., cum laude, 1981). Omicron Delta Kappa. National Order of Barristers. Legal Writing and Moot Court Instructor, Southern Illinois University School of Law, 1978-1981. Articles Editor, Southern Illinois University Law Journal, 1980-1981. Law Clerk to Hon. James L. Foreman, Chief Judge, U.S. District Court, Southern District of Illinois, 1981-1983. Co-Author: "Retaliatory Discharge: Its Applicability to Employees Protected by a 'Just Cause' Provision," 72 Illinois Bar Journal 480, 1984. *Member:* Bar Association of Metropolitan St. Louis; St. Clair County and Illinois State Bar Associations; The Missouri Bar; Illinois Association of Defense Trial Counsel; Missouri Organization of Defense Lawyers; Adjusters Association of Central Illinois. ***PRACTICE AREAS:*** Professional Negligence; Personal Injury; Insurance Defense. ***Email:*** trichards@nrw-law.com

ROBERT G. WULLER, JR., born East St. Louis, Illinois, September 24, 1947; admitted to bar, 1972, Illinois; 1983, Missouri and U.S. District Court, Eastern District of Missouri. *Education:* University of Notre Dame (A.B., 1969); St. Louis University (J.D., 1972). Delta Theta Phi. *Member:* The Bar Association of Metropolitan St. Louis; St. Clair County, Illinois State (Member, Committee on the Unauthorized Practice of Law, 1981-1986) and American Bar Associations; American Bar Foundation; The Missouri Bar (Member, Missouri Bar Association Worker's Compensation Committee); Illinois Association of Defense Trial Counsel; Missouri Organization of Defense Lawyers; Adjusters Association of Central Illinois; Leading Lawyers Network. ***PRACTICE AREAS:*** Professional Negligence; Insurance Defense; Corporate; Real Estate; Real Estate Taxation; Probate. ***Email:*** bwuller@nrw-law.com

ASSOCIATES

MATTHEW C. ZITTEL, born Belleville, Illinois, August 28, 1971; admitted to bar, 1997, Illinois and U.S. District Court, Central and Southern Districts of Illinois; 1998, Missouri and U.S. District Court, Eastern of Missouri. *Education:* McKendree College (B.B.A., cum laude, 1994); Southern Illinois University (J.D., 1997). Co-Author: "1997 Evidence Update," 18th Annual Seminar, September 1997, Illinois Association of Defense Trial Counsel. *Member:* Bar Association of Metropolitan St. Louis; St. Clair County, Madison County and Illinois State Bar Associations; The Missouri Bar; Illinois Association of Defense Trial Counsel; Adjusters Association of Central Illinois. ***PRACTICE AREAS:*** Insurance Defense; Medical Malpractice; Personal Injury; Product Liability. ***Email:*** mzittel@nrw-law.com

CHRISTOPHER B. BORTZ, born La Porte, Indiana, January 16, 1974; admitted to bar, 2000, Illinois and Missouri; U.S. District Court, Southern District of Illinois. *Education:* Purdue University (B.A., 1996); St. Louis University (J.D., 1999). *Member:* The Bar Association of Metropolitan St. Louis; St. Clair County, Madison County and Illinois State Bar Associations; The Missouri Bar; Illinois Association of Defense Trial Counsel; Missouri Organization of Defense Lawyers; Adjusters Association of Central Illinois. ***PRACTICE AREAS:*** Insurance Defense; Product Liability; Medical Malpractice. ***Email:*** cbortz@nrw-law.com

PAUL J. CHAPKIN, born South Bend, Indiana, March 8, 1978; admitted to bar, 2003, Missouri; 2005 Illinois. *Education:* St. Louis University (B.A., Political Science, 2000); University of Missouri at Kansas City (J.D., 2003). *Member:* Bar Association of Metropolitan St. Louis; St. Clair County, Madison County, Illinois State and American Bar Associations; The Missouri Bar. ***PRACTICE AREAS:*** Personal Injury Defense; Medical Malpractice Defense; Insurance Defense; Workers Compensation. ***Email:*** pchapkin@nrw-law.com

REPRESENTATIVE CLIENTS: Illinois State Medical Inter-Insurance Exchange; Norfolk-Southern Corporation; Terminal Railroad Association of St. Louis; Illinois Bell Telephone; Great American Insurance Companies; Travelers Insurance; Risk Administration & Management Company; Professional Service Industries, Inc.; Trafalgar House; Elgin National Industries, Inc.; CIGNA Property and Casualty Companies; Zurich-American Insurance Group; The Equitable Life Assurance Company; General American Life Insurance Company; The St. Paul Insurance Company; Allstate Insurance Company; Lloyds of London; General Casualty; Transport Insurance Company; Employers Mutual of Wausau; Continental Insurance Companies; St. Paul Economy Fire & Casualty Company; Davy International; Rockford Mutual

(This Listing Continued)

Insurance Company; The Doctors' Company; Standard Mutual Insurance; Golden Rule Insurance Company; World Marine Transport; CNA Insurance Companies; Network America Life Insurance Company; Seaboard Underwriters, Inc.; Farm Bureau Insurance Company; Hermitage Insurance Company; Prudential Insurance Company of America; Reliable Life Insurance Company; Medical Claims Management Group; Lumberman's Mutual Casualty Company; Land-O-Sun Dairies, Inc.; The Belleville News Democrat; Orgulf Transport; Kaskaskia Water District; McBride & Sons; Country Companies, National Companies; National Emergency Services, Inc.; Columbia Insurance Group; Gateway Insurance Company; Liberty Mutual Insurance.

THOMAS J. NOONAN, P.C.

BELLEVILLE, ILLINOIS

(See St. Louis, Missouri)

Asbestos Litigation, Bankruptcy Litigation, Civil Litigation, Commercial Bankruptcy, Creditor Bankruptcy, Foreclosures, General Liability Defense, Insurance, Insurance Defense, Insurance Litigation, Litigation, Personal Injury, Personal Injury Defense, Products Liability, Mold Litigation, Motor Carrier Defense, Real Estate Bankruptcy, Real Estate Foreclosure, Tort Defense, Workers Compensation Defense.

O'GARA, GOMRIC & SCHULTZ, P.C.

6 EAST WASHINGTON STREET
BELLEVILLE, ILLINOIS 62220
Telephone: 618-234-2788
Fax: 618-234-0670
Email: o'gara@compu-type.net
URL: http://www.lawyers.com/ogaralaw

Criminal Defense, Personal Injury Law. Capital Offenses, Murder, Felonies, Misdemeanors, Driving While Intoxicated, Traffic Violations, Automobile Accidents and Injuries, Federal Criminal, White Collar Crime.

JOHN J. O'GARA, JR., born Harrisburg, Pennsylvania, March 15, 1961; admitted to bar, 1987, Illinois; 1988, U.S. District Court, Central District of Illinois; 1994, U.S. District Court, Southern District of Illinois; 1995, U.S. Court of Appeals, Seventh Circuit. *Education:* Quincy College (B.A, 1983); St. Louis University (J.D., 1987). Assistant Public Defender, 1987-1989 and Public Defender, 1989-1991, Knox County. Assistant Public Defender, St. Clair County, 1991-1994. *Member:* East St. Louis, St. Clair County (Member, Board of Directors, 1998—) and Illinois State Bar Associations (Member, Special Committee on Public Defenders Appointment Standard, 1996—); Illinois Public Defenders Association (Member, Board of Directors, 1995—); National Association of Criminal Defense Lawyers; Illinois Attorneys for Criminal Justice (Member, Board of Directors, 1998-2000). ***PRACTICE AREAS:*** State and Federal Criminal Defense; Personal Injury Law; Capital Offenses; Felonies; Misdemeanors; Driving While Intoxicated; Traffic Violations; Automobile Accidents and Injuries Law; White Collar Crime.

JAMES A. GOMRIC, born Belleville, Illinois, November 26, 1969; admitted to bar, 1995, Illinois; 2001, U.S. District Court, Southern District of Illinois; 2002, U.S. Court of Appeals, Seventh Circuit. *Education:* St. Louis University (B.S., 1992; J.D., 1995). Assistante State's Attorney, 1995-1997, Assistant Public Defender, 1998-2001 and Chief Assistant, 2000-2001, St. Clair County. *Member:* East St. Louis, St. Clair County and Illinois State Bar Associations; Illinois Capitol Litigation Trial Bar; National Association of Criminal Defense Attorneys. ***PRACTICE AREAS:*** Criminal Defense; Personal Injury Law; Workers Compensation; Capital Offenses; Felonies; Misdemeanors; Driving While Intoxicated; Traffic Violations; Automobile Accidents and Injuries; White Collar Crime. ***Email:*** gomric@compu-type.net

TODD M. SCHULTZ, born Indianapolis, Indiana, May 3, 1974; admitted to bar, 2000, Illinois. *Education:* University of Notre Dame (B.A., 1996); University of Illinois, Urbana-Champaign (J.D., 2000). *Member:* American Bar Association; NACOL. ***PRACTICE AREAS:*** Criminal Defense. ***Email:*** schultz@compu-typc.net

RABBITT, PITZER & SNODGRASS, P.C.

23 SOUTH FIRST STREET
BELLEVILLE, ILLINOIS 62222-8336
Telephone: 314-421-5545
Fax: 314-421-3144

St. Louis, Missouri Office: 100 South Fourth Street, Suite 400, 63102-1821. Telephone: 314-421-5545. Facsimile: 314-421-3144.

General Civil Trial and Appellate Litigation in State and Federal Courts of Eastern Missouri and Southern Illinois, including Personal Injury Defense, Professional Liability (Medical, Legal Architectural and Engineering), Products Liability, Environmental, Construction, Employment, Fire and Marine and General Business Litigation.

FIRM PROFILE: Rabbitt, Pitzer & Snodgrass, P.C. serves its local, national and international clients by professionally handling their litigation needs in Eastern Missouri and Southern Illinois.

MICHAEL J. PITZER, admitted to bar, 1973, Missouri; 1976, Illinois. *Education:* St. Louis University (B.S., 1970; J.D., 1973). *Member:* The Missouri Bar; Illinois State Bar Association; American Board of Trial Advocates; Illinois Association of Defense Counsel; Missouri Organization of Defense Lawyers. ***PRACTICE AREAS:*** General Liability; Products Liability; Professional Malpractice Defense. ***Email:*** pitzer@rabbittlaw.com

(For biographical data on all personnel, see Professional Biographies at St. Louis, Missouri)

REED, ARMSTRONG, GORMAN, MUDGE & MORRISSEY

PROFESSIONAL CORPORATION

BELLEVILLE, ILLINOIS

(See Edwardsville)

General Civil Trial and Appellate practice in all State and Federal Courts, including Missouri, Personal Injury, Negligence, Premises Liability, Products Liability, Insurance, Automobile, Construction, Commercial Litigation, Workers Compensation, Employment, Discrimination, Dram Shop/Liquor Liability, Marine/Water Recreational Boating, Wrongful Discharge, Extra Contractual Liability/Bad Faith, Property Damage, Fraud/Arson/Fire, Non-Vehicle General Liability, Eminent Domain, Civil Rights, Class Action, Environmental, Toxic Tort, School, Corporate, Probate, Estate Planning, Real Estate Law.

THE REX CARR LAW FIRM, LLC

7012 W. MAIN STREET
BELLEVILLE, ILLINOIS 62223
Telephone: 618-397-9191
800-333-5297
URL: http://www.rexcarr.com
URL: http://www.lawyers.com/rexcarr

St. Louis, Missouri Office: 1 Metropolitan Square, 211 North Broadway, Suite 2970, 63102. Telephone: 1-800-333-5297.
East St. Louis, Illinois Office: 412 Missouri Avenue, 62201. Telephone: 618-274-0434. Fax: 618-274-8369.

Railroad, Medical Malpractice, Product Liability, Toxic Torts, Nursing Home Negligence, General Negligence, Trial Practice, Workers Compensation, Class Actions, Complex Litigation, Automobile Litigation.

FIRM PROFILE: The firm serves both Missouri and Illinois in a specialized Tort Practice maintaining three staffed offices in East St. Louis, Illinois, Belleville, Illinois and St. Louis, Missouri. Its partners are instructors at both National Seminars and those conducted on State levels in Missouri and Illinois.

The firm is included in the Martindale-Hubbell Bar Register of Preeminent Lawyers.

(See East St. Louis, Illinois)

RIPPLINGER & ZIMMER L.L.P.

2215 WEST MAIN STREET
BELLEVILLE, ILLINOIS 62226
Telephone: 618-234-2440; 800-733-8333
Telecopier: 618-234-6728
URL: http://www.lawyers.com/ripplinger&associates
URL: http://georgeripplinger.wld.com

Legal Malpractice, Plaintiffs Personal Injury, Wrongful Death, Medical Malpractice, Products Liability.

GEORGE R. RIPPLINGER, JR., born April 19, 1945; admitted to bar, 1970, Illinois; 1976, Missouri. *Education:* University of Illinois (A.B., 1967; J.D., 1970). Phi Delta Phi. Member Board of Visitors, 1979-1986 and President, 1983-1984, College of Law, University of Illinois. Member, Board of Directors, 1983-1988 and Vice President, 1987-1988, Land of Lincoln Legal Assistance Foundation. *Member:* Illinois State (Secretary, 1991-1992, Member, Board of Governors, 1981-1983; 1987-1994; Assembly Representative, 1978-1996; Member, Illinois Task Force on Gender Bias in the Courts, 1988-1994; ISBA-CBA Joint Committee on Judicial Compensation, 1983—; Member, Civil Practice Section Council, 1994-1999; Professional Responsibility Committee, 1987-1988 and 1994-2002; Chair, 2000-2001); and American (Member of Council, 1989-1993 and 1994-2003; Division Director, 1988-1989, 1995-1997, 1998-1999; Chair, 2001-2002, General Practice Solo and Small Firm Section; Member, House of Delegates, 1989-1993; 1996-1999) Bar Associations; The Missouri Bar (Member: Civil Practice and Procedure Committee, 1977-1985; Tort Law Committee, 1980—); Illinois Trial Lawyers Association (Member: Board of Advocates, 1993—); The Bar Association of Metropolitan St. Louis (Member: Professional Ethics and Methods of Practice Committee, 1984-1987, 2000—). [Colonel, U.S. Army Reserve, 1970-2001]. ***PRACTICE AREAS:*** Legal Professional Liability; Civil Litigation; Catastrophic Injury; Professional Liability; Insurance. ***Email:*** george@ripplingerlaw.com

PATRICIA A. ZIMMER, born April 7, 1953; admitted to bar, 1992, Illinois; 1993, Missouri. *Education:* St. Louis University (B.S., cum laude, 1975; J.D., cum laude, 1992). Managing Editor, St. Louis University Public Law Review, 1991-1992. *Member:* Illinois State Bar Association (Member, Insurance Law Section Council, 1999—); The Missouri Bar. ***PRACTICE AREAS:*** Medical Malpractice; Legal Negligence; Federal Civil Litigation; Automobile Accidents and Injuries; Uninsured and Underinsured Motorists. ***Email:*** pat@ripplingerlaw.com

ASSOCIATE

JAMIE BAS, born Eldorado, Illinois, August 26, 1977; admitted to bar, 2002, Illinois and U.S. District Court, Northern, Central and Southern Districts of Illinois. *Education:* Southern Illinois University at Carbondale (B.A., magna cum laude, 1999); DePaul University College of Law (J.D., 2002). *Member:* Chicago and Illinois State Bar Associations; Illinois Trial Lawyers Association; The Association of Trial Lawyers of America. ***PRACTICE AREAS:*** Negligence; Personal Injury; Products Liability; Torts; Class Actions. ***Email:*** jamie@ripplinglaw.com

A list of Representative Clients provided on request.
REFERENCE: First Bank of Belleville, Illinois.

SANDBERG, PHOENIX & VON GONTARD

A PROFESSIONAL CORPORATION

Established in 1979

23 SOUTH 1ST STREET

BELLEVILLE, ILLINOIS 62220

Telephone: 618-397-2721; 800-225-5529

Email: spvg.com

URL: http://www.spvg.com

St. Louis, Missouri Office: 15th Floor, One City Centre. Telephone: 314-231-3332. Telecopier: 314-241-7604.

Carbondale, Illinois Office: Westowne Centre, 2015 West Main, Suite G, 62901. Telephone: 618-351-7200. Toll Free: 866-351-5529. Fax: 618-351-7604.

Trial and Appellate Practice in Federal and State Courts, Product Liability, Health Law, Medical Malpractice Defense, Class Action Litigation, Employment Law, Banking, Commercial and Corporate Law, Admiralty, Aviation, Insurance, Bankruptcy and Reorganization, Estate Planning and Probate, Real Estate, Family Law.

FIRM PROFILE: Sandberg, Phoenix & von Gontard, P.C. was founded in 1979 with nine attorneys. The firm has grown steadily to become one of the leading law firms in the St. Louis metropolitan area and the midwest. Sandberg, Phoenix & von Gontard, P.C. combines experience, innovation and aggressiveness to deliver legal services that are responsive to the needs of our clients. Sandberg, Phoenix & von Gontard, P.C. recruits outstanding students from top law schools of the region and the country. The firm is honored to have been nominated and elected into membership of The Network of Trial Law Firms. The Network of Trial Law Firms is a national organization comprised of a select number of premier law firms from around the country with practices concentrated in civil litigation.

LAW FIRM ALLIANCES/ASSOCIATIONS: **THE NETWORK OF TRIAL LAW FIRMS, INC.**

SHAREHOLDERS

JOHN S. SANDBERG, born Minneapolis, Minnesota, September 1, 1948; admitted to bar, 1972, Missouri; 1973, Illinois. *Education:* University of Missouri (A.B., 1970; J.D., cum laude, 1972). Phi Delta Phi; Order of the Coif. Managing Editor, Missouri Law Review, 1971-1972. Author: "Loss of Profit Damages," Missouri Bar CLE Damages Deskbook (1987); "Cross-examination of the Plaintiff," Missouri Products Liability Handbook (1988); "Loss of Profit Damages," Damages Deskbook, Second Edition 2001, Missouri Bar Association; and the Missouri law chapter in "Architects, Engineers & Builders Liability" published by Aspen Press. *Member:* American Bar Association; American Judicature Society; Maritime Law Association of the United States (Proctor, 1982—); Lawyer-Pilots Bar Association; American Board of Trial Advocates (Advocate). (Certified as a Civil Trial Advocate by the National Board of Trial Advocacy). ***PRACTICE AREAS:*** Business Litigation. ***Email:*** jsandberg@spvg.com

G. KEITH PHOENIX, born Centralia, Illinois, August 13, 1946; admitted to bar, 1974, Missouri and Illinois. *Education:* Southern Illinois University (B.A., 1968); St. Louis University (J.D., cum laude, 1973). Member, Order of Woolsack. Co-Author: "Hospital Liability for the Acts of Independent Contractors: The Ostensible Agency Liability Theory," Vol. 30, No. 3, St. Louis University Law Journal Health Law Symposium, 1986. Legal Consultant, American Academy of Pediatrics, 1985-1991. *Member:* American Bar Association; American Board of Trial Advocates; Lawyers Association of St. Louis (President, 1986). [1st Lt., U.S. Army, Military Police Corps, 1969-1971]. ***PRACTICE AREAS:*** Products Liability; Medical Malpractice. ***Email:*** kphoenix@spvg.com

PETER VON GONTARD, born St. Louis, Missouri, March 20, 1948; admitted to bar, 1973, Missouri; 1974, Illinois; 1975, Florida. *Education:* St. Louis University (B.S., 1970; J.D., 1973). *Member:* St. Clair County, Madison County and American Bar Associations; The Florida Bar; Missouri Organization of Defense Lawyers; Defense Research Institute. ***PRACTICE AREAS:*** Medical Malpractice; Products Liability. ***Email:*** vongontard@spvg.com

JONATHAN RIES, born South Bend, Indiana, April 15, 1948; admitted to bar, 1974, Missouri; 1975, Illinois. *Education:* Duke University (B.A., 1971); University of Manchester, England; University of Notre Dame (J.D., 1974). *Member:* American Bar Association. ***PRACTICE AREAS:*** Medical Malpractice; Business Litigation. ***Email:*** jries@spvg.com

KENNETH W. BEAN, born Lexington, Kentucky, November 14, 1952; admitted to bar, 1977, Missouri; 1978, Illinois. *Education:* Washington University (A.B., 1974; J.D., 1977). Order of the Coif. Member, Editorial Board, Washington University Law Quarterly, 1976-1977. *Member:* Missouri Society of Hospital Attorneys. ***PRACTICE AREAS:*** Health Law; Medical Malpractice; Franchise Litigation; Employment Law. ***Email:*** kbean@spvg.com

REED W. SUGG, born Morganfield, Kentucky, December 1, 1952; admitted to bar, 1978, Missouri; 1979, Illinois. *Education:* Furman University (B.A., summa cum laude, 1975); Vanderbilt University (J.D., 1978). Phi Beta Kappa; Order of the Coif. Patrick Wilson Scholar in Law. *Member:* American Bar Association; Lawyer-Pilots Bar Association. ***PRACTICE AREAS:*** Products Liability; Aviation and Aerospace; Asbestos Defense. ***Email:*** rsugg@spvg.com

WARREN W. DAVIS, born St. Louis, Missouri, July 8, 1946; admitted to bar, 1971, Missouri; 1980, U.S. Tax Court; 1984, U.S. Court of Appeals, Eighth Circuit; U.S. Supreme Court (Not admitted in Illinois). *Education:* Washington University (A.B., 1968); Boston University (J.D., 1971). *Member:* American Bar Association. ***PRACTICE AREAS:*** Real Estate Law; Corporate Organization and Disputes Law; Banking Law; Representation of Lenders Law. ***Email:*** wdavis@spvg.com

MARY ANNE MELLOW, born Chicago, Illinois, June 9, 1957; admitted to bar, 1982, Illinois; 1984, Missouri. *Education:* Duke University (B.A., magna cum laude, 1979); Washington University (J.D., cum laude, 1982). *Member:* American Bar Association; Missouri Organization of Defense Lawyers. ***PRACTICE AREAS:*** Medical Malpractice; Products Liability; Business Litigation. ***Email:*** mmellow@spvg.com

KATHLEEN L. PINE, born Urbana, Illinois, May 2, 1957; admitted to bar, 1982, Missouri; 1984, Illinois. *Education:* Illinois State University (B.S., 1978); Southern Illinois University (J.D., 1982). Member: Mortar Board; National Moot Court. *Member:* American Bar Association. (Also at Carbondale, IL and St. Louis, MO Offices). ***PRACTICE AREAS:*** Medical Malpractice. ***Email:*** kpine@spvg.com

KEVIN P. KRUEGER, born Clayton, Missouri, October 13, 1959; admitted to bar, 1985, Missouri; 1988, U.S. District Court, Eastern District of Missouri, U.S. District Court, Southern District of Illinois, U.S. Court of Appeals, Eighth Circuit (Not admitted in Illinois). *Education:* University of Missouri-Columbia (A.B., 1982); Washington University (J.D., 1985). *Member:* American Bar Association. ***PRACTICE AREAS:*** Products Liability. ***Email:*** kkrueger@spvg.com

SCOTT GREENBERG, born Kansas City, Missouri, April 1, 1958; admitted to bar, 1983, Missouri; U.S. District Court, Eastern and Western Districts of Missouri; U.S. Court of Appeals, Eighth Circuit; U.S. Supreme Court (Not admitted in Illinois). *Education:* University of Missouri at Columbia (B.S.B.A., cum laude, 1980; J.D., 1983). Co-Author: "Chapter 11 Reorganization: Pre-Filing and Confirmation Issues," The St. Louis Bar Journal, Spring 1995. ***PRACTICE AREAS:*** Bankruptcy Law; Reorganization Law; Banks and Banking; Real Estate Law; Corporate Law; Commercial Law. ***Email:*** sgreenberg@spvg.com

ANDREW R. KASNETZ, born St. Louis, Missouri, March 20, 1956; admitted to bar, 1982, Missouri; 1983, U.S. District Court, Eastern District of Missouri and U.S. Court of Appeals, Eighth Circuit; 2001, Illinois. *Education:* University of Kansas (B.A., 1978); St. Louis University (J.D., 1981). Law Clerk to the Honorable John M. Karns, Jr., Illinois Appellate Court, Fifth Judicial District, 1981-1982. *Member:* American Bar Association. ***PRACTICE AREAS:*** Business Litigation; Appellate Practice; Family Law. ***Email:*** akasnetz@spvg.com

RODNEY M. SHARP, born Decatur, Illinois, February 19, 1960; admitted to bar, 1985, Illinois; 1987, Missouri. *Education:* Southern Illinois University, Carbondale (B.A., with honors, 1982; J.D., cum laude, 1985). Notes and Comments Editor, Southern Illinois University Law Journal, 1984-1985. Law Clerk, Hon. A. G. Webber, III, Appellate Court of Illinois, Fourth District, 1985-1986. *Member:* American Bar Association; Missouri Organization of Defense Lawyers. ***PRACTICE AREAS:*** Medical Malpractice; Business Litigation. ***Email:*** rsharp@spvg.com

STEPHEN M. STRUM, born Springfield, Illinois, October 14, 1963; admitted to bar, 1988, Missouri; 1989, Illinois. *Education:* Lincoln Land Community College (A.A., 1983); University of Illinois (B.A., 1985); St. Louis University (J.D., 1988). Recipient, Lon O. Hocker Memorial Trial Lawyer Award, 1999. Student Law Clerk to Hon. Charles W. Chapman, Circuit Judge, Illinois Circuit Court, Third Judicial Circuit, 1987. *Member:* American Bar Association; The Association of Trial Lawyers of America; Missouri Organization of Defense Lawyers; Product Liability Advisory Council. ***PRACTICE AREAS:*** Products Liability; Nursing Home Litigation; Medical Malpractice. ***Email:*** sstrum@spvg.com

LYNDON P. SOMMER, born Pana, Illinois, November 2, 1964; admitted to bar, 1992, Illinois; 1993, Missouri. *Education:* Southern Illinois University (B.S., 1987; M. Acct., 1989; J.D., 1992). Phi Delta Phi. Member, National Moot Court Team, 1990-1992. Member, Order of the Barristers. Editor-in Chief, Southern Illinois University Law Journal, 1991-1992. Certified Public Accountant, Illinois, 1991. *Member:* American Institute of Certified Public Accountants; Illinois Society of Certified Public Accountants. ***PRACTICE AREAS:*** Business Litigation; Professional Malpractice; Products Liability. ***Email:*** lsommer@spvg.com

ANTHONY L. MARTIN, born Ottawa, Illinois, December 18, 1952; admitted to bar, 1982, Illinois; 1984, Missouri. *Education:* Harding University; Illinois State University (B.S., with honors, 1975); Southern Illinois University (J.D., 1982). Order of Barristers. Research Editor, Southern Illinois University Law Journal, 1981-1982. *Member:* Illinois State and American Bar Associations; The Missouri Bar. ***PRACTICE AREAS:*** Class Actions; Products Liability; Insurance. ***Email:*** amartin@spvg.com

TERESA D. BARTOSIAK, born Alton, Illinois, March 26, 1969; admitted to bar, 1993, Missouri; 1994, Illinois. *Education:* University of Illinois (B.A., with high distinction, 1990); Washington University (J.D., 1993). Member, Moot Court Board. Judicial Law Clerk, Hon. William H. Crandall, Missouri Court of Appeals, Eastern District, 1993-1994. ***PRACTICE AREAS:*** Products Liability; Medical Malpractice. ***Email:*** tbartosiak@spvg.com

KEITH D. PRICE, born Mt. Vernon, Illinois, October 18, 1963; admitted to bar, 1989, Missouri; 1990, Illinois and U.S. District Court, Eastern District of Missouri; 1995, U.S. Court of Appeals, Eighth and Fourth Circuits. *Education:* University of Illinois (B.S., in Accounting, cum laude, 1985); Baylor University (J.D., 1988). Phi Alpha Delta. Research and Topics Editor, Baylor University Law Review, 1988. *Member:* American Bar Association. ***PRACTICE AREAS:*** Commercial Litigation; Bankruptcy Law; Reorganization Law. ***Email:*** kprice@spvg.com

ANTHONY SOUKENIK, born Gates Mill, Ohio, June 2, 1960; admitted to bar, 1986, Missouri; 1987, Illinois; 1988, United States Tax Court and U.S. District Court, Eastern District of Missouri. *Education:* St. Louis University (B.S.B.A., Accounting, cum laude, 1982; J.D., 1986); Washington University (LLM, Taxation, 1993). Phi Alpha Delta. Jesuit Honors Program, 1982. Law Clerk, for the Honorable James Reinhart and Honorable Kent Karohl, Missouri State Court of Appeals, Eastern District. Former Lecturer, St. Louis University. Past Member: Old Jamestown Area Planning Study, St. Louis County Planning Department; Metropolitan Sewar District, Stormwater System Improvement Plan, Public Advisory Committee. Member: Advisory Board Member, First National Bank of St. Louis; Trustee of the Metropolitan Sewer District, St. Louis, 2001; City of Hazelwood Board of Appeals; Missouri Department of Revenue Advisory Committee. President, Community Association Institute, St. Louis Chapter, 1988. National Association of Security Dealer Arbitrator. *Member:* Bar Association of Metropolitan St. Louis (Member: Board of Governors, 1995-1997; Budget Committee, 1993-1995, 1996-1999; Chair: Real Estate Committee, 1994-1995; Clayton Facility Task Force, 1997-1999; Co-Chair, Economic Develop-

(This Listing Continued)

ment Committee, 1997-1999; Director, DePaul Hospital Foundation); Illinois State Bar Association; The Missouri Bar. **PRACTICE AREAS:** Banking; Corporate; Estate Planning; Real Estate; State Taxation; Federal Taxation. **Email:** asoukenik@spvg.com

MICHAEL E. BUB, born St. Louis, Missouri, July 9, 1962; admitted to bar, 1987, Missouri; 1990, Illinois. *Education:* St. Louis University (B.S., 1984; J.D., 1987). Articles Editor, St. Louis University Law Journal, 1985-1987. Law Clerk to the Hon. Gary M. Gaertner, Missouri Court of Appeals, 1987-1989. *Member:* The Missouri Bar; Illinois State Bar Association. **PRACTICE AREAS:** Products Liability. **Email:** mbub@paulhastings.com

STEPHEN P. NIEMIRA, born St. Louis, Missouri, September 13, 1967; admitted to bar, 1992, Missouri; 1995, Illinois; U.S. District Court, Eastern District of Missouri, U.S. District Court, Southern and Central Districts of Illinois, U.S. Court of Appeals, Seventh and Eighth Circuits and U.S. Supreme Court. *Education:* University of Missouri (A.B., 1989; J.D., 1992). Judicial Law Clerk to the Hon. Paul J. Simon, Missouri Court of Appeals, Eastern District, 1992-1994. *Member:* Bar Association of Metropolitan St. Louis; The Missouri Bar (Member: Professionalism Committee; Insurance Law Committee); Maritime Law Association of the United States. **PRACTICE AREAS:** Business Litigation.

Our lawyers are members of the Missouri and Illinois State Bar Associations and all the major local bar associations in the St. Louis metropolitan area, including those in southern Illinois.

(For complete biographical data on all personnel, see Professional Biographies at St. Louis, Missouri)

WILLIAM W. SCHOOLEY

BELLEVILLE, ILLINOIS

(See Granite City)

Plaintiff, Trial and Appellate Practice. Workers Compensation Law.

THOMPSON COBURN LLP

525 WEST MAIN STREET
BELLEVILLE, ILLINOIS 62222-0730
Telephone: 618-277-4700; 314-271-1800
Telecopier: 618-236-3434
For attorney e-mail use: first initial of first name, last name@thompsoncoburn.com, e.g. aallred@thompsoncoburn.com
Email: info@thompsoncoburn.com
URL: http://www.thompsoncoburn.com

St. Louis, Missouri Office: One US Bank Plaza. Telephone: 314-552-6000. Telecopier: 314-552-7000.
Washington, D.C. Office: 1909 K Street N.W., Suite 600. Telephone: 202-585-6900. Telecopier: 202-585-6969.

Admiralty, Appellate Litigation, Bankruptcy, Environmental, Government Contracts, Government, Health Care, Human Resources, Intellectual Property, Litigation, Municipal, Product Liability, Railroad, Real Estate, Toxic Tort.

PARTNERS

THOMAS W. ALVEY, JR., admitted to bar, 1966, Illinois; 1985, Missouri; 1994, West Virginia. *Education:* Virginia Military Institute (B.A., 1961); Washington University (J.D., 1966). Fellow, American College of Trial Lawyers. **PRACTICE AREAS:** Litigation; Personal Injury; Railroad Law. **Email:** talvey@thompsoncoburn.com

HARLAN A. HARLA, admitted to bar, 1985, Illinois; 1986, Missouri. *Education:* Southern Illinois University (B.S., 1978; J.D., cum laude, 1985). **PRACTICE AREAS:** Railroad Litigation; Personal Injury Defense. **Email:** hharla@thompsoncoburn.com

THOMAS E. JONES, admitted to bar, 1979, Illinois; 1981, U.S. District Court, Southern District of Illinois; 1985, Missouri and U.S. District Court, Eastern District of Missouri; 1995, U.S. District Court, Central District of Illinois. *Education:* Southern Illinois University (B.S., 1976; J.D., 1979). **PRACTICE AREAS:** Railroad Litigation; Products Liability; Transportation. **Email:** tjones@thompsoncoburn.com

KURT E. REITZ, admitted to bar, 1984, Illinois; 1985, Missouri. *Education:* University of Illinois (B.A., with high distinction, 1981; J.D., 1984). **PRACTICE AREAS:** Products Liability; Railroad Law; Class Actions. **Email:** kreitz@thompsoncoburn.com

ASSOCIATES

CORRINE M. GARNHART, admitted to bar, 2002, Illinois; 2003, Missouri and U.S. District Court, Southern District of Illinois. *Education:* University of Kentucky (B.A., 1999); Southern Illinois University (J.D., 2002). **PRACTICE AREAS:** Toxic Tort; Railroad Law. **Email:** cgarnhart@thompsoncoburn.com

HEATH H. HOOKS, admitted to bar, 1993, Illinois; 1999, Missouri. *Education:* Southern Illinois University (B.A., 1990; J.D., 1993). **PRACTICE AREAS:** Railroad Law; Defense Litigation; Appellate Practice. **Email:** hhooks@thompsoncoburn.com

KEVIN C. McGINLEY, (admission pending). *Education:* University of Illinois (B.A., 2002); Washington University (J.D., 2005). **PRACTICE AREAS:** Litigation; Railroad Law. **Email:** kmcginley@thompsoncoburn.com

CRYSTAL M. PIPHER, admitted to bar, 2005, Illinois and Missouri. *Education:* Eastern Illinois University (B.A., summa cum laude, 2002); Southern Illinois University (J.D., magna cum laude, 2004). **PRACTICE AREAS:** Railroad Litigation. **Email:** cpipher@thompsoncoburn.com

MARIE SPACCAROTELLA, admitted to bar, 2004, Illinois; 2005, Missouri, U.S. District Court, Northern and Southern Districts of Illinois and U.S. District Court, Eastern and Western Districts of Missouri. *Education:* University of Michigan (B.A., Economics, 2001); Washington University School of Law (J.D., 2004). (Member, Associate Committee). **PRACTICE AREAS:** Litigation; Torts; Railroad Law. **Email:** mspaccarotella@thompsoncoburn.com

(This Listing Continued)

ERICK E. VANDORN, admitted to bar, 1998, Illinois; 1999, Missouri. *Education:* Eastern Illinois University (B.A., cum laude, 1995); University of Illinois (J.D., cum laude, 1998). **PRACTICE AREAS:** Railroad Law; Labor Law; Tort Defense; Litigation. **Email:** evandorn@thompsoncoburn.com

REPRESENTATIVE CLIENTS: Ameren UE; Ameritech; Anderson Hospital; Burlington Northern Santa Fe; Canadian National/Illinois Central Railroad Co.; Clark Oil & Refining Corporation; Deere & Company; Diamond-Star Motors Corporation; FKG, Oil; Freightliner Corporation; General Motors Corp.; The Goodyear Tire & Rubber Company; Harcros Pigments, Inc.; Holland-Hinrichs, Inc.; The Kilian Corporation; Mitsubishi Corporation; Montgomery Kone, Inc.; New Holland North America, Inc.; Nissan Motor Corporation in U.S.A.; Norfolk Southern Corp.; Peabody Coal Company; Shoney's Inc.; Shop N Save Warehouse Foods, Inc.; Supervalue, Inc.; Toyota Motor Sales, U.S.A. Inc.; U-Haul International, Inc.; Union Pacific Railroad Company; Union Planters Banks; The Upjohn Company; Volkswagen of America, Inc.

WALKER & WILLIAMS

PROFESSIONAL CORPORATION
Established in 1970
4343 WEST MAIN STREET
BELLEVILLE, ILLINOIS 62226
Telephone: 618-274-1000; 277-1000
Telecopier: 618-233-1637
Email: waw@wawpc.net
URL: http://www.lawyers.com/walkerwilliams

General Trial and Appellate Practice in Federal and State Courts, including Automobile, Environmental, Civil Rights, Products Liability, Fire and Insurance Law, Railroad Defense, Governmental Liability, Professional Liability and Third Party Insurance Defense.

RALPH D. WALKER (1906-1988)
WAYNE P. WILLIAMS (1904-1990)
JOHN B. GUNN (1933-2001)

DAVID B. STUTSMAN, born St. Louis, Missouri, January 1, 1929; admitted to bar, 1953, Illinois. *Education:* University of Oklahoma; Washington University; University of Illinois (B.S., 1951; LL.B., 1953). Phi Alpha Delta. *Member:* East St. Louis, St. Clair County and American Bar Associations. Fellow, American College of Trial Lawyers; American Board of Trial Advocates; National Association of Railroad Trial Counsel. **PRACTICE AREAS:** Insurance; Railroad Defense; Environmental Law.

DONALD J. DAHLMANN, born Belleville, Illinois, February 21, 1948; admitted to bar, 1973, Illinois. *Education:* Southern Illinois University (B.A., 1970); St. Louis University (J.D., 1973). *Member:* St. Clair County (President, 1997-1998), Illinois State and American Bar Associations; National Association of Railroad Trial Counsel; Defense Research Institute; Illinois Association of Defense Trial Counsel. **PRACTICE AREAS:** Railroad; Insurance Defense; Products Liability. **Email:** djd@wawpc.net

DALE L. BODE, born Edwardsville, Illinois, September 13, 1945; admitted to bar, 1976, Illinois; 1985, Missouri. *Education:* Southern Illinois University (B.A., 1967; M.A., 1969); University of Missouri (J.D., 1976). *Member:* Madison County, St. Clair County and Illinois State Bar Associations; American Judicature Society; National Association of Railroad Trial Counsel. **PRACTICE AREAS:** Insurance; Railroad Defense; Automobile Accidents and Injuries. **Email:** dlb@wawpc.net

JAMES C. COOK, born Quincy, Illinois, October 4, 1951; admitted to bar, 1976, Illinois; 1984, Missouri. *Education:* Quincy University ; University of Illinois (B.A., 1973); Loyola University of Chicago (J.D., 1976). Law Clerk to Justice John T. Reardon, Illinois Appellate Court, Fourth District, 1976-1978. *Member:* The Bar Association of Metropolitan St. Louis; Chicago and Illinois State Bar Associations; The Missouri Bar; Defense Research Institute; Illinois Association of Defense Trial Counsel; Illinois Institute for Local Government Law. **PRACTICE AREAS:** Insurance; Civil Rights; Governmental Liability. **Email:** jcc@wawpc.net

PAUL P. WALLER III, born East St. Louis, Illinois, January 20, 1955; admitted to bar, 1980, Illinois. *Education:* University of Notre Dame (B.A., 1977); St. Louis University (J.D., 1980). Law Clerk to U.S. District Judge William Beatty, Southern District of Illinois, 1980-1981. *Member:* St. Clair County and Illinois State Bar Associations. **PRACTICE AREAS:** Insurance Defense; Litigation. **Email:** ppw@wawpc.net

---

LESLIE OFFERGELD, born Hinsdale, Illinois, November 9, 1962; admitted to bar, 1987, Illinois; 1988, Missouri. *Education:* Black Hawk College (A.A.S., 1982); University of Illinois (B.A., 1984); Southern Illinois University (J.D., 1987). Phi Alpha Delta. *Member:* St. Clair County, Illinois State and American Bar Associations; The Missouri Bar; National Association of Railroad Trial Counsel. **PRACTICE AREAS:** Insurance Defense; Railroad Defense; Appeals. **Email:** lgo@wawpc.net

CHRISTIAN CAGAS, born Manila, Philippines, April 30, 1968; admitted to bar, 2002, Illinois. *Education:* University of Illinois (B.S., 1990); St. Louis University (J.D., 1999). *Member:* St. Clair County, Illinois State and American Bar Associations; Illinois Association of Defense Trial Counsel. **PRACTICE AREAS:** Insurance Defense; Real Estate; Corporate Law. **Email:** cc@wawpc.net

J. KENNETH GRAHAM, III, born Wiesbaden, Germany, June 25, 1970; admitted to bar, 1999, Missouri; 2000, Illinois and U.S. District Court, Eastern District of Missouri; 2003, U.S. District Court, Southern District of Illinois. *Education:* University of Central Oklahoma (B.A., 1993); St. Louis University (J.D., 1999). **Email:** jkg@wawpc.net

REPRESENTATIVE CLIENTS: AlliedSignal Inc.; Allstate Insurance Co.; The Alton & Southern Railway Co.; Consolidated Rail Corp.; CSX Transportation, Inc.; Farmers Insurance Group; Firemen's Fund American Insurance Cos.; Governmental Insurance Managers; Governmental Interinsurance Exchange; Hanover Insurance Co.; Madison Mutual Insurance Co.; National Casualty Insurance Co.; National Fire & Casualty Co.; Nautilus Insurance Co.; St. Louis Southwestern Railway Co.; St. Paul Fire & Marine Insurance Co.; Scottsdale Insurance Co.; Sears, Roebuck & Co.; Standard Mutual Insurance Co.; Titan Indemnity Co.; United States Fidelity & Guaranty Co.; Union Pacific Railroad Co.

WILLIAMS VENKER & SANDERS LLC

Established in 2001

23 SOUTH FIRST STREET
BELLEVILLE, ILLINOIS 62220
Telephone: 314-345-5000
Fax: 314-345-5055
URL: http://www.lawyers.com/wvslaw
Email: wvs@wvslaw.com
URL: http://www.wvslaw.com

St. Louis, Missouri Office: 10 South Broadway, Suite 1600, 63102. Phone: 314-345-5000. Fax: 314-345-5055.

Edwardsville, Illinois Office: 111 E. Vandalia Street, Suite 3, 62025. Phone: 618-659-9100. Fax: 618-659-9125.

Aviation, Business Litigation, Employment Discrimination Litigation, Environmental Litigation, FELA, Health Care Litigation, Insurance Defense, Labor and Employment, Maritime, Medical Malpractice Defense, Occupational Disease Litigation, Premises Liability Defense, Product Liability Defense, Railroad Litigation, Toxic Torts, Transportation Litigation.

REPRESENTATIVE CLIENTS: AIG Insurance; AIMCO, Anheuser-Busch Companies; Baker-Hughes, Inc.; Bayer Corporation; BJC Health System; Caterpiller Inc.; CNA (Encompass) Insurance; General Electric Co.; Goodyear Tire and Rubber Company; Group Health Plan; Harrah's, Inc.; Kraft Foods, Inc.; Marathon Oil Company; Maxon Corp.; National Railroad Passenger Corporation (Amtrak); Rockwell International; Shell Oil Co.; Unilever; Union Pacific Railroad Company; Unity Health System; Waste Management, Inc.

(For complete biographical data on all personnel, see Professional Biographies at St. Louis, Missouri)

SUSAN PARNELL WILSON

14 SOUTH SECOND STREET
BELLEVILLE, ILLINOIS 62220
Telephone: 618-235-1600
Fax: 618-235-1617
Email: susanwilsonlaw@norcom2000.com
URL: http://www.susanpwilson.com

Child Custody, Child Support, Divorce, Family Law, Paternity.

SUSAN PARNELL WILSON, born Olney, Illinois, November 19, 1950; admitted to bar, 1985, Illinois; 1986, Missouri. *Education:* Greenville College (B.A., 1972); Southern Illinois University (M.S., 1978); Saint Louis University (J.D., 1985). *Member:* St. Clair County and Illinois State (Member, Section: Family Law) Bar Associations; The Missouri Bar. **PRACTICE AREAS:** Child Custody; Child Support; Divorce; Family Law; Paternity.

TIMOTHY S. WILTSIE

120 WEST MAIN STREET, SUITE 207
BELLEVILLE, ILLINOIS 62220
Telephone: 618-235-5750
Fax: 618-257-9300
Email: wiltsielaw@peaknet.net
URL: http://www.wiltsielaw.com

Civil Trial and Appellate Practice, Family Law, Divorce, Child Support, Child Custody, Business Litigation, Business Transactions, Real Estate, Personal Injury, Wills, Trusts and Estates.

TIMOTHY S. WILTSIE, born Lackland Air Force Base, Texas, August 29, 1963; admitted to bar, 1990, California and U.S. District Court, Southern District of California; 1992, U.S. District Court, Northern District of California; 1994, Illinois and U.S. District Court, Southern District of Illinois; 1996, U.S. District Court, Eastern District of Missouri; 1999, Missouri and U.S. Court of Appeals, Seventh Circuit. *Education:* Georgetown University (B.S.F.S., 1985); Northwestern University (J.D., 1989). Pro-Bono Volunteer, Land of Lincoln Legal Assistance Foundation, Inc., 1995. Agent for Attorney's Title Guaranty Fund, Inc., 2000. Adjunct Instructor: McKendree College, 2003; Paralegal Program, Southwestern Illinois College, 1996. Adjunct Professor, Civil Practice, St. Louis University School of Law, 1998. Arbitrator, Illinois Supreme Court Mandatory Arbitration Program, 20th Judicial Circuit, 1996. Member, St. Clair County Bar Association Public Relations/Law Day Committee, 1995. *Member:* American and Illinois State Bar Associations; Bar Association of Metropolitan St. Louis.

ABATE & SMITH

BELVIDERE, ILLINOIS

(See Rockford)

Family Law including Divorce, Child Custody, Child Support, Spousal Support, Alimony, Visitation Rights, Distribution of Property, Paternity, Adoption Law, Personal Injury including Automobile Accidents and Injuries, Real Estate, Contracts.

STEVEN J. BRODY & ASSOCIATES, LTD

BELVIDERE, ILLINOIS

(See Crystal Lake)

Family Law including Divorce, Separation Agreements, Child Custody, Child Support, Visitation Rights, Spousal Support, Restraining Orders, Paternity, Adoptions, Pre-nuptial / post-nuptial Agreements, Bankruptcy including Chapter 7 & 13, Consumer Bankruptcy, Small Business Bankruptcy, Foreclosures, Repossessions.

CICERO & FRANCE, A PROFESSIONAL CORPORATION

BELVIDERE, ILLINOIS

(See Rockford)

Insurance Defense, First and Third Party Insurance Defense, Property and Casualty Defense, Automobile Insurance Defense, Business Law and Litigation including Family Owned Businesses, Fraud, Contracts, Employment Agreements, Business Sales and Acquisitions, Commercial Litigation, Family Law including Divorce, Child Custody, Child Support, Spousal Support, Alimony, Adoptions, Visitation Rights, Separation Agreements and Parenting Plans.

DANIEL A. CWYNAR

BELVIDERE, ILLINOIS

(See Rockford)

Bankruptcy including individual and small business, foreclosures, repossessions, chapter 7, chapter 13; Residential and Commercial Real Estate, Buying and Selling, Contracts, Criminal Defense, DUI, Traffic, Misdemeanors.

THE LAW FIRM OF FRANKS, GERKIN & McKENNA, P.C.

BELVIDERE, ILLINOIS

(See Marengo)

General, Civil & Criminal Trial Practice, Banking, Business Law, Commercial Real Estate, Corporate Law, Criminal Law, Debt Collections, Family Law, Personal Injury, Real Estate, Trusts & Estates, Immigration, Wills, Workers Compensation, Municipal Law, Traffic, Zoning, Planning and Land Use.

O'BRIEN, HEALY & ZUBA

BELVIDERE, ILLINOIS

(See Rockford)

Family Law including Divorce, Child Custody, Child Support, Visitation Rights, Spousal Support, Alimony, Paternity, Adoption Law, Qualified, Domestic Orders, QDRO's, Criminal Defense including White Collar, Criminal Defense, Felonies, Fraud, Litigation.

POLLOCK, MEYERS, EICKSTEADT & PULAK, LTD.

BELVIDERE, ILLINOIS

(See Marengo)

General Trial Practice, Appellate Practice, Estate Planning, Probate Law, Trust Law, Real Estate, Banking Law, Bankruptcy Law, Personal Injury, Workers Compensation, Administrative Law, Corporate Law, Contracts, Civil Litigation, Trusts and Estates, Real Estate Law.

CURT P. REHBERG

BELVIDERE, ILLINOIS

(See Crystal Lake)

Real Estate, including Commercial and Residential, Contracts, Closings, Land Acquisition and Sales, Land Trusts, Development, Investment, Joint Ventures, Partnerships; Wills, Trusts and Estate Planning, including Family Trusts, Living Trusts, Powers of Attorney, Business Succession Planning, Retirement Planning, Wealth Preservation; Business Law, including Contracts, Business Formation, Sole Proprietorships, Partnerships, Business Incorporation, Joint Ventures, Business Fraud, Buy-Sell Agreements.

LAW OFFICES OF HENRY REPAY

405 1/2 SOUTH STATE STREET
BELVIDERE, ILLINOIS 61008-3706
Telephone: 815-547-3369
Fax: 815-544-5429
Email: repaylawfirm@ithink2.net
URL: http://www.lawyers.com/repaylawfirm

General Practice, Real Estate, Commercial Real Estate, Residential Real Estate, Mortgages, Personal Bankruptcy, Consumer Bankruptcy, Debtor Bankruptcy, Chapter 7, Chapter 13, Nonprofit and Charitable Organizations, Guardianship, Adoptions.

HENRY REPAY, born Chicago, Illinois, February 14, 1963; admitted to bar, 1988, Illinois; 1989, U.S. District Court, Northern District of Illinois. *Education:* Loyola University of Chicago (B.A., 1985; J.D., 1988). Lecturer, American Government, Judson College, 1992. *Member:* Winnebago, Boone County and Illinois State Bar Associations; Christian Legal Society. **LANGUAGES:** Hungarian.

THE SZYMANSKI KOROLL LITIGATION GROUP

BELVIDERE, ILLINOIS

(See Rockford)

Personal Injury, Wrongful Death, Medical Malpractice including Birth Injuries, Cancer, Failure to Diagnose and Misdiagnosis, Bar iatric Weight Loss Surgery, Obstetric, Surgical, Cardiac, Orthopedic, Nursing Malpractice, Nursing Home Abuse and Neglect including Bedsores,

(This Listing Continued)

Malnutrition, Falls, Physical Abuse, Medication Errors, Automobile Accidents and Injuries, Head, Neck and Back Injuries, Burns.

TOBIN & RAMON

530 SOUTH STATE STREET
SUITE 200
BELVIDERE, ILLINOIS 61008
Telephone: 815-544-0316
Fax: 815-544-4398
Email: tobinramon@mwci.net

General Practice. Business Litigation. Probate, School Law, Real Estate, Estate and Business Planning, Zoning and Family Law.

FIRM PROFILE: Tobin & Ramon was founded by Owen M. Johnson in 1935. Serving clients with a combined experience of over 70 years in the community. The geographic scope of the firm is throughout Boone, Winnebago and McHenry counties. The firm engages in a general practice with emphasis in Estate Administration and Planning, General Real Estate and Tax Law.

MEMBERS OF FIRM

CURTIS R. TOBIN, II, born Belvidere, Illinois, August 15, 1941; admitted to bar, 1965, Illinois. *Education:* Illinois Wesleyan University (B.S., 1963); University of Illinois (J.D., 1965). Counsel: School District #100, Belvidere, School District #200. . ATGF, Director, 1985—. *Member:* Boone County, Winnebago County and Illinois State (Member: Real Estate Law Section; General Assembly, 1980-1986; School Law Section, 1984-1986; Long Range Planning Committee, 1983-1987) Bar Associations. ***PRACTICE AREAS:*** Business Law; Estate Planning; Real Estate; Zoning Law; School Law; Estate Administration. **Email:** tobinramon@mwci.net

LOIS CANNELL RAMON, born Belvidere, Illinois, December 1, 1949; admitted to bar, 1974, Illinois. *Education:* Eastern Illinois University (B.S., with high honors, 1971); University of Illinois (J.D., 1974). Notes and Comments Editor, University of Illinois Law Forum, 1973-1974. Author: "Recent Development, Trusts and Trustees, Right of a Surviving Spouse to Have a Totten Trust Included in His Deceased Spouse's Estate for Purposes of Determining His Statutory Share, 1973 University of Illinois Law Forum 775; Comment, "Criminal Law: Concurrent and Consecutive Sentencing," 1973 University of Illinois Law Forum 423. *Member:* Boone County, Winnebago County and Illinois State Bar Associations. ***PRACTICE AREAS:*** Estate Planning; Estate Administration; Real Estate; Family; Business. **Email:** tobinramon@mwci.net

REPRESENTATIVE CLIENTS: Belvidere National Bank; Community Unit School District 100; Community Unit School District 200; Garden Prairie Grain Co.; Gallano Farms, Ltd.; Heritage Engineering, Ltd.; Growth Dimensions for Belvidere-Boone County, Inc.; Boone County Housing Authority; M & R Rubber Co., Inc.; Charles F. Lee & Sons, Inc.; Buck-Wheeler-Hyland Funeral Home, P.C.; Concordia Lanes, Inc.; Youngberg Industries; Rockford Toolcraft, Inc.; Wolf Chevrolet; Belvidere Construction Company; Elmhurst-Chicago Stone Company, Inc.; K-B Farms, Inc.; Louis Silver Scrap Iron & Metal Co; Edwards Apple Orchard; Jack Wolf Pontiac/Cadillac.; Poplar Grove Airport; Dare Cloud Development, Inc.; Landmark Development, Inc.; Kennedy Homes Limited Partnership; All World Machinery Supply, Inc.

PRATO & ASSOCIATES, P.C.

BENSENVILLE, ILLINOIS

(See Oak Brook)

Real Estate Transactions, Bankruptcy, Small Businesses, Corporate, Criminal, DUI, Personal Injury and Immigration Law.

BARRETT, TWOMEY, BROOM, HUGHES & HOKE, LLP

BENTON, ILLINOIS

(See Carbondale)

Banking, Estate Planning, Real Estate, Civil Trials and Appeals.

CRAIG & CRAIG

BENTON, ILLINOIS

(See Mount Vernon)

General Practice in State and Federal Courts. Coal, Oil, Gas, Mining, Insurance, Drainage and Levee Law, Environmental, Corporation, Labor Relations, Workers Compensation and Real Estate Law. Estate Planning and Probate. Trials and Appeals.

FEIRICH/MAGER/GREEN/RYAN

BENTON, ILLINOIS

(See Carbondale)

General Trial and Appellate Litigation, Business, Probate, Trust, Real Estate, Insurance Law, Worker's Compensation, Banking and Corporation Law, Intellectual Property and Healthcare Law.

HART AND HART

Established in 1887
602 WEST PUBLIC SQUARE
P.O. BOX 937
BENTON, ILLINOIS 62812-0937
Telephone: 618-435-8123
Telecopier: 618-435-2962
URL: http://www.harthart.com

General Trial and Appellate Practice in State and Federal Courts. Probate, Trust, Real Estate Deeds and Title Insurance, Bankruptcy (Creditors), Traffic, Banking, Business, Commercial and Corporation Law and Creditor Collections, Employment Law.

WILLIAM H. HART (1862-1941)
WILLIAM W. HART (1894-1968)
MARION M. HART (1896-1964)
WILLIAM W. HART, JR. (1925-1996)

RICHARD O. HART, born Benton, Illinois, December 13, 1927; admitted to bar, 1954, Illinois; U.S. District Court, Southern District of Illinois; 1986, U.S. Court of Appeals, Seventh Circuit. *Education:* University of Illinois (A.B., 1951); Washington University (J.D., 1954). Phi Delta Phi. State Representative, Illinois General Assembly, 59th District, 1968-1978. *Member:* Franklin County, Illinois State Bar Association (Member, Elder Law Section Council; Member, Legislation Committee). Fellow: American College of Trust and Estate Counsel; American Law Institute. ***PRACTICE AREAS:*** Litigation; Real Estate; Probate; Trusts and Estates; Estate Planning; Elder Law; Banking Law. ***Email:*** dickh@harthart.com

MURPHY C. HART, born Benton, Illinois, April 6, 1957; admitted to bar, 1983, Illinois; U.S. District Court, Southern District of Illinois; 1986, U.S. Court of Appeals, Seventh Circuit; 1991, Missouri. *Education:* Eastern Illinois University (B.A., 1980); Southern Illinois University (J.D., 1983). Director, Illinois State Bar Mutual Insurance Company. *Member:* Franklin County and Illinois State (Chair, Judicial Polling) Bar Associations; The Illinois Creditors Bar Association; Commercial Law League of America; Illinois Real Estate Lawyers Association. ***PRACTICE AREAS:*** Creditor Collections; Real Estate; Title Insurance; Traffic Violations. **Email:** murphyh@harthart.com

A. COURTNEY COX, born Christopher, Illinois, July 26, 1952; admitted to bar, 1982, Illinois and U.S. District Court, Central District of Illinois; 1984, U.S. District Court, Southern District of Illinois; 1986, U.S. Court of Appeals, Seventh Circuit; U.S. Supreme Court. *Education:* Illinois Wesleyan University (B.M., 1974); Southern Methodist University (M.M., 1976); Southern Illinois University (J.D., 1982). *Member:* Franklin County and Illinois State Bar Associations. ***PRACTICE AREAS:*** Federal Litigation; ERISA; Employment Discrimination. **Email:** courtc@harthart.com

REPRESENTATIVE CLIENTS: State Bank of Whittington; Credit Bureau Systems, Inc.; Walgreen Co.; Asset Acceptance, LLC; Old National Bank; Canter-Jones Lumber.

McMAHON, BERGER, HANNA, LINIHAN, CODY & McCARTHY

A PROFESSIONAL CORPORATION

BENTON, ILLINOIS

(See Collinsville)

Labor Relations, Civil Rights and Administrative Law, Employment Litigation in all Courts.

LAW OFFICE OF TERRY SHARP, P.C.

105 NORTH MAIN STREET
BENTON, ILLINOIS 62812
Telephone: 618-435-5109
Fax: 618-242-1170
Email: law@lotsharp.com
URL: http://www.lawyers.com/tsharp

Mailing Address: 1115 Harrison Street, P.O. Box 906, Mount Vernon, IL 62864

Mount Vernon, Illinois Office: 1115 Harrison Street, P. O. Box 906. Telephone: 618-242-0246. Telecopier: 618-242-1170.

Bankruptcy, Creditor's Rights, Commercial, Banking, Real Estate, Corporate, Probate and Estate Planning Law. No small collections.

FIRM PROFILE: The firm has extensive experience in creditor's remedies, inside and outside of bankruptcy, has represented most of the bankruptcy trustees who serve in the Southern District of Illinois, and has also represented a large number of debtors. In addition to bankruptcy law, the firm also practices in the areas of commercial, banking, real estate, corporate, probate and estate planning law throughout its geographic area. Firm is issuing agent for 4 title insurance companies and has a staff of abstractors providing real estate title searches throughout Southern Illinois. The firm maintains its main office in Mt. Vernon with a branch office in Benton. The firm's central location allows easy access to all bankruptcy and circuit courts in the Southern District of Illinois. Terry Sharp, senior attorney, has lectured at numerous professional and trade seminars, has published several articles dealing with bankruptcy and accounting issues.

TERRELL LEE SHARP, born Mt. Vernon, Illinois, July 28, 1944; admitted to bar, 1973, Illinois and U.S. District Court, Southern District of Illinois; 1986, U.S. Court of Appeals, Seventh Circuit; 1991, U.S. Supreme Court. *Education:* University of Illinois (B.S., 1970; J.D., 1973). Certified Public Accountant, Illinois, 1969. Certified Fraud Exam-

(This Listing Continued)

LAW OFFICE OF TERRY SHARP, P.C., Benton—Continued

iner, 1993. Author: "Bridging the Gap," Illinois Institute for Continuing Legal Education, 1978; "The Chapter 12 Trustee," Agricultural Bankruptcy Practice. . . A Field of Transition, 1987, Illinois Institute of Continuing Legal Education; "Ten Reasons to Lessen the Fears of Ag Lenders About Chapter 12 Bankruptcy," The Journal of Commercial Bank Lending, August, 1987; "Do You Need Bankruptcy Advice?" Northwest Oil World, May, 1987; "Make My Day: Ten Reasons Why a Banker Should Not Necessarily Fear a Chapter 12 Bankruptcy Proceeding," Norton Bankruptcy Law Advisor, June, 1987; "Defining Value," The Journal of Commercial Lending, January 1996. Planning Chairman, Secured Transaction Procedures in Illinois, Basic and Advanced Course, I.I.C.L.E., 1988. Lecturer, Commercial Bankruptcy and Banking Seminar, IICLE, 1989. Editor, Southern Illinois Bankruptcy Institute, 1991—. *Member:* Jefferson County (President, 1975), Illinois State Bar Associations; Illinois Trial Lawyers Association. ***REPORTED CASES:*** In re Atchison, 925 F.2d 209 (7th Cir. 1991), US Cert. Den. 112 S.Ct. 178; In re Tomer, 128 B.R. 746 (Bankr. S.D. Ill. 1991); In re McDowell, 87 B.R. 554 (Bankr. S.D. Ill. 1988); Veath vs. Specialty Grains, Inc., 190 Ill.App.3d 787, 137 Ill.Dec. 892, 546 N.E.2d 1005 (5th Dist. 1989); Home Federal Sav. & Loan Ass'n of Centralia vs. Cook, 170 Ill.App.3d 720, 121 Ill.Dec. 345, 525 N.E.2d 151 (5th Dist. 1988); Anna National Bank vs. Prater, 154 Ill.App.3d 6, 107 Ill.Dec. 26, 506 N.E.2d 769 (5th Dist. 1987); In re Tomer, 147 B.R. 461 (S.D.Ill. 1992); In re Chenoweth, 132 B.R. 161 (Bankr. S.D.Ill. 1991), aff'd 143 B.R. 527 (S.D.Ill. 1992), aff'd 3 F.3d 1111 (7th Cir. 1993); Deason vs. Gutzler, 622 N.E.2d 1276 (Ill.App. 5th Dist. 1993); Farm Credit Bank of St. Louis v. Dorr, 620 N.E.2d 549 (Ill. App. 5th Dist. 1993); Knight's Prairie Hunting Club, Inc. vs. Holmes, 636 N.E.2d 29 (Ill.App.5th Dist. 1994). ***PRACTICE AREAS:*** Bankruptcy (30%); Creditor; Real Estate (8%); Real Estate Title Insurance (20%); Banks and Banking (15%); Foreclosure Law (15%); Litigation (5%); Collections (5%); Estate Planning (2%). ***Email:*** law@lotsharp.com

JOHN T. HUNDLEY, born Abilene, Kansas, October 13, 1948; admitted to bar, 1979, Illinois and U.S. District Court, Northern District of Illinois, including Trial Bar; 1980, U.S. Court of Appeals, Seventh Circuit; 1981, U.S. District Court, Northern District of California; 1983, U.S. District Court, Central District of Illinois; 2001, U.S. District Court, Southern District of Illinois. *Education:* University of Illinois (B.S., with honors, 1970); DePaul University (J.D., with honors, 1979). Author: "'Inadvertent Waiver' of Evidentiary Privileges: Can Reformulating the Question Lead to More Sensible Decisions?" 19 S. Illinois Univ. L. J. 263 (1995); "Business Expansion Through Asset Acquisition: Some Problems Posed By Product Liability Doctrines," 77 Ill. B. J. 492 (1989); "White Knights, Pre-Nuptial Confidences, and the Morning After: The Effect of Transaction-Related Disclosures on the Attorney-Client and Related Privileges," 5 DePaul Bus. L. J. 59 (1992-1993); "Waiver of Evidentiary Privilege by Inadvertent Disclosure-State Law," 51 A.L.R. 5th 603 (1997); "Waiver of Evidentiary Privilege by Inadvertent Disclosure-Federal Law," 159 A.L.R. Fed. 153 (2000); "Long Arms and Foreign Pockets: Can Multinational Financial Organizations Be Used To Subject Alien Defendants to the Enforcement of Illinois Judgments?" Chi. Bar Assn. Record 24 (Sept. 1990); "Assignments of Wages in Illinois: Pitfalls for Employer Businesses," 14 DePaul Bus. L.J. 21 (2001). Lecturer: Pretrial Civil Litigation, DePaul University College of Law (1990-1991); Debt Collection in Illinois, National Business Institute, Schaumburg, IL (2004). Partner, 1986-1990; Associate, 1979-1986, Mayer, Brown & Platt. *Member:* Illinois State and American Bar Associations; American Trial Lawyers Association. ***REPORTED CASES:*** Noyola v. Board of Ed. of City of Chicago, 179 Ill.2d 121, 688 N.E.2d 81 (1997); In re Fine Paper Antitrust Litigation, 685 F.2d 810 (3rd Cir. 1983); Grant v. Board of Ed. of City of Chicago, 282 Ill.App.3d 1011, 668 N.E.2d 1188 (1996); Stewart v. EGNEP (Pty) Limited, 581 F.Supp. 788 (C.D.Ill. 1983); Ford Motor Credit Co. v. Aaron Lincoln-Mercury, Inc., 563 F.Supp. 1108 (N.D.Ill. 1983); Ford Motor Credit Co. v. Aaron Lincoln-Mercury, Inc., 563 F.Supp. 1118 (N.D.Ill. 1983); In re Torres, 191 B.R. 735 (Bankr. N.D.Ill. 1996). ***PRACTICE AREAS:*** Civil Litigation (75%); Business Law; Collections; Commercial Law; Contracts; Chancery and Equity. ***Email:*** jhundley@lotsharp.com

REPRESENTATIVE CLIENTS: Housing Authority of the City of Mt. Vernon; N.E. Mt. Vernon Water Co.; Peoples National Bank; South Pointe Bank; Preferred Bank; Illinois Community Bank.
LOCAL COUNSEL FOR: Agco; Farm Credit Leasing; Case Credit Corp.; Fifth Third Bank; Daimler Chrysler; Bombardier Capital, Inc.

TROUTT POPIT & WARNER, P.C.

Established in 1977

105 NORTH MAIN STREET
P.O. BOX 548
BENTON, ILLINOIS 62812
Telephone: 618-439-9427; 438-2200
Fax: 618-435-3916
Email: bentonlaw@onecliq.net
URL: http://www.lawyers.com/trouttalexander

General Civil and Criminal Practice in all State and Federal Courts. Trials and Appeals. Personal Injury, Worker's Compensation, Criminal/Traffic Defense, Municipal Law, Probate Cases and Wills, Real Estate, Collections, Creditor Litigation, Adoptions, Family Law and Mediations.

JEFF TROUTT, born Du Quoin, Illinois, December 29, 1939; admitted to bar, 1969, Illinois; 1970, U.S. District Court, Southern District of Illinois. *Education:* Southern Illinois University (B.A., 1961); University of Illinois (J.D., 1969).

PETER E. POPIT, born Waukegan, Illinois, June 17, 1951; admitted to bar, 1978, Illinois and U.S. District Court, Southern District of Illinois. *Education:* University of Notre Dame (B.A., cum laude, 1973); Southern Illinois University (J.D., cum laude, 1977).

EDWINA DAUM WARNER, born Decatur, Illinois, October 5, 1948; admitted to bar, 1981, Illinois; 1982, U.S. District Court, Southern District of Illinois. *Education:* Illinois State University (B.S., 1970); Memphis State University (J.D., 1981).

PRATO & ASSOCIATES, P.C.

BERWYN, ILLINOIS

(See Oak Brook)

Real Estate Transactions, Bankruptcy, Small Businesses, Corporate, Criminal, DUI, Personal Injury and Immigration Law.

THE LAW OFFICES OF MICHAEL J. VITALE

6332 W. 26TH STREET
BERWYN, ILLINOIS 60402
Telephone: 708-795-0055
Fax: 708-795-0059
Email: mvitale1@sbcglobal.net
URL: http://www.michaelvitalelaw.com

Family Law, Child Support, Domestic Relations, Divorce, Criminal Law, Felonies, Driving While Intoxicated.

MICHAEL J. VITALE, admitted to bar, 1980, Illinois. *Education:* Loyola University (B.A., 1975; LL.M., Child and Family Law, 2002); Northern Illinois University, DeKalb (J.D., 1981).

LAW OFFICES OF LEASA J. BAUGHER, LTD.

Established in 2005

125 EAST LAKE STREET, SUITE 304
BLOOMINGDALE, ILLINOIS 60108
Telephone: 630-529-2050
Fax: 630-529-2051
Email: lbaugher@baugherlaw.com
URL: http://www.baugherlaw.com

Estate Planning, Elder Law, Wills and Trusts, Powers of Attorney, Probate and Trust Administration, Real Estate, Employee Benefits (ERISA).

LEASA J. BAUGHER, born Shelbyville, Illinois, August 22, 1963; admitted to bar, 2002, Illinois, U.S. District Court, Northern District of Illinois and U.S. Tax Court. *Education:* Northeastern Illinois University (B.S., 1997); John Marshall Law School (J.D., 2001; LL.M., Employee Benefits, 2001). *Member:* Chicago, Du Page County, Illinois State and American Bar Associations. ***PRACTICE AREAS:*** Estate Planning; Wills; Trust Law; Probate; Guardianship; Business Law; Retirement Planning; Employee Benefits; ERISA; Employment Law. ***Email:*** lbaugher@baugherlaw.com

---

LAW OFFICE OF GREGORY J. MARTUCCI, P.C.

BLOOMINGDALE, ILLINOIS

(See Roselle)

Bankruptcy, Criminal Law, Driving While Intoxicated, Juvenile Criminal Law, Traffic Violations, Domestic Violence, Personal Injury, Automobile Accidents and Injuries, Slip and Fall, Workers Compensation.

LAW OFFICES OF WARREN PRESCOTT

181 S. BLOOMINGDALE ROAD, SUITE 103
BLOOMINGDALE, ILLINOIS 60108
Telephone: 630-924-8052
Fax: 630-924-8057
Email: prescott@lawyer.com
URL: http://www.livingrevocabletrusts.com

Estate Planning, Probate and Wills, Real Estate.

WARREN PRESCOTT, born Chicago, Illinois, May 6, 1951; admitted to bar, 1978, Illinois; 1981, California; 1994, U.S. Supreme Court. *Education:* University of Illinois (B.A., 1973); John Marshall Law School (J.D., 1978). Arbitrator, Eighteenth Judicial Circuit, 1998-2004. ***PRACTICE AREAS:*** Estate Planning; Probate; Wills; Real Estate.

JOHN M. QUINN & ASSOCIATES, LTD.

Established in 1999

125 SOUTH BLOOMINGDALE ROAD, SUITE 11
BLOOMINGDALE, ILLINOIS 60108-1216
Telephone: 630-529-2000
Toll Free: 877-NO-WALKIN
Fax: 630-894-2528
URL: http://www.jmqlaw.com
Email: drive@jmqlaw.com
URL: http://www.lawyers.com/jmqlaw

Drivers License Suspension, Administrative Hearings, Driving While Intoxicated, Criminal Law, Traffic Violations, Criminal Defense, Misdemeanors.

(This Listing Continued)

JOHN M. QUINN, born Mount Greenwood, Illinois, May 28, 1966; admitted to bar, 1993, Illinois. *Education:* Valparaiso University (B.S., Accounting, 1988); DePaul University (J.D., 1992). Pi Kappa Alpha. Instructor, Rules of Evidence, Illinois State Police Academy, 1998. Judicial Legal Assistant, Office of the Chief Judge, Cook County, 1993-1995. Assistant States Attorney, DuPage County States Attorney's Office, 1995-1999. *Member:* DuPage County and Illinois State Bar Associations. ***LANGUAGES:*** Spanish. **Email:** drive@jmqlaw.com

Language: Spanish.

LAW OFFICE OF JONATHAN A. BACKMAN

Established in 2001

117 NORTH CENTER

BLOOMINGTON, ILLINOIS 61701-1640

Telephone: 309-820-7420

Fax: 309-820-7430

URL: http://www.BackLawOffice.com

Email: jbackman@BackLawOffice.com

URL: http://www.lawyers.com/backmanlaw

Trial Practice, Appellate Practice, Bankruptcy, Corporate Reorganization, Civil Rights, Criminal Defense and Employment Law.

JONATHAN A. BACKMAN, born Brooklyn, New York, October 30, 1962; admitted to bar, 1987, Illinois and U.S. District Court, Northern and Central Districts of Illinois; 1990, U.S. Court of Appeals, Fifth Circuit; 1992, U.S. District Court, Eastern District of Michigan; 2001, U.S. Court of Appeals, Fourth Circuit; 2004, U.S. Court of Appeals, Seventh Circuit. *Education:* Harvard University (B.A., magna cum laude, 1984; J.D., cum laude, 1987). Judicial Clerkship to Judge Brian Barnett Duff, U.S. District Court, Northern District of Illinois, 1987-1989. Associate, Schopf & Weiss, 1989-1991. Senior Associate, Mayer, Brown & Platt, 1991-1995. Partner: Gould & Ratner, 1995-1997; Rudnick & Wolfe, 1997-1999. Counsel, Schopf & Weiss, 1999-2000. Board of Director, Central Illinois Center for Indepentant Living. Legal Analyst for WJBC Radio 1230AM Bloomington Bankruptcy Strategist, Board of Contributors. Author: Kaplan and Backman, "Civil RICO Claims in Bankruptcy"; Civil RICO Practice: Causes of Action, 1991 and 1993 Supp.; Gilford, Backman and Rosenthal, "Alternatives to Insurance Liquidation, a U.S. Perspective," 4 Int'l J. Ins. L. 218, October 1994; Prager and Backman, "Pursuing Alter-Ego Liability Against Non-Bankrupt Third Parties: Structuring a Comprehensive Conceptual Framework," 35 St. Louis J. J. 657, Spring 1991; Backman, "Hartford Insurance Revisited: Sellers Beware," Bankruptcy Strategist, September 2001; Backman and Naughton, "Challenges to Secured Creditor's Voted Remain Open," XIV Bankruptcy Strategist 1, September 1997; Backman and Ellsworth, "Subordination of Tax Penalties: Dead or Alive," XVII Bankruptcy Strategist 1, March 1996; and Backman and Ellsworth, "Banks May Freeze Funds Subject to Setoff," XV Bankruptcy Strategist 1, November 1995. *Member:* Mclean County, Central Federal District of Illinois, Illinois State and American Bar Associations. ***REPORTED CASES:*** People v. Bruer, 335 Ill. App. 3d 422, 780 N.E.2d 1128 (4th District, 2002).

JOEL E. BROWN, ATTORNEY AT LAW

BLOOMINGTON, ILLINOIS

(See Peoria)

Personal Injury, Medical Malpractice, Criminal Law.

COSTIGAN & WOLLRAB, P.C.

Established in 1917

308 EAST WASHINGTON STREET

BLOOMINGTON, ILLINOIS 61701

Telephone: 309-828-4310

Telecopier: 309-828-4325

URL: http://www.cwlawoffice.com

Civil and Criminal Litigation in Federal and State Courts, Banking and Finance Law, Business and Commercial Law, Corporate Law, Divorce and Family Law, Eminent Domain, Estate Planning and Probate, Insurance Law, Mergers and Acquisitions, Personal Injury Litigation, Real Estate and Worker's Compensation Law.

FIRM PROFILE: Founded in 1916, Costigan & Wollrab, P.C. provides efficient and quality representation for their clients' unique legal needs. While proficient in handling a broad range of legal matters, the firm has a strong emphasis in personal injury litigation, business and commercial litigation, corporate law, business and estate planning and worker's compensation. Members of the firm maintain leadership roles in professional and civic organizations, reflecting their quest to impact the legal profession and the greater community.

JAMES C. WOLLRAB (1919-1989)

PAUL R. WELCH (1936-2004)

DAVID C. WOCHNER, born Bloomington, Illinois, November 14, 1939; admitted to bar, 1964, Illinois. *Education:* University of Notre Dame (B.B.A., 1961); University of Illinois (LL.B., 1964). *Member:* McLean County and Illinois State Bar Associations. ***PRACTICE AREAS:*** Real Estate; Estate Planning; Corporate Law. **Email:** dwochner@cwlawoffice.com

ROBERT W. NEIRYNCK, born Bloomington, Illinois, March 25, 1944; admitted to bar, 1969, Illinois. *Education:* University of Illinois at Urbana-Champaign (A.B., cum laude, 1966); University of Notre Dame (J.D., cum laude, 1969). Member, Notre Dame Lawyer, 1967-1968. Articles Editor, Notre Dame Lawyer, 1968-1969. Law Clerk, Appellate Court Judge Leland Simkins, 1973-1975. Author: Note, "Teachers' Strikes—A New Militancy," 43 *Notre Dame Lawyer*, 367, 1968, reprinted, *Labor Law Journal*, May, 1968 and *Journal of the Florida Education Association*, December, 1968. Chapter Author: *Illinois Eminent Domain Practice,* Illinois Institute of Continuing Legal Education, 1985. Lecturer, IICLE, Civil Procedure and Eminent Domain. Participant, Allerton House Conference on Civil Procedure, 1982; 1984. Special Assistant Attorney General, 1984—. *Member:* McLean County and Illinois State (Member: Assembly, 1974-1980; Tort Council, 1980-1984; Insurance Law Council, 1986-1988; Chairman, 1988-1989) Bar Associations; Illinois Association of Defense Trial Counsel (Member, Board of Governors, 1983-1994); Defense Research Institute. Fellow: American College of Trial Lawyers. **Email:** rneirynck@cwlawoffice.com

DAWN L. WALL, born Aurora, Illinois, June 9, 1962; admitted to bar, 1987, Illinois. *Education:* Kentucky Wesleyan College (B.S., 1981); Southern Illinois University (J.D., 1987). Phi Delta Phi. Robert C. Underwood Inn of Court. Member: Prairie State Legal Services, 1988-1990; Bloomington Rotary Club, 1994-1997. *Member:* McLean County and Illinois State Bar Associations; Illinois Association of Defense Trial Counsel. ***LANGUAGES:*** French. ***PRACTICE AREAS:*** Civil Litigation; Insurance Defense; Workers Compensation; Employment Law. **Email:** dwall@cwlawoffice.com

ROBERT S. WHITE, born Peoria, Illinois, July 25, 1943; admitted to bar, 1985, Illinois. *Education:* Knox College (A.B., 1965); University of Illinois at Champaign-Urbana (M.A., 1968); Southern Illinois University at Carbondale (J.D., 1985). Barrister, Robert C. Underwood Inn of Court. Instructor, Business Law, Richland Community College, Decatur, Illinois, 1988-1989. *Member:* McLean County and Illinois State Bar Associations. ***PRACTICE AREAS:*** Civil Litigation; Insurance Defense; Family Law; Landlord and Tenant Law; Collections. ***Email:*** rwhite@cwlawoffice.com

J. CASEY COSTIGAN, born Bloomington, Illinois, November 18, 1965; admitted to bar, 1991, Illinois. *Education:* Indiana University (B.A., 1988); Thomas M. Cooley Law School (J.D., 1991). Barrister, Robert C. Underwood Inn of Court. Member, Greater Peoria Claims Adjusters Association. Assistant Attorney General for Condemnation. *Member:* McLean County and Illinois State Bar Associations; Illinois Association of Defense Trial Counsel. ***PRACTICE AREAS:*** Civil Litigation. **Email:** ccostigan@cwlawoffice.com

---

CARRIE L. BOROWSKI, born Bloomington, Illinois, October 1, 1978; admitted to bar, 2003, Illinois; U.S. District Court, Central District of Illinois and U.S Court of Appeals, Seventh Circuit. *Education:* Illinois State University (B.A., summa cum laude, 1999); University of Illinois (J.D., 2003). Phi Alpha Theta. Recipient: Senior Thesis in History Scholarship; Appellate Defender Clinic Fall, 2002. *Member:* McLean County and Illinois State Bar Associations; Robert C. Underwood Inn of Court. ***LANGUAGES:*** French. ***PRACTICE AREAS:*** Employment Law; Criminal Defense; Real Estate; Traffic Violations; Family Law; Civil Litigation. **Email:** cborowski@cwlawoffice.com

BRIAN L. CURTIS, born February 4, 1979; admitted to bar, 2004, Illinois and U.S. District Court, Central District of Illinois. *Education:* McKendree College (B.B.A., 2001); Southern Illinois University (J.D., 2004). *Member:* Mclean County and Illinois State Bar Associations; Robert C. Underwood Inns of Court. ***PRACTICE AREAS:*** Trusts and Estates; Real Estate; Corporate; Municipal Law; Collections. **Email:** bcurtis@cwlawoffice.com

DOMINIC SALVATI, born Streator, Illinois, May 10, 1976; admitted to bar, 2004, Illinois and U.S. District Court, Central District of Illinois. *Education:* Augustana College (B.A., 1999); John Marshall Law School (J.D., 2004). Chief Justice, Moot Court. *Member:* McLean County and Illinois State Bar Association; Robert C. Underwood Inns of Court. ***PRACTICE AREAS:*** Civil Litigation; Personal Injury; Workers Compensation; Corporate Law; Business Law. **Email:** dsalvati@cwlawoffice.com

OF COUNSEL

WILLIAM F. COSTIGAN, born Bloomington, Illinois, 1926; admitted to bar, 1951, Illinois. *Education:* University of Illinois (B.A., 1950; LL.B., 1951). Phi Delta Phi. Assistant Attorney General for Condemnation, 1964-1968, 1984-1991. *Member:* McLean County, Illinois State (Member: Board of Governors, 1985-1991; Defense Counsel) and American Bar Associations; American Judicature Society; Defense Research Institute; Illinois Association of Defense Trial Counsel. Fellow: American College of Trial Lawyers; American Bar Foundation; Illinois Bar Foundation.

WILLIAM S. BACH, born Normal, Illinois, April 24, 1937; admitted to bar, 1962, Ohio; 1964, Illinois. *Education:* Northwestern University and Ohio Wesleyan University (B.A., 1959); University of Michigan (J.D., 1962). Phi Delta Phi. *Member:* McLean County, Illinois State and American Bar Associations. ***PRACTICE AREAS:*** Estate Planning; Probate; Estate Litigation; Taxation. **Email:** wbach@cwlawoffice.com

JOSEPH M. AMBROSE, born Peoria, Illinois, July 28, 1957; admitted to bar, 1982, Illinois; 1983, Florida. *Education:* University of Illinois (B.S., 1979); Indiana University (J.D., 1982); Northwestern University (M.B.A., 2001). Chapter Author: *Advising Illinois Financial Institutions,* Illinois Institute for Continuing Legal Education, 1997. *Member:* McLean County, Illinois State and American Bar Associations; The Florida Bar. ***PRACTICE AREAS:*** Banking Law; Corporate Law; Financial Services Law; Mergers and Acquisitions. **Email:** jambrose@cwlawoffice.com

REPRESENTATIVE CLIENTS: Farmer's Auto Insurance Co., of Pekin; General Casualty Insurance Co.; CIGNA; Employers Mutual Insurance Co.; The Norfolk & Southern Railroad; MFA Insurance Co.; Aetna Life & Casualty; Farmland Insurance; Commercial Union; Cincinnati Insurance; St. Paul Insurance; Travelers Insurance; West Bend Insurance; USF & G Insurance; Crawford & Co.; County of McLean; Central Illinois Bank; BankOne, Illinois N.A.; Busey Bank, FSB; Shelter Insurance Co.; University of Illinois at Urbana-Champaign; State Farm Bank; State Farm Mutual Automobile Insurance Company; Public Building Commission of McLean County, Illinois; Freedom Oil Company; Corm Belt Energy Corporation.

(This Listing Continued)

DUNN, WILLARD, ARKELL & BUGG

Established in 1915
1001 NORTH MAIN STREET, SUITE A
BLOOMINGTON, ILLINOIS 61701
Telephone: 309-828-6241
Fax: 309-828-8321
Email: MTD@DunnLaw.com
URL: http://www.DunnLaw.com
Mailing Address: P.O. Box 3488, Bloomington, IL 61702-3488

General Civil Trial and Appellate Practice. General Practice, Litigation, Business Law, Business Litigation, Business Enterprises, Insurance, Intellectual Property, Licensing Agreements, Trade Secrets, Contracts, Commercial Law, Commercial Litigation, Civil Litigation, Copyright, Trademark, Bankruptcy, Banking Law, Corporate, Real Estate, Buying or Selling, Construction, Probate, Trusts and Estates, Municipal, University, Civil Rights, Immigration, Labor, Employment, Human Resources, Internet.

FIRM PROFILE: Dunn, Willard, Arkell & Bugg was founded by Richard F. Dunn in 1915. The firm handles a wide variety of legal issues in various fields of law with its primary focus being employment, immigration and labor law issues as they pertain to business, universities, professionals and governmental entities. Dunn, Willard, Arkell & Bugg is listed in the Bar Register of Preeminent Lawyers.

MEMBERS OF FIRM

RICHARD F. DUNN (1888-1963)

MARK T. DUNN, born Bloomington, Illinois, December 14, 1945; admitted to bar, 1972, Illinois, U.S. District Court, Northern District of Illinois including Trial Bar, U.S. District Court, Central District of Illinois, U.S. Court of Appeals, Seventh Circuit and U.S. Supreme Court. *Education:* University of Notre Dame (B.A., 1967; J.D., 1972). Member, Notre Dame Lawyer, 1970-1972. Law Clerk to Judge Rodger J. Kiley, U.S. Circuit Court of Appeals, 7th Circuit, 1972-1973. Ch. 7 Trustee, Central District of Illinois Bankruptcy Court, 1985-2005. Author: "Ch. 12 of the U.S. Bankruptcy Code, Recent Issues and Cases," Vol. 76 Ill. Bar. J., 1988. Member, Robert C. Underwood Inn of Court. *Member:* McLean County, Illinois State and American Bar Associations. ***PRACTICE AREAS:*** Business Law; Employment Law; School Law; Commercial Litigation. ***Email:*** MTD@DunnLaw.com

DONALD A. WILLARD, born Normal, Illinois, January 14, 1952; admitted to bar, 1978, Virginia and Illinois. *Education:* University of Illinois (B.S., 1974); International School of Law (J.D., 1978). *Member:* McLean County (Secretary, 1979-1980) and Illinois State Bar Associations; Virginia State Bar. ***PRACTICE AREAS:*** Estate Planning; Probate; Real Estate; Commercial Law; Trust Law. ***Email:*** DAW@DunnLaw.com

THOMAS J. ARKELL, born Dawson Creek, British Columbia, April 17, 1970; admitted to bar, 1997, Illinois; 1998, District of Columbia and Minnesota; U.S. District Court, Northern and Central Districts of Illinois; U.S. Court of Appeals, Seventh Circuit. *Education:* University of Notre Dame (B.A., 1994; J.D., 1997). Special Assistant Attorney General, Illinois, 1997-2001. Member: National Association of College and University Attorneys; Association of International Educators; Society for Human Resource Management. *Member:* Chicago, Illinois State and Minnesota State Bar Associations; The District of Columbia Bar; American Immigration Lawyers Association. ***PRACTICE AREAS:*** Immigration Law; Employment Law; Litigation; Technology; Contracts. ***Email:*** TJA@DunnLaw.com

TODD E. BUGG, born Decatur, Illinois, May 1, 1965; admitted to bar, 1990, Illinois. *Education:* Illinois Wesleyan University (B.A., 1987); University of Illinois, College of Law (J.D., 1990). *Member:* McLean County and Illinois State Bar Associations. ***PRACTICE AREAS:*** Commercial Real Estate; Residential Real Estate; Estate Planning; Special Needs Trusts; Small Business Planning; Corporate Law; Landlord and Tenant Law. ***Email:*** TEB@DunnLaw.com

ASSOCIATE

CLAYTON J. PATTERSON, born Springfield, Illinois, May 20, 1979; admitted to bar, 2004, Illinois. *Education:* Eastern Illinois University (B.A., summa cum laude, 2001); University of Illinois (J.D., cum laude, 2004). ***PRACTICE AREAS:*** Civil Litigation; Commercial Litigation; Contracts; Corporations; Real Estate. ***Email:*** CJP@DunnLaw.com

OF COUNSEL

LOUIS F. ULBRICH, born Bloomington, Illinois, October 3, 1928; admitted to bar, 1952, Illinois. *Education:* Illinois Wesleyan University (Ph.B., 1949); University of Illinois (J.D., 1952). Phi Delta Phi. Assistant Attorney General, Illinois, 1961-1969. *Member:* McLean County, Illinois State and American Bar Associations. ***PRACTICE AREAS:*** Real Estate Law; Trust Law; Taxation Law.

RICHARD T. DUNN, born Normal, Illinois, August 21, 1918; admitted to bar, 1947, Illinois. *Education:* University of Illinois (A.B., 1940; J.D., 1947). Phi Alpha Delta. Member, 1971-1975 and Chairman, 1972-1975, Judicial Inquiry Board, State of Illinois; Member, 1982-1992 and Chairman, 1985-1990, Illinois Supreme Court Committee on Professional Responsibility. *Member:* McLean County, Illinois State and American Bar Associations; American Judicature Society; National Association of College and University Attorneys. Fellow, American Bar Foundation. [Brig. General, A.U.S. Ret.; active duty, 1940-1946; 1952-1953; 1970]

F. JAMES ARKELL, born Dawson Creek, B.C., Canada, July 30, 1962; admitted to bar, 1990, Texas, U.S. District Court, Western, Eastern, Northern and Southern Districts of Texas and U.S. Court of Appeals, Fifth Circuit (Not admitted in Illinois). *Education:* Texas Tech University (B.A., 1986; J.D., 1989). Professor of Law, Shenzhen University School of Law, Shenzhen, China. *Member:* State Bar of Texas (Inactive). ***PRACTICE AREAS:*** Business Law; Intellectual Property; Technology; Contracts; Commercial Litigation.

(This Listing Continued)

GENERAL COUNSEL FOR: Illinois Wesleyan University; Northeastern Illinois University; Midwest Electronic Specialties, Inc.
ATTORNEYS FOR: Commerce Bank; Bluestem National Bank; Bloomington Housing Authority; McLean County; Illinois Branch Office, Farm Loan and Commercial Division, Metropolitan Life Insurance Co.; Western Illinois University; Chicago State University; Southern Illinois University; Southern Illinois University, School of Medicine; Illinois State University; University of Illinois at Urbana-Champaign; Bradley University; Hoffman Tool & Die, Inc.; Frichtl Steel & Welding, Inc.; Pfister Hybrid Corn Company; STL Technology Partners; Community Merchant Services, Inc.; Kahuna Business Group, Inc.; W.M. Putnam Company; Guthoff & Company, C.P.A.'s; Striegal Knoblach & Company L.L.C.

LAW OFFICE OF RANDALL B. EHLERS

Established in 1983
103 NORTH MAIN STREET
BLOOMINGTON, ILLINOIS 61701
Telephone: 309-827-8084
Fax: 309-828-6948
URL: http://www.ehlerslaw.com
Email: rehlers@ehlerslaw.com
URL: http://www.lawyers.com/ehlerslaw

General Civil Practice. Trial Practice in State and Federal Courts. Family Law, Personal Injury, Real Estate, Municipal, Wills, Estate Administration, Small Business.

FIRM PROFILE: Dedicated to providing knowledgeable, prompt, complete and compassionate legal services on behalf of our clients. The firm serves McLean, DeWitt, Livingston and Woodford counties.

The law offices of Randall B. Ehlers engages in a general practice with a focus on Domestic Relations. Mr. Ehlers has been practicing law in Bloomington, Illinois for more than 30 years, practicing in the very same office in which David Davis and Abraham Lincoln once practiced.

RANDALL B. EHLERS, born Oak Park, Illinois, August 31, 1948; admitted to bar, 1973, Illinois; 1974, U.S. District Court, Central District of Illinois; 1977, U.S. Supreme Court; 1981, U.S. Court of Appeals, 7th Circuit. *Education:* University of Illinois (B.S., in Psychology, 1970; J.D., 1973). *Member:* McLean County, Illinois State (Family Law Council, 1977-1980 and 1987-1990; Chairman, 1979-1980) and American (Member, General Practice Section; Family Law Section; Litigation Section) Bar Associations; Illinois Trial Lawyers Association (Member, Matrimonial Law Committee, 1982-1993). [U.S. Army ROTC, 1971-1973]

JAMES P. GINZKEY

221 E. WASHINGTON
BLOOMINGTON, ILLINOIS 61701
Telephone: 309-821-9707
Fax: 309-821-9708
Email: jim@jimginzkey.com
URL: http://www.lawyers.com/jimginzkey

Personal Injury, Medical Malpractice, Products Liability.

JAMES P. GINZKEY, born St. Joseph, Missouri, February 17, 1953; admitted to bar, 1979, Illinois; U.S. District Court, Northern and Central Districts of Illinois; U.S. Court of Appeals, Seventh Circuit and U.S Supreme Court. *Education:* University of Illinois (B.S., 1975); St. Mary's University (J.D., 1979). *Member:* McLean County and Illinois State (ISBA Civil Practice Section Council; ISBA Tort Law Section; ISBA General Assembly, 1984-1990) Bar Associations; Illinois Trial Lawyers Association. ***PRACTICE AREAS:*** Personal Injury; Medical Malpractice; Products Liability.

RONDA D. TAYLOR GLENN

115 WEST JEFFERSON, SUITE 303A
BLOOMINGTON, ILLINOIS 61701
Telephone: 309-827-3535
FAX: 309-828-2574

Family Law, Trial and Appellate Practice in State and Federal Courts, Divorce, Child Custody, Name Changes, Juvenile Law, Adoptions, Interstate and Intrastate Adoptions, Juvenile Abuse, Neglect and Delinquency Cases.

FIRM PROFILE: Ronda D. Taylor Glenn has been practicing law in Bloomington, IL since 1986. Serving clients throughout McLean, Logan, Livingston, Tazewell, Peoria, Will, DeWitt and surrounding counties. The firm has a focus and expertise in all types of family Law.

RONDA D. TAYLOR GLENN, born Bloomington, Illinois, September 27, 1961; admitted to bar, 1986, Illinois; 1988, U.S. District Court, Central District of Illinois; 1989, U.S. Court of Appeals, Seventh Circuit. *Education:* Bradley University (B.S., 1982); Washington University (J.D., 1986). Assistant Public Defender, McLean County, 1986-1987. *Member:* McLean County, Illinois State (Member, Family Law Section) and American (Member, Sections on: Family Law; Litigation) Bar Associations; McLean County Family Law Bar; Robert C. Underwood Inns of Court. ***PRACTICE AREAS:*** Family Law; Juvenile Law; Appeals.

CHRIS GRAMM
ATTORNEY AT LAW

2422 E. WASHINGTON STREET, SUITE 101
BLOOMINGTON, ILLINOIS 61704
Telephone: 309-275-6677
Fax: 309-663-6164
Email: chris@getgramm.com
URL: http://www.lawyers.com/getgramm

Criminal Defense, DUI, Traffic Violations, Felonies, Misdemeanors, Drug Crimes, Sex Crimes, Real Estate, Wills, Trust and Estates and Immigration Law.

CHRIS GRAMM, born Normal, Illinois, August 25, 1971; admitted to bar, 2001, Illinois. *Education:* Illinois State University (B.A., 1991); Northern Illinois University (J.D., 2001). Member, Federalist Society, 1998—. Assistant State's Attorney, McLean County, 2001-2003. *Member:* McLean County Bar Association. ***LANGUAGES:*** Japanese. ***PRACTICE AREAS:*** DUI; Criminal Law; Real Estate; Wills.

HARTWEG, TURNER, WOOD & SIMKINS, P.C.

Established in 1977

207 WEST JEFFERSON STREET, SUITE 400
P.O. BOX 397
BLOOMINGTON, ILLINOIS 61701-0397
Telephone: 309-827-0044
Telecopier: 309-829-0328
Email: HTWSLAW.COM

Civil Practice in all Courts. Trials and Appeals in Personal Injury, Insurance, Commercial and Family Law. Estate Planning, Probate, Real Estate, Corporate, Commercial and Transactional Law.

FIRM PROFILE: Hartweg, Turner, Wood & Simkins, P.C. was originally established in 1977 as Luedtke, Hartweg & Turner. The firm continues to conduct a general practice with emphasis in civil/personal injury litigation, business and commercial law, probate/estate planning, family law and real estate. Members of the firm specialize among themselves in these areas. The firm is active in American, Illinois and local Bar Association committees and activities. The firm maintains a high community profile; members of the firm are active in a wide range of community volunteer organizations.

DARRELL L. HARTWEG, born Keokuk, Iowa, July 10, 1942; admitted to bar, 1968, Illinois. *Education:* University of Illinois (B.A., 1964; J.D., 1968); University of Iowa (M.A., 1965). *Member:* McLean County (Member, Board of Governors, 1979-1983) and Illinois State (Member, General Assembly, 1978-1984; Member of Council, Law Office Economics Section, 1984-1987; Chairman, 1986-1987). Fellow, Illinois Bar Foundation. Robert C. Underwood Inn of Court (Master Bencher). ***PRACTICE AREAS:*** Business Law; Estate Administration; Construction Law; Civil Litigation. ***Email:*** DLHARTWEG@HTWSLAW.COM

RALPH T. TURNER, born Lincoln, Illinois, May 27, 1946; admitted to bar, 1973, Illinois. *Education:* Tulane University of Louisiana (B.A., 1968); Illinois State University (M.A., 1970); University of Illinois College of Law (J.D., 1973). Member, Board of Directors, 1985-1996 and Chairman, 1994-1995, Illinois Institute of Continuing Legal Education. *Member:* McLean County (Member, Board of Governors, 1987-1990), Illinois State (Member, Board of Governors, 1982-1984; Member of Council, Young Lawyers Section, 1976-1981; Chairman, 1981-1982) and American (Member: Executive Council, Young Lawyers Division, 1978-1980; Agriculture Committee, Taxation Section, Chairman, 1988-1989; Administration of Decedent's Estates Committee, Real Property, Probate and Trust Section, Chairman, 1987-1993) Bar Associations. Life Fellow: American Bar Foundation. Fellow: Illinois Bar Foundation. Fellow: American College of Trust and Estate Counsel. ***PRACTICE AREAS:*** Federal Estate and Gift Taxation; Fiduciary Income Tax; Probate; Trusts and Estates; Wills. ***Email:*** RTTURNER@HTWSLAW.COM

GEORGE C. WOOD, born Winona, Minnesota, June 25, 1964; admitted to bar, 1989, Illinois; 1990, U.S. District Court, Central and Northern Districts of Illinois. *Education:* Illinois State University (B.S., 1986); Southern Illinois University School of Law (J.D., 1989). McLean County Assistant States Attorney, 1989-1990. *Member:* McLean County and Illinois State Bar Associations (Committee on Professionalism, 1994-1995). ***PRACTICE AREAS:*** Commercial Litigation; Business Litigation; Insurance Law; Labor and Employment; Personal Injury. ***Email:*** GWOOD@HTWSLAW.COM

BRENDA H. SIMKINS, born Hammond, Louisiana; admitted to bar, 1995, Illinois; 1997, U.S. District Court, Central District of Illinois. *Education:* University of Mississippi (B.B.A., 1992; J.D., 1995). *Member:* McLean County and Illinois State Bar Associations; Robert C. Underwood Inn of Court. ***PRACTICE AREAS:*** Civil Appeals; Adoption Law; Civil Litigation; Guardianship; Estate Litigation; Family Law. ***Email:*** BSIMKINS@HTWSLAW.COM

ERIN L. BERRY, born Bloomington, Illinois, February 1, 1979; admitted to bar, 2004, Illinois. *Education:* Illinois State University (B.A., 2001); University of Missouri, Columbia (J.D., 2004). *Member:* McLean County and Illinois State Bar Associations. ***PRACTICE AREAS:*** Family Law; Civil Litigation; Real Estate. ***Email:*** eberry@htwslaw.com

REPRESENTATIVE CLIENTS: The Bank of Illinois; Mechanical Devices, Co.; Heritage Enterprises, Inc.; BBA Engineering, P.C.; Sulaski and Webb, CPAs; McLean County Apartment and Management Co.; Busey Bank; Donovan Commercial Industries, Inc.; Nu-Way Transportation Services, Inc.; New Life Air, Inc.; Barker's Collison, Inc.; BroMenn Health Care Systems; Commerce Bank; Conrad Sheet Metal, L.L.C.

HAYES, HAMMER, MILES & COX, LLP

202 N. CENTER
BLOOMINGTON, ILLINOIS 61701
Telephone: 309-828-7331
Fax: 309-827-7423
URL: http://www.hhmcg.com

General Civil Practice, Commercial, Corporate, Pension and Profit Sharing, Estate Planning, Real Estate, Probate, Taxation, Trust, Litigation, Family Law, Divorce, Adoption Law, Land Use, Zoning, Municipal, Alternative Dispute Resolution, Mediation, Collaborative Law.

MEMBERS OF FIRM

MERRICK C. HAYES, born Minneapolis, Minnesota, October 13, 1937; admitted to bar, 1960, Illinois. *Education:* Drake University (B.S., 1959; J.D., 1960). Phi Alpha Delta. *Member:* McLean County, Illinois State (Chairman, Estate Planning, Probate and Trust Council, 1990-1991) and American (Chair, Valuation Subcommittee, Estate and Gift Tax Section) Bar Associations; Illinois Society of Public Accountants. ***PRACTICE AREAS:*** Tax; Corporate Law; Estate Planning; Probate. ***Email:*** merrickhay@aol.com

FRANK MILES, born Des Moines, Iowa, June 13, 1946; admitted to bar, 1972, Illinois. *Education:* University of Illinois (B.S., 1968; J.D., 1971). *Member:* McLean County, Illinois State and American Bar Associations. ***PRACTICE AREAS:*** Real Estate; Municipal; Zoning, Planning and Land Use; Probate; Nonprofit and Charitable Organizations. ***Email:*** fmiles@hhmcg.com

DON C. HAMMER, born Peoria, Illinois, July 13, 1945; admitted to bar, 1975, Illinois; 1977, District of Columbia. *Education:* The Ohio State University (B.A., 1967); John Marshall Law School (J.D., with high distinction, 1975). Editor in Chief, John Marshall Journal of Practice and Procedure, 1974-1975. Member, Order of John Marshall. Law Clerk to Justice Howard Ryan, Illinois Supreme Court, 1975-1976. *Member:* McLean County and Illinois State Bar Associations. [Lt., USN, 1967-1972]. ***PRACTICE AREAS:*** Family Law; Commercial Law; Corporate Law; Alternative Dispute Resolution; Adoption Law; Mediation; Collaborative Law. ***Email:*** dhammer@hhmcg.com

A. CLAY COX, born Quincy, Illinois, November 17, 1954; admitted to bar, 1979, Illinois. *Education:* University of Missouri at Columbia (B.S.B.A., magna cum laude, 1976); University of Illinois (J.D., 1979). Beta Gamma Sigma; Phi Kappa Phi; Phi Eta Sigma; Beta Alpha Psi. Author: "Employee Benefits and Bankruptcy," Ch. 24, IICLE Employee Benefits Handbook, 1987 and 1994. *Member:* McLean County and Illinois State (Chairman, Council of Employee Benefits Section, 1987-1988) Bar Associations; Illinois Society of Certified Public Accountants. ***PRACTICE AREAS:*** Corporate; Taxation Law; Business Planning; Employee Benefits; Estate Planning. ***Email:*** claycox@hhmcg.com

REPRESENTATIVE CLIENTS: Beer Nuts, Inc.; Bloomington Radiology; Brock Oil Company; Habitat for Humanity; Heritage Enterprises; McLean County Orthopedics; Nussbaum Trucking, Inc.; McLean County Anesthesiology, Bloomington/Normal ENT; Johnston Contractors.
REFERENCE: Commerce Bank, Bloomington, Illinois.

HOWARD & HOWARD ATTORNEYS, P.C.

BLOOMINGTON, ILLINOIS

(See Peoria)

Administrative, Business, Commercial, Corporate, Creditors Rights, Education, Employee Benefits, Environmental, Financial Institutions, Government Relations, Immigration, Intellectual Property (Patents, Trademarks, Copyrights, and Gaming), Labor and Employment, Litigation, Probate, Public Finance, Real Estate, Securities, Taxation (Federal, State and Local), Trusts and Estates.

JOHNSON LAW GROUP

BLOOMINGTON, ILLINOIS 61701
Telephone: 309-827-3670
Fax: 309-827-3991
Email: johnson.law@verizon.net

Okemos, Michigan Office: 3474 Alaiedon Parkway, 47764. Telephone: 877-333-2889.
Canton, Ohio Office: 4571 Stephen Circle N.W., 44718. Telephone: 877-333-2889.
South Bend, Indiana Office: 218 W. Washington Street, 46601. Telephone: 877-333-2889.

Felonies, Murder, White Collar Crime, Drugs, Domestic Violence, DWI.

FIRM PROFILE: Johnson Law Group provides aggressive criminal defense representation throughout the entire States of Illinois, Indiana, Michigan and Ohio. Our Criminal Defense Attorneys are recognized in Illinois, Indiana, Michigan and Ohio for providing premier criminal defense services. The attorneys at Johnson Law Group place cutting edge aggressive defensive strategies at the top of their priority list. Johnson Law Group has developed a process that allows a client 24 hours a day, 7 days a week access to a client service representative who will work closely with the client and our experienced criminal defense lawyers to make sure that every possible angle in a case is covered. To learn more about our process, visit our website at johnsoncriminaldefenselawgroup.com.

MARK D. JOHNSON, admitted to bar, 1992, Illinois; 1993, Alabama; 1994, U.S. District Court, Central and Southern Districts of Illinois; 1997, U.S. District Court, Northern District of Illinois. *Education:* Illinois State University (B.A.,1989); Northern Illinois University College of Law (J.D., 1992). Founded Johnson Law Group, 1996. Arbitrator, Eleventh Judicial Circuit. Former Assistant Attorney General, Springfield, Illinois. Former First Assistant State's Attorney, Eureka, IL. Counsel, several Illinois Municipalities. Former Adjunct Professor, Lincoln College, Normal, Illinois, 1993-1995. *Member:* Illinois State, Michigan State, Ohio State, Indiana State, American and Federal Bar Associations; Association of Trial Lawyers of America; National Association of Criminal Defense Lawyers; Ohio Association of Criminal Defense Lawyers; Michigan Trial Lawyers Association; Il-

(This Listing Continued)

JOHNSON LAW GROUP, Bloomington—Continued

linois Bar Foundation. (Managing Director). ***PRACTICE AREAS:*** Felonies; Murder; White Collar Crime; Drug Crimes; Domestic Violence; Driving While Intoxicated. ***Email:*** mark@johnson-law.net

PETER C. SAMOURIS, admitted to bar, 1995, Michigan, Illinois, U.S. District Court, Eastern, Southern, Northern, Central and Western Districts of Michigan. *Education:* University of San Francisco (1992); Thomas M. Cooley Law School (J.D., 1994). *Member:* Hellenic and Michigan State Bar Associations; Michigan Trial Lawyers Association. (Resident Member, Okemos, Michigan). ***LANGUAGES:*** Greek. ***PRACTICE AREAS:*** Felonies; Murder; White Collar Crime; Drug Crimes; Domestic Violence; Driving While Intoxicated. ***Email:*** michigandefense@yahoo.com

P. STEVEN MAASZ, admitted to bar, 1991, Ohio; 1992, U.S. District Court, Northern District of Ohio. *Education:* Ohio University (B.A., History, summa cum laude, 1987); Boston University Law School (J.D., 1991). Phi Beta Kappa. *Member:* Stark County and Ohio State Bar Associations. [1st Lt., USAR (Armor) 1987-1995]. (Resident Member, Canton, Ohio). ***LANGUAGES:*** Japanese. ***PRACTICE AREAS:*** Felonies; Murder; White Collar Crime; Drug Crimes; Domestic Violence; Driving While Intoxicated. ***Email:*** ohiodefense@yahoo.com

SEAN P. HILGENDORF, admitted to bar, 1997, Indiana, U.S. District Court, Northern and Southern Districts of Indiana. *Education:* University of Notre Dame (B.A., 1990); Cleveland-Marshall College of Law (J.D., 1996). *Member:* St. Joseph County and Indiana State Bar Associations. (Resident Member, South Bend, Indiana). ***PRACTICE AREAS:*** Felonies; Murder; White Collar Crime; Drug Crimes; Domestic Violence; Driving While Intoxicated. ***Email:*** indianadefense@yahoo.com

ASSOCIATES

Thomas A. Sobecki
James M. Ansbro
Andy Scharf
Michael R. Puterbaugh (Not admitted in IL).
Jeffrey T. Abbott
K. Robert Toy
Carl Jordan (Not admitted in IL).
William F. McGinnis (Not admitted in IL).
Jeffrey A. Kline
Matthew J. McQuaid
Michael T. Maddaloni (Not admitted in IL).
Anthony R. Cicero (Not admitted in IL).
Robert J. Carter
John A. Goodridge (Not admitted in IL).
David A. Merchant, II (Not admitted in IL).
Shawn R. Dominy (Not admitted in IL).
Gregory Kaufman (Not admitted in IL).
Douglas R. Smith
Andrew M. Liefer
Michael J. Rousseau

Languages: Japanese and Greek.

KELLY LAW OFFICES, P.C.

121 NORTH MAIN STREET
3RD FLOOR
BLOOMINGTON, ILLINOIS 61701
Telephone: 309-661-2558; Chicago and Toll Free: 866-727-6507
Fax: 309-662-7443
Email: tw.kelly@verizon.net
URL: http://www.kellylawoffices.com

Chicago, Illinois Office: 222 N. Columbus Drive, Suite 408, 60601.

Personal Injury, Products Liability, Torts, Medical Malpractice, and Insurance cases in State and Federal Courts.

FIRM PROFILE: Kelly Law Offices, P.C. serves clients throughout Illinois.

TIMOTHY W. KELLY, born Chicago, Illinois, April 27, 1953; admitted to bar, 1978, Illinois. *Education:* University of Dayton (B.S., 1975; J.D., 1978). Named by "Business to Business" Magazine, Top 3 Lawyers in McLean County, March, 1997. Named by Leading Lawyers Network as Top 5% of Ill. Lawyers. Assistant Professor, Political Science, Illinois State University, 1980-1983. Staff Attorney, Prairie State Legal Services, 1978-1981. Assistant Public Defender, McLean County, 1981-1983. IICLE Faculty Member: Ill. Civil Litigation, 1989; Proof of Damages, 1989; Negotiating Personal Injury Cases, 1990; Vehicle Accident Cases, 1995; How to Introduce Evidence, 1996; Laying Foundation for Evidence, 1997; Product Defects in Auto Cases, 1999; How to Prove-up Damages, 2000; Bridge-the-Gap Seminar, 2001; How to Depose A Medical Expert, 2001; Jury Selection, 2003; ISBA Law-ed Series Faculty Member: Mechanics of Preparing Exhibits, 1991; How to Present a Personal Injury Case, 1991; Products Liability, an in-depth Study, 1992; Hot Tips - Proven Winning Ways in Personal Injury Cases, 1993; Civil Practice Update, 1995. Tort Reform Issues, 1995; Anatomy of Pretrial Preparations, 1995; Trial Techniques, 1996; Tort Law Update, 1996, General Practice Update, 1997; Civil Practice Update, 1997; Settlement Seminar, 1997; Litigating Personal Injury Cases, Civil Practice Update Seminar, 1998; How to Protect Against Malpractice, 1998, Civil Practice Update, 1999, Mandatory Arbitration, Case Law Update, 1999: Municipal Liability, 1999; Arbitration Case Law Review, 1999; Tort Law Seminar, 1999; Liens in UM & UIM Cases, 2002; Civil Practice Update and Review, 2002; Automobile Cases A to Z, 2003; Vehicular Accidents, Chicago, 2004; Rule 216 Admissions, 2005, ITLA; Faculty Member: Shotgun Seminar, 1995; Pretrial Techniques and Strategies, 1996; Evidence, Update & Review, 1997, Evidence Seminar, 1999; Evidence Seminar, 1999: Automobile Accident Claims, 2000; Products Liability Seminar, 2000; Demonstrative EUI Seminar, 2001: Medical Malpractice, 2002; Shotgun Seminar 2003; Automobile Litigation Update, 2003; Automobile Litigation Seminar, Springfield, 2004; UM/UIM Coverages, 2005; C.I.P.A. Personal Injury Law, 1999. Author: Laying Foundations for Introducing Evidence, IICLE, 1991, revised, 1996, 2000, 2004; Proving Damages in Personal Injury Cases, IICLE 1994. Review of Recent Cases, Trial Briefs, ISBA Vol. 34, 1989; Review of Recent Cases, Tort Trends, ISBA Vol. 31, 1995; Affirmation of the Common Fund Doctrine, Trial Briefs, ISBA Vol. 42, 1996; IPI 5.01 & Expert Witnesses, Tort Trends, ISBA Vol. 4, 1997; Special Duty Exception to Local Governmental Tort Immunity, Trial Briefs, ISBA Vol. 44, 1999. Mandatory Arbitration Case Review, Illinois Bar Journal, March 2000. Co-Author, 2 volume treatise, Illinois Pretrial Practice, James Publishing Co., 2002. Co-Editor, Ill. Causes of Action, 2 volume text, 2003, IICLE. Certified as McLean County Civil Case Mediator, 1996; Certified as a McLean County Civil Case Arbitrator, 1997. *Member:* Chicago, McLean County (Secretary, 1984-1985), Illinois State (Member, Civil Practice and Procedure Section Council, 1987-1989, 1992-1999; Vice-Chair, 1997-1998; Chair, 1998-1999; Tort Law Section Council, 1989-1992, 1995-1997, 2000—; Allerton House Steering Committee, 1994, 1996, 1998, 2000; Assembly, 1995-2001; Special Committee on Judicial Discipline, 1997-1998; Task Force on Allocation of Judges, 1998-2000; Building Committee, 2000-2001); and American Bar Associations; Illinois Trial Lawyers Association (Elected Manager, 1992—; Member, Executive Committee, 1998-1999; Seminar Director, 2001-2002; Chairman, Medical Malpractice Committee, 2003-2004); The Association of Trial Lawyers of America; McLean County Inns of Court (Master Bencher). Fellow, Illinois Bar Foundation. (Board of Directors, Illinois Inst. of Continuing Legal Education IICLE, 2000—; Executive Committee, 2002-2004). ***PRACTICE AREAS:*** Personal Injury; Medical Malpractice. ***Email:*** tw.kelly@verizon.net

KOEPKE & HILTABRAND, P.C.

BLOOMINGTON, ILLINOIS

(See Springfield)

General Civil Trial and Appellate Practice in all Courts, Insurance Defense, Workers' Compensation Defense, Professional Liability Defense, Insurance Coverage, Self Insured Defense, Employment/Discrimination Defense.

LIVINGSTON, BARGER, BRANDT & SCHROEDER

115 WEST JEFFERSON, SUITE 400
P.O. BOX 3457
BLOOMINGTON, ILLINOIS 61702-3457
Telephone: 309-828-5281
Fax: 309-827-3432
URL: http://www.lbbs.net

Champaign, Illinois Office: 2506 Galen Drive, Suite 108. Telephone: 217-351-7479. Fax: 217-351-6870.

Corporate, Business, Business Litigation, Real Estate Transactions, Creditors' Rights, Employment Law EEOC, ERISA, Estate Planning, Partnerships, Joint Ventures, Estates and Probate. Insurance Litigation, Product Liability, Medical Negligence Defense, Pharmaceutical Litigation, Construction Disputes, Environmental Litigation, Financial Litigation, Employment, Health Care to Physicians and Hospitals, Professional Liability, Officer's and Director's Liability, Environmental Law, Administrative Agency Procedures, Governmental Law, General Counsel Representation, Eminent Domain, Land Use Law, Subdivision and Zoning.

HERBERT M. LIVINGSTON (1898-1987)
RALPH SCHROEDER (1927-1991)
THOMAS M. BARGER, JR. (1912-1992)

OF COUNSEL

WILLIAM R. BRANDT
JAMES T. FOLEY

MEMBERS OF FIRM

WILLIAM C. WETZEL, born Bloomington, Illinois, December 16, 1939; admitted to bar, 1964, Illinois. *Education:* University of Notre Dame (B.A., 1961); University of Illinois (LL.B, 1964). Phi Delta Phi. *Member:* McLean County, Illinois State and American Bar Associations. ***PRACTICE AREAS:*** Probate Law; Trust Law; Taxation Law; Real Estate Law; Commercial Law including Litigation. ***Email:*** wwetzel@lbbs.com

THOMAS M. BARGER III, born Bloomington, Illinois, July 6, 1940; admitted to bar, 1965, Illinois and U.S. District Court, Central District of Illinois. *Education:* Northwestern University (B.S. in B.A., 1962); DePaul University (J.D., 1965). Delta Theta Phi. Commissioner, State of Illinois Appellate Defender, 1983-1989. *Member:* McLean County, Illinois State and American Bar Associations; American Bank Attorneys. ***PRACTICE AREAS:*** Probate Law; Trust Law; Real Estate Law. ***Email:*** tbarger@lbbs.com

CHRISTOPHER L. NYWEIDE, born Chicago, Illinois, March 11, 1951; admitted to bar, 1977, Illinois. *Education:* Illinois Wesleyan University (B.A., 1973); John Marshall Law School (J.D., 1976). Phi Alpha Delta. *Member:* McLean County, Illinois State and American Bar Associations; Illinois Association of Defense Trial Counsel; Defense Research Institute; International Association of Defense Council. ***PRACTICE AREAS:*** Insurance Defense Law; Medical Malpractice Defense Law; Real Estate Law. ***Email:*** cnyweide@lbbs.com

SUSAN H. BRANDT, born Bloomington, Illinois, December 20, 1950; admitted to bar, 1977, Illinois. *Education:* University of Colorado (B.A., 1973); University of Georgia (J.D., 1977). *Member:* McLean County, Illinois State and American Bar Associations; Illinois Association of Defense Trial Counsel. **PRACTICE AREAS:** Employment Law; Personal Injury Defense; Real Estate; Contracts; Family Law. ***Email:*** sbrandt@lbbs.com

RICHARD E. STITES, born Marshall, Michigan, June 7, 1954; admitted to bar, 1979, Illinois; 1980, U.S. District Court, Central District of Illinois; 1982, U.S. Court of Appeals,

(This Listing Continued)

Seventh Circuit; 1984, U.S. Supreme Court. *Education:* University of Illinois (A.B., cum laude, 1976); Indiana University (J.D., magna cum laude, 1979). Phi Beta Kappa; Phi Kappa Phi; Order of the Coif; Phi Alpha Delta. Administrative Editor, Board of Editors, Indiana Law Journal, 1977-1979. Author: "The Moment of Inadvertence Concept in Strict Products Liability; The Seed of Destruction For The Assumption of the Risk Defense?" Indiana Law Journal, Vol. 53, No. 3, 1977-1978; "Instructions and Special Interrogations," Illinois Civil Practice, Vol. III, Ch. 11, 1991, 1995 Supp., 1997, 1999 and 2003 (Illinois Institute for Continuing Legal Education); "Catastrophic Injury and Structured Verdicts-Confronting the Healing Art Malpractice Act," IDC Quarterly, Vol. 2 No. 2 (1992). *Member:* McLean County, Illinois State and American Bar Associations; Illinois Association of Defense Trial Counsel; Federation of Insurance and Corporate Counsel; International Association of Defense Counsel; The Society of Trial Lawyers. ***PRACTICE AREAS:*** Insurance Law; Medical Malpractice Defense Law; Products Liability Law; Business Litigation. ***Email:*** rstites@lbbs.com

PETER W. BRANDT, born Bloomington, Illinois, October 25, 1955; admitted to bar, 1983, Illinois. *Education:* University of Illinois (B.A., 1978); Southern Illinois University (J.D., 1983). Author: "Instructions and Special Interrogatories," Illinois Civil Practice, Vol. III, Ch. 11, 1991, 1995 Supp., 1997, 1999 and 2003 (Illinois Institute of Continuing Legal Education); "Catastrophic Injury and Structured Verdicts - Confronting The Healing Arts Malpractice Act," IDC Quarterly Vol. 2, No. 2 (1992); "Defending Misdiagnosed Ovarian Cancer," IDC Quarterly, Vol. 4 No. 2 (1994); "Making the Case for the Discovery Deposition," IDC Quarterly, Vol. 9, No. 3 (1999). Member, Civil Justice Reform Act Committee for The Federal District Court for the Central District of Illinois. Member, Illinois Supreme Court Committee on jury Instructions in Civil Cases (1997-2001). Past Editor-in-Chief, Illinois Association of Defense Trial Counsel Quarterly. *Member:* McLean County, Illinois State, and American Bar Associations; Illinois Association of Defense Trial Counsel (Member, Board of Directors, 1989—; President, 2000); International Association of Defense Counsel; Federation of Insurance and Corporate Counsel. ***PRACTICE AREAS:*** Insurance Law; Medical Malpractice Defense Law; Business Law. ***Email:*** pbrandt@lbbs.com

THOMAS B. BORTON, born Champaign, Illinois, September 12, 1963; admitted to bar, 1988, Missouri and U.S. District Court, Eastern District of Missouri; 1989, Illinois and U.S. District Court, Southern District of Illinois; 1994, U.S. District Court, Central District of Illinois. *Education:* Illinois Wesleyan University (B.A., 1985); Washington University School of Law (J.D., 1988). Articles Editor, Washington University Law Quarterly, 1987-1988. Author, "The IDC Monograph: Standard of Care Witnesses," IDC Quarterly, Vol. 8, No. 3 (1998). Formerly with Bryan, Cave, LLP (St. Louis, Missouri, 1988-1992). *Member:* McLean County, Champaign County, Illinois State, Missouri, and American Bar Associations; Bar Association of Metropolitan St. Louis; Illinois Association of Defense Trial Counsel (Co-Chair, Medical Liability Committee, 1997—). (Resident, Champaign Office). ***PRACTICE AREAS:*** Insurance Law; Medical Malpractice Defense; Products Liability; Commercial Litigation. ***Email:*** tborton@lbbs.com

RICHARD T. MARVEL, born Bloomington, Illinois, November 15, 1975; admitted to bar, 2001, Illinois. *Education:* Illinois Wesleyan University (B.A., 1998); St. Louis University School of Law (J.D., 2001). Phi Alpha Delta. *Chicago, McLean County, Illinois State and American Bar Associations; McLean County Inns of Court, Illinois Defense Counsel and Defense Research Institute.*

ASSOCIATES

KIRK A. HOLMAN, born Joliet, Illinois, July 30, 1961; admitted to bar, 1986, Illinois and U.S. District Court, Northern District of Illinois; 1987, U.S. District Court, Central District of Illinois. *Education:* Monmouth College (B.A., 1983); John Marshall Law School (J.D., 1986). Co-editor, Securities and Exchange Law Journal. Formerly with: Stephens and Schlickshup; Hinshaw & Culbertson; State Farm Mutual Automobile Insurance Companies. *Member:* McLean County, Illinois State and American Bar Associations; Defense Research Institute. ***PRACTICE AREAS:*** Insurance Defense; Professional Liability; Product Liability. ***Email:*** kholman@lbbs.com

MICHAEL A. WOZNIAK, born Chicago, Illinois, April 10, 1959; admitted to bar, 1984, Illinois; 2001, Ohio; 1985, U.S. District Court, Central District of Illinois and U.S. Court of Appeals, Seventh Circuit. *Education:* Illinois State University (B.S., high honors, 1981); University of Illinois College of Law (J.D., 1984). Recipient, Alice Ebel Honor Graduate Award. Author: "The IDC Monograph: HIPAA's Dilemma," IDC Quarterly Vol. 13, No. 3 (2003). Illinois Special Assistant Attorney General (1985-1992). Corporate Counsel and General Counsel, TTC Holdings, Inc. and TTC Illinois, Inc. (1992-2001). *Member:* Champaign, Illinois State and Ohio Bar Associations; Illinois Association if Defense Trial Counsel. ***PRACTICE AREAS:*** Corporate; Business; Employment; ERISA; Litigation. ***Email:*** mwozniak@lbbs.com

KENNETH S. WEISS, born New York, N.Y., August 27, 1949; admitted to bar, 2001, Illinois. *Education:* University of Michigan (B.S., 1971; M.D., 1975); Northwestern University (OTOL, 1979); University of Illinois College of Law (J.D., cum laude, 2001). Attending Emeritus Surgeon, Head Division of Otolaryngology/Head and Neck Surgery, 1979-1987 and Chairman, Department of Surgery (Chief of Surgery), 1987-1994, Carle Clinic Association. Clinical Assistant Professor, University of Illinois College of Medicine. Publications: "Serratia Marcescens in Tracheotomy Cultures," Laryngoscope, 1979. Co-Author: "Dermatofibrosarcoma Protuberans of the Face," Ear Nose and Throat Monthly, March 1979; "Airway Management in Craniofacial Anomalies," Otolaryngologic Clinics of North America, 1981; Otolaryngolic Lighting Bolts," American Journal of Otolaryngology, August 1981; "Transient Heating Loss with Metrinidazole," Laryngoscope, January 1985; "Velopalatine Incompetence After Tonsillectomy," Otolaryngology - Head and Neck Surgery, January 2000; "Life in Enemy Camp: A Surgeon Goes to Law School," Care Selected Paper, Vol. 44, Spring 2001; "Physician Unionization in America," University of Illinois College of Law, Law Review, Fall 2002. Member: President's Council, University of Illinois; Presidents Club, University of Michigan. Past Board Member, Champaign West Rotary Senior Active. *Member:* Champaign County and Illinois State (Member, Health Law Section) Bar Associations. Fellow: American Academy of Otolaryngology; American Academy of Facial Plastics and Reconstructive Surgery; American Society of Head and Neck Surgeons; American College of Surgeons. (Resident, Champaign Office). ***PRACTICE AREAS:*** Medical Malpractice; Health Law. ***Email:*** kweiss@lbbs.com

(This Listing Continued)

REPRESENTATIVE CLIENTS: AmerenIP; American International Group; American States Insurance Company; Aon Corporation; Associated Physicians Insurance Group; Bituminous Casualty Company; Bloomington-Normal Airport Authority; Bloomington-Normal Water Reclamation Dist.; Bloomington School District #87; Brandt Truck Lines, Inc.; BroMenn Healthcare; The Budd Company; Carle Clinic Association, P.C.; Cincinnati Insurance Company; Citizens Savings Bank; Colonial Insurance Company; Constitution States Insurance Company; DPIC Companies, Inc.; Digital Teleport Inc.; The Eaton Charitable Trust; Employers Insurance of Wausau; The Eureka Company; Federal Land Bank; Federated Insurance; Financial Security Insurance Groups; General Accident Group; General Motors Corporation; Glaxo Wellcome Company; Grinnell Mutual Reinsurance Company; Hamilton Resources Co.; Illinois Central Gulf Railroad; Illinois Provider Trust; Illinois State Medical Insurance Services, Inc; Indiana Insurance Company; Interstate Insurance Cos.; Kemper Insurance; Laidlaw Transit, Inc.; Lederle Laboratories, div. of American Home Products; MMI; Medical Claims Management Group; Miller's Mutual Insurance Company; Mitsubishi Motor Mfg, of America, Inc.; National Guard; Northern Illinois Gas Company; Novartis Pharmaceuticals Corporation; Ohio Casualty Company; Ohio Hospital Insurance Company; Pantagraph Printing & Stationery Company; Pekin Insurance; Pronational Insurance Company; Royal Globe Insurance Company; St. Paul Insurance Company; Self Insurance Service, Inc.; Sentry Cos.; State Farm Insurance Cos.; The Bank of Illinois in Normal; Travelers Insurance Companies/ Aetna; Underwriters Adjustment Company; Union Oil Company of California; Union Planters Bank; United Fire and Casualty; USF & G Company; Utica; Windsor Group.

JEROME MIRZA AND ASSOCIATES, LTD.

Established in 1973

705 EAST WASHINGTON STREET

BLOOMINGTON, ILLINOIS 61701

Telephone: 309-827-8011

Facsimile: 309-829-8638

URL: http://www.mirzalawfirm.com

Chicago, Illinois Office: Three First National Plaza. Telephone: 312-368-1903. Facsimile: 312-368-0528.

Trial and Appellate Practice. Products Liability, Malpractice and Railroad Law.

FIRM PROFILE: A small law office that handles only a select number of major personal injury cases throughout the state of Illinois and in adjoining states. The law firm has frequently secured verdicts for its clients which are among the largest awarded in the nation.

JEROME MIRZA, born Chicago, Illinois, November 3, 1937; admitted to bar, 1963, Illinois; 1972, U.S. Supreme Court; 1980, U.S. Court of Appeals, 7th Circuit. *Education:* Illinois Wesleyan University (B.S., 1960); University of Illinois (LL.B., 1963). Phi Alpha Delta. Author: "Preparation and Trial of a Railroad Crossing Case," *Illinois Bar Journal,* August 1970 and *The Practical Lawyer,* January 1971; The Practical Lawyer's Negligence Law Manual No. 2, November 1972; "Proving Damages to the Self-Employed Plaintiff," *Handbook on Damages* , Illinois Institute for Continuing Legal Education, 1974, 1981, 1987; "The Standard of Care," *Handbook on Medical Malpractice* , Illinois Institute for Continuing Legal Education, 1975; "Standard of Care and Duties," Handbook on Plaintiff's Medical Malpractice Litigation, Illinois Institute for Continuing Legal Education, 1981, 1984; "Malpractice Problems—Plaintiff's View," Representing Health Care Institutions Handbook, Illinois Institute for Continuing Legal Education, 1982; "Introduction—Some General Trial Techniques in Proving Damages," Handbook on Proof of Damages, Illinois Institute for Continuing Legal Education, 1987; "Railroad Crossing Litigation," American Jurisprudence Trials, 1976; "Illinois Tort Law and Practice," Lawyers Cooperative Publishing Company, 1974; "Illinois Tort Law and Practice, 2d Edition," Lawyers Cooperative Publishing Company, 1988; "Illinois Tort Law and Practice, 3d Edition," West Publishing, 2004; "Illinois Personal Injury," (10 Volumes), Lawyers Cooperative Publishing Company, 1989. "Winning Litigation The Mirza Way," The West Group, 1992. Co-Editor, 1972, and Editor, 1973-1976, *Tort Trends,* published by the Illinois State Bar Association. Editor, Trial Lawyers Journal, published by the Illinois Trial Lawyers Association, 1977-1981. Director and Principal Instructor: Illinois Trial Lawyers Association College of Advocacy, 1980-1987; Illinois Trial Lawyers Association—Association of Trial Lawyers of America College of Advocacy, 1988-1989, Jerome Mirza Professional Trial Lawyers College of Advocacy at the University of Illinois College of Law, 2000-2003. Member, Board of Directors, Illinois Institute for Continuing Legal Education, 1986-1988. *Member:* Illinois State (Member, 1970-1977, and Chairman, 1980-1981, Executive Council on Tort Law; Chairman, Committee on Specialization, 1975-1976; Third Vice President, 1985-1986; Second Vice President, 1986-1987; President Elect, 1987-1988; President, 1988-1989) and American (Member, House of Delegates, 1985-1989) Bar Associations; Illinois Trial Lawyers Association (Member: Board of Managers, 1967-1978; Chairman, Amicus Curiae, 1975-1978; Executive Committee, 1975-1977; Vice President, 1978-1980; President-Elect, 1980-1981; President, 1981-1982); The Association of Trial Lawyers of America (Member, Board of Governors, 1972-1975, 1981-1989); American Board of Trial Advocates (Advocate). Founder and Lifetime Member, Trial Lawyers for Public Justice; Inner Circle of Advocates (Member). Fellow: International Society of Barristers; International Academy of Trial Lawyers.

THOMAS M. HARRIS, JR., born Lincoln, Illinois, May 10, 1963; admitted to bar, 1988, Illinois. *Education:* University of Illinois (B.A., 1985); University of Colorado (J.D., 1988). Author: "Survey of Illinois Law: Tort Developments," Southern Illinois University Law Journal, Vol. 19, Summer 1995; "Zen and the Art of Motorcycle-Injury Litigation," Illinois Bar Journal, Vol. 88 No. 7, July 2000. Member, Editorial Board, Illinois Bar Journal. Assistant States' Attorney, Logan County, Illinois, 1989-1991. Faculty, Jerome Mirza Professional Trial Lawyers College of Advocacy at the University of Illinois College of Law, 2000-2003. Board of Directors, Illinois Bar Foundation. *Member:* Logan County, McLean County and Illinois State Bar Associations (Tort Law Section Council, Chair, 1995-1996; Civil Practice and Procedure Section Council: Chair, 1999-2000, Vice-Chair, 1998-1999, Secretary, 1997-1998; Allerton Conference, Chair, 2000; Committee on Legislation, 1996-1998; Standing Committee on Legal Education; Standing Committee on Supreme Court Rules); Illinois Trial Lawyers Association (Co-Chair, 1995-1996, Seminar Planning). ***Email:*** tomharrisjr@hotmail.com

REFERENCE: National City Bank, Bloomington, Illinois.

MUELLER & REECE, LLC

202 NORTH CENTER STREET
BLOOMINGTON, ILLINOIS 61701
Telephone: 309-827-4055
Fax: 309-829-6742
URL: http://www.muellerreece.com

Commercial Law, Civil and Commercial Litigation, Real Estate, Business Formations and Incorporations, Business Transactions, Personal Injury, Banking Law, Estate Planning, Trusts and Probate, Family Law.

WILLIAM A. MUELLER, JR., born Watseka, Illinois, November 5, 1945; admitted to bar, 1972, Illinois. *Education:* University of Illinois (B.A., 1969; J.D., 1972). Assistant States Attorney, McLean County, Illinois, 1972-1973. Member, Bloomington District No. 87 Board of Education, 1991-1994. *Member:* McLean County (Member, Board of Governors, 1974-1978, 1995-1999), Illinois State (Member, Voluntary Fee Arbitration Committee, 2001—) and American (Member, Section of Business Law, 1978—) Bar Associations; Robert C. Underwood Inn of Court (Master); Leading Lawyers Network. ***PRACTICE AREAS:*** Commercial Law; Civil Litigation; Commercial Litigation; Business Formation; Business Transactions; Personal Injury; Real Estate; Mechanics Liens; Estate Planning; Trust Law; Probate. ***Email:*** bmueller@muellerreece.com

JAY D. REECE, born Kirksville, Missouri, December 14, 1960; admitted to bar, 1992, Illinois. *Education:* Illinois State University (B.S., Economics, 1983); Chicago-Kent College of Law (J.D., with honors, 1992). *Member:* McLean County, Illinois State (Member, Standing Committee on Law Related Education for the Public, 1995—; Secretary, 2003-2004; Chair, 2004—) and American Bar Associations; Robert C. Underwood Chapter of the American Inns of Court. ***PRACTICE AREAS:*** Real Estate; Business Formation; Business Transactions; Nonprofit Organizations Law; Tax Exempt Organizations; Civil Litigation; Commercial Litigation; Estate Planning; Trusts; Probate; Personal Injury; Elder Law. ***Email:*** jreece@muellerreece.com

---

GENE CARSON BRUCKER, born Rensselaer, Indiana, January 21, 1975; admitted to bar, 2001, Illinois. *Education:* Illinois State University (B.S., 1997); Dickinson School of Law of the Pennsylvania State University (J.D., 2001). Co-Author: "Using DNA Evidence to Overcome the Presumption of Paternity," Illinois Bar Journal, Vol. 90, September 2002. *Member:* McLean County, Illinois State and American Bar Associations; Robert C. Underwood Inns of Court. ***PRACTICE AREAS:*** Matrimonial Law; Divorce; Child Custody; Visitation Rights; Child Support; Adoption; Civil Litigation; Collections; Criminal Law. ***Email:*** gbrucker@muellerreece.com

REPRESENTATIVE CLIENTS: Heartland Bank and Trust Company; House of Wesley, Inc.; Burgess Seed and Plant Company; Richard Owen Nursery, Inc.; Four Seasons Nursery, Inc.; Farmers Seed and Nursery, Inc.; Stark Excavating, Inc.; Isaacson Construction, Inc.; Passini Concrete Services, Inc.; Carrie Scharf Trucking, Inc.; Mid-America Siding, Inc.; Nordine Remodeling, LLC; U.S. Mechanical Services, Inc.; American Fire Systems, Inc.; Floor Covering Associates of Bloomington, Inc.; Illinois Special Olympics; Illinois Reading Council; Easter Seals/UCP of Central Illinois; Agra-Process Pelleting, Inc.; Central Illinois Medicare Equipment and Supply, Inc.; Merle Pharmacy, Inc.; Gould Marketing and Advertising, Inc.; D.J. Peters Orthopedics, Inc.; Slotky and Santiago, M.D.'s; Medical Hills Internists, LLC; Pinnacle Actuarial Resources, Inc.; Central Illinois Arena Management, Inc.; Terry Winn Tire and Auto Service, Inc.; Baum Chevrolet-Buick, Inc.; Dennison Ford; Toyota BMW, Inc.; Sud's Mercedes Benz; Volvo Audi, Inc.; Phoenix Paper Products, Inc.; Concord Engineering and Science, Inc.; Domestic Uniform and Linen Rental; Normal Township (Normal, Illinois); Easterbrook Drainage District.

THE PRIOR LAW FIRM, P.C.

1210 TOWANDA AVENUE, SUITE 15
P.O. BOX 5968
BLOOMINGTON, ILLINOIS 61702-5968
Telephone: 309-827-4300
Fax: 309-827-4111
Email: johnprior@insightbb.com
URL: http://www.thepriorlawfirm.com

Criminal Defense, Driving While Intoxicated, Traffic Violations, Juvenile Law, Family Law, Personal Injury, Collections and Insurance Subrogation.

FIRM PROFILE: The Prior Law Firm has a full-time Arbitration Writer/Subrogation Specialist on staff, Michel "Mike" Watkins. The firm also represents Spanish-speaking individuals looking for representation regarding their legal matters in which the firm focuses.

JOHN G. PRIOR, JR., admitted to bar, 1990, Illinois. *Education:* Coe College (B.A.); University of Northern Iowa (M.A.); John Marshall Law School (J.D.). Former Elected State's Attorney. *Member:* McLean County and Illinois State Bar Associations; National Association of Subrogation Professionals. ***PRACTICE AREAS:*** Criminal Defense; Driving While Intoxicated; Traffic Violations; Civil Litigation; Juvenile Law; Family Law; Personal Injury; Subrogation. ***Email:*** johnprior@insightbb.com

LARRY J. SPEARS, born Webb, Mississippi, January 10, 1953; admitted to bar, 1980, Illinois. *Education:* University of Illinois, Champaign (B.S., 1976); University of Illinois, Urbana (J.D., 1979); Southern Illinois University (M.S., Administration of Justice, 1991). Lecturer, Sangamon State University. Former Assistant Attorney General. Assistant Public Defender. Associate Director Attorney, Illinois State University. Assistant State Attorney. *Member:* McLean County Bar Association. ***PRACTICE AREAS:*** Criminal Defense; Driving While Intoxicated; Traffic Violations; Civil Litigation; Landlord and Tenant Law; Family Law; Personal Injury. ***Email:*** larryspears@insightbb.com

PRUSAK, WINNE & GORMAN, LTD.

BLOOMINGTON, ILLINOIS

(See Peoria)

General Practice. Trial, Insurance, Workers Compensation, Personal Injury, Probate, Corporate, Construction Litigation, Fire Loss, Professional Liability, Real Estate Law, Automobile Liability Defense, Insurance Coverage, Uninsured and Underinsured Motorists Arbitration, Products Liability Defense, Professional Liability Defense.

ADELE M. SAAF

121 NORTH MAIN STREET, 4TH FLOOR
BLOOMINGTON, ILLINOIS 61701
Telephone: 309-827-3700
Fax: 309-828-3536
Email: a.saaf@insightbb.com

Family Law, Wills, Living Trusts, Real Estate.

ADELE M. SAAF, born Waialua, Hawaii, October 31, 1949; admitted to bar, 1996, Illinois. *Education:* Vassar College (B.A. with honors, 1971) Phi Beta Kappa; Harvard University (M.A., 1973); Thomas M. Cooley Law School (J.D., cum laude, 1995). Dean's List. Honors Scholar. Recipient: American Jurisprudence Award; Certificate of Merit. Assistant Editor, Cooley Law Review, 1994-1995. Author: Casenote, Anywhere but Here: May Neighbors Prevent Group Homes for the Mentally Disabled?, T.M. Cooley Law Review, 1995. ***LANGUAGES:*** Russian, French and Japanese. ***REPORTED CASES:*** In re R.E., 738 N.E.2d 1007 (2000); In re S.B., M.B., and G.B., 736 N.E.2d 1164 (2000); In re K.H., 730 N.E.2d 131 (2000). ***PRACTICE AREAS:*** Divorce; Child Custody; Child Support; Paternity; Adoption Law; Juvenile Law; Name Changes; Residential Real Estate; Estate Planning for the Disabled; Estate Planning for the Elderly; Estate Planning for Unmarried Couples; Civil Appeals.

ROBERT C. STRODEL, LTD.

BLOOMINGTON, ILLINOIS

(See Peoria)

General Practice. Personal Injury Claims, with specialty in Medical Malpractice.

THOMSON & WEINTRAUB

Established in 1941
105 NORTH CENTER STREET
P.O. BOX 3577
BLOOMINGTON, ILLINOIS 61702-3577
Telephone: 309-829-7069
Facsimile: 309-827-3458
URL: http://www.thomsonandweintraub.com

General Civil and Trial Practice in all State and Federal Courts. Personal Injury, Auto Accidents, Workers Compensation, Family Law, Divorce, Adoptions, Bankruptcy, Real Estate, Criminal Law, Probate and Corporate Law, Civil Rights, Discrimination Law, Employment Law, Labor Law, School Law, Immigration Law.

FIRM PROFILE: Thomson & Weintraub was founded in 1941. Serving clients over 60 years throughout Central Illinois. The firm engages in a General Practice with a concentration on all types of litigation.

MEMBERS OF FIRM

CHESTER THOMSON (1910-1977)

ALAN I. WEINTRAUB, born Chicago, Illinois, March 16, 1947; admitted to bar, 1972, Illinois and U.S. Court of Appeals, Seventh Circuit. *Education:* University of Illinois (B.A., 1968; J.D., 1972). Associate Professor, Family Law and Real Estate Law, Illinois State University, 1978-1998. Instructor, Family Law, Illinois State Bar Association, Family Law Section. Speaker, Illinois State Bar Association, Family Law Update. *Member:* McLean County, Illinois State and American Bar Associations. ***REPORTED CASES:*** In re Marriage of Swanson, 275 Ill. App.3d 519, 656 N.E.2d 215 (4th Dist. 1995); In re Marriage of Gustavson, 247 Ill. App.3d 797, 617 N.E.2d 1313 (4th Dist. 1994); In re Marriage of Hobson, 220 Ill. App. 3d 1006, 581 N.E.2d 388 (4th Dist. 1991), as corrected Jan. 29, 1992; In re Marriage of Bush, 191 Ill. App.3d 249, 547 N.E.2d 590, 138 Ill. Dec. 423 (4th Dist. 1989); In re Marriage of Pauley, 104 Ill. App.3d 100, 432 N.E.2d 661, 59 Ill. Dec. 875 (4th Dist. 1982); Doyle v. Doyle, 62 Ill. App.3d 786, 379 N.E.2d 387, 19 Ill. Dec. 723 (4th Dist. 1978); Burton v. Lee, 43 Ill. App.3d 305, 356 N.E.2d 1310, 2 Ill. Dec. 23 (4th Dist. 1976); McClure v. McClure, 29 Ill. App.3d 930, 331 N.E.2d 829 (4th Dist. 1975). ***PRACTICE AREAS:*** Family Law; Real Estate Law.

KATHLEEN McDONALD KRAFT, born Bitburg Air Force Base, Bitburg, Germany, April 11, 1966; admitted to bar, 1991, Illinois and U.S. District Court, Northern District of Illinois; 1992, U.S. District Court, Central District of Illinois. *Education:* University of Illinois (B.A., 1988; J.D., cum laude, 1991). Omicron Delta Kappa. Harno Scholar. *Member:* McLean County (Secretary, 1993-1994), Illinois State and American Bar Associations. American Inns of Court, R.C. Underwood Chapter (Associate and Board Member). Fellow, American Academy of Matrimonial Lawyers. ***PRACTICE AREAS:*** Family Law; General Civil Litigation; Business Law; Real Estate Law.

GINA L. WOOD, born Rochester, Minnesota, February 14, 1968; admitted to bar, 1994, Illinois and U.S. District Court, Northern and Central Districts of Illinois. *Education:* Illinois State University (B.S., 1986); John Marshall Law School (J.D., 1994). Moot Court Participant, Best Brief, Chicago Bar Association Competition. Author: "Preparing Your Client for Divorce Mediation," ISBA General Practice, Vol. 26, No. 4, March 1998. Assistant State's Attorney, McLean County, 1994-1995. Board of Directors, Heartland Head

(This Listing Continued)

Start. Chair, FVCC, Eleventh Circuit. Co-Chair, Domestic Violence Task Force of McLean County. *Member:* McLean County, Illinois State (Member, General Practice Section, 1995-1998) and American Bar Associations; American Inns of Court, R.C. Underwood Chapter (Associate). ***PRACTICE AREAS:*** Family Law; Criminal Defense; Juvenile Law; Probate; General Civil Litigation.

TERENCE B. KELLY, born Camden, New Jersey, October 6, 1962; admitted to bar, 1989, Wisconsin and U.S. District Court, Eastern and Western Districts of Wisconsin; 1995, U.S. Court of Appeals, Seventh Circuit, Illinois and U.S. District Court, Northern, Southern and Central Districts of Illinois. *Education:* Kutztown University (B.A., 1985); University of Iowa (J.D., with distinction, 1989). Author: "Condition Verses Cause: A Doctrine Whose Time Has Passed?" Ill. Bar Journal, Vol. 84, March 1996. *Member:* McLean County and Illinois State Bar Associations; State Bar of Wisconsin; Illinois Trial Lawyers Association. ***REPORTED CASES:*** Seaman v. Thompson Electronics, 325 Ill. App.3d 560, 758 N.E.2d 454, 259 Ill. Dec. 331 (3rd Dist. 2001); Gallianetti v. Industrial Commission, 315 Ill. App. 3d 721, 734 N.E.2d 482, 248 Ill. Dec. 554 (3rd Dist. 2000); Tom Lange Co. v. A. Gagliano Co., 61 F.3d 1305 (7th Cir. 1995); Smith v. Industrial Commission, 308 Ill. App. 3d 260, 719 N.E.2d 329, 241 Ill. Dec. 468 (3rd Dist. 1999). ***PRACTICE AREAS:*** Litigation; Personal Injury; Medical Malpractice; Employment Discrimination; Workers Compensation.

MELISSA M. McGRATH, born Chicago, Illinois, March 25, 1958; admitted to bar, 1991, Illinois, U.S. District Court, Central District of Illinois and U.S. Court of Appeals, Seventh Circuit. *Education:* Illinois State University (B.S., 1980); Southern Illinois University (J.D., cum laude, 1991). Lead Articles Editor, Southern Illinois University Law Journal, 1990-1991. *Author:* "Federal Sentencing Law: Prosecutorial Discretion in Determining Departures Based on Defendant's Cooperation Violates Due Process," Southern Illinois University Law Journal, Vol. 15, Winter 1991; "Employment Discrimination: Title VII Protections Under Disparate Impact Analysis Drastically Diminished?" Southern Illinois University Law Journal, Vol. 15, Fall 1990. Clerk, Justice James A. Knecht, Illinois Appellate Court, Fourth District, 1991-1993. *Member:* McLean County, Illinois State and American Bar Associations. American Inns of Court, R.C. Underwood Chapter (Associate); National Employment Lawyer's Association; Illinois Employment Lawyer's Association. ***REPORTED CASES:*** Szmaj v. AT&T, 291 F.3d 955 (7th Cir. 2002); Thompson v. Archer Daniels Midland Co., 174 F. Supp. 2d 833 (C.D. Ill. 2001); Rewerts v. Reliance Ins. Co., 170 F. Supp. 2d 847 (C.D. Ill. 2001); Szmaj v. AT&T Inc., No. 2001 U.S. Dist. LEXIS 22601, 12 Am. Disabilities Case 1116 (C.D. Ill. 2001); In re Marriage of Shaddle, 317 Ill. App. 3d 428, 740 N.E.2d 525, 251 Ill. Dec. 444 (4th Dist. 2000); In re Marriage of Mayhall, 311 Ill. App. 3d 765, 725 N.E.2d 22, 244 Ill. Dec. 227 (4th Dist. 2000); In re Marriage of Claydon, 306 Ill. App. 3d 895, 715 N.E.2d 1201, 240 Ill. Dec. 144 (4th Dist. 1999); Stockton v. Oldenburg, 305 Ill. App. 3d 897, 713 N.E.2d 259, 238 Ill. Dec. 1013 (4th Dist. 1999); In re Marriage of Fields, 288 Ill. App. 3d 1053, 681 N.E.2d 166, 224 Ill. Dec. 184 (4th Dist. 1997); Kruse v. Kuntz, 288 Ill. App. 3d 431, 683 N.E.2d 1185, 225 Ill. Dec. 522 (4th Dist. 1996); Carmody v. Carmody, 274 Ill. App. 3d 46, 653 N.E.2d 977, 210 Ill. Dec. 782 (4th Dist. 1995); People v. Herbolsheimer, 272 Ill. App. 3d 140, 650 N.E.2d 287, 208 Ill. Dec. 830 (4th Dist. 1995); Tiffin v. Tiffin, 269 Ill. App. 3d 581, 646 N.E.2d 285, 206 Ill. Dec. 918 (4th Dist. 1995); People v. Katz (In re Katz), 267 Ill. App. 3d 692, 642 N.E.2d 893, 205 Ill. Dec. 28 (3rd Dist. 1994); People v. Lutrell (In re Lutrell), 261 Ill. App. 3d 221, 633 N.E.2d 74, 198 Ill. Dec. 612 (4th Dist. 1994). ***PRACTICE AREAS:*** Litigation; Appellate Practice; Employment Discrimination; Civil Rights; Personal Injury; Medical Malpractice; Family Law.

ASSOCIATE

DREW R. QUITSCHAU, born Austin, Texas, February 16, 1977; admitted to bar, 2002, Illinois; 2003, U.S. District Court, Central District of Illinois. *Education:* Gustavus Adolphus College (B.A., 1999); University of Arkansas (J.D., 2002). Articles Editor, Arkansas Law Review, 2001-2002. *Author:* "Anastasoff v. United States: Uncertainty in the Eighth Circuit - Is There A Constitutional Right to Cite Unpublished Opinions?" 54 Ark. L. Rev. 739, 847 (2002). ***PRACTICE AREAS:*** Family Law; Probate; Creditors Rights; Collections; Wills; Debtor and Creditor; Civil Litigation.

REFERENCE: Commerce Bank, Bloomington, Illinois.

TURNER LAW OFFICE

BLOOMINGTON, ILLINOIS

(See Springfield)

Criminal Defense, Driving While Intoxicated, Driving Under the Influence, Traffic Violations, Felonies, Misdemeanors, Drug Crimes, Appeals, Forfeiture, Search and Seizure, Sex Crimes.

WALKER & WYLDER, LTD

Established in 1975

207 W. JEFFERSON STREET
BLOOMINGTON, ILLINOIS 61701
Telephone: 309-828-5044
Fax: 309-827-2742
Email: info@walkerwylder.com
URL: http://www.walkerwylder.com

Toxic Torts, Asbestos, Chrome, Personal Injury, Automobile Accidents, Wrongful Death, Medical Malpractice, Employment Wrongful Discharge, Worker's Compensation.

FIRM PROFILE: The firm represents people with mesothelioma and other cancers and diseases caused by asbestos, cancer caused by chrome, nickel, and other toxic substances, injuries from medical malpractice, vehicle collisions, and employment.

The firm has handled asbestos and other cases for injured people and their families throughout the state of Illinois.

JAMES G. WALKER, born Lincoln, Illinois, October 12, 1944; admitted to bar, 1968, Illinois; 1973, U.S. Supreme Court. *Education:* University of Illinois (B.A., 1966; J.D., 1968). Note and Comments Editor, University of Illinois Law Forum. Law Clerk, Chief Justice Robert C. Underwood, Illinois Supreme Court, 1968-1969. Author: "Constitutionality of Adventitious Segregation in the Public Schools," U. Of Ill. Law Forum 685, 1967. *Member:* McLean County, Illinois State (Member: Legislative Committee, 1992-1994; Civil Practice Section, 1992-1995) and American Bar Associations; Illinois Trial Lawyers Association, (Board of Managers, 1992—); Association of Trial Lawyers of America; American Inns of Court (President, 2000-2002 and Board of Directors, 1996—, Robert C. Underwood Inn). ***PRACTICE AREAS:*** Toxic Torts; Personal Injury. ***Email:*** jwalker@walkerwylder.com

JAMES R. WYLDER, born Peoria, Illinois, January 31, 1953; admitted to bar, 1978, Illinois. *Education:* University of Illinois (A.B., A.B., 1975; J.D., 1978). *Member:* McLean County, Illinois State and American Bar Associations; Illinois Trial Lawyers Association; Association of Trial Lawyers of America; American Inns of Court. ***PRACTICE AREAS:*** Toxic Torts; Medical Malpractice; Personal Injury.

LISA R. CORWIN, born Cadillac, Michigan, November 29, 1971; admitted to bar, 1997, Illinois. *Education:* Kalamazoo College (B.A., 1994); University of Illinois (J.D., 1997). *Member:* McLean County (Treasurer, 1998; Member, Board of Governors, 2002—), Illinois State and American Bar Associations; East Central Illinois Women Attorneys Association; Illinois Trial Lawyers Association (Member: Civil Practice and Rules Committee, 2001—; Young Lawyers Committee, 2002—); Association of Trial Lawyers of America; American Inns of Court. ***PRACTICE AREAS:*** Toxic Torts; Medical Malpractice; Personal Injury; Workers Compensation. ***Email:*** lcorwin@walkerwylder.com

ANDREW J. KELLY, born London, Ontario, February 28, 1974; admitted to bar, 1999, Michigan; 2000, Illinois and U.S. District Court. *Education:* University of Western Ontario (B.A., 1996); Michigan State University (J.D., cum laude, 1999). Moot Court Board, 1998-1999. Editor-in-Chief, Journal of International Law and Practice, 1998-1999. Author: "The GATT Obstacle: International Trade as a Barrier to Enforcement of Environmental Conservation on the High Seas," Florida Journal of International Law, Vol 12, No.1, Spring 1998. *Member:* McLean County, Illinois State and American Bar Associations; State Bar of Michigan; Illinois Trial Lawyers Association; Association of Trial Lawyers of America; American Inns of Court. ***PRACTICE AREAS:*** Toxic Torts; Medical Malpractice; Personal Injury. ***Email:*** akelly@walkerwylder.com

CYNTHIA L. PETERSEN

12757 S. WESTERN AVENUE, SUITE 201
BLUE ISLAND, ILLINOIS 60406
Telephone: 708-388-2250
Fax: 708-388-2150
Email: attypetersen@sbcglobal.net
URL: http://www.attypetersen.com

Divorce, Qualified Domestic Relations Order (QDRO), Paternity, Premarital Agreements, Child Support.

FIRM PROFILE: Cynthia L. Petersen is there for you, providing excellent service and honest answers. Ms. Petersen concentrates her practice in the areas of divorce, paternity, family law, wills, trusts, powers of attorney and residential real estate. She has the knowledge and the ambition to protect your rights and interests.

CYNTHIA L. PETERSEN, born Alexandria, Indiana, 1965; admitted to bar, 1997, Illinois and U.S. District Court, District of Illinois. *Education:* Northwestern College (B.A., 1987); Loyola University (J.D., cum laude, 1997). Chair, Board of Directors, Well Spring Center for Hope. *Member:* Chicago, South Suburban, Illinois State and American Bar Associations.

M. HEDAYAT & ASSOCIATES, P.C.

Established in 1995

425 QUADRANGLE DRIVE, SUITE 101
BOLINGBROOK, ILLINOIS 60440
Telephone: 630-378-2200
Fax: 630-578-2878
URL: http://www.mha-law.com
Email: mmhedayat@mhu-law.com
URL: http://www.lawyers.com/mhedayat

Commercial Litigation, Commercial Transactions, Construction Law and Mechanics Liens, Debtor and Creditor Law, Commercial and Personal Bankruptcy, Commercial and Residential Real Estate.

FIRM PROFILE: The Firm has concentrated its activities in the areas of Real Property law, Construction law and Complex Commercial litigation since 1995, and in Bankruptcy law and litigation since 1997. While high-tech the Firm also remains high-touch, providing Clients with regular, frequent status updates and open lines of communication. The keys to achieving this balance are a relentless emphasis on quality and extensive use of technology in both Inter-office and Client-oriented systems. The Firm utilizes a combination of methods to leverage results for its Clients including:

- *Comprehensive, redundant Office Management systems;*
- *A high-speed internal network and "always-on" client-server environment;*
- *E-mail and Instant Messaging;*
- *Customized Client Extranets;*
- *Online meeting capabilities; and*
- *Proprietary Protocols for case intake, management and follow up.*

(This Listing Continued)

M. HEDAYAT & ASSOCIATES, P.C., Bolingbrook—Continued

MAZYAR M. HEDAYAT, born February 12, 1966; admitted to bar, 1995, Illinois; 1996, U.S. District Court, Northern District of Illinois. *Education:* University of Michigan (B.A., with distinction, 1987; M.B.A., 1990); DePaul University College of Law (J.D., 1995). Registered: Illinois Title Agent, Illinois Securities Representative, 1997-1999. Formerly With: eLawCentral.com LLC, 2000-2002; Securities and Exchange Commission, Midwest Regional Office, 1994; Office of Illinois Commissioner of Savings & Residential Finance, 1993; Miller, Shakman, Kurtzon & Schlifke, 1991-1992; Windstar Acquisitions, Ltd., 1991. *Member:* American Bankruptcy Institute; DuPage County Bar Association; Illinois Real Estate Lawyers' Association. ***LANGUAGES:*** Farsi. ***PRACTICE AREAS:*** Commercial Litigation; Commercial Transactions; Construction Law; Mechanics Liens; Commercial Bankruptcy; Personal Bankruptcy; Commercial Real Estate; Residential Real Estate; Collections. ***Email:*** mmhedayat@hotmail.com

---

ANDREW R. KREAMER, admitted to bar, 2002, Illinois. *Education:* Coe College (History and Political Science, 1998); University of Tulsa (J.D., 2001). ***PRACTICE AREAS:*** Construction Law; Bankruptcy; Personal Injury; Real Estate.

LEGAL SUPPORT PERSONNEL

Della Partovi Human Resources/Accounts Receivable/Accounts Payable.

Language: Farsi.

REPRESENTATIVE CLIENTS: Available upon request.

LAW OFFICES OF JOHN J. LYNCH

BOLINGBROOK, ILLINOIS

(See Woodridge)

Bankruptcy, Wills and Trusts, Probate, Real Estate, Business Law.

MITCHELL, BOLDEN & MELTON, P.C.

BOLINGBROOK, ILLINOIS

(See Joliet)

Criminal Law, Civil Law, Traffic Violations, Real Estate, Employment Law, Family Law.

MOSS AND BLOOMBERG, LTD.

BOLINGBROOK, ILLINOIS

(See Tressler, Soderstrom, Maloney & Priess)

TRESSLER, SODERSTROM, MALONEY & PRIESS

305 WEST BRIARCLIFF ROAD, SUITE 201
BOLINGBROOK, ILLINOIS 60440-0858
Telephone: 630-759-0800
Telecopier: 630-759-8504
URL: http://www.tsmp.com

Chicago, Illinois Office: 233 Wacker Drive, Sears Tower, 22nd Floor, 60606. Telephone: 312-627-4000. Fax: 312-627-1717.

Wheaton, Illinois Office: 2100 Manchester Road, Suite 950, 60187. Telephone: 630-668-2800. Fax: 630-668-3003.

Newark, New Jersey Office: 744 Broad Street, Suite 1510, 07102. Telephone: 973-848-2900. Fax: 973-623-0405.

Los Angeles, California Office: 1901 Avenue of the Stars, Suite 450, 90067. Telephone: 310-203-4800. Fax: 310-203-4850.

Costa Mesa, California Office: 3070 Bristol Street, Suite 450, 92626. Telephone: 714-429-2900. Fax: 714-429-2901.

General Civil Litigation and Trial Practice, Insurance, Reinsurance, Litigation, Insurance Bad Faith, Appellate Practice, Business Litigation, Business Transactions, Class Action Defense, Commercial Litigation, Complex Litigation, Directors and Officers Liability, Construction Law, Architects and Engineers, Fidelity and Surety, Real Estate Litigation and Transactions, Alternative Dispute Resolution, Product Liability, Intellectual Property, Internet Law, Electronic Commerce, Environmental Law, Asbestos Litigation, Health Care, ERISA, Labor and Employment, Technology Law, Securities Litigation, Health Care, Bankruptcy, Advertising Law, Personal Injury, Trusts and Estates, Contracts, Professional Liability, Regulatory, White Collar Crime, Corporate Law, Mergers and Acquisitions, Commodities, Condominium and Common Interest Community Law, Municipal Law.

LAW FIRM ALLIANCES/ASSOCIATIONS: **HARMONIE GROUP**

RESIDENT MEMBERS

BARRY L. MOSS, born Chicago, Illinois, February 3, 1943; admitted to bar, 1968, Illinois. *Education:* Bradley University (B.S., 1964); Northwestern University Law School (J.D., 1967). ***PRACTICE AREAS:*** Municipal Law; School Law; Local Government Law; Litigation; Corporate; Real Estate; Zoning. ***Email:*** bmoss@tsmp.com

STEVEN P. BLOOMBERG, born Chicago, Illinois, November 13, 1943; admitted to bar, 1969, Illinois. *Education:* University of Wisconsin (B.S., 1965); DePaul University (J.D., 1968). ***PRACTICE AREAS:*** Condominium Law; Municipal Law; Local Government Law; Corporate Law; Litigation; Real Estate. ***Email:*** sbloomberg@tsmp.com

GEORGE A. MARCHETTI, born Chicago, Illinois, September 27, 1948; admitted to bar, 1978, Illinois. *Education:* University of Notre Dame (B.A., 1970); University of Chicago (M.A., 1972); Chicago-Kent College of Law (J.D., 1978). ***PRACTICE AREAS:*** Municipal Law; School Law; Local Government Law; Litigation; Zoning. ***Email:*** gmarchetti@tsmp.com

DAVID J. FREEMAN, born Brooklyn, New York, December 14, 1958; admitted to bar, 1983, New Jersey and Pennsylvania; 1988, Illinois. *Education:* Georgetown University (A.B., 1979); Delaware Law School of Widener University (J.D., 1983). ***PRACTICE AREAS:*** Litigation; Insurance Defense; Condominium; Municipal. ***Email:*** dfreeman@tsmp.com

JAMES BOAN, born Milwaukee, Wisconsin, May 27, 1951; admitted to bar, 1983, Illinois. *Education:* University of Illinois (B.S.L.A., 1973); Northern Illinois University (J.D., 1983). ***PRACTICE AREAS:*** Municipal Law; Local Government Law; Zoning Law; Land Use; Litigation. ***Email:*** jboan@tsmp.com

RESIDENT ASSOCIATES

LARA A. ANDERSON, born Chicago, Illinois, August 19, 1967; admitted to bar, 1992, Illinois. *Education:* Northern Illinois University (B.S., 1989; J.D., 1992). ***Email:*** landerson@tsmp.com

JAMES P. ARRIGO, born Chicago, Illinois, February 6, 1960; admitted to bar, 1994, Illinois. *Education:* University of Illinois (B.S., 1982); DePaul University College of Law (J.D., 1994). ***Email:*** jarrigo@tsmp.com

(For Complete Biographical Data on all Personnel, see Professional Biographies at Chicago, Illinois)

ALAN F. SMIETANSKI

236 NORTH INDUSTRIAL DRIVE
BRADLEY, ILLINOIS 60915
Telephone: 815-935-2100
FAX: 815-935-2121
Email: afslaw@ameritech.net
URL: http://www.afslawfirm.com

General Civil and Trial Practice. Corporate, Real Estate, Probate, Collections, Personal Injury, Municipal and Domestic Relations Law, Estate Planning, Wills, Probate, Trusts and Estates, Adoption Law, Child Custody, Child Support, Wrongful Death Automobile Accidents, Medical Malpractice.

FIRM PROFILE: Alan F. Smietanski established his own firm in 1977. He has been serving clients throughout Kankakee, Iroquois and surrounding counties for over 20 years. Mr. Smietanski engages in a General Practice.

ALAN F. SMIETANSKI, born Kankakee, Illinois, September 20, 1951; admitted to bar, 1976, Illinois; 1977, U.S. District Court, Central District of Illinois; 1983, Florida; 1986, U.S. District Court, Northern District of Illinois including Trial Bar. *Education:* University of Illinois (B.A., 1973); John Marshall Law School (J.D., 1976). Assistant Public Defender, Kankakee County, 1977-1980. Municipal Counsel to Village of Bradley, Illinois, 1981—. *Member:* Chicago, Kankakee County and Illinois State Bar Associations; The Florida Bar.

REPRESENTATIVE CLIENTS: Adjustment Services, Inc.; American States Insurance Co.; Amerisure Cos.; Village of Bradley; Bradley-Bourbonnais Community High School District 307; Bourbonnais Township; Court Street Ford, Inc.; G & G Studios/Broadway Printing, Inc.; Guaranty National Insurance Co.; Illinois Insurance Guaranty Fund; International Association of Bridge, Structural and Ornamental Iron Workers; Iron Workers Local 465 Health and Welfare Fund; Bell Financial Community Credit Union; Ranger Insurance Co.; Spieth's Markets, Inc.; Illiana Financial Credit Union; Village of Bonfield.

LAW OFFICES OF JAMES D. STOUT

324 NORTH MAIN STREET
P.O. BOX 8
BRIDGEPORT, ILLINOIS 62417
Telephone: 618-945-2911
Fax: 618-945-3941
Email: jds1@shawneelink.net
URL: http://www.lawyers.com/stoutholtzhouser

Robinson, Illinois Office: 309 South Jefferson, P.O. Box 714, 62454. Telephone: 618-546-5404. Fax: 618-544-3659.

General Civil Practice. Trials. Corporation, Real Estate, Oil and Gas, Probate and Estate Planning Law.

(For complete biographical data on all personnel, see Professional Biographies, Robinson, Illinois)

ADLER LAW OFFICES, LTD.

BUFFALO GROVE, ILLINOIS

(See Arlington Heights)

Personal Injury, Automobile Accidents, Medical Malpractice, Products Liability, Wrongful Death.

LOIS KULINSKY & ASSOCIATES, LTD.

BUFFALO GROVE, ILLINOIS

(See Wheeling)

Family Law, Divorce, Adoptions, Child Custody, Child Support, Real Estate, Domestic Violence, Visitation Rights, Buying or Selling a Home, Trusts and Estates, Estate Planning, Wills and Probate, Incorporation.

PINZUR, COHEN & KERR, LTD.

BUFFALO GROVE, ILLINOIS

(See Long Grove)

Administrative Matters, Adoption Law, Annexation, Appellate Practice, Arbitration, Asset Acquisitions and Sales, Banking and Loan Documentation, Banking Law, Business Law, Business Litigation, Business Planning and Formation, Business Successions, Buying and Selling of Businesses, Child Custody, Child Support, Civil Litigation in State and Federal Courts, Civil Rights, Class Actions, Closings, Collections, Commercial and Residential Development, Commercial Litigation, Commercial Real Estate, Community Association Law, Condemnation, Condominium Law, Contractual Disputes, Construction Law, Construction Arbitration, Construction Defects, Construction Litigation, Consumer Law, Contested Wills, Contracts, Cooperative Housing Law, Copyrights, Corporate Law, Corporations, Creditors Rights, Debtor and Creditor, Developer Disputes, Discrimination, Divorce, Domestic Violence, Elder Law, Employment Agreements, Employment Law, Entrepreneurial Ventures, Environmental Law, Equipment Leasing, Equitable and Injunctive Remedies, Estate Planning, Family Law, Family Business Law, Forcible Eviction Law, Foreclosures, Franchise Law, General Practice, Guardianship, Harassment, Homeowner's Association Law, Incorporation, Institutional Lending, Insurance Regulations, Workouts, Insurance, Land Development and Zoning, Landlord and Tenant Law, Leases and Leasing, Limited Liability Companies, Litigation, Matrimonial Law, Mechanics Liens, Mergers and Acquisitions, Mortgages, Municipal, Partnership Law, Personal Injury, Premarital Agreements, Probate Law, Real Estate, Real Estate Finance, Real Estate Litigation, Real Estate Tax Appeals, Real Estate Tax Assessment, Residential Real Estate, Sales Acquisitions, School Law, Secured Transactions, Small Business Law, Social Security, Spousal Support, Stock Acquisitions and Sales, Trademarks, Trusts and Estates, Uniform Commercial Code, Wills, Zoning, Planning and Land Use.

MARTIN B. ROBINS

1110 LAKE COOK ROAD, SUITE 355
BUFFALO GROVE, ILLINOIS 60089
Telephone: 847-229-8710
Fax: 847-229-8839
Email: mrobins@mr-laws.com

MARTIN B. ROBINS, admitted to bar, 1980, Illinois. *Education:* University of Pennsylvania, Wharton School of Finance and Commerce (B.S., summa cum laude, 1977); Harvard University (J.D., cum laude, 1980). Author: "Cyberfinance: Raising Capital for the E-Business," CCH, 2001; "Patching the Leaky Umbrella: How to Cope with Drafting Anomalies in UCC Article 2A," Journal of Equipment Lease Finance, April 1997; "One Size Doesn't Fit All: A Primer (or Refresher) on Negotiating Commercial Loan Transactions and Documentation on Behalf of Borrowers," Chicago Bar Record, May 1997; "A Happy Medium: How to Acquire a Medium-Sized Business," 85 Illinois Bar Journal, September 1997; "Making Nice: Help Your Client Nurture Good Relations in Contract Negotiations," Business Law Today, May 1998; Matthew Bender Monograph "Commercial Equipment Leasing," March 2000; "Recipe for an Overdue Change: Why Corporate Lawyers Sometimes Need to Give Business Advice," Business Law Today, July/Aug., 2003; "Computing the Contract: Getting that tech stuff from the User Prospective," Business Law Today, May/June, 2004. Panelist: American Bar Association Teleconferences: Lawyers' Obligation to Give Business Advice, August 2003; Representing Technology Users' in Contract Negotiations, June 2004. Adjunct Professor, DePaul University College of Law, 2005. ***PRACTICE AREAS:*** Business Formation; Limited Liability Company Law; Small Business Law; Business Law; S Corporations; Executive Compensation; Employment Contracts; Leveraged Leasing; Technology Law; Technology Licensing; Mergers and Acquisitions; Corporate Finance; Asset Based Finance; Corporate Contracts; Information Technology Contracts; Computer Law; Equipment Leasing; Securities Offerings; Commercial Credit; Business Start-Ups; Buying and Selling of Businesses; Software Licensing.

LAW OFFICES OF ROGER W. STELK

BUFFALO GROVE, ILLINOIS

(See Arlington Heights)

Family Law, Divorce, Real Estate, Buying and Selling a Home, Civil Litigation.

WILLIAM G. PINTAS & ASSOCIATES, LTD.

CALUMET CITY, ILLINOIS

(See Chicago)

Personal Injury, Workers Compensation, Accidents, Automobile Accidents and Injuries, Automobile Negligence, Bodily Injury, Brain Injury, Plaintiffs Personal Injury, Motorcycle Accidents, Head Injury, Electrical Injury, Slip and Fall, Spinal Injury, Medical Malpractice, Birth Trauma, Gynecology Malpractice, Medical Negligence, Physicians Professional Liability, Psychiatric Malpractice, Surgeons Liability.

GREGORY R. SKUBISZ

1461 RING ROAD
CALUMET CITY, ILLINOIS 60409
Telephone: 708-862-0101
Fax: 708-862-0202
URL: http://www.lawyers.com/gregoryrskubisz

Criminal, Personal Injury, General Civil Litigation, Family, Real Estate, Estate Planning and Probate, Driving Under Influence, Traffic and Felonies.

GREGORY R. SKUBISZ, born 1951; admitted to bar, 1979, Illinois. *Education:* St. Joseph College (B.A., 1973); John Marshall Law School (J.D., 1979). Driving License Reinstatement and Secretary of State Hearing. ***PRACTICE AREAS:*** Criminal Law; Personal Injury; Family; Real Estate; Estate Planning; Probate.

(This Listing Continued)

ASSOCIATE

JOHN F. PELKEY, born San Antonio, Texas, July 7, 1951; admitted to bar, 1984, Illinois. *Education:* University of Illinois (B.A., 1976); John Marshall Law School (J.D., 1984). *Member:* Chicago, Illinois State and American Bar Associations. ***PRACTICE AREAS:*** Criminal Law; Personal Injury; Family; Real Estate; Estate Planning; Probate.

BROWN AND RAY

CAMBRIDGE, ILLINOIS

(See Geneseo)

General Civil Practice. Real Estate, Estate Planning and Probate, Drainage and Levee, Family and Taxation Law, Domestic Relations, Divorce, Wills and Trusts.

THOMAS W. MONTGOMERY

Established in 1975

127 NORTH PROSPECT STREET
P.O. BOX 176
CAMBRIDGE, ILLINOIS 61238-0176
Telephone: 309-937-3313
Fax: 309-937-3314
Email: twmlaw@theinter.com

Criminal Law, Traffic Violations, Driving While Intoxicated, Real Estate, Estate Planning, Wills, Trusts, Probate, Family Law, Divorce, Adoption, Personal Injury, Child Support, General Practice.

THOMAS W. MONTGOMERY, born Lincoln, Illinois, November 9, 1945; admitted to bar, 1972, Illinois. *Education:* University of Illinois (B.S., 1969; J.D., 1972). Finalist, University of Illinois Moot Court Team. Certified Public Accountant, Illinois, 1970. Co-Author: "Limited Partnerships, Some Legal and Tax Aspects," Illinois Banker, December, 1971. Public Defender, Henry County, Illinois, 1976-1977. *Member:* Henry County (President, 1980-1981), Illinois State and American Bar Associations.

BRYCEDOWNEY, LLC

P.O. BOX 100
CANTON, ILLINOIS 61520
Telephone: 309-789-2839
Fax: 309-789-2840
URL: http://www.brycedowney.com

Chicago, Illinois Office: 200 North LaSalle Street, Suite 2700, 60601. Telephone: 312-377-1501. Fax: 312-377-1502.

General Practice.

FIRM PROFILE: The professionals of the Chicago the law firm of BryceDowney, LLC are dedicated to the delivery of world-class service to the firm's Clients. Located in the heart of Chicago's loop BryceDowney, LLC is a diversified full service Chicago-based law firm. BryceDowney, LLC represent commercial, construction, banking, real estate development, manufacturing, advertising and insurance companies. Our practice includes creation and management of business organizations, financial transactions, real estate transactions, business transactions, accounts receivable management, personal injury defense, workers' compensation, transportation, business advice, employment advice and litigation.

As a full service firm, our trial attorneys, with nearly a century of combined trial experience efficiently and professionally manage and present cases for resolution to jury, judge or arbitration panel. The firm's trial attorneys are trial bar certified by the federal court and have for decades tried diverse cases to diverse fact finders. The trial attorneys' experience includes, construction, commercial, employment, personal injury and worker's compensation trials.

World-class service is accomplished in our business and transactional practice by decades of business entity formation, transactional document preparation, negotiation, drafting and execution. The firm's library of completed contracts, case law and business entity formation models provide a wealth of references for your business goals.

The firm also utilizes an Integrated Management System which allows business managers to make informed decisions about their litigation. Once a business decision is made, the strategy is executed and the results tracked and documented. The Integrated Management System is an on-going computer based data driven decisional matrix capturing the economics of litigation. The goal of Integrated Management System is to return the litigation decisions to the Client for integration into the Client's business objectives.

DAWN M. TARTER, born Illinois, October 6, 1963; admitted to bar, 1994, Illinois and U.S. District Court, Northern, Southern and Central Districts of Illinois. *Education:* Beloit College (B.A., 1985); Chicago-Kent College of Law (J.D., 1994). *Member:* Illinois State Bar Association. ***PRACTICE AREAS:*** Workers Compensation. **Email:** dtarter@brycedowney.com

BARRETT, TWOMEY, BROOM, HUGHES & HOKE, LLP

100 NORTH ILLINOIS AVENUE
P.O. BOX 3747
CARBONDALE, ILLINOIS 62902-3747
Telephone: 618-457-0437
Facsimile: 618-457-0411
Email: mail@btbhw.com
URL: http://www.lawyers.com/btbh&w

Banking, Estate Planning, Real Estate, Civil Trials and Appeals.

FIRM PROFILE: Barrett, Twomey, Broom, Hughes & Hoke, LLP is a general practice firm with an emphasis in business, banking, real estate, civil litigation and estate planning. Our practice covers the entire state of Illinois.

MEMBERS OF FIRM

WILLIAM L. BROOM III, born Effingham, Illinois, June 25, 1947; admitted to bar, 1972, Illinois; 1976, U.S. District Court, Southern District of Illinois; 1980, U.S. Court of Appeals, 7th Circuit; 1988, U.S. District Court, Central District of Illinois; 2000, U.S. Supreme Court. *Education:* University of Illinois (B.S., 1969; J.D., 1972). Author: Estate Planning Handbook, Chapter 8, Planning Techniques, Illinois Institute for Continuing Legal Education, 2005. Co-Author: Eminent Domain Handbook, Chapter 8, "Trial Procedure and Technique," Illinois Institute of Continuing Legal Education, 2002. Author: Advising Elderly Clients and Their Families, Chapter 4, Planning for Incapacity, Powers of Attorney, Living Trusts and Forms of Ownership, Illinois Institute of Continuing Legal Education, 2000. Registered Emergency Medical Technician, Illinois, 1982-1984. Special Assistant Attorney General, Illinois Departments of Transportation and Natural Resources, 1983—. Member, 1985-1997, Board of Trustees, Southern Illinois Hospital Services. *Member:* Jackson County, Illinois State (Member, Health Care Section Council, 1986-1991; Chairman, 1989 and Member, 1987-1993, Standing Committee on Continuing Legal Education; Chair, 1992; Member, Special Committee on Ethics, 2000—; Special Committee on Ancillary Services, 2001—; Standing Committee on Professional Responsibility, 2005—) and American Bar Associations; Illinois C.P.A. Society; The Association of Trial Lawyers of America; Illinois Trial Lawyers Association; Leading Lawyer Network. [U.S. Navy, 1972-1976, Lieut, J.A.G.C.]. ***REPORTED CASES:*** City of Carbondale v. Yehling, 96 Ill. 2d 495, 451 N.E. 2d 495; Norman v. American National First Insurance Company 198 Ill. App. 3d 269, 555 N.E. 2d 1087; Department of Conservation v. Fairless, 273 Ill. App. 3d 705, 653 N.E. 2d 446. ***PRACTICE AREAS:*** Trial Practice; Appellate Law; Eminent Domain; Estate Planning. ***Email:*** WmLBroom@aol.com

MICHAEL R. TWOMEY, born Jacksonville, Florida, October 22, 1954; admitted to bar, 1980, Illinois and U.S. District Court, Southern District of Illinois. *Education:* University of Illinois; Southern Illinois University (B.A., 1977; J.D., 1980). Trained Mediator, Northern Illinois University, 1995. *Member:* Jackson County (Secretary, 1983-1984; President, 1985-1986) and Illinois State (Member, Young Lawyers Division, Liaison, 1981-1982) Bar Associations; Leading Lawyer Network. ***PRACTICE AREAS:*** Banking Law; Real Estate; Creditors Rights Law; Bankruptcy; Water District Law; Mediation. ***Email:*** mtwomey@btbhw.com

KENNETH R. HUGHES, born Carbondale, Illinois, October 7, 1948; admitted to bar, 1982, Illinois and U.S. District Court, Southern District of Illinois; 1996, U.S Court of Appeals, 7th Circuit; 2000, U.S. Supreme Court. *Education:* University of Illinois (B.A., 1970); Troy State University (M.B.A., 1978); Southern Illinois University Law School (J.D., magna cum laude, 1982). Phi Kappa Phi; Phi Alpha Delta. Editor, Southern Illinois University Law Review, 1981-1982. Adjunct Professor of Law, Southern Illinois University School of Law, 1986. Instructor, Civil Procedure, Southern Illinois University, 1984—; Carbondale Housing Board of Appeals, 1995-2003. *Member:* Jackson County, Illinois State and American Bar Associations; Illinois Trial Lawyers Association; The Association of Trial Lawyers of America (Board of Visitors, SIU School of Law, 2000—); Leading Lawyer Network. [Captain, USAF, 1970-1978]. ***PRACTICE AREAS:*** Banking Law; Creditors Rights Law; Real Estate; Corporate Law; Trusts and Estates; Trial Practice. ***Email:*** khughes@btbhw.com

PATRICIA A. HOKE, born Fairfield, Illinois, September 6, 1953; admitted to bar, 1991, Illinois. *Education:* Southern Illinois University (B.S., 1988; J.D., magna cum laude, 1991; M.A., Accounting, 2003). Phi Kappa Phi; Phi Delta Phi. Recipient: Natural Resources Law Award, 1991; Journal of Legal Medicine Award, 1991. Research Editor, Southern Illinois University Law Review, 1990-1991. Author: "Handout, Family Law Section Education Series," Court Awards and Standards, December 8 and 15, 1990, Panelist Wenona Y. Whitfield, SIU School of Law; "A Further Analysis of Bush v. Turner," Family Law Newsletter, Vol. 33, No. 5, p. 6, June, 1990, Illinois State Bar Association; "DNA Tests in Criminal Prosecutions - Too Much Evidence or Not Enough?" 11 J. Legal Med. 481, 1990; "Estate Planning: Schools Out: A Practice Primer for New Attorneys, IICLE, 1999 Edition; "Estate Planning", Starting Points: The Fundamentals of Practice in Illinois, IICLE, 2001 Edition; "Premarital Agreements," Illinois Family Law, IICLE, 2003 Edition. Instructor, Southern Illinois University, School of Accountancy, Master of Accountancy Program, State and Local Taxation, 2005—. Member, Board of Directors, 1998— and Chair, 2004-2005, Illinois Institute for Continuing Legal Education. ***PRACTICE AREAS:*** Estate Planning; Probate; Real Estate; Corporate Law; Banking Law. ***Email:*** phoke@btbhw.com

ASSOCIATES

CRAIG R. REEVES, born St. Louis, Missouri, November 17, 1958; admitted to bar, 1985, Illinois; 1986, U.S. Claims Court; 1996, U.S. Court of Appeals, Seventh Circuit; 1997, U.S. District Court, Southern District of Illinois; 2000, U.S. Supreme Court. *Education:* Southern Illinois University (B.A., 1982; J.D., 1985). Phi Alpha Delta. Student Articles Editor, Southern Illinois University Law Journal, 1984-1985. Author: Casenote, "Kaske v. City of Rockford," 1984 Southern Illinois University Law Journal 205. Instructor, Real Estate Law, Southern Illinois University Division of Continuing Education, 1991-1994. Board of Directors, 1999— and President, 2003, Carbondale Main Street, Inc. *Member:* Jackson County, Illinois State (Member, Young Lawyers Division Section Council, 1991-1998; Community Involvement Committee, 1995-1996) and American (State Chair, Disaster Legal Assistance Committee, 1991-1999) Bar Associations. ***PRACTICE AREAS:*** Civil Appeals; Business Law; Corporate Law; Real Estate. ***Email:*** Lawhog@aol.com

(This Listing Continued)

PATRICIA A. SMALL, born Chicago, Illinois, December 25, 1960; admitted to bar, 1988, Nebraska; 1991, Illinois; U.S. District Court, Southern District of Illinois; 1999, South Carolina; 2000, U.S. Supreme Court. *Education:* University of Nebraska at Omaha (B.S., summa cum laude, 1984); University of Nebraska at Lincoln (J.D., with high distinction, 1988). Phi Kappa Phi. Delta Theta Phi. Order of the Coif. Member, University of Nebraska Law Review, 1986-1988. Author, Illinois Eminent Domain Practice, Chapter 14, "Appeals," Illinois Institute of Continuing Legal Education, 2002; Co-Author: Illinois Causes of Action, in Chapter 12, "Motor Vehicle Actions: Automobiles and Heavy Trucks," Illinois Institute of Continuing Legal Education, 2002. Law Clerk to Justice William C. Hastings, Nebraska Supreme Court, 1988-1990. Special Assistant Attorney General, Illinois Departments of Transportation and Natural Resources. *Member:* Nebraska State, Illinois State, South Carolina State and American Bar Associations. ***REPORTED CASES:*** Ritter v. Stanton, 745 N.E. 2d. 828 (Ind. App. 2001), transfer denied, cert. denied; Magna Trust Company, Administrator of The Estate of James C. Jones, Deceased v. Illinois Central Railroad Company, 313 Ill. App. 3d 375, 378 N.E. 2d 797 (2000). ***PRACTICE AREAS:*** Appellate Practice; Eminent Domain; Trial Practice. ***Email:*** psmall@mindspring.com

CAREY C. GILL, born Dennison, Iowa, June 9, 1976; admitted to bar, 2001, Illinois; 2002, Missouri and U.S. District Court, Central District of Illinois. *Education:* Monmouth College (B.A., summa cum laude, 1998); Southern Illinois University School of Law (J.D., summa cum laude, 2001). Managing Editor, Southern Illinois Law Journal, 2000-2001. Author: "You've Got Mail: Privacy Rights in the Workplace," Southern Illinois University Law Journal, Vol. 25, Issue 3. *Member:* Jackson County Bar; Illinois State Bar; American Bar Association. ***PRACTICE AREAS:*** Banking Law; Corporate Law; Civil Litigation; Eminent Domain; Estate Planning. ***Email:*** cgill@btbhw.com

SARAH J. TAYLOR, born Seattle, Washington, May 14, 1974; admitted to bar, 2002, Illinois. *Education:* Southern Illinois University, Carbondale (B.A., cum laude, 1997; J.D., magna cum laude, 2002). Student Articles Editor, Southern Illinois University Law Journal, 2001-2002. *Member:* Jackson County, Illinois State and American Bar Associations. ***PRACTICE AREAS:*** Creditors Rights; Civil Litigation; Estate Planning; Eminent Domain; Municipal. ***Email:*** staylor@btbhw.com

REPRESENTATIVE CLIENTS: Old National Bank, Carbondale, Illinois; Egyptian Electric Cooperative Association; First Bank of Carbondale, Illinois; Banterra Bank, State of Illinois Departments of Transportation and Natural Resources; S.I.U. Credit Union; Union Planters Bank; Carbondale Park District; Millstone Water District; U.S. Bancorp; First Bank & Trust Co., Murphysboro, Illinois; Murdale Water District; Ora Township; Vergennes Township; Village of DeSoto; Twin County Service Co., A Farm Service (FS) Cooperative; Illinois Agricultural Association, FS Credit Corp.; Egyptipan Water Company; Lakeside Water District.
REFERENCES: Old National Bank, Carbondale, Illinois; First Bank of Carbondale, Illinois.

BRANDON, SCHMIDT & GOFFINET

Established in 1977
916 WEST MAIN STREET
P.O. BOX 3898
CARBONDALE, ILLINOIS 62902-3898
Telephone: 618-549-0777
Telecopier: 618-457-4691
Email: inquiry@carbondalelaw.com
URL: http://www.carbondalelaw.com

General and Trial Practice. Insurance, Malpractice, Workers Compensation and Personal Injury Law.

FIRM PROFILE: The firm has been in the practice of general law and trial practice since 1977 and serves the entire Southern Illinois area in both State and Federal Courts. All firm partners and associates participate in continuing legal education seminars.

MEMBERS OF FIRM

WM. KENT BRANDON, born Carbondale, Illinois, August 25, 1939; admitted to bar, 1965, Illinois and U.S. District Court, Southern District of Illinois; U.S. Court of Appeals, Seventh Circuit; U.S. Supreme Court. *Education:* Southern Illinois University (B.A., 1961); Northwestern University (J.D., 1964). Author: "Magistrate Practice in Civil Matters," Federal Civil Practice, 1974; U.S. Magistrate, Eastern District of Illinois, 1971-1975. *Member:* Jackson County (Secretary, 1965-1966; President, 1975) and Illinois State Bar Associations; American Judicature Society; American College of Trial Lawyers. ***Email:*** wkbrandon@carbondalelaw.com

CHARLES E. SCHMIDT, born Munich, Germany, August 18, 1952; admitted to bar, 1977, Illinois and U.S. District Court, Southern District of Illinois; U.S. Court of Appeals, Seventh Circuit; U.S. Supreme Court. *Education:* Southern Illinois University (B.S., 1974; J.D., magna cum laude, 1977). Phi Alpha Delta. Author: "Survey of Illinois Law: Medical Malpractice," Southern Illinois University Law Journal, Vol. 22, 1998; "Recovery for Loss of Society and Companionship in Wrongful Death and Personal Injury Actions," Southern Illinois University Law Journal, Vol. 13, P. 319, 1989. *Member:* Jackson County, Illinois State and American Bar Associations; American Bar Foundation; Illinois Association of Defense Trial Counsel; Defense Research Institute. ***Email:*** cschmidt@carbondalelaw.com

JEFFREY A. GOFFINET, born Benton, Illinois, June 7, 1959; admitted to bar, 1984, Illinois, U.S. District Court, Southern District of Illinois and U.S. Court of Appeals, Seventh Circuit. *Education:* Southern Illinois University (B.A., 1981; B.S., 1981; J.D., cum laude, 1984). Phi Kappa Phi; Phi Alpha Delta. Adjunct Professor of Law, Southern Illinois University, Carbondale, 1992. *Member:* Franklin County, Jackson County and Illinois State Bar Associations; Illinois Association of Defense Trial Counsel. ***Email:*** jgoffinet@carbondalelaw.com

(This Listing Continued)

ASSOCIATES

KENTON J. OWENS, born Benton, Illinois, June 9, 1971; admitted to bar, 1999, Illinois and U.S. District Court, Southern District of Illinois; 2000, Missouri. *Education:* University of Illinois (A.B., 1995); Southern Illinois University (J.D., 1998). *Member:* The Missouri Bar. ***Email:*** kowens@carbondalelaw.com

AARON L. WRIGHT, born Seattle, Washington; admitted to bar, 2003, Illinois. *Education:* Toccoa Falls College (B.A., 1990); Southern Illinois University (J.D., 2003). Member, Moot Court, Appellate Division. *Member:* Illinois State Bar Association; Christian Legal Society (Vice President, 2001-2002; President, 2002-2003); Lincoln's Inn. ***Email:*** awright@carbondalelaw.com

REPRESENTATIVE CLIENTS: State Farm Mutual Automobile Insurance Co.; State Farm Fire & Casualty Co.; Pekin Insurance Co.; Grinnel Mutual Reinsurance Co.; Western Casualty & Surety Co. (The Western Insurance Cos.); National Indemnity Co.; Reliance Insurance Co.; Fireman's Fund American Insurance Co.; Illinois State Medical Insurance Services, Inc.; The St. Paul Insurance Co.; Ford Motor Co.; Continental Insurance Co.; The Hartford Insurance Co.; Commercial Union Insurance Co.; Madison Mutual Insurance Co.; U.S.A.A.; John Deere Insurance Co.; Progressive Insurance Co.; Hanover Insurance Co.; Lenders Service, Inc.; Bordel Corp.; PICOM Insurance; MetLife Insurance; Unitrin Insurance Company; RML Insurance; Liberty Mutual Group.
REFERENCE: Old National Bank, Carbondale, Illinois.

FEIRICH/MAGER/GREEN/RYAN

2001 WEST MAIN STREET
P.O. BOX 1570
CARBONDALE, ILLINOIS 62903-1570
Telephone: 618-529-3000
Telecopier: 618-529-3008

General Trial and Appellate Litigation, Business, Probate, Trust, Real Estate, Insurance Law, Worker's Compensation, Banking and Corporation Law, Intellectual Property and Healthcare Law.

MEMBERS OF FIRM

JOHN K. FEIRICH (1909-1998)

T. RICHARD MAGER (1934-2002)

RICHARD A. GREEN, born Murphysboro, Illinois, March 5, 1946; admitted to bar, 1972, Illinois. *Education:* Southern Illinois University (B.A., 1968); University of Illinois (J.D., 1972). Phi Alpha Delta; Order of the Coif. Adjunct Professor, Creditor's Rights, 1976 and Trial Advocacy, 1981-1996, Southern Illinois University. Instructor: Trial Advocacy Center for Continuing Legal Education, Western Michigan University, 1979-1982; Trial Advocacy, National Institute for Trial Advocacy, Midwest Regional Session, 1980—; National Institute for Trial Advocacy, Negotiations, 1981-1985. *Member:* Jackson County, Illinois State and American Bar Associations. ***PRACTICE AREAS:*** Personal Injury Defense Law; Products Liability Defense Law; Medical Malpractice Defense Law; Insurance Law. ***Email:*** rgreen@fmgr.com

JOHN C. RYAN, born Jacksonville, Illinois, July 25, 1951; admitted to bar, 1976, Illinois; 1979, U.S. District Court, Southern District of Illinois; 1982, U.S. Court of Appeals, Seventh Circuit; 1990, U.S. Supreme Court; 1994, Kentucky; 1998, Missouri and U.S. District COurt, Western District of Kentucky. *Education:* University of Denver (B.A., 1973); Southern Illinois University (J.D., 1976); National Institute for Trial Advocacy. *Member:* Jackson County (President, 1982-1983), Illinois State (Member, Young Lawyers Division Council, 1979-1985), Kentucky and American (Member, Lawyers Division Executive Council, 1984-1985) Bar Associations; The Missouri Bar; American Society of Law and Medicine. ***PRACTICE AREAS:*** Local Government Torts Defense; Local Government Civil Rights Defense; Medical Malpractice Defense; Product Liability Defense; Personal Injury Law; Employment Discrimination. ***Email:*** jryan@fmgr.com

MICHAEL F. DAHLEN, born Chicago, Illinois, April 30, 1949; admitted to bar, 1974, Illinois and U.S. District Court, Northern District of Illinois; 1979, U.S. District Court, Southern District of Illinois; 1982, U.S. Court of Appeals, Seventh Circuit; 1989, U.S. Supreme Court; 1991, U.S. Court of Appeals, Eighth Circuit; 1994, Kentucky. *Education:* Loras College (B.A., magna cum laude, 1971); DePaul University (J.D., 1974); National Institute for Trial Advocacy. Phi Alpha Delta; Delta Epsilon Sigma. Recipient, American Jurisprudence Award for Contracts. Member, De Paul Law Review, 1972-1974. Author: "People v. Dollen and United States v. Russell: New Developments in the Defense of Entrapment," 23 De Paul Law Review 570, 1973; "Common Errors in Appellate Practice," 7 Judicial Administration 1, Illinois State Bar Association, May, 1977; "Dismissal of a Complaint or Counts Thereof: A Few Appellate and Jurisdictional Ramifications," 69 Illinois Bar Journal 160, 1980; "Supreme Court Rule 24: Appellate Court Research Departments," 69 Illinois Bar Journal 766, 1981; Appellate Practice Skills Handbook, Section 8, "Procedural Considerations," Illinois Institute for Continuing Legal Education, 1982; Section II, "Scope and Powers of Review," Illinois Civil Appeals: The Current Law and Practice Clinic, Course Materials and Practice Handbook (IICLE, 1988); Section II, "Perfecting the Appeal," Appellate Practice for Illinois Lawyers, Course Materials and Practice Handbook (IICLE, 1989); "Supreme Court Rule 237 (b): Requiring the Corporate Defendant to Produce Employees or Officers at Trial," in Program Casebook, Hot Tips on Handling and Avoiding Common Settlement and Trial Problems, 63-89 (ISBA Law Ed Series, April, 1991); "The Appellate Timetable: a Procedural Checklist For the General Practitioner," 90 Illinois Bar Journal 188 (2002). Co-Author: "Scope and Powers of Review," Civil Appeals, Chapter 13, Illinois Institute for Continuing Legal Education, 1984, 1987 and 1989; "Supreme Court Rule 272: What Every Appellate Attorney Must Know Regarding Entry of a Final Judgement," 1 Appellate Law Review 6 (1989); "Reverse Apparent Agency in Medical Malpractice Cases, or Can the Plaintiff Have It Both Ways?' Defense Newsletter, Illinois Association of Defense Trial Counsel (October, 2002). Instructor, Illinois Institute for Continuing Legal Education, 1984-1990, 1993 and Illinois State Bar Association, Law Ed. Series (1991, 1997, 2002). Research Director and Court Administrator, Illinois Appellate Court, Fifth District, 1975-1981. Member: National Committee of Appellate Court Staff Counsel, 1978-1981, Board of Commissioners, State Appellate Defender Commission, 1979-1981; Illinois Supreme Court Judicial Information System Committee, 1980-1981. *Member:* Jackson County (President, 1987-1989), Illinois State (Secretary, Bench and Bar Section Council, 1986-1987; Member, Civil Practice and Procedure Section Council, 1988-1992; Member, Special Committee on Merit Selection of Judges by Appointment, 1987; Special Committee on Appellate Practice, 2001-2002) and American (Member, Tort and Insurance Practice, Litigation and Appellate Advocacy Committee, 1982—) Bar Associations; Illinois Appellate Lawyers Association (Board of Directors, 1991-1993); Defense Research Institute; Illinois Association of Defense Trial Counsel; Bar Association of the Central and Southern Federal Districts of Illinois; Illinois Association of Healthcare Attorneys; Transporatation Lawyers Association; Illinois Volunteers for Justice. ***PRACTICE AREAS:*** Appellate Practice; Insurance Defense Law; Medical Malpractice; Civil Litigation; Workers' Compensation Law. ***Email:*** mdahlen@fmgr.com

KEVIN L. MECHLER, born Belleville, Illinois, October 11, 1957; admitted to bar, 1982, Illinois and U.S. District Court, Central and Southern Districts of Illinois; 1991, North Carolina; 1993, Kentucky. *Education:* Southern Illinois University (B.S., 1979; J.D., 1982). Beta Gamma Sigma. Recipient, American Jurisprudence Award in Torts, 1979. *Member:* Jackson County, Illinois State (Member, Sections on: Workers' Compensation; Tort Law), Kentucky and American (Member, Section on Tort and Insurance Practice) Bar Associations; Defense Research Institute. ***PRACTICE AREAS:*** Personal Injury; Workers' Compensation; Insurance Law. ***Email:*** klmechler@fmgr.com

PIETER N. SCHMIDT, born Rockford, Illinois, May 17, 1956; admitted to bar, 1988, Illinois and U.S. District Court, Southern District of Illinois. *Education:* Southern Illinois University (B.A., 1981; J.D., cum laude, 1988). Member, 1986-1987 and Notes and Comments Editor, 1987-1988, Southern Illinois University Law Journal. Author: "PUNITIVE DAMAGES-Willful & Wanton Breach of Contract-Illinois Rejects the Extension of Tort Remedies into Contract Causes of Action-Morrow v. L.A. Goldschmidt Associates," 12 S. Ill. U.L.J. 495, 1988. Co-Author: "Survey of Illinois Law-Municipal Corporations," 15 Southern Illinois Law Journal 1021, 1991. *Member:* Jackson County (Member, Workers Compensation Law Section Council, 1997—), Illinois State and American Bar Associations. ***PRACTICE AREAS:*** Insurance Defense; Workers Compensation. ***Email:*** pschmidt@fmgr.com

JOHN S. RENDLEMAN, III, born Carbondale, Illinois, December 15, 1958; admitted to bar, 1987, Illinois and U.S. District Court, Southern and Central Districts of Illinois. *Education:* Southern Illinois University (B.A., 1984; J.D., 1987). Member, Order of Barristers. Recipient, American Jurisprudence Awards in Contracts and Municipal Law. Student Trustee, Southern Illinois University, 1983-1984. Co-Author: "Survey of Illinois Law-Municipal Corporations," 15 Southern Illinois University Law Journal 1021, 1991. *Member:* Jackson County, Illinois State and American (Business Law Section Council; Illinois Secretary of State Business and Advisory Committee) Bar Associations. ***PRACTICE AREAS:*** Commercial Transactions; Real Estate Transactions; Municipal Law; Business Litigation; Labor Law. ***Email:*** jrendleman@fmgr.com

GARY B. NELSON, born Dubuque, Iowa, January 14, 1963; admitted to bar, 1991, Illinois; 1992, U.S. District Court, Southern District of Illinois; 1995, U.S. Court of Appeals, Seventh Circuit. *Education:* University of Iowa (B.A., 1986); Southern Illinois University (J.D., 1991). *Member:* Jackson County, Illinois State and American Bar Associations. ***PRACTICE AREAS:*** Insurance Defense; Workers Compensation; Black Lung; Appellate Practice. ***Email:*** gnelson@fmgr.com

EDWARD E. RENSHAW, born Strasburg, Illinois, March 13, 1956; admitted to bar, 1992, Illinois; 1995, U.S. District Court, Southern District of Illinois; 1998, U.S. Court of Appeals, Seventh Circuit; 1999, U.S. Supreme Court. *Education:* Greenville College (B.S., cum laude, 1978); Southern Illinois University (J.D., cum laude, 1992). Phi Alpha Theta. Recipient, American Jurisprudence Award in Agency and Partnership. Student Articles Editor, Southern Illinois University Law Journal, 1991-1992. Author: "Equal Access - The New Life of the First Amendment in Secondary Education," 16 S.Ill. U.L.J. 531 (1992). *Member:* Jackson County, Illinois State and American Bar Associations. ***PRACTICE AREAS:*** Commercial Law; Banking Law; Real Estate; Employment Law. ***Email:*** erenshaw@fmgr.com

KARA L. JONES, born Belleville, Illinois, March 15, 1969; admitted to bar, 1994, Illinois; 1996, U.S. District Court, Southern District of Illinois. *Education:* St. Louis University (B.S.B.A., 1991); Southern Illinois University (J.D., 1994). *Member:* Jackson County, Illinois State and American Bar Associations. ***PRACTICE AREAS:*** Insurance Defense; Civil Rights Defense; Local Government Torts Defense; Medical Malpractice; Products Liability; Personal Injury; Appellate Practice. ***Email:*** kjones@fmgr.com

R. JAMES GIACONE, II, born Benton, Illinois, January 21, 1973; admitted to bar, 1998, Illinois and U.S. District Court, Central and Southern Districts of Illinois. *Education:* Southeast Missouri State University (B.S.B.A., 1995); University of Missouri (J.D., 1998). Phi Delta Phi. *Member:* Franklin County, Jackson County and Illinois State Bar Associations. ***PRACTICE AREAS:*** Workers Compensation; Litigation; Family Law. ***Email:*** jgiacone@fmgr.com

ASSOCIATES

JOHN R. DALY, born Taylorville, Illinois, August 10, 1967; admitted to bar, 1997, Illinois; 2001, U.S. District Court, Southern District of Illinois; 2002, U.S. Tax Court. *Education:* Southern Illinois University (B.S., 1990; M.Acct., 1994; J.D., 1997). Certified Public Accountant, 1993. *Member:* Jackson County, Illinois State and American Bar Associations; American Institute of Certified Public Accountants; Illinois CPA Society. ***PRACTICE AREAS:*** Taxation; Estate Administration and Planning; Corporate Law; Real Estate; Business Valuation. ***Email:*** jdaly@fmgr.com

THOMAS R. FRENKEL, born Chicago, Illinois, April 7, 1953; admitted to bar, 2000, Illinois and U.S. District Court, Southern District of Illinois; 2001, U.S. Court of Appeals, Seventh Circuit; 2002, Minnesota; 2002, District of Columbia Court of Appeals. *Education:* Southern Illinois University (B.A., 1975; J.D., 2000). Phi Delta Phi. Editor-in-Chief, Southern Illinois University Law Journal. Emergency Medical Technician, 1973. Commercial Pilot Airplane Single/Multiengine Land; former Certified Flight Instructor/Instrument Flight Instructor. Author: "Criminal Record Expungement: The Fifth Circuit Addresses a Split in Authority Regarding the Modification of Executive Branch Records," 24 S.Ill.U.L.J. 627, 2000. Contributing Feature Author, "Legally Speaking," American Bus Exchange Magazine. Past President, National Tour Association, Inc. Past Director, Travel In-

(This Listing Continued)

FEIRICH/MAGER/GREEN/RYAN, Carbondale—Continued

dustry Association of America. Member: Jackson County, Illinois State and American Bar Associations; Bar Association of the Central and Southern Federal Districts of Illinois (with service on Education Committee); Transportation Lawyers Association. ***PRACTICE AREAS:*** Insurance Law; Litigation; Personal Injury; Medical Malpractice; Transportation. ***Email:*** tfrenkel@fmgr.com

CHERYL L. ERDMAN, born Indianapolis, Indiana, August 3, 1968; admitted to bar, 2002, Illinois. *Education:* University of Illinois, Urbana-Champaign (B.A., 1990); Southern Illinois University (J.D., 2001). Member, Southern Illinois University Law Journal. Author, "The Medicolegal Dangers of Telephone Triage in Mental Health Care," 22 Journal of Legal Medicine 4, 2001. *Member:* Illinois State and American Bar Associations. ***PRACTICE AREAS:*** Workers Compensation; Real Estate; Business Litigation. ***Email:*** cerdman@fmgr.com

WILLIAM B. LEVANTI, born West Frankfort, Illinois, August 18, 1976; admitted to bar, 2002, Illinois; 2004, U.S. District Court, Southern District of Illinois. *Education:* Murray State University (B.S., 1999); Southern Illinois University (J.D., 2002). Phi Alpha Delta. *Member; Jackson County, Illinois State (Counsel Member, Young Lawyers Section, 2005) and American Bar Associations.* ***PRACTICE AREAS:*** Personal Injury; Workers Compensation; Contracts; Insurance Defense; Employment Law. ***Email:*** blevanti@hotmail.com

REPRESENTATIVE CLIENTS: Capital Crossing Bank; Center Home Equity Corp.; Combank, Inc.; Community National Bank; First National Bank of Jonesboro; First Southern Bank; G.E. Capital Credit Corp.; ACE/USA Ins.; Addison Insurance Co.; American Family Insurance; Aid Association for Lutherans; Allstate Life Insurance; Assury Mutual Insurance Co.; Associated Physician Insurance Company; Bierman-Condray; Bishop Township Mutual Insurance Co.; Celina Insurance Co.; Central States Health and Life Insurance Co. of Omaha; Chrysler Life; Chubb Insurance Group; Continental Insurance Co.; Country Mutual Insurance Co.; Diamond Insurance; Employers Mutual; Employers Reinsurance Co.; Equitable Life Assurance Society; Farmers Insurance; Federated Insurance Co.; GAB Business Services, Inc.; General Accident Insurance; General Casualty Insurance Co.; Great American Insurance Co.; Great Central Insurance Co.; Grinnell Mutual Reinsurance Co.; Hanover Insurance Co.; Illinois Compensation Trust; Illinois Fair Plan Association; Illinois Mun. League - Risk Mgmt. Assoc.; Iuka Mutual Insurance Co.; Jackson National Life Insurance Co.; Ky. Assoc. Gen. Contractors Self-Ins. Fund; Martin Boyer/Cambridge; Metropolitan Property & Liab. Insurance Co.; Jefferson County Mutual; National General Insurance Co.; North Central Life Insurance Co.; Northland Insurance Co.; Ohio Hospital Insurance Co.; Old Republic Companies; Providian Insurance; Prudential Insurance Company of America; Randolph Mutual Insurance Co.; Rockford Mutual Life Insurance Co.; Royal and Sun Alliance Ins. St. Paul Insurance Co.; Safeco Insurance Companies; Sentry Insurance Co.; Silvey Cos.; Standard Mutual Insurance Co.; Tokio Marine & Fire Insurance Co.; Transport Life Insurance; United Fire Group; Universal Fire and Casualty Co.; Viking Insurance Company of Wisconsin; Westfield Cos.; Willis Corroon; Zurich-American Ins.; Am. Elec. Power - Cook Coal Terminal; Big Ridge, Inc.; Consolidation Coal Co.; Kerr-McGee Corp.; Peabody Energy; R&G American Coal Co,; Rigsby & Barnard Quarries; AT&T; Central Illinois Public Service Co.; Electric Energy, Inc.; Indiana and Michigan Power Co.; Midwest Electric Power, Inc.; American Healthcare Financial Services; Carbondale Clinic, S.C.; Chamness Care Inc.; City of Carbondale; Continental Tire North America, Inc.; Health Services of Southern Illinois; Met-South, Inc.; Pilot House of Cairo, Inc.; Player's Island Casino; Saline Care Center; The Sollami Co.; So. Illinois Healthcare Enterprises, Inc.; Southern Illinois Hospital Services; So. Illinois Medical Properties, Inc.; Southern Illinois Regional Social Services; Reverly Farm Foundation; Bugher Foundation; Colonial Plaza, Inc.; Countryside Terrace, Inc.; Crypton, Inc.; Five Star Industries; Gilster Mary Lee Corp.; Glenbrook of Vienna, Inc.; Hardin County Materials Co.; Heartland Investigations; Holly Hill, Inc.; Joppa & Eastern Railroad Co.; JR's Centre, Inc.; KelTech Management, Inc.; Lincoln Square, Inc.; Mayflower Contract Services, Inc.; Mulberry Manor, Inc.; RDK Management, Inc.; Stone Creek Golf Course; UNIDOM Corp.; Allied Signal Corp.; Liberty Mutual; Canon Cochran Management Services, Inc.; Cincinnati Insurance Companies.

HOWERTON, DORRIS & STONE

CARBONDALE, ILLINOIS

(See Marion)

Plaintiff's Personal Injury, Workers Compensation Law, Insurance Bad Faith, Breach of Contract, Criminal Defense, Medical Malpractice, General Civil and Trial Practice.

EUGENIA C. HUNTER

905 WEST CHERRY STREET
CARBONDALE, ILLINOIS 62901
Telephone: 618-457-0476
Fax: 618-457-0477
Email: ech99@msn.com

Bankruptcy, Real Estate, Wills and Trusts, Probate, Elder Law, Guardianship, Adoption, Expungements.

EUGENIA C. HUNTER, born Waterbury, Connecticut, February 18, 1941; admitted to bar, 1977, Illinois and U.S. District Court, Southern District of Illinois; 1986, U.S. Court of Appeals, Seventh Circuit. *Education:* Southern Illinois University (B.A., 1963; M.S., 1970; J.D., 1976). Assistant States Attorney, 1978. *Member:* Jackson County (Vice-President, 1985-1986; President, 1986-1987) and Illinois State (Member, Standing Committee on Judicial Advisory Polls, 1987-1993; Standing Committee on Delivery of Legal Services, 1996—) Bar Associations; Southern Illinois Bankruptcy Institute; National Academy of Elder Law Attorneys, Inc.

MITCHELL & MITCHELL

CARBONDALE, ILLINOIS

(See Marion)

General Trial and Appellate Practice. Insurance, Personal Injury, Medical Malpractice, Products Liability, Commercial Law, Litigation and Divorce.

RUSIN MACIOROWSKI & FRIEDMAN, LTD.

Established in 1984

239 SOUTH LEWIS LANE, SUITE A
CARBONDALE, ILLINOIS 62901-3443
Telephone: 618-351-8100
Fax: 618-351-8109
URL: http://www.rusinlaw.com

Chicago, Illinois Office: Suite 1530, 10 South Riverside Plaza, 60606. Telephone: 312-454-5110. Fax: 312-454-6166.
Champaign, Illinois Office: 2506 Galen Drive, Suite 104, 61821-7047. Telephone: 217-351-1700. Fax: 217-351-1732.

Workers Compensation Law. Insurance Defense, Personal Injury, Products Liability, Auto and Trucking Liability, Structural Work Act, Commercial Litigation, Subrogation, Contract Insurance, Employment Discrimination. Wrongful Discharge.

FIRM PROFILE: Rusin Maciorowski & Friedman, Ltd. was founded in 1984 by Douglas F. Stevenson, Michael E. Rusin and Stephen J. Friedman (as Stevenson, Rusin & Friedman, Ltd.) with the goal of establishing a specialty firm focusing on representing employers and their insurance carriers in all of the varied legal aspects of the workplace injury, including Worker's Compensation, OSHA, personal injury, contribution liability and lien recovery, wrongful discharge and employment discrimination.

Through dedication to aggressive, result-oriented file handling and prompt, thorough client reporting, the firm grew from the original seven lawyers and continued to expand to serve its clients' needs throughout the state of Illinois and northern and northwestern Indiana. With the opening of our Champaign, Illinois office in 1999, and our Carbondale, Illinois office in 2003, the firm reinforced its commitment to efficient representation in our downstate venues.

With Douglas Stevenson's appointment to the Illinois Industrial Commission in 1998, the firm changed its name to reflect its current mission on providing a full service litigation practice to its client base of employers, industry and insurance carriers.

The firm's leadership role in Workers' Compensation and Employer Liability has carried over to its civil department. Initially developed to handle the claims evolving from the workplace accident, the firm has acquired a depth of experience in employment discrimination and wrongful discharge, product liability, and coverage issues. We have the unique ability to coordinate the handling of the Workers' Compensation claim and related civil actions including lien protection, third party practice including extensive remedy defenses and related insurance coverage issues, including the handling of Declaratory Judgement actions.

Our current civil department, managed by Gregory Vacala, has grown and provides seasoned trial attorneys handling cases throughout Illinois and surrounding states. These attorneys have a depth of experience in managing all phases of civil practice including transportation law (automobiles and trucking liability), commercial litigation, and insurance coverage.

The firm has earned a preeminent rating from Martindale-Hubbell.

(For Biographical data on all Personnel, see professional Biographies at Chicago, Illinois)

SANDBERG, PHOENIX & VON GONTARD

A PROFESSIONAL CORPORATION

Established in 1979

WESTOWNE CENTRE
2015 WEST MAIN, SUITE G
CARBONDALE, ILLINOIS 62901
Telephone: 618-397-2721; 800-225-5529
Fax: 618-351-7604

St. Louis, Missouri Office: 15th Floor, One City Centre. Telephone: 314-231-3332. Telecopier: 314-241-7604.
Belleville, Illinois Office: 23 South 1st Street. Telephone: 618-397-2721.

Trial and Appellate Practice in Federal and State Courts, Product Liability, Health Law, Medical Malpractice Defense, Class Action Litigation, Employment Law, Banking, Commercial and Corporate Law, Admiralty, Aviation, Insurance, Bankruptcy and Reorganization, Estate Planning and Probate, Real Estate, Family Law.

FIRM PROFILE: Sandberg, Phoenix & von Gontard, P.C. was founded in 1979 with nine attorneys. The firm has grown steadily to become one of the leading law firms in the St. Louis metropolitan area and the midwest. Sandberg, Phoenix & von Gontard, P.C. combines experience, innovation and aggressiveness to deliver legal services that are responsive to the needs of our clients. Sandberg, Phoenix & von Gontard, P.C. recruits outstanding students from top law schools of the region and the country. The firm is honored to have been nominated and elected into membership of The Network of Trial Law Firms. The Network of Trial Law Firms is a national organization comprised of a select number of premier law firms from around the country with practices concentrated in civil litigation.

LAW FIRM ALLIANCES/ASSOCIATIONS: **THE NETWORK OF TRIAL LAW FIRMS, INC.**

KATHLEEN L. PINE, born Urbana, Illinois, May 2, 1957; admitted to bar, 1982, Missouri; 1984, Illinois. *Education:* Illinois State University (B.S., 1978); Southern Illinois University (J.D., 1982). Member: Mortar Board; National Moot Court. *Member:* American Bar Association. (Resident). ***PRACTICE AREAS:*** Medical Malpractice. ***Email:*** kpine@spvg.com

REONA J. DALY, born Marion, Illinois, January 17, 1969; admitted to bar, 1994, Illinois and U.S. District Court, Southern District of Illinois. *Education:* Illinois Wesleyan

(This Listing Continued)

University (B.A., magna cum laude, 1991); Southern Illinois University (J.D., cum laude, 1994). Phi Delta Phi. *Member:* Jackson County and Illinois State Bar Associations. ***PRACTICE AREAS:*** Medical Malpractice; Business Litigation. ***Email:*** rdaly@spvg.com

Our lawyers are members of the Missouri and Illinois State Bar Associations and all the major local bar associations in the St. Louis metropolitan area, including those in southern Illinois.

(For complete biographical data on all personnel, see Professional Biographies at St. Louis, Missouri)

WINTERS, BREWSTER, CROSBY AND SCHAFER LLC

CARBONDALE, ILLINOIS

(See Marion)

General Practice. Trials in State and Federal Courts. Plaintiffs Personal Injury, Workers' Compensation. Probate, Estate Planning, Real Estate, Corporation, Environmental Law, Wills, Trusts, Estates, Probate and Class Actions.

LAW OFFICE OF KIM L. MOORE

CARLINVILLE, ILLINOIS

(See Virden)

Family Law, Divorce, Spousal Support, Child Support, Domestic Violence, Alimony, Real Estate, Title, Contracts, Business Law, Corporate Law, Estate Planning, Litigation, Commercial.

PHELPS, KASTEN, RUYLE, BURNS, SIMS & MEYER, P.C.

Established in 1966

130 EAST MAIN STREET
P.O. BOX 587
CARLINVILLE, ILLINOIS 62626
Telephone: 217-854-3283
FAX: 217-854-9527
Email: pkrb@accunet.net
URL: http://www.lawyers.com/pkrb

General Civil Practice in State and Federal Courts. Negligence, Wills and Trusts, Probate and Real Estate Law.

FIRM PROFILE: Since the firm's establishment in 1966, the firm has maintained a general civil practice. The firm primarily represents corporations, small businesses and individuals throughout the state of Illinois. The firm is listed in the Bar Register of Preeminent Lawyers.

EDWARD R. PHELPS (1904-1985)

THOMAS P. BURNS (1952-2001)

JOHN W. RUSSELL (Retired)

CARL E. KASTEN, born Carlinville, Illinois, February 8, 1944; admitted to bar, 1969, Illinois; 1975, U.S. Supreme Court. *Education:* Illinois State University (B.A., cum laude, 1966); Northwestern University (J.D., cum laude, 1969). Phi Eta Sigma; Pi Gamma Mu. Winner, Wigmore Key, Northwestern University School of Law, 1969. *Member:* Macoupin County, Illinois State and American Bar Associations; Illinois Trial Lawyers Association (Manager, 1978-1987); The Association of Trial Lawyers of America. ***PRACTICE AREAS:*** Civil Litigation; Probate; Real Estate; Appeals. ***Email:*** pkrb@accunet.net

NANCY L. RUYLE, born Chicago, Illinois, August 12, 1959; admitted to bar, 1983, Illinois. *Education:* St. Louis University; St. Ambrose College (B.A., summa cum laude, 1980); St. Louis University (J.D., 1983). *Member:* Macoupin County and Illinois State Bar Associations. ***PRACTICE AREAS:*** Civil Litigation; Probate; Real Estate; Appeals. ***Email:*** pkrb@accunet.net

BYRON J. SIMS, born Jacksonville, Illinois, May 20, 1965; admitted to bar, 1991, Illinois. *Education:* Manatee Junior College (1983); Illinois College (B.A., cum laude, 1987); Southern Illinois University (J.D., 1990). Member, National Fraternal Society For the Deaf. *Member:* Macoupin County and Illinois State Bar Associations; Illinois Trial Lawyers Association. ***LANGUAGES:*** American Sign Language. ***PRACTICE AREAS:*** Civil Litigation; Probate; Appeals; Domestic Relations. ***Email:*** pkrb@accunet.net

JOSHUA A. MEYER, born Fon du Lac, Wisconsin, September 3, 1975; admitted to bar, 2001, Illinois. *Education:* Blackburn University (B.A., summa cum laude, 1998); St. Louis University (J.D., 2001). *Member:* Macoupin County and Illinois State Bar Associations; Illinois Trial Lawyers Association. ***PRACTICE AREAS:*** Civil Litigation; Appellate Practice; Probate; Real Estate. ***Email:*** pkrb@accunet.net

REPRESENTATIVE CLIENTS: Carlinville National Bank; Blackburn University; Area Diesel Service, Inc.; H & H Construction Services, Inc.
REFERENCE: Carlinville National Bank.

WHAM & WHAM

CARLYLE, ILLINOIS

(See Centralia)

General Trial and Appellate Practice. Insurance Defense including Medical Malpractice, Automobile Accidents, Premises Liability, Products Liability, Personal Injury, Probate, Wrongful Discharge from Employment.

JELLIFFE, FERRELL, MORRIS & DOERGE

CARMI, ILLINOIS

(See Harrisburg)

Insurance Law, Negligence and Personal Injury, Litigation, Workers' Compensation Law, and Employment Law. Commercial Collection and DUI's. General Civil Practice in State and Federal Courts. Trials and Appeals.

PATRICK MAZZA & ASSOCIATES

290 SOUTH MAIN PLACE
CAROL STREAM, ILLINOIS 60188-2476
Telephone: 630-933-9200
Fax: 630-933-9824
Email: schodera@mcminc.net

Chicago, Illinois Office: 33 N. La Salle, Suite 1800. By Appointment Only.

Construction, Commercial, Contract and Mechanics Lien Law. Trial Practice.

PATRICK MAZZA, born Chicago, Illinois, August 10, 1940; admitted to bar, 1967, Illinois, U.S. District Court, Northern District of Illinois and U.S. Court of Appeals, 7th Circuit; 1971, U.S. Supreme Court; 1982, U.S. Claims Court. *Education:* University of Notre Dame (A.B., 1962); DePaul University (J.D., 1967). *Member:* Chicago, Du Page County, Illinois State and American (Member, Construction Litigation Committee, 1975—) Bar Associations; The Association of Trial Lawyers of America. ***PRACTICE AREAS:*** Construction Law; Mechanic's Lien Law; Commercial Law; Trial Practice.

LAW OFFICES OF RICHARD E. TRAVIS

CARPENTERSVILLE, ILLINOIS

(See Elgin)

General Practice in all Courts. Personal Injury, Wrongful Death, Commercial Litigation, Medical Malpractice, Products Liability and Worker's Compensation Law. Civil Litigation Practice, Automobile Accidents, Dog Bites, Slip and Fall.

HARTZELL, GLIDDEN, TUCKER AND HARTZELL

1852 as Ferris and Manier

WILLIAMS BUILDING
P.O. BOX 70
CARTHAGE, ILLINOIS 62321
Telephone: 217-357-3121
FAX: 217-357-2027
Email: firm@adams.net

Macomb, Illinois Office: Old Bailey House, 100 South Campbell Street. Telephone: 309-833-3121.

General Civil Trial and Appellate Practice in all State and Federal Courts. Real Estate, Estate Planning and Probate, Trust, Banking Law, Taxation, Personal Injury, Family Law, Municipal Law and Agricultural Law.

FIRM PROFILE: The firm was established in 1852 as Ferris & Manier and has conducted a general practice in Western Illinois, representing individuals, corporate, banking and business interests in local and regional matters and taxation. The firm's practice for individuals includes personal injury, family law, estate planning, probate, and personal legal affairs. The firm has maintained an active litigation practice in trial and appellate courts since its inception.

MEMBERS OF FIRM

HOMER H. WILLIAMS (1894-1965)

FRANKLIN M. HARTZELL, born Carthage, Illinois, August 24, 1923; admitted to bar, 1950, Illinois; 1956, U.S. Tax Court. *Education:* University of Illinois (B.S., 1948; LL.B., 1950). Phi Delta Phi. Author: "Ancillary Administration in Illinois," Illinois Estate Administration, Illinois Institute of Continuing Legal Education, 1989, 1993 and 1997. City Attorney, City of Carthage, 1955-1969. President, Board of Visitors, College of Law, University of Illinois, 1981-1982. *Member:* Hancock County, Illinois State (Member, Trust and Estate Section Council, 1986-1990, 1997—) and American Bar Associations; Society of Hospital Attorneys. Fellow, American College of Trust and Estate Counsel. ***REPORTED CASES:*** Kennedy v. Commissioner, (1986, C.A. 7) 804 F.2d 1332. ***PRACTICE AREAS:*** Estate Planning; Probate; Federal Taxation; State Taxation; Real Estate; Banking. ***Email:*** fmhlaw@adams.net

JOHN R. GLIDDEN, born Sanford, Maine, July 24, 1936; admitted to bar, 1961, Iowa; 1965, Illinois. *Education:* University of Wisconsin; Coe College (B.A., 1958); University of Iowa (LL.B., 1961). Phi Delta Phi. Carthage City Attorney, 1969—. *Member:* Hancock County, Iowa State, Illinois State (Member, Assembly of Delegates, 1982-1988) and American Bar Associations; Illinois Trial Lawyers Association (Member, Board of Managers, 1973-1981); The Association of Trial Lawyers of America. [Judge Advocate, U.S. Air Force, 1961-1965]. ***PRACTICE AREAS:*** Personal Injury; Domestic Relations; Litigation; Insurance Defense. ***Email:*** jrglaw@adams.net

STANLEY L. TUCKER, born Decatur, Illinois, August 20, 1942; admitted to bar, 1970, Illinois; 1976, U.S. Supreme Court. *Education:* University of Illinois (B.S., 1965; J.D., 1969). Author: "Judicial Review-Administrative Review Act," Illinois Administrative Law, IICLE, 1991; "Improving the Jury Decision Process," Illinois Bar Journal, November, 1984. Phi Alpha Delta (Justice, 1969). *Member:* Hancock County, Illinois State (Member: Section Council on Civil Practice and Procedure, 1981-1985; Assembly of Delegates, 1976-1982; Member, 1985 and Chairman, 1990, Standing Committee Judicial Advisory

(This Listing Continued)

HARTZELL, GLIDDEN, TUCKER AND HARTZELL, Carthage—Continued

Polls; Section Council on Administrative Law, 1986—) and American Bar Associations; Illinois Trial Lawyers Association; The Association of Trial Lawyers of America; Appellate Lawyers Association. ***PRACTICE AREAS:*** Litigation; Family; Estate Planning; Probate; Banking; Tax. ***Email:*** sltlaw@frontiernet.net

THOMAS F. HARTZELL, born Peoria, Illinois, March 1, 1959; admitted to bar, 1984, Illinois and U.S. Tax Court. *Education:* Illinois Wesleyan University (B.S., 1981); Southern Illinois University (J.D., 1984). Author: Chapter 16, "Ancillary Administration," Illinois Estate Administration, Illinois Institute for Continuing Legal Education. Co-Editor, Agricultural Law Section Council Newsletter, 2000-2001. *Member:* Hancock County, Illinois State (Member: Agricultural Law Section Council, 1996-2005; General Practice Solo and Small Firm Section Council, 2000-2004) and American Bar Associations. ***PRACTICE AREAS:*** Estate Planning and Probate Law; Real Estate; Banking Law; Taxation; Agricultural Law. ***Email:*** tfhlaw@frontiernet.net

All members of this firm are admitted to practice before the United States District Court, Central District of Illinois and the United States Court of Appeals, Seventh Circuit.

COUNSEL FOR: Marine Bank and Trust; Bowen State Bank; State Bank of Colusa; State Bank of Lima; First Federal Bank, Colchester; City of Hamilton; Memorial Hospital Assn.; Hancock County Nursing Assn.; City of Nauvoo; City of Carthage; Carthage Park District; Western Illinois Electrical Co-op.
LOCAL COUNSEL FOR: State Farm Mutual Insurance Co.; The Prudential Insurance Company of America; Methode Electronics, Inc.
REFERENCE: Marine Bank and Trust.

SHEEHAN & LOWER

6 SPRING STREET
CARY, ILLINOIS 60013
Telephone: 847-516-3200; Toll Free: 800-RIDE LAW
Fax: 847-516-3443
Email: ridelaw@aol.com

Civil Trial Practice, Product Liability, Insurance Coverage, Defense of the Amusement Industry, Defense of Roller Skating Establishments, Aviation, Employment Discrimination and Employment Law.

MEMBERS OF FIRM

THOMAS M. SHEEHAN, admitted to bar, 1984, Illinois and U.S. District Court, Northern District of Illinois. *Education:* Lewis University (A.A. in Aircraft Mechanics, 1975); University of Illinois (B.S. in Technical and Vocational Education, with high honors, 1978); Loyola University (J.D., 1984). NAARSO Certified Level Two Amusement Ride Safety Inspector. AIMS Level Two Certified Ride Mechanic. Author: "How to Prepare Your Fact Witness for a Deposition," Federal Discovery News (January, 1995). Frequent Amusement Industry Lecturer. Member: International Amusement and Leisure Defense Association (IALDA); National Association of Amusement Ride Safety Officials (NAARSO); Amusement Industry Manufacturers and Suppliers International (AIMS International); International Association of Amusement Parks and Attractions (IAAPA). *Member:* Chicago and American Bar Associations. ***PRACTICE AREAS:*** Civil Trial Litigation; Insurance Coverage; Products Liability; Amusement Park Liability; Defense of Roller Skating Establishments; Aviation; U.S. Consumer Product Safety Commission. ***Email:*** ridelaw@aol.com

JACQUELINE H. LOWER, admitted to bar, 1982, Illinois; 1984, U.S. District Court, Northern District of Illinois. *Education:* DePaul University (B.A., with high honors, summa cum laude, 1974); University of Chicago (M.A., 1976); Loyola University (J.D., 1982). Author: "The Pregnant Employee's Appearance as a BFOQ Under the Pregnancy Discrimination Act," 14 Loyola University Chicago Law Journal 195 (1982). *Member:* Chicago Bar Association; National Employment Lawyers Association. ***PRACTICE AREAS:*** Employment Discrimination; Employment Law; Civil Trial Litigation. ***Email:*** ridelaw@aol.com

ASSOCIATE

STEPHEN J. TASCH, admitted to bar, 1984, Illinois; 1986, U.S. District Court, Northern District of Illinois. *Education:* Lawrence University (B.A., 1977); John Marshall Law School (J.D., 1984). Member, John Marshall Law Review, 1983. President, Village of Fox River Grove, 1997-2005. Director, Legal/Insurance, Recreation Board, Village of Fox River Grove, 1993-2005. *Member:* Illinois State Bar Association. ***PRACTICE AREAS:*** Product Liability; Negligence; Civil Litigation; Insurance Defense; Insurance Coverage; Real Estate. ***Email:*** ridelaw@aol.com

JAMES M. GRANT

Established in 1998
101 NORTH CENTRAL
CASEY, ILLINOIS 62420
Telephone: 217-932-5885
Fax: 217-932-5889
Email: jmgrant@jamesmgrantlaw.com
URL: http://www.lawyers.com/jamesmgrantlaw

Charleston, Illinois Office: 611 6th Street, 61920. Telephone: 217-345-2510. Fax: 217-348-0082.

Real Estate, Real Estate Title, Wills & Estates.

FIRM PROFILE: Sole Practitioner.

Language: English.

(This Listing Continued)

REPRESENTATIVE CLIENTS: Casey State Bank; Preferred Bank; First Neighbor Bank, Charleston; Attorneys Title Guaranty Fund.

(For complete biographical data on all personnel, see Professional Biographies at Charleston, Illinois)

WHAM & WHAM

Established in 1888
212 EAST BROADWAY
CENTRALIA, ILLINOIS 62801
Telephone: 618-532-5621
Fax: 618-532-5055
Email: whamlawyers@aol.com
URL: http://www.lawyers.com/wham&wham

General Trial and Appellate Practice. Insurance Defense including Medical Malpractice, Automobile Accidents, Premises Liability, Products Liability, Personal Injury, Probate, Wrongful Discharge from Employment.

FIRM PROFILE: The firm has been in existence for more than 100 years, having been founded in 1888 by William F. Bundy. In 1912, Mr. Bundy was joined in practice by Charles Wham. Fred L. Wham joined the firm in 1917 and was a partner until he became a Federal Judge in 1925. John Page Wham joined the firm in 1929. In 1947 James B. Wham and William B. Wham returned from World War II and became partners. Richard A. Cary joined the firm in 1973, followed by Jennifer W. Price and Daniel R. Price.

Wham & Wham is a general litigation firm practicing throughout Southern Illinois in all State and Federal Courts.

CHARLES WHAM (1887-1963)
JOHN P. WHAM (1902-1992)
WILLIAM B. WHAM (Retired)

MEMBERS OF FIRM

JAMES B. WHAM, born Centralia, Illinois, October 10, 1918; admitted to bar, 1946, Illinois. *Education:* University of Illinois (B.S., 1946; J.D., 1947). Order of the Coif; Phi Delta Phi. Judge, Illinois Court of Claims, 1953-1961. *Member:* Marion County, Illinois State and American Bar Associations; Illinois Trial Lawyers Association; Illinois Association of Defense Trial Counsel; American Trial Lawyers Association; American Bar Foundation (Life Member); Appellate Lawyers Association; Society of Trial Lawyers; Illinois Oil and Gas Association. Fellow: American College of Trial Lawyers; International Society of Barristers. ***PRACTICE AREAS:*** Personal Injury; Appellate Practice. ***Email:*** whamlawyers@aol.com

RICHARD A. CARY, born Salem, Illinois, December 15, 1944; admitted to bar, 1973, Illinois. *Education:* Eastern Illinois University (B.S. in Education, 1968); St. Louis University (J.D., 1973). *Member:* Marion County and Illinois State Bar Associations; Illinois Association of Defense Counsel. Fellow, American College of Trial Lawyers. ***PRACTICE AREAS:*** Insurance Defense; Personal Injury. ***Email:*** whamlawyers@aol.com

JENNIFER W. PRICE, born Centralia, Illinois, November 30, 1955; admitted to bar, 1984, Illinois. *Education:* University of Arizona (B.A., 1978); Southern Illinois University (J.D., 1984). *Member:* Marion County, Illinois State and American Bar Associations. ***PRACTICE AREAS:*** Real Estate; Wills; Trusts; Probate. ***Email:*** whamlawyers@aol.com

DANIEL R. PRICE, born Chicago, Illinois, June 17, 1959; admitted to bar, 1984, Illinois. *Education:* University of Illinois (B.S., 1981); Southern Illinois University (M.S. 1984; J.D., 1984). Certified Public Accountant, Illinois, 1981. *Member:* Illinois State and American Bar Associations; Illinois Certified Public Accountant Society; American Institute of Certified Public Accountants; American Judicature Society. ***PRACTICE AREAS:*** Defense; Medical Malpractice; Insurance Defense; Worker's Compensation; Wrongful Termination. ***Email:*** whamlawyers@aol.com

OF COUNSEL

JANIE F. SMITH

REPRESENTATIVE CLIENTS: State Farm Insurance Cos.; Auto-Owners Insurance Co.; St. Mary's Hospital of Centralia, Illinois; Western and Southern Insurance; CNA; St. Paul-Economy; Chubb Services Corporation.

ALLEN & KORKOWSKI & ASSOCIATES

CHAMPAIGN, ILLINOIS

(See Rantoul)

Business Law, Real Estate, Estate Planning, Administrative Law, Family Law, Bankruptcy and Commercial Collections.

LAW OFFICE OF ANSEL & SMALL, LTD.

41 EAST UNIVERSITY AVENUE
CHAMPAIGN, ILLINOIS 61820
Telephone: 217-359-0200
Fax: 217-359-0888
Email: mjalaw@shout.net

Mailing Address: P.O. Box 468, Champaign, IL 61824-0468

Business Law, Commercial Litigation, Intellectual Property, Personal Injury, Insurance Litigation, and Insurance Defense. Civil Litigation and Civil Trial Practice Appeals.

(This Listing Continued)

FIRM PROFILE: The Firm's attorneys concentrate in civil litigation, including business and commercial, intellectual property, injury and insurance matters. The partners have focused their practice in these areas for more than thirty years, accepting referrals from local and out-of-area counsel needing assistance or representation in and around East Central Illinois. Admissions to practice include all trial and appellate courts in Illinois state and federal venues, as well as the United States and Illinois Supreme Courts.

MARC J. ANSEL, born Chicago, Illinois, June 8, 1949; admitted to bar, 1974, Illinois and U.S. District Court, Central District of Illinois; U.S. Court of Appeals, Seventh Circuit; 1983, U.S. Supreme Court. *Education:* University of Illinois (B.S., 1971; J.D., 1974). *Member:* Champaign County, Illinois State (Member, Inquiry Board, Attorney Registration and Disciplinary Commission, 1984-1986) and American Bar Associations. ***PRACTICE AREAS:*** Business Litigation; Commercial Litigation; Intellectual Property; Unfair Competition; Personal Injury; Insurance Litigation; Insurance Defense. ***Email:*** mjalaw@shout.net

HOWARD W. SMALL, born Chicago, Illinois, May 24, 1948; admitted to bar, 1974, Illinois; 1977, California. *Education:* University of Illinois and University of Arizona (B.A., 1970); University of Illinois (J.D., 1974). Phi Kappa Phi. *Member:* Champaign County and Illinois State Bar Associations; State Bar of California. [With U.S. Army Reserves, 1970-1976]. ***PRACTICE AREAS:*** Civil Litigation; Insurance Defense Law. ***Email:*** hwslaw@shout.net

---

STANLEY E. FREEMAN, born Rantoul, Illinois, September 3, 1959; admitted to bar, 1988, Illinois and U.S. District Court, Southern District of Illinois; 1991, U.S. Court of Appeals, Seventh Circuit; 2001, U.S. District Court, Central District of Illinois. *Education:* University of Illinois (B.A., 1982); Southern Illinois University (J.D., 1988). Member, Executive Committee, Southern Illinois American Inns of Court, 1992-1994. *Member:* Champaign County, Jefferson County (President, 1991-1992) and Illinois State Bar Associations. ***PRACTICE AREAS:*** Insurance Defense; Insurance Coverage; Civil Litigation; Commercial Litigation; Personal Injury. ***Email:*** sfreeman@shout.net

---

BECKETT & WEBBER, P.C.

CHAMPAIGN, ILLINOIS

(See Urbana)

General, Trial, Appellate and Federal Practice, Criminal, Personal Injury, Family, Probate and Estate Planning Law, DWI, Traffic Violations, Wills, Child Support, Divorce, Child Custody, Adoption, Workers Compensation, Real Estate, Elder Law.

DOBBINS, FRAKER, TENNANT, JOY & PERLSTEIN

A PROFESSIONAL CORPORATION

Established in 1894

215 NORTH NEIL

CHAMPAIGN, ILLINOIS 61820-4012

Telephone: 217-356-7233

Telecopier: 217-356-3548

Email: dftjp@dobbinslaw.com

URL: http://www.dobbinslaw.com

General Practice, Trial and Appellate Practice in State and Federal Courts. Health Care, Privacy Law, Real Estate, Corporate, Estate Planning, Probate, Insurance Defense, Alternative Dispute Resolution, Family, Personal Injury, Medical Malpractice, Professional Liability, Products Liability, Commercial Litigation, Workers Compensation, Municipal and Drainage and Levee Law.

FIRM PROFILE: Dobbins, Fraker, Tennant, Joy & Perlstein, P.C., is a general practice firm with special emphasis on civil litigation in state and federal courts, healthcare law and drainage law. The firm was founded in 1894 by Oliver B. Dobbins. One of its former partners, D. C. Dobbins, was the first lawyer from Champaign County to be elected to the U.S. House of Representatives. During the past century, the firm has played a significant role in the development of health care law and drainage law in the State of Illinois.

DONALD V. DOBBINS (1913-1981)

TODD M. TENNANT (1954-1997)

FRENCH L. FRAKER (1914-2005)

RICHARD M. JOY, born Elmhurst, Illinois, September 11, 1943; admitted to bar, 1969, Illinois; 1973, U.S. District Court, Central District of Illinois. *Education:* University of Michigan (B.A., 1966); University of Illinois (J.D., 1969). Member, Board of Editors, University of Illinois Law Forum, 1968-1969. Law Clerk to Chief Justice Robert O. Underwood, Illinois Supreme Court, 1969-1971. *Member:* Champaign County (Member, Real Estate Committee, Chairman, 1983-1991 and 1996—; Member, Board of Governors, 1989-1991, Vice President, 1990-1991) and Illinois State Bar Associations. ***PRACTICE AREAS:*** Business Law; Real Estate; Workers' Compensation. ***Email:*** rjoy@dobbinslaw.com

GUY C. HALL, born Chicago, Illinois, August 11, 1958; admitted to bar, 1983, Illinois; 1984, U.S. District Court, Central District of Illinois. *Education:* University of Illinois (B.A., 1980); University of Tulsa (J.D., 1983). Certified Mediator, Champaign County, Circuit Court Mediation Program. *Member:* Champaign County (Vice President, 1993-1994), Illinois State (Member: Law Office Economics Section, 1995-1996; Health Care Section, 1998—, Secretary 2003-2004; Vice Chairman, 2004-2005) and American (Member, Editorial Board of the Forum on Health Law, 1989-1991) Bar Associations; Illinois Association of Health Care Attorneys; Health Care Compliance Association. ***PRACTICE AREAS:*** Health Care; Business Law; Civil Trials and Appeals; Real Estate; Municipal. ***Email:*** ghall@dobbinslaw.com

(This Listing Continued)

RENEE L. MONFORT, born Champaign, Illinois, February 14, 1964; admitted to bar, 1990, Florida; 1991, Illinois; 1994, U.S. District Court, Central District of Illinois and U.S. Court of Appeals, Seventh Circuit. *Education:* Murray State University (B.S., 1986); Stetson University Law School (J.D., 1990). Guest Lecturer, Trial Advocacy Program, University of Illinois, 1998—. Member, Board of Directors, St. Jude Children's Research Hospital, Midwest Affiliate, 1997-1999. *Member:* Champaign County (Member, Medical Liability Committee, 1995—), DeWitt County and Illinois State Bar Associations; The Florida Bar; East Central Illinois Women Attorneys Association; Illinois Association of Healthcare Attorneys; Illinois Society of Healthcare Risk Managers; Illinois Association of Defense Trial Counsel (Member, Mediation/Arbitration Committee, 2000); The Association of Trial Lawyers of America; American Health Lawyers Association; Defense Research Institute. ***PRACTICE AREAS:*** Civil Trials and Appeals; Professional Liability Defense; Health Care. ***Email:*** rmonfort@dobbinslaw.com

JAMES D. COTTRELL, born Urbana, Illinois, December 12, 1955; admitted to bar, 1983, Illinois; 1986, U.S. District Court, Central District of Illinois and U.S. Court of Appeals, Seventh Circuit; 1987, U.S. Supreme Court. *Education:* University of Illinois (B.S., 1979); Drake University (J.D., 1982). Author: Environmental Law Chapter, 2001 and 2005 Supplement, Illinois Institute of Continuing Legal Education publication, Illinois Law and Agri-business; Drainage and Water Rights Chapter, 2001 and 2005 Supplement, Illinois Institute of Continuing Legal Education publication, Illinois Law and Agri-business; Riparian Rights - Drainage Actions Chapter, 2002 and 2005 Supplement, Illinois Institute of Continuing Legal Education publication, Illinois Causes of Action - Elements, Forms and Winning Tips. Member, Society for Human Resources. *Member:* Champaign County and Illinois State (Council Member and Co-Editor, ISBA Local Government Law, 1994-1996) Bar Associations; Institute of National Employment Law Association; Environmental Law Institute. ***PRACTICE AREAS:*** Civil Litigation; Employment Law; Municipal Law; Workers Compensation; Drainage and Levee Law; Environmental Law. ***Email:*** jcottrell@dobbinslaw.com

STEPHEN J. LeSUEUR, born Evanston, Illinois, March 17, 1955; admitted to bar, 1980, Illinois and U.S. District Court, Central District of Illinois. *Education:* Lawrence University (B.A., 1977); University of Illinois (J.D., 1980). *Member:* Champaign County (Member, Board of Governors, 1994-1996; Vice President, 1995-1996) and Illinois State Bar Associations. ***PRACTICE AREAS:*** Civil Litigation; Family; Real Estate; Business. ***Email:*** slesueur@dobbinslaw.com

DANIEL P. WURL, born Vandalia, Illinois, June 10, 1956; admitted to bar, 1981, Ohio; 1982, U.S. District Court, Southern District of Ohio; 1985, Illinois and U.S. Court of Appeals, Sixth Circuit; 1987, U.S. District Court, Central District of Illinois; 1992, U.S. Court of Appeals, Seventh Circuit. *Education:* University of Illinois (B.A., 1978; J.D., 1981). Author: "The Dos and Don'ts of Rule 213 Opinion Witness Discovery," Illinois State Bar Journal, January, 2001; "Institutional Negligence Claims against Hospitals and Other Health Care Entities," ISBA Tort Trends Newsletter, November, 2001; "HMO Liability and the Fiduciary Duty of Physicians," ISBA Tort Trends Newsletter, May, 2000. *Member:* Champaign County and Illinois State (Member, Civil Practice and Procedure Council, 1990-1998; Vice Chair, 1994-1996, Chair, 1996-1997; Member, Tort Law Section Council, 1997-2003; Member, Insurance Law Section Council, 1997-2003; Secretary, 1999-2000; Vice Chair, 2000-2001; Chair, 2001-2002) Bar Associations. ***PRACTICE AREAS:*** Commercial Litigation; Civil Trials and Appeals; Professional Liability Defense. ***Email:*** dwurl@dobbinslaw.com

MAGGIE BEDNAR, born Port Huron, Michigan, December 23, 1971; admitted to bar, 2003, Illinois and U.S. District Court, Central District of Illinois. *Education:* Southern Illinois University (B.A.,B.S., 1996); Southern Illinois University School of Law (J.D., 2003). Phi Delta Phi, 2001-2003. Author: "Medical Expert Witness Bias Due to Commonality of Insurance," Journal of Legal Medicine, Vol. 23, #3. *Member:* Champaign County and Illinois State Bar Associations; East Central Illinois Women Attorneys Association; Defense Research Institute; Illinois Trial Lawyers Association; American College of Legal Medicine. ***PRACTICE AREAS:*** Professional Liability Defense; Civil Practice; Appellate Practice; Business Law. ***Email:*** mbednar@dobbinslaw.com

OF COUNSEL

DONALD M. TENNANT

CREED D. TUCKER

D. CAMERON DOBBINS

DUNN, WILLARD, ARKELL & BUGG

CHAMPAIGN, ILLINOIS

(See Bloomington)

General Civil Trial and Appellate Practice. General Practice, Litigation, Business Law, Business Litigation, Business Enterprises, Insurance, Intellectual Property, Licensing Agreements, Trade Secrets, Contracts, Commercial Law, Commercial Litigation, Civil Litigation, Copyright, Trademark, Bankruptcy, Banking Law, Corporate, Real Estate, Buying or Selling, Construction, Probate, Trusts and Estates, Municipal, University, Civil Rights, Immigration, Labor, Employment, Human Resources, Internet.

ERWIN, MARTINKUS & COLE, LTD.

Established in 1975

411 WEST UNIVERSITY AVENUE

P.O. BOX 1098

CHAMPAIGN, ILLINOIS 61824-1098

Telephone: 217-351-4040

Telecopier: 217-351-4314

General Civil Trial and Appellate Practice. Business and Corporate Practice including Securities and Banking Law. Tort and Insurance Litigation. Medical Malpractice, Probate and Estate Planning, Real Estate, Family Law, Bankruptcy and Immigration and Naturalization.

FIRM PROFILE: The firm was established in 1975. The practice emphasizes general business matters, including securities law and maintains a strong litigation practice in State and Federal Courts.

General Civil Practice in State and Federal Court, Trials and Appeals, Estate Planning and Probate, Real Estate, Negligence, Family Law, Taxation Law, Insurance Coverage and Defense and Immigration and Naturalization.

SAM ERWIN (1935-2002)

JAMES A. MARTINKUS, born Chicago, Illinois, May 7, 1950; admitted to bar, 1977, Illinois. *Education:* University of California at Los Angeles (B.A., magna cum laude, 1972); University of Illinois (J.D., 1977). *Member:* Champaign County, Illinois State and American Bar Associations. ***LANGUAGES:*** Lithuanian, Russian. ***PRACTICE AREAS:*** Medical Malpractice; Personal Injury Law; Divorce Law; Criminal Law. ***Email:*** jim.martinkus@erwinlaw.com

PAUL R. COLE, born Hamilton, Ohio, August 11, 1945; admitted to bar, 1977, Illinois and U.S. District Court, Central District of Illinois. *Education:* Kenyon College (B.A., 1967); University of Chicago (M.B.A., 1971); University of Illinois (J.D., 1977). *Member:* Champaign County and Illinois State Bar Associations. [Sgt., U.S. Army, 1969-1970, Vietnam Service]. ***PRACTICE AREAS:*** Corporate Law; General Business Matters; Bankruptcy Law; Real Estate Law. ***Email:*** paul.cole@erwinlaw.com

RICHARD C. KIRBY, born Danville, Illinois, April 30, 1948; admitted to bar, 1980, Illinois. *Education:* University of Illinois (B.A., 1970); Oklahoma City University; Southern Illinois University (J.D., magna cum laude, 1980). Editor-in-Chief, Oklahoma City University Law Review, 1979-1980. *Member:* Champaign County, Illinois State and American Bar Associations. ***PRACTICE AREAS:*** Corporate Law; General Business Matters; Estate Planning Law; Securities Law; Real Estate. ***Email:*** rick.kirby@erwinlaw.com

SARAH B. TINNEY, born Elkins, West Virginia, July 6, 1952; admitted to bar, 1977, Illinois. *Education:* University of Florida (A.A., 1972); University of California at Berkeley (B.A., 1974); University of Illinois (J.D., 1977). *Member:* The Bar Association of the Central District of Illinois; Illinois State and American Bar Associations. ***PRACTICE AREAS:*** Divorce Law; Real Estate Law; Personal Injury Law; Civil Litigation; Workers Compensation.

JEFFERY B. WAMPLER, born Bloomington, Indiana, October 19, 1961; admitted to bar, 1986, Illinois; U.S. District Court, Southern and Northern Districts of Indiana; U.S. District Court, Central District of Illinois. *Education:* Indiana University (B.A., 1983); Valparaiso University (J.D., 1986). Phi Delta Phi. *Member:* Champaign County Bar Association. ***PRACTICE AREAS:*** General Business Matters; Real Estate Law; Commercial Litigation; Banking Law. ***Email:*** jeff.wampler@erwinlaw.com

LYNNE R. FELDMAN, born Brooklyn, New York, August 8, 1947; admitted to bar, 1975, California, U.S. District Court Northern District of California and U.S. Court of Appeals, Ninth Circuit; 1985, U.S. District Court, Central District of California; 1988, Illinois; 1989, U.S. District Court, Central District of Illinois. *Education:* Mills College (B.A., 1969); University of California, Hastings College of Law (J.D., 1974). Faculty and Author, Immigration, Illinois Continuing Legal Education. *Member:* Champaign County and Illinois State Bar Associations; American Immigration Lawyers Association; Chicago Chapter of American Immigration Lawyers Association. ***PRACTICE AREAS:*** Immigration and Naturalization. ***Email:*** lynne.feldman@erwinlaw.com

R. MICHAEL BROWN, born Danville, Illinois, September 5, 1948; admitted to bar, 1980, Illinois. *Education:* University of Illinois (B.S., Accounting, 1970); Valparaiso University (J.D., 1980). Beta Alpha Psi; Beta Gamma Sigma; Phi Eta Sigma. Edmund James James Scholar. Certified Public Accountant, Illinois, 1971; Hawaii, 1976. Certified Financial Planner. *Member:* Illinois State and American Bar Associations; American Institute of Certified Public Accountants; Eastern Illinois Estate Planners Council. ***PRACTICE AREAS:*** Taxation; Estate Planning; Wills and Probate; Corporate Law; General Business Matters. ***Email:*** r.michael.brown@erwinlaw.com

WAYNE O. SMITH, born Champaign, Illinois, February 10, 1962; admitted to bar, 1987, Illinois. *Education:* Illinois State University (B.S., Finance, 1984); Southern Illinois University (J.D., 1987). International Order of Barristers. Contributor, "Tort Trends," Tort Law Section, Illinois State Bar Association, 1997, 1998. Formerly with Dilks, Rocen, Gibson & Smith, Paxton, Illinois. *Member:* Ford County (President, 1997-1998), Champaign County and Illinois State (Member, Tort Law Section Council, 1996-2000) Bar Associations; Illinois Trial Lawyers Association. ***PRACTICE AREAS:*** Civil Litigation; Federal Civil Litigation; Personal Injury; Workers Compensation; Business Litigation; Family Law; Criminal Law. ***Email:*** wayne.smith@erwinlaw.com

JEFFREY L. HAYS, born Champaign, Illinois, September 13, 1947; admitted to bar, 1993, Illinois. *Education:* University of Illinois (B.S., 1969; J.D., 1993). *Member:* Champaign County and Illinois State Bar Associations. [Sgt., Illinois National Guard, 1968-1974]. ***PRACTICE AREAS:*** General Business Matters; Real Estate Law; Immigration and Naturalization. ***Email:*** jeff.hays@erwinlaw.com

---

ANNE M. MARTINKUS, born Champaign, Illinois, May 11, 1967; admitted to bar, 1996, Illinois. *Education:* University of Illinois (B.S., 1989); Thomas Cooley Law School (J.D., cum laude, 1996). Member, Special Committee to Implement Proposed Revision of

(This Listing Continued)

Illinois Custody Act. *Member:* Illinois State Bar Association (Member, General Practice Section). ***PRACTICE AREAS:*** Divorce; Real Estate; Estate Planning; Adoption Law. ***Email:*** anne.martinkus@erwinlaw.com

MIKE McCORMICK, born Metropolis, Illinois, May 22, 1959; admitted to bar, 1984, Illinois. *Education:* University of Illinois (B.S., with honors, 1981); Southern Illinois University (J.D., magna cum laude, 1983). States Attorney, Johnson County, 1988-1992. Senior Counsel and Advisor, Governor Jim Edgar, 1995-1999. Formerly Mike McCormick, Attorney at Law, Vienna, Illinois. *Member:* Champaign County Bar Association. ***PRACTICE AREAS:*** Corporate Law; Business Law; Real Estate; Estate Planning. ***Email:*** mike.mccormick@erwinlaw.com

BRIAN EDWARD KING, born Belleville, Illinois, March 16, 1972; admitted to bar, 2000, Illinois; 2002, U.S. District Court, Central District of Illinois. *Education:* Illinois State University (B.S., Political Science, 1996); Northern Illinois University (J.D., 2000). *Member:* Champaign County and Illinois State Bar Associations. ***PRACTICE AREAS:*** Personal Injury; Landlord and Tenant Law; Family Law; Criminal Defense; Traffic Violations; Workers Compensation. ***Email:*** brian.king@erwinlaw.com

RICK WAYNE AEILTS, born Lincoln, Illinois, December 13, 1965; admitted to bar, 1995, Illinois and U.S. District Court, Southern District of Illinois. *Education:* Southeast Missouri State University (B.A., 1989); Southern Illinois University (M.B.A., 1992; J.D., 1995). Phi Delta Phi. *Member:* Williamson County and Illinois State and American Bar Associations; The Association of Trial Lawyers of America; Illinois Trial Lawyers Association. ***PRACTICE AREAS:*** Personal Injury; Workers' Compensation; Collections; Real Property; Probate. ***Email:*** rick.aeilts@erwinlaw.com

L. JOHN CLAUSEN, born Decatur, Illinois, October 11, 1977; admitted to bar, 2002, Illinois. *Education:* University of Illinois (B.A., 1999); Valparaiso University School of Law (J.D., 2002). Phi Delta Phi. Associate Editor, Valparaiso University Law Review, 2001-2002. *Member:* Champaign County and Illinois State Bar Associations. ***PRACTICE AREAS:*** Corporate Law; Employment Law; Estate Planning; Real Estate; Mortgage Foreclosure; Traffic Violations; Litigation. ***Email:*** john.clausen@erwinlaw.com

LEGAL SUPPORT PERSONNEL

CAROLYN S. PITTS, C.L.A., born Anna, Illinois, September 11, 1959. *Education:* University of Illinois (B.A., 1981); Roosevelt University (Lawyer's Asst. Cert., 1982). Certified Legal Assistant, 1986; Recertified, 2001. President, Central Illinois Paralegal Association, 1992-1993; NALA Liaison, 1991-1992, 1993-1994; Secretary, 1995-1996. *Member:* Illinois State and American Bar Associations (Associate Member); National Association of Legal Assistants; Central Illinois Paralegal Association. ***PRACTICE AREAS:*** Personal Injury Law; Medical Malpractice; Commercial Litigation. ***Email:*** carolyn.pitts@erwinlaw.com

PETER G. PAOL, born Newport, Rhode Island, February 29, 1970. *Education:* Arizona State University (B.A., 1995); West Chester University of Pennsylvania (M.A., 1999); Arizona Paralegal Training Program (Paralegal Certificate, 2002). *Member, National Association of Legal Assistants.* ***PRACTICE AREAS:*** Family Law; Civil Litigation. ***Email:*** peter.paol@erwinlaw.com

REPRESENTATIVE CLIENTS: BankChampaign; BankIllinois; Bank One of Champaign-Urbana; The Bankvertising Co. (Publishing); Central Data Corporation (High Tech Manuf.); Computer Teaching Corp. (Computer Programs); McGladrey and Pullen (Accounting Firm); MDI (Nursing Homes); Allied Title Services, Inc. (Abstract Company and Title Insurance Agent); Human Kinetics Publishers, Inc. (Publishing); First Savings & Loan Association of South Holland, Illinois; Urbana & Champaign Sanitary District (Government); Horizon Hobby Distributors, Inc. (Distribution); Jimmy John's Enterprises (retail food); Flex-N-Gate (Auto Parts Mfg.).
REFERENCES: Bank Illinois; Bank One of Champaign-Urbana; BankChampaign.

EVANS, FROEHLICH, BETH & CHAMLEY

A Partnership including Professional Corporations

44 MAIN STREET

P.O. BOX 737

CHAMPAIGN, ILLINOIS 61820

Telephone: 217-359-6494

Telecopier: 217-359-6468

URL: http://www.efbclaw.com

General Practice. Real Estate, Banking, Bankruptcy and Collection Law. Corporate, State, Municipal and Public Authority Financing and Municipal Law, Taxation, Trust and Probate Law. Litigation in Federal and State Courts.

FIRM PROFILE: Evans, Froehlich, Beth & Chamley is a firm recognized throughout Illinois for its success with such complex matters as Banking, Bankruptcy, Municipal and Public Authority Finance Law and Municipal and Local Government Law. Dedication to continual education within each attorney's practice areas guarantees their clients pre-eminent representation.

MEMBERS OF FIRM

JAMES W. EVANS, (LTD.), born Hamilton, Missouri, August 22, 1937; admitted to bar, 1962, Illinois. *Education:* Beloit College (B.A., 1959); University of Illinois (LL.B., 1962). Phi Delta Phi. Co-Author: "Agricultural and Agri-Business Loans," Chapter 9, Advising Illinois Financial Institutions, Illinois Institute of Continuing Legal Education, 1987, revised, 1993. Assistant City Attorney, City of Champaign, Illinois, 1964-1975. Village Attorney: Mahomet, Illinois, 1976—. *Member:* Champaign County (President, 1969-1970), Illinois State (Assembly Member, 1978-1984) and American Bar Associations. ***PRACTICE AREAS:*** Real Estate Law; Bankruptcy Law; Banking Law.

KURT P. FROEHLICH, (LTD.), born Moline, Illinois, March 23, 1943; admitted to bar, 1973, Illinois; 1977, U.S. Supreme Court. *Education:* University of Illinois (B.S., 1966; M.Ed., 1968; J.D., 1973). City Attorney, City of Champaign, 1975-1980. Visiting Professor of Architecture, University of Illinois at Urbana-Champaign, Illinois, 1978-1993. *Member:* Champaign County, Illinois State (Chair, Local Government Law Section Council, 1991-1992) and American (Member, Committee on Tax Exempt Finance, 1987—) Bar Associa-

(This Listing Continued)

tions; National Institute of Municipal Law Officers (Chair, Finance Section, 1990-1993; now, International Municipal Lawyers Association); National Association of Bond Lawyers. ***PRACTICE AREAS:*** Municipal and Public Authority Finance; Local Government Law; Municipal Law.

KENNETH N. BETH, (LTD.), born Elgin, Illinois, January 13, 1943; admitted to bar, 1968, Illinois; 1972, U.S. Supreme Court. *Education:* Valparaiso University (B.A., 1965; J.D., 1968); University of Illinois (M.B.A., 1979). Village Attorney, Village of Rantoul, Illinois, 1990—. City Attorney, City of Urbana, Illinois, 1975-1990. *Member:* Champaign County, Illinois State and American Bar Associations; National Association of Bond Lawyers; International Municipal Lawyers Association. [Lieut. Cmdr., JAGC, U.S. Navy, 1969-1973]. ***PRACTICE AREAS:*** Municipal and Public Authority Finance Law; Municipal Law; Local Government Law; Real Estate Law.

JOSEPH P. CHAMLEY, (LTD.), born Monroe, Wisconsin, July 22, 1969; admitted to bar, 1994, Illinois, U.S. District Court, Central District of Illinois and U.S. Court of Appeals, Seventh Circuit; U.S. Supreme Court. *Education:* University of Illinois (B.A., cum laude, 1991; J.D., cum laude, 1994). Phi Beta Kappa. *Member:* Champaign County and Illinois State (Member, Commercial, Banking and Bankruptcy Law Section Council, 1999—) Bar Associations. ***PRACTICE AREAS:*** Banking Law; Bankruptcy Law; Litigation; Real Estate Law. ***Email:*** jpcefb@shout.net

LEGAL SUPPORT PERSONNEL

PEGGY A. SMITH

REPRESENTATIVE CLIENTS: BankIllinois; University of Illinois Employees Credit Union; Village of Rantoul, Illinois; Champaign Township, Illinois; Village of Mahomet, Illinois; Village of Bondville, Illinois.
REFERENCE: BankIllinois.

FLYNN, PALMER & TAGUE

Established in 1932

402 WEST CHURCH STREET
P.O. BOX 1517
CHAMPAIGN, ILLINOIS 61824-1517
Telephone: 217-352-5181
Telecopier: 217-352-7964
Email: fpt5law@aol.com

General Civil Practice in State and Federal Courts. Trials and Appeals. Banking, Estate Planning and Probate, Personal Injury, Real Estate, Family and Taxation Law.

FIRM PROFILE: Flynn, Palmer & Tague (formerly Meyer & Franklin 1932-1954; Franklin & Flynn 1959; Franklin, Flynn & Palmer 1964) is a business oriented firm representing the farming, business, banking and academic sectors of the East Central Illinois community. All of its members are involved in the active practice of law and are supporters of, and participate in, continuing legal education as well as pro-bono activities. This firm is included in The Bar Register of Preeminent Lawyers.

MEMBERS OF FIRM

MICHAEL J. TAGUE, born Alton, Illinois, January 30, 1955; admitted to bar, 1980, Illinois. *Education:* Bradley University (B.A., summa cum laude, 1977); University of Illinois (J.D., 1980). *Member:* Champaign County, Illinois State and American Bar Associations. ***PRACTICE AREAS:*** Civil Trials and Appeals; School Law; Insurance Law; Estate Planning; Probate; Business Law.

JEROME P. LYKE, born Evergreen Park, Illinois, May 20, 1957; admitted to bar, 1982, Illinois. *Education:* University of Notre Dame (B.A., 1979); University of Illinois (J.D., 1982). *Member:* Champaign County, Illinois State and American Bar Associations. ***PRACTICE AREAS:*** Civil Practice; Trials and Appeals; Insurance Defense; Local Government Law; Personal Injury; Workers Compensation.

ROBERT E. JACOBSON, born Rockford, Illinois, September 16, 1971; admitted to bar, 1996, Illinois; 1997, U.S. District Court, Central District of Illinois. *Education:* Trinity College (B.A., 1993); University of Illinois (J.D., 1996). *Member:* Champaign County and Illinois State Bar Associations. ***PRACTICE AREAS:*** General Practice; Civil Practice; Real Estate; Family Law. ***Email:*** rjacobsonfpt@aol.com

OF COUNSEL

CHARLES L. PALMER, born Champaign, Illinois, May 18, 1931; admitted to bar, 1957, Illinois. *Education:* University of Illinois (B.A., 1953; J.D., 1957). Phi Delta Phi. *Member:* Champaign County (President, 1971-1972), Illinois State (Member, Assembly, 1972-1976) and American Bar Associations. Fellow, American College of Trial Lawyers. Laureate, Academy of Illinois Lawyers.

REPRESENTATIVE CLIENTS: Bituminous Insurance Co.; Standard Mutual Insurance Company; Main Street Bank & Trust Co.; Champaign Asphalt Company; Champaign Board of Education; County of Champaign; General Growth Inc.; University of Illinois; Shelter Insurance Companies; First Federal Savings Bank.
REFERENCE: Main Street Bank & Trust Co.

HALLIHAN INTELLECTUAL PROPERTY LAW, LTD.

CHAMPAIGN, ILLINOIS

(See Chicago)

Litigation, Intellectual Property Law, Patents, Trademarks, Copyrights, Trade Secrets and Entertainment Law.

HARRINGTON & TOCK

Established in 1922

SUITE 601 HUNTINGTON TOWERS
201 WEST SPRINGFIELD AVENUE
P.O. BOX 1550
CHAMPAIGN, ILLINOIS 61824-1550
Telephone: 217-352-4167
Telecopier: 217-352-8707
URL: http://www.lawyers.com/harringtont&rlaw

Delray Beach, Florida Office: 100 East Linton Boulevard, Suite 215B, 33486. Telephone: 561-279-1840. Fax: 561-279-7842.

General Practice. Business, Partnership Law, Small Business Law, Family Business Law, Business Formation, Commercial Litigation, Probate, Tax, Corporation, Real Estate, Eminent Domain and Drainage Law, Shopping Center Law, Commercial Leasing, Commercial Landlord and Tenant Law, Tax Planning, IRS Controversies, Trials, Appeals and Commercial Arbitration.

FIRM PROFILE: Since its founding, the firm has been dedicated to providing high quality, personalized legal representation. The firm provides services to businesses, institutions and individuals in a range of complex business transactions and general counseling.

MEMBERS OF FIRM

EARL C. HARRINGTON (1895-1981)
LOUIS A. BUSCH (1886-1946)
ROBERT F. BUSCH (1914-1969)
W. KENNETH PORTER (1919-1996)
J. C. ERMENTROUT (1912-1998)

THOMAS E. HARRINGTON, born Urbana, Illinois, March 2, 1931; admitted to bar, 1955, Illinois. *Education:* University of Illinois (B.S., 1953; J.D., 1955). Phi Delta Phi. Public Defender, 1957-1959. *Member:* Champaign County, Illinois State and American Bar Associations. ***PRACTICE AREAS:*** Tax Planning Law; Corporate Law; Real Estate Law; Eminent Domain Litigation. ***Email:*** tharrington@harringtontock.com

DANIEL G. HARRINGTON, born Urbana, Illinois, August 2, 1957; admitted to bar, 1982, Florida and Illinois. *Education:* University of Illinois (B.S., 1979); Stetson University (J.D., 1981). *Member:* Champaign County and Illinois State Bar Associations; The Florida Bar. ***PRACTICE AREAS:*** Real Estate Law; Real Estate Development; Leasing; Corporate. ***Email:*** dharrington@harringtontock.com

JEFFREY W. TOCK, born Urbana, Illinois, June 4, 1948; admitted to bar, 1980, Illinois and U.S. District Court, Northern District of Illinois; 1982, U.S. District Court, Central District of Illinois. *Education:* University of Illinois (B.S., 1970; M.A., Urban Planning, 1975); Illinois Institute of Technology (J.D., 1980). ***PRACTICE AREAS:*** Litigation; Real Estate; Corporation; Drainage Law; Eminent Domain Litigation; Zoning, Planning and Land Use; Construction Law. ***Email:*** jtock@harringtontock.com

OF COUNSEL

KIP RANDOLPH POPE, born Urbana, Illinois, March 18, 1947; admitted to bar, 1974, Illinois. *Education:* University of Illinois (A.B., cum laude, 1969); Indiana University (J.D., cum laude, 1974). Omicron Delta Kappa. *Member:* Champaign County, Illinois State and American Bar Associations; Illinois Trial Lawyers Association. [1st Lt., U.S. Army, 1969-1971]. ***PRACTICE AREAS:*** Commercial Litigation.

CHAPIN ROSE, born Jacksonville, Illinois, December 27, 1973; admitted to bar, 2000, Illinois. *Education:* University of Illinois (B.S., 1997; J.D., 2000). Phi Alpha Delta. Assistant State's Attorney, 2000-2003. *Member:* Illinois State Bar Association. ***PRACTICE AREAS:*** Real Estate Law; Litigation; Corporate; Traffic; Estate Planning. ***Email:*** crose@harringtontock.com

REPRESENTATIVE CLIENTS: The University of Illinois; The Carle Foundation; Vesuvius USA; Round Barn Shopping Centre; Coldwell Banker; Devonshire Realty, Ltd.; Prairie Gardens, Inc.; Jeffrey Alans Stores; Interstate Research Park; Dodds Athletic Tours; Camp Farm Management, Inc.; Becknell Development, LLC; Shapland Management; Robeson's Inc.; HDC Engineering, Inc.; Architectural Spectrum, Inc.; Creek Development; Beaver Lake Drainage District; Big Slough Special Drainage District; Embarras River Special Drainage Distrct; Kankakee Drainage District; Kaskaskia Special Drainage District; Drainage District No. 2 of the Town of Sidney; Union Drainage District By User #1 of the Township of Raymond-Murdock; Upper Salt Fork Drainage District.

HINSHAW & CULBERTSON LLP

Hinshaw & Culbertson LLP is an Illinois registered limited liability partnership that has elected to be governed by the Illinois Uniform Partnership Act (1997)

Established in 1934

1802 FOX DRIVE
CHAMPAIGN, ILLINOIS 61820
Telephone: 217-352-1400
Facsimile: 217-352-1401
Telex: 880248
Email: kfox@hinshawlaw.com
URL: http://www.hinshawlaw.com

Other Office Locations: Chicago, Illinois; Appleton, Wisconsin; Belleville, Illinois; Boston, Massachusetts; Crystal Lake, Illinois; Edwardsville, Illinois; Fort Lauderdale, Florida; Jacksonville, Florida; Joliet, Illinois; Lisle, Illinois; Los Angeles, California; Miami, Florida; Milwaukee, Wisconsin; Minneapolis, Minnesota; New York, New York; Peoria, Illinois; Phoenix, Arizona; Portland, Oregon; Providence, Rhode Island; Rockford, Illinois; St. Louis, Missouri; San Francisco, California; Schererville, Indiana; Springfield, Illinois; Tampa, Florida; Waukegan, Illinois.

(This Listing Continued)

HINSHAW & CULBERTSON LLP, Champaign—Continued

Appellate, Banking & Financing, Bankruptcy & Creditors' Rights, Class Action Litigation, Civil Rights Defense, Commercial Litigation, Corporate, Construction Law, Director & Officer Liability, Employee Benefits, Environmental, Fidelity & Surety, General Liability Litigation, Government, Health Care, Insurance Coverage, Insurance and Reinsurance, Labor & Employment, Legal Malpractice, Medical Malpractice, Mergers & Acquisitions, Municipal Liability, Personal Injury Defense, Public Law, Products Liability Litigation, Professional Liability, Regulatory, Real Estate, School Law, Securities, Taxation, Transportation, White Collar Crime and Workers' Compensation Defense.

FIRM PROFILE: Hinshaw & Culbertson LLP is a national AMLaw 200 firm with 425 lawyers in 27 offices coast-to-coast. The firm offers a full-service practice, with an emphasis in commercial and defense litigation, corporate, environmental, employment and construction law, as well as the representation of professionals in their liability and risk management matters.

Hinshaw provides services to a range of clients in financial services, construction, health care, not-for-profit, insurance, legal, manufacturing, real estate, transportation and other industries. Firm clients also include government agencies, municipalities and schools.

Hinshaw was founded in 1934. The firm is headquartered in Chicago, and maintains offices in 12 states: Arizona, California, Florida, Illinois, Indiana, Massachusetts, Minnesota, Missouri, New York, Oregon, Rhode Island and Wisconsin.

PARTNER

RICHARD A. CHAPIN, born Danville, Illinois, July 14, 1953; admitted to bar, 1978, Illinois; 1979, U.S. District Court, Central District of Illinois; 1985, U.S. Court of Appeals, Seventh Circuit. *Education:* University of Illinois (B.S., cum laude, 1975; J.D., 1978). *Member:* Champaign County and American Bar Associations; Defense Research Institute. ***PRACTICE AREAS:*** Products Liability; Premises Liability; General Liability. ***Email:*** rchapin@hinshawlaw.com

ASSOCIATE

MATTHEW M. SEBEK, born Evergreen Park, Illinois, October 15, 1975; admitted to bar, 2003, Illinois and U.S. District Court, Northern District of Illinois. *Education:* Illinois Wesleyan University (B.A., Political Science and History, cum laude, 1998); University of Illinois (J.D., cum laude, 2003). Harno Scholar. Participant, Chicago Bar Association Moot Court Competition, 2002. Member, Trial Team, 2003. *Member:* American Bar Association. ***PRACTICE AREAS:*** General Liability Litigation; Transportation Litigation; Employment Litigation. ***Email:*** msebek@hinshawlaw.com

THOMAS Z. HODSON

701 DEVONSHIRE DRIVE, C-21
CHAMPAIGN, ILLINOIS 61820-7330
Telephone: 217-239-6652
Fax: 217-398-0413
Email: thodson@aol.com
URL: http://www.lawyers.com/thodsonlaw

Commercial Law, Agricultural Law, Real Estate.

THOMAS Z. HODSON, born Highland, Illinois, May 22, 1947; admitted to bar, 1975, Illinois; 1978, Maine. *Education:* Northwestern University (B.S.B.A., 1969); University of Illinois (J.D., with honors, 1975). Order of the Coif; Phi Alpha Delta. *Member:* Champaign County and Illinois State Bar Associations. ***PRACTICE AREAS:*** Commercial Law; Real Estate; Agricultural Law.

LIETZ, BANNER & FORD

1605 S. STATE STREET, SUITE 103
CHAMPAIGN, ILLINOIS 61820-7264
Telephone: 217-353-4900
Facsimile: 217-353-4901
URL: http://www.lawyers.com/lbf

Employment Law, Wills and Estates, Agricultural Law, Real Estate, General Litigation, Personal Injury, Securities.

FIRM PROFILE: We at Lietz, Banner & Ford are dedicated to exceeding our client's expectations. Our firm offers a full service business practice. We specialize in personalized legal representation for individuals and businesses in all state and federal courts. Our practice emphasizes the areas of business organizations and operations and complex transactions, securities law, employment law, real estate, agricultural law, secured transactions, and estate planning and administration.

MEMBERS OF FIRM

GARY R. LIETZ, born Urbana, Illinois, November 30, 1951; admitted to bar, 1977, Illinois. *Education:* Denison University (B.A., 1973); John Marshall Law School (J.D., 1976). *Member:* Champaign County (President, 1985-1987) and Illinois State (Member of Sections Counsel on Employment and Labor Law, 2000-2004; Economics Committee, 1978-1979; Member of Section Counsel on Management and Economics of Practice of Law, 1979; Chairman, 1982-1983) Bar Associations. ***PRACTICE AREAS:*** Employment Law; Employment Discrimination; Employment Litigation; Business Litigation; General Liability. ***Email:*** glietz@lbflaw.com

DELMAR K. BANNER, born Urbana, Illinois, August 10, 1945; admitted to bar, 1971, Illinois; 1972, Missouri. *Education:* University of Illinois (B.S., 1967; J.D., 1971). Adjunct Professor, Agricultural Law and Finance, University of Illinois, 1986—; Principal, Vice-Chair, Center for Farm and Rural Business Finance, 1991—. General Counsel, 1975-1980,

(This Listing Continued)

Senior Vice President of Operations, 1981-1983, Federal Intermediate Credit Bank of St. Louis. Special Counsel to the Farm Credit System Legislative Committee and the Farm Credit Administration, 1980. President and Chief Executive Officer, Farm Credit Council, Washington, D.C., 1983-1986. *Member:* Champaign County and Illinois State Bar Associations; The Missouri Bar; American Agricultural Law Association (Board Member, 1992-1995). ***PRACTICE AREAS:*** Estate Planning; Business Planning; Probate; Agribusiness; Cooperative Association Law; Nonprofit Organizations Law; Secured Transactions; Real Estate. ***Email:*** dbanner@lbflaw.com

KELLY E. FORD, born Burlington, Iowa, July 23, 1963; admitted to bar, 1988, Illinois; 1993, U.S. District Court, Central District of Illinois. *Education:* Monmouth College (B.A., 1985); University of Illinois (J.D., 1988). *Member:* Champaign County (Treasurer, 1995-1996), Illinois State and American Bar Associations. ***PRACTICE AREAS:*** Real Estate; Business Organization; Securities; Estate Planning; Estate Administration. ***Email:*** kford@lbflaw.com

REPRESENTATIVE CLIENTS: The University of Illinois; Farm Credit Services of Illinois; 1st Farm Credit Services; Fisher National Bank; Illini Pella, Inc.; Centrec Consulting Groups, L.L.C.; Illinois Farm Business Farm Management Association; Illinois Concrete Company; Federation of Animal Science Societies; American Dairy Science Association; Royal Properties; Ironwood Homes, Inc.; Ironwood Builders, Inc.; Signature Construction, Inc.; Stonecrest Builders, Inc.; Busey Bank; First Federal Savings Bank of Champaign-Urbana; Champaign Asphalt Co.; Grand Prairie Cooperative, Inc.; Top Flight Grain.

LIVINGSTON, BARGER, BRANDT & SCHROEDER

2506 GALEN DRIVE
SUITE 108
CHAMPAIGN, ILLINOIS 61821
Telephone: 217-351-7479
Fax: 217-351-6870

Bloomington, Illinois Office: 115 West Jefferson, Suite 400, P.O. Box 3457. Telephone: 309-828-5281. Fax: 309-827-3432.

Corporate, Business, Business Litigation, Real Estate Transactions, Creditors' Rights, Employment Law EEOC, ERISA, Estate Planning, Partnerships, Joint Ventures, Estates and Probate. Insurance Litigation, Product Liability, Medical Negligence Defense, Pharmaceutical Litigation, Construction Disputes, Environmental Litigation, Financial Litigation, Employment, Health Care to Physicians and Hospitals, Professional Liability, Officer's and Director's Liability, Environmental Law, Administrative Agency Procedures, Governmental Law, General Counsel Representation, Eminent Domain, Land Use Law, Subdivision and Zoning.

MEMBER OF FIRM

THOMAS B. BORTON (Resident, Champaign Office)

ASSOCIATES

MICHAEL A. WOZNIAK
KENNETH S. WEISS

REPRESENTATIVE CLIENTS: American International Group; American States Insurance Company; Aon Corporation; Associated Physicians Insurance Group; Bituminous Casualty Company; Bloomington-Normal Airport Authority; Bloomington-Normal Water Reclamation Dist.; Bloomington School District #87; Brandt Truck Lines, Inc.; BroMenn Healthcare; The Budd Company; Carle Clinic Association, P.C.; Cincinnati Insurance Company; Citizens Savings Bank; Colonial Insurance Company; Constitution States Insurance Company; DPIC Companies, Inc.; Digital Teleport Inc.; The Eaton Charitable Trust; Employers Insurance of Wausau; The Eureka Company; Federal Land Bank; Federated Insurance; Financial Security Insurance Groups; General Accident Group; General Motors Corporation; Glaxo Wellcome Company; Grinnell Mutual Reinsurance Company; Hamilton Resources Co.; Illinois Central Gulf Railroad; Illinois Power Company; Illinois Provider Trust; Illinois State Medical Insurance Services, Inc; Indiana Insurance Company; Interstate Insurance Cos.; Kemper Insurance; Laidlaw Transit, Inc.; Lederle Laboratories, div. of American Home Products; MMI; Medical Claims Management Group; Miller's Mutual Insurance Company; Mitsubishi Motor Mfg, of America, Inc.; Northern Illinois Gas Company; Novartis Pharmaceuticals Corporation; Ohio Casualty Company; Ohio Hospital Insurance Company; Pantagraph Printing & Stationery Company; Pekin Insurance; Pronational Insurance Company; Royal Globe Insurance Company; St. Paul Insurance Company; Self Insurance Service, Inc.; Sentry Cos.; State Farm Insurance Cos.; The Bank of Illinois in Normal; Travelers Insurance Companies/Aetna; Underwriters Adjustment Company; Union Oil Company of California; Union Planters Bank; United Fire and Casualty; USF & G Company; Utica; Windsor Group.

(For complete biographical data on all personnel, see Professional Biographies at Bloomington)

LAW OFFICE OF SHAYLA MAATUKA

CHAMPAIGN, ILLINOIS

(See Urbana)

Real Estate: Litigation, Residential, Commercial, Contracts, Closings, Land Trusts, Landlord Tennant, Evictions, Foreclosures; Business Law including Contracts, Incorporations, LLC's, Small Business, Advertisement, Corporate; Taxation; Family Law & Divorce; Immigration.

MEYER CAPEL

A PROFESSIONAL CORPORATION
Established in 1961
306 WEST CHURCH STREET
P.O. BOX 6750
CHAMPAIGN, ILLINOIS 61826-6750
Telephone: 217-352-1800
Telecopier: 217-352-1083
Email: attorneys@meyercapel.com
URL: http://www.meyercapel.com

General Civil Litigation, Corporate Law, Business Law, Estate Planning, Estate Administration, Real Estate, Tax, Telecommunications and Public Utility, Intellectual Property Law, Labor and Employment Law (Management), Municipal Law, Family Law, Health Care Law, Personal Injury, Products Liability Law, Criminal Law, Social Security Disability, Software Licensing, Education Law.

(This Listing Continued)

FIRM PROFILE: Meyer Capel is based in Champaign-Urbana, Illinois and is one of the largest law firms in Downstate Illinois. The firm represents clients throughout the United States and overseas and offers a wide range of legal services generally provided only by firms in major metropolitan areas. The firm is listed in the Bar Register of Preeminent Lawyers.

JAMES L. CAPEL, JR. (1933-1991)

DENNIS K. MUNCY, born Taylorville, Illinois, July 12, 1942; admitted to bar, 1967, Illinois and U.S. District Court, Central District of Illinois. *Education:* Northwestern University (B.S., 1964); University of Illinois (J.D., 1967). *Member:* Champaign County and Illinois State (Member, Public Utilities Section) Bar Associations. ***PRACTICE AREAS:*** Public Utilities Law; Telecommunications Law. ***Email:*** dmuncy@meyercapel.com

FRANCIS J. JAHN, born Harrisburg, Illinois, September 19, 1942; admitted to bar, 1967, Illinois; 1968, U.S. District Court, Central District of Illinois; 1976, U.S. Supreme Court; 1984, U.S. Tax Court. *Education:* University of Illinois (B.A., 1964; J.D., 1967). Omicron Delta Kappa; Phi Delta Phi. Winner, Moot Court Competition. Member, Corporate Acts Advisory Committee for Illinois Secretary of State, 1986-2003. *Member:* Champaign County and Illinois State Bar Associations. ***PRACTICE AREAS:*** Corporate Law; Business Law; Commercial Real Estate Law. ***Email:*** fjahn@meyercapel.com

DONALD R. ALDEEN, born Joliet, Illinois, December 18, 1934; admitted to bar, 1962, Illinois and U.S. District Court, Central District of Illinois; 1970, U.S. Court of Appeals, 7th Circuit and U.S. Supreme Court. *Education:* University of Illinois (B.A., 1960; J.D., 1962). Phi Delta Phi. Certified Title Examiner: Chicago Title Insurance Company; St. Paul Title Corporation; Attorney's Title Guaranty Fund, Inc. Member, Panel of Arbitrators, American Arbitration Association. Hearing Officer, Illinois Universities Civil Service System. *Member:* Champaign County (Secretary-Treasurer, 1964-1968; President, 1969), Illinois State and American Bar Associations. [With U.S. Army, 1954-1956]. ***REPORTED CASES:*** Tillitson v. City of Urbana, 29 Ill. 2d22, 193N.E. 2d1 (1963). ***PRACTICE AREAS:*** Real Estate Law; College and School Law; Zoning and Municipal Law; Real Estate; Estate Planning; Estate Administration. ***Email:*** daldeen@meyercapel.com

DAVID B. SHOLEM, born Champaign, Illinois, October 5, 1953; admitted to bar, 1978, Illinois. *Education:* Brown University (B.A., 1975); Case Western Reserve University (J.D., 1978); University of Illinois. *Member:* Champaign County (President, 1984-1985), Illinois State and American (Member, Sections on: Communications and Real Property Law) Bar Associations. ***PRACTICE AREAS:*** Real Estate Law; Corporate and Business Law. ***Email:*** dsholem@meyercapel.com

JOHN H. ELDER, born Pekin, Illinois, February 2, 1947; admitted to bar, 1972, Illinois. *Education:* Purdue University (B.S.I.M., 1969); University of Illinois (J.D., 1972). *Member:* Champaign County (Member, Probate Section) and Illinois State Bar Associations. ***PRACTICE AREAS:*** Real Estate; Trusts and Estates; Wills; Probate; Estate Planning.

MARK D. LIPTON, born Chicago, Illinois, February 25, 1947; admitted to bar, 1975, Illinois; 1976, U.S. District Court, Central District of Illinois; 1979, U.S. Court of Appeals, Seventh Circuit. *Education:* Knox College (B.A., 1968); Northwestern University (J.D., cum laude, 1975). Order of the Coif. Executive Editor, Journal of Criminal Law & Criminology, 1974-1975. Assistant State's Attorney, Champaign County, 1975-1982; First Assistant, 1981-1982. *Member:* Champaign County (President, 1998-2000), Illinois State and American Bar Associations; Illinois Trial Lawyers Association; The Association of Trial Lawyers of America. [With U.S. Army, 1968-1971; Vietnam, 1969-1970]. ***PRACTICE AREAS:*** Criminal Law; Felonies; Misdemeanors; Traffic Violations; Personal Injury; Civil Litigation; Business Litigation. ***Email:*** mlipton@meyercapel.com

TRACY J. NUGENT, born Champaign, Illinois, November 18, 1956; admitted to bar, 1984, Illinois and U.S. Tax Court; 1986, U.S. District Court, Central District of Illinois; 1993, U.S. Court of Appeals, Seventh Circuit; 1996, U.S. Supreme Court. *Education:* University of Illinois (B.S., with honors, 1979; M.B.A.; J.D., 1984). *Member:* Champaign County, Illinois State (Member, Section Council on Corporation, Securities and Business Law) and American (Member, Sections of: Science and Technology; Intellectual Property Law; Business Law) Bar Associations. ***PRACTICE AREAS:*** Corporate and Business Law; Intellectual Property Law; Securities Law; Banking Law; Real Estate Law. ***Email:*** tnugent@meyercapel.com

RICHARD T. WEST, born Chicago, Illinois, August 7, 1944; admitted to bar, 1969, Illinois and Indiana. *Education:* University of Illinois (B.S., 1966; J.D., 1969). Author: "'Immunity' from the Tort Immunity Act," Illinois Bar Journal, May, 1974. Co-Author: "Slamming the Door on Insureds: The Illinois Supreme Court's Lapham-Hickey Decision," Illinois Bar Journal, October, 1996. *Member:* Champaign County, Illinois State (Member, Section Council on Tort Law, 1972-1975; Insurance Law Section Council, 1975-1977), Indiana State and American Bar Associations; The Association of Trial Lawyers of America; International Association of Defense Counsel. [1st Lieut., U.S. Army, 1969-1971; Vietnam, 1970-1971]. ***PRACTICE AREAS:*** State and Federal Trial and Appellate Practice; Business Transactions; Business Litigation; Intellectual Property Law and Litigation; Corporate Law; Health Care; Personal Injury and Products Liability; Insurance Coverage; Class Actions. ***Email:*** rwest@meyercapel.com

RUSTY W. FREELAND, born Highland, Illinois, February 9, 1958; admitted to bar, 1985, Missouri and U.S. Tax Court; 1986, Illinois. *Education:* University of Illinois (B.A., 1980); Washington University (J.D., 1985). Phi Alpha Theta. Recipient, James Scholar. Certified Public Accountant, Illinois, 1980. *Member:* Champaign County and Illinois State Bar Associations; The Missouri Bar; American Institute of Certified Public Accountants; Illinois Certified Public Accountant Society. ***PRACTICE AREAS:*** Corporate Law; Mergers and Acquisitions; Intellectual Property Licensing; Venture Capital Transactions. ***Email:*** rfreeland@meyercapel.com

LORNA K. GEILER, admitted to bar, 1986, Illinois, U.S. District Court, Northern, Central and Southern Districts of Illinois, U.S. Court of Appeals, Seventh Circuit and U.S. Supreme Court. *Education:* Illinois State University (B.S., cum laude, 1983); University of Illinois (J.D., 1986). Author: Chapter 20: "Retaliatory Discharge," in IICLE 2002 Causes of Action Handbook. *Member:* Champaign County, Illinois State (Member, Employment and Labor Law Section Council) and American Bar Associations; The Association of Trial Lawyers of America. ***PRACTICE AREAS:*** Labor and Employment Law; Federal Civil Litigation; Civil Litigation. ***Email:*** lgeiler@meyercapel.com

PATRICK T. FITZGERALD, born Des Plaines, Illinois, August 28, 1963; admitted to bar, 1989, Illinois. *Education:* University of Illinois (B.A., 1986; J.D., 1989). *Member:* Champaign County, Illinois State and American Bar Associations. ***PRACTICE AREAS:*** Real Estate Law. ***Email:*** pfitzgerald@meyercapel.com

TODD J. BLACK, born Chicago, Illinois, November 30, 1959; admitted to bar, 1986, Illinois. *Education:* University of Illinois (B.S., 1983); John Marshall Law School (J.D., with distinction, 1985). Adjunct Professor of Law, Estate Planning, University of Illinois College of Law. *Member:* Champaign County, Illinois State and American Bar Associations. ***PRACTICE AREAS:*** Estate Planning; Estate Administration; Trust Administration; Business Planning. ***Email:*** tblack@meyercapel.com

JOSEPH D. MURPHY, born Urbana, Illinois, July 1, 1960; admitted to bar, 1986, Illinois; 1987, District of Columbia, New York, U.S. Court of Appeals, Seventh, District of Columbia and Federal Circuits and U.S. District Court, Central and Northern Districts of Illinois and the District of Columbia. *Education:* Boston College (B.A., magna cum laude, 1982); The American University (J.D.,cum laude, 1985). Member and Editor, The American University Law Review, 1983-1985. Law Clerk to the Honorable Stanley J. Roszkowski, U.S. District Judge for the Northern District of Illinois, 1985-1987. Author, Casenote, "Paper Converting Machine Company v. Magna-Graphics Corporation: Increased Protection Against Making and Using Combination Patents," 34 Am. U. L. Rev. 761, 1985. Adjunct Professor of Law, University of Illinois College of Law (course in trade secrets, copyright and trademark). *Member:* District of Columbia Bar; Illinois State, New York State and American Bar Associations. ***LANGUAGES:*** Japanese, German and Spanish. ***PRACTICE AREAS:*** Telecommunications Law; Intellectual Property; Franchise Law; Civil Litigation; Business Transactions. ***Email:*** jmurphy@meyercapel.com

JAMES M. MULLADY, born Kankakee, Illinois, May 27, 1952; admitted to bar, 1991, Illinois. *Education:* Illinois State University (B.S., 1974; M.S., 1975); University of Illinois (Adv. Cert., 1983); Indiana University (J.D., 1991). Phi Delta Kappa; Delta Kappa Pi. Member, Board of Directors, Illinois Pro Bono Center, 1998-2000. *Member:* Champaign County (Member, Board of Governors, 1994-1997; Chairman, Family Law Committee, 1996-1997), Illinois State and American (Member, Family Law Section) Bar Associations. ***PRACTICE AREAS:*** Family Law; Adoption; Social Security Disability; Landlord-Tenant Law. ***Email:*** jmullady@meyercapel.com

WILLIAM B. MOORE, born Los Angeles, California, February 29, 1956; admitted to bar, 1982, California; 1984, New York and U.S. Tax Court; 1996, Illinois; 2002, Colorado and Utah. *Education:* Utah State University (B.S., summa cum laude, 1978); University of California School of Law, Los Angeles (J.D., 1982); Pace Law School (LL.M., Environmental Law, 1994). Member: Moot Court Honors Program; UCLA Law Review, 1981-1982. Visiting Assistant Professor, University of Illinois School of Law, 1994-1996. Visiting Assistant Professor of Engineering, University of Illinois, 2002—. Co-Author: "The Case For State Pollution Taxes," 12 Pace Environmental Law Review, 1994. ***PRACTICE AREAS:*** Business Law; Corporate Law; Venture Capital; Business Start-Ups; Tax Law. ***Email:*** wmoore@meyercapel.com

EVAN D. COOBS, born Oelwein, Iowa, November 11, 1963; admitted to bar, 1989, Minnesota; 1991, U.S. District Court, District of Minnesota; 1993, U.S. Tax Court; 1995, Illinois. *Education:* University of Iowa (B.B.A., with distinction, 1986; M.A., 1989; J.D., with high distinction, 1989). Certified Public Accountant, Iowa, 1986. *Member:* Illinois State, Minnesota State and American Bar Associations. ***PRACTICE AREAS:*** Business Law; Corporate Law; Tax Law; Finance; Partnership Law. ***Email:*** ecoobs@meyercapel.com

JOHN J. POWERS, born Blue Island, Illinois, July 12, 1955; admitted to bar, 1980, Texas; 1984, Illinois. *Education:* University of Illinois (B.S., highest honors, 1977); University of Michigan (J.D., magna cum laude, 1980). Member, Order of the Coif. Certified Public Accountant, Illinois, 1977. *Member:* Champaign County and Illinois State Bar Associations. ***PRACTICE AREAS:*** Banking Law; Corporate Law. ***Email:*** jpowers@meyercapel.com

ROCHELLE A. FUNDERBURG, born Lincoln, Illinois, September 14, 1956; admitted to bar, 1981, Illinois; 1982, U.S. District Court, Central District of Illinois; 1986, U.S. District Court, Southern District of Illinois and U.S. Court of Appeals, Seventh Circuit. *Education:* University of Illinois (B.A., 1978; J.D., 1981). Phi Delta Phi; Phi Kappa Phi. *Member:* Champaign County (Member, Board of Governors, 1995), Illinois State (Member, Sections on: Tort; Administrative; Workers' Compensation) and American Bar Associations. ***PRACTICE AREAS:*** Litigation; Municipal Law; Workers Compensation; Labor and Employment. ***Email:*** rfunderburg@meyercapel.com

JEFFREY M. DAVIS, born Joliet, Illinois, November 20, 1970; admitted to bar, 1996, Illinois. *Education:* University of Illinois (B.S., with honors, 1993; J.D., 1996). *Member:* Champaign County (Member, Board of Governors, 2003, 2004), Illinois State and American Bar Associations. [with Illinois Army National Guard, 1990-1996]. ***PRACTICE AREAS:*** Estate Planning Law; Estate Administration Law; Real Estate Law; Corporate Law. ***Email:*** jdavis@meyercapel.com

KEITH E. EMMONS, born Pekin, Illinois, March 28, 1947; admitted to bar, 1974, Illinois and U.S. District Court, Central District of Illinois and U.S. Court of Appeals, Seventh Circuit. *Education:* Southern Illinois University (B.A., 1971); Loyola University of Chicago (J.D., 1974); University of Illinois (A.M., 1981). Member, Loyola University Law Journal, 1973-1974. Assistant States Attorney, DeWitt County, Illinois, 1978-1983. Co-Author, "National Practitioner Data Bank: Final Regulations," Illinois State Bar Journal, April, 1990. Co-Author, "Conflict Resolution Under the Health Care Surrogate Act, Private Decision-Making and the Continuing Role of the Guardian," Health Care Lawyer, October/December, 1991. Author: "Ex-Parte Communications With Health Care Providers," American Bar Association National Institute, New Orleans, Louisiana, May, 1993. Contributing Author and Editor: Health Care Law Section for the Illinois State Bar Association, Southern Illinois University Law School Annual Survey of Illinois Law. Co-Author and Principal Editor: "The Survey of Illinois Law Health Care," Southern Illinois University Law Journal, Vol. 18, 1994. Participating Author: "Continuing Course of Negligent Treatment and the Medical Malpractice Statute of Repose." Author: "Risk Management Implications of

(This Listing Continued)

MEYER CAPEL, A PROFESSIONAL CORPORATION, Champaign—Continued

Petrillo and its Progeny," Health Law News, Volume II, Issue 4, Fall, 1994. Author: "Evidence Update," presented at Illinois Association of Defense Trial Counsel Fall Seminar, St. Louis, Missouri, September, 1995. Author: "Corporate Practice of Medicine and Fee Splitting," presented at Illinois State Bar Association Law Ed. Series; "Health Care: Representing Physicians in Changing Health Environment," Chicago, Illinois, April, 1996. Co-Author, with D. Cameron Dobbins: "Corporate Practice of Medicine - Hospital Employment of Physicians, The Survey of Illinois Law: Health Care," Southern Illinois University Law Journal, Vol. 20, Summer, 1996. Author: "Contribution and Indemnity," Vol. 2, Chap. 5, Sec. 5.35, The Law of Medical Practice in Illinois, 2nd Ed., 1996-2000, by LeBlang, Basanta and Kane. Co-Author: "The Corporation of the Practice of Medicine: Is it Legal?" presented at the American Academy of Health Care Attorneys Annual Meeting, Toronto, Canada, June, 1997; Co-Author: "Are You Your Own Worst Enemy? How Hospitals Help and Hurt Their Defense in Medical Malpractice Cases," presented at the Illinois Association of Healthcare Attorneys Annual Meeting, Chicago, IL (October, 1998). Author: "Corporate Practice of Medicine, Survey of Illinois Law: Health Care Law," published in the Southern Illinois University Law Journal, Vol. 22, Summer, 1998. Co-Author: "Managed Care Reform and Patient Rights Act: Implications for Patients, Providers and Plans," Illinois Bar Journal, Vol. 87, No. 12, December 1999. Author: "Compliance and Implementation of the Health Insurance Portability and Accountability Act of 1996 (HIPAA)": the Final Privacy Regulations presented at HIPAA, Health Information Compliance, 2001, Springfield, IL August, 2001. Author: "HMO Liability for the Provision of Healthcare Affirmed Survey of Illinois Law: Healthcare Law," Southern Illinois Law Journal, Vol. 25, Summer 2001. Certified Mediator, Champaign County, Circuit Court Mediation Program. *Member:* Champaign County, Illinois State (Council Chair, 1997-1998; Member, Council, Health Care Section, 1988-2005) and American Bar Associations; American Health Lawyers Association; Illinois Association of Healthcare Attorneys (Member: Board of Directors and Past President); American Society of Medical Association Counsel; Appellate Lawyers Association; Illinois Association of Defense Trial Counsel. ***PRACTICE AREAS:*** Health Care; Privacy; Professional Liability Defense; Civil Trial Practice; Appellate Practice. ***Email:*** kemmons@meyercapel.com

MATT C. DEERING, born Beeville, Texas, November 6, 1968; admitted to bar, 1996, Illinois. *Education:* University of Kentucky (B.A., 1991); Ohio Northern University (J.D., 1996). *Member:* Champaign County, Illinois State and American Bar Associations. ***PRACTICE AREAS:*** Business Law; Real Estate; Intellectual Property; Telecommunications Regulation; Licensing. ***Email:*** mdeering@meyercapel.com

HAROLD N. ADAMS, born Lincoln, Illinois, December 2, 1970; admitted to bar, 1996, Illinois. *Education:* University of Illinois, Urbana-Champaign (B.A., Finance, with distinction, 1993; J.D., 1996). Phi Delta Phi. *Member:* Champaign County, Illinois State and American Bar Associations. ***PRACTICE AREAS:*** Residential Real Estate; Commercial Real Estate; Business Law; Corporate Law; Estate Administration; Estate Planning. ***Email:*** hadams@meyercapel.com

WARD F. McDONALD, born Decatur, Illinois, March 26, 1942; admitted to bar, 1969, Illinois. *Education:* University of Illinois (B.S., 1964; J.D., 1969). Adjunct Professor, Finance & Law, University of Illinois, 1990—. American College of Real Estate Lawyers, Charter Member, 1980. Co-Founder, Board of Directors, Land Conservation Foundation. President, Arrowhead Council, Boy Scouts of America, 1987-1989. Board of Directors, Prairie Rivers Network. *Member:* Illinois State Bar Association (Chairman, Real Estate Law Section Council, 1976-1977); Illinois Bar Foundation (Charter Member); American Bar Foundation; Attorneys Title Guaranty Fund (Board of Directors). ***PRACTICE AREAS:*** Real Estate; Real Estate Finance; Corporate Law; Estate Planning; Banking Law.

MARJORIE A. HARRIS, born Atlanta, Georgia, July 20, 1958; admitted to bar, 1984, New York; 1988, Illinois. *Education:* Brown University (B.S., magna cum laude, 1980); University of Michigan (J.D ., cum laude, 1983). Phi Delta Phi. Member, Michigan Law Review, 1981-1983. Visiting Instructor, University of Illinois College of Law, 1989, 1991-1993. *Member:* Illinois State Bar Association. ***PRACTICE AREAS:*** Estate Planning; Estate Administration; Charitable Gift Planning; Not-For-Profit Corporations. ***Email:*** mharris@meyercapel.xom

REBECCA E.P. WADE, born Herrin, Illinois, April 1, 1971; admitted to bar, 1998, Illinois. *Education:* University of Illinois, Urbana-Champaign (B.A., Economics, 1993; J.D., magna cum laude, 1998). Member, 1996-1997 and Articles Editor, 1997-1998, Elder Law Journal. Law Clerk, Hon. James A. Knecht, Fourth District Appellate Court, State of Illinois. Author: "The Face of Social Security in The 21st Century," Elder Law Journal, 1998. *Member:* Illinois State Bar Association. ***PRACTICE AREAS:*** Estate Planning; Estate Administration; Real Estate. ***Email:*** rwade@meyercapel.com

JENNY H. PARK, born Seoul, South Korea, February 27, 1973; admitted to bar, 2001, Indiana; 2002, Illinois. *Education:* University of Illinois (B.S., 1993); Indiana University School of Law (J.D., 2001). *Member:* Champaign County, Indianapolis, Indiana State and American Bar Associations. ***LANGUAGES:*** Korean. ***PRACTICE AREAS:*** Commercial Real Estate; Residential Real Estate; Condominium Law; Land Development; Landlord and Tenant Law. ***Email:*** jpark@meyercapel.com

BROOKE A.M. DIDIER, born Galesburg, Illinois, March 10, 1978; admitted to bar, 2003, Illinois. *Education:* Monmouth College (B.A., 2000); University of Illinois, College of Law (J.D., 2003). *Member:* Illinois State and Champaign County Bar Associations. ***PRACTICE AREAS:*** Estate Planning; Estate Administration. ***Email:*** bdidier@meyercapel.com

STEVEN A. AMJAD, born St. Louis, Missouri, January 8, 1974; admitted to bar, 2001, Missouri; 2002, Illinois. *Education:* St. Louis University (B.S., 1997; J.D., 2001); University of Illinois, Urbana-Champaign (M.B.A., 1998). City of St. Louis Office of the Circuit Attorney. Missouri Real Estate Broker, 2004. *Member:* Illinois State Bar Association; The Missouri Bar; St. Louis Association of Realtors. ***PRACTICE AREAS:*** Business Litigation; Commercial Litigation; Criminal Law; Real Estate. ***Email:*** samjad@meyercapel.com

(This Listing Continued)

TAMARA K. HACKMANN, born Mexico, Missouri, February 12, 1962; admitted to bar, 1995, Michigan; 1996, Illinois; 1998, Iowa; U.S. District Court, Southern District of Iowa and Central District of Illinois; U.S. Court of Appeals, Eighth Circuit. *Education:* University of Missouri-Columbia (B.S., summa cum laude, 1985); University of Michigan (J.D., magna cum laude, 1995). Member, Order of the Coif. *Member:* Illinois State, Iowa State and American Bar Associations. ***PRACTICE AREAS:*** Professional Liability; Commercial Litigation. ***Email:*** thackmann@meyercapel.com

SCOTT E. PERKINS, born Urbana, Illinois, March 23, 1979; admitted to bar, 2004, Illinois. *Education:* University of Illinois (B.S., Finance, highest honors, 2001; J.D., magna cum laude, 2004). Bronze Tablet. Illinois Real Estate Broker, 2002. *Member:* Champaign County and Illinois Bar Associations. ***PRACTICE AREAS:*** Business Law; Commercial Real Estate; Residential Real Estate. ***Email:*** sperkins@meyercapel.com

OF COUNSEL

RICHARD J. WINKEL, JR., born Kankakee, Illinois, September 25, 1956; admitted to bar, 1982, Illinois and U.S. District Court, Northern and Central Districts of Illinois. *Education:* University of Illinois (B.A., 1979); DePaul University (J.D., 1982). Omicron Delta Epsilon; Omicron Delta Kappa. Recipient, Edmund J. James Scholarship. Author: "Covenants Not To Compete: A State-By-State Survey," American Bar Association, 1991; "Employee Duty of Loyalty: A State-By-State Survey," American Bar Association, 1995. Member: Champaign County Board, 1992-1994; House Representative, Illinois, 1995-2003; State Senate, Illinois, 2003—. *Member:* Champaign County and Illinois State Bar Associations. ***PRACTICE AREAS:*** General Civil Practice. ***Email:*** rickwinkel@rickwinkel.com

REPRESENTATIVE CLIENTS: American Crop Protection Association; American Oil Chemists Society; Apartment MediaWorks, L.L.C.; Artwick Consulting, Inc.; The Atkins Group; Bank of Ivesdale; BASF Plant Science, LLC; Bell Foods, Inc.; Busey Bank; Cambridge Telephone Company; Cannon Cochran Management Services, Inc.; Carle Clinic Association; Cass Telephone Company; Champaign County; Champaign-Urbana Venture Fund, LLC; Champaign County Forest Preserve District; C.H.I. Overhead Doors, Inc.; Cingular Wireless LLC; Cookson America, Inc.; Cozad/Westchester; Duce Construction Company (DUCE); ExSeed Genetics, L.L.C.; Farm Management Company-Midwest; Foremost Insurance Co.; Fox Development Corp.; Franchise Management Systems, Inc.; Genesco Telephone Company; Gill Athletics, Inc.; Conseco Financial Vendor Services; EpiWorks, Inc.; Harris Industries; Hobbico, Inc.; Communication Management, Inc.; Housing Authority of Champaign County; Illinois Archaeological Survey; Illinois Fertilizer and Chemical Association; Illinois Foundation Seeds, Inc.; Illinois Independent Telephone Assn.; Incobrasa Industries, Inc.; Ivesdale Fire Protection District; Kirby Foods, Inc.; The Larson Co.; Lopax, Inc.; Main Street Bank & Trust Co.; McLane Co.; Midwest Television, Inc.; Monical Pizza Corp.; Nexus, Inc.; Illinois-American Water Co.; Parkland College; Plastic Container Corp.; Premiere Partners; Equistar Chemical, L.P.; Raindrop Geomagic, Inc.; Sangamon Valley Public Water District; Shawnee Telephone Company; SOMAT; Southwest Recreational Industries, Inc.; SBC Communications, Inc.; Stanton Township; Sullivan-Parkhill Holdings, Inc.; Thomasboro School District No. 130; Tolono Township Road District; Urbana Township; Valenti Management; Vesuvius, USA; Wal-Mart Stores, Inc.; Westchester Group, Inc.

PHEBUS & KOESTER

CHAMPAIGN, ILLINOIS

(See Urbana)

Civil trial practice in all courts, including class actions, mass torts, personal injury, including products liability, medical malpractice, automobile accidents, slip and fall, and railroad.

JOHN T. PHIPPS LAW OFFICES, P.C.

Established in 1970

303 LINCOLN BUILDING
44 MAIN STREET
P.O. BOX 1220
CHAMPAIGN, ILLINOIS 61824-1220
Telephone: 217-359-2929
Fax: 217-359-5329
URL: http://www.lawyers.com/johnphippslaw

General Civil Trial Practice, Family, Personal Injury, Corporate, Banking, Paternity, Child Custody, Visitation, Divorce, Wills and Estate Planning, Domestic Relations, Probate, Elder Law, Traffic Defense, Business Fraud, White Collar Crimes, Mediation, Arbitration, Real Estate, Criminal Law, Domestic Violence, DUI.

JOHN T. PHIPPS, born Chicago, Illinois, September 20, 1937; admitted to bar, 1965, Illinois. *Education:* DePauw University (B.A., 1959); University of Illinois (J.D., 1965). Phi Alpha Delta. Author: "Modifications of Divorce Judgements," Illinois State Bar Family Law Handbook (1995). Co-Author: "Going to Trial, A Step-by-Step Guide to Trial Practice and Procedure," ABA, 1989. Member, Board of Directors, Illinois Institute for Continuing Legal Education, 1989-1998. Arbitrator, American Arbitration Association, 1970—. Hearing Officer, State Universities Civil Service System Merit Board. Member, Illinois Supreme Court Alternative Dispute Resolution Committee, 1991—. *Member:* Illinois State (Member: Alternative Dispute Resolution Section Council, 1990-1997; Chairman, 1994-1995; General Practice Section Council, 1997—; Chairman, 2001—; Co-Editor Section Newsletter, 1999—; Assembly, 1998—) and American (Editor, General Practice Section Newsletter, 1990-1996; Member, General Practice Section Council, 1993-1997) Bar Associations. Charter Fellow, Illinois Bar Foundation. Fellow, American Bar Foundation. ***REPORTED CASES:*** Saldeen v. Hamelberg, et al. 555 N.E.2d 743 (Ill. App. 4th Dist. 1990); Harris v. Manor Healthcare Corporation, et al. 489 N.E.2d 1374 (Ill. Supreme Ct. 1986); Baily v. Timpone 389 N.E.2d 1193 (Ill. Supreme Ct. 1979); Cessna v. Montgomery 344 N.E.2d 447 (Ill. Supreme Ct. 1976); Okaw Homes, Inc. v. Industrial Commission 237 N.E.2d 510 (Ill. Supreme Ct. 1968). ***Email:*** jphipps@net66.com

REPRESENTATIVE CLIENTS: National Bank of Monticello; Farmer City State Bank; Auto-Owners Insurance Co.; Shelby Motors, Inc.; Petrolane, Inc.; T.V. Associates, Inc.; Bash & Lambert, Inc. Builders.
REFERENCE: Bank Illinois.

RAWLES, O'BYRNE, STANKO & KEPLEY, P.C.

Established in 1950

501 WEST CHURCH STREET
P.O. BOX 800
CHAMPAIGN, ILLINOIS 61824-0800
Telephone: 217-352-7661
Telecopier: 217-352-2169
URL: http://www.lawyers.com/rosklaw
URL: http://www.rosklaw.com

General practice in all State and Federal Courts, Trials and Appeals, Personal Injury, Product Liability, Estate and Business Planning, Probate, Real Estate, Hospital and Health Law, Commercial Litigation, Insurance Defense, Malpractice, Criminal Law, Taxation, Domestic Relations, Employment Law, Bankruptcy, Worker's Compensation, and General Counseling.

FIRM PROFILE: Founded in 1931 by Donald M. Reno, Sr., the firm established an early emphasis in the field of personal injury, civil litigation, and criminal defense. The firm became known as Reno & O'Byrne in 1952 when Michael O'Byrne became a partner. It became Reno, O'Byrne & Kepley in 1962, and then incorporated as Reno, O'Byrne & Kepley, P.C. in 1984. The firm is included in the Bar Register of Preeminent Lawyers.

EDWARD H. RAWLES, born Chicago, Illinois, May 7, 1945; admitted to bar, 1970, Illinois; 1974, U.S. Supreme Court; 1984, Colorado. *Education:* University of Illinois (A.B., 1967); Illinois Institute of Technology/Chicago-Kent College of Law (J.D., summa cum laude, 1970). Member, Kent Society of Honor Men, Chicago-Kent College of Law. Member, Chicago-Kent Law Review, 1968-1970. Listed in "Who's Who in American Law," 4th Edition. Contributing Author: "Deposing the Medical Witness," Chapter 1302, Lawyers Guide to Medical Proof, Matthew-Bender, 1982. Hearing Officer, Illinois Fair Employment Practice Commission, 1973-1975. Member, Panel of Arbitrators, American Arbitration Association. Member, University of Illinois Student Legal Services Advisory Board, 1979—. Member, Illinois State Supreme Court Committee on Character and Fitness, 2004. *Member:* Champaign County (President, 1994-1995), Illinois State, Colorado State and American (Member, Special Committee on Insurance Company Taxation, 1985-1986) Bar Associations; Illinois Trial Lawyers Association (Member, Civil Practice Committee, 1982—); Colorado Trial Lawyers Association; The Association of Trial Lawyers of America (sustaining member); Bar Association of the Seventh Federal Circuit; Charter Fellow, Illinois Bar Foundation. (Board Certified as a Specialist in Civil Trial Advocacy by the National Board of Trial Advocacy). ***PRACTICE AREAS:*** Malpractice; Civil Litigation; Insurance Law; Federal Practice; Personal Injury Law. ***Email:*** ehrawles@rosklaw.com

STEPHEN M. O'BYRNE, born Chicago, Illinois, October 6, 1950; admitted to bar, 1975, Illinois; 1980, U.S. Supreme Court. *Education:* University of Illinois (B.A., 1972; J.D., 1975). *Member:* Champaign County, Illinois State and American Bar Associations; American Society of Hospital Attorneys. ***PRACTICE AREAS:*** Corporate Law; Business Law; Hospital Law; Health Care; Probate and Estate Planning; Commercial Defense Law; Real Estate Law. ***Email:*** sobyrne@rosklaw.com

GLENN A. STANKO, born Canton, Illinois, May 5, 1949; admitted to bar, 1976, Illinois; 1982, U.S. Supreme Court. *Education:* Western Illinois University (B.S., 1971); University of Illinois (J.D., 1976). *Member:* Champaign County (Member, Board of Governors, 1988-1990), Illinois State and American Bar Associations; The Association of Trial Lawyers of America; Illinois Trial Lawyers Association; Champaign County Criminal Defense Lawyers Association. ***PRACTICE AREAS:*** Employment Law; Employment Discrimination Law; Personal Injury Law; Civil Litigation; Criminal Law. ***Email:*** gastanko@rosklaw.com

BRETT A. KEPLEY, born Champaign, Illinois, June 1, 1961; admitted to bar, 1986, Illinois. *Education:* University of Illinois (B.A., 1983); Northern Illinois University (J.D., 1986). Phi Alpha Delta. *Member:* Champaign County, Illinois State and American Bar Associations; Illinois Association of Defense Trial Counsel. ***PRACTICE AREAS:*** Commercial Litigation; Insurance Law; Personal Injury; Civil Litigation; Federal Practice; Bankruptcy Law; Real Estate Law; Leasing; Collections; Traffic Violations; Worker's Compensation. ***Email:*** bakepley@rosklaw.com

TIMOTHY S. JEFFERSON, born Bloomington, Illinois, March 29, 1961; admitted to bar, 1986, Missouri; 1990, Illinois. *Education:* Indiana University (B.S., 1983); University of Missouri-Columbia Law School (J.D., 1986). Recipient, American Jurisprudence Award in Torts. Certified Public Accountant, Missouri, 1988. *Member:* Illinois State Bar Association; The Missouri Bar. ***PRACTICE AREAS:*** Real Estate; Business Law; Corporate Taxation; Estate Planning; Probate Administration. ***Email:*** tsjeffer@rosklaw.com

OF COUNSEL

J. MICHAEL O'BYRNE

LEGAL SUPPORT PERSONNEL

ROSE M. LANTER, born Urbana, Illinois, September 16, 1953. *Education:* Parkland College. Certified Legal Assistant, 1987. *Member:* Association of Legal Assistants, Inc. (Member, Board of Directors, 1990-1994); Illinois State Bar Association (Associate). (Legal Assistant). ***PRACTICE AREAS:*** Civil Litigation at State and Appellate Levels; Real Estate; Probate. ***Email:*** rmlanter@rosklaw.com

KAREN B. JUDD, born Effingham, Illinois, February 23, 1948. *Education:* University of Illinois (B.S., 1973). Certified Legal Assistant, 1979. Author: "Beyond the Bar: Legal Assistants and the Unauthorized Practice of Law," Facts and Findings, 1983; "Legal Assistant Time in Attorney Fee Awards: A Separate and Distinct Compensation," Facts and Findings, 1988. *Member:* National Association of Legal Assistants, Inc. (President, 1988-1990; Member, Board of Directors, 1985-1990); Illinois State Bar Association (Associate). (Legal Assistant). ***PRACTICE AREAS:*** State and Federal Civil Litigation at Trial and Appellate Levels. ***Email:*** kbjudd@rosklaw.com

(This Listing Continued)

LOCAL COUNSEL FOR: American International Group; Construction Industry Welfare Fund of Central Illinois; Daily & Associates, Engineers, Inc.; New Hampshire Insurance Group; Pekin Insurance Co.; PKD, Inc. Construction Managers; Provena Covenant Medical Center; ServiceMaster of Champaign; Unitrin Insurance Group; University Construction.

RUSIN MACIOROWSKI & FRIEDMAN, LTD.

2506 GALEN DRIVE, SUITE 104
CHAMPAIGN, ILLINOIS 61821-7047
Telephone: 217-351-1700
Fax: 217-351-1732
Email: mcosimini@rusinlaw.com
URL: http://www.rusinlaw.com

Chicago, Illinois Office: Suite 1530, 10 South Riverside Plaza, 60606. Telephone: 312-454-5110. Fax: 312-454-6166.
Carbondale, Illinois Office: 239 South Lewis Lane, Suite A, 62901-3443. Telephone: 618-351-8100. Fax: 618-351-8109.

Workers Compensation Law. Insurance Defense, Personal Injury, Products Liability, Auto and Trucking Liability, Structural Work Act, Commercial Litigation, Subrogation, Contract Insurance, Employment Discrimination. Wrongful Discharge.

FIRM PROFILE: Rusin Maciorowski & Friedman, Ltd. was founded in 1984 by Douglas F. Stevenson, Michael E. Rusin and Stephen J. Friedman (as Stevenson, Rusin & Friedman, Ltd.) with the goal of establishing a specialty firm focusing on representing employers and their insurance carriers in all of the varied legal aspects of the workplace injury, including Worker's Compensation, OSHA, personal injury, contribution liability and lien recovery, wrongful discharge and employment discrimination.

Through dedication to aggressive, result-oriented file handling and prompt, thorough client reporting, the firm grew from the original seven lawyers and continued to expand to serve its clients' needs throughout the state of Illinois and northern and northwestern Indiana. With the opening of our Champaign, Illinois office in 1999, and our Carbondale, Illinois office in 2003, the firm reinforced its commitment to efficient representation in our downstate venues.

With Douglas Stevenson's appointment to the Illinois Industrial Commission in 1998, the firm changed its name to reflect its current mission on providing a full service litigation practice to its client base of employers, industry and insurance carriers.

The firm's leadership role in Workers' Compensation and Employer Liability has carried over to its civil department. Initially developed to handle the claims evolving from the workplace accident, the firm has acquired a depth of experience in employment discrimination and wrongful discharge, product liability, and coverage issues. We have the unique ability to coordinate the handling of the Workers' Compensation claim and related civil actions including lien protection, third party practice including extensive remedy defenses and related insurance coverage issues, including the handling of Declaratory Judgement actions.

Our current civil department, managed by Gregory Vacala, has grown and provides seasoned trial attorneys handling cases throughout Illinois and surrounding states. These attorneys have a depth of experience in managing all phases of civil practice including transportation law (automobiles and trucking liability), commercial litigation, and insurance coverage.

The firm has earned a preeminent rating from Martindale-Hubbell.

(For Biographical data on all Personnel, see professional Biographies at Chicago, Illinois)

SECREST WARDLE

Established in 1912

2919 CROSSING COURT, SUITE 11
CHAMPAIGN, ILLINOIS 61822
Telephone: 217-378-8002
Fax: 217-378-8003
Email: info@secrestwardle.com
URL: http://www.secrestwardle.com

Farmington Hills, Michigan Office: 30903 Northwestern Highway, P.O. Box 3040. Telephone: 248-851-9500. Telefacsimile: 248-851-2158.
Lansing, Michigan Office: 6639 Centurion Drive, Suite 130. Telephone: 517-886-1224. Facsimile: 517-886-9284.
Mount Clemens, Michigan Office: 94 Macomb Place. Telephone: 586-465-7180. Telefacsimile: 586-465-0673.
Grand Rapids, Michigan Office: 2025 E. Beltline, S. E., Suite 103. Telephone: 616-285-0143. Fax: 616-285-0145.

Appellate, Commercial and Business, Construction, Drug and Medical Device, Employment, Environmental and Toxic Tort, Governmental Litigation, Insurance Coverage, Intellectual Property/Advertising Injury, Motor Vehicle Litigation, Municipal, Premises Liabilty, Product Liability, Malpractice and Professional Liability.

FIRM PROFILE: Secrest Wardle specializes in defense litigation and as counsel for insurance, municipal and commercial clients. For detailed information on each practice visit www.secrestwardle.com.

JOHN B. HENSLEY, admitted to bar, 1982, Illinois and U.S. District Court, Northern District of Illinois; 1983, U.S. District Court, Central District of Illinois. *Education:* University of Illinois (B.S., 1973); DePaul University College of Law (J.D., 1982).

JENNIFER N. PAHRE, admitted to bar, 1986, California; 1987, U.S. District Court, Northern and Southern Districts of California; 1988, U.S. Court of Appeals, Sixth and Ninth Circuits; 1992, Michigan; 2000, Illinois; U.S. District Court, Eastern and Western Districts of Michigan. *Education:* Harvard University; Stanford University (B.A., 1983); Loyola Law School (J.D., 1986).

(For complete professional biographies, please see Farmington Hills, Michigan)

SINGLETON LAW FIRM, P.C.

ONE EAST MAIN, SUITE 215
CHAMPAIGN, ILLINOIS 61820
Telephone: 217-352-3900
Fax: 217-352-4900
URL: http://www.singletonlaw.pro

Corporate Law, Securities, Intellectual Property, Patents, Real Estate, Health Care.

ALAN R. SINGLETON, born Urbana, Illinois, October 21, 1964; admitted to bar, 1991, Illinois; 1992, U.S. District Court, Central District of Illinois; registered to practice before U.S. Patent and Trademark Office. *Education:* University of Illinois (B.S., 1988; J.D., 1991). Recipient, Chemical Rubber Company Chemistry Award. Academic Appointment: University of Illinois College of Medicine, 1998—. Guest Speaker, University of Illinois Technology Entrepreneur Center. Member, Advisory Council, EKOS Materials Corporation. *Member:* Champaign County, Illinois State and American (Member, Business and Intellectual Property Law Sections) Bar Associations; Bar Association Central and Southern Federal Districts of Illinois; American Intellectual Property Law Association; Intellectual Property Law Association of Chicago; Illinois Association of Healthcare Attorneys. ***PRACTICE AREAS:*** Corporate Law; Securities; Intellectual Property; Patents; Real Estate; Health Care.

THOMAS, MAMER & HAUGHEY, LLP

Established in 1946
NATIONAL CITY BANK BUILDING
30 E. MAIN STREET, SUITE 500
CHAMPAIGN, ILLINOIS 61820-3629
Telephone: 217-351-1500
Fax: 217-355-0087; 217-351-2017
217-351-2169
Email: tmh@tmh-law.com
URL: http://www.tmh-law.com
Mailing Address: P.O. Box 560, Champaign, IL 61824-0560

General Practice, Federal and State Trials, Probate, Trusts, Taxation, Real Estate, Business and Commercial Law, Insurance Defense, Employment and Employment Discrimination, Elder Law, Discrimination, Construction Accident, Adoptions, Premarital Agreements, Long Term Care, American with Disabilities Act, Family and Medical Leave Act, Sexual Harassment, Wrongful Termination, Medical practice, Automobile Accidents, Slip and Fall, Wrongful Death, Condominium Law, Landlord and Tenant Law, Residential Real Estate, Estate and Gift Taxation, Income Tax, Estate Litigation, Estate Planning, Guardianship and Conservatorship, Wills and Probate, Workers Compensation, Business Formation, Business Litigation, Buying and Selling of Business, Limited Liability Company Law, Partnership Law, Small Business Law, Construction Accidents, Breach of Contract, Employment Contracts, Personal Policies, Commercial Leasing, Commercial Real Estate, Landlord and Tenant Law.

FIRM PROFILE: Thomas, Mamer & Haughey, LLP serves clients throughout east central Illinois. The firm was founded by James G. Thomas and Wallace M. Mulliken in 1946, joined by Stuart M. Mamer in 1947. A full-service firm, with all lawyers concentrating in different areas.

JAMES G. THOMAS (1901-1990)

MEMBERS OF FIRM

STUART M. MAMER, born East Hardin, Illinois, February 23, 1921; admitted to bar, 1947, Illinois. *Education:* University of Illinois (A.B., 1942; J.D., 1947). Order of Coif; Phi Delta Phi. Commissioner, Attorney Registration and Disciplinary Commission, 1976-1982. *Member:* Champaign County, Illinois State and American Bar Associations. Fellow: American Bar Foundation; American College of Trust and Estate Counsel (Member, Board of Regents, 1984-1990). ***PRACTICE AREAS:*** Probate; Trusts; Real Estate. ***Email:*** smamer@tmh-law.com

ROGER E. HAUGHEY, born Normal, Illinois, April 28, 1928; admitted to bar, 1952, Illinois. *Education:* Illinois State Normal University; University of Illinois (J.D. 1951). Phi Alpha Delta. Fellow, Illinois Bar Foundation. *Member:* Champaign County, Illinois State and American Bar Associations. ***PRACTICE AREAS:*** Real Estate; Probate; Commercial Law. ***Email:*** haughey@tmh-law.com

LOTT H. THOMAS, born Champaign, Illinois, October 3, 1934; admitted to bar, 1962, Illinois. *Education:* DePauw University (B.A., 1956); University of Illinois (J.D., 1962). Phi Delta Phi. *Member:* Champaign County, Illinois State and American Bar Associations. ***PRACTICE AREAS:*** Probate; Trusts; Real Estate Law; Elder Law. ***Email:*** lthomas@tmh-law.com

WILLIAM J. BRINKMANN, born Chicago, Illinois, April 27, 1948; admitted to bar, 1974, Illinois. *Education:* University of Illinois (B.S., 1970; J.D., 1974). Phi Alpha Delta. *Member:* Champaign County, Illinois State and American Bar Associations; Illinois Association of Defense Trial Counsel; International Association of Defense Counsel. Fellow, American College of Trial Lawyers. ***PRACTICE AREAS:*** Civil Trials; Professional Liability; Hospital Law. ***Email:*** wjbrinkm@tmh-law.com

DAVID A. BAILIE, born Evanston, Illinois, December 21, 1948; admitted to bar, 1975, Illinois. *Education:* Westminster College (B.A., cum laude, 1970); University of Illinois (J.D., 1975). Adjunct Professor of Trial Advocacy, University of Illinois, College of Law. Assistant State Attorney, Champaign County, 1975-1981. *Member:* Champaign County, Illinois State and American Bar Associations; Federation of Insurance and Corporate Counsel. ***PRACTICE AREAS:*** Civil Litigation; Professional Liability Defense; Insurance Defense Law. ***Email:*** bailie@tmh-law.com

CRAIG J. CAUSEMAN, born Chicago, Illinois, March 30, 1955; admitted to bar, 1980, Illinois. *Education:* University of Illinois (A.B., in Economics, 1977); Southern Illinois University (J.D., 1980). *Member:* Champaign County and Illinois State Bar Associations. ***PRACTICE AREAS:*** Workers Compensation Law; Civil Litigation; Insurance Defense Law. ***Email:*** craig@tmh-law.com

RICHARD R. HARDEN, born Oak Park, Illinois, April 22, 1958; admitted to bar, 1983, Illinois. *Education:* Knox College (B.A., cum laude, 1980); University of Illinois (J.D., cum laude, 1983). Phi Beta Kappa. Roy W. LeClere Award; Hunter Trophy; John W. Burgess Prize. Author, "Uses of Medical Evidence," Chapter 5 of Medical Evidence, Illinois Institute of Continuing Legal Education, 1997, Supplement, 2000. Co-Author, "Risk Management Strategies and Advice About Deposition Testimony," Carle Selected Papers, Spring, 2000. *Member:* Champaign County and Illinois State Bar Associations; Defense Research Institute; Illinois Association of Defense Trial Counsel. ***PRACTICE AREAS:*** Civil Litigation; Medical Malpractice Law; Personal Injury Defense Law. ***Email:*** riharden@tmh-law.com

DAVID E. KRCHAK, born Elgin, Illinois, December 21, 1950; admitted to bar, 1980, Illinois. *Education:* University of Illinois (B.A., high honors in Economics, 1973; J.D., 1980). Urban Mass Transportation Fellow, Northwestern University. Author: "Advising Employers About Wrongful Discharge Under Illinois Contract and Tort Law," Illinois Bar Journal, March, 1999. Assistant State's Attorney, Champaign County, 1983-1985; Assistant City Attorney, City of Champaign, 1985-1990. *Member:* Champaign County (Member, Board of Governors, 1986-1987), Illinois State (Member, Labor and Employment Law Section Council, 1991-1999; Chair, Labor and Employment Law Section Council, 1998) and American Bar Associations. ***PRACTICE AREAS:*** Management Labor Law; Employment and Employment Discrimination; Business Law. ***Email:*** krchak@tmh-law.com

BRUCE E. WARREN, born Philadelphia, Pennsylvania, December 17, 1954; admitted to bar, 1986, Illinois; 1987, U.S. District Court, Southern District of Illinois and U.S. Court of Appeals, Seventh Circuit; 1992, U.S. District Court, Central District of Illinois. *Education:* University of Illinois (B.A., 1977); Southern Illinois University (M.A., 1983; J.D., 1986). *Member:* Champaign County and Illinois State Bar Associations; Illinois Association of Defense Trial Counsel. ***PRACTICE AREAS:*** Workers Compensation Law; Insurance Law; Civil Litigation. ***Email:*** nottd@tmh-law.com

JOHN M. STURMANIS, born Springfield, Illinois, June 14, 1967; admitted to bar, 1992, Illinois, U.S. District Court, Central District of Illinois and U.S. Court of Appeals, Seventh Circuit. *Education:* Southern Illinois University (B.S., 1989; J.D., 1992). Phi Delta Phi. Articles Editor, Southern Illinois Law Journal. *Member:* Champaign County and Illinois State Bar Associations. ***PRACTICE AREAS:*** Workers Compensation Law; Civil Litigation; Insurance Defense. ***Email:*** jms@tmh-law.com

BIANCA T. GREEN, born Urbana, Illinois, May 29, 1968; admitted to bar, 1994, Illinois. *Education:* University of Illinois (B.S., 1991); Southern Illinois University (J.D., 1994). Southern Illinois University Law Journal; Student Articles Editor, Journal of Legal Medicine. Member, American Bar Association, Oral Advocacy Moot Court Team. Author: Commentary, "Injured Consumers and the FDA: Should Federal Preemption Protect Medical Device Manufacturers Under a Quasi-Governmental Immunity?" Vol. 15 J. Legal Med. 155 (1994). *Member:* Champaign County (Secretary, 1998-2000) and Illinois State Bar Associations. ***PRACTICE AREAS:*** Civil Litigation; Insurance Defense; Medical Malpractice. ***Email:*** bianca@tmh-law.com

KENNETH D. REIFSTECK, born Champaign, Illinois, October 29, 1965; admitted to bar, 1991, Illinois; 1992, U.S. District Court, Central and Southern Districts of Illinois; U.S. Court of Appeals, Seventh Circuit; U.S. Supreme Court. *Education:* Illinois State University (B.S., 1988); Southern Illinois University (J.D., 1991). 1st Vice President, Student Bar Association, 1990-1991. Assistant Illinois Attorney General, 1996. *Member:* Champaign County and Illinois State Bar Associations; Illinois Association of Defense Trial Counsel. ***PRACTICE AREAS:*** Civil Litigation; Insurance Defense; Civil Rights. ***Email:*** kdr@tmh-law.com

MELISSA A. THOMAS, born Champaign, Illinois, May 26, 1969; admitted to bar, 1994, Illinois. *Education:* University of Illinois (B.S., Psychology, 1991; J.D., 1994). Phi Beta Kappa. Phi Kappa Phi. *Member:* Champaign County, Illinois State (Member, Corporation, Securities and Business Law Section Council, 2000-2003) and American Bar Associations. ***PRACTICE AREAS:*** Probate; Trust Law; Estate Planning; Corporate Law; Real Estate. ***Email:*** mat@tmh-law.com

ASSOCIATES

CHARLES A. LEFEBVRE, born Carbondale, Illinois, November 1, 1969; admitted to bar, 1998, Illinois; 2000, U.S. District Court, Central and Southern Districts of Illinois. *Education:* University of Illinois (B.S., 1992; J.D., summa cum laude, 1998). Order of the Coif. *Member:* Illinois State and American Bar Associations. ***PRACTICE AREAS:*** Elder Law; Probate; Trusts; Real Estate. ***Email:*** charles@tmh-law.com

DAMIAN P. MARSHALL, born Urbana, Illinois; admitted to bar, 2004, Illinois; 2005, U.S. District Court, Southern and Central Districts of Illinois. *Education:* Northwestern University (B.S., Communications, 2000);University of Illinois College of Law (J.D., 2004). Member, Illinois Law Review, Member, Moot Court Team. Instructor, "Legal Aspects of Sports," Department of Recreation, Sport, University of Illinois, 2004 and 2005. *Member:* Champaign County and Illinois State Bar Associations. ***PRACTICE AREAS:*** Medical Malpractice; Insurance Defense. ***Email:*** dpmarshall@tmh-law.com

JAMES D. GREEN, born Urbana, Illinois, May 7, 1961; admitted to bar, 1989, Missouri; 1990, Illinois; 1992, U.S. District Court, Central and Southern Districts of Illinois; 1994, U.S. Court of Appeals, Seventh Circuit. *Education:* Illinois Wesleyan University (B.S., 1983); St. Louis University (J.D., 1989). Member, Champaign Plan Commission, 1997-1999; Member, Champaign City Council, 1999-2005. *Member:* Champaign County, Illinois State and American Bar Associations; The Missouri Bar. ***PRACTICE AREAS:*** Civil Litigation; Real Estate; General Practice. ***Email:*** jim@tmh-law.com

JENNIFER E. DICKEN, born Danville, Illinois; admitted to bar, 2004, Illinois. *Education:* Indiana University, Bloomington (B.A., 2001; J.D., 2004). *Member:* Champaign County, Cook County and Illinois Bar Associations. ***PRACTICE AREAS:*** Civil Litigation; Insurance Defense. ***Email:*** jennifer@tmh-law.com

(This Listing Continued)

OF COUNSEL

GEORGE S. MILLER, born Chicago, Illinois, March 20, 1928; admitted to bar, 1956, Illinois. *Education:* Northwestern University (B.S., 1950); Harvard Law School (J.D., 1955). Adjunct Professor, University of Illinois College of Law, 1976-1998. Circuit Judge, Sixth Judicial Circuit, Illinois, 1981-1999. *Member:* Illinois State Bar Association (Assembly Member; Chair: Insurance Council Section; Bench and Bar Council Section). ***PRACTICE AREAS:*** Civil Litigation; Mediation; Arbitration. ***Email:*** gmiller@tmh-law.com

COUNSEL FOR: American States Insurance Co.; Auto Owners Insurance Co.; Bituminous Insurance Co.; Capitol Indemnity Co.; Cannon Cochran Management Services Inc.; The Carle Foundation; The Carle Foundation Hospital; Chicago Motor Insurance Co.; Economy Fire & Casualty Co.; Federated Insurance; Hanover Insurance Co.; Illinois Foundation Seeds; Illinois Founders Insurance Co.; Illinois Provider Trust; Illinois State Bar Association Mutual Insurance Company; Illinois State Medical Services; Indiana Consolidated Insurance Co.; Interstate Insurance Co.; Kemper Insurance Co.; Kraft General Foods; Lumbermen's Underwriting Alliance; Martin Boyer Co.; The Medical Protective Co.; Medmarc; Milwaukee Insurance Co.; MSI Insurance Co.; Progressive Insurance Co.; Prudential Insurance Co. of America; St. Paul Insurance Co.; Sangamon Homes, Ltd; Scottsdale Insurance Co.; State Auto Insurance Co.; States Universities Retirement System; Thompson Land Co.; Ulica Casualty Co.; Board of Trustees of the University of Illinois; Wasau Insurance; Westfield Insurance Co.

TUMMELSON BRYAN & KNOX

CHAMPAIGN, ILLINOIS

(See Urbana)

General Practice in all Courts including Trials and Appeals, Insurance, Workers' Compensation, Corporation, Administrative, Probate, Banking, Real Estate, Creditor's Rights and Mortgage Law.

WEBBER & THIES, P.C.

CHAMPAIGN, ILLINOIS

(See Urbana)

General, Appellate, Trial and Federal Practice, Complex Litigation, Probate, Trust, Family, Corporation, Labor/Employment (Management), Taxation, Real Estate, Zoning, Environmental, Health, Banking and Intellectual Property Law.

WEITH LAW OFFICE

SUITE 230
116 NORTH CHESTNUT STREET, C-U STATION
CHAMPAIGN, ILLINOIS 61820
Telephone: 217-398-1200
Facsimile: 217-398-0078
Email: glennaweith@hotmail.com
URL: http://www.lawyers.com/illinoisadoptionlaw

Adoption Law, Interstate Adoption, International Adoptions, Step-parent Adoptions, Grandparent Adoptions, Contested Adoptions, Guardianship, Surrogacy Law, Child Sexual Abuse, Child Abuse and Neglect, Childrens Rights, Child Advocacy, Assisted Reproductive Technology, Agency Adoptions, Child Support, Child Welfare, Termination of Parental Rights, Family Mediation, Foster Care, Divorce, Separation Agreements, Prenuptial Agreements, Post-Divorce Modification, Domestic Violence, Interstate Support, Parental Rights, Immigration Adoption Issues.

FIRM PROFILE: Since 1984, Glenna J. Weith has dedicated her practice to issues involved with children's rights, adoptions and child custody and welfare. Ms. Weith frequently lectures on child advocacy and provides vital public support for children's constitutional rights. The firm represents families, children, parents and others seeking legal advice and counsel for domestic and international adoptions and children's issues.

GLENNA J. WEITH, born Bement, Illinois, January 29, 1945; admitted to bar, 1984, Illinois and U.S. District Court, Central District of Illinois. *Education:* Illinois State University (B.S., 1981); University of Illinois (J.D., 1984). *Member:* Champaign County, Illinois State (Member: Family Law Section Council 1987-1990; Family Law Handbook Editorial Board) and American (Member, Family Law Section) Bar Associations; American Academy of Adoption Attorneys (Board of Trustees, 1991-1993; Vice President, 1994-1995; Chair, Interstate Adoption Committee, 2001—; Chair, Committee on Families in Fact); Member, Advisory Committee, Project Heart, State of Illinois.

THE BRAINARD LAW OFFICES

Established in 1935
BRAINARD BUILDING
600 JACKSON AVENUE
CHARLESTON, ILLINOIS 61920
Telephone: 217-345-3929
Fax: 217-345-6501
URL: http://www.brainardlaw.com

General Practice. Insurance Defense, Personal Injury, Products Liability, Probate, Trusts, Real Estate, Taxation, Municipal, Family and Health Law. Trials in all State and Federal Courts.

MEMBERS OF FIRM

H. OGDEN BRAINARD (1905-1992)

WILLIAM A. SUNDERMAN, born Charleston, Illinois, January 24, 1946; admitted to bar, 1972, Illinois; U.S. Court of Appeals, Seventh Circuit; U.S. District Court, Central District of Illinois; U.S. District Court, Southern District of Illinois. *Education:* Eastern Illinois University (B.S., with highest honors, 1968); University of Illinois (J.D., 1972). Graduate, National Institute of Trial Advocacy. Member, Illinois Judicial Inquiry Board, 1998—. *Member:* Coles-Cumberland and Illinois State Bar Associations; Illinois Trial Lawyers Association; The Association of Trial Lawyers of America; Illinois Appellate Lawyers Association. ***PRACTICE AREAS:*** Plaintiff Law; Defense Litigation; Insurance Defense Law; Commercial Law; Banking Law; Insurance Coverage. ***Email:*** wasunderman@brainardlaw.com

HENRY E. KRAMER, born Edgewood, Illinois, May 19, 1941; admitted to bar, 1965, Illinois. *Education:* Springfield Junior College (A.A., 1961); University of Illinois (J.D., 1965). Phi Alpha Delta. President, Charleston Area Chamber of Commerce, 1983. *Member:* Coles-Cumberland (President, 1985-1986) and Illinois State (Member, 1965— and Chairman, 1972, Executive Council, School Law Section) Bar Associations; Illinois Association of Hospital Attorneys. ***PRACTICE AREAS:*** Probate Law; Real Estate Law; Commercial Law; Corporate Law. ***Email:*** hekramer@brainardlaw.com

BRIAN L. BOWER, born Charleston, Illinois, April 9, 1958; admitted to bar, 1983, Illinois and U.S. District Court, Central District of Illinois. *Education:* Northwestern University (B.S.S., 1980); Northern Illinois University (J.D., cum laude, 1983). Graduate, National College of Advocacy, Basic Trial Advocacy College. *Member:* Coles-Cumberland and Illinois State (Member, Assembly, 2004—) Bar Associations; Illinois Trial Lawyers Association. ***PRACTICE AREAS:*** Litigation; Domestic Relations Law; Municipal Law. ***Email:*** blbower@brainardlaw.com

WILLIAM J. WARMOTH, born Charleston, Illinois, February 1, 1949; admitted to bar, 1974, Illinois, U.S. Court of Appeals, Seventh Circuit and U.S. District Court, Central District of Illinois; 1977, U.S. Supreme Court. *Education:* Michigan State University and Eastern Illinois University (B.S., 1971); University of Illinois (J.D., 1974). Sigma Pi Sigma; Pi Sigma Alpha; Phi Alpha Delta. Assistant Attorney General, 1975-1983. Board of Directors, 1981-1984 and President, 1983-1984, Eastern Illinois University Alumni Association. *Member:* Coles-Cumberland (President, 1993-1994; Secretary, 1975-1976), Illinois State (Member, General Practice Section Council, 1977-1982; Member, Assembly, 1978-1984 and 1986-1987) and American Bar Associations. ***PRACTICE AREAS:*** School Law; Appellate Litigation; Commercial Law. ***Email:*** wjwarmoth@brainardlaw.com

MARK R. KARPUS, born Mattoon, Illinois, September 22, 1960; admitted to bar, 1989, Illinois. *Education:* Eastern Illinois University (B.S., 1983); Thomas Cooley Law School (J.D., cum laude, 1989). *Member:* Coles-Cumberland County and Illinois State Bar Associations. ***PRACTICE AREAS:*** Personal Injury; Insurance Defense; Insurance Litigation; Commercial Law. ***Email:*** mrkarpus@brainardlaw.com

KRISTIN L. WILSON, born Rockford, Illinois, January 11, 1967; admitted to bar, 1991, Illinois and U.S. District Court, Central District of Illinois. *Education:* Creighton University (B.S.B.A., cum laude, 1989; J.D., cum laude, 1991). Omicron Delta Epsilon. *Member:* Coles-Cumberland and Illinois State Bar Associations. ***PRACTICE AREAS:*** Landlord and Tenant Law; Creditors Rights. ***Email:*** klwilson@brainardlaw.com

OF COUNSEL

J. LEEDS BOWER, born Mattoon, Illinois, October 21, 1931; admitted to bar, 1957, Illinois. *Education:* University of Illinois (B.A., 1953; J.D., 1957). Phi Alpha Delta. Assistant Attorney General, State of Illinois, Condemnation, 1969-1983. *Member:* Coles County (President, 1975-1976) and Illinois State (Member, Executive Council, Probate and Trust Section, 1970-1976) Bar Associations. ***PRACTICE AREAS:*** Probate Law; Real Estate Law; Taxation Law.

REPRESENTATIVE CLIENTS: Community Bank & Trust Savings Bank; Agri Bank FCB; Sarah Bush Lincoln Health Center; The Country Cos.; Prudential Insurance Co.; Protection Mutual Insurance Co.; St. Paul Insurance; Shelter Insurance Companies; Indiana Lumbermen's Mutual Ins. Co.; Firstar Bank; Neighborhood Bankshares; First Mid-IL Bank & Trust, N.A.
WILLIAM J. WARMOTH IS GENERAL COUNSEL FOR: Charities of the Grand Lodge A.F.& A.M. of Illinois.
J. Leeds Bower and Henry E. Kramer are approved attorneys for and agents of Attorney's Title Guaranty Fund.
William A. Sunderman serves as Chairman of the Illinois Judicial Inquiry Board.

MURRAY R. CHOATE II, ATTORNEY AT LAW

Established in 2004
622 JACKSON AVENUE
CHARLESTON, ILLINOIS 61920
Telephone: 217-345-4452
Fax: 217-348-7522
Email: rickchoate@choatelawyers.com
URL: http://www.choatelawyers.com

Real Estate, Resort and Planned Community Development, Condominiums, Property Owners Associations, Interstate and International Real Estate Offerings, Regulated Real Estate Product Disclosure and Registration, Real Estate Brokerage, Real Estate Broker Licensing, Franchise Law, International Travel and Tourism, International Commerical Transactions, U.S.-Australia Free Trade Agreement Opportunities.

FIRM PROFILE: Mr. Choate established this boutique firm after serving more than twenty years as in-house counsel to leading private and public companies engaged in planned community development, international resort development and management, hospitality, franchising, and travel.

The mission of the firm is to combine legal expertise, international experience, and industry knowledge to identify and evaluate client options, and to develop customized solutions to achieve client business objectives in a timely and cost efficient manner.

MURRAY R. CHOATE, II, born Anna, Illinois, January 27, 1954; admitted to bar, 1979, Indiana; 1982, Illinois; 1985, Arkansas. *Education:* Dartmouth College (B.A., Government, cum laude, 1976); Vanderbilt University (J.D., 1979). Phi Alpha Delta. Rufus Choate Scholar. Licensed Real Estate Broker, Illinois, 1987—. Associate Attorney, Cadick, Burns, Dick & Peterson, Indianapolis, Indiana, 1979-1980. Associate Attorney, Barnes & Thornburg, Indianapolis, Indiana, 1980-1982. General Counsel, Resort Condominiums In-

(This Listing Continued)

MURRAY R. CHOATE II, ATTORNEY AT LAW, Charleston—Continued

ternational, Inc., 1982-1984. Corporate Counsel, Fairfield Communities, Inc., Little Rock, Arkansas, 1984-1988. Vice-President and General Counsel, Vistana Resort Development, Inc., Lake Buena Vista, Florida, 1988-1990. Senior Vice-President and General Counsel, Euroactividade Corporation, Orlando, Florida, 1990-1991. Attorney, (1991); Senior Attorney, (1991-1992); Director-Legal, (1992-1994); Executive Counsel, (1994-1996), The Walt Disney Company, Lake Buena Vista, Florida, 1991-1996. Managing Director-Asia Pacific and Special Counsel, Interval International, Inc., Singapore, Republic of Singapore, 1996-2000. Executive Vice President and Global General Counsel, Resort Condominiums International LLC, 2000-2001. Managing Director and Corporate Counsel, The HMI and CVC Group, Gold Coast, Australia, 2002-2004. Founder and principal, Murray R. Choate II, Attorney At Law, Charleston, Illinois, 2004—. Speaker on various resort/community development and real estate timesharing subjects at meetings of the International Bar Association, the American Bar Association, the Urban Land Institute, the Pacific Asia Travel Association, the American Resort Development Association, the Association of Real Estate License Law Officials, the Thai Management Association, the Timeshare Association (Singapore), the Malaysian Holiday Timeshare Developer's Federation, the Timeshare Association of Thailand, the Sarawak Economic Development Corporation, the Vietnam National Administration of Tourism, Saigon Tourist, and the Australian Timeshare and Holiday Owners Council. Member, Virginia Real Estate Board Timeshare Advisory Council, 1983-1996. Director, National Land Council, 1992-1996. Director, Florida ARDA 1992-1996. Director, Timeshare Association (Singapore) 1996-2000. Director, Malaysian Holiday Timeshare Developers Federation 1997-1999. Adjunct Professor, School of Hospitality and Tourism, Griffith University, Gold Coast Campus, Gold Coast, Australia 2002-2003. *Member:* Indiana State Bar Association; Illinois State Bar Association; Arkansas Bar Association; American Bar Association. Registered Foreign Lawyer, Law Society of New South Wales, Australia. ***PRACTICE AREAS:*** Real Estate Development; International Law; Community Development; Contracts; Breach of Contract; Commercial Contracts; International Commercial Contracts; International Contracts; Franchises and Franchising; Franchise Law; Franchise Distribution; Franchise Licensing; Franchise Regulation; Franchise Termination; International Franchising; Property Law; International Property Law; Real Estate; Boundary Disputes; Common Interest Community Law; Community Association Law; Condominium Association Law; Condominium Conversions; Condominium Development; Condominium Law; Easements; Homeowners Association Law; International Real Estate; Land Acquisitions; Land Sales; Planned Unit Development Law; Property Management; Real Estate Acquisitions; Real Estate Brokerage Law; Real Estate Brokers and Agents Liability; Real Estate Brokers Licensing; Real Estate Brokers Malpractice; Real Estate Brokers Malpractice Defense; Real Estate Contracts; Real Estate Sales; Real Estate Trade Association Law; Real Property; Real Property Acquisitions; Real Property Development; Residential Real Estate Development; Resorts and Leisure; Amusement Park Liability; Country Club Law; Golf Course Development; Hospitality Law; Hotel and Resort Development; Hotel and Resort Law; Hotel Franchise Law; Hotel Liability; International Hotels and Resorts; Recreational Property Law; Resort Timeshares; Travel and Tourism; Australia - U.S. Free Trade Agreement.

CRAIG & CRAIG

CHARLESTON, ILLINOIS

(See Mattoon)

General Practice in State and Federal Courts. Coal, Oil, Gas, Mining, Oil and Gas Transportation, Insurance, Drainage and Levee Law, Environmental, Corporation, Labor Relations, Workers Compensation and Real Estate Law. Estate Planning, Probate and Bankruptcy Law. Trials and Appeals.

JAMES M. GRANT

Established in 1998

611 6TH STREET

CHARLESTON, ILLINOIS 61920

Telephone: 217-345-2510

Fax: 217-348-0082

Email: jmgrant@jamesmgrantlaw.com

URL: http://www.lawyers.com/jamesmgrantlaw

Casey, Illinois Office: 101 North Central, 62420. Telephone: 217-932-5885. Fax: 217-932-5889.

Real Estate, Real Estate Title, Wills & Estates.

FIRM PROFILE: Sole Practitioner with 2 offices.

JAMES M. GRANT, born Charleston, Illinois, May 28, 1950; admitted to bar, 1975, Illinois; 1979, U.S. District Court, Central District of Illinois; 1986, U.S. Tax Court. *Education:* Eastern Illinois University (B.A., 1972); St. Louis University (J.D., 1975). Director, Attorney's Title Guaranty Fund, 1989—. *Member:* Coles-Cumberland, Clark County and Illinois State (Member, General Practice Section Council, 1986-1991) Bar Associations; Illinois Township Attorney's Association (President, 1985-1986). ***LANGUAGES:*** English. ***PRACTICE AREAS:*** Municipal Law; Real Estate Law; Title Insurance; Wills & Estates.

Language: English.

REPRESENTATIVE CLIENTS: Casey State Bank; Preferred Bank; First Neighbor Bank, Charleston; Attorneys Title Guaranty Fund.

HELLER, HOLMES & ASSOCIATES, P.C.

CHARLESTON, ILLINOIS

(See Mattoon)

General Civil and Trial Practice in all State, Federal and Appellate Courts. Personal Injury, Medical Negligence, Criminal Defense, Insurance, Litigation, Probate, Workers Compensation, Corporation, Commercial, Family Law, Oil and Gas.

RYAN, BENNETT & RADLOFF

CHARLESTON, ILLINOIS

(See Mattoon)

General, Civil and Criminal Practice. Trials in all Courts. Insurance Defense, Workers Compensation, Negligence, Corporation, Probate, Estate Planning, Bankruptcy, Taxation and Oil and Gas Law. Domestic Relations, Divorce, Child Custody and Adoption Law.

LAW OFFICES OF WINTER-BLACK & LIVESAY

CHARLESTON, ILLINOIS

(See Mattoon)

Family Law, Foreclosures, Collections, Probate and Wills, Real Estate Contracts and Closings, Estate Planning, Bankruptcy, Appellate Practice.

BROWN & ASSOCIATES

CHESTER, ILLINOIS

(See Belleville)

Civil Litigation, Personal Injury, Medical Malpractice, Products Liability, Admiralty Law, Railroad Law and Commercial Law.

ABRAHAMSON VORACHEK & LEVINSON

Established in 1985

120 NORTH LA SALLE STREET, SUITE 1050

CHICAGO, ILLINOIS 60602

Telephone: 312-263-2698

Facsimile: 312-419-6770

Email: attorneys@avmlaw.com

URL: http://www.lawyers.com/avmlaw

Civil Rights, Employment Discrimination, Employees' Individual Rights, Equal Opportunity, Equal Employment, Labor (or Relations), Labor (Management or Employees) and Wage and Hour Law.

FIRM PROFILE: Small boutique labor and employment law practice, concentrating on employees' individual rights.

VICKI LAFER ABRAHAMSON, born Detroit, Michigan, December 8, 1953; admitted to bar, 1980, Illinois, U.S. District Court, Northern District of Illinois and U.S. Court of Appeals, Seventh and Fourth Circuits. *Education:* University of Michigan (B.A., with distinction, 1976; J.D., 1979). Contributing Author, Employee Rights Litigation -- Pleading and Practice, August 1991. Author, "A Primer For Proving Damages In An Age Discrimination Case," Trial Magazine, June 1989. Instructor, Women and the Law, University of Michigan, 1978-1979. Member: Board of Advisors, Corporate Counsel's Guide to the Americans With Disabilities Act (Business Laws, Inc.); Board of Editors, Law Firm Partnership and Benefits Report (Leader Publications). Featured as one of Chicago's "30 Tough Lawyers," Chicago Magazine, March 2002; Leading Plaintiff's Employment Lawyers, Chambers USA, 2003-2004. Member, Leading Lawyers Network, 2003—. Panel of Neutral Arbitrators, American Arbitration Association, 2005—. *Member:* Chicago (Member, Labor and Employment Law Committee), Illinois State and American (Council Member, Labor and Employment Law Section, 1994-2002; Past Co-Chair, Committee on Employee Rights and Responsibilities; Council Liaison to Employee Rights & Responsibilities Committee; Co-Chair, International Labor Law Committee) Bar Associations; National Employment Lawyers Association; College of Labor and Employment Lawyers (President, 2000-2001; Fellow and Member, Board of Governors, 1997—). ***PRACTICE AREAS:*** Labor and Employment; Contracts; Discrimination. ***Email:*** attorneys@avmlaw.com

DARLENE A. VORACHEK, born Allegan, Michigan, June 24, 1956; admitted to bar, 1982, Maryland, U.S. District Court, District of Maryland an d U.S. Court of Appeals, Fourth Circuit; 1984, Illinois, U.S. District Court, N orthern District of Illinois and U.S. Court of Appeals, Seventh Circuit; 1986, U.S. Supreme Court. *Education:* University of Michigan (B.A., with honors, 1978); George Washington University (J.D., with high honors, 1982). Bibliographic Notes Editor, Journal of International Law and Economics, James Publishing, Inc., 1981-1982. Author, "Effective Depositions in Employment and Other Cases," The Practical Litigator, July 2005. Contributing Author, BNA Retaliatory Discharge Supplemental Chapter, 1999. Contributor and Speaker, ABA 2nd Annual National Institute on the ADA 1999, Council on Education in Management Personnel Law Update 1999, 2002, 2004. Speaker and Contributor, ABA Employee Rights & Responsibilities Midwinter Meeting, 1999—; National Alliance Mediation Program 2002; ABA Young Lawyers Division Midwest Regional Conference, 2003; ABA 2003 Section Officers Conference Fall Meeting 2003; Law Education Institute 2004; Practising Law Institute 2004-2005. Member, Leading Lawyers Network, 2003—. *Member:* Chicago (Member, Chair, Labor and Employment Section, 2001-2002; Prior Chair, IDHR/HRC Subcommittee, 1996-1999), Maryland State and American (Member, Labor and Employment Section; Past Plaintiff's Co-Chair, Health Issues Subcommittee, Committee on Employee Rights & Responsibilities; Co-Chair, Employment Rights and Responsibilities Committee, 2001-2004;

(This Listing Continued)

Plaintiff Membership Chair, 2004—; Employee Co-Chair, Recruitment and Retention Subcommittee, Labor and Employment Section) Bar Associations; National Employment Lawyers Association. Fellow, College of Labor and Employment Lawyers, 2005—. **PRACTICE AREAS:** Labor and Employment.

ROBERTA A. LEVINSON, born Chicago, Illinois, August 30, 1951; admitted to bar, 1975, Illinois; 1986, U.S. District Court, Northern District of Illinois; 1991, U.S. Court of Appeals, 7th Circuit. *Education:* University of Illinois (B.A., cum laude, 1972; J.D., 1975). Phi Beta Kappa. Recipient, James Scholar. Member: National Moot Court Team Alternate; Moot Court Board. Research Assistant, Prof. Paul Marcus. Contributor Author: "Sex Discrimination: Title VII and the Bona Fide Occupational Qualification," 55 Texas Law Review 1025, 1977. Member, Leading Lawyers Network, 2003—. *Member:* Chicago Bar Association; National Employment Lawyers Association. **PRACTICE AREAS:** Labor and Employment. **Email:** ralevinson@avmlaw.com

ASSOCIATE

LORI L. DEEM, born Columbus, Ohio, November 7, 1972; admitted to bar, 1998, Illinois and U.S. District Court, Northern District of Illinois. *Education:* Xavier University (B.A., summa cum laude, 1995); Loyola University Chicago School of Law (J.D., 1998). Member, 1996-1997; Student Articles Editor, 1997-1998, Loyola University Chicago School of Law Journal, 1996-1997. Editor, "Litigation Strategy: Summary Judgment, Including Views From the Bench," 33rd Annual Institute on Employment Law, Practising Law Institute, Volume 1, p. 851 (October 2004). Co-Author: "Mediation as a Model for Resolving Employment Disputes in the New Millennium," 1 Employee Rights Quarterly 4 (Spring 2001); "Employment Law Year in Review, 32nd Annual Institute on Employment Law, Practising Law Institut, Volume 1, p. 153 (October 2003). *Member:* Chicago Bar Association; National Employment Lawyers Association (Illinois Chapter). **PRACTICE AREAS:** Employment Law. **Email:** attorneys@avmlaw.com

ABRAMSON & FOX

Established in 1892

ONE EAST WACKER DRIVE
CHICAGO, ILLINOIS 60601
Telephone: 312-644-8500
Fax: 312-644-0798
Email: AandF1@aol.com
URL: http://www.abramsonandfox.com

General Civil Trial and Appellate Practice, Commodity Futures, Federal and State Securities Registration and Regulation, Antitrust, Intellectual Property and Trademark Law, Employment Law, Health, Immigration, Commercial, Corporate, State and Federal Taxation and Real Estate, Banking, Finance, Estate Planning and Probate, Housing Discrimination, Bankruptcy and Reorganization.

MEMBERS OF FIRM

FLOYD H. ABRAMSON, born Omaha, Nebraska, July 1, 1931; admitted to bar, 1956, Illinois; 1958, U.S. District Court, Northern District of Illinois; 1963, U.S. Supreme Court. *Education:* Yale University (B.A., 1953); Harvard Law School (J.D., 1956). *Member:* Chicago (Member, Financial Institutions Committee, 1973—), Illinois State and American Bar Associations. **PRACTICE AREAS:** Banking Law; Corporate Law; Real Estate Law. **Email:** fhabramson@aol.com

DONALD P. COLLETON, born Newark, New Jersey, July 4, 1942; admitted to bar, 1967, New Jersey; 1968, Illinois; 1973, District of Columbia; 1975, U.S. Supreme Court. *Education:* Georgetown University (A.B., 1964); New York University (LL.B., 1967). *Member:* Illinois State Bar Association. **PRACTICE AREAS:** State and Federal Litigation; General Corporate Law; Health Law; Commodity Law; Intellectual Property Law; Employment Law; Advertising Law. **Email:** dpcolleton@aol.com

JOSEPH C. GRAYSON, born Chicago, Illinois, September 23, 1949; admitted to bar, 1976, Illinois. *Education:* University of Wisconsin (B.A., with distinction, 1971); John Marshall Law School (J.D., with distinction, 1976). Member, Order of John Marshall. *Member:* American Bar Association. **PRACTICE AREAS:** Banking and Financial Services; Corporate Law; Real Estate Law. **Email:** jcgrayson@aol.com

RICHARD S. HARTFORD, born Chicago, Illinois, August 15, 1946; admitted to bar, 1972, Illinois; 1973, U.S. Tax Court. *Education:* Loyola University (B.B.A., 1968); DePaul University (J.D., 1972). Member, Chicago Office of District Director of Internal Revenue Service, 1968-1973. *Member:* Chicago and Illinois State Bar Associations. **PRACTICE AREAS:** Corporate Law; Estates Law; Trusts Law; State and Federal Taxation Law. **Email:** rshartford@aol.com

ANTHONY P. JANIK, born Chicago, Illinois, February 5, 1955; admitted to bar, 1979, Illinois. *Education:* College of St. Francis (B.A., summa cum laude, 1976); Loyola University (J.D., 1979). Delta Epsilon Sigma. Recipient, Loyola University Law Scholarship. Member, Loyola University Law Journal, 1978-1979. *Member:* Illinois State Bar Association. **PRACTICE AREAS:** Real Estate Law; Real Estate Taxation Law; Corporate Law; Commercial Transactions; Trademark and Copyright Law; Licensing. **Email:** apjanik@aol.com

OF COUNSEL

JOHN J. ALIOTO, born Milwaukee, Wisconsin, March 12, 1949; admitted to bar, 1974, Illinois and U.S. District Court, Northern District of Illinois; 1976, U.S. Court of Appeals, Seventh Circuit; 1978, U.S. Supreme Court; 1987, Wisconsin. *Education:* Creighton University (B.A., 1971); Illinois Institute of Technology/Chicago-Kent College of Law (J.D., 1974). Co-Author: The State's Attorney's Pre-Trial Handbook, Chapter 4: (1978) Court Call Procedures (Manual distributed to all Cook County Trial Assistants). Cook County Assistant States Attorney, 1975-1979. *Member:* Chicago, West Suburban (President, 1990), Illinois State (Member, Assembly, 1991-1993) and American Bar Associations; Justinian Society of Lawyers. **PRACTICE AREAS:** Federal and State Criminal Defense; Plaintiff's Personal Injury.

(This Listing Continued)

RENATO L. AMPONIN, born Mindoro, Philippines, July 23, 1938; admitted to bar, 1963, Philippines; 1972, Illinois. *Education:* San Beda College and Lyceum of the Philippines; Far Eastern University (LL.B., 1962). *Member:* Chicago Bar Association (Member, Immigration Law Committee, 1973—); American Immigration Lawyers Association. **PRACTICE AREAS:** Immigration and Naturalization Law.

JAMES L. FOX, born Chicago, Illinois, November 30, 1920; admitted to bar, 1956, Illinois. *Education:* Loyola University (B.S., 1941; J.D., 1956). *Member:* Illinois State Bar Association. **PRACTICE AREAS:** Corporate Law; Commodity Law; State and Federal Litigation. **Email:** jlf128427@aol.com

RICHARD HIRSCHTRITT, born 1934; admitted to bar, 1958, Illinois; 1959, U.S. District Court, Northern District of Illinois; 1972, U.S. Tax Court; 1983, U.S. Court of Appeals, Seventh Circuit; 1994, U.S. Court of Federal Claims. *Education:* Northwestern University (B.S., 1955; J.D., 1958). Phi Alpha Delta. *Member:* Chicago and Illinois State Bar Associations. **PRACTICE AREAS:** Employee Benefits Law; Estate Planning Law; Probate Law; Federal and State Taxation; Partnership Law; Business Law.

MALCOLM S. KAMIN, born 1939; admitted to bar, 1964, Illinois. *Education:* Yale University (B.A., 1961); University of Chicago (J.D., 1964). Delegate to VIth Illinois Constitutional Convention, 1969-1970. First Place, Illinois State Bar Lincoln Award Legal Writing Contest, 1972 ("Constitutional Abolition of Ad Valorem, Personal Property Taxes" Illinois Bar Journal, Vol. 60, p. 432, Feb., 1972). Author: "School Finance Language of the Education Article," John Marshall Journal of Practice and Procedure, Vol. 6, p. 331, Spring 1973. Hearing Examiner, Illinois Fair Employment Practices Commission, 1971-1975. Director, Chicago Lawyers Committee for Civil Rights Under the Law, 1978-1991. *Member:* Chicago (Chairman: Constitutional Revision Committee, 1975-1976; Legislative Committee, 1983-1984; Secretary, Labor Law Committee, 1972) and Illinois State (Vice-Chairman, 1967-1968 and Chairman, 1969-1970, Bill of Rights Committee; Chairman, Section on Individual Rights and Responsibilities, 1973-1974; Delegate to ISBA Delegate Assembly, 1972-1978; Chairman, Rules Committee, 1975-1978; Parliamentarian, 1977-1978) Bar Associations. Fellow, American Bar Foundation. **PRACTICE AREAS:** Litigation; Real Estate Law; Labor Law. **Email:** mskamin@aol.com

JURIS KINS, born Jelgava, Latvia, April 24, 1942; admitted to bar, 1969, Wisconsin and Illinois; 1970, U.S. District Court, Northern District of Illinois; 1982, U.S. District Court, Northern District of Illinois including Trial Bar. *Education:* University of Wisconsin (B.S., Chem. Eng., 1964); University of Michigan (M.S., Chem. Eng., 1965); University of Wisconsin (J.D., 1969). Managing Editor, University of Wisconsin Law Review, 1969. *Member:* Chicago Bar Association; State Bar of Wisconsin; Latvian Bar Association. **LANGUAGES:** Latvian. **PRACTICE AREAS:** Commercial Law; Litigation; Antitrust. **Email:** juriskins@aol.com

ALLAN A. ACKERMAN, P.C.

Established in 1961

2000 NORTH CLIFTON AVENUE
CHICAGO, ILLINOIS 60614-4120
Telephone: 312-332-2891; 332-2863
Fax: 773-871-3304
Email: profaaa@aol.com
URL: http://www.lawyers.com/allanaackerman

Criminal Trial and Appellate Practice.

FIRM PROFILE: Over 200 reported decisions including United States v. Veltman, 6 F.3d 1483 (11th Cir. 1993) and United States v. Alt, 996 F.2d 827 (6th Cir. 1993); Illinois v. Pamon, 1-99-0711 (UNP-Rev); Aleman v. Circuit Court Judges, 138 F.3d 302 (7th Cir. 1998); Illinois v. Macejak, 1-99-1507 (UNP.Supp.App.-Aff'd); Liuna v. Caruso, 197 F.3d 1195 (7th Cir. 1999). Multiple publications including Chicago Daily Law Bulletin and Criminal Justice Section, Illinois State Bar Association, Illinois Appellate Lawyers Association.

ALLAN A. ACKERMAN, born Chicago, Illinois, December 17, 1937; admitted to bar, 1961, Illinois and U.S. Court of Appeals, 1st, 4th, 5th, 6th, 7th, 8th, 9th and 11th Circuits; 1964, U.S. District Court, Northern District of Illinois including Trial Bar; U.S. Supreme Court. *Education:* Wright Jr. College; University of Chicago; John Marshall Law School (J.D., 1961). *Member:* Illinois State and Federal Bar Associations; National College of Criminal Defense Lawyers; The Association of Trial Lawyers of America. **PRACTICE AREAS:** Criminal Trial Law; Appellate Practice. **Email:** profaaa@aol.com

LAW OFFICES OF HALL ADAMS LLC

Established in 2003

77 WEST WACKER DRIVE, SUITE 4800
CHICAGO, ILLINOIS 60601
Telephone: 312-606-8711
Fax: 312-444-9658
URL: http://www.adamslegal.net
Email: hall@adamslegal.net
URL: http://halladams.com

Trial Practice, State and Federal Courts, Personal Injury, Catastrophic Injury, Automobile Accidents, Premise Liability, Professional Negligence, Wrongful Death, Consumer Fraud, Business Litigation.

FIRM PROFILE: Hall Adams LLC has successfully tried over 100 cases to verdict including several record-breaking verdicts of plaintiffs and in novel cases of first impression. Recoveries over $25 million for clients in first year in solo practice. Applying substantial previous experience defending business and insurance companies to assist current clients.

HALL ADAMS, born Evanston, Illinois, November 26, 1962; admitted to bar, 1987, Illinois; U.S. Court of Appeals, Seventh and Eighth Circuits and U.S. District Court, North-

(This Listing Continued)

LAW OFFICES OF HALL ADAMS LLC, Chicago—Continued

ern and Central Districts of Illinois. *Education:* Colby College (B.A., cum laude, 1984); Loyola University, Chicago (J.D., 1987). Associate, 1990-1995, Partner, 1995-2003, Williams Montgomery & John Ltd. *Member:* Chicago and Illinois State Bar Associations. [Captain, USMC, 1987-1990]

ADAMSKI & CONTI

100 N. LA SALLE STREET
SUITE 1520
CHICAGO, ILLINOIS 60602
Telephone: 312-332-7800
Fax: 312-332-7818;
URL: http://www.adamskiandconti.com
Email: gaadamski@adamskiandconti.com
URL: http://www.lawyers.com/adamski&conti

Civil and Criminal Trial Practice in all State and Federal Courts.

FIRM PROFILE: Adamski & Conti was established in 1990 by Gregory A. Adamski and Karen Conti. Mr. Adamski was a civil and criminal trial partner of Winston & Strawn at its Chicago and Phoenix offices. Ms. Conti was a civil litigator with Peterson & Ross and with Tressler, Soderstrom, Maloney & Priess.

Adamski & Conti takes a creative, aggressive approach to litigation. The members of the firm are accessible and responsive to clients needs. Its goal is efficient, economical, and equitable dispute resolution. With their staff, Mr. Adamski and Ms. Conti provide their clients with large firm experience and expertise at substantially decreased costs.

Adamski & Conti is engaged in a national practice of trial law in all areas. Mr. Adamski and Ms. Conti have successfully litigated before the United States Supreme Court, various federal and state appellate courts, and trial courts throughout the United States. Ms. Conti is a member of the California Bar. Mr. Adamski and Ms. Conti are Adjunct Professors at the University of Illinois.

Adamski & Conti welcomes inquiries from out-of-state lawyers and clients seeking an initial consultation or referral to attorneys in other practice areas.

MEMBERS OF FIRM

GREGORY A. ADAMSKI, born Chicago, Illinois, October 14, 1948; admitted to bar, 1973, Illinois and U.S. District Court, Northern District of Illinois including Trial Bar; 1975, U.S. Court of Appeals, Seventh Circuit; 1978, U.S. Supreme Court; 1998, U.S. District Court, Central District of Illinois. *Education:* Xavier University (A.B., 1970; M.A., 1971); Catholic University of America (J.D., 1973). Alpha Sigma Nu; Delta Theta Phi. Articles and Book Review Editor, Catholic University Law Review, 1972-1973. Law Clerk, Hon. Richard B. Austin, U.S. District Court, Northern District of Illinois, 1973-1975. Member, Federal Defender Program, 1976-1988 and 1997—. Adjunct Professor of Law, University of Illinois College of Law, 2000—. Radio Talk Host "Chicago Law," WJJD, AM 1160, 1994-1997. Associate, Chicago, 1975-1979 and Partner, Chicago and Phoenix, 1979-1983, Winston & Strawn. *Member:* Chicago, Illinois, American and Federal Bar Associations. ***PRACTICE AREAS:*** Commercial and Criminal Litigation; Commercial Contracts; Trade Secrets; Business Torts; Restrictive Covenants; Defamation; Employment Discrimination; Antitrust; Securities; Professional Negligence and Malpractice; Civil Rights; Hospital Medical Privilege; Medical Peer Review; Professional Licensing. ***Email:*** gaadamski@adamskiandconti.com

KAREN CONTI, born Berwyn, Illinois, February 3, 1962; admitted to bar, 1986, Illinois and U.S. District Court, Northern District of Illinois including Trial Bar; 1990, U.S. Court of Appeals, Seventh Circuit; 1991U.S. Supreme Court; 1994, California; 1998, U.S. District Court, Central District of Illinois. *Education:* Northern Illinois University (B.A., magna cum laude, with University honors, 1983); University of Illinois (J.D., 1986). Adjunct Professor of Law, University of Illinois College of Law, 1994-1997. Radio Talk Show Host, "Chicago Law," WJJD AM 1160. Recipient: Chicago Daily Law Bulletin's, "40 Illinois Attorney's Under 40 to Watch," 2001; Today's Chicago Woman "The 100 Most Influential Woman in Chicago; Outstanding Recent Alumni of the Year, 1998; Distinguished Advocate Award, 2001-2002. *Member:* Chicago, Illinois and American Bar Associations. ***PRACTICE AREAS:*** Commercial and Criminal Litigation; Commercial Contracts; Insurance Coverage; Trade Secrets; Business Torts; Restrictive Covenants; Family Law; Defamation; Employment Severance and Discrimination; Professional Negligence; Professional Malpractice; Personal Injury; Civil Rights. ***Email:*** kconti@adamskiandconti.com

ASSOCIATES

SAMANTHA R. ENGEL, born Chicago, Illinois, April 18, 1976; admitted to bar, 2001, Illinois and U.S. District Court, Northern District of Illinois. *Education:* University of Michigan (B.A., 1998) Phi Beta Kappa; University of Chicago (J.D., with honors, 2001). Associate: Winston & Strawn, LLP, 2001-2003; Perkins Coie LLP, 2003-2005. *Member:* Chicago, Illinois and American Bar Associations. ***LANGUAGES:*** Spanish. ***PRACTICE AREAS:*** Commercial and Criminal Litigation; Commercial Contracts; Trade Secrets; Business Torts; Restrictive Covenants; Defamation; Employment Discrimination; Antitrust; Securities; Professional Negligence and Malpractice; Civil Rights; Hospital Medical Privilege; Medical Peer Review; Professional Licensing; Family Law. ***Email:*** sengel@adamskiandconti.com

ANDREA M. WEISER, born Chicago, Illinois, May 31, 1977; admitted to bar, 2002, Illinois; 2003, U.S. District Court, Northern District of Illinois. *Education:* University of Illinois (B.A., 1999); Chicago-Kent College of Law (J.D., 2002). *Member:* Chicago, Illinois State and American Bar Associations. ***PRACTICE AREAS:*** Commercial and Criminal Litigation; Commercial Contracts; Trade Secrets; Business Torts; Restrictive Covenants; Defamation; Employment Discrimination; Antitrust; Securities; Professional Negligence and Malpractice; Civil Rights; Hospital Medical Privilege; Medical Peer Review; Professional Licensing; Family Law. ***Email:*** sweiser@adamskiandconti.com

ADDUCCI, DORF, LEHNER, MITCHELL & BLANKENSHIP, P.C.

150 NORTH MICHIGAN AVENUE, SUITE 2130
CHICAGO, ILLINOIS 60601-7524
Telephone: 312-781-2800
Facsimile: 312-781-2811
Email: mblankenship@adlmb.com
URL: http://www.lawyers.com/adlmb

Commercial Litigation, Complex Litigation, Intellectual Property Litigation, Securities and Commodities Litigation, Employment and Labor Counseling and Litigation, Insurance Law, Business Law, Commercial Transactions, Legislative and Government Relations.

FIRM PROFILE: The firm offers a full range of counseling and litigation services. We provide sound and creative legal advice tempered with experience and common sense. We learn our client's objectives and tailor our approach to meet each client's unique needs. Our clients appreciate our responsiveness and direct approach.

JAMES D. ADDUCCI, born Chicago, Illinois, December 2, 1951; admitted to bar, 1976, Illinois; 1977, U.S. District Court, Northern District of Illinois, Trial Bar, and U.S. Court of Appeals, Seventh Circuit; 1990, U.S. Court of Appeals, Eighth Circuit; 1991, U.S. Court of Appeals, Third and Federal Circuits; 1995, U.S. Court of Appeals, Eleventh Circuit; 1998, U.S. Court of Appeals, Ninth Circuit; 2004, U.S. Court of Appeals, Fifth Circuit. *Education:* Loyola University of Chicago (B.A., summa cum laude, 1973); Harvard University (J.D., 1976). Law Clerk, Honorable Bernard M. Decker, U.S. District Court, Northern District of Illinois, 1976-1977. Arbitrator: National Association of Securities Dealers, Inc., 1988; National Futures Association, 1987; New York Stock Exchange, 1987. ***REPORTED CASES:*** Borowiec v. Gateway 2000, Inc., 808 N.E. 2d 957 (Ill. Sup. Ct. 2004); Mangren Research & Development Corp. v. National Chemical Co., 87 F.3d 937 (7th Cir. 1996); Beckett v. H&R Block, Inc., et al, 1994 U.S. Dist. Lexis 17714 (N.D. Ill. Dec. 8, 1994); Trans Union Credit Information Co. v. Associated Credit Services, Inc., 805 F.2d 188 (6th Cir. 1986); Winterland Concessions Company v. Edwin S. Trela, Jr., 735 F.2d 257 (7th Cir. 1984); Daniel F. McCarthy v. PaineWebber, Inc., 618 F.Supp. 933 (N.D. Ill. 1985); Danekas v. Wise, 381 N.E. 2d 1160 (Ill. App. 1978). ***PRACTICE AREAS:*** Commercial Litigation; Intellectual Property Litigation; Securities and Commodities Litigation. ***Email:*** jadducci@adlmb.com

MICHAEL C. DORF, born Chicago, Illinois, August 8, 1952; admitted to bar, 1976, Illinois; 1980, District of Columbia; 1980, U.S. District Court, Northern District of Illinois. *Education:* University of Chicago (B.A., 1973); Columbia University (J.D., 1976). Executive Editor, Columbia Journal of Law and Social Problems, 1975-1976. Author: "Disbarment in the United States: Who Shall Do The Noisome Work?" 12 Columbia Journal L. Soc. Prob. 1, 1976. Law Clerk, Hon. Hubert L. Will, U.S. District Judge, Northern District of Illinois, 1976-1978. Special Counsel, United States Representative Sidney R. Yates, 1978-1984. Director, Chicago Cultural Plan, City of Chicago, 1984-1987. Legal Affairs Consultant, President's Independent Commission on the National Endowment for the Arts, 1990; Adjunct Professor, School of the Art Institute of Chicago, 1997—. *Member:* Chicago Bar Association; Lawyers For The Creative Arts (Honors Council). ***PRACTICE AREAS:*** General Corporate; Commercial Transactions; Legislative and Government Relations; Estate Planning; Nonprofit and Charitable Organizations. ***Email:*** mdorf@adlmb.com

PAUL E. LEHNER, born St. Louis, Missouri, March 30, 1948; admitted to bar, 1975, District of Columbia; 1978, Illinois; U.S. District Court, Northern District of Illinois, Trial Bar, 1982; U.S. Court of Appeals, Seventh, Eleventh and District of Columbia Circuits. *Education:* Columbia University (B.A., 1970); Georgetown University (J.D., 1975). *Member:* Chicago, Illinois State and American (Member: Litigation Section; Section on Labor and Employment Law) Bar Associations. ***REPORTED CASES:*** Champion Parts Rebuilders, Inc. v. Cormier Corp., et al, 650 F. Supp. 87 (N.D. Ill. 1986), and 661 F. Supp. 825 (N.D. Ill. 1987); Horton v. CIGNA Individual Financial Services Company, 825 F.Supp. 852 (N.D. Ill. 1993); Sindermann v. Civil Service Commission, 657 N.E. 2d 41 (2d Dist. 1995); Chisholm v. Foothill Capital Corp., 940 F.Supp. 1273 (N.D. Ill. 1996) and 3 F.Supp.2d 925 (N.D. Ill. 1998); Otto v. Valic, 134 F.3d 841 (7th Cir. 1998); United States ex rel. Totten v. Bombardier Corp., 286 F.3d 542 (D.C. Cir. 2002). ***PRACTICE AREAS:*** Commercial Litigation; Labor and Employment Counseling and Litigation. ***Email:*** plehner@adlmb.com

RANDALL L. MITCHELL, born Chicago, Illinois, June 15, 1942; admitted to bar, 1967, Illinois; 1971, U.S. District Court, Northern District of Illinois including Trial Bar and U.S. Court of Appeals, Seventh Circuit; 1977, U.S. Supreme Court; 1984, U.S. District Court, Eastern District of Wisconsin ; 1985, U.S. Tax Court; 1988, U.S. Court of Appeals, Eleventh Circuit; 2001, U.S. Court of Appeals, District of Columbia Circuit. *Education:* University of Michigan (B.A., 1964); University of Illinois College of Law (J.D., 1967). Arbitrator, Cook County Mandatory Arbitration Program, 1990—. Certified Mediator, Part 20, Cook County Ruler. Member, Chicago Lincoln American Inn of Court. *Member:* Seventh Circuit and American (Member, Sections on: Litigation; Business Law; Labor and Employment Law; Torts and Insurance Practice) Bar Associations. [Lt., U.S. Navy, 1968-1971]. ***REPORTED CASES:*** United States ex rel. Totten v. Bombardier Corp., 380 F.3d 488 (D.C. Cir. 2004); Bilow v. Much Shelist Freed, 277 F.3d 882 (7th Cir. 2001); Otto v. Valic, 134 F.3d 841 (7th Cir. 1998); Illinois J. Livingston Co. v. Illinois Human Rights Commission, 302 Ill. App.3d 141, 704 N.E.2d 797 (1st Dist. 1998); Susman v. Lincoln American Corp., 561 F.2d 86 (7th Cir. 1977); Samuels v. Wilder, 906 F.2d 272 (7th Cir. 1990). ***PRACTICE AREAS:*** Commercial Litigation; Employment Litigation and Counselling; Insurance Litigation; Complex Litigation. ***Email:*** rmitchell@adlmb.com

MARSHALL L. BLANKENSHIP, born Chelsea, Massachusetts, March 13, 1961; admitted to bar, 1986, Illinois and U.S. District Court, Northern District of Illinois including Trial Bar; U.S. Court of Appeals, Fourth, Seventh, Ninth, Eleventh and Federal Circuits. *Education:* University of Notre Dame (B.A., 1983); University of Illinois (J.D., cum laude, 1986). Board Member, Chicago Council of Lawyers, 2001—. ***REPORTED CASES:*** Borowiec v. Gateway 2000, Inc., 808 N.E. 2d 957 (Ill. Sup. Ct. 2004); Mangren Research &

(This Listing Continued)

Development Corp. v. National Chemical Co., 87 F.3d 937 (7th Cir. 1996); Perdomo v. Browner, 67 F.3d 140 (7th Cir. 1995); Edwards v. Cabrera, 58 F.3d 290 (7th Cir. 1995); Competitive Strategies Group v. IP Communications Corp., 2000 U.S. Dist. LEXIS 3198 (N.D. Ill. March 10, 2000); Dorsey v. H.C.P. Sales, 46 F.Supp.2d 804 (N.D. Ill. 1999); Chisolm v. Foothill Capital Corp., 3 F.Supp.2d 925 (N.D. Ill. 1998); Skyview Film & Video, Inc. v. Safeco Life Insurance Co., 864 F.Supp. 755 (N.D. Ill. 1994). ***PRACTICE AREAS:*** Commercial Litigation; Intellectual Property; Insurance Law; Employment Litigation. ***Email:*** mblankenship@adlmb.com

ADELMAN & GETTLEMAN, LTD.

SUITE 1050, 53 WEST JACKSON BOULEVARD
CHICAGO, ILLINOIS 60604
Telephone: 312-435-1050
Fax: 312-435-1059
URL: http://www.adelmangettlemanlaw.com

Insolvency, Bankruptcy and Reorganization Law. General Civil and Trial Practice. Corporation, Commercial, Real Estate.

FIRM PROFILE: Adelman & Gettleman, Ltd. was founded in March, 1983 by Howard L. Adelman and Chad H. Gettleman, both of whom have devoted their entire professional career to the areas of bankruptcy, corporate reorganization and insolvency, and commercial litigation. In 1990, Henry B. Merens became a partner in the firm and has likewise devoted his entire professional career to the foregoing areas of concentration. In addition to commercial litigation in the state and federal courts, the firm has participated in major bankruptcy and reorganization cases, representing debtors, secured creditors and committees. The firm has an extensive internal continuing legal education program. Members of the Firm participate as speakers in seminars and commercial litigation programs, and author articles on areas of their concentration on a regular basis.

HOWARD L. ADELMAN, born Chicago, Illinois, June 27, 1952; admitted to bar, 1977, Illinois; 1978, Missouri and U.S. Court of Appeals, Eighth Circuit; 1979, U.S. District Court, Northern District of Illinois including Trial Bar; 1982, U.S. Supreme Court and U.S. Court of Appeals, Seventh Circuit. *Education:* Illinois State University (B.S., 1974); St. Louis University (J.D., cum laude, 1977). Phi Alpha Theta. Student Law Clerk to Honorable George Moran, Fifth District Appellate Court of Illinois, 1975-1976. Law Clerk to Honorable Robert G. Dowd, Chief Judge of the Missouri Court of Appeals, St. Louis District, 1977. Executive Judicial Assistant to the Missouri Court of Appeals, St. Louis District, 1978. Co-Author: "Mortgage Liens in Bankruptcy," Financing Real Estate Handbook, Illinois Institute of Continuing Legal Education, 1988; "Law of Guaranty," Secured Transactions Handbook, Illinois Institute of Continuing Legal Education, 1988; "Burnside: A Clear and Present Threat to the Availability of Debtor Representation," Bankruptcy Law Advisor 1989 Norton. Member, Judicial Conference, United States Advisory Committee, Federal Rules of Bankruptcy Procedure. Listed in "The Best Lawyers in America," Woodward/White, 1995-1996 and 1997-1998. *Member:* Chicago (Member, Bankruptcy and Reorganization Committee) and Illinois State Bar Associations; The Missouri Bar. ***PRACTICE AREAS:*** Insolvency; Bankruptcy; Reorganization; Commercial; Litigation. ***Email:*** hadelman@ag-ltd.com

CHAD H. GETTLEMAN, born Chicago, Illinois, May 31, 1951; admitted to bar, 1976, Wisconsin and U.S. District Court, Eastern and Western Districts of Wisconsin; 1978, Illinois and U.S. District Court, Northern District of Illinois including Trial Bar. *Education:* University of Illinois (B.S., Accounting, 1973); Marquette University (J.D., 1976). Tau Epsilon Rho (Secretary, 1975-1976). Certified Public Accountant, Illinois, 1974. *Member:* Chicago (Member, Bankruptcy and Reorganization Committee), Illinois State and American (Member, Section on Corporation, Banking and Business Law) Bar Associations; State Bar of Wisconsin. ***PRACTICE AREAS:*** Insolvency; Bankruptcy; Reorganization; Commercial; Litigation. ***Email:*** cgettleman@ag-ltd.com

HENRY B. MERENS, born Chicago, Illinois, July 28, 1956; admitted to bar, 1981, Illinois and U.S. District Court, Northern District of Illinois including Trial Bar; 1991, U.S. Court of Appeals, Seventh Circuit. *Education:* Trinity College (B.A., with honors in English, 1978); Washington University (J.D., 1981). Staff Member, Washington University Law School Urban Law Annual, 1979-1981. Author: "Private Cause Of Action Under Title IX: Cannon v. University Of Chicago," Vol. 20, Washington University Law School Urban Law Annual, pgs. 273-286, 1980. Co-Author: "Mortgage Liens in Bankruptcy," Financing Real Estate Handbook, Illinois Institute of Continuing Legal Education, 1988; "Law of Guaranty," Secured Transactions Handbook, Illinois Institute of Continuing Education, 1988; "Burnside: A Clear and Present Danger to The Availability of Debtor Representation," Bankruptcy Law Advisor, 1989, Norton. *Member:* Chicago Bar Association. ***PRACTICE AREAS:*** Insolvency; Bankruptcy; Reorganizations; Commercial; Litigation; Real Estate. ***Email:*** hmerens@ag-ltd.com

BRAD A. BERISH, born Chicago, Illinois, July 1, 1962; admitted to bar, 1989, Illinois and U.S. District Court, Northern District of Illinois. *Education:* Indiana University (B.S. Accounting, 1984); Emery University (J.D., 1989). Phi Delta Phi (President, 1987-1988). Recipient, Student Honors, Indiana University. Certified Public Accountant, Illinois, 1985. *Member:* Chicago Bar Association. ***PRACTICE AREAS:*** Insolvency; Bankruptcy; Reorganizations; Commercial; Litigation. ***Email:*** bberish@ag-ltd.com

MARK A. CARTER, born Joliet, Illinois, January 6, 1963; admitted to bar, 1988, Illinois and U.S. District Court, Northern District of Illinois. *Education:* University of Illinois (B.S., with honors, 1985; J.D., 1988). Alpha Lambda Delta; Phi Eta Sigma. Law Clerk, Hon. Richard N. DeGunther, U.S. Bankruptcy Court, Northern District of Illinois. Author: "Secured Interests in Bankruptcy," Advanced Commercial Finance and Creditors Rights in Illinois, IICLE, 1993. *Member:* Chicago, Illinois State and American Bar Associations. ***PRACTICE AREAS:*** Bankruptcy Law; Reorganization Law; Real Estate Law; Commercial Litigation; Secured Transactions; Commercial Transactions. ***Email:*** mcarter@ag-ltd.com

ADAM P. SILVERMAN, born Chicago, Illinois, December 27, 1970; admitted to bar, 1998, Illinois and U.S. District Court, Northern District of Illinois; 2001, Arizona. *Education:* University of Illinois (B.A., 1993); DePaul University (M.B.A., 1995); Chicago-Kent College of Law, Illinois Institute of Technology (J.D., with honors, 1998). Judicial Extern, Hon. Joan B. Gottschall, U.S. District Court, Northern District of Illinois. *Member:* Chicago and Illinois State Bar Associations. ***PRACTICE AREAS:*** Insolvency; Bankruptcy; Reorganizations; Commercial; Litigation. ***Email:*** APS@ag-ltd.com

NATHAN Q. RUGG, born Urbana, Illinois, July 23, 1975; admitted to bar, 2000, Illinois; U.S. District Court, Northern and Central Districts of Illinois and U.S. Court of Appeals, Seventh Circuit. *Education:* Dartmouth College (B.A., History, cum laude, 1997); University of Illinois College of Law, Urbana-Champaign (J.D., 2000). *Member:* Chicago Bar Association. ***PRACTICE AREAS:*** Bankruptcy; Corporate Reorganization; Commercial Litigation. ***Email:*** nrugg@ag-ltd.com

STANLEY F. ORSZULA, born Arlington Heights, Illinois, December 15, 1972; admitted to bar, 1998, Illinois; 2001, U.S. District Court, Northern District of Illinois. *Education:* Boston College (B.A., 1995); Loyola University (J.D., cum laude, 1998). Recipient, CALI Award in Trusts and Estates, 1997. Author: Business Credit, "The Unfriendly Skies for Aircraft Financiers in the United Airlines Bankruptcy," September, 2003. Trial Judiciary, Department of Defense, 1998. *Member:* Chicago Bar Association (Member, Young Lawyers Section Bankruptcy Committee; Vice-Chair, 2002-2003; Co-Chair, 2003-2004, Director of Young Lawyer Section, 2004—). [Lieutenant, U.S. Navy JAG Corps., 1998-2001]. ***LANGUAGES:*** German. ***PRACTICE AREAS:*** Bankruptcy; Banking; Finance; Business; Commercial Litigation. ***Email:*** sfo@ag-ltd.com

MICHAEL I. FEINBERG, born Skokie, Illinois, October 16, 1977; admitted to bar, 2004, Illinois. *Education:* Brandeis University (B.A., 1999); Northwest University (J.D., 2004). ***LANGUAGES:*** German, Italian. ***PRACTICE AREAS:*** Corporate Restructuring; Commercial Litigation.

(This Listing Continued)

ADLER, MURPHY & McQUILLEN

Established in 1995
ONE NORTH LA SALLE STREET
SUITE 2300
CHICAGO, ILLINOIS 60602
Telephone: 312-345-0700
Telefax: 312-345-9860
Email: amm-law.com
URL: http://www.amm-law.com

Civil Litigation, Aviation and Space Law, Products Liability, Premises Liability, Professional Liability, Insurance Defense and Coverage Matters, Environmental and Toxic Tort Litigation, Construction Claims and Litigation.

FIRM PROFILE: The firm carries the highest legal ability rating in Martindale-Hubbell.

MEMBERS OF FIRM

JOHN W. ADLER, admitted to bar, 1961, District of Columbia; 1965, U.S. Court of Military Appeals; 1967, Illinois; 1971, Colorado and U.S. Supreme Court; 1973, U.S. District Court, Northern District of Illinois including Trial Bar. *Education:* Georgetown University (B.S., 1958; LL.B., 1961). *Member:* Chicago, Colorado and Federal Bar Associations; The District of Columbia Bar; Law Club of Chicago. Fellow, American College of Trial Lawyers. ***PRACTICE AREAS:*** Aviation Accident Litigation; Products Liability Defense; Insurance Coverage. ***Email:*** jadler@amm-law.com

JAMES F. MURPHY, admitted to bar, 1981, Illinois and U.S. District Court, Northern District of Illinois including Trial Bar; 1992, U.S. District Court, District of Arizona; 2001, U.S. District Court, Western District of Michigan. *Education:* Northern Illinois University (B.S., with honors, 1976); DePaul University (J.D., 1981). Kappa Tau Alpha. Mock Trial Instructor, Chicago Coalition for Law Related Education, 1984—. *Member:* American Bar Association; Defense Research Institute. [U.S. Navy, 1970-1974]. ***REPORTED CASES:*** Darras v. Trans World Airlines, Inc., 617 F.Supp. 1068 (N.D. Ill. 1985); Darras v. Trans World Airlines, Inc., 622 F.Supp. 215 (N.D. Ill. 1985); Forum Ins. Co. v. Seitz Aviation, 241 Kan. 334, 737 P.2d. 29 (Kan. 1987); Fischer v. Northwest Airlines, Inc., 623 F.Supp. 1064 (N.D.Ill. 1988); Forum Ins. Co. v. Aviation Enter, Inc., 722 F.Supp. 1525 (W.D. Tenn.1988); Sweis v. Trans World Airlines, Inc., 681 F.Supp. 501 (N.D. Ill. 1988); Bahrs v. Hughes Aircraft Co., 795 F.Supp. 965 (D.Ariz. 1992); Tucson Airport Authority v. General Dynamics Corp., 922 F.Supp. 273 (D.Ariz. 1996); Yslava v. Hughes Aircraft Co., 188 Ariz. 380, 936 P.2d 1274 (Ariz. 1997); Tucson Airport Authority v. General Dynamics Corp., 136 F.3d 641 (9th Cir. 1998); Anderson v. Alberto-Culver et al 337 IL App 3d 643, 789 N.E. 2d 304 (1st Dist 2003); Alberto-Culver Company v. Aon Corporation, et al 351 IL App 3d 123; 812 N.E. 2d 369 (1st Dist 2004). ***PRACTICE AREAS:*** Complex Litigation; Toxic Torts; Environmental Regulation; Products Liability Defense; Insurance Coverage. ***Email:*** jmurphy@amm-law.com

MICHAEL G. McQUILLEN, admitted to bar, 1984, Illinois; U.S. District Court, Northern District of Illinois including Trial Bar; U.S. Court of Appeals, Sixth and Eleventh Circuits. *Education:* Illinois State University (B.S., 1980); John Marshall Law School (J.D., with distinction, 1984). Executive Candidacy Editor, The John Marshall Law Review, 1983-1984. Author: "Solar Rights and Nuisance Law: Prah v. Maretti," Volume 16 of John Marshall Law Review, 1983; "The Deception About The Inception Rule: Coverage For VFR Pilots IFR Conditions," 60 Journal of Air Law and Commerce, 179 (199). Former Writer for The Air and Space Lawyer (an ABA newsletter). Life Member of the National Registry of Who's Who, 2001 edition. Commercial Pilot Certificate, Airplane Single and Multi Engine Land with Sea Plane and Instrument Rating, Lifeline Pilot. *Member:* Illinois State and American (Member, Tort and Insurance Practice Section) Bar Associations; Lawyer/Pilots Bar Association. ***REPORTED CASES:*** In re Air Crash at Little Rock, Arkansas, June 1, 1999, 109 F.Supp.2d 1022 (E.D. Ark. 2000); Nippon Fire & Marine Ins. Co., Ltd. v. Skyway Freight Systems, Inc., 235 F.3d 53 (2nd Cir. N.Y., Dec. 06, 2000); Reliance Nat. Ins. Co. v. Great Lakes Aviation, Ltd., 12 F.Supp.2d 854 (C.D. Ill. 1998); Epps Flying Services, Inc. v. Hartzell Propeller, Inc., 1995 WL 612590, Prod.Liab.Rep. (CCH) P 14,423 (E.D.Pa. 1995);

(This Listing Continued)

ADLER, MURPHY & McQUILLEN, Chicago—Continued

Mio v. Alberto-Culver Co., 306 Ill.App.3d 822, 715 N.E.2d 309,239 Ill.Dec. 864 (Ill.App. 1999); In re Air Crash Disaster at Sioux City, Iowa, July 19, 1989, 133 F.R.D. 515 (N.D.Ill. 1990); Chung v. Tarom, S.A., 990 F.Supp. 581 (N.D.Ill. 1998); Anderson v. Alberto-Culver USA, Inc., 317 Ill.App.3d 1104, 740 N.E.2d 819, 251 Ill.Dec. 533 (Ill.App. 2000); North American Specialty Ins. Co. v. Myers, 111 F.3d 1273, (6th Cir. 1997); Brown v. North American Specialty Ins. Co., 235 Ga.App. 299, 508 S.E.2d 741, 98 FCDR 4146 (Ga.App. 1998); American Continental Ins. Co. v. Estate of Gerkens, 69 Ohio App.3d 697, 591 N.E.2d 774 (Ohio App. 3 Dist. 1990); Massie v. AAR Western Skyways, Inc., 4 Cal.App.4th 405, 5 Cal.Rptr.2d 654 (Cal.App. 4 Dist. 1992); In re Air Crash Disaster at Sioux City, Iowa, July 19, 1989, 259 Ill.App.3d 231, 631 N.E.2d 1302, 197 Ill.Dec. 843 (Ill.App. 1994); Anderson v. Alberto-Culver et at 337 IL App 3d 643, 789 N.E. 2d 304. ***PRACTICE AREAS:*** Products Liability Defense; Aviation Accident Litigation; Insurance Coverage. ***Email:*** mmcquillen@amm-law.com

LAWRENCE S. GOSEWISCH, admitted to bar, 1983, Illinois, U.S. District Court, Northern, Central and Southern Districts of Illinois including Trial Bar; U.S. Court of Appeals, Sixth, Seventh, Ninth and Eleventh Circuits. *Education:* Lewis University (B.A., with high honors, 1980); DePaul University (J.D., with honors, 1983). Recipient: Certificate in Mediation Training, DePaul University, 1999. *Member:* American Bar Association (Member, Litigation Section). ***REPORTED CASES:*** Bankhead v. Lucas Aerospace, Ltd., 878 F.Supp. 221 (N.D.Ga., Oct. 20, 1994); Uehlein v. Shwachman, 156 Ill.App.3d 274, (Ill.App. 1 Dist. 1987); Matter of Estate of Jacobs, 189 Ill.App.3d 625, (Ill.App.1 Dist. 1989); In re Estate of Carroll, 192 Ill.App.3d 202, 548 N.E.2d 650, 139 Ill.Dec. 265 (Ill.App. 1 Dist. 1989); Davila v. Arlasky, 857 F.Supp. 1258 (N.D.Ill. 1994); Davila v. Arlasky, 141 F.R.D. 68 (N.D.Ill. 1991). ***PRACTICE AREAS:*** Litigation; Insurance; Construction Law; Design Professionals Liability; Aviation Law. ***Email:*** lgosewisch@amm-law.com

KEVIN W. MURPHY, admitted to bar, 1989, Illinois and Georgia. *Education:* University of Illinois (B.S., 1986); University of Georgia (J.D., 1989). Panel Moderator, "NTSB Investigations: Who is Invited to the Party and What are They Supposed to Do?" 6th Annual American Bar Association Aviation Litigation Seminar. Speaker: "Discovery From Foreign Defendants," NTSB Bar Association Aviation Law Seminar; "Airline Liability Update," 8th Annual American Bar Association Aviation Litigation Seminar. Publication: NTSB Bar Association Newsletter, Spring 2003, Analysis of Recent Air Carrier Cases. Private Pilot, 1988. Instrument Rating, 1989. *Member:* State Bar of Georgia (Aviation Section); National Transportation Safety Board Bar Association; Aircraft Owners and Pilots Association. [U.S. Coast Guard Auxiliary, Skills & Seamanship (1997) Basic Coastal Navigation (1997) Advanced Coastal Navigation (1998)]. ***PRACTICE AREAS:*** Aviation Defense Litigation; Admiralty Law; Insurance Coverage. ***Email:*** kmurphy@amm-law.com

MARK S. SUSINA, admitted to bar, 1989, Illinois and U.S. District Court, Northern District of Illinois; 1991, U.S. Court of Appeals, Seventh Circuit. *Education:* Marquette University (B.A., 1986); Loyola University of Chicago (J.D., 1989). Managing Editor, Loyola University of Chicago Law Journal, 1988-1989. *Member:* Chicago Bar Association. ***REPORTED CASES:*** Nippon Fire & Marine Ins. Co. Ltd. v. Skyway Freight Systems, Inc., 235 F.3d 53 (2d Cir. 2000); Mio v. Alberto-Culver Co., 306 Ill.App.3d 822, 715 N.E.2d 309 (Ill.App. 1999); Lurzer v. AlliedSignal Inc. 1998 WL 102637 (N.D. Ill. 1998); Alberto-Culver Co. v. Aon Corp. 351 111 App 3rd 123, 812 N.E.2d 369 (Ill.App. 2004). ***PRACTICE AREAS:*** Aviation Accidents; Products Liability Defense; Insurance Defense. ***Email:*** msusina@amm-law.com

ERIC A. CUNNINGHAM III, admitted to bar, 1992, Illinois and U.S. Court of Appeals, Seventh Circuit; 1995, U.S. District Court, Eastern District of Michigan and U.S. Court of Appeals, Sixth Circuit; 1999, U.S. District Court, Central District of Illinois; U.S. District Court, Northern District of Illinois, including Trial Bar. *Education:* Vanderbilt University (B.A., cum laude, 1989); Washington University (J.D., 1992). Associate Editor, Washington University Law Quarterly, 1991-1992. Private Pilot License, 1990; Instrument Rating, 1991. Author, "Negligent Infliction of Emotional Distress in Air Crash Cases: A New Flight Path?" 70 Washington University Law Quarterly 935, 1992. Teaching Assistant, Legal Research and Writing, 1991-1992. *Member:* American and Lawyer-Pilots Bar Associations. ***REPORTED CASES:*** Mio v. Alberto-Culver Co., 715 N.E.2d 309 (Ill. App. 1999); North Am. Specialty Ins. Co. v. Myers, 111 F.3d 1273 (6th Cir. 1997); Epps Flying Service v. Hartzell Propeller, Inc., Prod. Liab. Rep. (CCH) P 14, 423, 1995 U.S. Dist. Lexis 15293 (E.D. Pa. 1995); Cheng v. United Airlines, Inc., 1995 U.S. Dist. Lexis 1140 (N.D. Ill. 1995). ***PRACTICE AREAS:*** Aviation Accident Litigation; Product Liability Defense; Commercial Litigation; Insurance Coverage; General Civil Litigation; Music Law. ***Email:*** ecunningham@amm-law.com

THOMAS S. FLANIGON, admitted to bar, 1993, Florida; 1994, Illinois; 1996, U.S. District Court, Northern District of Illinois. *Education:* University of Colorado at Boulder (B.A., 1990); Stetson University (J.D., 1993). *Member:* Chicago and Illinois State Bar Associations; The Florida Bar. ***REPORTED CASES:*** Anderson v. Alberto-Culver, et al, 337 IL App. 3d 643, 789 N.E. 2d 304 (1st Dist. 2003). ***PRACTICE AREAS:*** Civil Litigation; Aviation Defense. ***Email:*** tflanigon@amm-law.com

JOHN M. KELLY, born McHenry, Illinois, October 31, 1968; admitted to bar, 1994, Illinois. *Education:* Arizona State University (B.S., 1990); DePaul University (J.D., 1994). *Member:* Chicago, Illinois State and American Bar Associations; Illinois Association of Defense Trial Counsel; National Association of Railroad Trial Counsel. ***PRACTICE AREAS:*** Civil Litigation; Aviation Litigation; Commercial Litigation; Railroad Litigation. ***Email:*** jkelly@amm-law.com

PAULA LoMONACO WEGMAN, admitted to bar, 1996, Arizona; 1997, Illinois and U.S. District Court, District of Arizona; 1998, U.S. District Court, Northern District of Illinois including Trial Bar. *Education:* Arizona State University (B.A., 1992); Chicago-Kent College of Law, Illinois Institute of Technology (J.D., 1996). *Member:* State Bar of Arizona; Justinian Society of Lawyers; Defense Research Institute. ***REPORTED CASES:*** Anderson et al v. Alberto-Culver USA, Inc., et al, 251 111 Dec. 533, 740 Ne2d 819 (1st Dist. 2000). ***PRACTICE AREAS:*** Litigation; Aviation Law; Products Liability. ***Email:*** pwegman@amm-law.com

(This Listing Continued)

ASSOCIATES

NICHOLAS C. BART, admitted to bar, 1998, Wisconsin and U.S. District Court, Eastern District of Wisconsin; 1999, Illinois; 2001, U.S. District Court, Northern and Central Districts of Illinois and U.S. Court of Appeals, 7th Circuit; 2003, U.S. District Court, Southern District of Illinois. *Education:* Eastern Illinois University (B.A., 1995); Marquette University (J.D., 1998). *Member:* American Bar Association; State Bar of Wisconsin. [Sergeant, U.S. Army, National Guard, 1989-1995]. ***PRACTICE AREAS:*** Litigation. ***Email:*** nbart@amm-law.com

T. PATRICK BYRNES, admitted to bar, 1999, Illinois; U.S. District Court, Northern District of Illinois. *Education:* University of Illinois (B.A., 1996); DePaul University College of Law (J.D., 1999). Member, DePaul University College of Law Moot Court Society. Author: "Schafer v. Time, Inc." DePaul University College of Law Journal of Art and Entertainment Law, Fall 1998 Volume IX Number 1. *Member:* Chicago, Illinois and American Bar Associations. ***PRACTICE AREAS:*** Aviation; Civil Litigation; Insurance Defense. ***Email:*** tbyrnes@amm-law.com

AUSTIN W. BARTLETT, admitted to bar, 2000, Illinois. *Education:* Northern Illinois University (B.S., magna cum laude, 1997; J.D., magna cum laude, 2000). Lead Articles Editor, Law Review, 1999-2000. Recipient: Greatest Contribution to Advocacy Programs, graduation award, May 27, 2000; Outstanding Contribution to the College of Law Community, graduation award, May 27, 2000; First Place, Best Oralist, Second Best Brief, 17th Annual NIU College of Law Prize Moot Court; Second Place, Second Best Oralist, Sixteenth Annual Midwest Moot Court Competition, 2000; Philip C. Jessup International Law Moot Court Competition, 2000; Quarterfinalist, 19th Annual John Marshall International Moot Court Competition in Information Technology and Privacy Law, 1999; National Finals, ABA National Negotiation Competition, 1999; Regional Finalist, ABA Law Student Division Negotiation Competition, 1998. Co-Author: With Jeffrey A. Parness, *The Authority of Illinois Lawyers to Settle Their Clients' Civil Claims:* On Principles Not Quite Settled, 31 Loy. U. Chi. L. J. 199 (2000); With Jeffrey A. Parness, *Unsettling Questions Regarding Lawyer Civil Claim Settlement Authority,* 78 Or. L. Rev. 1061 (1999); With Jeffrey A. Parness and Amy M. Leonetti, *The Substantive Elements in the New Special Pleading Laws,* 78 Neb. L. Rev. 412 (1999); *Lease Resolution Corporation v. Larney,* The Counselor 3 (Nov. 1999); *Pope v. First of America N.A.,* The Counselor 5 (Sept. 1999); With Emily A. Chen, *Golden v. McDermott, Will & Emery,* The Counselor 4 (Sept. 1999); *Baldwin v. Wolff,* The Counselor 7 (Dec. 1998). *Member:* Chicago Bar Association. ***REPORTED CASES:*** Alberto-Culver Co. v. Aon Corp., 351 ILL. App 3d 123, 812 NE 2d 369 (1st Dist. 2004). ***PRACTICE AREAS:*** Appellate Practice; Products Liability Defense; Insurance Defense. ***Email:*** abartlett@amm-law.com

SARAH JAYNE CONDON, admitted to bar, 2000, Illinois and U.S. District Court, Northern District of Illinois. *Education:* University of Illinois (B.A., 1997); Loyola University (J.D., 2000). Recipient, Award in Appellate Advocacy. *Member:* Chicago and American Bar Associations. ***PRACTICE AREAS:*** Aviation; Litigation; Products Liability Defense. ***Email:*** scondon@amm-law.com

DAVID J. ALTSCHULER, admitted to bar, 2002, Illinois; 2004, U.S. District Court, Northern District of Illinois. *Education:* Washington University (B.A., 1998); Vanderbilt University (J.D., 2002). Sports Notes Editor, Vanderbilt Journal of Entertainment Law and Practice, 2001-2002. Author: "On the Ropes: New Regulations and State Cooperation Step Into the Ring to Protect Boxing From Itself," Vanderbilt Journal of Entertainment Law and Practice, Winter 2002. *Member:* Chicago and American Bar Associations.

PETER C. KIM, admitted to bar, 2003, Illinois. *Education:* University of Illinois at Chicago (B.S., 1997); Loyola University at Chicago (J.D., 2003). *Member:* Chicago Bar Association. ***PRACTICE AREAS:*** Aviation; Litigation; Insurance Defense. ***Email:*** pkim@amm-law.com

JOHN G. McAULEY, born Pittsburgh, Pennsylvania, November 10, 1952; admitted to bar, 1988, Illinois. *Education:* University of Pittsburgh (B.S., 1975); John Marshall Law School (J.D., 1988). Member, John Marshall Law Review. [Capt., USAF, 1978-1985]. ***Email:*** jmcauley@amm-law.com

WILLIAM F. MOORE, admitted to bar, 2004, Illinois. *Education:* Northern Michigan University (B.S., 2000); John Marshall Law School (J.D., 2004). Participant, ABA Negotiation Competition, 2003; John J. Gibbons National Criminal Procedure Moot Court Competition, 2004. *Member:* Chicago and American Bar Associations. ***PRACTICE AREAS:*** Aviation Law; Litigation; Insurance Coverage; Insurance Defense; Products Liability Defense. ***Email:*** wmoore@amm-law.com

KERRY BUTE, born Ottawa, Illinois, May 11, 1981; admitted to bar, 2005, Illinois. *Education:* Miami University (B.A., 2002); Northern Illinois University (J.D., 2005). Phi Delta Phi; Moot Court Society. Member, Northern Illinois University Law Review. *Member:* American Bar Association; American Trial Lawyers Association. ***PRACTICE AREAS:*** Aviation Defense; Products Liability; Insurance Defense. ***Email:*** kbute@amm-law.com

LISA A. IADEVAIA, born Providence, Rhode Island, June 29, 1979; admitted to bar, 2005, Illinois. *Education:* University of Rhode Island (B.A., summa cum laude, 2001); DePaul University College of Law (J.D., 2005). Phi Beta Kappa. Lead Articles Editor, DePaul-LCA Journal of Art & Entertainment Law. *Member:* Chicago and American Bar Association; Justinian Society of Lawyers. ***PRACTICE AREAS:*** Aviation; Insurance Coverage; Products Liability; Litigation. ***Email:*** liadevaia@amm-law.com

JULIE B. AIMEN

407 S. DEARBORN STREET
SUITE 1675
CHICAGO, ILLINOIS 60605
Telephone: 312-697-0022
Fax: 312-697-0812
Email: julie.aimen@juliebaimen.com
URL: http://www.juliebaimen.com

Criminal Defense, Criminal Appellate Practice, Family Law. Child Custody, Child Support, Divorce, Domestic Violence, Spousal Support, Driving Under the Influence, Drug Crimes, Felonies, Homicides, Misdemeanors, Probation, Parole, Sexual Assault, Traffic Violations.

(This Listing Continued)

FIRM PROFILE: The firm has a national trial practice, primarily representing clients throughout the state of Illinois. Ms. Aimen is an outspoken advocate for her clients. The firm's philosophy is based on the act of advocacy, negotiation and mediation to achieve the desired goal. Ms. Aimen is active in various professional organizations, committees and board positions. She has also organized seminars and published various articles.

JULIE B. AIMEN, born Highland Park, Illinois, February 1, 1957; admitted to bar, 1984, Illinois and U.S. Court of Appeals, Seventh Circuit. *Education:* University of Wisconsin-Madison (B.A.S.W., with honors, 1979); Chicago-Kent College of Law (J.D., with honors, 1984). Certified Arbitrator, Circuit Court of Cook County, 1990. Instructor: Trial Advocacy Workshop, Mandel Legal Clinic, University of Chicago, 1993—; Wisconsin Public Defender Trial Advocacy Program, 1999. Past Member, Fund For Justice. *Member:* Chicago (Past Chairperson, Criminal Law Committee) and Illinois State Bar Associations; Chicago Council of Lawyers (Past Member of Board of Governors; Chair, Indingency Panel; Past Co-Chair, State Evaluation Committee); Illinois Attorneys for Criminal Justice (Past President); National Association of Criminal Defense Lawyers (Past Member Board of Directors).

AINSWORTH & ASSOCIATES, P.C.

203 NORTH LA SALLE STREET, SUITE 2100
CHICAGO, ILLINOIS 60601
Telephone: 312-984-0398
Fax: 847-556-0648
Email: funny21@prodigy.net
URL: http://www.lawyers.com/ainsworthlaw

Trusts and Estates, Estate Planning, Guardianship, Wills, Probate, Civil Rights, Criminal Law, Felonies, Misdemeanors, Contested Estates, Contested Wills, Estate Tax, Conservatorships, Heir Property, Land Trusts, Living Wills, Power of Attorney, Fiduciary Litigation, Breach of Contracts, Chancery, Complaint for Declaratory Judgment, Quiet Title, Joint Tenancy Accounts, Policy Brutality, Probate, Dependency, Wrongful Death, Spousal Awards, Minors Awards, Minors Estates, Minor Guardianships, Gift to Minors, Small Estate, Convenience Accounts, Criminal Appeals, Civil Appeals, Employment Discrimination, Race Discrimination, Sex Discrimination.

DIANE AINSWORTH, born Queens, New York; admitted to bar, 1985, Illinois and U.S. District Court, Northern District of Illinois including Trial Bar. *Education:* Emma Willard School; State University of New York at Purchase (B.A., 1981); Northwestern University (J.D., 1985). Recipient: Community Service Award, Cook County Bar Association, 1986 and 1996; Outstanding Young Woman of America, 1986. ALTA Regional Moot Court Judge, 2003. Listed in: Who's Who in U.S. Executives, 1989, 1990. FACULTY: Adjunct Professor, Introduction to Trial Advocacy, Northwestern University School of Law, 2004—Adjunct Professor, Estates and Trusts, Roosevelt University Lawyer Assistant Program, 1997-1998. Certified Circuit Court Arbitrator. Volunteer, Chicago Volunteer Legal Services, 1990-2000. *Member:* Cook County (Member, Board of Directors, 1990-1992), Chicago (Co-Chair, Estate Planning Committee, 1995) and Illinois State (Member, Public Utilities and Transportation Law Section Council, 1989-1990) Bar Associations; The Association of Trial Lawyers of America; Black Women's Lawyers Association. ***LANGUAGES:*** French. ***SPECIAL AGENCIES:*** Board of Commissioners, Historic Preservation Commission, City of Hammond. Appointed as a Special Administrator and Guardian by the Probate Courts. ***PRACTICE AREAS:*** Trusts and Estates; Estate Planning; Guardianship; Wills; Probate; Civil Rights; Contested Trusts and Estates; Estate Administration; Estate Litigation; Trust Administration; Trust Litigation; Criminal Litigation; Chancery and Equity; Civil Litigation; Evictions; Commercial Leasing; Contract Litigation; Corporate Litigation.

OF COUNSEL

ZEDRICK T. BRADEN, III, born Chicago, Illinois, May 18, 1956; admitted to bar, 1985, Illinois. *Education:* Centre College of Kentucky (B.A., 1978); Thurgood Marshall School of Law (J.D., 1982). *Member:* Cook County Bar Association.

REPRESENTATIVE CLIENTS: Homart Corporation; Leadership Council of Metropolitan Open Communities; Pullman Bank and Trust Company (Trust Department).

ALBERT, WHITEHEAD, P.C.

10 NORTH DEARBORN STREET, SUITE 600
CHICAGO, ILLINOIS 60602
Telephone: 312-357-6300
Fax: 312-357-6219
URL: http://www.albertwhiteheadpc.com

Corporate, Business, Creditors' Rights, Financial Services, Labor and Employment, Litigation, Municipal Finance and Real Estate.

FIRM PROFILE: Albert, Whitehead, P.C. is a full-service minority-owned firm that is unique because of the extensive experience that its principals gained while practicing virtually all of its principals formerly practiced at large national law firms. The firm's attorneys have experience in handling sophisticated commercial transactions and litigation matters for some of the nation's largest corporations. The firm is a participant in the American Bar Association Minority Counsel Demonstration Program. In 1993 the firm became the first minority owned law firm in the United States to be selected as a voting member of a Resolution Trust Corporation Strategic Workout Asset Team.

CHARLES G. ALBERT, born Chicago, Illinois, May 12, 1955; admitted to bar, 1979, Illinois; U.S. Supreme Court; Illinois Supreme Court; U.S. Court of Appeals, Second and Seventh Circuits; U.S District Court, Northern and Central Districts of Illinois including Trial Bar; U.S. District Court, Northern District of Texas; U.S. District Court, District of North Dakota. *Education:* Princeton University (A.B., 1976); Harvard University (J.D., 1979). Bell, Boyd & Lloyd, 1979-1992 (Partner, 1987-1992). *Member:* Cook County, Chicago and American Bar Associations; Illinois Association of Defense Trial Counsel; National Association of Railroad Trial Counsel. ***PRACTICE AREAS:*** General Commercial Litigation; Securities/Litigation; Lender Liability Litigation; Employment Litigation; Insurance Litigation; Petroleum Industry Litigation. ***Email:*** calbert@awm-law.com

STEPHANIE S. GREEN, born Birmingham, Alabama, January 5, 1965; admitted to bar, 1997, Illinois. *Education:* University of California, Davis (B.A., 1993); Chicago-Kent College of Law, Illinois Institute of Technology (J.D., 1997). Member, Moot Court Honor Society. Dean's List. Formerly with, Sachnoff & Weaver Ltd. ***PRACTICE AREAS:*** Affordable Housing (60%); Commercial Real Estate (20%); Institutional Investment Law (20%). ***Email:*** sgreen@awm-law.com

PATRICIA C. HOLLAND, born Pittsburgh, Pennsylvania; admitted to bar, 1983, Illinois; U.S. District Court, Northern District of Illinois including Trial Bar. *Education:* University of Illinois (B.A., 1980); University of Chicago (J.D., 1983). Adjunct Professor, Chicago-Kent College of Law, 1986-1992. *Member:* Chicago and Illinois State (Chair, Corporation, Business and Securities Law Council) Bar Associations. ***PRACTICE AREAS:*** Securities; Corporate Law. ***Email:*** pholland@awm-law.com

LAURIE D. JAFFE, born Chicago, Illinois, January 15, 1954; admitted to bar, 1985, Illinois; U.S. District Court, Northern District of Illinois including Trial Bar; U.S. District Court, Central District of Illinois; U.S. District Court, District of North Dakota; U.S. Court of Appeals, Seventh Circuit. *Education:* Oberlin College (B.A., 1975); University of Michigan (M.S.W., 1977); Loyola University (J.D., 1985). Recipient, American Jurisprudence Award in Estates, 1984-1985. Lead Articles Editor, Loyola Law Journal, 1984-1985. Author: Note, "Pennhurst State School and Hospital v. Halderman: Federal Equity Jurisdiction Restricted by Eleventh Amendment Immunity," Vol. 16:1, Loyola University of Chicago Law Journal, Fall, 1984. Bell, Boyd & Lloyd, 1985-1993, Partner, 1993. *Member:* Chicago Bar Association. ***PRACTICE AREAS:*** General Commercial Litigation; Insurance Litigation; Lender Liability Litigation; Petroleum Litigation. ***Email:*** ljaffe@awm-law.com

GREGORY C. WHITEHEAD, born Portsmouth, Virginia, May 17, 1960; admitted to bar, 1985, Illinois and U.S. District Court, Northern District of Illinois. *Education:* University of Virginia (B.A., 1982; J.D., 1985). Associate, Seyfarth, Shaw, Fairweather & Geraldson, 1985-1991; Senior Associate, Carney & Brothers, Ltd., 1991-1992. Chairman, 2000-2005 and Board Member, 1994-2000, Broward Hospital and Heart Care Center, Chicago, Illinois. Co-Founder and Chairman, Chicago Committee on Minorities in Large Law Firms, 1990. *Member:* Chicago (Co-Chairman, Young Lawyers Section, Minorities in the Profession Committee, 1988-1989 and 1989-1990), American (Chairman, Young Lawyers Division, Young Lawyer Development Committee, 1989) and National Bar Associations. ***PRACTICE AREAS:*** Real Estate; Real Estate Finance; Financial Services; General Corporate Practice. ***Email:*** gwhitehead@awm-law.com

JOHNER T. WILSON III, born Chicago, Illinois, October 22, 1977; admitted to bar, 2002, Illinois and U.S. District Court, Northern District of Illinois. *Education:* University of Illinois (B.A., 1999); DePaul University (J.D., 2002). Recipient, Illinois Judicial Council Scholarship, 2001. Member, Board of Directors, New Zion Missionary Baptist Church, 2002—. Member, Executive Board, Black Law Students Association of DePaul University, 1999-2001. Chairman, Student Mentor Program, Student Bar Association of DePaul University, 2000. *Member:* Chicago and Cook County Bar Associations. ***PRACTICE AREAS:*** Commercial Litigation; Municipal Defense; Real Estate.

REPRESENTATIVE CLIENTS: American Bar Association; AM Corporation; Bank of America; Bank One; Baxter Healthcare; Blockbuster, Inc.; BP North America; Citibank, F.S.B.; City of Chicago; Cole Taylor Bank; Denny's; Exelon; Federal Deposit Insurance Corp.; General Electric Co.; GlaxoSmith Kline; Harris Bank; Heritage Bank; Kraft Foods, Inc.; LaSalle Partners Bank National Association; National Equity Fund; Nexster Financial Corp.; The Prudential Insurance Co.; Ryerson Tull, Inc.; Sears, Roebuck and Co.; Speigel; Square D.

ALHOLM, MONAHAN, KLAUKE, HAY & OLDENBURG, L.L.C.

Established in 1989

221 N. LASALLE, SUITE 450
CHICAGO, ILLINOIS 60601
Telephone: 312-704-8444
Fax: 312-704-1352
Email: info@illinois-law.com
URL: http://www.illinois-law.com

Legal Malpractice, Medical Malpractice, Professional Licensure, Employment Litigation and Workers' Compensation.

FIRM PROFILE: At Alholm, Monahan, Klauke, Hay & Oldenburg, L.L.C., we have not forgotten that the practice of law is a service profession. We are first and foremost committed to providing an unsurpassed level of legal representation and personal service to our clients. We believe that maintaining close ties and providing open lines of communication with our clients ensures the most efficient and effective handling of files and the elimination of excessive or duplicative fees.

We attribute our success to our expertise in the area of defense and our ability to establish close relationships with our clients. We have developed the unique set of skills required to meet the demands of challenging, sensitive and complex cases presented by our clients.

ANTHONY J. ALHOLM (1949-1999)

MEMBERS OF FIRM

PETER A. MONAHAN, admitted to bar, 1981, Illinois and U.S. District Court, Northern District of Illinois; U.S. Court of Appeals, Seventh Circuit; 1989, Federal Trial Bar; 2001 U.S. Supreme Court; U. S. District Court, Southern District of Illinois. *Education:* Knox College (B.A., 1976); DePaul University (J.D., 1981). Editor, De Paul Law Review, 1980-1981. Law Clerk to Justice Maurice Perlin, Illinois Appellate Court, First District, 1981-1982. Author: "Nursing Home Litigation: Defense Perspective"; "Defending Wrongful Discharge Claims Under Illinois Law"; "The Restatement of Law Governing Lawyers

(This Listing Continued)

ALHOLM, MONAHAN, KLAUKE, HAY & OLDENBURG, L.L.C., Chicago—Continued

What It Says and Where It Stands," TIPS Committee News, Professionals', Officers' & Directors' Liability Committee, Winter 1998; "Long-Arm Jurisdiction in Legal Malpractice," DRI, April 1997; "Ethical Dilemmas for the Attorney Defending Employment Cases," Labor and Employment Law Newsletter, February 1996; "Pre-Trial Litigation Sanctions Exposure in the Federal Courts: The Effects of the Amendments to the Federal Rules of Civil Procedure on the Defense Practice," I.D.C. Quarterly 21, 1994; "The New House Implied Warranty Comes to Illinois: Peterson vs. Hubschman Construction Company," 29 DePaul Law Review 617 - 1980," DePaul Law Review, 1980. Adjunct Assistant Professor, Legal Profession, DePaul University College of Law, 1993—. Faculty Member, Attorney Registration and Disciplinary Commission, Illinois Professional Responsibility Institute, 1996—. *Member:* Chicago, DuPage County, Illinois State and American Bar Associations; Illinois Association of Defense Trial Counsel; Defense Research Institute; Professional Liability Underwriters Society; American Trial Lawyers Association. ***PRACTICE AREAS:*** Legal Malpractice; Medical Malpractice; Employment Litigation; Professional Liability. ***Email:*** pmonahan@illinois-law.com

GEORGE F. KLAUKE, JR., admitted to bar, 1985, Illinois; 1986, U.S. District Court, Northern District of Illinois and U.S. Court of Appeals, Seventh Circuit; 1994, Wisconsin. *Education:* Indiana University (B.S., 1982); DePaul University (J.D., 1985). Presentations: Annual Construction Safety Conference, Strategies to Cope with the New Reality in Illinois Workers' Compensation, Chicago, 2004; Fourteenth Annual Road and Transportation Builders Conference, Strategies to Cope with the New Reality in Illinois Workers' Compensation, February, 2004; Risk Managers and Adjusters Conference, Las Vegas, Nevada, sponsored by Harrah's Entertainment Corporation (July 1997); Fireman's Fund, "The Interplay between the Illinois Workers' Compensation Act and the Federal Jones Act" (April 1997); E.C. Fackler, Inc. "Subrogation and Loss Recovery Practice" (April 1997). Speaker and Panel Member: "Managing Workers' Compensation Claims and Costs" 1996 Electrical Contractors Association Conference (August 1996); "Managing Workers' Compensation Claims" (March 1996) and "How to Reduce Workers' Compensation Costs" (February 1996), 1996 Safety Zone Conference. Speaker: "Workers Compensation and the Jones Act" Riverboat Risk Manager's Conference, Harrah's Casino. Co-Author: "Stacking the Deck - A Guide to Illinois Workers' Compensation and the Jones Act" Risk Manager's Reference, (July 1996). Co-Author: Update, "Trial Practice in the Law Division - 1986" Judges Symposium. Co-Author: "The Road to Understanding Workers' Compensation" Journal of Workers' Compensation. Lecturer and Presenter: LRP Publications Annual National Workers' Compensation and Disability Conference, 1995—; Presentation Materials, 1997, Organizing Claims Programs for Effective Defense; Presentation Materials, 1995, Selected Topics in Controlling Litigation Costs in Workers' Compensation; Annual Construction Safety Conference, 1995—; Build Safe '98, 1998 Chicagoland Construction Safety Seminar, Lunch workshop on Workers' Compensation in the Construction Industry; Lorman Educational Services Seminars, Workers' Compensation in Illinois; Safety Prevention, Cost Control and Workers' Compensation, 1999—; Tenth Annual Road Builders Conference, Managing Workers' Compensation Claims, February, 2000; 11th Annual Road Builders Conference, Saving Costs in Workers' Compensation. Co-Chair, 1988 and Director, 1989, Trial Techniques Committee. Director, Workers' Compensation Committee, 1989. *Member:* Chicago (Member, Trial Technique Committee, 1986-1990), Illinois State and American Bar Associations; State Bar of Wisconsin; Workers' Compensation Lawyers Association. ***PRACTICE AREAS:*** Workers Compensation; Maritime Law; Litigation. ***Email:*** gklauke@illinois-law.com

LINDA J. HAY, admitted to bar, 1986, Illinois and U.S. District Court, Northern District of Illinois; 1992, Federal Trial Bar; 2003, U.S. Court of Appeals, Seventh Circuit. *Education:* University of Illinois (B.A., 1982); John Marshall Law School (J.D., 1986). Co-Author: *The Burden of Proof on Proximate Cause: Should Illinois Take a Chance?* 4 IDC Quarterly 2, (1994); *Legal Malpractice: Recent Developments and Trends in the Law,* 6 IDC Quarterly 3 (1996). Author: *Legal Malpractice Claim Appropriate When Underlying Case Settles: McCarthy v. Pedersen & Houpt, et al.,* 4 IDC Quarterly 1 (1994); *Testimony of Plaintiff is Proper Support for Element of Causation Under Objective Standard in Informed Consent Case,* 5 IDC Quarterly 4 (1995); *The Pruning of Petrillo:* Practical Aspects for Defense Practitioners, 10 IDC Quarterly 2; "The 10 Biggest Mistakes Physicians Make Regarding Risk Management," SEAK, Inc., 2005; The 10 Biggest Mistakes Physicians Make which Could Lead to Liability for Failure to Provide Informed Consent," SEAK, Inc., 2005. Executive Editor, IDC Quarterly. *Member:* American, Chicago and Illinois State Bar Associations; Illinois Association of Defense Trial Counsel (Editor in Chief, IDC Quarterly; Chair, Medical Liability Committee; Member, Professional Liability Committee); Defense Research Institute; American Society for Healthcare Risk Management of the American Hospital Association; Chicagoland Healthcare; Risk Management Society; Illinois Association of Healthcare Attorneys. ***PRACTICE AREAS:*** Professional Liability Law; Medical Malpractice; Civil Litigation; Legal Malpractice. ***Email:*** lhay@illinois-law.com

ANNE MARIE OLDENBURG, admitted to bar, 1987, Illinois and U.S. District Court, Central District of Illinois; 1989, Missouri and U.S. District Court, Southern District of Illinois; 1990, U.S. District Court, Northern District of Illinois; 1993, Federal Trial Bar. *Education:* Ripon College (B.A., Cum Laude, 1983); John Marshall Law School (J.D., with Distinction, 1986). Associate Justice, Moot Court Board. Presentations: Recent Developments, Trends, Legislation, Verdicts, Decisions and the Harvard Study, DRI Nursing Home Litigation Conference, September 2003; Anatomy of a Claim: You be the Judge, SITE National Conference, 2003; Computerized Medical Office Records: Can They Reduce Your Practice's Malpractice Risk and Improve Patient Safety?, ISMIE Mutual Insurance Company Reducing Errors in Family Practice, 2003; Structural Work Act: Repeal, Revival, Repercussions, Illinois Road and Transportation Builders Association National Conference, 2003; Nurses on Trial, American Association of Critical Care Nurses Regional Meetings, 2000-2001; The Impact of Electronic Records on Medical Negligence Issues, ASHRM, 2000; Confidentiality of Medical Records, Lorman Education Services, 1998-1999; The Impact of Electronic Records on Medical Negligence Issues, Wisconsin Society of Health Care Risk Managers Annual Convention, 1999; Return to Work Issues in Illinois, Lorman Continuing Legal Education Programs, 1998-1999; Medical Evidence: Law and Technique, Illinois Insurance and Tort Law Update, Professional Education Systems, Inc., 1998; Litigation: Plaintiff vs. Defense Practice, Valparaiso University School of Law, Valparaiso, Indiana, 1998; Dental Malpractice: Learning the Rules of the Road, Various Dental Societies in Illinois and Wisconsin, 1998—; The Impact of Electronic Records in Medical Negligence Litigation, Lorman Educational Seminars, 1999—; Various Health Care Risk Management Seminars to Physicians, Residents, Nurses, Catholic Health Partners and Affiliated Groups, 1995—. *Member:* Chicago and Illinois State Bar Associations; Defense Research Institute; Illinois Association of Defense Trial Counsel (Board of Directors); American Society of Healthcare Risk Managers; Chicagoland Healthcare Risk Management Society; Illinois Association of Healthcare Attorneys. ***PRACTICE AREAS:*** Medical Malpractice; Professional Liability Law; Civil Litigation. ***Email:*** aoldenburg@illinois-law.com

MARC J. CAIRO, admitted to bar, 1995, Illinois and U.S. District Court, Northern District of Illinois. *Education:* University of Illinois (B.A., 1992); DePaul University College of Law (J.D., 1995). Author: Five Things Every Lawyer Should Know About Workers' Compensation Practice," CBA Record, Volume 18, Number 3, April 2004; "Can You Speak with the Treating Doctor?" MES Times, Volume 1, Issue 1, June 1, 2001. Co-Author: Chapter 3, "Employer/Employee Relationship," Workers Compensation Notebook, Illinois Trial Lawyers Association, 1997. Member, Chicagoland Chamber of Commerce. *Member:* Chicago Bar Association (Chair, Workers' Compensation Section, 2004-2005; Legislative Liaison, Workers' Compensation Section, 2003-2005); Illinois Trial Lawyers Association; Workers' Compensation Claims Association. ***PRACTICE AREAS:*** Workers Compensation; Employment Law. ***Email:*** mcairo@illinois-law.com

---

MELVIN G. HOBBS, admitted to bar, 1999, Illinois and U.S. District Court, Northern District of Illinois. *Education:* Southern College (A.S., 1984; B.S.N., 1988); University of Tennessee (M.S.N., 1992); DePaul University (J.D., 1999). Registered Professional Nurse 1984—. Lecturer and Presenter: East Tennessee Chapter of Critical Care Nurses, "Ballistics: Implications in the Trauma Patient." Co-presenter: Lorman Education Services "The Legalities of Utilizing and Maintaining Computerized Medical Records in Illinois," December 2000. Publications: Co-author, "The Pruning of Petrillo." IDC Quarterly, Second Quarter 2000; "A Patient's Guide to Congestive Heart Failure," St. Mary's of Nazareth Hospital Patient Education Booklet (1997); "A Patient's Guide to Pneumonia," St. Mary's of Nazareth Patient Education Booklet (1997). *Member:* Chicago, Illinois State and American Bar Associations; American Association of Nurse Attorneys; Illinois Association of Defense Trial Counsel; Defense Research Institute. ***PRACTICE AREAS:*** Medical Malpractice; General Liability; Professional Licensure Defense. ***Email:*** mhobbs@illinois-law.com

LISA A. TRULL, admitted to bar, 1994, Illinois. *Education:* Bryn Mawr College (A.B., 1978); Chicago-Kent College of Law (J.D., 1994). Phi Alpha Delta. Member, Illinois State Dental Society Dental Hygiene.*Member:* Chicago, Illinois State and American Bar Associations. ***PRACTICE AREAS:*** Dental Malpractice Defense; Medical Malpractice Defense. ***Email:*** ltrull@illinois-law.com

ADNAN A. ARAIN, admitted to bar, 2000, Illinois. *Education:* University of Chicago (B.A., 1995, with honors); Northwestern University (J.D., 2000). Recipient of 1996 Fulbright Scholarship. ***LANGUAGES:*** Spanish, Arabic. ***PRACTICE AREAS:*** Medical Malpractice Defense; General Liability Defense. ***Email:*** aarain@illinois-law.com

DANIEL G. ALHOLM, admitted to bar, 2003, Illinois. *Education:* Southern Methodist University (B.A., 1999); Loyola University (J.D., 2003). ***PRACTICE AREAS:*** Professional Liability Defense. ***Email:*** dalholm@illinois-law.com

MARK DINOS, admitted to bar, 2002, Illinois. *Education:* Benedictine University, Lisle, Illinois (B.A., Communications, 1999); John Marshall Law School, Chicago (J.D., 2002). *Member:* Chicago and Illinois State Bar Associations; Illinois Trial Lawyers Association. ***LANGUAGES:*** Greek. ***PRACTICE AREAS:*** Workers Compensation. ***Email:*** mdinos@illinois-law.com

MARY HASSE, admitted to bar, 2000, Illinois. *Education:* Catholic University of America (B.S.N., 1976); Rush University (M.S., 1981); Chicago-Kent College of Law (J.D., 1999). *Member:* Chicago and Illinois State Bar Associations; Chicago Association of Nurse Attorneys. ***PRACTICE AREAS:*** Medical Malpractice Insurance Defense. ***Email:*** mhasse@illinois-law.com

TAMMERA E. BANASEK, admitted to bar, 1993, Illinois and U.S. District Court, Northern District of Illinois. *Education:* Northern Illinois University (B.S., 1985); John Marshall Law School (J.D., cum laude, 1993). *Member:* Illinois State Bar Association. ***PRACTICE AREAS:*** Insurance Defense; Litigation. ***Email:*** tbanasek@illinois-law.com

LAWRENCE R. STOLBERG, born Chicago, Illinois, September 12, 1963; admitted to bar, 1988, Illinois. *Education:* University of Illinois (B.A., 1985); Chicago Kent College of Law, Illinois Institute of Technology (J.D., 1988). ***Email:*** lstolberg@illinois-law.com

SUSAN ANN WAGENER, born Iowa City, Iowa, June 29, 1959; admitted to bar, 1985, Wisconsin and Illinois. *Education:* University of Wisconsin-Madison (B.S., Nursing, 1982) Marquette University (J.D., 1985). Registered Nurse, Wisconsin, 1982. *Member:* State Bar of Wisconsin; Illinois State Bar Association. ***PRACTICE AREAS:*** Personal Injury; Medical Malpractice; General Liability. ***Email:*** swagener@illinois-law.com

OF COUNSEL

PATRICIA M. NOONAN, admitted to bar, 1988, Illinois; 1989, U.S. District Court, Northern District of Illinois. *Education:* Chicago State University (B.A. 1985); University of Illinois (J.D., 1988). Member, 1986-1988 and Administrative Editor; 1987-1988, University of Illinois Law Review. Author: "State Personal Jurisdictional Requirements and the Non aggregation Rule in Class Actions," University of Illinois Law Review, 1988; "The Case Within the Case: A Political Solution to Speculative Damage Claims," 6 IDC Quarterly 3 (1996); "Limits to the Statutory Bar on Punitive Damages in Legal Malpractice Actions," 6 IDC Quarterly 3 (1996). Co-Author, "Long-Arm Jurisdiction in Legal Malpractice," DRI, April 1997. *Member:* Illinois State Bar Association. ***PRACTICE AREAS:*** Medical Malpractice; Legal Malpractice; Appellate Practice; Insurance Coverage Defense. ***Email:*** pnoonan@illinois-law.com

(This Listing Continued)

ALTER AND WEISS

19 SOUTH LASALLE STREET, SUITE 1650
CHICAGO, ILLINOIS 60603
Telephone: 312-337-2100
Fax: 312-236-1365
Email: alterandweiss@yahoo.com
URL: http://www.alterandweiss.com

Patent, Trademark, Copyright, Unfair Competition and Related Antitrust Practice.

IRWIN C. ALTER, born Chicago, Illinois, June 19, 1934; admitted to bar, 1958, Illinois; 1959, U.S. Court of Appeals, 5th, 7th and 9th Circuits; 1976, U.S. Supreme Court; 1982, U.S. Court of Appeals for the Federal Circuit; 1983, U.S. District Court, Northern District of Illinois, Trial Bar; registered to practice before U.S. Patent and Trademark Office. *Education:* University of Illinois (B.S.M.E., 1955); University of Illinois and DePaul University (J.D., 1958). Winner, Second Place, Moot Court Competition at De Paul University, 1957. Named 2004 and 2005 Leading Illinois Lawyer by the Leading Lawyers Network. Author: "The Franchise Business and the Law," Vol. 21, Decalogue Journal 9, January, 1972—; "Crazy Legs Hirsch Runs Away With The Rights to His Name," National Law Journal, March 24, 1980. Panelist on topic of "Recent Developments in Trademark Law," Annual Trademark and Tradesecret Institute of Illinois, Institute of Continuing Legal Education, 1981—. Member, American Arbitration Association Chicago Advisory Council, 1981-1983; 1985. *Member:* Chicago Bar Association (Panelist, The First Amendment and Intellectual Property Rights, 1981); Bar Association of the Seventh Federal Circuit (Member: Committee on Study for Revision of Federal Rules on Diversity, 1978-1979; Speaker, 1979 Judicial Conference, Revision of Federal Rules of Civil Procedure; Ad Hoc Committee on High Cost of Litigation, 1978-1979); American Bar Association (Member, Sections on: Antitrust Law; Patent, Trademark and Copyright Law; Litigation Law; Committee on Franchising, 1978; Panelist, Annual Meeting, Trial Demonstration involving Intentional Interference with Existing Contract and Prospective Advantage, Litigation Section, 1980; Chairman, Program on Trial Demonstration, "Obtaining Injunctive Relief in Unfair Competition Cases," Annual Meeting Litigation Section, 1981); American Intellectual Property Law Association; Patent Law Association of Chicago (Chairman: Trade Secrets Committee, 1974—; Law Office Economics, 1975-1976). **Email:** alterandweiss@yahoo.com

OF COUNSEL

PHILLIP A. WEISS, born Chicago, Illinois, January 22, 1927; admitted to bar, 1960, Illinois. *Education:* Armour Institute of Technology (B.S.E.E.); Chicago-Kent College of Law (J.D.). retired.

NORA A. PREECE, born Chicago, Illinois, October 11, 1970; admitted to bar, 2002, Illinois; 2003, U.S. District Court, Northern District of Illinois. *Education:* University of Illinois, Chicago (B.A., English, 1992); Chicago-Kent College of Law, Illinois Institute of Technology (J.D., 2002; Certificate in Intellectual Property Law). *Member:* American Bar Association. **PRACTICE AREAS:** Trademarks; Unfair Competition; Copyrights; Internet Law; Trade Secrets. **Email:** np@norapreece.com

AMBROSE & CUSHING, P.C.

221 NORTH LASALLE STREET, SUITE 1748
CHICAGO, ILLINOIS 60601
Telephone: 312-726-1470
Fax: 312-726-3505
Email: bcolbert@ambrosecushing.com
URL: http://www.ambrosecushinglaw.com

Personal Injury, Medical Malpractice, Products Liability, Workers Compensation, Medical Negligence, Premises Liability, Automobile Accidents and Injuries, Slip and Fall, Spinal Injury, Wrongful Death, Construction Accidents and Commercial Litigation, Real Estate Law.

JOHN C. AMBROSE, born Chicago, Illinois, March 25, 1935; admitted to bar, 1959, Illinois and U.S. District Court, Northern District of Illinois. *Education:* Loyola University (B.S., 1956; J.D., 1959). *Member:* Illinois State Bar Association; American Trial Lawyers Association; Illinois Trial Lawyers Association. **PRACTICE AREAS:** Personal Injury; Medical Malpractice; Products Liability; Workers Compensation; Medical Negligence; Premises Liability; Automobile Accidents and Injuries; Slip and Fall; Spinal Injury; Wrongful Death; Construction Accidents; Commercial Litigation. **Email:** JAmbrose@ambrosecushing.com

F. JOHN CUSHING, born Chicago, Illinois, March 3, 1951; admitted to bar, 1976, Illinois; 1977, U.S. Court of Appeals, Fifth Circuit and U.S. District Court, Northern District of Illinois; 1979, U.S. Court of Appeals, Seventh Circuit; 1996, U.S. District Court, Central District of Illinois. *Education:* Loyola University (B.A., 1973; J.D., 1976). *Member:* Illinois State and Chicago Bar Associations; Illinois Trial Lawyers Association. **PRACTICE AREAS:** Personal Injury; Medical Malpractice; Products Liability; Workers Compensation; Medical Negligence; Premises Liability; Automobile Accidents and Injuries; Slip and Fall; Spinal Injury; Wrongful Death; Construction Accidents; Commercial Litigation. **Email:** bcolbert@ambrosecushing.com

---

THOMAS M. CUSHING, born Evanston, Illinois, November 3, 1961; admitted to bar, 1988, Illinois and U.S. District Court, Northern District of Illinois; 1991, U.S. Court of Appeals, Seventh Circuit. *Education:* University of Notre Dame (B.A., with honors, 1983); Loyola University (J.D., 1988). Faculty, Loyola Law School, 1989-1993, 2001-2003. *Member:* Chicago and Illinois State Bar Associations; Illinois Trial Lawyers Association; The Association of Trial Lawyers of America; Society of Trial Lawyers. **PRACTICE AREAS:** Personal Injury (65%); Medical Negligence (30%); Commercial Litigation (5%). **Email:** TCushing@ambrosecushing.com

JOSEPH F. VITU, JR., born Sommerville, New Jersey, January 2, 1971; admitted to bar, 1997, Illinois and U.S. District Court, Northern District of Illinois; U.S. Court of Appeals, Seventh Circuit. *Education:* University of Illinois (B.A., 1993); Creighton University (J.D., 1996). Lambda Pi Eta; Lambda Sigma; Phi Delta Phi (Magister; Member of Counsel, 2003—); Order of Omega. Arbitrator, Cook County Circuit Courts, 2002—. *Member:* Chicago, American and Federal Trial Bar Associations; Association of Trial Lawyers of America; Illinois Trial Lawyers of America (Member, Civil Practice Committee, 2003—). **PRACTICE AREAS:** Premises Liability; Construction; Personal Injury; Workers Compensation; Real Estate. **Email:** JVitu@abmrosecushing.com

MICHAEL M. CUSHING, born Evanston, Illinois, March 22, 1978; admitted to bar, 2003, Illinois and U.S. District Court, Northern District of Illinois. *Education:* University of Dayton (B.A., 2000); Loyola University, Chicago (J.D., 2003). *Member:* Chicago and American Bar Associations; Illinois Trial Lawyers Association; American Trial Lawyers Association. **PRACTICE AREAS:** Personal Injury; Medical Malpractice; Products Liability; Workers Compensation; Medical Negligence; Premises Liability; Automobile Accidents and Injuries; Slip and Fall; Spinal Injury; Wrongful Death; Construction Accidents; Commercial Litigation. **Email:** MCushing@ambrosecushing.com

JAMES J. RYAN, born Chicago, Illinois, December 25, 1956; admitted to bar, 1984, Illinois, U.S. District Court, Northern District of Illinois and U.S. Court of Appeals, Seventh Circuit. *Education:* Loyola University of Rome; Illinois Benedictine College; University of Illinois (B.A., 1979); John Marshall Law School (J.D., 1984). *Member:* American Trial Lawyers Association (Member, Insurance and Nursing Home Committees, 2005—). **PRACTICE AREAS:** Personal Injury; Medical Malpractice; Products Liability; Workers Compensation; Medical Negligence; Premises Liability; Automobile Accidents and Injuries; Slip and Fall; Spinal Injury; Wrongful Death; Construction Accidents; Commercial Litigation. **Email:** JRyan@ambrosecushing.com

MARILYN J. MARTIN, born Yuma, Arizona, July 9, 1945; admitted to bar, 1977, California; 1978, Illinois. *Education:* University of California (B.A., 1974); Loyola Marymount University (J.D., 1977). **PRACTICE AREAS:** Personal Injury; Medical Malpractice; Products Liability; Workers Compensation; Medical Negligence; Premises Liability; Automobile Accidents and Injuries; Slip and Fall; Spinal Injury; Wrongful Death; Construction Accidents; Commercial Litigation. **Email:** MMartin@ambrosecushing.com

AMIN LAW

217 NORTH JEFFERSON STREET, 5TH FLOOR
CHICAGO, ILLINOIS 60661
Telephone: 312-466-1033; 312-286-3925
Fax: 312-466-0808
URL: http://www.amin-law.com

Administrative Law, Food and Drug Administration, Federal Trade Commission, US Customs, Drug Enforcement Agency, USDA and related Federal and State Attorney General Regulatory Compliance and Litigation matters; Food, Beverage, Drug, Pharmaceutical, Cosmetic, Dietary Supplement, Medical Device, Animal Feed and Biotechnology Law; Restaurant, Liquor and Wine Law, Organic and Proposition 65 Law; Advertising, Marketing and Direct Seller Law, Healthcare Law, Intellectual Property, Patent, Trademark, Copyright, Trade Secret, Licensing, Internet, Entertainment and Unfair Competition Law; Telemedicine and Internet Pharmacy Law; Compounding Pharmacy Law; Practice of Medicine Law; Practice of Pharmacy Law; Bioterrorism Act Law; Manufacturer and Distributor Agreements; Corporate Law and Contracts and Business Litigation.

RAKESH M. AMIN, born Kalamazoo, Michigan, June 23, 1967; admitted to bar, 1995, Illinois and U.S. District Court, Northern District of Illinois; 2003, U.S. Court of Appeals, Seventh Circuit; U.S. Supreme Court. *Education:* Ferris State University (B.S., Pharmacy, 1991); John Marshall Law School (J.D., 1995); DePaul University College of Law (LL.M., 1998). Editor, DePaul Journal of Health Care Law. Member, Moot Court Council. Registered Pharmacist, Illinois, 1991-2005. Adjunct Professor, Food and Drug Law, DePaul University College of Law. Vice-President, Asian-Pacific American Law Students Association, 1993-1994. Member, National Nutritional Foods Association. *Member:* Chicago Bar Association (Member, Food, Drug and Consumer Product Regulation Committee); International Trademark Association; Food and Drug Law Institute; National Nutritional Foods Association; American Botanical Council; National Association of Boards of Pharmacy; American Pharmacists Association; Consultants Association for the Natural Products Industry. **PRACTICE AREAS:** Regulatory Law; Intellectual Property; Business Litigation; Business Transactions. **Email:** Rakesh@amin-law.com

ASSOCIATES

CHRISTINA KOLLINIATIS, born Oak Lawn, Illinois, July 29, 1979; admitted to bar, 2004, Illinois and U.S. District Court, Northern, Central and Southern Districts of Illinois. *Education:* University of Illinois (B.S., 2001); California Western School of Law (J.D., 2004). *Member:* Chicago, Illinois State and American Bar Associations; Hispanic Bar Association; Women's Bar Association. **PRACTICE AREAS:** Regulatory Law; Intellectual Property; Business Litigation. **Email:** Christina@amin-law.com

LAURA A. CHUBB, born Indianapolis, Indiana, December 29, 1977; admitted to bar, 2003, Illinois and U.S. District Court, Northern District of Illinois; registered to practice before U.S. Patent and Trademark Office. *Education:* Vanderbilt University (B.A., 2000); Indiana University School of Law - Indianapolis (J.D., 2003). *Member:* Chicago, Illinois State and American Bar Associations. **PRACTICE AREAS:** Regulatory Law; Intellectual Property; Business Litigation. **Email:** Laura@amin-law.com

LAW OFFICES OF MARINA E. AMMENDOLA, P.C.

33 NORTH LASALLE STREET, SUITE 900
CHICAGO, ILLINOIS 60602
Telephone: 312-220-9100
Fax: 312-220-9110
URL: http://www.lawyers.com/marinaammendola

Plaintiffs Personal Injury Law, Medical Malpractice Law.

(This Listing Continued)

LAW OFFICES OF MARINA E. AMMENDOLA, P.C., Chicago—Continued

MARINA E. AMMENDOLA, born Chicago, Illinois, January 27, 1960; admitted to bar, 1989, Illinois and U.S. District Court, Northern District of Illinois. *Education:* Rosary College (B.A., cum laude, 1982); IIT, Chicago Kent College of Law (J.D., with honors, 1989); National Institute of Trial Advocacy, 1991. Psi Chi; Phi Alpha Theta; Kappa Gamma Pi. Member, Theotokeion Honor Society. Recipient, Justinian Society Scholarship, 1988-1989. Recipient: American Jurisprudence Award in Business Associations, 1988; Chicago-Kent Class Awards, Tort Theory, 1989 and Medical Legal Problems, 1988. *Member:* Chicago (Mentor, The Pathways Mentoring Program, 1991-1992), and Illinois State Bar Associations; Illinois Trial Lawyers Association; Women's Bar Association; Association of Trial Lawyers of America. ***PRACTICE AREAS:*** Plaintiffs Personal Injury Law; Medical Malpractice Law.

ALAN O. AMOS & ASSOCIATES, P.C.

Established in 1982

SUITE 3150
180 NORTH LASALLE STREET
CHICAGO, ILLINOIS 60601
Telephone: 312-419-1300
Telecopier: 312-419-0302

Real Estate Law and Development, Probate and Estate Litigation.

ALAN O. AMOS, born Chicago, Illinois, December 1, 1937; admitted to bar, 1963, Illinois; 1965, U.S. Court of Appeals, Seventh Circuit and U.S. District Court, Northern District of Illinois including Trial Bar; 1972, Florida and U.S Tax Court; 1973, U.S. Supreme Court. *Education:* DePaul University (B.A., 1960; J.D., 1963). Phi Alpha Delta; Blue Key. Member, Board of Editors, De Paul Law Review, 1962-1963. *Member:* Chicago and Illinois State Bar Associations; The Florida Bar. ***REPORTED CASES:*** Kreiss v. Salsitz, 198 Ill. 2d 1, Ill. Sup. 2001; Royal Imperial vs. Blumburg, 608 NE 2d 178 Ill. App. 1992; Balla vs. Gambro 584 NE 2d 104 Ill. Sup. 1991; Royal Elm vs. Northern Ill. Gas 526 NE 2 376 Ill. App. 1988; RNR Realty vs. Burlington Coat Factory 522 NE 2 679 Ill. App. 1988. ***TRANSACTIONS:*** Conversion and sale of units of The State Parkway Condominium, 1993 (developer's counsel); Conversion and sale of units of 33 East Cedar Condominium, 1996 (developer's counsel); Conversion and sale of units of River Bank Lofts Condominium, 1995 (developer's counsel); Conversion and Sale of Units of River Plaza Condominium, Conversion and sale of units of Columbus on the Park Condominiums, 1999 (developer's counsel). Acquisition and lease of numerous nursing home facilities on behalf of affiliates of Zevco Enterprises, Inc. and Karell Capital Ventures, 1993-2000 (purchaser's counsel).

OF COUNSEL

THOMAS H. BOERSCHINGER, born Evanston, Illinois, November 9, 1937; admitted to bar, 1963, Illinois; 1968, U.S. District Court, Northern District of Illinois, 1970, U.S. Supreme Court; 1971, U.S. Court of Claims. *Education:* DePaul University (LL.B.). Member, Board of Editors, Law Review. Instructor, Antitrust Law, Loyola University of Chicago School of Law, 1978-1981. Author: "Dental Ethics," Chapter 10, Lea & Febiger Phil, 1993, edited by Bruce Weinstein; "Charging Patients Interest, The Federal Truth in Lending Act Can Bite You," American Dental Association, 1993. ***REPORTED CASES:*** U.S. vs Alston, 1992 Lexus 217065, -F.2d- (9th Cir. 1992); Stapleton vs. $2,438,110, 454 F.2d 1210 (4th Cir. 1971), cert. den. 409 U.S. 894; U.S. vs. Harris Trust & Savings Bank, 390 F.2d 285 (7th Cir. 1968).

REPRESENTATIVE CLIENTS: Zevco Enterprises, Inc.; Karell Capital Ventures; Enterprise Development Co.; Atlantis Properties Ltd.; MCZ Development Corp.; Intergroup Associates, Inc.
REFERENCE: Bank Leumi USA.

ANDERSON & ASSOCIATES, P.C.

166 W. WASHINGTON STREET, SUITE 640
CHICAGO, ILLINOIS 60602
Telephone: 312-236-5599

Wheaton Office: 400 S. County Farm Road, Suite 120, 60187. Telephone: 630-653-9400. Fax: 630-653-9450.
Schaumburg Office: 1701 East Woodfield Road, Suite 1050. Telephone: 847-995-9999. Fax: 847-995-0117.

Family Law, Bankruptcy, Real Estate Litigation and Transactions, Estate Planning and Probate.

JONATHAN G. ANDERSON, born Joliet, Illinois, June 16, 1953; admitted to bar, 1981, Florida, Illinois and U.S. District Court, Northern District of Illinois. *Education:* University of Wisconsin-Madison (B.A., 1975); University of Florida (J.D., 1980). *Member:* Du Puge County Bar Association (Family Law Section); Northwest Suburban Bar Association (Family Law Section). ***PRACTICE AREAS:*** Family Law; Bankruptcy; Real Estate Litigation; Estate Planning; Probate. ***Email:*** andrsnlaw@aol.com

ROBIN M. ZANDRI, born New York, N.Y., August 10, 1956; admitted to bar, 1997, Illinois; 2001, U.S. District Court, Northern District of Illinois. *Education:* University of Illinois at Chicago (B.S., 1993); Northern Illinois University (J.D., 1997). *Member:* Northwest Suburban Bar Association. ***PRACTICE AREAS:*** Family Law; Bankruptcy. ***Email:*** andrsnlaw@aol.com

ANDREA C. LAWRENCE, born Oak Lawn, Illinois, February 13, 1972; admitted to bar, 1997, Illinois and U.S. District Court, Northern District of Illinois. *Education:* Northern Illinois University (B.A., 1994); DePaul University (J.D., 1997). *Member:* Du Page County Bar Association. ***PRACTICE AREAS:*** Family Law; Bankruptcy; Real Estate. ***Email:*** andrsnlaw@aol.com

(This Listing Continued)

CHRISTOPHER J. MAURER, born Park Ridge, Illinois, August 5, 1972; admitted to bar, 1997, Illinois. *Education:* University of Illinois at Urbana-Champaign (B.S., 1994); Loyola University, Chicago (J.D., 1997). ***PRACTICE AREAS:*** Family Law; Plaintiffs Personal Injury. ***Email:*** andrsnlaw@aol.com

MIA DO, born Seoul, South Korea; admitted to bar, 2004, Illinois. *Education:* University of Illinois (B.A., 1999); University of Chicago (M.M., 2001); Chicago-Kent College of Law (J.D., 2004). *Member:* Christian Legal Society; Asian Pacific American Law Student Association. ***LANGUAGES:*** Korean. ***PRACTICE AREAS:*** Family Law; Immigration. ***Email:*** andrsnlaw@aol.com

ANDERSON & BOBACK

20 NORTH CLARK STREET, SUITE 1400
CHICAGO, ILLINOIS 60602
Telephone: 312-920-0870
Email: lawyers@illinoislawforyou.com
URL: http://www.illinoislawforyou.com

Child Custody, Adoption, Divorce, Domestic Violence and Paternity. Criminal Defense.

KIMBERLY J. ANDERSON, born Hammond, Indiana, January 25, 1964; admitted to bar, 1998, Illinois; 2002, U.S. Supreme Court. *Education:* Elmhurst College (B.S., Business, 1995); John Marshall Law School (J.D., with honors, 1998). Child Representative, 2003—. Former Assistant State Attorney, Cook County. *Member:* Chicago (Member, Adoption and Family Law Divisions; Chair, Matrimonial Subcommittee, Judiciary and the Courts, 2002-2004), Illinois State (Member: Committee on Membership and the Bar, 2000—; Committee on Women and The Law, 2000—; Standing Committee on Judicial Evaluations, Cook County, 2002—; Assembly Member, 2002—) and American (Co-Chair, Children and the Law, 2000-2001) Bar Associations; National Association of Counsel for Children. ***PRACTICE AREAS:*** Child Custody; Adoption; Divorce; Domestic Violence; Paternity; Criminal Defense.

JANICE L. BOBACK, born Ottawa, Illinois, November 21, 1961; admitted to bar, 1998, Illinois. *Education:* University of Illinois (B.S., Finance, 1994); John Marshall Law School (J.D., 1998). Coach, The John Marshall Law School, Civil Rights Litigation, St. John's School of Law, Queens, New York, 2003. Child Representative, 2001—. *Member:* Chicago, Illinois State and American Bar Associations; American Trial Lawyers Associations. ***PRACTICE AREAS:*** Domestic Relations.

ANDERSON KILL & OLICK

Established in 1998

230 WEST MONROE STREET, SUITE 2540
CHICAGO, ILLINOIS 60606
Telephone: 312-201-9516
Fax: 312-201-8548; 312-201-9553
Email: AKO@andersonkill.com
URL: http://www.andersonkill.com

New York, N.Y. Office: Anderson Kill & Olick, P.C., 1251 Avenue of the Americas. Telephone: 212-278-1000. Fax: 212-278-1733.
Washington, D.C. Office: Anderson Kill & Olick, L.L.P., 2100 M Street, N.W. Telephone: 202-218-0040. Fax: 202-218-0055.
Newark, New Jersey Office: Anderson Kill & Olick, P.C. One Gateway Center, Suite 901. Telephone: 973-642-5858. Fax: 973-621-6361.
Philadelphia, Pennsylvania Office: Anderson Kill & Olick, P.C., 1600 Market Street. Telephone: 215-568-4202. Fax: 215-568-4573.
Greenwich, Connecticut Office: Anderson Kill & Olick, P.C., Two Sound View Drive, Suite 100. Telephone: 202-622-7668. Fax: 202-622-0321.

Litigation, Insurance Coverage (Exclusively for Policyholders), Environmental Law, Trial and Appellate.

JAMES M. DAVIS, born Paige, Arizona; admitted to bar, 1995, Illinois; 2002, Colorado and Washington. *Education:* University of Washington (B.A., 1991); Chicago-Kent College of Law, Illinois Institute of Technology (J.D., 1995). *Member:* Chicago, Illinois State, Washington State and American (Co-Chair, Insurance Coverage Subcommittee on Emerging Issues, 2003-2005) Bar Associations. [Captain, U.S. Army Reserves, Corp of Engineers, 1991-1999]. ***PRACTICE AREAS:*** Insurance Recovery; Commercial Litigation. ***Email:*** jdavis@andersonkill.com

PAUL R. WALKER-BRIGHT, born San Diego, California; admitted to bar, 1994, Illinois. *Education:* University of Chicago (B.A., 1990); Chicago-Kent College of Law, Illinois Institute of Technology (J.D., 1994). *Member:* American Bar Association. ***PRACTICE AREAS:*** Insurance Coverage; Litigation; Bankruptcy; Appellate. ***Email:*** pwalkerbright@andersonkill.com

(For complete biographical data on New York, New York personnel, Washington, D.C. personnel, Philadelphia, Pennsylvania personnel, and Newark, New Jersey personnel, see Professional Biographies at their respective offices)

PETER ANDJELKOVICH, & ASSOCIATES

Established in 1980

39 SOUTH LA SALLE STREET, SUITE 200
CHICAGO, ILLINOIS 60603
Telephone: 312-782-8345
Fax: 312-782-6517
Email: PAlaw@sbcglobal.net
URL: http://www.lawyers.com/pandjelkovich

Personal Injury, Lottery Law, Commercial Litigation, Employment Litigation Defense, Executive Compensation and Severance, Wrongful Termination, ERISA, Civil Rights, Shareholder and Employee Disputes, Union/Labor Organizing Issues, Corporate Bankruptcy Modification Bargaining Agreements, White Collar Criminal Defense.

FIRM PROFILE: Over the last decade, Peter Andjelkovich & Associates has routinely appeared in federal and state courts, federal, state, and local civil rights administrative tribunals and various arbitration proceedings. The firm has successfully prosecuted and defended several lawsuits which received prominent national and local media attention.

PETER ANDJELKOVICH, born 1946; admitted to bar, 1980, Illinois; U.S. District Court, Eastern and Northern Districts of Illinois including Trial Bar; U.S. Supreme Court; U.S. Court of International Trade; U.S. Court of Appeals, 7th Circuit. *Education:* University of Illinois (B.S., Ec., 1969); John Marshall Law School (J.D., 1980). *Member:* Chicago, DuPage County, Lake County and Illinois State Bar Associations. ***LANGUAGES:*** German. ***PRACTICE AREAS:*** Employment Discrimination Law; Labor Law; Personal Injury Law; Corporate Law; Lottery Law; White Collar Criminal Defense.

ASSOCIATE

BRADLEY J. WARTMAN, born Hammond, Indiana, November 5, 1960; admitted to bar, 1987, Illinois; 1996, Indiana and U.S. District Court, Northern District of Illinois including Trial Bar; 1989, U.S. Tax Court; 1988, U.S. Court of International Trade; U.S. Court of Appeals, 7th Circuit. *Education:* Chicago State University (B.S.B.A., 1983); John Marshall Law School (J.D. 1987). *Member:* Chicago Bar Association (Member, Labor and Employment Committee). ***PRACTICE AREAS:*** Labor and Employment; Corporate Law; Employee Benefits; Personal Injury; Tax. ***Email:*** PAlaw@sbcglobal.net

ANESI, OZMON, RODIN, NOVAK & KOHEN, LTD.

161 NORTH CLARK STREET, 21ST FLOOR
CHICAGO, ILLINOIS 60601
Telephone: 312-372-3822
Fax: 312-372-3833
URL: http://www.anesilaw.com

Civil Trial and Appellate Practice. Workers Compensation and Personal Injury Law. General Practice.

NAT P. OZMON, born Davenport, Iowa, 1925; admitted to bar, 1954, Illinois; 1956, U.S. District Court, Northern District of Illinois; 1964, U.S. Court of Appeals, 7th Circuit; 1973, U.S. Supreme Court. *Education:* New York University; Northwestern University (J.D., 1954). Order of the Coif. Fellow, Roscoe Pound Foundation, 1969—. Recipient: Leonard M. Ring Lifetime Achievement Award, Illinois Trial Lawyers Association, 1994; American ORT Jurisprudence Achievement Award, 1998. Adjunct Professor, Loyola University of Chicago, 1976-1983. Member, Advisory Council, Loyola University School of Law, 1984—. American Board of Professional Liability Attorneys. Advocate, 1977—, Chapter Secretary, 1988, American Board of Trial Advocates. Founder: Trial Lawyers for Public Justice, 1983; Institute for Injury Reduction, 1988. Associate Director, Illinois College of Advocacy, 1984-1987. Member, Board of Directors, Illinois Institute for Continuing Education. Member, Visiting Committee, 1993—, Member, Dean's Advisory Committee, 1997—, Northwestern University School of Law. *Member:* Illinois Trial Lawyers Association (President, 1969-1970); The Association of Trial Lawyers of America (Member, Board of Governors, 1973-1975; Vice Chairman, Education Department, 1986-1987). ***PRACTICE AREAS:*** Personal Injury; Civil Torts.

CURT N. RODIN, born Chicago, Illinois, June 15, 1950; admitted to bar, 1975, Illinois and U.S. District Court, Northern District of Illinois; 1979, U.S. Court of Appeals, 7th Circuit and U.S. Supreme Court. *Education:* University of Illinois (B.A., 1972); Loyola University (J.D., 1975). Recipient, Trial Advocacy Award, Loyola University. Finalist, Trial Lawyer of the Year (1998) - Trial Lawyers For Public Justice. Adjunct Professor of Law, Loyola University of Chicago, 1999—. Chairman, Illinois Supreme Court Committee on Jury Instructions. *Member:* Chicago, Illinois State and American Bar Associations; Illinois Trial Lawyers Association (President, 1994-1995); The Association of Trial Lawyers of America; American Board of Trial Advocates; Society of Trial Lawyers - Illinois (President). (Certified as a Civil Trial Advocate by the National Board of Trial Advocacy, 1983, Re-Certified, 1988, 1993, 1998). ***PRACTICE AREAS:*** Personal Injury; Civil Torts.

MARK NOVAK, born Buffalo, New York, January 28, 1952; admitted to bar, 1977, Illinois and U.S. District Court, Northern District of Illinois; 1978, U.S. Court of Appeals, 7th Circuit. *Education:* University of Rochester (B.A., 1974); Loyola University (J.D., 1977). Trial Advocacy Award, Loyola University. *Member:* Chicago, Illinois State and American Bar Associations; Illinois Trial Lawyers Association; The Association of Trial Lawyers of America. ***PRACTICE AREAS:*** Personal Injury; Civil Torts Litigation.

BRUCE M. KOHEN, born Chicago, Illinois, November 17, 1953; admitted to bar, 1979, Illinois and U.S. District Court, Northern District of Illinois; 1980, U.S. Court of Appeals, Seventh Circuit; 1983, U.S. Supreme Court. *Education:* University of Illinois (B.S., in Accountancy, 1975); Illinois Institute of Technology, Chicago-Kent College of Law (J.D., 1979). Listed in: Trial Lawyer of the Year Finalist - Trial Lawyers For Public Justice, 1998; Best Lawyers in America, 2000—Leading Illinois Attorneys, 1996—Strathmores Who's Who, 1998— Author: "The Structural Work Act Proper Parties," IICLE, 1993; "Construction Negligence: Out From the Shadow of the Illinois Structural Work Act," Illinois Bar Journal, 1999; "Construction Negligence," ITLA Trial Journal, 2000. *Member:* Chicago, Illinois State (Elected Assemblyman, 1994-2000) and American Bar Associations; Illinois Trial Lawyers Association (Board of Managers, 1992—; Secretary, Treasurer, Chairman, Legislative Committee, 1993— Executive Committee, 1994—); The Association of Trial Lawyers of America (State Delegate, 1993-1996); The Decalogue Society of Lawyers. ***PRACTICE AREAS:*** Personal Injury; Civil Torts; Wrongful Death; Medical Malpractice; Products Liability; Construction Injuries. ***Email:*** bkohen@anesilaw.com

DOUGLAS A. COLBY, born Chicago, Illinois, July 9, 1957; admitted to bar, 1982, Illinois. *Education:* Northern Illinois University (B.S., cum laude, 1979); John Marshall Law School (J.D., 1982). *Member:* Chicago, Illinois State and American Bar Associations; Illinois Trial Lawyers Association; The Association of Trial Lawyers of America; Workmens Compensation Lawyers Association. ***PRACTICE AREAS:*** Worker's Compensation; Social Security.

MARC A. TAXMAN, born Chicago, Illinois, December 28, 1962; admitted to bar, 1988, Illinois; 1989, Minnesota and U.S. District Court, Northern District of Illinois. *Education:* University of Illinois (B.S., 1985); IIT/Chicago-Kent College of Law (J.D., 1988). Co-Author: "Illinois Structural Work Act Practice Handbook, Chap. 1, Overview of Statute and Case Law," 11CLE, 1992. *Member:* Chicago, Illinois State and American Bar Associations; Illinois Trial Lawyers Association. ***PRACTICE AREAS:*** Personal Injury; Civil Torts.

DANIEL V. O'CONNOR, born Chicago, Illinois, March 22, 1967; admitted to bar, 1992, Illinois. *Education:* Loyola University (B.S., 1989; J.D., 1992). *Member:* Chicago, Illinois State and American Bar Associations; Illinois Trial Lawyers Associations; The Association of Trial Lawyers of America. ***PRACTICE AREAS:*** Personal Injury; Civil Tort.

DAVID J. COMEAU, born Detroit, Michigan, August 19, 1955; admitted to bar, 1981, Illinois. *Education:* Miami University (B.A., 1977); John Marshall Law School (J.D., with honors, 1981). Member, National Moot Court Competition. Author: "The Abortion Arena-Recent Activity," The Journal of Legal Medicine, 1982; "Pleading and Proving Special Damages," IICLE, 1981; "Hearsay," IICLE, 1982. Member, National Million Dollar Verdict Society. Listed in Marquis Who's Who in American Law, 10th Ed., 1998-1999; Leading Illinois Attorneys, 1999. *Member:* Chicago and American Bar Associations; Illinois Trial Lawyers Association; The Association of Trial Lawyers of America. ***PRACTICE AREAS:*** Civil Torts; Personal Injury.

TELLY C. NAKOS, born Fort Wayne, Indiana, July 26, 1965; admitted to bar, 1990, Illinois and U.S. District Court, Northern and Central Districts of Illinois. *Education:* Wabash College (B.A., 1987); Keble College (CMRS), Oxford University, Oxford, England; Case Western Reserve University (J.D., 1990). Delta Theta Phi. Eli Lilly Scholar. Recipient: American College of Trial Lawyer Justice Lewis F. Powell Award for Trial Advocacy, 1989 and 1990; International Academy of Trial Lawyers Award for Excellence in Trial Advocacy, 1990; American Jurisprudence Award of Excellence in Trial Advocacy, 1990. Co-Author: "Damages in Wrongful Death Case," Proving & Disproving Damages in Personal Injury Cases, IICLE, December/1993. Instructor, Trial Tactics, Chicago Bar Association/Chicago Board of Education Project, January-April, 1991. Lecturer, Illinois Trial Lawyers Association, 2000 Civil Practice Update and Review Seminar (Construction Litigation). *Member:* Chicago, Illinois State and American Bar Associations; Illinois Trial Lawyers Association; American Trial Lawyers Association. ***LANGUAGES:*** Greek. ***REPORTED CASES:*** George Ratkovich, et al v. W.M. Wrigley Co.; Flora Rose Wood v. K-Mart Corp.; Donald Soderlund v. City of Chicago. ***PRACTICE AREAS:*** Construction Negligence; Products Liability; Personal Injury; Medical Malpractice.

JOHN M. POPELKA, born Appleton, Wisconsin, August 15, 1961; admitted to bar, 1987, Illinois and U.S. District Court, Northern District of Illinois; 1989, Iowa and Wisconsin. *Education:* Marquette University (B.A., 1983); John Marshall Law School (J.D., 1986). *Member:* Chicago Bar Association; State Bar of Wisconsin; Illinois Trial Lawyers Association; Worker's Compensation Lawyers Association; The Association of Trial Lawyers of America. ***REPORTED CASES:*** Jetson Midwest Maintenance v. Ill. Industrial Commission; Edward Gray Corp. v. Ill. Industrial Commission; Timothy L. Sauders v. Ill. Industrial Commission. ***PRACTICE AREAS:*** Worker's Compensation; Social Security Disability.

ALAIN LEVAL, born Paris, France, June 25, 1949; admitted to bar, 1975, Illinois; 1981, California. *Education:* University of Illinois (B.A., 1971); DePaul University (J.D., 1975). *Member:* Chicago, Illinois State and American Bar Associations; Illinois Trial Lawyers Association. ***LANGUAGES:*** French. ***PRACTICE AREAS:*** General Practice; Real Estate; Probate.

JOHN A. SALZEIDER, born Waukegan, Illinois, January 13, 1963; admitted to bar, 1988, Illinois. *Education:* Illinois State University (B.S., 1985); Northern Illinois University (J.D., 1988). *Member:* Chicago, Illinois State and American Bar Associations; Illinois Trial Lawyers Association (Member, Board of Advocates); Illinois Workers' Compensation Lawyers Association. ***PRACTICE AREAS:*** Workers Compensation; Social Security.

MARTIN J. LUCAS, born Evergreen Park, Illinois, December 12, 1963; admitted to bar, 1991, Illinois. *Education:* John Carroll University (B.A., 1986): Illinois Institute of Technology (J.D., 1991). Recipient, American Jurisprudence Award in Torts, 1988. *Member:* Chicago and Illinois State Bar Associations; Illinois Trial Lawyers Association; The Association of Trial Lawyers of America. ***PRACTICE AREAS:*** Personal Injury; Employment Discrimination.

MARK MURNANE, born Chicago, Illinois, January 27, 1967; admitted to bar, 1992, Illinois and U.S. District Court, Northern District of Illinois. *Education:* College of the Holy Cross (B.A., 1989); Loyola University (J.D., 1992). Member, Loyola University Law Journal. *Member:* Chicago and Illinois State Bar Associations; Illinois Trial Lawyers Association. ***PRACTICE AREAS:*** Illinois Structural Work Act; Products Liability; General Tort; Medical Malpractice.

STEVEN A. BERMAN, born Skokie, Illinois, September 25, 1969; admitted to bar, 1994, Illinois. *Education:* Bradley University (B.S., 1991); Chicago-Kent, College of Law,

(This Listing Continued)

ANESI, OZMON, RODIN, NOVAK & KOHEN, LTD., Chicago—Continued

Illinois Institute of Technology (J.D., 1994). *Member:* Chicago, Illinois State and American Bar Associations; Illinois Trial Lawyers Association. ***PRACTICE AREAS:*** Torts; Personal Injury Litigation.

STEVEN W. BURROWS, born Chicago, Illinois, January 7, 1973; admitted to bar, 1998, Illinois and U.S. District Court, Northern District of Illinois. *Education:* Illinois Wesleyan University (B.A., 1995); Chicago-Kent College of Law, Illinois Institute of Technology. *Member:* Chicago, Illinois and American Bar Associations; Justinian Society; Illinois Trial Lawyers Association. ***PRACTICE AREAS:*** Personal Injury. ***Email:*** sburrows@anesilaw.com

BRADLEY MICHAEL ARNOLD, born Skokie, Illinois, February 28, 1973; admitted to bar, 1998, Illinois and U.S. District Court, Northern District of Illinois. *Education:* University of Iowa (B.A., 1995); The John Marshall Law School (J.D., 1998). Phi Alpha Delta. *Member:* Chicago (Member, Tort Litigation and Trial Techniques) and American (Member, Tort Law) Bar Associations; Illinois Trial Lawyers Association. ***PRACTICE AREAS:*** Personal Injury.

MICHAEL P. HELLMAN, born Park Ridge, Illinois, November 24, 1972; admitted to bar, 1999, Illinois. *Education:* Roosevelt University (B.A., 1995); The John Marshall Law School (J.D., 1999). *Member:* Illinois State and American Bar Associations; Illinois Trial Lawyers Association; Workers' Compensation Lawyers Association. ***PRACTICE AREAS:*** Workers' Compensation; Social Security Disability.

STEPHEN J. CUMMINGS, born Chicago, Illinois, December 4, 1969; admitted to bar, 1998, Illinois. *Education:* University of Chicago (B.A., 1992); Loyola University (J.D., 1998). ***PRACTICE AREAS:*** Workers Compensation; Personal Injury; General Practice.

JEFFREY MARC ALTER, born Chicago, Illinois, October 10, 1971; admitted to bar, 1999, Illinois and U.S. District Court, Northern District of Illinois. *Education:* Loyola University (B.S., with honors, 1993); Loyola University (J.D., 1999). *Member:* Chicago and American Bar Associations; Illinois Trial Lawyers Association; Workers' Compensation Lawyers Association. ***PRACTICE AREAS:*** Workers' Compensation; Social Security Disability.

SEAN P. MURRAY, born Winfield, Illinois, October 19, 1976; admitted to bar, 2001, Illinois; U.S. District Court, Northern District of Illinois. *Education:* Western Illinois University (B.A., 1998); Loyola University (J.D., 2001). *Chicago, Illinois State and American Bar Associations; Illinois Trial Lawyers Association; Association of Trial Lawyers of America; Chicago Council of Lawyers.* ***PRACTICE AREAS:*** Personal Injury; Negligence; Medical Malpractice.

JONATHAN BECKET SCHLACK, born Detroit, Michigan, February 22, 1971; admitted to bar, 2001, Wisconsin (Not admitted in Illinois). *Education:* Augustana College (B.A., 1995); University of Wisconsin Law School (J.D., 1999). Dean's List. Member, Aresteia Honor Society. Recipient, CALI Award, 1996. ***LANGUAGES:*** Spanish. ***PRACTICE AREAS:*** Workers Compensation; Personal Injury. ***Email:*** jonschlack@hotmail.com

JEFFREY S. JORDAN, born Racine, Wisconsin, February 1, 1979; admitted to bar, 2004, Illinois. *Education:* Loyola University (B.A., 2001; J.D., 2004). Recipient: Trial Advocacy Certificate; National Champions, First Place, National Robert F. Wagner Labor & Employment Law Moot Court Competition, 2003; CALI Excellence for the Future Awards for earning highest grade in the following courses: Criminal Law, Illinois Litigation, Complex Issues in a Personal Injury Case. Author: "Construction Negligence: The Past, Present and Future Application of Section 414 of the Restatement (Second) of Torts in Illinois," published in Trial Journal of the Illinois Trial Lawyer's Association, Volume 7, Number 1, Winter, 2005. *Member:* Cook County, Chicago, American and Illinois State Bar Associations; Illinois Trial Lawyers Association; The Association of Trial Lawyers of America. ***PRACTICE AREAS:*** Personal Injury; Torts; Negligence. ***Email:*** jjordan@anesilaw.com

JAMES B. HARDY, born Chicago, Illinois, June 29, 1966; admitted to bar, 2004, Illinois. *Education:* Northwestern University (B.A., 1994); Valparaiso University (J.D., 2004). *Member:* Chicago Bar Association. ***PRACTICE AREAS:*** Workers Compensation.

HOWARD H. ANKIN

200 N. LASALLE STREET, SUITE 1810
CHICAGO, ILLINOIS 60601
Telephone: 312-346-8780
Fax: 312-346-8681
Email: howard@ankinlaw.com
URL: http://www.lawyers.com/hankin

Workers Compensation, Personal Injury, Automobile Accidents, Wrongful Death, Medical Malpractice, Slip and Fall, Dog Bites.

HOWARD H. ANKIN, born San Francisco, California, March 7, 1968; admitted to bar, 1993, Illinois and U.S. District Court, Central and Northern Districts of Illinois. *Education:* University of Illinois (B.S., 1990); John Marshall Law School (J.D., 1993). ***PRACTICE AREAS:*** Workers Compensation; Personal Injury; Automobile Accidents and Injuries; Wrongful Death; Medical Malpractice; Slip and Fall; Dog Bites.

LAW OFFICES OF SCOTT M. ANNES

CHICAGO, ILLINOIS

(See Park Ridge)

Commercial Litigation with focus on Small Business Law, Small Business Litigation, Family Business Law, Partnership Law, Breach of Contract, Employment Law and Wrongful Termination, Elder Law and Real Estate.

ANTHONY G. ARGEROS, L.L.C.

10 SOUTH LA SALLE STREET, SUITE 3300
CHICAGO, ILLINOIS 60603
Telephone: 312-332-1100
Fax: 312-332-0644
URL: http://www.argeroslaw.com
Email: aga@ArgerosLaw.com
URL: http://www.anthonyargeros.com

Personal Injury, Wrongful Death, Products Liability, Diesel Exposure, Toxic Mold, Automobile Accidents, Medical Malpractice, Birth Trauma, Traumatic Head Injuries, Nursing Home Litigation, Workers' Compensation, Civil Litigation, Appellate Practice.

ANTHONY G. ARGEROS, born Moline, Illinois, December 1, 1964; admitted to bar, 1990, Illinois. *Education:* Illinois State University (B.S., 1987); DePaul University College of Law (J.D., 1990). Phi Alpha Delta. Order of the Barristers. Member: Editorial Board, Journal of Health and Hospital Law; National Team Member, New York Bar Association National Moot Competition; National Team Member, Georgetown University Bioethics and the Law National Moot Court Competition; American College of Legal Medicine. Co-Author: "Preparing Treating Physicians for Deposition and Trial," 1998; "Evidentiary Issues in Products Liability Cases," 2000, Illinois Trial Lawyers Association Seminar Handbook. *Member:* Illinois Trial Lawyers Association. ***LANGUAGES:*** Greek. ***Email:*** aga@ArgerosLaw.com

ARNETT GAUBERT, LLP

Established in 1998

311 SOUTH WACKER DRIVE
SUITE 5600
CHICAGO, ILLINOIS 60606
Telephone: 312-922-0900
Facsimile: 312-922-2255
Email: info@aghalaw.com
URL: http://www.aghalaw.com

Dallas, Texas Office: 4650 Trammell Crow Center, 2001 Ross Avenue, 75201. Telephone: 214-760-0900. Facsimile: 214-760-0905.

Christiansted, St. Croix, Virgin Islands Office: Moore & Sopuch, P.C., 2108 Company Street, Lot 55-A, 2nd Floor, 00820-4936. Telephone: 340-773-4150. Facsimile: 340-778-7168.

Civil and Commercial Litigation.

PARTNER

BART F. HIGGINS, born Worcester, Massachusetts, May 18, 1965; admitted to bar, 1990, Virginia (inactive) and U.S. District Court, Eastern District of Virginia; 1991, District of Columbia; 1992, U.S. District Court, District of Columbia; 1995, U.S. District Court, Northern District of Illinois including Trial Bar; 1997, Illinois. *Education:* University of Virginia (B.S., 1987); George Mason University (J.D., 1990). *Member:* Illinois State Bar Association; The District of Columbia Bar; Virginia State Bar; Trial Lawyers Association of Metropolitan Washington, D.C. ***PRACTICE AREAS:*** Complex Commercial Litigation; Hospitality Law; Employment Litigation. ***Email:*** bhiggins@sopuchlaw.com

REPRESENTATIVE CLIENTS: American Realty Investors, Inc.; Basic Capital Management, Inc.; Chadwick Hospitality Management; China Resources (Holdings) Co., Ltd.; CROSSMARK, Inc.; Global Commerce Systems; GN Mortgage Corporation; Government of the United States Virgin Islands; Heller Healthcare Financial, Inc.; Henry Building, Inc.; Hyatt Corporation; Miami Cigar & Company; Production Group International, Inc.; Quickturn Design Systems, Inc.; Regis Hotel Corporation; Shelter Mortgage Corporation; Sunshine Mortgage Corp.; Tokyo Green Ltd.; Transcontinental Realty Investors, Inc.; Vartec Telecom.

(For complete biographical data on other personnel, see Professional Biographies at Dallas, Texas and Moore & Sopuch, P.C., Christiansted, St. Croix, Virgin Islands)

ARNOLD, WHITE & DURKEE

CHICAGO, ILLINOIS

(See Howrey LLP, Washington, D.C.)

ARNSTEIN & LEHR LLP

SUITE 1200
120 SOUTH RIVERSIDE PLAZA
CHICAGO, ILLINOIS 60606-3910
Telephone: 312-876-7100
Fax: 312-876-0288
Email: mail@arnstein.com
URL: http://www.arnstein.com

West Palm Beach, Florida Office: 515 North Flagler Drive, Suite 600, 33401-4323. Telephone: 561-833-9800. Fax: 561-655-5551.

Boca Raton, Florida Office: 2424 North Federal Highway, Suite 462, 33431. Telephone: 561-322-6900. Fax: 561-322-6940.

Miami, Florida Office: Miami Center, 201 South Biscayne Boulevard, Fourth Floor, 33131. Telephone: 305-374-3330. Fax: 305-374-4744.

Tampa, Florida Office: 300 South Hyde Park Avenue, Suite 180, 33606. Telephone: 813-259-9964. Fax: 813-259-9724.

Hoffman Estates, Illinois Office: 2800 West Higgins Road, Suite 425, 60195-5224. Telephone: 847-843-2900. Fax: 847-843-3355.

Milwaukee, Wisconsin Office: 7161 North Port Washington Road, 53217. Telephone: 414-351-2440. Fax: 414-352-6901.

(This Listing Continued)

General Practice, including Litigation in State and Federal, Trial and Appellate Courts, Products Litigation, Medical Malpractice, Litigation Management, Business Transactions, Real Estate, Employee Benefits, Creditors' Rights and Bankruptcy, Criminal Law, Commercial Finance, Commercial Litigation, Not-for-Profit Corporations, Estate Planning, Trust Administration and Probate, Taxation, Employment, Consumer Credit, Securities Law, Transportation Law, International Law, Insurance Law, Local Government, Intellectual Property, Environmental Law, Health Care and Practice before Federal and State Administrative Bodies.

FIRM PROFILE: Since its founding in 1893, Arnstein & Lehr LLP has served clients, large and small, throughout the United States and in many foreign countries. With offices in Illinois, Florida and Wisconsin, the firm engages in the general practice of law with attorneys in five basic service areas - Business, Litigation, Local Government, Personal Services and Real Estate. While the Firm is large enough to staff the most complex matters, it is small enough to give each client and every matter personal and careful attention, resulting in legal services of the highest quality. For further information concerning our firm and its personnel, see our website: http://www.arnstein.com.

LEO H. ARNSTEIN (1906-1993)

MEMBERS OF FIRM

MICHAEL A. ABRAMSON, admitted to bar, 1974, Illinois and U.S. District Court, Northern District of Illinois including Trial Bar; 1976, U.S. Court of Appeals, 7th Circuit; 1994, U.S. Tax Court. *Education:* DePaul University (B.A., 1971; J.D., 1974). ***PRACTICE AREAS:*** Business Transactions; Closely Held Corporations; Probate. ***Email:*** maabramson@arnstein.com

WILLIAM J. ANAYA, admitted to bar, 1981, Illinois and Indiana; U.S. District Court, Northern District of Illinois; U.S. Court of Appeals, 7th Circuit; U.S. Tax Court; U.S. Supreme Court. *Education:* Purdue University (B.A., 1978); Indiana University School of Law (J.D., 1981). ***PRACTICE AREAS:*** Environmental Law; Real Estate Law; Litigation. ***Email:*** wyanaya@arnstein.com

GEORGE P. APOSTOLIDES, admitted to bar, 1995, Illinois and U.S. District Court, Northern District of Illinois. *Education:* Princeton University (A.B., magna cum laude, 1992); Northwestern University (J.D., 1995). ***PRACTICE AREAS:*** Litigation. ***Email:*** gpapostolides@arnstein.com

KONSTANTINOS ARMIROS, admitted to bar, 1977, Illinois. *Education:* University of Wisconsin-Madison (B.A., cum laude, 1974); Boston University (J.D., 1977). ***PRACTICE AREAS:*** Corporate Law; Business Law; Litigation; Real Estate; Commercial Law; Banking; Restaurant Law. ***Email:*** karmiros@arnstein.com

BRUCE H. BALONICK, admitted to bar, 1974, Illinois. *Education:* University of Denver (B.S.B.A., 1970); DePaul University (J.D., cum laude, 1974). ***PRACTICE AREAS:*** Corporate Law; Estate Planning; Taxation; Real Estate. ***Email:*** bbalonick@arnstein.com

BRANDON E. BELL, admitted to bar, 1996, Wisconsin and Illinois. *Education:* Oberlin College (B.A., 1992); University of Wisconsin, Madison (J.D., 1996). ***PRACTICE AREAS:*** Corporate. ***Email:*** bebell@arnstein.com

ROY L. BERNSTEIN, admitted to bar, 1983, Illinois; 1984, U.S. District Court, Northern District of Illinois. *Education:* University of Wisconsin (B.A., with honors, 1980); George Washington University (J.D., with highest honors, 1983). ***PRACTICE AREAS:*** Environmental Law; Real Estate. ***Email:*** rlbernstein@arnstein.com

WILLIAM K. BLOMQUIST, admitted to bar, 1972, New York; 1973, U.S. District Court, Southern and Eastern Districts of New York; 1974, U.S. Court of Appeals, Second Circuit; 1977, U.S. Supreme Court; 1980, Illinois, U.S. Court of Appeals, Seventh Circuit and U.S. District Court, Northern District of Illinois. *Education:* Yale University (B.A., cum laude, 1967; J.D., 1971). ***PRACTICE AREAS:*** Corporate Law; General Business Law; International Law. ***Email:*** wkblomquist@arnstein.com

J. WILLIAM BRAITHWAITE, admitted to bar, 1956, Illinois, Connecticut and U.S. District Court, Northern District of Illinois; 1960, U.S. Court of Appeals, 7th Circuit. *Education:* University of Santo Tomas, Manila and University of Connecticut (B.A., 1950); Columbia University (J.D., 1955). ***PRACTICE AREAS:*** Municipal and Land Use Law; Estate Planning; General Civil Practice; Real Estate (Property) Law. ***Email:*** jwbraithwaite@arnstein.com

ROBERT D. BUTTERS, admitted to bar, 1977, Illinois; 1978, District of Columbia; 1980, U.S. District Court, Northern District of Illinois, and U.S. Court of Appeals, Seventh Circuit; 1981, U.S. Supreme Court; 1989, U.S. Court of Appeals, Fifth Circuit. *Education:* Trinity College (B.A., 1973); Vanderbilt University (J.D., 1977). ***PRACTICE AREAS:*** Professional Liability Defense; Civil Rights; Trade and Professional Associations; Computer and Database Licensing; Antitrust. ***Email:*** rdbutters@arnstein.com

BARRY A. CHATZ, admitted to bar, 1987, Illinois; 1989, California. *Education:* University of Wisconsin, Madison (B.A., 1984); DePaul University College of Law (J.D., 1987). ***PRACTICE AREAS:*** Bankruptcy; Creditors Rights; Commercial Litigation. ***Email:*** bachatz@arnstein.com

JAMES A. CHATZ, admitted to bar, 1958, Illinois; 1981, Colorado. *Education:* Michigan State University and Northwestern University (B.Sc., 1956); Northwestern University (LL.B., 1958). ***PRACTICE AREAS:*** Bankruptcy; Corporate and Business Law; Commercial Reorganization; Mergers and Acquisitions; Financial Planning. ***Email:*** jachatz@arnstein.com

STEPHEN R. CHESLER, admitted to bar, 1966, Illinois and U.S. District Court, Northern District of Illinois. *Education:* Grinnell College (B.S., 1962); Northwestern University (J.D., 1965). ***PRACTICE AREAS:*** Business; Real Estate; Corporate; Estate Planning; Shopping Center Development; Leasing; Finance Law. ***Email:*** srchesler@arnstein.com

COLLEEN ADAMS CHINDLUND, admitted to bar, 1999, Illinois. *Education:* University of Florida (B.S., 1993); John Marshall Law School (J.D., 1999). ***PRACTICE AREAS:*** Estate Planning; Probate; Corporate Law; Real Estate Law. ***Email:*** cachinlund@arnstein.com

(This Listing Continued)

ANNA-KATRINA S. CHRISTAKIS, admitted to bar, 1997, Illinois and U.S. District Court, Northern District of Illinois; 1998, Wisconsin; 1999, U.S. Court of Appeals, Seventh Circuit; 2002, U.S. Court of Appeals, Eleventh Circuit. *Education:* Cornell University (B.A., cum laude, 1991); University of Wisconsin-Madison (J.D., 1997). ***PRACTICE AREAS:*** Commercial Litigation. ***Email:*** aschristakis@arnstein.com

ROBERT T. CICHOCKI, admitted to bar, 1976, Illinois. *Education:* Wayne State University (B.A., 1972); John Marshall Law School (J.D., 1976). ***PRACTICE AREAS:*** Business; Estate Planning; Trade Association; Education; Real Estate. ***Email:*** rtcichocki@arnstein.com

THOMAS P. CONLEY, admitted to bar, 1980, Illinois and U.S. District Court, Northern District of Illinois. *Education:* Carleton College (B.A., 1977); DePaul University (J.D., 1980). ***PRACTICE AREAS:*** Health Care; State Government; Transactional. ***Email:*** tpconley@arnstein.com

BRIAN J. COOKE, born New York, NY., April 22, 1948; admitted to bar, 1974, New York and New Jersey; 1978, Florida. *Education:* Colby College (B.A., 1970); Brooklyn Law School (J.D., 1974); New York University (LL.M., 1975). (Resident, West Palm Beach, Florida Office). ***PRACTICE AREAS:*** Corporate Law; Commercial Law; Securities Law; Commercial Litigation; Matrimonial Law. ***Email:*** bjcooke@arnstein.com

PATRICK J. COTTER, admitted to bar, 1983, New York; 1990, Illinois. *Education:* Illinois State University (B.S., 1978); New York University (J.D., 1982). ***PRACTICE AREAS:*** Criminal. ***Email:*** pjcotter@arnstein.com

STEVEN L. DANIELS, admitted to bar, 1982, Florida; 1983, U.S. Court of Appeals, Eleventh Circuit. *Education:* Duke University (B.A., 1979); Washington University (J.D., 1982). (Resident, West Palm Beach and Boca Raton, Florida Offices). ***PRACTICE AREAS:*** Real Estate; Landlord-Tenant; Zoning; Corporation; Condominium and Community Association Law; Commercial Law. ***Email:*** sldaniels@arnstein.com

DAVID C. DUNKIN, admitted to bar, 1985, Illinois. *Education:* University of Illinois (B.A., 1982); Loyola University (J.D., 1985). ***PRACTICE AREAS:*** Real Estate Tax Assesment. ***Email:*** dcdunkin@arnstein.com

KENNETH EDELMAN, admitted to bar, 1980, New York; 1989, Florida (Not admitted in Illinois). *Education:* State University of New York at Stony Brook (B.A., 1976); St. Johns University (J.D., 1979); New York University (LL.M. in Taxation, 1983). ***PRACTICE AREAS:*** Estate Planning; Trusts. ***Email:*** kedelman@arnstein.com

MARK E. ENRIGHT, admitted to bar, 1983, Illinois and U.S. District Court, Northern District of Illinois including Trial Bar; 1992, U.S. Court of Appeals, Fifth Circuit. *Education:* University of Illinois-Urbana/Champaign (B.A., 1980); Loyola University (J.D., 1983). ***PRACTICE AREAS:*** Litigation; Products Liability Law (Defective Products); Commercial Litigation; Construction Law. ***Email:*** meenright@arnstein.com

LUIS A. ESPINO, admitted to bar, 1994, Florida; U.S. District Court, Southern and Northern Districts of Florida; U.S. Bankruptcy Court, Southern District of Florida and U.S. Court of Appeals, Eleventh Circuit. *Education:* University of Chicago (B.A., with honors, 1991); Florida State University (J.D., 1994); Oxford University (Graduate, Legal Studies). (Resident, Miami, Florida Office). ***PRACTICE AREAS:*** Commercial Litigation; Creditor's Rights; Bankruptcy; Real Estate Transactions; Real Estate Title Insurance; Real Estate. ***Email:*** laespino@arnstein.com

WILLA A. FEARRINGTON, admitted to bar, 1973, North Carolina; 1974, Florida. *Education:* University of North Carolina (B.A., 1971; J.D., 1973). (Resident, West Palm Beach Office). ***PRACTICE AREAS:*** Ad Valorem Taxation Law; Appellate Practice; Real Estate Law; Complex Litigation; Family Law. ***Email:*** wafearrington@arnstein.com

THADFORD A. FELTON, admitted to bar, 1994, Illinois and U.S. District Court, Northern District of Illinois including Trial Bar; 1996, U.S. Court of Appeals, 7th Circuit; U.S. Court of Appeals, 8th Circuit. *Education:* Denison University (B.A., 1989); Chicago Kent College of Law (J.D., 1994). ***PRACTICE AREAS:*** Commercial Litigation; Employment Law; Real Estate Law; Civil Rights Law. ***Email:*** tafelton@arnstein.com

RICHARD C. GERING, admitted to bar, 1977, Illinois and U.S. District Court, Northern District of Illinois; 1982, Florida; 1984, U.S. Court of Appeals, District of Columbia Circuit and U.S. Court of Appeals, 7th Circuit; 1985, U.S. Court of Appeals, 1st Circuit. *Education:* University of Notre Dame (B.A., 1974); Northwestern University (J.D., 1977). ***PRACTICE AREAS:*** Medical Malpractice Law; Unfair Competition Law; Products Liability Law. ***Email:*** rcgering@arnstein.com

ALLAN GOLDBERG, admitted to bar, 1970, Illinois and U.S. District Court, Northern District of Illinois including Trial Bar. *Education:* University of New Mexico (B.A., 1966); Loyola University of Chicago School of Law (J.D., 1969). ***PRACTICE AREAS:*** Real Estate Law; Community Association Law; Commercial Litigation; Financial Institutions. ***Email:*** agoldberg@arnstein.com

MATTHEW J. GOLDBERG, admitted to bar, 2001, Illinois; U.S. District Court, Northern District of Illinois. *Education:* University of Iowa (B.B.A., 1997); Chicago-Kent College of Law (J.D., 2001). ***PRACTICE AREAS:*** Condominium Law; Litigation. ***Email:*** mjgoldberg@arnstein.com

JAMES F. GOSSETT, admitted to bar, 1976, Illinois and U.S. District Court, Northern District of Illinois; 1981, U.S. Supreme Court. *Education:* Northwestern University (B.S.J., with honors, 1973; J.D., 1976). ***PRACTICE AREAS:*** Antitrust; Corporate; Intellectual Property; Taxation. ***Email:*** jfgossett@arnstein.com

JOHN F. GRADY, admitted to bar, 1996, Illinois and U.S. District Court, Northern District of Illinois. *Education:* University of Iowa (B.A., 1992); Northwestern University (J.D., 1996). ***PRACTICE AREAS:*** Civil Litigation; Criminal Litigation. ***Email:*** jfgrady@arnstein.com

LAWRENCE E. GRELLE, admitted to bar, 1968, Illinois. *Education:* Arizona State University and Northwestern University (B.S., 1965); University of Illinois (J.D., 1968). (Also at Hoffman Estates Office). ***PRACTICE AREAS:*** Business Law; Real Estate (Property); Estate Planning. ***Email:*** legrelle@arnstein.com

(This Listing Continued)

ARNSTEIN & LEHR LLP, Chicago—Continued

MAUREEN B. GRZESKIEWICZ, admitted to bar, 1999, Illinois and U.S. District Court, Northern District of Illinois. *Education:* Marquette University (B.A., 1994); DePaul University (J.D., 1998). ***PRACTICE AREAS:*** Trusts and Estates; Probate; Real Estate. ***Email:*** mbgrzeskiewicz@arnstein.com

JOHN C. HANSON, II, admitted to bar, 1992, Florida, U.S. District Court, Southern District of Florida and U.S. Court of Appeals, Eleventh Circuit; 1993, U.S. District Court, Middle District of Florida. *Education:* Florida State University (B.S., 1978); Washington University (M.A., 1983; Ph.D., 1985); University of Miami (J.D., cum laude, 1991). (Resident, Miami, Florida Office). ***PRACTICE AREAS:*** Civil Litigation; Commercial Litigation; Eminent Domain; Appellate Practice. ***Email:*** jchanson@arnstein.com

NANCY S. HARBOTTLE, admitted to bar, 1987, Illinois and Massachusetts. *Education:* DePauw University; Northern Illinois University, DeKalb (B.A., magna cum Laude, 1984); Chicago-Kent College of Law; Illinois Institute of Technology (J.D., 1987). (Resident, Hoffman Estates Office). ***PRACTICE AREAS:*** Local Government Law; Land Use; Real Estate; Estate Planning. ***Email:*** nsharbottle@arnstein.com

R. KYMN HARP, admitted to bar, 1978, Illinois and U.S. District Court, Northern District of Illinois including Trial Bar; 1986, Indiana, U.S. District Court, Northern and Southern Districts of Indiana; 2001, New Mexico. *Education:* Wabash College (B.A., 1975); John Marshall Law School (J.D., 1978). ***PRACTICE AREAS:*** Real Estate. ***Email:*** rkharp@arnstein.com

KURT J. HEINZ, admitted to bar, 1980, Illinois and U.S. District Court, Northern District of Illinois; 1984, U.S. Court of Appeals, 4th Circuit; 1994, U.S. Court of Appeals, Seventh Circuit. *Education:* University of Notre Dame (B.A., 1974); Emory University (J.D., 1980). ***PRACTICE AREAS:*** Commercial Litigation; Product and Premises Liability Law; Civil Trial and Appellate Practice; Litigation Management. ***Email:*** kjheinz@arnstein.com

RICHARD K. HELLERMAN, admitted to bar, 1987, Illinois and U.S. District Court, Northern District of Illinois including Trial Bar, 1995. *Education:* Washington University (B.A., 1984); Emory University (J.D., with distinction, 1987). ***PRACTICE AREAS:*** Litigation; Employment Litigation; Tort Law; Medical Malpractice Law; Commercial Litigation. ***Email:*** rkhellerman@arnstein.com

DAVID S. HORWITCH, admitted to bar, 1997, Illinois. *Education:* University of Illinois (B.A., with distinction, 1994; J.D., 1997). ***PRACTICE AREAS:*** Real Estate; Litigation; Business Law. ***Email:*** dshorwitch@arnstein.com

PHILLIP M. HUDSON, III, admitted to bar, 1985, Florida; U.S. Bankruptcy Court, Southern and Middle Districts of Florida; U.S. District Court, Southern District of Florida including Trial Bar; U.S. District Court, Middle District of Florida including Trial Bar;. *Education:* University of Maryland (B.A., 1982); University of Miami School of Law (J.D., 1985). (Resident, Miami, Florida Office). ***PRACTICE AREAS:*** Bankruptcy. ***Email:*** pmhudson@arnstein.com

JOEL M. HURWITZ, admitted to bar, 1976, Illinois and U.S. District Court, Northern District of Illinois including Trial Bar. *Education:* University of Pittsburgh (B.A., magna cum laude, 1973); University of Oslo, Oslo, Norway; University of Chicago Graduate School of Business (M.B.A., 1975); University of Chicago Law School (J.D., 1976). ***PRACTICE AREAS:*** Commercial Transactions; Real Estate Transactions; Business Law; Probate and Trusts. ***Email:*** jmhurwitz@arnstein.com

RICHARD B. IVANS, admitted to bar, 1969, New York; 1971, Florida. *Education:* City College of the City University of New York (B.B.A., 1966); Brooklyn Law School (J.D., 1968). (Resident, Miami, Florida Office). ***PRACTICE AREAS:*** Business Law; Corporate Law; Finance Law; Real Estate Transactions. ***Email:*** rbivans@arnstein.com

NORMAN P. JEDDELOH, admitted to bar, 1971, Illinois and U.S. District Court, Northern District of Illinois including Trial Bar; 1980, U.S. Supreme Court. *Education:* University of Notre Dame (B.A., with honors, 1968); Northwestern University (J.D., 1971). ***PRACTICE AREAS:*** Labor Law; Health Care Law; Insurance Law; Intellectual Property Litigation. ***Email:*** npjeddeloh@arnstein.com

MICHAEL N. JONAS, admitted to bar, 1980, Florida; 1981, U.S. District Court, Southern District of Florida. *Education:* Cornell University (B.S., 1977); University of Miami (J.D., 1980). (Resident, West Palm Beach, Florida Office). ***PRACTICE AREAS:*** Real Estate; Business Transactions; Corporate Transactions; Labor and Employment.

SCOTT H. KAPP, admitted to bar, 1998, Illinois. *Education:* University of Wisconsin (B.A., with honors, 1994); Northwestern University (J.D., 1998). ***Email:*** shkapp@arnstein.com

BARRY R. KATZ, admitted to bar, 1978, Illinois and U.S. District Court, Northern District of Illinois. *Education:* University of Michigan (B.A., 1975); Northwestern University School of Law (J.D., 1978). ***PRACTICE AREAS:*** Real Estate; Real Estate Transactions; Environmental Law; Corporate Law. ***Email:*** brkatz@arnstein.com

EUGENE J. KELLEY, JR., admitted to bar, 1963, Illinois and U.S. District Court, Northern District of Illinois including Trial Bar; 1964, U.S. Court of Appeals, 7th Circuit and U.S. District Court, Southern District of Wisconsin; 1975, U.S. Supreme Court. *Education:* University of Notre Dame (B.S., 1959); Northwestern University (J.D., 1963). ***PRACTICE AREAS:*** Commercial and General Litigation; Consumer Credit Litigation and Counselling; Common Carrier Litigation; Land Use Matters; Municipal Matters; Product Liability; Risk Pooling and Risk Management. ***Email:*** ejkelley@arnstein.com

STEPHANIE J. KIM, admitted to bar, 1996, Illinois and U.S. District Court, Northern District of Illinois. *Education:* Northwestern University (B.A., 1993); John Marshall Law School (J.D., cum laude, 1996). ***PRACTICE AREAS:*** Real Estate. ***Email:*** sjkim@arnstein.com

ARTHUR L. KLEIN, admitted to bar, 1962, Illinois and U.S. District Court, Northern District of Illinois; 1967, U.S. Court of Appeals, 7th Circuit; 1975, U.S. Supreme Court; 1979, U.S. Court of Appeals, 5th Circuit; 1983, U.S. Court of Appeals, 3rd Circuit; 1984, U.S. Court of Appeals, 4th Circuit; 1986, U.S. Court of Appeals, 8th Circuit; 1987, U.S. Court of Appeals, 10th Circuit; 1988, U.S. Court of Appeals, 11th Circuit; 1989, U.S. District Court, Eastern District of Wisconsin and U.S. Court of Appeals, 6th Circuit; 1991, U.S. Court of Appeals, Ninth Circuit. *Education:* University of Wisconsin and Northwestern University (B.S.L., 1960); Northwestern University (LL.B., 1962). ***PRACTICE AREAS:*** Appellate Practice Law; Insurance Coverage Law; Litigation. ***Email:*** alklein@arnstein.com

KATHLEEN M. LACH, admitted to bar, 1997, Illinois and U.S. District Court, Northern District of Illinois. *Education:* Oral Roberts University (B.A., 1983); State University of New York at Buffalo (J.D., 1997); Northwestern University School of Law (Visiting Student, 1997). ***PRACTICE AREAS:*** Tax Controversies; Tax Litigation; Litigation. ***Email:*** kmlach@arnstein.com

ROBERT J. LASKY, admitted to bar, 1962, Illinois; 1963, U.S. District Court, Northern District of Illinois. *Education:* Northwestern University; DePaul College of Law (J.D., 1962). ***PRACTICE AREAS:*** Business Law; Real Property Law; International Business Law; Estate Planning and Probate. ***Email:*** rjlasky@arnstein.com

LOUIS A. LEHR, JR., admitted to bar, 1951, Illinois; 1954, U.S. District Court, Northern District of Illinois and U.S. Court of Appeals, 7th Circuit; 1968, U.S. Court of Appeals, 6th Circuit; 1971, U.S. Court of Appeals, 10th Circuit; 1980, U.S. Court of Appeals, 3rd Circuit; 1983, U.S. District Court, Eastern District of Michigan; 1986, U.S. Court of Appeals, 8th Circuit; 1988, U.S. District Court, Eastern District of Wisconsin; 1992, U.S. Court of Appeals, 5th Circuit. *Education:* Loyola University (J.D., 1951). ***PRACTICE AREAS:*** Litigation; Products Liability Law; Civil Trial Practice; Litigation Management. ***Email:*** lalehr@arnstein.com

NEVILLE M. LESLIE, admitted to bar, 1997, Florida; 1998, U.S. District Court, Southern District of Florida; 2000, U.S. District Court, Middle District of Florida and U.S. Court of Appeals, Eleventh Circuit. *Education:* University of Miami (B.A., with honors, 1994); Nova Southeastern University (J.D., cum laude, 1996). (Resident, Miami, Florida Office). ***PRACTICE AREAS:*** Personal Injury Litigation; Commercial Litigation; Insurance Litigation; Civil Litigation. ***Email:*** nmleslie@arnstein.com

SAMUEL H. LEVINE, admitted to bar, 1981, Illinois. *Education:* Washington University (B.A., 1978); Chicago-Kent College of Law (J.D., 1981). ***PRACTICE AREAS:*** Construction Law; Mechanics Liens; Real Estate Litigation; Mortgage Foreclosure. ***Email:*** shlevine@arnstein.com

PATTI S. LEVINSON, admitted to bar, 1996, Illinois and U.S. District Court, Northern District of Illinois; 2002, U.S. District Court, Eastern District of Wisconsin. *Education:* State University of New York at Binghamton (B.A., 1979); Chicago-Kent College of Law, Illinois Institute of Technology (J.D., 1996). ***PRACTICE AREAS:*** Commercial Litigation; Employment Litigation; Appellate Practice; Litigation. ***Email:*** pslevinson@arnstein.com

STEVEN N. MALITZ, admitted to bar, 1995, Illinois and U.S. District Court, Northern District of Illinois; 1997, U.S. District Court, Northern District of Illinois Trial Bar; U.S. Court of Appeals, 7th Circuit. *Education:* Indiana University (B.A., Criminal Justice, magna cum laude, 1991); Albany Law School of Union University (J.D., 1995). ***PRACTICE AREAS:*** Commercial Litigation; Real Estate Litigation; Creditors Rights. ***Email:*** snmalitz@arnstein.com

ALFREDO J. MARQUEZ-STERLING, admitted to bar, 1984, Florida; 1988, U.S. District Court, Southern District of Florida; 1990, U.S. District Courts, Northern and Middle Districts of Florida. *Education:* Southern Illinois University (B.A., with highest honors, 1980; J.D., summa cum laude, 1984). (Resident, Miami, Florida Office). ***PRACTICE AREAS:*** Product Liability; Insurance Coverage Defense. ***Email:*** ajsterling@arnstein.com

THOMAS F. McGUIRE, admitted to bar, 1985, Illinois; 1991, Arizona and U.S. Tax Court. *Education:* University of Illinois-Urbana (B.S., Accountancy, 1982); University of Illinois College of Law (J.D., 1985). ***PRACTICE AREAS:*** Estate Planning Law; Probate Law; Taxation Law. ***Email:*** tfmcguire@arnstein.com

ROBERT E. McKENZIE, admitted to bar, 1979, Illinois, Supreme Court of Illinois, U.S. District Court, Northern District of Illinois and U.S. Tax Court; 1980, U.S. Court of Appeals, Seventh Circuit; 1983, Trial Bar of U.S. District Court, Northern District of Illinois and U.S. Supreme Court; 1991, U.S. Court of Federal Claims. *Education:* Michigan State University (B.A., 1970); Chicago-Kent College of Law, Illinois Institute of Technology (J.D., with high honors, 1979). ***PRACTICE AREAS:*** Taxation Law; Litigation. ***Email:*** remckenzie@arnstein.com

RONALD D. MENAKER, admitted to bar, 1970, Illinois; 1981, U.S District Court, Northern District of Illinois; 1986, U.S. Court of Appeals, Seventh Circuit. *Education:* Southern Illinois University (B.A., 1965); IIT/Chicago-Kent College of Law (J.D., 1970). ***PRACTICE AREAS:*** Criminal Law. ***Email:*** rdmenaker@arnstein.com

MARK F. MILLER, admitted to bar, 1979, Illinois, U.S. District Court, Northern District of Illinois and U.S. Court of Appeals, 7th Circuit; 1980, U.S. Tax Court. *Education:* Washington & Lee University; Northwestern University (B.A., with distinction, 1976; J.D., 1979). ***PRACTICE AREAS:*** Closely Held Corporation Law; Closely Held Businesses Law; Business Law. ***Email:*** mfmiller@arnstein.com

TREV M. MINNAERT, admitted to bar, 1993, Illinois. *Education:* University of Illinois at Urbana-Champaign (B.A., 1988); Loyola University of Chicago School of Law (J.D., 1991). ***PRACTICE AREAS:*** Corporate Law; Education Law. ***Email:*** tmminnaert@arnstein.com

HAL R. MORRIS, admitted to bar, 1985, Illinois; U.S. District Court, Northern District of Illinois including Trial Bar; 1988, U.S. Court of Appeals, Seventh Circuit; 1989, U.S. District Court, Northern District of California and Eastern District of Wisconsin; 1990, U.S. Court of Appeals, Sixth Circuit; 1991, U.S. Court of Appeals, Ninth Circuit; 1997, U.S. Supreme Court. *Education:* University of Chicago (B.A., 1978; M.B.A., 1979); IIT/Chicago-Kent College of Law (J.D., with high honors, 1985). ***PRACTICE AREAS:*** Appellate Practice; Civil Litigation; Real Estate Litigation; Insurance Coverage Law; Commercial Litigation; Litigation. ***Email:*** hrmorris@arnstein.com

CYNDE HIRSCHTICK MUNZER, admitted to bar, 1983, Illinois and U.S. District Court, Northern District of Illinois. *Education:* University of Illinois (B.S., 1979); ITT/

(This Listing Continued)

Chicago-Kent College of Law (J.D., with high honors, 1983). ***PRACTICE AREAS:*** Business Law; Closely Held Corporation Law; Property Leasing Law. ***Email:*** chmunzer@arnstein.com

CHRISTOPHER S. NAVEJA, admitted to bar, 1995, Illinois and U.S. District Court, Northern District of Illinois; 1998, U.S. Court of Appeals, 7th Circuit; 1999, U.S. District Court, Central District of Illinois. *Education:* Indiana University (B.S., 1992); University of Illinois (J.D., cum laude, 1995). ***PRACTICE AREAS:*** Litigation; Commercial Litigation; Consumer Credit Litigation; Municipal Litigation; Products Liability. ***Email:*** csnaveja@arnstein.com

WILLIAM G. NOSEK, admitted to bar, 1971, Illinois. *Education:* Loyola University (A.B., magna cum laude, 1967); University of Chicago (J.D., 1971). ***PRACTICE AREAS:*** Corporate Law. ***Email:*** wgnosek@arnstein.com

JOE OURTH, admitted to bar, 1988, Illinois. *Education:* Graceland College (B.A., summa cum laude, 1981); University of Illinois (J.D., magna cum laude, 1988). ***PRACTICE AREAS:*** Legislation and Administrative Law; Public Finance; Health Law. ***Email:*** jourth@arnstein.com

R. DELACY PETERS, JR., admitted to bar, 1989, Illinois. *Education:* University of Baltimore (B.S., 1985; J.D., 1988). ***PRACTICE AREAS:*** Litigation. ***Email:*** rdpeters@arnstein.com

JEFFREY D. PILGRIM, admitted to bar, 1999, Illinois and U.S. District Court, Northern District of Illinois. *Education:* University of Iowa (B.B.A., 1993); Chicago-Kent College of Law, Illinois Institute of Technology (J.D., with high honors, 1999). Author: "Collateral Protection Insurance: Current Issue and Defenses, " Consumer Finance Law Quarterly Report, Vol. 54, No. 1, 2000. ***PRACTICE AREAS:*** Litigation. ***Email:*** jdpilgrim@arnstein.com

HILDA PILOTO, admitted to bar, 1998, Florida; U.S. District Court, Southern and Middle Districts of Florida. *Education:* University of Miami (B.A., 1995; J.D., 1998). (Resident, Miami, Florida Office). ***PRACTICE AREAS:*** Litigation. ***Email:*** hpiloto@arnstein.com

PHILIP L. POMERANCE, admitted to bar, 1981, Illinois and U.S. District Court, Northern District of Illinois; 1982, U.S. Court of Appeals, 7th Circuit and U.S. District Court, Eastern District of Wisconsin. *Education:* Northwestern University (B.A., 1978; J.D., 1981). ***PRACTICE AREAS:*** Health Care; Corporate Law; Administrative Law. ***Email:*** plpomerance@arnstein.com

GUY E. QUATTLEBAUM, admitted to bar, 1996, Florida; 1997, U.S. District Court, Southern District of Florida and U.S. Court of Appeals, Eleventh Circuit. *Education:* Florida State University (B.A., 1991); St. Thomas University School of Law (J.D., 1996). (Resident, West Palm Beach, Florida Office). ***PRACTICE AREAS:*** Civil Litigation; Tort Defense; Commercial Litigation. ***Email:*** gequattlebaum@arnstein.com

JOHN L. ROPIEQUET, admitted to bar, 1972, Illinois; 1973, U.S. District Court, Northern District of Illinois and U.S. Court of Appeals, 7th Circuit; 1981, U.S. Court of Appeals, 3rd Circuit; 1984, U.S. Court of Appeals, 5th Circuit and U.S. Claims Court; 1986, U.S. Supreme Court and U.S. Court of Appeals, 8th Circuit; 1989, U.S. District Court, Eastern District of Wisconsin. *Education:* Johns Hopkins University (B.A., 1969); Northwestern University (J.D., cum laude, 1972). ***PRACTICE AREAS:*** Consumer Credit Litigation; Medical Malpractice Law; Environmental Law; Toxic Torts; Commercial Litigation. ***Email:*** jlropiequet@arnstein.com

JEFFREY B. SHAPIRO, admitted to bar, 1977, New York and U.S. District Courts, Southern and Eastern Districts of New York; 1985, Florida; 1986, U.S. District Courts, Southern and Middle Districts of Florida; 1988, U.S. Court of Appeals, Eleventh Circuit; 1990, U.S. District Court, Northern District of Florida; 2000, U.S. Supreme Court. *Education:* Queens College of the City University of New York (B.A., cum laude, 1973); St. John's University (J.D., 1976); New York University (LL.M., 1979). (Resident, Miami, Florida Office). ***PRACTICE AREAS:*** Trial Practice; Commercial Litigation; Product Liability; Medical Malpractice; Intellectual Property Litigation. ***Email:*** jbshapiro@arnstein.com

JEROLD N. SIEGAN, admitted to bar, 1972, Illinois, U.S. District Court, Northern District of Illinois and U.S. Court of Appeals, Seventh Circuit; 1973, District of Columbia. *Education:* University of Illinois (B.A., 1968); DePaul University (J.D., 1972). ***PRACTICE AREAS:*** Securities; Corporate. ***Email:*** jnsiegan@arnstein.com

A. THOMAS SKALLAS, admitted to bar, 1998, Illinois. *Education:* University of Illinois (B.S., Finance, 1995); DePaul University (J.D., M.B.A., 1998). ***PRACTICE AREAS:*** Tax; Estate Planning; E-Commerce; Corporate; Closely Held Business Law. ***Email:*** atskallas@arnstein.com

EDWARD A. SNYDER, admitted to bar, 1980, Illinois, U.S. District Court, Northern District of Illinois and U.S. Court of Appeals, 7th Circuit; 1981, U.S. Tax Court. *Education:* Wichita State University (B.B.A., magna cum laude, 1967); University of Virginia (J.D., 1980). ***PRACTICE AREAS:*** Federal Income Tax Law; State and Local Tax Matters; Tax-Exempt Organizations; ERISA. ***Email:*** easnyder@arnstein.com

JOSE D. SOSA, admitted to bar, 1998, Florida; 1999, U.S. District Court, Southern District of Florida. *Education:* Harvard University (A.B., cum laude, 1995); Georgetown University (J.D., 1998). (Resident, West Palm Beach, Florida Office). ***PRACTICE AREAS:*** Civil Litigation; Appellate Practice. ***Email:*** jdsosa@arnstein.com

WALTER J. STARCK, admitted to bar, 1976, Illinois. *Education:* Harvard University (A.B., with honors, 1972); Tulane University (J.D., 1976). ***PRACTICE AREAS:*** Real Estate; Construction Law; Business Law. ***Email:*** wjstarck@arnstein.com

PAUL E. STARKMAN, admitted to bar, 1984, Illinois and U.S. District Court, Northern District of Illinois including Trial Bar; 1987, U.S. Court of Appeals, Seventh Circuit; 1995, U.S. District Court, Central District of Illinois. *Education:* University of Wisconsin-Madison (B.A., 1980); DePaul University (J.D., 1984). ***PRACTICE AREAS:*** Employment Discrimination Law; Appellate Practice (Appeals) Law; Civil (or General Civil) Practice. ***Email:*** pestarkman@arnstein.com

(This Listing Continued)

MIRIAM R. STEIN, admitted to bar, 1996, Illinois and U.S. District Court, Northern District of Illinois. *Education:* Northwestern University (B.A., 1991); Chicago-Kent College of Law (J.D., 1996). ***PRACTICE AREAS:*** Bankruptcy; Creditor Rights; Insolvency; Commercial Litigation. ***Email:*** mrstein@arnstein.com

DAVID SUGAR, admitted to bar, 1976, Illinois and U.S. District Court, Northern District of Illinois. *Education:* University of Illinois, Chicago (B.A., with honors, 1972); Northwestern University (J.D., 1976). ***PRACTICE AREAS:*** Corporate; Condominium and Homeowners Association; Litigation. ***Email:*** dsugar@arnstein.com

HOWARD J. SWIBEL, admitted to bar, 1975, Illinois and U.S. District Court, Northern District of Illinois; 1978, U.S. Court of Appeals, 7th Circuit. *Education:* Harvard University (A.B., cum laude, 1972; J.D., cum laude, 1975). ***PRACTICE AREAS:*** Business Law; Health and Hospital Law; Litigation. ***Email:*** hjswibel@arnstein.com

JAY P. TARSHIS, admitted to bar, 1980, Illinois and U.S. District Court, Northern District of Illinois. *Education:* Northwestern University (B.S., 1976); University of Illinois (J.D., cum laude, 1980). ***PRACTICE AREAS:*** Employee Benefits; Estate and Gift Taxation; Income Taxation. ***Email:*** jptarshis@arnstein.com

ROBERT J. TAYLOR, admitted to bar, 1996, Illinois. *Education:* University of Illinois (B.S., 1991); Chicago-Kent College of Law, Illinois Institute of Technology (J.D., 1996). ***PRACTICE AREAS:*** Real Estate; Business Law. ***Email:*** rjtaylor@arnstein.com

JESSICA TOVROV, admitted to bar, 1990, Illinois and U.S. District Court, Northern District of Illinois. *Education:* University of Chicago (B.A.; M.A.; Ph.D); Illinois Institute of Technology, Chicago-Kent College of Law (J.D., cum laude). ***PRACTICE AREAS:*** Insurance; Insurance Insolvency; Bankruptcy; Litigation. ***Email:*** jtovrov@arnstein.com

HARRY N. TURK, admitted to bar, 1968, Wisconsin; 1971, New York; 1997, Florida and U.S. District Court, Southern and Middle Districts of Florida; U.S. District Court, Southern District of New York; U.S. Court of Appeals, Second, Third, Seventh, Tenth and District of Columbia Circuits. *Education:* University of Wisconsin (B.S., 1965; J.D., 1968). (Resident, Miami, Florida Office). ***PRACTICE AREAS:*** Arbitration Law; Collective Bargaining Law; Civil Rights Law; Employer-Employee Relations; Labor Law. ***Email:*** hnturk@arnstein.com

JOHN A. TURNER, admitted to bar, 1994, Florida and U.S. District Court, Southern and Middle Districts of Florida. *Education:* Pennsylvania State University (B.A., 1989); University of Florida (J.D., 1993). (Resident, West Palm Beach, Florida Office). ***PRACTICE AREAS:*** Commercial Litigation; Corporate Practice. ***Email:*** jaturner@arnstein.com

MICHAEL R. TUROFF, admitted to bar, 1964, Illinois and U.S. District Court, Northern District of Illinois including Trial Bar; 1973, U.S. Court of Appeals, 7th Circuit; 1974, U.S. Court of Appeals, 6th Circuit and U.S. Supreme Court; 1977, U.S. Court of Appeals, 2nd Circuit; 1983, U.S. Claims Court; 1984, U.S. Court of Appeals, 5th Circuit; 1989, U.S. District Court, Northern District of California and Eastern District of Michigan. *Education:* University of Michigan (B.B.A., 1961); University of Chicago (J.D., 1964). ***PRACTICE AREAS:*** Business Litigation; Complex Commercial Litigation; Business Law; Insurance Coverage. ***Email:*** mrturoff@arnstein.com

ROBERT I. URY, admitted to bar, 1964, Illinois; 1970, U.S. Tax Court; 1974, U.S. Supreme Court; 1981, U.S. Court of Appeals, 7th Circuit; 1999, U.S. Court of Appeals, 11th Circuit. *Education:* DePaul University (B.S., 1960); Northwestern University (J.D., 1964). ***PRACTICE AREAS:*** Federal Income, Estate and Gift Taxation Law; Probate, Trusts and Estates; Estate Planning Law; ERISA. ***Email:*** riury@arnstein.com

MARY CANNON VEED, admitted to bar, 1977, Nebraska and U.S. District Court, District of Nebraska and for the Federal District; 1987, U.S. Court of Appeals, Eighth Circuit; 1990, Illinois and U.S. District Court, Northern District of Illinois, including Trial Bar and U.S. Court of Appeals, Seventh Circuit; 1999, U.S. Supreme Court and U.S. Court of Appeals, Ninth Circuit. *Education:* University of Nebraska (B.A., 1974); Creighton University (J.D., cum laude, 1977); The Hague Academy of International Law (1982); University of Amsterdam, Europa Institute (Diploma in European Integration, 1983). ***PRACTICE AREAS:*** Insurance; Insurance Insolvency; Bankruptcy; Insurance Regulation. ***Email:*** mcveed@arnstein.com

JOHN T. WAGENER, admitted to bar, 1983, Illinois and U.S. District Court, Northern District of Illinois; 1988, U.S. Court of Appeals, 11th Circuit; 1990, U.S. District Court, Central District of Illinois. *Education:* Spring Hill College (B.A., magna cum laude, 1980); University of Illinois (J.D., magna cum laude, 1983). ***PRACTICE AREAS:*** Litigation; Risk Management; Products Liability Law; Tort Law; Landlord and Tenant Law; Commercial Litigation. ***Email:*** jtwagener@arnstein.com

DAVID S. WAXMAN, admitted to bar, 1985, Illinois and U.S. District Court, Northern District of Illinois including Trial Bar. *Education:* Indiana University (B.S., with distinction, 1982); University of Pennsylvania (J.D., 1985). ***PRACTICE AREAS:*** Litigation; Medical Malpractice Law; Commercial Litigation. ***Email:*** dswaxman@arnstein.com

DAVID S. WAYNE, admitted to bar, 1996, Illinois. *Education:* Northwestern University (B.A., 1993); Loyola University (J.D., 1996). ***PRACTICE AREAS:*** Labor and Employment; Insurance Coverage; Litigation. ***Email:*** dwayne@arnstein.com

RAYMOND J. WERNER, admitted to bar, 1971, Illinois, U.S. District Court, Northern District of Illinois and U.S. Court of Appeals, 7th Circuit; U.S. Court of Appeals, 9th Circuit. *Education:* DePaul University (B.S.C., 1967); IIT/Chicago-Kent College of Law (J.D., 1971). ***PRACTICE AREAS:*** Real Estate Law. ***Email:*** rjwerner@arnstein.com

DAWN C. WRONA EBY, admitted to bar, 1992, Illinois and U.S. District Court, Northern District of Illinois. *Education:* Princeton University (B.S.E., 1989); Indiana University (J.D., 1992). ***PRACTICE AREAS:*** Litigation; Products Liability; Medical Malpractice. ***Email:*** dcwronaeby@arnstein.com

THOMAS P. YARDLEY, admitted to bar, 1991, Wisconsin and Illinois. *Education:* University of Michigan (B.A., 1986); University of Essex, Colchester, England; Marquette University (J.D., 1991); Loyola University. ***PRACTICE AREAS:*** Litigation. ***Email:*** tpyardley@arnstein.com

(This Listing Continued)

ARNSTEIN & LEHR LLP, Chicago—Continued

MICHAEL J. ZDEB, admitted to bar, 1976, Illinois; 1977, U.S. Tax Court. *Education:* Loyola University (B.A., 1972; M.A., 1977); Loyola School of Law (J.D., cum laude, 1976). ***Email:*** mjzdeb@arnstein.com

SPECIAL COUNSEL

THERESIA E. WOLF-McKENZIE, admitted to bar, 1977, Illinois and U.S. District Court, Northern District of Illinois; 1978, U.S. Court of Appeals, 7th Circuit and U.S. Tax Court; 1983, U.S. District Court, Northern District of Illinois including Trial Bar and U.S. Supreme Court; 1991, U.S. Court of Claims. *Education:* University of Illinois (B.A., 1972); John Marshall Law School (J.D., 1977). ***PRACTICE AREAS:*** Real Estate Planning; Probate Law; Commercial Real Estate; Residential Real Estate; Tax Controversies; Hospital Law. ***Email:*** tewolfmckenzie@arnstein.com

ASSOCIATES

SHEKAR ADIGA, admitted to bar, 2003, Illinois. *Education:* Macalester College (B.A., 1995); Washington University (J.D., 2003). ***PRACTICE AREAS:*** Litigation. ***Email:*** sadiga@arnstein.com

KEVIN BRENNER, admitted to bar, 2002, Illinois. *Education:* University of Wisconsin (B.A., 1999); Chicago-Kent College of Law, Illinois Institute of Technology (J.D., 2002). ***PRACTICE AREAS:*** Litigation. ***Email:*** kbrenner@arnstein.com

RAY H. BURGAN, admitted to bar, 2002, Illinois; U.S. District Court, Northern District of Illinois. *Education:* Indiana University (B.S., 1998); Chicago-Kent College of Law, Illinois Institute of Technology (J.D., 2002); Northwestern University School of Law (LL.M., Taxation, 2003). ***PRACTICE AREAS:*** Closely Held Business Law; Business Taxation; Business Succession Planning. ***Email:*** rhburgan@arnstein.com

KRISTINA M. CANDIDO, admitted to bar, 1999, Florida; 2000, U.S. District Court, Southern and Northern Districts of Florida (Not admitted in Illinois). *Education:* University of Massachusetts (B.A., 1994); Nova Southeastern University (J.D., 1999). ***PRACTICE AREAS:*** Commercial Litigation; Civil Litigation; Marital Law. ***Email:*** kmcandido@arnstein.com

JENIFER L. CARACCIOLO, admitted to bar, 2003, Illinois. *Education:* University of Texas (B.A., high honors, 2000); Chicago-Kent College of Law, Illinois Institute of Technology (J.D., 2003). ***PRACTICE AREAS:*** Litigation. ***Email:*** jhcaracciolo@arnstein.com

ANDREA J. DURKIN, admitted to bar, 2001, Illinois. *Education:* University of Illinois (B.A., 1997); Chicago-Kent College of Law, Illinois Institute of Technology (J.D., 2000). ***Email:*** ajdurkin@arnstein.com

JASON C. HILL, admitted to bar, 2001, Florida. *Education:* University of Florida (B.S., with honors, 1994); Florida State University (J.D., 2001). (Resident, West Palm Beach, Florida Office). ***PRACTICE AREAS:*** Litigation; Transactional Law; Real Estate. ***Email:*** jchill@arnstein.com

JASON B. HIRSH, admitted to bar, 2004, Illinois; U.S. District Court, Northern District of Illinois. *Education:* Miami University, Ohio (B.S., with honors, 2001); Chicago-Kent College of Law, Illinois Institute of Technology (J.D., with honors, 2004). ***PRACTICE AREAS:*** Commercial Litigation; Antitrust; Employment Law. ***Email:*** jbhirsh@arnstein.com

ERIK L. KANTZ, admitted to bar, 2000, Illinois; 2001, District of Columbia. *Education:* Illinois Wesleyan University (B.A., 1994); DePaul University (J.D., 2000). ***PRACTICE AREAS:*** Commercial Law; Corporate Law; Business Acquisitions. ***Email:*** elkantz@arnstein.com

SHARILEE KEMPA, admitted to bar, 2002, Illinois. *Education:* University of Illinois, Urbana-Champaign (B.S., 1999); DePaul University of College of Law (J.D., 2002). ***PRACTICE AREAS:*** Litigation. ***Email:*** skempa@arnstein.com

LAURA L. LAU, admitted to bar, 2003, Illinois. *Education:* Winona State University (B.S., 1998); University of Wisconsin (J.D., 2003). ***PRACTICE AREAS:*** Litigation. ***Email:*** lllau@arnstein.com

JOY E. LEVY, admitted to bar, 2001, California; 2003, Illinois. *Education:* University of Southern California (B.S., 1998); Southwestern University School of Law (J.D., 2001). ***PRACTICE AREAS:*** Bankruptcy. ***Email:*** jelevy@arnstein.com

MARTHA K. MILIA, admitted to bar, 2000, Illinois and U.S. District Court, Northern District of Illinois; 2001, Michigan. *Education:* University of Michigan (B.A., 1997); DePaul University (J.D., 2000). ***PRACTICE AREAS:*** Litigation. ***Email:*** mkmilia@arnstein.com

ELIZABETH M. PERRY, admitted to bar, 2001, Illinois and U.S. Tax Court. *Education:* Michigan State University (B.A., 1997); Loyola University Chicago, School of Law (J.D., 2001). ***PRACTICE AREAS:*** Estate Planning; Tax Law. ***Email:*** emperry@arnstein.com

DANIEL I. SCHLADE, admitted to bar, 2000, Illinois and U.S. District Court, Northern District of Illinois. *Education:* University of Illinois, Urbana-Champaign (B.S., Advertising, 1996); Chicago-Kent College of Law, Illinois Institute of Technology (J.D., high honors, 2000). ***PRACTICE AREAS:*** Litigation. ***Email:*** dischlade@arnstein.com

IRINA SHELEST, admitted to bar, 2001, Illinois. *Education:* Northwestern University (B.A., 1998); Loyola University (J.D., 2001). ***PRACTICE AREAS:*** Health Care; HIPPA; Health Care Contracts. ***Email:*** ishelest@arnstein.com

HARLEY STORRINGS, admitted to bar, 2004, Florida. *Education:* University of Florida (B.A.); University of Miami (J.D., 2004). (Resident, Miami, Florida Office). ***PRACTICE AREAS:*** Bankruptcy; Employment Law; Commercial Law. ***Email:*** *hstorrings@arnstein.com*

E. JASON TREMBLAY, admitted to bar, 2000, Illinois. *Education:* Franklin & Marshall College (B.A., 1996); Chicago-Kent College of Law, Illinois Institute of Technology (J.D., 2000). ***PRACTICE AREAS:*** Litigation. ***Email:*** ejtremblay@arnstein.com

KELI M. VIDETTO, admitted to bar, 2001, Wisconsin; 2002, Illinois. *Education:* Transylvania University (B.A., 1998); University of Wisconsin (J.D., 2001). ***PRACTICE AREAS:*** Litigation. ***Email:*** kmvidetto@arnstein.com

OF COUNSEL

JOSEPH T. GANZER, admitted to bar, 2000, Wisconsin and U.S. District Court, Western and Eastern Districts of Wisconsin. *Education:* St. Norbert College (B.A., 1992); University of Wisconsin-Madison (J.D., 2000). (Resident, Milwaukee, Wisconsin Office; Also Associate, Hodan, Doster & Ganzer, S.C.)

MICHAEL J. GANZER, admitted to bar, 1981, Wisconsin, U.S. District Court, Eastern and Western Districts of Wisconsin and U.S. Court of Appeals, Seventh Circuit. *Education:* Marquette University (B.A., 1978); University of Dayton (J.D., 1981). (Resident, Milwaukee, Wisconsin Office; Also Member, Hodan, Doster & Ganzer, S.C.). ***PRACTICE AREAS:*** Litigation.

THEODORE J. HODAN, admitted to bar, 1963, Wisconsin and U.S. District Court, Eastern District of Wisconsin; 1966, U.S. Court of Military Appeals and U.S. Supreme Court; 1977, U.S. Court of Appeals, Seventh Circuit. *Education:* Marquette University (B.S.M.E., 1960; J.D., 1963). (Resident, Milwaukee, Wisconsin Office; Also Member, Hodan, Doster & Ganzer, S.C.). ***PRACTICE AREAS:*** Business Law; Litigation; Probate; Estate Planning.

STANLEY M. LIPNICK, admitted to bar, 1960, District of Columbia (inactive); 1966, Colorado (inactive); 1968, Illinois; 1983, Florida; U.S. Supreme Court; U.S. Court of Appeals, 2nd, 3rd, 6th, 7th, 10th and District of Columbia Circuits; U.S. District Court, Northern District of Illinois (including Trial Bar) and Eastern District of Wisconsin. *Education:* Columbia University (B.A., 1956); George Washington University (J.D., with honors, 1960). ***PRACTICE AREAS:*** Commercial Litigation; Trade Regulation Law; Antitrust Law; White Collar Crime Law. ***Email:*** smlipnick@arnstein.com

MARTIN PICO, admitted to bar, 1996, Florida. *Education:* University of Miami (B.B.A., 1992; J.D., cum laude, 1996). (Resident, Miami, Florida Office). ***PRACTICE AREAS:*** Commercial Litigation; Dispute Resolution. ***Email:*** mpico@arnstein.com

DAVID T. RALLO, admitted to bar, 1975, Illinois and U.S. District Court, Northern District of Illinois. *Education:* American University (B.A., 1971); John Marshall Law School (J.D., 1975). ***PRACTICE AREAS:*** Business Litigation; Contracts; Real Estate; Tax; Arbitration; ERISA; Labor and Employment. ***Email:*** dtrallo@arnstein.com

L. TRENT STINSON, admitted to bar, 1985, Illinois; 1999, Florida. *Education:* Princeton University (B.A., 1982); Harvard University Law School (J.D., 1985). (Resident, Miami, Florida Office). ***PRACTICE AREAS:*** Mergers and Acquisitions; International Law; Venture Capital; Public Finance. ***Email:*** ltstinson@arnstein.com

PATRICK A. TUITE, admitted to bar, 1961, Illinois; 1964, U.S. Court of Appeals, Seventh Circuit; 1969, U.S. District Court, Northern District of Illinois; 1992, U.S. Supreme Court; 1993, U.S. Court of Appeals, Sixth Circuit. *Education:* University of Illinois (B.A., 1958; LL.B., 1961). ***PRACTICE AREAS:*** Criminal Defense and Appeals, State and Federal. ***Email:*** patuite@arnstein.com

(This Listing Continued)

ARONBERG GOLDGEHN DAVIS & GARMISA

Established in 1892

SUITE 3000 ONE IBM PLAZA
CHICAGO, ILLINOIS 60611
Telephone: 312-828-9600
Telecopier: 312-828-9635
Email: agdg@agdglaw.com
URL: http://www.agdglaw.com

Schaumburg, Illinois Office: 10 North Martingale Road, Fourth Floor, 60173. Telephone: 847-985-4060.

Corporate, Banking and General Business Practice. Insurance Coverage, General Civil, Insurance Defense, Products Liability, Trial and Appellate Practice in all Courts. Real Estate Transactions, Estate Planning and Probate, Federal Taxation, Employee Benefits, Domestic Relations, Employment, Trademark, Copyright and Unfair Competition, Health Care and Government Relations.

FIRM PROFILE: At Aronberg Goldgehn Davis & Garmisa, we are proud of our long term and personalized relationships with our clients. Our approach to our clients' needs for legal services is tailored to meet their specific business goals. Our small firm efficiencies combined with our depth of experience have been the key to our success in attracting and keeping our clients for more than a century.

Throughout our history, we have been sought out by individuals and corporations for our experience in a wide range of practice areas, including corporate, healthcare, banking, tax, estate planning, real estate and domestic relations. Our membership in Legal Network Alliance (www.legalnetlink.net) allows us to offer clients the services of premier law firms in the United States, Canada, Mexico, South America, Europe, China and the Pacific Rim.

Highly experienced in complex commercial litigation matters, the firm's trial lawyers have expertise in a number of fast-changing areas of concern to clients in today's business world, including employment covenants, environmental litigation, intellectual property rights, construction, creditors' rights and bankruptcy matters. We are also a leading insurance coverage litigation firm, representing clients in major, multi-party coverage cases throughout the United States.

At Aronberg Goldgehn Davis & Garmisa, we combine creative solutions with sound legal analysis. Relying on thoughtful planning, experienced lawyers and modern technology, we handle the legal needs of our clients efficiently, at reasonable rates and with no sacrifice in the quality of legal representation.

(This Listing Continued)

MEMBERS OF FIRM

CHRISTOPHER J. BANNON, born Blue Island, Illinois, June 17, 1962; admitted to bar, 1987, Illinois and U.S. District Court, Northern District of Illinois including Trial Bar; 1996, U.S. Court of Appeals, Seventh Circuit. *Education:* University of Illinois-Chicago (B.A., with honors, 1984); Loyola University (J.D., 1987). Recipient, American Jurisprudence Awards in Illinois Civil Litigation, Civil Procedure and Legislation. *Member:* Chicago, Illinois State and American Bar Associations. ***PRACTICE AREAS:*** Litigation; Insurance Coverage; Construction Law; Professional Liability; Banking Law. ***Email:*** cbannon@agdglaw.com

ERIC M. BROWN, born Atlantic, Iowa, July 18, 1966; admitted to bar, 1991, Illinois. *Education:* Drake University (B.A., 1988); Syracuse University (J.D., cum laude, 1991); Chicago-Kent College of Law (LL.M., Taxation, with honors, 1995). *Member:* Chicago (Member, Federal Tax Committee) Bar Association. ***PRACTICE AREAS:*** Taxation; Corporate Law; Estate Planning; Real Estate. ***Email:*** ebrown@agdglaw.com

HOWARD J. FISHMAN, born Chicago, Illinois, February 19, 1968; admitted to bar, 1993, Illinois and U.S. District Court, Northern District of Illinois; 1994, U.S. Court of Appeals, Seventh Circuit. *Education:* University of Illinois (B.A., 1990); Chicago-Kent College of Law (J.D., with honors, 1993). *Member:* Chicago and Illinois State Bar Associations. ***PRACTICE AREAS:*** Insurance Coverage; Commercial Litigation. ***Email:*** hfishman@agdglaw.com

JAY A. FRANK, born Chicago, Illinois, April 6, 1943; admitted to bar, 1969, Illinois; 1970, U.S. District Court, Northern District of Illinois; 1971, U.S. Supreme Court. *Education:* University of Illinois (B.S., with honors, Political Science, 1965; J.D., 1968). Author: "Dissolution Proceedings by a Guardian on Behalf of a Ward," 2000 Illinois Family Law Report 202; "The Court Cannot Restrict a Spouse's Visitation by Excluding a Companion Absent a Finding of Serious Endangerment," 2003 Illinois Family Law Report 154; "How to Collect an Interim Fee Award," 2003 Illinois Family Law Report 209; "Does the Move Issuance of a Rule to Show Cause in a Contempt Proceeding Shift the Burden to the Alleged Contemnor," 2004 Illinois Family Law Report 186; "Application of the Fifth Amendment in Family Law Cases," 2005 Illinois Family Law Report 2. President, Advisory Board of Harbor Light, The Salvation Army, 1980-1984. Member, Chicago Advisory Board, 1986-1990, The Salvation Army. Board Member, One-To-One Learning Associates and Lilac Tree. Past Arbitrator, American Arbitration Association. Panel Speaker, Asset Protection Estate Planning For Professionals and Business Owners and Asset Protection Family Law Considerations. Chairman and Trustee, Legal Netlink Alliance. *Member:* Chicago (Member, Civil Practice and Matrimonial Law Committees), Northwest Suburban, Illinois State and American Bar Associations; American Academy of Matrimonial Lawyers. ***REPORTED CASES:*** In re Excello Press, Inc., 96 B.R. 840 (Bnkr. N.D. Ill. 1989); In re Marriage of Blunda, 702 N.E.2d 993 (Ill.App.2nd Dist. 1998). ***PRACTICE AREAS:*** Family Law; Litigation. ***Email:*** JFrank@agdglaw.com

WILLIAM J. GARMISA, born Chicago, Illinois, October 25, 1943; admitted to bar, 1968, Illinois. *Education:* University of Illinois (B.A., 1965); University of Michigan (J.D., 1968). *Member:* Chicago Bar Association. ***PRACTICE AREAS:*** Business Law; Corporate Law; Real Estate Law; Intellectual Property. ***Email:*** wgarmisa@agdglaw.com

PAUL A. GILMAN, born Chicago, Illinois, September 5, 1963; admitted to bar, 1989, Illinois. *Education:* University of Illinois (B.A., 1985); Loyola University (J.D., cum laude, 1989). Certified Public Accountant, 1985. ***PRACTICE AREAS:*** Corporate Law; Healthcare Law; Taxation; Estate Planning; Employee Benefits. ***Email:*** pgilman@agdglaw.com

MITCHELL S. GOLDGEHN, born Chicago, Illinois, March 15, 1931; admitted to bar, 1953, Illinois and U.S. District Court, Northern District of Illinois including Trial Bar; 1966, U.S. Court of Appeals, Seventh Circuit; 1966, U.S. Supreme Court; 2001, U.S. Court of Appeals, Fifth Circuit. *Education:* DePaul University (J.D., 1953). *Member:* Chicago, Illinois State Seventh Circuit and American Bar Associations; Illinois Association of Defense Trial Counsel; Defense Research Institute. ***PRACTICE AREAS:*** Insurance Coverage; Insurance Defense; Litigation. ***Email:*** mgoldgehn@agdglaw.com

JAMES S. JARVIS, born Chicago, Illinois, December 4, 1938; admitted to bar, 1962, Illinois; U.S. Tax Court, 1971. *Education:* St. Mary's College (B.A., 1959); Northwestern University (J.D., 1962). Phi Alpha Delta. Speaker, Asset Protection, Estate Planning and Offshore Trusts for Physicians, ISMIE Mutual Insurance Company. *Member:* Illinois State Bar Association. [Lt., U.S. Navy, Legal Specialist, 1962-1966]. ***PRACTICE AREAS:*** Probate; Trust Law; Estate Planning; Federal Taxation. ***Email:*** jjarvis@agdglaw.com

ELIZABETH OLEN LAZZARA, born Evanston, Illinois, March 24, 1964; admitted to bar, 1990, Louisiana; 1991, Illinois. *Education:* John Carroll University (B.A., 1986); Loyola University (J.D., 1989). *Member:* Chicago (Member, Family Law Section) and Illinois State (Member, Family Law Section Council) and Northwest Suburban Bar Associations. ***PRACTICE AREAS:*** Domestic Relations; Family Law; Estate Planning; Tax Planning. ***Email:*** elazzara@agdglaw.com

NATHAN H. LICHTENSTEIN, born Chicago, Illinois, June 12, 1953; admitted to bar, 1977, Illinois, Florida, U.S. District Court, Northern District of Illinois including Trial Bar and U.S. Court of Appeals, Seventh Circuit. *Education:* Northwestern University (B.A., 1974); DePaul University (J.D., cum laude, 1977); John Marshall Law School (LL.M., cum laude, 1983). *Member:* Decalogue Society (Chairman, Alternative Dispute Resolution Committee). ***REPORTED CASES:*** Trippe Mfg. Co. v. Nites Audio Corp., 401 F3d 529 (3rd Cir. 2005); Rose v. Mony Life Insurance Co., 82 F.Supp.2d 920 (N.D. Ill. 2000); Saunders v. Michigan Ave. National Bank, 278 Ill. App. 3d 307 (1st Dist. 1996); Maywood Proviso State Bank v. York State Bank, 625 N.E.2d 83 (Ill.App. 1st Dist. 1993); Graue Mill Development Corp. v. Colonial Bank, 927 F2d 988 (7th Cir. 1991); U.S. v. Northwest Commerce Bank, 727 F.Supp 403 (N.D. Ill. 1989); Slovick v. All American Bank, 516 N.E.2d 947 (Ill. App. 1st Dist. 1987); Marco Holding Co. v. Lear Siegler, Inc., 606 F.Supp. 204 (N.D. Ill. 1985). ***PRACTICE AREAS:*** Litigation; Creditor; Appellate Practice. ***Email:*** nlichtenstein@agdglaw.com

MITCHELL J. MELAMED, born Chicago, Illinois, November 10, 1943; admitted to bar, 1968, Illinois and U.S. District Court, Northern District of Illinois; 1991, Wisconsin. *Education:* University of Illinois (B.S., 1965; J.D., 1968); DePaul University School of Law (Masters in Health Law, 1996). Phi Delta Phi (President, 1967-1968). Trustee, Village of Glencoe, 2001—. Director, Friends of Glencoe Park District, Nominating Committee Chairman, Glencoe Caucus, 1984. Senior Housing Committee, Village of Glencoe, 1985. Glencoe Caucus Advisory Council, 1985-1991. Salvation Army Advisory Board, Harbor Light, 1988—; Ambassador, World Cup, 1994, Chicago Venue. Attorney for: Northwest Suburban Alliance for Commerce and Industry. Board of Visitors, University of Illinois College of Law, 1997-2000 *Member:* Chicago (Member, Judicial Evaluation Committee, 1988-1994), Illinois State and American (Member, Health Care) Bar Associations. ***PRACTICE AREAS:*** Health Care; Business Law; Corporate Law; Labor and Employment. ***Email:*** mmelamed@agdglaw.com

HENRY M. MORRIS, born Chicago, Illinois, January 21, 1939; admitted to bar, 1962, Illinois. *Education:* DePaul University and Northwestern University (B.S.L., 1960); Northwestern University (J.D., 1962). Member, Editorial Board, Northwestern Law Review, 1961-1962. *Member:* Chicago (Member, Real Property Law Committee, 1982-1984), Illinois State (Member: Estate Planning, Probate and Trust and Real Estate Sections) and American (Member, Real Property, Probate and Trust Law and Center for Professional Responsibility) Bar Associations. ***PRACTICE AREAS:*** Estate Planning; Wills; Probate; Estate and Trust Administration; Commercial Real Estate; Real Estate Finance; Land Use Law; Legal Ethics. ***Email:*** hmorris@agdglaw.com

JOHN M. RICCIONE, born Buffalo, New York, September 10, 1964; admitted to bar, 1989, Florida and U.S. District Court, Southern District of Florida; 1991, Illinois; U.S. District Court, Northern District of Illinois including Trial Bar and U.S. Court of Appeals, Seventh and Eleventh Circuits. *Education:* Canisius College (B.A., 1986); Syracuse University (J.D., 1989). *Member:* Palm Beach County and Illinois State Bar Associations; The Florida Bar. ***PRACTICE AREAS:*** Commercial Litigation; Trade Secrets; Labor and Employment; Construction Law. ***Email:*** jriccione@agdglaw.com

NED S. ROBERTSON, born Chicago, Illinois, May 5, 1945; admitted to bar, 1971, Illinois. *Education:* Hobart College (B.A., 1967); Chicago-Kent College of Law (J.D., 1971). Co-Author: "Reviewing Estate Plans — A Checklist," 28 CLU Journal 54, 1974; "Employment Contracts with Executive Personnel," Illinois Institute for Continuing Legal Education, 1979; "Valuation of the Professional Practice," Illinois Institute for Continuing Legal Education, 1986. Member, Franchise Advisory Board to the Illinois Attorney General. *Member:* Chicago (Past Chairman, Trust Law Committee) and Illinois State Bar Associations. ***PRACTICE AREAS:*** Commercial Real Estate; Trusts and Estates; Corporate Law; Banking Law; Franchises and Franchising. ***Email:*** nrobertson@agdglaw.com

DAVID H. SACHS, born Chicago, Illinois, August 13, 1963; admitted to bar, 1988, Illinois and U.S. District Court, Northern District of Illinois. *Education:* University of Illinois (B.A., 1985); IIT - Chicago Kent College of Law (J.D., 1988). Co-Author, "Defaults and Remedies," IICLE Commercial Landlord Tenant, Supp. 1996. *Member:* American Bar Association. ***PRACTICE AREAS:*** Real Estate; Creditor's Rights; Corporate Law; Business Law; Bankruptcy. ***Email:*** dsachs@agdglaw.com

BERNARD A. SCHLIFKE, born Chicago, Illinois, December 25, 1940; admitted to bar, 1966, Illinois. *Education:* University of Illinois and Northwestern University (B.S., 1962); University of Chicago (J.D., 1965). *Member:* American Bar Association. ***PRACTICE AREAS:*** Banking Law; Business Law; Corporate Law; General Practice; Real Estate.

WILLIAM J. SERRITELLA, JR., born Chicago, Illinois, April 17, 1967; admitted to bar, 1992, Illinois, U.S. District Court, Northern District of Illinois and U.S. Court of Appeals, Seventh Circuit. *Education:* Illinois Benedictine College (B.A., magna cum laude, 1988); DePaul University (J.D., summa cum laude, 1992). Order of the Coif. Member DePaul Law Review. Law Clerk, Illinois Appellate Court Justice Anthony J. Scariano, 1992-1993. Author: "Kelly vs. Lee's Old Fashioned Hamburgers: A Step Back From Certainty Under Rule 54 (b)," 41 DePaul L. Rev. 257 (1991). Co-Author: "Three Recent United States Supreme Court Decisions for Professionals Who Testify In Child Sexual Abuse Cases," Journal of Child Sexual Abuse, Vol. 1 (3), p. 15 (1992). ***PRACTICE AREAS:*** Litigation; Appellate Practice; Banking Law; Labor and Employment. ***Email:*** wserritella@agdglaw.com

ROBERT N. SODIKOFF, born Chicago, Illinois, August 21, 1948; admitted to bar, 1973, Illinois. *Education:* University of Illinois (B.A., with honors, 1970); Northwestern University (J.D., cum laude, 1973). Member, Northwestern Journal of Criminal Law, Criminology and Police Science. Author: "Letters of Credit," Illinois Institute for Continuing Legal Education, 1990 (revised 2001). Chairman, Plan Commission, Zoning Board of Appeals, 1990-1999 and Trustee, 1999—, Village of Burr Ridge. Member, Real Estate Council. *Member:* Illinois State (Labor and Employment Section Council); American Bar Association. ***PRACTICE AREAS:*** Corporate Law; Business Law; Real Estate; Labor and Employment; Health Care; Banking Law. ***Email:*** rsodikoff@agdglaw.com

BLOOMA STARK, born Breslau, Poland, February 12, 1947; admitted to bar, 1981, Illinois. *Education:* Northern Illinois University (B.S., summa cum laude, 1978); Northwestern University (J.D., cum laude, 1981). Phi Kappa Phi; Beta Gamma Sigma; Beta Alpha Psi. Certified Public Accountant, 1978. *Member:* Chicago (Trust Law Committee; Chairman, 1999), Illinois State and American Bar Associations; Chicago Estate Planning Council. ***PRACTICE AREAS:*** Estate Planning; Wills; Probate; Taxation. ***Email:*** bstark@agdglaw.com

ANDREW S. WILLIAMS, born Cincinnati, Ohio, May 24, 1945; admitted to bar, 1973, Illinois and U.S. District Court, Northern District of Illinois including Trial Bar. *Education:* Wabash College (B.A., magna cum laude, 1967); University of Michigan (J.D., cum laude, 1973). Phi Beta Kappa. Member, Plan Commission, Village of Hinsdale, 2003—. *Member:* Chicago Bar Association (Member, Employee Benefits Committee). ***PRACTICE AREAS:*** Employee Benefits; Employment Law; Corporate Law; Business Law; Banking Law. ***Email:*** awilliams@agdglaw.com

OF COUNSEL

RONALD J. ARONBERG, born Chicago, Illinois, June 22, 1932; admitted to bar, 1957, Illinois. *Education:* Northwestern University (B.S., 1954); University of Chicago (J.D., 1957). Phi Alpha Delta. Member, Board of Editors, University of Chicago Law Review, 1956-1957. (Retired)

MELVIN A. BLUM, born Chicago, Illinois, December 10, 1932; admitted to bar, 1957, Illinois; 1964, U.S. Supreme Court. *Education:* University of Michigan (B.A., 1954);

(This Listing Continued)

ARONBERG GOLDGEHN DAVIS & GARMISA, Chicago—Continued

Northwestern University (J.D., 1957). Assistant State's Attorney of Cook County, 1959-1962. ***PRACTICE AREAS:*** Corporate Law; Business Law; Banking Law. ***Email:*** mblum@agdglaw.com

JOEL C. LEVIN, born Evanston, Illinois, January 23, 1949; admitted to bar, 1974, Illinois. *Education:* University of Illinois (B.A., 1971); Washington University (J.D., 1974); New York University (LL.M., in Taxation, 1975). ***PRACTICE AREAS:*** Taxation; Corporate; Shareholders Agreements; Mergers and Acquisitions. ***Email:*** jlevin@agdglaw.com

STEVEN H. NEMEROVSKI, born Oak Park, Illinois, November 9, 1951; admitted to bar, 1977, Illinois and U. S. District Court, Northern District of Illinois. *Education:* University of Pennsylvania (B.A., 1972); University of Illinois (J.D., 1976). Certified Public Accountant, Illinois, 1976. Parliamentarian, Illinois House of Representatives, 1995-1996; Special Counsel to the Speaker, 1996-1997. *Member:* Chicago Bar Association. ***PRACTICE AREAS:*** Government Relations; Health Care; Medicaid. ***Email:*** snemerovski@agdglaw.com

WILLIAM P. ROSENTHAL (1923-2004)

CHARLES E. ZEITLIN, born Wilkes-Barre, Pennsylvania, January 19, 1932; admitted to bar, 1956, Illinois. *Education:* Harvard University (A.B., cum laude, 1953); Harvard Law School (J.D., 1956). (Retired)

ASSOCIATES

ANDREA AYCINENA, born Guatemala City, Guatemala, C.A.; admitted to bar, 2003, Illinois. *Education:* Miami University (B.A., 1998); DePaul University (J.D., 2003). *Member:* Chicago Bar Association; Women's Bar Association of Illinois; Hispanic Lawyers' Association of Illinois. ***LANGUAGES:*** Spanish. ***PRACTICE AREAS:*** Commercial Litigation; Professional Liability Defense; Appellate Practice.

LISA J. BRODSKY, born Evanston, Illinois, June 15, 1961; admitted to bar, 1986, Illinois. *Education:* Macalester College (B.A., 1983); Loyola University (J.D., 1986). *Member:* American Bar Association. ***PRACTICE AREAS:*** Insurance Coverage; Insurance Defense; Commercial Litigation; Health Care. ***Email:*** lbrodsky@agdglaw.com

DAVID C. GOLDSTEIN, born Long Island, New York, January 1, 1962; admitted to bar, 1993, Illinois; 1994, U.S. District Court, Northern District of Illinois; 1999, U.S. Tax Court; U.S. Court of Federal Claims, U.S. Court of Appeals, Seventh Circuit, U.S. Court of the Armed Forces and U.S. Supreme Court; 2000, New York; 2002, Florida. *Education:* Northeastern Illinois University (B.S., 1988); John Marshall Law School (J.D., cum laude, 1993). ***PRACTICE AREAS:*** Family Law; Domestic Relations. ***Email:*** dgoldstein@agdglaw.com

ELVIS D. GONZALEZ, born Chicago, Illinois, July 19, 1977; admitted to bar, 2003, Illinois and U.S. District Court, Northern District of Illinois. *Education:* University of Illinois at Chicago (B.S. with highest distinction in Economics, 2000); Loyola University Chicago School of Law (J.D., 2003). *Member:* Chicago Bar Association. ***LANGUAGES:*** Spanish. ***PRACTICE AREAS:*** Commercial Litigation; Employment Law. ***Email:*** egonzalez@agdglaw.com

PAUL A. GREENBERG, born Chicago, Illinois, September 6, 1969; admitted to bar, 1997, Illinois; 1998, U.S. District Court, Northern District of Illinois and U.S. Court of Appeals, Seventh Circuit. *Education:* University of Iowa; DePaul University (B.A., with honors, 1993); Chicago-Kent College of Law, Illinois Institute of Technology (J.D., with honors, 1997). *Member:* Illinois State and American (Member, Section on Litigation) Bar Associations. ***REPORTED CASES:*** Methode Electronics, Inc. v. Adam Technologies, Inc., 371 F.3d 923 (7th Cir. 2004); Superior Environmental Corp. v. Mangan, 247 F.Supp 2d 1001 (N.D. Ill. 2003); In re O'Shaughnessy, 252 B.R. 722 (N.D. Ill. 2000). ***PRACTICE AREAS:*** Business Litigation; Appellate Practice. ***Email:*** pgreenberg@agdglaw.com

MARY VIDAL HAYS, born St. Louis, Missouri, May 16, 1970; admitted to bar, 1995, Illinois. *Education:* University of Illinois (B.S., 1992); University of Denver (J.D., 1995). *Member:* Chicago Bar Association; Illinois CPA Society. ***PRACTICE AREAS:*** Taxation; Corporate Law; Probate; Estate Planning; Real Estate; Trademarks; Copyrights; Unfair Competition. ***Email:*** mhays@agdglaw.com

JENNIFER PAPAHRONIS, born Marburg, Germany, August 14, 1972; admitted to bar, 1998, Illinois. *Education:* Tufts University (B.A., with honors, 1994); DePaul University (J.D., 1998). *Member:* Chicago and Illinois State Bar Associations. ***LANGUAGES:*** German. ***PRACTICE AREAS:*** Family Law; Domestic Relations. ***Email:*** jpapahronis@agdglaw.com

CHRISTINA B. PEREZ, born Arlington Heights, Illinois, June 16, 1978; admitted to bar, 2003, Illinois. *Education:* University of Illinois (B.S., with honors, 2000); Chicago-Kent College of Law, Illinois Institute of Technology (J.D., with honors, 2003). Golden Key. ***LANGUAGES:*** German and French. ***PRACTICE AREAS:*** Real Estate. ***Email:*** cperez@agdglaw.com

ROBERT H. ARONSON

Established in 1958

SUITE 714, 100 WEST MONROE STREET
CHICAGO, ILLINOIS 60603
Telephone: 312-372-7123
FAX: 312-372-1247
Email: rharonson35@yahoo.com
URL: http://www.lawyers.com/robertharonson

General Criminal Trial and Appellate Practice in all State and Federal Courts.

FIRM PROFILE: Robert H. Aronson has concentrated in the practice of Criminal Defense, both trials and appeals, in both state and federal courts over 40 years. He is a member of the National Association of Criminal Defense Lawyers. The firm carries the highest legal ability rating in Martindale-Hubbell.

(This Listing Continued)

ROBERT H. ARONSON, born Chicago, Illinois, March 9, 1935; admitted to bar, 1958, Illinois and U.S. District Court, Northern District of Illinois; 1965, U.S. Court of Appeals, Seventh Circuit. *Education:* Northwestern University (B.S.L., 1956; J.D., 1958). Tau Epsilon Rho. Panel Attorney, Federal Defender Program, 1973-1977. *Member:* Chicago Bar Association (Member, Criminal Law Committee, 1995-1998); Chicago Association of Defense Lawyers (Member, Board of Governors, 1975-1977); National Association of Criminal Defense Lawyers.

ASH, ANOS, FREEDMAN & LOGAN, L.L.C.

Established in 1951

SUITE 1211, 77 WEST WASHINGTON STREET
CHICAGO, ILLINOIS 60602
Telephone: 312-346-1390
Fax: 312-346-7847

General Trial Practice. Products Liability, Malpractice, Probate, Corporate, Zoning, Municipal, Real Estate and Condominium Law.

MEMBERS OF FIRM

GEORGE J. ANOS (Retired)

JOSEPH ASH, born Poland, June 15, 1927; admitted to bar, 1949, Illinois; 1960, U.S. Supreme Court. *Education:* University of Illinois; DePaul University (LL.B., 1949). *Member:* Chicago (Member, Real Property Law Committee), Illinois State and American Bar Associations; Decalogue Society of Lawyers. ***PRACTICE AREAS:*** Transactional Real Estate and Land Use. ***Email:*** joeash@aflaw.com

LAWRENCE M. FREEDMAN, born Chicago, Illinois, December 25, 1943; admitted to bar, 1969, Illinois; 1976, U.S. Supreme Court. *Education:* Northwestern University (B.S., 1966); Loyola University (J.D., 1969). *Member:* Chicago (Member, Real Property Law Committee), Illinois State and American Bar Associations; Appellate Lawyers Association. ***PRACTICE AREAS:*** Transactional Real Estate; Land Use and Civil Appeals. ***Email:*** lmfreedman@aflaw.com

BRUCE T. LOGAN, born Abilene, Texas, April 6, 1943; admitted to bar, 1970, Illinois; 1982, U.S. District Court, Northern District of Illinois; 1990, U.S. Court of Federal Claims, U.S. Court of Appeals, Seventh Circuit. *Education:* DePaul University (B.S.C., 1965; J.D., 1969). Phi Alpha Delta. Arbitrator, Circuit of Cook County, Illinois, Court Annexed (1990-1997). Former General Counsel and Director Century Federal Savings Bank. Author, "Is it Time to Revise the Illinois Mechanics Lien Act?," Illinois Bar Journal, Nov. 2003, Vol. 91, Page 566. *Member:* Chicago (Member: Circuit Court Committee; Former Member Insurance Law Committee), Illinois State and American Bar Associations; Association of Trial Lawyers of America; Chicago Trial Lawyers Club. ***PRACTICE AREAS:*** Construction Litigation; Construction Contracting; Chancery and Special Remedies Litigation; Corporate and Partnership Dissolution Litigation; Business Organizations; Commercial Practice; Real Estate Acquisitions and Structuring; Civil Appeals. ***Email:*** btlogan@aflaw.com

BARRY ASH, born Chicago, Illinois, January 17, 1961; admitted to bar, 1987, Illinois and U.S. District Court, Northern District of Illinois. *Education:* Indiana University (B.S., 1983); IIT/Chicago-Kent College of Law (J.D., 1986). *Member:* Chicago (Member, Real Property Law and Local Government Committees), Illinois State and American Bar Associations; HomeBbuilders Association of Greater Chicago. ***PRACTICE AREAS:*** Transactional Real Estate and Land Use. ***Email:*** barryash@aflaw.com

REPRESENTATIVE CLIENTS: AMC Theatres; Bil-Jax, Inc.; Black Box Collotype Studios, Inc.; Burger King; Camelot Homes, Inc.; C. R. Bard, Inc.; City Wide Produce Distributors, Inc.; Cleaners Midwest Equipment Co.; Concord Homes; Design Galleries, Inc.; Great West Electrical Supply, Inc.; Brian Properties, Inc.; Keystone Aniline Corp.; Lexington Homes; McDonald's; Mobil Oil Co.; Restaurants Unlimited, Inc.; Shell Oil Co.; Pace; The Suburaban Bus Division of the Regional Transportation Authority; Storagemart, Inc.; Petsmart; The Alter Group; Wendy's; Westchester Public Library; Mt. Prospect Park District; Workforce Products, Inc.; Pritzker Realty Group, Inc.; Northern Builders; Pasquinelli Construction Co.; Prime Hospitality Corp.; New England Builders, Inc.; Solo Laboratories, Inc.

ASHCRAFT & ASHCRAFT, LTD.

Established in 1887

TWO PRUDENTIAL PLAZA
180 NORTH STETSON AVENUE
SUITE 5510
CHICAGO, ILLINOIS 60601
Telephone: 312-819-4010
Telecopier: 312-819-4009
URL: http://www.lawyers.com/ashcraft&ashcraft

Trust and Estates, Wills and Probate, Estate Planning, Elder Law, Trust Administration, Liquidity Planning, Asset Protection, Taxation, Tax Planning, Business Law, Contract Law, Corporate Law, Real Estate, Commercial Real Estate, Residential Real Estate, Buying and Selling a Home, Condominium Law.

FIRM PROFILE: The firm was founded over 100 years ago in 1887 and has, from its inception, represented family business interests and individuals. Today, the firm continues to serve closely held businesses and individual clients, providing a range of legal services, including, corporate and commercial, trust and estate, real estate, mergers and acquisitions, and Probate services.

RUFUS DAWES BEACH (1903-1989)

CHARLES H. G. KIMBALL (1909-1997)

CHARLES F. MOLES, born Detroit, Michigan, May 20, 1953; admitted to bar, 1979, Illinois and U.S. District Court, Northern District of Illinois. *Education:* Michigan State University (B.A., with honors, 1975); Wayne State University and DePaul University (J.D., 1979). ***PRACTICE AREAS:*** Estate Planning; Trust Administration; Taxation; Probate. ***Email:*** cfm@ashcraftandashcraft.com

(This Listing Continued)

RANDALL C. ROMEI, born Chicago, Illinois, December 29, 1954; admitted to bar, 1981, Illinois and U.S. District Court, Northern District of Illinois. *Education:* University of Illinois (B.A., 1976); DePaul University (J.D., 1981). ***PRACTICE AREAS:*** Wills; Real Estate; Estate Planning; Commercial Law; Corporate; Probate. ***Email:*** rcr@ashcraftandashcraft.com

THE LAW OFFICES OF DEBORAH S. ASHEN, LTD.

217 NORTH JEFFERSON STREET, SUITE 600
CHICAGO, ILLINOIS 60661
Telephone: 312-655-0800
Fax: 312-655-0801
Email: dsa@ashenlaw.com

Equipment Leasing, Finance, Commercial Litigation, Collection Litigation and Real Estate.

DEBORAH S. ASHEN, born Chicago, Illinois, June 17, 1961; admitted to bar, 1989, Illinois and U.S. District Court, Northern District of Illinois. *Education:* Arizona State University (B.S., 1984); DePaul University (J.D., 1989). Member: Equipment Leasing Association; Lease Enforcement Attorney Network. *Member:* Chicago, Illinois State and American Bar Associations; Commercial Law League of America. ***LANGUAGES:*** English. ***PRACTICE AREAS:*** Equipment Leasing; Finance; Commercial Litigation; Collection Litigation; Real Estate. ***Email:*** dsa@ashenlaw.com

ASHER, GITTLER, GREENFIELD & D'ALBA, LTD.

Established in 1951
200 WEST JACKSON BOULEVARD, SUITE 1900
CHICAGO, ILLINOIS 60606
Telephone: 312-263-1500
Fax: 312-263-1520
Email: firm@ulaw.com

Labor Relations, Employment and Employee Benefit Law, General Trial Practice in all Courts.

LESTER ASHER (1910-1990)

MICHAEL C. GREENFIELD, born Chicago, Illinois, May 4, 1934; admitted to bar, 1957, Illinois; 1982, Indiana. *Education:* University of Illinois (B.A., 1955); Northwestern University (J.D., 1957). Assistant States Attorney, Cook County, Illinois, 1957-1959. *Member:* Chicago, Illinois State and American Bar Associations. ***PRACTICE AREAS:*** Labor Law; Employment Benefits Law; Health Care Law. ***Email:*** mcg@ulaw.com

MARVIN GITTLER, born Bronx, New York, October 7, 1938; admitted to bar, 1963, Illinois. *Education:* Syracuse University (A.B., 1960); University of Chicago (J.D., 1963). Attorney, National Labor Relations Board, 1963-1967. *Member:* Chicago, Illinois State and American Bar Associations. Fellow, College of Labor and Employment Lawyers. ***PRACTICE AREAS:*** Labor Law; Employment Rights (Plaintiff) Law; Employee Benefits. ***Email:*** mg@ulaw.com

JOEL A. D'ALBA, born Charleston, South Carolina, July 22, 1944; admitted to bar, 1971, Illinois; 1972 Michigan. *Education:* Washington University (A.B., 1966); Illinois Institute of Technology (M.S., 1969); University of Illinois (J.D., 1971). Co-Author with Marvin Gittler: "Affirmative Action Plans," Ohio Legislative Institute, Midwest Labor Law Conference, 1973. Author: "Health Care Decisions of the National Labor Relations Board Since 1974 Amendments to the National Labor Relations Act," ABA National Institute, 1977; "Labor Relations Law Problems in Hospitals and the Health Care Industry," Report of 1976 Proceedings, Section of Labor Relations Law, American Bar Association, 1977; "The Nature of the Duty to Bargain in Good Faith, In Portrait of a Process-Collective Negotiations in Public Employment," Public Employment Relations Services, 1979. Administrative Assistant to Hon. Robert G. Howlett, Chairman, Michigan Employment Relations Commission, 1971-1973. Member, Advisory Committee, Labor Law Curriculum, Illinois Institute of Continuing Legal Education, 1990-1992. Member, Board of Advisors, Institute of Industrial Relations, Loyola University, 1987-1994. Member, CCH Panel of Labor Law Experts. *Member:* American Bar Association (Member, Labor and Employment Law Section, 1974-1980; Co-Chairman: Committee on State and Local Government Bargaining, Labor and Employment Law Section, 1989-1995; Assistant Editor, Labor and Employment Law Section Newsletter; Council Member, Labor and Employment Law Section, 2002—). Fellow, College of Labor and Employment Law. ***PRACTICE AREAS:*** Labor Law; Employment Rights (Plaintiff) Law. ***Email:*** jad@ulaw.com

ROBERT B. GREENBERG, born Chicago, Illinois, May 25, 1939; admitted to bar, 1964, Illinois. *Education:* University of Illinois and Roosevelt University; DePaul University (J.D., 1964). *Member:* Chicago, Illinois State and American (Member, Employee Rights and Responsibilities Committee) Bar Associations. [With USAFR, 1960-1966]. ***PRACTICE AREAS:*** Labor Law; Employment Benefits Law; Health Care Law; Collections; Federal Litigation. ***Email:*** rbg@ulaw.com

LEONARD J. ELBERTS, born Joliet, Illinois, April 1, 1948; admitted to bar, 1974, Illinois 1978, U.S. Court of Appeals, Seventh Circuit and U.S. District Court, Northern District of Illinois. *Education:* Loyola University (B.A., 1970); DePaul University (J.D., 1974). Member, De Paul University Law Review, 1972-1973. *Member:* Chicago, Illinois State and American Bar Associations. ***PRACTICE AREAS:*** Labor Law; Employment Benefits Law; Health Care Law. ***Email:*** lje@ulaw.com

BARRY G. COLLINS, born Chicago, Illinois, December 8, 1948; admitted to bar, 1980, Illinois and U.S. District Court, Northern District of Illinois; 1983, U.S. Court of Appeals, 7th Circuit. *Education:* Tolentine College (B.A., summa cum laude, 1971); Governors State University (M.A., 1975); John Marshall Law School (J.D., with highest distinction, 1980). Order of John Marshall. Member, The John Marshall Law Review, 1979-1980. Law Clerk to Justice John J. Stamos, Illinois Appellate Court, 1980-1982. *Member:* Chicago and American Bar Associations. ***PRACTICE AREAS:*** Labor Law; Employment Benefits Law; Health Care Law. ***Email:*** bgc@ulaw.com

(This Listing Continued)

PATRICIA A. COLLINS, admitted to bar, 1978, Illinois and U.S. District Court, Northern District of Illinois; 1983, U.S. Supreme Court. *Education:* Marietta College (B.A., 1969); Northwestern University (M.A., 1970); DePaul University (J.D., 1978). *Member:* Chicago, (Vice-Chair, 1994-1995; Chair, 1995-1996, Labor Employment Law Committee), Illinois State (Chair, 1986-1987, Labor Law Section) and American Bar Associations; Womens Bar Association of Illinois (Secretary, 1994-1996). ***PRACTICE AREAS:*** Labor Law; Employment Rights Law.

MARGARET ANGELUCCI, born Detroit, Michigan, June 20, 1969; admitted to bar, 1994, Illinois, U.S. District Court, Northern District of Illinois and U.S. Court of Appeals, 7th Circuit. *Education:* Michigan State University (B.A., 1991); DePaul University (J.D., 1994). *Member:* Chicago and American Bar Associations; Womens Bar Association of Illinois (Member, Judicial Evaluation Committee, 1997-1999; Contributing Editor, Discipline & Discharge in Arbitration). ***PRACTICE AREAS:*** Labor Law; Employment Rights Law.

RYAN A. HAGERTY, born Saginaw, Michigan, June 13, 1976; admitted to bar, 2001, Illinois. *Education:* Illinois State University (B.A., 1998); DePaul University (J.D., 2001). *Member:* Chicago, Illinois and American Bar Associations. ***PRACTICE AREAS:*** Labor and Employment. ***Email:*** rah@ilaw.com,

LIBRADO ARREOLA VEGA, born Guanajuato, Mexico, January 26, 1963; admitted to bar, 1990, Illinois, U.S. District Court, Northern and Central Districts of Illinois and U.S. Court of Appeals, 7th Circuit. *Education:* University of Illinois, Urbana-Champaign (B.A., 1986); Northeastern University School of Law (J.D., 1989). *Member:* Chicago and American Bar Associations; Hispanic Lawyers Association of Illinois. ***LANGUAGES:*** Spanish. ***SPECIAL AGENCIES:*** Attorney, National Labor Relations Board, 1990-1999. ***PRACTICE AREAS:*** Labor Law; Plaintiff Employment Rights; ERISA Collection Litigation. ***Email:*** la@ulaw.com

MICHELE COTRUPE, born Chantilly, Virginia, April 13, 1975; admitted to bar, 2000, Illinois; 2001, U.S. District Court, Northern District of Illinois. *Education:* Virginia Polytechnic Institute and State University (B.A., 1996); DePaul University (J.D., 2000). Administrative Law Judge, Illinois Labor Relations Board, 2000-2004. *Member:* Chicago, Illinois State and American Bar Associations. ***PRACTICE AREAS:*** Labor Law; Employment Rights.

OF COUNSEL

STEPHEN J. FEINBERG, born Chicago, Illinois, January 24, 1951; admitted to bar, 1975, Illinois. *Education:* University of Illinois (B.S.E.E., with high honors, 1972); University of Chicago (J.D., 1975). Tau Beta Pi; Sigma Tau. *Member:* Chicago, Illinois State and American Bar Associations. ***PRACTICE AREAS:*** Labor Law; Employment Rights Law; Civil Litigation.

ASHMAN LAW OFFICES, LLC

161 NORTH CLARK STREET
SUITE 3575
CHICAGO, ILLINOIS 60601
Telephone: 312-596-1700
Facsimile: 312-873-3800
Email: info@ashmanlawoffices.com
URL: http://www.ashmanlawoffices.com

New York, New York Office: 270 Madison Avenue, Suite 1203, 10016. Telephone: 212-581-9700. Facsimile: 312-873-3800. URL: http://www.AshmanLawOffices.com.
Riverwoods, Illinois Office: 2801 Orange Brace Road, 60015. Telephone: 847-444-1366. Facsimile: 312-873-3800.

Business, Corporate and Commercial Litigation, Securities Litigation, Class Actions, Internet Law, Insurance Litigation, Employment Litigation, Civil Rights, Intellectual Property Litigation, Corporate Counseling, and Foreign Corrupt Practices Act Litigation and Counseling.

FIRM PROFILE: Ashman Law Offices, LLC is a business law and litigation boutique, offering its clients the same quality legal representation found at the nation's largest and most prestigious law firms, for its principal has years of experience working at such firms. The firm was founded upon and adheres to the principle that attorneys can offer superior quality legal representation at affordable rates, through the use of the latest in law office technology, lean staffing, flexible billing approaches, and a commitment to excellence. The firm has a nationwide practice, litigating matters in both state and federal courts in virtually any jurisdiction, and representing clients in transactional matters in a variety of jurisdictions.

KENNETH J. ASHMAN, born Chicago, Illinois, February 21, 1961; admitted to bar, 1990, New Jersey and U.S. District Court, District of New Jersey; 1991, Illinois, New York and U.S. District Court, Southern and Eastern Districts of New York; 1996, U.S. District Court, District of Hawaii; 1997, U.S. Supreme Court and U.S. District Court, Northern District of Illinois; 1998, U.S. Court of Appeals, Second Circuit; 2000, U.S. Court of Appeals, Seventh Circuit; 2002, U.S. District Court, Northern District of Illinois Trial Bar. *Education:* Arizona State University (B.A.E., cum laude, 1983); New York University School of Law; Boston University (J.D., 1990). Member, New York University Mock Trial Team. Recipient, American Jurisprudence Awards, Excellence in Trial Advocacy and International Trade Law. Topics Development Editor, Boston University International Law Journal. Law Clerk to the Honorable Frederic Block, U.S. District Judge, Eastern District of New York, 1994-1995. Author: *The Sky is Falling; Recovery of Lost Profit Caused by Construction Disasters,* Outside Counsel, N.Y.L.J., Aug. 9, 1999, at 1, col. 1; *Class Action Settlements After Amchem, Outside Counsel,* N.Y.L.J., Aug. 11, 1997 at 1, col. 1; *The Omnibus Trade and Competitiveness Act of 1988 - The Section 301 Amendments: Insignificant Changes From Prior Law,* B.U. Intl. L.J. 115, 1989. Co-Author: *The Foreign Corrupt Practices Act, in* White Collar Crime: Business and Regulatory Offenses, Chapter 16 (Obermaier & Morvillo eds, 2003); *Delaware Supreme Court Decides Landmark GM-Perot Case, in* Corporation (Prentice Hall Law & Bus. June 11, 1991). Assisted in Preparation: *The Internal Af-*

(This Listing Continued)

ASHMAN LAW OFFICES, LLC, Chicago—Continued

fairs Doctrine and Choice of Law Issues, N.Y. L.J., May 16, 1991 at 5, col. 1. Associate: Weil, Gotshal & Manges, LLP, 1990-1994; LeBoeuf, Lamb, Green & MacRae, L.L.P., 1995-1997. Member, Ashman & Griffin, LLC, 1997-2001. ***PRACTICE AREAS:*** Business Litigation; Class Actions; Securities Litigation; Internet Law; Insurance Litigation. ***Email:*** info@ashmanlawoffices.com

NEAL D. KITTERLIN, admitted to bar, 2005, Illinois. *Education:* Louisiana Tech University (B.S., 2001); Chicago-Kent College of Law (J.D., 2004). Tau Beta Pi Engineering Honor Society. Member, Chicago-Kent Law Review. ***PRACTICE AREAS:*** Business Litigation; Intellectual Property; Small Business Corporations; Computer Law; Debtor and Creditor Collections. ***Email:*** nkitterlin@ashmanlawoffices.com

ASKOUNIS & BORST, P.C.

Established in 1992

303 EAST WACKER DRIVE, SUITE 1000
CHICAGO, ILLINOIS 60601
Telephone: 312-861-7100
Facsimile: 312-861-0022
Email: attorneys@askborst.com
URL: http://www.askborst.com:

General Practice. Commercial Litigation, Commercial Transactions, Bankruptcy Workouts and Litigation, Intellectual Property, Franchise Law, Telecommunications, Commercial Finance/Commercial Equipment Leasing, Corporate Law.

FIRM PROFILE: Askounis & Borst, P.C. is a full service law firm representing corporate clients, equipment lessors and secured lenders on a nationwide and international basis. The firm counsels its clients in all types of transactional, litigation, bankruptcy, workout, environmental, intellectual property and telecommunications matters.

THOMAS V. ASKOUNIS, born Chicago, Illinois, May 17, 1951; admitted to bar, 1975, Illinois; 1976, U.S. District Court, Northern District of Illinois; 1986, Tennessee; 1993, U.S. District Court, Eastern District of Wisconsin; 1994, U.S. District Court, Eastern District of Michigan; 2001, U.S. District Court, Northern District of Indiana. *Education:* Knox College; Northwestern University (B.A. 1972); Vanderbilt University (J.D., 1975). Recipient, American Jurisprudence Award in Constitutional Law. Licensed Real Estate Broker, Illinois, 1981. Author: "Power of Attorney Clauses: A Trap for the Unwary," Equipment Leasing Today, Feb. 1999; "Are You Authorized to Transact Business in Other States?" Equipment Leasing Today, April, 1997; "Grammatical Ambiguity Results in Unexpected Decision," Equipment Leasing Today, April, 1996; "New Hazards for Commercial Lenders," WAEL Newsletter, Winter, 1994. *Member:* American Bar Association (Member, UCC and Equipment Leasing Sections); Hellenic Bar Association (Member, Board of Directors, 1982-1992; President, 1990-1991); Equipment Leasing Association of America (Past, Bank Committee; Legal Committee; Membership Committee; Credit and Collections Committee); United Association of Equipment Lessors (Member, Board of Directors, 1996); Mid-America Association of Equipment Lessors (Member, Board of Directors & Secretary, 2000). ***LANGUAGES:*** Greek and French. ***PRACTICE AREAS:*** Bankruptcy Workouts and Litigation; Commercial Transactions; Real Estate. ***Email:*** taskounis@askborst.com

VINCENT T. BORST, born Memphis, Tennessee, November 10, 1958; admitted to bar, 1986, Illinois and U.S. District Court, Northern, including Trial Bar; Central and Southern Districts of Illinois; U.S. District Court, District of Colorado; U.S. District Court, Eastern District of Wisconsin; U.S. Court of Appeals, Seventh and Eleventh Circuits. *Education:* University of Tennessee at Knoxville (B.S.M.E., 1981); Keller Graduate School of Management (M.B.A., 1982); John Marshall Law School (J.D., 1986). Delta Theta Phi. Editor, John Marshall Law Review, 1985-1986. Author: "The Right To Die: An Extension of The Right to Privacy," 18 John Marshall Law Review 895, 1985. *Member:* American Bar Association (Member: Section on Litigation; Section of Business Law; Forum Committee on Air and Space Law); Equipment Leasing Association of America. ***REPORTED CASES:*** Stromberg Metal Works, Inc. v. Press Mechanical, Inc., 77F.3d 928 (7th Cir., 1996); General Electric Capital Corp. v. Palutsis, 1995 WL 263959 (N.D. Ill. 1995); Great America Leasing Company, LLC v. Balboa Capital Corp., 1999 WL35318 (N.D. Ill. 1999); Linc Equipment Services, Inc. v. Sign 1 Medical Services, Inc., 319 F.3d 288 (7th Cir. 2003). ***PRACTICE AREAS:*** Commercial Litigation; Intellectual Property; Franchise Law; Commercial Transactions. ***Email:*** vtborst@askborst.com

DANIEL L. COLLINS, born Pittsburgh, Pennsylvania, June 26, 1945; admitted to bar, 1991, Illinois and U.S. District Court, Northern District of Illinois; 1999, U.S. District Court, Eastern District of Wisconsin. *Education:* Kent State University (B.S., 1969); John Marshall Law School (J.D., 1991). Listed in Who's Who in American Colleges and Universities. *Member:* Chicago Bar Association (Chairman, Administrative Law Committee, 1992-1993); Federal Communications Bar Association. ***SPECIAL AGENCIES:*** Illinois Commerce Commission. ***PRACTICE AREAS:*** Telecommunications; Commercial Litigation; Bankruptcy Workouts and Litigation. ***Email:*** dcollins@askborst.com

D. ALEXANDER DARCY, born Westminster, Maryland, June 4, 1965; admitted to bar, 1993, Maryland; 1994, Illinois; 1997, California; U.S. District Court, Northern District of Illinois; U.S. District Court, Northern, Central, Southern and Eastern Districts of California; U.S. District Court, District of Colorado and Eastern District of Wisconsin; U.S. Court of Appeals, Seventh and Ninth Circuits. *Education:* Hamilton College (B.A., 1987); Washington University (J.D., 1993). *Member:* Chicago, Illinois State, Maryland State and California State Bar Associations. ***LANGUAGES:*** French and Japanese. ***REPORTED CASES:*** Line Equipment Services, Inc. v. Signal Medical Services, Inc., 319 F.3d 288 (7th Cir. 2003); Stromberg Mechanical, Inc. v. Press Mechanical, Inc., 77 F.3d 928 (7th Cir. 1996); In re: County Collector, Ajax Financial, L.P. v. ABN-AMRO Incorporated Leasing and Financial Services, 318 Ill.App.3d 641, 742 N.E.2d 839 (1st Dist. 2000); Lease Partners Corporation v. R&J Pharmacies, Inc., 329 Ill.App.3d 69, 768 N.E.2d 54 (1st Dist. 2002). ***PRACTICE AREAS:*** Commercial Litigation; Commercial Transactions; Bankruptcy Workouts; Real Estate. ***Email:*** adarcy@askborst.com

KENNETH D. PETERS, born Wilmington, Delaware, September 22, 1957; admitted to bar, 1983, Illinois; 1984, U.S. District Court, Central District of Illinois; 1988, U.S. District Court, Northern District of Illinois; 2000, U.S. District Court, Western District of Michigan; 2001, U.S District Court, Southern District of Illinois and Illinois Trial Bar. *Education:* Middlebury College (B.A., cum laude, 1979); University of Illinois (J.D., 1983). Co-Author: "Enhanced Recovery of Oil," Eastern Mineral Law Institute, Chapter 13, 1984. Author: Cover Story Article, "Illinois Law on Informed Consent Medical Malpractice Actions," Illinois Bar Journal, March, 1988; "Don't Delay on Deficiency Judgments" Equipment Leasing Today, May, 2004. Instructor, 1996-2004 and Member, Curriculum Council, 1999-2000, Lake Forest Graduate School of Management. Senior Manager and Counsel, Homan Corporation and Laser Oil Company, 1990-1998. Organize and Moderate, Chicago Bar Association Continuing Legal Education Seminar, "Representing The Small Business," April 23, 2002. Co-Author and Presenter: "Protecting Your Company Before Your Customer or Distributor is Unable to Pay," Continuing Legal Education Seminar, for Texas and Virginia CLE Credit, April 26, 2005. *Member:* Chicago Bar Association. ***REPORTED CASES:*** Sowers v. Illinois Central Gulf Railroad Company, 152 Ill.App.3d 163, 503 N.E. 2d 1082 (Fifth Dist. 1987); Forthenberry v. Franciscon Sister Health Care Corporation, 156 Ill.App.3d 634, 509 N.E. 2d 166 (Fourth Dist. 1987); Graves v. Daley, 172 Ill.App.3d 35, 526 N.E. 2d 679 (Third Dist. 1988); Dabbs v. Arthur Andersen L.L.P., 2002 WL 31729019 (N.D.Ill); Dabbs v. Arthur Andersen L.L.P., 2003 WL 21011742 (N.D.Ill);. ***PRACTICE AREAS:*** Commercial Collections (Nationwide); Secured Transactions; Uniform Commercial Code; Creditor Bankruptcy (Nationwide); Equipment Leasing; Real Estate Litigation; Equipment Replevin (Nationwide). ***Email:*** kpeters@askborst.com

DENNIS A. DRESSLER, born St. Louis, Missouri, April 30, 1969; admitted to bar, 1997, Missouri; 2000, Illinois; U.S. District Court, Northern, Central and Southern Districts of Illinois; U.S. District Court, Western District of Missouri and U.S. District Court, Northern District of Indiana. *Education:* Missouri State University (B.S., 1993); St. Louis University (J.D., cum laude, 1997). *Member:* Chicago and Illinois State Bar Associations; The Missouri Bar. ***LANGUAGES:*** Spanish. ***PRACTICE AREAS:*** Bankruptcy Litigation; Workouts; Commercial Litigation; Commercial Leasing; Secured Transactions; Real Estate. ***Email:*** ddressler@askborst.com

JENNIFER L. JERZY, born Rochester, Michigan, June 13, 1971; admitted to bar, 2001, Illinois and U.S. District Court, Northern, Central and Southern Districts of Illinois. *Education:* Michigan State University, James Madison College (B.A., 1993); Loyola University (J.D., 1998). *Member:* Chicago Bar Association. ***PRACTICE AREAS:*** Commercial Litigation. ***Email:*** jjerzy@askborst.com

D. ANN COKER, born Tokyo, Japan, 1972; admitted to bar, 2002, Illinois; 2003, U.S. District Court, Northern District of Illinois. *Education:* Northwestern University (B.A., 1995); DePaul University (J.D., cum laude, 2002). *Member:* Chicago and American Bar Associations. ***LANGUAGES:*** Japanese and German. ***PRACTICE AREAS:*** Commercial Litigation. ***Email:*** acoker@askborst.com

C. RANDALL WOOLLEY, II, born Peoria, Illinois, 1977; admitted to bar, 2003, Illinois. *Education:* DePaul University (B.S., 1999); Loyola University (J.D., 2003). *Member:* Chicago and Illinois Bar Associations. ***PRACTICE AREAS:*** Commercial Litigation; Bankruptcy. ***Email:*** rwoolley@askborst.com

DEBRA ROSE DEVASSY, born Kingston, Ontario, May 8, 1979; admitted to bar, 2004, Illinois; U.S. District Court, Northern District of Illinois; U.S. Court of Appeals, Seventh Circuit. *Education:* University of Illinois (B.A., English, 2001; J.D., 2004). Recipient, Best Overall, 2002, Editor, 2003-2004, and Executive Member, 2003-2004, Frederick Douglass Moot Court Competition. ***LANGUAGES:*** Malayalam. ***PRACTICE AREAS:*** Bankruptcy; Commercial Litigation. ***Email:*** ddevassy@askborst.com

OF COUNSEL

KENNETH B. DROST, born Peoria, Illinois, December 9, 1953; admitted to bar, 1978, California; 1979, Illinois. *Education:* Knox College (B.A., 1975); Hastings College of Law, University of California (J.D., 1978). Order of the Coif. Thurston Scholar. Research Editor, Hastings Law Journal, 1977-1978. *Member:* Chicago and American Bar Associations; State Bar of California. ***PRACTICE AREAS:*** Collections; Business Law.

REPRESENTATIVE CLIENTS: ABN AMRO Incorporated ; AGFA Corporation; AIM Financial Corporation; Alternate Power Inc.; Ameritech Credit Corp.; Barrington Medical; Bodi; Wachs Aviation Insurance Agency, Inc.; Bank of America; Bayer Corporation; Canon Financial Services, Inc.; Center Capital Corporation; Cisco Systems Capital Inc.; The CIT Group; Citicorp North America, Inc.; Cash Recovery LLC; Citicapital; Citicorp Vendor Finance; Commercial Bank, NA; Cura Capital; De Lage Landen; DVI Financial Services, Inc.; Equilease Financial Service, Inc.; Fidelity Leasing, Inc.; Financial Pacific Co.; Fleet Capital Leasing; FNF Capital, Inc.; First Portland Corporation; Fleet Business Credit Corp.; Focus Financial Corp.; Forsythe McArthur Associates, Inc.; General Electric Capital Auto Leasing Inc.; General Electric Capital Corporation; General Electric Healthcare Financial Services; General Electric/Telecom Financial Services Corporation; Gulf Coast Workstation Corporation; Great American Leasing Co., LLC; HPSC, Inc.; Ilford Imaging USA, Inc.; IMC Financial, LLC; Imperial Business Credit, Inc.; Information Leasing Corp.; JLA Credit Corporation; LFC Capital Inc.; Linc Capital, Inc.; Marquette Bank; Millenium Financial Group; Minolta Business Systems, Inc.; National Machine Tool Corp.; Neopost Leasing, Inc.; Northern Leasing Systems, Inc.; Oncology Therapeutics Network; Peoples' Capital & Leasing Corporation; Pitney Bowes Credit Corporation; Pullman Bank and Trust; Relational Funding Corporation; Resun Leasing Inc.; Starwood Corporation; Transmedia Restaurant Co.; Transamerica Commercial Finance Corporation; US Bancorp Leasing & Financial; Volvo Commercial Finance LLC; WFS Financial Inc.; Wells Fargo Financial Leasing, Inc.

(This Listing Continued)

ASONYE & ASSOCIATES

Established in 1993

11 SOUTH LA SALLE STREET, SUITE 2140
CHICAGO, ILLINOIS 60603
Telephone: 312-795-9110
Fax: 312-795-9114
Email: uche@aa-law.com
URL: http://www.aa-law.com

Employment Law, Immigration Law, Workers Compensation and Civil Rights.

FIRM PROFILE: Asonye and Associates represents individuals and small businesses in employment matters concerning sexual and racial harassment, sex, race, national origin, age and disability discrimination. We also represent individuals and businesses in immigration matters. Examples include non-immigrant visas, green cards, permanent visa, national interest waivers, labor certifications, J-1 waivers and, H-1B visas.

UCHE O. ASONYE, admitted to bar, 1992, Illinois. U.S. District Court, Northern District of Illinois, U.S. Tax Court, Federal Trial Bar. *Education:* DePaul University (B.Sc., with honors, 1985); Loyola University (J.D., 1992). Certified Public Accountant, 1987. Selected as a Leading American Attorney. ***PRACTICE AREAS:*** Employment Law; Immigration Law; Workers Compensation; Civil Rights; Civil Rights Defense; Discrimination; Race Discrimination; Sex Discrimination; Womens Rights. ***Email:*** uche@aa-law.com

ASSOCIATE

MARK PANDO, born Chicago, Illinois; admitted to bar, 2004, Illinois. *Education:* Northwestern Business College (A.A., 1998); Loyola University (B.A., 2001); Chicago-Kent College of Law (J.D., 2004). ***LANGUAGES:*** Spanish. ***PRACTICE AREAS:*** Employment Law; Immigration Law; Workers Compensation; Civil Rights. ***Email:*** mark@aa-law.com

Languages: Polish, Spanish.

ASPERGER ASSOCIATES, LLC

303 EAST WACKER DRIVE, SUITE 1000
CHICAGO, ILLINOIS 60601
Telephone: 312-856-9901
Fax: 312-856-9905
Email: jasperger@asplaw.net

Construction Products Liability, Complex and Multi-District Litigation, Commercial Torts, Admiralty and Maritime Law, Construction Liability, Negligence, Personal Injury, Products Liability, Torts, Insurance and Mold Litigation.

JEFFREY J. ASPERGER, born Youngstown, Ohio, September 18, 1952; admitted to bar, 1979, Illinois and U.S. District Court, Northern District of Illinois including Trial Bar; U.S. District Court, Northern District of Indiana. *Education:* Kent State University (B.A., 1975; M.A., with honors, 1976); John Marshall Law School (J.D., with honors, 1979). Best Oralist, National Appellate Advocacy Team. Member, National Moot Court Team. Delta Theta Phi. Lecturer, Loyola University Trial Workshop. *Member:* Chicago, Illinois State and American (Member, Sections on: Litigation; Tort and Insurance Practice Section; Discovery and Evidence Section; Products Liability Section; Construction Law Section) Bar Associations; The Association of Trial Lawyers of America; Trial Lawyers Club of Chicago; Blue Goose International; Economic Club of Chicago; The Propeller Club of the United States; National Registry of Who's Who. ***REPORTED CASES:*** Folkstone Maritime, Ltd. v. CSX Corp., 64 F.3d 1037 (7th Cir. 1995); Sovereign Chem. & Petroleum Prods. v. Ameropan Oil Corp., 148 F.R.D. 208 (N.D. Ill. 1992); Ball Corp. v. Bohlin Bldg. Corp., 543 N.E.2d 106 (Ill. App. Ct. 1st Dist. 1989); Chem-Pac, Inc. v. Simborg, 495 N.E.2d 1124 (Ill. App. Ct. 1st Dist. 1986); Gabrenas v. R.D. Werner Co., 451 N.E.2d 1307 (Ill. App. Ct. 1st Dist. 1983); Catalano v. Aetna Cas. & Sur. Co., 434 N.E.2d 31 (Ill. App. Ct. 2d Dist. 1982); J.B. Stein & Co. v. Sandberg, 419 N.E.2d 652 (Ill. App. Ct. 2d Dist. 1981); Textile Mach. v. Continental Ins. Co., 409 N.E.2d 1 (Ill. App. Ct. 1st Dist. 1980); Eddington v. Touchy, 793 S.W.2d 335 (Tex. Ct. App. 1st Dist. 1990); Continental Paper & Supply Co. v. City of Detroit, 521 N.W.2d 844 (Mich. Ct. App. 1994), 545 N.W.2d 657 (Mich. 1996). ***PRACTICE AREAS:*** Construction Products Liability; Complex and Multi-District Litigation; Commercial Torts; Admiralty and Maritime Law; Construction Liability; Negligence; Personal Injury; Products Liability; Torts; Insurance; Mold Litigation. ***Email:*** jasperger@asplaw.net

---

KELLY A. SAINDON, born Joliet, Illinois, June 15, 1971; admitted to bar, 1998, Illinois; 2003, U.S. District Court, Northern District of Illinois including Trial Bar. *Education:* University of Michigan (B.A., 1993); Drake University School of Law (J.D., 1996). *Member:* Chicago and American Bar Associations; The Association of Trial Lawyers of America; Illinois Trial Lawyers Association. ***REPORTED CASES:*** Bonert v. Village of Schiller Park, 322 Ill. App.3d 557, 750 N.E.2d 273, 2001 Ill. App. LEXIS 356, 255 Ill. Dec. 692, May 15, 2001; Decided, Released for Publication June 28, 2001. ***PRACTICE AREAS:*** Construction Products Liability; Complex and Multi-District Litigation; Commercial Torts; Admiralty and Maritime Law; Construction Liability; Negligence; Personal Injury; Torts; Insurance; Mechanics Liens; Contracts; Mold Litigation. ***Email:*** ksaindon@asplaw.net

DAILE V. GRIGAITIS, born Chicago, Illinois, December 20, 1971; admitted to bar, 1997, Illinois. *Education:* University of Wisconsin-Madison (B.S., 1993); DePaul University (M.B.A.; J.D., 1997). ***PRACTICE AREAS:*** Construction Products Liability; Complex and Multi-District Litigation; Commercial Torts; Admiralty and Maritime Law; Construction Liability; Negligence; Personal Injury; Products Liability; Torts; Insurance. ***Email:*** dgrigaitis@asplaw.net

(This Listing Continued)

ANTONIA HAYS, born 1974; admitted to bar, 2001, Illinois; 2002, U.S. District Court, Northern District of Illinois. *Education:* Loyola University (B.S., 1996); Loyola University Chicago School of Law (J.D., 2001). *Member:* Chicago, Illinois State and American Bar Associations. ***PRACTICE AREAS:*** Commercial Litigation.

ATKINSON & ATKINSON

CHICAGO, ILLINOIS

(See Evanston)

Association Law, Business Law including Corporate, Real Estate, Estate Planning, Estate and Trust Administration, Labor and Employee Benefits, Professional Associations, Professional Licensure and Certification, Administrative, Tax and Litigation related to these areas of practice.

MARSHALL J. AUERBACH & ASSOCIATES, LTD.

30 NORTH LASALLE STREET, SUITE 3400
CHICAGO, ILLINOIS 60602
Telephone: 312-853-3300
Fax: 312-853-1043
URL: http://www.auerbachlawoffice.com

Family, Domestic Relations, Divorce, Matrimonial. General Civil Practice.

FIRM PROFILE: Mr. Auerbach has represented clients and litigated matrimonial matters throughout the United States. He was the Principal Drafter of the Illinois Marriage and Dissolution of Marriage Act enacted in 1977 and has lectured extensively on matrimonial law. The Illinois Institute for Continuing Legal Education has described him as the Dean of Illinois matrimonial lawyers. He handles complex financial matrimonial litigation.

MARSHALL J. AUERBACH, born Chicago, Illinois, September 5, 1932; admitted to bar, 1955, Illinois. *Education:* University of Illinois; John Marshall Law School (J.D., 1955). Author: Principal Drafter of Illinois Marriage and Dissolution of Marriage Act, 1977. Co-Author with Albert E. Jenner, Jr. of Historical and Practice Notes to Illinois Marriage and Dissolution of Marriage Act and to Husband and Wife Act in Smith-Hurd Illinois Annotated Statutes, 1980 and Supplements through 1988. Author: "Trying A Contested Divorce Case," 1967 (Revised, 1972, 1973 and 1975), "Separate Maintenance," 1969 (Revised, 1973 and 1976), "Property Rights and Maintenance," 1978 and 1981, "Property Considerations Upon Dissolution of Marriage," 1982-1995, Illinois Matrimonial Law Handbook; "Division of Assets," Drafting Marital Separation Agreements Handbook, 1981 and 1982, Illinois Institute for Continuing Legal Education; "Pitfalls of Using National Service Life Insurance in Divorce Settlements," American Bar Association Law Notes, January 1971; "An Introduction to the New Illinois Marriage and Dissolution of Marriage Act," Illinois Bar Journal, November 1977. Conducted Matrimonial Law Skills Course for Illinois Institute for Continuing Legal Education, 1974, 1976, 1979, 1980 and 1984. Conducted Illinois Divorce Practice Before Trial for Illinois Institute of Continuing Legal Education, 1993. *Member:* Illinois State (Member of Council, 1968-1970; Secretary and Vice Chairman of Council, 1970-1971; Chairman, 1972-1973, Family Law Section; Member, Family Study Commission on Marriage, Divorce and Parental Responsibility, 1971—; Elected as a Delegate to the Assembly, 1973-1978; Member, 1973—and Chairman, 1976-1978, Credentials Committee of Assembly; Editor, Family Law Section Newsletter, 1973-1974; Delegate to Long Range Planning Conference, 1978; Conferee to 1982 Allerton House Conference on "The Cost of Civil Litigation") and American (Vice Chairman, Family Law Section Committee for Liaison with the Tax Section, 1972-1973) Bar Associations. Fellow, American Academy of Matrimonial Lawyers. ***PRACTICE AREAS:*** Family; Domestic Relations; Matrimonial; General Civil Practice.

AVERY CAMERLINGO KILL, LLC

Established in 2000

218 NORTH JEFFERSON, SUITE 200
CHICAGO, ILLINOIS 60661
Telephone: 312-648-9707
Fax: 312-648-9713

Family Law including Divorce, Child Custody, Child Support, Visitation Rights, Spousal Support (Alimony), Maintenance, Adoptions, Step Parent Adoptions, Marital Property Settlements, Modifications of Decree, Name Changes, Separation Agreements, Qualified Domestic Relations Orders (QDRO'S), Paternity, Guardianship, Employment Law including Wrongful Termination, Sexual and Racial Discrimination/Harassment, Age Discrimination, Disability Discrimination, Whistleblower Litigation, Family and Medical Leave Act, Retaliatory Discharge.

MEMBERS OF FIRM

MARY KATHERINE AVERY, born Kalamazoo, Michigan, March 17, 1968; admitted to bar, 1993, Illinois. *Education:* University of Michigan (B.A., 1989); Loyola University (J.D., 1993). *Member:* Chicago and Illinois State Bar Associations; Womens Bar Association; Council of Lawyers. ***PRACTICE AREAS:*** Domestic Relations; Family Law; Paternity; Child Support; Child Custody. ***Email:*** mavery@averycamerlingokill.com

PEPI CAMERLINGO, born Washington, D.C., February 8, 1969; admitted to bar, 1995, Illinois. *Education:* University of Nebraska at Omaha (B.S., 1992); DePaul University (J.D., 1995). Certified Public Accountant, 2000. Member, Illinois CPA Society. *Member:* Chicago Bar Association; Illinois State Bar Association; Womens Bar Association. ***PRACTICE AREAS:*** Family Law; Divorce; Adoption Law; Child Custody. ***Email:*** pcamerlingo@averycamerlingokill.com

ANNEMARIE E. KILL, born Chicago, Illinois, February 10, 1970; admitted to bar, 1995, Illinois. *Education:* Illinois State University (B.S., 1992); DePaul University (J.D., 1995). Mensa: Member, Illinois Task Force on Grandparents Raising Grandchildren. Presi-

(This Listing Continued)

AVERY CAMERLINGO KILL, LLC, Chicago—Continued

dent, GRANDFamilies Program of Chicago Board of Directors. *Member:* Chicago and Illinois State Bar Associations (Young Lawyer's Division Section Council, 1996-2003; Member, Women and the Law Committee, 2002—); Womens Bar Association (Member, Joint Task Force on Issues Affecting Women as the Age, 2001—); National Employment Lawyers Association. ***PRACTICE AREAS:*** Family Law; Qualified Domestic Relations Orders (QDROs); Employment Law. ***Email:*** akill@averycamerlingokill.com

DAVID A. AXELROD & ASSOCIATES, P.C.

Established in 2001

20 SOUTH CLARK, SUITE 2200
CHICAGO, ILLINOIS 60603
Telephone: 312-782-4600
Fax: 312-782-3015
Email: daa@axelrodpc.com
URL: http://www.axelrodpc.com

Commercial Litigation, Professional Negligence, Fraud Litigation.

FIRM PROFILE: David A. Axelrod & Associates, P.C. was founded by David Axelrod to provide elite trial and litigation services. The firm represents numerous business clients in commercial litigation. The firm also represents individuals and businesses in professional negligence and fraud cases.

DAVID A. AXELROD, born Chicago, Illinois, August 6, 1957; admitted to bar, 1983, Missouri; 1984, Illinois, U.S. Court of Appeals, 7th Circuit, U.S. District Court, Northern District of Illinois including Trial Bar, and U.S. Supreme Court. *Education:* Michigan State University (B.A., with honors, 1979); Washington College of Law, American University (J.D., 1983). *Member:* Chicago and Illinois State Bar Associations; Association of Trial Lawyers of America; Illinois Trial Lawyers Association. ***REPORTED CASES:*** Israel Travel Advisory Service, Inc. v. Israel Identity Tours, Inc., 61 F.3d 1250, 1995-2 Trade Cases P 71,063, RICO Bus.Disp.Guide 8854 (7th Cir.(Ill.), July 20, 1995; Video Views, Inc. v. Studio 21, Ltd., 797 F.2d 538 (7th Cir.(Ill.), August 4, 1986; Andren v. General Fiberglass Supply, Inc., 980 F.Supp. 975 (E.D.Wis., October 9, 1997); McKnight v. Gingras, 966 F.Supp. 801, 74 Fair Empl.Prac.Case.(BNA) 867 (E.D.Wis., June 15, 1997); Petre v. Kucich, 356 Ill.App.3d 57, February 17, 2005; Kim v. State Farm Fire and Cas. Co., 312 Ill.App.3d 770, March 24, 2000; Otto Wratschko, et al. v. Pavlovic, 205 Ill.2d 590, February 28, 2003. ***PRACTICE AREAS:*** Commercial Litigation; Professional Negligence; Fraud Litigation. ***Email:*** daa@axelrodpc.com

ROBERT A. COHEN, born Los Angeles, California, June 2, 1959; admitted to bar, 1985, California; 1988, North Carolina; 1994, Illinois. *Education:* University of California at Berkeley (A.B., with high honors in English, 1981); Boalt Hall School of Law, University of California (J.D., 1985). ***PRACTICE AREAS:*** Commercial Litigation. ***Email:*** rac@axelrodpc.com

STACEY L. LEINHEISER, born Berwyn, Illinois, March 27, 1976; admitted to bar, 2002, Illinois. *Education:* Illinois Wesleyan University (B.A., 1998); DePaul University (J.D., 2002). ***PRACTICE AREAS:*** Professional Negligence; Commercial Litigation. ***Email:*** sll@axelrodpc.com

H. DAVID ROSETH, born Chicago, Illinois, February 19, 1960; admitted to bar, 2001, Illinois; 2002, U.S. District Court, Northern District of Illinois. *Education:* University of Michigan, Ann Arbor (B.A., cum laude, 1982); New York University School of Law (J.D., 2001). ***PRACTICE AREAS:*** Litigation. ***Email:*** droseth@axelrodpc.com

AXELROD, GOODMAN, STEINER & BAZELON

Established in 1948

39 SOUTH LASALLE STREET, SUITE 920
CHICAGO, ILLINOIS 60603
Telephone: 312-236-9375
Fax: 312-236-2877
Email: jhs1@worldnet.att.net
URL: http://www.trans-law.com

Civil and Appellate Litigation, Transportation Law. Administrative, Real Estate, Business, Insurance Defense.

FIRM PROFILE: The firm of Axelrod, Goodman, Steiner & Bazelon has focused its practice in the area of transportation law with an emphasis on motor carrier related law, for fifty years.

DAVID AXELROD (1910-1976)

JOEL H. STEINER, born 1946; admitted to bar, 1971, Illinois, U.S. Supreme Court, U.S. Court of Appeals, 5th, 6th, 7th, 11th Circuits and Illinois Supreme Court. *Education:* University of Wisconsin-Madison (B.A., 1968; J.D., 1971). Past Chairman, Traffic Commission, City of Highland Park, Illinois. Member, Illinois Commerce Commission's Motor Advisory Committee. *Member:* Chicago and Illinois State Bar Associations; Transportation Lawyers' Association. ***PRACTICE AREAS:*** Transportation Law. ***Email:*** jhs1@att.net

PAUL A. GAJEWSKI, born 1960; admitted to bar, 1985, Illinois, Illinois Supreme Court, U.S. Court of Appeals, 7th Circuit and U.S. District Court, Northern District of Illinois. *Education:* Purdue University (B.S.); John Marshall Law School (J.D.). *Member:* Chicago, Illinois State and American Bar Associations. ***PRACTICE AREAS:*** Transportation Law. ***Email:*** paglaw@att.net

BABBITT & MELTON LLP

332 SOUTH MICHIGAN AVENUE, SUITE 710
CHICAGO, ILLINOIS 60604
Telephone: 312-427-5555
Fax: 312-427-5556
URL: http://www.babbittandmelton.com

College and University Law, Labor and Employment Law, Appellate Practice, Counseling, and Complex Commercial Litigation.

PARTNERS OF FIRM

ELLEN M. BABBITT, born Red Bank, New Jersey, December 9, 1955; admitted to bar, 1981, Illinois and U.S. District Court, Northern District of Illinois; 1983, U.S. Court of Appeals, Seventh Circuit; 1989, U.S. Supreme Court. *Education:* Vanderbilt University (B.A., magna cum laude, 1977); Northwestern University (J.D., cum laude, 1980). Phi Beta Kappa; Order of the Coif. Editor-in-Chief, Northwestern University Law Review, 1979-1980. Law Clerk to the Honorable Carl McGowan, U.S. Court of Appeals, District of Columbia Circuit, 1980-1981. Adjunct Professor, Northwestern University School of Law. Faculty Member, National Institute of Trial Advocacy. *Member:* Chicago, Illinois and American Bar Associations; Women's Bar Association; National Association of College and University Attorneys. ***PRACTICE AREAS:*** College and University Law; Labor and Employment; Complex Commercial Litigation; Appellate Practice. ***Email:*** ebabbitt@babbittandmelton.com

BRUCE W. MELTON, born Evanston, Illinois, December 22, 1960; admitted to bar, 1986, Illinois and U.S. District Court, Northern District of Illinois. *Education:* Cornell College (B. Phil., magna cum laude, 1982); University of Chicago (J.D., 1986). Phi Beta Kappa. Associate Editor, University of Chicago Law Review, 1985-1986. Teaching Associate, Northwestern University. Faculty Member, National Institute of Trial Advocacy. *Member:* National Association of College and University Attorneys. ***PRACTICE AREAS:*** College and University Law; Labor and Employment; Complex Commercial Litigation; Real Estate Law. ***Email:*** bmelton@babbittandmelton.com

PETER G. LAND, born Highland Park, Illinois, July 9, 1968; admitted to bar, 1995, Illinois and U.S. District Court, Northern District of Illinois; 1999, U.S. Court of Appeals, Seventh Circuit. *Education:* DePauw University (B.A., cum laude, 1990); Northwestern University (J.D., cum laude, 1995). Associate Editor, Notes and Comments, Northwestern University Law Review, 1994-1995. *Member:* American Bar Association; National Association of College and University Attorneys. ***PRACTICE AREAS:*** College and University Law; Labor and Employment; Complex Commercial Litigation; Appellate Practice. ***Email:*** pland@babbittandmelton.com

ASSOCIATES

ZACHARY B. SILVERSTEIN, born New Haven, Connecticut, March 7, 1968; admitted to bar, 1999, Illinois; 2000, U.S. Court of Appeals, Sixth Circuit, U.S. District Court, Northern District of Illinois and U.S. District Court, Southern District of Ohio. *Education:* Yale College (B.A., magna cum laude, 1990); Northwestern University (J.D., cum laude, 1999). Order of the Coif. Coordinating Comment Editor, Journal of Criminal Law and Criminology, 1998-1999. Law Clerk to the Honorable R. Guy Cole, Jr., U.S. Court of Appeals for the Sixth Circuit, 1999-2000. *Member:* Chicago and Illinois State Bar Associations. ***PRACTICE AREAS:*** Appellate Practice; College and University Law; Labor and Employment; Complex Commercial Litigation. ***Email:*** zsilverstein@babbittandmelton.com

STEVEN J. WINGER, born Evanston, Illinois, December 25, 1967; admitted to bar, 2000, Illinois; 2001, U.S. District Court, Northern District of Illinois and U.S. Court of Appeals, Seventh Circuit; 2003, U.S. Supreme Court. *Education:* Williams College (B.A., cum laude, 1990); University of Illinois at Urbana-Champaign (M.A., Philosophy, 1994); Northwestern University (J.D., cum laude, 2000). Note and Comment Editor, Journal of Criminal Law and Criminology, 1999-2000. Law Clerk to the Hon. William J. Bauer, U.S. Court of Appeals, Seventh Circuit, 2000-2001. Instructor, Loyola University Chicago School of Law. *Member:* Chicago, Illinois State and American Bar Associations. ***PRACTICE AREAS:*** Appellate Practice; College and University Law; Labor and Employment; Complex Commercial Litigation. ***Email:*** sjwinger@babbittandmelton.com

BRIAN C. BOARDMAN, born Denville, New Jersey, April 15, 1976; admitted to bar, 2003, Illinois and U.S. District Court, Northern District of Illinois. *Education:* Northwestern University (B.S., magna cum laude, 1998); Stanford University Law School (J.D., 2003). Fifth Grade Teacher, Teach For America, Washington, DC, 1998-2000. Participant, Stanford University Education Advocacy Clinic. *Member:* Chicago, Illinois State and American Bar Associations. ***PRACTICE AREAS:*** Employment Law; Appellate Practice; College and University Law. ***Email:*** bboardman@babbittandmelton.com

BAILEY & BAILEY

20 N. CLARK STREET, SUITE 3600
CHICAGO, ILLINOIS 60602
Telephone: 312-252-2800
Fax: 312-372-0511
URL: http://www.baileyandbaileylaw.com

Civil Litigation and Appellate Practice, Business Litigation, Breach of Contract, Labor and Employment, Employment Discrimination, Sexual Harassment, Wrongful Termination, Civil Rights, Pension and Profit Sharing, Insurance Law, Personal Injury, Automobile Accidents, Libel, Slander and Defamation, Consumer Law Defense.

BRIAN T. BAILEY, born Oak Park, Illinois, November 15, 1964; admitted to bar, 1989, Illinois and U.S. District Court, Northern District of Illinois; 1993, Nebraska; 1995, Federal Trial Bar and U.S. District Court, Central District of Illinois; 1999, U.S. Court of Appeals, Seventh Circuit; 2002, U.S. Court of Appeals, Eighth Circuit. *Education:* Creighton University (B.A., 1986); Loyola University (J.D., 1989). Co-Author: "The Factual Investigation from the Viewpoint of the Insurance Company Defendant," Property Insurance,

(This Listing Continued)

Illinois Institute for Continuing Legal Education. *Member:* Chicago and Illinois State Bar Associations. ***PRACTICE AREAS:*** Commercial Litigation; Personal Injury; Breach of Contract; Mechanics Liens; Municipal Law; Libel, Slander and Defamation; Consumer Law; Labor and Employment; Discrimination; Harassment; Wrongful Death; Insurance.

JULIE LINE BAILEY, born Fremont, Nebraska, October 15, 1965; admitted to bar, 1990, Illinois and U.S. District Court, Northern District of Illinois; 1991, Nebraska; 2002, U.S. Court of Appeals, Eighth Circuit. *Education:* Creighton University (B.A., summa cum laude, 1987); Northwestern University (J.D., 1990). Pi Sigma Alpha; Phi Alpha Theta. Note and Comment Editor, Journal of Criminal Law and Criminology. Law Clerk, Hon. John F. Grady, U.S. District Court, Northern District of Illinois, 1991. Author: "Further Erosion of the Fourth Amendment's Warrant Requirement: The Warrantless Trash Search Exception in California v. Greenwood," J. Crim. Law & Criminology Vol. 79:3. Assistant State's Attorney, Cook County, 1994-2002. *Member:* Chicago, Illinois State, Nebraska State and American Bar Associations. ***PRACTICE AREAS:*** Appellate Practice; Business Litigation; Personal Injury; Civil Rights; Labor and Employment.

OF COUNSEL

JAMES M. BAILEY, born Chicago, Illinois; admitted to bar, 1958, Illinois and U.S. District Court, Northern District of Illinois. *Education:* Loyola University (B.S., 1955; J.D., 1958). Instructor: National Judicial College, Reno, Nevada, 1965-1993; Illinois Judicial Conference, 1989-1990. Assistant Corporate Counsel, City of Chicago, 1958-1961. Assistant U.S. Attorney, Northern District of Illinois, 1962-1965. Circuit Court Judge, Cook County, 1965-1993. *Member:* Chicago and Illinois State Bar Associations. [1st Lt., U.S. Army Counterintelligence, 1957-1959; Captain, U.S. Army Reserves Counterintelligence, 1959-1965]. ***PRACTICE AREAS:*** Arbitration; Mediation; Litigation; Real Estate. **Email:** baileylawoffice@aol.com

BAILEY BORLACK NADELHOFFER LLC

Established in 1992

135 SOUTH LA SALLE STREET, SUITE 3950
CHICAGO, ILLINOIS 60603
Telephone: 312-629-2700
Facsimile: 312-629-0174
Email: bbn@bbn-law.com
URL: http://www.bbn-law.com

Commercial Real Estate, Landlord and Tenant Law, Real Estate Sales, Real Estate Acquisitions, Real Estate Secured Lending, Real Estate Development, Construction Law, Zoning Law, Corporate Law, Commercial Law, Business Law, Commercial Litigation, Business Litigation, Complex Litigation, Arbitration, Civil Litigation, Alternative Dispute Resolution, Mergers, Acquisitions and Divestitures.

FIRM PROFILE: Bailey Borlack Nadelhoffer LLC is both a real estate boutique, offering extensive experience in complex real estate transactions on local and national levels, and a full service law firm, advising and representing small to medium sized companies and ownership in sophisticated commercial transactions and separations, dispute resolution including negotiation, arbitration and all phases of litigation and in business planning and administration.

All matters are handled by one of the firm's five partners, who average more than 33 years of experience (none less than 20), much of that gained at large law firms and businesses. The firm's philosophy is to provide superior quality legal representation at affordable rates, through the use of the latest in law office technology, lean staffing, control of expenses, flexible billing approaches and a commitment to excellence. Many commercial real estate and litigation matters are referred by other attorneys, with absolute respect for the original client relationship assured by the firm.

ROBERT C. BAILEY, born Chicago, Illinois, June 1, 1935; admitted to bar, 1960, Illinois and U.S. District Court, Northern District of Illinois. *Education:* Loyola University; Loyola University School of Law (J.D., 1960). ***TRANSACTIONS:*** The Chicago Mercantile Exchange; Hyatt Regency Chicago Hotel; Chicago Fairmont Hotel; Illinois Center development; Franklin Point development. ***PRACTICE AREAS:*** Commercial Real Estate; Real Estate Leasing; Construction Law; Real Estate Partnerships; Real Estate Joint Ventures; Real Estate Settlements; Easements. **Email:** rbailey@bbn-law.com

ALAN R. BORLACK, born Detroit, Michigan, August 3, 1947; admitted to bar, 1972, Illinois; U.S. District Court, Northern District of Illinois including Trial Bar; 1987, U.S. Supreme Court. *Education:* University of Michigan (B.A., with high distinction, 1969); Harvard Law School (J.D., cum laude, 1972). Life Member, Strathmore's Who's Who, 2000-2001 Edition. Speaker: Depositions in Commercial Litigation, Illinois Institute for Continuing Legal Education, April 4, 1984; A Litigator's Viewpoint of Arbitration: The Benefits, Detriments, and Betterments, Chicago Bar Association, Arbitration and Alternative Dispute Resolution Committee, February, 1987; To Arbitrate or Not to Arbitrate: Is That the Question? A Litigator's Perspective, Chicago Bar Association, Young Lawyers Section, Corporate Practice Committee, September, 1987; Litigation of Computer Acquisitions, Today and Tomorrow, Bar Association of Metropolitan St. Louis, Computer Law Committee, April 30, 1991; Moderator, Illinois Legal Time's Roundtable on Arbitration and Alternative Dispute Resolution, Sept. 1992; Speaker: Taking Effective Depositions, Lorman Education Services, Chicago, Illinois, October 30, 1998, October 29, 1999, October 27, 2001, March 20, 2002, July 13, 2005 and Oak Brook Terrace, Illinois, March 10, 1999, March 9, 2000, March 23, 2001, October 27, 2001, April 11, 2003, May 28, 2003, January 28, 2005; Discovery of Confidential Records, Lorman Education Services, Itasca, Illinois, January 20, 1999; Litigation Skills in Illinois, Lorman Education Services, Chicago, Illinois, March 20, 2002 and Oak Brook, Illinois, March 18, 2003. *Member:* Chicago and Illinois State Bar Associations. ***PRACTICE AREAS:*** Business Litigation; Commercial Litigation; Arbitration; Securities Litigation; Real Estate Litigation; Federal Litigation; Intellectual Property Litigation; Complex Litigation; Employment Litigation; Trade Secrets; Civil Litigation. **Email:** aborlack@bbn-law.com

RICHARD D. COHLER, born Milwaukee, Wisconsin, December 13, 1942; admitted to bar, 1970, Illinois, U.S. District Court, Northern District of Illinois and U.S. Tax Court. *Education:* Roosevelt University (B.S., 1967); University of Chicago (J.D., 1970). Beta Gamma Sigma. ***PRACTICE AREAS:*** Business Transactions; Real Estate; Partnership Law; Real Estate Secured Lending; Entrepreneurial Business Law; Business Separations; Business Development; Business Planning; Joint Ventures; Small Business Law; Sole Proprietorships; Strategic Alliances; Commercial Real Estate Development; Construction Contracts; Corporate Contracts; Corporate Partnerships; Corporate Real Estate; Real Estate Development; Real Estate Leasing; Hotel and Resort Development. **Email:** rcohler@bbn-law.com

SARAH NADELHOFFER, born Naperville, Illinois, May 20, 1959; admitted to bar, 1985, Missouri and U.S. District Court, District of Missouri; 1986, Illinois and U.S. District Court, Northern District of Illinois. *Education:* Bowdoin College (B.A., cum laude, 1981); Washington University (J.D., 1985). Recipient, Award, Urban, State and Local Government Law Section, American Bar Association for Land Use Planning. ***PRACTICE AREAS:*** Commercial Real Estate; Real Estate Leasing; Real Estate Development; Zoning, Planning and Land Use. **Email:** snadelhoffer@bbn-law.com

KENNETH S. PERLMAN, born Chicago, Illinois, June 8, 1947; admitted to bar, 1972, Illinois. *Education:* University of Illinois (A.B., cum laude, 1968); Harvard Law School (J.D., cum laude, 1972). Phi Beta Kappa; Phi Kappa Phi. James Scholar. Author: "Business Assets Acquisition Agreement," IICLE, Illinois Business Documents Series, 1993 and 1995. Co-Author: "Stock Appreciation Rights," 33 Business Lawyer 749, January, 1978. Member, Regional Executive Directory, Anti-Defamation League. *Member:* Chicago Bar Association. ***PRACTICE AREAS:*** Corporate Law; Mergers, Acquisitions and Divestitures; Business Law; Real Estate; Banking Law; Finance. **Email:** kperlman@bbn-law.com

REPRESENTATIVE CLIENTS: Real Estate Counsel to - Harris, N.A. and Hitachi High Technologies America, Inc.; Sardee Industries, Inc.; Air Stores, Inc.; Carlson Environmental, Inc.; AmeriSource Corporation; Alpha Thought, Inc.; Smart Document Solutions, LLC; Sipi Metals Corp.; Belmont Trading Co., Inc.; Transolutions, Inc.

JOSEPH A. BALDI & ASSOCIATES, P.C.

19 SOUTH LASALLE STREET
SUITE 1500
CHICAGO, ILLINOIS 60603
Telephone: 312-726-8150
Fax: 312-332-4629
Email: jabaldi@ameritech.net

Bankruptcy, Insolvency, Creditors' Rights, Workouts.

JOSEPH A. BALDI, born Chicago, Illinois, April 11, 1949; admitted to bar, 1977, Illinois; 1978, U.S. Court of Appeals, 7th Circuit. *Education:* Western Illinois University (B.A., 1971); DePaul University College of Law (J.D., 1977). Attorney, United States Trustee Office, Department of Justice, 1982-1987. *Member:* Chicago Bar Association (Member, Bankruptcy and Reorganizations Subcommittee), American Bankruptcy Institute; National Association of Bankruptcy Trustees. ***PRACTICE AREAS:*** Bankruptcy; Insolvency; Creditors' Rights; Workouts. **Email:** jabaldi@ameritech.net

ELIZABETH C. BERG, born Glen Ridge, New Jersey, September 3, 1958; admitted to bar, 1989, Illinois and U.S. District Court, Northern District of Illinois. *Education:* Brown University (B.A., 1983); Loyola University of Chicago (J.D., 1989). Instructor, Paralegal Studies Department, Northwestern Business College, 2000-2001. ***LANGUAGES:*** French. ***PRACTICE AREAS:*** Bankruptcy. **Email:** ecberg@ameritech.net

DONNA B. WALLACE, born Reading, Pennsylvania, November 10, 1949; admitted to bar, 1989, Illinois and U.S. District Court, Northern District of Illinois. *Education:* Kutztown University (B.A., 1972); John Marshall Law School (J.D., with highest distinction, 1989). Recipient: Order of John Marshall; West Publishing Award; Wall Street Journal Scholastic Achievement Award. Staff, John Marshall Law Review, 1988-1989. Author: "Lender's Liability - The Shift From Contract To Tort Doctrine Deters Banks From Enforcing Unjustified and Detrimental Contract Provisions," 21 John Marshall Law Review 369, 1988. Associate Professor, Paralegal Studies, Northwestern Business College, 1998-2002. ***PRACTICE AREAS:*** Bankruptcy; Insolvency; Creditors Rights; Workouts. **Email:** dbwallace@ameritech.net

BANIAK PINE & GANNON

150 NORTH WACKER DRIVE, SUITE 1200
CHICAGO, ILLINOIS 60606
Telephone: 312-673-0360
Fax: 312-673-0361
URL: http://www.bpglaw.com

Intellectual Property, Patent, Trademark, Copyright and Trade Secret Law, Litigation, Licensing.

FIRM PROFILE: Baniak Pine & Gannon is a full service intellectual property firm providing prosecution, counseling, licensing and litigation expertise in all fields. The firm's attorneys have a wide range of technical degrees. They include published authors, teachers, lecturers, as well as testifying experts. The firm's attorneys are admitted to practice in federal courts throughout the United States, in various State Courts, and as patent attorneys/agents before the United States Patent and Trademark Office.

MEMBERS OF FIRM

MICHAEL H. BANIAK, born Troy, New York, January 4, 1955; admitted to bar, 1980, Ohio; 1985, Illinois; registered to practice before U.S. Patent and Trademark Office. *Education:* University of Dayton (B.S., Physics, cum laude, 1977); Indiana University (J.D., cum laude, 1980). Sigma Pi Sigma. Adjunct Professor, Patent and Copyright Law, Northwestern School of Law, 1986—. *Member:* American Bar Association; American Intellec-

(This Listing Continued)

BANIAK PINE & GANNON, Chicago—Continued

tual Property Law Association; Licensing Executives Society (Plenary Speaker; Member, Board of Trustees); The Association of Trial Lawyers of America. ***PRACTICE AREAS:*** Litigation; Intellectual Property; Licensing; Trademark; Copyright; Patents. ***Email:*** baniak@bpglaw.com

JEFFREY A. PINE, born Anaheim, California, August 7, 1962; admitted to bar, 1991, Illinois; registered to practice before U.S. Patent and Trademark Office. *Education:* University of Illinois (B.S.E.E., 1984); Loyola University of Chicago (J.D., 1991). Speaker: "Developments in Intellectual Property for the General Business Lawyer," Third Annual Advising Illinois Businesses Conference; "The Latest Developments in Intellectual Property Law," Executive Management and Computer Conference. Author: "How to Avoid Legal Entanglement When Weaving Your Web," b3 Build Better Business. *Member:* Chicago, Illinois State and American Bar Associations; American Intellectual Property Law Association; Intellectual Property Law Association of Chicago. ***PRACTICE AREAS:*** Litigation; Intellectual Property; Licensing; Trademarks; Copyrights; Patents. ***Email:*** pine@bpglaw.com

MICHAEL D. GANNON, born Chicago, Illinois, May 3, 1965; admitted to bar, 1991, Illinois and Wisconsin; registered to practice before U.S. Patent and Trademark Office. *Education:* Marquette University (B.S.E.E., 1988; J.D., 1991). *Member:* Chicago and American Bar Associations; State Bar of Wisconsin; American Intellectual Property Law Association. ***PRACTICE AREAS:*** Litigation; Intellectual Property; Licensing; Trademarks; Copyrights; Patents. ***Email:*** gannon@bpglaw.com

CHRISTINA L. BROWN, born Middletown, Ohio, February 3, 1965; admitted to bar, 1991, Ohio; 1992, U.S. District Court, Northern District of Ohio; 1994, U.S. Court of Appeals, Sixth Circuit; 1999, U.S. Court of Appeals for the Federal Circuit; 2003, Illinois. *Education:* Adrian College (B.S., 1987); University of Toledo (J.D., 1990). Beta Beta Beta, Biology Honorary Society. Dean's Scholar. Outstanding Advocate, Charles W. Fornoff Moot Court Competition. Member, Moot Court Board. Co-founder, The University of Toledo Environmental Law Society. Speaker: "Spies, Lies, and Dies: Protecting Technology at Home and Abroad," Women's Entrepreneurial Network; "Intellectual Property: How To Know It When You See It;" "What Attorneys Look For In An Expert Witness;" Trademarks and Unfair Competition, Licensing Executives Society. *Member:* Ohio State and Illinois State Bar Associations; American Intellectual Property Law Association; Intellectual Property Owners Association. ***PRACTICE AREAS:*** Litigation; Intellectual Property; Licensing; Trademarks; Copyrights; Patents. ***Email:*** clbrown@bpglaw.com

CHARLES C. VALAUSKAS, born Chicago, Illinois, November 14, 1952; admitted to bar, 1981, Illinois and U.S. District Court, Northern District of Illinois; registered to practice before U.S. Patent and Trademark Office. *Education:* University of Illinois (B.S., 1977); DePaul University College of Law (J.D., 1981); Northwestern University School of Law(LL.M., 1985). Recipient: State of Illinois Governor's Fellowship, 1979; Schweppe Foundation Grant, 1982. Co-Author: C. Valauskas and C. Innes, "Copyright Protection of Software, Multimedia, and Other Works: An Author's Guide," AUTM Educational Series no. 4 (Association of University Technology Managers, 2000); C. Innes and C. Valauskas, "Development and Deployment of Digital Works in Universities: A Guide for Authors and Licensing Officers," AUTM Educational Series no. 5 (Association of University Technology Managers, 2000). Publications: "Defective Reissue Application May be Corrected to Obtain Broadened Claims: An In Banc Ruling," 3 CAFC Newsletter 1 (1985); "Right to a Jury Trial in 'Complex' Patent Matters," 3 CAFC Newsletter 84 (1985). Author of other articles appearing in: Boston College International and Comparative Law Review, Hastings International and Comparative Law Review, the Review of Socialist Law, Land Use & Zoning Digest, Proceedings of the Institute of Medicine of Chicago, and Chicago Medicine. Adjunct Professor, Intellectual Property Law and Commercialization, DePaul University College of Law. *Member:* Illinois State Bar Association; Intellectual Property Law Association of Chicago; Licensing Executives Society; Association of University Technology Managers. ***PRACTICE AREAS:*** Litigation; Intellectual Property; Licensing; Trademarks; Copyrights; Patents. ***Email:*** ccv@bpglaw.com

CHARLES C. KINNE, born Pittsburgh, Pennsylvania, April 10, 1958; admitted to bar, 1984, Illinois and U.S. District Court, Northern District of Illinois; 1985, U.S. Court of Appeals for the Federal Circuit; 1987, U.S. Court of Appeals, Eleventh Circuit; 1988, U.S. Court of Appeals, Ninth Circuit; registered to practice before U.S. Patent and Trademark Office. *Education:* University of Rochester (B.S., in Chemical Engineering, 1980); University of Texas (J.D., 1984). Winner, Client Counselling Competition, 1984. C.J. Wrightsman Scholar. New York Regents Scholar; Rochester Prize Scholar. Director of Trial Advocacy, Board of Advocates, 1983-1984. ***PRACTICE AREAS:*** Patent, Trademark, Copyright and Trade Secret Litigation; Patent, Trademark and Copyright Procurement and Analyses. ***Email:*** ckinne@bpglaw.com

ASSOCIATES

ALLISON DUDLEY, born Highland Park, Illinois; admitted to bar, 2002, Illinois and U.S. District Court, Northern District of Illinois; registered to practice before U.S. Patent and Trademark Office. *Education:* University of Illinois (B.S.M.E., 1996); Chicago-Kent College of Law, Illinois Institute of Technology (J.D., 2001). ***PRACTICE AREAS:*** Intellectual Property; Litigation; Intellectual Property Licensing; Patent Prosecution. ***Email:*** adudley@bpglaw.com

CHRISTOPHER E. HAIGH, admitted to bar, 2000, Indiana and U.S. District Court, Southern and Northern Districts of Indiana; registered to practice before U.S. Patent and Trademark Office (Not admitted in Illinois). *Education:* Purdue University (B.S.E., 1994); Indiana University - Indianapolis (J.D., 1999). Sidney J. Eskenazi Scholarship Recipient. Head Rowing Coach, International School of Indiana. *Member:* Illinois State Bar Association; American Intellectual Property Law Association. ***PRACTICE AREAS:*** Patent Litigation; Trademark Litigation; Copyright Litigation; Trade Secrets Litigation; Patents Procurement and Analyses; Trademark Procurement and Analyses; Copyright Procurement and Analyses. ***Email:*** chaigh@bpglaw.com

ANDREW F. PRATT, born Los Angeles, California, March 22, 1970; admitted to bar, 1998, Washington; 2003, Illinois; registered to practice before U.S. Patent and Trademark Office. *Education:* University of Washington (B.S. in Microbiology, 1993); Temple University School of Law (J.D., 1998). Associate Editor, Temple Environmental and Technology Law Journal. Norwegian American Chamber of Commerce. *Member:* Washington State, Illinois State, Chicago and American Bar Associations; American Intellectual Property Law Association. ***PRACTICE AREAS:*** Patent Litigation; Trademark Litigation; Trade Secrets Litigation; Patent Prosecution. ***Email:*** apratt@bpglaw.com

ANUJ K. WADHWA, born Chicago, Illinois, December 24, 1975; admitted to bar, 2000, Ohio; 2002, Illinois; registered to practice before U.S. Patent and Trademark Office. *Education:* Benedictine University (B.S., 1997); Case Western Reserve University (J.D., 2000). *Member:* American Bar Association; American Intellectual Property Law Association; Computer Law Association. ***PRACTICE AREAS:*** Intellectual Property; Litigation; Intellectual Property Licensing; Patent Prosecution. ***Email:*** awadhwa@bpglaw.com

WILLIAM F. WARD, III, born Chicago, Illinois, July 31, 1976; admitted to bar, 2002, Illinois; registered to practice before U.S. Patent and Trademark Office. *Education:* Marquette University (B.S.C.E., 1998); The John Marshall Law School (J.D., cum laude, 2002). Order of John Marshall, Law Review. *Member:* Illinois State and American Bar Associations; American Intellectual Property Law Association; Intellectual Property Lawyers' Association of Chicago. ***PRACTICE AREAS:*** Intellectual Property; Litigation; Patent Prosecution; Intellectual Property Licensing. ***Email:*** wward@bpglaw.com

COUNSEL

GARY E. HOOD, born Spokane, Washington; admitted to bar, 1996, Washington and U.S. District Court, Western District of Washington; 2003, U.S. Court of Appeals, Ninth Circuit, U.S. District Court, Eastern District of Washington; 2004, Illinois, U.S. District Court, Northern District of Illinois, including Trial Bar; registered to practice before U.S. Patent and Trademark Office. *Education:* University of Southern California (B.S., Electrical Engineering, 1988); Gonzaga University School of Law (J.D., magna cum laude, 1996). Editor-in-Chief, Gonzaga Law Review, 1995-1996. National Moot Court, Regional Champion & National Competitor, 1995-1996. Guest Presenter, Pacific Lutheran University, Residence Programs, Copyright/P2P/File Sharing Issues on College Campuses, April 2003. Guest Lecturer, Pacific Lutheran University, MBA legal course, IP Basics, March 2003 and July 2003; University of Puget Sound, Business Leadership Program, "Intellectual Property Primer", November 2002. Co-author, 1998 Cumulative Supp. to Wash. Motor Vehicle Accident Deskbook Chap. 13. Author, "Campbell v. Wood: The Death Penalty in Washington State - 'Hanging' on to a Method of Execution", 30 Gonz. L. Rev. 163 (1994). Member, Professional Advisory Committee, Bridges Center for Grieving Children, 2003. Member, American Legion, 2002—; Member, United States Masters Swimming, 1999—. Trustee, Brown's Point Improvement Club, 1999-2000. Member, City of Federal Way Ethics Board, 1997-2000. Recipient, Navy Commendation Medal, Navy Achievement Medal, National Defense Service Medal, Southwest Asia Service Medal (with bronze service star), and Kuwait Liberation Medal. *Member:* Washington State, Illinois State, and American Bar Associations; American Intellectual Property Law Association; Intellectual Property Law Association of Chicago (Vice-Chair, Trade Secrets and Unfair Competition Committee, 2005). [Lt., U.S. Navy, 1988-1993, active duty, 1993-1996, drilling reserve]. ***LANGUAGES:*** German. ***REPORTED CASES:*** State v. Martin, 137 Wash.2d 774 (1999) (interpreting Washington's priest-penitent privilege statute). ***PRACTICE AREAS:*** Intellectual Property; Litigation; Patents; Copyrights; Trademarks; Trade Secrets; Unfair Competition; White Collar Crime. ***Email:*** ghood@bpglaw.com

PATENT AGENT

STEVEN B. COURTRIGHT, born Washington, D.C., September 12, 1958. registered to practice before U.S. Patent and Trademark Office. *Education:* Bradley University (B.S., Environmental Science/Biology, 1980). ***PRACTICE AREAS:*** Patent Prosecution; Mechanical Patent Prosecution; Chemical Patent Prosecution. ***Email:*** scourtright@bpglaw.com

MARK A. BANKS-GOLUB

Established in 2004

10 SOUTH LA SALLE STREET
SUITE 3500
CHICAGO, ILLINOIS 60603-1025
Telephone: 312-781-9310
Fax: 312-781-9312
Email: mark.banks-golub@banks-golub.com
URL: http://www.banks-golub.com

Business Law, Real Estate, Taxation, Trusts and Estates, Wills and Probate.

FIRM PROFILE: Mark's practice is currently concentrated in investigations and due diligence reviews for private and public real estate and securitization transactions on behalf of broker-dealers, acquirers, and acquisition targets; providing reasoned opinions to individual investors in tenant in common and like-kind exchange transactions; independent counseling of audit committees under Sarbanes-Oxley; representation of corporate officers and directors in private and public investigations under the Internal Revenue Code, Sarbanes-Oxley, and securities laws; defense of civil and criminal tax and securities litigation; advising on mergers, acquisitions, and dispositions; tax planning; and structuring business ventures.

Mark has advised clients in restructuring their corporate groups, including spin-offs of corporate entities. He is frequently called upon to assist other attorneys and clients in selecting the correct form of business entity and planning the formation and structure of joint business ventures. Mark has also participated in advising clients in state and federal audits with respect to income, sales, and franchise taxes. In addition, he has represented clients in the US Tax Court, the Court of Federal Claims, federal district courts, and state courts.

MARK A. BANKS-GOLUB, born Chicago, Illinois, September 22, 1961; admitted to bar, 1989, Illinois; U.S. District Court, Northern District of Illinois; 1997, U.S. Tax Court; U.S. Court of Federal Claims. *Education:* Lake Forest College (B.A., 1984); Chicago Kent College of Law, Illinois Institute of Technology (J.D., 1989); University of Houston Law

(This Listing Continued)

of Law; Adjunct Professor in Mergers and Acquisitions of The J.L. Kellogg Graduate School of Management at Northwestern University. Director, Harvard Law Society, 1975-1978. Planning Director, Corporate Counsel Institute, 1977-1980. *Member:* Chicago (Member: Securities Law Committee, 1974-1978; International Law Committee, 1974-1978), Illinois State and American Bar Associations; Chicago Council of Lawyers. ***PRACTICE AREAS:*** Corporate Law; International Business Law; Securities Law. ***Email:*** peter.barack@bfkpn.com

WILLIAM J. BARRETT, born Elmhurst, Illinois, September 3, 1958; admitted to bar, 1985, Michigan; 1991, Illinois. *Education:* Michigan State University (B.A., 1980); University of Southern California (J.D., 1985).

MARK J. BEAUBIEN, born Chicago, Illinois, May 2, 1967; admitted to bar, 1994, Illinois. *Education:* Cornell University (A.B., 1984); J.L. Kellogg Graduate School of Management (M.M., 1994); Northwestern University (J.D., magna cum laude, 1994). Phi Beta Kappa; Phi Kappa Phi; Order of the Coif; Golden Key. ***LANGUAGES:*** Spanish. ***Email:*** mark.beaubien@bfkpn.com

MARK S. BERNSTEIN, born Chicago, Illinois, November 4, 1963; admitted to bar, 1988, Illinois, U.S. District Court, Northern District of Illinois including Trial Bar, U.S. Court of Appeals, Seventh Circuit and U.S. Supreme Court; U.S. Court of Appeals, Sixth Circuit; U.S. District Court, Eastern District of Michigan. *Education:* University of Illinois (B.S., with honors, 1985); University of Michigan (J.D., cum laude, 1988). Order of the Coif. Associate and Contributing Editor, Michigan Law Review. Author, Chapter 18: Class Action Lawsuits in Advising Illinois Financial Institutions (Illinois Institute for Continuing Legal Education, 2002). Certified Public Accountant, Illinois, 1985. *Member:* Illinois State and American Bar Associations. ***PRACTICE AREAS:*** Commercial Litigation. ***Email:*** mark.bernstein@bfkpn.com

SARAH M. BERNSTEIN, born Northampton, Massachusetts, January 20, 1966; admitted to bar, 1991, Illinois. *Education:* The American University (B.A., magna cum laude, 1988); Northwestern University (J.D., 1991). Note and Comment Editor, Journal of Criminal Law and Criminology, 1990-1991. Author, Note, "Fourteenth Amendment-Police Failure to Preserve Evidence and Erosion of the Due Process Rights to a Fair Trial," 80 J. of Crim. Law and Criminology, 1256, 1990. ***PRACTICE AREAS:*** Corporate Law; Securities Law; Banking Law. ***Email:*** sarah.bernstein@bfkpn.com

SUZANNE BESSETTE-SMITH, born Montclair, New Jersey, October 5, 1956; admitted to bar, 1980, Illinois. *Education:* North Central College (B.A., cum laude, 1977); University of Illinois College of Law (J.D., 1980). Instructor, Northwestern University Law School, 2001—. *Member:* American College of Real Estate Lawyers; American Land Title Association (Associate Member; Member and Secretary, Lender's Counsel Group, 2002—); International Association of Attorneys and Executives in Corporate Real Estate. ***PRACTICE AREAS:*** Real Estate Law; Business Law. ***Email:*** suzanne.bessette-smith@bfkpn.com

EDWIN S. DEL HIERRO, born Nanegal, Ecuador, January 30, 1962; admitted to bar, 1986, Illinois and U.S. District Court, Northern District of Illinois. *Education:* Loyola University of Chicago (B.B.A., magna cum laude, 1983); University of Illinois (J.D., 1985). Beta Alpha Psi. *Member:* Chicago (Member: Financial Institutions Committee, 1988—; Chairman, Legislation Subcommittee, 1989-1990), Illinois State and American Bar Associations. ***PRACTICE AREAS:*** Banking Law; Securities Law; Corporate Law. ***Email:*** ed.delhierro@bfkpn.com

DANIEL L. DOMINGUEZ, born Washington, D.C., July 9, 1972; admitted to bar, 1997, Illinois. *Education:* Houghton College (B.A., summa cum laude, 1994); University of Chicago (J.D., with honors, 1997). Vice President, Latino Law Students Association, 1995-1996. *Member:* Chicago, Illinois State and American Bar Associations. ***PRACTICE AREAS:*** Corporate Law; Mergers and Acquisitions; Securities Law. ***Email:*** dan.dominguez@bfkpn.com

DENNIS A. FERRAZZANO, born Paterson, New Jersey, November 25, 1946; admitted to bar, 1971, District of Columbia; 1972, Illinois; 1994, Wisconsin. *Education:* Johns Hopkins University (B.A., 1968); Northwestern University (J.D., magna cum laude, 1971). Order of the Coif. Notes and Comments Editor, Northwestern University Law Review, 1970-1971. Author: "Political Activity and the Public Employee," 64 Northwestern University Law Review 736, 1969; "Jury Trial in a Stockholders Derivative Suit," 65 NW. U. L. Rev. 697, 1970. Adjunct Professor in Real Estate Law, 1979-1999. William H. Trumbull Lecturer, 1986-1999. Northwestern University School of Law. Recipient: Robert Childres Memorial Award for Teaching Excellence, 1985; Outstanding Adjunct Professor, 1996, 1997, 1998. *Member:* American Bar Association (Member, Sections of: Business Law; Real Property, Probate and Trust Law; Member, Committee on Leases 1975-1977). ***Email:*** dennis.ferrazzano@bfkpn.com

JOHN E. FREECHACK, born Brownsville, Pennsylvania, December 5, 1950; admitted to bar, 1975, Illinois. *Education:* Northwestern University (B.A., 1972); Northwestern University School of Law (J.D., 1975). Law Clerk to the Hon. Daniel J. McNamara, Justice, Illinois Appellate Court, 1975-1977. Chairman-Financial Institutions Group. Recipient: Illinois Bankers Association 1992 Distinguished Bank Counsel Award. Adjunct Professor of Banking Law, Northwestern University School of Law, 2001—. Frequent speaker at programs and seminars in the financial institutions area. Guest Lecturer on banking law, University of Iowa College of Law, 2001. Adjunct Professor of Law: graduate program in financial services law at the Chicago-Kent College of Law, 1992—. Member: Illinois Task Force on Financial Services, Safety and Soundness Subcommittee, 1985-1986; Advisory Committee, Bank Administration Institute, "Acquiring Savings and Loans," 1990. *Member:* American Bar Association (Member: Corporation, Banking and Business Law Section; Banking Law Committee, 1981—; Community Bank Matters Subcommittee, 1989—Chairman -- Community Bank Matters Subcommittee, 1992-1997). ***PRACTICE AREAS:*** Banking Law. ***Email:*** john.freechack@bfkpn.com

DAVID E. GORDON, born Chicago, Illinois, January 24, 1965; admitted to bar, 1991, Illinois and U.S. District Court, Northern District of Illinois including Trial Bar; 1994, U.S. Court of Appeals, Seventh Circuit; 1997, U.S. District Court, Eastern District of Michigan; 2001, U.S. Court of Appeals, Sixth Circuit. *Education:* University of Illinois (B.S., with high honors); University of Chicago Law School, University of Illinois College of Law (J.D., magna cum laude, 1991). Dean's List. Harno Fellow. Recipient, Rickert Award for

(This Listing Continued)

Excellence, Illinois Moot Court Team. Certified Public Accountant, Illinois, 1988. *Member:* American Bar Association. ***PRACTICE AREAS:*** Commercial Litigation; Civil Trial Practice. ***Email:*** david.gordon@bfkpn.com

MARC M. JACOBS, born Livonia, Michigan, August 3, 1960; admitted to bar, 1985, Illinois and U.S. District Court, Northern District of Illinois. *Education:* University of Michigan (A.B., 1982; J.D., 1985). Phi Beta Kappa. Note Editor, University of Michigan Journal of Law Reform, 1984-1985. *Member:* Chicago and American Bar Associations. ***Email:*** marc.jacobs@bfkpn.com

HOWARD J. KIRSCHBAUM, born Detroit, Michigan, June 19, 1955; admitted to bar, 1979, Illinois. *Education:* Northwestern University (B.A., with distinction, 1976); University of Michigan (J.D., magna cum laude, 1979). Phi Beta Kappa; Order of the Coif. ***PRACTICE AREAS:*** Real Estate Law; Land Use Law. ***Email:*** howard.kirschbaum@bfkpn.com

AMY LISTICK KOENIG, born Chicago, Illinois, January 24, 1962; admitted to bar, 1987, Illinois. *Education:* University of Illinois (B.A., 1984); Northwestern University (J.D., 1987). Phi Beta Kappa; Phi Kappa Phi; Omicron Delta Epsilon; Golden Key National Honorary. *Member:* Chicago Bar Association. ***PRACTICE AREAS:*** Real Estate Law. ***Email:*** amy.koenig@bfkpn.com

ALEXANDER LOURIE, born Boston, Massachusetts, March 8, 1957; admitted to bar, 1983, Illinois and U.S. District Court, Northern District of Illinois. *Education:* Duke University (B.S., magna cum laude, 1979); University of Chicago (J.D., 1983; M.B.A., 1983). Co-Author: "Application of the Hart-Scott-Rodino Act to Transactions in Japan," International Legal Strategy, May 1998; "International Commercial Arbitration in China: History, New Developments, and Current Practice," 28 J. Marshall L. Rev. 539, 1995; "Private Rights of Action Under the Proxy Rules and the Williams Act," Practising Law Institute, 1984; "Problems of Insider Trading During a Control Contest," Practising Law Institute, 1984. With Mori Sogo Law Offices, Tokyo, Japan, 1990-1991. *Member:* Chicago, American, International and Inter-Pacific Bar Associations. ***PRACTICE AREAS:*** Corporate Law; Securities Law; International Law. ***Email:*** alourie@bfkpn.com

LYNNE D. MAPES-RIORDAN, born Chicago, Illinois, January 28, 1963; admitted to bar, 1989, Illinois; U.S. District Court, Northern District of Illinois. *Education:* University of Michigan (B.A., 1985); Georgia State University (J.D., cum laude, 1989). Author, "Sex Discrimination and Employer Weight and Appearance Standards," 16 Employee Relations L.J. 493, 1991. Co-Author, "The Arbitrability of Age-Discrimination Claims: A Split in the Circuits," 16 Employee Relations L.J. 139, 1990. *Member:* Illinois State Bar Association (Member, Sections on Employee Benefits and Labor and Employment Law). ***PRACTICE AREAS:*** Employee Benefits Law; Labor and Employment Law. ***Email:*** lynne.mapes-riordan@bfkpn.com

MALCOLM McCALEB, JR., admitted to bar, 1971, Illinois. *Education:* Colgate University (B.A., 1967); Northwestern University (J.D., 1971). Member, 1977-1982 and Chairman, 1981-1982, Northfield, Illinois Village Caucus. Member, Northfield, Illinois School and Park Board Caucus, 1980-1987. Member, 1972-1982 and Board President, 1977-1979, Volunteers of America. Member, 1983-1988 and Chairman, 1985-1988, Village of Northfield Zoning Commission. *Member:* Chicago Bar Association; Bar Association of the Seventh Federal Circuit; Intellectual Property Law Association of Chicago; International Trademark Association. ***PRACTICE AREAS:*** Intellectual Property Law; Trademarks; Copyrights; Unfair Competition. ***Email:*** mac.mccaleb@bfkpn.com

ELLIOT I. MOLK, born New York, N.Y. August 24, 1964; admitted to bar, 1989, Illinois. *Education:* University of Michigan (B.B.A., with high distinction, 1986); University of Chicago (J.D., with honors, 1989). Certified Public Accountant, Illinois, 1987. *Member:* Illinois State and American Bar Associations. ***PRACTICE AREAS:*** Corporate Law; Business Law; Securities Law. ***Email:*** elliot.molk@bfkpn.com

DAVID H. NADOFF, born Des Moines, Iowa, November 12, 1954; admitted to bar, 1982, Illinois and U.S. District Court, Northern District of Illinois; 1985, U.S. District Court, Northern District of Illinois including Trial Bar. *Education:* Loyola University of Chicago (A.B., summa cum laude, 1976; A.M., 1979); Northwestern University (J.D., summa cum laude, 1982). Order of the Coif. Member, Editorial Board, Northwestern University Law Review, 1980-1982. ***PRACTICE AREAS:*** Real Estate Law; Corporate Law. ***Email:*** david.nadoff@bfkpn.com

HOWARD A. NAGELBERG, born Chicago, Illinois, October 31, 1947; admitted to bar, 1973, Illinois. *Education:* University of Michigan (B.A., 1969); University of Chicago (J.D., 1973). Member, 1970 and Associate Editor, 1971-1972, University of Chicago Law Review. Adjunct Professor of Real Estate Law, Northwestern University School of Law, 2000—. Guest Lecturer, Legal Aspects of Real Estate Financing, Kellogg Graduate School of Management, Northwestern University, 1994-1997. Member, American College of Real Estate Lawyers, 1986—. Member, American College of Mortgage Attorneys, 2000—. Member, Urban Land Institute, 1991—. Associate Member, American Land Title Association (Member, Lenders' Counsel Group, 1980—). *Member:* Chicago, Illinois State and American Bar Associations (Member of following ABA Sections and Committees: Real Property, Probate and Trust Law Section; Title Insurance Committee; Forum Committee on the Construction Industry; Real Estate Finance Committee). ***PRACTICE AREAS:*** Real Estate; Corporate. ***Email:*** howard.nagelberg@bfkpn.com

CHRISTINE K. NICHOLS, born East Chicago, Indiana, January 29, 1971; admitted to bar, 1996, Illinois; 2000, New York. *Education:* Purdue University (B.A., 1993); Indiana University School of Law (J.D., summa cum laude, 1996). Member, Indiana Law Review, 1994-1996.

RICHARD S. NIKCHEVICH, born Chicago, Illinois, February 7, 1962; admitted to bar, 1987, Illinois and U.S. District Court, Northern District of Illinois. *Education:* Carthage College (B.A., 1984); University of Chicago (J.D., 1987). *Member:* Chicago Bar Association (Real Property Committee); Chicago Mortgage Attorneys Association; Federal Communications Bar Association. ***PRACTICE AREAS:*** Real Estate Law; Telecommunications Law. ***Email:*** rich.nikchevich@bfkpn.com

DONALD L. NORMAN, JR., born Arlington Heights, Illinois, February 23, 1961; admitted to bar, 1986, Illinois. *Education:* University of Illinois (B.A., 1983); University of Kansas (J.D., 1986). ***Email:*** donald.norman@bfkpn.com

(This Listing Continued)

BARACK FERRAZZANO KIRSCHBAUM PERLMAN & NAGELBERG LLP, Chicago—Continued

RANDALL L. OYLER, admitted to bar, 1992, Illinois; 1993, U.S. District Court, Northern District of Illinois; 1992, U.S. Court of Appeals, Seventh Circuit. *Education:* Wheaton College (B.A., summa cum laude, 1989); University of Chicago (J.D., 1992). Developments Editor, University of Chicago Legal Forum, 1991-1992. ***REPORTED CASES:*** ING (U.S.) Securities, Futures & Options, Inc. v. Bingham Investment Fund, L.L.C., 934 F. Supp. 987 (N.D. Ill. 1996). ***PRACTICE AREAS:*** General Litigation; Commercial Litigation; Creditors Rights; Distributorship Litigation; Securities Litigation; Franchise Law. ***Email:*** randall.oyler@bfkpn.com

THOMAS H. PAGE, born Detroit, Michigan, September 7, 1952; admitted to bar, 1978, Illinois and U.S. District Court, Northern District of Illinois. *Education:* University of Michigan (B.A., with high distinction, 1974; J.D., magna cum laude, 1978). Phi Beta Kappa; Order of the Coif. Associate Editor, 1976-1977 and Notes Editor, 1977-1978, Michigan Law Review. ***PRACTICE AREAS:*** Real Estate Law; Business Law; Partnership Law. ***Email:*** tom.page@bfkpn.com

CHARLES H. PERLMAN, born Chicago, Illinois, August 2, 1945; admitted to bar, 1971, Illinois. *Education:* University of Wisconsin-Madison (B.B.A., with high honors, 1967); Northwestern University (J.D., magna cum laude, 1971). Beta Gamma Sigma; Order of the Coif; Tau Epsilon Rho. *Member:* Chicago Bar Association. ***PRACTICE AREAS:*** Corporate Law; Mergers and Acquisitions Law; Securities Law. ***Email:*** chuck.perlman@bfkpn.com

W. SCOTT PORTERFIELD, born Philadelphia, Pennsylvania, January 18, 1954; admitted to bar, 1979, Illinois, U.S. District Court, Northern, including Trial Bar and Central Districts of Illinois and U.S. Court of Appeals, Seventh and Eighth Circuits. *Education:* Northwestern University (B.A., 1976; J.D., 1979). Phi Beta Kappa. Notes and Comments Editor, Northwestern Journal of International Law and Business, 1978-1979. Participant in and Co-author of IICLE seminar materials for Illinois Contract Law, 1982 and 1986 Supplement. Co-author: "Contracts and Sales of Goods," chapter in IICLE book, 1990. Arbitrator, National Futures Association, 1988—. *Member:* American Bar Association. ***PRACTICE AREAS:*** Commercial Litigation; Arbitration; Civil Trial Practice. ***Email:*** scott.porterfield@bfkpn.com

JULIE K. RADEMAKER, born Peoria, Illinois, April 23, 1961; admitted to bar, 1986, Illinois. *Education:* Knox College (B.A., magna cum laude, 1983); Northwestern University (J.D., 1986). Phi Beta Kappa. Executive Editor, Northwestern University Law Review, 1985-1986. Author: "Alliance To End Repression v. City of Chicago: Judicial Abandonment of Consent Decree Principles," Northwestern University Law Review, 1986. ***PRACTICE AREAS:*** Real Estate Law; Business Law. ***Email:*** julie.rademaker@bfkpn.com

RAY G. REZNER, born Burlington, Iowa, January 6, 1951; admitted to bar, 1977, Illinois; U.S. District Court, Northern District of Illinois including Trial Bar; 1981, U.S. Court of Appeals, Seventh Circuit; 1991, U.S. Court of Appeals, Eight Circuit; 1993, U.S. Supreme Court. *Education:* University of Iowa (B.G.S., 1974; J.D., 1977). Participant in Seminars and Co-Author of IICLE publications, Illinois Contract Law Update, Sale of Goods Under Article 2; "Takeover Litigation and the Business Judgement Rule," PLI Banking Law and Regulation; "Buyer's and Seller's Remedies"; "The Supreme Court's Review of RICO," IBA LAWwatch; "Civil RICO Post Sedima and Attempts to Kill The Beast," IBA LAWwatch. Lecturer: The Bank Regulating Process, Illinois Banker Association; CBA, Trial Advocacy; ABA Civil RICO Workshop. Arbitrator, National Futures Association. *Member:* Chicago and American Bar Associations. ***PRACTICE AREAS:*** Commercial Litigation; Securities Law; Banking Law. ***Email:*** ray.rezner@bfkpn.com

JOHN W. ROBERTS, born Ft. Thomas, Kentucky, June 9, 1957; admitted to bar, 1982, Illinois; 1998, U.S. Supreme Court. *Education:* Lake Forest College (B.A., 1979); Harvard University (J.D., cum laude, 1982). Phi Beta Kappa. ***REPORTED CASES:*** Rutgerswerke v. Pneumo Abex, 2002 WL 1203836 (S.D.N.Y. June 4, 2002); Pneumo Abex v. Bessemer and Lake Erie Railroad, Inc. et. al., 921 F. Supp. 336, 936 F. Supp. 1250 (E.D. Va. 1996); 142 F.3d 769 (4th Cir. 1998); H & H Sand and Gravel v. Coyne Cylinder, 632 N.E.2d 697 (Ill. App. 1994); Hines v. Vulcan, 658 F. Supp. 651 (N.D.Ill. 1988); Inland Steel v. Koppers Company, 498 N.E.2d 1247 (Ind.App. 1986); Richman v. Chicago Bears, 468 N.W.2d 487 (Ill.App. 1984).

KIMBERLY J. ROBINSON, born Spencer, Iowa, December 6, 1960; admitted to bar, 1986, Illinois; 1987, U.S. District Court, Northern District of Illinois. *Education:* Iowa State University (B.S., with distinction, 1983); University of Iowa (J.D., with distinction, 1986). Phi Beta Kappa; Phi Kappa Phi. Member, Mortar Board. Law Clerk to: Judge William J. Lasarow and Judge Calvin K. Ashland, U.S. District Court, Central District of California; Judge Eugene R. Wedoff, U.S. District Court, Northern District of Illinois. Author: "Ninth Circuit Ratifies Formula Approach in Determining Appropriate Market Interest Rate Under 11 U.S.C.E. 12256," 5V.B. 1990 Norton Bankruptcy Law Advisor No. 9; "Non-core Determination Forecloses Ninth Circuits Opportunity to Rule on Contested Jury Trial Issue," 1990 Norton Bankruptcy Law Advisor No. 12. *Member:* Chicago (Member, Bankruptcy Committee, 1992-2000, 2003—), Illinois State and American (Member, Business Law Section) Bar Associations. ***PRACTICE AREAS:*** Bankruptcy (60%); Creditors Rights (40%). ***Email:*** kim.robinson@bfkpn.com

BRYAN SEGAL, born Chicago, Illinois, October 1, 1967; admitted to bar, 1994, Illinois and U.S. District Court, Northern District of Illinois. *Education:* University of Illinois (A.B., 1990); Northwestern University (J.D., cum laude, 1994). Order of the Coif. ***PRACTICE AREAS:*** Real Estate Law; Business Law. ***Email:*** bryan.segal@bfkpn.com

DAVID R. SELMER, born Huntington, Indiana, May 25, 1953; admitted to bar, 1978, Illinois. *Education:* Western Michigan University (B.A., summa cum laude, 1975); University of Michigan (J.D., 1977). Author: "The FDA's Over-The-Counter Drug Review: Expeditious Enforcement by Rulemaking," Vol. 11 University of Michigan Journal of Law Reform 142, 1977-1978; "Customer Suitability," Vol. 1, The Journal of Futures Markets 527, 1981, Supplement. Co-Author: "Hostile Corporate Takeovers: History and Overview," 8 Northern Illinois University Law Review 203, 1988. Illinois Secretary of State Business Corporation Acts Advisory Committee Chairman, 1999-2001. *Member:* Chicago (Member: Corporation and Business Law Committee, 1981—; Chairman, Corporation Law Committee, 1990-1991) and American (Member, Section of Business Law) Bar Associations. ***PRACTICE AREAS:*** Business Law; Corporate Law; Securities Law. ***Email:*** david.selmer@bfkpn.com

JEFFREY S. SHAMBERG, born St. Louis, Missouri, December 15, 1967; admitted to bar, 1995, Illinois; 1999, U.S. Tax Court. *Education:* University of Illinois (B.S., with honors, 1990); Northwestern University (J.D., 1995). Certified Public Accountant, Illinois, 1990. Co-Author: "Considerations in Electing S Corporation Status," in Limited Liability Companies and S Corporations, 13-1, Ill. Inst. for CLE, 2000; "New S Corporation Provisions Provide Tax-Saving Opportunities for Banks," Vol. 10/No. 3, Journal of Bank Taxation 99, Spring 1997. ***PRACTICE AREAS:*** Tax. ***Email:*** jeff.shamberg@bfkpn.com

ROBERT E. SHAPIRO, born Cambridge, Massachusetts, December 15, 1950; admitted to bar, 1979, Illinois and U.S. District Court, Northern District of Illinois including Trial Bar; 1980, U.S. Court of Appeals, Seventh Circuit; 1983, U.S. Supreme Court. *Education:* Harvard University (A.B., cum laude, 1972); University of Toronto, Toronto, Ontario, Canada (M.A., 1975; M. Phil., 1976); University of Chicago (J.D., cum laude, 1979). Order of the Coif. Article Editor, University of Chicago Law Review, 1978-1979. Law Clerk to Hon. Walter J. Cummings, Jr., U.S. Court of Appeals, 7th Circuit, 1979-1980. Special Assistant Attorney General (representing Illinois Gaming Board -- various matters), 1999—. Merit Selection Panel for U.S. Magistrates, United States District Court for the Northern District of Illinois, 1996-1997. Associate Editor, Litigation, 1988—. Review, "Resignation In Protest," 1997 Osgoode Hall Law Journal; "Interview with Morris Dees," Litigation, Vol. 16, No. 4 (1990); "Wrestling With The Discovery Demons," Litigation, Vol. 18, No. 1 (1992); Interview with Judge Hubert L. Will, Litigation, Vol. 20, No. 1, (1993); "Can a Litigator be a Problem-Solver," Litigation, Vol. 20, No. 4, (1994); "Advance Sheet," 2000 to present (quarterly). Visiting Faculty, DePaul University, School for New Learning (political philosophy). *Member:* American Bar Association. ***Email:*** rob.shapiro@bfkpn.com

WENDI E. SLOANE, born Kansas City, Missouri, March 9, 1957; admitted to bar, 1982, Illinois and U.S. District Court, Northern District of Illinois; 1983, U.S. Court of Appeals, Seventh and Eighth Circuits, U.S. Court of Appeals for the Federal Circuit and U.S. Supreme Court. *Education:* Brown University (B.A., magna cum laude, 1979); University of Chicago (J.D., 1982). Co-Author: "Illinois Contract Law," Ch. 10, (IICLE 1990), Common Law Remedies for Breach. Participant, IICLE Seminar: Seller's Remedies for Buyer's Breach, Uniform Commercial Code - Article 2, March 21, 1990. Arbitrator: National Futures Association. *Member:* Illinois State and American Bar Associations. ***PRACTICE AREAS:*** Commercial Litigation; Intellectual Property; Trademarks; Copyrights; Unfair Competition. ***Email:*** wendi.sloane@bfkpn.com

KAROL K. SPARKS, born Indianapolis, Indiana, September 11, 1951; admitted to bar, 1979, Indiana; 1992, California; 1993, New York (Not admitted in Illinois). *Education:* Sweet Briar College and Butler University (B.A., 1973); Indiana University (J.D., magna cum laude, 1979). Author, Insurance Activities of Banks, 1998; "After *'Nationsbank'*- An update on the National Bank Insurance Cases," The Investment Lawyer, Vol. 2. No. 2; "A Look Beyond Barnett: State Regulation of Bank Insurance Activities," The Review of Banking and Financial Services (Standard & Poors), Vol. 12, No. 5; "Is it an Antitrust Problem?" ABA Banking Journal White Paper, August 1995. Adjunct Professor of Banking Law and Commercial Transactions, University of Iowa College of Law, 2001—. *Member:* American Bar Association (Chair, Banking Law Committee, 1998-2002).

KATHERINE S. SPRENGER, born Evanston. Illinois, December 25, 1968; admitted to bar, 1994, Illinois. *Education:* Williams College (B.A., magna cum laude, 1991); Northwestern University (J.D., cum laude, 1994). Phi Beta Kappa. Academic All-American. Author: "Continuing Implicit Discrimination in Real Estate Advertisements: A Call for the Issuance of Human Model Injunctions," Northwestern University Law Review, Volume 88:3, Spring 1994. ***PRACTICE AREAS:*** Real Estate Law. ***Email:*** katherine.sprenger@bfkpn.com

GRETCHEN ANNE TROFA, born Ithaca, New York, November 16, 1963; admitted to bar, 1988, Illinois. *Education:* Duke University (A.B., cum laude, 1985); Northwestern University (J.D., cum laude, 1988). Order of the Coif. Member, Editorial Board, Journal of International Law and Business, 1986-1988. ***Email:*** gretchen.trofa@bfkpn.com

WILLIAM E. TURNER II, born San Diego, California, August 13, 1970; admitted to bar, 1995, Illinois and U.S. District Court, Northern District of Illinois. *Education:* University of Chicago (B.A., with honors, Economics, 1992); Northwestern University (J.D., cum laude, 1995). Articles Editor, Northwestern University Law Review. ***PRACTICE AREAS:*** Corporate Law; Securities Law; Mergers and Acquisitions. ***Email:*** will.turner@bfkpn.com

JAMES R. VOGLER, admitted to bar, 1977, Illinois and U.S. District Court, Northern District of Illinois (and Trial Bar); 1984, U.S. Supreme Court; 1996, U.S. District Court, Central District of Illinois. *Education:* Harvard University (B.A., magna cum laude, 1974); Southern Illinois University (J.D., 1977). Notes and Comments Editor, 1976-1977 and Lawyer's Advisory Board, 1985—, Southern Illinois University Law Journal. Member, Southern Illinois University School of Law, Board of Visitors. *Member:* Illinois State and American (Franchise Law Section) Bar Associations. ***PRACTICE AREAS:*** Commercial Litigation; Franchise Law; Intellectual Property Law. ***Email:*** jvogler@bfkpn.com

DENNIS R. WENDTE, born Effingham, Illinois, October 19, 1957; admitted to bar, 1982, Illinois and U.S. District Court, Northern District of Illinois. *Education:* University of Illinois (B.S., with highest distinction, 1978); University of Michigan (J.D., cum laude, 1982). Phi Kappa Phi; Order of the Coif; Phi Alpha Delta. Adjunct Professor, Banking Law, Northwestern University School of Law, 2001—. *Member:* American Bar Association (Member, Business Law Section). ***PRACTICE AREAS:*** Banking Law; Corporate Law; Securities Law. ***Email:*** dennis.wendte@bfkpn.com

ADEDAPO A. ADEDEJI, born Silver Spring, Maryland, April 8, 1973; admitted to bar, 2000, Illinois. *Education:* Obafemi Awolowo University, Osun Nigeria (LL.B., 1994); Northwestern University School of Law (J.D., 2000). ***PRACTICE AREAS:*** Real Estate; Finance. ***Email:*** adedapo.adedeji@bfkpn.com

JEREMY TODD BUNNOW, born Green Bay, Wisconsin, June 6, 1974; admitted to bar, 1999, Wisconsin and Illinois. *Education:* University of Wisconsin-Madison (B.A.,

(This Listing Continued)

with distinction, 1995); University of Wisconsin Law School (J.D., cum laude, 1999). Order of the Coif. Senior Managing Editor of Wisconsin Law Review, University of Wisconsin Law School, 1998-1999. Published: Note, Reinventing the Lemon: Agostini v. Felton and the Changing Nature of Establishment Clause Jurisprudence, Wisconsin Law Review (1998). *Member:* State Bar of Wisconsin. ***PRACTICE AREAS:*** Real Estate Law; Corporate Law. ***Email:*** jeremy.bunnow@bfkpn.com

KARYN L. DOERFLER, born Yonkers, New York, June 23, 1971; admitted to bar, 1998, Illinois. *Education:* DePaul University (B.S., 1995); Northwestern University (J.D., magna cum laude, 1998). Order of the Coif. *Member:* Chicago, Illinois State and American Bar Associations. ***PRACTICE AREAS:*** Corporate Law; Securities Law. ***Email:*** karyn.doerfler@bfkpn.com

BRETT FEINBERG, born Chicago, Illinois, August 3, 1974; admitted to bar, 1999, Illinois. *Education:* University of Michigan at Ann Arbor (B.S., 1995); Northwestern University (J.D., 1999). Order of the Coif. *Member:* Chicago and American Bar Associations. ***PRACTICE AREAS:*** Real Estate Law; Corporate Law. ***Email:*** brett.feinberg@bfkpn.com

ROBERT M. FLEETWOOD, born Grand Rapids, Michigan, October 25, 1972; admitted to bar, 1998, Illinois. *Education:* University of Michigan (B.A., 1995); Northwestern University School of Law (J.D., cum laude, 1998). Associate Articles Editor, Journal of Criminal Law and Criminology, 1997-1998. Guest Lecturer on Banking and Technology - Northwestern University School of Law, 2001. *Member:* Chicago (Member, Financial Institutions Committee) and American Bar Associations. ***PRACTICE AREAS:*** Corporate Law; Securities Law; Banking Law. ***Email:*** robert.fleetwood@bfkpn.com

ANNALIESE F. FLEMING, born Milwaukee, Wisconsin, December 21, 1973; admitted to bar, 1999, Illinois, U.S. Court of Appeals, Seventh Circuit, U.S. District Court, Northern and Central Districts of Illinois and Eastern and Western Districts of Wisconsin. *Education:* University of Wisconsin-Madison (B.A., with distinction, 1996); Northwestern University School of Law (J.D., cum laude, 1999). Author, "Louisiana's Newest Capital Crime," Journal of Criminal Law and Criminology, Vol. 89:2 (1999). *Member:* Chicago, Illinois State and American Bar Associations.

JOHN M. GEIRINGER, born Chicago, Illinois, November 29, 1970; admitted to bar, 1996, Illinois. *Education:* The American University (B.A., 1992); DePaul University College of Law (J.D., 1995). Legal Counsel, Illinois Office of Banks and Real Estate, 1997-1998. Author, "Harmonizing the Illinois and Federal Privacy Laws," Illinois Banker, Vol. 86, No. 5 (2001). *Member:* Chicago (Chairman: Financial Institutions Committee, 2002—, Vice Chairman and Legislative Liaison, 2000-2002), Illinois State and American Bar Associations; Decalogue Society of Lawyers. ***PRACTICE AREAS:*** Banking Law; Administrative Law; Legislative Law. ***Email:*** john.geiringer@bfkpn.com

T. RANDALL GRAEB, born Ridgewood, New Jersey, December 21, 1967; admitted to bar, 2000, Illinois. *Education:* George Washington University (B.A., cum laude, 1990); Northwestern University (J.D., cum laude, 2000). Senior Articles Editor, Journal of Criminal Law and Criminology, 1999-2000. ***PRACTICE AREAS:*** Real Estate. ***Email:*** randy.graeb@bfkpn.com

ANDREW R. GROSSMANN, born Chicago, Illinois, August 14, 1975; admitted to bar, 2000, Illinois. *Education:* University of Illinois (B.A., with highest honors, 1997); Northwestern University (J.D., magna cum laude, 2000). Order of the Coif. Articles Editor, Northwestern Law Review. ***PRACTICE AREAS:*** Corporate; Mergers and Acquisitions; Tax. ***Email:*** andrew.grossmann@bfkpn.com

MICHAEL R. HALL, born Edmonds, Washington, May 10, 1972; admitted to bar, 2002, Illinois. *Education:* University of Washington (B.A., with honors, 1994); University of Chicago Law School (J.D., 2002).

RANDY J. HEINIG, born Lansing, Michigan, May 29, 1971; admitted to bar, 2002, Illinois. *Education:* Wheaton College (B.A., 1993); Yale Law School (J.D., 2002).

JACKSON HWU, born Sao Paulo, Brazil, August 7, 1974; admitted to bar, 1997, Sao Paulo, Brazil; 2004, New York and Illinois. *Education:* Universidade de San Paulo-USP, School of Law (LL.B, 1996); Northwestern University (LL.M-K, 2000; J.D., 2004). ***LANGUAGES:*** English, Portuguese and French. ***PRACTICE AREAS:*** Corporate. ***Email:*** jackson.hwu@bfkpn.com

SHERMIN IZADPANAH, born Tehran, Iran, May 12, 1977; admitted to bar, 2002, Illinois and U.S. District Court, Northern District of Illinois. *Education:* University of Toronto (B.S., with honors, 1999); University of Michigan Law School (J.D., cum laude, 2002). *Member:* Chicago Bar Association; Chicago Council of Lawyers; Chicago's Public Interest Bar Association.

PETER B. JURGELEIT, born Boston, Massachusetts, September 20, 1968; admitted to bar, 1998, Illinois. *Education:* Dartmouth College (A.B., 1991); Indiana University, Bloomington (J.D., cum laude, 1998). Editor-in-Chief, Indiana Law Journal, 1997-1998. *Member:* Chicago and American Bar Associations. ***PRACTICE AREAS:*** Commercial Litigation; Franchise Law; Banking Law. ***Email:*** peter.jurgeleit@bfkpn.com

MYRIAM BENHAMOU KAPLAN, born Marrakech, Morocco, February 18, 1957; admitted to bar, 1984, New York; 1991, Illinois. *Education:* Assas Law School, Paris, France (License, with honors, 1979; Maîtrise with honors, 1980; Degree of Extensive Studies, 1982); Institut Libre d'Etudes des Relations Internationales, Paris, France (D.E.S., with honors, 1980); University of Pennsylvania (LL.M., 1982); Illinois Institute of Technology/Chicago-Kent College of Law (J.D., 1991). *Member:* Chicago Bar Association. ***LANGUAGES:*** French. ***PRACTICE AREAS:*** Real Estate Law. ***Email:*** myriam.kaplan@bfkpn.com

JOSEPH D. LAMBERT, born Fairfax, Virginia, June 14, 1974; admitted to bar, 2000, Illinois. *Education:* Michigan State University (B.A., with high honors, 1996); Harvard University (J.D., 2000). ***PRACTICE AREAS:*** Corporate Law; Real Estate. ***Email:*** joe.lambert@bfkpn.com

HEATHER J. MACKLIN, born Joliet, Illinois, August 14, 1974; admitted to bar, 1999, Illinois and U.S. District Court, Northern District of Illinois. *Education:* North Central College (B.A., summa cum laude, 1996); University of Chicago (J.D., 1999). 2000, 2001, appointed as Special Assistant to the Illinois Gaming Board. ***PRACTICE AREAS:*** Commercial Litigation. ***Email:*** heather.macklin@bfkpn.com

(This Listing Continued)

BRADLEY W. MARZULLO, born Santa Monica, California, September 18, 1978; admitted to bar, 2004, Illinois. *Education:* Washington University (B.A., 1996); University of Michigan (J.D., 2004). ***LANGUAGES:*** French. ***Email:*** bradley.marzullo@bfkpn.com

GEORGE R. MESIRES, born Watertown, New York, January 29, 1969; admitted to bar, 1995, New York; 2002, Illinois. *Education:* Colgate University (B.A., 1991); Syracuse University College of Law (J.D., 1995); Syracuse University School of Management (M.B.A., 1995). ***PRACTICE AREAS:*** Bankruptcy; Commercial Litigation. ***Email:*** george.mesires@bfkpn.com

GILLIAN E. MUNITZ, born Skokie, Illinois, October 2, 1974; admitted to bar, 2002, New York (Not admitted in Illinois). *Education:* University of Michigan (B.A., with high distinction, 1996); University of California at Los Angeles (J.D., 1999). Phi Beta Kappa. Law Clerk to Hon. Hector M. Laffitte, U.S. District Court, Puerto Rico, 1999-2000. ***PRACTICE AREAS:*** Bankruptcy. ***Email:*** gillian.munitz@bfkpn.com

JESSICA M. PEREZ, born Waukegan, Illinois, January 28, 1975; admitted to bar, 2003, Minnesota (Not admitted in Illinois). *Education:* University of Notre Dame (B.B.A., 1997); University of Illinois College of Law (J.D., 2003). ***Email:*** jessica.perez@bfkpn.com

CHARLES E. PICTON III, born Winfield, Illinois, September 22, 1972; admitted to bar, 2002, Illinois. *Education:* University of Illinois, Urbana/Champaign (B.A., 1994; J.D., 2002); The George Washington University (M.A., 1998). ***PRACTICE AREAS:*** Commercial Real Estate. ***Email:*** charles.picton@bfkpn.com

JEFFREY S. RINKOV, born Columbus, Ohio, March 9, 1978; admitted to bar, 2004, Illinois. *Education:* University of Wisconsin-Madison (B.S., 2000); University of Chicago (J.D., 2004). ***PRACTICE AREAS:*** Corporate. ***Email:*** jeffrey.rinkov@bfkpn.com

J.D. RUBIN, born Chicago, Illinois, August 10, 1976; admitted to bar, 2003, Illinois. *Education:* University of Wisconsin (B.A., with distinction, 1998); Northwestern University School of Law (J.D., cum laude, 2003). Articles Board Editor, Northwestern Law Review, 2002-2003. ***PRACTICE AREAS:*** Corporate. ***Email:*** j.d.rubin@bfkpn.com

JANELLE M. SAVAGE, born Overland Park, Kansas, January 23, 1974; admitted to bar, 2000, Illinois. *Education:* Miami University (B.S., magna cum laude, 1996); Northwestern University (J.D., cum laude, 2000). Phi Beta Kappa; Order of the Coif. Note and Comment Editor, Northwestern University Law Review. ***PRACTICE AREAS:*** Real Estate; Commercial Litigation; Corporate. ***Email:*** janelle.savage@bfkpn.com

ANDREA L. SILL, born Rochester, New York, June 9, 1971; admitted to bar, 1996, Maryland; 1997, Illinois; 1999, District of Columbia. *Education:* Bucknell University (B.A., 1993); American University, Washington College of Law (J.D., cum laude, 1996); Chicago Kent College of Law/Center for Law and Financial Services (LL.M. in Financial Services Law, 2003). ***PRACTICE AREAS:*** Regulatory Banking.

ROGER H. STETSON, born Ypsilanti, Michigan, February 21, 1978; admitted to bar, 2003, Illinois. *Education:* University of Southern California, Los Angeles (B.A., magna cum laude, 2000); University of Michigan (J.D., 2003). Phi Beta Kappa. ***PRACTICE AREAS:*** Litigation. ***Email:*** roger.stetson@bfkpn.com

CATHERINE M. THOMSON, born Chicago, Illinois, September 3, 1968; admitted to bar, 1996, Illinois. *Education:* University of Michigan (B.A., 1990); Chicago-Kent College of Law/Illinois Institute of Technology (J.D., 1996). *Member:* American Bar Association.

JUDITH A. VAN HOOSE, born Granite City, Illinois, May 6, 1975; admitted to bar, 1994, Illinois. *Education:* Northwestern University (B.A., 1997); University of Michigan (J.D., 2003). ***Email:*** judith.vanhoose@bfkpn.com

MELISSA M. VILLALOBOS, born St. Louis, Missouri, October 30, 1976; admitted to bar, 2004, Illinois. *Education:* Washington University (A.B., magna cum laude, 1999); Northwestern University (J.D., 2004). ***PRACTICE AREAS:*** Litigation. ***Email:*** melissa.villalobos@bfkpn.com

DAVID M. WIESE, born Elmhurst, Illinois, January 13, 1970; admitted to bar, 2001, Illinois and U.S. District Court, Northern District of Illinois. *Education:* University of Illinois (B.S., 1994); University of Iowa (M.A., 1998; J.D., with distinction, 2001). *Member:* Chicago and American Bar Associations. ***PRACTICE AREAS:*** Litigation.

STEVEN J. YATVIN, born Harvey, Illinois, March 26, 1973; admitted to bar, 1999, Illinois. *Education:* Indiana University (B.A., 1995); University of Illinois (J.D., magna cum laude, 1999). Member and Executive Administration Editor, University of Illinois Law Review, 1997-1999. Member, Recent Alumni Advisory Board, University of Illinois. *Member:* American Bar Association (Member, Forum on Franchising).

OF COUNSEL

BRUCE JAY BAKER, born Chicago, Illinois, June 18, 1954; admitted to bar, 1979, Illinois and U.S. District Court, Northern District of Illinois including Trial Bar. *Education:* University of Leeds, Leeds, England; University of Illinois (B.S., 1976); Washington University (J.D., 1979). Presently Senior Vice President and General Counsel, Illinois Bankers Association. Received the Illinois Bankers Association's Distinguished Bank Counsel Award in 1991 and 1997. Previously General Counsel to the Illinois Commissioner of Banks & Trust Companies and Senior Counsel with Dean Witter Financial Services Group, Inc. and Discover Card Services, Inc. Principal author of numerous Illinois banking laws, including the Illinois Financial Institution Insurance Sales Law. Published regularly in banking periodicals, and a frequent lecturer to bank officers, directors, regulators and inside counsel. *Member:* Chicago (Financial Institutions Committee), Illinois State (Commercial, Banking and Bankruptcy Section) and American (Banking Committee) Bar Associations; Bankers Club of Chicago.

GAYLE YEATMAN FISHER, admitted to bar, 1994, Illinois; 1994, U.S. District Court, Northern District of Illinois. *Education:* Northwestern University (B.A, 1991; J.D., cum laude, 1994) Kennedy Scholar. ***PRACTICE AREAS:*** Business Litigation. ***Email:*** gayle.fisher@bfkpn.com

(This Listing Continued)

BARACK FERRAZZANO KIRSCHBAUM PERLMAN & NAGELBERG LLP, Chicago—Continued

JOSHUA S. KANTER, born Chicago, Illinois, May 27, 1962; admitted to bar, 1987, Illinois. *Education:* Emory University (B.A., with high honors in Economics, magna cum laude, 1984); University of Chicago Law School (J.D., 1987). ***PRACTICE AREAS:*** Corporate Law; Securities Law; Real Estate Law. ***Email:*** josh.kanter@bfkpn.com

JUDITH K. MUNCY, born Fargo, North Dakota, August 6, 1955; admitted to bar, 1980, District of Columbia; 1992, Illinois. *Education:* The College of St. Catherine (B.A., 1977); Notre Dame Law School (J.D., 1980). Phi Beta Kappa. Member, Notre Dame National Moot Court Team. Co-author: "State Nonmember Bank and Savings and Loan Securities Activities," Banking Expansion Reporter, Vol. 8, No. 15 (1989). Author: "Extensions of Credit by Savings Associations to Executive Officers, Directors and Principal Shareholders," Consumer Finance Law Quarterly Report, Vol. 44, No. 3 (1990); "The New Capital Requirements for Banks and Bank Holding Companies," IBA LAW-watch, Vol. 4, No. 2 (1991). *Member:* Chicago Bar Association; The District of Columbia Bar.

BETH S. RUBIN, admitted to bar, 1987, Florida; 1988, Illinois; 1993, Michigan. *Education:* University of Michigan (A.B.Ed., with distinction, 1978; J.D., 1987). *Member:* The Florida Bar; State Bar of Michigan. ***PRACTICE AREAS:*** Commercial Real Estate; Real Estate Finance. ***Email:*** beth.rubin@bfkpn.com

PAUL J. BARGIEL, P.C.

100 WEST MONROE, SUITE 902
CHICAGO, ILLINOIS 60603
Telephone: 312-263-0888
Fax: 312-236-1065
Email: monsuite@aol.com

General Civil Appellate Practice, Family, Divorce, Child Custody, Commercial, Personal Injury and Medical Malpractice.

PAUL J. BARGIEL, born Chicago, Illinois, March 18, 1943; admitted to bar, 1972, Illinois and U.S. Court of Appeals, Seventh Circuit; 1975, U.S. Supreme Court; 1978, U.S. Court of Appeals, Eighth Circuit; 1979, U.S. Court of Appeals, Ninth Circuit. *Education:* Lewis University (B.A., 1970); John Marshall Law School (J.D., 1972). Member, John Marshall Journal of Practice and Procedure, 1971-1972. Author: "Leopold vs. Levin: Privacy 1970," John Marshall Journal of Practice and Procedure, 1971; Brief Writing, IICLE, 1984, Supplement, 1986. Lecturer, Appellate Procedure, Appellate Lawyers Association, 1979; 1981 and IICLE 1986, 1987. Instructor, Advanced Research and Writing, John Marshall Law School, 1972-1981. Assistant Attorney General, Chief Civil Appeals Division, 1972-1981. Special Assistant Attorney General, 1981-1985. *Member:* Chicago, Du Page County, Illinois State and American Bar Associations; Appellate Lawyers Association (President, 1982-1983).

BARLOW, KOBATA & DENIS

222 S. RIVERSIDE PLAZA
CHICAGO, ILLINOIS 60606
Telephone: 312-648-5570
Fax: 312-648-9697
Email: bkdlaw@bkd-law.com

Los Angeles, California Office: 2049 Century Park East, Suite 2270, 90067. Telephone: 310-277-7556. Fax: 310-277-2982.

Management Labor, Employment Discrimination Litigation.

MEMBERS OF FIRM

MARTY DENIS, born Chicago, Illinois, April 25, 1947; admitted to bar, 1970, Illinois; 1977, District of Columbia. *Education:* University of Illinois (B.A., with honors, 1967); Northwestern University (J.D., 1970). Author: "Implications of Offering Early Retirement Benefits in Exchange for a Release from Employment Claims," Employment Relations Today, Autumn 1996; "ERISA Plans-How Informal Can They Be?" Employee Relations Law Journal, Spring 1993; "Defamation-Do You Tell Employees Why a Coworker Was Discharged?" Employee Relations Law Journal, Spring 1991; "The Attorney-Client Privilege: Using It or Losing It," Employment Relations Today, Spring 1989; "Employee Health Screening: A Legitimate Need or Unnecessary Risk," Employment Relations Today, Summer 1988; "Employers' Procedural Rights in the Disclosure of Affirmative Action Plans," Employee Relations Journal, Spring 1988; "Privacy Rights and Medical Disclosures: An Employer's Dilemma," Spring 1987, Employment Relations Today; "Binding Arbitration—An Attractive Alternative To Litigation," Employment Relations Today, Autumn, 1987; "Privacy Rights and Medical Disclosures: An Employer's Dilemma," Employment Relations Today, Spring, 1987; "Privacy Rights and Drug Testing: Is There A Conflict?" Employment Relations Today, Autumn, 1986 and Winter, 1986-1987; "Releases: Maintaining Enforceability," Employee Relations Law Journal, Summer, 1986; "Avoiding and Defending Wrongful Discharge Claims," American Bar Association Tort and Insurance Practice Section Journal, Spring, 1986; "Subjective Decision Making: Does It Have A Place In The Employment Process," Employee Relations Law Journal, Autumn, 1985; Trial Attorney: Equal Employment Opportunity Commission, Regional Litigation Office, Philadelphia, Pennsylvania, 1972-1976. *Member:* American Bar Association (Member, Sections on: Labor and Employment Law; Litigation). ***PRACTICE AREAS:*** Labor Law; Employment Law. ***Email:*** mdenis@bkd-law.com

DANIEL R. MADOCK, born Woodstock, Illinois, September 29, 1958; admitted to bar, 1986, Illinois and U.S. District Court, Northern District of Illinois; 1988, California. *Education:* Southern Illinois University; University of Illinois, Chicago, Illinois (B.A., 1982); John Marshall Law School (J.D., 1986). *Member:* Chicago, Illinois State, California and American (Member, Sections on: Litigation and International Law) Bar Associations. ***PRACTICE AREAS:*** Commercial Litigation; General Business Law. ***Email:*** drmadock@bkd-law.com

(This Listing Continued)

ASSOCIATE

BETHANY A. HILBERT, born Hamilton, Ohio, June 7, 1978; admitted to bar, 2003, Illinois. *Education:* Wittenberg University (B.A., 2000); DePaul University College of Law (J.D., 2003). *Member:* Chicago, Illinois State and American Bar Associations. ***PRACTICE AREAS:*** Employment Law. ***Email:*** bhilbert@bkd-law.com

OF COUNSEL

LAWRENCE M. COHEN, born Chicago, Illinois, August 13, 1935; admitted to bar, 1960, Illinois; 1970, U.S. Supreme Court. *Education:* University of Michigan (B.B.A., 1957); University of Chicago (J.D., 1960). Phi Eta Sigma. Teaching Associate, Indiana University School of Law, 1960-1961. Adjunct Professor and Lecturer in Law, Illinois Institute of Technology/Chicago-Kent College of Law, 1977-1999. Author: "Prune Yard Shopping Center v. Robins: Past, Present and Future," 57 Chicago-Kent Law Review 373, 1981. Co-Author: "The Future of the American Labor Movement: The Role of Federal Law," 57 Chicago-Kent Law Review 21, 1981. Attorney, National Labor Relations Board, Washington, D.C. and Chicago, 1962-1966. Arbitrator, Federal Mediation and Conciliation Service, 1970—. Hearing Officer, Chicago Commission on Human Rights, 1995—. Arbitrator, American Arbitration Association, 1969—. Mediator, Equal Employment Opportunity Committee ADR Consortium. *Member:* Chicago (Member, Labor Law Committee; Chairman, 1976-1977) and American (Member, Section on Labor Law) Bar Associations; Chicago Council of Lawyers; American Judicature Society. Fellow, College of Labor and Employment Lawyers. ***PRACTICE AREAS:*** Labor Relations Law; Employment Discrimination Litigation; Alternative Dispute Resolution. ***Email:*** lmcohen@bkd-law.com

BARNES, RICHARDSON & COLBURN

Established in 1948
303 EAST WACKER DRIVE
SUITE 1100
CHICAGO, ILLINOIS 60601
Telephone: 312-565-2000
Facsimile: 312-565-1782
Email: barnes@brc-chi.com
URL: http://www.barnesrichardson.com

New York, New York Office: 475 Park Avenue South, 10016. Telephone: 212-725-0200.
Washington, D.C. Office: 1420 New York Avenue, N.W., Suite 700, 20005. Telephone: 202-628-4700.

Customs and International Trade Law, Administrative Law. General Federal Litigation and Appellate Practice.

RESIDENT MEMBERS OF FIRM

ROBERT E. BURKE, born Milwaukee, Wisconsin, 1942; admitted to bar, 1966, Wisconsin; 1971, Illinois; 1975, District of Columbia; 1981, New York; 1991, Texas. *Education:* Marquette Univ. (B.S., 1964; J.D., 1966). ***PRACTICE AREAS:*** Customs; International Trade. ***Email:*** rburke@brc-chi.com

DONALD J. UNGER, born Springfield, Illinois, 1950; admitted to bar, 1976, Illinois; 1979, District of Columbia. *Education:* Univ. of Illinois (B.A., 1972); John Marshall Law School (J.D., 1976). ***PRACTICE AREAS:*** Customs; International Trade. ***Email:*** dunger@brc-chi.com

BRIAN F. WALSH, born Evergreen Park, Illinois, 1960; admitted to bar, 1985, Illinois. *Education:* Michigan State Univ. (B.A., 1982); Loyola Univ. of Chicago (J.D., 1985). *Member:* Customs Brokers and Foreign Freight Forwarders Association of Chicago (Advisory Member, Board of Directors, 1995—, Chair, Broker Education Committee, 1994—). ***PRACTICE AREAS:*** Customs; International Trade. ***Email:*** bwalsh@brc-chi.com

KAZUMUNE V. KANO, born Chicago, Illinois, 1954; admitted to bar, 1986, Illinois; 1987, U.S. Court of International Trade; 1988, U.S. Court of Appeals for the Federal Circuit. *Education:* Illinois Institute of Technology (B.A., 1976); Sophia Univ. (certificate, 1981); Illinois Institute of Technology/Chicago-Kent (J.D., 1986). ***LANGUAGES:*** Japanese. ***PRACTICE AREAS:*** Customs; International Trade. ***Email:*** kkano@brc-chi.com

LAWRENCE M. FRIEDMAN, born Worcester, Massachusetts, 1963; admitted to bar, 1989, Illinois. *Education:* Univ. of Illinois (B.A., 1986); John Marshall Law School (J.D., with distinction, 1989; LL.M., Intellectual Property, with honors, 2001). *Member:* Chicago and American Bar Associations; Customs and International Trade Bar Association. ***PRACTICE AREAS:*** Customs; NAFTA; International Trade. ***Email:*** lfriedman@brc-chi.com

DAVID G. FORGUE, born Chicago, Illinois, 1971; admitted to bar, 1996, Illinois. *Education:* Univ. of Illinois (B.A., magna cum laude, 1993; J.D., magna cum laude, 1996). Harno Scholar. Recipient, Rickert Award. *Member:* Chicago and American Bar Associations. ***LANGUAGES:*** German. ***PRACTICE AREAS:*** Customs; International Trade. ***Email:*** dforgue@brc-chi.com

NON-RESIDENT MEMBERS OF FIRM

James S. O'Kelly (N.Y.)
Sandra Liss Friedman (N.Y.)
Matthew T. McGrath (D.C.)
Frederic D. Van Arnam, Jr. (N.Y.)
Alan Goggins (N.Y.)

RESIDENT ASSOCIATES

CAROLYN D. AMADON, born Denver, Colorado; admitted to bar, 1999, Illinois. *Education:* Baylor Univ. (B.A., 1987); Texas A & M Univ. (M.P.A., 1989); Loyola Univ. (J.D., 1999). Member, Intl. Law Society (President, 1998-1999). Co-Editor-In-Chief, YLS Journal of the CBA Record, 2001-2003. *Member:* Chicago Bar Association (Chair, Young Lawyers Section, 2005-2006). ***LANGUAGES:*** French. ***PRACTICE AREAS:*** Customs; International Trade. ***Email:*** camadon@brc-chi.com

(This Listing Continued)

ILYA A. BAKKE, admitted to bar, 2002, Illinois. *Education:* Wheaton College (B.A., 1999); University of Illinois (J.D., 2002). Member, Board of Directors, OWIT-Chicago, 2003-2005. ***LANGUAGES:*** Spanish. ***PRACTICE AREAS:*** Customs; International Trade Law. ***Email:*** ibakke@brc-chi.com

LOUISA VASSILEVA CARNEY, born Riga, Latvia, 1977; admitted to bar, 2002, Illinois. *Education:* Lyon College (B.A., 1999); University of Arkansas (J.D., 2002); John Marshall Law School (LL.M., 2004). Member and Vice President, International Law Society, 2001-2002. ***LANGUAGES:*** Bulgarian, Latvian and Russian. ***PRACTICE AREAS:*** Customs Law; International Trade. ***Email:*** lcarney@brc-chi.com

DIANE A. MACDONALD, admitted to bar, 1990, Illinois; 1994, California; 2003, New York. *Education:* Bucknell Univ. (B.A., 1981); London School of Econ. (M.Sc., 1983); IIT, Chicago-Kent College of Law (J.D., with honors, 1990); Golden Gate Univ. (LL.M., Tax, with honors, 1997). Licensed Customs Broker. Member of Board, OWIT-Chicago, 2003-2005. President, OWIT-NY, 2001-2003. *Member:* Chicago Bar Association (Member, 1990-1994 and Chair, 1993-1994, Customs and U.S. Law Committee). ***PRACTICE AREAS:*** Customs; International Trade. ***Email:*** dmacdonald@brc-chi.com

CHRISTINE H. MARTINEZ, born South Bend, Indiana; admitted to bar, 2003, Illinois. *Education:* Loyola Univ. (B.A., with honors, 1995; J.D., cum laude, 2003). Alpha Sigma Nu. Editor-at-Large and Member, Loyola Law Journal. ***LANGUAGES:*** German and Spanish. ***PRACTICE AREAS:*** International Trade; Customs Law.

WILLIAM J. MURPHY, born Chicago, Illinois, 1970; admitted to bar, 1995, Minnesota; 2000, Illinois. *Education:* St. John's Univ. (B.A., 1992); Hamline Univ. (J.D., 1995). ***LANGUAGES:*** Japanese. ***PRACTICE AREAS:*** Customs; International Trade Law. ***Email:*** wmurphy@brc-chi.com

NIKOLAY A. OUZOUNOV, born Veliko Tarnovo, Bulgaria, 1975; admitted to bar, 2004, Illinois. *Education:* Truman State Univ. (B.A., magna cum laude, 1999); John Marshall Law School (J.D., cum laude, 2004). Lead Articles Editor, Law Review. Member, Order of John Marshall. *Member:* Chicago and American (Member, International Law Section) Bar Associations. ***LANGUAGES:*** Bulgarian and Russian. ***PRACTICE AREAS:*** Customs Law; International Trade Law. ***Email:*** nouzounov@brc-chi.com

(For Complete Personnel and Biographical Data, See Professional Biographies at New York, N.Y. and Washington, D.C.)

BARNES & THORNBURG LLP

ONE NORTH WACKER DRIVE, SUITE 4400
CHICAGO, ILLINOIS 60606-2833
Telephone: 312-357-1313
FAX: 312-759-5646
URL: http://www.btlaw.com

Indianapolis, Indiana Office: 11 South Meridian Street, 46204. Telephone: 317-236-1313. FAX: 317-231-7433.

Fort Wayne, Indiana Office: 600 One Summit Square, 46802. Telephone: 260-423-9440. FAX: 260-424-8316.

South Bend, Indiana Office: 600 1st Source Bank Center, 100 North Michigan, 46601-1632. Telephone: 574-233-1171. FAX: 574-237-1125.

Elkhart, Indiana Office: 121 West Franklin Street, Suite 200, 46516. Telephone: 574-293-0681. FAX: 574-296-2535.

Washington, D.C. Office: Suite 900, 750 17th Street, N.W., 20006. Telephone: 202-289-1313. FAX: 202-289-1330.

Grand Rapids, Michigan Office: 300 Ottawa Avenue, N.W., Suite 500, 49503. Telephone: 616-742-3930. FAX: 616-742-3999.

Acquisitions and Divestitures, Ad Valorem Tax, Administrative Law, Affirmative Action, Agriculture Law, Americans with Disabilities Act, Antidumping, Antitrust, Antitrust and Trade Regulation, Appellate Practice, Attorney Grievances, Automotive Warranty Law, Aviation and Aerospace, Aviation Law, Banking Law, Banking Regulations, Bankruptcy, Bankruptcy Reorganization, Banks and Banking, Biochemical Patents, Biomedical Products Liability, Biomedical Technology, Biotechnology Patent Prosecution, Bond Law, Brain Injury, Breach of Warranty, Brown Fields Redevelopment, Business Immigration, Business Law, Business Litigation, Business Planning, Business Regulatory and Administrative, Business Start-ups, Business Succession Planning, Business Taxation, Business Torts, Business Transactions, Business Transfers, Buying and Selling of Businesses, Cable TV, Cargo Claims, Charitable Trusts and Foundations, Chemical Intellectual Property, Chemical Patent Prosecution, Chemical Patents, Chemical Products Liability, Civil Appeals, Civil Litigation, Civil Practice, Civil RICO, Class Action Defense, Clean Air Act, Clean Water Act, Closely Held Business Estate Planning, Closely Held Businesses, Closely Held Business Law, Closely Held Corporations, Collective Bargaining, Commercial Bankruptcy, Commercial Finance Law, Commercial Law, Commercial Leasing and Financing, Commercial Litigation, Commercial Conveyancing, Commercial Real Estate, Commercial Real Estate Acquisition, Commercial Real Estate Development, Commercial Real Estate Finance, Commercial Transactions, Commodities Fraud, Communications and Media, Complex Commercial Litigation, Complex Litigation, Computer and Software Patents, Computer Law, Computers and Software, Conflicts of Interest, Construction Labor Law, Construction Law, Consumer Credit, Contract Litigation, Cooperatives, Copyrights, Corporate Finance, Corporate Formation, Corporate Law, Corporate Taxation, Corporate Tax Planning, Countervailing Duties, Covenants Not To Compete, Creditors Rights, Creditors Rights in Bankruptcy, Criminal Defense, Criminal Law, Criminal Tax Audits, Customs Law, Dealer and Distributor Termination, Debt and Equity Finance, Decedents Estates, Defense Litigation, Design Patents, Disability Insurance Defense, Discrimination, Distribution, Drug and Medical Device Defense, Economic Development, Education Law, Elder Law, Election, Campaign and Political Law, Electric Power, Electric Utilities, Electrical Intellectual Property, Electrical Patents, Electro-mechanical Patents, Electronic Commerce, Electronic Patents, Eminent Domain, Employee Benefits, Employee Stock Ownership Plans, Employment Defense, Employment Discrimination, Employment Law, Employment Litigation, Energy, Energy Contracts, Energy Regulation, Environmental Administrative Law, Environmental Cleanup, Environmental Compliance, Environmental Criminal Defense, Environmental Law, Environmental Litigation, Environmental Permitting, Environmental Real Estate, Environmental Regulation, Environmental Risk Management, Equal Employment Opportunity Law, ERISA Litigation, Estate Administration, Estate and Gift Taxation, Estate Planning, Estate Planning and Taxation, Estate Planning and Administration, Estate Planning and Probate, Estate Planning for Parents of Handicapped Children, Estate Planning for Unmarried Individuals, Executive Compensation, Executive Severance Contracts, Export Regulation, Fair Employment Practices, Family and Medical Leave Act, Family Business Successions, Family Wealth Transfer, Federal and State Administrative Regulatory Practice, Federal and State Legislative Practice, Federal Civil Litigation, Federal Civil Practice, Federal Criminal Law, Federal Estate and Gift Taxation, Federal Litigation, Federal Tax Controversies, Federal Taxation, Fiduciary Income Tax, Finance, Financial Transactions, First Party Insurance, Foreign Investment in the United States, Freight Claims, Freight Loss and Damage, Gaming Law, Gaming Licensing, Gas Utilities, General Litigation, Government, Government Affairs, Government Agency Practice, Government Contracts, Government Investigations, Government Relations, Groundwater Contamination, Hazardous Materials and Substances, Hazardous Waste, Hazardous Waste Liability, Head Injury, Health Care, Health Care Corporate Law, Health Care Contracts, Health Care Fraud, Health Care Licensing, Health Care Litigation, Health Care Mergers and Acquisitions, Health Care Regulation, Health Care Reimbursement, Health Law, Heavy Equipment Products Liability, Immigration Law, Industrial Revenue Bond Law, Inheritance Tax, Initial Public Offerings, Insurance, Insurance Bad Faith, Insurance Coverage, Insurance Litigation, Insurance Regulation, Integrated Health Care Delivery Systems, Intellectual Property, Intellectual Property General Prosecution, Intellectual Property Infringement, Intellectual Property Licensing, Intellectual Property Litigation, Intellectual Property Procurement, Intellectual Property Protection, Intellectual Property Rights, International Business Law, International Intellectual Property, International Law, International Patents, International Trade, International Transportation Law, Internet Law, Internet Trademark Law, Joint Ventures, Labor and Employment, Labor Arbitration, Labor Law, Labor Relations, Land Use, Lease Law, Leasing, Legal Ethics and Professional Responsibility, Legal Malpractice Defense, Legislative Practice, Licensing, Life Insurance Defense, Limited Liability Company Law, Limited Partnerships, Liquor Licensing, Litigation, Loans, Lobbying, Local Government Law, Logistics, Long Term Care, Managed Care, Managed Care Contracts, Management Employment Law, Management Labor Law, Manufacturers Liability, Maritime Regulations, Mechanical Intellectual Property, Mechanical Patents, Media Law, Mediation, Medical Antitrust, Medical Intellectual Property, Medical Patents, Mental Health Law, Mergers, Acquisitions and Divestitures, Mergers and Acquisitions, Mineral Taxation, Molecular Biology Patents, Motor Carrier Law, Motor Carrier Regulation, Multi-Employer Pensions, Municipal Bonds, Municipal Bonds Taxation, Municipal Finance, Municipal Law, Municipal Leasing, Municipal Redevelopment, Municipal Securities, Municipal Taxation, National Labor Relations Act, Neurolaw, Nonprofit and Charitable Organizations, Nonprofit Organizations Law, North American Free Trade Agreement, Occupational Safety and Health, OSHA, Partnership Law, Partnership Taxation, Patent Infringement, Patent Interference Practice, Patent Litigation, Patent Prosecution, Patents, PCT Legal Export, Personal Injury, Personal Injury Defense, Pesticide Litigation, Pharmaceutical Intellectual Property, Pharmaceutical Patents, Physician Contracts, Physician Practices, Planning and Land Use, Power Line Contact Injury, Probate, Probate Litigation, Products Liability, Products Liability Defense, Professional Liability, Property Law, Property Tax, Property Tax Abatement, Property Tax Appeals, Psychological Injury, Public Finance, Public Sector Labor Relations, Public Utility Law, Railroad Law, Real Estate, Real Estate Acquisitions, Real Estate Contracts, Real Estate Development, Real Estate Finance, Real Estate Licensing, Real Estate Secured Lending, Real Estate Title Insurance, Real Property, Real Property Acquisitions, Real Property Finance, Reorganizations, Resource Conservation and Recovery Act (RCRA), Retirement Benefit Plans, School Law, Securities, Securities Litigation, Securitization, Semiconductor Technology, Sexual Harassment, Small Business Corporations, State Government Law, State Tax Controversies, State Taxation, Structured Finance, Succession Planning, Superfund, Tax Controversies, Tax Exempt Finance, Tax Exempt Organizations, Tax Increment Finance, Tax Law, Tax Litigation, Taxation, Technology and Science, Technology Law, Technology Licensing, Technology Transfers, Telecommunications Competition, Telecommunications Law, Theft of Trade Secrets, Title VII Discrimination, Title IX Discrimination, Tort Defense, Toxic Exposure, Toxic Tort Class Actions, Toxic Torts, Toxic Tort Defense, Trade Dress, Trade Secrets, Trademark Litigation, Trademarks, Trademark Prosecution, Trademark Protection, Trademark Registration, Transportation, Transportation Safety, Trial Practice, Trusts and Estates, Unfair Competition, Unfair Trade, Uniform Commercial Codes, Union Contract Negotiations, Union Elections, Utilities, Utility Law, Wage and Hour Law, WARN Act, Water Pollution, Water Quality, Water Utilities, Wetland Regulation, White Collar Crime, White Collar Criminal Defense, Wills, Workers Compensation, Workouts, World Trade Organization, Wrongful Death, Wrongful Termination, Wrongful Termination Defense, Zoning, Planning and Land Use.

FIRM PROFILE: Quality. Service. Efficiency. Communication. These are the cornerstones of the firm's culture and the keys to its success.

Established on January 1, 1982, Barnes & Thornburg LLP is relatively young; however, its founding date belies the firm's rich history. The firm's roots can be traced to two cities, South Bend and Indianapolis. Our northern Indiana presence began in 1926 with the establishment of Seebirt Oare & Omacht, and later grew when they merged with an Elkhart firm, Cawley and Harman. In Indianapolis, four partners opened Barnes Hickam Pantzer & Boyd on September 13, 1940. They began the firm with 13 people in an office of 13 rooms on the 13th floor of the Merchants Bank Building, the tallest in Indiana at that time. The number 13 has proven to be a lucky number for Barnes & Thornburg LLP.

Since 1982, the firm has opened offices in Chicago, Fort Wayne, Washington, D.C., Grand Rapids and merged with Jenkins, Coffey, Hyland, Badger & Conard, an intellectual property firm; Roberts, Ryder, Rogers & Scism, a labor and employment law firm; Church, Nilsson & Paulen of Elkhart; Roemer & Mintz, LLP, of South Bend and, most recently, Lee, Mann, Smith, McWilliams, Sweeney & Ohlson of Chicago. The firm has also been joined by Gallucci, Hopkins & Theisen, P.C., a Fort Wayne firm with an extensive labor and employment practice, and Johnson Lawhead Buth & Pope, P.C., an Indianapolis firm with a concentration in estate planning. Today Barnes & Thornburg LLP is the largest law firm in Indiana and one of the largest in the Midwest. More than 390 attorneys provide legal services to more than 11,000 international, national, regional and local clients.

(This Listing Continued)

BARNES & THORNBURG LLP, Chicago—Continued

With offices in Indianapolis, Fort Wayne, South Bend, Elkhart, Chicago, Washington, D.C., and Grand Rapids, we are a business-minded law firm serving clients ranging from Fortune 100 companies and governmental entities to individuals and nonprofit organizations. We represent the interests of businesses in our primary practices: business, tax and real estate, creditors' rights, energy, telecommunications and utilities, environmental law, governmental services and finance, healthcare, intellectual property, labor and employment law, litigation, appellate, business and technology, construction law, e-commerce, economic development, entrepreneurial services, financial institutions, international, media, pension and benefits litigation, property tax, transportation and white collar crime. Each of our offices offers a unique blend of services which collectively make Barnes & Thornburg LLP a diverse and dynamic legal resource for our clients and communities.

We have lawyers involved at city, state and national levels of the legal profession as officers, chairpersons and committee members in legal organizations. Others are authors, presenters and drafters of legislation. Most of our lawyers are active in their communities and provide civic leadership. Each office sponsors, contributes to, and often leads, an array of community activities.

LAW FIRM ALLIANCES/ASSOCIATIONS: ***TERRALEX, THE WORLDWIDE NETWORK OF INDEPENDENT LAW FIRMS***
TECHLAW GROUP

PARTNERS

SIDNEY G. SALTZ, admitted to bar, 1963, Illinois. *Education:* Northwestern University, Phi Beta Kappa (B.A., with highest distinction, 1959); Yale University (LL.B., 1962). Order of the Coif. Member, Board of Editors, Yale Law Journal, 1960-1962. Law Clerk, Chief Judge Lumbard, U.S. Court of Appeals, Second Circuit, 1962-1963. *Member:* Chicago (Chairman, Agribusiness Committee, 1991-1993) and American (Council Member, Real Property, Probate and Trust Section, 2000—; Vice Chair, 1997-1998 and Co-Chair, 1998-2000, CLE Committee, Real Property Division; Chair, Remedies and Miscellaneous Clauses Committee, 1995-1998) Bar Associations. ***PRACTICE AREAS:*** Real Estate Law; Commercial Leasing; Commercial Finance. ***Email:*** sidney.saltz@btlaw.com

LARRY D. BLUST, admitted to bar, 1968, Illinois. *Education:* University of Illinois (B.S., with high honors, 1965; J.D., with high honors, 1968). Order of the Coif. Certified Public Accountant, Illinois, 1965. Member, Illinois Board of CPA Examiners, 1978-1981. Co-Author: "32nd Annual Federal Tax Course," 1975; "33rd Annual Federal Tax Course," 1976; 38th Annual Federal Tax Course," 1981; "Pension Reform, ERISA," 1975; "Estate Planning Skills," Coursebook, 1975; "Pension Administration," 1977, 1981 and 1983; "Tax Aspects of Sheltered Investments," 1979; "Sales, Exchanges and Other Transfers of Partnership Interests," 1980, 1981; "ESOP and the Smaller Employer," 1979. *Member:* Illinois State and American (Member, Tax Section) Bar Associations. ***PRACTICE AREAS:*** Taxation Law; Financial Transactions; Mergers and Acquisitions Law. ***Email:*** larry.blust@btlaw.com

DENNIS M. McWILLIAMS, admitted to bar, 1968, Illinois; U.S. District Court, Northern District of Illinois; U.S. Court of Appeals, Second, Seventh and Federal Circuits; registered to practice before U.S. Patent and Trademark Office. *Education:* University of Notre Dame (B.A., 1963; B.S.M.E., 1969); Loyola University (J.D., 1968). *Member:* American Bar Association. ***PRACTICE AREAS:*** Intellectual Property Law; Patents; Trademarks; Litigation. ***Email:*** dennis.mcwilliams@btlaw.com

LEE T. POLK, admitted to bar, 1970, Illinois; 1972, U.S. Court of Military Appeals; 1983, U.S. Claims Court, U.S. Tax Court and U.S. Court of Appeals, 3rd, 6th and 7th Circuits. *Education:* Coe College (A.B., 1967); University of Chicago (J.D., 1970). Phi Kappa Phi; Phi Beta Kappa. Author: "ERISA Practice & Litigation," West Group (updated annually). Member, 1982—, Chair, 1986, Executive Committee, Midwest Pension Conference. Member, Illinois Institute of Continuing Legal Education, Editorial Board for the Employee Benefits Law Handbook, 1986—. Author: Chapter 25, "Litigation Involving Benefit Plans," and Co-Author: Chapter 14, "Multiemployer Plans," Illinois Institute of Continuing Legal Education, Employee Benefits Law Handbook, 1987. Author: Chapter 11, "Pensions and the Elderly," Illinois Institute of Continuing Legal Education, Advising Elderly Clients and Their Families, 1991. *Member:* Chicago (Chair, Employee Benefits Committee, 1987-1988), Illinois State and American (Member, Real Property, Probate and Trust Law; Member, 1991— and Chair, 2001—, Qualified Plans Committee; Taxation-Employee Benefits Committee, 1984—) Bar Associations; American Health Lawyers Association. Charter Fellow, American College of Employee Benefits Counsel. American Bar Foundation. [Captain, JAGC, U.S. Army, 1972-1975]. ***PRACTICE AREAS:*** Employee Benefits; Civil Litigation; Tax; Corporate; Health Care. ***Email:*** lee.polk@btlaw.com

WILLIAM M. LEE, JR., admitted to bar, 1975, Virginia; 1976, Illinois; 1979, U.S. Court of Appeals, Seventh and Federal Circuits; registered to practice before U.S. Patent and Trademark Office. *Education:* Cornell University (B.S., 1970; M.E.E., 1971); George Washington University School of Law (J.D., 1975). *Member:* Illinois State and American Bar Associations; American Intellectual Property Law Association; Intellectual Property Law Association of Chicago; Licensing Executives Society. ***PRACTICE AREAS:*** Intellectual Property Law; Patents; Trademarks; Copyrights; Litigation; Patent Licensing; Trade Secrets. ***Email:*** william.lee@btlaw.com

PAULA COZZI GOEDERT, admitted to bar, 1976, Illinois. *Education:* Mundelein College (B.A., summa cum laude, 1973); Northwestern University (J.D., magna cum laude, 1976). ***PRACTICE AREAS:*** Association Law; Tax; Corporate. ***Email:*** paula.goedert@btlaw.com

GLENN W. OHLSON, admitted to bar, 1976, Illinois and U.S. District Court, Northern District of Illinois; 1981, U.S. Court of Appeals, Seventh and Federal Circuits; registered to practice before U.S. and Canadian Patent and Trademark Offices. *Education:* University of Illinois (B.S.C.E., 1969); Elmhurst College; The John Marshall Law School (J.D., with honors, 1976; LL.M., 1989). Licensed Professional Engineer, Illinois, 1974. ***PRACTICE AREAS:*** Intellectual Property Law; Patents; Trademarks; Copyrights; Litigation; Patent Licensing. ***Email:*** glenn.olson@btlaw.com

DAVID C. BREZINA, admitted to bar, 1978, Illinois; U.S. District Court, Northern District of Illinois; U.S. District Court, Northern District of Indiana, U.S. District Court, Central District of Illinois and U.S. Court of Appeals, Seventh, Ninth and Federal Circuits; U.S. District Court, Northern District of Illinois including Trial Bar; registered to practice before U.S. Patent and Trademark Office. *Education:* Cornell College (B.S.S., 1975); Chicago Kent College of Law (J.D., with honors, 1978); John Marshall Law (LL.M., 1988). Articles, presentations and bar association work relating to patents include: "Protecting Corporate Value in the Patent Infringement Environment," "Advanced Patents and Trade Secrets," "Patent Basics," "Intellectual Property Basics for the General Practitioner and Beginning Intellectual Property Lawyer"; serving as a Judge in Trial Advocacy programs and Association Position Papers on patent issues. Lectures, articles, interviews, activities and presentations include: "Survey Types In Likelihood of Confusion Cases — Examining Confusion In Competitive and Noncompetitive Products," "Trade Dress Decision, The Supreme Court Reverses Based on Expired Utility Patent and Ducks Constitutional Issue," "The 'Gray Market' Goods Nightmare," "Numerals as Trademarks," "An Overview of Trademark Protection," "Costco: The Empire Built on Bargains - Selling Calvin Klein jeans, Trek bikes got Costco sued," "Protecting Your Package Innovations," "Trademark Fair Use and Parody," "The Expanding Scope of Section 43 (a) of the Lanham Act" and a Chicago Bar Association position paper in support of Trademark Revision Act of 1988. Author: Article on database licensing, "Navigating to Successful Database Licensing". Instructor: "Entrepreneurship: Basic Business Principles" and "Entertainment Law" in the Management Department of Columbia College in Chicago; "Legal Aspects of Entertainment, Publishing and the Arts"; "Antitrust and Misuse Aspects of Intellectual Property Law". Adjunct professor in the Center for Intellectual Property Law of the John Marshall Law School, Chicago (taught classes in Licensing, Patent Appeals, Reissues and Reexaminations and participated in other academic activities including judging the John Marshall accelerated trial advocacy class and reviewing papers for the Gerald Rose Memorial Legal Writing competition). *Member:* Chicago, Illinois State and American Bar Associations; American Intellectual Property Law Association; Bohemian Lawyers Association of Chicago. ***REPORTED CASES:*** Thriftimart, Inc. v. Scot Lad Foods, Inc. 207 USPQ 330 (TTAB 1980); DBA Products Co. v. Salamon, 1981 U.S. Dist. LEXIS 10802, (ND Ill , 1981); Pate Co. v. RPS Corp., 685 F.2d 1019, 216 U.S.P.Q. 571 (7th Cir. 1982); Plastiques Anchor v. Quinn David, 1992 U.S. Dist. LEXIS 12536, (N.D. Ill, 1982); Compania Cervecera De Nicaragua v. Cervezas Victoria y Tona Beers Inc. 28 USPQ 2d 1870 (MD Fla 1993); HWB, Inc. v. Braner, Inc., 1993 U.S. Dist. LEXIS 13757, (ND Ill, 1993); In Re Wm. W. Meyer, VII No. 2, Allen's Trademark Digest 7, (TTAB 1993) , Rasmussen v. The West, Inc. 28 USPQ 2d 1958 (N.D.Ill, 1993); Carbonara v. Olmos 1994 WL 370031 (CD Cal 1994); Respect Inc. v. Fremgen 897 F. Supp. 361; 889 F. Supp. 340; 36 U.S.P.Q.2d 1278, (ND Ill, 1995); Polillo v. Protel, Inc., 998 F. Supp. 958; 46 U.S.P.Q.2d 1722, (ND Ill, 1998); Trek Bicycle Corp. v. Alyx Fier, 56 U.S.P.Q. 2d 1527 (TTAB, 2000); Holland Co. v. Zeftek, Inc., 2001 U.S. Dist. LEXIS 13015 (ND Ill, 2001); Thane Int'l, Inc. v. Trek Bicycle Corp., 305 F.3d 894, 64 USPQ2d 1564 (9th Cir, 2002). ***PRACTICE AREAS:*** Intellectual Property Law (90%); Patents; Trademarks; Copyrights; Litigation (5%); Antitrust Law (5%). ***Email:*** david.brezina@btlaw.com

WILLIAM M. McERLEAN, admitted to bar, 1978, Illinois and U.S. District Court, Northern District of Illinois including Trial Bar; 1981, California; 1983, U.S. Court of Appeals, Seventh Circuit; 1989, U.S. Court of Appeals, Fifth Circuit; 1993, U.S. Court of Appeals, Ninth Circuit; 1995, U.S. Court of Appeals, Tenth Circuit; 2000, U.S. Court of Appeals, Second and Eleventh Circuits. *Education:* University of Notre Dame (B.A., magna cum laude, 1975); Georgetown University (J.D., with honors, 1978). Co-Author: "The Impact of Federal Rule 11 on Franchise Litigation," ABA Franchise Law Journal, 1989; "What to Do When Your Client Lies," ABA Litigation Magazine, 1989; "Privileges: How to Uncover the Facts," ABA Litigation Magazine, 1997; "From Kahn to Carlton: Recent Developments in Special Litigation Committee Practice," The Business Lawyer, Vol. 53, November 1997; "Training An Associate: Garbage In, Garbage Out", American Bar Association Litigation Magazine, 1998. ***Email:*** wmcerlean@btlaw.com

DAVID G. EDWARDS, admitted to bar, 1980, Pennsylvania; 1989, Illinois. *Education:* Duke University (B.A., magna cum laude, 1975); Cornell University (J.D., 1980). ***PRACTICE AREAS:*** Securities; Corporate Law. ***Email:*** david.edwards@btlaw.com

DANIEL P. ALBERS, admitted to bar, 1983, Illinois; registered to practice before U.S. Patent and Trademark Office. *Education:* University of Illinois (B.S., Biology, 1980; J.D., 1983). Arbitrator, AAA. *Member:* American Bar Association; APLAC; IPLAC. ***PRACTICE AREAS:*** Products Liability; Professional Liability; Commercial Litigation; Litigation; Patent Litigation; Personal Injury Defense. ***Email:*** daniel.albers@btlaw.com

DEBORAH L. THORNE, admitted to bar, 1983, Illinois; U.S. District Court, Northern District of Illinois. *Education:* Macalester College (B.A., 1975); Duke University (M.A.T., 1976); Chicago-Kent College of Law (J.D., with honors, 1983). Author: "New Law Gives Trade Creditors Help: Reclamation Creditors Gain Significant Advantage in Section 546(c)," ABI Journal, May 2005; "Bankruptcy Practice," Illinois Institute for Continuing Legal Education, General Practice Manual, 2005; "'Who's on First?'—The Eighth Circuit Highlights the Interplay of 'Circular Priority' and Bankruptcy Law," ABI Journal, December-January 2004; "Are All Creditor 'Animals' Equal?—Treatment of New Value Uner Section 547," ABI Journal April 2004; "Involuntary Bankruptcy: The Last Word on When the Dispute is Bona Fide!" Business Credit, May 2004; "Bank's Security Interests in Checking Accounts and Check-Kiting Schemes," ABI Journal, October 2002; "Representing Unsecured Creditors," Illinois Institute For Continuing Legal Education Bankruptcy Practice, 1990; "Representing Parties in Bankruptcy Cases," Illinois Institute for Continuing Legal Education, Starting Points. Member, Board of Editors, American Bankruptcy Journal, 2004—. Extern to the Honorable Robert L. Eisen, Bankruptcy Judge, U.S. District Court, Northern District of Illinois, 1982-1983. President, Evanston United Way Board, 1998-2000; Board Member, Women Employed, 2001—. *Member:* Chicago (Bankruptcy and Reorganization Committee; Vice Chair, 1994-1995; Chair, 1995-1996) and Seventh Circuit (Chair, Bankruptcy Committee) Bar Associations; American Bankruptcy Institute (Co-Chair, Unsecured Trade Creditors Committee; Board of Editors, American Bankruptcy Journal); Chicago Council of Lawyers (Co-Chair, Women's Rights Committee, 1990-

(This Listing Continued)

1991); International Women's Insolvency Confederation; Turnaround Management Association. ***PRACTICE AREAS:*** Bankruptcy; Creditors Rights; Secured Lending; Financial Reorganization. ***Email:*** deborah.thorne@btlaw.com

CHARLES J. SCHULTZ, admitted to bar, 1985, Illinois. *Education:* Northwestern University (B.A., 1982); Chicago-Kent (J.D., 1985; LL.M., Tax, 1986). ***PRACTICE AREAS:*** Corporate Law; Health Care; Business Law; Taxation; Mergers, Acquisitions and Divestitures. ***Email:*** chuck.schultz@btlaw.com

DONALD J. McNEIL, admitted to bar, 1986, Illinois; 1997, California; U.S. District Court, Northern District of Illinois including Trial Bar, U.S. District Court, Central District of Illinois, U.S. District Court, Northern District of Indiana, U.S. District Court, Western and Eastern Districts of Michigan, U.S. District Court, Northern District of Texas, U.S. District Court, Eastern District of Wisconsin, U.S. District Court, Central, Southern, Northern and Eastern Districts of California, U.S. Court of Appeals, Seventh and Ninth Circuits and U.S. Supreme Court. *Education:* Georgetown University (B.S., Lang., 1971); University of Missouri at Columbia (M.A., 1973); Loyola University, Chicago (J.D., magna cum laude, 1986). Kappa Tau Alpha. Recipient, Chief Justice Edward D. White Scholarship Award. Executive Editor, Student Articles, Loyola University of Chicago Law Journal, 1985-1986. Superintendent, Wage Claims Division, Illinois Department of Labor, 1975-1986. *Member:* Chicago, Los Angeles County and American Bar Associations. Fellow, American Bar Foundation. ***REPORTED CASES:*** Waters v. Churchill, 511 U.S 661 (1994); Franzoni v. Hartmarx Corp., 300 F.3d 767 (7th Cir. 2002); O'Regan v. Arbitration Forums, Inc., 121 F.3d 1060 (7th Cir. 1997); Ost v. West Suburban Travelers Limousine, Inc., 88 F.3d 435 (7th Cir. 1996); Walters v. United States Gypsum Co., 537 N.W.2d 708 (Iowa 1995); Franzoni v. Hart Schaffner & Marx, 312 Ill.App.3d 394, 726 N.E.2d 719 (1st Dist. 2000); Folbert v. Department of Human Rights, 303 Ill.App.3d 13, 707 N.E.2d 590 (1st Dist. 1999); Anderson v. U.S. Gypsum Co., 42 Ohio App.3d 112, 536 N.E.2d 1180 (11th Dist. 1987). ***PRACTICE AREAS:*** Employment Law; Covenants Not To Compete; Civil Litigation; Wage and Hour Law; Management Labor Law; Civil Appeals. ***Email:*** donald.mcneil@btlaw.com

THOMAS J. DONOVAN, admitted to bar, 1987, Illinois, U.S. District Court, Northern District of Illinois including Trial Bar and U.S. Court of Appeals for the Federal Circuit; 1988, registered to practice before U.S. Patent and Trademark Office. *Education:* University of Illinois (B.S.Mechanical Engineering, 1978); Illinois Institute of Technology/Chicago-Kent College of Law (J.D., 1987). Faculty Member, Illinois Institute of Technology/Chicago-Kent College of Law, 1992-1994. *Member:* Chicago, Illinois State and American Bar Associations; Intellectual Property Law Association of Chicago. ***PRACTICE AREAS:*** Intellectual Property; Patents; Trademarks; Copyrights; Trade Secrets; Unfair Competition. ***Email:*** thomas.donovan@btlaw.com

JEFFREY R. GRAY, admitted to bar, 1988, Illinois; 1989, U.S. District Court, Northern District of Illinois; 1990, U.S. Court of Appeals, Seventh and Federal Circuits; registered to practice before U.S. Patent and Trademark Office. *Education:* Illinois Institute of Technology (B.S.C.E., 1979); The John Marshall Law School (J.D., 1988; LL.M., in Intellectual Property Law, 1992). Licensed Professional Engineer, Illinois, 1985. ***PRACTICE AREAS:*** Intellectual Property Law; Patents; Trademarks; Copyrights; Litigation; Patent Licensing. ***Email:*** jeffrey.gray@btlaw.com

MARK E. RUST, admitted to bar, 1989, Illinois; U.S. District Court, Northern District of Illinois and U.S. Supreme Court. *Education:* University of Notre Dame (B.A., 1981); Loyola University (J.D., 1989). *Member:* Chicago (Chair, Health and Hospital Law Committee, 1998-1999), Illinois State (Chair, Health Law Section Council, 1999-2000) and American (Chair, Medicine and Law Committee, Tort and Insurance Practice Section, 1993-1994) Bar Associations; American Health Lawyers Association. ***PRACTICE AREAS:*** Healthcare Corporate Law; Healthcare Fraud; Healthcare Mergers and Acquisitions; Managed Care Contracts; Medical Antitrust; Physicians Contracts. ***Email:*** mark.rust@btlaw.com

BRADLEY B. FALKOF, admitted to bar, 1978, Illinois. *Education:* Brown University (B.A., 1974); Northwestern University (J.D., 1978). Member, Editorial Board, Journal of Criminal Law and Criminology. *Member:* American Bar Association; Appellate Lawyers Association. ***PRACTICE AREAS:*** Civil Litigation; Products Liability Defense; Breach of Warranty; Appellate Practice. ***Email:*** brad.falkof@btlaw.com

ALICE O. MARTIN, admitted to bar, 1990, Illinois; registered to practice before U.S. Patent and Trademark Office. *Education:* University of Michigan (M.S.,1963); Case Western Reserve University (Ph.D., 1969; Fellow in Anatomy 1973-1975); Loyola Law School of Chicago (J.D.,1989). Certified, American Board of Medical Genetics, 1982. Director, Clinical Cytogenetics Laboratory and Ph.D. Medical Geneticist. Member: Board of Directors, Illinois Biotechnology Industry Organization; Amicus Committee and Patent Committee, Biotechnology Industry Organization. *Member:* Illinois State, Federal and American Bar Associations; Illinois Trial Lawyers Association; The Association of Trial Lawyers of America; American Intellectual Property Association; Intellectual Property Law Association of Chicago. ***PRACTICE AREAS:*** Patent Prosecution; International Patent Prosecution; Litigation; Biotechnology; Medical; Plant; Genetics; Molecular Biology; Immunology. ***Email:*** alice.martin@btlaw.com

GRANT H. PETERS, admitted to bar, 1991, Illinois and U.S. District Court, Northern District of Illinois; 1992, registered to practice before U.S. Patent and Trademark Office; 1993, U.S. Court of Appeals for the Federal Circuit, 7th Circuit Court of Appeals and U.S. District Court, Central District of Illinois. *Education:* The University of Iowa (B.S. Industrial Engineering, 1986); Loyola School of Law-Chicago (J.D., 1991). Sigma Phi Epsilon; Theta Tau. Recipient: American Jurisprudence Award in Professional Responsibility; Loyola University Commendation for Leadership and Service. Member, Pace University Environmental Law Moot Court Team. Author: position paper submitted to the United States Patent and Trademark Office on proposed "Changes to the Hague Agreement Concerning the International Registration of Industrial Designs." Speaker: Industrial Design Society of America, "The Benefits of Intellectual Property in Industrial Design"; American Society of Association Executives, "Managing Technology Issues." Vice President, Board of Directors of the Suzuki-Orff School for Young Musicians. *Member:* Chicago and American Bar Associations; Intellectual Property Law Association of Chicago; American Intellectual Property Law Association; Industrial Designers Society of America. ***PRACTICE AREAS:*** Intellectual Property; Patent, Trademark and Copyright Law; Design Patents; Trade Secrets; Unfair Competition. ***Email:*** grant.peters@btlaw.com

(This Listing Continued)

FREDRIC P. ANDES, admitted to bar, 1980, Illinois; 1986, District of Columbia; 1990, U.S. Court of Appeals, Sixth Circuit and U.S. District Court, Northern District of Illinois; 1992, U.S. Court of Appeals, Tenth Circuit; 1995, U.S. Court of Appeals, Seventh and District of Columbia Circuits; 1996, U.S. District Court for the District of Columbia; 2001, U.S. Court of Appeals, Eleventh Circuit; 2003, U.S. Court of Appeals, Fourth Circuit. *Education:* Northwestern University (B.A., 1977); Harvard Law School (J.D., cum laude, 1980). *Member:* Illinois State (Member, Environmental Law Section) and American (Member, Environment, Energy and Resources Section) Bar Associations. ***PRACTICE AREAS:*** Clean Water Act; Environmental Compliance; Environmental Permitting; Water Pollution; Water Quality. ***Email:*** fredric.andes@btlaw.com

MARI YAMAMOTO REGNIER, admitted to bar, 1993, Illinois. *Education:* Ochanomizu University, Tokyo, Japan (B.A., 1983); University of Wisconsin (M.A.); Indiana University School of Law (J.D., 1993). ***LANGUAGES:*** Japanese. ***PRACTICE AREAS:*** Corporate; Mergers and Acquisitions; Financing; Pacific Rim. ***Email:*** mari.regnier@btlaw.com

TIMOTHY J. ENGLING, admitted to bar, 1995, Illinois; U.S. District Court, Northern District of Illinois; U.S. Court of Appeals, Seventh and Federal Circuits; registered to practice before U.S. Patent and Trademark Office. *Education:* United States Military Academy (B.S., 1988); IIT Chicago-Kent College of Law (J.D., 1995); John Marshall Law School (LL.M., 1999). [Capt., Army Aviation]. ***PRACTICE AREAS:*** Intellectual Property Law; Patents; Trademarks; Copyrights; Litigation; Patent Licensing. ***Email:*** timothy.engling@btlaw.com

JAMES B. CONTE, admitted to bar, 1993, California; 1995, Illinois; U.S. District Court, Northern District of Illinois; U.S. District Court, Central District of California; U.S. Court of Appeals, Seventh, Ninth and Federal Circuits; registered to practice before U.S. Patent and Trademark Office. *Education:* University of Illinois, Urbana (B.S., with high honors, 1987); University of California, Los Angeles (J.D., 1992). ***PRACTICE AREAS:*** Unfair Competition; Patent Litigation; Trademark Litigation; Intellectual Property Portfolio Management. ***Email:*** james.conte@btlaw.com

HOWARD B. ROCKMAN, admitted to bar, 1963, Maryland; 1969, Illinois and U.S. District Court, Northern District of Illinois; 1988, U.S. Court of Appeals for the Federal Circuit; registered to practice before U.S. Patent and Trademark Office. *Education:* Drexel Institute of Technology (B.S.M.E., 1959); George Washington University (J.D., with honors, 1963). Patent Examiner, U.S. Patent and Trademark Office, 1959-1963. Trial Attorney, U.S. Department of Justice, Washington, D.C., 1963-1968. Vice President, General Counsel, Jovan, Inc., 1979-1982. Adjunct Professor, Intellectual Property Practice Course, John Marshall Law School, 1988—. ***Email:*** howard.rockman@btlaw.com

PETER J. SHAKULA, admitted to bar, 1990, Illinois; 1993, Indiana; 1995, U.S. District Court, Northern District of Indiana,; 1998, U.S. District Court, Northern District of Illinois; registered to practice before U.S. Patent and Trademark Office. *Education:* Purdue University (B.S., 1986); Indiana University (J.D., 1989). ***PRACTICE AREAS:*** Intellectual Property Law; Patents; Trademarks; Copyrights; Litigation; Patent Licensing; Unfair Competition. ***Email:*** peter.shakula@btlaw.com

SCOTT T. LONGMAN, admitted to bar, 1993, Illinois. *Education:* Northwestern University (B.A., 1987); University of Illinois College of Law (J.D., magna cum laude, 1993). Harno Scholar. Recipient, American Jurisprudence Award for Contracts. Associate Editor, University of Illinois Law Review. *Member:* Defense Research Institute. ***PRACTICE AREAS:*** Litigation; Complex Litigation; Products Liability Defense; Toxic Tort Defense. ***Email:*** scott.longman@btlaw.com

CAROLYN S. HESSE, admitted to bar, 1983, Illinois. *Education:* University of Illinois (B.S., 1971; M.S., 1977); DePaul University (J.D., 1983). *Member:* Chicago and American (Member, Environmental Section) Bar Associations. ***PRACTICE AREAS:*** Environmental Law; Administrative Law; OSHA. ***Email:*** carolyn.hesse@btlaw.com

MELISSA A. VALLONE, admitted to bar, 1996, Illinois; 1997, Indiana. *Education:* Purdue University (B.S., 1993); Valparaiso University (J.D., summa cum laude, 1996). *Member:* American Bar Association; International Trademark Association; American Intellectual Property Law Association; Intellectual Property Law Association of Chicago. ***PRACTICE AREAS:*** Trademarks; Copyrights; Intellectual Property Litigation. ***Email:*** melissa.vallone@btlaw.com

MARC S. SILVER, admitted to bar, 1996, Illinois. *Education:* University of Rochester (B.A., cum laude, 1992); University of Illinois (J.D., cum laude, 1996). ***PRACTICE AREAS:*** Commercial Litigation; Products Liability Defense; Litigation; Real Estate Litigation; Fraud and Deceit. ***Email:*** marc.silver@btlaw.com

DAVID R. SCHENK, admitted to bar, 1968, Illinois. *Education:* University of Michigan (B.B.A., 1963; M.B.A., with distinction, 1965); John Marshall Law School (J.D., with honors, 1968). Editor-in-Chief, John Marshall Law Review, 1967-1968. ***PRACTICE AREAS:*** Real Estate; Construction; Alternative Dispute Resolution. ***Email:*** dschenk@btlaw.com

OF COUNSEL

STEPHEN M. FATUM, admitted to bar, 1985, Illinois. *Education:* College of the Holy Cross (B.A., 1981); Emory University School of Law (J.D., 1985). *Member:* Illinois State Bar Association (Health Care Section Council, 1988-1996, Chair, 1994-1995, Past Chair, 1995-1996; Chair, Legislative Committee, 1989-1992); Illinois Association of Healthcare Attorneys; American Health Lawyers Association. ***PRACTICE AREAS:*** Health Law; Managed Care Contracts; Physician Contracts; Managed Care; Health Care Corporate Law. ***Email:*** stephen.fatum@btlaw.com

MICHAEL J. MUELLER, admitted to bar, 1986, Illinois and U.S. District Court, Northern District of Illinois; 1989, U.S. Court of Appeals, Seventh Circuit; 1999, U.S. District Court, Eastern District of Michigan and U.S. District Court, Eastern District of Wisconsin. *Education:* University of Illinois (B.A., with honors, 1981); DePaul University College of Law (J.D., 1986). [U.S. Navy, 1972-1978]. ***LANGUAGES:*** Japanese. ***PRACTICE AREAS:*** Employment; Labor; Commercial Litigation. ***Email:*** michael.mueller@btlaw.com

(This Listing Continued)

BARNES & THORNBURG LLP, Chicago—Continued

ERIKA K. POWERS, admitted to bar, 1994, Michigan and U.S. District Court, Eastern District of Michigan; 1996, Illinois and U.S. District Court, Northern District of Illinois. *Education:* Alma College (B.A., summa cum laude, 1990); University of Michigan (J.D., cum laude, 1994). *Member:* Chicago (Past Chair, Environmental Law Committee); Illinois State (Environmental Law Section) and American (Section on Environment, Energy and Resources) Bar Associations; State Bar of Michigan (Environmental Section). ***PRACTICE AREAS:*** Environmental; Water. ***Email:*** epowers@btlaw.com

NORMA W. ZEITLER, admitted to bar, 1995, Illinois. *Education:* Southern Illinois University (B.S., 1982); Defense Intelligence College (M.S., Strategic Intelligence, 1989); Loyola University (J.D., cum laude, 1995). Recipient, President's Medal for service and academic excellence, Loyola University Chicago School of Law, 1995. Editor-in-Chief, Loyola University of Chicago Law Journal, 1994-1995. Author, Note, "St. Mary's Honor Center v. Hicks: The Shifting Burden Stays Put," Loyola University Chicago School of Law Journal, Volume 25, Issue 2, Winter, 1994. *Member:* American Bar Association (Member, Labor and Employment Section). [Captain, Company Commander, Platoon Leader and Intelligence Officer, U.S. Army, 1984-1992]. ***REPORTED CASES:*** O'Regan v. Arbitration Forums, Inc., 121 F.3d 1060 (7th Cir. 1997); Jones v. United States Gypsum Co., 126 F. Supp. 2d 1172 (N.D. Iowa 2000). ***PRACTICE AREAS:*** Labor and Employment; Litigation. ***Email:*** norma.zeitler@btlaw.com

JASON M. CAIN, admitted to bar, 1994, Illinois; 1995, Wisconsin and U.S. Tax Court. *Education:* Illinois State University (B.S., 1990); Widener University (J.D., 1993); DePaul University (LL.M., Taxation, 1995). ***PRACTICE AREAS:*** Business Law; Trusts and Estates; Wills; Taxation; Asset Protection. ***Email:*** jason.cain@btlaw.com

GERALD S. GEREN, admitted to bar, 1966, Illinois; 1969, U.S. District Court, Northern District of Illinois; 1979, U.S. Court of Appeals, Seventh and Federal Circuits; registered to practice before U.S. Patent and Trademark Office. *Education:* Illinois Institute of Technology (B.S. Metallurgical Engineering, 1961); DePaul University (J.D., 1966). ***PRACTICE AREAS:*** Intellectual Property Law; Patents; Trademarks; Copyrights; Litigation; Prosecution Law. ***Email:*** gerald.geren@btlaw.com

DARREN C. COLLIER, admitted to bar, 2000, Illinois. *Education:* Indiana University (B.A., 1989); Capital University (J.D., 1994). ***PRACTICE AREAS:*** Municipal Finance; Government Services. ***Email:*** darren.collier@btlaw.com

JOHN W. MORSE, admitted to bar, 1998, Illinois. *Education:* DePauw University (B.A., cum laude, 1995); Northwestern University (J.D., 1998). Co-Author, "Commercial Real Estate Sale Contracts," IICLE on Commercial Real Estate. Co-Author and Contributor, "Loan Commitment Litigation and the Illinois Credit Agreements Act," IICLE on Real Estate Litigation. *Member:* Cook County, Illinois State and American Bar Associations. ***PRACTICE AREAS:*** Commercial Real Estate (40%); Construction Contracts (5%); Construction Finance (30%); Asset Based Finance (10%); Commercial Finance (5%); Secured Finance (10%). ***Email:*** jmorse@btlaw.com

MARK J. McANDREW, admitted to bar, 1980, Illinois; U.S. District Court, Northern District of Illinois; U.S. Court of Appeals, Seventh Circuit. *Education:* University of Illinois (1972); John Marshall Law School (1980). *Member:* Chicago, DuPage County and Illinois State Bar Associations. ***PRACTICE AREAS:*** Civil Litigation; Trial Practice; Commercial Law; Labor and Employment; Employment Litigation; Commercial Litigation; Intellectual Property. ***Email:*** mmcandrew@btlaw.com

ASSOCIATES

JONATHAN P. FROEMEL, admitted to bar, 1996, Illinois; 1997, U.S. District Court, Northern District of Illinois; 2003, U.S. District Court, Western District of Michigan and Northern District of Indiana. *Education:* Washington University (B.A., with honors, 1993); University of Illinois (J.D., magna cum laude, 1996). ***PRACTICE AREAS:*** Intellectual Property Litigation; Trademark Litigation; Trademark Prosecution; Commercial Litigation. ***Email:*** jonathan.froemel@btlaw.com

ELLEN L. LUEPKE, admitted to bar, 1997, Illinois. *Education:* Valparaiso University (B.A., cum laude, 1994); University of Iowa College of Law (J.D., with distinction, 1997); Loyola University Chicago School of Law (LL.M. in Health Law, 1998). ***PRACTICE AREAS:*** Health Law; Health Care Regulation; Physician Practices. ***Email:*** ellen.luepke@btlaw.com

MARK A. HAGEDORN, admitted to bar, 1998, Illinois; 2002, U.S. District Court, Northern District of Illinois; U.S. District Court, Eastern District of Wisconsin; U.S. Court of Appeals, Seventh and Federal Circuits; registered to practice before U.S. Patent and Trademark Office. *Education:* Purdue University (B.S.Ch.E., 1994); Indiana University School of Law (J.D., 1998). Member, Intellectual Property Advisory Board, Indiana University. *Member:* Chicago and American Bar Associations; American Intellectual Property Law Association. ***PRACTICE AREAS:*** Intellectual Property; Patents; Trademarks. ***Email:*** mark.hagedorn@btlaw.com

MARK J. NAHNSEN, admitted to bar, 2000, Illinois; U.S. Court of Appeals, Seventh and Federal Circuits; registered to practice before U.S. Patent and Trademark Office. *Education:* Purdue University (B.S.C.E., 1994); John Marshall School of Law (J.D., 1999). *Member:* Illinois State and American Bar Associations; American Intellectual Property Law Association. ***REPORTED CASES:*** Barnett v. Strom 265 F.Supp.2d 946 (N.D. Ill 2003); Barnett v. Strom 243 F.Supp.2d 833 (N.D. Ill 2003); Allen Engineering v. Bartell 299 F.3d 1336 (Fed. Cir. 2002). ***PRACTICE AREAS:*** Intellectual Property; Patents; Trademarks; Copyrights; Litigation. ***Email:*** mark.nahnsen@btlaw.com

CHARLA L. HAUSLER, admitted to bar, 2000, Illinois. *Education:* University of Illinois (B.S., 1992); Valparaiso University (J.D., summa cum laude, 2000). Editor-in-Chief, Valparaiso Law Review, 1999-2000. ***PRACTICE AREAS:*** Commercial Litigation; Products Liability Defense. ***Email:*** charla.hausler@btlaw.com

KEVIN C. DRISCOLL, JR., admitted to bar, 2000, Illinois. *Education:* University of Illinois (A.B., 1992; J.D., magna cum laude, 2000). Member, University of Illinois Law Review. Author, "Eradicating the 'Discharge by Declaration' for Student Loan Debt in Chapter 13," 2000 University of Illinois Law Review 1311. ***PRACTICE AREAS:*** Bankruptcy; Commercial Litigation. ***Email:*** kevin.driscoll@btlaw.com

(This Listing Continued)

VLADIMIR KHODOSH, admitted to bar, 2002, Illinois; registered to practice before U.S. Patent and Trademark Office. *Education:* University of Illinois (B.A., Political Science, 1998; J.D., cum laude, 2001). *Member:* Intellectual Property Law Association of Chicago; American Intellectual Property Law Association. ***PRACTICE AREAS:*** Intellectual Property; Computers and Software; Copyrights; Patents; Intellectual Property Licensing. ***Email:*** vladimir.khodosh@btlaw.com

DAVID T. BALLARD, admitted to bar, 2001, Illinois and U.S. District Court, Northern District of Illinois 2003, U.S. Court of Appeals, Seventh Circuit and U.S. District Court, Central District of Illinois. *Education:* Chicago-Kent College of Law, Illinois Institute of Technology (J.D.). *Member:* Chicago, Cook County, Illinois State and American Bar Associations. ***PRACTICE AREAS:*** Civil Litigation; Commercial Litigation; Products Liability; Manufacturers Liability; Environmental Administrative Law; Environmental Litigation; Administrative Litigation; Complex Litigation; Federal Civil Litigation; Trial Practice; Lemon Law; Warranty Law; Toxic Torts. ***Email:*** david.ballard@btlaw.com

KELLY M. BELLINGER, admitted to bar, 2001, Illinois. *Education:* Vanderbilt University (B.A., 1995); University of Notre Dame (J.D., 2001). ***PRACTICE AREAS:*** Business Law; Corporate Law; Health Care. ***Email:*** kelly.murphy@btlaw.com

BRAD E. RAGO, admitted to bar, 2001, Illinois and U.S. District Court, Northern District of Illinois 2005, U.S. District Court, Central District of Illinois. *Education:* Purdue University (B.A., 1998); University of Illinois College of Law (J.D., 2001). ***PRACTICE AREAS:*** Litigation. ***Email:*** brad.rago@btlaw.com

JEREMY B. LEWIN, admitted to bar, 1999, Illinois. *Education:* DePaul University (B.A., high honors, 1993); London School of Economics (Economics Program, 1994); Loyola University Chicago School of Law (J.D., 1999). Recipient, American Jurisprudence Award in Employment Law Clinic, 1998. ***PRACTICE AREAS:*** Labor and Employment. ***Email:*** jeremy.lewin@btlaw.com

WESLEY W. BROQUARD, admitted to bar, 2002, Illinois and U.S. District Court, Northern District of Illinois. *Education:* University of Illinois, Urbana (B.A., magna cum laude, 1999); DePaul University College of Law (J.D., summa cum laude, 2002). *Member:* Chicago, Illinois State and American (Member, Real Property Section) Bar Associations. ***PRACTICE AREAS:*** Commercial Real Estate (80%); Business Law (20%). ***Email:*** wesley.broquard@btlaw.com

EVAN J. HAIM, admitted to bar, 2002, Illinois and U.S. District Court, Northern District of Illinois. *Education:* Ohio Wesleyan University (B.A., 1994); DePaul University College of Law (J.D., cum laude, 2002). ***PRACTICE AREAS:*** Commercial Litigation; Creditor. ***Email:*** evan.haim@btlaw.com

MARC E. DARNELL, admitted to bar, 2002, Ohio; 2003, U.S. District Court, Northern District of Ohio and U.S. Court of Appeals, Sixth Circuit; 2004, U.S. District Court, Northern District of Illinois; 2005, Illinois. *Education:* The College of William & Mary (B.A., 1999); Case Western Reserve University (J.D., 2002). *Member:* Cleveland (Member, Litigation Section), Ohio State (Member, Litigation Section) and American (Member, Litigation Section) Bar Associations. ***PRACTICE AREAS:*** Business Litigation; Complex Litigation; Class Actions. ***Email:*** marc.darnell@btlaw.com

PASCALE J. BISHOP, admitted to bar, 2001, Illinois. *Education:* University of Missouri-Columbia (B.A., summa cum laude, 1998); University of Michigan (J.D., cum laude, 2000). *Member:* Illinois State Bar Association. ***PRACTICE AREAS:*** Litigation (100%). ***Email:*** pascale.bishop@btlaw.com

JOHN P. WAPPEL, admitted to bar, 2004, Illinois, U.S. District Court, Northern District of Illinois, 2005, U.S. Court of Appeals, Seventh and Federal Circuits; registered to practice before U.S. Patent and Trademark Office. *Education:* University of Illinois, Urbana-Champaign (B.S.M.E., 1991); Chicago-Kent College of Law, Illinois Institute of Technology (J.D., 2004). *Member:* Chicago and American Bar Associations; American Intellectual Property Law Association. ***PRACTICE AREAS:*** Intellectual Property. ***Email:*** john.wappel@btlaw.com

JAMES E. MICHEL, admitted to bar, 2004, Illinois. *Education:* Purdue University, West Lafayette (B.A.); Loyola University, Chicago (J.D., 2004). *Member:* Chicago, Illinois State and American Bar Associations. ***PRACTICE AREAS:*** Commercial Litigation; Class Actions Litigation; Warranty Litigation; Patent Litigation. ***Email:*** james.michel@btlaw.com

DOUGLAS M. OLDHAM, admitted to bar, 2004, Illinois. *Education:* Northwestern University (B.A., 2001; J.D., 2004). *Member:* Chicago and Illinois State Bar Associations. ***LANGUAGES:*** French. ***PRACTICE AREAS:*** Labor and Employment. ***Email:*** douglas.oldham@btlaw.com

REPRESENTATIVE CLIENTS: 1st Source Bank; American National Bank & Trust Company; AMPRO, Inc.; Bank One; Chicago Football, L.L.C. (Rush); CIGNA Healthcare, Inc.; Citizens Commercial Leasing Corporation; Colonna's Shipyard, Inc.; Commonwealth Edison Company; Congress Financial Corporation; Edward Hospital Medical Staff; Equitable Life Assurance Society; Everen Securities, Inc.; Galaxie Lumber & Construction Company, Ltd.; Greater Cincinnati Cardiovascular Consultants, Inc.; Hallen Products, LTD. (Inc.); Harley-Davidson Motor Company; Ingersoll Products Corporation; International Facilities Group, L.L.C.; Lake Forest Orthopaedics, S.C.; LaSalle National Bank; Marchesan Implementos E Maquinas Agricoles Tatu SA; Marin Medical Management Company, Inc.; Massachusetts Mutual Life Insurance Company; Mercantile Real Estate Services, Inc.; National Steel Corporation; PACCAR Financial Corporation; Parkland Partners Ltd.; Pennsylvania Public Employe's Pension Fund; Physician's Anesthesia Care of Iowa City, P.C.; Physicians Healthcare Network; Pollution Controls, Inc.; Porter Athletic Equipment Company; ProAction, L.L.C.; Ron Weber & Associates of Illinois, Inc.; Transtech Products Corporation; Tri-State Heart Network, L.L.C.; West Virginia Physicians Management Services, L.L.C.; Whirlpool Corporation.

BARNOW AND ASSOCIATES, P.C.

Established in 1950

ONE NORTH LASALLE STREET, SUITE 4600
CHICAGO, ILLINOIS 60602
Telephone: 312-621-2000
Fax: 312-641-5504
Email: b.barnow@barnowlaw.com

General Civil Practice in all Courts. Civil Action Litigation, Class Actions.

(This Listing Continued)

WILLIAM T. McNEILL (1907-1983)

BEN BARNOW, born Milwaukee, Wisconsin, November 11, 1944; admitted to bar, 1969, Illinois; 1982, U.S. District Court, Northern District of Illinois; 1982, U.S. Court of Appeals, 7th Circuit; 1989, New York; 1994, U.S. Supreme Court. *Education:* University of Wisconsin (B.B.A., 1966); University of Michigan (J.D., 1969). Member: Panel of Arbitrators, American Arbitration Association. *Member:* Chicago, Illinois State and American Bar Associations; The Association of Trial Lawyers of America. ***PRACTICE AREAS:*** Litigation; Appellate Practice; Class Actions. ***Email:*** b.barnow@barnowlaw.com

---

SHARON A. HARRIS, born Pittsburgh, Pennsylvania, December 3, 1967; admitted to bar, 1998, Illinois. *Education:* Michigan State University (B.S., 1990); DePaul University (J.D., 1998). ***PRACTICE AREAS:*** Class Actions. ***Email:*** s.harris@barnowlaw.com

BARTLIT BECK HERMAN PALENCHAR & SCOTT LLP

COURTHOUSE PLACE
54 WEST HUBBARD STREET
CHICAGO, ILLINOIS 60610
Telephone: 312-494-4400
Facsimile: 312-494-4440
Email: bartlit-beck.com
URL: http://www.bartlit-beck.com

Denver, Colorado Office: 1899 Wynkoop Street. Telephone: 303-592-3100. Facsimile: 303-592-3140.

General Civil and Trial Practice in all Courts and Corporate Transactional Practice.

FIRM PROFILE: Bartlit Beck Herman Palenchar & Scott LLP was founded in 1993 with a goal of improving both quality and efficiency in business litigation through enhanced use of technology, staffing that is leaner and relies more on experienced lawyers, and innovative fee structures that provide alternatives to the traditional hourly rate system. The founding partners of Bartlit Beck Herman Palenchar & Scott LLP have over 120 years of litigation experience and have tried cases in over twenty states, the District of Columbia, the Virgin Islands, and Scotland. Since the Firm was founded, it has won seven of the top defense verdicts selected each year by "The National Law Journal." The Firm was ranked as one of the top ten law firms in the United States by "International Commercial Litigation" in its World Litigation Survey. The Firm also has extensive experience as principals in corporate counselling, securities regulations and transactions.

PARTNERS

FRED H. BARTLIT, JR. (P.C.), born Chicago, Illinois, August 1, 1932; admitted to bar, 1960, Illinois; 1995, Colorado. *Education:* United States Military Academy (B.S., Engineering, 1954); University of Illinois (LL.B., 1960). Editor, University of Illinois Law Review. Profiled in "The Trial Lawyers," by Emily Couric, St. Martin's Press, 1988; profiled in "America's Top Trial Lawyers: Who They Are & Why They Win," by Donald E. Vinson, Glasser LegalWorks, 1996; identified as one of the top ten litigation lawyers in the United States in a survey conducted by "International Commercial Litigation." *Member:* American Bar Association. Fellow, American College of Trial Lawyers; International Academy of Trial Lawyers. (Also at Denver, Colorado). ***PRACTICE AREAS:*** Commercial Litigation; Antitrust; Intellectual Property; Corporate Control/Mergers; Technical and Product Litigation; Environmental Litigation; Financial/Securities; Insurance Coverage; White Collar Criminal. ***Email:*** fred.bartlit@bartlit-beck.com

PHILIP S. BECK, born Chicago, Illinois, April 30, 1951; admitted to bar, 1977, Illinois; 1998, Colorado; 1999, Arizona; 2001, U.S. District Court, Western District of Wisconsin. *Education:* University of Wisconsin (B.A., with distinction, 1973); Boston University (J.D., magna cum laude, 1976). Editor-in-Chief, Boston University Law Review. Clerkship, United States Court of Appeals for the District of Columbia Circuit, 1976-1977. Lead Trial Lawyer for George W. Bush in 2000 Florida recount litigation. Named as one of the top ten trial lawyers in Illinois by the National Law Journal. Special Trial Counsel, U.S. Department of Justice. *Member:* Illinois State and American Bar Associations; American College of Trial Lawyers; International Academy of Trial Lawyers. ***PRACTICE AREAS:*** Commercial Litigation; Antitrust; Intellectual Property; Corporate Control/Mergers; Technical and Product Litigation; Environmental Litigation; Insurance Coverage; Financial/Securities. ***Email:*** philip.beck@bartlit-beck.com

SIDNEY N. HERMAN, born Chicago, Illinois, May 14, 1953; admitted to bar, 1978, Illinois; 1998, Colorado. *Education:* Haverford College (B.A., honors, 1975); Northwestern University (J.D., cum laude, 1978). Articles Editor, Northwestern University Law Review. Member, Northwestern Law Board, 1998—. Member, Board of Directors, Global Material Technologies, 1994—. Member, Board of Directors, Todd Shipyards Corp., 1992. Member, Board of Trustees, Francis W. Parker School, 1998—. Member, Board of Directors, Chicago Lawyers' Committee for Civil Rights Under Law, 1996—. *Member:* Chicago, Illinois State and American Bar Associations. Managing Partner of Firm. ***PRACTICE AREAS:*** Antitrust; Securities Litigation; Commercial Litigation; Contested Corporate Control/Mergers; Corporate Counseling. ***Email:*** skip.herman@bartlit-beck.com

MARK E. FERGUSON, born Kansas City, Missouri, June 6, 1958; admitted to bar, 1983, Illinois. *Education:* Northwestern University (B.S.J., 1980); University of Michigan (J.D., magna cum laude, 1983). Order of the Coif. Senior Editorial Board, Michigan Law Review. Adjunct Professor, Northwestern University School of Law. *Member:* American Bar Association. ***PRACTICE AREAS:*** Patent and Intellectual Property Litigation; Securities Litigation; Financial Services Litigation; Accounting Litigation; Antitrust Litigation; Commercial Litigation. ***Email:*** mark.ferguson@bartlit-beck.com

REBECCA WEINSTEIN BACON, born Edmonton, Alberta, Canada, March 27, 1972; admitted to bar, 1998, New York; 1999, Illinois; U.S. Court of Appeals for the Federal Circuit. *Education:* University of California, Los Angeles (B.A., magna cum laude, 1994);

(This Listing Continued)

Columbia University (J. D., 1997). Phi Beta Kappa. Kent Scholar; Harlan Fiske Stone Scholar. *Member:* Chicago and American Bar Associations. ***PRACTICE AREAS:*** Commercial Litigation. ***Email:*** rweinstein.bacon@bartlit-beck.com

PETER B. BENSINGER, JR., born New Haven, Connecticut, May 1, 1958; admitted to bar, 1989, New York; 1993, Illinois. *Education:* Stanford University (A.B., with distinction, 1980); New York University (J.D., 1989). Phi Beta Kappa; Pi Mu Io Ta, Italian Honor Society. Recipient, Myron J. Greene Award for Preeminent Achievement in Advocacy. Featured Speaker on legal technology at the ABA Tech Show, the ABA Annual Meeting, Legal Tech, Glasser LegalWorks, LawTech Plus in Canada and the American Inns of Court. Featured in "The Mobile Lawyer," a supplement to the "American Lawyer," as "The Most Wired Lawyer in America." *Member:* Chicago and American Bar Associations. ***PRACTICE AREAS:*** Patent Litigation; Commercial Litigation. ***Email:*** peter.bensinger@bartlit-beck.com

STEVEN E. DERRINGER, born De Kalb, Illinois, September 9, 1969; admitted to bar, 1997, Illinois and U.S. District Court, Northern District of Illinois; 2000, U.S. Court of Appeals, Seventh Circuit. *Education:* University of Michigan (B.A., with highest distinction and highest honors, 1991); Yale University (J.D., 1996). Phi Beta Kappa. James B. Angell Scholar. Managing Editor, Yale Law Journal. Law Clerk to the Honorable Dorothy W. Nelson, U.S. Court of Appeals, Ninth Circuit, 1996-1997. *Member:* American Bar Association. ***PRACTICE AREAS:*** Litigation. ***Email:*** steven.derringer@bartlit-beck.com

SEAN W. GALLAGHER, admitted to bar, 1997, Illinois. *Education:* University of Michigan (B.A., 1990; J.D., magna cum laude, 1994). Law Clerk to: Honorable Sandra Day O'Connor, Associate Justice, U.S. Supreme Court, 1995-1996; Honorable Alex Kozinski, U.S. Court of Appeals, Ninth Circuit, 1994-1995. ***PRACTICE AREAS:*** Commercial Litigation. ***Email:*** sean.gallagher@bartlit-beck.com

ANDREW L. GOLDMAN, born Chicago, Illinois, August 29, 1965; admitted to bar, 1995, Illinois and U.S. District Court, Northern District of Illinois. *Education:* University of Michigan (B.A., 1987); Northwestern University (J.D., cum laude, 1994). Order of the Coif. Northwestern Trial Team Regional Champion. ***PRACTICE AREAS:*** Commercial Litigation. ***Email:*** andrew.goldman@bartlit-beck.com

JEFFREY A. HALL, born Junction City, Kansas, September 4, 1960; admitted to bar, 1989, Illinois. *Education:* University of Pennsylvania (B.S., cum laude, Economics, 1982); University of Michigan (J.D., magna cum laude, 1988). Order of the Coif. Articles Editor, University of Michigan Law Review. Law Clerk to Honorable James L. Ryan, U.S. Court of Appeals, Sixth Circuit, 1988-1989. Certified Public Accountant, Michigan, 1982-1985. ***PRACTICE AREAS:*** Commercial Litigation. ***Email:*** jeffrey.hall@bartlit-beck.com

JAMES B. HEATON, III, born Quincy, Illinois, January 6, 1969; admitted to bar, 1999, Illinois and U.S. District Court, Northern District of Illinois. *Education:* University of Illinois (A.B., 1990); University of Chicago (J.D., M.B.A. & Ph.D., Finance, 1999). Phi Beta Kappa. Member, American Finance Association, 1994—. Adjunct Assistant Professor, Finance, University of Chicago, 2000-2001. Adjunct Associate Professor of Finance, Duke University, 2001-2003. ***PRACTICE AREAS:*** Complex and Multi-District Litigation; Professional Liability; Investment Litigation; Private Investment Funds; Trust Litigation. ***Email:*** jb.heaton@bartlit-beck.com

ADAM L. HOEFLICH, born New York, N.Y., July 9, 1964; admitted to bar, 1992, Illinois; 1994, U.S. District Court, Northern District of Illinois and U.S. Court of Appeals, Seventh Circuit. *Education:* Colgate University (B.A., 1987); University of Illinois (J.D., summa cum laude, 1991). Order of the Coif. Articles Editor, University of Illinois Law Review. Law Clerk: Hon. Milton I. Shadur, Senior Judge, U.S. District Court, Northern District of Illinois, 1992-1993; Hon. Thomas J. Meskill, Chief Judge, U.S. Court of Appeals, Second Circuit, 1991-1992. ***PRACTICE AREAS:*** Commercial Litigation. ***Email:*** adam.hoeflich@bartlit-beck.com

TAREK ISMAIL, born Alexandria, Egypt, September 22, 1969; admitted to bar, 1994, Illinois; 1995, U.S. District Court, Northern District of Illinois. *Education:* Carleton College (B.A., 1991); University of Illinois (J.D., summa cum laude, 1994). ***PRACTICE AREAS:*** Litigation. ***Email:*** tarek.ismail@bartlit-beck.com

CHRISTOPHER D. LANDGRAFF, born Pittsburgh, Pennsylvania, October 11, 1968; admitted to bar, 1994, Illinois. *Education:* University of North Carolina (B.A., 1991); University of California School of Law, Los Angeles (J.D., 1994). Phi Beta Kappa. Editor, UCLA Law Review. ***PRACTICE AREAS:*** Litigation. ***Email:*** chris.landgraff@bartlit-beck.com

MARK L. LEVINE, born Chicago, Illinois, December 20, 1964; admitted to bar, 1990, Illinois and U.S. District Court, Northern District of Illinois; 1999, U.S. Court of Appeals for the Federal Circuit; 2000, U.S. Court of Appeals, Second Circuit. *Education:* Princeton University (A.B., summa cum laude, 1986); Yale University Law School (J.D., 1989). Law Clerk, Honorable Nathaniel R. Jones, U.S. Court of Appeals, Sixth Circuit. ***PRACTICE AREAS:*** Commercial Litigation; Antitrust; Intellectual Property Litigation. ***Email:*** mark.levine@bartlit-beck.com

CHRIS LIND, born Minneapolis, Minnesota, October 5, 1968; admitted to bar, 1994, Illinois; 1995, U.S. District Court, Northern District of Illinois; 1996, Colorado; 2000, U.S. District Court, Western District of Michigan, U.S. District Court, Western District of Wisconsin and U.S. Court of Appeals for the Federal Circuit. *Education:* University of Michigan (B.A., with highest honors, 1990) Northwestern University (J.D., summa cum laude, 1994). Phi Beta Kappa. Northwestern University Law Review. Law Clerk, Honorable A. Raymond Randolph, U.S. Court of Appeals for the District of Columbia Circuit, 1994-1995. ***PRACTICE AREAS:*** Commercial Litigation; Intellectual Property Litigation. ***Email:*** chris.lind@bartlit-beck.com

MARK S. OUWELEEN, born Rochester, New York, March 13, 1964; admitted to bar, 1996, Illinois. *Education:* Georgetown University (A.B., magna cum laude, 1986); Yale University (J.D., 1994); Oxford University, Oxford, England. Phi Beta Kappa. Alpha Sigma Nu. Recipient: Coakely Medal; Spronck Medal; Bellarmine Scholarship. Oxford University, Rhodes Scholar. Yale Law School, Coker Fellow. Editor-in-Chief, Yale Journal of Law and Humanities. Senior Editor, Yale Law Journal. Law Clerk to Hon. Alex Kozinski, U.S. Court of Appeals, Ninth Circuit, 1994-1995. ***PRACTICE AREAS:*** Commercial Litigation. ***Email:*** mark.ouweleen@bartlit-beck.com

(This Listing Continued)

BARTLIT BECK HERMAN PALENCHAR & SCOTT LLP, Chicago—Continued

ANDRE M. PAUKA, born New York, New York, November 9, 1966; admitted to bar, 1996, Illinois and U.S. District Court, Northern District of Illinois. *Education:* United States Military Academy (B.S., Distinguished Cadet, 1988); Northwestern University (J.D., cum laude, 1996). Order of the Coif. Senior Articles Editor, Journal of Criminal Law and Criminology. [1st. Lt., U.S. Army Corps of Engineers, 1988-1992]. ***REPORTED CASES:*** Swiss Bank Corp. v. Dresser Indus., 141 F.3d 689 (7th Cir. 1998). ***PRACTICE AREAS:*** Commercial Litigation; Products Liability. ***Email:*** andre.pauka@bartlit-beck.com

JASON L. PELTZ, born Royal Oak, Michigan, September 6, 1967; admitted to bar, 1992, Illinois and U.S. District Court, Northern District of Illinois; 1993, Michigan and U.S. District Court, Eastern District of Michigan. *Education:* University of Michigan (A.B., with high distinction, 1989); University of Chicago (J.D., with honors, 1992). Law Clerk, Honorable Gerald E. Rosen, U.S. District Court, Eastern District of Michigan. *Member:* Chicago and American Bar Associations; State Bar of Michigan. ***PRACTICE AREAS:*** Commercial Litigation; Intellectual Property Litigation; Antitrust; Securities. ***Email:*** jason.peltz@bartlit-beck.com

ELIZABETH L. THOMPSON, born Tyler, Texas, March 12, 1957; admitted to bar, 1989, Illinois. *Education:* Indiana University (B.A., 1979; M.A., Uralic & Altaic Studies, 1985; J.D., magna cum laude, 1989). Order of the Coif. Articles Editor, Indiana Law Journal. ***PRACTICE AREAS:*** Commercial Litigation; Corporate; Contract; Employment Relations. ***Email:*** elizabeth.thompson@bartlit-beck.com

MICHAEL J. VALAIK, born Buffalo, New York, July 7, 1965; admitted to bar, 1997, Indiana and U.S. District Court, Southern and Northern Districts of Indiana; 2002, Illinois. *Education:* United States Naval Academy (B.S., with honors in History, 1988); University of Maryland (M.A., Modern European History, 1988); Georgetown University (J.D., cum laude, 1996). [Captain, U.S. Navy and U.S. Marine Corps., 1984-1996]. ***PRACTICE AREAS:*** Litigation. ***Email:*** michael.valaik@bartlit-beck.com

ASSOCIATES

ALLISON W. FREEDMAN, born Boston, Massachusetts, February 24, 1971; admitted to bar, 2002, Illinois. *Education:* Bowdoin College (B.A., 1993); University of Utah S. J. Quinney College of Law (M.A., 1998; J.D., 2002). Order of the Coif. Member, University of Utah Law Review. Author: "The Electronic Signatures Act: Preempting State Law by Legislating Contradictory Technology Standards," 2001 Utah Law Rev. 807. ***PRACTICE AREAS:*** Commercial Litigation. ***Email:*** allison.freedman@bartlit-beck.com

HAMILTON H. HILL, born Wichita, Kansas, August 30, 1975; admitted to bar, 2001, Illinois and U.S. District Court, Northern District of Illinois. *Education:* University of Kansas (B.G.S., 1998); University of Chicago (J.D., with honors, 2001). Member, University of Chicago Law Review. ***PRACTICE AREAS:*** Commercial Litigation. ***Email:*** hamilton.hill@bartlit-beck.com

CARRIE A. JABLONSKI, born Wichita, Kansas; admitted to bar, 2003, Illinois. *Education:* Harvard College (A.B., cum laude, 1998); Harvard Law School (J.D., cum laude, 2003). ***PRACTICE AREAS:*** Commercial Litigation. ***Email:*** carrie.jablonski@bartlit-beck.com

ALAN E. LITTMANN, born Detroit, Michigan, May 28, 1974; (admission pending). *Education:* University of Chicago (A.B., 1996; J.D., with honors, 2003). Editor-in-Chief, University of Chicago Law Review. Law Clerk to the Honorable Frank H. Easterbrook, U.S. Court of Appeals for the 7th Circuit, 2003-2004. ***PRACTICE AREAS:*** Commercial Litigation. ***Email:*** alan.littmann@bartlit-beck.com

J. SCOTT McBRIDE, born Indiana, June 12, 1970; admitted to bar, 2002, Illinois; 2003, U.S. Court of Appeals, Seventh Circuit. *Education:* Dartmouth College (A.B., summa cum laude, high honors in Chemistry, 1992); Northwestern University (M.S.Ed. 1994); University of Chicago Law School (J.D., high honors, 2002). Phi Beta Kappa. Order of the Coif. Member, University of Chicago Law Review. Law Clerk to the Honorable Richard D. Cudahy, U.S. Court of Appeals, Seventh Circuit, 2002-2003. ***PRACTICE AREAS:*** Litigation. ***Email:*** scott.mcbride@bartlit-beck.com

STEVEN J. NACHTWEY, born Green Bay, Wisconsin, February 15, 1975; admitted to bar, 2000, Minnesota; 2001, U.S. Court of Appeals, Eighth Circuit; 2002, Illinois; U.S. District Court, Northern District of Illinois. *Education:* University of Wisconsin-Madison (B.S., 1997); University of Minnesota at Minneapolis (J.D., 2000). Phi Beta Kappa; Order of the Coif. Law Clerk to the Honorable Diana E. Murphy, U.S. Court of Appeals, Eighth Circuit, 2000-2001. ***Email:*** steven.nachtwey@bartlit-beck.com

ANDREW K. POLOVIN, born Chicago, Illinois, June 12, 1973; admitted to bar, 2001, Illinois, U.S. District Court, Northern District of Illinois and U.S. Court of Appeals, Seventh Circuit. *Education:* Colgate University (B.A., cum laude, 1995); Northwestern University (J.D., magna cum laude, 2001). Order of the Coif. Member, Northwestern University Law Review. Law Clerk, Chief Judge Joel M. Flaum, U.S. Court of Appeals, Seventh Circuit, 2001-2002. *Member:* Illinois State and American Bar Associations. ***PRACTICE AREAS:*** Commercial Litigation. ***Email:*** andrew.polovin@bartlit-beck.com

REEGHAN RAFFALS, born Chicago, Illinois, March 19, 1967; admitted to bar, 2000, Massachusetts (Not admitted in Illinois). *Education:* University of Chicago (A.B., 1989); Harvard University (M.A./J.D., magna cum laude, 2000). *Member:* American Bar Association. ***PRACTICE AREAS:*** Litigation. ***Email:*** reeghan.raffals@bartlit-beck.com

PAUL J. SKIERMONT, born Blackfoot, Idaho, August 22, 1973; admitted to bar, 2001, Texas; 2002, Illinois. *Education:* University of Kentucky (B.A., cum laude, 1997); University of Chicago (J.D., high honors, 2001). Pi Sigma Alpha. Member, National Political Science Honor Society, University of Kentucky. ***PRACTICE AREAS:*** Litigation. ***Email:*** paul.skiermont@bartlit-beck.com

BRIAN C. SWANSON, born Merced, California, December 26, 1971; admitted to bar, 2001, Illinois. *Education:* Amherst College (B.A., 1994); Northwestern University (J.D., 2001). ***PRACTICE AREAS:*** Commercial Litigation. ***Email:*** brian.swanson@bartlit-beck.com

(This Listing Continued)

JILL R. TRUMBULL-HARRIS, born Tucson, Arizona, August 1, 1975; admitted to bar, 2001, Illinois; 2003, U.S. District Court, Northern District of Illinois. *Education:* University of Arizona (B.A., magna cum laude, 1997); Northwestern University (J.D., cum laude, 2000). Law Clerk to Judge Robert W. Gettleman, Northern District of Illinois, 2000-2002. Co-Author, with Steven Lubet: "Mock Trials: Preparing, Presenting and Winning Your Case," National Institute for Trial Advocacy, 2001. Adjunct Professor, Trial Advocacy, Northwestern University School of Law. ***PRACTICE AREAS:*** Litigation (100%). ***Email:*** jill.trumbull-harris@bartlit-beck.com

OF COUNSEL

MARY SZEWS MOORE, born Madison, Wisconsin, December 8, 1962; admitted to bar, 1988, Illinois; 1989, U.S. District Court, Northern District of Illinois; registered to practice before U.S. Patent and Trademark Office. *Education:* Marquette University (B.S.E.E., magna cum laude, 1985); Stanford University (J.D., 1988). Tau Beta Pi; Eta Kappa Nu. Notes Editor, Stanford Law Review, 1987-1988. ***PRACTICE AREAS:*** Intellectual Property Litigation; Commercial Litigation. ***Email:*** mary.moore@bartlit-beck.com

REPRESENTATIVE CLIENTS: Hewlett-Packard Company; Micron Technologies; Bayer A.G.; Ernst & Young; Verizon Wireless; Department of Justice, Government of Canada; BISSELL, Inc.; Forstmann Little & Co.; Brunswick Corporation; RealNetworks, Inc.; E.I. du Pont de Nemours & Company; United Technologies Corporation; Infineon Technologies AG; Morgan Stanley Dean Witter Co.; ABB, Inc; NL Industries; 3M Company; QUALCOMM, Inc.; Arthur Andersen & Co.; Tyco International Ltd.; Navistar International Corporation; University of Chicago; Deloitte & Touche USA LLP; NICOR Inc.

DANIEL L. BASKES

300 WEST ADAMS STREET, SUITE 529
CHICAGO, ILLINOIS 60606
Telephone: 312-236-2696
Fax: 312-236-2699
Email: dbaskes@yahoo.com
URL: http://www.lawyers.com/dbaskes

Real Estate, Commercial Real Estate, Residential Real Estate, Condominium Law, Commercial Leasing.

DANIEL L. BASKES, born Chicago, Illinois, July 16, 1965; admitted to bar, 1990, Illinois. *Education:* Grinnell College (B.A., History, 1987); University of Illinois (J.D., 1990). Associate: Rosenberg & Liebentritt, P.C., Chicago, Illinois, 1990-1997; Katten, Muchin & Zavis, Chicago, Illinois, 1997-1998. *Member:* Chicago and American Bar Associations. ***PRACTICE AREAS:*** Real Estate.

BEAULIEU LAW OFFICES

Established in 1980
5339 WEST BELMONT
CHICAGO, ILLINOIS 60641
Telephone: 773-545-9339
Fax: 773-545-8819
URL: http://www.beaulieulawfirm.com

Real Property Law, Commercial Litigation, Personal Injury.

MEMBER OF FIRM

ROBERT NEIL BEAULIEU, born Chicago, Illinois, 1951; admitted to bar, 1978, Illinois; 1983, Florida. *Education:* DePaul University (B.A., 1973); John Marshall Law School (J.D., 1978). ***PRACTICE AREAS:*** Corporate Law (10%); Real Property Law (50%); Probate Law (15%); Litigation.

ASSOCIATE

ELAINE A. LLERENA, born Miami, Florida, 1975; admitted to bar, 2003, Illinois. *Education:* Florida State University (B.S., Criminology and English, 1997); John Marshall Law School (J.D., 2002). ***PRACTICE AREAS:*** Real Estate.

OF COUNSEL

RORY D. CASSIDY, born Oneida, New York, September 24, 1950; admitted to bar, 1978, Illinois and U.S. District Court, Northern and Central Districts of Illinois. *Education:* Villanova University (B.A., 1972); John Marshall Law School (J.D., 1978). ***PRACTICE AREAS:*** General Insurance Defense; Commercial Transactions; RICO; Business Consumer Fraud Defense; AIDS/Blood Transfusion Defense; Environmental/Soil Remediation Litigation; Lanham Act Litigation; Mechanics Liens; Probate.

Languages: English, Spanish.

REPRESENTATIVE CLIENTS: LaSalle Bank; Standard Federal Bank; Heritage Title Company; Century 21 Beaulieu; First Guaranty Mortgage Corp.; American Pioneer Title Insurance Company; Sheridan Road Property Corp.

BEEM PATENT LAW FIRM

53 WEST JACKSON BOULEVARD, SUITE 1352
CHICAGO, ILLINOIS 60604-3787
Telephone: 312-201-0011
Fax: 312-201-0022
Email: patents@beemlaw.com
URL: http://www.beemlaw.com

Patents, Patent Law, Opinions, Litigation, Appellate Practice, Intellectual Property.

FIRM PROFILE: Acting on instructions and referrals in patent applications, prosecution, opinions and litigation.

(This Listing Continued)

RICHARD P. BEEM, born Chicago, Illinois; admitted to bar, 1985, Texas; 1986, District of Columbia; 1987, Illinois; U.S. District Court, Northern District of Illinois including Trial Bar; U.S. Court of Appeals, Federal and Seventh Circuits; U.S. Supreme Court; registered to practice before U.S. Patent and Trademark Office. *Education:* Iowa State University (B.S. Ch.E., 1979); University of Houston (J.D., cum laude, 1985). Order of the Coif. Editor, Houston Law Review, 1984-1985. Law Clerk to Hon. Edward S. Smith, Circuit Judge, U.S. Court of Appeals for the Federal Circuit, 1985-1987. *Member:* Chicago (Chair: Patents, Trademarks and Copyrights Committee, 1997-1998) and American (Co-chair, IPL Committee on Amicus Curiae Briefs, 2002-2004; Co-chair, IPL Alternative Dispute Resolution Committee, 2004—) Bar Associations; Intellectual Property Law Association of Chicago (Secretary, 1992-1994). ***SPECIAL AGENCIES:*** U.S. Patent and Trademark Office. ***PRACTICE AREAS:*** Patents; Patent Law; Patent Applications; Patent Prosecution; Patent Litigation; Intellectual Property. ***Email:*** Richard@beemlaw.com

ROGER J. FRENCH, born Oak Park, Illinois; admitted to bar, 1974, Illinois; registered to practice before U.S. Patent and Trademark Office. *Education:* Northwestern University (B.S.E.E., 1969); John Marshall Law School (J.D., with honors, 1974). *Member:* Chicago, Illinois State and American Bar Associations; American Intellectual Property Law Association; Intellectual Property Law Association of Chicago. ***SPECIAL AGENCIES:*** U.S. Patent and Trademark Office. ***PRACTICE AREAS:*** Intellectual Property; Patent; Patent Applications; Patent Prosecution. ***Email:*** rfrench@beemlaw.com

---

MICHAEL T. GRIGGS, born Milwaukee, Wisconsin; admitted to bar, 2003, Illinois, U.S. District Court, Northern District of Illinois, U.S. District Court, Western District of Wisconsin; registered to practice before U.S. Patent and Trademark Office. *Education:* University of Notre Dame (B.S., Mechanical Engineering, 2000); University of Wisconsin School of Law (J.D., 2003). ***SPECIAL AGENCIES:*** U.S. Patent and Trademark Office. ***PRACTICE AREAS:*** Intellectual Property; Patents; Patent Litigation. ***Email:*** mgriggs@beemlaw.com

GRACE I. LIU, born Taichung, Taiwan; admitted to bar, 2004, Illinois. *Education:* Harvard University (A.B., Molecular/Cellular Biology, cum laude, 2000); University of Chicago School of Law (J.D., 2004). *Member:* Chicago Bar Association (Chair, Intellectual Property Committee, 2005—); American Intellectual Property Law Association. ***LANGUAGES:*** Chinese (Mandarin). ***PRACTICE AREAS:*** Intellectual Property; Patents; Patent Applications. ***Email:*** gliu@beemlaw.com

---

BEERMANN SWERDLOVE WOLOSHIN BAREZKY BECKER GENIN & LONDON

Established in 1958

161 NORTH CLARK STREET, SUITE 2600
CHICAGO, ILLINOIS 60601-3221
Telephone: 312-621-9700
Telefax: 312-621-0909
Email: info@beermannlaw.com
URL: http://www.beermannlaw.com

Highland Park, Illinois Office: 1700 Greenbay Road, 60035.

Commercial, Insurance and Banking Litigation. Family (Divorce; Adoption), General Civil Trial and Appellate, Corporate, Real Estate and Condominium, Estate Planning and Probate, Personal Injury, Negligence, Plaintiff's Trial Law, Tort, Insurance, Business, Products Liability, and Business Organization and Transactions.

FIRM PROFILE: Founded in 1958, the firm of Beermann Swerdlove Woloshin Barezky Becker Genin & London, currently has 26 attorneys with many years of experience and expertise in a variety of fields of law. They are divided into departments which cover a wide range of legal services. Our clients range from individuals and small businesses to large corporations, insurance companies, banks and real estate concerns. The firm has over 220 reported Appellate and Supreme Court decisions.

MEMBERS OF FIRM

LAWRENCE R. BAREZKY, born Chicago, Illinois; admitted to bar, 1963, Illinois. *Education:* Roosevelt University (B.S.B.A., 1959); Northwestern University (J.D., 1962). Member of Panel, American Arbitration Association. *Member:* Chicago (Member, Sections on: Insurance Law; Civil Practice; Negligence Law), Illinois State and American Bar Associations; Illinois Trial Lawyers Association; The Association of Trial Lawyers of America. ***PRACTICE AREAS:*** Negligence Law; Plaintiff's Trial Practice; Tort Law.

ALVIN R. BECKER, born Chicago, Illinois; admitted to bar, 1962, Illinois; 1970, U.S. Supreme Court. *Education:* Roosevelt University (B.A., 1959); DePaul University (J.D., 1962). Instructor, John Marshall Law School, 1971-1973. Co-author, "Stays of Enforcement of Judgments or Orders Appealed From," IICLE and Appellate Lawyers Association Civil Appeals Handbook, 1984 Edition. Certificates of Insurance and Additional Insureds, 2002. Member, Chairman, Circuit Court Rules Committee, 1974-1979; 1983-1984. ***PRACTICE AREAS:*** Litigation; Appellate Practice; Insurance Law; Business Litigation.

MILES N. BEERMANN, born Chicago, Illinois; admitted to bar, 1958, Illinois; 1971, U.S. Supreme Court. *Education:* University of Illinois; DePaul University (J.D., 1958). Nu Beta Epsilon. Adjunct Professor of Law, DePaul University College of Law. Editor-in-Chief, Illinois Journal of Family Law, Mason Publishing Company, 1984-1986. Recipient of the Samuel S. Berger Award from the Illinois Chapter of the American Academy of Matrimonial Lawyers, 2002. Author: "Winning an Appeal, A How-to Guide for the Family Law Practitioner," Family Advocate Journal of the ABA Family Law Section, Summer 1980, Vol. 3, No. 1; "Grounds for the Dismissal of an Appeal," Appellate Practice Handbook, 1981 and 1982 Editions, Appellate Lawyers Association. Co-Author: "Stays of Enforcement of Judgments or Orders Appealed From," IICLE and Appellate Lawyers Association Civil Appeal Handbook, 1984, 1987 and 1989 Editions; "Rehabilitative Maintenance in Illinois," Illinois Bar Journal, August 1987, Vol. 75, No. 12. Lecturer for numerous organizations: Illinois Trial Lawyers Association; IICLE; Chicago Bar Association; American Academy of Matrimonial Lawyers; Appellate Lawyers Association; Northwest Suburban Bar Association; DuPage County Bar Association; Illinois State Bar Association; Lawyers Shrine Club; Annual Conference of Family and Conciliation Courts. Member of Faculty: Mental Health Evaluation of the Family in a Child Custody Dispute, Division of Forensic Psychiatry, Northwestern University Medical School, 1995; Psychiatry and Law, Northwestern School of Law, 1995; College of Advocacy, Illinois Trial Lawyers Association, Illinois Wesleyan University, Bloomington, Illinois and Northwestern University, Chicago, 1982-1990. Member, Board of Directors, IICLE, 1984-1986. *Member:* Chicago (Member: Board of Managers, 1984-1986; Committee on Evaluation of Candidates, 1977-1980; Chairman, Civil Practice Committee, 1979-1980; Member, 1980—; Secretary, 1984-1986, Vice Chairman, 1986-1987; Chairman, 1987-1988, Matrimonial Law Committee; Member, Nominating Committee, 1982; Co-Chairman, Supreme and Appellate Court Rules Sub-Committee of Matrimonial Law Committee, 1982-1984; Chairman, Division III, Legislative Committee, 1983-1984; Member, Matrimonial Law Committee, 1984—; Standing Committee on Litigation, 1984-1990) and Illinois State Bar Associations; Illinois Trial Lawyers Association (Vice Chairman, Family Law Committee, 1980-1981; Chairman, Amicus Curiae Committee, 1980-1983; Member, Legislative Committee, 1980-1983; Board of Directors, 1983-1985, 1989-1992; Treasurer, 1986; Secretary, 1987; Parliamentarian, 1988); The Association of Trial Lawyers of America; Appellate Lawyers Association (Member, Board of Directors, 1977-1980; Treasurer, 1980-1981; Secretary, 1981-1982; Vice President, 1982-1983; President, 1983-1984); American Board of Trial Advocates. Fellow: American Academy of Matrimonial Lawyers (Member, Board of Governors, Illinois Chapter, 1984-1991). ***REPORTED CASES:*** Trimble vs. Gordon U.S. S. Ct. 430 US 762, 52 L.Ed 2d 31, 97 SCT 1459; 65 Reported Appellate and Supreme Court Decisions. ***PRACTICE AREAS:*** Trial and Appeal of Matrimonial Law Cases. ***Email:*** mnbeermann@beermannlaw.com

LYLE S. GENIN, born Chicago, Illinois; admitted to bar, 1972, Illinois; 1977, U.S. Supreme Court and U.S. Tax Court. *Education:* University of Illinois (B.S., 1967); Illinois Institute of Technology/Chicago-Kent College of Law (J.D., 1972). Outside Counsel, ISMIE Mutual Insurance Co., 1982—. *Member:* Chicago (Real Property Committee, 1980; Probate Practice Committee, 1980; Chairman, 1988-1989), Illinois State and American Bar Associations. ***PRACTICE AREAS:*** Business Law; Employment Law; Estate Administration. ***Email:*** lgenin@beermannlaw.com

PAMELA J. HUTUL, born Chicago, Illinois; admitted to bar, 1975, Illinois. *Education:* Lake Forest College (B.A., 1970); John Marshall Law School (J.D., 1975); Northwestern University (M.A., 1990; Ph.D., A.B.D., 1991). ***PRACTICE AREAS:*** Family Law. ***Email:*** pjhutul@beermannlaw.com

HERBERT A. KESSEL, born Chicago, Illinois; admitted to bar, 1968, Illinois and U.S. District Court, Northern District of Illinois. *Education:* University of Illinois (A.B., with honors, 1964); Northwestern University (J.D., 1967). ***PRACTICE AREAS:*** Real Estate (Property) Law; Real Estate Development Law; Condominium Law and Practice.

HOWARD A. LONDON, born Chicago, Illinois; admitted to bar, 1978, Illinois; 1979, U.S. Court of Appeals, 7th Circuit; 1983, Arizona; 1984, U.S. District Court, Northern District of Illinois including Trial Bar. *Education:* Northwestern University (B.A., 1975); George Washington University (J.D., 1978). Adjunct Professor of Law, John Marshall Law School, 1984-1986. Author and Lecturer: American, Illinois State and Chicago Bar Associations; Illinois Institute for Continuing Legal Education. Selected, Leading Lawyers Network, Family Law. Reported Appellate Decisions: 79. *Member:* Chicago (Co-Chairman, Supreme Court Rules Committee of Matrimonial Law Section, 1985; Chairman, 1986-1987; Vice Chairman, 1988-1989; Member, Liaison Committee to the Circuit Court of Cook County, 1987-1988), Illinois State (Member, Family Law Section Council, 1996-1998) and American Bar Associations; State Bar of Arizona; Appellate Lawyers Association of Illinois (Member, Board of Directors, 1983-1985; Secretary, 1988-1989; Vice President, 1989-1990; President, 1990-1991). ***PRACTICE AREAS:*** Civil Trial and Appeals; Commercial Law; Matrimonial Law. ***Email:*** halondon@beermannlaw.com

WILLIAM WOLOSHIN, born Chicago, Illinois; admitted to bar, 1959, Illinois; 1960, U.S. District Court, Northern District of Illinois; 1977, U.S. Supreme Court. *Education:* Roosevelt University; DePaul University (J.D., 1959). Nu Beta Epsilon. *Member:* Chicago (Member: Real Property Committee, 1977—; Condominium Sub-Committee, 1978—; Contracts Subcommittee, 1986—) and Illinois State Bar Associations; Decalogue Society of Lawyers; Illinois Lawyers Real Estate Association. ***PRACTICE AREAS:*** Business Law; Real Estate Law; Estate Planning Law.

DEANE B. BROWN, born Elizabeth, New Jersey; admitted to bar, 1990, Illinois; 1991, U.S. District Court, Northern District of Illinois. *Education:* Johns Hopkins University (B.A., 1986); University of Cambridge, England (M.Phil., 1987); Boston University (J.D., 1990). Author: "From Office Sharing to Letterhead: The Ethics of Holding Yourself Out to the Public," 89 Illinois Bar Journal 369, July 2001. *Member:* Illinois State Bar Association (Member and Officer, Standing Committee on Professional Conduct, 2000—). ***PRACTICE AREAS:*** Commercial Litigation; Professional Responsibility. ***Email:*** dbrown@beermannlaw.com

HOWARD C. EMMERMAN, born Chicago, Illinois; admitted to bar, 1970, Illinois and U.S. District Court, Northern District of Illinois (Trial Bar); 1974, U.S. Tax Court; 1993, U.S. Court of Appeals, Seventh Circuit. *Education:* University of Illinois (B.S., 1967); DePaul University (J.D., 1970). Phi Alpha Delta. Member, Board of Editors, DePaul Law Review, 1968-1970. Certificate of Professional Achievement in Mediation, DePaul University Dispute Resolution Center (June, 2000). Court Appointed Trustee, Illinois Rollback Tax Fund, 1983-1986. ***PRACTICE AREAS:*** Commercial Litigation; Trial Practice; Business Organization; Intellectual Property; Construction Law; Executive Compensation. ***Email:*** hemmerman@beermannlaw.com

ROGER A. RUBIN, born Chicago, Illinois; admitted to bar, 1971, Illinois. *Education:* Indiana University (B.A., 1967); University of Illinois (J.D., 1971). *Member:* Illinois State and American Bar Associations. [With U.S.M.C., Reserve, 1969-1975]. ***PRACTICE AREAS:*** Family Law; Litigation. ***Email:*** rrubin@beermannlaw.com

JAMES M. QUIGLEY, born Green Bay, Wisconsin, October 30, 1966; admitted to bar, 1992, Illinois. *Education:* University of Wisconsin-Madison (B.A., 1989); DePaul University (J.D., 1992). (Also with Law Offices of Quigley & Associates, P.C.). ***PRACTICE AREAS:*** Family Law.

(This Listing Continued)

BEERMANN SWERDLOVE WOLOSHIN BAREZKY BECKER GENIN & LONDON, Chicago—Continued

ASSOCIATES

JULIE P. BRETT, born Fort Bragg, North Carolina; admitted to bar, 1987, Illinois, U.S. District Court, Northern District of Illinois and Supreme Judicial Court of Massachusetts. *Education:* Tufts University (B.A., cum laude, 1984); State University of New York at Buffalo (J.D., 1987). *Member:* Chicago Bar Association. ***PRACTICE AREAS:*** Family Law. ***Email:*** jpbrett@beermannlaw.com

MARIBETH OLENSKI, born Chicago, Illinois; admitted to bar, 1986, Illinois and U.S. District Court, Northern District of Illinois. *Education:* Loyola University (B.A., 1977); John Marshall Law School (J.D., 1985). *Member:* Illinois State Bar Association; Illinois Trial Lawyers Association. ***PRACTICE AREAS:*** Negligence Law; Plaintiff's Trial Practice; Tort Law.

JACQUELINE J. TORSHEN, born Chicago, Illinois; admitted to bar, 1998, Illinois and U.S. District Court, Northern District of Illinois. *Education:* University of Pennsylvania (B.A., cum laude, 1995); Chicago-Kent College of Law (J.D., 1998). *Member:* Chicago and Illinois State Bar Associations. ***LANGUAGES:*** French. ***PRACTICE AREAS:*** Family Law. ***Email:*** jjtorshen@beermannlaw.com

KATHERINE A. GROSH, born Chicago, Illinois; admitted to bar, 2002, Illinois and U.S. District Court, Northern District of Illinois. *Education:* University of Michigan (B.A., with honors, 1999); University of Illinois (J.D., 2002). *Member:* Chicago and Illinois State Bar Associations. ***PRACTICE AREAS:*** Commercial Litigation; Civil Litigation; Appellate Practice; Family Law. ***Email:*** kagrosh@beermannlaw.com

MARTIN W. BURZAWA, born Gdynia, Poland; admitted to bar, 2002, Illinois. *Education:* Loyola University (B.A., 1998); Chicago-Kent College of Law (J.D., 2002). ***LANGUAGES:*** Polish. ***PRACTICE AREAS:*** Personal Injury. ***Email:*** mwburzawa@beermannlaw.com

WILLIAM A. ZOLLA, II, born Chicago, Illinois; admitted to bar, 1997, New York; 2001, Illinois; 2002, U.S. Court of Appeals, Seventh Circuit. *Education:* University of Michigan (A.B., with distinction, 1990); Boston University (J.D., 1995). *Member:* Chicago Bar Association (Committee on Constitutional Law; Chair, Editorial Board, CBA Record, 2003-2004). ***PRACTICE AREAS:*** Litigation; Appellate Practice. ***Email:*** wazolla@beermannlaw.com

BRADLEY T. CHESKES, admitted to bar, 1995, Illinois and U.S. District Court, Northern District of Illinois. *Education:* University of Kansas (B.A., 1991); John Marshall Law School (J.D., 1995). *Member:* Chicago and Illinois State Bar Associations. ***PRACTICE AREAS:*** Plaintiffs Personal Injury.

STEFANIA PIALIS, born Toronto, Ontario, Canada; admitted to bar, 1996, Illinois. *Education:* University of Toronto (B.A., 1992); Michigan State University Detroit College of Law (J.D., cum laude, 1996). *Member:* Chicago, Illinois State and American Bar Associations. ***PRACTICE AREAS:*** Litigation; Insurance Coverage. ***Email:*** spialis@beermannlaw.com

CHARLES PHILLIPS, born Evanston, Illinois, May 26, 1979; admitted to bar, 2004, Illinois. *Education:* Miami University (B.S.A., 2001); Emory University (J.D., 2004). ***PRACTICE AREAS:*** Family Law. ***Email:*** cphillips@beermannlaw.com

RHONDA E. DEFREITAS, born Toronto, Ontario, Canada, February 17, 1963; admitted to bar, 1994, Illinois. *Education:* Florida International University (B.A., 1987); Loyola University, Chicago (J.D., 1993). Formerly with Jenner & Block, 1993-1995. ***PRACTICE AREAS:*** Family Law.

SHANA L. VITEK, born Crystal Lake, Illinois, October 25, 1979; admitted to bar, 2003, Illinois and U.S. District Court, Northern District of Illinois. *Education:* Western Illinois University (B.S., 2000); John Marshall Law School (J.D., 2003). *Member:* Chicago, Illinois State and American Bar Associations. ***PRACTICE AREAS:*** Family Law.

KATARINNA McBRIDE, admitted to bar, 2000, North Carolina; 2002, District of Columbia; 2005, Illinois; registered to practice before U.S. Patent and Trademark Office. *Education:* Wilkes University (B.A., magna cum laude, 1990); University of Dayton (J.D., magna cum laude, 1998). ***LANGUAGES:*** Russian. ***PRACTICE AREAS:*** Estate Planning; Estate Administration; Business Successions. ***Email:*** kmcbride@beermannlaw.com

TANYA L. AKINS, born Freeport, Illinois, June 18, 1970; admitted to bar, 2005, Illinois. *Education:* Northern Illinois University (B.S., 1992); University of Illinois, Chicago (M.S.W., 1996); DePaul University (J.D., 2004). ***PRACTICE AREAS:*** Family Law (100%). ***Email:*** tlakins@beermannlaw.com

OF COUNSEL

NATHAN B. SWERDLOVE, admitted to bar, 1958, Illinois; 1971, U.S. Supreme Court. *Education:* University of Illinois; DePaul University (LL.B., 1958). *Member:* Chicago (Member: Matrimonial Law Committee, 1970—; Continuing Legal Education Committee, 1979; Legislation Sub-Committee, 1979; Federal Tax Sub-Committee, 1980—; Supreme and Appellate Rules Sub-Committee, 1980—) and Illinois State (Lecturer, Matrimonial Workshop, 1972) Bar Associations. ***PRACTICE AREAS:*** Family Law. ***Email:*** nbswerdlove@beermannlaw.com

REPRESENTATIVE CLIENTS: American Country Insurance Co.; American Service Insurance Co.; Babco Construction Co.; Bisco, Inc.; CECO Concrete Construction, LLC; Douglas Press, Inc.; EMC Distribution Corporation; Empeco, Inc.; Groundwork, Ltd.; H & S Realty, LLC; Illinois State Medical Society; Infotrac, Inc.; ISMIE Mutual Insurance Co.; National Diamond Syndicate, Ltd.; Purity Wholesale Grocers, Inc.; Safeway Insurance Co.; Top Shelf Distributors, L.L.C.; Universal Casualty Company.

BELGRADE AND O'DONNELL

A PROFESSIONAL CORPORATION

20 NORTH WACKER DRIVE, SUITE 1900
CHICAGO, ILLINOIS 60606
Telephone: 312-422-1700
Facsimile: 312-422-1717
URL: http://www.belgradeodonnell.com
URL: http://www.bodpc.com
URL: http://www.belgradeodonnelllaw.com

Civil Trial and Appellate Practice. Tort and Commercial Law including General Negligence, Admiralty, Transportation, Insurance Defense, Insurance Coverage, Construction Injuries, Products Liability, Professional Malpractice and Environmental Insurance Litigation.

STEVEN B. BELGRADE, born Chicago, Illinois, August 4, 1950; admitted to bar, 1975, Illinois; 1999, Indiana; U.S. District Court, Northern and Central Districts of Illinois including Trial Bar; U.S. District Court, Northern and Southern Districts of Indiana; U.S. District Court, Eastern District of Wisconsin; U.S. District Court, Western District of Michigan; U.S. District Court, Eastern District of Missouri; U.S. Court of Appeals, Sixth, Seventh and Eighth District of Columbia Circuits; U.S. Supreme Court. *Education:* Loyola University of Chicago (B.A., 1972); Loyola University of Chicago School of Law (J.D., 1975). Author, "Litigating Riverboat Casino-Related Injuries in Illinois," Illinois Bar Journal, May, 1996. Law Instructor, Admiralty Law, Loyola University of Chicago, 1977-1994. Speaker: Illinois Bar Association Annual Meeting, Tort Law Seminar, 1995; Transportation Lawyers Association Annual Meeting; Transportation Law Update, 1994, 1996 and 1999; Greater New Orleans Barge Fleeting Association, River and Marine Industry Seminar, Maritime Law, 1996. *Member:* Chicago (Chairman, Admiralty and Maritime Law Committee, 1981-1982), Seventh Circuit, Illinois State (Chairman, Section on Admiralty and Maritime Law, 1985-1987 and 1992-1993; Editor of Admiralty Section Newsletter, 1983-1993), Indiana State, Federal and American Bar Associations; American Board of Trial Advocates; Maritime Law Association of the United States (Proctor in Admiralty); Transportation Lawyers Association, (Executive Committee, 1995-1997); Propeller Club of the United States (Port of Chicago President, 1993-1994); American Institute of Marine Underwriters; Chicago Ocean Marine Association. ***PRACTICE AREAS:*** Admiralty and Maritime Law; Insurance Coverage; Insurance Defense; Transportation Law. ***Email:*** sbelgrade@bodpc.com

JOHN A. O'DONNELL, born Chicago, Illinois, March 5, 1956; admitted to bar, 1981, Illinois; 1999, Indiana and U.S. District Court, Northern and Southern Districts of Indiana; U.S. District Court, Northern and Central Districts of Illinois including Trial Bar; U.S. District Court Western District of Michigan; U.S. District Court, Eastern District of Missouri; U.S. Court of Appeals, Sixth and Seventh Circuits. *Education:* St. John's University (B.A., 1978); Loyola University (J.D., 1981). Assistant State's Attorney, Cook County State's Attorney's Office, Chicago, Illinois, 1981-1986. Speaker: "Defense of Automobile Cases," Illinois Bar Association Continuing Legal Education, 1996 and Transportation Lawyers Association Annual Meeting. Transportation Law Update, 2000 and Transportation Lawyers Association Regional Meeting Regarding Trucking Litigation Law. *Member:* Chicago, Illinois State (Chairman, Section on Admiralty and Maritime Law, 1996-1997) and Indiana State Bar Associations; Maritime Law Association of the United States; Propeller Club of the United States (President, Port of Chicago, 1995-1997) American Institute of Marine Underwriters. ***PRACTICE AREAS:*** Admiralty and Maritime Law; Construction Injuries; Professional Malpractice Law; Insurance Defense. ***Email:*** jodonnell@bodpc.com

GEORGE M. VELCICH, born Chicago, Illinois, May 11, 1955; admitted to bar, 1980, Illinois; U.S. District Court, Northern and Central Districts of Illinois including Trial Bar; U.S. Court of Appeals, Sixth and Seventh Circuits. *Education:* University of Notre Dame (B.A., 1977); Loyola University of Chicago (J.D., 1980). Faculty Member, National College of District Attorneys, Houston, Texas, 1987. Instructor, Certified Trial Practice Instructor, National Institute for Trial Advocacy, Cambridge, Massachusetts, 1989. Adjunct Professor of Law, Trial Advocacy, John Marshall Law School, Chicago, 1991—. Trial Practice Instructor, Dupage County State's Attorney's Office, Wheaton, Illinois, 1988. Assistant State's Attorney, Cook County State's Attorney's Office, Chicago, Illinois, 1981-1991. Chairman, License Appeals Commission, City of Chicago, 1996-1998. Member, Chicago Police Board, 1998—. *Member:* Chicago Bar Association. ***PRACTICE AREAS:*** General Negligence; Construction Injuries; Admiralty and Maritime Law; Insurance Coverage. ***Email:*** gvelcich@bodpc.com

PATRICK J. CULLINAN, born Chicago, Illinois, July 22, 1959; admitted to bar, 1986, Illinois; 2001, Indiana; 1987, U.S. District Court, Northern District of Illinois including Trial Bar; 1993, U.S. Court of Appeals, Seventh Circuit; 1998, U.S. District Court, Southern District of Illinois; U.S. District Court, Northern and Southern Districts of Indiana. *Education:* Loyola University of Chicago (B.A., 1981); John Marshall Law School (J.D., 1986). *Member:* Chicago Bar Association. ***PRACTICE AREAS:*** Negligence; Construction Liability; Admiralty and Maritime Law. ***Email:*** pcullinan@bodpc.com

---

RICHARD P. GIRZADAS, born Oak Lawn, Illinois, October 17, 1965; admitted to bar, 1997, Illinois; 2001, Indiana; 1999, U.S. District Court, Northern District of Illinois; U.S. District Court, Northern and Southern Districts of Indiana. *Education:* George Washington University (B.A., 1987); John Marshall Law School (J.D., 1997); Tulane University (LL.M., Admiralty, 1998). ***PRACTICE AREAS:*** Admiralty Law; Maritime Law; Transportation Law; Insurance Defense. ***Email:*** rgirzadas@bodpc.com

JAMES SARANTEAS, born 1969; admitted to bar, 1999, Illinois, U.S. District Court, Northern District of Illinois and U.S. Court of Appeals, Seventh Circuit. *Education:* Knox College (B.A., 1991); Loyola University (J.D., 1999). ***Email:*** jsaranteas@bodpc.com

BRIAN A. CORBY, born Mexico City, Mexico, December 6, 1976; admitted to bar, 2003, Illinois. *Education:* Boston College, Chestnut Hill (B.S., 1999); Loyola University (J.D., 2003). ***PRACTICE AREAS:*** Commercial Litigation; Insurance Defense; Admiralty Law. ***Email:*** bcorby@bodpc.com

(This Listing Continued)

JOHN C. COYNE, born March 16, 1966; admitted to bar, 1998, Illinois; 2001, Ohio; U.S. District Court, Northern District of Ohio, U.S. District Court, Northern District of Indiana. *Education:* John Carroll University (B.A., 1988), Cleveland State University (M.A., 1991); Cleveland Marshall College of Law (J.D., 1997). Member, National Moot Court Team, 1996. Assistant State's Attorney, Criminal Division, Cook County State's Attorney's Office, 1998-2001.

KATHRYN RIVES BAND, born October 7, 1965; admitted to bar, 2004, Illinois; 2005, U.S. District Court Northern District of Illinois and U.S. Court of Appeals, Seventh Circuit. *Education:* University of Illinois (B.A., 1990); John Marshal Law School (J.D., 2004). *Member:* Chicago and Illinois Bar Associations. ***Email:*** krbriand@bodpc.com

BELL, BOYD & LLOYD LLC

Established in 1888

70 WEST MADISON STREET
SUITE 3100
CHICAGO, ILLINOIS 60602
Telephone: 312-372-1121
FAX: 312-827-8000
Email: attorneys@bellboyd.com
URL: http://www.bellboyd.com

Washington, D.C. Office: Bell Boyd & Lloyd, PLLC, 1615 L Street, N.W., Suite 1200. Telephone: 202-466-6300. Fax: 202-463-0678.

General Practice, Corporate and Securities Law; Litigation; Antitrust; Trade Regulation; Intellectual Property; Labor and Employment Law; Employee Benefits; Environmental Law; Real Estate; Healthcare Law; Food, Drug and Device Law; Business Taxation; Personal Tax and Estate Planning; Banking and Financial Services; Insurance Law; Bankruptcy and Business Reorganization; Investment Management and Financial Markets; Communications Law; Government Contracts, Construction Law.

MEMBERS OF FIRM

JEFFREY B. AARONSON, born November 17, 1957; admitted to bar, 1984, Illinois. *Education:* Washington University (A.B., 1979); University of Illinois (J.D., cum laude, 1983). ***PRACTICE AREAS:*** Litigation; Antitrust; White Collar Criminal Defense; Health Care. ***Email:*** attorneys@bellboyd.com

MICHAEL J. ABERNATHY, born August 7, 1956; admitted to bar, 1982, Illinois, U.S. District Court, Northern District of Illinois and U.S. District Court, Eastern District of Wisconsin; U.S. Court of Appeals, First, Second, Third, Fourth, Fifth, Seventh, Ninth and Eleventh Circuits; U.S. Supreme Court. *Education:* Illinois Benedictine College (B.A., magna cum laude, 1979); DePaul University (J.D., with honors, 1982). ***PRACTICE AREAS:*** Commercial Litigation; Intellectual Property Litigation; Antitrust. ***Email:*** attorneys@bellboyd.com

GREGORY R. ANDRE, born February 16, 1960; admitted to bar, 1985, Illinois. *Education:* Boston College (B.S., magna cum laude, 1982); George Washington University (J.D., with honors, 1985). ***PRACTICE AREAS:*** Real Estate Law; Construction Law. ***Email:*** attorneys@bellboyd.com

ANDREW R. ANDREASIK, born May 28, 1966; admitted to bar, 1991, Missouri and U.S. District Court, Eastern District of Missouri; 1992, Illinois; 1994, U.S. District Court, Northern District of Illinois. *Education:* Duke University (A.B., 1988); Washington University (J.D., 1991). ***PRACTICE AREAS:*** Real Estate; Commercial Litigation; Torts. ***Email:*** attorneys@bellboyd.com

CAMERON S. AVERY, born May 9, 1938; admitted to bar, 1963, Illinois. *Education:* Princeton University (B.S.E., cum laude, 1960); Harvard Law School (J.D., 1963). ***PRACTICE AREAS:*** Corporate; Securities; Financing; Investment Companies. ***Email:*** attorneys@bellboyd.com

ROBERT M. BARRETT, born April 11, 1956; admitted to bar, 1981, Illinois; U.S. District Court, Northern District of Illinois including Trial Bar; U.S. District Court, Western District of Wisconsin; U.S. Court of Appeals, Seventh Circuit; 1982, U.S. Court of Appeals for the Federal Circuit; registered to practice before U.S. Patent and Trademark Office. *Education:* University of Oklahoma (B.S., 1977; J.D., with honors, 1981). ***PRACTICE AREAS:*** Intellectual Property Litigation; Patent Infringement; Patent Licensing; Patent Prosecution; Patent Protection. ***Email:*** attorneys@bellboyd.com

ALAN L. BARRY, born June 3, 1956; admitted to bar, 1981, Illinois, U.S. District Court, Northern District of Illinois, Trial Bar; 1982, U.S. Court of Appeals, 11th Circuit; 1983, U.S. Court of Appeals, Federal Circuit; 1989, U.S. Court of Appeals, 7th Circuit; 1994, U.S. Supreme Court; registered to practice before U.S. Patent and Trademark Office. *Education:* University of Illinois (B.S., 1978); IIT/Chicago-Kent College of Law (J.D., with honors, 1981). ***PRACTICE AREAS:*** Patents; Intellectual Property. ***Email:*** attorneys@bellboyd.com

PATRICK S. BELVILLE, born May 13, 1970; admitted to bar, 1995, Illinois. *Education:* Illinois State University (B.S., 1992); University of Chicago (J.D., 1995). ***PRACTICE AREAS:*** Mergers and Acquisitions; Private Equity; Corporate Reorganization; Securities. ***Email:*** attorneys@bellboyd.com

NANCY E. BERTOGLIO, born March 6, 1948; admitted to bar, 1973, Illinois. *Education:* Purdue University; Valparaiso University (B.A., 1969); Loyola School of Law (J.D., cum laude, 1973). (Chief Operating Officer). ***PRACTICE AREAS:*** Labor and Employment Law. ***Email:*** attorneys@bellboyd.com

ROBERT J. BEST, born April 15, 1950; admitted to bar, 1975, Illinois. *Education:* Northwestern University (B.A., 1972); DePaul University (J.D., 1975). ***PRACTICE AREAS:*** Real Estate; Municipal Law; Zoning Law. ***Email:*** attorneys@bellboyd.com

DONALD J. BINGLE, born April 22, 1954; admitted to bar, 1979, Illinois; 1995, Colorado. *Education:* University of Chicago (A.B., 1976; J.D., 1979). ***PRACTICE AREAS:*** Securities; Corporate Law; Franchise Law; Mergers and Acquisitions. ***Email:*** attorneys@bellboyd.com

(This Listing Continued)

JOHN H. BITNER, born February 27, 1940; admitted to bar, 1964, Illinois. *Education:* Northwestern University (B.A., 1961); Columbia University (J.D., cum laude, 1964). ***PRACTICE AREAS:*** Corporate; Securities; Mergers and Acquisitions. ***Email:*** attorneys@bellboyd.com

JOHN C. BLEW, born August 9, 1941; admitted to bar, 1966, Illinois. *Education:* Dartmouth College (A.B., summa cum laude, 1962); Harvard University (J.D., 1966). ***PRACTICE AREAS:*** Corporate; Securities; Business Law. ***Email:*** attorneys@bellboyd.com

CHRISTOPHER A. BLOOM, born May 25, 1951; admitted to bar, 1975, Indiana; 1976, Illinois and Pennsylvania. *Education:* Kenyon College (B.A., cum laude, 1973); Indiana University (J.D., 1975). ***PRACTICE AREAS:*** Corporate Law; Intellectual Property Law; Computer Law. ***Email:*** attorneys@bellboyd.com

RANDY A. BRIDGEMAN, born January 13, 1967; admitted to bar, 1992, Michigan; 1995, Illinois. *Education:* University of Notre Dame (B.A., with honors, 1989); University of Michigan (J.D., 1992). ***PRACTICE AREAS:*** Corporate Law; Securities; Mergers and Acquisitions. ***Email:*** attorneys@bellboyd.com

ROBERT RAYMOND BROWN, born February 26, 1968; admitted to bar, 1993, Illinois. *Education:* Vanderbilt University (B.A., 1990); University of Chicago (J.D., 1993). ***PRACTICE AREAS:*** Labor Law; Employment Law. ***Email:*** attorneys@bellboyd.com

WILLIAM G. BROWN, born October 30, 1942; admitted to bar, 1969, New York; 1972, Illinois. *Education:* Princeton University (B.A., 1964); Harvard University (LL.B., 1967). ***PRACTICE AREAS:*** Corporate. ***Email:*** attorneys@bellboyd.com

TERRENCE E. BUDNY, born February 14, 1950; admitted to bar, 1976, Illinois. *Education:* Boston College (A.B., summa cum laude, 1972); University of Chicago (J.D., 1976). ***PRACTICE AREAS:*** Real Estate; Creditors Rights. ***Email:*** attorneys@bellboyd.com

THOMAS R. CAREY, born June 19, 1960; admitted to bar, 1990, Illinois and U.S. District Court, Northern District of Illinois. *Education:* Oakland University (B.S., with honors, 1983); University of Michigan (M.S., 1985); IIT/Chicago-Kent College of Law (J.D., with honors, 1990). ***PRACTICE AREAS:*** Environmental Law. ***Email:*** attorneys@bellboyd.com

LISA A. CARROLL, born December 15, 1967; admitted to bar, 1998, Illinois; 2000, U.S. District Court, Northern District of Illinois. *Education:* University of Illinois (B.S., 1990); John Marshall Law School (J.D., 1998; LL.M., 2000). Executive Student Publications Editor, The John Marshall Law Review. Author: "A Better Way to Skin the Cat: Resolving Domain Name Disputes Using State Unfair Competition Law," American Bar Association, Section of Intellectual Property Law Newsletter, Winter 2000. *Member:* Chicago and American Bar Associations; Intellectual Property Law Association of Chicago. ***PRACTICE AREAS:*** Intellectual Property Litigation; Trademark Prosecution; Intellectual Property Licensing. ***Email:*** attorneys@bellboyd.com

PAWEL CHUDZICKI, born March 13, 1971; admitted to bar, 1998, Illinois. *Education:* Yale College (B.A., 1995); Loyola University Chicago (J.D., 1998). Executive Editor, Loyola University Chicago Law Journal. Author, "The European Union's Response to the Libertad Act and the Iran-Libya Act: Extraterritoriality Without Boundaries," Loyola University Chicago Law Journal, Vol. 28, No. 3, Spring 1997. Member, Chicago-Warsaw Sister Cities Committee, by appointment of Hon. Richard M. Daley, Mayor of Chicago, 2001—. ***PRACTICE AREAS:*** Corporate Finance; Securities; Mergers and Acquisitions; Aircraft Finance; International Law. ***Email:*** attorneys@bellboyd.com

JAMES W. COLLINS, born December 10, 1942; admitted to bar, 1968, Illinois; U.S. Supreme Court; U.S. District Court, Northern District of Illinois including Trial Bar; U.S. Court of Appeals, Seventh and Eighth Circuits. *Education:* Marquette University (A.B., 1964); Loyola University Chicago (J.D., 1967). ***PRACTICE AREAS:*** Commercial Litigation; Financial Services Litigation; Securities Litigation. ***Email:*** attorneys@bellboyd.com

RANDY J. CURATO, born November 5, 1958; admitted to bar, 1984, Illinois, U.S. District Court, Northern District of Illinois and U.S. Court of Appeals, Seventh Circuit. *Education:* Manhattanville College (B.A., cum laude, 1981); University of Notre Dame (J.D., cum laude, 1984). ***PRACTICE AREAS:*** Litigation; Professional Malpractice; Product Liability Defense. ***Email:*** attorneys@bellboyd.com

JAMES P. DALEY, born November 14, 1948; admitted to bar, 1974, Illinois. *Education:* DePaul University (B.S., 1971; J.D., 1974). ***PRACTICE AREAS:*** Labor and Employment Law; Litigation. ***Email:*** attorneys@bellboyd.com

LEE A. DANIELS, born April 15, 1942; admitted to bar, 1967, Illinois. *Education:* University of Iowa (B.A., 1965); John Marshall Law School (J.D., 1967). ***PRACTICE AREAS:*** Corporate Law; Health Care. ***Email:*** attorneys@bellboyd.com

JOHN S. DELNERO, born October 13, 1961; admitted to bar, 1987, Illinois. *Education:* DePaul University (B.A., 1984; J.D., 1987). ***PRACTICE AREAS:*** Bankruptcy Law; Creditors Rights Law. ***Email:*** attorneys@bellboyd.com

WILLIAM F. DOLAN, born May 9, 1957; admitted to bar, 1982, Illinois; U.S. District Court, Northern District of Illinois; U.S. District Court, Northern District of California; U.S. District Court, Southern District of New York; U.S. Court of Appeals, Seventh Circuit. *Education:* Columbia University (A.B., cum laude, 1979; J.D., 1982). ***PRACTICE AREAS:*** Antitrust Law; Copyright; Litigation. ***Email:*** attorneys@bellboyd.com

RAYMOND H. DRYMALSKI, born June 1, 1936; admitted to bar, 1962, Illinois. *Education:* Georgetown University (A.B., 1958); University of Michigan (J.D., 1961). ***PRACTICE AREAS:*** Corporate Law; Health Care. ***Email:*** attorneys@bellboyd.com

JULIETTE GREGORY DUARA, born July 26, 1960; admitted to bar, 1995, Illinois. *Education:* Whitman College (B.A., 1986); University of Chicago (J.D., 1995). ***PRACTICE AREAS:*** Trusts and Estates. ***Email:*** attorneys@bellboyd.com

STEVEN E. DUCOMMUN, born July 24, 1958; admitted to bar, 1986, Illinois and U.S. District Court, Northern District of Illinois. *Education:* Drake University (B.S.B.A., summa cum laude, 1979); The University of Chicago Law School; Cornell Law School (J.D., cum laude, 1986). ***PRACTICE AREAS:*** Corporate Law; Securities. ***Email:*** attorneys@bellboyd.com

(This Listing Continued)

BELL, BOYD & LLOYD LLC, Chicago—Continued

ERIK F. DYHRKOPP, born April 23, 1965; admitted to bar, 1990, Illinois. *Education:* University of New Orleans (B.A., with honors, 1987); Northwestern University (J.D., 1990). ***PRACTICE AREAS:*** Trade Regulation; Antitrust; Franchise Law. ***Email:*** attorneys@bellboyd.com

PAUL H. DYKSTRA, born July 13, 1943; admitted to bar, 1968, Illinois; 1977, District of Columbia. *Education:* Princeton University (A.B., 1965); Yale Law School (LL.B., 1968). ***PRACTICE AREAS:*** Corporate Law; Investments; Investment Management; Mutual Funds; Securities. ***Email:*** attorneys@bellboyd.com

LAWRENCE A. EIBEN, born June 28, 1972; admitted to bar, 1997, Illinois; 1998, U.S. District Court, Northern District of Illinois. *Education:* University of Notre Dame (B.B.A., 1994); Loyola University Chicago (J.D., 1997). *Member:* Chicago and Illinois State Bar Associations. ***PRACTICE AREAS:*** Real Estate Law. ***Email:*** attorneys@bellboyd.com

LAWRENCE C. EPPLEY, born January 2, 1960; admitted to bar, 1985, Illinois and U.S. District Court, Northern District of Illinois. *Education:* University of Illinois (B.S., 1982; M.A.S., 1982; J.D., 1985). ***PRACTICE AREAS:*** Public Finance; Real Estate. ***Email:*** attorneys@bellboyd.com

NICHOLAS J. ETTEN, born February 19, 1942; admitted to bar, 1967, Illinois and U.S. District Court, Northern District of Illinois; 1968, U.S. Court of Appeals, Seventh Circuit; 1977, U.S. Court of Military Appeals; 1980, U.S. Supreme Court. *Education:* University of Notre Dame (A.B., 1964); Loyola University (J.D., 1967). ***PRACTICE AREAS:*** Litigation; White Collar Criminal Defense; Securities Litigation. ***Email:*** attorneys@bellboyd.com

JERRY K. FELLOWS, born March 19, 1946; admitted to bar, 1971, Illinois. *Education:* University of Wisconsin (B.A., 1968); University of Minnesota (J.D., 1971). ***PRACTICE AREAS:*** Employee Benefits; Employee Relations. ***Email:*** attorneys@bellboyd.com

NICOLA FIORDALISI, born August 24, 1962; admitted to bar, 1991, Italy; 1994, Illinois and U.S. District Court, Northern District of Illinois. *Education:* University of Bologna (J.D., 1988); Loyola University Chicago (J.D., 1993). ***PRACTICE AREAS:*** International Business Law; Corporate Law (U.S. and Italian); Commercial Law (U.S. and Italian); Italian Law. ***Email:*** attorneys@bellboyd.com

SANFORD R. GAIL, born July 24, 1943; admitted to bar, 1968, Illinois and U.S. District Court, Northern District of Illinois; 1971, U.S. Tax Court; 1972, U.S. Court of Appeals, Seventh Circuit; 1973, U.S. Supreme Court; 1974, U.S. Court of Appeals for the District of Columbia Circuit; 1982, District of Columbia; 1984, Florida. *Education:* University of Illinois (B.S., 1965); DePaul University (J.D., 1968); John Marshall Law School (LL.M., 1974). ***PRACTICE AREAS:*** Corporate Law; Real Estate; Estate Planning. ***Email:*** attorneys@bellboyd.com

STANLEY J. GARBER, born December 31, 1941; admitted to bar, 1973, Illinois. *Education:* Boston University (A.B., magna cum laude, 1963); Loyola University (J.D., cum laude, 1972). ***PRACTICE AREAS:*** Labor and Employment Law; Municipal Law. ***Email:*** attorneys@bellboyd.com

LAWRENCE M. GAVIN, born December 29, 1947; admitted to bar, 1972, Illinois and U.S. District Court, Northern District of Illinois including Trial Bar; 1973, U.S. Court of Appeals, Seventh Circuit; 1978, U.S. Supreme Court. *Education:* Maryknoll College (A.B., 1969); University of Michigan (J.D., cum laude, 1972). ***PRACTICE AREAS:*** Commercial Litigation. ***Email:*** attorneys@bellboyd.com

CAROL A. GENIS, born March 9, 1963; admitted to bar, 1988, Illinois and U.S. District Court, Northern District of Illinois. *Education:* Northwestern University (B.A., 1985; J.D., 1988); Phi Beta Kappa; University of Sussex, Brighton, England; Universite de Laval, Quebec. ***PRACTICE AREAS:*** Litigation; Securities Litigation; Intellectual Property. ***Email:*** attorneys@bellboyd.com

ALAN P. GOLDBERG, born 1964; admitted to bar, 1990, New York and New Jersey; 1991, Pennsylvania; 1998, Illinois. *Education:* University of Pennsylvania (B.A., 1986); Temple University (J.D., 1989). ***PRACTICE AREAS:*** Corporate Law; Securities; Investment Company Law. ***Email:*** attorneys@bellboyd.com

GRAHAM C. GRADY, born May 2, 1957; admitted to bar, 1984, Illinois and U.S. District Court, Northern District of Illinois. *Education:* University of Illinois (B.A., 1980); Northwestern University (J.D., 1983). ***PRACTICE AREAS:*** Government Relations; Zoning and Land Use; Real Estate; Litigation. ***Email:*** attorneys@bellboyd.com

VICTOR E. GRIMM, born January 28, 1937; admitted to bar, 1961, Illinois. *Education:* Bradley University (B.S., 1958); Northwestern University (J.D., 1961). ***PRACTICE AREAS:*** Antitrust; Litigation. ***Email:*** attorneys@bellboyd.com

SANA HAKIM, born November 4, 1970; admitted to bar, 1994, Illinois. *Education:* Northwestern University (B.A., 1991); University of Tulsa (J.D., 1994). ***PRACTICE AREAS:*** Litigation; Trademark, Copyright; Intellectual Property. ***Email:*** attorneys@bellboyd.com

MERRICK D. HATCHER, born May 13, 1968; admitted to bar, 1996, Illinois. *Education:* University of Michigan (B.A., with honors, 1990; M.B.A., 1996; J.D., 1996). ***PRACTICE AREAS:*** Mergers and Acquisitions; Corporate Law; Securities; Public Finance; Investments. ***Email:*** attorneys@bellboyd.com

BONITA L. HATCHETT, born June 14, 1970; admitted to bar, 1996, New Jersey and U.S. District Court, District of New Jersey; 2000, Illinois. *Education:* University of Michigan (B.A., 1992); Rutgers University (J.D., 1996); Georgetown University (LL.M., 1997). ***PRACTICE AREAS:*** Executive Compensation; Employee Benefits. ***Email:*** attorneys@bellboyd.com

DANIEL J. HAYES, born January 5, 1972; admitted to bar, 1997, Illinois and U.S. District Court, Northern District of Illinois; 1999, U.S. Court of Appeals, Seventh Circuit. *Education:* Boston College (B.A., 1994); University of Notre Dame Law School (J.D., magna cum laude, 1997). ***PRACTICE AREAS:*** Commercial Litigation. ***Email:*** attorneys@bellboyd.com

(This Listing Continued)

MICHAEL J. HAYES, SR., born November 29, 1946; admitted to bar, 1974, Illinois and U.S. District Court, Northern District of Illinois; 1979, U.S. Court of Appeals, Seventh Circuit; 1980, U.S. Supreme Court. *Education:* Loyola University Chicago (B.A., 1968); DePaul University (J.D., cum laude, 1974). ***PRACTICE AREAS:*** Commercial Litigation; Consumer Litigation; Government; Regulatory Law; Injunctive Practice; Civil Litigation; Administrative Litigation. ***Email:*** attorneys@bellboyd.com

THOMAS Z. HAYWARD, JR., born April 21, 1940; admitted to bar, 1966, Illinois and Ohio. *Education:* Northwestern University (B.A., 1962; J.D., 1965); University of Chicago, Graduate School of Business (M.B.A., 1970). ***PRACTICE AREAS:*** Real Estate; Land Use/Zoning; Corporate Law. ***Email:*** attorneys@bellboyd.com

DAVID F. HEROY, born July 13, 1951; admitted to bar, 1976, Illinois. *Education:* University of Michigan (A.B., 1973; J.D., cum laude, 1976). ***PRACTICE AREAS:*** Bankruptcy; Creditors Rights Law; Corporate Law; Commercial Litigation. ***Email:*** attorneys@bellboyd.com

FRANCIS J. HIGGINS, born December 31, 1936; admitted to bar, 1961, Illinois. *Education:* College of the Holy Cross (A.B., magna cum laude, 1958); Harvard University (LL.B., cum laude, 1961). Fellow, American College of Trial Lawyers. ***PRACTICE AREAS:*** Complex Litigation; Securities; Professional Liability; Products Liability; Commercial Arbitration. ***Email:*** attorneys@bellboyd.com

PATRICIA S. HOFSTRA, born 1952; admitted to bar, 1978, Ohio; 1980, Illinois. *Education:* Pennsylvania State University (B.S., 1973); Ohio Northern University (J.D., 1978). ***PRACTICE AREAS:*** Health Care. ***Email:*** attorneys@bellboyd.com

THOMAS C. HOMBURGER, born 1941; admitted to bar, 1966, Illinois. *Education:* Columbia University (B.A., 1963; LL.B., cum laude, 1966). ***PRACTICE AREAS:*** Real Estate; Financing; Non-Profit Corporations. ***Email:*** attorneys@bellboyd.com

GREGORY W. HUMMEL, born February 25, 1949; admitted to bar, 1974, Illinois and U.S. District Court, Northern District of Illinois. *Education:* MacMurray College (B.A., cum laude, 1971); Northwestern University (J.D., 1974). ***PRACTICE AREAS:*** Real Estate (Property) Law; Public-Private Partnerships Law; Construction Law; Project Finance. ***Email:*** attorneys@bellboyd.com

THOMAS F. JOYCE, born November 12, 1952; admitted to bar, 1981, Illinois, U.S. Tax Court, U.S. Claims Court, U.S. Court of Appeals, Fifth, Seventh, Ninth, Tenth, Eleventh, Federal Circuits and U.S. Supreme Court. *Education:* University of Chicago (B.S., with honors, 1973); Harvard University (J.D., cum laude, 1981). ***PRACTICE AREAS:*** Federal Taxation Law. ***Email:*** attorneys@bellboyd.com

THOR W. KETZBACK, born June 6, 1970; admitted to bar, 1995, Illinois. *Education:* DePaul University (B.A., 1992; J.D., 1995); George Washington University (LL.M., 1997). ***PRACTICE AREAS:*** Environmental; Litigation. ***Email:*** attorneys@bellboyd.com

BRYAN E. KEYT, born September 30, 1966; admitted to bar, 1993, Illinois. *Education:* Colgate University (B.A., 1988); DePaul University (J.D., with honors, 1993). ***PRACTICE AREAS:*** Environmental; Litigation. ***Email:*** attorneys@bellboyd.com

MARK THOMAS KINDELIN, born November 29, 1957; admitted to bar, 1982, Ohio; 1986, Illinois. *Education:* Bowling Green State University (B.S., 1979); Case Western Reserve University (J.D., 1982). ***PRACTICE AREAS:*** Mergers and Acquisitions; Financial Institutions. ***Email:*** attorneys@bellboyd.com

STEVEN M. KOWAL, born May 2, 1949; admitted to bar, 1974, Illinois, U.S. District Court, Northern District of Illinois including Trial Bar and U.S. Court of Appeals, Seventh Circuit. *Education:* St. Procopius College (B.A., magna cum laude, 1971); Northwestern University (J.D., cum laude, 1974). ***PRACTICE AREAS:*** Federal Criminal Defense Litigation; Antitrust Practice; Trade Practice; Civil Litigation; Food and Drug Law. ***Email:*** attorneys@bellboyd.com

JEFFREY R. LADD, born April 10, 1941; admitted to bar, 1973, Illinois. *Education:* University of Vienna and Loras College (B.A., cum laude, 1963); IIT/Chicago-Kent College of Law (J.D., cum laude, 1973). ***PRACTICE AREAS:*** Public Finance; Health Care. ***Email:*** attorneys@bellboyd.com

DANIEL J. LAWLER, born February 6, 1955; admitted to bar, 1981, Illinois; 1983, U.S. District Court, Central District of Illinois; 1986, U.S. District Court, Northern District of Illinois; 1990, U.S. Court of Appeals for the Federal Circuit. *Education:* Purdue University (B.S., 1977); Southern Illinois University (J.D., 1981). ***PRACTICE AREAS:*** Litigation; Health Care. ***Email:*** attorneys@bellboyd.com

JOSH M. LEAVITT, born May 6, 1960; admitted to bar, 1985, Illinois and U.S. District Court, Northern District of Illinois. *Education:* Yale University (B.A., 1982); New York University (J.D., 1985). ***PRACTICE AREAS:*** Commercial Litigation; Design and Construction Law. ***Email:*** attorneys@bellboyd.com

JOHN F. LEMKER, JR., born August 17, 1938; admitted to bar, 1971, Illinois; U.S. District Court, Northern District of Illinois, U.S. Court of Appeals, Eighth and Ninth Circuits and U.S. Supreme Court. *Education:* Northwestern University (B.A., 1960; J.D., 1971). ***PRACTICE AREAS:*** Food and Drug Regulation. ***Email:*** attorneys@bellboyd.com

IRVING B. LEVINSON, born September 13, 1947; admitted to bar, 1974, Illinois and U.S. District Court, Northern District of Illinois. *Education:* Washington University of St. Louis (B.A., 1969); Loyola University Chicago (J.D., 1974). ***PRACTICE AREAS:*** Litigation. ***Email:*** attorneys@bellboyd.com

BRUCE E. LITHGOW, born March 26, 1967; admitted to bar, 1994, Illinois; 1995, U.S. District Court, Northern District of Illinois. *Education:* Utah State University (B.A., summa cum laude, 1991); University of Chicago (J.D., 1994). ***PRACTICE AREAS:*** Bankruptcy. ***Email:*** attorneys@bellboyd.com

CARMEN H. LONSTEIN, admitted to bar, 1988, Florida; 1994, Illinois. *Education:* Hunter College (B.A., 1984); New York University (J.D., 1987). ***PRACTICE AREAS:*** Bankruptcy; Corporate Restructuring; Creditors Rights; Mortgage Banking Law. ***Email:*** attorneys@bellboyd.com

FRANCIS X. LYONS, born Evanston, Illinois, 1962; admitted to bar, 1988, Illinois; 1989, U.S. District Court, Northern and Central Districts of Illinois; 1994, U.S. Court of Appeals for the District of Columbia Circuit. *Education:* University of Minnesota (B.A.,

(This Listing Continued)

1984); Loyola University (J.D., 1988). Regional Administrator, U.S. Environmental Protection Agency, Region V, 1999-2001. Trial Attorney, Environmental Enforcement Section, Environment and Natural Resources Division, U.S. Department of Justice, 1994-1999. Assistant Attorney General, Office of the Illinois Attorney General, General Law and Environmental Control Divisions, 1988-1994. *Member:* Chicago, Illinois State and American (Member, Section on Environmental, Natural Resources and Energy Law) Bar Associations. ***PRACTICE AREAS:*** Environmental Law; Environmental Litigation.

LAWRENCE M. MAGES, born July 30, 1943; admitted to bar, 1968, Illinois. *Education:* Dartmouth College (B.A., cum laude, 1965); Harvard University (J.D., 1968). ***PRACTICE AREAS:*** Real Estate; Corporate Law. ***Email:*** attorneys@bellboyd.com

PATRICK J. MALONEY, born August 13, 1957; admitted to bar, 1984, New York; 1994, Illinois. *Education:* University of Chicago (B.A., cum laude, 1979; J.D., cum laude, 1982). ***PRACTICE AREAS:*** Corporate Law; Securities. ***Email:*** attorneys@bellboyd.com

BRIAN E. MARTIN, born March 16, 1956; admitted to bar, 1982, Illinois. *Education:* University of Connecticut (B.A., 1978); DePaul University (J.D., 1982). ***PRACTICE AREAS:*** Litigation. ***Email:*** attorneys@bellboyd.com

MICHAEL E. MARTÍNEZ, born December 26, 1972; admitted to bar, 1997, Minnesota and U.S. District Court, District of Minnesota; 1998, Wisconsin; 2000, U.S. District Court, Eastern District of Wisconsin; 2001, Illinois and U.S. Court of Appeals, Seventh Circuit. *Education:* Purdue University (B.A., 1994); University of Wisconsin-Madison Law School (J.D., 1997). ***PRACTICE AREAS:*** Antitrust; Franchise Distribution; Litigation. ***Email:*** attorneys@bellboyd.com

ADAM H. MASIA, born March 10, 1965; admitted to bar, 1990, Illinois; registered to practice before U.S. Patent and Trademark Office. *Education:* State University of New York at Binghamton (B.S., 1987); IIT Chicago-Kent (J.D., with high honors, 1990). ***PRACTICE AREAS:*** Intellectual Property; Patents; Copyrights; Trademarks. ***Email:*** attorneys@bellboyd.com

JANE K. McCAHILL, born October 25, 1953; admitted to bar, 1978, Illinois. *Education:* Bradley University (B.S., 1975); Washington University (J.D., 1978). ***PRACTICE AREAS:*** Health Care. ***Email:*** attorneys@bellboyd.com

JOHN T. McCARTHY, born September 11, 1941; admitted to bar, 1966, Illinois. *Education:* St. Joseph's College (B.S., 1963); Northwestern University (J.D., cum laude, 1966). (Chairman). ***PRACTICE AREAS:*** Corporate Law; Securities; Mergers and Acquisitions. ***Email:*** attorneys@bellboyd.com

KEVIN J. McCARTHY, born March 26, 1966; admitted to bar, 1991, Illinois. *Education:* University of Notre Dame (B.B.A., 1988); University of Illinois (J.D., magna cum laude, 1991). ***PRACTICE AREAS:*** Banking; Corporate Law; Securities. ***Email:*** attorneys@bellboyd.com

S. PATRICK McKEY, born December 31, 1960; admitted to bar, 1989, Illinois and Wisconsin; U.S. District Court, Northern, Central and Southern Districts of Illinois, U.S. District Court, Western District of Wisconsin and U.S. District Court, Eastern District of Michigan; U.S. Supreme Court. *Education:* University of Wisconsin (B.S., 1984; J.D., 1989). ***PRACTICE AREAS:*** Litigation; Intellectual Property; International; Products Liability; Public Law; Alternative Dispute Resolution. ***Email:*** attorneys@bellboyd.com

D. MARK McMILLAN, born January 30, 1963; admitted to bar, 1989, Illinois and U.S. District Court, Northern District of Illinois. *Education:* Wheaton College (B.A., 1985); Loyola University Chicago (J.D., 1989). ***PRACTICE AREAS:*** Corporate Law; Securities. ***Email:*** attorneys@bellboyd.com

CARRIE C. McNALLY, born April 5, 1969; admitted to bar, 1995, Illinois. *Education:* Duke University (B.A., 1991); Georgetown University (J.D., 1995). ***PRACTICE AREAS:*** Corporate Law. ***Email:*** attorneys@bellboyd.com

SCOTT M. MENDEL, born August 13, 1952; admitted to bar, 1976, Illinois. *Education:* University of Wisconsin and Northwestern University (B.A., 1973); Northwestern University (J.D., magna cum laude, 1976). ***PRACTICE AREAS:*** Antitrust. ***Email:*** attorneys@bellboyd.com

PAUL T. METZGER, born May 26, 1950; admitted to bar, 1976, Illinois; 1978, U.S. Tax Court. *Education:* Harvard University (B.A., magna cum laude, 1971; J.D., cum laude, 1976). ***PRACTICE AREAS:*** Federal Taxation; Mergers and Acquisitions; Corporate Law. ***Email:*** attorneys@bellboyd.com

JOHN P. (PETE) MORRISON, born August 15, 1956; admitted to bar, 1982, Illinois; 1985, U.S. District Court, Northern District of Illinois including Trial Bar, U.S. District Court, Western District of Michigan, U.S. District Court, Eastern District of Wisconsin and U.S. Court of Appeals, Seventh and Ninth Circuits. *Education:* Yale University (B.A., cum laude, 1978); Georgetown University (J.D., cum laude, 1982). ***PRACTICE AREAS:*** Labor and Employment Law; Litigation. ***Email:*** attorneys@bellboyd.com

ROBERT M. MOYE, born October 7, 1967; admitted to bar, 1994, Illinois and U.S. District Court, Northern District of Illinois. *Education:* Brigham Young University (B.A., cum laude, 1991); Northwestern University (J.D., 1994). ***PRACTICE AREAS:*** Litigation. ***Email:*** attorneys@bellboyd.com

SANDRA K. NEWMAN, born February 10, 1964; admitted to bar, 1992, Illinois. *Education:* Northeast Missouri State University (B.A., cum laude, 1986); Syracuse University (J.D., cum laude, 1992). ***PRACTICE AREAS:*** Probate; Estate Planning. ***Email:*** attorneys@bellboyd.com

DAVID M. NOVAK, born May 2, 1948; admitted to bar, 1982, Illinois. *Education:* University of Chicago (B.A., 1970; M.A., 1972; Ph.D., 1976; J.D., 1982). ***PRACTICE AREAS:*** Labor; Employment; ERISA Litigation; Patents; Medical Liens. ***Email:*** attorneys@bellboyd.com

KIMBERLY D. NOVOTNY, born September 16, 1972; admitted to bar, 1998, Illinois. *Education:* DePauw University (B.M., 1994); DePaul University (J.D., with honors, 1998). Order of the Coif. *Member:* Chicago and Illinois State Bar Associations. ***PRACTICE AREAS:*** Corporate Law. ***Email:*** attorneys@bellboyd.com

(This Listing Continued)

MICHAEL K. OHM, born January 2, 1960; admitted to bar, 1985, Illinois; 1987, U.S. District Court, Northern District of Illinois and Eastern District of Wisconsin. *Education:* University of Illinois (B.S.W., 1982); DePaul University (J.D., 1985). ***PRACTICE AREAS:*** Environmental Law. ***Email:*** attorneys@bellboyd.com

STEPHEN J. O'NEIL, born May 3, 1955; admitted to bar, 1980, Illinois; 1984, Wisconsin; U.S. District Court, Northern District of Illinois including Trial Bar; U.S. Court of Appeals, Fifth and Seventh Circuits. *Education:* University of Notre Dame (B.A., magna cum laude, 1977); George Washington University (J.D., with honors, 1980). ***PRACTICE AREAS:*** Commercial Litigation; Professional Liability. ***Email:*** attorneys@bellboyd.com

MICHAEL R. OSTERHOFF, born April 2, 1972; admitted to bar, 1998, Illinois; registered to practice before U.S. Patent and Trademark Office. *Education:* University of Illinois (B.S., 1994); University of Missouri (J.D., 1997). ***PRACTICE AREAS:*** Patent Prosecution; Patent Litigation; Technology Law. ***Email:*** attorneys@bellboyd.com

AMY G. O'TOOLE, born July 6, 1968; admitted to bar, 1995, Illinois, U.S. Court of Appeals, Federal Circuit and U.S. District Court, Northern District of Illinois; registered to practice before U.S. Patent and Trademark Office. *Education:* Indiana University (B.A., 1990); John Marshall Law School (J.D., 1995). ***PRACTICE AREAS:*** Antitrust; Patents; Copyrights; Intellectual Property; Trademarks. ***Email:*** attorneys@bellboyd.com

MICHAEL L. OWEN, born February 3, 1963; admitted to bar, 1988, Illinois; 1989, U.S. District Court, Northern District of Illinois. *Education:* Northwestern University (B.A., 1985); Indiana University (J.D., 1988). ***PRACTICE AREAS:*** Banks and Banking; Finance; Communications and Media; Real Estate; Business Law; Secured Lending. ***Email:*** attorneys@bellboyd.com

KENNETH A. PETERSON, JR., born September 14, 1966; admitted to bar, 1991, Illinois. *Education:* Purdue University (B.A., with honors, 1988); Indiana University (J.D., magna cum laude, 1991). ***PRACTICE AREAS:*** Corporate Law; Finance. ***Email:*** attorneys@bellboyd.com

PAULITA A. PIKE, born January 30, 1971; admitted to bar, 1996, Illinois. *Education:* University of Notre Dame (B.A., 1993; J.D., 1996). ***PRACTICE AREAS:*** Corporate Law; Investments; Investment Management; Mutual Funds; Securities. ***Email:*** attorneys@bellboyd.com

WILLIAM S. PRICE, born May 9, 1942; admitted to bar, 1968, Illinois. *Education:* Denver University (B.S.B.A., 1965); Northwestern University (J.D., cum laude, 1968). ***PRACTICE AREAS:*** Corporate Law; Securities; Public Finance; Insurance. ***Email:*** attorneys@bellboyd.com

KENNETH E. RECHTORIS, born January 28, 1961; admitted to bar, 1985, Illinois, U.S. District Court, Northern District of Illinois including Trial Bar, U.S. Court of Appeals, Seventh Circuit and U.S. Supreme Court. *Education:* University of Iowa (B.B.A., 1982; J.D., with high distinction, 1985). ***PRACTICE AREAS:*** Commercial Litigation; Environmental Litigation; Professional Liability; Insurance Litigation; Appellate Work. ***Email:*** attorneys@bellboyd.com

PAULA WILSON RENDER, born March 27, 1962; admitted to bar, 1996, Illinois and U.S. District Court, Northern District of Illinois. *Education:* American University (B.A., 1983); University of Chicago (J.D., 1996). ***PRACTICE AREAS:*** Trade Regulation; Antitrust; Complex Litigation. ***Email:*** attorneys@bellboyd.com

JOHN T. ROACHE, born September 24, 1968; admitted to bar, 1993, Illinois, U.S. District Court, Northern and Central Districts of Illinois and U.S. District Court, Eastern District of Wisconsin. *Education:* University of Notre Dame (B.B.A., high honors, 1990); University of Illinois (J.D., magna cum laude, 1993). ***PRACTICE AREAS:*** Commercial Litigation; Employment Litigation; Intellectual Property Litigation. ***Email:*** attorneys@bellboyd.com

JOHN W. ROTUNNO, born August 3, 1951; admitted to bar, 1976, Illinois; U.S. District Court, Northern District of Illinois, including Trial Bar; U.S. District Court, Eastern District of Michigan; U.S. Court of Appeals, Seventh Circuit and U.S. Tax Court. *Education:* University of Illinois (B.A., 1973); James Scholar; University of Chicago (J.D., 1976). ***PRACTICE AREAS:*** Securities; Business Torts; Commercial Litigation; Professional Liability. ***Email:*** attorneys@bellboyd.com

PETER G. RUSH, born November 15, 1959; admitted to bar, 1985, Indiana; 1989, Illinois, U.S. Court of Appeals, Seventh and Eleventh Circuits, U.S. District Court, Southern and Northern Districts of Indiana and U.S. District Court, Northern District of Illinois including Trial Bar. *Education:* University of Notre Dame (B.A., magna cum laude, 1982); Duke University (J.D., with honors, 1985). ***PRACTICE AREAS:*** Commercial Litigation; Corporate Law. ***Email:*** attorneys@bellboyd.com

DAVID M. SALTIEL, born June 14, 1954; admitted to bar, 1980, Illinois. *Education:* University of Michigan (B.B.A., with distinction, 1975); University of Illinois (J.D., 1979). ***PRACTICE AREAS:*** Real Estate; Corporate Law; Entertainment Law. ***Email:*** attorneys@bellboyd.com

PATRICIA KANE SCHMIDT, born October 27, 1964; admitted to bar, 1995, Illinois and U.S. District Court, Northern District of Illinois; registered to practice before U.S. Patent and Trademark Office. *Education:* Villanova University (B.S.E.E., 1986); University of Dayton (J.D., 1995). ***PRACTICE AREAS:*** Patents; Intellectual Property; Trade Secret. ***Email:*** attorneys@bellboyd.com

GREGORY J. SCHROEDTER, born October 26, 1946; admitted to bar, 1972, Wisconsin, Illinois and U.S. District Court, Southern and Northern Districts of Illinois including Trial Bar; U.S. Court of Appeals, Sixth and Seventh Circuits; U.S. Supreme Court. *Education:* University of Wisconsin (B.A., honors, 1969; J.D., 1972). ***PRACTICE AREAS:*** Labor and Employment Law. ***Email:*** attorneys@bellboyd.com

JOHN P. SCOTELLARO, born September 27, 1943; admitted to bar, 1968, Illinois, U.S. District Court, Northern District of Illinois including Trial Bar, U.S. Court of Appeals, Second, Fifth, Sixth and Seventh Circuits and U.S. Supreme Court. *Education:* Marquette University (B.A., 1965); Evans Scholar; New York University (J.D., cum laude, 1968). ***PRACTICE AREAS:*** Corporate and Commercial Litigation; Professional Liability; Products Liability. ***Email:*** attorneys@bellboyd.com

(This Listing Continued)

BELL, BOYD & LLOYD LLC, Chicago—Continued

MICHAEL SENNETT, born October 24, 1951; admitted to bar, 1977, Illinois; 1984, U.S. Supreme Court. *Education:* Quincy University (A.B., with honors, 1973); Loyola University Chicago (J.D., cum laude, 1977). ***PRACTICE AREAS:*** Antitrust; Complex Litigation; International. ***Email:*** attorneys@bellboyd.com

ALAN M. SERWER, born August 31, 1944; admitted to bar, 1969, Illinois; 1970, U.S. District Court, Northern District of Illinois; 1979, U.S. Court of Appeals, Seventh Circuit and U.S. Supreme Court; 1980, District of Columbia; 1982, U.S. Court of Appeals, Sixth Circuit; 1983, U.S. Court of Appeals, Fifth Circuit; 1984, U.S. Court of Appeals, Eleventh Circuit; 1987, U.S. Court of Appeals, Ninth Circuit. *Education:* University of Michigan (B.A., 1966); Northwestern University (J.D., 1969). ***PRACTICE AREAS:*** Labor and Employment Law; Age Discrimination. ***Email:*** attorneys@bellboyd.com

RICHARD L. SEVCIK, born May 1, 1960; admitted to bar, 1985, Illinois. *Education:* University of Iowa (B.A., with highest distinction, 1982); University of Chicago (J.D., 1985). ***PRACTICE AREAS:*** Corporate Law; Tax Exempt Organizations; Taxation; Health Care. ***Email:*** attorneys@bellboyd.com

PETER M. SFIKAS, born August 9, 1937; admitted to bar, 1962, Illinois; 1963, U.S. District Court, Northern District of Illinois including Trial Bar and U.S. Court of Appeals, 7th Circuit; 1970, U.S. Supreme Court. *Education:* Indiana University (B.S., 1959); Northwestern University (J.D., 1962). ***PRACTICE AREAS:*** Litigation; Insurance; Antitrust. ***Email:*** attorneys@bellboyd.com

ROBERT V. SHANNON, born January 16, 1951; admitted to bar, 1978, District of Columbia; 1980, Illinois. *Education:* Elmhurst College (B.A., 1972); Purdue University (M.A., 1974); University of Illinois (J.D., cum laude, 1977). ***PRACTICE AREAS:*** Bankruptcy; Banking and Financial Services. ***Email:*** attorneys@bellboyd.com

THOMAS C. SHIELDS, born April 26, 1941; admitted to bar, 1966, Illinois. *Education:* Georgetown University (A.B., 1963); Northwestern University (J.D., cum laude, 1966). ***PRACTICE AREAS:*** Health Care Law; Estate Planning Law; General Corporate Law. ***Email:*** attorneys@bellboyd.com

DAVID C. SIENKO, born August 8, 1968; admitted to bar, 1994, Wisconsin; 2000, Illinois; U.S. District Court, Northern District of Texas; U.S. District Court, Eastern District of Wisconsin. *Education:* Oberlin College (B.A., 1990); Marquette University (J.D., 1994); Georgetown University (LL.M., 1997). ***PRACTICE AREAS:*** Securities; Corporate; Mergers and Acquisitions. ***Email:*** attorneys@bellboyd.com

WOON-WAH SIU, born October 23, 1951; admitted to bar, 1993, Illinois. *Education:* Tilburg University, Tilburg, The Netherlands (Kandidaat, cum laude, 1984); University of Warwick, Coventry, England, (M.A., 1986); University of Illinois (J.D., magna cum laude, 1993). ***PRACTICE AREAS:*** Corporate Law; Mergers and Acquisitions; Securities. ***Email:*** attorneys@bellboyd.com

STANLEY P. SKLAR, born April 25, 1938; admitted to bar, 1964, Illinois. *Education:* University of Illinois (B.S., 1960); Northwestern University (J.D., 1964). ***PRACTICE AREAS:*** Construction Law; Alternative Dispute Resolution; Real Estate. ***Email:*** attorneys@bellboyd.com

RENATO L. SMITH, born July 3, 1972; admitted to bar, 1997, Illinois; registered to practice before the U.S. Patent and Trademark Office. *Education:* University of Illinois (B.S., 1994; J.D., 1997). ***PRACTICE AREAS:*** Intellectual Property Law; Patents; Intellectual Property Licensing. ***Email:*** attorneys@bellboyd.com

CORNELIUS J. TANIS, born September 13, 1958; admitted to bar, 1983, Illinois; 1986, New Jersey. *Education:* Calvin College (B.A., 1980); Rutgers University (J.D., with honors, 1983). ***PRACTICE AREAS:*** Computer Law; Intellectual Property. ***Email:*** attorneys@bellboyd.com

PAMELA L. TAYLOR, born April 6, 1965; admitted to bar, 1990, Massachusetts; 2001, Illinois. *Education:* Wellesley College (B.A., cum laude, 1987); Boston University (J.D., 1990). ***PRACTICE AREAS:*** Antitrust. ***Email:*** attorneys@bellboyd.com

SANDRA L. WALDIER, born September 9, 1973; admitted to bar, 1997, Illinois. *Education:* University of Illinois (B.A., cum laude, 1994; J.D., magna cum laude, 1997). ***PRACTICE AREAS:*** Real Estate. ***Email:*** attorneys@bellboyd.com

JOHN CRAIG WALKER, born November 20, 1957; admitted to bar, 1983, Illinois. *Education:* Stanford University (A.B., 1979); University of Michigan (J.D., 1983). ***PRACTICE AREAS:*** Corporate Law; Securities. ***Email:*** attorneys@bellboyd.com

PAUL J. WALSEN, born December 20, 1966; admitted to bar, 1994, Illinois and U.S. District Court, Northern District of Illinois. *Education:* University of Illinois (B.A., 1988; M.B.A., 1989; J.D., cum laude, 1994). ***PRACTICE AREAS:*** Commercial Litigation. ***Email:*** attorneys@bellboyd.com

NEAL H. WEINFIELD, born August 13, 1961; admitted to bar, 1987, Illinois. *Education:* Cornell University (B.A., B.F.A., magna cum laude, 1984); Vanderbilt University (J.D., 1987). ***PRACTICE AREAS:*** Environmental Law; Administrative Law. ***Email:*** attorneys@bellboyd.com

DONALD S. WEISS, born November 23, 1944; admitted to bar, 1971, District of Columbia; 1979, Illinois; 1983, U.S. District Court, Northern District of Illinois including Trial Bar. *Education:* Brown University (A.B., 1967); George Washington University (J.D., 1970). ***PRACTICE AREAS:*** Securities Futures and Options. ***Email:*** attorneys@bellboyd.com

ROBERT L. WIESENTHAL, born September 22, 1939; admitted to bar, 1964, Illinois; 1965, U.S. Court of Military Appeals; 1968, U.S. Supreme Court. *Education:* Wheaton College (B.A., 1961); Northwestern University (J.D., 1964). ***PRACTICE AREAS:*** Estates and Trusts. ***Email:*** attorneys@bellboyd.com

RICHARD O. WOOD, born February 19, 1948; admitted to bar, 1976, Illinois and Florida. *Education:* Trinity College (B.A., 1971); John Marshall Law School (J.D., with high distinction, 1976). ***PRACTICE AREAS:*** Administrative Law; OSHA. ***Email:*** attorneys@bellboyd.com

(This Listing Continued)

FENG XUE, born November 11, 1967; admitted to bar, 1998, Illinois. *Education:* Peking University, Peking, China (B.A., 1990); Duke University (LL.M., 1995; J.D., 1998). ***PRACTICE AREAS:*** Corporate Law; International Law.

OF COUNSEL

LAIRD BELL (1910-1965)

JAMES D. BENAK, born January 22, 1954; admitted to bar, 1980, Nebraska; 1990, Illinois and U.S. District Court, Northern District of Illinois. *Education:* University of Nebraska (B.S., 1977); Creighton University School of Law (J.D., 1980). ***PRACTICE AREAS:*** Litigation; Corporate; Securities; Intellectual Property Litigation; Insurance Coverage Litigation; Transportation. ***Email:*** attorneys@bellboyd.com

MARK H. BERENS, born August 4, 1928; admitted to bar, 1951, Illinois; 1955, District of Columbia. *Education:* University of Notre Dame (B.S.C., magna cum laude, 1950; J.D., magna cum laude, 1951). ***PRACTICE AREAS:*** Corporate; Insurance; International Law. ***Email:*** attorneys@bellboyd.com

STANTON H. BERLIN, born May 24, 1934; admitted to bar, 1959, Illinois and Michigan. *Education:* University of Michigan (B.B.A., 1955; M.B.A., 1956; J.D., 1959). ***Email:*** attorneys@bellboyd.com

DARRELL S. BOYD (1919-1971)

ALAN R. BRODIE, born November 13, 1930; admitted to bar, 1954, Illinois. *Education:* Reed College (B.A., 1951); University of Chicago (J.D., 1954). ***Email:*** attorneys@bellboyd.com

GEORGE M. BURDITT, born September 21, 1922; admitted to bar, 1949, Illinois; 1981, District of Columbia, U.S. District Court, Northern District of Illinois, Trial Bar, U.S. Court of Appeals, Second, Fourth, Seventh, Eighth, Ninth and District of Columbia Circuits and U.S. Supreme Court. *Education:* Harvard University (A.B., 1944; J.D., 1948). ***PRACTICE AREAS:*** Food, Drug and Medical Device Law; Administrative Law; Product Liability Law. ***Email:*** attorneys@bellboyd.com

WILLIAM G. BURNS (1907-1988)

RICHARD L. CURRY (Retired)

PAUL F. DONAHUE, born 1943; admitted to bar, 1976, Indiana; 1982, Illinois and Florida. *Education:* University of Massachusetts (B.A., 1966; M.A., 1970); Indiana University (J.D., magna cum laude, 1976). ***PRACTICE AREAS:*** Antitrust; Litigation. ***Email:*** attorneys@bellboyd.com

R. JAMES GORMLEY (1921-2001)

WILLIAM N. HADDAD (1903-2001)

WILLIAM B. HANLEY (1933-2005)

DOLORES K. HANNA, admitted to bar, 1952, Illinois. *Education:* Ohio University (B.A., 1949); IIT/Chicago-Kent College of Law (J.D., 1952). ***PRACTICE AREAS:*** Trademark Law; Unfair Competition Law; Mediation Law. ***Email:*** attorneys@bellboyd.com

WARREN C. HASKIN, born January 16, 1933; admitted to bar, 1958, Illinois. *Education:* Northwestern University (B.A., 1955; J.D., 1958). (Retired). ***PRACTICE AREAS:*** Corporate Law. ***Email:*** attorneys@bellboyd.com

J. WILLIAM HAYTON (1926-1994)

FRANK K. HEAP, born June 28, 1941; admitted to bar, 1966, Illinois. *Education:* Northwestern University (B.S., 1963); University of Chicago (J.D., 1966). ***PRACTICE AREAS:*** Litigation; Insurance Law. ***Email:*** attorneys@bellboyd.com

JAMES P. HEMMER, born March 28, 1942; admitted to bar, 1967, Illinois. *Education:* Marquette University (A.B., summa cum laude, 1964); Harvard University (LL.B., 1967). ***PRACTICE AREAS:*** Corporate Law; Securities; Banking. ***Email:*** attorneys@bellboyd.com

ROLLIN C. HUGGINS, JR., born October 11, 1931; admitted to bar, 1958, Illinois; 1960, U.S. Tax Court. *Education:* Knox College (A.B., magna cum laude, 1953); Harvard University (LL.B., cum laude, 1958). ***Email:*** attorneys@bellboyd.com

GLEN A. LLOYD (1931-1975)

ALICE S. LONOFF, born May 14, 1950; admitted to bar, 1977, Massachusetts; 1985, Illinois. *Education:* Oberlin College (B.A., 1972); Boston College (J.D., cum laude, 1977); Boston University (LL.M., 1983). ***PRACTICE AREAS:*** Estates and Trusts. ***Email:*** attorneys@bellboyd.com

CHARLES T. MARTIN, born March 9, 1915; admitted to bar, 1941, Indiana; 1943, Illinois. *Education:* Wabash College (A.B., 1937); Northwestern University (J.D., 1941). ***Email:*** attorneys@bellboyd.com

CHARLES T. PRICE, born February 11, 1944; admitted to bar, 1969, Ohio; 1974, U.S. District Court, Northern District of Ohio; 1981, U.S. Court of Appeals, Sixth Circuit; 1982, U.S. Supreme Court; 1989, Illinois. *Education:* Ohio Wesleyan University (B.A., 1966); Harvard University (J.D., 1969). ***PRACTICE AREAS:*** Labor and Employment; Media Law. ***Email:*** attorneys@bellboyd.com

JAMES T. RHIND, born July 21, 1922; admitted to bar, 1950, Illinois. *Education:* Hamilton College, Ohio State University (A.B., cum laude, 1944); University of Michigan; Harvard University (LL.B., cum laude, 1950). ***PRACTICE AREAS:*** Corporate Law. ***Email:*** attorneys@bellboyd.com

ALLEN R. SMART, born July 3, 1934; admitted to bar, 1961, Illinois. *Education:* Princeton University (A.B., magna cum laude, 1956); Harvard University (LL.B., 1961). ***Email:*** attorneys@bellboyd.com

DANIEL P. WARD (1918-1995)

JACK M. WHITNEY, II (1922-1995)

(This Listing Continued)

ASSOCIATES

HOLBY M. ABERN, born March 20, 1977; admitted to bar, 2002, Illinois; registered before U.S. Patent and Trademark Office. *Education:* University of Illinois (1999); Loyola University Chicago (J.D., 2002). ***PRACTICE AREAS:*** Intellectual Property. ***Email:*** attorneys@bellboyd.com

TED J. BARTHEL, born March 19, 1964; admitted to bar, 2000, Illinois and U.S. District Court, Northern District of Illinois; registered to practice before the U.S. Patent and Trademark Office. *Education:* Universitat Freiburg, Germany; Carroll College (B.A., 1987); DePaul University (J.D., 2000). ***PRACTICE AREAS:*** Intellectual Property; Patents; Trademarks; Copyrights; Litigation. ***Email:*** attorneys@bellboyd.com

THOMAS C. BASSO, born June 21, 1967; admitted to bar, 1999, Illinois and U.S. District Court, Northern District of Illinois; 2000, U.S. District Court, Northern District of Texas. *Education:* Albion College; Northwestern University (B.A., 1989; M.S., 1991); IIT/Chicago-Kent College of Law (J.D., 1999). ***PRACTICE AREAS:*** Patent Law; Copyright Law; Trademark Law; Litigation. ***Email:*** attorneys@bellboyd.com

PATRICE A. BAZIANOS, born May 18, 1972; admitted to bar, 1999, Illinois. *Education:* Loyola University Chicago (B.S., cum laude, 1995; J.D., 1999). ***Email:*** attorneys@bellboyd.com

MICHAEL A. BECKETT, born June 12, 1973; admitted to bar, 2004, Illinois. *Education:* University of Illinois (B.S., 1996; M.S., 1998); Purdue University (Ph.D., 2001); Washington University (J.D., 2004). ***PRACTICE AREAS:*** Intellectual Property; Patents; Trademarks; Copyrights. ***Email:*** attorneys@bellboyd.com

DIANE E. BELL, born March 16, 1978; admitted to bar, 2003, Illinois. *Education:* Washington University (B.A., 2000); University of Chicago (J.D., 2003). ***PRACTICE AREAS:*** Corporate. ***Email:*** attorneys@bellboyd.com

TIMOTHY W. BOARINI, born June 15, 1979; admitted to bar, 2004, Illinois. *Education:* Middlebury College (B.A., 2001); George Washington University; University of Iowa (J.D., 2004). ***PRACTICE AREAS:*** Corporate Law; Securities. ***Email:*** attorneys@bellboyd.com

HEATHER A. BOICE, born October 8, 1973; admitted to bar, 2000, Illinois and U.S. District Court, Northern District of Illinois; 2001, U.S. Court of Appeals, Federal Circuit. *Education:* Purdue University (B.S.E.E., 1996); John Marshall Law School (J.D., 2000). ***PRACTICE AREAS:*** Intellectual Property Litigation. ***Email:*** attorneys@bellboyd.com

CAROL CACHEY, born December 26, 1957; admitted to bar, 1983, Illinois. *Education:* University of Michigan (A.B., 1980); Loyola University (J.D., 1983). ***PRACTICE AREAS:*** Employee Benefits; ERISA; Health Care; Tax Law. ***Email:*** ccachey@bellboyd.com

CHRISTOPHER I. CEDILLO, born December 1, 1970; admitted to bar, 2001, Illinois. *Education:* Michigan State University (B.A., 1991); Northwestern University (J.D., 2001). ***PRACTICE AREAS:*** Trademarks; Copyrights. ***Email:*** attorneys@bellboyd.com

ROBERT W. CONNORS, born May 22, 1967; admitted to bar, 2000, Illinois. *Education:* Purdue University (B.S., 1989); Loyola University Chicago (J.D., 2000). ***PRACTICE AREAS:*** Patent Prosecution; Intellectual Property Litigation; Intellectual Property Licensing; Patent Litigation. ***Email:*** attorneys@bellboyd.com

BRADLEY E. DAVIS, born February 2, 1966; admitted to bar, 2002, Illinois. *Education:* University of Pittsburgh (B.S., 1989); University of Illinois; DePaul University (J.D., 2002). ***PRACTICE AREAS:*** Intellectual Property. ***Email:*** attorneys@bellboyd.com

AMY S. DOLGIN, born May 24, 1975; admitted to bar, 2000, Illinois and U.S. District Court, Northern District of Illinois. *Education:* University of Chicago (B.A., 1996); Northwestern University (J.D., 2000). ***PRACTICE AREAS:*** Litigation; Commercial Litigation. ***Email:*** attorneys@bellboyd.com

ANIA DOMAGALA-PIERGA, born October 13, 1973; admitted to bar, 1999, Illinois. *Education:* Loyola University Chicago (B.A., 1996); IIT/Chicago-Kent College of Law (J.D., 1999). ***PRACTICE AREAS:*** Real Estate; Construction Law. ***Email:*** attorneys@bellboyd.com

STEVEN DOMANOWSKI, born April 14, 1977; admitted to bar, 2003, Illinois. *Education:* State University of New York at Buffalo (B.A., 1999); DePaul University (J.D., 2002). ***PRACTICE AREAS:*** Litigation. ***Email:*** attorneys@bellboyd.com

MARY M. DONNERS, born September 16, 1952; admitted to bar, 1984, Illinois. *Education:* Loyola University Chicago (B.A., 1975); John Marshall Law School (J.D., 1984). ***PRACTICE AREAS:*** Real Estate Taxation; Public Law. ***Email:*** attorneys@bellboyd.com

KARA A. ELGERSMA, born March 11, 1976; admitted to bar, 2000, Illinois; 2001, U.S. District Court, Northern District of Illinois and U.S. Court of Appeals, Third Circuit; 2002, U.S. Court of Appeals, Seventh Circuit; 2003, U.S. Court of Appeals, Tenth Circuit; 2004, U.S. Supreme Court. *Education:* University of Kansas (B.A., 1997); Georgetown University (J.D., 2000). ***PRACTICE AREAS:*** Antitrust Litigation. ***Email:*** attorneys@bellboyd.com

JASON A. ENGEL, born December 28, 1974; admitted to bar, 2001, Illinois. *Education:* University of Dayton (B.S., 1998; J.D., cum laude, 2001). ***PRACTICE AREAS:*** Intellectual Property; Patents. ***Email:*** attorneys@bellboyd.com

NICHOLAS I. FINK, born October 24, 1974; admitted to bar, 1999, Illinois. *Education:* Institut D'Etudes Des Relations Internationales (D.E.S., 1995); Northwestern University (J.D., cum laude, 1999). ***PRACTICE AREAS:*** Corporate. ***Email:*** attorneys@bellboyd.com

JOHN M. FITZGERALD, born October 11, 1978; admitted to bar, 2004, Illinois. *Education:* University of Chicago (B.A., 2001; J.D., 2004). ***PRACTICE AREAS:*** Antitrust. ***Email:*** attorneys@bellboyd.com

MAURA FORDE O'MEARA, born April 3, 1976; admitted to bar, 2001, Illinois; 2002, District of Columbia. *Education:* Georgetown University (B.A., 1998); Loyola University Chicago (J.D., 2001). ***PRACTICE AREAS:*** Litigation. ***Email:*** attorneys@bellboyd.com

(This Listing Continued)

JEFFREY S. GARDNER, born November 1, 1976; admitted to bar, 2003, Illinois. *Education:* The Ohio State University (B.S., cum laude, 2000; M.B.A., 2000); Georgetown University (J.D., 2003). ***PRACTICE AREAS:*** Corporate. ***Email:*** attorneys@bellboyd.com

JAMES F. GOEDKEN, born October 24, 1966; admitted to bar, 2002, Illinois; registered to practice before U.S. Patent and Trademark Office. *Education:* Iowa State University (B.S., 1991); John Marshall Law School (J.D., 2001). ***PRACTICE AREAS:*** Patents; Trademarks; Copyrights. ***Email:*** attorneys@bellboyd.com

ROBERT M. GOULD, born April 16, 1958; admitted to bar, 1996, Texas; 2000, Illinois and U.S. District Court, Northern District of Illinois; registered to practice before U.S. Patent and Trademark Office. *Education:* University of Illinois (B.S., 1981); University of Iowa (Ph.D., 1988); University of Houston (J.D., 1996). ***PRACTICE AREAS:*** Patents; Trademarks; Trade Secrets; Contracts; Franchise Law. ***Email:*** attorneys@bellboyd.com

EDWARD M. GRAHAM, born November 21, 1959; admitted to bar, 1987, Illinois and U.S. District Court, Northern District of Illinois. *Education:* University of Wisconsin (B.A., 1983); Washington and Lee University (J.D., 1987). ***PRACTICE AREAS:*** Litigation. ***Email:*** attorneys@bellboyd.com

JOEL C. GRISWOLD, born May 5, 1977; admitted to bar, 2002, Illinois and U.S. District Court, Northern District of Illinois; 2003, U.S. District Court, Eastern District of Michigan. *Education:* Northwestern University (B.A., 1999); University of Minnesota (J.D., cum laude, 2002). ***PRACTICE AREAS:*** Litigation. ***Email:*** attorneys@bellboyd.com

ANIS H. HA, born May 8, 1978; admitted to bar, 2004, Illinois. *Education:* University of Illinois (B.S., 1999); University of Michigan (J.D., 2004). ***PRACTICE AREAS:*** Corporate Law. ***Email:*** attorneys@bellboyd.com

DOUGLAS J. HATLESTAD, born August 28, 1972; admitted to bar, 2000, Illinois. *Education:* University of Illinois (B.S., 1993); Loyola University Chicago (J.D., magna cum laude, 2000). ***PRACTICE AREAS:*** Finance; Mergers and Acquisitions; Securities. ***Email:*** attorneys@bellboyd.com

VEENA K. JAIN, born November 7, 1968; admitted to bar, 1994, Illinois; 1997, District of Columbia. *Education:* Northwestern University (B.A., 1991); University of Michigan (J.D., 1994). ***PRACTICE AREAS:*** Investment Management. ***Email:*** attorneys@bellboyd.com

DAWN L. JOHNSON, born June 6, 1974; admitted to bar, 2001, Illinois. *Education:* University of Illinois (B.A., 1996; J.D., 2001). ***PRACTICE AREAS:*** Litigation. ***Email:*** attorneys@bellboyd.com

DEANNA L. KEYSOR, born December 30, 1973; admitted to bar, 1999, Illinois and U.S. Court of Appeals, Sixth Circuit; 2000, U.S. District Court, Northern District of Illinois; 2003, U.S. Court of Appeals, Federal Circuit. *Education:* Miami University (B.A., summa cum laude, 1996); Yale University (J.D., 1999). Phi Beta Kappa. ***PRACTICE AREAS:*** Antitrust; Intellectual Property; Appellate Practice.

DAVID KIM, born September 4, 1977; admitted to bar, 2003, Illinois. *Education:* University of Michigan (B.A., 1999; J.D., 2002). ***PRACTICE AREAS:*** Corporate. ***Email:*** attorneys@bellboyd.com

MARCUS M. LEE, born August 24, 1973; admitted to bar, 1999, Illinois. *Education:* Northern Illinois University (B.S., 1995); Washington University (J.D., 1999). ***Email:*** attorneys@bellboyd.com

JEANA R. LERVICK, born January 4, 1977; admitted to bar, 2002, Illinois and U.S. District Court, Northern District of Illinois. *Education:* Montana State University (B.S., 1999); DePaul University (J.D., 2002). ***PRACTICE AREAS:*** Intellectual Property.

COLLEEN D. LUNDGREN, born January 12, 1964; admitted to bar, 1997, Michigan; 2000, Illinois. *Education:* Eastern Michigan University (B.S., magna cum laude, 1991); Wayne State University (J.D., magna cum laude, 1996). ***PRACTICE AREAS:*** Corporate Law; Securities. ***Email:*** attorneys@bellboyd.com

CYNTHIA S. MANGIAFORTE, born February 13, 1964; admitted to bar, 1990, Illinois and U.S. District Court, Northern District of Illinois. *Education:* Southern Illinois University (B.A., with honors, 1986); University of Notre Dame (J.D., 1990). ***PRACTICE AREAS:*** Real Estate. ***Email:*** attorneys@bellboyd.com

KARL L. MARSCHEL, born April 26, 1978; admitted to bar, 2003, Illinois. *Education:* University of Missouri (B.A., 2000); Washington University (J.D., 2003). ***PRACTICE AREAS:*** Real Estate. ***Email:*** attorneys@bellboyd.com

ERIC P. MARTIN, born January 17, 1976; admitted to bar, 2001, Illinois and U.S. District Court, Northern District of Illinois; 2002, U.S. District Court, Central District of Illinois and U.S. District Court, Eastern District of Wisconsin; registered to practice before U.S. Patent and Trademark Office. *Education:* University of Wisconsin (B.S., 1998); University of Notre Dame Law School (J.D., 2001). ***PRACTICE AREAS:*** Patent Litigation; Intellectual Property Licensing; Intellectual Property. ***Email:*** attorneys@bellboyd.com

ANDREW P.R. McDERMOTT, born September 12, 1976; admitted to bar, 2003, Illinois. *Education:* University of Minnesota (B.A., Phi Beta Kappa, 1998); Northwestern University (J.D., 2003). ***PRACTICE AREAS:*** Bankruptcy. ***Email:*** attorneys@bellboyd.com

MARIA A. MENDOZA, born September 12, 1978; admitted to bar, 2004, Illinois. *Education:* University of Oklahoma (B.A., 2001); University of Notre Dame (J.D., 2004). ***PRACTICE AREAS:*** Labor and Employment. ***Email:*** attorneys@bellboyd.com

ABRAM I. MOORE, born June 10, 1974; admitted to bar, 2002, Illinois. *Education:* University of Montana (B.A., 1998); University of Notre Dame (J.D., 2002). ***PRACTICE AREAS:*** Litigation. ***Email:*** attorneys@bellboyd.com

SANJAY K. MURTHY, born July 29, 1975; admitted to bar, 2000, California and U.S. District Court, Southern District of California; 2003, Illinois and U.S. District Court, Northern District of Illinois. *Education:* Loyola University (B.S., 1997); California Western School of Law (J.D., 2000); George Washington University Law School (LL.M., 2003). ***PRACTICE AREAS:*** Patent Litigation; Patent Prosecution.

(This Listing Continued)

BELL, BOYD & LLOYD LLC, Chicago—Continued

SEAN R. ODENDAHL, born August 1, 1972; admitted to bar, 2001, Illinois. *Education:* University of Illinois (B.A., magna cum laude, 1997; J.D., magna cum laude, 2001). ***PRACTICE AREAS:*** Corporate Law; Securities; Mergers and Acquisitions. ***Email:*** attorneys@bellboyd.com

CURT A. PAISON, born October 13, 1973; admitted to bar, 2000, Illinois. *Education:* DePauw University (B.A., 1996); Loyola University Chicago (J.D., 2000). ***PRACTICE AREAS:*** Estate Planning; Tax Exempt Organizations. ***Email:*** attorneys@bellboyd.com

KEVIN Y. PAK, admitted to bar, 1995, Illinois. *Education:* University of Illinois (B.A., 1990); Vanderbilt University (J.D., 1994). ***PRACTICE AREAS:*** Litigation; Bankruptcy. ***Email:*** attorneys@bellboyd.com

TODD E. PENTECOST, born June 9, 1972; admitted to bar, 1999, Illinois. *Education:* Marquette University (B.A., magna cum laude, 1994); University of Chicago (J.D., cum laude, 1999). ***PRACTICE AREAS:*** Commercial Litigation. ***Email:*** attorneys@bellboyd.com

ALICIA A. PERLA, born March 16, 1970; admitted to bar, 1999, California; 2002, Illinois. *Education:* Columbia University (B.A., 1992); University of Michigan (J.D., 1999). ***PRACTICE AREAS:*** Corporate Law; Securities Law; Mergers and Acquisitions. ***Email:*** attorneys@bellboyd.com

JEFFREY T. PETERSEN, born January 25, 1971; admitted to bar, 2001, California, Illinois and U.S. District Court, Central District of California. *Education:* University of Wisconsin (B.B.A., 1994); Georgetown University Law Center (J.D., 1998). ***PRACTICE AREAS:*** Litigation. ***Email:*** attorneys@bellboyd.com

COURTNEY RATZBURG, born November 9, 1977; admitted to bar, 2003, Illinois. *Education:* Vanderbilt University (B.S., with honors, 2000); Washington University (J.D., 2003). ***PRACTICE AREAS:*** Intellectual Property. ***Email:*** attorneys@bellboyd.com

FRANCES P. REYNOLDS, born January 29, 1975; admitted to bar, 2004, Wisconsin and Illinois. *Education:* University of Wisconsin-Madison (B.A., 1997; J.D., 2004). ***PRACTICE AREAS:*** Intellectual Property. ***Email:*** attorneys@bellboyd.com

MATTHEW T. RIDSDALE, born September 21, 1971; admitted to bar, 2002, Illinois. *Education:* University of Michigan (B.S.M.E., 1993); Keller Graduate School of Management (M.B.A., 1996); Chicago-Kent College of Law (J.D., 2001). ***PRACTICE AREAS:*** Intellectual Property; Patents.

DANIEL G. ROSENBERG, born December 24, 1975; admitted to bar, 2001, Illinois. *Education:* Miami University (B.S., Finance, 1998); Loyola University (J.D., 2001). ***PRACTICE AREAS:*** Litigation; Securities Litigation; Class Action Defense.

MICHAEL J. ROTH, JR., born May 18, 1976; admitted to bar, 2004, Illinois. *Education:* Truman State University (B.A., 1998); Washington University (J.D., 2004). ***PRACTICE AREAS:*** Real Estate. ***Email:*** attorneys@bellboyd.com

WENDY J. SAWYER, born November 26, 1974; admitted to bar, 2001, Illinois. *Education:* Indiana University (B.A., 1997); DePaul University (J.D., 2001). ***PRACTICE AREAS:*** Intellectual Property. ***Email:*** attorneys@bellboyd.com

SARAH E. SCHAEFER, born September 26, 1968; admitted to bar, 1999, Illinois. *Education:* Universitaet Augsburg (1st jur. Staatsexamen, 1992); Northwestern University (J.D., 1999). ***PRACTICE AREAS:*** Antitrust; Trade Regulation. ***Email:*** attorneys@bellboyd.com

ADAM R. SCHAEFFER, born August 15, 1978; admitted to bar, 2003, Illinois. *Education:* State University of New York College at Geneseo (B.A., 2000); University of Chicago (J.D., 2003). ***PRACTICE AREAS:*** Bankruptcy. ***Email:*** attorneys@bellboyd.com

JAMES R. SCHUELLER, born December 28, 1974; admitted to bar, 2000, Illinois. *Education:* University of Notre Dame (B.B.A., 1997; J.D., 2000). ***PRACTICE AREAS:*** Real Estate. ***Email:*** attorneys@bellboyd.com

LAURA E. SIMPSON, born December 12, 1975; admitted to bar, 2003, Illinois. *Education:* Amherst College (B.A., magna cum laude, 1998); Vanderbilt University (J.D., 2003). ***PRACTICE AREAS:*** Corporate. ***Email:*** attorneys@bellboyd.com

GREGORY P. SITRICK, born October 5, 1976; admitted to bar, 2003, Illinois. *Education:* University of Arizona (B.S.E.E., 2000); Northwestern University (J.D., 2003). ***PRACTICE AREAS:*** Intellectual Property; Patent. ***Email:*** attorneys@bellboyd.com

WALLACE C. SOLBERG, born February 2, 1960; admitted to bar, 1986, Illinois. *Education:* University of Illinois (B.A., 1983); IIT/Chicago-Kent College of Law (J.D., 1986). ***PRACTICE AREAS:*** Commercial Litigation; Governmental Regulation; Civil Rights Section 1983; Appellate Practice; Zoning. ***Email:*** attorneys@bellboyd.com

KATHRYN STARSHAK, born March 22, 1976; admitted to bar, 2002, Illinois. *Education:* DePaul University (B.A., 1998; J.D., 2002). ***PRACTICE AREAS:*** Intellectual Property. ***Email:*** attorneys@bellboyd.com

SAREN K. SUDEL, born June 8, 1974; admitted to bar, 2003, Illinois. *Education:* University of Minnesota (B.A., 1998); University of Chicago (J.D., 2003). ***PRACTICE AREAS:*** Antitrust. ***Email:*** attorneys@bellboyd.com

JOHN SUSORENY, born December 29, 1971; admitted to bar, 2004, Illinois. *Education:* Purdue University (B.S., 1994); University of Maryland School of Law (J.D., cum laude, 2004). ***PRACTICE AREAS:*** Antitrust and Trade Regulation. ***Email:*** attorneys@bellboyd.com

AARON K. TANTLEFF, born January 18, 1977; admitted to bar, 2004, Illinois. *Education:* Northwestern University (B.A., 1998); Chicago-Kent College of Law, Illinois Institute of Technology (J.D., 2004). ***PRACTICE AREAS:*** Intellectual Property; Patents; Intellectual Property Litigation. ***Email:*** attorneys@bellboyd.com

JOHN E. "JAY" TRUTY, born April 8, 1974; admitted to bar, 1999, Illinois and U.S. District Court, Northern District of Illinois. *Education:* Illinois Wesleyan University (B.A., 1996); University of Missouri (J.D., 1999). ***PRACTICE AREAS:*** Environmental Law; Occupational Health and Safety. ***Email:*** attorneys@bellboyd.com

(This Listing Continued)

BRENT W. VINCENT, born March 22, 1972; admitted to bar, 1999, Illinois and U.S. District Court, Northern District of Illinois. *Education:* Washington and Lee University (B.A., 1994); Northwestern University (J.D., 1999). ***PRACTICE AREAS:*** Commercial Litigation; Products Liability; Tort Defense. ***Email:*** attorneys@bellboyd.com

KAREN E. WALTHER, born May 29, 1975; admitted to bar, 2001, Illinois. *Education:* Michigan State University (B.A., 1997); Loyola University Chicago (J.D., 2001). ***PRACTICE AREAS:*** Corporate; Securities. ***Email:*** attorneys@bellboyd.com

BROOKE P. WEINSTEIN, born November 25, 1977; admitted to bar, 2003, Illinois. *Education:* University of Wisconsin (B.A., 1999); University of Chicago (J.D., 2003). ***PRACTICE AREAS:*** Antitrust. ***Email:*** attorneys@bellboyd.com

TRAYNE S. WHEELER, born September 12, 1973; admitted to bar, 2000, Massachusetts; 2001, District of Columbia; 2004, Illinois. *Education:* University of Chicago (A.B., 1995); Boston University (J.D., 2000). ***PRACTICE AREAS:*** Financial Services Law; Investment Management. ***Email:*** attorneys@bellboyd.com

ALLYSON L. WILCOX, born December 31, 1977; admitted to bar, 2003, Illinois and U.S. District Court, Northern District of Illinois. *Education:* University of California at San Diego (B.A., 2000); Pepperdine University School of Law (J.D., 2003). ***PRACTICE AREAS:*** Environmental Litigation.

JOSEPH C. WYLIE, II, born September 12, 1974; admitted to bar, 1999, Illinois and U.S. District Court, Northern District of Illinois. *Education:* University of California, Berkeley (B.A., 1996); Georgetown University (J.D., 1999). ***PRACTICE AREAS:*** Litigation. ***Email:*** attorneys@bellboyd.com

PETER ZURA, born November 1, 1967; admitted to bar, 1997, Michigan; 2003, District of Columbia; registered to practice before U.S. Patent and Trademark Office (Not admitted in Illinois). *Education:* Oakland University (B.S.E.E., 1990); Detroit College of Law at Michigan State University (J.D., 1997); George Washington University (LL.M., 2002). ***PRACTICE AREAS:*** Patents; Trademarks; Copyrights; Licensing. ***Email:*** attorneys@bellboyd.com

---

BRIGITTE SCHMIDT BELL, P.C.

Established in 1993

53 WEST JACKSON BOULEVARD, SUITE 702
CHICAGO, ILLINOIS 60604
Telephone: 312-360-1124
Fax: 312-360-1126;
Email: mediators@BSBPC.com
Email: lawyers@BSBPC.com
URL: http://www.mediate.com/brigittebell

Evanston, Illinois Office: 500 Davis Street, Suite 1006, 60201.
Lake Forest, Illinois Office: One Westminster Place, 60045.(By appt. only).

Family, Domestic Relations, Matrimonial, Adoption and Mediation Law, Mediation of Family, Adoption, Employment and Business issues, Collaborative Law.

BRIGITTE SCHMIDT BELL, born Hamburg, Germany, January 5, 1948; admitted to bar, 1979, Illinois and U.S. District Court, Northern District of Illinois; 1981, U.S. Court of Appeals, Seventh Circuit. *Education:* Swarthmore College (B.A., with high honors, 1970); University of Chicago (J.D., 1979). Co-Author: with Gemma B. Allen, "Child Support," Illinois Family Law (IICLE 1992); with Sandra R. Murphy, "Pleadings in Matrimonial Actions Under the Illinois Marriage and Dissolution of Marriage Act," Illinois Family Law, 3--1-3--154 (IICLE 1988); "QDROPHOBIA and Answers to Frequently Asked Tax Questions About Retirement Benefits in the Divorce Context," (IICLE Presentations, November and December 1989). Presentations: Academy of Family Mediators, July, 1994 Conference; July, 1995 Conference; February, 1996 Conference; July, 1996 Conference; July, 1997 Conference and July, 1998 Conference; July, 1999 Conference; Mediation Council of Illinois, April, 1994 Conference; MCI, 1995 Conference, 1996 Conference, April 1997 Conference; 1998 Conference; Wisconsin Association of Mediators, November, 1993 Conference; November, 1994 Conference; November, 1996 Conference; November, 1998 Conference; Academy of Legal Studies in Business, August 1995 Conference; NBI, Equitable Distribution in Illinois, March, 1997 Child Custody Litigation November 1998, Family Law March 1999; Aurora University, January, 2000. ACR Conference 2001; ACR Family Section Conference, 2002 and 2003. Extern Law Clerk to the Honorable George N. Leighton, U.S. District Court, Northern District of Illinois, 1978-1979. Adjunct Professor, Consensual Dispute Resolution, Loyola School of Law, 1986-1996. Visiting Faculty, DePaul University School for New Learning, 1992-1999. Legal Assistance Foundation's Children's Rights Project Advisory Board, 1985-1993. Certified Arbitrator, Cook County Mandatory Arbitration Program, 1990—. Volunteer Facilitator, Cook County Domestic Relations Division, 1998—. Certified Mediator and Trainer for the Neighborhood Justice Center of Chicago (now "Center for Conflict Resolution"), 1985—. Member, Board of Directors, 1987—; Chair, Long Range Planning Committee; Secretary, 1993-1996. Member: Mediation Council of Illinois, 1987— (Board of Directors, 1994-1999; Vice President, 1997-1999; Academy of Family Mediators, 1988—; (Practitioner Member, 1997). Approved Consultant, 1998—. Member, Panel of Arbitrators, American Arbitration Association, 1987—. Approved Consultant 1998—. Panel Member, National Arbitration Forum, 2002—. Member, Society of Professionals in Dispute Resolution, 1986—. Approved Mediator: Lake County; Illinois Dept. of Educational, Special Education Services, 2002—. *Member:* Chicago, Lake County, DuPage County, Illinois State and American (Member, Committee on ADR) Bar Associations; Women's Bar Association; Chicago Council of Lawyers. Fellow, Collaborative Law Institute of Illinois (First Co-President; Member, Board of Directors). ***LANGUAGES:*** German, Hungarian. ***PRACTICE AREAS:*** Mediation; Collaborative Law; Litigation; Family Law; Adoption; Employment; Business. ***Email:*** Lawyers@bsbpc.com

BELL JONES & QUINLISK

200 WEST ADAMS STREET
SUITE 2600
CHICAGO, ILLINOIS 60606-5233
Telephone: 312-425-2700
Fax: 312-960-9560

Estate Planning, Estate and Trust Administration, Taxation, Employee Benefits, Tax Exempt Organizations, Real Estate, Corporate and Business Matters, Insurance Law, Civil Litigation.

WALTER W. BELL, born Chicago, Illinois, March 25, 1947; admitted to bar, 1971, Illinois; 1974, U.S. Tax Court. *Education:* Northwestern University (B.A., 1968; J.D., magna cum laude, 1971). Order of the Coif; Phi Alpha Delta. Member, Editorial Board, Northwestern University Law Review, 1970-1971. Author: "Transactions Between a Trust and Its Grantor and Beneficiaries," Estate Planning Magazine, January, 1993; Note, "An Expansion of the Divided Damages Rule in Admiralty," 64 Northwestern University Law Review 765, 1969; Note, "Texas Gulf Sulphur: The Question of Remedy," 65 Northwestern University Law Review 486, 1970; Note, "Minors and the Guest Statute," 65 Northwestern University Law Review 1018, 1971. *Member:* Chicago (Member, Federal Taxation Committee, 1971), Illinois State (Member, Probate and Trust Law Section) and American (Member, Taxation Section) Bar Associations. ***PRACTICE AREAS:*** Income, Estate and Gift Taxation; Estate Planning; Trust and Estate Administration. ***Email:*** wwbell@bjq-law.com

JERRY D. JONES, born Peoria, Illinois, November 1, 1942; admitted to bar, 1967, Illinois. *Education:* Spoon River College and University of Illinois (A.B., 1964); University of Illinois (J.D., 1967). Order of the Coif. Author: "The Lanham Act: A Method for the Registration and Protection of a Trademark Plus a Statutory Remedy for False Advertisement," 1966 University of Illinois Law Review. Member: Public Interest Law Initiative. *Member:* Chicago (Chair, Probate Practice Executive Committee, 1992-1993; Chair, Probate Practice Legislative Committee, 1993-1994), Illinois State and American Bar Associations. ***PRACTICE AREAS:*** Estate Planning; Probate and Trust Administration; Estate Litigation; Taxation. ***Email:*** jjones@bjq-law.com

JOHN J. QUINLISK, born Chicago, Illinois, November 19, 1943; admitted to bar, 1970, Illinois; 1974, U.S. District Court, Northern District of Illinois and U.S. Tax Court. *Education:* Loyola University (B.B.A., 1966; J.D., 1969). Dean's Key and Blue Key. Editor, *Mertens Law of Federal Income Taxation,* Callaghan & Company, 1972-1982. Author: "Retirement Payments Made Easy-Not!," National Conference of Bar Foundations' Foundation Forum, Spring, 1993; "Retirement Payments Made Easy-Not Part II," National Conference of Bar Foundations' Foundation Forum, Summer, 1993; "New Rules for Directed Investments for Pension Plans," National Conference of Bar Foundations' Foundation Forum, Winter, 1993. *Member:* Chicago Bar Association (Member, Employee Benefit Section). [Capt., U.S. Army, 1970-1971]. ***PRACTICE AREAS:*** Federal Income Tax; Employee Benefits. ***Email:*** jquinlisk@bjq-law.com

GINA M. ANDERSON, born Akron, Ohio, August 7, 1965; admitted to bar, 1995, Illinois and U.S. District Court, Northern District of Illinois. *Education:* The Ohio State University (B.A., 1987); DePaul University (J.D., 1995). *Member:* Chicago (Secretary, Young Lawyers Section Estate Planning Committee, 1995-1997) and American Bar Associations. ***PRACTICE AREAS:*** Estate Planning; Trusts; Probate; Business. ***Email:*** ganderson@bjq-law.com

ASSOCIATE

MICHAEL H. ALLEN, born Joliet, Illinois, December 12, 1969; admitted to bar, 1995, Illinois. *Education:* University of Illinois (B.A., magna cum laude, 1992; J.D., 1995). Phi Beta Kappa. *Member:* Chicago and Illinois Bar Associations. ***PRACTICE AREAS:*** Corporate and Business Law; Real Estate Transactions. ***Email:*** mhallen@bjq-law.com

OF COUNSEL

KENT CHANDLER, JR., born Chicago, Illinois, January 10, 1920; admitted to bar, 1949, Illinois. *Education:* Yale University (B.A., 1942); University of Michigan (J.D., with distinction, 1949). Phi Beta Kappa; Phi Delta Phi. *Member:* Chicago, Lake County, Illinois State and American Bar Associations; Law Club of Chicago (President, 1985-1986); Legal Club of Chicago. [With U.S.M.C., 1942-1946; Ret. Major, U.S.M.C.R.]. ***PRACTICE AREAS:*** Banking; Employee Benefits; Federal Taxation.

BELL & PENSYL

111 W. WASHINGTON STREET, SUITE 1640
CHICAGO, ILLINOIS 60602
Telephone: 312-580-1940
Fax: 312-580-1943

Business, Corporate, Real Estate and Employment.

IRA BELL, born Chicago, Illinois, August 4, 1935; admitted to bar, 1960, Illinois. *Education:* University of Illinois and Northwestern University (B.A., 1957); University of Chicago (J.D., 1960). *Member:* Chicago Bar Association. ***PRACTICE AREAS:*** Corporate; Employment Law. ***Email:*** bell@bellpensyl.com

CLAIRE E. PENSYL, born Pittsburgh, Pennsylvania; admitted to bar, 1978, Illinois. *Education:* University of Chicago (B.A., with honors, 1973; M.A., 1973; J.D., 1978). *Member:* Chicago and American Bar Associations; National Network of Commercial Real Estate Women (Delegate, 1990-1992, 1994; Director, 1992); Chicago Real Estate Executive Women. ***PRACTICE AREAS:*** Corporate; Real Estate; Finance. ***Email:*** pensyl@bellpensyl.com

LAW OFFICES KENNETH D. BELLAH

222 SOUTH RIVERSIDE PLAZA
SUITE 1410
CHICAGO, ILLINOIS 60606
Telephone: 312-648-9878
Fax: 312-648-0438
Email: kenbellah@aol.com

Palos Heights, Illinois Office: 12750 South Harlem Avenue, 60463. Telephone: 708-448-1520.

Sanderson, Texas Office: 119 West Oak Street, P.O. Box 175, 79848. Telephone: 915-345-2914. Fax: 915-345-2926.

Estate Planning, Estate Administration, Real Estate, Commercial Litigation, Corporate Law.

KENNETH D. BELLAH, born Joliet, Illinois, August 17, 1955; admitted to bar, 1980, Illinois; 1981, U.S. District Court, Northern District of Illinois and U.S. Court of Appeals, Seventh Circuit; 2000, Texas. *Education:* Augustana College (B.A., 1977); Chicago-Kent College of Law (J.D., 1980). *Member:* Illinois State Bar Association; State Bar of Texas. ***REPORTED CASES:*** Howalt v. Ohio Casualty Insurance Co. 142 Ill.App.3d. 435, 491 N.E.2d. 1207, 96 Ill.Dec. 747 (First Dist., 1986); ADCO Services, Inc. v. Bullard, et. al. 256 Ill.App.3d. 655, 628 N.E.2d. 772, 195 Ill.Dec. 308 (First Dist., 1993). ***PRACTICE AREAS:*** Estate Planning; Estate Administration; Real Estate; Commercial Litigation; Corporate Law.

BELLOWS AND BELLOWS

A PROFESSIONAL CORPORATION
Established in 1971
209 SOUTH LASALLE STREET, SUITE 800
CHICAGO, ILLINOIS 60604
Telephone: 312-332-3340
Fax: 312-332-1190

Los Angeles, California Office: 601 South Figueroa Street, 27th Floor. Telephone: 213-485-1555.

Administrative Law, Advertising/Marketing; Aged and Aging; Business Law, Civil Practice, Class Actions, Commercial Law, Commodities, Contracts, Copyrights, Corporate Law, Family Law, General Practice, Labor and Employment Litigation, Partnership Law, Intellectual Property, Securities Law, Real Estate, Taxation, Torts, Trusts and Estates, Wills.

FIRM PROFILE: Boutique Chicago law firm concentrating in corporate/securities law, including, but not limited to commercial litigation, arbitration, NASD matters, employment benefits law, class actions, tax law, estates/probate matters.

JOEL J. BELLOWS, born Chicago, Illinois, September 27, 1939; admitted to bar, 1965, California and Illinois; 1969, U.S. Court of Appeals, Ninth, Seventh and Second Circuits; 1974, U.S. District Court, Northern District of Indiana; 1978, U.S. Court of Appeals, Fifth Circuit; 1988, U.S. District Court, Northern District of California; U.S. District Court, Northern District of Illinois; U.S. District Court, Central District of California; U.S. District Court, Northern District of Georgia and U.S. District Court, Southern District of New York; 1995, U.S. District Court, Central District of Illinois. *Education:* Massachusetts Institute of Technology; University of Chicago; John Marshall Law School (J.D., Tax, with honors); University of Chicago Graduate School of Business and Harris School of Public Policy (M.B.A., 2000; M.P.P., 2000). Author: "Primer for the Neophyte Attorney in Juvenile Matters," Chicago Bar Record (February, 1992); "Representing Brokers and Public Customers in Commodity Litigation," IICLE. Authored supplement of IICLE Handbook on "Handling Business and Commercial Litigation," Trial Techniques. Visiting Lecturer: University of Chicago Graduate School of Business; Stanford University School of Law. Faculty Member, Skills for Practicing Attorneys, IICLE Federal Trial Bar Course. Chairman, Cook County Task Force on Youth Welfare, 1991. Arbitrator, National Association of Securities Dealers, 1974—. Member, Panel of Arbitrators, American Arbitration Association, 1970—. Member: Chicago, Illinois State and American Bar Associations; Illinois Society of Lawyers-Certified Public Accountants. ***PRACTICE AREAS:*** Investment Fraud; Commodity Regulation and Registration; Securities Broker Fraud; Employment Discrimination. ***Email:*** jbellows@bellowspc.com

LAUREL G. BELLOWS, born Chicago, Illinois, April 9, 1948; admitted to bar, 1974, Illinois and U.S. District Court, Northern District of Illinois; 1975, Florida; 1977, U.S. Court of Appeals, Seventh Circuit; 1978, U.S. Court of Appeals, Fifth Circuit; 1979, U.S. District Court, Northern District of Georgia; 1980, U.S. District Court, Central District of California; 1981, California; 1995, U.S. District Court, Central District of Illinois. *Education:* University of Pennsylvania (B.A., 1969); Loyola University (J.D., 1974). Member, Loyola University Law Review, 1973-1974. Author: "Extortion 'Under Color of Official Right': Federal Prosecution of Official Corruption Under the Hobbs Act," Loyola University of Chicago Law Journal, 1974; Supplement of IICLE Handbook on "Handling Business and Commercial Litigation," Trial Technique, 1987-2003. Chair, ABA Commission on Women in the Profession, 1995-1998. President, National Caucus of Metropolitan Bar Associations, 1990-1992. President: National Conference of Bar Presidents, 1999-2000; National Conference of Women's Bar Associations Board, 1989-1991. Arbitrator, Circuit Court of Cook County, Mandatory Arbitration Panel, 1990. Board: Women's Business Development Center; Senate Judicial Nominations Committee. Chair, The Chicago Network, 1996. Member: The Economic Club of Chicago; The Commercial Club of Chicago. *Member:* Chicago (President, 1991-1992; Chairman, Membership Committee, 1982-1983; Chairman, Sustaining Member Program, 1984; Chairman, Public Relations Committee, 1985-1986; Chairman, Long Range Planning, 1986-1987), Illinois State and American (Member, Board of Governors, 2000-2003; Member, Standing Committee on Federal Judiciary, 1999-2000) Bar Associations; Women's Bar Association of Illinois Foundation (Director, 1988—). ***LANGUAGES:*** Spanish. ***SPECIAL AGENCIES:*** American Arbitration Association; New York Stock Exchange; National Association of Securities Dealers; National Futures Association; Chicago Mercantile Exchange; Commodity Futures Trading

(This Listing Continued)

BELLOWS AND BELLOWS, A PROFESSIONAL CORPORATION, Chicago—Continued

Commission; Chicago Board of Trade. ***PRACTICE AREAS:*** Business Litigation; Employment Law; Contracts; Separation Agreements; Executive Compensation. ***Email:*** lbellows@bellowspc.com

---

CHRISTOPHER L. GALLINARI, born New York, N.Y., October 12, 1965; admitted to bar, 1991, New York; 1993, Illinois, U.S. Court of Appeals, Seventh Circuit, Eighth Circuit and District of Columbia Circuit; U.S. District Court, Southern, Eastern and Western Districts of New York; U.S. District Court, Central, Southern and Northern Districts of Illinois including Trial Bar, Northern District of Indiana, Eastern and Western Districts of Michigan and Western District of Wisconsin. *Education:* Drew University (B.A., magna cum laude, 1987); New York University (J.D., 1990). Phi Alpha Delta. Speaker: "Liability of BBS Operators and On-Line Service Providers for Piracy by Subscribers," Indiana Continuing Legal Education Forum, Indianapolis, Indiana, October, 1994; "Ease on Down the Electronic Road," Midwest Computer Show sponsored by the Illinois CPA Society and Foundation, Chicago, Illinois, August, 1995. *Member:* Chicago and Illinois State Bar Associations. ***PRACTICE AREAS:*** Commercial Litigation; Business Law; Investment Fraud; Commodities Regulation; Securities; Intellectual Property. ***Email:*** cgallinari@bellowspc.com

LESLIE P. POOLE, born Brooklyn, New York, August 3, 1954; admitted to bar, 1981, Illinois; U.S. Court of Appeals, Federal Circuit. *Education:* Loyola University (B.B.A., Economics, 1976; J.D., 1980). Tau Epsilon Rho; Delta Sigma Pi (Past Treasurer; Vice President, 1974—). *Member:* Chicago, Illinois State and Federal Bar Associations; Illinois Trial Lawyers Association; Federal Trial Bar Association; The Association of Trial Lawyers of America. ***REPORTED CASES:*** Prodromos v. Poulos, 202 Ill. App.3d 1024; Sam Sianis v. Kettler, 168 Ill. App.3d 1071; Herr v. Chicago Park District, 1-00-1446; Dean Kordopitoulas v. Illinois Farmers Insurance Co. 1-00-4258. ***PRACTICE AREAS:*** Commercial Litigation; Business Law; Commercial Real Estate Litigation; Domestic Relations; Personal Injury; Insurance Coverage. ***Email:*** lpoole@bellowspc.com

HELEN BLOCH, born Evanston, Illinois, October 8, 1973; admitted to bar, 1998, Illinois. *Education:* Yeshiva University (B.A., magna cum laude, 1995); Chicago-Kent College of Law, Illinois Institute of Technology (J.D., International and Comparative Law, 1998). Dean's List. Recipient: Benjamin H. & Jennie Hammer Memorial Award for Excellence in Political Science; Stern College Alumnae Association Award for Academic Achievement and Service to the College; CALI Award for Academic Excellence. Author: "Should Sexually Provocative Advertisements Sell Law?" 1 DePaul Women's L.J. 10 (1988). Vice-President, 2002-2004 and Second Vice-President, 2000-2002, Decalogue Society of Lawyers. Member, Alliance of Bar Association for Judicial Screening, 1999-2004. Co-Chair, Associates Committee, 2003-2004 and Co-Chair, Specialties Committee, 2002-2003, Lawyers Division, Jewish Federation of Metropolitan Chicago. Formerly with, City of Chicago Law Department. ***PRACTICE AREAS:*** Business Litigation; Commercial Transactions; Divorce; Family Law; Employment; Estate Planning; Land Use Litigation; Workers Compensation Defense. ***Email:*** hbloch@bellowspc.com

GRETCHEN L. GRADINGER, born Kansas City, Missouri, May 15, 1976; admitted to bar, 2001, Illinois. *Education:* University of Kansas (B.S., 1998); John Marshall Law School (J.D., 2001). ***PRACTICE AREAS:*** Employment Law; Employment Litigation; Securities Litigation; Commercial Litigation. ***Email:*** ggradinger@bellowspc.com

CONNIE S. PIKE, born Sioux City, Iowa, June 23, 1977; admitted to bar, 2004, Illinois. *Education:* Benedictine College (B.A., 1999); University of Missouri at Kansas City (J.D., 2004). ***PRACTICE AREAS:*** Litigation; Securities; Employment Law. ***Email:*** cpike@bellowspc.com

LEGAL SUPPORT PERSONNEL

CINTHIA M. LEGRAND, (Firm Administrator)

RICHARD L. BERDELLE, JR., P.C.

THE ROOKERY BUILDING
209 SOUTH LASALLE STREET, SUITE 501
CHICAGO, ILLINOIS 60604-1447
Telephone: 312-726-0400
Fax: 312-726-0401
Email: dberdelle@sbcglobal.net
URL: http://www.berdellelaw.com

Medical Malpracticing including: Surgical and Physician Malpractice, Obstetric Malpractice, Hospital Malpractice, Birth Defects and Birth Trauma. Plaintiff Personal Injury including: Automobile Accidents, Trucking Accidents, Motorcycle Accidents, Head Injuries, Catastrophic Accidents and Wrongful Death.

RICHARD L. BERDELLE, JR., born Chicago, Illinois, October 19, 1953; admitted to bar, 1978, Wisconsin; 1978, Illinois and U.S. District Court, Northern District of Illinois. *Education:* Miami University of Ohio (B.S., Business, 1975); Marquette University (J.D., 1978). *Member:* Chicago and Illinois State Bar Associations; Illinois Trial Lawyers Association; Society of Trial Lawyers. ***PRACTICE AREAS:*** Medical Malpractice; Personal Injury. ***Email:*** dberdelle@sbcglobal.net

BERGER SCHATZ

A Partnership including Professional Corporations
161 NORTH CLARK STREET, SUITE 2800
CHICAGO, ILLINOIS 60601
Telephone: 312-782-3456
Fax: 312-782-8463
Email: info@bergerschatz.com
URL: http://www.bergerschatz.com

Lake County Office: 2333 Waukegan Road, Suite 260, Bannockburn, Illinois 60015. Telephone: 847-405-9500. Fax: 847-405-9563.

Matrimonial, Family, Domestic Relations Law, Trial and Appellate Practice: Including Divorce, Child Custody, Child Support, Paternity, Spousal Support and Visitation Rights.

FIRM PROFILE: Berger Schatz dedicates its practice solely to matrimonial and family law, and is one of the largest firms of its kind in the country.

On both the trial and appellate levels, the Firm's 25 attorneys handle cases involving substantial estates, valuation, tax, custody and issues of paternity. Members of the Firm are also proficient in drafting prenuptial and postnuptial agreements.

The Firm includes Fellows, Board Members and the Past President of the Illinois Chapter of the American Academy of Matrimonial Lawyers as well as three recent chairs of the Illinois State Bar Association Family Law Section Council and the past President of the Lake County Bar Association.

MEMBERS OF FIRM

JASON G. ADESS, born Skokie, Illinois, November 27, 1970; admitted to bar, 1995, Illinois and U.S. District Court, Northern District of Illinois. *Education:* University of Maryland (B.A., 1992); DePaul University (J.D., 1995). *Member:* Chicago and Illinois State (Council Member, Family Law Section) Bar Associations; Leading Lawyers Network. ***PRACTICE AREAS:*** Family Law; Domestic Relations; Matrimonial Law; Divorce. ***Email:*** jadess@bergerschatz.com

MICHAEL J. BERGER, (P.C.), born Chicago, Illinois, October 19, 1949; admitted to bar, 1973, Illinois. *Education:* Roosevelt University (B.A., 1970); Illinois Institute of Technology/Chicago-Kent College of Law (J.D., 1973). ***PRACTICE AREAS:*** Family Law; Domestic Relations; Matrimonial Law; Divorce. ***Email:*** mberger@bergerschatz.com

MARY J. CLARK, born Elmhurst, Illinois, December 14, 1954; admitted to bar, 1979, Illinois. *Education:* Barat College (B.A., 1976); Northern Illinois University (J.D., 1979). *Member:* Lake County (President, 1994) and Illinois State Bar Associations, Associations Women Attorneys (President, 1990-1991), Jefferson Inns, American Inns of Court (President, 2000) (Resident Partner-in-Charge, Bannockburn Office). (Resident Partner-in-Charge, Bannockburn Office). ***Email:*** mclark@bergerschatz.com

AMANDA B. CLAYMAN, born Boston, Massachusetts, December 2, 1971; admitted to bar, 1996, Arizona; 1999, Illinois. *Education:* Middlebury College (B.A., 1993); Northwestern Univ. School of Law (J.D., 1996). *Member:* Illinois State Bar and Chicago Bar Associations. ***PRACTICE AREAS:*** Family Law; Domestic Relations; Matrimonial Law; Divorce. ***Email:*** aclayman@bergerschatz.com

MICHAEL S. COHEN (1954-2004)

ANDREW D. EICHNER, born New York, N.Y., August 30, 1955; admitted to bar, 1980, Illinois and U.S. District Court, Northern District of Illinois. *Education:* Duke University (A.B., magna cum laude, 1977); Loyola University of Chicago (J.D., 1980). *Member:* Chicago (Member, Matrimonial Law Committee, 1985), Illinois State (Member, Law Section) and American Bar Associations. ***PRACTICE AREAS:*** Family Law; Domestic Relations; Matrimonial Law; Divorce. ***Email:*** aeichner@bergerschatz.com

LEON I. FINKEL, born Chicago, Illinois, February 3, 1958; admitted to bar, 1983, Illinois. *Education:* Northern Illinois University (B.S., magna cum laude, 1980); Loyola University (J.D., 1983). *Member:* Illinois State (Member, Family Law Section) and American (Member, Family Law Section) Bar Associations. ***PRACTICE AREAS:*** Family Law; Domestic Relations; Matrimonial Law; Divorce. ***Email:*** lfinkel@bergerschatz.com

P. ANDRÉ KATZ, born October 2, 1964; admitted to bar, 1989, Illinois; 1991, U.S. District Court, Northern District of Illinois. *Education:* University of Wisconsin (B.A., with distinction, 1985); Loyola University of Chicago (J.D., 1989). *Member:* Illinois State Bar, Chicago Bar and American Bar Associations. ***PRACTICE AREAS:*** Family Law; Domestic Relations; Matrimonial Law; Divorce. ***Email:*** akatz@bergerschatz.com

DEBBIE K. LERNER, born New York, N.Y.; admitted to bar, 1992, Wisconsin and U.S. District Court, Eastern District of Wisconsin; U.S. District Court, Western District of Wisconsin; 1994, California; 1999, Illinois. *Education:* San Diego State University (B.A. in history, cum laude, 1986); Marquette University (J.D., cum laude, 1992). Phi Alpha Theta. Sutherland Memorial Scholarship. Judge Noel Fox Scholarship. *Member:* State Bar of California, Illinois State and American Bar Associations; State Bar of Wisconsin. (Resident, Bannockburn Office). ***Email:*** dlerner@bergerschatz.com

DAVID H. LEVY, (P.C.), born Chicago, Illinois, April 16, 1951; admitted to bar, 1976, Illinois, U.S. District Court, Northern District of Illinois and U.S. Court of Appeals, Seventh Circuit. *Education:* Ohio University (B.G.S., 1973); Illinois Institute of Technology/Chicago-Kent College of Law (J.D., 1976). *Member:* Illinois State (Family Law Section Council, Secretary, 1993-1994, Vice-Chairman, 1995, Chairman, 1995-1996) and American (Family Law Section) Bar Associations. ***PRACTICE AREAS:*** Family Law; Domestic Relations; Matrimonial Law; Divorce. ***Email:*** dlevy@bergerschatz.com

NORMAN RUBER, born Chicago, Illinois, September 17, 1952; admitted to bar, 1978, Illinois. *Education:* Northeastern Illinois University (B.A., with honors, 1974); John Marshall Law School (J.D., 1978). *Member:* Illinois State and American (Member, Family Law Section); Bar Associations. ***PRACTICE AREAS:*** Family Law; Domestic Relations; Matrimonial Law; Divorce. ***Email:*** nruber@bergerschatz.com

MICHAEL S. SABATH, born Chicago, Illinois, December 15, 1966; admitted to bar, 1992, Illinois and U.S. District, Northern District of Illinois. *Education:* University of

(This Listing Continued)

Colorado at Boulder (B.A., 1989); Chicago-Kent College of Law, Illinois (J.D., with honors, 1992). *Member:* Chicago (Member, Matrimonial Law Committee) and Illinois State Bar Associations. **PRACTICE AREAS:** Family Law; Domestic Relations; Matrimonial Law; Divorce. **Email:** msabath@bergerschatz.com

BARRY A. SCHATZ, (P.C.), born Philadelphia, Pennsylvania, June 22, 1946; admitted to bar, 1974, Illinois and Pennsylvania. *Education:* Pennsylvania State University (B.A., 1968); John Marshall Law School (J.D., 1974). *Member:* Illinois State and American Bar Associations; American Academy of Matrimonial Lawyers. **PRACTICE AREAS:** Family Law; Domestic Relations; Matrimonial Law; Divorce; Prenuptial Agreements. **Email:** bschatz@bergerschatz.com

TRACEY A. WERTMAN, born Pittsburgh, Pennsylvania, February 20, 1966; admitted to bar, 1991, Ohio; 1994, U.S. District Court, Northern District of Ohio and U.S. Court of Appeals, Sixth Circuit; 1999, Illinois. *Education:* Duquesne University (B.A., 1988); The University of Akron School of Law (J.D., 1991). *Member:* Illinois State and Chicago (Matrimonial Law Committee and Young Lawyer's Family Law Committee) Bar Associations. **PRACTICE AREAS:** Family Law; Domestic Relations; Matrimonial Law; Divorce. **Email:** twertman@bergerschatz.com

---

BRIAN J. BLITZ, born Park Ridge, Illinois, May 11, 1977; admitted to bar, 2002, Illinois. *Education:* University of Texas (B.A., 1999); University of Illinois (J.D., 2002). *Member:* Illinois and Chicago Bar Associations. **PRACTICE AREAS:** Family Law; Domestic Relations; Matrimonial Law; Divorce. **Email:** bblitz@bergerschatz.com

CATHERINE M. DUNN, born Lansing, Michigan, November 6, 1973; admitted to bar, 1999, Illinois. *Education:* University of Michigan (B.A., 1996; J.D., 1999). *Member:* Illinois State and American Bar Associations. **PRACTICE AREAS:** Family Law; Domestic Relations; Divorce. **Email:** cdunn@bergerschatz.com

LAURENCE B. HIRSCH, born Springfield, Pennsylvania, May 28, 1974; admitted to bar, 1999, Illinois; 2000, U.S. District Court, Northern District of Illinois; 2004, Arizona. *Education:* University of Iowa (B.A., 1996); Chicago-Kent College of Law, Illinois Institute of Technology (J.D., 1999). Member: University of Iowa Alumni Association; Human Rights Campaign; Standard Club. *Member:* Chicago, Maricopa County and Illinois State Bar Associations; State Bar of Arizona; Decalogue Society of Lawyers. **PRACTICE AREAS:** Family Law; Domestic Relations; Matrimonial Law; Divorce. **Email:** lhirsch@bergerschatz.com

JOSHUA E. HORNADAY (Resident, Bannockburn Office)

KRISTINA L. JARVIS, born St. Louis, Missouri, September 28, 1972; admitted to bar, 2000, Illinois. *Education:* University of South Carolina (B.A., 1994) Chicago-Kent College of Law (J.D., 1999). *Member:* Chicago, Illinois State and American Bar Associations. **PRACTICE AREAS:** Family Law; Divorce; Matrimonial Law; Domestic Relations. **Email:** kjarvis@bergerschatz.com

MARGARET E. KEANE, born Chicago, Illinois, September 6, 1971; admitted to bar, 1999, Illinois. *Education:* DePaul University (B.A., 1993); Chicago-Kent College of Law (J.D., 1999). *Member:* Chicago and Illinois Bar Associations. **PRACTICE AREAS:** Family Law; Domestic Relations; Matrimonial Law; Divorce. **Email:** mkeane@bergerschatz.com

MARCELLE R. KOTT, born Illinois, April 15, 1967; admitted to bar, 1992, Illinois. *Education:* Indiana University (B.A., 1989); John Marshall Law School (J.D., 1992). *Member:* Chicago and Illinois State Bar Associations. **PRACTICE AREAS:** Family Law; Domestic Relations; Matrimonial Law; Divorce. **Email:** mkott@bergerschatz.com

KAREN ROSE KREHBIEL, born Red Bank, New Jersey, July 14, 1976; admitted to bar, 2002, New York and Illinois. *Education:* Dartmouth College (B.A., 1998); University of Michigan (J.D., 2001). *Member:* Illinois State and American Bar Associations. **PRACTICE AREAS:** Family Law; Domestic Relations; Matrimonial Law; Divorce.

SHARON STEINBERG MOBLEY, born New York, N.Y., June 22, 1970; admitted to bar, 2000, Illinois; 2002, New York. *Education:* University of Michigan (B.A., 1992); University of California at Los Angeles (J.D., 2000). *Member:* Illinois State and Chicago Bar Associations. **PRACTICE AREAS:** Family Law; Domestic Relations; Matrimonial Law; Divorce. **Email:** smobley@bergerschatz.com

MELINDA C. ROGERS, born Durham, North Carolina, 1968; admitted to bar, 1995, Illinois. *Education:* Southwestern University (B.A., 1990); DePaul University College of Law (J.D., 1995). **PRACTICE AREAS:** Family Law; Domestic Relations; Matrimonial Law; Divorce.

DINA WARNER, born New Brunswick, New Jersey, September 18, 1967; admitted to bar, 1992, Massachusetts and New York; 2002, Illinois. *Education:* Columbia University (B.A., 1988); Yale University Law School (J.D., 1991). **PRACTICE AREAS:** Family Law; Domestic Relations; Matrimonial Law; Divorce. **Email:** dwarner@bergerschatz.com

---

BERLIN & ASSOCIATES

222 NORTH COLUMBUS DRIVE
SUITE 4102
CHICAGO, ILLINOIS 60601
Telephone: 312-297-9000
Fax: 312-297-9000
Email: berlinlaw@sbcglobal.net
URL: http://www.berlinlawfirm.com

General Practice and Real Estate.

GERALD L. BERLIN, born New York, N.Y., November 6, 1958; admitted to bar, 1984, Illinois. *Education:* Ohio University (B.S., 1980); DePaul University (J.D., 1984). *Member:* Chicago, Illinois State and American Bar Associations. **PRACTICE AREAS:** Real Estate.

MICHAEL H. BERMAN, P.C.

180 NORTH LASALLE STREET, SUITE 2108
CHICAGO, ILLINOIS 60601
Telephone: 312-726-0531
Fax: 312-726-4928
Email: mhbermanpc@yahoo.com

Personal Injury, Torts, Medical Malpractice, Professional Liability, Automobile Accidents, Wrongful Death, Premises Liability, Civil Litigation.

MICHAEL H. BERMAN, born Brooklyn, New York, March 28, 1945; admitted to bar, 1969, Illinois. *Education:* Loyola University (B.S., 1966); John Marshall Law School (J.D., 1969). Partner, Berman and Trachtman, 1979-1995. *Member:* The Association of Trial Lawyers of America. [Capt., U.S. Army, 1969-1971]

PETER J. BERMAN, LTD.

Established in 1985

SUITE 1000
332 SOUTH MICHIGAN AVENUE
CHICAGO, ILLINOIS 60604-4398
Telephone: 312-408-1114
Fax: 312-408-1936
Email: pberman@pbermanlaw.com
URL: http://www.pbermanlaw.com

Business Litigation, Securities Arbitration, Broker-Dealer Arbitration, Commodities Arbitration, Federal Civil Practice, Shareholder Disputes, Trial Practice, Civil Appeals, Employment Litigation, Commercial Litigation.

FIRM PROFILE: The firm represents clients involved in business disputes before state and federal courts, and different arbitration, reparation, and disciplinary bodies, including the National Association of Securities Dealers ("NASD"), National Futures Association ("NFA"), Commodity Futures Trading Commission ("CFTC"), Securities and Exchange Commission ("SEC"), various exchanges, and the American Arbitration Association ("AAA").

Many of the disputes involve securities, commodities, derivatives, stocks, corporate bonds, government issues, stock options, warrants, options on futures contracts, variable and fixed annuities, securitized assets, private placements, registered securities, as well as the practices of broker-dealers, futures commission merchants, introducing brokers, investment advisers, commodity trading advisers, commodity pool operators, and their associated persons or registered representatives, floor traders, floor brokers, specialists, market makers, clearing brokers, exchange members, hedge funds, money mangers, asset managers, certified financial planners, financial consultants, insurance companies, insurance agents and brokers, accountants, banks, and other financial institutions.

The firm also represents firms and individuals in connection with registration matters before these bodies. The firm also represents employers and employees in raiding cases where restrictive covenants are at issue (e.g., non-compete agreements, non-solicitation agreements, and confidentiality agreements) and where claims involving the misappropriation of trade secrets, breach of fiduciary, fraud and compensation issues duty have been made. Many, but not all, of these cases involve brokerage firms.

The firm also represents clients involved in shareholder-disputes involving closely held corporations, general partnerships, limited liability companies or limited liability partnerships and other commercial matters.

PETER J. BERMAN, born New York, N.Y., June 10, 1946; admitted to bar, 1974, Illinois and U.S. District Court, Northern District of Illinois; 1975, U.S. Court of Appeals, Seventh Circuit; 1979, U.S. Supreme Court. *Education:* University of Wisconsin (B.A., 1968); DePaul University (J.D., cum laude, 1974). Member, De Paul University Law Review, 1973-1974. Author: "How to Resolve Business Disputes Without Going Broke," Altschuler, Melvoin & Glasser Ledger, Summer 1994; "Solving Disputes Without Litigation," Shopping Centers Today, May, 1994; "The Attorney/Client Privilege and the IRS: Assessing the Currency Transaction Reporting Regulations," Illinois Bar Journal, Vol. 77, No. 10, 530, June, 1989; "Resolving Business Disputes Through Mediation and Arbitration," The CPA Journal, November, 1994; "Alternative Fee Agreements With Counsel," The CPA Journal, Dec., 1994. Co-Author with Weiner: "Section 17 Registered Futures Associations," Journal of Futures Markets, Vol. 1, 1981 Supp.; "Mediation and Arbitration," the American Institute of Certified Public Accountants' *The Management of an Accounting Practice Handbook,* Chapter 214, Section 7 (May 1997). Trial Attorney, Commodity Futures Trading Commission, 1977-1979; *Member:* Chicago (Member, Futures Trading Committee, 1978—; Chairman, Litigation Sub-Committee, 1986; Securities Law committee, 1985—) and American (Member: Business Law Section; Futures and Derivatives Law Committee, 1979—) Bar Associations; Arbitrator for National Futures Association. **Email:** pberman@pbermanlaw.com

---

JAMES E. BETKE

161 NORTH CLARK STREET, SUITE 4950
CHICAGO, ILLINOIS 60601-3238
Telephone: 312-346-5050
Fax: 312-332-0515
Email: jebetke@imsif.com

Commercial Litigation, Insurance Law, Arbitration, Class Actions, Insurance Coverage, Professional Liability.

JAMES E. BETKE, born March 20, 1940; admitted to bar, 1966, Illinois; 1967, U.S. District Court, Northern District of Illinois. *Education:* Hope College (B.A., 1961); Uni-

(This Listing Continued)

JAMES E. BETKE, Chicago—Continued

versity of Chicago (M.A., 1963; J.D., 1966). *Member:* Chicago, Illinois State and American Bar Associations. ***PRACTICE AREAS:*** Commercial Litigation; Insurance; Arbitration; Class Actions; Insurance Coverage; Professional Liability.

BISCHOFF PARTNERS, LLC

217 NORTH JEFFERSON STREET
SUITE 600
CHICAGO, ILLINOIS 60661
Telephone: 312-466-9100
Facsimile: 312-466-1186

Corporate Law, Business Law, Transactional, Secured Transactions, Federal and State Civil Trial Practice, Commercial and Residential Real Estate, Estate Planning and Estate Administration, Zoning & Land Use.

MARK P. BISCHOFF, born Chicago, Illinois, February 22, 1947; admitted to bar, 1974, Illinois. *Education:* University of Illinois (B.A., 1969); University of San Diego (J.D., 1973). Author: "Parental Corporate Alter Ego Liability: How to Avoid Veil Piercing," Corporation, Securities and Business Law, March, 1993; Numerous Estate Planning and Wealth Preservation Planning articles for UBS Financial Services, Inc. President: Crossings Homeowners Association, 1978-1979; Zoning Board of Appeals, Village of Kildeer, IL, 1990-1994; Planning Commission, Kildeer, 1994-1995. Police Commissioner, Village of Kildeer, IL, 1997-2002. Director, 1981-1989, Second Vice President, 1986, First Vice President, 1987 and President, 1988, Arlington Heights Chamber of Commerce. Member, Attorney Network, UBS Financial Services, Inc., 1996—. Director, Planned Giving Committee, Chicago Anti Cruelty Society, 2002—. *Member:* Chicago Bar Association; Illinois State Bar Association (Member, Corporation and Securities Law Section Council, 1989-1993); American Bar Association (Member: Section on Taxation; Committees on Partnerships; Business Law; Law Practice Management). ***PRACTICE AREAS:*** Corporate; Business Succession Planning; Estate Planning; Estate Administration; Wealth Preservation Planning; Real Estate. ***Email:*** mbischoff@bis-law.com

THOMAS J. SWABOWSKI (1951-1999)

MONICA A. FORTE, born Chicago, Illinois, November 20, 1966; admitted to bar, 1994, Illinois and U.S. District Court, Northern District of Illinois; 1995, U.S. Court of Appeals, 6th Circuit. *Education:* University of Illinois (B.A., with distinction, 1989); Loyola University (J.D., 1994). Recipient, L.U. Legal Scholars Scholarship. Board Member, Lane Tech High School Alumni Association. *Member:* Chicago and Illinois State Bar Associations. ***LANGUAGES:*** French and Spanish. ***PRACTICE AREAS:*** Commercial Litigation. ***Email:*** mforte@bis-law.com

TED A. KOESTER, born Effingham, Illinois, June 2, 1972; admitted to bar, 1998, Illinois. *Education:* Eastern Illinois University (B.S., Finance, 1994); Seton Hall University (J.D., 1998). *Member:* Chicago (Member: Committees on: Trust Law; Corporation and Business Law; Probate Practice; YLS Estate Planning; YLS Corporate Practice), Illinois State (Member: Sections on: Trusts and Estates; Business Advice; Financial Planning) and American (Member: Sections on: Real Property, Probate and Trust Law) Bar Associations. ***PRACTICE AREAS:*** Estate Planning; Business Succession Planning; Wealth Preservation; Probate; Taxation; Business Law. ***Email:*** tkoester@bis-law.com

SCOTT A. WEINSTEIN, born Rochester, New York, August 6, 1968; admitted to bar, 1994, New York; 1998, Florida; 2000, Illinois and U.S. District Court, Northern District of Illinois. *Education:* University of Maryland (B.A., 1990); Temple University (J.D., 1993). *Member:* Chicago, Illinois State and New York State Bar Associations; The Florida Bar. ***PRACTICE AREAS:*** Corporate Law; Real Estate; Estate Planning. ***Email:*** sweinstein@bis-law.com

REPRESENTATIVE CLIENTS: UBS Financial Services, St. Mark's Missionary Baptist Church; Al Piemonte Automobile Dealerships; The Art Institute of Chicago; Freedom Mortgage Team, Inc.

BLAKE, CASSELS & GRAYDON (U.S.) LLP

Established in 1856
181 WEST MADISON STREET, SUITE 3610
CHICAGO, ILLINOIS 60602-4645
Telephone: 312-739-3610
Facsimile: 312-739-3611
Email: chicago@blakes.com
URL: http://www.blakes.com

The Firm maintains other offices in: Montréal, Québec; Toronto, Ottawa, Ontario; Calgary, Alberta; Vancouver, British Columbia; New York, New York; London, England and Beijing, China.

Alternate Dispute Resolution, Aviation, Business, China Practice, Class Actions (Class Action), Commodity Tax and Trade, Communications, Competition and Trade, Constitutional and Charter of Rights, Construction, Corporate Governance, Criminal, Electronic Commerce (E-commerce), Energy, Environmental, Estates and Trusts, Financial Services, First Nations Law (Aboriginal Law), Forestry, Franchising, Gaming, Health, Hospitality and Tourism, Immigration, Information Technology, Insurance, Intellectual Property, International, Labour and Employment, Linguistics, Litigation, Marketing and Advertising, Media, Mergers and Acquisitions, Mining, Municipal and Planning, Oil and Gas, Outsourcing, Pension and Employee Benefits (Pensions), Privacy, Procurement, Product Liability (Products Liability), Real Estate, Research, Restructuring and Insolvency, Securities, Sports and Entertainment, Structured Finance, Tax Litigation and Controversy Resolution, Tax (Taxation).

(This Listing Continued)

FIRM PROFILE: Firm's practice restricted to Canadian law. Assists U.S.-based clients wishing to conduct business in Canada, whether by building, investing in, or acquiring and operating Canadian businesses, as well as Canadian clients conducting business in the U.S., including facilitating access to the U.S. capital markets.

Blake, Cassels & Graydon LLP is one of Canada's leading business law firms, with more than 500 lawyers in offices in Montréal, Ottawa, Toronto, Calgary, Vancouver, New York, Chicago, London, England and Beijing, China.

LAW FIRM ALLIANCES/ASSOCIATIONS: ***LEX MUNDI***
TECHLAW GROUP
CHINA ALLIANCE

PARTNER

GEOFFREY S. BELSHER, born Regina, Saskatchewan, 1966; admitted to bar, 1992, British Columbia (Not admitted in Illinois). *Education:* Simon Fraser University (B.A., 1988); Osgoode Hall Law School (LL.B., 1991). ***PRACTICE AREAS:*** Mergers and Acquisitions; Securities; Business; Corporate Governance. ***Email:*** geoff.belsher@blakes.com

(For biographical data on other personnel, see Professional Biographies at Montréal, Québec; Ottawa and Toronto, Ontario; Calgary, Alberta; Vancouver, British Columbia; New York, New York; London, England and Beijing, China)

BLAU & BONAVICH

140 SOUTH DEARBORN STREET, SUITE 1610
CHICAGO, ILLINOIS 60603-5202
Telephone: 312-443-1600
Fax: 312-443-1665
Email: lesblau@aol.com
URL: http://www.blauandbonavich.com

Civil and Commercial Litigation, Commodity Futures Litigation, Securities Litigation, Employment Litigation.

LESLIE A. BLAU, admitted to bar, 1973, New York; 1981, Illinois. *Education:* Columbia University (J.D., 1972). Harlan Fiske Stone Scholar. Chief, Division of Enforcement, Commodity Futures Trading Commission, New York Office, 1976-1978. *Member:* Chicago Bar Association (Member, Futures Regulation Committee, 1980—; Chair, Federal Civil Procedure Committee, 1992-1993). ***PRACTICE AREAS:*** Commodity Futures Litigation; Securities Litigation.

PETER R. BONAVICH (Retired)

LAW OFFICES OF SHELL J. BLEIWEISS

321 SOUTH PLYMOUTH COURT, SUITE 1200
CHICAGO, ILLINOIS 60604
Telephone: 312-360-8782
Fax: 312-360-9212
Email: sbleiweiss@shell-bleiweiss.com
URL: http://www.shell-bleiweiss.com

Barrington, Illinois Office: 25840 Indian Trail Road, 60010. Telephone: 312-360-8782.

Environmental Law, Occupational Safety and Health, OSHA, Chemical Regulation, Alternative Dispute Resolution, Litigation.

SHELL J. BLEIWEISS, born March 7, 1950; admitted to bar, 1982, Illinois. *Education:* Northwestern University (J.D., 1982). Member, Editorial Board, Journal of Criminal Law and Criminology, 1981-1982. *Member:* American Bar Association (Member, Sections on: Litigation; Environment; Former Chair, Coordinating Group on ADR). ***REPORTED CASES:*** Argued before Illinois Supreme Court on behalf of Appellants, People v. Brockman, 143 Ill.2d 751 (1991). ***PRACTICE AREAS:*** Environmental Law; Occupational Safety and Health; OSHA; Chemical Regulation; Alternative Dispute Resolution; Litigation.

ALVIN W. BLOCK, & ASSOCIATES

33 NORTH LA SALLE STREET, SUITE 3000
CHICAGO, ILLINOIS 60602
Telephone: 312-346-5656
Fax: 312-78 BLOCK
URL: http://www.chicagolawyers.com
Email: attorneys@chicagolawyers.com
URL: http://www.lawyers.com/chicagolawyers

Federal and State Civil, Trial and Appellate Practice, Trials, Corporate, Business, Contracts, Breach of Contract, Insurance, Catastrophic Injury, Automobile Accidents, Commercial Insurance, Insurance Bad Faith, Life and Health Insurance, Property Insurance, Chancery and Class Actions, Personal Injury, Airplane Crash Litigation, Railroad Accidents, Sexual Abuse, Construction Accidents, Product Liability, Consumer, Civil Rights, Wrongful Death, Probate, Wills, Trust and Estates, Asset Protection, Contested Wills, Guardianship, Real Estate, Commercial Real Estate, Condominium, Cooperative Housing, Landlord and Tenant Mortgages, Commercial, Commercial Banking, Buying and Selling Business, Family Business, Limited Liability Company, Minority Business, Partnership, Professional Practices and Small Business Law.

FIRM PROFILE: We are an aggressive civil litigation firm, founded in 1958 as Block & Levy. The firm has also been known as Block, Levy & Becker, Block, Levy & Associates and for the last fifteen years, as Alvin W. Block & Associates. Representing primarily individuals and small to mid-size businesses, the firm practices in state and federal courts in Chicago, as well as the collar-county courts of the Chicago metropolitan area. Our seasoned trial lawyers are expe-

(This Listing Continued)

rienced in civil areas ranging from torts to class actions and commercial litigation. A tenacious law firm with an outstanding trial and appellate practice, we have distinguished ourselves among the smaller firms in Chicago.

ALVIN W. BLOCK, born Chicago, Illinois, August 27, 1930; admitted to bar, 1956, Illinois; 1957, U.S. District Court, Northern District of Illinois including Trial Bar; 1963, U.S. Supreme Court and U.S. Court of Appeals, Seventh Circuit. *Education:* Roosevelt University (B.S.C., 1954); John Marshall Law School (J.D., 1956). Lecturer: "Class Actions--Practical Considerations In Their Commencement And Prosecution," Chicago Bar Association Seminar on Chancery And Special Remedies, 1989. *Member:* Chicago and Illinois State Bar Associations; The Association of Trial Lawyers of America; Decalogue Society of Lawyers. ***REPORTED CASES:*** Kellerman, et al. vs. MCI Telecommunications Corp., 112 Ill. 2d 428, 493 N.E. 2d 1045 (1986); Carroll vs. Preferred Risk Ins. Co., 34 Ill. 2d 310, 215 N.E. 2d 801 (1966); In Re: Agathos, 194 Ill. App. 3d 168, 550 N.E. 2d 1161 (1st Dist. 1990); O-Kay Shoes, Inc. vs. Rosewell, 129 Ill. App. 3d 405, 472 N.E. 2d 883 (1st Dist. 1984); Meggison vs. Stevens, 21 Ill. App. 3d 505, 316 N.E. 2d 297 (1st Dist. 1974). ***PRACTICE AREAS:*** Civil Trial Practice; Class Actions; Chancery and Special Remedies.

ASSOCIATES

BERNARD N. BLOCK, born Evanston, Illinois, January 5, 1957; admitted to bar, 1985, Illinois; 1987, U.S. District Court, Northern District of Illinois; U.S. Supreme Court. *Education:* Northern Illinois University; Drake University (B.S., Business Administration, 1979); John Marshall Law School (J.D., 1984). *Member:* Chicago Bar Association; Decalogue Society of Lawyers; American Trial Lawyers Association; Illinois Trial Lawyers Association. ***PRACTICE AREAS:*** Secured Financing; Business Litigation; Class Actions; Personal Injury; Wrongful Death; Technology Law; Business Law. ***Email:*** bblock@chicagolawyers.com

JEROME E. BOYLE, born Chicago, Illinois, December 18, 1956; admitted to bar, 1983, Illinois, U.S. District Court, Northern District of Illinois including Trial Bar; U.S. Court of Appeals, Seventh Circuit; U.S. Supreme Court; U.S. Court of Appeals, Seventh Circuit. *Education:* Loyola University of Chicago (B.A., 1979); University of Illinois (J.D., 1983); National Institute for Trial Advocacy (Midwest Regional, 1988). Author: "Splitting Fees Without Splitting Hairs: A Primer on Referrals," CBA Record (YLS Journal), May-June, 1993, reprinted in Law Office Economics & Management, Vol. XXXIV, No. 4 (1994). Lecturer: "Ethical Referral And Fee Sharing Arrangements," Y.L.S./C.B.A. Committee on Professional Responsibility, 1993; "Surviving As An Associate," Y.L.S./C.B.A. Law Student Committee, 1993; "Class Action Lawyering: A Practical Guide," IIT/Chicago-Kent College of Law ATLA Chapter, 1995. Treasurer, 1991-1992; Vice-President, 1992-1993 and Secretary, 1993—, Irish Immigration Service. Charter Member, Rotary Club of Chicago-Midwest, 1996—. Member: Founding Committee, Chicago Lawyers for International Human Rights, 1992; Counsel, Institute for Economic Justice, 1989—. *Member:* Chicago (Mentor, The Pathways Mentoring Program, 1991-1992) and American (Member, Sections of Litigation, Individual Rights and Responsibilities) Bar Associations; Appellate Lawyers Association of Illinois. ***REPORTED CASES:*** Johnson vs. American Airlines, Inc., 261 Ill.App. 3d 622, 633 N.E. 2d 978 (1st Dist. 1994) vac'd. and remanded, 514 U.S., 131 L.Ed. 2d 129, 115 S.Ct. 1247 (1995), on remand, 278 Ill.App. 3d 624, 663 N.E.2d 54 (1st Dist. 1996); David Spitz et al., etc. vs. Goldome Reality Credit Corporation, 151 Ill.2d 71, 600 N.E. 2d 1185 (1992), affirming 210 Ill.App. 3d 215, 569 N.E.2d 43 (1st Dist. 1991); Dolan vs. Gawlicki, 256 Ill.App.3d 153, 628 N.E.2d 1188 (3d Dist., 1994) appeal after remand, 272 Ill.App 3d 165, 650 N.E.2d 286 (3d Dist. 1995); Beermann vs. Graff, 250 Ill.App.3d 632, 621 N.E.2d 173 (1st Dist. 1993); American States Insurance Company vs. Gawlicki & Hussey, Inc., 231 Ill.App.3d 199, 596 N.E.2d 720 (3d Dist. 1992); American Country Insurance Company vs. Efficient Construction Corporation et al., 225 Ill.App.3d 177, 587 N.E.2d 1073 (1st Dist. 1992); Mid-America National Bank Of Chicago, etc., et al. vs. First Savings & Loan Association of South Holland et al., 161 Ill.App.3d 531, 515 N.E.2d 176 (1st Dist. 1987). ***PRACTICE AREAS:*** Complex Commercial Litigation; Tort Litigation; Trial Practice; Appellate Practice; Chancery; Class Actions. ***Email:*** jboyle@chicagolawyers.com

LEGAL SUPPORT PERSONNEL

ROGER DELEOZ, (Legal Assistant)

REPRESENTATIVE CLIENTS: Damian Services Corp.; 1st National Bank of Wheaton; Sun Eco-Systems, Inc.; Transportation Capital Corp.; Checker Taxi Association; Illinois Transportation Leasing; Tower Oldsmobile, Inc.; Frank Clesen & Sons, Inc.; Medallion Financial Corp.; Bancopopular; E.H. Lynn Industriesl Advance Financial Corp.

LAW OFFICE OF MARC N. BLUMENTHAL

19 SOUTH LASALLE STREET, SUITE 1500
CHICAGO, ILLINOIS 60603
Telephone: 312-641-0616
Fax: 312-332-4629
Email: mnblawyer@cs.com
URL: http://www.blumenthalfranchiselaw.com

Franchise Law, Start-Up Franchisors and Franchisees, Leasing, Licensing, Trademarks, Trademark Information, Copyrights, Breach of Contract, Corporate Law, Business Formations, Business Transactions, Litigation, Arbitration.

MARC N. BLUMENTHAL, born Brooklyn, New York, December 13, 1953; admitted to bar, 1981, Louisiana; 1986, Illinois. *Education:* Tulane University (B.A., 1975); Tulane University Law School (J.D., 1981). Licensed Real Estate Broker, Illinois, 1994. Corporate Counsel, Chart House, Inc. (Divers Foods, Inc.) and Entre Computer Centers, Inc., 1981-1985. Speaker and Co-Author: "Avoiding and Addressing Wrongful Termination of Your Franchise," and "Don't Give Away The Store - The Purchase and Sale of a Franchise,", American Franchise Association Legal Symposium, 2001. Co-Author: "To Litigate, Arbitrate or Mediate...That is the Question!," American Franchise Association Quarterly (Volume 1, Issue 3, Autumn, 1993; "The Covenant of Good Faith and Fair Dealing," November 1994 VIEWS-Periodical for the National Association of 7-Eleven Franchises. Founding Affiliate Member, American Franchise Association. *Member:* Louisiana State Bar Association. ***REPORTED CASES:*** Collier v. Murphy, 2002 U.S. Dist. Lexis 23632; Genin, Trudeau & Co., Limited v. Integra Development International and Zak Designs, Inc. 845 F. Supp. 611 (N.D. IL. 1994); Hengel vs. Hot 'n Now, Inc. et al, 825 F.Supp. 1311 N.D. IL (1993). ***PRACTICE AREAS:*** Franchises and Franchising; Franchise Agreements; Buying and Selling of Businesses; Trademarks; Copyrights; Business Formation; Contracts; Litigation; Arbitration.

(This Listing Continued)

SUSAN BOGART

30 NORTH LA SALLE STREET
SUITE 2900
CHICAGO, ILLINOIS 60602
Telephone: 312-263-0900
Fax: 312-263-5013
URL: http://www.lawyers.com/bogart

Civil and Criminal Litigation. Labor and Employment Litigation, Counseling and Executive Coaching-Public and Private Sector, Representation of Officers and Directors, White Collar Federal Criminal Defense, Civil and Criminal Civil Rights and Privacy Litigation, Business Litigation, Representation of Private Parties in Disputes with Governmental and other Regulatory Authorities.

SUSAN BOGART, born Toledo, Ohio, May 14, 1952; admitted to bar, 1978, Illinois, U.S. District Court, Northern District of Illinois including Trial Bar, U.S. Court of Appeals, Seventh Circuit and U.S. Supreme Court. *Education:* Miami University; University of Michigan (B.A., with distinction, 1974); Loyola University of Chicago School of Law (J.D., 1978). Listed in Strathmore's Who's Who. Recipient, Special Achievement Award, Department of Justice, 1988. Senior Investigative Counsel, Committee on The Judiciary, U.S. House of Representatives, 1998-1999. Assistant United States Attorney, Northern District of Illinois, 1981-1988. Law Clerk, U.S. District Judge Stanley J. Roszkowski, 1979-1981. Adjunct Professor of Legal Writing, Moot Court and Appellate Advocacy, Loyola University of Chicago School of Law, 1978-1984. Director of Legal Writing Programs, Loyola University of Chicago School of Law, 1981-1982. Adjunct Professor of Trial Advocacy, John Marshall Law School, 1984—. Instructor, National Institute for Trial Advocacy, 1984-1990. Presenter, "Glass Ceiling Issues in the Law Firm," American Bar Association, Midyear National Meeting, February 1996. Co-Author and Presenter, "A Practical Guide to Federal Court Rules and Procedures in Illinois," National Business Institute, February 1996. Author and Presenter, "Evolving Areas of Expertise in Sexual Harassment Cases: Repressed Memory and 'Relevant Reporters'," ABA/PLI Litigation Sexual Harassment Claims, 1996. Assistant Reporter for the Illinois Judicial Conference on Fiduciary Responsibilities of Court Appointed Lawyers, 1978. Arbitrator and Mediator, Association of Securities Dealers, 2000—. Conciliator, Chicago Commission on Human Relations, 1992-1998. Certified Chairperson, Cook County Mandatory Arbitration Program, 1990-1997. Mediator, Center for Conflict Resolution, 1990-1993. Advisory Board and Academic Committee Member, Loyola University Center for Information Management and Technology, 2000. *Member:* Chicago, Illinois State, Federal and American Bar Associations; National Association of Women Lawyers; Chicago Council of Lawyers; Markey-Wigmore Inn of Court; Judge Howard T. Markey Inn of Court (Officer); Better Government Association Board. ***LANGUAGES:*** French.

BOLLINGER, RUBERRY & GARVEY

500 WEST MADISON STREET, 23RD FLOOR
CHICAGO, ILLINOIS 60661
Telephone: 312-466-8000
Fax: 312-466-8001

Insurance Coverage Analysis and Litigation, Bad Faith, Declaratory Actions, Toxic Tort Defense, Commercial Litigation, Construction Litigation, Product Liability, Insurance Defense, Transportation, Medical Malpractice, Rental Car Industry, Construction, School and Municipal Liability, Environmental Law, Director's and Officer's Liability.

FIRM PROFILE: Founded in 1986, the law firm of Bollinger, Ruberry & Garvey has dedicated itself to providing clients with the highest quality counseling and litigation services. The firm prides itself on the quality and talent of its attorneys, which includes some of the finest trial lawyers in the nation. Due to the demands and the needs of our clients, the firm has notably grown from 5 members to their present size in just a few short years. Our litigators handle large, complex cases on a daily basis and the practice has expanded to a national scope, with experience before the United States Supreme Court, as well as numerous state and federal courts and government agencies.

PARTNERS OF FIRM

BARRY G. BOLLINGER, born Peoria, Illinois, March 7, 1943; admitted to bar, 1973, Wisconsin and Illinois. *Education:* University of Wisconsin (B.S., 1965; J.D., cum laude, 1973). Editor, Wisconsin Law Review, 1971-1973. *Member:* Illinois State and American Bar Associations; Society of Trial Lawyers. ***PRACTICE AREAS:*** Medical Malpractice; Directors and Officers Liability; Products Liability; Toxic Torts; Pollution; Property Damage.

EDWARD F. RUBERRY, born Chicago, Illinois, August 7, 1947; admitted to bar, 1973, Illinois, U.S. District Court, Northern District of Illinois and U.S. Court of Appeals, 7th Circuit; 1978, U.S. Court of Appeals, 5th Circuit; 1980, U.S. Supreme Court. *Education:* Coe College (B.A., 1969); Loyola University (J.D., 1973). Editor, Loyola University Law Journal, 1972-1973. Law Clerk to the Honorable Daniel P. Ward, Chief Justice of the Supreme Court of Illinois, 1973-1975. Visiting Professor, Illinois Institute of Technology/Chicago-Kent College of Law, 1973-1975. *Member:* Chicago (Member, Antitrust Section), Illinois State and American (Member, Sections on: Antitrust, Securities, Professional Liability and Insurance Law) Bar Associations. ***PRACTICE AREAS:*** Corporate Law; Commercial Litigation; Insurance Coverage; Insurance; Asbestos Litigation; Construction Litigation. ***Email:*** ed.ruberry@brg-law.net

(This Listing Continued)

BOLLINGER, RUBERRY & GARVEY, Chicago—Continued

MAURICE J. GARVEY, born Chicago, Illinois, September 16, 1933; admitted to bar, 1960, Wisconsin and Illinois. *Education:* St. Joseph College, Collegeville, Indiana (B.A., 1955); Marquette University (J.D., 1960). Delta Theta Phi. Member, Marquette University Moot Court Team. Staff Member, Marquette University Law Review, 1959-1960. *Member:* Chicago, Illinois State and American Bar Associations; Legal Club of Chicago; Society of Trial Lawyers (President, 1985-1986); International Association of Insurance Counsel; Defense Research Institute; Illinois Defense Counsel. Fellow, American College of Trial Lawyers. ***PRACTICE AREAS:*** Professional Liability; Medical Malpractice.

JEREMIAH P. CONNOLLY, born Chicago, Illinois, October, 17, 1954; admitted to bar, 1979, Illinois. *Education:* Loyola University (B.S., 1976); DePaul University (J.D., 1979). *Member:* Chicago, Illinois State and American (Member, Sections on: Tort; Insurance) Bar Associations; The Society of Trial Lawyers. ***PRACTICE AREAS:*** Products Liability; Casualty Insurance; Professional Negligence; Construction Litigation; School District Liability; Municipal Liability.

NICHOLAS A. RIEWER, born Chicago, Illinois, October 23, 1955; admitted to bar, 1984, Illinois. *Education:* Loyola University (B.A., 1981); John Marshall Law School (J.D., 1984). *Member:* Chicago, Illinois State and American Bar Associations. ***PRACTICE AREAS:*** Environmental Law; Employment Discrimination; Construction Litigation; Professional Malpractice.

MARK F. WOLFE, born Chicago, Illinois, February 17, 1958; admitted to bar, 1983, Wisconsin and Illinois. *Education:* University of Wisconsin (B.S., 1980); Marquette University (J.D., 1983). Phi Delta Phi. Author: "Special Project, Interest on Lawyers Trust Accounts: A Proposal for Wisconsin," 66 Marquette Law Review 835, 1983. *Member:* Chicago, Illinois State and American Bar Associations; State Bar of Wisconsin. ***PRACTICE AREAS:*** Professional Liability; Professional Malpractice; Products Liability; Property Damage Litigation; Construction Law; Real Estate Law; Commercial Litigation.

JEFFREY A. GOLDWATER, born Highland Park, Illinois, March 28, 1959; admitted to bar, 1985, Illinois and U.S. District Court, Northern District of Illinois. *Education:* Northwestern University (B.A., 1981); University of Illinois (J.D., magna cum laude, 1984). Order of the Coif. Associate Editor, University of Illinois Law Review, 1983-1984. *Member:* Chicago and Illinois State Bar Associations. ***PRACTICE AREAS:*** Insurance Coverage; Professional Liability; Arbitration; Environmental Litigation; Employment Litigation; Civil Rights Litigation.

FRANCIS R. PETREK, JR., born Joliet, Illinois, May 24, 1949; admitted to bar, 1977, Illinois; 1979, Michigan. *Education:* University of Illinois (B.S., 1971); DePaul University (J.D., 1977). Psi Chi. Edmund James Scholar. Member, De Paul Law Review, 1976-1977. *Member:* Chicago, Illinois State and American Bar Associations; State Bar of Michigan; Defense Research Institute; Legal Club of Chicago; American Board of Trial Advocates. Fellow: Illinois Society of Trial Lawyers; American College of Trial Lawyers. ***PRACTICE AREAS:*** Toxic Tort Litigation; Product Liability; Commercial Litigation; Professional Negligence; Construction Litigation.

WILLIAM J. ROGERS, born Philadelphia, Pennsylvania, August 17, 1950; admitted to bar, 1975, Illinois. *Education:* Fairfield University (B.A., cum laude, 1972); Northwestern University (J.D., 1975). Article Editor, Northwestern University Journal of Criminal Law and Criminology, 1974-1975. Author: "Perjury: The Forgotten Offense," 65 J.Crim. L.&C. 361, 1974; "Border Searches: Almeida-Sanchez v. U.S.," 64 J.Crim. L.&C. 424, 1973. Co-Author: "Discovery," Medical Malpractice, IICLE, 1989, Supplement 1992. Member of Faculty, National Institute of Trial Advocacy, 1989, 1990, 1992. *Member:* Chicago, Illinois State and American (Member, Litigation, Tort and Insurance Sections) Bar Associations; Chicago Council of Lawyers; Trial Lawyers Club of Chicago; The Association of Trial Lawyers of America; The Society of Trial Lawyers. Fellow: Illinois Society of Trial Lawyers; American College of Trial Lawyers. ***PRACTICE AREAS:*** Products Liability; Medical Malpractice; Construction Litigation; Commercial Litigation.

JOHN M. STALMACK, born Chicago, Illinois, April 4, 1947; admitted to bar, 1974, Illinois; 1975, District of Columbia. *Education:* Coe College (B.A., cum laude, 1971); Loyola University (J.D., 1974); George Washington University (LL.M., 1976). Blue Key. Staff Member, 1972-1973 and Associate Editor, 1973-1974, Loyola University Law Journal. Member, Criminal Division, U.S. Department of Justice, 1974-1976. *Member:* The District of Columbia Bar; Illinois State and American Bar Associations. Fellow: Illinois Society of Trial Lawyers; American College of Trial Lawyers. ***PRACTICE AREAS:*** Medical Malpractice; Products Liability; Governmental Liability.

MICHAEL S. KNIPPEN, born Geneva, Illinois, December 5, 1955; admitted to bar, 1983, Illinois and U.S. District Court, Northern District of Illinois including Trial Bar. *Education:* St. Norbert College (B.A., 1978); DePaul University (J.D., 1983). *Member:* Chicago, Illinois State and American Bar Associations. ***PRACTICE AREAS:*** Insurance Litigation; Insurance Coverage Litigation; Environmental Litigation; Products Liability; Environmental Law.

BRYAN G. SCHUMANN, born Oak Park, Illinois, December 19, 1958; admitted to bar, 1985, Illinois; U.S. District Court, Northern District of Illinois. *Education:* Northern Illinois University (B.S., with honors, 1981); IIT/Chicago-Kent College of Law (J.D., with honors, 1985). Recipient, Political Science Scholar Award. *Member:* Chicago, Illinois State and American Bar Associations. ***PRACTICE AREAS:*** Insurance; Insurance Bad Faith; Insurance Coverage Litigation.

ROBERT J. FRANCO, II, born Hackensack, New Jersey, August 27, 1957; admitted to bar, 1984, Illinois, U.S. District Court, Northern District of Illinois including Trial Bar; U.S. District Court, Central and Southern Districts of Illinois, U.S. District Court, Eastern District of Wisconsin, U.S. District Court, Southern District of Texas and U.S. Court of Appeals, Sixth, Seventh and Tenth Circuits. *Education:* Grinnell College; Southern Illinois University (B.A., Economics, 1980); Rutgers University (M.A., Institute of Management and Labor Relations, 1983), Reuthers Scholar; IIT/Chicago-Kent College of Law (J.D., 1984). Publications: *Damages Under the Illinois Wrongful Death Act,* (update) (Ill. Inst. for CLE, 1996); *Advertising Injury Claims and the General Liability Insurance Policy,* Fed of Ins. & Corp. Csl. Q., 47 (Fall 1996); *Insurance Coverage for Construction Claims,* Construction Law In Illinois (Ill. Inst. for CLE, 1997); *Types of Insurance Coverage Available to Contractors,* Construction-Related Insurance Coverage Issues, (DRI, 1997); *Personal Injury Defense and Insurance Coverage Following Repeal Of the Tort Reform And Structural Work Acts,* (Ill. Inst. for CLE, 1998); *Insurance and Risk Shifting Under the 1997 A201 Form,* (PESI, 1998); *Insurer Liability for Judgements in Excess of Limits,* (Lorman, 1998). *Member:* Chicago, Illinois State (Sections on: Insurance Law and Tort Law), Federal (Board of Directors, Chicago Chapter, 1998) and American (Sections on: Litigation, Construction Litigation, Tort and Insurance Practice, Excess, Surplus Lines and Reinsurance Insurance Coverage Litigation Committees, and the Forum on the Construction Industry) Bar Associations; Defense Research Institute; Appellate Lawyers Association. ***PRACTICE AREAS:*** Construction; Commercial Law; Employment Law; Complex Litigation; Insurance Coverage; Bad Faith Litigation.

ROBERT M. COLLINS, born Chicago, Illinois, August 6, 1958; admitted to bar, 1983, Illinois and U.S. District Court, Northern District of Illinois. *Education:* University of Illinois (B.A., with honors, 1980); Illinois Institute of Technology/Chicago-Kent College of Law (J.D., with high honors, 1983). *Member:* Chicago, Illinois State and American Bar Associations. ***PRACTICE AREAS:*** Medical Malpractice; Products Liability; Governmental Litigation; Environmental Law; Toxic Torts Litigation.

DARCY LYNN IBACH, born Chicago, Illinois, April 27, 1960; admitted to bar, 1986, Illinois; 1987, U.S. District Court, Northern District of Illinois; 1991, U.S. Court of Appeals, Seventh Circuit; 1995, U.S. District Court, Northern District of Illinois including Federal Trial Bar; 2000, U.S. District Court, Central District of Illinois and U.S. District Court, Eastern District of Wisconsin; 2001, U.S. District Court, Southern District of Illinois; 2002, U.S. District Court, District of Nebraska; 2003, U.S. Court of Appeals, Eighth Circuit and U.S. District Court, District of Colorado; 2004, U.S. Court of Appeals, Tenth Circuit. *Education:* University of Illinois (B.S., 1982); DePaul University (J.D., 1986). Phi Eta Sigma; Alpha Lambda Delta. Registered Record Administrator, 1983. *Member:* Illinois State and American Bar Associations; American Medical Records Association; Illinois Medical Records Association. ***PRACTICE AREAS:*** Insurance Coverage Litigation; Professional Errors and Omissions; Public Law; Directors and Officers Liability; Employment Litigation. ***Email:*** darcy.ibach@brg-law.net

CLAY H. PHILLIPS, born Kirksville, Missouri, June 26, 1951; admitted to bar, 1976, Illinois and U.S. District Court, Northern District of Illinois including Trial Bar; 1981, U.S. Court of Appeals, 3rd Circuit; 1983, U.S. Court of Appeals, 7th Circuit; 1991, U.S. District Court, Central District of Illinois. *Education:* University of Missouri (A.B., with honors, 1973); Georgetown University (J.D., 1976). Editor, Law and Policy in International Business, 1975-1976. Trial Attorney, U.S. Dept. of Justice, 1976-1977. *Member:* Chicago (Chairperson, Antitrust Law Committee, 1988-1989), Illinois State and American Bar Associations; Legal Club of Chicago. ***PRACTICE AREAS:*** Insurance Coverage; Commercial Litigation.

AMY L. MINER, born Sigourney, Iowa; admitted to bar, 1990, Iowa and Illinois. *Education:* University of Iowa (B.B.A., with highest distinction, 1987; J.D., 1990). Beta Gamma Sigma; Beta Alpha Psi; Phi Eta Sigma; Mortar Board. Member, Moot Court Board. Associate Editor, Iowa Law Review, Vol. 75, member, Vol. 74, 1989-1990. *Member:* Iowa State and Illinois State Bar Associations. ***PRACTICE AREAS:*** Commercial Litigation; Insurance Coverage Litigation.

SCOTT C. BENTIVENGA, born Chicago, Illinois, February 14, 1963; admitted to bar, 1988, Illinois and U.S. District Court, Northern District of Illinois; 1989, U.S. Court of Appeals, Seventh Circuit. *Education:* University of Notre Dame (B.A., 1985); Loyola University (J.D., 1988). Co-Author, with Hartman, J.: "Civil Procedure," 1986-1987 Illinois Law Survey, 19 Loyola University of Chicago Law Journal 271, 293-338. ***PRACTICE AREAS:*** Torts Law.

MICHAEL T. WALSH, born Chicago, Illinois, December 15, 1962; admitted to bar, 1991, Illinois. *Education:* St. John's University (B.S., 1985); John Marshall Law School (J.D., 1991). Member, National Moot Court. Member, Law Review, John Marshall Law School, 1990-1991. *Member:* Chicago, Illinois State and American Bar Associations. ***PRACTICE AREAS:*** Commercial Litigation; Insurance Coverage; Medical Malpractice Defense.

JOHN J. MORONEY, IV, born Milwaukee, Wisconsin, August 18, 1964; admitted to bar, 1991, Illinois and U.S. District Court, Northern District of Illinois. *Education:* Marquette University (B.A., 1986); Trinity College; John Marshall Law School (J.D., 1991). *Member:* Chicago, Illinois State and American Bar Associations; The Association of Trial Lawyers of America; Illinois Trial Lawyers Association. ***LANGUAGES:*** French. ***PRACTICE AREAS:*** Medical Malpractice; Premises Liability; Torts Law.

GEORGE J. MANOS, born Chicago, Illinois, September 26, 1961; admitted to bar, 1986, Illinois and U.S. District Court, Northern District of Illinois; 1994, U.S. District Court, District of Arizona; 1996, U.S. Court of Appeals, Third and Eleventh Circuit; 1999, U.S. District Court, District of Colorado; 2000, U.S. District Court, Central District of Illinois and U.S. District Court, Eastern District of Wisconsin. *Education:* DePaul University (B.A., with honors, 1983; J.D., 1986). ***LANGUAGES:*** Greek. ***PRACTICE AREAS:*** Automobile Litigation; Tort Litigation; Asbestos Litigation; Insurance Coverage.

CAROL L. JOHNSON, born Chicago, Illinois, December 9, 1957; admitted to bar, 1984, Illinois. *Education:* University of Illinois (B.A., 1980); University of Illinois (J.D., cum laude, 1984). Member, University of Illinois Law Review. ***PRACTICE AREAS:*** Insurance Coverage; Insurance Counseling; Insurance Litigation; Environmental Litigation; Employment Litigation; Professional Liability; Public Officials Policies.

LUISA F. TRUJILLO, born Manizales, Columbia, November 17, 1968; admitted to bar, 1993, Illinois. *Education:* Cornell University (B.A., 1990); Washington University (J.D., 1993); DePaul University (LL.M., Healthcare Law, 1999). Member, Mock Trial Team. Winner, Regional Trial Competition, 1993. Guest Speaker: Association of Illinois Defense Counsel Meeting, 1999; Kent College of Law Healthcare Symposium, 1999. ***LANGUAGES:*** Spanish. ***PRACTICE AREAS:*** Tort Litigation; Products Liability; Premises Liability; Medical Malpractice.

JOHN P. SULLIVAN, born Chicago, Illinois, April 28, 1963; admitted to bar, 1989, Illinois. *Education:* The Ohio State University (B.S., 1989); Capital University (J.D., 1989).

(This Listing Continued)

Phi Alpha Delta. Member, Capital University Law Review. *Member:* Chicago, Illinois State and Federal Bar Associations; Illinois Trial Lawyers Association. ***PRACTICE AREAS:*** Medical Malpractice; Products Liability; Torts Law.

MICHELLE M. BRACKE, born Springfield, Illinois, November 18, 1966; admitted to bar, 1994, Illinois. *Education:* Northwestern University (B.G.S., 1991); King's College Faculty of Laws, University of London, London, England; Loyola University (J.D., 1994). Former Claims Broker, Lloyds of London. ***PRACTICE AREAS:*** Insurance Coverage; Fine Arts; Insurance Defense.

ROBERT W. BRUNNER, born Urbana, Illinois, October 11, 1961; admitted to bar, 1991, Illinois and District of Columbia. *Education:* University of Illinois (B.A., with honors, 1985; J.D., 1990); University of Wisconsin-Madison (M.A., 1986). *Member:* Champaign County, Illinois State and American Bar Associations; District of Columbia Bar.

ROBERT ALLEN CHANEY, born Decatur, Illinois, October 27, 1946; admitted to bar, 1981, Illinois. *Education:* University of Illinois (B.A., 1969); John Marshall Law School (J.D., 1981). ***PRACTICE AREAS:*** Insurance Coverage; Insurance Litigation.

JAMES MICHAEL EASTHAM, born Chicago, Illinois, December 31, 1968; admitted to bar, 1994, Illinois. *Education:* University of Illinois (B.S., 1991; J.D., 1994). ***PRACTICE AREAS:*** Insurance Coverage.

RICHARD M. KUNTZ, born Huntington, West Virginia, November 20, 1950; admitted to bar, 1984, Pennsylvania; 1985, Illinois. *Education:* West Virginia University (B.A., magna cum laude, 1972); George Washington University (J.D., 1984). Monthly Columnist, Environmental Law, Chicago Daily Law Bulletin. Author of over 50 articles in the areas of environmental defense and coverage and psychopharmacological drug development and liability. Moderator, Counsel Connect on-line environmental forum. ***REPORTED CASES:*** Citizens For A Better Environment v. Illinois Pollution Control Board 152 Ill.App.3rd 105 (1st Dist. 1987; Chavariet v. Williams Pipeline Co., 11 F.3d 7420 (7th Cir. 1993). ***PRACTICE AREAS:*** Environmental Insurance Coverage; Commercial Insurance.

ALISON L. MINER, born Sigourney, Iowa; admitted to bar, 1996, Illinois. *Education:* University of Iowa (B.B.A., with honors, 1993; J.D., 1996). Member, Moot Court Board. Member, Iowa Law Review, 1994-1995. ***PRACTICE AREAS:*** Insurance Coverage.

MITCHELL D. ROSE, born Highland Park, Illinois, November 26, 1965; admitted to bar, 1990, Wisconsin; 1991, Illinois. *Education:* University of Michigan (B.G.S., 1987); University of Wisconsin-Madison (J.D., 1990). Recipient: International Moot Court Award, University of Wisconsin; Law Alumni Award, University of Wisconsin. Law Clerk to the Hon. Moria Krueger and the Hon. Mark Frankel, Madison, Wisconsin. Legal Writing Instructor, University of Wisconsin. ***PRACTICE AREAS:*** Commercial Litigation; Medical Malpractice; Torts.

KRISTA R. FRICK, born Edison, New Jersey, July 26, 1971; admitted to bar, 1996, New Jersey and Illinois. *Education:* University of New Haven (B.A., cum laude, 1993); Hofstra University (J.D., 1996). First Place Winner, International Association of Defense Counsel Legal Writing Competition, 1996. Intern Clerk to the Hon. Thomas H. Dilts, Superior Court of New Jersey, 1994. Author, "Silicone, Science, and Settlements: Breast Implants and a Search for Truth," International Association of Defense Counsel Journal, Vol. 63, October 1996. ***PRACTICE AREAS:*** Appellate Practice; Torts.

KARIE J. VALENTINO, born Iowa City, Iowa, August 19, 1971; admitted to bar, 1996, Illinois. *Education:* University of Iowa (B.A., Psychology and English, 1993); John Marshall Law School (J.D., 1996). ***PRACTICE AREAS:*** Torts; Professional Liability; Medical Malpractice; Attorney Discipline.

MARTIN P. HEAD, born Chicago, Illinois, November 19, 1967; admitted to bar, 1992, Illinois and U.S. District Court, Northern District of Illinois. *Education:* Georgetown University (A.B., 1989); Northwestern University (J.D., 1992). *Member:* Chicago (Member, Young Lawyers Section, 1993—), Illinois State and American Bar Associations; Legal Club of Chicago. ***PRACTICE AREAS:*** Medical Malpractice Defense Law; Torts Law; Litigation; Insurance.

MICHAEL P. LATZ, born Chicago, Illinois, March 14, 1963; admitted to bar, 1989, Illinois; U.S. District Court, Northern District of Illinois including Trial Bar and U.S. Court of Appeals, Seventh Circuit. *Education:* University of Notre Dame (B.A., 1985; J.D., 1989). Prosecutor, Criminal Prosecutions Bureau, State's Attorney's Office, Cook County, Illinois, 1989-1994. *Member:* West Suburban Bar Association; National Employment Law Association. ***PRACTICE AREAS:*** Employment Defense; Civil Rights Defense; Torts.

RUTH GOLDWATER McCOY, born Chicago, Illinois, November 1, 1964; admitted to bar, 1989, Illinois. *Education:* University of Illinois (B.A., 1986); Chicago-Kent College of Law, Illinois Institute of Technology (J.D., 1989). ***PRACTICE AREAS:*** Insurance Coverage; Commercial Litigation; Environmental Law; Land Use; Zoning Law.

VINCENT P. TOMKIEWICZ, born Cleveland, Ohio, August 29, 1961; admitted to bar, 1986, Wisconsin and U.S. District Court, Western District of Wisconsin; 1987, U.S. District Court, Eastern District of Wisconsin; 1989, Illinois; 1991, U.S. District Court, Northern District of Illinois. *Education:* University of Wisconsin-Madison (B.A., 1982; J.D., 1986). *Member:* Chicago Bar Association; State Bar of Wisconsin.

PERRY M. SHORRIS, born Chicago, Illinois, January 29, 1968; admitted to bar, 1993, Illinois. *Education:* University of Michigan (A.B., 1990); University of Illinois (J.D., 1993). ***PRACTICE AREAS:*** Insurance Coverage; Defense Litigation; Medical Malpractice; Torts.

JAMES E. ABBOTT, born Chicago, Illinois, November 21, 1973; admitted to bar, 1998, Illinois. *Education:* University of Illinois at Urbana-Champaign (B.A., 1995); Chicago-Kent College of Law (J.D., 1998). ***REPORTED CASES:*** In re Estate of William Shanon Powless, 734 N.E.2d 111 (5th Dist. Ill. 2000); Selby v. GMC, 2001 U.S. Dist. Lexis 15477 (N.D. Ill. 2001); Mielour v. Cicero, 2002 U.S. Dist. Lexis 5914 (N.D. Ill. 2002); Panos v. Foley & Lardner, No. 00 C 6138 (N.D. Ill. Sept. 4, 2002). ***PRACTICE AREAS:*** Medical Malpractice; Products Liability; Toxic Tort Liability; Commercial Litigation.

JOHN J. RIEWER, born Chicago, Illinois, November 27, 1964; admitted to bar, 1999, Illinois. *Education:* Loyola University (B.A., 1993); John Marshall Law School (J.D., 1999). ***PRACTICE AREAS:*** Medical Malpractice; Products Liability; Torts.

(This Listing Continued)

OF COUNSEL

BETH ANN BERGER ZERMAN, born Chicago, Illinois, October 29, 1964; admitted to bar, 1993, Illinois. *Education:* University of Iowa (B.B.A., 1986); Chicago-Kent College of Law (J.D., 1993). ***PRACTICE AREAS:*** Insurance Coverage.

DAVID W. KANE, born Evanston, Illinois, 1967; admitted to bar, 1993, Illinois. *Education:* University of Illinois (B.A., 1989); DePaul University (J.D., 1993). *Member:* Chicago and American Bar Associations. ***PRACTICE AREAS:*** Insurance Coverage; Complex Litigation.

JAMES A. LUPO, JR., born Chicago, Illinois, June 15, 1964; admitted to bar, 1989, Illinois and U.S. District Court, Northern District of Illinois. *Education:* Northwestern University (B.A., 1985); Loyola University School of Law (J.D., 1989). *Member:* Illinois State and American Bar Associations; Defense Research Institute.

Cynthia Arrotti-Carter	***Sarah E. Heidenreich***
Michelle Bacher	***Rachel Kiley***
Sara K. Barnes	***Carla P. Larned***
Jagady Blue	***David A. Larson***
Walter Leonard Brown III	***Sarah E. Lopez***
Christopher G. Buenik	***Marc E. McCallister***
Jayne Megan Cadice	***Alison Milnamow***
Diane Karp Ehrhart	***Amanu M. Nwaomah***
Ahmed El-Ganzouri	***Adewale A. Oduye***
W. Grant Farrar	***Tanya Poth***
Janet A. Flynn	***Zachary M. Raimi***
Jordan E. Frank	***Sharon Rice***
James M. Freeman	***Aaron J. Shuler***
Gregory V. Ginex	***Lisa Smuckler***
Gena Gruss	***Rostyslaw J. Smyk***
Charles A. Hafner	***Kelly Link Stoltz***
Michael S. Haggerty	***Richard P. Tauras***
Michael L. Hahn	***Lisa Thaviu***
Katherine L. Hartley	***Brett L. Warning***
Jeffrey I. Young	

LAURENCE J. BOLON

19 SOUTH LA SALLE STREET, SUITE 1500
CHICAGO, ILLINOIS 60603
Telephone: 312-782-1272
Fax: 312-782-9870
URL: http://www.bolonlaw.com

Family Law, Divorce, Child Custody, Child Support, Visitation Rights, Criminal Law, Federal Criminal Law, White Collar Crime, Bank Fraud, Electronic Fraud, Felonies, Drug Offenses, Driving While Intoxicated, Civil Litigation, Business and Probate Litigation.

LAURENCE J. BOLON, born Chicago, Illinois, January 21, 1944; admitted to bar, 1969, Illinois and U.S. District Court, Northern District of Illinois; 1970, U.S. Court of Appeals, 7th Circuit; 1977, U.S. Supreme Court; 2000, U.S. Court of Appeals, 4th Circuit. *Education:* University of Illinois (B.S., 1965); John Marshall Law School (J.D., 1969). *Member:* Chicago and Illinois State Bar Associations; Northwest Suburban Bar; Illinois Association of Criminal Defense Lawyers.

BOODELL DOMANSKIS & SAIPE, LLC

205 N. MICHIGAN AVENUE, SUITE 4307
CHICAGO, ILLINOIS 60601
Telephone: 312-938-4070
Fax: 312-540-1162
URL: http://www.boodlaw.com

Business Law, Real Estate, International Law, Dispute Resolution, Trusts and Estates, Wills and Probate, Asset Protection, Finance, Banking Law, Corporate Law, Immigration.

THOMAS J. BOODELL, JR., born Chicago, Illinois, September 29, 1935; admitted to bar, 1964, Illinois. *Education:* Princeton University (A.B., 1957); Harvard Law School (J.D., 1964). *Member:* Chicago, American, International and Inter-Pacific Bar Associations; Lawyers Club of Chicago. Fellow, American Bar Foundation; Adlai Stevenson Institute of International Affairs (1968-1971). ***PRACTICE AREAS:*** Corporate Law; International Business Law; Alternative Dispute Resolution. ***Email:*** tboodell@boodlaw.com

ALEXANDER R. DOMANSKIS, born Chicago, Illinois, June 3, 1952; admitted to bar, 1977, Illinois. *Education:* University of Michigan (A.B., with high distinction, 1973; J.D., with distinction, 1977). Administrative Editor, University of Michigan Journal of Law Reform, 1976-1977. Member, Panel of Arbitrators, American Arbitration Association. Author: "Small Claims Courts: An Overview and Recommendation," 9 University of Michigan Journal of Law Reform 590, 1976; "The Journal: After A Decade," 11 University of Michigan Journal of Law Reform 1, 1977. Law Clerk to Hon. Edwin A. Robson, Judge, U.S. District Court, Northern District of Illinois, 1977-1979. Member, Title Insurance Task Force, Illinois Department of Financial Institutions, 1988-1989. Past Chairman, Board of Directors and Past President, Lithuanian World Center, Lemont, Illinois. *Member:* Chicago, Illinois State and American (Member, Sections on: Business; Probate and Real Property; International) Bar Associations. ***LANGUAGES:*** Lithuanian and Spanish. ***PRACTICE AREAS:*** Business Law; Real Estate; Zoning Law; Land Use; Buy-Sell Agreements; Finance; International Business Law. ***Email:*** domanskis@boodlaw.com

GARY SCOTT SAIPE, born Chicago, Illinois, September 15, 1948; admitted to bar, 1974, Illinois. *Education:* University of Illinois (B.S. with high honors, 1970); Northwest-

(This Listing Continued)

BOODELL DOMANSKIS & SAIPE, LLC, Chicago—Continued

ern University (J.D., 1974). Articles Editor, Journal of Criminal Law & Criminology, 1973-1974. Author: "Argersinger v. Hamlin: For Better or For Worse," 64 Journal of Criminal Law & Criminology 290, 1973. Instructor, First Yeal Legal Writing Course, Northwestern University School of Law, 1973-1974. *Member:* Illinois State Bar Association. ***PRACTICE AREAS:*** Real Estate Law; Financing; Banking Law; Corporate Law. ***Email:*** gsaipe@boodlaw.com

ASSOCIATES

JAE CHOI KIM, born Seoul, Korea, November 23, 1961; admitted to bar, 2002, Illinois. *Education:* University of Chicago (B.A., 1983); DePaul College of Law (J.D., Business Law, Intellectual Property Law, 2002). *Member:* Chicago and American Bar Associations. ***LANGUAGES:*** Korean. ***PRACTICE AREAS:*** Trusts and Estates; Real Estate; International Law; Corporate Law; Business Immigration. ***Email:*** jaekim@boodlaw.com

DAINIUS R. DUMBRYS, born Chicago, Illinois, October 4, 1977; admitted to bar, 2003, Illinois. *Education:* University of Iowa (B.A., 1999); University of Illinois College of Law (J.D., 2002). *Member:* Chicago, Illinois and American Bar Associations. ***LANGUAGES:*** Lithuanian. ***PRACTICE AREAS:*** Real Estate; Corporate Law; Business Law; Trusts and Estates. ***Email:*** ddumbrys@boodlaw.com

LAW OFFICE OF JAMES X. BORMES, P.C.

8 SOUTH MICHIGAN AVENUE
CHICAGO, ILLINOIS 60603
Telephone: 312-201-0575
Fax: 312-332-0600

Construction Law, Construction Defects, Mechanics Liens, Consumer Law, Consumer Fraud, Business Law, Business Litigation, Breach of Contract, Employment Contracts, Landlord and Tenant Law, Securities Fraud.

JAMES X. BORMES, born Aberdeen, South Dakota, September 19, 1962; admitted to bar, 1988, Illinois; 1989, U.S. District Court, Southern District of Illinois; 1993, U.S. District Court, Northern District of Illinois including Trial Bar and U.S. Court of Appeals, Seventh Circuit. *Education:* Saint Louis University (B.A., cum laude, 1984; J.D., 1988). Member, Saint Louis University Law Journal, 1987-1988. Law Clerk to Hon. William L. Beatty, U.S. District Court, Southern District of Illinois. Listed in Marquis Who's Who in American Law. *Member:* Chicago, Illinois State, Federal and American Bar Associations. (Also Of Counsel, Shannon & Associates). ***PRACTICE AREAS:*** Construction Law; Construction Defects; Mechanics Liens; Consumer Law; Consumer Fraud; Business Law; Business Litigation; Breach of Contract; Employment Contracts; Landlord and Tenant Law; Securities Fraud.

BOROVSKY & EHRLICH

Established in 1964
111 EAST WACKER DRIVE, SUITE 1325
CHICAGO, ILLINOIS 60601
Telephone: 312-861-0800
Fax: 312-819-0948

Labor Relations and Equal Opportunity Law. Labor Antitrust Law. Occupational Safety and Health Law. Pension and Employee Benefit Law. Related Trial and Appellate Practice, Matrimonial Law, Real Estate, Bankruptcy, Criminal Defense, Personal Injury, Civil Litigation, Consumer, Immigration.

LAWRENCE D. EHRLICH, born Chicago, Illinois, November 29, 1929; admitted to bar, 1956, Illinois; 1969, U.S. Court of Appeals, 7th Circuit; 1973, U.S. Supreme Court; 1976, U.S. Court of Appeals, District of Columbia Circuit and U.S. Court of Appeals, 5th Circuit. *Education:* University of Chicago (A.B., 1949); DePaul University (J.D., 1956). Editor, De Paul Law Review, 1955-1956. Attorney, Trial Specialist, National Labor Relations Board, 1960-1964. Assistant Regional Attorney, National Labor Relations Board, 1964-1965. *Member:* Chicago and American Bar Associations. ***PRACTICE AREAS:*** Labor Relations; Equal Opportunity; Labor Antitrust; Health; Pension and Employee Benefits.

JULIAN D. SCHREIBER, born Muskegon, Michigan, November 7, 1933; admitted to bar, 1960, Michigan; 1963, Illinois; 1976, District of Columbia, U.S. Supreme Court and U.S. Court of Appeals, 5th, 7th, 9th and District of Columbia Circuits; U.S. District Court, Northern District of Illinois including Trial Bar. *Education:* Muskegon Junior College and University of Michigan (A.B., 1956); University of Michigan (LL.B., 1959). Phi Beta Kappa; Phi Kappa Phi. Author: "The Relocation of Work Performed By Union Employees," Employee Relations Law Journal, Autumn, 1983. Supervising Attorney and Trial Specialist, National Labor Relations Board, Thirteenth Region, 1960-1973. *Member:* Chicago and Illinois State Bar Associations; State Bar of Michigan; District of Columbia Bar. ***PRACTICE AREAS:*** Labor Relations; Equal Opportunity; Labor Antitrust; Health; Pension and Employee Benefits.

THOMAS CANAFAX, JR., born Ponca City, Oklahoma, September 12, 1936; admitted to bar, 1960, Oklahoma; 1966, U.S. Court of Appeals, 10th Circuit; 1967, U.S. Court of Appeals, 4th Circuit; 1969, U.S. District Court for the District of Columbia; 1972, U.S. District Court, District of Maryland; 1973, District of Columbia; 1974, Illinois and U.S. District Court, Northern District of Illinois. *Education:* University of Oklahoma (B.A., 1958; LL.B., 1960). Phi Alpha Delta. Trial Attorney, 21st Region, National Labor Relations Board, 1961-1964. Attorney and Supervising Attorney, Division of Litigation, National Labor Relations Board, 1964-1969. *Member:* Chicago (Chairman, Constitutional Law Committee, 1985-1986), Illinois State and American Bar Associations; The District of Columbia Bar. ***PRACTICE AREAS:*** Labor Relations; Equal Opportunity; Labor Antitrust; Health; Pension and Employee Benefits.

(This Listing Continued)

JACQUELYN C. HAYNES, born Eugene, Oregon, December 17, 1952; admitted to bar, 1980, Illinois and U.S. District Court, Northern District of Illinois; 1987, U.S. District Court, Western District of Wisconsin; 1989, U.S. Tax Court. *Education:* University of Oregon (B.A., with honors, 1977); Northwestern University (J.D., 1980). Phi Beta Kappa. *Member:* Chicago (Member, Matrimonial Law Committee) Bar Association. ***PRACTICE AREAS:*** Matrimonial Law; Real Estate; Civil Litigation.

ARI M. TRUBITT, born Chicago, Illinois, September 21, 1962; admitted to bar, 1987, Illinois and U.S. District Court, Northern District of Illinois; 1988, U.S. Court of Appeals, Seventh Circuit; 1990, U.S. District Court, Eastern District of Wisconsin. *Education:* Western Illinois University; University of Illinois (B.A., 1984); John Marshall Law School (J.D., 1987). *Member:* Chicago, Illinois State and American Bar Associations. ***PRACTICE AREAS:*** Criminal Defense; Immigration Law.

DONALD J. MOCK, born Elgin, Illinois, March 27, 1958; admitted to bar, 1983, Illinois. *Education:* Wabash College (B.A., 1979); John Marshall Law School (J.D., 1983). ***PRACTICE AREAS:*** Civil Litigation.

SAMUEL Z. GOLDFARB, born 1951; admitted to bar, 1975, Illinois. *Education:* University of Illinois (B.A.); Loyola University, Chicago (J.D.). ***PRACTICE AREAS:*** Bankruptcy; Consumer Law; Civil Litigation.

SHELLÉ E. RILEY, born December 1, 1972; admitted to bar, 1999, Kansas; 2001, Illinois. *Education:* Lake Forest College (B.A., 1995); Washburn University (J.D., 1998). *Member:* Chicago Bar Association. ***PRACTICE AREAS:*** Matrimonial Law; Civil Litigation; Consumer Law.

JACK R. LEVIN, born Chicago, Illinois, February 10, 1950; admitted to bar, 1981, Illinois. *Education:* University of Illinois at Chicago (B.A., 1972); John Marshall Law School (J.D., 1981). *Member:* Chicago Bar Association. ***PRACTICE AREAS:*** Real Estate; Civil Litigation.

JOHN O. WALSH, born Chicago, Illinois, October 17, 1950; admitted to bar, 1989, Illinois; U.S. District Court, Northern District of Illinois; 1990, U.S. Court of Appeals, 7th Circuit. *Education:* St. Xavier College (B.A., 1972); Chicago-Kent College of Law, Illinois Institute of Technology (J.D., 1989). *Member:* Chicago Bar Association. ***PRACTICE AREAS:*** Matrimonial Law.

BOTTI, MARINACCIO & DELONGIS, LTD.

CHICAGO, ILLINOIS

(See Oak Brook)

Trial and Appellate Practice in State and Federal Courts, Civil, Criminal, Personal Injury, Family, Zoning, Corporation, Probate, Commercial and Government Litigation.

BOUNDAS SKARZYNSKI WALSH & BLACK LLC

Established in 2003
200 EAST RANDOLPH DRIVE, SUITE 7200
CHICAGO, ILLINOIS 60601-7719
Telephone: 312-946-4200
Fax: 312-946-4272
URL: http://www.bswb.com

New York, New York Office: One Battery Park Plaza, 22nd Floor, 10004. Telephone: 212-820-7750. Fax: 212-820-7740; 820-7788.
London, England Office: 37-39 Lime Street, EC3M 7AY. Telephone: +011-44-020-7929-5588. Fax: +011-44-020-7929-5999.

Insurance, Reinsurance, Commercial Litigation, Arbitration, Counseling, Directors and Officers Liability, E-Commerce, Internet, Technology, Employment Liability, Environmental Liability, Fidelity Insurance, Fiduciary Liability, Financial Insurance, Financial Institution Liability, Mutual Fund Liability, Finite Risk, Alternative Risk Transfer Products, Insurance Company Professional Liability, Insurance Regulation, Intellectual Property, Trademarks, Patents, Copyrights, Managed Care Liability, Health Care Liability, Municipal, School Board, Non-Profit Liability, Products Liability, Professional Liability, Securities Liability, Specialty Lines Insurance, Commercial Lines Insurance, Personal Lines Insurance, Alternative Dispute Resolution, Appellate Litigation, Corporate Governance, Corporate Compliance, Privacy Compliance.

FIRM PROFILE: Boundas, Skarzynski, Walsh & Black LLC is a law firm specializing in the insurance and financial services industry. Our attorneys are experienced and innovative leaders in the industries we serve. We have many years of experience and possess expertise in areas listed in the statement of practice section. Our attorneys have worked with each other for many years, most recently at Peterson & Ross, LLC. With offices in Chicago, London and New York, so we are well-positioned to meet the needs of your organization. Please contact one of our attorneys for further information.

PRINCIPALS

THEODORE A. BOUNDAS, born Chicago, Illinois, December 21, 1938; admitted to bar, 1964, Illinois and U.S. District Court, Northern District of Illinois; 1993, New York. *Education:* Villanova University (A.B., 1961); Harvard University (J.D., 1964; LL.B., 1964). Delta Epsilon Sigma. Author: *Directors' and Officers' Insurance: A Digest of Cases*, 4th Edition, 1995; "The U.S. Savings & Loan Rescue: Implications for D&O Insurance and the Liabilities of Directors, Offices and Affiliated Professionals," Part I and Part II, Japan Insurance News, 1990. Co-Author, "Insurance for A-Side D&O Exposures After Enron - A Riskier Proposition?", Expert Commentary, IRMI.com, November, 2002. Attorney, Federal Trade Commission, 1964-1966. Senior Legal Advisor, Professional Liability Insurance, published by the International Risk Management Institute. *Member:* Chicago, Illinois State, New York State and American (Business and Insurance Committee, Section of Busi-

(This Listing Continued)

ness Law; Excess, Surplus Lines and Reinsurance Committee, Section of Tort and Insurance Practice; Fidelity and Surety Law Committee, Section of Tort and Insurance Practice; Professional, Officers' and Directors' Liability Law Committee, Section of Tort and Insurance Practice) Bar Associations; Federal Trial Bar of the Northern District of Illinois; Professional Liability Underwriting Society (Member, Board of Directors, 2001-2004); Asia Pacific Lawyers Association. (Also at London, England Office). ***PRACTICE AREAS:*** Insurance; Reinsurance; Directors and Officers Liability; Professional Liability; Litigation; Insurance Underwriting. ***Email:*** tboundas@bswb.com

PETER F. LOVATO, III, born Milwaukee, Wisconsin, December 17, 1950; admitted to bar, 1976, Illinois and U.S. District Court, Northern District of Illinois, 1982, Trial Bar; 1978, U.S. Claims Court and U.S. Tax Court; 1987, U.S. Supreme Court and U.S. Court of Appeals, Fifth and Sixth Circuits; 1988, U.S. Court of Appeals, Eighth Circuit and U.S. District Court, Northern District of Texas; 1990, Texas, U.S. Court of Appeals, Eleventh Circuit; 1992, U.S. Court of Appeals, District of Columbia Circuit; 1997, U.S. Court of Appeals, Third Circuit; 1998, U.S. District Court, Western District of Michigan; 1999, U.S. District Court, District of Colorado; 2000, U.S. District Court, District of Wisconsin. *Education:* Princeton University (A.B., magna cum laude, 1973); Yale University (J.D., 1976). Phi Beta Kappa. *Member:* American Bar Association; National Legal Malpractice Data Center (Associate). ***PRACTICE AREAS:*** Insurance; Professional Liability; Employee Benefits; ERISA Litigation; Commercial Litigation; Securities Litigation; Securities Arbitration. ***Email:*** plovato@bswb.com

JOHN E. BLACK, JR., born Chicago, Illinois, March 12, 1958; admitted to bar, 1983, Illinois and U.S. District Court, Northern District of Illinois. *Education:* Illinois College (A.B., 1980); University of Illinois (J.D., 1983). Moot Court Board. Member, University of Illinois Law Review, 1982-1983. Author: "Tightening the Reins on Corporate Governance: The Increasing Judicial Scrutiny of Director Care and Independence," Expert Commentary, IRMI.com, August 2003; "Liability in the U.S. for Release of Private Information on E-Commerce Web Sites," *International Legal Studies,* November, 2000 and December 1999. Co-Author: Supplement to "Employment Liability," March, 2003 and "Directors' and Officers' Liability," December, 2002, Professional Liability Insurance, published by the International Risk Management Institute, Inc.; "Policy Limitations on Coverage: A D&O Trend in a Hard Market," Expert Commentary, IRMI.com, April, 2003; "Insurance for A-Side D&O Exposures After Enron-A Riskier Proposition?," Expert Commentary, IRMI-.com, November, 2002; "Dangers Lurk in Cyberspace," *Business Lawyers,* July, 2002. *Member:* American Bar Association (Member, Sections on: Labor and Employment Law; Law Practice Management; Tort and Insurance Practice; Corporation, Banking and Business Law; Cyberspace Law Committee; Corporate Aspects of Internet Technology Sub-Committee; Intellectual Property Subcommittee; Privacy in Commerce Working Group). ***PRACTICE AREAS:*** Insurance Regulation; Internet Law; Privacy Law; Insurance; Employment Law; Directors and Officers Liability; Insurance Products; Professional Liability. ***Email:*** jblack@bswb.com

DAVID T. BURROWES, born Seattle, Washington, February 17, 1960; admitted to bar, 1986, California and U.S. District Court, Central District of California; 1990, Illinois. *Education:* University of California at Los Angeles (B.A., 1983); Vanderbilt University (J.D., 1986). *Member:* American Bar Association (Member: Tort and Insurance Practice Section; Professionals, Officers' and Directors' Liability Law Committee; Insurance Coverage Litigation Committee; Non-Profit Organizations Committee; Dispute Resolution Practice Section); Professional Liability Underwriting Society. ***PRACTICE AREAS:*** Directors and Officers Liability; Employment Law; Professional Liability; Labor Law; Insurance. ***Email:*** dburrowes@bswb.com

MICHAEL J. ROSEN, born New York, N.Y., January 26, 1961; admitted to bar, 1986, Illinois and U.S. District Court, Northern District of Illinois. *Education:* Pitzer College (B.A., 1983); Washington University (J.D., 1986). Associate Editor, Washington University Journal of Urban and Contemporary Law, 1985-1986. ***PRACTICE AREAS:*** Directors and Officers Liability Insurance; Professional Liability; Underwriting Counseling; Labor and Employment; Health Care; Managed Care. ***Email:*** mrosen@bswb.com

R. NATHAN RANDALL, born Atlanta, Georgia, May 5, 1958; admitted to bar, 1988, Illinois and U.S. District Court, Northern District of Illinois. *Education:* Northwestern University (B.A., 1980; J.D., 1987). *Member:* American Bar Association (Member, Section on Business Law, Cyberspace Law Committee). ***PRACTICE AREAS:*** Directors and Officers Liability; Underwriting Counseling; Professional Liability. ***Email:*** rrandall@bswb.com

TERI LEE FERRO, born Chicago, Illinois; admitted to bar, 1990, Illinois and U.S. District Court, Northern District of Illinois. *Education:* University of Chicago (B.A., 1987); Northwestern University School of Law (J.D., 1990). Formerly with: Winston & Strawn, 1990-1995; Attorneys' Liability Assurance Society, Inc., 1995-2000. *Member:* Professional Liability Underwriting Society. ***PRACTICE AREAS:*** Directors and Officers Liability Insurance; Transactional Insurance Products; Underwriting Counseling; Commercial Litigation; Professional Liability. ***Email:*** tferro@bswb.com

ELLEN D. JENKINS, born Argentia, Newfoundland, Canada, June 20, 1963; admitted to bar, 1993, Maryland; 1996, Illinois and U.S. District Court, Northern District of Illinois. *Education:* College of William and Mary (B.A., 1985; J.D., 1993). Phi Beta Kappa. *Member:* Illinois State Bar Association; Maryland State Bar Association, Inc. ***LANGUAGES:*** German. ***PRACTICE AREAS:*** Insurance Coverage; Insurance Litigation; Directors and Officers Liability; Employment Practices Liability Insurance; Corporate Governance. ***Email:*** ejenkins@bswb.com

OF COUNSEL

REGINA K. McCABE, born Taylorville, Illinois, May 14, 1956; admitted to bar, 1981, Illinois and U.S. District Court, Northern District of Illinois including Trial Bar; 1995, U.S. Court of Appeals, Second Circuit; 1997, U.S. Court of Appeals, Third Circuit; 2001, New York, U.S. District Court, Southern District of Illinois and U.S. District Court, Southern and Eastern Districts of New York. *Education:* University of Illinois (B.A., summa cum laude, 1978); Edmund J. James Scholar, Bronze Tablet; Northwestern University (J.D., 1981). Executive Editor, Northwestern Journal of International Law and Business, 1980-1981. *Member:* Chicago, New York State and American (Member: Litigation Section; Committee on Insurance Coverage Litigation) Bar Associations; Legal Club of Chicago (President, 1998-1999); The Lawyer's Club of Chicago. ***REPORTED CASES:*** Certain Underwriters and Lloyd's, London vs. St. Joe Mincrols, 90 F.3d 671 (2nd Cir. 1996); McDonald vs. Prudential Ins. Co., 95 C 5186 CN.D.III 1999. ***PRACTICE AREAS:*** Insurance; Class Actions; Products Liability; Commercial Torts; Business Torts; Litigation. ***Email:*** rmccabe@bswb.com

NORBERT J. WEGERZYN, born Chicago, Illinois, September 2, 1939; admitted to bar, 1964, Illinois; 1966, U.S. District Court, Northern District of Illinois including Trial Bar; 1970, U.S. Court of Appeals, Seventh Circuit. *Education:* University of Michigan (A.B., 1961); Northwestern University School of Law (J.D., cum laude, 1964). Member, Board of Editors, Northwestern University Law Review, 1963-1964. Author: "Computer Generated Check Coverage Under Forgery Bonds," Midwinter Meeting, Fidelity and Surety Law Committee, American Bar Association, 1998; "Fidelity Insurance Policies: Yesterday, Today and Tomorrow," American Bar Association, 1999; "Violating Intellectual Property Rights — Internet Policies," Soundwaves — Navigating the Future, 2001. *Member:* American (Note Editor, Fidelity and Surety Newsletter; Vice-Chair, Fidelity and Surety Law Committee; Member, Uniform Commercial Code and Electronic Funds Payment Committees) and International Bar Associations. ***PRACTICE AREAS:*** Fidelity and Surety Bonds; Directors and Officers Insurance Coverage; Complex Litigation; E-Commerce Insurance. ***Email:*** n.wegerzyn@bswb.com

ASSOCIATES

PATRICK W. CARLSON, born Two Harbors, Minnesota, March 27, 1968; admitted to bar, 1994, Minnesota; 1995, Illinois. *Education:* University of North Dakota (B.A., 1990); Chicago-Kent College of Law (J.D., 1993). ***REPORTED CASES:*** In re A.H. 748 NE2d 183 (Ill.2001); In re N.B. 730 NE2d 1086 (Ill 2000). ***PRACTICE AREAS:*** Insurance; Professional Liability; Employee Benefits; ERISA Litigation; Commercial Litigation; Securities Litigation; Securities Arbitration. ***Email:*** pcarlson@bswb.com

AMANDA F. FAYNE, born Highland Park, Illinois, 1977; admitted to bar, 2002, Illinois. *Education:* University of Wisconsin-Madison (B.A., 1999); Chicago-Kent College of Law, Illinois Institute of Technology (J.D., 2002). ***Email:*** afayne@bswb.com

DAVID A. SHEDD, admitted to bar, 2002, Illinois; U.S. District Court, Northern District of Illinois. *Education:* University of Arkansas (B.A., 1977); Washington University (J.D., 2002). ***Email:*** dshedd@bswb.com

THOMAS M. SHEFFIELD, born Boise, Idaho, July 7, 1971; admitted to bar, 1999, Illinois and U.S. District Court, Northern District of Illinois; 2003, Florida and Solicitor in England and Wales. *Education:* University of Idaho (BS, 1994); DePaul University College of Law (JD, 1999). *Member:* Chicago, American and International Bar Associations. ***LANGUAGES:*** Spanish. ***PRACTICE AREAS:*** Insurance Coverage; Directors and Officers Liability; Professional Liability; International Law; Reinsurance. ***Email:*** tsheffield@bswb.com

BRIAN A. WHITE, born Davenport, Iowa, March 23, 1977; admitted to bar, 2002, Illinois and U.S. District Court, Northern District of Illinois. *Education:* University of Iowa (B.A.; 1999; J.D., 2002). *Member:* Illinois State and American Bar Associations. ***PRACTICE AREAS:*** Insurance; Reinsurance; Professional Liability; Insurance Litigation. ***Email:*** bwhite@bswb.com

(For complete biographical data on other personnel, see Professional Biographies at New York, New York and London, England)

LAW OFFICE OF TZVETELINA T. BOYNOVSKA

1834 WEST NORTH AVENUE, SUITE 1-SE
CHICAGO, ILLINOIS 60622
Telephone: 773-342-8671
Fax: 773-342-8680
Email: tboynovska@yahoo.com
URL: http://www.lawyers.com/tboynovska

Immigration, Family Law, Divorce, Residential Real Estate.

TZVETELINA T. BOYNOVSKA, born Russe, Bulgaria, May 6, 1967; admitted to bar, 1997, Illinois and U.S. District Court Northern District of Illinois; 1999, District of Columbia. *Education:* Sofia University, Bulgaria (Law, 1992); Loyola University (J.D., 1996). *Member:* Chicago Bar Association; American Immigration Lawyers Association. ***LANGUAGES:*** Bulgarian and Russian. ***PRACTICE AREAS:*** Immigration and Naturalization; Visas; Green Cards; Employment Immigration; Family Law; Divorce; Premarital Agreements; Real Estate; Residential Real Estate; Buy-Sell Agreements; Buying and Selling of Homes.

Languages: Bulgarian and Russian.

BRAUN STROBEL LORENZ BERGIN & MILLMAN, P.C.

Established in 1916
33 NORTH LA SALLE STREET
SUITE 2800
CHICAGO, ILLINOIS 60602
Telephone: 312-726-3877
FAX: 312-332-0039
Email: info@bslbm.com
URL: http://www.bslbm.com

General Civil and Trial Practice. State and Federal Workers Compensation Law. Litigation and Appellate Practice.

FRANCIS J. LYNCH (1921-2000)

MARK A. BRAUN, born Athens, Wisconsin; admitted to bar, 1950, Illinois. *Education:* Loyola University (J.D., 1949). Adjunct Professor of Law, Loyola University Law

(This Listing Continued)

BRAUN STROBEL LORENZ BERGIN & MILLMAN, P.C., Chicago—Continued

School, 1968-1999. Member and former chair, of Workers Compensation Committees, (ISBA, DRI, FICC and officer (V.P.) FICC). *Member:* American and Illinois State Bar Associations; Illinois State Workers Compensation Lawyers Association; Illinois Workers Compensation Bar Association. ***PRACTICE AREAS:*** Civil Trial; Workers Compensation; Appellate Practice. ***Email:*** mbraun@bslbm.com

JOHN A. STROBEL, born Chicago, Illinois, May 24, 1941; admitted to bar, 1967, Illinois. *Education:* University of Michigan (B.A., 1963); Loyola University, Chicago, Illinois (J.D., 1966). *Member:* Chicago, Illinois State and American Bar Associations; Workers Compensation Lawyers Association. ***PRACTICE AREAS:*** Civil Trial Practice; Workers Compensation; Appellate Practice. ***Email:*** jstrobel@bslbm.com

PETER J. LORENZ, born Evanston, Illinois, August 11, 1963; admitted to bar, 1989, Nebraska; 1991, Illinois and U.S. District Court, Northern District of Illinois. *Education:* Loyola University of Chicago (B.A., 1986); Creighton University (J.D., 1989). Member, Moot Court Board. *Member:* Chicago, Illinois State, Nebraska State and American Bar Associations; Worker's Compensation Lawyers Association. ***PRACTICE AREAS:*** Civil Trial Practice; Workers Compensation; Appellate Practice. ***Email:*** plorenz@bslbm.com

JOHN P. BERGIN, born Great Bend, Kansas, March 27, 1967; admitted to bar, 1992, Illinois and U.S. District Court, Northern District of Illinois. *Education:* Loyola University, Chicago (B.A., 1989; J.D., 1992). *Member:* Chicago, Illinois State and American Bar Associations; Workers' Compensation Lawyers Association. ***PRACTICE AREAS:*** Civil Trial Practice; Workers Compensation; Appellate Practice. ***Email:*** jbergin@bslbm.com

CRAIG MILLMAN, born New York, New York; admitted to bar, 1975, Illinois. *Education:* St. John's University (B.A., 1972); John Marshall Law School (J.D., 1975). *Member:* Illinois State Bar Association; Workers' Compensation Lawyers Association. ***Email:*** cmillman@bslbm.com

REPRESENTATIVE CLIENTS: ACE-USA; 21st Century Insurance; ESIS; Allstate Insurance Co.; BP Amoco Corp.; Chesterfield Services USA; Chicago Rawhide; Employers' Claim Service; Gallagher Bassett Services; General Casualty Insurance; GuideOne Insurance; Labor Ready, Inc.; Liberty Mutual Insurance Co.; Loyola University Chicago; Loyola University Health System; Ohio Casualty Gr.; Old Republic Insurance Co.; RSK Co.; Secura Insurance; Siemens Corporation; SKF USA, Inc.; St. Paul Fire and Marine; Travelers Insurance.
REFERENCE: Harris Trust & Savings Bank, Chicago.

BRENNER, FORD, MONROE & SCOTT, LTD.

Established in 1986

33 NORTH DEARBORN STREET, SUITE 300
CHICAGO, ILLINOIS 60602-3102
Telephone: 312-781-1970
Fax: 312-781-9202
URL: http://www.brennerlawfirm.com

Insurance Defense, Personal Injury, Medical Malpractice, Construction Law, Product Liability, Uninsured/Underinsured Motorist Arbitrations and Litigation of Contested Coverage Issues.

FIRM PROFILE: Brenner, Ford, Monroe & Scott, Ltd. has offices in the Chicago loop. The firm concentrates its practice in litigation and trial work. The firm has represented clients throughout Illinois and Northern Indiana. The firm takes pride in its record of success, and the personalized service that we provide for our clients. Clients of Brenner, Ford, Monroe & Scott, Ltd. are primarily insurers and managers of self-insureds with high standards and expectations of efficient, high-quality legal work. We strive to provide early and accurate evaluations of our cases to our clients, to thoroughly and vigorously prepare them for trial, to keep the clients informed of the status of their case, and to use our experience and hard work to obtain a favorable result on behalf of the client.

AMY L. ANDERSON, born Dixon, Illinois, March 16, 1965; admitted to bar, 1990, Illinois and U.S. District Court, Northern District of Illinois; 1994, Federal Trial Bar. *Education:* University of Illinois, Champaign-Urbana (B.A., 1987; J.D., 1990). *Member:* Chicago and Illinois State Bar Associations; Defense Research Institute. ***PRACTICE AREAS:*** Medical Malpractice; Insurance Coverage; Premises Liability; Automobile Litigation. ***Email:*** aanderson@brennerlawfirm.com

SHELDON A. BRENNER, born Chicago, Illinois, August 25, 1944; admitted to bar, 1969, Illinois; 1970, U.S. District Court, Northern District of Illinois including Trial Bar; 1996, U.S. Court of Appeals, Seventh Circuit; 1997, U.S. Supreme Court. *Education:* DePaul University (B.S., 1966; J.D., 1969). Consultant to the Illinois Supreme Court Committee to Recommend Rules for Court-Annexed Mandatory Arbitration. Member of the Select Cook County Committee to Draft Local Rules for Court-Annexed Mandatory Arbitration. *Member:* Chicago (Past Secretary, Insurance Law Committee) and Illinois State Bar Associations; Illinois Association of Defense Trial Counsel; American Arbitration Association (Committee on Accident Claim Resolution). ***PRACTICE AREAS:*** Medical Malpractice Defense; Arbitration; Alternative Dispute Resolution. ***Email:*** sbrenner@brennerlawfirm.com

SCOTT R. BRITTON, born Decatur, Illinois, November 12, 1960; admitted to bar, 1985, Illinois; U.S. District Court, Northern District of Illinois including Trial Bar; 1988, U.S. Court of Appeals, Seventh Circuit; 2000, U.S. Supreme Court. *Education:* Millikin University (B.A., summa cum laude, 1982); University of Illinois (J.D., 1985). Phi Kappa Phi. *Member:* Chicago Bar Association; Illinois Association of Defense Trial Counsel. ***PRACTICE AREAS:*** Civil Trial Practice; Appeals. ***Email:*** sbritton@brennerlawfirm.com

JAMES W. FORD, born Detroit, Michigan, September 20, 1949; admitted to bar, 1976, Illinois; U.S. District Court, Northern District of Illinois including Trial Bar; 1988, U.S. Court of Appeals, Seventh Circuit. *Education:* Loyola University (B.A., 1971; J.D., 1976). Member, Loyola University Law Journal, 1975-1976. Author: "Worker's Compensation Practice: Trial Preparation-Respondent's Viewpoint," IICLE, 1982-1996. *Member:* Chicago, Illinois State and American Bar Associations; Illinois Association of Defense Trial Counsel. ***PRACTICE AREAS:*** Civil Trial Practice; Appeals. ***Email:*** jford@brennerlawfirm.com

(This Listing Continued)

STEPHEN A. KOLODZIEJ, born St. Louis, Missouri, June 19, 1968; admitted to bar, 1993, Illinois and U.S. District Court, Northern District of Illinois; 2003, U.S. Court of Appeals, 7th Circuit, U.S. Supreme Court. *Education:* University of Illinois, Champaign-Urbana (B.A., 1990; J.D., 1993). *Member:* Chicago and Illinois State Bar Associations. ***PRACTICE AREAS:*** Civil Practice; Appellate Practice; Medical Malpractice Defense. ***Email:*** skolodziej@brennerlawfirm.com

TERESA R. MAHER, born Joliet, Illinois, November 20, 1955; admitted to bar, 1990, Illinois; 1992, U.S. District Court, Northern of Illinois. *Education:* University of Notre Dame (B.S., 1977); University of Illinois College of Dentistry (D.D.S., 1981); I.I.T. - Chicago-Kent College of Law (J.D., with honors, 1990). Licensed, Dentistry, Illinois. *Member:* Illinois State and American Bar Associations. ***PRACTICE AREAS:*** Medical Malpractice; Dental Malpractice. ***Email:*** tmaher@brennerlawfirm.com

RANDALL C. MONROE, born Gary, Indiana, February 7, 1959; admitted to bar, 1984, Illinois and U.S. District Court, Northern District of Illinois. *Education:* Valparaiso University (B.A., with distinction, 1981); University of Illinois (J.D., 1984). Who's Who Among American Law Students (3d ed. 1984). Editor, Illinois Bar Journal, Recent Decisions Section, 1983-1984. Author: Casenote, "Wrongful Death/Damages," 72 Illinois Bar Journal 36 (Sept. 1983); "Rule 220 and the Treating Physician," 26 Tort Trends 4 (Jan. 1991); "Limitations on Medical Malpractice Actions: The Continuous Course of Treatment Doctrine," 28 Tort Trends 5 (Dec. 1992). *Member:* Chicago, Illinois State and American Bar Associations. ***Email:*** rmonroe@brennerlawfirm.com

MARY KAY SCOTT, born Decatur, Illinois, April 12, 1959; admitted to bar, 1984, Illinois and U.S. District Court, Northern District of Illinois, Trial Bar, 1993. *Education:* University of Illinois, Champaign-Urbana (B.A., 1981; J.D., 1984). *Member:* Chicago, Illinois State and American Bar Associations; Defense Research Institute. ***PRACTICE AREAS:*** Medical Malpractice; Construction Litigation; Personal Injury Litigation. ***Email:*** mscott@brennerlawfirm.com

ASSOCIATES

KENNETH M. BATTLE, born Chicago, Illinois, December 26, 1973; admitted to bar, 1999, Illinois and U.S. District Court, Northern District of Illinois. *Education:* University of Illinois (B.A., 1996); Case Western Reserve University (J.D., 1999). ***Email:*** kbattle@brennerlawfirm.com

JOSHUA C. BELL, born Vincennes, Indiana, April 20, 1974; admitted to bar, 1999, Illinois and U.S. District Court, Northern District of Illinois. *Education:* Illinois State University (B.S., 1996); John Marshall Law School (J.D., 1999). ***Email:*** jbell@brennerlawfirm.com

ROBERT A. BRAUN, born Skokie, Illinois, August 28, 1970; admitted to bar, 1997, Wisconsin; 1999, Illinois. *Education:* University of Notre Dame (B.A., 1993); University of Wisconsin (M.S., 1997); University of Wisconsin Law School (J.D., 1997). ***Email:*** rbraun@brennerlawfirm.com

KATHERINE AMY LEMON, born Louisville, Kentucky, October 23, 1975; admitted to bar, 2002, Illinois; 2003, Indiana. *Education:* Indiana University, Bloomington (B.A., 1998); Indiana University School of Law, Indianapolis (J.D., 2002). ***Email:*** alemon@brennerlawfirm.com

MELISSA A. LYNOTT, born Dixon, Illinois, November 22, 1979; admitted to bar, 2004, Illinois and U.S. District Court, Northern District of Illinois. *Education:* Illinois State University (B.S., 2001); Valparaiso University School of Law (J.D., 2004). ***PRACTICE AREAS:*** Medical Malpractice Defense; Insurance Defense. ***Email:*** mlynott@brennerlawfirm.com

FRED A. NICKL, born Chicago, Illinois, April 28, 1973; admitted to bar, 1998, Illinois. *Education:* University of Illinois, Chicago (B.A., 1995); DePaul University (J.D., 1998). ***Email:*** fnickl@brennerlawfirm.com

EYDIE R. PERRY, born Chicago, Illinois, April 29, 1976; admitted to bar, 2001, Illinois, U.S. District Court, Northern District of Illinois. *Education:* University of Michigan (B.A., 1998); Loyola University (J.D., 2001). ***Email:*** eperry@brennerlawfirm.com

ERIC ALAN RYWALSKI, born Toledo, Ohio, August 23, 1974; admitted to bar, 2001, Illinois and U.S. District Court, Northern District of Illinois. *Education:* Miami University (B.S., Business, 1997); University of Toledo (J.D., 2001). ***Email:*** erywalski@brennerlawfirm.com

LANNY VANDAELE, born Davenport, Iowa, September 2, 1974; admitted to bar, 2003, Illinois and U.S. District Court, Northern District of Illinois. *Education:* University of Iowa (B.A., 1998; M.A., 2000); Valparaiso University (J.D., 2003). ***Email:*** lvandaele@brennerlawfirm.com

LEGAL SUPPORT PERSONNEL

VICTORIA A. REIDL, born Harvey, Illinois, September 20, 1961. (Paralegal). ***Email:*** treidl@brennerlawfirm.com

REPRESENTATIVE CLIENTS: The Guide One Insurance Group; ISMIE Mutual Insurance Co.; CIGNA; National Chiropractic Mutual Insurance Co.; Scottsdale Insurance Co.; Rush-Presbyterian-St. Luke's Medical Center; Amica Mutual Insurance Co.; Chesterfield Services, Inc.; Rockford Mutual; RLI/Mt. Hawley Insurance; Associated Insurance Co.; Westfield Group; United Fire Co.; AAO Services, Inc.; Berkeley Risk Services, Inc.; Nationwide Insurance; North Pointe Insurance Co. of Illinois; Indiana Insurance Co.; St. Paul Fire and Marine; Ophthalmic Mutual Insurance Co.; Mid-Plaines Insurance Co.; Contractors Bonding & Insurance Co.; Preferred Physicians Medical Risk Retention Group, Inc.; First Mercury Insurance; AXA Assurances; American Continental Insurance Co.; AP Specialty Corp.; Shelter Insurance Companies; Brotherhood Mutual Insurance Co.; Everest National Insurance Co.; American Physicians Insurance.

LEONARD J. BRENNER, LTD.

CHICAGO, ILLINOIS

(See Northbrook)

Business and Corporate Law, Tax Controversies, Estate Planning and Probate.

WARREN J. BRESLIN LAW OFFICES

CHICAGO, ILLINOIS

(See Schaumburg)

Criminal Law (All Felonies & Misdemeanors); DUI & All Traffic Violations (Major & Minor); Revoked & Suspended Licenses, Driver's License Reinstatement; Petitions for Executive Clemency (Governor Pardons); Expungements (Clearing Criminal & Traffic Arrest Records).

BRINKS HOFER GILSON & LIONE

A PROFESSIONAL CORPORATION

Established in 1917

NBC TOWER, SUITE 3600

455 NORTH CITYFRONT PLAZA DRIVE

CHICAGO, ILLINOIS 60611-5599

Telephone: 312-321-4200

Facsimile: 312-321-4299

Email: iplaw@usebrinks.com

URL: http://www.usebrinks.com

Indianapolis, Indiana Office: One Indiana Square, Suite 1600. Telephone: 317-636-0886. Facsimile: 317-634-6701.

Ann Arbor, Michigan Office: 524 South Main Street, Suite 200. Telephone: 734-302-6000. Facsimile: 734-994-6331.

Arlington, Virginia Office: 2001 Jefferson Davis Highway, Suite 208. Telephone: 703-415-0303. Facsimile: 703-415-0304.

Patent, Trademark, Copyright, Trade Secret and Internet Work, Unfair Competition, Technology and Licensing Agreements, Intellectual Asset Management and Intellectual Property Litigation.

FIRM PROFILE: Brinks Hofer Gilson & Lione serves the intellectual property needs of clients from around the world. As one of the largest IP law firms in the country, Brinks litigates on behalf of U.S. and international clients in all fields of intellectual property law in state and federal courts and before the International Trade Commission. The firm also counsels clients in all areas of intellectual property law, prosecutes patent, trademark and copyright applications in the U.S. and throughout the world, and negotiates licenses and other technology-transfer agreements. Firm lawyers are frequent participants in professional meetings and seminar programs. Several firm lawyers have written treatises which are recognized as standard works on patent, trademark, trade secret and licensing law.

Wilkinson & Huxley	(1917-1920)
Wilkinson, Huxley, Byron & Knight	(1920-1947)
Wilkinson, Huxley, Byron & Hume	(1947-1956)
Byron, Hume, Groen & Clement	(1956-1963)
Hume, Groen, Clement & Hume	(1963-1966)
Hume, Clement, Hume & Lee	(1966-1970)
Hume, Clement, Hume & Lee, Ltd.	(1970-1972)
Hume, Clement, Brinks, Willian, Olds & Cook, Ltd.	(1973-1976)
Hume, Clement, Brinks, Willian & Olds, Ltd., A Professional Corporation	(1977-1983)
Willian Brinks Olds Hofer Gilson & Lione, Ltd.	(1983-1988)
Willian Brinks Olds Hofer Gilson & Lione, A Professional Corporation	(1988-1993)
Willian Brinks Hofer Gilson & Lione	(1993-1996)

HENRY L. BRINKS, born Grundy Center, Iowa, December 22, 1924; admitted to bar, 1951, District of Columbia; 1952, Ohio; 1955, Illinois; 1981, U.S. Supreme Court; registered to practice before U.S. Patent and Trademark Office. *Education:* Wheaton College (A.B., 1948); George Washington University (J.D., 1951). Examiner, U.S. Patent Office, 1948-1951. Attorney, Oberlin and Limbach, Cleveland, Ohio, 1951-1954. Member, Brinks Hofer Gilson & Lione, 1954—. *Member:* Chicago, Federal Circuit, Illinois State and Federal Bar Associations; District of Columbia Bar; Intellectual Property Law Association of Chicago; American Intellectual Property Law Association; Intellectual Property Owners Association; Licensing Executive Society. ***REPORTED CASES:*** LITIGATION: Preformed Line Products Co. v. Fanner Mfg. Co., 328 F.2d 265, 140 U.S.P.Q. 500 (6th Cir. 1964); Yardley Created Products Co. v. Clopay Corp., 324 F.2d 932, 139 U.S.P.Q. 218 (7th Cir. 1963); James B. Clow & Sons, Inc. v. U.S. Pipe & Foundry Co., 313 F.2d 46, 136 U.S.P.Q. 397 (5th Cir. 1963); Store Decor Division of JAS International Inc. v. Stylex Worldwide Industries Ltd., 767 F.Supp. 181, 20 USPQ2d 1536 (N.D.Ill. 1991); Kimberly-Clark Corp. v. James River Corp., 131 F.R.D. 607, 14 U.S.P.Q.2D 2070 (N.D.Ga. 1989); Calgon Corp. v. Nalco Chemical Co., 726 F. Supp. 983, 13 U.S.P.Q.2D 1529 (D.Del. 1989); Crane Co. v. Goodyear Tire & Rubber Co., 577 F. Supp 186, 219 U.S.P.Q. 1100 (N.D. Ohio 1983); Carpigiani v. Beatrice Foods Co., 205 U.S.P.Q. 414 (N.D.Ill. 1979); Crane Co. v. Goodyear Tire & Rubber Co., 204 U.S.P.Q. 502 (N.D. Ohio 1979); Republic Industries, Inc. v. Schlage Lock Co., 433 F. Supp. 666, 196 U.S.P.Q. 351 (N.D.Ill. 1977); Crane Co. v. Aeroquip Corp., 180 U.S.P.Q. 126 (N.D.Ill. 1973); Broadview Chemical Corp. v. Loctite Corp., 162 U.S.P.Q. 139 (D. Conn. 1969); Preformed Line Products Co. v. Fanner Mfg. Co., 225 F. Supp. 762, 124 U.S.P.Q. 288 (N.D. Ohio 1962). EX PARTE APPEALS: In re Glaug, 283 F.3d 1335, 62 U.S.P.Q.2D 1151 (Fed. Cir. 2002); Echo Travel Inc. v. Travel Associates Inc., 870 F2d 1264, 10 USPQ2d 1368 (7th Cir. 1989); Republic Industries, Inc. v. Schlage Lock Co., 592 F.2d 963, 200 U.S.P.Q. 769 (Fed. Cir. 1979); In re Kanter, 399 F.2d 249, 158 U.S.P.Q. 331 (CCPA 1968); In re Peterson, 390 F.2d 735, 156 U.S.P.Q. 504 (CCPA 1968); In re Preformed Line Products Co., 359 F.2d 907, 149 U.S.P.Q. 569 (CCPA 1966); In re Hume, 346 F.2d 594, 145 U.S.P.Q. 710 (CCPA 1965); In re Flint, 330 F.2d 363, 141 U.S.P.Q. 299, 51 C.C.P.A. 1230 (CCPA 1966); In re Preformed Line Products Co., 323 F.2d 1007, 139 U.S.P.Q. 271 (CCPA 1963); In re Alexander, 311 F.2d 585, 136 U.S.P.Q. 165 (CCPA 1963). PATENT INTERFERENCES: Kellenberger v. Duenk, 18 USPQ2d 1573 (Comm'r Pats. 1991); Lawson v. Enloe 26 USPQ2d 1594 (Bd. Pat. App. & Int. 1992). ***PRACTICE AREAS:*** Patent Counseling; Patent Litigation; Patent Prosecution; Interferences. ***Email:*** hbrinks@usebrinks.com

(This Listing Continued)

ROY E. HOFER, born Cincinnati, Ohio, October 10, 1935; admitted to bar, 1961, Virginia and Illinois; registered to practice before U.S. Patent and Trademark Office. *Education:* Purdue University (B.Ch.E., 1957); Georgetown University (J.D., with honors, 1961). Tau Beta Pi; Phi Eta Sigma; Omega Chi Epsilon. Member, Board of Editors, Georgetown Law Journal, 1960-1961. Author: "Trade Secrets: Protection and Remedies," BNA Corporate Practice Series Monograph, 1985; "The Obviousness Issue: The Jury Takes Over!" Journal of Patent & Trademark Society, 1989; "Our Patent System: Catalyst For Technology," CBA Record, February, 1987; "Jury Selection In A Patent Case," Patent Litigation, PLI 1983; "Presenting The Trade Secret Owner's Case," Protecting Trade Secrets, PLI 1985; "Business Warfare Over Trade Secrets," ABA Litigation Journal, Summer 1983; "Experts in Patent Cases," ABA Litigation Journal, Winter 1982; "Should You Patent Your Idea?" Legal Aspects of Medical Practice, April 1980. Assistant Examiner, U.S. Patent Office, 1957-1959. Member, Board of Directors, 1986-1988, Illinois Institute of Continuing Legal Education. Member, Board of Directors, Center for Conflict Resolution, 1983-1988 and 1990-1991 and President, 1991-1997. Chairman, Citizens Committee on the Juvenile Court of Cook County, 1994-1995. Member, Civil Justice Reform Act Advisory Committee, 1991-1994 and Merit Selection Panel, Northern District of Illinois, 1996-1998. *Member:* Chicago (President, 1988-1989; First Vice President, 1987-1988; Second Vice President, 1986-1987; Member, Board of Managers, 1979-1981), and American (Chairman, Intellectual Properties Litigation Committee, 1979-1982; Division Director, 1982-1987, Litigation Section) Bar Associations; Seventh Circuit Bar Association; Intellectual Property Law Association of Chicago (Member, Board of Managers, 1974-1976); American Intellectual Property Law Association; The Federal Circuit Bar Association (Member, Board of Governors, 1989-1992; President, 1993-1994). ***PRACTICE AREAS:*** Intellectual Property. ***Email:*** rhofer@usebrinks.com

RICHARD G. LIONE, born Milwaukee, Wisconsin, June 14, 1931; admitted to bar, 1960, Illinois; U.S. Supreme Court; U.S. District Court, Northern District of Illinois including Trial Bar; registered to practice before U.S. Patent and Trademark Office. *Education:* University of Wisconsin (B.S., 1954); George Washington University (LL.B., 1959). Examiner, U.S. Patent and Trademark Office, 1957-1959. *Member:* Chicago and American Bar Associations; International Federation of Industrial Property Attorneys (FICPI); American Intellectual Property Law Association; Licensing Executives Society (USA/Canada); Intellectual Property Law Association of Chicago. [First Lieut., USAF, 1954-1956]. ***Email:*** rlione@usebrinks.com

JEROME GILSON, born Chicago, Illinois, January 12, 1931; admitted to bar, 1958, Illinois. *Education:* University of Missouri (A.B., 1952); Northwestern University (J.D., 1958). Member, Board of Editors, Northwestern University Law Review, 1957-1958. Counsel, United States (International) Trademark Association, 1991-1994. *Member:* American Bar Association; International Trademark Association; Chicago Intellectual Property Alliance. ***PRACTICE AREAS:*** Trademarks. ***Email:*** jgilson@usebrinks.com

JACK C. BERENZWEIG, born Brooklyn, New York, September 29, 1942; admitted to bar, 1968, Virginia; 1969, Illinois; registered to practice before U.S. Patent and Trademark Office. *Education:* Cornell University (B.E.E., 1964); American University (J.D., 1968). Delta Theta Phi. Member, Editorial Staff, American University Law Review, 1966-1968. Author: "Counterfeiting Unpatented Products May Once Again be Stopped," Vol. 7, No. 3 and Vol. 8, No. 1, State Bar of California Section of Patent, Trademark and Copyright New Matter, 1982-1983; Note, 15 American University Law Review 126, 1965. Member, Board of Directors: Brand Names Education Foundation, 1994-2000; U.S. Trademark Association, 1983-1985. *Member:* Chicago, Illinois State and American Bar Associations; Seventh Circuit Bar Association; Virginia State Bar. ***REPORTED CASES:*** Kennecott Corp. v. Kyocera Intern, Inc., 835 F.2d 1419 (Fed. Cir. 1987), cert. denied, 486 U.S. 1008 (1988); Munsingwear Inc. v. Jockey International Inc., 31 USPQ2d 1146 (D.C. Minn. 1994), aff'd 39 F.3d 1184 (8th Cir. 1994); Red Baron-Franklin Park, Inc. v. Taito Corp., 883 F.2d 275 (4th Cir. 1989); Williams & Humbert Ltd. v. Ruiz-Mateos, 18 USPQ2d 2041 (D.C.D.C. 1991); Pizzazz Pizza & Restaurant, et al. v. Taco Bell Corporation and Pepsico, Inc. et al., 642 F.Supp. 88 (N.D. Ohio 1986); Jockey International, Inc. v. Burkard, 185 USPQ 201 (S.D. Ca. 1975); North American Philips Corp. v. American Vending Sales Inc., 29 USPQ2d 1817 (N.D. Ill. 1993); Signode Corporation v. Weld-Loc Systems, Inc. et al., 216 USPQ 310 (N.D. Ill. 1982); Signode Corporation v. Weld-Loc Systems, Inc. and Strapex AG, 00 F.2d 1108 (7th Cir. 1983). ***PRACTICE AREAS:*** Intellectual Property. ***Email:*** jcb@usebrinks.com

JEROLD A. JACOVER, born Chicago, Illinois, March 20, 1945; admitted to bar, 1972, Ohio; 1973, Illinois; registered to practice before U.S. Patent and Trademark Office. *Education:* University of Wisconsin (B.S.E.E., 1967); Georgetown University (J.D., 1972). Editor, Georgetown Law Journal, 1971-1972. *Member:* American Intellectual Property Law Association (Member, Board of Directors, 1994-1998; Committee Chairman, 1981-1986); Intellectual Property Law Association of Chicago (Member, Board of Directors, 1993-1994; President, 2000; Treasurer, 1983-1984); IPLAC Educational Foundation (President, 1991-1993); Decalogue Society of Lawyers. ***Email:*** jjacover@usebrinks.com

GARY M. ROPSKI, born Erie, Pennsylvania, April 19, 1952; admitted to bar, 1976, Illinois; registered to practice before U.S. Patent and Trademark Office. *Education:* Carnegie-Mellon University (B.S., 1972); Northwestern University School of Law (J.D., cum laude, 1976). Tau Beta Pi. Executive Editor, Journal of Criminal Law and Criminology, 1975-1976. Member, Editorial Board of the Trademark Reporter, 1981-1984; 1987-1989; 1991-1992. Editor: "Butterworths Patent Litigation: Enforcing a Global Patent Portfolio," (December 1994). Author: "En Banc Decision-Making in the Federal Circuit," co-author (2005); "Will An Admission of Patent Validity Preclude A Later Validity Challenge," BNA Patent, Trademark and Copyright Journal (2003); "Civil Law, Uncivil Lawyers," An International Who's Who of Patent Lawyers 7 (1998); "Important Decisions, Trends, and Events in United States Patent Trademark Law: 1993 and 1994," Mitteilungen der Deutschen Patenanwaelte (October 1995); "Damages in U.S. Patent Litigation," 21 International Business Lawyer 467 (November 1993); "Claim Interpretation and Patent Infringement Under United States Patent Law," Mitteilungen der Deutschen Patentanwaelte (February 1993);

(This Listing Continued)

BRINKS HOFER GILSON & LIONE, A PROFESSIONAL CORPORATION, Chicago—Continued

"The Stars' Wars: Names, Pictures and Lookalikes," Schweizerische Mitteilungen Uber Immaterialgueterrecht (August 1990); "Damages in USA Intellectual Property Litigation," 72 Journal of the Patent and Trademark Office Society 181, March 1990; "The Stars' Wars: Names, Pictures and Lookalikes," 17 A.I.P.L.A. Quarterly Journal 81 (1989); "The Right of Publicity and the Celebrity Look-Alike: Now Section 43(a) Proscribes Faces That Deceive," 77 Trademark Reporter 31, January-February, 1987; "A Primer on Intellectual Property Rights," 50 Albany Law Review 405, Spring 1986; "A 'Non-Obvious' Framework for Analyzing Proof of Secondary Meaning," 11 A.P.L.A. Journal 211 (1983); "Further Comments on the Development of the Right of Publicity —A Matter of Life, Death, and Sometimes the First Amendment," 73 Trademark Reporter 278, May-June 1983; "The Right of Publicity—The Trend Towards Protecting a Celebrity's Celebrity," 72 Trademark Reporter 251, May-June 1982; "The Federal Trademark Jury Trial—Awakening of a Dormant Constitutional Right," 70 Trademark Reporter 177, May-June 1980; "Constitutional and Procedural Aspects of the Use of Juries in Patent Litigation," 58 Journal of the Patent Office Society 609, 673, October, November 1976. Adjunct Professor, Patent and Copyright Law, Northwestern University School of Law, 1981-1997. *Member:* Chicago, Federal, Federal Circuit, American and International Bar Associations; Intellectual Property Law Association of Chicago; American Intellectual Property Law Association; Intellectual Property Owners; International Trademark Association; International Patent and Trademark Association (AIPPI); International Trade Commission Trial Lawyers Association; Licensing Executives Society. ***LANGUAGES:*** German. ***PRACTICE AREAS:*** Patent Litigation; Trademark Litigation; Copyright Litigation. ***Email:*** gropski@usebrinks.com

JOEL W. BENSON, born Oak Harbor, Washington, April 10, 1949; admitted to bar, 1978, District of Columbia; 1979, U.S. District Court for the District of Columbia; 1980, Illinois, U.S. District Court, Northern District of Illinois including Trial Bar and U.S. Court of Appeals, Seventh Circuit; 1982, U.S. Court of Appeals for the Federal Circuit and U.S. Court of Appeals, Third Circuit; 1993, U.S. District Court, Western District of Michigan; 1996, U.S. District Court, Northern District of Indiana; 2001, U.S. Court of Appeals, Eleventh Circuit; 2003, U.S. District Court, Eastern District of Wisconsin; registered to practice before U.S. Patent and Trademark Office. *Education:* Delta College (A.A.S., summa cum laude, 1969); University of Michigan (B.S.E.E., cum laude, 1971); Georgetown University (J.D., 1978). Eta Kappa Nu; Phi Theta Kappa. Associate Editor, American Bar Association Tax Lawyer, 1977. *Member:* District of Columbia Bar; Chicago, Illinois State and American Bar Associations; American Intellectual Property Law Association. ***PRACTICE AREAS:*** Patent Litigation; Patent Prosecution; Trade Secrets; Copyrights. ***Email:*** jbenson@usebrinks.com

JOHN K. LUCAS, born Chicago, Illinois, July 9, 1946; admitted to bar, 1972, Illinois; registered to practice before U.S. Patent and Trademark Office. *Education:* Illinois Institute of Technology (B.S., with distinction, 1968); DePaul University (J.D., 1972). Tau Beta Pi; Eta Kappa Nu; Phi Alpha Delta. Adjunct Professor, De Paul University College of Law, 1986-1993. *Member:* Chicago, Illinois State and American Bar Associations; The Federal Circuit Bar Association; Seventh Circuit Bar Association; American Intellectual Property Law Association; Intellectual Property Law Association of Chicago; Legal Club of Chicago; Licensing Executives Society. ***PRACTICE AREAS:*** Intellectual Property Law. ***Email:*** jlucas@usebrinks.com

RAYMOND W. GREEN, born Detroit, Michigan, October 5, 1940; admitted to bar, 1966, Ohio; 1971, New York; 1972, U.S. Supreme Court; 1975-1982, U.S. Court of Customs and Patent Appeals; 1980-1982, U.S Court of Claims; 1982, U.S. Court of Appeals for the Federal Circuit; 1983, Illinois; registered to practice before U.S. Patent and Trademark Office; registered to practice before Canadian Patent Office. *Education:* University of Michigan (B.S., Chem., 1963; J.D., 1966). Phi Eta Sigma; Phi Alpha Delta (Vice Justice, 1964-1965). Member, 1971-1982 and President, 1979-1980, Niagara Frontier Patent Law Association. *Member:* Chicago and American Bar Associations; Intellectual Property Law Association of Chicago; American Intellectual Property Law Association (Chair, Interference Committee, 1998-2000); Federal Circuit Bar Association; Intellectual Property Institute of Canada; American Chemical Society. ***REPORTED CASES:*** Nitz v. Ehrenreich, 537 F.2d 539, 190 USPQ 413 (CCPA 1976); Shurie v. Richmond, 699 F.2d 1156, 216 USPQ 1042 (Fed. Cir. 1983); Lawson v. Enloe, 26 USPQ2d 1594 (Bd. of Pat. App. & Int. 1992). ***PRACTICE AREAS:*** Patents; Litigation. ***Email:*** rgreen@usebrinks.com

CYNTHIA A. HOMAN, born Evanston, Illinois, July 7, 1954; admitted to bar, 1981, Illinois. *Education:* University of Illinois (B.A., 1976); University of Pittsburgh (M.L.S., 1977); DePaul University (J.D., 1981). Federal Circuit Editor, Appellate Practice Journal, 1998-2002. Co-Author: "Designing An Effective Intellectual Property Compliance Program," 1994. *Member:* Chicago, American and Federal Circuit Bar Associations; American Intellectual Property Law Association; Intellectual Property Law Association of Chicago. ***PRACTICE AREAS:*** Appeals; Intellectual Property Litigation. ***Email:*** choman@usebrinks.com

JAMES R. SOBIERAJ, born Detroit, Michigan, February 18, 1957; admitted to bar, 1982, Illinois; U.S. District Court, Northern District of Illinois including Trial Bar; registered to practice before U.S. Patent and Trademark Office. *Education:* University of Michigan (B.S.E.E., magna cum laude, 1979; J.D., 1982). Tau Beta Pi; Eta Kappa Nu. *Member:* Federal Circuit and Federal Bar Associations; Licensing Executives Society (President, 2003; President Elect, 2002; Secretary, 1999-2001; Member, Board of Trustees, 1996-2004; International Delegate, 1997—); Intellectual Property Law Association of Chicago (Vice President, 2005); National Inventors Hall of Fame Foundation (Board of Directors, 2004—); American Intellectual Property Law Association; The Lawyers Club of Chicago. (Chair, Litigation Practice Group). ***REPORTED CASES:*** Procter & Gamble v. Haugen and Amway Corp., 317 F.3d 1121 (10th Cir. 2003); Procter & Gamble v. Haugen and Amway Corp., 22 F.3d 1262 (10th Cir. 2000); Wolverine World Wide Inc. v. Nike Inc., 38 F.3d 1192 (Fed. Cir. 1994); Amway Corp. v. Nartron Corp., 25 USPQ2d 1944 (W.D. Mich. 1992). ***PRACTICE AREAS:*** Litigation; Patents; Trade Secrets; Intellectual Property; Unfair Competition; Antitrust; Commercial Litigation. ***Email:*** jsobieraj@usebrinks.com

RICHARD A. KAPLAN, born New York, N.Y., May 27, 1957; admitted to bar, 1982, Illinois; registered to practice before U.S. Patent and Trademark Office. *Education:* Princeton University (B.S.E., magna cum laude, 1979); Albany Law School of Union University

(This Listing Continued)

(J.D., cum laude, 1982). Member, 1980-1982 and Executive Editor, 1981-1982, Albany Law Review. Author: Kaplan, "Trade Secrets: Protection and Remedies," 43-2nd C.P.S. (BNA); Kaplan, "California Makes Life Tough for Trade Secret Owners," Intellectual Property Law Update, Aspen Publishers, Chapter 8, 2003; Sternstein, Homan, Kaplan and Frankel, "Designing an Effective Intellectual Property Compliance Program," Corp. Compl. Series (Intell. Prop. vol.) West Group; Note, "Close Corporation Shareholders' Agreements and the Signal of Zion v. Kurtz: Frustration of the Statutory Notice Requirement," 46 Albany Law Review 198, Fall 1981. *Member:* Chicago, Federal Circuit, Illinois State and American (Member, Sections on: Patent, Trademark and Copyright Law; Litigation) Bar Associations; American Intellectual Property Law Association; Intellectual Property Law Association of Chicago; Intellectual Property Owners Association; The Decalogue Society of Lawyers. ***PRACTICE AREAS:*** Intellectual Property Litigation; Patents; Trade Secrets. ***Email:*** rkaplan@usebrinks.com

STEVEN P. SHURTZ, born Panguitch, Utah, January 23, 1956; admitted to bar, 1983, Illinois and U.S. District Court, Northern District of Illinois; 1997, Utah and U.S. District Court, District of Utah; registered to practice before U.S. Patent and Trademark Office. *Education:* University of Utah (B.S.Ch.E., magna cum laude, 1980; J.D., 1983). Order of the Coif. Author: "Community Communications Company v. City of Boulder: Denial of Parker Exemption to Home Rule Cities," 1983 Utah Law Review, 139. *Member:* Utah State Bar; American Bar Association; American Intellectual Property Law Association. ***PRACTICE AREAS:*** Chemical Patents; Design Patents; International Patents; Mechanical Patents; Metallurgical Patents; Medical Patents; Electro-Mechanical Patents; Patent Prosecution; Patent Licensing; Patent Litigation; Chemical Patent Prosecution; Mechanical Patent Prosecution; International Patent Prosecution; Patent Interference Practice. ***Email:*** sshurtz@usebrinks.com

JEFFERY M. DUNCAN, born Evanston, Illinois, September 4, 1956; admitted to bar, 1984, Illinois; registered to practice before U.S. Patent and Trademark Office. *Education:* Brigham Young University (B.S., Chem., 1981; J.D., 1984). Head, Biotechnology/Pharmaceutical Practice Group. *Member:* American Bar Association; American Intellectual Property Law Association; Licensing Executives Society; Intellectual Property Law Association of Chicago; J. Reuben Clark Law Society. ***PRACTICE AREAS:*** Intellectual Property Licensing; Chemical Intellectual Property; Pharmaceutical Intellectual Property; Biotechnology; Intellectual Property. ***Email:*** jduncan@usebrinks.com

JEFFERY A. HANDELMAN, born Evanston, Illinois, May 31, 1959; admitted to bar, 1984, Illinois. *Education:* University of Illinois (B.A., 1981); Georgetown University (J.D., 1984). Instructor, Legal Research and Writing, Georgetown University Law Center, 1983-1984. *Member:* Chicago Bar Association; International Trademark Association. ***PRACTICE AREAS:*** Intellectual Property. ***Email:*** jhandelman@usebrinks.com

HAROLD V. JOHNSON, born Clearwater, Florida, October 22, 1956; admitted to bar, 1984, Illinois; registered to practice before U.S. Patent and Trademark Office. *Education:* Michigan Technological University (B.S.E.E., 1978); Albany Law School of Union University (J.D., cum laude, 1984). *Member:* Chicago, Federal Circuit and American Bar Associations; American Intellectual Property Law Association; Licensing Executives Society. ***PRACTICE AREAS:*** Patent Prosecution and Counseling; Antitrust Litigation. ***Email:*** hjohnson@usebrinks.com

RODNEY A. DANIEL, born Middletown, Ohio, March 1, 1954; admitted to bar, 1985, Illinois; 2000, Colorado; registered to practice before U.S. Patent and Trademark Office. *Education:* Purdue University (B.S., with honors, 1976); University of Illinois (M.S., 1978; J.D., magna cum laude, 1985). Phi Beta Kappa; Sigma Pi Sigma. ***PRACTICE AREAS:*** Intellectual Property. ***Email:*** rdaniel@usebrinks.com

GLEN P. BELVIS, born Pittsburgh, Pennsylvania, October 26, 1958; admitted to bar, 1985, Illinois and U.S. District Court, Northern District of Illinois; 1992, U.S. District Court, Western District of Michigan and U.S. Court of Appeals for the Federal Circuit; 1997, U.S. District Court, Northern District of Illinois including Trial Bar; 2001, U.S. Supreme Court; registered to practice before U.S. Patent and Trademark Office, 1984. *Education:* University of Notre Dame (B.S., in Chemistry, 1980); DePaul University (J.D., with honors, 1985). Editor, De Paul Law Review, Vol. 34. Extern, Honorable William J. Bauer, Seventh Circuit Court of Appeals, 1984. Associate Editor, Licensing Law and Business Report, Vols. 9-11. Editor: 2003 Aspen IP Update. Author: "Amend Federal Rule 68," National Law Journal, March 14, 2005; "Better Things Come to a Patent Owner Who Waits - The Need to Fully Assess the Strategic Risks of Seeking Preliminary Injunctive Relief in Patent Cases," co-author, Intellectual Property Litigation, American Bar Association, Vol. 16, No. 4, Winter 2005; "Pitfalls of Electronic Communications," Managing Intellectual Property, September 2003; "The Doctrine of Equivalents and §112 Equivalents," 2003 Aspen IP Update; "An Analysis of the En Banc Decision in Festo Corp. v. Shoketsu Kinzoku Kogyoki Co.," Federal Circuit Bar Journal, Vol. 11, 2001 (awarded West Publishing outstanding IP article for 2001); "The Doctrine of Equivalents and 112 Equivalents," 2002 Aspen IP Update; "The Doctrine of Equivalents and 112 Equivalents," 2001 Aspen IP Update; "The Doctrine of Equivalents and §112 Equivalents," 1999 Wiley Intellectual Property Law Update; "The Federal Circuit Creates a New Depth Charge in the Arsenal Against Submarine Patent," Vol. 24, No. 1 IPLAC Newsletter, 1998; "IP Poses Opportunities Daring Economic Straits," The National Law Journal, June 22, 1998; "Computer Copyright and Tying Agreements: An Argument for the Abandonment of the Presumptions of Market Power," 28 Boston College Law Review 265, 1987. Volunteer Attorney, Office of the Public Guardian, 1993-1994. *Member:* American Bar Association (Member, Sections on: Litigation; Antitrust; Intellectual Property); American Intellectual Property Law Association; Intellectual Property Law Association of Chicago (Vice Chair, Patent Antitrust Committee). ***REPORTED CASES:*** Engate v. Esquire Depostion Services, 2003 U.S. Dist. LEXIS 10050 (N.D. Ill.); Crown v. Continental PET, 232 F.Supp. 294 (D. Del. 2002); Ferag v. Grapha, 935 F. Supp 1238 (D.DC. 1996), aff'd mem, 129 F.3d 135 (Fed. Cir. 1997); Haworth v. Herman Miller, 37 U.S.P.Q.2d 1094 (W.D. Mich. 1995); Haworth v. Herman Miller, 12 F.3d 1090 (Fed. Cir 1993); Haworth v. Herman Miller, 998 F.2d 975 (Fed. Cir. 1993); W.R. Grace v. Viskase, 21 U.S.P.Q.2d 1114 (N.D. Ill. 1991); Cuno v. Pall, 729 F. Supp. 234 (1989); Cuno v. Pall, 121 F.R.D. 198 (E.D.N.Y. 1988); Panduit v. Dennison, 810 F.2d 1561 (Fed. Cir. 1987); Panduit v. Dennison, 475 U.S. 809 (1986). ***PRACTICE AREAS:*** Litigation; Intellectual Property; Antitrust Trade Regulation; Patents; Copyrights; Trade Secrets;

(This Listing Continued)

Trademarks; Licensing; Biotechnology and Pharmaceutical; Chemical; Computers and Software; Forest and Paper Products; Internet/E-Commerce; Manufacturing. ***Email:*** gbelvis@usebrinks.com

THOMAS J. FILARSKI, born Illinois, October 20, 1956; admitted to bar, 1986, Illinois; registered to practice before U.S. Patent and Trademark Office. *Education:* Loyola University, Chicago (B.A., 1978); Michigan Technological University (M.S., 1980); DePaul University (J.D., 1986). Co-Author: "Patent Defenses, Patent Litigation Strategies Handbook," Ch. 20 (BNA Books, 2000); "Patent Enforcement in the Courts of the United States," Butterworths Patent Litigation, 1995; "Claim Interpretation And Patent Infringement Under United States Patent Law," Mitteilungen Der Deutschen Patentanwälte, February, 1993. *Member:* Chicago and American Bar Associations; American Intellectual Property Law Association; Intellectual Property Law Association of Chicago; Licensing Executives Society. ***PRACTICE AREAS:*** Intellectual Property; Patents; Chemical; Biotechnology and Pharmaceutical; Internet/E-Commerce. ***Email:*** tfilarski@usebrinks.com

WILLIAM H. FRANKEL, born New York, New York, December 11, 1955; admitted to bar, 1980, Illinois and U.S. District Court, Northern District of Illinois, including Trial Bar; registered to practice before U.S. Patent and Trademark Office. *Education:* Tulane University of Louisiana (B.S.M.E., cum laude, 1977; J.D., cum laude, 1980). Phi Eta Sigma; Tau Beta Pi. Member, Board of Editors, Maritime Lawyer, 1978-1980. Co-Author of *Designing An Effective Intellectual Property Compliance Program*, Vol. 8 of Corporate Compliance Series, West Group 1993—; Co-author of the 2005 Intellectual Property Handbook published by the Illinois Institute for Continuing Legal Education. Adjunct Professor of Patent Law, De Paul University College of Law, 1993-1995. *Member:* Chicago, Federal Circuit and American (Member: Patent, Trademark and Copyright Law and Litigation Sections) Bar Associations; American Intellectual Property Law Association; Intellectual Property Law Association of Chicago (Board of Managers, 1999-2001; Secretary, 2001-2003); International Patent and Trademark Association; Lawyers for the Creative Arts (Board of Directors; Vice-President, 2000-2003; President, 2004—); The Decalogue Society of Lawyers. ***PRACTICE AREAS:*** Intellectual Property Litigation and Counseling; Patent Litigation; Copyright Litigation; Trademark Litigation; Unfair Competition. ***Email:*** wfrankel@usebrinks.com

GUSTAVO SILLER, JR., born Monterey, Mexico, August 22, 1956; admitted to bar, 1983, Illinois and U.S. District Court, Northern District of Illinois; registered to practice before U.S. Patent and Trademark Office. *Education:* Northwestern University (B.S.M.E., 1979); DePaul University (J.D., 1983). Adjunct Professor, De Paul University College of Law, 1995-1997. Co-Author: "Patent and Trade Secret Protection of Computer Technology," Siller et al, Vol. VI No. 2, April 1993. *Member:* Chicago and American Bar Associations; American Intellectual Property Law Association. ***LANGUAGES:*** Spanish. ***Email:*** gsiller@usebrinks.com

JAMES P. NAUGHTON, born Chicago, Illinois, August 26, 1957; admitted to bar, 1981, Illinois, U.S. District Court, Northern District of Illinois, including Trial Bar and U.S. Court of Appeals for the Federal Circuit; registered to practice before U.S. Patent and Trademark Office. *Education:* University of Illinois (B.S.E.E., with highest honors, 1978; J.D., cum laude, 1981). Tau Beta Pi; Eta Kappa Nu. *Member:* Chicago and American Bar Associations; American Intellectual Property Law Association; Lawyers for the Creative Arts; Institute of Electrical and Electronics Engineers. ***Email:*** jnaughton@usebrinks.com

TIMOTHY Q. DELANEY, born Evergreen Park, Illinois, September 25, 1960; admitted to bar, 1988, Illinois and U.S. District Court, Northern District of Illinois; 1991, U.S. Court of Appeals, Federal Circuit; 1992, U.S. District Court, Western District of Michigan; 1999, U.S. Court of Appeals, Tenth Circuit; 2001, U.S. Court of Appeals, Sixth Circuit; registered to practice before U.S. Patent and Trademark Office. *Education:* University of Illinois (B.S., General Engineering, 1983); George Washington University (J.D., with honors, 1988). *Member:* Federal Circuit and American Bar Associations; American Intellectual Property Law Association; Intellectual Property Law Association of Chicago. ***PRACTICE AREAS:*** Patents; Intellectual Property; Litigation. ***Email:*** tdelaney@usebrinks.com

RALPH J. GABRIC, born Glen Ellyn, Illinois, July 13, 1962; admitted to bar, 1988, Illinois; 1989, U.S. District Court, Northern District of Illinois; 1996, U.S. Court of Appeals, Federal Circuit; registered to practice before U.S. Patent and Trademark Office. *Education:* Boston College (B.S., Chemistry, 1985); DePaul University (J.D., 1988). Member, De Paul Law Review, 1987-1988. Chambers USA: America's Leading Lawyers for Business; Leading Illinois Intellectual Property Lawyer, 2004, 2005. Leading Intellectual Property Lawyer, Leasing Lawyers Network, Law Bulletin Publishing Co., 2004. *Member:* American Bar Association; American Intellectual Property Law Association; Chicago Inn of Court; The Lawyers Club of Chicago. ***PRACTICE AREAS:*** Intellectual Property; Litigation; Trials; Copyright; Interference; Chemical; Internet/E-Commerce; Electrical and Computer; Software; Biotechnology and Pharmaceutical. ***Email:*** rgabric@usebrinks.com

BRADLEY G. LANE, born Chicago, Illinois, July 12, 1963; admitted to bar, 1988, Illinois and U.S. District Court, Northern District of Illinois; 1992, U.S. Court of Appeals for the Federal Circuit; 1996, U.S. District Court, Northern District of Illinois including Trial Bar; 2002, U.S. District Court, Eastern District of Michigan; registered to practice before U.S. Patent and Trademark Office. *Education:* University of Illinois (B.S.G.E., with highest honors, 1985); University of Michigan (J.D., 1988). Tau Beta Pi. James Scholar. Member, 1986-1988 and Managing Editor, 1987-1988, University of Michigan Journal of Law Reform. *Member:* Chicago, Federal Circuit and American Bar Associations; American Intellectual Property Law Association. ***REPORTED CASES:*** Sidel v. Uniloy Milacron Inc., 61 USPQ2d 1480 (N.D. Ga. 2001); Tec Air, Inc. v. Denso Corp., 49 USPQ2d 1944 (N.D. Ill. 1998), aff'd, 192 F.3d 1353 (Fed. Cir. 1999); Valley Recreation Prods. Inc. v. Arachnid, Inc., 35 USPQ2d 1218 (Fed. Cir. 1994)(unpublished); Tri-Seal Int'l Inc. v. J.S. Plastics Inc., 1991 U.S. Dist. LEXIS 19603 (N.D. Ill. 1991). ***PRACTICE AREAS:*** Litigation; Intellectual Property; Patents; Copyrights; Trademarks. ***Email:*** blane@usebrinks.com

G. PETER NICHOLS, born Colorado Springs, Colorado, September 18, 1958; admitted to bar, 1989, Illinois; 1996, U.S. Court of Appeals, Federal Circuit; registered to practice before U.S. Patent and Trademark Office. *Education:* University of Minnesota (B.S. Ch.E., 1981); DePaul University (J.D., 1989). *Member:* Chicago, Federal Circuit, Illinois State and American Bar Associations; American Intellectual Property Law Association. ***REPORTED CASES:*** Richardson-Vicks Inc. v. Upjohn Co., 122 F3d 1476 (Fed. Cir. 1997).

(This Listing Continued)

PRACTICE AREAS: Chemical Intellectual Property (40%); Mechanical Intellectual Property (25%); International Intellectual Property (25%); Intellectual Property Portfolio Management (10%). ***Email:*** gpn@usebrinks.com

MICHAEL E. MILZ, born Chicago, Illinois, December 12, 1960; admitted to bar, 1990, Illinois; 1991, U.S. District Court, Northern District of Illinois; registered to practice before U.S. Patent and Trademark Office. *Education:* University of Illinois (B.S., 1983); Illinois Institute of Technology, Chicago-Kent College of Law (J.D., with honors, 1990). Registered Professional Engineer, Illinois, 1987. *Member:* Chicago and American Bar Associations; American Intellectual Property Law Association. ***Email:*** mmilz@usebrinks.com

DOMINIC P. ZANFARDINO, born Chicago, Illinois, July 24, 1960; admitted to bar, 1990, Illinois; U.S. District Court, Northern District of Illinois; U.S. District Court, Western District of Michigan; U.S. District Court, Eastern District of Wisconsin; U.S. Court of Appeals for the Federal Circuit; U.S. District Court, District of Colorado; U.S. Court of Appeals for the Tenth Circuit; registered to practice before U.S. Patent and Trademark Office. *Education:* Loyola University (B.S., Biology, cum laude, 1982; J.D., 1990). *Member:* Chicago, Federal Circuit and American Bar Associations; Intellectual Property Law Association of Chicago; American Intellectual Property Law Association; Licensing Executives Society. ***PRACTICE AREAS:*** Intellectual Property. ***Email:*** dzanfardino@usebrinks.com

ROBERT S. MALLIN, born Chicago, Illinois, February 28, 1963; admitted to bar, 1990, Illinois; registered to practice before U.S. Patent and Trademark Office. *Education:* University of Illinois (B.S. Ch.E., 1985); Loyola University (J.D., 1990). ***PRACTICE AREAS:*** Intellectual Property. ***Email:*** rmallin@usebrinks.com

WILLIAM F. PRENDERGAST, born Evergreen Park, Illinois, August 27, 1965; admitted to bar, 1990, Illinois; U.S. District Court, Northern District of Illinois and U.S. Court of Appeals for the Federal Circuit; registered to practice before U.S. Patent and Trademark Office. *Education:* Loyola University (B.S., Physics, 1987); University of Illinois (J.D., cum laude, 1990). ***PRACTICE AREAS:*** Intellectual Property. ***Email:*** wprendergast@usebrinks.com

JOHN C. FREEMAN, born Ottawa, Illinois, June 22, 1959; admitted to bar, 1990, Illinois; U.S. District Court, Northern District of Illinois; U.S. Court of Appeals for the Federal Circuit; registered to practice before U.S. Patent and Trademark Office. *Education:* University of Illinois (B.S., Physics, cum laude, 1981); University of Wisconsin (M.S., Physics, 1983); George Washington University (J.D., 1990). Examiner, U.S. Patent and Trademark Office, 1985-1990. *Member:* Chicago, Illinois State and American Bar Associations; Intellectual Property Law Association of Chicago; American Intellectual Property Law Association. ***PRACTICE AREAS:*** Patent Prosecution; Patent Applications; Patent Litigation; Patent Licensing; Computer and Software Patents; Design Patents; Electro-Mechanical Patents; International Patents; Patent Infringement. ***Email:*** jfreeman@usebrinks.com

DAVID S. FLEMING, born Oak Park, Illinois, June 16, 1955; admitted to bar, 1981, Illinois and U.S. District Court, Northern District of Illinois including Trial Bar, 1985; 1984, U.S. Court of Appeals, 9th Circuit; 1985, U.S. Court of Appeals, 7th Circuit; 1990, U.S. Supreme Court. *Education:* Georgetown University; Northwestern University (B.A., 1978); University of Illinois (J.D., 1981). Member, University of Illinois Law Review, 1980-1981. Author: Note, "Prejudgment Interest: An Element of Full Compensation in Wrongful Death Cases," University of Illinois Law Review 453-484, 1981; "What Every Lawyer Should Know About Trademarks," DCBA Brief, Dec., 1993; "Intellectual Property Insurance," Managing Intellectual Property, May, 1998; "Is U.S. Advertising Of Foreign Services 'Use In Commerce'?" Intellectual Property Worldwide, November/December, 1998; "Wal-Mart Puts Pressure On Trade Dress Owners," Managing Intellectual Property, May, 2000. Co-Author: Ch. 7, "Trademarks/Unfair Trade Practice," In Business, Law and the Internet, Illinois Institute for Continuing Legal Education, 2002. Contributor, World Trademark Law Report (Globe Business Publishing), 2002—. Member of Faculty: LexisNexis Advanced Trademark Strategies Program, Chicago, Il., April 2002; International Trademark Association Trademark Trial Advocacy Program, Chicago, Il., July 2000. Faculty Member or Speaker: Mock jury trial, International Trademark Associational Annual Meeting, San Diego, California, May 17, 2005; "Trademarks in Internet Advertising: Banners, Pop-Ups, Paid Search," Georgetown University Advanced Computer and Internet Law Program, Washington, D.C., March 17, 2005; (co-chair) Trademark Administrators Forum, International Trademark Association, Arlington, Virginia, October 3-6, 2004; "U.S. Dilution Law," Famous and Well-Known Trademark Forum, International Trademark Association, Brussels, Belgium, September 20, 2004; "Internet Update: Domain Name Disputes and Cyber Infringement," IP Summer Conference, Michigan Institute of Continuing Legal Education, July 23, 2004; "Internet Advertising: Expanding Frontiers of Trademark Law," Intellectual Property Law Association of Chicago Seminar, Chicago, Illinois, November 21, 2003; "Trademarks on the Internet: Expanding Frontiers," LexisNexis Advanced Trademark Program, New York, New York, October 23-24, 2003; Intellectual Property Owners Association Annual Meeting, "Dilution: Open Issues After Moseley," Chicago, IL, September 2003; Georgetown University Continuing Legal Education Advanced Computer and Internet Law Program, "Trademarks and the Internet: Hot Topics," Washington, D.C., March 2003; International Trademark Association Advanced Dilution Forum, "Qualifying for Dilution Protection" (moderator), Arlington, VA, March 2003; Chicago International IP Conference, "Hot Topics In U.S. Trademark Law," Chicago, IL, October 2002; LexisNexis Advanced Trademark Strategies Program, "Effective Enforcement Strategies," Chicago, Il., April 2002; International Trademark Association Trademark Trial Advocacy Program, Chicago, Il., July 2000. *Member:* American Bar Association; International Trademark Association; American Intellectual Property Law Association; Intellectual Property Law Association of Chicago. ***REPORTED CASES:*** GoTo.com, Inc. v. The Walt Disney Company, et al., 202 F.3d 1199 (9th Cir. 2000). ***PRACTICE AREAS:*** Trademarks; Litigation. ***Email:*** dfleming@usebrinks.com

LAURA BETH MILLER, born August 22, 1960; admitted to bar, 1985, Illinois; U.S. District Court, Northern District of Illinois; U.S. District Court, Western District of Michigan; U.S. District Court, Eastern District of Wisconsin; U.S. Court of Appeals, Federal and Seventh Circuits; registered to practice before U.S. Patent and Trademark Office. *Education:* University of Virginia (B.A., 1982); Marshall Wythe School of Law College of Will-

(This Listing Continued)

BRINKS HOFER GILSON & LIONE, A PROFESSIONAL CORPORATION, Chicago—Continued

iam and Mary (J.D., 1985). *Member:* Chicago and American Bar Associations; American Intellectual Property Law Association; International Trademark Association; National Association of Women Lawyers. ***Email:*** lmiller@usebrinks.com

MICHAEL P. CHU, born Chicago, Illinois, September 13, 1967; admitted to bar, 1992, Illinois, U.S. District Court, Northern District of Illinois and U.S. Court of Appeals, Federal and Fourth Circuits; registered to practice before U.S. Patent and Trademark Office. *Education:* University of Illinois (B.S.M.E., 1989); College of William & Mary (J.D., 1992). Executive Editor, Professional Articles, William & Mary Law Review, 1991-1992. Author: "An Antitrust Solution to the New Wave of Predatory Patent Infringement Litigation," 33 William and Mary L. Rev. 1341, 1992. *Member:* Chicago and American Bar Associations; National Asian Pacific American Bar Association (President 2004-2005); American Intellectual Property Law Association; Asian-American Bar Association; The NAPABA Law Foundation. ***PRACTICE AREAS:*** Intellectual Property. ***Email:*** mchu@usebrinks.com

MEREDITH MARTIN ADDY, born Atlanta, Georgia, February 21, 1968; admitted to bar, 1993, Georgia and Illinois; 1995, District of Columbia; 1997, U.S. Court of Appeals for the Federal Circuit; 2001, U.S. Supreme Court; registered to practice before U.S. Patent and Trademark Office. *Education:* Rice University (B.S.E.E., 1990; B.A., Fine Arts, 1990); University of Georgia (J.D., cum laude, 1993); John Marshall Law School (LL.M., Intellectual Property, with honors, 1997). Law Clerk to Hon. Paul R. Michel, U.S. Court of Appeals for the Federal Circuit, 1997-1998. Author: "Brevity: The Key To Success At The Federal Circuit," Managing Intellectual Property Americas Enforcement Focus 2005, co-author with Cynthia A. Homan; "Is the Federal Circuit Ready to Accept Plenary Authority for Patent Appeals?" John Marshall Law School Review of Intellectual Property Law, Vol. 4, Issue 4 (Summer 2005); "Holistic Approach Works," The National Law Journal, Vol. 27 No. 45, p. 31 (July 18, 2005); "New Bill Aims To Curtail Forum Shopping In Patent Cases," IP Law Bulletin Online (June 30, 2005); "Dissecting Views of Judges on Written Description: Federal Circuit Includes 'Separatists,' 'Fusionists' and 'Clarificationists'," The National Law Journal, Vol. 26, No. 87 (June 13, 2005) co-author with Jeffery M. Duncan and C. Noel Kaman; "Claim Interpretation Under Post-Markman Precedent," 2003 Intellectual Property Law Update at 1 (2003), co-author with David H. Bluestone; "A View from the Crowd at Festo," Intellectual Property Strategist (March 2001); "Time Well Spent, Tommy," A Lawyers's Guide to Veterans Affairs, Issue 3 (2001). Co-Author with the Honorable Paul R. Michel, *State and Federal Court Adjudication of Federal Patent Issues*, published in Donald S. Chisum et al., *Principles of Patent Law* at 1410 (1998); "Claim Interpretation Under Post-Markman Precedent," 2003 Intellectual Property Law Update, 1 (2003). Adjunct Professor, John Marshall Law School, 2000—. Member: Federal Circuit Advisory Counsel; Editorial Board, AIPLA Quarterly Journal (Editorial Board). *Member:* Intellectual Property Law Association of Chicago (Board of Managers); Federal Circuit Bar Association (Member, Patent Subcommittee); American Intellectual Property Law Association (Member, Federal Litigation Committee). ***REPORTED CASES:*** Chiron Corp. v. Genentech, Inc., 363 F. 3d 1247 (Fed. Cir. 2004); In re Doyle, 293 F. 3d 1355 (Fed. Cir. 2002); In re Glaug, 283 F. 3d 1335 (Fed. Cir. 2001). ***PRACTICE AREAS:*** Intellectual Property Portfolio Management; Intellectual Property Litigation; Intellectual Property Procurement. ***Email:*** maddy@usebrinks.com

KENT E. GENIN, born Lafayette, Indiana, September 7, 1966; admitted to bar, 1993, Illinois; registered to practice before U.S. Patent and Trademark Office. *Education:* Stanford University (B.S.E.E., 1988); University of Cincinnati (J.D., 1993). Business Manager, University of Cincinnati Law Review, 1992-1993. ***PRACTICE AREAS:*** Intellectual Property. ***Email:*** kgenin@usebrinks.com

CRAIG A. SUMMERFIELD, admitted to bar, 1993, Illinois; registered to practice before U.S. Patent and Trademark Office. *Education:* University of Kansas (B.S.E.E., with honors, 1990); IIT/Chicago-Kent College of Law (J.D., with highest honors, 1993). Author: "Color as a Trademark and the Mere Color Rule: The Circuit Split for Color Alone," 68 Chi.-Kent L. Rev. 973 (1993). ***PRACTICE AREAS:*** Intellectual Property. ***Email:*** csummerfield@usebrinks.com

PHILIP A. JONES, born Kobe, Japan, January 19, 1966; admitted to bar, 1993, Illinois. *Education:* Princeton University (A.B., magna cum laude, 1988); Boston University (J.D., cum laude, 1993). ***PRACTICE AREAS:*** Intellectual Property. ***Email:*** pjones@usebrinks.com

MARC V. RICHARDS, born New York, N.Y., October 19, 1960; admitted to bar, 1993, Illinois; registered to practice before U.S. Patent and Trademark Office. *Education:* Washington University, St. Louis (B.S.Ch.E., 1982); University of Chicago (M.B.A., with honors, 1993); Loyola University of Chicago (J.D., cum laude, 1993). Editor-at-Large, Loyola Law Journal, 1992-1993. Professional Engineer, Illinois, 1989. Author: "Patenting Inventions," Chapter 1 of 2005 Intellectual Property Law Handbook published by Illinois Institute for Continuing Legal Education. *Member:* Chicago and American Bar Associations; American Intellectual Property Law Association; Intellectual Property Law Association of Chicago (Board of Managers 2002-2004). ***PRACTICE AREAS:*** Patent Prosecution; Biotechnology and Pharmaceutical; Chemical; International Patents and Trademarks; Internet/E-Commerce; Licensing; Litigation; Mechanical; Nanotechnology. ***Email:*** mrichards@usebrinks.com

JOHN T. GABRIELIDES, born Chicago, Illinois, August 12, 1963; admitted to bar, 1988, Illinois. *Education:* University of Illinois (B.A., 1985); DePaul University (J.D., 1988). ***PRACTICE AREAS:*** Intellectual Property Litigation; Intellectual Property Counseling. ***Email:*** jgabrielides@usebrinks.com

ANDREW D. STOVER, born Montreal, Quebec, Canada, July 10, 1965; admitted to bar, 1994, Illinois and U.S. District Court, Northern District of Illinois; 1995, U.S. Court of Appeals for the Federal Circuit; registered to practice before U.S. Patent and Trademark Office. *Education:* Washington University (B.S.M.E., 1987; M.S.M.E., 1991); Northwestern University (J.D., cum laude, 1994). Pi Tau Sigma. Note and Comment Editor, Journal of International Law & Business. Adjunct Professor, Patent and Copyright Law, Northwestern University School of Law, 1997-2000. *Member:* Chicago, Illinois State, Federal Circuit and American Bar Associations. ***Email:*** astover@usebrinks.com

(This Listing Continued)

JOSEPH V. NORVELL, admitted to bar, 1994, Illinois; U.S. District Court, Northern and Central Districts of Illinois. *Education:* University of Illinois (B.S., Finance, with highest honors, 1991); Georgetown University Law Center (J.D., 1994). *Member:* Chicago Bar Association; International Trademark Association; The Copyright Society of the U.S.A.; Intellectual Property Law Association of Chicago; Intellectual Property Owners Association. ***PRACTICE AREAS:*** Trademark; Copyright; Unfair Competition; Internet Law; Litigation. ***Email:*** jnorvell@usebrinks.com

K. SHANNON MRKSICH, born Somerville, New Jersey, 1966; admitted to bar, 1997, Illinois; registered to practice before U.S. Patent and Trademark Office. *Education:* Houghton College (B.S., cum laude, 1987); California Institute of Technology (Ph.D., 1992); Georgetown University (J.D., 1997). *Member:* Chicago Bar Association; American Intellectual Patent Law Association; American Chemical Society; Association of University Technology Management. ***Email:*** smrksich@usebrinks.com

JASON C. WHITE, born Elkhorn, Wisconsin, November 11, 1970; admitted to bar, 1996, Illinois; U.S. District Court, Northern District of Illinois and Eastern District of Michigan; registered to practice before U.S. Patent and Trademark Office. *Education:* Marquette University (B.S.E.E., 1992); University of Dayton (J.D., cum laude, 1996). Member, Dayton Law Review. *Member:* Chicago and Illinois State Bar Associations; American Intellectual Property Law Association. ***PRACTICE AREAS:*** Intellectual Property; Patent Prosecution; Litigation. ***Email:*** jwhite@usebrinks.com

THOMAS M. WILLIAMS, admitted to bar, 1996, Illinois. *Education:* University of Wisconsin (B.A., 1993); University of Illinois (J.D., 1996). Member, University of Illinois Law Review. *Member:* Chicago and American Bar Associations; International Trademark Association. ***PRACTICE AREAS:*** Intellectual Property; Trademarks; Unfair Competition; International Trademarks. ***Email:*** twilliams@usebrinks.com

JOSEPH F. HETZ, born Chicago, Illinois, June 29, 1972; admitted to bar, 1996, Illinois; U.S. District Court, Northern District of Illinois; registered to practice before U.S. Patent and Trademark Office. *Education:* Northwestern University (B.S.E.E., with Distinction and Departmental Honors, 1993)Tau Beta Pi; Eta Kappa Nu; University of Michigan (J.D., 1996). Executive Article Editor, Michigan Telecommunications and Technology Law Review. ***Email:*** jhetz@usebrinks.com

JOHN G. RAUCH, born Cincinnati, Ohio, March 15, 1961; admitted to bar, 1992, Illinois and U.S. District Court, Northern District of Illinois; registered to practice before U.S. Patent and Trademark Office. *Education:* Purdue University (B.S.E.E., 1984); Illinois Institute of Technology, Chicago-Kent College of Law (J.D., 1992). Order of the Coif. Author: "The Semiconductor Chip Protection Act," 3 Fordham Ent., Media & Intel. Prop. L.J. (1993). Adjunct Professor, Illinois Institute of Technology, Chicago-Kent College of Law, 1994-2000. ***PRACTICE AREAS:*** Patent Prosecution; Patent Counseling; Intellectual Property Licensing. ***Email:*** jrauch@usebrinks.com

MARK H. REMUS, born Elk Grove Village, Illinois, October 13, 1972; admitted to bar, 1997, Illinois and U.S. District Court, Northern District of Illinois; 1998, U.S. Court of Appeals, Federal Circuit; 2002, U.S. Supreme Court. *Education:* University of Illinois (B.S.Ch.E., with distinction, 1994; J.D., cum laude, 1997). ***PRACTICE AREAS:*** Patent Litigation. ***Email:*** mremus@usebrinks.com

TADASHI HORIE, admitted to bar, 1998, Illinois; registered to practice before U.S. Patent and Trademark Office; certified Japanese Patent attorney (Benrishi). *Education:* Nagoya Institute of Technology (B.E., 1979); Rensselaer Polytechnic Institute (M.B.A., 1992); Loyola University (J.D., 1998). *Member:* Chicago Bar Association. ***PRACTICE AREAS:*** Intellectual Property. ***Email:*** thorie@usebrinks.com

JONATHAN E. RETSKY, born Chicago, Illinois, April 22, 1962; admitted to bar, 1989, Illinois; 1990, U.S. District Court, Northern District of Illinois; registered to practice before U.S. Patent and Trademark Office. *Education:* Bradley University (B.S., Electrical Eng., 1984); University of Texas (J.D., 1989). Delta Theta Phi. Adjunct Professor, John Marshall Law School, Contemporary Technology and Intellectual Property Law (IP 421), (1995—). Author: "Computer Software Protection in 1996: A Practitioner's Nightmare," 29 J. Marshall L. Rev. 853 (1996); "Six Steps to Negotiating Successfully Through a Software Audit," XIII Computer Law Strategist, Aug. 1996, at 1,3. Co-Author: with Gustavo Siller, "Patent and Trade Secret Protection of Computer Technology," VI Software L.J. 239 (1993). Speaker: *Computer Software Protection—A Practitioner's Nightmare,* 40th Annual Conference on Developments in Intellectual Property, Feb. 22, 1996 (Chicago, Illinois); *Licensing in the Electronics Industry*, Licensing Executives Society (USA & Canada) Annual Meeting, Oct. 1996 (Las Croabas, Puerto Rico); *International Strategies for Patenting Software,* International Bar Association Annual Meeting, Oct. 1996 (Berlin, Germany). Licensing Executives Society. Corporate Vice President and Director, Patent Operations, Motorola, Inc., 2000-2004; Chairman, Intellectual Asset Management Practice Group; Panelist for "Maxing Out," roundtable, IP Law & Business, Feb. 2005; "Panning for Golden Nuggets in Your Patent/IP Portfolio," Interview on SkyRadio; Speaker (Case Study: Transforming the Large Company Portfolio) and Master of Ceremonies, Intellectual Asset Management Update, April 12, 2005 and Sept. 7, 2005. ***LANGUAGES:*** Hebrew. ***Email:*** jretsky@usebrinks.com

JAMES A. COLLINS, admitted to bar, 1997, Wisconsin and Illinois; registered to practice before U.S. Patent and Trademark Office. *Education:* University of Wisconsin-Platteville (B.S., Electrical Engineering, 1985; B.S., Business Administration, 1993); Marquette University (J.D., cum laude, 1996). ***PRACTICE AREAS:*** Intellectual Property; Copyrights; Patent Prosecution; Litigation. ***Email:*** jcollins@usebrinks.com

VINEET GAURI, admitted to bar, 1997, Illinois; U.S. District Court, Northern District of Illinois including Trial Bar, U.S. District Court, Eastern District of Wisconsin and U.S. District Court, Western District of Michigan; U.S. Court of Appeals, Federal Circuit; registered to practice before U.S. Patent and Trademark Office. *Education:* University of Michigan (B.S.Ch.E., 1994); Boston University (J.D., 1997). Board of Directors, Asian American Bar Association of Chicago; Panelist, Chicago Committee on Minorities in Large Law Firms; Adjunct Professor, Chicago-Kent College of Law; Volunteer Attorney, Cabrini Green Legal Aid Clinic and Legal Assistance Foundation of Metropolitan Chicago; Executive Editor, Boston University Journal of Science and Technology Law. ***PRACTICE AREAS:*** Intellectual Property; Patent Litigation. ***Email:*** vgauri@usebrinks.com

(This Listing Continued)

THOMAS L. HOLT, born Sikeston, Missouri, October 4, 1971; admitted to bar, 1997, Illinois; U.S. District Court, Northern District of Illinois; registered to practice before U.S. Patent and Trademark Office. *Education:* University of Missouri-Rolla (B.S., 1993); Loyola University Chicago (J.D., 1997). *Member:* Illinois State and American Bar Associations; International Trademark Association. ***Email:*** tholt@usebrinks.com

JAMES L. KATZ, born Southfield, Michigan, April 26, 1968; admitted to bar, 1998, Illinois and U.S. District Court, Northern District of Illinois; 2000, Michigan; registered to practice before U.S. Patent and Trademark Office. *Education:* University of Michigan (B.S.C.E., 1990); Indiana University School of Law (J.D., 1998). Website Editor, Federal Communications Law Journal. ***PRACTICE AREAS:*** Intellectual Property; Patent Prosecution; Patent Opinions; Litigation; Electrical and Computer; Intellectual Asset Management; Interference; Internet/E-Commerce; Licensing; Mechanical. ***Email:*** jkatz@usebrinks.com

COUNSEL

MARY M. SQUYRES, born Chicago, Illinois, January 12, 1950; admitted to bar, 1982, Illinois and U.S. District Court, Northern District of Illinois. *Education:* Manhattanville College (A.B., 1971); University of Chicago (M.A., 1972); Valparaiso University (J.D., 1982); John Marshall Law School (LL.M., 1994). *Member:* International Trademark Association; Marques, European Communities Trade Mark Association. (Head of International Trademark Practice Group). ***PRACTICE AREAS:*** International Trademarks; International Litigation. ***Email:*** msquyres@usebrinks.com

AMIR N. PENN, born Cincinnati, Ohio, September 30, 1967; admitted to bar, 1994, Illinois and U.S. District Court, Northern District of Illinois; registered to practice before U.S. Patent and Trademark Office. *Education:* University of Cincinnati (B.S.E.E., 1990); Stanford University, Graduate School (M.S.E.E., 1991); Northwestern University (J.D., magna cum laude, 1994). Associate Editor, Northwestern University Law Review, 1993-1994. ***PRACTICE AREAS:*** Intellectual Property Infringement; Intellectual Property Licensing; Intellectual Property Litigation; Electrical Patent Prosecution; Mechanical Patent Prosecution. ***Email:*** apenn@usebrinks.com

DONALD J. SILVERT, born Chicago, Illinois, 1953; admitted to bar, 1992, Illinois and U.S. District Court, Northern District of Illinois; 1996, New Jersey; registered to practice before U.S. Patent and Trademark Office. *Education:* Princeton University (A.B., Biochemical Sciences, 1975); University of California at Berkeley (Ph.D., Genetics, 1981); California Institute of Technology (Postdoctoral Fellow in Chemistry and Biology, 1981-1983); New York University (J.D., 1992). ***PRACTICE AREAS:*** Intellectual Property; Biotechnology; Pharmaceutical; Agricultural Law; Chemical; Interference; Licensing; Litigation; Nanotechnology; Patent Prosecution. ***Email:*** dsilvert@usebrinks.com

JEFFREY H. CANFIELD, born February 27, 1963; admitted to bar, 1993, Illinois; registered to practice before U.S. Patent and Trademark Office. *Education:* Michigan Technological University (B.S.E.E., 1986); John Marshall Law School (J.D., 1993). *Member:* Intellectual Property Law Association of Chicago. ***PRACTICE AREAS:*** Intellectual Property. ***Email:*** jcanfield@usebrinks.com

J. WILLIAM DOCKREY, born Denver, Colorado, March 14, 1953; admitted to bar, 1996, Illinois; registered to practice before U.S. Patent and Trademark Office (1989). *Education:* University of South Dakota (B.S., 1979); Colorado State University (M.S., 1982); The John Marshall Law School (J.D., 1996). Phi Delta Phi. *Member:* Chicago and American Bar Associations; Intellectual Property Law Association of Chicago; American Intellectual Property Law Association. ***PRACTICE AREAS:*** Patent Law. ***Email:*** jdockrey@usebrinks.com

CHRISTOPHER A. HARKINS, born Ottawa, Illinois, 1965; admitted to bar, 1990, New York; 1992, U.S. District Court, Southern and Eastern Districts of New York; 1995, Illinois and U.S. District Court, Northern District of Illinois including Trial Bar; registered to practice before U.S. Patent and Trademark Office. *Education:* Illinois State University (B.S., summa cum laude, 1987; B.S., Chemistry, summa cum laude, 1999); University of Illinois (J.D., cum laude, 1990). Member: Moot Court: Civil Rights Team. Articles Editor, University of Illinois Law Review. Author: "Overcoming the Extraterritorial Bar to Bringing Copyright Actions: On Pleading Copyright Infringement to Protect Copyrighted Works from the Defendant that Ships Overseas for Distribution Abroad," Intellectual Property & Technology Law Journal, Vol. 17, No. 5, 2005, pp. 1-9. Co-author: "An Anti-Subrogation Rule is Extended," Nat'l L.J. Jan. 17, 1994, pp. 19-23. Author: "The Pinocchio Defense Witness Impeachment Exception to the Exclusionary Rule: Combatting a Defendant's Use of the Perjurious Testimony of Defense Witnesses," 1990 U. Ill. L. Rev., 375-473. ***PRACTICE AREAS:*** General Practice; Federal Litigation; Patent Litigation; Trade Secrets. ***Email:*** charkins@usebrinks.com

JANET A. PIOLI, born Peru, Illinois, September 20, 1959; admitted to bar, 1984, Illinois; registered to practice before U.S. Patent and Trademark Office. *Education:* Illinois State University (B.S., 1981); Northern Illinois University (J.D., cum laude, 1984). Member, Northern Illinois Law Review. Member, Illinois Bar Foundation Research Fellow. ***PRACTICE AREAS:*** Intellectual Property. ***Email:*** jpioli@usebrinks.com

ROBERT B. POLIT, born Chicago, Illinois, May 1, 1962; admitted to bar, 1991, Illinois and U.S. District Court, Northern District of Illinois; U.S. Court of Appeals for the Federal Circuit; registered to practice before U.S. Patent and Trademark Office, 1988. *Education:* University of Illinois at Chicago, Honors College (B.S.E.E., 1984); John Marshall Law School (J.D., magna cum laude, 1991). Tau Beta Pi. James Scholar. *Member:* American Intellectual Property Law Association; Intellectual Property Law Association of Chicago. ***PRACTICE AREAS:*** Patent Prosecution; Trademarks; Copyrights. ***Email:*** rpolit@usebrinks.com

---

HOWARD S. MICHAEL, born April 1, 1970; admitted to bar, 1998, Illinois. *Education:* University of Michigan (B.A., 1993); Boston University School of Law (J.D., 1998). G. Joseph Tauro Scholar. *Member:* International Trademark Association. ***PRACTICE AREAS:*** Trademark; Unfair Competition; Copyright and Trade Secret Litigation; Trademark Conseling; Clearance; Prosecution; Licensing. ***Email:*** hmichael@usebrinks.com

(This Listing Continued)

SCOTT J. SLAVICK, born October 25, 1973; admitted to bar, 1998, Illinois. *Education:* Northwestern University (B.A., 1995); Georgetown University (J.D., 1998). Senior Notes Editor, Georgetown Journal of Legal Ethics, 1997-1998. Author: "Illinois and the McKay Commission: A Match Made in Heaven?" Georgetown Journal of Legal Ethics, 129, 1997. *Member:* International Trademark Association (Member, Public Relations Sub-Committee; Trademark Trends). ***REPORTED CASES:*** Thomas & Betts Corp. v. Panduit Corp., 55 U.S.P.Q.2d 1698 (N.D. Ill. 2000); Ameritech Corp. v. Quaterra Communications Corp., 60 U.S.P.Q.2d 1603 (D.C. E.Wis. 2001). ***PRACTICE AREAS:*** Trademark; Copyright; Internet Law; Unfair Competition; False Advertising; Trade Secret Law; Trademark Licensing. ***Email:*** sslavick@usebrinks.com

VINCENT J. GNOFFO, born Chicago, Illinois, March 19, 1969; admitted to bar, 1998, Illinois, U.S. District Court, Northern District of Illinois, U.S. District Court, Eastern District of Wisconsin, U.S. Court of Appeals, Seventh Circuit and U.S. Court of Appeals for the Federal Circuit; registered to practice before U.S. Patent and Trademark Office. *Education:* University of Illinois at Chicago (B.S.E.E., 1992); John Marshall Law School (J.D., cum laude, 1998). Member: Moot Court Council, 1996; John Marshall Law Review, 1996-1997. *Member:* Chicago Bar Association; Intellectual Property Law Association of Chicago; American Intellectual Property Law Association. ***PRACTICE AREAS:*** Intellectual Property; Patent Prosecution; Electrical and Computer; Litigation. ***Email:*** vgnoffo@usebrinks.com

RICHARD E. STANLEY, JR., born Pensacola, Florida, November 7, 1967; admitted to bar, 1999, Illinois; registered to practice before U.S. Patent and Trademark Office. *Education:* South Dakota School of Mines and Technology (B.S.M.E, 1990); University of Northern Iowa (M.B.A., 1996); Baylor University School of Law (J.D., 1999). ***PRACTICE AREAS:*** Intellectual Property; Patent Prosecution; Patent and Trade Secret Litigation; Mechanical; Electrical and Computer. ***Email:*** rstanley@usebrinks.com

DAVID H. BLUESTONE, born Skokie, Illinois, July 27, 1974; admitted to bar, 1999, Illinois; registered to practice before U.S. Patent and Trademark Office. *Education:* University of Illinois (B.S.E.E., 1996); Northwestern University (J.D., 1999). Eta Kappa Nu; Tau Beta Pi; Phi Eta Sigma; Phi Alpha Delta. Golden Key. ***PRACTICE AREAS:*** Intellectual Property; Litigation; Patent Prosecution; Copyrights; Trademarks; Unfair Competition. ***Email:*** dbluestone@usebrinks.com

CHRISTOPHER M. DOLAN, born Sandwich, Illinois, July 1, 1970; admitted to bar, 1999, Illinois. *Education:* Illinois State University (B.S., 1992; M.S., 1994); George Washington University (J.D., 1999). Executive Articles Editor, American Intellectual Property Law Association Quarterly Journal. *Member:* American Intellectual Property Law Association; International Trademark Association (Member, Regulatory Analysis Committee). ***PRACTICE AREAS:*** Intellectual Property. ***Email:*** cdolan@usebrinks.com

CHARLES M. McMAHON, born Fort Dodge, Iowa, April 6, 1974; admitted to bar, 1999, Illinois; 2002, Minnesota; registered to practice before U.S. Patent and Trademark Office. *Education:* University of Notre Dame (B.S.E.E., 1996); The George Washington University (J.D., 1999). Executive Production Editor, American Intellectual Property Law Association Quarterly Journal, 1998-1999. Author: "Intent to Commit Fraud on the USPTO: Is Mere Negligence Once Again Inequitable?" AIPLA Quarterly Journal, Volume 27, Issue 1. Co-Author: "The Unresolved Question: Does Private Digital Copying Constitute Fair Use?" 2003 Intellectual Property Law Update, Aspen Law & Business; "Jumping Over the Evidentiary Hurdle at Trial," NAT'L L.J., Aug. 7, 2000, at B11. *Member:* American Bar Association; Intellectual Property Law Association of Chicago; American Intellectual Property Law Association; Licensing Executives Society; Institute of Electrical and Electronics Engineers. ***PRACTICE AREAS:*** Intellectual Property. ***Email:*** cmcmahon@usebrinks.com

NICHOLAS G. DE LA TORRE, born Warrensburg, Missouri, October 3, 1973; admitted to bar, 1999, Illinois. *Education:* Pennsylvania State University (B.A., 1996); Boston University (J.D., 1999). *Member:* American Bar Association (Intellectual Property); International Trademark Association. ***PRACTICE AREAS:*** Intellectual Property. ***Email:*** ndelatorre@usebrinks.com

DAVID W. OKEY, born Dubuque, Iowa, September 3, 1946; admitted to bar, 2000, Illinois, U.S. Court of Appeals, Seventh Circuit, U.S. Court of Appeals for the Federal Circuit and U.S. District Court, Northern District of Illinois; registered to practice before U.S. Patent and Trademark Office. *Education:* University of Colorado (B.A., cum laude, 1972); John Marshall Law School (J.D., cum laude, 2000). Professional Engineer, Illinois, 1982. ***PRACTICE AREAS:*** Patent Prosecution; Litigation; Licensing; Chemical; Electrical and Computer; Mechanical; Intellectual Asset Management; International Patents and Trademarks. ***Email:*** dokey@usebrinks.com

JOSEPH W. FLERLAGE, admitted to bar, 2000, Illinois. *Education:* University of Illinois (B.S.E.E., 1989); DePaul University (J.D., 2000). Licensed Professional Engineer, 1995. *Member:* Chicago and Illinois State Bar Associations; Intellectual Property Law Association of Chicago; American Intellectual Property Law Association. ***PRACTICE AREAS:*** Intellectual Property; Patent Prosecution; Copyrights; Litigation; Electrical and Computer. ***Email:*** jflerlage@usebrinks.com

ANASTASIA HEFFNER, born Chicago, Illinois, July 31, 1969; admitted to bar, 2000, Illinois and U.S. District Court, Northern District of Illinois; registered to practice before U.S. Patent and Trademark Office. *Education:* University of Illinois (B.S., Mechanical Engineering, 1991); DePaul University (J.D., 2000). Order of the Coif. Member, DePaul Law Review. Professional Engineer in Training, 1990. *Member:* Chicago and American Bar Associations (Member, Sections on: Intellectual Property; Science and Technology; Litigation). ***LANGUAGES:*** Greek. ***PRACTICE AREAS:*** Patent Prosecution; Electro-Mechanical Patents; Patent Litigation; Copyright Litigation; Copyright Prosecution. ***Email:*** aheffner@usebrinks.com

JEFFRY M. NICHOLS, born Elk Grove Village, Illinois, October 27, 1975; admitted to bar, 2000, Illinois, U.S. District Court, Northern District of Illinois, U.S. District Court, Eastern District of Wisconsin and U.S. District Court, Eastern District of Michigan; U.S. Court of Appeals, Seventh Circuit; registered to practice before U.S. Patent and Trademark Office. *Education:* Northeast Missouri State University (B.S., Chemistry, 1997); University of Connecticut School of Law (J.D., with honors, 2000). *Member:* Chicago, Illinois State and American Bar Associations; American Chemical Society; American Intellectual

(This Listing Continued)

BRINKS HOFER GILSON & LIONE, A PROFESSIONAL CORPORATION, Chicago—Continued

Property Law Association; Intellectual Property Law Association of Chicago. ***PRACTICE AREAS:*** Patent Litigation; Patent Prosecution; Trademarks. ***Email:*** jnichols@usebrinks.com

JUSTIN B. RAND, born Greenville, Pennsylvania, May 2, 1975; admitted to bar, 2000, Illinois; registered to practice before U.S. Patent and Trademark Office, 2001. *Education:* Indiana University (B.S., Biology. 1997); Boston University (J.D., 2000). Managing Editor, American Journal of Law and Medicine, 1999-2000. *Member:* Chicago, Illinois State and American Bar Associations; American Intellectual Property Law Association. ***PRACTICE AREAS:*** Intellectual Property. ***Email:*** jrand@usebrinks.com

LIZABETH K. VITELLARO, born Hinsdale, Illinois, April 21, 1975; admitted to bar, 2000, Illinois; 2001, U.S. District Court, Northern District of Illinois. *Education:* Kenyon College (A.B., Chemistry, cum laude, with high honors and distinction, 1997); The John Marshall Law School (J.D., cum laude, 2000). Phi Alpha Delta. The John Marshall Law Review. Co-President, Kenyon College Chapter, American Chemical Society, 1996-1997. ***PRACTICE AREAS:*** Intellectual Property; Patent Prosecution; Patent Litigation. ***Email:*** lvitellaro@usebrinks.com

TIMOTHY P. LUCIER, born Detroit, Michigan, March 15, 1971; admitted to bar, 1998, Illinois and U.S. District Court, Northern District of Illinois; 2003, U.S. District Court, Western District of Michigan; registered to practice before U.S. Patent and Trademark Office. *Education:* GMI Engineering and Management Institute (B.S.M.E., 1994); Loyola University (J.D., 1998). ***PRACTICE AREAS:*** Intellectual Property. ***Email:*** tlucier@usebrinks.com

ELISA M. VALENZONA, born Chicago, Illinois, May 11, 1968; admitted to bar, 1998, Illinois. *Education:* University of Illinois (B.A., 1991); Chicago-Kent University (J.D., 1998). ***LANGUAGES:*** Spanish. ***PRACTICE AREAS:*** Trademark and Unfair Competition; International Intellectual Property. ***Email:*** evalenzona@usebrinks.com

WILLIAM D. JACKSON, born Chicago, Illinois, January 18, 1964; admitted to bar, 1991, Illinois. *Education:* University of Illinois at Urbana-Champaign (B.A., 1986); De-Paul University (J.D., 1991); Cornell University (M.B.A., 1996). Member, De Paul Law Review. Trademark Examining Attorney, U.S. Patent and Trademark Office, 1997-1999. *Member:* American Bar Association. ***PRACTICE AREAS:*** Trademarks. ***Email:*** wjackson@usebrinks.com

A. JOHN MURRAY, PH.D., born Portadown, Northern Ireland, September 30, 1953; admitted to bar, 1999, Illinois. *Education:* University of Manchester (B.S.C., 1975; Ph.D., 1979); Chicago-Kent College of Law (J.D., 1999). ***PRACTICE AREAS:*** Intellectual Property. ***Email:*** jmurray@usebrinks.com

C. NOEL KAMAN, born Milwaukee, Wisconsin; admitted to bar, 2001, Illinois. *Education:* University of Kentucky (B.S., cum laude, 1998); George Washington University (J.D., cum laude, 2001). ***PRACTICE AREAS:*** Intellectual Property; Patent Prosecution; Litigation; Appellate; Biotechnology and Pharmaceutical; Chemical. ***Email:*** nkaman@usebrinks.com

DAYMON L. RUTTENBERG, admitted to bar, 2001, Illinois. *Education:* John Carroll University (B.S., 1998); John Marshall Law School (J.D., cum laude, 2001). Staff Editor, The John Marshall Law Review. ***PRACTICE AREAS:*** Patent Litigation; Trademark Litigation; Copyright Litigation; Patent Prosecution; Chemistry; Biotechnology; Mechanical Arts. ***Email:*** druttenberg@usebrinks.com

SEAN P. SPRINGMAN, born February 17, 1975; admitted to bar, 2001, Illinois; registered to practice before U.S. Patent and Trademark Office. *Education:* Rose-Hulman Institute of Technology (B.S.M.E., 1997); Indiana University School of Law - Bloomington (J.D., magna cum laude, 2001). Managing Editor, Indiana Law Journal. ***PRACTICE AREAS:*** Patent Prosecution; Patent Litigation. ***Email:*** sspringman@usebrinks.com

MIRCEA A. TIPESCU, admitted to bar, 2001, Illinois. *Education:* Princeton University (B.S.E., Mechanical Engineering, 1992); Northwestern University (M.S., Mechanical Engineering, 1994); The George Washington University Law School (J.D., 2001). Member, Trial Court Board. Intern for the Honorable Randall R. Rader, United States Court of Appeals for the Federal Circuit, 2001. ***LANGUAGES:*** Romanian. ***PRACTICE AREAS:*** Intellectual Property; Patent Prosecution; Litigation; Electrical and Computer; Internet/E-Commerce; Mechanical. ***Email:*** mtipescu@usebrinks.com

SCOTT W. BRIM, born Dayton, Ohio, August 6, 1976; admitted to bar, 2002, Illinois; registered to practice before U.S. Patent and Trademark Office. *Education:* University of Dayton (B.S.E.E., 1999); University of Illinois (J.D., 2002). ***PRACTICE AREAS:*** Intellectual Property. ***Email:*** sbrim@usebrinks.com

AMANDA M. MILLER, born Chillicothe, Ohio, August 19, 1977; admitted to bar, 2002, Illinois and U.S. District Court, Northern District of Illinois; registered to practice before U.S. Patent and Trademark Office. *Education:* Capital University (B.A., Chemistry, 1999); The Ohio State University (J.D., 2002). Recipient, CALI Award for Excellence in Trial Practice, 2002. Symposium Editor, Ohio State Law Journal, 2001. ***PRACTICE AREAS:*** Patent Prosecution; Patent Litigation; Patent Licensing. ***Email:*** amiller@usebrinks.com

BENJAMIN B. COTTON, born January 24, 1976; admitted to bar, 2002, Illinois; registered to practice before U.S. Patent and Trademark Office. *Education:* Rose-Hulman Institute of Technology (B.S.M.E., cum laude, 1998); The John Marshall Law School (J.D., 2002). Author: "Prospecting or Cybersquatting: Registering Your Name Before Someone Else Does," 35 J. Marshall L. Rev. 287 (Winter 2002). ***PRACTICE AREAS:*** Intellectual Property. ***Email:*** bcotton@usebrinks.com

HEIDI A. DARE, born Pontiac, Michigan; admitted to bar, 2002, Illinois; registered to practice before U.S. Patent and Trademark Office. *Education:* Albion College (B.A.); University of Michigan (M.S.); Wayne State University (J.D., 2002). ***PRACTICE AREAS:*** Intellectual Property; Patent Prosecution; Biotechnology Patents; Licensing. ***Email:*** hdare@usebrinks.com

ROBERT G. PLUTA, admitted to bar, 2002, Illinois; registered to practice before U.S. Patent and Trademark Office. *Education:* Marquette University (B.S., Biomedical Engi-

(This Listing Continued)

neering, 1999); DePaul University (J.D., 2002). *Member:* National Order of Barristers. ***PRACTICE AREAS:*** Intellectual Property Litigation; Patent Prosecution; Patent Applications; Antitrust. ***Email:*** rpluta@usebrinks.com

JENNIFER A. PRIOLEAU, born New York, N.Y.; admitted to bar, 2002, Illinois; 2005, New Jersey; U.S. District Court, Northern District of Illinois; U.S. District Court, District of New Jersey. *Education:* Tufts University (B.A., International Relations, Russian Area Studies, 1995); Northwestern University School of Law (J.D., 2002). *Member:* Chicago, Cook County and American Bar Associations. ***LANGUAGES:*** French and Russian. ***PRACTICE AREAS:*** Trademarks; Unfair Competition; Copyrights; Patent Litigation; Internet Law. ***Email:*** jprioleau@usebrinks.com

RAYMOND R. RICORDATI, III, born Chicago, Illinois, June 27, 1977; admitted to bar, 2002, Illinois. *Education:* University of Notre Dame (B.S., Computer Engineering, 1999); John Marshall Law School (J.D., 2002). Executive Production Editor, John Marshall Review of Intellectual Property Law, 2001-2002. ***PRACTICE AREAS:*** Intellectual Property Litigation; Patents; Computer and Software Patents. ***Email:*** rricordati@usebrinks.com

SAMUEL E. SHEHADEH, admitted to bar, 2002, Illinois; registered to practice before U.S. Patent and Trademark Office. *Education:* The University of Wisconsin-Madison (B.S., 1996); George Washington University School of Law (J.D., 2002). ***PRACTICE AREAS:*** Patent Prosecution; Patent Litigation. ***Email:*** sshehadeh@usebrinks.com

JOSEPH A. YOSICK, admitted to bar, 2002, Illinois and U.S. District Court, Northern District of Illinois; registered to practice before U.S. Patent and Trademark Office. *Education:* University of Illinois (B.S. Ch.E., 1994; J.D., magna cum laude, 2002); University of Wisconsin (M.S. 1995). Internet Editor, University of Illinois Law Review. Author: "Compulsory Patent Licensing for Efficient Use of Inventions," 2001 ILL. L. REV 1275 (2001); "The Retroactive Effect of Prosecution History in Claim Construction," Computer & Internet Litigation Reporter, Vol 21, Issue 22, April 6, 2004 at 10. ***PRACTICE AREAS:*** Intellectual Property; Patent Prosecution; Patent Litigation. ***Email:*** jyosick@usebrinks.com

JILL HUBBARD BOWMAN, born Brigham City, Utah, November 28, 1962; admitted to bar, 1998, California; 2000, Texas; 2003, Illinois. *Education:* Brigham Young University (B.S., 1984); University of Michigan (J.D., 1998). ***PRACTICE AREAS:*** Intellectual Property Litigation. ***Email:*** jbowman@usebrinks.com

ANTHONY P. CURTIS, born Princeton, New Jersey, April 29, 1966; admitted to bar, 2003, Illinois; registered to practice before U.S. Patent and Trademark Office. *Education:* Massachusetts Institute of Technology (B.S.E.E.; B.S., Physics); Princeton University (M.S.E.E.); University of Illinois, Champaign-Urbana (M.S. Physics; Ph.D.E.E.); Loyola University (J.D.). *Member:* Chicago, Illinois State and American (Member, Intellectual Property Section) Bar Associations; Institute of Electrical and Electronic Engineers. ***PRACTICE AREAS:*** Intellectual Property; Computer Technology; Information Technology; Electrical Intellectual Property; Electrical Patent Prosecution; Electrical Patents; Electro-Mechanical Patents; Electronic Patents; Mechanical Patent Prosecution; International Patent Prosecution; Internet Patents; Patent Applications; Patent Prosecution. ***Email:*** acurtis@usebrinks.com

TIMOTHY J. LE DUC, born Chippewa Falls, Wisconsin, March 7, 1969; admitted to bar, 2003, Illinois and U.S. District Court, Northern District of Illinois; registered to practice before U.S. Patent and Trademark Office. *Education:* University of Wisconsin-Madison (B.S., Electrical and Computer Engineering, 1991); University of Minnesota (J.D., cum laude, 2002). Staff Member, Minnesota Intellectual Property Review, 2001-2002. Author: "The Application of Collateral Estoppel to Markman Rulings," 3 Minn. Intell. Prop. Rev. 297, 2002. [Nuclear Submarine Officer, U.S. Navy, 1991-1997]. ***PRACTICE AREAS:*** Intellectual Property. ***Email:*** tleduc@usebrinks.com

JOHN F. NETHERY, born Reading, Pennsylvania, June 25, 1968; admitted to bar, 1997, Illinois; registered to practice before U.S. Patent and Trademark Office. *Education:* Iowa State University (B.S. in Computer Engineering, with distinction, 1990; B.S. in Computer Science, with distinction, 1990); University of Illinois (M.S. in Computer Engineering, 1993; J.D., 1997). Phi Beta Kappa; Tau Beta Pi. Harno Fellow, University of Illinois, 1996. Former Editor in Chief, Recent Decisions section of the Illinois Bar Journal. Co-Author: with Mike Kiklis, "Business Methods Patents—Strategic Claiming for Business Method Inventions," Business Method Patents: How to Protect Your Clients' Interests 159, Practicing Law Instutute, 2002. ***PRACTICE AREAS:*** Patents. ***Email:*** jnethery@usebrinks.com

TREVOR K. COPELAND, born Montana, October, 1971; (admission pending). *Education:* Arkansas State University (B.S.Ed., Biology, 1993); University of Minnesota (M.S., Molecular, Cellular, Developmental Biology and Genetics, 2003; J.D., Joint Degree Program, 2003). Member: Center for Bioethics and Human Dignity; Federalist Society. *Member:* American Intellectual Property Law Association. ***PRACTICE AREAS:*** Patents; Biotechnology Patent Prosecution; Biotechnology Patents; Molecular Biology Patents; Patent Prosecution; Biotechnology; Patent Litigation; Design Patents. ***Email:*** tcopeland@usebrinks.com

STEPHANIE J. FELICETTY, born Warren, Ohio, July 31, 1974; admitted to bar, 2003, Illinois; U.S. District Court, Northern District of Illinois; U.S. Court of Appeals, Federal Circuit; registered to practice before U.S. Patent and Trademark Office. *Education:* Youngstown State University (B.E., summa cum laude, Chemical Engineering, 1996); University of Akron (J.D., summa cum laude, 2003). Recipient: Donald Othmer Sophomore Academic Excellence Award; AICHE Professional Promise Award; Dean's Academic Achievement Award for Highest Scholastic Achievement, 2000 and 2001. Assistant Editor, 2001 and Associate Editor, 2002, University of Akron Law Review. Giles Sutherland Rich Intellectual Property Competition, 2003. Certificate in Intellectual Property (University of Akron). ***PRACTICE AREAS:*** Patent Law. ***Email:*** sfelicetty@usebrinks.com

BRIAN A. GARCIA, born Willits, California; admitted to bar, 2003, Illinois. *Education:* Lake Forest College (B.A., 1995); University of Illinois (Ph.D., 2001; J.D., 2003). *Member:* American Bar Association; American Chemical Society. ***PRACTICE AREAS:*** Patent Prosecution. ***Email:*** bgarcia@usebrinks.com

MIYOUNG SHIN, born Seoul, Korea, September 11, 1971; admitted to bar, 2003, Illinois; registered to practice before U.S. Patent and Trademark Office, 2004. *Education:*

(This Listing Continued)

Korea University (B.S., 1995); Northwestern University (J.D., cum laude, 2003). Order of the Coif. Extern to Hon. Charles R. Norgle, U.S. District Court, Northern District of Illinois, 2002. Registered Korean Paten Attorney, 1996. ***LANGUAGES:*** Korean and Japanese. ***PRACTICE AREAS:*** Patents; Intellectual Property. ***Email:*** mshin@usebrinks.com

YOLANDA M. KING, born September 21, 1976; admitted to bar, 2002, Illinois. *Education:* Indiana University (B.A., Journalism, with highest distinction, 1999); Harvard University (J.D., 2002). ***PRACTICE AREAS:*** Intellectual Property. ***Email:*** yprice@usebrinks.com

NILAY S. DALAL, born January 29, 1979; admitted to bar, 2004, Illinois. *Education:* Ohio State University (B.S., Chemical Engineering, 1994; J.D., 2004); University of Akron (M.S., Chemical Engineering, 2004). ***PRACTICE AREAS:*** Intellectual Property. ***Email:*** ndalal@usebrinks.com

ANDREA L. EVENSEN, born 1979; admitted to bar, 2004, Illinois. *Education:* Purdue University (B.S., Computer Science, with distinction, 2001); John Marshall Law School (J.D., 2004). ***PRACTICE AREAS:*** Intellectual Property. ***Email:*** aevensen@usebrinks.com

JULIE L. LEICHTMAN, born August 27, 1977; admitted to bar, 2004, Illinois. *Education:* University of Chicago (B.A., Biological Sciences, with honors, 1999); Loyola University Chicago School of Law (J.D., with honors, 2004). ***PRACTICE AREAS:*** Intellectual Property. ***Email:*** jleichtman@usebrinks.com

DAVID P. LINDNER, admitted to bar, 2004, Illinois. *Education:* University of Illinois (B.S., Electrical Eng., with honors, 1997); DePaul University College of Law (J.D., summa cum laude, 2004). Registered to practice before the U.S. Patent and Trademark Office. ***PRACTICE AREAS:*** Intellectual Property. ***Email:*** dlindner@usebrinks.com

STEPHEN CONRAD SMITH, admitted to bar, 2004, Illinois; 2005, U.S. District Court, Eastern District of Wisconsin. *Education:* Purdue University (B.S., Mechanical Engineering, 1997); Georgetown University Law Center (J.D., 2004). *Member:* Chicago and American Bar Associations; American Intellectual Property Law Association. ***PRACTICE AREAS:*** Intellectual Property. ***Email:*** sxsmith@usebrinks.com

SCOTT A. TIMMERMAN, born January 1, 1979; admitted to bar, 2004, Illinois. *Education:* University of Iowa (B.S., with honors, Physics, Computer Science, Mathematics, 2001; J.D., with distinction, 2004). ***PRACTICE AREAS:*** Intellectual Property. ***Email:*** stimmerman@usebrinks.com

JASON M. WEJNERT, admitted to bar, 2004, Illinois. *Education:* Cornell University (B.S., Engineering Physics, with distinction, 1995); Columbia University (M.S., Electrical Engineering; Certificate Telecommunications Eng., 1999); Arizona State University (J.D., Certificate Law, Science, & Technology Program, 2004); Arizona State University (M.B.A., Technology Program, 1999). *Member:* Institute of Electrical and Electronics Engineers; American Physical Society. Center Fellow, Arizona State University College of Law, Center for Law, Science and Technology. ***LANGUAGES:*** Spanish and French. ***PRACTICE AREAS:*** Intellectual Property. ***Email:*** jwejnert@usebrinks.com

RAYNARLDO K. WHITTY, born Jacksonville, Florida, 1974; admitted to bar, 2001, Florida (Not admitted in Illinois). *Education:* Florida State University (B.S., Chemical Engineering/Bio-Engineering); University of Miami (J.D.). ***PRACTICE AREAS:*** Intellectual Property. ***Email:*** rwhitty@usebrinks.com

THOMAS J. WRONA, admitted to bar, 2002, Illinois; registered to practice before U.S. Patent and Trademark Office. *Education:* University of Illinois, Urbana-Champaign (B.S., Microbiology, 1991); University of Texas (Ph.D., Microbiology, 1997); John Marshall Law School (J.D., 2002). ***PRACTICE AREAS:*** Intellectual Property Law. ***Email:*** twrona@usebrinks.com

BRATISLAV STANKOVIC, admitted to bar, 2004, Wisconsin (Not admitted in Illinois). *Education:* University of St. Cyril and Methodius, Skopje, Macedonia (B.S., Agricultural Engineering, 1987); University of Novi Sad, Yugoslavia (M.S., Plant Physiology, 1991); University of Nebraska at Lincoln (Ph.D., with honors, Plant Molecular Biology, 1994); University of Wisconsin-Madison (J.D., with honors, 2004). ***PRACTICE AREAS:*** Intellectual Property. ***Email:*** bstankovic@usebrinks.com

MICHAEL K. HENDERSHOT, born Columbus, Ohio, December 15, 1975; admitted to bar, 2001, Illinois and U.S. District Court, Northern District of Illinois; 2003, U.S. Court of Appeals, Ninth Circuit. *Education:* The Ohio State University (B.S., Molecular Genetics, summa cum laude, 1998); University of Virginia School of Law (J.D., 2001). ***PRACTICE AREAS:*** Intellectual Property. ***Email:*** mhendershot@usebrinks.com

JAY BURGETT, born 1977; admitted to bar, 2005, Illinois. *Education:* University of Illinois (B.S., Electrical Engineering, 2001); Chicago-Kent College of Law, Illinois Institute of Technology (J.D., 2005). ***PRACTICE AREAS:*** Intellectual Property. ***Email:*** jburgett@usebrinks.com

ROCHELLE CLAERBAUT, admitted to bar, 2005, Illinois. *Education:* University of Illinois (B.A., French, 1992); George Washington University (J.D., 2005). ***PRACTICE AREAS:*** Intellectual Property. ***Email:*** rclaerbaut@usebrinks.com

JOSH GARFIELD, admitted to bar, 2005, Illinois. *Education:* University of Pennsylvania (B.S.E., Computer Science and Engineering, 2002; B.A., International Relations, 2002); Case Western Reserve University (J.D., 2005). ***PRACTICE AREAS:*** Intellectual Property. ***Email:*** jgarfield@usebrinks.com

JEFFREY A. MARX, born 1978; admitted to bar, 2005, Illinois and Wisconsin; registered to practice before U.S. Patent and Trademark Office. *Education:* Boston University (B.S., cum laude, Biomedical Engineering, 2001); University of Wisconsin Law School (J.D., cum laude, 2005). *Member:* State Bar of Wisconsin; American Bar Association; American Intellectual Property Law Association. ***PRACTICE AREAS:*** Intellectual Property Prosecution; Intellectual Property Litigation; Patents; Copyrights; Trademarks. ***Email:*** jmarx@usebrinks.com

DOUGLAS A. OGUSS, born 1977; admitted to bar, 2005, Illinois. *Education:* Vanderbilt University (B.E., cum laude, 1999); Stanford University (M.S., 2001); Santa Clara University (J.D., 2005). *Member:* American Bar Association. ***PRACTICE AREAS:*** Patents; Design Patents; Electro-Mechanical Patents; Electronic Patents; Internet Patents; Mechanical Patent Prosecution; Mechanical Patents; Medical Patents; Patent Applications; Patent Infringement; Patent Litigation; Patent Prosecution; Patent Protection; Trademarks. ***Email:*** doguss@usebrinks.com

HEATHER N. SCHAFER, admitted to bar, 2005, Illinois. *Education:* University of Iowa (B.S., 1997); Georgia State University (B.S., 2002); Georgia State University College of Law (J.D., magna cum laude, 2005). ***PRACTICE AREAS:*** Intellectual Property; Biotechnology. ***Email:*** hschafer@usebrinks.com

JASON W. SCHIGELONE, born Detroit, Michigan; admitted to bar, 2005, Illinois. *Education:* University of Michigan (B.S., Chemical Engineering, 1994; M.S., Chemical Engineering, 2000); Wayne State University (J.D., 2005). ***PRACTICE AREAS:*** Intellectual Property; Patents. ***Email:*** jschigelone@usebrinks.com

RICHARD D. WATKINS, born Memphis, Tennessee, 1975; admitted to bar, 2000, Pennsylvania; 2001, U.S. District Court, Eastern District of Pennsylvania; registered to practice before U.S. Patent and Trademark Office (Not admitted in Illinois). *Education:* Morehouse College (B.S., magna cum laude, with honors in Chemistry, 1997); Georgetown University (J.D., 2000). Coach, Lefkowitz Moot Court Team, 1999-2000 (1st Place Regional, 2nd Place National). Member, Frederick Douglass Moot Court Team, 1999 (Mid-Atlantic Regional Best Oralist and Team Oralist; Mid-Atlantic Regional 2nd Place Team, National Competition Runner-up Best Brief, National Competition 4th Place Team). Student Counsel, Georgetown Appellate Litigation Clinic. Co-Author: "Rio Case Oks Carnival of Music Copying," The National Law Journal, October 18, 1999. Member: Black Law Students Association, 1997-2000; Student Intellectual Property Law Association. Member, Executive Board, 2003-2004; Treasurer, 2005, Barrister's Association of Philadelphia (affiliate of the National Bar Association). Vice-President, Greater Philadelphia Chapter, Morehouse College Alumni Association, 2005. *Member:* Pennsylvania and American Bar Associations; American Intellectual Property Law Association. ***REPORTED CASES:*** Salazar v. Ballesteros, 2001 U.S. App. LEXIS 19183 (4th Cir. 2001); Rhoads v. FDTC, 27 F.3d 373 (4th Cir. 2001). ***PRACTICE AREAS:*** Intellectual Property; Chemical Intellectual Property; Intellectual Property Litigation; Intellectual Property Prosecution; International Intellectual Property; Pharmaceutical Intellectual Property; Medical Intellectual Property; Intellectual Property Portfolio Management. ***Email:*** rwatkins@usebrinks.com

RICKARD K. DEMILLE, born 1976; admitted to bar, 2005, Illinois. *Education:* Brigham Young University (B.S., Electrical Engineering; Minor, Mathematics, 2002); University of Illinois College of Law (J.D., 2005). ***LANGUAGES:*** Spanish. ***PRACTICE AREAS:*** Patents; Electrical Patent Prosecution; Mechanical Patent Prosecution; Patent Litigation; Patent Prosecution. ***Email:*** rdemille@usebrinks.com

INDIANAPOLIS SHAREHOLDER

A. JAMES RICHARDSON, born Toronto, Ontario, October 14, 1943; admitted to bar, 1974, Virginia; 1981, Indiana; registered to practice before U.S. Patent and Trademark Office. *Education:* Colorado State College (A.B., 1964; M.A., 1968); Indiana State University (M.A., 1969); George Washington University (J.D., 1974). Member: Conference Faculty, Advanced Computer Law Seminar 2000, University of Dayton; Conference on Licensing Intellectual Property 2001, University of Dayton; Midwestern Intellectual Property Law Symposium 2001, I.C.L.E.F.; Member, Board of Advisors to Intellectual Property Counselor. *Member:* Virginia State and Indiana State Bar Associations; American Intellectual Property Law Association. (Managing Attorney, Indianapolis Office). ***REPORTED CASES:*** Primedia Intertec Corp. v. Technology Marketing Corp. (DC Kan) 50 USPQ2d 1079 (11/6/1998). ***PRACTICE AREAS:*** International Patent and Trademark; Licensing; Patent Prosecution; Technology Transfer; Mechanical; Industrial and Intellectual Property Law. ***Email:*** jrichardson@usebrinks.com

INDIANAPOLIS OF COUNSEL

DAVID H. BADGER, born Indianapolis, Indiana, June 16, 1931; admitted to bar, 1964, Indiana Supreme Court and U.S. District Court, Southern District of Indiana; 1964-1982, U.S. Court of Customs and Patent Appeals; 1982, U.S. Court of Appeals for the Federal Circuit; registered to practice before U.S. Patent and Trademark Office. *Education:* Rose-Hulman Institute of Technology (B.S.E.E., with honors, 1953); Indiana University (J.D., 1964). Tau Beta Pi. Member, Indiana Law Review, 1963-1964. Licensed Professional Engineer, Indiana, 1958. *Member:* Indianapolis (Member, Intellectual Property Section), Indiana State (Member, Sections on: International; Patent, Trademark and Copyright) and American (Member, Section on: Patent, Trademark and Copyright Law) Bar Associations; American Intellectual Property Law Association; Licensing Executives Society; Association Internationale Pour La Protection De La Propriété Industrielle. ***Email:*** dbadger@usebrinks.com

INDIANAPOLIS COUNSEL

LAWRENCE A. STEWARD, born Columbus, Ohio, May 12, 1950; admitted to bar, 1979, Ohio; 1988, Indiana, U.S. District Court, Southern and Northern Districts of Indiana, U.S. District Court, Northern District of Ohio, U.S. District Court, Eastern District of Michigan and U.S. Court of Appeals for the Federal Circuit; registered to practice before U.S. Patent and Trademark Office. *Education:* University of Toledo (B.S., 1972; J.D., 1979). *Member:* Indianapolis and Indiana State Bar Associations; American Intellectual Property Law Association. ***PRACTICE AREAS:*** Intellectual Property; Patent Prosecution; Patent Litigation; Biotechnology and Pharmaceuticals; Chemical. ***Email:*** lsteward@usebrinks.com

INDIANAPOLIS ASSOCIATES

SANDERS N. HILLIS, born Milwaukee, Wisconsin, September 6, 1964; admitted to bar, 1999, Indiana; U.S. District Court, Northern and Southern Districts of Indiana; registered to practice before U.S. Patent and Trademark Office. *Education:* Ohio University (B.S.E.E., cum laude, 1987); Indiana University (J.D., magna cum laude, 1999). Licensed Professional Engineer, Illinois, Indiana, Ohio and Kentucky, 1993. *Member:* Indianapolis and Indiana State Bar Associations; American Intellectual Property Law Association; Li-

(This Listing Continued)

BRINKS HOFER GILSON & LIONE, A PROFESSIONAL CORPORATION, Chicago—Continued

censing Executive Society. ***PRACTICE AREAS:*** Intellectual Property; Patents; Trademarks; Copyrights; Trade Secrets; Licensing; Right to Use Issues; Patent Prosecution; Internet/E-Commerce; Electrical; Software. ***Email:*** shillis@usebrinks.com

NICHOLAS M. BOIVIN, admitted to bar, 2003, Illinois; registered to practice before U.S. Patent and Trademark Office. *Education:* Northwestern University (B.A., Chemistry, honors, 1996); Princeton University (M.A., Chemistry, 1998); University of Virginia School of Law (J.D., 2003). ***PRACTICE AREAS:*** Patents; Federal Litigation. ***Email:*** nboivin@usebrinks.com

MICHAEL E. WEVER, born Fort Wayne, Indiana, February 14, 1972; admitted to bar, 1997, South Carolina; registered to practice before U.S. Patent and Trademark Office. *Education:* Rose-Hulman Institute of Technology (B.S., Computer Engineering, 1994); University of South Carolina (J.D., 1997). Recipient, Cali Award in Intellectual Property. First Place, University of South Carolina School of Law, Nathan Burkin Memorial Competition, 1997. Author: "Patent Law: Protecting Software," National Law Journal, May 8, 2000. Member, Intellectual Property and Unfair Trade Practices Committee, South Carolina Bar. *Member:* Carolina Patent, Trademark and Copyright Law Association. ***PRACTICE AREAS:*** Intellectual Property. ***Email:*** mwever@usebrinks.com

ANN ARBOR SHAREHOLDERS

DAVID D. MURRAY, born Ann Arbor, Michigan, September 14, 1945; admitted to bar, 1977, Ohio; 1985, U.S. Court of Appeals for the Federal Circuit; 1999, Michigan; registered to practice before U.S. Patent and Trademark Office. *Education:* University of Michigan (B.S.M.E., 1970); University of Toledo (J.D., 1977). Adjunct Professor: Patent, Trademark and Copyright Law, University of Toledo College of Law, 1994— and Ave Maria School of Law, Ann Arbor, Michigan, 2002-2004. *Member:* Washtenaw County and American Bar Associations; State Bar of Michigan; American Intellectual Property Law Association; Licensing Executives Society (Toledo Chair, 1993-2001). [U.S. Army, Signal Corps (1966-1968)]. (Senior Partner, Ann Arbor Office). ***LANGUAGES:*** German. ***PRACTICE AREAS:*** Patents; Trademarks; Copyrights; Trade Secrets. ***Email:*** dmurray@usebrinks.com

STEVEN L. OBERHOLTZER, born Fort Wayne, Indiana, July 13, 1954; admitted to bar, 1981, Michigan; U.S. District Court, Eastern District of Michigan; registered to practice before U.S. Patent and Trademark Office. *Education:* General Motors Institute (B.S.M.E., 1977); Detroit College of Law (J.D., 1981). Author: "How to Negotiate Successfully," IAM 2004; "The Basics of Intellectual Property Law," 2005. *Member:* Washtenaw County and American Bar Associations; State Bar of Michigan; Michigan Patent Law Association. ***PRACTICE AREAS:*** Patent, Trademark and Intellectual Property. ***Email:*** soberholter@usebrinks.com

ERIC J. SOSENKO, born Weirton, West Virginia, November 11, 1963; admitted to bar, 1990, Michigan and U.S. District Court, Eastern District of Michigan; registered to practice before U.S. Patent and Trademark Office. *Education:* West Virginia University (B.S.M.E., 1986; J.D., 1989). *Member:* Washtenaw County Bar Association (Member and Past Chair, Intellectual Property Law Section); State Bar of Michigan (Member, Intellectual Property Law Section); Michigan Patent Law Association; American Intellectual Property Law Association. ***PRACTICE AREAS:*** Patents; Trademarks; Intellectual Property. ***Email:*** esosenko@usebrinks.com

ANN ARBOR COUNSEL

MARGARET DOBROWITSKY, born Detroit, Michigan, October 16, 1953; admitted to bar, 1992, Michigan; registered to practice before U.S. Patent and Trademark Office, 1992. *Education:* Wayne State University (B.S.E.E., summa cum laude, 1986); Detroit College of Law (J.D., magna cum laude, 1992). *Member:* State Bar of Michigan. ***PRACTICE AREAS:*** Patents; Licensing; Information Technology; Telecommunications; Copyrights; Trademarks; Commercial Transactions. ***Email:*** mdobrowitsky@usebrinks.com

ANN ARBOR ASSOCIATES

RAYMOND J. VIVACQUA, born Philadelphia, Pennsylvania, December 15, 1965; admitted to bar, 1998, Michigan and U.S. District Court, Eastern District of Michigan; registered to practice before U.S. Patent and Trademark Office. *Education:* Pennsylvania State University (B.S.M.E., 1990); Wayne State University (M.S., Electronics & Computer Controls, 1993); University of Detroit Mercy (J.D., 1998). *Member:* State Bar of Michigan; Federal and American Bar Associations; Michigan Patent Law Association. ***PRACTICE AREAS:*** Intellectual Property. ***Email:*** rvivacqua@usebrinks.com

DAN L. THOMPSON, born June 2, 1968; admitted to bar, 2001, Michigan. *Education:* Michigan Technological University (B.S.M.E., 1993); Wayne State University (J.D., 2000). *Member:* State Bar of Michigan. ***PRACTICE AREAS:*** Intellectual Property Law. ***Email:*** dthompson@usebrinks.com

LAWRENCE G. ALMEDA, born Staten Island, New York, November 30, 1967; admitted to bar, 1997, Michigan and U.S. District Court, Eastern District of Michigan; registered to practice before U.S. Patent and Trademark Office. *Education:* Purdue University (B.S.Ch.E., 1991); University of Detroit Mercy (J.D., 1997); John Marshall Law School (LL.M., Intellectual Property, 1999). Senior Member, University of Detroit Mercy Law Review, 1996-1997. Author: "Michigan's Ban on Partial-Birth Abortions: Balancing Competing Interests," 74 U. Det. Mercy L. Rev. 685 (Summer 1997). *Member:* State Bar of Michigan; American Bar Association; Michigan Patent Law Association. ***PRACTICE AREAS:*** Intellectual Property. ***Email:*** lalmeda@usebrinks.com

MICHAEL N. SPINK, born Rochester, Michigan, June 3, 1974; admitted to bar, 1999, Illinois; 2003, Michigan. *Education:* University of Michigan (B.S.E., Mechanical Engineering, 1996); John Marshall Law School (J.D., 1999). Staff Editor, John Marshall Law Review. Author: "Authors Stripped of Their Electronic Rights in Tasini v. New York Times Co.," 32 J. Marshall L. Rev. 409 (1999). ***PRACTICE AREAS:*** Intellectual Property; Intellectual Property Licensing; Client Counseling; Patent Prosecution; Trademark Prosecution; Patent Litigation; Trademark Litigation. ***Email:*** mspink@usebrinks.com

(This Listing Continued)

JOHN M. CARD, born April 26, 1960; admitted to bar, 2001, Massachusetts; 2003, Michigan; registered to practice before U.S. Patent and Trademark Office. *Education:* University of California, Berkeley (B.S.M.E., 1983; M.S.M.E., 1984); University of California, San Diego (Ph.D., Engineering Physics, 1992); Vermont Law School (J.D., 2000). Phi Tau Sigma. *Member:* American Intellectual Property Law Association; Michigan Intellectual Property Law Association. ***PRACTICE AREAS:*** Patents; Intellectual Property. ***Email:*** jcard@usebrinks.com

ROBERT K. FERGAN, born Detroit, Michigan, January 27, 1968; admitted to bar, 2003, Michigan; registered to practice before U.S. Patent and Trademark Office (Not admitted in Illinois). *Education:* General Motors Institute (B.S.E.E., 1991); Wayne State University (J.D., 2002). *Member:* State Bar of Michigan (Vice Chair and Council Member, Young Lawyers Section); American Bar Association (Intellectual Property Section; Business Law Section; Young Lawyers Section, Vice Chair, Intellectual Property Law Committee; Liaison to Intellectual Property Section); Washtenaw County Bar Association; American Intellectual Property Law Association; Michigan Intellectual Property Law Association. ***PRACTICE AREAS:*** Intellectual Property; Patents; Trademarks; Copyrights; Trade Secrets; Technology and Science. ***Email:*** rfergan@usebrinks.com

JON H. BEAUPRE, born August 30, 1977; admitted to bar, 2003, Michigan; registered to practice before U.S. Patent and Trademark Office. *Education:* University of Michigan (B.S., cum laude, 2000); University of Wisconsin-Madison (J.D., magna cum laude, 2003). Registered to practice before U.S. Patent and Trademark Office. ***PRACTICE AREAS:*** Intellectual Property; Patent Law; Trademark Law; Copyright Law. ***Email:*** jbeaupre@usebrinks.com

JOHN A. LINGL, born Howell, Michigan, October 11, 1976; admitted to bar, 2004, Michigan; registered to practice before U.S. Patent and Trademark Office. *Education:* Kettering University (B.S., Computer Engineering, 2000); Arizona State University (J.D., 2004). *Member:* Washtenaw County Bar Association; Michigan Intellectual Property Bar Association. ***PRACTICE AREAS:*** Intellectual Property. ***Email:*** jlingl@usebrinks.com

JAMES K. CLELAND, born Lansing, Michigan, May 4, 1972; admitted to bar, 1997, Illinois and U.S. District Court, Northern District of Illinois; 2000, U.S. Court of Appeals for the Federal Circuit; registered to practice before U.S. Patent and Trademark Office. *Education:* University of Michigan (B.S., cum laude, Chemical Engineering, 1994); Indiana University (J.D., cum laude, 1997). *Member:* Chicago Bar Association (Member, Young Lawyers Section); Illinois State Bar Association; American Bar Association (Member, Intellectual Property Section); American Intellectual Property Law Association. ***PRACTICE AREAS:*** Intellectual Property. ***Email:*** jcleland@usebrinks.com

DAVID P. HUDYMA, born Detroit, Michigan, 1975; (admission pending). *Education:* University of Michigan (B.S.E., Aerospace Engineering, cum laude, 1998); Indiana University (J.D., cum laude, 2005). Summer Associate and Winter Clerk, Brinks, Hofer, Gilson & Lione, 2004-2005. Sherman Minton Moot Court Competition, 2003. Test Engineer and Mechanical Designer, Williams International, 1998-2002. Summer Intern, General Motors Powertrain, 1997. Engineering Co-op, Hayes Wheels Corporation, 1996. Summer Intern, Detroit Diesel Corporation, 1995. ***PRACTICE AREAS:*** Patents. ***Email:*** dhudyma@usebrinks.com

Languages: Arabic, Croatian, French, German, Greek, Hebrew, Japanese, Korean, Latvian, Macedonian, Polish, Romanian, Russian, Serbian and Spanish.

BRODSKY & ODEH

Established in 2003

8 SOUTH MICHIGAN AVENUE, 32ND FLOOR
CHICAGO, ILLINOIS 60603
Telephone: 312-701-3000
Fax: 312-701-3088
Email: brodsky-odeh@sbcglobal.net
URL: http://www.brodskyodeh.com

Criminal Defense, Commercial Litigation, Immigration Law, Family Law and Real Estate Law.

FIRM PROFILE: We provide aggressive representation in criminal defense, immigration, commercial litigation and real estate cases. We get results when other attorneys can't.

MEMBERS OF FIRM

JOEL A. BRODSKY, born Chicago, Illinois, July 24, 1957; admitted to bar, 1982, Illinois; 1983, U.S. District Court, Northern District of Illinois; 1985, U.S. Court of Appeals, Seventh Circuit; 1986, U.S. Supreme Court. *Education:* Drake University (B.A., 1979); DePaul University (J.D., 1982). Author: Chapter, "Attachment, Replevin and Detinue," *Creditors Rights in Illinois,* Illinois Institute for Continuing Legal Education, 1986. *Member:* National Association of Criminal Defense Lawyers. ***REPORTED CASES:*** Collins v. St. Jude Temple No. 1, 157 Ill. App. 3d 708, 510 N.E.2d 979 (1987); LaSalle National Bank v. Hadi Kahn, 191 Ill. App. 3d 41, 547 N.E.2d 472 (1989); Joseph Bucci v. Paul Rustin, 227 Ill. App. 3d 779, 592 N.E.2d 297 (1992); Candice Company v. Ricketts, 281 Ill. App. 3d 359, 666 N.E.2d 722 (1996); People v. Jason Tomes, 284 Ill. App. 3d 514, 672 N.E.2d 289 (1996); In Re Boomgarden 708 F.2d 657 (1985); Volpert v. Ellis 110 F.3d 494 (1997). ***PRACTICE AREAS:*** Criminal Defense; Commercial Litigation; Immigration Law; Family Law; Real Estate. ***Email:*** joelbrodsky@sbcglobal.net

REEM H. ODEH, born Fairfax, Virginia; admitted to bar, 2003, Illinois and U.S. District Court, Northern District of Illinois; 2004, U.S. Court of Appeals, Seventh Circuit. *Education:* St. Xavier College (B.A., 1998); John Marshall Law School (J.D., 2003). *Member:* Illinois State and American Bar Associations; Arab-American Bar Association; Association of Trial Lawyers of America; American Immigration Lawyers Association; National Association of Criminal Defense Lawyers. ***LANGUAGES:*** Arabic. ***PRACTICE AREAS:*** Immigration Law; Criminal Defense; Family Law; Real Estate; Commercial Law. ***Email:*** reemodeh@sbcglobal.net

Languages: English, Arabic.

BRONSON & KAHN LLC

150 NORTH WACKER DRIVE, SUITE 1400
CHICAGO, ILLINOIS 60606
Telephone: 312-553-1700
FAX: 312-553-1733
URL: http://www.bronson-kahn.com
URL: http://www.lawyers.com/bronson&kahn

Real Estate, Real Estate Development, Condominium Law, Residential Real Estate Development, Commercial Leasing, Shopping Center Leasing, Construction Contracts, Construction Law, Office Leasing, Corporate Finance, Contracts, Real Estate Finance, Business and Corporate Law, Business Acquisitions, Business Divestitures, Commercial Loans, Commercial Finance, Private Placement, Estate Planning, Trust and Probate Administration, Tax, and Commercial Litigation.

DANIEL R. BRONSON, born Detroit, Michigan, April 22, 1959; admitted to bar, 1984, Illinois. *Education:* University of Michigan (A.B., with high distinction, Branstrom Prize, 1981; J.D., 1984). *Member:* Chicago (Member: Real Estate Law Committee; Condominium Law Subcommittee), Illinois State and American (Member, Real Property and Trust Committee) Bar Associations. ***PRACTICE AREAS:*** Real Estate; Real Estate Development; Construction Contracts; Condominium Development; Real Estate Finance; Business Law; Corporate Law. ***Email:*** dbronson@bronson-kahn.com

HARLAN D. KAHN, born Detroit, Michigan, March 30, 1961; admitted to bar, 1986, Illinois. *Education:* University of Michigan (A.B., with distinction, 1983; J.D., 1986). *Member:* Chicago, Illinois State (Member, Corporation and Securities Law Committee) and American Bar Associations. ***PRACTICE AREAS:*** Business Law; Corporate Law; Mergers, Acquisitions and Divestitures; Real Estate; Leases and Leasing; Commercial Finance; Private Placement. ***Email:*** hkahn@bronson-kahn.com

MARC W. O'BRIEN, born Connellsville, Pennsylvania, December 27, 1951; admitted to bar, 1984, Illinois; 1985, U.S. District Court, Northern District of Illinois including Trial Bar. *Education:* Hope College (B.A., 1979); John Marshall Law School (J.D., with highest distinction, 1984). ***PRACTICE AREAS:*** Commercial Litigation; Real Estate Law; Corporate Law; Business Law. ***Email:*** mobrien@bronson-kahn.com

ANTHONY BERGAMINO, JR., born East Patchogue, New York, January 13, 1963; admitted to bar, 1988, Illinois. *Education:* State University of New York at Stony Brook (B.A., summa cum laude, 1985); University of Chicago (J.D., 1988). Phi Eta Sigma; Phi Beta Kappa; Pi Sigma Alpha. ***PRACTICE AREAS:*** Real Estate; Construction Contracts; Leases and Leasing; Commercial Transactions; Commercial Finance. ***Email:*** abergamino@bronson-kahn.com

JOHN A. STRYE, born Milwaukee, Wisconsin, September 11, 1966; admitted to bar, 1992, District of Columbia, Wisconsin, Illinois, U.S. District Court, Northern District of Illinois, U.S. Tax Court and U.S. Court of Appeals, Seventh Circuit. *Education:* University of Wisconsin-Madison (B.B.A., 1989); John Marshall Law School (J.D., 1992); Georgetown University Law Center (LL.M., Taxation, 1993). *Member:* Chicago and American (Member, Taxation Section) Bar Associations; District of Columbia Bar; State Bar of Wisconsin. ***PRACTICE AREAS:*** Estate Planning; Probate; Taxation. ***Email:*** jstrye@bronson-kahn.com

BROOKS, ADAMS AND TARULIS

CHICAGO, ILLINOIS

(See Naperville)

General Practice including Trial and Appellate Litigation. General Business, Business/Commercial Litigation, Employment, Corporation, Municipal, School, Park, Condemnation, Real Estate, Environmental, Land Developments, Zoning, Probate, Wills, Trusts, Special Needs Trusts, Adoptions, Estate Planning, Banking, Commercial, Personal Injury, Condominium Law and Civil Rights Law, Consumer Protection, Consumer Fraud, Consumer Litigation, Family Law, Divorce, Matrimonial Law, Criminal/Traffic Defense, Juvenile Representation and School Law Matters.

PATRICIA BROSTERHOUS, LTD.

ONE NORTH LASALLE STREET
SUITE 1350
CHICAGO, ILLINOIS 60602
Telephone: 312-629-9629
Fax: 630-434-2844
Email: TRUSTLAW@AMERITECH.NET

Trusts and Estates, Estate Planning and Estate Administration.

PATRICIA BROSTERHOUS, born Long Beach, California, April 16, 1950; admitted to bar, 1983, Illinois. *Education:* University of California at Berkeley (B.A., 1974); Loyola University of Chicago (J.D., cum laude, 1983). Author: "Draft Statement of Principles Comes Not a Moment Too Soon," 127 *Trusts & Estates,* No. 12, 12 December, 1988; "Life, Death and Taxes Under H.R. 3838," 125 *Trusts & Estates,* No. 3, 36 March, 1986. Member, Chicago Estate Planning Council. *Member:* Chicago Bar Association (Probate Practice Chairman, Division III, 1990-1991; Chairman, Trust Law Committee, Division I, 1999-2000). Fellow, American College of Trust and Estate Counsel. ***PRACTICE AREAS:*** Estate Planning; Trust Administration; Probate; Charitable Organizations.

THE LAW OFFICES OF MARC L. BROWN

CHICAGO, ILLINOIS

(See Park Ridge)

Elder Law, Real Estate, Trusts and Estates, Wills, Probate, Living Trusts, Guardianship, Nursing Home Abuse and Neglect, Health Care.

BROYLES LAW OFFICE

3435 N. SHEFFIELD, SUITE 206
CHICAGO, ILLINOIS 60657
Telephone: 773-348-3101
Fax: 773-348-3181
URL: http://www.broyleslawoffice.com
Email: beth@broyleslawoffice.com
URL: http://www.lawyers.com/broyleslawoffice

Immigration Law, Employer Rights, Investors Visas, Immigration and Naturalization Law.

BETH ANN BROYLES, born July 2, 1969; admitted to bar, 1998, Illinois. *Education:* Northern Illinois University (B.A., 1994); Illinois Institute of Technology, Chicago-Kent College of Law (J.D., 1997). *Member:* Chicago Bar Association; American Immigration Lawyers Association. ***PRACTICE AREAS:*** Immigration Law (100%, 700); Employer Rights; Investor Visas; Immigration and Naturalization. ***Email:*** beth@broyleslawoffice.com

BRYAN CAVE LLP

Established in 2001

161 NORTH CLARK STREET, SUITE 4800
CHICAGO, ILLINOIS 60601-3206
Telephone: 312-602-5000
Facsimile: 312-602-5050
URL: http://www.bryancave.com

St. Louis, Missouri Office: One Metropolitan Square, 211 North Broadway, Suite 3600, 63102-2750. Telephone: (314) 259-2000. Facsimile: (314) 259-2020.
Washington, D.C. Office: 700 Thirteenth Street, N.W., 20005-3960. Telephone: (202) 508-6000. Facsimile: (202) 508-6200.
New York, N.Y. Office: 1290 Avenue of the Americas, 10104-3300. Telephone: (212) 541-2000. Facsimile: (212) 541-4630.
Kansas City, Missouri Office: 3500 One Kansas City Place, 1200 Main Street, 64105-2100. Telephone: (816) 374-3200. Facsimile: (816) 374-3300.
Leawood, Kansas Office: 4707 W. 135th Street, Suite 210, 66224-9800. Telephone: (913) 338-7700. Facsimile: (913) 338-7777.
Jefferson City, Missouri Office: 221 Bolivar Street, 65101-1574. Telephone: (573) 556-6620. Facsimile: (573) 556-6630.
Phoenix, Arizona Office: Two North Central Avenue, Suite 2200, 85004-4406. Telephone: (602) 364-7000. Facsimile: (602) 364-7070.
Santa Monica, California Office: 120 Broadway, Suite 300, 90401-2386. Telephone: (310) 576-2100. Facsimile: (310) 576-2200.
Irvine, California Office: 2020 Main Street, Suite 600, 92614-8226. Telephone: (949) 223-7000. Facsimile: (949) 223-7100.
London, England Office: 33 Cannon Street, EC4M 5TE. Telephone: 44-20-7246-5800. Facsimile: 44-20-7246-5858.
Khaldiya, Kuwait Office: Mashora Advocates & Legal Consultants, Al Mashora Tower, Second Floor, Abu Bakar Siddiq Street, P.O. Box 17469, 72455. Telephone: 965-240-4470. Facsimile: 965-242-4047.
Hong Kong Office: Suite 1109, Gloucester Tower, The Landmark, 11 Pedder Street, Central Hong Kong. Telephone: 852-2522-2821. Facsimile: 852-2522-3830.
Shanghai 200040, People's Republic of China Office: Suite 448, Shanghai Centre, 1376 Nan Jing West Road. Telephone: 8621-6279-8166. Facsimile: 8621-6279-8165.

Agency and Distributorships, Agricultural Law, Alternative Dispute Resolution, Antitrust and Trade Regulation, Appellate Practice, Aviation and Aerospace, Bankruptcy, Banks and Banking, Biotechnology, Class Actions, Commercial Real Estate, Complex and Multi-District Litigation, Construction Law, Copyrights, Eminent Domain, Employee Benefits, Environmental Law, Finance, Franchises and Franchising, Government Contracts, Health Care, Insurance, Insurance Defense, Intellectual Property, International Law, International Trade, Labor and Employment, Litigation, Merger, Acquisitions and Divestitures, Nonprofit and Charitable Organizations, Patents, Products Liability, Public Finance, Real Estate, Regulatory Law, Securities, Taxation, Trademarks, Trusts and Estates, White Collar Crime, Zoning, Planning and Land Use.

PARTNERS

MARY CLARE BONACCORSI, admitted to bar, 1989, Illinois; U.S. District Court, Northern District of Illinois; U.S. Court of Appeals, Third and Seventh Circuits. *Education:* Colgate University (B.A., cum laude, 1986); Northwestern University (J.D., 1989). ***PRACTICE AREAS:*** Commercial Litigation; Health Care.

JULES I. CRYSTAL, admitted to bar, 1971, Illinois; 1975, U.S. Court of Appeals, 4th and 7th Circuits; 1977, U.S. Supreme Court; 1983, U.S. Court of Appeals, Federal Circuit; 1996, U.S. Court of Appeals, 9th Circuit. *Education:* University of Michigan (B.A., 1968; J.D., 1971). ***PRACTICE AREAS:*** Labor and Employment; Collective Bargaining; Labor Strikes; Unfair Labor Practices; Management Labor Law. ***Email:*** jules.crystal@bryancave.com

ALAN J. DIXON, admitted to bar, 1949, Illinois and Missouri. *Education:* University of Illinois (B.S., 1946); Washington University (LL.B., 1949). ***PRACTICE AREAS:*** Corporate Law; Litigation; Appellate Practice. ***Email:*** ajdixon@bryancave.com

DONALD E. FIGLIULO, admitted to bar, 1978, Illinois. *Education:* St. Mary's University (B.A., cum laude, 1974); Chicago-Kent College of Law (J.D., with high honors, 1978). ***PRACTICE AREAS:*** Corporate Finance and Securities; Transactions. ***Email:*** don.figliulo@bryancave.com

D. SCOTT HARGADON, admitted to bar, 1983, Illinois. *Education:* University of Virginia (B.A., with high distinction, 1980); University of Pennsylvania (J.D., 1983). Chairman, Real Estate Department. Board Member and Chairman, Chicago Association for the

(This Listing Continued)

BRYAN CAVE LLP, Chicago—Continued

Performing Arts. Member, Board of Directors: North American Folk Music Alliance; Old Town School of Folk Music. *Member:* Urban Land Institute. ***PRACTICE AREAS:*** Real Estate. ***Email:*** scott.hargadon@bryancave.com

SCOTT HODES, admitted to bar, 1959, Illinois; 1963, U.S. Supreme Court; 1981, New York; 1991, District of Columbia;. *Education:* University of Chicago (A.B., 1956); University of Michigan (J.D., 1959) Northwestern University (LL.M., 1961). ***PRACTICE AREAS:*** Banking; Entrepreneurial, Technology and Commercial Practice; Transactions; Art Law.

MARY MARGARET MOORE, admitted to bar, 1991, Illinois; U.S. Supreme Court; U.S. Court of Appeals, 7th Circuit; U.S. District Court, Central and Northern Districts of Illinois; U.S. District Court, Eastern District of Michigan; U.S. District Court, Northern District of Indiana. *Education:* St. Mary's College (B.A., magna cum laude, 1988); Northwestern University (J.D., 1991). ***PRACTICE AREAS:*** Employment Law; Counseling; Litigation. ***Email:*** mimi.moore@bryancave.com

JEFFREY W. MOROF, admitted to bar, 1979, Missouri; 1982, California (Not admitted in Illinois). *Education:* University of Michigan (A.B., 1976); Washington University (J.D., 1979). ***PRACTICE AREAS:*** Civil Practice; Aviation Law; Products Liability Law. ***Email:*** jwmorof@bryancave.com

CHRISTIAN M. POLAND, admitted to bar, 1992, California; 1994, Illinois. *Education:* Wheaton College (B.A., 1988); University of Notre Dame (J.D., 1992). ***PRACTICE AREAS:*** Labor and Employment; Employment Discrimination; Employment Litigation; Wrongful Termination Defense; Education Law. ***Email:*** christian.poland@bryancave.com

BRIAN A. SHER, admitted to bar, 1987, Illinois, U.S. District Court, Northern District of Illinois and U.S. Court of Appeals, Seventh Circuit; 1998, U.S. Court of Appeals, Fourth Circuit. *Education:* University of Michigan (B.A., with high honors, 1984); Duke University (J.D., cum laude, 1987). ***PRACTICE AREAS:*** Commercial Litigation; Health Care.

STEVEN R. SMITH, admitted to bar, 1980, Illinois; U.S. District Court, Northern District of Illinois; U.S. Court of Appeals, Seventh Circuit. *Education:* University of Chicago (B.A., 1975); University of Santa Clara (J.D., 1980). ***PRACTICE AREAS:*** Commercial Litigation; Securities Litigation; Professional Liability Litigation. ***Email:*** srsmith@bryancave.com

WILLIAM J. WORTEL, admitted to bar, 1996, Illinois and U.S. District Court, Northern and Central Districts of Illinois; U.S. District Court, Northern District of Indiana; U.S. Court of Appeals, Third, Seventh and Eighth Circuits. *Education:* University of Illinois (B.S., with honors, 1993); DePaul University (J.D., 1996). ***PRACTICE AREAS:*** Labor and Employment; Employer Rights; Employment Discrimination; Employment Litigation; Wrongful Termination Defense. ***Email:*** bill.wortel@bryancave.com

OF COUNSEL

TIMOTHY C. KLENK, admitted to bar, 1967, Illinois; 1968, U.S. District Court, Northern District of Illinois; 1976, U.S. District Court, Eastern District of Wisconsin; 1979, U.S. Court of Appeals, Seventh Circuit; 1980, U.S. Supreme Court and U.S. District Court, Central District of Illinois; 1985, U.S. Tax Court; 1989, U.S. Court of Appeals, Fifth Circuit; 1999, U.S. District Court, Northern District of Indiana; 2000, U.S. Court of Appeals, Eighth and Fourth Circuits; 2000, U.S. District Court, Western District of Wisconsin. *Education:* Wheaton College (B.A., 1961); Northwestern University (J.D., 1967) Order of the Coif. ***PRACTICE AREAS:*** Labor and Employment; Employment Litigation; Commercial Litigation; Federal Civil Litigation; Nonprofit and Charitable Organizations. ***Email:*** tim.klenk@bryancave.com

JAMES M. STAULCUP, JR., admitted to bar, 1968, Illinois. *Education:* Wabash College (B.A., 1964); DePaul University (J.D., 1968). ***PRACTICE AREAS:*** Labor and Employment; Litigation. ***Email:*** jmstaulcup@bryancave.com

COUNSEL

MONICA A. CARROLL, admitted to bar, 1979, Illinois. *Education:* University of Illinois (B.A., 1974); Harvard University (J.D., cum laude, 1979). ***PRACTICE AREAS:*** Banking; Business Finance; Entrepreneurial, Technology and Commercial Practice; Health Care.

TAMMIE G. KRAUSKOPF, admitted to bar, 1987, Pennsylvania; 1989, District of Columbia; 1999, Illinois. *Education:* Pennsylvania State University (B.A., 1984); University of Pittsburgh (M.P.I.A., with honors, 1987; J.D., 1987). Licensed Customs Broker, 1995. ***PRACTICE AREAS:*** International Trade. ***Email:*** tammie.krauskopf@bryancave.com

PAUL A. LUTTER, admitted to bar, 1971, Illinois. *Education:* Carleton College (B.A., magna cum laude, 1968); Yale University (J.D., 1971). ***PRACTICE AREAS:*** Estate Administration; Estate Planning; Estate Planning for Unmarried Couples; Family Wealth Transfer; Living Trusts. ***Email:*** paul.lutter@bryancave.com

ASSOCIATES

CRAIG D. JEFFREY, admitted to bar, 2000, Missouri; 2005, Illinois. *Education:* Baruch College of the City University of New York (B.A., 1997); University of Iowa (J.D., 2000). Phi Alpha Delta. ***Email:*** cdjeffrey@bryancave.com

ERIN F. MARTIN, admitted to bar, 2001, Illinois; U.S. District Court, Northern District of Illinois. *Education:* University of Notre Dame (B.A., 1997); Northwestern University (J.D., 2001). ***Email:*** erin.martin@bryancave.com

SHONDA K. MAUPIN, admitted to bar, 2001, Missouri; 2002, Kansas (Not admitted in Illinois). *Education:* Southwest Baptist University (B.A., 1998); University of Notre Dame (J.D., 2001). ***PRACTICE AREAS:*** Transactions. ***Email:*** skmaupin@bryancave.com

MARK A. PASKAR, admitted to bar, 1999, Missouri; 2000, Illinois; U.S. District Court, Eastern District of Missouri. *Education:* Duke University (A.B., 1996); George Washington University (J.D., 1999). ***Email:*** mapaskar@bryancave.com

(This Listing Continued)

RODNEY PERRY, admitted to bar, 1998, Missouri; 2001, Illinois. *Education:* Tennessee State University (B.A., 1994); Washington University School of Law (J.D., 1998). Managing Editor, Washington University Journal of Urban and Contemporary Law, 1997-1998.

CHRISTY E. PHANTHAVONG, admitted to bar, 1999, Illinois; U.S. Court Of Appeals, Fourth and Tenth Circuits; U.S. District Court, Central and Northern Districts of Illinois, District of Colorado, Eastern and Western Districts of Wisconsin and Northern District of Indiana. *Education:* Wheaton College (B.A., summa cum laude, 1995); University of Illinois, Urbana-Champaign (J.D., summa cum laude, 1999). ***Email:*** christy.phanthavong@bryancave.com

DMITRY SHIFRIN, admitted to bar, 2002, Missouri; 2003, Illinois; U.S. District Court, Eastern District of Missouri; 2005, U.S. District Court, Northern District of Illinois. *Education:* University of Missouri-Columbia (B.A., 1998; J.D., 2002). ***Email:*** ddshifrin@bryancave.com

CAROLINE S. SOODEK, admitted to bar, 1997, Illinois. *Education:* University of Minnesota (B.A., 1994); Northwestern University (J.D., 1997).

WILLIAM F. ZIESKE, admitted to bar, 1997, Illinois and U.S. District Court, Northern District of Illinois; 2003, U.S. District Court, Southern District of Illinois. *Education:* Washington University in St. Louis (B.A., magna cum laude, 1991); University of Chicago (Graduate Studies); University of Notre Dame (J.D., summa cum laude, 1997).

All Partners and Associates of the Firm are Members of the American Bar Association

REPRESENTATIVE CLIENTS: A.G. Edwards & Sons Inc.; Arch Coal, Inc.; Bank of America; The Bank of New York; BJC; The Boeing Company; Brown Group, Inc.; Citigroup; Civic Progress, Inc.; DaimlerChrysler; EdwardJones; Emerson Electric Co.; ESCO Corp.; The First American Corporation; Ford Motor Company; Government of Kuwait; H&R Block; Heartland Bank; Lucent Technologies; Marriott International; Merck; Michelin USA; Monsanto; Nestle; Payless Shoe Source; Saint Louis University; Sigma Aldrich Corp.; Stifel, Nicolaus & Company, Inc.; The Washington University; Washington University Medical Center; Webster University.

BRYCEDOWNEY, LLC

200 NORTH LASALLE STREET, SUITE 2700
CHICAGO, ILLINOIS 60601
Telephone: 312-377-1501
Fax: 312-377-1502
URL: http://www.brycedowney.com

Central Illinois Office: P.O. Box 100, Canton, Illinois, 61520. Telephone: 309-789-2839. Fax: 309-789-2840.

General Practice.

FIRM PROFILE: The professionals of the Chicago the law firm of BryceDowney, LLC are dedicated to the delivery of world-class service to the firm's Clients. Located in the heart of Chicago's loop BryceDowney, LLC is a diversified full service Chicago-based law firm. BryceDowney, LLC represent commercial, construction, banking, real estate development, manufacturing, advertising and insurance companies. Our practice includes creation and management of business organizations, financial transactions, real estate transactions, business transactions, accounts receivable management, personal injury defense, workers' compensation, transportation, business advice, employment advice and litigation.

As a full service firm, our trial attorneys, with nearly a century of combined trial experience efficiently and professionally manage and present cases for resolution to jury, judge or arbitration panel. The firm's trial attorneys are trial bar certified by the federal court and have for decades tried diverse cases to diverse fact finders. The trial attorneys' experience includes, construction, commercial, employment, personal injury and worker's compensation trials.

World-class service is accomplished in our business and transactional practice by decades of business entity formation, transactional document preparation, negotiation, drafting and execution. The firm's library of completed contracts, case law and business entity formation models provide a wealth of references for your business goals.

The firm also utilizes an Integrated Management System which allows business managers to make informed decisions about their litigation. Once a business decision is made, the strategy is executed and the results tracked and documented. The Integrated Management System is an on-going computer based data driven decisional matrix capturing the economics of litigation. The goal of Integrated Management System is to return the litigation decisions to the Client for integration into the Client's business objectives.

GEOFFREY A. BRYCE, born Petoskey, Michigan, October 6, 1949; admitted to bar, 1981, Illinois. *Education:* University of Toledo (B.B.A., 1971); DePaul University (M.S.T., 1976); John Marshall Law School (J.D., 1981). Member, Brookfield, Illinois Zoning Board of Appeals, 1985-1990. Author: "Responsibilities and Liabilities of General Contractors, Subcontractors, Construction Managers and Material Suppliers for Construction Failures," Illinois Institute for Continuing Legal Education Construction Litigation Course Handbook, 1982—. Author and Speaker: "Advanced Construction Law in Illinois," National Business Institute, February 2003; Illinois Construction Law: What Do You Do When...?" National Business Institute, July 2002; "Management of Mold Risk," Bryce, Downey, Murray, Jensen & Milkus LLC, June 2002; "Illinois Construction Defect and Mold Litigation," National Business Institute, May 2002; "Advanced Construction Law in Illinois," National Business Institute, September 2001; "Project Delivery Methods;" "Construction Defects," and Kotecki," National Business Institute, August 22, 2000, and August 2001; "What Do You Do With A Defective Bid?", "What Do You Do When Conditions On The Job Change?," and "What Do You Do If You Do Not Get Paid?," National Business Institute, January 20, 2000 and May 1, 2001. *Member:* American Bar Association (Forum Committee for the Construction Industry); Illinois Society of Construction Attorneys. ***PRACTICE AREAS:*** Commercial Law; Construction Law; Insurance Coverage; Products Liability; Workers Compensation. ***Email:*** gbryce@brycedowney.com

(This Listing Continued)

STORRS W. DOWNEY, born Evanston, Illinois, October 8, 1957; admitted to bar, 1982, Illinois and U.S. District Court, Northern District of Illinois; 1983, Indiana. *Education:* Ripon College (A.B., magna cum laude, 1979); Drake University (J.D., with high honors, 1982). Phi Beta Kappa. *Member:* Chicago, Lake County, Illinois State and Indiana State Bar Associations; Defense Research Institute; Chicago and Indiana Bar Employment Law Divisions; Illinois Workers' Compensation Lawyers Association. ***REPORTED CASES:*** Short v. Keebler Co., 94 C 415 (N.D. Ill. 3/5/96); Fernandez v. Tempel Steel Corp., 1-93-3818 (Ill. App. Ct. 5th Div. 12/29/95); Honegger v. Wickes Furniture Corp. Inc., 94 C 1584 (N.D. Ill. 10/20/95); Chasko v. USX Corp., H91-299 (N.D. Ind. 1993); United States Steel Corp.- Gary Works v. Industrial Commission, 161 Ill. App. 2d 437, Ill. 3d Dist. 1987). ***PRACTICE AREAS:*** Employment Law; Construction Litigation; Workers Compensation; Products Liability; Complex Litigation. ***Email:*** sdowney@brycedowney.com

RICHARD W. LENKOV, born Montreal, Quebec, Canada, July 30, 1970; admitted to bar, 1996, Illinois and U.S. District Court, Northern District of Illinois. *Education:* McGill University (B.A., 1992); Northern Illinois University (J.D., 1995). *Member:* Chicago, DuPage County and Illinois State Bar Associations. ***PRACTICE AREAS:*** Defense Litigation; Workers' Compensation. ***Email:*** rlenkov@brycedowney.com

DAWN M. CASSIE, born Evanston, Illinois, May 28, 1956; admitted to bar, 1981, Illinois and U.S. District Court, Northern District of Illinois, including Trial Bar; 1985, Colorado and U.S. Court of Appeals, Seventh Circuit; 1989, U.S. District Court, Eastern District of Wisconsin; 1990, U.S. Court of Appeals for the Federal Circuit. *Education:* Cornell University (B.A., 1978); Loyola University (J.D., 1981). Regional Champion, National Mock Trial Team, 1981. CBA Alliance for Women, 2003-2004. *Member:* Chicago Bar Association. ***PRACTICE AREAS:*** Intellectual Property; Employment Law. ***Email:*** dcassie@brycedowney.com

JEANNE M. HOFFMANN, born Chicago, Illinois, April 8, 1965; admitted to bar, 1989, Illinois and U.S. District Court, Northern District of Illinois. *Education:* University of Illinois (B.A., with honors, 1986); DePaul University (J.D., 1989). Member, De Paul University Law Review, 1986-1989. *Member:* Chicago and American Bar Associations. ***PRACTICE AREAS:*** Commercial Litigation; Intellectual Property Litigation; Insurance Coverage. ***Email:*** jhoffmann@brycedowney.com

TERRENCE J. MADDEN, born Chicago, Illinois, January 26, 1948; admitted to bar, 1973, Illinois; 1975, U.S. District Court, Northern District of Illinois; 1982, U.S. Court of Appeals, Seventh Circuit. *Education:* St. Louis University (B.A., cum laude, 1970); University of Illinois College of Law (J.D., cum laude, 1973). Member, Order of the Coif. Assistant Editor, University of Illinois Law Forum, 1972-1973. Law Clerk, Illinois Supreme Court, 1973-1974. ***PRACTICE AREAS:*** Insurance Defense Litigation; Medical Malpractice; Insurance Coverage; Products Liability; Appellate Practice; Commercial Litigation. ***Email:*** tmadden@brycedowney.com

ROBERT C. BRAMLETTE, JR., born Birmingham, Alabama, November 11, 1949; admitted to bar, 1975, Illinois. *Education:* University of Notre Dame (B.B.A., magna cum laude, 1971); Northwestern University (J.D., 1974). Dean's List. Certified Public Accountant, Illinois, 1971. Instructor, Legal Writing, Northwestern University, 1973-1974. Member, Flossmoor, Illinois Police and Fire Commission, 2005. *Member:* Chicago and American Bar Associations. [Capt., U.S. Army, 1971-1979]. ***PRACTICE AREAS:*** Corporate Law (40%); Real Estate (40%); Employment Law (10%); Litigation (10%). ***Email:*** rbramlette@brycedowney.com

---

YASIR S. ALEEMUDDIN, born India, January 11, 1973; admitted to bar, 1999, Illinois. *Education:* University of Illinois-Champaign (B.A., 1996); University of Iowa (J.D., 1999). Member, Jessup International Law Moot Court Team. *Member:* Chicago Bar Association. ***LANGUAGES:*** Hindi and Urdu. ***PRACTICE AREAS:*** Construction Litigation; Commercial Litigation; Real Estate. ***Email:*** yaleemuddin@brycedowney.com

W. MATTHEW BRYANT, born Chicago, Illinois; admitted to bar, 1995, Illinois and U.S. District Court, Northern District of Illinois; 1998, U.S. District Court, Central District of Illinois. *Education:* University of Chicago (B.A., 1992); Loyola University, Chicago (J.D., 1995). *Member:* Chicago Bar Association. ***Email:*** wmbryant@brycedowney.com

JENNIFER B. CROMHEECKE, born New York, New York, September 27, 1966; admitted to bar, 1994, Georgia; 1997, Illinois. *Education:* Dartmouth College (A.B., cum laude, 1989); Tulane University of Louisiana (J.D., cum laude, 1993). *Member:* Illinois State Bar Associations; State Bar of Georgia. ***PRACTICE AREAS:*** Litigation; Construction; Insurance Defense. ***Email:*** jcromheecke@brycedowney.com

SAMANTHA H. HORWITZ, born Birmingham, Alabama, November 15, 1974; admitted to bar, 1999, Illinois; U.S. District Court, Northern District of Illinois. *Education:* University of Virginia (B.A., 1996; J.D., 1999). ***PRACTICE AREAS:*** Insurance Coverage; Commercial Litigation; Intellectual Property. ***Email:*** shorwitz@brycedowney.com

YVONNE M. KATO, born Oak Park, Illinois, December 15, 1973; admitted to bar, 1999, Illinois and U.S. District Court, Northern District of Illinois; 2001, U.S. Court of Appeals, Seventh Circuit. *Education:* University of Chicago (A.B., 1995); Chicago-Kent College of Law (J.D., 1998). *Member:* Illinois State Bar Association (Vice Chair, 2004-2005, Secretary, 2003-2004 and Editor, 2001-2002, Committee on Women and Minority Participation). ***PRACTICE AREAS:*** Insurance Defense; General Liability Defense; Labor and Employment. ***Email:*** ykato@brycedowney.com

MARTHA A. NILES, born Somerville, Massachusetts, August 12, 1954; admitted to bar, 1992, Illinois; 1999, U.S. District Court, Northern District of Illinois; 2002, Indiana. *Education:* University of Maryland at College Park (B.A., 1976); Chicago-Kent College of Law/IIT (J.D., with honors, 1992). Adjunct Professor of Appellate Advocacy, Chicago-Kent College of Law, 1994-1995. *Member:* Illinois State Bar Association; Worker's Compensation Lawyers Association. ***PRACTICE AREAS:*** Workers Compensation Defense; Litigation; Appellate Practice. ***Email:*** mniles@brycedowney.com

CHRISTOPHER M. PUCKELWARTZ, born Chicago, Illinois, March 7, 1972; admitted to bar, 1997, Illinois and U.S. District Court, Northern District of Illinois. *Education:* University of Illinois at Urbana-Champaign (B.A., 1994); Loyola University School of Law (J.D., 1997). Dean's List. Phi Alpha Delta. *Member:* Illinois State and Chicago Bar Associations. ***PRACTICE AREAS:*** Insurance Defense; Personal Injury; Insurance Coverage; Commercial Litigation; Consumer Fraud. ***Email:*** epuckelwartz@brycedowney.com

FRANK C. ROWLAND, born Chicago, Illinois, September 13, 1954; admitted to bar, 1976, Illinois; U.S. District Court, Northern District of Illinois including Trial Bar; U.S. Court of Appeals, Seventh Circuit; U.S. Supreme Court. *Education:* Marquette University (B.A., 1973); John Marshall Law School (J.D., with distinction, 1976). Phi Alpha Delta. Executive Editor, The John Marshall Journal of Practice and Procedure, 1975-1976. Assistant States Attorney of Cook County, 1976-1977. Law Clerk to U.S. District Judge Julius Hoffman, Northern District of Illinois, 1977-1978. *Member:* Chicago (Member, Federal Civil Procedure Committee, 1977—, Civil Practice Committee, 1977—) and American Bar Associations. ***PRACTICE AREAS:*** Appellate Practice; Insurance Defense Litigation; Products Liability; Workers Compensation. ***Email:*** frowland@brycedowney.com

IOANA SALAJANU, born Oradea, Romania, September 22, 1974; admitted to bar, 2000, Illinois and U.S. District Court, Northern District of Illinois. *Education:* University of Michigan (B.A., Political Science, 1996); Loyola University School of Law (J.D., 2000). Dean's List. *Member:* Chicago and American Bar Associations. ***LANGUAGES:*** Romanian, French, Italian and Spanish. ***PRACTICE AREAS:*** Commercial Litigation. ***Email:*** isalajanu@brycedowney.com

TYANIKA L. SAUNDERS, born Centralia, Illinois, March 13, 1973; admitted to bar, 2000, Ohio; 2005, Illinois and U.S. District Court, Northern District of Illinois. *Education:* University of Illinois at Urbana-Champaign (B.A., 1995); Capital University Law School (J.D., 1998). *Member:* Illinois State Bar Association. ***PRACTICE AREAS:*** Criminal Law; Workers Compensation. ***Email:*** nsaunders@brycedowney.com

CAROLINE WATSON, born Melrose Park, Illinois, November 13, 1965; admitted to bar, 2001, Illinois; 2002, Georgia; 2003, Ohio; 2004, New York. *Education:* Illinois State University (B.S., 1987); Cleveland State University (J.D., 2000). ***PRACTICE AREAS:*** Workers Compensation.

JENNIFER VAN BLARGAN, born Euclid, Ohio, 1977; admitted to bar, 2003, Illinois. *Education:* University of Dayton (B.S., 1999); Loyola University (J.D., 2003). Phi Alpha Delta (Treasurer, 2000-2001). Recipient, CALI Excellence for Future Award. ***PRACTICE AREAS:*** Intellectual Property; Business Law.

OF COUNSEL

PHILIP W. ENGLE, born London, England, January 28, 1955; admitted to bar, 1986, District of Columbia; 1994, Florida; 1998, Georgia (Not admitted in Illinois). *Education:* University of Vermont (B.A., 1976); American University (M.P.A., 1978; J.D., 1986); Emory University (M.B.A., 1999). Phi Alpha Alpha. Author: "Crafting International Commercial Arbitration Clauses," The ACCA Docket Journal of the American Corporate Counsel Association, July, August 1995. Instructor: International Business Law, American University, 1988-1992; Principles of Law in International Procurement and Business Transactions, University of Virginia, 1991. *Member:* The Florida Bar (Member, International Law Section, 1994—); State Bar of Georgia (Member, International Law Section); International Association of Corporate Real Estate Executives. (Resident, Roswell, Georgia Office).(Also Vice President, General Counsel and Secretary, Prenova, Inc., Energy Management, Marietta, Georgia). ***LANGUAGES:*** French, Spanish, German and Arabic. ***TRANSACTIONS:*** Involve major contracts for services in the U.S., Canada, Malaysia and single contracts for multiple countries ("Global"). ***PRACTICE AREAS:*** International Business Law; Contracts; Labor and Employment; Intellectual Property.

BUDIN LAW OFFICES

Established in 1990

ONE NORTH LA SALLE STREET
SUITE 1560
CHICAGO, ILLINOIS 60602
Telephone: 312-377-0700
Fax: 312-377-0707
Email: budinlaw@aol.com
URL: http://www.budinlaw.com

Automobile Accidents, Catastrophic Accidents and Injuries, Head Trauma, Spinal Cord Injuries, Construction Site Accidents, Work Related Injuries.

JOHN JOSEPH BUDIN, born St. Louis, Missouri, September 19, 1956; admitted to bar, 1985, Illinois and U.S. District Court, Northern District of Illinois. *Education:* Northeastern Illinois University (B.A., 1981); DePaul University (J.D., 1985). *Member:* Chicago and Illinois State Bar Associations; Illinois Trial Lawyers Association; Association of Trial Lawyers of America. ***PRACTICE AREAS:*** Automobile Accidents and Injuries; Catastrophic Injury; Head Trauma; Spinal Injury; Construction Accidents; Work Related Injuries. ***Email:*** budinlaw@aol.com

Language: Spanish; Arabic.

BULLWINKEL PARTNERS, LTD.

19 SOUTH LA SALLE STREET, SUITE 1300
CHICAGO, ILLINOIS 60603-1493
Telephone: 312-201-0777
Fax: 312-201-0737
URL: http://www.bullwinkel.com

General Practice, Litigation, Intellectual Property, Patents, Entrepreneurial Law.

GEORGE E. BULLWINKEL, born Chicago, Illinois, November 15, 1936; admitted to bar, 1964, Illinois; U.S. District Court, Northern District of Illinois and U.S. Court of Appeals, Seventh Circuit; registered to practice before U.S. Patent and Trademark Office. *Education:* Cornell University (B.M.E., 1959); Harvard Law School (LL.B., 1964). *Mem-*

(This Listing Continued)

BULLWINKEL PARTNERS, LTD., Chicago—Continued

ber: Chicago and American Bar Associations. ***PRACTICE AREAS:*** Intellectual Property Law; Trial Practice; Appellate Practice; Computer Law; Aviation Law. ***Email:*** geb@bullwinkel.com

CONSTANTINE D. KASSON, born Chicago, Illinois, August 14, 1929; admitted to bar, 1955, Illinois and U.S. District Court, Northern District of Illinois. *Education:* DePaul University (B.A., 1951); University of Michigan (J.D., 1954). Delta Theta Phi. Adjunct Professor, John Marshall Law School. Arbitrator, Circuit Court, Cook County, Illinois. *Member:* Chicago and American Bar Associations; The Association of Trial Lawyers of America; Illinois Trial Lawyers Association. ***Email:*** cdk@bullwinkel.com

BURKE, WARREN, MACKAY & SERRITELLA, P.C.

22ND FLOOR-IBM PLAZA
330 NORTH WABASH AVENUE
CHICAGO, ILLINOIS 60611-3607
Telephone: 312-840-7000
Facsimile: 312-840-7900
Email: info@burkelaw.com
URL: http://www.burkelaw.com

General Corporate and Business Matters including Real Estate, Eminent Domain, Financial Institutions, Mortgage Banking, Debtor-Creditor Relations, Bankruptcy, Automotive Franchises and Dealerships, Civil Practice in all State and Federal Courts. Litigation, including Complex and Class Action Defense, Securities, Mergers and Acquisitions, Health Care, Religious, Non-Profit, Educational and Social Services Organizations, Public Finance, Municipal Law, Employment and Labor, ERISA/Employee Benefits, Taxation, Estate Planning, Probate and Trust.

FIRM PROFILE: Burke, Warren, MacKay & Serritella, P.C., is committed to providing superior legal counsel with personal, responsive and efficient service.

Our clients range from international and publicly traded companies to closely held entrepreneurial enterprises, as well as the individuals who own and manage them. We offer significant experience in various industries including real estate, banking and finance, mortgage banking, labor and employment, civil litigation, tax, estate planning, automotive dealerships and franchises, health care, tax-exempt organizations, such as religious, educational and social service entities, general corporate representation and the unique concerns of closely held businesses and their owners.

PATRICK J. BRUKS, born Evansville, Indiana, May 7, 1968; admitted to bar, 1994, Illinois. *Education:* University of Notre Dame (B.A., with honors, 1990); University of Illinois (J.D., magna cum laude, 1994). ***PRACTICE AREAS:*** Corporate Law; Mergers and Acquisitions; Securities; Emerging Growth Companies. ***Email:*** pbruks@burkelaw.com

RICHARD W. BURKE, born Chicago, Illinois, October 3, 1933; admitted to bar, 1959, Illinois and U.S. District Court, Northern District of Illinois; 1965, U.S. Court of Appeals, Seventh Circuit; 1977, U.S. Supreme Court. *Education:* University of Notre Dame (A.B., 1955); University of Chicago Law School (J.D., 1958). *Member:* Chicago and Illinois State (Member, Trial Practice, Corporation and Real Estate Sections) Bar Associations. ***PRACTICE AREAS:*** Corporate Law; Employee Benefits; Litigation. ***Email:*** rburkesr@burkelaw.com

BARBARA CONDIT CANNING, born Toledo, Ohio, October 17, 1962; admitted to bar, 1988, Ohio; 1989, Illinois, U.S. District Court, District of Ohio and U.S. Court of Appeals, Sixth Circuit. *Education:* University of Michigan (B.A., 1984); Loyola University-Chicago (J.D., 1988). Member and Research Editor, Loyola University-Chicago Law Review, 1986-1988. *Member:* Chicago and American Bar Associations. ***PRACTICE AREAS:*** Real Estate. ***Email:*** bcanning@burkelaw.com

PATRICIA B. CARLSON, born Pasadena, California, March 11, 1953; admitted to bar, 1980, Illinois. *Education:* Princeton University (A.B., cum laude, 1975); University of Minnesota (M.A., 1980); Northwestern University School of Law (J.D., cum laude, 1980). Phi Beta Kappa; Order of the Coif. Note and Comment Editor, Journal of Criminal Law and Criminology, 1979-1980. Author: "Illinois Laws Concerning Non-Profit Organizations," 22 The Exempt Organization Tax Review 135, October, 1998. *Member:* Chicago Bar Association. ***PRACTICE AREAS:*** Tax Exempt Organizations; Corporate Law; Religious Organizations Law. ***Email:*** pcarlson@burkelaw.com

JOHN A. DARROW, born Champaign, Illinois, November 6, 1965; admitted to bar, 1990, Illinois and U.S. District Court, Northern District of Illinois; 1998, U.S. Supreme Court. *Education:* University of Notre Dame (B.A., cum laude, 1987); Georgetown University (J.D., cum laude, 1990). Omicron Delta Epsilon. *Member:* Chicago Bar Association; National Health Lawyers Association. ***PRACTICE AREAS:*** Corporate Law; Health Care; Mergers, Acquisitions and Divestitures. ***Email:*** jdarrow@burkelaw.com

STEPHANIE H. DENBY, born New Rochelle, New York, December 20, 1962; admitted to bar, 1988, Illinois. *Education:* University of Chicago (B.A., with honors, 1985); University of Michigan (J.D., cum laude, 1988). ***PRACTICE AREAS:*** Trusts and Estates; Wills; Probate; Closely Held Business Planning; Charitable Giving; Nonprofit and Charitable Organizations; Probate Litigation; Guardianship; Asset Protection; Taxation; Investment Structuring. ***Email:*** sdenby@burkelaw.com

JAY S. DOBRUTSKY, born Hartford, Connecticut, February 8, 1957; admitted to bar, 1996, Illinois and U.S. District Court, Northern and Central Districts of Illinois. *Education:* Boston University (B.A., 1981); University of Virginia (M.A., 1984; Ph.D., English, 1993); Loyola University School of Law (J.D., 1996). *Member:* Chicago and Illinois State Bar Associations. ***PRACTICE AREAS:*** Commercial Litigation; Construction Law; Mortgage Banking Law; Labor and Employment. ***Email:*** jdobrutsky@burkelaw.com

ROBERT J. EMANUEL, born Washington, D.C., August 19, 1969; admitted to bar, 1995, Illinois; U.S. District Court, Northern District of Illinois. *Education:* University of Iowa (B.A., 1991); Chicago-Kent College of Law (J.D., 1995). *Member:* Chicago (Member, Employment Law Committee, 1995-1997) and American Bar Associations. ***PRACTICE AREAS:*** Class Action Defense; Complex Commercial Litigation. ***Email:*** remanuel@burkelaw.com

(This Listing Continued)

JAMES C. GEOLY, born Manhasset, New York, October 30, 1960; admitted to bar, 1985, Illinois and U.S. District Court, Northern District of Illinois; 1993, U.S. Court of Appeals, Seventh Circuit; 1995, U.S. Court of Appeals, Fifth Circuit; 1996, U.S. Court of Appeals, Ninth Circuit and U.S. Supreme Court. *Education:* Columbia University (B.A., magna cum laude, 1982); University of Chicago Law School (J.D., 1985). Phi Beta Kappa. *Member:* Chicago (Member, Interfaith Law Committee) and American Bar Associations (Member, Section on Litigation). ***REPORTED CASES:*** Cady v. City of Chicago, 43 F.3d 326 (7th Cir. 1994) (argued); United States of America v. SCA Services, et al., 865 F. Supp. 533 (N.D. Ind. 1994); Evangelical Lutheran Church in America v. Atlantic Mutual Ins. Co., 973 F. Supp. 820; 173 F.R.D. 507 (N.D. Ill. 1997); Zipper v. Todd, 1997 WL 181044 (S.D.N.Y. 1997); South Jersey Catholic School Teachers Org. v. St Teresa of the Infant Jesus Elementary School, et al., 696 A.2d 709 (N.J. 1997); Ragavskene v. Edgebrook Motel, et al., 299 Ill. App. 3d 1125, 740 N.E.2d 98 (Ill. App. 1st Dist. 1998), appeal denied 182 Ill.2d 571, 707 N.E.2d 1245 (1999); Stein v. Rio Parismina Lodge, 296 Ill.App.3d 520, 695 N.E.2d 518 (1st Dist. 1998) (argued); Witzel v. CIS, 531 U.S. 1101, 121 S. Ct. 851 (mem) (2001); Nissan North America, Inc. v. Jim M'Lady Oldsmobile, Inc., 307 F.3d 601 (7th Cir. 2002) (argued); Brownlow v. Richards, 328 Ill.App.3d 833, 767 N.E.2d 482 (Ill. App. 1st Dist. 2002); Zawadzka v. Catholic Bishop of Chicago, 337 Ill. App. 3d 66, 785 N.E.2d 71 (Ill. App. 1st Dist.), appeal denied 204 Ill 2d 685, 792 N.E.2d 314 (2003); Friends of the Parks v. Chicago Park District, 203 Ill. 2d 312, 786 N.E.2d 161 (2003). ***PRACTICE AREAS:*** Litigation; Appellate Practice; Constitutional Law; Church and State; Commercial Litigation; Religious Institutions; Civil Rights; Nonprofit and Charitable Organizations. ***Email:*** jgeoly@burkelaw.com

TERRY D. JEFFREY, born Harvey, Illinois, September 2, 1949; admitted to bar, 1975, Illinois. *Education:* University of Illinois (B.S., 1971); DePaul University College of Law (J.D., 1974). *Member:* Chicago Bar Association. ***PRACTICE AREAS:*** Banking; Real Estate; Corporate; Business Law. ***Email:*** tjeffrey@burkelaw.com

WILLIAM H. KELLY, JR., born Chicago, Illinois, July 20, 1940; admitted to bar, 1966, Illinois and U.S. District Court, Northern District of Illinois. *Education:* Regis University (B.S., 1962); DePaul University (J.D., 1966). *Member:* Chicago and Illinois State Bar Associations. ***PRACTICE AREAS:*** Automotive Franchises and Dealerships; Financing; Real Estate; Corporate; Real Estate Tax. ***Email:*** wkelly@burkelaw.com

MARTIN K. LAPOINTE, born June 12, 1952; admitted to bar, 1987, Illinois; U.S. District Court, Eastern District of Wisconsin; U.S. District Court, Northern District of Illinois; U.S. District Court, Northern District of California; U.S. District Court, District of Arizona; U.S. Court of Appeals, Second, Fourth, Fifth, Sixth, Seventh and Eighth Circuits. *Education:* Wright State University (B.A., summa cum laude, 1981); IIT/Chicago-Kent College of Law (J.D., with high honors, 1987). Member, Chicago-Kent Chapter of the Order of the Coif. Staff Member and Member, Editorial Board, Chicago-Kent Law Review, 1984-1986. Judicial Law Clerk, Hon. Charles R. Norgle, U.S. District Court, Northern District of Illinois, 1987-1989. Member, Editorial Board and Contributor/Writer, *The Journal of Employment Discrimination Law, CCH, Inc., Fall, 1999-Spring 2001. Member, Editorial Board, Labor Law Journal,* (CCH, Inc.) Summer 2002—. ***PRACTICE AREAS:*** Labor and Employment; Insurance Defense. ***Email:*** mlapointe@burkelaw.com

EDWARD J. LESNIAK, born Chicago, Illinois, August 30, 1949; admitted to bar, 1974, Illinois; U.S. District Court, Northern and Central Districts of Illinois; U.S. Court of Appeals, Seventh Circuit. *Education:* DePaul University (B.S.C., 1971); Duke University (J.D., 1974). Blue Key. *Member:* American Bar Association. ***PRACTICE AREAS:*** Business Law; Banks and Banking; Commercial Litigation; Commercial Foreclosure; Creditors Rights; Bankruptcy. ***Email:*** elesniak@burkelaw.com

IRA M. LEVIN, born Baltimore, Maryland, May 17, 1960; admitted to bar, 1986, Illinois. *Education:* University of Miami (B.B.A., cum laude, 1982); Illinois Institute of Technology, Chicago-Kent College of Law (J.D., 1986). *Member:* Chicago, Illinois State and American Bar Associations. ***PRACTICE AREAS:*** Commercial Litigation; Motor Vehicle Franchise Litigation. ***Email:*** ilevin@burkelaw.com

GEORGE J. LYNCH, born Chicago, Illinois, January 7, 1948; admitted to bar, 1973, Illinois and U.S. District Court, Northern District of Illinois; U.S. Court of Appeals for the Seventh Circuit. *Education:* University of Dayton (B.A., 1970); University of Notre Dame (J.D., 1973). Assistant State's Attorney, Cook County, 1973-1977. ***PRACTICE AREAS:*** Litigation; Criminal Law; Labor Law; Eminent Domain; Municipal Law. ***Email:*** glynch@burkelaw.com

KAREN K. MACKAY, born Annapolis, Maryland, August 15, 1944; admitted to bar, 1971, Illinois. *Education:* Smith College (B.A., magna cum laude, 1966); University of Michigan (J.D., 1971) Phi Beta Kappa. *Member:* Chicago (Chair, Trust Law Committee, 1987-1988) and American Bar Associations; Chicago Estate Planning Council (Director, 1990-1997; President, 1995-1996; Member, Board of Directors, 1996-1998). Fellow, American College of Trust and Estate Counsel. ***PRACTICE AREAS:*** Trusts and Estates; Family Business Law; Tax Exempt Organization Law. ***Email:*** kmackay@burkelaw.com

CHRISTOPHER R. MANNING, born River Forest, Illinois, April 21, 1949; admitted to bar, 1974, Illinois and U.S. District Court, Northern District of Illinois. *Education:* Georgetown University (A.B., 1971); University of Chicago Law School (J.D., 1974). Phi Beta Kappa. Attorney, Textron, Inc., 1978-1980. Member, Illinois Secretary of State Business Corporation Acts Advisory Committee, 1989-1997. ***PRACTICE AREAS:*** Business Law; Corporate Law; Biotechnology; Securities Law; Public Finance. ***Email:*** cmanning@burkelaw.com

MICHAEL J. MARTIN, born Evergreen Park, Illinois, January 29, 1960; admitted to bar, 1985, Illinois. *Education:* University of Notre Dame (B.A., with honors, 1982); Loyola University of Chicago School of Law (J.D., cum laude, 1985). Articles Editor, Loyola University Law Journal, 1984-1985. Author: "Prejudgment Interest: Implementing Its Compensatory Purpose," 15 Loyola University of Chicago Law Journal 541, 1984. *Member:* International Council of Shopping Centers. ***PRACTICE AREAS:*** Commercial Real Estate; Contracts; Corporate Law; Commercial Transactions. ***Email:*** mmartin@burkelaw.com

(This Listing Continued)

STEPHEN R. MEINERTZHAGEN, born Newport, Rhode Island, August 8, 1968; admitted to bar, 1994, Illinois. *Education:* Wesleyan University (B.A., with departmental honors, 1990); University of Illinois (J.D., cum laude, 1994). *Member:* Federal Trial Bar. ***PRACTICE AREAS:*** Commercial Litigation; Class Actions; Consumer Lending. ***Email:*** smeinertzhagen@burkelaw.com

FREDERIC A. MENDELSOHN, born Chicago, Illinois, May 20, 1960; admitted to bar, 1986, Wisconsin and Illinois; 1991, U.S. District Court, Northern District of Illinois including Trial Bar. *Education:* Brandeis University (B.A., cum laude, honors in Economics, 1983); Marquette University (J.D., 1986); John Marshall Law School (L.L.M., Taxation, 1992). *Member:* Chicago and Illinois State Bar Associations. ***Email:*** fmendelsohn@burkelaw.com

JONATHAN W. MICHAEL, born Hialeah, Florida, July 19, 1968; admitted to bar, 1994, Florida; 1995, Illinois; 1996, U.S. District Court, Southern District of Florida and U.S. Tax Court; 1998, District of Columbia. *Education:* Miami University (B.S., 1990); University of Miami (J.D., cum laude, 1994); New York University (LL.M., in Taxation, 1995). *Member:* Chicago and Illinois State Bar Associations; The Florida Bar; The District of Columbia Bar. ***PRACTICE AREAS:*** Internet Commerce; Estate Planning; Taxation; Business Planning. ***Email:*** jmichael@burkelaw.com

THOMAS W. MURPHY, born Chicago, Illinois, January 8, 1954; admitted to bar, 1977, Illinois; 1978, U.S. District Court, Northern District of Illinois, U.S. Tax Court and U.S. Claims Court; 1984, New York. *Education:* Georgetown University (B.A.B.S., 1974); John Marshall Law School (J.D., with distinction, 1977). Instructor, John Marshall Law School, 1980-1985. Member of the Board of Directors, Colonial Bank, 1987-1993. Member of the Board of Directors, Archbishop Weber High School, 1998-1999. Speaker, National Association of Realtor's Radio Program. Legal Editorial Consultant, *Journal of Property Management,* National Association of Realtors. ***PRACTICE AREAS:*** Banking; Real Estate; Commercial Law; Business Law. ***Email:*** tmurphy@burkelaw.com

LEANN PEDERSEN POPE, born Harlan, Iowa, June 16, 1957; admitted to bar, 1983, Illinois; U.S. District Court, Northern District of Illinois including Trial Bar; U.S. Court of Appeals, First, Second, Seventh, Ninth and Eleventh Circuits. *Education:* Carthage College (B.A., 1979); The John Marshall Law School (J.D., with high honors, 1983). *Member:* American Bar Association (Class Actions and Derivative Suits Committee, Litigation Section); Mortgage Bankers Association of America (Legal Issues Committee). ***REPORTED CASES:*** Hosfield v. Weyerhaeuser Mortg. Co., 2003 WL 22229255 (N.D.Ill., Sep 26, 2003); Mongelli v. Columbia Equities, Ltd., 2003 WL 22229256 (N.D.Ill., Sep 26, 2003); Lester v. Percudani, - F.R.D. -, 2003 WL 221327890 (M.D.Pa., Sep 15, 2003); Stein v. JP Morgan Chase Bank, - F.Supp.2d -, 2003 WL 22016927 (S.D.N.Y., Aug 27, 2003); Mann v. Chase Manhattan Mortgage Corp., 2002 WL 32157516 (N.D. Ill. Aug 28, 2001), affirmed, Mann v. Chase Manhattan Mortg. Corp., 316 F.3d 1 (1st Cir. 2003) (argued); Lester v. Percudani, 2002 WL 1460763 (M.D.Pa., Apr 18, 2002); Ploog v. Homeside Lending, Inc., 2001 WL 987889 (N.D.Ill., Aug 28, 2001); Westfall v. Chase Lincoln First Bank, N.A., 258 A.D.2d 299, 685 N.Y.S.2d 181 (1st Dept. 1999) (argued). ***PRACTICE AREAS:*** Business Litigation; Mortgage Banking; Class Action Defense. ***Email:*** lpope@burkelaw.com

KENNETH H. RICHMAN, born Chicago, Illinois, March 28, 1947; admitted to bar, 1973, Wisconsin and Illinois. *Education:* Bradley University (B.S., 1969); University of Wisconsin-Madison (J.D., 1973). *Member:* Illinois State Bar Association. ***Email:*** krichman@burkelaw.com

GERARD D. RING, born Evergreen Park, Illinois, November 2, 1957; admitted to bar, 1986, Illinois; U.S. District Court, Northern District of Illinois including Trial Bar. *Education:* University of Illinois at Chicago (B.A., 1980); The John Marshall Law School (J.D., with high distinction, 1986). Order of John Marshall. Staff Editor, The John Marshall Law Review, 1985-1986. Author: "Unmasking the Criminal: A Proposal to Prevent the Accessibility of False Identification," 18 The John Marshall Law Review 789, 1985; "Reorganization and Liquidation in Landlord/Tenant Relationships," Commercial Landlord/Tenant Practice, Illinois Institute for Continuing Legal Education, 1990. Faculty Advisor, The John Marshall Law School Trial Advocacy Competition (The Association of Trial Lawyers of America Regionals), 1993-1998. Member, Board of Education, Palos Consolidated School District 118, 1994-1995; 2001-2003. *Member:* Chicago Bar Association; Federal Trial Bar. ***PRACTICE AREAS:*** Commercial Litigation; Trusts and Estates Litigation; Real Estate Litigation; Bankruptcy. ***Email:*** gring@burkelaw.com

KEVIN J. RYAN, born Fort Wayne, Indiana, October 10, 1956; admitted to bar, 1987, Illinois. *Education:* University of Notre Dame (B.S., 1979); University of Chicago (M.B.A., 1981); Illinois Institute of Technology/Chicago-Kent College of Law (J.D., 1987). Local School Council, Lenart Regional Gifted Center, 1996-2003. ***PRACTICE AREAS:*** Health Care Law; Corporate Law. ***Email:*** kryan@burkelaw.com

MARTIN P. RYAN, born Chicago, Illinois, January 29, 1967; admitted to bar, 1992, Illinois and U.S. District Court, Northern District of Illinois. *Education:* University of Illinois (B.A., Economics, 1989); Loyola University (J.D., 1992). Certified Public Accountant, Illinois, 1989—. Past Member: American Institute of Certified Public Accountants; Illinois Certified Public Accountants Society. *Member:* Chicago Bar Association (Member, Committees on: Trust Law; Assest Protection); Chicago Estate Planning Council; Little Brothers - Friends of the Elderly, Chicago (Member, Board of Directors). ***PRACTICE AREAS:*** Estate Planning; Taxation; Closely Held Businesses; Trusts and Estates. ***Email:*** mryan@burkelaw.com

JAMES A. SERRITELLA, born Chicago, Illinois, July 8, 1942; admitted to bar, 1971, Illinois and U.S. District Court, Northern District of Illinois, Eastern Division; 1976, U.S. Supreme Court; 1985, U.S. Tax Court; 1992, U.S. Court of Appeals, Sixth Circuit; 1993, U.S. Court of Appeals, Seventh Circuit; 1995, U.S. Court of Appeals, Fifth Circuit; 1996, U.S. Court of Appeals, Ninth Circuit. *Education:* State University of New York (St. Charles Seminary, B.A., 1965); Pontifical Gregorian University, Rome, Italy (B.A., 1966); University of Chicago (M.A., 1968; J.D., 1971). Partner, Kirkland & Ellis, Chicago, Illinois, 1978. Senior Partner, Reuben & Proctor, Chicago, Illinois, 1978-1986. Partner, Mayer, Brown & Platt, Chicago, Illinois, 1986-1997. Recipient: Outstanding Leaders Award, Carmelite Order, 1979; John Courtney Murray Award, DePaul University College of Law, 1988; *Pax et Bonum* Award, St. Peter's Church, Franciscan Friars, 1992; Honorary Doctor of Laws Degree, North Park College and Theological Seminary, 1996; *Rerum Novarum* Award of St. Joseph's Seminary, 1999. Member: Business Executives in Economic Justice, 1988—; Cook County State's Attorney's Task Force on the Foregoing of Life-Sustaining Treatment, 1989; North American College Board of Advisors, 1990-1992; Statewide Citizens' Committee on Child Abuse and Neglect, 1988-1994. Member, Board of Trustees, St. Xavier College, 1987-1992. Member, De Paul University College of Law Dean's Visiting Committee, 1982—. Chairman of Advisory Committee, De Paul University College of Law Center for Church/State Studies, 1982—. Member, Board of Advisors, Alzheimer's Center, Rush-Presbyterian-St. Luke's Medical Center, 1990—. Founder and Chairman of the Board, The Chicago Center for Peace Studies, 1990-1996. Member: Advisory Committee on Church, State and Taxation, National Conference of Christians and Jews; Law and Legislation Committee, National Catholic Cemetery Conference; The Park Ridge Center, Catholic Health Association; American Association of Homes for the Aging. Board of Governors, Illinois State Bar Association, 1982-1986. Member, Board of Directors, Catholic Lawyers Guild, 1982—. *Member:* Chicago, Illinois State and American Bar Associations; Canon Law Society of America; Diocesan Attorneys Association (Member, Executive Committee); The National Health Lawyers Association. Charter Fellow: Illinois Bar Foundation. Fellow, American Bar Foundation. ***PRACTICE AREAS:*** General Practice; Constitutional Law; Church and State; Religious Institutions; Tax Exempt Organizations. ***Email:*** jserritella@burkelaw.com

TERRENCE W. STEIN, admitted to bar, 1986, Wisconsin; 1988, Illinois. *Education:* University of Wisconsin (B.B.A., 1983); Harvard Law School (J.D., 1986). ***PRACTICE AREAS:*** Taxation; Executive Compensation; Partnership Law; Limited Liability Company Law; Mergers, Acquisitions and Divestitures. ***Email:*** tstein@burkelaw.com

JOHN P. STEPHENS, born Fort Jackson, South Carolina, March 20, 1956; admitted to bar, 1983, Illinois. *Education:* University of Notre Dame (B.A., cum laude, 1978; J.D., 1982). Omicron Delta Epsilon. *Member:* Chicago and Illinois State Bar Associations. ***PRACTICE AREAS:*** Real Estate Law; Construction Law; Zoning, Planning and Land Use. ***Email:*** jstephens@burkelaw.com

MARK O. STERN, born Highland Park, Illinois, September 20, 1972; admitted to bar, 1996, Illinois; 1997, U.S. District Court, Central District of Illinois; 2002, U.S. Tax Court and U.S. Court of Appeals, Seventh Circuit; 2003, U.S. District Court, Northern District of Illinois. *Education:* University of Illinois (B.A., 1993); University of Chicago (J.D., 1996). *Member:* Du Page County, Sangamon County and Illinois State Bar Associations; Federalist Society. ***PRACTICE AREAS:*** Corporate Law. ***Email:*** mstern@burkelaw.com

MICHAEL S. VIRGIL, born Elgin, Illinois, November 14, 1942; admitted to bar, 1967, Illinois. *Education:* Valparaiso University (B.A., with distinction, 1964; J.D., 1967). Phi Alpha Delta. Executive Editor, Valparaiso University Law Review, 1966-1967. Author: Chapter 19, *Withholding Tax,* in Illinois Tax Service, Matthew Bender, 1985. Teaching Associate, Valparaiso School of Law, 1967-1969. *Member:* Chicago Bar Association (Member, Committee on Employee Benefits, 1982—). ***PRACTICE AREAS:*** ERISA; Employee Benefits; Business; Estate Planning. ***Email:*** mvirgil@burkelaw.com

STEPHEN C. VORIS, born Chicago, Illinois, January 5, 1954; admitted to bar, 1979, Illinois, U.S. District Court, Northern District of Illinois and Eastern District of Michigan and U.S. Court of Appeals, Seventh Circuit; 1986, U.S. Supreme Court. *Education:* Boston College (A.B., cum laude, 1976); DePaul University College of Law (J.D., 1979). Editor, DePaul Law Review, 1979. Arbitrator, National Futures Association. *Member:* Chicago (Member, Litigation Committee, 1979—), Seventh Circuit and American (Member, Litigation Section) Bar Associations; Securities Industry Association; Chicagoland Chamber of Commerce (Member, Board of Directors). ***PRACTICE AREAS:*** Litigation; Arbitration; Securities; Commodities; Corporate. ***Email:*** svoris@burkelaw.com

DOUGLAS E. WAMBACH, born Chicago, Illinois, February 4, 1956; admitted to bar, 1981, Illinois; 1982, Arizona. *Education:* Georgetown University (B.S., cum laude, 1978; J.D., 1981). *Member:* Chicago Bar Association (Member: Real Estate Law Committee; Real Estate Finance Subcommittee). ***PRACTICE AREAS:*** Real Estate Law; Municipal Law; Zoning, Planning and Land Use. ***Email:*** dwambach@burkelaw.com

JEFFREY D. WARREN, born Chicago, Illinois, December 27, 1946; admitted to bar, 1972, Illinois and U.S. District Court, Northern District of Illinois; 1977, U.S. Court of Appeals, Seventh Circuit; 1978, U.S. Supreme Court. *Education:* Carleton College and Northwestern University (B.A., 1968); University of Chicago Law School (J.D., 1972). *Member:* Illinois Mortgage Bankers Association (Chairman, Legislative Committee); Mortgage Bankers Association of America (Member, Legal Issues Committee and Regulatory Compliance Committee); International Council of Shopping Centers. ***PRACTICE AREAS:*** Commercial Real Estate; Finance; Commercial Transactions; Closely Held Corporations. ***Email:*** jwarren@burkelaw.com

GREGORY M. WINTERS, born Chicago, Illinois, May 17, 1969; admitted to bar, 1994, Illinois; 1997, U.S. Tax Court. *Education:* University of Illinois (B.S., 1991); Loyola University (J.D., 1994). Certified Public Accountant, Illinois, 1991. ***PRACTICE AREAS:*** Taxation; Estate Planning; Corporate Law. ***Email:*** gwinters@burkelaw.com

MELANIE L. WITT, born Chicago, Illinois, February 2, 1963; admitted to bar, 1992, Illinois. *Education:* University of Michigan (B.A., 1986); University of Notre Dame (J.D., 1991); DePaul University (LL.M. in Taxation, 1993). ***PRACTICE AREAS:*** Estate Planning; Trusts and Estates. ***Email:*** mwitt@burkelaw.com

---

NORA E. FLAHERTY, born Chicago, Illinois, December 2, 1976; admitted to bar, 2003, Illinois. *Education:* Marquette University (B.A., 1999); University of Illinois (J.D., 2003). Phi Alpha Delta. *Member:* Chicago, Illinois State and American Bar Associations. ***PRACTICE AREAS:*** Commercial Litigation.

JOHN G. FOGARTY, JR., born Springfield, Illinois, June 14, 1969; admitted to bar, 1999, Illinois. *Education:* Northwestern University (B.S., Political Science, International Studies, 1991); Chicago-Kent College of Law (J.D., 1999). *Member:* Chicago and Illinois State Bar Associations. ***PRACTICE AREAS:*** Commercial Litigation; Employment Law; Election Law. ***Email:*** jfogarty@burkelaw.com

REBECCA HEINZ HUSTON, born Evanston, Illinois, October 7, 1976; admitted to bar, 2003, Illinois. *Education:* University of Wisconsin at Madison (B.A., with distinction,

(This Listing Continued)

BURKE, WARREN, MACKAY & SERRITELLA, P.C., Chicago—Continued

1998); University of Illinois (J.D., cum laude, 2003). *Member:* Chicago and American Bar Associations. ***PRACTICE AREAS:*** Real Estate; Corporate Law. ***Email:*** rheinzhuston@burkelaw.com

KRISTIN J. LEMMON, born July 22, 1976; admitted to bar, 2001, Illinois. *Education:* Augustana College (B.A., magna cum laude, 1998); Loyola University (J.D., cum laude, 2001). Phi Beta Kappa; Omicron Delta Kappa. *Member:* Chicago and American Bar Associations. ***REPORTED CASES:*** Brownlow v. Richards, 328 Ill.App.3d 833, 767 N.E.2d 482, 263 Ill.Dec. 31, Ill.App. 1 Dist., Mar 22, 2002. ***PRACTICE AREAS:*** Litigation; Labor and Employment. ***Email:*** klemmon@burkelaw.com

ALEXANDER D. MARKS, born Sterling, Illinois, January 12, 1979; (admission pending). *Education:* University of Illinois (B.S. in Business Administration, with high honors, 1997; J.D., magna cum laude, 2001). ***PRACTICE AREAS:*** Litigation; Labor and Employment. ***Email:*** amarks@burkelaw.com

ANDREW S. PAINE, born Los Alamos, New Mexico, June 20, 1973; admitted to bar, 1998, Illinois and U.S. District Court, Northern District of Illinois. *Education:* University of Michigan (B.A., with distinction, 1995); Indiana University (J.D., cum laude, 1998). University of Michigan Angell Scholar. Commissioner, City of Evanston, Illinois, Civil Service Commission, 2001—. Author, "Religious Fundamentalism and Legal Systems: Methods and Rationales in the Fight to Control the Political Apparatus," Indiana Journal of Global Legal Studies, vol. 5, p 263. *Member:* Chicago and Illinois State Bar Associations. ***PRACTICE AREAS:*** Commercial Litigation; Bankruptcy; Class Actions; Complex and Multi-District Litigation; Mortgages; Municipal Law. ***Email:*** apaine@burkelaw.com

CHRISTOPHER J. SCHAFER, born Ravenna, Ohio, October 9, 1976; admitted to bar, 2002, California, U.S. District Court, Northern District California and U.S. Court of Appeals, Ninth Circuit; 2004, Illinois. *Education:* University of Oklahoma (B.S., magna cum laude, 1999); University of California at Berkeley, Boalt Hall (J.D., 2002). *Member:* Illinois State Bar Association; State Bar of California.

BRADLEY I. SCHECTER, born Skokie, Illinois, July 24, 1976; admitted to bar, 2001, Illinois. *Education:* Miami University (B.A., magna cum laude, 1998); University of Illinois (J.D., magna cum laude, 2001). Phi Beta Kappa. *Member:* Chicago, Illinois State and American Bar Associations. ***PRACTICE AREAS:*** Litigation; Commercial Litigation; Constitutional Law; Church and State.

BRETT D. SMITH, born Skokie, Illinois, November 19, 1974; admitted to bar, 1999, Illinois. *Education:* University of Illinois (B.S., Finance, 1996); Loyola University School of Law (J.D., cum laude, 1999). Member, Chicago Real Estate Council. *Member:* Chicago and Illinois State Bar Associations. ***PRACTICE AREAS:*** Real Estate; Corporate Law; Sports Law; Zoning, Planning and Land Use. ***Email:*** bsmith@burkelaw.com

KIMBERLY A. SMITH, born Munster, Indiana, August 28, 1977; admitted to bar, 2002, Illinois. *Education:* Indiana University, Bloomington (B.A., high distinction, 1999; J.D., cum laude, 2002). Phi Beta Kappa. *Member:* Chicago and American Bar Associations. ***PRACTICE AREAS:*** Litigation; Employment Law. ***Email:*** ksmith@burkelaw.com

DANIELLE J. SZUKALA, admitted to bar, 1999, Illinois. *Education:* University of Iowa (B.A., 1996; J.D., 1999). *Member:* Chicago Bar Association. ***PRACTICE AREAS:*** Class Action Defense; Commercial Litigation. ***Email:*** dszukala@burkelaw.com

JOSEPH E. VON MEIER, born Ann Arbor, Michigan, September 14, 1972; admitted to bar, 2002, Illinois and Wisconsin. *Education:* University of Michigan (B.B.A., 1995); University of Wisconsin (J.D., cum laude, 2002). *Member:* Chicago and Illinois State Bar Associations; State Bar of Wisconsin. ***PRACTICE AREAS:*** Real Estate; Corporate Law. ***Email:*** jmeiers@burkelaw.com

CHRISTINA M. YEAGER, born Cherry Point, North Carolina, December 12, 1972; admitted to bar, 1999, Florida and U.S. District Court, Middle District of Florida; 2002, Illinois; 2003, U.S. District Court, Northern District of Illinois; 2004, U.S. District Court, Central and Southern Districts of Illinois. *Education:* University of Florida (B.A. in Political Science and Russian, with honors, 1993); University of Florida Levin College of Law (J.D., with honors, 1999). *Member:* Chicago, Illinois State and American Bar Associations. ***PRACTICE AREAS:*** Commercial Litigation; Product Liability; Employment Defense. ***Email:*** cyeager@burkelaw.com

BUTLER RUBIN SALTARELLI & BOYD LLP

70 WEST MADISON STREET, SUITE 1800
CHICAGO, ILLINOIS 60602
Telephone: 312-444-9660
Fax: 312-444-9287
Email: info@butlerrubin.com
URL: http://www.butlerrubin.com

Complex Commercial Litigation, including Trial, Appellate and Administrative Proceedings. Insurance Coverage and Reinsurance Arbitration and Litigation, Employment, Antitrust, Franchise and Distribution, Intellectual Property Litigation, Securities Litigation, and Products Liability and Class Action, Legacy Liability Litigation and Mass Tort. Corporate and Business Matters, including Finance, Venture Capital, Mergers and Acquisitions, Contracts, Executive Employment Law, Separation Agreements, Real Estate and Land Use.

FIRM PROFILE: Since the firm's inception in 1980, Butler, Rubin has developed a reputation for providing the quality of representation expected from the largest firms with the responsive and cost-effective service that characterizes the best small firms. Attracting lawyers from Chicago's top firms and the nation's finest law schools, the firm has carefully assembled a talented group of attorneys with sound judgment and exceptional skills. The firm's diverse and growing client base includes many national and multinational publicly held enterprises, family and entrepreneurial businesses, and individuals.

(This Listing Continued)

PARTNERS

LOUIS J. AURICHIO, born Bronx, New York, March 22, 1961; admitted to bar, 1989, California; 1993, Illinois and U.S. District Court, Northern District of Illinois including Trial Bar. *Education:* Connecticut College (1979-1981); Colgate University (B.A., magna cum laude, 1984); Northwestern University (J.D., 1989). Phi Beta Kappa. Note and Comment Editor, Northwestern University Law Review. U.S. Department of Justice Honor Program, Commercial Litigation Branch, Civil Division, 1989-1991. Law Clerk to the Honorable James B. Zagel, U.S. District Court, Northern District of Illinois, 1991-1993. *Member:* Chicago and American Bar Associations. ***PRACTICE AREAS:*** Reinsurance Law; Commercial Litigation; Appellate Litigation. ***Email:*** laurichio@butlerrubin.com

IRA J. BELCOVE, born Chicago, Illinois, March 31, 1963; admitted to bar, 1987, Illinois; 1988, U.S. District Court, Northern District of Illinois including Trial Bar; 1993, U.S. Court of Appeals, Seventh Circuit. *Education:* Columbia University (B.A., summa cum laude, 1984); University of Chicago (J.D., 1987). Phi Beta Kappa. Law Clerk to Honorable Bernard M. Decker, Northern District of Illinois, 1987-1988. Secretary-Treasurer, International Association of Insurance Law (U.S. Chapter), 1990-1994. ***PRACTICE AREAS:*** Reinsurance Arbitration; Litigation; Commercial Litigation; Appellate Litigation. ***Email:*** ibelcove@butlerrubin.com

R. DOUGLASS BOND, born Amsterdam, N.Y., December 20, 1954; admitted to bar, 1990, Illinois and U.S. District Court, Northern District of Illinois; 1992, U.S. Court of Appeals, Seventh Circuit. *Education:* Middlebury College (B.A., cum laude, highest honors, 1977); Brown University (M.A.T., 1978); University of Chicago (M.A., 1985); University of Michigan (J.D., cum laude, 1990). Articles Editor, Michigan Law Review. *Member:* Chicago and Illinois State Bar Associations. ***PRACTICE AREAS:*** Reinsurance Law; Insurance Insolvency; Commercial Litigation; Appellate Litigation. ***Email:*** dbond@butlerrubin.com

CRAIG T. BOYD, born Teaneck, New Jersey, March 1, 1947; admitted to bar, 1973, Illinois. *Education:* Brown University (B.S. Eng., cum laude, 1969); Northwestern University (M.B.A., Finance, with distinction, 1973; J.D., cum laude, 1973). Beta Gamma Sigma; Order of the Coif. *Member:* Chicago Bar Association. ***PRACTICE AREAS:*** General Business Law; Finance; Venture Capital; Mergers and Acquisitions; Contracts; Executive Employment Law; Separation Agreements. ***Email:*** cboyd@butlerrubin.com

RANDI L. ELLIAS, born New York, N.Y., July 24, 1971; admitted to bar, 1996, Illinois and U.S. District Court, Northern District of Illinois; 1999, Oregon. *Education:* Franklin & Marshall College (B.A., cum laude, 1993) Marshall Scholar; Phi Beta Kappa; Northwestern University (J.D., cum laude, 1996). Wigmore Scholar. Note and Comment Editor, Journal of Criminal Law and Criminology, 1995-1996. ***PRACTICE AREAS:*** Commercial Litigation; Reinsurance Law; Employment Litigation. ***Email:*** rellias@butlerrubin.com

KIRK T. HARTLEY, born Champaign, Illinois; admitted to bar, 1983, Illinois and U.S. District Court, Northern District of Illinois, including Trial Bar; 1987, U.S. Supreme Court. *Education:* University of Illinois (B.S., 1980); The John Marshall Law School (J.D., with honors, 1983). Managing Editor, The John Marshall Law Review, 1982-1983. Law Clerk to the Honorable Howard C. Ryan, Justice, Supreme Court of Illinois, 1983-1984. *Member:* Illinois State and American Bar Associations; Defense Research Institute. ***PRACTICE AREAS:*** Legacy Liabilities; Toxic Torts; Mass Torts; Products Liability; Class Action Litigation; Commercial Litigation; Alternative Dispute Resolution. ***Email:*** khartley@butlerrubin.com

DAVID I. HERBST, born Chicago, Illinois, September 22, 1940; admitted to bar, 1964, Illinois; 1966, U.S. District Court, Northern District of Illinois including Trial Bar; 1975, U.S. Court of Appeals, Seventh Circuit; 1989, U.S. Court of Appeals, 11th Circuit and U.S. District Court, Eastern District of Wisconsin. *Education:* University of Illinois (B.A., 1961); University of Chicago (J.D., 1964). *Member:* Chicago, Illinois State and American Bar Associations. ***PRACTICE AREAS:*** Commercial Litigation. ***Email:*** dherbst@butlerrubin.com

ROBERT N. HERMES, born Evanston, Illinois, October 29, 1954; admitted to bar, 1979, Illinois and U.S. District Court, Northern District of Illinois including Trial Bar; 1983, U.S. District Court, Northern District of California; 1989, U.S. Court of Appeals, Seventh Circuit; 1990, U.S. District Court, Eastern District of Wisconsin; 1996, U.S. Court of Appeals, Fifth Circuit. *Education:* Indiana University (B.A., 1976); De Paul University (J.D., 1979). Editor-in-Chief, De Paul Law Review, 1978-1979. Faculty Member, National Institute of Trial Advocacy, 1997. *Member:* Chicago and American Bar Associations. ***PRACTICE AREAS:*** Commercial Litigation; Reinsurance Law; Insurance Insolvency; Employment Law; Employment Litigation. ***Email:*** rhermes@butlerrubin.com

PATRICK J. LAMB, born Detroit, Michigan, May 7, 1957; admitted to bar, 1982, Illinois and U.S. District Court, Northern District of Illinois, including Trial Bar; 1983, U.S. Court of Appeals, Seventh Circuit; 1987, U.S. Supreme Court; 1991, U.S. Court of Appeals, Eleventh Circuit. *Education:* Northwestern University (B.S., with distinction, 1978); University of Michigan (J.D., cum laude, 1982). *Member:* Chicago and American Bar Associations; International Association of Defense Counsel; Economic Club of Chicago. ***PRACTICE AREAS:*** Legacy Liabilities; Toxic Torts; Business Litigation; Business Fraud; Products Liability. ***Email:*** plamb@butlerrubin.com

CATHERINE E. LAMSENS, born Winter Park, Florida, December 30, 1966; admitted to bar, 1996, Illinois; 1997, U.S. District Court, Northern District of Illinois, including Trial Bar; 2000, U.S. Court of Appeals, Seventh Circuit. *Education:* Duke University (B.A., 1988); Northwestern University School of Law (J.D., 1996). Member: National Trial Team, Northwestern University, 1994-1996. ***PRACTICE AREAS:*** Commercial Litigation; Reinsurance Law; Products Liability. ***Email:*** clamsens@butlerrubin.com

JAMES A. MORSCH, born LaGrange, Illinois, August 14, 1965; admitted to bar, 1992, Illinois and U.S. District Court, Northern District of Illinois including Trial Bar; 1993, U.S. Court of Appeals, Seventh and Third Circuits. *Education:* University of Notre Dame (B.A., cum laude, 1987); Northwestern University (J.D., 1992). Book Review Editor, Journal of Criminal Law and Criminology, 1991-1992. Author: "The Problem of Motive in Hate Crimes Statutes," Journal of Criminal Law and Criminology, Winter 1992. *Member:* Chicago and American (Member, Section on Antitrust Law) Bar Associations. ***LANGUAGES:*** Spanish. ***PRACTICE AREAS:*** Commercial Litigation; Antitrust; Franchise Distribution Law. ***Email:*** jmorsch@butlerrubin.com

(This Listing Continued)

KEVIN J. O'BRIEN, born Hartford, Connecticut, July 5, 1961; admitted to bar, 1986, Illinois; 1987, U.S. District Court, Northern District of Illinois including Trial Bar. *Education:* University of Notre Dame (B.A., with high honors, 1983); University of Chicago (J.D., with honors, 1986). Phi Beta Kappa. Associate Editor, University of Chicago Law Review, 1985-1986. Law Clerk to the Honorable John F. Grady, U.S. District Court, Northern District of Illinois, 1986-1987. ***PRACTICE AREAS:*** Commercial Litigation; Reinsurance Law; Environmental Law. ***Email:*** kobrien@butlerrubin.com

JAMES I. RUBIN, born Chicago, Illinois, March 16, 1946; admitted to bar, 1971, Illinois, U.S. District Court, Northern District of Illinois including Trial Bar and U.S. Court of Appeals, Seventh Circuit; 1983, U.S. District Court, Northern District of California and U.S. Supreme Court. *Education:* University of Illinois (A.B., 1967); Loyola University (J.D., 1971). Member, Loyola University Law Review, 1970-1971. Assistant Attorney General, State of Illinois, 1971-1974. Assistant Chief, Environmental Division, 1973-1974. *Member:* Illinois State and American Bar Associations; Chicago Council of Lawyers. ***PRACTICE AREAS:*** Commercial Litigation; Reinsurance Law. ***Email:*** jrubin@butlerrubin.com

GERALD G. SALTARELLI, born Buffalo, New York, October 17, 1947; admitted to bar, 1973, Illinois and U.S. District Court, Northern District of Illinois including Trial Bar; 1980, U.S. District Court, Eastern District of Wisconsin and Central District of Illinois; 1982, U.S. Court of Appeals, Seventh Circuit. *Education:* Princeton University (A.B., 1969); State University of New York at Buffalo (M.S., 1970); University of Chicago (J.D., 1973). Associate Editor, University of Chicago Law Review, 1972-1973. *Member:* Chicago and American (Member, Sections on: Antitrust Law and Litigation) Bar Associations. ***PRACTICE AREAS:*** Toxic Torts; Commercial Litigation; Antitrust; Arbitration. ***Email:*** gsaltarelli@butlerrubin.com

TERESA SNIDER, born Des Plaines, Illinois, May 17, 1967; admitted to bar, 1992, Illinois and U.S. District Court, Northern District of Illinois; 2000, U.S. Court of Appeals, Seventh Circuit. *Education:* University of Illinois (B.A., summa cum laude, 1989); University of Michigan (J.D., magna cum laude, 1992). Phi Beta Kappa; Order of the Coif. Executive Editor, Michigan Journal of International Law, 1991-1992. Law Clerk to the Honorable Harry D. Leinenweber, U.S. District Court, Northern District of Illinois, 1993. *Member:* Chicago and American Bar Associations. ***PRACTICE AREAS:*** Commercial Litigation; Insurance Insolvency; Reinsurance Law. ***Email:*** tsnider@butlerrubin.com

MICHAEL A. STICK, born Kitty Hawk, North Carolina, June 2, 1954; admitted to bar, 1981, Illinois; 1982, U.S. District Court, Northern District of Illinois including Trial Bar; 1983, U.S. Court of Appeals, Seventh Circuit; 1986, U.S. Court of Appeals, Eighth Circuit. *Education:* Davidson College (B.A., 1976); University of North Carolina (J.D., with honors, 1981). Member, University of North Carolina Law Review, 1979-1980. *Member:* Chicago and American Bar Associations. ***PRACTICE AREAS:*** Commercial Litigation; Business Fraud; Unfair Competition; Trade Secrets; Trademark Litigation. ***Email:*** mstick@butlerrubin.com

HAROLD C. WHEELER, born Oak Ridge, Tennessee, September 11, 1945; admitted to bar, 1974, Illinois; U.S. District Court, Northern District of Illinois, including Trial Bar; U.S. Court of Appeals, Second, Fifth, Seventh, Ninth and Eleventh Circuits; Federal Circuit Court of Appeals; U.S. Supreme Court. *Education:* Harvard University (A.B., 1967); University of Virginia (J.D., 1974). Managing Editor, Virginia Journal of International Law, 1973-1974. *Member:* Chicago and American Bar Associations. ***PRACTICE AREAS:*** Commercial Litigation; Reinsurance Law. ***Email:*** hwheeler@butlerrubin.com

SENIOR COUNSEL

JULIE P. SHELTON, born Minneapolis, Minnesota, March 13, 1955; admitted to bar, 1982, Illinois, U.S. District Court, Northern District of Illinois; 1989, Wisconsin and U.S. District Court, Central District of Illinois. *Education:* Hampshire College (B.S., 1977); DePaul University (J.D., 1982). Member, De Paul Law Review, 1981-1982. *Member:* Chicago, American and International Bar Associations. ***LANGUAGES:*** Italian. ***PRACTICE AREAS:*** Litigation; Products Liability; Legacy Liabilities. ***Email:*** jshelton@butlerrubin.com

OF COUNSEL

FRANK L. BUTLER, born Chicago, Illinois, December 29, 1937; admitted to bar, 1965, Illinois and U.S. District Court, Northern District of Illinois including Trial Bar; 1977, U.S. Supreme Court and U.S. Court of Appeals, Seventh Circuit; 1981, U.S. Court of Appeals, Second Circuit. *Education:* Loyola University (B.S., cum laude, 1961; J.D., cum laude, 1965). Editor-in-Chief, Loyola University Law Review, 1964-1965. Adjunct Faculty, Trial Practice, Northwestern University School of Law, 1981-1984. *Member:* Chicago, Illinois State and American Bar Associations. ***PRACTICE AREAS:*** Commercial Litigation; Arbitration; Mediation. ***Email:*** fbutler@butlerrubin.com

BARBARA J. PUTTA, born Barrington, Illinois, November 22, 1946; admitted to bar, 1975, Illinois and U.S. District Court, Northern District of Illinois. *Education:* University of Illinois (B.A., magna cum laude, 1968); Columbia University (M.A., 1969); Northwestern University (J.D., cum laude, 1975). Notes and Comments Editor, Northwestern University Law Review, 1974-1975. City of Evanston Zoning Board of Appeals, 1995—, Economic Development Committee, 2002—. *Member:* American Bar Association. Fellow, American Bar Foundation. ***PRACTICE AREAS:*** Real Estate Law; Land Use; Computer Law; General Corporate Law. ***Email:*** bputta@butlerrubin.com

ASSOCIATES

JULIE RODRIGUEZ ALDORT, born Los Angeles, California, January 18, 1972; admitted to bar, 1999, California; 2000, Illinois. *Education:* Claremont McKenna College (B.A., magna cum laude, 1994); University of Michigan (J.D., cum laude, 1998). Associate and Contributing Editor, Michigan Law Review, 1995-1997; Note Editor, Michigan Journal of Race and Law. Law Clerk, the Hon. Joan B. Gottschall, U.S. District Court, Northern District of Illinois. ***PRACTICE AREAS:*** Commercial Litigation; Trademark Litigation; Reinsurance Law. ***Email:*** jaldort@butlerrubin.com

STEVEN A. BLOCK, born Milwaukee, Wisconsin, January 9, 1974; admitted to bar, 1999, Illinois. *Education:* Northwestern University (B.S., 1996; J.D., 1999). Editor, Journal of Criminal Law and Criminology, 1998-1999. *Member:* American Bar Association (Member, Antitrust Section). ***PRACTICE AREAS:*** Commercial Litigation; Antitrust. ***Email:*** sblock@butlerrubin.com

KAREN MINKOFF BORG, born Park Ridge, Illinois, April 12, 1966; admitted to bar, 1995, Illinois and U.S. District Court, Northern District of Illinois; 1999, U.S. District Court, Central District of Illinois. *Education:* Duke University (B.A., 1988); Chicago-Kent College of Law, Illinois Institute of Technology (J.D., with honors, 1995). ***PRACTICE AREAS:*** Legacy Liabilities; Toxic Torts; Products Liability; Commercial Litigation. ***Email:*** kborg@butlerrubin.com

KRISTEN E. BROWN, born McCall, Idaho, November 23, 1964; admitted to bar, 1998, Illinois, U.S. District Court, Northern District of Illinois including Trial Bar and U.S. District Court, Central District of Illinois; 1999, U.S. Court of Appeals, Seventh Circuit. *Education:* College of Idaho (B.A., cum laude, 1987); Northwestern University (J.D., cum laude, 1998). Senior Articles Editor, Journal of Criminal Law and Criminology, 1997-1998. ***PRACTICE AREAS:*** Commercial Litigation; Reinsurance Law. ***Email:*** kbrown@butlerrubin.com

JASON S. DUBNER, born Cincinnati, Ohio, May 3, 1970; admitted to bar, 1998, Illinois and U.S. District Court, Northern District of Illinois; 1999, District of Columbia. *Education:* Swarthmore College (B.A., 1992); University of Chicago (J.D., 1998). *Member:* The District of Columbia Bar; Chicago (Vice-Chairman, Antitrust Committee), Illinois State (Member, Antitrust and Unfair Competition Law Section Council) and American Bar Associations (Member, Antitrust Section). ***PRACTICE AREAS:*** Commercial Litigation; Antitrust; Franchise Distribution Law; Reinsurance Law. ***Email:*** jdubner@butlerrubin.com

ELIZABETH AWE HAFKEY, born Elgin, Illinois, April 29, 1971; admitted to bar, 1996, Illinois and U.S. District Court, Northern District of Illinois. *Education:* University of Illinois (B.A., with highest honors, 1993; J.D., magna cum laude, 1996). Phi Beta Kappa. Harno Scholar. Member, University of Illinois Law Review. *Member:* Chicago Bar Association. ***PRACTICE AREAS:*** Commercial Litigation. ***Email:*** ehafkey@butlerrubin.com

AMY B. KELLEY, born Ann Arbor, Michigan, January 2, 1973; admitted to bar, 1997, Illinois; 1998, U.S. District Court, Northern District of Illinois. *Education:* Northwestern University (B.A., 1994); University of Michigan (J.D., 1997). Contributing Editor, Michigan Journal of International Law, 1995-1997. *Member:* Chicago and American Bar Associations. ***PRACTICE AREAS:*** Commercial Litigation; Reinsurance Law. ***Email:*** akelley@butlerrubin.com

BRIAN E. KONCIUS, born Detroit, Michigan, February 1, 1978; admitted to bar, 2003, Illinois and U.S. District Court, Northern District of Illinois; 2004, U.S. District Court, Central District of Illinois; 2005, U.S. Court of Appeals, Seventh Circuit. *Education:* Duke University (A.B., 2000); University of Michigan Law School (J.D., 2003). Assistant Editor, Michigan Telecommunications and Technology Law Review, 2001-2002. ***LANGUAGES:*** Spanish. ***PRACTICE AREAS:*** Litigation. ***Email:*** bkoncius@butlerrubin.com

NOAH B. MILLER, born Detroit, Michigan, August 19, 1978; admitted to bar, 2003, Pennsylvania (Not admitted in Illinois). *Education:* University of Michigan (B.A., 2000; J.D., 2003). Associate Editor, University of Michigan Journal of Law Reform, 2001-2002. ***PRACTICE AREAS:*** Commercial Litigation; Reinsurance Litigation. ***Email:*** nmiller@butlerrubin.com

KEVIN J. MUELLER, born St. Paul, Minnesota, May 10, 1979; admitted to bar, 2005, Illinois. *Education:* Miami University (B.S., magna cum laude, 2001); Northwestern University School of Law (J.D., cum laude, 2004). Managing Editor, Northwestern Journal of International Human Rights, Inaugural Edition, 2003-2004. Law Clerk to Honorable Mark Rinder, Alaska Superior Court, Third Judicial District, 2004-2005. ***PRACTICE AREAS:*** Commercial Litigation; Reinsurance Litigation. ***Email:*** kmueller@butlerrubin.com

JOSEPH P. NOONAN, III, born Garden City, Michigan, January 13, 1970; admitted to bar, 2002, Illinois. *Education:* Catholic University of America (B.A., magna cum laude, 1992); Northwestern University (J.D., cum laude, 2002); University of Utah (A.B.D., in Ph.D. Program, 1996). Note and Comment Editor, Northwestern University Law Review, 2001-2002. ***PRACTICE AREAS:*** Commercial Litigation; Reinsurance Law; Contracts. ***Email:*** jnoonan@butlerrubin.com

MARK A. SCHWARTZ, born Detroit, Michigan, April 15, 1972; admitted to bar, 1999, Illinois and U.S. District Court, Northern District of Illinois. *Education:* University of California at Los Angeles (B.A., summa cum laude, 1995); University of Michigan (J.D., cum laude, 1999). ***PRACTICE AREAS:*** Commercial Litigation; Reinsurance Law. ***Email:*** mschwartz@butlerrubin.com

JOHN DAVID WINTERS, born Gloucester, Virginia, June 9, 1968; admitted to bar, 2002, Illinois, U.S. District Court, Northern District of Illinois and U.S. Tax Court; 2004 U.S. District Court, Northern District of Indiana 2004 and U.S. Court of Appeals, Seventh Circuit. *Education:* University of South Florida (B.A., 1999; M.A., 1999); Northwestern University (J.D., 2002). Member, Northwestern University Law Review. ***PRACTICE AREAS:*** Commercial Litigation; Reinsurance. ***Email:*** dwinters@butlerrubin.com

LEGAL SUPPORT PERSONNEL

AUDREY H. RUBIN, born Chicago, Illinois, August 7, 1955; admitted to bar, 1978, Illinois. *Education:* Yale University (B.A., cum laude, 1975); Northwestern University (J.D., 1978). *Member:* Chicago, Illinois State and American Bar Associations; Association of Legal Administrators; Decalogue Society of Lawyers. (Chief Operating Officer). ***PRACTICE AREAS:*** Firm Management; Operations; Finance. ***Email:*** arubin@butlerrubin.com

(This Listing Continued)

CATHERINE M. BYRNE

77 WEST WASHINGTON STREET, SUITE 1711
CHICAGO, ILLINOIS 60602
Telephone: 312-332-5100
Fax: 312-332-5105
Email: catherinebyrne@ameritech.net
URL: http://www.cbyrnefamilylaw.com

Family Law including Child Custody, Child Support, Divorce, Domestic Violence, Premarital Agreement, Removal, Orders of Protection and Spousal Support.

FIRM PROFILE: Catherine M. Byrne practices throughout Du Page, Cook and Will counties.

CATHERINE M. BYRNE, born Chicago, Illinois, November 17, 1960; admitted to bar, 1987, Illinois. *Education:* Creighton University (B.A., 1983; J.D., 1986). Member, Foreign Language Honor Society. Certified Arbitrator. Certified Mediator. *Member:* DuPage County and Chicago Bar Associations. ***LANGUAGES:*** Spanish. ***PRACTICE AREAS:*** Family Law; Divorce; Child Custody; Child Support; Orders of Protection.

MICHAEL T. BYRNE

CHICAGO, ILLINOIS
(See Clarendon Hills)

Criminal Law, Driving While Intoxicated, Drug Crimes, Felonies, Homicide, Sexual Assault, Traffic Violations and Probation Violations.

LAW OFFICE OF WILLIAM J. CADIGAN, P.C.

180 N. WACKER DRIVE, SUITE 600
CHICAGO, ILLINOIS 60606
Telephone: 312-279-0520
Fax: 312-946-0470
Email: wcadigan@cadiganlaw.net

Health Care, Corporate Law, Government.

WILLIAM J. CADIGAN, born July 9, 1964; admitted to bar, 1993, Illinois. *Education:* Eastern Illinois University (B.A., 1986); John Marshall Law School (J.D., 1993). Commissioner, Illinois Medical District, 1999—. Board of Directors, Chicago Technology Park. *Member:* Chicago and Illinois State Bar Associations; American Health Lawyers; Lawyers Club of Chicago. ***PRACTICE AREAS:*** Health Care; Corporate Law; Government. ***Email:*** wcadigan@cadiganlaw.net

DENNIS J. CALLAHAN & ASSOCIATES, P.C.

4801 WEST PETERSON AVENUE
CHICAGO, ILLINOIS 60646
Telephone: 773-481-5386
Fax: 773-481-5387
Email: Dennisjcallahan@aol.com
URL: http://www.lawyers.com/callahan

Domestic Relations, Divorce, Family, Separation, Child Support, Child Custody, Paternity, Adoption, Guardianship, Personal Injury, Workers Compensation, Slip and Fall, Wrongful Death, Product Liability, Premises Liability, Railroad Accidents, Bus Accidents, Motorcycle Accidents, Automobile Accidents, Construction Accidents, Real Estate, Wills, Estate Planning, Criminal, Driving While Intoxicated, Drug Crimes, Felonies and General Practice, Commercial Litigation, Collection Litigation, Modifications, Mediation.

DENNIS J. CALLAHAN, born Chicago, Illinois, October 3, 1953; admitted to bar, 1979, Illinois; U.S. District Court, Northern District of Illinois including Trial Bar. *Education:* Illinois Benedictine College (B.A., 1975); DePaul University (J.D., 1978). Certified Child Representative, Cook County, Illinois, 2001. *Member:* Chicago Bar Association. ***Email:*** dennisjcallahan@aoc.com

CANEL, DAVIS & KING

10 SOUTH LA SALLE STREET, SUITE 3400
CHICAGO, ILLINOIS 60603
Telephone: 312-372-4142
Fax: 312-372-6737
URL: http://www.cdk-law.com

Trial and Appellate Practice, Commercial Litigation, Civil Rights, Environmental Law, Business Law, Construction Law, Contracts, Copyrights.

FIRM PROFILE: We have appeared as counsel in trial, appellate and arbitration proceedings in many states. We have handled contract, fraud, breach of fiduciary duty, employment, RICO, civil rights, Lanham Act, injunction, insurance coverage, environmental, antitrust and serious property damage and personal injury cases. This background provides an uncommon breadth of experience in this age of specialization.

MEMBERS OF FIRM

STEPHEN D. DAVIS, born Kansas City, Missouri, July 17, 1956; admitted to bar, 1982, Illinois and U.S. District Court, Northern District of Illinois. *Education:* University of Missouri (B.A., 1978); University of Michigan (J.D., 1982). Phi Beta Kappa. *Member:* Chicago, Illinois State and American Bar Associations. ***PRACTICE AREAS:*** Litigation. ***Email:*** sdavis@daviskinglaw.com

PETER M. KING, born Fort Carson, Colorado, November 22, 1956; admitted to bar, 1982, Illinois and U.S. District Court, Northern District of Illinois. *Education:* University of Illinois, Chicago (B.S., 1978); Illinois Institute of Technology/Chicago-Kent College of Law (J.D., with honors, 1982). Member, National Trial Advocacy Team, 1982. Certified Public Accountant, Illinois, 1979. Co-Author, "Crimes of the State: Obtaining Justice for the Wrongfully Imprisoned," ABA Litigation Magazine, Fall 2002. *Member:* Chicago, Illinois State and American Bar Associations. ***PRACTICE AREAS:*** Litigation. ***Email:*** pking@daviskinglaw.com

WILLIAM H. JONES, born Oak Park, Illinois, June 26, 1963; admitted to bar, 1989, Illinois and U.S. District Court, Northern District of Illinois. *Education:* University of Iowa (B.B.A., 1985); John Marshall Law School (J.D., 1989). Associate Lead Articles Editor, John Marshall Law Review, 1988-1989. Law Clerk to Justice Howard C. Ryan, Illinois Supreme Court, 1989-1990. Co-Author, "Crimes of the State: Obtaining Justice for the Wrongfully Imprisoned," ABA Litigation Magazine, Fall 2002. *Member:* Chicago, Illinois State and American Bar Associations. ***PRACTICE AREAS:*** Litigation. ***Email:*** wjones@daviskinglaw.com

CANTWELL & CANTWELL

SUITE 2850, THIRTY NORTH LA SALLE STREET
CHICAGO, ILLINOIS 60602
Telephone: 312-372-3000
Fax: 312-346-8300

Civil and Trial Practice. Litigation, Securities, Commodities and Securities Regulation, Commercial and Real Estate, Family Law, Estate Planning, Banking, Corporate Law, Creditors Rights and Bankruptcy.

PETER A. CANTWELL, born Oak Park, Illinois, February 9, 1950; admitted to bar, 1974, Illinois and U.S. District Court, Northern District of Illinois; 1977, U.S. Tax Court; 1985, U.S. Court of Appeals, 6th Circuit; 1987, U.S. Court of Appeals, 7th Circuit; 1988, U.S. Supreme Court. *Education:* Washington University (A.B., 1971; J.D., 1974). *Member:* Chicago, Illinois State (Member, Sections on: Commercial Law; Banking Law; Bankruptcy; Family Law; Securities Law) and American (Member, Sections on: Corporation and Securities Law; Family Law; Tort Law; Real Estate Law) Bar Associations. ***PRACTICE AREAS:*** Securities; Commodities; Litigation; Commercial Law; Securities Regulation; Divorce; Family Law; Real Estate.

PAUL H. SCHEUERLEIN, born Saint Albans, New York, March 12, 1952; admitted to bar, 1984, Illinois; 1986, U.S. District Court, Northern District of Illinois including Trial Bar; 1990, U.S. Court of Appeals, 7th Circuit. *Education:* Syracuse University (B.S., cum laude, 1975; J.D., 1984). Member, Lawyers for the Creative Arts, 1986—. *Member:* Chicago, Illinois State and American Bar Associations. ***PRACTICE AREAS:*** Commercial Litigation; Securities; Commodities; Securities Regulation; Commercial Law; Entertainment Law; Family Law.

STEPHEN F. BOULTON, born Ridgewood, New Jersey, August 28, 1958; admitted to bar, 1983, Ohio; 1984, Illinois and U.S. District Court, Northern District of Illinois; 1987, U.S. Court of Appeals, 6th Circuit; 1992, U.S. Court of Appeals, 7th Circuit. *Education:* University of Pennsylvania (B.A., 1980); Case Western Reserve University (J.D., 1983). *Member:* Chicago and American Bar Associations. ***PRACTICE AREAS:*** Securities; Commodities; Employment Law; Litigation; Commercial Law; Personal Injury.

ASSOCIATES

TELLY STEFANEAS, born Chicago, Illinois, August 17, 1972; admitted to bar, 1997, Illinois; 2002, U.S. District Court, Northern District of Illinois. *Education:* DePaul University (B.A., 1994; J.D., 1997). ***PRACTICE AREAS:*** Litigation; Personal Injury; Securities; Family Law.

MICHAEL J. CRONIN, born Evergreen Park, Illinois, February 2, 1961; admitted to bar, 1989, Illinois. *Education:* Harvard University (B.A., 1983); Northwestern University (J.D., 1989). *Member:* Chicago Bar Association; Illinois Association of Defense Trial Counsel; Illinois Appellate Lawyers Association; Defense Research Institute. ***PRACTICE AREAS:*** Litigation; Appellate Practice.

ROBERT D. LAPORTE, born Trenton, Michigan; admitted to bar, 2004, Illinois. *Education:* Western Michigan University (B.S., 1993; M.A., 1998); Thomas Jefferson School of Law (J.D., 2003).

WILLIAM LI, born New York, N.Y., October 5, 1978; (admission pending). *Education:* Washington University (B.A., 2000); DePaul University (J.D., 2004).

OF COUNSEL

ROBERT E. CANTWELL, III (1925-1995)

L. YAGER CANTWELL (1918-2000)

REPRESENTATIVE CLIENT: Merrill Lynch, Pierce, Fenner & Smith Inc.
REFERENCES: Bank One; Trust Company of Chicago.

DEAN CARAS & ASSOCIATES

320 W. ILLINOIS STREET, SUITE 2216
CHICAGO, ILLINOIS 60610
Telephone: 312-494-1500
Fax: 312-822-0955
Email: dean.caras@deanjcaras.com
URL: http://www.deanjcaras.com

Personal Injury, Catastrophic Injuries, Birth Trauma, Automobile Accidents, Railroad Accidents, Slip and Fall, Wrongful Death, Workers Compensation and Products Liability.

(This Listing Continued)

FIRM PROFILE: Dean Caras is an accomplished trial attorney who has enjoyed success in serving his clients for the past 18 years. He welcomes referrals of personal injury cases from other attorneys from other jurisdictions within the United States as well as abroad.

DEAN J. CARAS, born Chicago, Illinois; admitted to bar, 1985, Illinois and U.S. District Court, Northern District of Illinois; 1986, New York; 1992, U.S. District Court, Southern District of New York; 2000, U.S. Court of Appeals, Seventh Circuit; 2001, U.S. Supreme Court; U.S. Court of Federal Claims. *Education:* American University (B.A., International Studies, 1982); Southern Methodist University (J.D., 1985). ***LANGUAGES:*** Greek, Spanish, Russian and Romanian. ***PRACTICE AREAS:*** Plaintiffs Personal Injury. **Email:** dean.caras@deanjcaras.com

CARDINAL LAW GROUP, LTD.

720 SOUTH DEARBORN STREET, SUITE 503
CHICAGO, ILLINOIS 60605
Telephone: 847-905-7111
Fax: 847-905-7113
URL: http://www.cardinallawgroup.com/lawyers/cook/
Email: info@cardinallawgroup.com
URL: http://www.cardinallawgroup.com

Evanston, Illinois Office: 1603 Orrington Avenue, 60201. Telephone: 847-905-7111. Fax: 847-905-7113. URL: http://www.cardinallawgroup.com

Technology and Intellectual Property Law Including U.S. and International Patents, Patent Preparation, Patent Prosecution, Patent Litigation, Intellectual Property Licensing, Intellectual Property Litigation, Trademark, Copyright, Trade Dress, Trade Secret, Unfair Competition, Antitrust, Cyberlaw, Biotech, Mechanical, Electrical, Computer and Software Patents.

FIRM PROFILE: Cardinal Law Group specializes in intellectual property law including patent, trademark, copyright, trade secret and related areas.

With more than 20 lawyers and specialized professionals of varying backgrounds and experience, Cardinal Law Group is prepared to prosecute patent applications in all fields, including mechanical, electrical, software, biotech, and Internet related matters.

Our client base ranges from Fortune 500 companies to individual inventors.

REPRESENTATIVE CLIENTS: General Motors; Motorola; SBC; Philips Electronics; IBM; Medtronic; Agilent Technologies; Gritwire; Clear Lam Packaging.

(For complete biographical data, see Professional Biographies at Evanston)

CAREY, FILTER, WHITE & BOLAND

Established in 1886

33 WEST JACKSON BOULEVARD, FIFTH FLOOR
CHICAGO, ILLINOIS 60604
Telephone: 312-939-4300
Fax: 312-939-4285

General, Banking, Corporation, Real Estate, Probate Practice. Construction, Estate Planning, Horse Racing.

MEMBERS OF FIRM

ROBERT F. CAREY (1904-1980)

THOMAS F. CAREY, born Chicago, Illinois, November 10, 1932; admitted to bar, 1959, Illinois. *Education:* University of Notre Dame (B.A.A., 1955); Northwestern University (J.D., 1958). Phi Alpha Delta.

EDWARD M. WHITE, born Chicago, Illinois, August 28, 1928; admitted to bar, 1951, Illinois and U.S. District Court, Northern District of Illinois including Trial Bar. *Education:* Loyola University (J.D., 1951). Phi Alpha Delta; Alpha Sigma Nu. Assistant Attorney General, Illinois, 1951-1960. *Member:* Chicago Bar Association.

EDMUND P. BOLAND, born Evergreen Park, Illinois, January 24, 1942; admitted to bar, 1967, Illinois and U.S. District Court, Northern District of Illinois including Trial Bar. *Education:* St. Procopius College (B.A., 1964); Loyola University (J.D., 1967). *Member:* Chicago, Illinois State and American Bar Associations. **Email:** pboland@careyfilter.com

ANTHONY CAREY, born Chicago, Illinois, December 24, 1943; admitted to bar, 1969, Illinois. *Education:* University of Notre Dame (B.A., 1966); DePaul University (J.D., 1969). *Member:* Illinois State Bar Association. **Email:** acarey@careyfilter.com

F. KEVIN MURNIGHAN, born Evanston, Illinois, March 10, 1950; admitted to bar, 1976, Illinois and U.S. District Court, Northern District of Illinois including Trial Bar. *Education:* Brown University (A.B., 1972); John Marshall Law School (J.D., 1976). Member, Law Review, 1975-1976. *Member:* Chicago Bar Association. **Email:** kevin@careyfilter.com

MICHAEL E. WHITE, born Chicago, Illinois, September 14, 1954; admitted to bar, 1979, Illinois and U.S. District Court, Northern District of Illinois. *Education:* University of Notre Dame (B.B.A., 1976); John Marshall Law School (J.D., 1979). *Member:* Chicago Bar Association. **Email:** mwhite@careyfilter.com

MICHAEL J. MURRAY, born Chicago, Illinois, October 31, 1956; admitted to bar, 1982, Illinois and U.S. District Court, Northern District of Illinois including Trial Bar. *Education:* Loyola University of Chicago (B.B.A., 1979; J.D., 1982). *Member:* Chicago Bar Association. **Email:** mmurray@careyfilter.com

PATRICK S. FILTER (1915-1999)

CARPENTER & CAPT, CHTD.

53 WEST JACKSON BOULEVARD, SUITE 1752
CHICAGO, ILLINOIS 60604
Telephone: 312-803-5110
Fax: 312-803-5112
URL: http://www.lawyers.com/cncchtd
Email: c&clawyers@carpenterandcapt.com
URL: http://www.carpenterandcapt.com

The firm's immigration practice includes representation on family-based and work-based visas, all non-immigrant visas, and asylum applications. We also practice plaintiff's personal injury including auto and truck accidents, slip and falls, construction-related accidents, and wrongful death actions, real estate and probate law.

FIRM PROFILE: Carpenter and Capt's mission is to provide quality legal representation to each and every client. We believe that each client is equally important and deserving of individual attention. We strive to keep all of our clients informed and up-to-date on the progress of his/her file. The firm utilizes all available technology in order to accomplish this goal. The firm has won over $1.5 million in settlements and verdicts for personal injury clients since its inception. Robert Carpenter is best known in the immigration community not only for the overall quality and success of general applications, but also for his ongoing successful litigation against the INS in federal court for inaction and malfeasance on files.

ROBERT T. CARPENTER, born Chicago, Illinois, November 5, 1967; admitted to bar, 1992, Illinois. *Education:* University of Florida (B.S., 1989); DePaul University (J.D., 1992). *Member:* Chicago and American Bar Associations; American Immigration Lawyers Association. ***LANGUAGES:*** Spanish. ***PRACTICE AREAS:*** Immigration Law; Personal Injury. **Email:** rcarpenter@carpenterandcapt.com

PATRICIA E. CAPT, born San Antonio, Texas, May 29, 1966; admitted to bar, 1993, Illinois. *Education:* St. Mary's University of San Antonio (B.S., with honors, 1988); DePaul University (J.D., 1992). ***LANGUAGES:*** Spanish. ***PRACTICE AREAS:*** Personal Injury; Real Estate; Probate. **Email:** pcapt@carpenterandcapt.com

---

JOHN W. MUG, born Evanston, Illinois, April 11, 1946; admitted to bar, 1977, Illinois; 1978, District of Columbia. *Education:* Loyola University (A.B., 1968; J.D., 1977). *Member:* The District of Columbia Bar. ***PRACTICE AREAS:*** Immigration Law; Personal Injury.

CARPONELLI & KRUG

Established in 1973

230 W. MONROE STREET, SUITE 250
CHICAGO, ILLINOIS 60606
Telephone: 312-372-2707
Fax: 312-641-6174
Email: eastonlaw@aol.com
URL: http://www.carponellikrug.com

General Practice. Civil and Criminal Trial and Appellate Practice in all Courts. Antitrust, Hospital, Commercial, Corporate, Personal Injury, Workers Compensation, Estate Planning, Real Property Law, Trade Secrets, Trademark and Copyright Law, Dissolution, Professional Negligence, Environmental and Various Business and Real Estate Transactions.

FIRM PROFILE: The firm was established in 1973. From its inception an emphasis on trial work found the firm working on a wide variety of cases. The firm has successfully tried to verdict criminal, personal injury, condemnation, civil RICO, trade secret, hospital privilege and libel cases. In addition, the firm has continued to maintain a strong emphasis on injunctive and equitable remedies having combined successfully law and equitable counts. The firm also engages in the representation of parties involved in various business and real estate transactions.

STEPHEN P. CARPONELLI, born Chicago, Illinois, December 11, 1947; admitted to bar, 1972, Illinois and U.S. District Court, Northern District of Illinois including Trial Bar; 1974, U.S. Court of Appeals, Seventh Circuit; 1979, U.S. Supreme Court; 1980, U.S. Tax Court. *Education:* Drake University (B.S., 1969); John Marshall Law School (J.D., with honors, 1972). Order of John Marshall; Phi Alpha Delta. Associate Editor, John Marshall Journal of Practice and Procedure, 1971-1972. Instructor: John Marshall Law School, 1973-1974; Trial Practice Course, Chicago Bar Association, 1985-1990 and Illinois Institute of Continuing Legal Education, 1986-1990. *Member:* Chicago, Illinois State and American Bar Associations; The Association of Trial Lawyers of America. ***REPORTED CASES:*** Riley v. World Hockey Association, 427 N.E.2d 290 (1st Dist. Ill.App. 1981); Knapp v. Palos Community Hospital, 465 N.E.2d 554 (1st Dist. Ill. 1984) ("Knapp I"); Knapp v. Palos Community Hospital, 531 N.E.2d 989 (1st Dist. 1988) ("Knapp II"); George Szczerbaniuk, M.D. v. McHenry Memorial Hospital, 536 N.E.2d 138 (2d Dist. Ill.App. 1989); Rockwell Graphic Systems, Inc. v. Dev Industries, Inc., 730 F.Supp. 171 (N.D. Ill. 1990) and 925 F.2d 174 (7th Cir. 1991); Weiland v. Telectronics Pacing Sys., 721 N.E. 2d 1149, 1999; Garibaldi v. Applebaum, 742 N.E. 2d 279, 2000; Hojnacki v. Klein-Acosta, 285 F. 3d 544, 2002, Native American Arts, Inc. v. The Waldron Corporation, 339 F.3d 871 (7th Cir. 2005). ***PRACTICE AREAS:*** Civil and Criminal Trial Practice; Injunction Prosecution and Defense; Professional Negligence; Unfair Competition; Intellectual Property; Trade Secret; Torts; Hospital Privileges; Medical Peer Review; Defamation; Employment; Environmental Law; Family Law.

ROBERT F. KRUG, JR., born Chicago, Illinois, August 9, 1948; admitted to bar, 1973, Illinois; 1979, U.S. Supreme Court. *Education:* Northern Illinois University (B.S., 1970); University of Illinois (J.D., 1973). *Member:* Chicago, Illinois State and American Bar Associations. ***PRACTICE AREAS:*** Civil Litigation; Negligence; Corporate; Commercial Law; Real Estate; Estate Planning and Probate.

(This Listing Continued)

CARPONELLI & KRUG, Chicago—Continued

BRIAN M. OZOG, born Chicago, Illinois, July 18, 1973; admitted to bar, 1999, Illinois and U.S. District Court, Northern District of Illinois; 2001, U.S. Court of Appeals, Seventh Circuit. *Education:* University of Illinois at Urbana - Champaign (B.A., 1996); Chicago-Kent College of Law, Illinois Institute of Technology (J.D., 1999). *Member:* Chicago, Illinois State and American Bar Associations. ***PRACTICE AREAS:*** Corporate Law; Commercial Litigation; Trademark Litigation; Copyright Litigation; Trade Secret. ***Email:*** bozog@hotmail.com

RAYMOND M. RUDNICK, born Arlington Heights, Illinois, March 21, 1973; admitted to bar, 2000, Illinois; U.S. District Court, Northern District of Illinois. *Education:* Western Illinois University (B.S., 1995); John Marshall Law School (J.D., 2000). *Member:* Chicago, Illinois State and American Bar Associations. ***PRACTICE AREAS:*** General Practice; Personal Injury; Criminal Law; Probate; Family Law. ***Email:*** eastonlaw@aol.com

DON F. TAYLOR, born Washington D.C., September 7, 1961; admitted to bar, 1998, Illinois. *Education:* University of Michigan at Ann Arbor (B.S.M.E., 1983); Detroit College of Law at Michigan State University (J.D., magna cum laude, 1998). ***PRACTICE AREAS:*** General Practice. ***Email:*** eastonlaw@aol.com

REPRESENTATIVE CLIENTS: Putman Publishing Co.; Harris Steel Co.; The Ryland Group, Inc.; Illinois State Bar Mutual Insurance Co.; Advanced Flexible Composites, Inc.; DSK Premium Supplies Limited; Illinois Harness Horsemen Association, several law firms, attorneys and physicians.

THE LAW OFFICES OF GWEN VERONICA CARROLL, LTD.

53 WEST JACKSON BOULEVARD
SUITE 205
CHICAGO, ILLINOIS 60604
Telephone: 312-939-4000
Fax: 312-939-4100
Email: gvcarroll@gvc-law.com
URL: http://www.gvc-law.com

Labor and Employment Law.

GWEN V. CARROLL, born Milwaukee, Wisconsin, April 22, 1954; admitted to bar, 1980, Illinois. *Education:* Georgetown University (B.S., 1977); DePaul University (J.D., with honors, 1980). Editor-in-Chief, De Paul Law Review, 1979-1980. Partner and Chair of Labor and Employment Law Practice, Ungaretti & Harris (previously Coffield, Ungaretti & Harris), 1990-1997; Partner (Labor and Employment), Katten Muchin & Zavis, 1987-1990; Associate (Labor and Employment), Katten Muchin & Zavis, 1986-1987; Associate (Labor and Employment), Seyfarth, Shaw, Fairweather & Geraldson, 1980-1984. Author: Note, "Insurance Subrogation Actions No Longer Barred By General Releases In Illinois—Home Insurance Co. v. Hertz Corporation," 28 De Paul Law Review 189 (1978). Lecturer, Labor Law, Loyola University School of Law, 1988. Contributing Author: Supplement to Sexual Harassment In Employment Law. *Member:* Chicago (Chair, Client Development and Firm Economics Committee, Young Lawyers Section 1991) and American (Member, Labor and Employment Law Section, Employee Rights and Responsibilities Committee) Bar Associations; Women's Bar Association of Illinois. ***PRACTICE AREAS:*** Labor and Employment. ***Email:*** gvcarroll@aol.com

CARROLL, HARTIGAN & CERNEY, LTD.

Established in 1938
30 NORTH LA SALLE STREET
SUITE 1200
CHICAGO, ILLINOIS 60602
Telephone: 312-236-3575
Fax: 312-236-3584
Email: info@chc-law.com
URL: http://www.chc-law.com

Commercial Transactions, Business Law, Banks and Banking, Civil Litigation, Insurance, Trusts and Estates, Probate, Real Estate, Nonprofit Organization Law.

FIRM PROFILE: We are designed to provide prompt, aggressive and cost efficient representation.

JOHN M. HARTIGAN, born Chicago, Illinois, May 6, 1932; admitted to bar, 1958, Illinois and U.S. District Court, Northern District of Illinois. *Education:* University of Notre Dame (B.S., cum laude, 1955); Northwestern University (J.D., 1958). Phi Delta Phi. Member, Chicago Crime Commission. Economic Club of Chicago. *Member:* Chicago, Illinois State and American Bar Associations. ***PRACTICE AREAS:*** Commercial Transactions; Business Planning; Probate; Nonprofit Organizations Law; Banking Law. ***Email:*** jmh@chc-law.com

JOHN S. CARROLL, born Evergreen Park, Illinois, July 7, 1945; admitted to bar, 1972, Illinois; 1983, U.S. District Court, Northern District of Illinois, Trial Bar. *Education:* Loras College (B.A., 1967); University of Illinois (J.D., 1972). *Member:* Chicago, Illinois State and American Bar Associations. ***PRACTICE AREAS:*** Business Law; Financial Institution Law; Real Estate.

J. TIMOTHY CERNEY, born Chicago, Illinois, March 12, 1953; admitted to bar, 1979, Illinois and U.S. District Court, Northern District of Illinois; 1981, U.S. Court of Appeals, Seventh Circuit; 1983, U.S. District Court, Northern District of Illinois, Trial Bar. *Education:* University of Iowa (B.S., cum laude, 1975; J.D., 1979). Phi Delta Phi. *Member:* Chicago, Illinois State (Member, Insurance Law Section) and American Bar Associations; Defense Research Institute; Illinois Association of Defense Trial Counsel; Illinois Trial Lawyers Association; The Association of Trial Lawyers of America. ***REPORTED CASES:*** Mi-Jack Products v. Chamberlain Mfg. Co. 145 IL App 3d 1159, 511 N.E. 2d 277 (1986); Comark v. The Highland Group 932 F 2d 1196 (1991); Adame v. Munoz, 287 IL App 3d 181, 678 N.E. 2d 26 (1997); First Bank & Trust v. Firstar Corporation, 276 F. 3d 317 (2001). ***PRACTICE AREAS:*** Civil Litigation; Insurance. ***Email:*** jtc@chc-law.com

(This Listing Continued)

MARY K. HARTIGAN, born Chicago, Illinois, June 14, 1962; admitted to bar, 1991, California; 1992, Illinois. *Education:* Georgetown University (B.S.F.S., 1984); University of Notre Dame (J.D., 1991). *Member:* Chicago, California, Illinois State and American Bar Associations. ***PRACTICE AREAS:*** Commercial Transactions; Business Litigation; Unfair Competition; Insurance Coverage. ***Email:*** mkh@chc-law.com

CAROL SHARPE McMAHAN, born Columbia, South Carolina, September 23, 1951; admitted to bar, 1985, Utah; 1986, Illinois. *Education:* University of Utah (J.D., 1985). *Member:* Chicago, Illinois State and American Bar Associations. ***PRACTICE AREAS:*** Business Law; Securities. ***Email:*** csm@chc-law.com

PHILIP E. OLD, born San Diego, California, May 12, 1964; admitted to bar, 1993, Illinois and U.S. District Court, Northern District of Illinois. *Education:* Marquette University (B.S., 1986); Loyola University (J.D., 1993). *Member:* American Bar Association. [U.S. Navy, 1986-1990; Commander, U.S. Naval Reserve, 1990—]. ***REPORTED CASES:*** Euro Motors, Inc. v. Southwest Financial Bank & Trust Co., 297 Ill. App. 3d 246, 696, N.E. 2d 711 (1998). ***PRACTICE AREAS:*** Civil Litigation; Insurance; Commercial Litigation.

OF COUNSEL

DAVID M. HARTIGAN, born Chicago, Illinois, December 28, 1940; admitted to bar, 1966, Illinois; 1970, U.S. District Court, Northern District of Illinois. *Education:* Georgetown University (A.B., 1963); Loyola University (J.D., 1966). Assistant U.S. Attorney, Northern District of Illinois, 1968-1992. Assistant Chief, Civil Division, 1970-1971 and Chief, Tax Division, 1971-1972, Deputy License Commissioner, City of Chicago, 1972-1974. President, Chicago Chapter, Federal Bar Association, 1983. Catholic Lawyers Guild of Chicago, Chairman, 1993—; Attorney Registration and Disciplinary Committee for the Illinois Supreme Court, 1988-1999; Chairman, 1996-1999. *Member:* Chicago, Bar Association. ***PRACTICE AREAS:*** Real Estate Tax Consulting.

REPRESENTATIVE CLIENTS: Thomas W. Dower Foundation; B.B.C. Fasteners, Inc.; Titan Security Services, Inc.; Suburban Bank & Trust Co.; First Evanston Bancorp, Inc.; First Bank & Trust; Harris Bank, Westchester; New City Bancorp, Inc., New City Bank; TIG Insurance Co.; Liberty Mutual Insurance Co.; Chicago Title Insurance Co.; Crawford & Co.; Vericlaim; Absolute Architecture, Inc.; Werner Martin Enterprises; Steel Services Co.; Tailored Tours, Inc.; The Habitat Co.; Sensophonics, Inc.; Millis Transfer; Academy of Model Aeronautics; Scotts Lawn Service/The Scotts Company; NCB Holdings, Inc.; New Century Bank.
REFERENCES: Suburban Bank & Trust Co.; First Bank & Trust; J.P. Morgan Chase Bank, NA.

CASSIDAY, SCHADE & GLOOR, LLP

Established in 1979
20 NORTH WACKER DRIVE, SUITE 1040
CHICAGO, ILLINOIS 60606-2903
Telephone: 312-641-3100
Fax: 312-444-1669
URL: http://www.cassiday.com

Libertyville, Illinois Office: 1870 West Winchester Road, Suite 148, 60048-5353. Telephone: 847-932-6922. Fax: 847-932-6947.
Naperville, Illinois Office: 1230 East Diehl Road, Suite 202, 60563-9362. Telephone: 630-328-2970. Fax: 630-328-2979.
Rockford, Illinois Office: 120 West State Street, Suite 401, 61101-1159. Telephone: 815-962-8301. Fax: 815-962-8401.

General Practice. Civil Trial Practice, Civil Appellate Practice, Insurance Coverage, Environmental, Medical and Professional Malpractice, Products Liability, Structural Work Act, Railroad, Employment, Corporate and Health Care Law, Commercial Litigation, Construction, Workers Compensation, Intellectual Property, Municipalities, Transportation, Patent Law.

FIRM PROFILE: Cassiday Schade & Gloor, LLP was founded in 1979. The firm specializes in civil trial litigation, representing corporations, hospitals, and insurers. It maintains offices in Chicago, Libertyville, Naperville, and Rockford, Illinois. The firm has expertise in virtually all areas of civil litigation, including health care litigation, product liability, construction law, insurance law, environmental and toxic injury litigation, employment practices, workers compensation, intellectual property, municipalities, patent law and intellectual property.

The firm also has an established Quality Control Department.

MEMBERS OF FIRM

JAMES D. AHERN, born Chicago, Illinois, November 21, 1955; admitted to bar, 1989, Illinois; U.S. Court of Appeals, Seventh Circuit; U.S. District Court, Northern District of Illinois. *Education:* Marquette University (B.A., 1977); John Marshall Law School (J.D., 1989). Member, John Marshall Law Review. *Member:* Illinois Association of Defense Trial Counsel; Defense Research Institute. ***PRACTICE AREAS:*** Medical Malpractice Defense. ***Email:*** jda@cs-g.com

RICHARD A. BARRETT, JR., born Evanston, Illinois, July 12, 1951; admitted to bar, 1976, Illinois; U.S. District Court, Northern District of Illinois including Trial Bar. *Education:* University of Notre Dame (B.S., 1973); Georgetown University (J.D., 1976). Author: "Apparent Agency: How Can Hospitals Combat the Appearance?" Journal of American Medical Record Association. Certified Arbitrator (Chair Eligible). *Member:* Illinois State Bar Association; Illinois Association of Defense Trial Counsel. ***PRACTICE AREAS:*** Professional Liability Defense; Medical Malpractice Defense. ***Email:*** rab@cs-g.com

MARC F. BENJOYA, born Chicago, Illinois, July 3, 1958; admitted to bar, 1983, Illinois including Federal Trial Bar, U.S. District Court, Northern District of Illinois and Wisconsin; 1999 U.S. District Court, Southern District of Indiana. *Education:* Northern Illinois University (B.A., cum laude, 1980); IIT/Chicago-Kent College of Law (J.D., 1983). *Mem-*

(This Listing Continued)

ber: Lake County, Illinois State and Wisconsin State Bar Associations; Illinois Association of Hospital Attorneys; Illinois Association of Defense Trial Counsel. (Libertyville and Rockford Offices). ***PRACTICE AREAS:*** Professional Negligence; Professional Liability Defense; Insurance Defense. ***Email:*** mfb@cs-g.com

THOMAS P. BOYLAN, born Evergreen Park, Illinois, April 4, 1961; admitted to bar, 1986, Illinois and U. S. District Court, Northern District of Illinois. *Education:* University of Illinois (B.A., 1983); Loyola University of Chicago (J.D., 1986). *Member:* Chicago Bar Association; Defense Research Institute. ***PRACTICE AREAS:*** ERISA Litigation; Professional Liability Defense; Insurance Defense. ***Email:*** tpb@cs-g.com

MARK M. BRENNAN, born Chicago, Illinois, May 16, 1967; admitted to bar, 1993, Illinois and U.S. District Court, Northern District of Illinois. *Education:* DePaul University (B.A., with honors, 1989; M.A., with distinction, 1990); Loyola Law School (J.D., 1993). Co-Author: "Jury Selection: Defendant's Perspective," Point/Counterpoint Seminar of the Illinois Trial Lawyers Association Education Fund, October 11, 1993. *Member:* Chicago, Illinois State and American Bar Associations. ***PRACTICE AREAS:*** Professional Liability Defense; Personal Injury Defense; Insurance Defense. ***Email:*** mmb@cs-g.com

SCOTT J. BROWN, born Sacramento, California, November 27, 1964; admitted to bar, 1991, Illinois. *Education:* Northwestern University (B.A., 1987); Boston University (J.D., 1991). *Member:* Chicago and Illinois State Bar Associations. ***PRACTICE AREAS:*** Insurance Defense; Personal Injury Defense; Professional Liability Defense. ***Email:*** sjb@cs-g.com

JENNIFER S. BURKE, born South Bend, Indiana, February 25, 1972; admitted to bar, 1997, Illinois. *Education:* University of Dayton (B.A., 1994); Indiana University (J.D., 1997). *Member:* Chicago and Illinois State Bar Associations; Workers' Compensation Lawyer's Association. ***PRACTICE AREAS:*** Workers Compensation; Workers Compensation Defense; Workers Compensation Appeals. ***Email:*** jsb@cs-g.com

KYLE R. BURKHARDT, born El Paso, Texas, December 29, 1970; admitted to bar, 1997, Illinois. *Education:* University of Michigan (B.A., 1994); John Marshall Law School (J.D., 1997). *Member:* Chicago and Illinois State Bar Associations; Illinois Association of Trial Defense Counsel. ***PRACTICE AREAS:*** Medical Malpractice Defense. ***Email:*** krb@cs-g.com

ROBERT S. BURTKER, born Chicago, Illinois, January 26, 1955; admitted to bar, 1981, Illinois; U.S. District Court, Northern District of Illinois. *Education:* University of Illinois (B.A., 1978); IIT/Chicago-Kent College of Law (J.D., 1981). *Member:* Illinois State Bar Association. ***PRACTICE AREAS:*** Professional Liability Defense; Medical Malpractice Defense; Insurance Defense. ***Email:*** rsb@cs-g.com

JOSEPH A. CAMARRA, born Utica, New York, January 11, 1946; admitted to bar, 1970, Illinois; U.S. District Court, Northern District of Illinois. *Education:* St. Bernardine of Siena College (B.A., 1967); University College of Law, University of London, London, England (Certificate in English and American Law, 1969); University of Notre Dame (J.D., 1970). Co-Author: "Hospital Liability: Apparent Agency or Agency by Estoppel," Illinois Bar Journal, March, 1988. Elected as a leading American Attorney in Medical & Professional Malpractice, 1998. Lecturer, Medical Malpractice Issues, World Federation of Neurosurgeons, Agra, India. *Member:* Chicago and Illinois State Bar Associations. ***PRACTICE AREAS:*** Medical Malpractice Defense; Insurance Defense. ***Email:*** jac@cs-g.com

SUSAN E. SEIWERT CONNER, born Aurora, Illinois, March 1, 1959; admitted to bar, 1984, Illinois and U.S. District Court, Northern District of Illinois. *Education:* Gustavus Adolphus College (B.A., magna cum laude, 1981); Loyola University of Chicago (J.D., 1984). *Member:* Chicago and Illinois State Bar Associations; Illinois Defense Counsel; Defense Research Institute; Women Health Executive Network. ***PRACTICE AREAS:*** Professional Liability Defense; Medical Malpractice Defense; Insurance Defense. ***Email:*** sec@cs-g.com

MICHAEL J. CUCCO, born Chicago, Illinois, August 8, 1959; admitted to bar, 1986, Illinois; U.S. District Court, Northern District of Illinois including Trial Bar. *Education:* Denison University (B.A., 1981); Loyola University (J.D., 1986). Co-Author of IICLE Chapter: "Limitations on Discovery," 1987. *Member:* Chicago and Illinois State Bar Associations. ***PRACTICE AREAS:*** Products Liability; Dental Malpractice; Insurance Defense; Professional Liability Defense; Medical Malpractice Defense. ***Email:*** mjc@cs-g.com

JOHN R. DAVIS, born Sterling, Kansas, December 19, 1951; admitted to bar, 1983, Illinois; U.S. District Court, Northern District of Illinois; U.S. District Court, Eastern District of Wisconsin; U.S. Court of Appeals, Seventh Circuit. *Education:* University of Illinois (B.S., 1974); John Marshall Law School (J.D., 1983). *Member:* Illinois State Bar Association; Defense Research Institute; Christian Legal Society. (Resident, Libertyville Office). ***PRACTICE AREAS:*** Personal Injury Defense; Professional Liability Defense; Insurance Defense. ***Email:*** jrd@cs-g.com

JAMES A. FOSTER, born Chicago, Illinois, March 17, 1957; admitted to bar, 1983, Illinois. *Education:* University of Michigan (B.A., 1979); University of Illinois (J.D., 1983). Co-Author: B. Schroeder, "Manufacturers Beware: The Attack on Product Warnings in the Restatement (third) Products Liability," For the Defense, Vol. 42, No. 4, April 2001. Speaker: Assessment of Claims, REBEX 1998, Chicago, sponsored by Chicago, Northeastern Illinois and Wisconsin Chapters of Risk and Insurance Management Society Inc.; Eleventh Annual Product Liability Conference, University of Wisconsin-Madison (Department of Engineering, November 18-19, 1999). *Member:* Chicago Bar Association; Trucking Industry Defense Association; Transportation Lawyers Association. ***PRACTICE AREAS:*** Products Liability Defense; Trucking Law; Transportation. ***Email:*** jaf@cs-g.com

WILLIAM J. FUREY, born Chicago, Illinois, October 1, 1948; admitted to bar, 1973, Illinois; 1984, Wisconsin; U.S. District Court, Northern District of Illinois; U.S. Supreme Court. *Education:* Northern Illinois University (B.S., 1970); DePaul University (J.D., 1973); Rosary College (M.B.A., 1983). Named to Top 20 Tort Defense Trial Lawyers, Chicago Lawyer, January 2003. Arbitrator, American Arbitration Association. Author: "Safety Considerations in Job Specifications," Jean Golden and William Furey, *The Construction Specifier,* Vol. 47 11-94. *Member:* Chicago, Illinois State and American Bar Associations; Defense Research Institute. ***PRACTICE AREAS:*** Products Liability Defense; Construction Litigation Defense; Professional Liability Defense. ***Email:*** wjf@cs-g.com

(This Listing Continued)

CATHERINE L. GARVEY, born Chicago, Illinois, July 16, 1961; admitted to bar, 1990, Illinois; U.S. District Court, Northern District of Illinois. *Education:* University of Illinois (B.S.N., 1984); DePaul University (J.D., 1990). Editor, Journal of Health and Hospital Law, 1988-1989. Member, Board of Directors, Ronald McDonald House, Chicago. *Member:* Chicago, Illinois State Bar Association; Illinois Nurses' Association; American Association of Nurse Attorneys. ***PRACTICE AREAS:*** Medical Malpractice Defense; Insurance Defense; Professional Liability Defense. ***Email:*** clg@cs-g.com

JOSEPH A. GIANNELLI, born Chicago, Illinois, August 17, 1956; admitted to bar, 1982, Illinois and U.S. District Court, Northern District of Illinois, including Trial Bar. *Education:* Loyola University (B.A., 1978); John Marshall Law School (J.D., 1982). Guest Lecturer, Health Care and Medical Malpractice Issues, University of Chicago Residents in Emergency Medicine and Chicago area hospitals. Selected as having obtained one of the top ten defense verdicts in the country by *The National Law Journal. Member:* Chicago and Illinois State Bar Associations. ***PRACTICE AREAS:*** Professional Liability Coverage; Medical Malpractice Defense. ***Email:*** jag@cs-g.com

D. PATTERSON GLOOR, born Oak Park, Illinois, October 7, 1941; admitted to bar, 1966, Michigan; 1970, Illinois; U.S. District Court, Northern District of Illinois. *Education:* Miami University (B.S., 1963); University of Michigan (J.D., 1966). Lecturer, various legal seminars, most recently, "Illinois Tort Reform," ICLE, Chaired by Justice Michael Gallagher, Cook County Circuit Court. Instructor, Products Liability, Chicago-Kent School of Law, 1976. Midwest Regional Counsel to the Welding Industry, 1987—. Author: "The Real Story Behind Welding Rod Litigation: Why Elam is an Aberration," Harris Martin Litigation Watch: Welding Rods Newsletter, 2004. *Member:* Illinois State Bar Association; Defense Research Institute. ***PRACTICE AREAS:*** Civil Litigation; Toxic Torts; Environmental Litigation. ***Email:*** dpg@cs-g.com

JEAN M. GOLDEN, born Evanston, Illinois; admitted to bar, 1977, Illinois; U.S. District Court, Northern District of Illinois. *Education:* Boston College (B.A., magna cum laude); Loyola University (J.D.). Co-Author: "Safety Considerations and Job Specifications," Construction Specifier, with W. Furey, November, 1994; "The Outside Counsel's Role in Litigation Management" with J. Berkeley, Law Department Management Adviser, Business Laws Inc. (Issue 107, February, 1993); "Insurance Law Update," with J. Berkeley, Illinois Defense Trial Counsel Publication (Fall, 1992); "The Attorney's Role in Claims Management," American Contractors Insurance Group Taped Publication (Spring 1992); "Foundations - The Art of Presenting and Objecting to Evidence at Trial," with G. Saltarelli, IICLE, Evidence Advocacy (July, 1990); "Illinois Medicaid Fraud-Curbing Vendor Abuses," 60 Chicago Bar Record 155 (1978); Frequent Law Lecturer. *Member:* Chicago and Illinois State Bar Associations; Women's Bar Association; Defense Research Institute; Lawyers Trust Fund of Illinois (President, 2000-2002; Member, Board of Directors, 1997—); Illinois Association of Defense Trial Counsel. ***PRACTICE AREAS:*** Complex Insurance Coverage. ***Email:*** jmg@cs-g.com

JOHN D. HACKETT, born Oak Park, Illinois, July 3, 1962; admitted to bar, 1987, Illinois and U.S. District Court, Northern District of Illinois. *Education:* Northern Illinois University (B.A., magna cum laude, 1984); DePaul University (J.D., 1987). Notes and Comment Editor, DePaul Law Review, 1987. Author: Casenote, "Conservatorship of Valerie N.," Vol. 36 DePaul Law Review. Received Chartered Property and Casualty Underwriters (CPCU) designation, 1999. *Member:* Chartered Property and Casualty Underwriters Society (Chicago Chapter). ***PRACTICE AREAS:*** Complex Insurance Coverage. ***Email:*** jdh@cs-g.com

MICHAEL J. HENNIG, born Chicago, Illinois, February 12, 1956; admitted to bar, 1981, Illinois; U.S. District Court, Northern District of Illinois and Eastern District of Wisconsin; U.S. Court of Appeals, 7th Circuit. *Education:* St. John's University (B.S., cum laude, 1978); John Marshall Law School (J.D., with high distinction, 1981). Member, John Marshall Law Review. Author: "Hospital Risk Managers and the Structural Work Act," The Occurrence, 1993. Co-Chairman, "Rookie Seminar," Illinois Association of Defense Trial Counsel. Lecturer: CBA; IDC; IICLE; 1997 Annual Conference of the Environmental Claims Managers' Association, Seattle, Washington. *Member:* Chicago Bar Association; Illinois Association of Defense Trial Counsel. ***PRACTICE AREAS:*** Medical Malpractice Defense; Insurance Defense; Environmental Litigation; Toxic Torts. ***Email:*** mjh@cs-g.com

BRIAN J. HICKEY, born Oak Park, Illinois, November 8, 1963; admitted to bar, 1988, Illinois, U.S. District Court, Northern District of Indiana and Northern District of Illinois including Trial Bar. *Education:* University of Illinois, Champaign/Urbana (B.S., 1985); DePaul University (J.D., 1988). *Member:* DuPage County and Chicago Bar Associations. (Resident, Naperville Office). ***PRACTICE AREAS:*** Personal Injury Defense; Professional Liability Defense. ***Email:*** bjh@cs-g.com

PATRICIA J. HOGAN, born Sumner, Iowa, February 25, 1959; admitted to bar, 1990, Illinois and U.S. District Court, Northern District of Illinois. *Education:* Illinois State University (B.S., 1981); University of Illinois (M.S.W., 1984; J.D., cum laude, 1990). *Member:* Chicago Bar Association; Defense Research Institute; Society of Trial Lawyers; Illinois Association of Defense Trial Counsel (Committee Chair, 2001—). ***PRACTICE AREAS:*** Construction Litigation Defense; Professional Liability Defense. ***Email:*** pjh@cs-g.com

RICHARD C. HUETTEL, born Wilmette, Illinois, February 3, 1960; admitted to bar, 1985, Illinois; U.S. District Court, Northern District of Illinois. *Education:* The University of Michigan (B.A., 1982); DePaul University (J.D., 1985). Co-Author: IICLE Chapter, "Jurisdiction of the Subject Matter," 1987-1996; "Organization of Courts," Supplement 1997; The Law and Where You Find it: Statutory & Case Law, Supplement 1997. *Member:* Illinois State Bar Association. ***PRACTICE AREAS:*** Professional Liability Defense; Medical Malpractice Defense. ***Email:*** rch@cs-g.com

CHRISTOPHER R. KEARNS, born Washington, D.C., February 23, 1971; admitted to bar, 1997, New Jersey; 1999, Illinois and U.S. Court of Appeals, Seventh Circuit. *Education:* Marquette University (B.A., 1993); John Marshall Law School (J.D., 1997). *Member:* Chicago Bar Association; Defense Research Institute; Illinois Association of Defense Counsel. ***PRACTICE AREAS:*** Construction Insurance Defense; Products Liability Defense; Toxic Tort Defense. ***Email:*** crk@cs-g.com

JAMES W. KOPRIVA, born Evanston, Illinois, August 20, 1951; admitted to bar, 1979, Illinois, U.S. District Court, Northern District of Illinois including Federal Trial Bar. *Education:* University of Illinois (B.A., 1973); Lewis University College of Law (J.D.,

(This Listing Continued)

CASSIDAY, SCHADE & GLOOR, LLP, Chicago—Continued

1979). President, Bohemian Lawyers Association, 1985. Lecturer, Illinois Institute of Continuing Legal Education "Deposition School". *Member:* Illinois State Bar Association; Society of Trial Lawyers. ***PRACTICE AREAS:*** Insurance Defense; Medical Malpractice Defense. ***Email:*** jwk@cs-g.com

KATHLEEN M. McCABE, born Des Plaines, Illinois, June 18, 1964; admitted to bar, 1990, Illinois and U.S. District Court, Northern District of Illinois including Trial Bar. *Education:* University of Illinois (B.S., cum laude, 1986); University of Copenhagen; John Marshall Law School (J.D., 1990). Assistant Attorney General, Illinois. *Member:* Chicago (Judicial Evaluation Committee) and Illinois State Bar Associations; Illinois Association of Defense Trial Counsel. ***PRACTICE AREAS:*** Products Liability Defense; Professional Liability Defense; Commercial Litigation Defense. ***Email:*** kmm@cs-g.com

MICHAEL J. MORRISSEY, born Chicago, Illinois, January 14, 1948; admitted to bar, 1974, Illinois; U.S. District Court, Northern District of Illinois. *Education:* Loyola University (B.A., 1970); DePaul University (J.D., cum laude, 1974). Named to Top 20 Tort Defense Trial Lawyers, Chicago Lawyer, January 2003. Author: "Handling the Medical Malpractice Case Before Trial," Chapter in IICLE Defense of Medical Malpractice, 1981. *Member:* Chicago, Illinois State and American Bar Associations; Trial Lawyers Club of Chicago; Society of Trial Lawyers; American Academy of Hospital Attorneys. ***PRACTICE AREAS:*** Medical Malpractice Defense; Professional Liability Defense. ***Email:*** mjm@cs-g.com

WILLIAM W. RANARD, born Helena, Montana, November 7, 1966; admitted to bar, 1992, Illinois; 1993, Missouri; 1995, Indiana; 2000, Wisconsin. *Education:* Northwestern University (B.A., 1989); University of Missouri (J.D., 1992). Treasurer, Grievance Committee and Chair, Faculty Appointments Committee, University of Missouri. Board Member, Harbor Light Salvation Army, 1993-1994. *Member:* Winnebago County and Illinois State Bar Associations; The Missouri Bar; State Bar of Wisconsin. (Also at Rockford, Illinois Office). ***PRACTICE AREAS:*** Insurance; Medical Malpractice; Personal Injury; Civil Rights Defense; Medical Malpractice Defense. ***Email:*** wwr@cs-g.com

JOHN J. REID, born Park Ridge, Illinois, January 17, 1971; admitted to bar, 1996, Illinois. *Education:* Northwestern University (B.A., 1993); IIT/Chicago-Kent College of Law (J.D., 1996). *Member:* Lake County and Illinois State Bar Associations; Defense Research Institute; Illinois Association of Defense Trial Counsel. (Resident, Libertyville Office). ***PRACTICE AREAS:*** Medical Malpractice Defense; Products Liability Defense. ***Email:*** jjr@cs-g.com

KIMBERLY L. ROBINSON, born Chicago, Illinois, April 26, 1964; admitted to bar, 1989, Illinois; U.S. District Court, Northern District of Illinois. *Education:* Northern Illinois University (B.S., 1986); Northern Illinois University College of Law (J.D., 1989). *Member:* Illinois State Bar Association. ***PRACTICE AREAS:*** Medical Malpractice Defense; Personal Injury Defense. ***Email:*** klr@cs-g.com

BRADFORD D. ROTH, born Chicago, Illinois, April 13, 1952; admitted to bar, 1979, Illinois; U.S. District Court, Northern and Central Districts of Illinois (Trial Bar); U.S. District Court, Eastern and Western Districts of Wisconsin and Northern District of Indiana; U.S. Court of Appeals, Seventh Circuit. *Education:* University of Iowa (B.B.A., 1974); IIT/Chicago-Kent College of Law (J.D., with high honors, 1979). *Member:* Illinois State Bar Association; Illinois Association of Defense Trial Counsel; Defense Research Institute; Illinois Association of Health Care Attorneys. ***PRACTICE AREAS:*** Professional Liability; Products Liability; Environmental Law; Commercial Litigation. ***Email:*** bdr@cs-g.com

PATRICIA A. RYAN, born Chicago, Illinois, October 22, 1969; admitted to bar, 1994, Illinois. *Education:* University of Illinois (B.A., 1991); Loyola University (J.D., 1994). *Member:* Illinois State Bar Association. ***PRACTICE AREAS:*** Insurance Coverage; Insurance Defense. ***Email:*** par@cs-g.com

JEFFREY R. SANDLER, born Skokie, Illinois, November 15, 1968; admitted to bar, 1993, Illinois and U.S. District Court, Northern District of Illinois. *Education:* University of Illinois (B.A., 1990); John Marshall Law School (J.D., 1993). Author: "Prejudgment Interest in Personal Injury Claims: A Proposal for the Illinois General Assembly," 25 J. Marshall L.Rev. 595 (1992). *Member:* Chicago and Illinois State Bar Associations. ***REPORTED CASES:*** Moorehead v. Metropolitan Water Reclamation District of Greater Chicago, 749 N.E.2d 443, Ill.App.3rd, 635 (1st Dist. 2001). ***PRACTICE AREAS:*** Toxic Torts; Construction Liability Defense; Environmental Litigation. ***Email:*** jrs@cs-g.com

RUDOLF G. SCHADE, JR., born New York, N.Y., September 26, 1941; admitted to bar, 1968, Illinois. *Education:* Heidelberg College (B.A., 1963); John Marshall Law School (J.D., with honors, 1968). Author: Chapter, "Trial Technique in the Medical Malpractice Defense," IICLE Book "Defense of Medical Malpractice," 1981. Lecturer, "Negotiating Personal Injury Settlements," IICLE Program, 1984. Director, 1972-1981, 1983-1990 and Chairman, 1975-1978, Evangelical Health Systems. Adjunct Professor, John Marshall Law School. Director, *Advocate* Health Care (1995—). Director, Plymouth Place, Inc., 1984-1995. Trustee, Elmhurst College, 1996—. Arbitrator, American Arbitration Association. *Member:* Chicago, Illinois State and American Bar Associations; Trial Lawyers Club of Chicago; American Society of Hospital Attorneys; Illinois Society of Hospital Attorneys; Defense Research Institute; The Lawyers Club of Chicago; The Economic Club; Illinois Association of Defense Trial Counsel (Director 1974-1992; President, 1992-1993); Society of Trial Lawyers; International Association of Defense Counsel (Served on Trial Academy, Boulder, Colorado, 1996); American Board of Trial Advocates (Advocate; Former President, Illinois Chapter; Participant, "Masters in Trial" Program); American College of Trial Lawyers; International Society of Barristers. ***PRACTICE AREAS:*** Medical Malpractice Defense; Professional Liability Defense. ***Email:*** rgs@cs-g.com

BRIAN A. SCHROEDER, born Blue Island, Illinois, August 24, 1967; admitted to bar, 1992, Illinois; 1998, U.S. District Court, Northern and Southern Districts of Illinois; 2000, U.S. Court of Appeals, Seventh Circuit. *Education:* University of Illinois (B.A., with honors, 1989); Northern Illinois University (J.D., cum laude, 1992). *Member:* Illinois State Bar Association; Appellate Lawyers Association. ***REPORTED CASES:*** Moorehead v. Metropolitan Water Reclamation District of Chicago, No. 1-00-1285 (Ill. App. Ct. 1st Dist. May 2001); Harris v. Old Kent Bank, 315 Ill. App.3d 894, 735 N.E.2d 758 (2nd Dist. 2000); Grehan v. Illinois State Labor Relations Board, 315 Ill. App.3d 459, 734 N.E.2d 33 (3rd Dist. 2000); Rohe v. CNA Insurance, 312 Ill. App.3d 123, 726 N.E.2d 38 (1st Dist. 2000). ***PRACTICE AREAS:*** Appellate Practice. ***Email:*** bas@cs-g.com

THERESE S. SEELEY, born Grand Rapids, Michigan, November 26, 1955; admitted to bar, 1982, Illinois; 1983, U.S. District Court, Northern District of Illinois including Trial Bar. *Education:* University of Notre Dame (B.B.A., 1977); DePaul University (J.D., 1982). Arbitrator, DuPage County Circuit Court. *Member:* DuPage County and Illinois State Bar Associations; Defense Research Institute. (Resident, Naperville Office). ***PRACTICE AREAS:*** Insurance Defense; Professional Liability Defense. ***Email:*** tss@cs-g.com

JOHN N. SEIBEL, born Detroit, Michigan, November 29, 1952; admitted to bar, 1978, Michigan; 1981, Illinois; U.S. District Court, Northern District of Illinois including Trial Bar. *Education:* Michigan State University (B.S., with honors, 1975); University of Detroit (J.D., magna cum laude, 1978). Lecturer: Palmer Associates, Inc., Medical Practice Management Workshop, 1986; Illinois State Medical Society, Impaired Physicians Committee on Legal Issues for Advanced Intervention Training, 1988, 1990 and 1992; Civil Litigation for Illinois Institute of Continuing Legal Education, 1987 and 1990. *Member:* Chicago and Illinois State Bar Associations; Trial Lawyers Club of Chicago (Director, 1990—). ***PRACTICE AREAS:*** Professional Liability Defense; Medical Malpractice Defense. ***Email:*** jns@cs-g.com

A. JEFFREY SEIDMAN, born Peoria, Illinois, August 5, 1946; admitted to bar, 1974, Illinois; U.S. District Court,Northern District of Illinois including Trial Bar. *Education:* Purdue University (B.S., 1969); IIT/Chicago-Kent College of Law (J.D., with highest honors, 1974). Author, recent article on first-party environmental coverage issues, *For the Defense,* Defense Research Institute. *Member:* Illinois State and American Bar Associations; Illinois Association of Defense Trial Council; Trial Lawyers Club of Chicago. ***PRACTICE AREAS:*** Directors and Officers Liability; Intellectual Property Litigation. ***Email:*** ajs@cs-g.com

STEPHANIE R. STOMBERG, born Chicago, Illinois, January 28, 1970; admitted to bar, 1997, Illinois and U.S. District Court, Northern District of Illinois. *Education:* Purdue University (B.A., 1992); Loyola University, Chicago (J.D., 1997). *Member:* Chicago and Illinois State Bar Associations. ***PRACTICE AREAS:*** Environmental Insurance Defense; Professional Liability Defense; Medical Malpractice Defense. ***Email:*** srs@cs-g.com

DOUGLAS S. STROHM, born Fort Collins, Colorado, November 15, 1964; admitted to bar, 1991, Illinois. *Education:* University of Iowa (B.S., 1987; J.D., 1990). *Member:* DuPage County Bar Association; Illinois Association of Trial Counsel. (Resident, Naperville Office). ***PRACTICE AREAS:*** Insurance Defense; Municipal Entities; Public Entities. ***Email:*** dss@cs-g.com

DAVID C. VAN DYKE, born Garner, Iowa, November 14, 1957; admitted to bar, 1990, Illinois and U.S. District Court, Northern District of Illinois including Trial Bar; registered to practice before U.S. Patent and Trademark Office. *Education:* University of Iowa (B.S., Pharmacy, 1983); Drake University (J.D., 1990). Registered Pharmacist, Iowa, 1983; Illinois, 1990. *Member:* Illinois State Bar Association; American Intellectual Property Law Association; American Society of Pharmacy Law. ***PRACTICE AREAS:*** Products Liability Defense; Pharmaceutical Intellectual Property; Patent; Trademark. ***Email:*** dvd@cs-g.com

MARIA L. VERTUNO, born Portsmouth, Virginia, January 9, 1968; admitted to bar, 1993, Illinois. *Education:* Loyola University of Chicago (B.A., with honors, 1990); University of Notre Dame (J.D., 1993). ***Email:*** mlv@cs-g.com

BRUCE M. WALL, born Chicago, Illinois, May 22, 1951; admitted to bar, 1976, Illinois; U.S. District Court, Northern District of Illinois; U.S. Court of Appeals, Seventh Circuit. *Education:* DePaul University (B.S.C., 1973); IIT/Chicago-Kent College of Law (J.D., 1976). Lecturer, "Regulating Duties and Liabilities for Hospitals," Evangelical Health Systems, February, 1988. Arbitrator, American Arbitration Association. *Member:* Chicago and Illinois State Bar Associations; Illinois Association of Hospital Attorneys; Illinois Association of Defense Trial Counsel; Society of Trial Lawyers; Illinois Society of Hospital Attorneys. ***PRACTICE AREAS:*** Products Liability Insurance Coverage; Insurance Defense; Automobile Insurance Defense. ***Email:*** bmw@cs-g.com

SALLY J. ZIMMERMAN, born East Liverpool, Ohio, April 29, 1954; admitted to bar, 1991, Illinois; U.S. District Court, Northern District of Illinois. *Education:* Bethesda Hospital School of Nursing (Nsg., 1975); Illinois Benedictine College (B.S.N., 1986); Northern Illinois University (J.D., 1991). Registered Nurse, Illinois. *Member:* Illinois State Bar Association. (Also at Rockford, Illinois Office). ***PRACTICE AREAS:*** Medical Malpractice Defense; Professional Liability Defense. ***Email:*** sjz@cs-g.com

ASSOCIATES

PHILIP M. ABELLERA, born Manila, Philippines, September 20, 1971; admitted to bar, 1999, Illinois. *Education:* University of Illinois at Chicago (B.A., 1994); John Marshall Law School (J.D., 1999). ***Email:*** pma@cs-g.com

MATTHEW K. ABRAMS, born Skokie, Illinois, September 11, 1976; admitted to bar, 2001, Illinois. *Education:* University of Michigan-Ann Arbor (B.A., 1998); Illinois Institute of Technology, Chicago-Kent College of Law (J.D., 2001). *Member:* Chicago, Illinois State and American Bar Associations. ***PRACTICE AREAS:*** Insurance Defense; Commercial Litigation. ***Email:*** mka@cs-g.com

ERIK L. ANDERSEN, born Ann Arbor, Michigan, December 31, 1968; admitted to bar, 1998, Illinois. *Education:* University of Wisconsin-Madison (B.A., 1991); Chicago-Kent College of Law, Illinois Institute of Technology (J.D., 1998). ***Email:*** ela@cs-g.com

MELISSA A. ANDERSON, born Chicago, Illinois, April 15, 1977; admitted to bar, 2002, Illinois. *Education:* University of Iowa (B.A., 1999); Chicago-Kent College of Law, Illinois Institute of Technology (J.D., 2002). ***Email:*** mas@cs-g.com

JAMES A. BERGLUND, born Chicago, Illinois, March 5, 1961; admitted to bar, 1986, Illinois. *Education:* Drake University (B.A., 1983); Chicago-Kent College of Law, Illinois Institute of Technology (J.D., 1986). (Resident, Libertyville Office). ***PRACTICE AREAS:*** Defense Litigation. ***Email:*** jb@cs-g.com

(This Listing Continued)

EHREN V. BILSHAUSEN, born Hinsdale, Illinois, August 18, 1977; admitted to bar, 2002, Illinois and U.S. District Court, Northern District of Illinois. *Education:* DePaul University (B.S., 1999); John Marshall Law School (J.D., 2002). *Member:* Illinois Trial Lawyers Association. ***Email:*** evb@cs-g.com

JENNIFER A. BOLLOW, born Darien, Illinois, July 25, 1973; admitted to bar, 1998, Illinois. *Education:* Illinois State University (B.S., 1995); Loyola University (J.D., cum laude, 1998). (Resident, Naperville Office). ***Email:*** jab@cs-g.com

BARBARA F. BROWN, born Chicago, Illinois, January 1, 1954; admitted to bar, 2002, Illinois. *Education:* Graceland College (B.S.N., 1976); University of Missouri-Kansas City (J.D., 2002). ***Email:*** bfb@cs-g.com

BROOK M. CAREY, born Elgin, Illinois, 1978; admitted to bar, 2003, Illinois. *Education:* Lewis University (B.A., with highest honors, 2000); Loyola University (J.D., cum laude, 2003). (Resident, Naperville Office). ***Email:*** bmc@cs-g.com

JULIE A. FLAHERTY-CHEATHAM, born LaSalle, Illinois, August 2, 1974; admitted to bar, 1999, Illinois. *Education:* DePaul University (B.S., 1996); IIT/Chicago-Kent College of Law (J.D., 1999). ***Email:*** jfc@cs-g.com

STACEY A. CISCHKE, born Seoul, South Korea, June 1, 1975; admitted to bar, 2000, Illinois. *Education:* Michigan State University (B.A., 1997); Loyola University (J.D., 2000). ***Email:*** sac@cs-g.com

KIMBERLY A. CRAFT, born Woodhaven, Michigan, January 1, 1976; admitted to bar, 2001, Illinois and U.S. District Court, Northern District of Illinois. *Education:* Michigan State University (B.A., 1998); Loyola University (J.D., 2001; Certificate in Health Law, 2001). Law Clerk, Tressler, Soderstrom, Maloney & Priess. Temporary Law Clerk to the Hon. Ronald A. Guzmán, U.S. District Court, Northern District of Illinois, 2001. ***Email:*** kac@cs-g.com

MARY C. CRAWFORD, born Minneapolis, Minnesota, April 9, 1969; admitted to bar, 1998, Illinois. *Education:* University of Minnesota (B.A., 1993); Pepperdine University School of Law (J.D., 1998). Recipient, Manuel P. Wiley Award for Pro Bono Service. ***Email:*** mcc@cs-g.com

THOMAS G. CRONIN, born Evanston, Illinois, December 31, 1978; admitted to bar, 2004, Illinois. *Education:* Miami University (B.A., 2000); Loyola University (J.D., cum laude, 2004). ***Email:*** tgc@cs-g.com

ALEXANDRA L. DAMES, born Chicago, Illinois, May 7, 1973; admitted to bar, 2000, Illinois. *Education:* Washington University (B.F.A., 1995); Loyola University (J.D., 2000). ***Email:*** ald@cs-g.com

ANDREW M. DeLUCA, born Youngstown, Ohio, May 2, 1973; admitted to bar, 1998, Illinois and U.S. District Court, Northern District of Illinois. *Education:* University of Notre Dame (B.A., magna cum laude, 1995); Vanderbilt University (J.D., 1998). *Member:* Chicago, Illinois State and American Bar Associations; Illinois Trial Lawyers Association. ***Email:*** amd@cs-g.com

STEPHEN P. ELLENBECKER, born Sturgeon Bay, Wisconsin, June 28, 1971; admitted to bar, 2002, Illinois. *Education:* University of Wisconsin at Whitewater (B.S.E., 1994); Chicago-Kent College of Law, Illinois Institute of Technology (J.D., with honors, 2002). ***Email:*** spe@cs-g.com

DENISE P. ERLICH, born Chicago, Illinois, August 3, 1964; admitted to bar, 1999, Illinois. *Education:* University of Illinois (B.S., 1986); DePaul University (M.B.A., 1995); IIT/Chicago-Kent College of Law (J.D., with honors, 1999). ***LANGUAGES:*** Spanish. ***Email:*** dpe@cs-g.com

RONALD D. FIET, born Rockford, Illinois, March 17, 1966; admitted to bar, 1996, Illinois. *Education:* Augustana College (B.A., 1988); Valparaiso University (J.D., 1995). *Member:* Winnebago County (Treasurer, Young Lawyers Division, 1998-1999), Illinois State and American Bar Associations. (Also at Rockford Office). ***Email:*** rdf@cs-g.com

ANDREW T. FLEISHMAN, born Boston, Massachusetts, September 15, 1968; admitted to bar, 2001, Illinois. *Education:* New York University (B.A., 1991); Illinois Institute of Technology, Chicago-Kent College of Law (J.D., 1995). (Also at Libertyville Office). ***Email:*** atf@cs-g.com

JAMIE H. GOLDSTEIN, born Skokie, Illinois, January 28, 1979; admitted to bar, 2004, Illinois. *Education:* University of Wisconsin-Madison (B.S., 2001); Illinois Institute of Technology, Chicago-Kent College of Law (J.D., 2004). Order of the Coif. (Also at Libertyville Office). ***Email:*** jhg@cs-g.com

PATRICK E. HALLIDAY, born Peoria, Illinois, June 28, 1978; admitted to bar, 2004, Illinois. *Education:* Northern Illinois University (B.A., 2000); DePaul University (J.D., 2003). ***Email:*** peh@cs-g.com

TRISHA M. HART, born Oak Park, Illinois, February 2, 1977; admitted to bar, 2001, Illinois and U.S. District Court, Northern District of Illinois. *Education:* Dominican University (B.A., with honors, 1998); John Marshall Law School (J.D., cum laude, 2001). John Marshall Distinguished Scholar. Member, John Marshall Law Review, 2000-2001. ***Email:*** tmh@cs-g.com

JEFFREY A. HESSER, born Skokie, Illinois, February 26, 1972; admitted to bar, 1998, Illinois. *Education:* University of Missouri-Columbia (B.A., 1994); DePaul University (J.D., 1998). ***Email:*** jah@cs-g.com

JAMES B. HILLER, born Royal Oak, Michigan, December 1, 1974; admitted to bar, 2002, Illinois. *Education:* Oakland University (B.A., 1998); DePaul University (J.D., 2002). ***Email:*** jbh@cs-g.com

JAMIE L. HULL, born Cincinnati, Ohio, May 26, 1975; admitted to bar, 2001, Illinois; 2002, U.S. Court of Appeals, Seventh Circuit. *Education:* Miami University (B.A., 1997); John Marshall Law School (J.D., 2000). ***Email:*** jlh@cs-g.com

PAUL T. KLEPPETSCH, born Hinsdale, Illinois, September 4, 1978; admitted to bar, 2003, Illinois and U.S. District Court, Northern District of Illinois. *Education:* University of Dayton (B.A., summa cum laude, 2000); John Marshall Law School (J.D., cum laude, 2003). Member, The John Marshall Law School Law Review. Author, "In the Wake of Kyllo v. United States: The Future of the Real Imaging Cameras," 36 J.Marshall L.R.CV 507 (2003). *Member:* American Bar Association. ***Email:*** ptk@cs-g.com

(This Listing Continued)

BRANDON J. KROFT, born Valparaiso, Indiana, October 24, 1972; admitted to bar, 1999, Illinois; 2002, Indiana. *Education:* Valparaiso University (B.A., 1995); DePaul University College of Law (J.D., 1999). ***PRACTICE AREAS:*** Insurance Coverage; Commercial Litigation; Civil Litigation; Construction Litigation; Insurance Litigation. ***Email:*** bjk@cs-g.com

BRIAN F. LANSU, born Villa Park, Illinois, June 6, 1972; admitted to bar, 1999, Illinois. *Education:* DePauw University (B.A., 1994); Northern Illinois University (J.D., 1999). ***Email:*** bfl@cs-g.com

ROBIN B. LEVIN, born Skokie, Illinois, June 7, 1968; admitted to bar, 1999, Illinois. *Education:* University of Illinois (B.S., 1990); John Marshall Law School (J.D., 1999). (Resident, Libertyville Office). ***Email:*** rbl@cs-g.com

THOMAS M. LOMBARDO, born Park Ridge, Illinois, 1977; admitted to bar, 2003, Illinois. *Education:* DePaul University (B.A., 2000): Loyola University (J.D., 2002). ***Email:*** tml@cs-g.com

ANTHONY J. LONGO, born Evanston, Illinois, March 22, 1979; admitted to bar, 2005, Illinois. *Education:* Loyola University (B.A., cum laude, 2001); John Marshall Law School (J.D., 2004). Dean's Scholar. ***Email:*** ajl@cs-g.com

GINA M. LUKOWSKI, born Chicago, Illinois, September 29, 1978; admitted to bar, 2003, Illinois. *Education:* DePaul University (B.A., 2000); John Marshall Law School (J.D., 2003). ***Email:*** gml@cs-g.com

MICHAEL T. LYNCH, born Queens, New York, February 10, 1978; admitted to bar, 2004, New York and Illinois. *Education:* Cornell University (B.A., 2000); Boston College (J.D., 2004). ***Email:*** mtl@cs-g.com

SARA F. MARZULLO, born Berkeley, California, April 21, 1975; admitted to bar, 2000, Illinois. *Education:* University of California at Los Angeles (B.A., 1996); Loyola University (J.D., 2000). ***Email:*** sfm@cs-g.com

YARO M. MELNYK, born Guadalajara, Mexico, April 4, 1973; admitted to bar, 2000, Illinois. *Education:* Loyola University (B.S., magna cum laude, 1995); Chicago-Kent College of Law, Illinois Institute of Technology (J.D., with honors, 1999). ***Email:*** ymm@cs-g.com

JONATHAN P. MINCIELI, born Brooklyn, New York, February 6, 1971; admitted to bar, 1997, New York; 2000, New Jersey; 2001, Illinois. *Education:* State University of New York at Oswego (B.A., 1993); St. John's University (J.D., cum laude, 1996). (Resident, Naperville Office). ***Email:*** jpm@cs-g.com

DONNA L. MOORE, born Chicago, Illinois, 1965; admitted to bar, 2004, Illinois. *Education:* Roosevelt University (B.G.S., 1995); University of Phoenix (M.B.A., 2001); John Marshall Law School (J.D., 2004). ***Email:*** dlm@cs-g.com

NATHAN I. NEFF, born Essen, West Germany, April 16, 1972; admitted to bar, 2000, Illinois. *Education:* University of Southern California (B.A., 1995); Loyola University (J.D., 2000). ***Email:*** nin@cs-g.com

HENRY ORTIZ, born Gary, Indiana, September 13, 1973; admitted to bar, 2001, Illinois. *Education:* Purdue University (B.A., 1996); Valparaiso University (J.D., 2001). ***Email:*** ho@cs-g.com

TANYA PARK, born Grand Rapids, Michigan, June 25, 1967; admitted to bar, 1998, Illinois. *Education:* University of Michigan (B.A., cum laude, 1989); Valparaiso University (J.D., 1998). ***Email:*** tb@cs-g.com

JORI L. POLISNER, born Elk Grove Village, Illinois, November 25, 1973; admitted to bar, 2000, Illinois. *Education:* University of Wisconsin at Madison (B.A., 1995); IIT/Chicago-Kent College of Law (J.D., 2000). ***Email:*** jlp@cs-g.com

JENNIFER T. RHOADES, born Goshen, Indiana, May 19, 1975; admitted to bar, 2001, Illinois. *Education:* Indiana University (B.A., 1997); Loyola University (J.D., 2001). ***Email:*** jtr@cs-g.com

J. HAYES RYAN, born Chicago, Illinois, March 27, 1974; admitted to bar, 2001, Illinois. *Education:* Kenyon College (B.A., 1996); John Marshall Law School (J.D., 2000). ***Email:*** jhr@cs-g.com

MARK A. SANSONE, born Evergreen Park, Illinois, April 27, 1975; admitted to bar, 2000, Illinois. *Education:* St. Joseph's College (B.S., 1997); Valparaiso University School of Law (J.D., 2000). (Resident, Naperville Office). ***Email:*** mas@cs-g.com

LYNDE SELDEN, III, born N.Y., N.Y., October 21, 1972; admitted to bar, 2000, California; 2003, Illinois. *Education:* University of California at Davis (B.A., 1994); University of San Diego (J.D., 1999). ***Email:*** ls3@cs-g.com

STEVEN M. SHEAR, born Grand Haven, Michigan, June 25, 1974; admitted to bar, 2001, Illinois and U.S. District Court, Northern District of Illinois. *Education:* Michigan State University (B.A., 1996); DePaul University (J.D., 2001). *Member:* Chicago Bar Association (Member, Young Lawyers Section); Illinois Trial Lawyers Association. ***Email:*** sms@cs-g.com

OTTO J. SHRAGAL, born Merrillville, Indiana, December 4, 1978; admitted to bar, 2005, Illinois. *Education:* Tri-State University (B.A., 2001); John Marshall Law School (J.D., cum laude, 2005). ***Email:*** ojs@cs-g.com

TRISHA K. TESMER, born LaGrange, Illinois, September 28, 1976; admitted to bar, 2001, Illinois. *Education:* Indiana University (B.S., 1998); DePaul University (J.D., 2001). Order of the Barristers. Member: DePaul University Law Review; Moot Court Society. ***PRACTICE AREAS:*** Civil Litigation. ***Email:*** tkt@cs-g.com

CHRISTINE L. TRIMARCO, born Park Ridge, Illinois, May 13, 1972; admitted to bar, 1997, Illinois. *Education:* DePaul University (B.A., 1994); John Marshall Law School (J.D., 1997). ***Email:*** clt@cs-g.com

TIFFANIE B. TUCKER, born Chicago, Illinois, November 8, 1975; admitted to bar, 2000, Illinois. *Education:* Truman State University (B.S., 1997); University of Missouri (J.D., 2000). Order of the Barristers. ***Email:*** tbt@cs-g.com

(This Listing Continued)

CASSIDAY, SCHADE & GLOOR, LLP, Chicago—Continued

LISA VELEZ, born Chicago, Illinois, May 4, 1972; admitted to bar, 1998, Illinois; 2002, U.S. District Court, Northern District of Illinois. *Education:* University of Illinois (B.A., 1994); University of California School of Law, Los Angeles (J.D., 1997). *Member:* Illinois State Bar Association. ***Email:*** lv@cs-g.com

MATTHEW H. WELLER, born Columbus, Ohio, November 25, 1975; admitted to bar, 2002, Illinois. *Education:* Elmhurst College (B.A., 1998); Illinois Institute of Technology, Chicago-Kent College of Law (J.D., 2002). ***Email:*** mhw@cs-g.com

CHRISTOPHER M. WELLING, born St. Louis, Missouri, January 16, 1975; admitted to bar, 2000, Missouri; 2003, Illinois. *Education:* St. Louis University (B.A., summa cum laude, 1997); St. Louis University School of Law (J.D., 2000); DePaul University (LL.M., 2003). ***Email:*** cmw@cs-g.com

DANIEL E. WIESCH, born Chicago, Illinois, March 4, 1975; admitted to bar, 2001, Illinois. *Education:* Northwestern University (B.A., 1997); University of Illinois (J.D., cum laude, 2001). (Resident, Libertyville Office). ***Email:*** dew@cs-g.com

SHANTEL D. WOOD-BILL, born Silvis, Illinois, September 24, 1976; admitted to bar, 2001, Illinois. *Education:* Illinois State University (B.S., 1998); DePaul University (J.D., 2001). Order of Barristers. ***Email:*** sdb@cs-g.com

OF COUNSEL

BRADFORD A. BURTON, born Philadelphia, Pennsylvania, November 4, 1957; admitted to bar, 1984, Illinois and U.S. District Court, Northern District of Illinois. *Education:* Denison University (B.A., 1980); John Marshall Law School (J.D., 1983). *Member:* Chicago and Illinois State Bar Associations. ***PRACTICE AREAS:*** Insurance Defense; Construction Law. ***Email:*** bab@cs-g.com

JOHN D. CASSIDAY, born Springfield, Illinois, February 19, 1937; admitted to bar, 1962, Illinois; U.S. District Court, Northern District of Illinois; U.S. Court of Appeals, Seventh Circuit. *Education:* Northwestern University (B.A., 1959); University of Virginia (LL.B., 1962). Author: "The Prescription Drug Exception to The Doctrine of Strict Liability," published in the Illinois State Bar Journal, December, 1969. Member, Attorney Registration and Disciplinary Commission of the Illinois Supreme Court, 1975-1976. *Member:* Chicago and Illinois State Bar Associations; Defense Research Institute. ***PRACTICE AREAS:*** Professional Liability Insurance Coverage. ***Email:*** jdc@cs-g.com

SHARON T. DOHERTY, born Evergreen Park, Illinois, August 25, 1963; admitted to bar, 1987, Illinois; 1988, U.S. District Court, Northern District of Illinois including Trial Bar. *Education:* Creighton University (B.S.B.A., 1985; J.D., 1987). Guest Lecturer, Illinois Association of Defense Trial Counsel. Arbitrator, Circuit Court of Cook County. *Member:* Chicago and Illinois State Bar Associations; Women's Bar Association; Illinois Association of Defense Trial Counsel. ***PRACTICE AREAS:*** Insurance Defense. ***Email:*** std@cs-g.com

WILLIAM M. DUNN, born Decatur, Illinois, November 20, 1967; admitted to bar, 1995, Illinois and U.S. District Court, Northern District of Illinois. *Education:* University of Notre Dame (B.A., 1989); John Marshall Law School (J.D., 1995). *Member:* Chicago and Illinois State Bar Associations. ***PRACTICE AREAS:*** Medical Malpractice Defense; Commercial Insurance Defense. ***Email:*** wmd@cs-g.com

DONALD F. IVANSEK, born Chicago, Illinois, July 14, 1961; admitted to bar, 1990, Illinois. *Education:* St. Mary's College of Minnesota (B.A., 1983); The John Marshall Law School (J.D., cum laude, 1990). Order of John Marshall. *Member:* Chicago and Illinois State Bar Associations; Appellate Lawyers Association of Illinois. ***REPORTED CASES:*** Common v. West Suburban Hosp. Med. Center, 1998 W.L. 813114, 704 NE2d 731 (1st Dist. 1998); Pepper Const. Co. v. Transcontinental Ins. Co., 285 Ill.App. 3d 573, 673 NE2d 1128 (1st Dist. 1996); Geraghty v. Continental Western Life Ins. Co., 281 Ill.App. 3d 669, 667 NE2d 510 (1st Dist. 1996); Butkiewicz v. Loyola University Medical Center, 244 Ill-.Dec.149, W.L. 137119 (1st Dist. 2000); Rohe v. CAN Ins. Co., W.L. 140923 (1st Dist. 2000). ***PRACTICE AREAS:*** Appellate Practice; Insurance Coverage Defense; Professional Liability Defense. ***Email:*** dfi@cs-g.com

SANDRA E. KUPELIAN, born Elmhurst, Illinois, February 1, 1965; admitted to bar, 1990, Illinois; 1993, U.S. District Court, Northern District of Illinois; 1994, U.S. District Court, Central District of Illinois; 1995, U.S. District Court, Western District of Michigan and U.S. Court of Appeals, Seventh Circuit; 1996, U.S. Supreme Court. *Education:* Northern Illinois University (B.A., 1987); University of Illinois (J.D., cum laude, 1990). Clerkships: Justice Marvin D. Dunn, Illinois Appellate Court, Second District, 1990-1992; Justice James F. Quetsch, Illinois Appellate Court, Second District, 1993. *Member:* Illinois State Bar Association; Appellate Lawyers Association. ***PRACTICE AREAS:*** Appellate Practice; Products Liability Defense; Complex and Multi-District Litigation. ***Email:*** sek@cs-g.com

CONSTANCE R. O'NEILL, born Rockford, Illinois, November 8, 1961; admitted to bar, 1986, Illinois and U.S. District Court, Northern District of Illinois. *Education:* University of Illinois-Champaign (B.S., 1983); IIT/Chicago-Kent College of Law (J.D., 1986). Co-Author: "Apparent Agency: How Can Hospitals Combat the Appearance?" Journal of American Medical Record Association, May 1988; Chapter, "Expert Evidence," Medical Malpractice Volume of the Illinois Institute for Continuing Education, 1989, Supplement, 1992. *Member:* Chicago and Illinois State Bar Associations; American Trial Lawyers Association. ***PRACTICE AREAS:*** Medical Malpractice Defense; Civil Practice. ***Email:*** cro@cs-g.com

TAMI J. REDING-BRUBAKER, born Chicago, Illinois, November 20, 1958; admitted to bar, 1983, Illinois. *Education:* North Central College (B.A., cum laude, 1980); IIT/Chicago-Kent College of Law (J.D., 1983). *Member:* Lake County and Illinois State Bar Associations. (Resident, Libertyville, Illinois Office). ***PRACTICE AREAS:*** Medical Malpractice Defense. ***Email:*** tjr@cs-g.com

DEBORAH M. SHERIDAN, born St. Andrews, Scotland, August 3, 1968; admitted to bar, 1994, Illinois; 1996, New York. *Education:* Hofstra University (B.B.A., 1989; J.D., 1993). *Member:* Nassau County Bar Association. ***LANGUAGES:*** French. ***PRACTICE AREAS:*** Insurance Coverage; Complex Insurance Coverage. ***Email:*** dms@cs-g.com

(This Listing Continued)

JULIE A. TEUSCHER, born Monroe, Wisconsin, July 18, 1960; admitted to bar, 1985, Illinois and U.S. District Court, Northern District of Illinois; 1993, Trial Bar. *Education:* University of Illinois (B.A., 1982); DePaul University (J.D., with honors, 1985). Member, Regional Moot Court Competition. ***PRACTICE AREAS:*** Medical Malpractice Defense; Products Liability Defense; Premises Liability Defense.

A list of Representative Clients will be made available upon request.

FRANK CECE, JR.

53 WEST JACKSON BOULEVARD
SUITE 1460
CHICAGO, ILLINOIS 60604
Telephone: 312-922-0400
Fax: 312-362-9907
Email: frank@cecelaw.com
URL: http://www.cecelaw.net

Criminal Defense, Federal Crimes, Felonies, Misdemeanors and Traffic including DUI, Battery, Domestic, Drugs, Possession, Theft, Forgery, Burglary, Robbery, Criminal Sexual Assault, Reckless Homicide, Murder, Probation Violations, Bond Hearings, Preliminary Hearings, Personal Injury, Automobile Accidents, Wrongful Death, Construction Accidents, Truck Accidents.

FRANK CECE, JR., born Chicago, Illinois, October 11, 1964; admitted to bar, 1991, Illinois; 1992, U.S. District Court, Northern District of Illinois. *Education:* Loyola University (B.A., 1987); John Marshall Law School (J.D., 1991). Member, Justinian Society of Lawyers. *Member:* Chicago Bar Association; National Association of Criminal Defense Lawyers; Federal Trial Bar; Capital Litigation Trial Bar. ***LANGUAGES:*** Spanish.

LAW OFFICES OF CHADWICK & LAKERDAS

5300 SOUTH SHORE DRIVE
SUITE 100
CHICAGO, ILLINOIS 60615
Telephone: 773-955-1088
Fax: 773-955-9511
URL: http://www.chadwicklakerdaslaw.com
URL: http://www.chadwicklakerdas.com

Criminal Law, Driving While Intoxicated, Drug Crimes, Felonies, Homicide, Juvenile Law, Misdemeanors, Parole and Probation, Sexual Assault, Traffic Violations, Personal Injury, Airplane Crash Litigation, Automobile Accidents, Dog Bites, Railroad Accidents, Sexual Abuse, Slip and Fall, Wrongful Death.

MEMBERS OF FIRM

STURGIS E. CHADWICK, III, born Buffalo, New York, December 26, 1957; admitted to bar, 1984, Illinois; 1987, Florida. *Education:* Southern Illinois University (B.A., 1981); John Marshall Law School (J.D., 1984). *Member:* The Florida Bar; Illinois State Bar Association. ***PRACTICE AREAS:*** Personal Injury; Medical Malpractice; Criminal Defense. ***Email:*** schadwick@chadwicklakerdas.com

JAMES G. LAKERDAS, born Charleroi, Pennsylvania, August 11, 1953; admitted to bar, 1984, Illinois. *Education:* Duquesne University (B.A., 1975); Southern Illinois University (M.S., Counseling, 1979); John Marshall Law School (J.D., 1984). *Member:* Chicago; Illinois State and American Bar Associations. ***LANGUAGES:*** Greek. ***PRACTICE AREAS:*** Personal Injury; Workers Compensation; Real Estate. ***Email:*** jlakerdas@chadwicklakerdas.com

ASSOCIATE

MICHAEL G. KELLY, born Gary, Indiana, 1974; admitted to bar, 2001, Illinois. *Education:* Knox College (B.A., 1997); DePaul University School of Law (J.D., 2001). *Member:* Illinois State Bar Association. ***PRACTICE AREAS:*** Personal Injury; Consumer Fraud. ***Email:*** mkelly@chadwicklakerdas.com

DAYNA WHEATLEY CHANG, LLC

SUITE 640
166 W. WASHINGTON STREET
CHICAGO, ILLINOIS 60602
Telephone: 312-236-9911
Fax: 312-236-9500
Email: daynachg@aol.com

Troy, Michigan Office: 100 Big Beaver Road, Suite 200, 48084. Telephone: 248-680-8408. Fax: 248-680-6699.

Immigration Law, Mediation, Employment Law, Discrimination, Sexual Harassment, Wrongful Termination, Family Law, Real Estate.

FIRM PROFILE: The mission of Dayna Wheatley Chang, LLC is to provide excellent representation for its clients and to work for the betterment of its client communities. Because of its emphasis on mediation, however, the law practice is also geared to helping clients avoid the costs of litigation.

Languages: Translators for nearly any language may be arranged with advance notice. Depending on the language, an additional fee may be required.

DAYNA CHANG, born Highland Park, Michigan, March 31, 1965; admitted to bar, 2003, Illinois and U.S. District Court, Northern District of Illinois. *Education:* Wayne State University (B.A., Political Science, 1989); Wheaton College (M.A., Intercultural Studies, 1995); Chicago-Kent College of Law, Illinois Institute of Technology (J.D., 2003). Phi Delta Phi. Certified Mediator, Center For Conflict Resolution (CCR), Chicago, Illinois, 2004.

(This Listing Continued)

Law Clerk, Tressler, Soderstrom, Maloney & Priess, 2001-2002. Judicial Extern, U.S. Department of Justice, Executive Office of Immigration Review, Chicago Immigration Court, 2003. Associate, Law Offices of MaryLu Cianciolo, 2003-2004. President, Diversity Group, Inc. 1998-2001. Adjunct Faculty, Cultural Diversity and Sociology Courses, Joliet Junior College, 1995-1997 and 1999-2000. English Teacher, Hsinchu International School in Taiwan, 1992-1994. Claims Representative, Social Security Administration, 1990-1992. *Member:* Chicago and Illinois State Bar Associations; American Immigration Lawyers Association (AILA); Association for Conflict Resolution (ACR). ***PRACTICE AREAS:*** Immigration Law; Mediation; Employment Law; Discrimination; Sexual Harassment; Wrongful Termination.

CHAPMAN AND CUTLER LLP

Established in 1913

111 WEST MONROE STREET
CHICAGO, ILLINOIS 60603
Telephone: 312-845-3000
Fax: 312-701-2361
Email: postmaster@chapman.com
URL: http://www.chapman.com

San Francisco, California Office: 26th Floor, 595 Market Street, 94105. Telephone: 415-541-0500. Fax: 415-541-0506.

Salt Lake City, Utah Office: One Utah Center, Suite 2000, 201 South Main Street, 84111. Telephone: 801-533-0066. Fax: 801-533-9595.

General Practice. Corporate, State, Municipal and Public Authority Financing. Corporation Law and Corporate Financing, Securities, Intellectual Property, Public Utilities, Real Estate, Banking, Lease Financing, Asset Securitization, State and Federal Taxation, Estate Planning, Trust and Probate Law. Bankruptcy Law. Practice before State and Federal Administrative and Regulatory Agencies. Litigation in Federal and State Courts.

ANN E. ACKER, admitted to bar, 1973, Illinois. *Education:* St. Mary's College; Loyola University Chicago School of Law. ***Email:*** acker@chapman.com

SCOTT R. ANDERSON, admitted to bar, 1993, Illinois. *Education:* Augustana College; Loyola University Chicago School of Law. ***Email:*** scanders@chapman.com

LEAH F. ARNER, admitted to bar, 1981, Colorado; 1987, Pennsylvania; 1990, Illinois. *Education:* University of Kansas; University of Denver College of Law. ***Email:*** arner@chapman.com

DAVID T. B. AUDLEY, admitted to bar, 1985, Illinois and Wisconsin. *Education:* University of Wisconsin-Madison; University of Wisconsin Law School. ***Email:*** audley@chapman.com

ANDREA G. BACON, admitted to bar, 1979, Illinois. *Education:* University of Illinois; Northwestern University School of Law. ***Email:*** bacon@chapman.com

CYNTHIA A. BAKER, admitted to bar, 1990, New York; 1999, Illinois. *Education:* Oakland University; University of Michigan Law School.

DANIEL W. BAKER, admitted to bar, 1995, Illinois. *Education:* Amherst College; University of Chicago Law School. ***Email:*** dbaker@chapman.com

MICHAEL P. BARRETT, admitted to bar, 1975, Illinois. *Education:* University of Illinois; University of Illinois College of Law. ***Email:*** barrett@chapman.com

DAVID S. BARRITT, admitted to bar, 1981, Illinois. *Education:* DePauw University; Indiana University School of Law-Bloomington. ***Email:*** barritt@chapman.com

ERIN P. BARTHOLOMY, admitted to bar, 1993, Illinois. *Education:* University of Notre Dame; University of Notre Dame Law School. ***Email:*** bartholo@chapman.com

WALTER P. BEGLEY, admitted to bar, 1984, Illinois. *Education:* Indiana University; University of Notre Dame Law School. ***Email:*** begley@chapman.com

MICHAEL T. BENZ, admitted to bar, 1986, Illinois. *Education:* University of Illinois; Loyola University Chicago School of Law. ***Email:*** benz@chapman.com

JEFFREY D. BERRY, admitted to bar, 1980, Illinois. *Education:* University of Cincinnati; Georgetown University Law Center; DePaul University College of Law. ***Email:*** berry@chapman.com

DEBORAH T. BOYE, admitted to bar, 1980, Illinois; 1988, Georgia. *Education:* University of Arkansas; University of Notre Dame Law School. ***Email:*** dboye@chapman.com

JAMES M. BREEN, admitted to bar, 1968, Illinois. *Education:* St. Francis College; Catholic University of America-Columbus School of Law. ***Email:*** breen@chapman.com

JEFFREY A. BURGER, admitted to bar, 1979, Illinois. *Education:* Lafayette College; Indiana University School of Law-Bloomington. ***Email:*** burger@chapman.com

NANCY A. BURKE, admitted to bar, 1987, Illinois. *Education:* University of Notre Dame; University of Notre Dame Law School. ***Email:*** burke@chapman.com

PAUL D. CARMAN, admitted to bar, 1986, Illinois. *Education:* Kansas Wesleyan University; Northwestern University School of Law. ***Email:*** carman@chapman.com

THEODORE S. CHAPMAN (1877-1943)

DAVID J. CHOLST, admitted to bar, 1983, Illinois. *Education:* Harvard University; University of Chicago Law School. ***Email:*** cholst@chapman.com

STEVEN L. CLARK, admitted to bar, 1968, Illinois. *Education:* Indiana University; University of Chicago Law School. ***Email:*** sclark@chapman.com

JEFFREY G. CLOSE, admitted to bar, 1994, Illinois. *Education:* DePaul University; Northwestern University School of Law. ***Email:*** jclose@chapman.com

MARLA CHERNOF COHEN, admitted to bar, 1977, Illinois. *Education:* Northwestern University; Loyola University School of Law. ***Email:*** cohen@chapman.com

RAFAEL L. COOK, admitted to bar, 1983, Illinois. *Education:* Ohio Wesleyan University; Harvard Law School. ***Email:*** cook@chapman.com

(This Listing Continued)

RICHARD A. COSGROVE, admitted to bar, 1977, Illinois. *Education:* Coe College; University of Iowa College of Law. ***Email:*** cosgrove@chapman.com

ROBERT M. CRISWELL, admitted to bar, 1994, Illinois. *Education:* University of Wisconsin-Madison; DePaul University College of Law. ***Email:*** criswell@chapman.com

JOHN R. CROSSAN, admitted to bar, 1974, Illinois; registered to practice before U.S. Patent and Trademark Office. *Education:* University of Virginia; University of Chicago Law School. ***Email:*** crossan@chapman.com

DAVID S. CROSSETT, admitted to bar, 1980, Illinois. *Education:* University of Notre Dame; University of Notre Dame Law School; DePaul University College of Law. ***Email:*** crossett@chapman.com

PATRICIA M. CURTNER, admitted to bar, 1979, Illinois. *Education:* University of Michigan; University of Michigan Law School. ***Email:*** curtner@chapman.com

HENRY E. CUTLER (1879-1959)

STATHY DARCY, admitted to bar, 1991, California; 1994, Illinois. *Education:* University of Illinois at Urbana-Champaign; Pepperdine University School of Law. ***Email:*** darcy@chapman.com

DANIEL J. FAVERO, admitted to bar, 1989, Illinois. *Education:* University of Illinois at Springfield (Sangamon State University); DePaul University College of Law. ***Email:*** favero@chapman.com

ERIC F. FESS, admitted to bar, 1978, Illinois. *Education:* Southern Methodist University; University of Illinois College of Law. ***Email:*** fess@chapman.com

J. RICHARD FISHER, JR., admitted to bar, 1971, Illinois. *Education:* Ohio State University; Northwestern University School of Law. ***Email:*** fisher@chapman.com

FELICE R. FOUNDOS, admitted to bar, 1990, Illinois. *Education:* Loyola University, Chicago; University of Notre Dame Law School. ***Email:*** foundos@chapman.com

AUGUST J. FRANCIS, admitted to bar, 1994, Illinois. *Education:* DePaul University; Chicago-Kent College of Law. ***Email:*** francis@chapman.com

MARC P. FRANSON, admitted to bar, 1980, Iowa; 1984, Illinois. *Education:* Drake University; Drake University Law School. ***Email:*** franson@chapman.com

BRIAN D. FREE, admitted to bar, 1991, Illinois. *Education:* Miami University; Chicago-Kent College of Law. ***Email:*** free@chapman.com

STEVEN G. FROST, admitted to bar, 1983, Illinois. *Education:* University of Colorado at Boulder; DePaul University; DePaul University College of Law. ***Email:*** frost@chapman.com

LYNDA K. GIVEN, admitted to bar, 1980, Illinois. *Education:* Miami University; Ohio State University College of Law. ***Email:*** given@chapman.com

RONALD J. HACKER, admitted to bar, 1988, Illinois. *Education:* University of Illinois; University of Iowa College of Law. ***Email:*** hacker@chapman.com

HEATHER L. HANSCHE, admitted to bar, 1980, Michigan; 1981, Illinois. *Education:* University of Michigan; University of Detroit Mercy School of Law. ***Email:*** hansche@chapman.com

STEVEN G. HASTINGS, admitted to bar, 1987, Illinois. *Education:* University of Illinois; University of Illinois College of Law. ***Email:*** hastings@chapman.com

KYLE W. HENDERSON, admitted to bar, 1986, Illinois. *Education:* Kenyon College; University of Chicago; University of Michigan Law School. ***Email:*** khenderson@chapman.com

WILLIAM C. HERMANN, admitted to bar, 1990, Illinois. *Education:* University of Notre Dame; Indiana University School of Law-Bloomington. ***Email:*** whermann@chapman.com

JOHN C. HITT, JR., admitted to bar, 1990, Illinois. *Education:* Yale University; University of Virginia School of Law. ***Email:*** hitt@chapman.com

DOUGLAS R. HOFFMAN, admitted to bar, 1982, Illinois; 2005, New York. *Education:* Illinois Benedictine College; Chicago-Kent College of Law. ***Email:*** hoffman@chapman.com

VAN E. HOLKEBOER, admitted to bar, 1983, Illinois. *Education:* Calvin College; University of Michigan Law School. ***Email:*** holkrboer@chapman.com

CHARLES S. HUGHES, admitted to bar, 1976, Illinois. *Education:* Augustana College; Northwestern University School of Law. ***Email:*** hughes@chapman.com

R. WILLIAM HUNTER, admitted to bar, 1991, Illinois. *Education:* Southern Methodist University; University of Illinois College of Law. ***Email:*** hunter@chapman.com

CHARLES L. JARIK, admitted to bar, 1978, Illinois. *Education:* Duke University; Vanderbilt University Law School. ***Email:*** jarik@chapman.com

DANIEL L. JOHNSON, admitted to bar, 1975, Illinois. *Education:* Cornell University; University of Illinois College of Law. ***Email:*** djohnson@chapman.com

CHRISTIAN T. JONES, admitted to bar, 1968, Illinois; 1984, California. *Education:* Occidental College; Northwestern University School of Law. ***Email:*** cjones@chapman.com

GREGORY A. KLAMRZYNSKI, admitted to bar, 1995, Illinois. *Education:* DePaul University; University of Illinois College of Law. ***Email:*** klamrzyn@chapman.com

RICHARD F. KLEIN, admitted to bar, 1981, Illinois. *Education:* University of Illinois; University of Notre Dame Law School. ***Email:*** klein@chapman.com

MARK J. KNEEDY, admitted to bar, 1972, Illinois. *Education:* University of Illinois; University of Illinois College of Law. ***Email:*** kneedy@chapman.com

JONATHAN A. KOFF, admitted to bar, 1985, Illinois. *Education:* University of Illinois; DePaul University College of Law. ***Email:*** koff@chapman.com

PAUL C. KOSIN, admitted to bar, 1968, Illinois. *Education:* Northwestern University; Northwestern University School of Law. ***Email:*** kosin@chapman.com

KELLY K. KOST, admitted to bar, 1986, Illinois. *Education:* Monmouth College; Vanderbilt University Law School. ***Email:*** kost@chapman.com

(This Listing Continued)

CHAPMAN AND CUTLER LLP, Chicago—Continued

DARRELL R. LARSEN, JR., admitted to bar, 1976, Utah; 1977, California; 1995, Illinois; 2002, New York. *Education:* University of Utah; University of Utah College of Law. ***Email:*** larsen@chapman.com

THOMAS C. LEE, admitted to bar, 1989, New York; 2005, Illinois. *Education:* New York University; Columbia University; University of Pennsylvania Law School. ***Email:*** thomlee@chapman.com

MATTHEW R. LEWIN, admitted to bar, 1981, Illinois. *Education:* State University of New York at Albany; Indiana University School of Law-Bloomington. ***Email:*** lewin@chapman.com

WILLIAM M. LIBIT, admitted to bar, 1985, Illinois; 2001, New York. *Education:* Emory University; Northwestern University School of Law. ***Email:*** libit@chapman.com

FREDERICK V. LOCHBIHLER, admitted to bar, 1976, Illinois. *Education:* University of Notre Dame; University of Chicago Law School. ***Email:*** lochbihl@chapman.com

ROBERT E. LOCKNER, admitted to bar, 1979, Illinois. *Education:* University of Minnesota; Harvard Law School. ***Email:*** lockner@chapman.com

JAMES E. LUEBCHOW, admitted to bar, 1973, Illinois. *Education:* Northern Illinois University; Duke University School of Law. ***Email:*** luebchow@chapman.com

DAVID A. LULLO, admitted to bar, 1987, Illinois. *Education:* University of Illinois; University of Michigan Law School. ***Email:*** lullo@chapman.com

NEIL R. MANN, admitted to bar, 1975, Illinois. *Education:* University of Michigan; University of Michigan Law School. ***Email:*** mann@chapman.com

STEVEN C. MASON, admitted to bar, 1988, Texas; 1996, Illinois. *Education:* University of Notre Dame; University of Illinois College of Law; Lewis and Clark College-Northwestern School of Law. ***Email:*** mason@chapman.com

MICHAEL G. McGEE, admitted to bar, 1977, Illinois. *Education:* Roosevelt University; University of Michigan Law School. ***Email:*** mcgee@chapman.com

TIMOTHY V. McGREE, admitted to bar, 1973, Illinois. *Education:* University of Chicago; University of Chicago Law School. ***Email:*** mcgree@chapman.com

TERRY A. McILROY, admitted to bar, 1970, Illinois. *Education:* University of Washington; University of Chicago Law School. ***Email:*** mcilroy@chapman.com

TIMOTHY P. MOHAN, admitted to bar, 1985, Illinois. *Education:* Michigan State University; DePaul University College of Law. ***Email:*** mohan@chapman.com

ROBERT C. NASH, admitted to bar, 1969, Illinois. *Education:* Dartmouth College; Harvard Law School. ***Email:*** nash@chapman.com

JAMES R. NELSON, admitted to bar, 1991, Illinois. *Education:* Coe College; University of Iowa College of Law. ***Email:*** nelson@chapman.com

ROBERT W. OLLIS, JR., admitted to bar, 1974, Illinois. *Education:* University of Missouri; University of Michigan Law School. ***Email:*** ollis@chapman.com

LISA A. OLSEN, admitted to bar, 1989, Illinois. *Education:* University of Michigan-Dearborn; University of Michigan Law School. ***Email:*** mccormic@chapman.com

TERENCE T. O'MEARA, admitted to bar, 1973, Illinois. *Education:* University of Wisconsin-Whitewater; Loyola University Chicago School of Law. ***Email:*** omeara@chapman.com

EDWARD J. PELICAN, admitted to bar, 1993, Illinois. *Education:* University of Notre Dame; Northwestern University School of Law. ***Email:*** epelican@chapman.com

STACY K. PIKE, admitted to bar, 1987, Illinois and Wisconsin. *Education:* Oxford University; Troy State University; University of Wisconsin-Madison Law School. ***Email:*** pike@chapman.com

GARY R. POLEGA, admitted to bar, 1988, Illinois. *Education:* Bradley University; DePaul University College of Law. ***Email:*** polega@chapman.com

MARK D. RASMUSSEN, admitted to bar, 1992, Illinois. *Education:* University of Michigan; University of Michigan Law School. ***Email:*** rasmusse@chapman.com

JAMES R. RICHARDSON, admitted to bar, 1969, Illinois. *Education:* DePauw University; University of Chicago Law School. ***Email:*** richards@chapman.com

DIANNE E. RIST, admitted to bar, 1992, Illinois. *Education:* Converse College; University of Iowa College of Law. ***Email:*** rist@chapman.com

ERIC M. ROBERSON, admitted to bar, 1991, Illinois. *Education:* Bradley University; University of Illinois College of Law. ***Email:*** roberson@chapman.com

RONALD E. ROKOSZ, admitted to bar, 1969, Illinois. *Education:* Loyola University, Chicago; Northwestern University School of Law. ***Email:*** rokosz@chapman.com

ANTHONY R. ROSSO, admitted to bar, 1985, Wisconsin; 1986, Illinois. *Education:* University of Wisconsin; University of Michigan Law School; DePaul University College of Law. ***Email:*** rosso@chapman.com

SUZANNE M. RUSSELL, admitted to bar, 1990, Illinois. *Education:* College of the Holy Cross; University of Notre Dame; University of Notre Dame Law School; Loyola University Chicago School of Law. ***Email:*** russell@chapman.com

ROBERT J. SCHNEIDER, admitted to bar, 1973, Illinois; registered to practice before U.S. Patent and Trademark Office. *Education:* University of Cincinnati; University of Cincinnati College of Law. ***Email:*** iplaw@chapman.com

DAVID I. SCHRODT, admitted to bar, 1990, Illinois; 1999, Michigan. *Education:* University of Illinois at Urbana-Champaign; University of Virginia School of Law. ***Email:*** schrodt@chapman.com

SUSAN SHALLENBERGER, admitted to bar, 1986, Illinois. *Education:* University of Dayton; University of Illinois College of Law. ***Email:*** shallenb@chapman.com

SUZANNE L. SHIER, admitted to bar, 1985, Illinois. *Education:* University of Michigan; Loyola University, Chicago; DePaul University College of Law. ***Email:*** shier@chapman.com

(This Listing Continued)

EDWARD V. SOMMER, admitted to bar, 1982, Illinois. *Education:* Hamilton College; University of Notre Dame Law School. ***Email:*** sommer@chapman.com

JAMES E. SPIOTTO, admitted to bar, 1972, Illinois. *Education:* St. Mary of the Lake Seminary; University of Chicago Law School. ***Email:*** spiotto@chapman.com

JAMES R. THEISS, JR., admitted to bar, 1979, Illinois. *Education:* University of Notre Dame; DePaul University College of Law. ***Email:*** theiss@chapman.com

CAROL K. THOMPSON, admitted to bar, 1989, Illinois. *Education:* University of Iowa; University of Iowa College of Law. ***Email:*** mcalpine@chapman.com

FRANKLIN H. TOP III, admitted to bar, 1988, Illinois. *Education:* Kenyon College; Ohio State University College of Law. ***Email:*** top@chapman.com

M. JOHN TROFA, admitted to bar, 1981, Illinois. *Education:* Boston College; University of Illinois College of Law. ***Email:*** trofa@chapman.com

ROBERT G. TUCKER, admitted to bar, 1992, Wisconsin and Illinois. *Education:* Emory University; University of Wisconsin Law School. ***Email:*** tucker@chapman.com

WILLIAM F. TUETING, admitted to bar, 1969, New York; 1984, Illinois. *Education:* Columbia University; Columbia University School of Law. ***Email:*** tueting@chapman.com

CHRISTOPHER F. WALRATH, admitted to bar, 1991, Illinois. *Education:* Northern Illinois University; DePaul University College of Law. ***Email:*** walrath@chapman.com

MORRISON C. WARREN, admitted to bar, 1991, Illinois. *Education:* Occidental College; University of Notre Dame Law School. ***Email:*** warren@chapman.com

LAWRENCE E. WHITE, admitted to bar, 1990, Illinois. *Education:* University of Texas at Austin; University of Pennsylvania Law School. ***Email:*** white@chapman.com

KARL T. WILLIAMS, admitted to bar, 1986, Illinois. *Education:* Yale University; University of Michigan Law School. ***Email:*** kwilliam@chapman.com

STEVEN N. WOHL, admitted to bar, 1970, Illinois. *Education:* Miami University; Northwestern University School of Law. ***Email:*** wohl@chapman.com

RICHARD A. WOHLLEBER, admitted to bar, 1979, Illinois. *Education:* University of Illinois; University of Chicago Law School. ***Email:*** wohllebe@chapman.com

DAVID E. WORSLEY, admitted to bar, 1974, Iowa; 1975, Illinois. *Education:* University of Iowa; University of Iowa College of Law. ***Email:*** worsley@chapman.com

ANTHONY D. YAGER, admitted to bar, 1989, Illinois. *Education:* University of Michigan; University of Illinois College of Law. ***Email:*** yager@chapman.com

---

KIMBERLY L. AHLGRIM, admitted to bar, 1996, Illinois. *Education:* Illinois State University; University of Illinois College of Law. ***Email:*** ahlgrim@chapman.com

LISA M. ANAGNOSTOPOULOS, admitted to bar, 1997, Illinois. *Education:* Bradley University; DePaul University College of Law. ***Email:*** anagnos@chapman.com

ALI O. ANEKWE, admitted to bar, 2003, Illinois. *Education:* Southern Illinois University at Carbondale; University of Michigan Law School. ***Email:*** anekwe@chapman.com

EDUARDO AVILES, admitted to bar, 2004, Illinois. *Education:* University of Illinois; University of Michigan Law School. ***Email:*** eaviles@chapman.com

EMILY TODD BASTEDO, admitted to bar, 2003, Illinois. *Education:* University of Notre Dame; DePaul University College of Law. ***Email:*** emtodd@chapman.com

JANE S. BERMAN, admitted to bar, 1987, Illinois; registered to practice before U.S. Patent and Trademark Office. *Education:* University of Illinois; University of Illinois College of Law. ***Email:*** berman@chapman.com

CHARLES M. BIGGAM III, admitted to bar, 1996, Illinois. *Education:* University of Redlands; Chicago-Kent College of Law. ***Email:*** biggam@chapman.com

GREGORY S. BLOEDORN, admitted to bar, 2004, Illinois. *Education:* Cornell University; University of Illinois College of Law.

S. TODD CUBBAGE, admitted to bar, 1993, Oklahoma; 1994, Illinois. *Education:* Oklahoma State University; University of Tulsa College of Law; Chicago-Kent College of Law. ***Email:*** cubbage@chapman.com

KEITH M. CYZEN, admitted to bar, 1997, Illinois. *Education:* University of Illinois; DePaul University College of Law. ***Email:*** cyzen@chapman.com

JENNIFER A. DeVRIENDT, admitted to bar, 2002, Illinois. *Education:* University of Iowa; Chicago-Kent College of Law. ***Email:*** devriend@chapman.com

RICHARD J. DiLALLO, admitted to bar, 2001, Illinois. *Education:* Northern Illinois University; Chicago-Kent College of Law. ***Email:*** dilallo@chapman.com

WALTER L. DRANEY, admitted to bar, 1999, Illinois. *Education:* University of Illinois; University of Illinois College of Law. ***Email:*** draney@chapman.com

AARON J. EFTA, admitted to bar, 2004, Illinois. *Education:* Montana State University; University of Michigan Law School. ***Email:*** ajefta@chapman.com

BRENT L. FELLER, admitted to bar, 1998, New Jersey; 1999, New York; 2001, Pennsylvania; 2004, Illinois. *Education:* University of Utah; University of Montana School of Law; New York University School of Law. ***Email:*** feller@chapman.com

DAVID M. FIELD, admitted to bar, 1999, Arizona; 2001, Illinois. *Education:* University of Iowa; University of Iowa College of Law. ***Email:*** dfield@chapman.com

TODD E. FREIER, admitted to bar, 2003, Illinois. *Education:* University of Michigan; University of Notre Dame Law School. ***Email:*** freier@chapman.com

SCOTT R. FRYZEL, admitted to bar, 1994, Illinois. *Education:* Eureka College; Loyola University Chicago School of Law. ***Email:*** fryzel@chapman.com

ROSE E. GALLAGHER, admitted to bar, 1999, Indiana; 2004, Illinois. *Education:* Indiana University; Indiana University School of Law-Bloomington. ***Email:*** gallaghe@chapman.com

(This Listing Continued)

MARIA CLARA GARCIA, admitted to bar, 1999, Illinois. *Education:* University of Minnesota; Northwestern University School of Law. ***Email:*** kgarcia@chapman.com

T. KELLAN GRANT, admitted to bar, 2000, Illinois. *Education:* Purdue University; University of Chicago Law School. ***Email:*** kgrant@chapman.com

H. RICHARD HAGEN, admitted to bar, 1997, Illinois. *Education:* College of St. Francis; University of Illinois College of Law.

JAMES HEISER, admitted to bar, 2003, Illinois. *Education:* Drexel University; University of Notre Dame Law School. ***Email:*** heiser@chapman.com

JANE C. HONG, admitted to bar, 2001, Illinois and Wisconsin. *Education:* Boston College; University of Wisconsin-Madison Law School. ***Email:*** janehong@chapman.com

THOMAS F. HOWARD, admitted to bar, 1999, Illinois. *Education:* Lake Forest College; North Central College; University of Illinois College of Law.

CHARLES J. KOLIN, admitted to bar, 1999, Illinois. *Education:* John Carroll University; John Marshall Law School. ***Email:*** ckolin@chapman.com

COLLEEN A. KUSHNER, admitted to bar, 1992, Illinois. *Education:* University of Illinois at Urbana-Champaign; Villanova University School of Law. ***Email:*** gartland@chapman.com

DAVID J. LASOTA, admitted to bar, 1998, Illinois. *Education:* University of Illinois at Urbana-Champaign; University of Notre Dame Law School. ***Email:*** lasota@chapman.com

WILLIE F. LEWIS, JR., admitted to bar, 1999, Illinois. *Education:* DePaul University; DePaul University of Law. ***Email:*** wlewis@chapman.com

LORELLE L. LINDO, admitted to bar, 2004, Illinois. *Education:* University of Iowa; University of Iowa College of Law. ***Email:*** llindo@chapman.com

PHILLIP LODATO, admitted to bar, 2003, Illinois. *Education:* Indiana University; Indiana University School of Law-Bloomington. ***Email:*** lodato@chapman.com

JOSEPH P. LOMBARDO, admitted to bar, 1999, Ohio; 2000, Illinois. *Education:* University of Dayton; Duke University School of Law. ***Email:*** lombardo@chapman.com

JIL L. MARTIN, admitted to bar, 2001, Illinois. *Education:* University of Wisconsin-Madison; Loyola University at Chicago School of Law. ***Email:*** jlmartin@chapman.com

JOHN J. MARTIN, admitted to bar, 2000, Illinois. *Education:* University of Dayton; DePaul University College of Law. ***Email:*** jjmartin@chapman.com

LAURA L. McKINNEY, admitted to bar, 2000, Arizona; 2004, Illinois. *Education:* Rhodes College; University of Arizona-James E. Rogers College of Law. ***Email:*** mckinney@chapman.com

JANE E. NAGLE, admitted to bar, 1993, Pennsylvania; 1994, New Jersey; 1995, Illinois. *Education:* La Salle University; University of Notre Dame Law School. ***Email:*** jnagle@chapman.com

NATHAN H.B. ODEM, admitted to bar, 2003, Illinois. *Education:* University of Iowa; University of Iowa College of Law. ***Email:*** odem@chapman.com

AMY L. OLSHANSKY, admitted to bar, 1998, Illinois. *Education:* Cornell University; University of Notre Dame Law School. ***Email:*** olshansky@chapman.com

SCOTT H. OLSON, admitted to bar, 2000, Illinois. *Education:* Stanford University; University of Notre Dame Law School. ***Email:*** olson@chapman.com

MARK R. O'MEARA, admitted to bar, 1996, Illinois. *Education:* Ohio University; Chicago-Kent College of Law, Illinois Institute of Technology. ***Email:*** momeara@chapman.com

PEGGY JOYCE OSTERMAN, admitted to bar, 2002, Illinois. *Education:* Creighton University; Georgetown University Law Center.

MARK A. PARTIN, admitted to bar, 2002, Illinois. *Education:* Indiana University; DePaul University College of Law.

DAVID M. PEDERSON, admitted to bar, 2002, Illinois. *Education:* University of Minnesota; University of Minnesota Law School.

CHRISTOPHER A. PESCH, admitted to bar, 1995, Washington; 2004, Illinois. *Education:* Lake Forest College; Seattle University School of Law. ***Email:*** pesch@chapman.com

MICHAEL D. ROBSON, admitted to bar, 1999, Illinois. *Education:* University of Notre Dame; University of Notre Dame Law School. ***Email:*** robson@chapman.com

MATTHEW B. SCHMANSKI, admitted to bar, 2004, Illinois. *Education:* University of Miami; University of Notre Dame Law School. ***Email:*** schmanski@chapman.com

RYAN T. SCHULTZ, admitted to bar, 2003, Nevada (Not admitted in Illinois). *Education:* Purdue University; University of Chicago Law School.

SHELLY A. SCINTO, admitted to bar, 1993, Illinois. *Education:* Eastern Illinois University; Chicago-Kent College of Law, Illinois Institute of Technology. ***Email:*** scinto@chapman.com

JORDAN M. SICKMAN, admitted to bar, 2001, California; 2004, Illinois. *Education:* University of California at Los Angeles; Vanderbilt University Law School. ***Email:*** sickman@chapman.com

JULIA J. SINGH, admitted to bar, 2004, Illinois. *Education:* Baruch College of the City University of New York; University of Minnesota Law School. ***Email:*** jsingh@chapman.com

STEPHEN TODD SIPE, admitted to bar, 1991, Texas; 1993, Washington; 1998, Illinois. *Education:* Georgetown University; University of Washington; Northwestern University; University of Michigan Law School.

TIMOTHY A. STRATTON, admitted to bar, 1999, Illinois. *Education:* Ball State University; Thomas M. Cooley Law School.

JAMES P. SULLIVAN, admitted to bar, 1998, Illinois. *Education:* University of Illinois; DePaul University College of Law. ***Email:*** jsullivan@chapman.com

(This Listing Continued)

TARA WAGNER TILBURY, admitted to bar, 2001, Illinois. *Education:* Lawrence University; University of Minnesota Law School. ***Email:*** tilbury@chapman.com

JEFFREY L. TROXCLAIR, admitted to bar, 2004, Illinois. *Education:* North Carolina State University; University of Notre Dame Law School. ***Email:*** troxclair@chapman.com

REBECCA WALLENFELSZ, admitted to bar, 1997, Illinois. *Education:* University of Notre Dame; Loyola University at Chicago Law School. ***Email:*** schmucke@chapman.com

LISA M. WEIER, admitted to bar, 2000, Illinois. *Education:* University of Illinois; Chicago-Kent College of Law, Illinois Institute of Technology. ***Email:*** weier@chapman.com

GLENN E. WEINSTEIN, admitted to bar, 1991, Illinois. *Education:* Brown University; Northwestern University School of Law. ***Email:*** weinstei@chapman.com

ANDREW L. WOOL, admitted to bar, 2004, Illinois. *Education:* University of Wisconsin; University of Illinois College of Law. ***Email:*** andwool@chapman.com

KERRY E. ZARLEY, admitted to bar, 2001, Illinois. *Education:* Truman State University; University of Illinois College of Law. ***Email:*** zarley@chapman.com

OF COUNSEL

LEE A. BOYE, admitted to bar, 1961, Illinois. *Education:* University of Illinois; University of Illinois College of Law. ***Email:*** lboye@chapman.com

BECKY BRUECKEL, admitted to bar, 1977, Massachusetts and Illinois. *Education:* Yale University; Boston University School of Law. ***Email:*** brueckel@chapman.com

F. B. HUBACHEK, JR., admitted to bar, 1950, Illinois. *Education:* Yale University; University of Chicago Law School.

CHARLES A. KELLY, admitted to bar, 1956, District of Columbia and Illinois. *Education:* Amherst College; Harvard Law School. ***Email:*** ckelly@chapman.com

BARBARA C. KLABACHA, admitted to bar, 1987, Illinois; 1997, Kentucky. *Education:* St. Mary's College; University of Chicago; Northwestern University School of Law.

ROBERT V. LEWIS, admitted to bar, 1964, Illinois; 1972, Florida; 1975, U.S. Tax Court; U.S. District Court, Northern District of Illinois; U.S. Court of Appeals, Seventh Circuit. *Education:* Princeton University; University of Michigan Law School. ***Email:*** rlewis@chapman.com

EILEEN STRANG, admitted to bar, 1954, Illinois. *Education:* Antioch College (B.A.); University of Michigan (J.D.). ***Email:*** strang@chapman.com

KENNETH J. VAUGHAN, admitted to bar, 1961, District of Columbia; 1966, Illinois. *Education:* Georgetown University; Georgetown University Law Center.

DANIEL W. WEIL, admitted to bar, 1965, Illinois. *Education:* London School of Economics, London, England; University of Wisconsin-Madison; Northwestern University.

SENIOR COUNSEL

SUSAN E. ROLLINS, admitted to bar, 1977, Illinois. *Education:* Northwestern University; Cornell University Law School. ***Email:*** rollins@chapman.com

CHAPMAN & SPINGOLA, LLP

Established in 1992

77 WEST WACKER DRIVE, SUITE 4800
CHICAGO, ILLINOIS 60601
Telephone: 312-630-9202
Facsimile: 312-630-9233
Email: rchapman@chapmanspingola.com
Email: pspingola@chapmanspingola.com

Civil Trial and Appellate Practice including General Commercial, Complex Commercial, Intellectual Property Litigation, Plaintiff's Personal Injury, Professional Liability, Transactional and Counseling Matters relating to Intellectual Property.

MEMBERS OF FIRM

ROBERT A. CHAPMAN, born Chicago, Illinois, October 8, 1960; admitted to bar, 1985, Illinois and U.S. District Court, Northern District of Illinois including Trial Bar; 1996, U.S. Court of Appeals, Seventh Circuit; 1997, U.S. Supreme Court. *Education:* University of California at Berkeley (B.A., 1982); Boalt Hall School of Law (J.D., 1985). Associate Editor, California Law Review, 1984-1985. Co-Editor, Trial Lawyer's Guide, West, 1997-1999. Author: "Recent Decisions Concerning the Use of Experts--Rules 703 and 705 do have their Limitations," 39 Illinois State Bar Association Trial Briefs 1, 1994. Panelist, "Tipping the Scales in Favor of One Side?: The Jury is Still out on the Motivations of Using Trial Consultants," 10 Illinois Legal Times 1, 1996; "Trial as a Law School Exam: Esser v. McIntyre," 41 Trial Lawyer's Guide No. 3 1997, 2000; "Confronting Breach of Settlement Agreement 8," Illinois Bar Journal 217, 1999; "Litigating the Legal Malpractice Case," Attorneys' Legal Liability, Illinois Institute for Continuing Legal Education, 2002. Member, Hearing Board, Illinois Attorney Registration and Disciplinary Commission, 2001-2003. *Member:* Chicago (Chairperson, Committee on Prevention of Attorney Malpractice, 1998-1999) and Illinois State (Member, Civil Practice and Procedure Section Council, 1994-1995, 1996-2003; Judicial Evaluation Committee, 1998-2003) Bar Associations; Illinois Trial Lawyers Association; The Association of Trial Lawyers of America; Appellate Lawyers Association of Illinois. ***PRACTICE AREAS:*** Civil Practice; Trial Practice; Appellate Practice; Commercial Law; Professional Liability; Personal Injury. ***Email:*** rchapman@chapmanspingola.com

PETER M. SPINGOLA, born Melrose Park, Illinois, April 7, 1971; admitted to bar, 1997, Illinois. *Education:* Dartmouth College (B.A., 1993); Chicago-Kent College of Law, Illinois Institute of Technology (J.D., with highest honors, 1997). Order of the Coif. Member, Chicago-Kent Law Review, 1996-1997. Member, Chicago-Kent Trial Advocacy Team, 1997. Author, "Knapp v. Northwestern University: Seventh Circuit Slam Dunks the Rights

(This Listing Continued)

CHAPMAN & SPINGOLA, LLP, Chicago—Continued

of the Disabled," 73 Chi-Kent L. Rev. 709. Co-Author: "Assignability of Intellectual Property Licenses in Bankruptcy: Navigating the Murky Waters of Section 365," Fall 2002 Issue of ABA's Intellectual Property Newsletter; "After the Fall: What Happens to IP Licenses During Bankruptcy," August 2002 Issue of IP Worldwide; "Confronting Breach of Settlement Agreement," 8 Illinois Bar Journal 217, 1999. Formerly of Kirkland & Ellis LLP. *Member:* Chicago Lincoln American Inn of Court. ***PRACTICE AREAS:*** Civil Practice; Trial Practice; Appellate Practice; Commercial Law; Intellectual Property. ***Email:*** pspingola@chapmanspingola.com

REPRESENTATIVE CLIENTS: Administrative Management Group; American Automobile Association; Bank of Lincolnwood; Chicago Motor Club; ConAgra, Inc.; Kreg Therapeutics, Inc.; Laidlaw Transportation, Inc.; Lyon & Healy, Inc.; Mesirow Financial; National Emergency Services, Inc.; Nautilus International, Inc.; Orix Real Estate Equities, Inc.; Remax Exclusive Properties; Remodeling Consultants Home Improvement, Inc.; Security Associates International, Inc.; Swift Engineering Inc.; The Alter Group; The Thresholds, Inc.; Umbrella Bank, fsb; URS Greiner, Inc.; Creative Intellectual Property Management, LLC; Epilepsy Association of Central Florida.

CHARITY & ASSOCIATES, P.C.

Established in 1994

20 NORTH CLARK STREET, SUITE 700
CHICAGO, ILLINOIS 60602
Telephone: 312-849-9000
Fax: 312-849-9001
URL: http://www.charityandassociates.com

Real Estate, Corporate and Public Finance.

FIRM PROFILE: Charity & Associates, P.C. was established in January of 1994 by Elvin E. Charity. The attorneys of Charity & Associates, P.C. have handled sophisticated matters for a variety of large and small clients, ranging in size from sole proprietorships to Fortune 500 corporations. Charity & Associates, P.C. is committed to providing these clients with high quality and cost effective legal services.

ELVIN E. CHARITY, born Youngstown, Ohio, May 19, 1953; admitted to bar, 1979, Ohio; 1982, Illinois. *Education:* Yale University (B.A., 1975); Harvard University (J.D., 1979). Lambda Alpha. Fellow, Leadership Greater Chicago, Class of 1988-1989. Chairman, Community Development Commission of Chicago, 1992-2000. Member: The Economic Club of Chicago, 1995—; Economic Development Commission of Chicago, 1992-2000; Commercial District Development Commission, 1988-1992. With, Hopkins & Sutter, 1981-1992 (Partner, 1987-1992). *Member:* Cook County, American and National Bar Associations. ***PRACTICE AREAS:*** Real Estate; Corporate Law; Public Finance. ***Email:*** elvin.charity@charity-associates.com

ALAN M. BELL, born East Chicago, Indiana, October 12, 1963; admitted to bar, 1991, Illinois and U.S. District Court, Northern District of Illinois. *Education:* University of Notre Dame (B.B.A., 1986; J.D., 1989). Executive Articles Editor, Notre Dame Journal of Legislation, 1988-1989. Member, Project Management Institute. *Member:* National Association of Bond Lawyers. ***PRACTICE AREAS:*** Real Estate; Project Finance; Public Finance. ***Email:*** alan.bell@charity-associates.com

TIMOTHY K. HINCHMAN, born Hinsdale, Illinois, February 16, 1967; admitted to bar, 1994, Illinois and U.S. District Court, Northern District of Illinois. *Education:* University of Illinois (B.S., 1990); The John Marshall Law School (J.D., 1993). ***PRACTICE AREAS:*** Real Estate; Zoning Law; Public Finance. ***Email:*** tim.hinchman@charity-associates.com

REPRESENTATIVE CLIENTS: McDonalds Corporation; Bank of America N.A.; Boulevard Realty Services Corp.; City of Chicago; Harris Trust and Savings Bank; Yum! Brands; Chicago Transit Authority; Chicago Board of Education; Chicago Metropolitan Housing Development Corporation; Prairie Mortgage Company; Thrush Realty, Inc.; Chicago Housing Authority.

MYRON M. CHERRY & ASSOCIATES, LLC

30 NORTH LA SALLE STREET, SUITE 2300
CHICAGO, ILLINOIS 60602-2504
Telephone: 312-372-2100
Telecopier: 312-853-0279
Email: mcherry@cherry-law.com

Trial and Appellate Practice in all State and Federal Courts. Business, Commercial, Entertainment, Antitrust, Contract, Copyright, Environmental and Administrative Law.

MYRON M. CHERRY, born Chicago, Illinois, January 25, 1939; admitted to bar, 1962, Illinois; 1972, California and District of Columbia; 1982, Wisconsin. *Education:* University of Illinois and Northwestern University (B.S.L., 1960); Northwestern University (LL.B., 1962). Order of the Coif. Editor, Northwestern University Law Review, 1962. *Member:* The District of Columbia Bar; Chicago, Illinois State and American (Member, Special Committee on Energy Law, 1975-1986) Bar Associations; State Bar of California; Chicago Council of Lawyers. ***PRACTICE AREAS:*** Litigation; Business Litigation; Commercial Litigation; Antitrust Litigation; Environmental Litigation; Administrative Litigation.

ASSOCIATES

DANIEL J. BECKA, born Cleveland, Ohio, December 12, 1962; admitted to bar, 1988, Illinois; 1996, California; 1998, U.S. Court of Appeals, Ninth Circuit; U.S. Court of Federal Claims, U.S. District Court, Northern District of Illinois, Eastern District of Michigan, District of Arizona, Central District of California and Southern, Middle and Northern Districts of Florida. *Education:* Case Western Reserve University (B.S., in Accounting, cum laude, 1985); University of Pennsylvania (J.D., 1988). Recipient, G. Joseph Tauro Distinguished Scholar Award. Associate Editor, University of Pennsylvania Law Review, 1987-1988. ***PRACTICE AREAS:*** Securities Litigation; Securities Arbitration; Complex Commercial Litigation; Appellate Practice. ***Email:*** dan@dbeckalaw.com

JACIE ZOLNA, admitted to bar, 2002, Illinois and U.S. District Court, Northern District of Illinois. *Education:* University of Minnesota Duluth (B.A., 1999); DePaul University (J.D., 2002). Member, DePaul Law Review. Recipient, Dean's Scholarship. *Member:* Chicago, Illinois State and American Bar Associations. ***PRACTICE AREAS:*** Commercial Litigation; Employment Litigation; Class Actions. ***Email:*** jzolna@cherry-law.com

OF COUNSEL

CARY N. GOLDBERG, born Chicago, Illinois, November 29, 1959; admitted to bar, 1984, Illinois and U.S. District Court, Northern District of Illinois. *Education:* Cornell University (B.A., 1981); University of Chicago (J.D., 1984). *Member:* Illinois State and American Bar Associations. ***PRACTICE AREAS:*** Litigation; Business Litigation; Commercial Litigation. ***Email:*** cgoldberg@cherry-law.com

CHERSKOV & FLAYNIK

Established in 1992

THE CIVIC OPERA BUILDING
20 NORTH WACKER DRIVE, SUITE 1447
CHICAGO, ILLINOIS 60606
Telephone: 312-621-1330
Telefax: 312-621-0088
Email: mail@cherskov.com

Intellectual Property and Technology Related Law including Patents, Trademarks, Trade Secrets, Copyrights, Unfair Competition, Entertainment and Related Litigation.

MEMBERS OF FIRM

DONALD G. FLAYNIK, JR., born Joliet, Illinois, August 18, 1952; admitted to bar, 1980, Illinois and U.S. District Court, Northern District of Illinois; registered to practice before U.S. Patent and Trademark Office. *Education:* University of Illinois (B.S.E.E., 1974); Chicago-Kent College of Law (J.D., 1979). Professional Engineer, Illinois, 1980. *Member:* Illinois State Bar Association; Instruments Society of America; Institute of Electrical and Electronic Engineers. ***Email:*** dflaynik@cherskov.com

MICHAEL J. CHERSKOV, born Chicago, Illinois, August 6, 1958; admitted to bar, 1988, Illinois, U.S. District Court, Northern District of Illinois and U.S. Court of Appeals, Seventh Circuit; registered to practice before U.S. Patent and Trademark Office. *Education:* Maryville College (B.A. Chemistry, 1980); Boston University (M.S. Science Communications, 1982); Loyola University of Chicago (J.D., 1988). *Member:* American Chemical Society. ***Email:*** mcherskov@cherskov.com

OF COUNSEL

CHARLES NISSIM-SABAT, PH.D., born Sofia, Bulgaria, February 1, 1938; admitted to bar, 1995, Illinois; 1996, U.S. District Court, Northern District of Illinois and U.S. Court of Appeals, 7th Circuit; registered to practice before U.S. Patent and Trademark Office. *Education:* Columbia University (B.A., Physics, 1959; M.S., Physics, 1960; Ph.D., Physics, 1965); Chicago-Kent College of Law (J.D., 1994). ***Email:*** cnissim-sabat@cherskov.com

LEGAL/TECHNICAL SUPPORT PERSONNEL

DANA P. MCDERMOTT, PH.D., born Huntington, West Virginia, November 16, 1948; admitted to bar, 1997, West Virginia and U.S. District Court, Southern District of West Virginia; 1998, Maryland and U.S. District Court, Northern District of West Virginia; 1999, Illinois. *Education:* Centre College (B.A., Chemistry, 1970); University of California at Berkeley (Ph.D., Chemistry, 1974); University of Pittsburg School of Law (J.D., 1996). *Member:* Chicago, West Virginia State, Maryland State, Illinois State and American Bar Associations. ***Email:*** dmcdermott@cherskov.com

ALBERT Y. TSUI, born Chicago, Illinois, January 16, 1977; admitted to bar, 2003, Illinois and U.S. District Court, Northern District of Illinois. *Education:* Knox College (B.A., Biochemistry, Philosophy, 1999); DePaul University College of Law (J.D., 2002). Admitted to practice before U.S. Patent and Trademark Office. ***Email:*** atsui@cherskov.com

THOMAS J. MOTZNY, born Oak Park, Illinois, July 11, 1978; admitted to bar, 2003, Illinois, U.S. District Court, Northern District of Illinois. *Education:* DePaul University (B.A., English, 2000; J.D., 2003). Order of the Coif. ***Email:*** tmotzny@cherskov.com

JILLIAN M. SZAFRANSKI, born Evergreen Park, Illinois, August 2, 1978. *Education:* Massachusetts Institute of Technology (B.S., Chemistry, 2000); DePaul University College of Law (J.D., 2005). ***Email:*** jszafranski@cherskov.com

CHICAGO INTERNET ATTORNEYS

105 WEST MADISON, SUITE 1300
CHICAGO, ILLINOIS 60602
Telephone: 312-782-6463
Fax: 312-855-1177

Personal Injury, Spinal Cord Injury, Automobile Accidents, Wrongful Death, Products Liability, Medical Malpractice, Corporate, Business, Real Estate, Criminal and Civil Litigation.

DENNIS J. KELLOGG, born 1949; admitted to bar, 1975, Illinois, U.S. District Court, Northern District of Illinois, U.S. Court of Appeals, Seventh Circuit, U.S. Supreme Court, U.S. Federal Court of Claims. *Education:* University of Illinois (B.A., 1971); Illinois Institute of Technology (J.D., 1974). Certified arbitrator, Circuit Court Program. *Member:* Chicago and Illinois State Bar Associations; Illinois Trial Lawyers Association; Association of

(This Listing Continued)

Trial Lawyers of America; American Arbitration Association. **PRACTICE AREAS:** Litigation; Personal Injury; Real Estate.

CHITKOWSKI LAW OFFICES

CHICAGO, ILLINOIS

(See Lisle)

Business, Construction, Transportation, Corporate, Labor and Employment and Real Estate, Litigation and Transactions.

CHITTENDEN, MURDAY & NOVOTNY, LLC

303 WEST MADISON STREET, SUITE 1400
CHICAGO, ILLINOIS 60606
Telephone: 312-281-3600
Fax: 312-281-3678

Appellate Practice, Business and Commercial Litigation, Business and Corporate Law, Class Action Defense, Employee Benefits Law, Employment and Labor Law, Insurance Tax Litigation, Life, Health & Disability Insurance Law, Managed Health Care Law, Medical Malpractice Defense, Product Liability Law, Securities Litigation and Arbitration.

WILLIAM A. CHITTENDEN, III, born Elmhurst, Illinois, July 4, 1957; admitted to bar, 1982, Illinois and U.S. District Court, Northern, Central and Southern Districts of Illinois including Trial Bar; 1984, U.S. Supreme Court and U.S. Court of Appeals, Seventh Circuit; 1988, U.S. District Court, Northern District of Indiana. *Education:* University of Illinois (B.S., 1979); Southern Methodist University (J.D., 1982). Order of the Coif. Member, Southwestern Law Journal, 1981-1982. *Member:* Seventh Circuit, Chicago and American (Member, Life Insurance Law Committee; Sections on: Litigation; Tort Trial and Insurance Practice) Bar Associations; Society of Trial Lawyers; Defense Research Institute (Member, Life, Health and Disability Insurance Committee); Lawyer's Club of Chicago; Association of Life Insurance Counsel. **PRACTICE AREAS:** Litigation.

ELIZABETH GWYNN DOOLIN, born Detroit, Michigan, May 25, 1966; admitted to bar, 1992, Illinois and U.S. District Court, Northern District of Illinois Including Trial Bar; 1993, U.S. District Court, Central District of Illinois; 1997, U.S. Court of Appeals, Seventh Circuit. *Education:* University of Michigan (B.A., 1989); Washington University (J.D., 1992). Recipient, American Jurisprudence Award, Trial Practice. *Member:* American Bar Association; Defense Research Institute; Illinois Association of Defense Trial Counsel. **PRACTICE AREAS:** Litigation; Insurance; Employment Law.

JOSEPH J. HASMAN, born Chicago, Illinois, July 19, 1941; admitted to bar, 1966, Illinois; 1967, U.S. District Court, Northern District of Illinois including Trial Bar; 1968, U.S. Court of Appeals, Seventh Circuit; 1974, U.S. Supreme Court; 1994, U.S. District Court, Central and Southern Districts of Illinois. *Education:* University of Illinois (A.B., 1964; J.D., 1966). Co-Chairperson, National Conference of Lawyers and Life Insurance Companies, 1988-1991. Member, Law Committee, International Claim Association. *Member:* American Bar Association (Chairperson, Tort Trial and Insurance Practice Section, Life Insurance Law Committee, 1986-1987); Association of Life Insurance Counsel; National Conference of Lawyers & Life Insurance Companies. **PRACTICE AREAS:** Life, Health, Disability, AD&D, and ERISA claims and counseling; Civil Litigation; Employment Discrimination Litigation.

SEAN PATRICK MacCARTHY, born Oak Park, Illinois, September 6, 1963; admitted to bar, 1988, Illinois and U.S. District Court, Northern District of Illinois, including Trial Bar; 1994, U.S. District Court, Central District of Illinois; U.S. Court of Appeals, Seventh Circuit. *Education:* University of Illinois (B.A., 1985) Phi Beta Kappa; Loyola University (J.D., 1988). Member, Philip C. Jessup International Law Moot Court Competition. Arbitrator, Circuit Court of Cook County Mandatory Arbitration Program. Member, Board of Directors, Broader Urban Involvement Leadership Development, Inc. (BUILD). *Member:* Chicago, Illinois State and American Bar Associations; Defense Research Institute; Illinois Association of Defense Trial Counsel. **REPORTED CASES:** Evangelou v. Children's Memorial Hospital, 227 Ill.App.3d 909, 592 N.E.2d 329 (1st Dist. 1992); Vincent v. Williams, 279 Ill.App.3d 1, 664 N.E.2d 650 (1st Dist. 1996); Chmiel v. JC Penney Life Insurance Company, 158 F.3d 966 (7th Cir. 1998). **PRACTICE AREAS:** Commercial Litigation; Medical Malpractice; Life, Health and Disability Litigation; Products Liability; Employment Law.

DONALD A. MURDAY, born San Antonio, Texas, June 9, 1960; admitted to bar, 1985, Illinois; 2001, Indiana; U.S. District Court, Northern, Central and Southern Districts of Illinois, including Trial Bar; U.S. Court of Appeals, Seventh Circuit; U.S. District Court, Northern and Southern Districts of Indiana U.S. District Court, Eastern and Western Districts of Michigan; U.S. District Court, Eastern and Western Districts of Wisconsin. *Education:* University of Notre Dame (B.B.A., 1982); Catholic University of America (J.D., 1985). *Member:* Indiana State and American (Member, Sections on: Litigation; Tort and Insurance Practice) Bar Associations; Defense Research Institute; Association of Life Insurance Counsel. **PRACTICE AREAS:** Litigation.

DAVID J. NOVOTNY, born Melrose Park, Illinois, October 3, 1953; admitted to bar, 1978, Illinois and U.S. District Court, Northern District of Illinois including Trial Bar; U.S. District Court, Central District of Illinois; U.S. Court of Appeals, Seventh Circuit; U.S. District Court, Northern District of Indiana. *Education:* DePaul University (B.S.C., with high honors, 1975; J.D., with honor, 1978). Executive Editor, De Paul Law Review, 1977-1978. Law Clerk to Hon. John J. Sullivan, Illinois Appellate Court, 1978-1980. Member, Panel of Arbitrators, American Arbitration Association. *Member:* American Bar Association; Seventh Circuit Bar Association; The Lawyers Club of Chicago; Society of Trial Lawyers; Defense Research Institute; Lawyer-Pilots Bar Association. **PRACTICE AREAS:** Litigation.

DAVID F. SCHMIDT, born Detroit, Michigan, January 1, 1958; admitted to bar, 1990, Illinois and U.S. District Court, Northern District of Illinois, 1994, Trial Bar; 1995, U.S. Court of Appeals, Seventh Circuit and U.S. District Court, Central District of Illinois; 1999, U.S. District Court, Southern District of Illinois; 2002, U.S. District Court, Southern District of Indiana and U.S. District Court, Eastern District of Michigan; 2003, U.S. District Court, Northern District of Indiana, U.S. District Court, Eastern District of Texas, U.S. Court of Appeals, Sixth Circuit; 2004, U.S. District Court, Southern District of Texas. *Education:* Coe College (B.A., 1978); Loyola University School of Law (J.D., cum laude, 1990). Senior Member, Loyola Law Journal, 1988-1990. President, Student Bar Association. Recipient, American Jurisprudence Award in Remedies, 1989. Co-Author: "Recent Developments in Health Insurance and Life Insurance Case Law," Tort and Insurance Law Journal, Winter 1991, Winter 1994, Winter 1995. *Member:* Illinois State Bar Association. **PRACTICE AREAS:** Commercial Litigation; Insurance Litigation; Employee Benefits; Workers Compensation.

(This Listing Continued)

CRAIG M. BARGHER, born Sidney, New York, June 26, 1968; admitted to bar, 1993, Illinois and U.S. District Court, Northern District of Illinois; 1997, New York. *Education:* Brown University (A.B., 1990); DePaul University (J.D., 1993). Member, DePaul Law Review. Assistant Casenote Editor, Journal of Health and Hospital Law. Member, DePaul LCA Journal of Art and Entertainment Law. Author: "Understanding Section 2-619(a)(3) Motions to Dismiss or Stay," 87 Ill. B.J. 327 (1999). **PRACTICE AREAS:** Litigation.

MICHAEL BRIAN GALIBOIS, born Natick, Massachusetts, May 8, 1974; admitted to bar, 2000, Illinois and U.S. District Court, Northern District of Illinois; 2001, U.S. District Court, Central District of Illinois; 2003, U.S. District Court, Northern District of Indiana. *Education:* Georgetown University (B.S.F.S., 1996); University of Notre Dame (J.D., 2000). Editor-in-Chief, Journal of Legislation. *Member:* Chicago, Illinois State and American Bar Associations; Chicago Council of Lawyers. **PRACTICE AREAS:** Commercial Litigation; Securities; Employment Law; Employee Benefits.

MATTHEW W. GASAWAY, born Mason City, Iowa, November 25, 1975; admitted to bar, 2001, Illinois. *Education:* University of Notre Dame (B.B.A., 1998); University of Iowa (J.D., 2001). **PRACTICE AREAS:** Commercial Litigation; Insurance Coverage.

JOSEPH R. JEFFERY, born West Point, New York, May 25, 1970; admitted to bar, 1997, Illinois and U.S. District Court, Northern District of Illinois; U.S. District Court, Western District of Michigan; 1998, U.S. Court of Appeals, Seventh Circuit; 2002, Missouri; U.S. District Court, Eastern District of Michigan; 2003, U.S. District Court, Northern District of Indiana; U.S. District Court, Eastern and Southern Districts of Texas; U.S. Court of Appeals, Sixth Circuit. *Education:* University of Iowa (B.A., 1992); St. Louis University (J.D., 1996). Author: "Temporary Presidential Immunity," 40 St. Louis L. Jou. 833, 1996. *Member:* American Bar Association. **PRACTICE AREAS:** ERISA Litigation; Commercial Litigation.

JENNIFER S. STEGMAIER, born Skokie, Illinois, December 18, 1970; admitted to bar, 1998, Illinois. *Education:* University of Illinois, Chicago (B.S., 1992); Chicago-Kent College of Law, Illinois Institute of Technology (J.D., 1998). *Member:* Chicago Bar Association. **PRACTICE AREAS:** Litigation.

JULIE FREUND WALL, born Hazel Crest, Illinois, June 6, 1974; admitted to bar, 1999, Illinois and U.S. District Court, Northern District of Illinois; 2001, U.S. District Court, Central District of Illinois, U.S. District Court, Southern District of Illinois and U.S. District Court, Northern District of Indiana; U.S. Court of Appeals, Seventh Circuit. *Education:* University of Dayton (B.S., Economics and Finance, 1996); University of Illinois (J.D., magna cum laude, 1999). Phi Delta Phi. *Member:* Illinois State and American Bar Associations. **PRACTICE AREAS:** Civil Litigation.

GEORGIA L. JOYCE, born Indianapolis, Indiana, December 2, 1955; admitted to bar, 1994, Illinois and U.S. District Court, Northern District of Illinois. *Education:* University of Illinois (B.S. Finance, 1978); DePaul University (M.B.A. Finance, 1981); Chicago-Kent College of Law (J.D., 1994). *Member:* Chicago and American (Member, D&O/Professional Liability, Fidelity and Surety Law) Bar Associations. **PRACTICE AREAS:** Litigation; Insurance Law. **Email:** gjoyce@cmn-law.com

JENNIFER L. NOLAND, born Fort Wayne, Indiana; admitted to bar, 2003, Illinois and U.S. District Court, Northern District of Illinois. *Education:* DePauw University (B.A., English Literature, 2000); DePaul University (J.D., 2003). *Member:* Chicago Bar Association. **PRACTICE AREAS:** Civil Litigation. **Email:** jnoland@cmn-law.com

MORGAN J. MILNER, admitted to bar, 2004, Illinois; 2005, U.S. District Court, Northern District of Illinois. *Education:* Colby College (B.A., 2000); Catholic University of America (J.D., 2004). Technology Editor, Journal of Contemporary Health Law and Policy. *Member:* Chicago and Illinois State Bar Associations; Illinois Association of Defense Trial Counsel. **PRACTICE AREAS:** Commercial Litigation; Insurance. **Email:** mmilner@cmn-law.com

OF COUNSEL

DONALD B. LEVENTHAL, born Topeka, Kansas, April 8, 1960; admitted to bar, 1986, Illinois; 1991, U.S. District Court, Northern District of Illinois. *Education:* Michigan State University (B.A., 1983); The Ohio State University (J.D., 1986). Member, Phillip C. Jessup International Law Moot Court Competition. Member, Ohio State Law Journal. *Member:* Chicago Bar Association. **PRACTICE AREAS:** Business Law; Corporate Law.

MURRAY R. CHOATE, II
ATTORNEY AT LAW

CHICAGO, ILLINOIS

(See Charleston)

CHRISTENSEN & EHRET, LLP

222 WEST ADAMS STREET
21ST FLOOR
CHICAGO, ILLINOIS 60606
Telephone: 312-634-1014
Facsimile: 312-634-1018
Email: law@christensenehret.com
URL: http://www.christensenehret.com

Pasadena, California Office: 55 South Lake Avenue, Suite 560, 91101. Telephone: 626-793-7526. Facsimile: 626-793-7744.

Admiralty and Maritime Law, Appellate Practice, Commercial Litigation, Construction Liability, Excess and Reinsurance, Insurance Coverage, Products Liability, Professional Malpractice, Transportation, Trial Practice.

MEMBERS OF FIRM

MARK E. CHRISTENSEN, born Oak Park, Illinois, May 2, 1956; admitted to bar, 1982, Illinois and U.S. District Court, Northern District of Illinois including Trial Bar; 1988, U.S. Court of Appeals, Sixth and Seventh Circuits; 1989, U.S. Supreme Court; 1992, U.S. District Court, District of North Dakota; 1993, U.S. District Court, Eastern and Western Districts of Michigan and U.S. District Court, Western District of Wisconsin; 1994, U.S. District Court, Southern District of Illinois; 2003, California. *Education:* Wheaton College (B.A., high honors, 1977); Northwestern University (J.D., cum laude, 1982). *Member:* Chicago, Illinois State and American Bar Associations; National Association of Railroad Trial Counsel (Treasurer, Secretary and President, Illinois Division, 1992-1994). (Also at Pasadena, California Office). ***PRACTICE AREAS:*** Commercial Litigation; Construction Liability; Insurance Coverage; Admiralty and Maritime Law; Transportation; Trial Practice. ***Email:*** mchristensen@christensenehret.com

JOHN B. EHRET, born Cleveland, Ohio, August 28, 1929; admitted to bar, 1958, Illinois and U.S. District Court, Northern District of Illinois. *Education:* Cornell University (B.M.E., 1952); Northwestern University (J.D., 1958). *Member:* Chicago, Illinois State and American Bar Associations. [Lieut., U.S. Navy, Bureau of Ordinance, 1952-1955]. ***PRACTICE AREAS:*** Commercial Litigation; Products Liability; Trial Practice. ***Email:*** jehret@christensenehret.com

JACK C. HSU, born Boston, Massachusetts, May 30, 1968; admitted to bar, 1993, Illinois and U.S. District Court, Northern District of Illinois; 2002, U.S. Court of Appeals, Sixth Circuit; 2003, California, U.S. District Court, Northern, Central and Southern Districts of California and U.S. Court of Appeals, Seventh Circuit. *Education:* University of Chicago (A.B., 1990); Indiana University (J.D., 1993). *Member:* Chicago, Illinois State and American (Vice Chair, Economics of Tort and Insurance Law Practice Committee, Tort and Insurance Practice Section, 1998-2001) Bar Associations; Chinese American Bar Association; National Asian Pacific American Bar Association. (Also at Pasadena, California Office). ***PRACTICE AREAS:*** Excess and Reinsurance; Insurance Coverage. ***Email:*** jhsu@christensenehret.com

ERIC D. STUBENVOLL, born Milwaukee, Wisconsin, November 6, 1966; admitted to bar, 1992, Michigan and U.S. District Court, Western District of Michigan and Western District of Wisconsin; 1993, Illinois and U.S. District Court, Northern District of Illinois, and U.S. Court of Appeals, Sixth Circuit; 1996, U.S. Court of Appeals, Seventh Circuit; 2002, U.S. District Court, Western District of Colorado and Eastern District of Michigan; 2005, U.S. Supreme Court. *Education:* University of Illinois (B.A., 1989; J.D. cum laude, 1992). Harno Fellow. Moot Court Board. Recipient, American Jurisprudence Award. *Member:* Chicago, Illinois State and American Bar Associations; State Bar of Michigan. ***PRACTICE AREAS:*** Commercial Litigation; Products Liability; Construction Litigation; Professional Malpractice.

ASSOCIATES

KATHERINE A. JONES, born Kenosha, Wisconsin, April 19, 1972; admitted to bar, 1998, West Virginia and U.S. District Court, Southern District of West Virginia; 1999, U.S. Court of Appeals, Fourth Circuit; 2002, Illinois and U.S. Court of Appeals, Third Circuit. *Education:* Lawrence University (B.A., 1994); Washington and Lee University (J.D., 1998). *Member:* Chicago, Illinois State and American Bar Associations. ***PRACTICE AREAS:*** Excess and Reinsurance; Construction Liability; Products Liability. ***Email:*** kjones@christensenehret.com

MIMI Y. KIM, born Toledo, Ohio, February 19, 1975; admitted to bar, 2000, Michigan; 2002, U.S. District Court, Eastern and Western Districts of Michigan; 2003, Illinois. *Education:* Miami University (B.S., cum laude, 1997); The Ohio State University (J.D., 2000). *Member:* Detroit, Oakland County and Illinois State Bar Associations. ***PRACTICE AREAS:*** Construction Liability; Products Liability; Transportation. ***Email:*** mkim@christensenehret.com

KIRSTEN RADLER WAACK, born Salem, Ohio, October 10, 1969; admitted to bar, 1994, Ohio; 1999, Illinois, U.S. District Court, Northern District of Illinois and U.S. District Court, Northern District of Ohio; 2002, U.S. Court of Appeals, Sixth Circuit. *Education:* Duquesne University (B.A., cum laude, 1991); Wake Forest University (J.D., 1994). Phi Alpha Delta. Recipient, Law Faculty Scholarship. Co-Editor-in-Chief, *The Jurist.* Law Clerk, Judge John W. Reece, Ohio Court of Appeals, Ninth District, 1995-1997; Justice Deborah L. Cook, Supreme Court of Ohio, 1998-1999. *Member:* Chicago, Illinois State and Ohio State Bar Associations. ***PRACTICE AREAS:*** Appellate Practice; Excess and Reinsurance. ***Email:*** kwaack@christensenehret.com

OF COUNSEL

JAY M. SMYSER (1933-2003)

WILLIAM G. OLDFORD, JR., born Port Huron, Michigan, November 18, 1965; admitted to bar, 1991, California and U.S. District Court, Southern District of California; 1992, Illinois and U.S. District Court, Northern District of Illinois; 1993, Michigan. *Education:* University of Michigan (B.A., 1988); California Western School of Law (J.D., 1991). *Member:* Chicago, Illinois State and American Bar Associations. ***PRACTICE AREAS:*** Insurance Coverage; Products Liability. ***Email:*** woldford@christensenehret.com

(This Listing Continued)

CHUHAK & TECSON, P.C.

Established in 1987

30 SOUTH WACKER DRIVE, 26TH FLOOR
CHICAGO, ILLINOIS 60606-7413
Telephone: 312-444-9300
FAX: 312-444-9027
URL: http://www.chuhak.com

Corporate, Employee Benefits, Estate Planning, General Business, Health Care, Litigation, Appellate Practice, Municipal, Probate, Real Estate, Taxation and Medical Malpractice.

FIRM PROFILE: Since 1987, Chuhak & Tecson has grown to become one of the 50 largest legal firms in Illinois by serving as valued business partners with our clients.

We regard the performance of legal service as a uniquely personal business. At Chuhak & Tecson, responsive professionals with a broad base of experience and exceptional creativity address your needs with a sense of ownership to clarify objectives, often identifying issues that may have been overlooked. We examine every potential strategy, looking beyond traditional solutions to achieve the most favorable possible outcome. This is ultimately the true measure of the quality and value of our service.

Our reputation rests upon the trust and open lines of communication we have established with the individuals, businesses, communities and professional colleagues we serve.

THOMAS S. CHUHAK (1920-1995)

DAVID S. ARGENTAR, born Chicago, Illinois, October 6, 1968; admitted to bar, 1993, Illinois and U.S. District Court, Northern District of Illinois; 2000, U.S. District Court, Central District of Illinois; 2001, U.S. District Court, Eastern District of Michigan. *Education:* University of California, Los Angeles (B.A., 1990); Northwestern University (J.D., 1993). *Member:* Chicago Bar Association. ***PRACTICE AREAS:*** Commercial Litigation; Trademarks; Trademark Litigation. ***Email:*** dargentar@chuhak.com

JERALYN H. BARAN, admitted to bar, 1990, Illinois. *Education:* Marquette University (B.A., magna cum laude, 1984; M.A., 1986); University of Illinois (J.D., 1990). Phi Beta Kappa; Order of the Coif. Recipient: Rickerts Scholarship for Academic Excellence; American Jurisprudence Award in Products Liability. *Member:* Chicago, Illinois State and American Bar Associations. ***PRACTICE AREAS:*** Civil and Commercial Litigation; Employment Litigation. ***Email:*** Jbaran@chuhak.com

FRED C. BEGY, III, born Springfield, Ohio, May 5, 1947; admitted to bar, 1973, Illinois and U.S. District Court, Northern District of Illinois including Trial Bar; 1975, U.S. District Court, Eastern District of Wisconsin and U.S. Court of Appeals, 7th Circuit; 1978, U.S. Supreme Court and U.S. District Court, Western District of Texas; 1979, U.S. District Court, Eastern District of Kentucky; 1981, U.S. Court of Appeals, 5th, 10th and 11th Circuits; 1982, U.S. District Court, District of South Carolina; 1983, U.S. Court of Appeals, 8th Circuit; 1984, U.S. District Court, Eastern District of Michigan; 1989, U.S. Court of Appeals, 6th and 9th Circuits; 1990, U.S. District Court, Northern District of California; 1993, U.S. District Court, District of Arizona. *Education:* University of South Florida (B.A., 1970); University of Notre Dame (J.D., 1973). Member, Gold Key. Commercial Pilot's Certificate, Airplane Single and Multi-Engine, Instrument, Certified Flight Instructor, Instruments Ground Instructor, Advanced and Instruments, 1965. Author: "Defending Aerial Applicator Chemical Liability Claims: An Overview," Annual SMU Air Law Symposium, 1986. Director, Aviation Insurance Association, 1982. *Member:* Member: Chicago (Member, Aviation Committee, 1974), Illinois State and American (Member: Aviation and Space Law Committee, Tort and Insurance Practice Law Section, 1975—; Committee on Litigation, Litigation Section, 1980—) Bar Associations; National Aeronautic Association; Regional Airline Association; National Association of Flight Instructors; Aviation Insurance Association; National Business Aviation Association, Inc.; Helicopter Association International. ***PRACTICE AREAS:*** Aviation; Insurance Defense; Toxic Torts.

THOMAS F. BENNINGTON, JR., born Morris, Illinois, April 23, 1962; admitted to bar, 1987, Illinois and U.S. District Court, Northern District of Illinois. *Education:* North Central College (B.A., 1984); DePaul University (J.D., 1987). Phi Alpha Delta (Justice, 1985-1987). Member, De Paul Moot Court Executive Board, 1986-1987. Lecturer, Business Law, North Central College, 1992-1997. Assistant Editor, Chicago Bar Record, Young Lawyers Section, 1992-1993. Commissioner, DuPage County Board, 1998—. Commissioner, DuPage County Forest Preserve District, 1998-2002. Member: Community Service Block Grant Advisory Board, 1998; DuPage County Community Development Commission, 1998—; DuPage Workforce Development Board, 2003—; University of Illinois Cooperative Extension Board, DuPage Unit, 2000—; Illinois Prairie Trail Authority, 2001—; DuPage Convention and Tourism Bureau, 2004—; Homeland Security Task Force, National Association of Counties 2004—; Energy, Environment and Land Use Steering Committee, National Association of Counties. Chairman: DuPage County Economic Development Committee. Board Member: United Way of Metropolitan Chicago, United Way of South DuPage, 2000-2003; United Way of Suburban Chicago, 2001-2003. Trustee, North Central College Board of Trustees, 1998-2000. President, 1998-2000 and Member, 1995-2001, North Central College Alumni Association. Director, Willowbrook - Burr Ridge Kiwanis. Volunteer: Our Lady of Mount Carmel Catholic Church, Darien, Illinois; Cub Scouts, Des Plaines Valley Council; Woodridge Community Resource Center, Conservation Foundation, Naperville, Illinois; Good Samaritan Hospital, Downers Grove, Illinois. *Member:* Chicago (Vice Chairman, Young Lawyers Section, Environmental Law and Energy Committee, 1991, 1992; Contributing Editor, CBA Record), DuPage County, Illinois State and American Bar Associations. ***PRACTICE AREAS:*** General Business and Corporate Law; Mergers and Acquisitions; Real Estate Law; Environmental Law. ***Email:*** Tbennington@chuhak.com

(This Listing Continued)

MARK BROADDUS, born Lexington, Kentucky, August 9, 1963; admitted to bar, 1991, Illinois. *Education:* University of Kentucky (B.A., 1986); University of Louisville (J.D., 1991). ***PRACTICE AREAS:*** Probate Administration; Probate Litigation; Guardianship; Estate Planning. ***Email:*** Mbroaddus@chuhak.com

WILLIAM F. DeYOUNG, born 1953; admitted to bar, 1980, Illinois; 1985, Arizona, U.S. District Court, Northern District of Illinois, U.S. District Court, District of Arizona and U.S. Court of Appeals, Seventh Circuit. *Education:* Northwestern University (B.S., 1977); University of Illinois (J.D., magna cum laude, 1980). Order of the Coif. Associate Editor, University of Illinois Law Review, 1979-1980. *Member:* Chicago and American Bar Associations. ***Email:*** wdeyoung@chuhak.com

JOHN P. FADDEN, born Scranton, Pennsylvania, March 15, 1948; admitted to bar, 1973, Pennsylvania; 1974, Illinois; 1993, U.S. Tax Court. *Education:* Pennsylvania State University (B.A., 1970); Georgetown University (J.D., 1973). Certified Public Accountant, Illinois, 1980. *Member:* Chicago (Member, Committee on Employee Benefits, 1975—) and American (Member, Section of Taxation, 1980—) Bar Associations. ***PRACTICE AREAS:*** Corporate and Tax Law (60%); Real Estate Law (10%); Estate Planning (20%); Tax Exempt Revenue Bonds (5%); Employee Benefits Law (5%). ***Email:*** Jfadden@chuhak.com

BARRY A. FEINBERG, born Chicago, Illinois, December 24, 1944; admitted to bar, 1971, Illinois and U.S. District Court, Northern District of Illinois including Trial Bar. *Education:* DePaul University (B.A., 1967); John Marshall Law School (J.D., 1971). Counsel to the Public Administrator of Cook County, 1993—. *Member:* Chicago, Illinois State and American Bar Associations. ***PRACTICE AREAS:*** Probate Administration; Contested Trusts and Estates; Estate Planning; Corporate Law. ***Email:*** Bfeinberg@chuhak.com

MITCHELL S. FEINBERG, born Chicago, Illinois, August 8, 1972; admitted to bar, 1997, Illinois. *Education:* University of Michigan (B.A., 1994); Northwestern University (J.D., 1997). *Member:* Chicago, Illinois State and American Bar Associations. ***PRACTICE AREAS:*** Estate Planning; Contested Trusts and Estates; Probate Litigation and Administration. ***Email:*** Mfeinberg@chuhak.com

DENNIS A. FERRARO, born Rockford, Illinois, October 13, 1946; admitted to bar, 1981, Illinois and U.S. District Court, Northern District of Illinois. *Education:* Northern Illinois University (B.A., 1969); John Marshall Law School (J.D., 1981). Phi Eta Sigma. Co-Author: "Hospital Liability: Apparent Agency or Agency by Estoppel," Illinois Bar Journal, March, 1988; "Apparent Agency: Estoppel/Detrimental Reliance/Proximate Cause - An Evolution From Case Law to Statute," Journal of Health and Hospital Law, Jan./Feb. 1996. *Member:* Chicago, Illinois State and American Bar Associations; Illinois Trial Lawyers Association; Illinois Association of Defense Trial Counsel; Illinois Appellate Lawyers Association. ***PRACTICE AREAS:*** Medical Malpractice (90%); Civil Appeals (2%); Personal Injury (2%); Civil Litigation (Plaintiff and Defendant) (2%); Commercial Litigation (1%); General Liability (1%); Products Liability (1%); Insurance Coverage (1%). ***Email:*** Dferraro@chuhak.com

CARY S. FLEISCHER, born Chicago, Illinois, May 6, 1950; admitted to bar, 1976, Illinois, U.S. District Court, Northern District of Illinois and U.S. Court of Appeals, Seventh Circuit; U.S. Court of Appeals, Sixth Circuit; U.S. Federal Circuit Court of Appeals. *Education:* Washington University (B.A., 1972); John Marshall Law School (J.D., highest distinction, 1976). Member, John Marshall Law Review, 1974-1976. Author: "The Vanishing Right of Plaintiff to Voluntarily Dismiss His Actions," The John Marshall Law Journal, Spring, 1976. *Member:* Chicago and American Bar Associations. ***PRACTICE AREAS:*** Trade Secrets Law; Appellate Practice; Litigation. ***Email:*** Cfleischer@chuhak.com

VALERIE J. FREIREICH, born Chicago, Illinois, July 14, 1952; admitted to bar, 1977, Illinois. *Education:* University of Illinois (B.S., 1974; J.D., 1977). *Member:* Chicago, Illinois State and American Bar Associations. ***PRACTICE AREAS:*** Real Estate; Corporate. ***Email:*** Vfreireich@chuhak.com

DANIEL J. FUMAGALLI, born Brockton, Massachusetts, May 4, 1957; admitted to bar, 1982, Illinois and U.S. District Court, Northern District of Illinois; 1988, U.S. Court of Appeals for the Federal Circuit, 1989; 1989, U.S. District Court, Northern District of Illinois, including Trial Bar and U.S. Court of Appeals, Seventh Circuit. *Education:* College of the Holy Cross (B.A., cum laude, 1979); Cornell University (J.D., 1982). Phi Beta Kappa. Member, Moot Court Board. ***PRACTICE AREAS:*** Commercial Litigation; Employment Law; Corporate Law. ***Email:*** dfumagalli@chuhak.com

JAMES B. GOTTLIEB, born Chicago, Illinois, December 16, 1943; admitted to bar, 1968, Illinois. *Education:* Miami University (B.A., 1965); Northwestern University (J.D., 1968). Co-Author: "Customers in Financial Difficulty," I.C.L.E. Handbook, 1981. Lecturer: Illinois Institute for Continuing Legal Education, Annual Commercial, Banking and Bankruptcy Short Course, 1980, 1981, 1982 and 1983; New Approaches to Multi-Bank Credits, 1987; Resolving the Non-Performing Loan, 1990. *Member:* Chicago (Member: Commercial Law Committee, 1976—) and American (Member, Section of Corporation, Banking and Business Law) Bar Associations. ***PRACTICE AREAS:*** Secured Transactions; Bankruptcy Law; Creditor Rights Law. ***Email:*** Jgottlieb@chuhak.com

ALBERT L. GRASSO, born Woodbury, New Jersey, May 5, 1946; admitted to bar, 1973, District of Columbia; 1974, Illinois, U.S. Tax Court and U.S. District Court, Northern District of Illinois; 1980, U.S. Court of Appeals, Seventh Circuit; 1982, U.S. Supreme Court. *Education:* Georgetown University (B.S.F.S., 1968; J.D., 1973; LL.M. in Taxation, 1974). Editor, Journal of Law & Policy in International Business, 1972-1973. Author: "AICPA Experts' Premier Federal Tax Update," AICPA, 1998; "Al Grassos's Tax Briefs, Creative Tax Planning for Closely Held Businesses," AICPA, 2000; "Compensation Issues in Not-For-Profit Organizations," AICPA, 1997; "S Corporation or Limited Liability Company," Warren, Gorham, 1997; "Tax Reform Act of 1986: Pension and Deferred Compensation Plans," Prentice-Hall, 1986; "Retirement Planning," Federal Tax Workshops, Inc., 1984; "Compensating Employees of Tax-Exempt Organization," Illinois CPA Foundation, 1990; "Unrelated Business Taxable Income," Illinois CPA Foundation, 1992. Co-author: "Tax Reform Act of 1986," AICPA, 1986; "1987/1988 Annual Tax Update," AICPA, 1987; "Tax Planning Issues After TRA '86," AICPA, 1987; "Partnerships—Taxable Income and Distributive Shares," BNA Tax Management Portfolio 282-2nd, 1982; "TAMRA-Technical Corrections Topics," AICPA, 1988; "Mastering the Tax Season," AICPA, an annual update 1988-1994; "Closely Held Corporations," Practitioners Pub. Co., 1993. Visiting Assistant Professor, Pensions, Profit Sharing Plans and Employees Benefits, Roosevelt University, 1978-1987. Lecturer, American Institute of Certified Public Accountants, 1979—. *Member:* Chicago, Illinois State and American Bar Associations; The District of Columbia Bar. [With U.S. Army, 1968-1970]. ***PRACTICE AREAS:*** Tax Law; Employee Benefits Law; General Business Law. ***Email:*** Agrasso@chuhak.com

(This Listing Continued)

JOSHUA S. HYMAN, born Washington, D.C., January 18, 1963; admitted to bar, 1989, Illinois; 1990, U.S. District Court, Northern District of Illinois. *Education:* University of Wisconsin-Madison (B.A., 1985); Washington University (J.D., 1989). ***PRACTICE AREAS:*** Banking Law; Creditors Rights; Business Law; Commercial Litigation. ***Email:*** jhyman@chuhak.com

TERRELL J. ISSELHARD, born Belleville, Illinois, March 12, 1942; admitted to bar, 1967, Illinois. *Education:* St. Joseph College (B.S., cum laude, 1964); University of Illinois (J.D., 1967). Phi Alpha Delta. Lectures: Before Illinois Institute of Continuing Legal Education seminars on various occasions regarding professional corporations, from 1969; Chairman, 33rd Annual Federal Tax Course 1975 and lectured; Lectured at the Illinois Corporate Assistance 1977 Course, topic: Impact of the Tax Reform Act of 1976; The Pension Practice 1978 Course, topic: Self-employed vs. Corporate Plans; Advanced Estate Planning 1979, 1980, 1981 and 1982 Courses, topic: Use of the Closely Held Corporation as an Estate Planning Tool; The Closely Held Corporation as an Estate and Income Tax Planning Tool 1981 Course, topics; The General Plan Design Within a Closely Held Corporation, and Profit Sharing Plans and Estate Taxation of Distributions From Qualified Pension and Profit Sharing Plans; Federal Taxation Skills, November, 1981, Course, topic: Corporate Taxation-Professional Corporations; Retirement Planning Under the 1982 Course, topic: Choice of Form of Business Organizations and Income Taxation of Distributions from Qualified Pension and Profit Sharing Plans Under the 1982 Tax Act; 40th Annual Federal Tax Course, December 1983, topic: Professional Service Corporations After TEFRA; Illinois Institute of Continuing Legal Education Seminar, November 3, 1983, topic: Special Problems and Techniques in Organizing Professional Corporations; 27th Annual Estate Planning Short Course, 1984, topic: Retirement Planning After TEFRA; Financial Planning for Attorneys and Clients, Illinois Institute for Continuing Legal Education, 1985, topic: Insurance Alternatives, Lectured before the Chicago Bar Association on Use of Trusts in Estate Planning for the Owner of a Closely Held Corporation, topic: Structuring and Benefit Plans with a View to Use Trusts in the Estate Plan, April, 1983; Professional Management Research Institute Inc., 1994, topic: Structural and Legal Issues In Group Practice Formation. Professional Seminars from 1994 on the following topics: 1994: "Positioning your Practice and Planning for the 90"s"; "Tax Advantaged Wealth Planning"; "Tax and Financial Strategies for Investment and Asset Protection"; "The Dynamics of Business Succession Planning". 1996-1999: September 1996; The Airport Ground Transportation Association, conference in Las Vegas, Nevada, topic: "Business Planning for Owners of Closely Held Businesses"; February 10, 1997, February 10, 1998, Owners of Closely Held Businesses, topic: Business Succession Planning"; January 1998, The Chicago Medical Society, topic: "Taking Control of Managed Care."; February 4, 1999, Chicago Medical Society, topic: "Fraud, Abuse and Billing Compliance"; April 18, 1999; North Suburban Branch of The Chicago Medical Society, topic: "Estate Planning"; April 28, 1999, topic: "Fraud, Abuse, Billing Compliance—Who Me?"; May 15, 1999, July 22, 1999 and October 27, 1999, topic: "Managed Care Trends, Are You Compliant? Are You Protected, Avoid the consequences"; November 3, 1999, topic: "Negotiating Physician Employment Agreements"; November 13, 1999, topic: "Medical Practice Solutions. . . Newly Recognized Areas of Unprotected Liability Exposure." 2000—: February 9, 2000, December 14, 2000, topic: Business Succession Planning"; March 22, 2000, November 13, 2000, topic: Medical Practice Solutions . . . Newly Recognized Areas of Unprotected Liability Exposure"; April 3, 2000, topic: Asset Protection Planning, Preserving Wealth, Harmony and Business Continuity"; June 26-28, 2000, June 18-20, 2001, topic: the "Dynamics of Auto Dealership Business Planning: Preserving Wealth, Harmony and Business Continuity"; February 22, 2001, Navy Pier, Chicago, IL, topic: Why Risk It? 7 Ways to Prevent Fraud & Abuse; April 18, 2001 "2001—New Administration Healthcare Legislation, topic: What"s In, What"s Out, What"s on Hold?"; October 6, 2001, topic: "What is HIPAA?" December 7, 2001, topic: "Medical Practice Crisis: Could you Financially Survive a Multi Million Dollar Malpractice Settlement"; December 12, 2001, topic: HIPAA Regulations, with BDO Seidman Group. February 8, 2002, February 25, 2002, topic: "The Dynamics of Business Succession Planning: Preserving Wealth, Harmony and Business Continuity." April 23, 2002, topic: "Estate and Asset Protection Planning;" February 26, 2003, topic: HIPAA Practical and Legal Issues; April 15, 2003, April 26, 2003, topic:, "Covenants Not to Compete: Are they still enforceable?" May, 2003 through April, 2005, - 31 Professional Seminars in the Greater Chicago area - topic: "Crisis: Could You Financially Survive a Multi Million Dollar Malpractice Settlement." Author: Group Practice Journal, "Planning for the Medical Building," September/October, 1982; Group Practice Journal, "Benefit Packages for the 80"s," September/October 1983; Pension Practice, Illinois Institute for Continuing Legal Education, Chapter Four: Self-Employed vs. Corporate Plans and Considerations for Top-Heavy Plans, 1983; Employee Benefits Law, Illinois Institute for Continuing Legal Education, Chapter Five: Self-Employed vs. Corporate Plans, 1987; 1988-1989 ISBA Law Ed Series: Estate Planning, Probate and Trust "Distributions From Qualified Plans of Deferred Compensation under the New 15% "Excess Contribution/Accumulation Rules," February 9, 1989; The Journal of Medical Practice Management, "Physician Equity Medical Groups: Preserving Independence in the New Health Care Environment," January/February 1995; as advisor to Medical Economics Magazine, February 24, 1997, concerning new physicians entering the profession and the issues that they should be aware when joining an existing medical practice; The Chicago Medical Society publication Chicago Medicine, September 7, 1998, "Legal trends in the evolving managed care environment", and January 21, 1999, "Strategic/succession planning for medical practices,"; Will Grundy Medical Society publication, September 1998, "The Chronic Mismanagement of Managed Care Practices"; Will-Grundy Dental Society publication, Spring 1999, "Strategic/Succession Planning for the Dental Practice", "The Effect of CLIA Regulations on Physicians on-site Laboratories, August, 2001; "Status Of Tort Reform—Or Lack Thereof," published September 2004 by The Chicago Medical Society; "Employment Agreements & Restrictive Covenants for Physician," published February 2005 by The Chicago Medical Society; "Professional Liability Coverage After Termination," published May 2005 by The Chicago Medical Soc. *Member:* Chicago, Illinois State and American Bar Associations; Illinois Association of Hospital Attorneys; National Health Lawyers Association. ***PRACTICE AREAS:*** Health Care; Professional Corporation Law; Estate Planning; Asset Protection; Federal Taxation; Corporate and Business Planning; Employee Benefits. ***Email:*** Tisselhard@chuhak.com

(This Listing Continued)

CHUHAK & TECSON, P.C., Chicago—Continued

EDWIN I. JOSEPHSON, born Chicago, Illinois, 1944; admitted to bar, 1968, Illinois and U.S. District Court, Northern District of Illinois; 1973, U.S. Tax Court; 1999, U.S. Supreme Court. *Education:* Roosevelt University (B.S., with honors, 1965); DePaul University (J.D., with honors, 1968). Member, De Paul Law Review, 1967-1968. Certified Public Accountant, Illinois, 1965. Lecturer on matters affecting Taxation, Closely-Held Businesses and Estate Planning before various Accounting Groups, including the Illinois Society of Certified Public Accountants. *Member:* Chicago (Past Chairman, Federal Tax Committee, Division C) and Illinois State Bar Associations; Decalogue Society of Lawyers; Chicago Estate Planning Council. ***PRACTICE AREAS:*** Corporate Law; Business Law; Tax Law; Estate Planning. ***Email:*** Ejosephson@chuhak.com

ARNOLD E. KAROLEWSKI, born Chicago, Illinois, June 17, 1952; admitted to bar, 1976, Illinois and U.S. District Court, Northern District of Illinois. *Education:* Northern Illinois University (B.S.Ed., cum laude, 1973); Illinois Institute of Technology/Chicago-Kent College of Law (J.D., 1976). *Member:* Illinois State Bar Association. ***PRACTICE AREAS:*** Real Estate Law; Municipal Law; Lending Law. ***Email:*** Akarolewski@chuhak.com

LORETTO M. KENNEDY, admitted to bar, 1988, Illinois. *Education:* Loyola University of Chicago (B.S., 1985); University of Illinois-Champaign (J.D., 1988). *Member:* Chicago and American Bar Associations. ***PRACTICE AREAS:*** Litigation; Construction Litigation; Aviation Litigation. ***Email:*** lkennedy@chuhak.com

STEPHEN M. MARGOLIN, born Chicago, Illinois, December 23, 1935; admitted to bar, 1964, Illinois and U.S. District Court, Northern District of Illinois; 1996, Wisconsin. *Education:* University of Illinois (B.S., 1957); John Marshall Law School (J.D., 1964). Author: "Dynasty Trusts and the Rule Against Perpetuities," March 1999, Illinois Bar Journal; "Contingent Beneficiaries and Crummey Powers: The Battle Lines are Drawn," July 1997, Journal of The American Society of CLU & CHFC; "Not So Irrevocable Trust Revisited," June 1996, NAPFA News; "The Flexible Irrevocable Trust," January 1996, Journal of The American Society of CLU & CHFC; "The Gift Tax Annual Exclusion: The Code, The Commissions and The Courts," July/August, 1994, Lifeline; "That Crummey Feeling & Exclusive Relief," NAPFA News, 1994; "Feeling Crummey? Try the Annual Exclusion," Life Association News, 1993; "ESOP -- No Fable, It's Fabulous," NAPFA News, 1993; Who's Who In American Law. Former Internal Revenue Agent. Member: Estate and Gift Taxes Committee of the American Bar Association Section of Taxation; Employee Benefit Section of the Illinois State Bar Association, Federal Taxation Section of the Illinois State Bar Association; Estate Planning Council; Financial Planning Association. [1st Lt., U.S. Army]. ***PRACTICE AREAS:*** Estate Planning; Corporate Law; Asset Protection; Employee Benefits; Taxation. ***Email:*** Smargolin@chuhak.com

JAMES R. PRANGER, born Yakima, Washington, October 10, 1960; admitted to bar, 1985, Illinois and U.S. District Court, Northern District of Illinois including Trial Bar; U.S. Court of Appeals, Seventh Circuit. *Education:* Loyola University of Chicago (B.A., magna cum laude, 1982); University of Illinois (J.D., cum laude, 1985). Phi Alpha Theta; Alpha Sigma Nu; Delta Theta Phi. ***PRACTICE AREAS:*** Litigation (50%); Labor and Employment (50%). ***Email:*** Jpranger@chuhak.com

EDWARD C. RICHARD, born Chicago, Illinois, May 21, 1949; admitted to bar, 1974, Illinois; 1975, U.S. District Court, Northern District of Illinois; 1980, U.S. Supreme Court. *Education:* Tulane University (B.A., 1971); Washington University (J.D., 1974). Recipient, American Jurisprudence Award in Civil Procedure, 1972 and Estate Planning, 1974. Notes Editor, Washington University Urban Law Annual, 1973-1974. ***PRACTICE AREAS:*** Commercial Litigation; Chancery Practice; Bankruptcy; Creditors Rights. ***Email:*** erichard@chuhak.com

ALAN B. RONSON, born Bronx, New York, October 17, 1967; admitted to bar, 1992, California and U.S. District Court, Central District of California; 1993, U.S. District Court, Southern District of California; 1994, Illinois and U.S. District Court, Northern District of Illinois; 2001, U.S. Court of Appeals, Ninth Circuit. *Education:* Johns Hopkins University (B.A., 1989); Washington University (J.D., 1992). *Member:* Chicago, Illinois State and American Bar Associations. ***PRACTICE AREAS:*** Medical Malpractice; Professional Liability; Negligence; Commercial Litigation. ***Email:*** Aronson@chuhak.com

LISA A. ROTHSTEIN, born Springfield, Missouri, June 7, 1964; admitted to bar, 1993, Illinois; 1994, Ohio and U.S. District Court, Southern District of Ohio. *Education:* University of Michigan (A.B., with high honors, History, 1987); The Ohio State University (J.D., with honors, 1993). Chief Managing Editor, 1992-1993 and Staff, 1991-1992, Ohio State Journal on Dispute Resolution. *Member:* Chicago and American (Member, Business Law Section) Bar Associations. ***PRACTICE AREAS:*** Corporate Law; Business Law; Trademarks. ***Email:*** Lrothstein@chuhak.com

DONALD J. RUSS, JR., born Champaign, Illinois, November 16, 1952; admitted to bar, 1977, Texas; 1980, Illinois. *Education:* Western Illinois University (B.B.A., 1974); University of Houston (J.D., 1976). Instructor, Individual and Corporate Tax, Roosevelt University, 1980-1982. Co-Author "Partnerships - Taxable Income and Distributive Shares," BNA Tax Management Portfolio 282-2d, 1982. *Member:* Chicago, Illinois State and American Bar Associations; State Bar of Texas. ***PRACTICE AREAS:*** Corporate Law; Estate Planning Law; Tax Law. ***Email:*** Druss@chuhak.com

STEVEN M. SCHOLL, born Chicago, Illinois, February 24, 1960; admitted to bar, 1985, Illinois and U.S. District Court, Northern District of Illinois. *Education:* University of Illinois (B.S., 1982); Loyola University (J.D., 1985). Certified Public Accountant, Illinois, 1982. ***PRACTICE AREAS:*** Business Planning; Entertainment Law; Real Estate; Corporate Transactional. ***Email:*** Sscholl@chuhak.com

GARY J. STERN, born Jamaica, New York, January 6, 1959; admitted to bar, 1983, Illinois and U.S. District Court, Northern District of Illinois. *Education:* Cornell University (B.A., cum laude, 1980); University of Chicago (J.D., 1983). Phi Beta Kappa. *Member:* Chicago (Member, Federal Taxation Committee, 1984—), Illinois State and American (Member, Real Property, Probate and Trust Law Sections) Bar Associations. ***PRACTICE AREAS:*** Wealth Protection; Estate Planning; Tax Planning; Corporate Law; Real Estate Law. ***Email:*** Gstern@chuhak.com

(This Listing Continued)

TRACY E. STEVENSON, born Birmingham, Michigan, January 24, 1966; admitted to bar, 1991, Illinois; 1992, Michigan; 1994, U.S. District Court, Northern District of Illinois; 1998, U.S. District Court, Eastern District Michigan. *Education:* Purdue University (B.A., 1988); University of Detroit (J.D., 1991). Order of the Barristers. Author: "Tort Reform In The Wake of Petrillo," IDC Quarterly, Vol. 7, No. 3; Columnist IDC Quarterly. Instructor: National Insurance Crime Bureau Basic Academies. Arbitrator, Cook County Arbitration. *Member:* Chicago and Illinois State Bar Associations; State Bar of Michigan; Illinois Trial Lawyers Association; Federal Trial Bar. ***PRACTICE AREAS:*** Insurance Defense; Medical Malpractice; Tort; Construction; Commercial. ***Email:*** Tstevenson@chuhak.com

ANDREW P. TECSON, born Oak Park, Illinois, August 12, 1955; admitted to bar, 1980, Illinois and U.S. District Court, Northern District of Illinois. *Education:* University of Munich; Northwestern University (B.A., 1977); University of Chicago (J.D., 1980). *Member:* Chicago Bar Association; Illinois Association of Health Care Attorneys; American Health Lawyers Association. ***PRACTICE AREAS:*** Health Care Law; Corporate Law; Estate Planning; Finance Law. ***Email:*** Atecson@chuhak.com

DAVID J. TECSON, born Berwyn, Illinois, February 24, 1961; admitted to bar, 1988, Illinois; 1991, U.S. District Court, Northern District of Illinois including Trial Bar. *Education:* Macalester College (B.A., Economics, with honors, 1983); University of Illinois (J.D., cum laude, 1987). *Member:* Illinois State Bar Association; American Health Lawyers Association. ***LANGUAGES:*** Spanish. ***PRACTICE AREAS:*** Commercial Litigation; Health Care; Employment Law; Environmental Law; Class Actions. ***Email:*** dtecson@chuhak.com

MITCHELL D. WEINSTEIN, born Skokie, Illinois, October 29, 1968; admitted to bar, 1992, Illinois and U.S. District Court, Northern District of Illinois. *Education:* University of Illinois (B.S., with highest honors, 1989); Northwestern University (J.D., cum laude, 1992). Certified Public Accountant, Illinois, 1989. Recipient, Elijah Watt Sells certiicate from AICPA, 1989. Named One of 40 Attorneys Under Age Forty to Watch, 2005, by Law Bulletin Publishing Company. Author: "Dynasty Trusts and the Rule Against Perpetuities," Illinois Bar Journal, March, 1999. Speaker: "Using Non-Qualified Plans to Retain Key Employees," AICPA National Conference on Federal Taxes, 1998; "Do You Trust Trusts," New Jersey Society of Certified Public Accountants, June, 1998. *Member:* Chicago and Illinois State Bar Associations. ***PRACTICE AREAS:*** Estate Planning; Asset Protection; Federal and State Taxation; Real Estate; Corporate; General Business. ***Email:*** Mweinstein@chuhak.com

ALAN S. WERNICK, born Columbus, Ohio; admitted to bar, 1978, Ohio; 1979, U.S. District Court, Southern District of Ohio; 1987, New York and District of Columbia; 1989, U.S. District Court, Northern District of Ohio, U.S. Court of Appeals, Sixth Circuit and U.S. Supreme Court; 1999, Illinois, U.S. District Court, Northern District of Illinois and U.S. Court of Appeals, Seventh Circuit; 2001, U.S. Court of Appeals, Fifth Circuit. *Education:* Ohio State University (B.S., Accounting, 1974); Capital University (J.D., 1978). Phi Alpha Delta (President, Central Ohio Alumni Chapter, 1978-1979). Author: "Rights in a Database Don't Extend to Inputted Information, Court Held," The National Law Journal, January 2004; "Consider Your Intellectual Capital Assets," Retail Register, Illinois Merchant Association, March 2002; "Perfecting Security Interests in Computer Programs - Collateral Protection," Business Law News, State Bar of Wisconsin, December 2001; "Copyrights and Codes: Model Building Codes as Protectable Works Under the U.S. Copyright Laws," CCH Guide to Computer Law, June 2001; "ISPs Could Not Rely on Immunity in Two Cases: CDA Defense Ruled Out in Trademark Case; Safe-Harbor Defense Nixed in DMCA Case," The National Law Journal, May 2001; "Trademark Owners Receive New Federal Law in Their Fight Against Cyberpirates and Cybersquatters," E-Commerce Law Report, March 2000; "Internet: Fundamental Legal Issues C Domain Name," Computer Law Briefs, BAR-briefs, May 1996. Member, Advisory Board, BNA's Electronic Commerce & Law Report, Washington, 1996. Chairman of the Board, CCH Advisory Council, Guide to Computer Law, 2001—. Lecturer: Information Quality Conference, 2004 and 2005; Chicago tech-Congress, 2004; Toronto techCongress, 2004; LSI, 2003—; The Conference Board, 2000; Glasser Legal Works, 2000. Member: North American Legal Working Group, 2001—; Board of Directors, 2001—, Recording Secretary, 2003-2004 and Member, Congregation Beth Shalom Men's Club; Technology Panel, Member, Regional Advisory Committee for Commercial Arbitration, 1999—; Commercial Panel of Arbitrators, 1984—, American Arbitration Association. *Member:* Ohio State (Founding Chairman, 1985-1986 and Member, 1985—, Computer Law Committee) and American (Member, Sections on: Intellectual Property Law; Science and Technology) Bar Associations; Computer Law Association (Member: Board of Directors, 1990-1996, 1998-2001; Committee on Contracting for Computers, 1984-2000; Chair: Publications Committee, 2000-2001; Technology Use Committee, 1996-2000). ***PRACTICE AREAS:*** Information Technology; Computer Law; Copyrights; Trademarks; Trade Secrets; Intellectual Property Licensing; E-Commerce; Outsourcing; Alternative Dispute Resolution. ***Email:*** awernick@chuhak.com

BARI D. WOOD, born Skokie, Illinois, January 19, 1968; admitted to bar, 1993, Illinois and U.S. District Court, Northern District of Illinois. *Education:* Michigan State University (B.A., magna cum laude, 1990); University of Illinois (J.D., magna cum laude, 1993). Phi Kappa Phi. Author: Obtaining Mental Health Records," IDC Quarterly, Third Quarter, Volume 12, Number 3, 2002; "Defense Attorney's Role with Matters Before the Illinois Department of Professional Regulation," IDC Quarterly, Fourth Quarter, Volume 12, Number 4, 2002. *Member:* Chicago, Illinois State and American Bar Associations. ***PRACTICE AREAS:*** Corporate Transactional; Corporate Healthcare. ***Email:*** Bwood@chuhak.com

JOSEPH A. ZARLENGO, born February 18, 1959; admitted to bar, 1985, Illinois. *Education:* California State University at Northridge (B.A., 1982); John Marshall Law School (J.D., with distinction, 1985); New York University (LL.M., Taxation, 1986). National Moot Court Competitor. Staff Editor, 1983-1984 and Special Editor, 1984-1985, John Marshall Law Review. *Member:* Chicago, Illinois State and American Bar Associations. ***PRACTICE AREAS:*** Estate Planning; Business Law; Corporate Law; Partnership Law; Tax Planning. ***Email:*** jzarlengo@chuhak.com

---

JOHN P. ADAMS, born Detroit, Michigan, January 5, 1960; admitted to bar, 1986, Illinois. *Education:* Valparaiso University (B.S., 1982); Ohio Northern University (J.D.,

(This Listing Continued)

1986); DePaul University (LL.M., 1991). Ohio Northern University Law Review, 1985-1986. Certified Public Accountant, Illinois, 1988. *Member:* Chicago Bar Association. ***PRACTICE AREAS:*** Federal and State Taxation; Estate Planning; Estate and Trust Administration; Corporate. ***Email:*** Johnadams@chuhak.com

STACEY C. BROMBERG, born Chicago, 1972; admitted to bar, 1997, Illinois. *Education:* University of Illinois Urbana-Champaign (B.A., 1994); Chicago-Kent College of Law (J.D., 1997). Order of the Coif. Member, Moot Court Honor Society. *Member:* Illinois State and American Bar Associations. ***PRACTICE AREAS:*** Estate Administration; Trust Administration; Estate Litigation; Trust Litigation; Estate Planning. ***Email:*** sbromberg@chuhak.com

CARRI A. CONLON, born St. Joseph, Michigan, January 29, 1971; admitted to bar, 1998, Illinois and U.S. District Court, Northern District of Illinois. *Education:* Western Michigan University (B.S., 1994); Widener University (J.D., 1998). *Member:* Chicago and Illinois State Bar Associations. ***PRACTICE AREAS:*** Insurance Coverage; Insurance Defense; Commercial Litigation; General Litigation. ***Email:*** Cconlon@chuhak.com

DIMITRA A. DALLAS, born November 30, 1978; admitted to bar, 2002, Illinois. *Education:* University of Illinois (B.S., 1999); Chicago-Kent College of Law (J.D., 2002). ***Email:*** ddallas@chuhak.com

RUDY A. FIGUEROA JR., born 1973; admitted to bar, 2000, Illinois and U.S. District Court, Northern District of Illinois. *Education:* Purdue University (B.A., 1995); Chicago-Kent College of Law, Illinois Institute of Technology (J.D., 1999). *Member:* Chicago and American (Member, Business Law Section) Bar Associations. ***PRACTICE AREAS:*** Business Law. ***Email:*** Rfigueroa@chuhak.com

JEANNE M. KERKSTRA, born Oak Lawn, Illinois, May 14, 1965; admitted to bar, 1992, Illinois. *Education:* University of Illinois (B.S. in Accounting, 1988); Chicago-Kent College of Law (J.D., 1992). Certified Public Accountant, Illinois, 1991. ***PRACTICE AREAS:*** Asset Protection; Tax; Succession Planning. ***Email:*** Jkerkstra@chuhak.com

DANIEL F. MARREN, born Evanston, Illinois, August 11, 1961; admitted to bar, 1988, Illinois; 1989, U.S. District Court, Northern District of Illinois; 1993, Trial Bar and U.S. Court of Appeals, Seventh Circuit. *Education:* Marquette University (B.A., 1984); Loyola University of Chicago (J.D., 1988). Author, "Estates, Trusts and Guardianship Litigation," Chapter 9: Oral Contracts to Make Wills," 2002 IICLE. Speaker, IICLE Seminar: Estates, Trusts and Guardianship Litigation (East Peoria, October 2, 2002; Chicago October 3, 2002); Organized and Moderated, Fall, 2001 CBA Probate Practice Committee Seminar, November 7 and 13, 2001. Expert in contested attorney and executor fee disputes, Circuit Court of Cook County, Illinois. *Member:* Chicago Bar Association (Secretary, 1994-1995; Vice Chairman, 1995-1996; Chairman, 1996-1997; Chair of overall Probate Practice Committee, 2002-2003; Chair of Executive Comittee, Probate Practice, 2002-2003; Member, Legislative Roundtable consisting of Chairs and Vice-Chairs of Probate Pratice, ISBA Trusts & Estates Section, and Corporate Fiduciaries, 2002-2003), Illinois State and American Bar Associations. ***REPORTED CASES:*** Estate of Wrage, 194 Ill.App.3d 117, 550 N.E.2d 1115 (1st Dist. 1990); Estate of Lum, 298 Ill.App.3d 791, 699 N.E.2d 1049 (1st Dist. 1998); Estate of Malbrough, 329 Ill.App.3d 77, 768 N.E.2d 120 (1st Dist. 2002); Estate of Charlotte E. Barth, 339 Ill.App.3d 651; 792 N.E.2d 315 (1st Dist. 2003). ***PRACTICE AREAS:*** Estate Litigation; Trust Litigation; Estate Administration; Trust Administration; Estate Planning; Real Estate; Civil Practice. ***Email:*** Dmarren@chuhak.com

DAVID B. SHINER, born Chicago, Illinois, September 15, 1969; admitted to bar, 1996, Illinois. *Education:* Boston University (B.S.B.A., 1992); John Marshall Law School (J.D., 1996); Chicago-Kent College of Law (LL.M., 2001). Certified Public Accountant, Illinois, 1995. ***PRACTICE AREAS:*** Taxation; Estate Planning; Corporate. ***Email:*** Dshiner@chuhak.com

DAVID C. STROSNIDER, born Camden, New Jersey, June 8, 1973; admitted to bar, 1999, Illinois. *Education:* Dickinson School of Law of the Pennsylvania State University (J.D., 1999); Georgetown University Law Center (LL.M., Taxation, 2000). Phi Gamma Mu. Volunteer Income Tax Assistant (VITA). *Member:* Chicago and Illinois State Bar Associations. ***PRACTICE AREAS:*** Federal Income Tax Planning; Federal Income Tax Controversies; Employee Benefits; Qualified and Non-Qualified Retirement Plans; Welfare Benefit Plans. ***Email:*** dstrosnider@chuhak.com

MATTHEW THOMPSON, born Kenosha, Wisconsin, January 19, 1979; admitted to bar, 2004, Illinois. *Education:* University of Wisconsin (B.B.A., 2001); Loyola University, Chicago School of Law (J.D., magna cum laude, 2004). Phi Alpha Delta. Recipient: CALI Excellence of the Future Award in Legal Writing, 2002; Civil Procedure, 2002. Member, Loyola University Chicago Law Journal, 2002-2004. *Member:* American Bar Association. ***PRACTICE AREAS:*** Business; Corporate Law; Estate Planning. ***Email:*** mthompson@chuhak.com

MOLLY A. WARD, admitted to bar, 2002, Illinois. *Education:* University of Illinois, Urbana-Champaign (B.A.); DePaul University College of Law (J.D.). *Member:* Chicago and Illinois State Bar Associations. ***PRACTICE AREAS:*** Estate Administration; Probate Litigation. ***Email:*** mward@chuhak.com

KENDALL E. WOODS, admitted to bar, 2002, Illinois; 2004, U.S. District Court, Northern District of Illinois. *Education:* Indiana University (B.S., Finance and Marketing, 1998); Loyola University Chicago School of Law (J.D., cum laude, 2002). Member, National Moot Court Team. Member, Consumer Law Review. Judicial Extern to the Honorable Judge Ronald Guzman, U.S. District Court, Northern District of Illinois. *Member:* Chicago and Illinois State Bar Associations. ***PRACTICE AREAS:*** Aviation Defense; Construction Defense; Products Liability Defense. ***Email:*** kwoods@chuhak.com

OF COUNSEL

LAWRENCE E. GLICK, admitted to bar, 1954, Florida; 1955, Illinois. *Education:* University of Miami (B.B.A., 1951; J.D., 1954). Assistant States' Attorney, 1955-1957. Member, Chicago Estate Planning Council, 1979—. *Member:* Chicago (Member, Probate Practice Committee, 1968-1973), Illinois State and American Bar Associations; The Florida Bar. ***PRACTICE AREAS:*** Estate Planning; Estate Administration; Trust Administration. ***Email:*** Lglick@chuhak.com

(This Listing Continued)

LAURA A. JOSEPHSON BERNAT, admitted to bar, 1993, Illinois; 1998, Colorado. *Education:* Indiana University (B.S., with distinction, 1990); Loyola University, Chicago (J.D., cum laude, 1993; M.B.A., 1993). ***PRACTICE AREAS:*** Corporate Law; Electronic Commerce; Franchising. ***Email:*** Ljosephson@chuhak.com

JOSEPH O. RUBINELLI, born Chicago, Illinois, May 26,; admitted to bar, 1940, Illinois; 1977, Florida. *Education:* DePaul University (B.S., 1937; J.D., 1940). Assistant Illinois Attorney General, 1952-1970. Chief, Tax Division, Attorney General's Office, 1960-1970. *Member:* Chicago, Illinois State and American Bar Associations; The Florida Bar; American Judicature Society. ***PRACTICE AREAS:*** Estate Planning; Estate and Trust Administration. ***Email:*** Jrubinelli@chuhak.com

JOSEPH A. TECSON, born Chicago, Illinois, April 4, 1928; admitted to bar, 1955, Illinois, U.S. District Court, Northern District of Illinois and U.S. Court of Appeals, Seventh Circuit. *Education:* Ripon College (B.A., 1952); University of Wisconsin (LL.B. and J.D., 1954). Author: "The Executive Article of the Illinois Constitution," Chicago Bar Record, 1970; "The Regional Transportation Authority in Illinois," Chicago Bar Record, 1975; "Legal Services and the Poor in Urban America: The Delivery of Legal Aid in Cook County," Chicago Bar Record, 1977. Special Assistant Attorney General of Illinois, 1969-1973. Delegate and Chairman, Executive Article Committee, Illinois Constitutional Convention, 1969-1970. Special Counsel, Illinois Department of Insurance, 1969-1973. Member, Board of Directors, 1974-1976 and Acting Chairman, 1974-1975, Regional Transportation Authority. Member and Vice Chairman, Board of Directors, MacNeal Hospital, 1968-1989. Commissioner: Cook County Board of Commissioners, 1976-1982. Special Counsel: Illinois Department of Professional Regulation, 1977-1990; Illinois Medical Disciplinary Board, 1979-1988. Secretary, Illinois State Toll Highway Authority, 1982-1987. Special Counsel: Illinois Department of Public Aid, 1982-1983; Illinois Department of Public Health, 1983-1984. Member, Cook County Zoning Board of Appeals, 1987-1993. Member, Board of Trustees of Brookfield Zoo, 1991-2000; Board of Directors of Metra, 1995—. Member, The Illinois Redistricting Process Review Commission, 1992-1994. Member, Board of Trustees, The Lincoln Academy of Illinois, 1999—. Member, Panel of Arbitrators, American Arbitration Association. *Member:* Chicago, Illinois State and American Bar Associations; Trial Lawyers Club of Chicago; American Academy of Hospital Attorneys. ***PRACTICE AREAS:*** Hospital; Health Care; Corporate; Municipal and Governmental Law. ***Email:*** Jtecson@chuhak.com

LAW OFFICES OF MARYLU CIANCIOLO

823 SOUTH WESTERN AVENUE
CHICAGO, ILLINOIS 60612
Telephone: 312-455-1940
Fax: 312-455-0183
URL: http://www.cianciololaw.com
Email: mcianciolo@cianciololaw.com
URL: http://www.lawyers.com/fraudaudit

Family Immigration, Employment Immigration and Visas, Labor Certifications and Permanent Residency, Deportation, Asylum, Health Care Law including, Health Care Fraud, Health Care Licensing, Reimbursement, Medicare and Medicaid, Alternative Health Care Delivery Systems, Home Health Care, Long Term Care, Managed Care, Medical Ethics, Physical Therapist Licensing, Nursing Home Regulations, Physicians Contracts and Licensing. Business Immigration, Employment Immigration and Visas, Labor Certifications and Permanent Visas.

MARYLU CIANCIOLO, born Milwaukee, Wisconsin, January 14, 1963; admitted to bar, 1987, Illinois; 1988, New York; 1989, U.S. District Court, Northern District of Illinois. *Education:* University of Denver (B.A., with honors in Psychology, 1983); Valparaiso University (J.D., 1986); University of Chicago (M.B.A., 1992). Phi Alpha Delta. Member, Jessup Moot Court Team. Instructor: Corporations and Paralegalism, American Institute of Paralegal Studies, New York, 1987-1988; Legal Liability and Medical Scope of Practice, Therapy Team Educational Services, 1995—. *Member:* Illinois State and New York State Bar Associations; American Immigration Lawyers Association. ***LANGUAGES:*** Spanish. ***PRACTICE AREAS:*** Immigration; Medicare and Medicaid; Health Law. ***Email:*** cianciololaw@hotmail.com

ASSOCIATE

BERNADETTE C. McGUIRE, born Denver, Colorado, March 18, 1974; admitted to bar, 2003, Colorado (Not admitted in Illinois). *Education:* University of Colorado (B.A., 1997); William Mitchell College of Law (J.D., 2002). Staff Member, William Mitchell Law Review, 2001-2002. *Member:* Colorado and Denver Bar Associations; Colorado Womens Bar Association. ***PRACTICE AREAS:*** Immigration Law. ***Email:*** cianciololaw2@hotmail.com

CIARDELLI AND CUMMINGS

19 WEST JACKSON BOULEVARD
SUITE 300
CHICAGO, ILLINOIS 60604
Telephone: 312-346-2522
Fax: 312-922-0631
URL: http://www.lawcicu.com

Criminal Law, Personal Injury, Medical Malpractice, Products Liability.

MEMBERS OF FIRM

VICTOR F. CIARDELLI, admitted to bar, 1960, Illinois. *Education:* DePaul University (B.A., 1956; LL.B., 1960).

PATRICK M. CUMMINGS, admitted to bar, 1980, Illinois. *Education:* John Caroll University (B.A., 1977); John Marshall Law School (J.D., 1980).

KELLY Q. BENNETT, born Los Angeles, California, October 2, 1969; admitted to bar, 1998, Illinois. *Education:* University of Wisconsin-Milwaukee (B.A., Political Sci-

(This Listing Continued)

CIARDELLI AND CUMMINGS, Chicago—Continued

ence, 1994); Chicago-Kent College of Law (J.D., 1998). *Member:* Chicago and Illinois State Bar Associations. ***PRACTICE AREAS:*** Criminal Law; Personal Injury; Litigation. ***Email:*** KB@KQBLAW.COM

MARC R. CAMPAGNA, admitted to bar, 2002, Illinois. *Education:* University of Illinois (B.A., 1999); DePaul University College of Law (J.D., 2002).

CIRIGNANI HELLER HARMAN & LYNCH LLP

Established in 1980
SUITE 2600
150 SOUTH WACKER DRIVE
CHICAGO, ILLINOIS 60606
Telephone: 312-346-8700
Facsimile: 312-346-5180
Email: info@cirignani.com
URL: http://www.cirignani.com

Medical Malpractice, Wrongful Death, Cerebral Palsy, ERBS Palsy, Brain Damage, Anesthesia Injury, Improper Medication, Operating Room Death, Misdiagnosis, Birth Injuries, Retardation, Surgical Error, Medical Product Failure, Nursing Errors, Hospital Negligence, Head and Spinal Injuries, Automobile Accidents, Truck Accidents, Construction Accidents, Product Liability, Labor and Employment Litigation, Commercial Litigation, Insurance Coverage, Torts. Litigation.

STANLEY J. HELLER, born Philadelphia, Pennsylvania, May 10, 1941; admitted to bar, 1988, Illinois and U.S. District Court, Northern District of Illinois; 1996, Georgia and U.S. District Court, Northern District of Georgia. *Education:* Johns Hopkins University (A.B., 1962); Johns Hopkins University School of Medicine (M.D., 1965); Northwestern University (J.D., 1988). Listed in: Who's Who in America; Who's Who in the World. Intern, Presbyterian-St. Luke's Medical Center, 1965-1966; Resident, Internal Medicine, Rush-Presbyterian St. Luke's Medical Center, 1966-1968; USPHS Fellow, Cardiovascular Diseases, Rush-Presbyterian-St. Luke's Medical Center, 1968-1970. Medical Certifications and Appointments: Current Licensure, Illinois; Prior Licensure - Maryland: Board Certified in Cardiovascular Disease, 1973; Board Certified in Internal Medicine, 1973; Instructor, Internal Medicine -University of Illinois School of Medicine, 1968-1970; Assistant Professor, Loyola-Stritch College of Medicine, 1970-1972; Associate Professor, Loyola-Stritch College of Medicine, 1972-1975; Associate Professor of Clinical Medicine, Northwestern University School of Medicine, 1975-1990. Fellowships and Awards: Fellow Emeritus: American College of Physicians; American College of Cardiology; Council on Clinical Cardiology; of the American Heart Association. Fellow, American College of Legal Medicine. *Member:* Illinois State and American Bar Associations; Illinois Trial Lawyers Association; Georgia Trial Lawyers Association; The Association of Trial Lawyers of America. ***LANGUAGES:*** English. ***PRACTICE AREAS:*** Medical Malpractice. ***Email:*** sjh@cirignani.com

JAMES C. HARMAN, born Evergreen Park, Illinois, May 10, 1958; admitted to bar, 1987, Illinois and U.S. District Court, Northern District of Illinois; 1998, Georgia and U.S. District Court, Northern District of Georgia. *Education:* Southern Illinois University (B.S., 1980); Northwestern University (Certificate in Respiratory Therapy, 1982); John Marshall Law School (J.D., with distinction, 1987). *Member:* Chicago Bar Association; Illinois State Bar Association; American Bar Association; American Trial Lawyers Association. ***LANGUAGES:*** English. ***PRACTICE AREAS:*** Medical Malpractice; Catastrophic Injury; ERBS Palsy; Cerebal Palsy. ***Email:*** jim@cirignani.com

WILLIAM A. CIRIGNANI, born Chicago, Illinois, October 29, 1960; admitted to bar, 1988, Arizona; 1993, Illinois; U.S. District Court, Northern District of Illinois; U.S. Court of Appeals, Seventh Circuit; 2003, Georgia and U.S. District Court, Northern District of Georgia. *Education:* Loyola University (B.B.A., 1984); Northwestern University (J.D., 1988). *Member:* Chicago, Illinois State and American Bar Associations; State Bar of Georgia; State Bar of Arizona; The Association of Trial Lawyers of America. ***LANGUAGES:*** English. ***PRACTICE AREAS:*** Medical Malpractice; Catastrophic Injury; Commercial Litigation; Torts; Product Liabilities Litigation. ***Email:*** wac@cirignani.com

DANIEL LYNCH, born Boulder, Colorado, December 23, 1959; admitted to bar, 1988, Colorado and U.S. District Court, District of Colorado; 1989, Illinois, U.S. District Court, Northern District of Illinois including Trial Bar and U.S. Court of Appeals, Seventh Circuit; 1993, U.S. District Court, Central District of Illinois; 1994, U.S. Court of Appeals, Eighth Circuit; 1998, U.S. Court of Appeals, Second Circuit; 2000, U.S. Court of Appeals, Tenth Circuit. *Education:* University of Colorado at Boulder (B.A., 1985); University of Denver; Northwestern University (J.D., 1988). *Member:* Chicago, Illinois State and American Bar Associations. ***LANGUAGES:*** English. ***PRACTICE AREAS:*** Commercial Litigation; Class Actions; Consumer Fraud; Complex Litigation; Securities Litigation; Real Estate Litigation. ***Email:*** daniellynch@cirignani.com

ASSOCIATES

DEBORAH ALROTH, born Lake Forest, Illinois, August 3, 1971; admitted to bar, 1995, Illinois and U.S. District Court, Northern District of Illinois; 1997, Georgia and U.S. District Court, Northern District of Georgia. *Education:* Indiana University (B.S., 1992); Chicago-Kent College of Law, Illinois Institute of Technology (J.D., 1995). *Member:* Chicago, Illinois State and American Bar Associations. ***LANGUAGES:*** English. ***PRACTICE AREAS:*** Medical Malpractice. ***Email:*** debbie@cirignani.com

BENJAMIN P. BERINGER, born Chicago, Illinois, October 19, 1965; admitted to bar, 1990, Illinois. *Education:* Wabash College (B.A., summa cum laude, 1987); Indiana University (J.D., cum laude, 1990). Phi Beta Kappa. Delta Theta Phi. Member, Indiana Law Journal, 1988-1990. Editor in Chief, Indiana University Exordium, 1987-1989. Member, Indiana University Trial Team, 1990. *Member:* Illinois State (Member, Health Care Section; Insurance Law Section) and Chicago (Member, Insurance Law Committee; Professional Responsibility Committee) Bar Associations; Defense Research Institute; Illinois Association of Healthcare Attorneys: Chicagoland Healthcare Risk Management Society. ***LANGUAGES:*** English. ***PRACTICE AREAS:*** Litigation; Health Care Litigation; Medical Law; Medical Malpractice. ***Email:*** bpb@cirignani.com

(This Listing Continued)

SCOTT C. PATTON, born Flint, Michigan, December 6, 1971; admitted to bar, 2001, Illinois and U.S. District Court, Northern District of Illinois. *Education:* Oakland University (B.S., 1998); Chicago-Kent College of Law (J.D., 2001). *Member:* Chicago, Illinois State and American Bar Associations. ***PRACTICE AREAS:*** Medical Malpractice; Labor and Employment Litigation; Commercial Litigation. ***Email:*** scottpatton@cirignani.com

CLARK & JOHNSON, LLC

446 NORTH WELLS STREET, SUITE 340
CHICAGO, ILLINOIS 60610
Telephone: 312-593-2009
Fax: 312-416-0312

Corporate Law, Commercial Real Estate, Business Litigation, Mergers and Acquistions, International Law.

LANCE E. CLARK, born Houston, Texas, May 4, 1970; admitted to bar, 1998, Michigan and U.S. District Court, Western and Eastern Districts of Michigan; 1999, Illinois, District of Columbia and U.S. District Court, Northern District of Illinois; 2001, U.S. Court of Appeals, Seventh Circuit. *Education:* Trinity International University (B.A., 1994); University of Illinois College of Law (J.D., magna cum laude, 1997). Recipient, Harno Fellow Award. Member, University of Illinois Law Review. *Member:* Chicago and American Bar Associations. ***PRACTICE AREAS:*** Business Litigation; Arbitration; Insurance; Reinsurance. ***Email:*** lclark@lordbissell.com

TIGE C. JOHNSON, born Morris, Illinois, October 20, 1970; admitted to bar, 1998, Michigan; 1999, District of Columbia; 2000, Illinois. *Education:* University of New Mexico (B.A., with distinction, 1992); Vanderbilt University (J.D., 1996); London School of Economics and Political Science, London, England (LL.M., in International Business Transactions, with merit, 1997). Deans List; Phi Beta Kappa; Phi Eta Sigma (President); Phi Alpha Delta (Chief Justice, 1994-1995); Golden Key; Moot Court Board, Justice for Traveling Teams. Member, International Law Association, British Branch, 1996-1997. Adjunct Professor: Grand Valley State University, Allendale, MI, 1999; Columbia College Chicago, Chicago, IL, 2002. ***LANGUAGES:*** French and Spanish. ***PRACTICE AREAS:*** Corporate Law; Private Equity; Mergers and Acquisitions; International Law. ***Email:*** johnsont@allheimer.com

WILLIAM G. CLARK, JR. & ASSOCIATES, LTD.

350 N. LA SALLE STREET, SUITE 800
CHICAGO, ILLINOIS 60610
Telephone: 312-329-0830
Fax: 312-329-1830
Email: wmclarkjrassoc@aol.com
URL: http://www.williamgclarkjrassociates.com

Family Law, Divorce, Support, Custody, Prenuptial Agreements.

FIRM PROFILE: William G. Clark, Jr. & Associates, Ltd. has been providing legal services since 1982. In the early years of the law firm's existence, Clark & Associates handled a wide range of legal matters in the Supreme, Appellate and Circuit Courts. For the past 15 years, the firm has specialized in Family Law matters, including Divorce, Premarital Agreements, Child Custody, and Support.

WILLIAM G. CLARK, JR., born Chicago, Illinois, April 16, 1949; admitted to bar, 1977, Illinois; 1978, U.S. District Court, Northern District of Illinois; 1982, U.S. Court of Appeals, 7th Circuit; 1988, U.S. Supreme Court. *Education:* Loyola University (B.A., 1972); DePaul University (J.D., 1976). Recipient: Certificate of Dedication, Illinois Trial Lawyers Board of Managers, 2004; Commendation, De Paul College of Law, Family Law Center, 2003-2004; Distinguished Service Award, Chicago Volunteer Legal Services Foundation, 2002-2003; Certificate of Appreciation, Family Law Section, Illinois State Bar Association, 1992. Author: Introduction to "Suggested Guidelines for Supervised Visitation," 74 Ill. Bar Journal 224. Lecturer: "The Trial of A Divorce Case," Chicago Bar Association, Young Lawyers Committee, December 1993; "Effective Use of Experts in Matrimonial Cases," Illinois Institute for Continuing Education, September 1989; "Special Circumstances Involving Child Support and Maintenance," Chicago Bar Association, January 1986. Member: Leading Lawyers Network (Family Law), 2003-2004. *Member:* Chicago Bar Association; Illinois State Bar Association; American Bar Association; Illinois Trial Lawyers Association; American Academy of Matrimonial Lawyers; Catholic Lawyers Guild of Chicago; Celtic Lawyers of Chicago (President, 1992). ***PRACTICE AREAS:*** Family Law; Divorce; Child Support; Child Custody; Premarital Agreements.

LISA MARIE ZAHN, born Chicago, Illinois, 1967; admitted to bar, 1993, Illinois; U.S. District Court, Northern District of Illinois. *Education:* University of Wisconsin-Madison (B.S., Psychology, 1989); IIT Chicago-Kent College of Law (J.D., 1993). Recipient, Certificate of Appreciation for Contributors to the Court Facilitator Program, June 2003. *Member:* Chicago Bar Association. ***PRACTICE AREAS:*** Family Law; Divorce; Child Custody; Child Support.

CLAUSEN MILLER P.C.

Established in 1936

10 SOUTH LA SALLE STREET
SUITE 1600
CHICAGO, ILLINOIS 60603-1098
Telephone: 312-855-1010
Fax: 312-606-7777
Email: info@clausen.com
URL: http://www.clausen.com

Wheaton, Illinois Office: Building C, Suite 1700, 2100 Manchester Road, 60187-2402. Telephone: 630-668-9100. Fax: 630-668-9169.

European Affiliated Law Firm—Clausen Miller Europe: Tetaud-Lambard-Jami & Associés, 83, boulevard Raspail, 75006, Paris, France. Telephone: +33.1.45.48.62.63. Fax: +33.1.45.48.42.57. Studio Legale Corapi, Via Flaminia, 318 00196- Roma. Telephone: 39.06.32.18.563. Fax: 39.06.32.00.992. van Cutsem-Wittamer-Marnef & Partners, Avenue Louise 137/1, B-1050 Brussels, Belgium. Telephone: +32-2-543-02-00. Fax: +32-2-538-13-78.

European Affiliated Law Firm—Clausen Miller, L.L.P.: 148 Leadenhall Street, London, EC3V 4QT England. Telephone: +44.20.7648.8460. Fax: +44.20.7648.8461.

New York, N.Y. Office: One Chase Manhattan Plaza, 10005. Telephone: 212-805-3900. Fax: 212-805-3939.

Parsippany, New Jersey Office: One Gatehall Drive, Suite 203, 07054. Telephone: 973-401-0470. Fax: 973-401-0513.

Irvine, California Office: 2040 Main Street, Suite 500, 92614. Telephone: 949-474-3100. Fax: 949-474-3190.

Admiralty, Appellate, Banking and Secured Lending, Business/Corporate, Construction, Employment, Environmental/OSHA, Fidelity and Surety, First-Party Property, Insurance Coverage, Intellectual Property, International Law, Liability Defense, Medical Malpractice, Mold, Municipal Liability, Premises Liability, Products Liability, Professional Liability, Subrogation, Transportation.

FIRM PROFILE: Clausen Miller P.C., a full-service civil litigation and general practice firm with more than 175 proven trial attorneys nationwide, is headquartered in the heart of the business, financial and legal district of downtown Chicago. Clausen Miller's five additional offices span from coast to coast, with affiliate offices in England, France and Italy.

During our 70-year history, we've built a solid reputation as an insurance defense firm, while expanding our practice areas to include everything from admiralty to corporate transactions and litigation to Intellectual Property. This expansion has allowed us to better serve the needs of our diverse client base. To enhance client relationships, our attorneys participate in various community projects and professional activities as well as sponsoring industry conferences.

We at Clausen Miller have always stressed the important role our clients play in the success of the firm. This spirit of partnership is the basis for our creative and hard-working legal style. Because many of our lawyers and paralegals have additional degrees, they are able to understand the industries our clients are working in and provide fast, effective solutions. This strong legal scholarship allows us to provide proven results in or out of the courtroom.

At Clausen Miller, the needs of the client dictate the direction we take.

IVAR R. AZERIS, born Tübingen, Germany, April 2, 1948; admitted to bar, 1974, Illinois; 1975, U.S. District Court, Northern District of Illinois including Trial Bar. *Education:* University of Illinois (B.A., 1970); Boston College (J.D., 1973). *Member:* Chicago (Member, Civil Practice Committee), Illinois State and American Bar Associations. ***PRACTICE AREAS:*** Real Estate; Business; Commercial Litigation; Employment Law; Estate Planning; Probate. ***Email:*** iazeris@clausen.com

KURT D. BAER, born Syracuse, New York, October 16, 1948; admitted to bar, 1981, Illinois and U.S. District Court, Northern District of Illinois including Trial Bar; 1984, U.S. Court of Appeals, Seventh Circuit. *Education:* Lawrence University (B.A., magna cum laude, 1970); Northwestern University (M.S., 1971); IIT Chicago-Kent College of Law (J.D., with honors, 1980). *Member:* American Bar Association. ***PRACTICE AREAS:*** Products Liability; Subrogation; Construction Litigation; Business Litigation; Commercial Litigation; Alternative Dispute Resolution; Casualty/Liability Defense. ***Email:*** kbaer@clausen.com

JAMES S. BARBER, born Chicago, Illinois, January 31, 1946; admitted to bar, 1977, Illinois, U.S. District Court, Northern District of Illinois and U.S. Court of Appeals, Seventh Circuit. *Education:* DePaul University (B.A., 1967; M.B.A., 1974; J.D., 1977). *Member:* Chicago, Illinois State and American (Member, Labor and Employment Committee) Bar Associations. ***PRACTICE AREAS:*** Employment Law; Commercial Litigation; Bankruptcy; Business; Intellectual Property; Securities. ***Email:*** jbarber@clausen.com

DIANE M. BARON, born Chicago, Illinois, September 19, 1953; admitted to bar, 1984, Illinois and U.S. District Court, Northern and Central Districts of Illinois; 1997, New York. *Education:* Northwestern University (B.S., with honors, 1981; J.D., 1984). *Member:* Chicago Bar Association. ***PRACTICE AREAS:*** Medical Malpractice; Health Care; Professional Liability; Insurance; Business; Commercial Litigation; Liability Insurance Coverage; Employment Law; Casualty/Liability Defense. ***Email:*** dbaron@clausen.com

MICHAEL W. BASIL, born Saginaw, Michigan, May 7, 1968; admitted to bar, 1995, Missouri; 1996, Illinois; U.S. District Court, Northern District of Illinois; U.S. District Court, Western District of Michigan; U.S. Court of Appeals, Fifth, Seventh and Eighth Circuits. *Education:* University of Michigan (B.A., 1990); St. Louis University (J.D., cum laude, 1995); Loyola University (M.B.A., 2001). ***PRACTICE AREAS:*** Construction Litigation; Subrogation; Business; Commercial Litigation; First Party Property; Casualty/Liability Defense. ***Email:*** mbasil@clausen.com

JAMES JOSEPH BIGONESS, born Detroit, Michigan; admitted to bar, 1982, Illinois; U.S. District Court, Northern District of Illinois including Trial Bar and U.S. Court of Appeals, Seventh Circuit. *Education:* St. Joseph's College (B.S., 1976); DePaul University (J.D., 1982). ***PRACTICE AREAS:*** Subrogation; Construction Litigation; Premises Liability; Products Liability; Casualty/Liability Defense. ***Email:*** jbigoness@clausen.com

(This Listing Continued)

PETER G. BORA, born Chicago, Illinois, December 4, 1962; admitted to bar, 1989, Illinois; 1990, U.S. District Court, Northern District of Illinois. *Education:* Illinois State University (B.S., 1984); John Marshall School of Law (J.D., with distinction, 1989). ***PRACTICE AREAS:*** Insurance Coverage; Insurance; Environmental Coverage; Liability Insurance Coverage. ***Email:*** pbora@clausen.com

PAUL BOZYCH, born Joliet, Illinois, August 14, 1963; admitted to bar, 1988, Illinois; 1989, U.S. District Court, Northern District of Illinois. *Education:* University of Illinois (A.B., 1985); DePaul University (J.D., with honors, 1988). ***PRACTICE AREAS:*** Torts; Products Liability; Business; Commercial Litigation; Casualty/Liability Defense; Construction Litigation; Insurance Coverage. ***Email:*** pbozych@clausen.com

RICHARD A. BUCHANAN, born Martinsville, Virginia, July 16, 1951; admitted to bar, 1976, Illinois. *Education:* Bradley University (B.A., 1973); Loyola University of Chicago College of Law (J.D., 1976). Member, National Moot Court Team, 1976. *Member:* Chicago, Illinois State and American (Member, Property Insurance and Insurance Coverage Subcommittees) Bar Associations; Defense Research Institute. ***PRACTICE AREAS:*** Insurance; Insurance Coverage; First Party Property; Liability Insurance Coverage. ***Email:*** rbuchanan@clausen.com

SUSAN J. CONDON, born Chicago, Illinois; admitted to bar, 1977, Illinois and U.S. District Court, Northern District of Illinois; U.S. Court of Appeals, Second, Fourth, Sixth, Seventh, Tenth and Eleventh Circuits; 1994, U.S. Supreme Court. *Education:* University of Illinois (B.S., 1974); DePaul University (J.D., magna cum laude, 1977). Assistant State's Attorney, Civil Action Bureau, Cook County, Illinois, 1979-1991; Supervisor, Chancery-General Litigation, 1983-1991. *Member:* Appellate Lawyers Association (Director, 1996-1997). ***PRACTICE AREAS:*** Appellate Litigation; Environmental Coverage. ***Email:*** scondon@clausen.com

MARGARET HUPP FAHEY, born Chicago, Illinois, February 19, 1961; admitted to bar, 1986, Illinois and U.S. District Court, Northern District of Illinois. *Education:* University of Missouri at Columbia (B.J., with high honors, 1983); University of Illinois (J.D., 1986). Kappa Tau Alpha. *Member:* Chicago, Illinois State and American Bar Associations. ***PRACTICE AREAS:*** Professional Liability; Construction Litigation; Insurance Coverage; First Party Property. ***Email:*** mfahey@clausen.com

DENNIS D. FITZPATRICK, born Chicago, Illinois, November 8, 1964; admitted to bar, 1989, Illinois; 1990, U.S. District Court, Northern District of Illinois, including Trial Bar; 1991, District of Columbia; 1992, Minnesota and U.S. District Court, Eastern District of Wisconsin. *Education:* Marquette University (B.A., 1986); DePaul University (J.D., 1989). *Member:* Chicago, Illinois State and American Bar Associations; The District of Columbia Bar. ***PRACTICE AREAS:*** Insurance; Subrogation; Construction Litigation; Products Liability; Professional Liability; First Party Property; Environmental Coverage; Insurance Coverage; Casualty/Liability Defense. ***Email:*** dfitzpatrick@clausen.com

ROBERT E. GILMARTIN III, born Chicago, Illinois, January 3, 1950; admitted to bar, 1975, Illinois; U.S. District Court, Northern District of Illinois including Trial Bar. *Education:* Northwestern University (B.A., 1972); Loyola University of Chicago (J.D., 1975). Author: "When to Use Polygraph Evidence," American Bar Association's *The Brief,* Winter, 1988 ed., Vol. 17, No. 2; "Subrogation," Illinois Institute of Continuing Legal Education's Handbook on Chancery and Special Remedies, 1992 ed.; "International Multimodal Shipments of Goods—The Inland Truck and Rail Segments," Midwest Conference on Marine Claims and Insurance, 1990. Law Clerk, Illinois Appellate Court, 1975-1977. Lecturer, Legal Writing, Loyola University School of Law, 1976-1978. *Member:* Chicago, Illinois State and American (Member, Litigation and Tort and Insurance Practice Sections; Property Insurance Committee; Vice Chair, Rail Motor Carriers Committee, 1989-1990) Bar Associations. ***REPORTED CASES:*** National Tea v. Gaylord Discount Dept. Stores, 427 N.E.2d 345; Kondourajian v. Millers National Ins. Co., 503 N.E.2d 775; Complaint of Midwest Equipment Leasing Corp., 703 F. Supp. 727; In re Fernstrom Storage and Van Co., 100 B.R. 1017; San Antonio Press v. Custom Built Machinery, 852 S.W.2d 64 (Tex. 1993); St. Paul Insurance Co. v. Estate of Venute, 656 N.E.2d 113 (Ill. App. Ct. 1995). ***PRACTICE AREAS:*** Subrogation; Environmental Coverage; Insurance; Insurance Coverage; Products Liability; First Party Property; Liability Insurance Coverage; Casualty/Liability Defense. ***Email:*** rgilmartin@clausen.com

MICHAEL R. GRIMM, SR., born Cleveland, Ohio, December 24, 1951; admitted to bar, 1978, Illinois, U.S. District Court, Northern District of Illinois including Trial Bar, U.S. Supreme Court, U.S. Court of Appeals, Seventh Circuit and U.S. District Court, Northern District of Indiana. *Education:* MacMurray College and University of Illinois (B.A., with honors, 1973); The John Marshall Law School (J.D., with distinction, 1978). *Member:* Chicago, Illinois State and American Bar Associations; Illinois Defense Counsel; Defense Research Institute; NSBA Council of School Attorneys; Illinois Council of School Attorneys; International Association of Defense Counsel. ***PRACTICE AREAS:*** International; Insurance; Reinsurance; Business; Commercial Litigation; Employment Law; Insurance Coverage; Professional Liability; Securities; Casualty/Liability Defense. ***Email:*** mgrimm@clausen.com

THOMAS S. GOZDZIAK, born Hinsdale, Illinois, November 24, 1968; admitted to bar, 1995 Illinois and U.S. District Court, Northern District of Illinois. *Education:* Bradley University (B.S., 1990); John Marshall Law School (J.D., 1995). ***PRACTICE AREAS:*** First Party Property; Insurance Coverage; Professional Liability; Subrogation; Products Liability; Environmental Defense. ***Email:*** tgozdziak@clausen.com

JOHN T. GROARK, born Evanston, Illinois, November 18, 1951; admitted to bar, 1979, Illinois and U.S. District Court, Northern District of Illinois including Trial Bar. *Education:* Loyola University (B.S., 1976); John Marshall Law School (J.D., 1979); DePaul University (LL.M., 1984). Assistant State's Attorney, Cook County, Illinois, 1980-1987. *Member:* Chicago Bar Association. ***PRACTICE AREAS:*** Business; Commercial Litigation; OSHA Defense; Subrogation; Casualty/Liability Defense. ***Email:*** jgroark@clausen.com

SUSAN N. K. GUMMOW, born Beloit, Wisconsin; admitted to bar, 1991, Louisiana; 1993, Texas; 2000, Illinois. *Education:* Baylor University (B.B.A., 1984); Louisiana State

(This Listing Continued)

CLAUSEN MILLER P.C., Chicago—Continued

University (J.D., 1991). ***PRACTICE AREAS:*** Banking; Secured Lending; Bankruptcy; Business; Commercial Litigation; Securities; Insurance. ***Email:*** sgummow@clausen.com

WILLIAM J. HACKER, born Chicago, Illinois, July 26, 1951; admitted to bar, 1976, Illinois and U.S. District Court, Northern District of Illinois. *Education:* DePaul University (B.S., 1973); John Marshall Law School (J.D., 1976). *Member:* Chicago, Illinois State and American Bar Associations; International Association of Defense Counsel. ***LANGUAGES:*** Spanish. ***PRACTICE AREAS:*** Construction Litigation; Banking Law; Secured Lending; Fidelity and Surety; Subrogation; Business; Commercial Litigation; Employment Law; Real Estate; Estate Planning; Probate. ***Email:*** whacker@clausen.com

MARYLU HAHN, born Chicago, Illinois, August 15, 1949; admitted to bar, 1987, Illinois and U.S. District Court, Northern District of Illinois; 1992, U.S. District Court, Eastern District of Michigan; U.S. District Court, Eastern District of Wisconsin. *Education:* Loyola University (B.S., 1972); John Marshall Law School (J.D., 1987). ***PRACTICE AREAS:*** Insurance; Reinsurance; First Party Property; Insurance Coverage. ***Email:*** mhahn@clausen.com

DAVID M. HEILMANN, born Evergreen Park, Illinois, October 10, 1962; admitted to bar, 1987, Illinois and U.S. District Court, Northern District of Illinois including Trial Bar; U.S. District Court, Central District of Illinois. *Education:* University of Illinois (B.S., 1984); DePaul University (J.D., 1987). *Member:* Chicago, Illinois State and American Bar Associations. ***PRACTICE AREAS:*** Environmental Coverage; Business; Commercial Litigation; Construction Litigation; Municipal Defense; Casualty/Liability Defense; Toxic Torts. ***Email:*** dheilmann@clausen.com

HARVEY R. HERMAN, born Jersey City, New Jersey, May 15, 1955; admitted to bar, 1982, Illinois; U.S. District Court, Northern and Central Districts of Illinois. *Education:* University of Michigan (B.A., 1977; J.D., 1982). ***PRACTICE AREAS:*** Subrogation; Fidelity and Surety. ***Email:*** hherman@clausen.com

CELESTE A. HILL, born McLeansboro, Illinois, November 6, 1960; admitted to bar, 1986, Illinois; 1987, U.S. District Court, Northern District of Illinois including Trial Bar. *Education:* University of Illinois (A.B., 1982); Northwestern University (J.D., 1986). Phi Beta Kappa; Phi Kappa Phi. *Member:* Chicago and American Bar Associations. ***PRACTICE AREAS:*** Insurance; Subrogation; Construction Litigation; Products Liability; First Party Property; Insurance Coverage; Casualty/Liability Defense. ***Email:*** chill@clausen.com

JAMES M. HOEY, born Baltimore, Maryland, November 29, 1952; admitted to bar, 1977, Illinois and U.S. District Court, Northern District of Illinois; registered to practice before U.S. Patent and Trademark Office. *Education:* Purdue University (B.S.M.E., with honors, 1974); Loyola University (J.D., 1977). *Member:* Chicago and American Bar Associations. ***PRACTICE AREAS:*** First Party Property; Professional Liability; Construction Litigation; Subrogation; Reinsurance; Intellectual Property; Casualty/Liability Defense. ***Email:*** jhoey@clausen.com

RICHARD G. HOWSER, born Tulsa, Oklahoma, April 5, 1951; admitted to bar, 1977, Illinois and U.S. District Court, Northern District of Illinois including Trial Bar. *Education:* University of Illinois (B.A., 1973); Loyola University of Chicago (J.D., 1977). Phi Alpha Delta. *Member:* Chicago, Illinois State and American Bar Associations; Defense Research Institute; Illinois Defense Counsel; Society of Trial Lawyers. ***PRACTICE AREAS:*** Construction Litigation; Medical Malpractice; Health Care; Products Liability; Casualty/Liability Defense. ***Email:*** rhowser@clausen.com

JOHN M. HYNES, born Evergreen Park, Illinois, September 6, 1954; admitted to bar, 1979, Illinois and U.S. District Court, Northern District of Illinois; U.S. Court of Appeals, Seventh Circuit. *Education:* Northwestern University (B.A., 1976); Loyola University (J.D., 1979). Assistant State's Attorney, Illinois, 1979-1985. *Member:* Chicago Bar Association. ***PRACTICE AREAS:*** Medical Malpractice; Health Care; Professional Liability; Casualty/Liability Defense. ***Email:*** jhynes@clausen.com

TRACEY A. JORDAN, born Cincinnati, Ohio, May 25, 1967; admitted to bar, 1992, Florida; 1993, Pennsylvania and West Virginia; 1996, U.S. District Court, Northern District of West Virginia; 1998, Illinois; 1999, U.S. District Court, Northern District of Illinois. *Education:* Miami University (B.A., 1989); Case Western Reserve University (J.D., 1992). ***PRACTICE AREAS:*** Insurance; Subrogation; First Party Property; Insurance Coverage. ***Email:*** tjordan@clausen.com

COLE S. KAIN, born Park Ridge, Illinois, March 12, 1963; admitted to bar, 1990, Illinois and U.S. District Court, Northern District of Illinois; 1991, U.S. Court of International Trade; 1992, District of Columbia and U.S. Court of Appeals, Federal Circuit; 1995, U.S. District Court, Eastern District of Michigan. *Education:* The University of Iowa (B.A., 1985); The John Marshall Law School (J.D., with high distinction, 1990); New York University School of Law (LL.M., 1992). Law Clerk to Honorable Dominick L. DiCarlo, Chief Judge, U.S. Court of International Trade, 1990-1992. ***PRACTICE AREAS:*** Fidelity and Surety; Banking; Secured Lending; Business; Commercial Litigation. ***Email:*** ckain@clausen.com

RICHARD M. KAPLAN, born Queens, New York, March 15, 1950; admitted to bar, 1975, Illinois and U.S. District Court, Northern District of Illinois. *Education:* Johns Hopkins University (B.A., 1972); Northwestern University (J.D., 1975). *Member:* Chicago Bar Association. ***PRACTICE AREAS:*** Construction Litigation; Professional Liability; Casualty/Liability Defense. ***Email:*** rkaplan@clausen.com

EDWARD M. KAY, born Chicago, Illinois, October 10, 1952; admitted to bar, 1979, Illinois; U.S. Court of Appeals, First, Second, Fifth, Sixth, Seventh, Ninth, Tenth and Eleventh Circuits and U.S. Supreme Court. *Education:* Loyola University (B.A., 1974); Northern Illinois University (J.D., 1979). *Member:* Appellate Lawyers Association. Fellow, American Academy of Appellate Lawyers. ***PRACTICE AREAS:*** Dispostive Trial Briefing; Complex Litigation; Post Trial Litigation; Appellate Litigation. ***Email:*** ekay@clausen.com

KIMBLEY A. KEARNEY, born Chicago, Illinois, July 1, 1958; admitted to bar, 1984, Louisiana; 1991, Illinois; U.S. District Court, Northern District of Illinois including Trial Bar; U.S. District Court, Northern District of Indiana; U.S. District Court, Eastern, Western and Middle Districts of Louisiana; U.S. Court of Appeals, Fifth, Sixth and Seventh Circuits; U.S. Supreme Court. *Education:* St. Mary's College (B.A., 1980); Tulane University of Louisiana (J.D., cum laude, 1984; M.B.A., 1984). *Member:* Maritime Law Association of the United States. ***PRACTICE AREAS:*** Admiralty and Maritime Law; Business; Commercial Litigation; Employment Law; Appellate; Casuality/Liability Defense. ***Email:*** kkearney@clausen.com

MELINDA S. KOLLROSS, born Park Ridge, Illinois, May 28, 1967; admitted to bar, 1992, Illinois and U.S. District Court, Northern District of Illinois; 1994, U.S. Court of Appeals, Sixth and Seventh Circuits; 1999, New York; 2000, U.S. District Court, Northern District of Indiana. *Education:* DePaul University (B.A., with highest honor, 1989); IIT Chicago-Kent College of Law (J.D., with high honors, 1992). Order of the Coif. *Member:* Chicago and Illinois State Bar Associations; Illinois Appellate Lawyers Association. ***PRACTICE AREAS:*** Appellate; Insurance; Insurance Coverage. ***Email:*** mkollross@clausen.com

ILENE M. KOREY, born Chicago, Illinois, October 31, 1957; admitted to bar, 1983, Illinois and U.S. District Court, Northern District of Illinois including Trial Bar, and Southern District of Illinois. *Education:* University of Colorado at Boulder (B.A., 1979); DePaul University (J.D., 1983). Arbitrator, Circuit Court of Cook County, 1990—; Arbitrator, National Futures Association, 1989—. *Member:* Chicago (Member, 1984—, Co-Chair, Trial Techniques Committee, 1989-1990; Board of Directors, 1990-1991; Chair, Young Lawyers Section, 1993-1994; Board of Managers, 1995-1997) and American (Member 1990, YLD Membership Chair, 1990-1991; YLD District Representative, 1991-1994) Bar Associations; Chicago Bar Foundation (Board Member, 1994—). ***LANGUAGES:*** French. ***PRACTICE AREAS:*** Insurance; Environmental Coverage; Business; Commercial Litigation; Construction Litigation; Employment Law; Insurance Coverage; Medical Malpractice; Health Care; Premises Liability; Products Liability; Professional Liability; Liability Insurance Coverage; Casualty/Liability Defense. ***Email:*** ikorey@clausen.com

STEPHEN D. MARCUS, born Buffalo, New York, May 12, 1941; admitted to bar, 1967, Illinois. *Education:* Harvard University (B.A., 1963; J.D., 1967); King's College, Cambridge University, England (Certificate of Research, 1964). Registered Foreign Lawyer. Fellow, American College of Trial Lawyers. Author: "Actual Cash Value, Illinois and the Broad Evidence Rule," Illinois Bar Journal, August, 1971; "How Big an Umbrella? The Illinois Structural Work Act's Extent of Coverage," 53 Chicago Bar Record, January, 1972; "The Presidium Crisis: A Study of Power Allocation in United States Government," 4 Loyola University of Chicago Law Journal, Summer, 1973; Chapter 10, Quo Warranto and Mandamus, ICLE, Equitable Remedies in Chancery, 1978 (Revised, 1982, 1983, 1989, 1992, 1994, 1999); "Goals and Objectives for Alternative Dispute Resolution," 1992 Journal of Performance of Constructed Facilities—American Society of Civil Engineers—Technical Council on Forensic Engineering, Vol. 2, No. 1, February, 1988. Lecturer in Law, Chicago-Kent College of Law, 1970-1979. Member, Loss Executives Association. *Member:* Chicago, Illinois State and American Bar Associations. [Capt., U.S. Army, Adjutant, 509th Radio Research Group (ASA), Vietnam, 1969]. ***LANGUAGES:*** French. ***PRACTICE AREAS:*** Insurance; First Party Property; Insurance Coverage; International; Reinsurance; Professional Liability; Subrogation; Casualty/Liability Defense. ***Email:*** smarcus@clausen.com

RANDALL I. MARMOR, born Chicago, Illinois, December 8, 1953; admitted to bar, 1978, Illinois, U.S. District Court, Northern District of Illinois and U.S. Court of Appeals, Seventh Circuit. *Education:* Eastern Illinois University (B.A., 1975); John Marshall Law School (J.D., 1978). *Member:* Chicago and American (Member, Tort and Insurance Practice Section; Fidelity and Surety Committee) Bar Associations; International Association of Defense Counsel; Defense Research Institute. ***PRACTICE AREAS:*** Fidelity and Surety; Commercial Litigation; Directors and Officers Liability. ***Email:*** rmarmor@clausen.com

BARBARA I. MICHAELIDES, born Queens, New York, November 26, 1961; admitted to bar, 1996, Illinois; 1999, U.S. Court of Appeals, Seventh Circuit; 2001, U.S. Court of Appeals, District of Columbia Circuit; 2002, U.S. Court of Appeals, Fifth Circuit. *Education:* State University of New York (B.A., 1984); Loyola University (J.D., cum laude, 1996). ***PRACTICE AREAS:*** Appellate; Insurance Coverage. ***Email:*** bmichaelides@clausen.com

ERIN E. MORAN, born Chicago, Illinois, September 1, 1973; admitted to bar, 1998, Illinois. *Education:* Benedictine University (B.A., magna cum laude, 1994); John Marshall Law School (J.D., cum laude, 1998). ***PRACTICE AREAS:*** Insurance; First Party Property; Insurance Coverage. ***Email:*** emoran@clausen.com

RICHARD L. MURPHY, born Chicago, Illinois, January 27, 1951; admitted to bar, 1976, Illinois, U.S. District Court, Northern District of Illinois and U.S Court of Appeals, Seventh Circuit. *Education:* University of Notre Dame (B.A., 1973); Boston College (J.D., 1976). *Member:* Chicago and American Bar Associations; DRI; Illinois Defense Council; Society of Trial Lawyers. ***PRACTICE AREAS:*** Medical Malpractice; Health Care; Casualty/Liability Defense; Products Liability; Construction Litigation. ***Email:*** rmurphy@clausen.com

MELISSA A. MURPHY-PETROS, born Bloomington, Indiana, October 30, 1965; admitted to bar, 1995, Illinois; 1996, New York. *Education:* Indiana University (B.A., 1987); University of Notre Dame (M.A., 1989); Loyola University (J.D., 1995). ***PRACTICE AREAS:*** Appellate. ***Email:*** mmurphy-petros@clausen.com

STEVEN N. NOVOSAD, born St. Louis, Missouri, January 8, 1953; admitted to bar, 1984, Illinois and U.S. District Court, Northern, Southern and Central Districts of Illinois. *Education:* Southern Illinois University (B.S., 1977); John Marshall Law School (J.D., 1984). *Member:* Chicago, Lake County and Illinois State Bar Associations; Illinois Association of Defense Trial Counsel; Defense Research Institute. ***PRACTICE AREAS:*** Liability Insurance Coverage; Casualty/Liability Defense; Insurance Coverage; Bankruptcy; Construction Litigation; Municipal Defense; Professional Liability; Insurance; Business; Commercial Litigation; Premises Liability; Products Liability. **Email:** snovosad@clausen.com

SONIA V. ODARCZENKO, born Chicago, Illinois, May 18, 1964; admitted to bar, 1988, Illinois; 1989, U.S. District Court, Northern District of Illinois. *Education:* Bradley University (B.A., magna cum laude, 1984); Loyola University (J.D., 1988). *Member:* Chi-

(This Listing Continued)

cago and Illinois State Bar Associations. ***LANGUAGES:*** Ukrainian and French. ***PRACTICE AREAS:*** Medical Malpractice; Health Care; Professional Liability; Liability Insurance Coverage; Casualty/Liability Defense. ***Email:*** sodarczenko@clausen.com

MARGARET J. ORBON, born Chicago, Illinois, January 21, 1951; admitted to bar, 1976, Illinois and U.S. District Court, Northern District of Illinois. *Education:* Institute of European Studies; St. Mary's College (B.A., cum laude, 1973); Loyola University (J.D., 1976). *Member:* Chicago, Illinois State and American Bar Associations; Defense Research Institute. ***PRACTICE AREAS:*** Mass Torts; Insurance; Liability Insurance Coverage; Environmental Coverage; Insurance Coverage; Casualty/Liability Defense. ***Email:*** morbon@clausen.com

EDWARD J. OZOG, born Chicago, Illinois, June 13, 1948; admitted to bar, 1973, Illinois; 1980, U.S. Supreme Court. *Education:* DePaul University (B.A., 1970; J.D., 1973). Registered Foreign Lawyer. Member, 1970-1973 and Business Manager, 1971-1973, De Paul University Law Review. Recipient of 1992 International Association of Arson Investigators and a Partner with Clausen Miller Europe. Distinguished Service Award. Special Assistant Attorney General/Editor of Arson Prosecution and Training Manual for use by all Illinois State Prosecutors, State of Illinois (1987). Assistant State's Attorney, Cook County, 1973-1980. *Member:* Chicago, Illinois State and American (Vice-Chairman, Property Law Committee, Tort and Insurance Practice Section, 1988—) Bar Associations; International Association of Defense Counsel; Advocates Society; International Association of Arson Investigators (Illinois Chapter). ***PRACTICE AREAS:*** Insurance; Construction Litigation; First Party Property; Reinsurance; Subrogation; Insurance Coverage. ***Email:*** eozog@clausen.com

MARK D. PAULSON, born Decatur, Illinois; admitted to bar, 1992, Illinois. *Education:* Southern Illinois University; John Marshall Law School. ***PRACTICE AREAS:*** Insurance; Environmental Coverage; Liability Insurance Coverage; Insurance Coverage; First Party Property; Casualty/Liability Defense. ***Email:*** mpaulson@clausen.com

AMY RICH PAULUS, born Chicago, Illinois, December 19, 1963; admitted to bar, 1989, Illinois and U.S. District Court, Northern District of Illinois. *Education:* Northwestern University (B.A., 1985); Northern Illinois University (J.D., magna cum laude, 1989). Chartered Property and Casualty Underwriter (CPCU). *Member:* Chicago Bar Association. ***PRACTICE AREAS:*** Liability Insurance Coverage; First Party Property Insurance Coverage; Reinsurance; Insurance Coverage Litigation; Environmental Coverage; Toxic Torts. ***Email:*** apaulus@clausen.com

WILLIAM P. PISTORIUS, born Springfield, Illinois, May 19, 1962; admitted to bar, 1987, Illinois and U.S. District Court, Northern District of Illinois; 1988, U.S. Court of Appeals, Seventh Circuit. *Education:* University of Illinois (B.A., 1984); DePaul University (J.D., 1987). ***PRACTICE AREAS:*** Commercial Litigation; Medical Malpractice; Municipal Defense; Products Liability; Professional Liability; Casualty/Liability Defense. ***Email:*** wpistorius@clausen.com

DEAN S. RAUCHWERGER, born New York, N.Y., May 14, 1959; admitted to bar, 1984, Connecticut; 1985, New York and Illinois; U.S. District Court, Northern District of Illinois; U.S. Court of Appeals, Fifth and Seventh Circuits; U.S. District Court, District of Arizona; 1997, U.S. District Court, Southern District of New York; 2001, U.S. District Court, Northern District of Indiana; 2003, U.S. District Court, Western District of Michigan; 2004, U.S. District Court, Western District of Wisconsin. *Education:* Washington University (B.A., 1981; J.D., 1984). ***PRACTICE AREAS:*** Mass Torts; Subrogation; Business Litigation; Commercial Litigation; Products Liability; Toxic Torts. ***Email:*** drauchwerger@clausen.com

ROBERT L. REIFENBERG, born Evanston, Illinois, December 19, 1956; admitted to bar, 1981, Illinois; 1982, U.S. District Court, Northern District of Illinois including Trial Bar. *Education:* St. Mary's College (B.S., cum laude, 1978); Northern Illinois University (J.D., cum laude, 1981). Executive Editor, Northern Illinois University Law Review, 1980-1981. Law Clerk to Hon. Philip G. Reinhard, Illinois Appellate Court, Second District, 1981-1982. *Member:* Chicago Bar Association. ***PRACTICE AREAS:*** Liability Insurance Coverage; Business; Commercial Litigation; Mass Torts; Medical Malpractice; Construction Litigation; Products Liability; Insurance Coverage; Professional Liability; Casualty/Liability Defense. ***Email:*** rreifenberg@clausen.com

BRIAN J. RIORDAN, born Oak Lawn, Illinois, April 9, 1971; admitted to bar, 1996, Illinois. *Education:* Eastern Illinois University (B.A., 1993); Loyola University (J.D., 1996). ***PRACTICE AREAS:*** Mass Torts; Medical Malpractice; Health Care; Municipal Defense; Premises Liability; Professional Liability; Casualty/Liability Defense. ***Email:*** briordan@clausen.com

PAUL SCOTT RITCHIE, born Ravenna, Ohio, December 5, 1960; admitted to bar, 1989, Illinois and U.S. District Court, Northern and Central Districts of Illinois. *Education:* Purdue University (B.S., 1983); DePaul University (J.D., 1989). Order of Barristers. National Moot Court Team Member, 1988. ***SPECIAL AGENCIES:*** Specialized Carriers and Rigging Association. ***PRACTICE AREAS:*** Construction Litigation; Business; Commercial Litigation; Premises Liability; Products Liability; Casualty/Liability Defense. ***Email:*** pritchie@clausen.com

DOMINICK W. SAVAIANO, born Chicago, Illinois, July 17, 1956; admitted to bar, 1981, Illinois; 1982, U.S. District Court, Northern District of Illinois. *Education:* University of Illinois (B.A., 1978); Loyola University (J.D., 1981). *Member:* Illinois State and American Bar Associations; Illinois Association of Defense Trial Counsel; Defense Research Institute; Society of Trial Lawyers; American Board of Trial Advocates; Professional Liability Underwriters Society. ***PRACTICE AREAS:*** Products Liability; Liability Insurance Coverage; Business; Commercial Litigation; Construction Litigation; Medical Malpractice; Health Care; Insurance Coverage; Professional Liability; Casualty/Liability Defense. ***Email:*** dsavaiano@clausen.com

K. CLARK SCHIRLE, born Decatur, Illinois, October 7, 1963; admitted to bar, 1988, Illinois and U.S. District Court, Northern District of Illinois; 1992, U.S. Court of Appeals, Seventh Circuit. *Education:* University of Illinois (B.A., 1985); University of California at Los Angeles (J.D., 1988). ***PRACTICE AREAS:*** First Party Property; Commercial Litigation; Business; Bankruptcy. ***Email:*** cschirle@clausen.com

SCOTT L. SCHMOOKLER, born Poughkeepsie, New York, October 12, 1971; admitted to bar, 1996, Illinois. *Education:* Bradley University (B.A., 1993); Chicago-Kent College of Law (J.D., 1996). ***LANGUAGES:*** Spanish. ***PRACTICE AREAS:*** Fidelity and Surety; Banking Litigation; Commercial Litigation; Insurance Coverage; Insurance Litigation. ***Email:*** sschmookler@clausen.com

GILBERT J. SCHROEDER, born Chicago, Illinois, July 13, 1945; admitted to bar, 1970, Illinois. *Education:* DePaul University (A.B., 1967; J.D. 1970). *Member:* Chicago, Illinois State and American (Member: Torts and Insurance Practice Section; Fidelity and Surety Committee, 1970-2002) Bar Associations; International Association of Defense Counsel (Member, Fidelity and Surety Committee, 1980-2002); Federation of Insurance and Corporate Counsel (Member, Fidelity and Surety Committee). ***PRACTICE AREAS:*** Fidelity and Surety. ***Email:*** gschroeder@clausen.com

MARTIN C. SENER, born Chicago, Illinois, November 27, 1959; admitted to bar, 1984, Illinois and U.S. District Court, Northern District of Illinois including Trial Bar; 1991, U.S. District Court, Northern District of California. *Education:* Northwestern University (B.S., Engineering, 1981); The John Marshall Law School (J.D., 1984). *Member:* Chicago and American (Member, Torts and Insurance Practice Section) Bar Associations. ***PRACTICE AREAS:*** Construction Litigation; Products Liability; First Party Property; Subrogation; Casualty/Liability Defense. ***Email:*** msener@clausen.com

JAMES F. SMITH, born New York, N.Y., January 6, 1960; admitted to bar, 1989, Illinois and U.S. District Court, Northern District of Illinois; 1990, Pennsylvania and U.S. District Court, Western District of Pennsylvania. *Education:* University of Virginia (B.S., Commerce, 1982); University of Maryland (B.A., German, 1986); University of Notre Dame (J.D., 1989); Matthias Concannon Program of International Law, England (1987-1988); Naval War College (M.A., National Security, 2000). *Member:* Chicago, Illinois State and American Bar Associations. [Col., USAF, active duty, 1982-1986; USAF Reserves, 1986—]. ***PRACTICE AREAS:*** Intellectual Property; Subrogation; Professional Liability; First Party Property; Casualty/Liability Defense. ***Email:*** jsmith@clausen.com

MARY F. STAFFORD, born Cook County, Illinois, October 18, 1951; admitted to bar, 1976, Illinois; U.S. District Court, Northern, Central and Southern Districts of Illinois; U.S. Court of Appeals, Sixth, Seventh, and Eleventh Circuits; 1989, U.S. District Court, Eastern District of Michigan. *Education:* University of Illinois (B.A., 1973); John Marshall Law School (J.D., with highest distinction, 1976). *Member:* Chicago Bar Association; Women's Bar Association of Illinois; Appellate Lawyers Association; DRI. ***PRACTICE AREAS:*** Insurance; Insurance Coverage; Professional Liability; Liability Insurance Coverage; Environmental Coverage; Casualty/Liability Defense. ***Email:*** mstafford@clausen.com

RICHARD WM STRAWBRIDGE, born Akron, Ohio, October 31, 1947; admitted to bar, 1978, Illinois and U.S. District Court, Northern District of Illinois including Trial Bar. *Education:* Colgate University (B.A., 1970); John Marshall Law School (J.D., with distinction, 1978). Member, Moot Court National Competition Team. Contributing Editor, "Fire and Explosion Liability," Section to IICLE Premises Liability. *Member:* Chicago and American (Member, Torts and Insurance Practice Section) Bar Associations. [1st Lt., U.S. Army Field Artillery, 1970-1974]. ***PRACTICE AREAS:*** Subrogation; Environmental Coverage; Products Liability; Professional Liability; First Party Property; Casualty/Liability Defense. ***Email:*** rstrawbridge@clausen.com

JAMES R. SWINEHART, born Grand Rapids, Michigan, August 22, 1957; admitted to bar, 1982, Illinois and U.S. District Court, Northern District of Illinois including Trial Bar. *Education:* University of Notre Dame (B.A., cum laude, 1979); University of Toledo (J.D., 1982). Member, University of Toledo Law Review, 1981-1982. Author: "Business Travel Insurance: The Rules of the Road," 56 Defense Counsel Journal 325, July, 1989. *Member:* Chicago and American Bar Associations. ***REPORTED CASES:*** Stanton Road Associates v. Pacific Employers Ins. Co., 43 Cal. Rptr. 2d 1 (Cal. App. 1995); Leafland Group-II, Montgomery Tower United Partnership Ins. Co. of North America, 118 N.M. 281, 881 P.2d (1994). ***PRACTICE AREAS:*** Insurance; First Party Property; Environmental Coverage; Insurance Coverage. ***Email:*** jswinehart@clausen.com

MICHELLE R. VALENCIC, born Cleveland, Ohio, June 10, 1970; admitted to bar, 1996, Ohio; 1997, Illinois and U.S. District Court, Northern District of Ohio; 1998, U.S. District Court, Northern District of Illinois. *Education:* Ohio University (A.B., summa cum laude, 1992); Case Western Reserve University (J.D., cum laude, 1996; M.S.S.A., 1996). ***PRACTICE AREAS:*** Insurance; Environmental Coverage; Insurance Coverage; Liability Insurance Coverage; Casualty/Liability Defense. ***Email:*** mvalencic@clausen.com

SAVA ALEXANDER VOJCANIN, born Oak Lawn, Illinois, October 15, 1964; admitted to bar, 1988, Illinois; U.S. District Court, Northern District of Illinois and U.S. District Court, Northern District of Texas. *Education:* DePauw University (B.A., with distinction, 1985); Washington University (J.D., 1988). *Member:* Chicago Bar Association; Serbian Bar Association of America (President, 2002-2003; Vice President, 2001-2002; Secretary, 2000-2001; Treasurer, 1999-2000; Director, 1992—). ***LANGUAGES:*** Serbian. ***PRACTICE AREAS:*** First Party Property; Insurance Coverage; Insurance; Construction Litigation; Products Liability; Professional Liability. ***Email:*** svojcanin@clausen.com

DEBRA B. WALKER, born Carthage, Illinois, May 27, 1960; admitted to bar, 1987, Illinois and U.S. District Court, Northern District of Illinois; 1999, U.S. District Court, Central District of Illinois; 2002, U.S. Supreme Court. *Education:* University of Illinois (B.S., with high honors, 1982; J.D., 1987). *Member:* Chicago and Illinois State Bar Associations; Women's Bar Association of Illinois (Past President); Illinois Bar Foundation (Member, Board of Directors). ***PRACTICE AREAS:*** Medical Malpractice; Health Care; Professional Liability; Casualty/Liability Defense. ***Email:*** dwalker@clausen.com

GORDON K. WALTON, born Miami, Florida, August 26, 1968; admitted to bar, 1994, Illinois. *Education:* University of Chicago (B.A.); John Marshall Law School (J.D.). ***PRACTICE AREAS:*** Toxic Torts; Environmental; Insurance Coverage. ***Email:*** gwalton@clausen.com

ROBERT E. WILENS, born Highland Park, Illinois, January 22, 1965; admitted to bar, 1990, Illinois; U.S. District Court, Northern, Central and Southern Districts of Illinois and U.S. District Court, Western District of Wisconsin; U.S. Court of Appeals, Seventh Circuit; 1995, U.S. Supreme Court; 1997, Missouri and U.S. District Court, Northern District of Illinois Trial Bar. *Education:* University of Michigan (B.G.S., 1987); Washington University (J.D., 1990). ***PRACTICE AREAS:*** Subrogation; Real Estate; Business; Commercial Litigation; Products Liability; First Party Property; Casualty/Liability Defense. ***Email:*** rwilens@clausen.com

(This Listing Continued)

CLAUSEN MILLER P.C., Chicago—Continued

KIRK ZAPP, born Gary, Indiana, April 22, 1968; admitted to bar, 1994, Illinois, U.S. District Court, Northern District of Illinois. *Education:* Arizona State University (B.A., 1991); Loyola University, Chicago (J.D., 1994). *Member:* Chicago Bar Association. ***PRACTICE AREAS:*** Subrogation; First Party Property. ***Email:*** kzapp@clausen.com

MARK W. ZIMMERMAN, born Hinsdale, Illinois, October 13, 1961; admitted to bar, 1993, Illinois and U.S. District Court, Northern District of Illinois. *Education:* Southern Illinois University (B.S., 1983); DePaul University (J.D., with honors, 1993). Order of the Coif. Author: "Opening the Door to Race-Based Real Estate Marketing," Vol 41:4 DePaul Law Review. *Member:* Chicago, DuPage County and Illinois State Bar Associations. ***REPORTED CASES:*** Chrysler Credit Corp. v. Marino, 63 F3d 574 (7th Cir. 1995). ***PRACTICE AREAS:*** Insurance; Business; Commercial Litigation; Environmental Coverage; Insurance Coverage; Liability Insurance Coverage. ***Email:*** mzimmerman@clausen.com

OF COUNSEL

JAMES T. FERRINI, born Chicago, Illinois, January 14, 1938; admitted to bar, 1963, Illinois; U.S. Court of Appeals, Third, Fourth, Sixth, Seventh, Eighth, Ninth, Tenth, and Eleventh Circuits; U.S. Supreme Court. *Education:* Loyola University (B.S., 1960; J.D. cum laude, 1963). Member, Illinois Supreme Court Committee on Pattern Jury Instructions, 1979-1994. *Member:* Appellate Lawyers Association (President, 1978-1979); American Academy of Appellate Lawyers. ***PRACTICE AREAS:*** Appellate; Insurance; Insurance Coverage. ***Email:*** jferrini@clausen.com

FRANCIS A. HEROUX, born River Forest, IL, December 15, 1934; admitted to bar, 1959, Illinois and U.S. District Court, Northern District of Illinois. *Education:* St. Mary's College (B.A., cum laude, 1956); Northwestern University (J.D., 1959). Phi Alpha Delta. Hardy Scholar. Member, Board of Legal Publications of Northwestern University Law Review, 1957-1959. Assistant Editor-in-Chief, Journal of Criminal Law and Criminology, 1958-1959. Assistant Editor-in-Chief, Journal of Air Law and Commerce, 1958-1959. *Member:* Chicago, DuPage County and Illinois State Bar Associations. ***PRACTICE AREAS:*** Real Estate; Business; Commercial Litigation.

JAMES O. NOLAN, born Chicago, Illinois, November 22, 1939; admitted to bar, 1966, Illinois. *Education:* DePaul University (B.A., 1961; LL.B., 1966). Lecturer, National Institute of Trial Advocacy. *Member:* Chicago, Illinois State and American Bar Associations; Defense Research and Trial Lawyers Association; International Association of Insurance Counsel; Society of Trial Lawyers. ***PRACTICE AREAS:*** Professional Liability; Employment Law; Insurance; Reinsurance; Construction Litigation; Mass Torts; Municipal Defense; Medical Malpractice; Health Care; International; Business; Commercial Litigation; Intellectual Property; Products Liability; Insurance Coverage; Liability Insurance Coverage; Securities; Casualty/Liability Defense. ***Email:*** jnolan@clausen.com

HARRY L. WILSON, born Hutchinson, Kansas, December 13, 1942; admitted to bar, 1973, Illinois. *Education:* Michigan State University (B.A., summa cum laude, 1970); University of Michigan (J.D., 1973). ***PRACTICE AREAS:*** Admiralty and Maritime Law; Construction Litigation; Medical Malpractice; Health Care; Products Liability; Professional Liability; Casualty/ Liability Defense. ***Email:*** hwilson@clausen.com

SENIOR ASSOCIATE

WILLIAM J. FLORIANO II, born Buffalo, New York, 1958; admitted to bar, 1983, Illinois; U.S. District Court, Northern and Central Districts of Illinois; U.S. District Court, Eastern District of Wisconsin; U.S. Court of Appeals, Seventh Circuit. *Education:* University of Notre Dame (B.A., 1980); Loyola University (J.D., 1983). Recipient, Leadership and Service Award, 1983. *Member:* Chicago and Illinois State Bar Associations; National Association of Subrogation Professionals. ***PRACTICE AREAS:*** Subrogation; Liability Insurance Coverage; Premises Liability; First Party Property; Casualty Liability Defense. ***Email:*** wfloriano@clausen.com

---

W. GREGORY AIMONETTE, admitted to bar, 1998, Illinois and U.S. District Court, Northern District of Illinois, including Trial Bar; 2003, U.S. District Court, Central District of Illinois, U.S. District Court, Eastern District of Michigan and U.S. District Court, Northern District of Indiana. *Education:* DePauw University (B.A., 1994); Northern Illinois University (J.D., 1997). *Member:* Chicago, DuPage County and Illinois State (Member, Civil Practice and Procedure Committee) Bar Associations; Justinian Society of Lawyers. ***PRACTICE AREAS:*** Subrogation; First-Party Property; Insurance Coverage; Casualty/Liability Defense; Products Liability; Environmental Coverage. ***Email:*** waimonette@clausen.com

JOSHUA A. ALDORT, born Chicago, Illinois, September 4, 1970; admitted to bar, 1997, Illinois. *Education:* Purdue University (B.A., Political Science, 1992); Chicago-Kent College of Law (J.D., 1996; Certificate of International Law, 1996). ***PRACTICE AREAS:*** Intellectual Property; Business; Commercial Litigation. ***Email:*** jaldort@clausen.com

CHERI L. BADEN, admitted to bar, 2003, Illinois. *Education:* Carroll College (B.S., 1999); Valparaiso University (J.D., 2003). ***Email:*** cbaden@clausen.com

COLLEEN A. BROWN, born Chicago, Illinois, March 23, 1974; admitted to bar, 1999, Illinois. *Education:* University of Illinois (B.S., 1996); DePaul University (J.D., 1999). ***PRACTICE AREAS:*** Insurance Coverage; Insurance; Liability Insurance Coverage; Business; Commercial Litigation; Environmental Coverage. ***Email:*** cbrown@clausen.com

PAULA M. CARSTENSEN, born Chicago, Illinois, May 12, 1954; admitted to bar, 1981, Illinois, U.S. District Court, Northern District of Illinois; 1982, U.S. Court of Appeals, Seventh Circuit. *Education:* University of Denver (B.A., with honors, 1976); Illinois Institute of Technology (J.D., with high honors, 1981). ***PRACTICE AREAS:*** Appellate; Employment Law; Employment Litigation; Civil Litigation. ***Email:*** pcarstensen@clausen.com

(This Listing Continued)

ANN C. CHALSTROM, born Rochester, Minnesota, January 1, 1972; admitted to bar, 1997, Illinois; 1999, U.S. District Court, Northern District of Illinois; 2001, U.S. Court of Appeals, Sixth and Seventh Circuits. *Education:* Illinois Wesleyan University (B.A., magna cum laude, Economics, 1994); University of Illinois (J.D., magna cum laude, 1997). Order of the Coif. ***PRACTICE AREAS:*** Appellate. ***Email:*** achalstrom@clausen.com

JAMES W. DAVIDSON, admitted to bar, 2003, Illinois. *Education:* Ball State University (B.S. 2000); Loyola University Chicago (J.D., 2003). ***PRACTICE AREAS:*** Professional Liability; Casualty / Liability Defense; Premises Liability. ***Email:*** jdavidson@clausen.com

BRIAN E. DeVILLING, admitted to bar, 2002, Illinois. *Education:* University of Michigan (B.A., 1999), Loyola University, Chicago (J.D., 2002). ***PRACTICE AREAS:*** Products Liability; Medical Malpractice; Health Care; Business; Commercial Litigation; Casualty; Liability Defense. ***Email:*** bdevilling@clausen.com

RODD E. ELGES, born Dayton, Ohio; admitted to bar, 1998, Illinois. *Education:* Illinois State University (B.S., 1988); Northern Illinois University (M.A., 1991); John Marshall Law School (J.D., 1998). ***PRACTICE AREAS:*** Medical Malpractice; Health Care; Casualty/Liability Defense. ***Email:*** relges@clausen.com

MICHAEL S. ERRERA, admitted to bar, 1998, Illinois. *Education:* Emory University (B.A., 1995); Stetson University College of Law (J.D., 1998). ***PRACTICE AREAS:*** Subrogation. ***Email:*** merrera@clausen.com

PAUL V. ESPOSITO, born Oak Park, Illinois, June 4, 1950; admitted to bar, 1975, Illinois. *Education:* St. Norbert College (B.A., magna cum laude, 1972); Loyola University (J.D., 1975). Assistant Attorney General, Illinois, 1975-1978. Lewis Overbeck & Furman, 1978-1999, Partner, 1988-1999. ***PRACTICE AREAS:*** Appellate. ***Email:*** pesposito@clausen.com

COLLEEN M. FEENEY, admitted to bar, 2003, Illinois; U.S. District Court, Northern District of Illinois. *Education:* University of Notre Dame (B.S., 2000); Loyola University, Chicago (J.D., 2003). *Member:* Chicago Bar Association; Women's Bar Association of Illinois. ***Email:*** cfeeney@clausen.com

KEITH G. FLANAGAN, born Newark, New Jersey, January 26, 1973; admitted to bar, 1998, New York; 1999, Georgia and Massachusetts (Not admitted in Illinois). *Education:* Georgetown University (B.A., 1995); Boston University (J.D., 1998). ***PRACTICE AREAS:*** Fidelity and Surety; Business; Commercial Litigation. ***Email:*** kflanagan@clausen.com

GEORGE K. FLYNN, admitted to bar, 1997, Illinois. *Education:* Illinois State University (B.S., 1993); Thomas M. Cooley Law School (J.D., 1997). *Member:* Chicago Bar Association. ***PRACTICE AREAS:*** Construction Litigation; Medical Malpractice; Health Care; Insurance Coverage; Professional Liability; Casualty/Liability Defense; Products Liability. ***Email:*** gflynn@clausen.com

LISA N. FONTANA, admitted to bar, 2002, Illinois and Michigan. *Education:* Miami University, Ohio (B.A., 1997); Loyola University, Chicago (J.D., 2002). *Member:* Chicago and American Bar Associations; Women's Bar Association of Illinois. ***PRACTICE AREAS:*** Casualty; Liability Defense; Premises Liability; Products Liability; Business; Commercial Litigation; Medical Malpractice; Health Care; Liability Insurance Coverage. ***Email:*** lfontana@clausen.com

SHANNON M. GEIER, admitted to bar, 2002, Illinois. *Education:* St. Norbert College (B.A., 1993); National - Louis University (M.Ed., 1999); Loyola University, Chicago (J.D., 2002). *Member:* Chicago and American Bar Associations; Women's Bar Association of Illinois. ***PRACTICE AREAS:*** Medical Malpractice; Health Care; Professional Liability; Casualty; Liability Defense. ***Email:*** sgeier@clausen.com

KATHLEEN A. JOHNSON, admitted to bar, 1987, Illinois. *Education:* Elmhurst College (B.A., 1972); The John Marshall Law School (J.D., 1987). ***PRACTICE AREAS:*** Insurance Coverage; Liability Coverage; Liability Casualty Defense. ***Email:*** kjohnson@clausen.com

SHAWN K. JONES, admitted to bar, 1997, Illinois. *Education:* Brigham Young University (B.A., 1994); Illinois Institute of Technology-Chicago/Kent College of Law (J.D., 1997). ***PRACTICE AREAS:*** Business; Commercial Litigation. ***Email:*** sjones@clausen.com

KELLY A. JORGENSEN, admitted to bar, 2002, Illinois. *Education:* University of Iowa (B.B.A., 1999); DePaul University (J.D., 2002). Order of the Coif. ***PRACTICE AREAS:*** Insurance Coverage; First-Party Property; Subrogation. ***Email:*** kmcelvogue@clausen.com

PAUL D. KERPAN, born Chicago, Illinois, March 8, 1950; admitted to bar, 1978, Illinois and U.S. District Court, Northern, Central and Southern Districts of Illinois. *Education:* Western Illinois University (B.A., 1972); John Marshall Law School (J.D., 1978); Loyola University of Chicago (M.B.A., 1985). ***PRACTICE AREAS:*** Subrogation; Professional Liability; Casualty Defense. ***Email:*** pkerpan@clausen.com

BRADFORD S. KRAUSE, (admission pending). *Education:* University of Illinois at Urbana-Champaign (B.A., 1994); DePaul University (J.D., 1997). ***PRACTICE AREAS:*** Products Liability; Business Litigation; Commercial Litigation; Medical Malpractice; Health Care; Construction Litigation; Casualty Insurance Defense. ***Email:*** bkrause@clausen.com

JANINE E. KUTYLO, born Hyannis, Massachusetts, February 4, 1972; admitted to bar, 2000, Illinois; 2001, Massachusetts. *Education:* American University (B.A., 1994); Loyola University Chicago School of Law (J.D., 2000). ***PRACTICE AREAS:*** Commercial Litigation; Casualty/Liability Defense; Products Liability; Professional Liability; Construction Litigation; Medical Malpractice; Municipal Defense. ***Email:*** jdoherty@clausen.com

C. KYLE LANG, admitted to bar, 2003, Illinois. *Education:* Denison University (B.A., 1999); John Marshall Law School (J.D., 2003). *Member:* Chicago and American Bar Associations. ***Email:*** clang@clausen.com

(This Listing Continued)

MINDY M. MEDLEY, born Chicago, Illinois, July 19, 1976; admitted to bar, 2001, Illinois. *Education:* Washington University, St. Louis (B.A., 1998; J.D., 2001). *Member:* Chicago and Illinois State Bar Associations. ***PRACTICE AREAS:*** First Party Property; Insurance Coverage; Subrogation. ***Email:*** mmedley@clausen.com

TODD M. MURPHY, admitted to bar, 2003, Illinois. *Education:* University of Notre Dame (B.A., 1996); John Marshall Law School (J.D., 2003). ***PRACTICE AREAS:*** Casualty; Liability Defense; Insurance; Products Liability. ***Email:*** tmurphy@clausen.com

SALVATORE A. PELLEGRINO, admitted to bar, 2002, Illinois. *Education:* Northern Illinois University (B.A., 1999); John Marshall Law School (J.D., 2002). ***PRACTICE AREAS:*** Environmental Coverage; Liability Insurance Coverage. ***Email:*** spellegrino@clausen.com

AGELO L. REPPAS, born Cedar Falls, Iowa, September 27, 1973; admitted to bar, 2000, Illinois and U.S. District Court, Northern District of Illinois; 2001, U.S. Court of Appeals, Seventh Circuit. *Education:* University of Iowa (B.S., 1995; B.A., 1995); Washington University (J.D., 2000). *Member:* Appellate Lawyers Association. ***PRACTICE AREAS:*** Appellate. ***Email:*** areppas@clausen.com

ELLEN G. ROBINSON, born February 12, 1975; admitted to bar, 2001, Illinois. *Education:* University of Illinois (B.A., History, 1998); Chicago-Kent College of Law, Illinois Institute of Technology (J.D., 2001). ***PRACTICE AREAS:*** Fidelity and Surety. ***Email:*** erobinson@clausen.com

DAVID J. ROE, born Detroit, Michigan, 1963; admitted to bar, 1993, Michigan; 1994, U.S. District Court, Western and Eastern Districts of Michigan; 1995, U.S. Court of Appeals, Seventh Circuit; 1996, Illinois; 2000, U.S. District Court, Northern District of Illinois. *Education:* University of Iowa (B.A., 1989); Michigan State University - Detroit College of Law (J.D., cum laude, 1993). ***PRACTICE AREAS:*** Insurance; Business; Commercial Litigation; Insurance Coverage. ***Email:*** droe@clausen.com

BETSY R. ROSENBERG, admitted to bar, 2001, Illinois. *Education:* University of Wisconsin-Madison (B.A., 1998); Washington University (J.D., 2001). ***PRACTICE AREAS:*** Medical Malpractice; Health Care; Professional Liability. ***Email:*** brosenberg@clausen.com

TIFFANY J. TRACY, admitted to bar, 2002, Illinois and District of Columbia; U.S. District Court, Northern District of Illinois. *Education:* University of Illinois, Urbana-Champaign (B.A., 1999); Loyola University, Chicago (J.D., 2002). *Member:* Chicago, Illinois State and American Bar Associations; The Association of Trial Lawyers of America; Women's Bar Association. ***PRACTICE AREAS:*** Liability Insurance Coverage; Medical Malpractice; Health Care; Municipal Defense; Business; Commercial Litigation; Premises Liability; Professional Liability; Products Liability. ***Email:*** ttracy@clausen.com

ANTHONY P. ULM, born Toledo, Ohio, February 20, 1971; admitted to bar, 1997, Illinois and U.S. District Court, Central District of Illinois. *Education:* University of Illinois, Urbana-Champaign (B.A., 1994); Southern Illinois University (J.D., 1997). Pi Sigma Alpha; Phi Delta Phi. Casenote and Comment Editor, Southern Illinois Law Journal, 1996-1997. *Member:* Chicago, Illinois State and American Bar Associations. ***PRACTICE AREAS:*** Casualty; Liability Defense; Fidelity and Surety; Medical Malpractice; Health Care; Professional Liability. ***Email:*** aulm@clausen.com

MARIA Z. VATHIS, admitted to bar, 2002, Illinois, U.S. District Court, Northern District of Illinois. *Education:* University of Illinois at Urbana-Champaign (B.A., 1998); DePaul University College of Law (J.D., 2001). *Member:* Federal Bar Association. ***LANGUAGES:*** Greek. ***PRACTICE AREAS:*** First Party Insurance; Premises Liability. ***Email:*** mvathis@clausen.com

AMY L. WITT, admitted to bar, 2002, Michigan, Illinois and U.S. District Court, Northern District of Illinois. *Education:* Michigan State University (B.A., 1999); DePaul University (J.D., 2002). *Member:* Chicago, Illinois State and American Bar Associations; State Bar of Michigan; Women's Bar Association of Illinois. ***PRACTICE AREAS:*** Environmental Coverage; Liability Insurance Coverage; Insurance Coverage; Casualty; Liability Defense; Admiralty and Maritime. ***Email:*** awitt@clausen.com

KENNETH R. WYSOCKI, born January 25, 1972; admitted to bar, 1996, Illinois and U.S. District Court, Northern District of Illinois; 1999, U.S. District Court, Central District of Illinois; 2002, U.S. District Court, Eastern District of Wisconsin. *Education:* Indiana University (B.S., 1993); University of Virginia (J.D., 1996). *Member:* Illinois State Bar Association. ***PRACTICE AREAS:*** Insurance; Litigation. ***Email:*** kwysocki@clausen.com

REFERENCES: The First National Bank of Chicago; La Salle National Bank.

CLIFFORD LAW OFFICES, P.C.

120 NORTH LA SALLE STREET, 31ST FLOOR
CHICAGO, ILLINOIS 60602
Telephone: 312-899-9090; 1-800-899-0410
Fax: 312-251-1160
Email: info@CliffordLaw.com
URL: http://www.cliffordlaw.com

Airplane Crash Litigation, Aviation Accidents, Aviation Litigation (Commercial and General), Health Care, Helicopter Crash Litigation, Commercial Litigation, Construction Accidents, Construction Liability, Construction Litigation, Consumer Litigation, Consumer Protection, Nursing Home Litigation, Nursing Home Liability, Nursing Home Negligence, Patients Rights, Hospital Negligence, Complex Litigation, Trial Practice, Birth Trauma, Medical Negligence, Nursing Negligence, Nursing Malpractice, Accidents, Automobile Accidents and Injuries, Automobile Negligence, Brain Injury, Head Injury, Motor Vehicle Accidents and Injuries, Railroad Accidents and Injuries, Truck Accidents, Plaintiff's Personal Injury Litigation, Wrongful Death, Medical Malpractice, Transportation, Product Liability, Premises Liability, Vehicular Accident Law.

FIRM PROFILE: Robert A. Clifford founded a personal injury law firm in his name in 1984. For more than 20 years, the firm has worked to establish a national reputation. Clifford Law Offices now boasts 24 attorneys, who combined, represent over 300 years of practice in personal injury law. Since its inception, the entire staff of Clifford Law Offices is dedicated to the goal of representing the rights of plaintiffs concentrating on aviation liability, transportation liability, medical malpractice, health care, construction liability, premises liability, personal injury and wrongful death litigation.

Robert A. Clifford was selected in 2004 as one of the "five most respected and feared plaintiffs' attorneys" in the country by Corporate Legal Times, calling him "the best of the bad." The National Law Journal named Mr. Clifford's firm on the "Plaintiffs' Hot List: 25 Go-To Teams" in 2003 as well as one of the 20 firms on the plaintiffs' Hot List of 2004. Mr. Clifford also was named one of the Top Ten Litigators in Illinois in 1999, as well as one of the nation's Top Ten Litigators by the National Law Journal in 1993. American Lawyer Media recognized Mr. Clifford as one of the Top Ten Most Influential Lawyers in Illinois in 2000. He has consistently been voted one of the Best Lawyers in America; and he was named one of Chicago's "30 Toughest Lawyers" by Chicago Magazine in 2002. In 2005, he was inducted into the International Society of Barristers, an organization of outstanding trial lawyers chosen by their peers on the basis of excellence and integrity in advocacy.

Robert Clifford was named one of the 2005 Super Lawyers in Illinois by Law and Politics, a national organization that conducted independent research among thousands of his peers across the state. In the initial announcement of the top five percent of the state's lawyers, Mr. Clifford was selected as the cover photo of the inaugural issue where they called him "Chicago's Most Likeable Tough Guy." The feature story headlined him as "Chicago's Most-Feared Attorney - Bob Clifford is a lamb who turns into a lion when he's confronted by injustice."

The very nature of Clifford Law Offices involves a willingness to accept the challenges and responsibilities inherent in complex litigation. Clifford Law Offices has pioneered many of the modern courtroom techniques now considered standard practice in the presentation of tort cases. This has led attorneys from around the country to refer cases, particularly aviation cases involving mass tort disasters, to the firm.

The firm boasts a highly sophisticated, interactive web site, the first of its kind in Chicago developed by a personal injury firm which can be found at www.CliffordLaw.com.

The philosophy of Clifford Law Offices is based upon a dedication to protecting and preserving the dignity and the rights of all individuals. Toward that end, it is the commitment of Clifford Law Offices to seek justice for victims of injury — physical, intellectual, emotional, legal and financial. Experience has proven the power of a single lawsuit can eliminate the dangers caused by unsafe products and practices. Clifford Law Offices is committed to pursuing this philosophy on behalf of its clients.

ROBERT A. CLIFFORD, born Evergreen Park, Illinois, March 24, 1951; admitted to bar, 1976, Illinois and U.S. District Court, Northern District of Illinois including Trial Bar; 1981, U.S. Supreme Court; 1993, U.S. District Court, Eastern District of Wisconsin and Central District of Illinois; 1996, U.S. Court of Appeals, Seventh Circuit; 2005, U.S. Court of Appeals, Second Circuit. *Education:* DePaul University (B.S.C., 1973); DePaul College of Law (J.D., 1976; Doctor of Laws, honoris causa, 2003). Listings: Plaintiff's Hot List: Twenty-five Go-to Teams for When the Going Gets Tough, The National Law Journal, July 21, 2003; World's Leading Litigation Lawyers, 2002; Thirty Tough Lawyers, Chicago Magazine, Mar. 2002; Top Ten Most Influential Attorneys in Illinois, American Research Corporation, 2000; Top Ten Lawyers in Illinois, The National Law Journal, 1999; Leading Attorneys in Illinois, American Research Corporation, 1995-2001; The Best Lawyers in America and Top Ten Litigators, The National Law Journal, 1993; Who's Who in American Law, 1985. Honoree: "A Salute to Those Who Make a Difference," Illinois State Crime Commission, Illinois, June 21 2000. MEMBER: Chicago Bar Foundation (Fellow); Chicago Inn of Court (Master; President. 1994-1995); Illinois Attorneys for Criminal Justice; Illinois Institute for Continuing Legal Education (Board of Directors, 1989) Illinois State and Chicago Society of Physical Medicine and Rehabilitation; Society of Trial Lawyers of America; Trial Lawyers Club of Chicago; the Executive Club of Chicago Special Supreme Court Committee on Professionalism; American College of Trial Lawyers; International Academy of Trial Lawyers; The American Law Institute; Inner Circle of Advocates; The National Judicial College; American Inns of Court; American Judicature Society; Illinois Committee for Judicial Independence; American Society of Law and Medicine; American Institute for Aeronautics and Astronautics; Steering Committee, Northwestern University School of Education, Center for Social Policy, 1999; Board of Oversees, ICJ, Rand Institute for Civil Justice, 1998—; Advisoty Expert, Aviation Committee Studying NTSB, 1998; Board of Directors, Isaac Ray Center, 1992; Advisory Committee Meeting on Civil Jury Trial Symposium, The Brookings Institute, 1991—; Advisory Board of Judge James A. Geroulis Educational Foundation, 1990—; Roscoe Pound Foundation, 1990—; Board of Advisors, Mercy Hospital and Medical Center, 1988—; DePaul University College of Law, Advisory Council, 1987—; DePaul University, Board of Trustees, 1987—; Products Liability ADR Development Committee, Center for Public Resources, DePaul University, 1985-1986; President DePaul University Alumni Association, 1983-1985; Board of Directors, Chicago Executive Committee for University College, Galway, Ireland, 1983-1984; Board of Directors, Access Living of Metropolitan Chicago, 1982-1985; DePaul University College of Law Visiting Committee, Chair, Financial Aid Subcommittee and Executive Committee, 1982-1985; Commission on Alumni Affairs, DePaul University, 1982-1983; City of Hope Fund Raising Committees, Mike Royko and James Roberts Jr., Benefits, 1981-1982; Lex Legio Law Society of DePaul University College of Law, 1976-1983; Society of Fellows Foundation of DePaul University, 1976-1983. AUTHOR: CLIFFORD'S NOTES-CHICAGO LAWYER: "Proposed Rules Suggest Changes to Electronic Discovery," Sept. 2005; "Torts Provide Best Relief for Nursing Home Residents," Aug. 2005; "Patient's Plea to Stop Caps Legislation Fell on Deaf Ears," July 2005; "Servivemen's Cases Can, at Times, March Forward," June 2005; "ABA Guidelines Give Roadmap to Juries for 21st Century," May 2005; "Court Struggles with Good Samaritans in Hospitals," Apr. 2005; Law Leaves Jilted Lovers Out in Cold," Mar. 2005; "Rights Expanding for Plaintiffs with In Utero Injuries," Feb. 2005; "Only the Facts Will Get to Medical Reform," Jan. 2005; "2004 Served Up Plenty of Juicy Celebrity Litigation," Dec. 2004; Court's Split on Federal Preemption after FDA Approval," Nov. 2004; "Court Examining Limited Doctor/Patient Relationship," Oct. 2004; "Patients Deserve Informed Consent in Medical Research," Sept. 2004; "High Court Decision Keeps Patients From Suing HMO's," Aug. 2004; "Ruling

(This Listing Continued)

(This Listing Continued)

CLIFFORD LAW OFFICES, P.C., Chicago—Continued

Gives Guidance on Licensing of Expert Witness," July, 2004; "Confidentiality May Cost Plaintiffs Plenty in Taxes," June, 2004; "Changes to Med-Mal Rules Must Keep Fairness at Center," May, 2004; "Tort Debate Must Broaden to Address Health Safety," Apr. 2004; ""Major Med-Mal Rulings has Impact on Cases, Ethics," Mar. 2004; "High Court to Review Patients' Right to Sue," Feb. 2004; "New Rulings in Ozik Shows Court's Knowledge of Law," Jan. 2004; "Patients Lose Out with Arbitration Clause," Dec. 2003; "Case Will Clarify Immunity for State-Employed Doctors," Nov. 2003; "Ruling on Liability Promotes Good-Faith Settlements," Sept. 2003; "Jurors Questions Pose Tricky Balance," Aug. 2003; "Court Addresses Electronic Discovery," July 2003; "Insurance Decision May Help Plaintiffs," June 2003; "Back-up Asbestos Suit as Best as You Can," May 2003; "Use Checklists Before Settling," Feb. 2003; "Untangling Knots in State Discovery Rule," Jan. 2003; "Pitting Scalpel Against Scalpel," Dec. 2002; "Accountant's Liability," Oct. 2002; "Risk Allocation in Tort Cases," Sept. 2002; "Holding Hospitals Responsible for Doctors' Negligence," Aug. 2002; "Rule 213: Disclose, Disclose, Disclose," July 2002; "Forum Fights," June 2002; "Judges Should Let Juries Hear Reliable Expert Witnesses," May 2002; "Pretense is Gone in Sealing Court Records," Apr. 2002; "The Rules for Victims' Comp," Feb. 2002; "Does High Court Decision Hurt Petrillo Doctrine?" Jan. 2002; "Lots of Factors in Landowners Liability for Criminal Attacks," Dec. 2001; "Airline Relief Legislation Needs Scrutiny," Nov. 2001; "Fifth District Jumps into Trampoline Debate," Oct. 2001; "Do Lie Detectors Lie or Provide the Truth?" Sept. 2001; "Who Owns your DNA?" Aug. 2001; "Some Lawyers 'Selling Out' Rights in Product Liability Cases," July 2001; "Criminal Contempt Use May Prod Discovery," June 2001; "Experts' Capsule Summaries May be Hard Pills to Swallow," May 2001; "Will 'Miss Manners' be an Expert Witness?" Apr. 2001; "Rule 213 Changes Leading to Double Vision," Mar. 2001; "Online Medical Advice Raises Legal Concerns," Feb. 2001; "Use Rule 310 to Speed Appeals," Jan. 2001; "Yes, Virginia, California Can be Reasonable," Dec. 2000; "Proximate Cause," Nov. 2000; "Defining Bad Faith," Oct. 2000; "Courts Asking Whether Dangers are Excessive or Acceptable," Sept. 2000; "Educating Drug Companies about Learned Intermediaries," Aug. 2000; "Amusement Parks Take Consumers for a Ride," July 2000; "Courts Lower Gate on State Tort Laws Regarding Rail Crossings," June 2000; "Informed Consent Moves Beyond Risk to Participation," May 2000; "Consider Justice in Interpreting Rule 213," Apr. 2000; "Ten Tips for Successful P.I. Settlements," Mar. 2000; "The Conflict Between 'Disability' and 'Loss of Normal Life,'" Feb. 2000; "Case Raises Questions about Sanctions in 'Frivolous' Suits," Jan. 2000; "Allow Punitives in Wrongful Death Cases," Dec. 1999; "Right to Sue Prescribes the Necessary Treatment for HMO's," Nov. 1999; "Tort Deform Strips Constitutional Rights," Oct. 1999; Drawbacks to Using the Web to Settle PI Claims," Sept. 1999; "Some Doctors Stacking the Thermometers," Aug. 1999; "High-Low Deals Offer High Sophistication," July 1999; "Sneak Attacks Uncalled For," June 1999; "Court Parks Tire Ruling in Daubert's Garage," May 1999; "Are a Psychotherapist's Notes Confidential?" Apr. 1999; "Court's Eye Spoliation of Evidence Claims," Feb. 1999; "Judges and Juries Should Target Gun Policies," Feb. 1999; "This is Not the Right Time for a Time Clock," Jan. 1999; "Insurance Issue Grows in Intentional Torts," Dec. 1998; "Why Should Venue Changes to the Next County be Allowed?" Nov. 1998; "Why Double the Deposition Work?" Oct. 1998; "AMA Proposal Would Protect Bad Doctors," Sept. 1998; "Who Owns Notes and Reports?" Aug. 1998; "Builders: Be Upright and Fix SUV Rollovers," July 1998; "Restatement Reflect Biases," May 1998; "Tampering with the Evidence Rule," Apr. 1998; "Juries Use Awards to Make Bold Statements," Mar. 1998; "High Court Right in Tort Reform Decision," Feb. 1998; "The Duty to Warn," Jan. 1998; "Family Members Deserve More," Dec. 1997; "Doctors Should Have a Duty to Admit Errors," Nov. 1997; "Cellular Phones May Drive Drivers to Dangerous Distraction," Oct. 1997; "The Value of an Individual," Sept. 1997; "Question Raised About Daubert," Aug. 1997; Victory Adds Up to Loss in High Court Case," July 1997; "Zipped Up Documents Zapping the Public," June 1997; "Lights, Cameras, ... Action?" May 1997; "Getting Weight Loss Centers to Fork Over," Apr. 1997; "Red Rover, Dead Rover, I Send This Suit Over," Feb, 1997; "Sorting Out the Confusion in Cramer," Jan. 1997; "Where Should Plane Crash Cases Land?" Dec. 9, 1996; "Tort Fight at the Accountability Corral," Dec. 1996; "Care Needed in Managed Care Revolution," Oct. 1996; "Clearing the Haze Around College Hazing," Sept. 1996; "Covenants Ignore the Duty to Public Interest," Aug. 1996; "State Bombs Out in Fireworks Laws," July 1996; "Certify Candidates, But Keep the Ballot Box," June 1996; "Getting Teed Off Over Golf Balls," May 1996; "Accountant's Facing More Tort Actions in Malpractice Cases," Apr. 1996; "Families Target Therapists in Memory Cases," Mar. 1996; "Fevered Debate Over Inconsistent Coverage," Feb. 1996; "Health Effects of Cellular Phones on Hold," Jan.1996; "Two States Give Battered Women Tort Option," Dec. 1995; "Charting the Court of Nurse's Liabilty," Nov. 1995; "Expansion of Good Samaritan Act Not an Act of Kindness," Aug. 1995; "ABA Needs More Than PR to Polish Tarnished Legal Image," Aug. 1995; "When Does Death Occur?" July 1995; "Hot Pursuit Car Chases Lead to Pursuit of Chase Standards," June 1995; "Short-Sighted Legislators Wearing I-Glasses," May 1995; "Gramm Bill Aids Industry for the Health of It," April, 1995; "Court, IRS Disagree on Whether Punitive Damages Taxable," Mar. 1995; "Forecast: Storm Warning for Meteorologists," Feb. 1995; "With Product Liability, What You Don't Know Can Hurt You," Jan. 1995; "Toy Industry Needs to Stop Playing Around With Child Safety," Dec. 1994; "New Liability Infects Hospitals that Catch Marketing Fever," Nov. 1994; "Government is Best that Plays Sports Least," Oct. 1994; "Skill at Taking Depositions Brings Victory in the Courtroom," Sept. 1994; "Like Travel, Travel Litigation is Broadening," Aug. 1994; "Tort Surgery Will Fail to Excise Health Costs," July 1994; "Aviation Industry Putting its Head in Clouds," June 1994; "All Lawyers Face Urgent Need for Restoration of Mentoring," May 1994. AUTHOR: "Popular Media Paints Unrealistic Portrait of Lawyers (and what we can do about it)," Viewpoint, CBA Record, Jan. 2005; "County Fire Tragedy Could Have Been Avoided," Voice of the People, Chicago Tribune, Oct. 25, 2004; "Mediating Malpractice," Letter to the Editor, Chicago Sun-Times, Sept. 27,2004; "Jury Duty," Letter to the Editor, Chicago Tribune, Aug. 23, 2004; "Insurance Regulation is the Better Solution," Letter to the Editor, The Daily Herald, Apr. 25, 2004; "Look at Insurance Industry," Letter to the Editor, Chicago Tribune, Apr. 23, 2004; "Deselecting the Jury in a Civil Case," ABA, Litigation Magazine, Winter, 2004; "Malpractice Facts," Voice of the People, Chicago Tribune, Jan. 17, 2004; "Medical Malpractice," Voice of the People, Chicago Tribune, Feb. 24, 2003; "Wrong Remedy, Doc," Letter to the Editor, Chicago Sun-Times, Nov. 26, 2002; "Personal Injuries," Book Review, CBA Record, Apr. 2002; "Now More Than Ever," Opening Statement, ABA, Litigation Magazine, Spring 2002; Task Force Examines Legal Issues Relating to Terrorism," ABA Partner, Winter 2002; "Confronting our Critics," Opening Statement, ABA, Litigation Magazine, Winter 2002; "Harsh Judgment," Letter to the Editor, Chicago Sun-Times, Dec. 7, 2001; "The Impact of Popular Culture on the Perception of Lawyers," Opening Statement, ABA, Litigation Magazine, Fall 2001; "Are Lawyers Capable of Behaving Nobly?" Voice of the People, Chicago Tribune, Oct. 14, 2001; "Raising the Bar," Opening Statement, ABA, Litigation Magazine, Summer 2001; "Living by the Decision of the Supreme Court," Voice of the People, Chicago Tribune, June 8, 2001; "Opening and Closing Argument in Barton v. Northeast Illinois Regional Commuter Railroad Corp. and Chicago & Northwestern Transportation Co.," ITLA, Trial Journal, Winter 2000; "Praising Cook County's Judges," Voice of the People, Chicago Tribune, Nov. 5, 2000; Media Effort on Tires Will Save Lives," Letter to the Editor, Chicago Sun-Times, Aug. 14, 2000; "Making Amusement Rides Safer," Voice of the People, Chicago Tribune, July 19, 2000; "Personal Injuries," Book Review, CBA Record, Apr. 2000; "Runaway Juries? The Facts Say No," The National Law Journal, Feb. 21, 2000; "Mammograms, Reliability Under Question: Should This Be a Cause for Alarm?" Medical Malpractice Law and Strategy, Jan. 2000; "Judiciary's Place in Democracy," Voice of the People, Chicago Tribune, Jan. 15, 2000; "Clinton Should Make Recess Appointment to Federal Bench," Letter to the Editor, Chicago Daily Law Bulletin, Dec. 27, 1999; "Justice Can Cure Ills," Chicago-Sun Times, Letters to the Editor, Oct. 7, 1999; "Jury Selection in a Civil Case: A Plaintiff's Perspective," CBA Brief, Oct. 1999; "Risk of Rollovers in SUV's," Chicago Tribune, Voice of the People, July 3, 1999; "Issues to Examine in Cases Against Common Carriers," Product Liability Law and Strategy, 1999; "Just Crossing Street a Hazard to Our Health," Letter to the Editor, Chicago Sun-Times, Apr. 29, 1999, "Railroads Indifferent Despite Verdict," and "Barton Gave Jury Fair Verdict Based on Fact," Chicago Sun-Times, Letters to the Editor, Mar. 5, 1999; "Road Warriors, The Best Alternative," Women Attorney Magazine, 1999; "Turnabout Fair Play and 'Dishonest' Judicial Ratings," Letter to the Editor, Chicago Daily Law Bulletin, Oct. 26, 1998; "Electorate Should Ignore Judicial Ratings by Business Group," Letter to the Editor, Chicago Daily Law Bulletin, Oct. 13, 1998; "Are Physician Expert Witnesses Practicing Medicine?" A Plaintiff's Perspective and "AMA Proposal to Require Experts to be Licensed in the State," Medical Malpractice Law & Strategy, Sept. 1998; "Power of the People: The Jury in Flight 4184," Chicago Lawyer, May 1998; "Cash Now: Needs Regulating Fast," Voice of the People, Chicago Tribune, May 16, 1998; "Restatement 3rd of Torts: Reasonable Alternative Design, A Plaintiff's Perspective," Product Liability Law & Strategy, May 1998; "Stream of Payments Shields Some Injury Victims from Unwise Decision, Maximizes Compensation," Law Day Issue, Chicago Daily Law Bulletin, Apr. 25, 1998; "Column on Tort Reform Elicits Strong Responses," Letter to the Editor, Illinois Legal Times, Mar. 1998; "Bill of Rights for Patient's Step Toward Improving Health Care," USA Today, Letter to the Editor, Feb. 22, 1998; "Overhauled Federal Rule of Evidence 407 Poses Problems for Plaintiff," Product Liability Law and Strategy, Feb. 1998; "When a Plane Goes Down," The Washington Post, Dec. 9, 1997; "Governments Must Act Safely," Voice of the People, Chicago Tribune, Nov. 3, 1997; "Litigating the Power Tool Case," Trial Magazine, Nov. 1997; "Lawyers with Civility Born, Not Legislated," Chicago Sun-Times, Oct. 15, 1997; "Good Samaritans Needn't Fear Helping," Chicago Sun-Times, Sept. 12, 1997; "Heart of Justice Beats Anew," Commentary, Chicago Sun-Times, Feb. 9, 1997; "Physician Liability in a Managed Care Enviroment," The Journal of Medical Practice Management, 1997; "Full Justice Means Assigning Blame," Voice of the People, Chicago Tribune, Nov. 1996; "Battling for Big Bucks," ABA, Litigation Magazine, Fall 1996; "ValuJet Crash Shows Flawed System," Voice of the People, Chicago Tribune, June 11, 1996; "An Electric Complex: Wire Service or Powered Product?" Product Liability Law Strategy, Apr. 1996; ""Judging the Way We Chose Judges," Commentary, Chicago Sun-Times, Apr. 13, 1996; "Beware Real Costs of Managed Care," Voice of the People, Chicago Tribune, Feb. 20, 1996; "Illinois Personal Injury Practice Forms," West Law, Feb. 1996; "Dollar Signs at Railroad Crossing," Chicago Tribune, Voice of the People, Dec. 1, 1995; "O.J. Faces Different Set of Rules in Civil Cases," The Forum, Chicago Sun-Times, Oct. 1995; "When Lightning Struck," Chicago Bar Association Journal, July 1995; "To Be a Trial Lawyer," F. Lee Bailey Book Review, Trial Magazine, June 1995; "Whatever Happened to Debate, Compromise?" Lawyers' Forum, Chicago Daily Law Bulletin, May 22, 1995; "Workplace Violence Generates Two Kinds of Tort," National Law Journal, Apr. 17, 1995; "Victims Lose in Capping Damages," Voice of the People, Chicago Tribune, Mar. 26, 1995; "Mock Trials Offer Virtual Reality," National Law Journal, Feb. 27, 1995; "Capping Damages Hurt Victims Rights," Voice of the People, Chicago Tribune, Dec. 27, 1994; "The Malpractice Damages Debate," Letters to the Editor, Wall Street Journal, Nov. 11, 1994; "Negligent Tort Reform," Chicago Daily Law Bulletin, Nov. 3, 1994; "Marketing Tools May Increase Hospitals' Liability Exposure," Illinois State Bar Newsletter, Oct. 1994; "Litany of Litigation Survey of Lawyers Can't be Called Objective," Chicago Sun-Times, Commentary, Oct. 8, 1994; "Justice System Corrects Its Outrage," Chicago Tribune, Voice of the People, Sept. 29, 1994; It's Duck Season: Public's Safety Under the Gun," National Law Journal, Podium, Aug. 22, 1994; "Malpractice Suits Do Not Inflate Health Costs," National Law Journal, May 16, 1994, reprinted in Illinois Medicine, June 3, 1994; "The False Issue of Malpractice Costs," The Wall Street Journal, May 10, 1994; "Proposal on Physician-Patient Privilege Would Send Public Policy up in Smoke," Law Day Issue, Chicago Daily Law Bulletin, Apr. 23, 1994; "Must Hold Purveyors of Gun Liable," Voice of the People, Chicago Tribune, Mar. 7, 1994; "Petrillo Doctrine, The Latest from the Supreme Court," Chicago Lawyer, Jan. 1994; "The Malpractice Damages Debate," The Wall Street Journal, Nov. 1994; "Is It Ethical for Experts to Work Both Sides?" and "Collagen Ruling Illogical, Unsupported," Product Liability Law and Strategy, 1993; "Malpractice Damage Caps Won't Help," The Wall Street Journal, Oct. 13, 1993; "Criticism of Malpractice Suits is Undeserved," National Law Journal, Aug. 2, 1993; "The Art of Cross-Examining an Expert," Chicago Lawyer, Sept. 1993; "Can Experts be IME's for Both Sides? Should They?" Medical Malpractice Law and Strategy, New York, July 1993; "Injured Patients Deserve to Sue," Personal View, Chicago Sun-Times, June 24, 1993; "Court Tackles Making Sense of Rule 220," and "Practice Tips," Chicago Lawyer, May 1993; "Getting Picky Picking Jurors," Chicago Lawyer, 1993; "Certification Masks Competency, Could be Guise for Higher Fees," Chicago Daily Law Bulletin, Apr. 24, 1993; "Positive Benefit in Punitive Damages," Chicago Tribune, Voice of the People, Apr. 24, 1993; "Wrongful Adoption Gains Acceptance," Sept. 28, 1992, reprinted in Illinois State Bar Journal Tort Trends publication, Dec. 1992; "Tort Reform is Based on False Assumptions," National Law Journal, October 19, 1992; "Beefy 'Meat and Potatoes' Trial Book Should Allow for Spice," Chicago Lawyer, Sept. 1992; "Little Sympathy for Defense," Chicago Daily Law Bulletin, July 14, 1992; "Great Flood Sinks Premise of Tort Reform," Crain's Chicago Business, June 29,

(This Listing Continued)

1992; "Win the Write Way With Mirza," Chicago Lawyer, June 1992; "Legal Reformers Haven't Made Case," Voice of the People, Chicago Tribune, Apr. 12, 1992; "War Stories and Maxims Target Book to Young Trial Lawyers," Chicago Lawyer, Apr. 1992; "PI Lawyer Calls Foul Ball on Baseball Act," Chicago Lawyer, 1992; Consulting Editor, Medical Malpractice Newsletter, 1992—; Products Liability Newsletter, 1991—; "Insurance Companies Lied," Merrill's Illinois Legal Times, May 1988; Contributing Author: "Damages as an Element of Proof," Medical and Hospital Negligence, 1988; "Does Rule 11 Give Judges Too Much Discretion?" Chicago Daily Law Bulletin, June 3, 1987; "The Current Status of the Medical Malpractice Statute," Chicago Daily Law Bulletin, Apr. 7, 1986; "Demonstrative Evidence," Master Advocates Handbook, 1986, National Institute for Trial Advocacy; Book Review, "Preparing Products Liability Cases by Terrence F. Kiely," Journal of the ABA, May 1986; "Tort Reform, Details of Legislation Approved as Response to Insurance 'Crisis'," Chicago Daily Law Bulletin, Aug. 9, 1986; "Tort Reform, New Law Adopts Strict Federal Rule on Attorney Sanctions," Chicago Daily Law Bulletin, Oct. 10, 1986; "The 1985 Illinois Medical Malpractice Reform Legislation Explained," Chicago Daily Bulletin, Aug. 1985; "Comparative Negligence and the Jury," The Law of Comparative Negligence, 1984; "Study of Jury Verdicts Yields Interesting Overview," Legal Times, 1982; "Hospital Malpractice and the Independent Contractor Defense: Hospitals Do Practice Medicine," Personal Injury Manual, 1981; "Venue in Federal Civil Litigation," Federal Civil Practice, (1981) and updating Supplements, 1983, 1985, (IICLE, 1983, 1985, 1987,Rewritten 1988, Supplement, 1989); "Organizing a Plaintiff's Personal Injury and Wrongful Death Law Office," ABA Litigation Magazine, Summer 1979; "Proof of Damages in Amputation Cases - Plaintiffs Treating Physician, Rehabilitation Physician and Certified Prosthetist," Personal Injury Manual, 1979; "Use and Presentation of Demonstrative Evidence," Proof of Fault in Auto Accident Cases, (1979) and Updating Supplements, 1983, 1985 (ILLCE, 1983, 1985, Rewritten 1988, Updated Supplement 1990). SPONSOR: Clifford Symposium of Tort Law and Social Policy, DePaul University College of Law : "Who Feels Their Pain? The Challenge of Non-Economic Damages in Civil Litigation," 11th Annual, Apr. 2005; ""Starting Over?: Redesigning the Medical Malpractice System," 10th Annual, Apr. 2004; "After Disaster: The September 11th Compensation Fund and the Future of Civil Justice," 9th Annual, Apr. 2003; "Is Tort Law Exportable?" 8th Annual, Apr. 2002; "Smoke Signals: The Changing Landscape of the Practice, Financing and Ethics of Civil Litigation in the Wake of the Tobacco Wars," 7th Annual, Apr. 2001; "The Impact of Pop Culture on the Civil Justice System," 6th Annual, Apr. 2000; "Judges as Tort Law Makers," 5th Annual, Apr. 1999; "The American Civil Jury: Illusion and Reality," 4th Annual, 1998; "A Conference on the Contingency Fee," 3rd Annual, Apr. 1997; "Tort Law and the Science of the 21st Century," 2nd Annual, May 1996; "Experiments in Creative ADR," ADR and Torts: Implications for Practice and Reform, 1st Annual, May 1995; DePaul University College of Law, 50th Anniversary of the DePaul Law Review, May 17, 2001. FACULTY: University of Chicago College of Law; Loyola University School of Law; DePaul University College of Law; IIT/Chicago-Kent Law School; John Marshall Law School. LECTURER: Testified before Illinois State Legislature, House Judiciary Committee, Pending Medical Malpractice Reform Litigation, May 10, 2005; "2005 Advocacy Showcase, The Business Torts Case: A One Day Trial," Illinois Trial Lawyers Association (ITLA) Chicago, May 7, 2005; "The American Jury Trial-Do We Allow Its Death or Lead Its Rebirth?" A National Summit on the Present State of the Seventh Amendment Right to Trial by Jury, American Board of Trial Advocates, Las Vegas, April 1, 2005; "Medical Liability: The New Legal Landscape," Professional Liability Underwriting Society, Chicago, March 16, 2005; "Trial Tools in the Courtroom," Tort Litigation Committee, Chicago Bar Association (CBA), Chicago, April 16, 2004; "Advanced Techniques of Direct and Cross Examination," Advanced Trial Institute Program, American Bar Association (ABA), San Francisco, Aug. 7, 2003; "Ethics in the Media: The Ever-Growing Thirst for Information," ABA Section of Litigation, New York, June 5, 2003; "The Medical Negligence Case: A One-Day Trial," 2003 Advocacy Showcase, ITLA, Chicago, May 3, 2003; "Jury Trials after Enron and WorldCom: How Do We Regain Corporate Credibility," 2003 Corporate Counsel College Program, International Association of Defense Counsel, Apr. 24, 2003; Keynote Speaker, Korean American Bar Association, Chicago, Mar. 2002; Testified before the Illinois Senate Health and Human Services Subcommittee on Health Care, Impact of the Civil Justice System on Medical Malpractice and Health Care Insurance, Chicago, Mar. 17, 2003; "Anatomy of a Malpractice Case from a Litigator's Perspective," DePaul Journal of Health Care Law, DePaul University College of Law, Chicago, Feb. 21, 2003; "The Rachel Barton Trial: Perspective from the Plaintiff's Attorney," Trial Attorney Superstar Series, CBA and John Marshall Law School, Chicago, Feb. 12, 2003; "Cross Examining the Scientific Expert," All Star Cross-Examination, CBA and the Seventh Circuit Bar Association, Chicago, Oct. 25, 2002; "Civility in the Courtroom," The Abraham Lincoln Marovitz American Inn of Court Meeting with the Chicago Inn of Court, Chicago, Oct. 22, 2002; "Use of Demonstrative Evidence in Complex Litigation: From Argument to Trial: What Really Works," Complex Litigation, The Sedona Conference, Arizona, May 2, 2002; "Legal Issues Arising from Acts of Terrorism and Anti-Terrorism Efforts," The Association of the Federal Bar of the State of New Jersey Annual Judicial Conference, New Jersey, Mar. 20, 2002; "Land Owner Liability," Winning Trial Techniques from Voir Dire to Closing, ITLA, Chicago, Feb. 18, 2002; "Foreign Plaintiffs-Issues and Problems," Aviation Issues in the Real Millennium, ABA Tort and Insurance Practice, Washington, D.C., Oct. 18, 2001; "Ethics in the Media: Are you Crossing the Line?" ABA, Chicago, Aug. 6, 2001; "Hands on Learning at the Federal Courthouse - The Art of Cross Examination," ABA, Chicago, Aug. 4, 2001; "Civility in the Practice of Law," The Roger K. O'Reilly Symposium on Civility and Advocacy, Illinois, Aug. 1, 2001; "The Criminalization of Aviation 'Accidents' - Is it Here to Stay?" ABA Section of Litigation, New York, June 7, 2001; "Leading Lawyers Pursuing Justice," and "Winning Arguments and the Psychology of Jury Decision-Making," ABA Section of Litigation, Phoenix, May 2001; "Ten Settlement Truisms," University of Illinois, College of Law Bootcamp, Chicago, Jan. 11, 2001; "The Future of Technology and Jury Consultation in Federal Trials in the 21st Century, Federal Litigation in the 21st Century," Chicago, Nov. 28, 2000; "Products Over the Pond: Is U.S. Style Litigation Invading the U.K.?" ABA Annual Meeting, London, July 2000; "When Your Own Trial Witness Blows a Gaping Hole in Your Case, How Far Can You Go to Keep your Case from Sinking Like the Titanic," ABA Section of Litigation, New York, July 2000; "Mock Trial," Department of Obstetrics and Gynecology, Georgetown University Hospital Seminar, Colorado, June 3, 2001; "Medical Malpractice in Women's Imaging," Radiological Society of North America, Chicago, Nov. 2001; Comparing British and American Civil Justice Systems, Moderator, ABA Annual Meeting, Oxford University, Cambridge, England, July 18, 2000; "Task Force on the Judiciary," ABA,

(This Listing Continued)

Section of Litigation, Seattle, Apr. 7, 2000; "Settlements and Negotiations," ITLA Past Presidents Seminar, Chicago, Jan. 8, 2000; "Raconteuring," Chicago Inn of Court, Oct. 20, 1999; "Medical Malpractice from a Plaintiff Attorney's Perspective," Am. Society for Healthcare Risk Management, Chicago, 1999; "State-of-the-Art Courtroom Technology in the Courtroom," DuPage County Bar Association, Illinois, June 10, 1999; "Aviation on Trial—In the Trenches with Aviation Accident Litigation," ABA Section of Litigation, New York, N.Y., May 13, 1999; "Aveon '99, Debate—Plaintiff's Perspective After an Airline Crash," London, England, Apr. 27, 1999; "The Advocate's Art, Voir Dire by the Masters," and "Dodging Friendly Fire—Know Thy Enemy," A Plaintiff's Perspective, ABA, Section of Litigation, Dallas, Apr. 1999; "A Plaintiff's Perspective on Limiting the Scope of Practice & Procedure," Federal Judicial Conference Committee on Practice and Procedure, Chicago, Jan. 28, 1999; "Jury Selection," Under the Microscope: The Anatomy of a Malpractice Trial," ITLA, Chicago, Dec. 5, 1998; "Maximizing Damages," Trial Technique Seminar, ITLA, Chicago, Oct. 12, 1998; "The Trial of the Titanic," ABA, Montreal, Canada, Aug. 3, 1998; "Jury Selection and Jury Appeal: What We Learn From Focus Groups," ABA, Section of Litigation, June 4, 1998; "Getting the Most Out of Insurers at Settlement and Trial," Illinois Institute for Continuing Legal Education, Chicago, Apr. 17, 1998; "Presenting the Complex Civil Case to a Jury," ABA, Section of Litigation, Moderator and Panel Member: "High Tech/High Costs," Chicago, Feb. 26, 1998; "To Settle or Not to Settle Your Malpractice Lawsuit — Why? When? For How Much?: Those Are the Questions," Chicago Radiological Society, Jan. 15, 1998; "Standard Care in Psychiatry," Am. Academy of Psychiatry & Law, 1998; "Judicial Management of Mass Torts Through Class Actions and MDL," ABA, Hilton Head, Nov. 21, 1997; "Aviation Liability Into the 21st Century," ABA Section of Litigation, New York, June 20, 1997; "Aviation Litigation: Trial Evidence Issues After ValuJet and TWA 800," ABA, Washington, D.C., Apr. 18, 1997; "Unique Aspects of Handling Motor Vehicle Products Liability Cases," National Practice Institute's Conference on Products Liability Law, Chicago, Apr. 1997; "Consumers and Alternate Dispute Resolution," CPR Institutefor Dispute Resolution, New York, Jan. 31, 1997; "Maximizing Results Through Settlement and Trial," ITLA, Chicago, Feb. 17, 1997; "The Do's and Don'ts of Videos as Demonstrative Evidence," CBA, Chicago, Jan. 9, 1997; "Disclosure in a Law Firm: A Sexual Harassment Mock Trial," Trial Tactics and Employment, Chicago, Oct. 1996; "The Plaintiff's Perspective on Exclusive Federal Jurisdiction," Aviation Liability Into the 21st Century, ABA, Washington, D.C., Oct. 1996; "Understanding Jurors, the Key to Winning Cases," Ann Arbor, May 1996; "The Ultimate Mentoring Seminar," Jury Selection, ITLA, Chicago, May 4, 1996; "Airplane Design," Product Liability Litigation, ITLA Jan. 13, 1996; "Opening Statements," Young Lawyers Section Trial Practice Course, CBA, Oct. 10, 1995; "Hurray for Hollywood: How the Masters Try Cases," ABA Section of Litigation, Chicago, Aug. 1995; Traumatic Brain Injury Litigation Group, American College of Trial Lawyers, New York, July 18, 1995; Plaintiff's Case/Defendant's Case Panel, College of Health Sciences, Health Systems Management, Rush-Presbyterian St. Luke, Chicago, Illinois, Apr. 12, 1995; "Jury Persuasion in a Hostile Environment - The Case for Credibility," Indiana Trial Lawyers Association, Nov. 1994; "Trying a Case from the Plaintiff's Perspective," CBA, Nov. 1994; "Product Liability," CBA Young Lawyers Section, Oct. 1994; "Treatment Decisions in a Litigious Society, What is the Human Cost?" DuPage Ethics Conference, Sept. 1994; "Drawing First Blood: Depositions - How to Use Them Effectively," Advanced Trial Techniques, CLE International, Oct. 1993; "Presidential Face-Off, Medical Malpractice," ITLA, June 1993; "'Opening Statement: Plaintiff's Program Point/Counterpoint,' Trial Advocacy From Both Sides," ITLA, May 1993; Breast Implant Support Group, Franklin Park, Oct. 1993, "Medical Malpractice-Closing Argument," ITLA, Dec. 5, 1992; "A Plaintiff Attorney's Approach to Malpractice Suits," Program for American Colleges of General Practitioners Education & Research Foundation, Sept. 19, 1992; "The Art of Cross Examination," CBA Young Lawyers Section, Sept. 17, 1992; "Discovery Practice in the 90's," Program for "A How-To Seminar Focusing on Competency, Efficiency & Civility, CBA, May 21, 1992; "Discovery," Program for Products Liability: In-Depth Study of Litigation Involving Products, Illinois State Bar Association (ISBA), Apr. 16, 1992; "Objections at Trial and How to Deal with the Difficult Lawyer," National Practice Institute, Nov. 15, 1991; American Board of Trial Advocates, "The Masters in Trial Demonstration," 1993; American College of General Practitioners Education & Research Foundation, "A Plaintiff Attorney's Approach to Malpractice Suits," 1992; "Federal Civil Practice," Illinois Institute for Continuing Legal Education, Dec. 1992; ISBA, Products Liability, In-Depth Study of Litigation Involving Products, Similar Occurrences and Discovery, 1992; "Secrecy Within the Civil Justice System," Association of Trial Lawyers of America, New Orleans, 1990; "Maximizing Damages in Products Cases," and "Working with Experts: Translation of Engineers into English," National Conference on Product Liability Law, 1988; "Overview and Judicial Trends in Strict Liability Cases Involving Defective Products," CBA, 1988; "Riskey Claims," New Areas of Litigation Seminar, ITLA, 1988; "Handling the Reality of a Malpractice Suit: Plaintiff's Perspective," Am. College of Surgeons, 1988; "The Law, Insurance & Rehabilitation: Partnership for the Catastrophically Injured," Chicago Medical Society, 1988; Mediator, Circuit Court of Cook County, CBA, Special Mediation Program for the Law Division, 1988-1989. Trial by Jury Program, Illinois State Fair, 1988; "Settlement from the Plaintiff's Perspective," Professional Education Systems, 1987; "The Adverse Witness," "Legislator, Judge and Executioner, Problems with the Imposition of Sanctions on the Court's Own Initiative," and "New Law and Practice Respective Changes in Comparative Negligence Standards and Joint and Several Liability," Illinois Institute for Continuing Legal Education, 1987; Conference on Post Traumatic Stress Disorders, Professional Education Systems, 1985; "Cross Examination of Expert Witnesses," Professional Education Systems,1983; "Medical Malpractice," Moderator, ABA Section of Litigation, 1982; "Trial Strategy Under Comparative Negligence, The Plaintiff's Perspective," Civil Litigation Short Course, 1982. Mediation panelist, Endispute of Chicago, 1982-1984. *MEMBER:* American Bar Association (Illinois State Delegate, ABA House of Delegates, 2005-2008; ABA Task Force on Hurricane Katrina, 2005; Co-Chair, 2005 ABA Annual Meeting Advisory Committee, 2004-2005; Member, Task Force on Gatekeeper Regulation and the Profession, 2003—; CBA Delegate, ABA House of Delegates, 2003-2005; Vice-Chair, Commission on the 50th Anniversary of Brown vs. Board of Education, 2003; Task Force on Asbestos Litigation, 2003-2004; Board of Directors, ABA Museum of Law, 2002-2005; Chair, Task Force on Terrorism and the Law, 2001-2002; Governmental Affairs Standing Committee, 2000-2006; Section of Litigation: Chair, Task Force on Hurrican Katrina, 2005—; Image of the Profession Task Force, 2004-2005; Judicial Intern Opportunity Program Working Group, 2004-2005; Former Chair, Council Member, 2003-2005; Civil Justice Initiatives, 2003-2005; Civil Justice Institute, 2002-

(This Listing Continued)

CLIFFORD LAW OFFICES, P.C., Chicago—Continued

2004; Immediate Past Chair, Executive Committee, 2002-2003; Chair, 2001-2002; Chair-Elect, 2000-2001; Vice Chair, 1999-2000; Special Committee on Reserves, 1999-2000; Discovery Standards Task Force, 1998-1999; Founder, Co-Editor, Tips from the Trenches, 1998-1999; Institute for Trial Practice, 1997-1999; Discovery Task Force, 1997-1998; Co-Chair, Membership Committee, Task Force on the Recruitment of Plaintiffs' Lawyers, 1997-1998; Stregic Planning Implementation Committee, 1996-1997; Co-Chair, 1995 ABA Annual Meeting, Chicago, 1993-1996; Federal Initiatives Task Force, 1995-1996; Task Force on the Justice System, 1994-1995; Strategic Planning Committee, 1993-1994; Task Force on State of the Justice System, 1993-1994; Coordinating Group on Civil Justice Reform, 1992-1993; Co-Chair, Task Force on the Adversary System, 1991-1992; Liaison, American Inns of Court, 1991-1992; Co-Director, Division IV, Prodedural, 1986-1987; Task Force on Tort Reform, 1986-1987; Council, 1983-1986; Chair, Professional Liability Litigation, 1982-1983; Co-Director, Division III, 1981-1982; Co-Chair, Manufacturers' Liability, 1980-1981; Chair, Communications, 1978-1980); Chicago (Delegate to ABA House of Delegates, 2003-2004; Board of Managers, 1992-1994; ADR Coordinating Committee, 1990; Committee on Disaster Relief, 1990; Chip Bytes Committee, 1990; Committee on Committees, 1984-1986; Tort Litigation Committee, Chair, 1983-1984; Vice Chair, 1982-1983; Secretary, 1981-1982; Chair, Tort Litigation Subcommittee on Pre-Judgment Interest, 1981-1982; Chair, Tort Litigation Subcommittee on Products Liability, 1979-1981; Lawyer Referral Panel Screening Committee, 1979—; Tort Litigation, Civil Practice, and Health and Hospital Care Committee, 1976), Illinois State (Advisory Board, Illinois Bar Foundation Fellows, 1989—; Offer of Judgment Committee, 1983-1985; Special Committee on Reduction of Court Costs, Delays and Involvement; 1983-1985; Action Commission on Court Costs, Delays and Involvement, 1983-1985; General Assembly, 1981-1985); Association of Trial Lawyers of America (Membership Committee, 1989—; Dean, Advanced College of Advocacy, 1986-1988); Kane County; Lake County; Northwest Suburban and Federal Bar Associations; Illinois Trial Lawyers Association (Director, College ofAdvocacy, 1990—; President, 1990; President-Elect, 1989; Second Vice President, 1988; Third Vice President, 1987; Excutive Committee, 1986—; Chair, Legislative Committee, 1985-1987; Committee on Medical Malpractice Legislation, 1984-1985; Co-Chair, Public Relations Committee, 1984-1985; Political Action Committee, 1983-1984; Membership Committee, 1980-1981). ***PRACTICE AREAS:*** Airplane Crash Litigation; Aviation Accidents; Aviation Litigation (Commercial and General); Health Care; Helicopter Crash Litigation; Commercial Litigation; Construction Accidents; Construction Liability; Construction Litigation; Consumer Litigation; Consumer Protection; Nursing Home Litigation; Nursing Home Liability; Nursing Home Negligence; Patients Rights; Hospital Negligence; Complex Litigation; Trial Practice; Birth Trauma; Medical Negligence; Nursing Negligence; Nursing Malpractice; Accidents; Automobile Accidents and Injuries; Automobile Negligence; Brain Injury; Head Injury; Motor Vehicle Accidents and Injuries; Railroad Accidents and Injuries; Truck Accidents; Plaintiffs Personal Injury Litigation; Wrongful Death; Medical Malpractice; Transportation; Product Liability; Premises Liability; Vehicular Accident Law. ***Email:*** RACA@CliffordLaw.com

KEITH A. HEBEISEN, born Elgin, Illinois, September 14, 1953; admitted to bar, 1983, Illinois and U.S. District Court, Northern District of Illinois including Trial Bar, 1987; 1990, U.S. District Court, Eastern District of Wisconsin and U.S. District Court, Western District of Michigan; 1992, U.S. Court of Appeals, Sixth Circuit; 1994, U.S. Supreme Court; 1996, U.S. Court of Appeals, Seventh Circuit. *Education:* University of Illinois (B.A., 1976); DePaul University (J.D., with honor, 1983). PUBLICATIONS: Contributing Author, Illinois Trial Lawyers Association (ITLA) Trial Notebook, 1989 ; Editor, ITLA Medical Malpractice Trial Notebook, 1992-2004, Co-Editor, 1990 and 1991; "Third-Party Litigation/Kotecki," Worker's Compensation Notebook - II, Nov. 1992; "Part III, Postpartum, The Third Stage," Legal Commentary, In/Operative Obstetrics, 1995; "Third-Party Litigation/Kotecki," Worker's Compensation Notebook Update, November 1996, 1999, 2002, 2004; "FRE 407: Even After Recent Amendment, the Prohibition Against the Admission of Evidence of Subsequent Remedial Measures in Product Liability Cases is "Swallowed Up" By the Exceptions," Products Liability Advisory, West Group, Sept. 1998; Editor, Illinois Bar Journal, Editor, 2002-2004; "How New SCR 213 Will Affect Your Practice: A Trial Lawyer's Prespective," Illinois State Bar Association (ISBA), Bench & Bar. Sept. 2002. Member: Society of Trial Lawyers; Trial Lawyers for Public Justice. RECIPIENT: Weidemann Wysocki Award, 1999-2000, 2001-2002, 2003-2004; ITLA, Amicus Volunteer Award, June 2002; William J. Harte Amicus Volunteer Award, June 2003. TEACHING: Adjunct Lecturer, DePaul University School of Law, "Medical Malpractice Law," Fall 1992, 1993, 1999, 2000, 2001, 2002 and Spring 2002. LECTURER/WRITTEN MATERIALS: "Medical Evaluation of Damages and Disability," Illinois Institute of Continuing Legal Education (IICLE), Chicago, Feb. 13, 1985; "Demonstrative Evidence and Experts," Trial Evidence Committee, ABA Section of Litigation, Chicago, Oct. 24, 1987; "Current Trends and Recent Developments in Litigation in Illinois," and "Interviewing Witnesses," Illinois Civil Litigation Techniques: Active Roles for Legal Assistants, Chicago, Mar. 9, 1988; "Products Liability," Update and Review Seminar, ITLA, Sept. 9, 1989; "The Wrongful Death Act: Obtaining the Successful Result, 'Procedural Aspects'," Chicago Bar Association (CBA), Feb.15, 1990; "Proving Fault and Defending Auto Accident Cases-How to Handle Particular Types of Collision Cases," IICLE, Chicago, Mar. 5, 1990; "How to Argue Liability in the Injury Case," ITLA Trial Notebook Seminar, St. Louis, Apr. 21, 1990; Seminar Planning Chair, ITLA, June 1990-1991; "Slip and Fall Cases - From the Plaintiff's Perspective - Preparation Before Trial," CBA, Feb. 4, 1991; "Third-Party Litigation/Kotecki," Worker's Compensation Seminar, ITLA, Illinois, Nov. 9, 1991; "Products Liability: In Depth Study of Litigation Involving Products," Jury Instructions/Pleadings/Summary Judgment, ISBA Law Education Series, Chicago, Apr.16, 1992; "Advanced Claims Management," MMI Companies, Inc. Focus Training Workshops, Illinois, Nov. 21, 1992; Seminar Planning Chair, Expert Witnesses, ITLA, Feb. 17, 1992; "Economic Loss," ITLA Shotgun Seminar, Chicago, Feb.15, 1993; "Expert Witnesses and Rule 220," ITLA Civil Practice Update and Review Seminar, Chicago, Sept.11, 1993; "Handling the Defendant's Expert," ITLA Point/Counterpoint Seminar, Chicago, Oct.10, 1994; "Anesthesiology Malpractice Cases," ITLA Medical Malpractice Seminar, Chicago, Dec. 3, 1994; Program Chair and Moderator, ITLA Medical Malpractice Seminar, Chicago, Dec. 1994, 1995 and 2001; "Trial Demonstration - Closing Arguments," 13th Annual Defense Tactics Seminar, Chicago, Mar. 5, 1995; "'Apparent Agency", Life Before and After House Bill 20," ITLA Chicago, Illinois, May 6, 1995. Round Table Discussion, Workers' Compensation Seminar, ITLA, Illinois, Nov. 1995; "Pretrial Trade Secrets of the Pros - Winning Your Case Before Trial, and Move Over Columbo," ITLA, Chicago, Feb. 19, 1996; "Where Will We Be A Year From Now? Tort Law Change," DuPage County Bar Association, Illinois, Oct. 30, 1996; "Surgery Cases," ITLA Medical Malpractice Seminar, Chicago, Dec. 7, 1996; "Expert Testimony—Effective Cross-Examination," ITLA Product Liability Seminar, Chicago, Jan. 11, 1997; "Cutting-Edge Issues in Health Care, Bringing Medical Negligence Case in the MCO Setting — The Plaintiff's Perspective," The John Marshall Law School, Mar.17, 1997; Presentation of "Plaintiff's Case/Defendant's Case," Health Law Course, Health Systems Management, College of Health Sciences, Rush University, Apr.16, 1997; "Maximizing Damages," ITLA Trial Technique Seminar, Chicago, Oct.13, 1997; "215 Exam and Deposing the Defense Expert," ITLA Automobile Accident Cases Seminar, Illinois, Feb. 7, 1998; "Medical Malpractice Update," Tort Trends; Approaching the Millennium, CBA, Chicago, Mar.10, 1998. "Admissibility of Subsequent Design Changes in Product Liability Cases: The New Federal Rule," National Conference on Products Liability Law, Chicago, May 29, 1998; "Damages: Obtaining the Best Outcome on Your Release or Verdict Form," ISBA Tort Law Update, St. Louis, June 19, 1998; "Neuropsychological and Legal Aspects of Mild Traumatic Brain Injury and the Post Concussion Syndrome, Plaintiff Attorneys' Prospective," DePaul University School of Law, Chicago, Oct.1998; "Under the Microscope: The Anatomy of a Malpractice Trial," Program Chair and Moderator, ITLA, Chicago; "Trying the Technologically Savvy Malpractice Case," IICLE Modern Medical Malpractice Litigation Seminar, Chicago, Mar. 26, 1999; Medical Negligence," ITLA Civil Practice Update & Review Seminar, Chicago, Sept.18, 1999; "Medical Negligence: Identifying the Viable Case," ITLA Medical Negligence Seminar, Chicago, Dec.11, 1999; "Closing Argument-You Are the Jury," and "How to Testify in Court, Be It as a Defendant or Expert: Perspectives of a Plaintiff's Attorney and a Defense Attorney," Malpractice Issues in Radiology Seminar, The International Institute for Continuing Medical Education, Chicago, Apr.1, 2000; "Making an Impact with Exhibits," ITLA Practicing with the Best & Avoiding the Rest Seminar, Oct. 8, 2001; "Depositions of Doctors: How to Avoid the Land Mines," IICLE's, Chicago, Nov. 29, 2001; "Civil Trial Procedures: Learn How New SCR 213 Will Affect Your Practice," CBA June 13, 2002; "What are the Feds Up To?" ITLA Medical Practice Seminar, Chicago, Dec. 7, 2002; "Evidence Depositions," ITLA Evidence Seminar, Chicago, Feb. 17, 2003; "HIPAA," ITLA Update and Review Seminar, Chicago, Sept. 13, 2003; "Deposing Defendants & Defendant Experts," ITLA Medical Malpractice Seminar, Chicago, Dec. 6, 2003; "Malpractice Tort Reform: Is Malpractice Tort Reform Really Necessary?" 89th Scientific Assembly and Annual Meeting of the Radiological Society of North America, Chicago, Dec. 4, 2003. *Member:* Illinois Trial Lawyers Association (Civil Practice Committee, 1984; Elected Board of Managers, 1989—; Seminar Planning Chair, 1990-1991; Vice Chair, Publications Committee, 1992; Medical Negligence Committee, 1992, and Co-Chair, 1998-2003; Nominating Committee, 1994-1995; Membership Committee, 1995-2001; Executive Committee, 1995-1996, 1999—; Legislative Committee, 1996—; Co-Chair, 2003-2004; Long Range Planning Committee, 2001; Third Vice President, 2002-2003; Second Vice President, 2003-2004; President-Elect, 2004-2005; President, 2005-2006); Chicago (Civil Practice Committee, 1997; Tort Litigation Committee, 2003); Kane County, Illinois State (Civil Practice, Insurance & Tort Law, 1990—; Standing Committee on the Illinois Bar Journal Editorial Board, Secretary, 1998-2000; Vice Chair, 2000-2003; Associate Editor, 2001-2002; Editor, 2002-2004; Ex-offcio, 2004); American Bar Associations; The Association of Trial Lawyers of America (State Delagate - Delegate, 1995-2000; Secretary, 1996-1997; Vice-Chair, 1997-1998; Chair-Elect, 1998-1999; Chair, 1999-2000; Presidents' Club Charter Member, 1999; List Advisory Committee, 1999—; Coordinating Committee on State Relations, 1999-2000; Executive Committee, 1999-2000; State Affairs Liaison Committee, 2000-2001; Insurance Committee, 2000-2001; Board of Governors, 2001-2002); Northwest Suburban Bar. ***PRACTICE AREAS:*** Airplane Crash Litigation; Aviation Accidents; Aviation Litigation (Commercial and General); Health Care; Helicopter Crash Litigation; Commercial Litigation; Construction Accidents; Construction Liability; Construction Litigation; Consumer Litigation; Consumer Protection; Nursing Home Litigation; Nursing Home Liability; Nursing Home Negligence; Patients Rights; Hospital Negligence; Complex Litigation; Trial Practice; Birth Trauma; Medical Negligence; Nursing Negligence; Nursing Malpractice; Accidents; Automobile Accidents and Injuries; Automobile Negligence; Brain Injury; Head Injury; Motor Vehicle Accidents and Injuries; Railroad Accidents and Injuries; Truck Accidents; Plaintiffs Personal Injury Litigation; Wrongful Death; Medical Malpractice; Transportation; Product Liability; Premises Liability; Vehicular Accident Law. ***Email:*** KAH@CliffordLaw.com

KEVIN P. DURKIN, born Chicago, Illinois, July 22, 1955; admitted to bar, 1980, Illinois, U.S. District Court, Northern District of Illinois, 1993, U.S. District Court, Central District of Illinois; 1995, U.S. Court of Appeals, Seventh Circuit; 2000, U.S. District Court, Western District of Michigan. *Education:* University of Illinois (B.S., 1977); DePaul College of Law (J.D., 1980). FACULTY: National Institute of Trial Advocacy, Certified Instructor, 1989. Adjunct Faculty, DePaul University College of Law, 1988-1994. Member: DePaul College of Law, Advisory Board Member, 2005—; Center for Conflict Resolution, Board of Directors, 2001—; International Aviation Law Institute; Chicago Bar Foundation, Board of Directors, 2000—. *Member:* Chicago (Membership Committee, 2005—, 1st Vice President, 2005—; 2nd Vice President, 2004-2005; Aviation Law Committee, 2003—; Treasurer, 2002-2004; Chair, Finance Committee, 2002-2004; Chair, Appellate Review Committee, 2001; Board of Managers, 1998-2000; Judicial Evaluation Committee, 1989-1998 - Vice Chair, 1993-1995, Chair, 1995-1997, General Chair, 1997-1998, Hearing Division, 1991-1993, Investigation Division, 1989-1991; Tort Litigation Committee, 1988—); Illinois State (Tort Law Committee, Civil Practice and Procedure Committee, 1989—) and American Bar (Section of Litigation, Co-Chair, Mass Torts Committee, 2004—, Co-Chair, Aviation Litigation Committee, 2000-2004; Products Liability Committee, 1992—; Tort Trial & Insurance Practice Section, Vice Chair, Aviation & Space Law Committee, 2005—; Commercial Transportation Litigation; Products General Liability & Consumer Law) Associations; Illinois Trial Lawyers Association (Board of Managers, 2001, Board of Advocates, 1993-2001, Legislative Committee, 1993—); Association of Trial Lawyers of America (Motor Vehicle Collision, Highway and Premises Liability, Products Liability, Railroad Law, Federal Tort Liability and Military Advocacy, 1999—; Aviation Law, 1996—). ***PRACTICE AREAS:*** Airplane Crash Litigation; Aviation Accidents; Aviation Litigation (Commercial and General); Health Care; Helicopter Crash Litigation; Commercial Litigation; Construction Accidents; Construction Liability; Construction Liti-

(This Listing Continued)

(This Listing Continued)

gation; Consumer Litigation; Consumer Protection; Nursing Home Litigation; Nursing Home Liability; Nursing Home Negligence; Patients Rights; Hospital Negligence; Complex Litigation; Trial Practice; Birth Trauma; Medical Negligence; Nursing Negligence; Nursing Malpractice; Accidents; Automobile Accidents and Injuries; Automobile Negligence; Brian Injury; Head Injury; Motor Vehicle Accidents and Injuries; Railroad Accidents and Injuries; Truck Accidents; Plaintiffs Personal Injury Litigation; Wrongful Death; Medical Malpractice; Transportation; Product Liability; Premises Liability; Vehicular Accident Law. **Email:** KPD@CliffordLaw.com

THOMAS K. PRINDABLE, born Belleville, Illinois, September 24, 1943; admitted to bar, 1973, Illinois and U.S. District Court, Northern District of Illinois. *Education:* St. Mary of the Lake (B.A., Philosophy, 1965); Illinois Institute of Technology Chicago-Kent College of Law (J.D., 1973). *Member:* Chicago, Kane County (Civil Procedure Committee, 1990—; President, 1979); Illinois State; American Bar Associations; Illinois Trial Lawyers Association (Legislative Committee, 1991—); Association of Trial Lawyers of America. ***PRACTICE AREAS:*** Airplane Crash Litigation; Aviation Accidents; Aviation Litigation (Commercial and General); Health Care; Helicopter Crash Litigation; Commercial Litigation; Construction Accidents; Construction Liability; Construction Litigation; Consumer Litigation; Consumer Protection; Nursing Home Litigation; Nursing Home Liability; Nursing Home Negligence; Patients Rights; Hospital Negligence; Complex Litigation; Trial Practice; Birth Trauma; Medical Negligence; Nursing Negligence; Nursing Malpractice; Accidents; Automobile Accidents and Injuries; Automobile Negligence; Brain Injury; Head Injury; Motor Vehicle Accidents and Injuries; Railroad Accidents and Injuries; Truck Accidents; Plaintiffs Personal Injury Litigation; Wrongful Death; Medical Malpractice; Transportation; Products Liability; Premises Liability; Vehicular Accident Law. **Email:** TKP@CliffordLaw.com

ROBERT P. WALSH, JR., born Oak Park, Illinois, April 12, 1959; admitted to bar, 1986, Illinois and U.S. District Court, Northern District of Illinois. *Education:* St. John's University (B.A., 1981); Loyola University (J.D., 1986). *Member:* Chicago (Judicial Evaluation Committee, Investigations Division, 1995-1999), Illinois State and American Bar Associations; Illinois Trial Lawyers Association; Association of Trial Lawyers of America; Fenwick Bar (Treasurer, 1995-1999; Vice President, 2000-2004; President, 2005—). ***PRACTICE AREAS:*** Airplane Crash Litigation; Aviation Accidents; Aviation Litigation (Commercial and General); Health Care; Helicopter Crash Litigation; Commercial Litigation; Construction Accidents; Construction Liability; Construction Litigation; Consumer Litigation; Consumer Protection; Nursing Home Litigation; Nursing Home Liability; Nursing Home Negligence; Patients Rights; Hospital Negligence; Complex Litigation; Trial Practice; Birth Trauma; Medical Negligence; Nursing Negligence; Nursing Malpractice; Accidents; Automobile Accidents and Injuries; Automobile Negligence; Brain Injury; Head Injury; Motor Vehicle Accidents and Injuries; Railroad Accidents and Injuries; Truck Accidents; Plaintiffs Personal Injury Litigation; Wrongful Death; Medical Malpractice; Transportation; Product Liability; Premises Liability; Vehicular Accident Law. **Email:** RPW@CliffordLaw.com

SUSAN A. CAPRA, born Chicago, Illinois, January 19, 1960; admitted to bar, 1990, Illinois, U.S. District Court, Northern District of Illinois and Eastern District of Wisconsin. *Education:* DePaul University (B.S.N., 1982; J.D., with honors, 1990). Registered Nurse, Illinois, 1982. *AUTHOR:* "The Evaluation of a Medical Negligence Case," Women Attorney, July/August, 1999; "Cocaine Babies: Meeting the Challenge," Illinois Bar Journal, 1992; "Third Party Litigation - Kotecki," ITLA Workers' Compensation Notebook, 1990; "Settlement/Empty Chair Defenses," ITLA Medical Malpractice Trial Notebook, 1990; "Expert Witnesses," ITLA Medical Malpractice Trial Notebook, 1990, 1992, 1997, 1998, 1999; . FACULTY: DePaul College of Law, Medical Malpractice, Fall 1999, 2000, 2001. LECTURER: "Evaluating a Medical Negligence Case," Loyla University Law School, Chicago, Feb. 27, 2001; "Venue Forum Non Conveniens," ITLA, Sept. 9, 2000; "Nursing Negligence," American Academy of Pediatrics, Chicago, Oct. 27, 2000; "Deposition Strategies in Medical Negligence Cases," CBA, Dec. 2000 and Dec. 1999; "Analyzing Medical Records for the Illinois Paralegal," Institute for Paralegal Education, Illinois, Oct. 1999 and Nov. 1997; "Deposing the Defendent Physician in a Medical Malpractice Case," CBA, Dec, 1997. *Member:* Illinois Trial Lawyers Association (Medical Negligence Committee, 1998 -); American Bar Association; Association of Trial Lawyers of America. ***PRACTICE AREAS:*** Airplane Crash Litigation; Aviation Accidents; Aviation Litigation (Commercial and General); Health Care; Helicopter Crash Litigation; Commercial Litigation; Construction Accidents; Construction Liability; Construction Litigation; Consumer Litigation; Consumer Protection; Nursing Home Litigation; Nursing Home Liability; Nursing Home Negligence; Patients Rights; Hospital Negligence; Complex Litigation; Trial Practice; Birth Trauma; Medical Negligence; Nursing Negligence; Nursing Malpractice; Accidents; Automobile Accidents and Injuries; Automobile Negligence; Brain Injury; Head Injury; Motor Vehicle Accidents and Injuries; Railroad Accidents and Injuries; Truck Accidents; Plaintiffs Personal Injury Litigation; Wrongful Death; Medical Malpractice; Transportation; Product Liability; Premises Liability; Vehicular Accident Law. **Email:** SAC@CliffordLaw.com

JEFFREY J. KROLL, born Chicago, Illinois, February 24, 1964; admitted to bar, 1990, Illinois; 1991, U.S. District Court, Northern District of Illinois; 2000, U.S. District Court, Northern District of Indiana. *Education:* DePaul University (B.S., 1987; J.D., 1990). Recipient: Judge Olga Jurco Award for Outstanding Trial Advocacy; 40 Under 40 to Watch, Law Bulletin Publishing Company, 2000. 40 Under 40: Promising Young Advocates, National Law Journal, 2002. Member, Chicago Inns of Court (Barrister). LECTURER: "Tort Immunity Act: Pleadings, Standard of Care and Burden of Proof," CBA, 1992; "Winning with the Masters: Maximizing Damages in Catastrophic Injury Cases," Louisiana Trial Lawyers Association, Dec. 1992; Medical Malpractice Law, DePaul University College of Law, Fall 1992, Spring 1993; "Maximizing Damages in Wrongful Death Cases," Louisiana Trial Lawyers Association, Dec. 1993; "Motor Vehicles Collision, Highway and Premises Liability, Child Death Cases Stemming from Auto Crashes," Association of Trial Lawyers of America, July, 1994; "Bad Faith Litigation," ITLA, Sept. 1994; "Overview of Health Law as Field of Practice - Plaintiff's Perspective," Health & Hospital Law Committee of the CBA, Oct.1994; "Preparing Plaintiff for Deposition," ITLA, Feb. 1995; "Products Liability Trial Lawyers Workshop: Recent Trends in Products Liability Law," CBA, Feb.1995; "Maximizing Damages in Death Cases," Southwest Bar Association, Mar.1995; "Proving a Products Liability Case - When the Product Has Disappeared," ITLA, Apr.1995; "Proof of Damages," Wyoming Trail Lawyers Association, June, 1995; "North American Agricultural Equipment Conference: Is Agriculture Winning the Blame Game?" Nov.1995; American Society of Trial Consultants, Batson and J.E.B.: "The Challenge Continued: Lecture and Demonstration of How to Argue and Defend a Challenge in Civil Cases," May, 1995; "Effective Damage Presentation," Trial Techniques—Getting the Case Ready; Getting a Verdict, ISBA, Nov.1996; "Winning with the Masters: Obtaining a Multi-Million Dollar Verdict in a Knee Injury Case," Louisiana Trial Lawyers Association, Dec.1996; Rush Presbyterian-St. Luke's Medical Center, Health Systems Management, College of Health Sciences, Health Law Course, Apr.1996; "Get Caught Up—An Update of Civil Practice, Insurance, Mental Health and Tort Law Issues—Damages: Making the Most of Our Case," ISBA, Dec.1997; "Basic Evidence," Illinois Paralegal Association, Oct.1997; "1997 Post-Legislative Retreat: Effective Damages Arguments in Catastrophic Injury and Wrongful Death Cases," Louisiana Trial Lawyers Association, July 1997; "How to Deal with Insurance Carriers and Great Results: Educating Insurers About the Value of Your Case," Illinois Institute of Continuing Legal Education, Apr. 1998; "Presenting the Complex Civil Case to a Jury Utilizing Focus Groups in Personal Injury and Wrongful Death Cases," ABA, Feb. 1998; "Point-Counterpoint Damages Seminar—Fractures and Joint Injuries—Plaintiff's Perspective," ITLA, May, 1998; "Litigating Personal Injury Cases: Recent Decisions Including *Taylor Machine Works* et al.: The Petrillo and Kunkel Decisions," ISBA, Illinois, Feb.1998; "Maximizing Damages Through the Use of Expert Witnesses: Help Us Help You," and "What Experts and Attorneys Need to Know About Working with Justice," SEAK, Hyannis, MA, June, 1998; "How to Depose a Treating Physician," IICLE, Dec.1998; Moderator, Trial Techniques Seminar, ITLA, Oct.1998; "Staying on Top of Tort Issues in Your Practice: Litigating Soft Tissue Cases: Proving Your Damages," ISBA, Dec.1998; "100 Days to Trial," Illinois Paralegal Association, Nov.1998; "Anatomy of Nursing Home Malpractice—Demonstrative Evidence in Nursing Home Litigation Cases," ABA, Mar.1999; Medical Witness Summit, SEAK, Ft. Lauderdale, Florida, Feb.1999; Evidence Seminar: Evidence Depositions, ITLA, May 1999; Nuts and Bolts for the Tort Practitioner-Demonstrative Evidence: Bringing Your Case to Life, ISBA, Lake Geneva, WI, June 1999; "Nursing Homes-Tort and Contract Litigation," Second Annual Elder Law Institute, Pennsylvania Bar Institute, Philadelphia, July 1999; Moderator, Update and Review Seminar, ITLA, Sept.1999; Basics of Handling an Auto Accident Case: Evidence Concerning Damages in Auto Accident Cases, IICLE, Illinois, Oct.1999; Litigating Tort Cases Without going Bankrupt: Cost Effective Exhibits, ISBA, Illinois, Oct.1999; New Theories of Liability: Will Your Industry be in the Crosshairs Next?, ABA, LaQuinta, CA, Feb. 2000; Mealey's Emerging Coverage Issues; Elder Care, ABA, Boston, Apr. 2000; Moderator, Evidence Seminar, ITLA, May 2000; Multi-Media Medical Trial: New Developments in Malpractice Litigation - Plaintiff Perspective, ABA, New York, July 2000; Trial Advocacy Program: Selling your Case in Opening Statement and Closing Argument, Colorado Trial Lawyers Association, Colorado Springs, Aug. 2000; Supreme Court Rule 213 and Its Impact in Tort Litigation - Damage Testimony: What Are the Elements?, ISBA, Oct. 2000; Moderator, The Art of Maximizing (or Minimizing) Damages in a Personal Injury Action, IICLE, Dec. 2000; 90 Days Before Trial: The Final Countdown Detailing your Case for Trial, CBA, Dec. 2000; Moderator, Point/Counter-Point Seminar, ITLA, Jan. 2001; Minimizing and Maximizing Damage Awards in Personal Injury Cases: Open/Close for the Plaintiff, CBA, Apr. 2001; "Direct Testimony of Experts: Good, Bad & Ugly," and "Demonstrative Evidence & Expert Witnesses," 10th Anniversary National Expert Witness & Litigation Seminar, SEAK, Hyannis, MA, June 2001; "The Masters on Deposition-Demonstrations from America's Leading Trial Attorneys," ABA, Philadelphia, Feb. 2002; "Central Illinois Civil Practice Update and Review Seminar: Demonstrative Evidence," ITLA, Feb. 2002; "Nursing Home Negligence-The Trial of a Nursing Home Negligence Case: Plaintiff's Perspective," Professional Education Systems Institute, June 2002; Moderator: "101 Tips from the Trenches," and "Jurors' Attitudes and Perceptions in a Time of Crises: Trying Cases after September 11th and the Enron Collapse," ABA Section of Litigation, Washington, D.C., August 2002; "90 Days Before Trial: The Final Countdown - Detailing Your Case for Trial," CBA, Sept. 2002; "Medical Witness Summit," SEAK, Chicago, Nov. 2002; "Maximizing Damages in a Catastrophic Injury or Death Case," and "Use of Themes and Analogies in a Personal Injury Trial," National CLE Conference, Aspen, Jan. 2003; "Demonstrative Evidence and Expert Witnesses," and "Cross Examination: Bending But Not Breaking," 1st Annual California Expert Summit, Newport Beach, CA, Mar. 2003; Moderator, Voir Dire: "Winning Before You Begin," and Impact Direct: "Making the Most of Your Direct Examination," ABA Section of Litigation, Houston, Apr. 2003; "Effective Illinois Jury Selection: Illinois Law Practice Realities," IICLE, Chicago, Apr. 2003; "Using Themes and Analogies to Persuade at Trial," and "Proof and Argument of Mental Pain and Anguish," The Absolute Litigators Conference VIII, Las Vegas, May 2003; "90 Days Before Trial: The Final Countdown, Detailing Your Case for Trial," CBA, Dec. 2003; "Winning With the Masters Seminar: Using Themes and Analogies to Persuade at Trial," Louisiana Trial Lawyers Association, Dec. 2003; "Maximizing Damages in a Catastrophic Injury or Death Case," National CLE Conference, Law Education Institute, Aspen, , Jan. 2004; AUTHOR: "Loss of Society and Punitive Damages Are Recoverable in Action Under Maritime Law," ISBA, Soundings Newsletter, Dec.1995; "Rescue Doctrine Saves Plaintiff," and "Wild Bore Gets One Free Bite," ISBA Tort Trends Newsletter, January 1997; "Lights, Camera, Action—Using Videotapes at Trial in Illinois," Jan.1998; "Litigation the Power Tool Case," Trial, Nov. 1997; "No Medical Testimony? No Problem—Or Is It?" Tort Trends, Newsletter, June 1997; "Slip and Fall Verdict for Head Chef Upheld," ISBA, Soundings Newsletter, Apr.1997; "High-Low Deals: In Vogue or In Trouble?" ISBA, Tort Trends Newsletter, Jan.1999; "Closing Arguments in Civil Trials: How Far Can Lawyers Go?" Illinois Bar Journal, Dec.1998; "Offering Evidence of Prior Occurrences," ATLA Products Liability Section Newsletter, Spring 1998; "Itemized Verdicts: When are They to be Used and How Are the Various Elements of Damages Itemized?" ISBA, Tort Trends Newsletter, Apr.1998; "Using Focus Groups to Prepare for Trial," ISBA Tort Trends, Newsletter, March 2000, ISBA; "Maximizing Damaging in Soft-Tissue Injury Cases," Illinois Bar Journal, July 1999; "Reheating Old Soup: Taking a Case to Verdict...A Second Time," ABA Section of Litigation, Tips from the Trenches Newsletter, June 2000; "The Case for Making Pre-Impact Fear Compensable in Survival Actions," Illinois Bar Journal, August 2000; "The Use and Presentation of Demonstrative Evidence in the Trial of an Automobile Negligence Case," Proving Fault in Auto Accident Cases, IICLE, 2001; "Using Demonstrative Evidence to Maximize Damages: A Plaintiff's Perspective," Trial Technique Committee Newsletter, and "Demonstrative Evidence in Medical Malpractice Actions: Lead, Follow or Get Out of the Way," The Brief, Tort and Insurance Practice Section, Spring 2001; "Using Technology to Enhance Medical Demonstrative Evidence," The Practical Litigator,

(This Listing Continued)

(This Listing Continued)

CLIFFORD LAW OFFICES, P.C., Chicago—Continued

July 2001; "Adverse Examination of Former Employees in Illinois," Illinois Bar Journal, June 2003; "Effective Use of Depositions at Trial," ABA, Litigation, Fall 2003; "No Damage? No Expert? No Defense!!" ISBA, Tort Trend Newsletter, Oct. 2003; "Using Themes at Trial," Automobile Law Committee Newsletter, Tort Trial Insurance Practice Section, Spring 2004; "Revisiting Bulger v. CTA: The Case for Admitting Transportation Company Investigation Results," Illinois Bar Journal, Apr. 2004; "The Fear Factor," Trial, Feb.2004. FACULTY: Northwestern School of Law, Trial Advocacy, Fall 2001, 2002, 2004, 2005; DePaul College of Law, Trial Advocacy, Spring 1999, 2000, Medical Malpractice Law, Fall 1992 & Spring 1993. *Member:* Chicago (Tickets for Kids Subcommittee, 1996-1997; CBA/YLS Health & Hospital Law Committee, 1995-1996; Public Affairs Committee, 1993-1995); DuPage County (Medical Legal Committee, 1997-1998), Illinois State (Special Committee on Mentoring, 2003-2004; Assembly, 1998-2001; Legislative Liaison, Tort Litigation Committee, Young Lawyers, 1996; Tort Law Section Council, 1996-2000; Admiralty and Maritime Law, Section Council, 1995-1997; Chair, 1995-1996) and American (Section of Litigation - Co-Chair, Expert Witness, 2005-2006; Co-Chair, 2005 ABA Annual Meeting, 2003-2005; Representative, 2003 Section Offices Conference, CLE Task Force, 2003; Co-Chair, Trial Evidence Committee, 2002-2003; Co-Chair, Tips from the Trenches Publication, 1999-2002; Program Co-Chair, Section Annual Meeting, 1995; Task Force, State of the Justice System, 1993; Tort Trial and Insurance Practice Section, Vice Chair, Trial Techniques Committee, 1999-2001; General Liability and Consumer Law Committee, 1996; Public Relations Committee, 1993-1995; Liaison between the Public Relations Committee and Medicine & the Law; Workers' Compensation and Employers' Liability Law; Admiralty & Maritime; Charitable, Religious & Non-Profit Organizations, 1993-1995. Long Range Planning Group in Civil Justice System Improvement, 1993) Bar Associations; Illinois Trial Lawyers Association (Board of Advocates, 2000—; Co-Chair, Seminar Planning, 1999-2001; Civil Practice and Rules, 1997-1998; Amicus Curiae Committee, 1993-1995; Board of Advocates, 1993-2000; Medical Malpractice Committee, 1992-1994; Publications Committee, 1992-1995) Association of Trial Lawyers of America (Executive Committee, Products Liability Section, 1994-1997); Southwest Bar Association of Chicago. Fellow, Illinois Bar Foundation, 1998—. ***PRACTICE AREAS:*** Airplane Crash Litigation; Aviation Accidents; Aviation Litigation (Commercial and General); Health Care; Helicopter Crash Litigation; Commercial Litigation; Construction Accidents; Construction Liability; Construction Litigation; Consumer Litigation; Consumer Protection; Nursing Home Litigation; Nursing Home Liability; Nursing Home Negligence; Patients Rights; Hospital Negligence; Complex Litigation; Trial Practice; Birth Trauma; Medical Negligence; Nursing Negligence; Nursing Malpractice; Accidents; Automobile Accidents and Injuries; Automobile Negligence; Brain Injury; Head Injury; Motor Vehicle Accidents and Injuries; Railroad Accidents and Injuries; Truck Accidents; Plaintiffs Personal Injury Litigation; Wrongful Death; Medical Malpractice; Transportation; Product Liability; Premises Liability; Vehicular Accident Law. ***Email:*** JJK@CliffordLaw.com

RICHARD F. BURKE, JR., born Chicago, Illinois, September 10, 1953; admitted to bar, 1978, Illinois, U.S. District Court, Northern District of Illinois including Trial Bar; 1988, U.S. Court of Appeals, Seventh Circuit. *Education:* Loyola University (B.S., 1975); DePaul University (J.D., 1978); University of Chicago (M.B.A., 1988). *LECTURES/ARTICLES:* "Maximizing Damages," Illinois State Bar Association (ISBA), 1996; "Opening Statement in Medical Malpractice Cases," Illinois Trial Lawyers Association (ITLA), 1997; ISBA Tort Law Update-Product Liability Cases, Dec. 1997; Litigating Personal Injury Cases, 1998; Cost Effective Trial Exhibits, 1999; Motor Vehicle Product Liability Cases, ITLA, Feb. 2000; Law of Closing Argument, Chicago Bar Association (CBA), March 2000; Lecture on Anatomy of a Trial, Maximizing Damages, ITLA, Oct. 2000; Trial Techniques Course, "Objections During Trial," ISBA, 2000; Cook County States' Attorney's Office, Experts in Civil Cases, 2001; Post Trial Motions, ISBA, 2002. INSTRUCTOR: CBA Federal Trial Bar Advocacy Training, 1993-1995. Member, Illinois Supreme Court Committee on Jury Instructions in Civil Cases, 2004. *Member:* Chicago (Judicial Evaluation Committee, 1993-2004; Co-Chair, Investigation Division, 2002-2003; Chair, Judicial Evaluation Committee, 2003-2004), Illinois State and American Bar Associations; Illinois Trial Lawyers Association; Association of Trial Lawyers of America. ***PRACTICE AREAS:*** Airplane Crash Litigation; Aviation Accidents; Aviation Litigation (Commercial and General); Health Care; Helicopter Crash Litigation; Commercial Litigation; Construction Accidents; Construction Liability; Construction Litigation; Consumer Litigation; Consumer Protection; Nursing Home Litigation; Nursing Home Liability; Nursing Home Negligence; Patients Rights; Hospital Negligence; Complex Litigation; Trial Practice; Birth Trauma; Medical Negligence; Nursing Negligence; Nursing Malpractice; Accidents; Automobile Accidents and Injuries; Automobile Negligence; Brain Injury; Head Injury; Motor Vehicle Accidents and Injuries; Railroad Accidents and Injuries; Truck Accidents; Plaintiffs Personal Injury Litigation; Wrongful Death; Medical Malpractice; Transportation; Product Liability; Premises Liability; Vehicular Accident Law. ***Email:*** RFB@CliffordLaw.com

ROBERT A. STRELECKY, born Chicago, Illinois, April 28, 1953; admitted to bar, 1980, Illinois and U.S. District Court, Northern District of Illinois including Trial Bar. *Education:* University of Illinois (B.S., 1975); DePaul University (J.D., 1980). *Member:* American Bar Association; Illinois Trial Lawyers Association, Association of Trial Lawyers of America. ***PRACTICE AREAS:*** Airplane Crash Litigation; Aviation Accidents; Aviation Litigation (Commercial and General); Health Care; Helicopter Crash Litigation; Commercial Litigation; Construction Accidents; Construction Liability; Construction Litigation; Consumer Litigation; Consumer Protection; Nursing Home Litigation; Nursing Home Liability; Nursing Home Negligence; Patients Rights; Hospital Negligence; Complex Litigation; Trial Practice; Birth Trauma; Medical Negligence; Nursing Negligence; Nursing Malpractice; Accidents; Automobile Accidents and Injuries; Automobile Negligence; Brain Injury; Head Injury; Motor Vehicle Accidents and Injuries; Railroad Accidents and Injuries; Truck Accidents; Plaintiffs Personal Injury Litigation; Wrongful Death; Medical Malpractice; Transportation; Product Liability; Premises Liability; Vehicular Accident Law. ***Email:*** RAS@CliffordLaw.com

PAMELA S. MENAKER, admitted to bar, 1984, Illinois. *Education:* Medill School of Journalism, Northwestern University (B.S.; M.S.); Loyola University of Chicago School of Law (J.D., 1984). Community Service: Center for Disability and Elder Law, Board Member, 2002— Chair, Marketing Committee, 2003—. LECTURER: "Law and Ethics of Marketing," Northwestern University, McDill School of Journalism. *Member:* Chicago (Chicago Bar Record Editorial Board, 1994—; Summary Judgments Editor, 2000—; Pro Bono Committee, 2005—) and American (2005 Annual Meeting Advisory Committee; Section of Litigation, Chair, Media Relations, 2001-2002; Town Hall Meeting, Apr. 2002; Editorial Board, Litigation Magazine, 2002—; Chair, Unpublished References Committee, 2002-2003; Chair, Written Materials Committee, 2003-2004; Co-Chair, Written Materials Programming 2005 Annual Meeting) Bar Associations; Illinois Trial Lawyers Association. ***PRACTICE AREAS:*** Airplane Crash Litigation; Aviation Accidents; Aviation Litigation (Commercial and General); Health Care; Helicopter Crash Litigation; Commercial Litigation; Construction Accidents; Construction Liability; Construction Litigation; Consumer Litigation; Consumer Protection; Nursing Home Litigation; Nursing Home Liability; Nursing Home Negligence; Patients Rights; Hospital Negligence; Complex Litigation; Trial Practice; Birth Trauma; Medical Negligence; Nursing Negligence; Nursing Malpractice; Accidents; Automobile Accidents and Injuries; Automobile Negligence; Brain Injury; Head Injury; Motor Vehicle Accidents and Injuries; Railroad Accidents and Injuries; Truck Accidents; Plaintiffs Personal Injury Litigation; Wrongful Death; Medical Malpractice; Transportation; Product Liability; Premises Liability; Vehicular Accident Law. ***Email:*** pammenaker@aol.com

MICHAEL S. KRZAK, born Chicago, Illinois, September 1, 1970; admitted to bar, 1997, Illinois and U.S. District Court, Northern District of Illinois. *Education:* Northeastern Illinois University (B.A., summa cum laude, 1992); DePaul University (J.D., 1997). Listings: 40 Under 40 to Watch, Law Bulletin Publishing Company, 2001. Member, Million Dollar Advocate's Forum. AUTHOR: "Medical Malpractice Network," Illinois Trial Lawyers Association, 1997-1999; "Wrapping Up and Structured Settlements;" Feb. 16, 1998. LECTURER: "What You Should Know About High/Low Agreements & Structured Settlements," Illinois Institute for Continuing Legal Education, Oct. 1999. *Member:* Chicago (Vice-Chair, Aviation Law Committee, Judicial Evaluation Committee); Illinois State (Tort Law Committee) and American Bar Associations; Illinois Trial Lawyers Association; Association of Trial Lawyers of America. ***PRACTICE AREAS:*** Airplane Crash Litigation; Aviation Accidents; Aviation Litigation (Commercial and General); Health Care; Helicopter Crash Litigation; Commercial Litigation; Construction Accidents; Construction Liability; Construction Litigation; Consumer Litigation; Consumer Protection; Nursing Home Litigation; Nursing Home Liability; Nursing Home Negligence; Patients Rights; Hospital Negligence; Complex Litigation; Trial Practice; Birth Trauma; Medical Negligence; Nursing Negligence; Nursing Malpractice; Accidents; Automobile Accidents and Injuries; Automobile Negligence; Brain Injury; Head Injury; Motor Vehicle Accidents and Injuries; Railroad Accidents and Injuries; Truck Accidents; Plaintiffs Personal Injury Litigation; Wrongful Death; Medical Malpractice; Transportation; Product Liability; Premises Liability; Vehicular Accident Law. ***Email:*** MSK@CliffordLaw.com

TIMOTHY S. TOMASIK, born Evanston, Illinois, January 7, 1964; admitted to bar, 1989, Colorado and U.S. District Court, District of Colorado; 1990, Illinois and U.S. District Court, Northern District of Illinois including Trial Bar. *Education:* University of Colorado (B.S., 1986); University of Denver (J.D., 1989). RECIPIENT: 40 Illinois Attorneys Under 40 to Watch, Law Bulletin Publishing Company, 2000; American Legion Expert Litigator Award, 1999. INSTRUCTOR: University of Virginia Law School, Institute of Trial Advocacy, 2002-2004; Chicago Bar Association, Federal Trial Bar, Trial Advocacy, 2000; Trial Advocacy, National Advocacy Center, 1998; Trial Advocacy, National College of District Attorneys, 1997-1998; LECTURER: "Supreme Court Rule 213," Illinois Trial Lawyers Association (ITLA), Oct. 2005; "You're Sued for Malpractice! Should you Defend or Settle?" Illinois Radiological Society, Chicago, May 2002; ; "Third Party Liability for the Criminal Assaults of Others," ITLA, Sept. 2001; "Malpractice Issues Involving Gynecological Radiology," The Radiological Society of North America, Chicago, Nov. 2001; "Jury Selection," Maximizing Damages, Illinois Institute for Continuing Legal Education; Federal Rules of Evidence, American Law Institute - American Bar Association , Chicago, 2000 & 2005. *Member:* Chicago (Judicial Evaluation Committee, 1997—, Vice Chair, 2003-2005; General Chair, 2005-2006), Illinois State and American Bar Associations; Illinois Trial Lawyers Association; Chicago Bar Foundation (Grant Committee); Chicago Inns of Court. ***PRACTICE AREAS:*** Airplane Crash Litigation; Aviation Accidents; Aviation Litigation (Commercial and General); Health Care; Helicopter Crash Litigation; Commercial Litigation; Construction Accidents; Construction Liability; Construction Litigation; Consumer Litigation; Consumer Protection; Nursing Home Litigation; Nursing Home Liability; Nursing Home Negligence; Patients Rights; Hospital Negligence; Complex Litigation; Trial Practice; Birth Trauma; Medical Negligence; Nursing Negligence; Nursing Malpractice; Accidents; Automobile Accidents and Injuries; Automobile Negligence; Brain Injury; Head Injury; Motor Vehicle Accidents and Injuries; Railroad Accidents and Injuries; Truck Accidents; Plaintiffs Personal Injury Litigation; Wrongful Death; Medical Malpractice; Transportation; Product Liability; Premises Liability; Vehicle Accident Law. ***Email:*** TST@CliffordLaw.com

JOHN T. KARNEZIS, born July 23, 1966; admitted to bar, 1991, Illinois. *Education:* University of Illinois (B.S., 1988); Loyola University School of Law (J.D., 1991). FACULTY: National College of District Attorneys, Houston, Norfolk, San Francisco, San Diego; National Advocacy Center, Columbia, S.C.; Adjunct Professor, Trial Advocacy, John Marshall Law School, Chicago. LECTURER/ARTICLES: Chicago Bar Association (CBA) Federal Bar Training Course, "Tips on Cross Examination," Apr. 2004 and "Closing Statements," Apr. 2005; "Perspective of Deposition Practice," DePaul School of Law, Chicago, Apr. 2005; "Actions Speak Louder than Words," National Association of Criminal Defense Lawyers, Las Vegas, Oct. 2002 ; "Theme Development in Jury Trials," "Analytical Advocacy and the Visual Trial," "Theory of Cross Examination, Proactive and Reactive Methodology," "Cross Examination of Expert Witnesses," U.S. Naval Judge Advocate General Trial Enhancement Program, San Diego, Apr. 2000; "Coffee is for Closers - The Fundamentals of Effective Closing Argument," National Advocacy Center, Columbia, S.C., 2000; "Oh Yeah, That's What you Say - Proactive and Reactive Cross Examination Techniques" and "May I Have Your Attention Please - Effective Opening Statements in Jury Trials," U.S. Naval Judge Advocate General Trial Enhancement Program, Norfolk; "Handling Mitigation Experts," Cook County States Attorneys Office, Capital Litigation, June 2000; "More Lethal Than Bullets, More Valuable Than Gold - Effective Presentation of Narcotics Trials to Juries," Montana County Attorneys Association, Montana, July 2000; "Just Win, Baby - Theme Development in Jury Trials," Career Prosecutor Course, National College of District Attorneys, Charleston, S.C., June 2000; "Do's & Don't's of Opening Statements," CBA, June 2000; "Are They Really Experts?" Illinois Institute of Continuing

(This Listing Continued)

Legal Education, Expert Witness Seminar; "The Usual Suspects - Prosecuting Gang Homicides" and "The Paper Chase - Effective Pre-trial Motion Practice," National College of District Attorneys Homicide Course, San Francisco; "What's Up, Doc - Cross Examination of Mental Health Experts," Technical Cross Examination, National Advocacy Center, Columbia, S.C., Feb. 1999. *Member:* Chicago, Illinois State and American Bar Associations; Illinois Trial Lawyers Association; Association of Trial Lawyers of America. ***PRACTICE AREAS:*** Airplane Crash Litigation; Aviation Accidents; Aviation Litigation (Commercial and General); Health Care; Helicopter Crash Litigation; Commercial Litigation; Construction Accidents; Construction Liability; Construction Litigation; Consumer Litigation; Consumer Protection; Nursing Home Litigation; Nursing Home Liability; Nursing Home Negligence; Patients Rights; Hospital Negligence; Complex Litigation; Trial Practice; Birth Trauma; Medical Negligence; Nursing Negligence; Nursing Malpractice; Accidents; Automobile Accidents and Injuries; Automobile Negligence; Brain Injury; Head Injury; Motor Vehicle Accidents and Injuries; Railroad Accidents and Injuries; Truck Accidents; Plaintiffs Personal Injury Litigation; Wrongful Death; Medical Malpractice; Transportation; Product Liability; Premises Liability; Vehicular Accident Law. ***Email:*** JTK@CliffordLaw.com

---

BRIAN THOMAS NASH, born Chicago, Illinois, February 10, 1971; admitted to bar, 1999, Illinois and U.S. District Court, Northern District of Illinois; 2000, U.S. District Court, Western District of Wisconsin; 2003, U.S. Supreme Court. *Education:* University of Illinois (B.S., 1993); DePaul University (J.D., 1999). President, DePaul University College of Law Student Chapters, 1997-1998. *Member:* Chicago (Judicial Evaluation Committee), Illinois State and American Bar Associations; Illinois Trial Lawyers Association; Association of Trial Lawyers of America. ***PRACTICE AREAS:*** Airplane Crash Litigation; Aviation Accidents; Aviation Litigation (Commercial and General); Health Care; Helicopter Crash Litigation; Commercial Litigation; Construction Accidents; Construction Liability; Construction Litigation; Consumer Litigation; Consumer Protection; Nursing Home Litigation; Nursing Home Liability; Nursing Home Negligence; Patients Rights; Hospital Negligence; Complex Litigation; Trial Practice; Birth Trauma; Medical Negligence; Nursing Negligence; Nursing Malpractice; Accidents; Automobile Accidents and Injuries; Automobile Negligence; Brain Injury; Head Injury; Motor Vehicle Accidents and Injuries; Railroad Accidents and Injuries; Truck Accidents; Plaintiffs Personal Injury Litigation; Wrongful Death; Medical Malpractice; Transportation; Product Liability; Premises Liability; Vehicular Accident Law. ***Email:*** BTN@CliffordLaw.com

KATHERINE L. DZIK, born Chicago, Illinois, September 10, 1972; admitted to bar, 2000, Illinois and U.S. District Court, Northern District of Illinois. *Education:* DeVry Institute of Technology (B.S., 1993); DePaul College of Law (J.D., 2000). *Member:* Chicago, Illinois State and American Bar Associations; Illinois Trial Lawyers Association; Association of Trial Lawyers of America. ***PRACTICE AREAS:*** Airplane Crash Litigation; Aviation Accidents; Aviation Litigation (Commercial and General); Health Care; Helicopter Crash Litigation; Commercial Litigation; Construction Accidents; Construction Liability; Construction Litigation; Consumer Protection; Nursing Home Litigation; Nursing Home Liability; Nursing Home Negligence; Patients Rights; Hospital Negligence; Complex Litigation; Trial Practice; Birth Trauma; Medical Negligence; Nursing Negligence; Nursing Malpractice; Accidents; Automobile Accidents and Injuries; Automobile Negligence; Brain Injury; Head Injury; Motor Vehicle Accidents and Injuries; Railroad Accidents and Injuries; Truck Accidents; Plaintiffs Personal Injury Litigation; Wrongful Death; Medical Malpractice; Transportation; Product Liability; Premises Liability; Vehicular Accident Law. ***Email:*** KLD@CliffordLaw.com

J. RYAN POTTS, born April 30, 1977; admitted to bar, 2002, Illinois and U.S. District Court, Northern District of Illinois. *Education:* University of Illinois (B.S., 1999); DePaul University College of Law (J.D., 2002). *Member:* Chicago, DuPage County; Illinois State and American (Section of Litigation- 2005 Annual Meeting Host Committee, Young Lawyers Website Advisory Group) Bar Associations; Illinois Trial Lawyers Association (Governmental Affairs Committee); Association of Trial Lawyers of America. ***PRACTICE AREAS:*** Airplane Crash Litigation; Aviation Accidents; Aviation Litigation (Commercial and General); Health Care; Helicopter Crash Litigation; Commercial Litigation; Construction Accidents; Construction Liability; Construction Litigation; Consumer Litigation; Consumer Protection; Nursing Home Litigation; Nursing Home Liability; Nursing Home Negligence; Patients Rights; Hospital Negligence; Complex Litigation; Trial Practice; Birth Trauma; Medical Negligence; Nursing Negligence; Nursing Malpractice; Accidents; Automobile Accidents and Injuries; Automobile Negligence; Brian Injury; Head Injury; Motor Vehicle Accidents and Injuries; Railroad Accidents and Injuries; Truck Accidents; Plaintiffs Personal Injury Litigation; Wrongful Death; Medical Malpractice; Transportation; Product Liability; Premises Liability; Vehicular Accident Law. ***Email:*** JRP@CliffordLaw.com

CRAIG J. SQUILLACE, born Chicago, Illinois, December 17, 1973; admitted to bar, 2002, Illinois. *Education:* Illinois State University (B.S.,1996); John Marshall Law School (J.D., 2002). *Member:* Chicago (Judicial Evaluation Committee, 2005); Illinois State and American (Trial Techniques Committee, 2005) Bar Associations; Illinois Trial Lawyers Association; Association of Trial Lawyers of America. ***PRACTICE AREAS:*** Airplane Crash Litigation; Aviation Accidents; Aviation Litigation (Commercial and General); Health Care; Helicopter Crash Litigation; Commercial Litigation; Construction Accidents; Construction Liability; Construction Litigation; Consumer Litigation; Consumer Protection; Nursing Home Litigation; Nursing Home Liability; Nursing Home Negligence; Patients Rights; Hospital Negligence; Complex Litigation; Trial Practice; Birth Trauma; Medical Negligence; Nursing Negligence; Nursing Malpractice; Accidents; Automobile Accidents and Injuries; Automobile Negligence; Brian Injury; Head Injury; Motor Vehicle Accidents and Injuries; Railroad Accidents and Injuries; Truck Accidents; Plaintiffs Personal Injury Litigation; Wrongful Death; Medical Malpractice; Transportation; Product Liability; Premises Liability; Vehicular Accident Law. ***Email:*** CJS@CliffordLaw.com

HEATHER A. BEGLEY, born Evergreen Park, Illinois; admitted to bar, 2003, Illinois. *Education:* University of Illinois (B.S., 1999); DePaul University College of Law (J.D., 2002). *Member:* Chicago, Illinois State and American Bar Associations; Illinois Trial Lawyers Association; Association of Trial Lawyers of America. ***PRACTICE AREAS:*** Airplane Crash Litigation; Aviation Accidents; Aviation Litigation (Commercial and General); Health Care; Helicopter Crash Litigation; Commercial Litigation; Construction Accidents; Construction Liability; Construction Litigation; Consumer Protection; Nursing Home Litigation; Nursing Home Liability; Nursing Home Negligence; Patients Rights; Hospital Negligence; Complex Litigation; Trial Practice; Birth Trauma; Medical Negligence; Nursing Negligence; Nursing Malpractice; Accidents; Automobile Accidents and Injuries; Automobile Negligence; Brain Injury; Head Injury; Motor Vehicle Accidents and Injuries; Railroad Accidents and Injuries; Truck Accidents; Plaintiffs Personal Injury Litigation; Wrongful Death; Medical Malpractice; Transportation; Product Liability; Premises Liability; Vehicular Accident Law. ***Email:*** HAB@CliffordLaw.com

SHANNON M. McNULTY, born Evergreen Park, Illinois, October 8, 1971; admitted to bar, 2004, Illinois and U.S. District Court, Northern District of Illinois. *Education:* Loyola University (B.S., 1993); DePaul University (J.D., 2004). *Member:* Chicago, Illinois State and American (Section of Litigation- 2005 Annual Meeting Advisory Committee) Bar Associations; Illinois Trial Lawyers Association; Association of Trial Lawyers of America. ***PRACTICE AREAS:*** Airplane Crash Litigation; Aviation Accidents; Aviation Litigation (Commercial and General); Health Care; Helicopter Crash Litigation; Commercial Litigation; Construction Accidents; Construction Liability; Construction Litigation; Consumer Litigation; Consumer Protection; Nursing Home Litigation; Nursing Home Liability; Nursing Home Negligence; Patients Rights; Hospital Negligence; Complex Litigation; Trial Practice; Birth Trauma; Medical Negligence; Nursing Negligence; Nursing Malpractice; Accidents; Automobile Accidents and Injuries; Automobile Negligence; Brain Injury; Head Injury; Motor Vehicle Accidents and Injuries; Railroad Accidents and Injuries; Truck Accidents; Plaintiffs Personal Injury Litigation; Wrongful Death; Medical Malpractice; Transportation; Product Liability; Premises Liability; Vehicular Accident Law. ***Email:*** SMM@CliffordLaw.com

MATTHEW L. WILLENS, born Chicago, Illinois, October 24, 1969; admitted to bar, 1995, Illinois and U.S. District Court, Northern District of Illinois, including Trial Bar, 2004; 1998, U.S. District Court, Central District of Illinois. *Education:* Northern Illinois University (B.S., 1991) Loyola University (J.D., 1995). *Member:* Chicago, Illinois State and American Bar Associations; Illinois Trial Lawyers Association; Association of Trial Lawyers of America. ***PRACTICE AREAS:*** Airplane Crash Litigation; Aviation Accidents; Aviation Litigation (Commercial and General); Health Care; Helicopter Crash Litigation; Commercial Litigation; Construction Accidents; Construction Liability; Consumer Litigation; Consumer Protection; Nursing Home Litigation; Nursing Home Liability; Nursing Home Negligence; Patients Rights; Hospital Negligence; Complex Litigation; Trial Practice; Birth Trauma; Medical Negligence; Nursing Negligence; Nursing Malpractice; Accidents; Automobile Accidents and Injuries; Automobile Negligence; Brain Injury; Head Injury; Motor Vehicle Accidents and Injuries; Railroad Accidents and Injuries; Truck Accidents; Plaintiffs Personal Injury Litigation; Wrongful Death; Medical Malpractice; Transportation; Product Liability; Premises Liability; Vehicular Accident Law. ***Email:*** MLW@CliffordLaw.com

BRIAN SHALLCROSS, born Winfield, Illinois, December 16, 1972; admitted to bar, 2005, Illinois and U.S. District Court, Northern District of Illinois. *Education:* DePaul University (B.A., 2001; J.D., 2004). *Member:* Chicago, Illinois State and American Bar Associations; Illinois Trial Lawyers Association; Association of Trial Lawyers of America. ***PRACTICE AREAS:*** Airplane Crash Litigation; Aviation Accidents; Aviation Litigation (Commercial and General); Health Care; Helicopter Crash Litigation; Commercial Litigation; Construction Accidents; Construction Liability; Construction Litigation; Consumer Litigation; Consumer Protection; Nursing Home Litigation; Nursing Home Liability; Nursing Home Negligence; Patients Rights; Hospital Negligence; Complex Litigation; Trial Practice; Birth Trauma; Medical Negligence; Nursing Negligence; Nursing Malpractice; Accidents; Automobile Accidents and Injuries; Automobile Negligence; Brain Injury; Head Injury; Motor Vehicle Accidents and Injuries; Railroad Accidents and Injuries; Truck Accidents; Plaintiffs Personal Injury Litigation; Wrongful Death; Medical Malpractice; Transportation; Product Liability; Premises Liability; Vehicular Accident Law.

VIVIAN T. TARVER, born Illinois; admitted to bar, 2003, Illinois and U.S. District Court, Northern District of Illinois. *Education:* Olive Harvey College (A.A., Nursing, 1979); Governors State University (B.A., 1999); The John Marshall Law School (J.D., 2003). *Member:* Chicago (Civil Litigation Committee, 2004—) and Illinois State Bar Associations; Illinois Trial Lawyers Association; Association of Trial Lawyers of America; Black Women's Lawyer Association. ***PRACTICE AREAS:*** Airplane Crash Litigation; Aviation Accidents; Aviation Litigation (Commercial and General); Health Care; Helicopter Crash Litigation; Commercial Litigation; Construction Accidents; Construction Liability; Construction Litigation; Consumer Litigation; Consumer Protection; Nursing Home Litigation; Nursing Home Liability; Nursing Home Negligence; Patients Rights; Hospital Negligence; Complex Litigation; Trial Practice; Birth Trauma; Medical Negligence; Nursing Negligence; Nursing Malpractice; Accidents; Automobile Accidents and Injuries; Automobile Negligence; Brain Injury; Head Injury; Motor Vehicle Accidents and Injuries; Railroad Accidents and Injuries; Truck Accidents; Plaintiffs Personal Injury Litigation; Wrongful Death; Medical Malpractice; Transportation; Product Liability; Premises Liability; Vehicular Accident Law. ***Email:*** VTT@CliffordLaw.com

OF COUNSEL

ROBERT P. SHERIDAN, born Chicago, Illinois, May 16, 1946; admitted to bar, 1975, Illinois, U.S. District Court, Northern District of Illinois, U.S. Court of Appeals, Seventh Circuit and U.S. Supreme Court. *Education:* University of Iowa; Roosevelt University; DePaul University (J.D., 1974). *Member:* Chicago, Illinois State; American Bar Associations; Illinois Trial Lawyers Association; Association of Trial Lawyers of America. ***PRACTICE AREAS:*** Airplane Crash Litigation; Aviation Accidents; Aviation Litigation (Commercial and General); Health Care; Helicopter Crash Litigation; Commercial Litigation; Construction Accidents; Construction Liability; Construction Litigation; Consumer Litigation; Consumer Protection; Nursing Home Litigation; Nursing Home Liability; Nursing Home Negligence; Patients Rights; Hospital Negligence; Complex Litigation; Trial Practice; Birth Trauma; Medical Negligence; Nursing Negligence; Accidents; Automobile Accidents and Injuries; Automobile Negligence; Brain Injury; Head Injury; Motor Vehicle Accidents and Injuries; Railroad Accidents and Injuries; Truck Accidents; Plaintiffs Personal Injury Litigation; Wrongful Death; Medical Malpractice; Transportation; Product Liability; Premises Liability; Vehicular Accident Law. ***Email:*** RPS@CliffordLaw.com

(This Listing Continued)

MICHAEL W. COFFIELD, & ASSOCIATES

77 WEST WACKER DRIVE
SUITE 4800
CHICAGO, ILLINOIS 60601
Telephone: 312-444-9696
Fax: 312-444-9658
Email: mike@bigdoglaw.com

Litigation includes both Civil and Criminal Antitrust, RICO, Environmental, Labor, Products Liability, Trademark and Copyright, Constitutional and First Amendment Litigation, Admiralty, Tax, Bankruptcy, Wills and Trust Litigation, Corporate Internal Investigations.

MICHAEL W. COFFIELD, born Evanston, Illinois, January 28, 1940; admitted to bar, 1967, Illinois and U.S. District Court, Northern District of Illinois, including Trial Bar and U.S. Supreme Court. *Education:* Dartmouth College (A.B., 1962); University of Michigan (J.D., 1967). Listed in "Best Lawyers in America," Corporate Litigation Attorneys Section in Illinois, 1999-2004. Named Chicago Lawyer of the Year, 1999 and Leading Lawyers, 2004. *Member:* Chicago, Seventh Judicial Circuit, Illinois State and American Bar Associations; Chicago Council of Lawyers; Illinois Trial Lawyers Association; Legal Club of Chicago (Member, Executive Committee); National Association of Criminal Defense Lawyers; Illinois Association of Criminal Defense Lawyers; American Judicature Society; Barristers Society; The Chicago Inn of Court (President, 1988-1990); American Inns of Court (Trustee, 1990-1997). ***PRACTICE AREAS:*** Litigation; Civil Law; Criminal Law.

COGAN & McNABOLA, P.C.

Established in 1992

55 WEST WACKER DRIVE, 9TH FLOOR
CHICAGO, ILLINOIS 60601
Telephone: 312-629-2900; 800-704-2900
Fax: 312-629-2916
URL: http://www.cogenandmcnabola.com
Email: info@coganmcnabola.com
URL: http://www.cogan-mcnabola.com

Personal Injury, Medical Malpractice, Products Liability, Professional Negligence.

FIRM PROFILE: Attorneys Michael Cogan and Mark McNabola founded Cogan & McNabola, P.C. in 1992. The firm's attorneys represent injured men, women and children in a wide variety of injury and medical malpractice cases throughout state and federal courts in Illinois.

At this Chicago law firm, attorneys take responsibility for effective, aggressive investigation and legal representation. This allows injured clients to attend to their immediate health, safety, and welfare concerns while the attorneys pursue a variety of legal methods to obtain the highest possible financial recovery.

The attorneys at Cogan & McNabola, P.C. have obtained over $200 million dollars in verdict and settlement for their clients. Because of this stellar reputation, over 70 percent of the firm's cases are referred by other attorneys. The partners at the firm are members of the "Leading Lawyers Network," and "Super Lawyers." The founding partners have received the highest possible rating from Martindale Hubble. One partner is also included in the Chicago Daily Law Bulletin's "Forty Under Forty Lawyers to Watch.".

MEMBERS OF FIRM

MARK E. McNABOLA, born Chicago, Illinois, July 11, 1959; admitted to bar, 1985, Illinois and U.S. District Court, Northern District of Illinois. *Education:* DePaul University (B.A., English/Communication, 1981; J.D., 1985). Top 5% of all Personal Injury Attorneys in the State of Illinois. Professor, Business Law, Chicago College of Commerce, 1983-1985. Named an Illinois Super Lawyer for 2005, representing the top 5% of practicing attorneys in Illinois and selected by peers. Adjunct Professor, Law, DePaul University College of Law. Contributing Author: ITLA Trial Notebook Series, 1989-1991; ITLA Notebook Series; Post-Traumatic Stress Disorder; Proof of Facts. Guest Lecturer, ITLA: "The Anatomy of an Automobile Accident Lawsuit," 1990. Contributing Author: "Deposition Taking and Establishing Accountability;" "Damages and Its Impact on the Trial of a Premises Liability Case;" "Trial Strategy Regarding the Use of Economic Damages"; Journal of ATLA, 2001: "The Special Interrogatory." Associate, Motherway & Glenn, P.C., Chicago, Illinois, 1985-1992. President, 1987-1992, Executive Director. Children's Charities of Chicago. Member and Legal Counsel, The Knapp Burn Foundation. Member, Society of Trial Lawyers. Member, Million Dollar Advocate Forum. Member, Prevent Child Abuse America, Chicago Board. *Member:* Chicago (Member: Judicial Administration and Reform Committee; Trial Techniques Committee), Illinois State and American Bar Associations; North Suburban Bar Association; Illinois Trial Lawyers Association; (Member: Board of Managers, Parliamentarian; Member, Executive Board; Civil Procedures Committee; Medical Malpractice Committee); The Association of Trial Lawyers of America; Fellow, American Bar Foundation. ***PRACTICE AREAS:*** Personal Injury; Aviation Law; Medical Malpractice. ***Email:*** markm@cogan-mcnabola.com

MICHAEL P. COGAN, born Chicago, Illinois, May 30, 1956; admitted to bar, 1981, Illinois; 1983, U.S. District Court, Northern District of Illinois and U.S. District Court, Eastern District of Wisconsin; 2002, U.S. District Court, District of Colorado;. *Education:* University of Illinois (B.A., Accounting, 1978); John Marshall Law School (J.D., 1981). Judge, National Moot Court Trial Competition, 1998. Judge, National Criminal Trial Advocacy Competition, 1998. Named an Illinois Super Lawyer for 2005, representing the top 5% of practicing attorneys in Illinois and selected by peers. Invited Speaker: "How Not to Get Sued," University of Illinois at Chicago Third-year Resident Retreat, 2005. "International Screening Guidelines for Colon Cancer," Crones and Colitis Foundation of America, 2000; Annual Meeting, Gastroenterological Association, 1999; "Medical Malpractice Deposing the Defense Expert," and "Medical Malpractice Settlement Strategy", ITLA. Guest Lecturer, "Evidence in Wrongful Death Actions," Grand Rounds Legal Issue, St. Francis Hospital; Grand Rounds Legal Issue, University of Chicago. Contributing Author: "The Governmental Tort Anomaly," ISBA Journal, Sept. 2002. Associate, Motherway & Glenn, P.C., Chicago, Illinois, 1983-1991. Formerly, Associate General Counsel, Michael Reese Hospital & Medical Center, Chicago, Illinois. Member and Legal Counsel, The Knapp Burn Foundation. President, The University of Chicago's Gastrointestinal Research Foundation (GIRF). Member, National Criminal Trial Advocacy, Illinois Leading Attorney's, 1998. Member, Million Dollar Advocate Forum. Commissioner, Village of Glencoe Baseball Association. *Member:* Chicago and Illinois State Bar Associations; Illinois Trial Lawyers Association; The Association of Trial Lawyers of America. ***PRACTICE AREAS:*** Medical Malpractice; Personal Injury; Federal Tort Claims. ***Email:*** michaelc@cogan-mcnabola.com

EDWARD W. McNABOLA, born Evanston, Illinois, June 10, 1966; admitted to bar, 1992, Illinois and U.S. District Court, Northern District of Illinois including Trial Bar. *Education:* Miami University (M.A., with honors, 1989); Loyola University (J.D., 1992; M.A., 1995). Pi Sigma Alpha; Order of Omega. Member: Chicago Inn of Court, 1993-1995; American Inn of Court, 1993-1995. Selected: by the Illinois Law Bulletin Publishing Company as one of the 40 Attorneys Under 40 To Watch in the State of Illinois; Circle of Advocates at Loyola University of Chicago School of Law, 1992. Elected to General Assembly, Illinois State Bar Association, 2001—. Author: "The Latest on Liens: An Illinois Tort Lawyers Guide," Illinois Bar Journal, March, 2002; "Tort Immunity: A Trial Lawyer's Guide," Illinois Bar Journal, June, 2003. Assistant to Author: Callahan's Appellate Advocacy Manual. Adjunct Professor: Trial Advocacy, Northwestern University School of Law, 2001—; Trial Techniques, Loyola University of Chicago School of Law, 1999—; National Institute of Trial Advocacy; Midwest Trial Techniques, 1994; Regional Trial Techniques, 1996, and Teacher Training Program, Harvard Law School, 1995. Professor, Civil Law, Chicago College of Commerce, 1993-1995. Guest Lecturer, Illinois Trial Lawyers Association, "Understanding Illinois Lien Law," and "Governmental Immunity Law." Member, Board of Directors, Metro Board, Metropolitan Family Services, 2000—. *Member:* Chicago Bar Association (Member, Tort Law, Moot Court and Medical-Legal Relations Committees) and American Bar Association; Illinois Trial Lawyers Association. ***PRACTICE AREAS:*** Personal Injury; Medical Negligence; Class Actions; Mass Torts; Aviation Law; Products Liability; Premises Liability; Professional Negligence. ***Email:*** ted@cogan-mcnabola.com

---

JAMES P. NAVARRE, born Toledo, Ohio; admitted to bar, 1993, Illinois and U.S. District Court, Northern District of Illinois. *Education:* University of Illinois (B.S., magna cum laude, 1990); Loyola University (J.D., cum laude, 1993). ***PRACTICE AREAS:*** Construction Law; Municipal; Products Liability; Professional Liability; Criminal Defense.

JOHN M. POWER, born Chicago, Illinois, February 14, 1962; admitted to bar, 1988, Illinois and U.S. District Court, Northern District of Illinois including Trial Bar. *Education:* Loyola University (B.B.A., cum laude, 1984; J.D., 1988). Beta Gamma Sigma; Alpha Sigma Nu. Member, National Mock Trial Competition Team, 1987. Guest Speaker, Medical Negligence, De Paul University School of Law. *Member:* Chicago and Illinois State Bar Associations; Illinois Trial Lawyers Association; Association of Trial Lawyers of America. ***PRACTICE AREAS:*** Medical Malpractice; Personal Injury; Wrongful Death; Professional Negligence; Products Liability; Premises Liability; Construction Accidents. ***Email:*** johnp@cogan-mcnabola.com

JODY B. PRAVECEK, born Boston, Massachusetts, September 15, 1970; admitted to bar, 1995, Illinois. *Education:* Lehigh University (B.A., 1992); The John Marshall Law School (J.D., 1995). Co-Author: "Informed Consent," Illinois Trial Lawyers Association Medical Malpractice Trial Notebook, 1996 Addendum; "Investigation and Pre-suit Preparation-Develop Your Theme," Illinois Trial Lawyers Association Seminar, February 17, 1997; "Economic Evidence," Illinois Trial Lawyers Association Evidence Seminar, 1999; "Damages and Its Impact on the Trial of a Premises Liability Case," ITLA Premises Liability Seminar, 2000. *Member:* Chicago, Illinois State and American Bar Associations; Women's Bar Association (Co-Chair, Torts Division, 2001); The Association of Trial Lawyers of America; Illinois Trial Lawyers Association. ***PRACTICE AREAS:*** Plaintiff's Personal Injury Litigation; Medical Negligence; Premises Liability; Professional Negligence; Construction Accidents; Vehicular Accident Law; Products Liability; Wrongful Death Law. ***Email:*** jody@cogan-mcnabola.com

ADRIA EAST MOSSING, born Arlington Heights, Illinois, June 6, 1961; admitted to bar, 1988, Illinois and U.S. District Court, Northern District of Illinois. *Education:* Northwestern University (B.A., 1983); DePaul University (J.D., 1988). Managing Editor, Notes and Comments, De Paul Law Review, 1987-1988. Named an Illinois Super Lawyer for 2005, representing the top 5% of practicing attorneys in Illinois and selected by peers. Adjunct Professor, DePaul University College of Law. Contributing Editor, IICLE "Pleadings," Chapter. *Member:* Illinois State and Chicago Bar Associations; Womens Bar Association. ***PRACTICE AREAS:*** Medical Malpractice; Personal Injury; Professional Negligence. ***Email:*** adria@cogan-mcnabola.com

PATTI L. TUTTLE, born Mendota, Illinois, February 10, 1949; admitted to bar, 1993, Illinois; 1994, U.S. District Court, Northern District of Illinois. *Education:* Northwestern University (B.A., Spanish, 1971); Wesley Passavant School of Nursing (R.N., 1975); Loyola University (J.D., 1993). Recipient, American Jurisprudence Award, Professional Responsibility. *Member:* Illinois State Bar Association; Women's Bar Association. ***PRACTICE AREAS:*** Medical Malpractice; Personal Injury; Products Liability. ***Email:*** ptuttle@coganmcnabola.com

OF COUNSEL

THOMAS R. CANHAM, born Jacksonville, Illinois, April 29, 1958; admitted to bar, 1983, Arizona; 1992, Nevada; 1995, U.S. Supreme Court (Not admitted in Illinois). *Education:* University of Michigan (B.A., with honors, 1980); DePaul University (J.D., 1983). Phi Alpha Delta; Sigma Nu. Mortar Board. Editor-in-Chief, De Paul Law Review, 1982-1983. Arbitrator, National Futures Association, Chicago. 1985—. *Member:* State Bar of Arizona; State Bar of Nevada; The Association of Trial Lawyers of America. ***PRACTICE AREAS:*** General Commercial; Construction; Real Property; Business Tort Litigation.

DEBORAH BLEICH COGAN, born Philadelphia, Pennsylvania, March 25, 1957; admitted to bar, 1985, New York; 1986, Illinois. *Education:* Yale University (B.A., 1979);

(This Listing Continued)

University of Virginia (J.D., 1984). J. Hardy Dillard Fellow. Author: "Hellerstein & Bleich, When Clients Are in Conflict," Nat. L.J., April, 1985. The Office of the General Counsel, Chicago Board of Options Exchange, Chicago, Illinois, 1990-1993. Associate, Hopkins & Sutter, Chicago, Illinois, 1987-1989. *Member:* Chicago Bar Association. ***PRACTICE AREAS:*** Medical Malpractice; Personal Injury; Products Liability.

COGHLAN KUKANKOS COOK LLC

Established in 1929

55 WEST WACKER DRIVE, SUITE 1210
CHICAGO, ILLINOIS 60601-1612
Telephone: 312-357-9200
Fax: 312-357-0961

Civil Trial and Appellate Practice in State and Federal Courts. Administrative Law and Procedure, ERISA Compliance and Litigation; Pension, Labor, Employment, Commercial Litigation, Trade Secrets, Antitrust, Health Care, Employee Benefit Plan Design and Subrogation, Real Estate and Corporate.

MEMBERS OF FIRM

JOHN P. COGHLAN (1903-1968)

JAMES L. COGHLAN, born Chicago, Illinois, June 3, 1932; admitted to bar, 1955, Illinois. *Education:* Georgetown University; DePaul University (LL.B., 1955). Member: Illinois Supreme Court Committee on Civil Jury Instructions, 1973-1979; Illinois Supreme Court Committee on Arbitration, 1985-1987; Attorney Registration and Disciplinary Commission, 1984-1995; Inquiry Board, 1984-1986; Hearing Board, 1986-1988; Review Board, 1988-1995; Chairman, Review Board, 1990-1995. *Member:* Chicago, Illinois State (Member, House of Delegates, 1974-1980) and American Bar Associations; American Board of Trial Advocates. ***PRACTICE AREAS:*** Civil Trials and Appeals; ERISA; Employee Benefits. **Email:** JLC@CKC-Law.com

JOHN A. KUKANKOS, born Holyoke, Massachusetts, September 21, 1946; admitted to bar, 1974, Illinois. *Education:* University of Notre Dame (B.A., with honors, 1968); Northwestern University (J.D., 1974). Co-Author, "Estoppel by Verdict, the Multidistrict Litigation Act, and Constitutional Rights of Litigants—Can They Co-Exist?" 20 Trial Lawyers Guide 279, 1976. *Member:* Chicago and Illinois State Bar Associations. ***LANGUAGES:*** Spanish. ***PRACTICE AREAS:*** ERISA; Corporate Law; Real Estate; Employee Benefits; Civil Trials and Appeals. **Email:** JAK@CKC-Law.com

BARBARA J. COGHLAN, born Chicago, Illinois, November 2, 1961; admitted to bar, 1988, Illinois and U.S. District Court, Northern District of Illinois. *Education:* University of Illinois (B.A., 1983); DePaul University (J.D., 1986). *Member:* Chicago, Illinois State and American Bar Associations. ***PRACTICE AREAS:*** ERISA; Employee Benefits; Civil Trials and Appeals. **Email:** BJC@CKC-Law.com

ELIZABETH A. LONGO, born Detroit, Michigan, June 26, 1965; admitted to bar, 1991, Illinois and U.S. District Court, Northern District of Illinois. *Education:* Loyola University (B.B.A., 1987); DePaul University (M.B.A., J.D., 1990). *Member:* Chicago, Illinois State and American Bar Associations. ***PRACTICE AREAS:*** Civil Trials and Appeals; ERISA; Employee Benefits. **Email:** EAL@CKC-Law.com

FRANCIS E. STEPNOWSKI, born Chicago, Illinois, October 27, 1959; admitted to bar, 1984, Illinois, U.S. District Court, Northern District of Illinois, U.S. District Court, Eastern District of Michigan and U.S. Supreme Court. *Education:* University of Dallas (B.A., 1981); Northwestern University (J.D., 1984). Author, "Less Than Perfected: Uncertainty in Illinois Judgment Lien Law," 13 N. Ill. U.L.R. 33 (1993). ***PRACTICE AREAS:*** Civil Trials and Appeals; ERISA; Employee Benefits; Insurance; Bankruptcy. **Email:** FES@CKC-Law.com

SUSAN H. COGHLAN, born Chicago, Illinois, December 9, 1968; admitted to bar, 1993, Illinois; 1994, U.S. District Court, Northern District of Illinois. *Education:* University of Illinois (B.S., 1990); DePaul University (J.D., 1993). *Member:* Chicago, Illinois State and American Bar Associations. ***PRACTICE AREAS:*** ERISA; Employee Benefits; Personal Injury; Civil Trials and Appeals. **Email:** SHC@CKC-Law.com

MARK J. COGHLAN, born Chicago, Illinois, September 3, 1957; admitted to bar, 1984, Illinois and U.S. District Court, Northern District of Illinois. *Education:* University of Illinois (B.A., with honors, 1981); DePaul University (J.D., 1984). *Member:* Chicago, Illinois State and American Bar Associations. ***PRACTICE AREAS:*** Civil Trials and Appeals; ERISA; Employee Benefits; Corporate Law. **Email:** MJC@CKC-Law.com

CATHERINE C. COOK, born Chicago, Illinois, January 25, 1934; admitted to bar, 1974, Maryland; 1975, District of Columbia; 1991, Illinois. *Education:* Loyola University (B.A., with highest honors, 1954; M.A., 1960); George Washington University (J.D., with honors, 1974); Georgetown University (LL.M., 1975). Trial Attorney, U.S. Consumer Product Safety Commission, 1975-1983. Assistant and Deputy General Counsel for Litigation, U.S. Dept. of Energy, 1983-1986. General and Special Counsel, Federal Energy Regulatory Commission, 1986-1991. General Counsel, U.S. Railroad Retirement Board, 1991-1998. Member, Illinois Supreme Court Committee on Character and Fitness, 1999-2000. *Member:* Illinois State Bar Association; The District of Columbia Bar. ***PRACTICE AREAS:*** Civil Trials and Appeals; ERISA; Administrative Law. **Email:** CCC@CKC-Law.com

MICHAEL A. BRESSLER, II, born Fort Collins, Colorado, August 19, 1973; admitted to bar, 2003, Illinois and U.S. District Court, Northern District of Illinois. *Education:* University of Texas-El Paso (B.B.A., Economics, 1998); University of Denver (J.D., 2001). *Member:* Chicago, Illinois State and American Bar Associations. ***LANGUAGES:*** Spanish. ***PRACTICE AREAS:*** Civil Litigation; Personal Injury; ERISA; Employee Benefits. **Email:** MAB@CKC-Law.com

---

KRISTINE A. MUELLER, born Moline, Illinois, April 16, 1977; admitted to bar, 2004, Illinois. *Education:* Illinois State University (B.S., 1999); DePaul University (J.D., 2004). Member, De Paul Journal of Sports Law & Contemporary Practices Vol. 2 No 1, Spring 2004. *Member:* Chicago, Illinois State and American Bar Associations. ***PRACTICE AREAS:*** Subrogation; ERISA. **Email:** KAM@CKC-Law.com

REFERENCE: JPMorgan Chase Bank, N.A.

NEIL H. COHEN

2000 NORTH CLIFTON AVENUE
CHICAGO, ILLINOIS 60614
Telephone: 773-871-4814
24 hours Telephone: 312-246-1734
Fax: 773-871-3304
Email: slim2@prodigy.net
URL: http://www.lawyers.com/neilcohenlaw

State and Federal Criminal and Civil Trial Practice. White Collar Crime, Capital Litigation, Homicide, Felonies, Driving While Intoxicated, Traffic Violations, Misdemeanors, Criminal Appeals, RICO Defense and Commercial Law.

NEIL H. COHEN, born Chicago, Illinois, June 16, 1950; admitted to bar, 1976, Florida, Illinois and U.S. District Court, Northern District of Illinois including Trial Bar; 1981, U.S. Supreme Court and U.S. Court of Appeals, Seventh Circuit. *Education:* American University (B.A., 1972); University of Miami (J.D., 1975). Phi Delta Phi. Member, Bar and Gavel. Adjunct Professor, Kent School of Law, Clinical Program, 1984-1989. Senior Associate, Lord, Bissell & Brook, 1987-1990. States Attorney, Cook County: Deputy Supervisor, Narcotics Division, 1984-1987; Trial Assistant, Felony Division, 1978-1987. *Member:* Chicago, Northwest Suburban, Illinois State and Federal Bar Associations; Illinois Criminal Justice Authority.

COHEN, MILSTEIN, HAUSFELD & TOLL, P.L.L.C.

39 SOUTH LASALLE STREET, SUITE 308
CHICAGO, ILLINOIS 60603
Telephone: 312-357-0370
Fax: 312-357-0369
URL: http://www.cmht.com

Washington, D.C. Office: 1100 New York Avenue, N.W., Suite 500 West, 20005-3964. Telephone: 202-408-4600. Facsimile: 202-408-4699. Email: lawinfo@cmht.com. URL: http: //www.cmht.com.
New York, New York Office: 150 East 52nd Street, 30th Floor, 10019-6004. Telephone: 212-838-7797. Fax: 212-838-7745.
Philadelphia, Pennsylvania Office: One South Broad Street, Suite 1850, 19107. Telephone: 215-825-4010. Fax: 215-825-4001.

General Civil Trial and Appellate Practice in State and Federal Courts. Antitrust and Unfair Trade Practices, Securities, Civil Rights and Employment Law, Consumer Product Liability, Franchising, Mass Torts, and Toxic Tort Litigation. Complex, Multi-District and Class Action Litigation.

FIRM PROFILE: The firm is one of a handful of firms in the United States litigating plaintiffs' class actions as a regular part of its business, with a specialty in antitrust, securities, civil rights and employment law, environmental toxic tort, consumer and product liability cases. The firm has been involved in many of the major complex class action cases litigated in the United States and has a national reputation in this area. Members of the firm have concluded numerous securities and antitrust class actions in which they have played a principal or lead role or served on the Executive Committee of plaintiffs' counsel.

(For Complete Biographical Data on all personnel, See Professional Biographies at Washington, D.C.)

COHON RAIZES & REGAL LLP

SUITE 1860, 208 SOUTH LA SALLE STREET
CHICAGO, ILLINOIS 60604
Telephone: 312-726-2252
Telecopier: 312-726-0609
URL: http://www.lawyers.com/cohonraizes
Email: crrlaw@CohonRaizes.com
URL: http://www.CohonRaizes.com

General Civil and Trial Practice in all State and Federal Courts. Corporation, Bankruptcy, Creditors Rights, Secured Transactions, Antitrust, Probate, Estate Planning, Wills and Trusts, Real Estate, Health Care, Employee Benefits, Family Law, Divorce, Federal Tax and Appellate Practice.

MEMBERS OF FIRM

JACK A. COHON (1905-1981)

GERALD D. CHISS (1941-1990)

MAURICE P. RAIZES, born Newton, Iowa, October 3, 1929; admitted to bar, 1953, Illinois; 1954, U.S. Court of Military Appeals; 1957, U.S. Tax Court; 1969, U.S. Supreme Court. *Education:* University of Illinois (B.S., 1951; J.D., 1953). President, Board of Visitors, University of Illinois, 1981. Faculty Member, Illinois Institute for Continuing Legal Education, 1975-1980. *Member:* Chicago (Chairman, Federal Civil Procedure Committee, 1974), 7th Circuit, Illinois State (Delegate, General Assembly, 1978-1984), Federal and American Bar Associations; Decalogue Society of Lawyers; Appellate Lawyers Association (Director, 1979-1981, 1987-1989). **Email:** MRaizes@CohonRaizes.com

HARRY S. WOLIN, born Chicago, Illinois, March 19, 1933; admitted to bar, 1959, Illinois. *Education:* Michigan State University (B.A., 1953); Northwestern University (J.D., 1956). Member, Preservation Commission, Evanston, Illinois, 1983-1989. *Member:* Chicago and Illinois State Bar Associations.

(This Listing Continued)

COHON RAIZES & REGAL LLP, Chicago—Continued

JEFFREY M. BRICKMAN, born Chicago, Illinois, April 29, 1951; admitted to bar, 1976, Illinois and U.S. District Court, Northern District of Illinois; 1981, U.S. Tax Court; 1982, U.S. Court of Appeals, Seventh Circuit. *Education:* University of Illinois (B.A., with honors, 1973); DePaul University School of Law (J.D., 1976). Phi Beta Kappa. Editorial Associate, De Paul Law Review, 1975-1976. *Member:* Chicago, Illinois State and American Bar Associations. ***Email:*** JBrickman@CohonRaizes.com

BRUCE J. WALDMAN, born Chicago, Illinois, October 19, 1952; admitted to bar, 1977, Illinois; 1978, U.S. District Court, Northern District of Illinois and U.S. Court of Appeals, 7th Circuit; 1981, U.S. Tax Court. *Education:* University of Iowa (B.S., 1974); University of Illinois (J.D., 1977). Phi Beta Kappa. *Member:* Chicago and Illinois State Bar Associations. ***Email:*** BWaldman@CohonRaizes.com

CORNELIUS P. BROWN, born Evanston, Illinois, March 5, 1953; admitted to bar, 1978, Illinois, U.S. District Court, Northern District of Illinois and U.S. Court of Appeals, 7th Circuit; 1986, U.S. Supreme Court. *Education:* University of Notre Dame (A.B., 1975); DePaul University (J.D., 1978). *Member:* Chicago and Illinois State Bar Associations. ***Email:*** NBrown@CohonRaizes.com

ANDREA S. BRYER, born Chicago, Illinois, October 2, 1950; admitted to bar, 1979, Illinois. *Education:* Indiana University and University of Illinois (B.A., with Honors, 1972); De Paul University (J.D., 1979). *Member:* Chicago (Member, Committees on: Estate Planning; Hospital and Health Care Law; Employee Benefits, 1984—) and Illinois State Bar Associations. ***Email:*** ABryer@CohonRaizes.com

J. MICHAEL WILLIAMS, born Detroit, Michigan; admitted to bar, 1986, Illinois and U.S. District Court, Northern District of Illinois. *Education:* Arizona State University (B.A., 1973; M.A., 1978); University of Chicago (M.A., 1983; J.D., 1986). *Member:* Chicago (Chair, Civil Practice Committee, 1997-1998) and American Bar Associations. ***PRACTICE AREAS:*** Business Litigation; ERISA; Litigation; Employee Benefit Plans; Bankruptcy Litigation. ***Email:*** MWilliams@CohonRaizes.com

CARRIE A. DOLAN, born Evanston, Illinois, August 5, 1969; admitted to bar, 1994, Illinois and U.S. District Court, Northern District of Illinois. *Education:* University of Wisconsin at Madison (B.S., 1991); DePaul University (J.D., 1994). Recipient, The Samuel & Dorothy Sweig Award for Excellence in Legal Writing, 1991. Public Interest Law Association, Vice President, DePaul Chapter, 1991-1992. *Member:* Illinois State and American Bar Associations; Women's Bar Association. ***Email:*** CDolan@CohonRaizes.com

---

CHERYL A. PERRY, born Olympia Fields, Illinois, July 3, 1979; admitted to bar, 2004, Illinois and Wisconsin; U.S. District Court, Eastern District of Wisconsin; 2005, U.S. District Court, Northern District of Illinois. *Education:* Marquette University (B.A., with honors, 2001); Marquette University Law School (J.D., 2004). *Member:* Chicago, Illinois State and American Bar Associations; State Bar of Wisconsin. ***Email:*** cperry@cohonraizes.com

ROBERT F. COLEMAN & ASSOCIATES

Established in 1984

77 WEST WACKER DRIVE
SUITE 4800
CHICAGO, ILLINOIS 60601
Telephone: 312-444-1000
Telecopier: 312-444-1028
Email: rcoleman@colemanlawfirm.com
URL: http://www.colemanlawfirm.com

Complex Business Litigation and Appellate Practice in all Courts. Legal Malpractice, Class Actions, Commercial, Labor and Employment, Intellectual Property, Professional Liability, Civil Rights, Antitrust and Insurance Law.

PRINCIPAL

ROBERT F. COLEMAN, born Chicago, Illinois, December 14, 1944; admitted to bar, 1969, Illinois; 1971, U.S. Court of Appeals, Ninth Circuit; 1974, U.S. Court of Appeals, Seventh Circuit; 1977, U.S. Supreme Court; 1979, U.S. Court of Appeals, Sixth Circuit; 1994, U.S. Court of Appeals, Eighth Circuit. *Education:* DePaul University (B.S., 1966; J.D., 1969). Phi Alpha Delta. Assistant Attorney General, Antitrust Division, State of Illinois, 1969-1974. Assistant Chief, Antitrust Division, Office of the Illinois Attorney General, 1973-1974. *Member:* Chicago (Member: Antitrust and Trade Regulations Committee, 1969—; Civil Practice Committee, 1976—; Federal Laws of Civil Procedure Committee, 1976—) and American (Member, Sections of: Antitrust Law; Economics of Law Practice) Bar Associations; Illinois Trial Lawyers Association; The Association of Trial Lawyers of America; American Inns of Court. ***PRACTICE AREAS:*** Complex Litigation; Legal Malpractice; Accountants Malpractice; Professional Liability; Bankruptcy Litigation; Trial Practice; Insurance Litigation; Civil Appeals.

ASSOCIATES

KENNETH P. ROSS, born Chicago, Illinois, August 16, 1951; admitted to bar, 1977, Illinois, U.S. District Court, Northern District of Illinois including Trial Bar and U.S. Court of Appeals, Seventh Circuit; 1982, U. S. Supreme Court; 1983, U.S. Court of Appeals, Eleventh Circuit; 1985, U.S. Tax Court; 1994, U.S. Court of Appeals, Eighth Circuit. *Education:* University of Wisconsin-Madison (B.A., cum laude, 1973); Northeastern University (J.D., 1977). Author: "Constitutional Challenges to the Massachusetts Sexually Dangerous Persons Act," *4 New England Law Review 253,* 1978: "Multistate Consumer Class Actions in Illinois," 57 Chicago Kent Law Review 397, 1981. Adjunct Professor of Law, Chicago-Kent College of Law, 1979-1983. Instructor, Columbia College, 1995—. Law Clerk to Hon. Abraham L. Marovitz, United States District Court, Northern District of Illinois, 1977-1979. *Member:* Chicago Bar Association; Decalogue Society of Lawyers. ***PRACTICE AREAS:*** Trial Practice; Civil Appeals; Labor and Employment law; Civil Rights; Intellectual Property. ***Email:*** kross@colemanlawfirm.com

EUGENE J. SCHILTZ, born Chicago, Illinois, August 7, 1956; admitted to bar, 1981, Illinois and U.S. District Court, Northern District of Illinois; 1982, U.S. Court of Appeals, Seventh Circuit; 1987, U.S. Supreme Court; 1994, U.S. Court of Appeals, Eighth Circuit. *Education:* Illinois State University (B.S., with high honors, 1977); University of Chicago (J.D., 1981). Adjunct Instructor, The John Marshall Law School, 1988—. Arbitrator, Circuit Court, Cook County Illinois Mandatory Arbitration Program (1990—). *Member:* Chicago, Illinois State and American Bar Associations. ***PRACTICE AREAS:*** Complex Litigation; Legal Malpractice; Accountants Malpractice; Class Actions; Civil Appeals; Trial Practice. ***Email:*** eschiltz@colemanlawfirm.com

JERRY S. MENGE, born Chicago, Illinois, October 11, 1959; admitted to bar, 1986, Illinois and U.S. District Court, Northern District of Illinois; 1987, U.S. Court of Appeals, Seventh Circuit. *Education:* DePaul University (B.A., with honors, 1983); Illinois Institute of Technology/Chicago-Kent College of Law (J.D., with honors, 1986). Member: Mundelein, Illinois Plan Commission, 1990-1992; Libertyville, Illinois Zoning Board and Plan Commission, 1998-2000. *Member:* Chicago, Illinois State and American Bar Associations. ***PRACTICE AREAS:*** Legal Malpractice; Business Litigation; Complex Litigation; Class Actions. ***Email:*** jmenge@colemanlawfirm.com

SEAN B. CROTTY, born Chicago, Illinois, September 27, 1972; admitted to bar, 1997, Illinois, U.S. District Court, Northern District of Illinois and U.S. Court of Appeals, Seventh Circuit. *Education:* Indiana University (B.A., 1994); DePaul University (J.D., 1997). *Member:* Chicago (Member, Civil Practice Committee; Young Lawyers Section), Illinois State and American (Member, Litigation Section) Bar Associations; The Association of Trial Lawyers of America (Member, Commercial Litigation Section). ***PRACTICE AREAS:*** Legal Malpractice; Business Litigation; Complex Litigation. ***Email:*** scrotty@colemanlawfirm.com

CASSANDRA A. CROTTY, born Chicago, Illinois, September 6, 1972; admitted to bar, 1998, Illinois and U.S. District Court, Northern District of Illinois. *Education:* Indiana University (B.A.J., 1994); DePaul University (J.D., 1998). *Member:* Chicago, Illinois State and American Bar Associations; The Association of Trial Lawyers of America; The Women's Bar Association. ***PRACTICE AREAS:*** Legal Malpractice; Business Litigation; Civil Litigation. ***Email:*** ccrotty@colemanlawfirm.com

ELIZABETH E. RICHERT, born Claremont, California, June 28, 1976; admitted to bar, 2001, Illinois and U.S. District Court, Northern District of Illinois. *Education:* Wheaton College (B.A., 1998); Duke University (J.D., 2001). *Member:* Chicago, Illinois State and American Bar Associations; American Bankruptcy Institute. ***PRACTICE AREAS:*** Bankruptcy; Legal Malpractice; Business Litigation; Civil Litigation. ***Email:*** erichert@colemanlawfirm.com

RYAN S. ZELLER, born Kalamazoo, Michigan, July 14, 1977; admitted to bar, 2004, Illinois and U.S. District Court, Northern District of Illinois. *Education:* Indiana University, Bloomington (B.A., 1999); DePaul University College of Law, Kellstadt Graduate School of Business (J.D. / M.B.A., 2003). *Member:* Chicago, Illinois State and American Bar Associations. ***PRACTICE AREAS:*** Bankruptcy; Legal Malpractice; Business Litigation; Civil Litigation. ***Email:*** rzeller@colemanlawfirm.com

OF COUNSEL

STEVEN R. JAKUBOWSKI, born Syracuse, New York, October 27, 1957; admitted to bar, 1985, Illinois. *Education:* Union College (B.S., 1980); University of Chicago Law School (J.D., 1985). Co-Author, with John William Butler, Jr. and Kelly A. Chesney: "Standards for Awarding Attorney's Fees Under Section 506(c) to Secured Creditors," *Norton Annual Review of Bankruptcy,* 1991. Chairman and Chief Executive Officer, Commonwealth Snack Company, Inc., State Line Snacks Corporation, Boyd Acquisition Corporation, Lynn, Massachusetts, 1996-1997. Chief Operating Officer and Director, Magic Restaurants, Inc., Yonkers, New York, 1995-1996. Associate Attorney, Bankruptcy and Reorganization Group: Skadden, Arps, Slate, Meagher & Flom, Chicago, Illinois, 1989-1992; Kirkland & Ellis, Chicago, Illinois, 1986-1989. Principal, Lindner-Jakubowski Films, Inc., Washington, D.C., 1985-1986. (Also Practicing Individually). ***PRACTICE AREAS:*** Bankruptcy. ***Email:*** sjakubowski@colemanlaw.com

COLKY & KIRSH, LTD.

1 NORTH LA SALLE STREET, SUITE 3100
CHICAGO, ILLINOIS 60602
Telephone: 312-558-9700
Fax: 312-558-9899
Email: scolky@colkyandkirsh.com
URL: http://www.colkyandkirsh.com

Family Law, Child Custody, Divorce, Post Divorce Litigation, Adoptions, Postnuptial Agreements, Paternity, Surrogacy, Premarital Agreements, Grandparents Rights and Litigation.

FIRM PROFILE: Scott C. Colky and Matthew A. Kirsh have a combined 40 years of trial experience with a significant amount of that time having been devoted to divorce, child custody disputes, adoptions and obtaining custody for grandparents. Mr. Colky is well known for his presentation and cross-examination of psychological and psychiatric witnesses. He has recently handled a high profile contested adoption case that received national media attention.

Colky & Kirsh believes in minimizing the trauma of divorce and works effectively with mental health professionals who respect this philosophy. Mr. Kirsh is frequently appointed by judges to represent children because of his ability to protect the best interests of children.

SCOTT C. COLKY, born Chicago, Illinois, December 15, 1952; admitted to bar, 1977, Illinois; 1994, Montana. *Education:* University of Illinois (B.A., 1974); Loyola University (J.D., 1977). Publications: "Priveleged Communication Under The Mental Health and Developmental Disabilities Confidentiality Act and Family Law Issue, ISBA Family Law Newsletter, December 2003; "The Child Representative Statute is Unconstitutional, ISBA

(This Listing Continued)

Family Law Newsletter, December 2002; ISBA Family Law Newsletter Restricting Visitation, "What Evidence is Sufficient," May 1998; ISBA Family Law, "Modification of Custody Within Two Years after Davis," published by Illinois State Bar Association, March 1999; "The Forgotten Writ," ISBA Family Law Newsletter, January 2000; "Problems In The Enrollment of Foreign Judgment," ISBA Family Law Newsletter, May 2001. Presentations: "Illinois Child Custody Act is Unconstitutional," Loyola School of Law, October 2003 and December 2003. Custody Tidbits, ISBA Mid Year Meeting, 6/2002; I.C.L.E. (I.S.B.A. Mid Year Meeting) Supervised and Restricted Visitation in Illinois, the Role of Forensic Experts in Child Custody Dispute, Illinois Council of Child and Adolescent Psychiatrists, A.F.C.C. National Conference, the Role of the Pro-Active Guardian ad Litem, 1993, A.F.C.C. National Conference, 1996; Third Party Standing in Custody Cases; Evanston Northwestern Hospital, Divorce - The Role of the Psychologist and Psychiatrist, An Attorney Perspective; I.C.L.E. (Family Law Update, 1999), Pre and Post-Nuptial Agreements and Drafting Tips; "Child Custody and Time Sharing in Illinois," National Business Institute, March 2000. Faculty Member, Trial Practice Court, Loyola University School of Law, Trial Seminar Practice Civitas (Child Law Center Loyola) Faculty 1995, 1996. *Member:* Illinois State (Counsel, 1997—, Vice Chairman, 2005, Family Law Section) and Montana State Bar Associations. Fellow, American Academy of Matrimonial Lawyers (Member, Board of Managers, Illinois Chapter). ***PRACTICE AREAS:*** Family Law; Child Custody; Divorce; Postnuptial Agreements; Paternity; Surrogacy; Premarital Agreements; Litigation; Mediation. ***Email:*** scolky@colkyandkirsh.com

MATTHEW A. KIRSH, born Chicago, Illinois, March 18, 1964; admitted to bar, 1989, Illinois. *Education:* University of Illinois (B.A., 1986; J.D., 1989). Author: "The Use of the Fifth Amendment Privilege Against Self Incrimination in Domestic Relations Cases," ISBA Family Law Newsletter, 2000. Presenter, Chicago Bar Association, Young Lawyers Section Family Law Committee Seminar, 1996. Adjunct Professor, Legal Drafting for Family Law, De Paul College of Law. Moderator, Cook County, Illinois Continuing Legal Education for Children's Representative, Drug and Alcohol Addiction and Its Effects on Families, 2000. *Member:* Chicago (Member, Matrimonial Law Committee) and Illinois State (Member, Family Law Section) Bar Associations. Fellow, American Academy of Matrimonial Lawyers (Associate Member, Family Law Section Counsel, 1999-2000). ***PRACTICE AREAS:*** Family Law; Divorce; Child Custody; Premarital Agreements; Postnuptial Agreements; Litigation. ***Email:*** mkirsh@colkyandkirsh.com

Joshua J. Beyer
Jennifer M. Byrd
Alison G. Turoff
Amy M. Kesselring

COLLINS & BARGIONE

Established in 1957

ONE NORTH LASALLE STREET
SUITE 2235
CHICAGO, ILLINOIS 60602
Telephone: 312-372-7813
Fax: 312-372-7840
Email: email@cb-law.com

General Trial and Appellate Practice in all State and Federal Courts. Corporate, Criminal and Civil RICO, Criminal, Professional Discipline, Securities, Probate, Medical Malpractice, Banking Law and Federal Practice.

MEMBERS OF FIRM

GEORGE B. COLLINS, born Kansas City, Missouri, April 23, 1931; admitted to bar, 1953, Arkansas; 1955, Illinois; 1970, U.S. Tax Court; 1972, U.S. Supreme Court; 1982, U.S. District Court, Northern District of Illinois, Trial Bar; U.S. District Court, Eastern District of Arkansas; U.S. District Court, Eastern District of Wisconsin; U.S. Court of Appeals, Second, Seventh, Eighth and Ninth Circuits. *Education:* Arkansas A. & M. College (B.S., 1952); University of Arkansas (LL.B., 1954). Omicron Delta Kappa. Associate Editor, Arkansas Law Review, 1951-1952. Author: "Usury," 8 Arkansas Law Review, September, 1954. Teaching Associate, Northwestern University School of Law, 1954-1955. Co-Author: "Defending White Collar Crimes," Practicing Law Institute, 1976; "White Collar Crimes: Defense Strategies," Practicing Law Institute, 1977; "White Collar Crimes," Practicing Law Institute, 1978; "White Collar Crimes," Practicing Law Institute, 1980. *Member:* Chicago (Member, 1955-1978, Vice Chairman, 1967 and Chairman, 1968, Committee on Legal Education; Member, Committee on Professional Fees, 1966—; Vice Chairman, 1973; 1974-1975; Chairman, 1975, Member, Committees on: Environmental Law, 1973; Circuit Court Operations, 1976—; Member, 1976-1986, Vice Chairman, 1979-1980; 1981— and Chairman, 1980-1981, Lawyers Referral Plan Committee), Illinois State, Arkansas and American Bar Associations; Association of Professional Responsibility Lawyers. ***PRACTICE AREAS:*** Attorney Discipline; Legal Malpractice; Civil Litigation; Criminal Litigation.

CHRISTOPHER BARGIONE, born Franklin Square, New York, July 12, 1958; admitted to bar, 1983, Illinois; 1985, U.S. District Court, Northern District of Illinois; 1990, U.S. Court of Appeals, Seventh Circuit. *Education:* St. John's University (B.A., 1980); John Marshall Law School (J.D., summa cum laude, 1983). *Member:* Chicago and Illinois State Bar Associations. ***PRACTICE AREAS:*** Probate; General Litigation; Real Estate; Discrimination; Medical Malpractice; Products Liability; Commercial Litigation.

ADRIAN M. VUCKOVICH, born Chicago, Illinois, April 3, 1965; admitted to bar, 1991, Illinois and U.S. District Court, Northern District of Illinois; 1993, U.S. Court of Appeals, Seventh Circuit. *Education:* University of Wisconsin at Madison (B.A., with distinction, History and International Relations, 1987); Loyola University (J.D., 1991). Recipient, Best Petitioner's Brief Award. Niagara Moot Court Team, 1990. Judicial Conference Symposium Editor, Loyola Law Journal, 1990-1991. Author: "Diminskis v. CTA: Circumventing Expert Witness Discovery," Vol. 21:3 Loyola Law Journal. *Member:* Chicago and Illinois State Bar Associations. ***PRACTICE AREAS:*** Litigation.

(This Listing Continued)

ASSOCIATE

JAMES J. LESSMEISTER, born Chicago, Illinois, February 7, 1967; admitted to bar, 1994, Arkansas; 2002, Illinois. *Education:* Illinois State University (B.S., 1989); University of Arkansas at Little Rock (J.D., 1993). ***PRACTICE AREAS:*** Civil Litigation; Real Estate; Probate.

OF COUNSEL

THERESA GRONKIEWICZ, born Chicago, Illinois, May 9, 1956; admitted to bar, 1982, Illinois and U.S. District Court, Northern District of Illinois; 1986, U.S. Court of Appeals, 7th Circuit. *Education:* University of Illinois at Chicago (B.A., 1978); John Marshall Law School (J.D., 1982). Phi Alpha Delta. Former Senior Counsel, The Attorney Registration and Disciplinary Commission. *Member:* DuPage County, Chicago, Illinois State and American Bar Associations; Association of Professional Responsibility Lawyers. ***PRACTICE AREAS:*** Attorney Discipline/Professional Responsibility; Civil Litigation.

COUNSEL FOR: First National Bank of Lincolnwood; Chatham Corporation; Altair Corporation; Harvest Industries, Inc.; E & W Railroad Co.

CONNELLY ROBERTS & McGIVNEY LLC

ONE NORTH FRANKLIN STREET, SUITE 1200
CHICAGO, ILLINOIS 60606-3421
Telephone: 312-251-9600
Fax: 312-251-9601
Email: info@crmlaw.com
URL: http://www.crmlaw.com

Commercial Litigation, Corporate Transactions, Mergers and Acquisitions, Securities, Technology Law, Licensing, Intellectual Property, Commercial Real Estate, Healthcare, Antitrust, Professional Liability, Product Liability, Employment Disputes, Transportation, Rail and Aviation Law, Insurance and Reinsurance Disputes, Construction Defect Litigation, Copyright and Trademark Law, and Employment Litigation.

FIRM PROFILE: Connelly Roberts & McGivney LLC has attained Martindale-Hubbell's highest rating for legal ability and ethical standards.

MICHAEL P. CONNELLY, born Chicago, Illinois, March 16, 1941; admitted to bar, 1966, Illinois; U.S. District Courts, Northern and Central Districts of Illinois including Trial Bar, U.S. Court of Appeals, Seventh Circuit and U.S. Supreme Court. *Education:* Loyola University (B.S., 1963; J.D., 1966). Alpha Sigma Nu; Blue Key. Associate Editor, "Recent Decisions," Section, Illinois Bar Journal, 1965-1966. Board of Managers, Federal Bar Association, Northern District of Illinois, 1995-1996. *Member:* Chicago, Illinois State (Assembly Member, First Judicial District, 1982-1985; Committees: Council Member, Civil Practice and Procedure; Tort Law) and American (Member, Committees on Litigation and Aviation Law) Bar Associations; Trial Lawyers Club of Chicago (President, 1981-1982); Illinois Trial Lawyers Association (Member, Civil Practice Committee); The Association of Trial Lawyers of America; National Association of Railroad Trial Counsel. [Capt., USMC, 1966-1969]. ***PRACTICE AREAS:*** Commercial Litigation; Insurance; Reinsurance; Aviation; Products Liability; Professional Liability. ***Email:*** mconnelly@crmlaw.com

MICHAEL S. ROBERTS, born Chicago, Illinois, July 6, 1961; admitted to bar, 1987, Illinois. *Education:* Northern Illinois University (B.S., 1983); DePaul University (J.D., 1987). Member, De Paul Law Review, 1986-1987. Certified Public Accountant. ***PRACTICE AREAS:*** Mergers and Acquisitions; Corporate Law; Securities Law; Technology Law; Intellectual Property Law; Real Estate Law; International Outsourcing. ***Email:*** mroberts@crmlaw.com

CATHERINE McGIVNEY, born Chicago, Illinois, January 2, 1960; admitted to bar, 1986, New York; 1992, Illinois. *Education:* University of Illinois (B.A., 1981); New York University (J.D., 1985). Phi Kappa Phi. Recipient, American Judicature Society Award. Author: "Annual Survey of American Law," Labor Law, 1984; "United Kingdom: Regulation of Investigatory Powers Act 2000," BNA Corporate Counsel Weekly, December 2000. *Member:* Chicago and Illinois State Bar Associations. ***PRACTICE AREAS:*** Mergers and Acquisitions; Corporate Law; Securities Law; Technology Law; Intellectual Property Law; Business Law; Real Estate Law. ***Email:*** cmcgivney@crmlaw.com

MATTHEW PATRICK CONNELLY, born Oak Park, Illinois, July 15, 1970; admitted to bar, 1995, Illinois and U.S. District Court, Northern District of Illinois; 1996, U.S. Court of Appeals, Seventh Circuit and U.S. Court of Appeals for the Federal Circuit, U.S. District Court, Eastern District of Wisconsin. *Education:* Western Illinois University (B.S., 1992); John Marshall Law School (J.D., 1995). Named, One of the 40 Attorneys Under the Age of 40 to Watch in Illinois, Chicago Lawyer, 2004. *Member:* Chicago, Illinois State and American Bar Associations; Illinois Association of Defense Trial Counsel; Association of Trial Lawyers of America; Illinois Trial Lawyers Association; Chicago Trial Lawyers Association; The Missouri Bar. ***PRACTICE AREAS:*** Commercial Litigation; Coverage Disputes; Directors and Officers Liability; Railroad Liability; Contractor Liability; Professional Liability; Employment Disputes; Contract Litigation; Breach of Contract; Construction Law; Products Liability. ***Email:*** mpconnelly@crmlaw.com

THOMAS R. RAKOWSKI, born Chicago, Illinois, January 14, 1943; admitted to bar, 1970, Illinois and U.S. District Court, Northern District of Illinois. *Education:* DePaul University (B.S.C., 1967); John Marshall Law School (J.D., 1970). Member, Law Review. Assistant States Attorney, Cook County, Illinois, 1970-1972. Associate Judge, 1977-1980 and Circuit Judge, 1980-1989, Circuit Court of Cook County. Justice, Illinois Appellate Court, 1989-2000. Member and Alternate Member, Illinois Courts Commission, 1994-1998. Chairman, 1993, and Member, 1998-2000, Executive Committee, Illinois Appellate Court, First District. Member, Supreme Court Committee on Judicial Education, 1992-1993. *Member:* Chicago, Illinois State and American Bar Associations. ***PRACTICE AREAS:*** Appeals; Litigation; Alternative Dispute Resolution; General Practice. ***Email:*** TRakowski@crmlaw.com

TERRY M. SCHLADE, born Chicago, Illinois, March 15, 1942; admitted to bar, 1966, Illinois. *Education:* University of Illinois (B.S., Accounting; B.S., Economics, with high honors, 1963); Harvard University (LL.B., cum laude, 1966). Beta Gamma Sigma. Certi-

(This Listing Continued)

CONNELLY ROBERTS & McGIVNEY LLC, Chicago—Continued

fied Public Accountant, Illinois, 1963. Former Co-Franchise Editor, Hotel & Motel Management Magazine. Former Board Member, Not for Profit Corporation administering the Trade Adjustment and Assistance Act for U.S. Department of Commerce. *Member:* American, Chicago and Illinois State Bar Associations. ***PRACTICE AREAS:*** Commercial Transactions; Intellectual Property; Finance; Software and Technology Licensing; Franchise and Dealership Law; Corporate Law; Native American Transaction and Gaming Law. ***Email:*** tschlade@crmlaw.com

WILLIAM E. SNYDER, born Evanston, Illinois, November 3, 1944; admitted to bar, 1969, Illinois; 1973, U.S. Court of Appeals, Seventh Circuit; 1982, U.S. District Court, Northern District of Illinois including Trial Bar. *Education:* Northwestern University (B.S., 1966; J.D., cum laude, 1969). Articles Editor, Northwestern University Law Review, 1968-1969. Law Clerk to Judge Julius J. Hoffman, 1969-1971. *Member:* Chicago, Illinois State and American Bar Associations. ***PRACTICE AREAS:*** Antitrust; Securities; Intellectual Property; Complex Business Litigation. ***Email:*** wsnyder@crmlaw.com

RAYMOND E. STACHNIK, born Chicago, Illinois, September 17, 1949; admitted to bar, 1975, Illinois and U.S. District Court, Northern District of Illinois including Trial Bar; U.S. Supreme Court and U.S. Court of Appeals, Seventh and Tenth Circuits. *Education:* University of Montana (B.A., 1971); The John Marshall Law School (J.D., 1975). *Member:* Chicago, Seventh Circuit, Illinois State, Federal and American Bar Associations. ***PRACTICE AREAS:*** Complex Business Litigation; Trial Practice; Appellate Practice. ***Email:*** rstachnik@crmlaw.com

---

CORY D. ANDERSON, born Dell Rapids, South Dakota, December, 5 1974; admitted to bar, 2001, Illinois and U.S. District Court, Northern District of Illinois. *Education:* University of Wisconsin-LaCrosse (B.S., 1998); John Marshall Law School (J.D., 2001). *Member:* Chicago, Illinois State and American Bar Association. ***PRACTICE AREAS:*** Torts; Civil Litigation; Commercial Litigation; Products Liability; Toxic Torts; Professional Negligence. ***Email:*** canderson@crmlaw.com

STACIA A. BUECHLER, born Green Bay, Wisconsin, October 23, 1977; admitted to bar, 2002, Illinois and U.S. District Court, Northern District of Illinois. *Education:* Butler University (B.A., 1999); Chicago-Kent College of Law, Illinois Institute of Technology (J.D., 2002) Dean's List. Recipient: Richard A. Lewin Memorial Scholarship; CALI Award in Advanced Legal Drafting. *Member:* Chicago, Illinois State and American Bar Associations. ***PRACTICE AREAS:*** Corporate Law; Intellectual Property; Real Estate; Mergers and Acquisitions; Securities. ***Email:*** sbuechler@crmlaw.com

GARRETT C. CARTER, born Southfield, Michigan, January 9, 1978; admitted to bar, 2003, Illinois, U.S. District Court, Northern District of Illinois, U.S. District Court, Eastern District of Wisconsin. *Education:* Michigan State University (B.A., 2000); Loyola University (J.D., 2003). *Member:* Chicago and Illinois State Bar Associations. ***PRACTICE AREAS:*** Commercial Litigation; Business Litigation; Civil Litigation; Employment Law. ***Email:*** gcarter@rmlaw.com

JOHN D. FITZPATRICK, born East Lansing, Michigan, April 18, 1974; admitted to bar, 2002, Illinois; 2003, U.S. District Court, Northern District of Illinois. *Education:* Michigan State University (B.A., 1996); University of Texas at Austin (J.D., 2002). Author: "Advanced Employment Law: Review of Whistleblower Act," Texas Bar CLE Course Book (2002). *Member:* Chicago and Illinois State Bar Associations. ***PRACTICE AREAS:*** Commercial Litigation; Tort; Products Liability Law; Civil Litigation. ***Email:*** jfitzpatrick@crmlaw.com

SARA D. LUND, born Evergreen Park, Illinois, March 30, 1972; admitted to bar, 1998, Illinois; 1999, U.S. District Court, Northern District of Illinois. *Education:* University of Illinois, Urbana (B.A., 1994); John Marshall Law School (J.D., 1998). *Member:* Chicago and American Bar Associations. ***LANGUAGES:*** French. ***PRACTICE AREAS:*** Commercial Litigation; Business Law; Products Liability; Aviation Law. ***Email:*** slund@crmlaw.com

STEVEN J. SCOTT, born East Chicago, Indiana, June 3, 1974; admitted to bar, 1999, Illinois and U.S. District Court, Northern District of Illinois; 2001, Indiana. *Education:* Calvin College (B.A., 1996): Valparaiso University (J.D., 1999). ***PRACTICE AREAS:*** Commercial Litigation; Civil Litigation; Torts; Business Litigation; Toxic Torts. ***Email:*** sscott@crmlaw.com

OF COUNSEL

ROBERT M. CAPUA, born Evergreen Park, Illinois, November 15, 1962; admitted to bar, 1988, Illinois; 1989, U.S. District Court, Northern District of Illinois. *Education:* De Paul University (B.A., 1984; J.D., 1988). Teaching Assistant, De Paul University College of Law, 1985-1987. *Member:* Chicago, Illinois State and American Bar Associations. ***PRACTICE AREAS:*** Trademarks; Copyrights; Computer Law; Unfair Competition; Trade Secrets; Intellectual Property Law. ***Email:*** rcapua@crmlaw.com

---

CONNELLY SHEEHAN HARRIS

150 SOUTH WACKER DRIVE, SUITE 1600
CHICAGO, ILLINOIS 60606
Telephone: 312-372-1969
Fax: 312-372-1968
URL: http://www.csh-law.com

Labor and Employment Law. Litigation.

FIRM PROFILE: Connelly Sheehan Harris represents management exclusively in all types of labor and employment matters. We handle employment litigation and advise clients everywhere in the United States. We think with both sides of the brain. We get the New York Times crossword puzzle right. We draw cartoons as well as conclusions. We do our own dishes. We throw on first down. We quote Dylan as well as Darrow. We even have a philosophy: don't waste time or resources; approach each case or question creatively; and whenever possible, enjoy it.

(This Listing Continued)

PARTNERS

P. KEVIN CONNELLY, born Chicago, Illinois, April 29, 1950; admitted to bar, 1975, Illinois; 1978, U.S. Supreme Court. *Education:* Georgetown University (B.S.F.S., 1972); Loyola University (J.D., 1975). Adjunct Professor, Labor and Employment Law, Loyola University School of Law, 1977-1997; 2001—. *Member:* American Bar Association (Member, Sections of: Labor and Employment Law; Litigation). ***PRACTICE AREAS:*** Labor and Employment Law; Litigation. ***Email:*** kconnelly@csh-law.com

MICHAEL J. SHEEHAN, born Evanston, Illinois, April 12, 1959; admitted to bar, 1984, Ohio; 1987, Illinois. *Education:* Hillsdale College (B.A., cum laude, 1981); Wake Forest University (J.D., 1984). Omicron Delta Kappa. Member, Wake Forest Law Review, 1982-1984. Author: "Employment Discrimination-Good Faith As A Defense In Title VII Actions-Stoller v. Marsh," Wake Forest Law Review, Vol. 19, No. 2, April, 1983. Co-author: "Employment-At-Will Doctrine in Illinois: The Effect of Employee Handbooks," 76 Illinois B.J. 268 (1988). *Member:* Chicago, Illinois State and American (Member, Sections of: Labor and Employment Law; Litigation) Bar Associations. ***PRACTICE AREAS:*** Labor and Employment Law; Litigation. ***Email:*** msheehan@csh-law.com

MARTIN HARRIS, born Philadelphia, Pennsylvania, September 19, 1963; admitted to bar, 1987, Ohio; 1993, Illinois. *Education:* Princeton University (A.B., cum laude, 1984); University of Michigan (J.D., magna cum laude, 1987). Order of the Coif. Campbell Moot Court Champion, 1985-1986. Associate Editor, University of Michigan Law Review. ***PRACTICE AREAS:*** Labor and Employment Law; Litigation. ***Email:*** mharris@csh-law.com

RACHEL B. COWEN, born Chicago, Illinois; admitted to bar, 1993, Illinois. *Education:* Eastern Illinois University (B.A., 1990); Chicago-Kent College of Law (J.D., with high honors, 1993). Order of the Coif. Member, Chicago-Kent Law Review. ***PRACTICE AREAS:*** Labor and Employment Law; Litigation. ***Email:*** rcowen@csh-law.com

WILLIAM HENRY BARRETT, born Boston, Massachusetts, December 4, 1953; admitted to bar, 1980, Illinois and U.S. District Court for Northern District of Illinois; 1981, U.S. District Court, Central District of Illinois. *Education:* Harvard College (A.B., cum laude, 1975); Loyola University of Chicago (J. D., 1980). Formerly with: Michael Best & Friedrich, LLP. ***REPORTED CASES:*** Pruitt, et al. v. City of Chicago, 2004 WL 1146110; Marting v. Crawford & Co., 2004 WL 305724; McCabe v. Crawford & Co., 272 F. Supp. 2d 736; L&W Supply Co., Inc. v. Bryant (Appeal of Chicago Metallic Corp.), 1998 WL 904964; Selcke v.Bove, 258 Ill. App. 3d 932, 629 N.E.2d 747. ***PRACTICE AREAS:*** Commercial Litigation; Corporate Law; Employment Benefits Law; Business Piracy. ***Email:*** whbarrett@csh-law.com

ALLISON ZOUSMER STEIN, born New York, New York, April 21, 1965; admitted to bar, 1990, Illinois; 1991, Michigan. *Education:* University of Michigan (B.A., with high distinction, 1987; J.D., cum laude, 1990). Contributing Editor, Journal of International Law, University of Michigan. Author: "Comparison: Japanese and American Plant Closing Laws," Michigan Journal of International Law, Summer, 1989, Vol. 10, No. 3. Law Clerk to Judge Ryan, U.S. Court of Appeals, Sixth Circuit, 1990-1991. ***PRACTICE AREAS:*** Labor and Employment Law; Litigation. ***Email:*** astein@csh-law.com

ASSOCIATES

KRISTINE AUBIN, born Minneapolis, Minnesota, December 3, 1971; admitted to bar, 1997, Wisconsin, Illinois and U.S. District Court, Eastern and Western Districts of Wisconsin. *Education:* University of Wisconsin-Madison (B.A., 1994; J.D., 1997). Phi Alpha Delta. Member, Moot Court Board, 1995-1997. Member, International Law Journal, 1995-1996. *Member:* Chicago, Illinois State and American (Member, Labor and Employment Section, 1997—) Bar Associations; State Bar of Wisconsin. ***PRACTICE AREAS:*** Labor and Employment Law; Litigation. ***Email:*** kaubin@csh-law.com

HEATHER A. BAILEY, born Lakewood, Ohio, June 29, 1970; admitted to bar, 2001, Illinois and U.S. District Court, Northern District of Illinois. *Education:* Bowling Green State University (B.A., Communications, 1992); John Marshall Law School (J.D., 2001). *Member:* Chicago, Illinois State and American Bar Associations. ***PRACTICE AREAS:*** Labor and Employment Law; Litigation. ***Email:*** hbailey@csh-law.com

JOHN ANTON BERG, born Kansas City, Missouri, October 24, 1971; admitted to bar, 1998, Illinois and U.S. District Court, Northern District of Illinois. *Education:* Miami University of Ohio (B.A., 1994); Loyola University (J.D., cum laude, 1998). Author: "Venue, Federal Civil Practice," Iicle, 2000. *Member:* Chicago and American Bar Associations. ***PRACTICE AREAS:*** Labor and Employment Law; Litigation. ***Email:*** jberg@csh-law.com

JENNIFER L. CAMDEN, born Murphysboro, Illinois, May 7, 1976; admitted to bar, 2002, Illinois; 2003, U.S. District Court, Northern District of Illinois and U.S. Court of Appeals, Sixth and Seventh Circuits. *Education:* Southern Illinois University, Carbondale (B.S., 1999); University of Notre Dame (J.D., cum laude, 2002). Articles Editor, Notre Dame Law Review, 2001-2002. Law Clerk to Judge Carr, U.S. District Court, Northern District of Ohio. *Member:* Chicago, Illinois State and American Bar Association. ***PRACTICE AREAS:*** Labor and Employment; Litigation. ***Email:*** jennifercamden@earthlink.net

KEVIN V. DUNPHY, born Naperville, Illinois, August 22, 1965; admitted to bar, 1996, Illinois and U.S. District Court, Northern District of Illinois; 1997, U.S. Court of Appeals, Seventh Circuit; 2003, U.S. Court of Appeals, Eighth Circuit. *Education:* University of Illinois (B.A., 1987); Loyola University, Chicago (J.D., 1996). ***PRACTICE AREAS:*** Labor Law; Litigation. ***Email:*** kdunphy@csh-law.com

ZACHARY C. JACKSON, born Chicago, Illinois, April 20, 1979; admitted to bar, 2003, Illinois; 2003, U.S. District Court, Northern District of Illinois; 2004, U.S. District Court, Central and Southern Districts of Illinois. *Education:* Vanderbilt University (B.A., 2000); Washington University (J.D., 2003). Moot Court. Member, Washington University Global Studies Law Review, 2001-2003. *Member:* Chicago and American Bar Associations. ***PRACTICE AREAS:*** Labor and Employment; Litigation. ***Email:*** zjackson@csh-law.com

KYLE D. KICKHAEFER, born Abilene, Kansas, August 19, 1971; admitted to bar, 1999, California (Not admitted in Illinois). *Education:* University of Kansas (B.G.S.,

(This Listing Continued)

1994); Boalt Hall School of Law, University of California, Berkeley (J.D., 1999). Member, Law Review. Moot Court Best Brief; Moot Court Board. *Member:* State Bar of California. ***PRACTICE AREAS:*** Labor and Employment. ***Email:*** kkickhaefer@csh-law.com

TERENCE P. SMITH, born New York, New York, May 30, 1968; admitted to bar, 2000, Illinois; U.S. District Court, Northern District of Illinois; U.S. District Court, Northern District of Indiana. *Education:* University of Scranton (B.A., 1990); Loyola University Chicago (M.S.I.R.,1997); Chicago-Kent College of Law, Illinois Institute of Technology (J.D., with honors, 2000). *Member:* Chicago, Illinois State and American Bar Associations. ***PRACTICE AREAS:*** Labor and Employment Law; Litigation. ***Email:*** tsmith@csh-law.com

BRIAN EDWARD SPANG, born West Chester, Pennsylvania, March 22, 1972; admitted to bar, 1997, Illinois. *Education:* College of William and Mary (A.B., with honors, 1994); University of Illinois (J.D., magna cum laude, 1997). Law Clerk, U.S. Magistrate Judge Roger B. Cosbey, U.S. District Court for the Northern District of Indiana, 1997-1999. ***PRACTICE AREAS:*** Labor and Employment Law; Litigation. ***Email:*** bspang@csh-law.com

ELLEN D. STUART, born Atlanta, Georgia; admitted to bar, 2003, California (Not admitted in Illinois). *Education:* University of Denver (B.A., 1998); California Western School of Law (J.D., 2002). *Member:* State Bar of California; American Bar Association. ***PRACTICE AREAS:*** Labor and Employment Law. ***Email:*** estuart@csh-law.com

JACQUELINE J. WADE, born Hammond, Indiana, 1971; admitted to bar, 2002, Indiana and Illinois. *Education:* Harvard University (A.B., 1993;); Indiana University School of Law (J.D., 1995). Member, Indiana Law Journal. *Member:* Illinois State and Indiana State Bar Associations. ***PRACTICE AREAS:*** Labor and Employment.

REPRESENTATIVE CLIENTS: American International Group, Inc.; Luster Products, Inc.; Mars, Inc.; Metropolitan Life Insurance Co.; National Automatic Merchandising Assn.; Robert Bosch Corp.; US Freightways; VWR Scientific.

CONWAY & CHIAVIELLO, LTD.

Established in 1998

77 WEST WASHINGTON BOULEVARD
SUITE 1601
CHICAGO, ILLINOIS 60602
Telephone: 312-782-3553
Fax: 312-782-3552
Email: conchiltd@yahoo.com

Personal Injury and Workers Compensation.

MICHAEL F. CONWAY, born Chicago, Illinois, November 19, 1952; admitted to bar, 1980, Illinois and U.S. District Court, Northern District of Illinois and Indiana; U.S. Court of Appeals, Seventh Circuit. *Education:* Georgetown University (B.S.F.S., 1974); Northern Illinois University (J.D., 1978); University of Paris/Pantheon-Sorbonne. Member, American Arbitration Association, 1982-1990. Arbitrator, Cook County Mandatory Arbitrator Project, 1990. *Member:* Chicago and American (Attorney/Lobbyist for Private Bar Involvement Project, 1983-1987) Bar Associations; The Association of Trial Lawyers of America. ***PRACTICE AREAS:*** Premises Liability; Personal Injury; Civil Litigation; Workers Compensation; Complex Commercial Litigation.

PHILIP S. CHIAVIELLO, born Jacksonville, Florida, November 20, 1956; admitted to bar, 1983, Illinois and U.S. District Court, Northern District of Illinois; 1986, Arizona; 1995, U.S. District Court, Northern District of Indiana. *Education:* Ramapo College of New Jersey (B.A., 1980); John Marshall Law School (J.D., 1983). *Member:* Chicago Bar Association; State Bar of Arizona; Justinian Society of Lawyers. ***PRACTICE AREAS:*** Automobile Accidents and Injuries; Personal Injury; Product Liability; Wrongful Death; Workers Compensation; Medical Malpractice. ***Email:*** philipc672@aol.com

TODD P. KLEIN, born Park Ridge, Illinois, August 2, 1976; admitted to bar, 2001, Illinois and U.S. District Court, Northern District of Illinois. *Education:* Illinois State University (B.S., 1998); John Marshall Law School (J.D., cum laude, 2001). Member, John Marshall Law Review. *Member:* Chicago and Illinois State Bar Associations; Illinois Trial Lawyers Association; The Association of Trial Lawyers of America. ***PRACTICE AREAS:*** Premises Liability; Personal Injury; Products Liability; Workers Compensation. ***Email:*** tpklein5@yahoo.com

PAUL GAMBOA, born Chicago, Illinois, September 27, 1977; admitted to bar, 2004, Illinois. *Education:* University of Illinois, Urbana-Champaign (B.A., 1999; J.D., cum laude, 2004). *Member:* Chicago, Fenwick and Illinois State Bar Associations; Catholic Lawyers Guild of Chicago. ***PRACTICE AREAS:*** Personal Injury; Workers Compensation; Products Liability; Premises Liability.

Language: Spanish.

CONWAY & MROWIEC

Established in 2000

20 SOUTH CLARK, SUITE 750
CHICAGO, ILLINOIS 60603
Telephone: 312-658-1100
Fax: 312-658-1201
URL: http://www.cmcontractors.com

Construction, Mechanics Liens, Arbitration, Government Contracts, Insurance, Complex Litigation and Construction Related Bankruptcy.

FIRM PROFILE: The firm Conway & Mrowiec concentrates its practice in Construction and Public Contracts Law and Litigation. Conway & Mrowiec has broad experience in achieving successful, cost-effective results for contractors, construction managers, design/builders, trade contractors, architects, engineers, owners and sureties, in contract drafting, bidding and performance issues through claim prosecution or defense.

(This Listing Continued)

MEMBERS OF FIRM

TIMOTHY R. CONWAY, born Chicago, Illinois, November 14, 1956; admitted to bar, 1980, Illinois. *Education:* DePaul University (B.A., 1977); Northwestern University (J.D., summa cum laude, 1980). Order of the Coif. Executive Editor, Northwestern Law Review, 1979-1980. Speaker: "Construction Management/Design-Build: Contracting & Claims Avoidance," AIA Contracts, March 2003, April 2003; "Construction Issues," 2002; "Construction Delay Claims in Illinois," Aug. 2002, June, 2004, and May, 2005; "Fundamentals of Construction Contracts Understanding the Issues," March, 2004 and March, 2005; "Illinois Construction Law: Creative Strategies for Project Completion and Litigation Avoidance," 2002; "Illinois Construction Lien Law," 2002; "Protecting Your Construction Industry Clients," Illinois Institute for Continuing Legal Education, 1996. Author, "Mechanics Liens and Surety Bonds," *Illinois Construction Law,* Aspen, 2003. Co-Author: "Requirements for the Original Contractor's Lien on Private Projects," Illinois Institute of Continuing Education, 1994, 2000, 2004 eds. *Member:* Chicago and American (Member, Fidelity and Surety Law Committee, 2005) Bar Associations; Builders Association of Greater Chicago; Fox Valley General Contractors Association; Society of Illinois Construction Lawyers; Leading Lawyers Network. ***REPORTED CASES:*** Builders Association of Greater Chicago v. City of Chicago, 298 F.Supp. 2d 725 (N.D. Ill. 2003); Builders Association of Greater Chicago v. County of Cook, 256 F.3d 642 (7th Cir. 2001), 123 F.Supp.2d 1087 (N.D. Ill. 2000); Mellon Stuart Construction, Inc. v. Metropolitan Water Reclamation District, 1995 U.S. Dist. LEXIS 5376 (N.D.Ill. 1995); Chase Commercial Corp. v. Brandt, 1999 U.S. Dist. LEXIS 16441 (N.D.Ill. 1999); Builders Association of Greater Chicago v. County of Cook, 2000 U.S. Dist. LEXIS 144 (N.D.Ill. 2000); 1998 U.S. Dist. LEXIS 2991 (N.D.Ill. 1998); 1996 U.S. Dist. LEXIS 13142 (N.D.Ill. 1996); Dunne v. County of Cook, 483 N.E.2d 13 (1984); Amalgamated Trust & Savings Bank v. Silha, 460 N.E.2d 372 (1984); Builders Association of Greater Chicago v. City of Chicago, 170 F.R.D. 435 (N.D.Ill. 1996); Prisco Serena Sturm Architects, Ltd. v. Liberty Mutual Insurance Co., 1995 U.S. Dist. LEXIS 9904 (N.D.Ill. 1995); 1996 U.S. Dist. LEXIS 7278 (N.D.Ill. 1996); U.S. Dist. LEXIS 4350, 3021, 2216 (N.D.Ill.1996). ***PRACTICE AREAS:*** Construction Law; Insurance Coverage Law; Mechanics Liens. ***Email:*** trc@cmcontractors.com

JOHN S. MROWIEC, born Rockford, Illinois, November 11, 1954; admitted to bar, 1983, Illinois; 1985, U.S. District Courts, Northern District of Illinois including Trial Bar, U.S. District Court, Eastern District of Wisconsin and Northern District of Indiana. *Education:* Northern Illinois University (B.A., cum laude, 1980); DePaul University (J.D., 1983); Marshall-Wythe Law School, College of William & Mary, Exeter, Devonshire, England. Lead Articles and Notes Editor, DePaul Law Review, 1982-1983. Author: "Mechanics Lien Rights in Illinois, A Practical Guide to Enforcement." Co-Author: "Requirements for the Original Contractor's Lien on Private Projects," in Illinois Mechanics Liens, IICLE (1994, 2000, 2004 eds). Law Columnist, Midwest Construction News, McGraw-Hill, May, 2000—. Speaker and Author: "U.S. Electronic Discovery Issues: Zubulake v. UBS Warburg, Locating and Preserving, Retrieving and Producing Electronic Documents," Canadian College of Construction Lawyers, Inc., 8th Annual Conference, May, 2005; "The Nelson Energy Project" or "The Contractor's Perfect Storm," Canadian College of Construction Lawyers, Inc., 8th Annual Conference, May 2005; AIA Contracts, Sept. 2005, Sept. 2004, Mar. 2003; "Public Construction Contracting: Bidding and Building in Illinois," Oct. 2004, Mar. 2002, Aug. 2001, Mar. 2001; "Illinois Construction Issues," Mar. 2005, Mar. 2004, Oct. 2002, May 2002, Mar. 2002, Feb. 2002, Feb. 2001; "Construction Management/ Design-Build: Contracting & Claims Avoidance," Apr. 2005, Nov. 2004, Apr. 2004, Apr. 2003, Apr. 2002, Mar. 2002, Nov. 2001, Nov. 2000; "Construction Delay Claims in Illinois," May 2005, June 2004, Aug. 2002, Sept. 2000; "Illinois Construction Law: Creative Strategies for Project Completion and Litigation Avoidance, 2000 (three locales); "Construction Law, Associated General Contractor Superintendent Certification," 1999. Co-Author: "Changes That Result from Delays and Interferences," Construction Change Order Claims, 2d ed. Aspen 2005. Instructor, DePaul University, Real Estate Center, Construction Law and Contracts, Mar. 2005, Mar. 2004, Mar. 2003, Dec. 2002. Member, Advisory Board, Leading Lawyers Network. *Member:* Chicago and American (Member, Construction Industry Forum, Public Contracts and Litigation Sections) Bar Associations; Builders Association of Greater Chicago; Associated General Contractors; American Institute of Architects; Society of Illinois Construction Lawyers. ***REPORTED CASES:*** Downey, Inc. v. Bradley Center Corp., 524 N.W.2d 915 (Wis.Ct.App. 1994); Mellon Stuart Construction, Inc. v. MWRDGC, 1995 U.S. Dist. LEXIS 3493 (N.D.Ill. 1995); Southwest Financial Bank & Trust Co. v. George Hyman Construction Co., 940 F.Supp. 1331 (N.D.Ill. 1996); United States f/u/b DJM Construction, Inc. v. Rust Engineering Co., 1996 WL 204318 (N.D.Ill. 1996); Mellon Stuart Construction, Inc. v. MWRDGC, 1990 U.S. Dist. LEXIS 7669 (N.D.Ill. 1990); Acme Metals, Inc. v. Raytheon Engineers & Constructors, Inc. (In re Acme Metals, Inc.), 257 B.R. 714 (Bankr. Ct.D. Del. 2000); In re KNM Roswell LP, 126 B.R. 548 (Bankr. Ct. N.D. Ill.1991); In Re Highland Park Associates LP, 130 B.R. 55 (Bankr. Ct. N.D. Ill. 1991). ***PRACTICE AREAS:*** Construction Law; Arbitration; Mechanics Liens; Government Contracts. ***Email:*** jsm@cmcontractors.com

EDWARD B. KEIDAN, born Detroit, Michigan, January 24, 1970; admitted to bar, 1995, Illinois and U.S. District Court, Northern District of Illinois including Trial Bar; 2001, U.S. Court of Appeals, Seventh Circuit; U.S. District Court, Northern District of Indiana. *Education:* University of Michigan (B.A., with distinction, 1992; J.D., cum laude, 1995). Speaker: "Public Construction Contracting: Bidding and Building in Illinois"; "Construction Issues: "Illinois Construction Law: Creative Strategies for Project Completion and Litigation Avoidance"; "Illinois Construction Lien Law." ; "Construction management/Design Build" ; "AIA Contracts"; "Fundamentals of Construction Contracts". *Member:* Chicago and American Bar Associations (Member, Construction Industry). ***REPORTED CASES:*** Builders Association of Greater Chicago v. City of Chicago, 298 F.Supp. 2d 725 (N.D. Ill. 2003); Builders Association of Greater Chicago v. County of Cook, 256 F.3d 642 (7th Cir. 2001), 123 F.Supp.2d 1087 (N.D. Ill. 2000); Delaney v. DeTella, 123 F.Supp2d 429 (N.D. Ill. 2000); Chase Commercial Corp. v. Brandt, 1999 U.S. Dist. LEXIS 16441 (N.D. Ill. 1999). ***PRACTICE AREAS:*** Construction Law; Commercial Litigation; Securities Litigation. ***Email:*** ebk@cmcontractors.com

ASSOCIATES

KENNETH A. CRIPE, born Elmhurst, Illinois, June 28, 1967; admitted to bar, 1999, Illinois. *Education:* Illinois State University (B.S., Business, 1989); DePaul University

(This Listing Continued)

CONWAY & MROWIEC, Chicago—Continued

College of Law (J.D., 1999). *Member:* Chicago, Illinois State and American Bar Associations. ***PRACTICE AREAS:*** Construction Law; Construction Litigation. ***Email:*** kac@cmcontractors.com

MARK R. BECKER, born 1974; admitted to bar, 2000, Illinois. *Education:* Northwestern University (B.S., Civil Engineering, cum laude, 1997); University of Iowa (J.D., with high distinction, 2000). Recipient, Faculty Scholar Award, University of Iowa College of Law. Member, University of Iowa Law Review. Co-Author: "Judicial Scrutiny of Expert Testimony by Engineers"; "Responsible Use of Computer Technology by Engineers." Author: "Basic Copyright for Engineers." *Member:* American Bar Association (Member, Construction Law Forum); American Society of Civil Engineers. ***PRACTICE AREAS:*** Construction Law; Construction Litigation. ***Email:*** mrb@cmcontractors.com

BRIAN W. MORRIS, born Portage, Michigan, 1975; admitted to bar, 2002, Illinois. *Education:* Alma College (B.A., Philosophy, Sociology, 1998); University of Illinois (J.D., magna cum laude, 2002). Member and Editor, University of Illinois Law Review, 2001-2002. ***PRACTICE AREAS:*** Construction Law; Construction Litigation. ***Email:*** bwm@cmcontractors.com

COOK, ALEX, McFARRON, MANZO, CUMMINGS & MEHLER

200 WEST ADAMS, SUITE 2850
CHICAGO, ILLINOIS 60606
Telephone: 312-236-8500
Fax: 312-236-8176
Email: firm@cammcm.com
URL: http://www.cammcm.com

Patent, Trademark, Copyright and Unfair Competition Law, Intellectual Property Practice.

FIRM PROFILE: The firm of Cook, Alex, McFarron, Manzo, Cummings & Mehler, was formed on August 1, 1999. The firm is the result of attorneys coming together from the firms formerly known as Cook, McFarron & Manzo and Lockwood, Alex, FitzGibbon & Cummings, both of which have enjoyed a national practice in the field of intellectual property law. The Lockwood, Alex, FitzGibbon and Cummings firm traces its roots to the 1916 formation of "Cromwell, Greist & Warden." The predecessors of the Cook, McFarron & Manzo firm date to 1977, when "Cook, Wetzel and Egan was formed.

GRANGER COOK, JR., born Chicago, Illinois, August 31, 1926; admitted to bar, 1955, Illinois and U.S. District Court, Northern District of Illinois, including Trial Bar; 1962, U.S. Court of Appeals, Seventh Circuit; 1963, U.S. Supreme Court; 1966, U.S. Court of Federal Claims; 1968, U.S. Court of Appeals, Second Circuit; 1971, U.S. Court of Appeals, First Circuit; 1975, U.S. Court of Appeals, Third Circuit; 1978, U.S. Court of Customs and Patent Appeals; 1978, U. S. Court of Appeals, Tenth Circuit; 1982, U.S. Court of Appeals, Ninth Circuit; 1985, U.S. Court of Appeals, Federal Circuit; registered to practice before U.S. Patent and Trademark Office. *Education:* Northwestern University (B.S.E.E., 1951); University of Michigan (J.D., 1954). Phi Delta Phi. Member, Board of Directors, 1975—, Member, Board of Trustees, 1984—, President, 1983 and 1984, Better Government Association. Chairman, Plan Commission, City of Lake Forest, 1979-1984. President and Founder, Phi Chapter Educational Foundation, 1960—. Member, Mayor Washington's Ethics Committee, 1985-1987. Chairman, Advisory Board, Lake Forest Symphony, 1991—. *Member:* Chicago and American Bar Associations; Intellectual Property Law Association of Chicago (Past Chairman of Taxation Committee); American Intellectual Property Law Association; International Trade Commission Trial Lawyers Association; The Law Club of Chicago; Legal Club of Chicago; The Lawyers Club of Chicago; Barristers of the Patent Law (Chairman). ***PRACTICE AREAS:*** Intellectual Property; Patent; Trademarks; Copyrights; Unfair Competition; Antitrust. ***Email:*** gcook@cammcm.com

JOHN L. ALEX, born Chicago, Illinois, July 25, 1936; admitted to bar, 1962, Illinois; U.S. District Court, Northern District of Illinois including Trial Bar; U.S. Supreme Court; U.S. Court of Appeals for the Federal Circuit; U.S. Court of Appeals, First, Seventh and Eighth Circuits; registered to practice before U.S. Patent and Trademark Office. *Education:* Northwestern University (B.S., Ch.E., 1959; J.D., 1962). *Member:* Chicago, Seventh Circuit, Illinois State and American Bar Associations; Intellectual Property Law Association of Chicago; The Lawyers Club of Chicago. ***PRACTICE AREAS:*** Intellectual Property; Patents; Trademarks; Copyrights; Unfair Competition. ***Email:*** jalex@cammcm.com

DANIEL M. RIESS, born Evanston, Illinois, July 28, 1936; admitted to bar, 1968, Illinois; U.S. District Court, Northern District of Illinois, including Trial Bar; U.S. Court of Appeals, Seventh and Federal Circuits; U.S. Supreme Court; registered to practice before U.S. Patent and Trademark Office. *Education:* Northwestern University (B.S. Ch.E., 1959); Georgetown University (J.D., 1967). *Member:* Chicago, Illinois State and American Bar Associations; Bar Association of the Seventh Circuit; Bar Association of the Federal Circuit; American Intellectual Property Law Association; Intellectual Property Law Association of Chicago. ***PRACTICE AREAS:*** Patent; Trademark; Copyright; Unfair Competition. ***Email:*** driess@cammcm.com

EUGENE M. CUMMINGS, born Princeton, Illinois, April 3, 1941; admitted to bar, 1970, Illinois and U.S. District Court, Northern District of Illinois; 1988, U.S. Court of Appeals for the Federal Circuit; 1998, U.S. Supreme Court; registered to practice before U.S. Patent and Trademark Office. *Education:* Northwestern University (B.S.E.E., 1963); Loyola University (J.D., 1969). *Member:* Chicago, Illinois State and American Bar Associations; Intellectual Property Law Association of Chicago (Member, Board of Managers, 1976-1977); American Intellectual Property Law Association; Institute of Electrical and Electronics Engineers. ***PRACTICE AREAS:*** Patent; Trademark; Copyright; Unfair Competition. ***Email:*** ecummings@emcpc.com

JAMES S. PRISTELSKI, born Marinette, Wisconsin, April 12, 1943; admitted to bar, 1973, Illinois and U.S. District Court, Northern District of Illinois; 1982, U.S. Court of Appeals, Seventh and Federal Circuits; registered to practice before U.S. Patent and Trademark Office. *Education:* University of Wisconsin-Madison (B.S.E.E., 1966); University of Iowa (J.D., with distinction, 1972). Tau Beta Pi. Eta Kappa Nu. Phi Alpha Delta. *Member:* Intellectual Property Law Association of Chicago; American Intellectual Property Law Association. ***PRACTICE AREAS:*** Intellectual Property; Patents; Trademarks; Copyrights; Unfair Competition. ***Email:*** jpristelski@cammcm.com

GARY W. McFARRON, born Evansville, Indiana, October 16, 1948; admitted to bar, 1974, Illinois and U.S. District Court, Northern District of Illinois including Trial Bar; 1983, U.S. Court of Appeals for the Federal Circuit; 1985, U.S. Supreme Court; 1990, U.S. Court of Appeals, Seventh Circuit; 1974, registered to practice before U.S. Patent and Trademark Office. *Education:* Purdue University (B.S.M.E., with distinction, 1971); Northwestern University (J.D., cum laude, 1974). Tau Beta Pi; Phi Kappa Phi. Member, Northwestern University Law Review, 1973-1974. *Member:* Chicago and American Bar Associations; Intellectual Property Law Association of Chicago; American Intellectual Property Law Association. ***PRACTICE AREAS:*** Intellectual Property; Patents; Trademarks; Copyrights; Unfair Competition; Antitrust. ***Email:*** gmcfarron@cammcm.com

RAYMOND M. MEHLER, born Chicago, Illinois, December 16, 1944; admitted to bar, 1974, Illinois; 1977, U.S. District Court, Northern District of Illinois; 1983, U.S. Court of Appeals for the Federal Circuit; registered to practice before U.S. Patent and Trademark Office. *Education:* Illinois Institute of Technology (B.S., with distinction, 1970); University of Chicago (J.D., 1974). *Member:* Chicago Bar Association; Intellectual Property Law Association of Chicago; American Intellectual Property Law Association. ***PRACTICE AREAS:*** Patents; Trademarks; Copyrights; Unfair Competition. ***Email:*** rmehler@cammcm.com

EDWARD D. MANZO, born New York, N.Y., November 23, 1950; admitted to bar, 1976, New York, U.S. District Court, Southern District of New York; 1979, Illinois and U.S. District Court, Northern District of Illinois including Trial Bar; 1982, U.S. Court of Appeals for the Federal Circuit; 1983, U.S. Supreme Court; registered to practice before U.S. Patent and Trademark Office. *Education:* Polytechnic Institute of Brooklyn (B.S. in Physics, 1972); State University of New York at Buffalo (J.D., cum laude, 1975). Sigma Pi Sigma. Editor and Co-author, "Federal Circuit Review of Markman Issues (2001)," "Federal Circuit Review of Markman Issues (2002), (Intellectual Prop. L. Assoc. of Chicago 2003). Author: *Intellectual Property Law in Illinois,* (co-author), Cambridge Institute, 1988; "Means Claims in Patent Infringement Litigation," *J.P.T.O.S.,* March, 1986; "Does Your Programmed Computer Infringe the Patent?" IEEE Compcon, 1984. Co-Author, "The Testimony of Patent Examiners," (PLI 1974). Instructor, De Paul University, "Legal Aspects of Data Processing," (Computer Science Department), 1989-1991. Member, Panel of Arbitrators, American Arbitration Association, 1986-1994. *Member:* Intellectual Property Law Association of Chicago; American Intellectual Property Law Association; Law Club of Chicago (Member, Board of Directors, Concertante di Chicago, 1997—). ***LANGUAGES:*** French. ***PRACTICE AREAS:*** Intellectual Property; Patents; Trademarks; Copyrights; Unfair Competition. ***Email:*** emanzo@cammcm.com

JOEL H. BOCK, born Hammond, Indiana, May 30, 1952; admitted to bar, 1977, Illinois; 1978, U.S. District Court, Northern District of Illinois. *Education:* University of Michigan (B.S., 1974); Indiana University (J.D., 1977). *Member:* Chicago Bar Association. ***PRACTICE AREAS:*** Patent, Trademark and Copyright Law; Unfair Competition Causes. ***Email:*** jbock@cammcm.com

STEPHEN B. HELLER, born Chicago, Illinois, August 12, 1955; admitted to bar, 1980, Illinois and U.S. District Court, Northern District of Illinois; 1982, U.S. Court of Appeals for the Federal Circuit; registered to practice before U.S. Patent and Trademark Office. *Education:* Iowa State University (B.S. Aero E., with honors, 1977); University of Illinois (J.D., cum laude, 1980). Tau Beta Pi. *Member:* Intellectual Property Law Association of Chicago. ***PRACTICE AREAS:*** Intellectual Property; Patents; Trademarks; Unfair Competition. ***Email:*** sheller@cammcm.com

DAVID LESHT, born Chicago, Illinois, November 29, 1951; admitted to bar, 1981, Illinois; U.S. District Court, Northern District of Illinois including Trial Bar; U.S. Court of Appeals for the Federal Circuit, U.S. Supreme Court; registered to practice before U.S. Patent and Trademark Office. *Education:* University of Illinois (B.S., 1973); University of Missouri at Columbia (M.A., 1977); Illinois Institute of Technology, Chicago-Kent College of Law (J.D., with honors, 1981). *Member:* Chicago and American Bar Associations; Intellectual Property Law Association of Chicago; American Chemical Society. ***PRACTICE AREAS:*** Patents; Trademarks; Copyrights; Unfair Competition. ***Email:*** dlesht@cammcm.com

ANDREW G. KOLOMAYETS, born Chicago, Illinois, October 30, 1961; admitted to bar, 1988, Illinois; 1989, U.S. District Court, Northern District of Illinois and U.S. Court of Appeals for the Federal Circuit; registered to practice before U.S. Patent and Trademark Office. *Education:* Loyola University (B.A. in Chemistry, 1984); University of Illinois (J.D., 1988). *Member:* Intellectual Property Law Association of Chicago; American Chemical Society; Ukrainian-American Bar Association. ***LANGUAGES:*** Ukrainian. ***PRACTICE AREAS:*** Intellectual Property; Patents; Trademarks; Copyrights; Unfair Competition. ***Email:*** akolomayets@cammcm.com

MARK J. MURPHY, born Janesville, Wisconsin, February 20, 1964; admitted to bar, 1989, Wisconsin, Illinois and U.S. District Court, Eastern District of Wisconsin; 1990, U.S. District Court, Northern District of Illinois; 1991, U.S. Court of Appeals for the Federal Circuit; registered to practice before U.S. Patent and Trademark Office. *Education:* University of Notre Dame (B.S., Ch.Eng., 1986); Marquette University (J.D., 1989). *Member:* American Bar Association; State Bar of Wisconsin; Intellectual Property Law Association of Chicago. ***PRACTICE AREAS:*** Intellectual Property; Patents; Trademarks; Copyrights; Unfair Competition; Antitrust. ***Email:*** mmurphy@cammcm.com

MICHAEL J. McGEE, born Dunedin, Florida, October 19, 1970; admitted to bar, 1997, Illinois; registered to practice before U.S. Patent and Trademark Office. *Education:* Florida State University (B.S.E.E., 1993; M.S.E.E., 1994); John Marshall Law School (J.D., magna cum laude, 1997). Tau Beta Pi. Recipient, Dean's Scholar, John Marshall Law School. Staff Editor, John Marshall Law Review. Judicial Extern for Magistrate Judge Ronald Guzman, 1996-1997. *Member:* Chicago Bar Association; Intellectual Property Law Association of Chicago; American Intellectual Property Law Association. ***PRACTICE AREAS:*** Patent; Trademark; Copyright; Unfair Competition Law. ***Email:*** mmcgee@cammcm.com

(This Listing Continued)

DAVID MICHAEL MUNDT, born Chicago, Illinois, September 13, 1970; admitted to bar, 1997, Illinois and U.S. District Court, Northern District of Illinois; 1998, U.S. Court of Appeals for the Federal Circuit; U.S. Supreme Court; registered to practice before U.S. Patent and Trademark Office. *Education:* University of Iowa (B.S.B.M.E., 1993); John Marshall Law School (J.D., 1997). *Member:* Chicago and American Bar Associations; Intellectual Property Law Association of Chicago. ***PRACTICE AREAS:*** Intellectual Property; Patent; Trademark; Copyrights; Unfair Competition Law. ***Email:*** dmundt@emcpc.com

ASSOCIATES

RENEE C. BARTHEL, born Chicago, Illinois, December 11, 1973; admitted to bar, 2000, Illinois; 2001, U.S. District Court, Northern District of Illinois; registered to practice before U.S. Patent and Trademark Office. *Education:* University of Florida (B.S. ENE, 1997); Chicago-Kent College of Law (J.D., 2000). Certified Engineering Intern, Florida State Board of Professional Engineers, 1999. ***PRACTICE AREAS:*** Intellectual Property; Patents; Trademarks; Copyrights. ***Email:*** rbarthel@cammcm.com

LOUIS JOHN ALEX, born Chicago, Illinois, June 6, 1968; admitted to bar, 2001, Illinois. *Education:* Cornell University (B.S., Chemical Engineering, 1992; B.A., Psychology, 1992); Georgetown University (J.D., 2001). ***PRACTICE AREAS:*** Intellectual Property; Patents; Trademarks; Copyrights. ***Email:*** lalex@cammcm.com

MICHAEL D. ZARONIAS, born Gary, Indiana, October 6, 1965; admitted to bar, 2002, Illinois; 2003, Indiana. *Education:* Indiana University (B.A., Chemistry, 1998); Valparaiso University School of Law (J.D., magna cum laude, 2002). Member, American Bar Association, 2002-2003. *Member:* American Intellectual Property Law Association; Intellectual Property Law Association of Chicago. ***LANGUAGES:*** Greek. ***PRACTICE AREAS:*** Intellectual Property. ***Email:*** mzaronias@cammcm.com

PANASARN AIM JIRUT, born Chicago, Illinois, September 15, 1978; admitted to bar, 2004, Illinois; registered to practice before U.S. Patent and Trademark Office. *Education:* Vanderbilt University (B.E., B.M.E., 2000); DePaul University College of Law (J.D., 2003). Recipient: Vanderbilt University Chancellor's Scholar; Certificate of Specialization in General Intellectual Property Law, DePaul University College of Law. ***PRACTICE AREAS:*** Intellectual Property; Patents; Trademarks; Copyrights; Unfair Competition. ***Email:*** ajirut@cammcm.com

PAUL RAYA, born Chicago, Illinois, December 16, 1972; admitted to bar, 2004, Illinois. *Education:* Knox College (B.C., Chemistry, 1995); John Marshall Law School (J.D., magna cum laude, 2004). ***PRACTICE AREAS:*** Intellectual Property. ***Email:*** praya@cammcm.com

JOSEPH R. FREUND, born Woodstock, Illinois, November 17, 1980; admitted to bar, 2004, Illinois. *Education:* University of Illinois, Urbana-Champaign (B.S., 2001); DePaul University (J.D., 2004). Certificate of Specialization in General Intellectual Property Law, DePaul University College of Law. *Member:* Chicago and American Bar Associations. ***PRACTICE AREAS:*** Intellectual Property; Patents; Trademarks; Copyrights; Unfair Competition. ***Email:*** jfreund@cammcm.com

BETSY J. LEVSTIK, born Willoughby, Ohio, December 26, 1978; admitted to bar, 2004, Illinois. *Education:* College of William and Mary (B.S., 2001); DePaul University (J.D., 2004). *Member:* Chicago and American Bar Associations; Intellectual Property Law Association of Chicago (IPLAC). ***PRACTICE AREAS:*** Intellectual Property. ***Email:*** blevstik@cammcm.com

OF COUNSEL

FRED S. LOCKWOOD, (P.C.), born North Hannibal, New York, 1916; admitted to bar, 1942, District of Columbia and Illinois; registered to practice before U.S. Patent and Trademark Office. *Education:* Syracuse University (B.Ch.E., 1937); John Marshall Law School (J.D., 1943). Tau Beta Pi; Pi Mu Epsilon. *Member:* Chicago, Seventh Circuit and American Bar Associations; Intellectual Property Law Association of Chicago; American Intellectual Property Law Association; American Chemical Society. ***PRACTICE AREAS:*** Patents; Trademarks; Copyrights; Unfair Competition. ***Email:*** flockwood@cammcm.com

WILLIAM H. MAGIDSON, born 1931; admitted to bar, 1956, Illinois. *Education:* Northwestern University (B.S., 1952; J.D., 1956). ***PRACTICE AREAS:*** Patents. ***Email:*** wmagidson@cammcm.com

DANIEL C. McEACHRAN, born Oak Park, Illinois, March 20, 1932; admitted to bar, 1959, Illinois; 1982, U.S. District Court, Northern District of Illinois, Trial Bar. *Education:* Iowa State University (B.S.E.E., 1953); Loyola University, Chicago (J.D., cum laude, 1959). Tau Beta Pi. *Member:* American Bar Association. ***PRACTICE AREAS:*** Patent, Trademark and Copyright Law; Unfair Competition Causes. ***Email:*** dmceachran@cammcm.com

EDWARD M. KEATING, born Chicago, Illinois, December 14, 1930; admitted to bar, 1960, Illinois; 1982, U.S. District Court, Northern District of Illinois, Trial Bar. *Education:* Illinois Institute of Technology (B.S., 1952); DePaul University (J.D., 1960). Phi Alpha Delta. *Member:* Chicago Bar Association; Intellectual Property Law Association of Chicago. ***PRACTICE AREAS:*** Patent, Trademark and Copyright Law; Unfair Competition Causes. ***Email:*** ekeating@cammcm.com

LISA A. COPLAND, P.C.

2600 S. MICHIGAN AVENUE, SUITE 405
CHICAGO, ILLINOIS 60616
Telephone: 312-881-9225
Fax: 312-881-9226
Email: Coplandlaw@aol.com
URL: http://www.lawyers.com/coplandlaw

Family Law, Divorce, Adoptions, Child Custody, Child Support, Domestic Violence, Premarital Agreements, Spousal Support, Visitation Rights, Juvenile Law, Wills.

(This Listing Continued)

LISA A. COPLAND, born Fort Eustis, Virginia, August 16, 1972; admitted to bar, 1997, Illinois and U.S. District Court, Northern District of Illinois. *Education:* Princeton University (A.B., 1994); Northwestern University (J.D., 1997). *Member:* Chicago, Cook County and Illinois State Bar Associations. ***PRACTICE AREAS:*** Family Law; Civil Litigation.

JOHN J. CORBETT & ASSOCIATES

Established in 1987

33 NORTH LA SALLE STREET
CHICAGO, ILLINOIS 60602
Telephone: 312-558-1900
Telefax: 312-750-0632
Email: john.corbett@corbettlawoffices.com
URL: http://www.corbettlawoffices.com

Personal Injury, Medical Malpractice, Products Liability, Negligence, Construction Accidents, Wrongful Death and Automobile Accidents, Nursing Home Litigation, Airplane Crash Litigation, Maritime Personal Injury, Railroad Accidents, Police Misconduct, Sexual Harassment.

JOHN J. CORBETT, born Chicago, Illinois, June 2, 1953; admitted to bar, 1980, Illinois; 1982, U.S. District Court, Northern District of Illinois. *Education:* Southern Illinois University (B.S., 1977); Northern Illinois University (J.D., 1980). *Member:* Chicago, Illinois State and American Bar Associations; American Trial Lawyers Association; Illinois Trial Lawyers Association (Member, Malpractice Committee, 1994—); Society of Trial Lawyers. ***PRACTICE AREAS:*** Personal Injury; Medical Malpractice; Products Liability; Negligence; Construction; Wrongful Death; Automobile Accidents and Injuries; Nursing Home Litigation; Airplane Crash Litigation; Maritime Personal Injury; Railroad Accidents and Injuries; Police Misconduct; Sexual Harassment.

ASSOCIATE

PAUL L. JACOBS, born Hammond, Indiana, February 1, 1971; admitted to bar, 1996, Illinois and U.S. District Court, Northern District of Illinois. *Education:* Eastern Illinois University (B.A., 1993); Creighton University School of Law (J.D., 1996). Formerly with: Lowis & Gellen. *Member:* Chicago and Illinois State Bar Associations. ***PRACTICE AREAS:*** Personal Injury; Medical Malpractice; Products Liability; Negligence; Construction Law; Wrongful Death; Automobile Accidents and Injuries; Nursing Home Litigation; Airplane Crash Litigation; Maritime Personal Injury; Railroad Accidents and Injuries; Police Misconduct; Sexual Harassment.

CORBOY & DEMETRIO, P.C.

33 NORTH DEARBORN STREET
21ST FLOOR
CHICAGO, ILLINOIS 60602
Telephone: 312-346-3191
FAX: 312-346-5562
TDD: 312-236-3191
Email: phc9@corboydemetrio.com
URL: http://www.corboydemetrio.com

Plaintiff's Personal Injury and Wrongful Death Litigation, with an emphasis on Commercial and General Aviation, Professional and Hospital Negligence, FELA, Product Liability, Premises, Construction, Vehicular, Railroad and Commercial Litigation.

FIRM PROFILE: Corboy & Demetrio was founded by nationally acclaimed trial lawyer Philip H. Corboy. Since 1974, the firm has attained more than 400 verdicts and settlements of $1 million or more for its clients and, since 1980, has successfully acquired almost $3 billion in settlements and verdicts for its clients.

Mr. Corboy has been named one of the country's 100 most influential lawyers in The National Law Journal "Profiles in Power" survey in every listing since 1985, when the NLJ began the triennial survey. One of only 13 lawyers nationwide to hold that distinction, Mr. Corboy also has been listed in The Best Lawyers in America since its inception in 1987.

Name partner, Thomas A. Demetrio, who has garnered honorable mentions in the last three NLJ Profiles in Power surveys, is a nationally recognized trial lawyer and has also been listed in The Best Lawyers in America since its inception. In 1990, he was named one of the country's top 10 trial lawyers by The National Law Journal and in 1999, the NLJ also names him as one of the top four plaintiff's trial lawyers in Illinois. He has acquired over $100 million in jury verdicts, including the largest personal injury verdict ever upheld by the Illinois Supreme Court.

The firm has been actively involved in every major aviation disaster over the past 30 years and represents Cook County, Illinois, against the country's major tobacco companies to recoup public monies paid out for treatment of tobacco-related illnesses.

PHILIP H. CORBOY, born Chicago, Illinois, August 12, 1924; admitted to bar, 1949, Illinois, U.S. District Court, Northern District of Illinois and Indiana and Illinois Supreme Courts; 1956, U.S. Court of Appeals, Seventh Circuit; 1960, U.S. District Court, Northern District of Indiana; 1965, U.S. Supreme Court; 1975, U.S. District Court, Eastern District of Wisconsin; 1983, U.S. Court of Appeals, Tenth Circuit. *Education:* St. Ambrose College; Baylor University; Sacramento Junior College; University of Notre Dame; Loyola University (J.D., cum laude, 1949). Awarded: LL.D., St. Ambrose College, 1978; Honorary Doctorate of Humane Letters, Loyola University, Chicago, 1996. Alpha Sigma Nu Jesuit Honorary Society. Awarded Medal of Excellence, Loyola Law Alumni Association, 1967. Author: "From Relocation Camp to St. Ambrose as Told by Yone Tanaka to Phil Corboy," The Ambrosian, May, 1943; "Illinois System of Instructing Jurors in Civil Cases," De Paul Law Review, Spring, 1959; "Objections to Jury Instructions, Why, When, How," Illinois Bar Journal, May, 1959; "Discovery Practice in Illinois—Documents, Tangible Articles and

(This Listing Continued)

CORBOY & DEMETRIO, P.C., Chicago—Continued

Real Estate," University of Illinois Forum, Fall, 1959: "Closing Argument for Plaintiff Severely Injured," 1962 Annual Trial Lawyer's Guide; "Will Split Trial Solve Court Delay? A Negative Response," Illinois Bar Journal, August, 1964; "Backlog Not Reduced by Routine Application of Severance Rule," American Bar Association Section of Insurance, Negligence and Compensation Law Proceedings, 1964; "Argument to the Jury on Dollar Amount of Damages," ABA Section of Insurance, Negligence and Compensation Law Proceedings, 1965; "Pattern Jury Instructions," Insurance Counsel Journal, January, 1965; "Proof of Distance Objects Can Be Seen," 1965 Annual Trial Lawyer's Guide; "Use of Written Authorities in Cross-Examination of Expert Witnesses," 1966 Annual Trial Lawyer's Guide; "A Practitioner's View of the Revised Federal Tort Claims Act," The Forum, published by American Bar Association Section of Insurance, Negligence and Compensation Law, January, 1967; "Use of Engineers as Experts," American Jurisprudence, Volume 6, 1967; "The Nonmedical Expert Witness," 1967 Annual Trial Lawyer's Guide; "Interpleader," University of Illinois Law Forum, 1967; "Negligent Destruction of a Racehorse-Proof of Damages," 1968 Annual Trial Lawyer's Guide; "The Basic Protection Plan-Panacea or Inequity," Notre Dame Lawyer, Volume 44, Number 1, October, 1968; "Proving Earning Capacity (Also Pecuniary Loss): Personal Injury and Wrongful Death Action," Third Annual Trial Evidence Seminar, Institute on Continuing Education of the Illinois Bar; "Economist Testimony: Proof of Economic Loss Suffered by Youth Severely Injured While Diving," The Trial Lawyer's Guide, Volume 13, Number 2, May, 1969; "What Should be Taught in Torts: A Practitioner's View," Torts and Retorts, December, 1973; "Lawyers' Contingent Fees," A & C Medical Challenge, August, 1973; "Defending Insurance Companies and the Insured-Can Two Masters Be Served?" Chicago Bar Record, Volume 55 Number 3, December, 1973; "The National Institute for Trial Advocacy - Innovation and Excellence in the Teaching of Trial Advocacy," International Society of Barristers Quarterly, Volume 9, Number 2, April 1974; "Should Judgments Be Reduced to Present Cash Value," Advocacy in the No-Fault Era, The Institute for Continuing Legal Education, 1974; "The Jury System-Perspectives from the Bar," The Jury System in America: A Critical Overview, Volume 4, Sage Criminal Justice System Annuals, 1975; "Adequate Legal Representation for the Professional Who is Sued, As Viewed by a Plaintiff's Lawyer," Medico-Legal, American Medical Association, 1975; "Actions Against Surgeons, Radiologists and Other Specialists," Medical Malpractice, Illinois Institute for Continuing Legal Education, 1975; "The Expanding Universe of Jeffrey O'Connell: Backing Into a Brave New World," University of Illinois Law Forum, 1976; "Contingency Fees: The Individual's Key to the Courthouse Door," Litigation Journal of American Bar Association, Volume 2, Number 4, Summer, 1976: "Has Illinois Adopted the Federal Rules of Evidence? Maybe Yes, Maybe No," Chicago Bar Record, Volume 59, Number 3, November/December, 1977; "Evidence," Chicago-Kent Law Review, Volume 54, Number 2, 1977; "Structuring the Presentation of Proof of Evidence," Trial Diplomacy Journal, Volume 1, Number 2, Summer, 1978; "Shielding the Plaintiff's Achilles' Heel: Tort Claim Notices to Governmental Entities," De Paul Law Review Volume 28, Number, 3, Spring 1979; "Organizing a Plaintiff's Personal Injury and Wrongful Death Law Office," Litigation Journal, American Bar Association, Volume 5, Number 4, Summer, 1979; "A Tale of Two Airplane Crashes," Chicago Bar Record, Volume 61, Number 2, September/October, 1979; "Justice James A. Dooley," Loyola University Law Journal, Volume 10, Number 2, Winter, 1979; "Reading the Jury," ABA Consortium for Professional Education, *Picking and Persuading a Jury -- A Workbook*, "Selecting a Jury," 1980; "American Courts Do Not Need English Solutions," The National Law Journal, January 21, 1980; "The Right to Trial by Jury," Trial Magazine, Volume 16, Number 5, May, 1980; "Brill's Idea Doubles the Injustice," The American Lawyer, September, 1980; "Structured Injustice: Compulsory Periodic Payment of Judgment," American Bar Association Journal, December 1980; "Economic Experts in Tort Litigation," Litigation Journal, American Bar Association, Volume 8, Number 2, Winter, 1982; "The Hostile Juror: An Approach," The National Law Journal, Volume 5, Number 46, July 25, 1983; "The Impact of Economic Theory on the Determination of Damages in a Wrongful Death Case: Income Taxes and Inflation Affect the Estimation of Future Loss of Earnings," The Trial Lawyer's Guide, Volume 28, Number 4, Winter, 1984; "The Impact of Economic Theory on the Determination of Damages in a Wrongful Death Case," The Forum, American Bar Association, Volume XX, Number 4, Summer, 1985; "Demonstrative Evidence," Master Advocates' Handbook, National Institute for Trial Advocacy, 1986; "AIDS: A Legal Challenge of the 1980s and Beyond," CBA Record, May, 1987; "Cross-Examination: Walking the Line Between Proper Prejudice and Unethical Conduct," American Journal of Trial Advocacy, Volume 10:1, Summer, 1986. "CTA must be held accountable for ineffective security," Chicago Sun-Times, October 20, 1988; "An 'Immunized' CTA endangers the public," Chicago-Daily Law Bulletin, October 21, 1988; "Closing Argument Masters of Trial Practice," pp. 101-119, John Wiley and Sons, 1988; "Final Arguments," Components of a Trial, The Association of Trial Lawyers of America, 1989; "A punishment that fits the crime," Chicago Tribune, May 10, 1989; "Defending Product Liability Laws," Crain's Chicago Business, May 29, 1989; "No Need to Fix Product Liability Law," Chicago Tribune, September 15, 1989; "License To Do Evil?," The National Law Journal, November 6, 1989; "Straight Talk on Annuity Cost Evidence," Illinois Bar Journal, Volume 77, Number 16, December 1989; "Masked and Muzzled, Litigants Tell No Evil: Is This Blind Justice?" Legal Times, January 8, 1990; "Product Liability: The Other Side," Chicago Lawyer, March 1990; "Going the Distance, How To Perfect the Trial Record and Win on Appeal," ABA Journal, Volume 76, April 1990; "Ex Parte Contacts Between Plaintiff's Physician And Defense Attorneys: Protecting the Patient-Litigant's Right to A Fair Trial," Loyola University of Chicago Law Journal, Volume 21, Number 4, Summer 1990; "The Discovery Dilemma: Advancing Justice or Hindering It?" Senior Lawyers Division, American Bar Association, Annual Meeting, August 4, 1990; "United Airlines Flight 232: Forty Minutes of Pre-Impact Terror," The Association of Trial Lawyers of America Mid-Year Meeting, January 1994; "No: Corporations Must Be Accountable," ABA Journal, January 1991; "The Case for Punitive Damages," Chicago Tribune, April 1, 1991; "Pain and Suffering in Bush Plan," Chicago Tribune, June 4, 1991; "Ignorance is not bliss," Crain's Chicago Business, July 22, 1991; "The Medical Expert-Chapter 13," Expert Witnesses, pp. 287-333, 1991 American Bar Association; "Rambo-Style Discovery Common in High-Stakes Cases," de facto Bar Press Verdict Reporter, August 1, 1991; "Court Secrecy: The Closed Circle and the Public Interest," Maryland Journal of Contemporary Legal Issues, Volume III, No. 1, Fall 1991; "Vicarious Liability for Punitive Damages -- Effort to Constitutionalize 'Tort Reform'," Constitutional Law Journal, Seton Hall Law School, Fall 1991; "Trial by Jury - Questioning

(This Listing Continued)

by Jurors? A Tentative Yes," Trial Magazine, October 1991; "Final Argument," Anatomy of a Personal Injury Lawsuit, 3rd Edition, pp. 361-379; ATLA Press, 1991; "Trust Juries in Awarding Damages," Chicago Tribune, December 31, 1991; "Ethical Rules Restricting Sexual Relations Between Attorneys and Their Clients," ABA Journal, January, 1992; "Final Argument: Earning the Jury's Trust," Trial Magazine, February, 1992; "An Open Letter to Vice President Quayle," International Society of Barristers, Volume 26, Number 3; "Federal Preemption of Product Liability Law: Federalism and the Theory of Implied Preemption," American Journal of Trial Advocacy, Volume 15:3, Spring, 1992; "Jury System Ain't Broke, So Leave It," The National Law Journal, August 31, 1992; "Counsel for the Plaintiff: Bart 'Bull's Eye' Wilson," Picking Juries, The American Lawyer, January/February 1993; "Automobile No-Fault: A Proven Failure," Legal Times, Week of January 11, 1993; "Who Should Be Liable for Gun Violence? Manufacturers, Importers Ought to Be Accountable," Chicago Sun-Times, February 20, 1993; "Secret Settlements: The Challenges Remain," Trial Magazine, June 1993; "Medical Malpractice Insurance and Defensive Medicine - The Myth of Tort-Reform 'Savings'," National Forum, The Phi Kappa Phi Journal, Summer 1993, Volume LXXIII, Number 3; "'Reform' And Constitutional Change," The Journal of the Section of Litigation, American Bar Association, Volume 20, Number 1, Fall 1993; "No need to change liability laws," Chicago Tribune, Voice of the People, April 25, 1994; "Casinos for Tort Reform a Bad Deal," Chicago Sun-Times, Sunday Commentary/Letters, Personal View, October 9, 1994; "The Case of the Napping Partner," Law Office Management, Navigating the Nineties, TRIAL, January 1995; "The Not-So-Quiet Revolution: Rebuilding Barriers to Jury Trial in the Proposed *Restatement (Third) of Torts: Products Liability*," Tennessee Law Review, a Symposium of the Ali's Proposed Restatement (Third) of Torts: Products Liability, Volume 61, Summer 1994, Number 4; "Steamrolling Tort Reform," Legal Times, Points of View, Opinion and Commentary, pp. 20, 24, week of March 27, 1995; "Newt is Cooking the Numbers," Texas Lawyer, Commentary, April 17, 1995; "The Common Sense of American Juries," Chicago Daily Law Bulletin, April 20, 1995; "Tort Reform No Friend to Consumers," Chicago Tribune, May 8, 1995; "Corporations afraid of the light," Chicago Tribune, June 14, 1995; "New Technology May Boost the Jury's Role," TRIAL, October 1995; "Looking back: The lessons of the Simpson trial: Beleaguered jurors did their job well; the police did not," Chicago Tribune, October 10, 1995; "Bit o'Luck," Trial Magazine, July, 1996; "How I Solved My Evidence Problem," ABA Journal, (contributor), July, 1997; "Football Won't Have Tragic End, But Some Players Will," Chicago Tribune, September 24, 1997; "Proof of Damages," Institute for Continuing Education of the Illinois Bar, reprinted from Negligence Law Forum; "Liability May Get Through to HMOs," Voice of the People, Chicago Tribune, Section 1, p. 24, July 1, 1998; "Illinois Courts: Vital Developers of Tort Law as Constitutional Vanguards, Statutory Interpreters, and Common Law Adjudicators," Illinois Judicial Conference Symposium, Loyola University Chicago Law Journal, Winter, 1999; "Holding Managed Care Accountable," Chicago Tribune, Voice of the People, Section 1, p. 22, July 22, 1999; "Abolishing Jury Awards Takes a Step Backwards," Illinois Legal Times, p. 8, August 1999. *Structured for a Reason*, ABA Journal, June 2000. *Profiles: Chicago and the American Century*, Contemporary Books, by F. Richard Ciccone, pp. 231, 258-259, 1999; *The Power 100*, Chicago Magazine, January, 1998; "Profiles in Power - 100 - The Most Influential Lawyers in America," The National Law Journal, April 28, 1997; "The Best Lawyers in America," Woodward/White, by Steven Naifeh and Gregory White Smith, pg. 283; 1997-1998; "Profiles in Power - 100 - The Most Influential Lawyers in America," The National Law Journal, April 4, 1994; "Fighting for 'the brave ' Personal injury lawyer loves to take on deep pockets," USA TODAY, December 12, 1995; "America's Top Trial Lawyers, Who They Are & Why They Win," Prentice Hall Law & Business, by Donald E. Vinson, 1994; "The Elite Registry of Extraordinary Professionals," Oxford's Who's Who, 1992-1993; "The Best Lawyers in America," Woodward/White, by Steven Naifeh and Gregory White Smith, 1993, pg. 283; "Philip H. Corboy, Legal Dynamo," Vital Times, September 1992; "Chicago Law," Inside Chicago, November/December 1991; "CHICAGO PROFILE/Philip H. Corboy," Chicago Sun-Times, May 3, 1991; "Profiles in Power - 100 - The Most Influential Lawyers in America," The National Law Journal, March 25, 1991; "First Person - Corboy Hits Hard at Misuse of Discovery," Merrill's Illinois Legal Times, September 1990; "What a Lawyer Looks for Before Suing You," Physician's Management, March 1990; "Million Dollar Lawyer - Phil Corboy, Chicago's Hottest Litigator," Blackacre, Loyola University of Chicago Law School, November 1989, Vol. 22, No. 3; "The Litigators: Inside the Powerful World of America's High Stakes Trial Lawyers," by John A Jenkins, Doubleday, New York, 1989, pp. 315 to 371; "A Talk with..Philip Corboy," Visual Evidence, August 1989; Philip Corboy's Three C's," Trial Excellence, August 1989; "Courting Disaster - Flamboyant Corboy wins trials, praise, big income," Crain's Chicago Business, July 31-August 6, 1989, Vol. 12, No. 31; "Expert witnesses - Philip Corboy tells 'em how to choose 'em, how to use 'em," Chicago Lawyer, April 18, 1989; "High Stakes," The Reader, March 3, 1989; "The Trial Lawyers," by Emily Couric, St. Martin's Press, 1988, pp. 221 to 261; "Profiles in Power - 100 - The Most Influential Lawyers in America," The National Law Journal, May 2, 1988; "Mock trials, community attitude surveys, shadow juries: A round table discussion," Trial Diplomacy Journal, Spring 1988; "The Best Lawyers in America," Woodward/White, New York, by Steven Naifeh and Gregory White Smith, 1987, pg. 561; "Philip Corboy: Mastering The Science of P.I.," The American Lawyer, June 1987; "Profile," The Loyola Patron, Summer 1987; "Winning - 15 of the nation's top trial lawyers talk about their winning tips and techniques," The National Law Journal, April 15, 1985; "Profiles in Power, The Nation's 100 Most Powerful Lawyers," The National Law Journal, April 15, 1985; "Trial lawyers learn by osmosis from mentor," Chicago Daily Law Bulletin, December 22, 1983; "King of the Personal Injury Lawyers," Loyola Magazine, Fall 1983; "The Best Lawyers in America," Seaview/Putnam, by Steven Naifeh and Gregory White Smith, 1983; "How Phil Corboy turned a ruined weekend into a $208,000 judgment," Chicago Lawyer, November 1981, Vol. 4, Num. 11; "The Million-Dollar Lesson in Lawyering," The National Law Journal, May 11, 1981; "Windy City's Wizard - Phil Corboy: Ten Years Without a Loss," The National Law Journal, July 21, 1980; "Who Runs Chicago," Michael Kilian, Connie Fletcher and F. Richard Ciccone, St. Martin's Press, New York, pp. 260 to 261, 1979; "What Happens If You Sue The Bastards," Money, November 1978; "The million-dollar attorney for the maimed," Chicago Tribune Magazine, April 3, 1977; "For the Plaintiff .Lawyers Specializing in Personal-Injury Suits Find Business is Good," The Wall Street Journal, August 2, 1972. Honorary Lifetime Trustee, The Roscoe Pound Foundation. Professional Safety Service Member, National Safety Council. Member, Loyola University's Citizen's Board. Past Editor, American Trial Lawyers Association Law Journal. Member, Board of Editors, Trial Diplomacy Journal. Co-Chairman, Committee to Study Case Flow Management in the Law Di-

(This Listing Continued)

vision of the Circuit Court of Cook County. Member, Board of Directors, Center for Elder & Disability Law. Member, Trial Advocacy Board, Loyola University School of Law. Member, National Advisory Board, American Journal of Trial Advocacy. Past Member, Board of St. Mary's College, 1981-1983. Member, Institute for Injury Reduction. Past Chairman, Cook County State's Attorney's Task Force on Life Sustaining Treatment. Former General Counsel, Illinois Democratic Party. Past Member, Illinois Supreme Court Committee on Jury Instructions. Past Chairman, National Institute for Trial Advocacy. Chicago Bar Association: President, 1972-1973; 1st Vice President, 1971-1972; 2nd Vice President, 1970-1971; Board Member, Aviation Law Committee, 1969-1972; Member, Board of Managers, 1969-1971; Member/Vice Chair, Committee on Candidates, 1963-1969; Member, Chicago Host Committee for 1978 ABA Annual Meeting, 1977; Member, Civil Practice Committee, 1955-1968 (Vice Chairman, 1963-1965; Chairman, 1965-1966); Member, ISBA/CBA Com. to Recommend Arbitration/Mediation Pilot Program, 1983; Chair, Liaison Special Committee, 1971-1972; Member, Committee on Negligence Law, 1962-1969; Member, Special No-Fault Committee, 1972; Member, Nominating Committee, 1966, 1975-Chairman, 1980 and 1985; Member, Committee on Operations of Circuit Court, 1974-1976; Board Member, Public Relations Advisory Committee, 1973-1974; Board Member, Committee on Revision of Circuit Court Rules, 1970-1973; Board Member, Unauthorized Practice Committee, 1969-1970; Member, Young Members Committee, 1950-1952. Illinois State Bar Association: Member, Civil Practice and Procedures Section Counsel, 1967-1969; Member, Special Committee for Medical/Legal Co-Op, 1960-1972; Member, Section of Negligence Law, 1959-1965 (Exec. Chair, 1959-1961; Vice Chair, 1963-1965); Member, Tort Law Section Counsel, 1965-1967 and Chairman, 1965-1966. American Bar Association: Member and Chairman, Special Committee on Medical Professional Liability; Past Chairman, Litigation Section; Past Member, House of Delegates; Past Chairman, Insurance Section, Committee on Rules and Procedures; Past Member, Special Committee on the Tort Liability System; Past Chairman, Insurance Section, Trial Techniques Committee. Illinois Trial Lawyers Association: President, 1963-1964; President-Elect, 1962-1963; Second Vice President, 1961-1962; Third Vice President, 1960-1961; Member, Public Relations Committee, 1983-1984; Member, Membership Committee, 1987-1988; Member, Legislative Committee, 1988-1990; Member, Executive Committee, 1992-1993. Association of Trial Lawyers of America: Committee Member, Bar Liaison Committee, 1993-1998; Chair, Stalwarts Committee, 1994-1995; Committee Member, Public Affairs Committee, 1994-1998. Awards and Honors: *Medal of Excellence,* Loyola University School of Law, 1967; *The Lasallian Award,* Christian Brothers of the Midwest Province, 1972; *Signum Fidei Honor,* Chicago Province of the Christian Brothers, 1995; *Philip H. Corboy Fellowship in Trial Advocacy,* Loyola University Chicago School of Law, est. 1995; *Leonard Ring Lifetime Achievement Award,* ITLA, 1995; *Big Shoulders Humanitarian Award,* 1996; *Champion of Justice Award,* ATLA, 1996; *Crystal Shamrock Award,* St. Patrick's H.S., 1996; *Chicago Street Dedication,* 1998; *The John Marshall Law School Freedom Award,* 1998; *Carl Rolewick Award,* LAP/CBA, 1998; *Distinguished Leadership Award,* Hazelden Chicago, 1999; *Laureate, Initial Class,* Academy of Illinois Lawyers, ISBA, 1999; *Richard J. Daley Medal of Honor,* Chicago Police Dept., 2000; Justice John Paul Stevens Award, *Inaugural Class,* CBA, September 13, 2000. *Member:* Chicago (Vice Chair, Judicial Evaluation Committee; Member: Past Presidents' Committee, 1973—; Senior Lawyers Committee, 1973—; Sustaining Member, 1983—; Chairman, Association Meetings Committee), Illinois State (Special Counsel to the Executive Committee, 1986—; Member, Special Advisory Committee to the Constitutional Challenge Committee, 1996—) and American (Member: Commission on Standards of Judicial Administration; House of Delegates; Insurance, Negligence, Compensation Law; AIDS Coordinating Committee; Torts and Insurance Practice Section; Special Committee on Product Liability) Bar Associations; Bar Association of the Seventh Federal Circuit; Illinois Trial Lawyers Association (Special Counsel to the Executive Committee, 1986—; Member, Special Advisory Committee to the Constitutional Challenge Committee, 1996—); The Association of Trial Lawyers of America (Trustee, Civil Justice Foundation, 1994—); Law Science Academy, Society of Trial Lawyers; American Judicature Society (Member, Board of Directors); American Board of Professional Liability Attorneys (Past President); Inner Circle of Advocates. Fellow: American College of Trial Lawyers; American Bar Foundation; Chicago Bar Foundation (Life Fellow). Charter Fellow, Illinois State Bar Foundation. ***PRACTICE AREAS:*** Plaintiff's Personal Injury Litigation; Aviation Litigation; Commercial Litigation; Medical Negligence; Professional Negligence; FELA; Product Liability; Premises Liability; Construction Accidents; Wrongful Death Law; Vehicular and Railroad Accident Law. ***Email:*** phc9@corboydemetrio.com

THOMAS A. DEMETRIO, born Evanston, Illinois, September 4, 1947; admitted to bar, 1973, Illinois, Florida and U.S. Court of Appeals, Fifth, Seventh and Ninth Circuits. *Education:* University of Notre Dame (B.A., 1969); Illinois Institute of Technology, Chicago-Kent College of Law (J.D., 1973). Profiles: Steven Naifeh and Gregory White Smith, *The Best Lawyers in America* , Woodward/White (1987—); Janine Warsaw, *Elements of a $12 Million Personal Injury Case,* ABA Journal - Litigation Techniques; Emily Couric, *50 Under 50, The National Law Journal* (June 5, 1989 (50 of the nation"s top lawyers under the age of 50); Marshall Sella, *The 10 Largest Jury Verdicts of 1988, The ABA Journal* (March, 1989); Margaret Cronin Fisk, *Winning - Successful Strategies from 10 of the Nation's Top Litigators, The National Law Journal* (February 12, 1990); Paul C. Gerber, *What a Lawyer Looks for Before Suing You, Physicians Management* (March 1990); David M. Beam, *Profile: Thomas A. Demetrio: A Lawyer with a Heart, The CBA Record* (September, 1992); Margaret Cronin Fisk, *Profiles in Power - 100 of the Most Influential Lawyers in America, The National Law Journal* (March 25, 1991; April 4, 1994; April 28, 1997) (listed as one of the three dozen lawyers deserving of an honorable mention); Jim Bell, *An Interview with Thomas A. Demetrio: "Because I Know You"re a Trial Lawyer" Trial Excellence* (Vol. 8, No. 7 July 1996, and Vol. 8, No. 8, August 1996); Margaret Cronin Fisk, *The NLJ Visits Illinois: Big Shoulders - The State's Top 10 Litigators, The National Law Journal* (November 8, 1999); *Tragedy's Bottom Line: When a plane crashes, lawyers embark on a painstaking and often gruesome exercise to decide who should pay for lost lives,* USA Today (January 5, 2000). Author: "Principles of Illinois Discovery: An Overview," and "Medical Malpractice Discovery," Illinois Civil Discovery Practice, Illinois Institute for Continuing Legal Education, 1983, Supplements: 1984, 1992, 1994, 1996 and 1999; "Comparative Fault in Illinois: Its Past, Present and Future," Illinois Trial Lawyers Journal, Vol. 6, No. 1, Fall-Winter, 1983; "The Due Process Clause of the Fifth Amendment Mandates that the Right to Trial by Jury, Guaranteed by the Seventh Amendment be Preserved," ABA-Tort and Insurance Practice Section Manual, 1985, Trial Magazine, August, 1985; "Video Depositions:

(This Listing Continued)

How and When to Use Them," CBA, Tort Litigation Committee, 1987; "The Practical Application of Illinois Discovery Rules," and "A Practical Guide to Discovery in Medical Negligence Litigation," Illinois Civil Discovery Practice (IllCLE, 1987, Supp. 1989); "Medical Malpractice," ABA Journal (An Interview) March, 1988; "Finding and Using Experts," ABA Tort and Insurance Practice Section Manual, 1988; "Look for the Silver Lining"—An Analysis of Weather-Related Air Crash Disasters, *Trial* Magazine, August 1998; "But Compared to What? Comparative Fault, Contribution and Joint and Several Liability" in *Illinois Bar Journal* April 1998 (co-authored with Michael Reagan); "The Key to Final Argument?—Persuasion," The CBA Record, March 1998; "Demetrio on Trial Practice—Batson: A Black and White Issue—Or Is It?" The CBA Record, June/July 1999; "Demetrio on Trial Practice—Motions *In Limine:* Why, When and How to Use Them" *CBA Record,* October 1999; *Demetrio on Trial Practice—Opening Statement:* Some Initial Thoughts an Bullet Points, *CBA Record, November 1999;* "Demetrio on Trial Practice—Striving for Excellence" *CBA Record,* December 1999; "More Cases We Remember-A Lesson In Credibility," *Trial* Magazine, April, 2000; "Demetrio on Trial Practice-Offers of Proof, Why, When & How," *CBA Record,* June/July 2000; "Loss of Consortium-A Continuing Evolution," *Trial* Magazine, Sept. 2000; "Demetrio on Trial Practice-Attorney/Client Privilege-Oh Really?" *CBA Record,* October 2000; "Demetrio on Trial Practice-Daubert-Its Early Years," *CBA Record,* April 2001; "Your Witness: Lessons on Cross-Examination and Life from Great Chicago Trial Lawyers: Cross-Examination and Its Impact on Credibility," Law Bulletin Publishing, Spring 2004. Faculty Member: ABA-Litigation Section, 1977—; The New York Law Journal, 1978; Illinois Institute for Continuing Legal Education, 1978—; Instructor, Product Liability, I.I.T. Chicago-Kent College of Law, 1979-1980; National Institute for Trial Advocacy Regional, 1978—; National, 1983—; National Institute for Trial Advocacy Annual Program on Negotiations and Counseling, 1983, 1986; Plaintiff"s co-counsel in two videotape series, "Training the Advocate," 1983 and "Training the Advocate: The Pre-Trial Stage," 1983, produced by NITA and The ABA Consortium for Professional Education; Federal Trial Bar Advocacy Program, 1983—; American Law Institute - American Bar Association Committee on Continuing Professional Education, 1983—; Chicago Bar Association, 1983—; Illinois Trial Lawyers Association, 1983—; ATLA National College of Advocacy Program, 1984—. Teaching and Lecturing: "Cross Examination," Litigation Section, American Bar Association, 1977; National Institute for Trial Advocacy, Regional, 1978—; National, 1983—; "Determining and Proving Damages," New York Law Journal, Colorado, 1978; "The Expert Witness in the Courtroom," American Society of Safety Engineers, 1979; "Illinois Product Liability Practice," Illinois Institute for Continuing Legal Education, 1980; "Deposition Strategy and Technique," Chicago Bar Association - Young Lawyers Section, 1983; "Recent Developments in Evaluating and Proving Damages," "Litigating Medical Malpractice Claims," ALI-ABA, California, 1983; "Plaintiff"s Final Argument in a Comparative Negligence Case," Association of Trial Lawyers of Iowa, 1983; "Plaintiff"s Final Argument," Illinois Defense Counsel"s Tactics Seminar, 1983; "How to Establish the Medical Opinion," Illinois Trial Lawyers Association Second Annual Comprehensive Evidence Seminar, 1983; "Effective Persuasion at Trial," Illinois Trial Lawyers Association Second Annual Presidents Seminar, 1983; "Evaluating, Proving and Arguing Damages," "Litigating Medical Malpractice Claims," ALI-ABA, California, 1984; "Closing Argument-The Plaintiff"s Perspective," Illinois Trial Lawyers Association, The Practical Approach to Trial Advocacy, 1984; "Assessment of Damages," "Third Annual Symposium on Head Trauma, Spinal Cord and Amputation for the Litigator," The Rehabilitation Institute of Chicago, 1984; "Trial Tactics in Governmental Liability Suits," Association of Trial Lawyers of Iowa, 1984; "How to Prove Loss of Companionship in the Case of a Deceased Spouse, Parent or Child," Illinois Institute for Continuing Legal Education, Proving and Disproving Damages in Personal Injury and Wrongful Death Cases, 1985; "Consulting the Appropriate Witness and Assessment of Damages," The Thorough Representation of the Catastrophically-Injured, The Rehabilitation Institute of Chicago, 1985; "Final Argument," The Ohio Academy of Trial Lawyers, 1985; "Anatomy of an Automobile Accident Trial," Practicing Law Institute, 1985; "Litigating Medical Malpractice Claims," ALI-ABA and Massachusetts CLE, 1985; "Jury De-Selection," Trial Superstars Seminar, Chicago Bar Association - Young Lawyers Section, 1985; "Closing Argument," ATLA"s Roscoe Pound Foundation Workshop, 1985; "How to Present the Expert Economist," Illinois Trial Lawyers Association, 1985; "Changes in Recovery Under the Illinois Wrongful Death Act," CBA-Tort Litigation Committee, 1986; "Proper Negotiation Techniques," NITA"s Annual Program on Negotiations and Counseling, 1986; "Our Tort System Must Be Preserved," 21st Annual Meeting of the Congress of Organizations of the Physically Handicapped, 1986; "Today"s Civil System of Justice," National Association of Independent Insurers, 1986; "Persuasive Trial Techniques," Hispanic National Bar Association 1986 Annual Convention; "Proper Evaluation of Product Liability Cases," Illinois Trial Lawyers Association - Pick the Best, Decline the Rest, 1986; "Lawyers and Doctors: A Time for Harmony," Illinois State Medical Society, 1986; "Ethics and Attorneys" Fees," Northwestern University Law School, 1986 and 1987; "How Proof Relates to the Final Argument," Association of Trial Lawyers of America 1987 Mid-Winter Convention; "Recent Trends in Evaluating, Proving and Arguing Damages," Litigating Medical Malpractice Claims, ALI-ABA and California CLE, 1987; "Assessment of Damages," "The Thorough Representation of the Catastrophically-Injured: Causation, Expert Assessments of Damages and Long Term Care Issues," The Rehabilitation Institute of Chicago, 1987; "Video Depositions: How and When to Use Them," Chicago Bar Association, Tort Litigation Committee, 1987; "The Art of Deposition Taking," Chicago Bar Association, Tort Litigation Committee, 1987; "How to Find and Use the Expert Recreational and Sports Witness," Illinois Trial Lawyers Association, 1987; "Negotiations," Chicago Bar Association - Young Lawyers Section, 1988; "Finding and Using Experts in Crash Cases," ABA-TIPS, Massachusetts, 1988; "Comparative Fault," Indiana State Bar Association, 1988; "The Medical Malpractice Case," The 39th Annual Advocacy Institute, Ann Arbor, Michigan, 1988; "ITLA College of Advocacy," 1988; "Closing Argument," CBA-YLS, 1988; "Litigating Medical Malpractice Claims," ALI-ABA, South Carolina, 1988; Tort Expo "Masters of Advocacy," Tennessee Trial Lawyers Association, 1988; "Tort Reform or Deform? A Public Debate," Illinois State Bar Association, 1988; "Proving and Disputing Liability in Tort Cases," Chicago Bar Association - Young Lawyers Section, 1989; "The Persuasive Final Argument," Illinois Trial Lawyers Association, 1989; "Ideas on Final Argument," A Weekend with the Masters, Georgia Trial Lawyers Association, 1989; The 46th Annual Belli Seminar, 1989; "Non-Economic Damages: The Persuasive Final Argument," The Workhorse Seminars, Association of Trial Lawyers of America, 1989; "Using Final Argument to Enhance Damages," Alabama Trial Lawyers Association, 38th Annual Mid-Winter Con-

(This Listing Continued)

CORBOY & DEMETRIO, P.C., Chicago—Continued

ference, 1990; "Do"s and Don"ts of Direct Examination," Trial Notebook Series, Illinois Trial Lawyers Association, 1990; "Trial Symposium-Advocacy into the 90"s," Ohio Academy of Trial Lawyers, 33rd Annual Convention, 1990; Address to the Professional Liability Committee of the American Bar Association, ABA Annual Meeting, Chicago, 1990; "How to Address Damages in the Opening Statement and Closing Argument," Chicago Bar Association, 1990; "Arguing Medical Negligence," Illinois Trial Lawyers Association, 1990; "Arguing and Maximizing Damages," Kansas Trial Lawyers" Association, 1990; "A Collection of Great Closing Arguments: Techniques and Demonstrations," California Trial Lawyers Association 26th Annual Tahoe Seminar, 1991; "1991 Best Evidence Seminar," American Bar Association, Section of Litigation, Chicago, 1991; "Developing and Defending Employment Discrimination Cases," 42nd Annual Advocacy Institute, Ann Arbor, Michigan, 1991; "Final Argument," Joint Seminar of the Association of Florida Trial Lawyers and Georgia Trial Lawyers Association, Bermuda, 1991; "Effective Trial Techniques - From Pre-Trial Proceedings Through Summation," Chicago Bar Association, Chicago, 1991; "Delivering a Knock-Out Punch in Opening Statement," Third Annual Tort Masters Seminar, sponsored by Alabama Trial Lawyers Association, Academy of Florida Trial Lawyers and Georgia Trial Lawyers Association, Atlanta, 1991; "Winning with the Masters: Louisiana Trial Lawyers Association, "Last Chance Seminar," New Orleans, 1991; "Art of Summation" New York State Trial Lawyers Institute, New York, 1992; "Plaintiff"s Perspective: Closing," Federation of Insurance and Corporate Counsel Winter Program, Boca Raton, 1992; "Bad Faith in the "90s - How to Avoid It," Rollins Burdick Hunter Co. National Leadership Conference, Chicago, 1992; "Discovery Practice in the 90"s: A How-To Seminar Focusing on Competency, Efficiency & Civility," (Moderator) Chicago Bar Association, Chicago, 1992; Presentation of Plaintiff"s Perspective in a Product Liability Case (Opening Statement), Federal Bar Association, 1992; National Convention, Cleveland, 1992; "Is a Cap on Damages Socially Desirable?" Plaintiff"s Perspective, Illinois Provider Trust Annual Risk Management Meeting, Bloomington, 1992; "Jury Selection: Plaintiff"s Perspective" Point/Counterpoint Seminar, Illinois Trial Lawyers Association, Chicago, 1992, 1993; "Medical Experts: Effective Direct and Cross Examination-Plaintiff"s Perspective"-Illinois Association of Defense Trial Counsel, 1993; "Winning Closing Arguments"-ITLA Annual Seminar, 1993; "Practical Problems of Litigating with Foreign Defendants"-ABA Section of Tort and Insurance Practice, Washington, DC, 1993; "Aspects of American Product Liability Law"-International Institute, University of College Dublin, Dublin, Ireland, 1993; "Aftermath of an Error"-The NBC/GM Truck-Safety Broadcast Controversy, Loyola University"s Communication Department, Chicago, 1993; "Product Liability," Illinois Trial Lawyers Association, Chicago, 1994; "Product Liability: Third Restatement Torts," American Bar Association, Phoenix, Arizona, 1994; "Effective Direct and Cross-Examination"- Summer Boot Camp for Aspiring Litigators, CBA, Chicago, 1994; "Closing Arguments"-YLS Trial Practice Course, CBA, Chicago 1994; "Jury Selection in the Industrial Product Liability Case," The 13th Annual Conference on Product Liability Law - National Practice Institute, Chicago, 1995; "Direct and Re-Direct Examination — Trial Demonstration," ICLE"s 46th Annual Advocacy Institute - The Institute of Continuing Legal Education - Ann Arbor, Michigan, 1995; "House Bill 20 - Redefining Tort Practice in Illinois," CBA, 1995; "Litigation Management: Manage Dollars or Activities?" Johnson Controls Annual Law Department Meeting, Chicago, 1995; "The Art of Persuasion," Demonstration: Plaintiff"s Closing Argument, Defense Research Institute, Trial Techniques Seminar, Chicago, 1995; "Litigating Medical Malpractice Claims - Plaintiff"s Perspective," Annual American Law Institute-American Bar Association Committee on Continuing Professional Education, Charleston, South Carolina, 1995; "Winning with the Masters," Last Chance Seminar - Louisiana Trial Lawyers Association, New Orleans, 1995; "Closing Arguments," Ultimate Mentor Interactive Seminar, ITLA, Chicago, 1996; "The Obligations of Lawyering in Today"s World," Featured Speaker at the Annual Luncheon Meeting of the Franklin County Trial Lawyers Association, Columbus, Ohio, 1996; "Lessons Learned at Trial," CBA/YLS Seminar, Trial Superstars, CBA, Chicago, 1997; "Shaping the Jury"s Verdict — Winning in the Age of Tort Reform," ICLE"s 48th Annual Advocacy Institute - The Institute of Continuing Legal Education - Ann Arbor, Michigan, 1997; "How to Value the Personal Injury Case: Negotiating Strategies & Settlement Techniques"-ABA, Washington, D.C., 1998; "Trial Practice in the 90"s: Jury Selection, Focus Groups and Computer Graphics Animation" IICLE, Chicago, 1998; "Computer Graphics and Animation" International Academy of Trial Lawyers Annual Convention, Chicago, 1998; "Rebuttal Argument," ITLA Past President Seminar, Chicago, 2000; "Mentoring," Professionalism Day, IIT Chicago-Kent College of Law, Chicago, 2000. Federalist Society, Chicago 2000; "Rebuttal Argument," ATLA Convention, Chicago, 2000; "Anatomy of a Trial Seminar-Final Argument," Illinois Trial Lawyers Association, Chicago, 2000; "The Past, Present and Future of Product Liability," ABA Litigation Section, Chicago, 2000; "Views of a Trial Lawyer," Rotary Club of Chicago, 2000; "Jury Selection—Or Is It?" Chicago Bar Association, October 2001; "Trial Superstars—One Lawyer"s Perspective," John Marshall Law School, Chicago, November 2002; "Jury Persuasion," Northwestern University School of Law, Chicago, February 2003; "2003 Advocacy Showcase—The Medical Negligence Case: A One-Day Trial," Illinois Trial Lawyers Association, Chicago, May 2003; "Electronics in the Courtroom," Inner Circle of Advocates, Chicago, 2003; "Tort Reform Wars: The Future of the Civil Jury System in a Litigious Nation," The Economic Club of Chicago, March 2004; "Tort Reform: Its Economic Impact Nationally and in Illinois," The Executives" Club of Chicago, October 2004; "Breaking Barriers, Building Bridges—Masters at Trial," Chicago Bar Association, October 2004; "Opening Statement—Telling the Story," Lessons from the Stars, D.C. Trial Lawyers Association, March 2005; "2005 Advocacy Showcase—A One-Day Trial," Illinois Trial Lawyers Association, May 2005; "Tort Reform Summit," Chicago Daily Law Bulletin, May 2005; "Opening Statement and Final Argument: Is There Really a Difference?" Academy of Florida Trial Lawyers, June 2005. Dean, ATLA"s National College of Advocacy-Specialized College on Damages, Colorado, 1987. Member, Illinois Supreme Court Committee on Pattern Civil Jury Instructions, 1978-1996. IIT Chicago-Kent College of Law: Chairman IIT Downtown Center Campaign Committee, 1989—; President, Alumni Association, 1988-1989; Chairman Partnership Program, 1987-1988; Vice-President of Finance, 1987-1988; Treasurer, 1986-1987; Board of Directors, Alumni Association, 1986-1989; The President"s Council, 1984—; Board of Trustees, St. Ignatius College Prep, 1990-1995; Board of Advisors, Mundelein Seminary, 1992-1997; Board of Directors, Big Shoulders, Archdioceses of Chicago, 1993—; Dispute Resolution Research Center Advisory Committee, J.L. Kellogg Graduate School of Management, Northwestern Univ., Chicago, 1993—; Chairman, Chicago Neurosurgical Center Leadership Committee, 1991—; IIT Chicago-Kent Advisory Committee on. *Member:* Chicago (Sustaining Member; Treasurer, 1989-1990; Second Vice President, 1990-1991; First Vice President, 1991-1992; President, 1992-1993; Board of Directors, Chicago Bar Association Television Products, Inc. 1990—; Public Relations Committee, 1990—; Task Force on Mandatory CLE, 1998; Chairman, Finance Committee, 1989-1990; Board of Managers, 1987-1989; Permanent Home Committee, 1987-1990; Board Subcommittees: Recommendations Regarding the Law Division, 1989—, Evaluation of Special Commission Recommendations, 1989; General Counsel Search Committee, 1988; Commentator, L.A. Law-Fact or Fiction" CBA TV, 1988, 1990; Participant, CBA Settlement Project, 1988, 1989; Committee on Bicentennial of the United States Constitution, 1986-1987; Evaluation of Judicial Candidates Committee, 1978-1982, 1983-1986; Implementation Commission for the Lawyers Trust Fund of Illinois, 1983-1984; Law Library Committee, 1974-1975), Illinois State (Member: General Assembly, 1981-1984; Offer of Judgment Committee, 1983-1985), Federal and American Bar Associations; The Florida Bar; Illinois Trial Lawyers Association (President, 1988-1989; President-Elect, 1987-1988; Second Vice-President, 1986-1987; Third Vice President, 1985-1986; Member: Board of Managers, 1978—; Amicus Curiae Committee, 1982; Vice Chairman, 1983-1985, Legislative Committee, 1984; ITLA-PAC Committee, 1984—; Public Relations Committee, Chairman, 1985-1987; Executive Committee, 1985—); The Association of Trial Lawyers of America (Member; Discovery Abuse Committee, 1989-1990; National College of Advocacy Faculty Training ATLA Basic and Advanced Colleges and Seminars Committee, 1989-1990; Chairman: Advanced Seminars, 1987-1988; National Seminar Programs, 1986-1987); The American Board of Professional Liability Attorneys (Convention Program Co-Chairman, 1984); The Society of Trial Lawyers-Illinois; Trial Lawyers for Public Justice (Member, Board of Directors, 1988—). The Seventh Circuit Bar Association; Chicago Inn of Court (Master of the Bench); The Law Club of Chicago; Trial Lawyers Club of Chicago; Center for Elder & Disability Law (Board of Directors, 1990—); Illinois Public Action Counsel (Board of Directors, 1988-1997); The Center for Conflict Resolution (Board of Directors, 1990-1993); Legal Aid Society United Charities (Board of Directors, 1991—); Metropolitan Family Services Legal Aid Bureau; Handgun Committee on Violence. Life Fellow: Illinois Bar Foundation (Charter Member). Fellow, American College of Trial Lawyers (Upstate Illinois State Committee, 1997-2002; National Trial Competition Committee, 2004-); International Academy of Trial Lawyers; Inner Circle of Advocates; American Bar Foundation; Chicago Bar Foundation (Board of Directors, 1994-1996, Lend-A-Hand Advisory Board, 1994-); Illinois Law Foundation. ***PRACTICE AREAS:*** Personal Injury; Wrongful Death; Aviation Litigation; Commercial Litigation; Medical Negligence; Professional Negligence; Federal Employers Liability Act (FELA); Product Liability; Premises Liability; Construction Liability; Automobile Liability. ***Email:*** tad9@corboydemetrio.com

PHILIP HARNETT CORBOY, JR., born Evanston, Illinois, November 11, 1950; admitted to bar, 1978, Illinois and U.S. District Court, Northern District of Illinois; 1994, U.S. Court of Appeals, Seventh Circuit. *Education:* Villanova University (B.S., Political Science, 1973); DePaul University (J.D., 1977). Appointments: Cook County Circuit Court Committee to Recommend Local Rules for Court-Annexed Mandatory Arbitration, 1988; Vice President, Variety Club Children"s Charity, Tent No. 26, 1987-1994; Board of Trustees, Presidents" Club, De Paul University, 1987—; Democratic National Committee, Permanent Committee on Credentials, 1992; Capital Development Committee, De Paul University College of Law, 1992—; Oxford"s "Who"s Who", 1992—; Law Advisory Council, De Paul University College of Law, 1996—; Board of Directors, Legal Assistance Foundation of Chicago, 1997—; Board of Directors, The Chicago Lighthouse for the Blind, 2000—. Lecturer: John Marshall Law School, Intensive Trial Advocacy Program, 1984; Kent College of Law, Student Intern Program, 1984-1985; ABA Annual Convention, New York City, Torts and Insurance Practice Section, 1986; Chicago Bar Association Trial Practice Course, 1988; Illinois Trial Lawyers Association Annual Update Seminar, 1988; Illinois Trial Lawyers Association, "Trial by Jury", 1988; American Trial Lawyers Association, National Law School Trial Advocacy Competition, 1989 (Judge); Chicago Bar Association, "Proof of Damages," Seminar, 1989; De Paul University Moot Court Competition, Judge, 1984-1989; Tennessee Trial Lawyers Association Annual Convention, "Increasing Damages Through Closing Arguments," July 1989; NALI Regions II and V Seminar, "Airline Accidents", October 1989; Illinois Trial Lawyers Association, Trial Notebook Seminar, "Demonstrative Evidence", 1989; Chicago Bar Association, "Tort Litigation" Seminar, 1990; Northwestern University School of Law Moot Court Competition Judge, 1990; Continuing Legal Education Satellite Network, Video Presentation "Litigation Trends in the 1990"s," February 1990; Chicago Cable Access Television Panelist, "Judicial Evaluation," March 1990; Chicago Bar Association, Proof of Facts Seminar, "Proving Injury," May 1991; De Paul University, "Career Day Programs" Seminar, Personal Injury Litigation, September 1991; John Marshall Moot Court and American Bar Association Joint National Criminal Justice Trial Advocacy Program, Judge, March 1992; American Bar Association, "Emerging Issues in Automobile Product Liability Litigation," April 1992; Chicago Bar Association "Summation in a Civil Case," May 1992; De Paul University "Career Day Programs" Seminar, Personal Injury Litigation, September 1992; Illinois Trial Lawyers Association Seminar, "Evidence," May 1993; De Paul University "Career Day Programs" Seminar, Personal Injury Litigation, September 1993; Chicago Bar Association, Trial Lawyers Workshop, "Product Liability" March 1993; Illinois Trial Lawyers Association, Shotgun Seminar, "Taking the Defendant"s Deposition" February 1994; De Paul University College of Law, "The Art of Persuasion," February 1996; Chicago Bar Association, YLS Group "Enhancing Your Practice Through Public Speaking," May 1996; Business Executives for Economic Justice "A Christian Perspective on Litigation in America" Panel, Chicago, Illinois, November 1996; DuPage County Bar Association, "Collecting, Analyzing and Preserving the Evidence," October 1997; John Marshall Law School and American Bar Association Criminal Justice Trial Advocacy Competition, Judge, Spring, 1998; Illinois State Bar Association Young Lawyers Division, "Motions-in-Limine," Speaker, May, 1998; Illinois Trial Lawyers Association Seminar, "Forum Non Conveniens," September 1998; Medical Educational Services, Inc. Confidentiality of Medical Records Seminar, "AIDS/HIV Patient Records," September, 1998; Western Trial Lawyers Association, Sun Valley, Idaho, "Daubert & Kumho: A Review and Their Practical Application," February, 2000; Illinois Trial Lawyer Association, "Economic Damages," May, 2000; Crittenden Medical Conference, Washington, DC, Panelist, "Plaintiff Attorneys v. Defense Attorneys," May, 2001; Chicago Bar Association, Continuing Legal Education Seminars, "Civil Liability for Injuries During a Sporting Event," May, 2001; Crittenden Medical Conference, Las Vegas,

(This Listing Continued)

Panelist, "Severity of Verdict—Where is it going & how do we stop it?" May 2003; "Winning Strategies for Disability Jury Trials" American Conference Institute, December 2003; "Update on Intrastate Forum Non Conveniens," ITLA Update & Review Seminar, October 2004; "Recognizing & Preventing the $10 Million Verdict," Crittenden Medical Conference, May 2005. Continuing Legal Education: Various Seminars by the Cook County State"s Attorney"s Office, Criminal Division, 1978-1985; ATLA Annual Convention, July 1985; ITLA Seminar Medical Malpractice, August 1985; ITLA Update and Review Seminar, September 1985; ITLA Shotgun Seminar, October 1985; IICLE Medico-Legal Symposium Seminar, 1985; ITLA Superstar Seminar, February 1986; ITLA Comprehensive Experts Seminar, December 1987; Architect - Engineer Liability under Illinois Law, 1987; Chicago Bar Association Trial Practice Course, 1988; ITLA Annual Update Seminar, 1988; ITLA "Trial by Jury," 1988; Chicago Bar Association "Proof of Damages" Seminar, 1989; Chicago Bar Association "Tort Litigation: Important Answers to New Questions" Seminar, 1990; ITLA Seminar on New Discovery Rules, Fall, 1995; ITLA Seminar on Evidence, Winter, 2000; Profiled in "Civil Excellence, De Paul Personal Injury Litigators," Dialogue, The Magazine of De Paul College of Law, Winter, 2000 Annual Convention, The Association of Trial Lawyers of America, July 1985; Medical Malpractice Seminar, Illinois Trial Lawyers Association, August 1985; Update and Review Seminar, Illinois Trial Lawyers Association, September 1985; Shotgun Seminar, Illinois Trial Lawyers Association, October 1985; IICLE Medico-Legal Symposium Seminar, 1985; Superstar Seminar, Illinois Trial Lawyers Association, February 1986; Comprehensive Experts Seminar, Illinois Trial Lawyers Association, December 1987; "Architect-Engineer Liability Under Illinois Law," 1987; "Trial Practice Course, Chicago Bar Association, 1988; Annual Update Seminar, Illinois Trial Lawyers Association, 1988; "Trial by Jury," Illinois Trial Lawyers Association, 1988; "Proof of Damages" Seminar, Chicago Bar Association, 1989; "Tort Litigation: Important Answers to New Questions" Seminar, Chicago Bar Association, 1990; Seminar on New Discovery Rules, Illinois Trial Lawyers Association, Fall, 1995. Profiles: "Civil Excellence, De Paul Personal Injury Litigators," Dialogue, The Magazine of De Paul College of Law, Winte. *Member:* Chicago (Board of Managers 1994-1996; Judicial Evaluation Committee, 1980; Vice-Chair, 1984-1987; Chairman, 1987-1990; General Chairman, 1989-1990; House Committee Chairman, 1990-1991; Long Range Planning Committee Chairman, 1999—; Cook County Circuit Court Settlement Program, Mediator, 1988-1989), Illinois State and American Bar Associations; Illinois Trial Lawyers Association (Member: Board of Managers 1997—; Legislative Committee, 1997—; Nominating Committee, 2000); The Association of Trial Lawyers of America (Illinois State Delegate, 2001-2002; Delegate 2002—); Society of Trial Lawyers Association. ***PRACTICE AREAS:*** Personal Injury; Wrongful Death; Aviation Litigation; Commercial Litigation; Medical Negligence; Professional Negligence; FELA; Product Liability; Premises Liability; Construction Liability; Automobile and Railroad Liability. ***Email:*** fhc@corboydemetrio.com

---

ROBERT J. BINGLE, born Toledo, Ohio, August 15, 1951; admitted to bar, 1981, Illinois. *Education:* University of Notre Dame (B.A., 1973); University of Chicago (M.A., 1975); Loyola University (J.D., 1981). Author: The National Law Journal: "Winning the Verdict with Video and Virtual Reality," June 15, 1998; "How to Try a Personal Injury Case—Strategies and Techniques from the Experts—A Satellite Program," Chair and Editor, Practicing Law Institute, 1998; "When Can the Government Be Sued Under the Illinois Tort Immunity Act? The Conundrum of Discretionary Versus Ministerial Acts," ITLA Journal, June 1999; "The Liability of Non-Operator Defendant," ITLA Publication, Automobile Litigation in Illinois, Spring 2002; "Motor Vehicle Actions," Illinois Causes of Action - Elements, Forms and Winning Tips: Tort Actions, IICLE Handbook, 2002. Faculty Member: National Institute for Trial Advocacy Program on Negotiations: A Systematic Approach, 1985-1988, 1990-1991, 1993-1994, 1996-1997; Loyola Appellate Advocacy, March 1986. Judge, Loyola Moot Court Competition, 1986 and 1987. Lecturer: "Careful Habits, Reputation Evidence" ITLA Evidence Seminar, December 3, 1988; National Business Institute, Personal Injury Litigation Practice in Illinois, January 1989; ITLA Evidence Seminar, December 3, 1988; Trial Notebook Series, ITLA, February 19, 1990; "Overcoming Governmental Immunity, The Plaintiff's Perspective," Young Lawyers Section of the CBA, February 20, 1990; Illinois Institute for Continuing Legal Education: Defending Auto Accident Cases - Proving One Car Accident Cases, March 5, 1990; Aetna Insurance Company Claims Representatives Regional Conference, Negotiation Seminar, May 24, 1990; CBA - Young Lawyers Section, Comparative Negligence, February, 1991; CBA - Young Lawyers Section, Committee on Professional Responsibility, April 22, 1991; ITLA Civil Practice Update and Review Seminar: "Negligence," September 7, 1991; ABA Litigation Section, Voir Dire Program, October 25, 1991; CBA, Slip and Fall - A Plaintiff"s Perspective, November 11, 1991; CBA, Proving Injury: Pain & Suffering, Loss of Consortium and Earnings, November 21, 1991; ITLA, Products Liability/Wrongful Death Seminar: Proof & Argument in the Courtroom, Loss of Consortium and Society, January 11, 1992; ISBA, Law Education Series, Civil Practice: Products Liability, April 16, 1992; New Mexico Trial Lawyers Association. The Ultimate Trial Seminar II: Final Argument, June 12, 1992; ATLA, Melvin Belli Seminar, July, 1994; Texas Trial Lawyers Association Annual Meeting: Ten Reasons Why Lawyers are Hated and Loved, September 9, 1994; De Paul University, National Symposium on the Legal and Business Issues of Tort Reform, February 2, 1996; ITLA, Practice Update and Review Seminar: The Settlement Dilemma, February 19, 1996; ITLA, Practice Seminar: The Art of Persuasion, presented at De Paul College of Law and Kent College of Law, February 29, 1996; Illinois Civil and Criminal Justice, Inside Insights Panel Discussion, March 5, 1996; ITLA, Maximizing Results Through Settlement and Trial: Prosecuting the Negligence Case - Handling Coverage and Bad Faith Issues to Maximize Settlement, February 17, 1997; ITLA, Point-Counterpoint: Trial Advocacy from Both Sides with Views from the Bench, "Constructing and Presenting Plaintiff"s Case-In-Chief," April 11, 1997; Loyola University School of Law, Health Conference in Dublin, Ireland, June 24-26, 1997; Illinois Defense League, Multi-District Litigation Discussion Panel, September 13, 1997; Office of the Illinois Attorney General, Expert Witness Foundations for Expert Opinions, September 25, 1997; ITLA, Trial Techniques Seminar: Opening Statements, October 13, 1997; Chicago Bar Association - Young Lawyers Section, Enhancing Your Law Practice Through Public Speaking, December 5, 1997; Federalist Society Debate, September 1999; ISBA Civil Practice Update Seminar, April 1999; Evidence Seminar, ITLA, *Empty Chair Defense,* May 2000; *Enhancing Your Practice Through Public Speaking,* CBA-YLS, January 2000. Faculty Chair, "How to Try a Personal Injury Case," Practicing Law Institute, October 15, 1998. Panelist, Jury Selection, CBA—

(This Listing Continued)

Bench/Bar Relations Committee Seminar, October 27, 1998. Lecture, Trial Practice, ISBA—Civil Practice Update Seminar, April 23, 1999. Moderator and Program Planner, ITLA Evidence Seminar, May 8, 1999; ITLA Evidence Seminar, May 1999; "Maximizing Damages," ITLA, 2001; "Evidence Seminar-Opening Remarks," ITLA, 2001. Continuing Legal Education: Illinois Institute of Continuing Legal Education, Trial Bar Skills Seminar, 1983; Motion Practice in the Law Division of the Circuit Court of Cook County, January 1983; Chicago Bar Association - Young Lawyers Section, Trial Techniques Seminar, April 1983; ITLA, Past President"s Seminar, February 1984; Chicago Bar Association, Probate Seminar, March 1985; American Trial Lawyers Association, Annual Convention, July 1985; ITLA, Medical Malpractice Seminar, August 1985; ITLA, Update and Review Seminar, September 1985; ITLA, Shotgun Seminar, October 1985; NATLE/ATLA State Legislative Conference, November 1985; ITLA, Superstar Seminar, February 1986; American Trial Lawyers Association, Sports" Injuries and the Law - A Safety Conference and Trial Seminar, June 1986; Chicago Bar Association, Effective Trial Seminar, June 1986; ITLA, Education Fund Seminar, December 1986; ITLA Comprehensive Experts Seminar, December 1987; Institute of Continuing Legal Education, Trial Skills Workshop Seminar, May 1988; ITLA, Annual Convention - Torts Seminar, June 1988; ITLA, Annual Evidence Seminar: Careful Habits, Character & Reputation, December 3, 1988; Illinois Institute of Continuing Legal Education, Persuasive Techniques in Personal Injury Cases Seminar, September 1995; De Paul University, National Symposium on the Legal and Business Issues of Tort Reform, February 2, 1996; ITLA, Practice Update and Review Seminar: The Settlement Dilemma, February 19, 1996; Illinois Civil and Criminal Justice - Inside Insights Panel Discussion, March 5, 1996; American Trial Lawyers Association, Summer Convention, July 21-24, 1997. Member, State of Illinois Supreme Court Committee on Character and Fitness, First District, 1993-2. *Member:* Chicago (Chairman, House Committee, 1992-1993, 1993-1994), Illinois State (Standing Committee on Judicial Appointments, 1994-1995) and American (Member, Section on Litigation) Bar Associations; Illinois Trial Lawyers Association (President, 2002-2003; 2nd Vice President, 2001-2002; Third Vice President, 2000-2001; Board of Managers, 1987-2000; Chairman, Membership Committee, 1988-1990, 1992-1994; Member, Executive Committee, 1995- ; Chairman, Legal Education Program; Co-Chairman, Legislative Committee, 1997-1999; Public Relations Committee, 1985-1987; Editorial Board, Journal, 1999); The Association of Trial Lawyers of America (Railroad Law Section, 1995-1998); National Institute for Trial Advocacy; Illinois Supreme Court Committee on Jury Instructions in Civil Cases (2004—). (Managing Partner). ***PRACTICE AREAS:*** Personal Injury Litigation; Aviation Litigation; Commercial Litigation; Medical Negligence; Professional Negligence; FELA; Product Liability; Premises Liability; Construction Accidents; Wrongful Death Law; Vehicular Accident Law. ***Email:*** rjb9@corboydemetrio.com

FRANCIS PATRICK MURPHY, born Berea, Ohio, February 3, 1948; admitted to bar, 1975, Illinois and U.S. District Court, Northern District of Illinois. *Education:* Northwestern University (B.S.B.A., 1970); Illinois Institute of Technology, Chicago-Kent College of Law (J.D., 1975). Author: "Practical Approach for Uninsured/Underinsured Motorist Claims," Professional Education Systems, Inc.; "Wrongful Death Cases - Procedural Aspects," Chicago Bar Association; "Jury Selection Practice and Procedure," The Art & Science of Jury Selection, Illinois Institute of Continuing Legal Education, 1988; "How to Direct Examine the Economist," Chicago Bar Association, 1989; "Masters in Trial," American Bar Association Tort and Insurance Practice Section, April 24, 1998; "A Shattered Bottle...a Shattered Life" *Packaging Forensics: Package Failure in the Courts,* Lawyers & Judges Publishing Company, Inc. (2000); 18 "Intentional Infliction of Emotional Distress," Illinois Causes of Action, Illinois Institute of Continuing Legal Education (2001). Faculty Member: Guest Instructor, De Paul College of Law, 1984-1986; IIT Chicago-Kent College of Law, National Mock Trial Competition Regional Evaluator, February 1986; Guest Instructor, Loyola University School of Law, 1987; Lecturer of Law, Loyola University School of Law, 1987-1996. Adjunct Professor, Loyola University School of Law, 1997—. Lecturer: "Gun Control - Illinois Perspective," Criminal Justice Institute, 1983; "Bill 1200 - Overview of Tort Reform Affecting Corporations," American Society of Corporate Secretaries, 1987; "Proving Injury - Pain & Suffering, Loss of Consortium and Earnings," Chicago Bar Association, November 9, 1992; "Wrongful Death Cases - Procedural Aspects," Chicago Bar Association, February 11, 1993; "Pretrial Trade Secrets of the Pros - Those Precious Few Interrogatories," Illinois Trial Lawyers of America, February 19, 1996; "The Use of Demonstrative Evidence in Trial: The Millennium and Beyond," American Bar Association Tort and Insurance Practice, April 24, 1998; "Masters in Trial," ABA Tort and Insurance Practice Section, April 24, 1998; Guest Speaker, PriceWaterhouseCoopers 1998 Legal Tech Conference, October 1998. American Bar Association Judge for National Appellate Court Competition, Law Student Division, 1990; "Making the Defense Medical Expert Your Expert in a MIST Case Using a Ben Franklin Balance Sheet," ATLA, July 2004. *Member:* Chicago, Illinois State and American Bar Associations; Illinois Trial Lawyers Association; The Association of Trial Lawyers of America; Society of Trial Lawyers. ***PRACTICE AREAS:*** Personal Injury; Wrongful Death; Aviation Litigation; Commercial Litigation; Medical Negligence; Professional Negligence; FELA; Product Liability; Premises Liability; Construction Liability; Automobile and Railroad Liability. ***Email:*** fpm@corboydemetrio.com

SUSAN J. SCHWARTZ, born Chicago, Illinois, June 27, 1956; admitted to bar, 1980, Illinois and U.S. District Court, Northern District of Illinois. *Education:* Georgetown University (B.S.F.S., 1977); Loyola University (J.D., 1980). Author: "Final Argument," Anatomy of a Personal Injury Lawsuit, 3rd Edition, 1990; "Going the Distance, How to Perfect the Trial Record and Win on Appeal," ABA Journal, Vol. 76, April 1990; "Res Ipsa Loquitur," Illinois Trial Lawyers Association, Malpractice Trial Notebook, 1997 and 1999 issues; "Tort Actions: Loss of Consortium," Chapter 12, IICLE Illinois Causes of Action - Elements, Forms & Winning Tips, 2002; "Pain and Suffering and Non-Economic Damages," Chapter 24, ATLA"s Litigating Tort Cases, 2003, 2004. Co-Author: "Medical Professional Negligence: Building a Prima Facie Case," Chapter 2 of 1996 IICLE Medical Malpractice Practice Handbook; "Cervical Insufficiency," Operative Obstetrics, 1995; "Illinois Courts: Vital Developers of Tort Law as Constitutional Vanguards, Statutory Interpreters, and Common Law Adjudicators," Loyola University Chicago Law Journal, Winter 1998. Lecturer: "The Medical Malpractice Crisis: Federal Efforts, States" Rules and Private Responses—Patient Perspective with a Focus on Compensatory Harm," Loyola University School of Law Annual Health Law & Policy Colloquium, November 14, 2003; "Reducing Your Malpractice Risk: A Plaintiff"s Lawyer"s Insight," Evanston Northwestern

(This Listing Continued)

CORBOY & DEMETRIO, P.C., Chicago—Continued

HealthCare Physicians Group, February 4, 2004; "Pleadings and Written Discovery," Tort Litigation Seminar, Illinois Trial Lawyers Association, January 19, 2002; "Cancer Cases," Medical Malpractice Seminar, Illinois Trial Lawyers Association, December 8, 2001; "Disclosure of Medical Errors: Demonstrated Strategies to Enhance Communication," American Society for Healthcare Risk Management of the American Hospital Association, June 20, 2001; "Evidence Privileges," Illinois Trial Lawyers Association, May 8, 1999; "Trial of a Medical Malpractice Case," Loyola University Chicago, March 2, 1999; "Federal Bar Training Course," Exhibits, Young Lawyers Section, Chicago Bar Association, October 27, 1998. Moderator: Damages Seminar, Illinois Trial Lawyers Association, May 9, 1998; "Closing Arguments," Federal Trial Bar Training Course, Young Lawyers Section, Chicago Bar Association, November 4, 1997; "Six Days to Trial: Trial of a Medical Malpractice Case for the Plaintiff," Chicago Bar Association, June 4, 1997; "How to Make Money and Sleep at Night Handling Plaintiff"s Litigation," Avoiding Legal Malpractice, Illinois State Bar Association, CLE Seminar, January 20, 1997; "Effective Use of Expert Witnesses," Chicago Bar Association Young Lawyers Section, Trial Techniques, January 24, 1994; "A Different Standard of Care for Physicians in Training?" Participant, Panel Discussion, Institute for Health Law, Loyola University of Chicago School of Law, October 27, 1993; "How to Get a Verdict," Northwest Suburban Bar Association, Civil Litigation Seminar, Third District Courthouse, Rolling Meadows, Illinois, March 13, 1993; "Evaluating Our System of Justice: Is Our Judicial and Litigation System Delivering Justice to all the Public?" American Bar Association, 1992 Annual Meeting, San Francisco, California; "Fundamentals of Trial Preparation," Illinois Trial Lawyers Association Education Fund, Young Lawyers" Seminar, Chicago, May 2, 1992; "Medical Malpractice Trends - North and South of the Border," Comparative Health Law and Policy Conference, Loyola University of Chicago School of Law, Institute for Health Law, July 13, 1990; Illinois Medical Record Association co-sponsored by Illinois State Bar Association, Legal Issues Workshops, Medical Records as Evidence - A Trial Attorney"s Perspective, Hillside, Illinois, June 20, 1989; "Insurance Law for Plaintiffs," Seminar, The Insurance Contract, Illinois Trial Lawyers Association, June 10, 1989; Illinois Trial Lawyers Association, "Insurance Law for Plaintiffs," The Insurance Contract, Oak Book Hills, Illinois, June 10, 1989; Illinois Society of Oral and Maxillofacial Surgery, Anesthesia Committee, "What is Dental Malpractice? Oak Brook, Illinois, April 30, 1989; Proof of Negligence in Medical Negligence Cases - Plaintiff"s Perspective, Sponsored by Chicago Bar Association, January 25, 1989; Legal Systems Influencing the Quality of Medical Care, Loyola University of Chicago, School of Law, Institute for Health Law, February 1 and 8, 1989. Participant, Round Table discussion on Gender Bias in the Courts, sponsored by Illinois Task Force on Gender Bias in the Courts, November 21, 1988. Instructor, American Bar Association/National Institute for Trial Advocacy Video Series, Cross-Examination of Experts, October 24 - 27, 1987, Minneapolis, Minnesota. Lecturer, Named Insureds and Members of Family - What is "Resident of Household?" Illinois Trial Lawyers Association, October 18, 1986. Judge, Interschool Appellate Advocacy Competition, at Loyola University School of Law, 1984, 1985, 1986. Lecturer, Illinois Trial Lawyers Association Past President"s Seminar, "Arbitration & Mediation in Cook County," 1985. Guest Lecturer, Street Law Program, Loyola University of Chicago School of Law, Chicago, Illinois, 19. *Member:* Chicago, Illinois State and American Bar Associations; Illinois Trial Lawyers Association; The Association of Trial Lawyers of America. ***PRACTICE AREAS:*** Personal Injury; Wrongful Death; Aviation Litigation; Commercial Litigation; Medical Negligence; Professional Negligence; FELA; Product Liability; Premises Liability; Construction Liability; Automobile and Railroad Liability. ***Email:*** sjs9@corboydemetrio.com

RENÉ A. TORRADO, JR., born Miami Beach, Florida, August 4, 1947; admitted to bar, 1973, Florida; 1985, District of Columbia; 1981, Illinois; U.S. Court of Appeals for the District of Columbia Circuit; U.S. District Court, Northern District of Illinois; U.S. Court of Appeals for the Seventh Circuit; U.S. District Court, Southern District of Florida. *Education:* University of Notre Dame (B.A., 1969); Georgetown University (J.D., 1973). *Member:* Chicago (President, 1995-1996; First VP, 1994-1995; General Counsel, 1998-1995) and American Bar Associations; The Florida Bar; District of Columbia Bar; Illinois Trial Lawyers Association; Chicago Inn of Court. ***PRACTICE AREAS:*** Personal Injury; Wrongful Death; Aviation Litigation; Commercial Litigation; Medical Negligence; Professional Negligence; FELA; Product Liability; Premises Liability; Construction Liability; Automobile Liability; Railroad Liability.

MICHAEL K. DEMETRIO, born Evanston, Illinois, July 26, 1954; admitted to bar, 1979, Illinois; 1987, U.S. District Court, Northern District of Illinois; 1992, U.S. District Court, Eastern District of Wisconsin. *Education:* University of Notre Dame (B.B.A., 1976); Illinois Institute of Technology, Chicago-Kent College of Law (J.D., 1979). Author: "Aviation Causes of Action," IICLE, June 2002 Edition. Lecturer: "Motion Practice in the Law Division Circuit Court of Cook County," Chicago Bar Association Continuing Legal Education Committee Seminar, 1986; "Vehicular Design Liability Litigation," Illinois Institute for Continuing Legal Education, 1986; "Proof of Defect in a Product Liability Case," National Law Journal, 1986; "Superstar Seminar," Illinois Trial Lawyers Association, 1986; Graduate National Institute of Trial Advocacy Faculty Training Program, Harvard Law School, 1989; "Art of Cross-Examination," Chicago Bar Association, 1991; "Trial Evidence and Hearsay Seminar," Illinois Trial Lawyers Association, 1991; "The Problems and Procedures of Jury Selection," Chicago Bar Association, 1991; Presidential Face-Off Seminar/Handling Personal Injury Cases, Illinois Trial Lawyers Association, 1993; The Trial of Automobile Collision Cases, 1991-1996, Chicago Bar Association; ITLA, Product Liability Litigation, Spoliation, January, 1995; CBA, Joint & Several Liability and Contribution: Pre and Post P.A. 89-7, January, 1996; "Spoliation of Evidence," Inner Circle, October, 1997; "Trial Practice in the '90s: Jury Selection, Focus Groups and Computer Graphics & Animation," IICLE, April, 1998; "Evaluating and Handling Spinal Cord Injuries, Brain Injuries and Wrongful Death Cases," CBA, October 1998; "Successful Automobile Trials," CBA Young Lawyers Section, January 2000; NTSB Transportation Safety & The Law Symposium, Washington, DC, April 2000; "Deposition Strategy," CBA, October 2000; "Trial Techniques Seminar," CBA Young Lawyers Section, March 2001; "Handling the Commercial Airline Crash Case," ATLA Annual Convention, July 2001; "Trial Strategy," ITLA Past President's Seminar, April 2002; "Identification of the Anchor and Reference Points," Identifying and Overcoming Jury Bias, ITLA, January 2003; "What's New in Tort & Trial," ITLA Construction Accidents, September 2003; "Great Trials Panel: Lessons Learned by

(This Listing Continued)

the Experts," ABA/YLS, September 2003; Law Student Division Competition Judge, ABA, April 2004. Appointed Lead Counsel, MDL No. 1084. Participant, PSC, Pittsburgh/US Air Disaster, MDL and Cook County. National Faculty Member, National Institute of Trial Advocacy. Certified Arbitrator, Cook County Mandatory Arbitration Program and American Arbitration Association. *Member:* Chicago (Board of Managers, 1996-1998; Treasurer, 1999-2001; 2nd Vice-President, 2001-2002; 1st Vice-President, 2002-2003; President, 2003-2004; Finance Committee, 1998—, Chair, 1999-2001; Chair, Long Range Planning Committee, 1995-1996; Chair, Judiciary Committee, 1994-1995; Co-Chair Appellate Judicial Evaluation Committee, 1993-1994; Judicial Evaluation Committee, 1984-1990); Illinois State and American (Member, Litigation Section) Bar Associations; Chicago Bar Foundation (Board of Directors, 1998—; Lend-A-Hand Annual Fundraising Event, Co-Chair, 1998—); Illinois Trial Lawyers Association (Member, Board of Managers, 1990—; Co-Chair, Membership Committee, 1996-2000; Secretary, 1995-1996; Treasurer, 1994-1995; Parliamentarian, 1993-1994); The Association of Trial Lawyers of America; American Arbitration Association (Panel Member of Neutral Arbitrator). International Academy of Trial Lawyers; The Society of Trial Lawyers. ***PRACTICE AREAS:*** Personal Injury; Wrongful Death; Aviation Litigation; Commercial Litigation; Medical Negligence; Professional Negligence; FELA; Product Liability; Premises Liability; Construction Liability; Automobile and Railroad Liability. ***Email:*** mkd9@corboydemetrio.com

SHAWN S. KASSERMAN, born Champaign, Illinois, May 28, 1965; admitted to bar, 1990, Illinois and U.S. District Court, Northern District of Illinois; 1994, U.S. District Court, Eastern District of Wisconsin; 1999, U.S. Court of Appeals, Ninth Circuit; 2001, U.S. District Court, Northern District of Indiana; 2002, U.S. District Court, Central District of Illinois. *Education:* Western Illinois University (B.A., 1987); DePaul University (J.D., 1990). Co-Author, "Jury Selection," 1993 Callahan's Supplement. Host, Midwest Sectional National Moot Court Competition, 1991, 1992. Lecturer: "Negligence," Illinois Trial Lawyers Association, 1992; "Taking Defendants' Depositions," Chicago Bar Association, December 1993; "Plaintiff Personal Injury Law," Illinois State Bar Association, February 1997; "Vehicle Rollovers, Latch Failures, Air Bags and More," Illinois Trial Lawyers Association January 1998; "Establishing Negligence & Rebutting the Defense of Contributory Negligence," Young Lawyers Section, Chicago Bar Association, October 1998; "Wrongful Death and Minor's Litigation," Young Lawyers Section, Chicago Bar Association, January 1999; Toxic Tort Seminar, National Business Institute, July 2000; "Maximizing Your Clients' Recovery Through Proper Allocation of Settlement," Potpourri of Civil Practice, Tort and Insurance Law Program, ISBA, June 2003. Contributor, Civil Practice and Procedure Section, Illinois State Bar Association, May 1999. Moderator, Illinois State Bar Association Leadership Conference, 1994, 1995. *Member:* Chicago (Judicial Evaluation Committee, 1998-1999; Interfaith Law Committee, 2000; Homeless and Runaway Youth Committee, Young Lawyers Section, 1992-1993), Illinois State (Young Lawyers Division Council; Past Chair, Young Lawyers Section, 1998-1999; Organizational Committee for the Leadership Conference, 1995-1996; Ad Hoc Committee for the First Annual Illinois State Bar Association Leadership Conference, 1993-1994); DuPage County (Civil Practice Committee, 1995-1996; Association Legal Aid Committee, 1995-1996); American (Young Lawyers Division Assembly, 1997); Illinois Trial Lawyers Association (Legislative Committee; Amicus Curiae Committee); The Association of Trial Lawyers of America (Advisory Committee, New Lawyers Division). ***PRACTICE AREAS:*** Personal Injury; Wrongful Death; Aviation Litigation; Commercial Litigation; Medical Negligence; Professional Negligence; FELA; Product Liability; Premises Liability; Construction Liability; Automobile and Railroad Liability. ***Email:*** ssk9@corboydemetrio.com

BARRY R. CHAFETZ, born Chicago, Illinois, December 16, 1946; admitted to bar, 1972, Illinois and U.S. District Court, Northern and Central Districts of Illinois. *Education:* University of Illinois (B.A., 1969; M.A., 1970; J.D., 1972). Listed in Who's Who in America, Leading Lawyers Network (Medical Malpractice). *Member:* American, Chicago, Illinois State, Association of Trial Lawyers of America, Illinois Trial Lawyers Association. ***PRACTICE AREAS:*** Personal Injury; Wrongful Death; Aviation Litigation; Commercial Litigation; Medical Negligence; Professional Negligence; FELA; Product Liability; Premises Liability; Construction Liability; Automobile and Railroad Liability. ***Email:*** brc9@corboydemetrio.com

DANIEL M. KOTIN, born Chicago, Illinois, December 24, 1965; admitted to bar, 1991, Illinois and U.S. District Court, Northern District of Illinois; 1998, Trial Bar, U.S. District Court, Northern District of Illinois. *Education:* Boston College (B.A., cum laude, 1988); Loyola University (J.D., cum laude, 1991). National Institute for Trial Advocacy, Midwest Regional Program, Chicago, Illinois, 1994. Member: Loyola University National Mock Trial Team, 1991; Senior Member, Loyola University of Chicago Law Review, 1989-1991. Coach, Loyola University National Mock Trial Team, 1994—. Instructor, Chicago Bar Association Federal Trial Bar Training Course, November 1996-1998; National Institute for Trial Advocacy, Midwest Regional Program, March, 2001; Intensive Advocacy Program, CBA, September 2000. Program Planning Chair: "ITLA Overcoming Jury Bias Seminar" (2003). Moderator: "ITLA Medical Malpractice Seminar" (2003); "Deposition Strategies and Techniques," CBA, 1993, 2004; "Preparation and Trial of Automobile Cases Seminar," CBA, January 1995; "Trial Superstars Seminar," CBA, May 1997; "Evidence Seminar," ITLA, May 1999; "Avoiding Common Pitfalls Seminar," ITLA (2002); "Evidence Seminar," ITLA (2003). Lecturer: Institute of Real Estate Management, Seminar on Building Security and Civil Liability, 1994; "Effective Cross-Examination," CBA *Proving Facts at Trial* Seminar, November 1995; "Proving Damages in a Personal Injury Case," CBA *Proving Facts in Trial* Seminar, December 1996; "The Plaintiff"s Perspective," Evaluating a Personal Injury Case," CBA, 1997; "Negotiating and Settling Personal Injury Cases," ITLA, 1998; "Proving Damages in a Personal Injury Case," CBA Association Proof of Facts Seminar, November 1998; "Liability to Particular Persons, Product and Premises Liability Seminar," ITLA, February 2000; "Preparing and Litigating Premises Liability Cases," CBA, April 2000; "Midwest Product Liability Workshop," ABA Litigation Section Committee on Corporate Counsel (2000); "Pleadings and Discovery," ITLA Product Liability Seminar, February 2001; "Deposition Strategy, Taking and Defending Depositions in State and Federal Courts Seminar," CBA (2002); "Settlement: Liens, Right of Subrogation, Good Faith Findings and Set-Offs," Getting to Trial Seminar, ISBA (2003); "Hands-on Discovery Workshop: Successfully Managing Legal and Strategic Challenges Seminar," Illinois Institute of Continuing Legal Education (2003); "Opening Statements," 39th Annual Trial Institute (2003); "Opening Statements," Anatomy of a Trial Seminar, ITLA (2004); "Lawyers Forum," Chicago Daily Law Bulleting Career Day (2004); "Re-

(This Listing Continued)

ducing the Costs of Civil Litigation in Illinois Circuit Courts," Allerton Conference, ISBA (2004); "How Plaintiffs Push Verdicts Higher," Crittenden Medical Insurance Conference, San Diego (2004); "All Schools Reception," CBA, Young Lawyers Section (2004); "Deposition Strategy," Taking and Defending Depositions in State and Federal Court Seminar, CBA (2004); "Deposing Fact Witnesses, Taking and Defending Effective Depositions in Illinois," Lorman Education Services (2005); "Liens," Tort Law Trends, ITLA (2005); "How Plaintiff Lawyers Perceive Insurance Companies," Chartered Property Casualty Underwriters Association (March 2005); "Career Advancement through Pro Bono Work, "Chicago Daily Law Bulletin Career Day (April 2005). Host, "You and the Law," CBA Cable Television Program, February 2001. Instructor, Jury Selection Workshop, Chicago Bar Association College of Trial Lawyers (October 2001). Author: "Ten Rules of Successful Cross Examination," CBA Record, March, 1996, reprinted as "The Art of Litigation: Ten Tips for Successful Cross-Examination," *Cleveland Bar Journal,* November 1997; "Premises Liability: Actions Against Landowner (Homeowner)," Illinois Institute of Continuing Legal Education, Causes of Action (2002); "Premises Liability: Actions Against Landlord," Chapter 21, Illinois Institute of Continuing Legal Education, Causes of Action, (2002); "Special Considerations in a Medical Negligence Case," Illinois Civil Discovery Practice, Ill. Ins. for Continuing Legal Education (2003); "The Practical Application of Civil Discovery Rules," Illinois Civil Discovery Practice, Illinois Institute for Continuing Legal Education (2003); Contributor, Jacob A. Stein, "Closing Argument, The Art and the Law," Clark, Boardman, Calahan, 1995; Lane, Scott D. and Lee, Stephanie Hoit, "Illinois Motions in Limine," Litigation One Publishing (2004). Evaluator, National High School Mock Trial Championship, 1994; Loyola University Trial Advocacy Program, 1994. Vice President, Partners of Misericordia, 1994-1997. Class Representative, Loyola University Chicago School of Law Alumni Association, 1993—. Profile: "40 Lawyers Under 40 to Watch," Chicago Lawyer (June 2002). *Member:* Chicago (Member, Executive Council, Young Lawyers Section, 1994—; Co-Chair, Trial Techniques Committee, 1994-1995; Special Projects Coordinator, 1995-1996; Director, YLS, 1996-1997; Vice-Chair, Television Committee, 2000-2001; Judicial Evaluation Committee Investigator, 2003), Illinois State and American Bar Associations; Illinois Trial Lawyers Association (Member; Board of Managers, 2001—; Board of Advocates, 2000-2001; Publications Committee, 1994-1996); The Association of Trial Lawyers of America; The Society of Trial Lawyers (Board of Directors, 2003—); Loyola Univ. School of Law Circle of Advocates (Member, 2002—); Leading Lawyers Network (Member, 2003—). ***PRACTICE AREAS:*** Personal Injury; Wrongful Death; Aviation Litigation; Commercial Litigation; Medical Negligence; Professional Negligence; FELA; Product Liability; Premises Liability; Construction Liability; Automobile and Railroad Liability. ***Email:*** dmk@corboydemetrio.com

DAVID R. BARRY JR., born Evanston, Illinois, June 14, 1956; admitted to bar, 1981, Illinois; 1985, Wisconsin. *Education:* St. Norbert College (B.A., 1978); Northwestern University (J.D., 1981). Author, "Proving and Disproving Damages in Personal Injury Cases," IICLE, 1996; "Damages in a Wrongful Death Case: Defendant's Perspective," IICLE, 2000. Lecturer, "Illinois Civil Discovery Practice," IICLE, July 21, 1988; "Discovery Tools and Tactics for the Personal Injury Lawyer," IICLE, January 26, 1990; "Depositions," ITLA Young Lawyers Seminar, May 2, 1992; "Mock Malpractice Trial for Medical Students," University of Illinois, April 15, 1993; "How to Depose a Medical Expert," IICLE, November 20, 2003; "Neuroimaging: The Latest Developments in Determining the Etiology and Timing of the Events Leading to Irreversible Brain Damage," ITLA Medical Malpractice Seminar, December 6, 2003; "Knowing When To Say No," CBA, Taking and Defending Depositions in State and Federal Court, December 17, 2003. *Member:* Chicago, Illinois State, Federal and American Bar Associations; Illinois Trial Lawyers Association; Association of Trial Lawyers of America; Trial Lawyers Club of Chicago (President, 1993-1994). Society of Trial Lawyers. ***PRACTICE AREAS:*** Personal Injury; Wrongful Death; Aviation Litigation; Commercial Litigation; Medical Negligence; Professional Negligence; FELA; Product Liability; Premises Liability; Construction Liability; Automobile Liability; Railroad Liability. ***Email:*** drb@corboydemetrio.com

---

THOMAS F. BOLEKY, born Pittsburgh, Pennsylvania, October 29, 1963; admitted to bar, 1993, Illinois and U.S. District Court, Northern District of Illinois; 1998, U.S. District Court, Northern District of Colorado; 1999, U.S. District Court, District of Arizona; 2000, Federal Trial Bar, U.S. District Court, Northern District of Illinois. *Education:* Spring Hill College (B.S., 1986); DePaul University (J.D., 1993). Judge, De Paul University Moot Court Competition, 1996. Regional Coordinator, ATLA Student Trial Advocacy Competition, February 28-March 2, 2003. Planning Chair & Moderator, IICLE Seminar "Effective Illinois Jury Selection," April 24, 2003. Lecturer: "Legal Issues Arising from September 11," ISBA, March 26, 2002; "How to Negotiate a Case in Civil Litigation," IICLE Success Skills Seminar, August 8, 2002; "Preparing and Presenting Your Expert at Trial," CBA, October 3, 2002; "How to Use Motion Practice to Get the Discovery You Want," CBA, November 21, 2002; "Jury Instructions," ITLA Shotgun Seminar, February 8, 2003; "How to Negotiate a Case in Civil Litigation," IICLE Success Skills Seminar, August 22, 2003. *Member:* Chicago, Illinois State and American (Member, Forum on Air and Space Law) Bar Associations; Illinois Trial Lawyers Association; The Association of Trial Lawyers of America. ***PRACTICE AREAS:*** Personal Injury; Wrongful Death; Aviation Litigation; Commercial Litigation; Medical Negligence; Professional Negligence; Federal Employers Liability Act (FELA); Product Liability; Premises Liability; Construction Liability; Automobile Liability. ***Email:*** tfb9@corboydemetrio.com

WILLIAM T. GIBBS, born Chicago, Illinois, January 2, 1975; admitted to bar, 2004, Illinois; 2005, U.S. District Court, Northern District of Illinois. *Education:* University of Notre Dame (B.A., 1997); University of Portland (M.A., 1999); IIT Chicago-Kent College of Law (J.D., 2004). Judge: National Collegiate Trial Advocacy Competition, 2005; American Trial Lawyers Advocacy Competition, 2005. *Member:* Chicago Bar Association; American Trial Lawyers Association; Illinois Trial Lawyers Association; Notre Dame Law Association; Fenwick Bar Association Scholarship (Treasurer, 2005-2006). ***PRACTICE AREAS:*** Personal Injury. ***Email:*** bgibbs@corboydemetrio.com

DANIEL S. KIRSCHNER, born Baltimore, Maryland, December 19, 1971; admitted to bar, 1998, Illinois and U.S. District Court, Northern District of Illinois; 1999, U.S. Court of Appeals, Ninth Circuit. *Education:* University of Wisconsin (B.A., 1994); Illinois Institute of Technology, Chicago-Kent College of Law (J.D., 1998). Appointment: Committee on Character & Fitness, Illinois Board of Admission to the Bar, 1999-2002; Illinois Supreme Court Rules Committee, 2003— ; Ad Hoc Committee of the Law Division of the Circuit Court of Cook County, 2003— . Author, "Standing Room Only: An Analysis of Jasniowski v. Rushing," Young Lawyers, ISBA Newsletter, Vol. 42, No. 2, January 1998. Profile: "40 Lawyers Under 40 to Watch" Law Bulletin Publishing, July 2003. Lecturer: "Subrogation and Common Fund Doctrine," ISBA, May 2003; "Special Settlement Problems," ITLA Past Presidents' Seminar, May 2004; "Handling Liens," ITLA Settlement on Settlements Seminar, January 2004. *Member:* Chicago (Investigator, Judicial Evaluation Committee, 2003; Fellow, CBA College of Trial Lawyers, 2001; Special Project Coordinator, Young Lawyers Section, 2001-02; Executive Counsel, Young Lawyers Section, 2001-02); Illinois State and American Bar Associations; Illinois Trial Lawyers Association (Member, Amicus Committee, 1999—); The Association of Trial Lawyers of America. ***PRACTICE AREAS:*** Personal Injury; Wrongful Death; Aviation Litigation; Commercial Litigation; Medical Negligence; Professional Negligence; FELA; Product Liability; Premises Liability; Construction Liability; Automobile and Railroad Liability. ***Email:*** dsk@corboydemetrio.com

KENNETH T. LUMB, born Hinsdale, Illinois, February 17, 1966; admitted to bar, 1991, Illinois; 1992, U.S. Army Court of Military Review; 2000, U.S. District Court, Northern District of Illinois; 2005, U.S. Court of Appeals, Seventh Circuit. *Education:* University of Notre Dame (B.A., 1988); DePaul University (J.D., 1991); National Institute for Trial Advocacy, Midwest Regional Program, 1996. Medical Malpractice Claims Attorney, Legal Advisor to Risk Management and Quality Improvement Committees, Faculty, Forensic Psychiatry Fellowship Program, Walter Reed Army Medical Center (WRAMC), Washington, D.C., 1992-1995. Assistant Professor, Military Science, Wheaton College, 2000—. Author: "Defamation," Illinois Causes of Action, IICLE, 2002; "The Federal Tort Claims Act," Illinois Causes of Action, IICLE, 2005; "A Medical Literature Primer," Trial Journal of the Illinois Trial Lawyers Association, Vol. 7, No. 2, Summer 2005. Lecturer: "Aids and the Law," WRAMC Department of Nursing, 1992; "Legal Aspects of Military Medicine," WRAMC, 1992-1995; "Tort Law - Basic Legal Research," WRAMC Forensic Psychiatry Fellowship Program, 1992-1995; "Medical and Psychiatric Malpractice" and "Emotional Injuries," WRAMC Forensic Psychiatry Fellowship Program, 1993-1995; "Preparing to be an Expert Witness," WRAMC Physical Medicine and Rehabilitation Service Short Course, 1995; "Legal Aspects of Military Psychiatry," WRAMC Department of Psychiatry, 1995; "Department of Defense Standards of Conduct," WRAMC, 1995; "Army Medical Records," WRAMC Directorate of Patient Administration, 1995; "Basics of Handling an Auto Accident Case: Initial Investigation and Preservation of Evidence Through Discovery," IICLE, 1999; "Defense Dept. Standards of Conduct," University of Illinois at Chicago Army ROTC, 1999; "Law of Land Warfare," University of Illinois at Chicago Army ROTC, 1999; "Military Law," Wheaton College, Wheaton, Illinois, 2000; Claims Against the Federal Government, "Avoiding Common Pitfalls-Including the New Rule 213," ITLA, Chicago 2002; "Proving Deviation from the Standard of Care," Medical Malpractice Seminar, ITLA, 2002; "Independent Contractors and Medical Malpractice," Understanding and Litigating FTCA Cases, Federal Tort Liability & Military Advocacy Section, ATLA, 2005. *Member:* Chicago, Illinois State (Standing Committee on Military Affairs) and American Bar Associations; Illinois Trial Lawyers Association; The Association of Trial Lawyers of America. [Capt., U.S. Army, Judge Advocates General's Corp, 1992-1995; Major, U.S. Army Reserve, 1998]. ***PRACTICE AREAS:*** Personal Injury; Wrongful Death; Aviation Litigation; Commercial Litigation; Medical Negligence; Professional Negligence; FELA; Product Liability; Premises Liability; Construction Liability; Automobile and Railroad Liability. ***Email:*** ktl9@corboydemetrio.com

DOUGLAS PETROVIC, born Oxford, England, June 5, 1969; admitted to bar, 1995, Indiana and U.S. District Court, Northern and Southern Districts of Indiana; 1998, U.S. Court of Appeals, Seventh Circuit; 2002, Illinois; 2004, U.S. District Court, Northern District of Illinois and U.S. Supreme Court. *Education:* Northwestern University (B.A., magna cum laude, 1991), Indiana University School of Law (J.D., 1994). Recipient: 2002 U.S. Attorney Commendation for Excellent Performance; 2000, FBI Commendation for Outstanding Performance; 1998, U.S. Dept. of Justice Special Achievement Award for Superior Performance. *Member:* Chicago (Judicial Evaluation Committee, 2003-2005), Illinois (Legislative Committee, 2003-2004), and American Bar Associations; Illinois Trial Lawyers Association; Association of Trial Lawyers of America (New Lawyers Committee, 2004-2005). ***PRACTICE AREAS:*** Personal Injury; Wrongful Death; Aviation Litigation; Commercial Litigation; Medical Negligence; Professional Negligence; FELA; Product Liability; Premises Liability; Construction Liability; Automobile Liability; Railroad Liability. ***Email:*** ddp9@corboydemetrio.com

MARGARET M. POWER, born Chicago, Illinois, September 16, 1943; admitted to bar, 1986, Illinois. *Education:* St. Francis Hospital School of Nursing (Diploma in Nursing, 1964); Fordham University (B.A., 1977); Loyola University (J.D., 1986). Seminars: "Birth Trauma," Litigating Catastrophically Injured Infant Cases, Atlanta Trial Lawyers Association, April 11-12, 1997; "Medical Negligence Seminar," Illinois Trial Lawyers Association, December, 1996; "The Winning Brief," Law Prose Seminar presented by Bryan A. Garner, Chicago, Illinois, June 24, 1996; "Ontario Birth Trauma Litigation Program," Co-chaired by Atlanta Trial Lawyers Association Birth Trauma Litigation Section and Ontario Trial Lawyers Association Medical Malpractice Section, Speaker on Preparing Plaintiff's Experts for Direct Examination, Toronto, Ontario, Canada, June 21 and June 22, 1996; "Ultimate Mentor Interactive Seminar," Illinois Trial Lawyers Association, May 4, 1996; "Birth Trauma Litigation Group," Seminar, Atlanta Trial Lawyers Association, March 31 - April 1, 1995. "Trial of an Obstetrical Malpractice Case," Law Journal Seminars Press, 1993; Illinois Trial Lawyers Association Medical Malpractice Seminar, 1992; "Expert Witnesses - Courtroom Warriors: Their Weapons and Weaknesses," Illinois Trial Lawyers Association, 1992; "Under the Jury's Microscope: Medical Malpractice Scrutinized and the Medical Malpractice Trial Notebook," Illinois Trial Lawyers Association, 1990; "Obstetrics/Gynecology Prenatal Medicine and the Law Including Emergency Medicine, Anesthesiology and Surgery," American Society of Law and Medicine, 1989; "Medical and Legal Frontiers in Obstetrics and Perinatal Medicine," Boston University School of Medicine and the American Society of Law and Medicine, 1987; "College of Trial Advocacy," Illinois Trial Lawyers Association, 1986; "Obstetrics, Perinatal Medicine and the Law," Boston University and American Society of Law and Medicine, 1985. *Member:* Chicago, Illinois State and American Bar Associations; Illinois Trial Lawyers Association; The Association of Trial Lawyers of America (Treasurer, Birth Trauma Litigation Group, 1998—). ***PRACTICE AREAS:*** Personal Injury; Wrongful Death; Aviation Litigation; Commercial Litigation;

(This Listing Continued)

CORBOY & DEMETRIO, P.C., Chicago—Continued

gation; Medical Negligence; Professional Negligence; FELA; Product Liability; Premises Liability; Construction Liability; Automobile and Railroad Liability. ***Email:*** mmp@corboydemetrio.com

EDWARD G. WILLER, born Chicago, Illinois, August 17, 1948; admitted to bar, 1973, Illinois and U.S. District Court, Northern District of Illinois; 1992, U.S. District Court, Central District of Illinois. *Education:* DePaul University (B.A., 1970; J.D., 1973). Blue Key. *Member:* Chicago (Member: Circuit Court Committee, 1990—; Civil Practice Committee, 1991—); Illinois State and American (Vice-Chair, Committee on Product General Liability and Consumer Law, Section on Tort and Insurance Practice, 1989-1990) Bar Associations; Illinois Trial Lawyers Association (Member, Product Liability Committee); The Association of Trial Lawyers of America (Member: Stalwarts Committee, 1999—; Hall of Fame Committee, 2000—); American Judicature Society. ***PRACTICE AREAS:*** Personal Injury; Wrongful Death; Aviation Litigation; Commercial Litigation; Medical Negligence; Professional Negligence; FELA; Product Liability; Premises Liability; Construction Liability; Automobile and Railroad Liability. ***Email:*** egw9@corboydemetrio.com

MICHELLE M. KOHUT, born Milwaukee, Wisconsin, June 26, 1974; admitted to bar, 2002, Illinois. *Education:* Loyola University, Chicago (B.A., 1996); Loyola University, Chicago School of Law (J.D., 2002). Certification, Loyola University Chicago, Institute for Paralegal Studies, 1997. Reporter, Public Interest Law, 2000-2001. *Member:* Chicago and Illinois State Bar Associations; Illinois Trial Lawyers Association; Women's Bar Association. ***PRACTICE AREAS:*** Personal Injury; Wrongful Death; Premises Liability; Construction Liability; Automobile Liability; Aviation Litigation; Commercial Litigation; Professional Negligence; FELA; Product Liability; Railroad Liability. ***Email:*** mmk@corboydemetrio.com

MICHAEL J. MATHEW, born Louisville, Kentucky, December 24, 1976; admitted to bar, 2003, Illinois and U.S. District Court, Northern District of Illinois. *Education:* Loyola University, Chicago (B.A., 1998, M.A., 1999); DePaul University, College of Law (J.D., 2002),. *Member:* Chicago and Illinois State Bar Associations; Illinois Trial Lawyers Association; Association of Trial Lawyers of America; Indian-American and Asian-American Bar Associations. ***LANGUAGES:*** Malayalam. ***PRACTICE AREAS:*** Personal Injury; Wrongful Death; Premises Liability; Construction Liability; Automobile Liability; Aviation Litigation; Commercial Litigation; Professional Negligence; FELA; Product Liability; Railroad Liability. ***Email:*** mmathew@corboydemetrio.com

REFERENCE: The American National Bank & Trust Company, Chicago, Illinois.

CORNFIELD AND FELDMAN

Established in 1962

25 EAST WASHINGTON STREET, SUITE 1400

CHICAGO, ILLINOIS 60602

Telephone: 312-236-7800

FAX: 312-236-6686

Labor Relations, Employment and Employee Benefit Law. General Practice. Workers Compensation. Trials. Appellate Practice.

MEMBERS OF FIRM

ARNOLD E. CHARNIN (1933-1978)

MELISSA J. AUERBACH, born New York, N.Y., August 29, 1955; admitted to bar, 1980, Illinois. *Education:* Yale University (B.A., 1977); Harvard University (J.D., 1980). *Member:* Chicago Bar Association. ***PRACTICE AREAS:*** Labor Law. ***Email:*** mauerbach@cornfieldandfeldman.com

J. DALE BERRY, born Roswell, New Mexico, January 17, 1943; admitted to bar, 1970, Illinois; U.S. District Court, Northern, Central and Southern Districts of Illinois. *Education:* Michigan State University (B.A., cum laude, 1965); University of Michigan (J.D., 1970). *Member:* Chicago Bar Association (Member, Board of Directors, McHenry County Defenders, 1985-1994; Associated Firefighters of Illinois (AFFI), (General Counsel, 1990—). ***REPORTED CASES:*** City of Decatur v. AFSCME, 122 Ill. 2d 353 (1988); City of Freeport v. ISLRB, 135 Ill. 2d 499 (1990); City of Evanston v. ISLRB, 227 Ill.App.3d 955 (1st Dist. 1992); Town of Cicero v. IAFF Local 717, 338 Ill.App.3d 364 (1st Dist. 2003). ***PRACTICE AREAS:*** Labor Law. ***Email:*** jdberry@cornfieldandfeldman.com

GILBERT A. CORNFIELD, born Chicago, Illinois, July 6, 1931; admitted to bar, 1954, Illinois. *Education:* University of Chicago (B.A., 1951; J.D., 1954). Associate Editor, University of Chicago Law Review, 1954. Author: "Developing Standards for Determining Arbitrability of Labor Disputes by Federal Courts," Labor Law Journal, 1963; "The Partial Strike," Vol. 21, University of Chicago Law Review; "The Significance of the Supervisory and Managerial Definitions in the Illinois Educational Labor Relations Act and the Public Labor Relations Act of Illinois," Vol. 60, No. 4, Chicago Kent Law Review, 1984; "Arthur J. Goldberg's Legacies to American Labor Relations," 32 The John Marshall Law Review No. 3 (1999). *Member:* Chicago, Illinois State and American Bar Associations. ***PRACTICE AREAS:*** Labor Law. ***Email:*** gcornfield@cornfieldandfeldman.com

GILBERT FELDMAN, born Chicago, Illinois, May 7, 1931; admitted to bar, 1955, Illinois; 1956, U.S. District Court, Northern District of Illinois. *Education:* Northwestern University (B.S., 1952, with distinction,; J.D., 1955). Comment Editor, Northwestern Law Review. Author: "The Illinois Supreme Court's *Stahulak* Decision Establishes A Further Departure Under The IPLRA From The Federal Model In Duty of Fair Representation Cases," The Illinois Public Employee Relations Report, Vol. 17, No.1; "The Illinois Judiciary and Public Employee Labor Disputes: A Return To An Imperial Judiciary?" Chicago-Kent Law Review, Vol. 53, No. 3, 1977; "The Scope of Review, Due Process, and The Conscientious Objector--Some Unresolved Problems," Northwestern Law Review, Vol. 50, No. 5, November-December, 1955; "The Quantity Discount and Now The Quantity Limit", Northwestern Law Review, Vol. 49, No. 2, May-June, 1954; "Unclean Hands in Anti-Trust Cases: An Uncertain Future," Northwestern Law Review, Vol. 48, No. 5, November-December, 1953. *Member:* Chicago Bar Association; Chicago Council of Lawyers. ***PRACTICE AREAS:*** Labor Law. ***Email:*** gfeldman@cornfieldandfeldman.com

(This Listing Continued)

DAVID M. GOLDBERG, born Chicago, Illinois, March 17, 1954; admitted to bar, 1980, Illinois. *Education:* Northwestern University (B.A., 1976); The John Marshall Law School (J.D., 1980). Member, The John Marshall Law Review, 1979-1980. ***LANGUAGES:*** Spanish. ***PRACTICE AREAS:*** Labor Law; Workers Compensation.

BARBARA J. HILLMAN, born Chicago, Illinois, August 11, 1942; admitted to bar, 1967, Illinois, U.S. District Court, Northern, Central and Southern Districts of Illinois, U.S. District Court, Northern District of Indiana, U.S. District Court, Western District of Pennsylvania, U.S. District Court, Southern District of New York, U.S. District Court, District of Columbia, U.S. Court of Appeals, Second, Third, Fourth, Seventh, Eighth and Tenth Circuits and U.S. Supreme Court. *Education:* University of Chicago (B.A., with honors, 1963; J.D., 1966). Member, Welfare Council, Metropolitan Chicago, 1970-1971. Board Member, 1972-1979 and General Counsel, 1975-1977, Committee on Illinois Government. Secretary to the Board of TASC, Inc., 1976—. Member, Board of Directors, Illinois ACLU, 1981-1983. *Member:* Chicago and American Bar Associations. ***PRACTICE AREAS:*** Labor Law; ERISA.

JACOB POMERANZ, born Hesse, Germany, August 22, 1946; admitted to bar, 1973, Illinois; 1978, California. *Education:* University of Wisconsin-Madison (B.S., 1968); Yale University (J.D., 1973). Assistant General Counsel, New York City Health Services Administration, 1971-1972. *Member:* Chicago, Illinois State and American Bar Associations. ***PRACTICE AREAS:*** Labor Law. ***Email:*** jpomeranz@cornfieldandfeldman.com

ROBERT A. SELTZER, born Madison, Wisconsin, January 14, 1953; admitted to bar, 1992, Maryland (Inactive); 1993, Illinois, District of Columbia, U.S. District Court, District of Maryland and U.S. Court of Appeals, Fourth and Ninth Circuits; 1995, U.S. District Court, Northern District of Illinois; 1996, U.S. District Court, Southern District of Illinois and U.S. Court of Appeals, Seventh Circuit; 1997, U.S. District Court, Central District of Illinois. *Education:* University of Wisconsin (B.A., with distinction, 1976); University of Michigan (J.D., cum laude, 1992). *Member:* American Bar Association. ***PRACTICE AREAS:*** Labor and Employment Law; ERISA.

RICHARD J. TUPPER, born Muskegon, Michigan, August 30, 1957; admitted to bar, 1986, Illinois; U.S. District Court, Northern and Central Districts of Illinois, U.S. Court of Appeals, Second and Seventh Circuits. *Education:* Calvin College (B.A., 1979); Yale University (M.A., 1981); Harvard Law School (J.D., 1986). ***PRACTICE AREAS:*** Labor Law.

JIM M. VAINIKOS, born Melrose Park, Illinois, July 21, 1963; admitted to bar, 1990, Illinois. *Education:* Northwestern University (B.A., 1985); American University (J.D., 1988). Alpha Lambda Delta. Member, Administrative Law Journal, American University, 1987-1988. *Member:* Chicago, Illinois State, American and Hellenic Bar Associations; Workers Compensation Lawyers Association; Illinois Trial Lawyers Association. ***LANGUAGES:*** Greek. ***PRACTICE AREAS:*** Labor Law; Workers Compensation. ***Email:*** jvainikos@cornfieldandfeldman.com

STEPHEN A. YOKICH, born Detroit, Michigan, July 19, 1957; admitted to bar, 1982, Illinois, U.S. Court of Appeals, Third, Fourth, Sixth, Seventh and Eighth Circuits and U.S. District Court, Northern, Central and Southern Districts of Illinois; 1998, U.S. Supreme Court. *Education:* Northwestern University (B.A., 1978); University of Michigan (J.D., cum laude, 1981). Law Clerk to Honorable George C. Edwards, United States Court of Appeals, Sixth Circuit, 1981-1982. General Counsel, U.S. House of Representatives, Committee on Education and Labor, 1993-1994. Associate General Counsel, United Automobile, Aerospace and Agricultural Implement Workers, International Union, 1995-1998. ***PRACTICE AREAS:*** Labor Law. ***Email:*** syokich@cornfieldandfeldman.com

---

GAIL E. MROZOWSKI, born Chicago, Illinois, September 2, 1955; admitted to bar, 1981, Illinois. *Education:* DePaul University; Northern Illinois University (B.S., 1977); Chicago-Kent College of Law (J.D., 1981). *Member:* Chicago, Illinois State and American Bar Associations. ***PRACTICE AREAS:*** Labor Law. ***Email:*** gmrozowski@cornfieldandfeldman.com

PETER C. SWANSON, born Anoka, Minnesota, December 22, 1969; admitted to bar, 1998, Illinois and U.S. District Court, Northern District of Illinois; 2000, U.S. District Court, Central District of Illinois. *Education:* University of Iowa (B.A., 1992); Northeastern University (J.D., 1998). Contributing Editor: The Developing Labor Law, 2002 Cumulative Supplement. President, Board of Directors, The Musical Offering. *Member:* Chicago, Illinois and American Bar Associations. ***PRACTICE AREAS:*** Labor and Employment Law; ERISA.

OF COUNSEL

BROUDY SIMONS, born Detroit, Michigan, May 3, 1925; admitted to bar, 1952, Illinois. *Education:* University of Michigan (B.S., 1947; M.S., 1948); Northwestern University (J.D., 1952). Associate Editor, Northwestern Law Review, 1951-1952. *Member:* Chicago and Illinois State Bar Associations. ***PRACTICE AREAS:*** Real Estate; Probate; Trust Law.

REPRESENTATIVE CLIENTS: Bakery, Confectionery and Tobacco Workers; American Federation of State, County and Municipal Employees; Oil, Chemical and Atomic Workers International Union; International Typographical Union; American Federation of Teachers; International Association of Fire Fighters; International Brotherhood of Electrical Workers; United Mine Workers of America; Retail, Wholesale, Department Union (RWSDU); American Guild of Musical Artists; American Federation of Television & Radio Artists; International Brotherhood of Teamsters; Service Employees International Union.
REFERENCE: Amalgamated Bank & Trust Co.

JAMES A. CORRIGAN, LTD.

Established in 1986

39 SOUTH LA SALLE, SUITE 610
CHICAGO, ILLINOIS 60603
Telephone: 312-853-2771
Fax: 312-853-3180
Email: jacorr@aol.com

Personal Injury, Negligence, Products Liability and Workers Compensation Law. Civil Trial Practice in all State and Federal Courts.

JAMES A. CORRIGAN, born Evergreen Park, Illinois, September 6, 1945; admitted to bar, 1971, Illinois and U.S. District Court, Northern District of Illinois; 1980, U.S. Court of Appeals, 7th Circuit and U.S. Supreme Court. *Education:* Loyola University (B.B.A., 1968); John Marshall School of Law (J.D., 1971). Author: "Comments Regarding Distinction Between Substantive and Procedural Law," 16 Tr. L. Guide 62, 1972; "Trial of a Constructive Trust Case," 17 Tr. L. Guide 7, 1973; "Remandment from Federal Court to State Court," 19 Tr. L. Guide 222, 1975. Member, Trial Lawyers for Public Justice. *Member:* Chicago, Illinois State and American Bar Associations; Illinois Trial Lawyers Association; The Association of Trial Lawyers of America; Workers Compensation Lawyers Association.

COTSIRILOS, TIGHE & STREICKER, LTD.

Established in 1974

SUITE 600
33 NORTH DEARBORN STREET
CHICAGO, ILLINOIS 60602
Telephone: 312-263-0345
Facsimile: 312-263-4670

White Collar Criminal Trial and Appellate Practice, Complex Civil Litigation, Administrative Enforcement Actions, Corporate Investigations.

FIRM PROFILE: Cotsirilos, Tighe & Streicker, Ltd. has seven attorneys, all of whom specialize in the representation of individual and corporate clients in white collar criminal, civil and administrative cases in the federal and state courts throughout the United States at both the trial and appellate levels. Each of the firm's attorneys has extensive trial experience, and has represented clients in a wide variety of cases including antitrust, health care fraud and abuse, securities violations, commercial litigation, environmental enforcement, taxation, customs and public corruption. The attorneys at Cotsirilos, Tighe & Streicker are experienced in representing and advising clients in all phases of investigations conducted by government agencies, including the U.S. Department of Justice, the U.S. Attorney's offices throughout the country, the Securities and Exchange Commission, the Commodities Futures Trading Commission, the U.S. Customs Service, the Department of Health and Human Services, the Internal Revenue Service, and the Environmental Protection Agency. In addition, Cotsirilos, Tighe & Streicker has expertise conducting internal corporate and other investigations. The firm also represents clients in a wide range of civil litigation.

More information about the firm and its attorneys is available at our website, http://ctslawltd.lawoffice.com.

GEORGE J. COTSIRILOS, born Chicago, Illinois, October 17, 1920; admitted to bar, 1942, Illinois; 1946, U.S. District Court, Northern District of Illinois; 1964, U.S. Court of Appeals, Seventh Circuit; 1966, U.S. Court of Appeals, Fifth Circuit; 1970, U.S. Supreme Court. *Education:* University of Chicago (B.A., 1941); University of Chicago Law School (LL.B., 1942). Co-Author: "Judge Aspen and the Case of the Severed Indictments," 6 Criminal Justice 18 (ABA Summer 1991); "Birds Of A Feather: Defending Multiple Defendant Prosecutions," 4 Criminal Justice 2 (ABA Winter 1990); "Cameras In The Courtroom-An Opposing View," Illinois Trial Lawyers Journal, Fall-Winter, 1982; "Basic Strategy In Federal Criminal Defense Litigation," ABA Journal of the Section of Litigation, Fall, 1981. Author: "Plea Bargaining & Pre-Trial Diversion," Federal Criminal Practice Handbook, Illinois Institute for Continuing Legal Education, 1980; "Handling Witnesses," Illinois Criminal Practice Handbook, Illinois Institute for Continuing Legal Education, 1977. Instructor in Criminal Law, John Marshall Law School, 1960-1963. Assistant State Attorney, 1949-1952. Appointed to Supreme Court Committee on Jury Instructions in Criminal Cases, 1961-1963. Commissioner, Attorney Registration and Disciplinary Commission of the Supreme Court of Illinois, 1973-1984. *Member:* Chicago (Member: Board of Managers, 1962-1964; Committee on Candidates, 1966-1973), Illinois State (Chairman, Section on Criminal Law, 1970-1971) and American (Chairman, Complex Crimes Litigation Committee, Section on Litigation, 1979-1981) Bar Associations: American Judicature Society; Law Club of Chicago; Illinois Trial Lawyers Association; Bar Association of the Seventh Federal Circuit (Member, Committee on Federal Criminal Jury Instructions of the Seventh Circuit, 1976-1980); National Association of Criminal Defense. Fellow: American College of Trial Lawyers (Regent, 1988-1994; Member, Committee on Legal Ethics and Discipline, 1979-1983; Chairman, 1981-1983; Co-Chairman, Illinois State Committee, 1982-1984); Chicago Bar Foundation; American Bar Foundation; International Academy of Trial Lawyers. ***PRACTICE AREAS:*** White Collar Criminal Defense; Criminal Defense; Criminal Appeals. ***Email:*** cotsirilos@ameritech.net

JOHN POWERS CROWLEY (1936-1989)

ANN C. TIGHE, born Evanston, Illinois, January 26, 1940; admitted to bar, 1973, Illinois; 1974, U.S. District Court, Northern District of Illinois and U.S. Court of Appeals, Seventh Circuit; 1980, U.S. Supreme Court; 1989, U.S. Tax Court. *Education:* Mt. Holyoke College and Stanford University (A.B., 1961); Northwestern University (J.D., 1973). Member, Editorial Board, Northwestern University Law Review, 1971-1973. Co-Author: "Cameras In The Courtroom-An Opposing View," Illinois Trial Lawyers Journal, Fall-Winter, 1982. Author, "Qui Tam Actions Under the False Claims Statute," 67 Northwestern University Law Review 446, 1972. Assistant U.S. Attorney, Northern District of Illinois, 1974-1979 (Deputy Chief, Appellate Division, 1975-1976; Chief, Government Fraud Division,

(This Listing Continued)

1976-1977. Chief, Criminal Receiving and Appellate Division, 1977-1979). Member, Board of Directors, Chicago Bar Foundation, 1998—. *Member:* Chicago, Illinois State and American Bar Associations. Fellow, American College of Trial Lawyers (Co-Chair, Illinois State Committee, 2000-2001). ***PRACTICE AREAS:*** Criminal Defense; Civil Litigation; White Collar Criminal Defense; Environmental Law; Appellate Practice. ***Email:*** atighe@ameritech.net

JAMES R. STREICKER, born Chicago, Illinois, November 9, 1944; admitted to bar, 1969, Illinois; 1970, U.S. District Court, Northern District of Illinois; 1971, U.S. Court of Appeals, Seventh Circuit; 1980, U.S. Supreme Court; 1986, U.S. District Court, Eastern District of Wisconsin and U.S. District Court, Northern District of Indiana; 1989, U.S. Tax Court. *Education:* Miami University (A.B., 1966); University of Illinois (J.D., 1969). Instructor: Trial Advocacy, John Marshall Law School, 1979-1980; U.S. Attorney General's Advocacy Institute, 1978-1980. Teaching Assistant, National Institute for Trial Advocacy 1981-1984. Lecturer: Federal Bar Association, Federal Sentencing Guidelines, 1990; Illinois Institute For Continuing Legal Education, Sentencing, New Techniques and Attitudes, 1986; Compliance Center Seminar, Prosecutions of Doctors, Hospitals and Nursing Homes, 1998. Assistant Attorney General, State of Illinois, 1970-1971. Assistant Appellate Defender State of Illinois, 1971-1975. Deputy Appellate Defender, First District, 1975. Assistant U.S. Attorney, Northern District of Illinois, 1975-1980. Chief, Criminal Receiving and Appellate Division, U.S. Attorney's Office, Northern District of Illinois, 1979-1980. *Member:* Chicago, Illinois State and American Bar Associations; National Association of Criminal Defense Lawyers. Fellow: American College of Trial Lawyers; American Board of Criminal Lawyers. ***PRACTICE AREAS:*** White Collar Criminal Defense; Antitrust; Corporate Investigations; Professional Liability; Civil Litigation; Regulatory Agency Practice; Appellate Practice. ***Email:*** jstreicker@ameritech.net

THEODORE T. POULOS, born Kalavrita, Greece, June 9, 1961; admitted to bar, 1987, Illinois; U.S. District Court, Northern District of Illinois; U.S. Court of Appeals, Seventh Circuit. *Education:* Purdue University (B.A., 1983); Loyola University (J.D., cum laude, 1987). Recipient, Department of Justice Director's Award for Superior Service as an Assistant U.S. Attorney, 1992 and Special Achievement Award of the U.S. Attorney's Office 1989. Assistant U.S. Attorney, Northern District of Illinois, 1987-1992. *Member:* Chicago, Illinois State, Federal and American Bar Associations; Chicago Council of Lawyers. ***PRACTICE AREAS:*** Federal Criminal Defense; Attorney Discipline. ***Email:*** ttpoulos@aol.com

TERENCE H. CAMPBELL, born New York, N.Y., July 21, 1967; admitted to bar, 1995, Illinois; U.S. District Court, Northern District of Illinois; 1998, U.S. District Court, District of Arizona; 1999, U.S. Court of Appeals, Seventh and Third Circuits. *Education:* University of Notre Dame (B.B.A., 1989); Northwestern University (J.D., magna cum laude, 1995). Order of the Coif. *Member:* Chicago, Illinois State and American Bar Associations; Chicago Council of Lawyers. ***PRACTICE AREAS:*** White Collar Criminal Defense; Criminal Defense; Criminal Appeals; Civil Litigation. ***Email:*** tcwolfram@aol.com

TYSON K. HARPER, born Evanston, Illinois, March 4, 1976; admitted to bar, 2001, Massachusetts; 2002, Illinois and U.S. District Court, Northern District of Illinois. *Education:* University of Michigan (B.A., 1998); Harvard University (J.D., 2001). *Member:* Chicago, Illinois State and American Bar Associations. ***PRACTICE AREAS:*** Criminal Defense; White Collar Criminal Defense; Criminal Appeals; Civil Litigation. ***Email:*** tharper@ctslawfirm.com

OF COUNSEL

PRENTICE H. MARSHALL (1926-2004)

GEORGE M. COVINGTON

CHICAGO, ILLINOIS

(See Lake Forest)

Real Estate, Land Use and Zoning Law, Conservation Law.

COZEN O'CONNOR

A PROFESSIONAL CORPORATION

222 SOUTH RIVERSIDE PLAZA, SUITE 1500
CHICAGO, ILLINOIS 60606
Telephone: 312-382-3100
Fax: 312-382-8910
Email: postmaster@cozen.com
URL: http://www.cozen.com

Philadelphia, Pennsylvania Office: 1900 Market Street, 19103. Telephones: 215-665-2000; 800-523-2900. Fax: 215-665-2013.

Charlotte, North Carolina Office: One First Union Center, Suite 2100, 301 S. College Street, 28202. Telephones: 704-376-3400; 800-762-3575. Fax: 704-334-3351.

Dallas, Texas Office: 2300 BankOne Center, 1717 Main Street, 75201. Telephones: 214-462-3000; 800-448-1207. Fax: 214-462-3299.

New York, N.Y. Offices: 45 Broadway Atrium, 16th Floor, 10006. Telephones: 212-509-9400; 800-437-7040. Fax: 212-509-9492. Midtown Office: 909 Third Avenue, 17th Floor, 10022. Telephones: 212-509-9400; 800-437-7040. Fax: 212-207-4938.

West Conshohocken, Pennsylvania Office: 200 Four Falls Corporate Center, Suite 400, P.O. Box 800, 19428. Telephone: 610-941-5400; 800-379-0695. Fax: 610-941-0711.

San Diego, California Office: Suite 1610, 501 West Broadway, 92101. Telephones: 619-234-1700; 800-782-3366. Fax: 619-234-7831.

Los Angeles, California Office: 777 South Figueroa Street, Suite 2850, 90017. Telephones: 213-892-7900; 800-563-1027. Fax: 213-892-7999.

Seattle, Washington Office: Suite 5200, Washington Mutual Tower, 1201 Third Avenue, 98101. Telephones: 206-340-1000; 800-423-1950. Fax: 206-621-8783.

(This Listing Continued)

COZEN O'CONNOR, A PROFESSIONAL CORPORATION, Chicago—Continued

Newark, New Jersey Office: One Newark Center, Suite 1900, 07102. Telephone: 973-286-1200; 888-200-9521. Fax: 973-242-2121.
Atlanta, Georgia Office: Suite 2200, SunTrust Plaza, 303 Peachtree Street, N.E., 30308. Telephones: 404-572-2000; 800-890-1393. Fax: 404-572-2199.
London, England Office: Fountain House, 130 Fenchurch Street, London EC3M 5DJ. Telephone: 011-44-20-7864-2000. Fax: 011-44-20-7864-2013.
Wilmington, Delaware Office: Chase Manhattan Centre, 1201 North Market Street, Suite 1400, 19801. Telephone: 302-295-2000; 888-207-2440. Fax: 302-295-2013.
Las Vegas, Nevada Office (Affiliated with the Law Offices of J. Goldberg & D. Grossman): 601 South Rancho, Suite 20, 89106. Telephone: 800-782-3366.
San Francisco, California Office: 425 California Street, Suite 2400, 94104-2203. Telephone: 415-617-6100; 800-818-0165. Fax: 415-617-6101.
Washington, D.C. Office: 1667 K Street, NW, 20006. Telephone: 202-912-4800; 800-540-1355. Fax: 202-912-4830.
Cherry Hill, New Jersey Office: LibertyView, Suite 300, 457 Haddonfield Road, P.O. Box 5459, 08002-2220. Telephone: 856-910-5000; 800-989-0499. Fax: 856-910-5075.
Wichita, Kansas Office: 8415 E. 21st Street, Suite 220, 67206. Telephone: 316-609-3380. Fax: 316-634-3837.
Denver, Colorado Office: 707 17th Street, Suite 3100, 80202. Telephone: 303-292-9080. Fax: 303-292-9650.
Trenton, New Jersey Office: 144-B West State Street, 08608. Telephone: 609-989-8620.
Houston, Texas Office: 1 Houston Center, 1221 McKinney Street, Suite 2900, 77010. Telephone: 800-448-8502; 832-214-3900. Fax: 832-214-3905.
Toronto, Ontario Office: One Queen Street East, Suite 2000, M5C 2W5. Telephone: 416-361-2000. Fax: 416-361-1405.
Santa Fe, New Mexico Office: 125 Lincoln Avenue, Suite 400, 87501. Telephones: 505-820-3346; 866-231-0144. Fax: 505-820-3347.

Advertising Liability/Personal Injury, Alternative Dispute Resolution, Agent/Broker Liability, Antitrust and Unfair Competition, Appellate Practice, Arbitration and Alternative Dispute Resolution, Arson and Fraud, Aviation Litigation, Bad Faith Litigation, Bankruptcy, Insolvency and Restructuring, Business Torts, Cargo Losses, Class Actions, Multi-District Litigation and Other Consolidated Claims, Commercial General Liability, Commercial Litigaion, Construction Law and Litigation, Construction Liability, Corporate and Partnership Law, Corporate Planning, Crisis Management, Cross Border Transactions, Directors' and Officers' Liability, E-Commerce, Internet and Cyber-Peril Insurance, Emerging Business and Venture Capital, Employee Benefits and Executive Compensation, Employment, Labor and Employee Benefits, Environmental Coverage, Environmental Litigation, Estate Planning and Administration, Excess and Surplus Lines, Family Law, Fidelity and Surety, Financial Services, Health Law, Health Care Malpractice, Insurance Corporate and Regulatory Law, Intellectual Property, Intellectual Property Litigation, International Tax and Estate Planning, Labor and Employment, Life, Health and Disability Maritime Law, Medical Device and Drug Litigation, Mergers and Acquisitions, Personal Lines, Privacy Law and Regulation, Private Wealth Services, Products Liability, Professional Liability, Property Insurance, Public and Project Finance, Public Utilities and Energy, Punitive Damages, Real Estate, Real Estate Litigation, Reinsurance, Securities, Securities Litigation and Civil RICO, Security and Premises Liability, Tax, Tax Litigation, Toxic and Other Mass Torts, White Collar Crime.

FIRM PROFILE: Cozen O'Connor is a dynamic, full-service client-oriented firm actively engaged in a diverse business and litigation practice. Headquartered in Philadelphia, Pennsylvania, the firm consists of over 530 lawyers practicing from twenty-four offices in the United States, London and Canada. The firm's practice is divided into four areas: business, business litigation, insurance and intellectual property.

Cozen O'Connor is dedicated to and focused on providing each client with the highest level of legal services rendered in the most efficient and cost-effective manner. Our philosophy acknowledges the paramount importance of each client's interests and we recognize that effective attorney-client relationships not only exist between institutions but with individuals as well. We endeavor to develop trust and confidence through close personal working relationships between our attorneys and the individual representatives of each client. This attention to the specific needs of each client explains our ability to represent a diverse clientele. Our clients range from individuals to corporations, including major utility companies, banks, real estate investment trusts, professional corporations, public companies, domestic insurance companies and foreign insurance syndicates.

FIRM MEMBERS IN CHICAGO

RICHARD L. BLATT, born Oak Park, Illinois, May 24, 1940; admitted to bar, 1968, Illinois, U.S. District Court, Northern District of Illinois and U.S. Court of Appeals, Seventh Circuit; 1974, U.S. Supreme Court; 1977, U.S. District Court, Southern District of Illinois; 1987, U.S. Court of Appeals, Fourth Circuit; 1989, New York; U.S. Court of Appeals, Third Circuit. *Education:* University of Illinois (B.A., 1962); University of Michigan (J.D., 1965) Phi Beta Kappa; Phi Kappa Phi. Co-Author: "Punitive Damages: A State-By-State Guide To Law And Practice," published in 1991 by West Publishing Company, with subsequent supplements. (New Editions published in 2002, 2003, 2004 and 2005) (This book has also been published in a Japanese language edition by Hoken-Mainichi Shinbun-sha, Tokyo, 1995, Professor Kazutake Okuma, Seinan Gakuin University, Translator); "@ Risk: Internet and E-Commerce Insurance and Reinsurance Legal Issues," Reactions Publishing Company Group Limited, London, 2000; "@ Risk: Version 2.0, The Definitive Guide to Legal Issues of Insurance and Reinsurance of Internet, E-Commerce and Cyber Perils," Reactions Publishing Company Group Limited, London, 2002; "Insurability of Punitive Damages, Liability, Risk & Insurance," (London), 1990; "Hazardous Waste Cleanup Costs As Damages: An Analysis of Outboard Marine Corporation v. Liberty Mutual Insurance Company," Lloyds Environmental Law International, 1991. Author: "Supreme Court Rules on Alabama Punitive Damages Case," published by Alexander & Alexander, Inc. Global Financial Services Group, New York, New York, in Currency Magazine, Vol. 5, No. 2, 1991; "Pollution Exclusion Reaches the High Court," published in the Illinois Legal Times, Vol. 5, No. 54, 1991. Co-Author: "Emotional Distress Damages Due to Fear of Failure of Medical Products," Legal Mind, 1993; "Paying for Pollution," Post Magazine and Insurance Week, (London), 1993; "Comments About Punitive Damages in American Law," The Journal of the Japanese Institute of International Business Law, (Tokyo), 1993; "Further Comments About Punitive Damages in American Law," The Journal of the Japanese Institute of International Business Law, (Tokyo), 1993; "Tort Reform in The United States," Mealeys Litigation Reports Product Liability, 1995; "U.S. Punitive Damages, Insurance Law & Claims," 1995. Author: "There is More to Coverage Suits Than the Verdict," National Law Journal, 1995. Co-Author: "Tort Reform In The United States," published in Mealeys Appellate Reports, Wayne, Pennsylvania, Vol. 1, No. 12, 1995; "Punitive Damages in the United States: BMW v. Gore," International Insurance Law Review, 1996; "Supreme Court of the United States Limits Excessive Punitive Damage Verdict," The Journal of the Japanese Institute of International Business Law, (Tokyo), 1996 (Translated by Professor Kazutake Okuma). Author: "Punitive Damages," published in Casualty Insurance Companies General Institute, Vol. 57, No. 4, 1996. (This article is based on a paper given at Tokyo, Japan on November 2, 1995 by Richard L. Blatt, and published by The Non-Life Insurance Institute of Japan); "The Only Certainty is Change: The Challenge of Providing Legal Services in the New Century," International Financial Law Review, 1997. Co-Author: "Legal Attraction: The Bid of Singapore to Become the Risk Transfer Hub of Asia," Asia Cover, 2000; "Being There: Licensing Insurance Companies in the Peoples Republic of China," Asia Cover, 2000; "More Reform to Come," Asia Cover, 2000; "Alternative Dispute Resolution in the United States," a ten-part series of introductory articles published in The Journal of the Japanese Institute of International Business Law, (Tokyo), 2000-2001. Author: "ADR Can Help Fend Off Big Punitive Awards," Crains Business Insurance, 2001; "Asbestos Today in the U.S.A.," Journal of the Japanese Institute of International Business Law, (Tokyo), 2001. Co-Author: "Defining Property Loss, Risk & Insurance, 2001; chapter entitled "Alternative Dispute Resolution, @ Risk, Version 2 - The Definitive Guide to Legal Issues of Insurance and Reinsurance of Internet, E-Commerce and Cyber Perils," 2002. Papers, Speeches and Presentations: "The Insurers View of Alternative Dispute Resolution," given at the Alternative Dispute Resolution Seminar sponsored by Alexander Howden Group Limited, Sedgwick Centre, London, U.K., May 8, 1991; "Punitive Damages: The Risks Faced by Manufacturers Selling Products in the United States," given to the Japanese Institute of International Business Law, Tokyo, Japan, November 15, 1991; "How a London Underwriter Views American Coverage Claims," given at the American Bar Association, Section of Litigation, Insurance Coverage Litigation Committee Annual Meeting, Tucson, Arizona, March 27, 1993; "Punitive Damages," given to The Non-Life Institute of Japan, Tokyo, Japan, November 2, 1995; "An Overview of Product Liability in the United States and Selected Topics In Product Liability Insurance Coverage," given to the Insurance School of the Pacific, sponsored by the Insurance Educational Association, St. Marys College, Moraga, California, August 8, 1996; "Tort Reform In The United States," given to The Chiyoda Fire and Marine Insurance Company, Ltd.; "Risk Management Seminar," Tokyo, Japan, November 5, 1996; "Contemporary Issues In Case Law and Insurance," panel presenter, Illinois State University - Lloyds of London Study Tour, Normal, Illinois, July 15, 1997; "Insurance - The Role of Antitrust In Japan and In The United States," given to the Insurance School of the Pacific, sponsored by the Insurance Educational Association, St. Marys College, Moraga, California, August 6, 1997; "USA Revisited; A Signpost For The Future," given at The Fourth Insurance Market Conference Liability Insurance Conference, Liability Insurance In a Changing World, arranged on behalf of the Liability Underwriters Group, Exeter College, Oxford, U.K., September 9, 1997; "Aspects of Tort Reform In The United States," presentation given to Terra Nova Insurance Company Ltd., London, U.K., February 17, 1998; "Punitive Damages," panel presentation to The American Corporate Counsel Association, Chicago, Illinois, May 20, 1998; "Contemporary Issues In American Case Law And Insurance," panel moderator and presenter, Illinois State University - Lloyds of London Study Tour, Normal, Illinois, July 16, 1998; "Corporate Environmental Exposures: The Impact On Your Bottom Line," presentation given at the Illinois State University Breakfast Seminar for Insurance Professionals and Risk Managers, Chicago, Illinois, November 4, 1998; "Alternative Dispute Resolution: What Is It? Why Do It?" panel moderator and presenter, Illinois State University - Lloyds of London Study Tour, Normal, Illinois, July 15, 1999; "Y2K In The U.S.A.," paper given by Richard L. Blatt and Scott W. Wright at The Japan Industrial Management and Accounting Institute, Tokyo, Japan, August 4, 1999; "Y2K In The U.S.A. - An Overview of Commercial, Legal and Insurance Aspects," paper given at The Non-Life Insurance Institute of Japan, Tokyo, Japan, August 6, 1999; "Alternative Dispute Resolution In The U.S.," presentation given to Terra Nova Insurance Company, Ltd., London, U.K., March 1, 2000; "Punitive Damages: Early Detection and Avoidance, presentation given to Aegis Claims Roundtable," Kansas City, Missouri, March 30, 2000; "The U.S. Legal Environment After Y2K," paper given at The Non-Life Insurance Institute of Japan, Tokyo, Japan, April 10, 2000; "Financial Services Modernization in the United States: An Overview for Insurance Companies," paper jointly prepared with Scott W. Wright and Elliot S. Orol and given at The Non-Life Insurance Institute of Japan, Tokyo, Japan, April 10, 2000; "Defending The High Risk Punitive Damages Case," presentation given by Richard L. Blatt and Kristy L. Allen to AEGIS Claims Seminar 2000: New Tools, Proven Strategies, Palm Beach, Florida, May 9, 2000; "E-Commerce: The Challenges Facing Business without Borders," Richard L. Blatt, Moderator and Panelist, Illinois State University - Lloyds Study Tour, Union League Club of Chicago, July 10, 2000; "Fraud and Insurance Fraud In The United States," paper given by Richard L. Blatt, Zacarias R. Chacon and Robin C. Dusek to The Insurance Educational Association Insurance School of The Pacific, St. Marys College, Moraga, California, July 17, 2000; "Successful Defense of The High Risk Punitive Damages Case: Identifying and Containing The Risk," presentation given by Richard L. Blatt and Lori S. Nugent to AEGIS 2000 Claims Roundtable Seminar, Jersey City, New Jersey, September 7, 2000; "The Ball Is In Court - Whose Court?" Panel presentation given by Richard L. Blatt, Robert W. Hammesfahr and Ryan M. Henderson on reinsurance insolvencies at Excess/Surplus Lines Claims Association Annual Conference - 2000, Naples, Florida, September 17-20, 2000; "ADR In A Dotcom World," keynote luncheon address given by Richard L. Blatt to Dispute Resolution 2000, DePaul University, Chicago, Illinois, December 1, 2000; "Getting the Money Back: Insurance Subrogation and Recovery in the United States," presentation given by James I. Tarman and Richard L. Blatt for the Lloyds - Illinois State University 2001 Study Tour at the Illinois State University (Normal, Illinois) July 12, 2001; "E-Commerce: The Framework and Management of Risk," seminar series given by Richard L. Blatt at DePaul University, Chicago, Illinois, November - December, 2001; "Getting the Money Back: In-

(This Listing Continued)

surance Subrogation and Recovery in the United States: a Prototype for London?" presentation given by James I. Tarman, Joseph G. Lyons and Richard L. Blatt for the Lloyds - Illinois State University 2002 Study Tour at the Illinois State University (Normal, Illinois) July 10, 2002; "Corporate Governance Today," given for the Lloyds - Illinois State University 2003 Study Tour at the Illinois State University, (Normal, Illinois), July 8, 2003; "A Lawyer"s Introduction to Alternative Dispute Resolution (ADR)," presentation given at the University of Illinois College of Law, Champaign, Illinois, October 15, 2003; "Current Developments in International Arbitration and Mediation," presentation given as a co-panelist at the Chicago Bar Association Alternative Dispute Resolution Committee Program, November 21, 2003. *Member:* Chicago, Illinois State, New York State and American (Member, Alternative Dispute Resolution Committee) Bar Associations. North American Branch of the Chartered Institute of Arbitrators (London); Center for Public Resources Institute for Dispute Resolution (Representative Member and Distinguished Neutral Panelist); Chicago International Dispute Resolution Association (Member, Planning Committee); National Association of Securities Dealers Regulation Board of Arbitrators (Public Arbitrator Member); Court-Annexed Mandatory Arbitration Program, Circuit Court of Cook County, Illinois (Chair-Qualified Arbitrator); Court-Annexed Mediation Committee, Circuit Court of Cook County, Illinois (Practitioner Member); Court-Annexed Mediation Program, Circuit Court of Cook County, Illinois (Court-Certified Mediator). [Captain, Infantry, USAR; Active Duty, 1965-1967]. ***PRACTICE AREAS:*** Business Litigation; Arbitration; Alternative Dispute Resolution; Insurance Litigation; Environmental Coverage; Insurance Coverage; Products Liability; Reinsurance; Toxic; Mass Torts. ***Email:*** rblatt@cozen.com

KEVIN P. CARAHER, born Evanston, Illinois, August 17, 1956; admitted to bar, 1981, Illinois and U.S. District Court, Northern District of Illinois including Trial Bar; 1990, U.S. District Court, Central District of Illinois; 1993, U.S. Court of Appeals, Seventh Circuit; 1997, U.S. District Court, Southern District of Illinois; 2001, U.S. District Court, District of Colorado; 2003, U.S. Court of Appeals, Tenth Circuit. *Education:* Lawrence University (B.A., 1978); Northwestern University School of Law (J.D., 1981). Law Clerk to the Hon. Justice Daniel P. Ward, Illinois Supreme Court, 1981-1984. *Member:* Lake County and Illinois State Bar Associations; The Association of Trial Lawyers of America. ***PRACTICE AREAS:*** Property Subrogation; Construction Law; Complex and Multi-District Litigation; Commercial Litigation; Insurance Coverage; Transportation. ***Email:*** kcaraher@cozen.com

ZACARIAS R. CHACON, born Hutchinson, Kansas, July 31, 1956; admitted to bar, 1981, Illinois and U.S. District Court, Northern District of Illinois; 1984, U.S. Court of Appeals, Seventh Circuit. *Education:* University of Texas at Austin (B.A., with honors, 1978; J.D., 1981). Phi Alpha Delta. Co-Author: "@ Risk: Internet and E-commerce Insurance and Reinsurance Legal Issues," a Reactions Publishing, 2000; "Insurers Develop New Products to Cover Web Perils," National Law Journal, August 20, 2001; "Cyberproperty Losses and Traditional First Party Property Coverages," Journal of Insurance Coverage, Vol. 5, No. 2, page 52, Spring 2002. *Member:* Chicago, Illinois State, Seventh Circuit and American Bar Associations; Latin American Bar Association; Mexican American Legal Association. ***LANGUAGES:*** Spanish. ***PRACTICE AREAS:*** Insurance Litigation (40%); Arson and Fraud Defense (20%); Insurance Coverage (40%). ***Email:*** zchacon@cozen.com

MARTHA E. CONLIN, born Ann Arbor, Michigan, September 3, 1971; admitted to bar, 1996, Illinois and U.S. District Court, Northern District of Illinois. *Education:* St. Mary's College (B.A., magna cum laude, 1993); Northwestern University (J.D., 1996). *Member:* Chicago and American Bar Associations. ***PRACTICE AREAS:*** Insurance Litigation; Insurance Coverage; Commercial Litigation; Reinsurance Arbitration. ***Email:*** mconlin@cozen.com

LARRY R. EATON, born Quincy, Illinois, August 18, 1944; admitted to bar, 1968, Illinois; 1976, U.S. District Court, Northern District of Illinois; 1978, U.S. Supreme Court; 1984, U.S. Court of Appeals for the District of Columbia Circuit; 1989, U.S. Court of Appeals, 7th Circuit; 1994, U.S. Court of Appeals, 3rd Circuit; 1997, New York. *Education:* Western Illinois University (B.A., 1965); University of Michigan (J.D., 1968). Instructor of Law, University of Liberia School of Law, 1969-1970. Instructor of Environmental Law, Quincy College, 1973-1975. Illinois Assistant Attorney General (Chief, Environmental Control Law Division), 1971-1975. Member, Illinois Industrial Pollution Control Financing Authority, 1979. Special Hearing Officer for Governor James R. Thompson under Section 125 of Federal Clean Air Act, 1978. Listed in Who's Who in America, 1988-2000. Who's Who in American Law, 1985-2000. *Member:* Chicago (Member, Environmental Law Section, 1990—), Illinois State (Chairman, Environmental Control Law Section, 1977-1978; Member: Environmental Control Law Section, 1971-1978, 1990—; Assembly 1980-1986, 1989-1992) and American (Member, Environmental Coverage Litigation Task Force, 1990—) Bar Associations; Bar Association of the Seventh Judicial Circuit; Law Club of Chicago; Atticus Finch Inn of Court. Fellow, Illinois Bar Foundation (Charter Member). ***PRACTICE AREAS:*** Business Litigation; Commercial Litigation; Construction Litigation; Insurance Litigation; Insurance Coverage; Products Liability; Environmental Insurance Coverage; Environmental Insurance Defense; Property Subrogation. ***Email:*** leaton@cozen.com

JAY M. GOLDSTEIN, born Philadelphia, Pennsylvania, April 29, 1948; admitted to bar, 1973, Pennsylvania; 1989, California; 1996, North Carolina (Not admitted in Illinois). *Education:* Temple University (B.B.A., 1970); Villanova University (J.D., 1973). *Member:* American Bar Association; State Bar of California; The Association of Trial Lawyers of America. ***PRACTICE AREAS:*** Subrogation; Property Insurance Coverage. ***Email:*** jgoldstein@cozen.com

TIA C. GLASS, born Ft. Wayne, Indiana, May 22 1971; admitted to bar, 1999, Illinois. *Education:* St. Joseph's College (B.S., 1993); John Marshall Law School (J.D., 1999). Inducted in to the St. Joseph's College Sports Hall of Fame, 1999. *Member:* Chicago, Illinois State and American (Former Lieutenant Governor, 7th Circuit, Law Student Division) Bar Associations. ***PRACTICE AREAS:*** Litigation. ***Email:*** tglass@cozen.com

ROBERT W. HAMMESFAHR, born Pittsfield, Massachusetts, May 17, 1954; admitted to bar, 1978, Illinois and U.S. District Court, Northern District of Illinois; 1989, U.S. Court of Appeals, Seventh Circuit and U.S. Supreme Court; 1990, New York. *Education:* Colgate University (B.A., magna cum laude, Political Science, with honors, 1975); Northwestern University (J.D., 1978). Phi Beta Kappa. Listed in Who's Who in America, 1994—. Author: "Watch Out for Web Loopholes," Lloyd's.com, July 7, 2001; "Are Insurers and Reinsurers at Risk from the Growing Number of Information, Internet and E-Commerce Claims?" Cozen O'Connor London Insurance Seminar, June 13, 2001; "How Do Claims Handling Decisions Impact on Reinsurance Claims Resolutions?" Defense Research Institute Insurance and Claims Institute, May 18, 2001; "Deconstructing a Reinsurance Contract," Mealey's Reinsurance 101 Conference, April 30, 2001; "Legal Risks in E-Business and Technology - Liability Exposures and Insurance Coverage," Andrews Publication Seminar, February 2001; "New New Risks and Liabilities for Insurers," Cozen and O'Connor National Insurance Seminar, November 14, 2000; "The Ball's in Court - Who's Court," Excess Surplus Lines Claims Association, September 2000; "@Risk - Insurance Risks of the New Economy," Chapter 6 of "E-Insurance and the Internet Revolution," Reactions, 2000; "Point-Counterpoint on Cedent and Market Viewpoint Regarding Claim Payments," BRMA's 5th Annual Committee Rendezvous, March 25, 1999. Co-Author: "Punitive Damages: A State-by-State Guide to Law and Practice," West Publishing Company, 1991, current Supplement; Japanese Language Edition published by Hoken-Mainichi Shinbun-sha, 1995, "The Law of Reinsurance Claims," Andrews Professional Books, 1994 and Supplement, 1997; Co-Author: "@ Risk: Internet and E-commerce Insurance and Reinsurance Legal Issues," a Reactions Publishing, 2000. Chair, Cyber Risks 2000 Conference, June 2000. *Member:* Chicago and American Bar Associations; Defense Research Institute. (Also at New York, New York Office). ***PRACTICE AREAS:*** Insurance Litigation; Reinsurance. ***Email:*** rhammesfahr@cozen.com

(This Listing Continued)

GREGORY D. HOPP, born Winchester, Massachusetts, April 30, 1959; admitted to bar, 1984, Illinois; 1985, U.S. District Court, Northern District of Illinois; 1992, U.S. District Court, Eastern District of Michigan; 1993, U.S. Supreme Court. *Education:* University of Illinois (B.A., cum laude, 1981); University of Michigan (J.D., 1984). Co-Author: "@ Risk: Internet and E-commerce Insurance and Reinsurance Legal Issues," a Reactions Publishing, 2000. *Member:* American Bar Association. ***PRACTICE AREAS:*** Insurance Litigation; Reinsurance. ***Email:*** ghopp@cozen.com

JOSH M. KANTROW, born Baton Rouge, Louisiana, February 22, 1965; admitted to bar, 1991, Louisiana, U.S. District Court, Eastern, Middle and Western Districts of Louisiana and U.S. Court of Appeals, Fifth Circuit; 1996, Illinois, U.S. District Court, Northern District of Illinois and U.S. Court of Appeals, Seventh Circuit; 2000, New York. *Education:* Louisiana State University (B.S., Finance, 1987; J.D., 1990). Member, Moot Court Board. Intern to the Honorable Randall R. Rader, U.S. Claims Court, 1989. Author and Lecturer, Speech and Paper on various insurance and legal topics, including panel discussion to Lloyd's Study Group Participants at the Katie School of Insurance, Illinois State University, July 1998, July 1999 and July 2004. International Underwriting Association, London, England, October 16, 2000; Panel Discussion Participant and Author, Paper on "Defending Indefensible Casualty Claims - Aggressive Motion Practice," delivered at Cozen O'Connor 2001 Insurance Litigation Seminar, Chicago, IL, May 22, 2001; Author, Article: "Defending Mold Claims," National Underwriter Magazine, March 2002; Speaker and Author of Paper on "Defending Complex Maritime Claims," delivered at Cozen O'Connor 2004 Seminars in New York, London, and Paris in June, 2004. Served Secondment with Faraday Underwriting Ltd., May through October, 2002. Co-Founder and Co-Chair, Young Leadership Board-Chicago, American Israel Public Affairs Committee, 2000-2002. Member, Jewish United Fund of Metropolitan Chicago Lawyers Division Campaign Cabinet, 2002—. Selected for Inclusion in Who's Who in Finance and Industry, Thirty-First Edition, 1999. *Member:* Illinois State and American Bar Associations. ***REPORTED CASES:*** Stein v. Seadog Ventures, Circuit Court of Cook County, Illinois; Rooney and Hennessey v. Sutterlin, Circuit Court of Cook County, Illinois. ***PRACTICE AREAS:*** Insurance Coverage Litigation; Commercial Litigation; Admiralty and Maritime; Subrogation and Recovery. ***Email:*** jkantrow@cozen.com

BRUCE M. LICHTCSIEN, born Norwalk, Ohio, March 7, 1964; admitted to bar, 1990, Illinois and U.S. District Court, Northern District of Illinois; 2001, U.S. Court of Appeals, Seventh Circuit; 2002, U.S. District Court, Eastern District of Wisconsin. *Education:* Northwestern University (B.A., 1986); Case Western Reserve University School of Law (J.D., 1990). *Member:* Chicago and Illinois State Bar Associations. ***PRACTICE AREAS:*** Insurance Litigation; Commercial Litigation; Environmental Coverage; Products Liability; Life Insurance; Disability Insurance. ***Email:*** blichtcsien@cozen.com

JOSEPH G. LYONS, born Hinsdale, Illinois, April 12, 1962; admitted to bar, 1987, Michigan; 1988, Illinois; 2002, Wisconsin. *Education:* Hope College (B.A., 1984); University of Detroit (J.D., 1987); DePaul University. Delta Theta Phi. *Member:* Chicago, Cook County and Illinois State Bar Associations; State Bar of Michigan. ***PRACTICE AREAS:*** Subrogation and Recovery. ***Email:*** jlyons@cozen.com

ANTHONY J. MORRONE, born Oak Lawn, Illinois, June 24, 1974; admitted to bar, 1999, Illinois and U.S. District Court, Northern District of Illinois. *Education:* University of Illinois Urbana-Champaign (B.A., Economics, 1996); John Marshall Law School (J.D., 1999). Phi Alpha Delta. ***PRACTICE AREAS:*** Subrogation; Insurance Recovery. ***Email:*** amorrone@cozen.com

CATHERINE A.T. NELSON, born Chicago, Illinois, June 27, 1961; admitted to bar, 1986, Illinois, U.S. District Court, Northern District of Illinois, U.S. Court of Appeals, Sixth and Seventh Circuits and U.S. Supreme Court. *Education:* University of Illinois (B.S., 1983); John Marshall Law School (J.D., 1986). Staff Editor, John Marshall Law Review, 1985-1986. Author: *Privacy in Photographs,* 18 J.M.L.R., 969 (1985). Judicial Clerk to Hon. Michael A. Bilandic, First District Appellate Court, 1986-1989. *Member:* Defense Research Institute. ***PRACTICE AREAS:*** Insurance Litigation; Appellate Practice; Insurance Coverage. ***Email:*** cnelson@cozen.com

LORI S. NUGENT, born Peoria, Illinois, April 24, 1962; admitted to bar, 1987, Illinois. *Education:* Knox College (B.A., cum laude, 1984); Northwestern University (J.D., 1987). Named "Attorney to Watch in 2002," Best's Review. Co-Author: "Punitive Damages: A State-by-State Guide to Law and Practice," West Publishing Company, 1991, current edition, 2002; Japanese Language Edition published by Hoken-Mainichi Shinbun-sha, 1995; Co-Author: "@ Risk: Internet and E-commerce Insurance and Reinsurance Legal Issues," a Reactions Publishing, 2000. *Member:* American Bar Association. ***PRACTICE AREAS:*** Insurance Litigation; Reinsurance; Reinsurance Arbitration; Appellate Practice; Technology Law. ***Email:*** LNugent@cozen.com

MARC A. POLANSKY, born Altoona, Pennsylvania, October 4, 1966; admitted to bar, 1994, Illinois and U.S. Court of Appeals, Seventh Circuit. *Education:* University of

(This Listing Continued)

COZEN O'CONNOR, A PROFESSIONAL CORPORATION, Chicago—Continued

Maryland (B.A., 1989); Chicago-Kent College of Law (J.D., 1994). Co-Author: "@ Risk: Internet and E-commerce Insurance and Reinsurance Legal Issues," a Reactions Publishing, 2000. *Member:* Chicago and Illinois State Bar Associations. ***PRACTICE AREAS:*** Insurance Litigation; Arson and Fraud Defense; Insurance Coverage; Subrogation and Recovery. ***Email:*** mpolansky@cozen.com

MARGARET A. REETZ, born La Grange, Illinois, December 27, 1960; admitted to bar, 1987, California and Illinois; 1992, New York. *Education:* University of Illinois (B.A., Econ., 1983); DePaul University (J.D., 1986). ***PRACTICE AREAS:*** Reinsurance; Insurance Coverage. ***Email:*** mreetz@cozen.com

LEENA SONI, born Rajasthan, India, December 26, 1966; admitted to bar, 1992, Illinois; 1993, U.S. District Court, Northern District of Illinois; 1999, U.S. Court of Appeals, Seventh Circuit; 2002, U.S. Court of Appeals, Sixth Circuit. *Education:* University of Missouri (B.J., 1989); University of Iowa (J.D., 1992). Member, Iowa Law Review. Moot Court Board; Association of Professional Insurance Women. *Member:* Chicago and American Bar Associations. ***PRACTICE AREAS:*** Insurance Coverage. ***Email:*** lsoni@cozen.com

JAMES I. TARMAN, JR., born Bellefonte, Pennsylvania, December 28, 1960; admitted to bar, 1987, Pennsylvania and New Jersey; 1998, Texas; 2001, Illinois; U.S. District Court, District of New Jersey, Eastern District of Pennsylvania, Western District of Michigan, Northern, Southern, Eastern and Western Districts of Texas and U.S. District Court, Northern, Southern and Central Districts of Illinois. *Education:* Pennsylvania State University (B.S., 1982); Dickinson School of Law of the Pennsylvania State University (J.D., 1987). *Member:* Chicago and American Bar Associations; State Bar of Texas. ***PRACTICE AREAS:*** Fire Insurance Subrogation; Property Damage; Property Loss; Property Subrogation; Subrogation. ***Email:*** jtarman@cozen.com

MATTHEW T. WALSH, born Naperville, Illinois, July 10, 1963; admitted to bar, 1990, Illinois; 2000, California. *Education:* University of Illinois (B.S., 1985); University of San Diego (J.D., 1990). *Member:* American Bar Association. ***PRACTICE AREAS:*** Aviation Litigation; Insurance Coverage; Products Liability; Class Actions. ***Email:*** mwalsh@cozen.com

FIRM ASSOCIATES IN CHICAGO

JEREMY S. BAKER, born Akron, Ohio, August 18, 1976; admitted to bar, 2002, Illinois; 2004, Minnesota. *Education:* University of California, Santa Barbara (B.A., Law and Society, with honors, 1999); Tulane University School of Law (J.D., cum laude, 2002). Litigation Associate, 2002—. Judicial Extern to Chief United States District Judge Emeritus, Morey L. Sear, United States District Court for the Eastern District of Louisiana, 2001-2002. Law Clerk, Office of the Corporation Counsel, Washington, D.C., 1999. *Member:* Chicago, Illinois State, Minnesota State and American Bar Associations. ***PRACTICE AREAS:*** Construction Law; Civil Litigation; Products Liability; Insurance. ***Email:*** jsbaker@cozen.com

JEFFREY C. CALABRESE, admitted to bar, 2002, Illinois and U.S. District Court, Northern District of Illinois. *Education:* Texas A & M University (B.B.A., 1987); United States Naval Academy; Southwestern University School of Law (J.D., 2002). *Member:* Chicago, Illinois State and American Bar Associations. [Lieutenant, U.S. Navy, 1987-1999]. ***PRACTICE AREAS:*** Property Insurance Coverage; Fire Insurance Subrogation; Subrogation; Insurance Litigation; Civil Litigation. ***Email:*** jcalabrese@cozen.com

D. CHRISTINE DUCAT, born Mt. Clemens, Michigan, July 5, 1976; admitted to bar, 2003, Illinois, U.S. District Court, Northern District of Illinois and U.S. District Court, Eastern District of Wisconsin. *Education:* University of Detroit Mercy (B.A., cum laude, 1976) Temple University (J.D., 2003). Recipient: Barrister Award, 2001 and 2002; Best Advocate, National Civil Trial Competition, 2002; Victor A. Jaczun Award, 2003; Lenard Sigal Memorial Award, 2003. Member, Temple Law Review, 2001-2003. Member, Temple's National Trial Team, 2002-2003. Listed in Who's Who of American Law Students, 2001. *Member:* Chicago and Illinois State Bar Associations; Association of Trial Lawyers of America. ***PRACTICE AREAS:*** Subrogation. ***Email:*** cducat@cozen.com

S. ELLYN FARLEY, born Roanoke, Virginia November 13, 1972; admitted to bar, 1998, Illinois; 2002, U.S. District Court, Northern District of Illinois. *Education:* Purdue University (B.A., with honors, 1995); Loyola University, Chicago (J.D., 1998). ***PRACTICE AREAS:*** Subrogation; Insurance Defense; Professional Liability. ***Email:*** efarley@cozen.com

JOHN E. FLAHERTY, born Evergreen Park, Illinois; admitted to bar, 1991, Illinois and U.S. District Court, Northern District of Illinois. *Education:* University of Illinois (B.A., 1988); Loyola University (J.D., 1991). *Member:* Chicago Bar Association. ***PRACTICE AREAS:*** Insurance Subrogation. ***Email:*** jflaherty@cozen.com

MAYA HOFFMAN, born Chicago, Illinois, May 18, 1974; admitted to bar, 2001, Illinois and U.S. District Court, Northern District of Illinois. *Education:* University of Illinois (B.A., 1996); The John Marshall Law School (J.D., 2000). Delta Theta Phi. Participant: John J. Gibbons National Criminal Procedure Moot Court Competition; The Cathy Bennett 10th Annual Criminal Trial Competition. Editor-in-Chief, The John Marshall Law Review, 1999-2000. Law Clerk to Justices Allen Hartman and Patrick J. Quinn, Illinois Appellate Court, First District, 2000-2004. Author: "A Game of High Stakes Roulette: Credit Card Companies Cash In On Gamblers' Bad Luck," The John Marshall Law Review, Summer 1999. *Member:* Chicago Bar Association. ***PRACTICE AREAS:*** Appellate Practice; Insurance Litigation; Technology Law; Reinsurance. ***Email:*** mhoffman@cozen.com

KEITH E. HORTON, admitted to bar, 2004, Illinois. *Education:* Yale University (B.A.); University of Illinois (J.D.). Editor-in-Chief, The Elder Law Journal, 2003-2004. *Member:* Chicago and American Bar Associations. ***Email:*** khorton@cozen.com

DANIEL R. JOHNSON, admitted to bar, 2004, Illinois. *Education:* Amherst College (B.A., cum laude, 2001); Northwestern University School of Law (J.D., 2004). ***PRACTICE AREAS:*** Insurance Coverage. ***Email:*** djohnson@cozen.com

CHRISTOPHER H. MURPHY, born February 2, 1974; admitted to bar, 1999, Massachusetts; 2000, New York; 2002, Illinois. *Education:* University of Michigan (B.A., 1996); Boston College (J.D., 1999). *Member:* American Bar Association. ***PRACTICE AREAS:*** Products Liability; Admiralty and Maritime Law; Aviation; Commercial Litigation; Insurance Coverage; Reinsurance. ***Email:*** chmurphy@cozen.com

THEODORE W. PANNKOKE, born Oak Park, Illinois, December 20, 1971; admitted to bar, 2000, Illinois and U.S. District Court, Northern District of Illinois. *Education:* University of Illinois (B.A., History, 1996; J.D., 2000). [With: United States Army, 1989-1991; Illinois Army National Guard, 1991-1997]. ***PRACTICE AREAS:*** Civil Appeals; Excess Coverage; General Liability; Insurance Bad Faith; Reinsurance; Punitive Damages. ***Email:*** tpannkoke@cozen.com

BETH A. STROUP, born Michigan City, Indiana, July 15, 1971; admitted to bar, 1998, Illinois. *Education:* Central Michigan University (B.S., 1994); DePaul University (J.D., 1998). Phi Alpha Delta. *Member:* Chicago, Illinois State and American Bar Associations. ***PRACTICE AREAS:*** International Insurance; Reinsurance; Punitive Damages; E-Commerce; Internet Insurance. ***Email:*** bstroup@cozen.com

---

DONALD M. CRAVEN, P.C.

CHICAGO, ILLINOIS

(See Springfield)

Media and First Amendment, Libel Defense, Intellectual Property, Commercial Transactions, Commercial Litigation, Appellate Practice and Legislative Law.

JAMES CRAWLEY & ASSOCIATES, LTD.

2 NORTH LA SALLE STREET, SUITE 1776
CHICAGO, ILLINOIS 60602
Telephone: 312-750-1300
Toll Free: 1-866-324-2896
Fax: 312-873-3705
Email: info@312law.com
URL: http://www.312law.com

Plaintiff's Personal Injury Liability, Medical Malpractice, Birth Trauma, Aviation Liability, Product Liability, Premises Liability, Construction Accidents, Wrongful Death, Vehicular Accident Law, Appellate Practice, ADR, Professional Liability, Torts; Toxic Torts, Workers Compensation.

FIRM PROFILE: James P. Crawley & Associates, Ltd., represents individuals and families for tragedies that occured due to the conduct of another in personal injury and wrongful death cases arising out of vehicular accidents, medical malpractice, product liability, premises liability, and construction accidents. James P. Crawley & Associates, Ltd., and its trial lawyers have obtained settlements of over $1,000,000 for its clients.

JAMES P. CRAWLEY, born Joliet, Illinois, February 27, 1964; admitted to bar, 1989, Illinois; 1990, U.S. District Court, Northern District of Illinois, including Trial Bar. *Education:* Loyola University (B.A., cum laude, 1986); St. Louis University School of Law (J.D., 1989). Alpha Sigma Nu; Editorial Staff, Saint Louis University Public Law Review. Staff Assistant to United States Senator Paul Simon (D-IL), 1985-1986; Assistant to the Honorable Myron H. Bright, Senior Judge, 8th Circuit United States Court of Appeals, 1989; Deputy Cook County Treasurer, 1994-1997 and Deputy General Counsel, Cook County, Illinois, 1992-1993; Election Lawyer, Cook County Board of Elections, 1993—; Board of Directors, Jane Addams Hull House, Chicago, and AIDS Care, Chicago; Citizens Advisory Council to the Chicago Police Department *Member:* Illinois State and American Bar Associations; Illinois Trial Lawyers Association; Association of Trial Lawyers of America. ***PRACTICE AREAS:*** Plaintiffs Personal Injury Liability; Medical Malpractice; Birth Trauma; Aviation Liability; Products Liability; Premises Liability; Construction Accidents; Wrongful Death; Vehicle Accidents; Election Law; Appellate Practice; ADR; Professional Liability; Torts; Toxic Torts; Workers Compensation. ***Email:*** jpc@312Law.com

---

CREMER, KOPON, SHAUGHNESSY & SPINA, LLC

180 NORTH LASALLE STREET, SUITE 3300
CHICAGO, ILLINOIS 60601
Telephone: 312-726-3800
Fax: 312-726-3818
URL: http://www.cksslaw.com

Complex Civil Litigation Defense, including Product Liability, Construction Law, Insurance Coverage, Commercial Litigation, Drug and Medical Device Litigation, Employment Law, Toxic Torts, Commercial Real Estate, University and College Law and all aspects of Trial and Appellate work in both State and Federal Courts.

WILLIAM J. CREMER, born Chicago, Illinois, September 4, 1956; admitted to bar, 1981, Illinois. *Education:* Lewis University (B.A., 1978); Loyola University; Hamline University (J.D., 1981). *Member:* Defense Research Institute (Member: Steering Committee, DRI; Drug and Medical Device Litigation Committee); Illinois Association of Defense Trial Counsel; Federation of Insurance and Corporate Counsel. ***PRACTICE AREAS:*** Products Liability; International Law; Construction Litigation; Commercial Litigation. ***Email:*** wcremer@cksslaw.com

ANDREW KOPON, JR., born Newark, New Jersey, July 6, 1954; admitted to bar, 1980, Illinois; 1982, New Jersey. *Education:* Providence College (B.A., 1976); John Marshall Law School (J.D., with distinction, 1980). *Member:* Illinois Association of Defense Trial Counsel; International Association of Defense Counsel (Past Chairman, Product Liability Committee); Defense Research Institute; National Association of College and University Attorneys. ***PRACTICE AREAS:*** Products Liability; College and University Law; Employment Law. ***Email:*** akopon@cksslaw.com

BRIAN P. SHAUGHNESSY, born Evergreen Park, Illinois, December 2, 1952; admitted to bar, 1979, Illinois. *Education:* Marquette University (B.S., 1974); Illinois Institute of Technology (J.D., with honors, 1979). *Member:* DuPage County Bar Association; Illinois

(This Listing Continued)

Association of Defense Trial Counsel; Defense Research Institute. ***PRACTICE AREAS:*** Tort Defense Litigation; Products Liability; Toxic Torts; Construction Litigation. ***Email:*** bshaughnessy@ckslaw.com

FRANCIS A. SPINA, born Evanston, Illinois, April 15, 1955; admitted to bar, 1980, Illinois. *Education:* University of Notre Dame (B.A., 1977); University of Denver; DePaul University (J.D., 1980). *Member:* American Bar Association; Illinois Association of Defense Trial Counsel; Defense Research Institute. ***PRACTICE AREAS:*** Insurance Coverage; Insurance Litigation; Employment Law; Tort Defense Litigation; Appellate Practice Litigation. ***Email:*** fspina@cksslaw.com

EDMUND J. SIEGERT, born Dubuque, Iowa, September 4, 1960; admitted to bar, 1986, Iowa and Illinois. *Education:* Loras College (B.S., 1983); DePaul University (J.D., with honors, 1986). *Member:* Chicago Bar Association; Defense Research Institute; Illinois Association of Defense Trial Counsel. ***PRACTICE AREAS:*** Products Liability; International Law; Commercial Litigation. ***Email:*** esiegert@cksslaw.com

GARY T. JANSEN, born Oak Park, Illinois, January 17, 1959; admitted to bar, 1984, Illinois. *Education:* Northern Illinois University (B.S., summa cum laude, 1981); DePaul University (J.D., 1984). *Member:* Chicago and Illinois State Bar Associations; Illinois Association of Defense Trial Counsel; Defense Research Institute. ***PRACTICE AREAS:*** Construction Litigation; Products Liability; Professional Liability; Premises Liability; Insurance Coverage. ***Email:*** gjansen@cksslaw.com

JOHN P. LYNCH, JR., born South Holland, Illinois, October 26, 1963; admitted to bar, 1988, Illinois and U.S. District Court, Northern District of Illinois including Trial bar; 1997, U.S. District Court, Eastern District of Wisconsin; 2001, U.S. District Court, Northern District of Indiana. *Education:* St. Norbert College (B.B.A., 1985); DePaul University (J.D., 1988). *Member:* Defense Research Institute; Illinois Association of Defense Trial Counsel (Board Member, 2003—); National Association of Insurance Litigation Management. ***PRACTICE AREAS:*** Commercial Litigation; Construction Litigation; Transportation Litigation; Products Liability. ***Email:*** jlynch@cksslaw.com

THOMAS R. PENDER, born Cincinnati, Ohio, March 10, 1962; admitted to bar, 1988, Illinois. *Education:* Miami University; Washington & Lee University. *Member:* Defense Research Institute. ***PRACTICE AREAS:*** Commercial Litigation; Creditors Rights Law; Torts Litigation. ***Email:*** tpender@cksslaw.com

MICHAEL A. AIRDO, born Westchester, Illinois, September 14, 1971; admitted to bar, 1996, Illinois. *Education:* DePaul University (B.A., 1993; J.D., 1996). Illinois Trustee, Village of Bartlett, 2001—. ***PRACTICE AREAS:*** Construction Litigation; Products Liability; Premises Liability; College and University Law. ***Email:*** mairdo@cksslaw.com

BRIAN A. O'GALLAGHER, born Chicago, Illinois, November 1, 1967; admitted to bar, 1992, Illinois; 1993, Wisconsin. *Education:* University of Illinois at Urbana-Champaign (B.S., 1989); University of Notre Dame (J.D., 1992). *Member:* Chicago, Dupage County and Illinois State Bar Associations. ***PRACTICE AREAS:*** Insurance Law; Torts. ***Email:*** bogallagher@cksslaw.com

KIMBERLY A. ROSS, born Lansing, Michigan, May 18, 1970; admitted to bar, 1996, Illinois. *Education:* University of Michigan (B.A., 1992); DePaul College of Law (J.D., 1996). ***PRACTICE AREAS:*** Insurance Defense Litigation; Employment Law. ***Email:*** kross@cksslaw.com

---

KRISTINA M. BECK, born Chula Vista, California, July 26, 1976; admitted to bar, 2001, Illinois and U.S. District Court, Northern District of Illinois; 2002, California. *Education:* Arizona State University (B.A., 1998); John Marshall Law School (J.D., 2001; LLM, 2002). ***PRACTICE AREAS:*** Insurance (100%). ***Email:*** kbeck@cksslaw.com

DAVID T. BROWN, born Davenport, Iowa, June 3, 1977; admitted to bar, 2002, Illinois. *Education:* University of Iowa (B.B.A., 1999; J.D., 2002). ***PRACTICE AREAS:*** Insurance Coverage. ***Email:*** dbrown@cksslaw.com

BRADLEY M. BURD, born Cincinnati, Ohio, June 19, 1977; admitted to bar, 2002, Illinois. *Education:* Miami University (B.S., 1999); University of Cincinnati College of Law (J.D., 2002). ***PRACTICE AREAS:*** Litigation; International; Insurance. ***Email:*** bburd@cksslaw.com

JEREMY T. BURTON, born Rochester, Michigan, August 12, 1973; admitted to bar, 2001, Wisconsin, Illinois and U.S. District Court, Northern District of Illinois. *Education:* Loyola University (B.A., 1995); University of Wisconsin-Madison (J.D., 2001). ***PRACTICE AREAS:*** Commercial Litigation; Construction Litigation; Tort Defense. ***Email:*** jburton@cksslaw.com

PAUL PATRICK CELLA, born Chicago, Illinois, January 27, 1977; admitted to bar, 2002, Illinois and U.S. District Court, Northern District of Illinois. *Education:* Miami University (B.A., 1999); DePaul University College of Law (J.D., 2002). ***PRACTICE AREAS:*** Tort Litigation. ***Email:*** pcella@cksslaw.com

JENNIFER COLVIN, born Mankato, Minnesota, September 19, 1975; admitted to bar, 2001, Illinois. *Education:* Marquette University (B.A., 1998); DePaul University College of Law (J.D., 2001). ***Email:*** jcolvin@cksslaw.com

COLLEEN COSTELLO, born Harvey, Illinois, September 5, 1975; admitted to bar, 2001, Illinois. *Education:* Purdue University (B.A., 1997); Loyola University School of Law (J.D., 2001). ***PRACTICE AREAS:*** Insurance Coverage. ***Email:*** ccostello@cksslaw.com

STACY DOLAN FULCO, born Dayton, Ohio, January 20, 1971; admitted to bar, 1997, Illinois and U.S. District Court, Northern District of Illinois; 1999, U.S. Court of Appeals, Seventh Circuit; 2000, U.S. District Court, Central District of Illinois. *Education:* Illinois State University (B.A., 1993); DePaul University (J.D., 1997; M.B.A., 1997). ***PRACTICE AREAS:*** Professional Liability; Personal Injury Defense; Wrongful Death Defense; Commercial Litigation. ***Email:*** sfulco@cksslaw.com

KEVIN GEORGERIAN, born Alexandria, Virginia, October 18, 1978; admitted to bar, 2004, Illinois. *Education:* University of Richmond (B.A., 2001); Washington & Lee University (J.D., 2004). ***PRACTICE AREAS:*** Litigation. ***Email:*** kgeorgerian@cksslaw.com

(This Listing Continued)

SCOTT M. GILBERT, born St. Louis, Missouri, June 10, 1979; (admission pending). *Education:* Wittenberg University (B.A., 2001); Loyola College (J.D., 2004). ***Email:*** sgilbert@cksslaw.com

TIMOTHY E. HOERMAN, born Bethesda, Maryland, September 1, 1964; admitted to bar, 1998, Illinois; 2001, U.S. District Court, Northern District of Illinois; registered to practice before the U.S. Patent and Trademark Office. *Education:* Loyola University (B.S., 1987); Southern Illinois University at Carbondale (J.D., 1998). ***REPORTED CASES:*** People v. Holloman, 304 Ill. App. 3D 177; People v. Bowden, 313 Ill. App. 3D 666. ***PRACTICE AREAS:*** Commercial Litigation; Tort Litigation; Commercial Real Estate; Appellate Practice; Business Transactions. ***Email:*** thoerman@cksslaw.com

MARIO M. IVELJIC, born Hammond, Indiana, November 22, 1977; admitted to bar, 2003, Illinois. *Education:* Yale University (B.A., 1999); Chicago-Kent College of Law (J.D., 2003). ***LANGUAGES:*** Croatian. ***PRACTICE AREAS:*** Products Liability; Premises Liability; Torts; International Law. ***Email:*** miveljic@cksslaw.com

GREGORY JAMES McKENNA, born White Plains, New York, February 9, 1974; admitted to bar, 2001, Illinois. *Education:* University of Notre Dame (B.A., magna cum laude, 1996); Georgetown University (M.S., 1997); Loyola University School of Law (J.D., with honors, 2001). ***PRACTICE AREAS:*** Products Liability; Construction Law; Insurance Coverage. ***Email:*** gmckenna@cksslaw.com

MATTHEW W. MILLER, born Chicago, Illinois, August 23, 1977; admitted to bar, 2003, Illinois. *Education:* Indiana University (B.A., 1999); Chicago-Kent College of Law (J.D., 2003). ***Email:*** mmiller@cksslaw.com

NICOLE D. MILOS, born Chicago, Illinois, December 12, 1976; admitted to bar, 2001, Illinois. *Education:* St. Mary's College (B.S., 1998); John Marshall Law School (J.D., 2001). ***PRACTICE AREAS:*** Tort Defense. ***Email:*** nmilos@cksslaw.com

JACOB C. MUROV, born Newport News, Virginia, August 7, 1978; admitted to bar, 2004, Illinois. *Education:* Indiana University, Bloomington (B.S., 2000); DePaul University College of Law (J.D., 2004). ***PRACTICE AREAS:*** Tort Litigation; Insurance Coverage; Products Liability. ***Email:*** jmurov@cksslaw.com

SHANON SHUMPERT, born Houston, Texas, July 17, 1970; admitted to bar, 1997, Illinois. *Education:* DePaul University (B.A., 1993; LL.M., Health, 2005); Howard University (J.D., 1997). ***PRACTICE AREAS:*** Labor and Employment; Education Law.

MATTHEW TIBBLE, born Winfeld, Illinois, July 17, 1977; admitted to bar, 2004, Illinois. *Education:* DePaul University (B.A., 1999; J.D., 2003). ***Email:*** mtibble@ckkslaw.com

DENNIS N. VENTURA, born Chicago, Illinois, January 17, 1979; admitted to bar, 2004, Illinois; 2005, U.S. District Court, District of Illinois. *Education:* University of Illinois (B.S., 2000); John Marshall Law School (J.D., 2004). ***Email:*** dventura@cksslaw.com

HEATHER WATTERSON, born Cleveland, Ohio, April 14, 1973; admitted to bar, 2001, Illinois. *Education:* Wittenberg University (B.A., 1995); DePaul University (J.D., 1997). ***PRACTICE AREAS:*** Insurance Defense. ***Email:*** hwatterson@cksslaw.com

JOSHUA D. YEAGER, born Waukegan, Illinois, July 25, 1974; admitted to bar, 2000, Illinois; 2001, U.S. District Court, Northern District of Illinois. *Education:* Illinois State University (B.S., summa cum laude, 1997); Chicago-Kent College of Law (J.D., 2000). ***PRACTICE AREAS:*** Products Liability; Tort Defense; Commercial Litigation. ***Email:*** jyeager@cksslaw.com

STEVEN A. CRIFASE, LTD.

8 SOUTH MICHIGAN
SUITE 2000
CHICAGO, ILLINOIS 60203
Telephone: 312-855-0511
FAX: 312-855-0537
Email: crifase@aol.com
URL: http://www.stevencrifase.com

Personal Injury including Auto Negligence, Medical Negligence, Products Liability and Worker's Compensation.

STEVEN A. CRIFASE, born Chicago, Illinois, June 3, 1957; admitted to bar, 1982, Illinois. *Education:* Drake University (B.S.B.A., 1979); Loyola University (J.D., 1982). *Member:* Chicago, Illinois State and American Bar Associations; Illinois Trial Lawyers Association; The Association of Trial Lawyers of America.

REFERENCE: American National Bank.

CRISHAM & KUBES, LTD.

30 NORTH LASALLE STREET, SUITE 2800
CHICAGO, ILLINOIS 60602
Telephone: 312-327-2500
Fax: 312-327-2450
URL: http://www.crishamlaw.com

General Civil Trial Practice, Complex Litigation, Commercial Law, Construction Law, Professional Liability, Environmental Litigation, Product Liability, Insurance/Reinsurance Coverage and Litigation, Labor and Employment, ERISA Litigation, Constitutional and Local Government Law, Appellate Law, Alternative Dispute Resolution, Intellectual Property Law, Trademark, Copyright, Unfair Competition, and Trade Secret Litigation.

FIRM PROFILE: Crisham & Kubes, Ltd. is a mid-sized firm of experienced trial and appellate lawyers. It was founded in 2001 by Thomas M. Crisham 30-year veteran of Hinshaw & Culbertson and a member of its executive committee for more than 15 years, and Jeffrey T. Kubes a 20-year litigator, also a Hinshaw & Culbertson veteran. Most recently, Crisham and Kubes were principals in the firm Quinlan & Crisham, Ltd. Crisham & Kubes attorneys are accomplished trial and appellate lawyers. They have tried numerous cases to juries, conducted many successful bench trials, won countless appeals before state and federal tribunals and have en-

(This Listing Continued)

CRISHAM & KUBES, LTD., Chicago—Continued

joyed success in serving their clients. The firm is committed to the highest professional standards and to the efficient and cost-effective representation of clients in trial and appellate proceedings, as well as in alternative dispute resolution matters.

THOMAS M. CRISHAM, born Chicago, Illinois; admitted to bar, 1965, Illinois and U.S. District Court, Northern District of Illinois; 1971, U.S. Supreme Court; 1978, U.S. Court of Appeals, Seventh Circuit. *Education:* Loyola University (B.B.A., 1962; J.D., cum laude, 1965). Alpha Sigma Nu. Recipient, Medal of Excellence, Loyola Law Alumni Association, 1993. Listed: "Pillar of the Legal Community," and among top 5% of Illinois Attorneys by Leading Lawyers Network, 2003, 2004 and 2005; Named by peers as one of Illinois' Top 100 Super Lawyers, 2005. Associate Editor, Loyola Law Review. Member: Editorial Advisory Board, *Insurance Outlook*, 1989-1990; Board of Advisors, *Expert Evidence Reporter*, 1989-1990. Contributing Author: *Architects/Engineers Liability:* Claims Against Design Professionals , John Wiley & Sons, Spring 1987, Second Edition, June 1995; *Prosecuting and Defending Insurance Claims*, John Wiley & Sons, 1989. President, Trial Lawyers Club of Chicago, 1975-1976. Member, Panel of Arbitrators, American Arbitration Association. Member, Board of Directors, Lawyers for Civil Justice, 1988-1990. *Member:* Chicago, Illinois State and American Bar Associations; Appellate Lawyers Association; Product Liability Advisory Council; Defense Research Institute (President, 1989-1990; Chairman of the Board, 1990-1991; Honorary Chairman, 1991-1992); Society of Trial Lawyers of Illinois; Law Club of Chicago; International Association of Defense Counsel; Association of Defense Trial Attorneys; Illinois Association of Defense Trial Counsel. Fellow, American College of Trial Lawyers; Diplomate, American Board of Trial Advocates. Fellow, International Society of Barristers; Master of the Bench, Judge Howard T. Markey Chapter, 1989—; American Inn of Court. ***PRACTICE AREAS:*** Professional Liability Litigation; Product Liability; Complex Commercial Litigation; Insurance and Reinsurance Litigation; Insurance Coverage; Construction Law; Environmental Litigation; Alternative Dispute Resolution. ***Email:*** tcrisham@crishamlaw.com

JEFFREY T. KUBES, born Minneapolis, Minnesota; admitted to bar, 1981, Illinois; 1988, U.S. District Court, Northern District of Illinois including Trial Bar; 1999, U.S. Court of Appeals, Fifth, Sixth and Seventh Circuits; 2002, U.S. Supreme Court. *Education:* Loyola University; Eastern Illinois University (B.S., 1978); Northern Illinois University (J.D., with Honors, 1981). Author: "Tort Trends Publication," for ISBA Tort Litigation Committee, 1992-1995; "My Insurance Company is Insolvent - Now What...," Hinshaw Reports: Torts, 1991-1995; "Perils of Third Party Practice in Construction Litigation," IADC, 2004. Faculty: John Marshall Law School, 1997-1998; Paralegal Institute, 1992-1994. Member: American Institute of Architects - Chicago Chapter; American Society of Civil Engineers. *Member:* DuPage, Chicago (Officer and Chairman, Tort Litigation Committee, 1993-1996), Illinois State and American Bar Associations; Defense Research Institute; International Association of Defense Counsel (Vice Chair, Construction Law Committee, 2004-2005); Association of Defense Trial Attorneys; Illinois Association of Defense Trial Counsel; Society of Trial Lawyers; Professional Liability Underwriting Society; Society of Illinois Construction Attorneys. ***PRACTICE AREAS:*** Construction Law; Complex Commercial Litigation; Professional Liability Litigation; Products Liability; Alternative Dispute Resolution. ***Email:*** jkubes@crishamlaw.com

MICHAEL C. BRUCK, born Elmhurst, Illinois; admitted to bar, 1988, Illinois; U.S. Court of Appeals, 7th Circuit; U.S. District Court, Northern District of Illinois; U.S. District Court, Central District of Illinois; Federal Trial Bar. *Education:* Purdue University (B.S., 1984); DePaul University (J.D., 1988). Faculty, Insurance School of Chicago for CPCU Course. Columnist, IDC Quarterly, Technology Law. Member: DePaul College of Law Alumni Board; DePaul College of Law Dean's Council. Member, Illinois Liaison and Chair, Third-Party Audit and Civility Subcommittees of Committee, Professionalism and Ethics. Author: "Defending Claims Against Accountants." Co-Author: DRI Symposium on Litigation Involving Accountants, Directors and Officers and Failed Financial Institutions, April 1992; The Do's and Don'ts of Corporate Documentation, Illinois CPS Society & Foundation 1996 fraud conference; Providing Damages in a Commercial Case, Chicago Bar Association, November 1996; Managing Your Accounting Firm in the Year 2000 and Beyond, Quinlan & Crisham, Ltd. Symposium; The Year 2000 Computer Problem and Accountant Litigation Exposure, The Certificate, Vol. 57, No. 1, April 1999, republished in The Magazine of the Illinois CPA Society, April 1999; Accounting Today, Vol. 13, No. 8, May 10-23, 1999; Part 1, The Wisconsin CPA, Vol. 3, No. 5, May 1999; today's CPA, Texas Society of Certified Public Accountants, May/June, 1999 and Part 2, The Wisconsin CPA, Vol. 3, No. 6, June 1999; Avoiding Malpractice for Tax Services, Presentation to over 300 accountants at Illinois CPA Society Business & Technology Solutions Show, August 2004; Understanding and Making the Most of Section 230 of the Communications Decency Act in Illinois, IDC Quarterly, Second Quarter 2004, at 57; Nanotechnology - It's Small, But it May be the Next Big Thing, IDC Quarterly, Third Quarter 2004, at 44; A Long-Awaited First Interpretation of Section 1201(a) of the Digital Millennium Copyright Act, IDC Quarterly, Fourth Quarter 2004, at 37; Betamax Revisited, Again, IDC Quarterly, First Quarter 2005. *Member:* Chicago, Illinois State and American Bar Associations; 7th Circuit Bar Association; Illinois Association of Defense Trial Counsel; The Society of Trial Lawyers of Illinois; Defense Research Institute; Professional Liability Underwriting Society. ***PRACTICE AREAS:*** Complex Commercial Litigation; Professional Liability Litigation; Intellectual Property Litigation; Insurance Coverage Law and Litigation; Reinsurance Coverage Law and Litigation; Alternative Dispute Resolution. ***Email:*** mbruck@crishamlaw.com

JOHN P. O'MALLEY, born Evanston, Illinois; admitted to bar, 1991, Illinois and U.S. District Court, Northern District of Illinois; 1992, U.S. Court of Appeals, Seventh Circuit; 1998, U.S. Court of Appeals, Eighth Circuit. *Education:* Marquette University (B.S., 1987); DePaul University (J.D., with honors, 1991). Order of the Coif. *Member:* Illinois State Bar Association (Member, Insurance Coverage Committee); Society of Trial Lawyers of Illinois; Defense Research Institute. ***PRACTICE AREAS:*** Insurance Coverage; Litigation; Intellectual Property. ***Email:*** jomalley@crishamlaw.com

DANIEL L. STANNER, born Chicago, Illinois; admitted to bar, 1992, Illinois and U.S. District Court, Northern District of Illinois. *Education:* Boston College (B.A., cum laude, 1989); Loyola University of Chicago (J.D., cum laude, 1992). Member, Loyola University of Chicago, Law Journal. *Member:* Chicago and Illinois State Bar Associations. ***PRACTICE AREAS:*** Construction Litigation; Transportation Litigation; Products Liability; Commercial Litigation; Labor and Employment; Insurance Law. ***Email:*** dstanner@crishamlaw.com

EDWARD FITZSIMMONS DUNNE, born Evanston, Illinois, February 1, 1968; admitted to bar, 1994, Illinois. *Education:* University of Wisconsin-Madison (B.A., 1990); Illinois Institute of Chicago-Kent College of Law (J.D., 1994). *Member:* Chicago, Illinois State and American Bar Associations. ***PRACTICE AREAS:*** Construction Litigation; Commercial Litigation; Insurance Litigation; Intellectual Property. ***Email:*** edunne@crishamlaw.com

JEAN M. PRENDERGAST, born Oak Lawn, Illinois; admitted to bar, 1994, Illinois and U.S. District Court, Northern District of Illinois; 2000, U.S. Court of Appeals, Seventh Circuit; 2001, U.S. Supreme Court. *Education:* Loyola University (B.A., magna cum laude, 1993; J.D., 1994). Member: Chicago Bar Association Moot Court Team, 1993; Loyola National Trial Team, 1994. Recipient, American Jurisprudence Award for Trial Practice/Advocacy. Law Clerk: Hon. Mary Jane Theis, Illinois Appellate Court, 1994-1996; Hon. Mary Ann McMorrow, Illinois Supreme Court, 1996-1997. Author: "Foreign Legal Consultant Rules: Effective or Expendable?" 63 The Bar Examiner, No. 1 (Feb. 1994); "Making the Most of Your Oral Argument," 90 ILL. B. J. 207 (April 2002). Member, Illinois Supreme Court Committee on Character and Fitness. *Member:* Chicago Bar Association (Member, Young Lawyers Section; Co-Chair, Appellate Law Committee, 1994); Appellate Lawyers Association (Board of Directors, 2000-2002); Women's Bar Foundation (Board of Directors); Women's Bar Association of Illinois (Board of Directors, 2002-2003). ***PRACTICE AREAS:*** Complex Commercial Litigation; Professional Liability Litigation; Appellate Practice; Insurance Litigation. ***Email:*** jprendergast@crishamlaw.com

---

THOMAS W. MULCAHY, born Evergreen Park, Illinois, July 8, 1974; admitted to bar, 2000, Illinois. *Education:* Indiana University at Bloomington (B.A., 1997); John Marshall Law School (J.D., cum laude, 2000). Co-Author: "Conflicts of Interest in Document Authentication By Attorney-Notaries in Illinois," 87 B.J. 320, June 1999; "Perils of Third Party Practice in Construction Litigation," Defense Counsel Journal (Apr. 2005). ***PRACTICE AREAS:*** Commercial Litigation; Professional Liability; Construction Litigation; Maritime Law. ***Email:*** tmulcahy@crishamlaw.com

DAVID J. SULLIVAN, born Chicago, Illinois, March 17, 1971; admitted to bar, 1996, Illinois and U.S. District Court, Northern District of Illinois; 2004, U.S. Court of Appeals, Seventh Circuit. *Education:* University of Notre Dame (B.B.A., Accounting, 1993); Loyola University Chicago School of Law (J.D., cum laude, 1996). Certified Public Accountant, Illinois, 1996. *Member:* Chicago Bar Association. ***PRACTICE AREAS:*** Commercial Litigation; Professional Liability Defense; Real Estate. ***Email:*** dsullivan@crishamlaw.com

JOHN R. BOWLEY, born Orangeburg, South Carolina; admitted to bar, 2001, Illinois and U.S. District Court, Northern District of Illinois. *Education:* The Ohio State University (B.A., Journalism, 1996); John Marshall Law School (J.D., cum laude, 2001). Co-Author, "Understanding and Making the Most of the Communications Decency Act," IDC Quarterly, Vol. 14 No. 2, Second Qtr. 2004. *Member:* Chicago, Illinois State and American Bar Associations. ***PRACTICE AREAS:*** Commercial Litigation. ***Email:*** jbowley@crishamlaw.com

MICHAEL J. FALEY, born Chicago, Illinois, January 4, 1976; admitted to bar, 2002, Illinois. *Education:* University of Illinois (B.S., Accounting, 1998); John Marshall Law School (J.D., 2002). Illinois Certificate of Certified Public Account, 1999. *Member:* Illinois State Bar Association. ***PRACTICE AREAS:*** Litigation. ***Email:*** mfaley@crishamlaw.com

JOHN P. LYNCH, born Oak Lawn, Illinois, August 14, 1974; admitted to bar, 2001, Illinois and U.S. District Court, Northern District of Illinois. *Education:* Eastern Illinois University (B.S., 1997); John Marshall Law School (J.D., 2001).

JAMIE L. ROSS, born Centralia, Illinois, September 6, 1974; admitted to bar, 1999, Illinois. *Education:* Knox College (B.A., summa cum laude, 1996); Southern Illinois University (J.D., magna cum laude, 1998). Phi Beta Kappa. *Member:* Illinois State Bar Association. ***PRACTICE AREAS:*** Commercial Litigation; Appeals. ***Email:*** jross@crishamlaw.com

JOHN E. NEWTON, born Blue Island, Illinois, December 29, 1971; admitted to bar, 2001, Illinois. *Education:* Northwestern University (B.S., Economics, 1994); Chicago-Kent College of Law, Illinois Institute of Technology (J.D., 2001). *Member:* Illinois State and American Bar Associations. ***PRACTICE AREAS:*** Commercial Litigation; Professional Liability; Construction Litigation; Torts. ***Email:*** jnewton@crishamlaw.com

KATHLEEN J. DOYLE, born Oak Lawn, Illinois, October 30, 1979; admitted to bar, 2005, Illinois and U.S. District Court, Northern District of Illinois. *Education:* Marquette University (B.A., 2002); Loyola University Chicago School of Law (J.D., 2005). *Member:* Chicago, Illinois State and American Bar Associations. ***PRACTICE AREAS:*** Professional Liability Litigation; Complex Commercial Litigation; Insurance Coverage Law and Litigation. ***Email:*** kdoyle@crishamlaw.com

(This Listing Continued)

CRONIN, PETERS & COOK, P.C.

221 NORTH LA SALLE STREET, SUITE 1454
CHICAGO, ILLINOIS 60601
Telephone: 312-372-1872
Fax: 312-372-1733
Email: cpcworkcomp@aol.com
URL: http://www.lawyers.com/candplaw

Workers Compensation, Social Security Disability.

THOMAS G. CRONIN (1920-1999)

KENNETH D. PETERS, born Rockford, Illinois, December 23, 1948; admitted to bar, 1974 Illinois and U.S. District Court, Northern District of Illinois. *Education:* Purdue University (B.S., 1970); John Marshall Law School (J.D., 1974). *Member:* Chicago Bar Asso-

(This Listing Continued)

ciation; Illinois Trial Lawyers Association; Worker's Compensation Lawyers Association; The Association of Trial Lawyers of America. ***REPORTED CASES:*** Insulated Panel co. vs. Industrial Comm. 318 Ill. App.3d 100, 743 N.E. 2d 1038, 252 Ill. Dec. 882 (2nd Dist. 2001); Robert Lester v. Industrial Commission, 256 Ill.App.3rd 520, 628 N.E.2d 191, 194 Ill.Dec. 694 (1st Dist. 1993); Reliance Elevator v. Industrial Commission, 233 Ill.App.3d 956, 600 N.E.2d 4, 175 Ill.Dec. 381 (1st Dist. 1992). ***PRACTICE AREAS:*** Workers Compensation. ***Email:*** cpcworkcomp@aol.com

JOHN J. CRONIN, born Oak Park, Illinois, March 3, 1949; admitted to bar, 1976, Illinois; 1987, U.S. District Court, Northern District of Illinois. *Education:* John Carroll University (B.A., 1971); IIT/Chicago-Kent College of Law (J.D., 1975). Lecturer, Illinois Trial Lawyers Workers Compensation Seminar. Assistant Cook County State's Attorney, 1977-1988. *Member:* Chicago Bar Association (Member, Judicial Evaluation Committee, 1987—); Trial Lawyers Club of Chicago; Illinois Trial Lawyers Association; Workers Compensation Lawyers Association; The Association of Trial Lawyers of America. ***PRACTICE AREAS:*** Workers Compensation. ***Email:*** cpcworkcomp@aol.com

PATRICIA CRONIN COOK, born Chicago, Illinois, May 25, 1956; admitted to bar, 1984, California, U.S. District Court, Central District of California and U.S. Court of Appeals, Ninth Circuit; 1985, Illinois; 1986, U.S. District Court, Northern District of Illinois and U.S. Court of Appeals, Seventh Circuit; 1987, U.S. District Court, Central District of Illinois. *Education:* University of Illinois (B.S., 1978); Southwestern University School of Law (J.D., cum laude, 1984). Editor, Southwestern University Law Review, 1983-1984. Judicial Clerkship: U.S. District Judge Alicemarie H. Stotler, Central District of California; 1984-1985; U.S. Circuit Judge Arthur L. Alarcon, U.S. Court of Appeals, Ninth Circuit, 1985-1986. *Member:* Chicago and American Bar Associations; State Bar of California; Illinois Trial Lawyers Association; Workers Compensation Bar Association; The Association of Trial Lawyers of America. ***REPORTED CASES:*** Modern Drop Forge Corp. v. Industrial Commission, 284 Ill.App.3d 259, 671 N.E.2d 753, 219 Ill.Dec. 586 (1st Dist. 1996). ***PRACTICE AREAS:*** Workers Compensation; Social Security Disability. ***Email:*** cpcworkcomp@aol.com

REFERENCE: American National Bank and Trust Company of Chicago, Illinois.

CROWLEY BARRETT & KARABA, LTD.

Established in 1927

SUITE 2310
TWO FIRST NATIONAL PLAZA
20 SOUTH CLARK STREET
CHICAGO, ILLINOIS 60603
Telephone: 312-726-2468
Fax: 312-726-2741
URL: http://www.cbklaw.com

Acquisitions, Divestitures and Mergers, Banking and Corporate, Business Law, Commercial Litigation, Real Estate, Domestic Relations, Probate and Estate Planning Law. General Practice.

MEMBERS OF FIRM

ALAN RAUH ORSCHEL, born Chicago, Illinois, 1939; admitted to bar, 1966, Illinois. *Education:* Dartmouth College (B.A., 1961); University of Chicago (J.D., 1964). *Member:* Chicago, Illinois State and American Bar Associations. ***PRACTICE AREAS:*** Real Estate Law; Corporate Law; Banking Law; Commercial Finance Law; Domestic Relations Law. ***Email:*** aorschel@cbklaw.com

GREGORY M. WHITE, born Chicago, Illinois, 1949; admitted to bar, 1975, Illinois. *Education:* DePaul University (B.A., 1971; J.D., summa cum laude, 1975); John Marshall Law School (LL.M., Taxation, 1982). Comment Editor, De Paul Law Review, 1974-1975. Certified Financial Planner. Instructor in Law, Illinois Institute of Technology—Chicago-Kent College of Law, 1980-1982. *Member:* Illinois State and American Bar Associations. ***PRACTICE AREAS:*** Mergers, Acquisitions and Divestitures; Banking Law; Commercial Finance Law; Business Law; Real Estate Law; Estate Planning. ***Email:*** gwhite@cbklaw.com

CHARLES W. SIRAGUSA, born New York, New York, 1949; admitted to bar, 1974, Illinois and U.S. District Court, Northern District of Illinois; 1983, Trial Bar for the Northern District of Illinois. *Education:* Northwestern University (B.A., 1971; J.D., cum laude, 1974). *Member:* Illinois State and American Bar Associations. ***PRACTICE AREAS:*** Civil Litigation; Appellate Practice. ***Email:*** csiragusa@cbklaw.com

THOMAS F. KARABA, born Chicago, Illinois, 1955; admitted to bar, 1980, Illinois. *Education:* Northwestern University (B.S., 1977; J.D., 1980). *Member:* Illinois State and American Bar Associations. ***PRACTICE AREAS:*** Banking Law; Commercial Finance Law; Corporate Law; Environmental Law; Estate Planning; Employment Law. ***Email:*** tkaraba@cbklaw.com

SCOTT D.H. REDMAN, born Urbana, Illinois, 1964; admitted to bar, 1989, Illinois. *Education:* University of Illinois (A.B., 1986; J.D., magna cum laude, 1989). Delta Theta Phi. Recipient, Rickert Award for Excellence. Harno Fellow. *Member:* Illinois State and American Bar Associations. ***PRACTICE AREAS:*** Banking Law; Commercial Finance Law; Corporate Law. ***Email:*** sredman@cbklaw.com

JEFFREY S. BURNS, born New Brunswick, New Jersey, 1968; admitted to bar, 1993, Illinois. *Education:* Miami University (B.A., 1990); The John Marshall Law School (J.D., 1993). *Member:* Chicago, Illinois State and American Bar Associations. ***PRACTICE AREAS:*** Litigation; Creditors Rights. ***Email:*** jburns@cbklaw.com

DAVID C. BIRKS, born Grand Rapids, Michigan, 1962; admitted to bar, 1993, Illinois; 1997, Michigan. *Education:* Michigan State University (B.A., 1984); University of Notre Dame (J.D., 1993). Certified Public Accountant, 1986. *Member:* Chicago and Illinois State Bar Associations. ***PRACTICE AREAS:*** Corporate Law; Real Estate. ***Email:*** dbirks@cbklaw.com

BRUNO W. TABIS, JR., born Chicago, Illinois, 1946; admitted to bar, 1973, Illinois and U.S. District Court, Northern District of Illinois. *Education:* University of Illinois

(This Listing Continued)

(B.S., 1973); Illinois Institute of Technology-Chicago-Kent College of Law (J.D., with distinction, 1973). Associate Editor, Chicago-Kent Law Review, 1972-1973. Instructor, IIT/Chicago-Kent College of Law, 1980-1981. Director, 1979-1988 and Secretary, 1980-1981, Lawyers for the Creative Arts. Commissioner, Lawyers Trust Fund Implementation Commission, 1983-1985. Director: Neighborhood Justice of Chicago, 1981-1983. *Member:* Chicago (Chairman, 1982-1983, Young Lawyers Section; Member, Board of Managers, 1984-1986; Editor-in-Chief, Communicator, 1983-1986) and Illinois State (Real Estate Law Section Council; Chairman, 1993-1994; Board of Editors, Illinois Bar Journal, 1994—) Bar Associations. ***PRACTICE AREAS:*** Real Estate; Environmental; Corporate.

PAUL F. MARKOFF, IV, born Grand Rapids, Michigan, 1970; admitted to bar, 1996, Illinois; 1997, District of Columbia; 1998, Colorado. *Education:* University of Michigan (A.B., 1992); Depaul University (J.D., 1996). *Member:* Chicago, Illinois State and American Bar Associations; The District of Columbia Bar. ***PRACTICE AREAS:*** Commercial Litigation; Appellate Practice; Products Liability Defense. ***Email:*** pmarkoff@cbklaw.com

KARL G. LEINBERGER, born Springfield, Illinois, 1969; admitted to bar, 1996, Illinois; 1997, U.S. District Court, Northern District of Illinois; U.S. Court of Appeals, Seventh Circuit. *Education:* University of Iowa (B.A., Finance, 1992); DePaul Law School (J.D., 1996). Recipient, American Jurisprudence Award for Legal Writing. Editor in Chief, DePaul Business Law Journal, 1995-1996. *Member:* Chicago, Illinois State and American Bar Associations. ***PRACTICE AREAS:*** Civil Litigation; Commercial Litigation. ***Email:*** kleinberger@cbklaw.com

ANDREW NICHOLAS PLASZ, born Waukegan, Illinois, 1974; admitted to bar, 1999, Illinois; 2000, Missouri; 2001, U.S. District Court, Northern District of Illinois including Trial Bar. *Education:* Washington University (A.B., 1996; J.D., 1999). Associate Editor, Washington University Law Quarterly, 1998-1999. *Member:* Chicago, Illinois State and American Bar Associations; The Missouri Bar. ***PRACTICE AREAS:*** Commercial Litigation. ***Email:*** aplasz@cbklaw.com

LAW OFFICES
CROWLEY & LAMB, P.C.

350 NORTH LA SALLE STREET
SUITE 900
CHICAGO, ILLINOIS 60610
Telephone: 312-670-6900
Fax: 312-467-5926
URL: http://www.crowleylamb.com

Commercial and Residential Real Estate Acquisition, Development, Contracts, Financing, Litigation and Dispute Resolution, Commercial Litigation, Banking Law.

JAMES M. CROWLEY, born Chicago, Illinois, January 8, 1957; admitted to bar, 1982, Illinois. *Education:* Moraine Valley Community College (A.A., 1977); Northern Illinois University (B.A., 1979); DePaul University (J.D., 1982). *Member:* Chicago and Illinois State Bar Associations. ***PRACTICE AREAS:*** Banking Law; Commercial Litigation.

PATRICK D. LAMB, born Chicago, Illinois, May 5, 1954; admitted to bar, 1980, Illinois and U.S. District Court, Northern District of Illinois. *Education:* University of Dayton (B.S.,1976); John Marshall Law School (J.D., 1980). *Member:* Chicago and Illinois State Bar Associations; Illinois Trial Lawyers Association; The Association of Trial Lawyers of America. ***PRACTICE AREAS:*** Real Estate Acquisitions; Residential Real Estate; Commercial Real Estate; Real Estate Development; Real Estate Litigation.

WILLIAM J. HURLEY, III, born Chicago, Illinois, January 5, 1956; admitted to bar, 1982, Illinois; 1983, U.S. District Court, Northern District of Illinois. *Education:* Knox College (B.A., 1977); John Marshall Law School (J.D., 1982). *Member:* Illinois State and American Bar Associations. ***PRACTICE AREAS:*** Banking Law; Real Estate Law; Environmental Law; Litigation.

FRANCIS J. PENDERGAST, III, born 1956; admitted to bar, 1980, Illinois. *Education:* Loyola University (B.S., 1977; J.D., 1980). ***PRACTICE AREAS:*** Mortgage Foreclosure (70%, 150); Bankruptcy Law (30%, 30).

JOSEPH BROWN, admitted to bar, 1998, Wisconsin (Not admitted in Illinois). *Education:* University of Minnesota (B.A., 1991; M.B.A., 1991); University of Minnesota Law School (J.D., 1998).

CHRISTOPHER S. FOWLER, admitted to bar, 2003, Nebraska; 2004, Illinois. *Education:* Creighton University (B.A., 2000); Creighton University Law School (J.D., 2003).

ADELA C. LUCCHESI, born Northridge, California, September 15, 1974; admitted to bar, 2000, Illinois, U.S. District Court, Northern and Central Districts of Illinois; U.S. Court of Appeals, Seventh Circuit; U.S. District Court, Southern District of Texas. *Education:* California State University (B.A., 1996) Loyola University (J.D., 1999).

OF COUNSEL

PHILIP J. BERENZ, LAW OFFICES OF PHILIP J. BERENZ, born St. Louis, Missouri, January 10, 1970; admitted to bar, 2000, Illinois and U.S. District Court, Northern District of Illinois. *Education:* Purdue University (B.S., 1992); Indiana University School of Law - Bloomington (J.D., 2000). Certified Public Accountant, Illinois, 1994. *Member:* American Institute of Certified Public Accountants; Illinois Certified Public Accountant Society. (Also practicing individually). ***PRACTICE AREAS:*** Health Care; Business Law; General Practice.

DAVID A. CULPEPPER

77 WEST WASHINGTON STREET, SUITE 1708
CHICAGO, ILLINOIS 60602
Telephone: 312-939-0779
Fax: 312-939-0875
Email: steaks2@aol.com
URL: http://www.davidculpepper.com

Bankruptcy, Personal Injury, Wrongful Death, Automobile Accidents, Truck Accidents, Negligence, Probate, Chapter 7, Foreclosures, Domestic Relations, Family Law, Divorce, Adoptions.

DAVID A. CULPEPPER, born 1947; admitted to bar, 1978, Illinois. *Education:* City College of the City University of New York (B.B.A., 1968; M.B.A., 1970); Northwestern University (J.D., 1978). ***PRACTICE AREAS:*** Bankruptcy; Personal Injury; Probate; Family Law; Divorce; Adoption Law.

CUMMINS & CRONIN, LLC

77 WEST WACKER DRIVE, SUITE 4800
CHICAGO, ILLINOIS 60601
Telephone: 312-578-0500
Fax: 312-578-1234

Trial Practice.

ROBERT P. CUMMINS, born Oak Park, Illinois, March 17, 1933; admitted to bar, 1962, Illinois; 1985, Colorado. *Education:* Purdue University (B.S. in E.E., with distinction, 1958); DePaul University (J.D., 1962). Eta Kappa Nu; Tau Beta Pi. Member, De Paul University Law Review, 1961-1962. Appointed Special Counsel Chicago Bar Association in Black Panther Case, 1970 and Supreme Court, Committee on Character and Fitness, First District, 1972-1974; 1999-2000. Member, Governing Board, Chicago Law Enforcement Study Group, 1971-1973. Lecturer, Trial Practice, John Marshall Law School, 1973-1974. Lecturer, Loyola University School of Law, 1979-1988. Gubernatorial Appointee as Member, 1979 and Chairman, 1980-1987, Illinois Judicial Inquiry Board. Member, Review Board, Attorney Registration and Disciplinary Commission of the Illinois Supreme Court, 1973-1980. Member, Board of Directors, Criminal Justice Project of Cook County, 1987-1989. Board Member, Lawyers Assistance Program, Inc., 1979—. Member, Dean's Visiting Committee, De Paul University Law School, 1982-1987. Member, De Paul University Law School Advisory Council, 1987-1993. Member, Performance Assistance Committee, United States District Court, Northern District of Illinois. Member, Fund Committee, Seventh Circuit Court of Appeals. Board Member, Legal Clinic for the Disabled, Inc., 1982-1987. Former Member: Editorial Board, ABA/BNA Lawyers, Manual on Professional Conduct; Performance Assistance Committee, Trial Bar of the U.S. District Court, Northern District of Illinois. Laureate, Academy of Illinois Lawyers, 2004. *Member:* Chicago (Member, Board of Managers, 1978-1980), Seventh Circuit, Illinois State (Member, Board of Governors, 1972-1977; Vice Chairman, Task Force on Professionalism, 1987-1989) and American (Member, Standing Committee on Professional Discipline, 1981-1987; Chairman, 1984-1987; Co-Chairman, Joint Committee on Professional Sanctions, 1984-1986; Member, Standing Committee on Lawyer Competence, 1987-1990; Member, Standing Committee on Lawyers' Professional Liability, 1992-1994. Member, Standing Committee on Professionalism, 1998—; Member, Task Force on the Independent Lawyer, Litigation Section; Chair, Task Force on Ethics 2000, Litigation Section, 2000—) Bar Associations; Chicago Council of Lawyers (Executive Vice President, 1972; Member, Board, 1972-1973); Law Club of Chicago; Legal Club of Chicago; American Judicature Society (Chairman, Advisory Committee, 1984-1986; Member, Board of Directors, 1985-1988; 1999—). [U.S. Marine Corps, 1952-1954]. ***Email:*** rpc@cumminscronin.com

THOMAS C. CRONIN, born Oak Park, Illinois, January 21, 1964; admitted to bar, 1990, Illinois, U.S. District Court, Northern District of Illinois, U.S. Court of Appeals, Seventh Circuit and U.S. Supreme Court; 1999, California. *Education:* Harvard (B.A., with honors, American Government and Political Theory, 1986); University of Chicago Law School and Graduate School of Business (J.D./M.B.A., Accounting, 1990). Bradley Fellow in Criminal Justice. Recipient, Pro Bono Commitment to Service Award, Winton & Strawn, 1997. Law Clerk, Chief Judge William J. Bauer, U.S. Court of Appeals, Seventh Circuit. Member: Board of Directors, John Howard Association for Prison Reform. Vice-chair and Member of the Board of Trustees, The Poetry Foundation. *Member:* Chicago Bar Association. ***PRACTICE AREAS:*** Complex Commercial Litigation; Trial Practice; Appellate Practice. ***Email:*** tcc@cumminscronim.com

---

CUMMINS & HESSION, P.C.

Established in 2000

415 NORTH LASALLE STREET, SUITE 603
CHICAGO, ILLINOIS 60610-4509
Telephone: 312-464-9840
Fax: 312-464-9845
Email: jcummins@cumminshession.com
URL: http://www.cumminshession.com

Corporate Law: including Mergers and Acquisitions, Venture Financing, Shareholder Agreements, Buy-Sell Contracts, Licensing, Franchising, Joint Ventures, Labor and Employment and Real Estate; Business Litigation and Counseling: Prosecution and Defense of Contractual, Statutory and Common Law Claims, including Business Contract Matters, Labor and Employment, Non-Competition Agreements, Severance Agreements, Restrictive Covenant Disputes and Risk Avoidance Counseling; Intellectual Property: including Analysis, Protection, Licensing and Sale of Patents, Trademarks, Copyrights and Trade Secrets; Counseling regarding Infringement and Theft.

FIRM PROFILE: Cummins and Hession, P.C. represents and counsels corporate and individual clients in corporate transactions, commercial litigation and intellectual property matters. The firm regularly represents emerging and established organizations in the technology,

(This Listing Continued)

health care, manufacturing, venture capital, private placement, professional and financial services, construction and real estate industries. The firm also represents entrepreneurs, owners, directors and executives of business organizations in their individual business ventures.

JOHN J. CUMMINS, born Geneva, Illinois, July 6, 1966; admitted to bar, 1992, Illinois, U.S. District Court, Northern and Central Districts of Illinois and U.S. Court of Appeals, Seventh and Federal Circuits. *Education:* DePaul University (B.A., 1988; J.D., 1992). *Member:* Chicago, Illinois State and American Bar Associations. ***PRACTICE AREAS:*** Corporate Law; Intellectual Property; Trade Secrets; Mergers and Acquisitions; Commercial Litigation. ***Email:*** jcummins@cumminshession.com

CHRISTOPHER D. HESSION, born Washington, D.C., July 7, 1971; admitted to bar, 1997, Illinois and U.S. District Court, Northern District of Illinois; 2005, Colorado. *Education:* Indiana University (B.S., 1993); DePaul University (J.D., and M.B.A., 1997). *Member:* Chicago, Illinois State and American Bar Associations. ***PRACTICE AREAS:*** Corporate; Employment; Commercial Litigation. ***Email:*** chession@cumminshession.com

---

DAAR & VANEK, P.C.

225 W. WASHINGTON STREET, 18TH FLOOR
CHICAGO, ILLINOIS 60606
Telephone: 312-224-1500
Telecopier: 312-224-1510
URL: http://www.DAARVANEK.com

Corporate Litigation and transaction practice. Insurance Law, Policyholder Representation and Uninsured Loss Recovery, Antitrust, Intellectual Property, Brand Review and Protection.

FIRM PROFILE: Daar & Vanek, P.C. is a law firm offering experienced advice and representation on a variety of legal matters throughout the world. Messrs. Daar and Vanek have been practicing law together since 1986.

HENRY R. DAAR, born Chicago, Illinois, July 7, 1955; admitted to bar, 1980, Illinois; U.S. District Court, Northern District of Illinois, including Trial Bar. *Education:* University of Illinois (B.S., 1977); Loyola University (J.D., 1980). Phi Kappa Phi; Phi Eta Sigma. Member, Loyola Law Review. Member, Securities Moot Court Team, 1980. Author: "Expansion of Tender Offers Under the Williams Act," 11 Loyola Law Journal 277, 1980; "A Revisit to the Environmental Claim and the Property Insurance Policy," Environmental Claims Journal, Vol. 3, No. 3, Spring 1991; "Property Policy Liability for Environmental Claims," Environmental Claims Journal, Vol. 1, No. 1, Autumn 1988. Co-Author: "Asbestos Removal Claims Under All Risk First-Party Insurance Policies," Environmental Claims Journal, Vol. 5, No. 1, Autumn 1992. *Member:* Chicago and American Bar Associations. ***PRACTICE AREAS:*** Insurance; Environmental Law; Loss Recovery. ***Email:*** hdaar@daarvanek.com

JOSEPH M. VANEK, born Minneapolis, Minnesota, November 25, 1961; admitted to bar, 1987, Illinois; 1988, Massachusetts and U.S. District Court, Northern District of Illinois; 1989, U.S. Court of Appeals, Ninth Circuit; 1994, U.S. Court of Appeals, Fifth Circuit; 1996, U.S. District Court, Central District of Illinois; 1997, U.S. Court of Appeals, Federal Circuit; 1998, U.S. Supreme Court. *Education:* Creighton University (B.A., magna cum laude, 1984); Boston College Law School (J.D., cum laude, 1987). *Member:* Chicago Bar Association. ***PRACTICE AREAS:*** Intellectual Property; Patents; Copyrights; Trademarks; Antitrust; Litigation; Business Law; Commercial Law; Professional Liability; Insurance.

THOMAS A. VICKERS, born Waukegan, Illinois, August 4, 1963; admitted to bar, 1994, Illinois and U.S. District Court, Northern District of Illinois; 1998, U.S. Court of Appeals, Seventh Circuit; 1999, U.S. District Court, Central District of Illinois and U.S. District Court, Eastern District of Wisconsin. *Education:* Eastern Illinois University (B.S., Energy Management, 1985); Illinois Institute of Technology, Chicago-Kent College of Law (J.D., 1994). ***PRACTICE AREAS:*** Intellectual Property; Commercial Litigation; Insurance; Loss Recovery; Antitrust. ***Email:*** tvickers@daarvanek.com

ANGELA C. WILCOX, born Decatur, Illinois, October 1, 1974; admitted to bar, 1999, Illinois. *Education:* University of Illinois (B.S., 1996); De Paul University (J.D., 1999). Author: "Should Right of Publicity Protection be Extended to Actors in the Characters Which They Portray?" De Paul Art & Entertainment Law Journal, 1999. *Member:* American Bar Association. ***PRACTICE AREAS:*** Trademarks; Patent Litigation; Antitrust. ***Email:*** awilcox@daarvanek.com

---

DAVID P. GERMAINE, born Chicago, Illinois, March 21, 1975; admitted to bar, 2001, Illinois and U.S. District Court, Northern District of Illinois; 2002, U.S. Court of Appeals, Federal Circuit. *Education:* John Carroll University (B.A., magna cum laude, 1997); De Paul University (J.D., 2001). Order of the Barristers. Member: Evidence Moot Court Team, 2000; Sports Law Moot Court Team, 2001; Moot Court Executive Board, De Paul University College of Law, 2000-2001. Author: "Regulating Rap Music: It Doesn't Melt You in Your Mouth," DePaul Journal of Art and Entertainment Law, Spring 2001. ***PRACTICE AREAS:*** Antitrust; Intellectual Property; Trademarks; Patents; Copyrights. ***Email:*** dgermaine@daarvanek.com

KELLEY A. BITTERLY, born Boston, Massachusetts, November 18, 1978; admitted to bar, 2003, Illinois and U.S. District Court, Northern District of Illinois. *Education:* University of Notre Dame (B.A., 2000); Boston College Law School (J.D., 2003). ***PRACTICE AREAS:*** Intellectual Property. ***Email:*** kbitterly@daarvanek.com

JEFFREY R. MORAN, JR., born Sacramento, California, May 17, 1979; admitted to bar, 2004, Illinois; 2005, U.S. District Court, Northern District of Illinois. *Education:* Boston College (B.A., cum laude, 2001; J.D., 2004). *Member:* American Bar Association. ***PRACTICE AREAS:*** Intellectual Property; Antitrust; Litigation; Patents; Insurance. ***Email:*** jmoran@daarvanek.com

DAGGETT LAW FIRM

CHICAGO TITLE TOWER, SUITE 4950
161 N. CLARK STREET
CHICAGO, ILLINOIS 60601
Telephone: 312-960-1600
Fax: 312-332-0515
Email: TWDaggett@Comcast.net

Environmental Law, Brownfields Redevelopment, Litigation, Toxic Torts, Chemical Regulation.

THOMAS W. DAGGETT, born 1951; admitted to bar, 1976, Illinois; U.S. Supreme Court; U.S. Court of Appeals, Sixth and Seventh Circuits; U.S. District Court, Central and Northern Districts of Illinois, Northern District of Indiana and Eastern and Western Districts of Michigan. *Education:* University of Illinois (B.S. Chemistry, 1973; J.D., 1976; M.S., Environmental Engineering, 1977). Equity Partner at Chicago litigation firm, Wildman Harrold, 1990-2003, associate 1988-1990. Section Chief, Office of Regional Counsel, U.S. Environmental Protection Agency, Chicago, 1979-1988. Special Assistant U.S. Attorney, Northern District of Illinois, 1982-1983. Expert Advisor to U.S. State Dept., Great Lakes Water Quality Agreement Negotiations, 1987. Regional Attorney, Illinois Environmental Protection Agency, 1977-1979. Special Assistant Illinois Attorney General, 1979. Author: "The Intent Element of A CERCLA Arranger Claim After U.S. v. Cello-Foil," Toxics Law Reporter, Vol. 11, No. 38 (1997); Author: "Steel Co. v. CBE: The U.S. Supreme Court Holds Citizen's Suits For Past Violations Unconstitutional," Environmental Litigation Committee Newsletter, ABA, Vol. 9, No. 1 (1998). *Member:* American (Member: Section on Environment, Energy and Resources; Environmental Committee, Section on Litigation) and Illinois Bar Associations; American Chemical Society.

DAHL & BONADIES

Established in 1984

225 WEST WASHINGTON STREET
SUITE 1640
CHICAGO, ILLINOIS 60606
Telephone: 312-641-3245
Fax: 312-641-1662
Email: dahlfirm@dahlfirm.com
URL: http://www.dahlfirm.com

Civil Litigation. Alternative Dispute Resolution. Probate and Civil Rights.

JAMES E. DAHL, born Chicago, Illinois, August 30, 1949; admitted to bar, 1974, Illinois. *Education:* University of Notre Dame (B.A., summa cum laude, 1971; J.D., magna cum laude, 1974). Phi Beta Kappa. Note and Comment Editor, Notre Dame Law Journal, 1973-1974. *Member:* Illinois Trial Lawyers Association; The Association of Trial Lawyers of America; American Board of Trial Advocates. ***PRACTICE AREAS:*** Civil Litigation; Alternative Dispute Resolution; Probate; Civil Rights. ***Email:*** jdahl@dahlfirm.com

PAUL N. BONADIES, born New Haven, Connecticut, January 29, 1966; admitted to bar, 1991, Illinois and U.S. District Court, Northern District of Illinois. *Education:* University of Notre Dame (B.A., 1988); DePaul University (J.D., 1991). *Member:* Chicago and Illinois State Bar Associations. ***PRACTICE AREAS:*** Civil Litigation; Alternative Dispute Resolution; Probate; Civil Rights. ***Email:*** pbonadies@dahlfirm.com

ASSOCIATES

RICHARD JOSEPH MURPHY, born New York, N.Y., October 20, 1971; admitted to bar, 1998, Illinois and New York; 2001, U.S. District Court, Northern District of Illinois. *Education:* State University of New York, Geneseo (B.A., 1993); University of Notre Dame (J.D., 1997). ***PRACTICE AREAS:*** Civil Litigation; Alternative Dispute Resolution; Probate; Civil Rights. ***Email:*** rmurphy@dahlfirm.com

PATRICK DAHL, born Winnetka, Illinois, March 13, 1977; admitted to bar, 2002, Illinois and U.S. District Court, Northern District of Illinois. *Education:* University of Notre Dame (B.A., 1999; J.D., 2002). ***PRACTICE AREAS:*** Civil Litigation; Alternative Dispute Resolution; Probate; Civil Rights.

OF COUNSEL

WALTER P. DAHL, born Chicago, Illinois, September 13, 1922; admitted to bar, 1948, Illinois; 1950, U.S. District Court, Northern District of Illinois. *Education:* Southwestern Louisiana State University; University of North Carolina; Northwestern University (LL.B., 1948). Judge, Circuit Court of Cook County, Illinois, 1962-1983. Presiding Judge: Juvenile Division, 1966-1969; Probate Division, 1976-1983. *Member:* Chicago and Northwest Suburban Bar Associations. [U.S. Marine Corps, 1942-1945]

DAHM & ELVIN, LLP

161 NORTH CLARK STREET, SUITE 1750
CHICAGO, ILLINOIS 60601
Telephone: 312-683-3900
Fax: 312-683-3911
URL: http://www.dahmandelvin.com

Fort Wayne Office: 9604 Coldwater Road, Suite 201, 46825. Telephone: 260-497-6000. Fax: 260-497-6019.

Drug & Medical Device Litigation, Product Liability, Class Action Defense, Federal Civil Litigation, Complex and Multi-District Litigation, Business Litigation.

ALBERT J. DAHM, born 1958; admitted to bar, 1983, Indiana and U.S. District Court, Northern and Southern Districts of Indiana; 1986, Arizona and U.S. District Court, District of Arizona; 1989, California and U.S. District Court, Central, Eastern, Northern and Southern Districts of California; 1997, U.S. Court of Appeals, Third Circuit; 1998, U.S. Court of Appeals, Fourth Circuit; 2005, U.S. Court of Appeals, Ninth Circuit (Not admitted in Illinois). *Education:* Xavier University (B.S.B.A., magna cum laude, 1980); Indiana University School of Law (J.D., 1983). Associate Editor, Indiana Law Review, 1982-1983. New York Bar National Moot Court Team. *Member:* Allen County, Indiana State and American Bar Associations; Product Liability Advisory Council; Defense Research Institute (Member, Medical Device Committee). ***PRACTICE AREAS:*** Drug and Medical Device Defense; Product Liability; Complex & Multi District Litigation; Federal Civil Litigation; Commercial Litigation; Business Litigation. ***Email:*** bert.dahm@dahmelvin.com

MICHAEL S. ELVIN, born 1963; admitted to bar, 1988, Illinois and U.S. District Court, Northern District of Illinois; 1991, U.S. Court of Appeals, Seventh Circuit; 1998, Indiana and U.S. District Court, Northern District of Indiana; 2002, U.S. Court of Appeals, Fifth Circuit. *Education:* Bucknell University (B.S.B.A., 1985); Northwestern University (J.D., 1988). ***PRACTICE AREAS:*** Drug and Medical Device Defense; Product Liability; Complex and Multi-District Litigation; Federal Civil Litigation; Commercial Litigation; Business Litigation. ***Email:*** michael.elvin@dahmelvin.com

MATTHEW S. ELVIN, born 1967; admitted to bar, 1992, Illinois and U.S. District Court, Northern District of Illinois; 1996, U.S. Court of Appeals, Seventh Circuit; 2004, U.S. District Court, Eastern and Western Districts of Wisconsin. *Education:* Bucknell University (B.A., 1989); The Dickinson School of Law of the Pennsylvania State University (J.D., cum laude, 1992). *Member:* Chicago, Illinois State and American Bar Associations. ***PRACTICE AREAS:*** Product Liability Litigation; Civil Litigation; Federal Civil Litigation; Insurance Litigation. ***Email:*** matthew.elvin@dahmelvin.com

SANDY L. MORRIS, born 1974; admitted to bar, 1999, Illinois; 2001, U.S. District Court, Northern District of Illinois; 2003, U.S. District Court, Southern District of Illinois. *Education:* Syracuse University (B.A., 1995); University of Chicago Law School (J.D., 1999). National Merit Scholar; Chancellor's Scholar. *Member:* Chicago, Illinois State and American Bar Associations; National Association of Women Lawyers. ***PRACTICE AREAS:*** Products Liability; Litigation; Civil Litigation; Federal Civil Litigation; Insurance Litigation. ***Email:*** sandy.morris@dahmelvin.com

T. MONIQUE JONES, born Detroit, Michigan, July 15, 1977; admitted to bar, 2002, Illinois and U.S. District Court, Northern District of Illinois including Trial Bar. *Education:* Michigan State University (B.A., with high honors, 1999); George Washington University Law School (J.D., 2002). Staff Member, Public Contract Law Journal, 2000-2001. Co-Author: "The Legal Power of Arbitrators to Grant and Limit Discovery," ARIAS Quarterly, Fourth Quarter, 2002. *Member:* Cook County Bar Association (Member, Lawyers in the Classroom Program, 2004—). ***PRACTICE AREAS:*** Business Torts; Commercial Litigation; Business Litigation; Fraudulent Conveyance; Insurance Coverage. ***Email:*** monique.jones@dahmelvin.com

OF COUNSEL

ANDREW M. SPANGLER, born January 21, 1962; admitted to bar, 1992, Illinois; 1993, U.S. District Court, Northern District of Illinois, including Trial Bar; 1997, U.S. Court of Appeals, Seventh Circuit; 1998, U.S. District Court, Western District of Michigan; 1999, U.S. District Court, District of Arizona; U.S. Court of Appeals, Ninth and Eleventh Circuits; 2000, U.S. Court of Appeals, Tenth Circuit; 2001, U.S. Court of Appeals, Sixth Circuit. *Education:* University of Cincinnati (B.F.A., 1984); Boston College (J.D., cum laude, 1992). *Member:* Chicago, Illinois State and American Bar Associations. ***PRACTICE AREAS:*** Complex Contracts; Insurance Coverage; Subrogation; Construction Law; Mechanics Liens; Trade Secrets; Class Actions; Telecommunications; Employment Discrimination; Defamation. ***Email:*** andrew.spangler@dahmelvin.com

DALEIDEN & TREMAINE, LTD.

CHICAGO, ILLINOIS

(See Arlington Heights)

General Practice, Corporate, Tax, Employee Benefits, Estate Planning, Probate, Real Estate, Litigation, Elder Law.

DALEY, DEBOFSKY & BRYANT

Established in 2002

1 NORTH LASALLE STREET, SUITE 3800
CHICAGO, ILLINOIS 60602
Telephone: 312-372-5200
Fax: 312-372-2778
URL: http://www.ddbchicago.com
Email: info@ddbchicago.com
URL: http://www.lawyers.com/ddbchicago

Social Security Disability including, Denial of Claims, Disability Insurance, Life and Health Insurance, ERISA, Employee Benefits, Employment Discrimination.

FIRM PROFILE: Daley, DeBofsky & Bryant is engaged in the representation of individuals seeking disability benefits from the Social Security Administration and from private insurance, as well as representation of individuals seeking employee benefits and involved in employment disputes.

MEMBERS OF FIRM

FREDERICK J. DALEY, JR., born Pawtucket, Rhode Island, 1948; admitted to bar, 1973, Rhode Island; 1974, Illinois; U.S. Court of Appeals, Seventh Circuit; U.S. Supreme Court. *Education:* University of Miami (B.A., 1970); New England School of Law (J.D., 1973). Speaker, Continuing Legal Education Seminars on Social Security Disability Law, Chicago Bar Association. ***PRACTICE AREAS:*** Social Security Disability; Civil Litigation. ***Email:*** fdaley@ddbchicago.com

MARK D. DEBOFSKY, born Chicago, Illinois, 1956; admitted to bar, 1980, Illinois; 1984, U.S. Supreme Court; U.S. Court of Appeals for Seventh Circuit, U.S. District Court,

(This Listing Continued)

DALEY, DEBOFSKY & BRYANT, Chicago—Continued

Northern and Central Districts of Illinois, U.S. District Court, Eastern District of Wisconsin; U.S. District Court, District of Arizona. *Education:* University of Michigan (B.A., with honors and high distinction, 1977); University of Illinois (J.D., 1980). Adjunct Professor: John Marshall Law School. Lecturer: American Bar Association, Association of Trial Lawyers of America; LEXIS-NEXIS/Mealey's; Chicago Bar Association; National Organization of Social Security Claimants' Representatives. *Member:* Chicago, Illinois State and American Bar Associations; Association of Trial Lawyers of America. ***REPORTED CASES:*** Hackett v. Xerox Corporation, 315 F.3d 771 (7th Cir. 2003), ERISA claim-appellate court overturned lower court ruling; ordered that judgment be entered in favor of claimant restoring payment of benefits; Herzberger v. Standard Insurance Company, 205 F.3d 327 (7th Cir. 2000). ERISA claim-court overturned prior precedent to issue sweeping ruling modifying standard of review applicable in employee benefit cases; Ladd v. ITT Corp., 148 F.3d 753 (7th Cir. 1998). ERISA disability insurance claim, summary judgment for defendant reversed on appeal, benefits awarded to plaintiff; Smith v. The Equitable Life Assurance Society, 67 F.3d 611 (7th Cir. 1995) (claim for disability income insurance-case tried/verdict for plaintiff for full indemnity as well as salutatory penalty for unreasonable and vexatious delay, affirmed by Court of Appeals, including award of prejudgment interest); Marcial v. Coronet Insurance Co., No. 89 CH 4476 (Cir.Ct.Cook County, Ill.) (Insurance claim--claim for consumer fraud/use of polygraph to evaluate claims of automobile theft). Filed as class action suit, Settlement for full payment of claims, penalty, and attorneys' fees; United States v. Clarence McClain, 934 F.2d 822 (7th Cir. 1991) (Criminal appeal-- major civic corruption case, Several changes reversed by Court of Appeals); Becker v. United Airlines, No. 90 C 7191 (U.S.D.Ct. N.D.Ill.) (personal injury--fractured leg from fall in United Airlines terminal at O'Hare Airport), Settlement: $157, 500; Castillo v. XLO Micromatic (Ex-Cello Corporation), No. 83 L 18654 (Cir.Ct.Cook County, Illinois) (products liability--die casting machine/catastrophic injury), Jury verdict: $1.2 million. ***PRACTICE AREAS:*** Disability Insurance; Employee Benefits; Employment Discrimination; Social Security Disability; ERISA; Insurance. ***Email:*** mdebofsky@ddbchicago.com

DAVID A. BRYANT, born May 17, 1968; admitted to bar, 1996, Illinois; U.S. Court of Appeals, Seventh Circuit. *Education:* University of Wisconsin-Madison (B.A., 1991); John Marshall Law School (J.D., 1995). Lecturer: Illinois Trial Lawyers Association; American Trial Lawyers Association; American Bar Association; Chicago Bar Association; Workers Compensation Lawyers Association; Work Place Injury and Litigation Group. Board of Directors: Chicago Volunteer Legal Services; Counsel for Disability Right; Legal Assistance Foundation. *Member:* Chicago and American Bar Associations; American Trial Lawyers Association; Illinois Trial Lawyers Association. ***PRACTICE AREAS:*** Social Security Disability; ERISA; Civil Litigation; Medicare and Medicaid; Insurance Litigation. ***Email:*** dabryant@ddbchicago.com

ASSOCIATES

MARCIE E. GOLDBLOOM, born Pittsburgh, Pennsylvania, November 6, 1961; admitted to bar, 1986, Illinois; 1990, U.S. Court of Appeals, Seventh Circuit; 1991, U.S. Court of Appeals, 6th Circuit; 1994, U.S. Supreme Court. *Education:* University of Michigan (B.A., 1983); Gonzaga University (J.D., 1986). Former Litigator, U.S. Department of Health and Human Services. Member, Government Relations Board, Chicago Area MS Society. *Member:* Chicago Bar Association; National Organization of Social Security Claimants' Representatives. ***PRACTICE AREAS:*** Social Security Disability; Disability Insurance; ERISA. ***Email:*** mgoldbloom@ddbchicago.com

JAMES R. COMERFORD, admitted to bar, 2002, Illinois. *Education:* University of Florida (B.S., 1998); John Marshall Law School (J.D., 2002). ***PRACTICE AREAS:*** ERISA Litigation; Social Security.

OF COUNSEL

DAVID R. BRYANT, born Evanston, Illinois, March 21, 1939; admitted to bar, 1965, Illinois and U.S. District Court, Northern District of Illinois. *Education:* Loyola University (B.S., 1961); Northwestern University (J.D., 1964). Adjunct Professor of Law, John Marshall Law School, 1997-2002. *Member:* American Bar Association. ***PRACTICE AREAS:*** Social Security. ***Email:*** drb7949@concentric.net

DALEY AND GEORGE, LTD.

TWO FIRST NATIONAL PLAZA
20 SOUTH CLARK, SUITE 400
CHICAGO, ILLINOIS 60603-1903
Telephone: 312-726-8797
Fax: 312-726-8819

General Civil, Trial and Appellate Practice in all Courts. Corporate, Probate, Labor, Real Estate, Land Development, Zoning, Land Use, Eminent Domain, Estate Planning, Welfare and Pension Funds, Employment and Discrimination Law.

MICHAEL DALEY, born Chicago, Illinois, April 18, 1943; admitted to bar, 1968, Illinois; 1971, U.S. Court of Appeals, Seventh Circuit and U.S. District Court, Northern District of Illinois. *Education:* Loyola University; DePaul University (LL.B., 1968). *Member:* Chicago, Illinois State and American Bar Associations. ***PRACTICE AREAS:*** Labor; Corporate Law; Probate; Estate Planning; Pension Plans. ***Email:*** mdaley@daleygeorge.com

JOHN J. GEORGE, born Chicago, Illinois, March 7, 1940; admitted to bar, 1967, Illinois, U.S. Court of Appeals, Seventh Circuit and U.S. District Court, Northern District of Illinois; 1977, U.S. Supreme Court. *Education:* Xavier University (B.S., 1963); DePaul University (J.D., 1967). Nu Beta Epsilon. *Member:* Chicago, Illinois State and American Bar Associations. ***PRACTICE AREAS:*** Land Use; Zoning Law; Condemnation; Trial Practice; Appellate Practice; Corporate Law. ***Email:*** jgeorge@daleygeorge.com

---

DENNIS J. AUKSTIK, born Chicago, Illinois, March 10, 1956; admitted to bar, 1982, Illinois, U.S. Court of Appeals, Seventh Circuit and U.S. District Court, Northern District of Illinois, Trial Bar, 1989; 1989, Wisconsin. *Education:* Loyola University (B.A., 1978; J.D., cum laude, 1982). *Member:* Chicago Bar Association; State Bar of Wisconsin. ***PRACTICE AREAS:*** Civil Litigation; Real Estate; Land Development; Zoning; Land Use. ***Email:*** daukstik@daleygeorge.com

ROBERT T. OLESZKIEWICZ, born Chicago, Illinois, May 21, 1960; admitted to bar, 1985, Illinois and U.S. District Court, Northern District of Illinois; 1996, U.S. Court of Appeals, Seventh Circuit. *Education:* Northwestern University (B.A., 1982); DePaul University (J.D., 1985). *Member:* Chicago and Illinois State Bar Associations. ***PRACTICE AREAS:*** Labor; Employee Benefit Law. ***Email:*** robert@daleygeorge.com

CHRIS A. LEACH, born Kokomo, Indiana, November 1, 1964; admitted to bar, 1991, Illinois and U.S. District Court, Northern District of Illinois. *Education:* Indiana University at Bloomington (B.S., 1987); John Marshall Law School, Chicago (J.D., 1991). *Member:* Illinois State Bar Association. ***PRACTICE AREAS:*** Estate Planning; Probate; Real Estate; Corporate Law; Civil Litigation. ***Email:*** cleach@daleygeorge.com

RICHARD A. TOTH, born Chicago, Illinois, September 25, 1965; admitted to bar, 1994, Illinois, U.S. District Court, Northern and Central Districts of Illinois and U.S. Court of Appeals, Seventh Circuit; 1995, District of Columbia, Minnesota, Nebraska. *Education:* University of Illinois at Urbana (B.S., 1988); Chicago-Kent College of Law (J.D., with honors, 1994). ***PRACTICE AREAS:*** Labor Law; Employee Benefits; Business Law. ***Email:*** rtoth@daleygeorge.com

KATHLEEN A. DUNCAN, born October 12, 1978; admitted to bar, 2003, Illinois and U.S. District Court, Northern District of Illinois. *Education:* Butler University (B.A., 2000); John Marshall Law School (J.D., 2003). *Member:* Chicago, Illinois State and American Bar Associations. ***Email:*** kduncan@daleygeorge.com

JILL P. CONROY, born New York, New York, September 17, 1977; admitted to bar, 2004, Illinois and U.S. District Court, Northern District of Illinois. *Education:* Fairfield University (B.A., 1999); Loyola University (J.D., 2003). *Member:* The Chicago Bar Association; Illinois State and American Bar Associations. ***Email:*** jconroy@daleygeorge.com

DALEY & MOHAN, P.C.

150 NORTH WACKER DRIVE, SUITE 1550
CHICAGO, ILLINOIS 60606
Telephone: 312-422-9999
Fax: 312-201-9368
Email: info@daleymohan.com
URL: http://www.daleymohan.com

General Corporate, Commercial Litigation, Casualty and Products Liability Litigation, Labor, Real Estate, Bankruptcy, Creditor's Rights.

FIRM PROFILE: Daley & Mohan, P.C. is a Chicago law firm concentrating in complex business and casualty litigation and sophisticated commercial and real estate transactions. Each of our partners brings a wealth of career experience from partnerships at major law firms and/or senior positions at prominent corporate law departments. We share a commitment to providing superior legal services with an understanding of the competitive environment in which both we and our clients operate. Our firm's structure and partnering relationships with long-term clients reflect this dedication to ensuring that we provide value to our clients.

JAMES P. DALEY, born 1927; admitted to bar, 1955, Illinois; U.S. Court of Appeals, Seventh Circuit; U.S. District Court, Northern District of Illinois; U.S. Supreme Court. *Education:* DePaul University (LL.B., J.D., 1955). Senior Vice President of Labor, Law, and Real Estate, Chicago and North Western Transportation Co., 1983-1995; General Counsel, 1979-1995. Former Chairman, Rail Amicus Committee. *Member:* Chicago, Illinois State and American Bar Associations; National Association of Railroad Trial Counsel (Member, Executive Committee; President, 1994). ***PRACTICE AREAS:*** Casualty Litigation; Commercial Litigation. ***Email:*** daley@daleymohan.com

RAYMOND H. GROBLE III, born Chicago, Illinois, October 3, 1951; admitted to bar, 1986, Illinois; 1987, U.S. District Court, Northern District of Illinois including Trial Bar, U.S. District Court, Central District of Illinois, U.S. Court of Appeals, Seventh Circuit and U.S. Supreme Court. *Education:* DePaul University (B.A., 1983); University of Illinois (J.D., magna cum laude, 1986). *Member:* Illinois State and American (Member, Litigation Section and Forum on the Construction Industry) Bar Associations; National Association of Railroad Trial Counsel; Defense Research Institute. ***PRACTICE AREAS:*** Commercial Litigation; Casualty Litigation; Corporate; Product Liability Litigation; Real Estate. ***Email:*** groble@daleymohan.com

DANIEL J. MOHAN, born Streator, Illinois, November 26, 1959; admitted to bar, 1984, Illinois; 1992, Wisconsin; U.S. Court of Appeals, Seventh and Ninth Circuits; U.S. District Court, Northern District of Illinois including Trial Bar. *Education:* University of Notre Dame (B.A., 1981); Loyola University (J.D., 1984). Former Trial Attorney and Assistant Vice President, Chicago and North Western Railway Co. *Member:* Chicago and Illinois State Bar Associations; National Association of Railroad Trial Counsel (President, Illinois Division; National Executive Counsel). ***PRACTICE AREAS:*** Casualty Litigation; Commercial Litigation. ***Email:*** mohan@daleymohan.com

BERNARD ROCCANOVA, born Paterson, New Jersey, February 3, 1946; admitted to bar, 1972, New Jersey, U.S. District Court, District of New Jersey, Illinois and U.S. District Court, Northern District of Illinois; 1979, U.S. Court of Appeals, Seventh Circuit. *Education:* Fairleigh Dickinson University (B.A., 1967); University of Illinois (J.D., 1971). Member, National Moot Court Team. *Member:* Chicago and Illinois State Bar Associations; National Association of Railroad Trial Counsel. ***PRACTICE AREAS:*** Casualty Litigation. ***Email:*** rocc@daleymohan.com

SEAN M. SULLIVAN, born Winona, Minnesota, February 4, 1960; admitted to bar, 1985, Illinois and U.S. District Court, Northern District of Illinois including Trial Bar; 1989, U.S. Court of Appeals, Third Circuit; 1990, U.S. Court of Appeals, Seventh and Ninth Circuits; 1991, U.S. Court of Appeals, Fifth Circuit; 1993, U.S. Supreme Court; 1996, U.S. Court of Appeals, Eleventh Circuit; 1997, U.S. Court of Appeals, Fourth Circuit. *Education:* Eastern Illinois University (B.A., cum laude, 1982); University of Illinois (J.D., cum

(This Listing Continued)

laude, 1985). Author: "Recent Trends In The Implied Duty of Good Faith," Commercial Lending Review, Fall, 1991. *Member:* Chicago and American Bar Associations; Defense Research Institute; Propane Gas Defense Association. ***PRACTICE AREAS:*** Complex Business Litigation; Product Liability Defense. ***Email:*** ssullivan@daleymohan.com

MARY L. KANDYBA, born Chicago, Illinois, July 16, 1956; admitted to bar, 1981, Illinois and U.S. District Court, Northern District of Illinois. *Education:* University of Illinois (B.S., 1978); DePaul University (J.D., 1981). Publications: "Protecting Railroad Workers with the ADA," TRIAL Magazine, March 1995; "On Your Own: Do You Have What It Takes?" TRIAL Magazine, March 1996; "The Lawyer and Her Slip Opinion," TRIAL Magazine, July 1996; "They Didn't Teach This in Law School," Reflections, TRIAL Magazine, August 1999; "Family Law, More Cases We Remember," TRIAL Magazine, April 2000; "Jury Selection: Why the Old School Methods Don't Work," presented at the National College of Advocacy's Program on Auto Collision Cases, Chicago, Illinois, September 15-16, 2000; "A Mother's Gift," TRIAL Magazine, June 2001; "Lazy B: Review of a Novel by Sandra Day O'Connor and H. Alan Day," TRIAL Magazine, July 2002; "The 'aha' Moment: Going Through the Motions," TRIAL Magazine, December 2002; "Life, Law and Laughter," TRIAL Magazine, July 2003, distributed at the Montana State Bar Continuing Education Seminar, October 11, 2003, reprinted, Sidebar, Oregon Trial Lawyers Association; "Mastiffs and Liability Insurance," Mastiff Club of America Journal No. 4, 2003; "Recognize the Strength of a Team of One," TRIAL Magazine, September 2004. *Member:* South Suburban (Member, Civil Practice Committee, 2002-2004) and Illinois State Bar Associations; The Association of Trial Lawyers of America (Member, Publications Committee, 2000-2004). ***PRACTICE AREAS:*** Civil Litigation. ***Email:*** mlkandyba@daleymohan.com

---

CHRISTOPHER R. KARSTEN, born Evanston, Illinois, January 13, 1967; admitted to bar, 1994, Indiana and U.S. District Court, Northern District of Indiana; 1995, Illinois. *Education:* Loyola University (B.A., 1989); Valparaiso University School of Law (J.D., cum laude, 1993). Member, Valparaiso University Moot Court Society. Author: "One Step Too Far: The Supreme Court Denies Criminal Defendants the Unfettered Use of the Peremptory Challenge in Georgia v. McCollum," 27 Val. U.L. Rev. 287 (1992). *Member:* Lake County and Indiana State Bar Associations. ***PRACTICE AREAS:*** Casualty Litigation; Commercial Litigation. ***Email:*** karsten@railaw.com

DANIEL MARKO, born Ann Arbor, Michigan, October 8, 1973; admitted to bar, 2000, Illinois. *Education:* University of Michigan (B.S.E., 1995); Chicago Kent College of Law (J.D., 2000). ***PRACTICE AREAS:*** Federal Employers Liability Act (FELA); Railway Labor Law. ***Email:*** dmarko@daleymohan.com

BLAKE A. BARRON, born Aurora, Colorado; admitted to bar, 2003, Wisconsin, Illinois and U.S. District Court, Eastern District of Wisconsin; 2004, U.S. District Court, Northern District of Illinois. *Education:* Colorado College (B.A., Biology, 2000); Marquette University (J.D., 2003). *Member:* State Bar of Wisconsin; American Bar Association. ***PRACTICE AREAS:*** Civil Litigation.

OF COUNSEL

ELIZABETH WEST SPEIDEL, born Fort Smith, Arkansas, October 27, 1948; admitted to bar, 1980, Illinois and U.S. District Court, Northern District of Illinois including Trial Bar. *Education:* Oklahoma State University (B.S., 1970); Indiana University (M.S.W., 1972); Northwestern University (J.D., 1980). *Member:* Chicago and American (Member, Sections on: Torts, Litigation and National Resources) Bar Associations. ***LANGUAGES:*** English. ***PRACTICE AREAS:*** Products Liability Defense. ***Email:*** espeidel@daleymohan.com

---

D'ANCONA & PFLAUM LLC

CHICAGO, ILLINOIS

(See Seyfarth Shaw LLP)

DASHIELL LAW OFFICES, LLC

70 WEST MADISON, SUITE 1400
CHICAGO, ILLINOIS 60602
Telephone: 312-214-3329
Fax: 312-214-3328
Email: jrdashlaw@yahoo.com

Casualty Defense Law, Employment Practice, Commercial Litigation.

JAMES R. DASHIELL, born Evanston, Illinois, November 30, 1947; admitted to bar, 1972, Michigan; 1982, Illinois. *Education:* University of Michigan (B.A., with distinction, 1969; J.D., 1972). *Member:* Chicago, Illinois State and American Bar Associations. ***PRACTICE AREAS:*** Commercial Litigation; Employment Practice; Casualty Defense Law.

REPRESENTATIVE CLIENTS: Tecumseh Products Co.; Reliance Insurance Co.; in Liquidation; Legion Insurance Co., Pennsylvania Department of Insurance; Burns Philip Foods, Inc.; APCapital, Inc.; Orange Crush, LLC; Midwest Fence Corp.; Zurich North America; First Capital Group; Ohio Casualty Insurance Company; Systems Resource Group, Ltd.

DASPIN & AUMENT, LLP

10 SOUTH RIVERSIDE PLAZA
SUITE 1220
CHICAGO, ILLINOIS 60606
Telephone: 312-258-1600
Fax: 312-258-1955
URL: http://www.daspinaument.com

Oak Brook Office: 210 W. 22nd Street, Suite 102, 60523. Telephone: 630-928-0430. Fax: 630-928-0392.

(This Listing Continued)

Real Estate, Commercial Real Estate Development, Estate Planning, Business Succession Planning, Tax Planning, Trust Administration, Estate Administration, Corporate Law and Financial Services Law. Intellectual Property including Patents, Trademarks, Copyrights and Computer Law.

MEMBERS OF FIRM

ROBERT C. AUMENT, born Chicago, Illinois, September 7, 1959; admitted to bar, 1989, Illinois. *Education:* Illinois State University (B.S., in Accounting, minor in Economics, 1981); Illinois Institute of Technology, Chicago-Kent College of Law (J.D., 1989). Certified Public Accountant, Illinois, 1983. *Member:* Illinois State and American Bar Associations; Illinois Society of Certified Public Accountants. (Resident, Oak Brook Office). ***PRACTICE AREAS:*** Estate and Income Tax Planning; Business Succession Planning; Estate and Income; Trust Administration; Estate Administration; Corporate Law; Real Estate. ***Email:*** raument@daspinaument.com

NICOLE RUDMAN BROWN, born Oak Lawn, Illinois, February 20, 1969; admitted to bar, 1996, Illinois. *Education:* Northern Illinois University (B.S., Finance, 1991); Loyola University (J.D., 1996). ***PRACTICE AREAS:*** Real Estate. ***Email:*** nbrown@daspinaument.com

D. ALBERT DASPIN, admitted to bar, 1987, Illinois. *Education:* Miami University (B.A., magna cum laude, 1983); Indiana University (M.B.A., 1987); Indiana University (J.D., magna cum laude, 1987). Phi Beta Kappa. Order of the Coif. Articles Editor, Indiana Law Journal. Author: "Of Hoops, Labor Dupes and Antitrust Ally-Oops: Fouling Out the Salary Cap," 62 Indiana Law Journal 95, 1986. Co-Author: "First Class Condition: Responsibilities, Rights and Remedies Respecting The Condition of Commercial Leasehold Premises," Real Property, Probate and Trust Journal, Vol. 29, No. 4, Winter, 1995; "Managing The Retail Anchor Tenant Lease," The Practical Real Estate Lawyer, Vol. 9, No. 1, January, 1993; "Negotiating Office Lease Operating Cost Pass-Throughs," Real Estate Review, Vol. 23, No. 4, Winter, 1994; "Cross-Use Agreements For Shopping Centers," Real Estate Review, Vol. 21, No. 4, Winter, 1992; "Prorating Real Estate Taxes At Closing of Sale of Shopping Center Property," Real Estate Review, Vol. 27, No. 2, Summer, 1997. Contributor: ALI-ABA's Practice Checklist Manual For Drafting Leases, March, 1994. Editorial Board Member: Commercial Leasing Law and Strategy; Shopping Center Legal Update; various ALI-ABA publications. *Member:* Chicago, Illinois State and American Bar Associations. ***PRACTICE AREAS:*** Real Estate; Corporate Law. ***Email:*** adaspin@daspinaument.com

JOHN G. CARUSO, admitted to bar, 1992, Illinois. *Education:* University of Texas (B.A., 1988); DePaul University (J.D., 1992). *Member:* Chicago and American (Member, Real Estate Section) Bar Associations. ***PRACTICE AREAS:*** Real Estate; Finance.

JAMES H. MARSHALL, admitted to bar, 1997, Illinois. *Education:* Northwestern University (B.A., with honors, 1994; J.D., cum laude, 1997). *Member:* Chicago and American Bar Associations. ***PRACTICE AREAS:*** Commercial Real Estate Development. ***Email:*** jmarshall@daspinaument.com

JEFFERSON PERKINS, born Evanston, Illinois, April 12, 1955; admitted to bar, 1983, Illinois; 1985, Texas; registered to practice before U.S. Patent and Trademark Office. *Education:* University of Illinois (B.S.E.E., B.S.L.A.S., 1978); The John Marshall Law School (J.D., with distinction, 1983). Order of John Marshall. *Member:* Chicago Bar Association; American Intellectual Property Law Association; Intellectual Property Law Association of Chicago; Federalist Society. (Resident, Oak Brook Office). ***PRACTICE AREAS:*** Patents; Trademarks; Copyrights; Computer Law. ***Email:*** jperkins@daspinaument.com

HOWARD S. THOMPSON, admitted to bar, 1988, Illinois. *Education:* University of Michigan (B.B.A., 1985); Duke University (J.D., 1988). ***PRACTICE AREAS:*** Real Estate. ***Email:*** hthompson@daspinaument.com

ASSOCIATES

MATTHEW C. ALSHOUSE, born 1973; admitted to bar, 1999, Illinois. *Education:* Duke University (A.B., 1996); University of Michigan (J.D., 1999). *Member:* Chicago and American Bar Associations. ***PRACTICE AREAS:*** Real Estate; Financial Services Law. ***Email:*** malshouse@daspinaument.com

MARIA TOLIOPOULOS, admitted to bar, 2001, Illinois. *Education:* Loyola University at Chicago (B.A., 1997); The John Marshall Law School (J.D., cum laude, 2001). Executive Production Editor, Journal of Computer and Information Law, John Marshall Law School, 2000-2001. Author: "Technology Arms Peeping Toms With a New and Dangerous Arsenal: Why States Must Adopt New Technology," 17 J. Marshall J. Computer & Info. L. 1167, 1999. Co-Author: "Whether the Provider of an Online Archive of Previously Published Information Can Be Considered the Publisher of That Information," 18 J. Marshall J. Computer & Info. L. 181, 1999. *Member:* Chicago, Illinois State and American Bar Associations. ***LANGUAGES:*** Greek, Spanish. ***PRACTICE AREAS:*** Commercial Real Estate; Health Insurance Portability and Accountability Act (HIPAA); Information Technology. ***Email:*** mtoliopoulos@daspinaument.com

DAWN K. LUCK, born Chicago, Illinois, May 26, 1971; admitted to bar, 2003, Illinois, U.S. District Court, Northern District of Illinois. *Education:* Northern Illinois University (B.A., 1993); Chicago-Kent College of Law (J.D., 2003). Formerly with Grant, Ross & Fanning, Chicago, Illinois. *Member:* Chicago, Illinois State and American Bar Associations. ***PRACTICE AREAS:*** Commercial Real Estate (60%); Corporate Law (40%). ***Email:*** dluck@daspinaument.com

CODY SALTER, born Spokane, Washington, October 8, 1975; admitted to bar, 2004, Illinois. *Education:* University of Illinois (B.S., 1998); University of California Los Angeles (J.D., 2004). ***PRACTICE AREAS:*** Real Estate.

OF COUNSEL

JOHN T. HUNTINGTON, born Evanston, Illinois, March 21, 1950; admitted to bar, 1975, Illinois. *Education:* Denison University (B.A., 1972); IIT Chicago-Kent College of Law (J.D., 1975). Instructor in Business Law, Illinois Benedictine College, 1977-1979. Adjunct Professor, Graduate School of Management, Lewis University, 1991. (Resident, Oak

(This Listing Continued)

DASPIN & AUMENT, LLP, Chicago—Continued

Brook Office). ***PRACTICE AREAS:*** Real Estate; Real Estate Finance; Corporate Law. ***Email:*** jhuntington@daspinaument.com

THE LAW OFFICES OF DAVID DAUDELL

30 N. LASALLE STREET
SUITE 2340
CHICAGO, ILLINOIS 60602
Telephone: 312-701-0012
Fax: 312-701-9056
URL: http://www.daudelllaw.com

Adoption Law, Bankruptcy, Business Organization, Contracts, Criminal Law, Driving While Intoxicated, Divorce, Family Law, Gaming Law, Landlord and Tenant Law, Medical Malpractice, Motor Vehicle Accidents and Injuries, Personal Injury, Probate, Estate Administration, Real Estate, White Collar Crime, Wills, Litigation.

DAVID DAUDELL, born April 15, 1963; admitted to bar, 1992, Illinois and U.S. District Court, Central, Southern and Northern Districts of Illinois. *Education:* Loyola University; John Marshall Law School (J.D., 1992). ***PRACTICE AREAS:*** Adoption Law; Bankruptcy; Business Organization; Contracts; Criminal Law; Driving While Intoxicated; Divorce; Family Law; Gaming Law; Landlord and Tenant Law; Medical Malpractice; Motor Vehicle Accidents and Injuries; Personal Injury; Probate; Estate Administration; Real Estate; White Collar Crime; Wills; Litigation.

KEITH L. DAVIDSON & ASSOCIATES

30 NORTH LA SALLE STREET, SUITE 3516
CHICAGO, ILLINOIS 60602
Telephone: 312-419-0544
Fax: 312-419-0758
Email: KLDLAW@ix.netcom.com

Product Liability, Medical Malpractice Law, Personal Injury Law, Tort Law and Wrongful Death Law.

KEITH L. DAVIDSON, born Chicago, Illinois, October 31, 1942; admitted to bar, 1968, Illinois; 1969, U.S. District Court, Northern District of Illinois including Trial Bar; 1971, U.S. Court of Appeals, 7th Circuit; 1973, U.S. Court of Appeals, 4th Circuit; 1978, U.S. Supreme Court. *Education:* University of Illinois (A.B., 1965); Loyola University (J.D., 1968). Participating Advocate, National Education TV Program, The Advocates, November, 1973. Member, American Law Institute, 1996—. Adviser, Restatement of the Law Third, Torts: General Principles. *Member:* Chicago (Member, Inquiry Board of Disciplinary Committee, 1973-1974), Illinois State (Council Member, Civil Practice and Procedure Section, 1977-1978; Member, Board of Governors, under age 37, First Judicial District, 1978-1980; Member, Board of Governors, 1980-1982; Chairman, Special Committee on Judicial Merit Selection, 1981-1982; Member, Joint Illinois State and Chicago Bar Associations Committee on Judicial Salaries, 1981-1989) and American (Member, Section of Tort and Insurance Practice; Program Chairman, Annual Meeting, 1980; Member of Council, 1980-1984; Section Vice Chairman, 1984-1985; Section Chairman-Elect, 1985-1986; Section Chairman, 1986-1987) Bar Associations; Illinois Trial Lawyers Association (Member: Board of Managers, 1976-1983; Amicus Curiae Committee, 1979; Co-Chairman, Legislative Committee, 1984-1985); The Association of Trial Lawyers of America; Chicago Council of Lawyers (Member, 1972-1973 and Vice President, 1974-1976); American Law Institute (Member, 1996—; Adviser, Restatement of the Law Third Torts: General Principles). Fellow: American Bar Foundation; International Academy of Trial Lawyers.

DAVIS & CAMPBELL L.L.C.

161 N. CLARK, SUITE 4700
CHICAGO, ILLINOIS 60601
Telephone: 312-523-2120; 773-404-5900
Fax: 312-523-2121; 773-404-6232
Email: jgbunge@dcamplaw.com
URL: http://www.dcamplaw.com

Home Office of Jonathan G. Bunge: 3014 North Racine Avenue, Chicago, Illinois, 60657. Telephone: 773-404-5900. Fax: 773-404-6232.
Peoria, Illinois Office: 401 Main Street, Suite 1600, 61602-1241 Telephone: 309-673-1681. Telecopier: 309-673-1690.
Washington, D.C. Office: 1828 L Street, N.W., Suite 660, 20036. Telephone: 202-293-5690. Fax: 202-296-5706.

Management Labor Law, Corporate Law, Trial Practice, Employee Benefits, Mergers and Acquisitions, Employer Rights, Local Government Rights, Employment Law, Commercial Law, Commercial Litigation, Complex Litigation, Intellectual Property, Securities Regulation, Antitrust, Immigration and Naturalization, Real Estate, Zoning Planning and Land Use, Tax Law, Estate Planning, Probate.

OF COUNSEL

JONATHAN G. BUNGE, born La Crosse, Wisconsin, October 20, 1936; admitted to bar, 1961, Illinois. *Education:* Princeton University (A.B., cum laude, 1958); Harvard University (J.D., 1961). Listed in, Who's Who in American Law. Professor, John Marshall Law School, 1968-1973. Formerly with: Lees & Bunge, 1961-1962; Keck, Mahin & Cate, 1964-1995; Ross & Hardies, 1995-2000. *Member:* Chicago, Judicial 7th Circuit and American Bar Associations; Maritime Law Association of the United States; Economic Club of Chicago. (Also Practicing Individually, Chicago, Illinois). ***PRACTICE AREAS:*** Commercial

(This Listing Continued)

Litigation; Complex Litigation; Antitrust and Trade Regulation; Intellectual Property Litigation; Securities Litigation. ***Email:*** jgbunge@dcamplaw.com

DAVIS FRIEDMAN ZAVETT KANE MacRAE MARCUS & RUBENS LLP

A Limited Liability Partnership including Professional Corporations
Established in 1985
135 SOUTH LA SALLE STREET, 36TH FLOOR
CHICAGO, ILLINOIS 60603
Telephone: 312-782-2220
Fax: 312-782-0464
Email: info@davisfriedman.com
URL: http://www.davisfriedman.com

Family Law. Trial and Appellate Practice, Divorce, Child Custody, Spousal Support, Pre- and Post-Marital Agreements, Alimony, Paternity.

FIRM PROFILE: All 14 of the lawyers in DAVIS FRIEDMAN ZAVETT KANE MacRAE MARCUS & RUBENS LLP, practice only family law. The firm was created in 1985 by the merger of three firms, one of which was founded in 1946. One of the partners, now Of Counsel, authored a book about divorce for laymen that has sold well for over 20 years (Friedman, The Divorce Handbook, Random House, 1982, 1984, 1999), another, with an associate, has written a sixth edition of a widely-praised book on Illinois family law practice for lawyers (Davis and Yazici, The Illinois Practice of Family Law, West Group, 2004-2005), several partners have written articles for the Illinois Institute for Continuing Legal Education (Zavett, Kane, Rubens, and Marcus), and two partners (Kane and Zavett) served as consulting editors for the Family Law Volume of Nichols' Illinois Civil Practice, West Publishing Co., 1999, among other publications. Lawyers in the firm frequently lecture other lawyers in Chicago and around the country on family law topics. Lawyers in the firm have led organized bar groups in their field, including President of the American Academy of Matrimonial Lawyers; President of the Illinois Chapter of the American Academy of Matrimonial Lawyers (2); Chairman of the Chicago Bar Association Matrimonial Committee (4); Chairman of the Illinois State Bar Association Family Law Section Council (2); etc. The partners have addressed family law seminars (usually sponsored by state bar associations) in many states. Ten of the firm's 14 active practitioners were named to Leading Lawyers Network for 2005.

MEMBERS OF FIRM

BENJAMIN B. DAVIS (1946-1977)
WILLIAM C. BOYDEN (1946-1965)

MULLER DAVIS, (P.C.), born Chicago, Illinois, April 23, 1935; admitted to bar, 1960, Illinois; 1961, U.S. District Court, Northern District of Illinois. *Education:* Phillips Exeter Academy and Yale University (B.A., magna cum laude, 1957); Harvard University (J.D., 1960). Pi Sigma Alpha. Member, Editorial Board, Equitable Distribution Journal, 1983—. Co-Author with Sherman C. Feinstein, "The Parental Couple In A Successful Divorce," 1984. Author: "The Davis Case Revisited," Illinois Bar Journal, November, 1982; "Valuation of Professional Practices in Dissolution Cases," Illinois Bar Journal, September, 1985; "Best Interest of the Child: The Case for Joint Custody Even in Contested Divorces," Illinois Bar Journal, July, 1996. Co-Author: with Jody Meyer Yazici, "The Illinois Practice of Family Law," West Group, 1995, 1996-1997, 1998-1999, 2000-2001, 2003-2004, 2005-2006 Editions. Contributing Author, "Marriage, Health and the Professions," 2002. Vice Chairman, 1995-1997 and Chair, 1997-1999, Legal Aid Society. Listed in "The Best Lawyers in America." Co-Chair, Committee to Study and Recommend a Comprehensive Rules Design for the Domestic Relations Division, Circuit Court of Cook County, Illinois, 2003—. *Member:* Chicago (Member, 1970-1986 and Chairman, 1981-1982, Committee on Civil Practice; Matrimonial Law, 1968-1983), Illinois State (Member, Family Law Section), Federal and American (Member, Section of Family Law) Bar Associations; American Judicature Society; The Association of Trial Lawyers of America; American Academy of Matrimonial Lawyers (Illinois Chapter, Member, Board of Managers, 1996-1999); The Lawyers Club of Chicago. Fellow, American Bar Foundation; Scribes, The American Society of Writers on Legal Subjects. ***PRACTICE AREAS:*** Family Law; Domestic Relations Law; Divorce; Appellate Practice; Child Custody; Premarital Agreements; Spousal Support. ***Email:*** mdavis@davisfriedman.com

ERROL ZAVETT, born Omaha, Nebraska, March 25, 1938; admitted to bar, 1964, Illinois and U.S. District Court, Northern District of Illinois. *Education:* University of Iowa (B.A., 1960); University of Illinois (J.D., 1963). Phi Delta Phi. Consulting Editor, Nichols Illinois Civil Practice, Family Law Volume, 1999. Co-Author: Chapter on Appeals, Illinois Family Law II, 1977, revised, 1981, 1985, 1986, 1988, 1989, 1992, 1995, 1998, 2001, and 2003; "Negotiating Settlements in Matrimonial Cases," Guide to Negotiations, 1979; "Practitioner's Introduction to the new Illinois Marriage and Dissolution of Marriage Act," General Practice Review, 1977. Member, Advisory Committee, Illinois Family Law Reporter, 1983—. Lecturer on Family Law, Illinois, Kansas, Nevada and South Carolina State Bar Associations. Listed in The Best Lawyers in America. Adjunct Professor of Law, De Paul Law School. *Member:* Chicago (Chairman, Matrimonial Law Committee, 1982-1983), Illinois State (Member, Family Law Section Council, 1980-1987; Editor, Family Law Newsletter, 1980-1981; Chairman, 1985-1986; Member, CLE Program, 1987-1990) and American Bar Associations; Illinois Trial Lawyers Association (Chairman, Family Law Committee, 1981-1983). Fellow, American Academy of Matrimonial Lawyers (Member: Bounds of Advocacy Committee; Client Relations Committee; Chairman, History Committee, 1997-2005; Governor, 1989-1992, 1998-2003; Board Journal of American Academy of Matrimonial Lawyers; Illinois Chapter, President, 1988-1989; Board of Managers, 1983-1992). ***PRACTICE AREAS:*** Family Law; Domestic Relations Law; Divorce; Appellate Practice; Spousal Support. ***Email:*** ezavett@davisfriedman.com

LARRY R. KANE, (P.C.), born Chicago, Illinois, August 27, 1940; admitted to bar, 1965, Illinois and U.S. District Court, Northern District of Illinois. *Education:* University of Illinois (B.S., 1962); DePaul University (J.D., 1965). Consulting Editor, Nichols Illinois

(This Listing Continued)

Civil Practice, Family Law Volume, 1999. Lecturer, Illinois Institute for Continuing Legal Education, Illinois State Bar Association and Chicago Bar Association, 1980—. Member, Domestic Relations Management Advisory Committee and Executive Committee and Chair, Calendar Management Subcommittee, Cook County Circuit Court, 1986-1993. Listed in: The Best Lawyers in America; Leading Lawyers of Illinois. Hearing Officer, Attorney Registration and Disciplinary Commission of the Supreme Court of Illinois, 2002—. Member, Board of Directors, Chicago Volunteer Legal Services. *Member:* Chicago (Member, Matrimonial Law Committee, 1972—; Chairman, 1983-1984; Member, Civil Practice Committee, 1976-1981; Member, Judicial Evaluation Committee, 1983-1987), Illinois State (Member: Section on: Family Law; Family Law Section Council, 1985-1994 and 1998-2004; Co-Editor, Newsletter, 1995-1998) and American (Member, Section on: Family Law) Bar Associations. Fellow: American Academy of Matrimonial Lawyers (Member, Illinois Chapter: Board of Managers, 1980-1996 and 1999—; Admissions Committee, 1980-1994 and 1998—; Seminar Chair, 1997-1999 and 2004; President, 1986-1987. National: Chair, Forensic Resource Guide Committee, 1995-1998; Chair, Certified List Committee, 1986-1988; Member, Focus on Forever Committee, 1998-2003). ***PRACTICE AREAS:*** Family Law; Domestic Relations Law; Divorce; Child Custody. ***Email:*** lkane@davisfriedman.com

DORENE MARCUS, born Chicago, Illinois, November 27, 1940; admitted to bar, 1978, Illinois. *Education:* University of Illinois; Roosevelt University (B.A., 1962); Loyola University (J.D., 1978). Author: "Valuation of Marital Property Right", Illinois Institute of Continuing Legal Education Family Law Handbook, 1986, revised 1989, 1992 and 1995. Co-Author: "The Continuing Jurisdiction Dilemma in Interstate Child Custody Disputes," 70 Illinois Bar Journal 304, 1982. Faculty, ABA Family Law Trial Advocacy Institute, U. of Houston Law School, 2002—. Certified Family Law Arbitrator. *Member:* Chicago (Chair, Matrimonial Law Committee, 1988-1989), Illinois State and American (Family Law Section, Member, Executive Council, 1993-1996, Chair Long Range Planning, 1994-1995; Publications Development Board, 1986-1993) Bar Associations; American Academy of Matrimonial Lawyers (Parlimentarian 2004-2005; Vice President, 2000-2003; Treasurer, 1997-2000; Secretary, 1995-1997; President, Illinois Chapter, 1996-1997); International Academy of Matrimonial Lawyers; American College of Family Trial Lawyers. ***PRACTICE AREAS:*** Family Law; Domestic Relations; Premarital Agreements; Spousal Support; Paternity; Divorce; Child Custody. ***Email:*** dmarcus@davisfriedman.com

JAMES L. RUBENS, born Chicago, Illinois, April 4, 1954; admitted to bar, 1979, Illinois and U.S. District Court, Northern District of Illinois. *Education:* Kenyon College; University of Illinois (B.A., 1976); DePaul University (J.D., 1979). Lecturer: American Academy of Matrimonial Lawyers; Illinois State Bar Association; Illinois Institute of Continuing Legal Education; Lorman Business Institute Family Law Custody and Placement Seminar, Chicago Bar Association. Author: "Guardian-Ad-Litem and Attorneys for the Child, and Child's Representatives," Child Custody Litigation Handbook and subsequent updates, Illinois Institute of Continuing Legal Education, 1992, 1998, 2000, 2004. Guest Lecturer, DePaul University College of Law School. Appeared on the Today Show television program, June 14, 1990. Interviewed in the New York Times, May 11, 1990. Member: Board of Directors, American Jewish Committee, 2004, 2005; Board of Directors, Young Men's Jewish Council, 1982. *Member:* Chicago (Member, Matrimonial Law Committee) and Illinois State (Co-Editor, ISBA Family Law Section Newsletter, 1994) Bar Associations; Chicago Council of Lawyers (Chairman, State Judicial Evaluation Committee, 1989-1994; Treasurer; Member, Board of Governors, 1989-1993). ***PRACTICE AREAS:*** Family Law; Domestic Relations; Divorce; Litigation; Spousal Support; Paternity; Premarital Agreements; Child Custody; Appellate Practice. ***Email:*** jrubens@davisfriedman.com

JOSHUA T. FRIEDMAN, born Chicago, Illinois, April 28, 1964; admitted to bar, 1991, Illinois. *Education:* Miami University (B.A., 1986); Washington University (J.D., 1991). Executive Articles Editor, Washington University Journal of Urban and Contemporary Law, 1990-1991. Author: Vol. 40 Washington University Journal of Urban and Contemporary Law p. 109, 1991. *Member:* Chicago (Member, Matrimonial Law Committee), Illinois State (Member, Family Law Section) and American (Member, Family Law Section) Bar Associations. ***PRACTICE AREAS:*** Family Law; Domestic Relations Law; Divorce; Spousal Support; Child Custody; Alimony. ***Email:*** jfriedman@davisfriedman.com

ROBERT D. SEGAL, born Philadelphia, Pennsylvania, October 27, 1961; admitted to bar, 1986, Pennsylvania, U.S. District Court, Eastern District of Pennsylvania and U.S. Court of Appeals, Third Circuit; 1987, New Jersey and U.S. District Court, District of New Jersey; 1994, Illinois and U.S. Court of Appeals, Second Circuit. *Education:* University of Pennsylvania (B.A., 1982); University of Pennsylvania Law School; Temple University (J.D., 1986). Author: "New Law Raising Old Questions Involving Maintenance and Work," Chicago Daily Law Bulletin, March 17, 1995; "Court Rejects Joint Custody Arrangement," Chicago Daily Law Bulletin, November 27, 1995; "Courts Reluctant to Enforce Pacts on Religion," Chicago Daily Law Bulletin, August 1996; "Partnership Law Edging Into Realm of Divorce Cases," Chicago Law Bulletin, August 25, 1997; "Harassment Prohibition in Order of Protection Has Broad Implications," Chicago Daily Law Bulletin, April, 2000. Lecturer, "Child Custody Trial-What You Need to Know," Chicago Bar Association, 2001. Guest Lecturer, "Business Interests and Divorce," Hinshaw & Culbertson, February 2002, Baker & McKenzie, May 2002. Lecturer, "Complex Divorce Issues for the Illinois Practitioner," National Business Institute, Chicago, Illinois, January 2003; Divorce Taxation, Illinois Institute for Continuing Legal Education (IICLE) 2nd Annual Family Law Conference, Champaign/Urbana and Chicago, Illinois, April 2003. Named, Top 5 Percent of Lawyers in Illinois, Leading Lawyers Network, February 2003 and 2004. Course Planner and Lecturer, Divorce Taxation and Malpractice Traps for the Unwary, IICLE 3rd Annual Family Law Conference, Champaign/Urbana and Chicago, Illinois, April 2004. Course Planner, IICLE 7th Annual Family Law Conference, Champaign/Urbana and Chicago, Illinois, April 2005. *Member:* Chicago, Illinois State and American Bar Associations. Fellow, American Academy of Matrimonial Lawyers. ***PRACTICE AREAS:*** Family Law; Domestic Relations; Divorce; Spousal Support; Paternity; Premarital Agreements; Child Custody. ***Email:*** rsegal@davisfriedman.com

DORIS SCHUMACHER McMORROW, born Tulsa, Oklahoma, June 25, 1951; admitted to bar, 1977, Illinois and U.S. District Court, Northern District of Illinois. *Education:* Vassar College (B.A., magna cum laude, 1973); Suffolk University (J.D., 1977). *Member:* Illinois State Bar Association. ***PRACTICE AREAS:*** Family Law; Domestic Relations Law; Child Custody; Divorce; Spousal Support; Premarital Agreements; Paternity. ***Email:*** dmcmorrow@davisfriedman.com

(This Listing Continued)

ASSOCIATES

MURIEL KUHS, born New York, N. Y., March 17, 1941; admitted to bar, 1978, Illinois. *Education:* Cornell University (A.B., 1961); Smith College (Graduate School of Social Work); John Marshall Law School (J.D., 1978). Contributing Author: The Illinois Practice of Family Law by Muller Davis, West Publishing, 1995. Member, Cornell University Council. President, Cornell Alumni Federation. Board of Directors, Legal Aid Bureau. *Member:* Illinois State Bar Association (Member, Family Law Section); Chicago Council of Lawyers (State Judicial Evaluation Committee Member, Board of Governors, 1994-2000). ***PRACTICE AREAS:*** Family Law; Domestic Relations; Divorce; Child Custody; Spousal Support. ***Email:*** mkuhs@davisfriedman.com

JODY MEYER YAZICI, born Fairmont, Minnesota, March 11, 1968; admitted to bar, 1994, Illinois. *Education:* Northwestern University (B.A., 1990); Cornell University (J.D., 1994). Author, with Muller Davis, The Illinois Practice of Family Law, West Group, 1995, 1996-1997, 1998-1999, 2000-2001, 2003-2004, 2005-2006 Editions. Author, with Muller Davis: "Best Interest of the Child: The Case for Joint Custody Even in Contested Divorces," 84 Ill. B.J. 348, 1996. Contributing Author, Illinois State Bar Association Family Law Section Newsletter, March, 1996. *Member:* Illinois State (Member, Family Law Section) Bar Association; Chicago Council of Lawyers (Member, Judicial Evaluation Committee). ***PRACTICE AREAS:*** Family Law; Domestic Relations Law; Divorce; Premarital Agreements; Child Custody; Spousal Support; Paternity. ***Email:*** jyazici@davisfriedman.com

DAVID CLYDE AINLEY, born Chicago, Illinois, January 29, 1967; admitted to bar, 1994, Illinois, U.S. District Court, Northern District of Illinois; 1999, U.S. District Court, Trial Bar. *Education:* Purdue University (B.S., 1990); John Marshall Law School (J.D., 1994). *Member:* Chicago (Member, Matrimonial Law Committee) and Illinois State (Member, Family Law Section) Bar Associations. ***PRACTICE AREAS:*** Family Law; Domestic Relations Law; Divorce; Child Custody. ***Email:*** dainley@davisfriedman.com

ZORKA RISTANOVIC, born Chicago, Illinois, October 10, 1970; admitted to bar, 1995, Illinois. *Education:* University of Illinois (B.A., Political Science, 1992); De Paul University (J.D., 1995). Formerly in-house counsel for Allstate Insurance Co. *Member:* Chicago, Illinois State (Member, Family Law Section) and Serbian Bar Associations. ***LANGUAGES:*** Serbian. ***PRACTICE AREAS:*** Family Law; Domestic Relations; Divorce; Child Custody; Spousal Support; Paternity. ***Email:*** zristanovic@davisfriedman.com

KAREN AUGUSTINE, born Chicago, Illinois, May 8, 1980; admitted to bar, 2004, Illinois. *Education:* Loyola University (B.A., 2002; J.D., 2004). ***PRACTICE AREAS:*** Family Law. ***Email:*** kaugustine@davisfriedman.com

OF COUNSEL

JAMES T. FRIEDMAN, (P.C.), born Oak Park, Illinois, May 28, 1936; admitted to bar, 1961, Illinois and U.S. District Court, Northern District of Illinois. *Education:* University of Michigan (B.A., 1958; J.D., 1961). Author: "Extension of the Illinois Long Arm Statute," De Paul Law Review, 1966; "Preparing for Trial in Child Custody Litigation," American Bar Association Law Notes, July, 1969; "No Fault Divorce Legislation-A Comparison," Chicago Bar Record, January and February, 1975; "A Practitioner's Introduction to the Illinois Marriage & Dissolution of Marriage Act," Illinois Institute for Continuing Legal Education, December, 1977; *The Divorce Handbook,* Random House, 1982. Editor and Publisher, Illinois Family Law Report, 1978-1982. *Member:* Chicago (Chairman, Family Law Committee, 1978), Illinois State (Editor, Illinois State Bar Family Law Newsletter, 1969-1975; Chairman, Family Law Council, 1981) and American (Member, Section on Family Law) Bar Associations; American Academy of Matrimonial Lawyers (Governor, 1968-1974; Vice President, 1974-1977; Counsel, 1977-1983; Treasurer, 1984-1985; President-elect, 1986-1987; President, 1987-1988). ***PRACTICE AREAS:*** Family Law; Domestic Relations Law; Child Custody; Divorce; Matrimonial Law.

RODERICK E. MacRAE, born Evanston, Illinois, September 7, 1945; admitted to bar, 1971, Illinois. *Education:* University of Colorado and Georgetown University (B.S., 1968); Vanderbilt University (J.D., 1971). Phi Delta Phi. *Member:* Chicago (Member: Committee on Matrimonial Law, 1972-2000; Young Lawyers Section) and Illinois State Bar Associations. ***PRACTICE AREAS:*** Family Law; Domestic Relations Law; Divorce; Child Custody; Paternity; Premarital Agreements.

DAVIS McGRATH LLC

125 SOUTH WACKER DRIVE, SUITE 1700
CHICAGO, ILLINOIS 60606
Telephone: 312-332-3033
Fax: 312-332-6376
URL: http://www.davismcgrath.com

Commercial Litigation and Alternative Dispute Resolution, Business Transactions, Intellectual Property, Trademark, Copyright, Trade Secret, Entertainment Law, Computer Law, Real Estate Litigation and Transactions, Antitrust, Employment Law, Trade Associations, Creditors' Rights.

FIRM PROFILE: Davis McGrath was formed by attorneys who were previously partners at large firms in Chicago. Our attorneys combine to provide a high level of experience and service in diverse areas of practice. Our clients range from individuals and small businesses to Fortune 500 Companies.

DAVID C. BOGAN (1946-1995)

CHAMP W. DAVIS, JR., born Springfield, Illinois, October 20, 1940; admitted to bar, 1966, Illinois; U.S. Supreme Court, U.S. Court of Appeals, 7th Circuit and U.S. District Court, Northern District of Illinois including Trial Bar. *Education:* University of Illinois (B.S., 1963; J.D., 1966). Order of the Coif. Associate Editor, University of Illinois Law Review. Adjunct Professor, Negotiations, Chicago Kent College of Law, 1992—. Participant: American Arbitration Association Arbitration Panel; National Association of Securities Dealers Arbitration Panel. Member: Illinois Attorney Registration and Disciplinary

(This Listing Continued)

DAVIS McGRATH LLC, Chicago—Continued

Commission Hearing Board. ***PRACTICE AREAS:*** Civil Litigation; Alternative Dispute Resolution; Business Counseling; Computer Law; Employment Law; Construction Law; Antitrust. ***Email:*** cdavis@davismcgrath.com

MARSHA K. HOOVER, born Imperial, Nebraska, January 30, 1955; admitted to bar, 1980, Illinois; U.S. Court of Appeals, 7th Circuit and U.S. District Court, Northern District of Illinois including Trial Bar. *Education:* Northwestern University (B.S., 1977; J.D., 1980). Law Clerk to Judge Thomas R. McMillen, U.S. District Court, Northern District of Illinois, 1980-1982. *Member:* Chicago and American Bar Associations; International Trademark Association. ***PRACTICE AREAS:*** Intellectual Property; Trademarks; Copyrights; Litigation. ***Email:*** mkhoover@davismcgrath.com

GINI S. MARZIANI, born Geneva, Illinois, April 28, 1955; admitted to bar, 1980, Illinois and U.S. District Court, Central and Northern Districts of Illinois including Trial Bar; U.S. District Court, Eastern District of Wisconsin; U.S. District Court, Northern District of Indiana. *Education:* North Central College (B.A., with honors, 1977); Chicago-Kent College of Law (J.D., 1980). *Member:* Chicago and American Bar Associations. ***REPORTED CASES:*** St. Louis North Joint Venture v P&L Enterprises, 116 F3d 262 (7th Circuit, 1997). ***PRACTICE AREAS:*** Civil Litigation; Commercial Law; Real Estate Law. ***Email:*** gsmarziani@davismcgrath.com

WILLIAM T. McGRATH, born Oak Park, Illinois, June 4, 1951; admitted to bar, 1976, Illinois; U.S. Supreme Court, U.S. Court of Appeals, Fifth, Seventh, Tenth and Federal Circuits and U.S. District Court, Northern District of Illinois, including Trial Bar. *Education:* University of Notre Dame (B.A., 1973); Washington University (J.D., 1976). Associate Director, Center for Intellectual Property Law. Adjunct Professor of Copyright Law, John Marshall Law School. *Member:* Chicago Bar Association (Chair, Patent, Trademark and Copyright Committee, 1992-1993); Intellectual Property Law Association of Chicago (President, 1999-2000); Lawyers for the Creative Arts (Board Member, 1996-1998); Copyright Society of the U.S.A. (Board of Trustees, 1999-2001). ***REPORTED CASES:*** In re Amsted Industries, Inc., 972 F.2d 1326 (Fed. Cir.1992); Roulo v Russ Berrie & Co., 886 F.2d 931 (7th Cir. 1989); Storm Impact, Inc. v. Software of the Month Club, 13 F. Supp.2d 782 (N.D. Ill.1998). ***PRACTICE AREAS:*** Intellectual Property; Copyright Law; Trademark; Computer Law; Civil Litigation. ***Email:*** wmcgrath@davismcgrath.com

JOHN B. ALSTERDA, born Chicago, Illinois, September 2, 1960; admitted to bar, 1988, Illinois; U.S. District Court, Northern and Central Districts of Illinois; U.S. Court of Appeals, 7th Circuit. *Education:* Colorado College (B.A., 1982); University of Illinois (J.D., 1988). *Member:* Chicago and Illinois State Bar Associations. ***REPORTED CASES:*** St. Louis Joint Venture v. P&L Enterprises 116 F. 3d 262 (7th Cir. 1997); Kaimowitz v. Board of Trustees 951 F. 2d 765 (7th Cir. 1992); Crum & Forster v. RTC, 156 Ill. 2d. 384 (Ill. 1993). ***PRACTICE AREAS:*** Real Estate; Business Transactions; Commercial Litigation. ***Email:*** jalsterda@davismcgrath.com

---

BARBARA J. MULVANNY, born Milwaukee, Wisconsin, July 17, 1952; admitted to bar, 1984, Illinois and U.S. District Court, Northern District of Illinois. *Education:* University of Wisconsin-Milwaukee (B.S., 1980); Loyola University (J.D., cum laude, 1984); John Marshall Law School (LL.M., Intellectual Property, 2002). Judicial Clerk to Hon. John J. Sullivan, Illinois Appellate Court, First District, 1984-1986. *Member:* Chicago and American Bar Associations. ***PRACTICE AREAS:*** Litigation; Copyrights; Trademarks. ***Email:*** bmulvanny@davismcgrath.com

JODI L. FLYNN, born Cloquet, Minnesota, November 6, 1966; admitted to bar, 1996, Illinois; 1997, U.S. District Court, Northern District of Illinois; 2001, U.S. District Court, Northern District of Indiana. *Education:* St. Mary's University of Minnesota (B.A., 1989); DePaul University College of Law (J.D., 1995). *Member:* Chicago Bar Association. ***PRACTICE AREAS:*** Civil Litigation; Commercial Law; Construction Law. ***Email:*** jlflynn@davismcgrath.com

KEVIN A. THOMPSON, born Madison, Wisconsin, January 13, 1971; admitted to bar, 1998, Illinois and U.S. District Court, Northern District of Illinois. *Education:* University of Wisconsin-Madison (B.A., 1993); DePaul University (J.D., with honors, 1998). Order of the Coif. *Member:* Chicago Bar Association; Intellectual Property Law Association of Chicago (Board of Directors, 2005-2006). ***PRACTICE AREAS:*** Trademarks; Copyrights; Internet Law; Computer Law; Intellectual Property; Commercial Litigation. ***Email:*** kthompson@davismcgrath.com

EVAN D. BROWN, born Bedford, Indiana, October 30, 1974; admitted to bar, 2001, Colorado; 2002, Illinois and U.S. District Court, Northern District of Illinois. *Education:* Wabash College (B.A., 1997); University of Denver (J.D., 2000). *Member:* Chicago, Illinois State and American Bar Associations. ***PRACTICE AREAS:*** Trademarks; Copyrights; Computer Law; Internet Law; Commercial Litigation. ***Email:*** ebrown@davismcgrath.com

BORIS UMANSKY, born Odessa, Ukraine, June 12, 1975; admitted to bar, 2000, Indiana; 2003, Illinois. *Education:* Indiana University (B.A., 1997; J.D., 2000). Phi Delta Phi. *Member:* Chicago Bar Association; Intellectual Property Law Association of Chicago. ***PRACTICE AREAS:*** Intellectual Property; Trademarks; Copyrights; Computer Law; Internet Law; Commercial Litigation. ***Email:*** bumansky@davismcgrath.com

OF COUNSEL

TERESA F. FRISBIE, born Evanston, Illinois, October 10, 1961; admitted to bar, 1986, Illinois and U.S. District Court, Northern District of Illinois. *Education:* University of Illinois (B.A., 1983); Loyola University of Chicago School of Law (J.D., 1986). Member, National Restaurant Association, 1996-1999. *Member:* Chicago Bar Association (Member, Alternative Dispute Resolution Committee). Fellow, Chartered Institute of Arbitrators. Executive Director, Chicago International Dispute Resolution Association (CIDRA). ***PRACTICE AREAS:*** Civil Litigation; Personal Injury; Domestic and International; Alternative Dispute Resolution. ***Email:*** tfrisbie@davismcgrath.com

CELESTE EBERS KRALOVEC, born Blue Island, Illinois, May 1, 1956; admitted to bar, 1981, Illinois; U.S. District Court, Northern District of Illinois including Trial Bar and U.S. Court of Appeals, Seventh Circuit. *Education:* University of Illinois (B.A., 1978); The John Marshall Law School (J.D., 1981). Member, The John Marshall Law Review, 1980-1981. ***PRACTICE AREAS:*** Civil Litigation; Guardianship; Estates. ***Email:*** ckralovec@davismcgrath.com

GERALD J. MANNIX, born Chicago, Illinois, June 26, 1930; admitted to bar, 1959, Illinois and U.S. District Court, Northern District of Illinois. *Education:* DePaul University (B.A., 1953; J.D., 1959). Adjunct Professor, Paralegal, Harper College, 1991-1998. Zoning Board of Appeals, River Forest, Illinois, 1987—. [Capt., U.S.M.C.R., 1952-1954]. ***PRACTICE AREAS:*** Probate Law; Trust Litigation. ***Email:*** gmannix@davismcgrath.com

MARGARET F. WOULFE, born Chicago, Illinois, February 14, 1957; admitted to bar, 1982, Illinois; U.S. Court of Appeals, 7th Circuit, U.S. District Court, Northern District of Illinois including Trial Bar, U.S. District Court, Eastern District of Wisconsin. *Education:* Illinois State University (B.S., with honors, 1979); University of Illinois (J.D., 1982). Member, National Moot Court Team, University of Illinois College of Law. Adjunct Professor, Chicago-Kent College of Law. Arbitrator, Circuit Court of Cook County. *Member:* Chicago, Illinois State and American Bar Associations; Women's Bar Association of Illinois. ***PRACTICE AREAS:*** Civil Litigation; Employment Law; Real Estate Law. ***Email:*** mwoulfe@davismcgrath.com

---

THOMAS D. DECKER AND ASSOCIATES, LTD.

Established in 1981

SUITE 1500, 321 S. PLYMOUTH COURT
CHICAGO, ILLINOIS 60604
Telephone: 312-922-4180
Fax: 312-922-4184
Email: deckerlawoffice@ameritech.net

Civil and Criminal Trial and Appellate Practice.

THOMAS D. DECKER, born Waukegan, Illinois; admitted to bar, 1963, Illinois. *Education:* Lake Forest College (B.A., 1955); Northwestern University (J.D., 1963). Law Clerk, U.S. District Court, Northern District of Illinois, 1963-1964. Assistant Attorney General, State of Illinois, 1964-1967. Deputy Director, Federal Defender Program, Inc., U.S. District Court, Northern District of Illinois, 1967-1976. *Member:* Chicago, Illinois State (Member, House of Delegates, 1973-1977), Federal and American Bar Associations; Bar Association of the Seventh Federal Circuit (Member: Board of Governors, 1984-1987; Advisory Committee on Circuit Rules); Illinois State Trial Lawyers Association; National Association of Criminal Defense Lawyers (Director, 1979-1986). Fellow, American College of Trial Lawyers. ***PRACTICE AREAS:*** Civil Practice; Criminal Defense; Civil Appeals; Criminal Appeals.

BARBARA M. DeCOSTER

4801 WEST PETERSON, SUITE 412
CHICAGO, ILLINOIS 60646
Telephone: 773-286-3800
Fax: 773-286-3504
Email: bdecoster@yahoo.com
URL: http://www.lawyers.com/bdecoster

Litigation in State and Federal Courts. Collections, Commercial and Contract, Negligence, Personal Injury, Automobile Accidents, Slip and Fall, Dog Bites, Probate, Trusts, Real Estate, Products Liability, Professional Negligence, Dental Malpractice.

BARBARA M. DeCOSTER, born Paterson, New Jersey, March 27, 1948; admitted to bar, 1978, Illinois; 1983, U.S. Court of Appeals, Seventh Circuit; 1990, U.S. District Court, Northern District of Illinois including Trial Bar; 1993, U.S. District Court, Central District of Illinois; 1997, U.S. U.S. District Court, Southern District of Illinois. *Education:* Smith College; George Washington University (B.A., 1971); Stanford University (M.A., 1973); University of Iowa (J.D., with high distinction, 1978). Phi Beta Kappa; Order of the Coif. Member, Board of Editors, Iowa Law Review, 1977-1978. *Member:* Chicago and Illinois State Bar Associations; Women's Bar Association of Illinois. ***PRACTICE AREAS:*** Personal Injury; Commercial Litigation; Trusts and Estates.

DEFREES & FISKE

Established in 1884

SUITE 1100
200 SOUTH MICHIGAN AVENUE
CHICAGO, ILLINOIS 60604
Telephone: 312-372-4000
Fax: 312-939-5617
Email: defrees@defrees.com
URL: http://www.defrees.com

General Practice including Business, Corporate Law, Finance, Mergers and Acquisitions, Public and Unregulated Utilities and Energy, Taxation, Employment Benefits, Labor and Employment Law, General Civil Litigation, Appellate Practice, Copyright and Trademark and Unfair Competition, Non Profit and Tax Exempt Organizations, Trade Association, Health Care and Hospital Law, Wills and Probate, Trusts and Estates, Real Estate Law, Construction Law and Environmental Law, Bankruptcy and Reorganizations, Creditors Rights, Music Law, Intellectual Property, Telecommunications.

FIRM PROFILE: Founded in 1884, Defrees & Fiske provides general and specialized legal services. Our clients include large, publicly-held corporations, but we also often serve as general counsel to closely-held businesses and as legal advisor to individuals.

(This Listing Continued)

Our commitment to professionalism, expertise and integrity has earned our clients' trust in local, regional and national matters ranging from the routine to the complex. Our attorneys' broad range of experience in transactional and litigation areas provide the base from which we serve the diversified needs of regulated and unregulated businesses and entrepreneurs.

Defrees & Fiske is a member of the International Society of Primerus Law Firms. Primerus is an international alliance of law firms prescreened for their adherence to high ethical standards, excellence of work product, reasonable fee structure and civility. A prospective Primerus law firm's clients and peers, along with members of the judiciary, participate in the strict screening process used by Primerus in selecting candidates for membership.

Law Firm Affiliations: Illinois Chamber of Commerce; Chicagoland Chamber of Commerce; The International Society of Primerus Law Firms.

MEMBERS OF FIRM

DONALD DEFREES (1915-1968)

KENNETH M. FISKE (1928-1978)

GREGORY E. NORWELL, born Memphis, Tennessee, April 25, 1943; admitted to bar, 1967, Illinois. *Education:* University of Chicago (B.A., 1963); Northwestern University (J.D., 1967). *Member:* Chicago (Member, Trust Law Committee, 1976—; Chairman, 1984-1985; Member, Probate Practice Committee, 1991—; Chairman, Subcommittee on Uniform Probate Legislation, 1994-1995) and Illinois State Bar Associations; Chicago Estate Planning Council. ***PRACTICE AREAS:*** Wills; Probate; Trusts and Estates. ***Email:*** gen@defrees.com

TIMOTHY J. RIORDAN, born Chicago, Illinois, March 25, 1941; admitted to bar, 1965, Illinois, U.S. District Court, Northern District of Illinois including Trial Bar and U.S. Court of Appeals, Seventh Circuit. *Education:* Loras College (B.A., 1962); Northwestern University (J.D., 1965). Phi Delta Phi. Assistant Attorney General, 1965-1966 and Special Assistant Attorney General, 1969-1975, State of Illinois. *Member:* Chicago (Member: Younger Members Committee, 1967-1975; Judicial Candidates Committee, 1974-1980; Probate Committee, 1974-1980; Circuit Court Committee, 1985-1987; Federal Court Committee, 1985-1987; Labor and Employment Law Committee, 1990—) and Illinois State Bar Associations. ***PRACTICE AREAS:*** Commercial Litigation; Labor and Employment; Construction Law; Trademarks; Copyrights; Unfair Competition; Corporate Law; Municipal Law. ***Email:*** tjriorda@defrees.com

HENRY J. UNDERWOOD, born Greensboro, North Carolina, January 8, 1944; admitted to bar, 1969, Illinois. *Education:* University of North Carolina (B.A., 1966); University of Chicago (J.D., 1969); University of London, London, England (LL.M., 1971). Assistant Professor of Business Law, Roosevelt University, 1969-1970. *Member:* Chicago (Member: Securities Law Committee, 1973-1978; Commercial Law Committee, 1979—), Illinois State and American Bar Associations. ***PRACTICE AREAS:*** Commercial Law; Corporate Law; Business Law; Commercial Contracts; Securities Law; Mergers and Acquisitions. ***Email:*** hju@defrees.com

KENNETH A. von KLUCK, born Chicago, Illinois, January 21, 1944; admitted to bar, 1968, Illinois. *Education:* Ripon College (A.B., 1965); University of Wisconsin (J.D., 1968). Phi Alpha Delta. *Member:* Chicago Bar Association (Member: Mental Health Law Committee, 1982-1985; Medico-Legal Relations Committee, 1982-1986); Vice-Chairman, 1984-1985; Chairman, 1985-1986); National Health Lawyers Association. ***PRACTICE AREAS:*** Health Care; Real Estate Law; Nonprofit Tax Law; Tax Exempt Organizations. ***Email:*** kavk@defrees.com

LESLIE RECHT, (MS.), born Chicago, Illinois, May 19, 1949; admitted to bar, 1974, Illinois. *Education:* University of Chicago (A.B., 1970); IIT/Chicago-Kent College of Law (J.D., with high honors, 1974). Adjunct Professor, Energy and Environmental Law, IIT/Chicago-Kent College of Law, 1991-1997. *Member:* Chicago Bar Association (Member, Public Utility Law Committee, 1975—; Chairman, 1984-1985; Real Property Law, Preservation and Architecture Subcommittee Chairman, 1986-1988); Women's Bar Association of Illinois (Board Member, 1984-1986; Lawyer Referral Service Commissioner, 1985-1987, 1991-2003); Federal Energy Bar Association. ***SPECIAL AGENCIES:*** Energy Regulatory Commission; Illinois Commerce Commission. ***PRACTICE AREAS:*** Energy Law; Public Utilities Law; Environmental Law; Commercial Litigation. ***Email:*** lrecht@defrees.com

W. MICHAEL SEIDEL, born Chicago Heights, Illinois, February 6, 1953; admitted to bar, 1978, Illinois. *Education:* University of Notre Dame (B.A., summa cum laude, 1975); University of Illinois (J.D., 1978). Phi Beta Kappa. Harno Fellow. *Member:* Chicago Bar Association (Chairman, 1985-1986; Vice-Chairman, 1984-1985, Public Utility Law Committee). ***PRACTICE AREAS:*** Public Utilities Law; Commercial Litigation; Contract Law; Real Estate Law. ***Email:*** wmseidel@defrees.com

MIRIAM LESKOVAR BURKLAND, born Chicago, Illinois, December 25, 1956; admitted to bar, 1981, Illinois. *Education:* University of Illinois (B.A., cum laude, 1978; J.D., 1981). Phi Beta Kappa; Phi Kappa Phi. *Member:* Chicago Bar Association. ***PRACTICE AREAS:*** Commercial Law; Corporate Law; Business Law; Commercial Contracts; Finance; Intellectual Property Law; Mergers and Acquisitions. ***Email:*** mburkland@defrees.com

CHARLES A. SEMMELHACK, born Milwaukee, Wisconsin, January 4, 1960; admitted to bar, 1985, Wisconsin and Illinois. *Education:* Northwestern University (B.A., Economics, 1982); University of Wisconsin-Madison (J.D., cum laude, 1985). Phi Beta Kappa; Alpha Lambda Delta; Phi Eta Sigma; Pi Sigma Alpha; Phi Alpha Delta. Senior Note and Comment Editor, 1984-1985 and Writer, 1983-1984, Wisconsin International Law Journal. *Member:* Chicago Bar Association; State Bar of California. ***PRACTICE AREAS:*** Commercial Law; Corporate Law; Finance; Commercial Contracts; Real Estate Law; Intellectual Property Law; Mergers and Acquisitions. ***Email:*** cas@defrees.com

MICHAEL J. POWERS, born Lake Bluff, Illinois, August 18, 1957; admitted to bar, 1984, Illinois; 1986, U.S. District Court, Northern District of Illinois; 1989, U.S. Tax Court. *Education:* Western Illinois University (B.B.A., with honors, 1980); University of Illinois (J.D., 1984). Beta Gamma Sigma, Phi Kappa Phi. *Member:* Chicago Bar Association (Member, Federal Taxation and Employee Benefits Committees). ***PRACTICE AREAS:*** Tax Law; Employee Benefit Law; Business Law; Pension and Profit Sharing; ERISA; Executive Compensation. ***Email:*** mjpowers@defrees.com

(This Listing Continued)

TIMOTHY S. BUCKLEY, born Chicago, Illinois, October 27, 1954; admitted to bar, 1981, Illinois and U.S. District Court, Northern District of Illinois. *Education:* University of Illinois, Chicago (B.A., 1976); John Marshall Law School (J.D., 1981). *Member:* Illinois State and American Bar Associations. ***PRACTICE AREAS:*** Business Law; Commercial Litigation; Appellate Practice; Commercial Law; Corporate Law; Real Estate; Labor and Employment; Trademarks; Unfair Competition. ***Email:*** tbuckley@defrees.com

PHILLIP B. BOWMAN, born Ames, Iowa, February 28, 1936; admitted to bar, 1961, Illinois; 1962, U.S. District Court, Northern District of Illinois. *Education:* Princeton University (B.S.E., 1958); University of Michigan (J.D., 1961). Phi Delta Phi. *Member:* American Bar Association; Lawyers Club of Chicago; Association Forum (Member: Education Committee, 1984-1989; Government Affairs Committee, 1995-1997). ***PRACTICE AREAS:*** Nonprofit Organizations; Tax Exempt Organizations; Commercial Contracts; Business Law; Corporate Law; Commercial Law; Environmental Law; Insurance Law. ***Email:*** pbb@defrees.com

L. JUDSON TODHUNTER, born Denver, Colorado, May 8, 1950; admitted to bar, 1976, Illinois, Colorado and U.S. District Court, Northern District of Illinois. *Education:* University of Colorado at Boulder (B.A., 1973); John Marshall Law School (J.D., 1976). *Member:* Chicago (Member, Bankruptcy Committee, 1981—) and American (Member, Section of Business Law, Bankruptcy Committee, Subcommittee on Avoidance Powers, 1985—) Bar Associations; American Bankruptcy Institute. ***PRACTICE AREAS:*** Corporate Law; Business Law; Commercial Law; Creditor's Rights; Bankruptcy Law; Business Reorganization. ***Email:*** ljt@defrees.com

SCOTT M. LEVIN, born Chicago, Illinois, May 18, 1954; admitted to bar, 1983, Illinois and U.S. District Court, Northern District of Illinois including Trial Bar; 1991, U.S. Court of Appeals, Seventh and Ninth Circuit. *Education:* University of Illinois (B.S., 1976; M.A., 1978); Chicago-Kent College of Law (J.D., with honors, 1983); John Marshall Law School (LL.M., Intellectual Property, 1994). Executive Assistant, Illinois Law Enforcement Commission, 1977-1982. Deputy Executive Director, Illinois Criminal Justice Information Authority, 1983-1986. *Member:* Chicago (Member, Patent, Trademark & Copyright Committee; Chairman, Police Lawyer Relations Committee), Illinois State (Member, Sections on: Civil Practice and Procedure; Banking and Bankruptcy; Corporations and Securities; General Practice; Intellectual Property) and American (Member, Sections on: General Practice; Intellectual Property; Business Law; Litigation) Bar Associations; State Bar of California; Illinois Association of Chiefs of Police. ***PRACTICE AREAS:*** Business Law; Commercial Law; Commercial Litigation; Intellectual Property Law. ***Email:*** levin@defrees.com

ASSOCIATES

DOUGLAS C. GIESE, born Brookfield, Illinois, November 2, 1965; admitted to bar, 1997, Illinois. *Education:* College of Dupage (A.A., 1985); Northern Illinois University (B.S., 1987); Chicago-Kent College of Law, Illinois Institute of Technology (J.D., 1997). *Member:* Chicago Bar Association. ***PRACTICE AREAS:*** General Practice; Commercial Litigation; Appellate Practice; Commercial Law; Creditors Rights; Alternative Dispute Resolution. ***Email:*** dcgiese@defrees.com

JENNIFER PAGANESSI FISHER, admitted to bar, 1995, Illinois and U.S. District Court, Northern District of Illinois. *Education:* Syracuse University (B.S., 1992); Chicago-Kent College of Law (J.D., 1995). *Member:* Chicago, Illinois State and American Bar Associations. ***PRACTICE AREAS:*** Business Law; Commercial Law; Real Estate Law; Commercial Litigation; Litigation. ***Email:*** fisher@defrees.com

STEVEN WISER, born Durham, North Carolina, April 12, 1969; admitted to bar, 1998, Illinois and U.S. District Court, Northern District of Illinois; 2004, New York. *Education:* Loyola University (B.A., 1993; J.D., 1997). Salzbury Scholar. *Member:* Chicago Bar Association (Member, Patent, Trademark and Copyright, Corporate and Business Law and Entertainment Law Committees); Intellectual Property Law Association of Chicago (Member, Copyright and U.S. Trademark Committees); National Academy of Recording Arts and Sciences. ***PRACTICE AREAS:*** Commercial Litigation; Intellectual Property; Business Law; Music Law. ***Email:*** wiser@defrees.com

MELANIE C. LEONARD, admitted to bar, 2002, Illinois and U.S. District Court, Northern District of Illinois. *Education:* University of Illinois (B.A., 1999); Chicago-Kent College of Law (J.D., 2002). *Member:* Chicago, Illinois State and American Bar Associations. ***PRACTICE AREAS:*** Business Law; Commercial Law; Real Estate; Commercial Litigation; Litigation; Intellectual Property. ***Email:*** mleonard@defrees.com

OF COUNSEL

EDWARD J. GRIFFIN, born Evanston, Illinois, December 10, 1932; admitted to bar, 1956, Illinois. *Education:* University of Notre Dame (B.S., 1955; LL.B., 1956). *Member:* Chicago and Illinois State Bar Associations. ***PRACTICE AREAS:*** Public Utilities Law; Commercial Litigation. ***Email:*** egriffin@defrees.com

JOHN W. HUPP, born Chicago, Illinois, March 20, 1927; admitted to bar, 1953, Illinois. *Education:* Northwestern University (B.S., 1950); University of Michigan (J.D., 1953). Phi Beta Kappa; Delta Theta Phi. Assistant Editor, Michigan Law Review, 1952-1953. *Member:* Chicago (Chairman, Corporation Law Committee, 1974-1975), Illinois State and American Bar Associations; Lawyers Club of Chicago; American Judicature Society. ***PRACTICE AREAS:*** Corporate Law; Commercial Law. ***Email:*** jhupp@defrees.com

WILLIAM P. STEINBRECHER, born Chicago, Illinois, November 7, 1917; admitted to bar, 1943, Illinois. *Education:* University of Chicago (A.B., 1942; J.D., 1944). *Member:* Chicago Bar Association (Chairman, Probate Practice Committee, 1957); Lawyers Club of Chicago. ***Email:*** wps@defrees.com

MARVIN S. HELFAND, born Chicago, Illinois, June 29, 1936; admitted to bar, 1960, Illinois. *Education:* Northwestern University (B.S., 1957; J.D., 1960). Order of the Coif; Tau Epsilon Rho; Beta Gamma Sigma; Beta Alpha Psi. Note and Comment Editor, Northwestern University Law Review, 1959-1960. *Member:* Chicago Bar Association (Member,

(This Listing Continued)

DEFREES & FISKE, Chicago—Continued

Trust Law Committee, 1965—; Chairman, Division II, 1981-1982). ***PRACTICE AREAS:*** Corporations Law; Probate Law; Trust and Estates. ***Email:*** mshelfand@defrees.com

LUKE DeGRAND & ASSOCIATES, P.C.

20 NORTH CLARK STREET, SUITE 1450
CHICAGO, ILLINOIS 60602
Telephone: 312-236-9200
Fax: 312-236-9201
URL: http://www.lukedegrand.com

Civil Litigation, including Employment and Commercial Law.

LUKE DeGRAND, born Alton, Illinois, June 11, 1960; admitted to bar, 1985, Illinois. *Education:* University of Illinois (B.A., 1982; J.D., magna cum laude, 1985). Associate Editor, University of Illinois Law Review, 1984-1985. Member, Chicago Council of Lawyers. *Member:* Chicago, Illinois State and American Bar Associations. ***PRACTICE AREAS:*** Civil Litigation; Employment Law; Commercial Law. ***Email:*** ldegrand@lukedegrand.com

TRACEY L. WOLFE, born Dubuque, Iowa, September 15, 1972; admitted to bar, 1998, Illinois. *Education:* Illinois State University (B.A., cum laude, 1995); University of Illinois (J.D., 1998). Member, Chicago Council Lawyers. *Member:* Chicago and Illinois State Bar Association. ***PRACTICE AREAS:*** Civil Litigation; Employment Law; Commercial Law. ***Email:*** twolfe@lukedegrand.com

RONALD R. DELMENICO

30 NORTH LASALLE STREET, SUITE 3400
CHICAGO, ILLINOIS 60602
Telephone: 312-641-5311
Fax: 312-641-5520
Email: delmenico@aol.com
URL: http://www.lawyers.com/delmenicolaw

Corporate Law, Business Law, Real Property, Commercial Law and International Law.

RONALD R. DELMENICO, born Castlemaine, Victoria, Australia, July 7, 1938; admitted to bar, 1975, England and Wales; 1976, Illinois; 1985, Victoria, Australia. *Education:* Inns of Court School of Law and College of Law. Member, Lincoln's Inn, England. Former Member, Governmental Relations and International Committees of Cosmetics, Toiletries and Fragrances Association, 1993-1995. Former Chairman, Governmental Relations Committee of American Health and Beauty Aids Institute, 1995-1996. National President, Australian New Zealand American Chambers of Commerce. *Member:* Chicago, Illinois State (Chairman, International Law Section Council, 1980-1981; Council Member, 1977-1983; Program Committee Chairman for Illinois International Law Section/Illinois Institute for Continuing Legal Education's "National Conference on Practice and Procedure under the New Export Trading Company Act and U.S. Export Laws"), American and International Bar Associations; American Corporate Counsel Association.

DeSANTO, MORGAN & MITTELMAN

AN ASSOCIATION OF PROFESSIONAL CORPORATIONS
CHICAGO, ILLINOIS

(See Libertyville)

Plaintiff's Personal Injury, Automobile Accidents and Injuries, Slip and Fall, Wrongful Death, Insurance Bad Faith, Products Liability, Commercial Litigation, Employment Litigation, Discrimination, Harassment, Wrongful Termination.

DEUTSCH, LEVY & ENGEL

CHARTERED
225 WEST WASHINGTON STREET
SUITE 1700
CHICAGO, ILLINOIS 60606
Telephone: 312-346-1460
Fax: 312-346-1859
Email: Lawyers@dlec.com
URL: http://www.dlec.com

General Civil and Trial Practice in all State and Federal Courts. Corporation, Probate, Publishing and Libel Defense, Real Estate, Real Estate Taxation, Estate Planning, Deferred Compensation Planning, Taxation Law and Trademark and Copyright Law. Eminent Domain/Condemnation.

FIRM PROFILE: Deutsch, Levy & Engel, Chartered was founded more than 40 years ago and serves clients throughout the United States and in many foreign countries.

Members of the firm pride themselves on the ability to meet challenges and to complete a wide range of complicated legal transactions on an efficient and timely basis. The firm concentrates in the areas of commercial transaction, financing, corporations, litigation, real estate, federal, state and local taxation, estate planning and probate. The firm has a special emphasis on libel and slander law and First Amendment matters.

The firm's clients list includes publicly held as well as entrepreneurial and middle market companies engaged in a broad range of activities, financial institutions and state and local governmental agencies.

(This Listing Continued)

EARL A. DEUTSCH, born Chicago, Illinois, March 22, 1924; admitted to bar, 1950, Illinois and U.S. District Court, Northern District of Illinois; 1963, U.S. Supreme Court. *Education:* University of Illinois; John Marshall Law School (J.D., 1950). Assistant Corporation Counsel, City of Chicago Appeals Division, 1951-1954. Assistant States Attorney, County of Cook, 1954-1957. Master in Chancery, Circuit Court of Cook County, 1958-1968. Trustee, Metropolitan Sanitary District of Greater Chicago, 1964-1966. *Member:* Chicago, Illinois State and American Bar Associations. ***PRACTICE AREAS:*** Corporate Law. ***Email:*** Deutsch@dlec.com

PAUL M. LEVY, born Chicago, Illinois, December 22, 1935; admitted to bar, 1960, Illinois and U.S. District Court, Northern District of Illinois; 1976, Florida and U.S. Supreme Court. *Education:* Bowling Green State University (B.S., 1957); DePaul University (J.D., 1960). Assistant Professor, Torts and Damages, John Marshall Law School, 1966-1972. *Member:* Chicago, Illinois State and American (Member, Sections on: Litigation; Corporation, Banking and Business Law) Bar Associations; The Florida Bar. ***PRACTICE AREAS:*** Libel Defense; First Amendment Law; Publishing Law; Commercial Litigation. ***Email:*** Levy@dlec.com

TERRY L. ENGEL, born Chicago, Illinois, January 12, 1944; admitted to bar, 1967, Illinois and U.S. District Court, Northern District of Illinois; 1976, Florida and U.S. Supreme Court. *Education:* University of Illinois (B.S., 1964); DePaul University (J.D., 1967). Member, Board of Directors, Village of Skokie Library, 1971-1974. *Member:* Chicago, Illinois State and American Bar Associations; The Florida Bar. ***PRACTICE AREAS:*** Corporate Law; Local Taxation. ***Email:*** Engel@dlec.com

FRANK R. COHEN, born Chicago, Illinois, June 15, 1939; admitted to bar, 1966, Illinois, U.S. District Court, Northern District of Illinois and U.S. Tax Court. *Education:* University of Illinois; John Marshall Law School (J.D., cum laude, 1966). Certified Public Accountant, Illinois, 1961. *Member:* Chicago and Illinois State Bar Associations. ***PRACTICE AREAS:*** Corporate Tax Planning; Individual Taxation; Estate Planning; Mergers and Acquisitions. ***Email:*** Cohen@dlec.com

JERRY I. RUDMAN, born Chicago, Illinois, July 30, 1942; admitted to bar, 1968, Illinois; 1971, U.S. Tax Court; 1980, California. *Education:* University of Illinois (B.S., 1964); DePaul University (J.D., 1968). *Member:* Chicago, Illinois State and American Bar Associations; State Bar of California. ***PRACTICE AREAS:*** Corporate Law; Secured Transactions; Mergers and Acquisitions; Estate Planning. ***Email:*** Rudman@dlec.com

MICHAEL J. DEVINE, born Chicago, Illinois, July 22, 1952; admitted to bar, 1978, Illinois and U.S. District Court, Northern District of Illinois including Trial Bar. *Education:* John Carroll University (B.S.B.A., 1974); John Marshall Law School (J.D., 1978). Certified Public Accountant, 1977. Adjunct Professor, Lawyering Skills Program, John Marshall Law School, 1985. Member, Board of Directors: Montini Catholic High School; Our Childrens Homestead. *Member:* Chicago, Illinois State and American Bar Associations; American Institute of Certified Public Accountants; Illinois Society of Certified Public Accountants. ***PRACTICE AREAS:*** Commercial Litigation; Corporate Law; Transactional Law; Condemnation. ***Email:*** Devine@dlec.com

STUART BERKS, born Chicago, Illinois, December 28, 1941; admitted to bar, 1966, Illinois and U.S. District Court, Northern District of Illinois. *Education:* DePaul University (B.A., 1964; J.D., cum laude, 1966). Instructor, Contracts II, John Marshall Law School, 1972. *Member:* Chicago, Northwest Suburban, Illinois State and American Bar Associations. ***PRACTICE AREAS:*** Employment Law; Mergers and Acquisitions; Commercial Litigation; Appellate Practice.

KENNETH W. FUNK, born Chicago, Illinois, January 4, 1955; admitted to bar, 1982, Illinois, U.S. District Court, Northern District of Illinois and U.S. Court of Appeals, Seventh Circuit. *Education:* DePaul University (B.A., with highest honors, 1977; J.D., 1982), Delta Epsilon Sigma; Pi Gamma Mu. Special Assistant Attorney General, Illinois State Toll Highway Authority, 1991—. Counsel to Commonwealth Realty Advisors. Special Counsel: Metropolitan Water Reclamation District of Greater Chicago; Illinois Housing Development Authority. *Member:* Chicago (Member, Environmental Law Committee), Illinois State and American (Member, Environmental Law Section) Bar Associations. ***PRACTICE AREAS:*** Real Estate; Environmental Compliance. ***Email:*** Funk@dlec.com

PHILLIP J. ZISOOK, born Chicago, Illinois, June 22, 1953; admitted to bar, 1978, Illinois. *Education:* University of Illinois (B.A., 1975); Chicago-Kent College of Law, Illinois Institute of Technology (J.D., with honors, 1978). Member, Chicago-Kent Law Review, 1977-1978. Author, "First Amendment Beats RICO-Victory for a Free Press," 11 Communications Lawyer, No. 1 (Spring 1993). Co-Author, "Media Privacy and Related Law," Libel Defense Resource Center, Illinois Chapter, 1995-2001. Adjunct Professor of Law, The John Marshall Law School, 1993-1995. *Member:* Chicago and American (Member, Sections on: Litigation; Communications Law) Bar Associations; Appellate Lawyers Association. ***PRACTICE AREAS:*** Defamation; First Amendment Law; Commercial Litigation; Appellate Practice. ***Email:*** Zisook@dlec.com

DENNIS E. FRISBY, born Chicago, Illinois, August 22, 1954; admitted to bar, 1979, Illinois; 1980, U.S. Tax Court. *Education:* DePaul University (B.S.C., with highest honors, 1976; J.D., with honors, 1979). Beta Gamma Sigma; Phi Alpha Delta. Recipient, American Jurisprudence Award in Contracts. Certified Public Accountant, Illinois, 1976. Author: "Civil Tax Litigation—Injunctions," Illinois Institute for Continuing Legal Education, 1983, 1985, 1987; Aiding and Abetting Penalty Shelters Uncertainty (July 1989); IRS Delays, Don't Get Mad Get An Interest Abatement (Jan. 1989); Illinois CPA Society News Journal Articles: In an Emergency, File 911 (Feb. 1990). *Member:* Chicago Bar Association; Illinois CPA Society. ***REPORTED CASES:*** Chicago Merchantile Exchange v. Commissioner, TC Memo, 2000-67; Bertram Emanuel vs. United States 705 F.Supp. 434 (N.D. Ill. 1989); William Spencer vs. United States, 82-1 USTC Par 9102 (N.D. Ill. 1982). ***PRACTICE AREAS:*** Estate Planning; Federal Taxation. ***Email:*** Frisby@dlec.com

JOEL A. STEIN, born New York, N.Y., November 4, 1949; admitted to bar, 1978, Illinois and U.S. District Court, Northern District of Illinois; 1979, District of Columbia Court of Appeals; 1980, California and U.S. Court of Appeals, Seventh Circuit; 1986, New Jersey and U.S. District Court, District of New Jersey. *Education:* State University of New York at Buffalo (B.A., 1974); University of Chicago (J.D., 1978). *Member:* DuPage County and Illinois State Bar Associations; State Bar of California; The District of Columbia Bar;

(This Listing Continued)

Illinois Creditors Bar Associations. **PRACTICE AREAS:** Banking Law; Bankruptcy; Commercial Law; Litigation; Secured Transactions; Probate. **Email:** joelastein@dlec.com

ALVIN J. HELFGOT, born Chicago, Illinois, February 16, 1946; admitted to bar, 1974, Illinois. *Education:* University of Illinois (B.A., 1967); Northwestern University (M.A., 1968); Loyola University (J.D., magna cum laude, 1974). *Member:* Illinois State Bar Association. **PRACTICE AREAS:** Banking Law; Real Estate; Corporate Law. **Email:** Helfgot@dlec.com

JAMES E. O'HALLORAN, III, born Evanston, Illinois, February 8, 1966; admitted to bar, 1992, Illinois, Wisconsin, U.S. District Court, Northern District of Illinois, U.S. District Court, Eastern District of Wisconsin and U.S. Court of Appeals, Seventh Circuit. *Education:* Tulane University of Louisiana (B.A., 1988); Marquette University (J.D., 1992). Member, Marquette University Law Review, 1991-1992. Special Assistant Attorney General, Illinois Attorney General. *Member:* Chicago and Illinois State Bar Associations; State Bar of Wisconsin. **PRACTICE AREAS:** Commercial Litigation; Insurance Coverage; Employment Litigation. **Email:** jeo@dlec.com

AARON B. ZARKOWSKY, born St. Louis, Missouri, June 7, 1970; admitted to bar, 1995, Illinois. *Education:* University of Illinois (B.A., 1992); DePaul University (J.D., 1995). Author, De Paul/LCA Journal of Art and Entertainment Law, Winter, 1994, Spring, 1995. *Member:* Chicago, Illinois State and American Bar Associations. **PRACTICE AREAS:** Corporate Law; Real Estate; Limited Liability Company Law; Partnership Law; Mergers and Acquisitions; Finance. **Email:** Zarkowsky@dlec.com

LEO G. AUBEL, born Endicott, New York, December 23, 1960; admitted to bar, 1986, Illinois and U.S. District Court, Northern District of Illinois; 1987, U.S. Court of Appeals, Seventh and Eighth Circuits. *Education:* Carnegie-Mellon University (B.F.A., cum laude, 1983); IIT/Chicago-Kent College of Law (J.D., 1986). Margaret Morrison Carnegie Fellowship for Study Abroad. University Scholar. Moot Court Society. *Member:* Chicago and Illinois State (Chair, Corporation and Securities Law Section Council, 1993-1994; Special Task Force on Vicarious Liability of Attorneys, 1994; Illinois Liaison to American Bar Association Committee on the Model Corporation Act, 1990-1994) Bar Associations. **PRACTICE AREAS:** Real Estate; Business Law; Guardianship and Conservatorship; Probate. **Email:** laubel@dlec.com

---

KAREN KAVANAGH MACK, born Arlington Heights, Illinois, April 1, 1973; admitted to bar, 1998, Illinois; U.S. District Court, Northern District of Illinois. *Education:* Loyola University (B.A., 1995; J.D., 1998). Alpha Sigma Nu. Member, National Moot Court Team. Recipient: CALI Legal Writing Award; Academic Honors Scholarship; Leadership & Service Award. Legal Writing Tutor. Appellate Advocacy Instructor, Loyola University School of Law, 1999—. Special Assistant Attorney General, State of Illinois, 2000. Former Staff Attorney and Hearing Officer, Illinois Pollution Control Board. *Member:* Chicago and American Bar Associations. **PRACTICE AREAS:** Commercial Litigation; Environmental Law; Condemnation. **Email:** Mack@dlec.com

MOYENDA MUTHARIKA KNAPP, born Dar es Salaam, Tanzania, September 20, 1969; admitted to bar, 1994, Massachusetts; 1996, District of Columbia; 1998, Illinois; 2001, U.S. District Court, Northern District of Illinois. *Education:* Dartmouth College (A.B., 1991); Boston University School of Law (J.D., 1994). Certified Arbitrator, Cook County Mandatory Arbitration Program. *Member:* Cook County, Chicago, Illinois State and American Bar Associations. **PRACTICE AREAS:** Commercial Litigation; Discrimination; First Amendment Law. **Email:** Knapp@dlec.com

DAVID J. BEN-DOV, born Skokie, Illinois, April 11, 1972; admitted to bar, 1998, Illinois and U.S. District, Northern District of Illinois; 1999, U.S. District Court, Central District of Illinois. *Education:* University of Illinois (B.A., 1994); Chicago-Kent College of Law, Illinois Institute of Technology (J.D., 1998). Member, Chicago-Kent Moot Court Honor Society. Assistant Illinois Attorney General, 2000-2003. *Member:* Chicago and Illinois State Bar Associations. **PRACTICE AREAS:** Commercial Litigation; Employment Discrimination; Eminent Domain; Litigation; Environmental Litigation. **Email:** Bendov@dlec.com

LEE E. FARBMAN, born New York, N.Y., January 29, 1963; admitted to bar, 1999, Illinois and U.S. District Court, District of Illinois. *Education:* Williams College (B.A., 1984); Northwestern University (J.D., 1999). Recipient, Judging Committee Kogan Legal Writing Award, Chicago Bar Association, 1999—. Executive Editor, Journal of Criminal Law and Criminology, 1998-1999. Editor-in-Chief, "The Young Lawyer," 2002-2004, American Bar Association's. Editorial Board Member "The Young Lawyer," 2000-2002, American Bar Association's. Student Editor, "Student Lawyer," 1988-1999, American Bar Association's. *Member:* Illinois State, Chicago and American Bar Associations. **REPORTED CASES:** Kurczaba v. Pollock, 742 N.E.2d 425 (Ill. App. Ct. 2000); Citizen's Bank-Illinois, N.A. v. American Nat'l Bank & Trust Co. of Chicago, 761 N.E.2d 275 (Ill. App. Ct. 2001), appeal den'd, 770 N.E.2d 217 (2002); Allen v. Berger,—N.E.2d—, 2002 WL 3189012 (Ill. App. Ct. Dec. 31, 2002). **PRACTICE AREAS:** Litigation. **Email:** farbman@dlec.com

COUNSEL

MARSHALL D. KROLICK, born Chicago, Illinois, August 9, 1938; admitted to bar, 1962, Illinois and U.S. District Court, Northern District of Illinois. *Education:* Drake University (B.A., 1959); Northwestern University (J.D., 1962). Assistant States Attorney, County of Cook, 1963-1965. Member, Zoning Board of Appeals, Village of Northbrook, Illinois, 1975-1997. *Member:* Chicago, Illinois State and American Bar Associations. **PRACTICE AREAS:** Real Estate; Construction Law; Corporate Law. **Email:** Krolick@dlec.com

ARTHUR J. SABIN, born Chicago, Illinois, September 21, 1930; admitted to bar, 1959, Illinois and U.S. District Court, Northern and Eastern Districts of Illinois. *Education:* Northwestern University (A.M., 1953); John Marshall Law School (J.D., with highest honors, 1959). Author: "All About Suing and Being Sued," Anderson, 1981; "Red Scare in Court," University of Penn. Press, 1993. *Member:* Illinois State and American Bar Associations. **PRACTICE AREAS:** Automobile Liability (80%); Personal Injury; Products Liability (20%); Professional Malpractice.

DI FRANCO & ASSOCIATES, P.C.

CHICAGO, ILLINOIS

(See Park Ridge)

Criminal Defense, Civil Litigation.

LAW OFFICES OF DEBRA DIMAGGIO

Established in 1997

161 NORTH CLARK STREET, SUITE 4700
CHICAGO, ILLINOIS 60601
Telephone: 312-364-0404
Facsimile: 312-364-0250
URL: http://www.setufree.net
Email: deb@dimaggio-law.com
URL: http://www.lawyers.com/dimaggiolaw

Family Law, including all phases of Matrimonial Litigation, Divorce Litigation, Divorce Taxation, Financial Law and Finances, Financial Discovery and Analysis, Tax Considerations and Retirement Benefits, Business Valuation, Corporate Holdings and Stock Plans, Negotiation and Mediation, Joint Parenting Agreements, Enforcement & Modification of Judgments, Disproportionate Awards, Custody and Visitation, Pre-nuptial and Post-nuptial Agreements, Parentage Actions, Adoption, UCCJA, Same-Sex Unions, Entertainment and Residential Real Estate.

FIRM PROFILE: 24 years experience concentrating in all aspects of family law. Clients include: Local Business Owners, CEO'S, Professional Athletes, Newscasters, Musicians, Artists, Homemakers, Medical Doctors, Architects, Attorneys, Pilots, Flight Attendants, Police Officers, Firemen, Traders and Accountants.

DEBRA DIMAGGIO, born Chicago, Illinois; admitted to bar, 1983, Illinois and U.S. District Court, Northern District of Illinois. *Education:* DePaul University (B.S., with highest honors, 1979; J.D., 1983).

LESLIE J. FINEBERG, born Miami, Florida; admitted to bar, 1991, Illinois. *Education:* American University (B.A., with honors, 1988); University of Miami (J.D., 1991). **PRACTICE AREAS:** Domestic Relations (90%); Residential Real Estate (8%); Mediation (2%). **Email:** lfineberg@dimaggio-law.com

MELISSA ANN BELL, born Elmhurst, Illinois, May 17, 1976; admitted to bar, 2001, Illinois and U.S. District Court, Northern District of Illinois. *Education:* Washington University (B.A., with honors, 1998); DePaul University (J.D., 2001). **PRACTICE AREAS:** Domestic Relations; Guardianship. **Email:** mbell@dimaggio-law.com

---

DI MONTE & LIZAK

CHICAGO, ILLINOIS

(See Park Ridge)

Construction and Real Estate Development (Zoning, Mechanics' Lien, etc.), Banking, Bankruptcy and Insolvency, Corporate Law, Estate Planning, Probate and Trust Litigation, Employment Law, Health Care Law, Civil Litigation Trials and Appeals.

DLA PIPER RUDNICK GRAY CARY US LLP

203 NORTH LA SALLE STREET, SUITE 1900
CHICAGO, ILLINOIS 60601-1293
Telephone: 312-368-4000
FAX: 312-236-7516
URL: http://www.dlapiper.com

Annapolis, Maryland Office: 60 West Street, Suite 401, 21401-2434. Telephone: 443-482-3830. FAX: 443-482-3848.

Baltimore, Maryland Office (Downtown): 111 South Calvert Street, Suite 1950, 21202-6174. Telephone: 410-580-3000. FAX: 410-580-3665.

Baltimore, Maryland Office (Mt. Washington): 6225 Smith Avenue, 21209-3600. Telephone: 410-580-3000. FAX: 410-580-3001.

Boston, Massachusetts Office: One International Place, 21st Floor, 02110-2613. Telephone: 617-406-6000. FAX: 617-406-6100.

Dallas, Texas Office: 1717 Main Street, Suite 4600, 75201-4605. Telephone: 214-743-4500. FAX: 214-743-4545.

Easton, Maryland Office: 117 Bay Street, 21601-2703. Telephone: 410-820-4460. FAX: 410-820- 4463.

Edison, New Jersey Office: Piper Rudnick LLP, A New Jersey Limited Liability Partnership, Robert A. Assuncao, Managing Partner, 379 Thornall Street, Eighth Floor, 08837-2226. Telephone: 732-590-1850. FAX: 732-590-1860.

La Jolla, California Office: 1200 Prospect Street, Suite 575, 92037. Telephone: 858-638-6806. Fax: 858-456-3075.

Las Vegas, Nevada Office: Hughes Center, 3960 Howard Hughes Parkway, Suite 400, 89109. Telephone: 702-737-3433. FAX: 702-737-1612.

Los Angeles, California Office (Century City): 1999 Avenue of the Stars, Fourth Floor, 90067-6022. Telephone: 310-595-3000. FAX: 310-595-3300.

Los Angeles, California Office (Downtown): 550 South Hope Street, Suite 2300, 90071-2631. Telephone: 213-330-7700. FAX: 213-330-7701.

New York, New York Office: 1251 Avenue of the Americas, 10020-1104. Telephone: 212-835-6000. FAX: 212-835-6001.

Paris, France Office: Cariddi, Mee, Rue, Association d'Avocats au Barreau de Paris, Correspondants de Piper Rudnick LLP, 12 rue de la Paix, 75002 Paris, France. Telephone: +33-1 42.61.57.71. FAX: +33-1 42.61.79.21.

Philadelphia, Pennsylvania Office: One Liberty Place, 1650 Market Street, Suite 4900, 19103. Telephone: 215-656-3300. FAX: 215-656-3301.

(This Listing Continued)

DLA PIPER RUDNICK GRAY CARY US LLP, Chicago—Continued

Raleigh, North Carolina Office: Six Forks Center I, 4700 Six Forks Road, Suite 200, 27609. Telephone: 919-786-2000. FAX: 919-786-2200.
Reston, Virginia Office: 1775 Wiehle Avenue, Suite 400, 20190-5159. Telephone: 703-773-4000. FAX: 703-773-5000.
San Francisco, California Office: 333 Market Street, Suite 3200, 94105-2150. Telephone: 415-659-7000. FAX: 415-659-7300.
Tampa, Florida Office: 101 East Kennedy Boulevard, Suite 2000, 33602-5149. Telephone: 813-229-2111. FAX: 813-229-1447.
Washington, District of Columbia Office: 1200 Nineteenth Street, NW, Main Reception on 7th Floor, 20036-2412. Telephone: 202-861-3900. FAX: 202-223-2085.

Advertising, Promotion and Trade Practices; Aerospace and Defense; Antitrust and Trade Regulation; Aviation; Bankruptcy and Business Reorganization; Biosciences; Business and Technology; Class Action Litigation; Communications; Construction; Copyrights; Corporate Governance and Protective Practices; Corporate and Securities; Domain Name Practice; Drug and Medical Device; Electronic Commerce and Privacy; Employee Benefits and Executive Compensation; Energy; Environmental; Federal Affairs and Legislative; Finance; Finance, Financial Services and Bankruptcy; Franchise and Distribution; Franchise and Distribution-International; Franchise and Distribution-Litigation; Franchise and Distribution-Technology; Government Contracts; Government Controversies; Governmental Affairs, Land Use and Development; HIPAA Privacy and Security; Health Care; Homeland Security; Information Technology; Insurance and Reinsurance; Insurance and Surety Litigation; Intellectual Property; International Commerce and Litigation; Iraq Reconstruction; Labor and Employment Law; Leasing; Legislative Financial Services; Litigation; Lodging and Timeshare; Medical Malpractice Defense; Mergers and Acquisitions; Multifamily Housing and Community Development Law; Nonprofit Organizations; Outsourcing; Patent Litigation; Patent Prosecution; Pesticide; Private Client Services; Product Liability and Toxic Torts; Professional Liability; Project Finance; Public Finance; REITs and Real Estate Securitization; Real Estate; Real Estate Finance; Securities Litigation; Sports Facilities Development; State Legislation and Public Policy; Tax; Tax Policy and Legislation; Technology Transfer; Trademark Litigation; Trademarks; Transportation; Venture Capital and Emerging Companies; White Collar; Workout Experience.

FIRM PROFILE: As an organization, we place the highest value on building close working relationships with our clients. To accomplish that, we offer you lawyers who are culturally attuned to the business demands and legal requirements of their countries, who have excellent legal skills, and who are totally committed to our client service ethic. Our clients say that this commitment is what really sets us apart.

We provide an extensive range of legal services through seven global practice groups:

Corporate and Finance - On the corporate and finance side, we operate significant transactional-based practices and serve not only some of the world's largest companies but numerous middle and upper-mid market clients. The firm is on the panels of a number of major banks and financial institutions and has a substantial bankruptcy and restructuring practice.

We are relationship-driven lawyers meeting the ongoing legal needs of our clients wherever they choose to do business. Operating across the US, Europe and Asia, we offer you 2,700 lawyers in 49 cities in 18 countries. We act for enterprises across the full spectrum of business, including local, national and multinational companies in a wide range of business sectors. Our clients range from single-owner startups to household name companies known worldwide.

Commercial - The group will be a market leader in European Public Private Partnerships (PPPs) and the provision of infrastructure and project finance services to sponsors and funders internationally. The group has lawyers who are particularly experienced in energy, sports, water, defense, healthcare and transportation, and is also recognized worldwide for its top-ranked franchise and distribution practice.

Human Resources - With more than 200 lawyers located in key jurisdictions around the world, our human resources and labor lawyers are equipped to handle both local employment issues and complex cross-border transactions.

Legislative and Regulatory - At the federal and state level in the US, and in the individual countries of Europe as well as the EU, our people understand the legislative and regulatory process. To the strengths of our team, which includes our chairman, Senator George J. Mitchell, we add the firm's alliance with The Cohen Group, the international business consulting firm.

Litigation - The group brings together more than 800 top litigators in the US, Europe and Asia and offers lawyers experienced in patent, class action, securities, antitrust, banking and finance, technology, telecommunications and insurance disputes.

Real Estate - With over 200 real estate lawyers in both the US and the UK, our real estate practice is one of the most highly ranked in the world, serving the needs of developers, corporations, retailers and investors.

Technology, Media and Communications (TMC) - This global practice represents a combination of market-leading teams in information technology/outsourcing, telecommunications, patent, trademark, copyright, media, e-business, sport, data protection and privacy. With over 420 lawyers globally, it will be one of the leading global TMC/TMT practices.

THERESA D. CROPPER, (admission pending). *Education:* Ohio Wesleyan University (B.A., 1975); American University (J.D., 1979). ***Email:*** theresa.cropper@dlapiper.com

PARTNERS

STANLEY J. ADELMAN, born 1942; admitted to bar, 1967, Illinois and U.S. District Court, Northern District of Illinois; 1968, Wisconsin; 1971, U.S. Court of Appeals, Seventh Circuit; 1972, U.S. Supreme Court; 1979, U.S. District Court, Eastern District of Wisconsin; 1984, U.S. Court of Appeals, Tenth Circuit; 1987, U.S. Court of Appeals, Federal Circuit; 1996, U.S. District Court, Western District of Wisconsin and U.S. District Court, District of Arizona. *Education:* University of Wisconsin (B.S., with honors, 1964; J.D., 1967). Order of the Coif; Phi Kappa Phi. Member, Wisconsin National Moot Court Team, 1965-1966. Editor, Wisconsin Law Review, 1965-1967. Member of Faculty, National Institute of Trial Advocacy, 1985—. Past President and Member, American Inns of Court (Markey-Wigmore). Member, The Lawyers Club of Chicago. *Member:* Chicago Council of Lawyers (Committees on: State Judiciary; Federal Judiciary; Ethics and Professional Responsibility). ***PRACTICE AREAS:*** Litigation; Trial Practice. ***Email:*** stanley.adelman@dlapiper.com

STEPHEN L. AGIN, born Chicago, Illinois, January 18, 1957; admitted to bar, 1983, Illinois. *Education:* North Central College (B.A., Political Science, cum laude, 1980); De-Paul University (J.D., 1983). *Member:* Chicago and American Bar Associations. ***PRACTICE AREAS:*** Litigation; Class Action; Securities Litigation. ***Email:*** stephen.agin@dlapiper.com

ROSS J. ALTMAN, born 1956; admitted to bar, 1982, Illinois. *Education:* University of Michigan (B.S., 1978); George Washington University (J.D., 1981). ***PRACTICE AREAS:*** Real Estate. ***Email:*** ross.altman@dlapiper.com

RICHARD W. ASHLEY III, born 1966; admitted to bar, 1993, Illinois; 1995, New York. *Education:* Syracuse University (B.A., 1988); John Marshall Law School (J.D., cum laude, 1993); Georgetown University (LL.M., Taxation, 1994). Order of John Marshall. Staff Editor, Law Review. *Member:* Chicago, New York State, Illinois State and American Bar Associations. ***PRACTICE AREAS:*** Employee Benefits; Executive Compensation; Taxation. ***Email:*** richard.ashley@dlapiper.com

ANNE C. AUTEN, born 1970; admitted to bar, 1995, Illinois. *Education:* University of Pennsylvania (B.A., magna cum laude, 1992); University of Michigan (J.D., cum laude, 1995). Phi Beta Kappa. *Member:* Chicago Bar Association. ***PRACTICE AREAS:*** Commercial Litigation. ***Email:*** anne.auten@dlapiper.com

JAMES L. BEARD, born 1954; admitted to bar, 1980, Illinois. *Education:* University of Illinois (B.S., 1976); Illinois Institute of Technology (J.D., with highest honors, 1980). Member, Illinois Institute of Technology Law Review, 1979-1980. ***PRACTICE AREAS:*** Real Estate (Property) Law; Business Law. ***Email:*** james.beard@dlapiper.com

MICHAEL L. BEN-ISVY, born 1968; admitted to bar, 1993, Illinois and U.S. District Court, Northern District of Illinois. *Education:* University of Michigan (B.A., with high distinction, 1990); Northwestern School of Law (J.D., 1993). Phi Beta Kappa. *Member:* Chicago, Illinois State and American Bar Associations. ***PRACTICE AREAS:*** Real Estate. ***Email:*** michael.ben-isvy@dlapiper.com

ERIC BERG, born 1965; admitted to bar, 1992, Illinois and U.S. District Court, Northern District of Illinois. *Education:* Yale University (B.A., 1987); Northwestern University (J.D., 1992). Associate, Gessler, Hughes & Socol, Ltd., 1992-1995; Associate, Stein, Ray & Conway, 1995-1998; General Counsel, Greater Chicago Food Depository, 1999-2004; General Counsel, America's Second Harvest - The Nation's Food Bank Network, 2004—. *Member:* Chicago, Illinois State and American Bar Associations; Nordic Law Club (President, 1996-1997). ***PRACTICE AREAS:*** Construction Law; Commercial Litigation. ***Email:*** eric.berg@dlapiper.com

ADAM T. BERKOFF, born 1969; admitted to bar, 1994, Wisconsin and Illinois. *Education:* University of Wisconsin, Madison (B.A., with honors, 1991); Marquette University Law School (J.D., 1994). Executive Editor, Marquette Law Review. Member: Iron Cross Society; Golden Key. *Member:* State Bar of Wisconsin. ***PRACTICE AREAS:*** Real Estate. ***Email:*** adam.berkoff@dlapiper.com

MARK A. BERKOFF, born 1961; admitted to bar, 1987, Illinois. *Education:* University of Wisconsin-Madison (B.A., with honors and distinction, 1983); University of Chicago (J.D., 1986). Phi Beta Kappa; Phi Kappa Phi. ***PRACTICE AREAS:*** Bankruptcy Law; Litigation; Creditors Rights; Trial Practice. ***Email:*** mark.berkoff@dlapiper.com

DANIEL S. BRENNAN, born 1965; admitted to bar, 1990, Illinois; 1991, U.S. District Court, Northern District of Illinois and U.S. District Court, Western District of Wisconsin; 2001, U.S. Court of Federal Claims. *Education:* University of Notre Dame (B.A., cum laude, 1986); Georgetown University Law Center (J.D., cum laude, 1990). *Member:* Chicago, Illinois State and American (Forum on the Construction Industry) Bar Associations; Society of Illinois Construction Attorneys; American Association of Healthcare. ***PRACTICE AREAS:*** Construction; Litigation. ***Email:*** daniel.brennan@dlapiper.com

MICHAEL G. BRENNAN, born 1952; admitted to bar, 1979, Illinois. *Education:* Universite Catholique de l'Ouest, Angers, France; University of Notre Dame (B.A., with high honors, 1974); Graduate Institute of International Studies, Geneva, Switzerland; De-Paul University College of Law (J.D., 1979). Member, De Paul International Moot Court. Founding Chairman of Franchising and Distribution Law Subcommittee, International Young Lawyers Association; Former Vice Chairman of Intellectual Property Committee, Inter-Pacific Bar Association; Chairman of International Franchising Committee, International Bar Association. Listed in International Who's Who of Franchise Lawyers. ***LANGUAGES:*** French. ***PRACTICE AREAS:*** Domestic and International Business Law; Franchising and Licensing. ***Email:*** michael.brennan@dlapiper.com

LAURENCE R. BRONSKA, born 1962; admitted to bar, 1987, Illinois. *Education:* The University of Michigan (B.B.A., 1984); Boston University (J.D., 1987). *Member:* Chicago Bar Association. ***PRACTICE AREAS:*** Corporate; Securities. ***Email:*** laurence.bronska@dlapiper.com

HAL M. BROWN, born 1942; admitted to bar, 1967, Illinois. *Education:* Northwestern University (B.S., B.A., 1964; J.D., cum laude, 1967). Order of the Coif. ***PRACTICE AREAS:*** Mergers and Acquisitions; Securities Law; Public and Private Securities Offerings; Business Law; Real Estate; Capital Markets. ***Email:*** hal.brown@dlapiper.com

CATHERINE M. BURKHARDT, born 1971; admitted to bar, 1993, Illinois. *Education:* College of William & Mary (B.S., 1990); University of Virginia (J.D., 1993). [Lt., U.S. Navy, JAGC, 1993-1997]. ***PRACTICE AREAS:*** Litigation; Franchise and Distribution. ***Email:*** catherine.burkhardt@dlapiper.com

PETER C. B. BYNOE, born 1951; admitted to bar, 1982, Illinois. *Education:* Harvard University (B.A., 1972; J.D., 1976); Business School, Harvard University (M.B.A., 1976). Board of Directors/Member, Chairman, Commission on Chicago Historical and Architectural Landmarks, 1985-1997. Chairman, Eecutive Committee, Goodman Theatre, 1984—.

(This Listing Continued)

Director, Illinois Sports Facilities Authority, 1993-2005. Trustee, Rush-Presbyterian-St. Luke's Hospital, 1993—. Director, Uniroyal Technology Corporation, 1992-2002. Overseer, Harvard University, 1993-2002. Director: Economic Club, 1993-2000; Chicago Council on Foreign Relations, 1995-2000; Trans Africa Forum, 1995-1997. Chairman, Chicago Planning and Development Commission, 1997-2004. Director: JACOR Communications, Inc., 1997-1999; Blue Chip Broadcasting, 1999-2002; divine interVentures, inc., 2000-2001. Member: Chicago Art Institute Alliance; Commercial Club of Chicago, 1997-2000. Commercial Real Estate Broker, 1982. *Member:* The Lawyers Club of Chicago. ***TRANSACTIONS:*** Negotiated new stadium/arena deals for the Cincinnati Reds and Bengals, Miami Heat, Milwaukee Brewers, Washington Redskins, Columbus Blue Jackets, Chicago White Sox, Atlanta Braves and the Denver Nuggets. ***PRACTICE AREAS:*** Sports; Entertainment; Telecommunications. ***Email:*** peter.bynoe@dlapiper.com

WILLIAM J. CAMPBELL, JR., born 1948; admitted to bar, 1973, Illinois and U.S. District Court, Northern District of Illinois; 1974, U.S. Court of Appeals, Seventh Circuit, California and U.S. District Court, Central District of California; 1976, U.S. Court of Appeals, District of Columbia Circuit and U.S. Court of Military Appeals; 1978, U.S. Supreme Court; 1979, U.S. District Court, Central District of Illinois; 1980, U.S. Courts of Appeals, Second, Fifth and Ninth Circuits; 1983, U.S. District Court, Northern District of California. *Education:* University of Chicago (B.A., 1970); University of Michigan (J.D., 1973). [Judge Advocate General's Corps, U.S. Naval Reserve, 1970-1982, Active Duty, 1973-1976; Lt.]. ***PRACTICE AREAS:*** Litigation; Trial Practice. ***Email:*** william.campbell@dlapiper.com

CATHERINE J. CASEY, born 1967; admitted to bar, 1993, Illinois. *Education:* Princeton University (B.A., 1989); Georgetown University (J.D., 1993). ***PRACTICE AREAS:*** Litigation. ***Email:*** catherine.casey@dlapiper.com

DANIELLE MELTZER CASSEL, born 1970; admitted to bar, 1996, Illinois. *Education:* Yale University (B.A., summa cum laude, 1992) Phi Beta Kappa; John F. Kennedy School of Government at Harvard University (M.A., 1996) Harvard University (J.D., cum laude, 1996). ***PRACTICE AREAS:*** Real Estate; Zoning and Land Use; Affordable Housing. ***Email:*** danielle.cassel@dlapiper.com

STEVEN J. CHRISTENHOLZ, born 1969; admitted to bar, 1994, Illinois. *Education:* University of Illinois (B.S., with honors in Finance, 1991); DePaul University (M.B.A., with distinction, 1994; J.D., 1994). *Member:* Chicago and Illinois State Bar Associations. ***PRACTICE AREAS:*** Finance. ***Email:*** steven.christenholz@dlapiper.com

FREDRIC A. COHEN, born 1960; admitted to bar, 1988, Illinois; U.S. Supreme Court; U.S. Court of Appeals, First, Sixth, Seventh and Tenth Circuits; U.S. District Court, Northern, Central and Southern Districts of Illinois, Western District of Michigan; U.S. District Court, District of Colorado. *Education:* University of Chicago; Hebrew University of Jerusalem (B.S. Sc., 1985); DePaul University (J.D., with honors, 1988). Member: Order of Barristers. ***LANGUAGES:*** Hebrew. ***PRACTICE AREAS:*** Franchise Litigation; Commercial Litigation; Trial Practice. ***Email:*** fredric.cohen@dlapiper.com

LOUIS S. COHEN, born 1956; admitted to bar, 1981, Illinois. *Education:* Stanford University (B.A., 1978); Northwestern University (J.D., 1981). ***PRACTICE AREAS:*** Real Estate Development and Finance; Sports Law. ***Email:*** louis.cohen@dlapiper.com

MERLE TEITELBAUM COWIN, born 1954; admitted to bar, 1978, Illinois. *Education:* The Ohio State University (B.A., summa cum laude, 1974); Northwestern University (J.D., cum laude, 1978). Order of the Coif. Member, Journal of Criminal Law and Criminology, 1976-1978. *Member:* Chicago and Illinois State Bar Associations. ***PRACTICE AREAS:*** Real Estate Development Law; Real Estate Finance; Workouts; Banking Law. ***Email:*** merle.cowin@dlapiper.com

JOHN T. J. CUSACK, born 1958; admitted to bar, 1984, New York; 1986, Illinois. *Education:* Drew University (B.S., magna cum laude, 1980); George Washington University (J.D., 1983). ***PRACTICE AREAS:*** Real Estate Development Law; Finance Law; Real Estate Finance; Business Law; Real Estate Capital Markets. ***Email:*** john.cusack@dlapiper.com

GREGORY R. A. DAHLGREN, born 1957; admitted to bar, 1982, Illinois. *Education:* University of Illinois (B.S., with highest honors, 1979); University of Pennsylvania (J.D., 1982). Beta Gamma Sigma. Certified Public Accountant, Illinois, 1979. ***PRACTICE AREAS:*** Commercial Law; Taxation (Federal, State and Local) Law; Real Estate; Capital Markets. ***Email:*** gregory.dahlgren@dlapiper.com

ALAN S. DALINKA, born 1968; admitted to bar, 1993, Illinois and U.S. District Court, Central and Northern Districts of Illinois; 1994, U.S. Court of Appeals, Seventh Circuit; 1997, U.S. Court of Appeals, Sixth Circuit; 1998, Trial Bar, Northern District of Illinois; 1999, U.S. District Court, Eastern District of Wisconsin; 2000, U.S. District Court, Western District of Wisconsin; U.S. Court of Appeals, Federal Circuit; 2001, U.S. District Court, District of Colorado; 2002, U.S. Court of Appeals, Ninth Circuit; 2005, U.S. Supreme Court. *Education:* Northwestern University (B.S., 1989); Northwestern University (J.D., 1993). Member, Board of Directors, Lawyers For the Creative Arts, 1999—; Treasurer, 2003—. *Member:* Chicago Bar Association. ***PRACTICE AREAS:*** Intellectual Property Litigation; Trade Secrets. ***Email:*** alan.dalinka@dlapiper.com

BYRON S. DELMAN, born January 28, 1937; admitted to bar, 1961, Illinois and Indiana. *Education:* Northwestern University (B.A., with honors, 1958; J.D., 1961). ***PRACTICE AREAS:*** Corporate Finance Law. ***Email:*** byron.delman@dlapiper.com

PETER J. DONOGHUE, born 1964; admitted to bar, 1991, Illinois. *Education:* Georgetown University (B.A., 1986); Duke University (J.D., 1991). Phi Beta Kappa; Order of the Coif. *Member:* Chicago and American Bar Associations. ***PRACTICE AREAS:*** Commercial Litigation. ***Email:*** peter.donoghue@dlapiper.com

BRIAN K. DOYLE, born 1964; admitted to bar, 1993, Illinois. *Education:* Knox College (B.A., 1986); Loyola University (J.D., 1993). ***LANGUAGES:*** German. ***PRACTICE AREAS:*** Real Estate; Corporate Transactions; Bankruptcy. ***Email:*** brian.doyle@dlapiper.com

MARY KAY GARA DREYFUS, born 1965; admitted to bar, 1995, Illinois. *Education:* University of Illinois at Urbana-Champaign (B.F.A., highest honors, 1987); John Marshall Law School (J.D., cum laude, 1995). Bronze Tablet Scholar; Order of John Marshall; Staff Editor, John Marshall Law Review, 1993-1995. *Member:* Chicago and American Bar Associations. ***PRACTICE AREAS:*** General Corporate; Mergers and Acquisitions; Securities. ***Email:*** marykay.dreyfus@dlapiper.com

(This Listing Continued)

JANICE L. DUBAN, born 1951; admitted to bar, 1991, Illinois. *Education:* University of California at Los Angeles (B.A., 1974); Loyola University of Chicago (J.D., magna cum laude, 1991). Recipient, West Publishing Award for Outstanding Scholastic Achievement, 1990-1991. ***PRACTICE AREAS:*** Bankruptcy Law; Commercial Litigation. ***Email:*** janice.duban@dlapiper.com

ELIZABETH R. BACON EHLERS, admitted to bar, 1989, Illinois. *Education:* The College of Wooster (B.A., 1985) with Independent Thesis Honors; Loyola University School of Law (J.D., 1989) with Academic Achievement Award. Co-Chair: 1996 National Conference of Women Litigators. *Member:* American Bar Association (Member: Business Torts, Product Liability and Litigation Management Committees). ***PRACTICE AREAS:*** Trial Practice; Commercial Litigation; Electronic Commerce; Internet Law; Business Law; Securities; Health Care; Products Liability. ***Email:*** elizabeth.ehlers@dlapiper.com

STEVEN E. EHRLICH, born 1963; admitted to bar, 1990, Illinois. *Education:* University of Illinois (B.S., in Accountancy with honors, 1985; J.D., cum laude, 1990). Certified Public Accountant, Illinois, 1985. ***Email:*** steven.ehrlich@dlapiper.com

MICHAEL H. ELAM, born 1954; admitted to bar, 1980, Indiana and Illinois. *Education:* Macalester College (B.A., 1976); Colorado College; Universite Libre de Bruxelles, Brussels, Belgium; Indiana University (J.D., 1980). Phi Beta Kappa. Associate Instructor, Indiana University School of Law, 1980. Physical Scientist, U.S. EPA, 1976. Attorney, Senior Attorney, Branch Chief, Deputy Regional Counsel, Region V, U.S. EPA, Chicago, Illinois, 1989-1998. Special Assistant AA for Enforcement, U.S. EPA, Washington, D.C. (Co-Chairman, Environmental Law Practice Group). ***LANGUAGES:*** French. ***PRACTICE AREAS:*** Environmental; Natural Resources; Real Estate Transactions; Corporate; Litigation; International. ***Email:*** michael.elam@dlapiper.com

LESLI L. MANN FALK, born 1966; admitted to bar, 1999, Illinois. *Education:* University of Kansas (B.S., 1989); Vanderbilt University (J.D., 1993). Member, Vanderbilt University Journal of Transnational Law. *Member:* Illinois State and American Bar Associations. ***PRACTICE AREAS:*** Commercial Real Estate. ***Email:*** lesli.falk@dlapiper.com

MARK I. FELDMAN, born 1950; admitted to bar, 1974, Illinois, U.S. District Court, Northern District of Illinois and U.S. Court of Appeals, Seventh and Federal Circuits; registered to practice before U.S. Patent and Trademark Office. *Education:* University of Illinois (B.S.I.E., with high honors, 1971); Georgetown University (J.D., 1974). Tau Beta Pi; Phi Eta Sigma. Listed in: International Who's Who of Trademark Lawyers, 2003-2004; Guide to the World's Leading Trade Mark Practitioners, 2002-2004; Leading Lawyers, 2003-2004; Illinois Super Lawyers, 2005; 2005 Who's Legal: The International Who's Who of Business Lawyers. *Member:* Intellectual Property Law Association of Chicago (President 2005-2006; President-Elect, 2004-2005; Board of Managers, 1995-1997; Appointed to the National Public Advisory Committee for Trademark Affairs, 1997-2000); American Intellectual Property Law Association (Chairman, Franchise Law Committee, 1995-1997). ***PRACTICE AREAS:*** Intellectual Property Law. ***Email:*** mark.feldman@dlapiper.com

LAWRENCE J. FEY, born 1957; admitted to bar, 1986, Illinois. *Education:* University of Chicago (B.A., 1979); Washington University (J.D., 1986). Order of the Coif. Associate Editor, Washington University Law Quarterly, 1985-1986. ***PRACTICE AREAS:*** Real Estate (Property) Law. ***Email:*** lawrence.fey@dlapiper.com

MICHAEL B. FISCHER, born 1949; admitted to bar, 1972, Illinois and U.S. Court of Appeals, Seventh Circuit. *Education:* Syracuse University (B.A., 1969); New York University (J.D., 1972). Author, "Selection of the Business Entity, Organizing and Advising Illinois Businesses," (I.I.C.L.E., 1995). ***PRACTICE AREAS:*** Acquisitions and Mergers; Structured Finance; Hotel and Resort Law; Capital Formation; Electronic Commerce. ***Email:*** michael.fischer@dlapiper.com

HAROLD W. FRANCKE, born 1952; admitted to bar, 1979, Illinois and U.S. District Court, Northern District of Illinois. *Education:* University of Chicago (B.A., with special honors, 1974); University of Illinois (J.D., 1979). Member, National Moot Court Team. ***PRACTICE AREAS:*** General Real Estate; Land Use; Annexation; Zoning; Public Sector Financing; Real Estate Litigation. ***Email:*** harold.francke@dlapiper.com

ELIZABETH H. FRIEDGUT, born 1954; admitted to bar, 1981, District of Columbia; 1989, Illinois. *Education:* Middlebury College (B.A., cum laude, 1976); Washington University School of Law (J.D., 1980). With United States Department of Housing and Urban Development, Washington, D.C., 1980-1987. ***PRACTICE AREAS:*** Housing and Urban Development Law; Real Estate (Property) Law. ***Email:*** elizabeth.friedgut@dlapiper.com

WILLIAM M. GANTZ, born 1964; admitted to bar, 1990, Illinois and U.S. District Court, Northern District of Illinois; 1995, U.S. District Court, Eastern District of Wisconsin and Federal Trial Bar; 2000, U.S. District Court, Northern District of Indiana; 2002, U.S. Court of Appeals, Seventh Circuit. *Education:* The University of Chicago (B.A., 1987); The Ohio State University College of Law (J.D., 1990). *Member:* Illinois State Bar Association. ***PRACTICE AREAS:*** Trial Practice; Products Liability; Commercial Litigation; Construction Litigation; Mass Torts; Class Actions; Transportation; Trucking; Warranty; Toxic Torts; Intentional Torts; Professional Liability; Directors and Officers Liability; Medical Negligence; Risk Management; Insurance; Gaming Litigation; Intellectual Property. ***Email:*** william.gantz@dlapiper.com

DEBORAH L. GERSH, admitted to bar, 1983, Illinois. *Education:* Northwestern University (B.A., 1980); University of Madrid, Madrid, Spain; George Washington University (J.D., honors, 1983). Phi Beta Kappa. ***PRACTICE AREAS:*** Venture Capital; Technology Law; Health Care Law; Corporate Law. ***Email:*** deborah.gersh@dlapiper.com

MARK A. GERSHON, born 1961; admitted to bar, 1986, Illinois. *Education:* Northwestern University (B.S., 1983; J.D., 1986). Co-Author: *Illinois Zoning, Eminent Domain and Land Use Manual* (Lexis Law Publishing 1997) and Chapter 12, *Land Use and Development Controls* in Basic Real Estate Volume II, I.I.C.L.E. ***PRACTICE AREAS:*** Land Use Law; Real Estate Development Law; Electric Power; Energy Project Development; Land Annexation; Environmental Land Use; Zoning Law; Public Authority Finance. ***Email:*** mark.gershon@dlapiper.com

(This Listing Continued)

DLA PIPER RUDNICK GRAY CARY US LLP, Chicago—Continued

THOMAS F. GESELBRACHT, admitted to bar, 1979, Illinois and U.S. District Court, Northern District of Illinois; 1987, U.S. Court of Appeals, Seventh Circuit; 1998, U.S. District Court, District of Colorado. *Education:* Marquette University (A.B., 1976); University of Chicago (J.D., 1979). Phi Beta Kappa. Law Clerk to Justice Seymour Simon, Illinois Supreme Court, 1979-1981. Principal Author, *Illinois Zoning, Eminent Domain and Land Use Manual* Lexis Law Publishing, 1997. Co-Author, *Condemnation of Property: Practice and Strategies for Winning Just Compensation,* Wiley Law Publication, 1994. Member, Illinois Supreme Court Committee on Character and Fitness, 1985-1996; Vice-Chair, 1996; Director, Chicago Lawyers Committee for Civil Rights Under Law, Inc., 1985—; Secretary-Treasurer, 1996; Vice-Chair, 1997; Chair, 1998. ***PRACTICE AREAS:*** Litigation; Trial Practice; Real Estate. ***Email:*** thomas.geselbracht@dlapiper.com

ALLEN J. GINSBURG, (P.C.), born 1944; admitted to bar, 1969, Illinois; 1973, U.S. Tax Court. *Education:* Northwestern University (B.S., 1965; J.D., cum laude, 1968). Certified Public Accountant, Illinois, 1966. ***PRACTICE AREAS:*** Franchise Law; Franchise Relations Law; Acquisitions, Divestitures and Mergers Law; Corporate Law; Hotel and Resort Law; Resort Timeshares. ***Email:*** allen.ginsburg@dlapiper.com

DAVID GLICKSTEIN, born 1941; admitted to bar, 1967, Illinois and California. *Education:* University of Wisconsin (B.B.A., with honors, 1963); Northwestern University School of Law (J.D., 1966). Order of the Coif. Member, Board of Editors, Northwestern University Law Review, 1965-1966. Teaching Fellow, Stanford University School of Law, 1966-1967. *Member:* Chicago Bar Association; American College of Real Estate Lawyers. ***PRACTICE AREAS:*** Real Estate Law. ***Email:*** david.glickstein@dlapiper.com

LARRY S. GOLDBERG, born 1947; admitted to bar, 1971, Illinois. *Education:* Michigan State University (B.A., 1968); University of Illinois (J.D., 1971). Member, University of Illinois Law Forum, 1969-1971. *Member:* Chicago and American Bar Associations. ***PRACTICE AREAS:*** Corporate Law; Mergers and Acquisitions. ***Email:*** larry.goldberg@dlapiper.com

EDWARD S. GOLDMAN, born 1961; admitted to bar, 1986, Illinois. *Education:* University of Michigan (B.B.A., 1983); University of Chicago (J.D., 1986). Phi Beta Kappa; Beta Alpha Psi; Beta Gamma Sigma; Order of the Coif. Staff Member, University of Chicago Law Review, 1985-1986. Certified Public Accountant, Illinois, 1983. ***PRACTICE AREAS:*** Real Estate (Property) Law; Commercial Leasing Law. ***Email:*** edward.goldman@dlapiper.com

ROBERT H. GOLDMAN, born 1945; admitted to bar, 1969, Illinois and U.S. District Court, Northern District of Illinois. *Education:* University of Michigan (B.A., 1966; J.D., 1969). ***PRACTICE AREAS:*** Real Estate (Property) Law; Real Estate Development Law. ***Email:*** robert.goldman@dlapiper.com

STEPHEN M. GORDON, born 1962; admitted to bar, 1988, Illinois. *Education:* Michigan State University (M.B.A., 1986; B.A., with high honors, 1984); University of Michigan (J.D., cum laude, 1988). Phi Kappa Phi; Beta Alpha Psi; Beta Gamma Sigma. Certified Public Accountant, Illinois, 1985. ***PRACTICE AREAS:*** Taxation; REITS; Real Estate Securitization; Corporate Law; Partnership Law; Real Estate; Capital Markets. ***Email:*** stephen.gordon@dlapiper.com

SHEPARD GOULD, born 1956; admitted to bar, 1980, Illinois. *Education:* University of Illinois (B.A., 1977; J.D., magna cum laude, 1980). Phi Beta Kappa; Order of the Coif. ***PRACTICE AREAS:*** Real Estate (Property) Law. ***Email:*** shepard.gould@dlapiper.com

ROSS GREEN, born 1958; admitted to bar, 1984, Illinois. *Education:* Harvard University (B.A., cum laude, 1980); University of Chicago (J.D., 1984). ***PRACTICE AREAS:*** Real Estate (Property) Law; Real Estate Development Law. ***Email:*** ross.green@dlapiper.com

DAVID V. HALL, born 1966; admitted to bar, 1991, Illinois and U.S. District Court, Northern District of Illinois. *Education:* University of Southern California (J.D., 1991). ***PRACTICE AREAS:*** Real Estate Law. ***Email:*** david.hall@dlapiper.com

ERROL R. HALPERIN, born 1941; admitted to bar, 1968, Illinois; 1972, U.S. Tax Court. *Education:* DePaul University (B.S., 1964; J.D., 1967); New York University (LL.M. in Taxation, 1968). Member, De Paul Law Review, 1966-1967. Assistant Branch Chief, Legislation and Regulations Division, Office of the Chief Counsel, Internal Revenue Service, 1968-1972. Legislation Attorney, Joint Committee on Taxation, U.S. Congress, 1977-1979. ***PRACTICE AREAS:*** Corporate Mergers; Mergers, Acquisitions and Divestitures; Taxation (Federal, State and Local) Law; Real Estate (Property) Law; Real Estate Investment Trusts; Structuring and Taxation of International Transactions; Real Estate; Capital Markets. ***Email:*** errol.halperin@dlapiper.com

TIMOTHY S. HARRIS, born 1960; admitted to bar, 1988, Illinois and U.S. District Court, Northern District of Illinois; 1989, U.S. Court of Appeals, Seventh Circuit. *Education:* University of Toledo (B.A., magna cum laude, 1982); University of North Carolina (M.A., 1986); Ohio State University (J.D., with honors, 1988). Phi Kappa Phi; Phi Alpha Theta; Order of the Coif. Recipient, American Jurisprudence Award in Constitutional Law. Articles Editor, Ohio State Law Journal, 1987-1988. Author: "Protecting Personal Guarantees of Small Corporations' Leases," BOMA Newsletter, December, 1993. *Member:* Chicago Bar Association. ***REPORTED CASES:*** Harris v. Wally's World of Fun, Ltd., 279 Ill. App. 3d 61, 664 N.E. 2d 324 (1st Dist. 1996); LaSalle Nat'l Bank v. Skidmore, Owings & Merrill, 262 Ill. App. 3d 899, 635 N.E. 2d 564 (1st Dist. 1994); Delaney Elec. Co., Inc. v. Schiessle, 235 Ill. App. 3d 258, 601 N.E. 2d 978 (1st Dist. 1992). ***PRACTICE AREAS:*** Bankruptcy Litigation; Commercial Litigation; Real Estate Litigation. ***Email:*** timothy.harris@dlapiper.com

GREGORY W. HAYES, born 1970; admitted to bar, 1996, Illinois. *Education:* Northern Michigan University (B.S., summa cum laude, 1993); University of Michigan Law School (J.D., cum laude, 1996); University of Chicago (M.B.A., 2002). Member, Michigan Law Review, 1994-1996. *Member:* Chicago, Illinois State and American Bar Associations. ***PRACTICE AREAS:*** Corporate; Securities; Real Estate; Capital Markets. ***Email:*** gregory.hayes@dlapiper.com

STUART HERSHMAN, born 1959; admitted to bar, 1984, Illinois and U.S. District Court, Northern District of Illinois. *Education:* University of Michigan (B.A., with high distinction, 1981; J.D., cum laude, 1984). Recipient: Regents-Alumni Scholarship; Angell Scholarship. ***LANGUAGES:*** Hebrew. ***PRACTICE AREAS:*** Franchise Law; Antitrust Law; Trade Regulation. ***Email:*** stuart.hershman@dlapiper.com

JOHN H. HEUBERGER, born 1948; admitted to bar, 1974, Florida; 1977, Illinois and U.S. District Court, Northern District of Illinois. *Education:* Northern Illinois University (B.S., 1970); University of Miami (J.D., 1973); Georgetown University Law Center (LL.M., Taxation, 1976). Certified Public Accountant, Illinois, 1971. Attorney, Division of Corporation Finance, Securities and Exchange Commission, 1974-1976. Trustee, Village of Deerfield, Illinois, 1993-2001. ***PRACTICE AREAS:*** Business Law; Public/Private Partnerships; Securities Law. ***Email:*** john.heuberger@dlapiper.com

JENNIFER D. HOMER, born 1965; admitted to bar, 1995, Illinois. *Education:* Washington University (B.A., 1987; LL.M. in Taxation, 1996); Drake University (J.D., 1995). *Member:* Chicago, Illinois State and American Bar Associations. ***LANGUAGES:*** French. ***PRACTICE AREAS:*** Corporate Finance; Banking Law; Secured Lending; Aircraft Finance and Leasing. ***Email:*** jennifer.homer@dlapiper.com

PAUL HOMER, (P.C.), born 1923; admitted to bar, 1951, Illinois. *Education:* University of Chicago (B.A., 1947); Northwestern University (J.D., 1951). Order of the Coif. Note Editor, Northwestern Law Review, 1950-1951. ***PRACTICE AREAS:*** Business Law; Real Estate Law; General Litigation. ***Email:*** paul.homer@dlapiper.com

LEROY G. INSKEEP, born 1948; admitted to bar, 1973, Illinois and U.S. District Court, Northern District of Illinois. *Education:* University of Illinois (B.S., 1970; J.D., 1973). Order of the Coif. Member and Editor, University of Illinois Law Review, 1972-1973. ***PRACTICE AREAS:*** Bankruptcy Law; Debtor Creditor Law; Litigation; Trial Practice. ***Email:*** leroy.inskeep@dlapiper.com

SAMUEL B. ISAACSON, born 1957; admitted to bar, 1982, Pennsylvania; 1983, Illinois; 1985, District of Columbia. *Education:* Dickinson College (B.A., magna cum laude, 1979; J.D., 1982). Phi Beta Kappa. Member: Appellate Moot Court Board, 1981-1982. *Member:* Chicago, Illinois State and American (Member, Litigation Section) Bar Associations; Defense Research Institute; Federation of Insurance and Corporate Counsel; The Lawyer's Club of the City of Chicago. ***PRACTICE AREAS:*** Commercial Litigation; Products Liability. ***Email:*** samuel.isaacson@dlapiper.com

J. KENNETH JOUNG, born 1969; admitted to bar, 1994, Illinois. *Education:* Dartmouth College (A.B., magna cum laude, 1991); Northwestern University (J.D., 1994); Illinois Institute of Technology (B.S., Chem. E., with high honors, 1997). Phi Beta Kappa; Tau Beta Pi. ***PRACTICE AREAS:*** Intellectual Property. ***Email:*** ken.joung@dlapiper.com

HOWARD E. KANE, born 1927; admitted to bar, 1952, Illinois. *Education:* University of Michigan (B.B.A., 1949); Northwestern University (J.D., 1952). Order of the Coif. Editor, Illinois Law Review, 1951-1952. *Member:* American College of Real Estate Lawyers (former Governor); Anglo-American Real Property Institute (former Chairman). ***PRACTICE AREAS:*** Real Estate (Property) Law; Real Estate Development Law; Commercial and Transactional Law. ***Email:*** howard.kane@dlapiper.com

JASON N. KAPLAN, born 1970; admitted to bar, 1995, Illinois and U.S. District Court, Northern District of Illinois. *Education:* University of Texas, Austin (B.B.A., 1992); Chicago-Kent College of Law, Illinois Institute of Technology (J.D., 1995). Recipient, Ramsey-Burke Academic Scholarship. *Member:* Chicago and American Bar Associations. ***PRACTICE AREAS:*** Finance; Workouts; Debt Restructuring; Corporate. ***Email:*** jason.kaplan@dlapiper.com

C. OLIVIA KEATING, born 1963; admitted to bar, 1994, Illinois. *Education:* University of Illinois (B.A., 1985); Loyola University School of Law (J.D., 1994). ***PRACTICE AREAS:*** Finance; Real Estate Finance; Real Estate; Bankruptcy. ***Email:*** olivia.keating@dlapiper.com

SANDRA Y. KELLMAN, born 1952; admitted to bar, 1977, Illinois. *Education:* University of Illinois (B.A., with high honors, 1973); Northwestern University (J.D., cum laude, 1977). Note and Comment Editor, Journal of Criminal Law and Criminology, 1976-1977. ***PRACTICE AREAS:*** Real Estate; Property Law; Real Estate Development; Landlord and Tenant Law; Project Finance; Power Plant Development; Hospitality Industry. ***Email:*** sandra.kellman@dlapiper.com

MICHAEL L. KENAGA, born 1957; admitted to bar, 1990, Illinois; registered to practice before U.S. Patent and Trademark Office. *Education:* DeVry Institute (B.E.E.T., 1979); John Marshall Law School (J.D., 1989). *Member:* Chicago (Chairman, IP Committee, 2004-2005; Vice Chairman, Patent Trademark & Copyright Committee, 2003-2004; Chairman, Patent Subcommittee, 2001-2002) and American Bar Associations; Intellectual Property Law Association of Chicago (Treasurer, 1997-1999; Chairman, Foreign Patent Committee, 1996-1997, Vice Chairman, 1994-1996); American Intellectual Property Law Association; Licensing Executives Society. ***PRACTICE AREAS:*** Intellectual Property Law. ***Email:*** michael.kenaga@dlapiper.com

JONATHAN D. KING, born 1964; admitted to bar, 1989, Illinois. *Education:* University of Chicago (A.B., 1986); Northwestern University School of Law (J.D., 1989). Adjunct Professor, Trial Advocacy, Northwestern University School of Law, 1992-2000. ***PRACTICE AREAS:*** Litigation; White Collar Criminal Defense. ***Email:*** jonathan.king@dlapiper.com

RICHARD F. KLAWITER, born 1963; admitted to bar, 1990, Illinois. *Education:* St. Olaf College (B.A., 1985); Harvard University (M.A., 1987); Stanford Law School (J.D., 1990). Associate Editor, Stanford Law Review. ***LANGUAGES:*** Spanish. ***PRACTICE AREAS:*** Real Estate. ***Email:*** richard.klawiter@dlapiper.com

ROBERT W. KLEINMAN, born 1946; admitted to bar, 1971, Illinois. *Education:* University of Pennsylvania (B.S., 1968); Boston University (J.D., 1971). Note Editor, Boston University Law Review, 1970. ***PRACTICE AREAS:*** Finance. ***Email:*** robert.kleinman@dlapiper.com

IAN S. KOPELMAN, born 1949; admitted to bar, 1974, Illinois, U.S. District Court, Northern District of Illinois and U.S. Tax Court. *Education:* Knox College (B.A., cum laude, 1971); University of Iowa (J.D., with distinction, 1974). Pi Sigma Alpha; Omicron Delta Kappa; Phi Delta Phi. Listed in: "Who's Who in American Law; Who's Who in America, 2000. Author of numerous papers including: Chapter in book, "The Problem with

(This Listing Continued)

QDROs," Profit Sharing Council Journal p. 13, Sept./Oct., 1995; "Unemployment Compensation Amendments of 1992 New Rollover and Withholding Plans," Trusts & Estates, p. 8, November, 1992; "Section 410 (b) Minimum Coverage Rules," Profit Sharing Handbook, February, 1990; "Coping With 410 (b)," Profit Sharing Council Journal, July 1988; "New Limitations Applicable to Defined Contribution Plans," in Profit Sharing in the Eighties 44, 1988; "Disposition of Retirement Plans on an Athlete's Retirement," The Sports Lawyer, Summer 1988; "The Problems Involved in Qualified Domestic Relations Orders," Profit Sharing Council Journal, April, 1986; "Overview of Top Heavy Plans Under TEFRA," Profit Sharing Council Journal, January 1983; "Favorable Determination Letters and Vesting," Profit Sharing Council Journal, January 1982; "A Capsule View of Retirement Plans," Chicago Daily Law Bulletin, January 1982. Member, Advisory Committee, Leading Lawyers of Illinios, 2004—. Selected Illlinios "Super Lawyer," Chicago Magazine 2005. Frequent Speaker and Adjunct Professor of Law at the John Marshall Law School. *Member:* Chicago (Chairman, Employee Benefits Committee, 1985-1986), Illinois State and American Bar Associations; WEB, Inc.; Midwest Benefits Conference (Chairman, Legal and Legislative Committee, 1991-1993); Profit Sharing Council of America (Legal Counsel and Executive Office Member, Board of Directors, 1997-2005; Legal and Legislative Committee, 1991—, Communications Committee, 1988-1991); Chicago Association of Commerce and Industry (Member, Employee Benefits Committee, 1982—); Society for Human Resource Management. (Chair, Employee Benefits and Executive Compensation Group). ***PRACTICE AREAS:*** ERISA; Employee Benefits; Employee Benefits and Executive Compensation. ***Email:*** ian.kopelman@dlapiper.com

MICHAEL P. KUPPERSMITH, born 1959; admitted to bar, 1984, Texas; 1987, California; 1994, Illinois. *Education:* University of Georgia (B.A., magna cum laude, 1981); University of Texas (J.D., with honors, 1984). Phi Beta Kappa. Member, Order of the Coif. *Member:* State Bar of California; Illinois State Bar Association. ***PRACTICE AREAS:*** Commercial Real Estate Law. ***Email:*** michael.kuppersmith@dlapiper.com

STEPHEN A. LANDSMAN, born 1942; admitted to bar, 1967, Illinois and U.S. District Court, Northern District of Illinois; 1968, U.S. Court of Appeals, Seventh Circuit; 1975, U.S. Tax Court. *Education:* Wharton School of Finance at University of Pennsylvania (B.S., 1964); University of Michigan (J.D., cum laude, 1967). Order of the Coif. Member, Panel of Arbitrators, American Arbitration Association. ***PRACTICE AREAS:*** Corporate Law; Mergers and Acquisitions; Corporate Finance Law. ***Email:*** stephen.landsman@dlapiper.com

TY D. LAURIE, born 1961; admitted to bar, 1986, Illinois and U.S. District Court, Northern District of Illinois; 1989, U.S. Court of Appeals, Fifth Circuit; 1998, U.S. District Court, Western District of Michigan. *Education:* Northwestern University (B.A., with honors, 1983); University of Michigan (J.D., 1986). Chair, Zoning Board of Appeals, Village of Glenview. Chair, 1996-1999 and Governing Committee, 2001-2004, ABA Forum on Construction Industry Division, 2005. Chair-elect, ABA Forum on Construction. *Member:* American College of Construction Lawyers; American Arbitration Association (Arbitrator and Mediator). ***PRACTICE AREAS:*** Construction Law; Alternative Dispute Resolution; Arbitration; Mediation. ***Email:*** ty.laurie@dlapiper.com

NORMAN M. LEON, born 1966; admitted to bar, 1993, New York and U.S. District Court, Southern District of New York; 1997, Illinois and U.S. District Court, Eastern District of New York; 1998, U.S. District Court, District of Colorado; 1999, U.S. Court of Appeals, First Circuit; 2001, U.S. Court of Appeals, Seventh Circuit; 2002, U.S. Court of Appeals, Fourth Circuit, U.S. District Court, Western District of Michigan and U.S. District Court, Northern District of Texas; 2003, U.S. District Court, Northern District of Indiana. *Education:* Boston University (B.A., 1988); Brooklyn Law School (J.D., 1992). Comments Editor, Brooklyn Law Review. Member, Moot Court Honor Society. *Member:* American Bar Association (Forum on Franchising). ***PRACTICE AREAS:*** Antitrust; Trade Regulation; Litigation; Franchise and Distribution. ***Email:*** norman.leon@dlapiper.com

JASON W. LEVIN, admitted to bar, 1983, Illinois and U.S. District Court, Northern District of Illinois. *Education:* Indiana University (B.S., 1980; J.D., 1983). Associate Member, 1981-1982 and a Managing Editor, 1982-1983, Indiana Law Journal. *Member:* Chicago and American (Member, Sections on: Corporation, Banking and Business Law) Bar Associations. ***PRACTICE AREAS:*** General Corporate Law; Intellectual Property; Information Technology. ***Email:*** jason.levin@dlapiper.com

PETER A. LEVY, born 1949; admitted to bar, 1974, Illinois. *Education:* University of Illinois (B.A., 1971); University of Chicago (J.D., 1974). Phi Beta Kappa. ***PRACTICE AREAS:*** Real Estate (Property) Law; Time Sharing Law. ***Email:*** peter.levy@dlapiper.com

SUSAN GROB LICHTENFELD, born Baltimore, Maryland, August 4, 1952; admitted to bar, 1977, Illinois and U.S District Court, Northern District of Illinois, U.S. Court of Appeals, Fifth Circuit; U.S. Supreme Court. *Education:* George Washington University (B.A., with special honors and distinction, 1974); Washington University (J.D., 1977). Phi Beta Kappa. Assistant Editor, Washington University Urban Law Annual, 1976-1977. ***PRACTICE AREAS:*** Finance. ***Email:*** susan.lichtenfeld@dlapiper.com

JANET A. LINDEMAN, born 1963; admitted to bar, 1987, Illinois. *Education:* Gettysburg College (B.A., 1984); St. John's University (J.D., 1987). Senior Scholars Seminar. *Member:* Chicago Bar Association. ***PRACTICE AREAS:*** Real Estate. ***Email:*** janet.lindeman@dlapiper.com

ROGER L. LONGTIN, (P.C.), born 1945; admitted to bar, 1973, Illinois. *Education:* University of Notre Dame (B.A., 1967); University of Illinois (J.D., 1973). Editor of the Attorney General's Report for the Illinois State Police Journal, 1975-1976. First Amendment and Commercial Speech under the U.S. Constitution. Assistant Attorney General for the State of Illinois assigned to the Special Prosecutions Unit, 1973-1976. ***PRACTICE AREAS:*** Commercial Litigation; Class Actions; Regulatory Law; Privacy Law; First Amendment Law. ***Email:*** roger.longtin@dlapiper.com

GERALD B. LURIE, born 1944; admitted to bar, 1969, Illinois; 1974, U.S. District Court, Northern District of Illinois. *Education:* University of Michigan (B.A., 1966); DePaul University (J.D., 1969). ***PRACTICE AREAS:*** Commercial Litigation; Landlord and Tenant Law; Trial Practice. ***Email:*** gerald.lurie@dlapiper.com

DAVID G. LYNCH, born 1947; admitted to bar, 1974, Illinois and U.S. District Court, Northern District of Illinois; 1990, U.S. Court of Appeals, Third Circuit. *Education:* Northern Illinois University (B.A., 1971); University of Illinois (J.D., cum laude, 1974). Order of the Coif. Notes and Comments Editor, University of Illinois Law Forum, 1973-1974. ***PRACTICE AREAS:*** Litigation; Trial Practice. ***Email:*** david.lynch@dlapiper.com

ROBERT S. MARKIN, born 1959; admitted to bar, 1984, Illinois and U.S. District Court, Northern District of Illinois; 1987, U.S. Court of Appeals, Seventh Circuit; 1994, U.S. District Court, Eastern District of Wisconsin; 2001, U.S. District Court, Eastern District of Michigan. *Education:* Brown University (B.A., 1981); Georgetown University (J.D., magna cum laude, 1984). General Counsel and Chief of Staff, Chicago Board of Education, 1995-1997. *Member:* Chicago and American Bar Associations. ***PRACTICE AREAS:*** Litigation; Government. ***Email:*** robert.markin@dlapiper.com

CHRISTINA L. MARTINI, admitted to bar, 1994, Illinois. *Education:* University of Illinois at Chicago (B.S., Industrial Engineering, with University Honors (highest distinction), 1991); Northwestern University School of Law (J.D., 1994). Note and Comment Editor, Northwestern Journal of International Law and Business, 1993-1994. Author: "Medical Waste Regulation in the U.S.: a Dire Need for Recognition and Reform," Northwestern Journal of International Law and Business, Fall 1993. *Member:* Chicago and Illinois State Bar Associations; International Trademark Association; Brand Names Education Foundation. ***LANGUAGES:*** Spanish. ***PRACTICE AREAS:*** Intellectual Property; Advertising, Promotion, and Trade Practices; Copyrights; Domain Name Practice; Mergers and Acquisitions; Trademarks; Trademark Litigation. ***Email:*** christina.martini@dlapiper.com

ADRIANNE C. MAZURA, born 1951; admitted to bar, 1978, Illinois; 1985, U.S. Court of Appeals, Seventh Circuit. *Education:* University of Michigan (B.A., with distinction, 1973); Wayne State University (J.D., magna cum laude, 1978). Member, 1976-1977 and Note & Comment Editor, 1977-1978, Wayne State Law Review. Co-Author: "Drug Testing in the Workplace," BNA, 1989. Executive Committee, Board of Directors, Illinois Institute of Continuing Legal Education. Treasurer, Illinois Institute of Continuing Legal Education, 2005—. Named Illinios Leading Lawyer, 2004 and Super Lawyer, 2005, 2006. *Member:* American Bar Association (Member, Section on Labor Law); Life Fellow, American Bar Foundation. ***PRACTICE AREAS:*** Labor Law; Employment Law; Litigation; Trial Practice. ***Email:*** adrianne.mazura@dlapiper.com

ANDREW W. McCUNE, born 1963; admitted to bar, 1989, Illinois. *Education:* Washington University (A.B., summa cum laude, 1986); University of Chicago (J.D., 1989). Phi Beta Kappa. *Member:* American Bar Association. ***PRACTICE AREAS:*** Corporate; Securities. ***Email:*** andrew.mccune@dlapiper.com

SALLY J. McDONALD, born 1964; admitted to bar, 1990, Illinois. *Education:* Indiana University (B.S., 1986); Duke University (J.D., 1990). Member, Executive Committee, Moot Court Board. Authored Chapter in 1996 and 2000 Illinois Institute for Continuing Legal Education Employment Discrimination Handbook. *Member:* Chicago Bar Association (Board of Managers, 1999-2001; Chair, Young Lawyers Section, 1996-1997). ***PRACTICE AREAS:*** Labor Law; Employment Law. ***Email:*** sally.mcdonald@dlapiper.com

KEITH W. MEDANSKY, born 1961; admitted to bar, 1987, Illinois; U.S. District Court, Northern District of Illinois; U.S. Court of Appeals for the Federal Circuit. *Education:* Northwestern University (B.A., 1984); University of Illinois (J.D., magna cum laude, 1987). *Member:* American Bar Association; Intellectual Property Association of Chicago (Co-Chair, Trademark Committee); Brand Names Educational Foundation. ***PRACTICE AREAS:*** Intellectual Property Law; Litigation. ***Email:*** keith.medansky@dlapiper.com

DAVID E. MENDELSOHN, born 1964; admitted to bar, 1988, England and Wales; 1991, Illinois; U.S. District Court, Northern District of Illinois. *Education:* University College of London, Faculty of Laws, London, England (LL.B., with honors, 1985); Lancaster Gate College of Law, London, England (with honors, 1986); Illinois Institute of Technology, Chicago-Kent College of Law (J.D., 1991); Insurance School of Chicago (ARe., 1994); Insurance Institute of Americas (Certificate of Completion of Insurance Reinsurance Regulation, 1996). Publication: "Contracts, Regulatory and Coverage Issues of Global Import," The Euromoney Global Insurance Handbook, 2005; "Everybody Will Benefit from Spitzer," Insurance Day, February 11, 2005; "US Primary Risk Broker and Reinsurance," The Euromoney Global Insurance Handbook, 2004; "Terrorism and Security Issues: Management Responsibility," D&O Advisor (Summer 2003); "'Know-Your-Customer' Laws Come to Real Estate," USA Patriot Act, Real Estate Chicago (September 2002); "The Best Laid Y2K Plans...," Gen. Reins. Year 2000 (August 1999); "Y2K: A Reinsurance Perspective," 9 Mealey's Litig. Rep., Reinsurance No. 15, 17-37 (1998), reprinted as "Insurers, Reinsurers Grapple with Y2K Issues," Y2K Counselor, April 1999 at 5 Beware Common Account Reinsurance, 8 Mealey's Litig. Rep., Ins. Insol. No. 9 (1997); "The Year 2000 Software Problem: Reinsurers Beware," RAA Executive Newsletter Vol. 5, No. 11 (1997); "The Year 2000 Software Problem: The Most Ominous Legal Concern Facing Businesses Today," Insurance Specialist Vol. 2, Iss. 5 (1997) at 40; "The Year 2000 Software Problem: Reinsurers Beware," Mealey's Litigation Report Vol. 8, No. 4 (June 25, 1997); "Viatical Settlements and the Elderly: An Emerging Market," (unpublished 1996); "Insurer Receiverships," Longman's INT'L INS. LAW & REG. (D. Campbell ed., 1995); "Caught Between Rocks and Hard Places: The Plight of Reinsurance Intermediaries Under U.S. and English Law," 16 Mich. J. Int'l L. 485 (1995), reprinted in 8 Nat'l Ins. L.Rev. 79 (1996); "Derivatives in Insurer Receiverships," (unpublished 1995); "Insurance Company Receiverships: What Does the Future Hold?," ABA National Institute on Solvency Concerns with Foreign Insurers and Reinsurers/Recent Developments/U.S. Reform Efforts (1994); "Insurance Futures Contracts and Options: The Long and Short of It (excerpts only)," Financial Reinsurance & Futures Newsletter No. 32 (April 1994). Contributing Author to Reinsurance and Claims chapters of RECEIVER'S HANDBOOK FOR INSURANCE COMPANY INSOLVENCIES (1st and 2d eds. 1992, 1994); "Re Insurance Antitrust Litigation," 2 Ins. Law & Practice 112 (1992); Illinois, International Business Series, Legal Aspects of Doing Business in North America and Canada (Kluwer Law and Taxation Publishers, (Fall 1992, 1993) (3 part article); Franchise UPDATE 15 (Parts I-III) (1992) "Valuation of Contingent Claims and the Application of Set-Offs in Reinsurance Insolvencies," (5 part article), Ins. Law & Practice (Parts I-III) (1991) (Parts IV, V) (1992); "Cross-Border Insurance Insolvency: The Search for a Forum Concursus," 12 U. Pa. J. Int. Bus. Law 303 (1991), reprinted in Ins. Law & Practice (2 parts) (1992); "Onset of an Offset Revolution: The Application of Set-Offs in Insurance Insolvencies," 95 Dick. L. Rev. 449 (1991), 8 J. Ins. Reg. 446 (1990), reprinted in 5 Nat'l Ins. L. Rev. 813 (1992), and VI INSURANCE LAW ANTHOLOGY 107 (1992); "Launching an International Franchise Program, International Franchising: An In-Depth Treatment of Business and Legal Techniques," (Y. Gramatidis and D. Campbell ed. 1991);

(This Listing Continued)

DLA PIPER RUDNICK GRAY CARY US LLP, Chicago—Continued

"Amreco: A Step Towards International Rehabilitations," 7 J. Ins. Reg. 388 (1989). Contributing Author, Receivership Matters (Rudnick & Wolfe's semi-annual insurer receivership newsletter). Contributing Author, Health Care (Rudnick & Wolfe's health care law publication). *Member:* The Law Society, England and Wales; Association of Fellows and Legal Scholars of the Center for International Legal Studies; National Futures Association (Arbitrator). ***PRACTICE AREAS:*** Insurance and Reinsurance; Insurance Insolvency; Corporate; Transactional; Regulatory; Information Management; Technology; Transactional and Regulatory. ***Email:*** david.mendelsohn@dlapiper.com

LEE I. MILLER, born 1947; admitted to bar, 1973, Maryland; 1976, Illinois. *Education:* Georgetown University (B.S.B.A., 1969); Georgetown University (J.D., 1973). Co-Chairman, Piper Rudnick LLP. *Member:* American College of Real Estate Lawyers. ***PRACTICE AREAS:*** Real Estate (Property) Law. ***Email:*** lee.miller@dlapiper.com

NICHOLAS R. MINEAR, born 1956; admitted to bar, 1981, Illinois and U.S. District Court, Northern District of Illinois. *Education:* University of Iowa (B.B.A., with highest distinction, 1977); Stanford University (J.D., 1981). Adjunct Professor of Law, Chicago-Kent College of Law. ***PRACTICE AREAS:*** Taxation Law; Partnership Law; Corporate Law. ***Email:*** nicholas.minear@dlapiper.com

DAVID N. MISSNER, admitted to bar, 1967, Illinois; 2004, Colorado; U.S. District Court, Northern District of Illinois including Trial Bar; U.S. District Court, Central District of Illinois; U.S. District Court, Northern District of Indiana; U.S. District Court, Eastern District of Wisconsin; U.S. District Court, Western District of Wisconsin; U.S. Court of Appeals, Seventh Circuit; U.S. Supreme Court. *Education:* Miami University (A.B., 1963); Northwestern University School of Law (J.D., 1966). Listed in: Chambers, 2004; American Leading Business Lawyers, Chambers, 2003. Author: "Representing the Creditor with a Secured Claim," and "Chapter 11-Representing the Debtor," published Bankruptcy Practice, Illinois Institute of Continuing Legal Education, 1985, 1990. Lecturer, Bankruptcy Reorganization, IICLE, 1983-1990 and Chicago Bar Association, 1996. Attorney, National Labor Relations Board, Los Angeles, California, 1966-1968. *Member:* Chicago, Illinois State and American Bar Associations. ***PRACTICE AREAS:*** Litigation; Finance; Mergers and Acquisitions; Bankruptcy and Business Reorganization. ***Email:*** david.missner@dlapiper.com

ALISON M. MITCHELL, born 1965; admitted to bar, 1990, Illinois. *Education:* University of Michigan (B.A., 1987); Northwestern University (J.D., 1990, cum laude). ***PRACTICE AREAS:*** Real Estate (Property) Law. ***Email:*** alison.mitchell@dlapiper.com

ANITA T. MOLANO, born 1951; admitted to bar, 1976, Ohio; 1980, Illinois. *Education:* George Washington University (B.A., 1973); University of Cincinnati College of Law (J.D., 1976). *Member:* Chicago and American Bar Associations; American Health Lawyers Association. ***PRACTICE AREAS:*** Corporate Law; Securities; Health Care. ***Email:*** anita.molano@dlapiper.com

RICHARD J. MOREY, born 1971; admitted to bar, 1996, Illinois. *Education:* University of Illinois at Urbana (B.A., 1993); University of Pennsylvania (J.D., 1996). ***LANGUAGES:*** French. ***PRACTICE AREAS:*** Corporate Franchise; General Corporate; Mergers and Acquisitions. ***Email:*** richard.morey@dlapiper.com

PORTIA OWEN MORRISON, born 1944; admitted to bar, 1978, Illinois and U.S. District Court, Northern District of Illinois. *Education:* Agnes Scott College (B.A., with honors, 1966); University of Wisconsin-Madison (M.A., 1967); University of Chicago (J.D., 1978). *Member:* American College of Real Estate Lawyers. ***PRACTICE AREAS:*** Real Estate (Property) Law. ***Email:*** portia.morrison@dlapiper.com

SONYA D. NAAR, born 1970; admitted to bar, 1994, New Jersey and Pennsylvania; 1997, Illinois. *Education:* Smith College (A.B., with high honors in government, 1991); Rutgers University Law School - Camden (J.D., with high honors, 1994). Notes and Casenotes Editor, Rutgers Law Journal. ***PRACTICE AREAS:*** Commercial Litigation. ***Email:*** sonya.naar@dlapiper.com

DAVID M. NEFF, born 1960; admitted to bar, 1985, Illinois; U.S. District Court, Northern District of Illinois; U.S. District Court, Western and Eastern Districts of Wisconsin; U.S. District Court, Western District of Michigan. *Education:* Northwestern University (B.S.J., 1982); DePaul University (J.D., 1985). Member, De Paul Law Review, 1983-1985. Law Clerk to Hon. Robert E. Ginsberg, U.S. Bankruptcy Court, Northern District of Illinois, 1985-1986. Executive Editor to R. Ginsberg and R. Martin, *Bankruptcy:* Text, Statutes, Rules, Forms, 3d. Ed. Aspen Law & Business, 1986-1995. Contributing Editor, *Norton Bankruptcy Law and Practice,* Clark Boardman Callaghan Co., 1997. Author: "Law Firm and Other Professional Partnership Bankruptcies," 10 Journal of Bankruptcy Law & Practice 315, May/June 2001; "Denial of Title VII Protection to Transsexuals: Ulane v. Eastern Airlines, Inc.," 34 De Paul Law Review 553, 1985. Co-Author: "Bulk Transfers in Illinois," Creditors' Rights in Illinois, Illinois Institute for Continuing Legal Education, 1990; "Equitable Remedies," Creditors' Rights in Illinois, Illinois Institute for Continuing Legal Education, 1986; "Bankruptcy Rules of Procedure," Bankruptcy Practice, Illinois Institute for Continuing Legal Education, 1986 Supplement; "Rush to Judgment: Congressional Response to Judicial Recognition of Rejection of Collective Bargaining Agreements Under Chapter 11 of the Bankruptcy Code," 27 Arizona Law Review 617, 1985; "People of the State of Illinois v. John Gacy: The Functioning of the Insanity Defense at the Limits of the Criminal Law," 86 West Virginia Law Review 1169, 1984. Speaker: Norton Bankruptcy Litigation Institute I; Norton Bankruptcy Litigation Institute II; Midwestern Bankruptcy Conference; American Bar Association; Illinois State Bar Association; Chicago Bar Association; Illinois Institute for Continuing Legal Education; ABA Forum on Franchising; International Council of Shopping Centers U.S. Law Conference, 1993-1996. President, Association of Former Bankruptcy Law Clerks (N.D. Ill.), 1994. Chair, Bankruptcies and Reorganization Committee, Chicago Bar Association, 1998-1999. Member, International Society of Hospitality Consultants. ***PRACTICE AREAS:*** Bankruptcy; Insolvency. ***Email:*** *david.neff@dlapiper.com*

THEODORE J. NOVAK, (P.C.), born 1940; admitted to bar, 1967, Illinois and U.S. District Court, Northern District of Illinois. *Education:* University of Illinois (B.S., 1962); Chicago-Kent College of Law (J.D., 1967). Lamda Alpha (Ely Chapter). Co-Author: *Illinois Zoning, Eminent Domain and Land Use Manual* and *Condemnation of Property: Practice and Strategies for Winning Just Compensation.* Also Co-Authored "Land Use and Development Controls" *Basic Real Estate,* Vol. II; "Landowner Strategies in the Face of Condemnation," *National Law Journal,* and "Invitation to Abuse of Discretion: Aesthetic and Automatic Reviews," Land Use & Zoning Digest (Nov. 1990). Adjunct Professor at Northwestern University School of Law, teaching a course in Land Use, Zoning and Condemnation, 1998-1999 and 1999-2000; Lecturer, University of Chicago Law School, teaching a course in Land Use, Zoning and Condemnation, 2000-2001. Member: LaSalle Street Council; Chicago Development Council; Urban Land Institute. *Member:* Chicago, Illinois State and American Bar Associations; American College of Real Estate Lawyers (ACREL). ***PRACTICE AREAS:*** Real Estate (Property) Law; Zoning Law; Land Use; Condemnation; Government Affairs; Hospitality; Lodging and Timeshare; Energy; Public Utilities; Project Finance. ***Email:*** theodore.novak@dlapiper.com

MICHAEL C. O'NEIL, born 1961; admitted to bar, 1989, Illinois. *Education:* Brooklyn College (B.A., with high honors, 1986); DePaul University (J.D., with honors, 1989). Member, 1987-1989 and Article and Note Editor, 1988-1989, DePaul Law Review. ***PRACTICE AREAS:*** Litigation; Privacy Law; Insurance. ***Email:*** michael.oneil@dlapiper.com

JEFFREY N. OWEN, born 1954; admitted to bar, 1979, Illinois and U.S. District Court, Northern District of Illinois. *Education:* Kalamazoo College (B.A., 1976); John Marshall Law School (J.D., with distinction, 1979). Associate Candidacy Editor, John Marshall Law Review, 1978-1979. ***PRACTICE AREAS:*** Real Estate (Property) Law. ***Email:*** jeffrey.owen@dlapiper.com

ANNE M. PACHCIAREK, born 1957; admitted to bar, 1982, Illinois. *Education:* University of Illinois (B.A., 1979); Northwestern University (J.D., 1982). *Member:* Chicago and American (Member, Employee Benefits Committees) Bar Associations. ***PRACTICE AREAS:*** Employee Benefits; Executive Compensation. ***Email:*** anne.pachciarek@dlapiper.com

MARILYN A. PEARSON, admitted to bar, 1976, Minnesota; 1979, District of Columbia (Not admitted in Illinois). *Education:* University of Minnesota (B.A., Sociology, 1973; J.D., 1976). ***PRACTICE AREAS:*** Labor and Employment. ***Email:*** marilyn.pearson@dlapiper.com

JAMES M. PHIPPS, born 1952; admitted to bar, 1977, Illinois and U.S. District Court, Northern District of Illinois; 1978, U.S. Court of Appeals, Seventh Circuit. *Education:* Stanford University (B.S., 1973); Washington University (J.D., 1977). Order of the Coif. Author: "Action Forcing under NEPA-Beyond the Environmental Impact Statement," 14 Urb. L. Ann 137, 1977. *Member:* Chicago and American Bar Associations. ***PRACTICE AREAS:*** Real Estate; Capital Markets. ***Email:*** james.phipps@dlapiper.com

DOV J. PINCHOT, born 1967; admitted to bar, 1994, Illinois. *Education:* Yeshiva University (B.A., 1990); University of Chicago (J.D., 1994). Winner, Moot Court Competition. ***PRACTICE AREAS:*** Commercial Leasing; Real Estate. ***Email:*** dov.pinchot@dlapiper.com

RUTH A. PIVAR, born 1948; admitted to bar, 1991, Wisconsin and U.S. District Court, Eastern District of Wisconsin; 1997, Illinois. *Education:* University of Wisconsin-Milwaukee (B.B.A., 1986); Marquette University (J.D., cum laude, 1991). Beta Gamma Sigma; Phi Kappa Phi. *Member:* Chicago and Illinois State Bar Associations; State Bar of Wisconsin (Member, Real Property, Probate and Trust Law, General Practice, Business Law and Taxation Sections); Association of Women Lawyers. ***PRACTICE AREAS:*** Estate Planning; Probate and Estate Administration; Real Estate; Tax Planning; Marital Property. ***Email:*** ruth.pivar@dlapiper.com

GEORGE T. PLUMB, born 1950; admitted to bar, 1977, Illinois; 1985, Texas. *Education:* DePaul University (A.B., cum laude, 1972; J.D., magna cum laude, 1977). ***PRACTICE AREAS:*** Finance Law; Secured Transactions Law; Bankruptcy Law. ***Email:*** george.plumb@dlapiper.com

HAROLD B. POMERANTZ, born 1953; admitted to bar, 1979, Illinois and U.S. District Court, Northern District of Illinois. *Education:* Washington University (B.A., cum laude, 1975; Masters of Business Administration, 1979; J.D., 1979). ***PRACTICE AREAS:*** Real Estate Development Law; Commercial Leasing Law; Real Estate (Property) Law. ***Email:*** harold.pomerantz@dlapiper.com

MICHAEL S. POULOS, born 1961; admitted to bar, 1986, Ohio, U.S. District Court, Northern District of Ohio including Trial Bar; 1996, Illinois, U.S. District Court, Northern and Central Districts of Illinois including Trial Bar, U.S. District Court, Eastern District of Wisconsin and U.S. Court of Appeals, Sixth and Seventh Circuits. *Education:* Grinnell College (B.S., 1983); Case Western Reserve University (J.D., 1986). Order of the Coif. *Member:* American Bar Association; American Corporate Counsel Association. ***PRACTICE AREAS:*** Complex Commercial Litigation; Securities Litigation; Consumer Fraud Litigation; Professional Malpractice; Insurance Litigation; Employment Litigation. ***Email:*** michael.poulos@dlapiper.com

DENNIS J. POWERS, born 1958; admitted to bar, 1983, Illinois and U.S. District Court, Northern and Southern Districts of Illinois; 1990, U.S. Court of Appeals, Seventh and Sixth Circuits; U.S. District Court, Northern District of Indiana and Western District of Michigan. *Education:* Western Illinois University (B.S., with honors, 1980); DePaul University (J.D., 1983). Author: "Sub-Subcontractor's Lien: Requisites For and Perfection Of," Illinois Institute for Continuing Legal Education Mechanic's Liens; "Assessibility: Not Just The Owner's Responsibility," The Construction Lawyer, Vol. 21, No. 2 (2001); "Seeking Recovery for the Construction Defect Claims," The Real Estate Finance Journal, Winter 2005; "Design Professionals' Liability to the Contractort," Ch. 6. *Member:* Chicago and American (Construction Law Forum and Litigation Section) Bar Associations. ***PRACTICE AREAS:*** Commercial Litigation; Construction Law. ***Email:*** dennis.powers@dlapiper.com

WILLIAM L. RAWSON, born 1952; admitted to bar, 1979, Illinois. *Education:* Drake University (B.A., 1974); Tulane University School of Law (J.D., 1978); Georgetown University Law Center (LL.M., Taxation, 1979). ***PRACTICE AREAS:*** Corporate Finance; Secured Lending; Aircraft Finance; Mergers and Acquisitions. ***Email:*** william.rawson@dlapiper.com

(This Listing Continued)

DAVID L. REIFMAN, born 1959; admitted to bar, 1988, Illinois. *Education:* University of Illinois (B.A., 1981; M.A., 1985); Northwestern University (J.D., 1988). ***PRACTICE AREAS:*** Real Estate (Property) Law; Land Use Law; Zoning and Planning Law; Public Sector Financing. ***Email:*** david.reifman@dlapiper.com

JAMES D. ROBERTS, born 1959; admitted to bar, 1989, Illinois and U.S. District Court, Northern District of Illinois. *Education:* Wheaton College (B.A., 1982); John Marshall Law School (J.D., with distinction, 1989). Recipient, Scribes Award 1989. ***PRACTICE AREAS:*** Litigation; Trial Practice. ***Email:*** james.roberts@dlapiper.com

LAWRENCE A. ROBINS, (P.C.), born 1949; admitted to bar, 1973, Illinois, U.S. District Court, Northern District of Illinois and U.S. Court of Appeals, Seventh Circuit; 1974, U.S. Tax Court. *Education:* University of Illinois (B.A., with honors, 1970); George Washington University Law Center (J.D., with high honors, 1973). Trustee, Village of Wilmette, 1981-1985. ***PRACTICE AREAS:*** Estate Planning Law; Closely Held Businesses; Taxation Law; Trust Law. ***Email:*** lawrence.robins@dlapiper.com

PETER B. ROSS, born 1961; admitted to bar, 1986, Illinois. *Education:* Yale University (B.A., 1983); Northwestern University (J.D., cum laude, 1986). Order of the Coif. ***PRACTICE AREAS:*** Real Estate (Property) Law. ***Email:*** peter.ross@dlapiper.com

LEWIS G. RUDNICK, born 1935; admitted to bar, 1964, Illinois and U.S. District Court, Northern District of Illinois. *Education:* University of Illinois (A.B., with honors, 1957); Columbia University (M.B.A., 1960); Northwestern University (J.D., 1964). Co-Author: *Franchising, A Planning and Sales Compliance Guide,* Commerce Clearing House, 1987. Associate Editor, Journal of International Franchising and Distribution Law, 1987—. Counsel, International Franchise Association. Co-Author: *Negotiating an International Master Franchise Agreement,* Sweet & Maxwell Limited (2002) London). *Member:* American Bar Association (Governing Committee, 1977-1983 and Chairman, 1980-1982, Forum on Franchising; Illinois Franchise Advisory Board, 1974—). ***PRACTICE AREAS:*** Domestic and International Franchise and Distribution Law; Residential Mortgage Banking. ***Email:*** lewis.rudnick@dlapiper.com

WILLIAM A. RUDNICK, born 1964; admitted to bar, 1989, Illinois. *Education:* Tufts University (B.A., cum laude, 1986); Northwestern University (J.D., 1989); University of Chicago Graduate School of Business (M.B.A., with honors, 1997). ***PRACTICE AREAS:*** Real Estate (Property) Law; Corporate Finance; Corporate. ***Email:*** william.rudnick@dlapiper.com

JAMES P. RYTHER, born 1934; admitted to bar, 1961, Illinois and U.S. District Court, Northern District of Illinois; 1964, U.S. Court of Appeals, Seventh and Fifth Circuits; 1965, U.S. Court of Appeals, Eighth Circuit; 1975, U.S. Court of Appeals, Ninth Circuit; 1976, U.S. Court of Appeals, Sixth Circuit and U.S. Court of Federal Claims; 1983, U.S. Court of Appeals for the Federal Circuit; registered to practice before U.S Patent and Trademark Office. *Education:* University of Notre Dame (B.S., 1956); Georgetown University (J.D., 1960). *Member:* Chicago Bar Association; Intellectual Property Law Association of Chicago. Fellow, American College of Trial Lawyers. ***PRACTICE AREAS:*** Patent, Trademark and Copyright Law. ***Email:*** james.ryther@dlapiper.com

VINCENT A. SANCHEZ, born 1968; admitted to bar, 1994, Illinois. *Education:* University of Notre Dame (B.A., 1991); Notre Dame Law School (J.D., 1994). *Member:* American Bar Association; Computer Law Association. [1st Lt., USMCR, 1991-1995]. ***PRACTICE AREAS:*** Information Technology; Electronic Commerce; Venture Capital; Corporate Law; Securities. ***Email:*** vincent.sanchez@dlapiper.com

KENNETH L. SCHMETTERER, born 1963; admitted to bar, 1989, Illinois. *Education:* University of Wisconsin-Madison (B.A., with distinction, 1985); Harvard Law School (J.D., 1989). Member, Village of Deerfield Youth Council. *Member:* Chicago, Federal and American (Member, Sections on: Litigation; State and Local Government Law) Bar Associations; Lawyers Club of Chicago. ***PRACTICE AREAS:*** Commercial Litigation; Land Use Litigation; Constitutional Litigation. ***Email:*** kenneth.schmetterer@dlapiper.com

RENEE M. SCHOENBERG, born 1952; admitted to bar, 1976, Illinois and U.S. District Court, Northern District of Illinois. *Education:* Northwestern University (B.A., with distinction, 1973); University of Michigan (J.D., cum laude, 1976). Phi Beta Kappa. *Member:* Chicago Bar Association (Secretary, Trust Law Executive Committee, 1985-1987). ***PRACTICE AREAS:*** Closely Held Business Law; Estate Planning Law; Non-Profit Organizations. ***Email:*** renee.schoenberg@dlapiper.com

STEPHEN W. SCHWAB, admitted to bar, 1982, Illinois, U.S. Supreme Court, U.S. Court of Appeals, Seventh and Ninth Circuits, U.S. Tax Court, U.S. Claims Court and U.S. District Court, Northern District of Illinois including Trial Bar; 1994, District of Columbia. *Education:* Northwestern University (B.A., 1979); Dickinson School of Law of Pennsylvania State University (J.D., 1982); Insurance School of Chicago (A.Re., 1995). Phi Eta Sigma. Member, The Order of Barristers. Chairman, Trial Moot Court Board, 1981-1982. Author: "Bearable Alternatives for Reinsurance Arbitration Part One: Panel Selection," American Bar Association, Excess, Surplus Lines and Reinsurance Newsletter (Summer 2005); "Recent Developments in Excess, Surplus Lines and Reinsurance Law, " 39 ABA Tort Tr. & Ins. Pract. L.J. 375 (2004) (Introduction, Reinsurance Section, and Conclusion); *U.S. Primary Risk, Broker and Reinsurance Regulatory Issues in 2004* in The Euromoney Global Insurance Handbook 2005 89 (2004); *Insurer Receiverships in Oceana's* International Insurance Law & Regulations (D. Campbell ed., 2000); "Uninsured and Underinsured Motorists Coverage Remains Risky Business for Primary and Excess Carriers," Scor Re (Sept. 2001); "The Best Laid Year 2000 Plans: Planning and Preparation for the New Millenium," Gen. Reins. Year 2000 (August, 1999); *Y2K: A Reinsurance Perspective* IX Mealey's Lit. Rep. Rein. No. 15, 17-37 (1998); *Reinsurer Liability for Contingent Claims,* (1997) Int'l. J. of Ins. Law 28, 175; *Beware Common Account Reinsurance,* VIII Mealey's Lit. Rep. Ins. Insolv. No. 9 (1997); *Banks Selling Annuities May Cause a Turf Battle,* Nat'l L.J., May 22, 1995; *Caught Between Rocks and Hard Places: The Plight of Reinsurance Intermediaries Under U.S. and English Law,* 16 Mich. J. Int'l L. 485 (1995); *Should Receivers Sell, or Just Collect, Insurer Shells?,* VI Mealey's Litig. Rep., Ins., Insolv. No. 14 (1994); *Insurance Company Receiverships: What Does the Future Hold?,* A.B.A. National Institute, Sec. Bus. Law, Solvency Concerns with Foreign Insurers and Reinsurers/Recent Developments/U.S. Reform Efforts (1994); Contingent Claims: Has Their Time Finally Come? III Soc. of Ins. Rec. News. No. 3, p. 9 (1994); Supreme Court Decides Superpriority Case, II Soc. of Ins. Rec. News. No. 3, p. 3 (1993); U.S. Dept. of Treasury v. Fabe, 3 Ins. L. & Prac. 112 (1993); Editor and Contributing Author, Data Processing Investigation and

(This Listing Continued)

Asset Recovery, Claims, and Special Receiverships Chapters, National Association of Insurance Commissioners Receiver's Handbook for Insurance Company Insolvencies; An Overview of United States Reinsurance Regulation and Proposals for Reform (unpublished 1992); Cross-Border Insurance Insolvency: The Search for a Forum Concursus, 12 U. Pa. J. Int. Bus. Law 303 (1991), reprinted in Ins. Law & Practice (2 parts) (1992); Onset of an Offset Revolution: The Application of Set-Offs in Insurance Insolvencies, 95 Dick. L. Rev. 449 (1991), 8 J. Ins. Reg. 446 (1990), reprinted in 5 Nat'l Ins. L. Rev. 813 (1992) and VI Insurance Law Anthology 107 (1992); Unigard Security Ins. Co., Inc. v. North River Ins. Co., 1 Ins. L. & Practice 97 (1991); Searching for a Forum Concursus, 2 and 3 Europe 1992 Law & Strategy No. 3 (Mar. and Apr. 1991); Valuation of Contingent Claims and the Application of Set-offs in Reinsurance Insolvencies (5 part article), Ins. Law & Practice (Parts I-III) (1991) (Parts IV, V) (1992); Amreco: A Step Towards International Rehabilitations, 7 J. Ins. Reg. 388 (1989); Retaliatory Discharge: Insurable or Not?, 14 YLS Journal No. 4 (1985). ***PRACTICE AREAS:*** Insurance; Reinsurance; Regulation; Insolvency Law; Litigation. ***Email:*** stephen.schwab@dlapiper.com

ANDREW P. SCOTT, born 1966; admitted to bar, 1996, Illinois. *Education:* Tufts University (B.A., 1989); Chicago Kent University (J.D., with honors, 1996). Assistant Counsel to the Speaker of the House of Representatives, 1997. *Member:* Illinois State Bar Association. ***PRACTICE AREAS:*** Real Estate; Land Use; Zoning Law; Government Ethics. ***Email:*** andrew.scott@dlapiper.com

RANDAL J. SELIG, born 1956; admitted to bar, 1981, Illinois. *Education:* Indiana University (B.A., 1978); George Washington University (J.D., with honors, 1981). Articles Editor, George Washington Law Review, 1980-1981. Chicago, Illinois State and American Bar Associations. ***PRACTICE AREAS:*** Real Estate. ***Email:*** randal.selig@dlapiper.com

PAUL W. SHADLE, born 1964; admitted to bar, 1996, Illinois. *Education:* Carleton College (B.A., 1986); Harvard University Kennedy School of Government (M.P.P., 1991); University of Chicago (J.D., 1996). Member: Urban Land Institute, 2001; Metropolitan Planning Council, 2002. Leadership Greater Chicago Fellow, 2003-2004. *Member:* Chicago and American Bar Associations. ***LANGUAGES:*** French. ***PRACTICE AREAS:*** Real Estate; Land Use; Government Affairs; Affordable Housing Development; Housing Finance. ***Email:*** paul.shadle@dlapiper.com

JOSEPH W. SHEYKA, born 1946; admitted to bar, 1974, Illinois. *Education:* University of Illinois (B.A., 1968; Phi Beta Kappa); Northwestern University (J.D., 1974). Order of the Coif. Article Editor, Journal of Criminal Law & Criminology, 1973-1974. ***PRACTICE AREAS:*** Franchise Law; Franchise Relations Law. ***Email:*** jospeh.sheyka@dlapiper.com

DONALD A. SHINDLER, born 1946; admitted to bar, 1971, Louisiana and U.S. District Court, Eastern District of Louisiana; 1974, U.S. Tax Court; 1975, Illinois and U.S. District Court, Northern District of Illinois. *Education:* Washington University (B.S.B.A., with final honors, 1968); Tulane University of Louisiana (J.D., 1971). Beta Gamma Sigma; Order of the Coif. Member, Tulane Law Review, 1970-1971. Member, Tulane Moot Court, 1969-1970. Certified Public Accountant, Louisiana, 1979. [LT, JAGC, USNR, 1971-1975]. ***PRACTICE AREAS:*** Real Estate (Property) Law; Real Estate Development Law. ***Email:*** donald.shindler@dlapiper.com

DAVID B. SICKLE, born 1959; admitted to bar, 1986, Illinois. *Education:* University of Pennsylvania (B.S. Econ., cum laude, 1981; B.S. Eng., cum laude, 1981); University of Michigan (J.D., cum laude, 1986). Member, Barristers Society. ***PRACTICE AREAS:*** Real Estate Development Law; Commercial Leasing Law; Real Estate (Property) Law. ***Email:*** david.sickle@dlapiper.com

SEYMOUR F. SIMON, born 1915; admitted to bar, 1938, Illinois. *Education:* Northwestern University (B.S., 1935; J.D., 1938). Phi Beta Kappa; Order of the Coif. Alderman, 40th Ward, Chicago, 1955-1961 and 1967-1974. Member, Cook County Board of Commissioners, 1961-1966. President, Cook County Board of Commissioners, 1962-1966. Member, Public Building Commission, City of Chicago, 1962-1967. Judge, Illinois Appellate Court, 1974-1980. Judge, Illinois Supreme Court, 1980-1988. Chairman, Illinois Low Level Nuclear Waste Disposal Facility Siting Commission, 1990-1993. *Member:* Chicago, Illinois State and American Bar Associations; Illinois Judges Association. [U.S. Navy, 1942-1945]. ***PRACTICE AREAS:*** Trial Practice; Appellate Practice; Administrative Law; Arbitration; Mediation. ***Email:*** seymour.simon@dlapiper.com

MICHAEL L. SKLAR, born 1938; admitted to bar, 1963, Illinois. *Education:* University of Michigan (B.A., Economics, 1960); Harvard University (J.D., 1963). *Member:* Chicago, Illinois State and American Bar Associations. ***PRACTICE AREAS:*** Mergers and Acquisitions Law; Corporate Finance Law. ***Email:*** michael.sklar@dlapiper.com

PERRY J. SNYDERMAN, born 1932; admitted to bar, 1960, Illinois. *Education:* Bradley University (B.S., 1954); DePaul University (J.D., 1960). *Member:* Chicago (Member, Board of Managers), Illinois State and American Bar Associations; American College of Real Estate Lawyers. ***PRACTICE AREAS:*** Real Estate; Lodging and Timeshare; Land Use; Land Development; Multifamily Housing and Community Development; Insurance; Reinsurance. ***Email:*** perry.snyderman@dlapiper.com

MORTON M. STEINBERG, born 1945; admitted to bar, 1971, Illinois and U.S. District Court, Northern District of Illinois; 1972, U.S. Court of Appeals, 7th Circuit; 1974, U.S. Supreme Court; 1994, District of Columbia; 1998, U.S. District Court, District of Colorado; 2003, New York. *Education:* University of Illinois (A.B., with honors, 1967); Northwestern University (J.D., 1971). Senior Editor, Northwestern University Journal of Criminal Law and Criminology, 1969-1970. Pro-Bono Counsel to the Frank Lloyd Wright Preservation Trust, 1996—. *Member:* Chicago (Member, Real Property Law Committee, 1983—; Mortgage Financing Subcommittee, 1983—), Illinois State, New York State and American Bar Associations. ***PRACTICE AREAS:*** Real Estate (Property) Law; Commercial Law. ***Email:*** morton.steinberg@dlapiper.com

SAMUEL B. STEMPEL, born 1967; admitted to bar, 1992, Illinois. *Education:* University of Michigan (B.A., 1989); University of Illinois; Northwestern University (J.D., 1992). ***PRACTICE AREAS:*** Real Estate. ***Email:*** samuel.stempel@dlapiper.com

KELLY L. STONEBRAKER, born 1955; admitted to bar, 1981, Illinois. *Education:* Grinnell College; University of Chicago (B.A., 1977); New York University (J.D., 1981). *Member:* Chicago Bar Association. ***Email:*** kelly.stonebraker@dlapiper.com

(This Listing Continued)

DLA PIPER RUDNICK GRAY CARY US LLP, Chicago—Continued

ALEXANDER TERRAS, born 1952; admitted to bar, 1977, Illinois. *Education:* University of Chicago; DePaul University (J.D., 1977). ***PRACTICE AREAS:*** Finance. ***Email:*** alexander.terras@dlapiper.com

MONICA L. THOMPSON, (P.C.), born 1953; admitted to bar, 1981, Illinois. *Education:* University of Louisville (B.A., 1978); Washington University (J.D., 1981). ***PRACTICE AREAS:*** Litigation; Intellectual Property. ***Email:*** monica.thompson@dlapiper.com

BEDELL A. TIPPINS, born 1948; admitted to bar, 1978, Illinois, U.S. District Court, Northern District of Illinois including Trial Bar, U.S. Court of Appeals, Seventh Circuit and U.S. Supreme Court. *Education:* Rutgers University (B.A., 1970); John Marshall Law School (J.D., 1978). Editor-in-Chief, John Marshall Law Review, 1977-1978. *Member:* Chicago and American Bar Associations; Maritime Law Association of the United States. [Capt., U.S. Army, 1970-1974]. ***PRACTICE AREAS:*** Litigation. ***Email:*** buck.tippins@dlapiper.com

CHRISTOPHER J. TOWNSEND, born 1966; admitted to bar, 1991, Illinois; 1992, U.S. District Court, Northern District of Illinois. *Education:* Augustana College (B.A., Political Science, cum laude, 1988); University of Iowa College of Law (J.D., with honors, 1991). *Member:* Chicago, Illinois State and American (Administrative Law and Regulatory Practice Committee, Public Utility, Communications and Transportation Law Committee, and Natural Resources, Energy and Environmental Law Committee) Bar Associations. ***PRACTICE AREAS:*** Administrative Law; Appellate Practice; Communications and Media; Energy; Environmental Law; Government; Litigation; Natural Resources; Regulatory Law; Utility Law. ***Email:*** christopher.townsend@dlapiper.com

JOHN VERHEY, admitted to bar, 1988, Illinois. *Education:* Calvin College (B.A., 1985); Harvard University (J.D., cum laude, 1988). ***Email:*** john.verhey@dlapiper.com

RICHARD A. WENDY, admitted to bar, 1983, Illinois. *Education:* George Washington University (B.A., 1976; J.D., 1983); Washington University School of Architecture (M.Arch., 1983). ***PRACTICE AREAS:*** Real Estate. ***Email:*** richard.wendy@dlapiper.com

DENNIS E. WIECZOREK, born 1952; admitted to bar, 1977, Illinois and U.S. District Court, Northern District of Illinois. *Education:* Washington University (A.B., magna cum laude, 1974); Duke University (J.D., 1977) and Washington University. Chair, Governing Committee, American Bar Association Forum Committee on Franchising. Chair, Advisory Committee to North American Securities Administrators Association Franchise Project Group. Co-Author: "Annual Franchise and Distribution Law Developments 2002," ABA Press, 2002. ***PRACTICE AREAS:*** Franchise Law; Antitrust Law; Business Law. ***Email:*** dennis.wieczorek@dlapiper.com

MARK R. WILLIAMS, born 1966; admitted to bar, 1993, Illinois; 1994, District of Columbia. *Education:* University of Illinois (B.A., in Political Science, magna cum laude, 1988); The London School of Economics and Political Science (M.Sc. in Faculty of Economics-International Relations, 1989); Columbia Law School (J.D., 1992). Phi Beta Kappa. Intern, The Legal Resources Centre, Johannesburg, South Africa, 1990. Henry Luce Foundation Fellowship, Thailand Institute of Public and International Affairs, Bangkok, Thailand, 1992-1993. Foreign Legal Consultant, Lee & Ko, Seoul, South Korea, 1996-1997. *Member:* Chicago, Illinois State and American Bar Associations; District of Columbia Bar. ***LANGUAGES:*** Spanish. ***PRACTICE AREAS:*** Corporate Law; Mergers and Acquisitions; International Law; Franchise Law; Commercial Law. ***Email:*** mark.williams@dlapiper.com

DENNIS M. WILSON, born 1944; admitted to bar, 1969, Illinois. *Education:* University of Notre Dame (A.B., Economics, magna cum laude, 1966); Northwestern University (J.D., 1969). Executive Editor, Northwestern University Law Review, 1968-1969. *Member:* Chicago and American (Chairman, State and Local Taxation Committee, Section of Real Property, Probate and Trust Law, 1987-1993) Bar Associations. ***PRACTICE AREAS:*** Corporate Law; Real Estate. ***Email:*** dennis.wilson@dlapiper.com

LAWRENCE A. WOJCIK, born 1951; admitted to bar, 1977, Illinois. *Education:* DePaul University (B.S., with high honors, 1973; LL.M. in Taxation, 1981); Northwestern University (J.D., 1977). Beta Alpha Psi. Certified Public Accountant, Illinois, 1973. *Member:* Chicago, Illinois State (Committee on Professional Conduct Committee, 1995-2000; 2002—), Seventh Circuit and American Bar Associations; Chicago Council of Lawyers; American Institute of Certified Public Accountants; Illinois Society of Certified Public Accountants (Director, 2002—); The Lawyers Club of Chicago. ***PRACTICE AREAS:*** Accounting Law; Legal Malpractice Law; Securities and Commercial Litigation. ***Email:*** lawrence.wojcik@dlapiper.com

THEODORE I. YI, born 1957; admitted to bar, 1982, Illinois. *Education:* University of Illinois (B.S., B.A., 1979); Harvard University (J.D., 1982). Phi Beta Kappa. Editor, Harvard Environmental Law Review, 1979-1982. ***PRACTICE AREAS:*** Leasing Law; Shopping Center Law; Construction Law; Real Estate (Property) Law. ***Email:*** theodore.yi@dlapiper.com

MARK D. YURA, born 1953; admitted to bar, 1978, Illinois and U.S. District Court, Northern District of Illinois. *Education:* University of Michigan (B.A., with high honors, 1975; J.D., cum laude, 1978). Articles: *Structuring Commercial Real Estate Workouts: Alternatives to Foreclosures,"* 1995 Supplement, Editor; *"Legal Opinions in Illinois Real Estate Secured Loan Transactions,"* 1993, Chicago Bar Association (Co-Author). Adjunct Professor: Real Property Finance Law, John Marshall Law School, 1999-2002; University of Michigan Law School, 2003, 2005. *Member:* Chicago Bar Association (Member, Real Property Law Committee, Executive Council, 1991—; Past Chairman, Real Property Law Committee, 1996-1997; Past Chairman, Real Property Finance Subcommittee, 1991-1993); Chicago Mortgage Attorneys Association; American College of Mortgage Attorneys. ***PRACTICE AREAS:*** Mortgage Law; Real Estate (Property) Law. ***Email:*** mark.yura@dlapiper.com

ALISON N. ZIRN, admitted to bar, 1994, Illinois. *Education:* University of Michigan (B.A., 1984); Hastings College of the Law, University of California (J.D., 1987). ***PRACTICE AREAS:*** Real Estate; Property Law. ***Email:*** alison.zirn@dlapiper.com

(This Listing Continued)

WILLIAM A. ZOLLA, born 1940; admitted to bar, 1965, Illinois and U.S. District Court, Northern District of Illinois. *Education:* University of Michigan (B.A., with honors, 1962); University of Chicago (J.D., 1965). Law Clerk to Justice U.S. Schwartz, III Appellate Court, 1965-1967. ***PRACTICE AREAS:*** Real Estate Development Law; Hotel Law; Recreational Law; Resort Timeshares; Mortgage Law; Real Estate (Property) Law. ***Email:*** william.zolla@dlapiper.com

SENIOR COUNSEL

CHARLES L. EDWARDS, born 1940; admitted to bar, 1965, Illinois. *Education:* University of Wisconsin (B.B.A., with highest honors, 1962); University of Chicago (J.D., 1965). Phi Beta Kappa; Beta Gamma Sigma. Author: "Commercial Mortgage Loan Commitments: A Borrower's Perspective," *Probate & Property,* ABA (1994); Co-Author, "Hotel Room Revenues: Bates Motel Revisited," *Real Estate Law Journal,* (Summer, 1993). *Member:* Chicago Bar Association (Chair, Real Property Law Subcommittee on Real Property Finance, 1986-1988; Co-Chair, Real Property Law Subcommittee on Continuing Legal Education, 1989-1991; Vice-Chair, Real Property Law Committee, 1991-1992; Chair, Real Property Law Committee, 1992-1993); American College of Real Estate Lawyers; American College of Mortgage Attorneys; Adjunct Professor of Law, The John Marshall Law School, Real Estate Finance, LL.M. Program. ***PRACTICE AREAS:*** Finance Law; Real Estate Law. ***Email:*** charles.edwards@dlapiper.com

RICHARD S. HOMER, born 1934; admitted to bar, 1958, Illinois. *Education:* University of Chicago (B.A., 1955); Northwestern University (J.D., 1958). ***PRACTICE AREAS:*** Business Law; Real Estate Development Law. ***Email:*** richard.homer@dlapiper.com

CAROL S. LEPMAN, born 1961; admitted to bar, 1983, Michigan and U.S. District Court, Eastern District of Michigan; 1985, Illinois and U.S. Tax Court. *Education:* University of Michigan; Indiana University (LL.B., cum laude, 1983). Phi Alpha Delta. *Member:* American Bar Association; State Bar of Michigan; Profit Sharing Council of America (Member, Communication Committee, 1991—). ***PRACTICE AREAS:*** ERISA; Employee Benefits. ***Email:*** carol.lepman@dlapiper.com

OF COUNSEL

ELIZABETH H. BELKIN, born 1946; admitted to bar, 1979, Illinois. *Education:* University of Illinois (B.A., 1968; M.A., 1969); IIT., Chicago-Kent College of Law (J.D., with highest honors, 1979). Editor-in-Chief, Chicago-Kent Law Review, 1978-1979. Editor: Key Shopping Center Lease Issues, 1996. Adjunct Professor of Law (Real Estate Transactions), IIT/Chicago-Kent College of Law, 1986-1992. Law Clerk to the Honorable Joel M. Flaum: U.S. District Court for the Northern District of Illinois, 1982-1983; U.S. Court of Appeals for the Seventh Circuit, 1983. *Member:* American Bar Association (Member, Committee on Real Estate/Commercial Leasing, Co-Chair, Retail Leasing Subcommittee); International Council of Shopping Centers (Co-Chair, U.S. Law Conference, 1997-1999; Recipient, Trustee's Distinguished Service Award, 1996). ***PRACTICE AREAS:*** Real Estate Law; Partnership Law; General Business Law. ***Email:*** elizabeth.belkin@dlapiper.com

DAVID E. CHER, born 1957; admitted to bar, 1982, California (Not admitted in Illinois). *Education:* University of Chicago (B.A., 1979); Harvard University Law School (J.D., 1982). Phi Beta Kappa. Author: "Jurisdiction: Service of Process on Iran," 21 Harvard International Law Journal 775, 1980. ***PRACTICE AREAS:*** Finance; Financial Services; Bankruptcy; Real Estate Capital Markets. ***Email:*** david.cher@dlapiper.com

JONATHAN A. COHEN, born 1953; admitted to bar, 1981, Illinois. *Education:* Oberlin College (A.B., 1974); University of Chicago (J.D., 1981). ***PRACTICE AREAS:*** Commercial Real Estate Law; Leasing. ***Email:*** jonathan.cohen@dlapiper.com

RASHA ELGANZOURI, born 1971; admitted to bar, 1997, Illinois. *Education:* St. Mary's College, Notre Dame, Indiana (B.A., magna cum laude, 1993); Illinois Institute of Technology, Chicago-Kent College of Law (J.D. and M.B.A., 1997). ***LANGUAGES:*** Spanish and Arabic. ***PRACTICE AREAS:*** Real Estate; Financial Services; Anti-Money Laundering Compliance. ***Email:*** rasha.elganzouri@dlapiper.com

CARYN S. ENGLANDER, born 1957; admitted to bar, 1984, Illinois. *Education:* University of Wisconsin-Madison (B.S., 1979); Northwestern University (J.D., 1984). ***PRACTICE AREAS:*** Real Estate. ***Email:*** caryn.englander@dlapiper.com

TRACY L. FARLEY, born 1969; admitted to bar, 1995, Illinois. *Education:* Northwestern University (B.A., 1992); University of Illinois (J.D., 1995). ***PRACTICE AREAS:*** Labor and Employment. ***Email:*** tracy.farley@dlapiper.com

MARC I. FENTON, born 1953; admitted to bar, 1981, Illinois. *Education:* Loyola University (B.A., 1975); Northern Illinois University (J.D., 1981). ***PRACTICE AREAS:*** Finance. ***Email:*** marc.fenton@dlapiper.com

REYNALDO PRESTON GLOVER, born 1943; admitted to bar, 1970, New York; 1971, Illinois. *Education:* Fisk University (B.A., 1965); Harvard University (LL.B., 1968). President and Member, Board of Directors of TLC-LC, 1994—. Chairman, Board of Trustees, Fisk University, Nashville, TN. *Member:* Chicago and Cook County Bar Associations. ***PRACTICE AREAS:*** Corporate (80%); Real Estate (20%). ***Email:*** preston.glover@dlapiper.com

LISA GOYER, born 1961; admitted to bar, 1987, Illinois. *Education:* University of Missouri (B.A., magna cum laude, 1984); University of Illinois (J.D., 1987). ***PRACTICE AREAS:*** Employee Benefits; Executive Compensation. ***Email:*** lisa.goyer@dlapiper.com

DAVID T. HEJNA, born 1953; admitted to bar, 1978, Illinois. *Education:* University of Michigan (A.B.; J.D.). ***PRACTICE AREAS:*** Real Estate. ***Email:*** david.hejna@dlapiper.com

ROBERT G. HERTEL, admitted to bar, 1985, Illinois. *Education:* Michigan State University (B.S., 1972); University of Chicago (M.A., 1981); Washington University School of Law (J.D., 1985). ***PRACTICE AREAS:*** Real Estate Capital Merkets. ***Email:*** robert.hertel@dlapiper.com

KAREN LITSCHER JOHNSON, born 1961; admitted to bar, 1988, Illinois; 1989, U.S. District Court, Northern District of Illinois, Trial Bar, 1991; 1990, U.S. Court of Appeals, Seventh Circuit. *Education:* University of Wisconsin-Madison (B.A., with distinction, 1984); Cornell University (J.D., 1988). Phi Beta Kappa; Phi Kappa Phi. Co-editor in

(This Listing Continued)

chief, *Chicago Lawyer's Court Handbook,* 1997. Chair, Chicago Bar Association/Young Lawyers Section, 1998-1999. Chair-Elect, CBA/YLS, 1997-1998. Vice-chair, CBA/YLS, 1996-1997. Secretary, CBA/YLS, 1995-1996. Director, CBA/YLS, 1993-1995. Co-Chair, Environmental Law and Energy Committee, CBA/YLS, 1991-1993. Author, "Recovering Fees and Costs From the United States," Chicago Bar Association Record, November, 1994. Seminar Moderator: "Don't Wait Until the Inspector is at the Door -- Advance Planning for an Environmental Inspection," Chicago Bar Association, January 1993; Underground Storage Tanks: A Practical Approach, Chicago Bar Association, March 1992; Environmental Consultants: Understanding Their Role and Future Trends in Environmental Assessments, Chicago Bar Association, November, 1991. ***PRACTICE AREAS:*** Professional Development; Litigation. **Email:** karen.johnson@dlapiper.com

CHRISTINA KING LOUNDY, born 1968; admitted to bar, 1993, Illinois. *Education:* Carleton College (B.A., cum laude and with distinction, 1990); University of Iowa (J.D., with distinction, 1993). Symposium Editor, Transnational Law and Contemporary Problems, 1992-1993. *Member:* Chicago, Illinois State and American Bar Associations. ***PRACTICE AREAS:*** Environmental Law. **Email:** christina.loundy@dlapiper.com

CHARLES LYNN LOWDER, born 1945; admitted to bar, 1980, Illinois. *Education:* University of Illinois (B.A., 1976); DePaul University (J.D., 1980). ***PRACTICE AREAS:*** Litigation. **Email:** charles.lowder@dlapiper.com

MICHELE G. MAGNER, born 1951; admitted to bar, 1977, Illinois. *Education:* Knox College (B.A., 1973); Washington University (J.D., 1977). Order of the Coif. *Member:* Chicago Bar Association. ***PRACTICE AREAS:*** Real Estate; Property Law. **Email:** michele.magner@dlapiper.com

SUSAN M. PEDERSEN, admitted to bar, 1987, Illinois. *Education:* Saint Mary's College (B.B.A., 1981); Chicago-Kent College of Law (J.D., 1986). ***PRACTICE AREAS:*** Real Estate. **Email:** susan.pedersen@dlapiper.com

PATRICIA M. RELOSKY, born 1953; admitted to bar, 1981, Illinois. *Education:* University of Chicago Law School (J.D., 1981). ***PRACTICE AREAS:*** Real Estate. **Email:** patricia.relosky@dlapiper.com

DAVID J. RICHTER, born 1940; admitted to bar, 1970, Ohio; 1974, Illinois; 1988, Wisconsin; registered to practice before the U.S. Patent and Trademark Office. *Education:* University of Wisconsin-Madison (B.S.M.E., 1962); University of Illinois (M.B.A., 1967; J.D., 1970). Theta Tau. Patent Counsel, The Proctor-Gamble Company, Cincinnati, Ohio. Corporate Counsel and Assistant Secretary, Roper Corporation, Kankakee, Illinois. Corporate Counsel, Snap-on Tools Corporation, Snap-on Technologies, Inc. Arbitrator, City of Kankakee, Illinois, 1975. Chamber of Commerce, Kankakee, Illinois, Legislative Committee, 1976-1980, Airport Committee, 1981-1982. School Board, St. Patricks School, Kankakee, Illinois, 1979-1982, Chairman, 1981-1982. *Member:* Illinois State and American Bar Associations; State Bar of Wisconsin. [U.S. Army, 1963-1965]. ***PRACTICE AREAS:*** Patents; Trademarks; Trade Dress; Copyrights; Trade Secrets. **Email:** david.richter@dlapiper.com

LESTER ROSEN, born 1930; admitted to bar, 1955, New York; 1960, Illinois. *Education:* University of Pennsylvania (B.S., 1951); Harvard Law School (LL.B., cum laude, 1954). Member, National Panel, American Arbitration Association, 1970—. *Member:* Illinois State and American Bar Associations; American College of Real Estate Lawyers. ***PRACTICE AREAS:*** Finance; Commercial Real Estate. **Email:** lester.rosen@dlapiper.com

PAUL D. RUDNICK, born 1940; admitted to bar, 1965, Illinois and U.S. District Court, Northern District of Illinois. *Education:* Tulane University (B.S., 1962); Northwestern University (J.D., cum laude, 1965). Order of the Coif. Editor, Northwestern University Law Review, 1964-1965. Co-Author: "Illinois Real Estate Forms," Aspen Publications, 1989. Member, Pitkin County, Colorado Planning and Zoning Commission. *Member:* American College of Real Estate Lawyers. ***PRACTICE AREAS:*** Business Law; Commercial Law; Science Law; Technology Law; Business Organizations; Mortgages and Foreclosures. **Email:** paul.rudnick@dlapiper.com

MARC SEIDLER, admitted to bar, 1973, Illinois. *Education:* University of Chicago (B.A., with honors, 1970; J.D., 1973). Law Review. *Member:* American Bar Association (Forum Committee on Franchising). ***PRACTICE AREAS:*** Franchise and Dealership; Commercial Litigation; Insurance; Arbitration. **Email:** marc.seidler@dlapiper.com

JANET L. TRACY, born August 22, 1951; admitted to bar, 1981, Illinois. *Education:* University of Illinois (B.A., 1979); DePaul University (J.D., 1981). *Member:* Chicago and American Bar Associations. ***PRACTICE AREAS:*** Finance; Financial Services Law; Bankruptcy. **Email:** janet.tracy@dlapiper.com

JULIUS Y. YACKER, born 1925; admitted to bar, 1958, Illinois. *Education:* University of Chicago (M.A., 1952; J.D., 1958). *Member:* Chicago, Illinois State and American Bar Associations. ***PRACTICE AREAS:*** Housing-Affordable (70%); Community Economics Development (25%). **Email:** julius.yacker@dlapiper.com

ASSOCIATES

KARL M. AHLM, born Oak Lawn, Illinois, November 24, 1971; admitted to bar, 1996, Illinois. *Education:* Northwestern University (B.A., 1993); George Washington University (J.D., with honors, 1996).

BRIAN A. AUDETTE, born 1974; admitted to bar, 2002, Illinois. *Education:* Brown University (B.A., 1997); Loyola University of Chicago (J.D., cum laude, 2002). ***PRACTICE AREAS:*** Bankruptcy; Business Reorganization. **Email:** brian.audette@dlapiper.com

HEIDI J. AZULAY, born 1974; admitted to bar, 2000, Illinois. *Education:* University of Wisconsin-Madison (B.A., with honors, 1997); Chicago-Kent College of Law, Institute of Technology (J.D., 2000). ***PRACTICE AREAS:*** Real Estate. **Email:** heidi.azulay@dlapiper.com

JENNIFER J. BAUMANN, admitted to bar, 2003, Illinois; 2004, California. *Education:* University of Michigan (B.A., with honors, 2000); University of Michigan Law School (J.D., 2003). ***PRACTICE AREAS:*** Trademarks; Copyrights; New Media. **Email:** jennifer.baumann@dlapiper.com

(This Listing Continued)

ELIZABETH ROWNTREE BECK, born 1968; admitted to bar, 1995, Illinois. *Education:* Washington University (B.A., 1991; J.D., 1995). Order of the Coif. Member, Washington University Law Review. *Member:* Chicago and American Bar Associations. ***PRACTICE AREAS:*** Real Estate. **Email:** elizabeth.beck@dlapiper.com

ANDREW P. BLEIMAN, born 1973; admitted to bar, 1998, Illinois. *Education:* University of Texas at Austin (B.A., 1995); IIT/Chicago-Kent College of Law (J.D., with honors, 1998). ***PRACTICE AREAS:*** Commercial Litigation; Product Liability; Toxic Torts; Franchise Litigation; Construction Litigation. **Email:** andrew.bleiman@dlapiper.com

WILLIAM A. BORDERS, born 1969; admitted to bar, 2003, Illinois. *Education:* Allegheny College (B.A., English, 1992); Chicago-Kent College of Law (J.D., 2002). Author: "Learning from the Storm: Lessons for Illinois Following California's Experience with Electricity Restructuring," Chicago-Kent Law Review, Vol. 77, Number 1, 2001. *Member:* Chicago, Federal Energy and American Bar Associations. ***PRACTICE AREAS:*** Energy; Environmental Law; Litigation. **Email:** william.borders@dlapiper.com

ANN MARIE BREDIN, born 1974; admitted to bar, 1998, Illinois and U.S. District Court, Northern District of Illinois. *Education:* Northwestern University (B.S., 1995); Northwestern University School of Law (J.D., 1998). ***PRACTICE AREAS:*** Bankruptcy; Restructuring; Insolvency. **Email:** ann.bredin@dlapiper.com

MATTHEW F. CARMODY, admitted to bar, 2000, Illinois. *Education:* University of Illinois (B.S.); DePaul University (J.D.). *Member:* Chicago, Illinois State and American Bar Associations; Chicago Inns of Court. ***PRACTICE AREAS:*** Commercial Litigation; Appellate Practice. **Email:** matthew.carmody@dlapiper.com

CORINNE PAVLIS CARR, born 1969; admitted to bar, 1994, Illinois. *Education:* St. Mary's College, Notre Dame, Indiana (B.A., 1991); University of Notre Dame, School of Law, Notre Dame, Indiana (J.D., 1994). ***PRACTICE AREAS:*** Insurance Regulatory Law; Insurance Transactional. **Email:** corinne.carr@dlapiper.com

DENISE C. CASTILLO, born 1973; admitted to bar, 1999, Illinois. *Education:* DePauw University (B.A., magna cum laude, 1996); Boston College (J.D., 1999). **Email:** denise.castillo@dlapiper.com

DIANA CHAFEY, admitted to bar, 1994, Illinois. *Education:* Arizona State University (B.A., 1990); Valparaiso University (J.D., 1994). *Member:* Chicago, Illinois State and American Bar Associations. ***PRACTICE AREAS:*** Insurance Regulation; Reinsurance; Corporate Law. **Email:** diana.wazenberg@dlapiper.com

AMY CHENG, born 1971; admitted to bar, 1997, Illinois. *Education:* University of Michigan (B.A., 1994); American University, Washington College of Law (J.D., magna cum laude, 1997). Member, The American University Journal of International Law and Policy. *Member:* Chicago, Illinois State and American Bar Associations. ***LANGUAGES:*** Chinese, Japanese and French. ***PRACTICE AREAS:*** Franchise and Distribution; Franchise and Distribution - International; Mergers and Acquisitions; General Corporate. **Email:** amy.cheng@dlapiper.com

WILLIAM CHOSLOVSKY, admitted to bar, 1994, Illinois. *Education:* University of Illinois (B.S., 1990); Harvard Law School (J.D., 1994). ***PRACTICE AREAS:*** Bankruptcy; Litigation; Sports Law. **Email:** william.choslovsky@dlapiper.com

BRIAN ADAM COHEN, born 1978; admitted to bar, 2003, Illinois. *Education:* University of Illinois at Urbana-Champaign (B.A., 2000); Northwestern University (J.D., 2003). *Member:* Chicago Bar Association (Young Lawyers Section; Real Estate Law Committee). ***PRACTICE AREAS:*** Real Estate. **Email:** brian.cohen@dlapiper.com

JOSEPH E. COLLINS, born 1969; admitted to bar, 1996, Illinois. *Education:* Loyola University (B.A., 1991); Chicago-Kent College of Law, Illinois Institute of Technology (J.D., 1996). ***PRACTICE AREAS:*** Litigation. **Email:** joseph.collins@dlapiper.com

JESSE A. CRIZ, born 1973; admitted to bar, 1998, Illinois. *Education:* University of Illinois (B.S., Accountancy, 1995); Loyola University Chicago (J.D., 1998). ***PRACTICE AREAS:*** Real Estate; Capital Markets; Business Taxation; Corporate. **Email:** jesse.criz@dlapiper.com

MARIAH F. DIGRINO, born 1978; admitted to bar, 2004, Illinois. *Education:* Western Illinois University (B.A., 2000); University of Illinois College of Law (J.D., 2004). ***PRACTICE AREAS:*** Real Estate. **Email:** mariah.digrino@dlapiper.com

JESSE W. DODSON, born 1976; admitted to bar, 2003, Illinois. *Education:* University of Colorado at Boulder (B.S., 1999); Northwestern University (J.D., 2003). ***PRACTICE AREAS:*** Real Estate; Land Use; Zoning. **Email:** jesse.dodson@dlapiper.com

C. CRAIG DOLLY, JR., born 1970; admitted to bar, 2001, Illinois. *Education:* Vanderbilt University (B.A., 1993); John Marshall Law School (J.D., 2001). *Member:* Chicago and American Bar Associations. ***PRACTICE AREAS:*** Finance; Corporate; Bankruptcy. **Email:** craig.dolly@dlapiper.com

GINA L. DURHAM, born 1974; admitted to bar, 1999, Illinois. *Education:* Northwestern University (B.A., 1996); DePaul University (J.D., 1999). Order of the Coif. Article and Notes Editor, DePaul Business Journal. *Member:* Chicago Bar Association. ***PRACTICE AREAS:*** Intellectual Property. **Email:** gina.durham@dlapiper.com

PATRICE D'ZIIRE, admitted to bar, 2003, Illinois. *Education:* University of Illinois at Urbana-Champaign (B.A., 1996); New York University (J.D., 2001). ***PRACTICE AREAS:*** Litigation. **Email:** patrice.d'ziire@dlapiper.com

PETER M. ELLIS, born 1972; admitted to bar, 1998, Ohio; 1999, U.S. District Court, Northern and Southern Districts of Illinois and U.S. Court of Appeals, Sixth Circuit; 2000, Illinois; 2001, U.S. Court of Appeals, Seventh Circuit. *Education:* University of Michigan (B.A., 1994); The Ohio State University (J.D., 1998). ***PRACTICE AREAS:*** General Litigation; Franchise Distribution; Corporate. **Email:** peter.ellis@dlapiper.com

TIMOTHY M. ENRIGHT, born 1971; admitted to bar, 2002, Illinois. *Education:* Southern Illinois University (B.A., 1993); John Marshall (J.D., 2002). ***PRACTICE AREAS:*** Finance; Bankruptcy. **Email:** timothy.enright@dlapiper.com

DAVID J. FEINBERG, admitted to bar, 2003, Illinois. *Education:* Northwestern University (B.A., Political Science, 1999); Northwestern University School of Law (J.D., cum laude, 2003). *Member:* Chicago and American Bar Associations. ***PRACTICE AREAS:*** Real Estate. **Email:** david.feinberg@dlapiper.com

(This Listing Continued)

DLA PIPER RUDNICK GRAY CARY US LLP, Chicago—Continued

JEFFREY M. FRIEDMAN, admitted to bar, 2000, Illinois. *Education:* University of Michigan (B.A., 1997); Chicago-Kent College of Law, Illinois Institute of Technology (J.D., 2000); New York University School of Law (LL.M., Taxation, 2001); Stuart Graduate School of Business, Illinois Institute of Technology (M.B.A., 2002). ***PRACTICE AREAS:*** Real Estate Capital Markets; Tax; International Tax; Mergers and Acquisitions. ***Email:*** jeffrey.friedman@dlapiper.com

PAULA DAVIS FRIEDMAN, born 1967; admitted to bar, 1994, Maryland; 1997, Illinois. *Education:* Lehigh University (B.A., 1991); University of Baltimore School of Law (J.D., cum laude, 1994). Recent Development Editor, University of Baltimore Law Forum, 1992-1994. *Member:* Maryland State and Illinois State Bar Associations. ***PRACTICE AREAS:*** Commercial Litigation. ***Email:*** paula.friedman@dlapiper.com

MICHAEL S. GERSHOWITZ, born 1971; admitted to bar, 1997, Illinois. *Education:* University of Michigan (B.A., with distinction, 1993); Northwestern University (J.D., 1997). Author, "Waiver of the Plea-Statement Rules," Journal of Criminal Law and Criminology, 86:4, Summer, 1996. ***PRACTICE AREAS:*** Real Estate. ***Email:*** michael.gershowitz@dlapiper.com

LEAH D. GIDRON, born 1969; admitted to bar, 1996, Illinois and U.S. District Court, Northern District of Illinois; U.S. District Court, Central District of Illinois; U.S. District Court, Northern District of Indiana; U.S. Court of Appeals, Seventh Circuit. *Education:* University of California at Berkeley (B.A., with high distinction, 1991); Northwestern University School of Law (J.D., 1996). ***PRACTICE AREAS:*** Labor and Employment. ***Email:*** leah.gidron@dlapiper.com

JOSHUA M. GLAZOV, born 1970; admitted to bar, 1995, Florida; 1999, Illinois. *Education:* George Washington University (B.A., 1992); University of Miami (J.D., cum laude, 1995). ***PRACTICE AREAS:*** Real Estate; Timeshare. ***Email:*** joshua.glazov@dlapiper.com

EMILY S. GOTTLIEB, born 1975; admitted to bar, 2000, Illinois. *Education:* University of Michigan (B.A., 1997); Loyola University School of Law, Chicago (J.D., magna cum laude, 2000). Phi Beta Kappa. ***LANGUAGES:*** Hebrew. ***PRACTICE AREAS:*** Bankruptcy; Creditors' Rights. ***Email:*** emily.gottlieb@dlapiper.com

GREGG SETH GRAINES, born 1977; admitted to bar, 2002, Illinois. *Education:* University of Wisconsin-Madison (B.A., 1999); Chicago-Kent College of Law (J.D., 2002). Ohio Real Estate License, 1998. ***PRACTICE AREAS:*** Real Estate. ***Email:*** gregg.graines@dlapiper.com

DEBORAH M. GUTFELD, born 1976; admitted to bar, 2000, Illinois. *Education:* Indiana University (B.S., Marketing and International Business, with high distinction, 1997); Northwestern University (J.D., 2000). Beta Gamma Sigma. *Member:* Chicago Bar Association (Co-Chair, Young Lawyers Section, Bankruptcy Committee). ***PRACTICE AREAS:*** Bankruptcy; Business Reorganization; Corporate Law. ***Email:*** deborah.gutfeld@dlapiper.com

KRISTA S. HALLBERG, admitted to bar, 1998, Illinois and U.S. District Court, Northern District of Illinois. *Education:* Miami University (B.A., cum laude, 1995) Phi Beta Kappa; Loyola University (J.D., cum laude, 1998). Author: "Construction Industry Expert Testimony in the Aftermath of Kumho Tire Co., Ltd. v. Carmichael and Under amended Rule 702 of the Federal Rules of Evidence," ABA Forum on the Construction Industry 2001 Annual Meeting, Volume 2, April 26-28, 2001; "Five Steps an Owner Should Take to Terminate a Construction Contract Properly," 21 Shopping Center Legal Update 1, 11-13, Spring 2001; "Construction Site Safety," Structure Magazine, p.19, April 2001; "Contractual Protections Against Mechanics Liens and the Importance of Lien Waivers," Commercial Leasing Law and Strategy, November/December 2001. *Member:* Chicago and American Bar Associations. ***PRACTICE AREAS:*** Construction Law; Litigation. ***Email:*** krista.hallberg@dlapiper.com

ALBERT E. HARTMANN, born 1972; admitted to bar, 1998, Illinois and U.S. District Court, Northern District of Illinois, including Trial Bar, 2000. *Education:* University of Illinois at Urbana-Champaign (B.A., with distinction, 1994); University of Michigan Law School, Ann Arbor, Michigan (J.D., 1998). Note, "Crafting an Advocate for a Child," 31 U. Mich. J.L. Reform 237, 1997. ***PRACTICE AREAS:*** Civil Litigation; Fair Credit Reporting Act. ***Email:*** albert.hartmann@dlapiper.com

ROBERT T. HEFFERNAN, born 1971; admitted to bar, 2002, Illinois. *Education:* Tulane University (B.S., 1993); University of Illinois (J.D., 2002). [U.S. Navy, 1993-1999]. ***PRACTICE AREAS:*** Real Estate. ***Email:*** robert.heffernan@dlapiper.com

JONATHAN R. HELTON, born 1975; admitted to bar, 2001, Illinois. *Education:* University of Kentucky (B.A., 1998; J.D., cum laude, 2001). ***PRACTICE AREAS:*** Employee Benefits; Executive Compensation. ***Email:*** jonathan.helton@dlapiper.com

R. MATTHEW HILLER, born Atlanta, Georgia, November 27, 1975; admitted to bar, 2002, Illinois and U.S. District Court, Northern District of Illinois; 2003, U.S. Court of Appeals, Seventh Circuit. *Education:* University of Missouri (A.B., 1998); University of Illinois-Urbana-Champaign (J.D., 2002). ***REPORTED CASES:*** Moore v. Knight, 368 F. 3d 936 (7th Circuit 2004). ***PRACTICE AREAS:*** Litigation. ***Email:*** matthew.hiller@dlapiper.com

JOHN A. HUGHES, admitted to bar, 2001, Illinois. *Education:* Michigan State University (B.A., 1998); George Washington University (J.D., 2001). ***PRACTICE AREAS:*** Franchise Litigation; Litigation; Franchise Distribution. ***Email:*** john.hughes@dlapiper.com

STEVEN V. HUNTER, born 1977; admitted to bar, 2002, Illinois. *Education:* Brown University (A.B., 1999); Georgetown University Law Center (J.D., 2002). ***LANGUAGES:*** American Sign. ***PRACTICE AREAS:*** Product Liability; Toxic Torts. ***Email:*** steven.hunter@dlapiper.com

CHRISTINA HWANG, admitted to bar, 2003, Texas; 2004, Illinois; registered to practice before U.S. Patent and Trademark Office. *Education:* University of Texas (B.A., 1999; J.D., 2002). *Member:* American Intellectual Property Law Association. ***PRACTICE AREAS:*** Technology Sourcing. ***Email:*** christina.hwang@dlapiper.com

(This Listing Continued)

DOUGLAS W. HYMAN, born 1970; admitted to bar, 1995, Illinois. *Education:* Indiana University, Bloomington (B.A., 1992; J.D., 1995). Member, Moot Court Honors Board. Publications: Defense Research Institute Industry Liability News, "The Elimination of Direct Reliance in Fraud/Products Liability Actions," Vol. 1, No. 2 (Spring 1998); Washington Legal Foundation, "California Supreme Court Blocks EMF Lawsuits," Vol. 6, No. 30 (November 15, 1996); Food and Drug Law Journal, "The Regulation of Health Claims in Food Advertising: Have the FTC and FDA Finally Reached a Common Ground?" Vol. 51, No. 1 (1996). *Member:* Chicago and American Bar Associations; Securities Industry Association. ***PRACTICE AREAS:*** Securities Litigation; SEC Enforcement; Commercial Litigation. ***Email:*** douglas.hyman@dlapiper.com

UNMAISH JINDAL, admitted to bar, 2003, Illinois. *Education:* University of Michigan (B.A., 1998); Michigan State University College of Law (J.D., 2003). ***PRACTICE AREAS:*** Real Estate. ***Email:*** aj.jindal@dlapiper.com

RICHARD BLAKE JOHNSTON, born 1963; admitted to bar, 1997, Illinois and U.S. District Court, Northern District of Illinois; registered to practice before U.S. Patent and Trademark Office. *Education:* The Ohio State University (B.S.M.E., 1986); University of Nebraska (M.B.A., 1989); Loyola University (J.D., 1997). *Member:* Chicago, Illinois State and American Bar Associations; Intellectual Property Law Association of Chicago; American Intellectual Property Law Association. ***PRACTICE AREAS:*** Intellectual Property. ***Email:*** blake.johnston@dlapiper.com

AMANDA JONES, admitted to bar, 2005, Illinois. *Education:* University of Oklahoma (B.A./B.S., 2000); Vanderbilt University Law School (J.D., 2005). *Member:* American Bar Association; Association of Trial Lawyers of America; National Native American Law Student Assocation. ***PRACTICE AREAS:*** Litigation. ***Email:*** amanda.jones@dlapiper.com

MICHAEL KASDIN, admitted to bar, 2004, Illinois. *Education:* Cornell University (B.A., 1999); Chicago-Kent College of Law (J.D., 2004). ***LANGUAGES:*** French. ***PRACTICE AREAS:*** Litigation. ***Email:*** michael.kasdin@dlapiper.com

ALICE A. KELLY, born 1969; admitted to bar, 1996, Missouri; 2000, California (Not admitted in Illinois). *Education:* Saint Louis University (B.A., 1992; J.D., 1996). ***PRACTICE AREAS:*** Franchise and Distribution. ***Email:*** alice.kelly@dlapiper.com

ROBYN KOYNER, born 1974; admitted to bar, 2000, New York; 2001, Illinois. *Education:* Johns Hopkins University (B.A., 1996); University of Michigan (J.D., 1999). ***PRACTICE AREAS:*** Corporate Law; Securities. ***Email:*** robyn.koyner@dlapiper.com

ERIN KREJCI, born 1979; admitted to bar, 2004, Illinois. *Education:* University of Illinois (B.S., 2001); Georgetown University (J.D., 2004). ***PRACTICE AREAS:*** Litigation. ***Email:*** erin.krejci@dlapiper.com

JASON KRELLNER, born 1974; admitted to bar, 2000, Illinois. *Education:* State University of New York at Binghamton (B.A., 1996); University of Minnesota (J.D., 2000). ***PRACTICE AREAS:*** Corporate; Securities; Mergers and Acquisitions; Privacy. ***Email:*** jason.krellner@dlapiper.com

VILDANA KUJUNDJIC, born 1974; admitted to bar, 2000, Illinois. *Education:* University of Illinois at Urbana-Champaign (B.S., 1996); Chicago-Kent College of Law, Illinois Institute of Technology (J.D., with honors, 2000). Law Clerk to Magistrate Judge Arlander Keys, United States District Court, Northern District of Illinois, May 2002-May 2003. *Member:* Chicago and American Bar Associations. ***LANGUAGES:*** Serbo-Croatian. ***PRACTICE AREAS:*** Corporate Law; Securities. ***Email:*** vildana.kujundjic@dlapiper.com

PETER GIBBONS LAWRENCE, born 1972; admitted to bar, 1997, Illinois. *Education:* University of Notre Dame (B.A., cum laude, 1994); University of Illinois (J.D., summa cum laude, 1997). Order of the Coif. *Member:* Chicago Bar Association. ***PRACTICE AREAS:*** Corporate; Securities. ***Email:*** peter.lawrence@dlapiper.com

ROBERT J. LEDUC, born 1967; admitted to bar, 1997, Illinois; 1999, Massachusetts. *Education:* University of Wisconsin-Eau Claire (B.B.A., 1992); New York University (J.D., 1997). ***PRACTICE AREAS:*** Federal Income Tax. ***Email:*** robert.leduc@dlapiper.com

SANG-YUL LEE, born 1968; admitted to bar, 1996, Illinois. *Education:* Northwestern University (B.A., 1990); University of Illinois (J.D., 1995; A.M., 1995). Trial Attorney, National Labor Relations Board (1995-1999). ***LANGUAGES:*** Korean. ***PRACTICE AREAS:*** Labor and Employment Law; Litigation; Corporate Law. ***Email:*** sangyul.lee@dlapiper.com

SAL A. LELE, born 1971; admitted to bar, 1998, Illinois. *Education:* University of Illinois (B.A., Political Science, 1993; B.S., Finance, 1993); University of North Carolina (J.D., 1998). Editor, North Carolina Banking Journal, 1997-1998. Staff, North Carolina Law Review, 1996-1997. *Member:* Illinois State and American Bar Associations. ***PRACTICE AREAS:*** Information Technology; Technology and Science; Electronic Commerce; Internet Law; Computer Law; Telecommunications Law. ***Email:*** sal.lele@dlapiper.com

JAMIE LOCKHART, admitted to bar, 2002, Minnesota and Wisconsin (Not admitted in Illinois). *Education:* Boston College (B.A., 1999); University of Wisconsin Law School (J.D., 2002). ***PRACTICE AREAS:*** Corporate and Securities. ***Email:*** jamie.lockhart@dlapiper.com

GILLIAN D. MADSEN, born 1972; admitted to bar, 1997, Illinois and U.S. District Court, Northern District of Illinois; 2001, U.S. District Court, Central District of Illinois; U.S. Court of Appeals, Seventh Circuit; U.S. Court of Federal Claims. *Education:* Princeton University (B.S.E., cum laude, 1994); Northwestern University (J.D., 1997). Member, Northwestern University National Moot Court Team, 1996. Recipient: William Jennings Bryan Award and Lowden Wigmore Prize for winning the Julius H. Miner Moot Court Competition. Staff Member, 1995-1996; Associate Articles Editor, Northwestern University Law Review, 1996-1997. Co-Author: "Recent Supreme Court Rulings on the Americans with Disabilities Act," Trial Lawyer's Guide, Volume 43, Number 2, 1999. *Member:* Chicago Bar Association. ***PRACTICE AREAS:*** Litigation. ***Email:*** gillian.madsen@dlapiper.com

MICHELE K. MALIS, born 1970; admitted to bar, 1996, Illinois. *Education:* University of Southern California (B.A., 1992); Pepperdine University (J.D., 1996). ***PRACTICE AREAS:*** Estate and Gift Taxation. ***Email:*** michele.malis@dlapiper.com

(This Listing Continued)

KATHERINE F. MARZO, born 1976; admitted to bar, 2004, Illinois. *Education:* Northwestern University (B.A., 1998); Northwestern University School of Law (J.D., 2004). ***LANGUAGES:*** Spanish. ***PRACTICE AREAS:*** Real Estate. ***Email:*** kate.marzo@dlapiper.com

VAL D. MATHELIER, born 1975; admitted to bar, 2003, Illinois. *Education:* University of Wisconsin-Madison (B.A., 1997); Northwestern University School of Law (J.D., 2002). ***PRACTICE AREAS:*** Real Estate. ***Email:*** val.mathelier@dlapiper.com

SPIRIDOULA MAVROTHALASITIS, admitted to bar, 2003, Illinois. *Education:* Northwestern University (B.A., 1997); University of Michigan (J.D., 2003). ***PRACTICE AREAS:*** Litigation. ***Email:*** litza.mavrothalasitis@dlapiper.com

MICHAEL D. McCULLOUGH, born 1967; admitted to bar, 1995, Illinois and U.S. District Court, Northern District of Illinois. *Education:* Indiana University (B.S., in Finance, 1989); Loyola University Chicago School of Law (J.D., cum laude, 1995). Recipient: American Jurisprudence Award in Legal Writing and Secured Transactions, Loyola University Chicago School of Law. Lead Articles Editor, Loyola University of Chicago Law Journal, 1994. Author: "When First In Time Is Not First In Right: The Supreme Court Increases Problems for Judgment Creditors in United States v. McDermott," 25 Loy.U.Chi.L.J. 405 (1994). *Member:* Chicago and American (Litigation Section) Bar Associations. ***PRACTICE AREAS:*** Commercial Litigation. ***Email:*** michael.mccullough@dlapiper.com

COLLEEN E. McMANUS, born 1972; admitted to bar, 1997, Illinois. *Education:* Indiana University (B.A., 1994); DePaul University College of Law (J.D., 1997). ***PRACTICE AREAS:*** Bankruptcy; Commercial Litigation. ***Email:*** colleen.mcmanus@dlapiper.com

KARLA MITCHELL, admitted to bar, 2001, Illinois. *Education:* Spring Hill College (B.S., 1998); Washington University (J.D., 2001). ***PRACTICE AREAS:*** Corporate; Securities. ***Email:*** karla.mitchell@dlapiper.com

LAUREN JILL MUROV, admitted to bar, 2004, Illinois. *Education:* Indiana University (B.A., 2000); DePaul University (J.D., summa cum laude, 2004). Editor, DePaul University Law Review. *Member:* Chicago and American Bar Associations. ***PRACTICE AREAS:*** Franchise; Distribution; Corporate. ***Email:*** lauren.murov@dlapiper.com

AILEEN T. MURPHY, admitted to bar, 2002, Illinois. *Education:* Bryn Mawr College (B.A., 1995); University of Michigan (J.D., 2002). *Member:* Chicago and Illinois State Bar Associations. ***PRACTICE AREAS:*** Corporate and Securities; Health Law. ***Email:*** aileen.murphy@dlapiper.com

NICOLE CISZAK MURPHY, born 1971; admitted to bar, 2000, New Jersey; 2001, New York; 2003, Illinois. *Education:* Boston College (B.A., magna cum laude, 1994); Boston College Law School (J.D., magna cum laude, 2000). ***PRACTICE AREAS:*** Finance. ***Email:*** nicole.murphy@dlapiper.com

MATTATHIAS H. OBERMAN, born 1978; admitted to bar, 2004, Illinois. *Education:* University of Virginia (B.A., 2000; J.D., 2004). ***PRACTICE AREAS:*** Corporate; Securities. ***Email:*** matt.oberman@dlapiper.com

MICAH R. ONIXT, born 1972; admitted to bar, 1998, Illinois and U.S. District Court, Northern District of Illinois; registered to practice before U.S. Patent and Trademark Office. *Education:* University of Michigan (B.A., English, 1994); University of Illinois (B.S., Biology, cum laude, 1995); Loyola University (J.D., cum laude, 1998). Executive Lead Articles Editor, Loyola Law Journal. Member, Golden Key Honor Society. Newsletter Editor and Planning Board Member, Intellectual Property and Computer Law Committee, Young Lawyer's Division. Publication, Romer V. Evans: a Positive Portent of the Future, 28 Loy. U. Chi. L.J. 593 (1997). *Member:* Chicago, Illinois State and American Bar Associations; Intellectual Property Law Society. ***PRACTICE AREAS:*** Corporate; Securities. ***Email:*** micah.onixt@dlapiper.com

KIMBERLIE PEARLMAN, born 1973; admitted to bar, 2001, Illinois. *Education:* University of Illinois (B.A., 1995); John Marshall Law School (J.D., 2001). ***PRACTICE AREAS:*** Real Estate. ***Email:*** kimberlie.pearlman@dlapiper.com

ANN PILLE, born 1978; admitted to bar, 2004, Illinois. *Education:* Northwestern University (B.S., 2000); University of Michigan (J.D., 2004). ***PRACTICE AREAS:*** Finance. ***Email:*** ann.pille@dlapiper.com

GRACE Y. POE, born 1972; admitted to bar, 1997, Illinois. *Education:* Northwestern Univ. (B.S., 1994; J.D., cum laude, 1997). ***Email:*** grace.poe@dlapiper.com

CARL H. POEDTKE, III, born 1969; admitted to bar, 1996, Illinois and U.S. District Court, Northern District of Illinois. *Education:* Stetson University (B.A., 1992); John Marshall Law School (J.D., magna cum laude, 1996). Phi Delta Phi. Order of the Coif; Moot Court. Member, John Marshall Law Review. Law Clerk to: the Honorable Charles R. Norgle, Sr., U.S. District Court, Northern District of Illinois, 1998-1999; the Honorable Peg McDonnell Breslin, Illinois Appellate Court, Third District, 1996-1998. *Member:* Chicago, Illinois State and American Bar Associations. ***PRACTICE AREAS:*** Financial Services Law. ***Email:*** carl.poedtke@dlapiper.com

KALYNA A. PROCYK, born 1976; admitted to bar, 2004, Illinois. *Education:* Wesleyan University (B.A., 1997); Chicago-Kent College of Law (J.D., with honors, 2004). *Member:* Chicago, American and Federal Energy Bar Associations. ***LANGUAGES:*** Ukranian, French, Czech and Polish. ***PRACTICE AREAS:*** Litigation. ***Email:*** kalyna.procyk@dlapiper.com

MARIANNE RAIMONDI, born Chicago, Illinois; admitted to bar, 1999, Illinois, 2000, U.S. District Court, Northern District of Illinois. *Education:* Loyola University (B.B.A., 1993); John Marshall Law School (J.D., 1999). *Member:* Illinois State Bar Association; The Justinian Society; Illinois Real Estate Lawyer's Association. ***PRACTICE AREAS:*** Real Estate; Affordable Housing; Public Finance. ***Email:*** marianne.raimondi@dlapiper.com

ALEXANDRA D. ROSE, admitted to bar, 2001, Illinois and U.S. District Court, Northern District of Illinois. *Education:* University of Michigan (B.A., 1992); George Washington University (J.D., 2001). ***PRACTICE AREAS:*** Corporate and Securities. ***Email:*** alexandra.rose@dlapiper.com

(This Listing Continued)

SUZANNE KARBARZ ROVNER, born 1970; admitted to bar, 1995, Virginia; 1996, Illinois; 1997, District of Columbia. *Education:* University of Illinois (B.A., 1992); George Washington University (J.D., 1995). ***PRACTICE AREAS:*** Construction Law; Government Contracts; White Collar Crime. ***Email:*** suzanne.rovner@dlapiper.com

TERRY I. RYAN, admitted to bar, 2003, New York; 2005, Illinois. *Education:* Cornell University (B.A., 1999); Northwestern University School of Law (J.D., 2002). ***PRACTICE AREAS:*** Litigation. ***Email:*** terry.ryan@dlapiper.com

THOMAS W. RYAN, born 1969; admitted to bar, 1997, Ohio; 1998, Illinois and U.S. District Court, Northern District of Illinois; registered to practice before U.S. Patent and Trademark Office. *Education:* University of Wisconsin-Madison (B.S., 1991); University of Dayton (J.D., 1997). *Member:* Chicago and American Bar Associations; American Intellectual Property Law Association (AIPLA); Chicago Intellectual Property Law Association. ***PRACTICE AREAS:*** Intellectual Property; Intellectual Property Licensing. ***Email:*** thomas.ryan@dlapiper.com

ANDREW J. SANNES, admitted to bar, 2004, Illinois. *Education:* University of Wisconsin-Madison (B.A. 1998); John Marshall Law School (J.D., 2004). ***PRACTICE AREAS:*** Corporate Law; Securities. ***Email:*** andrew.sannes@dlapiper.com

MARIA SCHERER, admitted to bar, 2001, Illinois. *Education:* University of Notre Dame (B.A.); University of Virginia (J.D., 2001). ***PRACTICE AREAS:*** Real Estate. ***Email:*** maria.scherer@dlapiper.com

JENNIFER L. SCHILLING, born 1973; admitted to bar, 1998, Illinois. *Education:* University of Wisconsin, Milwaukee (B.A., 1995); Loyola University, Chicago (J.D., cum laude, 1998). National Moot Court. ***PRACTICE AREAS:*** Labor and Employment. ***Email:*** jennifer.schilling@dlapiper.com

JUDITH L. SCHUCH, born 1968; admitted to bar, 2000, Illinois. *Education:* University of Illinois (B.A., 1990); The John Marshall Law School (J.D., cum laude, 2000). Delta Theta Phi. Recipient: Baim Scholarship; Rosenberg Scholarship. Member, The John Marshall Law Review. Member, JMLS Alumni Advisory Board. *Member:* Chicago, Illinois State and American Bar Associations; Women's Bar Foundation (Member, Board of Director). ***PRACTICE AREAS:*** Commercial Litigation; TILA; Construction Law; Landlord and Tenant Law; Class Actions. ***Email:*** judith.schuch@dlapiper.com

RAJ N. SHAH, born 1973; admitted to bar, 1998, Illinois. *Education:* University of Michigan (B.B.A., 1995; J.D., 1997). Champion, University of Michigan Campbell Moot Court Competition, 1998. University of Michigan Journal of International Law. ***LANGUAGES:*** Gujarati. ***PRACTICE AREAS:*** Complex Commercial Litigation. ***Email:*** raj.shah@dlapiper.com

CHAD SHIFRIN, admitted to bar, 2004, Illinois. *Education:* University of Illinois-Champaign (B.A., 2001); Chicago-Kent College of Law (J.D., 2004). ***PRACTICE AREAS:*** Litigation. ***Email:*** chad.shifrin@dlapiper.com

JOHN P. SIEMSEN, born 1970; admitted to bar, 2000, Illinois. *Education:* Michigan State University (B.S., 1993); Chicago-Kent College of Law, Illinois Institute of Technology (J.D., 1999). Valedictorian; Order of the Coif. Notes and Comments Editor, Chicago-Kent Law Review. Member, Moot Court Honor Society. *Member:* Illinois State, Chicago and American Bar Associations. ***PRACTICE AREAS:*** Franchise; Distribution; Corporate; Securities; Mergers and Acquisitions. ***Email:*** john.siemsen@dlapiper.com

DAVID E. SINGER, born 1969; admitted to bar, 1996, Maryland; 2001, Illinois. *Education:* Princeton University (A.B., 1991); University of Maryland (J.D./M.B.A., 1996). ***PRACTICE AREAS:*** Corporate Finance; Railcar Finance; Corporation; Securities; Public Finance. ***Email:*** david.singer@dlapiper.com

ERICA S. SITKOFF, born 1979; admitted to bar, 2004, Illinois. *Education:* Northwestern University (B.A., 2001); Georgetown University Law Center (J.D., 2004). ***LANGUAGES:*** French. ***PRACTICE AREAS:*** Real Estate. ***Email:*** erica.sitkoff@dlapiper.com

CHRISTOPHER N. SKEY, born 1969; admitted to bar, 1997, Illinois; 1998, Florida. *Education:* Northwestern University, Evanston, Il. (B.A., 1991); Northwestern University School of Law, Chicago, Il. (J.D., cum laude, 1997). Law Clerk to the Honorable Steven D. Merryday, U.S. District Court, Middle District of Florida, 2000-2003. ***PRACTICE AREAS:*** Litigation. ***Email:*** christopher.skey@dlapiper.com

COREE SMITH, admitted to bar, 2001, Illinois. *Education:* University of Northern Iowa (B.A., summa cum laude, 1998); University of Iowa (J.D., with high honors, 2001). Phi Delta Phi. Captain, National Moot Court Competition Team. Best Advocate, Moot Court Competition. Managing Editor, Iowa Law Review. *Member:* American Bar Association. ***PRACTICE AREAS:*** Real Estate. ***Email:*** coree.smith@dlapiper.com

KATHLEEN E. STENDAHL, born 1975; admitted to bar, 2002, Illinois and U.S. District Court, Northern District of Illinois. *Education:* Northwestern University (B.A., 1998) University of Minnesota (J.D., 2001). Editor, Journal of Law and Inequality, 2000-2001. Author, "Vicarious Liability of Motor Vehicle Lessors," Business Lawyer, May 2004. *Member:* Chicago, Illinois State and American Bar Associations. ***LANGUAGES:*** Spanish. ***PRACTICE AREAS:*** Franchise and Distribution. ***Email:*** kathleen.stendahl@dlapiper.com

DARRELL W. TAYLOR, born 1964; admitted to bar, 2003, Indiana; 2005, Illinois. *Education:* The University of Texas Medical Branch, Galveston (B.S.M.T., 1994); University of Notre Dame Law School (J.D., 2003). Certified by American Society of Clinical Pathologists, 1990—. *Member:* American Bar Association (Member, Sections on: Health Law; IP; Business Law); American Society of Clinical Pathologists; Clinical Laboratory Management Association. [E-4, U.S. Army, 1982-1986]. ***PRACTICE AREAS:*** Corporate; Securities. ***Email:*** darrell.taylor@dlapiper.com

PATRICK DALEY THOMPSON, admitted to bar, 1999, Illinois. *Education:* St. Mary's College (B.A., 1991); John Marshall Law School (J.D., 1999). ***PRACTICE AREAS:*** Real Estate. ***Email:*** patrick.thompson@dlapiper.com

VASILIOS TOLIOPOULOS, admitted to bar, 2001, Illinois. *Education:* Loyola University (B.A., 1998); DePaul University (J.D., 2001). ***PRACTICE AREAS:*** Construction Litigation; Commercial Litigation. ***Email:*** bill.toliopoulos@dlapiper.com

(This Listing Continued)

DLA PIPER RUDNICK GRAY CARY US LLP, Chicago—Continued

KELLI A. TORONYI, admitted to bar, 1996, Illinois and U.S. District Court, Northern District of Illinois. *Education:* Elmhurst College (B.S., 1990); The John Marshall Law School (J.D., 1996); University of Chicago (M.B.A., 2004). Phi Delta Phi. Editor, John Marshall Law Review, 1994-1995. *Member:* Chicago Bar Association. ***PRACTICE AREAS:*** Employee Benefits; Executive Compensation; General Corporate. ***Email:*** kelli.toronyi@dlapiper.com

JULIA A. TURK, born 1968; admitted to bar, 1997, Illinois. *Education:* University of Michigan (B.A., 1990); Loyola University Chicago School of Law (J.D., cum laude, 1997); New York University School of Law (LL.M., Taxation, 1998). ***PRACTICE AREAS:*** Tax Law; Corporate Law; Real Estate; Capital Markets. ***Email:*** julia.turk@dlapiper.com

JARED M. WARNER, born 1977; admitted to bar, 2003, Illinois. *Education:* Hanover College (B.A., 2000); University of Michigan (J.D., 2002). ***PRACTICE AREAS:*** Finance. ***Email:*** jared.warner@dlapiper.com

JOYCELYNN WATKINS-ASIYANBI, admitted to bar, 2004, Illinois. *Education:* University of Wisconsin-Madison (B.A., Chemical Engineering and Economics, 1996); Kellog School of Management (M.B.A., Business Management, 2003); Northwestern University (J.D., 2003). ***PRACTICE AREAS:*** Corporate Finance; Financial Services; Bankruptcy. ***Email:*** joycelynn.watkins-aslyanbi@dlapiper.com

KAREN S. WAY, born 1968; admitted to bar, 1998, Illinois. *Education:* Penn State University (P.S.B.S. (Public Service Bachelor of Science), 1990); University of Illinois, Chicago (M.U.P.P. (Masters Urban Planning and Policy)); Chicago-Kent College of Law (J.D., 1998). ***PRACTICE AREAS:*** Public Utility Law; Energy; Environmental Law; Zoning Law; Real Estate. ***Email:*** karen.way@dlapiper.com

MEGAN WEBSTER, admitted to bar, 2001, Illinois. *Education:* University of Kentucky (B.B.A., 1998); DePaul University (J.D., 2001; M.B.A., 2001). *Member:* Chicago, Illinois State and American Bar Associations; Chicago Inns of Court. ***PRACTICE AREAS:*** Information Technology; Telecommunications Law; Commercial Litigation. ***Email:*** megan.webster@dlapiper.com

SARAH A. WEERSING, born 1971; admitted to bar, 1999, Illinois. *Education:* Northwestern University (B.S., 1992); Boston College (M.B.A., J.D., 1999). Member, Boston College Law Review, 1997-1999. *Member:* Chicago, Illinois State and American Bar Associations. ***PRACTICE AREAS:*** Mergers and Acquisitions; Corporate Law; Emerging Growth Companies. ***Email:*** sarah.weersing@dlapiper.com

KENNETH I. WEINER, admitted to bar, 2000, Illinois. *Education:* Northern Michigan University (B.S., 1992); Loyola University, Chicago (J.D., magna cum laude, 2000). Recipient: Loyola's Leadership and Service Award; Loyola's Pro Bono Recognition Award; The David C. Hilliard Award from the Chicago Bar Association for outstanding committee service. Member, Loyola Law Review. *Member:* Chicago Bar Association (Co-Chair, 2002-2004, Real Estate Law Committee, Young Lawyers Section). ***PRACTICE AREAS:*** Commercial Real Estate. ***Email:*** kenneth.weiner@dlapiper.com

KURT A. WINIECKI, born 1966; admitted to bar, 1997, Illinois and U.S. District Court, Northern District of Illinois; 2002, U.S District Court, Northern District of Indiana. *Education:* University of Illinois (B.S., Finance, 1988; M.S., Accounting, 1992); Loyola University (J.D., 1997). Certified Public Accountant, Illinois, 1993. Co-Author: "Bank's Security Interests in Checking Accounts and Check-Kiting Schemes," American Bankruptcy Institute Journal, Vol XXI, No. 8 (October 2002). *Member:* Chicago Bar Association (Member, Bankruptcy Section, 2002—); American Bankruptcy Institute. ***PRACTICE AREAS:*** Bankruptcy; Creditors Rights; Litigation; Corporate. ***Email:*** kurt.winiecki@dlapiper.com

CHRISTY M. YOUNG, admitted to bar, 2003, Illinois. *Education:* Ball State University (B.A., 1998); University of Virginia (J.D., 2003). ***PRACTICE AREAS:*** Labor and Employment. ***Email:*** christy.young@dlapiper.com

MYLA BAREFIELD YOUNG, born 1972; admitted to bar, 1998, Illinois. *Education:* Duke University (A.B., 1994; J.D./M.B.A., 1998). Duke Journal of Gender Law & Policy. *Member:* Chicago and American Bar Associations; Intellectual Property Law Association Chicago (IPLAC). ***PRACTICE AREAS:*** Trademarks; Copyrights; Contracts; Advertising Law; Marketing Law; Sweepstakes; Promotion Law. ***Email:*** myla.barefield@dlapiper.com

ATTORNEYS

MICHELLE D. KANE, born 1969; admitted to bar, 1995, Illinois. *Education:* Wellesley College (B.A., magna cum laude, 1992) Durant Scholar; University of Chicago (J.D., 1995). ***PRACTICE AREAS:*** Real Estate. ***Email:*** michelle.kane@dlapiper.com

MIA P. JIGANTI, born 1967; admitted to bar, 1994, Illinois. *Education:* Knox College (B.A., 1989); The John Marshall Law School (J.D., 1994). Supervising Counsel, Attorney Registration and Disciplinary Commission of the Supreme Court of Illinois. *Member:* Chicago Bar Association (Young Lawyers Section: Chair 2002-2003, Chair-Elect, 2001-2002, Vice-Chair, 1999-2001, Secretary, 1998-1999, Director, 1997-1998, Board of Managers 2002-2003 and 2004—). ***Email:*** mia.jiganti@dlapiper.com

LINDA URBANIK JOHNSON, born 1958; admitted to bar, 1993, Illinois and U.S. District Court, Northern District of Illinois; 1995, U.S. Court of Appeals, Seventh Circuit. *Education:* Purdue University (B.A., with distinction, 1980); Loyola University of Chicago Law School (J.D., 1993). Senior Member, 1992-1993; Member, 1991-1992, Loyola University of Chicago Law Journal. Author: "Executive Veto, Congressional Compromise, and Judicial Confusion: The 1991 Civil Rights Act--Does It Apply Retroactively?," Published: Fall, 1992. Cases Editor, 1991-1992; Cases Writer, two published case summaries, 1990-1991, Loyola Consumer Law Reporter. *Member:* Chicago and American Bar Associations; Intellectual Property Law Association of Chicago. ***REPORTED CASES:*** Roberts & Schaefer Company v. Merit Contracting, Inc., 99 F. 3d 248 (7th Cir. 1996). ***PRACTICE AREAS:*** Intellectual Property; Trademarks. ***Email:*** linda.johnson@dlapiper.com

AMY L. KURLAND, admitted to bar, 1985, Illinois and U.S. District Court, Northern District of Illinois. *Education:* University of Illinois (B.S., 1982); University of Wisconsin-Madison (J.D., 1985). *Member:* American Bar Association. ***PRACTICE AREAS:*** Real Estate. ***Email:*** amy.kurland@dlapiper.com

DOBBS AND HUTCHISON

Established in 1992

DEARBORN STATION, SUITE M-2
47 WEST POLK STREET
CHICAGO, ILLINOIS 60605
Telephone: 312-461-9800
Fax: 312-461-9008
Email: roghutch@prodigy.net
URL: http://www.dobbsandhutchison.com

Personal Injury, Automobile Accidents, Trucking Accidents, Motorcycle Accidents, Head Trauma, Spinal Cord Injuries, Premises Liability, Wrongful Death, Social Security, Social Security Disability Benefits, Children's Benefits.

MEMBERS OF FIRM

KENNETH PAUL DOBBS, admitted to bar, 1992, Illinois. *Education:* California State University (B.S., 1970); University of Oregon (M.A., 1976); Chicago-Kent College of Law (J.D., 1992). Member, National Organization of Social Security Claimants' Representatives. *Member:* Chicago, North Suburban, North-West Suburban, South Suburban and Illinois State Bar Associations; Illinois Trial Lawyers Association. ***PRACTICE AREAS:*** Personal Injury; Constitutional Law; Social Security. ***Email:*** kendobbslaw@prodigy.net

ROGER S. HUTCHISON, born Springfield, Illinois, March 18, 1967; admitted to bar, 1992, Illinois. *Education:* University of Illinois (B.A., 1989); Chicago-Kent College of Law (J.D., 1992). *Member:* Chicago, Will County, South Suburban (Member, Board of Directors) and Illinois State Bar Associations; The Association of Trial Lawyers of America; National Organization of Social Security Claimants' Representatives; Illinois Trial Lawyers Association. ***PRACTICE AREAS:*** Wrongful Death; Personal Injury; Social Security Disability. ***Email:*** roghutch@prodigy.net

ALICE E. DOLAN & ASSOCIATES LLC

Established in 2005

321 SOUTH PLYMOUTH COURT-14TH FLOOR
CHICAGO, ILLINOIS 60604
Telephone: 312-386-1600
Fax: 312-386-1616
Email: adolan@aedolanllc.com
URL: http://www.aedolanllc.com

Medical Malpractice, Personal Injury, Negligence, Products Liability.

FIRM PROFILE: Alice E. Dolan is the founder of Alice E. Dolan & Associates, LLC. in Chicago, Illinois. Previously, she was an owner of the law firm of Gogan, McNabola & Dolan, LLC. Ms. Dolan grew up in the North suburbs of Chicago where she graduated from Regina Dominican High School in 1973. She obtained her college degree from Marquette University in Milwaukee in 1977 where she was elected as President of the business school fraternity in her finial year. She earned her law degree from the John Marshall Law School in 1981. During her final year of law school, she became President of the Phi Delta Phi legal fraternity. She also obtained a temporary law license and worked for Chicago Volunteer Legal Services which provides free legal services to indigent clients. During law school, she also clerked for a law firm in Chicago. Her legal career since then has centered on representing injured plaintiffs in catastrophic injury and wrongful death cases.

ALICE E. DOLAN, born Morristown, New Jersey, July 26, 1955; admitted to bar, 1981, Illinois and U.S. District Court, Northern District of Illinois, U.S. District Court District of Colorado, Pro Hac Vice. *Education:* Marquette University (B.A., 1977); John Marshall Law School (J.D., 1981). Phi Delta Phi (President, Stevens Chapter, 1980-1981). Selected, Super Lawyers, 2005, merit based selection of only 5% of the Illinois Bar. Recipient: Million Dollar Advocate Forum; Selected by Peers Among Top 5% of Lawyers in Illinois, Leading Lawyers Network; Recognized as One of the Top 50 Female Lawyers in Illinois. Guest Lecturer, "Supreme Court Rule 213," DePaul University Law School. Invited Lecturer, "Closing Arguments, The Plaintiff's Perspective," Illinois Trial Lawyers Association. Adjunct Professor: Trial Advocacy, Northwestern University School of Law, 2003—; National Institute of Trial Advocacy Regional. Pro Hac Vice, District Court, Johnson County, Iowa. *Member:* Chicago, Illinois State and American Bar Associations; The Association of Trial Lawyers of America; Illinois Trial Lawyers Association; Women's Bar Association; National Association of Women Lawyers. ***LANGUAGES:*** English. ***REPORTED CASES:*** Waliczek v. Alexian Brothers Medical Center, Cook County, 97 L8110; Brettschneider v. Greyhound Lines, Inc., Cook County, 00L11550; Busche v. "ETC" et al, Johnson County, Iowa, LACV0 62989. ***PRACTICE AREAS:*** Medical Malpractice; Personal Injury; Negligence; Products Liability. ***Email:*** adolan@aedolanllc.com

LAW OFFICE OF PATRICK DALEY DOLAN

155 NORTH MICHIGAN AVENUE, SUITE 718
CHICAGO, ILLINOIS 60601
Telephone: 312-239-9336
Fax: 312-239-9337
Email: pddlaw@aol.com

Labor and Employment, Litigation, Civil Rights, Executive Severance and Employment Contracts, Civil Litigation, Business Litigation, Commercial Litigation.

PATRICK D. DOLAN, born Austin, Texas, December 6, 1964; admitted to bar, 1992, California and Wisconsin; 1998, Illinois. *Education:* University of Wisconsin-Madison (B.A., 1988; J.D., 1992). Phi Alpha Delta. Member, Moot Court Honor Board, 1991-1992. Managing Editor, Wisconsin Law Review, 1991-1992. Extern Law Clerk to Wisconsin Supreme Court Justice William A. Bablitch, 1992*Member:* Chicago, Illinois State, Federal and American Bar Associations; State Bar of California; State Bar of Wisconsin; National

(This Listing Continued)

Employment Lawyers Association (Member, Civil Practice/Procedure Committee, 1999); Illinois Association of Defense Counsel; American Corporate Counsel Association; Defense Research Institute; National Institute for Trial Advocacy. **REPORTED CASES:** Allen v. Sundstrand Corporation, 2000 U.S.Dist. LEXIS 13328; Messick v. Toyota Motor Mfg., Inc. 45 F. Supp. 2d 578; Miller Brewing Co. v. Dept. of Indus., Labor and Human Rels., Equal Rights Div., 563 N.W. 2d 460.

DOLGIN & FISCHER, LLC

30 NORTH LASALLE STREET, SUITE 4300
CHICAGO, ILLINOIS 60602-2516
Telephone: 312-705-2000
Fax: 312-705-2001

Estate Planning, Tax Planning, Probate, Guardianship, Trust Administration, Corporate Law, Business Planning, Succession Planning, Commercial Litigation, Business Law, Contested Estates, Probate Litigation, Elder Law and Asset Protection.

MEMBERS OF FIRM

JAY L. DOLGIN, born Chicago, Illinois, May 14, 1944; admitted to bar, 1969, Illinois and U.S. District Court, Northern District of Illinois; 1973, Florida; 1989, U.S. Tax Court. *Education:* University of Wisconsin-Madison (B.S., 1966); DePaul University (J.D., 1969). Adjunct Professor of Law, Estate Planning, Will Drafting, Trusts and Estates, John Marshall Law School, 1985—. Member, Professional Advisory Committee, Jewish United Fund, 1993—. *Member:* Illinois State and American Bar Associations; Chicago Bar Association; The Florida Bar; Chicago Estate Planning Council; North Shore Estate Planning Council; National Academy of Elder Law Attorneys; Illinois Elder Law Association; Illinois Guardianship Association. ***PRACTICE AREAS:*** Estate Planning; Tax Planning; Probate; Guardianship; Trust Administration; Corporate Law; Business Planning; Succession Planning; Elder Law. ***Email:*** jld@dnf-law.com

DAVID J. FISCHER, born Baltimore, Maryland, May 20, 1950; admitted to bar, 1979, Illinois; 1981, U.S. District Court, Northern District of Illinois. *Education:* University of Michigan (B.A., 1972); John Marshall Law School (J.D., 1979). Contributing Author: Chapter, "Mergers," book entitled "Savings and Loan Reorganization," Ticor Printing Group Inc., 1981. *Member:* Chicago and Illinois State Bar Associations. ***PRACTICE AREAS:*** Commercial Litigation; Business Law. ***Email:*** dfischer@dnf-law.com

OF COUNSEL

JOHN L. WAHLERS, born Sandusky, Ohio, October 10, 1951; admitted to bar, 1977, Illinois. *Education:* Amherst College (B.A., 1974); Vanderbilt University (J.D., 1977). Recipient, American Jurisprudence Award, Future Interests, 1977. *Member:* DuPage County and Illinois State (Member, Sections on: Business Advice and Financial Planning; Real Property Law; Commercial, Banking and Bankruptcy Law; Environmental Law; Trusts and Estates) Bar Associations. ***Email:*** jwahlers@aol.com

DOMMERMUTH, BRESTAL, COBINE AND WEST, LTD.

CHICAGO, ILLINOIS

(See Naperville)

General Civil Practice. Personal Injury, Worker's Compensation, Corporate, Banking, Municipal, Zoning and Development, Real Estate, Family and Probate Law, Litigation, Federal and State Taxation, Commercial Collection.

JOHN D. DONLEVY

30 NORTH LA SALLE STREET, SUITE 2040
CHICAGO, ILLINOIS 60602-2506
Telephone: 312-201-0227
Fax: 312-236-6906
Email: jdonlevy@core.com
URL: http://www.lawyers.com/jdonlevy

Diversified Trial Practice in State and Federal Courts, concentrating on Criminal Cases, Business Litigation and some Personal Injury. Criminal Law specialties include DUI, Drug Cases and White Collar Crime.

JOHN D. DONLEVY, admitted to bar, 1957, Illinois; U.S. District Court, Northern District of Illinois; U.S. Court of Appeals, Seventh Circuit; U.S. Supreme Court. *Education:* Stanford University, Northwestern University (B.S., 1954); University of Chicago (J.D., 1957). Listed in Who's Who in America. Awarded the highest rating from Martindale-Hubbell. Assistant State's Attorney, Cook County, Illinois (Criminal Division), 1958-1961. City Prosecutor, Evanston, Illinois, 1961. Mayer Brown & Platt, Chicago, 1962-1990 (Partner, 1973-1990). Author: "The Sixth Amendment Right to Counsel: Does Miranda Suffice?", Vol. 2, *CBA Record,* p. 13, 1988; "Vocational Rehabilitation Needs Legislative Rehabilitation", Vol. 1, *CBA Record,* p. 28, 1987. Profiled, *Illinois Police and Sheriffs News,* Fall 1995 ed., p. 4. *Member:* Chicago, (Defense of Prisoners Committee; Chair, 1993-1994), Illinois State and American Bar Associations; Astor Terrace Condominium Association (President).

GERALD T. DONOGHUE

20 NORTH CLARK STREET, SUITE 3600
CHICAGO, ILLINOIS 60602
Telephone: 312-332-3359
Fax: 312-419-6688
Email: gdonoghue@att.net
URL: http://www.donoghue-law.com

Civil Trial and Appellate Practice, Auto Accidents and Injuries, Personal Injury, Medical Malpractice, Legal Malpractice, Wrongful Death, Workers Compensation, Products Liability and Premises Liability Law.

GERALD T. DONOGHUE, born Chicago, Illinois, March 14, 1951; admitted to bar, 1977, Illinois; U.S. District Court, Northern District of Illinois, including Trial Bar. *Education:* University of Illinois, Champaign-Urbana (B.A., with honors, 1973); Loyola University (J.D., 1977). Associated with the late nationally- recognized trial lawyer, Leonard M. Ring, 1983-1994. Public Defender, Cook County, 1977-1983, Murder Task Force, 1979-1983. *Member:* Chicago Bar Association; Illinois Trial Lawyers Association; The Association of Trial Lawyers of America.

LAW OFFICE OF JOSEPH M. DOOLEY, III, P.C.

100 WEST MONROE STREET - SUITE 1900
CHICAGO, ILLINOIS 60603
Telephone: 312-236-7282
Fax: 312-346-6549
Email: dooleylaw@covad.net
URL: http://www.josephmdooley.com

Personal Injury, Catastrophic Injuries, Medical Malpractice, Products Liability, Wrongful Death, Automobile Accidents, Trucking Accidents, Birth Injury, Spinal Injury, Head Injury, Neurological Injuries, Construction Accidents, Railroad Accidents, Slip and Fall, Pedestrian Injuries, Litigation.

JOSEPH M. DOOLEY III, admitted to bar, 1988, Illinois; 1989, U.S. District Court, Northern District of Illinois including Trial Bar. *Education:* Southern Methodist University (B.A./B.S., 1983); IIT Chicago-Kent (J.D., 1988). *Member:* Illinois State and American Bar Associations. ***Email:*** dooleylaw@covad.net

DOWD & DOWD, LTD.

Established in 1950
617 WEST FULTON STREET
CHICAGO, ILLINOIS 60661
Telephone: 312-704-4400
Telecopier: 312-704-4500
URL: http://www.dowdanddowd.com

Fontana, Wisconsin Office: 632 Middleton, 53125. Telephone: 262-275-0057. Telecopier: 262-275-6786.

Highland, Indiana Office: 9721 Prairie Avenue, 46322. Telephone: 219-924-8122. Fax: 219-924-8125.

General Civil Trial Practice, Negligence and Products Liability, Insurance Coverage Litigation, Workers' Compensation, Appellate Practice, Employment Law, Municipal Law, Transportation Law.

JOSEPH V. DOWD, born Spring Valley, Illinois, July 9, 1922; admitted to bar, 1950, Illinois and U.S. Supreme Court. *Education:* DePaul University (LL.B., 1949). Graduate, U.S. Naval Justice School. Certified Trial and Defense Counsel, U.S. Military Courts. Delta Theta Phi. *Member:* Illinois State and American Bar Associations; American Judicature Society; Trial Lawyers Club of Chicago; Illinois Trial Lawyers Association; Workers' Compensation Lawyers Association; Celtic Legal Society of Chicago; The Association of Trial Lawyers of America.

MICHAEL E. DOWD (1957-1996)

PATRICK C. DOWD, born Chicago, Illinois, July 10, 1958; admitted to bar, 1985, Illinois; U.S. District Court, Northern, Central and Southern Districts of Illinois including Trial Bar; 1997, Wisconsin. *Education:* Northern Arizona University (B.S., cum laude, 1981); DePaul University (J.D., 1985) Phi Kappa Phi. Pi Sigma Alpha; Phi Alpha Delta. Listed: Martindale-Hubbell Bar Register of Preeminent Lawyers, 2000—; Crain's Chicago Business, "Leading Lawyers" in Illinois, January 2005. Elected to: "Leading Lawyers," for State of Illinois, December, 2004; Illinois Defense Council, Board of Directors, May 2005. Instructor: Chicago School of Commerce, 1984-1987. Lecturer: "Legal Terminology," Illinois State Court Reporter Convention, 1987; "Instruction on Debate," Chicago Bar Association, 1986; "Erosion of the Peremptory Challenge: Rule Against Jurors Based on Race Applies To Civil Cases," Illinois State Bar Association Trial Briefs, July, 1992; "Determination of Good Faith Findings", Illinois State Bar Association Trial Briefs, May, 1994. Participant: Annual Minority and Women Attorneys' Conference, 1993; Allerton House Conference, Monticello, Illinois, May, 1994. Guest Speaker: Illinois State Bar Association, Civil Practice Update, February, 1994, Rock Island, Illinois; Illinois State Bar Association, Law Ed Series, Anatomy of a Trial, Part II: Recurring Evidentiary Issues, Chicago, November, 1994. Presenter: Back to Basics Program, October 1999; A Panel Discussion of the How and Why of Catastrophic Investigation, October 1999; Answers to Commonly Asked Questions About the N.T.S.B. and U.S.D.O.T., November 2000; Industrial Commission and Courts More Skeptical of Employee Conduct, April 2001; Changes to Discovery Rules Under Illinois Supreme Court Rules, April 2002; Defense Perspective: Focus Groups and Mock Trials, October, 2002; Transportation Industry Seminar: Wrongful Death - Post Mortem, Fall, 2003; Update: Comparing and Contrasting Substantive Law of Illinois and Indiana, Fall, 2003; Defense Strategies for Bad Venues - Aftermath of Catastrophic Loss, Hous-

(This Listing Continued)

DOWD & DOWD, LTD., Chicago—Continued

ton, Texas, January, 2004; Duty to Defend: A Refresher, Summer 2004. Executive Director, Children's Charities of Chicago, 1985-1996. Member, Board of Advisors, Appointed by Cardinal George, and Legal Advisory Committee, Catholic Charities of the Archdiocese of Chicago, 1997. *Member:* Chicago, Illinois State (Member, Committees on: Trial Techniques, 1985-1986; Tort Litigation, 1985-1986; Civil Practice, 1991-1995; Elected Assembly Member, 1994-1996, Illinois State Hearing Committee; Member, Tort Law Section Council, 1996-1997; Allerton House Steering Committee, 1994) and American (Member: Tort and Insurance Practice Section; Commercial Transportation Litigation Committee) Bar Associations; American Trial Lawyers Association; The Association of Trial Lawyers of America; Trial Lawyers Club of Chicago; Transportation Lawyers Association (Member, Committee on Alternative Dispute Resolution, 1996-1999; Transportation Law, 1995—); Trucking Industry Defense Association; Association for Transportation Law; American Trucking Association; Defense Research Institute (Member, Trucking Sub-Committee, 1997—); Association for Transportation Law; International Association of Defense Counsel; Catholic Lawyers Guild of Chicago; Illinois Association of Defense Trial Counsel; Catholic Lawyers Guild of Chicago. ***Email:*** pdowd@dowdanddowd.com

ROBERT J. GOLDEN, born Chicago, Illinois, August 21, 1959; admitted to bar, 1986, Illinois and U.S. District Court, Northern, Central and Southern Districts of Illinois and U.S. Court of Appeals, Seventh Circuit. *Education:* University of Illinois at Chicago (B.A., 1981); The John Marshall Law School (J.D., 1986). Featured presentation at The Brain Injury Association's 19th Annual Symposium-At the Crossroads: The Future of Brain Injury 2000 and Beyond, Introduction to Medical-Legal Issues in Acquired Brain Injury (ABI)-a Defense Perspective, July 29, 2000. Featured Speaker, Wrongful Death Case Overview, Transportation Industry Seminar, Schneider National, Inc., September 2003. *Member:* Chicago, Illinois State and American Bar Associations; Defense Research Institute; Illinois Association of Defense Trial Counsel. ***Email:*** rgolden@dowdanddowd.com

PATRICK J. RUBERRY, born Chicago, Illinois, October 17, 1959; admitted to bar, 1984, Illinois and U.S. District Court, Northern District of Illinois including Trial Bar. *Education:* University of Illinois (B.A., summa cum laude, with all University honors, 1981, Phi Beta Kappa; J.D., 1984); University of Illinois College of Law. *Member:* Illinois Association of Defense Trial Counsel. ***REPORTED CASES:*** Farley Metals v. Barber Coleman, 269 Ill. App. 3rd 104, 645 N.E. 2d 964 (1st Dist. 1994). ***Email:*** pruberry@dowdanddowd.com

---

PHILIP F. CUEVAS, born Chicago, Illinois, August 23, 1970; admitted to bar, 2000, Illinois; 2001 Indiana. *Education:* Illinois State University (B.S., in Political Science, 1996); John Marshall Law School (J.D., 2000). *Member:* Chicago, Indianapolis, Kane County, DuPage County and Indiana State Bar Associations; Indiana Trial Lawyers Association. ***Email:*** pcuevas@dowdanddowd.com

S. ROBERT DEPKE, born Chicago, Illinois, January 13, 1929; admitted to bar, 1958, Illinois; 1962, U.S. District Court, Eastern District of Illinois; 1983, U.S. District Court, Northern District of Illinois including Trial Bar. *Education:* Loras College; Loyola University of Chicago (B.S., 1952; J.D., 1958). Delta Theta Phi.

JEANNINE GILLERAN-LUNT, born Chicago, Illinois, December 19, 1968; admitted to bar, 1993, Illinois. *Education:* University of Illinois, Champaign-Urbana (B.F.A., 1990); Chicago-Kent College of Law (J.D., 1993). Member, Moot Court. ***PRACTICE AREAS:*** Litigation. ***Email:*** jlunt@dowdanddowd.com

JANE E. HUGHES, born Valparaiso, Indiana. December 1, 1978; admitted to bar, 2004, Illinois. *Education:* Indiana University (B.S., Marketing, 2001; J.D., 2004). ***PRACTICE AREAS:*** Insurance Defense. ***Email:*** jhughes@dowdanddowd.com

THOMAS A. JACOBSON, born Chicago, Illinois, April 7, 1973; admitted to bar, 2003, Illinois. *Education:* DePaul University (B.A., 1998); DePaul University College of Law (J.D., summa cum laude, 2003). Member, DePaul University Law Review. ***Email:*** tjacobson@dowdanddowd.com

MATTHEW R. LINK, born Oak Lawn, Illinois, January 12, 1979; admitted to bar, 2004, Illinois and U.S. District Court, Northern District of Illinois. *Education:* Loyola University (B.A., magna cum laude, 2001); DePaul University (J.D., cum laude, 2004). Phi Beta Kappa. ***Email:*** mlink@dowdanddowd.com

KIMBERLY A. MALTBY, born LaGrange, Illinois, May 25, 1962; admitted to bar, 1991, Illinois; 2005, U.S. District Court, Eastern District of Wisconsin. *Education:* University of Illinois (B.A., 1985); Cornell Law School. University of Illinois (J.D., 1990). Phi Kappa Phi; Phi Alpha Delta; Sigma Iota Lambda. Mortar Board. Golden Key Society. Recipient, Student Leadership Award. *Member:* Chicago Bar Association. ***LANGUAGES:*** Russian, French. ***REPORTED CASES:*** Cooper v. Vicorp - Verdict Search Reptr. ***PRACTICE AREAS:*** Insurance Defense; Employment Law; Personal Injury; Corporate Law; Class Actions. ***Email:*** kmaltby@dowdanddowd.com

DANIEL L. POLSBY, born Baltimore, Maryland, March 3, 1972; admitted to bar, 1999, Illinois; 2000, U.S. District Court, Northern District of Illinois. *Education:* Bradford College (B.A., 1995); Northwestern University (J.D., 1999). *Member:* Illinois State Bar Association. [E-4, U.S.M.C.R, 1990-1996]. ***PRACTICE AREAS:*** Insurance Defense (50%); Condominium Association Law (10%); Trucking Defense (20%); Employment Law (5%); Insurance Coverage (15%). ***Email:*** dpolsby@dowdanddowd.com

PETER ZAVODNYIK, born Chicago, Illinois, April 21, 1969; admitted to bar, 1997, Illinois; 2000, U.S. District Court, District of Illinois. *Education:* University of Notre Dame (B.A., 1992; J.D., 1995). ***PRACTICE AREAS:*** Premises Liability; Insurance. ***Email:*** pzavodnyik@dowdanddowd.com

LEGAL SUPPORT PERSONNEL

AMY T. LEBEAU, born Carbondale, Illinois, July 30, 1960. *Education:* Southern Illinois University (B.S., Dietetics, 1983); Roosevelt University (Lawyers Assistant Program, 1989). ***Email:*** alebowl@aol.com

JENNIFER A. BRENDEL, born Chicago, Illinois, September 20, 1976. *Education:* University of Wisconsin-Madison (B.A., Political Science, 1999). ***Email:*** lawclerks@dowdanddowd.com

ROSANNE GALVEZ, born Chicago, Illinois, July 1, 1983. *Education:* Northwestern Business College (Associates, Applied Science, Certified Paralegal, 2004). ***Email:*** rgalvez@dowdanddowd.com

BRIDGET A. MELICHAREK, born Chicago, Illinois, May 24, 1979. *Education:* Fox Business College (1998). ***Email:*** bmelicharek@dowdanddowd.com

OF COUNSEL

RICHARD H. LUCY, born Chicago, Illinois, September 12, 1932; admitted to bar, 1959, Illinois and U.S. District Court, Northern District of Illinois including the Trial Bar. *Education:* Northwestern University (B.S., 1954; J.D., 1957). *Member:* Chicago (Past Chairman, Circuit Court Committee) and Southwest (Past President) Bar Associations; American Arbitration Association.

SAM L. MILLER, born Chicago, Illinois, September 12, 1926; admitted to bar, 1951, Illinois; 1971, U.S. Supreme Court. *Education:* Loyola University (1948); Chicago-Kent College of Law (J.D., 1951). Phi Delta Phi. Prosecutor, Village of Arlington Heights, 1956. President: Society of Trial Lawyers, 1986; Trial Lawyers Club of Chicago, 1963. *Member:* Chicago (Member, Judicial Investigative Committee), Illinois State and American Bar Associations; Federation of Insurance Counsel; International Association of Insurance Counsel. [U.S. Navy, 1944-1946]

NORMAN E. SAMELSON, born Chicago, Illinois, September 16, 1939; admitted to bar, 1967, Illinois; 1968, U.S. District Court, Northern District of Illinois. *Education:* DePauw University (B.A., 1963); Chicago Kent College of Law (J.D., 1967). (Also Member, Samelson & Knickerbocker). ***PRACTICE AREAS:*** Government Law; Land Use Law.

EDMUND A. STEPHAN, III, born Chicago, Illinois, July 7, 1966; admitted to bar, 1995, Maryland; 1996, Illinois; 1997, U.S. District Court, Northern District of Illinois; 2003, U.S. Court of Appeals, Seventh Circuit. *Education:* University of Notre Dame (B.A., 1988; J.D., 1994). ***Email:*** estephan@dowdanddowd.com

PAMELA K. HARMAN, born Chicago, Illinois, March 13, 1950; admitted to bar, 1978, Illinois and U.S. District Court, Northern District of Illinois. *Education:* University of Illinois (B.A., with high honors, 1971); DePaul University (J.D., with honors, 1978). Author: Course Handbooks, "Workmen's Compensation Skill," Illinois Institute for Continuing Legal Education, 1986, 1987; "Worker's Compensation Law Update," National Business Institute, 1992, 1996; "Employment Law Review," National Business Institute, 1995-2002. Lecturer: Workers Compensation Law, Advanced Workers Compensation Law, Worker's Compensation Skills, Illinois Institute for Continuing Legal Education, 1979-1990, 2005; Worker's Compensation Seminar, "Litigation Preparation for Health Care Professionals," Insurance Law Update, Rehabilitation Institute of Chicago, 1983-1990; "Medical/Legal Issues in Worker's Compensation, Pulmonary Occupational Disease Claims in Illinois," with Dr. David Cugell, Association of Law and Medicine, 1983; "Occupational Disease Claims in Illinois," with Dr. Peter Orris, Professional Education Systems, 1988; Employment Law Update and Workers Compensation Law, National Business Institute, 1992 and 1996; Vocational Rehabilitation Law and Vocational Expert Testimony, Illinois Rehabilitation Association, 1987-1990; "Expert Witness Preparation for Physicians," University of Illinois School of Public Health, 1991-1994; "Technical Expert Witness Preparation," American College of Occupational and Environmental Medicine (ACOEM), 1995-1996; "Legal Update on 'Kotecki' waiver," Sheet Metal Contractors Association, 1999. *Member:* Chicago (Member, Industrial Commission Committee, 1978-1990, Chairman, 1988-1989); Workers Compensation Lawyers Association. ***PRACTICE AREAS:*** Workers Compensation Defense; Tort Defense; Employer Liability; Labor and Employment Law. ***Email:*** pharman@dowdanddowd.com

REPRESENTATIVE CLIENTS: AIG American International Companies; Aldi, Inc.; American Bankers Insurance Company; American Limosine, Inc.; AON Corporation (Combined); Bakers Square Restaurants; Budget Rent a Car Systems, Inc.; Cambridge Integrated Services Group, Inc.; Catholic Charities of Chicago; Christian Brothers Risk Pool; City of Des Plaines; Clarendon National Insurance Company; Cook DuPage Transportation; Crawford Risk Management Services; Enterprise Rent-A-Car; Excel Insurance; Frozen Food Express Industries, Inc.; Gallagher Bassett Services, Inc.; Globe Life and Accident Insurance Company; Greenwich Insurance Company; Indian Harbor Insurance Company; Insurance Corporation of Hanover; Kentucky Farm Bureau Mutual Insurance Company; Landstar Inway, Inc.; Markel Insurance Company; Metropolitan Pier and Exposition Authority; National Express Corporation; Nationwide Insurance Enterprise; North American Risk Services; Pace; Royal & Sunalliance Insurance Company; Schneider National, Inc.; Scottsdale Insurance Company; The Travelers Insurance Company; Thrifty Rent-A-Car System, Inc.; TIG Insurance Corporation of America; U.S. Xpress Enterprises, Inc.; Wal-Mart; Western Heritage Insurance; Westport Insurance Corporation.

(This Listing Continued)

DOWNS LAW OFFICES, P.C.

Established in 1966

150 NORTH WACKER DRIVE
SUITE 1870
CHICAGO, ILLINOIS 60606
Telephone: 312-781-1963
Fax: 312-781-1962
URL: http://www.lawyers.com/downslaw
Email: Bob@Downslaw.com
URL: http://www.downslaw.com

Family Law, Divorce, Child Custody, Adoption, Domestic Violence, Premarital Agreements, Child Support, Trusts and Estates, Wills, Probate, Elder Law, Guardianship and Real Estate.

ROBERT K. DOWNS, admitted to bar, 1965, Florida; 1966, Illinois. *Education:* Stetson University (J.D., 1965). Former Chair, Family Law Section, Illinois State Bar Association. *Member:* Chicago Bar Association (Matrimonial Law Committee); Illinois State Bar Association. ***Email:*** Bob@Downslaw.com

JOHN T. DOYLE

10 SOUTH LA SALLE STREET, SUITE 3500
CHICAGO, ILLINOIS 60603-1002
Telephone: 312-332-5560; 708-352-8981
Fax: 312-332-5566
Efax: 708-575-8959
Email: jdoyle@doylelaw.com
URL: http://www.lawyers.com/doylelawfirm

Business Law and Transactions, Corporate Law, Mergers and Acquisitions, and Information Technology Law and Transactions.

JOHN T. DOYLE, born Oak Park, Illinois; admitted to bar, 1980, Illinois and U.S. District Court, Northern District of Illinois; 1981, U.S. Court of Appeals, Seventh Circuit; 1983, U.S. Supreme Court. *Education:* Loyola University (B.B.A.; M.B.A.); Loyola University (J.D.; LL.M.); Chicago-Kent College of Law, Illinois Institute of Technology (LL.M., Financial Services). Member, Loyola University Law Journal. Vice Chairman, Illinois Business Organizations Acts Advisory Committee, 2005 —. Illinois Secretary of State Business Organizations Acts Advisory Committee, Member, 1994—2005; Secretary, 2003—2005. Chairman, Corporations, Securities and Business Law Section, Illinois State Bar Association, 1995-1996. Editor, *Corporation, Securities and Business Law Forum,* Illinois State Bar Association, 1992-2000. Member, Corporation and Securities Law Section Council, Illinois State Bar Association, 1991-1998; 2000-2005. Member: Standing Committee on Legislation, 1993—; Chairman, Standing Committee on Legal Technology, Illinois State Bar Association, 2004-2005. *Member:* Chicago (Member, Committees on: Corporation and Business Law), Illinois State and American (Member, Section of Business Law) Bar Associations.

DOYLE & BOLOTIN, LTD.

A PROFESSIONAL CORPORATION
TEN SOUTH LA SALLE STREET
SUITE 3450
CHICAGO, ILLINOIS 60603
Telephone: 312-782-5600
Facsimile: 312-782-6660

Commodity Futures Regulation and Litigation, Managed Funds, Commodities and Securities Arbitration, Business Law.

BERNARD F. DOYLE, JR., born Chicago, Illinois, March 10, 1945; admitted to bar, 1971, Illinois and U.S. District Court, Northern District of Illinois. *Education:* Campion High School; Loyola University of Chicago (B.S., honors, 1968); Northwestern University Law School (J.D., 1971). Instructor, Legal Assistants Program, Roosevelt University, 1975. Law Clerk, Justice Glenn K. Seidenfeld, Illinois Appellate Court, Second District, 1971-1972. Chief Counsel, Chicago Board of Trade, 1976-1979. Arbitrator, Chicago Mercantile Exchange, National Futures Association, 1985—; National Association of Securities Dealers. *Member:* Chicago (Member, Commodity Law Section), Illinois State and American (Member, Commodity Law Section) Bar Associations. ***PRACTICE AREAS:*** Commodities; Securities; Arbitration; Managed Funds; Business Law. ***Email:*** bdoyle@d-b-law.com

WILLIAM J. BOLOTIN, born Evergreen Park, Illinois, October 13, 1958; admitted to bar, 1983, Illinois and U.S. District Court, Northern District of Illinois including Trial Bar; 1992, U.S. Court of Appeals, Seventh Circuit. *Education:* University of Notre Dame (B.B.A., Finance, 1980); University of Illinois College of Law (J.D., 1983). Author: Chapter 16, "Commodities Regulation Issues," Illinois Law and Agribusiness, Illinois Institute for Continuing Legal Education, 2001. Moderator: Chicago Bar Association Financial and Investment Services Symposium, March 2000. Speaker: "Futures Regulation Issues for the Agricultural Lawyer" presented at Illinois State Bar Association Agricultural Law Seminar, March 2000. Arbitrator, National Futures Association, 1985—. *Member:* Chicago (Futures and Derivatives Law Committee; Chairman, Financial and Investment Services Committee, 2000-2001) and Illinois State (Agricultural Law Section Council) Bar Associations. ***PRACTICE AREAS:*** Futures; Commodities; Securities; Arbitration; Business Law. ***Email:*** wbolotin@d-b-law.com

DRANE FREYER & LAPINS, LIMITED

150 NORTH WACKER DRIVE, 8TH FLOOR
CHICAGO, ILLINOIS 60606
Telephone: 312-827-7100
Fax: 312-827-7111

General Practice, Real Estate Law including Acquisitions and Dispositions, Financing, Leasing, Annexation, Zoning, Land Use, Land Development, and Property Management; Corporate and Securities Law, Venture Capital, Business Acquisitions, Sales and Divestitures, Technology Businesses, Litigation.

FIRM PROFILE: Founded in 2000 by partners from other Chicago firms, the firm provides a wide range of sophisticated legal services to businesses. In the business community, Drane Freyer & Lapins has quickly developed a reputation for skill, integrity and top-quality legal services. As a business-oriented law firm, we help our clients meet the challenges of today's complex business environment. Client service and individual attention to our clients' needs are our primary concerns. Our close working relationships with clients and efficient delivery of services make our representation especially effective. Legendary service is our continuing goal.

SCOTT A. DRANE, born Ramey AFB, Puerto Rico, May 13, 1955; admitted to bar, 1981, Illinois. *Education:* University of Illinois (B.A., cum laude, 1976); Northwestern University (M.M., with distinction, 1981; J.D., cum laude, 1981). Phi Kappa Phi; Phi Beta Kappa; Beta Gamma Sigma; Order of the Coif. Austin Scholar. Member, Editorial Board,

(This Listing Continued)

Northwestern University Law Review, 1979-1981. *Member:* American Bar Association. ***PRACTICE AREAS:*** Real Estate Law; Commercial Law; Corporate Law; Finance Law; Venture Capital Law. ***Email:*** scott_drane@transwestern.net

WENDY FREYER, born Chicago, Illinois, January 23, 1959; admitted to bar, 1985, Illinois. *Education:* London School of Economics, London, England; Smith College (A.B., cum laude, 1981); Northwestern University (J.D., 1985). *Member:* Chicago and American Bar Associations. Fellow, American College of Investment Counsel. ***PRACTICE AREAS:*** Real Estate Law; Commercial Law; Securities Law; Finance Law; Construction Law. ***Email:*** wendy_freyer@transwestern.net

DAVID A. LAPINS, born Chicago, Illinois, July 3, 1958; admitted to bar, 1983, Illinois. *Education:* University of Illinois (B.A., with distinction, 1980); Northwestern University (J.D., 1983). Member, Editorial Board, Northwestern Journal of International Law & Business, 1982-1983. Author: "Title Insurance Needed in Portfolio Acquisitions," The National Law Journal, January 23, 1995. Co-Author: "Illinois Statute 765 ILCS 5/31.5-Rent Assignment and Perfection"; "Legal Considerations Confronting the Shopping Center Industry," Shopping Centers and Other Retail Projects - Their Investment, Development, Financing and Management, 1996. *Member:* Chicago (Member, Real Property Law Committee, Real Property Finance Subcommittee) and American (Member, Real Property, Probate and Trust Law Section) Bar Associations. ***PRACTICE AREAS:*** Real Estate Law; Commercial Law; Corporate Law; Finance Law. ***Email:*** david_lapins@transwestern.net

DRINKER BIDDLE & REATH LLP

A Pennsylvania Limited Liability Partnership
115 S. LA SALLE STREET
23RD FLOOR
CHICAGO, ILLINOIS 60603-3862
Telephone: 312-977-1510
Telefax: 312-977-1511
Cable Address: "Debemac"
URL: http://www.drinkerbiddle.com

Philadelphia, Pennsylvania Office: One Logan Square, 18th & Cherry Streets. Telephone: 215-988-2700. Telefax: 215-988-2757. Cable Address: "Debemac."
Washington, D.C. Office: 1500 K Street, N.W., Suite 1100. Telephone: 202-842-8800. Telefax: 202-842-8465.
Wilmington, Delaware Office: 1100 N. Market Street, Suite 1000. Telephone: 302-467-4200. Fax: 302-467-4201.
Florham Park, New Jersey Office: 500 Campus Drive. Telephone: 973-360-1100. Fax: 973-360-9831.
Princeton, New Jersey Office: Suite 300, 105 College Road East. Telephone: 609-716-6500. Telefax: 609-799-7000.
Berwyn, Pennsylvania Office: Suite 300, 1000 Westlakes Drive. Telephone: 610-993-2200. Telefax: 610-993-8585.
San Francisco, California Office: 50 Fremont Street, 20th Floor. Telephone: 415-591-7500. Telefax: 415-591-7510.
Los Angeles, California Office: Wells Fargo Center, 333 South Grand Avenue. Telephone: 213-253-2300. Cable Address: "Debemac."
New York, N.Y. Office: 140 Broadway, 39th Floor. Telephone: 212-248-3140. Fax: 212-248-3141.

Products Liability, Toxic Torts, Environmental Litigation, Insurance Coverage, Antitrust, Intellectual Property, Commercial and Securities Litigation, Construction Litigation, Real Estate Litigation, Professional Error and Omissions, Employment Litigation and General Civil Litigation.

FIRM PROFILE: Drinker Biddle & Reath LLP practices nationally and internationally in three major areas: business and finance, litigation, and personal and fiduciary law. Our clients include Fortune 100 companies, emerging and prominent technological enterprises, healthcare companies, environmental businesses, private equity investors, financial institutions, real estate concerns, major academic institutions, individuals and fiduciaries. Headquartered since 1849 in Philadelphia, Pennsylvania, Drinker Biddle's more than 450 lawyers serve clients collaboratively from nine offices, including others in New York, NY, Washington, DC, Los Angeles, CA, San Francisco, CA, Florham Park, NJ, Princeton, NJ, Berwyn, PA, Wilmington, DE and Chicago, IL.

MEMBERS OF FIRM

JOHN DAMES, born 1946; admitted to bar, 1971, Illinois. *Education:* Washington Univ. (B.A., 1966); Indiana Univ. (M.A., 1968); Loyola Univ. (J.D., 1971). ***LANGUAGES:*** Russian, German, Greek and Spanish. ***PRACTICE AREAS:*** Products Liability; Toxic Tort Litigation. ***Email:*** john.dames@dbr.com

DAVID B. SUDZUS, born 1964; admitted to bar, 1990, Illinois. *Education:* Benedictine Univ. (B.A., 1987); Northwestern Univ. (J.D., 1990). ***PRACTICE AREAS:*** Products Liability; Medical Device, Complex and Multi-District Litigation. ***Email:*** david.sudzus@dbr.com

ASSOCIATES

WILLIAM V. ESSIG, born 1970; admitted to bar, 1996, Illinois. *Education:* Yale Univ. (B.A., 1992); Northwestern Univ. (J.D., 1996). ***PRACTICE AREAS:*** Products Liability. ***Email:*** william.essig@dbr.com

LARA C. OTSUKA, born 1971; admitted to bar, 1999, Illinois. *Education:* California State Univ. (B.A., 1993); Northwestern Univ. (J.D., 1999). ***PRACTICE AREAS:*** Products Liability. ***Email:*** lara.otsuka@dbr.com

STEPHANIE J. SYNOL, born 1966; admitted to bar, 2003, Illinois. *Education:* DePaul Univ. (B.A., 1999); Northwestern Univ. (J.D., 2003). ***PRACTICE AREAS:*** Products Liability. ***Email:*** stephanie.synol@dbr.com

B. TODD VINSON, born 1972; admitted to bar, 1998, Tennessee; 2001, Illinois. *Education:* Univ. of Florida (B.S., 1994); Vanderbilt Univ. (J.D., 1998). ***PRACTICE AREAS:*** Products Liability. ***Email:*** todd.vinson@dbr.com

(For Biographical data on all Personnel, see Professional Biographies at Philadelphia, Pennsylvania)

DRUNKEN DRIVING DEFENSE LAWYERS OF ILLINOIS, LTD.

Established in 1981

ONE NORTH LA SALLE STREET
SUITE 4200
CHICAGO, ILLINOIS 60602-4011
Telephone: 312-263-4422
Fax: 312-263-2803
URL: http://www. absolutely-100percent-not-guilty.com
URL: http://www.duidefense-law.com

Waukegan, Illinois Office: 25 North County Street, 2nd Floor, 60085.

Practice Limited to Criminal Defense, Driving While Intoxicated (DWI) and Other Offenses Arising Out of Operation of Motor Vehicles, Drug Crimes, Felonies, Homicide, Misdemeanors, Parole and Probation and Traffic Violations.

FIRM PROFILE: Statewide defense of allegations regarding drunken driving and reckless homicide. The firm maintains offices in Chicago, Cook County; Waukegan, Lake County; and Woodridge, Dupage County.

STEPHEN M. KOMIE, born Chicago, Illinois, 1949; admitted to bar, 1976, Illinois Supreme Court; 1985, U.S. Supreme Court, U.S. Court of Appeals, Sixth, Seventh and Eighth Circuits, U.S. District Court, Central, Northern and Southern Districts of Illinois, U.S. District Court, Northern District of Indiana, U.S. District Court, Eastern and Western Districts of Michigan, U.S. District Court, Eastern District of Missouri and U.S. Tax Court. *Education:* University of Arizona (B.A., M.A.); DePaul University (J.D., 1976). Recipient: Public Service Award for Pro Bono Service, American Trial Lawyers Association, 1994; Illinois State Bar Association Board of Governors Award, 1991; Illinois State Bar Association Certificates of Appreciation, June 1986, September, 1990, October 1990, August, 2005; Chicago Bar Certificate of Appreciation, June, 1984, February, 1987. Author: "Attorney's Bill of Rights," Adopted by the State Bar, June, 1990; "Illinois State Bar Association Legislation Proposed to Protect Attorney/Client Relationship," Chicago Law Bulletin, March 12, 1987; "Little RICO Bill Should Not Be Passed," The Bar News, June 1984; "Little RICO in Illinois, The Case Against It," Chicago Law Bulletin, April, 1984. Founding Member, Illinois Attorney's for Criminal Justice, 1984. Founder, National College of Drunken Driving Defense. Member, National College of Criminal Defense Lawyers and Public Defenders, 1977. *Member:* Chicago Bar Association (Chairperson: Criminal Law Committee; Defense of Prisoner Committee); Illinois State Bar Association (Secretary, 1996—; Member: Board of Governors, 1992-1998; 1999—; Assembly, 1985-1998; By-Laws Assembly Committee; Mandatory Continuing Legal Education Committee; Chairman: Credentials Committee, 1985; Criminal Justice Section, 1989; Professionalism Committee, 1991-1992; Traffic Courts and The Law Committee; Judicial Compensation Committee, 1990); American Bar Association (Elected Member, Criminal Justice Section Council 05-08, Small Firm and Solo Practice Task Force, 1990-1992); International Bar Association (Chairman, Family Law, 05-08). Fellow: Illinois Bar Foundation (Director; Diamond Fellow). (Also Member, Law Offices Komie and Associates). ***PRACTICE AREAS:*** Driving While Intoxicated; Homicide; Criminal Law; Traffic Violations; Vehicular Homicide; Drug Crimes; Felonies; Juvenile Law; Misdemeanors; Parole and Probation; Sexual Assault.

DARIUS R. DIRMANTAS, born Chicago, Illinois, 1968; admitted to bar, 2000, Illinois and U.S. District Court, Northern District of Illinois. *Education:* Massachusetts Maritime Academy (B.S., 1992); Loyola University (J.D., 2000). U.S. Coast Guard Chief Engineers License, 1995. Member, National College of DUI Defense, 2001. *Member:* Chicago, Illinois State and American Bar Associations. (Also Associate, Law Offices of Komie & Associates). ***LANGUAGES:*** Lithuanian. ***PRACTICE AREAS:*** Criminal Law; Internet Crimes; Drug Crimes; Felonies; Driving While Intoxicated. ***Email:*** darius_r_dirmantas@komie-and-associates.com

ELISABETH A. RITTER, born Evanston, Illinois, 1969; admitted to bar, 1994, Illinois; 1995, Missouri. *Education:* Northwestern University (B.A., 1991); Washington University (J.D., 1994). *Member:* Illinois State Bar Association; The Missouri Bar. (Also Associate, Law Offices of Komie and Associates, Chicago, Illinois). ***PRACTICE AREAS:*** Family Law; Civil Litigation; Probate. ***Email:*** elisabeth_a_ritter@komie-and-associates.com

BRIAN E. KING, born Chicago, Illinois, July 17, 1970; admitted to bar, 1996, Illinois, U.S. Court of Appeals, Seventh Circuit, U.S. District Court, Northern District of Illinois and U.S. District Court, Eastern District of Michigan. *Education:* Michigan State University (B.S., 1993); DePaul University (J.D., 1996). Phi Alpha Delta. Graduate, National College of DUI Defense, Harvard Law School, 1997. *Member:* Chicago, Illinois State and American Bar Associations. (Also Associate, Law Offices of Komie and Associates, Chicago, Illinois). ***LANGUAGES:*** German. ***PRACTICE AREAS:*** Driving While Intoxicated; Appellate Practice; Criminal Law.

SARAH E. TONEY, born Illinois, 1978; admitted to bar, 2004, Illinois and U.S. District Court, Northern District of Illinois. *Education:* Miami University (B.S., 2000); Loyola University (J.D., 2003). Member, National College for Driving Under the Influence Defense. *Member:* Chicago, Illinois State and American Bar Associations. (Also Associate, Law Offices of Komie and Associates, Chicago, Illinois). ***PRACTICE AREAS:*** Criminal Defense; Driving While Intoxicated; Child Abuse and Neglect; Drug Crimes; Internet Crimes. ***Email:*** stoney@komie-and-associates.com

OF COUNSEL

MARC D. WOLFE, born Los Angeles, California, 1951; admitted to bar, 1976, Illinois Supreme Court, U.S. Court of Appeals, Seventh Circuit, and U.S.District Court, Northern District of Illinois. *Education:* University of Denver (B.A.B.S., 1973); John Marshall Law

(This Listing Continued)

School (J.D., 1976). *Member:* Du Page County and Illinois State Bar Associations. (Also Of Counsel, Law Offices Komie and Associates). ***PRACTICE AREAS:*** Divorce; Commercial; Criminal; Real Estate; Driving While Intoxicated.

REPRESENTATIVE CLIENTS: National College of DUI Defense; Network of Illinois DUI Attorneys.

DUANE MORRIS LLP

227 WEST MONROE STREET, SUITE 3400
CHICAGO, ILLINOIS 60606
Telephone: 312-499-6700
Fax: 312-499-6701
URL: http://www.duanemorris.com

Philadelphia, Pennsylvania Office: 30 South 17th Street. Telephone: 215-979-1000. Fax: 215-979-1020.

New York, New York Office: 380 Lexington Avenue. Telephone: 212-692-1000. Fax: 212-692-1020.

Los Angeles, California Office: 333 South Hope Street. Telephone: 213-229-2900. Fax: 213-229-2999.

London, England Office: Duane Morris, 4 Chiswell Street, 5th Floor, EC1Y 4UP. Telephone: +44 0 20 7786 2100. Fax: +44 0 20 7786 2101.

Washington, D.C. Office: 1667 K Street, N.W., Suite 700. Telephone: 202-776-7800. Fax: 202-776-7801.

San Francisco, California Office: One Market, Spear Tower, Suite 2000. Telephone: 415-371-2200. Fax: 415-371-2201.

Boston, Massachusetts Office: 470 Atlantic Avenue, Suite 500. Telephone: 617-9200. Fax: 617-598-9201.

Atlanta, Georgia Office: 1180 West Peachtree Street, Suite 700. Telephone: 404-253-6900. Fax: 404-253-6901.

Miami, Florida Office: 200 South Biscayne Boulevard, Suite 3400. Telephone: 305-960-2200. Fax: 305-960-2201

Wilmington, Delaware Office: 1100 North Market Street, Suite 1200. Telephone: 302-657-4900. Fax: 302-657-4901.

Harrisburg, Pennsylvania Office: 305 North Front Street, 5th Floor, P.O. Box 1003. Telephone: 717-237-5500. Fax: 717-232-4015.

Newark, New Jersey Office: 744 Broad Street, Suite 1200. Telephone: 973-424-2000. Fax: 973-424-2001.

Allentown, Pennsylvania Office: 968 Postal Road, Suite 200, P.O. Box 90400. Telephone: 610-266-3650. Fax: 610-266-3651.

Houston, Texas Office: 3200 Southwest Freeway, Suite 3150. Telephone: 713-402-3900. Fax: 713-402-3901.

Hamilton, New Jersey Office: 240 Princeton Avenue, Suite 150. Mailing Address: P.O. Box 5203, Princeton, NJ. Telephone: 609-631-2400. Fax: 609-631-2401.

San Diego, California Office: 101 West Broadway, Suite 900. Telephone: 619-744-2200. Fax: 619-744-2201.

Pittsburgh, Pennsylvania Office: 600 Grant Street, Suite 5010. Telephone: 412-497-1000. Fax: 412-497-1001.

Administrative Law, Accountants Liability, Admiralty and Maritime Law, Affordable Housing, Alternative Dispute Resolution, Antitrust and Trade Regulation, Appellate Practice, Architects and Engineers Liability, Aviation and Aerospace, Aerospace Law, Banks and Banking, Banking Litigation, Bankruptcy, Bankruptcy Chapter 11, Bankruptcy Reorganization, Business Development, Business Law, Business Litigation, Business Reorganization, Business Start-Ups, Business Taxation, Charitable Giving, Chemical Intellectual Property, Chemical Patent Prosecution, Civil Litigation, Civil Rights, Class Actions, Closely Held Business Law, Closely Held Corporations, COBRA, College and University Law, Commercial Law, Commercial Litigation, Commercial Real Estate, Complex Commercial Litigation, Computers and Software, Computer and Software Patents, Computer Law, Condominium Law, Construction Law, Construction Litigation, Consumer Law, Content Licensing, Copyrights, Copyright Infringement, Copyright Prosecution, Copyright Protection, Corporate Banking Law, Corporate Commercial Law, Corporate Finance, Corporate Law, Creditor Bankruptcy, Criminal Law, Customs Law, Debt Finance, Debtor and Creditor, Debtor and Creditor Rights, Debtor Bankruptcy, Deportation, Disability Benefits, Disability Insurance, Domain Names, E-Commerce, Education Law, Elder Law, Emerging Growth Companies, Eminent Domain, Employee Benefits, Employee Benefits Litigation, Employment Authorizations, Employment Discrimination, Employment Law, Employment Litigation, Energy, Energy Regulation, Environmental Law, Equipment Finance and Leasing, Equine Law, Equity Finance, ERISA, Estates and Asset Planning, Estate and Gift Taxation, Fair Housing, Family Law, Federal Income Tax, Fidelity and Surety, Fidelity and Surety Bonds, Finance, Financial Planning, Franchise and Franchising, Franchise Law, General Practice, Government, Government Investigations, Government Relations, Health Care, Health Care Compliance, Health Care Fraud, Health Maintenance Organizations, Homeowners Association Law, Housing Development, Housing Finance, Housing Law, Immigration and Naturalization, Immigration Law, Independent School Law, Information Technology, Initial Public Offerings, Insurance, Insurance Coverage, Insurance Defense, Insurance Litigation, Integrated Health Care Delivery, Intellectual Property, Intellectual Property Infringement, Intellectual Property Litigation, Intellectual Property Procurement, Intellectual Property Rights, International Energy Law, International Finance, International Law, International Taxation, International Trade, Internet Intellectual Property, Internet Law, Internet Patents, Joint Ventures, Labor and Employment, Land Use, Land Use Litigation, Leveraged Buyouts, Life and Health Insurance, Litigation, Local Government Law, Local Taxation, Low Income Housing, Managed Care, Managed Care Contracts, Mechanical Intellectual Property, Mediation, Medical Malpractice, Medicare and Medicaid, Mergers, Acquisitions and Divestitures, Mortgages, Municipal Bonds, Municipal Finance, Municipal Law, Natural Gas, Natural Resources, Nonprofit and Charitable Organizations, Oil and Gas Law, Partnership Law, Patents, Patent Licensing, Patent Prosecution, Personal Injury, Personal Injury Defense, Piracy, Political Asylum, Privatization, Private Foundations, Probate, Probate Litigation, Products Liability, Professional Liability, Professional Malpractice, Professional Negligence, Proxy Contests, Public Finance, Public Housing, Public Policy, Public School Law, Real Estate, Real Estate Acquisitions, Real Estate Development, Real Estate Litigation, Real Estate Tax Assessment, Regulatory Compliance, Regulatory Law, Reinsurance, Reorganiza-

(This Listing Continued)

tion and Finance, RICO, Risk Management, Secured Creditors Rights, Securities, Securities Fraud, Securities Litigation, Securities Taxation and Telecommunications, Sexual Harassment, Shareholders Disputes, Shareholder Rights, Sports Law, State Government Law, Taxation, Torts, Toxic Torts, Trade Association Law, Trade Secrets, Trademarks, Trademark Licensing, Trademark Prosecution, Trademark Protection, Trusts and Estates, Unsecured Creditors Rights, Utility Law, Visas, Water Law, Water Rights, Web Site Development, White Collar Crime, Workers Compensation, Workouts, Wrongful Death, Zoning, Planning and Land Use.

FIRM PROFILE: Duane Morris LLP, among the 100 largest law firms in the United States, is a full-service firm of over 550 lawyers. In addition, Duane Morris affiliates have over 50 professionals engaged in a number of nonlegal service businesses. The firm represents clients across the nation and around the world through a combination of 18 offices and a relationship with an international network of independent law firms. For more information, visit the firm's Web site at: www.duanemorris.com.

Duane Morris refers to Duane Morris LLP and its affiliates, including Duane Morris in London, a law firm of solicitors and registered foreign lawyers regulated by the Law Society in the conduct of investment business.

RESIDENT PARTNERS

DAVID B. ALLSWANG, born Chicago, Illinois, September 6, 1967; admitted to bar, 1994, Illinois. *Education:* Boston University College of Communication (B.S., magna cum laude, 1990); Boston University School of Law (J.D., cum laude, 1994); Yeshiva University Gruss Institute. . ***Email:*** dballswang@duanemorris.com

DOUGLAS J. ANTONIO, born New York, New York, September 14, 1955; admitted to bar, 1980, Maryland; 1981, District of Columbia; 1983, Missouri; 1996, Illinois. *Education:* University of Maryland (B.S., and B.A., with highest honors, 1977; J.D., with honors, 1980; M.B.A., 1981); Georgetown University Law Center (LL.M., Taxation, 1983). Editor, International Trade Law Journal. Attorney Advisor, U.S. Department of Labor, 1980-1983. *Member:* Chicago Bar Association (Member, Executive Committee). ***PRACTICE AREAS:*** Affordable Housing; Community Development; Real Estate Law; Tax Law; Partnership Syndication; Partnership Law. ***Email:*** djantonio@duanemorris.com

FREDERICK R. BALL, born Akron, Ohio, October 28, 1964; admitted to bar, 1996, Illinois. *Education:* University of Colorado at Boulder (B.A., 1993); Cornell University (J.D., cum laude, 1996). Member, Editorial Board, Cornell Law Review. [U.S. Army, 1985-1987]. ***PRACTICE AREAS:*** Commercial Litigation; Class Actions; Civil Rights; Closely Held Corporations; Contracts. ***Email:*** frball@duanemorris.com

NEVILLE M. BILIMORIA, born Chicago, Illinois, November 22, 1970; admitted to bar, 1994, Illinois. *Education:* Northwestern University (B.A., 1991): Northwestern University School of Law (J.D., 1994). Note and Comment Editor, Journal of Criminal Law and Criminology. Moot Court Competition. Author: "Telemedicine: Laws Still Need a Dose of Efficiency," Journal of Medical Practice Management, May/June 2003. ***PRACTICE AREAS:*** Health Care Law; Health Care Corporate Law; Health Care Litigation; Health Care Fraud; Health Care Abuse; Health Care Compliance; HIPAA. ***Email:*** nmbilimoria@duanemorris.com

ROBERT P. BRAMNIK, born Brooklyn, New York, November 17, 1949; admitted to bar, 1974, New York; 1980, Illinois. *Education:* City College of the City University of New York (B.A., 1970); Brooklyn Law School (J.D., 1973). Co-Author, "Untoward Employee Whistleblower Claims Under Sarbanes-Oxley," Journal of Investment Compliance, Fall 2003. Author: "Clearing Firm Liability - Everything Old Is New Again," published by the American Bar Association, February 2003. Lecturer, Securities Industry Association Compliance and Legal Division, New York, 1980-1991, 1994-2001. Senior Trial Counsel, New York Stock Exchange, Inc., 1973-1975. Assistant General Counsel: E.F. Hutton & Co., Inc., 1975-1977; National Securities Clearing Corp., 1977-1979. Vice-Chairman, 1985-1988 and Chairman, 1989-1995, Illinois Advisory Committee on Commodity Regulation. Arbitrator: National Association of Securities Dealers, 1980—; National Futures Association, 1984—. Member, Business Conduct Committee, National Futures Association, 2001—. *Member:* Association of the Bar of the City of New York; Illinois State and American (Member, Subcommittee on Market Regulation, Committee on Federal Regulation of Securities, 1985— and Co-Chair, Subcommittee on Futures Commission Merchants, Committee on Regulation of Futures and Derivatives, 2001—) Bar Associations; Securities Industry Association (Member, Legal and Compliance Divisions). Fellow, Illinois Bar Foundation. ***PRACTICE AREAS:*** Financial Services Law; Strategic Business Planning; Investments; Securities; Securities Regulation; Futures Regulation; Compliance; Derivative Products. ***Email:*** rpbramnik@duanemorris.com

CHERYL BLACKWELL BRYSON, born Baltimore, Maryland, May 1, 1950; admitted to bar, 1977, Illinois. *Education:* Morgan State University (B.A., cum laude, 1972); The Ohio State University (J.D., 1977). Associate Editor, The Ohio State Law Journal. Co-Author, "Untoward Employee Whistleblower Claims Under Sarbanes-Oxley," Journal of Investment Compliance, Fall 2003. Deputy Corporation Counsel, Labor Relations Division, Law Department, City of Chicago. Head of the Chicago office's Employment Law and Management Labor Relations practice. ***PRACTICE AREAS:*** Labor Law; Employment Law; Employment Litigation; Title VII Discrimination; Employment Discrimination; Employment Claims; Equal Employment Opportunity Law; Collective Bargaining. ***Email:*** cbbryson@duanemorris.com

NEIL E. CASS, born Carthage, Illinois, January 8, 1952; admitted to bar, 1977, Iowa and Wisconsin; 1980, Illinois; 2002, Pennsylvania. *Education:* University of Puget Sound (B.A., 1974); University of Iowa (M.B.A., 1977; J.D., 1977); University of Miami (LL.M., Estate Planning, 1980). Certified Public Accountant, Illinois, 1981. *Member:* State Bar of Wisconsin; Iowa State, Illinois State and American Bar Associations. ***PRACTICE AREAS:*** Estate Planning; Estate Administration; Trust Administration. ***Email:*** necass@duanemorris.com

ROSANNE CIAMBRONE, born Chicago Heights, Illinois, July 14, 1963; admitted to bar, 1988, Illinois. *Education:* University of Michigan (B.A., 1985); University of Notre Dame (J.D., 1988). ***PRACTICE AREAS:*** Debt Restructuring; Recapitalization; Bankruptcy Reorganization. ***Email:*** rciambrone@duanemorris.com

(This Listing Continued)

JOHN COLLEN, born Chicago, Illinois, December 26, 1954; admitted to bar, 1980, Illinois. *Education:* Dartmouth College (A.B., summa cum laude, 1977); Georgetown University Law Center (J.D., 1980). Phi Beta Kappa. Winner, Leahy Moot Court Competition. Georgetown Law Fellow. Listed in Who's Who in American Law and Who's Who in America. Instructor, Legal Research and Writing, 1979-1980. Author: "Buying and Selling Real Estate In Bankruptcy," single volume treastise, West, 1997; "Bankruptcy and D&O Insurance," Journal of Bankruptcy Law and Practice, Vol. 11, No. 2, January/February 2002. Member, Editorial Advisory Board, Journal of Bankruptcy Law and Practice. Head of the Chicago office's bankruptcy practice. *Member:* American Bankruptcy Institute (Co-chair, Real Estate Bankruptcy Committee). Fellow, American College of Bankruptcy. ***PRACTICE AREAS:*** Bankruptcy Law; Loan Workouts; Corporate Reorganizations; Creditors Rights; Distressed Real Estate; Real Estate Bankruptcy; Real Estate Foreclosure; Real Estate Workouts. ***Email:*** jcollen@duanemorris.com

LAWRENCE I. DAVIDSON, born Chicago, Illinois, November 6, 1949; admitted to bar, 1975, Illinois. *Education:* University of Illinois (B.S., 1972); The John Marshall Law School (J.D., 1975; LL.M., Taxation, 1979). Certified Public Accountant, Illinois, 1975. ***PRACTICE AREAS:*** Employee Benefits; Executive Compensation; Retirement Benefit Plans; ERISA. ***Email:*** lidavidson@duanemorris.com

HOWARD M. HOFFMANN, born Chicago, Illinois, December 24, 1941; admitted to bar, 1968, Illinois. *Education:* Loyola University (B.S., 1965); Chicago-Kent College of Law (J.D., 1968). Author: "Eight Inches Below the Horizon: An Argument in the U.S. Supreme Court," NJ Lawyer Magazine, April, 2003; "History, Decision, and Aftermath of Thompson v. Western States - Drug Advertising and the First Amendment," Update Magazine, Food and Drug Law Institute, 2003. Member, Chicago-Kent Law Review. U.S. Attorney's Office, Northern District of Illinois: Assistant U.S. Attorney, 1968-1971; Chief, Criminal Division, 1971-1976; Chief, Tax Division, 1970-1977; Deputy U.S. Attorney, 1976-1977. ***PRACTICE AREAS:*** Commercial Litigation; Health Care Litigation; Fraud and Abuse; Appellate Litigation; White Collar Criminal Defense. ***Email:*** hmhoffmann@duanemorris.com

STANLEY R. KAMINSKI, born Chicago, Illinois, October 3, 1955; admitted to bar, 1980, Illinois. *Education:* DePaul University (B.S.C., with highest honors, 1977); DePaul University College of Law (J.D., 1980). Certified Public Accountant, Illinois. Chief Assistant Corporation Counsel for Taxation, City of Chicago Department of Law, 1987-1989. Author: "Illinois' New Tax Amnesty," Tax Trends, October 2003; "Analysis of Two Recent Tax Cases Decided by the Illinois Appellate Court," Tax Trends, August 2003; Illinois Tax Handbook, Research Institute of America; "Illinois Supreme Court Narrows Constitutional Protections of Taxpayers," State Tax Notes, April 7, 2003; "Case Synopses," Tax Trends, April 2003; Article summarizes two recent opinions from the Circuit Court of Cook County, Illinois: Mead Corporation v. Illinois Department of Revenue-Circuit Court of Cook County, Illinois (No. 00 CH 7854) December 2, 2002 and Groesbeck v. Bower, et al. ***PRACTICE AREAS:*** State Taxation; Local Taxation; Sales and Use Tax; Franchise Taxation; Corporate Income Tax. ***Email:*** srkaminski@duanemorris.com

CHARLES D. KATZ, admitted to bar, 1985, New York (Not admitted in Illinois). *Education:* Union College (B.A., 1981); Fordham University School of Law (J.D., 1984). ***PRACTICE AREAS:*** Commercial Finance; Municipal Finance; Affordable Housing; Community Development Law; Municipal Bonds. ***Email:*** cdkatz@duanemorris.com

DAVID J. KAUFMAN, born Detroit, Michigan, May 19, 1963; admitted to bar, 1990, Illinois. *Education:* University of Michigan (B.A., with distinction and honors, 1985; M.P.P., International, 1986; J.D., 1990). Member, Editorial Board, Michigan Journal of International Law, 1989-1990. Editor-in-Chief, Michigan Journal of Political Science. *Member:* American Bar Association (Chair, Standing Committee on Strategic Communications, Business Law Section, 2002-2004). ***PRACTICE AREAS:*** Corporate Law; Corporate Finance; Mergers and Acquisitions; Securities Law. ***Email:*** djkaufman@duanemorris.com

BRIAN P. KERWIN, born Detroit, Michigan, April 14, 1964; admitted to bar, 1989, Illinois; 1991, District of Columbia. *Education:* University of Michigan (B.A., magna cum laude, with honors, 1986); The National Law Center of The George Washington University (J.D., with honors, 1989); The John Marshall Law School (LL.M., Intellectual Property Law, 1996). Member, George Washington Law Review. Contributing Author: "Advanced Commercial Finance and Creditor's Rights," Illinois Institute of Continuing Legal Education. (Member, Chicago Office Management Committee, Duane Morris LLP). ***PRACTICE AREAS:*** Business Transactions; Mergers and Acquisitions; Venture Capital; Private Placement; Commercial Finance; Intellectual Property Licensing. ***Email:*** bpkerwin@duanemorris.com

DANIEL KOHN, born Chicago, Illinois, May 14, 1962; admitted to bar, 1987, Illinois. *Education:* Brandeis University (B.A., summa cum laude, 1984); Harvard University (J.D., 1987). ***PRACTICE AREAS:*** Real Estate; Real Estate Development; Real Estate Finance; Real Estate Sales; Mortgage Securitization. ***Email:*** dkohn@duanemorris.com

KENNETH A. LATIMER, born Chicago, Illinois, October 26, 1943; admitted to bar, 1969, District of Columbia; 1970, Illinois. *Education:* University of Wisconsin (B.S., 1966); The National Law Center of The George Washington University (J.D., with honors, 1969). Listed in, Chambers Global: The World's Leading Lawyers in the area of Banking and Finance. Founding Member and Member, Governing Board, Commercial Finance Association, Education Foundation. Fellow, American Bar Foundation. ***PRACTICE AREAS:*** Corporate Law; Business Law; Secured Finance; Asset Based Finance; Real Estate Finance; Loan Workouts; Mergers and Acquisitions; Loan Restructuring. ***Email:*** kalatimer@duanemorris.com

NICHOLAS J. LYNN, born Waukegan, Illinois, October 1, 1952; admitted to bar, 1980, Illinois. *Education:* Drake University College of Pharmacy (B.S., 1975); The John Marshall Law School (J.D., 1980). Registered Pharmacist, Illinois. Chief Counsel, Illinois Health Facilities Planning Board, 1984-1985. Chief and Assistant Chief Counsel, Department of Public Health Division, 1983-1985. General Counsel, Illinois Health Care Association. Head of the Chicago office's health law practice. (Member, Chicago Office Management Committee, Duane Morris LLP). ***PRACTICE AREAS:*** Health Care Litigation; Health Care Regulation; Health Care Compliance; Pharmacy Law. ***Email:*** njlynn@duanemorris.com

JOANNE J. MATOUSEK, born Wilkes-Barre, Pennsylvania, March 6, 1962; admitted to bar, 1987, Illinois. *Education:* Syracuse University (B.S., cum laude, 1984); Univer-

(This Listing Continued)

DUANE MORRIS LLP, Chicago—Continued

sity of Notre Dame (J.D., 1987). ***PRACTICE AREAS:*** Insurance; Insurance Coverage; Directors and Officers Liability; Subrogation. ***Email:*** jjmatousek@duanemorris.com

PAMELA J. MILLS, born Indianapolis, Indiana, August 2, 1958; admitted to bar, 1982, District of Columbia; 1985, Illinois. *Education:* Northwestern University (B.A., Economics, 1979); University of Notre Dame (J.D., 1982). ***PRACTICE AREAS:*** Franchising; Distribution; Commercial Law; Licensing; Antitrust. ***Email:*** pjmills@duanemorris.com

HOWARD L. MOCERF, born Louisville, Kentucky, April 13, 1946; admitted to bar, 1973, Illinois; 1976, District of Columbia. *Education:* Washington & Lee University (B.A., 1968); University of Louisville (J.D., 1971). Attorney, National Labor Relations Board, Cincinnati, Ohio, 1971-1973. ***PRACTICE AREAS:*** Employment Law; Labor Law; Unfair Labor Practices; National Labor Relations Act; Collective Bargaining; Labor Arbitration; Employment Discrimination; Wage and Hour Law; OSHA; Noncompete Agreements; Trade Secrets; Affirmative Action. ***Email:*** hlmocerf@duanemorris.com

VINCENT S. OLESZKIEWICZ, born Chicago, Illinois, August 24, 1957; admitted to bar, 1982, Illinois and U.S. District Court, Northern District of Illinois; 1990, U.S. District Court, Eastern and Western Districts of Michigan; 1991, Federal Trial Bar and U.S. District Court, Eastern District of Missouri; 1998, U.S. Court of Appeals, Seventh Circuit; 1999, U.S. Court of Appeals, Eleventh Circuit. *Education:* Michigan State University (B.A., cum laude, 1979); DePaul University College of Law (J.D., 1982). *Member:* Chicago, Illinois State and American Bar Associations. ***PRACTICE AREAS:*** Environmental; Corporate Compliance; Class Action Litigation; International; Manufacturing. ***Email:*** vsoleszkiewicz@duanemorris.com

MICHAEL A. REITER, born Pittsburgh, Pennsylvania, November 15, 1941; admitted to bar, 1967, Wisconsin; 1975, Illinois. *Education:* University of Wisconsin, Madison (B.S., 1963; M.S., 1964; J.D., 1967; Ph.D., 1969). ***PRACTICE AREAS:*** Commercial Litigation; White Collar Criminal Defense; Corporate Governance; Hostile Takeovers; Lender Liability. ***Email:*** mareiter@duanemorris.com

JOHN T. SCHRIVER, III, born Evanston, Illinois, May 18, 1945; admitted to bar, 1971, Illinois; 1972, Florida. *Education:* College of the Holy Cross (A.B., 1967); Georgetown University Law Center (J.D., 1971). Co-Author: "Fair Value Determinations Under Section12.56 of the Illinois Business Corporation Act," Illinois Bar Journal, April 2003. [Sgt. U.S. Air Force Reserve, 1975, Honorable Discharge]. ***PRACTICE AREAS:*** Civil Litigation; Corporate Litigation; Professional Liability; Trade Secret Litigation; Employment Claims; Labor Claims; Uniform Commercial Code; Construction Litigation; Securities Transactions. ***Email:*** jtschriver@duanemorris.com

LARRY SELANDER, born Chicago, Illinois, May 28, 1946; admitted to bar, 1972, Illinois and U.S. District Court, Northern District of Illinois; 1973, U.S. Court of Appeals, Seventh Circuit. *Education:* University of Notre Dame (B.S.Ch.Eng., 1967); University of Illinois (J.D., 1972). ***Email:*** lselander@duanemorris.com

MICHAEL J. SILVERMAN, born Chicago, Illinois, April 16, 1963; admitted to bar, 1990, Illinois. *Education:* University of Illinois (B.S., with highest honors, 1985); Northwestern University School of Law (J.D., cum laude, 1990). Certified Public Accountant, Illinois, 1985. Certified by the Association of Certified Fraud Examiners. Chair, Information Technologies and Telecommmunications Practice Group, Duane Morris LLP. Special Counsel to the City of Chicago regarding the Y2K computer issue. Member, Mayor's Council of Technology Advisors, City of Chicago. ***PRACTICE AREAS:*** Commercial Litigation; Computer Law; Technology Law; E-Commerce; Internet Law. ***Email:*** mjsilverman@duanemorris.com

CHRISTOPHER B. SULLIVAN, born Melrose Park, Illinois, March 6, 1967; admitted to bar, 1995, Illinois and U.S. District Court, Northern District of Illinois; 2000, U.S. Court of Appeals, Seventh Circuit. *Education:* Cornell University (A.B., 1989); Northwestern University School of Law (J.D., 1995). ***PRACTICE AREAS:*** Litigation; Health Care. ***Email:*** cbsullivan@duanemorris.com

MICHAEL A. WITT, born Skokie, Illinois, December 31, 1969; admitted to bar, 1995, Illinois. *Education:* University of Illinois (B.A., 1992); Loyola University, Chicago (J.D., 1995). Member, Loyola Law Journal. ***PRACTICE AREAS:*** Corporate Law; Lender Law; Mergers and Acquisitions. ***Email:*** mawitt@duanemorris.com

DAVID B. YELIN, born Akron, Ohio, January 31, 1957; admitted to bar, 1986, Illinois. *Education:* University of Akron (B.S., magna cum laude, 1980); Case Western Reserve University School of Law (J.D., magna cum laude, 1986). Order of the Coif. Articles Editor, Case Western Reserve Law Review. Certified Public Accountant, Ohio, 1982. (Partner-in-Charge, Chicago, Illinois Office, Duane Morris LLP; Member, Chicago Office Management Committee). ***PRACTICE AREAS:*** Real Estate Law; Commercial Real Estate; Loan Restructuring; Loan Workouts; Planned Unit Development Law; Zoning Variances; Real Estate Acquisitions; Real Estate Development; Real Estate Finance. ***Email:*** dbyelin@duanemorris.com

JON ZIMRING, born Chicago, Illinois, March 11, 1967; admitted to bar, 1992, Illinois. *Education:* University of Michigan (B.A., with highest distinction, 1989); Northwestern University (J.D., 1992). ***PRACTICE AREAS:*** Labor Law; Employment Law; Labor Relations; Collective Bargaining; Unfair Labor Practices. ***Email:*** jzimring@duanemorris.com

RESIDENT ASSOCIATES

RICHARD P. DARKE, born Southfield, Michigan, March 21, 1971; admitted to bar, 1998, Illinois. *Education:* Western Michigan University (B.A., 1994); University of Michigan School of Law (J.D., 1998). ***PRACTICE AREAS:*** Commercial Litigation; Construction Litigation. ***Email:*** rpdarke@duanemorris.com

CHRISTOPHER P. KELEHER, born Evergreen Park, Illinois, August 12, 1977; admitted to bar, 2002, Illinois and U.S. District Court, Northern District of Illinois; 2003, U.S. Court of Appeals, Seventh Circuit. *Education:* Marquette University (B.A., 1999); DePaul University (J.D., summa cum laude, 2002).

DIETRICH A. LOOS, born Milwaukee, Wisconsin, November 13, 1973; admitted to bar, 1998, Illinois. *Education:* Pepperdine University (B.A., summa cum laude, 1995); University of Chicago Law School (J.D., high honors, 1998). Order of the Coif. Member, Law Review, 1996-1997. ***PRACTICE AREAS:*** Corporate Law; Securities Offerings; Public Offerings; Business Acquisitions; Business Divestitures. ***Email:*** daloos@duanemorris.com

AMY E. McCRACKEN, born Detroit, Michigan, September 16, 1959; admitted to bar, 1991, Michigan; 1998, Illinois. *Education:* Wayne State University (B.S.N., cum laude, 1982); University of Michigan Law School (J.D., cum laude, 1990). Judicial Clerk, Honorable George R. Corsiglia, Forty Eighth Judicial Circuit Court, Allegan, Michigan, 1990-1991. ***PRACTICE AREAS:*** Products Liability; Complex Litigation; Toxic Torts; Professional Liability; Mechanics Liens. ***Email:*** aemccracken@duanemorris.com

RACHAEL G. PONTIKES, born Evanston, Illinois, June 10, 1974; admitted to bar, 2001, Illinois. *Education:* Wesleyan University (B.A., with honors, 1996); The University of Chicago Law School (J.D., 2001). ***LANGUAGES:*** Italian. ***PRACTICE AREAS:*** Commercial Litigation. ***Email:*** rgpontikes@duanemorris.com

RESIDENT SPECIAL COUNSEL

MICHELE J. BRAUN, born Long Beach, New York, March 8, 1959; admitted to bar, 1984, Illinois. *Education:* State University of New York at Binghamton (B.A., 1979); John Marshall Law School (J.D., 1984). ***PRACTICE AREAS:*** Health Care Law; Nursing Home Litigation; Assisted Living Litigation; Employment Law; Construction Litigation; Products Liability; Medical Malpractice; Civil Rights Litigation; Consumer Fraud; Tort Litigation; Breach of Contract; Commercial Litigation. ***Email:*** mjbraun-pritzker@duanemorris.com

DIRK E. EHLERS, born Clinton, Iowa, March 22, 1963; admitted to bar, 1988, Illinois. *Education:* Cornell College (B.A., summa cum laude, 1985); University of Chicago (J.D., 1988). ***PRACTICE AREAS:*** Insurance Law; Insurance Coverage; Directors and Officers Liability Insurance; Property Insurance; Casualty Insurance; Reinsurance; Insurance Defense Subrogation. ***Email:*** deehlers@duanemorris.com

JAMES F. DUNNEBACK, P.C.

CHICAGO, ILLINOIS

(See Orland Park)

Corporate, Business, Contracts, Estate Planning, Probate, Probate Litigation, Real Estate and Real Estate Development.

DURKIN & ROBERTS

53 WEST JACKSON BOULEVARD, SUITE 615
CHICAGO, ILLINOIS 60604
Telephone: 312-913-9300
Fax: 312-913-9235
Email: admin@durkinroberts.com
URL: http://www.lawyers.com/durkin&roberts

Criminal Trial, Appellate and Grand Jury Practice in all Federal and State Courts. International Extradition, Attorney Disciplinary Defense, Child Welfare and Juvenile Justice.

THOMAS ANTHONY DURKIN, born Chicago, Illinois, September 30, 1946; admitted to bar, 1973, California; 1974, Illinois; 1975, U.S. Court of Appeals, 7th and 9th Circuits, U.S. District Court, Northern District of California and U.S. District Court, Northern District of Illinois including Trial Bar; 1985, U.S. District Court, Northern District of Indiana; 1987, Indiana and U.S. District Court, Central District of Illinois ; 1988, U.S. Tax Court. *Education:* University of Notre Dame (A.B., 1968); University of San Francisco (J.D., 1973). Adjunct Professor of Law, John Marshall Law School, Advanced Trial Advocacy, 1978-1986. Faculty: Trial Advocacy Program, Loyola University, 1980; National Institute of Trial Advocacy, Southwest Regional, 1982; Attorney General's Advocacy Institute, U.S. Department of Justice, Washington, D.C., 1981-1984. Law Clerk, Hon. James B. Parsons, U.S. District Court, Northern District of Illinois, 1973-1974. Assistant United States Attorney, Special Prosecutions Division, Northern District of Illinois, 1978-1984. Member, Lawyers Assistance Program, Inc., 1983—. Member, Board of Directors, The John Howard Association, 1994—. Chairman, Panel for Capital Case Appointments, U.S. District Court for Northern District of Indiana, 1996—. Liaison, U.S. Court of Appeals, Seventh Circuit Committee to Study the Appointment of Counsel for Indigent Habeas Corpus Petitions Under a Sentence of Death, 1999—. *Member:* Chicago and American (Member, Criminal Justice, International Law and Practice Sections) Bar Associations; State Bar of California; National Association of Criminal Defense Lawyers (Member, Select Committee on Military Tribunals, 2004—). ***PRACTICE AREAS:*** Criminal Law; International Extradition; Attorney Disciplinary Defense. ***Email:*** tdurkin@durkinroberts.com

JANIS D. ROBERTS, born San Diego, California, November 13, 1948; admitted to bar, 1980, Wisconsin, U.S. District Court, Western and Eastern Districts of Wisconsin; 1981, U.S. District Court, Northern District of Illinois including Trial Bar; 1985, Illinois and U.S. Court of Appeals, Seventh Circuit. *Education:* Illinois State University (B.S., 1970); Marquette University (J.D., 1980). Executive Editor, Marquette University Law Review, 1979-1980. Staff Attorney, Federal Defender Program, Inc., Northern District of Illinois, 1981-1984. Supervisory Regional Counsel, Illinois Department of Children and Family Services, Child Protection and Juvenile Justices Divisions of the Circuit Court of Cook County, 1997-2000. *Member:* Illinois State Bar Association; State Bar of Wisconsin; National Association of Criminal Defense Lawyers. ***PRACTICE AREAS:*** Criminal Law; Child Welfare; Adoption; Juvenile Delinquency; Attorney Discipline Defense. ***Email:*** jdroberts@durkinroberts.com

---

MARIAH E. MORAN, born Hammond, Indiana, November 9, 1971; admitted to bar, 2000, Illinois; U.S. District Court, Northern District of Illinois. *Education:* Miami University (B.A., 1993); London School of Economics and Political Science (M.A., 1997); Indiana University School of Law (J.D., 2000). Senior Articles Editor, Federal Communications

(This Listing Continued)

Law Journal. Law Clerk, Hon. James T. Moody, U.S. District Court, Northern District of Indiana, 2002-2003; Hon. Allen Sharp, U.S. District Court, Northern District of Indiana, 2003-2005. ***PRACTICE AREAS:*** Criminal Law; Appellate Practice. ***Email:*** mmoran@durkinroberts.com

OF COUNSEL

MICHAEL BUCKLEY BOLAN, born Minneapolis, Minnesota, January 29, 1941; admitted to bar, 1966, Illinois; 1968, U.S. District Court, Northern District of Illinois; 1972, U.S. Supreme Court; 1977, U.S. Tax Court. *Education:* University of Colorado at Boulder (B.S., 1963); Loyola University (J.D., 1966). Law Clerk, Hon. Thomas Kluczynski, Illinois Supreme Court, 1967-1968. Author: "Misdemeanors and Moving Traffic Violations," IICLE Handbook '76-78 C9; "Batson v. Kentucky-Limitation of Preemptory Challenges," ITLA Journal '91; "Merit Selection Lacks the Merit of Elections," Chicago Lawyer. Assistant Illinois Attorney General, Charitable Trusts Division, 1996. Assistant States Attorney Cook County, Felony Trial Division, 1969-1972. Associate Asher, Greenfield, Gubbins and Segall, 1972-1974. General Practice, 1974-1983. Associate Judge, Circuit Court of Cook County, 1983-1991; Judge, Circuit Court of Cook County, 1991-2001. Judicial Assignment, Felony Trial Division Circuit Court of Cook County, 1990-2001. Partner, Paul B. Episcope, Ltd, 2001-2003. *Member:* Illinois State Bar Association; Chicago Bar Association; Illinois Trial Lawyers Association; Illinois Judges Association. (Also practicing individually as Law Offices of Michael Buckley Bolan). ***PRACTICE AREAS:*** Criminal Law; Civil Litigation; Law and Chancery; Mediation; State and Federal Appeals; Personal Injury; Commercial Litigation; Litigation. ***Email:*** mbolan@durkinroberts.com

CLARKE P. DEVEREUX, born Chicago, Illinois, May 25, 1962; admitted to bar, 1987, Illinois, U.S. District Court, Northern District of Illinois including Trial Bar. *Education:* Boston College (B.A., 1984); Loyola University School of Law (J.D., 1987). Assistant State's Attorney Cook County, Felony Trial Division, 1987-1994. *Member:* Chicago, Illinois State Bar Associations; National Association of Criminal Defense Lawyers. ***PRACTICE AREAS:*** Criminal Law; Appellate Practice. ***Email:*** cdevereux@durkinroberts.com

DEAN S. DUSSIAS

180 NORTH LASALLE STREET
SUITE 1800
CHICAGO, ILLINOIS 60601
Telephone: 312-263-9801
Fax: 312-855-0535
Email: esquire345@aol.com
URL: http://www.lawyers.com/deandussias

Divorce, Civil Litigation, Family Law Litigation.

DEAN S. DUSSIAS, born Chicago, Illinois, May 4, 1965; admitted to bar, 1991, Illinois and U.S. District Court, Northern District of Illinois. *Education:* Loyola University (B.A., 1987); John Marshall Law School (J.D., 1991). *Member:* Chicago (Former Co-Chair, Family Law Division; Young Lawyers Division), Illinois State and American Bar Associations. Board of Governors, American Academy of Matrimonial Lawyers. ***LANGUAGES:*** Greek. ***PRACTICE AREAS:*** Divorce; Civil Litigation; Pre-Nuptial Agreements.

ASSOCIATE

CHRISTOPHER S. SYREGELAS, born Maywood, Illinois, November 29, 1974; admitted to bar, 2000, Illinois. *Education:* University of Illinois (B.S., 1996); Chicago-Kent College of Law, Illinois Institute of Technology (J.D., 1999). *Member:* Hellenic and Illinois State Bar Associations. ***LANGUAGES:*** Greek. ***PRACTICE AREAS:*** Civil Litigation; Divorce. ***Email:*** csyregelas@dussiaslaw

DWYER, McCARTHY & ASSOCIATES, LTD.

Established in 1980

39 SOUTH LA SALLE, SUITE 610
CHICAGO, ILLINOIS 60603
Telephone: 312-782-7482
Fax: 312-782-7433
Email: pedts@aol.com
URL: http://www.patrickedwyerandassociatesltd.com

Auto Accidents, Construction Site Injuries, Product Liability, Dog Bites, Slip and Fall, Wrongful Death, Medical Malpractice, Construction Defects.

PATRICK E. DWYER, born Chicago, Illinois, July 9, 1940; admitted to bar, 1967, Illinois and U.S. District Court, Northern District of Illinois. *Education:* Loyola University (B.S., 1962); DePaul University (J.D., 1967). Recipient, President Award, 2004. Assistant Corporation Counsel, City of Chicago, 1967-1968. Commissioner, Village of Flossmoor Plan and Zone Commission, 1978-1984. Member: Panel of Arbitrators, American Arbitration Association; Mandatory Arbitration Panel, Circuit Court of Cook County, 1991—. *Member:* Chicago (Member, Industrial Commission Committee, 1980-1986; Tort Litigation Committee, 1981-2002), Illinois State and American Bar Associations; Illinois Trial Lawyers Association (Member, Board of Managers, 1985—); The Association of Trial Lawyers of America; Workers Compensation Lawyers Association; Illinois Trial Lawyers Association. ***PRACTICE AREAS:*** Civil Litigation; Products Liability; Personal Injury Law; Workers Compensation Law. ***Email:*** pedts@aol.com

JAMES G. McCARTHY, born Chicago, Illinois, October 31, 1966; admitted to bar, 1995, Illinois; 1996, Florida and U.S. District Court, Northern District of Illinois. *Education:* Georgetown University (A.B., 1988); DePaul University (J.D., 1995). Commissioner, Village of Skokie Zoning Board of Appeals, 2001—. *Member:* Illinois State Bar Association; Illinois Trial Lawyers Association. ***PRACTICE AREAS:*** Personal Injury (80%); Civil Litigation (10%); Workers' Compensation (10%).

(This Listing Continued)

WILLIAM M. WIPPOLD, born St. Louis, Missouri, July 8, 1943; admitted to bar, 1973, Missouri; 1974, Illinois; 1981 U.S. District Court, Northern District of Illinois and U.S. Court of Appeals, Seventh Circuit. *Education:* University of Illinois (A.B., 1969; J.D., 1972). *Member:* Illinois State Bar Association; Illinois Trial Lawyers Association; Workers' Compensation Lawyers Association. ***PRACTICE AREAS:*** Workers Compensation Law.

DYKEMA GOSSETT PLLC

Established in 1926

10 SOUTH WACKER DRIVE, SUITE 2300
CHICAGO, ILLINOIS 60606
Telephone: 312-876-1700
Fax: 312-876-1155
URL: http://www.dykema.com

Ann Arbor, Michigan Office: 2723 South State Street, Suite 400, 48104. Telephone: 734-214-7660. Fax: 734-214-7696.
Aurora, Illinois Office: 2 Hankes Road. Telephone: 630-844-2200. Facsimile: 630-844-2277.
Bloomfield Hills, Michigan Office: 39577 Woodward Avenue, Suite 300, 48304-2820. Telephone: 248-203-0700. Fax: 248-203-0763.
Detroit, Michigan Office: 400 Renaissance Center, 48243-1668. Telephone: 313-568-6800. Fax: 313-568-6545.
Grand Rapids, Michigan Office: Suite 700, 300 Ottawa Avenue, N.W., 49503-2306. Telephone: 616-776-7500. Fax: 616-776-7573.
Joliet, Illinois Office: 111 North Ottawa Street. Telephone: 815-727-4511. Facsimile: 815-727-1586.
Lansing, Michigan Office: 124 W. Allegan Street, Suite 800, 48933-1742. Telephone: 517-374-9100. Fax: 517-374-9191.
Lisle, Illinois Office: 4200 Commerce Court, Suite 300. Telephone: 630-245-0400. Facsimile: 630-245-0140.
Los Angeles, California Office: 333 South Grand Avenue, Suite 2100, 90071. Telephone: 213-457-1800. Fax: 213-457-1850.
Washington, D.C. Office: Franklin Square, Suite 300 West, 1300 I Street, N.W., 20005-3353. Telephone: 202-906-8600. Fax: 202-906-8669.

Antitrust and Trade Regulation, Automotive, Banking and Financial Services, Bankruptcy, Biotechnology and Life Sciences, Casino Gaming, Class Action Defense, Computer and Software Law, Construction, Consumer Financial Services, Corporate Finance, E-Commerce, Emerging Business and Technology, Employee Benefits, Entertainment and Sports, Environmental Law, Family Law, Franchise Law and Regulation, Government Contracts, Government Policy and Practice, HealthCare, Indian Law, Insurance, Intellectual Property, International Law, Labor and Employment, Litigation and Dispute Resolution, Mergers and Acquisitions, Products Liability Defense, Public Finance, Real Estate, Retail Law, Securities, Taxation and Estates, Trade Associations.

FIRM PROFILE: Dykema Gossett PLLC represents the interests of domestic and foreign-based companies and institutions on a broad array of matters. Our diversified practice and Midwest work ethic have long made Dykema the choice of Fortune 100 companies, privately-held businesses, entrepreneurial enterprises and emerging businesses. With offices in Michigan, California, Illinois and Washington, D.C., Dykema has expanded beyond its original Michigan roots to become one of the largest firms in the United States. Our recent merger with Rooks Pitts in Illinois, effective April 1, 2004, is a significant milestone in our continued growth in the Midwest. We are proud to be recognized by area businesses as a corporate leader, and our broad-based litigation practice is routinely chosen by clients and peers alike as one of the best in the nation. Dykema is equally well known for our experienced government relations specialists, whose experience at the national, state and local levels is unrivalled. From manufacturers and automotive suppliers to financial institutions, from patent and trademark disputes to complex class action defense, from startups to large multinational corporations, our clients repeatedly look to Dykema to help them navigate through an ever-increasing stream of complex litigation and changing business environments.

MEMBERS OF FIRM

HARRY N. ARGER, born Alton, Illinois, August 7, 1963; admitted to bar, 1988, Illinois and U.S. District Court, Southern District of Illinois; U.S. District Court, Central District of Illinois; 1989, Missouri; 1990, U.S. District Court, Northern District of Illinois; 1996, U.S. Court of Appeals, Seventh Circuit. *Education:* University of Illinois (A.B., 1985); Washington University (J.D., 1988). ***PRACTICE AREAS:*** Commercial Litigation; Torts; Business Law. ***Email:*** harger@dykema.com

JOHN J. BLASI, born Chicago, Illinois, April 29, 1943; admitted to bar, 1967, Illinois, U.S. District Court, Northern District of Illinois including Trial Bar and U.S. Court of Appeals, Seventh Circuit. *Education:* University of Notre Dame (B.B.A., 1966; J.D., 1967). Beta Gamma Sigma. Listed as "Illinois Super Lawyer," General Litigation, 2005. *Member:* Illinois State Bar Association; International Association of Defense Counsel. [Lieutenant, Judge Advocate General's Corps, U.S. Navy, 1968-1970]. ***PRACTICE AREAS:*** Litigation; Construction Law; Architects and Engineers Liability; Insurance; Insurance. ***Email:*** jblasi@dykema.com

MICHAEL C. BORDERS, born Tell City, Illinois, March 9, 1955; admitted to bar, 1981, Illinois, U.S. Court of Appeals, Seventh Circuit and U.S. District Court, Northern and Central Districts of Illinois including Trial Bar. *Education:* University of Notre Dame (B.B.A., 1977; J.D., 1981). Board Member: Lakefront Supportive Housing; Chicagoland Chamber of Commerce. *Member:* Chicago and American Bar Associations; Illinois Defense Counsel. ***PRACTICE AREAS:*** Litigation; Products Liability; Insurance Coverage. ***Email:*** mborders@dykema.com

(This Listing Continued)

DYKEMA GOSSETT PLLC, Chicago—Continued

TERRENCE M. BURNS, born Evergreen Park, Illinois, March 2, 1954; admitted to bar, 1978, Illinois and U.S. District Court, Northern District of Illinois including Trial Bar; 1979, U.S. Court of Appeals, Seventh Circuit; 1985, U.S. Supreme Court; 1989, U.S. District Court, Northern District of Indiana. *Education:* Loyola University (B.A., 1975); DePaul University (J.D., 1978). Phi Alpha Delta. *Member:* Chicago Bar Association (President, 2001-2002). ***PRACTICE AREAS:*** Civil Law; Medical Malpractice; Products Liability; Civil Rights Section 1983. ***Email:*** tburns@dykema.com

JEFFREY M. DALEBROUX, born Green Bay, Illinois, October 1, 1951; admitted to bar, 1976, Wisconsin; 1980, Illinois. *Education:* Marquette University (A.B., magna cum laude, 1973); Georgetown University (J.D., 1976). ***PRACTICE AREAS:*** Corporate; Mergers and Acquisitions; Banks and Banking; Securities. ***Email:*** jdalebroux@dykema.com

I. WALTER DEITCH, born Chicago, Illinois, February 1, 1945; admitted to bar, 1969, Wisconsin (inactive); 1970, Illinois; 1972, California. *Education:* University of Chicago (A.B., 1966); University of Wisconsin (J.D., with honors, 1969). Order of the Coif. Recipient, Salmon W. Dalberg Prize. Articles Editor, Wisconsin Law Review, 1969. Law Clerk, Chief Justice Roger J. Traynor, California Supreme Court, 1969-1970. *Member:* Chicago, Illinois State and American Bar Associations; State Bar of California. ***PRACTICE AREAS:*** Corporate; Securities; Real Estate; Public Finance. ***Email:*** wdeitch@dykema.com

DEAN A. DICKIE, admitted to bar, 1969, Illinois; 1971, U.S. District Court, Northern District of Illinois and U.S. Court of Appeals, Seventh Circuit; 1972, U.S. Claims Court; 1974, Michigan; 1977, U.S. Supreme Court; 1982, U.S. District Court, Eastern District of Michigan; 1983, U.S. District Court, Northern District of Illinois including Trial Bar; 1984, Wisconsin. *Education:* Northwestern University (B.A., 1966); Exeter College, Oxford, England, 1965; Georgetown University Law Center (J.D., 1969). ***PRACTICE AREAS:*** Antitrust; Directors and Officers Liability; Employment Discrimination Law; Labor Law; Medical Malpractice Law; Partnership Dissolutions; Securities Litigation; Title VII Discrimination; Civil Rights; Wrongful Discharge Litigation; Wrongful Termination-Employment at Will; Zoning Law; Shareholder Claims; Takeover Litigation; Corporate Law; Auditors Malpractice; Internal Investigations; Intellectual Property Litigation. ***Email:*** ddickie@dykema.com

GWEN M. GERAGHTY, born Chicago, Illinois, October 5, 1968; admitted to bar, 1993, Illinois and U.S. District Court, Northern District of Illinois. *Education:* Marquette University (B.A., 1990); Loyola University (J.D., 1993). ***REPORTED CASES:*** Robinson v. Johnson, 346 Ill. App. 3d 895 (1st Dist. Sept. 25, 2003), rehearing denied (Mar. 22, 2004), opinion supplemented on denial of rehearing (1st Dist. Mar. 25, 2004). ***PRACTICE AREAS:*** Commercial; Insurance Defense; Professional Liability Litigation. ***Email:*** ggeraghty@dykema.com

MARC D. GINSBERG, born Chicago, Illinois, August 14, 1951; admitted to bar, 1977, Illinois, U.S. District Court, Northern District of Illinois and U.S. Court of Appeals, Seventh Circuit; 1981, U.S. Supreme Court; 1991, U.S. Court of Appeals, Ninth Circuit. *Education:* University of Illinois (B.A., with honors, 1972); Indiana University (M.A., 1975); John Marshall Law School (J.D., with highest distinction, 1977); DePaul University (LL.M., 1992). ***PRACTICE AREAS:*** Insurance Defense; Medical Malpractice; Health Care; Appellate Practice. ***Email:*** mginsberg@dykema.com

RICHARD E. GOTTLIEB, born New York, N.Y., December 20, 1960; admitted to bar, 1986, New York and District of Columbia; 1992, Illinois. *Education:* Vanderbilt University (B.A., cum laude, 1981); State University of New York at Buffalo (J.D., 1985); Georgetown University Law Center (LL.M., 1986). *Member:* American Bar Association (Member, Consumer Financial Services Committee, Business Law Section). ***PRACTICE AREAS:*** Consumer Financial Services (50%); Class Action Defense (50%). ***Email:*** rgottlieb@dykema.com

JODI L. HENNINGER, born Winfield, Illinois, December 6, 1969; admitted to bar, 1995, Illinois. *Education:* University of Illinois (B.A., 1992); DePaul University (J.D., 1995). De Paul Business Law Journal, 1994-1995. Member, Commercial Real Estate Women - CREW Chicago, 2005. *Member:* DuPage County and Illinois State Bar Associations; International Council of Shopping Centers. ***PRACTICE AREAS:*** Real Estate. ***Email:*** jhenninger@dykema.com

GLENN Z. HERING, born Chicago, Illinois, March 29, 1952; admitted to bar, 1977, Illinois; 1978, U.S. District Court, Northern District of Illinois and U.S. Court of Appeals, Seventh Circuit. *Education:* American University (B.A., 1973); John Marshall Law School (J.D., with distinction, 1977). ***LANGUAGES:*** German, Czech. ***PRACTICE AREAS:*** Commercial Law; Corporate Law; International Law; Immigration Law; Real Estate. ***Email:*** ghering@dykema.com

LEE T. HETTINGER, born Aurora, Illinois, February 20, 1941; admitted to bar, 1966, Illinois; 1967, U.S. District Court, Northern District of Illinois. *Education:* Marquette University (B.A., cum laude, 1963); University of Michigan (J.D., 1966). Phi Delta Phi. ***PRACTICE AREAS:*** Litigation; Environmental Law; Railroad Law; Appellate Practice; Personal Injury. ***Email:*** lhettinger@dykema.com

THOMAS R. HILL, born Chicago, Illinois, September 27, 1960; admitted to bar, 1985, Illinois and U.S. District Court, Northern District of Illinois including Trial Bar; 1987, U.S. Court of Appeals, Seventh Circuit. *Education:* University of Illinois (B.A., 1982); Loyola University (J.D., 1985). Phi Alpha Delta. ***PRACTICE AREAS:*** Medical Malpractice; Commercial Litigation. ***Email:*** thill@dykema.com

JAMES H. IHRKE, born Chicago, Illinois, June 6, 1943; admitted to bar, 1968, Illinois. *Education:* Northwestern University (B.A., 1965); University of Michigan (J.D., 1968). ***PRACTICE AREAS:*** Taxation; Employee Benefits; Corporate; Probate; Trusts and Estates. ***Email:*** *jihrke@dykema.com*

GREGORY J. JORDAN, born South Bend, Indiana, December 20, 1958; admitted to bar, 1984, Indiana; 1991, Illinois. *Education:* University of Notre Dame (B.B.A., 1981); Indiana University (J.D., 1984). Member, Alumni Board, Indiana University School of Law - Bloomington. *Member:* Chicago, Illinois State and American Bar Associations; American Bankruptcy Institute; Turnaround Management Association. ***PRACTICE AREAS:*** Bankruptcy; Corporate Litigation; Creditors Rights. ***Email:*** gjordan@dykema.com

TERRENCE E. KIWALA, born Chicago, Illinois, February 23, 1945; admitted to bar, 1970, Illinois, Indiana and Wisconsin; 1977, U.S. Supreme Court; U.S. District Court, Northern District of Illinois including Trial Bar; U.S. District Court, Eastern District of Wisconsin; U.S. District Court, Northern District of Ohio; U.S. District Court, Central District of Illinois; U.S. Court of Appeals, Fifth, Sixth and Seventh Circuits. *Education:* University of Notre Dame (B.A., 1966); Northwestern University (J.D., 1970). ***PRACTICE AREAS:*** Environmental Law; Toxic Torts; Insurance Law. ***Email:*** tkiwala@dykema.com

CHARLES A. LeMOINE, born Chicago, Illinois, October 9, 1957; admitted to bar, 1987, Illinois, U.S. District Court, Northern District of Illinois including Federal Trial Bar, U.S. Court of Appeals, Seventh Circuit and U.S. Supreme Court. *Education:* University of Illinois (B.A., 1981); John Marshall Law School (J.D., with distinction, 1987). Arbitrator, Cook County Arbitration Program. *Member:* National Association of Railroad Trial Counsel. ***PRACTICE AREAS:*** Complex Commercial Litigation; Local Government Defense; Railroad Litigation; Manufacturers Liability; Medical Malpractice Defense; Construction Litigation. ***Email:*** clemoine@dykema.com

JOHN J. MANGAN, born Chicago, Illinois, May 26, 1951; admitted to bar, 1976, Illinois; 1982, U.S. District Court, Northern District of Illinois including Trial Bar; U.S. Court of Appeals, 7th Circuit and U.S. Tax Court. *Education:* University of Kansas (B.A., 1973); John Marshall Law School (J.D., with distinction, 1976). *Member:* DuPage County, Illinois State and American Bar Associations; American Health Lawyers Association; Society of Trial Lawyers. ***PRACTICE AREAS:*** Business Law; Corporate Law; Health Care; Litigation; Commercial Law. ***Email:*** jmangan@dykema.com

NICK MARSICO, born Chicago, Illinois, March 20, 1966; admitted to bar, 1991, Illinois. *Education:* DePaul University (B.S., with highest honors, 1988; J.D., 1991). Certified Public Accountant, Illinois, 1988. *Member:* Chicago Bar Association; Illinois CPA Society. ***PRACTICE AREAS:*** Business Law; Taxation; Limited Liability Company Law; Corporate Law; Trademarks; Mergers, Acquisitions and Divestitures; Securitizations; Commercial Law; Contracts. ***Email:*** nmarsico@dykema.com

JEROME I. MAYNARD, born Detroit, Michigan, September 20, 1947; admitted to bar, 1989, Michigan; 1991, Illinois. *Education:* Michigan Technological University (B.S., 1972); University of Wisconsin (J.D., 1988). *Member:* Chicago, Illinois State and American Bar Associations; State Bar of Michigan. ***PRACTICE AREAS:*** Environmental (100%); Administrative Law. ***Email:*** jmaynard@dykema.com

JAMES W. McCONKEY, born St. Louis, Missouri, November 4, 1963; admitted to bar, 1989, Illinois and U.S. District Court, Southern District of Illinois; 1990, Missouri; 1995, U.S. District Court, Central and Northern Districts of Illinois. *Education:* Davidson College (A.B., 1986); Seattle University (J.D., 1989). ***PRACTICE AREAS:*** Civil Litigation; Contract Litigation; Personal Injury Defense; Commercial Litigation. ***Email:*** jmcconkey@dykema.com

JOHN M. McGARRY, born Minneapolis, Minnesota, August 31, 1958; admitted to bar, 1983, Illinois; 1992, U.S. District Court, Northern District of Illinois including Trial Bar; 1994, U.S. District Court, Central District of Illinois; 1995, U.S. Court of Appeals, Seventh Circuit. *Education:* Kenyon College (B.A., cum laude, 1980); Washington & Lee University (J.D., 1983). ***PRACTICE AREAS:*** Civil Litigation. ***Email:*** jmcgarry@dykema.com

PAUL A. MICHALIK, born Chicago, Illinois, July 31, 1958; admitted to bar, 1988, Illinois and U.S. District Court, Northern District of Illinois. *Education:* Loyola University (B.S., 1980); IIT-Chicago Kent College of Law (J.D., with high honors, 1988). ***PRACTICE AREAS:*** Appellate Law; Civil Litigation; Products Liability; Civil Practice; Toxic Torts. ***Email:*** pmichalik@dykema.com

DAVID L. MILLER, born Detroit, Michigan, August 31, 1962; admitted to bar, 1987, Illinois and U.S. District Court, Northern District of Illinois; 1994, U.S. Court of Appeals, Seventh Circuit. *Education:* Amherst College (B.A., 1984); Wayne State University (J.D., 1987). ***PRACTICE AREAS:*** Labor and Employment; Workers' Compensation; Litigation. ***Email:*** dmiller@dykema.com

DANIEL M. NOLAND, born Elmhurst, Illinois, November 21, 1968; admitted to bar, 1996, Illinois and U.S. District Court, Northern District of Illinois; 1997, U.S. Court of Appeals, Seventh Circuit; 1999, U.S. Supreme Court. *Education:* University of Notre Dame (B.A., 1990); John Marshall Law School (J.D., magna cum laude, 1996). Member, Law Review. *Member:* Illinois State Bar Association. ***PRACTICE AREAS:*** Litigation. ***Email:*** dnoland@dykema.com

PATRICIA CARI NOWAK, born Chicago, Illinois, May 29, 1956; admitted to bar, 1986, Illinois and U.S. District Court, Northern District of Illinois. *Education:* Loyola University (B.S.N., 1978; J.D., 1986); Boston College (M.S.N., 1980); University of Notre Dame. Sigma Theta Tau. Registered Nurse, Illinois, 1978. ***PRACTICE AREAS:*** Medical Malpractice; Health Law. ***Email:*** pnowak@dykema.com

WAYNE F. PLAZA, born Chicago, Illinois, June 21, 1945; admitted to bar, 1970, Illinois; 1975, U.S. Supreme Court; 1990, Wisconsin; 1992, U.S. District Court, Northern and Central Districts of Illinois including Trial Bar. *Education:* Knox College (B.A., 1967); Illinois Institute of Technology/Chicago-Kent College of Law (J.D., 1970). ***PRACTICE AREAS:*** Business Litigation; Commercial Litigation; Entertainment Law; Civil Litigation; Public School Law; Products Liability; RICO. ***Email:*** wplaza@dykema.com

MARC A. PRIMACK, born Chicago, Illinois, April 29, 1952; admitted to bar, 1977, Illinois. *Education:* University of Chicago (B.A., with honors, 1973); Stanford University (J.D., 1977). Phi Beta Kappa. ***PRACTICE AREAS:*** Civil Litigation; Antitrust and Trade Regulation; Creditors Rights. ***Email:*** mprimack@dykema.com

ARTHUR F. RADKE, born Chicago, Illinois, December 30, 1952; admitted to bar, 1979, Illinois and U.S. District Court, Northern District of Illinois including Trial Bar; 1983, U.S. Court of Appeals, Seventh Circuit; 1984, U.S. District Court, Eastern District of Wisconsin; 1986, Wisconsin. *Education:* Marquette University (B.A., cum laude, 1974; M.B.A., 1976); University of California, Los Angeles (J.D., 1979). *Member:* Chicago, Seventh Circuit and American (Member, Sections on: Business Law; Real Property, Probate

(This Listing Continued)

and Trust Law) Bar Associations; State Bar of Wisconsin (Member, Litigation Section). ***PRACTICE AREAS:*** Civil Litigation; Business Law. ***Email:*** aradke@dykema.com

STEPHEN D. SAYRE, born Denver, Colorado, August 2, 1962; admitted to bar, 1992, Illinois and U.S. District Court, Northern District of Illinois. *Education:* University of Colorado (B.S., 1984); DePaul University (J.D., with honors, 1991). Order of the Coif. Law Clerk to the Hon. Mary L. Cooper, U.S. District Court, District of New Jersey, 1992-1993. *Member:* Illinois State and American (Member, Business Law Section) Bar Associations. ***PRACTICE AREAS:*** Corporate Law; Information Technology. ***Email:*** ssayre@dykema.com

MICHAEL F. SEXTON, born Springfield, Illinois, March 8, 1958; admitted to bar, 1983, Illinois. *Education:* Northwestern University; Millikin University (B.A., magna cum laude, 1980); University of Illinois (J.D., 1983). Phi Kappa Phi; Phi Alpha Theta. ***PRACTICE AREAS:*** Real Estate; Corporate. ***Email:*** msexton@dykema.com

IAN M. SHERMAN, born Chicago, Illinois, April 30, 1953; admitted to bar, 1978, Illinois and U.S. District Court, Northern District of Illinois including Trial Bar; 1984, U.S. Court of Appeals, Seventh Circuit; 1995, U.S. District Court, Eastern District of Wisconsin; 2000, U.S. District Court, Northern District of Indiana. *Education:* University of Illinois (A.B., cum laude, 1975); Boston University (J.D., cum laude, 1978). Phi Beta Kappa; Phi Kappa Phi. *Member:* Chicago and Illinois State Bar Associations; The Society of Trial Lawyers (Member, Illinois Chapter); American Board of Trial Advocates; Illinois Association of Healthcare Attorneys. ***PRACTICE AREAS:*** Medical Malpractice (75%); Commercial Litigation (10%); Defense Litigation (10%); Health Care Liability (5%). ***Email:*** isherman@dykema.com

JOHN M. STEED, born November 6, 1955; admitted to bar, 1980, Illinois and U.S. District Court, Northern District of Illinois; 1981, U.S. Court of Appeals, Seventh Circuit. *Education:* John Carroll University; Marquette University (B.S.B.A., 1977); DePaul University (J.D., 1980). Calles v. Scripto Tokai Corporation, 832 N.E.2d 409 (Ill.App. 1 Dist. 2005) Mathey v. Country Mutual Insurance, 321 Ill.App. 3d 805 (Ill. App. 1 Dist 2001) Valuzzi v. State of Illinios, 51 Ill.Ct. of Claims 126 (1998). ***PRACTICE AREAS:*** Medical Negligence Litigation (80%); Professional Negligence (10%); Professional Licensing Matters (10%). ***Email:*** jsteed@dykema.com

ALLAN J. STERNSTEIN, born Chicago, Illinois, June 7, 1948; admitted to bar, 1977, Illinois, U.S. District Court, Northern District of Illinois and U.S. District Court, Northern District of Ohio; 1979, U.S. Court of Appeals, Seventh Circuit; 1978-1982, U.S. Court of Customs and Patent Appeals; 1982, U.S. Court of Appeals for the Federal Circuit; 1986, U.S. District Court, Eastern District of Michigan; 1990, U.S. District Court, Western District of Michigan; registered to practice before U.S. Patent and Trademark Office. *Education:* University of Illinois (B.S., with honors, 1970); University of Michigan (M.S., 1972); Loyola University (J.D., 1977). Tau Beta Pi; Sigma Gamma Tau; Sigma Tau; Phi Eta Sigma. Midwest Regional Winner, Giles S. Rich Moot Court Competition, 1977. Adjunct Professor of Law: John Marshall Law School, 1989-1991; De Paul University, 1991-1993; University of Illinois, 1993—. *Member:* Chicago and American Bar Associations; Intellectual Property Law Association of Chicago (Chairman: Inventor Services Committee, 1981; Membership Committee, 1987-1989); American Intellectual Property Law Association; Licensing Executives Society. ***Email:*** asternstein@dykema.com

JANET A. STIVEN, born June 2, 1960; admitted to bar, 1985, Illinois and U.S. District Court, Northern District of Illinois. *Education:* University of Illinois (B.A., 1982); DePaul University (J.D., 1985). ***PRACTICE AREAS:*** Corporate Law; Securities; Trademarks; Copyrights; Computers and Software; Real Estate. ***Email:*** jstiven@dykema.com

ROBERT K. VILLA, born Chicago, Illinois, November 18, 1970; admitted to bar, 1995, Illinois; 1996, U.S. District Court, Northern and Southern Districts of Illinois and U.S. Court of Appeals, Seventh Circuit. *Education:* University of Illinois (B.S., 1992); DePaul University (J.D., 1995). Faculty, Moot Court, DePaul College of Law, 1999-2003. Member, City of Geneva Plan Commission, 2000-2002. *Member:* Chicago and American Bar Associations. ***PRACTICE AREAS:*** Commercial Litigation; Litigation; Insurance Coverage; Employment Law. ***Email:*** rvilla@dykema.com

CHERYL A. WARZYNSKI, born Evergreen Park, Illinois, October 21, 1972; admitted to bar, 1997, Illinois. *Education:* University of Illinois (B.A., with high distinction, 1994); Valparaiso University (J.D., cum laude, 1997); Loyola University (LL.M., 2002). Phi Alpha Delta; Phi Kappa Phi; Golden Key. *Member:* Chicago (Treasurer, Young Lawyer's Section) and Illinois State Bar Associations; Women's Bar Association. ***REPORTED CASES:*** Campos v. Campos, 342 Ill. App. 3d 1053, 796 N.E.2d 316 (1st Dist. 2003); McKinnon v. West Aurora School District 129, 325 Ill. App. 3d 241, 758 N.E.2d 316 (2d Dist. 2002); People v. Norris, 303 Ill. App. 3d 163, 707 N.E.2d 628 (1st Dist. 1999); Shadrall Associates v. Dominick's, 1-01-3022 (unpublished opinion). ***PRACTICE AREAS:*** School Law; Appellate Practice; Medical Malpractice; Premises Liability. ***Email:*** cwarzynski@dykema.com

MARK W. WEISBARD, born Washington, D.C., August 30, 1954; admitted to bar, 1979, Illinois. *Education:* Dartmouth College (B.A., magna cum laude, 1976); Northwestern University (J.D., cum laude, 1979). ***PRACTICE AREAS:*** Employee Benefits; Probate; Trusts and Estates. ***Email:*** mweisbard@dykema.com

OF COUNSEL

CLYDE O. BOWLES, JR., born Kansas City, Missouri, February 2, 1927; admitted to bar, 1951, Missouri; 1954, Illinois; 1955, U.S. District Court, Northern District of Illinois including Trial Bar; 1982, Hawaii; 1984, District of Columbia. *Education:* Northwestern University (B.S., with distinction, Phi Beta Kappa, 1948); Yale Law School (J.D., 1951). ***PRACTICE AREAS:*** Business Law; Civil Litigation; Arbitration; Mediation. ***Email:*** cbowles@dykema.com

JOHN C. CORRIGAN, born Cleveland, Ohio, January 8, 1967; admitted to bar, 1994, Illinois. *Education:* Bowling Green State University (B.A., cum laude, 1991); DePaul University (J.D., 1994). Order of the Coif. Member, DePaul University Law Review. *Member:* Chicago and American Bar Associations. [U.S. Army, 1986-1988]. ***REPORTED CASES:*** E B Harper & Co., Inc. v. Nortek, Inc., 104 E.3d 913 (7th Cir. 1997). ***PRACTICE AREAS:*** Government Relations; Procurement. ***Email:*** jcorrigan@dykema.com

(This Listing Continued)

JOHN ALDEN FRITCHEY, born Bossier City, Louisiana, March 2, 1964; admitted to bar, 1989, Illinois and U.S. District Court, Northern District of Illinois including Trial Bar; 1990, U.S. District Court, Central District of Illinois; 1991, U.S. Court of Appeals, Seventh Circuit. *Education:* University of Michigan (A.B., Economics, 1986); Northwestern University (J.D., 1989). Former Adjunct Lecturer, Northwestern University. Illinois State Representative, 1996—. Chairman, House Civil Judiciary Committee, 2003—. Member, Mayor's Advisory Task Force on Administrative Hearings. *Member:* Chicago, Illinois State and American Bar Associations. ***PRACTICE AREAS:*** Zoning, Planning and Land Use; Local Government. ***Email:*** jfritchey@dykema.com

ARTHUR I. GOULD, born Chicago, Illinois, July 31, 1929; admitted to bar, 1956, Illinois; 1957, U.S. Court of Appeals, Seventh Circuit; 1959, U.S. Claims Court; 1961, U.S. Supreme Court; 1963, U.S. District Court, Northern District of Illinois and U.S. Tax Court. *Education:* University of Illinois (B.S., 1951); Northwestern University (J.D., 1956). Beta Gamma Sigma; Phi Eta Sigma. ***PRACTICE AREAS:*** Taxation; Finance; Mergers, Acquisitions and Divestitures. ***Email:*** agould@dykema.com

MISTY S. GRUBER, born Spokane, Washington, February 3, 1950; admitted to bar, 1978, Arizona; 1982, U.S. District Court, District of Arizona and U.S. Court of Appeals, Ninth Circuit; 1984, California and U.S. District Court, Northern District of California; 1985, Illinois and U.S. District Court, Northern District of Illinois. *Education:* University of Arizona (B.S., Zoology, with distinction, 1972; M.S., Physiology, 1975; J.D., 1978). Certified Public Accountant, Arizona, 1981. Author: "Balancing Publication of Genomic Data Against Governmental Needs in Combating Bioterrorism," Conference on Terrorism: Its Impact on the Law, Commerce, and Human Rights, Salzburg, Austria, 2004; "Prospectus Perspective - Private Deliberations About Going Public," Shefsky, Froelich & Devine, Ltd., 1992; "Real Estate Programs (including Chapters on REITs and RELPs)," Matthew Bender & Co., Inc., 1992; "An Overview of Anti-Takeover Devices for REITs and RELPs," The Real Estate Investment Journal, April 1992; "Recent Developments in State Regulation of Public Real Estate Securities Offerings," The Business Lawyer, Vol. 47, No. 1, November 1991; "Anti-Takeover Devices Used by REITs and RELPs," Real Estate Review, Vol. 21, No. 3, Fall 1991; "The Model State Control Share Statute of the North American Securities Administrators Association," The Business Lawyer, Vol. 44, No. 1, February 1989; "Low Income Housing Programs," The Real Estate Securities Journal, Vol. 9, No. 1, 1988; "State Regulation of Publicly Offered Equipment Programs," The Business Lawyer, Vol. 43, No. 1, November 1987; "The New REMIC Amendments and Mortgage-Backed Securities - An Introduction," The Real Estate Securities Journal, Vol. 8, No. 1, 1987; "The Equipment Guidelines and Proposed Amendments," The Business Lawyer, Vol. 41, No. 4, August 1986. Member, Journal Editorial Board: National Association of Realtors Real Estate Securities Syndication Institute, 1988-1989; Real Estate Investment Association, 1989-1993. Co-Editor, State Regulation of Securities Newsletter, American Bar Association, 1988-1993. Counsel, The Capital Circle, 1993-1995. Member: Investors' Circle, 1995-1998; Honorary Council, Business Women's Network, 1996; Board of Advisors, Center for Biotechnology, Kellogg Graduate School of Management, Northwestern University; Board of Trustees, Center for Excellence in Education; Founders' Council, Field Museum of Natural History; James Henry Breasted Society, Oriental Institute of Chicago. Chairman, Board of Trustees, Pacific Forest Trust. *Member:* State Bar of Arizona; State Bar of California; American Bar Association (Member: Banking and Business Law Section; State Regulation of Securities Committee, 1982—; Federal Regulation of Securities Committee, 1986—); National Association of Real Estate Investment Trusts (Member, SEC Task Force). ***PRACTICE AREAS:*** Corporate Law. ***Email:*** mgruber@dykema.com

MARK LENZ, born Fort Wayne, Indiana, October 14, 1956; admitted to bar, 1986, Illinois. *Education:* University of Michigan (B.A., magna cum laude, 1979) Phi Beta Kappa; University of Texas (J.D., 1985). Phi Alpha Delta. *Member:* Chicago Bar Association. ***LANGUAGES:*** Spanish. ***PRACTICE AREAS:*** Real Estate. ***Email:*** mlenz@dykema.com

JAY A. LIPE, born Rockford, Illinois, October 14, 1930; admitted to bar, 1953, Virginia; 1956, Illinois; U.S. District Court, Northern District of Illinois; U.S. District Court, Northern District of Indiana; U.S. Court of Appeals, Seventh Circuit; U.S. Court of Appeals, Third Circuit; U.S. Supreme Court. *Education:* University of Chicago (A.B., 1950); University of Virginia (LL.B., 1953). Delta Theta Phi. ***PRACTICE AREAS:*** Corporate; Commercial Real Estate. ***Email:*** jlipe@dykema.com

ARNOLD A. SILVESTRI, admitted to bar, 1950, Illinois. *Education:* Morgan Park Jr. College (A.A., 1948); Universita per Stranieri, Perugia, Italy (Certificate, 1948); University of Chicago (J.D., 1949). ***Email:*** asilvestri@dykema.com

KATHLEEN J. SWAN, admitted to bar, 1985, Illinois. *Education:* Vanderbilt University (B.A., 1980); University of Miami (J.D., 1985). Chairman, Screening Committee, Springboard 2003. Member: Springboard Forum Committee, 2001, 2003; Judy Barr Topinka's Committee on the Status of Business in Illinois. Treasurer of Illinois. Former Member: Chicago Chapter, National Hemophilia Foundation; Young Alumni Visiting Committee, University of Miami School of Law. *Member:* National Association of Women Business Owners (Former Chairman). ***PRACTICE AREAS:*** Corporate Finance. ***Email:*** kswan@dykema.com

STANLEY R. WEINBERGER, born Troy, Ohio, October 5, 1930; admitted to bar, 1954, Ohio; 1957, Illinois. *Education:* University of Michigan (B.A., 1952; J.D., 1954). Member, Advisory Board, Housing and Development Reporter, 1973-1998; Member, 1973-1979 and President, 1977-1979, Glencoe, Illinois, Board of Education. Member, New Trier Township, Illinois, Trustees of Schools, 1981-1987. President, Chicago Chapter, 1987-1989, and Member, National Board of Governors, 1988-1991, American Jewish Committee. Member, Glencoe, Illinois Plan Commission, 1993-2001. Member, Board of Directors: North Shore Community Bank and Trust Company, 1995—; Wayne Hummer Trust Company, 1998—; Chicago Chamber Musicians, 1995—. Member, National Panel of Arbitrators, American Arbitration Association. *Member:* Chicago, Illinois State and American Bar Associations. [Enlisted Man, U.S. Army, 1954-1956]. ***PRACTICE AREAS:*** Business Law; Health Care; Corporate; Commercial Real Estate. ***Email:*** sweinberger@dykema.com

RETIRED PARTNERS

JAMES L. DONNELLY, admitted to bar, 1958, Illinois. *Education:* University of Notre Dame (A.B., 1951); Georgetown University; DePaul University (LL.B., 1957).

(This Listing Continued)

DYKEMA GOSSETT PLLC, Chicago—Continued

RAY F. DREXLER, admitted to bar, 1958, Illinois. *Education:* University of Notre Dame (Ph.B., cum laude, 1957; LL.B., 1958).

JEROME N. GROARK, admitted to bar, 1961, Illinois. *Education:* Loyola University, Chicago; University of Notre Dame (B.S., cum laude, 1956); DePaul University (J.D., 1961).

TIMOTHY J. GROARK, admitted to bar, 1966, Illinois. *Education:* Xavier University (A.B., 1961); DePaul University (J.D., 1966).

D. GLENN OFSTHUN, admitted to bar, 1950, Illinois. *Education:* Harvard University (A.B., cum laude, 1947; LL.B., cum laude, 1950).

HENRY L. PITTS, admitted to bar, 1939, Illinois. *Education:* University of Illinois (B.S., 1934); Illinois State University; University of Michigan (J.D., 1939).

JOHN G. POUST, admitted to bar, 1946, Illinois. *Education:* Northwestern University (B.S.L., 1942); Colorado University; Northwestern University (LL.B., 1946).

ASSOCIATES

ALLYSON R. BEHM, born Harvey, Illinois, January 20, 1977; admitted to bar, 2001, Illinois and U.S. District Court, Nothern District of Illinois. *Education:* Monmouth College (B.A., magna cum laude, 1998); Boston University (J.D., 2001). *Member:* Will County and Illinois State Bar Associations. ***PRACTICE AREAS:*** Litigation; Insurance Defense; Medical Malpractice Defense. ***Email:*** abehm@dykema.com

LAURA MARIE CALLAHAN, born Chicago, Illinois, March 12, 1969; admitted to bar, 1995, Illinois. *Education:* Marquette University (B.A., 1991); John Marshall Law School (J.D., 1995). *Member:* Illinois State and American Bar Associations. ***PRACTICE AREAS:*** Estate Planning; Estate Administration; Residential Real Estate; Tax Law. ***Email:*** lcallahan@dykema.com

DAVID T. CELLITTI, born Milwaukee, Wisconsin, February 21, 1974; admitted to bar, 2000, Illinois. *Education:* University of Illinois (B.A., 1997); Lewis and Clark Law School (J.D., 2000). *Member:* Chicago and American Bar Associations. ***PRACTICE AREAS:*** Corporate Law. ***Email:*** dcellitti@dykema.com

SONIA A. DESAI, born Evanston, Illinois, June 8, 1973; admitted to bar, 1998, Illinois; 2002, U.S. District Court, Northern District of Illinois. *Education:* University of Illinois, Urbana-Champaign (B.S., 1995; J.D., 1998). Recipient, CALI Excellence Award for highest achievement in Trial Advocacy Course. *Member:* Illinois State Bar Association; Asian-American Bar Association (Community Service Committee); The Association of Trial Lawyers of America; Defense Research Institute; Women's Bar Association. ***PRACTICE AREAS:*** Medical Negligence Defense; Health Care Litigation; Premises Liability; Tort Litigation; Commercial Litigation. ***Email:*** sdesai@dykema.com

EVANGELOS J. GEGAS, born Athens, Greece, October 17, 1967; admitted to bar, 1999, Illinois; 2000, Texas. *Education:* The Ohio State University (B.A., 1990; M.A., 1992; J.D., 1997). *Member:* American Bankruptcy Institute. ***LANGUAGES:*** French and Greek. ***PRACTICE AREAS:*** Bankruptcy. ***Email:*** egegas@dykema.com

JASON L. HOPP, born Elgin, Illinois, October 9, 1973; admitted to bar, 1998, Illinois and U.S. District Court, District of Illinois. *Education:* University of Illinois, Urbana-Champaign (B.A., 1995); John Marshall Law School (J.D., 1998). ***PRACTICE AREAS:*** Litigation; Civil Practice; Medical Malpractice. ***Email:*** jhopp@dykema.com

RAFI K. JAFRI, born New York, N.Y., May 5, 1976; admitted to bar, 2003, Illinois. *Education:* University of Chicago (B.A., with honors, 1998); DePaul University (J.D., cum laude, 2003). Recipient, CALI Excellence Award for highest achievement in Administrative Law and Labor Law. *Member:* Illinois State Bar Association. ***PRACTICE AREAS:*** Litigation. ***Email:*** rjafri@dykema.com

JULIE C. KELLER, born Decatur, Illinois, September 29, 1971; admitted to bar, 1998, Illinois and U.S. District Court, Central District of Illinois. *Education:* Marquette University (B.A., 1993); The Ohio State University (J.D., 1998). Member, The Ohio State University Law Journal, 1997-1998. *Member:* Decatur and Illinois State Bar Associations. ***Email:*** jkeller@dykema.com

JUSTIN T. LANGE, born Sterling, Illinois, June 2, 1978; admitted to bar, 2003, Iowa and U.S. Tax Court; 2005, Illinois. *Education:* University of Iowa (B.B.A., 2000); University of Iowa College of Law (J.D., 2003). Participant, Moot Court, University of Iowa College of Law. Student Judge, Moot Court Board. *Member:* Chicago, Polk County, Iowa State (Member, Young Lawyers Division), Illinois State and American (Member: Young Lawyers Division; Sections on: Business Law; Taxation) Bar Associations. ***PRACTICE AREAS:*** Corporate Law; Banking Law; Securities. ***Email:*** jlange@dykema.com

NAHRIN S. MARINO, born Baghdad, Iraq, May 13, 1974; admitted to bar, 2003, Illinois; 2004, U.S. District Court, Northern District of Illinois. *Education:* Illinois State University (B.S., 1997); John Marshall Law School (J.D., magna cum laude, 2003). ***LANGUAGES:*** Assyrian. ***PRACTICE AREAS:*** Litigation; Medical Malpractice Defense. ***Email:*** nmarino@dykema.com

TRICIA E. McVICKER, born Danville, Illinois, December 7, 1971; admitted to bar, 2002, Illinois. *Education:* Lakeview College of Nursing (B.S.N., 1994); John Marshall Law School (J.D., 2002). ***PRACTICE AREAS:*** Medical Malpractice; Civil Litigation; Health Care. ***Email:*** tmcvicker@dykema.com

SHARON A. SALINAS, born Chicago, Illinois, November 21, 1961; admitted to bar, 1989, Illinois and U.S. District Court, Northern District of Illinois. *Education:* Loyola University (B.S., 1985); IIT Chicago-Kent College of Law (J.D., with high honors, 1989). Order of the Coif. Member, Legal Advisory Board for the Institute of Paralegal Studies at Loyola University. *Member:* Chicago, Illinois State and American Bar Associations. ***PRACTICE AREAS:*** Environmental Law; Litigation. ***Email:*** ssalinas@dykema.com

PETER J. SCHMIDT, born July 26, 1971; admitted to bar, 1998, Illinois and U.S. District Court, Northern District of Illinois. *Education:* University of Illinois at Urbana (B.S., 1993); DePaul University College of Law (J.D., with honors, 1998). ***PRACTICE AREAS:*** Commercial Litigation; Bankruptcy; Mechanics Liens. ***Email:*** pschmidt@dykema.com

(This Listing Continued)

KATHLEEN E. SUROWIEC, born Detroit, Michigan, March 9, 1978; admitted to bar, 2003, Michigan and U.S. District Court, Eastern District of Michigan; 2004, Illinois. *Education:* Albion College (B.A., magna cum laude, 2000); University of Notre Dame (J.D., 2003). ***PRACTICE AREAS:*** Labor and Employment. ***Email:*** ksurowiec@dykema.com

ROSA TUMIALAN, born February 18, 1970; admitted to bar, 1994, Illinois. *Education:* University of Missouri (B.A./P.S., 1990); Loyola University (J.D., 1994). ***PRACTICE AREAS:*** Insurance Coverage; Litigation. ***Email:*** rtumialan@dykema.com

DAVID A. WHEELER, born St. Paul, Minnesota, February 3, 1963; admitted to bar, 1999, Illinois. *Education:* University of Maryland (B.S., Information Systems Management, 1987); Loyola College, Maryland (M.B.A., Finance, 1993); Loyola University (J.D., 1999). ***PRACTICE AREAS:*** Consumer Law; Litigation Law. ***Email:*** dwheeler@dykema.com

GREGORY M. WRIGHT, born Rochester, Michigan, September 3, 1980; admitted to bar, 2005, Illinois. *Education:* University of Notre Dame (B.A., magna cum laude, 2002; J.D., cum laude, 2005). Member, Notre Dame Immigration Clinic. Executive Articles Editor, 2004-2005 and Staff Member, Journal of College and University Law, University of Notre Dame. ***PRACTICE AREAS:*** Corporate Finance. ***Email:*** gwright@dykema.com

RENEÉ L. ZIPPRICH, born Detroit, Michigan, September 12, 1970; admitted to bar, 2003, Illinois; U.S. District Court, Northern and Western Districts of Illinois. *Education:* University of Michigan (B.A., 1993); Loyola University, Chicago (J.D., 2003). ***PRACTICE AREAS:*** Litigation; Consumer Finance; Class Actions Defense. ***Email:*** rzipprich@dykema.com

MARK R. ZITO, born January 23, 1972; admitted to bar, 1999, Ohio; 2000, Kentucky; 2001, Illinois; 2003, U.S. District Court, Northern District of Illinois. *Education:* University of Notre Dame (B.A., Philosophy, 1994); University of Iowa (J.D., with distinction, 1998). *Member:* Chicago and Illinois State Bar Associations. ***PRACTICE AREAS:*** Litigation; Commercial Litigation. ***Email:*** mzito@dykema.com

STAFF ATTORNEY

MARGARET J. RHIEW, admitted to bar, 2005, Illinois, U.S. District Court, Northern District of Illinois and U.S. District Court, Eastern District of Wisconsin. *Education:* University of Michigan (B.A.); Chicago-Kent College of Law, Illinois Institute of Technology (J.D.). *Member:* Chicago and Illinois State Bar Associations; Women's Bar Association of Illinois. ***PRACTICE AREAS:*** Litigation; Consumer Financial Services; Class Action Defense. ***Email:*** mrhiew@dykema.com

DZIEZAK LAW FIRM, P.C.

CHICAGO, ILLINOIS

(See Hoffman Estates)

Intellectual Property Law, including Patent, Trademark, Trade Secret, and Copyright Law, Licensing, and Unfair Competition.

DAVID ECKBERG

Established in 1974

39 SOUTH LASALLE STREET, SUITE 825
CHICAGO, ILLINOIS 60603
Telephone: 312-372-3448
Fax: 312-372-3099
Email: DavidEckberg@ameritech.net
URL: http://www.davideckberg.com

Criminal Law, Driving While Intoxicated, Drug Crimes, Juvenile Crimes, Parole and Probation, Traffic Violations, White Collar Crime, Child Custody, Child Support, Divorce, Domestic Violence, Visitation Rights, Automobile Accidents, Sexual Abuse, Wrongful Death, Condemnation and Fast Track Demolition, Employment Law, Domestic Relations, Bankruptcy, Discrimination, Employee Benefits, Wrongful Termination.

FIRM PROFILE: Mr. David Eckberg established his private practice in 1974. David Eckberg has over 30 years experience in litigation, criminal law, personal injury, condemnation and fast track demolition, employment law, domestic relations, family law, child custody and support. He has held numerous positions in the legal industry. He was former states attorney, former hearing officer-unemployment, former deputy sheriff, former legal assistant state-capital, state-federal court practitioner. Also, he is a member of the Chicago Bar Association and Illinois State Bar Association.

DAVID ECKBERG, admitted to bar, 1968, Illinois; 1971, U.S. District Court, Southern District of Illinois; 1978, U.S. District Court, Northern District of Illinois and U.S. Court of Appeals, Seventh Circuit. *Education:* Northern Illinois University (B.S., 1964); Chicago-Kent College of Law, Illinois Institute of Technology (J.D., 1967). Former Legal Assistant, Illinois State Capitol. Author: Illinois Snowmobile Registration and Safety Act, 625 ILCS 40/1-let seq. Former Assistant Prosecuting Attorney, Sangamon County, Illinois. Former Village Attorney, Sherman, Illinois. Former Deputy Sheriff, Cook County, Illinois. Former Hearing Officer, IDES. *Member:* Chicago (Member: Criminal, Domestic Relations and Unemployment Referral Panels; In Court Criminal Defense Panel) and Illinois State Bar Associations. ***REPORTED CASES:*** People v. Gary Dailey; D'Attomo v. D'Attomo. ***PRACTICE AREAS:*** Criminal; Drug Crimes; Divorce; Employment; Unemployment; Driving While Intoxicated; Traffic; Personal Injury; Condemnation; Bankruptcy; Discrimination; Employee Benefits; Wrongful Termination.

LAW OFFICE OF
LORI D. ECKER, PC

180 NORTH LA SALLE STREET, SUITE 2300
CHICAGO, ILLINOIS 60601
Telephone: 312-855-1880
Fax: 312-263-4609
URL: http://www.employmentlawyer.org
Email: loriecker@ameritech.net
URL: http://www.lawyers.com/employee_rights

Labor and Employment Law, Employment Contracts, Employment Arbitration, Employment Rights, Wrongful Termination Litigation, Family and Medical Leave Act, Sexual Harassment, Employment Discrimination and Americans with Disabilities Act.

FIRM PROFILE: Dedicated exclusively to employment law, the Law Office of Lori D. Ecker, PC provides consultation and legal services to employees on a wide variety of employment-related issues.

LORI D. ECKER, born Plymouth, Indiana; admitted to bar, 1982, Illinois and U.S. District Court, Northern and Central Districts of Illinois including Trial Bar. *Education:* Lake Forest College (B.A., 1979); DePaul University (J.D., 1982). Author: "Labor Law," Matthew Bender, Chapters 55 and 58, 1991 and 1992 revisions; "Proving Willful Violations Under the ADEA: The Evolving Law Since Thurston," *1989 National Employment Lawyers Association-Illinois Seminar Handbook; ADEA Commentaries for NITA, LEXIS, September 2003, January, 2004. Co-Author:* "Litigation at the Illinois Human Rights Commission," CBA Record, July/August 1992; "Handling Discrimination Cases in Illinois - A Practical Guide", CBA Record, February, 1991; "Privacy Issues", Employment Discrimination and Employment Termination, Illinois Institute for Continuing Legal Education, 1990. Presenter: "The Joys and Pitfalls of a Small Plaintiff's Employment Practice," Second Annual National Employment Lawyers Association Conference, Cape Cod, Massachusetts, June 1991; "Rights, Wrongs & Responses; Sexual Harassment, Discrimination & Stereotyping," March 1992 meeting of Food Executive Women; "Representing Employees in Sexual Harassment Cases," Decalogue Society of Lawyers Continuing Education Series, April 1993; "Representing Plaintiffs in Employment Litigation: Defeating Summary Judgment Motions," Young Lawyers Section of the Chicago Bar Association Seventh Annual Seminar on Litigating Employment Discrimination and Wrongful Discharge Cases, February 1994; Illinois Employment Tort Update: A Survey of Recent State and Federal Case Law," CBA YLS Labor and Employment Law Committee, March 1995; "Winning Employment Torts," Sixth Annual NELA Conference, June 1995; "Multiple Claims Available to Injured Employees," 1995 Annual Meeting, ABA General Practice Section, August 1995; "Winning Pre-Trial Preparation in the New World of Illinois Civil Litigation," IICLE, October 1995; "Profile of an Ideal Plaintiff," Equal Employment Advisory Council Membership Meeting, October 1996; "Employment Litigation in the 90's: Unemployment Compensation Claims as Pretrial Preparation," Fifth Annual National Workers Compensation & Disability Conference, November 1996; "Employment Litigation Preparing for a Jury Trial," CBA, January 1997; "Developing and Proving Damages," NELA/Illinois regional seminar on trial practice techniques, April 18, 1998; "Privacy in the Workplace," Institute for Business and Professional Ethics, DePaul University, May 13, 1998; "Legal Perspectives: Women in the Workplace," Chicago-Kent College of Law, March 6, 1998; "Employee Discharges: The Do's and Don'ts in Representing the Discharged Employee," Labor and Employment Section of the ISBA legal education program, June 5, 1998; "Terminating Employees Protected by the FMLA," Council on Education in Management, September 14, 1998; "Plaintiffs Attorney's Guide to Management Pitfall," Employment and Labor Law in Illinois, Lorman Education Services, January 6 and 13, 1999; "Hot Topics and Recent Developments in Employment Law," Dupage County Bar Association, January 23, 1999; "Privacy Interests and Defamation: Understanding the Issues," Privacy Law in Illinois, Lorman Education Services, March 5, 1999; "The Practical Effect of the Affirmative Defenses Enunciated in Farragher and Ellerth: What Plaintiffs Need to Plan For and Do, ABA Section of Labor and Employment Law, Employee Rights & Responsibilities Committee Midwinter Meeting, March 25, 1999, Stuart, Florida; "Lessons from the Real World: Best Practices for Avoiding Wrongful Discipline and Termination Liability," Progressive Discipline, Coaching and Termination Law, Council on Education in Management, October 4, 1999; "Mediation Preparation and Advocacy from A to Z," EEO Mediation Conclave and Workshop, October 25, 1999; "The New Wave of Backlash Lawsuits: Employer Liability to the Accused Harasser," Personnel Law Update, Council on Education in Management, November 30, 1999; "Claims and Defenses After Oncale, Ellerth, and Farragher, Perspectives After a Year and a Half: How Have the Courts Applied the Decisions?" ABA Section of Labor and Employment Law, ERR Committee Midwinter Meeting, March 18, 2000, La Jolla, California; "Cash Balance Pensions: Implication for Employment Lawyers," CBA Labor and Employment Law Committee Seminar, April 27, 2000; "Lessons from the Real World: Best Practices for Avoiding Wrongful Discipline and Termination Liability," Council on Education in Management Seminar: Progressive Discipline, Coaching and Termination Law, June 12, 2000, Oakbrook Terrace; "Preparing and Trying Jury Cases," NELA- Illinois luncheon meeting, February 13, 2001; "Mediation Preparation and Advocacy: A Plaintiff Representative's Perspective," CBA Meeting of the Alternative Dispute Resolution and Labor and Employment Law Committees, March 14, 2001; "Preparing Punitive Damages Claims in the Aftermath of Kolstad," ABA Section of Labor and Employment Law, ERR Committee, March 2001 Midwinter Meeting, St. Petersburg, Florida; "Understanding Executive Compensation Packages," ABA Annual Meeting, Chicago, Illinois, August 6, 2001; "Preparing Punitive Damages Claims in the Aftermath of Kolstad," CBA YLS Labor & Employment Law Committee luncheon meeting, February 1, 2002; "Family-Friendly State Laws," ABA Section of Labor and Employment Law, ERR Committee, March 2002 Midwinter Meeting, Puerto Vallarta, Mexico; "Coping With Disaster: Avoiding Enforcement of Non-Competition Agreements & Representing the Employee-Defending Against Injunction Actions," and "Refining Discovery Tactics," ABA Regional Institute, June 2002, Chicago, Illinois; "Who Are You? I Really Want to Know: Learning Enough to Hire, Fire and Otherwise Act Without Crossing the Legal Line," March 2003, ABA Section of Labor and Employment Law, ERR Committee, San Juan, Puerto Rico; "The Basics: Family and Medical Leave and "The Basics: Employment Rights and Responsibilities," August 2003, ABA Annual Meeting, San Francisco, California; "Employment Torts," September 2003, CBA Labor & Employment Law Committee luncheon; "Layoffs and Mass Termination," September 2003, American Employment Law Survey sponsored by the ABA and the Canadian Bar Association, Toronto, Canada; "Top Ten Employer Actions that Send Employees to a Lawyer," November 2003, Spencer Fane Britt & Browne Client Conferences, Kansas City, Missouri; "Independent Contractor or Employee? Determining Employee and Employer Status," January 2004, LEI Labor & Employment Conference, Snowmass, Colorado. *Member:* Chicago (Co-Chair, Young Lawyers Section, Labor and Employment Law Committee, 1991-1992 and 1992-1993; Vice-Chair, Labor and Employment Law Committee, 1996-1997; Chair, 1997-1998), Illinois State and American (Member, Sections On: Labor and Employment; Individual Rights and Responsibilities) Bar Associations; American Arbitration Association Roster of Neutrals. ***REPORTED CASES:*** Oblix v. Winiecki, No. 02 C 6878, 2003 WL 1964193, 2003 WL 21544030 (N.D. Ill. Apr. 24 and Jul 3, 2003); Lynn v. Acme Metals, Inc., No.94 C 5633, 1995 WL 472747, 1995 WL 370230 (ND. Ill. Aug. 8, 1995 and June 20, 1995) Dillard and Precoat Metal, Ch. No. 1990CF3737, 1994 WL 880297 (Ill. HRC Dec. 23, 1994) Bristow v. Drake Street Inc., 41 E3d 345 (7th Cir. 1994); Vajda v. Arthur Andersen & Co., 253 Ill. App.3d 345 (1st Dist. 1993).

(This Listing Continued)

ECKHART KOLAK LLC

Established in 1905

(Formerly Eckhart, McSwain, Silliman and Sears LLC)

55 WEST MONROE STREET, SUITE 1925
CHICAGO, ILLINOIS 60603
Telephone: 312-236-0646
Fax: 312-236-0105
Email: admin@eckhart.com
URL: http://www.eckhart.com

General Business Practice, including Corporate Law, Real Estate, Commercial Transactions, Litigation (State and Federal Courts), Federal Taxation, Probate, Estate Planning, Employment Law, and Not for Profit Corporations.

FIRM PROFILE: Eckhart Kolak LLC represents business owners and their companies, families with substantial assets, and cultural and educational organizations since its founding in 1905. The firm has particular strength in business law, taxation, estates and trusts, business and real estate transactions, and commercial litigation.

MEMBERS OF FIRM

PERCY B. ECKHART (1877-1969)

RAYMOND P. KOLAK, born 1952; admitted to bar, 1978, Illinois; 2003, U.S. Tax Court. *Education:* University of Chicago (B.A., 1975); George Washington University (J.D., with honors, 1978). Member, George Washington Law Review, 1977-1978. *Member:* Chicago (Co-Chair, Mergers and Acquisitions Sub-Committee), Illinois State and American Bar Associations. ***PRACTICE AREAS:*** Corporate Law; Real Estate; Taxation. ***Email:*** rkolak@eckhart.com

ANGELO J. LOUMBAS, born 1966; admitted to bar, 1993, Illinois; 2002, New York. *Education:* DePauw University (B.A., 1988); University of Notre Dame (M.B.A., with honors, 1990); Indiana University, Bloomington (J.D., 1993). Delta Theta Phi; Order of Barristers. *Member:* Chicago, Illinois State and American Bar Associations. ***PRACTICE AREAS:*** Corporate Law; Commercial Litigation; Estate Litigation; Employment Law. ***Email:*** aloumbas@eckhart.com

JASON S. ORNDUFF, born 1971; admitted to bar, 1996, Illinois; 2003, U.S. Tax Court. *Education:* University of Illinois (B.A., with high distinction, 1993; J.D., cum laude, 1996). Phi Delta Phi. Executive Administrative Editor, Elder Law Journal, 1996. *Member:* Chicago, Illinois State and American Bar Associations. ***PRACTICE AREAS:*** Probate; Estate Planning; Corporate Law; Real Estate; Taxation. ***Email:*** jornduff@eckhart.com

OF COUNSEL

ROY W. SEARS, born 1933; admitted to bar, 1961, Illinois, U.S. District Court, Northern and Central Districts of Illinois including Trial Bar, U.S. Court of Appeals, Seventh Circuit and U.S. Supreme Court. *Education:* Northwestern University (B.S., 1958; J.D., 1961). Phi Alpha Delta. Member, Journal of Criminal Law, Criminology and Police Science, 1960. *Member:* Chicago and Illinois State Bar Associations. ***PRACTICE AREAS:*** Litigation; State Taxation; Local Taxation; Employment Law; Commercial Transactions. ***Email:*** rsears@eckhart.com

REPRESENTATIVE CLIENTS: The Art Institute of Chicago; Ardent Health Services, Inc.; Chicago Maritime Society; Distribution Market Advantage, Inc.; The Metraflex Company; ORC Protel, Inc.; Rada Advertising, Inc.; Recycling Services, Inc.; Robert G. Burkhardt & Associates, P.E.; Selig Sealing Products, Inc.; Sutech Industries, Inc.; Terra Foundation for the Arts; Usach Technologies, Inc.; Val-Matic Valve and Manufacturing Corporation.

EDELMAN AND EDELMAN

CHARTERED
Established in 1940

100 WEST MONROE STREET, SUITE 306
CHICAGO, ILLINOIS 60603-1902
Telephone: 312-372-3535
Fax: 312-372-3815
Email: ledelman48@yahoo.com
URL: http://www.lawyers.com/edelmanandedelmanchtd

General Civil and Trial Practice. Probate, Estate Planning, Tax, Real Estate, Corporation, Medical Legal and Family Law, Domestic Relations, Divorce, Child Custody, Child Support.

LEON EDELMAN (1888-1949)

ALVIN EDELMAN (Retired)

(This Listing Continued)

EDELMAN AND EDELMAN, CHARTERED, Chicago—Continued

LEON F. EDELMAN, born Chicago, Illinois, July 20, 1951; admitted to bar, 1976, Illinois; 1980, U.S. Tax Court. *Education:* Amherst College (A.B., magna cum laude, 1973); Boston University; Northwestern University (J.D., 1976). Co-Author, "Informed Consent; The Patient's Dilemma and the Doctor's Problem," International Surgery Journal, 1976. Author, "Basic American," N.O.L.P.E. Law Journal, 1977. President, 1984-1985 and Director, 1985—, Amherst Club of Chicago. Commissioner, 1984-1985, Village of Wheeling Fire and Police Commission. Member: Board of Chicago Bar Foundation, 1986-1987; Board of Directors, Legal Assistance Foundation of Chicago, 1986-1995. Chair Qualified Arbitrator, Cook County Mandatory Arbitration Program. *Member:* Chicago (Chairman, Health and Hospital Law Committee, 1980-1981, Director, 1981-1982, Secretary, 1982-1983, Vice Chairman, 1983-1984, Chairman-Elect, 1984-1985 and Chairman, 1985-1986, Young Lawyers Section; Member, Board of Managers, 1987-1989; Chairman, Membership Committee, 1990-1991) and Illinois State Bar Associations. ***PRACTICE AREAS:*** Corporate Law; Real Estate; Family Law; Divorce; Child Custody; Child Support; Domestic Relations; Litigation; Elder Care; Estate Planning. ***Email:*** ledelman48@yahoo.com

GENERAL COUNSEL FOR: International College of Surgeons; American Taxi Dispatch, Inc.; Global Diamonds, Inc.; Pedian Rug, Inc.
REFERENCES: American National Bank & Trust Company of Chicago, Illinois; Bank of America/Illinois, Chicago, Illinois.

EICHHORN & EICHHORN

CHICAGO, ILLINOIS

(See Hammond, Indiana)

General Practice, Litigation in State and Federal Courts, Public Utility, Banking, Corporation, Health Care, Insurance, Commercial Transactions, Labor and Employment Law, Real Estate, Professional Liability and Tort Law. Mediation.

EIMER STAHL KLEVORN & SOLBERG LLP

224 SOUTH MICHIGAN AVENUE, SUITE 1100
CHICAGO, ILLINOIS 60604
Telephone: 312-660-7600
Fax: 312-692-1718
URL: http://www.eimerstahl.com

Complex Commercial Litigation, Antitrust, Mergers & Acquisitions, Securities Fraud, Toxic Tort, Environmental Litigation, Civil Litigation and General Litigation.

NATHAN P. EIMER, born Chicago, Illinois, June 26, 1949; admitted to bar, 1973, Illinois; 1985, New York; 1998, Texas. *Education:* University of Illinois (A.B., Economics, magna cum laude, with highest distinction in Economics, 1970); Northwestern University (J.D., cum laude, 1973). ***PRACTICE AREAS:*** Complex Commercial Litigation; Antitrust. ***Email:*** neimer@eimerstahl.com

DAVID M. STAHL, born Chicago, Illinois, September 22, 1946; admitted to bar, 1972, Illinois; U.S. Court of Appeals for the District of Columbia Circuit, Fifth, Seventh and Ninth Circuits. *Education:* University of Illinois (B.A., 1968); University of Michigan (J.D., magna cum laude, 1971; M.A., 1971). Order of the Coif. ***PRACTICE AREAS:*** Commercial Litigation; Energy Law.

ANDREW G. KLEVORN, born Herrin, Illinois, March 23, 1961; admitted to bar, 1987, Illinois, U.S. District Court, Northern District of Illinois, U.S. District Court, Northern District of Texas, U.S. District Court, Eastern District of Michigan, U.S. Court of Appeals, Seventh Circuit. *Education:* University of Chicago (B.A., with honors, 1983); University of Michigan (J.D., magna cum laude, 1986). Order of the Coif. Recipient, Campbell Moot Court Competition Award, University of Michigan. ***LANGUAGES:*** French. ***PRACTICE AREAS:*** Commercial Litigation; Antitrust; Securities; Mergers and Acquisitions.

SCOTT C. SOLBERG, born Rockford, Illinois, October 8, 1963; admitted to bar, 1990, Illinois and U.S. District Court, Northern District of Illinois; 1998, U.S. District Court, Eastern District of Wisconsin and U.S. Court of Appeals, Seventh and Tenth Circuits. *Education:* Augustana College (B.A., cum laude, 1986); Vanderbilt University (J.D., 1990). Phi Beta Kappa. ***REPORTED CASES:*** Draeger Oil Co. v. Uno-Ven, 314 F.3d 299 (7th Cir. 2002)' Stop-n-Go v. Uno-Ven, 184 F.3d 672 (7th Cir. 1999); Endo v. Albertine, 863 F.Supp. 708 (N.D.Ill. 1994); In re ECI, 173 B.R. 363 (N.D.Ill. 1994). ***PRACTICE AREAS:*** Complex Commercial Litigation; Toxic Torts; Antitrust; Securities Fraud; Litigation.

PAMELA R. HANEBUTT, born Mattoon, Illinois, August 18, 1959; admitted to bar, 1984, Illinois and U.S. District Court, Northern District of Illinois. *Education:* University of Illinois (B.A., magna cum laude, 1981); Tulane University (J.D., magna cum laude, 1984). Order of the Coif. ***PRACTICE AREAS:*** Environmental Litigation; Toxic Torts; Complex Commercial Litigation. ***Email:*** phanebutt@eimerstahl.com

LISA S. MEYER, born Knobnoster, Missouri, May 13, 1966; admitted to bar, 1994, Virginia and U.S. District Court, Northern District of Indiana; 1996, Illinois and U.S. District Court, Northern District of Illinois. *Education:* University of Virginia (B.A., 1988); Valparaiso University School of Law (J.D., magna cum laude, 1994). ***PRACTICE AREAS:*** Complex Commercial Litigation; Toxic Torts; Litigation.

ADAM B. DEUTSCH, born Cleveland, Ohio, December 12, 1970; admitted to bar, 1996, Illinois and U.S. District Court, Northern District of Illinois. *Education:* Rutgers University (B.A., with high honors, 1993); New York University (J.D., 1996). Member, Moot Court Board, Competitions Division. ***PRACTICE AREAS:*** Commercial Litigation; Antitrust. ***Email:*** adeutsch@eimerstahl.com

VANESSA G. JACOBSEN, born Chicago, Illinois, November 24, 1972; admitted to bar, 1997, Illinois and U.S. District Court, Northern District of Illinois. *Education:* Valparaiso University (B.A., magna cum laude, 1994); DePaul University College of Law (J.D., with honors, 1997). Order of the Coif. Member, Moot Court Society. Editor, DePaul Law Review. ***PRACTICE AREAS:*** Commercial Litigation; Antitrust; Securities Litigation. ***Email:*** vjacobsen@eimerstahl.com

(This Listing Continued)

OF COUNSEL

MICHAEL I. MILLER, born Chicago, Illinois, April 9, 1937; admitted to bar, 1960, District of Columbia and Illinois. *Education:* Northwestern University (B.A., 1957; J.D., 1960). Phi Beta Kappa. Order of the Coif. ***PRACTICE AREAS:*** Complex Litigation; Antitrust.

RONALD J. ALLEN, born Chicago, Illinois, July 14, 1948; admitted to bar, 1974, Nebraska; 1979, Iowa; 1984, Illinois. *Education:* Marshall University (B.S., mathematics, magna cum laude, 1970); University of Michigan (J.D., magna cum laude, 1973). Phi Eta Sigma. Order of the Coif. American Law Institute. John Henry Wigmore Professor of Law, Northwestern University, 1992—; Duke University, 1982-1983; Iowa University, 1978-1982; Nebraska., 1973-1974. Author: "Comprehensive Criminal Procedure," Aspen, 2001; "Evidence," Aspen 2002. *Member:* Illinois State, Iowa State and Nebraska State Bar Associations. ***PRACTICE AREAS:*** Complex Litigation; Government Investigations. ***Email:*** rallen@eimerstahl.com

J. CUNYON GORDON, born Atlanta, Georgia, July 6, 1953; admitted to bar, 1981, Illinois; 1984, U.S. Court of Military Appeals; 1985, U.S. Supreme Court; 1992, U.S. District Court, Northern District of Illinois including Trial Bar. *Education:* Yale College; University of Nebraska (B.A., with honors, 1976); Yale University (J.D., 1981). Author: "Visitor from Another Planet," Mich.L.Rev. 1993; "Painting by Numbers," upcoming Fordham L.Rev. 2003. Instructor: Boston University, 1992-1993; Boston College, 1998-1999; University of Oregon, 2002; Seattle University, Summer 1999, 2000, 2001. *Member:* American Bar Association (Member, Commission on Women, 1998-2000; Commission on Racial & Ethnic Diversity, 2001-2002). [U.S. Navy JAGC, 1981-1987; U.S. Navy, 1978-1981; Lieutenant, 2000-2003]. ***LANGUAGES:*** French. ***PRACTICE AREAS:*** Litigation; Commercial Law. ***Email:*** cgordon@eimerstahl.com

RONIT C. BARRETT, born La Mesa, California, January 5, 1975; admitted to bar, 1999, California; 2001, Illinois. *Education:* University of California, Santa Barbara (B.A., with high honors, 1996); University of Virginia (J.D., 1999). ***PRACTICE AREAS:*** Commercial Litigation. ***Email:*** rbarrett@eimerstahl.com

CHRISTINE M. JOHNSON, born Chicago, Illinois, June 10, 1951; admitted to bar, 1994, Illinois; U.S. District Court, Northern District of Illinois; 2003, U.S. Court of Appeals, Seventh Circuit. *Education:* University of Illinois (B.A., 1973; B.S.N., 1980; M.S.N., 1984); College of William and Mary (J.D., 1994). Order of the Coif. Recipient, Am Jur Awards, Torts & Civil Procedure. Staff Member, William & Mary Law Review. Staff Editor, William & Mary Journal of Women & The Law. ***PRACTICE AREAS:*** Commercial Litigation; Product Liability; Toxic Torts; Litigation. ***Email:*** cjohnson@eimerstahl.com

LINDA P. KURTOS, born Chesterton, Indiana, January 25, 1966; admitted to bar, 1991, Illinois, U.S. District Court, Northern District of Illinois including Trial Bar and U.S. Court of Appeals, Seventh Circuit. *Education:* Michigan State University (B.S., with honors, 1988); Northwestern University (J.D., 1991). Articles Editor, Journal of Criminal Law and Criminology. *Member:* Chicago Bar Association. ***PRACTICE AREAS:*** Complex Commercial Litigation; Toxic Torts; Product Liability. ***Email:*** lkurtos@eimerstahl.com

MICHELLE K. MORITZ, born Grand Rapids, Michigan, June 26, 1972; admitted to bar, 1997, Illinois and U.S. District Court, Northern District of Illinois. *Education:* Calvin College (B.A., 1994); Indiana University School of Law (J.D., magna cum laude, 1997). Order of the Coif. ***PRACTICE AREAS:*** Commercial Litigation. ***Email:*** mmoritz@eimerstahl.com

JONATHAN M. WIER, born Mequon, Wisconsin, September 29, 1974; admitted to bar, 1999, Wisconsin and Illinois. *Education:* University of Pennsylvania (B.S., Accounting, 1996); University of Wisconsin-Madison (J.D., 1999). ***PRACTICE AREAS:*** Commercial Litigation; Complex Litigation. ***Email:*** jwier@eimerstahl.com

GREG J. WEINTRAUB, born Philadelphia, Pennsylvania, September 24, 1975; admitted to bar, 2001, Pennsylvania; 2002, Illinois. *Education:* Boston University (B.S.B.A., summa cum laude, 1997); University of Chicago (J.D., with honors, 2000). Phi Beta Kappa. ***PRACTICE AREAS:*** Complex Commercial Litigation. ***Email:*** gweintraub@eimerstahl.com

RISHI AGRAWAL, born Chicago, Illinois, July 20, 1973; admitted to bar, 1998, Illinois. *Education:* Northwestern University (B.A., 1995); Loyola University (J.D., 1998). *Member:* Asian American Bar Association (Vice President, 2004-2005); Indian Bar Association (Board of Directors, 2004-2005). ***LANGUAGES:*** Hindi and Spanish. ***PRACTICE AREAS:*** Toxic Torts; Complex Commercial Litigation. ***Email:*** ragrawal@eimerstahl.com

WILLIAM S. BOOTH, born Oak Lawn, Illinois, March 19, 1969; admitted to bar, 2000, Illinois and U.S. District Court, Northern District of Illinois. *Education:* Eastern Illinois University (B.A.); DePaul University (J.D., 2000). Author: "Survival Under the ADA,: 2 De Paul J. Health Care L. 269 (Winter 1998). ***PRACTICE AREAS:*** Complex Commercial Litigation. ***Email:*** bbooth@eimerstahl.com

ADAM OYEBANJI, born Coatbridge, Lanarkshire, Scotland, August 1, 1963; admitted to bar, 2001, Illinois and U.S. Court of Appeals, Seventh Circuit. *Education:* University of Birmingham (LL.B., 1986); Harvard Law School (J.D., 2001); University of Bristol (LL.M., 2004). ***REPORTED CASES:*** Rickard v. Sternes, 44 Fed. Appx. 738 (7th Cir. 2002); People v. Griffith, 334 Ill. App.3d 98 (2002); RJB Mining (UK) Ltd. v. Hambleton and another, Court of Appeal (Civil Division), (Eng.), 27 July 1998; Cox Homes Ltd. v. Ideal Homes (Midlands) Ltd. and another, Court of Appeal (Civil Division) (Eng.), 10 February 1998; Swindle and others v. Harrison and another, Court of Appeal, Civil Division (Eng.), (1997) 4 All ER 705, 25 March 1997; W W Greener (Sporting Guns) Ltd. v. Thomas, Court of Appeal (Civil Division) (Eng.), 30 July 1997; R v. Slough Bourough Council, ex parte Green, Queen's Bench Division (Crown Office List) (Eng.), CO/410/96, 15 November 1996; Birmingham City Council v. Hayes, Court of Appeal (Civil Division) (Eng.), 6 June 1995; Miles v. Lintner, Court of Appeal (Civil Division) (Eng.), 25 October 1993; Airspeed Aviation Ltd. v. The Commissioners of Customs and Excise, Manchester VAT Tribunal (Eng.), MAN/91/1358, 2 December 1993; R v. Naylors (R&J) Ltd. Associated Heat Services PLC, Nickerson Investments Ltd. and Welshpool Justices ex parte National Rivers

(This Listing Continued)

Authority, Queen's Bench Division (Crown OFfice List) (Eng.), CO/0386/91, 13 November 1992. ***PRACTICE AREAS:*** Commercial Litigation. ***Email:*** aoyebanji@eimerstahl.com

LISA M. CIPRIANO, born Detroit, Michigan, June 1, 1970; admitted to bar, 1995, Illinois; U.S. District Court, Northern District of Illinois; 2000, U.S. Court of Appeals, Third Circuit; 2003, U.S. Tax Court; 2004, U.S. District Court, Northern District of Texas. *Education:* University of Michigan (B.A., 1992); Northwestern University (J.D., cum laude, 1995). *Member:* Chicago and American Bar Associations. ***PRACTICE AREAS:*** Commercial Litigation; Securities; Accountants Liability.

VANESSA D. McCLINTON, born Chicago, Illinois, August 25, 1973; admitted to bar, 1998, Illinois. *Education:* University of Michigan (B.A., 1994); Northewestern University (J.D., 1998). Previously with Sidley and Austin. ***PRACTICE AREAS:*** Litigation. ***Email:*** vmcclinton@eimerstahl.com

JILL M. BRADY, born Michigan, November 30, 1975; admitted to bar, 2003, Michigan; 2004, Illinois. *Education:* University of Michigan (B.A., 1999; J.D., 2002). ***PRACTICE AREAS:*** Commercial Litigation; Antitrust. ***Email:*** jbrady@eimerstahl.com

RYAN S. HEDGES, born Fort Wayne, Indiana, April 7, 1971; admitted to bar, 2001, California, U.S. District Court, Central and Eastern Districts of California, U.S. Court of Appeals, Ninth Circuit (Not admitted in Illinois). *Education:* Northwestern University (B.S., Speech, 1993); University of Southern California (J.D., 2001). Editor-in-Chief, Southern California Law Review, 2001. Recipient, Warren J. Ferguson Social Justice Writing Award. Previously with Alschuler Grossman Stein and Kahan LLP, Santa Monica, CA. *Member:* American Bar Association; State Bar of California. ***PRACTICE AREAS:*** Commercial Litigation (100%). ***Email:*** rhedges@eimerstahl.com

EMALFARB, SWAN & BAIN

CHICAGO, ILLINOIS

(See Highland Park)

Construction Law, Mechanics Liens, Construction Defects, Bankruptcy, Creditor Rights, Real Estate Law, Zoning Law, Contracts.

LAW OFFICES OF JULIE T. EMERICK, LTD.

105 WEST MADISON STREET, SUITE 2200
CHICAGO, ILLINOIS 60602
Telephone: 312-372-3380
Fax: 312-372-3392
Email: jtemerick@emigrate-immigrate.com
URL: http://www.emigrate-immigrate.com

Immigration and Naturalization Law.

JULIE T. EMERICK, born Detroit, Michigan, August 15, 1966; admitted to bar, 1992, Michigan and U.S. District Court, Eastern District of Michigan; 1998, Illinois and U.S. District Court, Northern District of Illinois; 2005 U.S. Court of Appeals, Seventh Circuit. *Education:* John Carroll University (B.A., 1988); University of Detroit (J.D., 1992). *Member:* Federal Bar Association; State Bar of Michigan; American Immigration Lawyers Association. ***LANGUAGES:*** French. ***Email:*** jtemerick@emigrate-immigrate.com

EMRICH & DITHMAR LLC

125 SOUTH WACKER DRIVE, SUITE 2080
CHICAGO, ILLINOIS 60606-4401
Telephone: 312-663-9800
FAX: 312-663-9822
URL: http://www.emrichdithmar.com

Patent, Trademark, Copyright, and Unfair Competition Law. Trials and Appeals before Federal and State Courts and Governmental Agencies.

MEMBERS OF FIRM

PAUL L. BROWN, born Paullina, Iowa, April 19, 1939; admitted to bar, 1966, New York and Iowa; 1973, Illinois; registered to practice before U.S. Patent and Trademark Office. *Education:* Monmouth College (B.A., 1961); DePauw University (M.A.Ch., 1963); University of Michigan (J.D., 1966). ***PRACTICE AREAS:*** Patents; Trademarks; Copyrights.

JAMES J. HILL, born Chicago, Illinois, January 21, 1937; admitted to bar, 1965, Illinois; 1971, U.S. Supreme Court; registered to practice before U.S. Patent and Trademark Office. *Education:* Marquette University (B.E.E., 1959); University of Pennsylvania (M.S.E.E., 1961); DePaul University (J.D., 1965). ***PRACTICE AREAS:*** Patents; Trademarks; Copyrights.

HARRY M. LEVY, born Chicago, Illinois, January 15, 1940; admitted to bar, 1965, Illinois; registered to practice before U.S. Patent and Trademark Office. *Education:* Purdue University (B.S. Ch.E., 1962); Northwestern University (J.D., 1965). ***PRACTICE AREAS:*** Patents; Trademarks; Copyrights.

ROBERT R. CALIRI, born New York, New York, December 22, 1946; admitted to bar, 1973, Illinois. *Education:* Cornell University (B.A., 1968); University of North Carolina at Chapel Hill (J.D., 1973). ***PRACTICE AREAS:*** Trademarks; Copyrights.

THOMAS E. HILL, born Oak Park, Illinois, January 14, 1944; admitted to bar, 1978, California; 1980, Illinois; registered to practice before U.S. Patent and Trademark Office. *Education:* Western Illinois University (B.S., 1967); Kansas State University (M.S., 1969); George Washington University (J.D., 1977). ***PRACTICE AREAS:*** Patents; Trademarks; Copyrights.

JONATHAN J. KRIT, born Chicago, Illinois, December 16, 1964; admitted to bar, 1989, Illinois; registered to practice before U.S. Patent and Trademark Office, 1993. *Education:* Northwestern University (B.S., 1986; J.D., 1989). ***PRACTICE AREAS:*** Patents; Trademarks; Copyrights.

(This Listing Continued)

DONALD F. ENGEL

320 WEST OHIO STREET, SUITE 501
CHICAGO, ILLINOIS 60610
Telephone: 312-229-7900
Fax: 312-229-7901
Email: chicagolaw@uscounsel.com
URL: http://www.uscounsel.com

Litigation, Real Estate, Bankruptcy, Corporate Finance, Business.

DONALD F. ENGEL, born Cincinnati, Ohio, July 27, 1943; admitted to bar, 1986, Illinois. *Education:* DePaul University (B.A., 1983); Loyola University (J.D., 1985). Real Estate Broker, Ohio, 1970; Illinois, 1996. Author: "Bankruptcy and Brokerage, Professional Report," (1993). Commercial Pilots License. Partner, Schwart and Freeman, 1993-1998. Partner, Gottieb and Schwartz, 1990-1993. *Member:* Chicago, Illinois State and American Bar Associations. [Capt., USMC, 1962-68]. ***PRACTICE AREAS:*** Litigation; Real Estate; Bankruptcy; Corporate Law; Structured Finance.

REPRESENTATIVE CLIENTS: Playboy Enterprises, Inc.; Abbott Labratories; Z Automation Company; Environmental Technology Soluctions, Inc.; CSM Fastener Products Co.; United IM-EX Corp.; Silk Road Oriental Restaurants.

ENTERTAINMENT LAW CHICAGO, P.C.

6441 N. BOSWORTH AVENUE, 3RD FLOOR
CHICAGO, ILLINOIS 60626
Telephone: 773-882-4912
Email: info@entertainmentlawchicago.com
URL: http://www.entertainmentlawchicago.com

Entertainment Law, Entertainment Contracts, Motion Picture Production and Distribution, Music Copyright, Music Law, Music Licensing, Art Law, Publishing Law, Intellectual Property, Copyrights, Trademarks, Licensing Agreement.

DONALD R. SIMON, born Joplin, Missouri, November 23, 1972; admitted to bar, 2003, Illinois. *Education:* Missouri Southern State University (B.A., 1999); John Marshall Law School (J.D., 2002; LL.M., Intellectual Property, 2003). *Member:* Chicago, Illinois State and American Bar Associations. ***PRACTICE AREAS:*** Entertainment Law; Entertainment Contracts; Motion Picture Production and Distribution; Music Copyright; Music Law; Music Licensing; Art Law; Publishing Law; Intellectual Property; Copyrights; Trademarks. ***Email:*** dsimon@entertainmentlawchicago.com

ENTWISTLE & CAPPUCCI LLC

123 N. WACKER DRIVE, SUITE 1800
CHICAGO, ILLINOIS 60606
Telephone: 312-474-7938
Facsimile: 312-474-7898
URL: http://www.entwistle-law.com

Austin, Texas Office: 98 San Jacinto Boulevard, Suite 1300, 78701. Telephone: 512-703-5705. Facsimile: 512-476-5139.
Florham Park, New Jersey Office: 30 Columbia Turnpike, P.O. Box 95, 07982. Telephone: 973-236-0666. Facsimile: 973-236-9565.
New York, New York Office: 299 Park Avenue, 14th Floor, 10171. Telephone: 212-894-7200. Facsimile: 212-894-7272.
Tallahassee, Florida Office: 400 North Meridian Street, 32301. Telephone: 850-222-9886. Facsimile: 850-671-4402.
Washington D.C. Office: 1735 New York Avenue, NW, 20006. Telephone: 202-661-3960. Facsimile: 202-331-1024.

General Corporate Practice, Commercial Litigation, Complex Business and Securities Litigation, Securities and Antitrust Class Action Litigation, Employment and Labor Law and Litigation, Insurance and Reinsurance Law and Litigation, Bankruptcy, Insolvency and Workouts, Executive Compensation, Estate Litigation and Administration, Commercial Transactions, Cyber Law and Intellectual Property and Product Liability Litigation.

CRAIG E. NELSON, admitted to bar, 1991, Illinois. *Education:* University of Notre Dame (B.B.A., 1981); University of Houston (M.B.A., 1987); University of Texas School of Law (J.D., 1991). (Resident). ***Email:*** cenelson@uhlaw.com

RICHARD E. NAWRACAJ, born 1968; admitted to bar, 1993, Illinois; 2002, registered to practice before U.S. Patent and Trademark Office. *Education:* University of Illinois (B.S., 1990); Loyola University School of Law (J.D., 1993); Northwestern University (M.B.A., 1999). ***PRACTICE AREAS:*** Intellectual Property; Corporate Law; Business Transactions; Commercial Litigation. ***Email:*** rnawracaj@entwistle-law.com

EPSTEIN BECKER & GREEN, P.C.

150 NORTH MICHIGAN AVENUE, SUITE 420
CHICAGO, ILLINOIS 60601-7553
Telephone: 312-499-1400
Facsimile: 312-845-1998
Email: martindale@ebglaw.com
URL: http://www.ebglaw.com

New York, N.Y. Office: 250 Park Avenue. Telephone: 212-351-4500.
Washington, D.C. Office: 1227 25th Street, N.W., Suite 700. Telephone: 202-861-0900.
San Francisco, California Office: One California Street, 26th Floor. Telephone: 415-398-3500.

(This Listing Continued)

EPSTEIN BECKER & GREEN, P.C., Chicago—Continued

Los Angeles, California Office: 1875 Century Park East, Suite 500. Telephone: 310-556-8861.
Dallas, Texas Office: Epstein Becker Green Wickliff & Hall, P.C., Lincoln Plaza, 500 North Akard Street, Suite 2700. Telephone: 214-397-4300.
Houston, Texas Office: Epstein Becker Green Wickliff & Hall, P.C., Wells Fargo Plaza, 1000 Louisiana, Suite 5400. Telephone: 713-750-3100.
Stamford, Connecticut Office: One Landmark Square, Suite 1800. Telephone: 203-348-3737.
Newark, New Jersey Office: Two Gateway Center, 12th Floor. Telephone: 973-642-1900.
Atlanta, Georgia Office: Resurgens Plaza, 945 East Paces Ferry Road, Suite 2700. Telephone: 404-923-9000.
Miami, Florida Office: Wachovia Financial Center, 200 South Biscayne Boulevard, Suite 2100. Telephone: 305-982-1520.

General Practice. Corporation, Securities and Commercial Law. Banking, Antitrust. Health Care and Hospital Law. Management Labor Relations and Employee Benefits Law. Equal Employment Opportunity and Affirmative Action Law and Practice. Taxation, Insurance, Government Procurement, Municipal Finance, Real Estate, Political Activities, Legislation and Election Law. Arbitration, Administrative Proceedings, State and Federal Civil and Appellate Practice. Estate Planning and Estate and Trust Administration.

LAW FIRM ALLIANCES/ASSOCIATIONS: **INTERNATIONAL LAWYERS NETWORK**

MEMBERS OF THE FIRM

JULIE BADEL, born Chicago, Illinois, September 14, 1946; admitted to bar, 1977, Illinois, U.S. District Court, Northern District of Illinois including Trial Bar, U.S. District Court, Eastern District of Michigan, U.S. Court of Appeals, 7th and District of Columbia Circuits, U.S. Supreme Court. *Education:* Knox College and Columbia College (B.A., 1967); DePaul University (J.D., summa cum laude, 1977). Pi Gamma Mu. Member, Writing Staff, 1975-1976 and Note and Comment Editor, 1976-1977, DePaul Law Review. Co-Author: "Hospital Restructuring: Employment Law Pitfalls," Pluribus Press and American College of Hospital Administrators, 1985, chapter author: Employers' Tax (Unemployment Insurance), Matthew Bender, 1985. *Member:* Chicago and American Bar Associations. ***REPORTED CASES:*** Ransom v. CSC Consulting, Inc., 217 F.3d 467 (7th Cir. 2000)(lack of direct evidence of age discrimination); Randle v. LaSalle Telecommunications, 876 F.2d 563 (7th Cir. 1989)(establishing the standard for direct evidence in discrimination cases). ***PRACTICE AREAS:*** Labor and Employment. ***Email:*** jbadel@ebglaw.com

STEPHEN R. DRAKE, admitted to bar, 1996, Idaho; 1997, Oregon; 1998, Colorado (Not admitted in Illinois). *Education:* Albertson College of Idaho (B.A., cum laude, 1991); Willamette University (J.D., cum laude, 1996). ***PRACTICE AREAS:*** Corporate; Securities Law; Biotechnology. ***Email:*** sdrake@ebglaw.com

LOLA MIRANDA HALE, born 1944; admitted to bar, 1969, Illinois. *Education:* Albertus Magnus College (B.A., 1965); Fordham University (J.D., 1968). Author: "Private Placement of Securities," published by Matthew Bender, 1988 (Last Revised 2002); "Exemptions From Registration Under Federal Law" (Securities Law Handbook 2002, Illinois Institute for Continuing Legal Education); "Securities Laws and the Internet" (Securities Law Handbook 2002, Illinois Institute for Continuing Legal Education); "New SEC Attorney Conduct Rules," (Supplement Securities Law Handbook 2003, Illinois Institute for Continuing Legal Education); "NYSE and NASDAQ Corporate Governance Proposals," (Supplement Securities Law Handbook, 2003, Illinois Insitute for Continuing Legal Education); "Beyond the Stock Issues: Securities Law Implications for Public Companies on the Internet," (E-Commerce Laws: "New Rules for a New Way of Doing Business," 2000, Illinois Institute for Continuing Legal Education); "Federal and State Securities Law Implications of Buying and Selling Businesses," (Buying and Selling Businesses Handbook, 1994, 1996 and 1998 Supplements, Illinois Institute for Continuing Legal Education); "Use of the Internet for Securities Offerings, Web Based Securities Exchanges and Electronic Disclosure Dissemination," (Securities Law Handbook 1997 Illinois Institute for Continuing Legal Education); "Introduction to Exempt Private Financing," 1997 Supplement (Securities Law Practice Handbook first published 1991, Illinois Institute for Continuing Legal Education); "Private Offering Exemptions Under Federal Law 1997 Supplement (Securities Law Practice Handbook first published 1991, Illinois Institute for Continuing Education); Chapter, "Federal and State Securities Law Considerations," Buying and Selling Businesses, 1992 (Last Revised 1996); Chapter, "Regulation A: Small Business Financing Exemption," 1997 Supplement (Securities Law Handbook first published 1991), published by the Institute of Continuing Legal Education of the Illinois Bar; "Identifying Securities Transactions and the Lawyers' Roles," (Chicago Bar Association Continuing Legal Education Program, 1988); "Common Pitfalls of Private Offerings, Securities Law Update," Illinois Institute of Continuing Legal Education, 1990; State Chapter: Regulation of Broker-Dealers and Agents in Private Offerings, published by the Practicing Law Institute, 1986; "Use of Regulation D by Reporting Companies and Related Recently Proposed Amendments to Regulation D," presented March 1987 to the American Society of Corporate Secretaries, Chicago Regional Group. Program Moderator and Faculty Member: Lawyers' Responsibilities in Securities Transactions, presented as part of the Continuing Legal Education Program of The Chicago Bar Association, 1988. Lecturer: "New SEC Rules for Attorneys Appearing and Practising Before SEC," Illinois Institute for Continuing Legal Education, 2003; "NYSE and NASDAQ Corporate Governance Proposals," Illinois Institute for Continuing Legal Education, 2003; "Raising Capital on the Internet: Opportunities and Risks for Lawyers and Their Clients," Chicago Bar Association, 1997. Author/Lecturer: American Conference Institute, Employee Stock Ownership Plans - "Securities Law Considerations," 1994. Lecturer and Author of Chapter: "Legal Access to U.S. Capital Markets by non-United States Companies," Center for International Legal Studies Seminar; "Globalizing Capital Markets: Cross-Border Financing and Access to Equity Funds," (Austria, 1995). Lecturer, 3rd Annual W. McNeil Kennedy Securities Law Seminar 1990. Lecturer and Author of Chapter: "Raising Capital," Corporation Law Seminar, Chicago Bar Association, 1991 (last revised 1994). Lecturer: "Blue Sky Laws," 1986 and 1988 Practicing Law Institute Seminar. Member: Executive Committee, 1990, 2001 and 2003; Planning Committee, 1991-2002, Ray Garrett Jr. Corporate and Securities Institute. *Member:* Chicago (Chair, 1988-1989 and Member, Securities Law Committee, 1976—; Member, 1976— and Subcommittee Chair, 1984-1985, Registration and Reporting, Section 16 Matters and Accounting Matters Subcommittee of the Securities Law Committee, 1978-1979; Sub-Committee Chair, 1934 Act Registration and Reports, 1984-1985; Subcommittee Chair, Exemptions from Securities Act of 1933, 1985-1987; Member, Corporation Law Committee, 1976—), Illinois State and American (Member: Corporation, Banking and Business Law Section; Federal Regulation of Securities Committee; Small Business Committee) Bar Associations; Latin American Bar Association. ***LANGUAGES:*** Spanish. ***PRACTICE AREAS:*** Corporate Law; Securities. ***Email:*** lhale@ebglaw.com

PAUL C. MILTONBERGER, born Huntington, Indiana, June 23, 1958; admitted to bar, 1983, Arizona; 1989, Illinois; U.S. District Court, Northern District of Illinois including Trial Bar. *Education:* University of Illinois (B.A., 1980; J.D., cum laude, 1983). ***PRACTICE AREAS:*** Litigation. ***Email:*** pmiltonberger@ebglaw.com

DIANE J. ROMA-KUTZ, admitted to bar, 1982, Illinois. *Education:* Western Illinois University (B.S., with honors); Northern Illinois University (J.D., with honors, 1981); Loyola University, Chicago (LL.M, 1994). Member: Child Advocacy, Executive Committee; Cook County Child Advocacy Board; Food and Drug Law Institute; Health Care Compliance Association; National Health Care Compliance Association. *Member:* American Bar Association (Member, Health Care Law Committee); American Health Lawyers Association (Vice Chair, Managed Care and Integrated Delivery Systems, 1998—); National Health Lawyers Association. ***PRACTICE AREAS:*** Health Law. ***Email:*** dromakutz@ebglaw.com

MICHAEL T. ROUMELL, born Detroit, Michigan, June 3, 1954; admitted to bar, 1981, Illinois, U.S. District Court, Northern District of Illinois including Trial Bar; U.S. Court of Appeals, 7th Circuit. *Education:* University of Michigan (B.A., magna cum laude, 1976); University of Detroit (M.B.A., 1978; J.D., cum laude, 1981). Author: "What Every Manager Needs to Know About Sexual Harassment," Amacom, 1999 Ed.; "Employee Committees," Labor Law Handbook, Illinois Institute for Continuing Legal Education, 2001 Ed. . *Member:* American Bar Association; College of Labor and Employment Lawyers. ***REPORTED CASES:*** Mein vs. Masonite Corporation, 485 N.E.2d 312 (Ill. S.Ct. 1985) (Leading Illinois case mandating administrative remedies for statutory state employment discrimination claims and prohibiting independent court actions). ***PRACTICE AREAS:*** Labor and Employment; Litigation. ***Email:*** mroumell@ebglaw.com

PETER A. STEINMEYER, born Texas City, Texas, August 2, 1965; admitted to bar, 1990, Missouri; 1991, U.S. District Court, Eastern District of Missouri; 1993, Illinois and U.S. District Court, Northern District of Illinois; 1997 Trial Bar; 1995, U.S. District Court, Western District of Michigan and U.S. Court of Appeals, Seventh Circuit; 1999, U.S. District Court, Southern District of Illinois and Northern District of Indiana; 2000, U.S. Supreme Court; 2003, U.S. District Court, Central District of Illinois. *Education:* University of Virginia (B.A., 1987); University of Chicago (J.D., 1990). *Member:* Chicago and American Bar Associations; Chicago Council of Lawyers (Board Member, 2002—). ***REPORTED CASES:*** Contempo Design v. Chicago & N.E.IL Carpenters, 226 F.3d 535 (7th Cir. 2000) (en banc). ***PRACTICE AREAS:*** Labor and Employment Law; ERISA Litigation. ***Email:*** psteinmeyer@ebglaw.com

HANS U. STUCKI, born Spiez, Switzerland, 1948; admitted to bar, 1974, Ohio; 1983, Illinois. *Education:* Ohio State University (B.A., 1970); University of Notre Dame Law School (J.D., 1974). Frequent writer and speaker on Alternate Dispute Resolution Systems and Litigation Case Cycle Management/Cost Controls. Former Chair, National Litigation Committee, Association of Corporate Counsel, 1992-1996. Member of the Year, Association of Corporate Counsel, 1995. *Member:* American Bar Association; Association of Corporate Counsel. [U.S. Marine Corps, 1969-1970]. ***LANGUAGES:*** German. ***PRACTICE AREAS:*** Litigation; Labor and Employment. ***Email:*** hstucki@ebglaw.com

SENIOR ATTORNEYS

MICHAEL P. BUTLER, admitted to bar, 1994, Illinois; 1995, Texas; U.S. Supreme Court; U.S. Court of Appeals, Fifth, Seventh and Tenth Circuits; U.S. District Court, Northern District of Illinois including Trial Bar, Central District of Illinois, Northern District of Indiana and Northern, Southern, Eastern and Western Districts of Texas. *Education:* Rice University (B.A., 1991); University of Illinois (J.D., 1994). Member, College of the State Bar of Texas, 1998-2000. *Member:* Chicago and Illinois State (Member, Sections on Labor and Employment Law and Appellate Law) Bar Associations; State Bar of Texas. ***PRACTICE AREAS:*** Labor and Employment Law; Business Litigation. ***Email:*** mbutler@ebglaw.com

HEATHER FESKO, admitted to bar, 1996, Indiana; 2000, Illinois. *Education:* DePauw University (B.A., 1993); Indiana University (J.D., 1996). *Member:* Indiana State Bar Association; American Health Lawyers Association. ***PRACTICE AREAS:*** Health Law. ***Email:*** hfesko@ebglaw.com

ASSOCIATES

AMY DOW, born Bloomington, Illinois, December 14, 1973; admitted to bar, 2004, Illinois; 2005, U.S. District Court, Northern District of Illinois. *Education:* University of Arizona (B.S., Microbiology, magna cum laude, 1996); Northwestern University (J.D., cum laude, 2004). ***PRACTICE AREAS:*** Health Law. ***Email:*** adow@ebglaw.com

CATHERINE KATILIUS, admitted to bar, 2004, Illinois; 2005, U.S. District Court, Northern District of Illinois and U.S. District Court, Northern District of Indiana. *Education:* Michigan State University (B.A., Business Administration-Marketing, 1988); Wayne State University (B.S.N., summa cum laude, 1991); University of Michigan (M.S., Acute and Critical Care, 1997); Loyola University, Chicago (J.D., cum laude, 2004; Health Law Certificate, 2004). Certified Nurse Practitioner, Acute & Critical Care, 1997. *Member:* Chicago and American Bar Associations; American Health Lawyers Association; National Association of Women Lawyers. ***PRACTICE AREAS:*** Health. ***Email:*** ckatilius@ebglaw.com

TANJA SAMARDZIJA, born Chicago, Illinois, September 20, 1974; admitted to bar, 2000, Illinois. *Education:* University of Illinois (B.S., Economics, 1996); Loyola University, Chicago (J.D., 2000). *Member:* Chicago and American Bar Associations. ***PRACTICE AREAS:*** Commercial Litigation; Labor and Employment. ***Email:*** tsamardzija@ebglaw.com

(This Listing Continued)

JASON SCHMIDT, born January 18, 1974; admitted to bar, 1999, Illinois. *Education:* University of Michigan (B.A., 1996; J.D., cum laude, 1999). ***PRACTICE AREAS:*** Labor and Employment. ***Email:*** jschmidt@ebglaw.com

(For other Personnel and Biographical Data, see Professional Biographies at Los Angeles and San Francisco, California, Stamford, Connecticut, Washington, D.C., Atlanta, Georgia, Newark, New Jersey, New York, New York, Dallas and Houston, Texas Offices)

MICHAEL H. ERDE & ASSOCIATES P.C.

Established in 1980

4801 WEST PETERSON AVENUE
SUITE 412
CHICAGO, ILLINOIS 60646
Telephone: 773-286-3800
Toll Free: 866-378-3800
Fax: 773-286-3504
URL: http://www.erdelaw.com
Email: MHErde@aol.com
URL: http://www.lawyers.com/erdelaw

Elder Law, Probate, Wills, Trusts and Estates, Guardianship, Asset Protection, Disabilities, Special Needs Trusts, Living Trusts.

FIRM PROFILE: Michael H. Erde & Associates, P.C. has been serving clients and their families since 1980. Clients receive comprehensive estate planning advice with respect to elder law issues, wills, living trusts, special needs trusts, disabilities and asset protection. The firm also offers experienced assistance with guardianships, probate estates, trust administration and other post-mortem matters.

MICHAEL H. ERDE, born Chicago, Illinois, April 28, 1943; admitted to bar, 1969, Illinois. *Education:* Washington University (B.S., 1965); University of Illinois (J.D., 1968); John Marshall Law School (Master, Tax Credits, 1974). Real Estate Broker, Illinois, 1979—. Author: "New Developments in Estate Planning, Probate, Taxes," Northwest Suburban Bar Journal, 1986; "Trustees Individuals or Institutions," Northwest Suburban Bar Journal, 1985; "Elder Abuse"; "Initiating Probate"; "Medicaid Transfer Strategies." Probate Chairman, Northwest Suburban Bar, 1986—. Lecturer, Elder Law, Estate Planning & Asset Protection on Radio, TV, Cruise Ships, Professional Education Systems Institute, Lorman & National Business Institute and Half Moon Company. Guardian Ad Litem, Lake County, Illinois, 1990. Director and Counsel: Edgebrook/Sauganash Chamber of Commerce, 1994—; Special Probate Administrator; Lake County Apartment Owners Association. Instructor, Seminars on Wills & Trusts, Adult Education and Professional Groups, 1972—. Appointed Probate Court Special Administrator and Guardian ad Litem. *Member:* Chicago (Probate, Trust Assembly; Chairman, Elder Law and Asset Protection Committees) and Illinois State (Member, Section Council Elder Law Committee) Bar Associations; Northwest Suburban Bar Association (Chairman of Wills, Trusts, Probate and Elder Law Committees); National Academy of Elder Law Attorneys (Director, Chicago Chapter); Illinois Alliance for Aging. Director and Secretary, Greater Northshore Estate and Financial Planning Council. ***SPECIAL AGENCIES:*** Agent, Attorneys Title Guaranty Company; Former Director, Irene Josselyn Center for Mental Health. ***PRACTICE AREAS:*** Estate Planning and Elder Law (48%, 175); Probate (25%, 70); Guardianship (20%, 30); Real Estate-Leases (2%, 12); Corporate-Business (5%, 100). ***Email:*** mherde@aol.com

JENNIFER HAHN AXELSEN, born Park Ridge, Illinois, May 31, 1969; admitted to bar, 1993, Illinois. *Education:* University of Illinois (B.S., 1990); DePaul University (J.D., 1993). Certified Trust and Financial Advisor (CTFA), 1999—. Member: ABA National Trust School, 1997; ABA National Graduate Trust School, 1999. *Member:* Illinois State Bar Association (Member, Trusts & Estates Section). ***PRACTICE AREAS:*** Estate Administration (60%); Guardianship (30%); Trust Administration (10%). ***Email:*** jenniferaxelsen@sbcglobal.net

REPRESENTATIVE CLIENTS: Devon Bank; Harris Bank; La Salle Bank; Waukegan Bank; Guaranty Title & Trust; Northern Trust Co.

EVAN LAW GROUP, LLC

566 WEST ADAMS, SUITE 350
CHICAGO, ILLINOIS 60661
Telephone: 312-876-1400
Fax: 978-268-8715
URL: http://www.evanlawfirmgroup.com

Intellectual Property.

MEMBER OF THE FIRM

PAUL E. RAUCH, PH.D., admitted to bar, 1998, Virginia; 2000, Illinois; U.S. Court of Appeals, Fourth Circuit; registered to practice before U.S. Patent and Trademark Office. *Education:* Oberlin College (B.A., with high honors, 1986); Cornell University (M.A., 1988; Ph.D., 1991); George Washington University (J.D., with honors, 1998). ***Email:*** paul.rauch@evanlawgroup.com

JONATHAN M. BLANCHARD, PH.D., born Fort Campbell, Kentucky, January 24, 1966; admitted to bar, 2000, Kentucky; 2001, Illinois, U.S. District Court, Northern District of Illinois and U.S. Court of Appeals for the Federal Circuit; registered to practice before U.S. Patent and Trademark Office. *Education:* Centre College of Kentucky (B.S., 1990); Syracuse University (M.S., 1992); Washington University (A.M., 1995; Ph.D., 1997); University of Kentucky College of Law (J.D., 2000). Fellow, Washington University. *Member:* Chicago and American Bar Associations; American Chemical Society; American Intellectual Property Law Association; Association of University Technology Managers. ***REPORTED CASES:*** In re Doyle, 293 F.3d 1355 (Fed. Cir. 2002). ***PRACTICE AREAS:*** Intellectual Property. ***Email:*** jonathan.blanchard@evanlawgroup.com

(This Listing Continued)

PATENT AGENT

JONATHAN P. TAYLOR, PH.D. *Education:* Bob Jones University (B.S. in Chemistry, 1995); Pennsylvania State University (Ph.D. in Chemistry, 2000) registered to practice before U.S. Patent and Trademark Office. *Member:* American Intellectual Property Law Association; Intellectual Property Association of Chicago; American Chemical Society (Division of Polymer Chemistry, Polymeric Materials: Science and Engineering, and Chemistry and Law); American Association for the Advancement of Science ***PRACTICE AREAS:*** Chemistry; Polymers; Semiconductor Technology; Consumer Protection. ***Email:*** jonathan.taylor@evanlawgroup.com

EVANS, LOEWENSTEIN, SHIMANOVSKY & MOSCARDINI, LTD.

Established in 1978

130 S. JEFFERSON STREET, SUITE 500
CHICAGO, ILLINOIS 60661
Telephone: 312-782-1850
Fax: 312-466-0819
URL: http://www.elsm.com

General Practice. Corporate, Federal and State Taxation, Estate Planning and Probate, Real Estate, Litigation in State and Federal Courts, Partnerships, Tort and Personal Injury Law, Mechanics Liens, Employee Benefits, Family Law, Commercial Litigation, Insurance and Labor.

FIRM PROFILE: The firm was founded by Arthur H. Evans in 1978; Daniel M. Loewenstein joined the firm in 1989, followed by David L. Shimanovsky in 1992 and Frank Moscardini, Jr., in 1994. At its inception, the firm concentrated in federal income tax, real estate, corporate, estate planning and probate matters and has now grown into a general practice firm providing a full range of legal services. In addition to the foregoing, Evans, Loewenstein, Shimanovsky & Moscardini, Ltd. is the Illinois Provider law firm for Pre-Paid Legal Services, Inc.

ARTHUR H. EVANS, born Chicago, Illinois, May 17, 1949; admitted to bar, 1974, Illinois and U.S. District Court, Northern District of Illinois; 1976, U.S. Tax Court. *Education:* University of Wisconsin-Madison; University of Illinois (B.S., Accounting, 1971); DePaul University (J.D., 1974). Certified Public Accountant, Illinois, 1971. *Member:* Chicago (Member, Tax Committee, 1976-1979), Illinois State and American Bar Associations. ***PRACTICE AREAS:*** Corporate; Tax; Estate Planning; Probate; Real Estate. ***Email:*** aevans@elsm.com

DANIEL M. LOEWENSTEIN, born Nashville, Tennessee, June 19, 1954; admitted to bar, 1980, Illinois and U.S. District Court, Northern District of Illinois. *Education:* Washington University (A.B., cum laude, 1976; J.D., 1980). Staff Member, Primary Editor, Urban Law Annual, 1979-1980. *Member:* Chicago, Illinois State and American (Member, Real Property Section) Bar Associations. ***PRACTICE AREAS:*** Real Estate; Business; Corporate Law. ***Email:*** dloewenstein@elsm.com

DAVID L. SHIMANOVSKY, born Chicago, Illinois, June 16, 1963; admitted to bar, 1988, Illinois and U.S. District Court, Northern District of Illinois. *Education:* Illinois State University (B.S., 1985); John Marshall Law School (J.D., 1988). Moot Court Council. Member, Graduate of the Fred Lane Trial Technique Course. *Member:* Chicago and Illinois State Bar Associations. ***PRACTICE AREAS:*** Civil Litigation; Real Estate; Probate; Corporate Law; Family Law; Tort Law; Employment Law. ***Email:*** dshimanovsky@elsm.com

FRANK A. MOSCARDINI, JR., born Chicago, Illinois, April 20, 1963; admitted to bar, 1988, Illinois and U.S. District Court, Northern District of Illinois. *Education:* DePaul University (B.A., summa cum laude, 1985); Loyola University of Chicago (J.D., 1988). Loyola Law Quarterly on Public Issues. *Member:* Chicago, Illinois State and American Bar Associations. ***PRACTICE AREAS:*** Civil Litigation; Tort Law; Personal Injury; Federal and State Taxation; Real Estate; Mechanics Lien; Estate Planning; Probate; Business and Corporate Law. ***Email:*** fmoscardini@elsm.com

NORA M. HERNANDEZ, born January 28, 1972; admitted to bar, 1998, Illinois. *Education:* Northwestern University (B.S., 1994); University of Iowa (J.D., 1997). ***LANGUAGES:*** Spanish. ***Email:*** nhernandez@elsm.com

FAGELHABER LLC

Established in 1962

55 EAST MONROE STREET, 40TH FLOOR
CHICAGO, ILLINOIS 60603
Telephone: 312-346-7500
FAX: 312-580-2201
URL: http://www.fagelhaber.com

Bankruptcy, Reorganization and Creditors' Rights, Business Law, Commercial Finance and Secured Transactions, Construction Law, Corporate and Securities, Corporate Governance, E-Commerce, Employee Benefits and Executive Compensation, Employment Law, Environmental, Equipment Leasing, Finance and Structured Finance, Financial Institutions, Financial Services, Governmental Relations, Health Care, Insurance Regulation, Intellectual Property, Intellectual Property Litigation, Investment Management, Licensing and Distribution, Litigation and Dispute Resolution, Mergers and Acquisitions, Private Equity, Public Finance, Real Estate, Real Estate Development, Real Estate Finance, Real Estate Litigation, Real Estate Taxation, Securities, Tax Planning and Litigation, Taxation of Financial Products, Technology, Trusts and Estates, Taxation, Estate Planning and Wealth Preservation.

FIRM PROFILE: The Firm now, FagelHaber LLC, was founded in 1962 and continues to be engaged primarily in general business representation, including planning, organization, transactions, and litigation. Our clients are best served when their lawyers are an integral tool in developing and implementing their business plans and tactics. Our strength is our ability to

(This Listing Continued)

FAGELHABER LLC, Chicago—Continued

draw upon the wide-ranging knowledge and experience of our lawyers in multiple practice areas. We collaborate with our clients, then formulate and implement creative strategies to achieve their objectives, all within budget. The clients of FagelHaber receive solutions, not surprises. We measure success not only by the results, but by our clients' satisfaction.

MEMBERS OF FIRM

ALLEN J. FAGEL, born Chicago, Illinois, March 7, 1938; admitted to bar, 1962, Illinois and U.S. District Court, Northern District of Illinois; 1963, U.S. Court of Appeals, 7th Circuit and U.S. Tax Court; 1989, Wisconsin. *Education:* University of Illinois (B.S., 1959); University of Illinois and DePaul University (J.D., 1962). Co-Author: "Selling on Consignment," Business Credit, October, 1996; "New Life for an Old Remedy — Reclamation from Insolvent Buyers and Bankruptcy Debtors," Business Credit, January 1998. Editor and Co-Author: "Secured Transactions," Credit Research Foundation, 2000; "Bad Check Laws — A 50 State Guide of Rights and Remedies," Credit Research Foundation, 2002; *Member:* Chicago, Illinois State and American (Member, Section of Corporation, Banking and Business Law, 1965—; Member, Committees on: Commercial Transactions Litigation, 1983—; Uniform Commercial Code, 1987—; Member, Subcommittee Secured Transactions, 1985—) Bar Associations. ***PRACTICE AREAS:*** Commercial Transactions; Asset Based Finance Law. **Email:** afagel@fagelhaber.com

JOEL A. HABER, born New York, N.Y., September 17, 1943; admitted to bar, 1967, Wisconsin; 1968, Illinois; 1973, U.S. Supreme Court and U.S. Court of Appeals, 7th Circuit; 1969, U.S. District Court, Northern District of Illinois. *Education:* State University of New York at Buffalo (B.S., 1964); University of Wisconsin (J.D., 1967). Formerly with Securities and Exchange Commission, 1967-1970. ***PRACTICE AREAS:*** Corporate Transactions; Securities Law; Insurance Regulation. **Email:** jhaber@fagelhaber.com

FLOYD BABBITT, born Chicago, Illinois, November 24, 1941; admitted to bar, 1973, Illinois and U.S. District Court, Northern District of Illinois; U.S. Court of Appeals, Seventh Circuit. *Education:* University of Missouri; North Park College (B.A., cum laude); Illinois Institute of Technology, Chicago-Kent College of Law (J.D.). Assistant U.S. Attorney, Northern District of Illinois, Civil Division, 1973-1977. *Member:* Chicago, Federal and Seventh Circuit Bar Associations; Commercial Law League of America. ***PRACTICE AREAS:*** Commercial Litigation; Bankruptcy; Creditor Rights. **Email:** fbabbitt@fagelhaber.com

DENNIS E. QUAID, admitted to bar, 1970, Illinois. *Education:* University of Illinois at Chicago (B.A., 1967); DePaul University (J.D., 1970). Phi Alpha Delta. *Member:* American Bar Association (Member, Business Bankruptcy Committee); American Bankruptcy Institute; Commercial Law League of America; Turnaround Management Association. ***PRACTICE AREAS:*** Creditors' Rights; Bankruptcy; Workouts; Commercial Litigation. **Email:** dquaid@fagelhaber.com

GLEN T. KEYSOR, born Lynn, Massachusetts, May 20, 1951; admitted to bar, 1976, Illinois and U.S. Court of Appeals, 7th Circuit; 1977, U.S. District Court, Northern District of Illinois including Trial Bar; 1990, Wisconsin. *Education:* University of Illinois (B.S., 1973); John Marshall Law School (J.D., with distinction, 1976). Member, The John Marshall Journal of Practice and Procedure, 1975-1976. *Member:* Chicago Bar Association (Member, Sections on: Corporate, Banking and Business Law; Litigation). ***PRACTICE AREAS:*** Real Estate Law; General Litigation; Construction Law. **Email:** gkeysor@fagelhaber.com

WALTER D. CUPKOVIC, born Cleveland, Ohio, July 30, 1952; admitted to bar, 1979, Illinois and U.S. District Court, Northern District of Illinois. *Education:* Northwestern University (B.A., 1974); Loyola University (J.D., 1979). *Member:* Chicago Bar Association. ***PRACTICE AREAS:*** Commercial Real Estate Law. **Email:** wcupkovic@fagelhaber.com

JOHN J. CULLERTON, born Chicago, Illinois, October 28, 1948; admitted to bar, 1974, Illinois. *Education:* Loyola University (B.A., 1970; J.D., 1974). Member of The Illinois General Assembly, 1979 —. Illinois State Senator, 1991 —. State Representative, Illinois House of Representatives, 1979-1991. Legislative Committees: Democratic Spokesman, Judiciary; Insurance, Financial Institutions, Rules. *Member:* Illinois State Bar Association. ***PRACTICE AREAS:*** Real Estate Taxation; Government Relations. **Email:** jcullerton@fagelhaber.com

RICHARD H. CHAPMAN, born Chicago, Illinois, November 17, 1957; admitted to bar, 1982, Illinois, U.S. Court of Appeals, Seventh and Ninth Circuits, U.S. District Court, Northern District of Illinois, including Trial Bar and U.S. District Court, Eastern District of Michigan. *Education:* University of Illinois (B.A., with high distinction in History, 1979); Loyola University (J.D., 1982). Student Articles Editor and Member, Loyola University Law Journal, 1981-1982. Co-Editor, The Trial Lawyer's Guide, (1997-2000) West. *Member:* Chicago Bar Association (Member, Board of Managers, 1994-1996). ***PRACTICE AREAS:*** Civil Litigation. **Email:** rhchapman@fagelhaber.com

HOWARD M. BERRINGTON, born Chicago, Illinois, August 31, 1953; admitted to bar, 1978, Illinois and U.S. District Court, Northern District of Illinois. *Education:* University of Illinois, Chicago (B.A., with honors, 1975); DePaul University College of Law (J.D., 1978). ***PRACTICE AREAS:*** Corporate Transactions; Commercial Finance and Creditor Rights. **Email:** hberrington@fagelhaber.com

NORTON N. GOLD, born Chicago, Illinois, February 9, 1934; admitted to bar, 1963, Illinois and U.S. District Court, Northern District of Illinois; 1974, U.S. Tax Court. *Education:* University of Illinois (B.S., with honors, 1955); DePaul University (J.D., 1962). Certified Public Accountant, Illinois, 1956. *Member:* Chicago, Illinois State and American Bar Associations. ***PRACTICE AREAS:*** Business Transactions; Corporate Taxation; Partnership and Limited Liability Company Tax Issues; Individual Taxation; Estate Planning. **Email:** ngold@fagelhaber.com

JAMES M. DRAKE, born October 18, 1961; admitted to bar, 1987, Illinois and U.S. District Court, Northern District of Illinois. *Education:* University of Michigan (B.A., 1983); DePaul University (J.D., 1987). Member, De Paul Law Review. ***PRACTICE AREAS:*** General Corporate Law; Intellectual Property Law; International Law. **Email:** jdrake@fagelhaber.com

VICTOR A. DES LAURIER, born Chicago, Illinois, August 6, 1965; admitted to bar, 1993, Illinois. *Education:* Northern Illinois University (B.S., 1987); DePaul University (J.D., with honors). Order of the Coif. ***PRACTICE AREAS:*** Commercial Finance; Workouts; Bankruptcy. **Email:** vdeslaurier@fagelhaber.com

EDWARD L. FILER, born South Bend, Indiana, November 26, 1964; admitted to bar, 1991, Illinois and Wisconsin. *Education:* University of Michigan (B.A., 1987); University of Wisconsin (J.D., 1991). *Member:* Chicago Bar Association and American Bar Associations; State Bar of Wisconsin; Society of Illinois Construction Attorneys. ***PRACTICE AREAS:*** Complex Commercial Litigation; Construction Law; Real Estate Law; Insurance Law. **Email:** elfiler@fagelhaber.com

ALAN JAY GOLDSTEIN, born Chicago, Illinois, May 28, 1959; admitted to bar, 1984, Illinois, U.S. District Court, Northern District of Illinois including Trial Bar and U.S. Court of Appeals, 7th Circuit. *Education:* University of Illinois (B.A., 1981); DePaul University (J.D., 1984). Recipient, American Jurisprudence Award. Law Clerk to Justice Dom J. Rizzi, Illinois Appellate Court, 1985. ***PRACTICE AREAS:*** Business Law; Corporate Health Care; Professional Licensure Compliance and Defense. **Email:** agoldstein@fagelhaber.com

CHRISTINA BROTTO, born Hickory Hills, Illinois, September 21, 1969; admitted to bar, 1995, Illinois. *Education:* Loyola University. *Member:* Chicago and American Bar Associations. ***PRACTICE AREAS:*** Commercial Real Estate. **Email:** cbrotto@fagelhaber.com

PATRICK J. CULLERTON, born St. Charles, Illinois, March 12, 1964; admitted to bar, 1990, Illinois. *Education:* Eastern Illinois University (B.A., 1986); Loyola University of Chicago (J.D., 1990). *Member:* Chicago Bar Association. ***PRACTICE AREAS:*** Real Estate Taxation; Government Relations. **Email:** pcullerton@fagelhaber.com

ROBERT H. LANG, born Wichita, Kansas, June 27, 1969; admitted to bar, 1994, Illinois; 1997, Federal Trial Bar. *Education:* University of Illinois (B.A., 1991); Wake Forest University (J.D., 1994). *Member:* Arab-American Bar Association. ***LANGUAGES:*** Spanish. ***REPORTED CASES:*** Krueger vs. Oberto, 309 Ill. App. 3d 358 (2d Dist 1999). ***PRACTICE AREAS:*** Commercial Litigation; Real Estate Litigation; Bankruptcy Litigation; Intellectual Property Litigation. **Email:** rlang@fagelhaber.com

ARTHUR B. STERNBERG, admitted to bar, 1980, Illinois and U.S. District Court, Northern District of Illinois including Trial Bar; U.S. Court of Appeals, 4th, 7th and 9th Circuits. *Education:* University of Illinois (J.D., 1980). ***PRACTICE AREAS:*** Labor and Employment; Litigation. **Email:** asternberg@fagelhaber.com

BARRY L. FISCHER, born May 29, 1968; admitted to bar, 1993, Illinois. *Education:* University of Sussex (1989); Northwestern University (B.A., 1990); University of Michigan (J.D., 1993). Recipient: Book Award, Contracts; Certificate of Merit, International Law Society; Certificate of Merit, Environmental Law Society. Four-Year National Merit Scholarship Winner. *Member:* Chicago and American Bar Associations. ***PRACTICE AREAS:*** Corporate; Finance. **Email:** bfischer@fagelhaber.com

GARY E. GREEN, admitted to bar, 1988, Illinois; 1989, U.S. District Court, Northern District of Illinois and U.S. Court of Appeals, Seventh Circuit; 1996, U.S. District Court, Central District of Illinois. *Education:* Loyola University (B.A., 1983; M.A., 1985); University of California, Hastings College of the Law (J.D., 1988). *Member:* Chicago and Illinois State Bar Associations; Equipment Leasing Association. ***PRACTICE AREAS:*** Equipment Finance; Banking; Commecial Litigation; Bankruptcy; Real Estate. **Email:** ggreen@fagelhaber.com

TINA M. BIRD, born Valdosta, Georgia, February 19, 1971; admitted to bar, 1996, Illinois and U.S. District Court, Northern District of Illinois. *Education:* University of Florida (B.S., 1993; J.D., 1996). Board Member, University of Florida Law Review, 1995-1996. *Member:* Chicago and American Bar Associations. ***REPORTED CASES:*** Metropolitan Property v. James McHugh, 1999 U.S. District Lexis 16475; Luise, Inc. v. Village of Skokie, 335 Ill. App. 3d 672, 781 N.E.2d 353 (1st Dist. 1992); Bohner v. Ace American Ins. Co., 2005 Ill. App. LEXIS 884 (2nd Dist. 2005). ***PRACTICE AREAS:*** Complex Commercial Litigation; Construction Law; Real Estate Law. **Email:** tbird@fagelhaber.com

DENEAN K. STURINO, admitted to bar, 1996, Illinois and U.S. District Court, Northern District of Illinois; 1997, Wisconsin, U.S. District Court, Eastern District of Wisconsin and U.S. District Court, Central District of Illinois; 1998, U.S. Court of Appeals, Seventh Circuit; 2003, U.S. District Court, Western District of Wisconsin. *Education:* University of Wisconsin-Parkside (B.A., Political Science/Sociology, magna cum laude, 1992); John Marshall Law School (J.D., magna cum laude, 1996). Member, Moot Court. Staff Editor, John Marshall Law Review, 1995-1996. *Member:* Chicago and American Bar Associations; State Bar of Wisconsin; Defense Research Institute; International Association of Lemon Law Administrators. ***PRACTICE AREAS:*** Litigation (100%). **Email:** dsturino@fagelhaber.com

MARK MACIASZ, admitted to bar, 1992, Illinois. *Education:* University of Illinois (B.S., 1989); DePaul University College of Law (J.D., 1992; LL.M., Taxation, 1998). *Member:* Illinois State Bar Association; American Institute of Certified Public Accountants; Illinois Society of Certified Public Accountants. ***PRACTICE AREAS:*** Estate Planning; Tax; Trusts. **Email:** mmaciasz@fagelhaber.com

ASSOCIATES

SEAN D. AUTON, born January 12, 1970; admitted to bar, 1995, Michigan; 2001, Illinois. *Education:* University of Michigan (B.A., 1992; J.D., 1995). ***PRACTICE AREAS:*** Commercial Transactions; Secured Transactions; Corporate Law; Finance; Creditors Rights; Intellectual Property; Copyrights; Licensing; E-Commerce. **Email:** sauton@fagelhaber.com

DAVID R. BASS, born December 3, 1969; admitted to bar, 1996, Illinois. *Education:* Washington University (A.B., 1992); John Marshall Law School (J.D., 1996). ***PRACTICE AREAS:*** Real Estate; Real Estate Taxation. **Email:** dbass@fagelhaber.com

(This Listing Continued)

CHRISTINA M. BERISH, born September 28, 1978; admitted to bar, 2003, Illinois. *Education:* University of Michigan (B.A., 2000; J.D., 2003). ***PRACTICE AREAS:*** Litigation; Bankruptcy. ***Email:*** cberish@fagelhaber.com

DARREN BERTRAM, born October 24, 1973; admitted to bar, 1998, Illinois. *Education:* University of Illinois (B.S., 1995; J.D., magna cum laude, 1998). ***PRACTICE AREAS:*** Litigation. ***Email:*** dbertram@fagelhaber.com

LINDSEY F. BROWN, admitted to bar, 2001, Illinois. *Education:* Stetson University (B.A., 1997); Chicago-Kent College of Law, Illinois Institute of Technology (J.D., 2001). *Member:* Chicago Bar Association. ***PRACTICE AREAS:*** Construction Litigation (100%). ***Email:*** lbrown@fagelhaber.com

RICHARD F. BRUEN, JR., born November 5, 1967; admitted to bar, 1997, Illinois. *Education:* Northern Illinois University (B.S., 1993); DePaul University (J.D., 1997). ***PRACTICE AREAS:*** Labor and Employment; Commercial Litigation; Construction Litigation; Business Torts; Contract Litigation; Tort Defense; Real Estate Litigation; Bankruptcy Litigation. ***Email:*** rbruen@fagelhaber.com

WILLIAM KENT CARTER, born March 1, 1972; admitted to bar, 1997, Illinois. *Education:* University of Illinois (B.A., 1994); Southern Illinois University (J.D., 1997). ***PRACTICE AREAS:*** Commercial Litigation; Banking Law; Bankruptcy; Secured Lending. ***Email:*** wcarter@fagelhaber.com

KATHLEEN T. CUNNINGHAM, admitted to bar, 2002, Illinois. *Education:* DePaul University (B.A., 1995); University of Illinois (J.D., 2002). *Member:* Chicago Bar Association. ***PRACTICE AREAS:*** Real Estate; Land Use.

JOEL S. DALINKA, born November 21, 1970; admitted to bar, 1996, Illinois. *Education:* University of Illinois (B.S., with high honors, 1992); Northwestern University (J.D., cum laude, 1996). ***PRACTICE AREAS:*** General Corporate; Secured Lending. ***Email:*** jdalinka@fagelhaber.com

GEORGIA LOUKAS DEMEROS, born September 6, 1972; admitted to bar, 1998, Illinois. *Education:* Loyola University (B.B.A., 1994); Chicago-Kent College of Law (J.D., 1998; LL.M., Taxation, 2003). ***PRACTICE AREAS:*** Tax; Real Estate; Estate Planning; Trusts. ***Email:*** gdemeros@fagelhaber.com

WILLIAM T. EVELAND, admitted to bar, 2005, Illinois. *Education:* University of North Alabama (B.S., magna cum laude, 1999); Loyola University Chicago (J.D., 2005). *Member:* American, Chicago and Illinois State Bar Associations. ***PRACTICE AREAS:*** Litigation. ***Email:*** weveland@fagelhaber.com

THOMAS BERNARD GOLZ, born May 29, 1950; admitted to bar, 1987, Illinois. *Education:* University of Illinois (B.S., 1971); University of Chicago (M.B.A., 1979); DePaul University (J.D., 1987). ***PRACTICE AREAS:*** Construction Law; Environmental Law. ***Email:*** tgolz@fagelhaber.com

CLINTON P. HANSEN, born April 10, 1972; admitted to bar, 2001, Illinois. *Education:* Valparaiso University (B.S., 1994; J.D., 2001). ***PRACTICE AREAS:*** Creditors Rights; Bankruptcy; Commercial Transactions; Secured Transactions; Real Estate. ***Email:*** chansen@fagelhaber.com

BETH L. HANSHER, born September 26, 1975; admitted to bar, 2000, Illinois and Wisconsin. *Education:* University of Wisconsin-Madison (B.A., with distinction, 1997); University of Wisconsin (J.D., 2000). ***PRACTICE AREAS:*** Litigation. ***Email:*** bhansher@fagelhaber.com

ROBERT N. KAMENSKY, born October 2, 1969; admitted to bar, 1998, Illinois. *Education:* University of Iowa (B.A., 1991); DePaul University (J.D., 1998). ***PRACTICE AREAS:*** Corporate Law; Mergers and Acquisitions; Information Technology Law. ***Email:*** rkamensky@fagelhaber.com

SUSAN M. LORENC, born April 10, 1976; admitted to bar, 2002, Illinois and Wisconsin. *Education:* University of Michigan (B.A., 1998); University of Wisconsin School of Law (J.D., 2002). ***PRACTICE AREAS:*** Litigation; Employment Law. ***Email:*** slorenc@fagehaber.com

JAMES P. MOORHEAD, born 1972; admitted to bar, 1999, Maryland; 2001, District of Columbia; 2002, Illinois. *Education:* Georgetown University (B.A., 1994); Loyola University, Chicago (J.D., 1999). *Member:* Chicago and Maryland State Bar Associations; The District of Columbia Bar. ***PRACTICE AREAS:*** Real Estate; Zoning, Planning and Land Use.

LAUREN NEWMAN, born January 8, 1957; admitted to bar, 1982, Missouri; 1984, Illinois. *Education:* Washington University (A.B., 1979); St. Louis University Law School (J.D., 1982). *Member:* Chicago Bar Association; The Missouri Bar; American Bankruptcy Institute. ***PRACTICE AREAS:*** Bankruptcy; Creditors Rights. ***Email:*** lnewman@fagelhaber.com

MICHELLE G. NOVICK, born January 30, 1967; admitted to bar, 1991, Illinois. *Education:* University of Illinois at Urbana-Champaign (B.S., Finance, with high honors, 1988; J.D., 1991). ***PRACTICE AREAS:*** Insolvency; Bankruptcy; Creditors Rights. ***Email:*** mnovick@fagelhaber.com

JAMES L. OAKLEY, born August 18, 1978; admitted to bar, 2003, Illinois and Wisconsin. *Education:* University of Pennsylvania (B.A., 2000); University of Wisconsin (J.D., 2003). ***PRACTICE AREAS:*** Litigation. ***Email:*** joakley@fagelhaber.com

JACK L. PARRINO, born March 27, 1974; admitted to bar, 2000, Illinois. *Education:* Northwestern University (B.S., 1996); DePaul University (J.D., with honors, 2000). ***Email:*** jparrino@fagelhaber.com

DAVID M. ROWND, born June 4, 1965; admitted to bar, 1991, Illinois. *Education:* Northwestern University (B.A., 1987); Washington University (J.D., 1991). Articles Editor, Washington University Journal of Urban and Contemporary Law, 1990-1991. ***PRACTICE AREAS:*** Commercial Litigation; Business Law; Computer Law; Insurance; Employment Law. ***Email:*** drownd@fagelhaber.com

JAMIE BROOKE SCHWARTZ, born March 27, 1972; admitted to bar, 1997, Illinois. *Education:* University of Wisconsin-Madison (B.A., 1994); Chicago-Kent College of Law (J.D., 1997). ***PRACTICE AREAS:*** Commercial Litigation. ***Email:*** jschwartz@fagelhaber.com

(This Listing Continued)

ADAM C. TOOSLEY, born October 18, 1974; admitted to bar, 2002, Illinois. *Education:* University of Illinois (B.A., 1996; J.D., 2002). *Member:* Chicago Bar Association. ***PRACTICE AREAS:*** Litigation. ***Email:*** atoosley@fagelhaber.com

OF COUNSEL

JAMES P. CHAPMAN, born December 28, 1929; admitted to bar, 1954, Illinois. *Education:* University of Colorado at Boulder (B.A., 1951); Harvard University (LL.B., 1954). Fellow: American College of Trial Lawyers; International Academy of Trial Lawyers; Illinois American College of Trial Lawyers. (Also Practicing Individually). ***Email:*** jamespchapman@aol.com

ROBERT B. CHAPMAN, admitted to bar, 1969, Missouri; 1974, Illinois. *Education:* Indiana University (A.B., 1966; J.D., 1969). Order of the Coif. *Member:* Chicago (Member, Sections on: Corporate Law; Securities, 1981—) and American (Member, Sections on: Business Law; Taxation Law) Bar Associations. [Lt. JAGC, U.S. Navy, 1969-1974]. ***PRACTICE AREAS:*** Corporate; Municipal Finance; Insurance Regulation; Securities Law. ***Email:*** rbchapman@fagelhaber.com

GORDON H. MILLNER, born Chicago, Illinois, March 2, 1934; admitted to bar, 1958, Illinois. *Education:* University of Illinois (B.A., 1955); Northwestern University (J.D., 1958). ***PRACTICE AREAS:*** Real Estate Taxation. ***Email:*** gmillner@fagelhaber.com

MAYNARD B. RUSSELL, born Chicago, Illinois, April 14, 1926; admitted to bar, 1958, Illinois and U.S. District Court, Northern District of Illinois. *Education:* Roosevelt University; University of Illinois (B.S., 1948); DePaul University (J.D., 1958). ***PRACTICE AREAS:*** Real Estate; Corporate Law. ***Email:*** mrussell@fagelhaber.com

---

NANCY FALLON-HOULE, P.C.

CHICAGO, ILLINOIS

(See Downers Grove)

Entrepreneur, Entrepreneurship, Starting a Business, Incorporation, Corporation, Corporations, Limited Liability Company, Limited Liability Companies, LLC, Entity, Partnership, Partnerships, Business Enterprises, Start-Up, Start Up, Early Stage, Early-Stage, Small Business, Business, Emerging Growth, Emerging Company, Corporate, Corporate Law, Corporate Lawyer.

Venture Capital, Raising Capital, Investor, Investing, Angel Investor, Seed Capital, Regulation D, Form D, Rule 506, Rule 504, SCOR, U-7, Form U-7, Business Plan, Business Planning, Disclosure, Due Diligence, Securities Disclosure, Private Placement, Private Offering, Private Offering Memo, Private Offering Memorandum, Private Placement Memo, Private Placement Memorandum, PPM, Subscription Agreement, Investor Agreement, Equity, Equity Financing, Financing, Stock, Shares, Stock Option, Option, Options, Warrants, Stock Offering. Securities Law, Securities Offering, Securities Exemption, Exemption, Exempt Offering, SEC, Securities and Exchange Commission, Securities Registration, Securities Regulation, Registration, Compliance, Reg D, Blue Sky, Blue Sky Law, State Securities, State Securities Law, State Registration, Federal Securities, Regulation A, Regulation SB, IPO, NASDAQ, Securities Lawyer, Securities and Investments.

Investment Adviser, Investment Advisor, Financial planner, Financial Planning, IARD, ADV, Form ADV, WebCRD, CRD, NASD, Finder, Money Finder, Private Placement Broker, NFA, Managed Funds, Hedge Fund, Trading Fund, Securities Fund, Futures Fund, Commodities Fund, Commodity Trading Advisor, CTA, Commodity Pool, CPO, Futures, Fund, Funds, CFTC, Disclosure Document, Compliance Audits, Regulatory Audits.

Business Law, Business Lawyer, Contract, Contracts, Agreement, Stockholder, Shareholder; Shareholder Agreement, Stockholder Agreement, LLC Agreement, Operating Agreement, Executive Agreement, Stock Option Agreement, Nondisclosure Agreement, Confidentiality Agreement, Closely-held, Closely held, Closely Held Businesses, Officers, Directors, Resolutions, Minute Book, Stock Ledger, Corporate Maintenance, Qualification, State Qualification, Business License, Annual Report.

Venture, Joint Venture, Joint Ventures, Strategic Alliance, Strategic Alliances, Film Financing.

ALAN S. FARNELL

10 SOUTH LA SALLE STREET, SUITE 3300

CHICAGO, ILLINOIS 60603

Telephone: 312-606-0655

Fax: 312-332-1811

Email: alan@farnelllaw.com

URL: http://www.farnelllaw.com

Bankruptcy, Civil Litigation, Railroad Law, Railcar Law.

ALAN S. FARNELL, born Hartford, Connecticut, March 14, 1948; admitted to bar, 1973, District of Columbia; 1974, New York; 1980, Illinois and U.S. District Court, Northern District of Illinois including trial bar; U.S. Court of Appeals, 7th Circuit. *Education:* Trinity College (B.A., with honors, 1970); Georgetown University (J.D., 1973). Editor, Georgetown Law Journal, 1972-1973. ***REPORTED CASES:*** Brunswick Leasing Corp. v. Wisconsin Central, Limited, 136 Fed. 3rd 521 (7th Circuit 1998).

LOCAL COUNSEL FOR: Chrysler Financial Company, General Motors Acceptance Corporation and Mercedes-Benz Credit Corporation LLC; Chapter 7, 11 and 13 matters in the Northern District of Illinois Bankruptcy Court.

COUNSEL FOR: *Railcar Leasing, Sale and Brokerage:* Transmatrix, Inc.; Quality Railway Service and Supply Co. *Railroad:* Wisconsin Central, Ltd. *Manufacturing:* Pennsylvania Precision Cast Parts, Inc. *Construction:* Best Homes, Inc.; Alpha Construction Co.; Lincoln Paving Co.

MICHAEL V. FAVIA

Established in 1982

5045 NORTH HARLEM AVENUE
CHICAGO, ILLINOIS 60656
Telephone: 773-631-4580
Fax: 773-631-7776
Email: Favia@lawyer.com
URL: http://www.michaelfavia.com

Civil Litigation, Personal Injuries, Automobile Accidents, Medical Malpractice, Products Liability, Work Injuries, Health Law, Medicare and Medicaid Fraud, Medical and Health Related Regulatory Issues, Professional Licensure Matters.

FIRM PROFILE: Favia Law Offices represents individuals, professionals and various business organizations with regard to healthcare, regulatory and injury matters. Mr. Favia and his affiliated attorneys, medical experts and other professionals provide experienced advice, consultations and litigation services for each client. Mr. Favia carries the highest legal ability rating in Martindale-Hubbell.

The firm is counsel to individuals; professional medical practices; regulatory boards and agencies.

MICHAEL V. FAVIA, born Chicago, Illinois, 1955; admitted to bar, 1982, Illinois and U.S. District Court, Northern District of Illinois; 1994, U.S. Supreme Court. *Education:* Loyola University (B.B.A., 1978); The John Marshall Law School (J.D., 1982). Highest Rating by Martindale-Hubbell. Selected by peers as a "Leading Attorney" in Health Law. Publications & Lectures: Newsletter Editor, Health Care Alert; Contributing Author, Justinian Society of Lawyers Newsletter; Co-Author: *An Attorney's Guide to the Illinois Department of Professional Regulation,* 82 Illinois Bar Journal 204, 1994; *A Common Guide to Controlled Substance Subscribing,* 94 Chicago Medical Journal 24, 1994; *A Pharmacists Guide to the Illinois Department of Professional Regulation,* Journal of Pharmacy Practice, Vol. VIII, April 1995; *Survey of Illinois Health Law,* Southern Illinois University Law Journal, 1997 and 1998. Lecturer: "Representing Health Care Providers in a Changing Environment, Illinois State Bar Association, 2003; "Regulatory Issues in the Practice of Podiatric Medicine, Federation of Podiatric Medical Boards, 2003; "A Review of Business and Legal Issues for the New Medical Practitioner, Illinois Eye Institute-Illinois College of Optometry, 2003; "State Regulation of the Health Related Professional, Lake County Medical Society, 2002; "State Regulation Health Related Professional," Northeast Illinois Pharmacist's Association, 2002; "Establishing a Medical Practice," Illinois Osteopathic Medical Society, 2002; "Legal Issues in the Practice of Medicine", Westlake Hospital, 2000; "The Practice of Health Law-An Overview", Chicago-Kent College of Law, 2000; "The Role of Arbitration and Mediation in Today's Law Practice, The Justinian Society of Lawyers, 1999; "Managed Care/Legal Risks", Chicago Medical Society, 1997, 1998 and 1999; "The State Regulation of Physicians", 1996, "Practice before the Illinois Department of Professional Regulation", 1995 and "Interprofessional Regulations and Cooperation", 1992, Illinois State Bar Association; "Representing Health Practitioners at the Illinois Department of Professional Regulations", Chicago Bar Association, 1994; Various Training Programs and Seminars for Health Prosecutors and Investigators, Illinois Department of Professional Regulations, 1988-1996; "Consumer Fraud Update Seminar", 1987 and "Real Estate and Mortgage Fraud Issues", 1988, Office of the Illinois Attorney General. Professional Background: Legal Counsel to the Law Firm of Goldberg, Zulkie & Frankenstein; Commissioner, Safety Commission Village of Northbrook; Chief of Medical and Health Related Prosecutions, Illinois Department of Professional Regulation, 1988-1996; Assistant Illinois Attorney General, 1986-1988; Counsel: Chicago City Council, Committee on Housing and Neighborhood Development, 1983-1986; International Association of Board Examiners in Optometry, 1996-1998; Association of Regulatory Boards of Optometry; Association of American Physicians and Surgeons; Hispanic Service Corporation of America. Member: Board of Trustees, Chairman of the Legal Affairs, Risk Management and the Real Estate Committees, Illinois College of Optometry; American Society of Law, Medicine and Ethics, The Northwestern Business College Advisory Board (Ret.); I.S.B.A. General Assembly; Tort Law Section Council; Health Care Section Council (Past Chair); Interprofessional Cooperation, (Past Chair); Voluntary Fee Arbitration (Past Chair); Business Advise and Financial Planning (Ret.); *Member:* Chicago and Illinois Bar Associations; Justinian Society of Lawyers (Past President, Executive Committee); The John Marshall Law Schools Alumni Association (Board of Directors); The Government Bar Association; Association of American Physicians and Surgeons; Illinois Police Association. (Also Of Counsel, Goldberg & Frankenstein, LLC). ***LANGUAGES:*** Italian, Polish & Spanish. ***PRACTICE AREAS:*** Civil Litigation; Personal Injury; Automobile Accidents and Injuries; Medical Malpractice; Products Liability; Health Law; Medicare Fraud and Abuse; Professional Licensing.

Languages: Spanish, Polish and Italian.

FEDOTA CHILDERS, P.C.

THREE FIRST NATIONAL PLAZA, SUITE 3900
CHICAGO, ILLINOIS 60602
Telephone: 312-236-5015
Fax: 312-236-8559

Insurance Defense, Excess and Reinsurance, Insurance Coverage, Medical Malpractice, Healthcare, Railroads, Product Liability, Professional Liability Insurance Coverage, Commercial Litigation, Family Law, Environmental, Business Law, Employment Law, Complex Litigation, General Civil Litigation, Directors and Officers Liability, Appellate Practice, Torts, Insurance Bad Faith International Dispute Resolution,.

FIRM PROFILE: Fedota Childers, P.C. provides custom services for all of its clients' legal needs. Combining the wisdom of collective experience with the energy and innovation of youth, Fedota Childers has the flexibility to adapt and respond to clients' specific legal needs in these dynamic times.

(This Listing Continued)

Fedota Childers represents a natural union of coverage and trial counsel. As coverage and claims counsel for domestic and international insurance and reinsurance companies, its members have arbitrated and litigated complex coverage disputes, resolved hundreds of cases nationwide involving potential exposure to insurers and reinsurers, performed claim audits, and managed loss portfolios. Its members have also engaged in product development, including drafting of policies, identifying and assisting in the development of new insurance vehicles and assisting with risk management. As litigation counsel, its members have successfully tried hundred of cases involving general liability, product liability, healthcare professional liability, railroad, toxic tort, professional indemnity and commercial litigation.

J. RICHARD CHILDERS, born Metropolis, Illinois, April 18, 1939; admitted to bar, 1967, Illinois; 1969, U.S. District Court, Northern District of Illinois. *Education:* University of Illinois and Southern Illinois University (B.A., 1962); University of Illinois (J.D., 1967). *Member:* Illinois State, American and International Bar Associations; American Academy of Hospital Attorneys; Defense Research Council; Illinois Association of Defense Trial Lawyers; Health Lawyers Association; American Society of Hospital Attorneys; American Society of Law and Medicine. ***PRACTICE AREAS:*** Excess and Reinsurance; Health Care; Insurance Coverage; Professional Liability Insurance Coverage; International Dispute Resolution. ***Email:*** jrc@fedotachilders.com

MARK C. FEDOTA, born Chicago, Illinois, April 15, 1944; admitted to bar, 1969, Illinois and U.S. District Court, Northern District of Illinois including Trial Bar. *Education:* Loyola University (A.B., 1966); Georgetown University Law Center (J.D., 1969). Editor-in-Chief, *Res Ipsa Loquitur,* 1968-1969. Lecturer: Strict Tort Liability/Statute of Repose, Travelers Insurance Company; Toxic Tort Litigation, Consolidated Rail; Trial Techniques, Loyola University of Chicago Law School. Member, Panel of Arbitrators, American Arbitration Association. *Member:* Chicago (Lecturer, Civil Practice), Illinois State (Lecturer, Punitive Damages in Mass Tort Litigation) and American (Past Chair, Rail and Motor Carrier Law Committee, Section of Tort and Insurance Practice, 1989-1990) Bar Associations; National Association of Railroad Trial Counsel (President, 2001—; Vice President, 1995-1996); Illinois Defense Counsel; International Association of Defense Counsel; Defense Research Institute; American Arbitration Association. ***PRACTICE AREAS:*** Medical Malpractice; Health Care; Railroads; Insurance Defense; Commercial Litigation. ***Email:*** mfedota@fedotachilders.com

JASON WILLIAM FURA, born Alexandria, Virginia, August 22, 1971; admitted to bar, 1998, Florida; 1999, Illinois; 2000, U.S. District Court, Northern District of Illinois. *Education:* University of Miami (B.B.A., International Finance and Marketing, 1993; J.D., 1998). Former Assistant Public Defender, Law Offices of the Public Defender, Eleventh Judicial Circuit of Florida. ***PRACTICE AREAS:*** Medical Malpractice Defense; Commercial Litigation; Criminal Defense. ***Email:*** jfura@fedotachilders.com

MELISSA L. KERCHNER, born Boston, Massachusetts, January 20, 1979; admitted to bar, 2004, Illinois. *Education:* Boston College (B.A., French and Philosophy, cum laude, 2001); Boston College Law School (J.D., 2004). Phi Delta Phi. *Member:* Chicago and Illinois State Bar Associations. ***LANGUAGES:*** French. ***PRACTICE AREAS:*** Medical Malpractice; Commercial Litigation; Insurance Coverage. ***Email:*** mkerchner@fedotachilders.com

JOHN D. KUHN, born Chicago, Illinois, October 26, 1936; admitted to bar, 1984, Illinois, California and U.S. District Court, Northern District of Illinois including Trial Bar. *Education:* Loyola University (B.S., 1960; J.D., 1984). Adjunct Faculty, Harper College, Business Law, 1987-1997. *Member:* Chicago, Illinois State and American Bar Associations; The State Bar of California. ***PRACTICE AREAS:*** Insurance Coverage; Appellate; Insurance Bad Faith; General Tort; Professional Malpractice. ***Email:*** jkuhn@fedotachilders.com

RUWAN C. PERERA, born October 31, 1976; admitted to bar, 2004, Illinois; 2005, U.S. District Court, Northern District of Illinois. *Education:* Ohio State University (B.S., Economics, 2000); Dominican University Graduate School of Business (M.B.A., 2003); John Marshall Law School (J.D., 2003). ***Email:*** rperera@fedotachilders.com

DAVID R. SCHMIDT, born Philadelphia, Pennsylvania, October 21, 1949; admitted to bar, 1979, Illinois and U.S. District Court, Northern District of Illinois; 1990, U.S. Court of Appeals, Seventh Circuit. *Education:* University of Notre Dame (A.B., 1971; M.A., 1972); Villanova University (J.D., 1979). *Member:* Chicago and American (Chair, Committee on Rail and Motor Carrier Law, 1992-1993) Bar Associations; National Association of Railroad Trial Counsel (Executive Committee). ***PRACTICE AREAS:*** Railroad Litigation; Tort Litigation.

PAUL D. STREICHER, born Chicago, Illinois, May 18, 1952; admitted to bar, 1980, Illinois and U.S. District Court, Northern District of Illinois including Trial Bar; 1992, U.S. District Court, Central District of Illinois. *Education:* University of Wisconsin-Madison (B.A., with honors, 1974); Tulane University (J.D., cum laude, 1980). *Member:* Chicago and Illinois State (Member, Sections on: Civil Practice; Tort; Family Law) Bar Associations. ***PRACTICE AREAS:*** Commercial Litigation; Business Law; Family Law. ***Email:*** streicher@fedotachilders.com

CHRISTINA S. VASILATOS, born Chicago, Illinois, December 13, 1975; admitted to bar, 2001, Illinois. *Education:* Arizona State University (B.A., 1997); John Marshall Law School (J.D., 2000). Member, Hellenic Professional, 2000. Mediator, American Academy of Alternative Dispute Resolution Attorneys (Chicago Chapter). ***LANGUAGES:*** Greek, French. ***PRACTICE AREAS:*** Medical Malpractice; Commercial Litigation; Insurance Coverage. ***Email:*** cvasilatos@fedotachilders.com

S. ANA WATSON, admitted to bar, 1990, Illinois and U.S. District Court, Northern District of Illinois; 1993, District of Columbia. *Education:* Northwestern University (B.A., 1987); Cornell University (J.D., 1990). *Member:* Chicago, Illinois State and American Bar Associations. ***LANGUAGES:*** Serbo-Croatian. ***PRACTICE AREAS:*** Excess and Reinsurance Coverage; Insurance Litigation; Health Care; Professional Liability; International Dispute Resolution. ***Email:*** aperich@fedotachilders.com

OF COUNSEL

KATHLEEN A. BROSNAN, born Evergreen Park, Illinois, June 4, 1960; admitted to bar, 1985, Illinois and U.S. District Court, Northern District of Illinois. *Education:* Knox

(This Listing Continued)

College (B.A., cum laude, 1982); University of Illinois (J.D., 1985). Phi Beta Kappa; Pi Sigma Alpha; Delta Theta Phi. *Member:* Chicago and Illinois State Bar Associations. ***PRACTICE AREAS:*** Excess and Reinsurance; Insurance Litigation; Professional Liability. ***Email:*** kbrosnan@fedotachilders.com

CECILIA M. CLARKE, born New York, New York, March 2, 1960; admitted to bar, 1987, Illinois; 1988, U.S. District Court, Northern District of Illinois; 1990, District of Columbia. *Education:* Brown University (B.A., 1982); Georgetown Law Center (J.D., 1987). Notes and Comments Editor, American Criminal Law Review, 1986-1987. Legal Research and Writing Fellow. *Member:* Chicago and American Bar Associations; The District of Columbia Bar. ***PRACTICE AREAS:*** Insurance Coverage; Excess and Reinsurance; Professional Liability Insurance Coverage; Directors and Officers Liability Insurance; Insurance Litigation. ***Email:*** cclarke@fedotachilders.com

FEELEY & ASSOCIATES, P.C.

Established in 1999

161 NORTH CLARK STREET
SUITE 2500
CHICAGO, ILLINOIS 60601
Telephone: 312-541-1200
Fax: 312-541-1260
Email: feeleypc@aol.com

Commercial Litigation, Creditors' Rights, Bankruptcy.

CYNTHIA SWIGER FEELEY, born Chicago, Illinois, September 8, 1950; admitted to bar, 1981, Illinois, U.S. District Court, Northern District of Illinois including Trial Bar; 1995, U.S. Court of Appeals, Seventh Circuit. *Education:* University of Illinois (B.S., Management Industrial Relations with honors and distinction, 1977); DePaul University (J.D., 1981). Seminar Speaker: National Business Institute, Inc., "Bankruptcy and the Secured Lender and/or Lessor"; Chicago Bar Association, "Chapter 11 Practice," Northern Illinois Industrial Association, "Bankruptcy and Creditor Rights- Both Sides of the Insolvency Issue". Workshop Chair, National Association of Women Business Owners, "Capital Ideas-Whose Got It - How to Find It." Author, "Basic Bankruptcy and Creditor Rights (or "7" and "11" Aren't Necessarily Lucky)," Listed, National Registry of Who's Who, 2001. Member, and Vice Chair, 2000-2001, Board of Directors: Workforce Development Council of Northern Cook County; Member, Board of Directors, Career Transitions Center of Chicago. *Member:* Chicago and Illinois State Bar Associations; American Bankruptcy Institute; National Association of Women Business Owners (Chair, Capital Development Committee, 1995-1997). ***PRACTICE AREAS:*** Creditor Rights; Bankruptcy and Commercial Litigation.

ELIZABETH M. FEELY, P.C.

401 N. MICHIGAN AVENUE, SUITE 1200
CHICAGO, ILLINOIS 60611
Telephone: 312-856-0306
Fax: 312-858-1812
Email: feelylaw@aol.com
URL: http://www.feelylaw.com

Family Law.

ELIZABETH M. FEELY, born Evergreen Park, Illinois, January 28, 1962; admitted to bar, 1987, Illinois, U.S. District Court, Northern District of Illinois, U.S. District Court for the District of Columbia and U.S. Court of Appeals, Seventh Circuit. *Education:* University of Notre Dame (B.A., with high honors, 1984); University of Illinois (J.D., magna cum laude, 1987). Phi Alpha Delta. *Member:* Chicago, Illinois State and American Bar Associations. ***PRACTICE AREAS:*** Domestic Relations. ***Email:*** feelylaw@aol.com

FEINBERG & BARRY, P.C.

Established in 1985

20 S. CLARK STREET, SUITE 500
CHICAGO, ILLINOIS 60603
Telephone: 312-444-1050
Fax: 312-444-1027
Email: joy@feinbergbarry.com
URL: http://www.feinbergbarry.com

South Suburban Office: 14315 South 108th Avenue, Suite 222, Orland Park, Illinois. Telephone: 708-349-2050. Fax: 312-444-1027.

Practice Limited to Matrimonial, Family, Divorce Law Trial and Appellate Practice.

JOY M. FEINBERG, born Chicago, Illinois, July 27, 1952; admitted to bar, 1977, Illinois; U.S. District Court, Northern District of Illinois and U.S Court of Appeals, 7th Circuit. *Education:* University of Illinois (B.A., 1974); DePaul University (J.D., 1977). Author: "Direct Exam of Business Valuation Expert" and "What the Judge Wants to Know," ABA Family Advocate, Winter 2003; "Pensions in Divorce," ABA Family Advocate, 2001; "Egelhoff's Effect on Divorce"; "Child Custody," Illinois Institute of Continuing Legal Education, 1988-2004; Survey Illinois Law "Review of Family Law Cases," Illinois Institute of Continuing Legal Education, 1988-1992; "Rule 220; Expert Witnesses and Psychological Testing," Child Custody, IICLE, 1992-2000; "Opinion Witnesses, Psychological Testing and The Mental Health Code", 2004; "Property Tax Issues in Divorce," Illinois State Bar Association Family Law Book, 1994; "Divorce Taxation Overview," Family Law Review, Wiley Publications, 1996; "Dependency Exemptions After Divorce," Wiley Publications, 1996; "The New Tax Effects IRA's", ABA Family Advocate, 1997. *Member:* Illinois State (Member, Section Council, Family Law, 1987, Chair, 1994-1995; Newsletter Editor, 1990-1991; Chair, Continuing Legal Education Committee, 1993-1994; Member, Bar Publications Board, 1992-1998; Legislation, 1996-1998) and American (Member: Domestic Relations Tax Problems-Tax Committee; Family Law Committee, 1980—; Co-Chair: Custody Committee, 1994-1996; Chair, 1998-1999; Domestic Violence, 1996-1997) Bar Associations. Fellow, American Academy of Matrimonial Lawyers (Illinois Chapter: President, 1995-1996; Vice-President, 1991-1994; Board of Governors; Admissions Committee, Illinois Chapter, 1989—; National: One of the Drafters, National Exam Committee, 1992—; Chair, 1994—); American Academy of Matrimonial Lawyers Foundation (Board of Governors, 1999-2000; President, 1997-1998); International Academy of Matrimonial Lawyers; Illinois Trial Lawyers Association. ***LANGUAGES:*** English. ***PRACTICE AREAS:*** Divorce; Paternity; Custody; International Child Abduction; Hague Convention Proceedings; Business Valuations in Divorce; Pre-Nuptial Agreements; Appellate Practice. ***Email:*** joy@feinbergbarry.com

CARROLL A. BARRY, born Ottawa, Illinois; admitted to bar, 1980, Illinois and U.S. District Court, Northern District of Illinois. *Education:* George Williams College (B.S., 1971); Northern Illinois University (J.D., 1980). Co-Author: "Survey of Illinois Law Review of Family Law Cases," Illinois Institute of Continuing Legal Education, 1989-1992. *Member:* Chicago (Member Matrimonial Law Committee; Legislative Committee) and American (Member, Family Law Section; Paternity Committee) Bar Associations; Southwest Suburban Bar (Member, Judicial Review Committee). Fellow, American Academy of Matrimonial Lawyers (Member, Illinois Chapter, 1993—; Board of Governors, 1998—; Admissions Committee, 1998-2000). Fellow, American Academy Foundation. ***LANGUAGES:*** English. ***PRACTICE AREAS:*** Divorce; Paternity; Custody; Matrimonial; Premarital Agreements; Appellate Practice. ***Email:*** carroll@feinbergbarry.com

DAVID M. GOLDMAN, born Chicago, Illinois, October 30, 1949; admitted to bar, 1981, Illinois and U.S. District Court, Northern District of Illinois. *Education:* University of Illinois (B.A., 1971); University of Chicago; DePaul University (J.D., 1981). *Fellow:* American Academy of Matrimonial Lawyers. ***LANGUAGES:*** English. ***PRACTICE AREAS:*** Family Law; Domestic Relations; Matrimonial Law; Divorce. ***Email:*** dgoldman@feinbergbarry.com

LEGAL SUPPORT PERSONNEL

CYNTHIA BRADFORD
TAMMY KAMMERER
JANET PENICONI
THERESA O'DONNEL
JEANNIE CHIN

PAUL L. FEINSTEIN, LTD.

10 SOUTH LASALLE STREET, SUITE 1420
CHICAGO, ILLINOIS 60603-1078
Telephone: 312-346-6392
Fax: 312-346-0810
Email: pfeinlaw@aol.com
URL: http://paulfeinstein.com

Family, Matrimonial, Divorce, Child Custody, Child Support, Visitation Rights, Family Law Appeals, Trials and Appellate Practice.

FIRM PROFILE: Paul L. Feinstein has practiced matrimonial law since 1980. He became a Fellow of the prestigious American Academy of Matrimonial Lawyers in 1991. He has spoken and written about numerous matrimonial law subjects and is currently on the Board of Editors of The Matrimonial Strategist, a national publication. He devotes a substantial portion of his practice to appellate and constitutional law, and in 1993 he was successful in overturning Illinois' automatic domestic relations asset freeze law in the Supreme Court of Illinois. In 2004, he was also successful in having the Supreme Court of Illinois declare the Illinois Child Representative Statute unconstitutional. He handles a complete range of family law issues, including divorce, custody, antenuptial agreements and parentage. Many of his cases contain complex procedural and substantive matters, and involve high profile people.

PAUL L. FEINSTEIN, born Chicago, Illinois, January 5, 1955; admitted to bar, 1980, Georgia and Illinois; 1997, U.S. Supreme Court. *Education:* Tulane University of Louisiana (B.A., 1977); Emory University (J.D., 1980). Pi Sigma Alpha; Phi Alpha Delta (Secretary, Vice President, 1977-1980). Listed in Who's Who in American Law. Speaker on Illinois Domestic Violence Act and Illinois Marriage and Dissolution of Marriage Act for Chicago Bar Association, 1982-1986. Speaker, Matrimonial Law Skills Course for Illinois Institute for Continuing Legal Education, 1987. Speaker, Estate Planning Skills Course for Illinois Institute for Continuing Legal Education, 1989-1990. Speaker, Child Custody Seminar, Illinois Institute for Continuing Legal Education, 2003, 2005. Board of Editors, Matrimonial Strategist, 1995—. Legal Publications: "Defining Income for Child Support Purposes," Matrimonial Strategist, February 2005; "Do You Know Your Federal Law? Conflicts of Law Affect Retirement Plan and Life Insurance Benefits," Matrimonial Strategist, June 2004; "Term Life Insurance in Divorce Cases: A New Deal," Matrimonial Strategist, November 2003; "A Case in Point," Matrimonial Strategist, August 2003; "Beyond DNA: Equitable Parentage," Matrimonial Strategist, May 2003; "How Matrimonial Lawyers Can Avoid Disqualification Due to Conflicts of Interest," Matrimonial Strategist, July 2000; "Creative Remedies for Problems Of Short-Term High-Income Earners," Matrimonial Strategist, May 1999; "Tenancy by The Entirety: A Means Of Protecting a Debtor Spouse," Matrimonial Strategist, January 1998; "State's Highest Court Says Workers' Comp Awards are Marital," Matrimonial Strategist, October 1996; "When are Workers' Comp/Personal Injury Awards Marital Property?", Matrimonial Strategist, July 1996; "Piercing the Corporate Veil in Matrimonial Proceedings," Matrimonial Strategist, March 1995; "Ramifications of Asserting the Privilege Against Self-Incrimination," Matrimonial Strategist, December 1994; "Interstate Custody Disputes: Deciphering the Statutory Maze," Matrimonial Strategist, January 1994; "Final Obituary for Percentage Child Support Orders," FairShare Magazine, December 1993; "The Automatic Dissolution Stay--Rest in Peace," Illinois State Bar Association Family Law Newsletter, November 1993; "Citations to Discover Assets," Illinois Family Law Report, September 1989. Certified to serve as Guardian Ad Litem, Child's Rep-

(This Listing Continued)

PAUL L. FEINSTEIN, LTD., Chicago—Continued

resentative and Attorney for the Child, Circuit Court of Cook County, Illinois. *Member:* Illinois State (Member, Sections on: Family Law, 1980—; Civil Practice and Procedure, 1982—) and American (Member, Section on, Family Law, 1980—) Bar Associations; State Bar of Georgia (Member, Family Law Section, 1980—). Fellow, American Academy of Matrimonial Lawyers, 1991—. (Co-Chair, Amicus Briefs Committee, 1996-1997; 2000-2001). ***SPECIAL AGENCIES:*** Illinois Marriage and Family Therapy Licensing and Disciplinary Board (Illinois Department of Professional Regulation), 1998-2003. ***REPORTED CASES:*** Messenger v. Edgar, 157 Ill.2d 162, 623 N.E.2d 310; In Re Marriage of Mostow, 95 Ill.App.3d 917, 420 N.E.2d 731; In Re Marriage of Rayfield, 221 Ill.App.3d 763, 583 N.E.2d 23; In Re Custody of Rose, 281 Ill.App.3d 423, 666 N.E.2d 1228; In Re Marriage of James, 259 Ill.App.3d 29, 630 N.E.2d 948; McNellis v. O'Connor, 266 Ill.App.3d 1063, 640 N.E. 2d 1354; In Re Marriage of Tyler, 230 Ill. App.3d 1009, 596 N.E.2d 119; Blair v. Mackoff, 284 Ill.App.3d 836, 672 N.E.2d 895; In Re Marriage of Yelton, 286 Ill.App.3d 436, 676 N.E.2d 993; In Re Marriage of Walker, 287 Ill.App.3d 634, 678 N.E.2d 705; Kaufman, Litwin & Feinstein v. Edgar, 301 Ill.App.3d 826, 704 N.E.2d 756; In Re Stella, 339 Ill. App.3d 610, 791 N.E.2d 187; In Re Marriage of Epsteen, 339 Ill. App.3d 586, 791 N.E.2d 175; In Re Marriage of Bates, 342 Ill. App.3d 207, 794 N.E.2d 868; affirmed, 212 Ill.2d 489, 819 N.E.2d 714; In Re Marriage of Johnson, 351 Ill. App.3d 88, 812 N.E.2d 661; Berdex International, Inc. v. Milfico Prepared Foods, Inc., 258 Ill.App.3d 738, 630 N.E.2d 998. ***PRACTICE AREAS:*** Matrimonial; Family; Divorce; Custody; Appellate.

THE LAW OFFICES OF ANTHONY B. FERRARO

CHICAGO, ILLINOIS

(See Rosemont)

Wills, Trusts, Estates, Estate Planning, Estate Taxation, Probate and Trust Administration, Medicaid, Guardianship, Elder Law, and Trust and Estate-Related Commercial Transactions including Business Acquisitions and Real Estate, Commercial Arbitration.

FERRIS, THOMPSON & ZWEIG, LTD.

CHICAGO, ILLINOIS

(See Gurnee)

Personal Injury, Airplane Crashes, Medical Malpractice, Construction Site Accidents, Nursing Home Abuse and Neglect, Property Damage, Railroad Accidents and Injuries, Slip and Fall, Unsafe Products, Wrongful Death, Automobile Accidents, Workers Compensation, Criminal Defense, Drug Crimes, Drunk Driving, Felonies, Homicides, Juvenile Crimes, Misdemeanors, Parole and Probation, Traffic Violations.

FIELD & GOLAN LLP

THREE FIRST NATIONAL PLAZA
70 WEST MADISON STREET, SUITE 1500
CHICAGO, ILLINOIS 60602-4206
Telephone: 312-263-2300
Fax: 312-263-0939
URL: http://www.fieldgolan.com

Business, Real Estate, Creditor Rights, Banking, Mergers and Acquisitions, Commercial Litigation, Civil Trial, Real Estate Valuation Litigation, Probate and Tax Law.

MEMBERS OF FIRM

ROBERT E. FIELD, born Chicago, Illinois, August 21, 1945; admitted to bar, 1973, Illinois. *Education:* Illinois Wesleyan University (B.A., 1967); Northwestern University (M.A., 1969; J.D., 1973). Phi Eta Sigma; Phi Kappa Phi; Blue Key. Senior Editor, Journal of Criminal Law & Criminology, 1973. Teaching Assistant, Northwestern University School of Law, 1971-1973. President, Village of Olympia Fields, 1991-1997. Member, State Banking Board of Illinois, 1993-1997. Trustee, Illinois Wesleyan University, 1990—; Treasurer, 1994—. *Member:* Chicago, Illinois State and American Bar Associations. ***PRACTICE AREAS:*** Business Law; Finance; Bank Regulatory Issues; Mergers and Acquisitions; Contracts. ***Email:*** refield@fieldgolan.com

STEPHEN L. GOLAN, born Chicago, Illinois, October 22, 1951; admitted to bar, 1978, Illinois. *Education:* Claremont Men's College (B.A., 1974); Northwestern University (M.B.A., 1978; J.D., 1978). Certified Public Accountant, Illinois, 1976. Lake Forest Caucus, 1994-1999. *Member:* Chicago, Illinois State and American Bar Associations; American Institute of Certified Public Accountants; Computer Law Association. ***PRACTICE AREAS:*** Business Law; Business Structures; Financing; Real Estate; Technology Law. ***Email:*** slgolan@fieldgolan.com

MARGARET A. CHRISTIE, born Elyria, Ohio, October 2, 1954; admitted to bar, 1978, Illinois and U.S. District Court, Northern District of Illinois. *Education:* Ohio Wesleyan University (B.A., summa cum laude, 1975); Northwestern University (J.D., 1978). Phi Beta Kappa. Member, Mortar Board. Member of Staff, 1976-1977, Executive Editor, 1977-1978, Northwestern University Law Review. *Member:* Illinois State and American Bar Associations. ***PRACTICE AREAS:*** Commercial Real Estate; Office, Shopping Center and Industrial Acquisitions; Financing; Leasing; Sales; General Business Law. ***Email:*** machristie@fieldgolan.com

DONNA F. HARTL, born Chicago, Illinois, June 26, 1958; admitted to bar, 1983, Illinois and U.S. District Court, Northern District of Illinois; 1988, U.S. Tax Court and U.S. Court of Claims. *Education:* North Central College (B.A., magna cum laude, 1979) Alumni Recognition Award, 1992; Loyola University (J.D., 1983). Recipient, American Jurisprudence Award. Certified Public Accountant, Illinois, 1980. Member, Board of Education, South Berwyn School District 100, 1989-1993. Director-at-Large, Illinois Association of School Boards, West Cook Division, 1991-1993. Chairperson, 1990-1991, Vice-President, 1991-1992, Legislation Committee, Business and Professional Women's Society, La Grange Chapter. Former Chair of the Federal Tax Section of the Illinois State Bar Association. Member, Board of Directors of the Chicago Chapter of Recording for the Blind & Dyslexic, 1995-1997. Member, Board of Directors, AIDSCARE, Inc. Panelist, "You and Your Money," 1998; "Illinois Law," 1997, Cable TV Shows. *Member:* Chicago, Illinois State and American Bar Associations; Illinois Certified Public Accountants Society; Bohemian Lawyers Bar Association. ***PRACTICE AREAS:*** Tax Law; Non-Profits; Corporate; Business and Personal Tax Planning. ***Email:*** dfhartl@fieldgolan.com

BARBARA L. YONG, born Chicago, Illinois, January 4, 1958; admitted to bar, 1982, Illinois and U.S. District Court, Northern District of Illinois including Trial Bar; 1987, U.S. Court of Appeals, Seventh Circuit; 1996, U.S. Supreme Court. *Education:* University of Illinois (B.A., 1979); Loyola University School of Law (J.D., 1982). Phi Beta Kappa; Phi Kappa Phi; Phi Eta Sigma; Phi Alpha Delta (President, 1981-1982). Commissioner, Park District of LaGrange, 1987-1995. Special Assistant Attorney General, Office of Illinois Attorney General, 1982-1986. *Member:* Chicago (Chair, Runaway and Homeless Youth Project, 1985-1986; Chair, Committee on Women's Rights, 1989-1991), DuPage County, Illinois State and American Bar Associations; Women's Bar Association of Illinois (Treasurer, 1992-1993); WILPOWER, Political Action Committee (PAC) of the Women's Bar Association of Illinois (Member, Board of Directors, 1999—); Illinois Federation of Business and Professional Women (State Parliamentary Advisor, 1999-2002); National Association of Women Business Owners. The Need Foundation (Board President, 1997-1999); BPW Illinois Educational Foundation (President, 2000—). ***PRACTICE AREAS:*** Commercial Litigation; Bankruptcy Law; Real Estate; Business Law; Estate Planning. ***Email:*** blyong@fieldgolan.com

DAVID K. SCHMITT, born Evanston, Illinois, April 23, 1955; admitted to bar, 1980, Illinois, U.S. District Court, Northern District of Illinois; 1981, U.S. Court of Appeals, Seventh Circuit; 1984, U.S. Tax Court; 1994, U.S. Court of Appeals, Eighth Circuit, U.S. District Court, Western and Eastern Districts of Michigan; 1997, U.S. Supreme Court. *Education:* University of Colorado at Boulder (B.A., cum laude, 1977); Loyola University of Chicago (J.D., 1980). *Member:* American and Chicago Bar Associations; Supreme Court Historical Society. ***PRACTICE AREAS:*** Business Litigation; Insurance Litigation. ***Email:*** dkschmitt@fieldgolan.com

MARGARET A. GISCH, born Westchester, Illinois, April 22, 1965; admitted to bar, 1990, Illinois; 1992, U.S. District Court, Northern District of Illinois including Trial Bar; 1994, U.S. Court of Appeals, Seventh Circuit. *Education:* St. Mary's College (B.A., 1987); University of Illinois College of Law (J.D., 1990). Recipient, Rickert Award for Excellence in Appellate Advocacy. Member, Illinois Moot Court Team, Spring and Fall, 1989. IICLE Board of Directors, 1995-2002, Executive Committee, 1997-1999. *Member:* Chicago, Kane County (Director, Board of Managers, 1994-1995; Co-Chair, New Lawyer's Division, 1992-1994); Illinois State and American Bar Associations. ***PRACTICE AREAS:*** Commercial Litigation; Employment; Corporate Law. ***Email:*** magisch@fieldgolan.com

ANTHONY R. TAGLIA, born Chicago, Illinois, September 7, 1969; admitted to bar, 1994, Illinois. *Education:* Northern Illinois University (B.S., 1991); DePaul University (J.D., 1994; M.B.A., 1994). Certified Public Accountant, 1991. *Member:* Chicago, Illinois State and American Bar Associations; American Institute of Certified Public Accountants. ***PRACTICE AREAS:*** Business Law; Mergers and Acquisitions; Taxation; Trusts and Estates. ***Email:*** artaglia@fieldgolan.com

ASSOCIATES

DARRIN S. BAIM, born Chicago, Illinois, March 21, 1970; admitted to bar, 1998, Illinois. *Education:* University of Illinois (B.S., 1992; M.S., 1995); Loyola University (J.D., cum laude, 1998). Editor-at-Large (1996-1998) and Board Member, Loyola University Chicago Law Journal. Articles Editor (1996) Annals of Health Law. *Member:* Chicago and Illinois State Bar Associations. ***PRACTICE AREAS:*** Business Law; Mergers and Acquisitions; Banking Regulation. ***Email:*** dsbaim@fieldgolan.com

KIMBERLY A. FIELD, born Blue Island, Illinois, December 9, 1977; admitted to bar, 2002, Illinois. *Education:* Illinois Wesleyan University (B.A., 1999); Loyola University School of Law (J.D., 2002). *Illinois State Bar Association; Womens Bar Association of Illinois.* ***LANGUAGES:*** Japanese. ***PRACTICE AREAS:*** Business Law; Banking Regulation; Trusts and Estates. ***Email:*** kafield@fieldgolan.com

OWEN P. QUINN, born Chicago, Illinois, December 21, 1975; admitted to bar, 2001, Illinois. *Education:* University of Illinois (B.A., 1998; J.D., 2001). ***PRACTICE AREAS:*** Litigation. ***Email:*** opquinn@fieldgolan.com

LIAT R. MEISLER, born December 23, 1972; admitted to bar, 1998, Illinois. *Education:* University of Michigan (B.A., 1993); University of Michigan Law School (J.D., 1997). Formerly with KMZ Rosenman. ***LANGUAGES:*** Hebrew. ***PRACTICE AREAS:*** Commercial Litigation. ***Email:*** lrmeisler@fieldgolan.com

MICHAEL J. OSTY, born Chicago, Illinois, May 25, 1968; admitted to bar, 1994, Illinois. *Education:* Purdue University (B.A., 1990); John Marshall Law School (J.D., 1994). *Member:* Chicago, Illinois State and American (Member, Business Law Section) Bar Associations. ***PRACTICE AREAS:*** Banking Law; Commercial Finance; Business Transactions; Mergers and Acquisitions. ***Email:*** mjosty@fieldgolan.com

CAREN A. LEDERER, born Irving, Texas, September 14, 1967; admitted to bar, 1998, Illinois and U.S. District Court, Northern District of Illinois; 2001, U.S. Court of Appeals, Seventh Circuit. *Education:* University of Texas at Austin (B.A., cum laude, 1988); John Marshall Law School (J.D., cum laude, 1998). Recipient, American Bankruptcy Institute Certificate of Excellence in Banking. *Member:* Chicago and Illinois State Bar Associations. ***PRACTICE AREAS:*** Commercial Litigation; Workouts; Real Estate; Bankruptcy; Corporate Law; Creditors Rights; Condominium Law; Business Law. ***Email:*** calederer@fieldgolan.com

STEVEN A. MARDEROSIAN, born Oak Park, Illinois, August 21, 1969; admitted to bar, 1996, Illinois and U.S. District Court, Northern District of Illinois. *Education:* University of Illinois (B.A., with honors, 1992); DePaul University (J.D., 1996). *Member:* Illinois State Bar Association. ***PRACTICE AREAS:*** Commercial Litigation; Business Litigation. ***Email:*** samarderosian@fieldgolan.com

(This Listing Continued)

JEFFREY M. GLASS, born Wichita, Kansas, July 16, 1966; admitted to bar, 1991, Illinois. *Education:* University of Illinois College of Commerce (B.S., with honors, 1988); DePaul University; University of Chicago Law School (J.D., 1991). *Member:* Chicago and Illinois State Bar Association. ***PRACTICE AREAS:*** Civil Litigation. ***Email:*** jmglass@fieldgolan.com

OF COUNSEL

JOAN E. MALONEY, born Evanston, Illinois, July 2, 1955; admitted to bar, 1994, Illinois. *Education:* Elmhurst College (B.S.R.N., 1989); John Marshall Law School (J.D., 1994). Sigma Theta Tau; Phi Delta Phi. Registered Nurse, Illinois, 1989. *Member:* Chicago and American Bar Associations. ***PRACTICE AREAS:*** Employment Law. ***Email:*** jemaloney@fieldgolan.com

LEONARD W. GOLAN, born Chicago, Illinois, 1923; admitted to bar, 1948, Illinois and U.S. District Court, Northern District of Illinois; 1951, U.S. Court of Appeals, Seventh Circuit; 1954, U.S. Court of Military Appeals; 1958, U.S. Supreme Court. *Education:* Northwestern University (B.S.L., 1947); Northwestern University School of Law (J.D., 1947). Phi Delta Phi. Master in Chancery, Superior Court of Cook County, Illinois, 1958-1965. Special Assistant Attorney General for Condemnation of Real Property, 1969-1984. *Member:* Chicago, Illinois State and American Bar Associations; The Legal Club of Chicago. ***PRACTICE AREAS:*** General Civil Trial Practice in all courts; Business and Corporate Law.

PATRICK C. DOODY, born Chicago, Illinois, April 29, 1949; admitted to bar, 1978, Illinois; 1988, Wisconsin. *Education:* DePaul University (B.S., 1971); Chicago-Kent College of Law (J.D., 1978). Certified Public Accountant, 1973. *Member:* Illinois State Bar Association; State Bar of Wisconsin. ***PRACTICE AREAS:*** Taxation Law; Property Law. ***Email:*** pcdoody@fieldgolan.com

JOHN E. VRANICAR, born Oak Park, Illinois, January 5, 1949; admitted to bar, 1984, Illinois; 1998, Indiana. *Education:* Northern Illinois University (B.A., with high honors, 1971); University of Minnesota (M.A., 1974; M.P., 1976); Loyola University (J.D., magna cum laude, 1984). Author: Note, "Illinois v. Gates: A Paradoxical Version of Common Sense," 15 Loyola University-Chicago Law Journal 153, 1983. Co-Author: "Into Harms' Way: Now That Harms v. Sprague Has Established The Lien Theory of Mortgages in Illinois, Does Foreclosure Cut Off Junior Leases Or Can A Mortgagee Elect to Preserve Them?" 34 De Paul Law Journal 449. *Member:* Chicago, Illinois State and Indiana State Bar Associations. ***PRACTICE AREAS:*** Real Estate; Land Use; Environmental. ***Email:*** jevranicar@fieldgolan.com

REPRESENTATIVE CLIENTS: Great Lakes Financial Resources, Inc.; Great Lakes Bank, N.A.; Mid-Continent Builders, Inc.; Romano Bros. Beverage Co.; B. Mueller Distributing Co.; Ferrostaal Inc.; (CPFL); Bell & Howell.

FIELD AND GOLDBERG, LLC

10 SOUTH LASALLE STREET, SUITE 2910
CHICAGO, ILLINOIS 60603
Telephone: 312-408-7200
Fax: 312-408-7201

Real Estate, Real Estate Tax, Finance, Mortgage Foreclosure, Real Estate Litigation, Commercial Real Estate.

MEMBERS OF THE FIRM

JAMES A. FIELD, born Chicago, Illinois, January 5, 1965; admitted to bar, 1991, Illinois. *Education:* Indiana University (B.S., 1987); Emory University (J.D., 1990); The John Marshall Law School (LL.M., Real Estate, 2001). ***Email:*** jfield@fieldandgoldberg.com

JAY RUSSELL GOLDBERG, born Queens, New York, November 16, 1954; admitted to bar, 1989, Illinois and U.S. District Court, Northern District of Illinois. *Education:* University of South Florida (B.A., 1976); Florida State University (M.Ed., 1978); Loyola University School of Law (J.D., 1989). ***Email:*** jgoldberg@fieldandgoldberg.com

JUSTIN M.. NEWMAN, born Skokie, Illinois, June 25, 1977; admitted to bar, 2002, Illinois. *Education:* University of Illinois (B.A., 1999); Washington University (J.D., 2002).

ROBERT GODNIK, admitted to bar, 1992, Illinois. *Education:* University of Illinois, Urbana-Champaign (B.S., Finance, with honors, 1989); University of Illinois College of Law (J.D., 1992). ***Email:*** rgodnik@fieldandgoldberg.com

ELIZABETH D. JENSEN, admitted to bar, 2001, Illinois. *Education:* DePaul University (B.A., 1996); DePaul University College of Law (J.D., with honors, 2001). ***Email:*** ejensen@fieldandgoldberg.com

FIGLIULO & SILVERMAN, P.C.

10 SOUTH LA SALLE STREET, SUITE 3600
CHICAGO, ILLINOIS 60603
Telephone: 312-251-4600
Fax: 312-251-4610
Email: law@fslegal.com
URL: http://www.fslegal.com

Trial and Appellate Practice in Federal and State Courts. Business and Corporate Litigation, Eminent Domain, Professional Liability, Bankruptcy, Construction, and Real Estate Related Litigation.

JAMES R. FIGLIULO, born Evergreen Park, Illinois, October 22, 1949; admitted to bar, 1975, Arizona and U.S. District Court, District of Arizona; 1977, U.S. Court of Appeals, Ninth Circuit; 1979, Illinois; 1980, U.S. Supreme Court; 1983, U.S. District Court, Northern District of Illinois including Trial Bar; 1984, U.S. Court of Appeals, Seventh Circuit. *Education:* St. Mary's College (B.A., cum laude, 1971); University of Arizona (J.D., 1974). Chairman, Moot Court Board. Recipient, William Spaid Memorial Scholar Award. Author: Article, "Breaking the Language Barrier," 10 Litigation, No. 2, Winter 1984.

(This Listing Continued)

Listed Recent Edition of "Best Lawyers in America." *Member:* Seventh Circuit (President, 2005-2006), Chicago, Illinois State (Member, Civil Practice Section)and American (Member, Litigation Section) Bar Associations; Arizona State Bar (Chairman, Civil Practice and Procedures Committee, 1979-1980); Chicago Inn of Court (President, 1992-1993; Master of the Bench). Fellow, American College of Trial Lawyers. ***PRACTICE AREAS:*** Trial Practice; Appellate Practice; Business Litigation; Corporate Litigation; Eminent Domain; Professional Liability; Real Estate Litigation. ***Email:*** jfigliulo@fslegal.com

PETER A. SILVERMAN, born Providence, Rhode Island, December 4, 1961; admitted to bar, 1987, Illinois and U.S. Court of Appeals, Seventh Circuit. *Education:* Northwestern University (B.A., 1984); Boston University (J.D., 1987). Member, American Journal of Law and Medicine, 1986. *Member:* Chicago (Member, Judicial Evaluation Committee), American and Federal Trial Bar Associations. ***PRACTICE AREAS:*** Commercial Litigation; Employment Law. ***Email:*** psilverman@fslegal.com

CARL A. GIGANTE, born Chicago, Illinois, July 2, 1957; admitted to bar, 1983, Illinois and U.S. District Court, Northern District of Illinois; 1984, U.S. Court of Appeals, Seventh Circuit; 1989, U.S. Supreme Court. *Education:* Northwestern University; Loyola University (B.A., magna cum laude, 1980; J.D., 1983). Member, Loyola Law Journal, 1983. *Member:* Chicago Bar Association; Chicago Inn of Court. ***PRACTICE AREAS:*** Eminent Domain. ***Email:*** cgigante@fslegal.com

MARC S. PORTER, born Chicago, Illinois, August 28, 1954; admitted to bar, 1979, Illinois. *Education:* Creighton University (B.S.B.A., 1976); Northern Illinois University (J.D., 1979). Administrative Hearing Officer, Department of Labor, 1980-1982. ***PRACTICE AREAS:*** Real Estate; Construction Law; Municipal; Corporate Law; Employment. ***Email:*** mporter@fslegal.com

JAMES H. BOWHAY, born Sacramento, California, May 8, 1959; admitted to bar, 1987, Wisconsin; 1990, Illinois. *Education:* Grinnell College (B.A., 1981); University of Illinois (J.D., cum laude, 1987). Phi Beta Kappa. *Member:* Chicago, Illinois State and American Bar Associations; State Bar of Wisconsin. ***PRACTICE AREAS:*** Commercial Litigation; Appellate Litigation; Professional Liability; Legal Malpractice. ***Email:*** jbowhay@fslegal.com

JOHN J. LYNCH, born Evergreen Park, Illinois, August 22, 1945; admitted to bar, 1973, Illinois and U.S. District Court, Northern District of Illinois including Trial Bar; 1976, U.S. Court of Appeals, Seventh Circuit. *Education:* St. Mary of the Lake Seminary (B.A., 1967); DePaul University (M.A., 1970; J.D., 1973). Member, Board of Editors, De Paul Law Review, 1972-1973. *Member:* Chicago, Illinois State and American Bar Associations; Federation of Defense and Corporate Counsel; Illinois Association of Defense Trial Counsel; Defense Research Institute; Professional Liability Underwriting Society. ***PRACTICE AREAS:*** Civil Litigation; Professional Liability; Insurance Coverage; Legal Malpractice; Medical Malpractice. ***Email:*** jlynch@fslegal.com

JEFF D. HARRIS, born Urbana, Illinois, October 22, 1953; admitted to bar, 1978, Illinois and U.S. District Court, Northern District of Illinois including Trial Bar; 1983, U.S. Court of Appeals, Seventh Circuit; 1989, U.S. Supreme Court. *Education:* Miami University (B.A., cum laude, 1975); Washington & Lee University (J.D., 1978). Phi Kappa Phi; Pi Sigma Alpha. *Member:* Chicago and American Bar Associations. ***PRACTICE AREAS:*** Commercial Litigation; Construction Law; Commercial Real Estate. ***Email:*** jharris@fslegal.com

MICHAEL K. DESMOND, born Chicago, Illinois, August 9, 1961; admitted to bar, 1992, Illinois and U.S. District Court, Northern District of Illinois. *Education:* Northern Illinois University (B.S., 1983); John Marshall Law School (J.D., 1992). Certified Public Accountant, 1985. Adjunct Faculty, De Paul University College of Law. *Member:* Chicago, Illinois State and American Bar Associations. ***PRACTICE AREAS:*** Commercial Litigation; Bankruptcy; Real Estate. ***Email:*** mdesmond@fslegal.com

STEPHEN A. VIZ, born Oak Lawn, Illinois, June 20, 1967; admitted to bar, 1992, Illinois and U.S. District Court, Northern District of Illinois. *Education:* University of Notre Dame (B.A., 1989); Chicago-Kent College of Law, Illinois Institute of Technology (J.D ., 1992). *Member:* Chicago Bar Association. ***PRACTICE AREAS:*** Eminent Domain; Real Estate. ***Email:*** sviz@fslegal.com

STEPHANIE D. JONES, born Miami, Florida, December 7, 1969; admitted to bar, 1994, Illinois. *Education:* Williams College (B.A., 1991); University of Michigan (J.D., 1993). *Member:* Chicago and American Bar Associations. ***PRACTICE AREAS:*** Litigation; Dispute Resolution; Antitrust; Intellectual Property Litigation. ***Email:*** sjones@fslegal.com

GREGORY L. STELZER, born Wisconsin Rapids, Wisconsin, February 8, 1973; admitted to bar, 1998, Illinois. *Education:* Northwestern University (B.S., 1995); University of Minnesota (J.D., magna cum laude, 1998). Phi Beta Kappa. ***PRACTICE AREAS:*** Commercial Litigation; Securities Litigation; Professional Liability. ***Email:*** gstelzer@fslegal.com

COLLEEN M. SCHMIEGE, born Los Angeles, California, August 19, 1976; admitted to bar, 2002, Illinois and U.S. District Court, Northern District of Illinois. *Education:* Boston College, Chestnut Hill (B.S., 1998); Loyola University School of Law, Chicago (J.D., 2002). *Member:* Chicago, Illinois State and American Bar Associations. ***PRACTICE AREAS:*** Commercial Litigation; Professional Liability. ***Email:*** cschmiege@fslegal.com

MICHAEL T. GRAHAM, born Elmhurst, Illinois, October 2, 1972; admitted to bar, 2003, Illinois. *Education:* University of Illinois, Urbana-Champaign (B.S., 1994); University of Michigan (M.S., 1998); University of Chicago (J.D., 2003). ***PRACTICE AREAS:*** Commercial Litigation. ***Email:*** mgraham@fslegal.com

THOMAS D. WARMAN, born Des Plaines, Illinois, July 29, 1978; admitted to bar, 2003, Illinois. *Education:* Carthage College (B.A., magna cum laude, 2000); University of Illinois College of Law (J.D., cum laude, 2003). *Member:* Chicago and Illinois State Bar Associations. ***PRACTICE AREAS:*** Commercial Litigation; Contract Disputes; Business Torts. ***Email:*** twarman@fslegal.com

FISCHEL & KAHN, LTD.

Established in 1919

190 SOUTH LA SALLE STREET, SUITE 2850
CHICAGO, ILLINOIS 60603-3412
Telephone: 312-726-0440
Fax: 312-726-1448

General Civil and Trial Practice. Corporation, Probate, Estate Planning, Tax, Insurance, Real Estate, Lending, Elder Law, Guardianships and Domestic Relations.

FREDERIC A. FISCHEL (1905-1956)

LOUIS L. KAHN (1912-1965)

MAX HESS WEINBERG (1936-1986)

DAN BRUSSLAN, born Chicago, Illinois, January 18, 1926; admitted to bar, 1950, Illinois and U.S. District Court, Northern District of Illinois including Trial Bar. *Education:* University of Illinois; Chicago-Kent College of Law (J.D., 1950). Nu Beta Epsilon. City Councilman, City of Highland Park, Illinois, 1969-1977. Chairman, Civil Service Commission, 1981—. *Member:* Chicago (Member, Inquiry Committee, 1971-1974), Illinois State and American (Member, Committees on: Family Law; Litigation) Bar Associations; Casualty Adjusters Association of Chicago); Defense Research Institute; Illinois Association of Defense Trial Counsel. ***PRACTICE AREAS:*** Civil Litigation; Insurance Litigation; Family Law; Zoning Law. ***Email:*** dbrusslan@fischelkahn.com

JOEL H. FENCHEL, born Chicago, Illinois, May 3, 1942; admitted to bar, 1966, Illinois and U.S. District Court, Northern District of Illinois including Trial Bar. *Education:* Northwestern University (B.S., 1963; J.D., cum laude, 1966). Tau Epsilon Rho. Member, 1975-1982 and Chairman, 1980-1982, Planning Commission, City of Highland Park, Illinois. Member, Inquiry Board, Attorney Registration and Disciplinary Commission, 1978-1982. Member, Panel of Arbitrators, American Arbitration Association. *Member:* Chicago (Member, Insurance Law Committee, 1971-1974), Illinois State and American Bar Associations. ***PRACTICE AREAS:*** Corporate Law; Business Law; Real Estate Law; Family Law. ***Email:*** jfenchel@fischelkahn.com

MORRIS G. DYNER, born Panama City, Panama, July 5, 1942; admitted to bar, 1967, Illinois and U.S. District Court, Northern District of Illinois. *Education:* University of Chicago (B.A., 1964; J.D., 1967). *Member:* Chicago (Member, Committees on: Corporation Law, 1981-1983; Real Property Law, 1981-1982), Illinois State and American (Member, Committees on: Commodities Regulation, 1976-1982; Business, Corporate and Taxation Law, 1983—) Bar Associations; Chicago Estate Planning Council. ***PRACTICE AREAS:*** Corporate Law; Business Law; Estate Planning; Probate; Real Estate. ***Email:*** mdyner@fischelkahn.com

DAVID W. INLANDER, born Chicago, Illinois, March 14, 1951; admitted to bar, 1975, Illinois and U.S. District Court, Northern District of Illinois including Trial Bar. *Education:* Vanderbilt University and University of Illinois (B.A., cum laude, 1972); Loyola University (J.D., with honors, 1975). Psi Chi. Note and Comment Editor, Loyola University Law Journal, 1974-1975. *Member:* Chicago, Illinois State (Member, Tort, Family and General Practice Sections) and American Bar Associations; Illinois Trial Lawyers Association; The Association of Trial Lawyers of America. ***PRACTICE AREAS:*** Civil Litigation; Medical Legal Practice; Family Law. ***Email:*** dinlander@fischelkahn.com

ROBERT W. KAUFMAN, born Chicago, Illinois, May 4, 1951; admitted to bar, 1977, Illinois and U.S. District Court, Northern District of Illinois; 1977, U.S. Tax Court. *Education:* University of Michigan (B.B.A., with distinction, 1973); University of Maryland (J.D., with honors, 1976); New York University (LL.M., in Taxation, 1977). Beta Alpha Psi. Certified Public Accountant, Illinois, 1974. *Member:* Chicago (Member, 1979—and Chairman, 1987-1988, Probate Practice Committee), Illinois State (Member, Estate Planning, Probate and Trust Section) and American (Member, Sections on: Real Property, Probate and Trust Law, Taxation) Bar Associations; Decalogue Society of Lawyers; National Academy of Elder Attorneys; Chicago Estate Planning Council. ***PRACTICE AREAS:*** Estate Planning Law; Elder Law; Probate Law; Taxation Law; Real Estate Law; Corporate Law. ***Email:*** rkaufman@fischelkahn.com

EDWARD F. (BUD) DOBBINS, born Brooklyn, New York, November 18, 1946; admitted to bar, 1972, New York; 1976, Illinois. *Education:* Providence College (B.A., 1968); St. John's University School of Law (J.D., 1972). Village Trustee, Willmette, 1987-1991. *Member:* Illinois State Bar Association. [Sgt., U.S. Army Reserves, 1971-1976]. ***PRACTICE AREAS:*** Lender Law; Real Estate; Banking. ***Email:*** bdobbins@fischelkahn.com

MARK R. ROSENBAUM, born Chicago, Illinois, September 10, 1951; admitted to bar, 1976, Illinois. *Education:* University of Michigan (A.B., with distinction, 1973); University of Chicago (J.D., 1976). Member, Community Associations Institute, 1996—. *Member:* Chicago (Member, Condominium Law Subcommittee), Illinois State and American Bar Associations. ***PRACTICE AREAS:*** Real Estate; Common Interest Communities; Condominium Law; Corporate Law; Litigation; Estate Planning. ***Email:*** mrosenbaum@fischelkahn.com

PETER J. SCHMIEDEL, born Orange, New Jersey, April 16, 1948; admitted to bar, 1974, Illinois. *Education:* Seton Hall University (B.A., History, 1970); John Marshall Law School (J.D., 1974). Member, Moot Court. Cook County Public Guardian. *Member:* American Bar Association. ***PRACTICE AREAS:*** Adult Guardianship; Elder Law; Childrens Rights; Litigation.

RONALD D. MENNA, JR., born Oak Park, Illinois, November 4, 1962; admitted to bar, 1988, Illinois and U.S. District Court, Northern District of Illinois including Trial Bar; 1993, U.S. Court of Appeals, Seventh Circuit. *Education:* University of the South (B.A., Political Science and Economics, 1984); University of Illinois (J.D., 1988). Appellate Law Clerk to Hon. Michael A. Bilandic, Justice, Illinois Appellate Court, First District, 1988-1990. Member, Milton Township Committee on Youth, 2005-2008). *Member:* Chicago, DuPage County and Illinois State Bar Associations. ***REPORTED CASES:*** Helms v. Local 705 I.B.T., 1999 WL 965230, N.D. Ill. September 30, 1999; In re Estate of Forrest, 302 Ill. App.3d 1021, 706 N.E.2d 1043 (3rd Dist. 1999), appeal denied, 184 Ill. 2d 557, 714 N.E.2d 527; Helms v. Local 705 I.B.T., 1998 WL 182513, N.D. Ill, April 16, 1998; Johnson v. DuPage Airport Authority, 268 Ill. App.3d 409, 644 N.E.2d 802 (2nd Dist. 1994); In re Marriage of Sloane, 255 Ill.App.3d 653, 628 N.E.2d 1198 (2nd Dist. 1994), appeal denied, 156 Ill. 2d 566, 638 N.E.2d 1125, Chicago Daily Law Bulletin, August 4, 1994; Kimber v. City of Warrenville, 248 Ill. App.3d 361, 617 N.E.2d 1263 (2nd Dist. 1993) appeal denied, 153 Ill. 2d 560, 624 N.E.2d 808; Sea-Land Services, Inc. v. Pepper Source, 993 F.2d 1309 (7th Cir. 1992). ***PRACTICE AREAS:*** Civil Litigation; Appellate Practice; Business Law; Corporate Law; Real Estate. ***Email:*** rmenna@fischelkahn.com

SUZANNE GLADE, born New Orleans, Louisiana, June 7, 1959; admitted to bar, 1982, Illinois. *Education:* Louisiana State University; Tulane University of Louisiana (J.D., cum laude, 1982). Adjunct Facility, U.S. Environmental Protection Agency Trial Advocacy Institute, 1988-2002. *Member:* Illinois State Bar Association. ***PRACTICE AREAS:*** Civil Litigation; Family Law. ***Email:*** sglade@fischelkahn.com

DEBORAH JO SOEHLIG, born Springerville, Arizona, July 2, 1963; admitted to bar, 1987, Illinois; 1988, U.S. District Court, Northern District of Illinois, including Trial Bar; 1994, Wisconsin. *Education:* University of New Mexico (B.A., cum laude, 1983); Washington University School of Law (J.D., 1987). Blue Key National Honor Fraternity. Presidential Scholar. Adjunct Professor, Legal Writing, John Marshall Law School, Chicago, IL, 1999—. *Member:* Chicago, Illinois State and American Bar Associations. ***PRACTICE AREAS:*** Civil Litigation; Corporate Law; Real Estate Law; Guardianship Law; Conservatorship Law. ***Email:*** dsoehlig@fischelkahn.com

(This Listing Continued)

FISHER KANARIS, P.C.

Established in 1992

200 SOUTH WACKER DRIVE, 22ND FLOOR
CHICAGO, ILLINOIS 60606
Telephone: 312-474-1400
Telecopier: 312-474-1410
URL: http://www.FISHERKANARIS.com

A National Civil Litigation Practice with emphasis in First-Party Property and Third-Party Liability Insurance and Reinsurance, Subrogation-Loss Recovery, Professional Liability Defense, Construction Law, Warehouseman's Legal Liability Defense, Design Professional Contract Formation-Risk Management, Business and Commercial Litigation and Product Liability.

FIRM PROFILE: Fisher Kanaris, P.C. is a civil litigation law firm that offers experienced advice, counsel and representation for a variety of legal matters throughout the world. Founded in 1992 by a diverse group of attorneys, the firm has steadily grown, building an exemplary reputation for cost-effective, innovative and well-prepared advocacy.

STEVEN B. FISHER, born Skokie, Illinois, June 27, 1962; admitted to bar, 1987, Illinois and U.S. District Court, Northern District of Illinois. *Education:* University of Illinois (B.S., 1984); IIT/Chicago-Kent College of Law (J.D., 1987). *Member:* Illinois State Bar Association. ***PRACTICE AREAS:*** Subrogation; Products Liability; Insurance. ***Email:*** sfisher@FISHERKANARIS.com

DAVID E. HEISS, born Oak Park, Illinois, December 16, 1970; admitted to bar, 1997, Illinois and U.S. District Court, Northern District of Illinois. *Education:* DePauw University (B.A., 1993); John Marshall Law School (J.D., 1997). Phi Delta Phi. *Member:* Chicago and Illinois State Bar Associations. ***PRACTICE AREAS:*** Insurance; Commercial Law; Subrogation. ***Email:*** dheiss@FISHERKANARIS.com

SUANNE P. HIRSCHHAUT, born Chicago, Illinois, July 14, 1956; admitted to bar, 1981, Illinois and U.S. District Court, Northern District of Illinois; 1982, U.S. Court of Appeals, 7th Circuit. *Education:* Indiana University (B.A., 1978); Illinois Institute of Technology-Chicago Kent College of Law (J.D., 1981). *Member:* Chicago Bar Association. ***PRACTICE AREAS:*** Architects and Engineers Liability; Construction Law; Professional Liability Defense. ***Email:*** shirschhaut@FISHERKANARIS.com

PETER E. KANARIS, born Chicago, Illinois, December 26, 1959; admitted to bar, 1985, Illinois, U.S. District Court, Northern District of Illinois including Trial Bar; U.S. Court of Appeals, Seventh and Tenth Circuits; 1992, New York and U.S. District Court, Southern District of New York. *Education:* Duke University (B.A., 1982); Washington University (J.D., 1985). Associate Editor, Journal of Urban and Contemporary Law, 1984-1985. Co-Author: "Asbestos Removal Claims Under All Risk First-Party Insurance Policies," Environmental Claims Journal, Vol. 5, No. 1, Autumn 1992; "Common Exclusions in the First-Party Property Insurance Policy and Their Application to Environmental Claims," Tort and Insurance Practice Journal, Spring 1995. *Member:* Chicago and American Bar Associations; The Association of Trial Lawyers of America. ***PRACTICE AREAS:*** Insurance; Environmental Law; Subrogation; Construction Law; Professional Liability; Business Law; Commercial Law. ***Email:*** pkanaris@FISHERKANARIS.com

MARC F. KATALINIC, born Chicago, Illinois, October 5, 1965; admitted to bar, 1990, Illinois and U.S. District Court, Northern District of Illinois. *Education:* DePaul University (B.S., 1987); The John Marshall Law School (J.D., cum laude, 1990). Associate Managing Editor, The John Marshall Law Review, 1989-1990. ***PRACTICE AREAS:*** Subrogation; Products Liability; Insurance. ***Email:*** mkatalinic@FISHERKANARIS.com

JON B. MASINI, born Benton Harbor, Michigan, September 15, 1960; admitted to bar, 1989, Illinois; 1990, U.S. District Court, Northern District of Illinois. *Education:* University of Notre Dame (B.A., 1984); Loyola University (J.D., 1989). Registered Professional Architect, Illinois, 1989. *Member:* Chicago and Illinois State Bar Associations; American Institute of Architects. ***PRACTICE AREAS:*** Construction Law; Professional Liability; Insurance; Subrogation; Warehouseman's Legal Liability. ***Email:*** jmasini@FISHERKANARIS.com

LAWRENCE D. MASON, born Chicago, Illinois, February 27, 1964; admitted to bar, 1989, Illinois and U.S. District Court, Northern District of Illinois; 1992, U.S. Court of Appeals, 7th Circuit; 1995, U.S. Supreme Court; 1996, New York; 1999, U.S. District Court, Central District of Illinois; 2001, U.S. Court of Appeals, 3rd Circuit; U.S. District Court, Eastern District of Virginia; 2002, U.S. Court of Appeals, 9th Circuit; 2004, Wisconsin and U.S. District Court, Eastern District of Wisconsin; 2005, U.S. District Court, Western District of Pennsylvania and Northern District of Indiana. *Education:* University of Illinois (B.A., 1986; J.D., 1989). Member, Products Liability Moot Court. Co-Author,

(This Listing Continued)

"Common Exclusions in the First-Party Property Insurance Policy and Their Application to Environmental Claims," Tort and Insurance Practice Journal, Spring 1995. Arbitrator, Cook County, Illinois Circuit Court. *Member:* Chicago, Illinois State, New York and American Bar Associations; State Bar of Wisconsin; Federal Trial Bar Association. ***PRACTICE AREAS:*** Insurance; Environmental Law; Subrogation; Business Litigation; Commercial Litigation; Construction Law; Professional Liability. ***Email:*** lmason@FISHERKANARIS.com

SCOTT A. RUKSAKIATI, born DeKalb, Illinois, February 1, 1968; admitted to bar, 1993, Illinois. *Education:* Indiana University (B.A., 1990); DePaul University (J.D., 1993). ***PRACTICE AREAS:*** Insurance; Construction Law; Professional Liability. ***Email:*** sruksakiati@FISHERKANARIS.com

JOHN R. SCHLEITER, born Chicago, Illinois, March 23, 1971; admitted to bar, 1996, Illinois and U.S. District Court, Northern District of Illinois; U.S. District Court, Eastern District of Wisconsin. *Education:* University of Illinois (B.A., 1993); John Marshall Law School (J.D., 1996). Phi Delta Phi. Member: Moot Court; ABA Moot Court Competition; Herzog Moot Court Competition. Recipient, Justinian Society Scholarship. *Member:* Chicago and Illinois State Bar Associations; Illinois Trial Lawyers Association; National Association of Subrogation Professionals. ***PRACTICE AREAS:*** Insurance; Subrogation; Products Liability; Commercial Litigation. ***Email:*** jschleiter@FISHERKANARIS.com

STEPHEN A. WHELAN, born Rochester, New York, March 2, 1967; admitted to bar, 1992, Illinois; U.S. District Court, Northern District of Illinois. *Education:* Boston College (B.A., cum laude, 1989); Loyola University (J.D., 1992). Omicron Delta Epsilon; Golden Key. ***PRACTICE AREAS:*** Professional Liability; Commercial Litigation; Subrogation. ***Email:*** swhelan@FISHERKANARIS.com

---

JEFFREY C. ARNOLD, born Pontiac, Illinois, February 23, 1971; admitted to bar, 1997, Illinois; U.S. District Court, Northern District of Illinois. *Education:* Hope College (B.A., 1993); Chicago-Kent College of Law (J.D., 1996). ***PRACTICE AREAS:*** Subrogation; Insurance; Litigation; Personal Injury; Products Liability. ***Email:*** jarnold@FISHERKANARIS.com

ERNEST L. CLIFFORD, born 1969; admitted to bar, 1995, Illinois and U.S. District Court, Northern District of Illinois. *Education:* Western Illinois University (B.A., 1992); Northern Illinois University (J.D., 1995). ***PRACTICE AREAS:*** Civil Litigation; Commercial Litigation; Subrogation. ***Email:*** eclifford@FISHERKANARIS.com

MARGARET M. DONNELL, born Chicago, Illinois, April 17, 1974; admitted to bar, 1999, Illinois and U.S. Court of Appeals, Seventh Circuit; 2001, U.S. District Court, Northern District of Illinois. *Education:* Arizona State University (B.S., magna cum laude, 1996); The John Marshall Law School (J.D., 1999). Delta Theta Phi. Member, American Bar Association Moot Court Competition. *Member:* Chicago, Illinois State and American Bar Associations. ***PRACTICE AREAS:*** Professional Liability; Construction Law; Business Litigation; Commercial Litigation. ***Email:*** mdonnell@FISHERKANARIS.com

DAVID L. HEATON, born Chicago, Illinois, October 19, 1971; admitted to bar, 1998, Illinois. *Education:* Northern Illinois University (B.A., 1995); DePaul University (J.D., 1998). ***PRACTICE AREAS:*** Insurance; Civil Litigation. ***Email:*** dheaton@FISHERKANARIS.com

CHERYL L. HEISS, born Oak Park, Illinois, July 29, 1975; admitted to bar, 2000, Illinois. *Education:* DePauw University (B.A., 1997); Chicago-Kent College of Law, Illinois Institute of Technology (J.D., with honors, 2000). ***PRACTICE AREAS:*** Insurance; Civil Litigation. ***Email:*** cheiss@FISHERKANARIS.com

ROBERT J. LENTZ, born Chicago, Illinois, August 2, 1964; admitted to bar, 1989, Illinois; 1992, U.S. District Court, Northern District of Illinois. *Education:* Western Illinois University (B.A., 1986); John Marshall Law School (J.D., 1989). ***PRACTICE AREAS:*** Insurance; Subrogation; Civil Litigation. ***Email:*** rlentz@FISHERKANARIS.com

AARON E. LUNT, born Elgin, Illinois, July 18, 1978; admitted to bar, 2004, Illinois. *Education:* Trinity Christian College (B.A., 2000); John Marshall Law School (J.D., 2004). ***PRACTICE AREAS:*** Insurance; Subrogation; Civil Litigation. ***Email:*** alunt@FISHERKANARIS.com

JEFFERSON D. PATTEN, born Chicago, Illinois, November 16, 1972; admitted to bar, 2001, Illinois; U.S. District Court, Northern and Central Districts of Illinois; U.S. District Court, Northern District of Indiana; U.S. District Court, District of Arizona; U.S. District Court, Eastern District of Wisconsin. *Education:* University of Illinois (B.S., 1998); John Marshall Law School (J.D., 2001). ***PRACTICE AREAS:*** Insurance; Subrogation; Civil Litigation. ***Email:*** jpatten@FISHERKANARIS.com

KEVIN MICHAEL PHILLIPS, born Detroit, Michigan, January 28, 1971; admitted to bar, 1997, Illinois and U.S. District Court, Northern District of Illinois. *Education:* George Washington University (B.B.A., 1993); John Marshall Law School (J.D., 1996). Phi Alpha Delta. Recipient, The Justinian Scholarship. *Member:* Chicago, Illinois State and American Bar Associations. ***PRACTICE AREAS:*** Subrogation; Loss Recovery; Construction; Professional Liability; Commercial Litigation; Personal Injury; Warehouseman's Legal Liability. ***Email:*** kphillips@FISHERKANARIS.com

KEVIN M. PUGLIESE, born Winfield, Illinois, May 29, 1969; admitted to bar, 1994, Illinois; 2004, U.S. District Court, Southern and Northern Districts of Illinois, including Trial Bar. *Education:* Marquette University (B.A., 1991); DePaul University (J.D., 1994). Arbitrator, Cook County. *Member:* Cook County and Illinois State Bar Associations. ***PRACTICE AREAS:*** Subrogation; Insurance Coverage. ***Email:*** kpugliese@FISHERKANARIS.com

DAVID M. ROACH, born Orlando, Florida, July 15, 1975; admitted to bar, 2001, Illinois. *Education:* State University of New York at Oswego (B.A., 1996); DePaul University College of Law (J.D., 2001). ***PRACTICE AREAS:*** Subrogation; Civil Litigation. ***Email:*** droach@FISHERKANARIS.com

(This Listing Continued)

JOHN M. SCHMIDT, born Winfield, Illinois, October 5, 1971; admitted to bar, 1998, Illinois. *Education:* Augustana College (B.A., 1994); John Marshall Law School (J.D., 1998). ***PRACTICE AREAS:*** Construction Law; Professional Liability. ***Email:*** jschmidt@FISHERKANARIS.com

STEVEN C. SWANSON, born Chicago, Illinois, 1969; admitted to bar, 2000, Illinois, Wisconsin (inactive), 2001, U.S. District Court, Western District of Wisconsin and Northern District of Illinois and Northern District of Indiana. *Education:* University of Illinois, Urbana-Champaign (B.S., 1991; M. 1993); University of Wisconsin (J.D., 2000). Registered Professional Architect, Illinois (inactive) and Wisconsin. Member: Championship Moot Court Team, Chicago Bar Association Competition, 1999. *Member:* Chicago Bar Association. ***PRACTICE AREAS:*** Construction Law; Professional Liability. ***Email:*** sswanson@FISHERKANARIS.com

MICHAEL A. WAX, born Chicago, Illinois, June 26, 1977; admitted to bar, 2002, Illinois and U.S. District Court, Northern District of Illinois. *Education:* DePauw University (B.A., 1998); Loyola University (J.D., 2002). ***PRACTICE AREAS:*** Insurance; Civil Litigation. ***Email:*** mwax@FISHERKANARIS.com

JONATHAN S. WEBER, born Detroit, Michigan, March 25, 1972; admitted to bar, 1998, Arizona; 2001, Illinois. *Education:* University of Arizona (B.A., 1994); DePaul University College of Law (J.D., 1998). *Member:* State Bar of Arizona. ***PRACTICE AREAS:*** Litigation; Insurance. ***Email:*** jweber@FISHERKANARIS.com

REPRESENTATIVE CLIENTS: Available Upon Request.

FISHER & PHILLIPS LLP

Established in 1943

1000 MARQUETTE BUILDING
140 SOUTH DEARBORN STREET
CHICAGO, ILLINOIS 60603
Telephone: 312-346-8061
Fax: 312-346-3179
Email: fp@laborlawyers.com
URL: http://www.laborlawyers.com

Atlanta, Georgia Office: 1500 Resurgens Plaza, 945 East Paces Ferry Road, 30326. Telephone: 404-231-1400. Fax: 404-240-4249.
Charlotte, North Carolina Office: Suite 2020, 227 West Trade Street, 28202. Telephone: 704-334-4565. Fax: 704-334-9774.
Columbia, South Carolina Office: Suite 1400, 1901 Main Street, 29201. Telephone: 803-255-0000. Fax: 803-255-0202.
Dallas, Texas Office: 4343 Thanksgiving Tower, 1601 Elm Street, 75201. Telephone: 214-220-9100. Fax: 214-220-9122.
Fort Lauderdale, Florida Office: Suite 800, 450 East Las Olas Boulevard, 33301. Telephone: 954-525-4800. Fax: 954-525-8739.
Irvine, California Office: Suite 400, 18400 Von Karman Avenue, 92612. Telephone: 949-851-2424. Fax: 949-851-0152.
Kansas City, Missouri Office: Suite 400, 104 West Ninth Street, 64105. Telephone: 816-842-8770. Fax: 816-842-8767.
Las Vegas, Nevada Office: Suite 650, 3993 Howard Hughes Parkway, 89109. Telephone: 702-252-3131. Fax: 702-252-7411.
New Orleans, Louisiana Office: Suite 3710, 201 St. Charles Avenue, 70170. Telephone: 504-522-3303. Fax: 504-529-3850.
Oakland, California Office: City Center Suite 200, 501 Fourteenth Street, 94612. Telephone: 510-763-4411. Fax: 510-763-4418.
Orlando, Florida Office: 1250 Lincoln Plaza, 300 South Orange Avenue, 32801. Telephone: 407-541-0888. Fax: 407-541-0887.
Portland, Oregon Office: Suite 1600, 1001 S.W. Fifth Avenue, 97204. Telephone: 503-242-4262. Fax: 503-242-4263.
San Diego, California Office: 4225 Executive Square, Suite 950, La Jolla, California, 92037. Telephone: 858-597-9600. Fax: 858-597-9601.
Somerset, New Jersey Office: Corporate Park III, Third Floor, 580 Howard Avenue, 08873. Telephone: 732-560-7100. Fax: 732-560-0788.
Tampa, Florida Office: Suite 2525, 401 East Jackson Street, 33602. Telephone: 813-769-7500. Fax: 813-769-7501.

Labor and Employment, Alternative Dispute Resolution, Arbitration, Business Immigration, Collective Bargaining, Employment Discrimination, Labor Relations, Mergers, Acquisitions and Divestitures, Sexual Harassment, Wage and Hour Law, Whistleblower Litigation, Wrongful Termination.

FIRM PROFILE: Fisher & Phillips LLP, a national law firm founded in 1943, was one of the first law firms to center its practice on representing employers in labor and employment matters. Now one of the largest in the field, the firm has maintained its commitment to helping employers find innovative legal and practical solutions to their business needs by offering management preventive advice and litigation defense. Working in many areas of employment law, the firm's attorneys offer a wide breadth of expertise covering such traditional subjects as NLRB practice, EEOC, wage and hour, and disability law, as well as business immigration, pension and benefits, education law and occupational safety and health. In addition to defending employers in labor cases, Fisher & Phillips attorneys help their clients to minimize litigation risks through the development of effective contracts, policies and procedures and through training supervisors and administrators in practical compliance strategies and dispute resolution. The firm's integrated communications systems and network of ten offices from coast to coast enable its attorneys to handle matters promptly and efficiently in any state. Its focus on labor law permits the firm to provide cost-effective services to employers ranging from large multi-national companies to small, family-owned businesses. Firm attorneys participate actively in state and local bar associations and in many charitable organizations and public service activities.

(This Listing Continued)

FISHER & PHILLIPS LLP, Chicago—Continued

Fisher & Phillips LLP represents employers in a broad range of industries including hospitality, health care, automotive, manufacturing, transportation and logistics, credit unions, banks and financial institutions, private schools, colleges and universities, state and local governments, legal and professional service firms, insurance and related services, and non-profit organizations.

MEMBERS OF FIRM

CRAIG R. ANNUNZIATA, born Chicago, Illinois, August 20, 1963; admitted to bar, 1992, Illinois; 1993, Florida. *Education:* DePaul University (B.S., 1985); Loyola University (M.B.A., 1987); John Marshall Law School-Chicago (J.D., 1992). Editor, John Marshall Law Review; Law Clerk to the Hon. William J. Castagna, U.S. District Judge, Middle District of Florida, Tampa, Florida (1992-1994). *Member:* The Justinian Society. ***PRACTICE AREAS:*** Labor and Employment; Age Discrimination in Employment Act (ADEA); Americans with Disabilities Act (ADA); Employment Litigation and Counseling; Employment Practices Liability Insurance (EPLI); Employment-Related Torts; Jury Trials; Restrictive Covenants; Retaliation and Wrongful Termination; Title VII Discrimination. ***Email:*** cannunziata@laborlawyers.com

JAMES F. HENDRICKS, JR., born Chicago, Illinois, November 18, 1944; admitted to bar, 1973, Illinois; U.S. Supreme Court. *Education:* Indiana University (B.S., 1966); Loyola University (M.S.I.R., 1968; J.D., 1973). Author: "Strikes," Labor Law for the General Practitioner, IICLE. *Member:* American Bar Association (Member, Practice and Procedure before the NLRB Subcommittee). Fellow, College of Labor and Employment Lawyers. ***PRACTICE AREAS:*** Labor and Employment; Collective Bargaining and Arbitration; Employment Practices Liability Insurance (EPLI); Fair Labor Standards Act (FLSA); Labor and Employment Litigation; Labor Contract Negotiations; Management Labor Law; National Labor Relations Board (NLRB); Strike Avoidance; Unfair Labor Practices (ULP); Wage and Hour. ***Email:*** jhendricks@laborlawyers.com

JANE M. McFETRIDGE, born Dixon, Illinois, June 28, 1958; admitted to bar, 1989, Illinois. *Education:* University of Illinois (B.S., with honors, James Scholar, 1980); Northwestern University (J.D., 1989). Certified Public Accountant, Illinois, 1980. Faculty Member, National Institute on Sexual Harassment, American Bar Association, 1997, 1998. Program Chair, Defense Research Institute's Annual Employment Law Seminar, 2004. Author: "When are Superiors Personally Liable for Employment Law Violations?" Illinois Bar Journal (Illinois State Bar Association, December, 2004); "After September 11th: Religious Discrimination in the Workplace," For the Defense, (Defense Research Institute, October 2002); "Avoiding and Attacking 'Junk Science' in Employment Litigation, Mental and Emotional Injuries in Employment Litigation," Second Edition, (Bureau of National Affairs, 2001). *Member:* Defense Research Institute (Employment Law Committee). ***PRACTICE AREAS:*** Labor and Employment; Class Actions; Employment Discrimination; Jury Trials; Non-Compete Contracts; Personnel and Supervisor Training; Race Discrimination; Title VII; Whistleblower and Retaliation. ***Email:*** jmcfetridge@laborlawyers.com

KEVIN S. SIMON, admitted to bar, 1992, California; 1993, Illinois. *Education:* College of the Holy Cross (B.A., 1989); University of California, Hastings College of the Law (J.D., 1992). ***PRACTICE AREAS:*** Employment Counseling; Employment Law and Benefits; Employment Litigation; ERISA Litigation. ***Email:*** ksimon@laborlawyers.com

MATT D. STRUBBE, born Jacksonville, Illinois, June 22, 1968; admitted to bar, 1993, Illinois; 2005, Indiana. *Education:* Northwestern University (B.A., Departmental Honors, 1990); Indiana University School of Law at Bloomington (J.D., 1993). [Judge Advocate, U.S. Marine Corps, 1991-1999]. ***PRACTICE AREAS:*** Labor and Employment; Employment Contracts; Equal Employment Opportunity Law; Federal Trial Practice; Multidistrict Litigation; Preventive Labor and Employment Law; Sexual Harassment; Workplace Audits; Wrongful Discharge. ***Email:*** mstrubbe@laborlawyers.com

OF COUNSEL

STEVE A. MILLER, born Davenport, Iowa, June 19, 1970; admitted to bar, 1997, Illinois. *Education:* University of Northern Iowa (B.A., 1992; M.A., 1993); University of Michigan Law School (J.D., 1997). ***PRACTICE AREAS:*** Labor and Employment; Federal and State Litigation; Labor Management Relations. ***Email:*** smiller@laborlawyers.com

JOEL W. RICE, born Gary, Indiana, April 5, 1957; admitted to bar, 1983, Illinois; 1986, Ohio. *Education:* Wabash College (B.A., summa cum laude, 1979); University of Chicago (J.D., 1983). Phi Beta Kappa. ***PRACTICE AREAS:*** Labor and Employment; Age Discrimination in Employment Act (ADEA); Civil Rights; Complex Litigation; Discrimination; Drug Testing; Employment Related Litigation; Federal Appellate Practice; Prevention and Compliance Programs; Severance/Separation Agreements. ***Email:*** jrice@laborlawyers.com

ASSOCIATES

NADINE C. ABRAHAMS, admitted to bar, 1992, Illinois. *Education:* University of Chicago (B.A., 1989); New York University (J.D., 1992). Phi Beta Kappa. ***PRACTICE AREAS:*** Labor and Employment; Defense Litigation; Discrimination; Employment Law; Harassment in the Workplace; Manager Training; Retaliatory Discharge; Title VII. ***Email:*** nabrahams@laborlawyers.com

TANY L. JACHIMIAK, born Oak Lawn, Illinois, June 17, 1970; admitted to bar, 1998, Illinois. *Education:* University of Illinois at Chicago (B.S., 1995); DePaul University College of Law (J.D., 1998). Phi Beta Kappa. ***PRACTICE AREAS:*** Labor and Employment; Contracts; Disability and Illness Discrimination; Employment Discrimination; Employment Release Agreements; Fair Labor Standards Act (FLSA); Litigation; National Origin Discrimination; Non-Compete Agreements; Sex Discrimination; Wage and Hour Litigation. ***Email:*** tjachimiak@laborlawyers.com

(This Listing Continued)

NESHEBA M. KITTLING, born Oakland, California, March 2, 1979; admitted to bar, 2004, Illinois. *Education:* Northwestern University (B.A., 2001); Northwestern University School of Law (J.D., 2004). ***PRACTICE AREAS:*** Labor and Employment; Discrimination; Employment Litigation; Title VII. ***Email:*** nkittling@laborlawyers.com

BRIAN K. LAFRATTA, born New York, N.Y., February 10, 1973; admitted to bar, 2001, Illinois. *Education:* Boston University (B.A., 1997); University of Illinois College of Law (J.D., 2001). ***PRACTICE AREAS:*** Labor and Employment; Appellate Practice; Breach of Employment Contract; Employment Litigation and Counseling; Immigration Law; Non-Competition Agreements. ***Email:*** blafratta@laborlawyers.com

BRIANNE L. MARRIOTT, born Fresno, California, October 26, 1980; (admission pending). *Education:* Northwestern University (B.S., 2002); University of Chicago (J.D., 2005). ***PRACTICE AREAS:*** Labor and Employment; Employee Relations Consulting; Employment-At-Will; Employment Policies and Procedures; Labor and Employment Defense; Non-Competition Law. ***Email:*** bmarriott@laborlawyers.com

(For complete biographical data on attorneys in other offices, see Professional Biographies at those locations)

FISK KART KATZ AND REGAN, LTD.

Established in 1937

SUITE 900, 77 WEST WASHINGTON STREET
CHICAGO, ILLINOIS 60602
Telephone: 312-726-1833
FAX: 312-726-4622
URL: http://www.proptax.com

Practice Limited to Property Taxation and Assessment Law. Ad Valorem Tax Law, Property Tax Law, Property Tax Appeals, Property Tax Assessments, Real Estate Taxation, Real Estate Tax Assessment, Tax Appeals.

FIRM PROFILE: Fisk Kart Katz and Regan, Ltd. has provided its clients with effective legal representation in the area of property tax and assessment law since 1937. Several of the firm's partners and associates previously served with the major governmental offices which are responsible for assessment and taxation.

Fisk Kart Katz and Regan is one of the founders and the Illinois member of American Property Tax Counsel (APTC), The National Affiliation of Property Tax Attorneys. This affiliation of independent law firms provides a platform from which Fisk Kart Katz and Regan can offer its clients professional, experienced, local representation in every state and throughout Canada.

JAMES P. REGAN, born Brooklyn, New York, March 8, 1934; admitted to bar, 1979, New York; 1995, Illinois. *Education:* Cathedral College, Catholic University of America (B.A., 1961); New School for Social Research (M.A., 1973); St. John's University Law School (J.D., 1978). Certified, Illinois Assessing Office, 1985. Author: " Malls Are more Than Real Estate," Retail Traffic, July 2004; "Why Deregulation Isn't Always The Best Solution," Real Estate Chicago, January/February 2003; "2003 Assessments Should Recognize Post-2001 Values, Real Estate Chicago, July/Aug 2003; "The Ongoing Injustice of Regional Mall Assessments," Real Estate Chicago, March, 2002; "Price Equals Market Value: Fact or Fiction?" Real Estate Chicago, July/August, 2001; "How Regional Malls Can be Overtaxed," Real Estate Chicago, April, 2001; Monthly Contributor GlobeSt.com Tax Talk Column, 2001-2004; "Refining Valuation Theories," Shopping Center World, April 1996; "Measuring Intangible Value: Building a Valuation Framework," Journal of Property Tax Management, Spring 1996; "Anchor Tenants and Other Tenants in Shopping Malls—Their Interrelationship," International Association of Assessing Officers Legal Council Seminar, 1993; "The Valuation of Resorts and Full Service Hotels," International Association of Assessing Officers Legal Council Seminar, 1996. Board Member, American Property Tax Counsel, 1993-2004. Chairman, APTC National Seminars, Real Estate Valuation of Regional Shopping Centers, 1996—; Real Estate Valuation of Hotels, 1997—; Reducing Real Estate Taxes on REIT'S and Trophy Properties, 1998—; Reducing Property Taxes on Industrial Properties in the Advancing Technologic Age, 2000; Removing Intangibles from the Real Estate Tax Bill, 2001; Emerging Theories on Intangibles and Obsolescence, Their Impact on the Taxation of Industrial and Office Properties, 2002; Old Questions Beget New Answers to Over Taxation, 2003; An Answer to Assessors' Runaway Sales Prices, 2004. Member: Tax Committee of Chicago Development Council; Real Estate Tax Forum, Cook County Assessor. *Member:* Illinois State and American Bar Associations; International Association of Assessing Officers; Institute of Property Taxation; Civic Federation of Chicago, Chicagoland Chamber of Commerce (Member, Real Estate Tax Committee); Real Estate Investment Association; National Association of Real Estate Investment Trusts; International Council of Shopping Centers. ***LANGUAGES:*** Spanish. ***PRACTICE AREAS:*** Property Tax Law. ***Email:*** jregan@proptax.com

JACK E. BOEHM, JR., born Peru, Illinois, October 17, 1956; admitted to bar, 1982, Illinois and U.S. District Court, Northern District of Illinois. *Education:* University of Notre Dame (B.B.A., 1978); John Marshall Law School (J.D., 1982). Phi Delta Phi. *Member:* Illinois State Bar Association. ***PRACTICE AREAS:*** Property Tax Law. ***Email:*** jboehm@proptax.com

JEFFREY A. BROWN, born Brooklyn, New York, December 10, 1952; admitted to bar, 1979, Illinois and U.S. District Court, Northern District of Illinois. *Education:* State University of New York at Buffalo (B.A., summa cum laude, 1975); George Washington University (J.D., with honors, 1979). Phi Beta Kappa. Special Assistant Attorney General, State of Illinois, 1979-1981. Author: "A Potential Limit on Property Taxes," Real Estate Chicago, July/August, 2002; "Lower Assessment in Cook County," Real Estate Chicago, November, 2000. *Member:* Chicago, Illinois State and American Bar Associations. ***PRACTICE AREAS:*** Property Tax Law. ***Email:*** jbrown@proptax.com

GEORGE J. RELIAS, born Berwyn, Illinois, May 7, 1964; admitted to bar, 1995, Illinois; U.S. District Court, Northern District of Illinois. *Education:* Marquette University (B.S., 1986); John Marshall Law School (J.D., 1995). *Member:* Chicago, Illinois State and American Bar Associations. ***PRACTICE AREAS:*** Property Tax Law. ***Email:*** grelias@proptax.com

(This Listing Continued)

WILLIAM J. SEITZ, born Royal Oak, Michigan, May 18, 1961; admitted to bar, 1986, Illinois. *Education:* University of Illinois (B.S., with high honors, 1983); Loyola University of Chicago (J.D., 1986); Georgetown University Law Center (LL.M., 1987). Special Assistant Attorney General, Administrative Hearings Division, State of Illinois Department of Revenue, 1989-1996. Member, State and Local Taxation Department. *Member:* Illinois State Bar Association. ***PRACTICE AREAS:*** State Taxation; Local Taxation; Property Tax Law. **Email:** wseitz@proptax.com

ROBERT J. TONOS, born Chicago, Illinois, 1942; admitted to bar, 1972, Illinois; 1975, New Mexico; 1987, Michigan. *Education:* University of Chicago (A.B., 1964; J.D., 1972). Assistant State's Attorney, Cook County, Illinois, 1980-1986. *Member:* Chicago (Chairman, Real Estate Taxation Committee, 2002-2003) and Illinois State Bar Associations; Bohemian Lawyers' Association of Chicago; State Bar of New Mexico; International Association of Assessing Officials (Member, Legal Committee); Civic Federation of Chicago; Institute of Property Taxation. ***LANGUAGES:*** French, Spanish, Russian. ***SPECIAL AGENCIES:*** Illinois Property Tax Appeal Board. ***REPORTED CASES:*** Fromm v. Rosewell, 771 F.2d 1089 (7th Cir. 1985). ***PRACTICE AREAS:*** Property Tax Law. **Email:** rtonos@proptax.com

ALBERT FISK (1941-1964)

MARTIN S. KATZ (1946-2000)

OF COUNSEL

EUGENE KART, born Chicago, Illinois, December 4, 1911; admitted to bar, 1936, Illinois; 1963, U.S. Supreme Court. *Education:* Northwestern University (B.S., 1933); Northwestern University School of Law (J.D., 1936). Phi Beta Kappa; Tau Epsilon Rho. Law Society (National President, 1957-1958). Special Assistant Attorney General, Illinois, 1964 and 1965. *Member:* Chicago, Illinois State and American Bar Associations; American Judicature Society; Law Club of Chicago.

GILBERT KART, born Chicago, Illinois, January 23, 1921; admitted to bar, 1951, Illinois. *Education:* North Park College; John Marshall Law School (J.D., 1951). Tau Epsilon Rho. Vice-President, John Marshall Law School Alumni Association, 1981—. *Member:* Chicago (Member, 1963— and Chairman, 1967-1968, State and Local Tax Committee), Illinois State and American Bar Associations.

REFERENCE: American National Bank & Trust Co., Chicago.

FITCH, EVEN, TABIN & FLANNERY

120 SOUTH LA SALLE, SUITE 1600
CHICAGO, ILLINOIS 60603
Telephone: 312-577-7000
Fax: 312-577-7007
Email: email@fitcheven.com
URL: http://www.fitcheven.com

San Diego, California Office: 9276 Scranton Road, Suite 250, 92121. Telephone: 858-552-1311. Telecopier: 858-552-0095.

San Luis Obispo, California Office: 1010 Peach Street, 93406-0031. Telephone: 805-541-2800. Fax: 805-541-2802.

Washington, D.C. Office: Suite 1801 K Street, N.W., Suite 401L, 20006-1201. Telephone: 202-419-7000. Fax: 202-419-7007.

Boulder, Colorado Office: 1942 Broadway, Suite 213, 80302. Telephone: 303-402-6966. Fax: 303-402-6970.

Los Angeles, California Office: Warner Center Towers, Suite 780, 21800 Oxnard Street, Woodland Hills, California, 91367. Telephone: 818-715-7025. Fax: 818-715-7033.

Intellectual Property and Technology-Related Law including United States and International Patents, Trademarks, Trade Secret, Copyrights and Unfair Competition, Antitrust and International Trade Commission Causes and Related Litigation.

FIRM PROFILE: Fitch, Even, Tabin & Flannery was founded in 1859 as Goodwin, Larned & Goodwin making it the senior established law firm in Chicago. Its practice is devoted to intellectual property and technology related law.

Fitch, Even, Tabin & Flannery practice areas include client counseling, licensing and litigation (of all forms of intellectual property rights), patent prosecution, protection and enforcement of patent rights, patent validity and infringement opinions, unfair competition and trade secrets, prosecution and maintenance of trademarks and copyrights, trademark registrability and infringement opinions. We advise and assist clients in the negotiation of all manner of agreements involving or related to the transfer of intellectual property, e.g., acquisitions/divestitures, assignments, research and development agreements, licenses, confidential disclosure agreements, consulting and employment agreements.

The firm's clients range from independent inventors to multi-national corporations. The firm regularly represents its clients in courts and governmental agencies in the U.S. as well as some 140 other countries.

Firm members have been leaders in their respective fields of technology as well as in the legal community, having served as expert witnesses, special masters in the Federal Courts, educators, authors and also founders and presidents of noteworthy legal associations including the Intellectual Property Law Association of Chicago and its predecessor.

Goodwin, Larned & Goodwin	1859-1867
Goodwin & Larned	1867-1869
Goodwin, Larned & Towle	1869-1874
Goodwin, Offield & Towle	1874-1880
Offield & Towle	1880-1886
Offield, Towle & Phelps	1886-1890
Offield, Towle & Linthicum	1890-1909
Offield, Towle, Graves & Offield	1909-1918
Offield, Towle, Graves & Soans	1918-1919
Fisher, Towle, Clapp & Soans	1919-1927
Fisher, Clapp, Soans & Pond	1927-1940
Soans, Pond & Anderson	1940-1950
Soans, Glaister & Anderson	1950-1956
Soans, Anderson, Luedeka & Fitch	1956-1962
Anderson, Luedeka, Fitch, Even & Tabin	1963-1970
Fitch, Even, Tabin & Luedeka	1970-1978
Fitch, Even & Tabin	1979-1980
Fitch, Even, Tabin, Flannery & Welsh	1981-1982
Fitch, Even, Tabin & Flannery	

MEMBERS OF FIRM

MORGAN L. FITCH, JR., born Chicago, Illinois, November 21, 1922; admitted to bar, 1948, Illinois; registered to practice before U.S. Patent and Trademark Office. *Education:* Illinois Institute of Technology (B.S. Ch.E., 1943); University of Michigan (J.D., 1948). Tau Beta Pi; Phi Lambda Upsilon. *Member:* Chicago, Illinois State and American Bar Associations; Seventh Circuit Bar Association; Lawyers Club of Chicago; Intellectual Property Law Association of Chicago; International Association for the Protection of Industrial Property. ***PRACTICE AREAS:*** Intellectual Property Law; Technology and Science; Licensing; Patents; Trademarks; Copyrights; Litigation; Trade Secrets Law; Contract Law; Antitrust Law; Unfair Competition. **Email:** mlfitc@fitcheven.com

FRANCIS A. EVEN, born Chicago, Illinois, September 8, 1920; admitted to bar, 1949, District of Columbia; 1950, Illinois; registered to practice before U.S. Patent and Trademark Office. *Education:* University of Illinois (B.S.M.E., 1942); George Washington University (J.D., 1949). Pi Tau Sigma; Phi Delta Phi; Order of the Coif. *Member:* Chicago, Illinois State (Chairman, Section on Patent, Trademark and Copyright Law, 1959-1960) and American Bar Associations; The District of Columbia Bar; Intellectual Property Law Association of Chicago (Member, Board of Managers, 1972-1974; 1982-1986; President, 1984); American Intellectual Property Law Association (Member, Board of Managers, 1963-1966); Seventh Circuit Bar Association. Fellow, American College of Trial Lawyers. ***PRACTICE AREAS:*** Intellectual Property Law; Litigation; Appellate Practice; Mechanical; Electro-Mechanical; Technologies and Sciences; Patents; Trademarks; Copyrights; Unfair Competition Law; Trade Secrets Law; Contract Law. **Email:** faeven@fitcheven.com

JULIUS TABIN, born Chicago, Illinois, November 8, 1919; admitted to bar, 1949, California and District of Columbia; 1950, Illinois; registered to practice before U.S. Patent and Trademark Office. *Education:* University of Chicago (B.S., 1940; Ph.D., Physics, 1946); Harvard Law School (LL.B., 1949). Sigma Xi. *Member:* Chicago, Illinois State and American Bar Associations; The State Bar of California; Intellectual Property Law Association of Chicago; American Physical Society. ***PRACTICE AREAS:*** Intellectual Property Law; Technology and Science; Biotechnology; Physics; Litigation; Technical Litigation; Licensing Law; Patents; Trademarks; Copyrights; Trade Secrets Law; Contract Law; Antitrust Law. **Email:** jtabin@fitcheven.com

JOHN F. FLANNERY, born Chicago, Illinois, October 15, 1928; admitted to bar, 1959, Illinois; registered to practice before U.S. Patent and Trademark Office. *Education:* University of Illinois (B.S.E.E., cum laude, 1950); Graduate study in E.E., Northwestern University, 1953-1954; Loyola University (J.D., 1959). Phi Alpha Delta; Eta Kappa Nu. Trustee, Village of Lincolnwood, 1978-1983. *Member:* Chicago, Illinois State and American Bar Associations; Intellectual Property Law Association of Chicago. Fellow, American College of Trial Lawyers. ***PRACTICE AREAS:*** Intellectual Property Law; Appellate Practice; Litigation; Technical Litigation; Licensing Law; Patents; Trademarks; Copyrights; Trade Secrets Law; Contract Law; Computer; Antitrust Law; Technologies and Science; Electronics; Electromechanical. **Email:** jfflan@fitcheven.com

ROBERT B. JONES, born Cresco, Iowa, February 7, 1932; admitted to bar, 1960, Illinois; registered to practice before U.S. Patent and Trademark Office. *Education:* Iowa State University (B.S. Ch.E., 1952); University of Michigan (J.D., with honors, 1960). Order of the Coif. Member, 1978-1984 and President, 1980-1984, River Forest Board of Education. President, Village of River Forest, 1989-1993. Past President, River Forest Tennis Club. *Member:* Chicago, Illinois State and American Bar Associations; American Intellectual Property Law Association; Intellectual Property Law Association of Chicago. ***PRACTICE AREAS:*** Intellectual Property Law; Intellectual Property Arbitration; Trademark Arbitration; Technology and Science; Chemical Litigation; Technical Litigation; Appellate Practice; Patents; Trademarks; Copyrights; Trade Secrets Law; Contract Law; Unfair Competition Law. **Email:** oljones@attbi.com

JAMES J. SCHUMANN, born Chicago, Illinois, May 31, 1934; admitted to bar, 1962, Illinois; registered to practice before U.S. Patent and Trademark Office. *Education:* Illinois Institute of Technology (B.S. Ch.E., 1955); Loyola University (J.D., cum laude, 1962). Tau Beta Pi; Phi Eta Sigma. *Member:* Chicago (Member, Board of Managers, 1980-1982), Illinois State and American Bar Associations; Intellectual Property Law Association of Chicago; San Diego Intellectual Property Association. (Resident, San Diego, California Office). ***PRACTICE AREAS:*** Intellectual Property Law; Biochemical Technology; Biomedical Technology; Biotechnology Patents; Chemical Intellectual Property; Licensing Law; Patents; Trademarks; Trade Secrets; Unfair Competition. **Email:** jjschu@fitcheven.com

JAMES J. HAMILL, born Cuba City, Wisconsin, February 1, 1933; admitted to bar, 1961, Illinois; registered to practice before U.S. Patent and Trademark Office. *Education:* Georgia Institute of Technology (B.M.E., 1957); George Washington University (LL.B., 1960). Pi Tau Sigma; Phi Alpha Delta. *Member:* Chicago and Illinois State Bar Associations; Intellectual Property Law Association of Chicago. ***PRACTICE AREAS:*** Intellectual Property Law; Licensing Law; Litigation; Patents; Trademarks; Copyrights; Trade Secrets Law; Contract Law; Unfair Competition Law; Technologies and Sciences; Mechanical; Electromechanical; Technical Litigation. **Email:** jjhami@fitcheven.com

TIMOTHY E. LEVSTIK, born Cleveland, Ohio, July 30, 1945; admitted to bar, 1970, Ohio; 1980, Illinois; registered to practice before U.S. Patent and Trademark Office. *Education:* Case Institute of Technology (B.S., Chem., 1967); University of Minnesota (J.D., 1970). Adjunct Professor of Law, Intellectual Property Law, Depaul University College of Law, 1999—. *Member:* American Bar Association; Intellectual Property Law Association of Chicago. ***PRACTICE AREAS:*** Intellectual Property Law; Technology and Science; Chemicals; Inorganic Chemistry; Coatings Technology; Chemical Patent Practice; Patents; Trademarks; Copyrights; Trade Secrets Law; Litigation; Technical Litigation; Appellate Practice. **Email:** televs@fitcheven.com

(This Listing Continued)

FITCH, EVEN, TABIN & FLANNERY, Chicago—Continued

JOSEPH E. SHIPLEY, born Chicago Heights, Illinois, May 25, 1956; admitted to bar, 1982, Illinois; registered to practice before U.S. Patent and Trademark Office. *Education:* Northwestern University (B.S.M.E., 1979); University of Illinois (J.D., 1982). Editor, Chicago Lawyer's Court Handbook, 1992. *Member:* Chicago, Illinois State and American Bar Associations; Intellectual Property Law Association of Chicago. ***PRACTICE AREAS:*** Intellectual Property Law; Patents; Trademarks; Copyrights; Litigation; Technology and Science Law. ***Email:*** jeship@fitcheven.com

KENNETH H. SAMPLES, born Aurora, Nebraska, June 21, 1946; admitted to bar, 1973, Illinois and U.S. District Court, Northern District of Illinois; 1982, U.S. Court of Appeals for the Federal Circuit; registered to practice before U.S. Patent and Trademark Office. *Education:* University of Nebraska (B.S.E.E., 1969); John Marshall Law School (J.D., with honors, 1973). Sigma Tau; Eta Kappa Nu; Pi Mu Epsilon. *Member:* American Intellectual Property Law Association; Intellectual Property Law Association of Chicago; International Association for the Protection of Industrial Property. ***PRACTICE AREAS:*** Intellectual Property; Technology and Science; International Technology and Science; Computer and Software; Electronics; Electromechanical; International Intellectual Property; Licensing; Patents. ***Email:*** khsamp@fitcheven.com

PHILIP T. PETTI, born Chicago, Illinois, July 27, 1958; admitted to bar, 1985, Illinois; U.S. District Court, Northern District of Illinois, including Trial Bar; U.S. District Court, Eastern District of Wisconsin; U.S. District Court, District of Colorado; U.S. Court of Appeals for the Federal, Seventh and Tenth Circuits; registered to practice before U.S. Patent and Trademark Office. *Education:* Carleton College (B.A., 1980); North Central College (B.S., Chem., 1982); Drake University (J.D., with high honors, 1985). Order of the Coif. Adjunct Professor of Law, Master of Intellectual Property Law Program (Patent Litigation); Center for Intellectual Property Law, John Marshall Law School, 1998—. *Member:* Chicago and American Bar Associations; American Intellectual Property Law Association; Intellectual Property Law Association of Chicago. ***PRACTICE AREAS:*** Intellectual Property Infringement; Patent Infringement; Patents; Trademarks; Copyrights; Trade Secrets; Complex Litigation; Technology and Science; Chemical Patents; Polymers; Medical Technology; Inorganic Chemistry; Organic Chemistry; Petroleum Chemistry. ***Email:*** ptpett@fitcheven.com

JOSEPH T. NABOR, born Japan, April 26, 1957; admitted to bar, 1989, Illinois and U.S. District Court, Northern District of Illinois. *Education:* Northeastern Illinois University (B.A., 1984); Illinois Institute of Technology, Chicago-Kent College of Law (J.D., 1989). *Member:* Chicago, Illinois State (Member, Intellectual Property Section Council) and American Bar Associations; Intellectual Property Law Association of Chicago. ***SPECIAL AGENCIES:*** Trademark Trial and Appeal Board. ***PRACTICE AREAS:*** Trademarks; Copyrights; Trade Dress; Unfair Competition; International Trademarks; Trademark Licensing; Litigation. ***Email:*** jtnabo@fitcheven.com

STEVEN C. SCHROER, born St. Cloud, Minnesota, November 7, 1948; admitted to bar, 1976, New York; 1979, Minnesota; U.S. District Court, District of Alaska, Central, Eastern and Northern Districts of California, District of Minnesota, Southern District of New York, Western District of Wisconsin, Southern District of Florida, Colorado; U.S. Court of Appeals, Second, Seventh, Eighth, Ninth and Federal Circuits and U.S. Supreme Court; 1998, Illinois. *Education:* St. Olaf College (B.A., 1971); Columbia University (J.D., 1974); University of Cambridge, Cambridge, England (LL.M., 1978). Member, Columbia Law Review, 1973-1974. Harlan Fiske Stone Scholar. Law Clerk to Honorable Murray I. Gurfein, Judge, U.S. Court of Appeals, Second Circuit, 1974-1975. *Member:* The Association of the Bar of the City of New York; The Federal Circuit Bar Association. ***Email:*** scschr@fitcheven.com

RICHARD A. KABA, born Charlotte, North Carolina, May 14, 1947; admitted to bar, 1989, Michigan; 1990, District of Columbia; registered to practice before U.S. Patent and Trademark Office (Not admitted in Illinois). *Education:* Clemson University (B.S., Chem., 1969) Phi Kappa Phi; Duke University (Ph.D., Phys.Chem., 1974) Phi Beta Kappa; University of Michigan (J.D., with honors, 1988). Order of the Coif. Executive Article Editor, Michigan Law Review, 1987-1988. *Member:* State Bar of Michigan; The District of Columbia Bar. ***PRACTICE AREAS:*** Biochemical Technology; Biomedical Technology; Biotechnology Licensing; Genetics; Immunology; Intellectual Property; Patents; Technology and Science; Chemicals; Medical Technology; Biotechnology. ***Email:*** rakaba@fitcheven.com

KARL R. FINK, born Hartford, Connecticut, July 24, 1956; admitted to bar, 1981, Illinois; 1982, U.S. District Court, Northern District of Illinois including Trial Bar; 1989, U.S. Court of Appeals, Seventh Circuit and U.S. Court of Appeals for the Federal Circuit; 1994, U.S. Supreme Court; registered to practice before U.S. Patent and Trademark Office. *Education:* University of Michigan (B.S.E., magna cum laude, 1978; J.D., 1981). Tau Beta Pi. *Member:* Chicago (Member, Patent, Trademark and Copyright Law Section), Illinois State (Member, Sections on: Trial Practice; Intellectual Property Law) and American Bar Associations; Chicago Lincoln American Inn of Court (Secretary, 1994-1995; Programming Chairman, 1995-1998; President, 1998-2000). ***PRACTICE AREAS:*** Civil Litigation; Trial Practice; Intellectual Property Litigation; Patent Litigation; Trademark Litigation; Copyrights; Theft of Trade Secrets. ***Email:*** krfink@fitcheven.com

MARK W. HETZLER, born Bismarck, North Dakota, December 6, 1966; admitted to bar, 1993, Illinois and U.S. District Court, Northern District of Illinois, 1998, Trial Bar; registered to practice before U.S. Patent and Trademark Office. *Education:* Northwestern University (B.S.M.E., with distinction, 1989); Loyola University of Chicago (J.D., 1993). Tau Beta Pi (Northwestern Chapter); Phi Eta Sigma; Alpha Lambda Delta; Phi Alpha Delta. *Member:* Chicago, Illinois State and American Bar Associations; Intellectual Property Law Association of Chicago. ***PRACTICE AREAS:*** Intellectual Property Law; Litigation; Patents; Trademarks; Copyrights; Licensing Law; Trade Secrets Law; Unfair Competition; Contract Law; Employment Agreements; Mechanical; Electromechanical. ***Email:*** mwhetz@fitcheven.com

TIMOTHY P. MALONEY, born Evergreen Park, Illinois, May 12, 1966; admitted to bar, 1993, Illinois, U.S. District Court, Northern District of Illinois and U.S. District Court, Eastern District of Michigan; U.S. Court of Appeals for the Federal and Ninth Circuits; registered to practice before U.S. Patent and Trademark Office. *Education:* University of Illinois (B.S.Ch.E., summa cum laude, 1988; J.D., summa cum laude, 1993). Alpha Chi Sigma; Phi Beta Kappa; Phi Alpha Delta; Order of the Coif; Bronze Tablet Scholar; National Moot Court. Editor, University of Illinois Law Review. Author: "The Enforcement of Patent Rights in the United States," 31 IIC 723, June 2000. *Member:* Chicago, Illinois State and American Bar Associations; Intellectual Property Law Association of Chicago; American Institute of Chemical Engineers; Licensing Executive Society; International Association for the Protection of Industrial Property. ***PRACTICE AREAS:*** Intellectual Property; Appellate Practice; Litigation; Patents; Trademarks; Copyrights; Trade Secrets; Technology and Science; Antitrust and Trade Regulation; Licensing; Business Law. ***Email:*** tpmalo@fitcheven.com

(This Listing Continued)

JAMES P. KRUEGER, born Blue Island, Illinois, August 11, 1958; admitted to bar, 1993, Illinois and U.S. District Court, Northern District of Illinois; registered to practice before U.S. Patent and Trademark Office. *Education:* Trinity Christian College (B.A., Bio., 1980); Illinois Institute of Technology (M.S., 1984; Ph.D., Microbio. and Biochem., 1989); Chicago-Kent College of Law (J.D., 1993). *Member:* Chicago Bar Association; Intellectual Property Law Association of Chicago; American Society for Microbiology; Society for Industrial Microbiology. ***PRACTICE AREAS:*** Intellectual Property Law; Chemical Intellectual Property; Inorganic Chemistry; Organic Chemistry; Medical Technology; Biotechnology; Polymens; Biomedical; Enzymology; Genetics; Immunology; Microbiology; Patents. ***Email:*** jpkrue@fitcheven.com

STEPHEN S. FAVAKEH, born Chicago, Illinois, April 6, 1964; admitted to bar, 1991, Illinois and U.S. District Court, Northern District of Illinois; registered to practice before U.S. Patent and Trademark Office. *Education:* University of Tulsa (B.S., 1985); University of Illinois (J.D., 1991). *Member:* American Bar Association; Intellectual Property Law Association of Chicago; Federal Circuit Bar Association. ***PRACTICE AREAS:*** Intellectual Property; Electromechanical; Mechanical; Infringement; Patents; Trademarks; Copyrights; Licensing. ***Email:*** ssfava@fitcheven.com

RICHARD E. WAWRZYNIAK, born St. Louis, Missouri, June 19, 1965; admitted to bar, 1991, California, U.S. District Court, Northern District of California and U.S. Court of Appeals, Ninth Circuit; registered to practice before U.S. Patent and Trademark Office. *Education:* University of Missouri-Rolla (B.S.E.E., summa cum laude, 1988); University of Missouri-Columbia (J.D., 1991). Associate Editor-in-Chief, Missouri Law Review, 1990-1991. *Member:* American Bar Association. (Resident, San Diego, California Office). ***PRACTICE AREAS:*** Patent Applications; Patent Prosecution; Electrical Patents; Electronic Patents; Computer and Software Patents; Patent Licensing; Patent Litigation. ***Email:*** rich@fitcheven.com

STEVEN G. PARMELEE, born San Francisco, California, April 24, 1953; admitted to bar, 1978, Minnesota; 1981, Nebraska; registered to practice before U.S. Patent and Trademark Office (Not admitted in Illinois). *Education:* Rose-Hulman Institute of Technology (B.S.E.E., 1975); Creighton University (J.D., magna cum laude, 1978). Adjunct Professor, Intellectual Property Law, Creighton University, 1984. (Resident at Omaha, Nebraska Office). ***PRACTICE AREAS:*** Intellectual Property; Electrical Intellectual Property; Intellectual Property Protection; Intellectual Property Rights; Computer and Software Patents; Design Patents; Electrical Patents; Electronic Patents; Mechanical Patents; Electro-Mechanical Patents.

THOMAS F. LEBENS, born Omaha, Nebraska, March 31, 1966; admitted to bar, 1993, California; U.S. District Court, Southern, Northern and Eastern Districts of California and California Supreme Court; 1994, U.S. Court of Appeals, Ninth Circuit, U.S. Court of Appeals for the Federal Circuit and U.S. District Court, Central District of California; 1997, U.S. Supreme Court; registered to practice before U.S. Patent and Trademark Office. *Education:* California Polytechnic State University (B.S.E.E., 1989); University of San Diego (J.D., cum laude, 1993). President, Associated Students Incorporated of California Polytechnic, San Luis Obispo, 1988-1989. Director, San Luis Obispo Chamber of Commerce, 1985-1986. Partner, Fitch, Even, Tabin & Flannery, San Diego, 1998-2000; Associate, Fitch, Even, Tabin & Flannery, San Diego, 1993-1997. Of Counsel, Fitch, Even, Tabin & Flannery, San Diego, 2000—. *Member:* Los Angeles County, San Diego County (Member, Intellectual Property Section), San Luis Obispo County and American (Member, Intellectual Property Section) Bar Associations; State Bar of California (Member, Intellectual Property Section); American Intellectual Property Law Association. (Also Member, Sinsheimer, Schiebelhut & Baggett, A Professional Corporation, San Luis Obispo, California Office). ***PRACTICE AREAS:*** Intellectual Property; Business Strategy; Licensing; Infringement and Validity Analysis; Patentability, Infringement and Validity Opinions; Trademark; Copyright Law, Artistic Property; Electrical Intellectual Property.

KENDREW H. COLTON, born St. Charles, Missouri, September 27, 1955; admitted to bar, 1980, District of Columbia; 1990, U.S. Supreme Court; registered to practice before U.S. Patent and Trademark Office. *Education:* Colby College (B.A., 1977); Case Western Reserve University (J.D., 1980). Member, Robert F. Wagner National Labor Law Moot Court Team; Moot Court Executive Board. Author: "Patent Pitfalls In Government Contracting," 25 ABA Public Contract Newsletter 5 (1990); "Generic Animal Drug Patent Term Extension Act of 1988—An Overview," Patent World, January, 1990; "New Judicial Interpretation of Product-By-Process Claims," Intellectual Property Business Briefing, July/August, 1991; "Experimental Use As An Exception or Defense In A Patent Infringement Action in the United Kingdom and Canada (II)," 37 Journal Japanese Group of AIPPI 28 (Jan. 1992); "The Solo Inventor Strikes Back," Chemical Innovations, 54 (Nov. 2001). Co-Author: "Patent Law Developments In The United States Court of Appeals for the Federal Circuit During 1992," 42 Am. Univ. L. Rev. 909 (1993). Member, Patent Trademark Institute of Canada, 1991-1996. Chair-Elect, Division of Chemistry and the Law, American Chemical Society, 2002. Member, Society of Plastic Engineers, 1988-1999. Advisory Board Member, Chemical Innovation/Chemtech, 1994-2001. *Member:* Bar Association of the District of Columbia; American Bar Association (Member: Patent, Trademark and Copyright Law Section; Administrative Law Section; Public Contract Law Section; Litigation Section; Standing Committees on: Environmental Law, 1982; Amicus Curiae Briefs, 1982-1984; Member, Inequitable Conduct and Antitrust Matters, Patent, Trademark and Copyright Law Section, 1983-1984); The Federal Circuit Bar Association; American Intellectual Property Law Association; Licensing Executives Society; American Chemical Society. (Resident, Washington, D.C. Office). ***PRACTICE AREAS:*** Intellectual Property Law; Patents; Biotechnology; Chemicals; Trade Secrets; Technology and Science; Litigation. ***Email:*** kcolton@fitcheven.com

(This Listing Continued)

G. PAUL EDGELL, born Dallas, Texas, March 9, 1937; admitted to bar, 1967, Virginia; 1968, District of Columbia; 1980, Illinois. *Education:* University of Illinois (B.S., Aero. Eng., 1960); Georgetown University (J.D., 1967); Roosevelt University (M.B.A., with honors, 1983; B.G.S., Computer Science, with honors, 1986). *Member:* The District of Columbia Bar; Illinois State, Virginia and American Bar Associations; American Intellectual Property Law Association. [U.S.M.C., 1960-1963, Capt.]. (Resident, Washington, D.C. Office). ***PRACTICE AREAS:*** Intellectual Property. ***Email:*** gpedgell@fitcheven.com

MICHAEL A. SANZO, PH.D., born Brooklyn, New York, May 4, 1952; admitted to bar, 1992, District of Columbia and U.S. Court of Appeals, Federal Circuit; registered to practice before U.S. Patent and Trademark Office. *Education:* University of Maryland (B.S., Biochemistry, 1977); Albany Medical College (Ph.D., Biochemistry, 1981); St. Louis University (J.D., cum laude, 1991); registered to practice before U.S. Patent and Trademark Office. (Resident, Washington, D.C. Office). ***PRACTICE AREAS:*** Intellectual Property; Counseling; Biotechnology. ***Email:*** msanzo@fitcheven.com

SCOTT J. MENGHINI, born Missoula, Montana, June 20, 1967; admitted to bar, 1998, California; registered to practice before U.S. Patent and Trademark Office. *Education:* Montana State University (B.S.E.E., 1991); University of San Diego (J.D., 1998). Recipient, International Academy of Trial Lawyers for Excellence in Advocacy Cause and Trial Court Work. *Member:* San Diego Intellectual Property Law Association. (Resident, San Diego, California Office). ***PRACTICE AREAS:*** Intellectual Property; Patent; Technology and Science; Computer Software; Electronics; Electro-Mechanical; Cable Communications; Cable TV; Cellular Communications; Cellular Telephone; Electronic Commerce; Wireless Communications; Computer Technology; Software Protection; Electrical Intellectual Property; Intellectual Property Prosecution; International Intellectual Property Patents; Mechanical Intellectual Property; International Patents; Patent Prosecution. ***Email:*** sjmeng@fitcheven.com

NORMAN KUNITZ, born Philadelphia Pennsylvania, July 18, 1935; admitted to bar, 1961, District of Columbia; 1962, U.S. Court of Appeals, District of Columbia Circuit; 1962, U.S. Court of Customs and Patent Appeals; 1970, California and U.S. Supreme Court; 1982, U.S. Court of Appeals, Federal Circuit; registered to practice before U.S. Patent and Trademark Office. *Education:* Drexel University (B.S.E.E., 1957); George Washington University (J.D., 1961). Phi Alpha Delta; Eta Kappa Nu. Patent Examiner, U.S. Patent Office, 1957-1962. *Member:* The District of Columbia Bar; Bar Association of the District of Columbia; State Bar of California; American Bar Association; American Intellectual Property Law Association; International Trade Commission Trial Lawyers Association. (Resident, Washington, D.C. Office). ***Email:*** nkunitz@fitcheven.com

RUDY I. KRATZ, born Park Ridge, Illinois, December 7, 1967; admitted to bar, 1993, Illinois; 1999, U.S. District Court, Northern District of Illinois; registered to practice before U.S. Patent and Trademark Office. *Education:* University of Illinois (B.S., Engineering Physics, 1990; B.A., Psychology, 1990; J.D., summa cum laude, 1993). Harno Scholar. Rickert Award for Academic Excellence. Member, University of Illinois Law Review. Co-Author: "Recent Decisions - Punitive Damages" in March, 2000 ISBA Trial Briefs. Contributed to "Sanctions under Rule 11," ALI-ABA, March, 2000. *Member:* Chicago and Illinois State Bar Associations. ***PRACTICE AREAS:*** Intellectual Property Litigation; Intellectual Property Prosecution. ***Email:*** rkratz@fitcheven.com

RAMON R. HOCH, born Emporia, Kansas, November 20, 1959; admitted to bar, 1991, Virginia; 1994, Minnesota; 2002, District of Columbia; registered to practice before U.S. Patent and Trademark Office (Not admitted in Illinois). *Education:* University of Kansas (B.S.Ch.E., 1983); George Mason University (J.D., 1991). Primary Patent Examiner, U.S. Patent & Trademark Office, 1983-1990. *Member:* Virginia State Bar; The District of Columbia Bar. (Also at Washington, D.C. Office). ***PRACTICE AREAS:*** Intellectual Property. ***Email:*** rhoch@fitcheven.com

JOHN D. BAUERSFELD, born Washington, D.C., February 23, 1940; admitted to bar, 1969, District of Columbia; 1971, California; registered to practice before U.S. Patent and Trademark Office. *Education:* George Washington University (B.M.E., 1965); Catholic University of America (J.D., 1969). Delta Theta Phi. *Member:* San Fernando Valley and American Bar Associations; State Bar of California; The District of Columbia Bar; American Intellectual Property Law Association; Los Angeles Patent Law Association. (Resident, Woodland Hills, California Office). ***PRACTICE AREAS:*** Intellectual Property Law; Patents, Trademark and Copyright Law; Litigation. ***Email:*** jbauer@fitcheven.com

GARY D. MANN, born Kalamazoo, Michigan, March 12, 1950; admitted to bar, 1980, Indiana; 1982, Texas; 1992, California, U.S. Court of Appeals, Fifth, Ninth and Federal Circuits and U.S. District Court, Northern, Central and Southern Districts of California; registered to practice before U.S. Patent and Trademark Office. *Education:* United States Naval Academy (B.S., Physics, 1972); Graduate, U.S. Naval Nuclear Power School, 1973; Indiana University (J.D., cum laude, 1980). National Team Member, Moot Court Society. Associate Editor, Indiana Law Review, 1979-1980. *Member:* State Bar of California; Los Angeles Intellectual Property Law Association. [Lieut., U.S. Navy, 1972-1977]. (Resident, Woodland Hills, California Office). ***PRACTICE AREAS:*** Patents; Trademarks; Copyrights. ***Email:*** gmann@fitcheven.com

EDWARD E. CLAIR, born Chicago, Illinois, December 23, 1972; admitted to bar, 1999, Illinois. *Education:* Marquette University (B.S.E.E., 1996); IIT Chicago-Kent College of Law (J.D., 1999). Phi Alpha Delta. Recipient, CALI Awards for Legal Drafting and Intellectual Property for Corp. Transactions. *Member:* Chicago, Illinois State and American Bar Associations; The Intellectual Property Law Association of Chicago; Institute of Electrical and Electronics Engineers; American Intellectual Property Law Association. ***PRACTICE AREAS:*** Intellectual Property; Patent Prosecution; Electrical Patents; Electronic Patents; Computer and Software Patents; Computer Software; Electro-Mechanical Patents; Mechanical Patents; Patent Licensing; Patent Litigation; Trademarks; Copyrights; Trade Dress; Trade Secret. ***Email:*** eclair@fitcheven.com

JOHN E. LYHUS, born Janesville, Illinois, October 18, 1957; admitted to bar, 1984, New York; 1989, U.S. District Court, Southern District of New York; 1995, Illinois. *Education:* University of Wisconsin at Madison (B.B.A., 1980); New York Law School (J.D., 1983). Member: Chicago and Illinois State Bar Associations, 1993-1997. ***PRACTICE AREAS:*** Trademark; Copyright. ***Email:*** jelyh@fitcheven.com

(This Listing Continued)

SAMUEL P. BURKHOLDER, born 1958; admitted to bar, 1994, New Jersey and Pennsylvania (inactive); 1999, District of Columbia; registered to practice before U.S. Patent and Trademark Office (Not admitted in Illinois). *Education:* Goshen College (B.A., 1980); Purdue University (M.S., 1987); Temple University (J.D., 1994).

DAVID W. MAHER, PH.D., born San Francisco, California, 1961; admitted to bar, 1999, California; registered to practice before U.S. Patent and Trademark Office (Not admitted in Illinois). *Education:* University of Notre Dame (B.S., 1983); University of the Pacific; University of California, San Diego (Ph.D., 1992); Santa Clara University (J.D., 1998).

JOHN J. GRESENS, born Springfield, Illinois, February 4, 1959; admitted to bar, 1986, Illinois and U.S. District Court, Northern District of Illinois; 1988, Minnesota; 1993, U.S. District Court, District of Minnesota, U.S. Court of Appeals for the Federal Circuit and U.S. Court of Appeals for the District of Columbia Circuit; registered to practice before U.S. Patent and Trademark Office. *Education:* St. John's University (B.S., Chemistry, 1981); Hamline University (J.D., 1986).

OF COUNSEL

GEORGE H. SPENCER, born June 21, 1928; admitted to bar, 1952, New York; 1953-1982, U.S. Court of Customs and Patent Appeals; 1953, U.S. Court of Military Appeals; 1957, U.S. District Court, Southern District of New York; 1958, U.S. Supreme Court; 1958-1982, U.S. Court of Claims; 1959, District of Columbia and U.S. Court of Appeals for the District of Columbia Circuit; 1973, U.S. Court of Appeals, Fourth Circuit; 1977, U.S. Court of International Trade; 1982, U.S. Court of Appeals for the Federal Circuit; registered to practice before U.S. Patent and Trademark Office. *Education:* Cheshire Academy; Yale University (B.E., 1948); Cornell University (J.D., 1952). Patent Examiner, U.S. Patent Office, 1952-1954. Arbitrator and Mediator, WIPO (World Intellectual Property Organization) Arbitration and Mediation Center. *Member:* The District of Columbia Bar; Bar Association of the District of Columbia; American Bar Association; American Intellectual Property Law Association; Federal Circuit Bar Association; German American Law Association; Judge Advocates Association; Lawyer-Pilots Bar Association; International Trade Commission Trial Lawyers Association; Intellectual Property Institute of Canada (Foreign Associate); American Inn of Court (Master of the Bench, The Prettyman-Leventhal). [U.S. Army Reserve, Signal Corps, 1948-1956, Judge Advocate General's Corps, 1956-1962]. (Resident, Washington, D.C. Office). ***LANGUAGES:*** German and French. ***PRACTICE AREAS:*** Intellectual Property Law; Patent Law; Trademark Law; Litigation. ***Email:*** ghspencer@fitcheven.com

---

JON A. BIRMINGHAM, born Alton, Illinois, June 4, 1975; admitted to bar, 2000, Illinois. *Education:* Northwestern University (B.S., 1997); University of Illinois (J.D., cum laude, 2000). ***Email:*** jbirmi@fitcheven.com

STEVEN M. FREELAND, admitted to bar, 1998, California. *Education:* Brigham Young University (B.S., 1992); University of San Diego (J.D., 1998). (Resident, San Diego, California Office). ***PRACTICE AREAS:*** Intellectual Property; Patents. ***Email:*** steve@fitcheven.com

BRIAN SOMMER CLISE, born June 17, 1972; admitted to bar, 1999, Missouri; 2000, Massachusetts; 2002, Illinois. *Education:* Duke University (B.S.E., 1993); Washington University (J.D., 1999). ***PRACTICE AREAS:*** Patent Prosecution; Patent Litigation; Mechanical Patents; Electrical Patents; Computer and Software Patents. ***Email:*** bclise@fitcheven.com

MARTIN R. BADER, born Santa Rosa, California, April 14, 1976; admitted to bar, 2002, California and U.S. District Court, Southern District of California; registered to practice before U.S. Patent and Trademark Office. *Education:* California Polytechnic State University (B.S., Electrical Engineering, 1999); University of San Diego (J.D., magna cum laude, 2002). Order of the Coif. Member, San Diego Law Review. (Resident, San Diego, California Office). ***PRACTICE AREAS:*** Patents; Trademarks; Licensing. ***Email:*** martin@fitcheven.com

MARK A. BORSOS, born Kalamazoo, Michigan, March 7, 1977; admitted to bar, 2002, Illinois and U.S. District Court, Northern District of Illinois; registered to practice before U.S. Patent and Trademark Office. *Education:* University of Michigan (B.S., with distinction, Biology, 1999; J.D., 2002). Recipient: Sophomore Honors Award; James B. Angell Scholar, University of Michigan. ***PRACTICE AREAS:*** Intellectual Property; Litigation. ***Email:*** mborsos@fitcheven.com

TIMOTHY R. BAUMANN, born Iowa Falls, Iowa, August 16, 1963; admitted to bar, 1995, Illinois; 1996, U.S. District Court, Northern District of Illinois and U.S. Court of Appeals for the Federal Circuit; registered to practice before U.S. Patent and Trademark Office. *Education:* Iowa State University (B.S.E.E., 1986; B.S.C.S., 1986); University of Illinois (J.D., magna cum laude, 1995). Eta Kappa Nu. Notes Editor, Elder Law Journal, 1994-1995. ***PRACTICE AREAS:*** Patent Litigation; Patent Prosecution; Electrical Engineering. ***Email:*** tbaumann@fitcheven.com

JEFFREY A. CHELSTROM, born St. Paul, Minnesota, 1969; admitted to bar, 2003, Illinois. *Education:* Iowa State University (B.S., Chemical Engineering, with honors, 1991); William Mitchell College of Law (J.D., magna cum laude, 2003). ***PRACTICE AREAS:*** Intellectual Property; Patents; Litigation. ***Email:*** jachel@fitcheven.com

NICHOLAS T. PETERS, born Chicago Heights, Illinois, 1976; admitted to bar, 2003, Illinois; registered to practice before U.S. Patent and Trademark Office. *Education:* Vanderbilt University (B.S., Mathematics and Engineering Science with a concentration in Applied Physics, magna cum laude, 1998; M.S., Physics, 2000); Loyola University (J.D., cum laude, 2003). ***PRACTICE AREAS:*** Intellectual Property; Litigation. ***Email:*** ntpete@fitcheven.com

KENNETH E. PLOCHINSKI, born Detroit, Michigan, 1955; admitted to bar, 2003, Illinois. *Education:* University of Michigan (B.S.E., Engineering, cum laude, 1981; M.A., Mathematics, 1983; J.D., cum laude, 2003). ***PRACTICE AREAS:*** Intellectual Property; Litigation. ***Email:*** kploch@fitcheven.com

(This Listing Continued)

FITCH, EVEN, TABIN & FLANNERY, Chicago—Continued

GRACE LAW O'BRIEN, born February 18, 1970; admitted to bar, 2000, Illinois and U.S. District Court, Northern District of Illinois; registered to practice before U.S. Patent and Trademark Office. *Education:* University of California (B.A., Pure Mathematics, with honors, 1996); Chicago-Kent College of Law (J.D., 1999). ***LANGUAGES:*** Chinese and Cantonese. ***PRACTICE AREAS:*** Intellectual Property. ***Email:*** glaw@fitcheven.com

CHRISTINE A. ABUEL, born Detroit, Michigan, January 13, 1979; admitted to bar, 2004, Illinois and U.S. District Court, Northern District of Illinois; registered to practice before U.S. Patent and Trademark Office. *Education:* Wayne State University (B.A., Biology; Minor in Chemistry, 2001); DePaul University College of Law (J.D., cum laude, 2004). ***PRACTICE AREAS:*** Intellectual Property; Litigation.

TARA M. REEDY, born Chicago, Illinois, May 22, 1978; admitted to bar, 2004, Illinois; 2005, U.S. District Court, Northern District of Illinois. *Education:* University of Arizona (B.A., summa cum laude); DePaul University (J.D.). ***PRACTICE AREAS:*** Trademark; Copyright; Litigation. ***Email:*** treedy@fitcheven.com

SARAH M. WALKINGTON, born Winfield, Illinois, March 26, 1976; admitted to bar, 2002, Illinois. *Education:* University of Iowa (B.S., Microbiology, 1998); John Marshall Law School (J.D., magna cum laude, 2002). Order of John Marshall; Dean's Scholar; Herzog Scholar. Editor and Co-Founder, The John Marshall Review of Intellectual Property Law.

JOEL H. BOOTZIN, born 1967; admitted to bar, 1996, Illinois; 1997, Wisconsin; U.S. District Court, Northern District of Illinois; U.S. Court of Appeals for the Federal Circuit; registered to practice before U.S. Patent and Trademark Office. *Education:* Milwaukee School of Engineering (B.S., 1989); Chicago-Kent College of Law, Illinois Institute of Technology (J.D., 1996). *Member:* Chicago and American Bar Associations; American Intellectual Property Law Association; Intellectual Property Law Association of Chicago.

MICHAEL P. FURMANEK, born Southfield, Michigan, 1977; admitted to bar, 2003, Michigan; 2004, Illinois. *Education:* University of Michigan (B.S.M.E., cum laude, 2000); DePaul University (J.D., cum laude, 2003). *Member:* State Bar of Michigan. ***PRACTICE AREAS:*** Intellectual Property; Patents.

JAMES M. WAKELY, born Park Forest, Illinois, August 19, 1975; admitted to bar, 2000, California (inactive); 2002, Illinois; registered to practice before U.S. Patent and Trademark Office. *Education:* Bradley University (B.S.E.E., cum laude, 1997); Northwestern University (J.D., 2000). National Merit Scholar. ***PRACTICE AREAS:*** Intellectual Property; Patents.

PATENT AGENTS

ERIC JAMES WHITESELL, born Berkeley, California, January 28, 1944; registered to practice before U.S. Patent and Trademark Office. *Education:* University of the South (A.B., Physics, 1966). Space and Naval Warfare Systems Center, San Diego. (Electronics Engineer, Patent Agent). ***LANGUAGES:*** German, Vietnamese. ***PRACTICE AREAS:*** Patents; Patent Applications; Patent Prosecution; Electronics. ***Email:*** eric@fitcheven.com

LILIA I. SAFONOV, born Kishinev, Moldova, USSR, May 31, 1953. *Education:* Moscow Institute of Electronics, Moscow, Russia (M.S.E.E., 1977); Central Institute of Patent Studies, Moscow, Russia (Patent Attorney, 1983). (Registered Patent Agent). ***LANGUAGES:*** Russian. ***PRACTICE AREAS:*** Patent Prosecution; Electrical Intellectual Property Prosecution; Electronic Intellectual Property Prosecution; Mechanical Intellectual Property Prosecution. ***Email:*** lisafo@fitcheven.com

NADA J. ARDELEANU, born St. Paul, Minnesota, November 25, 1974; registered to practice before the U.S. Patent and Trademark Office. *Education:* University of Minnesota (B.S., Chemical Engineering, minor in Chemistry, 1996). ***LANGUAGES:*** Serbian and Romanian. ***PRACTICE AREAS:*** Intellectual Property; Patent Prosecution. ***Email:*** nardeleanu@fitcheven.com

FLAHERTY & JACOBSON, P.C.

134 NORTH LASALLE STREET
SUITE 1600
CHICAGO, ILLINOIS 60602
Telephone: 312-782-4700
Fax: 312-782-4725
URL: http://www.lawyers.com/fjlaw
Email: lawyers@fjlaw.com
URL: http://www.fjlaw.com

Business and Financial Tort, Legal Malpractice, Construction and Complex Commercial Litigation.

FIRM PROFILE: Flaherty & Jacobson, P.C., founded in 1996, represents professionals and non-professionals in complex litigation, including legal and financial professional malpractice, business tort, commercial, construction and mass-tort claims.

MICHAEL J. FLAHERTY, born Peru, Illinois, November 15, 1958; admitted to bar, 1983, Illinois; 1986, U.S. District Court, Northern District of Illinois. *Education:* University of Illinois (B.A., 1980); Illinois Institute of Technology (J.D., 1983). Author/Co-Author: "Lawyers Liability and Discipline," 1992—; "Professional Liability and Ethics Flashpoints," 1999—; Illinois State Bar Association Annual Edition of Southern Illinois University Law Journal; "Transforming U.S. Law Firms, Law Firm Governance Review, Aspen, 1999; "A Perspective on Alcoholism In The Profession, Trial Lawyers Guide, Vol 43, No. 1 West, 1999; "Know The Fair Debt Law and Follow It," ABA Journal, p. 73, May, 1999; "Striking Out Free Agents," ABA Journal, p. 82 July 1997; "Subject of Defending Lawyers in Stimulating Work," Elaine McArdle Lawyers Weekly USA, 99LAUSA 415/ May 13, 1999. Featured in Presidential Lessons, John Gilbert, ABA Journal, p. 52 December 1988 and Avoiding Trouble at the Mill, John Gibeaut, ABA Journal, p. 48, March 1997. Speaker, 2002 Lloyds/Equitas Policyholder Conference on Aggregative Asbestos and Mass Tort Settlements. Adjunct Professor (Ethics), Northwestern University Law School, 1998—. Faculty, National Institute For Trial Advocacy, 1994—. Faculty, Professional Responsibility Institute of the Illinois Supreme Courts, 1988—. Past President, Association of Professional Responsibility Lawyers. Past-President, Lawyers' Risk Management Association. Co-Chair: 2002 Global Forum on International Legal Ethics and Risk Management, Florence, Italy; 2000 Global Forum on Multi-Discipline and Multi-Jurisdictional Practice, Cambridge, England. *Member:* Chicago (Chair, Committee on Preventing Legal Malpractice) and American (Editorial Board Member, Center for Professional Responsibility; member, Joint Committee on Lawyer Regulation; Reporter, 2000 U.S. Chief Justices Conference on Multi-Jurisdictional Practice) Bar Associations. Fellow, American Bar Foundation. ***PRACTICE AREAS:*** Legal Malpractice Defense; Financial Law; Business Torts; Construction Litigation; Insurance Litigation; Risk Management. ***Email:*** mflaherty@fjlaw.com

(This Listing Continued)

RICHARD J. JACOBSON, born Fort Benning, Georgia, July 12, 1943; admitted to bar, 1977, Virginia and Illinois and U.S. District Court, Northern District of Illinois; 1979, District of Columbia; 1991, U.S. Court of Appeals, Seventh Circuit. *Education:* Harvard University (A.B., magna cum laude, 1965; Ph.D., 1970); University of Virginia (J.D., 1977). Recipient: Woodrow Wilson National Fellowship, 1965; Briggs Prize; Porter Prize. Author, "The Letter: Responding to an Attorney Registration and Disciplinary Commission Investigation," Chicago Bar Association Record, January 1995. Co-Author: *Lawyers' Liability and Discipline* ; "Survey of Illinois Governing Lawyers," 25 Southern Illinois University Law Journal 841. Summer 2001; "Survey of Illinois Professional Responsibility Law," 23 Southern Illinois University Law Journal 1201, Summer 1999; "Transforming U.S. Law Firms," Law Governance, Vol. 4, No. 1, Autumn 1999; "A Perspective on Alcoholism in the Legal Profession," 1999 Trial Lawyers Guide, Vol. 43, No. 1 (West); "Billing Practices, Problems Can Create Costly Liability," Vol. 143, No. 241 Chicago Daily Law Bulletin, December 10, 1997; "Striking Out Free Agents," ABA Journal, p. 82, July 1997; "Left Holding the Bag," Counselor, vol. VI, issue II, 1997; "Revisiting Himmel Under the 1990 Illinois Rules of Professional Conduct," 78 Illinois Bar Journal 488, October 1990; "Talking to Juries: The Inner Game," Trial Diplomacy Journal, 1986; "Simplifying Complex Concepts for a Lay Fact Finder," *Transportation Negligence,* IICLE, 1984. Adjunct Professor of Law, Trial Advocacy, Northwestern University Law School, 1999—. Faculty Member: Deposition Skills Program, Northwestern University Law School, National Institute for Trial Advocacy, 1999; Professional Responsibility Institute of the Illinois Supreme Court, 1998—. *Member:* Chicago (Vice-Chair, Committee on Preventing of Legal Malpractice, 1999-2000; Chair, Committee on Preventing Legal Malpractice, 2000-2001) and American (Associate, National Legal Malpractice Data Center, Standing Committee on Lawyers Professional Liability, 1996-1998; Member, Law Practice Management Section: Committee on Professionalism, Ethics and Competency, 1998-1999; Section Liaison, Standing Committee on Lawyers Professional Liability, 1999-1999) Bar Associations; Legal Club of Chicago; Association of Professional Responsibility Lawyers. ***PRACTICE AREAS:*** Legal Malpractice; Financial Law; Business Torts; Construction Litigation; Insurance Litigation; Professional Discipline; Risk Management. ***Email:*** rjacobson@fjlaw.com

JEFFREY S. YOUNGERMAN, born Chicago, Illinois, May 8, 1961; admitted to bar, 1986, Illinois and U.S. District Court, Northern District of Illinois. *Education:* University of Illinois (B.S., Finance, 1983); DePaul College of Law (J.D., 1986). Recipient, American Jurisprudence Award in Torts. *Member:* Chicago (Member, Subcommittee on Commercial Litigation), Illinois State and American Bar Associations. ***PRACTICE AREAS:*** Construction Litigation; Civil Litigation; Community Association Law; Real Estate Law.

OF COUNSEL

STEPHEN D. SHARP, born LaPorte, Indiana, October 17, 1952; admitted to bar, 1978, Iowa and Illinois; 1980, U.S. District Court, Northern District of Illinois; 1985, U.S. District Court, Northern District of California; 1989, U.S. Court of Appeals, Third, Seventh and Ninth Circuits; 1988, Arizona. *Education:* DePauw University (B.A., with honors, 1975); University of Iowa (J.D., with distinction, 1978). *Member:* Illinois State and American Bar Associations. ***PRACTICE AREAS:*** Complex Litigation; Construction Law.

FLAMM & TEIBLOOM, LTD.

20 NORTH CLARK STREET, 22ND FLOOR
CHICAGO, ILLINOIS 60602
Telephone: 312-236-8400
Telecopier: 312-236-7660
Email: ft@flamm.com
URL: http://www.flamm.com

Organization, Acquisition, Representation and Sale of Businesses. Real Estate and Financial Transactions, Health Care Law and Regulation, Hospitals, Business, Real Estate and Insurance Litigation, Securities Law and Litigation, Antitrust and Trade Regulation, Federal, State and Local Taxation, Real Estate Tax Sale and Tax Deed Matters, Probate and Estate Planning.

FIRM PROFILE: Flamm & Teibloom, Ltd. is a Chicago law firm concentrating in business and real estate transactions and in related areas of civil litigation. Our firm has extensive experience in the organization, acquisition, representation and sale of corporations, partnerships and limited liability companies; commercial and residential real estate transactions, financing and development; securities law and litigation; antitrust and trade regulation; federal, state and local taxation; real estate tax sale and tax deed matters; health care law and litigation; estate planning and probate; and most types of business and real estate litigation. The firm represents prominent national and Illinois corporations and individuals, including Aurico Reports, Inc., Bank One, N.A.; Broadway Bank; Chicago Title Insurance Company; Commonwealth Land Title Insurance Company; Diamond Headache Clinic, Ltd.; the Village of Dolton; Fidelity National Title Insurance Company; JP Morgan; Chase Bank, N.A.; Loop Mortgage Corporation; The National Association for Spinal Care; Regent Investments, Inc.; The Roscoe Company; Southern Illinois Securities; and Transnation Title Insurance Company. The Martindale-Hubbell Law Directory has given our firm the highest possible ratings. Our goal is to provide our clients with expert advice and advocacy of the highest quality while being responsive to the needs of businesses and individuals.

(This Listing Continued)

MATTHEW A. FLAMM, born Chicago, Illinois, October 11, 1953; admitted to bar, 1978, Illinois. *Education:* University of Illinois; Northwestern University (B.A., 1975); Georgetown University (J.D., magna cum laude, 1978). Editor, Georgetown Law Journal, 1977-1978. Secretary and Attorney, Lighthouse Park District of Evanston, 1980—. *Member:* Chicago (Chairman, Tax Sale and Tax Deed Subcommittee, Committee on Real Estate Taxation, 1992-1994; Chairman, Committee on Real Estate Taxation, 1995-1996 and 2005-2006), Illinois State (Associate Editor, State and Local Taxation Council Newsletter, 2005—) and American Bar Associations; Chicago Council of Lawyers. ***PRACTICE AREAS:*** Business; Business Litigation; Real Estate Litigation; Real Estate Transfers; Tax Law. ***Email:*** mflamm@flamm.com

JOEL D. TEIBLOOM, born Chicago, Illinois, February 15, 1954; admitted to bar, 1980, Illinois. *Education:* Brandeis University (A.B., cum laude, 1976); Boston University School of Law (J.D., 1980). *Member:* Chicago Council of Lawyers; Decalogue Society. ***PRACTICE AREAS:*** Business; Real Estate; Business Litigation; Real Estate Litigation; Health Law; Hospitals; Probate; Estate Planning. ***Email:*** jteibloom@flamm.com

JOHN W. STANKO, JR., born Chicago, Illinois, September 1, 1962; admitted to bar, 1988, Illinois. *Education:* St. John's University (B.A., 1985); John Marshall Law School (J.D., 1988). *Member:* Chicago Bar Association. ***PRACTICE AREAS:*** Real Estate Transactions; Real Estate Litigation; Tax Sale and Tax Deed Matters. ***Email:*** jstanko@flamm.com

---

EMMETT R. McCARTHY, born 1973; admitted to bar, 1999, Illinois. *Education:* University of Illinois, Urbana-Champaign (B.S., 1995); DePaul University (J.D., 1999). Case Editor, DePaul Environmental Law Digest. Lecturer, Illinois Trial Lawyers Association. *Member:* Chicago Bar Association (Member, Legislation Liaison, 2003-2004; Chairman, Tax Sale and Tax Deed Sub Committee; Real Estate Taxation Committee). ***PRACTICE AREAS:*** Tax Law; Real Estate; Real Estate Litigation.

JOSE MOYA, admitted to bar, 2004, Illinois. *Education:* Marquette University (B.S., 1998); University of Illinois College of Law (J.D., 2003).

NATALIE P. NIMERALA, born Hobart, Indiana; admitted to bar, 2003, Illinois. *Education:* University of the South (B.A., 2000); Loyola University Chicago, School of Law (J.D., 2003). Dean's List. Member, American Bar Association Moot Court Team. Recipient, CALI Award in Sports and Entertainment Law. Member, 2000-2003, and Secretary, 2002, Women's Law Society. *Member:* Chicago and Illinois State Bar Associations; Women's Bar Association of Illinois. ***PRACTICE AREAS:*** Business Litigation; Real Estate Litigation. ***Email:*** nnimerala@flamm.com

OF COUNSEL

RICHARD ORLIKOFF, born Garfield, New Jersey, July 2, 1923; admitted to bar, 1950, Illinois; U.S. District Court, Northern District of Illinois; U.S. Court of Appeals, Seventh and Eighth Circuits; 1972, U.S. Supreme Court. *Education:* University of Michigan (B.A., 1943); University of Chicago (J.D., 1949). Member, Board of Editors, University of Chicago Law Review, 1948-1949. ***PRACTICE AREAS:*** Corporate Law; Mergers and Acquisitions. ***Email:*** rorlikoff@flamm.com

WILLIAM M. LAYTIN, born Fort Smith, Arkansas, February 10, 1947; admitted to bar, 1972, Oklahoma; 1973, Illinois. *Education:* University of Oklahoma (B.A., 1969; J.D., 1972). Phi Alpha Delta. *Member:* Illinois State and American Bar Associations. ***PRACTICE AREAS:*** Real Estate; Finance; Corporate; Partnership; Land Use; Municipal Law.

HENRY W. KENOE (1907-1998)

ARNOLD M. FLAMM (1925-1998)

REPRESENTATIVE CLIENTS: Chicago Title Insurance Co.; Commonwealth Land Title Insurance Co.; Community Nutrition Network, Inc.; Diamond Headache Clinic, Ltd.; Loop Mortgage Corp.; Fidelity National Title Insurance Co.; S.I. Securities; Lutheran General Hospital; The National Association for Spinal Care; The Roscoe Co.; Service Insurance Agency, Inc.

FLANAGAN / BILTON

Established in 1968

200 EAST RANDOLPH DRIVE, SUITE 6900
CHICAGO, ILLINOIS 60601
Telephone: 312-782-5000
Fax: 312-565-0821
URL: http://www.flanaganbilton.com

National Practice Limited to Real Estate Taxation. Ad Valorem Tax Law. Personal Property Tax Law.

FIRM PROFILE: Flanagan/Bilton, a thirty year-old firm, represents clients in ad valorem property tax matters only. As a property tax law firm, Flanagan/Bilton is unique in that it represents properties in many states throughout the country, with a high concentration in the states of Illinois, Florida, Minnesota and Texas. A number of the firm's clients are commercial and industrial property owners with properties in many states and jurisdictions.

The Flanagan/Bilton partners were local government lawyers, with tax, trial and appellate experience prior to forming the firm. In addition to the partners, the firm has appraisers on staff, all of whom have assessment experience in government offices. The firm employs paralegals, who are trained in assessment and valuation procedures, and who have appraisal certifications.

The services offered clients include rendering opinions concerning the accuracy or legality of property tax assessments, preparing and filing property tax schedules or renditions, filing and trying assessment complaints or protests before Assessors, Boards of Review, tax tribunals or courts, and monitoring and auditing tax assessments and bills. The multi-state activity of Flanagan/Bilton gives property owners the ability to concentrate this activity in one law firm, regardless of the location of the property.

(This Listing Continued)

MEMBERS OF FIRM

THOMAS D. FLANAGAN, born Chicago, Illinois, September 18, 1937; admitted to bar, 1963, Illinois; 1978, U.S. Supreme Court. *Education:* Loyola University (B.S., 1959); Chicago-Kent College of Law (J.D., 1963). Author: "Procedures in Appeals Before Cook County Board of Appeals," Illinois State Bar Association Local Government Law Newsletter, Vol. 10, No. 5, June, 1973; "Rising property taxes: Where's the real risk?" Apartment Finance Today, Vol. 8, No. 5, July/August 2004. Assistant State's Attorney, Cook County, 1963-1969. *Member:* Chicago, Illinois State and American Bar Associations. ***PRACTICE AREAS:*** Ad Valorem Property Taxation. ***Email:*** tflanagan@flanaganbilton.com

DEAN H. BILTON, born Chicago, Illinois, October 25, 1937; admitted to bar, 1960, Illinois; 1969, U.S. Supreme Court; 1981, Minnesota; 1989, Texas. *Education:* University of Arizona; University of Michigan; Loyola University; DePaul University (LL.B., 1960). Nu Beta Epsilon. Assistant State's Attorney, Cook County, 1961-1970. *Member:* Chicago, Illinois State and Minnesota State Bar Associations; State Bar of Texas. ***REPORTED CASES:*** Boyle v. Landy, 401 U.S. 77 (1971). ***PRACTICE AREAS:*** Ad Valorem Property Taxation. ***Email:*** dbilton@flanaganbilton.com

ASSOCIATE

HUAN D. CASSIOPPI TRAN, born Saigon, Vietnam, June 17, 1964; admitted to bar, 2001, Illinois and U.S. District Court, Northern District of Illinois; 2002, District of Columbia; 2003, California. *Education:* University of Iowa (B.A., 1990); Loyola University (J.D., 2001). Phi Alpha Delta. Author: "Internet Privacy: Whose Right is it Anyway?," Loyola Forum of International Law, Vol. VII, Issue 1, 1999. *Member:* Chicago and Illinois State Bar Associations; The District of Columbia Bar; State Bar of California; International Association of Assessing Officers; Institute for Professionals in Taxation. ***LANGUAGES:*** Vietnamese and Japanese. ***PRACTICE AREAS:*** Ad Valorem Taxation. ***Email:*** huan@flanaganbilton.com

LEGAL SUPPORT PERSONNEL

TAX ADMINISTRATORS

ORLANDO PELLEGRINO, born Chicago Heights, Illinois, December 23, 1934. *Education:* University of Iowa (B.A., 1957). Certified Illinois Assessing Officer. Certified Member, Institute of Property Taxation. Prior Position: Cook County Assessor's Office. ***Email:*** opellegrino@flanaganbilton.com

SPERO N. KOPITAS, born Chicago, Illinois, January 8, 1967. *Education:* DePaul University (B.S., 1991). State Licensed Tax Representative: Texas; Tennessee. Member: Appraisal Institute; Institute for Professionals in Taxation; International Association of Assessing Officers; National Multi-Housing Counsel. ***LANGUAGES:*** Greek. ***Email:*** skopitas@flanaganbilton.com

JAMES E. OWENS, born Evergreen Park, Illinois, July 10, 1959. *Education:* St. Xavier University (B.A., 1982). Certified Illinois Assessing Officer. Certified Assessment Expert Candidate. Prior Position: Director of Assessment Planning, Cook County Assessor's Office. ***Email:*** jowens@flanaganbilton.com

ROBERT E. PERNAI, born Chicago, Illinois, August 13, 1959. *Education:* DePaul University (B.S., 1981; M.B.A., 1988). Certified Public Accountant. Prior Position, Director of Real Estate Taxes for Balcor Management Services, Inc. ***Email:*** bpernai@flanaganbilton.com

PARALEGALS

ABBY MARKOWITZ, born Chicago, Illinois, September 8, 1963. *Education:* Indiana University (B.S., 1985); Roosevelt University (Certified Paralegal); Loyola University (M.B.A., 1997); Illinois Property Assessment Institute. Certified Illinois Assessing Officer. ***Email:*** amarkowitz@flanaganbilton.com

KRISTINE R. PETERSON, born Chicago, Illinois, July 11, 1967. *Education:* Northern Illinois University (B.A., 1989); Roosevelt University (Certified Paralegal). Certified Illinois Assessing Officer, Associate. Member: Illinois Property Assessment Institute; Institute for Professionals in Taxation. ***Email:*** kpeterson@flanaganbilton.com

CHERYL L. BEILKE, born Chicago, Illinois, April 21, 1968. *Education:* South Suburban College; Prairie State College. Affiliate Member, Appraisal Institute. *Member:* Illinois Coalition of Appraisal Professionals. ***Email:*** cbeilke@flanaganbilton.com

RYAN J. GIBBS, born Cincinnati, Ohio, February 29, 1976. *Education:* Washington & Lee University (B.A., 1998). Affiliated Member, Appraisal Institute. *Member:* Illinois Coalition of Appeals Professionals. ***Email:*** ryangibbs@flanaganbilton.com

REPRESENTATIVE CLIENTS: Alliance Holdings; Ameritech; American Express; BP Amoco Property; Brown & Williamson Tobacco Co., Inc.; Central States, Southeast & Southwest Areas Health & Welfare & Pension Funds; Columbia College; CNA Insurance Co.; Corn Products International;EPT Management Company; Fifth Third Bank; First Industrial Realty Trust Inc.; Gables Residential; Trammel-Crowe; GE Capital; Goodyear Tire and Rubber Company; Inland Real Estate Corp.; Invesco; Jones Lang LaSalle; Kensington Advisors; Lend Lease Real Estate Investments; Marshall Field & Co.; McShane Corporation; Metropolitan Life Insurance Co.; NiSource; Northrup; OPUS North Management Corporation; ORIX Real Estate Equities; Penguin Group; Prime Residential LP; Pritzker Residential; Regency Realty; Robert Sheridan & Partners; RREEF Funds; SBC; Target; Taubman Co.; Trammel Crow Company; USX Corp.

KENNETH N. FLAXMAN, P.C.

SUITE 1240, 200 SOUTH MICHIGAN AVENUE
CHICAGO, ILLINOIS 60604
Telephone: 312-427-3200
Fax: 312-427-3930
Email: knf@kenlaw.com
URL: http://www.kenlaw.com

Civil Rights Law. Federal Civil Litigation (Trial and Appellate).

(This Listing Continued)

KENNETH N. FLAXMAN, P.C., Chicago—Continued

KENNETH N. FLAXMAN, born New York, N.Y., April 30, 1948; admitted to bar, 1972, Illinois, North Carolina and U.S. District Court, Northern District of Illinois; 1975, U.S. Supreme Court; U.S. Court of Appeals, Third, Fourth, Seventh and District of Columbia Circuits. *Education:* City College of the City University of New York (B.E.E., 1968); IIT/Chicago-Kent College of Law (J.D., with distinction, 1972). *Member:* Chicago, Illinois State and American Bar Associations; The Association of Trial Lawyers of America. ***REPORTED CASES:*** Jaffe v. Redmond, 116 S.Ct. 1923 (1996); United States Parole Commission v. Geraghty, 445 V.S. 388 (1978); Doe v. Calumet City, 754 F.Supp 1211 (N.D. Ill 1990); Thomas v. Evanston, 610 F.Supp 422 (N.D. Ill 1985). ***Email:*** knf@kenlaw.com

REPRESENTATIVE CLIENT: Compuaction, Inc.; Evanston Black Police Assn.

KEVIN M. FLYNN & ASSOCIATES

77 WEST WACKER DRIVE
SUITE 4800
CHICAGO, ILLINOIS 60601
Telephone: 312-456-0240
Fax: 312-444-1028
URL: http://www.Kevinflynnlaw.com
Email: kevin@kmflynnlaw.com
URL: http://www.Kevinflynnlaw.com

Trial Practice in all State and Federal Courts and all Alternative Dispute Resolution Forums. Substantive litigation experience includes Antitrust and Trade Regulation, Banking, Complex Business and Commercial, Chancery and Equity, Employment, Franchise, Information Technology, Real Estate, Litigation, Securities, Trade Secrets, White Collar Criminal, Arbitration and Mediation.

FIRM PROFILE: Mr. Flynn is a seasoned trial lawyer with over 27 years of complex commercial litigation experience. In 1996 he resigned from the Chicago law firm now known as Ungaretti & Harris to form his own trial practice firm, having served as one of that firm's senior trial attorneys and having completed a three-year term as that firm's Managing Partner. Mr. Flynn has tried over 125 cases to final disposition in state and federal courts and numerous arbitration forums throughout the country. He also has wide-ranging trial and appellate experience in other substantive areas and forums.

Mr. Flynn is an active member of the Markey-Wigmore Chapter of the American Inns of Court, a nationwide association of judges, trial attorneys and law students dedicated to enhancing the quality and civility of American trial lawyers. He is a former Officer and Director of the Chicago Chapter of the Federal Bar Association, has recently served as Chapter President, a member of the federal trial bar for the United States District Court for the Northern District of Illinois and many other professional associations. In 1998, Mr. Flynn was appointed Special Counsel for the City of Chicago to prosecute charges of police misconduct involving physical abuse of subjects under arrest.

In 2000, Kevin was appointed to the Advisory Council to the Chicago Board of Education's Law and Public Safety Academy.

In 2004, Kevin was selected by his peers to be included in The Best Lawyers in America and the Directory of Illinois Super Lawyers.

KEVIN M. FLYNN, born Lafayette, Indiana, March 21, 1953; admitted to bar, 1978, Illinois and U.S. Supreme Court. *Education:* DePauw University (B.A., 1975); DePaul University (J.D., with honors, 1978). Member, DePaul Law Review, 1977-1978. *Member:* Chicago, Seventh Circuit, Illinois State, Federal (Officer and Director, Chicago Chapter, 1988—) and American Bar Associations; American Inns of Court, Markey-Wigmore Chapter; The Association of Trial Lawyers of America; Illinois Trial Lawyers Association; NITA Advocates Association (Representative). ***REPORTED CASES:*** Pillsbury v. Conboy, 459 U.S. 248 (1983) (fifth amendment/antitrust); Wilmette Park District v. Village of Wilmette, 112 Ill.2d 6 (1986) (home rule authority of Illinois municipalities); Haroco v. American National Bank, 38 F.3d 1429 (7th Cir. 1994) (civil RICO); Spicer v. Chicago Board Options Exchange, Inc., 977 F.2d 255 (7th Cir. 1992) (federal securities regulation); In Re: Corrugated Container Antitrust Litigation, 655 F.2d 748 (7th Cir. 1981) (antitrust); Stathis v. Geldermann, Inc., 692 N.E.2d 798 (Ill. App. 1998) (affirming jury verdict in commercial fraud claim); Travelers v. First National Bank of Blue Island, 621 N.E.2d 209 (1993) (commercial loan foreclosure); Travelers v. Holland Farms, Inc., 504 N.E.2d 532 (Ill. App. 1987) (conflict of laws); Rosin v. First Bank of Oak Park, 466 N.E.2d 1245 (Ill. App. 1984) (real estate auction); Denton Enterprises, Inc. v. Illinois State Toll Highway Authority, 396 N.E.2d 34 (Ill. App. 1979) (highway construction litigation); Ohio Casualty Insurance v. Bank One, et al., 1997 U.S. Dist. LEXIS 702 (N.D. Ill. 1997) (lender liability); Robbins Resource Recovery Partners, et al. v. James D. Edgar, et al. 947 F. Supp. 1205 (N.D. Ill. 1996) (unconstitutional impairment of contract); Nielsen v. Kidder, Peabody, et al., 1996 U.S. Dist. LEXIS 14441 (N.D. Ill. 1996) (securities class action); Taylor v. Bank One, et al. 932 F. Supp. 218 (N.D. Ill. 1996) (consumer lending class action); Sinclair v. Bloom, 1996 U.S. Dist. LEXIS 6701 (N.D. Ill. 1996) (lawyer conflict of interest); Industry Speciality Chemicals v. Cummins Engine, et al., 918 F. Supp. 1173 (N.D. Ill. 1996) (deceptive trade practices); Cusumano v. Mapco Gas Products, et al. 1994 U.S. Dist. LEXIS 7912 (N.D. Ill. 1994) (personal injury); U.S. v. 122, 942 Shares of Common Stock, 847 F. Supp. 105 (N.D. Ill. 1994) (RICO forfeiture); Robin v. Doctors Officenters Corp., 686 F. Supp. 199 (N.D. Ill. 1988) (securities class action); Coronet Insurance Company v. Seyfarth, et al., 665 F. Supp. 661 (N.D. Ill. 1987) (securities fraud).

FOLEY & LARDNER LLP

Established in 1842
321 NORTH CLARK, SUITE 2800
CHICAGO, ILLINOIS 60610
Telephone: 312-832-4500
Fax: 312-832-4700
Email: webmaster@foley.com
URL: http://www.foley.com

Los Angeles, California Office: 2029 Century Park East, 35th Floor. Telephone: 310-277-2223. Fax: 310-557-8475.
Palo Alto Office: 1530 Page Mill Road. Telephone: 650-856-3700. Facsimile: 650-856-3710.
Sacramento, California Office: 1215 K Street, Suite 1920. Telephone: 916-443-8005. Fax: 916-443-2240.
San Diego, California Office: 402 West Broadway, 23rd Floor. Telephone: 619-234-6655. Fax: 619-234-3510.
San Diego/North County, California Office: 11250 El Camino Real, Suite 200. Telephone: 858-847-6700. Facsimile: 858-792-6773.
San Francisco, California Office: One Maritime Plaza, Sixth Floor. Telephone: 415-434-4484. Fax: 415-434-4507.
Washington, D.C. Office: Washington Harbour, Suite 500, 3000 K Street, N.W. Telephone: 202-672-5300. Facsimile: 202-672-5399.
Jacksonville, Florida Office: One Independent Drive, Suite 1300. Telephone: 904-359-2000. Facsimile: 904-359-8700.
Orlando, Florida Office: Suite 1800, 111 North Orange Avenue, P.O. Box 2193. Telephone: 407-423-7656. Facsimile: 407-648-1743.
Tallahassee, Florida Office: 106 East College Avenue, Highpoint Center, Suite 900, P.O. Box 1819. Telephone: 850-222-6100. Facsimile: 850-561-6475.
Tampa, Florida Office: Suite 2700, 100 N. Tampa Street, P.O. Box 3391. Telephones: 813-229-2300; Pinellas County: 813-442-3296. Facsimile: 813-221-4210.
West Palm Beach, Florida Office: 777 South Flagler Drive, Suite 901, West Tower. Telephone: 561-655-5050. Facsimile: 561-655-6925.
Tokyo, Japan Office: JT Building 15F, 2-2-1 Toranomon Minato-ku, Tokyo, 105-0001. Telephone: +81 (03) 5114-8320. Facsimile: +81 (03) 5114-8321.
Detroit, Michigan Office: One Detroit Center, 500 Woodward Avenue, Suite 2700. Telephone: 313-234-7100. Fax: 313-234-2800.
New York, New York Office: 90 Park Avenue. Telephone: 212-682-7474. Facsimile: 212-687-2329; 212-490-3654.
Madison, Wisconsin Office: Verex Plaza, 150 East Gilman Street, P.O. Box 1497. Telephone: 608-257-5035. Facsimile: 608-258-4258.
Milwaukee, Wisconsin Office: 777 East Wisconsin Avenue. Telephone: 414-271-2400. Facsimile: 414-297-4900.
Brussels, Belgium Office: Avenue de Cortenbergh, 118. Telephone: +011-32-2-639-2710. Facsimile: +011-32-2-646-0311.
Boston, Massachusetts Office: 111 Huntington Avenue. Telephone: 617-342-4000. Facsimile: 617-342-4001.

General Practice. Bankruptcy and Insolvency, Domestic and International Patent, Trademark and Copyright, Corporate Law and Taxation, Corporate Securities, Broker/dealer matters, Commodities, Real Estate, Government Finance, Banking and Commercial Finance, Litigation, International and Health Law.

FIRM PROFILE: Foley & Lardner LLP provides the full range of corporate legal counsel. Our attorneys understand today's most complex business issues, including corporate governance, securities enforcement, litigation, mergers and acquisitions, intellectual property counseling and litigation, labor and employment, and tax. The firm offers total solutions in the automotive, e-business and information technology, energy, entertainment and media, financial services, food, golf and resort services, insurance, health care, life sciences, nanotechnology, and sports industries.

PARTNERS

LISA J. ACEVEDO, admitted to bar, 1995, Illinois. *Education:* Loyola University of Chicago (B.S., Dental Hygiene, 1992; Certificate in Dental Hygiene, 1983); DePaul University College of Law (J.D., with honors, 1995). Order of the Coif. Member, DePaul University Law Review. Casenote Editor, Journal of Health and Hospital Law. Assistant Note Editor, Business Law Journal. Author: "To Review or Not to Review: Antitrust Liabilities and Physician Peer Review," Journal of Health and Hospital Law, November 1994. Corporate Counsel, Baxter International, Inc., 1999-2001. Formerly associated with: McDermott, Will & Emery, Chicago, 1997-1999; Holleb & Coff, 1995-1997l *Member:* American Bar Association; American Health Lawyers Association. ***LANGUAGES:*** Spanish. ***PRACTICE AREAS:*** Health Care; Health Care Corporate Law; Life Sciences; Health Law. ***Email:*** lacevedo@foley.com

G. PETER ALBERT, JR., admitted to bar, 1993, Michigan; 1994, Illinois; U.S. District Court, Southern, Northern and Central Districts of California; U.S. District Court, Eastern District of Michigan; U.S. District Court, Northern District of Illinois; U.S. District, Eastern District of Wisconsin; U.S. Court of Appeals, Federal Circuit; registered to practice before U.S. Patent and Trademark Office. *Education:* Michigan Technological University (B.S.E.E., 1987); The John Marshall Law School (J.D., 1993). Frequent Lecturer on Intellectual Property. Adjunct Professor of law, Handong University, Korea. Faculty Member: Patent Resource Group; The Law Education Institute; The Center for International Legal Studies. Co-Chair, Content and Applications Special Interest Group and Intellectual Property Special Interest Group, San Diego Telecom Counsel, Wireless. *Member:* American Bar Association; American Intellectual Property Law Association. ***PRACTICE AREAS:*** Intellectual Property Litigation; Electronics; Trademarks; Copyrights; Intellectual Property. ***Email:*** palbert@foley.com

MICHAEL G. BAILEY, admitted to bar, 1981, California; 1998, Illinois. *Education:* Stanford University (A.B., with high honors, 1977); University of Chicago (J.D., 1981). *Member:* American Bar Association; National Association of Bond Lawyers. ***SPECIAL***

(This Listing Continued)

AGENCIES: Counsel to the Assistant Chief Counsel and Senior Reviewing Attorney, Financial Institutions and Products, Office of Chief Counsel, Internal Revenue Service, 1990-1997. ***PRACTICE AREAS:*** Taxation; Public Finance; Financial Law; Health Care Finance; Tax Litigation; Tax Valuation. ***Email:*** mbailey@foley.com

SHARON R. BARNER, admitted to bar, 1982, Ohio; 1986, Illinois. *Education:* Syracuse University (B.S., cum laude, 1979; B.A., cum laude, 1979); University of Michigan (J.D., 1982). *Member:* Chicago, Ohio State, Illinois State and American Bar Associations (Intellectual Property Section, Chairperson on Women and Minorities). ***REPORTED CASES:*** Hughes Aircraft Co. v. United States, No. 426-73 (Fed. Cl. Ct.); Celex Group v. The Executive Gallery, Inc. No. 94 C1087 (N.D. Ill.). ***PRACTICE AREAS:*** Intellectual Property Litigation; Patent Law (85%); Transportation; Food and Drug Regulation. ***Email:*** sbarner@foley.com

WESLEY N. BECKER, admitted to bar, 1983, Texas; 1986, Illinois. *Education:* Colorado State University (B.S., 1980); University of Chicago (J.D., 1983). *Member:* Illinois State Bar Association. ***PRACTICE AREAS:*** Real Estate Transactions; Secured Lending; Real Estate; Business Law. ***Email:*** wbecker@foley.com

STEPHEN P. BEDELL, admitted to bar, 1980, Illinois, U.S. District Court, Northern District of Illinois, including Trial Bar and U.S. Court of Appeals, Fifth, Seventh, Ninth and Tenth Circuits; 1986, U.S. Supreme Court; 1987, U.S. District Court, Northern District of Texas; 1988, Wisconsin; 1993, Pennsylvania. *Education:* Xavier University (H.A.B., with honors, magna cum laude, 1976); Northwestern University (J.D., 1979). Articles Editor, Northwestern Journal of International Law and Business, 1978-1979. Co-Author, with L. Harrison, S. Harvey and M. B. Cyze, Book, *Arbitration Practice,* Illinois Institute For Continuing Legal Education, 1989. Member, Inquiry Board, 1985-1988 and Hearing Board, 1989-1995, Attorney Registration and Disciplinary Commission of the State of Illinois. *Member:* Chicago, Illinois State and American Bar Associations; The Association of Trial Lawyers of America; American Judicature Society. ***PRACTICE AREAS:*** Securities; Finance; Litigation; Securities Litigation; Securities Regulation; SEC Enforcement; Investment Regulation. ***Email:*** sbedell@foley.com

MYLES D. BERMAN, admitted to bar, 1983, Illinois; 1991, U.S. District Court, Northern District of Illinois. *Education:* University of Illinois, Urbana-Champaign (A.B., with honors, 1974; M.U.P., 1979); Northwestern University (J.D., 1983). Adjunct Professor of Law, Northwestern University School of Law. Adjunct Professor of Urban and Regional Planning, University of Illinois at Urbana. Field Associate, Brookings Institution's study of the Community Block Grant Program. Research Associate, Northwestern University's Center for Urban Affairs and Policy Research. Chairman, Board of Directors, Chicago Lawyers' Committee for Civil Rights Under Law Inc. Board President, Public Interest Law Initiative. Co-author, chapter of the Attorney's Practice Guide to Negotiations (1995). *Member:* Chicago, Illinois State and American Bar Associations; Chicago Council of Lawyers. ***PRACTICE AREAS:*** Regulatory Law; Government Relations; Election Law; Campaign Law; Political Law; Energy Regulation. ***Email:*** mberman@foley.com

LAURA L. BILAS, admitted to bar, 1985, Illinois. *Education:* Valparaiso University (B.A., with high distinction and honors, 1982); University of Minnesota (J.D., cum laude, 1985). ***PRACTICE AREAS:*** Banking Law; Public Finance Law; Finance; Health Care Finance; Business Law. ***Email:*** lbilas@foley.com

RICHARD BROMLEY, admitted to bar, 1968, Iowa; 1969, Illinois. *Education:* University of Iowa (B.A., 1966; J.D., 1968). Order of the Coif; Delta Theta Phi. Member, Board of Editors, Iowa Law Review, 1967-1968. Law Clerk to Judge Donald P. Lay, U.S. Court of Appeals, Eighth Circuit, 1968-1969. Adjunct Professor, Taxation of Exempt Organizations, De Paul University College of Law, 1984-1989 and IIT Chicago-Kent College of Law, 1987-1989. Member of Board of Advisors of *The Insurance Tax Review,* 1988—. *Member:* American Bar Association (Member, Taxation Section; Chairman, Task Force on Property and Casualty Insurance Company Federal Income Tax Legislation, 1983-1984; Chairman, Subcommittee on Property and Casualty Companies, 1985-1988; Secretary, 1988-1990; Vice Chair, 1990-1992; Chair, Committee on Insurance Company Taxation, 1992-1994); Chicago Crime Commission (Vice Chairman). ***PRACTICE AREAS:*** Taxation Law; Insurance Law; Regulatory Law. ***Email:*** rbromley@foley.com

JOHN T. BROOKS, admitted to bar, 1989, Illinois; 1996, Florida. *Education:* University of Illinois (B.S., 1986; J.D., magna cum laude, 1989). ***PRACTICE AREAS:*** Trust and Estate Litigation; Corporate Tax Planning; Tax Valuation; Tax Litigation. ***Email:*** jbrooks@foley.com

R. LEE CHRISTIE, admitted to bar, 1984, District of Columbia; 1988, Illinois. *Education:* Illinois Wesleyan University (B.A., 1981); Harvard University (J.D., 1984). ***PRACTICE AREAS:*** Taxation Law; Insurance Law; Financial Services Law; Fiduciary Litigation; Regulatory Law; Tax Valuation; Tax Litigation. ***Email:*** lchristie@foley.com

MICHAEL M. CONWAY, admitted to bar, 1973, Illinois. *Education:* Northwestern University (B.S., cum laude, 1968); Yale University (J.D., 1973). Member, Board of Editors, Yale Law Journal, 1971-1973. Author: Notes, Vol. 80, 82 Yale Law Journal; "Enforcement of Restrictive Covenants in Illinois Employment Contracts," 60 Chicago Bar Record 142, 1978. Co-Author: "Libel and Slander Depositions" (Juris Publishing, Inc., 1999); Chapter 16, "Damages, Double Costs, and Fees," *Attorney's Guide to Seventh Circuit Court of Appeals.* Chairman, Yale Law School Barristers Union, 1972-1973. Counsel, U.S. House of Representatives Committee on Judiciary Impeachment Inquiry of Richard M. Nixon, 1974. *Member:* American Bar Association. Fellow, American College of Trial Lawyers. [United States Army, 1969-1971.]. ***PRACTICE AREAS:*** Commercial Litigation; Media Law; Federal Tax Litigation; Appellate Practice; Airport Regulation; Tax Litigation; Tax Valuation. ***Email:*** mconway@foley.com

ELIZABETH L. COREY, admitted to bar, 1982, Illinois. *Education:* St. Mary's College; Butler University (A.B., 1973); New York Law School (J.D., 1982). Author: "Illinois Real Estate Leasing Forms," Kane & Levy, Butterworths 1994, ABA Monogram, 1996. *Member:* Chicago and American Bar Associations; International Council of Shopping Centers. ***TRANSACTIONS:*** Commercial Real Estate Development, Financings and Leasing. ***PRACTICE AREAS:*** Commercial Real Estate; Commercial Financings; Sports Law; Golf Course Development; Hotel and Resort Law; Automotive Industry; Real Estate; Transportation. ***Email:*** ecorey@foley.com

(This Listing Continued)

DEWEY B. CRAWFORD, admitted to bar, 1967, Illinois. *Education:* Dartmouth College (A.B., 1963); University of Michigan (J.D., with distinction, 1966). *Member:* Chicago (Securities Law Committee) and Illinois State (Corporation and Securities Law Sections) Bar Associations. ***PRACTICE AREAS:*** Business Law; Mergers and Acquisitions; Securities. ***Email:*** dcrawford@foley.com

JAMES D. DASSO, admitted to bar, 1987, Illinois; 1988, U.S. District Court, Northern District of Illinois (Trial Bar); 1995, U.S. Court of Appeals, Seventh Circuit; 1999, U.S. Court of Appeals, Ninth Circuit; 2000, U.S. Court of Appeals, Federal Circuit. *Education:* University of Oregon (B.S., 1982); University of Michigan (J.D., magna cum laude, 1986). Order of the Coif. Executive Editor, Michigan Law Review, 1985-1986. Law Clerk to the Honorable J. Edward Lumbard, U.S. Court of Appeals, Second Circuit, 1986-1987. ***PRACTICE AREAS:*** Intellectual Property Litigation; Commercial Litigation; Appellate Practice; Litigation. ***Email:*** jdasso@foley.com

PAULINE E. DOOHAN, admitted to bar, 1989, Michigan; 1991, Illinois. *Education:* Michigan State University (B.A., with honors, 1986); Wayne State University (J.D., cum laude, 1989). Member, Mortar Board, Michigan State University. *Member:* Detroit, Illinois and American (Member, Business Law Section) Bar Associations; State Bar of Michigan (Member, Oil & Gas Law Committee, 1998-2001). ***PRACTICE AREAS:*** Corporate Law; Finance; Energy; Mergers and Acquisitions; Project Finance; Infrastructure Development; Business Law; Securities. ***Email:*** pdoohan@foley.com

BRUCE W. DOUGHTY, admitted to bar, 1990, Illinois and U.S. District Court, Northern District of Illinois. *Education:* Princeton University (A.B., with honors, 1985); University of Chicago (J.D., 1990). ***PRACTICE AREAS:*** Energy; Energy Regulation; Regulatory Law. ***Email:*** bdoughty@foley.com

SCOTT E. EARLY, admitted to bar, 1975, Illinois and U.S. District Court, Northern District of Illinois; 1979, U.S. Court of Appeals, Fifth Circuit; 1982, U.S. District Court, Northern District of Illinois, Trial Bar; 1983, U.S. Court of Appeals, Seventh Circuit; U.S. Supreme Court. *Education:* Princeton University (A.B., 1971); Vanderbilt University (J.D., 1975). Associate Articles Editor, Vanderbilt Law Review, 1974-1975. General Counsel, Board of Trade of the City of Chicago (1983-1994). *Member:* Chicago (Member and Past Chairman, Futures Regulation Section; Trial Techniques Section), Illinois State (Member, Litigation Section), Federal (Director) and American (Member, Litigation and Business Law Sections; Executive Committee, Committee of Futures and Derivatives Instruments Executive Committee) Bar Associations. ***PRACTICE AREAS:*** Financial Litigation; Futures Regulation; Securities Litigation; Securities Regulation; SEC Enforcement; Mergers and Acquisitions. ***Email:*** searly@foley.com

KEVIN J. EGAN, admitted to bar, 1975, Illinois; 1976, U.S. Court of Appeals, 7th Circuit; 1977-1982, U.S. Court of Customs and Patent Appeals; 1983, U.S. Court of Appeals for the Federal Circuit. *Education:* University of Illinois (B.A., with highest honors, 1972); Northwestern University (J.D., 1975). Phi Kappa Phi. Article Editor, Journal of Criminal Law and Criminology, 1974-1975. Author: "The Imposition of Administrative Penalties and The Right to Trial By Jury," 65 Journal of Criminal Law & Criminology, 345, 1974. Instructor, Legal Writing, Northwestern University, 1974-1975. Recipient, Hodes Prize, 1975. Law Clerk to Judge Richard B. Austin, U.S. District Court, Northern District of Illinois, 1975-1977. Assistant U.S. Attorney, Northern District of Illinois, 1978-1982. *Member:* Chicago (Member, Membership Committee, 1980-1981; Health Law Committee, 1982—; Committee on Evaluation of Judicial Candidates, 1984—) and American Bar Associations; Bar Association of the Seventh Federal Circuit. ***PRACTICE AREAS:*** Health Care Corporate Law; Health Care. ***Email:*** kegan@foley.com

FREDRIC J. ENTIN, admitted to bar, 1972, Illinois and U.S. District Court, Northern District of Illinois including Trial Bar. *Education:* University of Wisconsin, Madison (B.A., Psychology, 1968); DePaul University College of Law (J.D., 1972). Author: *Medical Legal Issues of Mechanical Ventilation,* Yearbook Publications (1980); *Reviewing the Contract, Managing Computer Systems,* American Journal of Hospital Pharmacy (1982); *Emergicenters, The New Kid on the Block,* Legal Aspects of Medical Practice (1983); *Emergicenters, A Health Care System in Evolution,* The Journal of Legal Medicine (1984); *Death, Dying and the Terminally Ill,* Illinois Institute for Continuing Legal Education (1983); and *DRG's, HMO's and PPO's: Introducing Economic Issues in the Medical Malpractice Case,* The Forum, Tort and Insurance Practice Section, American Bar Association (1983); *Preparation of the Medical Malpractice Defense Before Trial,* Illinois Institute for Continuing Legal Education (1987); *Ambulatory Care Facilities,* Medical and Hospital Negligence, Chapter 21, Callaghan & Company (1988); *Hospital Collaboration: The Need for an Appropriate Antitrust Policy,* Wake Forest Law Review (1994). *Member:* American Bar Association; Illinois Association of Hospital Attorneys (Board Member, 1981-1987; President, 1985-1986); American Health Lawyers Association (Board Member); American Society of Association Executives; Bureau of National Affairs (Health Law Reporter, Advisory Board). (Also Outside Legal Counsel, American Hospital Association). ***PRACTICE AREAS:*** Health Care; Trade Association Law; Health Care Legislation. ***Email:*** fentin@foley.com

BENNETT L. EPSTEIN, admitted to bar, 1975, Illinois; 1976, Missouri; 1979, U.S. Court of Appeals, Seventh Circuit; 1983, U.S. District Court, Northern District of Illinois, Trial Bar; 1992, U.S. District Court, Central District of Illinois. *Education:* University of Wisconsin; University of Michigan (B.A., with distinction, 1972); Washington University (J.D., 1975). Associate Editor, Urban Law Annual, 1974-1975. Trial Attorney, National Labor Relations Board, 1975-1978. *Member:* American Bar Association. ***PRACTICE AREAS:*** Employment Law; Labor Law; Labor and Employment. ***Email:*** bepstein@foley.com

JAY ERENS, admitted to bar, 1959, Illinois; 1968, U.S. Supreme Court; 1960, U.S. District Court, Northern District of Illinois; 1962, U.S. Court of Appeals, 7th Circuit. *Education:* Yale University (B.A., summa cum laude, 1956); Harvard University (LL.B., magna cum laude, 1959). Phi Beta Kappa. Member, 1957-1958 and Note Editor, 1958-1959, Harvard Law Review. Author: "Liability of a Corporation for Acts of a Subsidiary or Affiliate," 71 Harvard Law Review, 1122, 1958. Law Clerk to Mr. Justice John M. Harlan, U.S. Supreme Court, 1959-1960. Lecturer on Law, Northwestern University, 1961-1963. Special Assistant Attorney General, State of Illinois, 1964-1971. *Member:* Chicago and American

(This Listing Continued)

FOLEY & LARDNER LLP, Chicago—Continued

Bar Associations. ***PRACTICE AREAS:*** Corporate Law; Litigation; Commercial Transactions; Business Planning; Securities; Mergers and Acquisitions; Business Law. ***Email:*** jerens@foley.com

FREDERICK L. FELDKAMP, admitted to bar, 1971, Wisconsin; 1977, Michigan; 1996, Illinois. *Education:* University of Michigan (A.B., with distinction, 1968; J.D., magna cum laude, 1971). Order of the Coif. Listed in: *Guide to the World's Leading Securitization Lawyers,* Euromoney Publications PLC, March 1999; *The International Who's Who of Business Lawyers,* Law Business Research Ltd., 2002. Author: "It's Moving the Cash Flow-Stupid," Securitization Yearbook 1999 Supplement to *International Financial Law Review*, September 1999; "U.S. Developments: What is Menacing the Virtuous Economy?" The ISR Legal Guide to Securitisation, July 2000; "Asset Securitization: The Alchemist's Dream," Securitization Yearbook 2000 Supplement to *International Financial Law Review,* September 2000; "U.S. Developments: Protecting Goldilocks from the Bears," The ISR Legal Guide to Securitisation, July 2001; "Saving Private Intermediation," Structured Finance Yearbook 2001 Supplement to *International Financial Law Review,* October 2001; "From Depression to Prosperity but not Back -- U.S. Debt Trading Market Reform," The ISR Legal Guide to Securitisation, July 2002; "The New 2003 American Securitization Model: Isolation and Risk Diversification," Structured Finance Yearbook 2002 Supplement to *International Financial Law Review,* October 2002. Co-Author, "Rethinking the Role of Recourse in the Sale of Financial Assets," The Business Lawyer, Vol. 52, No. 1, November 1996. *Member:* Chicago and Illinois State Bar Association; State Bar of Wisconsin; State Bar of Michigan; American Bar Association. ***PRACTICE AREAS:*** Asset-Backed Securities; Financial Services; Mergers and Acquisitions; Corporate Law; International Law; Transportation; Energy; Business Law. ***Email:*** ffeldkamp@foley.com

JOHN N. GAVIN, admitted to bar, 1975, Illinois. *Education:* College of the Holy Cross (A.B., cum laude, 1968); Harvard University (J.D., cum laude, 1975). Author: "Competing Forums for the Resolution of Claims Against an Insolvent Insurer," XXIII Tort and Insurance Law Journal 604, 1988. Co-Author: "Mutual Holding Companies as a Strategic Alternative for Mutual Insurers," 1 Journal of International Insurance 1, 1999. Member, Board of Editors, Harvard Civil Rights, Civil Liberties Law Review, 1974-1975. Law Clerk to Judge Charles M. Merrill, U.S. Court of Appeals for the Ninth Circuit, 1975-1976. Office of Legal Counsel, Department of Justice, 1976-1979. *Member:* Chicago and American Bar Associations. [Lt., United States Navy 1968-1971.]. ***PRACTICE AREAS:*** Insurance; Corporate Law; Public Utilities Law; Energy; Regulatory Law. ***Email:*** jgavin@foley.com

DIANE GIANOS, admitted to bar, 1989, Illinois; 1990, U.S. District Court, Northern District of Illinois including Trial Bar; U.S. Court of Appeals, Sixth and Seventh Circuits. *Education:* DePaul University (B.S., 1984); Chicago-Kent College of Law (J.D., 1989). ***PRACTICE AREAS:*** Labor and Employment; Litigation. ***Email:*** dgianos@foley.com

JEANNE M. GILLS, admitted to bar, 1994, Illinois; registered to practice before U.S. Patent and Trademark Office. *Education:* Michigan State University (B.S., Electrical Engineering, with honors, 1991); University of Chicago Law School (J.D., 1994). Phi Kappa Phi; Golden Key National Honor Societies. Outstanding Student Engineer of the Year Nomination. Recipient, 1999 Foley & Lardner IP Founder's Award. *Member:* American Bar Association (Member, Intellectual Property Section); National Bar Association; AIPLA; IPLAC. ***LANGUAGES:*** French. ***PRACTICE AREAS:*** Intellectual Property Litigation (70%); Intellectual Property Transactions (30%); Industrial Models and Designs; Trademarks; Copyrights. ***Email:*** jmgills@foley.com

PHILLIP M. GOLDBERG, admitted to bar, 1983, Illinois. *Education:* Indiana University (B.A., 1980); University of Madrid; DePaul University (J.D., 1983). Author: "Settlement Process and Procedures," Report On Task Force on SRO matters, ABA committee on Securities Litigation, November 1994; "SRO Disciplinary Process," Futures, March 1993; "Arbitration Roundtable," Futures Industry, September/October 1993; "The Anatomy of a Corporate Internal Investigation," Insights, July 1994. *Member:* Chicago (Chairman, Aviation Law Committee, 1988-1989), Illinois State (Member, Corporate and Securities Law Committee, 1992-1995) and American (Member, Task Force on SRO Process; Co-Chair, Litigation Section Subcommittee on SRO Matters) Bar Associations; Chicago Inn of Court. ***PRACTICE AREAS:*** Litigation; Securities Litigation; Commercial Litigation; SEC Enforcement; Securities Regulation. ***Email:*** pgoldberg@foley.com

GEORGE R. GOODMAN, admitted to bar, 1987, Illinois, U.S. Tax Court, and U.S. District Court, Northern District of Illinois. *Education:* University of Montana (B.A., Mathematics, with highest honors, 1983); University of Chicago (J.D., 1986). Author: "Tax Return Compliance," 76 Tax Notes 1201 (Sept. 1, 1997); "Teasing the Limits of Interest Stripping," 71 Tax Notes 677 (Apr. 29, 1996); "The Latest Stock Hedging Regulations," 67 Tax Notes 1795 (June 26, 1995); "Employing a Corporation and Other Strategies to Reduce Taxes," 72 TAXES 174 (Apr. 1994). ABA Subcommittee Chair on Important Developments During 1995, Affiliated and Related Corporations, 49 Tax Lawyer 997 (Summer 1996). Organizer and Moderator, CBA YLS Tax Law Committee Seminars, "Surfing the Third Wave: Taxation of Ordinary Business on the Internet and Transfers of Technology" (June 6, 1997) and "Mergers and Acquisitions" (May 17, 1996). Panelist/Speaker: CBA YLS Corporate Law Committee Seminars, "Buying and Selling the Presently Held Company," (1997-1998); Federal Bar Association, Insurance Tax Seminar, "Insurance Company Investment: Options, Shareholders and Resent Legislation," (May, 1998); CBA YLS Real Estate Law Committee, "Commercial Real Estate Transactions," (Oct. 8, 1997); ABA Tax Section Committee on Affiliated and Related Corporations, "Parent Stock" (Jan. 19, 1996); CBA Federal Taxation Committee Divisions C and F, "Tax Analysis of Restructuring an Overly-Leveraged Company" (May 9, 1990). *Member:* Chicago Bar Association (Chair, Young Lawyers Section Tax Law Committee, 1995-1997; Member, Federal Taxation Committee). ***PRACTICE AREAS:*** Corporate Taxation; International Business Law; Tax Valuation; Tax Litigation; Taxation. ***Email:*** ggoodman@foley.com

DAVID B. GOROFF, admitted to bar, 1985, Illinois; 1986, U.S. District Court, Northern District of Illinois, U.S. Court of Appeals, Seventh, Second and Sixth Circuits and U.S. Supreme Court. *Education:* University of Illinois (B.A., summa cum laude, 1982); Columbia University (J.D., 1985). Bronze Tablet. Harlan Fiske Stone Scholar. Notes and Comments Editor, Columbia Law Review. Law Clerk to the Hon. Richard D. Cudahy, U.S. Court of Appeals, Seventh Circuit, 1985-1986. Adjunct Professor: University of Illinois College of Law; Chicago-Kent Law School. ***PRACTICE AREAS:*** Appellate Practice; Antitrust; Litigation; Bankruptcy. ***Email:*** dgoroff@foley.com

EDWARD J. GREEN, admitted to bar, 1993, Iowa and U.S. District Court, Northern District of Iowa; 1994, Illinois and U.S. District Court, Northern District of Illinois including Trial Bar. *Education:* University of Iowa (B.B.A., 1988; M.B.A., 1992; J.D., with high distinction, 1992). Associate Editor, University of Iowa Law Review, 1990-1991. Law Clerk to Honorable Michael J. Melloy, Chief U.S. District Court Judge, Northern District of Iowa, 1992-1994. ***PRACTICE AREAS:*** Health Care; Health Care Corporate Law; Health Care Finance; Energy; Health Law. ***Email:*** egreen@foley.com

BYRON L. GREGORY, admitted to bar, 1969, Illinois. *Education:* Northwestern University (B.A., 1966); Northwestern University School of Law (J.D., 1969). *Member:* Chicago, Illinois State and American Bar Associations. ***PRACTICE AREAS:*** Litigation; Commercial Litigation. ***Email:*** bgregory@foley.com

PAUL F. HANZLIK, admitted to bar, 1971, Illinois and U.S. District Court, Northern District of Illinois including Trial Bar; 1978, U.S. Supreme Court and U.S. Court of Appeals, Seventh Circuit. *Education:* Wesleyan University, Middletown, Connecticut (B.A., cum laude, with honors, 1964); Columbia University (LL.B., 1967). Chairman, Electric Power Committee, American Bar Association, Section of Natural Resources Energy and Environmental Law, 1990-1992. [First Lieut., U.S. Army, 1968-1971]. ***PRACTICE AREAS:*** Energy; Regulatory Law; Energy Regulation. ***Email:*** phanzlik@foley.com

JAMES R. HELLIGE, admitted to bar, 1976, Illinois and U.S. District Court for the Northern District of Illinois; 1977, U.S. Tax Court. *Education:* St. Mary's University of Minnesota (B.A., summa cum laude, 1973); University of Notre Dame (J.D., cum laude, 1976). Associate Articles Editor, Notre Dame Law Review, 1975-1976. Author: "The Right of A Creditor of an Heir to Contest the Will," 50 Notre Dame Law Review, 309, 1974; "Coping With the Generation-Skipping Transfer Tax," 69 Illinois Bar Journal, 166 and 228, 1980 and 16 Law Notes, 103, 1980 and 52 The Oklahoma Bar Journal, 2510, 2829 and 3093, 1981; "Strategies to Use While Awaiting Possible Repeal of the Generation-Skipping Tax," 125 Trusts & Estates, No. 2, 42, February, 1986; "An Overall Look at Planned Giving Options," 16 Fund Raising Management, No. 12, 74, February, 1986; "A New Set of Complexities," 126 Trusts and Estates, No. 3, 8 and No. 4, 10, March and April, 1987; "The New Generation-Skipping Tax: Analysis, Planning and Drafting," Northwestern University Estate Planning Advisory Council Press, June 1, 1987; "Temporary Regulations Help to Answer Some Questions," 128 Trusts & Estates, No. 2, 55, February, 1989; "Sophisticated Charitable Giving: Techniques and Problems," 41 Major Tax Planning ¶ 1100 Matthew Bender & Company, Inc., 1989; "Charitable Giving and the Generation-Skipping Tax," 130 Trusts & Estates, No. 5, 34, May, 1991. *Member:* Chicago (Member, Probate Practice Committee, Co-Chair, Division C, 1994-1995, Chair, Executive Subcommittee of Probate Practice Committee, 1997-1998; Chair, Legislative Subcommittee of Probate Practice Committee, 1998-1999), and American (Member, Sections on: Real Property, Probate and Trust Law; Taxation) Bar Associations; Chicago Estate Planning Council; Director, Chicago Council on Planned Giving; Advisory Board of Catholic Charities of the Archdiocese of Chicago. Fellow, American College of Trust and Estate Counsel. ***PRACTICE AREAS:*** Estate Planning Law; Probate Law; Estates Law; Trusts Law; Charitable Organizations Law; Related Taxation. ***Email:*** jhellige@foley.com

WM. CARLISLE HERBERT, admitted to bar, 1976, Illinois; 1977, U.S. Court of Appeals, 7th Circuit; 1978, Florida and U.S. District Court, Northern District of Illinois; 1980, U.S. Supreme Court; 1982, U.S. Tax Court and U.S. District Court, Northern District of Illinois, Trial Bar. *Education:* Princeton University (A.B., 1969); Northwestern University (M.S.J., 1970; J.D., cum laude, 1976). Executive Editor, Northwestern University Law Review, 1976. Law Clerk to Senior Judge Latham Castle, Seventh Circuit, U.S. Court of Appeals, 1976-1977. Co-Author, "Criminal Rights in Civil Antitrust Litigation: The Roles of Grand Jury Secrecy and the Right Against Self-Incrimination," and "Defamation, Deposition Strategy, Law and Forms," Chapters in Matthew Bender series. *Member:* Chicago, Illinois State and American Bar Associations; The Florida Bar. ***PRACTICE AREAS:*** Financial Litigation; Insurance Law; Libel Law; Antitrust Law; Media Law; Insurance Litigation; Litigation. ***Email:*** wherbert@foley.com

MARIANNE CRAIGMILE HOLZHALL, admitted to bar, 1990, Illinois. *Education:* Northwestern University (B.S.J., 1984); Loyola University (J.D., cum laude, 1990). Member, 1988-1989 and Editor, 1989-1990, Loyola University Law Journal. ***PRACTICE AREAS:*** Litigation; Intellectual Property; Intellectual Property Litigation. ***Email:*** mholzhall@foley.com

HEIDI H. JEFFERY, admitted to bar, 1996, Illinois. *Education:* Northwestern University (B.A., 1993); University of Iowa (J.D., with distinction, 1996). Managing Editor, Iowa Law Review, 1995-1996. *Member:* National Association of Bond Lawyers. ***PRACTICE AREAS:*** General Finance; Public Finance; Health Care Finance; Business Law; Finance; Health Care. ***Email:*** hjeffery@foley.com

DEAN M. JESKE, admitted to bar, 1989, Illinois and U.S. District Court, Northern District of Illinois; 1997, U.S. Court of Appeals, Seventh Circuit; 1999, U.S. Court of Appeals, Ninth Circuit. *Education:* University of Illinois (B.A., 1986; J.D., magna cum laude, 1989). ***PRACTICE AREAS:*** Securities Litigation; Employment Litigation; Commercial Litigation; SEC Enforcement; Litigation. ***Email:*** djeske@foley.com

C. RICHARD JOHNSON, admitted to bar, 1965, Illinois; 1976, U.S. Supreme Court. *Education:* Ripon College (A.B., cum laude, 1962); University of Chicago Law School (J.D., cum laude, 1965). Phi Beta Kappa. Order of the Coif. Member, University of Chicago Law Review, 1963-1964. Author: "Securities Law Duties of Bond Counsel," Duke Law Journal. *Member:* American Bar Association; Chicago Council of Lawyers; National Association of Bond Lawyers. [LTCDR, U.S. Navy Reserve, 1965-1972]. ***PRACTICE AREAS:*** Government Finance; Government Law; Constitutional Law; Finance; Health Care Finance; Public Finance; Sports Law; Business Law. ***Email:*** cjohnson@foley.com

BRYAN T. D. JUNG, admitted to bar, 1990, Illinois. *Education:* Illinois Wesleyan University (B.F.A., 1985); University of Chicago Law School (J.D., 1990). ***PRACTICE AREAS:*** Finance; General Corporate; Nanotechnology; Business Law. ***Email:*** bjung@foley.com

(This Listing Continued)

GLEN H. KANWIT, admitted to bar, 1968, Illinois and U.S. District Court, Northern District of Illinois; 1971, U.S. Court of Appeals, 7th Circuit; 1972, U.S. Tax Court; 1973, U.S. Claims Court and U.S. Court of Appeals, 2nd Circuit; 1974, U.S. Supreme Court; 1976, U.S. Court of Appeals, 10th Circuit; 1979, U.S. Court of Appeals, 1st Circuit; 1987, U.S. Court of Appeals, 4th Circuit; 1990, U.S. Court of Ap peals, 3rd and 5th Circuits; 1996, Federal Circuit. *Education:* Swarthmore College (B.A., cum laude, 1965); Columbia University (LL.B., cum laude, 1968). Co-Author: "Enforcement of Restrictive Covenants in Illinois Employment Contracts," 60 Chicago Bar Record 142, 1978; "The Corporate Client and the Attorney-Client Privilege," 66 Chicago Bar Record 84, 1984. Member of Faculty, National Institute of Trial Advocacy, 1990—. Adjunct Professor, Northwestern University Law School, 2000—. *Member:* Chicago (Chairman, Civil Practice Committee, 1982-1983) and American Bar Associations; Chicago Council of Lawyers (Chairman, Judiciary Committee, 1981; Vice President, 1981-1982; Member, Board of Governors, 1983-1985; Treasurer, 1985-1986). ***PRACTICE AREAS:*** Commercial Law; Financial Litigation; Insurance Litigation; Appellate Practice; Corporate Tax Planning; Tax Valuation; Tax Litigation. ***Email:*** gkanwit@foley.com

CHRISTOPHER N. KNIGHT, admitted to bar, 1971, Wisconsin; 1979, North Carolina; 1980, Minnesota and U.S. Supreme Court; 1982, Illinois; 1996, New York. *Education:* Yale University (B.A., 1968); Duke University (J.D., 1971). Member, Board of Editors, Duke Law Journal, 1970-1971. *Member:* Chicago, Illinois State, Minnesota State, New York State, North Carolina and American Bar Associations; State Bar of Wisconsin. ***PRACTICE AREAS:*** Public Finance; Banking Law; Finance; Health Care Finance; Business Law. ***Email:*** cknight@foley.com

THOMAS P. KREBS, admitted to bar, 1995, Illinois. *Education:* University of Notre Dame (B.A., magna cum laude, 1990); The Ohio State University College of Law (J.D., with honors, 1995). Phi Beta Kappa. *Member:* Chicago, Illinois and American Bar Associations. ***PRACTICE AREAS:*** Litigation; Securities Litigation; Securities Regulation; SEC Enforcement. ***Email:*** tkrebs@foley.com

JOHN R. LANDIS, admitted to bar, 1988, Oregon; 1990, New York; 1993, Minnesota; 1996, Illinois. *Education:* Lawrence University (B.A., cum laude, 1984); University of Minnesota (J.D., magna cum laude, 1988). Order of Coif. Member, University of Minnesota, Law Review, 1988. Clerk, Honorable James M. Rosenbaum, U.S. District Court, District of Minnesota, 1988-1990. *Member:* Minnesota State, New York State and Illinois State Bar Associations; Oregon State Bar. ***PRACTICE AREAS:*** Business Reorganization; Bankruptcy; Securites Litigation; Securities Regulation; SEC Enforcement; Litigation. ***Email:*** jrlandis@foley.com

JOHN D. LIEN, admitted to bar, 1968, Wisconsin; 1972, Illinois and U.S. District Court, Northern District of Illinois; 1978, U.S. Court of Appeals, Seventh Circuit. *Education:* University of Wisconsin-Madison (B.A., 1965); Harvard University (J.D., 1968). Trustee, Winnetka Public Library District, 1985-1993. Trustee, Village of Winnetka, 1997-2001. *Member:* Chicago and American Bar Associations; Seventh Circuit Bar Association. [Capt., USAF, 1968-1972]. ***PRACTICE AREAS:*** Litigation; Construction Law. ***Email:*** jlien@foley.com

J. CRAIG LONG, admitted to bar, 1978, Illinois. *Education:* Colgate University (B.A., 1975); DePaul University (J.D., 1978). Member, Board of Directors, Colgate University Alumni Corporation, 1992-1996. Member, Corporate Advisory Board, Salvation Army, 1989-1993. Former General Counsel, Chicago Stock Exchange. *Member:* Chicago (Member, Securities Law Committee), Illinois State and American Bar Associations. ***PRACTICE AREAS:*** Financial Markets; Securities; Corporate; Government Relations; Business Law; Mergers and Acquisitions; Securities Litigation; Securities Regulation; SEC Enforcement. ***Email:*** clong@foley.com

MARY KAY McCALLA MARTIRE, admitted to bar, 1985, Michigan and U.S. District Court, Northern District of Michigan; 1988, Illinois; 1989, U.S. Court of Appeals, Seventh Circuit and U.S. District Court, Northern District of Illinois including Trial Bar; U.S. District Court, Central District of Illinois. *Education:* Kalamazoo College, 1978-1979; Michigan State University (B.A., with high honors, 1982); University of Michigan (J.D., 1985). *Member:* Chicago and American Bar Associations. ***PRACTICE AREAS:*** Commercial Litigation; Tax Litigation; Intellectual Property; Antitrust; Insurance Litigation; Media Law; Litigation; Taxation. ***Email:*** mmartire@foley.com

EDWIN D. MASON, admitted to bar, 1980, Illinois. *Education:* University of Illinois (B.S., with highest honors, 1977); University of Michigan (J.D., with honors, 1980). *Member:* Chicago and American Bar Associations. ***PRACTICE AREAS:*** Mergers and Acquisitions; General Corporate and Securities; Securities; Emerging Growth Companies; Joint Ventures; Business Law. ***Email:*** emason@foley.com

JOHN W. McCAFFREY, admitted to bar, 1974, Illinois and U.S. District Court, Northern District of Illinois; 1983, U.S. Court of Appeals, Seventh Circuit; 1985, U.S. Supreme Court; 1989, U.S. Court of Appeals for the District of Columbia; 1991, U.S. District Court, Central District of Illinois. *Education:* Southern Illinois University (B.A., 1971); IIT Chicago Kent College of Law (J.D., 1974). Adjunct Professor of Law, Energy Law and Policy, IIT Chicago Kent College of Law, 1992-1997. Assistant Corporation Counsel, Law Department, City of Chicago, 1974-1983; Chief Assistant Corporation Counsel, 1977-1983; Senior Assistant Attorney General, Director of the Public Interest Bureau, Illinois Attorney General's Office, 1983-1993. Partner, Hopkins & Sutter, 1993-2001. *Member:* Chicago and American Bar Associations; American Judicature Society; Catholic Lawyers Guild; Federal Communications Bar Association; The Lawyers Club of Chicago; Economics Club of Chicago; National Strategy Forum. ***PRACTICE AREAS:*** Energy Regulation; Telecommunications; Government Relations; Energy. ***Email:*** jmccaffrey@foley.com

WILLIAM J. McKENNA, JR., admitted to bar, 1979, Illinois. *Education:* Middlebury College (B.A., cum laude, 1975); University of Illinois; University of Chicago (J.D., 1979). Harnow Scholar, 1977. Author: "Lender Liability, Secured Transactions," IICLE, 2001 Edition. Adjunct Professor of Law, Northwestern University. *Member:* American Bar Association. Fellow, American College of Trial Lawyers. ***PRACTICE AREAS:*** Commercial Litigation; Business Reorganization; Construction Law; Tax Valuation; Tax Litigation; Litigation. ***Email:*** wmckenna@foley.com

WILLIAM G. McMASTER, JR., admitted to bar, 1973, Illinois. *Education:* Miami University (B.A., cum laude, 1968); Northwestern University (J.D., cum laude, 1973). Phi Beta Kappa; Order of the Coif. Member, Board of Editors, Northwestern Law Review, 1972-1973. *Member:* Chicago and American Bar Associations. ***PRACTICE AREAS:*** General Corporate Law; Business Acquisitions Law; Venture Capital Law; Securities; Commercial Tansactions; Business Law; Mergers and Acquisitions. ***Email:*** wmcmaster@foley.com

GERALD J. NEAL, admitted to bar, 1968, Wisconsin; 1981, Florida; 1988, Illinois; 2001, Michigan. *Education:* Harvard College (B.A., magna cum laude, 1965); Yale University (LL.B., 1968). *Member:* Chicago, Illinois State and American Bar Associations; State Bar of Wisconsin; The Florida Bar; National Association of Bond Lawyers. ***PRACTICE AREAS:*** Health Care Law; Government Finance Law; Business Law; Finance; Financial Restructuring; Public Finance; Health Care. ***Email:*** gneal@foley.com

GREGORY S. NORROD, admitted to bar, 1988, Illinois. *Education:* Indiana University (B.A., with honors, 1985; J.D., cum laude, 1988). *Member:* Chicago (Member, Intellectual Property Section) and American (Member, Litigation Section) Bar Associations; American Intellectual Property Law Association. ***PRACTICE AREAS:*** Intellectual Property Litigation; Commercial Litigation; Litigation. ***Email:*** gnorrod@foley.com

WAYNE F. OSOBA, admitted to bar, 1985, Illinois and U.S. District Court, Northern District of Illinois. *Education:* University of Illinois (B.S., highest honors, 1982; J.D., summa cum laude, 1985). Order of the Coif. ***PRACTICE AREAS:*** Real Estate Law; Commercial Lending; Financial Institutions; Business Law. ***Email:*** wosoba@foley.com

JAMES D. OSSYRA, admitted to bar, 1983, Illinois; 1991, Colorado. *Education:* Harvard University (A.B., cum laude, 1978); Boston University (J.D., magna cum laude, 1983). Member and Notes and Comments Editor, American Journal of Law and Medicine, 1982-1983. *Member:* American Bar Association. ***PRACTICE AREAS:*** Litigation; Construction; Airport Regulation; Insurance Litigation. ***Email:*** jossyra@foley.com

JOHN B. PALMER III, admitted to bar, 1977, Illinois; 2001, U.S. Court of Claims and U.S. Court of Appeals for the Federal Circuit. *Education:* Michigan State University (B.A., with high honors, 1974); University of Michigan (J.D., magna cum laude, 1977). Order of the Coif. Member, University of Michigan Law Review, 1976-1977. Speaker and Writer on a variety of tax topics, including the taxation of partners and partnerships and tax accounting. Adjunct Professor, IIT/Chicago-Kent College of Law, Masters of Tax Program, 1984—. *Member:* American Bar Association (Member, Taxation Section). ***PRACTICE AREAS:*** Federal Income Taxation; Equipment Leasing; Partnerships; Corporations; Automobile Liability; Sports Law; Tax Valuation; Tax Litigation. ***Email:*** jpalmer@foley.com

KATHLEEN R. PASULKA-BROWN, admitted to bar, 1986, Illinois and California. *Education:* University of California at Los Angeles (B.A., 1983); Harvard University (J.D., 1986). ***PRACTICE AREAS:*** Litigation; Energy; Telecommunications; Employment; Insurance; Business Reorganization; Energy Regulation. ***Email:*** kpasulka-brown@foley.com

TODD B. PFISTER, admitted to bar, 1986, Wisconsin and U.S. District Court, Eastern and Western Districts of Wisconsin; 1994, Florida; 2000, Illinois. *Education:* Lake Forest College (B.A., summa cum laude, 1983); Yale University (J.D., 1986). Phi Beta Kappa. Editor, Yale Law & Policy Review, 1985-1986. Author: "Capitalization, Shares and Distributions," Chapter 5, *Florida Corporate Practice* (Fla. Bar 3rd ed. 1995). *Member:* Hillsborough County and American Bar Associations; State Bar of Wisconsin; The Florida Bar (Member, Business Law Section; Corporations and Securities Law Committee). ***PRACTICE AREAS:*** Corporate Law; Securities Law; Partnership Law; Banking Law; Commercial Law. ***Email:*** tpfister@foley.com

RICHARD J. PHELAN, admitted to bar, 1961, Illinois. *Education:* University of Notre Dame (Ph.B., 1958); Georgetown University (J.D., 1961). Listed in Best Lawyers in America. Member, Georgetown National Moot Court Team, 1960. Adjunct Professor, Torts, Insurance, Trial Practice and Products Liability, IIT/Chicago-Kent College of Law, 1963-1974 and 1979-1983. Special Assistant Corporation Counsel, City of Chicago, 1974-1976. Chairman, Practising Law Institute and New York Law Journal Programs, 1972-1988. Director: Public Interest Law Internship, 1983-1988; Constitutional Rights Foundation, 1984-1988. Member, Executive Advisory Board of Saint Joseph Hospital, 1985-1988. Special Outside Counsel to the U.S. House of Representatives, Committee on Standards of Official Conduct in the Matter of Speaker James C. Wright, Jr., 1988-1989. Director, Leadership Council for Metropolitan Open Communities, 1987-1990. President, Cook County Board of Commissioners, 1990-1994. Member, The Commercial Club of Chicago, 1996—. Trustee, Knox College, Galesburg, Illinois, 1992-1996. Member, Board of Visitors, John Marshall Law School, 1992—. *Member:* Chicago (President, 1985-1986; Chairman, Permanent Home Committee, 1986-1988), Illinois (Member, Federal Judicial Appointments Committee; Honorary Fellow) and American Bar Associations. Fellow: International Academy of Trial Lawyers (Director, 1982-1984 and Chairman, Admissions Committee, 1984-1988; Dean, 1989-1990); American College of Trial Lawyers (Chairman, Illinois State Committee, 1988-1990); American Bar Foundation. ***PRACTICE AREAS:*** Litigation; Intellectual Property; Products Liability. ***Email:*** rphelan@foley.com

MARK L. PRAGER, admitted to bar, 1976, Illinois; 1978, U.S. District Court, Northern District of Illinois including Trial Bar; 1980, U.S. Court of Appeals, Seventh Circuit; 1982, U.S. Supreme Court; 1985, U.S. Tax Court; 1998, Wisconsin. *Education:* University of Illinois (B.A., magna cum laude, 1973); Washington University, St. Louis, Mo. (J.D., 1976). Edmund James Scholar. Fellowship in State Government, State of Illinois, 1972. Internship, Hon. Robert L. Eisen, Bankruptcy Court, Northern District of Illinois, Eastern Division, 1975. Author: "Health Care Finance and Insolvency: The Lender's Perspective," 15 Commercial Lending Review, Winter 1999-2000; "Financing The Chapter 11 Debtor: The Lenders' Perspective," 45 The Business Lawyer, August 1990. Co-Author: "Pursuing Alter-Ego Remedies Against Non-Bankrupt Third Parties - Structuring a Comprehensive Conceptual Framework," 35 St. Louis University Law Journal, 657 Spring, 1991; "Protecting Secured Lenders in the Structuring and Workout of LBO Related Loans," 7 Commercial Lending Review, 11 Spring, 1992; "Litigation Strategies in Prosecuting or Contesting Involuntary Bankruptcy Petitions: The Creditor's Perspective," 9 Commercial Lending Review, 19 Fall 1993; "Environmental Lender Liability: Searching for Safe Harbors in the Wake of Kelly vs. EPA," 1 University of Wisconsin Environmental Law Journal, 1 Summer 1994; "Realizing Maximum Value When Holding and Liquidating Contaminated Property: Practical Considerations for the Secured Lender After Kelly vs. U.S. EPA," 9 Commercial Lending Review, Fall 1994; "No Band-Aid Approach Can Heal the Woes of CERCLA," 5 Corporate Legal Times, March 1995; "Getting to the Bottom Line: The Search for Cred-

(This Listing Continued)

FOLEY & LARDNER LLP, Chicago—Continued

ibility and Fraud in a Bankruptcy Case," 8 The Corporate Analyst, 3 May 1996; "Key Issues in Chapter 11 Retail Inventory Sales: The Lender's Perspective," 13 Commercial Lending Review, Winter 1997-1998; "The Growing Use of Liquidating Trusts in Chapter 11 Cases: Practical Considerations," 17 Commercial Lending Review, 2 March 2002; Speaker: The Robert Morris Associates, "Bankruptcy Review for Lenders," Chicago, 1991; The Robert Morris Associates, "New Developments in Fraudulent Conveyance Litigation," Chicago 1993; The National Business Institute, "Representing Creditors in Chapter 11 and Involuntary Bankruptcy Strategies," Winter 1994; Legal Education Institute, Inc. and The Bureau of National Affairs, Inc., "Analyzing the Debtor's Historical and Prospective Financial Information," Winter 1996; "Chicago Bar Association, Advanced Chapter 11 Seminar; Financing the Debtor-in-Possession and Cash Collateral Orders," Chicago, 1997; American Bankruptcy Institute, "Post Confirmation Problems: Failed Chapter 11's, Successor Liability and Creditor Trust," Winter Conference, 1997; Fulcrum Information Services, Inc., "The Telecommunications Industry Bankruptcy and Workouts Forum," Washington, D.C., Fall 1999; "Healthcare Reorganizations and Insolvencies," Chicago, Ill., Fall 1999; "Lending Issues in Health Care Insolvencies," Fulcrum Information Systems, Inc., New York, New York, Fall 2000; "Insolvencies from the Creditors Perspective," Chicago, Ill., March 2001; "Super Liquidations: Bridge Technology," Renaissance American Management, Inc., Chicago, Ill., September 2001; "Purchasing a Company of Uncertain Solvency or From a Bankruptcy Estate," Northwestern University School Of Law, Corporate and Securities Law Institute, Chicago, Ill., April 2002; "Unrolling the Roll Up, Private Equity Markets and the Reorganization Process," Renaissance American Management, Inc., Chicago, Ill., June 2002; Arbitrator, National Association of Securities Dealers, 1985-1988. United States Trustee, Private Panel, Northern District of Illinois, Eastern Division, 1990, 1992 and 1993. Elected, Village of Glencoe Nominating Committee (Chairman, 1995-1996). *Member:* Chicago, Illinois State and American Bar Associations; Chicago Council of Lawyers (Chairman, Legislative Committee, 1988-1990; Secretary to Board of Governors, 1989-1990); American Bankruptcy Institute. (Managing Partner, Chicago Office). ***PRACTICE AREAS:*** Bankruptcy Law; Commercial Litigation; Banking Law; Creditors Rights Law; Health Care; Litigation. ***Email:*** mprager@foley.com

JOHN P. RATNASWAMY, admitted to bar, 1985, Illinois; 1986, U.S. Court of Appeals, 7th Circuit; 1987, U.S. District Court, Northern District of Illinois and U.S. Court of Appeals, 4th Circuit; 1988, U.S. Supreme Court; 1992, U.S. District Court, Central District of Illinois; 2003, U.S. Court of Appeals, 5th Circuit. *Education:* Northwestern University (B.S., 1982; M.A., 1982; J.D., cum laude, 1985). ***PRACTICE AREAS:*** Energy; Litigation; Administrative Law; Legal Ethics; Professional Responsibility; Appellate Practice; Media Law; Regulatory Law. ***Email:*** jratnaswamy@foley.com

MICHAEL D. RECHTIN, admitted to bar, 1982, Illinois; 1988, Wisconsin; registered to practice before U.S. Patent and Trademark Office. *Education:* University of Illinois (B.S., 1966); Massachusetts Institute of Technology (Ph.D., 1970); Illinois Institute of Technology/Chicago-Kent College of Law (J.D., with honors, 1982). *Member:* Chicago, Milwaukee, Illinois State and American (Member, Trademark Committee) Bar Associations; State Bar of Wisconsin; Patent Law Association of Chicago; American Intellectual Property Law Association. ***PRACTICE AREAS:*** Patents; Trademarks; Intellectual Property Law; Trademark and Copyright Law; Energy; Nanotechnology. ***Email:*** mrechtin@foley.com

DANIEL S. REINBERG, admitted to bar, 1991, Illinois and U.S. District Court, Northern District of Illinois; 1994, U.S. District Court, Central District of Illinois; 1995, U.S. Court of Appeals, Seventh Circuit. *Education:* Miami University (B.S., Marketing/Decision Science, cum laude, 1988); Northwestern University (J.D., magna cum laude, 1991). Order of the Coif. Awarded Lowden-Wigmore Second Prize for Legal Writing. Managing Editor, Law Review. Law Clerk to the Hon. Marvin E. Aspen, U.S. District Court, Northern District of Illinois, 1991-1993. Author, Comment, "The Constitutionality of the Illinois Death Penalty Statute," 85 Northwestern Law Review 272 (1990). Formerly with: Sidley & Austin, 1993-1996; U.S. Attorney's Office, Northern District of Illinois, 1996-2001. *Member:* American Bar Association. ***PRACTICE AREAS:*** Compliance; Counseling; Government Enforcement; White Collar Criminal Defense; Health Care Reimbursement; Health Care Compliance; Litigation; Health Care. ***Email:*** dreinberg@foley.com

E. GLENN RIPPIE, admitted to bar, 1985, Illinois, including Trial Bar and U.S. District Court, Northern District of Illinois; 1986, U.S. Court of Appeals, Seventh Circuit; 1987, U.S. Tax Court; 1989, U.S. Supreme Court; 1990, U.S. District Court, Central District of Illinois. *Education:* Northwestern University (B.A., highest distinction in Economics and Mathematical Methods, 1982; M.A. in Economics, 1982); Yale University (J.D., 1985). Coker Fellow, 1985. Acting Associate General Counsel for Regulatory, Commonwealth Edison Company, 1999-2000. Special Assistant Corporation Counsel, City of Chicago, 1987-1990. *Member:* Chicago and American (Member, Sections on: Administrative Law; Energy and Natural Resources); Energy Bar Association. ***PRACTICE AREAS:*** Energy; Utility Law; Commercial Litigation; Energy Regulation; Regulatory Law. ***Email:*** grippie@foley.com

JOHN L. ROGERS, III, admitted to bar, 1974, Illinois. *Education:* University of Virginia (B.A., with high distinction, 1970); Harvard University (J.D., magna cum laude, 1973). Phi Beta Kappa. Member, Harvard Law Review, 1971-1973. Law Clerk to Judge Warren H. Young, District Court of the Virgin Islands, 1973-1974. *Member:* American Bar Association. ***PRACTICE AREAS:*** Commercial Litigation; Energy; Securities Litigation; Energy Regulation; Regulatory Law; SEC Enforcement; Securities Regulation. ***Email:*** jrogers@foley.com

CHARLES P. SHEETS, admitted to bar, 1983, Illinois; 1992, Wisconsin. *Education:* University of Illinois at Chicago (B.A., 1979): John Marshall Law School (J.D., 1983). *Member:* DuPage County Bar Association; State Bar of Wisconsin; American Health Lawyers Association; Illinois Healthcare Association. ***PRACTICE AREAS:*** Health Law; Health Care Corporate Law. ***Email:*** csheets@foley.com

GEORGE T. SIMON, admitted to bar, 1973, New York; 1982, Illinois. *Education:* Trinity College (B.A., 1969); Harvard University (J.D., 1972). Phi Beta Kappa. Associate Director, United States Securities and Exchange Commission, Division of Market Regulation, 1980-1981. General Counsel, Chicago Stock Exchange, 1993-1997. *Member:* American Bar Association (Member: Committee on Federal Regulation, 1980—). ***PRACTICE AREAS:*** Securities Law; Corporate Law; Financial Institutions Law; Business Law; Securities Litigation; Securities Regulation; SEC Enforcement; Securities; Mergers and Acquisitions. ***Email:*** gsimon@foley.com

MICHAEL J. SMALL, admitted to bar, 1991, Illinois. *Education:* Brown University (A.B., 1985); Jewish Theological Seminary of America (M.A., 1988); University of Chicago (J.D., 1991). Phi Beta Kappa. Published Writings: "Key Issues in Chapter 11 Retailer Inventory Sales: The Lender's Perspective," Commercial Lending Review, Vol. 13, No. 1, Winter 1997-1998; "Health Care and Insolvency: The Lender's Perspective," Commercial Lending Review, Vol. 15, No. 1, Winter 1999-2000. *Member:* Chicago and American Bar Associations; American Bankruptcy Institute. ***LANGUAGES:*** Hebrew. ***REPORTED CASES:*** *In re Corcoran Hospital District,* 233 B.R. 449 (Bankr. E.D. Cal. 1999); *In re DeMert & Dougherty, Inc.,* 232 B.R. 103 (N.D. Ill. 1999); *In re DeMert & Dougherty, Inc.,* 227 B.R. 508 (Bankr. N.D. Ill. 1998); *Westinghouse Electric Corp. v. McLean,* 938 F.Supp. 487 (N.D. Ill. 1996); *Avila v. Rubin,* 84 F.3d 222 (7th Cir. 1996); *Kale v. Obuchowski,* 985 F.2d 360 (7th Cir. 1993). ***PRACTICE AREAS:*** Creditors Rights; Bankruptcy Law; Commercial Litigation; Food and Agriculture; Litigation; Business Reorganization; Health Care. ***Email:*** msmall@foley.com

JEFFREY A. SOBLE, admitted to bar, 1996, Illinois and U.S. District Court, Northern District of Illinois; 1998, U.S. District Court, Central District of Illinois. *Education:* University of California at Los Angeles (B.A., Economics, 1993; B.A., History, 1993); Loyola University Chicago School of Law (J.D., cum laude, 1996). National Trial Competition National Champion. Best Oral Advocate. *Member:* Illinois State and American Bar Associations; The Association of Trial Lawyers of America; Illinois Trial Lawyers Association. ***PRACTICE AREAS:*** Litigation; General Commercial Litigation; Transportation; Products Liability; Insurance Coverage Litigation. ***Email:*** jsoble@foley.com

ROBERT M. STEPHENSON, admitted to bar, 1973, Illinois; 1974, U.S. District Court, Northern District of Illinois and U.S. Court of Appeals, Seventh Circuit; 1980, U.S. Supreme Court; 1988, U.S. Tax Court and U.S. District Court, Middle District of Florida; 1990, U.S. District Court, Southern District of Texas; 1992, U.S. Court of Appeals, Fifth Circuit; 1994, U.S. District Court, Northern District of Indiana and Southern District of Louisiana; 1995, U.S. District Court, Northern and Western Districts of Kentucky and Southern District of Ohio; 1997, U.S. Court of Appeals, Sixth Circuit; 1998, U.S. District Court, District of Arizona. *Education:* University of Illinois (B.A., 1970; J.D., 1973). Author: "Representing Persons in Criminal Antitrust Cases," Antitrust Institute, Ohio State Bar Associations Continuing Legal Education, Volume 00-71, Nov 3, 2000. Co-Author: "Basic Strategy In Federal Criminal Defense Litigation," ABA Journal of the Section of Litigation, Fall, 1981. Teaching Assistant, National Institute For Trial Advocacy, 1973-1974. Adjunct Professor, Trial Advocacy, John Marshall Law School, 1978. Visiting Lecturer, Trial Advocacy Program, Harvard University, Fall, 1980. Lecturer, Practicing Law Institute, Spring, 1985; American Law Institute/American Bar Association, Fall, 1987. Visiting Lecturer, Trial Advocacy, University of Illinois College of Law, 1997. Law Clerk to U.S. District Court Judge Prentice H. Marshall, 1973-1975. Assistant U.S. Attorney, Northern District of Illinois, 1975-1978 (Deputy Chief, Criminal Receiving and Appellate Division, 1976-1978). Recipient of the Department of Justice Director's Award for Superior Service as an Assistant U.S. Attorney, 1976 and Special Commendation for Outstanding Service as an Assistant U.S. Attorney, 1978. Member, Committee on Federal Criminal Jury Instructions of the Seventh Circuit, 1976 —; Chairman, Board of Commissioners, State Appellate Defender, 1983-1989. Formerly with: Cotsirilos, Stephenson, Tighe & Streicker, Ltd., 1978-1999. Listed in: Who's Who in American Law; The Best Lawyers in America. *Member:* Chicago, Illinois State, Federal and American (Member, Section on Criminal Justice) Bar Associations; American Judicature Society. Fellow, American College of Trial Lawyers. ***PRACTICE AREAS:*** White Collar Crime; Litigation; Antitrust and Trade Regulation; Regulatory Compliance; Civil Litigation; Criminal Litigation; Appellate Practice. ***Email:*** rstephenson@foley.com

KATHRYN M. TRKLA, admitted to bar, 1983, Illinois. *Education:* University of Chicago (B.A., 1980); Northwestern Law School (J.D., cum laude, 1983). Phi Beta Kappa. Associate, 1989-1991, Partner, 1991-1994, Coffield, Ungaretti & Harris, Chicago, Illinois. Associate General Counsel, 1994-1998, Senior Vice President and Associate General Counsel, 1998-2000, Chicago Board of Trade. *Member:* Chicago (Chair, Futures and Derivatives Law Committee, 1997-1998), Illinois State and American Bar Associations. ***PRACTICE AREAS:*** Business Law; Securities; Mergers, Acquisitions and Divestitures; SEC Enforcement; Securities Litigation; Securities Regulation. ***Email:*** ktrkla@foley.com

ROBERT J. VECHIOLA, admitted to bar, 1992, Illinois. *Education:* Illinois State University (B.S., 1983); DePaul University (M.B.A., 1985; J.D., with honors, 1992). Order of the Coif. *Member:* Chicago and American Bar Associations. ***PRACTICE AREAS:*** Corporate Law; Business Law; International Law; Commercial Transactions. ***Email:*** rvechiola@foley.com

WILLIAM C. WEINSHEIMER, admitted to bar, 1965, Illinois. *Education:* University of Notre Dame (B.B.A., 1962); Northwestern University (J.D., 1965). Phi Delta Phi. Co-Author: "Generation-Skipping Tax Strategies," Trusts & Estates, 1986; "Impact of Tax Reform Act on Fiduciary Income Taxes," Trusts & Estates, 1987; of Book "The New Generation-Skipping Tax: Analysis, Planning and Drafting," 1987, Northwestern University Press; "Drafting Wills and Trust Agreements," IICLE, 1990. Speaker: "Estate Planning for Business Owners: 'To Give or Not to Give? That Is the Question'!" Indiana Continuing Legal Education Forum, 1996 Midwest Estate, Tax & Business Planning Institute, June 6-7, 1996; "GRAT Ideas: Achieving Leverage in an Era of Changing Rates: Planning and Drafting," Notre Dame Tax and Estate Planning Institute, September 14-15, 1995; "Qualified Personal Residence Trusts — Planning and Drafting or 'Honey, I Shrunk the House'," Annual Notre Dame Tax and Estate Planning Institute, October 1993; Family Business Succession Planning Institute, Insight Information Co., "Using Testamentary and Inter Vivos Discretionary Trusts in Family Business Succession Planning," October 1998; "Estate Planning for Closely Held Business." President, 1981-1982, Board Member, 1972-1990, and Honors Council, 1990—, Lawyers for Creative Arts. Director, Illinois Bar Foundation, 1984-1990, and Chicago Bar Foundation, 1991-1998. *Member:* Chicago (Member, Probate Practice Committee, 1969—; Chair, 1988-1989; Chair, Division III, 1976-1977. Chair, Creative City Committee, 1973-1974), Illinois State and American (Estate Planning and Probate Editor, Law Notes, 1975-1983) Bar Associations; Northwestern University Estate Planning Advisory Council; Chicago Community Trust Professional Advisors Committee;

(This Listing Continued)

Chicago Symphony Orchestra Planned Giving Advisory Council; The Economic Club of Chicago. Fellow, American College of Trust and Estate Counsel (Editor, ACTEC Notes, 1991-1992; Illinois Chair, 1989-1992; Member, Board of Regents, 1992-1998; Chair, Editorial Board, 1993-1996); Member, International Academy of Estate and Trust Law. [Captain, U.S. Army, 1965-1967]. (Co-Chair of Firm's Estates and Trusts Practice). ***PRACTICE AREAS:*** Trusts Law; Related Taxation; Trusts and Estates; Taxation; Tax Litigation; Tax Valuation. ***Email:*** wweinsheimer@foley.com

TRACY D. WILLIAMS, admitted to bar, 1994, Illinois. *Education:* University of Illinois (B.A., magna cum laude, 1991); Harvard University (J.D., cum laude, 1994). Member, IRPAC, 1999-2000. *Member:* Chicago (Member, State and Local Tax Committee) and American (Member: Tax Section; Insurance Companies Committee). ***PRACTICE AREAS:*** Taxation; Insurance; Trusts and Estates; Tax Valuation; Tax Litigation. ***Email:*** twilliams@foley.com

MICHAEL H. WOOLEVER, (P.C.), admitted to bar, 1976, Illinois. *Education:* Kalamazoo College (B.A., 1971); Wayne State University; University of Michigan (J.D., magna cum laude, 1976). Staff Member, University of Michigan Journal of Law Reform, 1975-1976. Author: "Providing an Effective Remedy in Shareholder Suits against Officers, Directors and Controlling Persons," University of Michigan Journal of Law Reform, Vol. 9, No. 1, Fall 1975. *Member:* American Bar Association (Member: Closely-Held Business Committee and Employee Benefits Committee, Section of Taxation). ***PRACTICE AREAS:*** Taxation; Trusts and Estates; Employee Benefits; Tax Litigation; Tax Valuation. ***Email:*** mwoolever@foley.com

JOHN F. ZABRISKIE, admitted to bar, 1984, Illinois and U.S. District Court, Northern District of Illinois. *Education:* University of Michigan (B.A., with high honors, 1981; J.D., cum laude, 1984). ***PRACTICE AREAS:*** Complex Commercial Litigation; Litigation; Appellate Practice. ***Email:*** jzabriskie@foley.com

JANET E. ZEIGLER, admitted to bar, 1991, Illinois. *Education:* University of Illinois (B.A., Economics, 1988); Indiana University School of Law, Bloomington (J.D., magna cum laude, 1991). Order of the Coif. Managing Editor, The Indiana Law Journal, 1990-1991. *Member:* American Bar Association; National Association of Bond Lawyers; American Health Lawyers Association. ***PRACTICE AREAS:*** Health Care Finance; Health Care Reform; Finance; Business Law; Public Finance; Brownfields Redevelopment. ***Email:*** jzeigler@foley.com

CHRISTOPHER W. ZIBART, admitted to bar, 1984, Illinois and U.S. District Court, Northern District of Illinois. *Education:* Miami University (A.B., cum laude, 1981); University of Illinois (J.D., 1984). ***PRACTICE AREAS:*** Regulatory Law; Energy; Environmental Law; Project Finance; Infrastructure Development; Brownfields Redevelopment. ***Email:*** czibart@foley.com

ROBERT J. ZIMMERMAN, admitted to bar, 1976, Illinois. *Education:* Ripon College (A.B., magna cum laude, 1970); Vanderbilt University (J.D., 1975). Phi Beta Kappa. Personal Member, The Catholic Health Association of the United States. *Member:* Illinois State and American Bar Associations; American Health Lawyers Association; Healthcare Financial Management Association; Illinois Association of Healthcare Attorneys; National Association of Bond Lawyers. ***PRACTICE AREAS:*** Health Care Law; Finance; Public Finance; Health Care Finance; Health Care Reform; Business Law. ***Email:*** rzimmerman@foley.com

RETIRED PARTNER

STEPHEN M. SLAVIN, admitted to bar, 1964, Illinois and U.S. District Court, Northern District of Illinois; 1967, U.S. Court of Appeals, Seventh Circuit; 1983, New York. *Education:* Colgate University (A.B., 1961); University of Chicago (J.D., 1964). Trustee, Village of Deerfield, Illinois, 1969-1973. ***PRACTICE AREAS:*** Corporate; Mergers and Acquisitions; Corporate Finance; Securities; Business Law. ***Email:*** sslavin@foley.com

OF COUNSEL

MICHAEL K. CAVANAUGH, (P.C.), admitted to bar, 1960, Iowa; 1966, Illinois. *Education:* University of Portland and Creighton University (B.S.B.A., 1957); Georgetown University (J.D., 1960); New York University (LL.M. in Taxation, 1963). Beta Alpha Psi. Member, Georgetown Law Journal, 1959-1960. Trial Attorney, Tax Division, U.S. Department of Justice, 1961-1966. *Member:* Chicago, Illinois State and American Bar Associations; The Lawyers Club of Chicago. ***PRACTICE AREAS:*** Tax Law; Corporate Law; Estate Planning Law; Commercial Transactions; Business Law. ***Email:*** mcavanaugh@foley.com

SHELDON KARON, admitted to bar, 1955, Illinois; 1971, District of Columbia. *Education:* Northwestern University (B.S., summa cum laude, 1952); Harvard Law School (J.D., 1955). Phi Eta Sigma; Phi Beta Kappa. *Member:* Chicago, Illinois State, Federal Circuit and American Bar Associations; Illinois Supreme Court Special Commission on the Administration of Justice. Fellow: American College of Trial Lawyers; American Bar Foundation; Illinois State Bar Foundation. ***PRACTICE AREAS:*** Litigation; Intellectual Property Litigation; Arbitration; Mediation; Financial Institutions Law. ***Email:*** skaron@foley.com

JAY A. STEINBERG, admitted to bar, 1971, Illinois. *Education:* Roosevelt University (B.S.B.A., 1968); DePaul University (J.D., 1971). *Member:* Chicago, Illinois State and American Bar Associations. ***PRACTICE AREAS:*** Taxation; Bankruptcy; Litigation. ***Email:*** jsteinberg@foley.com

HELEN L. TOAL, admitted to bar, 1973, Illinois. *Education:* Smith College; University of Michigan (B.A., 1969); Stanford University (J.D., 1973). *Member:* Illinois State and American Bar Associations. ***PRACTICE AREAS:*** Business Law; Securities; Mergers, Acquisitions and Divestitures; Commercial Transactions; Business Planning. ***Email:*** htoal@foley.com

SENIOR COUNSEL

JONATHAN E. ABERMAN, admitted to bar, 1998, Illinois. *Education:* Duke University (B.A., cum laude, 1995); Northwestern University (J.D., 1998). Student Attorney, Northwestern University Legal Clinic. Member, National Moot Court Team. Extern, U.S. Attorney's Office, Northern District of Illinois. ***PRACTICE AREAS:*** Bankruptcy; Debtor and Creditor Rights; Commercial Litigation; Insurance Coverage; Insurance Defense; Environmental; Professional Liability (Insurance and Other Financial Agents, Brokers and Dealers). ***Email:*** jaberman@foley.com

ANDREA M. AUGUSTINE, admitted to bar, 1997, Illinois; 1998, U.S. District Court, Northern District of Illinois; registered to practice before U.S. Patent and Trademark Office. *Education:* University of Illinois (B.S., Electrical Engineering, 1987; J.D., 1997). ***PRACTICE AREAS:*** Intellectual Property; Intellectual Property Litigation; Life Sciences. ***Email:*** aaugustine@foley.com

MELISSA C. BROWN, admitted to bar, 1997, Illinois; 1998, U.S. District Court, Northern District of Illinois and U.S. Court of Appeals, Seventh Circuit. *Education:* Grand Valley State University (B.A., with high honors, 1977); Ohio University (M.S., 1990); Notre Dame Law School (J.D., cum laude, 1997). White Scholar. Recipient, A. Harold Weber Award for Excellence in Legal Writing. Managing Editor, Notre Dame Journal of Law, Ethics and Public Policy, 1996-1997. Author: "Equal Protection in a Mean World," Notre Dame Journal of Law, Ethics & Public Policy, Vol. II, Issue 1, 1997. Legal Writing and Moot Court Instructor, Notre Dame Law School, 1996-1997. *Member:* Chicago, Illinois State, Seventh Circuit and American Bar Associations. ***REPORTED CASES:*** Rapier v. Harris, 172 F.3d 999 (7th Cir. 1999). ***PRACTICE AREAS:*** Litigation; Securities; Commercial Litigation; Media Law. ***Email:*** mcbrown@foley.com

ADRIAN R. CYHAN, admitted to bar, 2000, Illinois and U.S. District Court, Northern District of Illinois; registered to practice before U.S. Patent and Trademark Office. *Education:* University of Notre Dame (B.S., 1991); University of Michigan (J.D., 2000). ***PRACTICE AREAS:*** Intellectual Property; Electrical Intellectual Property; Life Sciences. ***Email:*** acyhan@foley.com

CYNTHIA A. FONNER, admitted to bar, 1992, Illinois. *Education:* Emory University (B.A., 1989; J.D., 1992). Notes and Comments Editor, Emory International Law Review. [Capt., U.S. Air Force, 1993-1999]. ***PRACTICE AREAS:*** Energy Regulation; Energy; Business Reorganization; Litigation; Regulatory Services; Regulatory Law. ***Email:*** cfonner@foley.com

LaDALE K. GEORGE, admitted to bar, 1991, Missouri; 1992, Virginia; 1997, Illinois. *Education:* University of Kansas (B.A., 1987); Northwestern University (J.D., 1990). Author: "Economic Unification of the European Union and Africa," National Bar Association Journal, Vol. 5, No. 5. Recipient, 1987 Hilltopper Award. *Member:* Cook County, Muslim and National Bar Associations; American Health Lawyers Association. ***REPORTED CASES:*** CBIS Federal v. Va. Department of Health; Marilyn Mandel et al. v. Governor George Allen; Sue Choe v. Western State Hospital, Virginia; Louis Marks, et al. v. U.S. Social Security Administration, Virginia Department of Rehabilitative Services. ***TRANSACTIONS:*** Allegheny University Hospital/Tenet Health Systems Transaction. ***PRACTICE AREAS:*** Health Care; Health Care Corporate Law; Health Care Finance; Health Law. ***Email:*** lgeorge@foley.com

STEVEN GERENRAICH, admitted to bar, 1996, Illinois. *Education:* University of Michigan (B.A., 1989); University of Illinois (J.D., magna cum laude, 1996). ***PRACTICE AREAS:*** Securities; Mergers and Acquisitions; Commercial Transactions; Business Planning; Finance; Health Care Finance; Business Law; International Business Law. ***Email:*** sgerenraich@foley.com

JILL L. MURCH, admitted to bar, 1998, Illinois and U.S. District Court, Northern District of Illinois including Trial Bar. *Education:* University of Chicago (A.B., with honors, 1995); University of Illinois (J.D., cum laude, 1998). Editor, University of Illinois Elder Law Journal. American Bankruptcy Institute Medal of Excellence. Author: Illinois State Bar Association's The Challenge, Fraudulent Transfers under the Bankruptcy Code, August 2002; American Bankruptcy Institute's Cracking the Code, *Seventh Circuit Court of Appeals Holds Burden of Proof Remains with Taxpayers,* July 9, 1999. Author: University of Illinois Elder Law Journal, *Promises Made, Promises Broken, Securing Defined Benefit Pension Income in the Wake Of Employer Bankruptcy. Should we Rethink Priority Status for the Pension Benefit Guaranty Corporation?* 6 Elder L.J.77. *Member:* Chicago, Illinois State and American Bar Associations; American Bankruptcy Institute. ***PRACTICE AREAS:*** Bankruptcy; Creditors Rights; Business Reorganization; Litigation. ***Email:*** jmurch@foley.com

CATHERINE B. NELSON, admitted to bar, 1996, Illinois. *Education:* University of Illinois (B.S., 1988); Northwestern University School of Law (J.D., 1996). Member, Northwestern University Law Review. ***PRACTICE AREAS:*** Business Transactions; Securities; Commercial Transactions; Business Law; Emerging Business Law; Venture Capital; Mergers and Acquisitions; Business Planning. ***Email:*** cbnelson@foley.com

RICHARD L. PREBIL, admitted to bar, 1979, Missouri; 1980, Illinois. *Education:* University of Illinois (B.A., 1974); St. Louis University (M.H.A., J.D., cum laude, 1979). ***PRACTICE AREAS:*** Health Care; Health Care Corporate Law; Health Care Finance; Health Care Reform; Health Law. ***Email:*** rprebil@foley.com

GARY S. ROVNER, admitted to bar, 1995, Illinois; 1997, District of Columbia. *Education:* Dartmouth College (B.A., Government, 1992); George Washington University Law School (J.D., 1995). Former Member, Environmental Law Association. Executive Development Editor, The Environmental Lawyer. *Member:* Illinois State and American (Vice Chairman, Special Committe on Corporate Counsel and Member, Natural Resouces, Energy and Environmental Law Section) Bar Associations. ***PRACTICE AREAS:*** Regulatory Law; Environmental Regulation; Brownfields Redevelopment; Land Use. ***Email:*** grovner@foley.com

LISA L. THARPE, admitted to bar, 1998, Illinois. *Education:* University of California, Berkeley (B.A., 1994); Emory University Law School (J.D., 1998). Phi Beta Kappa; Order of the Coif. Law Review. ***PRACTICE AREAS:*** Securities; Regulatory Law; Media Law; White Collar Crime; Litigation; Securities Litigation; Securities Regulation; SEC Enforcement. ***Email:*** ltharpe@foley.com

DEAN M. VICTOR, admitted to bar, 1992, Illinois. *Education:* University of Wisconsin-Madison (B.A., 1989); John Marshall Law School (J.D., 1992). ***PRACTICE AREAS:*** Litigation; Commercial Litigation. ***Email:*** dvictor@foley.com

SAMANTHA E. WEISSBLUTH, admitted to bar, 1997, Illinois. *Education:* Northwestern University (B.A., 1994; J.D., 1997). Associate Articles Editor, Journal of Criminal

(This Listing Continued)

FOLEY & LARDNER LLP, Chicago—Continued

Law and Criminology. *Member:* Chicago (Probate Practice Committee), Illinois State and American Bar Associations; Association of Trial Lawyers of America. ***LANGUAGES:*** Spanish. ***PRACTICE AREAS:*** Trusts and Estates Litigation; Taxation; Tax Litigation; Tax Valuation. ***Email:*** sweissbluth@foley.com

ELLEN M. WHEELER, admitted to bar, 1997, Illinois. *Education:* Grinnell College (B.A., with honors, 1994); University of Michigan (J.D., 1997). ***PRACTICE AREAS:*** Litigation; Commercial Litigation; Securities; SEC Enforcement; Securities Litigation; Securities Regulation. ***Email:*** ewheeler@foley.com

SPECIAL COUNSEL

CHRISTINE GUSTAFSON, admitted to bar, 1997, Illinois. *Education:* DePaul University (J.D.). ***PRACTICE AREAS:*** Taxation; Insurance; Corporate Taxation. ***Email:*** cgustafson@foley.com

MIKI V. TESIJA, admitted to bar, 1997, Illinois and U.S. District Court, Northern District of Illinois; 1998, U.S. Court of Appeals, Seventh Circuit. *Education:* University of Illinois, Urbana-Champaign (B.A., 1993); George Washington University (J.D., with honors, 1997). *Member:* Chicago Bar Association. ***LANGUAGES:*** Croatian. ***PRACTICE AREAS:*** General Commercial Litigation; Media Law; Litigation. ***Email:*** mvucic@foley.com

ASSOCIATES

ERIKA A. ALLEY, admitted to bar, 2002, Illinois; U.S. District Court, Northern District of Illinois. *Education:* Wittenberg University (B.A., summa cum laude, 1999); Chicago-Kent College of Law, Illinois Institute of Technology (J.D., with high honors, 2002). *Member:* Chicago and Illinois State Bar Associations. ***Email:*** ealley@foley.com

THOMAS K. ANDERSON, admitted to bar, 2003, Illinois. *Education:* University of Notre Dame (B.A., magna cum laude, 2000; J.D., magna cum laude, 2003). Articles Editor, Notre Dame Journal of Law, Ethics & Public Policy, 2002-2003. Law Clerk to the Hon. Deborah Cook, United States Court of Appeals for the Sixth Circuit. *Member:* Chicago and American Bar Associations. ***PRACTICE AREAS:*** Litigation. ***Email:*** tanderson@foley.com

MICHAEL S. BAIG, admitted to bar, 1999, Illinois and U.S. District Court, Northern District of Illinois; 2000, U.S. District Court, Central District of Illinois; 2001, U.S. District Court, Southern District of Illinois. *Education:* University of Michigan (A.B., 1987; J.D., cum laude, 1999). *Member:* Chicago and American Bar Associations. ***PRACTICE AREAS:*** Litigation; Electronic Commerce; Commercial Litigation; Media Law. ***Email:*** mbaig@foley.com

HEIDI L. BELONGIA, admitted to bar, 2002, Illinois. *Education:* Marquette University (B.A., magna cum laude, 1999); DePaul University (J.D., summa cum laude, 2002). ***PRACTICE AREAS:*** Litigation; Intellectual Property Litigation; Trademarks; Copyrights. ***Email:*** hbelongia@foley.com

MARTIN J. BISHOP, admitted to bar, 1999, Illinois. *Education:* Florida Atlantic University (B.A., 1996); Boston University (J.D., 1999). Executive Editor, Boston University Law Review. ***PRACTICE AREAS:*** Complex Commercial Litigation; Computer Software; Licensing Litigation; Media Law; Litigation; Appellate Practice. ***Email:*** mbishop@foley.com

JASON A. BREMER, admitted to bar, 1999, Illinois. *Education:* University of Wisconsin (B.A., 1995); University of Iowa (J.D., with honors, 1999). ***PRACTICE AREAS:*** Tax; Insurance; Corporate Taxation; Tax Valuation; Tax Litigation. ***Email:*** jbremer@foley.com

MARSHALL J. BROWN, admitted to bar, 1999, Illinois; registered to practice before U.S. Patent and Trademark Office. *Education:* University of Michigan (B.S.M.E., 1996); University of Michigan Law School (J.D., 1998). ***PRACTICE AREAS:*** Intellectual Property; Copyrights; Trademarks. ***Email:*** mjbrown@foley.com

JAMES F. CIRINCIONE, admitted to bar, 2003, Illinois. *Education:* Colgate University (B.A., 1998); Vanderbilt University Law School (J.D., 2003). ***PRACTICE AREAS:*** Business Law; Health Care Finance; Finance. ***Email:*** jcirincione@foley.com

DANIEL M. CORDIS, (admission pending). *Education:* University of Illinois, Urbana-Champaign (B.S., with high honors, 2002); DePaul University (J.D., summa cum laude, 2005). ***PRACTICE AREAS:*** Commercial Litigation. ***Email:*** dcordis@foley.com

DANIEL A. DINGERSON, admitted to bar, 2004, Illinois; 2005, U.S. District Court, Northern District of Illinois. *Education:* University of Michigan (B.A., 2001); University of California School of Law, Los Angeles (J.D., 2004). ***PRACTICE AREAS:*** Litigation; Commercial Litigation. ***Email:*** ddingerson@foley.com

ANDERS W. FRANZON, admitted to bar, 2003, Illinois. *Education:* Bucknell University (B.A., cum laude, 2000); University of Illinois (J.D., magna cum laude, 2003). Order of the Coif. ***PRACTICE AREAS:*** Business Law; Business Reorganization; Finance; Securities; Mergers and Acquisitions. ***Email:*** afranzon@foley.com

GEOFFREY S. GOODMAN, admitted to bar, 1999, Maryland; 2000, Illinois; U.S. Court of Appeals, Fourth Circuit; U.S. District Court, District of Maryland; U.S. District Court, Northern District of Illinois. *Education:* Illinois Wesleyan University (B.A., 1996); University of Illinois (J.D., summa cum laude, 1999). Order of the Coif. Notes Editor, University of Illinois Law Review. ***PRACTICE AREAS:*** Litigation; Bankruptcy; Appellate Practice. ***Email:*** ggoodman@foley.com

KAREN A. KAWASHIMA, (admission pending). *Education:* University of Notre Dame (B.A., magna cum laude, 1999); Northwestern University (J.D., 2005). ***PRACTICE AREAS:*** Litigation; Commercial Law. ***Email:*** kkawashima@foley.com

JASON J. KEENER, admitted to bar, 2003, Wisconsin (Not admitted in Illinois). *Education:* University of Wisconsin-Madison (B.S., with distinctive scholastic achievement, 2000; J.D., summa cum laude, 2003). *Member:* State Bar of Wisconsin. ***PRACTICE AREAS:*** Litigation; Intellectual Property Litigation; Commercial Litigation. ***Email:*** jkeener@foley.com

(This Listing Continued)

KELLY L. KOEPPL, admitted to bar, 2003, Illinois. *Education:* Saint Norbert College (B.A., magna cum laude, 1991); The Fletcher School at Tufts Univeersity (M.A., 1996); Northwestern University School of Law (J.D., cum laude, 2003). ***PRACTICE AREAS:*** Litigation; Commercial Litigation. ***Email:*** kkoeppl@foley.com

JOANNE LEE, admitted to bar, 2004, Illinois. *Education:* University of Illinois (B.A., with honors, 2000); University of Chicago (J.D., 2004). ***LANGUAGES:*** Korean. ***PRACTICE AREAS:*** Litigation. ***Email:*** jlee@foley.com

JOSEPH J. LOTUS, admitted to bar, 2001, Illinois. *Education:* University of Iowa (B.A., with honors and distinction, 1998; J.D., with distinction, 2001). Member, Iowa Law Review. Member, Psychology Law Group. Member, Board of Directors, Camp Algonquin, Metropolitan Family Services. *Member:* Illinois State Bar Association (Former Student Government Representative); Environmental Law Society. ***PRACTICE AREAS:*** Litigation; Commercial Litigation. ***Email:*** jlotus@foley.com

MATTHEW E. MARTIN, admitted to bar, 2003, Illinois; registered to practice before U.S. Patent and Trademark Office. *Education:* Purdue University (B.S., Biology, 2000); John Marshall Law School (J.D., magna cum laude, 2003). Distinguished Scholar. Member, John Marshall Law Review. Editor-in-Chief, Review of Intellectual Property Law. ***LANGUAGES:*** Chinese, Latin. ***PRACTICE AREAS:*** Intellectual Property; Biotechnology; Intellectual Property Litigation; Energy Regulation. ***Email:*** memartin@foley.com

MICHAEL J. McMORROW, admitted to bar, 2000, Illinois. *Education:* Yale University (B.A., 1994); University of Illinois at Urbana (J.D., magna cum laude, 2000). ***PRACTICE AREAS:*** Litigation; Commercial Litigation. ***Email:*** mmcmorrow@foley.com

DAVID A. MOORE, admitted to bar, 2004, Illinois. *Education:* Indiana State University (B.S., cum laude, 2001); Indiana University School of Law - Bloomington (J.D., magna cum laude, 2004). ***PRACTICE AREAS:*** Litigation; Commercial Litigation. ***Email:*** dmoore@foley.com

BELINDA S. MORGAN, admitted to bar, 2000, Illinois and U.S. District Court, Northern District of Illinois; 2002, U.S. Court of Appeals, Fifth Circuit. *Education:* Purdue University (B.A., 1988; A.A.S., 1991) University of Illinois (J.D., summa cum laude, 2000). Order of the Coif. Business Manager, University of Illinois Law Review. *Member:* Chicago, Illinois State and American Bar Associations. ***PRACTICE AREAS:*** Tax; Corporate Law; Tax Valuation; Tax Litigation. ***Email:*** bmorgan@foley.com

SHARON C. NELSON, admitted to bar, 2001, Illinois. *Education:* Loyola University, Chicago (B.A., Communications, magna cum laude, 1998); University of Illinois College of Law (J.D., summa cum laude, 2001). Order of the Coif. Harno Scholar. Recipient, Rickert Award for Excellence in Academics. *Member:* Illinois Association of Business Communcators. ***PRACTICE AREAS:*** Tax Planning; Trusts and Estates. ***Email:*** snelson@foley.com

AMY P. PURCELL, admitted to bar, 2003, Illinois. *Education:* University of Michigan (B.A., 2000; J.D., cum laude, 2003). ***PRACTICE AREAS:*** Litigation; Commercial Litigation. ***Email:*** apurcell@foley.com

DAVID P. RESNICK, admitted to bar, 2000, Illinois. *Education:* University of Michigan (B.A., 1994); Northwestern University (J.D., 2000). *Member:* Illinois State Bar Association. ***PRACTICE AREAS:*** Real Estate; Business Law. ***Email:*** dresnick@foley.com

REAGEN C. ROBBINS ATWOOD, admitted to bar, 1997, Illinois. *Education:* Harvard University (A.B., Government, cum laude, 1988); University of Michigan (J.D., cum laude, 1997). ***PRACTICE AREAS:*** Public Law; Public Finance; Health Care; Health Law; Health Maintenance Organizations. ***Email:*** rrobbinsatwood@foley.com

MICHAEL S. SHAPIRO, admitted to bar, 2003, Illinois. *Education:* University of Illinois (B.S., 2000); Chicago-Kent College of Law (J.D., high honors, 2003). Order of the Coif. Editor-in-chief, Chicago-Kent College Law Review, 2002-2003. ***PRACTICE AREAS:*** Litigation; Commercial Litigation. ***Email:*** mshapiro@foley.com

KATHERINE ANN SIDDON O'BRIEN, admitted to bar, 1998, Illinois; 2003, U.S. District Court, Northern District of Illinois. *Education:* Kenyon College; University of Colorado at Boulder (B.A., 1994); Dickinson School of Law of the Pennsylvania State University (J.D., 1998). *Member:* Chicago, Illinois State, and American Bar Associations; Federal Communications Bar Association. ***PRACTICE AREAS:*** Energy; Public Utility Law; Telecommunications Law; Regulatory Law; Antitrust; Administrative Agency Practice; Administrative Hearings and Appeals; Administrative Litigation; Energy Regulation; Business Reorganization. ***Email:*** kobrien@foley.com

JONATHAN R. SPIVEY, admitted to bar, 1997, Texas; 2000, District of Columbia; 2004, Illinois; registered to practice before U.S. Patent and Trademark Office. *Education:* Prairie View A & M University (B.S., Electical Engineering, 1991); Thurgood Marshall School of Law (J.D., cum laude, 1997); George Washington University (LL.M., 1998). Pi Mu Epsilon. Author: "King Instruments Corp. v. Perego: Conflict in the Awarding of Patent Damages," 21 T. Marshall L. Rev. 369. Member, National Society of Black Engineers - Alumni Extension. *Member:* Federal Circuit Bar Association; State Bar of Texas; The District of Columbia Bar; National Bar Association; American Intellectual Property Law Association; Giles S. Rich American Inn of Court. ***PRACTICE AREAS:*** Intellectual Property Litigation. ***Email:*** jspivey@foley.com

AMY L. STRONG, (admission pending). *Education:* University of Southern Mississippi (B.M.E., 1997); Indiana University School of Law - Indianapolis (J.D., cum laude, 2005). ***PRACTICE AREAS:*** Commercial Litigation. ***Email:*** astrong@foley.com

NATHANIEL L. STRUP, admitted to bar, 2002, Illinois. *Education:* The Ohio State University (B.A., Political Science, 1999); DePaul University (J.D., magna cum laude, 2002). Phi Kappa Phi; Order of the Coif. Member, DePaul Law Review. ***PRACTICE AREAS:*** Litigation; Commercial Litigation. ***Email:*** nstrup@foley.com

MONA THAKKAR, admitted to bar, 2004, Illinois. *Education:* University of Illinois, Urbana-Champaign (B.S., 2001); DePaul University College of Law (J.D., magna cum laude, 2004). ***PRACTICE AREAS:*** Litigation; Commercial Litigation; Media Law. ***Email:*** mthakkar@foley.com

MICHAEL P. TOMLINSON, admitted to bar, 2003, Illinois. *Education:* University of Illinois (B.S., 1999); Illinois Institute of Technology, Chicago-Kent School of Law (J.D.,

(This Listing Continued)

high honors, 2003). Certificates in litigation and alternative dispute resolution. *Member:* American Bar Association. ***PRACTICE AREAS:*** Litigation; Commercial Litigation. ***Email:*** mtomlinson@foley.com

FRANCES "ALEXIS" TRETTER, admitted to bar, 2004, Illinois. *Education:* University of Kentucky (B.A., summa cum laude, 2001); Vanderbilt University (J.D., 2004). ***PRACTICE AREAS:*** Business Reorganizations; Litigation. ***Email:*** ftretter@foley.com

KARL W. VON DRATHEN, admitted to bar, 2000, Illinois. *Education:* University of Southern California (B.S., cum laude, 1996); University of Illinois (J.D., magna cum laude, 2000). ***PRACTICE AREAS:*** Business Law; Mergers, Acquisitions and Divestitures; Finance; Health Care Finance; Health Care Reform; Securities. ***Email:*** kvondrathen@foley.com

CHRISTOPHER J. WERNER, admitted to bar, 2002, Illinois. *Education:* Indiana University (B.A., Philosophy, 1997); George Washington University (J.D., 2002). Managing Editor, George Washington International Law Review. ***PRACTICE AREAS:*** Litigation; Commercial Litigation. ***Email:*** cwerner@foley.com

DEREK L. WRIGHT, admitted to bar, 2001, Illinois and Wisconsin. *Education:* University of Michigan (B.A., English, 1998); University of Wisconsin-Milwaukee (J.D., 2001). ***PRACTICE AREAS:*** Commercial Litigation; Litigation. ***Email:*** dlwright@foley.com

ANDREA K. ZOLLETT, (admission pending). *Education:* University of Arizona (B.A., summa cum laude, 2000); Vanderbilt University (J.D., 2004). Recipient: Law School Scholarship; Academic Award of Excellence. Author and Member, Vanderbilt Journal of Transnational Law. ***PRACTICE AREAS:*** Litigation; Bankruptcy. ***Email:*** azollett@foley.com

(See Foley & Lardner listings at Milwaukee and Madison, Wisconsin; Chicago, Illinois; Washington, D.C.; Jacksonville, Miami, Orlando, Tallahassee, Tampa and West Palm Beach, Florida; Los Angeles, Palo Alto, Sacramento, San Diego and San Francisco, California; New York, New York; Boston, Massachusetts; Tokyo, Japan and Brussels, Belgium for professional biographies information on attorneys resident in those offices)

FORAN GLENNON PALANDECH & PONZI PC

150 SOUTH WACKER DRIVE 11TH FLOOR
CHICAGO, ILLINOIS 60606
Telephone: 312-863-5000
Fax: 312-863-5099
URL: http://www.fgpp.com

Los Angeles, California Office: 12400 Wilshire Boulevard, 15th Floor, 90025. Telephone: 310-826-1810. Fax: 310-826-1821.

Civil Litigation, Property Insurance, Design Professional Liability, Construction Litigation, Products, Professional and Employment Liability, Bad Faith, Insurance Coverage Defense, Excess and Reinsurance, Subrogation and Liability Coverage.

ROBERT T. BOYLAN, born 1970; admitted to bar, 1995, Illinois and U.S. District Court, Northern District of Illinois. *Education:* University of Michigan (B.A., 1992); Boston University (J.D., 1995). ***PRACTICE AREAS:*** Construction; Products Liability; Professional Liability; First Party Property. ***Email:*** rboylan@fgpp.com

GEORGE M. FERRETI, born 1969; admitted to bar, 1994, Illinois and U.S. District Court, Northern District of Illinois. *Education:* University of Illinois (B.A., cum laude, 1991); University of Michigan (J.D., 1994). ***LANGUAGES:*** Spanish. ***PRACTICE AREAS:*** Product Liability; Subrogation; Civil Litigation; Construction Litigation. ***Email:*** gferreti@fgpp.com

MICHAEL L. FORAN, born 1961; admitted to bar, 1985, Illinois; 1986, U.S. District Court, Northern District of Illinois and U.S. District Court, Eastern District of Wisconsin; 1998, U.S. District Court, District of Colorado. *Education:* Colgate University (B.A., cum laude, 1982); Loyola University, Chicago (J.D., 1985). ***PRACTICE AREAS:*** Property Insurance; Environmental Insurance Claims; Insurance Bad Faith Defense; Reinsurance; Professional Liability; Civil Litigation; Mold Litigation. ***Email:*** mforan@fgpp.com

JAMES B. GLENNON, born 1963; admitted to bar, 1988, Illinois and U.S. District Court, Northern District of Illinois; 1998, Nevada and U.S. District Court, District of Nevada; 1999, Indiana and U.S. District Court, Northern District of Indiana. *Education:* University of Notre Dame (B.A., 1985); Loyola University, Chicago (J.D., 1988). *Member:* State Bar of Nevada. ***PRACTICE AREAS:*** Civil Litigation; Subrogation; Property Insurance; Products Liability; Construction Litigation. ***Email:*** jglennon@fgpp.com

MICHAEL H. McCOLL, born 1970; admitted to bar, 1994, Illinois. *Education:* Denison University (B.A., 1991); Northwestern University (J.D., 1994). ***PRACTICE AREAS:*** Medical Malpractice Defense; Personal Injury Defense; Products Liability Defense; Insurance Coverage. ***Email:*** mmccoll@fgpp.com

MARY C. O'CONNOR, born 1951; admitted to bar, 1976, Illinois; U.S. District Court, Northern District of Illinois inculing Trial Bar; U.S. Court of Appeals, Seventh Circuit. *Education:* University of Illinois (B.A., 1973); Northwestern University (J.D., 1976). Assistant State's Attorney, Cook County, 1976-1983. ***PRACTICE AREAS:*** Medical Malpractice Defense; Municipal Liability; Civil Rights Litigation; Products Liability Defense; Casualty Defense; Employer Liability; Insurance Coverage. ***Email:*** moconnor@fgpp.com

THOMAS B. ORLANDO, born 1965; admitted to bar, 1994, Illinois and U.S. District Court, Northern and Central Districts of Illinois; 1999, U.S. District Court, Eastern District of Wisconsin; 2000, U.S. District Court, Northern District of Ohio and U.S. District Court, Eastern District of Michigan. *Education:* Miami University (B.S., cum laude, 1988); University of Illinois (J.D., magna cum laude, 1994). Certified Public Accountant, Illinois, 1988. ***PRACTICE AREAS:*** Civil Litigation; Property Insurance; Reinsurance; Professional Liability; Products Liability; Construction Law. ***Email:*** torlando@fgpp.com

DOUGLAS J. PALANDECH, born 1951; admitted to bar, 1977, Illinois and U.S. District Court, Northern District of Illinois. *Education:* University of Texas (B.A. with high honors, 1973); Illinois Institute of Technology, Chicago-Kent College of Law (J.D. with

(This Listing Continued)

honors, 1977). Phi Beta Kappa; Pi Sigma Alpha. ***PRACTICE AREAS:*** Design Professional Liability; First-Party Insurance Defense; Construction Litigation; Products Liability; Mold Litigation. ***Email:*** dpalandech@fgpp.com

MATTHEW S. PONZI, born 1963; admitted to bar, 1988, Illinois; 1989, U.S. District Court, Northern District of Illinois. *Education:* DePauw University (B.A., 1985); George Washington University (J.D., 1988). ***PRACTICE AREAS:*** Property Insurance; Excess and Reinsurance; Insurance Coverage Defense; Extra Contractual Insurance Claims; Mold Litigation. ***Email:*** mponzi@fgpp.com

BRIAN T. PARSONS, born 1972; admitted to bar, 2000, Illinois. *Education:* Illinois State University (B.S., Health Sciences, 1994); Loyola University, Chicago (J.D., 2000). ***PRACTICE AREAS:*** Professional Malpractice; Construction Litigation; Products Liability; Mold Litigation. ***Email:*** bparsons@fgpp.com

GEORGE DANIEL PILJA, born 1971; admitted to bar, 1996, Florida; U.S. District Court, Southern District of Florida; 1997, Illinois: U.S. District Court, Northern District of Illinois. *Education:* North Central College (B.A., magna cum laude, 1993); University of Illinois (J.D., 1996). *Member:* The Florida Bar. ***PRACTICE AREAS:*** Commercial Litigation; Products Liability Litigation; Construction Litigation; Subrogation. ***Email:*** gpilja@fgpp.com

UJJVAL K. VYAS, born 1960; admitted to bar, 2003, Illinois. *Education:* Dickinson State College (B.A., 1981); Chicago-Kent College of Law (J.D., 2003).

JONATHAN FRAWLEY FIEGEN, born 1970; admitted to bar, 1996, Missouri; 2002, Illinois. ***PRACTICE AREAS:*** Construction Law; First Party Insurance; Personal Injury. ***Email:*** jfiegen@fgpp.com

GARRETT P. KERN, born Arlington Heights, Illinois, January 30, 1975; admitted to bar, 2001, Illinois. *Education:* University of Notre Dame (B.A., 1997); Loyola University (J.D., 2001). *Member:* Chicago and American Bar Associations. ***PRACTICE AREAS:*** Construction Litigation; Commercial Litigation; Professional Liability. ***Email:*** gkern@fgpp.com

JOHN O'GRADY, admitted to bar, 1990, Illinois and U.S. District Court, Northern District of Illinois. *Education:* University of Illinois at Urbana-Champaign (B.A., 1987); Illinois Institute of Technology, Chicago (J.D., 1990). ***PRACTICE AREAS:*** Medical Malpractice Defense; First Party Insurance; Casualty Insurance Defense.

C. ZACHARY RANSEL, born Elkhart, Indiana, May 2, 1975; admitted to bar, 2001, Illinois. *Education:* Miami University (B.S., Economics, 1997); Indiana University School of Law (J.D., 2001). ***PRACTICE AREAS:*** Litigation; Construction; Products Liability. ***Email:*** zransel@fgpp.com

NIZAM ARAIN, born Chicago, Illinois, April 30, 1974; admitted to bar, 2000, Illinois. *Education:* University of Illinois (B.A., 1996); University of Michigan (J.D., 1999). ***PRACTICE AREAS:*** Insurance Defense. ***Email:*** narain@fgpp.com

MAURA YUSOF, born Kabul, Afghanistan, June 8, 1976; admitted to bar, 2002, Illinois; 2003, Missouri. *Education:* Georgetown University (B.S.L.A., 1998); Washington University School of Law (J.D., 2002). Teaching Assistant, First Year Law Students Legal Research Writing, Fall, 2001-2002. ***LANGUAGES:*** Dari (dialect of Persian), Spanish and French. ***PRACTICE AREAS:*** Large Loss Subrogation; Construction Law; Commercial Litigation. ***Email:*** myusof@fgpp.com

JASON R. WILLIAMS, born Buffalo, New York, May 9, 1973; admitted to bar, 2003, Illinois; 2005, U.S. District Court, Northern District of Illinois. *Education:* DePaul University (B.A., International Studies with Honors, 1999); Chicago-Kent College of Law, Illinois Institute of Technology (J.D., 2002). Phi Delta Phi. *Member:* Chicago (Chair, Young Lawyers Section, 2005—); Veterans Legal Assistance & Military Law Committee. [U.S. Attorney, 82 Airborne Division, 1996-1997.]. ***PRACTICE AREAS:*** Medical Malpractice Defense; Hospital Representation. ***Email:*** jwilliams@fgpp.com

OF COUNSEL

PAUL T. LIVELY, born Olney, Illinois, June 7, 1948; admitted to bar, 1973, Illinois. *Education:* University of Illinois (A.B., with high honors, 1970); Northwestern University (J.D., with honors, 1973). Phi Beta Kappa. Recipient, Bronze Tablet, 1970. ***PRACTICE AREAS:*** Construction Law; Insurance Coverage; Professional Liability; Business Law; Corporate Law; Land Use; Zoning Law; Alternative Dispute Resolution; Appellate Practice.

SENIOR COUNSEL

KEVIN J. GLENN, born Syracuse, New York, May 27, 1951; admitted to bar, 1979, Illinois and U.S. District Court, Northern District of Illinois; 1984, California; 1990, U.S. District Court, Southern District of Illinois; 1991, New York. *Education:* University of Notre Dame (B.B.A., 1973); Lewis University (J.D., 1978). *Member:* Chicago, Illinois State, New York State and American Bar Associations; State Bar of California; Society of Trial Lawyers. ***PRACTICE AREAS:*** Medical Malpractice; Personal Injury. ***Email:*** kglenn@fgpp.com

FORAN, O'TOOLE & BURKE LLC

Established in 2004

321 NORTH CLARK STREET
SUITE 2450
CHICAGO, ILLINOIS 60610
Telephone: 312-644-1414
Facsimile: 312-644-1415
Email: attorneys@foblaw.com
URL: http://www.foblaw.com

Eminent Domain and Protection of Property Rights.

(This Listing Continued)

FORAN, O'TOOLE & BURKE LLC, Chicago—Continued

JOHN J. FORAN, born Chicago, Illinois, July 31, 1952; admitted to bar, 1985, Illinois and U.S. District Court, Northern District of Illinois. *Education:* Harvard University (B.A., cum laude, 1974); Northwestern University (M.A., 1975); John Marshall Law School (J.D., 1985). Lecturer: American Law Institute; American Bar Association; CLE International, various Eminent Domain topics, 1998 and 2000-2002. *Member:* Chicago, Illinois State and American (Midwest Regional Editor, Committee on Condemnation, Zoning and Land Use) Bar Associations. ***PRACTICE AREAS:*** Eminent Domain. ***Email:*** jforan@foblaw.com

MARK T. O'TOOLE, born Chicago, Illinois, July 5, 1960; admitted to bar, 1985, Illinois and U.S. District Court, Northern District of Illinois. *Education:* Miami University (B.S., 1982); Loyola University (J.D., 1985). Author: "New Judicial Subcircuiting Brings a Different Election Process," Chicago Bar Association Record, March, 1992. Law Clerk to Justice William G. Clark, Illinois Supreme Court, 1990. Lecturer: American Bar Association; CLE International; various Eminent Domain topics, 2001, 2002 and 2003. Staff Counsel to the Speaker of the Illinois House of Representatives, 1991. Licensed Lobbyist under State of Illinois regulations. *Member:* Chicago, Illinois State and American Bar Associations. ***PRACTICE AREAS:*** Eminent Domain. ***Email:*** motoole@foblaw.com

STEPHEN M. BURKE, born Chicago, Illinois, June 7, 1967; admitted to bar, 1993, Illinois. *Education:* Brown University (B.A., Philosophy, with honors, Economics, 1989); Loyola University (J.D., 1992). Lecturer: CLE International, Eminent Domain Damages, 2003. *Member:* Chicago, Illinois State, and American Bar Associations. ***PRACTICE AREAS:*** Eminent Domain. ***Email:*** sburke@foblaw.com

REPRESENTATIVE CLIENTS: Exxon Mobil Corp.; Vicorp Restaurants Inc./Baker's Square; Continental General Tire, Inc.; McDonald's Corp.; Freightliner LLC; Morgan Services, Inc.; Diamond Construction Co.; Loyola University of Chicago; Banner Wholesale Grocers; Bally Total Fitness Corp.; SWM Ventures, Inc.; Fraternal Order of Police, Lodge #7; Dearborn Restaurant, Inc.; Hulett Corp.; Standard Wire and Steel Works; Chicago Central Tire and Wheel, Inc.; Motive Parts Company of America; J&J Motor Services, Inc.; Hopkins Illinois Elevator Co.

KEVIN M. FORDE, LTD.

SUITE 1100, 111 WEST WASHINGTON STREET
CHICAGO, ILLINOIS 60602
Telephone: 312-641-1441
Fax: 312-641-1288

Trials and Appeals. Commercial Litigation, Constitutional Law, Class Actions, Business Torts, Products Liability, Antitrust, Securities Law, Chancery Practice, State and Local Taxation.

KEVIN M. FORDE, born Chicago, Illinois, September 5, 1938; admitted to bar, 1963, Illinois; U.S. Court of Appeals, Seventh Circuit; U.S. Supreme Court and U.S. Court of Appeals for the District of Columbia Circuit. *Education:* Marquette University (B.S., 1960); Loyola University (J.D., 1963). Counsel to President of Cook County (later Supreme Court Justice) Seymour Simon, 1964-1966. Law Clerk to Judge William J. Campbell, U.S. District Court, Northern District of Illinois, 1966-1970. Faculty Member, The John Marshall Law School, 1968-1970. General Counsel, Federal Judges Association, 1984—. Editor-in-Chief, Chicago Bar Record, 1972-1978. Consulting Editor, Class Actions, Illinois Institute Continuing Legal Education, 1979. Member, 1979—, Chair, 1997—, Board of Directors, Federal Defender Program, Inc., Northern District of Illinois. Member, Board of Directors, Lawyers Trust Fund of Illinois, 1983-1987. Chair, Compensation Review Board, State of Illinois, 1984—. *Member:* Chicago (Member, Board of Managers, 1973-1975; President, 1981-1982), Illinois State, Federal and American Bar Associations; National Conference of Bar Presidents; Appellate Lawyers Association (Member, Board of Governors, 1977-1979); American Judicature Society (Member, Board of Directors, 1987-1992); Celtic Legal Society of Chicago (President, 1983-1984). Fellow: American College of Trial Lawyers; International Academy of Trial Lawyers; American Academy of Appellate Lawyers. ***Email:*** kforde@fordeltd.com

---

JANICE R. FORDE, born Evergreen Park, Illinois, October 10, 1943; admitted to bar, 1984, Illinois; U.S. District Court, Northern District of Illinois; U.S. Court of Appeals for the Federal Circuit; U.S. Court of Appeals, Seventh Circuit. *Education:* St. Xavier (B.A., 1965); University of Chicago (M.A.T., in Mathematics, 1969); Loyola University (J.D., 1984). Member, Board of Trustees, Saint Xavier University, 1995—. Member, Board of Directors, Chicago Bar Foundation, 1993-1999. *Member:* Chicago (Member, Board of Managers, 1998-2000), Illinois State and American Bar Associations; Women's Bar Association of Illinois; Women's Bar Foundation (Board of Directors, 1998-2003). ***Email:*** jforde@fordeltd.com

KEVIN R. MALLOY, born Niagara Falls, New York, January 7, 1971; admitted to bar, 1997, Illinois and U.S. District Court, Northern District of Illinois; 1999, U.S. Court of Appeals for the Federal Circuit; 2000, U.S. Court of Appeals, Seventh Circuit. *Education:* University of Notre Dame (B.A., 1993); Washington College of Law, American University (J.D., cum laude, 1997). Co-author: "Special Considerations in a Class Action," Illinois Civil Discovery Practice, Illinois Institute for Continuing Legal Education, 2003; "State Practice: Illinois' Class Action Statute," Class Actions, Illinois Institute for Continuing Legal Education, 2001, 8 Supp. 2004. Author: "Procedural Aspects of Shareholder Derivative Suits in Illinois," Class Actions, Illinois Institute for Continuing Legal Education, Supplement, 2004. *Member:* Chicago, Illinois State and American Bar Associations. ***Email:*** kmalloy@fordeltd.com

JOANNE ROUZAN DRISCOLL, born Chicago, Illinois, August 20, 1952; admitted to bar, 1978, Illinois and U.S. District Court, Northern District of Illinois; 1983, U.S. Court of Appeals, Seventh Circuit. *Education:* DePaul University (B.S.C., summa cum laude, 1974; J.D., 1978). Note and Comment Editor, DePaul Law Review, 1977-1978. Law Clerk to Justice Joseph Gordon, Illinois Appellate Court, 1994-1999. Law Clerk to Justice Helen F. McGillicuddy, Illinois Appellate Court, 1979-1982. Executive Director, Lawyers' Assistance Program, Inc., 1991-1994; Associate, Driscoll & Driscoll, Schaumburg, Illinois, 1983-1990; Assistant Counsel, North American Company for Life & Health Insurance, Chicago, Illinois, 1978-1979. *Member:* Chicago and American (Co-Chair, Amicus Curiae Briefs Committee of Litigation Section, 2001—) Bar Associations; Women's Bar Association of Illinois; Women's Bar Foundation (Board of Directors, 1990—; President, 2003-2005; Vice President, 2001-2003; Secretary, 1999-2001); Appellate Lawyers Association; Illinois Lawyers' Assistance Program. ***PRACTICE AREAS:*** Appellate Practice; Civil Litigation. ***Email:*** jdriscoll@fordeltd.com

MELISSA GUINTA, born La Grange, Illinois, August 16, 1976; admitted to bar, 2001, Illinois; 2004, U.S. District Court, Northern District of Illinois. *Education:* Miami University (B.A., 1998); Loyola University (J.D., 2001; LL.M., Health Law, 2002). *Member:* Chicago and American Bar Associations. ***Email:*** mguinta@fordeltd.com

FOX, HEFTER, SWIBEL, LEVIN & CARROLL, LLP

321 NORTH CLARK STREET, SUITE 3300
CHICAGO, ILLINOIS 60610
Telephone: 312-224-1200
Facsimile: 312-224-1201
URL: http://www.fhslc.com

Business Transactions, Business Litigation and Real Estate Practice.

FIRM PROFILE: The firm's purpose is to provide clients with high-quality representation at reasonable fees for the resolution of their business disputes and the successful consummation of their commercial transactions. The firm's partners are graduates of top-rated law schools and formerly practiced at large, nationally-known, highly-respected firms. In forming a leading boutique firm, they continue to provide the same high quality of representation at lower cost to their clients with greater responsiveness. The firm's transactional group counsels clients in a wide range of corporate, real estate, banking and securities matters. The firm's dispute resolution group represents clients at all levels of state and federal courts as well as in arbitrations and mediations.

MARTIN B. CARROLL, born Chicago, Illinois, January 28, 1963; admitted to bar, 1989, Illinois and U.S. District Court, Northern District of Illinois; 1994, U.S. Court of Appeals, Seventh Circuit; 1998, U.S. District Court, Central District of Illinois and U.S. Supreme Court. *Education:* University of Illinois (B.A., magna cum laude, 1985); London School of Economics, London, England (M.A., 1987); University of Michigan (J.D., cum laude, 1989). Phi Beta Kappa. Selected as a "Leading Illinois Attorney" in Commercial Litigation and Banking Litigation. Chairman, Board of Directors, DuPage Theatre Foundation. *Member:* Illinois State Bar Association. ***REPORTED CASES:*** Liautaud v. Liautaud, 221 F.3d 981 (7th Cir. 2000); Helm v. Resolution Trust Corp., 84 F.3d 874 (7th Cir. 1996); Vasquez v. Hernandez, 60 F.3d 325 (7th Cir. 1995); Fischel & Kahn, Ltd. v. Van Straaten Gallery, Inc., 727 N.E.2d 240 (Ill. 2000); Walters v. National Properties, LLC, 699 N.W.2d 71 (WI 2005); Egidi v. Town of Libertyville, 578 N.E.2d (2d Dist. 1991); Morse v. Abbott Laboratories, 756 F. Supp. 1108 (N.D., Ill. 1991). ***PRACTICE AREAS:*** Banking Litigation; Business Litigation; Real Estate Litigation; Trade Secrets Litigation; Employment Litigation. ***Email:*** mcarroll@fhslc.com

MICHAEL E. FOX, born Chicago, Illinois, April 14, 1938; admitted to bar, 1962, Illinois, U.S. District Court, Northern District of Illinois and U.S. Supreme Court. *Education:* University of Illinois (B.S., with high honors, 1959); Harvard University (J.D., 1962). Phi Eta Sigma; Phi Kappa Phi; Beta Gamma Sigma; Beta Alpha Psi. Bronze Tablet. Selected as a "Leading Illinois Attorney" in Tax Law, Business and Small, Closely and Privately Held Business Law. Certified Public Accountant, Illinois, 1959. Attorney, Staff of the Joint Committee on Internal Revenue Taxation, 1965-1968. *Member:* Chicago, Illinois State and American Bar Associations. (Managing Partner). ***PRACTICE AREAS:*** Business Law; Private Business Law; Federal Tax Law; Restaurant Law. ***Email:*** mfox@fhslc.com

ROGER B. HARRIS, born Chicago, Illinois, February 4, 1938; admitted to bar, 1962, Illinois. *Education:* University of Michigan (B.A., 1959; LL.B., 1962). Barristers. Selected as a "Leading Illinois Attorney" in Commercial Litigation. Associate Editor, Michigan Law Review, 1961-1962. *Member:* Chicago (Member, Civil Practice Committee, 1983-1997, Division Chairman, 1992-1993 and Federal Civil Procedure Committee, 1968-1984; Chairman, 1977-1978), Illinois State and American Bar Associations. ***PRACTICE AREAS:*** Litigation. ***Email:*** rharris@fhslc.com

DANIEL S. HEFTER, born Chicago, Illinois, March 4, 1956; admitted to bar, 1980, Illinois and U.S. District Court, Northern District of Illinois; 1981, U.S. Court of Appeals, Seventh Circuit; 1983, U.S. Court of Appeals, District of Columbia Circuit; 1987, U.S. Supreme Court; 1999, U.S. District Court, Western District of Michigan. *Education:* University of Illinois (B.S., 1977); University of Michigan (J.D., cum laude, 1980). Selected as a "Leading Illinois Attorney" in Commercial Litigation. *Member:* Chicago, Illinois State and American (Member, Litigation Section) Bar Associations; Chicago Council of Lawyers. ***REPORTED CASES:*** Fischel & Kahn, Ltd. v. Van Straaten Gallery, Inc., 189 Ill. 2d 240, 727 N.E.2d 240 (2000); Weiss v. Wark, 202 F.3d 276 (7th Cir. 1999); Ross v. Fultz, 709 N.E. 2d 317 (2d Dist. 1997); Haynes v. Alfred A. Knopf, Inc., 8 F.3d 1222 (7th Cir. 1993); Altheimer & Gray v. Sioux Manufacturing Co., 983 F.2d 803 (7th Cir.); Resolution Trust Corporation v. Holtzman, 248 Ill. App. 3d 105, 618 N.E.2d 418 (1st Dist. 1993); Frazier v. Dettman, 212 Ill. App. 3d 139, 569 N.E.2s 1382 (2nd Dist. 1991); Dreyfuss Metal Co. v. Berg, 569 N.E.2d 19 (1st Dist. 1991); O'Donnell v. Field Enterprises, Inc., 491 N.E.2d 1212 (1st Dist. 1986); Ollman v. Evans, 750 F.2d 970 (D.C. Cir. 1984) (en banc). ***PRACTICE AREAS:*** Business Litigation; Real Estate Litigation; Trade Secrets Litigation; Unfair Competition Litigation; Defamation; Media and First Amendment; Appeals. ***Email:*** dhefter@fhslc.com

JOSEPH C. HUNTZICKER, born Ann Arbor, Michigan, September 24, 1973; admitted to bar, 2000, Michigan; 2001, Illinois; 2003, California. *Education:* University of Michigan (B.A., political science, 1996; JD., cum laude, 2000). ***PRACTICE AREAS:*** Commercial Finance; Real Estate; Corporate Law. ***Email:*** jhuntzicker@fhslc.com

HOWARD L. KASTEL, born June 11, 1932; admitted to bar, 1960, Illinois. *Education:* Harvard University (A.B., 1954); Loyola University of Chicago (J.D., cum laude, 1960). Member, Loyola University Law Review, 1958-1960. Selected as a "Leading Illinois Attorney" in Employment Law, International Law and Commercial Litigation. Member: Financial Accounting Standards Board Task Force on Non-Business Organizations, 1981-

(This Listing Continued)

1983; Accounting Standards Board and AcSEC Liaison Committees. Member, National Panel of Arbitrators, American Arbitration Assn. *Member:* Chicago (Member: Labor Law Committee, 1961-1972; Civil Practice Committee, 1971-1988; Securities Law Committee, 1981-1988; Judiciary Committee, 1983-1997), Illinois State and American (Member, Committees on: Labor Law, 1972-1988; Law and Accounting, 1977—, Chairman, Subcommittee on International Accounting; Federal Regulations of Securities, Subcommittee on SEC Practice and Enforcement Matters, 1979—; Chairman, Not For Profit Corporations, 1979-1983; Chairman, Subcommittee on Accounting and Auditing, 1979-1983; Litigation Subcommittee on Securities Litigation, 1980-1988; Chairman, Special Task Force on Emerging Issues, 1984-1988; Member, Task Force on SEC Rules of Practice Relating to Administrative Proceedings and Investigations, 1985—) Bar Associations. ***REPORTED CASES:*** First Stop Book Shop v. Matthews Book Co., Inc., 634 F.2d 625 (1980); McDasniel v. Frye, 536 F.2d 625 (1976); Telco Leasing, Inc. v. Allphin, 347 N.E.2d 729; Mesker Bros. Iron Co. v. Des Lauriers Col. Mould Co., 289 N.E.2d 223; Reilly v. Segert, 201 N.E.2d 444; Schwarz v. Folloder, 767 F.2d 125 (1985); Surowitz v. Hilton Hotels Corporation, 342 F.2d 596 (1965); Albert v. Grant Thornton, 735 F.Supp. 443 (W.D.Mo. 1990). ***TRANSACTIONS:*** Alexander Grant & Co./Fox & Co. ***PRACTICE AREAS:*** Business Litigation; Trial Practice; Securities Litigation; Employment Law; Employment Litigation; Arbitration; Mediation; Crisis Management. ***Email:*** hkastel@fhslc.com

TRACY E. KATZ, born Evanston, Illinois, April 6, 1976; admitted to bar, 2000, Illinois and U.S. District Court, Northern District of Illinois. *Education:* Georgetown University (B.S.F.S., 1997); University of Chicago (J.D., 2000). Co-author: "Judge Easterbrook's New Look at Proving Class Claims of Deception," Class Action Litigation, Dec., 22, 2000. *Member:* Illinois State Bar Association. ***PRACTICE AREAS:*** Litigation; Intellectual Property. ***Email:*** tzatz@fhslc.com

MARIA L. KING, born Minot, North Dakota, April 16, 1976; admitted to bar, 2002, Illinois; 2005, Minnesota. *Education:* University of North Dakota (B.A., summa cum laude, 1998); Harvard Law School (J.D., 2002). Phi Beta Kappa. ***PRACTICE AREAS:*** Corporate Finance; Real Estate; Corporate Law. ***Email:*** mking@fhslc.com

LAURIE A. LEVIN, born Queens, New York, February 15, 1956; admitted to bar, 1985, New York and U.S. District Court, Southern District of New York; 1986, Illinois. *Education:* The Juilliard School of Music (B.M., 1978; M.M., 1980); Fordham University (J.D., cum laude, 1984). Senior Articles Editor, Fordham University Law Review. Selected as a "Leading Illinois Attorney" in Real Estate. *Member:* Illinois State Bar Association. ***PRACTICE AREAS:*** Real Estate Law; Banking Law; Corporate Law. ***Email:*** llevin@fhslc.com

DAVID J. MORRIS, born St. Louis, Missouri, June 23, 1966; admitted to bar, 1991, Illinois; 1992, Missouri. *Education:* University of Illinois (B.S., with highest honors, 1988); London School of Economics, London, England; University of California School of Law, Los Angeles (J.D., 1991). Associate Editor, UCLA Law Review, 1990-1991. Selected as a "Leading Illinois Attorney" in Mergers and Acquisitions Law, Securities and Venture Financing Law, and Small, Closely and Privately Held Business Law. Intern, United States Securities and Exchange Commission, Washington, D.C., 1990. *Member:* Illinois State Bar Association. ***PRACTICE AREAS:*** Corporate Law; Mergers, Acquisitions and Divestitures; Securities Law; Finance; Commodities. ***Email:*** dmorris@fhslc.com

WILLIAM J. PELTIN, born Milwaukee, Wisconsin, February 10, 1962; admitted to bar, 1987, Illinois and Wisconsin. *Education:* University of Illinois (B.S., with honors, 1984); University of Wisconsin-Madison (J.D., 1987). Associate Editor, University of Wisconsin Law Review, 1986-1987. *Member:* Illinois State Bar Association; State Bar of Wisconsin. ***PRACTICE AREAS:*** Real Estate Law; Finance; Corporate Law. ***Email:*** wpeltin@fhslc.com

RICHARD L. SANDLER, born September 18, 1955; admitted to bar, 1980, Missouri; 1984, Illinois, U.S. District Court, Northern District of Illinois and U.S. Court of Appeals, Seventh, Eighth and Tenth. *Education:* Washington University (A.B., cum laude, 1977); University of Iowa (J.D., with high honors, 1980). Order of the Coif. *Member:* Illinois State and American Bar Associations; The Missouri Bar. ***PRACTICE AREAS:*** Commercial Litigation; Architects and Engineers Liability; Defamation; First Amendment Law. ***Email:*** rsandler@fhslc.com

AMANDA A. SCHWOB, admitted to bar, 2001, Illinois. *Education:* Lamar University (B.S., Speech, 1988); University of Texas (M.F.A., Acting, 1993); University of Illinois (J.D., cum laude, 2001). Articles Editor, The Elder Law Journal. Author: "Open Wide I Meant Your Pocketbook: Repercussions of the Dental Exclusion to the Medicare Act" (2001). Professor, Speech Communications, University of Illinois, 2000-2001. *Member:* Illinois State and American Bar Associations. ***PRACTICE AREAS:*** Real Estate; Corporate Law. ***Email:*** aschwob@fhslc.com

YURI M. SHIDENKO, born Moscow, Russian Federation, May 27, 1976; admitted to bar, 2002, New York (Not admitted in Illinois). *Education:* Kyiv National University, Kyiv, Ukraine (Master of International Law, with honors, 1998); Northwestern University School of Law (LL.M., with honors, 1999). *Member:* New York State and American Bar Associations. ***LANGUAGES:*** Ukrainian and Russian. ***PRACTICE AREAS:*** Corporate; Securities; International. ***Email:*** yshidenko@fhslc.com

DAVID B. SINGER, born Chicago, Illinois, December 19, 1977; admitted to bar, 2003, Illinois. *Education:* University of Michigan, Ann Arbor, (B.A., Political Science, 2000; J.D., 2002). ***PRACTICE AREAS:*** Litigation. ***Email:*** dsinger@fhslc.com

LAWRENCE B. SWIBEL, born Chicago, Illinois, March 20, 1954; admitted to bar, 1978, Illinois. *Education:* University of Rochester (B.A., 1975); Vanderbilt University (J.D., cum laude, 1978). Selected as a "Leading Illinois Attorney" in Real Estate. *Member:* Chicago, Illinois State and American Bar Associations. ***PRACTICE AREAS:*** Real Estate Law; Finance; Corporate Law; International Law. ***Email:*** lswibel@fhslc.com

DALE B. TAUKE, born Dubuque, Iowa, March 15, 1952; admitted to bar, 1977, Illinois; 1985, Missouri. *Education:* University of Iowa (B.B.A., 1974); University of Chicago (J.D., 1977). Beta Gamma Sigma. Member, University of Chicago Law Review. Selected as a "Leading Illinois Attorney" in Acquisition and Dispositions, Joint Ventures, Outsourcing and Commercial Transactions. Assistant Professor, St. Louis University School of Law. *Member:* Chicago, Illinois State and American Bar Associations. ***PRACTICE AREAS:*** Outsourcing; Complex Commercial Contracting; Corporate Finance; Securities; Mergers and Acquisitions. ***Email:*** dtauke@fhslc.com

(This Listing Continued)

ROBIN L. WOLKOFF, born Chicago, Illinois, May 12, 1966; admitted to bar, 1990, Illinois. *Education:* University of Illinois, Urbana-Champaign (B.S., with highest honors, 1987); Northwestern University School of Law (J.D., 1990). Dean's List; National Mock Trial Team. Co-Author: "Three Proposals for Interdisciplinary Study," Family Business Review, vol. XI, September 1998. Trustee, Board of Trustees, Chiaravalle Montessori School, Evanston, Illinois. *Member:* Illinois State Bar Association. ***PRACTICE AREAS:*** Business Litigation; Real Estate Litigation. ***Email:*** rwolkoff@fhslc.com

REPRESENTATIVE CLIENTS: The Firm's clients include publicly and privately held corporations, major lending institutions, real estate developers and asset managers, restaurant companies and restauranteurs, life insurance companies and wealthy individuals and investors. Some of the Firm's better known clients include: AthletiCo; Bank of America, N.A.; Barclays Bank PLC; Builders Bank; CB Richard Ellis; Cole Taylor Bank; Corus Bank; Cushman & Wakefield of Illinois, Inc.; Diamond Cluster International, Inc.; Fifth Third Bank; FMC Corporation; GE Capital Realty; H&R Block; Heitman Properties, Ltd.; ICON, LLC; JPMorganChase; Lettuce Entertain You Enterprises, Inc.; MONY Life Insurance Company; North Star Trust Company; Oversea Chinese Banking Corporation; Prentiss Properties; Priester Aviation LLC; Prime Group Realty Trust; Raymond James Financial; Sargent & Lundy, LLC; Walgreen Co.; Wells Fargo Bank.

FRAGOMEN, DEL REY, BERNSEN & LOEWY, LLP

200 WEST JACKSON BOULEVARD, SUITE 1800
CHICAGO, ILLINOIS 60606
Telephone: 312-263-6101
Facsimile: 312-346-1970
URL: http://www.fragomen.com

New York, New York Office: 515 Madison Avenue. Telephone: 212-688-8555. Facsimile: 212-758-7215; 212-319-5236.
Washington, D.C. Office: 1212 New York Avenue, N.W., Suite 850. Telephone: 202-223-5515. Facsimile: 202-371-2898.
Coral Gables, Florida Office: 241 Sevilla Avenue, Suite 802. Telephone: 305-774-5800. Facsimile: 305-774-6666.
San Francisco, California Office: 100 Spear Street, 10th Floor. Telephone: 415-986-1446. Facsimile: 415-986-7964.
Los Angeles, California Office: 12121 Wilshire Boulevard, Suite 1001. Telephone: 310-820-3322. Facsimile: 310-820-2702.
Santa Clara, California Office: 2804 Mission College Boulevard, 2nd Floor. Telephone: 408-919-0600. Facsimile: 408-919-0615.
Irvine, California Office: 18401 Von Karman Avenue, Suite 255. Telephone: 949-261-0209. Facsimile: 949-261-2821.
San Diego, California Office: 11238 El Camino Real, Suite 100. Telephone: 858-793-1600. Facsimile: 858-793-1686.
Stamford, Connecticut Office: One Atlantic Street. Telephone: 203-352-1871. Facsimile: 203-352-1874.
Iselin, New Jersey Office: 99 Wood Avenue South. Telephone: 732-906-1230. Facsimile: 732-906-9190.
Troy, Michigan Office: 2301 West Big Beaver Road, Suite 225. Telephone: 248-649-5404. Facsimile: 248-649-5121.
Dallas, Texas Office: 5000 Quorum Drive, Suite 215. Telephone: 972-233-6646. Facsimile: 972-233-3134.
Boston, Massachusetts Office: 31 Milk Street, Suite 201. Telephone: 617-574-0400. Facsimile: 617-574-0450.
Brussels, Belgium Office: Rue Des Colonies 11 1000 Brussels, Belgium. Telephone: 32-2 517 61-23. Fax: 32-2 517-65-92.
Singapore Office: Centennial Tower, Level 21 3 Temasek Avenue, Singapore 039190. Telephone: 65 6549-7284. Facsimile: 65 6549-7284.
Affiliated Offices:
Fragomen Australia: Waterfront Place Level 16, 1 Eagle Street, Brisbane, QLD 4000 Australia. Telephone: 61 7 3257 5177. Fax: 61 7 3257 8009.
Fragomen Australia: 215 Spring Street, Melbourne, VIC 3001 Australia. Telephone: 61 3 8603 3607. Fax: 61 3 8603 6347.
Fragomen Australia: Level 24 6 O'Connell Street Sydney, NSW 2000 Australia. Telephone: 61 2 8224 8555. Fax: 61 2 8224 8500.
Fragomen Great Britain: 75 Cannon Street, London EC4N 5BN. Telephone: 44 0 870 735 1490. Fax: 44 0 207 556 7001.
Fragomen Hong Kong: 1811, Level 18 One International Finance Centre 1 Harbour View Street, Central Hong Kong. Telephone: 852 2166 8660. Fax: 852 2166 8841.

Immigration; Visas; I-9 Compliance; Export Control; U.S. and Global Immigration and Nationality Law.

MICHAEL F. TURANSICK, born Trenton, New Jersey, August 14, 1957; admitted to bar, 1983, New York (Not admitted in Illinois). *Education:* Fordham University (B.A., 1979; J.D., 1982). Associate Editor, Fordham International Law Journal. Member, International Who's Who of Corporate Immigration Lawyers, 2003-2005. Director, Canadian Club of Chicago (2005). *Member:* New York State and American (Co-Chair, Immigration and Nationality Law Committee, Section of International Law 2003—) Bar Associations; American Immigration Lawyers Association (Chair, New York Chapter, 1999-2000); American Immigration Law Foundation (Trustee, 2002—). ***Email:*** mturansick@fragomen.com

ASSOCIATES

JILL M. GUZMAN, born Peoria, Illinois, June 10, 1970; admitted to bar, 1995, Illinois. *Education:* Valparaiso University (B.A., 1992); DePaul University College of Law (J.D., 1995). *Member:* Chicago and American Bar Associations; American Immigration Lawyers Association; Northern Federal District of Illinois Bar. ***LANGUAGES:*** Spanish. ***Email:*** jguzman@fragomen.com

SHAYDA A. SAFAPOUR, born Kalamazoo, Michigan, April 30, 1974; admitted to bar, 2001, Massachusetts; 2004, Illinois. *Education:* Western Michigan University, Honors College (B.A., 1995); Suffolk University Law School (J.D., 1999); Suffolk University School of Management (M.B.A., 2000). ***LANGUAGES:*** Persian, French.

(This Listing Continued)

FRAGOMEN, DEL REY, BERNSEN & LOEWY, LLP, Chicago—Continued

CYNTHIA L. SHEARN, born Park Ridge, Illinois, April 24, 1969; admitted to bar, 1996, Illinois. *Education:* Boston University (B.A., 1991); American University, Washington College of Law (J.D., 1996). Phi Beta Kappa. Harold C. Case Scholar. *Member:* Chicago Bar Association; American Immigration Lawyers Association. ***LANGUAGES:*** French. ***Email:*** cshearn@fragomen.com

CATERINA P. TASSONE, admitted to bar, 1997, Illinois. *Education:* Loyola University (B.A., 1994); Chicago-Kent College of Law (J.D., 1997). Judicial Law Clerk to the Honorable Justice John J. Bowman of the Illinois Appellate Court. Legal Writing Instructor at Loyola University School of Law. Co-author: "Staying Competitive in the Twenty-First Century: Visa Alternatives for Global Employers," Employee Relations Law Journal. Lecturer, Immigration briefings sponsored by the American Council on International Personnel. *Member:* American Immigration Lawyers Association.

ALEXANDER C. ELSBERG, born Hartford, Connecticut, July 27, 1970; admitted to bar, 1996, Ohio; 1999, Illinois. *Education:* Vassar College (B.A., 1992); Case Western Reserve University (J.D., cum laude, 1996). Articles Editor, Case Western Reserve University Law Review. Recipient, American Jurisprudence Award in Legal Research, Analysis, and Writing. Contributing Author, "The Visa Processing Guide," American Immigration Lawyers Association. *Member:* Chicago Bar Association; American Immigration Lawyers Association. ***Email:*** aelsberg@fragomen.com

ANNA MORZY, born Siemiatycze, Poland, July 25, 1974; admitted to bar, 2001, Illinois; U.S. District Court, Northern District of Illinois. *Education:* DePaul University (B.A., 1998); Loyola University (J.D., 2001). *Member:* Chicago and American Bar Associations; American Immigration Lawyers Association. ***LANGUAGES:*** Polish. ***Email:*** amorzy@fragomen.com

ISABEL A. KUGLER, born Oakland, California, August 23, 1971; admitted to bar, 2004, California (Not admitted in Illinois). *Education:* University of California, Los Angeles (B.A., 1995); Pepperdine University School of Law (J.D., 2003). *Member:* State Bar of California; American Bar Association; American Immigration Lawyers Assocation. ***LANGUAGES:*** Turkish.

ROBERT W. KRUG, born Chicago, Illinois, March 13, 1970; admitted to bar, 1999, Illinois. *Education:* University of Illinois, Chicago (B.A., 1993); DePaul University (J.D., 1998). ***LANGUAGES:*** German.

MARIA VENIAMINOVA, born Moscow, Russia, March 24, 1975; admitted to bar, 2001, Illinois and U.S. District Court, Northern District of Illinois. *Education:* Minnesota State University (B.S., 1998); DePaul University (J.D., 2001). *Member:* Chicago and American Bar Associations; American Immigration Lawyers Association. ***LANGUAGES:*** Russian. ***Email:*** mveniaminova@fragomen.com

SENIOR COUNSEL

ETHAN E. BENSINGER, born Tel Aviv, Israel, June 26, 1949; admitted to bar, 1976, Illinois and U.S. District Court, Northern District of Illinois. *Education:* University of Illinois (B.A. Sc., with honors, 1971); Illinois Institute of Technology (J.D., 1976). Clerk, Illinois Appellate Court, 1976. Member, International Who's Who of Corporate Immigration Lawyers, 2001. *Member:* Chicago, Illinois State and American Bar Associations; American Immigration Lawyers Association; Decalogue Society of Lawyers. ***LANGUAGES:*** German. ***Email:*** ebensinger@fragomen.com

COUNSEL

KEVIN C. AISTON, born Highland Park, Illinois, November 21, 1959; admitted to bar, 1984, Illinois. *Education:* Tulane University (B.A., 1980; J.D., summa cum laude, 1984). Phi Beta Kappa. Managing Editor, Tulane Law Review. Former: Deputy Chief, Legal Advisory Opinions Division, Visa Office, U.S. Department of State; Consular Officer, U.S. Embassies in Paris, France, and Victoria, Seychelles. ***LANGUAGES:*** French. ***Email:*** kaiston@fragomen.com

(For complete biographical data on Personnel at New York, New York and Washington, D.C., Coral Gables, Florida, San Francisco, Los Angeles, Santa Clara, Irvine and San Diego, California, Stamford, Connecticut, Iselin, New Jersey, Troy, Michigan, Dallas, Texas, Boston Massachusetts, Boston, Massachusetts, Brussels, Belgium and Singapore, see Professional Biographies at those locations)

FRANCZEK SULLIVAN P.C.

Established in 1994

300 SOUTH WACKER DRIVE
SUITE 3400
CHICAGO, ILLINOIS 60606-6785
Telephone: 312-986-0300
FAX: 312-986-9192
URL: http://www.franczek.com

Labor and Employment, Employment Discrimination, Labor Relations, Employment Litigation, Collective Bargaining, Equal Opportunity Law, Employee Benefits, OSHA, Education Law, Public Employment Relations.

FIRM PROFILE: Franczek Sullivan P.C. concentrates on representing management, both private and public, in all aspects of labor and employment law, as well as offering unsurpassed depth in education law.

Franczek Sullivan P.C. is among the most talented employment and education law firms in the country. Indeed, when it opened in 1994, Crain's Chicago Business characterized the firm as "a new labor law powerhouse composed of very good lawyers and very good people.".

SHELLI L. ANDERSON, born Farmington, Michigan, November 27, 1972; admitted to bar, 1997, Illinois. *Education:* Loyola University-Chicago (B.S., summa cum laude, 1994; J.D., magna cum laude, 1997). *Member:* Chicago, Illinois State and American Bar Associations. ***PRACTICE AREAS:*** Employment Law; School Law. ***Email:*** sla@franczek.com

TERRENCE T. CREAMER, born Chicago, Illinois, October 26, 1958; admitted to bar, 1990, Illinois and U.S. District Court, Northern District of Illinois; U.S. Court of Appeals, 6th, 7th and 9th Circuits. *Education:* Northern Illinois University (B.S., 1980; M.S., 1981) Illinois Institute of Technology (J.D., cum laude, 1990). Judicial Clerk to Honorable Thomas J. Moran, Illinois Supreme Court, 1990-1992. ***PRACTICE AREAS:*** Labor and Employment Law; Education Law. ***Email:*** tc@franczek.com

ANTHONY J. CREMENT, born Chicago, Illinois, March 15, 1944; admitted to bar, 1969, Illinois; U.S. District Court, Northern District of Illinois including Trial Bar; U.S. Court of Appeals, 1st, 6th and 7th Circuits. *Education:* St. Joseph's College (B.A., summa cum laude, 1966); Harvard Law School (J.D., 1969). Listed in Who's Who Among Students in American Colleges and Universities. Author: "Reductions in Force: Practical Problems and Legal Pitfalls," Illinois Reporter - Illinois League of Savings Institutions, May-June, 1990. Lecturer, Institute of Continuing Legal Education and other groups.*Member:* Chicago and American Bar Associations. Fellow, College of Labor and Employment Lawyers. ***PRACTICE AREAS:*** Labor and Employment Law; Employment Litigation; Collective Bargaining; Arbitration. ***Email:*** ajc@franczek.com

ARES G. DALIANIS, born Chicago, Illinois, June 4, 1964; admitted to bar, 1990, Illinois. *Education:* University of Illinois (A.B., 1986); University of Illinois College of Law (J.D., 1990). Phi Kappa Phi. ***REPORTED CASES:*** LaSalle Partners, Inc. v. Illinois Property Tax Appeal Board, 269 Ill.App.3d 621 (2nd Dist. 1995); In re Application of Anderson, 279 Ill.App.3d 593 (2nd Dist. 1996); Cook County Board of Review v. Property Tax Appeal Board, 339 Ill.App.3d 529 (1st Dist. 2002); Elmhurst Chicago Stone Co. v. Novak, 356 Ill.App.3d 180 (2nd Dist. 2005). ***PRACTICE AREAS:*** Real Estate Taxation; Education Law; Government Law. ***Email:*** agd@franczek.com

EDWARD N. DRUCK, born Scranton, Pennsylvania, November 29, 1965; admitted to bar, 1991, Illinois and U.S. District Court, Northern District of Illinois; 1992, U.S. Court of Appeals, 7th Circuit; 1994, U.S. District Court, Central District of Illinois. *Education:* University of Rochester (B.A., magna cum laude, 1988); Vanderbilt University School of Law (J.D., 1991). Phi Beta Kappa. *Member:* Chicago and American Bar Associations. ***PRACTICE AREAS:*** Labor and Employment; Litigation. ***Email:*** end@franczek.com

J. TODD FAULKNER, born Oak Park, Illinois, June 25, 1948; admitted to bar, 1977, Illinois and U.S. District Court, Northern District of Illinois including Trial Bar; 1987, U.S. Court of Appeals, Seventh Circuit. *Education:* Princeton University (A.B., 1970); DePaul University (J.D., magna cum laude, 1977). Author: "Formal Dismissal Procedures under Illinois Teacher Tenure Laws," Illinois Association of School Boards, 1977; "School Board Practices and Procedures," Illinois School Law, Illinois Institute of Continuing Legal Education, 1985, 1988, 1996 and 1999 Supplements. Member, Illinois Council of School Attorneys. *Member:* DuPage County Bar Association. ***PRACTICE AREAS:*** Education Law. ***Email:*** jtf@franczek.com

JAMES C. FRANCZEK, JR., born Hammond, Indiana, November 11, 1946; admitted to bar, 1971, Illinois and Supreme Court of Illinois; 1972, U.S. Court of Appeals, 7th Circuit; 1975, U.S. Court of Appeals, 6th Circuit; 1978, U.S. District Court, Northern District of Illinois including Trial Bar; 1987, U.S. Supreme Court. *Education:* University of Notre Dame (B.A., magna cum laude, 1968); University of Chicago (J.D., 1971). Listed in: The College of Labor and Employment Lawyers, 1998; Best Lawyers in America, 1990-2001; Who's Who Among Outstanding Americans. Author: "Labor Relations in the Trucking Industry," Trucking Employers (1977); "Proving & Defending the Claim," Age Discrimination Law Seminar, Federal Publications, Inc. (1983); "A Changing Road Ahead—The Future of Labor Relations in the Trucking Industry," 1982 Eastern Transportation Law Seminar, Papers and Proceedings (1983). Member, Board of Directors, Chicagoland Chamber of Commerce, 2001.*Member:* Chicago (Chairman, Labor and Employment Law Committee, 1981-1982), Illinois State and American Bar Associations; Chicago Association of Commerce and Industry (Co-Chairman, Committee on Public Sector Labor Law, 1981—). ***PRACTICE AREAS:*** Labor and Employment Law; Education Law. ***Email:*** jcf@franczek.com

RONALD J. HEIN, JR., born Moline, Illinois, February 26, 1950; admitted to bar, 1975, Illinois; 1980, U.S. Supreme Court; U.S. District Court, Central and Northern Districts of Illinois including Trial Bar; U.S. District Court, Northern District of Indiana; U.S. District Court, Eastern District of Wisconsin; U.S. Court of Appeals, Fifth, Sixth, Seventh and Eighth Circuits. *Education:* University of Notre Dame (B.A., cum laude, 1972; J.D., 1975). Omicron Delta Epsilon. *Member:* American Bar Association (Member, Labor and Employment Law Section); American Foundrymen's Society. ***PRACTICE AREAS:*** Labor and Employment Law. ***Email:*** rjh@franczek.com

MICHAEL J. HERNANDEZ, born Chicago, Illinois, November 25, 1958; admitted to bar, 1986, New York; 1988, U.S. District Court, Southern and Eastern Districts of New York; 1989, U.S. District Court, Northern District of Illinois; 1990, Illinois and U.S. District Court, Central District of Illinois. *Education:* Loyola University (B.A., 1981); University of Michigan (J.D., 1984). Delta Theta Phi. Instructor, Legal Writing, University of Michigan Law School, 1983-1984. Assistant District Attorney, Kings County, Brooklyn, 1984-1989. Assistant Attorney, 1991-1992, Supervising Assistant Attorney, 1992-1993 and Deputy General Counsel, 1994-1995, Chicago Board of Education. Member, Chicago Council on Foreign Relations. *Member; Chicago, Illinois State (Member, Education Law Section Council; Editor, Newsletter) and American Bar Associations; Hispanic Lawyers Association of Illinois.* ***Email:*** mjh@franczek.com

DARCY L. KRIHA, born Freeport, Illinois, March 7, 1968; admitted to bar, 1992, Illinois. *Education:* Mundelein College (B.A., magna cum laude, 1989); John Marshall Law School (J.D., 1992). *Member:* Chicago Bar Association (Chairperson, School Law Committee, 1997-1998). ***PRACTICE AREAS:*** School Law; Special Education Law. ***Email:*** dlk@franczek.com

LISA A. McGARRITY, born Appleton, Wisconsin, March 7, 1962; admitted to bar, 1988, Illinois. *Education:* University of Wisconsin-Madison (B.B.A., with honors, 1985); Northwestern University (J.D., 1988). ***REPORTED CASES:*** Iowa Mold Tooling Inc. v. Teamsters Local Union No. 828, 16 F3d 311 (8th Cir. 1994); Baulos and Schneider v. Road-

(This Listing Continued)

way Express Inc., 139 F3D 1147 (7th Cir. 1998); Wales v. Board of Education of Community Unit School District 300, 120 F3d 82 (7th Cir. 1997). ***PRACTICE AREAS:*** Labor Law; Employment Law. ***Email:*** lam@franczek.com

PAUL A. MILLICHAP, born London, England, January 29, 1952; admitted to bar, 1978, Illinois and U.S. District Court, Northern District of Illinois including Trial Bar; 1982, U.S. Court of Appeals, 7th Circuit. *Education:* University of Virginia (B.A., 1974); DePaul University School of Law (J.D., 1978). Assistant Illinois Attorney General, General Law Division, 1978-1984. *Member:* Illinois State Bar Association; National School Boards Association Council of School Attorneys. ***PRACTICE AREAS:*** Education Law; Municipal Law. ***Email:*** pam@franczek.com

JEREMY C. MORITZ, born Decatur, Illinois, December 24, 1971; admitted to bar, 1997, Illinois. *Education:* Wittenberg Univ. (B.A., 1994); Indiana Univ. (J.D., cum laude, 1997). ***PRACTICE AREAS:*** Labor; Employment Litigation. ***Email:*** jcm@franczek.com

DAVID P. RADELET, born Merrick, New York, December 7, 1955; admitted to bar, 1981, Illinois; U.S. District Court, Northern District of Illinois including Trial Bar; U.S. District Court, Central District of Illinois; U.S. Court of Appeals, Seventh, Eighth and Eleventh Circuits; U.S. Supreme Court. *Education:* Michigan State University (B.A., with high honors, 1978); University of Michigan (J.D., 1981). Phi Kappa Phi. *Member:* American Bar Association (Member, Labor and Employment Law Section). ***PRACTICE AREAS:*** Labor and Employment Law. ***Email:*** dpr@franczek.com

JOHN A. RELIAS, born Chicago, Illinois, April 2, 1946; admitted to bar, 1972, Illinois and U.S. District Court, Northern District of Illinois including Trial Bar; 1982, U.S. Court of Appeals, 7th Circuit; 1983, U.S. Court of Appeals, 9th Circuit; 1992, U.S. District Court, Central District of Illinois; 1997, U.S. Supreme Court. *Education:* Northwestern University (B.A., with highest distinction, 1968; J.D., cum laude, 1972). Phi Beta Kappa; Order of the Coif. Member, Northwestern University Law Review, 1971-1972. *Member:* National School Boards Association Council of School Attorneys. ***PRACTICE AREAS:*** Educational Law. ***Email:*** jar@franczek.com

MICHAEL I. RICHARDSON, born Chicago, Illinois, December 25, 1958; admitted to bar, 1987, Illinois and U.S. District Court, Northern and Central Districts of Illinois and Northern District of Indiana; U.S. Court of Appeals, 7th and 11th Circuits; U.S. Supreme Court. *Education:* University of Notre Dame (B.A., 1981; J.D., magna cum laude, 1987); Loyola University of Chicago (M.S., Industrial Relations, 1985). Staff Member, 1985-1986 and Articles Editor, 1986-1987, Notre Dame Law Review. Author: "Securing Employee Welfare Benefits Through ERISA," 61 Notre Dame Law Review 551, 1986; "Is the Conflict Between Title VII and Section 1983 Resolved?" 61 Notre Dame Law Review 88, 1986. Faculty Member, Loyola University of Chicago Institute of Human Resources and Industrial Relations, 1994. ***PRACTICE AREAS:*** Employee Benefits; Labor and Employment Law. ***Email:*** mr@franczek.com

CHARLES P. ROSE, born Fort Polk, Louisiana, June 2, 1957; admitted to bar, 1982, Illinois. *Education:* Villanova University (B.A., cum laude, 1978); DePaul University (J.D., 1982). Counsel, Illinois Association of School Boards, 1983-1984. *Member:* National School Boards Association Council of School Attorneys. ***PRACTICE AREAS:*** Labor and Employment Law; Educational Law. ***Email:*** cpr@franczek.com

SALLY J. SCOTT, born Fremont, Michigan, October 12, 1964; admitted to bar, 1990, Illinois. *Education:* Calvin College (B.A., 1987); University of Michigan (J.D., 1990). *Member:* Chicago and American Bar Associations. ***PRACTICE AREAS:*** Labor Law; Employment Law; OSHA. ***Email:*** sjs@franczek.com

WILLIAM R. SULLIVAN, JR., born Evanston, Illinois, July 22, 1943; admitted to bar, 1971, Illinois. *Education:* College of the Holy Cross (A.B., 1965); University of Chicago (J.D., 1971). Alpha Sigma Nu. *Member:* Chicago and American Bar Associations; Chicago Council of Lawyers. ***PRACTICE AREAS:*** Labor and Employment Law. ***Email:*** wrs@franczek.com

ANDREA R. WAINTROOB, born Chicago, Illinois, December 23, 1952; admitted to bar, 1978, Illinois and U.S. District Court, Central Northern Districts of Illinois including Trial Bar; 1982, U.S. Court of Appeals, 7th Circuit; 1989, U.S. Supreme Court. *Education:* Brown University (A.B., magna cum laude, 1975); University of Chicago (J.D., with honors, 1978). Phi Beta Kappa; Phi Delta Phi; Magister (1978). Member: University of Chicago Law Review, 1977-1978. Lecturer in Industrial Relations, University of Chicago Graduate School of Business, 1984-1996. Author: Comment, "Procedural Prerequisites to Private Suit Under the Age Discrimination in Employment Act," 44 University of Chicago Law Review 457 (1977); "The Developing Law of Equal Employment Opportunity at the White Collar and Professional Levels," 21 William & Mary Law Review 45 (1979); "Employee Benefits and Sex Discrimination," Pension World, January, 1981; "Comparable Worth: The Employer's Side," The Hospital Manager, July-August, 1985. Co-Author: "Illinois Labor Law Developments," IICLE 1988, 1989, 1990 and 1991 Annual Surveys of Illinois Law; "The Legal Status of Physicians and Unionization," The Journal of Medical Practice Management, Vol. 6, No. 1, Summer, 1990; "Remediating and Dismissing the Incompetent Teacher," The School Administrator, 1995. Co-Editor, "Guide to Illinois Statutes Affecting Schools." *Member:* Chicago Bar Association; National School Boards Association Council of School Attorneys; Chair, Illinois Council of School Attorneys. ***PRACTICE AREAS:*** Labor and Employment Law; Education Law; Civil Rights. ***Email:*** arw@franczek.com

MICHAEL A. WARNER, JR., born Chicago, Illinois, April 5, 1966; admitted to bar, 1991, Illinois; 1993, U.S. District Court, Northern District of Indiana; 1995, U.S. District Court, Northern District of Illinois. *Education:* Duke University (A.B., cum laude, 1988); Northwestern University (J.D., 1991). Editor, Journal of International Law and Business, 1990-1991. Lowden-Wigmore Prize Winner: Outstanding Published Article, Northwestern Journal of International Law and Business. Author: "Strangers in a Strange Land: Foreign Compulsion and the Extraterritorial Application of United States Employment Law," 11 Northwestern Journal of International Law and Business, 371 (1990). Law Clerk to Judge Robert L. Miller, U.S. District Court, Northern District of Indiana, 1991-1993. *Member:* American Bar Association (Member, Labor and Employment and Litigation Sections). ***PRACTICE AREAS:*** Labor and Employment; Litigation. ***Email:*** maw@franczek.com

PATRICIA J. WHITTEN, born Illinois, July 25, 1950; admitted to bar, 1974, Illinois and U.S. District Court, Northern District of Illinois including Trial Bar; 1975, U.S. Court of Appeals, 7th Circuit; 1982, U.S. Supreme Court. *Education:* Louisiana State University (B.S., 1971); Illinois Institute of Technology, Chicago-Kent College of Law (J.D., with honors, 1974). Member, Chicago-Kent College of Law Review, 1974. Author: "Conflict in the Circuits: Mainstreaming or Inclusion," NSBA Council of School Attorneys School Law in Review, 2003; "Inside or Outside? Considerations in the Decision to Employ In-House or Retain Outside Counsel," NSBA Council of School Attorneys (1997); "Recent Developments in Employee Dismissal," NSBA Council School of School Attorneys School Law in Review, 1994; "*Missouri v. Jenkins:* Taxation Without Representation or Remedy of Last Resort?" ABA Urban, State and Local Law Newsletter, Vol. 14, No 1, Fall 1990; "An Attack on Confession of Judgment Clauses in Residential Leases Through Section 2-302 of the UCC," 50 Chicago-Kent Law Review 482 (1973); "The Rights of Foster Parents to the Children in Their Care," Chicago-Kent Law Review 86 (1973). General Counsel, Chicago Board of Education, 1981-1990; Acting General Counsel, 1993-1995; Assistant Attorney, Chicago Board of Education, 1974-1980. *Member:* Chicago, Illinois State (Member, Education Law Section Council, Committee on Law Related Education, Chair, 1999-2000) and American (Member, Labor and Employment, Law Practice Management Sections) Bar Associations; Women's Bar Association of Illinois; Illinois Council of School Attorneys (Director, 1987-1994; Chair, 1992-1993; Vice-Chair, 1991-1992); National School Boards Association Council of School Attorneys. ***PRACTICE AREAS:*** Public Education Law (100%, 2000). ***Email:*** pjw@franczek.com

JAMES J. ZUEHL, born Milwaukee, Wisconsin, June 13, 1947; admitted to bar, 1981, Illinois; 1989, U.S. District Court, Northern District of Illinois; 1992, U.S. District Court, Central District of Illinois and U.S. Court of Appeals, 7th Circuit. *Education:* University of Wisconsin (B.S., 1969); University of Chicago (J.D., 1980). Visiting Assistant Professor, IIT/Chicago-Kent College of Law, 1985-1988. Bigelow Fellow, University of Chicago, 1984-1985. ***PRACTICE AREAS:*** Labor and Employment Law; Educational Law; Civil Rights. ***Email:*** jjz@franczek.com

---

KRISTI L. BOWMAN, born 1976; admitted to bar, 2001, Illinois. *Education:* Drake University (B.A., summa cum laude, 1998); Duke University Law School (J.D., magna cum laude, 2001; M.A., 2001). Phi Beta Kappa. ***PRACTICE AREAS:*** Education Law. ***Email:*** klb@franczek.com

BRIAN P. CROWLEY, born Chicago, Illinois, June 27, 1972; admitted to bar, 1997, Illinois. *Education:* Miami University (B.A., 1994); University of Illinois (J.D., 1997). ***PRACTICE AREAS:*** Education; Land Use; Government. ***Email:*** bpc@franczek.com

DANA FATTORE CRUMLEY, born Valparaiso, Indiana, March 20, 1966; admitted to bar, 2001, Illinois. *Education:* Northwestern University (B.A., 1988); Loyola University Chicago School of Law (J.D., 2001). *Member:* Chicago Bar Association. ***PRACTICE AREAS:*** Education Law. ***Email:*** dfc@franczek.com

SCOTT CRUZ, born Chicago, Illinois, September 2, 1977; admitted to bar, 2002, Illinois; 2003, Missouri. *Education:* Marquette University (B.A., English, cum laude, 1999); University of Illinois (J.D., 2002). ***LANGUAGES:*** Spanish. ***PRACTICE AREAS:*** Labor and Employment. ***Email:*** sc@franczek.com

PAUL A. DENHAM, born St. Louis, Missouri, June 3, 1977; admitted to bar, 2004, Illinois. *Education:* George Washington University (B.A., 1999); Northwestern University (J.D., 2004). ***PRACTICE AREAS:*** Labor and Employment; Education Law. ***Email:*** pad@franczek.com

NORA FITZGERALD MELDRUM, born Louisville, Kentucky, June 23, 1974; admitted to bar, 2000, Kentucky; 2001, District of Columbia and Illinois. *Education:* Georgetown University (B.A., 1996); University of Michigan (J.D., 1999). Recipient, Irving R. Stenn Award. *Member:* Louisville, Kentucky and Illinois State Bar Associations; The District of Columbia Bar. ***LANGUAGES:*** French. ***PRACTICE AREAS:*** Labor and Employment. ***Email:*** nef@franczek.com

WHITNIE D. HARDY, born Norfolk, Virginia, January 14, 1978; admitted to bar, 2004, Illinois. *Education:* Hampton University (B.A., 2000); Duke University (J.D., 2003). ***PRACTICE AREAS:*** Employment Law. ***Email:*** wdh@franczek.com

JULIE HEUBERGER YURA, born Chicago, Illinois, February 14, 1973; admitted to bar, 1998, Illinois and U.S. District Court, Northern and Central Districts of Illinois. *Education:* University of Iowa (B.A., 1995); DePaul University (J.D., 1998). *Member:* Chicago (Member, Local Government Committee) and Illinois State Bar Associations. ***Email:*** jhy@franczek.com

KAREN K. HYNES, admitted to bar, 2002, Illinois. *Education:* University of Illinois, Urbana-Champaign (B.A., 1992); Loyola University Chicago Law School (J.D., cum laude, 2002). Articles Editor, Children's Legal Rights Journal. Member, Juvenile Moot Court Team. ***PRACTICE AREAS:*** Education Law. ***Email:*** kkh@franczek.com

KYLE B. JOHANSEN, born Evanston, Illinois, August 29, 1976; admitted to bar, 2002, Illinois. *Education:* Northern Illinois University (B.A., 1999); Chicago-Kent College of Law, Illinois Institute of Technology (J.D., with high honors, 2002). ***PRACTICE AREAS:*** Labor and Employment. ***Email:*** kbj@franczek.com

PAMELA P. JONES, admitted to bar, 2002, Illinois. *Education:* Pace University (B.A., 1999); Chicago-Kent College of Law (J.D., 2002). *Member:* Chicago and Illinois State Bar Associations. ***PRACTICE AREAS:*** Education Law; Employment Law. ***Email:*** ppj@franczek.com

D. SANDERS LOWERY, born Jackson, Mississippi, August 10, 1974; admitted to bar, 1999, Illinois, U.S. District Court, Northern District of Illinois and U.S. District Court, Western District of Michigan. *Education:* Vanderbilt University (B.S., 1996); Loyola University Law School, Chicago (J.D., 1999). ***PRACTICE AREAS:*** Labor and Employment. ***Email:*** dsl@franczek.com

ANDREW A. MALAHOWSKI, born White Plains, New York, March 15, 1977; admitted to bar, 2002, Illinois. *Education:* University of Notre Dame (B.A., 1999; J.D., 2002). ***PRACTICE AREAS:*** Labor and Employment. ***Email:*** aam@franczek.com

TIMOTHY P. McGRORY, born Chicago, Illinois, October 6, 1970; admitted to bar, 1997, Illinois. *Education:* Northwestern University (B.A., 1992); Boston University

(This Listing Continued)

FRANCZEK SULLIVAN P.C., Chicago—Continued

School of Law (J.D., 1997). G. Joseph Tauro Scholar. *Member:* Chicago, Illinois State and American Bar Associations. ***PRACTICE AREAS:*** Employee Benefits; ERISA; Executive Compensation. ***Email:*** tpm@franczek.com

JEFFREY S. NOWAK, born December 17, 1972; admitted to bar, 1999, Illinois. *Education:* Indiana University (B.A., 1995; J.D., 1999). Federal Communications Law Journal, 1997-1999. Author, "Employer Liability for Employee Online Criminal Acts," published in *Federal Communications Law Journal,* March 1999 (51 Federal Communications Law Journal 467). ***Email:*** jsn@franczek.com

JULIA K. OLTMANNS, born Urbana, Illinois, April 26, 1975; admitted to bar, 2000, Illinois. *Education:* University of Illinois at Urbana-Champaign (B.S., 1997); Loyola University (J.D., cum laude, 2000). *Member:* Chicago and American Bar Associations. ***PRACTICE AREAS:*** Labor and Employment; Education Law. ***Email:*** jko@franczek.com

CORINNE S. O'MELIA, born Rock Island, Illinois, October 8, 1976; admitted to bar, 2001, Illinois. *Education:* University of Illinois (B.A., 1998); Northwestern University School of Law (J.D., 2001). *Member:* Chicago Bar Association. ***PRACTICE AREAS:*** Labor and Employment; Education Law. ***Email:*** cso@franczek.com

STEVEN J. PEARLMAN, born Evanston, Illinois, September 22, 1972; admitted to bar, 1998, California; 2002, Illinois. *Education:* University of Illinois, Champaign-Urbana (B.S., 1994); University of California School of Law, Los Angeles (J.D., 1998). ***PRACTICE AREAS:*** Labor and Employment; Trade Secrets and Unfair Competition; Litigation. ***Email:*** sjp@franczek.com

THOMAS J. POSEY, born Chicago, Illinois, November 26, 1971; admitted to bar, 2003, Illinois and U.S. District Court, Northern District of Illinois. *Education:* Illinois State University (B.S., 1994); University of Illinois (M.S.W., 1997); Chicago-Kent College of Law, Illinois Institute of Technology (J.D., 2003). *Member:* Chicago and American Bar Associations. ***PRACTICE AREAS:*** Employment; Labor; Commercial Litigation. ***Email:*** tjp@franczek.com

LISA M. SPIEGLER, born Oklahoma City, Oklahoma, December 8, 1972; admitted to bar, 1997, Illinois. *Education:* University of Kansas (B.A., 1994); Washington University (J.D., 1997). *Member:* Chicago, Illinois State and American Bar Associations. ***Email:*** lms@franczek.com

DAWN M. SPIVEY, born Appleton, Wisconsin, August 28, 1971; admitted to bar, 1998, Florida; 2002, Illinois. *Education:* Kansas State University (B.A., 1993); University of Illinois (M.Ed., 1997; J.D., cum laude, 1997). *Member:* Chicago Bar Association (Member, School Law Committee); The Florida Bar. ***LANGUAGES:*** Spanish. ***PRACTICE AREAS:*** Education Law. ***Email:*** dms@franczek.com

ANNE E. WILSON-LOKKEN, born Erie, Pennsylvania, September 1, 1972; admitted to bar, 1997, Illinois and U.S. District Court, Northern District of Illinois; 1999, U.S. District Court, Central District of Illinois; 2000, U.S. District Court, Southern District of Illinois. *Education:* Drake University (B.A., 1994); DePaul University College of Law (J.D., Certificate in Health Law, 1997). Note Editor, 1996-1997, Member, 1995-1997, DePaul Journal of Health College of Law. Co-author, "School Reconstruction and Its Labor Implications: A Survey of School Districts," National School Board Association, School Law Review, 1998. *Member:* Chicago and Illinois Bar Associations; National School Boards Association Council of School Attorneys; Illinois Council of School Attorneys. ***PRACTICE AREAS:*** Public Education Law; Special Education; Education Law; Employment Law; Litigation. ***Email:*** awl@franczek.com

OF COUNSEL

WESLEY A. WILDMAN, born Chicago, Illinois, May 22, 1931; admitted to bar, 1954, Illinois. *Education:* University of Chicago (A.B., 1951; M.A., 1956; J.D., 1954). *Member:* Chicago Bar Association. ***Email:*** waw@franczek.com

RESPICIO F. VAZQUEZ, born Chicago, Illinois, August 19, 1960; admitted to bar, 1986, Illinois. *Education:* DePaul University (B.S.C., Business Administration, 1982; J.D., 1985). General Counsel, Illinois State Board of Education, 2000-2004. State Superintendent of Education, Illinois, 2002. Former General Counsel and Former First Assistant General Counsel, City Colleges of Chicago. Fomer Assistant Attorney, Chicago Board of Education. Special Assistant Attorney General and Former Assistant Attorney General, Office of the Illinois Attorney General . *Member:* Illinois State Bar Association. ***LANGUAGES:*** Spanish. ***PRACTICE AREAS:*** Education; Government. ***Email:*** rfv@franczek.com

LEGAL SUPPORT PERSONNEL

CATY E. KEARNEY, born Chicago, Illinois, April 4, 1952. *Education:* Northern Illinois University (B.A., 1974); Roosevelt University (Paralegal Studies, 1994). *Member:* Illinois Paralegal Association. (Senior Paralegal). ***PRACTICE AREAS:*** Labor and Employment; School Law. ***Email:*** cek@franczek.com

GINA MANDARINO, born Chicago, Illinois, June 7, 1960. *Education:* Northern Illinois University (B.S., 1984); Roosevelt University (Paralegal Certification, with honors, 1995). (Paralegal). ***PRACTICE AREAS:*** Labor and Employment; Education Law. ***Email:*** gmm@franczek.com

FRANK/GECKER LLP

325 N. LASALLE STREET, SUITE 625
CHICAGO, ILLINOIS 60610
Telephone: 312-276-1400
Fax: 312-276-0035
URL: http://www.fgllp.com

Bankruptcy Litigation and Appeals, Creditors Rights, Valuation Disputes, Workouts, Preferential and Fraudulent Transfers, Officer and Director Liability and Contested Plan Confirmation, Asbestos and Mass Tort Bankruptcies, Financial Transactions, Distressed Debt and Asset Sales and Acquisitions, Trustee and Trust Representation and Preferential Transfer Litigation.

(This Listing Continued)

FIRM PROFILE: Frank/Gecker LLP has a national practice representing creditors' committees, trustees on their most complex litigation and more than one dozen major public and private companies as outside in-house bankruptcy counsel on both their complex bankruptcy matters and day-to-day debtor/creditor issues. We represent many other major corporations when they find themselves embroiled in bankruptcies and workouts in the Midwest or want to acquire assets from business in bankruptcy. In our experience, our clients do not like to see their names in listing by their bankruptcy Company, even though we usually work for them when they are on the creditor side of the table. When we look at long lists of other law firm's clients, it does not really tell us much. If you would like to hear about how we serve as outside in-house bankruptcy counsel to major corporations, just call and ask, we will tell you all about it, name names and even put you in touch with our clients so they can tell you about our good work.

JOSEPH D. FRANK, born Chicago, Illinois, 1964; admitted to bar, 1993, Illinois and U.S. District Court, Northern District of Illinois; U.S. Supreme Court; U.S. District Court, Western District of Michigan; U.S. Court of Appeals, Third, Seventh and Ninth Circuits. *Education:* Carleton College (B.A., magna cum laude, 1986); University of Chicago (J.D., with honors, 1993). Selected as one of the "Forty Illinois Attorneys to Watch Under Forty," by the Chicago Daily Law Bulletin and Chicago Lawyer, 2003. Retail Law Strategist, Editorial Board, 2001—. *Member:* American Bankruptcy Institute; International Counsel of Shopping Centers; Chicago Bar Association. ***PRACTICE AREAS:*** Insolvency; Restructuring; Creditors Rights; Business Law. ***Email:*** jfrank@fgllp.com

FRANCES GECKER, born 1953; admitted to bar, 1988, Illinois, U.S. District Court, Northern District of Illinois and U.S. Court of Appeals, First, Fifth, Seventh and Ninth Circuits. *Education:* University of Wisconsin-Madison (B.A., cum laude, 1974); Northwestern University (J.D., cum laude, 1988). Order of the Coif. Author: "Recovery of Lost Opportunity Costs as Adequate Protection," Northwestern Law Review, Winter 1987; "The Doctrine of Necessity," Marquette Law Review, Spring 1990; "Due Process and Bankruptcy; A Contradiction in Terms?" Bankruptcy Development Journal, Volume 10, No. 1, 1994. Appointed by the United States Trustee to serve as: Trustee, Northern District of Illinois and Member, Trustee Advisory Panel, 1999—. *Member:* American Bar Association; American Bankruptcy Institute. ***PRACTICE AREAS:*** Insolvency; Restructuring; Creditors Rights. ***Email:*** fgecker@fgllp.com

MICHAEL J. GOLDE, admitted to bar, 1983, Illinois and U.S. District Court, Northern District of Illinois. *Education:* Washington University (B.S.B.A., 1980); DePaul University (J.D., 1983). Former Staff Attorney, U.S. Department of Justice, Office of U.S. Trustee, Northern District of Illinois, 1983-1984. *Member:* Chicago Bar Association (Education Chair, Committee on Bankruptcy and Reorganization). ***PRACTICE AREAS:*** Bankruptcy; Reorganization Law; Commercial Litigation. ***Email:*** mgolde@fgllp.com

SENIOR COUNSEL

MICAH R. KROHN, born 1959; admitted to bar, 1993, New York and Illinois. *Education:* Brandeis University (B.A., 1982); Benjamin N. Cardozo School of Law, Yeshiva University (J.D., 1992). Law Clerk to the Hon. Erwin I Katz, U.S. Bankruptcy Judge, Northern District of Illinois, 1992-1994.*Member:* Chicago Bar Association. [U.S. Navy Lieutenant, 1982-1986]. ***PRACTICE AREAS:*** Insolvency; Loan Restructuring; Creditors Rights. ***Email:*** mkrohn@fgllp.com

ASSOCIATE

ZANE L. ZIELINSKI, admitted to bar, 2002, Illinois and U.S. District Court, Northern District of Illinois. *Education:* University of Chicago (B.A., with honors, 1996); Chicago-Kent College of Law (J.D., cum laude, 2002). Order of the Coif. Executive Articles Editor, Chicago-Kent Law Review. Recipient, Medal of Excellence, American Bankruptcy Institute, 2002. ***Email:*** zzielinski@fgllp.com

OF COUNSEL

DWIGHT B. PALMER, born Orange, New Jersey, April 1, 1949; admitted to bar, 1978, Illinois. *Education:* University of Colorado (B.A., Philosophy, 1973); IIT-Chicago Kent College of Law (J.D., with honors, 1978). *Member:* Chicago Bar Association. ***PRACTICE AREAS:*** Insurance Litigation; Commercial Litigation.

FREEBORN & PETERS LLP

311 SOUTH WACKER DRIVE
SUITE 3000
CHICAGO, ILLINOIS 60606-6677
Telephone: 312-360-6000
Fax: 312-360-6520
URL: http://www.freebornpeters.com

Springfield, Illinois Office: 217 E. Monroe Street, Suite 202, 62701. Telephone: 217-535-1060. Fax: 217-535-1069.

Business Litigation, Securities Litigation, Complex Commercial Disputes, Insurance Coverage Litigation, Products Liability, Professional Malpractice, Corporate Counseling and Transactions, Alternative Dispute Resolution, Compliance with Regulations by Government Agencies, Employment Law, Labor Law, Mergers and Acquisitions, Antitrust and Trade Regulation, Commercial Real Estate Transactions, Estate Planning, Government Relations, Environmental Law, Health and Safety Law, Railroad Law.

FIRM PROFILE: With offices headquartered in the heart of Chicago's downtown business district, Freeborn & Peters provides a wide array of sophisticated legal services to a clientele that is international in scope. Through the use of advanced technology and unsurpassed legal savvy, our attorneys offer perceptive, innovative counsel to both entrepreneurial start-ups as well as Fortune 500 companies.

(This Listing Continued)

Founded in 1983 by six attorneys, Freeborn & Peters is now comprised of over 100 attorneys and is listed among the top 35 law firms in Chicago as well as the top third of the one thousand largest firms in the country. We have been called a "litigation powerhouse" by the Chicago Tribune, and our acute understanding of the needs of technology and emerging growth companies has earned us the reputation as "the entrepreneur's law firm."

Our continued focus on the needs of our clients remains the cornerstone of the Firm's success, along with hard work, ingenuity and an unwavering standard of professional excellence. These are the qualities that have made us "One of America's Leading Law Firms to Business."

Freeborn & Peters focuses its practice in the following areas: business litigation, with an emphasis on antitrust, securities litigation, complex commercial disputes, insurance coverage litigation, products liability and professional malpractice; employment and labor law counseling and litigation, including ERISA and executive compensation; corporate and business services, with an emphasis on mergers and acquisitions, early stage, venture capital, and private placement financing, initial public offerings, secondary offerings, and public company reporting, taxation, intellectual property and information technology, antitrust and trade regulation, advertising and franchising, commercial real estate transactions, entity formation and structuring, and estate planning; and government relations, environmental, health and safety, and railroad law.

PARTNERS

DOUGLAS A. ALBRITTON, admitted to bar, 1995, Illinois and U.S. District Court, Northern District of Illinois; 1996, U.S. District Court, Central District of Illinois. *Education:* Illinois State University (B.S., 1992); University of Illinois (J.D., 1995). *Member:* Chicago, Illinois State and American Bar Associations. ***PRACTICE AREAS:*** Business Litigation. ***Email:*** dalbritton@freebornpeters.com

JILL C. ANDERSON, admitted to bar, 1995, Illinois; 1999, U.S. District Court, Northern District of Illinois and U.S. Court of Appeals, Seventh Circuit; 2000, U.S. Supreme Court. *Education:* University of Florida (B.A., with honors, 1991); Columbia University (J.D., 1995). Harlan Fiske Stone Scholar. Law Clerk: Hon. Norman C. Roettger, U.S. District Court, Southern District, Florida, 1995-1997; Hon. Martha Craig Daughtrey, U.S. Court of Appeals, Sixth Circuit, Tennessee, 2001-2002. *Member:* Chicago Bar Association. ***PRACTICE AREAS:*** Commercial Litigation; Appellate Practice. ***Email:*** janderson@freebornpeters.com

HELEN N. BAKER, admitted to bar, 1990, Indiana; 1993, Illinois. *Education:* Brown University (A.B., 1976); Indiana University School of Law (J.D., 1990). ***PRACTICE AREAS:*** Labor and Employment; Employee Benefits. ***Email:*** hbaker@freebornpeters.com

ROBERT M. BARATTA, JR., admitted to bar, 1990, Illinois. *Education:* Georgetown University (A.B., 1987; J.D., magna cum laude, 1990). ***PRACTICE AREAS:*** Environmental Law; Health and Safety Law. ***Email:*** bbaratta@freebornpeters.com

SCOTT B. BARNETT, admitted to bar, 1994, Illinois. *Education:* University of Illinois (B.S., 1990; J.D., 1994). ***Email:*** sbarnett@freebornpeters.com

ROGER H. BICKEL, admitted to bar, 1989, Illinois. *Education:* Indiana University (B.A., with honors, 1982); Loyola University of Chicago (J.D., 1989). Co-Author: "1991 Survey of Illinois Administrative Law," Illinois Institute for Continuing Legal Education; 1992-1996, Annual Surveys of Administrative Law. Member, Illinois Secretary of State's Corporate Acts Advisory Committee, 1991-1995. General Counsel, Illinois Secretary of State, 1991-1995. Special Assistant U.S. Attorney for the Central District of Illinois, 1992-1994. ***PRACTICE AREAS:*** Business Litigation; Administrative Law; Regulatory Compliance. ***Email:*** rbickel@freebornpeters.com

GERALD P. CALLAGHAN, admitted to bar, 1979, Illinois; 1990, Indiana. *Education:* University of Illinois (B.A., 1975; J.D., 1979). Assistant State's Attorney, Lake County, Illinois, 1981-1984. ***PRACTICE AREAS:*** Real Estate; Land Use.

ANTHONY J. CARBALLO, admitted to bar, 1986, Illinois. *Education:* Loras College (B.A., cum laude, 1983); Chicago-Kent College of Law (J.D., 1986). Assistant State's Attorney, Cook County State's Attorney's Office, Chicago, Illinois, 1986-1994. ***PRACTICE AREAS:*** Business Litigation. ***Email:*** tcarballo@freebornpeters.com

JOEL T. COOPER, admitted to bar, 1981, Illinois. *Education:* Purdue University (B.A., 1977; M.A., 1978); DePaul University (J.D., with honors, 1981). Phi Beta Kappa. ***PRACTICE AREAS:*** Real Estate; Land Use. ***Email:*** jcooper@freebornpeters.com

JEFFERY M. CROSS, admitted to bar, 1975, Illinois and U.S. District Court, Northern District of Illinois including Trial Bar; 1977, U.S. Court of Appeals, Seventh and Fifth Circuits; 1982, U.S. Court of Appeals, Eleventh Circuit; 1990, U.S. District Court, Central District of Illinois and U.S. Court of Appeals, Sixth Circuit; 1992, U.S. District Court, Eastern District of Wisconsin and U.S. Court of Appeals, Eighth Circuit; 1993, U.S. District Court, Northern District of Indiana and U.S. Supreme Court; 1997, U.S. District Court, Southern District of Illinois; 1998, U.S. District Court, Western District of Michigan. *Education:* University of Illinois (B.A., 1972); Syracuse University (J.D., magna cum laude, 1975). Order of the Coif. Research Editor, Syracuse Law Review, 1974-1975. Author: "Franchising: Antitrust Considerations," Ch. 9 and "Sentencing," Ch. 65, Antitrust Counseling and Litigation Techniques, Matthew Bender & Co., 1999. Adjunct Professor, John Marshall Law School, 2000. *Member:* Illinois State (Chairman, Antitrust Law Section, 1988-1989) and American (Chairman, Antitrust Section, Subcommittee on RICO and Other Offenses, 1985-1986; Vice Chairman, Antitrust Section, Criminal Practice and Procedure Committee, 1986-1987; Vice Chairman, Computer Technology Committee, 1989-1991; Member, Antitrust Section, Ad Hoc Committee on United States Sentencing Commission, 1986-1987; Member, Editorial Board, Antitrust Section, "Sample Jury Instructions in Criminal Antitrust Cases," 1979-1981) Bar Associations. ***PRACTICE AREAS:*** Antitrust and Trade Regulation; Business Litigation. ***Email:*** jcross@freebornpeters.com

DANIEL C. CURTH, admitted to bar, 1995, Illinois and U.S. District Court, Northern District of Illinois; 2000, U.S. Court of Appeals, 7th Circuit. *Education:* Michigan State University (B.A., with honors, 1992); University of Michigan (J.D., 1995). *Member:* Federal Bar Association. ***PRACTICE AREAS:*** Business Litigation. ***Email:*** dcurth@freebornpeters.com

STEVEN E. CYRANOSKI, admitted to bar, 1992, Illinois. *Education:* University of Illinois (B.S., 1986); Villanova University (J.D., cum laude, 1992). ***PRACTICE AREAS:*** Business Litigation; ERISA. ***Email:*** scyranoski@freebornpeters.com

JEFFREY L. DORMAN, admitted to bar, 1974, Ohio (inactive status); 1979, Illinois and U.S. District Court, Northern District of Illinois. *Education:* University of Michigan (B.A., with distinction, 1971); University of Wisconsin-Madison (M.S., 1976); Case Western Reserve University (J.D., 1974). Editor, Case Western Law Review, 1973-1974. Author: "Illinois Tax Agency Clarifies Unitary Business Issues Left Open After Allied Signal," 9 Journal of Multistate Taxation and Incentives 9 (1999); "Transfers of Liabilities to Controlled Corporations," Wisconsin Law Review 1016, 1976; "State Action Immunity—a Problem Under Cantor v. Detroit Edison," 27 Case Western Reserve Law Review 503, 1976. *Member:* Chicago and American (Member, Sections on: Antitrust; Tax; Litigation) Bar Associations. ***PRACTICE AREAS:*** Antitrust; State Tax Controversies; Local Tax Controversies; Corporate Litigation. ***Email:*** jdorman@freebornpeters.com

AREN L. FAIRCHILD, admitted to bar, 1995, Michigan; 1999, Illinois. *Education:* University of Michigan (A.B., 1992; J.D., cum laude, 1995). Managing Editor, University of Michigan Journal of Law Reform, Vol. 28. *Member:* Detroit Metropolitan and American Bar Associations; State Bar of Michigan. ***PRACTICE AREAS:*** Business Litigation. ***Email:*** afairchild@freebornpeters.com

RICHARD ANTHONY FIORE, admitted to bar, 1997, Illinois and U.S. District Court, Northern District of Illinois. *Education:* University of Illinois (B.S., 1994; J.D., magna cum laude, 1997). ***PRACTICE AREAS:*** Business Litigation; Antitrust and Trade Regulation; Labor and Employment Law. ***Email:*** rfiore@freebornpeters.com

JENNIFER L. FITZGERALD, admitted to bar, 1995, Illinois; registered to practice before U.S. Patent and Trademark Office. *Education:* University of Southern California (B.S., 1992); Loyola University (J.D., 1995). ***PRACTICE AREAS:*** Business Litigation. ***Email:*** jfitzgerald@freebornpeters.com

JOSEPH L. FOGEL, admitted to bar, 1986, Illinois. *Education:* University of California at San Diego (B.A., with honors, 1983); DePaul University (J.D., with honors, 1986). Staff Member and Article and Note Editor, De Paul Law Review. ***PRACTICE AREAS:*** Business Litigation. ***Email:*** jfogel@freebornpeters.com

MICHAEL D. FREEBORN, admitted to bar, 1972, Indiana and Illinois. *Education:* U.S. Air Force Academy (B.S., 1968); University of Chicago (M.B.A., 1975); Indiana University (J.D., 1972). Associate Editor, Indiana Law Review. Vice Chairman of the Board, Voices for Illinois Children. Director, Constitutional Rights Foundation. ***PRACTICE AREAS:*** Business Litigation; Products Liability Litigation; Securities Litigation. ***Email:*** mfreeborn@freebornpeters.com

ANDREW L. GOLDSTEIN, admitted to bar, 1984, Illinois. *Education:* University of Illinois (B.S., with highest honors, 1981; J.D., magna cum laude, 1984). Member, Management Committee, International Trademark Association. ***PRACTICE AREAS:*** Advertising Law; Computer Software Law; Intellectual Property Licensing; Trademark Protection; Information Technology. ***Email:*** agoldstein@freebornpeters.com

HARLEY J. GOLDSTEIN, admitted to bar, 1998, Illinois, New York, U.S. District Court, Northern District of Illinois including Trial Bar and U.S. Court of Appeals, Third Circuit; 1999, U.S. District Court, District of Colorado; U.S. District Court, Northern and Southern Districts of New York. *Education:* Arizona State University (B.A., 1994); Benjamin N. Cardozo School of Law, Yeshiva University (J.D., 1997). Law Clerk to the Hon. Erwin I. Katz, U.S. Bankruptcy Judge, Northern District of Illinois, 1997-1998. Author: "On-line Gambling: Down to the Wire?" 8 Marq. Sports L.J., Fall 1997; "On-line Wagering ensnared in Minnesota's Web," Chicago Daily Law Bulletin, June 23, 1998, p. 6.; "Can Ipso Facto Clauses Resolve the Discharge Debate? An Economic Approach to Novated Fraud Debt in Bankruptcy," 1 DePaul Bus. & Comm. L.J. (Spring 2003)(coauthored with Michael J. Di Gennaro); "Spending Other People's Money: Creditors' Remedies for the Misuse of Cash Collateral in Bankruptcy," published in the University of Miami Business Law Review (coauthored with Craig A. Sloane, Esq.). ***PRACTICE AREAS:*** Commercial Bankruptcy; Bankruptcy Reorganization; Bankruptcy Litigation; Out of Court Debt Restructuring; Creditors Rights. ***Email:*** hgoldstein@freebornpeters.com

JAMES S. GRAY, admitted to bar, 1969, Illinois. *Education:* Williams College (A.B., 1965); University of Chicago (J.D., 1968). *Member:* Chicago, Illinois State and American Bar Associations; International Council of Shopping Centers; Corenet; Industrial Asset Management Council; International Association of Attorneys and Executives in Corporate Real Estate (Founding Member and Past Chairman); The National Conference for Community and Justice (Member, Board of Directors, Chicago Chapter). ***PRACTICE AREAS:*** Real Estate Development; Real Estate Purchases and Sales; Construction Lending; Secured Lending; Corporate Real Estate Services; Commercial Transactions; Leasing. ***Email:*** jgray@freebornpeters.com

DAVID C. GUSTMAN, admitted to bar, 1979, Illinois, U.S. Supreme Court, U.S. Court of Appeals, Sixth, Seventh, Eighth and Federal Circuits, U.S. District Court, Northern, Central and Southern Districts of Illinois, Northern District including Trial Bar, U.S. District Court, Eastern and Western Districts of Wisconsin and U.S. District Court, Eastern District of Michigan. *Education:* University of Michigan (B.A. in Economics, with distinction, 1975); George Washington University National Law Center (J.D., 1979). Articles Editor, George Washington University Journal of International Law and Economics. Member, Board of Advisors, BNA Antitrust and Trade Regulation Report in Washington, DC. *Member:* Illinois and American (Member, Antitrust and Litigation Sections) Bar Associations. ***REPORTED CASES:*** In re Potash Antitrust Litigation, In Re Sulfuric Acid Antitrust Litigation, Congregation of the Passion v. Touche Ross & Co., MBI v. The Chronicle Publishing Co. ***PRACTICE AREAS:*** Complex Business Litigation; Antitrust and Trade Regulation; Antitrust; General Business Counseling. ***Email:*** dgustman@freebornpeters.com

AARON L. HAMMER, admitted to bar, 1997, Illinois and U.S. District Court, Northern District of Illinois; 2001, U.S. District Court, Eastern District of Michigan. *Education:* University of Michigan (A.B., with distinction, 1994); Northwestern University (J.D., magna cum laude, 1997). Order of the Coif. James B. Angell Scholar. *Member:* American

(This Listing Continued)

FREEBORN & PETERS LLP, Chicago—Continued

Bankruptcy Institute; Insol International. ***TRANSACTIONS:*** In re Lason, Inc. (Bankruptcy D. Del.) (01-11488 MWF); In re Metal Management, Inc. (Bankruptcy D. Del.) (00-4303 PJW). ***PRACTICE AREAS:*** Bankruptcy; Insolvency; Workouts; Out of Court Debt Restructuring. ***Email:*** ahammer@freebornpeters.com

EDWARD J. HANNON, admitted to bar, 1991, Illinois and U.S. Tax Court; 1993, District of Columbia. *Education:* St. Louis University (B.S., 1987); Loyola University, Chicago (J.D., 1991); Georgetown University (LL.M., with distinction, 1994). ***PRACTICE AREAS:*** Federal Taxation; State Taxation; Like Kind Exchanges. ***Email:*** ehannon@freebornpeters.com

STEVEN M. HARTMANN, admitted to bar, 1983, Illinois. *Education:* Northwestern University (B.A., 1980); University of Illinois (J.D., magna cum laude, 1983). Note Editor, Illinois Bar Journal, Recent Decisions Section. ***PRACTICE AREAS:*** Labor and Employment; Corporate; Business Litigation. ***Email:*** shartmann@freebornpeters.com

WILLIAM N. HOWARD, admitted to bar, 1985, Illinois and U.S. District Court, Northern District of Illinois; 1997, U.S. Court of Appeals, Seventh Circuit. *Education:* University of Illinois, Urbana-Champaign (B.S., 1982); Chicago-Kent College of Law (J.D., 1985). *Member:* Illinois State and American Bar Associations. ***PRACTICE AREAS:*** Business Litigation; Business Counseling; Employment Litigation; Corporate. ***Email:*** whoward@freebornpeters.com

ROBERT W. KARR, JR., born Evanston, Illinois, August 15, 1969; admitted to bar, 1999, Illinois. *Education:* University of Iowa (B.A., 1991); DePaul University School of Law (J.D., 1999). Board Member, Chicago Sister Cities International Program. Co-Chair, Osaka-Chicago Sister Cities Relationship. Vice Chairman, International Committee, Illinois Biotechnology Industry Organization. ***LANGUAGES:*** Japanese. ***PRACTICE AREAS:*** Corporate Law; Mergers, Acquisitions and Divestitures; Immigration. ***Email:*** rkarr@freebornpeters.com

MICHAEL J. KELLY, admitted to bar, 1980, Illinois. *Education:* University of Notre Dame (B.A., 1977); DePaul University College of Law (J.D., 1980). Member, Cook County State's Attorney's Office, 1981-1990. Special Assistant to the Illinois Attorney General. ***PRACTICE AREAS:*** Business Litigation. ***Email:*** mkelly@freebornpeters.com

KENNETH K. KNEUBUHLER, admitted to bar, 1975, Indiana; 1977, Illinois, U.S. District Court, Northern District of Illinois. *Education:* Ball State University (B.A., with honors, 1972); Northwestern University School of Law (J.D., cum laude, 1975). Blue Key. *Member:* Chicago (Member, Employee Benefits Committee; Chair, 1989-1990) and American Bar Associations. ***PRACTICE AREAS:*** Employee Benefits; Executive Compensation. ***Email:*** kkneubuhler@freebornpeters.com

MICHAEL P. KORNAK, admitted to bar, 1996, Illinois. *Education:* Indiana University (B.S., 1993); University of Illinois (J.D., summa cum laude, 1996). Order of the Coif. Law Clerk for the Honorable Alice M. Batchelder, U.S. Circuit Judge for the 6th Circuit Court of Appeals, 1996-1997. ***PRACTICE AREAS:*** Products Liability; Business Litigation. ***Email:*** mkornak@freebornpeters.com

WILLIAM N. KRUCKS, admitted to bar, 1976, Illinois and Mississippi. *Education:* Tulane University (B.A., 1972); University of Mississippi (J.D., with honors, 1976). Comment and Associate Editor, Mississippi Law Journal. General Counsel, Illinois Public Risk Fund, 1985—. Certified Arbitrator, Circuit Court of Cook County, Illinois. *Member:* National Council of Self-Insurers; Illinois Association of Self-Insurers; Defense Research Institute. (Also Vice Chairman, General Counsel and Secretary, Rauland-Borg Corporation, Skokie, Illinois). ***PRACTICE AREAS:*** Corporate; Insurance; Labor and Employment; Workers' Compensation Law; Occupational Disease. ***Email:*** bkrucks@freebornpeters.com

JOHN Z. LEE, admitted to bar, 1992, Illinois and U.S. District Court, Northern District of Illinois including Trial Bar; 1998, U.S. District Court, Eastern District of Michigan. *Education:* Harvard College (A.B., magna cum laude, 1989); Harvard Law School (J.D., cum laude, 1992). *Member:* Illinois State and American (Member, Environmental and Litigation Sections) Bar Associations. ***PRACTICE AREAS:*** Business Litigation; Antitrust and Trade Regulation; Environmental, Health and Safety Law. ***Email:*** jlee@freebornpeters.com

NEAL H. LEVIN, born Park Ridge, Illinois, August 21, 1962; admitted to bar, 1990, Illinois. *Education:* University of Denver (B.A., 1984); DePaul University (J.D., 1989). Member: Moot Court; Mock UN Conference, International Court of Justice. Adjunct Professor, Animal Law, De Paul University College of Law. General Counsel, Friends of Chicago's Animal Care and Control Commission. Director and Corporate Committee Chair, P.A.W.S. (Pets are Worth Saving). *Member:* Chicago, Illinois State and American Bar Associations; Seventh Circuit Bar Association. (Also practicing individually, Chicago, Illinois). ***REPORTED CASES:*** Delta Medical Supply v. Mid America Medical Supply, et al, WESTLAW 1245892, 331 Ill. App. 3d 777 (2002); Dubey v. Abam Building Corp., 266 Ill.App. 3d 44 (1994); Fabrica de Tejidos Imperial v. Brandon Apparel Group, et al., 218 F.Supp 2d 974 (N.D. Ill. 2002); LaSalle National Bank v. WFT, 1-01-3857, Appellate Court of Illinois, 2002; Chow v. AEGIS, et al., 185 F.Supp. 2d 914 (N.D. Ill. 2002). ***PRACTICE AREAS:*** Commercial Bankruptcy; Commercial Litigation; Creditors Rights; White Collar Fraud. ***Email:*** nhlevin@freebornpeters.com

RICHARD B. LEVY, admitted to bar, 1981, Illinois and U.S. District Court, Northern District of Illinois. *Education:* DePauw University (B.A., 1977); Chicago-Kent College of Law, Illinois Institute of Technology (J.D., 1980). *Member:* Chicago Bar Association (Executive Member, Judicial Evaluation Committee Prosecutors). (Assistant General Counsel). ***PRACTICE AREAS:*** Business Litigation; Mass Torts; Class Actions; Personal Injury. ***Email:*** rlevy@freebornpeters.com

WESTON W. MARSH, admitted to bar, 1976, Illinois. *Education:* Yale University (B.A., 1972); University of Illinois (J.D., with honors, 1976); University of Chicago (M.B.A., 1989). Associate Editor, Illinois Law Review. *Member:* National Association of Railroad Trial Counsel (President, Illinois Division, 1988). ***PRACTICE AREAS:*** Business Litigation; Personal Injury; Antitrust and Trade Regulation. ***Email:*** wmarsh@freebornpeters.com

(This Listing Continued)

PETER I. MASON, admitted to bar, 1976, Illinois; 1981, New York. *Education:* Bard College (A.B., 1973); Boston University (J.D., cum laude, 1976). ***PRACTICE AREAS:*** Business Law; Corporate Law; Finance. ***Email:*** pmason@freebornpeters.com

JEFFREY M. MATTSON, admitted to bar, 1990, Illinois; 1994, Florida. *Education:* University of Illinois (B.S., Finance, 1987); University of Chicago (J.D., 1990). ***PRACTICE AREAS:*** Securities; Corporate Law; Mergers, Acquisitions and Divestitures; Business Law; Contracts. ***Email:*** jmattson@freebornpeters.com

JEFFREY J. MAYER, admitted to bar, 1986, Illinois; 1987, U.S. District Court, Northern District of Illinois; 1991, Michigan; 1992, U.S. District Court, Eastern District of Michigan; 1993, U.S. Court of Appeals, Sixth and Seventh Circuits; 1995, U.S. Supreme Court; 1998, Ohio; 2000, U.S. Court of Appeals, Eighth Circuit. *Education:* Duke University (B.A., 1982); Washington University (J.D., 1986); University of Michigan (LL.M., 1993). Order of the Coif. Honor Scholar. Associate Editor, Washington University Law Quarterly. Author: Mayer, Practical Guidance On Service Warranties, Purchasing Law Report (April 2001); Mayer, "Online Dispute Resolution," Purchasing Today Magazine (February 2001); Mayer, "Crafting Clauses For Effective Arbitration," Purchasing Today Magazine (November 2000); "CEELI, Kazakhstan and The Ukraine," Michigan International Lawyer (Fall 2000); "Drafting and Implementationl of ADR Provisions in the United States," Croatian Arbitration Yearbook (1998); "You Can't Always Get What You Want," Purchasing Today Magazine (August 2000); "Understanding the Unusual Dynamics of Business Break-Up Litigation: Developing an Initial Litigation Checklist," 21 American Journal of Trial Advocacy 565 (1998); "Effective Drafting and Implementation of Alternative Dispute Resolution Provisions," State Bar of Michigan, Business Law Section (October, 1998); "How to Obtain and Maintain Control Over Business Break-Up Litigation," Michigan Institute for Continuing Legal Education (1995); "Recent Mexican Arbitration Reform: The Continued Influence Of The Publicistas," 47 University of Miami Law Review 913 (1993); "Individual Moral Responsibility And The Criminalization of Youth Gangs," 27 Wake Forest Law Review 943 (1993); "Prescribing Cooperation: The Mandatory Pretrial Disclosure Requirements Of Proposed Rules 26 and 27 Of the Federal Rules of Civil Procedure," 12 The Review of Litigation 77 (University of Texas) (1992); "Islamic Use of Practical Reason-Islamasizing The Preemption Doctrine in Pakistan," 16 Suffolk Transnational Law Journal 323 (1993); "A Critical Analysis of Judicial Attempts to Reconcile Title VII and The Japan-United States Treaty of Friendship, Commerce & Navigation," 13 Northwestern Journal of International Law and Business 328 (1992); "Thinking About Commercial Arbitration in Latin America," The ADR Newsletter (Fall 1993); Presenter: "Managing A Purchasing Crisis," National Association of Purchasing Management-International Conference, Orlando, Florida (April 2001); Invited Speaker: "Recent Developments in Franchise Litigation," The 4th Annual Restaurant Industry Mergers and Acquisitions Forum," Fulcrum Information Services, Inc., (New York City) (2000); Lecturer: "Drafting Alternate Dispute Resolution Clauses," Michigan Institute of Continuing Legal Education (1998); "Recent Developments in Shareholder Dispute Litigation," Michigan Institute for Continuing Legal Education (2000); State Bar of Michigan, "ADR? What to Include in Your Business and Employment Contracts," Michigan Institute for Continuing Legal Education (1998); Walsh College "Comparative Law for Business Persons," (1998); State Bar of Michigan "A Litigation Checklist for Corporate Break-Up Cases," (1996); State Bar of Michigan Business Law Section, "Drafting International Arbitration Clauses," (1994); Symposium "Legal Aspects of Doing Business in Mexico," February 1993; St. Mary's University School of Law, Topic: "Recent Mexican Arbitration Reform," San Antonio, Texas; Seminar "Doing Business in Mexico," May 1993, Topic: Legal and Cultural Differences Between The United States and Mexico," Troy, Michigan; Seminar, "Doing Business in Mexico," June 1993, Topic: "The United Nations Convention On Contracts For The International Sale of Goods," Troy, Michigan; Seminar, Central Michigan University, October 1993; Topic: "The Mexican Legal System," Panel Attorney, U.S. Court of Appeals for the Sixth Circuit; Expert Commentator: The ABA Central and East European Legal Initiative (Kazakhstan, Slovenia, Albania, Croatia and the Ukraine); Law Clerk to: The Honorable Jack D.H. Hays, The Arizona Supreme Court, 1986; The Honorable James Moeller, The Arizona Supreme Court, 1987; Student Intern, The Honorable Theodore McMillian, United States Court of Appeals For the Eight Circuit, 1985. Member, Board of Advisors, Purchasing Law Report; Natural Association of Purchasing Management. *Member:* Chicago, Seventh Circuit and Ohio State Bar Associations; State Bar of Michigan (Member, Section on Alternative Dispute Resolution). ***PRACTICE AREAS:*** Business Litigation; Employment Litigation; General Corporate. ***Email:*** jmayer@freebornpeters.com

ROBERT A. McWILLIAMS, admitted to bar, 1983, Wisconsin; 1986, Illinois. *Education:* Indiana University (B.S., with distinction, 1979); University of Illinois (M.B.A., 1983; J.D., cum laude, 1983). ***PRACTICE AREAS:*** Corporate and Securities Law; Mergers, Acquisitions and Restructuring. ***Email:*** rmcwilliams@freebornpeters.com

MICHAEL A. MOYNIHAN, admitted to bar, 1992, Illinois; 1993, U.S. District Court, Northern District of Illinois and U.S. Court of Appeals, Seventh Circuit; 1996, U.S. Supreme Court. *Education:* University of Notre Dame (B.S., 1989); Loyola University, Chicago (J.D., 1992). Member, National Moot Court Team. *Member:* Chicago, Illinois State and American Bar Associations; Chicago Real Estate Council; Chicago Association of Realtors. ***LANGUAGES:*** Spanish. ***PRACTICE AREAS:*** Real Estate Development; Real Estate Finance; Commercial Leasing. ***Email:*** mmoynihan@freebornpeters.com

BRIAN P. NORTON, admitted to bar, 1984, Illinois. *Education:* Loyola University (B.A., cum laude, 1981; J.D., cum laude, 1984). ***PRACTICE AREAS:*** Antitrust and Trade Regulation; Business Litigation. ***Email:*** bnorton@freebornpeters.com

TODD J. OHLMS, admitted to bar, 1995, Illinois. *Education:* University of Missouri-Rolla (B.S., 1992); Washington University School of Law (J.D., 1995). *Member:* American Institute of Aeronautics and Astronautics. ***PRACTICE AREAS:*** Business Litigation. ***Email:*** tohlms@freebornpeters.com

JORDAN H. PETERS, admitted to bar, 1972, Illinois. *Education:* Brown University (A.B., 1965); The John Marshall Law School (J.D., with honors, 1972). Editor-in-Chief, The John Marshall. Board of Trustees, John Marshall Law School. ***PRACTICE AREAS:*** Real Estate; Land Use. ***Email:*** jpeters@freebornpeters.com

JOSEPH P. RODDY, admitted to bar, 1990, Illinois. *Education:* College of the Holy Cross (B.A., 1986); Chicago-Kent College of Law, Illinois Institute of Technology (J.D,

(This Listing Continued)

with honors, 1990). Dean's List (Advisory Council). Recipient, J. W. Cavanaugh Scholarship. ***PRACTICE AREAS:*** Business Litigation; Government Relations. ***Email:*** jroddy@freebornpeters.com

WILLIAM E. RUSSELL, admitted to bar, 1984, Ohio; 1985, Illinois. *Education:* Duke University (B.A., magna cum laude, 1979); Washington University (M.B.A., 1984; J.D., 1984). *Member:* Chicago Bar Association (Vice-Chairman, Estate Tax Committee); Chicago Estate Planning Council. ***PRACTICE AREAS:*** Taxation; Corporate; Trusts and Estates. ***Email:*** brussell@freebornpeters.com

MICHAEL J. SCOTTI III, admitted to bar, 1991, Illinois. *Education:* Hillsdale College (B.A., 1985); University of Tulsa (J.D., 1990). *Member:* American Bar Association. ***PRACTICE AREAS:*** Business Litigation; Personal Injury Defense. ***Email:*** mscotti@freebornpeters.com

JOHN T. SHAPIRO, admitted to bar, 1991, Illinois; 1993, Minnesota. *Education:* Carleton College (B.A., 1985); University of Minnesota (J.D., cum laude, 1991). Law Clerk to Judge David S. Doty, U.S. District Court for the District of Minnesota, 1991-1993. *Member:* Illinois State and Minnesota State Bar Associations. ***PRACTICE AREAS:*** Labor and Employment; Business Litigation. ***Email:*** jshapiro@freebornpeters.com

RICHARD T. SIKES, JR., admitted to bar, 1980, Illinois. *Education:* Marquette University (B.S.B.A., 1976); DePaul University (J.D., 1980). Assistant State's Attorney, Cook County, Illinois, 1981-1989. Special Assistant to the Illinois Attorney General. ***PRACTICE AREAS:*** Business Litigation; Products Liability; Labor and Employment Law. ***Email:*** rsikes@freebornpeters.com

ROBERT J. SITKOWSKI, born Chicago, Illinois, February 15, 1961; admitted to bar, 1996, Pennsylvania; 1997, Connecticut (Not admitted in Illinois). *Education:* University of Illinois at Chicago (B.Arch. in Design, 1985); University of Pittsburgh (J.D., 1994; M.U.R.P., 1994). *Member:* American Bar Association (Chair, State and Local Government Law Section; Member, Forum on Affordable Housing and Community Development Law; New Urbanism Subcommittee); American Institute of Architects (AIA); American Institute of Certified Planners (AICP); American Planning Association (Member, Planning and Law Division and New Urbanism Division); Congress for the New Urbanism (CNU); National Association of Home Builders' LANDS Network. ***PRACTICE AREAS:*** Land Use. ***Email:*** rsitkowski@freebornpeters.com

HILLARD M. STERLING, born Chicago, Illinois, August 17, 1964; admitted to bar, 1989, District of Columbia; 1996, Illinois; U.S. District Court, Northern District of Illinois; U.S. District Court for the District of Columbia; U.S. District Court, Eastern District of Michigan. *Education:* Northern Illinois University (B.A., summa cum laude, 1986); Georgetown University (J.D., magna cum laude, 1989). Order of the Coif. *Member:* Chicago, Illinois State and American Bar Associations. ***PRACTICE AREAS:*** Technology Litigation; Complex Litigation; Antitrust. ***Email:*** hsterling@freebornpeters.com

JOHN E. STEVENS, admitted to bar, 1978, Illinois and U.S. District Court, Northern District of Illiniois; 1993, U.S. Supreme Court. *Education:* Loras College (B.A., 1975); Northern Illinois University (J.D., 1978). *Member:* Illinois State Bar Association. ***PRACTICE AREAS:*** Government Relations; Regulatory Law; Commercial Litigation. ***Email:*** jstevens@freebornpeters.com

JOHN C. STIEFEL, admitted to bar, 1965, Illinois. *Education:* University of Chicago (B.A., 1962); Northwestern University (J.D., 1965). *Member:* Chicago, Illinois State and American Bar Associations. ***PRACTICE AREAS:*** Corporate Law; Mergers and Acquisitions; Restructuring. ***Email:*** jstiefel@freebornpeters.com

KATHRYN C. THOMAS, admitted to bar, 1993, Illinois. *Education:* Illinois Wesleyan University (B.A., with honors, 1989); The John Marshall Law School (J.D., 1993). *Member:* Chicago, Illinois State and American Bar Associations. ***PRACTICE AREAS:*** Business Litigation. ***Email:*** kthomas@freebornpeters.com

RICHARD J. TRAUB, admitted to bar, 1987, Illinois. *Education:* University of Notre Dame (B.A., 1984; J.D., 1987). ***PRACTICE AREAS:*** Real Estate; Finance; Corporate Law. ***Email:*** rtraub@freebornpeters.com

RANDALL G. VICKERY, admitted to bar, 1988, Illinois. *Education:* Emory University (A.A., 1982; B.A., 1984); Harvard University (J.D., 1987). ***PRACTICE AREAS:*** Environmental Health and Safety Law; Real Estate; Land Use. ***Email:*** rvickery@freebornpeters.com

DANIEL J. VOELKER, admitted to bar, 1985, Illinois, U.S. District Court, Northern District of Illinois including Trial Bar; 1989, U.S. Court of Appeals, Seventh Circuit; 1998, U.S. Supreme Court. *Education:* University of Illinois (B.S., 1982; C.P.A., 1982); Chicago-Kent College of Law (J.D., high honors, 1985). *Member:* Illinois State and International Bar Associations. ***PRACTICE AREAS:*** Business Litigation; Business Counseling. ***Email:*** dvoelker@freebornpeters.com

CHARLES E. WATSON, II, born Arkansas City, Kansas, October 6, 1964; admitted to bar, 1990, Illinois. *Education:* University of Kansas (B.A., 1987); Georgetown University Law Center (J.D., 1990). Board of Directors, The Renaissance Collaborative, Inc. *Member:* Illinois State and American Bar Associations. ***PRACTICE AREAS:*** Government Affairs; Regulatory Law; Litigation. ***Email:*** cewatson@freebornpeters.com

CHARLES W. WEBSTER, admitted to bar, 1979, Indiana; 1981, Illinois; 1982, U.S. District Court, Northern District of Illinois; 1983, U.S. Court of Appeals, Seventh Circuit and U.S. Supreme Court. *Education:* Xavier University (A.B., cum laude, 1974); Indiana University (J.D., 1979). Law Clerk to: Hon. Stanley B. Miller, Court of Appeals of Indiana, Fourth District; Hon. V. Sue Shields, Court of Appeals of Indiana, Second District, 1981-1982. *Member:* Illinois State Bar Association; National Association of Railroad Trial Counsel; Defense Research Institute, Inc. ***PRACTICE AREAS:*** Railroad Law; FELA Occupational Hearing Loss. ***Email:*** cwebster@freebornpeters.com

JAMES M. WITZ, admitted to bar, 1992, Illinois. *Education:* Wesleyan University (B.A., 1987); University of California at Los Angeles (J.D., 1992). ***PRACTICE AREAS:*** Business Litigation. ***Email:*** jwitz@freebornpeters.com

EUGENE F. ZELEK, JR., admitted to bar, 1978, Illinois. *Education:* University of Illinois (B.S., with high honors, 1974); Northwestern University (M.B.A., with distinction, 1978; J.D., cum laude, 1978). Kappa Tau Alpha; Beta Gamma Sigma. Distinguished Scholar. Executive Editor, Northwestern University Law Review, 1977-1978. Author: "The

(This Listing Continued)

Legal Framework for Pricing," in Nagle and Holden, The Strategy and Tactics of Pricing (3d ed. 2001); "Role of Regulation in Setting Prices," in Kellogg on Marketing (Dawn Iacobucci, ed. 2001); "The Legal Framework for Pricing in the 1990's," The Journal of Professional Pricing, Fall 1995; "Legal Aspects of Sensory Analysis," Food Technology, November 1990 at 168. Adjunct Assistant Professor of Marketing, Kellogg School of Management, Northwestern University, "Marketing, Society and Public Policy: The Legal Aspects of Marketing Strategy," "The Legal Aspects of Pricing" and "Legal Issues in Channel Management," 1985—. Member, National Advisory Board, The Pricing Institute, 1997—. ***PRACTICE AREAS:*** Antitrust; Marketing; Trade Regulation; Intellectual Property; Information Technology; Corporate; Entertainment. ***Email:*** ezelek@freebornpeters.com

ANN M. ZWICK, admitted to bar, 1989, Illinois. *Education:* University of Illinois (B.S., with highest honors, 1986); Northwestern University (J.D., cum laude, 1989). Former Assistant Counsel with the Illinois Environmental Protection Agency. ***PRACTICE AREAS:*** Government Relations; Regulatory Law; Environmental, Health and Safety Law; Real Estate; Land Use. ***Email:*** azwick@freebornpeters.com

ASSOCIATES

RACHEL ATTERBERRY, born Peoria, Illinois, August 21, 1979; (admission pending). *Education:* DePauw University (B.A., cum laude, 2001); Washington University (J.D., 2004). ***PRACTICE AREAS:*** Litigation. ***Email:*** ratterberry@freebornpeters.com

DAVID BECKER, admitted to bar, 2000, Illinois. *Education:* University of Rochester (B.A., 1995); DePaul University (J.D., 2000). ***PRACTICE AREAS:*** Business Litigation; Products Liability; Antitrust. ***Email:*** dbecker@freebornpeters.com

MELISSA L. BENZON, born Omaha, Nebraska, January 1, 1974; admitted to bar, 2001, Illinois. *Education:* DePaul University (B.A., with highest honors, 1998); Northwestern University (J.D., 2001). Dean's List. ***PRACTICE AREAS:*** Litigation. ***Email:*** mbenzon@freebornpeters.com

STACI A. BURTON, admitted to bar, 1998, Illinois. *Education:* University of Illinois (B.S., 1995); Washington University (J.D., 1998). *Member:* Chicago Bar Association. ***PRACTICE AREAS:*** Trusts and Estates; Estate Planning; Taxation. ***Email:*** sburton@freebornpeters.com

GIA COLUNGA, born Chicago, Illinois, August 31, 1979; (admission pending). *Education:* Tulane University (B.A., cum laude, 2001); Loyola University (J.D., cum laude, 2004). ***PRACTICE AREAS:*** Litigation. ***Email:*** gcolunga@freebornpeters.com

GINA DI BELLA, born Chicago, Illinois, February 25, 1979; (admission pending). *Education:* Indiana University (B.S., magna cum laude, 2001); DePaul University College of Law (J.D., summa cum laude, 2004). ***PRACTICE AREAS:*** Litigation. ***Email:*** gdibella@freebornpeters.com

KELLYE L. FABIAN, born St. Joseph, Michigan, September 24, 1975; admitted to bar, 2000, Illinois and U.S. District Court, Northern District of Illinois; 2003, U.S. District Court, Eastern District of Michigan; 2004, U.S. District Court, District of Colorado and U.S. Court of Appeals, Ninth Circuit. *Education:* University of Illinois (B.A., 1997); DePaul University College of Law (J.D., 2000). *Member:* American Bar Association (Member, Litigation Section). ***PRACTICE AREAS:*** Litigation. ***Email:*** kfabian@freebornpeters.com

THOMAS R. FAWKES, admitted to bar, 2002, Illinois; 2003, U.S. District Court, Eastern District of Wisconsin; 2004, U.S. District Court, Northern District of Illinois. *Education:* Loyola University, Chicago (B.A., summa cum laude, 1999); Northwestern University School of Law (J.D., cum laude, 2002). Order of the Coif. ***PRACTICE AREAS:*** Bankruptcy. ***Email:*** tfawkes@freebornpeters.com

MICHELE L. FOSTER, admitted to bar, 1999, Illinois and U.S. District Court, Northern District of Illinois. *Education:* San Diego State University (B.A., with distinction, 1994); Loyola University, Chicago (J.D., 1999). *Member:* Chicago, Illinois State and American Bar Associations; American Intellectual Property Association. ***PRACTICE AREAS:*** Business Litigation; Intellectual Property; Information Technology. ***Email:*** mfoster@freebornpeters.com

MICHAEL T. FRANZ, admitted to bar, 1996, Florida; 1997, U.S. District Court, Middle District of Florida; 1998, Illinois; 2000, U.S. District Court, Northern District of Illinois. *Education:* University of Michigan (B.A., 1993); Detroit College of Law at Michigan State University (J.D., 1996). Tau Kappa Epsilon (President, 1991-1992); Delta Pi Chapter. ***LANGUAGES:*** German. ***PRACTICE AREAS:*** Business Litigation; Railroad Law; Federal Employers Liability Act (FELA) Litigation. ***Email:*** mfranz@freebornpeters.com

ELIZABETH T. FRIEDLANDER, admitted to bar, 1999, Illinois. *Education:* Vanderbilt University (B.S., 1996); Loyola University (J.D., 1999). Dean's List. *Member:* Chicago and American Bar Associations. ***PRACTICE AREAS:*** Business Litigation. ***Email:*** etolva@freebornpeters.com

AMI D. GANDHI, born August 24, 1980; (admission pending). *Education:* Indiana University (B.A., magna cum laude, 2001); The George Washington University (J.D., 2004). ***PRACTICE AREAS:*** Business Litigation. ***Email:*** agandhi@freebornpeters.com

JOHN C. HAMMERLE, born Pontiac, Michigan; admitted to bar, 2005, Illinois. *Education:* Butler University (B.S., magna cum laude, 2001); DePaul University (J.D, 2005). Order of the Coif. Associate Editor, DePaul Law Review. ***PRACTICE AREAS:*** Litigation. ***Email:*** jhammerle@freebornpeters.com

JEFFREY M. HANSEN, admitted to bar, 1999, Illinois. *Education:* Drake University (B.A., summa cum laude, 1995); Northwestern University School of Law (J.D., 1999). ***PRACTICE AREAS:*** Civil Litigation; Complex Litigation; Defense Litigation. ***Email:*** jhansen@freebornpeters.com

TONITA M. HELTON, admitted to bar, 2001, Illinois. *Education:* Drake University (B.A., International Relations & Political Science, cum laude, 1997); University of Iowa (J.D., with distinction, 2001). Phi Alpha Delta. ***PRACTICE AREAS:*** Business Litigation. ***Email:*** thelton@freebornpeters.com

JOHN F. JACOBS, admitted to bar, 1993, Illinois and U.S. District Court, Northern District Court of Illinois; 1994, U.S. Tax Court. *Education:* University of Illinois (B.A.,

(This Listing Continued)

FREEBORN & PETERS LLP, Chicago—Continued

1990); DePaul University College of Law (J.D., 1993). *Member:* Chicago, Illinois State and American Bar Associations. ***PRACTICE AREAS:*** Taxation; Estate Planning; Estate Administration; Business Organization. ***Email:*** jjacobs@freebornpeters.com

MARC H. KALLISH, admitted to bar, 1996, Illinois. *Education:* University of Illinois (B.A., Political Science, 1992); John Marshall Law School (J.D., 1996). *Member:* Chicago Bar Association; Defense Research Institute. ***PRACTICE AREAS:*** Civil Litigation; Complex Litigation; Medical Malpractice Defense. ***Email:*** mkallish@freebornpeters.com

DAVID L. KANE, admitted to bar, 2002, Illinois and U.S. District Court, Northern District of Illinois. *Education:* University of Wisconsin, Madison (B.A., 1999); Case Western Reserve University (J.D., 2002). ***PRACTICE AREAS:*** Commercial Bankruptcy; Bankruptcy Chapter 11; Creditors Rights; Bankruptcy Reorganization. ***Email:*** dkane@freebornpeters.com

JACOB D. KOERING, admitted to bar, 2001, Illinois; 2004, Minnesota. *Education:* University of Wisconsin at Madison (B.S., 1998); Loyola University (J.D., 2001). ***PRACTICE AREAS:*** Intellectual Property Litigation (100%). ***Email:*** jkoering@freebornpeters.com

THEODORE J. KOERTH, admitted to bar, 2002, Illinois. *Education:* University of Virginia (B.A., 1999); George Washington University (J.D., 2002). Order of Omega. *Member:* Chicago and American Bar Associations. ***LANGUAGES:*** Spanish. ***PRACTICE AREAS:*** Litigation; Commercial Litigation; Trade Secrets. ***Email:*** tkoerth@freebornpeters.com

MATTHEW J. KRAMER, born Joliet, Illinois, September 9, 1979; (admission pending). *Education:* University of Illinois (B.S., with honors, 2001); University of Illinois College of Law (J.D., magna cum laude, 2004). ***PRACTICE AREAS:*** Litigation. ***Email:*** mkramer@freebornpeters.com

HILLARY P. KRANTZ, born Hartford, Connecticut, April 8, 1971; admitted to bar, 2001, Illinois and U.S. District Court, Northern District of Illinois; 2003, U.S. Court of Appeals, Seventh Circuit. *Education:* Northwestern University (B.A., 1993; J.D., 2001). ***PRACTICE AREAS:*** Litigation. ***Email:*** hkrantz@freebornpeters.com

TODD A. LABINSKY, admitted to bar, 2000, Illinois. *Education:* University of Illinois (B.A., cum laude, 1996; M.B.A., 1997; J.D., 2000). Phi Beta Kappa. *Member:* Chicago and American Bar Associations. ***LANGUAGES:*** Japanese. ***PRACTICE AREAS:*** Mergers and Acquisitions; Private Equity; Venture Capital; Financing; Corporate Counseling. ***Email:*** tlabinsky@freebornpeters.com

ELENI S. LAMPERIS, born Chicago, Illinois, December 5, 1973; admitted to bar, 1998, Illinois. *Education:* DePaul University (B.S., with high honor, 1995; J.D., with honors, 1998). Member, Order of the Coif. *Member:* Chicago, Illinois State and American Bar Associations. ***LANGUAGES:*** Greek. ***PRACTICE AREAS:*** Real Estate Law. ***Email:*** elamperis@freebornpeters.com

DAVID M. MADDEN, admitted to bar, 2003, Illinois. *Education:* Michigan State University (B.A., 1998); DePaul University (J.D., 2003). Recipient: General Intellectual Property Certificate. [Corporal, U.S. Marine Corps Reserve, 1995-2001]. ***PRACTICE AREAS:*** Commercial Bankruptcy; Post Judgment Collections. ***Email:*** dmadden@freebornpeters.com

ERIC M. MADIAR, admitted to bar, 2000, Illinois. *Education:* Truman State University (B.A., 1995); Chicago-Kent College of Law, Illinois Institute of Technology (J.D., 2000). ***PRACTICE AREAS:*** State Legislative Practice; Government Agency Practice. ***Email:*** emadiar@freebornpeters.com

ROGER S. MALKI, admitted to bar, 2003, Illinois. *Education:* University of Montreal, Montreal, Quebec, Canada (B.A., 2000); Michigan State University College of Law (J.D., 2003). *Member:* Chicago and American Bar Associations. ***LANGUAGES:*** French and Arabic. ***PRACTICE AREAS:*** Commercial Litigation. ***Email:*** rmalki@freebornpeters.com

TRACY H. MICHAEL, admitted to bar, 2002, Illinois. *Education:* Emory University (B.A., 1998); Northwestern University (J.D., 2001). ***PRACTICE AREAS:*** Real Estate. ***Email:*** tmichael@freebornpeters.com

CATHERINE A. MILLER, admitted to bar, 1999, Illinois. *Education:* University of Illinois (B.A., 1993; J.D., cum laude, 1999); Depaul University (1996-1997). *Member:* Chicago and American Bar Associations. ***PRACTICE AREAS:*** Business Litigation. ***Email:*** cmiller@freebornpeters.com

JENNIFER L. MILOS, admitted to bar, 2001, Illinois. *Education:* University of Michigan (B.A., English Literature, 1998); University of Illinois (J.D., 2001). (Resident, Springfield Office). ***PRACTICE AREAS:*** Business Litigation. ***Email:*** jmilos@freebornpeters.com

KRIS R. MURPHY, admitted to bar, 1996, Illinois. *Education:* University of Notre Dame (B.A., 1989); College of William & Mary (M.A., 1993); Columbus School of Law, The Catholic University of America (J.D., 1996). Law Clerk to Hon. Ann O'Regan Keary, Superior Court of the District of Columbia, 1996-1997. ***PRACTICE AREAS:*** Business Litigation. ***Email:*** kmurphy@freebornpeters.com

ANDREW C. NORDAHL, admitted to bar, 1995, Illinois and U.S. District Court, Northern District of Illinois. *Education:* Loyola University of Chicago (B.A., 1989); John Marshall Law School (J.D., 1995). ***PRACTICE AREAS:*** Business Litigation. ***Email:*** ano-dahl@freebornpeters.com

RAYMOND H. PRUCHNICKI, admitted to bar, 1999, Illinois. *Education:* Iowa State University (B.S., 1989); University of Illinois at Champaign-Urbana (Master of Urban Planning, 1992); DePaul University (J.D., 1999). *Member:* Chicago Bar Association; American Planning Association; American Institute of Certified Planners. ***LANGUAGES:*** Polish. ***PRACTICE AREAS:*** Real Estate; Land Use; Zoning. ***Email:*** rpruchnicki@freebornpeters.com

VERONA M. SANDBERG, admitted to bar, 2003, Illinois. *Education:* University of Illinois (B.S., with honors, 1998); Northwestern University (J.D., 2003). ***PRACTICE AREAS:*** Business Litigation. ***Email:*** vsandberg@freebornpeters.com

(This Listing Continued)

TERRENCE J. SHEAHAN, admitted to bar, 1999, Illinois. *Education:* Indiana University (B.A., 1994); DePaul University (J.D., 1999). *Member:* Chicago Bar Association; Prosecutors Bar Association. ***PRACTICE AREAS:*** Business Litigation; Government Relations; Regulatory Law. ***Email:*** tsheahan@freebornpeters.com

BRIAN A. SMITH, admitted to bar, 1998, Illinois and U.S. Tax Court; 2002, U.S. District Court, Northern District of Illinois including Trial Bar. *Education:* Indiana University (B.S., 1994; J.D., 1998). Certified Public Accountant, Illinois, 1996. ***PRACTICE AREAS:*** Taxation. ***Email:*** bsmith@freebornpeters.com

JOJI TAKADA, admitted to bar, 2004, Illinois. *Education:* Whitman College (B.A., 1995); Doshisha University (M.A. 2000); Illinois Institute of Technology, Chicago-Kent College of Law (J.D., 2003). ***LANGUAGES:*** Japanese. ***PRACTICE AREAS:*** Bankruptcy. ***Email:*** jtakada@freebornpeters.com

DAVID TER MOLEN, born Dallas, Texas, October 1, 1968; admitted to bar, 1999, Illinois and U.S. District Court, Northern District of Illinois. *Education:* Dartmouth College (A.B., 1991); Northwestern University (J.D., magna cum laude, 1999). Order of the Coif. *Member:* Illinois State and American Bar Associations. ***PRACTICE AREAS:*** Intellectual Property Litigation; Civil Litigation. ***Email:*** dtermolen@freebornpeters.com

STEPHANIE TOWNER, admitted to bar, 2001, Illinois and U.S. District Court, Northern District of Illinois. *Education:* DePaul University (B.F.A., with honors, 1996; J.D., 2001). ***PRACTICE AREAS:*** Trademarks; Copyrights; Internet; E-Commerce. ***Email:*** stowner@freebornpeters.com

SUSAN E. WALSH, admitted to bar, 1998, Illinois. *Education:* University of Illinois (B.S., 1994); Chicago-Kent College of Law (J.D., 1998). *Member:* Chicago and American Bar Associations. ***PRACTICE AREAS:*** Labor and Employment Law; Workers' Compensation; Occupational Disease. ***Email:*** swalsh@freebornpeters.com

GARRY L. WILLS, admitted to bar, 2003, Illinois. *Education:* Yale University (B.A., 1983); Northwestern University (J.D., 2003). ***PRACTICE AREAS:*** Business Litigation. ***Email:*** gwills@frebornpeters.com

PATRICK J. WOYTEK, admitted to bar, 1998, Illinois. *Education:* DePaul University (B.A., with high honors, 1995; J.D., 1998). Recipient, Research and Writing Award, De Paul Law Review, 1996-1997. Member and Editor, De Paul Law Review, 1997-1998. *Member:* Chicago, Illinois State and American Bar Associations. ***PRACTICE AREAS:*** Business Litigation; Railroad Law; FELA Litigation. ***Email:*** pwoytek@freebornpeters.com

JANE D. YANOVSKY, born Moscow, Russia; admitted to bar, 2005, Illinois. *Education:* Northwestern University (B.A., 2001); George Washington University (J.D., 2005). ***LANGUAGES:*** Russian and French. ***PRACTICE AREAS:*** Litigation. ***Email:*** jyanovsky@freebornpeters.com

SHEILA ZELLER, admitted to bar, 1997, Illinois. *Education:* University of Alabama (B.A., 1993); The John Marshall Law School (J.D., 1997). ***PRACTICE AREAS:*** Commercial Bankruptcy; Postjudgment Collections; Fraudulent Conveyance; Commercial Litigation. ***Email:*** szeller@freebornpeters.com

STAFF ATTORNEY

JOHN R. FANONE, admitted to bar, 1975, Illinois; 1976, U.S. District Court, Northern District of Illinois; 1985, U.S. Court of Appeals, Seventh Circuit; 1990, U.S. District Court, District of Arizona; 1991, U.S. District Court, Central District of Illinois; 1993, Texas. *Education:* Purdue University (B.S.E.E., 1972); John Marshall Law School (J.D., 1975). Co-Author, "American Briefing," Product Liability International, Lloyds of London Press Limited (Monthly). Paralegal Instructor, William Rainey Harpers College, 1984, 1988. Lecturer, Defense Research Institute, 1988. Assistant Attorney General, Court of Claims Division, State of Illinois, 1978-1981. *Member:* Chicago Bar Association; State Bar of Texas; Defense Research Institute. ***REPORTED CASES:*** First National Bank of Dwight v. Regent Sports Corporation, 803 F.2d 1431 (1988); Kochin v. Eaton Corp., 986 F.2d 1424 (1993); Golden v. Montwood 107 F.3d 28 (1997). ***PRACTICE AREAS:*** Personal Injury (55%); Products Liability (15%); Construction Law (15%); Manufacturers Liability; Technology Law (15%). ***Email:*** jfanone@freebornpeters.com

SENIOR COUNSEL

RICHARD R. DENNERLINE, admitted to bar, 1989, Illinois. *Education:* Purdue University (B.S.I.E., with highest distinction, 1986); University of Michigan (J.D., magna cum laude, 1989). ***PRACTICE AREAS:*** Emerging Companies; Venture Capital; Securities; Corporate Law; Intellectual Property. ***Email:*** rdennerline@freebornpeters.com

KATHLEEN L. HOBBINS, born Phoenix, Arizona, January 2, 1956; admitted to bar, 1995, Illinois. *Education:* Wesleyan University (B.A., 1978); Chicago-Kent College of Law (J.D., with high honors, 1995). Order of the Coif. *Member:* Chicago (Member, Commercial Finance and Transactions Committee) and American Bar Associations. ***PRACTICE AREAS:*** Commercial Transactions; Banking Law; Bond Finance. ***Email:*** khobbins@freebornpeters.com

WILLIAM C. HOLMES, admitted to bar, 1973, California; 1975, Illinois. *Education:* Stanford University (B.A., with distinction, 1969); Harvard Law School (J.D., cum laude, 1973). Phi Beta Kappa. Author: treatise, "Intellectual Property and Antitrust Law," reference series "Antitrust Law Handbook," reference series "Antitrust Law Sourcebook for the United States and Europe." Member, Economic Club of Chicago. ***PRACTICE AREAS:*** Antitrust and Trade Regulation; Intellectual Property; Information Technology; Corporate. ***Email:*** wholmes@freebornpeters.com

LELAND W. HUTCHINSON, JR., admitted to bar, 1975, Illinois. *Education:* University of Illinois (A.B., 1972; J.D., with honors, 1975). Member, Board of Editors, University of Illinois Law Forum. ***PRACTICE AREAS:*** Business Litigation. ***Email:*** lhutchinson@freebornpeters.com

MICHAEL A. SMITH, admitted to bar, 1972, California, U.S. District Court, Northern and Eastern Districts of California and U.S. Court of Appeals, Ninth Circuit; 1988, Illinois. *Education:* University of California at Davis (A.B., Political Science, 1968; J.D., 1971). Instructor, Legal Research and Writing, University of California at Davis, 1970-1971. *Member:* Bar Association of San Francisco (Member, Corporate Section); State Bar of California; American Bar Association; Association of American Railroads (Economic

(This Listing Continued)

Regulation Working Group, 1990-1999; Antitrust Working Group, 1990-1999). ***PRACTICE AREAS:*** Railroad Law; Federal Employers Liability Act (FELA) Litigation; Real Estate; Land Use; Business Litigation. ***Email:*** msmith@freebornpeters.com

WILLIAM A. SPENCE, admitted to bar, 1971, Illinois. *Education:* Northwestern University (B.A., 1965); Loyola University (J.D., 1971). Foreign Advisor, State Pharmaceutical Administration of China. Assistant U.S. Attorney, Northern District of Illinois, 1979-1987. Law Professor, East China University of Politics and Law, Shanghai, China, 1994. Co-Chairman, Chicago Sister Cities International, China Committee, 1997. ***PRACTICE AREAS:*** Business Litigation. ***Email:*** bspence@freebornpeters.com

OF COUNSEL

AMORY CUMMINGS, admitted to bar, 1977, Illinois; 1984, Missouri. *Education:* Yale University (B.A., cum laude, 1974); University of Michigan (J.D., cum laude, 1977). University of Michigan Law Review. ***PRACTICE AREAS:*** Corporate; Corporate Finance; Securities; Mergers, Acquisitions and Restructuring. ***Email:*** acummings@freebornpeters.com

HARRY L. DeLUNG, JR., admitted to bar, 1968, Illinois; 1983, Texas. *Education:* University of North Carolina (A.B., 1964); Emory University (J.D., 1967). Associate Editor, Journal of Public Law, 1967. General Counsel, Santa Fe Pacific Corporation, 1988-1990. *Member:* Association of Transportation Law Practitioners (Chairman, Chicago Chapter, 1978-1979); American Corporate Counsel Association (Chairman, Outside Counsel Committee, 1989-1990). ***PRACTICE AREAS:*** Railroad Law; Federal Employers Liability Act (FELA) Litigation; Corporate; Business Litigation. ***Email:*** hdelung@freebornpeters.com

PAUL A. DUFFY, admitted to bar, 1992, Illinois; 1993, Massachusetts; 2003, California. *Education:* Elmhurst College (B.S., 1981); Loyola University of Chicago (M.B.A., 1987); DePaul University (J.D., cum laude, 1992). *Member:* Chicago and American Bar Associations. ***PRACTICE AREAS:*** Commercial Litigation; Environmental Law; Commercial Transactions; Commercial Crimes. ***Email:*** pduffy@freebornpeters.com

PAUL A. HYBEL, admitted to bar, 1988, Illinois. *Education:* Dartmouth College (B.A., 1979); Boston University; New York University (J.D., 1988). ***PRACTICE AREAS:*** Business Litigation; Antitrust and Trade Regulation; Securities Litigation. ***Email:*** phybel@freebornpeters.com

ANDY V. JONUSAITIS, admitted to bar, 1986, Illinois. *Education:* Northwestern University (B.A., 1982; M.A., 1982; J.D., 1986). ***PRACTICE AREAS:*** Corporate; Mergers and Acquisitions; Private and Public Equity Financing; Consumer Data Privacy. ***Email:*** ajonusaitis@freebornpeters.com

CHARLES E. KELLY, admitted to bar, 1982, Kansas; 1992, Nevada (Not admitted in Illinois). *Education:* Southern Illinois University (B.A., 1979); Washburn University School of Law (J.D., 1982). Phi Beta Kappa. (Also practicing individually in Las Vegas, Nevada). ***PRACTICE AREAS:*** Government Relations; Regulatory Law. ***Email:*** ckelly@freebornpeters.com

REPRESENTATIVE CLIENTS: 3Com; AIG; Acxiom Corporation; Baxter Health Care; The Boeing Company; Burlington Northern/Santa Fe; BP; Canadian National/Illinois Central Railway; Chicago Bears; Chicago Public Schools; City of Chicago; Commonwealth Edison; DuPont Pharmaceuticals; Fleet Business Credit Corporation; Harris Bank; Information Resources, Inc.; Johns-Manville Corporation; McDonalds Corporation; Microsoft; Motorola; Nissan; Noranda, Inc.; Northern Trust; RailMarketplace.com; Sprint; VoiceStream Wireless.

FREEMAN, FREEMAN & SALZMAN, P.C.

Established in 1968

401 NORTH MICHIGAN AVENUE, SUITE 3200

CHICAGO, ILLINOIS 60611-4207

Telephone: 312-222-5100

Facsimile: 312-822-0870

Email: freeman@ffspc.com

URL: http://www.ffspc.com

Antitrust Litigation, Securities and Commodity Litigation, General Commercial Litigation and Employment Litigation.

FIRM PROFILE: Freeman, Freeman & Salzman, P.C. was founded in 1968. Since then, our firm has specialized in prosecuting and defending antitrust, securities, commodities and other types of commercial litigation on behalf of major corporations, associations, and public agencies in trial and appellate courts throughout the country. We also appear regularly before administrative agencies including the CFTC, SEC and FTC. We represent clients in regulatory and disciplinary matters before commodities and securities exchange and other self-regulatory organizations; engage in the arbitration and mediation of securities and commodities claims; and serve as arbitrators, mediators and receivers. Representative clients include the Chicago Mercantile Exchange, Wabash Valley Power Association, Lockheed Martin Corporations, Kraft General Foods, Coca-Cola Enterprises, Sara Lee Corporation, PepsiCo, Ringier America and Deloitte & Touche.

LEE A. FREEMAN (1909-1995)

LEE A. FREEMAN, JR., born Chicago, Illinois, July 31, 1940; admitted to bar, 1966, Illinois and District of Columbia; 1986, Montana. *Education:* Harvard University (A.B., magna cum laude, 1962; LL.B., magna cum laude, 1965). Case Editor, Harvard Law Review, 1965. Law Clerk to Justice Tom Clark, 1965-1966. Assistant U.S. Attorney, Washington, D.C., 1966-1968. Special Assistant Attorney General: Illinois, Indiana, Tennessee and West Virginia, 1970-1981; Wisconsin, Minnesota, Michigan, Pennsylvania, Kentucky and Colorado, 1973-1978. Special Assistant Corporation Counsel, Chicago, 1971-1976. *Member:* Chicago and American (Council Member, Antitrust Section, 1975—) Bar Associations. ***PRACTICE AREAS:*** Commercial Litigation; Business Litigation; Antitrust; Utility Regulation. ***Email:*** lfreemanjr@ffspc.com

JERROLD E. SALZMAN, born Chicago, Illinois, October 11, 1940; admitted to bar, 1965, Illinois. *Education:* University of Michigan (A.B., with high distinction, 1962); Harvard University (LL.B., cum laude, 1965). Phi Beta Kappa. Member, Harvard Law Review, 1965. *Member:* Chicago and American Bar Associations; Chicago Council of Lawyers. ***Email:*** jsalzman@ffspc.com

(This Listing Continued)

JOHN F. KINNEY, born Milwaukee, Wisconsin, November 19, 1948; admitted to bar, 1973, Illinois. *Education:* Georgetown University (A.B., magna cum laude, 1970; J.D., 1973). Phi Beta Kappa. *Member:* Chicago, Illinois State and American (Member, Antitrust Section) Bar Associations. ***Email:*** jkinney@ffspc.com

JAMES T. MALYSIAK, born Berwyn, Illinois, May 31, 1946; admitted to bar, 1976, Illinois. *Education:* Dartmouth College (B.A., summa cum laude, 1968); Oxford University (M.A., 1970); Yale University (J.D., 1973). Phi Beta Kappa. Fulbright Scholar. Editor, Yale Law Journal, 1972-1973. Author: Note, "Toward a Substantive Private International Law of Trademarks," 82 Yale Law Journal 1072, 1973; Article, "Justice White on Antitrust: Protecting Freedom to Compete," 58 University of Colorado Law Review 497, 1987. Law Clerk to: Judge Charles B. Renfrew, U.S. District Court for the Northern District of California, 1973-1974; Justice Byron R. White, U.S. Supreme Court, 1974-1975. ***Email:*** jmalysiak@ffspc.com

PHILLIP L. STERN, born Chicago, Illinois, September 10, 1949; admitted to bar, 1975, Illinois and U.S. District Court, Northern District of Illinois; 1984, U.S. Court of Appeals, Seventh Circuit. *Education:* DePaul University (B.S.C., 1971; J.D., cum laude, 1975). Instructor, Securities Regulation, IIT/Chicago-Kent College of Law, 1982-1983. Staff Attorney, Branch of Investment Company Examination, 1975-1976, Staff Attorney, Branch of Enforcement, 1976-1978, Chief, Branch of Enforcement, 1978-1980 and Assistant Regional Administrator, Enforcement, Securities and Exchange Commission, Chicago Regional Office. Special Assistant U.S. Attorney, 1981-1993. *Member:* Chicago and American (Member, Securities Regulation Committee, 1985—, Sections on: Human Rights, Litigation and Corporation, Banking and Business Law) Bar Associations; The Decalogue Society of Lawyers. ***Email:*** pstern@ffspc.com

---

JOSEPH P. ADAMCZYK, born Park Ridge, Illinois, August 20, 1976; admitted to bar, 2001, Illinois and U.S. District Court, Northern District of Illinois. *Education:* DePaul University (B.S., 1998); Loyola University Chicago School of Law (J.D., 2001). *Member:* Chicago and American Bar Associations. ***PRACTICE AREAS:*** Antitrust; Securities Litigation; Commercial Litigation. ***Email:*** jadamczyk@ffspc.com

KEVIN M. JONES, born Buffalo, New York, August 2, 1976; admitted to bar, 2001, Illinois; 2002, U.S. District Court, Northern District of Illinois. *Education:* Canisius College (B.A., summa cum laude, 1998); DePaul University College of Law (J.D., with honors, 2001). Author: "A Jurisdictional Survey of Community of Interest States," Distribution Newsletter, May 2004. *Member:* American Bar Association (Member, Antitrust Law Section, 2001; Franchise and Dealership Committee, 2004). ***PRACTICE AREAS:*** Antitrust; Commercial Litigation; Securities; Franchise Distribution. ***Email:*** kjones@ffspc.com

OF COUNSEL

GLYNNA W. FREEMAN, born Midland, Texas, November 7, 1945; admitted to bar, 1971, Illinois. *Education:* Smith College (B.A., 1968); Northwestern University (J.D., 1971). Assistant U.S. Attorney, Northern District of Illinois, 1972-1978. *Member:* Chicago and American (Member, Sections on: Corporation, Banking and Business Law; Litigation; Natural Resources Law) Bar Associations. ***Email:*** gfreeman@ffspc.com

RICHARD P. CAMPBELL, born Indianapolis, Indiana, January 24, 1940; admitted to bar, 1966, New Mexico and U.S. District Court, District of New Mexico; 1968, Illinois, U.S. District Court, District of Illinois and U.S. Supreme Court. *Education:* Northwestern University (B.S., with highest distinction, 1962); Harvard University (LL.B., 1965). Phi Eta Sigma; Beta Gamma Sigma. *Member:* Chicago Bar Association. ***PRACTICE AREAS:*** Commercial Litigation; Antitrust; Employment Litigation; Civil Rights. ***Email:*** rcampbell@ffspc.com

LAW OFFICES OF
ERIC S. FREIBRUN, LTD.

CHICAGO, ILLINOIS

(See Northbrook)

Intellectual Property, Intellectual Property Licensing, Intellectual Property Litigation, Internet Intellectual Property, Internet Law, Trademark Law, Proprietary Rights, Computers and Software, Computer Contracts, Computer Law, Computer Security, Computer Software Law, Information Technology, Information Technology Contracts, Information Technology Licensing, International Computer Law, Software Copyright, Software Licensing, Software Protection, Software Publishing Technology, E-commerce.

HOWARD FRIEDMAN

150 N. WACKER DRIVE, SUITE 1400

CHICAGO, ILLINOIS 60606

Telephone: 312-553-1700

Fax: 312-553-1733

Corporate, Mergers and Acquisitions, Real Estate, International Transactions.

HOWARD FRIEDMAN, born Chicago, Illinois, December 19, 1940; admitted to bar, 1964, Illinois. *Education:* Indiana University (B.S., 1960); Northwestern University (J.D., magna cum laude, 1964). Phi Eta Sigma; Beta Gamma Sigma; Order of the Coif. Managing Editor, Northwestern University Law Review, 1963-1964. Certified Public Accountant, Illinois, 1962. *Member:* Chicago, Illinois State and American Bar Associations. [Capt., JAGC, U.S. Naval Reserve]. ***PRACTICE AREAS:*** Corporate; Mergers and Acquisitions; Real Estate; International Transactions.

MICHAEL T. FRIEDMAN & ASSOCIATES

Established in 1996

155 NORTH MICHIGAN AVENUE, SUITE 600
CHICAGO, ILLINOIS 60601
Telephone: 312-616-8816
Fax: 312-938-8541
Email: mikefriedmanlaw@comcast.net
URL: http://www.lawyers.com/injurylawyer

Personal Injury, Wrongful Death, Automobile Accidents, Slip and Fall, Workers' Compensation, Airline Accidents, Products Liability, Construction Accidents, Bus Accidents, Railroad Accidents, Dog Bites, Medical Malpractice, Brain and Spinal Injuries, Catastrophic Injuries, Pedestrian Injuries, Real Estate, Commercial Real Estate, Mechanics Liens, Zoning and Land Use, Buying and Selling a Home, Family Law, Divorce, Child Custody and Support, Adoptions.

FIRM PROFILE: Michael T. Friedman established his solo practice in 1996. Mr. Friedman's primary focus is personal injury law. However, Mr. Friedman can assist clients with other legal matters. Michael T. Friedman's aggressive approach to win, along with his personalized attention to clients, has led to many successful cases.

MICHAEL T. FRIEDMAN, born Chicago, Illinois, November 13, 1967; admitted to bar, 1992, Illinois and U.S. District Court, Northern District of Illinois. *Education:* Indiana University (B.A., 1989); John Marshall Law School (J.D., 1992). Managing Editor, The Software Law Journal, 1991. Author: "The Misuse of Electronically Transferred Confidential Information in Interstate Commerce: How Well do Our Present Laws Address the Issue?" The Software Law Journal, Vol. 4, Oct. 1991, #3. *Member:* Chicago, Lake County, Illinois State and American Bar Associations; Illinois Trial Lawyers Association; The Association of Trial Lawyers of America.

FRIEDMAN & BONEBRAKE, P.C.

Established in 1996

150 N. WACKER DRIVE, SUITE 2020
CHICAGO, ILLINOIS 60606
Telephone: 312-466-8200
Fax: 312-466-8238
URL: http://www.attorneyillinois.net
Email: friedman@attorneyillinois.net
URL: http://www.lawyers.com/mattfriedman

Personal Injury, Automobile Accidents, Medical Malpractice, Products Liability, Workers Compensation, Toxic Torts and Insurance Coverage, Premises Liability, Wrongful Death, Consumer Fraud, Real Estate, Business Transactions.

FIRM PROFILE: Friedman & Bonebrake, P.C. represents individuals in personal injury litigation, including medical malpractice, automobile accidents, products liability, premises liability, toxic torts, wrongful death, and workers compensation. In addition, our firm represents individuals in consumer fraud cases, real estate transactions and insurance coverage litigation. We also represent businesses and individuals in business transactions and business litigation. We work on a contingency fee for most personal injury cases. Please call or email us to find out more about our firm.

MATTHEW C. FRIEDMAN, born Northbrook, Illinois, February 26, 1965; admitted to bar, 1993, Illinois and U.S. District Court, Northern District of Illinois. *Education:* Indiana University (B.S., 1987); DePaul University (J.D., 1993). *Member:* Chicago and Illinois State Bar Associations; Illinois Trial Lawyers Association; Association of Trial Lawyers of America; Illinois Trial Lawyers (Member, Medical Malpractice Committee, 1996—). ***REPORTED CASES:*** Stephens v. Trinity Medical Center, 685 NE2d 403 (3rd Dist. 1997). ***PRACTICE AREAS:*** Personal Injury; Automobile Accidents; Medical Malpractice; Products Liability; Toxic Torts. ***Email:*** friedman@attorneyillinois.net

JAMES G. BONEBRAKE, born Park Ridge, Illinois, January 31, 1965; admitted to bar, 1990, Illinois and U.S. District Court, Northern District of Illinois; 1994, U.S. Court of Appeals, Seventh Circuit. *Education:* DePauw University (B.A., magna cum laude, 1987); Northwestern University (J.D., 1990). Phi Beta Kappa. Author: "Sixth and Fourteenth Amendments: A Lost Role of the Peremptory Challenge in Securing an Accused's Right to An Impartial Jury," Journal of Criminal Law and Criminology Supreme Court Review Issue, Fall, 1988. Co-Author, "Medical Malpractice Handbook, Chapter 7: Specific Defenses," Illinois Institute of Continuing Legal Education. *Member:* Chicago Bar Association (Member, Tort Litigation Committee, 1996—). ***LANGUAGES:*** Spanish. ***REPORTED CASES:*** Northrop Corporation v. AIL Systems, 218 III. App. 3d 951, 578 N.E.2d 1208 (1st Dist. Il 1991); Neufville v. Diamond, 166 III. 2d 507, 655 N.E.2d 888 (III. S. Ct. 1995); The Northern Trust Company v. Frank E. Peters, 69 F.3d 123 (7th Cir. 1995); Board of Education of Township High School District 207 v. International Insurance Company, 292 III. App. 3d 14, 684 N.E.2d 978 (1st Dist. IL 1997). ***PRACTICE AREAS:*** Medical Negligence; Personal Injury; Insurance Coverage. ***Email:*** bonebreak@attorneyillinois.net

MICHAEL S. FROMAN

CHICAGO, ILLINOIS

(See Skokie)

Insurance Defense, General Liability Claims Defense, Subrogation, Workers Compensation Defense, Personal Injury. Arbitration and Alternative Dispute Resolution. Corporate and Business Litigation. Probate and Estate Planning. Legal Audit and Claims Review Services.

FUCHS & ROSELLI, LTD.

440 WEST RANDOLPH STREET, SUITE 500
CHICAGO, ILLINOIS 60606-1507
Telephone: 312-651-2400
FAX: 312-651-2499
URL: http://www.frltd.com

General Civil and Trial Appellate Practice. Corporation, Federal, State and Local Tax, Real Estate, Labor, Bankruptcy, Probate, Construction, Employee Benefits, Employment and Administrative Agency Law.

JOHN T. ROSELLI, born Virginia, Minnesota, November 14, 1949; admitted to bar, 1975, Illinois; 1976, U.S Courts of Appeals, Seventh Circuit; 1981, U.S. Supreme Court. *Education:* University of Notre Dame (A.B., 1971); John Marshall Law School (J.D., with high honors, 1975). *Member:* Chicago and Illinois State Bar Associations. ***PRACTICE AREAS:*** Real Estate. ***Email:*** JRoselli@FRLtd.com

MARK H. SCHIFF, born Chicago, Illinois, March 6, 1953; admitted to bar, 1977, Illinois; 1980, U.S. Court of Appeals, Seventh Circuit; 1981, U.S. Supreme Court; 1985, U.S. Tax Court. *Education:* University of Illinois (B.S., 1974); John Marshall Law School (J.D., 1977). Phi Delta Phi. Edmund James Scholar. Adjunct Professor, John Marshall Law School, 1984-1987. *Member:* Chicago (Member, Corporate Law Committee), Illinois State and American Bar Associations; Chicago Estate Planning Council. ***PRACTICE AREAS:*** Litigation; Corporate Law; Employment Law. ***Email:*** mschiff@frltd.com

SUSAN GHELERTER, born Jacksonville, Florida, February 7, 1955; admitted to bar, 1981, New York and Illinois. *Education:* Boston University (B.A., magna cum laude, 1977); Suffolk University Law School (J.D., 1980). *Member:* Chicago and Illinois State (Member, Real Estate Law Committee) Bar Associations. ***PRACTICE AREAS:*** Real Estate. ***Email:*** SGhelerter@FRLtd.com

THOMAS W. HAYES, born St. Paul, Minnesota, August 25, 1951; admitted to bar, 1976, Minnesota; 1977, Illinois; 1979, U.S. Tax Court. *Education:* College of St. Thomas (B.A., magna cum laude, 1973); University of Notre Dame (J.D., 1976). *Member:* Chicago, Illinois and American (Member, Taxation Section) Bar Associations; Chicago Estate Planning Council. ***PRACTICE AREAS:*** Estate and Financial Planning; Business Law; Tax Law. ***Email:*** THayes@FRLtd.com

STEVEN M. RUFFALO, born Chicago, Illinois, April 2, 1962; admitted to bar, 1989, Illinois and U.S. District Court, Northern District of Illinois; 1993 Trial Bar; 1995, Eastern District of Wisconsin; U.S. Court of Appeals, Seventh Circuit. *Education:* University of Illinois (B.S., 1984); Rosary College (M.B.A., with honors, 1988); John Marshall Law School (J.D., 1988). Appeals: Guarantor Liability - 240 Ill. App. 3d 578 (1st Dist. 1992); Commercial Forcible Entry & Detainer - 276 Ill App. 3d 433 (1st Dist. 1995); RICO - 175 F3d 534 (7th Cir. 1999). *Member:* DuPage County (Chair, Labor and Employment Law Committee, 2002-2003), Chicago (Member, Civil Practice Committee, 1990-1992; Vice-Chair, Business Law and Practice Committee, 2003-2004) and Illinois State Bar Associations. ***PRACTICE AREAS:*** Civil Trials and Appeals; Business and Commercial Law. ***Email:*** SRuffalo@FRLtd.com

MICHAEL T. O'CONNOR, born Chicago, Illinois, December 27, 1962; admitted to bar, 1988, Illinois and U.S. District Court, Northern District of Illinois. *Education:* Indiana University (B.S., 1985); Loyola University (J.D., 1988). *Member:* Chicago and Illinois State Bar Associations. ***PRACTICE AREAS:*** Real Estate; Secured Lending. ***Email:*** moconnor@frltd.com

RICHARD A. HARBAUGH, born Mansfield, Ohio, November 11, 1947; admitted to bar, 1972, Illinois and U.S. District Court, Northern District of Illinois; 1986, U.S. Tax Court. *Education:* Wheaton College (B.A., cum laude, 1969); Northwestern University (J.D., 1972). Certified Public Accountant, Illinois, 1978. *Member:* Chicago and Illinois State Bar Associations. [Second Lieutenant, U.S. Army, 1972-1973]. ***PRACTICE AREAS:*** Estate Planning; Taxation; Employee Benefits; Business Law; Nonprofit Organizations. ***Email:*** RHarbaugh@FRLtd.com

EDWARD J. McGILLEN, born Chicago, Illinois, January 17, 1957; admitted to bar, 1982, Illinois and U.S. District Court, Northern District of Illinois. *Education:* Marquette University (B.A., magna cum laude, 1979); Loyola University (J.D., 1982). Alpha Sigma Nu; Phi Alpha Theta. Associate Editor, Loyola University Law Journal, Chicago, Illinois, 1981-1982. *Member:* Chicago (Member, Probate and Trust Law Committee) and Illinois State Bar Associations. ***PRACTICE AREAS:*** Estate Planning; Trust Planning; Tax Planning; Estate Administration; Trust Administration; Business Law. ***Email:*** EMcGillen@FRLtd.com

RICHARD C. PERNA, born Chicago, Illinois, May 24, 1961; admitted to bar, 1986, Illinois and U.S. District Court, Northern District of Illinois; 1997, U.S. District Court, Central District of Illinois. *Education:* St. Mary's College (B.A., 1983); Hamline University (J.D., 1986). Beta Beta Beta; Phi Alpha Delta. ***PRACTICE AREAS:*** Commercial Litigation; Loan Workout; Bankruptcy; Commercial Transactions. ***Email:*** RPerna@FRLtd.com

DAVID R. BUETOW, born Chicago, Illinois, November 20, 1970; admitted to bar, 1995, Illinois. *Education:* University of Illinois (B.A., 1992; J.D., 1995). Phi Beta Kappa; University Honors Bronze Tablet. Author, "Organization of Courts," IICLE Civil Procedure, 1997. *Member:* Chicago and Illinois State Bar Associations. ***LANGUAGES:*** Spanish. ***PRACTICE AREAS:*** Commercial Litigation; Employment Litigation. ***Email:*** dbuetow@frltd.com

TERRENCE M. LaBANT, born Cleveland, Ohio, November 30, 1966; admitted to bar, 1992, Ohio; 1995, Illinois. *Education:* John Carroll University (B.A., summa cum laude, 1989); Northwestern University School of Law (J.D., 1992). *Member:* Chicago Bar Association; Chicago Estate Planning Council; Chicago Council on Planned Giving. ***PRACTICE AREAS:*** Estate Planning; Probate; Guardianship; Tax Exempt Organizations. ***Email:*** tlabant@frltd.com

MARK R. ANDERSON, born Valparaiso, Indiana, October 10, 1973; admitted to bar, 1999, Illinois, Indiana and U.S. District Court, Northern District of Illinois and Northern

(This Listing Continued)

and Southern Districts of Indiana. *Education:* Indiana University (B.S., 1996; J.D., 1999). ***PRACTICE AREAS:*** Trusts and Estates; Corporate Law; Business Law. ***Email:*** manderson@frltd.com

ALISA M. LEVIN, born San Bernardino, California, August 27, 1975; admitted to bar, 2004, Illinois. *Education:* Arizona State University (B.S., Justice Studies, 1998); Loyola University (J.D., 2003); John Marshall Law School (LL.M., 2004). ***PRACTICE AREAS:*** Civil Litigation.

J. MATTHEW PFEIFFER, born Queens, New York, July 26, 1974; admitted to bar, 2000, Illinois and U.S. District Court, Northern District of Illinois. *Education:* Purdue University (B.S., 1997); Northern Illinois University Law School (J.D., 2000). Phi Alpha Delta. Co-Author and Speaker: "Civil Litigation: Update and Overview of Civil Practice and Procedure," Illinois State Bar Association Law Ed. Series, 2005. *Member:* Chicago, DuPage County and Illinois State (Member: Civil Practice and Procedure Section Council, 2004—; Young Lawyers' Division Section Council, 2004-2005) Bar Associations. ***PRACTICE AREAS:*** Commercial Litigation; Construction Law; Business Torts; Creditors Rights; Appellate Practice. ***Email:*** mpfeiffer@frltd.com

JAY E. PRESSER, born Toronto Canada, March 3, 1970; admitted to bar, 1996, Ohio; 1999, Illinois. *Education:* State University of New York at Buffalo (B.A., 1992); Capital University Law School (J.D., 1996; L.L.M., Taxation, 1996). *Member:* Chicago, Illinois State and American Bar Associations. ***LANGUAGES:*** French. ***PRACTICE AREAS:*** Commercial Real Estate. ***Email:*** jpresser@frltd.com

JAMES B. TOOHEY, born Erie, Pennsylvania, January 28, 1970; admitted to bar, 2000, Illinois. *Education:* Gannon University (B.A., magna cum laude, 1992); Loyola University, Chicago (J.D., 2000). Executive Editor, Loyola University Law Review, 19999-2000. Author: "A Standard with N. Moxie." *Member:* Chicago (Member, Sections on: Young Lawyers; Real Property) and American (Member, Real Property Section) Bar Associations. ***PRACTICE AREAS:*** Real Estate. ***Email:*** jtoohey@frltd.com

JOHN A. TSOUTSIAS, born Evanston, Illinois, July 2, 1974; admitted to bar, 1999, Illinois. *Education:* Miami University (B.A., Political Science, 1996); Loyola University (J.D., 1999). ***PRACTICE AREAS:*** Corporate Law; Mergers and Acquisitions. ***Email:*** JTsoutsias@FRLtd.com

JOONHO YU, born Seoul, Korea, October 8, 1973; admitted to bar, 1999, Illinois. *Education:* University of Chicago (B.A., 1995); Loyola University, Chicago (J.D., 1999). ***LANGUAGES:*** Korean. ***PRACTICE AREAS:*** Civil Litigation; Corporate Law; Appellate Practice. ***Email:*** jyu@frltd.com

OF COUNSEL

ROBERT F. FUCHS, born Milwaukee, Wisconsin, January 25, 1924; admitted to bar, 1948, Illinois. *Education:* University of Wisconsin; Harvard Law School (J.D., 1948). Member, Board of Editors, Harvard Law Review, 1946-1948. *Member:* Chicago (Chairman, Civil Rights Committee, 1958-1960; Member, Committees on: Corporation Law, 1978—; State and Local Taxation, 1954-1956; Bankruptcy and Reorganization, 1974-1976), Illinois State and American Bar Associations; Bar Association of the Seventh Federal Circuit. [U.S. Army Air Force, 1942-1945]. ***PRACTICE AREAS:*** Corporate Law; Closely Held Corporations; Civil Trials; Appeals; Employment Law.

PAUL HANSFIELD, born Chicago, Illinois, April 13, 1930; admitted to bar, 1982, Illinois. *Education:* DePaul University (B.Sc., 1951; J.D., 1982). Certified Public Accountant, Illinois, 1953. *Member:* Chicago, Illinois State and American (Member: Forum Committee on Construction Law) Bar Associations; American Institute of CPA's; Illinois Society of CPA's; AAA National Panel of Construction Arbitrators. ***PRACTICE AREAS:*** Construction Law; Mechanic's Liens; Employment Law; Creditor Bankruptcy; Mergers and Acquisitions; Accounting Malpractice.

FULTZ LAW OFFICES

CHICAGO, ILLINOIS

(See Springfield)

Criminal Defense, Family Law, Estate Planning, Real Estate, Governmental Affairs.

FUNKHOUSER VEGOSEN LIEBMAN & DUNN LTD.

Established in 1981

(Formerly, Levin & Funkhouser, Ltd.)

55 WEST MONROE STREET
SUITE 2410
CHICAGO, ILLINOIS 60603-5008
Telephone: 312-701-6800
Facsimile: 312-701-6801
Email: info@fvldlaw.com
URL: http://www.fvldlaw.com

General Corporate Practice. Corporate Litigation and White Collar Criminal Trial and Appellate Practice, Banking, Labor and Employee Relations, Business Planning, Commercial, Antitrust, Trade Regulation, Intellectual Property, Securities, Mergers and Acquisitions, Real Estate Development and Financing, Taxation, Mortgage Banking, Construction Law, Estate Planning and Probate Law, Civil Trial Practice.

DAMON E. DUNN, born East Liverpool, Ohio, May 21, 1954; admitted to bar, 1981, Illinois and U.S. District Court, Northern District of Illinois including Trial Bar; 1986, U.S. Court of Appeals, Fifth Circuit; 1989, U.S. Supreme Court; 1990, U.S. Court of Appeals, Seventh Circuit; 1991, U.S. Court of Appeals, Sixth Circuit; 1993, U.S. District Court, Central District of Illinois and U.S. Court of Appeals, Ninth Circuit. *Education:* College of Wooster (B.A., with honors, 1976); Illinois Institute of Technology/Chicago-Kent College of Law (J.D., with high honors, 1981). Member, Bar and Gavel. Chief Justice, Moot Court Society, 1980-1981. National semi-finalist, Best Brief Award, 1980 National Moot Court Competition. Assistant Legal Writing Instructor, Illinois Institute of Technology/Chicago-Kent College of Law, 1981. Adjunct Professor of Appellate Advocacy, Illinois Institute of Technology/Chicago-Kent College of Law, 1993—. *Member:* Chicago, Illinois State and American Bar Associations. ***Email:*** ddunn@fvldlaw.com

ROCHELLE SECEMSKY DYME, born Chicago, Illinois, June 11, 1955; admitted to bar, 1979, Illinois and U.S. District Court, Northern District of Illinois including Trial Bar. *Education:* University of Illinois (B.A., cum laude, with distinction, 1976); Northwestern University (J.D., 1979). Phi Kappa Phi. *Member:* Chicago, Illinois State and American Bar Associations; Chicago Council of Lawyers; Women's Bar Association of Illinois. ***Email:*** rdyme@fvldlaw.com

WILSON P. FUNKHOUSER, born Roanoke, Virginia, November 15, 1946; admitted to bar, 1973, Illinois, U.S. District Court, Northern District of Illinois and U.S. Court of Appeals, Seventh Circuit; 1975, U.S. Court of Appeals, Fourth Circuit; 1978, U.S. Supreme Court and U.S. Court of Appeals for the District of Columbia Circuit; 1983, U.S. Tax Court; 1985, U.S. Court of Appeals, Federal, Fifth and Ninth Circuits; 1993, U.S. District Court, Central District of Illinois; 1994, U.S. Court of Appeals, Eleventh Circuit and U.S. District Court, Northern District of California. *Education:* Yale University (B.A., 1969); University of Chicago (J.D., 1973). Member, University of Chicago Law Review, 1971-1972. *Member:* Chicago, Illinois State and American Bar Associations; Chicago Council of Lawyers. ***Email:*** wfunkhouser@fvldlaw.com

DANIEL T. GRAHAM, born Ames, Iowa, July 15, 1965; admitted to bar, 1990, Illinois and U.S. District Court, Northern District of Illinois; 1991, U.S. District Court, Western District of Wisconsin; 1993, U.S. District Court, Western District of Michigan, U.S. District Court, Northern District of Indiana and U.S. District Court, Central District of Illinois; 1998, U.S. District Court, Eastern District of Wisconsin, U.S. District Court, Eastern District of Michigan. *Education:* Loras College (B.A., maxima cum laude, 1987); University of Iowa (J.D., with distinction, 1990). Phi Delta Phi. Recipient: Loras Presidential Scholarship. Best Advocate, Van Oosterhaut Memorial All-School Moot Court Competition, 1989. National Moot Court Team Captain, 1989-1990. Second Vice-Chairperson, Moot Court Board, 1990. Author: Comment, "An Economic Analysis of *Shapero v. Kentucky Bar Association:* Is There Any Possibility of Overreaching in Targeted Direct Mail Solicitation?" 14 J. Corp. Law 809, 1989; "Detente: The Great Illusion," DES All-College Writing, 1985; "Short Sheeted," Outlet Literary Magazine, 1987. *Member:* Chicago, Illinois State and American Bar Associations. ***Email:*** dgraham@fvldlaw.com

JAMES F. GROTH, born Madison, Wisconsin, February 8, 1967; admitted to bar, 1992, Illinois and U.S. District Court, Northern District of Illinois; 1996, U.S. Court of Appeals, Seventh Circuit. *Education:* University of Wisconsin-Madison (B.B.A., 1989); Northwestern University (J.D., cum laude, 1992). Order of the Coif. Note and Comment Editor, Northwestern University Law Review, 1991-1992. Author: Comment, "Can Regulators Force Bank Holding Companies to Bail Out Their Failing Subsidiaries? -- An Analysis of the Federal Reserve Board's Source-of-Strength Doctrine," 86 Northwestern University Law Review 112, 1991. *Member:* Chicago and American Bar Associations. ***Email:*** jgroth@fvldlaw.com

HAL "CORKY" KESSLER, born Chicago, Illinois, November 12, 1949; admitted to bar, 1974, Illinois and U.S. District Court, Northern District of Illinois; 1985, U.S. Court of Appeals, Seventh Circuit. *Education:* The Ohio State University (B.S.B.A., 1971); John Marshall Law School (J.D., cum laude, 1974). Adjunct Professor, Entertainment and Business Law, John Marshall Law School. *Member:* Chicago and American Bar Associations. ***Email:*** ckessler@fvldlaw.com

VANCE L. LIEBMAN, born Milwaukee, Wisconsin, August 12, 1952; admitted to bar, 1977, Illinois and U.S. District Court, Northern District of Illinois including Trial Bar; 1983, U.S. Tax Court; 1985, U.S. Court of Appeals, Fifth Circuit; 1989, U.S. Supreme Court; 1991, U.S. Court of Appeals, Seventh Circuit. *Education:* Grinnell College (B.A., with honors, 1974); Northwestern University (J.D., cum laude, 1977). *Member:* Chicago, Illinois State and American Bar Associations. ***Email:*** vliebman@fvldlaw.com

GLENN A. RICE, born Chicago, Illinois, November 11, 1959; admitted to bar, 1985, Illinois; 1986, U.S. District Court, Northern District of Illinois. *Education:* Northern Illinois University (B.S., 1982); Illinois Institute of Technology/Chicago-Kent College of Law (J.D., with honors, 1985). Member, Chicago-Kent Law Review, 1984-1985. Co-Author: "Evidence: Application and Refinement of the Federal Rules of Evidence in the Seventh Circuit," 61 Chicago-Kent Law Review 395, 1985. Legal Writing Teaching Assistant, Chicago-Kent College of Law, 1984-1985. Law Clerk to the Honorable William G. Clark, Illinois Supreme Court, 1986-1988. *Member:* Chicago and American Bar Associations. ***Email:*** grice@fvldlaw.com

JONATHAN VEGOSEN, born Long Branch, New Jersey, November 18, 1949; admitted to bar, 1976, Illinois; 1977, U.S. District Court, Northern District of Illinois and U.S. Court of Appeals, Seventh Circuit; 1983, U.S. Tax Court; 1985, U.S. Court of Appeals, Fifth Circuit. *Education:* Northwestern University (B.A., with distinction, 1973; J.D., cum laude, 1976). Phi Beta Kappa. Member, Editorial Board, Journal of Criminal Law and Criminology, 1975-1976. Author: "Schneckloth v. Bustamonte: The Question of Noncustodial and Custodial Consent Searches," 66 Journal of Criminal Law and Criminology 286, 1975. Law Clerk to the Honorable Edwin A. Robson, U.S. District Court, Northern District of Illinois, 1976-1978. *Member:* Chicago and American Bar Associations. ***Email:*** jvegosen@fvldlaw.com

OF COUNSEL

DENISE M. CHAN, born Chicago, Illinois, January 21, 1972; admitted to bar, 1998, Illinois. *Education:* Northwestern University (B.A., with honors, 1993); University of Illinois (J.D., 1998). Member and Notes Editor, University of Illinois Law Review. Co-Editor-in-Chief, Poetic Justice. Note Author: "ERISA Preemption: Immunity for HMOs," 98 U. ILL. L. Rev. 199, 1998. *Member:* Chicago Bar Association (Member, Trust Law Committee); Chicago Estate Planning Council (Associate Member). ***Email:*** dchan@fvldlaw.com

LAWRENCE R. LEVIN, born Chicago, Illinois, March 25, 1939; admitted to bar, 1965, Illinois; 1966, U.S. District Court, Northern District of Illinois including Trial Bar and Middle District of Alabama; U.S. Court of Appeals, Fifth and Seventh Circuits; 1969, U.S. Supreme Court; 1978, U.S. Court of Appeals for the District of Columbia Circuit; 1983, U.S. Tax Court; 1985, U.S. Court of Appeals, Federal, Ninth and Eleventh Circuits.

(This Listing Continued)

FUNKHOUSER VEGOSEN LIEBMAN & DUNN LTD., Chicago—Continued

Education: University of Arizona (B.A., 1962); Yale University (LL.B., 1965). Order of the Coif; Phi Alpha Theta. Assistant in Instruction, Yale University, 1964-1965, Law Clerk to the Honorable Richard T. Rives, U.S. Court of Appeals, Fifth Circuit, 1965-1966. *Member:* Chicago (Member, Anti-Trust Law Committee, 1970—) and American Bar Associations. ***Email:*** llevin@fvldlaw.com

SHARON BETH-HALACHMY, born Tel Aviv, Israel, May 23, 1968; admitted to bar, 1996, Illinois. *Education:* Claremont McKenna College (B.A., 1990); University of Illinois College of Law (J.D., magna cum laude, 1996). Co-Editor and Co-Founder, *Poetic Justice,* a literary journal of the College of Law. Participant, one semester, International Human Rights Seminar, Hebrew University/Tulane Law School, in Israel. *Member:* Chicago and American Bar Associations. ***Email:*** sbethhalachmy@fvldlaw.com

ERIC D. BOLANDER, born Des Plaines, Illinois, February 5, 1969; admitted to bar, 2002, Illinois. *Education:* University of Iowa (B.S., 1991); University of Illinois (J.D., 2002). Member and Administrative Editor, The Elder Law Journal. Teaching Assistant, College of Law Legal Research and Writing Department. *Member:* Chicago Bar Association. ***Email:*** ebolander@fvldlaw.com

DANIEL M. HINKLE, born Rochester, New York, September 24, 1975; admitted to bar, 2004, Illinois. *Education:* Brown University (A.B., magna cum laude, 1998); Harvard Law School (J.D., magna cum laude, 2004). *Member:* Chicago Bar Association. ***Email:*** dhinkle@fvldlaw.com

NEIL M. ROSENBAUM, born Detroit, Michigan, April 12, 1979; admitted to bar, 2004, Illinois. *Education:* University of Michigan (B.A., 2001); Chicago-Kent College of Law (J.D., 2004). *Member:* Chicago, Illinois State and American Bar Associations. ***Email:*** nrosenbaum@fvldlaw.com

DARA SAHEBJAMI, born Cincinnati, Ohio, September 22, 1973; admitted to bar, 1998, Illinois. *Education:* Northwestern University (B.A., with honors, 1995); Georgetown University (J.D., 1998). *Member:* Chicago, Illinois State and American Bar Associations. ***Email:*** dsahebjami@fvldlaw.com

GALARNYK & ASSOCIATES

70 W. MADISON STREET, SUITE 2100
CHICAGO, ILLINOIS 60602-4253
Telephone: 312-441-5800
Fax: 312-853-1169
Email: jgalarnyk@galarnykandassociates.com

Business Law, Commercial, Contract, Employment, Unfair Competition, Securities, White Collar Defense, General Civil Litigation.

MEMBER OF FIRM

JOHN D. GALARNYK, born Madison, Wisconsin, July 14, 1960; admitted to bar, 1985, Illinois. *Education:* University of Wisconsin-Madison (B.A., 1982); John Marshall Law School (J.D., 1985). *Member:* Chicago, Illinois State and American Bar Associations. ***PRACTICE AREAS:*** Business Law; Commercial Litigation; Civil Litigation. ***Email:*** jgalarnyk@galarnykandassociates.com

GARDNER CARTON & DOUGLAS LLP

191 NORTH WACKER DRIVE, SUITE 3700
CHICAGO, ILLINOIS 60606-1698
Telephone: 312-569-1000
Facsimile: 312-569-3000
Email: gcdinfo@gcd.com
URL: http://www.gcd.com

Washington, D.C. Office: Suite 900, East Tower, 1301 K Street, N.W. 20005-3317. Telephone: 202-230-5000. Facsimile: 202-230-5300.
Milwaukee, Wisconsin Office: 777 East Wisconsin Avenue, Suite 2000, 53202-5319. Telephone: 414-221-6040. Facsimile: 414-224-1025.
Albany, New York Office: 321 Great Oaks Boulevard, 12203-5971. Telephone: 518-452-8787. Facsimile: 518-452-8767.

Corporate Law, Corporate Restructuring, Environmental, Financial Markets Litigation, Government Relations, Health Law, Hedge Funds, HR Law (Employee Benefits and Labor and Employment), Indian Tribal Governments, Intellectual Property, Litigation and Dispute Resolution, Real Estate, Taxation, Wealth Planning and Philanthropy.

LAW FIRM ALLIANCES/ASSOCIATIONS: ***WORLD LAW GROUP***

PARTNERS OF FIRM

HENRY A. GARDNER (1883-1968)

ALFRED T. CARTON (1884-1968)

JAMES H. DOUGLAS, JR. (1899-1988)

RICHARD G. AGIN, born New York, New York, January 4, 1961; admitted to bar, 1988, Illinois and U.S. District Court, Northern District of Illinois; 1991, U.S. Court of Appeals, Seventh Circuit. *Education:* Princeton University (A.B., magna cum laude, 1983); Northwestern University (J.D., 1988). Legal Counsel, Office of the Governor (Illinois), 1993-1995. ***PRACTICE AREAS:*** Commercial Litigation. ***Email:*** ragin@gcd.com

KEITH R. ANDERSON, born Joliet, Illinois; admitted to bar, 1982, District of Columbia; 1989, U.S. Supreme Court; 1999, Illinois. *Education:* DePauw University (B.A., cum laude, 1979); George Washington University (J.D., 1982). Editor-in-Chief, George Washington Journal of International Law and Economics, 1981-1982. Law Clerk to Hon.

(This Listing Continued)

Norma Holloway Johnson, U.S. District Court for the District of Columbia, 1984. *Member:* The District of Columbia Bar; Illinois State and American Bar Associations; American Health Lawyers Association. ***PRACTICE AREAS:*** Health Care Law; Corporate Transactions; Corporate Law. ***Email:*** kanderson@gcd.com

CATHY KISELYAK AUSTIN, born Oak Harbor, Washington, April 9, 1954; admitted to bar, 1980, Illinois; 1989, Iowa. *Education:* Massachusetts Institute of Technology (S.B., 1976); Yale University (J.D., 1980). Chairman, Keokuk Zoning Board of Adjustment, 1990-1997. ***LANGUAGES:*** German. ***PRACTICE AREAS:*** Intellectual Property; Copyrights; E-Commerce; Technology Law; Privacy Law; Trade Secrets; Technology Joint Ventures. ***Email:*** caustin@gcd.com

WARREN von CREDO BAKER, born Philadelphia, Pennsylvania, October 18, 1948; admitted to bar, 1975, Illinois and U.S. District Court, Northern District of Illinois. *Education:* University of Pennsylvania (B.S., 1970); John Marshall Law School (J.D., 1975). Vice Chairman, Litigation Department. President, Andover/Abbot Regional Association, 1990. Executive Committee, Big Brothers Big Sisters of Chicago Campaign. ***PRACTICE AREAS:*** Domestic and International Complex Commercial Litigation; Intellectual Property; Employment Relations; Contracts; Securities; Business Torts; Products Liability; Higher Education; Antitrust; Health Care; Alternative Dispute Resolution; Internal Investigations; General Corporate Law. ***Email:*** wbaker@gcd.com

CHRISTOPHER J. BARBER, admitted to bar, 1986, Illinois. *Education:* Ohio State University (B.S.B.A., 1981); University of Mississippi (J.D., 1985). ***PRACTICE AREAS:*** Litigation; Arbitration. ***Email:*** cbarber@gcd.com

MICHAEL E. BARRY, born Peoria, Illinois, August 1, 1953; admitted to bar, 1978, Illinois; 1990, Wisconsin and U.S. District Court, Northern District of Illinois, including Trial Bar. *Education:* Harvard University (B.A., 1975); University of Notre Dame (J.D., 1978). *Member:* Chicago and American Bar Associations; State Bar of Wisconsin. ***PRACTICE AREAS:*** Antitrust and Trade Regulation; Antitrust; Business Law; Business Dispute Resolution; Litigation. ***Email:*** mbarry@gcd.com

THOMAS A. BELUSH, born Cincinnati, Ohio, December 10, 1964; admitted to bar, 1991, Illinois, Indiana, U.S. District Court, Northern District of Illinois and U.S. District Court, Northern and Southern Districts of Indiana; registered to practice before U.S. Patent and Trademark Office. *Education:* Purdue University (B.S.M.E., 1987); Indiana University (J.D., 1991). *Member:* American Intellectual Property Law Association. ***Email:*** tbelush@gcd.com

LUIS A. BERRONES, born Del Rio, Texas, July 25, 1957; admitted to bar, 1983, Illinois; U.S. District Court, Northern District of Illinois, including Trial Bar, U.S. District Court, Eastern District of Michigan, U.S. Court of Appeals, Sixth and Seventh Circuits and U.S. Supreme Court. *Education:* DePaul University (B.A., with high honors in Political Science, 1980; J.D., 1983). Pi Gamma Mu; Phi Alpha Delta; Blue Key. Member, De Paul Law Review, 1981-1982. Assistant State's Attorney, Lake County State's Attorney's Office, 1983-1987. Arbitrator, Lake County Mandatory Arbitration Programs. *Member:* American Bar Association; Defense Research Institute. ***LANGUAGES:*** Spanish. ***PRACTICE AREAS:*** Commercial Litigation; Products Liability; Complex Litigation. ***Email:*** lberrones@gcd.com

RICHARD P. BLESSEN, born 1961; admitted to bar, 1986, Illinois. *Education:* Valparaiso University (B.A., cum laude, 1983); University of Illinois (J.D., magna cum laude, 1986). *Member:* Chicago and American Bar Associations. ***PRACTICE AREAS:*** Corporate; Real Estate. ***Email:*** rblessen@gcd.com

W. DAVID BRAUN, born Chicago, Illinois, June 25, 1950; admitted to bar, 1975, Illinois; 1985, District of Columbia. *Education:* University of Illinois (B.A., with distinction, 1972); University of Notre Dame (J.D., 1975); Notre Dame London Centre for Legal Studies (1973-1974); University of Munich (1978-1979). Co-Author: with Dr. L. Ritter and F. Rawlinson "European Competition Law: a Practitioner's Guide," 2nd. ed. Kluwer, 2000. Trial Attorney, Midwest Field Office, Antitrust Division, U.S. Department of Justice, 1975-1978; Attorney, Office of Policy Planning, Antitrust Division, U.S. Department of Justice, 1979-1981; Trial Attorney, Foreign Commerce Section, Antitrust Division, U.S. Department of Justice, 1981-1984. Research Fellow, Max Planck Institute for Foreign and International Patent, Copyright and Competition Law, Munich, Germany, 1978-1979. ***LANGUAGES:*** German. ***PRACTICE AREAS:*** Antitrust and Trade Regulation; Corporate Law; International Trade. ***Email:*** dbraun@gcd.com

JENNIFER R. BREUER, born Chicago, Illinois, September 27, 1966; admitted to bar, 1995, Illinois. *Education:* Wesleyan University (B.A., 1988); Northwestern University (J.D., 1995). Strategy consultant to the worldwide pharmaceutical biotechnology and medical device industries at the Wilkerson Group (now IBM Consulting) New York, New York, 1988-1992. *Member:* Illinois Association of Healthcare Attorneys; American Health Lawyers Association. ***PRACTICE AREAS:*** Health Care Regulation; Corporate Compliance; Privacy; Medicare; Health Care Reimbursement; Health Law Fraud. ***Email:*** jbreuer@gcd.com

EDWIN E. BROOKS, admitted to bar, 1986, Illinois; U.S. District Court, Northern District of Illinois including Trial Bar; U.S. District Court, Southern District of Illinois; U.S. District Court, Eastern District of Wisconsin; U.S. District Court, District of Delaware; U.S. District Court, Eastern District of Michigan; U.S. Court of Appeals, Sixth and Seventh Circuits; U.S. Supreme Court. *Education:* Alma College (B.A.); DePaul University (J.D.). Adjunct Professor, Northwestern University Law School. ***PRACTICE AREAS:*** Litigation. ***Email:*** ebrooks@gcd.com

GREGORY K. BROWN, born December 9, 1951; admitted to bar, 1976, Illinois. *Education:* University of Kentucky (B.S., 1973); University of Illinois (J.D., 1976). Order of the Coif. *Member:* American (Chair, ESOP Subcommittee, Employee Benefits Committee, Taxation Section) and Illinois State (Past Chair, Employee Benefits Section Council) Bar Associations; ESOP Association (Past Member, Board of Directors; Past Chair, Legislative and Regulatory Committee); International Pension and Employee Benefits Lawyers Association (Past Member, Steering Committee). ***PRACTICE AREAS:*** ERISA; Executive Compensation Law; Employee Stock Ownership Plans (ESOPs). ***Email:*** gkbrown@gcd.com

L. EDWARD BRYANT, JR., born Olney, Illinois, December 2, 1941; admitted to bar, 1967, Illinois. *Education:* Northwestern University (B.S., Jour., 1963; J.D., 1967). Rated #1

(This Listing Continued)

by Chambers USA, Leading Lawyers, Best Lawyers and Super Lawyers, from their inception. Chairman: IICLE course on Health Law '74; frequent IICLE health law faculty; NU Law School Health Law Symposium, 1985-1986. Lecturer on health law, NU Kellogg School of Management and Loyola Law School, 1986-1992. Catholic Health Association Legal Advisory Committee. Named one of the nation's top health lawyers *National Law Journal,* 1985; Top health lawyers *Chicago Lawyer,* 1991. Co-founder: American Society of Hospital Attorneys, 1969. Co-founder, 1976 and President, 1979, Illinois Association of Healthcare Attorneys. Founder of the firm's Health Law Department, 1979. Firm's Management Committee, 1980-1989. Firm's Practice Council Chairman, 1995-1997. Chairman of the Firm's Practice Council, 1985-1987. Director and Chairman, Sisters of Charity of Leavenworth Health System, 1997-2004. Director, Rehabilitation Institute of Chicago. *Member:* American Health Lawyers Association; Illinois Association of Health Attorneys. ***PRACTICE AREAS:*** Health Care; Corporate Law; Antitrust and Trade Regulation; Administrative Law; Nonprofit and Charitable Organizations. ***Email:*** ebryant@gcd.com

THOMAS BURANOSKY, born McKees Rocks, Pennsylvania, June 11, 1963; admitted to bar, 1988, Illinois. *Education:* Yale University (B.A., 1985); University of Chicago (J.D., 1988). ***PRACTICE AREAS:*** Real Estate. ***Email:*** tburanosky@gcd.com

CRYSTAL PRUESS BUSH, born Chicago, Illinois, February 12, 1955; admitted to bar, 1979, Illinois. *Education:* Yale University (B.A., cum laude, 1976); Harvard University (J.D., cum laude, 1979). Co-Author: "1988-1989 Illinois Law Survey, Real Property and Real Estate Transactions," Loyola University of Chicago Law Journal, Vol. 21, Number 2, Winter, 1990. *Member:* Chicago Bar Association; Chicago Mortgage Attorneys' Association; Chicago Real Estate Executive Women. ***PRACTICE AREAS:*** Real Estate; Real Estate Acquisitions; Real Estate Brokerage Law; Real Estate Finance; Real Estate Leasing. ***Email:*** cbush@gcd.com

CHARLES L. BYRUM, born San Antonio, Texas, September 13, 1944; admitted to bar, 1969, Illinois. *Education:* DePauw University (A.B., 1966); Northwestern University (J.D., cum laude, 1969). *Member:* Chicago (Real Property Law Committee) and Illinois State Bar Associations. ***PRACTICE AREAS:*** Real Estate; Land Acquisitions; Land Sales; Real Estate Development; Real Estate Leasing. ***Email:*** cbyrum@gcd.com

DARREN S. CAHR, born Park Ridge, Illinois, October 31, 1968; admitted to bar, 1993, Illinois and U.S. District Court, Northern District of Illinois; 1996, U.S. District Court, Central District of Illinois, U.S. Court of Appeals, Seventh Circuit and U.S. Supreme Court. *Education:* Northwestern University (B.A., 1990; J.D., 1993). Author: "March Madness: Dual Use Trademarks, Reverse Confusion and First Amendment," Selected Legal Papers. *Member:* American Bar Association; Promotion Marketing Association of America. ***PRACTICE AREAS:*** Intellectual Property; Trade Regulation; Litigation. ***Email:*** dcahr@gcd.com

TROY M. CALKINS, admitted to bar, 1991, Illinois; 2001, District of Columbia. *Education:* Michigan State University (B.A., 1988); University of Michigan Law School (J.D., 1991). *Member:* American Bar Association (Member, Committee on Federal Regulation of Securities). ***PRACTICE AREAS:*** Corporate Law; Employee Benefits; Securities. ***Email:*** tcalkins@gcd.com

TIMOTHY J. CAREY, born 1951; admitted to bar, 1980, Georgia; 1981, Illinois. *Education:* University of Notre Dame (B.A., 1973; J.D., summa cum laude, 1980); Bryant College (M.B.A., with honors, 1977). ***PRACTICE AREAS:*** Commodities; Derivatives; Securities Litigation; Commercial Litigation. ***Email:*** tcarey@gcd.com

DENNIS J. CARLIN, born Chicago, Illinois, August 23, 1941; admitted to bar, 1967, Illinois. *Education:* University of Wisconsin (B.B.A., 1963); DePaul University (J.D., 1967); Georgetown University (LL.M., in Taxation, 1971). Beta Alpha Psi; Pi Gamma Mu. Editor-in-Chief, DePaul University Law Review, 1967. Certified Public Accountant, Illinois, 1963. Member and Lecturer, Advisory Committee, NYU Annual Institute on Federal Taxation, 1978-1983; National Real Estate Development Center, 1991-1995; National Institute of Tax Professionals, 1991; National Institute on Real Estate Taxation, 1991-1992. Lecturer, ALI-ABA Seminar, Creative Tax Planning for Real Estate, 1987-1991. Vice Chairman of the Board, Council for Jewish Elderly. *Member:* Chicago (Chairman, Committee on Federal Taxation, 1982-1983), Illinois State (Member, Federal Taxation Council, 1977-1979, 1985-1986) and American (Member, Section of Taxation, Committee on Real Estate Taxation, 1977) Bar Associations. Fellow, American College of Tax Counsel. ***PRACTICE AREAS:*** Business Law; Business Reorganization; Business Successions; Closely Held Business Law; Taxation. ***Email:*** dcarlin@gcd.com

TIMOTHY R. CASEY, born Evergreen Park, Illinois, June 7, 1956; admitted to bar, 1981, Illinois and U.S. District Court, Northern District of Illinois; 1990, U.S. District Court, Northern District of Illinois, Trial Bar. *Education:* John Carroll University (B.A., 1978); John Marshall Law School (J.D., 1981). *Member:* Chicago Bar Association. ***PRACTICE AREAS:*** Bankruptcy; Commercial Law; Debtor and Creditor. ***Email:*** tcasey@gcd.com

PATRICK S. COFFEY, born Madison, Wisconsin, February 14, 1958; admitted to bar, 1984, Illinois, U.S. District Court, Northern District of Illinois, including Trial Bar and U.S. Court of Appeals, Seventh Circuit; 1989, Wisconsin; 1993, U.S. District Court, Eastern District of Wisconsin and U.S. District Court, Eastern District of Michigan. *Education:* University of Wisconsin (B.A., 1980); IIT/Chicago-Kent College of Law (J.D., with high honors, 1984). *Member:* Chicago and American Bar Associations; State Bar of Wisconsin. ***PRACTICE AREAS:*** Civil Litigation; Commercial Litigation; Corporate Litigation; White Collar Crime; Litigation; White Collar Criminal Defense. ***Email:*** pcoffey@gcd.com

N. PAUL COYLE, born Chicago, Illinois, January 19, 1968; admitted to bar, 1994, Illinois. *Education:* DePaul University (B.S., 1991); John Marshall Law School (J.D., 1994). Certified Public Accountant, Illinois, 1992. Author: "Dissolution and Liquidation of Partnerships," I.I.C.L.E., 1994-1997. Adjunct Professor, Agency and Partnership Law, The John Marshall Law School, 1997-1998. *Member:* Chicago and American Bar Associations; Illinois Institute of Certified Public Accountants; American Association of Attorneys - Certified Public Accountants. ***PRACTICE AREAS:*** Corporate; Investment Management. ***Email:*** pcoyle@gcdc.com

BARBARA A. CRONIN, born Chicago, Illinois, February 2, 1946; admitted to bar, 1982, Illinois and U.S. District Court, Northern District of Illinois; 1987, U.S. Tax Court. *Education:* University of Illinois (B.A., 1967); DePaul University (J.D. with honors, 1982). Member, De Paul University Law Review, 1981-1982. Co-Author: "Taxation of Distributors: Planning for the Employee," Employee Benefits Law, Ill. Inst. for CLE, 1987; "Qualified Deferred Compensation Plans," Pub. Callaghan, 1990-1993. Instructor, Employee Benefits Law, Roosevelt University Paralegal Institute, 1991-1993. *Member:* Chicago and American Bar Associations. ***PRACTICE AREAS:*** Employee Benefits; Qualified Retirement Plans; Non-Qualified Benefits; Welfare Benefits; Mergers and Acquisitions. ***Email:*** bcronin@gcd.com

MICHAEL F. CSAR, born Chicago, Illinois, May 26, 1950; admitted to bar, 1977, Illinois. *Education:* Yale University (B.A., summa cum laude, 1972, Phi Beta Kappa); King's College; Cambridge University, Cambridge, England (B.A., 1974); Yale University (J.D., 1977). *Member:* American Bar Association (Member, Sections on: Corporation, Banking and Business Law; Real Property, Probate and Trust Law); Chicago District Council, Urban Land Institute; Building Owners and Managers Association; National Association of Real Estate Investment Trusts. ***PRACTICE AREAS:*** Real Estate; Corporate; Partnership. ***Email:*** mcsar@gcd.com

JOHN T. CUSACK, born Oak Park, Illinois, June 22, 1935; admitted to bar, 1960, Illinois; 1961, U.S. District Court, Northern District of Illinois, including Trial Bar; 1966, U.S. Supreme Court; 1973, U.S. Court of Appeals, Seventh Circuit; 1975, U.S. Courts of Appeals, Fifth and Ninth Circuits; 1982, U.S. District Court, Northern District of Indiana; 1984, U.S. Tax Court; 1986, U.S. Court of Appeals, Third Circuit; 1987, U.S. Court of Appeals, Tenth Circuit. *Education:* University of Notre Dame (A.B., cum laude, 1957); University of Michigan (J.D., 1960); Harvard University Graduate School of Business Administration, 1961-1962. Trial Attorney, Antitrust Division, U.S. Department of Justice, 1962-1970. *Member:* Chicago (Member, Antitrust Law Committee, 1971—) and American (Member, Sections on: Antitrust Law; Litigation; Health Law Committee) Bar Associations; Bar Association of the Seventh Federal Circuit. ***PRACTICE AREAS:*** Antitrust; Trade Regulations; Criminal Law; Criminal Antitrust; Litigation. ***Email:*** jcusack@gcd.com

ANTONIO DeBLASIO, born Oak Park, Illinois, April 26, 1969; admitted to bar, 1994, Illinois and U.S. District Court, Northern District of Illinois; 1997, U.S. District Court, Central District of Illinois; 1998, U.S. District Court, Southern District of Illinois including Trial Bar. *Education:* Purdue University (B.A., with highest distinction, 1991); The John Marshall Law School (J.D., cum laude, 1994). Editor, The John Marshall Law Review, 1993-1994. Judicial Extern, Hon. George W. Lindberg, U.S. District Court, Northern District of Illinois, 1992. *Member:* Chicago and American Bar Associations. ***LANGUAGES:*** Italian. ***REPORTED CASES:*** Federal Trade Comm'n v. Freeman Hospital, 911 F.Supp. 1213 (W.D. Mo. 1995), aff'd, 69 F.3d 260 (8th Cir. 1995). ***PRACTICE AREAS:*** Antitrust and Trade Regulation; Health Care Litigation; Intellectual Property Litigation; Civil Litigation; Commercial Litigation; Arbitration. ***Email:*** adeblasio@gcd.com

SHEILA H. DEELY, born Chicago, Illinois, December 5, 1970; admitted to bar, 1996, Illinois and U.S. District Court, Northern and Central Districts of Illinois. *Education:* Purdue University (B.A., 1992); Chicago-Kent College of Law, Illinois Institute of Technology (J.D., with honors, 1996). Member, Moot Court Honor Society. Member, Chicago-Kent Law Review, 1994-1996. Author, "Innocent Misrepresentation Voids Termination Agreement," Commercial Leasing Law & Strategy, July 1997. Co-Author: "Historic Preservation, The Year In Review," Section on Natural Resources, Environment, and Energy Law, SONREEL, 1996-1998; "Regulation of Wetlands," BNA Environmental Due Diligence Guide, July 1998 and Update, August 1998; Asbestos Chapter, "Asbestos, Environmental Aspects of Real Estate Transactions," American Bar Association, 1998; "Being Smart About Wetlands," The Practical Real Estate Lawyer, January 1999. *Member:* Chicago (Member, Environmental Law Committee), Illinois State and American (Member, Natural Resources, Energy and Environmental Law Section) Bar Associations. ***SPECIAL AGENCIES:*** U.S. Environmental Protection Agency; Illinois Pollution Control Board; U.S. Army Corps of Engineers; Illinois Environmental Protection Agency; Federal Emergency Management Agency. ***REPORTED CASES:*** United States v. Hallmark Construction Co., 30 F. Supp. 2d 1033 (N.D. IL 1998); United States v. United Homes of Illinois, 1998 U.S. Dist. Lexis 2354 (N.D. Il. 1999). ***PRACTICE AREAS:*** Real Estate; Environmental. ***Email:*** sdeely@gcd.com

STEPHANIE LEE DODGE, born Urbana, Illinois, May 6, 1968; admitted to bar, 1993, Illinois. *Education:* University of Illinois (B.S., 1990; J.D., 1993). *Member:* Chicago and Illinois State Bar Associations. ***PRACTICE AREAS:*** Labor and Employment. ***Email:*** sdodge@gcd.com

MICHAEL DUFFY, born Chicago, Illinois, October 3, 1951; admitted to bar, 1978, Illinois, U.S. District Court, Northern District of Illinois, District of Colorado, Eastern District of Wisconsin and U.S. Court of Appeals, Fifth and Seventh Circuits. *Education:* Kenyon College (A.B., 1973); Loyola University of Chicago (J.D., 1978). Assistant State's Attorney of Lake County, Illinois, 1979-1983. ***PRACTICE AREAS:*** Civil and Criminal Litigation; Product Liability Defense; Health Care Litigation; Real Estate Litigation. ***Email:*** mduffy@gcd.com

KAREN A. ERIKSON, born Santa Monica, California, June 18, 1967; admitted to bar, 1993, California; 1998, Illinois. *Education:* University of Southern California (B.S., 1989); George Washington University (J.D., 1993). *Member:* Chicago Bar Association. ***PRACTICE AREAS:*** Information Technology; E-Commerce; Technology Law; Privacy Law; Health Information Technology; Intellectual Property; Copyrights; Trade Secrets; Tech Ventures. ***Email:*** kerikson@gcd.com

WILLIAM P. FARRELL, JR., born Philadelphia, Pennsylvania, February 13, 1968; admitted to bar, 1993, Illinois; 1996, U.S. District Court, Northern District of Illinois including Trial Bar; U.S. Court of Appeals, Seventh Circuit; U.S. Tax Court. *Education:* Indiana University School of Business (B.S., 1990); University of Notre Dame (J.D., 1993). Thomas J. White Scholar. *Member:* Chicago and American Bar Associations; American Society of Association Executives; Association Forum of Chicagoland. ***PRACTICE AREAS:*** White Collar Criminal Defense; Non-Profit and Trade Associations; Corporate Transactions; Commercial Litigation. ***Email:*** wfarrell@gcd.com

GLENN E. FERENCZ, born Chicago, Illinois, June 23, 1950; admitted to bar, 1976, Illinois. *Education:* University of Illinois (B.A., with honors, 1973); University of Michigan (J.D., cum laude, 1976). Certified Public Accountant, Illinois, 1973. *Member:* Ameri-

(This Listing Continued)

GARDNER CARTON & DOUGLAS LLP, Chicago—Continued

can (Member, Section of Taxation) Bar Association. ***PRACTICE AREAS:*** Taxation; Tax Planning; Corporate Law; Corporate Tax Planning; Partnership Law. ***Email:*** gferencz@gcd.com

SCOTT J. FISHER, born Southfield, Michigan, October 11, 1971; admitted to bar, 1996, Illinois, U.S. District Court, Northern District of Illinois and U.S. Court of Appeals, Seventh Circuit; 1999, U.S. Court of Appeals, Sixth and Ninth Circuits. *Education:* The Ohio State University (B.A., 1993); Chicago-Kent College of Law, Illinois Institute of Technology (J.D., highest honors, 1996) Order of the Coif. Adjunct Faculty Member, Chicago-Kent College of Law, 2001-2002. *Member:* Chicago Bar Association (Member, Judicial Evaluation Committee, 2001—). ***REPORTED CASES:*** Zipser v. AccuFix Research Institute, FNC, 253 F. 3d 1180 (9th Cir. 2001). ***PRACTICE AREAS:*** Complex Commercial Litigation; Class Action Litigation; Bankruptcy Litigation. ***Email:*** sfisher@gcd.com

QUIN R. FRAZER, born Long Beach, California, March 14, 1945; admitted to bar, 1975, Illinois. *Education:* St. Pius X Seminary (A.A., 1965); Mount St. Paul College (B.A., 1968); University of Notre Dame (J.D., 1975). *Member:* Chicago, Illinois State and American Bar Associations. ***PRACTICE AREAS:*** Corporate Law; Closely Held Corporations; Nonprofit and Charitable Organizations; Tax Exempt Organizations; Taxation; Federal Estate and Gift Taxation; Trusts and Estates; Estate Planning; Family Wealth Transfer. ***Email:*** qfrazer@gcd.com

CHARLES A. FREEMAN, born Chicago, Illinois, April 28, 1938; admitted to bar, 1963, Illinois, U.S. District Court, Northern District of Illinois and U.S. Court of Appeals, Sixth and Seventh Circuits. *Education:* University of Illinois (B.S., 1959); DePaul University (J.D., 1963). Pi Gamma Mu. Phi Alpha Delta. Author: "Partial Plant Closure —Duty to Bargain," Illinois State Bar Association, Young Members Conference Newsletter, May, 1970; "Controlling Alcohol and Drug Abuse in the Work Place: Release of Information to Employers," Topics in Health Records Management, Aspen Publishers, Inc., September, 1987; "Aids in the Workplace," Topics in Health Record Management, Aspen Publishers, Inc., 1987. Co-Author: "NLRB's St. Francis Decision Signals Broader-Based Bargaining Units," Health Progress, May 1985; "Employment-Related Issues and Considerations," *Merging Health Care Institutions - A Guidebook for Buyers and Sellers,* American Hospital Publishing, Inc., 1987. *Member:* Chicago, Illinois State and American Bar Associations. ***PRACTICE AREAS:*** Labor and Employment; Collective Bargaining; Equal Employment Opportunity Law; Labor Relations; Management Labor Law. ***Email:*** cfreeman@gcd.com

KEVIN L. FREEMAN, born Chicago, Illinois, May 25, 1969; admitted to bar, 1994, Illinois; U.S. District Court, Northern District of Illinois. *Education:* Northwestern University (B.A., 1991); University of Chicago Law School (J.D., 1994). Board Member: Cook County Zoning Board of Appeals, 1998—; Illinois Property Tax Appeals Board, 2003—; American Cancer Society, 2004—; Public Interest Law Initiative, 2003—; Cook County Commission on Human Rights, 1996-1998; Street-Level Youth Media, 2002-2004; Parkways Foundation YPO, 2002-2004. Fellow: Leadership Greater Chicago, 2005-2006. Member: The Economic Club of Chicago, 2004—. Chairman: Gardner Carton & Douglas LLP Pro Bono Committee, 2003—. Commissioner: Committee on Character and Fitness, 1997-2002. *Member:* Chicago Bar Association. ***PRACTICE AREAS:*** Corporate and Securities; Mergers and Acquisitions. ***Email:*** kfreeman@gcd.com

MARK E. FURLANE, born Joliet, Illinois, August 2, 1949; admitted to bar, 1974, Illinois; 1979, U.S. Court of Military Appeals; 1985, U.S. District Court, Northern District of Illinois, including Trial Bar; 1983, U.S. Court of Appeals, Fifth, Sixth, Seventh, Ninth and Eleventh Circuits; 2001, U.S. Supreme Court. *Education:* Central College (B.A., magna cum laude, 1971); George Washington University (J.D., with honors, 1974); University of Chicago, Graduate School of Business (MBA, Finance Specialization, 1982). Author: "Mediation, Arbitration and Other ADR Techniques-Recent Developments in Litigation Avoidance"; "The Glass Ceiling, Affirmative Action, Pay Equity and Workplace Diversity-A Legal Analysis of Where They Are and Where They Are Going," Presented at The 5th Employment and Labor Law Institute for Corporate Counsel. Listed in Who's Who in America, Illinois Leading Attorneys. *Member:* Chicago (Member, Employment Law Committee, 1979—; Vice-Chair, 1993-1994; Chair, 1994-1995) and Federal (Member, Labor and Employment Law Committee; Board Member, 1999—) Bar Associations; Center for Disability and Elder Law (Board Member, 2000—; Chairman, Pro Bono Committee); Public Interest Law Initiative (Board Member, 2001—). [Capt., U.S. Marine Corps Reserves, 1971-1981; Active Duty, 1974-1979]. (Chairman, ERISA and Fiduciary Practice Group). ***PRACTICE AREAS:*** Labor and Employment; Employment Law; Employee Benefits Law; Employment Litigation; Executive Employment Law; Management Labor Law. ***Email:*** mfurlane@gcd.com

GARY W. GARNER, born Olney, Illinois, July 25, 1962; admitted to bar, 1988, Illinois; 1988, U.S. District Court, Northern District of Illinois; 1996, U.S. District Court, Western District of Michigan; 1997, U.S. Court of Appeals, Sixth Circuit. *Education:* University of Illinois (B.A., 1985); University of Kansas (J.D., 1988). Moot Court Council. Recipient, American Jurisprudence Award. *Member:* American Bar Association (Business Law and Litigation Sections). ***PRACTICE AREAS:*** Business Law; Business Litigation; Securities; Securities Fraud Class Action; Securities Litigation. ***Email:*** ggarner@gcd.com

EDWIN A. GETZ, born Johannesburg, South Africa, August 8, 1956; admitted to bar, 1985, Illinois. *Education:* Carleton College (B.A., 1977); Northwestern University Graduate School of Management (M.B.A., 1982); Washington University (J.D., 1985). Articles Editor, Washington University Journal of Urban and Contemporary Law, 1984-1985. Member, Panel of Arbitrators, American Arbitration Association. *Member:* Chicago Bar Association (Member, Computer Law Committee); Intellectual Property Law Association of Chicago; International Trademark Association; Lawyers for the Creative Arts. ***PRACTICE AREAS:*** Intellectual Property; Patent Infringement; Information Technology; E-Commerce; Online Intellectual Property Enforcement; Domain Name Infringement; Trademarks; Trademark Infringement; Data Privacy. ***Email:*** egetz@gcd.com

D. LOUIS GLASER II, *born Akron, Ohio, June 2, 1962; admitted to bar, 1989, Illinois* and U.S. District Court, Northern District of Illinois; 1990, U.S. Court of Appeals, 6th Circuit. *Education:* DePauw University (B.A., 1984); Ohio State University (M.H.A., 1986); Loyola University of Chicago (J.D., cum laude, 1989). Phi Kappa Phi; Alpha Sigma Nu. Selected as one of the "40 Illinois Attorneys Under 40," Law Bulletin Publishing Company, July 2001. Listed in: The Best Lawyers in America (Health), 2003-2005; Leading Lawyers Network (Health Law), 2004-2005. Named by Nightingale's Healthcare News as one of the Country's Outstanding Hospital Lawyers, 2003 and Outstanding Healthcare Transactional Lawyers, 2004. Editor-in-Chief, Loyola University Law Journal, 1988-1989. Author: "The Case for Parity Between Tax-Exempt and Non-Exempt Purchasers in Asset Acquisitions," 39 DePaul Law Review 753, 1990; "Unrelated Trade or Business Income and Hospitals: Reconciling Operating Losses and Charity Care," 19 Loyola University of Chicago Law Review, 1988. Member, Management Committee, 2000—. Member, Management Committee, 2000-2005. *Member:* Chicago Bar Association (Co-Chairman, Health and Hospital Law Committee, Young Lawyers Section, 1992-1993); American Health Lawyers Association; Illinois Association of Healthcare Attorneys. ***PRACTICE AREAS:*** Health Care; Health Care Mergers and Acquisitions; Health Law; Health Care Compliance; Integrated Health Care Delivery Systems; Managed Care. ***Email:*** lglaser@gcd.com

JOHN P. GOEBEL, born St. Louis, Missouri, March 17, 1966; admitted to bar, 1991, Illinois. *Education:* Middlebury College (B.A., magna cum laude, 1988); Harvard University (J.D., 1991). Phi Beta Kappa. Author: "Corporate Compliance Under the New Federal Sentencing Guidelines," 38 The Practical Lawyer 83 (June 1992) and Corporate Secretary's Guide (CCH) 48, 209 (September 1992); "Rules and Standards: A Critique of Two Critical Theorists", 31 Duquesne Law Review 51 (1992). *Member:* Chicago, Illinois State and American Bar Associations. ***PRACTICE AREAS:*** Corporate Law; Securities Law; Mergers and Acquisitions; Private Equity. ***Email:*** jgoebel@gcd.com

JOSEPH H. GREENBERG, born Chicago, Illinois, October 26, 1961; admitted to bar, 1988, Illinois. *Education:* Washington University (A.B., 1984); Harvard Law School (J.D., cum laude, 1988). Phi Beta Kappa. Law Clerk, Honorable Harry D. Leinenweber, U.S. District Court Judge, Northern District of Illinois, 1988-1990. *Member:* American Bar Association. ***PRACTICE AREAS:*** Emerging Growth Companies; Corporate Finance; Venture Capital; Mergers and Acquisitions; Securities. ***Email:*** jgreenberg@gcd.com

TERRY M. HACKETT, born Champaign, Illinois, September 6, 1965; admitted to bar, 1991, Illinois; U.S. District Court, Northern District of Illinois and U.S. Court of Appeals, Fifth Circuit. *Education:* University of Illinois (B.S., cum laude, 1988); Loyola University of Chicago (J.D., cum laude, 1991). Member, Loyola University of Chicago Law Journal, 1990-1991. Author, "Paramount Communications, Inc. v. Time, Inc.: Taking the Teeth Out of Proportionality Review, 22 Loyola University of Chicago Law Journal 229, 1990. *Member:* Chicago Bar Association. ***PRACTICE AREAS:*** Commercial Litigation; Products Liability; Intellectual Property Litigation. ***Email:*** thackett@gcd.com

ROY M. HARSCH, born Burlington, Iowa, June 30, 1946; admitted to bar, 1972, Iowa; 1973, Illinois. *Education:* Iowa State University (B.S., 1968); University of Iowa (M.S., 1973; J.D., with distinction, 1972). Lecturer, Environmental and Administrative Law, Illinois Continuing Legal Education, 1975-1978. Author: "The National Pollutant Discharge Elimination System in Illinois: The State Assumes Direct Authority," DePaul Law Review, 1978. *Member:* Chicago (Member, Environmental Law Committee, 1974—; Chairman: Legislative Subcommittee, 1976-1977; Seminar Committee, 1977-1978; Committee Chairman, 1978-1979) and Illinois (Member, Environmental Law Committee) Bar Associations. ***PRACTICE AREAS:*** Environmental Law; Clean Air Act; Clean Water Act; Environmental Permitting; Environmental Compliance; Environmental Litigation. ***Email:*** rharsch@gcd.com

VALERIE A. HAUGH, born Norfolk, Virginia, April 21, 1959; admitted to bar, 1988, Illinois and U.S. District Court, Northern District of Illinois. *Education:* Loyola University (B.A., 1981); John Marshall Law School (J.D., with highest distinction, 1988). Recipient, Illinois Women's Bar Scholarship. Managing Editor, John Marshall Law Review, 1986-1987. Author: Note, 20 John Marshall Law Review 169, 1986; Comment, 21 John Marshall Law Review 87, 1987. *Member:* American Bar Association. ***PRACTICE AREAS:*** Commercial Real Estate; Corporate. ***Email:*** vhaugh@gcd.com

MARK F. HEBBELN, born Chicago, Illinois, April 6, 1970; admitted to bar, 1997, Georgia; 2000, Illinois. *Education:* Wake Forest University (B.A., 1993); Emory University (J.D., 1997). ***PRACTICE AREAS:*** Bankruptcy; Creditors Rights. ***Email:*** mhebbeln@gcd.com

NANCY L. HENDRICKSON, born Evergreen Park, Illinois, April 4, 1961; admitted to bar, 1991, Illinois and U.S. District Court, Northern District of Illinois including Trial Bar; 1998, U.S. Court of Appeals, Seventh Circuit. *Education:* University of Illinois; Northwestern University (B.S., 1988); DePaul University College of Law (J.D., with honors, 1991). Order of the Coif. Managing Editor of Lead Articles, De Paul Univ. Law Review, 1990-1991. *Member:* Chicago and American Bar Associations. ***PRACTICE AREAS:*** Securities Litigation; Securities Arbitration; Complex Commercial Litigation. ***Email:*** nhendrickson@gcd.com

LAURIE A. HOLMES, born Brooklyn, New York, April 16, 1962; admitted to bar, 1993, New York; 1994, District of Columbia; 1996, Virginia; 1997, U.S. Supreme Court; U.S. District Court, District of Columbia, U.S. District Court, Eastern District of Virginia, U.S. District Court, Northern District of Illinois and U.S. Court of Appeals, District of Columbia Circuit (Not admitted in Illinois). *Education:* Manhattanville College (B.A., magna cum laude, 1984); Georgetown University (J.D., cum laude, 1992). Associate Editor, American Criminal Law Review, 1991-1992. Law Clerk to the Honorable Truman A. Morrison III, Superior Court of the District of Columbia, 1992-1993. ***PRACTICE AREAS:*** Employment Law; Litigation. ***Email:*** lholmes@gcd.com

KIRK A. HOOPINGARNER, born Grand Rapids, Michigan, September 8, 1958; admitted to bar, 1984, Illinois. *Education:* Hope College (B.A., 1981); University of Michigan (J.D. cum laude, 1984). ***PRACTICE AREAS:*** Estate Planning and Administration; Business and Financial Planning. ***Email:*** khoopingarner@gcd.com

GARY W. HOWELL, born Mediapolis, Iowa, August 7, 1950; admitted to bar, 1977, New York; 1985, Illinois. *Education:* University of Iowa (B.A., 1972; J.D., 1976). Note and Comment Editor, Iowa Law Review, 1975-1976. Adjunct Professor, University of Iowa College of Law, 1988—. *Member:* American Bar Association (Member, Employee Benefits Committee of Labor Section). ***PRACTICE AREAS:*** Employee Benefits; Employee Stock Ownership Plans; ERISA Compliance; Executive Compensation; Pension and Profit Sharing Plans. ***Email:*** ghowell@gcd.com

(This Listing Continued)

ELISSA L. ISAACS, born Chicago, Illinois, September 21, 1966; admitted to bar, 1991, District of Columbia; 1993, Illinois. *Education:* Northwestern University (B.S., 1988); George Washington University (J.D., with honors, 1991). Kappa Alpha Tau. Trustee Scholar. Full Merit Scholarship. Member, Moot Court Board. Member, George Washington University Law Review. *Member:* Illinois State and American Bar Associations. ***PRACTICE AREAS:*** Litigation. ***Email:*** eisaacs@gcd.com

IRA M. KALINA, born Arlington Heights, Illinois, June 11, 1969; admitted to bar, 1994, Illinois and U.S. District Court, Northern District of Illinois. *Education:* University of Michigan (B.A., 1991); University of Chicago (J.D., 1994). ***PRACTICE AREAS:*** Information Technology; Intellectual Property; Healthcare Information Technology; Licensing; Technology Licensing; Content Licensing; Software Development; Open Source; Hotel, Resort and Gaming Technology; Internet; Internet Law; E-Commerce; Web Site Development; Technology Transfers. ***Email:*** ikalina@gcd.com

HAROLD L. KAPLAN, admitted to bar, 1976, New York and U.S. District Court, Eastern and Southern District of New York; 1979, Illinois; 1980, U.S. District Court, Northern District of Illinois, U.S. Court of Appeals, Seventh Circuit and U.S. Supreme Court; U.S. Court of Appeals, Fifth Circuit. *Education:* University of Wisconsin (B.A., 1972; M.A., 1975); University of Chicago (J.D., 1975). ***PRACTICE AREAS:*** Bankruptcy Chapter 11; Bankruptcy Litigation; Bankruptcy Reorganization; Commercial Bankruptcy; Commercial Foreclosure; Commercial Workouts; Fraudulent Conveyance; Insolvency; International Insolvency; Bankruptcy; Liquidations; Our of Court Debt Restructuring; Workouts.

DAVID N. KAY, born Hertford, England, October 13, 1955; admitted to bar, 1979, London, England as Barrister; 1990, Illinois. *Education:* Kingston University, Kingston upon Thames, Surrey, England (B.A. Law, Hons.); IIT Chicago-Kent School of Law (J.D., 1989); King Saud University, Riyadh, Saudi Arabia (Cert. Arabic, 1981). Recipient, OBE (Officer of the Order of the British Empire) by Queen Elizabeth II in her Birthday Honors List in recognition of his services to British business interests and the British Community in the United States, 2003. Co-Author: with Ernest Kay, "Trading With America, A Practical Guide," Gower (USA), Gower Publishing Limited (UK), 1997. Chairman, Firm's Corporate Department. Hon. Society of Gray's Inn, London. Chairman and Director, British American Chamber of Commerce for the Midwest, Inc.. Honorary Legal Advisor to H.M. Consul General, Chicago, Illinois. Chambers of Christopher Morcom QC, Hogarth Chambers, 5 New Square, Lincoln's Inn, London, England. Member, Panel of Arbitrators: American Arbitration Association; London Court of International Arbitration. *Member:* Illinois State and American Bar Associations; Commercial Bar Association, England; International Bar Association. ***PRACTICE AREAS:*** Alternative Dispute Resolution; Business Law; International Corporate Law; Intellectual Property. ***Email:*** dkay@gcd.com

PATRICK J. KELLEHER, born Lake Placid, New York, October 28, 1968; admitted to bar, 1993, Illinois; U.S. Supreme Court; U.S. Court of Appeals, Federal, 6th, 7th, 8th and 10th Circuits; U.S. District Court, Northern District of Illinois including Trial Bar; U.S. District Court, Central District of Illinois; U.S. District Court, Southern District of Illinois; U.S. District Court, Western District of Michigan; U.S. District Court, Western District of Wisconsin. *Education:* Boston College (B.A., magna cum laude, 1990); Northwestern University (J.D., 1993). Publications with Hon. Paddy H. McNamara, Voir Dire in Civil Case (1995, update 1998). Law Clerk to Hon. Paddy H. McNamara, Circuit Court of Cook County, 1994-1996. *Member:* American Bar Association. ***PRACTICE AREAS:*** Litigation; Intellectual Property; Antitrust. ***Email:*** pkelleher@gcd.com

ALAN S. KING, born Chicago, Illinois, April 28, 1963; admitted to bar, 1988, Illinois; 1989, U.S. District Court, Northern District of Illinois; 1994, U.S. Court of Appeals, Seventh Circuit. *Education:* Augustana College (B.A., 1985); University of Illinois (J.D., 1988). Notes Editor, Illinois Bar Journal. *Member:* Chicago, Cook County and American Bar Associations. ***PRACTICE AREAS:*** Labor and Employment; Litigation; Civil Litigation; Sports Law. ***Email:*** aking@gcd.com

BRIGITTE T. KOCHENY, admitted to bar, 1993, Wisconsin and U.S. District Court, Western District of Wisconsin; 1994, U.S. Court of Appeals, Seventh Circuit; 1995, Illinois; 1996, U.S. District Court, Northern District of Illinois. *Education:* University of Wisconsin (B.A., with distinction, 1988; J.D., cum laude, 1993). Staff Attorney, U.S. Court of Appeals, Seventh Circuit, 1993-1995. *Member:* Chicago and Illinois State Bar Associations; State Bar of Wisconsin. ***LANGUAGES:*** German. ***PRACTICE AREAS:*** Litigation; Financial Markets. ***Email:*** bkocheny@gcd.com

TINA D. KOURASIS, born Freeport, New York, October 14, 1971; admitted to bar, 1997, Illinois. *Education:* University of Illinois (B.A. in Economics, summa cum laude, 1993) Phi Beta Kappa; University of Chicago (J.D., 1996). Recipient, Mandel Legal Aid Clinic Scholarship. Clerk to the Hon. Charles P. Kocoras, Northern District of Illinois, 1997-1998. ***PRACTICE AREAS:*** Intellectual Property; Trademark. ***Email:*** tkourasis@gcd.com

MARK A. LATHAM, born Chicago, Illinois, August 4, 1957; admitted to bar, 1989, Illinois and U.S. District Court, Northern District of Illinois; 1992, U.S. District Court, Western District of Michigan; 1993, U.S. District Court, Eastern District of Wisconsin; 1997, U.S. Court of Appeals, Seventh Circuit. *Education:* Illinois Wesleyan University (B.S., 1979); Boalt Hall, University of California at Berkeley (J.D., 1989). Chair, Visiting Committee, Northern Illinois University College of Law, 1997-1998. Panel Attorney, Illinois Capital Resource Center. *Member:* American Bar Association. ***PRACTICE AREAS:*** Environmental Law; Environmental Auditing; Environmental Cleanup; Environmental Compliance; Environmental Litigation. ***Email:*** mlatham@gcd.com

HOWARD J. LEVINE, born Kansas City, Missouri, August 14, 1951; admitted to bar, *1979, Florida; 1983, Illinois. Education:* University of Kansas (B.A., in Economics, 1973; M.B.A., 1975); University of Miami (J.D., 1978). Member, University of Miami Law Review, 1977-1978. *Member:* Chicago (Member, Employee Benefits Committee) and American Bar Associations; The Florida Bar. ***PRACTICE AREAS:*** Employee Benefits Law; Executive Compensation Law; ESOP Law. ***Email:*** hlevine@gcd.com

SUSAN J. MACAULAY, born Oceanport, New Jersey, February 18, 1952; admitted to bar, 1984, Illinois and U.S. District Court, Northern District of Illinois. *Education:* Oberlin Conservatory of Music (B. Mus., 1974); Loyola University Chicago School of Law (J.D., 1984); Chicago-Kent College of Law (LL.M., Financial Services Law, with high honors, 1990); University of Chicago (M.L.A., Humanities, 1995). Alpha Sigma Nu. Managing Editor, *Loyola Law Journal,* 1983-1984. Recipient, American Jurisprudence Award in Constitutional Law. Adjunct Professor of Law, Chicago-Kent College of Law, 1992—. *Member:* Chicago and American (Member, Securitizations and Derivatives, Loan Documentation, Loan Workout, Commercial Finance, Opinions of Counsel and Aircraft Financing Subcommittees) Bar Associations; American College of Investment Counsel. ***PRACTICE AREAS:*** Finance; Lending; Corporate Law. ***Email:*** smacaulay@gcd.com

RUTH I. MAJOR, admitted to bar, 1990, Illinois and U.S. District Court, Northern District of Illinois; 1996, Trial Bar; U.S. District Court, Eastern District of Wisconsin. *Education:* University of Illinois (B.S., with honors, 1985); University of Iowa (J.D., with distinction, 1990). *Member:* Chicago Bar Association. ***PRACTICE AREAS:*** Commercial Litigation; Employment Law; Securities Litigation; Securities Arbitration. ***Email:*** rmajor@gcd.com

DAVID M. MATTESON, born Rhinelander, Wisconsin; admitted to bar, 1977, Illinois. *Education:* Occidental College (B.A., 1974); Loyola School of Law (J.D., 1977). ***PRACTICE AREAS:*** Futures Law; Hedge Funds. ***Email:*** dmatteson@gcd.com

GEORGE C. McKANN, born Orange, New Jersey, January 20, 1942; admitted to bar, 1966, Illinois. *Education:* Lawrence University (B.A., with high honors, 1963); Northwestern University (J.D., 1966). *Member:* American (Member, Committee on Federal Regulation of Securities) and International Bar Associations. ***PRACTICE AREAS:*** Corporate; Securities; Corporate Governance; Mergers, Acquisitions and Divestitures; Foreign Corrupt Practices Act. ***Email:*** gmckann@gcd.com

HELEN J. McSWEENEY, born Chicago, Illinois, April 24, 1959; admitted to bar, 1984, Illinois. *Education:* Wellesley College; Yale University (B.A., magna cum laude, 1981); Northwestern University (J.D., 1984). *Member:* Chicago Bar Association. ***PRACTICE AREAS:*** Corporate Law; Securities. ***Email:*** hmcsweeney@gcd.com

MICHAEL E. MERMALL, admitted to bar, 1986, Illinois. *Education:* Miami University (B.A., 1982); University of Chicago (M.A., 1983); Washington University (J.D., 1986). ***PRACTICE AREAS:*** Real Estate; Environmental Law. ***Email:*** mmermall@gcd.com

JOYCE L. MEYER, born Gary, Indiana, November 30, 1953; admitted to bar, 1990, Illinois. *Education:* Indiana University (B.S., 1975); DePaul University (M.B.A., 1987); DePaul College of Law (J.D., 1990). Order of the Coif. ***PRACTICE AREAS:*** Executive Compensation; Qualified Retirement Plans. ***Email:*** jmeyer@gcd.com

PETER J. MEYER, born Milwaukee, Wisconsin, May 6, 1956; admitted to bar, 1984, Illinois, U.S. District Court, Northern District of Illinois including Trial Bar, U.S. District Court, Western District of Michigan, U.S. District Court, Eastern District of Wisconsin and U.S. Court of Appeals, Third, Sixth, Seventh and Federal Circuits. *Education:* University of Missouri (B.J., 1978); IIT/Chicago-Kent College of Law (J.D., with high honors, 1984). Adjunct Professor, IIT - Kent College of Law, 2002. Law Clerk for Justice Thomas J. Moran, Illinois Supreme Court, 1984-1986. Member of Staff, 1982-1983 and Executive Notes and Comments Editor, 1983-1984, Chicago Kent Law Review. *Member:* Chicago, Federal and American Bar Associations. ***PRACTICE AREAS:*** Complex Litigation; Federal Civil Litigation; Securities Litigation; Intellectual Property Litigation. ***Email:*** pmeyer@gcd.com

KATHLEEN M. MURPHY, admitted to bar, 1985, Illinois; U.S. District Court, Northern District of Illinois; U.S. Court of Appeals, Seventh Circuit; U.S. Court of International Trade; U.S. Court of Appeals, Federal Circuit. *Education:* St. Xavier College (B.A.); Loyola University-Chicago (M.A.; J.D.). *Member:* American Bar Association; American Association of Exporters and Importers (Member, Board of Directors); Customs and International Trade Bar Association; Joint Industry Group (JIG); Midwest Importers Trade Association; Women in International Trade. ***PRACTICE AREAS:*** International Trade; Customs Law; Antidumping; Customs Seizures; Export Complaince; Export Regulation; GATT; Import and Export Law; North American Free Trade Agreement; U.S. Foreign Trade Zones; World Trade Organization; Corporate Law. ***Email:*** kmurphy@gcd.com

GORDON B. NASH, JR., born Chicago, Illinois, February 24, 1944; admitted to bar, 1969, Illinois; 1972, U.S. Court of Appeals, Seventh Circuit. *Education:* University of Notre Dame (B.A., 1966); Loyola University (J.D., 1969). Assistant U.S. Attorney, Northern District of Illinois, 1971-1978. Chief, Special Prosecution Division (1978). Chief, Criminal Receiving and Appellate Division (1977). Instructor, John Marshall Law School, 1976. Chairman, State of Illinois Board of Ethics, 1980-1986. Co-author: "Grand Jury Practice," Federal Criminal Practice, Illinois Institute for Continuing Legal Education, 1980. Member, Board of Governors, Illinois Institute of Continuing Legal Education, 1988-1989. Board of Directors, Chicago Bar Foundation, 1983-1985 and 1987-1990. *Member:* Chicago (President, 1990-1991) and American Bar Associations; The Chicago Inn of Court (President, 1996-1997). Fellow, American College of Trial Lawyers. ***PRACTICE AREAS:*** Antitrust and Trade Regulation; Business Law; Criminal Law; Legal Ethics and Professional Responsibility; Securities. ***Email:*** gnash@gcd.com

MARK D. NELSON, born Rochester, Minnesota, February 14, 1957; admitted to bar, 1982, Illinois. *Education:* University of Illinois (B.A., 1979; J.D., 1982); Wake Forest University. Member, Illinois Hospital Association Task Force on AIDS, 1986-1988. *Member:* Illinois State Bar Association; Illinois Association of Hospital Attorneys. ***PRACTICE AREAS:*** Labor Law; Employment Law. ***Email:*** mnelson@gcd.com

JOHN K. NOTZ, JR., born Chicago, Illinois; admitted to bar, 1956, Illinois; 1957, Florida; 1989, Wisconsin. *Education:* Williams College (B.A., 1953); Northwestern University School of Law (J.D., 1956). Chairman of the Board of Directors, Illinois Institute for Continuing Legal Education, 1990-1991. Member, Illinois Secretary of State's Corporation Acts Advisory Committee, 1982-1995; Chairman, 1987-1989; Chairman, Not-for-Profit Act Subcommittee, 1984-1987. Member: Panels of Commercial and Construction Industry Arbitrators, American Arbitration Association; National Association of Securities Dealers; National Futures Association. Mediator, Trained by American Arbitration Association and Endispute, Inc.; CPR Institute for Dispute Resolution Panel of Distinguished Neutrals. Member, Business Conduct Committee, Chicago Board Options Exchange, Inc. Trustee, Beloit College. *Member:* Chicago (Chairman, Corporation Law, 1981-1982; Member, Committees on Corporation and Futures Law), Illinois State and American (Member: Dispute Resolution Section; Senior Lawyers Division; Vice Chair, Alternative Dispute Resolution Committee; Member, Nonprofit Corporation Committee; Co-Chairman, Subcom-

(This Listing Continued)

GARDNER CARTON & DOUGLAS LLP, Chicago—Continued

mittee on Model Nonprofit Corporation Act, 1990-1995) Bar Associations; The Florida Bar; State Bar of Wisconsin; American Law Institute. ***REPORTED CASES:*** CFTC vs. Weintraub USSC, 1986. ***PRACTICE AREAS:*** Corporate. ***Email:*** jnotz@gcd.com

STEPHEN O'DONNELL, born New York, N.Y., August 28, 1960; admitted to bar, 1986, Illinois and U.S. District Court, Northern District of Illinois. *Education:* Washington University (B.A., 1982); University of Illinois (J.D., magna cum laude, 1986). Steve concentrates his practice in complex commercial litigation involving insurance coverage, reinsurance, securities, and contract issues. Member, 1984-85 and Associate Editor, 1985-86, Univ. of Illinois Law Review. ***PRACTICE AREAS:*** Insurance; Reinsurance; Securities. ***Email:*** sodonnell@gcd.com

NEIL S. OLDERMAN, born New Brunswick, New Jersey; admitted to bar, 1990, Pennsylvania; 1992, District of Columbia; 1993, Illinois. *Education:* Indiana University (B.A., 1985); Catholic University (J.D., 1990). Author, "Legal Aspects of Economic Credentialing," vol. 17, Physician Executive, 1991. Co-Author, "Overview of Legal Issues," Fundamental Medical Management: A Guide for the New Physician Executive, 1993. *Member:* Chicago, Illinois State, Pennsylvania and American Bar Associations; The District of Columbia Bar; American Health Lawyers Association; Illinois Association of Healthcare Attorneys. ***PRACTICE AREAS:*** Health Care Transactions; Health Care Corporate Law. ***Email:*** nolderman@gcd.com

ANITA J. PONDER, admitted to bar, 1985, Illinois and U.S. District Court, Northern District of Illinois. *Education:* Fisk University (B.A.); University of Florida (J.D.). ***PRACTICE AREAS:*** Corporate; Regulated Technology Transactions. ***Email:*** aponder@gcd.com

MICHAEL D. ROSENBAUM, born Madison, Wisconsin, July 19, 1962; admitted to bar, 1987, Wisconsin, Illinois and U.S. District Court, Northern District of Illinois and Western District of Wisconsin. *Education:* Michigan State University (B.A., 1984); University of Wisconsin (J.D., 1987). Certified Public Accountant, Illinois, 1985. *Member:* State Bar of Wisconsin. ***PRACTICE AREAS:*** Employee Benefits; COBRA; Deferred Compensation; Pension and Profit Sharing Plans; Health Benefits. ***Email:*** mrosenbaum@gcd.com

KIMBERLY K. RUBEL, born Oak Park, Illinois, October 15, 1968; admitted to bar, 1995, Illinois. *Education:* University of Illinois, Urbana-Champaign (B.S., in Finance, 1990); University of Chicago (J.D., 1995). *Member:* American Bar Association (Member, Committee on Federal Regulation of Securities); American College of Investment Counsel. ***PRACTICE AREAS:*** Corporate; Finance; Securities; Securities Offerings. ***Email:*** krubel@gcd.com

DAVID A. RUBENSTEIN, born Chicago, Illinois, March 2, 1958; admitted to bar, 1983, Illinois. *Education:* University of Illinois (B.A., 1980); University of Michigan (J.D., cum laude, 1983). Phi Beta Kappa. ***PRACTICE AREAS:*** Corporate Law; Closely Held Corporations; Mergers and Acquisitions; Business Law. ***Email:*** drubenstein@gcd.com

JESSE H. RUIZ, born Oak Lawn, Illinois, February 17, 1965; admitted to bar, 1995, Illinois and U.S. District Court, Northern District of Illinois. *Education:* University of Illinois (B.A., 1988); University of Chicago (J.D., 1995). Symposium Editor, University of Chicago Law School Roundtable, 1994-1995. Commissioner, Illinois Board of Admissions to the Bar Character and Fitness Committee, 1998—. Member, University of Chicago Law School Visiting Committee, 2001—. President, Hispanic Lawyers Association of Illinois, 2000-2001. Selected as one of the "40 Illinois Attorneys Under Forty to Watch," Chicago Daily Law Bulletin, July 2003. *Member:* Chicago and American (Member, Business Law Section) Bar Associations; Hispanic Lawyers Association of Illinois. ***LANGUAGES:*** Spanish. ***PRACTICE AREAS:*** Corporate and Securities; Mergers, Acquisitions and Divestitures; Corporate Governance; Commercial. ***Email:*** jruiz@gcd.com

BRIAN C. RUPP, born Chicago, Illinois, September 21, 1962; admitted to bar, 1990, Illinois; registered to practice before U.S. Patent and Trademark Office;. *Education:* DePaul University (B.S., 1984; J.D., 1990); Marquette University (M.S., Electrical Engineering, 1986). Patent Counsel, Samsung Display Devices and Samsung Aerospace Industries, 1995-1998. ***PRACTICE AREAS:*** Intellectual Property. ***Email:*** brupp@gcd.com

BARNETT P. RUTTENBERG, born Chicago, Illinois, December 11, 1945; admitted to bar, 1972, Illinois. *Education:* University of Illinois (B.A., 1967); University of Illinois and Northwestern University (J.D., cum laude, 1972). Co-Author: "Mixed-Use and Shared Use Developments, Advanced Uses of Reciprocal Agreements," for the American College of Real Estate Lawyers, 1981. ***PRACTICE AREAS:*** Real Estate Transactions. ***Email:*** bruttenberg@gcd.com

JAMES L. SAWYER, admitted to bar, 1994, Illinois; U.S. Court of International Trade; U.S. Court of Appeals, Federal Circuit; U.S. District Court, Northern District of Illinois. *Education:* Union College (B.A.); Chicago-Kent College of Law (J.D.). ***PRACTICE AREAS:*** International Trade; Customs Law; Corporate Law; Antidumping; Customs Seizures; Export Compliance; Export Regulation; GATT; Import and Export Law; North American Free Trade Agreement; U.S. Foreign Trade Zones; World Trade Organization. ***Email:*** jsawyer@gcd.com

DAVID S. SCHAFFER, born Chicago, Illinois, September 8, 1961; admitted to bar, 1989, New York; 1990, Illinois. *Education:* University of Chicago (B.A., highest honors, 1983); Harvard University (J.D., 1987). Author: "Disclosure Issues for Municipal Securities," Volume 24, Number 392, Securities Regulation Law Journal, 1997; "Delaware's Limit on Director Liability," 10 Harvard Journal of Law & Public Policy 665, 1987. Deputy Chief, State's Attorney of Cook County, 1991-1993. Law Clerk to Hon. Jack B. Jacobs, Court of Chancery, State of Delaware, 1987-1988. Secretary, Treasurer and Director, Lawyers Trust Fund of Illinois, 2000—. Member, Governor's Conference on Housing, 1991. Recipient: Marshall Fellowship, 2002; National MS Leadership Award, 2001. *Member:* American Bar Association. ***LANGUAGES:*** French. ***PRACTICE AREAS:*** Corporate Law; Securities; Municipal Law. ***Email:*** dschaffer@gcd.com

KATHLEEN SHEIL SCHEIDT, born December 27, 1972; admitted to bar, 1998, Indiana and U.S. District Court, Northern and Southern Districts of Indiana; 2001, Massachusetts; 2002, Illinois. *Education:* University of Notre Dame (B.A., cum laude, 1995); University of Iowa College of Law (J.D., with high distinction, 1998). Phi Alpha Delta. Managing Editor, Journal of Corporation Law, 1997-1998. Selected Publications: Author: "Special Considerations in Designing and Operating an ESOP" (BNA ERISA Compliance & Enforcement Strategy Guide); "Current Considerations and New Challenges for ERISA Section 404(c) Compliance" (BNA ERISA Compliance & Enforcement Strategy Guide); "Prudence and Diversification Revisited: ERISA Section 404(c) Protection in the Wake of Enron" (Employee Benefits Journal, 2003); "What Every Employer Needs to Know About the HIPAA Privacy Rules" (Employee Benefit Plan Review, 2003); "The Americans with Disabilities Act: Are Your Wrists Protected?" Volume 23:3 Journal of Corporation Law, Winter, 1998; *National Labor Relations Board v. Town & Country Electric, Inc.: Allowing a Trojan Horse to Trample Employer Rights*" Volume 24:1 Journal of Corporation Law, Fall, 1998. Co-author, monthly Regulatory Update column, Employee Benefit Plan Review. Co-editor, *International Employee Equity Plans: Participation Beyond Borders,* published by World Law Group (addressing the legal ramifications of offering equity compensation plans in multiple countries).*Member:* American Bar Association; The ESOP Association (Member, Administrative Advisory Committee); National Association of Stock Plan Professionals; Global Equity Organization. ***PRACTICE AREAS:*** Employee Benefits; Executive Compensation; Employee Stock Ownership Plans (ESOPs); ERISA. ***Email:*** kscheidt@gcd.com

JEFFREY M. SCHWARTZ, born Peoria, Illinois, May 7, 1967; admitted to bar, 1992, Illinois. *Education:* University of Illinois (B.S., 1989; J.D., magna cum laude, 1992). Order of the Coif. ***PRACTICE AREAS:*** Bankruptcy; Corporate Reorganization; Creditors' Rights. ***Email:*** jschwartz@gcd.com

STEPHANIE B. SHELLENBACK, born Milwaukee, Wisconsin; admitted to bar, 1982, Illinois and U.S. District Court, Northern District of Illinois. *Education:* University of Wisconsin-Madison (B.A., 1979); Emory University (J.D., 1982). Notes and Comments Editor, Emory Law Journal, 1981-1982. Member, Commercial Real Estate Executive Women - CREW Chicago, 1994—. *Member:* Chicago Bar Association. ***PRACTICE AREAS:*** Commercial Real Estate (100%). ***Email:*** sshellenback@gcd.com

S JONATHAN SILVERMAN, born 1961; admitted to bar, 1992, Illinois. *Education:* Yale University (B.A., 1986); University of Chicago (A.M., 1989; J.D., 1992). ***PRACTICE AREAS:*** Antitrust and Trade Regulation; Commercial Litigation. ***Email:*** jsilverman@gcd.com

JOHN A. SIMON, born Chicago, Illinois, June 24, 1960; admitted to bar, 1985, Illinois and U.S. District Court, Northern District of Illinois; 1986, Florida; 1991, U.S. Court of Appeals, Seventh Circuit and U.S. Supreme Court. *Education:* University of Santa Clara (B.S., cum laude, 1982); Loyola University (J.D., 1985). Member, Cook County Judicial Advisory Council, 1995—. *Member:* The Florida Bar; Defense Research Institute. ***LANGUAGES:*** Spanish and Portuguese. ***REPORTED CASES:*** Beverly Bank v. Illinois Dept. of Transportation 144 Ill. 2d 210; 579 N.E. 2d 815, 162 Ill. Dec. 1; Gade v. National Solid Works Management Assn., 112 S.Ct. 2374, 120 L. Ed. 2d 73; Lamar v. West Chicago, 355 Ill.App.3d 352, 823 N.E.2d 610 (2nd Dist. 2005). ***PRACTICE AREAS:*** Litigation; Complex Commercial; Toxic Torts; Labor and Employment; Appellate Practice; Real Estate Litigation; Drug and Medical Device Defense. ***Email:*** jsimon@gcd.com

TIMOTHY J. STANTON, born Milwaukee, Wisconsin, April 9, 1965; admitted to bar, 1994, Illinois and U.S. District Court, Northern District of Illinois. *Education:* University of Wisconsin (B.A., 1988); Loyola University of Chicago (J.D., 1994). Author: (with Gary Howell), "Moran Ruling Could Spur Increased Employer Costs, Employee Reviews, State Regulation," Employee Benefits Management Directions (CCH), August 6, 2002; "Confusion About HIPAA Privacy Rules," Business Insurance, June 24, 2002; (with Lisa Collins), "Proposed Nondiscrimination Rules for Wellness Programs Pose Challenges for Employers," Employee Benefits Management Directions (CCH), February 27, 2001; (with Lisa Collins), "New HIPAA Nondiscrimination Rules Provide Clear Guidance for Health Plan Administrators," Employee Benefits Management Directions (CCH), February 13, 2001; (with Lisa Collins), "New ERISA Claims Procedure Regulations Promise to Keep Health and Disability Plan Administrators Busy in the Coming Year," Health Plan Compliance Guide after HIPAA (CCH), January 2001; (with Lisa Collins), "Kinder, Gentler Election Change Rules for Cafeteria Plans," Health Plan Compliance Guide After HIPAA (CCH), June 2001. *Member:* Chicago and American Bar Associations. ***PRACTICE AREAS:*** Employee Benefits; Health and Welfare Plans; HIPAA. ***Email:*** tstanton@gcd.com

SANFORD M. STEIN, born Chicago, Illinois, October 18, 1949; admitted to bar, 1975, Illinois. *Education:* University of Illinois (B.S., cum laude, 1970); George Washington University (J.D., with honors, 1974). Commissioner, Lake County Regional Planning Commission, 1991-1996, 1999—. Board Member: Uptown Community Development Corporation, 2003—; Highland Park School District Board of Education, 1981-1983. Registered Lobbyist, Illinois, 1991—. Contributing Author: "Land Use Law Handbook," Illinois Institute for Continuing Legal Education, 2004-Update; "Legal Ethics for Environmental Lawyers: Real Problems, New Challenges and Old Values," William & Mary Environmental Law Review, Williamsburg, VA, Spring 2002. ***REPORTED CASES:*** The Steel Company v. Citizens for a Better Environment, 523 U.S. 83, 118 S.Ct. 1003 (1998); 3M v. Rolling Meadows, 789 F.2d 571 (7th Cir. 1986). ***PRACTICE AREAS:*** Land Use and Development; Environmental; Legislation and Government Affairs; Litigation. ***Email:*** sstein@gcd.com

NANCY L. STERN, born Saginaw, Michigan, March 16, 1970; admitted to bar, 1994, Michigan; 1995, Illinois. *Education:* University of Michigan (A.B., with distinction, 1991; J.D., 1994). Law clerk to the Honorable Robert H. Cleland, United States District Judge, Eastern District of Michigan, 1994-1996. ***PRACTICE AREAS:*** Corporate; Mergers, Acquisitions and Divestitures; Private Equity; Securities; Corporate Governance; Business Law. ***Email:*** nstern@gcd.com

K. BRUCE STICKLER, born Chicago, Illinois, January 3, 1946; admitted to bar, 1970, Texas; 1972, Illinois. *Education:* Southern Methodist University (B.A., 1967; J.D., 1970). Clinical Faculty Member, St. Louis University Department of Hospital and Health Care Administration, Center for Health Services Education and Research. Healthcare Advisory Board Member, DePaul University, College of Law. Member, Board of Directors, Illinois Association of Hospital Attorneys, 1991-1994. *Member:* Chicago, Illinois State (Chairman, Labor Law Section Council, 1983) and American Bar Associations; State Bar

(This Listing Continued)

of Texas; American Academy of Hospital Attorneys; National Health Lawyers Association; Illinois Association of Hospital Attorneys. ***PRACTICE AREAS:*** Labor Law; Employment Law; Health Care Law. ***Email:*** bstickler@gcd.com

RICHARD M. STOCK, born Chicago, Illinois, February 2, 1952; admitted to bar, 1977, Illinois. *Education:* University of Illinois (B.S., 1974); Loyola University, Chicago (J.D., 1977). Chicago Inn of Court, 1995—. Cook County State's Attorney's Office, 1977-1988. DuPage County State's Attorney's Office, 1988-1995. Illinois Attorney General's Office, 1995- 2003. *Member:* Chicago, DuPage County, Illinois State and American Bar Associations. ***PRACTICE AREAS:*** Regulatory Litigation; General Civil Litigation; Criminal Litigation; Government Relations. ***Email:*** rstock@gcd.com

BARRY W. SUFRIN, born Chicago, Illinois, July 20, 1948; admitted to bar, 1974, Illinois, U.S. Supreme Court, U.S. Court of Appeals for the Federal Circuit and Seventh Circuit and U.S. District Court, Northern District of Illinois including Trial Bar; registered to practice before U.S. Patent and Trademark Office. *Education:* University of Illinois, Urbana-Champaign (B.S., 1970; J.D., 1974). *Member:* Intellectual Property Law Association of Chicago; American Intellectual Property Law Association. ***PRACTICE AREAS:*** Intellectual Property. ***Email:*** bsufrin@gcd.com

DOUGLAS B. SWILL, born Brooklyn, New York, January 18, 1964; admitted to bar, 1989, Illinois and U.S. District Court, Northern District of Illinois; 1990, U.S. Court of Appeals, Seventh Circuit. *Education:* Muhlenberg College (B.A., 1986); Washington University (J.D., 1989); Loyola University School of Law (LL.M. in Health Care, 1990). Loyola University School of Law Fellowship in Health Care Law. Assistant State's Attorney, State Attorney's Office of Cook County, Federal Litigation and Hospital Divisions, 1990-1993. *Member:* American Health Lawyers Association. ***PRACTICE AREAS:*** Health Care; Joint Ventures; Health Care Contracts; Hospital and Physician Alliances and Arrangements. ***Email:*** dswill@gcd.com

LIISA M. THOMAS, born Helsinki, Finland, March 20, 1971; admitted to bar, 1996, Illinois; 1998, District of Columbia. *Education:* Haverford College (B.A., 1993); University of Chicago (J.D., 1996). *Member:* American Bar Association; International Trademark Association (Member, Law Firm Subcommittee, Membership Services Committee); Promotion Marketing Association. ***LANGUAGES:*** French, Spanish and Arabic. ***PRACTICE AREAS:*** Advertising; Privacy Law; Trademarks; Intellectual Property. ***Email:*** lthomas@gcd.com

TRACY L. TREGER, born Chicago, Illinois; admitted to bar, 1993, Illinois; 1994, U.S. District Court, Northern District of Illinois including Trial Bar. *Education:* University of Pennsylvania (B.A., 1989; M.S., 1990); Chicago-Kent College of Law, Illinois Institute of Technology (J.D., with honors, 1993). Law Clerk to the Honorable David H. Coar, U.S. Bankruptcy Court for the Northern District of Illinois, 1993-94. Author: "Is 'Lease' a Financing Agreement in Disguise? Rights of Both Sides Hinge on Answer," The Journal of Corporate Renewal, July 2004 (with Mark F. Hebbeln); "The Landlord's Post-filing Prerejection Limbo: The Treatment of Option Period Charges Under 11 U.S.C. §365(d)(3)," ABI Committee News, Real Estate Committee, February 2004; "Indenture Trustees and Lease Recharacterization," ABA Trust & Investments, March/April 2005 (with H. Kaplan and M. Hebbeln); "Dischargeability of Credit Card Debt Under 11 U.S.C. §523(a)," 1999 Wiley Bankruptcy Law Update; "Mixing Business and Law: Enforcing Contractual Damages Provisions," Fox Valley Business Journal, June 1998; "Avoiding the Preference Pitfall in Workouts," Commercial Lending Review, Spring 1997 (with Bradley S. Schmarak). *Member:* Chicago Bar Association; American Bankruptcy Institute; Turnaround Management Association. ***PRACTICE AREAS:*** Bankruptcy; Creditors; Corporate Restructuring. ***Email:*** ttreger@gcd.com

STEPHEN A. TSORIS, born Milwaukee, Wisconsin, July 26, 1957; admitted to bar, 1982, Illinois. *Education:* Marquette University (B.A., magna cum laude, 1979); Cornell Law School (J.D., 1982). Phi Beta Kappa. Editor-in-Chief, Cornell International Law Journal, 1981-1982. *Member:* Chicago Bar Association (Chairman, Corporation Law Committee, 1992-1993). ***PRACTICE AREAS:*** Corporate Law; Mergers, Acquisitions and Divestitures; Securities; Business Start-Ups; Emerging Growth Companies. ***Email:*** stsoris@gcd.com

CAROL HINES WACASER, admitted to bar, 1993, Illinois and U.S. District Court, Northern District of Illinois. *Education:* University of Vermont School of Business Administration (B.S., with honors, 1986); DePaul University (J.D., 1993). Author, "A Modest Proposal for Defining 'Gross Misconduct' for COBRA Coverage Disqualification," DePaul Law Review, Volume 42, Number 1. *Member:* Chicago and American Bar Associations. ***PRACTICE AREAS:*** Employee Benefits; Qualified Retirement Plans; Executive Compensation; Non-Qualified Arrangements; Health Benefits; Welfare Benefits; Mergers and Acquisitions. ***Email:*** chines@gcd.com

PRISCILLA A. (PAM) WALTER, born Chicago, Illinois, February 9, 1943; admitted to bar, 1978, Illinois. *Education:* Wellesley College (B.A., 1965); London School of Economics and Political Science, London, England (M.Sc., 1967); Northwestern University (J.D., 1978). Order of the Coif. Articles Editor, Northwestern Law Review, 1977-1978. Law Clerk to Honorable Walter J. Cummings, U.S. Court of Appeals, Seventh Circuit, 1978-1979. Trustee and Executive Committee, Illinois Institute of Technology; Executive Committee and Past Chairman, Board of Governors, Metropolitan Planning Council; Vice Chairman, Chicago Shakespeare Theater; Board of Overseers, IIT-Kent School of Law. *Member:* American Bar Foundation; Computer Law Association; Software and Information Industry Association. ***PRACTICE AREAS:*** Communication and Media; Internet Law; Computers and Software; Computer Law; Information Technology. ***Email:*** pwalter@gcd.com

JOHN W. WATSON III, born Chicago, Illinois, February 16, 1963; admitted to bar, 1988, Illinois. *Education:* St. Olaf College (B.A., 1985); IIT Chicago-Kent (J.D., 1988). Joyce Foundation Environmental Law Scholar. *Member:* Chicago and American Bar Associations. ***REPORTED CASES:*** AM Intern. v. International Forging Equip., 743 F.Supp. 525, aff'd in part, reversed in part, 982 F.2d 989 (6th Cir. 1993); AMI v. Data Card Corp., 146 B.R. 391 (N.D. Ill. 1992). ***PRACTICE AREAS:*** Environmental Law; Environmental Cleanup; Environmental Litigation; Underground Storage Tanks; Environmental Cost Recovery. ***Email:*** jwatson@gcd.com

ROBERT J. WILCZEK, born Chicago, Illinois, January 8, 1944; admitted to bar, 1968, Illinois; 1974, U.S. Supreme Court; 2002, Michigan. *Education:* University of Dayton (B.A., 1965); University of Notre Dame (LL.B., 1968). Note and Book Review Editor, Notre Dame Law Review, 1967-1968. Trustee, Chicago Cultural Foundation, 1995—; Trustee, St. Patrick High School, Chicago, 1996—. Member, Notre Dame Law School Advisory Council, 1997—. Director, Australian-American Chamber of Commerce of Chicago, 1991-1998; Director, Pacific Dunlop Holdings Inc., 1986-2000; Director, Southcorp Holdings (USA) Inc., 1995—. *Member:* State Bar of Michigan; American Bar Association (Member, Sections on: Business Law and International Law). ***PRACTICE AREAS:*** Corporate; Securities; Corporate Governance; Mergers, Acquisitions and Divestitures; Strategic Alliances. ***Email:*** rwilczek@gcd.com

ELIZABETH ANNE WILLIAMS, born St. Charles, Illinois, June 13, 1968; admitted to bar, 1996, Illinois. *Education:* Acadia University (B.A., Honors, 1992); Northwestern University (J.D., cum laude, 1996). *Member:* Chicago and Illinois State Bar Associations. ***PRACTICE AREAS:*** Real Estate. ***Email:*** ewilliams@gcd.com

DAVID L. WOLFE, born Kankakee, Illinois, July 24, 1951; admitted to bar, 1976, Illinois. *Education:* University of Illinois (B.S., with highest honors, 1973); University of Michigan (J.D., cum laude, 1976). Certified Public Accountant, Illinois, 1973. Member, Firm's Management Committee. Speaker/Author, Numerous Employee Benefits Topics. ***PRACTICE AREAS:*** Employee Benefits Law; Retirement Plans; Health Care; Executive Compensation; ERISA Litigation; Deferred Compensation. ***Email:*** dwolfe@gcd.com

RICHARD W. YOUNG, born Greenwich, Connecticut, January 26, 1956; admitted to bar, 1981, Illinois; 1996, U.S. Supreme Court; U.S. Court of Appeals, Third, Seventh, Tenth and Federal Circuits; registered to practice before U.S. Patent and Trademark Office. *Education:* Yale College (B.S., 1978); Indiana University (J.D., 1981). Executive Editor, Indiana Law Journal, 1980-1981. Author: "Constitutional Limitations on Government Disclosure of Private Trade Secret Information," 56 Indiana Law Journal 347 (1980); "U.S. Federal Circuits: Trademark Cases and the Judiciary" (INTA). *Member:* American Bar Association (Member, Sections on: Litigation; Intellectual Property); American Intellectual Property Law Association; Intellectual Property Law Association of Chicago; International Trademark Association (Member, Publications Committee). ***REPORTED CASES:*** Kos Pharmaceuticals v. Andrx Corp., 369 F.3d 700 (3d Cir. 2004); Ty Inc. v. Perryman, 306 F.3d 509 (7th Cir. 2002); Illinois High School Ass'n v. GTE Vantage Inc., 99 F.3d 244 (7th Cir. 1996). ***PRACTICE AREAS:*** Litigation; Intellectual Property Litigation; Advertising and Marketing; Literary Property. ***Email:*** ryoung@gcd.com

ALEX W. ZABROSKY, born Chicago, Illinois, August 18, 1953; admitted to bar, 1978, Illinois and U.S. District Court, Northern District of Illinois. *Education:* University of Chicago (A.B., with honors, 1975); Leningrad State University, Leningrad, U.S.S.R., St. Petersburg, Russia (Cert., 1974); George Washington University (J.D., 1978). Staff Associate, Journal of International Law and Economics, 1977. Author: "Consulting Law Update: Consulting Firm Hit for $1.6 Million in Damages," IMC Times, Summer 2002; (co-authored with Richard Hodgson), "LLPs In Great Britain," Consulting to Management, June 2002; (co-authored with George C. Glover, Jr.), "Consulting in Canada," Consulting to Management, September 2001; "Understanding the Legal ABCs of RIFs," Consultants News, July 2001; "The Art of Writing an Engagement Letter," Journal of Management Consulting, May 1999; "Court Rules Business Methods Patentable," Consultants News, February 1999; "Handling Deadbeat Clients Part II: Bankruptcy," Consultants News, August 1998. *Member:* Chicago and American (Member, Sections on: Corporate, Business and Banking Law, 1978—; International Law, 1977—) Bar Associations. ***PRACTICE AREAS:*** Business Law; International Business Law; Corporate Law; Investments; Foreign Investment. ***Email:*** azabrosky@gcd.com

HOWARD P. ZWEIG, born Minneapolis, Minnesota, July 17, 1954; admitted to bar, 1981, Illinois. *Education:* Cooper Union (B.Arch., 1978); University of Minnesota (J.D., cum laude, 1981). Member, 1979-1981 and Associate Editor, 1980-1981, Minnesota Law Review. *Member:* Chicago and Illinois State Bar Associations; National Association of College and University Attorneys. ***PRACTICE AREAS:*** Real Estate; Higher Education; Zoning, Planning and Land Use. ***Email:*** hzweig@gcd.com

OF COUNSEL

THOMAS ARTHUR, born Chicago, Illinois, June 12, 1930; admitted to bar, 1958, Illinois. *Education:* Hamilton College (B.A., 1952); Northwestern University (J.D., 1958). *Member:* Chicago and American Bar Associations. ***PRACTICE AREAS:*** Corporate Law; Securities Law; Health Law. ***Email:*** tarthur@gcd.com

EARL J. BARNES II, born Chicago, Illinois, April 18, 1964; admitted to bar, 1989, Illinois and U.S. District Court, Northern District of Illinois. *Education:* Lake Forest College (B.A., cum laude, 1986); University of Michigan (J.D., 1989). ***PRACTICE AREAS:*** Health Law.

RICHARD J. KISSEL, born Chicago, Illinois, November 27, 1936; admitted to bar, 1962, Illinois and U.S. Court of Appeals, Third, Seventh and District of Columbia Circuits; 1980, U.S. Supreme Court and U.S. District Court, Northern and Southern Districts of Illinois, Eastern District of New York and District of Kansas; 1984, U.S. Court of Appeals, Second Circuit; 1985, U.S. Court of Appeals, Third Circuit. *Education:* Northwestern University (B.A., 1958; J.D., 1961). Author: Water Pollution Chapter of Illinois Institute for Continuing Legal Education (IICLE) Handbook on Environmental Law, 1978, Updated, 1983 and 1988. Chairman, Environmental Affairs Committee of the Illinois State Chamber of Commerce, 1972-1976. Member, Visiting Committee, Northwestern University Law School Alumni Association, 1996-1999. Member, Committee on Courts for the 21st Century, Cook County. *Member:* Chicago, Lake County and Illinois State Bar Associations. Fellow, International Society of Barristers. Of Counsel, Gardner, Carton & Douglas, 2000—. ***PRACTICE AREAS:*** Environmental Law; Environmental Cleanup; Environmental Compliance; Environmental Insurance; Environmental Litigation. ***Email:*** rkissel@gcd.com

GORDON LANG, JR., born Evanston, Illinois, July 27, 1933; admitted to bar, 1960, Illinois. *Education:* Yale University (B.A., 1954); University of Arizona (M.A., 1958); Harvard Law School (LL.B., 1960). *Member:* Chicago (Member: Corporation Law Committee, 1975-1998; Financial Institutions Committee, 1985-1998), Illinois State and American (Member, Business Law Section) Bar Associations. [1st Lieutenant, U.S. Air Force, 1955-1957]. ***PRACTICE AREAS:*** General Corporate; Securities; Banking. ***Email:*** glang@gcd.com

(This Listing Continued)

GARDNER CARTON & DOUGLAS LLP, Chicago—Continued

JAMES J. McCLURE, JR., born Oak Park, Illinois, September 23, 1920; admitted to bar, 1950, Illinois. *Education:* University of Chicago (B.A., 1942); University of Chicago Law School (J.D., 1949). Order of the Coif. Editor-in-Chief, University of Chicago Law Review, 1948-1949. President, Village of Oak Park, 1973-1981. *Member:* Chicago, Illinois State and American Bar Associations; American College of Trust and Estate Counsel; American Law Institute. ***PRACTICE AREAS:*** HR Law; Wealth Planning. ***Email:*** jmcclure@gcd.com

PETER H. MERLIN, born Switzerland, November 3, 1928; admitted to bar, 1954, New York; 1955, Illinois; 2000, Colorado. *Education:* Collegium Marianum, Vaduz, Liechtenstein; University of Geneva, Switzerland, Law School (LL.B., 1950); University of Michigan Law School (J.D., 1953). *Member:* Chicago, Denver, Illinois State and Colorado Bar Associations. ***LANGUAGES:*** German and French. ***PRACTICE AREAS:*** Corporate Law; International Law. ***Email:*** pmerlin@gcd.com

WILLIAM L. MORRISON, born Nampa, Idaho, January 19, 1931; admitted to bar, 1958, Illinois. *Education:* Harvard University (A.B., 1952; LL.B., 1958). *Member:* Chicago Bar Association. ***PRACTICE AREAS:*** Tax Law. ***Email:*** wmorrison@gcd.com

GEOFFREY B. SHIELDS, admitted to bar, 1973, Vermont; 1975, District of Columbia; 1976, Illinois. *Education:* Harvard University; Yale Law School (J.D., 1972). Editor, Yale Law Journal. Law Clerk for Judge James L. Oakes, U.S. Court of Appeals, Second Circuit, 1972-1973. Assistant Counsel, Subcommittee on Multinational Corporations, United States Senate Foreign Relations Committee, 1973-1975. Counsel and Foreign Policy Advisor to U.S. Senator Frank Church, 1975-1976. Special Assistant to Secretary of HEW, 1977. Author: Over 40 articles on Mergers and Acquisitions, Finance and Securities issues. Co-Editor: *Merging Health Care Institutions,* AHA, 1987, and three other books on Healthcare Finance and Mergers and Acquisitions. Vice-Chairman, Chicago Counsel on Foreign Relations. Member, New York Council in Foreign Relations. Trustee, Shedd Aquarium. ***LANGUAGES:*** Spanish. ***PRACTICE AREAS:*** Securities Law; Corporate Law; Health Care; Antitrust and Trade Regulation. ***Email:*** gshields@gcd.com

GORDON H. SMITH, born Syracuse, New York, October 26, 1915; admitted to bar, 1939, New York; 1946, Illinois. *Education:* Princeton University (A.B., 1936); Yale University (LL.B., 1939). *Member:* Chicago, Illinois State and American Bar Associations. ***PRACTICE AREAS:*** Corporate and Securities Law. ***Email:*** gsmith@gcd.com

STEVEN M. WAGNER, admitted to bar, 1979, Illinois. *Education:* Eastern Illinois University (B.A., Economics, 1976); John Marshall Law School (J.D., with distinction, 1979). ***PRACTICE AREAS:*** Corporate Law; Corporate Trusts; Bankruptcy; Bankruptcy Reorganization. ***Email:*** swagner@gcd.com

COUNSEL

SUSAN BARNES DE RESENDIZ, born Athens, Ohio, July 6, 1947; admitted to bar, 1974, Ohio; 1975, District of Columbia; 1980, Florida; 1998, Texas (Not admitted in Illinois). *Education:* Ohio State University (B.A., cum laude, 1968; J.D., cum laude, 1974). Phi Beta Kappa. ***PRACTICE AREAS:*** Corporate Restructuring; Banking; Consumer Credit; Commercial Transactions; Corporate. ***Email:*** sderesendiz@gcd.com

CAROL LARCHER, born Hammond, Indiana, February 26, 1961; admitted to bar, 1994, Illinois; registered to practice before U.S. Patent and Trademark Office. *Education:* Murray State University (B.S., magna cum laude, 1983); University of Illinois at Urbana-Champaign (Ph.D., 1991); Loyola University of Chicago (J.D., 1994). ***PRACTICE AREAS:*** Intellectual Property; Biotechnology; Pharmaceuticals. ***Email:*** clarcher@gcd.com

MARK S. MELICKIAN, born Santa Monica, California, June 22, 1959; admitted to bar, 1995, Illinois; 1996, U.S. District Court, Northern District of Illinois. *Education:* Colorado State University (B.A., 1984); Northwestern University (J.D., 1995). *Member:* American Bar Association; American Bankruptcy Institute. ***PRACTICE AREAS:*** Corporate; Corporate Restructuring. ***Email:*** mmelickian@gcd.com

MICHAEL P. MORRISON, admitted to bar, 1972, Illinois. *Education:* University of Maine; Michigan State University (B.A., with honors, 1967); University of Texas at Austin (J.D., 1972). Phi Delta Phi; Lambda Alpha. Author: "U.S. Supreme Court Validates Landmark Laws," Illinois Bar Journal, 1979; "New Developments in the Use of Tax-Free Exchanges," Industrial Development, 1982. *Member:* Chicago, Illinois State and American (Executive Committee of the National Realty Committee) Bar Associations; Urban Land Institute (Full Member). ***PRACTICE AREAS:*** Real Estate Transactional and Securitization Practice. ***Email:*** mmorrison@gcd.com

KATHERINE N. O'CONNELL, born Park Ridge, Illinois, December 12, 1964; admitted to bar, 1993, Illinois. *Education:* University of Illinois (B.A., 1987); American University, Washington College of Law (J.D., 1993). *Member:* Chicago, Illinois State and American Bar Associations. ***PRACTICE AREAS:*** Real Estate; Environmental. ***Email:*** koconnell@gcd.com

ASSOCIATES

Kathleen O'Connor Adams; Terri Ahrens; Kelli Anne Alces; Kendra M. Allaband; David S. Almeida; Marla Anderson; Martin F. Barna; Christine S. Bautista; Carrie A. Beyer; Jeffrey R. Blumberg; Jarrett T. Bostwick; Mary Elizabeth Brown; Nicole M. Bulman; Julie A. Burger; Noreen H. Cull; Alice D. Czyzycki; John J. D'Attomo; Jennifer L. de Lyon; Melissa Skylas Dillenbeck; Shawna M. Doran; Sasha M. Engle; Kelly A. Fetzer; Ashley M. Fischer; Blake J. Fix; Noemi Flores; Lisa M. Formolo; David A. Frey; David P. Gearey; William L. Goldbeck; L. Robert Guenthner, III; Lawrence N. Hill; Scott M. Holmes; Jonathan E. Hyun; Alan A. Kelly; Ann M. Kim; Tina Kuska; Scott C. Lascari; Andrew D. McNair; Mina Mehta; Evan M. Meyers; Sarah Bassler Millar; David J. Moorhead; Steven J. Murawski; Douglas C. Murray; Nicole Murray; C. Brooks Newman; Michael A. Nicolas; Carrie E. O'Brien; Stephen R. Patterson; David W. Porteous; Kelly Powis; Tanvir A. Rahman; Rupal Raval; Howard J. Rosenburg; William R. Rucker; Heather Heath Ryan; Mary K. Samsa; Mark Schauerte; Arthur M. Scheller III; Daryl M. Schumacher; Wendy L. Seltzer; Lori L. Shannon; Steven S. Shonder; Annapurna Singh; David Neal Tanner; Laura Yates Taylor; Kevin Van Timmeren; Sally L. Venverloh; Virginia A. Walls; Krista L. Watson; Lionel W. Weaver; Andrew E. Weissman; John R. Wiktor; Richard A. Wulff.

CONTRACT ATTORNEY

BEATA K. SPUHLER, born Chicago, Illinois, 1974; admitted to bar, 1999, Illinois; U.S. Court of International Trade; U.S. Court of Appeals, Federal Circuit; U.S. District Court, Northern District of Illinois. *Education:* DePaul University (B.A., 1996); Chicago-Kent College of Law (J.D., 1999). ***PRACTICE AREAS:*** International Trade; Customs Law. ***Email:*** bspuhler@gcd.com

OFFICER

JACQUELINE M. SCHIMMEL, born Chicago, Illinois, June 13, 1964; admitted to bar, 1993, Wisconsin, Illinois and U.S. District Court, Western District of Wisconsin and Northern District of Illinois. *Education:* Rice University (B.A., 1987); University of Wisconsin-Madison (J.D., 1992). ***PRACTICE AREAS:*** Conflicts of Interest. ***Email:*** jschimmel@gcd.com

GARDNER LEGAL, P.C.

53 W. JACKSON BOULEVARD, SUITE 1524
CHICAGO, ILLINOIS 60604
Telephone: 312-788-1008
Fax: 312-788-1088
Email: gardner@gardnerlegal.com

Personal Injury, Criminal Defense, Traffic Violations, Commercial Litigation.

TIMOTHY J. GARDNER, born Maywood, Illinois, June 30, 1974; admitted to bar, 2000, Illinois. *Education:* Morehouse College (B.A., 1997); Loyola University (J.D., 2000). Psi Chi. *Member:* Chicago, Cook County and Illinois State Bar Associations. ***PRACTICE AREAS:*** Personal Injury; Criminal Defense; Litigation; Traffic Violations; Commercial Litigation. ***Email:*** gardner@gardnerlegal.com

GARFIELD & MEREL, LTD.

A PROFESSIONAL CORPORATION
223 WEST JACKSON BOULEVARD, SUITE 1010
CHICAGO, ILLINOIS 60606-6908
Telephone: 312-583-1600
Telecopier: 312-583-1700
URL: http://www.garfield-merel.com

Real Estate, Business Law and Commercial Litigation.

RICHARD A. MEREL, born Chicago, Illinois, November 26, 1950; admitted to bar, 1975, Illinois. *Education:* University of Illinois (B.S., 1972); DePaul University College of Law (J.D., 1975). *Member:* Chicago and Illinois State Bar Associations. ***PRACTICE AREAS:*** Real Estate; Business; Banking; Commercial Litigation. ***Email:*** rmerel@garfield-merel.com

ALAN H. GARFIELD, born Chicago, Illinois, September 4, 1949; admitted to bar, 1974, Illinois and U.S. District Court, Northern District of Illinois. *Education:* University of Illinois (B.A., 1974); DePaul University (J.D., 1974). *Member:* Chicago, Illinois State and American Bar Associations. ***PRACTICE AREAS:*** Real Estate; Business; Banking; Commercial Litigation. ***Email:*** garfield@garfield-merel.com

STEPHEN M. ALDERMAN, born Harvey, Illinois, May 13, 1959; admitted to bar, 1984, Illinois and U.S. District Court, Northern District of Illinois. *Education:* Michigan State University (B.A., with honors, 1981); University of Illinois (J.D., 1984). *Member:* Chicago, Illinois State and American Bar Associations; Decalogue Society of Lawyers; Equipment Leasing Association. ***PRACTICE AREAS:*** Secured Lending; Unsecured Finance; Corporate Law; Partnership Law; Equipment Leasing; Finance; Real Estate. ***Email:*** alderman@garfield-merel.com

---

KEITH A. CHADWICK, born August 31, 1964; admitted to bar, 1989, Illinois and U.S. District Court, Northern and Central Districts of Illinois. *Education:* Eastern Illinois University (B.A., 1986); Chicago-Kent College of Law (J.D., 1989). ***PRACTICE AREAS:*** Contracts; Medical Malpractice; Probate; Premises Liability; Commercial Litigation. ***Email:*** chadwick@garfield-merel.com

GREGORY A. McCORMICK, born Dallas, Texas, January 27, 1965; admitted to bar, 1989, Illinois and U.S. District Court, Northern District of Illinois. *Education:* DePaul University (B.A., with honors, 1986); IIT/Chicago Kent College of Law (J.D., with high honors, 1989). *Member:* Chicago, Illinois State and American Bar Associations; American Corporate Counsel Association. ***PRACTICE AREAS:*** Commercial Litigation; Labor and Employment Law; Insurance Law; Civil Practice. ***Email:*** mccormick@garfield-merel.com

GAROFALO, SCHREIBER, HART & STORM

CHARTERED
Established in 1997
55 WEST WACKER DRIVE, 10TH FLOOR
CHICAGO, ILLINOIS 60601
Telephone: 312-670-2000
Facsimile: 312-419-1336
URL: http://www.gshslaw.com

Insurance Defense Law, Employers' Liability, Workers Compensation-Defense, State and Federal, Trials and Appeals.

JOSEPH A. GAROFALO, born Chicago, Illinois, September 11, 1952; admitted to bar, 1977, Illinois and U.S. District Court, Northern District of Illinois including Trial Bar;

(This Listing Continued)

1987, U.S. Court of Appeals, Seventh Circuit. *Education:* North Park College (B.A., magna cum laude, 1974); DePaul University (J.D., 1977). Recipient, Louis Kokoris Memorial Scholarship in Political Science and Law, 1973-1974. Lecturer, Chicago Bar Association, "Trial of a Workers' Compensation Case," Spring, 1984 and "Case Developments in Workers' Compensation," Spring, 1988. Arbitrator, Circuit Court of Cook County, 1990. *Member:* Illinois State Bar Association; Workers' Compensation Lawyers Association; Chicago Bar Association; Will County Bar Association. ***PRACTICE AREAS:*** Insurance Defense; Workers Compensation Defense; Trials. ***Email:*** jgarofalo@gshslaw.com

SCOTT T. SCHREIBER, born Oak Park, Illinois, August 13, 1956; admitted to bar, 1981, Illinois. *Education:* Valparaiso University (B.A., 1978; J.D., 1981). Managing Editor, Valparaiso University Law Review, 1980-1981. Author: "The Unsupervised Child: Parental Negligence or Necessity," Valparaiso University Law Review, Vol. 15, P. 167, Fall, 1980. *Member:* Winnebago County Bar Association; Workers' Compensation Lawyers Association. ***PRACTICE AREAS:*** Insurance Defense; Workers Compensation Defense; Trials. ***Email:*** sschreiber@gshslaw.com

BENNETT F. HART, born Spencer, Iowa, July 22, 1954; admitted to bar, 1979, Illinois. *Education:* Iowa State University; University of Iowa (B.B.A., 1976; J.D., 1979). *Member:* Illinois State Bar Association; Workers' Compensation Lawyers Association. ***PRACTICE AREAS:*** Insurance Defense; Workers Compensation Defense; Trials. ***Email:*** bhart@gshslaw.com

DEREK A. STORM, born Mattoon, Illinois, July 28, 1959; admitted to bar, 1984, Illinois; 1987, U.S. District Court, District of Illinois. *Education:* Eastern Illinois University (B.A., with honor, 1981); DePaul University (J.D., 1984); University of London, England (LL.M., with merit, 1989). *Member:* Chicago Bar Association; Workers' Compensation Lawyers Association (Member, Board of Directors). ***PRACTICE AREAS:*** Insurance Defense; Workers Compensation Defense; Trials. ***Email:*** dstorm@gshslaw.com

GREGORY P. SUJACK, born Evergreen Park, Illinois, January 15, 1959; admitted to bar, 1984, Illinois; 1986, U.S. District Court, Central District of Illinois; 1987, U.S. Court of Appeals, Seventh Circuit; 1991, U.S. District Court, Northern District of Illinois, Trial Bar, 1992; 1992, U.S. Court of Appeals, Eighth Circuit; U.S. Supreme Court. *Education:* Boston College (B.S., 1981); Loyola University of Chicago (J.D., 1984). Clerk to Hon. William B. Wombacher, Illinois Appellate Court, Third District, 1985-1986. Lecturer, Peoria County Bar Association, Continuing Legal Education, 1988; Longshore Claims Association Seminar, 2002. *Member:* American Bar Association; State Bar of Wisconsin; Workers Compensation Lawyers Association; Longshore Claims Association. ***SPECIAL AGENCIES:*** U.S. Dept. of Labor; U.S. Benefits Review Board. ***PRACTICE AREAS:*** State and Federal Workers Compensation Defense; Employer's Liability; Appellate Advocacy; Insurance Defense. ***Email:*** gsujack@gshslaw.com

PHILIP G. BRINCKERHOFF, born Chicago, Illinois, June 3, 1958; admitted to bar, 1985, Illinois. *Education:* Marquette University (A.B., 1980); St. Louis University (J.D., 1985). Phi Alpha Theta. Member, Moot Court Board. *Member:* Chicago Bar Association; Illinois Association of Defense Trial Counsel. ***PRACTICE AREAS:*** Insurance Defense; Workers Compensation Defense; Employers Liability; Trials. ***Email:*** pbrinckerhoff@gshslaw.com

STEVEN R. SCARLATI, JR., born Paw Paw, Michigan, August 15, 1963; admitted to bar, 1990, Illinois. *Education:* Eastern Illinois (B.A., 1986); Western Michigan University; Chicago Kent College of Law (J.D., 1990). *Member:* Chicago Bar Association; Will County Bar Association; Workers' Compensation Lawyers Association. ***Email:*** sscarlati@gshslaw.com

JAMES R. CLUNE, born Springfield, Massachusetts, July 19, 1953; admitted to bar, 1978, Florida; 1980, Illinois, and U.S. District Court, Northern District of Illinois including Trial Bar. *Education:* University of Notre Dame (B.A., 1975); Stetson University (J.D., 1978). Phi Alpha Delta. Author: "Perfecting a Circuit Court Review and Appeal to the Appellate Court in a Workers' Compensation Proceeding," copyright 1993, Presented at the Chicago Bar Association Seminar, December 2, 1995; "Defending Against Malingerers," copyright 1993, Presented at the Workers' Compensation Claims Association Seminar, April 13, 1993; "The Impact of a Common Law Action on the Settlement Trial of a Workers' Compensation Claim-Respondent's Perspective," copyright 1993, Presented at the Chicago Bar Association Seminar, January 7, 1993. Co-Author: "Employer-Employee Problems," Illinois Workers' Compensation Practice, 1999 Edition, Illinois Institute for Continuing Legal Education. *Member:* The Florida Bar; Workers Compensation Lawyers Association (Board of Directors, 1989-1991). ***REPORTED CASES:*** Luttrell v. Industrial Comm., 154 Ill. App. 3d 943, 507 N.E. 2d 533, 107 Ill. Dec. 620 (Ill. App. 2 Dist., April 27, 1987). United Air Lines, Inc. v. CEI Industries of Illinois, Inc., 148 Ill. App. 3d 332, 499 N.E. 2d 558, 102 Ill, December 1, Prod. Liab. Rep. (CCH) P. 11, 218 (Ill. App. 1 Dist., Oct. 3, 1986). ***PRACTICE AREAS:*** Workers Compensation; Commercial Litigation; Tort Litigation. ***Email:*** jclune@gshslaw.com

ANDREW L. RANE, born Chicago, Illinois, June 27, 1967; admitted to bar, 1994, Illinois and U.S. District Court, Northern District of Illinois. *Education:* University of Illinois (B.A., 1990); Northern Illinois University (J.D., cum laude, 1994). Recipient, American Jurisprudence Award in Administrative Law. *Member:* Illinois State Bar Association; Workers' Compensation Lawyers Association. ***PRACTICE AREAS:*** Workers Compensation. ***Email:*** arane@gshslaw.com

JEFFREY C. HART, born Lincoln Park, Michigan, February 24, 1969; admitted to bar, 1995, Illinois and U.S. District Court, Northern District of Illinois. *Education:* Michigan State University (B.A., 1992); Loyola University of Chicago (J.D., 1995). Member, Outstanding College Students of American, 1990-1992. Case Editor, Loyola Consumer Law Reporter, 1994-1995. *Member:* American Bar Association; Workers' Compensation Lawyers Association. ***PRACTICE AREAS:*** Insurance Defense Litigation; Workers; Personal Injury Litigation. ***Email:*** jhart@gshslaw.com

TODD E. WEGMAN, born Aurora, Illinois, August 2, 1969; admitted to bar, 1996, Illinois. *Education:* Illinois State University (B.S., Public Relations, 1991); Chicago-Kent College of Law, Illinois Institute of Technology (J.D., 1996). *Member:* American Bar Association; Workers' Compensation Lawyers Association. ***PRACTICE AREAS:*** Workers Compensation; Trials. ***Email:*** twegman@gshslaw.com

(This Listing Continued)

CRAIG M. SCARPELLI, born Plainesville, New York, October 3, 1970; admitted to bar, 1996, Illinois and U.S. District Court, Northern District of Illinois. *Education:* University of Wisconsin, Madison (B.S., magna cum laude, 1992); DePaul University School of Law (J.D., 1996). Alumni Advisor, Phi Kappa Sigma. Recipient, American Jurisprudence Award in Legal Writing. DePaul Intramural Moot Court Competition, 1995. DePaul Legal Clinic (August 1997-May 1998). *Member:* Workers' Compensation Lawyers Association. ***PRACTICE AREAS:*** Workers Compensation; Personal Torts. ***Email:*** cscarpelli@gshslaw.com

KEVIN JAMES REID, born Farnborough Hants, England, December 12, 1968; admitted to bar, 1996, Illinois and U.S. District Court, Northern District of Illinois. *Education:* Boston College (B.A., 1991; B.A., 1991); DePaul University College of Law (J.D., 1996). Health Law Journal. Executive Editor, Environmental Law Digest. American Jurisprudence Award in Contracts. Legal Clinic, Staff Attorney. C0-author: "Taking a Claim Out of Comp-Reorganizing and Responding to Circumstances Which Make An Injury Non-Compensable," copyright 1998, Presented to the National Council on Education and Management, August 19, 1998. *Member:* Will County Bar Association; Workers' Compensation Lawyers Association. ***PRACTICE AREAS:*** Insurance Defense Litigation. ***Email:*** kreid@gshslaw.com

WILLIAM R. STANCZAK, born Waukegan, Illinois, November 14, 1971; admitted to bar, 1998, Illinois; 1999, Florida. *Education:* Michigan State University (B.A., 1995); DePaul University (J.D., 1998). *Member:* The Florida State Bar; Workers' Compensation Lawyers Association. ***PRACTICE AREAS:*** Workers Compensation. ***Email:*** wstanczak@gshslaw.com

DAVID P. HANSON, born Hobart, Indiana, May 25, 1974; admitted to bar, 2001, Illinois. *Education:* Indiana University (B.S., 1997); DePaul University (J.D., 2000). Phi Alpha Delta. *Member:* Chicago Bar Association; Workers' Compensation Lawyers Association. ***LANGUAGES:*** Japanese. ***PRACTICE AREAS:*** Workers Compensation. ***Email:*** dhanson@gshslaw.com

DANIEL L. GRANT, born Plano, Illinois; admitted to bar, 2002, Illinois. *Education:* Illinois State University (B.S., 1998); DePaul University College of Law (J.D., 2002). *Member:* American Bar Association; Workers' Compensation Lawyers Association. ***PRACTICE AREAS:*** Workers Compensation; Longshore and Harbor Workers Compensation Act. ***Email:*** dgrant@gshslaw.com

CHRISTOPHER P. CARR, born Washington, D.C.; admitted to bar, 1998, Illinois. *Education:* University of Michigan (B.A., 1992); DePaul University (J.D., 1998). *Member:* Illinois State Bar Association; Illinois Defense Trial Counsel. ***PRACTICE AREAS:*** Civil Litigation; Insurance Defense; Construction Law; Workers Compensation. ***Email:*** ccarr@gshslaw.com

JUAN A. RODRIGUEZ-DEL MORAL, born Chicago, Illinois, April 2, 1970; admitted to bar, 2004, Illinois. *Education:* DePaul University (B.A., 1993); Chicago-Kent College of Law, Illinois Institute of Technology (J.D., 2003). *Member:* Chicago, Illinois State and American Bar Associations. ***PRACTICE AREAS:*** Workers Compensation. ***Email:*** jrodriguez-delmoral@gshslaw.com

SHAWN F. LUEDDE, born Carbondale, Pennsylvania, September 9, 1977; admitted to bar, 2004, Illinois. *Education:* Wright State University (B.A., 2001); John Marshall Law School (J.D., 2004). Recipient, Public Interest Law Initiative Scholarship, 2002. *Member:* Chicago, Illinois State and American Bar Associations. ***PRACTICE AREAS:*** Workers Compensation; Employer Liability. ***Email:*** sluedde@gshslaw.com

RONAK T. JOSHI, born Toronto, Ontario, Canada, December 2, 1977; admitted to bar, 2004, Illinois. *Education:* University of Toronto (B.A., 2001); John Marshall Law School (J.D., 2004). Recipient, 5 Academic Scholarships, John Marshall Law School. Member, John Marshall Law School Law Review. Member, Moot Court. *Member:* American Bar Association (Lieutenant Governor, 7th Circuit, 2002-2003). ***LANGUAGES:*** English, French, Hindi and Gujarati. ***PRACTICE AREAS:*** Workers Compensation; Civil Practice. ***Email:*** rjoshi@gshslaw.com

ANITA S. OAK, born Toledo, Ohio, September 8, 1978; admitted to bar, 2003, Illinois. *Education:* The Ohio State University (B.A., 2000); John Marshall Law School (J.D., 2003). *Member:* Chicago and American Bar Associations. ***PRACTICE AREAS:*** Workers Compensation; Insurance Defense. ***Email:*** asoak@gshslaw.com

OF COUNSEL

RALPH L. BERKE, born Chicago, Illinois, April 7, 1950; admitted to bar, 1974, Illinois; 1981, U.S. District Court, Northern District of Illinois; 1986, U.S. Court of Appeals, Seventh Circuit; 1989, U.S. Supreme Court; 1990, U.S. Court of the Armed Forces. *Education:* Wheaton College (B.A., with high honors, 1971); Northwestern University (J.D., 1974). Pi Gamma Mu. [Lt. Col., U.S. Army Reserve]. ***PRACTICE AREAS:*** Litigation; Estate Planning; Business Transactions.

REPRESENTATIVE CLIENTS: Addison Insurance Company; Advocate Health Care; Aida; Alcoa; Allstate Insurance Company; American Airlines; American Bottling, Inc.; American Contractors Inc.; American Country Insurance Company; American Family Insurance; Amerisure Company; Arch Construction; Army Airforce Exchange Service; Broadspire; Cambridge Integrated Services Group; Chesterfield Services, Inc.; Chicago Sun Times, Inc.; Clark Construction Group, Inc.; CompManagement, Inc.; Continental Cable; Conway Central Express; Consolidated Freeways; Construction Program Group; Covenant Management; Corn Products International; Crawford and Company; Crum & Forster; Dick Corporation; Dominicks; Eagle Industries/Caron International; Edward Gray Corp.; Eichleay Corp.; Gallagher Bassett; Gates McDonald; G.E. Riddiford Company; Great Central Insurance Company; H.I.H. America; Edward Hines Lumber Company; Illinois Compensation Trust; Illinois Insurance Guaranty Fund; ITT Specialty Risk; J.A. Jones Construction Company; Jernberg Industries; Kenny Construction Company; Lakeside Building Maintenance; Lexington Homes; Lindsey Morden Claims Management, Inc.; Marinette Marine Corporation; Marmon-Keystone; McHugh Construction; McNulty Brothers Construction Company; Meccon Industries, Inc.; Minnesota Insurance Guaranty; New Breed Corporation; Northern American Specialty Insurance; Northwestern University; Ozinga; Pepper Construction Company; Pepsi-Cola General Bottlers; Power Maintenance & Constructors; Rail Terminal Services; Risk Enterprise Management; Rockford Headed Products; Rockford Memorial Hospital; Royal & SunAlliance; RSKCo.; Sentry Claims Service; Signal Administration, Inc.; Sisters of St. Francis/St. James Hospital; Snap On Tools; Southwest Airlines; St. Paul Insurance Company; St. Paul Seaboard; Tar Heel Insurance Management Services; Textron; Thatcher Engineering; Transguard Insurance of America; United Fire & Casualty; United Heartland; United Technologies Inc.; Unitrin Property & Casualty Insurance Group; Vanliner Insurance Company; Utica National Insurance Group; Vienna Beef; Virginia Surety Insurance Company; Vitran

(This Listing Continued)

GAROFALO, SCHREIBER, HART & STORM, CHARTERED, Chicago—Continued

Express; WabTec; Ward North America; Waste Management of North America; West Irving Dye Corporation; Wheatland; Williams Insurance Group; W.W. Grainger; Zurich-American Insurance Company.

AUDREY L. GAYNOR & ASSOCIATES, P.C.

20 SOUTH CLARK STREET, SUITE 1620
CHICAGO, ILLINOIS 60603
Telephone: 312-201-0030
Fax: 312-201-0608
Email: audreygaynor@earthlink.net
URL: http://www.lawyers.com/gaynor

Family Law, Divorce, Paternity, Child Custody, Child Support, Domestic Violence, Premarital Agreements, Spousal Support.

AUDREY L. GAYNOR, born Detroit, Michigan, January 28, 1961; admitted to bar, 1988, California; 1992, Illinois. *Education:* University of Michigan (B.A., with highest distinction, 1983; J.D., 1986). Law Clerk to the Hon. Clarence A. Brimmer, Chief Judge, U.S. District Court, District of Wyoming, 1986-1987. *Member:* Bar Association of San Francisco; Chicago, Illinois State and American Bar Associations; State Bar of California. ***PRACTICE AREAS:*** Family Law; Civil Litigation. **Email:** audreygaynor@earthlink.net

GEORGE M. SANDERS, born Geneva, Switzerland, November 14, 1964; admitted to bar, 1990, New York and U.S. District Court, Southern and Eastern Districts of New York; 1993, U.S. District Court, Northern District of Illinois and U.S. Court of Appeals, Second Circuit; 1994, Illinois. *Education:* St. John's University (B.A., summa cum laude, 1986); University of Chicago (J.D., 1989). Author: Chapter, "Antitrust," Business, Law, and the Internet: Essential Guidance for You, Your Clients, and Your Firm, IICLE, 2002 edition. *Member:* Illinois State and American Bar Associations. ***PRACTICE AREAS:*** Family Law; Commercial Litigation. **Email:** george_sanders@earthlink.net

MAUREEN A. MITCHEL, admitted to bar, 1978, Illinois; 2002, U.S. District Court, Northern District of Illinois. *Education:* Indiana University (B.A., with honors, 1975); Loyola University (J.D., 1978). ***PRACTICE AREAS:*** Family Law; Commercial Litigation. **Email:** maureenmitchel@earthlink.net

TAMI JAGGERS, born Indianapolis, Indiana, October 26, 1972; (admission pending). *Education:* Purdue University (B.A., 1996); Chicago-Kent College of Law (J.D., 2005). Director of Special Events for a radio station group in Indianapolis, Indiana. Assistant Publicist, Los Angeles Entertainment Public Relations Firm. Law Clerk: Chicago-Kent's Family Law Clinic; Audrey L Gaynor & Associates, P.C., January 2004. ***PRACTICE AREAS:*** Family Law; Divorce; Domestic Relations; Marital Agreements; Marital Property Distribution; Domestic Violence; Interstate Support; Marital Property Settlements; Paternity; Palimony; Post Divorce Modification; Postnuptial Agreements; Premarital Agreements; Qualified Domestic Relations Orders (QDROs); Restraining Orders; Separation Agreements; Spousal Support; Alimony; Equitable Distribution; Matrimonial Law; Uncontested Divorce. **Email:** tami&under;jaggers@earthlink.net

GEKAS & ASSOCIATES, LTD.

Established in 1997
11 SOUTH LA SALLE STREET, SUITE 1700
CHICAGO, ILLINOIS 60603
Telephone: 312-726-4501
Fax: 312-726-4505
Email: cjg@cjglaw.com
URL: http://www.cjglaw.com

State and Federal Civil and Criminal Litigation, Trials and Appellate Practice, Securities, Commodities, Intellectual Property, Bankruptcy, Employment and Real Estate Law.

CONSTANTINE JOHN (CHRIS) GEKAS, born Chicago, Illinois, March 1, 1946; admitted to bar, 1971, Illinois and U.S. District Court, Northern District of Illinois including Trial Bar; 1973, District of Columbia, Virginia and U.S. District Court, District of Columbia; 1974, U.S. Supreme Court; 1978, U.S. Court of Appeals for the District of Columbia Circuit; 1984, U.S. Court of Appeals, Seventh Circuit; 1988, U.S. Court of Appeals, Ninth Circuit; 1993, Arizona. *Education:* University of Chicago (B.A., 1967); University of Illinois (J.D., 1970). Partner, Harvitt & Gekas, Ltd., 1985-1997. Regional Counsel, Midwest Region, Division of Enforcement, United States Commodity Futures Trading Commission, 1980-1984. Assistant United States Attorney, District of Columbia, 1976-1980. Associate Counsel, Subcommittee on Crime, House Judiciary Committee, United States House of Representatives, 1974-1976. Counsel, Impeachment Inquiry, House Judiciary Committee, United States House of Representatives, 1974. Attorney, Criminal Division, United States Department of Justice, 1973-1974. Associate, Chadwell, Keck, Kayser & Ruggles, Chicago, Illinois, 1971-1972. [With USAR, Intelligence Corps, 1969-1975]. ***REPORTED CASES:*** Walters v. Metropolitan Educational Enterprises, Inc., 519 U.S. 202 (1997). ***PRACTICE AREAS:*** Securities; Commodities; Commercial Litigation; Employment Law. **Email:** cgekas@cjglaw.com

SHERYL RAE GHEZZI

CHICAGO, ILLINOIS

(See Lincolnwood)

Civil Litigation, Family Law, Child Custody, Divorce, Premarital Agreements, D.U.I., Drug Crimes, Juvenile Crimes, Misdemeanors, Traffic, DUI Defense, Immigration, Wills and Probate, Divorce, Child Support, Visitation Interference, Visitation Abuse, Personal Injury Defense, Property Damage Defense, Estate Planning, Real Estate Litigation.

GIGNILLIAT & HYMEN, P.C.

CHICAGO, ILLINOIS

(See Northbrook)

Corporate, Estate Planning, Trusts and Estates, Wills and Probate, Taxation and Real Estate Law, Commercial Real Estate.

GIORDANO & NEILAN, LTD.

Established in 1996
360 NORTH MICHIGAN AVENUE, SUITE 1005
CHICAGO, ILLINOIS 60601
Telephone: 312-580-5480
Fax: 312-580-5481
URL: http://www.dereglaw.com
Email: giordanoneilan@dereglaw.com
URL: http://www.lawyers.com/giordano_law

Energy and Telecommunications Law.

FIRM PROFILE: Giordano & Neilan, Ltd. is Chicago's first law firm devoted to representation of clients on energy and telecommunications matters. The firm was founded in 1996 by Patrick N. Giordano, previously a partner at the national law firm of Foley & Lardner and supervisor of the Public Utilities Division for then Cook County State's Attorney Richard M. Daley. Giordano & Neilan, Ltd. provides representation on regulatory, litigation, transactional and legislative matters pertaining to all aspects of the energy and telecommunications industries.

PATRICK N. GIORDANO, born New York, N.Y., August 16, 1952; admitted to bar, 1979, Oregon; 1980, Illinois. *Education:* Tufts University (B.A., 1974); Northwestern School of Law of Lewis and Clark College (J.D., 1979). Partner, Foley & Lardner, 1989-1996. Supervisor, Public Utilities Division, Cook County State's Attorney's Office, 1981-1989. Chairman, Legislative/Regulatory Committee, Chicago Area Clean Cities Program, 1993-1996. *Member:* Chicago (Chairman, Energy and Environment Committee, 1988-1989), Illinois State and American Bar Associations; Oregon State Bar. ***REPORTED CASES:*** County of Cook v. Midcon Corp., 773 F.2d 892 (7th Cir. 1983), People ex rel. Hartigan v. Illinois Com. Comm., 148 Ill. 2d 348 (1992); Business and Professional People v. Illinois Com. Comm., 146 Ill.2d 175 (1991); Business and Professional People v. Illinois Com. Comm., 136 Ill. 2d 192 (1989); People ex rel. Hartigan v. Illinois Com. Comm, 117 Ill. 2d 120 (1987); Central Illinois Light Co. v. Illinois Com. Comm., 255 Ill. App. 3d 876 (1993); City of Chicago v. Illinois Com. Comm., 233 Ill. App. 3d 992 (1992); Bloom Township High School, et al. v. Illinois Com. Comm., 309 Ill. App.3d 163 (1999). ***PRACTICE AREAS:*** Electric Power; Energy Regulation; Energy Competition; Energy Contracts; Cogeneration; Energy Deregulation; Energy Marketing; Energy Project Development; Alternative Energy; Energy Facility Siting; Independent Power; International Energy Law; Wholesale Power Contracts; Broadcast Regulation; Telecommunication Regulation; Telecommunication Competition; Telecommunication Contracts; Electric Utilities; Electric Utility Regulation; Telephone Utilities; Telephone Utility Regulation. **Email:** patrickgiordano@dereglaw.com

PAUL G. NEILAN, born Brooklyn, New York, May 9, 1958; admitted to bar, 1983, Illinois. *Education:* Columbia University (B.A., cum laude, 1980); University of Chicago Law School (J.D., 1983). Recipient, Ann Barber Outstanding Service Award. Author: Chapter 4, "Subordination Agreements," and Chapter 5, "Participations, Syndications and Assignments," in *Advanced Commercial Finance and Creditors' Rights in Illinois,* Illinois Institute for Continuing Legal Education 1993; "Secured Lender Wins on All Counts in Fraudulent Conveyance Attack," in *The Secured Lender,* May/June 1994. *Member:* Chicago (Chairman, Commercial Finance and Transactions Committee, 1993-1994) and American Bar Associations. ***PRACTICE AREAS:*** Telecommunications Law; Telephone Utilities; Energy Deregulation; Energy Contracts; Business Transactions; Commercial Loans; Secured Transactions; Commercial Real Estate Finance; Finance; Mergers and Acquisitions. **Email:** paulneilan@dereglaw.com

OF COUNSEL

LAWRENCE WEISS, born New Kensington, Pennsylvania, September 12, 1949; admitted to bar, 1974, Pennsylvania; 1975, District of Columbia (Not admitted in Illinois). *Education:* University of Virginia (B.A., 1971); University of Georgia (J.D., 1974). Phi Delta Phi. Member and Editor, Georgia Journal of International and Comparative Law, 1973. Author: "The International Legal Implications of Weather Modification Activities," 4 Georgia Journal of International and Comparative Law, 159, 1974; "The Role of The NRC in Export Licensing," Atomic Energy Law Journal, 1977; With William O. Doub, "International Nuclear Commerce in the Age of Interdependence," Vanderbilt Law Review, 1979; "Cogeneration and Small Power Production Manual", Fairmont, 1997; Wheeling and Transmission Manual, Fairmont, 1998. Attorney, Federal Energy Administration, 1974-1975. Assistant to the Commissioner, Nuclear Regulatory Commission, 1975-1977. *Member:* The District of Columbia Bar; Pennsylvania and Federal Bar Associations. ***PRACTICE AREAS:*** Electric Power; Cogeneration; Energy Competition; Energy Contracts; Energy Regulation; Federal Energy Regulation; Wholesale Power Contracts; Energy Deregulation. **Email:** lweiss@compowergroup.com

ASSOCIATES

ARTHUR Z. HANDELMAN, born Boston, Massachusetts, August 16, 1962; admitted to bar, 1989, Illinois; 1990, U.S. District Court, Northern District of Illinois. *Education:* Connecticut College (B.A., 1984); Emory University (J.D., 1988); Loyola University Chicago, School of Law (LL.M., Health Law, 2001). Phi Delta Phi. Recipient, American Jurisprudence Award in Entertainment. *Member:* American Bar Association (Member, Civil Litigation Section). ***REPORTED CASES:*** Maddox v. Rozek 203 11. Dec. 125, 639 N.E. 2s 164, 111. App. 1st Distr. 1994. ***PRACTICE AREAS:*** Energy Deregulation; Energy

(This Listing Continued)

Contracts; Electric Utilities; Electric Utility Regulation; Telecommunications Law; Telephone Utilities; Health Law; Civil Litigation; Commercial Litigation. **Email:** arthurhandelman@dereglaw.com

CHRISTINA A. PUSEMP, born Oak Park, Illinois, April 5, 1975; admitted to bar, 2003, Illinois. *Education:* DePaul University (B.A., cum laude, 2000); University of Oregon (J.D., 2003). Symposium Editor and Managing Board Member, Journal of Environmental Law and Litigation, 2002-2003. *Member:* Chicago and American Bar Associations. ***PRACTICE AREAS:*** Energy Deregulation; Energy Contracts; Business Transactions; Electric Utility Regulation; Telecommunications Law. **Email:** christinapusemp@dereglaw.com

REPRESENTATIVE CLIENTS: Trizec Properties, Inc.; Shorenstein Realty Services, L.P.; Chicago Public Schools; Draper and Kramer, Inc.; Tempel Steel Co.; Deutsche Financial Services Corp.; Gamesa Energia S.A.; MB Real Estate, Inc.; Handy Industries; Building Owners and Managers Association of Chicago.

GLEASON & MACMASTER, LLC

77 WEST WASHINGTON, SUITE 1218
CHICAGO, ILLINOIS 60602
Telephone: 312-578-9530
Fax: 312-578-9524
URL: http://www.gleasonmacmasterlaw.com

Bankruptcy, Divorce, Real Estate, Driving While Intoxicated (DUI).

MEMBERS OF FIRM

TROY L. GLEASON, born Defiance, Ohio, December 17, 1969; admitted to bar, 2002, Illinois. *Education:* University of Toledo (B.A., 1992; J.D., 1995). **Email:** troy@gleasonmacmaster.com

SARAH R. MACMASTER, born Harrisonburg, Virginia, August 1, 1974; admitted to bar, 1999, Illinois. *Education:* Miami University (B.A., 1995); The Ohio State University (J.D., 1999). **Email:** sarah@gleasonmacmaster.com

ASSOCIATE

JULIE M. GLEASON, born Toledo, Ohio, April 17, 1971; admitted to bar, 2000, Illinois. *Education:* Lourdes College (B.A., 1995); University of Toledo (J.D., 1999). ***PRACTICE AREAS:*** Bankruptcy; Divorce; Driving While Intoxicated. **Email:** julie@gleasonmacmaster.com

PAUL M. GLICK, CHARTERED

10 SOUTH LASALLE STREET, SUITE 1017
CHICAGO, ILLINOIS 60603
Telephone: 312-419-4770
Fax: 312-419-4771
Email: pmg@pglicklaw.com

Tax and Employee Benefits Law.

PAUL M. GLICK, born New York, N.Y., December 7, 1948; admitted to bar, 1973, Illinois and U.S. Tax Court; 1976, U.S. Supreme Court and U.S. Claims Court. *Education:* University of Wisconsin (B.A., with distinction, 1970); DePaul University (J.D., cum laude, 1973). Pi Sigma Alpha; Pi Gamma Mu. Professor, DePaul University Graduate School of Law, 1978-1984. Author: "When Should Rabbi Trusts Be Used to Secure Non-Qualified Deferred Compensation Arrangements?" *Estate Planning,* January/February, 1988; "Close Corps Must Reconsider Cafeteria Plan Benefits in Light of Proposed Regs.," Estate Planning, September/October, 1989. Member: Midwest Pension Conference, 1976—; Profit Sharing Council of America, 1980-1986. Associate Member, American Society of Pension Actuaries, 1982-1994. Public Member, Illinois Public Employees Pension Laws Commission, 1984-1985. Member, State of Illinois Retirement System Task Force, 1985. *Member:* Chicago (Member, Employee Benefits Committee, 1973—), Illinois State and American Bar Associations; American Judicature Society. ***PRACTICE AREAS:*** Employee Benefits. **Email:** pmg@pglicklaw.com

STEPHEN A. GLICKMAN, P.C.

225 WEST WASHINGTON STREET
SUITE 2300
CHICAGO, ILLINOIS 60606
Telephone: 312-960-9550
Fax: 312-960-9555
Email: sagpc@aol.com

Employment Law, Employment Discrimination, Litigation, Sexual Harassment, Wrongful Termination, Separation Agreements, Executive Severance, Employment Contracts, Human Resources, Business Lawsuits, and General Commercial Litigation.

FIRM PROFILE: Stephen A. Glickman, P.C. serves a broad range of clients, with an emphasis on employment law, commercial litigation and human resources advice and counseling.

STEPHEN A. GLICKMAN, born Chicago, Illinois, July 1, 1961; admitted to bar, 1987, Illinois and U.S. District Court, Northern District of Illinois; 1989, Federal Trial Bar and U.S. Court of Appeals, Seventh Circuit. *Education:* University of Wisconsin-Madison (B.A., 1983); DePaul University College of Law (J.D., 1987). Arbitrator, Circuit Court of Cook County. ***PRACTICE AREAS:*** Employment Law; Employment Discrimination; Litigation; Sexual Harassment; Wrongful Termination; Separation Agreements; Executive Severance; Employment Contracts; Human Resources; Business Lawsuits; General Commercial Litigation.

HERBERT A. GLIEBERMAN & ASSOCIATES

Established in 1956
19 SOUTH LA SALLE STREET, SUITE 600
CHICAGO, ILLINOIS 60603-1402
Telephone: 312-236-2879
Fax: 312-236-3417
URL: http//www.herbertgliebermandivorce.com
Email: hglieber@aol.com
URL: http://www.lawyers.com/hglieber

Divorce Law, Family Law, Domestic Relations, Child Custody.

FIRM PROFILE: Representing Clients from all counties in Illinois and in other states in association with local attorneys as co-counsel in all issues arising in family law, including divorce, custody, alimony, child support, visitation and paternity cases.

Frequent guest on radio and television programs across the country. Former host of Ask the Lawyer and Law and Controversy, two radio shows that aired in 38 states over NBC and WMAQ in Chicago.

HERBERT A. GLIEBERMAN, admitted to bar, 1954, Illinois; 1987, District of Columbia. *Education:* Chicago-Kent College of Law (J.D., 1953). Author: "Confessions of a Divorce Lawyer"; "Four Weekends to an Ideal Marriage"; "Closed Marriage"; "Know Your Legal Rights," *Consumer's Digest*; "Child Custody," *Illinois Family Law*; "Discovery Tactics in a Divorce Case," and "Trying a Divorce Case," *The Chicago Bar Record*; "No-Fault as Another Ground for Dissolution in Illinois," *Illinois Trial Lawyer Journal*; "Prenuptial Agreements," *Trial Magazine* ; "Marriage-Divorce-Disaster"; "Some Syndromes of Love"; "Depositions and Divorce Actions," *The Practical Lawyer* . Lecturer, Family Law: Chicago-Kent College of Law; Northwestern University Law School; Decalogue Society of Lawyers; American Bar Association; Illinois State Bar Association; Chicago Bar Association; American Academy of Matrimonial Lawyers; Association of Trial Lawyers of America; Illinois Trial Lawyers Association; North Carolina State Bar Association; Idaho State Bar Association; Northwest Suburban Bar Association; Illinois Certified Public Accountants Foundation; DuPage Estate Planning Council; Continuing Legal Education/Satellite Network, Inc.; International Law Institute. Listed in: Who's Who in the World; Who's Who in America; Who's Who in the Midwest; Who's Who in American Law; Who's Who in Finance and Industry; The Best Lawyers in America; Million Dollar Lawyers. *Member:* Chicago (Member, Matrimonial Law Committee), Illinois State (Member, Family Law Committee; Past Chair, Publicity Committee; Matrimonial Law Committee) and American (Member, Matrimonial Law Section) Bar Associations; American Academy of Matrimonial Lawyers (Chartered Member); The Association of Trial Lawyers of America (Past Chair, Family Law Litigation Section).

GOEDERT, HUNTINGTON & DEBOER

CHICAGO, ILLINOIS

(See Oak Park)

Business Law, Corporate Law, Mergers and Acquisitions, Contracts, Employee Benefits, Taxation, Trusts and Estates, Wills, Decedents Estates, Probate, Elder Law, Nonprofit and Charitable Organizations, Real Estate.

JEFFREY M. GOLDBERG LAW OFFICES

Established in 1975
20 NORTH CLARK STREET, SUITE 3100
CHICAGO, ILLINOIS 60602
Telephone: 312-236-4146
Fax: 312-236-5913
Fax: 1-800-564-1707
Email: firm@goldberglaw.com
URL: http://www.goldberglaw.com

Plaintiffs Personal Injury firm including Product Liability, Birth Injuries, Medical Malpractice, Aviation, Wrongful Death, Occupant Restraint and Seat Belt Accidents, F.E.L.A., Premises Liability, Class Action, Brain Injury.

FIRM PROFILE: The firm was formed in 1975 by Jeffrey M. Goldberg. Mr. Goldberg concentrates in the handling of catastrophic personal injury and wrongful death cases. The firm has handled a wide variety of product liability, aviation and major medical malpractice claims. Mr. Goldberg has regularly been involved in multiple multi-million dollar settlements and verdicts. The firm has in-house support of an investigator and full time nurse. A substantial portion of the firm's representation is based on referrals from other attorneys recognizing the firm's specialization and expertise in handling substantial matters.

JEFFREY M. GOLDBERG, born Chicago, Illinois, March 8, 1948; admitted to bar, 1974, Illinois and U.S. District Court, Northern District of Illinois. *Education:* Bradley University (B.S.,1970); John Marshall Law School (J.D., 1974). Member: Moot Court Team; Client Counseling Competition Team, 1973. Private Pilot, Instrument Rated, 1980. Co-Editor, Illinois Institute of Continuing Education, Medical Malpractice Handbook, 1989 and revision, 1992, 1995. Author: "Barring the Defendant from Using Annuity Trial Testimony," Illinois Trial Lawyers Journal, 1988. Author and Speaker: "Anatomy of Pre-Trial Preparation - Professional Negligence/Product Liability, Illinois State Bar Association, 1995; "Cross Examination of Defendant's Liability Expert," Illinois Trial Lawyers Association, October 14, 1996; "Handling Subsequent Treating Physicians," Illinois Trial Lawyers Association, December 7, 1996; "Proving that the Product is Unreasonably Dangerous," Illinois Trial Lawyers Association, January 11, 1997; "Option Evidence - What the Experts Can Testify To," Illinois Trial Lawyers Association, May 3, 1997; "Professional Negligence/Product Liability," Law Education Series, Illinois State Bar Association, 1995;

(This Listing Continued)

JEFFREY M. GOLDBERG LAW OFFICES, Chicago—Continued

"Proving Proximate Cause: Medical and Legal Considerations," Illinois Trial Lawyers Association, 1995; "Using the Power of Visual Persuasion - How to Prepare Admissible Demonstrative Evidence," Chicago Bar Association, September 24, 1997; "Closing Argument, Medical Negligence Trial: Winning the Plaintiff's Case in Chief," Illinois Trial Lawyers Association, December 6, 1997; "Examining Your Expert with Confidence," Illinois Trial Lawyers Association, January 10, 1998. Lecturer: ITLA Products Liability Seminar, 1995; ITLA Torts Update Seminar, 1994; Civil Practice Update, Chicago Bar Association, 1980 and 1981; Medical Malpractice, Illinois Institute of Continuing Legal Education, 1989, 1992, 1995; Hearsay Evidence, 1988, Expert Witnesses, 1989, Trial Techniques, 1987 and Medical Malpractice Seminar, 1991, Illinois Trial Lawyers Association; Chairman, Illinois Trial Lawyers Association 1992 Medical Malpractice Seminar. Moderator, 1993 ITLA Medical Malpractice Seminar. Speaker: ITLA, Update Seminar Speaker; ITLA 1994 Product Liability Seminar. Avoiding Medical Malpractice Claims, Midwest Podiatric Association, 1987; Product Liability in the Food Processing Industry, American Food Processing Association, 1987; Trial Practice Seminar, Lewis University, College of Law, 1980; Northwest Suburban Emergency Medical Services Seminar, For Emergency Physicians, Paramedics and Emergency Nurses, 1986, 1987, 1988, 1990; Medical — Legal Aspect of Neurosurgical Practice, American Association of Neurological Surgeon, 1991. Guest Speaker, Parents of Developmentally Disabled Children, 1990. Chairman, Trial Lawyers Association Medical Malpractice Seminar, 1992-1993. Panel Member on the "Mediating the Medical Malpractice Case" Seminar sponsored by the Health Care Risk Management Society of Metropolitan Chicago, February 8, 1996. *Member:* Chicago (Chairman, Committee on Legal Specialization, Young Lawyers Division, 1977; Vice Chairman, 1980 and Chairman, 1981, Tort Litigation Committee; Investigatory Member, Investigation Section, 1980-1983 and Member, Hearing Section, 1984-1987, Judicial Evaluation Committee) and Illinois State Bar Associations; Illinois Trial Lawyers Association (Member, Board of Managers, 1987-1991; Parliamentarian, 1991-1992; Treasurer, 1992-1994; Secretary, 1995; Chairman, Insurance Committee, 1992, 1994; Member, Medical Negligence Committee, 1992-1994; Chairman, Membership Committee, 1987-1988; Member, Legislative Committee, 1989, 1990, 1991, 1992); Lawyers-Pilots Bar Association; Roscoe Pound Foundation; American Bar Foundation; The Association of Trial Lawyers of America (Member: Board of Directors, Center for Disability and Elder Law; Board of Directors, Birth Trauma Litigation Group); The Society of Trial Lawyers (Member, Executive Board); Trial Lawyers for Public Justice (President). ***PRACTICE AREAS:*** Personal Injury; Aviation; Products Liability; Medical Malpractice; Negligence; Tort Law; Commercial Litigation. ***Email:*** jgoldberg@goldberglaw.com

GARY P. ANNES, born Chicago, Illinois, March 9, 1970; admitted to bar, 1995, Illinois. *Education:* University of Illinois, Urbana-Champaign (B.A., 1992); Loyola University School of Law (J.D., 1995). ***Email:*** gannes@goldberglaw.com

DAVID P. BUCHANAN, born Mexico City, Mexico, August 1, 1963; admitted to bar, 1992, Texas; 2001, Illinois. *Education:* Texas A & M University (B.A., Biology, 1986); University of Texas at Austin (B.S., 1988); Drake University (J.D.; M.A., 1992). Delta Theta Phi. *Member:* State Bar of Texas; Illinois State and American Bar Associations. ***LANGUAGES:*** Spanish. ***PRACTICE AREAS:*** Medical Malpractice. ***Email:*** dbuchanan@goldberglaw.com

GEOFFREY G. JOHNSON, born Chicago, Illinois, March 11, 1947; admitted to bar, 1974, Washington; 1975, Illinois. *Education:* University of Washington (B.A., 1970); John Marshall School of Law (J.D., 1974). *Member:* Illinois State Bar Association; Illinois Trial Lawyers Association. ***PRACTICE AREAS:*** Personal Injury; Litigation. ***Email:*** gjohnson@goldberglaw.com

MEGAN E. LASER, born Berwyn, Illinois, December 8, 1974; admitted to bar, 2004, Illinois; 2005, U.S. District Court, Northern District of Illinois. *Education:* University of Wyoming (B.S., 1998); Chicago-Kent College of Law (J.D., 2004). *Member:* DuPage County and Illinois State Bar Associations; Trial Lawyers for Public Justice. ***PRACTICE AREAS:*** Medical Malpractice; Personal Injury. ***Email:*** mlaser@goldenberglaw.com

DON M. SOWERS, JR., born Oak Park, Illinois, December 15, 1959; admitted to bar, 1986, Illinois and U.S. District Court, Northern District of Illinois including Trial Bar; 1990, U.S. Court of Appeals, Seventh Circuit. *Education:* DePauw University; Texas Christian University (B.B.A., 1982); John Marshall Law School (J.D., 1986). Author: "Vacating Default Judgments Entered Due Solely to Attorney Neglect" CBA Record, October, 1992, republished ISBA Young Lawyers Newsletter, April, 1993. *Member:* Trial Lawyers Club of Chicago; American Trial Lawyers Association; Illinois Trial Lawyers Association. ***PRACTICE AREAS:*** Medical Malpractice; Personal Injury; Products Liability. ***Email:*** dsowers@goldberglaw.com

GOLDBERG, KOHN, BELL, BLACK, ROSENBLOOM & MORITZ, LTD.

55 EAST MONROE STREET, SUITE 3700
CHICAGO, ILLINOIS 60603
Telephone: 312-201-4000
Telecopier: 312-332-2196
Email: info@goldbergkohn.com
URL: http://www.goldbergkohn.com

Business Law, Business Litigation, Corporate, Commercial Finance, Asset-Based Finance, Real Estate, Creditor Bankruptcy, Workouts, Securities, Tax, Labor and Employment, Intellectual Property, Environmental Law.

FIRM PROFILE: Founded in 1976 by young partners from other Chicago firms, the firm has grown fifteen-fold to become one of the most respected mid-sized firms in Chicago. The firm's hiring standards are competitive with the largest firms in Chicago. Its clientele includes large institutions, entrepreneurs and middle market companies. The firm strives to staff matters leanly and to give close personal attention to all matters, large and small.

(This Listing Continued)

PRINCIPALS

OSCAR L. ALCANTARA, born Grosse Pointe, Michigan, May 6, 1968; admitted to bar, 1993, Illinois. *Education:* Harvard University (A.B., magna cum laude, 1990); University of Michigan (J.D., cum laude, 1993). Co-Author: "Termination of Licenses: What Happens to License Rights if a Termination Was Wrongful," The Licensing Journal, September 2003; "The Sale of Trademarked Inventory in Bankruptcy: Pitfalls for Trademark Owners," International Trademark Association, May 2003; "The Dilution of the Federal Trademark Dilution Act," For the Defense, August 2001; "Study Concerning a Possible Convention on Financing Issues Pertaining to Intellectual Property," The Secured Lender, May/June 2001; "Trademark Infringement on the Internet," Market Focus: Toys, May/June 1997; "Class Certification Under Rule 23," ABA National Institute on Class Actions, June 1997. Author: "Ownership of Health Information in the Information Age," Journal of the American Health Information Management Association, Vol. 69, No. 3, March 1998; "The Legend of Avalon: Perfection in Unregistered Copyrights May Not Be Possible," CBA Record, January 1998; "Ideology, Historiography and International Legal Theory," Vol. IX, no. 25., International Journal for the Semiotics of Law, 1996. Panelist: "Understanding Basic Principles of Trademark and Unfair Competition," Practising Law Institute, August 2001; "New Technologies and the Rules of the Game," Defense Research Institute, Technology Litigation The Next Wave, November 2000; "Ethics on the Internet," American Intellectual Property Law Association, Mid-Winter Institute on the Law and Use of the Internet, February 1999; "Intellectual Property Audits and Financing Transactions," The Corporate Counsel Center of Northwestern University School of Law, Symposium on Intellectual Property Law, October 1998; "Consumer Protection and NSF Checks Under the Fair Debt Collection Practices Act," Chicago Bar Association Continuing Legal Education Seminar, October 1997; "Defending Class Actions under the Fair Debt Collection Practices Act," Illinois Institute for Continuing Legal Education Seminar, September 1997. Moderator, "Use of Survey Evidence in Trademark Litigation," International Trademark Association, Annual Conference, May 1997. Co-Conference Co-Moderator, Protection of Product Configuration and Design, Chicago Bar Association, March 1998. Conference Co-Moderator, Developments in Intellectual Property Counterfeiting, Chicago Bar Association, March 1997. Presenter: Illinois Paralegal Association, "Intellectual Property Audits in Loan Transactions," October 2001; "Avoiding a Legal Blowout on the Information Superhighway: Selling Toys on the Internet," Toy Marketing Association, American International Toy Fair, February 2001; "Comments on Passage of the Illinois Right Publicity Statute," Chicago Bar Association, November 1998. Member: Meetings Committee Member, International Trademark Association, 2002—; National Academy of Recording Arts & Sciences, 2001—; Steering Committee Member, International Anti-Counterfeiting Coalition, TRIPs Compliance Project, 1995-1996. Co-Chair, ABA Intellectual Property Section, Legislative Sub-Committee on Right of Publicity, 2001—; Meritas, Intellectual Property Section, 1999—; Chicago Bar Association-Young Lawyers Section, Intellectual Property Committee, 1996-1998. ***PRACTICE AREAS:*** Trademark Law; Copyright Law. ***Email:*** Oscar.Alcantara@goldbergkohn.com

RONALD BARLIANT, born Chicago, Illinois, August 25, 1945; admitted to bar, 1969, Illinois. *Education:* Roosevelt University (B.A., 1966); Stanford University School of Law (J.D., 1969). Member, Editorial Board, Stanford Law Review. Professor, Debtor-Creditor Relations, John Marshall Law School, Spring 1992 and Spring 1993. Member: Board of Governors, National Conference of Bankruptcy Judges, 1998-2000; Board, National Conference of Bankruptcy Judges' Endowment for Education, 1997-1998. Vista Volunteer and Staff Attorney, Cook County Legal Assistance Foundation, 1996-1972. *Member:* American Bankruptcy Institute; American Bar Association. ***PRACTICE AREAS:*** Creditors Rights; Bankruptcy. ***Email:*** Ronald.Barliant@goldbergkohn.com

STEPHEN B. BELL, born Bristol, Virginia, April 22, 1944; admitted to bar, 1969, Illinois. *Education:* Wheaton College, Illinois (A.B., with high honors, 1966); Harvard University (J.D., cum laude, 1969). ***PRACTICE AREAS:*** Real Estate Law; Workout Law. ***Email:*** Stephen.Bell@goldbergkohn.com

DENNIS B. BLACK, born Chicago, Illinois, May 29, 1944; admitted to bar, 1968, Illinois. *Education:* Cornell University (A.B., magna cum laude, 1965); Harvard University (J.D., magna cum laude, 1968). Phi Beta Kappa; Phi Kappa Phi; Phi Eta Sigma. Member, Harvard Law Review, 1966-1968. Law Clerk, Seventh Circuit Court of Appeals, 1968-1969. Vice Chairman, Meritas, Law Firms Worldwide. *Member:* Chicago and American (Member, Corporation, Banking and Business Law Section) Bar Associations; Chicago Council of Lawyers. ***PRACTICE AREAS:*** Corporate and Finance Law; Partnerships. ***Email:*** Dennis.Black@goldbergkohn.com

PHILIP M. BLACKMAN, born Chicago, Illinois, April 26, 1962; admitted to bar, 1987, Illinois. *Education:* University of Michigan (B.A., Political Science, with highest honors, 1984); University of Chicago (J.D., 1987). ***PRACTICE AREAS:*** Commercial Finance. ***Email:*** Philip.Blackman@goldbergkohn.com

JAMI L. BRODEY, born Indianapolis, Indiana, February, 5, 1971; admitted to bar, 1998, Illinois. *Education:* University of Pennsylvania (B.S., cum laude, 1993); Northwestern University (J.D., cum laude, 1998). ***PRACTICE AREAS:*** Real Estate. ***Email:*** Jami.Brodey@goldbergkohn.com

JOEL F. BROWN, born Chicago, Illinois, June 8, 1967; admitted to bar, 1992, Illinois and U.S. District Court, Northern District of Illinois. *Education:* Wesleyan University (B.A., 1989); New York University (J.D., 1992). Phi Beta Kappa. ***PRACTICE AREAS:*** Secured Lending; Corporate General. ***Email:*** Joel.Brown@goldbergkohn.com

DENISE B. CAPLAN, born Grand Rapids, Michigan, July 7, 1958; admitted to bar, 1983, Illinois. *Education:* University of Illinois (B.B.A., 1980); University of Chicago (J.D., 1983). *Member:* Chicago, Illinois State and American Bar Associations. ***PRACTICE AREAS:*** Corporate Law; Finance Law. ***Email:*** Denise.Caplan@goldbergkohn.com

ANDREW R. CARDONICK, born Philadelphia, Pennsylvania, July 24, 1967; admitted to bar, 1993, Massachusetts, New York, Illinois and U.S. District Court, Northern District of Illinois. *Education:* Pennsylvania State University (B.S., summa cum laude, 1989); University of Chicago (J.D., cum laude, 1993). ***PRACTICE AREAS:*** Corporate Bankruptcy; Corporate Workouts. ***Email:*** Andrew.Cardonick@goldbergkohn.com

DAVID J. CHIZEWER, born Chicago, Illinois, April 4, 1966; admitted to bar, 1991, Illinois. *Education:* Pomona College (B.A., magna cum laude, 1988); University of Chi-

(This Listing Continued)

cago (J.D., 1991). Phi Beta Kappa. Author: "Defense of Consumer Class Actions after Johnson v. Revenue Management Corporation," Defense Research Institute's Business Suit, Winter 1999. Panelist: Fourth Annual U.S. Department of Education's Charter Schools National Conference, June 2002; National Charter Financing Forum, June 2001; " 'World-Class Education' An Exploration of Substance, Entitlement and Implementation," Edison Schools National Client Conference, September 1999. Member: Founding Member, Illinois Network of Charter Schools; Board of Directors, Chicago Charter School Foundation and College Bound; Executive Committee, Daniel Murphy Scholarship Foundation. *Member:* Chicago and American Bar Associations; Defense Research Institute. ***PRACTICE AREAS:*** Commercial Litigation. ***Email:*** David.Chizewer@goldbergkohn.com

FREDERICK H. COHEN, born Chicago, Illinois; admitted to bar, 1990, Illinois; 1991, U.S. District Court, Northern District of Illinois and U.S. Court of Appeals, Seventh Circuit; 2001, U.S. Supreme Court. *Education:* University of Illinois (B.A., 1987); University of Chicago (J.D., with honors, 1990). Adjunct Professor, IIT-Kent College of Law. ***PRACTICE AREAS:*** Complex Business Litigation; Intellectual Property; State and Local Taxation. ***Email:*** Frederick.Cohen@goldbergkohn.com

JONATHAN M. COOPER, born Southfield, Michigan, June 12, 1968; admitted to bar, 1994, Illinois. *Education:* University of Michigan (B.S., Business Administration, with high distinction, 1996); Northwestern University (J.D., cum laude, 1994). Certified Public Accountant. Author: "NAFTA's Rule of Origin and its Effect on the North American Automotive Industry," Northwestern Journal of International Law and Business, Winter 1994. Co-prepared, "A Study Concerning a Possible Convention on Inventory Financing," for the 2001 UNCITRAL Convention in Vienna. Previously worked with United Nations Commissions on International Trade Law (UNCITRAL) in drafting portions of the United Nations Convention on the Assignment of Receivables in International Trade. Currently with UNCITRAL in preparing a Legislative Guide on Secured Transactions. ***PRACTICE AREAS:*** Commercial Finance. ***Email:*** Jonathan.Cooper@goldbergkohn.com

DAVID L. DRANOFF, born Princeton, New Jersey, October 23, 1955; admitted to bar, 1983, Illinois. *Education:* Wesleyan University (B.A., magna cum laude, 1977); Northwestern University (J.D., cum laude, 1983). Order of the Coif. Member, Staff, 1981-1982 and Notes and Comments Editor, 1982-1983, Northwestern Law Review. *Member:* Chicago and American Bar Associations. ***PRACTICE AREAS:*** Secured Transactions; Workout Law. ***Email:*** David.Dranoff@goldbergkohn.com

BARBARA M. FLOM, born Evergreen Park, Illinois, October 10, 1956; admitted to bar, 1987, Illinois. *Education:* Northwestern University; University of Chicago (J.D., cum laude, 1986). Member, Order of the Coif. Member, 1984-1986 and Articles Editor, 1985-1986, University of Chicago Law Review. Author: "Constructive Ownership Transactions: The Sound of one Shoe Dropping," Journal of Taxation of Financial Products, Vol. 1, No. 219 (Summer 2000). Lead Author: "Demystifying Derivatives: using Financial Products for Charitable Giving," 57th New York University Institute on Federal Taxation, Chapter 20, 1999; Co-Author: "An Abecedarium on Alphabet Stock," 66 TAXES — The Tax Magazine 954, December 1988. Lecturer in Law, University of Chicago Law School, 1991-2000. *Member:* American Bar Association. ***PRACTICE AREAS:*** Federal Taxation; Corporate Law. ***Email:*** Barbara.Flom@goldbergkohn.com

MICHAEL C. HAINEN, born Boston, Massachusetts, April 11, 1972; admitted to bar, 1997, Illinois. *Education:* Middlebury College (B.A., cum laude, 1994); Vanderbilt University (J.D., 1997). Member, Order of the Coif. Associate Articles Editor, Vanderbilt Law Review, 1995-1997. ***TRANSACTIONS:*** Senior Credit Facilities, Restructuring of Distressed Debt. ***PRACTICE AREAS:*** Commercial Finance; Mergers and Acquisitions. ***Email:*** Michael.Hainen@goldbergkohn.com

DEBORAH RZASNICKI HOGAN, born Pittsburgh, Pennsylvania, October 7, 1970; admitted to bar, 1995, Illinois. *Education:* Northwestern University (B.A., 1992; J.D., cum laude, 1995). ***PRACTICE AREAS:*** Litigation. ***Email:*** Deborah.Hogan@goldbergkohn.com

GERALD L. JENKINS, born San Francisco, California, September 10, 1948; admitted to bar, 1975, Illinois. *Education:* Eastern Illinois University (B.A., with high honors, 1971); Harvard University (J.D., cum laude, 1975). Presenter, "Collateral Consequences of the Privacy Rules Imposed on Financial Institutions," Institute for International Research, 2000. Presenter, "How to Negotiate with the dot com world," Seminar, Chicago, Illinois, 2000. Presenter, "Vertical Hubs and Exchanges: Disintermediation and Re-intermediation," Chicago Bar Association, 2000. Presenter, "Securities Law on the Internet," Chicago Bar Association, 1999. Panelist, "The Internet Changes Everything: Financing in the '.com' World," ABA Business Law Section, Commercial Financial Services Committee, 1999. Co-Author: "Income Tax Aspects of Organizing Corporations," *Organizing and Advising Illinois Business,* Illinois Institute for Continuing Legal Education, 1999. Presenter, "Media's Role in Informing the Public about Year 2000 Issues," World Future Society Y2K Conference, Washington, D.C., 1998. Presenter, "Financing the Small Business," Seminar, National Business Institute, Chicago, Illinois, 1998. Presenter, "Electronic Communications Policies," Institute of Internal Auditors, Chicago, Illinois, 1998. Author: "Domain Names and the Asset Based Lender," *The Secured Lender,* 1997. Co-Author: "My Borrower Has a Web Site - What Do I Do Now?" *The Secured Lender,* 1997. Adjunct Professor of Law, Information Technology and Privacy Law LLM Program, John Marshall Law School, 1982-1984, 1999-2001. *Member:* Chicago, Illinois State and American Bar Associations; Society of Information Managers. ***PRACTICE AREAS:*** Internet Law; E-Commerce; Federal and State Income Taxation; Business Acquisitions and Dispositions. ***Email:*** Gerald.Jenkins@goldbergkohn.com

MICHAEL D. KARPELES, born Minneapolis, Minnesota, May 15, 1958; admitted to bar, 1985, Illinois; 1986, U.S. District Court, Northern District of Illinois; 1997, U.S. Court of Appeals, Seventh Circuit. *Education:* Wheaton College (B.A., summa cum laude, 1981); Harvard University (J.D., cum laude, 1985). Member and current President: Salvation Army Correctional Services Program Advisory Council; Society for Human Resource Management (SHRM) Legislative Action Committee. Member, Human Resource Planning Society. *Member:* Chicago Bar Association. ***PRACTICE AREAS:*** Litigation; Employment Law. ***Email:*** Michael.Karpeles@goldbergkohn.com

FREDERIC R. KLEIN, born Brooklyn, New York, July 24, 1950; admitted to bar, 1980, Illinois and U.S. District Court, Northern District of Illinois; 1987, U.S. Court of Appeals, Seventh Circuit; 1988, U.S. Supreme Court. *Education:* Tufts University (B.A., magna cum laude, 1972); University of Michigan (J.D., magna cum laude, 1980). Law Clerk to U.S. District Judge William T. Hart, U.S. District Court for the Northern District of Illinois, 1982-1983. *Member:* Chicago and American Bar Associations; Chicago Council of Lawyers. ***PRACTICE AREAS:*** Commercial Litigation; Real Estate Litigation. ***Email:*** Frederic.Klein@goldbergkohn.com

RANDALL L. KLEIN, born Detroit, Michigan, August 19, 1965; admitted to bar, 1990, Illinois; 1994, Florida. *Education:* University of Illinois (B.A., 1987); Northwestern University School of Law (J.D., cum laude, 1990). Member, Editorial Board, Journal of Criminal Law and Criminology. Co-Executive Editor, Ginsberg & Martin On Bankruptcy, 4th Ed., 1996—. Contributing Editor and Author, Norton's Annual Survey of Bankruptcy Law, 1993-2000. Co-Author: "Capital Call Agreements as Credit Enhancement," The Secured Lender, July/August 2002; "A Reply to Whether § 1111(b) Gives General Partners Exposure on Non-Recourse Debt," 7 Norton Bkrptcy. L. Adv. July 1993; "The Hotel Revenues Paradox: Taking a Prepetition Lien On Future Income Streams," Critical Issues in Chapter 11 Bankruptcies, ABA 1994. Panelist, "Cutting-Edge Legal Issues and Strategies in DIP Financings: What Are Lenders Asking for, What are Debtors and Committees Agreeing to and What are Courts Approving?" Commercial Finance Association Seminar, 2002. Speaker: "SM 104 and The New Value Corollary: A Secured Creditor's Blessing in Disguise?" CBA Advanced Bankruptcy Seminar, 1994; "Disjointed and Severed Liability: General Partners in Partnership-Debtors," ABI Central States Bankruptcy Workshop, 1999; "ABC's of Secured Claims: § 506(a), (b) and (c), "CBA Advanced Bankruptcy Seminar, 1999; National CLE Conference (Bankruptcy), 2001; "Last-Out Participations: Traps for the Unwary Lender," 01/10/01. Panelist, Commercial Loan Workouts, Executive Enterprises, 1999-2000. Law Clerk to Hon. Ronald Barliant, U.S. Bankruptcy Court, Northern District of Illinois, 1992-1993. *Member:* Chicago (Member: Bankruptcy Committee; Real Property Finance Subcommittee) and American Bar Associations. ***PRACTICE AREAS:*** Bankruptcy Law; Creditors' Rights; Commercial Finance. ***Email:*** Randall.Klein@goldbergkohn.com

RICHARD M. KOHN, born Chicago, Illinois, December 31, 1944; admitted to bar, 1969, Illinois. *Education:* University of Michigan (B.A., with distinction, 1966; J.D., cum laude, 1969). Fellow: American College of Commercial Finance Lawyers, 1994—; Associate General Counsel, Commercial Finance Association, 1995—. Editor, Prospectus, A Journal of Law Reform, 1968-1969. Author: "Further Reflections on International Asset-Based Lending," The Secured Lender, May/June 1999; "Reflections on International Asset-Based Lending," The Secured Lender, Jan/Feb 1991 at p. 8; "Preferential Transfers on the Eve of the Bankruptcy Amendments," 2 Prospectus 259, 1968; "Pure Debtor-In-Possession Financing," The Secured Lender, Nov/Dec., 1995; "Warranties Arising Under the UCC," Sales and Financing under the Revised Uniform Commercial Code (Illinois Institute for Continuing Legal Education, Chapter 2, 1978). Lecturer, Sperling Seminar, University of Michigan Law School, April 2001—. Lecturer and Panelist: National and Local Chapters of the Commercial Finance Association, 1986—; CFA/Wharton Institute of Secured Lending, 1987. Uniform Commercial Code Panelist, "Lawyers' Forum," Chicago Daily Law Bulletin, 1978-1980. Member, Board of Regents, American College of Commercial Finance Lawyers, 2000—. *Member:* Chicago and American Bar Associations; Chicago Council of Lawyers; American Bankruptcy Institute. ***PRACTICE AREAS:*** Finance. ***Email:*** Richard.Kohn@goldbergkohn.com

ADAM M. LASER, born Chicago, Illinois, May 5, 1969; admitted to bar, 1997, Illinois. *Education:* Northwestern University (B.A., 1991; J.D., 1997). ***PRACTICE AREAS:*** Real Estate; Corporate Law. ***Email:*** Adam.Laser@goldbergkohn.com

STEVEN A. LEVY, born Chicago, Illinois, September 24, 1963; admitted to bar, 1988, Illinois, U.S. Court of Appeals, Seventh and Ninth Circuits and U.S. District Court, Northern and Central Districts of Illinois. *Education:* Miami University (B.S., cum laude, 1985); University of Illinois (J.D., magna cum laude, 1988). Order of the Coif. ***PRACTICE AREAS:*** Commercial Litigation; Banking Litigation; Securities Litigation; Class Action Litigation. ***Email:*** Steven.Levy@goldbergkohn.com

ROGER A. LEWIS, born Chicago, Illinois, February 3, 1970; admitted to bar, 1995, Illinois. *Education:* Stanford University (B.A., with honors, 1992); Harvard University (J.D., cum laude, 1995). Law Clerk, Honorable James B. Moran, U.S. District Court, Northern District of Illinois. ***PRACTICE AREAS:*** Commercial Litigation. ***Email:*** Roger.Lewis@goldbergkohn.com

WILLIAM R. LOESCH, born Chicago, Illinois, November 23, 1965; admitted to bar, 1992, Illinois. *Education:* Princeton University (A.B., 1989); Northwestern University (J.D., 1992). ***PRACTICE AREAS:*** Corporate; Venture Capital; Technology; Education. ***Email:*** William.Loesch@goldbergkohn.com

MICHAEL B. MANUEL, born Akron, Ohio, October 27, 1960; admitted to bar, 1988, Illinois. *Education:* University of Michigan (B.S., 1983); Northwestern University (J.D., 1988). Member and Associate Editor, Northwestern University Law Review, 1987-1988. *Member:* Chicago and American Bar Associations. ***PRACTICE AREAS:*** Real Estate; Technology. ***Email:*** Michael.Manuel@goldbergkohn.com

DAVID M. MASON, born Chicago, Illinois, March 25, 1959; admitted to bar, 1984, Illinois. *Education:* University of Illinois (B.S., in Accountancy, 1981); Stanford University (J.D., 1984). Beta Gamma Sigma. Beta Alpha Psi. Bronze Tablet. Arthur Carter Scholarship. Recipient, Elijah Watt Sells Award. Certified Public Accountant, Illinois, 1981. Real Estate Documentation For Commercial Lenders, The Secured Lender Magazine, September/October, 1995. Co-Authored: "Those Third-Party Legal Opinions: Can Loan Transaction Costs be Reduced?" Business Law Today, September/October, 1997. Co-Authored: "Documenting Loans For Leveraged Buildups," Commercial Lending Review, Winter, 2000-2001. *Member:* Chicago and American (Opinion Committee, Business Law Section; Revised Article 9 Form Task Force, Business Law Section, 2002) Bar Associations. Fellow, American College of Commercial Finance Lawyers. ***PRACTICE AREAS:*** Commercial Finance; Loan Workouts and Restructurings. ***Email:*** David.Mason@goldbergkohn.com

WILLIAM C. MEYERS, born Cleveland, Ohio, September 7, 1962; admitted to bar, 1987, Illinois and U.S. District Court, Northern District of Illinois; 1989, U.S. Court of Appeals, Seventh Circuit. *Education:* Michigan State University (B.A., with honors, 1984); University of Michigan (J.D., 1987). Chapter Co-Author: "Marketing Toys on the Internet—Legal Issues," New Media for Kids, Market Focus Publications, 1997. Author: Author: "Trademark Rights At Risk," Candy Business (July/August, 2001); "The Dilution of

(This Listing Continued)

GOLDBERG, KOHN, BELL, BLACK, ROSENBLOOM & MORITZ, LTD., Chicago—Continued

the Federal Trademark Dilution Act," For The Defense (August, 2001); "Establishing a Trademark on the Internet," Market Focus: Toys (April, 1997); "Trademark Infringement on the Internet," Market Focus: Toys (May-June, 1997). Lecturer: "Federal Trademark Dilution," American Intellectual Property Law Association, October, 1999; "Electronic Discovery," DePaul College of Law, April, 2001, April, 2000 and September, 1999; "Discovery Issues in the Electronic Information Age," Itasca, Illinois, January, 1999; "Privilege, Work Product, and Discovery in the Electronic Information Age," Chicago, Illinois, June, 1998; "Electronic Communications Policies," Institute of Internal Auditors, Chicago, Illinois, May, 1998; "E-Mail, Voice Mail and Internet Communications: Avoiding the Hidden Risks," Chicago, Illinois, December, 1997. *Member:* Chicago and American Bar Associations. ***PRACTICE AREAS:*** Intellectual Property; Business Litigation. ***Email:*** William.Meyers@goldbergkohn.com

TERRY F. MORITZ, born Chicago, Illinois, December 24, 1942; admitted to bar, 1970, Illinois. *Education:* Loyola University (B.S., 1966; J.D., 1970). Law Clerk to Judge William J. Lynch, United States District Court, Northern District of Illinois, 1969-1971. Special Assistant Attorney General: Illinois, 1986-1989; Minnesota, 1985—. Author: "Business, Law and the Internet," 2002, the Illinois Institute for Continuing Legal Education Practice Handbook. Lecturer: "Taxing Telecommunications," Federation of Tax Administrators Annual Meeting, June 1989; "Recent Developments in Real Property Taxation: Public Utility Deregulation in the United States," International Association of Assessing Officers 17th Annual Legal Seminar, November 1996; "Impact of Electric Utility Deregulation," Commercial Law Affiliates Annual Meeting, March 1997; "Antitrust Issues and the Restructuring of the Power Industry," CBI's Power Plant Divestiture and Acquisition Conference, December 1998; "Utility Taxation in an Era of Deregulation," International Association of Assessing Officers Annual Legal Seminar, December 1998; "Deregulation: Power Plant Values and Property Taxes: Illinois' Experience," Lincoln Institute of Land Policy, Cambridge, Massachusetts, October 1999; "Antitrust Issues and the Restructuring of the Power Industry," The Electricity Journal, November 1999; "Deregulation: Power Plant Values and Property Taxes: Shifting Values-Shifting Rules," The 30th Annual Wichita Program, August 2000; "Techniques and Resources for Developing Proper Valuation of the Electric Power Generating Plants," CBI's 3rd Annual Electric Asset Valuation Seminar, February 2001. Member, Board of Directors: The Chicago Lighthouse, 1989—; The Big Shoulders Fund, 1994—. President, Society for Contemporary Art, The Art Institute of Chicago, 1991-1993. *Member:* Chicago (Board Member and Secretary, Young Lawyer Section, 1973-1976; Chairman, National Volunteer in Parole Program, 1974-1975; Member and Chairman, Long Range Planning Committee, 1982-1985; Member, Nominating Committee, 1985-1986) and American Bar Associations. ***PRACTICE AREAS:*** Litigation; Utility Regulation. ***Email:*** Terry.Moritz@goldbergkohn.com

DAVID E. MORRISON, born West Lafayette, Indiana, May 28, 1968; admitted to bar, 1993, Illinois and U.S. District Court, Northern District of Illinois; 1998, U.S. District Court, Western District of Michigan; 1999, U.S. District Court, Northern District of Illinois including Trial Bar; 2000, U.S. Court of Appeals, Seventh Circuit. *Education:* Indiana University (B.A., with honors, 1990); University of Michigan (J.D., cum laude, 1993). Associate Editor, 1991-1992, Executive Note Editor, 1992-1993, University of Michigan Journal of Law Reform. Author: "You've Built the Bridge, Why Don't You Cross It? A Call for State Labor Laws Prohibiting Private Employment Discrimination on the Basis of Sexual Orientation," 26 U. Mich. J.L. Ref. 245 (1992). Law Clerk to the Honorable Suzanne B. Conlon, U.S. District Court, Northern District of Illinois, 1995-1996. *Member:* Chicago Bar Association; Chicago Council of Lawyers. ***PRACTICE AREAS:*** Employment Litigation; Commercial Litigation. ***Email:*** David.Morrison@goldbergkohn.com

GERALD F. MUNITZ, born Jersey City, New Jersey, August 3, 1933; admitted to bar, 1960, Illinois; U.S. District Court, Northern District of Illinois including Trial Bar; U.S. Supreme Court; U.S. Court of Appeals, Sixth, Seventh, Ninth and Tenth Circuits. *Education:* University of Michigan (B.A., 1955); University of Chicago (J.D., 1960). Conferee, National Bankruptcy Conference, 1971—. Fellow, American College of Bankruptcy, 1990. Contributing Editor: Collier on Bankruptcy, 15th Ed. Rev., 1996—; Collier on Bankruptcy Practice Guide, 1981—, Aspen Law & Business Inc.; Bankruptcy Litigation Manual, 1980—. *Member:* Chicago (Member, 1964— and Chairman, 1967-1968, Bankruptcy and Reorganization Committee; Member, Committee on Character and Fitness, 1973-1985), Illinois State and American Bar Associations; The Lawyers Club of Chicago. ***PRACTICE AREAS:*** Insolvency and Reorganization. ***Email:*** gfm@goldbergkohn.com

ALICE G. OWINGS, born Ann Arbor, Michigan, April 10, 1966; admitted to bar, 1992, Illinois. *Education:* Duke University (A.B., 1988); University of Michigan (J.D., 1992). *Member:* American Bar Association. ***PRACTICE AREAS:*** Corporate; Securities. ***Email:*** Alice.Owings@goldbergkohn.com

KEITH G. RADNER, born Detroit, Michigan, August 11, 1968; admitted to bar, 1996, Illinois; U.S. District Court, Northern District of Illinois. *Education:* University of Michigan (A.B., 1990); University of Illinois (J.D., magna cum laude, 1996). Order of the Coif. Member and Associate Editor, University of Illinois Law Review, 1994-1996. *Member:* Chicago, Illinois State and American Bar Associations. ***PRACTICE AREAS:*** Commercial Finance. ***Email:*** Keith.Radner@goldbergkohn.com

JAMES B. ROSENBLOOM, born Chicago, Illinois, 1947; admitted to bar, 1972, Illinois. *Education:* Yale University (B.A., cum laude, 1969); University of Chicago (J.D., 1972). Law Clerk, Honorable Bernard M. Decker, U.S. District Court, Northern District of Illinois, 1972-1973. Lecturer in Law, University of Chicago Law School. *Member:* Chicago Bar Association (Member, Real Estate Committee; Real Estate Finance Subcommittee). Fellow, American College of Real Estate Lawyers. (Founding Partner). ***Email:*** James.Rosenbloom@goldbergkohn.com

GARY N. RUBEN, born Chicago, Illinois, April 19, 1957; admitted to bar, 1981, Illinois. *Education:* University of Illinois (B.S., highest honors, Bronze Tablet, 1978); Harvard University (J.D., magna cum laude, 1981). Recipient, Elijah Watt Sells Award. Certified Public Accountant Examination, Illinois, Spring, 1978. *Member:* Chicago and American Bar Associations. ***PRACTICE AREAS:*** Real Estate Business and Finance. ***Email:*** Gary.Ruben@goldbergkohn.com

(This Listing Continued)

DANIEL P. SHAPIRO, born Chicago, Illinois, July 7, 1957; admitted to bar, 1982, Illinois and U.S. District Court, Northern District of Illinois including Trial Bar. *Education:* University of Illinois (B.A., 1979); University of Chicago (J.D., 1982). Phi Beta Kappa; Bronze Tablet. Author: "Judge Easterbrook's New Look at Proving Class Claims of Deception," Class Action Litigation Report, BNA 2000; "Class Certification Under Rule 23," National Institute on Class Actions Publication, ABA, 1998; "Class Actions Are the '90s Form of Greenmail," The National Law Journal, Sept. 22, 1997; "'First Party' Collections: Vendors Collecting Consumer Debts in the Name of the Credit Grantor," The Agency Examiner, Vol. XII, Issue VII, July 1998; "How Will the Increase in Collection Industry Litigation Affect the Charged-Off Debt Market?, co-authored with Denise B. Caplan, The Debt Marketplace News, Vol. III, Issue II, March/April, 1999. Adjunct Faculty Member, Round Table Group, 2002—. Member, Advisory Board, Bureau of National Affairs Publication Class Action Litigation Report. *Member:* Chicago and American (Co-Chair, National Institute on Class Actions, 1997-2000; Co-Chair, Subcommittee on Consumer Class Actions, 1998-2001) Bar Associations. ***PRACTICE AREAS:*** Class Action Defense. ***Email:*** Daniel.Shapiro@goldbergkohn.com

KEITH A. SIGALE, born Chicago, Illinois, May 29, 1973; admitted to bar, 1997, Illinois. *Education:* University of Illinois, Urbana-Champaign (B.S., summa cum laude, 1994); Harvard University (J.D., cum laude, 1997). ***PRACTICE AREAS:*** Corporate; Securities; Tax. ***Email:*** Keith.Sigale@goldbergkohn.com

ALAN P. SOLOW, born Chicago, Illinois, 1954; admitted to bar, 1979, Illinois and U.S. District Court, Northern District of Illinois including Trial Bar; U.S. Court of Appeals, Seventh Circuit; U.S. Supreme Court. *Education:* University of Illinois (A.B., summa cum laude, 1976); Harvard University (J.D., cum laude, 1979). Phi Kappa Phi; Phi Eta Sigma; Pi Sigma Alpha; Phi Beta Kappa. Member, Bronze Tablet. Charles Merriam Scholar. Lecturer: "Representing a Creditor in Chapters 7 and 11," Illinois Institute for Continuing Legal Education, 1988; "Rejection, Assumption and Assignment of Executory Contracts and Unexpired Leases," Illinois Institute for Continuing Legal Education, 1990; "Legal Issues Confronting the Indenture Trustee in the Bankruptcy of the Obligor," Corporate Fiduciary Association of Illinois Education Committee, 1994; "Real Estate Bankruptcy Planning: What Works and What Doesn't," CBA Real Property Finance Subcommittee, 1996; "Creditors' Claims," Illinois Institute for Continuing Legal Education, 1998. Co-Editor: "Bankruptcy Practice," Illinois Institute for Continuing Legal Education, 1990. Co-Author: "Pure Debtor-In-Possession Financing," *The Secured Lender,* November/December, 1995; "Section 552 - Post-Petition Liens on Future Income Streams," Norton Ann. Sur. Bankr. L. 479, 1011, 1995 Ed.; "Section 552 - The Application and Adequate Protection of Post-Petition Rents," Norton Ann. Sur. Bankr. L., 479, 1996 Ed.; "The Impact of State Law on Interpreting Rents' and Proceeds' Under 552(b)," Norton Ann. Sur. Bkrptcy. L., 379, 1997 Ed.; "Section 364 - Recent Developments from the Lender's Perspective," Norton Ann. Sur., Bankr. L., 1998 Ed. Instructor, Commercial Finance Association, Workouts and Bankruptcy Workshops. *Member:* Chicago and American Bar Associations; American Bankruptcy Institute. Fellow, American College of Bankruptcy. ***PRACTICE AREAS:*** Creditors' Rights Law; Litigation. ***Email:*** Alan.Solow@goldbergkohn.com

MICHAEL L. SULLIVAN, admitted to bar, 1991, Illinois; U.S. District Court, Northern District of Illinois; 1996, U.S. District Court, Eastern District of Michigan; 1997, U.S. District Court, Central District of Illinois. *Education:* University of Illinois (B.S., with high honors, 1988; J.D., 1991). Dean's List. Harno Fellow. Recipient, Rickert Award for Excellence, Illinois Moot Court Team. Author: "No Tender-Back Clauses in Waivers of Age Claims," The National Law Journal, July, 2002; "Harassment Law Update: Prompt and Effective Remedial Action as a Defense to Harassment Claims," American Bar Association Tort and Insurance Practice Employer Employee Relations Committee Newsletter, Summer, 2001. Topic Author: "Elkouri and Elkouri, How Arbitration Works," BNA 6th Edition, 2001. *Member:* Chicago (Member, Labor and Employment Section), Illinois State (Member, Labor and Employment Section) and American (Member, Tort and Insurance Practice Section and Tort and Insurance Practice Section, Employee Relations Committee, 1993—) Bar Associations; Industrial Relations Research Association (Director, Chicago Chapter). ***REPORTED CASES:*** Solsberry v. Chicago Sun-Times, Inc. (N.D. Ill. 2005 No. 04 C 3611) Obtained summary judgment for defending employer against race discrimination, harassment and retaliation lawsuit; Linebek v. International Union of Operating Engineers, Local 150, Obtained a temporary restraining order in conjunction with the NLRB to stop illegal secondary picketing; MacDonald Machinery Co., Inc. and Local 150, International Union of Operating Engineers, AFL-CIO, Case 25-RC-9930 08/27/01; Greenslade v. Chicago Sun-Times, 112 F.3d 853 (7th Cir. 1997); Turner v. Claims Administration Corp., 993 F. Supp. 982 (W.D. Tex. 1998); Burton v. CNA Ins. Co., 978 F. Supp. 803 (N.D. Ill. 1997); Kahalas v. Claims Administration Corp., 69 Fair Employment Practices Cases 816 (BNA) (D.Md. 1995). ***PRACTICE AREAS:*** Labor and Employment Law. ***Email:*** Michael.Sullivan@goldbergkohn.com

CAROLE K. TOWNE, born Chicago, Illinois, October 9, 1951; admitted to bar, 1977, Illinois. *Education:* University of Michigan (B.G.S., 1973); Northwestern University Graduate School of Management (M.M., 1977); Northwestern University (J.D., cum laude, 1977). Faculty, Practicing Law Institute, 1983-1984. Lecturer, Commercial Real Estate, Chicago Bar Association Continuing Legal Education Seminar, 1990. Moderator, Construction Loan Financing, Illinois Institute of Continuing Legal Education, 1996. *Member:* Chicago and American Bar Associations. ***PRACTICE AREAS:*** Real Estate. ***Email:*** Carole.Towne@goldbergkohn.com

KENNETH S. ULRICH, born Colts Neck, New Jersey, March 7, 1963; admitted to bar, 1987, Illinois and U.S. District Court, Northern District of Illinois; 1991, U.S. Court of Appeals, Seventh Circuit. *Education:* Northwestern University (B.A., 1984; J.D., 1987). Author: "When You Find Yourself on the Board of Directors," The Brief, Summer 1990. *Member:* Chicago and American Bar Associations. ***PRACTICE AREAS:*** Commercial Litigation; Intellectual Property; Insurance Coverage; Construction Law. ***Email:*** Kenneth.Ulrich@goldbergkohn.com

MATTHEW A.C. ZAPF, born Saginaw, Michigan, January 13, 1962; admitted to bar, 1987, Illinois; 1988, U.S. District Court, Northern District of Illinois; 2000, U.S. District Court, Central Districts of Illinois. *Education:* University of Notre Dame (B.A., magna cum laude, 1984); Northwestern University School of Law (J.D., 1987). Author: "Waiver of Right to Arbitrate," Illinois Institute for Continuing Legal Education, 1989; "Judicial Review of Arbitration Awards - Vacature," Illinois Institute for Continuing Legal Education,

(This Listing Continued)

1989. ***PRACTICE AREAS:*** Alternative Dispute Resolution; Complex and Multi-District Litigation; Construction Law; Intellectual Property; Products Liability; Toxic Torts. ***Email:*** Matthew.Zapf@goldbergkohn.com

GARY T. ZUSSMAN, born St. Louis, Missouri, February 28, 1957; admitted to bar, 1982, Illinois. *Education:* The Wharton School, University of Pennsylvania (B.S., magna cum laude, 1979); University of Michigan (J.D., cum laude, 1982). ***PRACTICE AREAS:*** Commercial Finance Law. ***Email:*** Gary.Zussman@goldbergkohn.com

ASSOCIATES

STACY S. JAKOBE, admitted to bar, 2003, Illinois. *Education:* University of Michigan (B.A., with high distinction and honors, 1999; J.D., honors, 2002). ***PRACTICE AREAS:*** Labor and Employment; Litigation; Alternative Dispute Resolution. ***Email:*** stacy.jakobe@goldbergkohn.com

MAZEN ASBAHI, admitted to bar, 2000, Illinois. *Education:* University of Michigan (B.A., highest honors, 1996); Northwestern University School of Law (J.D., cum laude, 2000). ***PRACTICE AREAS:*** Corporate Law.

VANESSA A. BACHTELL, born December 27, 1974; admitted to bar, 1999, Illinois. *Education:* University of Arizona (B.A., 1996); Northwestern University (J.D., 1999). ***PRACTICE AREAS:*** Corporate. ***Email:*** Vanessa.Bachtell@goldbergkohn.com

CHAD A. BLUMENFIELD, (admission pending). *Education:* University of Wisconsin-Madison (B.A., with honors, 1999); University of Chicago (J.D., 2004). ***PRACTICE AREAS:*** Litigation. ***Email:*** chad.blumenfield@goldbergkohn.com

CATHERINE S. CARRIGAN, born Mobile, Alabama, July 14, 1977; admitted to bar, 2002, Illinois. *Education:* Vanderbilt University (B.S., magna cum laude, 1999); University of Michigan (J.D., 2002). *Member:* Chicago and American Bar Associations. ***PRACTICE AREAS:*** Commercial Litigation; Labor and Employment. ***Email:*** catherine.carrigan@goldbergkohn.com

RACHEL GENA CHISS, born Fresno, California, December 26, 1974; admitted to bar, 2000, Illinois. *Education:* Washington University (B.A., 1996); Northwestern University (J.D., 2000). Note and Comment Editor, Journal of Criminal Law, 1999-2000. ***PRACTICE AREAS:*** Commercial Finance. ***Email:*** Rachel.Genachiss@goldbergkohn.com

JESSICA DeBRUIN, born Oak Park, Illinois, February 25, 1975; admitted to bar, 2000, Illinois. *Education:* University of Illinois (B.S., 1997); New York University (J.D., 2000). ***PRACTICE AREAS:*** Commercial Finance. ***Email:*** jessica.debruin@goldbergkohn.com

JEREMY M. DOWNS, born Kankakee, Illinois, April 21, 1975; admitted to bar, 2000, Illinois; U.S. District Court, Northern District of Illinois, Eastern and Western Districts of Wisconsin and Eastern District of Michigan. *Education:* Harvard University (A.B., 1997); Northwestern University (J.D., 2000). ***PRACTICE AREAS:*** Bankruptcy (70%); Litigation (20%); Commercial Finance (10%). ***Email:*** Jeremy.Downs@goldbergkohn.com

HILLARY LEVITT DUNN, born Chicago, Illinois, July 16, 1973; admitted to bar, 1999, Illinois. *Education:* University of Wisconsin-Madison (B.A., 1995); Northwestern University (J.D., 1999). *Member:* Chicago and Illinois State Bar Associations. ***PRACTICE AREAS:*** Commercial Litigation; Employment. ***Email:*** Hillary.Dunn@goldbergkohn.com

MICHAEL D. EBNER, born June 15, 1973; admitted to bar, 2000, Illinois. *Education:* University of Michigan (B.A., 1995); Northwestern University (J.D., 2000). *Member:* Illinois State and American Bar Associations. ***PRACTICE AREAS:*** Commercial Finance. ***Email:*** michael.ebner@goldbergkohn.com

BRIAN D. FAGEL, born Skokie, Illinois, March 26, 1969; admitted to bar, 1994, Illinois. *Education:* Stanford University (A.B., 1991); University of Chicago (J.D., 1994; M.A. in English, 1995; Ph.D., 2000). *Member:* Chicago Bar Association. ***PRACTICE AREAS:*** Litigation; Intellectual Property. ***Email:*** Brian.Fagel@goldbergkohn.com

JEFFREY K. FLEISHMANN, born New Orleans, Louisiana, 1968; admitted to bar, 2002, Tennessee (Not admitted in Illinois). *Education:* University of Texas at Austin (B.A., 1991); University of Memphis (J.D., magna cum laude, 2002). Editor-in-Chief, University of Memphis Law Review. Recipient: Sam Myar Memorial Scholarship; Robert and Elaine Hoffman Scholarship; Phi Delta Phi Professional Responsibility Award. Judicial Clerk to Judge Holly M. Kirby, Tennessee Court of Appeals. Volunteer, Memphis Area Legal Services. Member, Board of Directors, Friends for Life, a Tennessee-based HIV/AIDS service organization. Campaign Coordinator, United Way. *Member:* Memphis, Tennessee and American Bar Associations. ***PRACTICE AREAS:*** Commercial Finance. ***Email:*** jeffrey.fleishmann@goldbergkohn.com

SETH H. GOOD, (admission pending). *Education:* University of Michigan (B.A., with highest distinction, 2000); Harvard Law School (J.D., 2003). *Member:* Chicago, Illinois State and American Bar Associations. ***PRACTICE AREAS:*** Commercial Finance. ***Email:*** seth.good@goldbergkohn.com

ALAIS L.M. GRIFFIN, born Amersham, Buckinghamshire, England; admitted to bar, 2002, New York; 2004, Illinois. *Education:* Harvard University (A.B., 1994); Northwestern University (J.D., cum laude, 2001). ***PRACTICE AREAS:*** Litigation. ***Email:*** alais.griffin@goldbergkohn.com

ALLISON G. HAMMER, born Chicago, Illinois, December 27, 1973; admitted to bar, 1998, Illinois. *Education:* University of Michigan (B.A., with distinction, 1995); Northwestern University (J.D., 1998). Author: "Are Scholars Better Teachers?" Symposium on the Relation Between Scholarship and Teaching; Chicago Kent L.Rev. Vol. 73, No. 3, 1998. ***PRACTICE AREAS:*** Commercial Finance. ***Email:*** Allison.Hammer@goldbergkohn.com

CAROLINE E. HAMMOND, born Columbus, Ohio, August 11, 1977; admitted to bar, 2002, Illinois; 2003, Michigan. *Education:* University of Michigan (B.A., high distinction, 1999; J.D., cum laude, 2002). *Member:* State Bar of Michigan; American Bar Association. ***PRACTICE AREAS:*** Real Estate. ***Email:*** Caroline.Hammond@goldbergkohn.com

(This Listing Continued)

JEFFERY D. HOFFENBERG, born Chicago, Illinois, May 28, 1975; (admission pending). *Education:* University of Michigan (B.A., 1997); University (J.D., 2001). ***PRACTICE AREAS:*** Real Estate. ***Email:*** Jeffery.Hoffenberg@goldbergkohn.com

SUSAN H. KANE, born Chicago, Illinois, November 17, 1970; admitted to bar, 1999, Illinois. *Education:* University of Wisconsin-Madison (B.A., with honors, 1993); University of Pennsylvania (J.D., 1999). *Member:* Chicago and American Bar Associations. ***PRACTICE AREAS:*** Litigation; Intellectual Property; Commercial Litigation; Insurance Recovery; Securities Litigation. ***Email:*** Susan.Kane@goldbergkohn.com

DIMITRI G. KARCAZES, born Evanston, Illinois, April 30, 1974; admitted to bar, 1999, Illinois. *Education:* University of Chicago (B.A., cum laude, 1996; J.D., cum laude, 1999). Phi Beta Kappa. ***PRACTICE AREAS:*** Creditors Rights; Bankruptcy; Commercial Finance. ***Email:*** Dimitri.Karcazes@goldbergkohn.com

SALVADOR K. KAROTTKI, born West Berlin, West Germany, November 23, 1974; admitted to bar, 2000, Illinois; 2001, U.S. District Court, Northern District of Illinois; registered to practice before U.S. Patent and Trademark Office. *Education:* Indiana University (B.S., 1997); Duke University School of Law (J.D., 2000). ***PRACTICE AREAS:*** Commercial Litigation; Trademark Litigation; Patent Litigation. ***Email:*** Sal.Karottki@goldbergkohn.com

JONATHON J.H. KIM, born Inchon, Korea, January 11, 1973; admitted to bar, 2000, Illinois. *Education:* Yale University (B.A., 1995); Washington University (J.D., 2000). ***LANGUAGES:*** German and Korean. ***SPECIAL AGENCIES:*** U.S. Trade Representative Intern. ***PRACTICE AREAS:*** Commercial Finance. ***Email:*** johathon.kim@goldbergkohn.com

JON ERIC KLINGHOFFER, born Trenton, New Jersey, March 29, 1970; admitted to bar, 1999, Illinois and U.S. District Court, Northern District of Illinois; 2002, U.S. Court of Appeals, Third Circuit. *Education:* Purdue University (B.S., 1992); University of Illinois (J.D., magna cum laude, 1999). ***PRACTICE AREAS:*** Labor and Employment; Litigation. ***Email:*** Jon.Klinghoffer@goldbergkohn.com

RACHAEL R. LAPE, born San Francisco, California, May 4, 1973; admitted to bar, 2000, Illinois. *Education:* University of Missouri, Columbia (B.J., magna cum laude, 1995; B.A., magna cum laude, 1995); University of Virginia (J.D., 2000). *Member:* American Bar Association. ***LANGUAGES:*** Russian. ***PRACTICE AREAS:*** Commercial Finance; Corporate Law; Securities. ***Email:*** rachael.lape@goldbergkohn.com

STEPHEN LOCHER, born Mason City, Iowa, March 28, 1978; admitted to bar, 2004, Illinois and U.S. Court of Appeals, Eighth and Sixth Circuits. *Education:* University of Notre Dame (B.A., 2000); Harvard Law School (J.D., 2003). ***PRACTICE AREAS:*** Litigation. ***Email:*** stephen.locher@goldbergkohn.com

JAMES P. MADIGAN, born Warren, Ohio, May 3, 1974; admitted to bar, 2002, Illinois. *Education:* Case Western Reserve University (B.A., 1997); University of Chicago (J.D., 2000). Phi Beta Kappa. Bigelow Teaching Fellow, University of Chicago Law School, 2000-2002. ***PRACTICE AREAS:*** Litigation. ***Email:*** James.Madigan@goldbergkohn.com

MAUREEN E. MERIN, (admission pending). *Education:* Williams College (B.A., magna cum laude, 1998); University of Mississippi (M.A., 2000); University of Chicago (J.D., with honors, 2004). ***PRACTICE AREAS:*** Litigation. ***Email:*** maureen.merin@goldbergkohn.com

ROBERT M. OBERLIES, born Rochester, New York, June 21, 1974; admitted to bar, 2002, Illinois. *Education:* College of the Holy Cross (B.A., 1996); Northwestern University (J.D., 2002). ***LANGUAGES:*** Mandarin Chinese. ***PRACTICE AREAS:*** Corporate Securities; Tax; Creditors Rights; Bankruptcy; Commercial Finance. ***Email:*** Robert.Oberlies@goldbergkohn.com

KATHRYN A. PAMENTER, born Milwaukee, Wisconsin, 1970; admitted to bar, 1995, Wisconsin (inactive) and U.S. District Court, Eastern District of Wisconsin; 1996, Illinois and U.S. District Court, Northern District of Illinois. *Education:* University of Notre Dame (B.B.A., magna cum laude, 1992; J.D., 1995). Author: "U.S. v. Dixon: The Supreme Court Returns to the Traditional Standard for Double Jeopardy Clause Analysis," 69 N.D.L.R. 575, 1994. Law Clerk to The Hon. Robert K. Rodibaugh, U.S. Bankruptcy Court, Northern District of Indiana, 1997-1998. *Member:* Illinois State Bar Association; State Bar of Wisconsin. ***PRACTICE AREAS:*** Bankruptcy Law. ***Email:*** Kathryn.Pamenter@goldbergkohn.com

ELAN PERETZ, born Chicago, Illinois; admitted to bar, 2003, Illinois. *Education:* Washington University (B.S., 1998); University of Chicago (J.D.,cum laude, 2003). ***LANGUAGES:*** Hebrew. ***PRACTICE AREAS:*** Real Estate. ***Email:*** elan.peretz@goldbergkohn.com

JOHN E. PESCHKE, admitted to bar, 2002, Illinois; 2003, District of Columbia. *Education:* University of Notre Dame (B.A., 1999); University of Chicago (J.D., 2002). *Member:* The District of Columbia Bar. ***PRACTICE AREAS:*** Commercial Finance. ***Email:*** john.peschke@goldbergkohn.com

ANNE MARIE PISANO, born Pittston, Pennsylvania; admitted to bar, 1999, Illinois. *Education:* Villanova University (B.A.H., summa cum laude, 1995); University of Chicago (J.D., with honors, 1999). ***PRACTICE AREAS:*** Commercial Finance. ***Email:*** Annemarie.Pisano@goldbergkohn.com

SHIRA ROTH, admitted to bar, 2001, California; 2003, Illinois. *Education:* University of California, Berkeley (B.A., 1997); University of California School of Law, Los Angeles (J.D., 2001). *Member:* State Bar of California; State Bar of Illinois. ***PRACTICE AREAS:*** Bankruptcy; Creditors Rights. ***Email:*** shira.roth@goldbergkohn.com

ANNE M. SHERRY, admitted to bar, 2002, Missouri; 2003, Illinois. *Education:* University of Missouri (B.A., 1999); University of Chicago (J.D., 2002). *Member:* Illinois State and American Bar Associations. ***LANGUAGES:*** French. ***PRACTICE AREAS:*** Bankruptcy; Creditors' Rights; Commercial Finance. ***Email:*** anne.sherry@goldbergkohn.com

CHANTE D. SPANN, born Chicago, Illinois, November, 1977; admitted to bar, 2001, Illinois and U.S. District Court, Northern District of Illinois. *Education:* Emory University

(This Listing Continued)

GOLDBERG, KOHN, BELL, BLACK, ROSENBLOOM & MORITZ, LTD., Chicago—Continued

(B.A., 1997); New York University (J.D., 2001). Dean's Scholar. *Member:* Cook County Bar Association. ***PRACTICE AREAS:*** Litigation. ***Email:*** chante.spann@goldbergkohn.com

WILLIAM A. STARSHAK, born Appleton, Wisconsin, October 24, 1972; admitted to bar, 2000, Illinois. *Education:* University of Virginia (B.A., History and Foreign Affairs, high distinction, 1994); Northwestern University (J.D., cum laude, 1999). *Member:* American Bar Association. ***LANGUAGES:*** German. ***Email:*** william.starshak@goldbergkohn.com

MARLA SWARTZ, born Detroit, Michigan, October 11, 1977; admitted to bar, 2003, Illinois. *Education:* Northwestern University (B.A., 2000); University of Michigan (J.D., 2003). ***PRACTICE AREAS:*** Litigation. ***Email:*** marla.swartz@goldbergkohn.com

ANDREW TORRE, admitted to bar, 2004, Illinois. *Education:* Georgetown Universtiy (B.A., summa cum laude, 2000); University of Chicago (J.D., 2004). *Member:* Chicago Bar Association; Hispanic National Bar Association. ***LANGUAGES:*** Spanish. ***PRACTICE AREAS:*** Real Estate Finance; Real Estate Leasing; Real Estate Development. ***Email:*** andrew.torre@goldbergkohn.com

JEANETTE K. TRUDELL, born Detroit, Michigan, March 12, 1978; admitted to bar, 2004, New York (Not admitted in Illinois). *Education:* University of Michigan (A.B., 2000); University of Chicago (J.D., 2003). *Member:* American Bar Association. ***PRACTICE AREAS:*** Commercial Finance. ***Email:*** jeanette.trudell@goldbergkohn.com

VANESSA B.M. VERGARA, born Chicago, Illinois; admitted to bar, 2000, Illinois; 2001, U.S. District Court, Northern District of Illinois. *Education:* Hamline University (B.A., summa cum laude, 1997); Northwestern University (J.D., cum laude, 2000). Phi Beta Kappa. Managing Editor, Northwestern Law Review, 1999-2000. Author, "Abusive Mail-Order Bride Marriage and the Thirteenth Amendment," Northwestern University Law Review, 2000. *Member:* American Bar Association; Asian American Bar Association; Filipino American Bar Association. ***PRACTICE AREAS:*** Litigation. ***Email:*** vanessa.vergara@goldbergkohn.com

MEGAN G. WALKER, born Holland, Michigan, February 5, 1975; admitted to bar, 2000, Illinois. *Education:* Michigan State University (B.S., 1997); University of Michigan (J.D., 2000). ***PRACTICE AREAS:*** Real Estate. ***Email:*** Megan.Walker@goldbergkohn.com

A. COLIN WEXLER, born Evanston, Illinois, October 3, 1972; admitted to bar, 1999, Illinois; 2000, U.S. District Court, Northern District of Illinois. *Education:* Yale University (B.A., 1995); University of Michigan (J.D., cum laude, 1999). Law Clerk to Judge Charles P. Sifton, U.S. District Court, Eastern District of New York, 1999-2000. ***PRACTICE AREAS:*** Commercial Litigation. ***Email:*** Colin.Wexler@goldbergkohn.com

OF COUNSEL

ROBIN S. KING, born Pittsburgh, Pennsylvania, March 31, 1958; admitted to bar, 1983, Illinois; 1988, California. *Education:* University of Virginia (B.A., 1980); Northwestern University (J.D., 1983). *Member:* Chicago and Illinois State Bar Associations. ***PRACTICE AREAS:*** Real Estate. ***Email:*** robin.king@goldbergkohn.com

JOSEPH M. MARTIN, born Oak Park, Illinois, October 18, 1966; admitted to bar, 1991, Illinois. *Education:* Eastern Illinois University (B.A., 1988); University of Illinois (J.D., 1991). ***PRACTICE AREAS:*** Commercial Finance. ***Email:*** Joseph.Martin@goldbergkohn.com

JAY S. GOLDENBERG

221 NORTH LA SALLE STREET, SUITE 240
CHICAGO, ILLINOIS 60601
Telephone: 312-346-7899
Fax: 312-896-5047
URL: http://www.chicplan.com
Email: Attyjsg@chicplan.com
URL: http://www.lawyers.com/chicplan

Probate, Trusts and Estates, Estate Planning and Wills, Elder Law, Living Trusts, Trust Planning, Asset Protection, Gift Tax, Family Limited Partnerships.

JAY S. GOLDENBERG, born 1938; admitted to bar, 1966, Illinois. *Education:* Shimer College (B.A., 1957); John Marshall Law School (J.D., 1966).

GOLDMAN & EHRLICH

19 SOUTH LASALLE STREET - FIFTEENTH FLOOR
CHICAGO, ILLINOIS 60603
Telephone: 312-332-6733
Facsimile: 312-332-4629
URL: http://www.goldmanandehrlich.com

Employment Law, Commercial Litigation, Discrimination, Disabled Access, Sexual Harassment, Wrongful Termination, Americans with Disabilities Act, Family and Medical Leave Act, Affirmative Action, Age Discrimination, Civil Service, Covenants Not To Compete.

MEMBERS OF THE FIRM

JONATHAN C. GOLDMAN, born Chicago, Illinois, July 22, 1967; admitted to bar, 1992, Illinois; 2003, Michigan; U.S. District Court, Northern District of Illinois including Trial Bar; U.S. District Court, Central District of Illinois; U.S. Court of Appeals, Seventh and Federal Circuits. *Education:* University of Michigan (B.A., 1989); Chicago-Kent College of Law (J.D., with honors, 1992). ***SPECIAL AGENCIES:*** Equal Employment Opportunity Commission; Merit Systems Protection Board; Illinois Department of Human Rights; Human Rights Commission (IL), State, City and County Civil Service Boards. ***PRACTICE AREAS:*** Employment Law; Discrimination; Disabled Access; Sexual Harassment; Wrongful Termination. ***Email:*** jon@goldmanehrlich.com

ARTHUR R. EHRLICH, born Newton, Massachusetts, March 29, 1959; admitted to bar, 1984, Illinois; U.S. District Court, Northern District of Illinois Trial Bar; U.S. Court of Appeals, Seventh Circuit; U.S. Court of Appeals for the Federal Circuit. *Education:* Hebrew University, Jerusalem, Israel; Boston University (B.A., magna cum laude, 1981); DePaul University (J.D., with honors, 1984). Recipient: American Jurisprudence Award, Civil Procedure, 1981; Administrative Process, 1984. Listed, Who's Who, 2000. *Member:* Chicago and Illinois State Bar Associations. ***SPECIAL AGENCIES:*** Equal Employment Opportunity Commission; Merit Systems Protection Board; Illinois Department of Human Rights; Human Rights Commission (IL).; State, City and County Civil Service Boards. ***PRACTICE AREAS:*** Employment Law; Commercial Litigation; Discrimination; Disabled Access; Sexual Harassment; Wrongful Termination. ***Email:*** arthur@goldmanehrlich.com

MARSHALL J. GOLDSMITH

Established in 1965

77 WEST WACKER DRIVE, SUITE 3200
CHICAGO, ILLINOIS 60601
Telephone: 312-346-6622
Toll Free: 877-346-6622
Fax: 312-346-1566
URL: http://www.mjgoldmithlaw.lawoffice.com
Email: goldsmithlaw@aol.com
URL: http://www.lawyers.com/goldsmithlaw

Highland, Indiana Office: 2546 45th Street, 46322. Telephone: 219-924-4101. Fax: 219-924-4104.

Corporations, Tax, Real Estate, Estate Planning, Wills, Trusts and Probate Law, Commercial Real Estate, Elder Law, Asset Protection.

MARSHALL J. GOLDSMITH, born East Chicago, Indiana, January 21, 1940; admitted to bar, 1965, Indiana, Illinois and U.S. Tax Court; 1976, U.S. Supreme Court. *Education:* Indiana University (B.A., 1962; J.D., 1965). Phi Delta Phi. *Member:* Chicago (Member, Tax Committee, 1965-1970), Illinois State, Indiana State (Member, Taxation Section) and American (Member, Taxation Section) Bar Associations.

RICHARD M. GOLDWASSER

20 NORTH CLARK, SUITE 1700
CHICAGO, ILLINOIS 60602
Telephone: 312-372-3300
Fax: 312-372-0531
Email: rmg@goldwasserlaw.com
URL: http://www.goldwasserlaw.com

Commercial Litigation, Criminal Law, Appellate Practice.

RICHARD M. GOLDWASSER, born Evanston, Illinois, February 21, 1965; admitted to bar, 1991, Illinois; 1997, U.S. District Court, Northern District of Illinois and U.S. Court of Appeals, Seventh Circuit; 2004, U.S. Supreme Court. *Education:* University of Illinois (A.B., 1987; J.D., 1990). Instructor, Advanced Civil Procedure, Loyola University College of Law, 1996. Judicial Clerk: Hon. Chief Justice, Meir Shamgar Supreme Court of Israel, 1991; Hon. Justice Dom J. Rizzi, Illinois Appellate Court, First District, 1993-1995. ***LANGUAGES:*** Hebrew. ***REPORTED CASES:*** McElmeel v. Village of Hoffman Estates, 2005 WL 2061017 (Ill. App. 1 Dist., Aug 26, 2005), Brooks v. State, 903 So.2d 691, 2005 WL 674817 (Miss. S. Ct. 2005); People v. Salgado, 353 Ill.App.3d 605, 818 N.E.2d 381 (Ill. App. 3 Dist. 2004); People v. Caballes, 207 Ill.2d 504, 802 N.E. 2d 202 (Ill. S. Ct. 2003); People v. Taher, 329 Ill.App.3d 1007, 769 N.E.2d 1021 (Ill. App. 3 Dist. 2002); People v. Miller, 327 Ill.App.3d 594, 763 N.E.2d 865 (Ill. App. 3 Dist. 2002); Garrison v. Choh, 308 Ill.App. 48, 719 N.E.2d 237 (Ill. App. 1 Dist. 1999); Kreykes v. Malk & Harris, 297 Ill.App.3d 936, 697 N.E.2d 885 (Ill. App. 1 Dist. 1998). ***PRACTICE AREAS:*** Commercial Litigation; Appellate Practice.

GOMBERG, SHARFMAN, GOLD AND OSTLER, P.C.

Established in 1969

208 SOUTH LA SALLE STREET, SUITE 1200
CHICAGO, ILLINOIS 60604
Telephone: 312-332-6194
FAX: 312-332-4083
Email: gsgo@gsgolaw.com
URL: http://www.lawyers.com/gsgolaw

General Corporation and business Matters, including Real Estate, Mortgage Banking, Debtor-Creditor Relations, Bankruptcy, General Practice in all State and Federal Courts, litigation, including Class Action Defense, Probate, Mortgages, Mortgage Foreclosure, Mechanic's Lien, Title Insurance, thrift Institution Regulations, Commercial Collections and Mortgage Broker Regulation.

OF COUNSEL

ROBERT J. SHARFMAN, born Chicago, Illinois, March 23, 1936; admitted to bar, 1960, Illinois. *Education:* University of Illinois (B.S., 1958); DePaul University (J.D., 1959). Phi Delta Phi. President, Moot Court Board. Author: "Replevin and Attachment," Creditors' Rights in Illinois, Illinois Institute for Continuing Legal Education, Revised, March, 1969; "Foreclosure of a Real Estate Mortgage," Creditors' Rights in Illinois, Illinois Institute for Continuing Legal Education, Revised, May, 1972; "Handling Mortgage Foreclosures," Mortgages and Foreclosures, Illinois Institute for Continuing Legal Education

(This Listing Continued)

Handbook #32, 1973. General Editor and Author, "Handbook on Administrative Law," Illinois Institute for Continuing Education, 1977. Lecturer: Financial Executives, University of Illinois Executive Development Center, 1976-1985; Real Estate Law and Commercial Law, Institute for Financial Education, 1971-1980. Adjunct Professor, IIT Chicago-Kent Graduate Program on Financial Services Law, 1986, 1996-1998. Goodyear Executive Professor of Business, Kent University, Kent, Ohio. General Counsel, Office of Savings and Loan Commissioner, State of Illinois, 1963-1965. *Member:* Chicago (Member, Committee for the Development of the Law, 1978—), Illinois State and American (President, Metropolitan Area II Committee on Savings and Loan, 1972) Bar Associations. ***PRACTICE AREAS:*** Savings and Loan Law; Thrift Institutions Law. ***Email:*** rsharfman@gsgolaw.com

PARTNERS

LAWRENCE A. GOLD, born Bronx, New York, February 1, 1946; admitted to bar, 1972, Illinois; 1973, Florida. *Education:* University of Wisconsin (B.S., 1967); Washington College of Law (J.D., 1972). Author: "Construction Loan Commitments," Underwriter, Spring, 1987. Co-Author: "Handling Mortgage Foreclosures," Creditors' Rights in Illinois, Illinois Institute for Continuing Legal Education, Revised, 1983. Consulting Attorney for The Law of Distressed Real Estate, Clark Boardman Co., Ltd., 1985. Lecturer, "Real Estate Participations," Banking Law Institute, October, 1986. Counsel, Illinois Association of Mortgage Brokers, 1990—. *Member:* Chicago and American Bar Associations. ***PRACTICE AREAS:*** Savings and Loan Law; Thrift Institutions Law; Mortgage Banking Law; Commercial Mortgages. ***Email:*** lgold@gsgolaw.com

RAYMOND J. OSTLER, born Philadelphia, Pennsylvania, December 29, 1950; admitted to bar, 1976, Illinois and U.S. District Court, Northern District of Illinois including Trial Bar; 1992, U.S. Court of Federal Claims. *Education:* University of Illinois (B.A., 1972); DePaul University (J.D., 1976). Co-author: "Due on Sale Clauses in Mortgages," The Underwriter Vol. I Issue II, June, 1981; "Evolution of Bankruptcy Law/Decline of Creditors Rights," The Quarterly Statement, July/September, 1984; "Bankruptcy Considerations in Foreclosures" Illinois Institute for Continuing Legal Education, 2003; "Foreclosure and Bankruptcy," ILCLE Illinois Mortgage Foreclosure Practice, 2003. Author: "Pitfalls and Roadblocks to Collection," Collecting Judgments, 1989, "How Does Bankruptcy Affect Foreclosure-Creditor Perspective," 1990 Illinois Continuing Legal Education. Consulting Editor, "Enforcement of Judgments," 1997 Nichols Illinois Civil Practice, Vol. 5; "Enforcing Judgments Against Real Estate," Illinois Bar Journal, May 2001. Lecturer, "Enforcement of Judgment," Illinois Institute for Continuing Education, 2000-2004. Member, Illinois Mortgage Bankers Association Legislative Committee, 1990-2000. *Member:* Chicago (Member, Real Estate Law Committee), Illinois State and American Bar Associations. ***PRACTICE AREAS:*** Commercial Litigation; Collections; Real Estate Litigation; Real Estate Title Insurance. ***Email:*** rostler@gsgolaw.com

ROBERT M. GOMBERG, born Chicago, Illinois, January 12, 1960; admitted to bar, 1986, Illinois. *Education:* Colorado State University (B.A., 1982, Phi Beta Kappa); Chicago-Kent College of Law (J.D., 1986). Phi Beta Kappa. *Member:* Chicago and Illinois State Bar Associations. ***PRACTICE AREAS:*** Litigation; Real Estate; Banking; Title Insurance. ***Email:*** robtg@gsgolaw.com

---

KIMBERLY A. OREL-PADJEN, born Chicago, Illinois, June 23, 1961; admitted to bar, 1987, Illinois; 1993, U.S. District Court, Northern District of Illinois. *Education:* St. Mary's College (B.A., 1983); Loyola University, Chicago (J.D., 1986). Speaker: "Handling Mortgage Foreclosures" 1990 Illinois Institute for Continuing Legal Education. *Member:* Chicago (Member, Financial Institutions Committee) and American Bar Associations. ***PRACTICE AREAS:*** Foreclosures; Real Estate and Banking. ***Email:*** kpadj@gsgolaw.com

JOHN J. LYDON, born Arlington Heights, Illinois, May 3, 1963; admitted to bar, 1989, Illinois and U.S. District Court, Northern District of Illinois; 1997, U.S. Court of Federal Claims. *Education:* Loyola University, Chicago (B.A., 1985); DePaul College of Law (J.D., 1989). *Member:* Chicago (Member, Probate Practice Committee) and American (Member, Litigation Division, Forum on Affordable Housing) Bar Associations. ***PRACTICE AREAS:*** Banking Litigation; Consumer Class Actions; Chancery Practice; Commercial Litigation; Nonprofit Corporations; Probate Administration; Real Estate Litigation. ***Email:*** lydonj@gsgolaw.com

MAURESETA T. HAWKINS, born Los Angeles, California, November 17, 1954; admitted to bar, 1997, Illinois, U.S. District Court, Northern District of Illinois; 1998, U.S. Court of Federal Claims. *Education:* Governor's State University (B.A.B.A., 1990); The John Marshall Law School (J.D., 1996). *Member:* Chicago, Cook County, Illinois State and American Bar Associations. ***PRACTICE AREAS:*** Collections. ***Email:*** mhawkins@gsgolaw.com

JOHN W. ROSSITER, born Michigan City, Indiana, September 8, 1964; admitted to bar, 2003, Illinois and U.S. District Court, Northern District of Illinois. *Education:* Albion College (B.A., 1987); Iowa State University (M.B.A., 1998); John Marshall Law School (J.D., 2003). Author: "The Legend Lives On: A Look at the Foreign Corrupt Practices Act of 1977," The Globe, Vol. 40, No. 5, May 2003. Certified Public Accountant, Iowa, 2000. *Member:* Chicago, Illinois State and American Bar Associations; American Institute of Certified Public Accountants; Illinois CPA Society. ***PRACTICE AREAS:*** Banking Law; Commercial Law; Trusts and Estates; Litigation; Federal Taxation. ***Email:*** johnr@gsgolaw.com

REFERENCE: MB Financial Bank.

GONZALEZ, SAGGIO & HARLAN, L.L.P.

Established in 1989

208 S. LASALLE STREET, SUITE 1460
CHICAGO, ILLINOIS 60604
Telephone: 312-236-0475
Facsimile: 312-236-1750
Email: main@gshllp.com
URL: http://www.gshllp.com

Milwaukee, Wisconsin Office: 225 East Michigan, 4th Floor, 53202. Telephone: 414-277-8500. Fax: 414-277-8521.
Indianapolis, Indiana Office: 201 North Illinois Street, Suite 1900, 46204. Telephone: 317-686-9800. Fax: 317-686-9821.
West Des Moines, Iowa Office: 1501 42nd Street, Suite 465, 50266. Telephone: 515-453-8509. Fax: 515-267-1408.
Cincinnati, Ohio Office: Carew Tower, 441 Vine Street, Suite 3615, 45202. Telephone: 513-651-3456. Fax: 513-651-3446.

Business and Corporate Law, Civil Litigation, Insurance Defense Law, Equal Opportunities and Employment, School Law, Municipal Finance, Business and Commercial Litigation, Real Estate, Construction, Condemnation Law, Environmental, Taxation, Utilities Law, Trials and Appeals, Government Relations.

FIRM PROFILE: Gonzalez, Saggio & Harlan, L.L.P. is one of the fastest growing law firms in the Midwest. This growth is a reflection of the firm's devotion to quality, efficiency and frank communication in servicing client needs. Furthermore, as a minority-owned law firm, we believe that our diverse backgrounds add value to those clients wanting to better serve a changing and dynamic environment.

ELIZABETH A. McDUFFIE, born Chicago, Illinois, June 8, 1963; admitted to bar, 1990, Wisconsin and U.S. District Court, Eastern and Western Districts of Wisconsin (Not admitted in Illinois). *Education:* Carroll College (B.S., 1984); Marquette University (J.D., 1990). Member, Moot Court Board. Author: "Absence Control Handbook," Milwaukee, Wisconsin, 1994. *Member:* State Bar of Wisconsin (Member, Labor and Employment Section); American Bar Association; Wisconsin Association for Women Lawyers; Wisconsin Association of Minority Attorneys. ***PRACTICE AREAS:*** Employee Benefits; Employment Law. ***Email:*** liz_mcduffie@gshllp.com

ASSOCIATE

PHILIP S. HOLLOWAY, born Chicago, Illinois, February 3, 1971; admitted to bar, 2000, Illinois. *Education:* University of Illinois, Chicago (B.S., 1996); University of Cincinnati (J.D., 1999). ***PRACTICE AREAS:*** Litigation; Labor and Employment; Housing Law. ***Email:*** philip_holloway@gshllp.com

OF COUNSEL

EMMITT C. HOUSE, born Oklahoma City, Oklahoma, 1949; admitted to bar, 1978, Illinois and U.S. Court of Appeals for the District of Columbia, Fifth, Seventh, Eighth, Tenth and Eleventh Circuits. *Education:* Carleton College (B.A., 1971); Northwestern University (J.D., 1978). Watson Fellow. *Member:* Chicago and Cook County Bar Associations. ***PRACTICE AREAS:*** Corporate Law; Energy; Energy Regulation; Business Law; Utility Law; Electric Power.

JERRY D. BROWN, born April 4, 1963; admitted to bar, 1992, Illinois; 1993, U.S. District Court, Northern District of Illinois, 2000, Trial Bar; 1998, U.S. Supreme Court; 2001, U.S. District Court, Eastern District of Wisconsin. *Education:* University of Chicago (A.B., Sociology, 1987); University of Minnesota (J.D., 1992). Member: Circuit Court of Cook County Committee on Racial and Ethnic Bias in the Courts, 1997; Chicago Council on Foreign Relations. *Member:* Chicago and Cook County (Chair, Job Fair Committee, 1996) Bar Associations. ***PRACTICE AREAS:*** Litigation. ***Email:*** jerry_brown@gshllp.com

REPRESENTATIVE CLIENTS: Accenture; Alliant Energy; Bear, Stears & Co.; Chubb Insurance Company; City of Milwaukee; CNH Global N.V.; Darden Restaurants, Inc.; Denny's; Eastman Kodak Company; E.I. du Pont de Nemours and Company; Family Dollar Stores, Inc.; Forest County Potawatomi Community; Harley-Davidson Motor Company; Kohl's Corporation; Luxottica Group; Menard, Inc.; Midwest Airlines; PepsiAmericas, Inc.; Starwood Hotels & Resorts Worldwide, Inc.; State of Wisconsin; Target Corporation; Time Warner Cable; We Energies; Wisconsin Housing and Economic Development Authority (WHEDA); Zale Corporation.

(For complete biographical data on all personnel, see Professional Biographies at Milwaukee, Wisconsin)

NEIL H. GOOD

30 N. LA SALLE, SUITE 3400
CHICAGO, ILLINOIS 60602
Telephone: 312-629-1212
Email: neil@neilgood.com
URL: http://www.neilgoodlawfirm.com

Palatine, Illinois Office: 800 E. Northwest Highway, Suite 814, 60074. Telephone: 847-577-4476.

Social Security Disability, Personal Injury, Medical Malpractice, Plaintiffs Personal Injury.

(For complete biographical data on all personnel, see Professional Biographies at Palatine, Illinois)

GOODSMITH GREGG & UNRUH LLP

Established in 1996

105 WEST ADAMS STREET, 26TH FLOOR
CHICAGO, ILLINOIS 60603
Telephone: 312-322-1981
Fax: 312-322-0056
Email: ggu@ggulaw.com
URL: http://www.ggulaw.com

Commercial Litigation, Employment Law, Real Estate and Finance, Mergers and Acquisitions, Corporate Law, Company Counseling.

FIRM PROFILE: GoodSmith Gregg & Unruh LLP was founded in 1996 by three former partners of Latham & Watkins who were joined by two additional former Latham partners in 2002. These attorneys, together with highly qualified associates and counsel, provide "big firm" quality legal services in a variety of practice areas without the inefficiencies, and attendant costs, often associated with large firms.

KENNETH S. GOODSMITH, born Newark, New Jersey, July 20, 1956; admitted to bar, 1981, Illinois, U.S. District Court, Northern District of Illinois including Trial Bar and U.S. Court of Appeals, First, Sixth, Seventh and Tenth Circuits. *Education:* Georgetown University (B.A., magna cum laude, 1978); Northwestern University (J.D., cum laude, 1981). Order of the Coif; Phi Beta Kappa. Notes and Comments Editor, Northwestern University Law Review, 1980-1981. Judicial Clerkship, Hon. Robert A. Sprecher, U.S. Court of Appeals, Seventh Circuit, 1981-1982. ***PRACTICE AREAS:*** Antitrust and Trade Regulation; Labor and Employment; Franchise Law; Commercial Litigation. **Email:** kgoodsmith@ggulaw.com

DAVID D. GREGG, born Chicago, Illinois, May 23, 1956; admitted to bar, 1981, Illinois. *Education:* University of Illinois (B.A., magna cum laude, 1978); London School of Economics, London, England; University of Michigan (J.D., magna cum laude, 1981). Order of the Coif; Phi Beta Kappa. Note Editor, University of Michigan Journal of Law Reform, 1980-1981. Judicial Clerkship, Hon. Anthony J. Celebrezze, U.S. Court of Appeals, Sixth Circuit, 1981-1982. ***PRACTICE AREAS:*** Business Law; Commercial Law; Corporate Law; Commercial Real Estate. **Email:** dgregg@ggulaw.com

MARILEE C. UNRUH, born Los Angeles, California, March 3, 1957; admitted to bar, 1981, California; 1983, Illinois. *Education:* Stanford University (B.A., 1978); University of California School of Law, Los Angeles (J.D., 1981). Chief Articles Editor, UCLA Law Review, 1980-1981. Judicial Clerkship, Hon. John M. Ferren, District of Columbia Court of Appeals, 1981-1982. ***PRACTICE AREAS:*** Business Law; Corporate Law; Mergers, Acquisitions and Divestitures. **Email:** munruh@ggulaw.com

LINDA S. SCHURMAN, born Portland, Maine, June 9, 1960; admitted to bar, 1985, Illinois. *Education:* Middlebury College (B.A., magna cum laude, 1982); University of Chicago (J.D., 1985). Phi Beta Kappa. ***PRACTICE AREAS:*** Finance; Real Estate; Business Law; Commercial Law. **Email:** lschurman@ggulaw.com

KENNETH D. CREWS, born Indianapolis, Indiana, February 24, 1966; admitted to bar, 1993, Illinois. *Education:* University of Pennsylvania (B.S.E., summa cum laude, 1988); University of Chicago (J.D., high honors, 1993). Order of the Coif. University of Chicago Law Review. *Member:* Illinois State and American Bar Associations. ***PRACTICE AREAS:*** Commercial Real Estate; Mergers, Acquisitions and Divestitures; Finance; Business Law. **Email:** kcrews@ggulaw.com

ASSOCIATES

CARRIE L. DEVALK, born Oak Lawn, Illinois, October 26, 1968; admitted to bar, 1993, Illinois. *Education:* Dartmouth College (A.B., cum laude, 1990); University of Illinois (J.D., magna cum laude, 1993). Order of the Coif. Member, University of Illinois Law Review, 1992-1993. Associate: Latham & Watkins, 1993-1995; Holleb & Coff, 1995-1996. **Email:** cdevalk@ggulaw.com

ELLEN K. FULTON, born Evanston, Illinois, November 30, 1971; admitted to bar, 2000, Illinois and District of Columbia. *Education:* Southern Methodist University (B.S., magna cum laude, 1993); University of Chicago Law School (J.D., 2000). Phi Beta Kappa. Member and Symposium Editor, The University of Chicago Law School Roundtable, 1998-2000. Investment Banking Analyst, Credit Suisse First Boston, 1993-1995. Manager, Financial Analysis, Holly Corporation, 1995-1997. Associate, Wilmer, Cutler & Pickering, 2000-2003. **Email:** efulton@ggulaw.com

JENNIFER L. HANSEN, born Davenport, Iowa, April 7, 1971; admitted to bar, 1997, Illinois. *Education:* University of Dayton (B.A., magna cum laude, 1993); Tulane University Law School (J.D., summa cum laude, 1997). Order of the Coif. Member, Tulane Law Review. Associate, Latham & Watkins, 1997-2000. **Email:** jhansen@ggulaw.com

CAMERON R. KRIEGER, born Honolulu, Hawaii, January 21, 1974; admitted to bar, 2001, Illinois. *Education:* Grinnell College (B.A., 1996); University of Chicago (J.D., 2001). Editor-in-Chief, Chicago Journal of International Law, 2000-2001. Associate, Latham & Watkins, 2001-2005. **Email:** ckrieger@ggulaw.com

KEREN L. WEISS, born Tel-Aviv, Israel, June 24, 1976; admitted to bar, 2002, District of Columbia and New York; 2003, Illinois. *Education:* Johns Hopkins University (B.A., 1998); George Washington University Law School (J.D., with high honors, 2001). Order of the Coif. Member, The George Washington Law Review. Associate, Jenner & Block LLP, 2003-2005; Wilmer, Cutler & Pickering, 2001-2003. ***LANGUAGES:*** Hebrew. ***PRACTICE AREAS:*** Corporate. **Email:** kweiss@ggulaw.com

OF COUNSEL

D. R. EDWARDS, born Beckley, West Virginia, February 11, 1953; admitted to bar, 1985, Illinois. *Education:* West Virginia University (B.F.A., magna cum laude, 1974; M.A., 1976); Northwestern University (J.D., 1985). Recipient: International Academy of Trial Lawyers, Best Speaker; Lowden-Wigmore Prize in Julius Minor Moot Court Competition. Associate, Latham & Watkins, 1985-1992. Senior Supervising Attorney, City of Chicago Department of Law, 1992-1995; Deputy Purchasing Agent, City of Chicago, 1995-1997. ***PRACTICE AREAS:*** Commercial Litigation; Construction Law; Municipal Contracts. **Email:** dredwards@ggulaw.com

GILBERT E. GILDEA, JR., born Ironton, Ohio, June 13, 1944; admitted to bar, 1969, Illinois; 1972, Michigan; 1973, Ohio; 1985, California; 1986, Florida. *Education:* Yale University (B.A., cum laude, 1966); University of Chicago Law School (J.D., 1969); Harvard University Business School (M.B.A., 1977); New York University (LL.M., Taxation, 1988). Adjunct Professor, University of Dayton Law School, 1979-1980. Assistant Professor, Michigan State University, 1969-1973. *Member:* Ohio State and Illinois State Bar Associations; State Bar of California; State Bar of Michigan; The Florida Bar.

LAW OFFICES OF BELLE LIND GORDON P.C.

33 NORTH LA SALLE STREET
SUITE 900
CHICAGO, ILLINOIS 60602
Telephone: 312-443-9700
Fax: 312-443-9777
Email: blglawoffice@aol.com

Divorce, Domestic Relations, Family Law, Child Custody, Paternity and Adoption.

FIRM PROFILE: The majority of her 29 year career has been devoted to negotiating settlements, litigating cases on the trial and appellate levels, and preparing pre and post-nuptial agreements. She has extensive experience with valuations, tax matters and mental health experts. She is a Fellow of the American Academy of Matrimonial Lawyers and was an Adjunct Professor of Matrimonial Law at Chicago-Kent College of Law. She has instructed attorneys in negotiation and mediation for the National Institute of Trial Advocacy (NITA). She was formerly a Partner at Schiller, Ducanto & Fleck, and at Beermann Swerdlove Woloshin Barezky Becker Genin & London.

BELLE LIND GORDON, born Manhattan, New York, June 26, 1950; admitted to bar, 1975, Illinois and U.S. District Court, Northern District of Illinois; 1981, U.S. Court of Appeals, Seventh Circuit. *Education:* University of Wisconsin-Madison; University of Illinois (B.S., with honors, 1972); Loyola University School of Law (J.D., 1975). Member, Loyola University Law Review, 1974-1975. Author: "Removal After Eckert," ISBA Family Law Section Journal, April, 1992; "Substitution of Judges as a Matter of Right," ISBA Family Law Section Journal, May 2001; "Recognizing and Protecting Against Conflicts of Interest," ISBA Family Law Section Journal, January 2002. Lecturer: "Confidentiality of Children's Records, Alcohol and Drug Abuse Records and Mental Health Patient Records," Medical Educational Series, 1995; "Tax Aspects of Divorce," National Business Institute, 1993; "Discovery and Finding Hidden Assets, Real World Conversations on Today's Successful Family Law Practice Techniques," IICLE, 1992; "Removal/Relocation Cases; Focusing on the Tough Issues," ISBA, 1991; "Effective Cross-Examination of Expert Witnesses on Business Valuations," IICLE, 1990; "Winning Child Custody, Support and Maintenance Cases: Cross Examination of an Expert Highlighting Issues of Privilege and Psychological Testing," IICLE, 1989; "Fighting the Sexual Abuse Allegation at Trial, What Every Practitioner Needs to Know to Defend Against the Ugliest Litigation," ITLA, 1989; "What Every Practitioner Needs to Know About the Three Most Difficult Areas in Custody Litigation," CBA, 1988; "Effective Cross-Examination of an Expert Witness," IICLE, 1988; "Effective Litigation Techniques and Strategies in a Matrimonial Case," 1988. Elected Member: ISBA Assembly, 1988-2001; Board of Directors, Greater Chicago Counsel, National Committee for Prevention of Child Abuse, 1988-1990. Appointed, ISBA Task Force on Specialization Certification. Appointed Member, ISBA Family Law Section Council, 2000-2003. Assistant State's Attorney, Cook County, Illinois, 1975-1979. ***PRACTICE AREAS:*** Divorce; Domestic Relations; Family Law; Child Custody; Paternity; Adoption Law. **Email:** blglawoffice@aol.com

GORDON & EINSTEIN, LTD.

Established in 1987

224 EAST ONTARIO
CHICAGO, ILLINOIS 60611
Telephone: 312-280-7766
Telecopier: 312-280-9599
URL: http://www.gordon-einstein.com

General Corporate, Business Mergers and Acquisitions, Real Estate and Finance Law.

FIRM PROFILE: Gordon & Einstein, Ltd. was founded in 1987 by its two principals, Raymond P. Gordon and Jean M. Einstein, with the primary focus of being a small firm which could provide sophisticated legal services in corporate, real estate and finance, whose principals would be accessible to and directly serve clients, but as a small firm could provide such services more efficiently and at a substantial cost savings to clients from rates they were receiving for comparable work at larger firms.

RAYMOND P. GORDON, born Chicago, Illinois, April 4, 1949; admitted to bar, 1974, Illinois. *Education:* Tulane University (B.A., 1971); Northwestern University (J.D., 1974). Phi Beta Kappa. President, John Henry Wigmore Alumni Club, Northwestern University School of Law, 1987-1988. President, Congregation Am Shalom, 1994-1996. Vice-Chair, Design Industry Foundation Fighting AIDS/Chicago, 1993-1994. *Member:* Chicago and American Bar Associations; Decalogue Society of Lawyers. ***PRACTICE AREAS:*** General Corporate; Business; Finance; Real Estate. **Email:** rgordon@gordon-einstein.com

JEAN M. EINSTEIN, born Cleveland, Ohio, January 29, 1949; admitted to bar, 1977, Ohio; 1983, Illinois. *Education:* University of Michigan (B.A., 1971); University of Cincinnati (J.D., 1977). Order of the Coif. Member, Editorial Board, University of Cincinnati

(This Listing Continued)

Law Review, 1976-1977. *Member:* Chicago and American Bar Associations. ***PRACTICE AREAS:*** General Corporate; Business; Finance. **Email:** einstein@gordon-einstein.com

LEGAL SUPPORT PERSONNEL

LAURA A. KOZICKI, born Chicago, Illinois, October 24, 1964. *Education:* Roosevelt University (B.S.B.A., with honors, 1986; Certificate, Legal Assistant Program, Corporate Secretary, with honors, 1986). Registrar, 2001—, and Co-Chair, 2001-2003, Ridgeland Association Girl Scouts. ***PRACTICE AREAS:*** General Corporate; Business; Finance and Real Estate. **Email:** lkozicki@gordon-einstein.com

GORDON, GLICKMAN, FLESCH & ROSENWEIN

A Partnership of Professional Corporations

Established in 1980

THE MARQUETTE BUILDING
140 SOUTH DEARBORN STREET, SUITE 404
CHICAGO, ILLINOIS 60603
Telephone: 312-346-1080
Fax: 312-346-3708
URL: http://www.lawggf.com

Trials and Appeals. Antitrust, Securities, Copyright and Commercial Litigation, Employment Law, Wrongful Discharge, Intellectual Property.

JAMES S. GORDON, (LTD.), born New York, N.Y., February 15, 1941; admitted to bar, 1965, Illinois; 1966, Florida; 1974, U.S. Supreme Court; U.S. District Court, Northern District of Illinois including Trial Bar. *Education:* University of Florida (B.A., 1962); Yale University (LL.B., 1965). Phi Beta Kappa; Phi Kappa Phi; Phi Alpha Delta; Order of the Coif; Florida Blue Key. Editor, Yale Law Journal, 1963-1965. Author: "An Experiment in Preventive Antitrust: Judicial Regulation of the Motion Picture Exhibition Market Under the Paramount Decrees," 74 Yale Law Journal 1041, 1965; "Horizontal and Vertical Restraints of Trade; The Legality of Motion Picture Splits Under the Antitrust Law," 75 Yale Law Journal 239, 1965; "Shipping Regulation and the Federal Maritime Commission, Part 1," 37 University of Chicago Law Review 90, 1969; "Shipping Regulation and the Federal Maritime Commission, Part 2," 37 University of Chicago Law Review 256, 1970. Assistant Professor, 1967-1968 and Associate Professor, 1969, Antitrust Law, Trademarks and Copyrights and Regulated Industries, Indiana University School of Law, Bloomington. International Trade and Development Fellow, Ford Foundation, University of Chicago Law School, 1965-1966. Member, Executive Committee, Yale Law School Association, 1987-1995. *Member:* The Lawyers Club of Chicago. ***REPORTED CASES:*** Zeitz v. Village of Glenview, 1999, Appellate Court of Illinois, 304 Ill. App. 3d 586, 710 N.E. 2d 849; Instrumentalist Co. v. Band, Inc., Neidig (Kenneth L.), 1985, Appellate Court of Illinois, First District, 480 N.E.2d 1273, 89 Ill.Dec. 530, 134 Ill.App.3d 884; In re Village of Kildeer, 112 Ill.2d 494, 493 N.E.2d 1075 (1988); Peter Wright and Beneficial Standard Corporation, Plaintiffs-Appellants, Cross Appellees, v. The Heizer Corporation, Defendant-Appellee, Cross-Appellant, and International Digisonics Corporation, Defendant-Appellee., 1977 United States Court of Appeals, Seventh Circuit, 560 F.2d 236, Fed. Sec. L. Rep. P 96, 101; Harold J. O'Brien et al., Plaintiffs-Appellants, v. Continental Illinois National Bank and Trust Company of Chicago, a National Banking Association, Defendant-Appellee., 1979 United States Court of Appeals, Seventh Circuit, 593 F2d 54, Fed. Sec. L. Rep. P 96, 780; Trabert & Hoeffer, Inc., an Illinois Corporation, Plaintiff Appellee, v. Piaget Watch Corporation, North American Watch Corporation and Concord Watch Corporation, Defendant Appellants., 1980, United States Court of Appeals, Seventh Circuit, 633 F.2d 477, 1980-81 Trade Cases P. 63,574. ***PRACTICE AREAS:*** Antitrust and Securities Litigation; Financial Restructuring; Litigation of Restrictive Covenants; Partnership Dissolutions; Municipal Zoning; Annexations; UCC; Stockholders Agreements; White Collar Fraud; Will Contests. **Email:** JGordon@lawggf.com

DON E. GLICKMAN, (LTD.), born March 9, 1947; admitted to bar, 1972, Illinois; 1982, Florida. *Education:* Miami University (A.B., magna cum laude, 1969); University of Chicago (J.D., 1972). Phi Beta Kappa. Member, University of Chicago Law Review, 1970-1971. Publication: Practices, Tactics and Considerations for the Zoning Litigator, 60 Chicago-Kent L. Rev. 89 (1984). *Member:* Chicago and American Bar Associations. ***REPORTED CASES:*** Zeitz v. Village of Glenview, 1999, Appellate Court of Illinois, 304 Ill. App.3d 586, 710 N.E.2d 849; Oak Park Trust and Savings Bank v. Village of Palos Park, Cook County, Illinois, 1982, Appellate Court of Illinois, First District, 435 N.E.2d 1265, 62 Ill.Dec. 293, 106 Ill.App.3d 394; Moylan (Ross T.) v. Meadow Club, Inc., 1992, United States Court of Appeals, Seventh Circuit, 979 F.2d 1246, 123 Lab.Cas. P 35,738, 37 Fed. R. Evid. Serv. 241, 1 Wage & Hour Cas. 2d (BNA) 171. ***PRACTICE AREAS:*** Employment Litigation; Wrongful Termination; Fair Labor Standards; Land Use Litigation; Real Estate Litigation; Commercial Litigation; Trial Practice. **Email:** DGlickman@lawggf.com

JAMES A. FLESCH, (LTD.), born July 9, 1955; admitted to bar, 1980, Illinois, U.S. District Court, Northern District of Illinois and U.S. Court of Appeals, Seventh Circuit. *Education:* University of Illinois (B.S., 1977; J.D., 1980). Certified Public Accountant, Illinois, 1977. ***REPORTED CASES:*** Krautsack v. Anderson, 2002, Appellate Court of Illinois, First District, 329 Ill.App.3d 666, 768 N.E.2d 133; McCormick Road Associates v. Taub, 1995, Appellate Court of Illinois, First District, 276 Ill.App.3d 780, 659 N.E.2d 52; Toys 'R' Us, Inc. v. NBD Trust Company of Illinois, 1990, United States Court of Appeals, Seventh Circuit, 904 F.2d 1172; Don Carrillo individually and on the behalf of all others similarly situated v. Jam Productions, Ltd., et al., 1988, Appellate Court of Illinois, First District, 173 Ill.App.3d 693, 527 N.E.2d 964; Capital Associates Development Corporation v. James E. Roberts-Ohbyashi Corporation, 1985, Illinois Appellate Court, First District, 138 Ill.App. 1031, 487 N.E.2d 7. ***PRACTICE AREAS:*** Commercial Litigation; Trial Practice; Appellate Practice; Arbitration; Employment Litigation; Restrictive Covenants. **Email:** JAFlesch@lawggf.com

THOMAS D. ROSENWEIN, (LTD.), born New York, N.Y., May 18, 1943; admitted to bar, 1978, Illinois and U.S. District Court, Northern District of Illinois; 1981, U.S. Supreme Court; 1982, U.S. Court of Appeals for the Federal Circuit; 1984, U.S. Court of Appeals, Seventh Circuit. *Education:* University of Chicago (A.B., with honors, 1965; M.A., 1968); DePaul University (J.D., with honor, 1978). Co-editor, Court of Appeals for the Federal Circuit Newsletter, 1983-1987. Co-Author: "Sanctions: Rule 11 and Other Powers," 2d Ed., ABA Pub., 1988; "The Federal Trademark Dilution Act: A Statute in Limbo," International Legal Strategy, Vol. IX-8, 2000; "Taming the Tiger: How Litigation is Bringing Discipline to Business Methods Patents, International Legal Strategy, Vol. X-6, June 2001; "Flirting With Fame: Another Year in the Life of the Federal Trademark Dilution Act," International Legal Strategy, Vol. X-8, August, 2001. Speaker: "The Very Latest in Trademark Insurance Coverage," Mealy's-LexisNexis Advanced Trademark Strategies Conference, Chicago, April 15, 2002. *Member:* Chicago Bar Association; Federal Circuit Bar Association (Board Member, 1988-1991); American Intellectual Property Law Association. ***LANGUAGES:*** French and Spanish. ***PRACTICE AREAS:*** Intellectual Property; Litigation; Labor and Employment. **Email:** TRosenwein@lawggf.com

(This Listing Continued)

GORDON & GLICKSON LLC

Established in 1974

444 NORTH MICHIGAN AVENUE, SUITE 3600
CHICAGO, ILLINOIS 60611-3903
Telephone: 312-321-1700
FAX: 312-321-9324
Email: gg@ggtech.com
URL: http://www.ggtech.com

Information Technology, Digital Strategies, Life Sciences, Computer Law, Online and Internet Law, Technology Licensing and Transactions, Outsourcing, Corporate and Securities, Finance, Venture Capital, Distribution, Marketing, Development, Intellectual Property, Multimedia and New Media, Telecommunications, Wireless, Commercial Law, Complex Commercial Litigation, Trials and Dispute Resolution.

FIRM PROFILE: Gordon & Glickson LLC is devoted exclusively to providing strategic legal counsel to the technology marketplaces. In the late 1970's, the firm was one of the first in the country to establish this sharply focused practice. Two decades later, Gordon & Glickson remains a leader in advising technology sectors from information technology to life sciences. Our clients range from Fortune 500 corporations to emerging enterprises, from not-for-profit organizations to state and local governmental agencies, and from local businesses to those operating globally. Like our clients, Gordon & Glickson's professionals are entrepreneurs and innovators, business people who are active contributors to the communities we serve. Our attorneys hold influential positions on technology-related organizations, committees and editorial boards; present at conferences across the globe; and publish frequently in noted journals and publications. At www.ggtech.com, we publish daily technology headlines, white papers, and informational resources. Visitors to the website may also register to receive the Law Forum, Gordon & Glickson's electronic newsletter of breaking technology legal issues and business strategy.

KENNETH K. DORT, born Chicago, Illinois, February 2, 1961; admitted to bar, 1986, Illinois; U.S. District Court, Northern District of Illinois including Trial Bar; U.S. Court of Appeals, Seventh, Ninth and Federal Circuits; U.S. District Court, District of Arizona; U.S. District Court, Northern and Central Districts of California; U.S. District Court, Southern District of Florida; U.S. District Court, Northern District of Indiana; U.S. District Court, Western District of Kentucky; U.S. District Court, Western District of Michigan; U.S. District Court, District of Minnesota; U.S. District Court, Southern District of New York; U.S. District Court, Northern District of Ohio; U.S. District Court, District of Oregon; U.S. District Court, Western District of Texas; U.S. District Court, Western District of Virginia; U.S. District Court, Western District of Washington. *Education:* Stanford University (A.B., with distinction and honors, 1983); University of Chicago (J.D., 1986). ***PRACTICE AREAS:*** Information Technology; Complex Commercial Litigation; Alternative Dispute Resolution; Intellectual Property; Trademark Protection; Trade Secrets; Trademark Licensing; Software Licensing. **Email:** kkdort@ggtech.com

SCOTT L. GLICKSON, born Chicago, Illinois, March 28, 1950; admitted to bar, 1975, Illinois; 1979, U.S. Supreme Court. *Education:* University of Illinois (B.A., with high honors, 1972); Northwestern University (J.D., 1975). ***PRACTICE AREAS:*** Corporate Finance; Business Formation; Commercial Law; Securities; Information Technology; Computer Law; Internet Law. **Email:** slglickson@ggtech.com

STEPHEN GOLD, born Cleveland, Ohio, May 31, 1959; admitted to bar, 1985, Ohio; 1997, Illinois. *Education:* University of Michigan (B.A., with distinction, 1981); Georgetown University (J.D., magna cum laude, 1985). ***PRACTICE AREAS:*** Securities Law; Corporate Law; Corporate Finance; Internet Law; Computer Law; Information Technology; New Technology. **Email:** sgold@ggtech.com

MARK L. GORDON, born Chicago, Illinois, February 20, 1951; admitted to bar, 1976, California; 1977, Illinois. *Education:* University of Michigan (B.A., with distinction, 1973); Northwestern University (J.D., cum laude, 1976). Texts: Computer Software: *Contracting for Development and Distribution,* John Wiley & Sons, Inc. (1986). ***PRACTICE AREAS:*** Information Technology; Computer Law; Outsourcing; Corporate Law. **Email:** mlgordon@ggtech.com

MICHAEL T. HEPBURN, born Hartford, Connecticut, February 16, 1968; admitted to bar, 1995, Illinois. *Education:* University of Connecticut (B.S., honors, 1990); DePaul University College of Law (J.D., 1995). ***PRACTICE AREAS:*** Information Technology; Internet Law; Computer Law; Corporate Law; Outsourcing. **Email:** mthepburn@ggtech.com

BENJAMIN D. KERN, born Bloomington, Indiana, January 28, 1970; admitted to bar, 1997, Illinois. *Education:* Indiana University (B.A., 1992); Cornell University (M.B.A., 1996; J.D., 1997). ***PRACTICE AREAS:*** Corporate Law; Information Technology; Internet Law; New Technologies. **Email:** bdkern@ggtech.com

JANET SMERLING LEVEE, born Chicago, Illinois, July 13, 1962; admitted to bar, 1988, Illinois. *Education:* University of Michigan (B.A., with high honors, 1984); North-

(This Listing Continued)

GORDON & GLICKSON LLC, Chicago—Continued

western University (J.D., 1988). ***PRACTICE AREAS:*** Information Technology; Business Law; Corporate Law; Commercial Law; Venture Capital; Corporate Finance; Equipment Finance and Leasing Law. ***Email:*** jslevee@ggtech.com

THOMAS O. LEVENBERG, born April 10, 1970; admitted to bar, 1996, Arizona; 1999, Illinois. *Education:* Stanford University (B.A., 1992); Northwestern University (J.D., cum laude, 1996). ***PRACTICE AREAS:*** Information Technology; Corporate Law; Internet Law; Computer Law. ***Email:*** tolevenberg@ggtech.com

PHILIP P. McGUIGAN, born New York, N.Y., August 28, 1944; admitted to bar, 1969, New York; 1975, U.S. Supreme Court and U.S. Court of Appeals for the District of Columbia Circuit; 1981, Utah; 1998, Illinois. *Education:* Brown University (A.B., 1966); University of Minnesota (J.D., 1969). ***PRACTICE AREAS:*** Venture Capital; Corporate Finance; Commercial Law; Securities; Healthcare IT; Corporate Law; Technology Licensing; Mergers and Acquisitions; Government Outsourcing. ***Email:*** ppmcguigan@ggtech.com

STUART SMITH, born Omaha, Nebraska, August 31, 1946; admitted to bar, 1972, Nebraska, Illinois and U.S. District Court, District of Nebraska; 1973, U.S. District Court, Northern District of Illinois; 1982, U.S. Court of Appeals, Seventh Circuit; 1983, U.S. District Court, Northern District of Illinois, including Trial Bar; 1989, U.S. Court of Appeals, Sixth Circuit; 1990, U. S. Court of Appeals for the Federal Circuit; 1996, U.S. Supreme Court; U.S. District Court, Eastern District of Michigan. *Education:* University of Nebraska (B.S. Ch.E., 1969; J.D., with distinction, 1972). Phi Delta Phi. [U.S. Army]. ***PRACTICE AREAS:*** Complex Commercial Litigation; Civil Litigation; Trials; Appellate Practice; Information Technology; Intellectual Property; Dispute Resolution. ***Email:*** ssmith@ggtech.com

---

STEPHANIE A. FISHMAN, born Royal Oak, Michigan, November 18, 1971; admitted to bar, 2001, Michigan, U.S. District Court, Eastern District of Michigan and U.S. Court of Appeals, Sixth Circuit (Not admitted in Illinois). *Education:* Syracuse University (B.A., 1993); Wayne State University (J.D., cum laude, 2001). Author: "Individuals with Disabilities But Without Mitigating Measures," 46 Wayne L. Rev., 2013, 2000. *Member:* State Bar of Michigan; American Bar Association (Member, Sections on: Business Law; Science and Technology Law; Taxation Law). ***PRACTICE AREAS:*** Commercial Law; Computer Law; Internet Law; Information Technology. ***Email:*** safishman@ggtech.com

JAMES A. KOVACS, born Livonia, Michigan, November 7, 1975; admitted to bar, 2000, Illinois and U.S. District Court, Northern District of Illinois. *Education:* University of Michigan (B.A., with high honors, 1997); Harvard University Law School (J.D., 2000). Phi Beta Kappa; Golden Key. James B. Angell Scholar, 1997. ***PRACTICE AREAS:*** Information Technology; Internet Law; Computer Law; Commercial Law. ***Email:*** jakovacs@ggtech.com

DEREK A. ROACH, born Alton, Illinois, May 16, 1974; admitted to bar, 1999, Illinois; registered to practice before U.S. Patent and Trademark Office. *Education:* Illinois Wesleyan University (B.A., magna cum laude, 1996); University of Chicago (J.D., 1999). ***PRACTICE AREAS:*** Intellectual Property; Software Licensing; Finance; Corporate Law. ***Email:*** daroach@ggtech.com

BRADLEY A. SALMON, born Euclid, Ohio, August 28, 1973; admitted to bar, 2000, Illinois. *Education:* Ohio State University (B.A., magna cum laude, 1996; J.D., with honors, 2000). ***PRACTICE AREAS:*** Information Technology; Internet Law; Outsourcing; Computer Law. ***Email:*** basalmon@ggtech.com

GEORGE R. SPATZ, born Kettering, Ohio, September 21, 1972; admitted to bar, 2002, Illinois; U.S. District Court, Northern District of Illinois. *Education:* Northwestern University (B.S.E.D, 1996); Texas A&M University (M.A., 1999); University of Chicago Law School (J.D., 2002). ***PRACTICE AREAS:*** Commercial Litigation; Intellectual Property; Trademark Protection; Copyright Protection; Contract Litigation; Software Protection. ***Email:*** grspatz@ggtech.com

---

GOULD & RATNER

Established in 1949

222 NORTH LA SALLE STREET
8TH FLOOR
CHICAGO, ILLINOIS 60601
Telephone: 312-236-3003
Fax: 312-236-3241
Email: info@gould-ratner.com
URL: http://www.gould-ratner.com

Family Business advisory and Planning, Entrepreneurial Business, Real Estate Law including Leasing, Annexation, Zoning, Land Development, Ground and Air Rights Leases, Condemnations, Property Taxes. Corporate and Securities Law. Business Acquisitions, Sales and Divestitures. Technology and E-Commerce Businesses. Mortgage Lending, Financing and Recapitalizations. Employment and Labor Law. ERISA and Employee Benefits. Bankruptcy, Workouts and Creditors Rights. Environmental Matters including Cost Recovery Actions and Allocations. Mining Law (stone, gravel, coal). Telecommunications Law. Federal and State Taxation including Income Taxes, Sales and Use Taxes and Other Taxes, Tax Compliance. Charitable Giving, Estate Planning, Probate and Guardianships. Civil Litigation including Trial Practice and Appellate Practice. Admiralty Law. Administration Law including Black Lung. Government Regulation. Mechanics Lien Law. Member of Law Exchange International.

FIRM PROFILE: A Family Business advisory law firm for over 60 years, Gould & Ratner has focused its legal and business services on representing fast-paced, entrepreneurial clients. Typically, these entrepreneurs own sophisticated closely held or family-owned businesses, working in diverse industries ranging from those which helped build our nation to the technology, telecommunications and new economy areas which should strengthen our future.

(This Listing Continued)

Often, the founders' entrepreneurial spirit still shines through in companies which have grown into multi-billion-dollar international corporations. In all cases, clients come to Gould & Ratner expecting sophisticated legal skills provided within the context of their business goals. They stay with us for our dedication to client service.

MEMBERS OF FIRM

GERALD RATNER, born Chicago, Illinois, December 17, 1913; admitted to bar, 1937, Illinois. *Education:* University of Chicago (Ph.B., 1935; J.D., cum laude, 1937). Phi Beta Kappa; Order of the Coif. *Member:* Chicago, Illinois State and American Bar Associations. ***PRACTICE AREAS:*** Real Estate Law; Land Use Law; Business Law. ***Email:*** gratner@gould-ratner.com

GERALD A. WEBER, born Chicago, Illinois, March 6, 1939; admitted to bar, 1963, Illinois. *Education:* University of Michigan (B.B.A., 1960; J.D., 1963). Certified Public Accountant, Illinois, 1962. *Member:* Chicago, Illinois State and American Bar Associations. ***PRACTICE AREAS:*** Taxation (Federal Income) Law; Estate Planning Law; Closely Held Businesses Law. ***Email:*** gweber@gould-ratner.com

RICHARD R. ELLEDGE, born Painesville, Ohio, January 8, 1934; admitted to bar, 1963, Illinois. *Education:* Carleton College (B.A., 1955); University of Chicago (J.D., 1961). *Member:* Chicago, Illinois State and American Bar Associations. ***PRACTICE AREAS:*** Environmental Law; Mining Law; Appellate Practice. ***Email:*** relledge@gould-ratner.com

STEPHEN P. SANDLER, born St. Louis, Missouri, May 14, 1939; admitted to bar, 1967, Illinois. *Education:* Washington University (B.S., 1961); Northwestern University (J.D., 1967). *Member:* Chicago, Illinois State and American Bar Associations. ***PRACTICE AREAS:*** Real Estate Law; Project Financing Law; Business Law. ***Email:*** ssandler@gould-ratner.com

DAVID M. RUBIN, born Chicago, Illinois, November 8, 1945; admitted to bar, 1971, Illinois. *Education:* University of Illinois and Roosevelt University (B.S.B.A., 1967); DePaul University (J.D., 1971). Certified Public Accountant, Illinois, 1967. With Office of District Director of Internal Revenue Service, 1967-1972. *Member:* Chicago, Illinois State and American Bar Associations. (Also General Counsel, Material Service Corporation, Henry Crown and Company, Great Dane L.P., Bush Hog, LLC, Woodard, LLC). ***PRACTICE AREAS:*** Business Acquisitions Law; Business Law; Taxation (Federal Income) Law; Estate Planning Law. ***Email:*** drubin@gould-ratner.com

THOMAS A. KORMAN, born Chicago, Illinois, February 15, 1948; admitted to bar, 1974, Illinois. *Education:* University of Illinois (B.S., cum laude, 1969); DePaul University (J.D., 1974). Certified Public Accountant, Illinois, 1970. *Member:* Chicago, Illinois State and American Bar Associations; Illinois Society of Certified Public Accountants; American Institute of Certified Public Accountants. ***PRACTICE AREAS:*** Taxation (Federal Income); Business Law; Closely Held Businesses. ***Email:*** tkorman@gould-ratner.com

DAVID M. ARNBURG, born Adel, Iowa, September 8, 1949; admitted to bar, 1974, Illinois. *Education:* Iowa State University (B.S., 1971); George Washington University (J.D., with highest honors, 1974). Order of the Coif. Notes Editor, George Washington Law Review, 1973-1974. Co-Author: "Interstate Commerce Commission: A Critical Overview," 41 George Washington Law Review 759, 1973. *Member:* Chicago, Illinois State and American (Member, Section on Taxation) Bar Associations. ***PRACTICE AREAS:*** ERISA; Commercial Leasing Law; Employee Benefits Law. ***Email:*** darnburg@gould-ratner.com

JOHN A. WASHBURN, born Rockford, Illinois, February 14, 1951; admitted to bar, 1976, Illinois. *Education:* Stanford University (B.A., with distinction, 1973); University of Chicago (J.D., 1976). Phi Beta Kappa. *Member:* Chicago, Illinois State and American Bar Associations. ***PRACTICE AREAS:*** Business Acquisitions Law; Business Law; Real Estate Law; Litigation. ***Email:*** jwashburn@gould-ratner.com

JOHN H. MAYS, born Chicago, Illinois, December 23, 1946; admitted to bar, 1974, Illinois. *Education:* DePaul University (B.S., in Finance, 1968; J.D., 1974). *Member:* Chicago, Illinois State and American Bar Associations. ***PRACTICE AREAS:*** Real Estate Law; Zoning Law; Real Estate Development Law; Municipal Law; Land Annexations and Disconnections. ***Email:*** jmays@gould-ratner.com

RONALD N. MORA, born Chicago, Illinois, July 27, 1933; admitted to bar, 1958, Illinois; 1972, California. *Education:* Indiana University (B.S., 1955); Northwestern University (J.D., 1958). Associate Editor, Journals Board, 1957-1958. Adjunct Instructor, Estate Planning and Administration, The John Marshall Law School, Fall, 1991. *Member:* Chicago, Illinois State and American Bar Associations; State Bar of California. ***PRACTICE AREAS:*** Estate Planning; Corporate; Taxation; Real Estate; General. ***Email:*** rmora@gould-ratner.com

JOHN S. WORTHEN, born Libertyville, Illinois, March 31, 1949; admitted to bar, 1975, Illinois; 1987, U.S. Tax Court. *Education:* University of Illinois (B.A., 1971); DePaul University (J.D., 1975). Certified Public Accountant, Illinois, 1979. *Member:* Chicago, DuPage County and American Bar Associations. ***PRACTICE AREAS:*** Taxation (Federal and State) Law; Estate Planning and Probate Law; Business Law. ***Email:*** jworthen@gould-ratner.com

GAIL POTYSMAN BLEY, born Chicago, Illinois, December 17, 1952; admitted to bar, 1979, Illinois. *Education:* Arizona State University (B.S., 1976); Illinois Institute of Technology, Chicago-Kent College of Law (J.D., 1979). Beta Alpha Psi; Delta Theta Phi (Treasurer, 1978). Lead Articles Editor, Chicago-Kent Law Review, 1978-1979. Author: "Federal Estate Tax Apportionment," 54 Chicago-Kent Law Review 943, 1978. *Member:* Chicago, Illinois State and American Bar Associations. ***PRACTICE AREAS:*** Taxation (Federal Income) Law; Estate Planning Law; Estate and Gift Taxation Law. ***Email:*** gbley@gould-ratner.com

ROBERT A. CARSON, born Elmhurst, Illinois, September 15, 1955; admitted to bar, 1980, Illinois. *Education:* University of Illinois (B.S., with high honors, 1977); Duke University (J.D., 1980). Author: "Evidentiary Motions at Trial," Illinois Institute for Continuing Legal Education Handbook on Civil Evidence. Member, Judicial Evaluation Commit-

(This Listing Continued)

tee, Chicago Bar Association. *Member:* Chicago, Illinois State and American Bar Associations. **PRACTICE AREAS:** Litigation and Trial Practice. **Email:** rcarson@gould-ratner.com

FREDRIC D. TANNENBAUM, born New York, New York, March 6, 1956; admitted to bar, 1981, Wisconsin, Illinois and U.S. District Court, Northern District of Illinois including Trial Bar and Western District of Wisconsin; 1982, U.S. Court of Appeals, Seventh Circuit and District of Columbia Circuit. *Education:* Ohio Wesleyan University (B.A., magna cum laude, 1978); University of Wisconsin (J.D., magna cum laude, 1981). Phi Beta Kappa. Author: "*Organizing, Financing, Growing and Selling Businesses:* Forms and Advice for Lawyers," ALI-ABA Press 2003. Author: "Restricted Stock and Stock Options: Tax and Other Consequences to the Family Business," Family Business Journal, Summer, 2001; "Major Battlegrounds in Venture Capital Transactions," ABA's The Practical Lawyer, March and April, 1999 Edition; "What Every Business Lawyer and Business Owner Should Know About Buy-Sell Agreements," ABA's The Practical Lawyer, November, 1999 and January, 2000, Editions; "Venture Capital Financing: The Lifeblood of Growing Entrepreneurial Businesses," Chapter in West's Treatise, Fall, 2001; "It's Time to Talk Turkey: Seller Strategies to Prevent a Buyer from Wriggling Away," Business Law Today, January/February, 2001. *Member:* Chicago, Illinois State and American Bar Associations. **PRACTICE AREAS:** Business Acquisitions Law; International Business Law; Venture Capital. **Email:** ftannenbaum@gould-ratner.com

EDWARD A. TRIO, born Newark, New Jersey, December 29, 1952; admitted to bar, 1977, Illinois and U.S. District Court, Northern District of Illinois; 1979, U.S. Tax Court; 1984, U.S. Supreme Court. *Education:* University of Notre Dame (B.B.A., 1974); Hamline University (J.D., 1977); IIT/Chicago-Kent College of Law (LL.M., in Taxation, with honors, 1984). Beta Alpha Psi. Certified Public Accountant, Illinois, 1975. *Member:* Chicago, Illinois State and American (Member, Sections on: Taxation, Real Property, Probate and Trust Law) Bar Associations; American Institute of Certified Public Accountants. **PRACTICE AREAS:** Estate Planning; Federal Income Taxation; Estate and Gift Taxation; Probate Law. **Email:** etrio@gould-ratner.com

LOUIS D. BERNSTEIN, born Boone, Iowa, January 2, 1958; admitted to bar, 1984, New York and U.S. District Court, Southern and Eastern Districts of New York; 1986, Illinois and U.S. District Court, Northern District of Illinois. *Education:* Indiana University (B.A., 1980); Hofstra University (J.D., 1983). Certified Mediator, Illinois, 2001. *Member:* Chicago, Nassau County, New York State, Illinois State and American Bar Associations. **PRACTICE AREAS:** Energy; Mineral Law; Arbitration; Mediation; Business Litigation; Commercial Litigation; Real Estate Litigation. **Email:** lbernstein@gould-ratner.com

AMY M. BLUMENTHAL, born New York, N.Y., March 21, 1956; admitted to bar, 1985, Illinois. *Education:* University of Rochester (B.S., with distinction, 1978); National Law Center, George Washington University (J.D., 1985). *Member:* Chicago, Illinois State and American Bar Associations; American Nursing Association. **PRACTICE AREAS:** Real Estate Law; Land Use Law; Secured Transactions; Project Financing Law. **Email:** ablumenthal@gould-ratner.com

STEVEN C. GUSTAFSON, born Yuma, Arizona, August 14, 1961; admitted to bar, 1986, Illinois. *Education:* DePaul University (B.S., 1983); IIT/Chicago-Kent College of Law (J.D., 1986). *Member:* Chicago, Illinois State and American Bar Associations. **PRACTICE AREAS:** Taxation (Federal Income) Law; Estate Planning; Closely Held Businesses Law. **Email:** sgustafson@gould-ratner.com

KARIN T. O'CONNELL, born Grand Rapids, Michigan, February 10, 1960; admitted to bar, 1986, Illinois and U.S. District Court, Northern District of Illinois. *Education:* University of Michigan (B.A., 1982); University of Notre Dame (J.D., 1986). Recipient, International Academy of Trial Lawyers Award for Outstanding Achievement in the Art of Advocacy. *Member:* Chicago, Illinois State and American Bar Associations. **PRACTICE AREAS:** Environmental Law; Commercial and Environmental Litigation. **Email:** koconnell@gould-ratner.com

BRIAN B. GILBERT, born Chicago, Illinois, August 12, 1962; admitted to bar, 1987, Illinois. *Education:* University of Illinois (B.S., with high honors, 1984); Duke University (J.D., 1987). *Member:* Chicago, Illinois State and American Bar Associations; Chicago Council of Lawyers. **PRACTICE AREAS:** Business Law; Business Acquisitions Law; Corporate Law. **Email:** bgilbert@gould-ratner.com

JOSEPH M. LAUB, born Bethlehem, Pennsylvania, September 16, 1960; admitted to bar, 1985, Illinois. *Education:* Temple University (B.B.A., 1982); John Marshall Law School (J.D., with distinction, 1985). Beta Alpha Psi. Member, John Marshall Law School Law Review, 1984-1985. *Member:* Chicago, Illinois State and American Bar Associations. **PRACTICE AREAS:** Taxation (Federal and State Income Tax, Individual and Corporate). **Email:** jlaub@gould-ratner.com

PAUL W. CARROLL, born Davenport, Iowa, May 19, 1962; admitted to bar, 1987, Illinois; U.S. District Court, Northern District of Illinois. *Education:* University of Illinois (B.A., 1984); DePaul University (J.D., 1987). *Member:* Chicago, Illinois State and American Bar Associations. **PRACTICE AREAS:** Civil Litigation. **Email:** pcarroll@gould-ratner.com

CHRISTOPHER J. HORVAY, born Erie, Pennsylvania, January 19, 1951; admitted to bar, 1976, Illinois and U.S. District Court, Northern District of Illinois; 1985, U.S. Court of Appeals, Seventh Circuit; 1991, U.S. District Court, Eastern and Western Districts of Wisconsin and U.S. District Court, Eastern District of Michigan. *Education:* Syracuse University (A.B., magna cum laude, 1973); Northwestern University (J.D., 1976). Phi Beta Kappa. *Member:* American Bankruptcy Institute. **PRACTICE AREAS:** Bankruptcy Law; Creditors' Rights; Corporate Reorganization. **Email:** chorvay@gould-ratner.com

FREDERICK R. DEMPSEY, born Chicago, Illinois, December 10, 1956; admitted to bar, 1989, Illinois. *Education:* Loyola University (A.B. with honors, 1978); Northwestern University (J.D., 1989). Licensed, Real Estate Broker, Illinois. Registered Title Insurance Agent. Member, Executive Committee and Secretary of Board of Directors, Institute on Religious Life. Knight of the Equestrian Order of the Holy Sepulchre of Jerusalem, Granted by the Holy See. *Member:* Chicago, Illinois State and American Bar Associations. **PRACTICE AREAS:** Property Taxation; Real Estate Litigation; Real Estate Transactions. **Email:** fdempsey@gould-ratner.com

(This Listing Continued)

THEODORE F. KOMMERS, born South Bend, Indiana, November 29, 1965; admitted to bar, 1992, Illinois; 1994, U.S. District Court, Northern District of Illinois. *Education:* University of Notre Dame (B.A, 1988; J.D., 1992). Thomas J. White, Law and Government Scholar. Editor-in-Chief, Notre Dame Journal of Law, Ethics and Public Policy, 1991-1992. Author: "Increased Press Access to Information--Limiting the Range of Government Classification" 6 Notre Dame Journal of Law Ethics and Public Policy 217 (1992). Law Clerk, Honorable Federico A. Moreno, U.S. District Judge, Southern District of Florida (1992-1993). *Member:* Chicago and American Bar Associations. **PRACTICE AREAS:** Litigation; Construction Law. **Email:** tkommers@gould-ratner.com

MARK E. LEIPOLD, born Belleville, Illinois, April 20, 1960; admitted to bar, 1986, Illinois. *Education:* Northwestern University (B.S., 1982); DePaul University (J.D., 1986). Clerk to The Honorable Robert E. Ginsburg, U.S. Bankruptcy Court, Northern District of Illinois, 1986-1987. Publications: Contributing Editor (1989—), Ginsburg and Martin on Bankruptcy (Ginsburg, R., Martin, R. 4th Ed. 1996) (Aspen Law and Business), Bankruptcy, Chapter 2: Proofs of Claim, Priorities in Distributions (Illinois Institute of Continuing Education 1990), Contributing Author, Bankruptcy Law Letter 1991 (Warren Gorham Lemont). *Member:* Chicago, Seventh and American Bar Associations; American Bankruptcy Institute. **PRACTICE AREAS:** Bankruptcy; Creditor-Debtor Rights; Commercial Litigation; Workouts; Secured Transactions. **Email:** mleipold@gould-ratner.com

DAVID N. MICHAEL, born Cincinnati, Ohio; admitted to bar, 1993, Illinois. *Education:* Indiana University (B.S., 1989); Loyola University (J.D., 1993). Recipient, American Jurisprudence Award in Property and Legal Writing. Wagner Moot Court Team, 1992. *Member:* Chicago and American Bar Associations. **PRACTICE AREAS:** Labor; Employment Law; Litigation. **Email:** dmichael@gould-ratner.com

JESSICA G. LINGERTAT, born Rockford, Illinois, January 26, 1972; admitted to bar, 1997, Illinois and Wisconsin. *Education:* University of Illinois (B.A., 1994); Marquette University (J.D., cum laude, 1997). Member, Marquette Law Review. Intern, Seventh Circuit Court of Appeals, 1996. Research Assistant, National Sports Law Institute, 1995-1996. *Member:* Chicago and American Bar Associations. **PRACTICE AREAS:** Real Estate Law. **Email:** jlingertat@gould-ratner.com

OF COUNSEL

VIRGINIA M. HARDING, born Spring Valley, Illinois, February 5, 1947; admitted to bar, 1972, Illinois. *Education:* Illinois Valley Community College (A.A., 1967); University of Illinois (B.A., 1969); University of Chicago (J.D., 1972). Phi Beta Kappa; Phi Delta Phi. *Member:* Chicago and American Bar Associations; Women's Bar Association; Chicago Mortgage Attorneys Association. **PRACTICE AREAS:** Land Development; Land Sales and Purchases; Environmental Matters. **Email:** vharding@gould-ratner.com

THEODORE M. SWAIN, admitted to bar, 1954, Illinois; 1956, U.S. District Court, Northern District of Illinois. *Education:* University of Illinois (A.B., Valedictorian, 1951); Harvard University (LL.B., cum laude, 1954). Phi Beta Kappa. Lecturer, State and Local Taxation, Loyola University Law School, 1980-1981. Chief Deputy Assessor, Cook County Assessor's Office, 1973-1976. Judge, Circuit Court of Cook County, 1976-1983. Chairman, Illinois Department of Revenue Advisory Committee for Recodification of the Illinois Property Tax Act, 1992. *Member:* Chicago, Illinois State and American Bar Associations; American Judicature Society. **PRACTICE AREAS:** Property Taxation Law; Taxation (Real Estate) Law. **Email:** tswain@gould-ratner.com

HOWARD M. TURNER, born Chicago, Illinois, November 22, 1936; admitted to bar, 1960, Illinois. *Education:* University of Chicago (A.B., 1956; J.D., 1959). Co-Author: Chapter 4 "Subcontractors' Lien-its Nature and Enforcement"; Chapter 9 "Trial Practice-Proof and Selected Issues"; Chapter 10 "Trial Practice-Breach and Damages;" Mechanics Liens in Illinois, Illinois Institute of Continuing Legal Education (1994). Author: "Construction Law in Illinois," Chapter 2 and 8, Illinois Institute of Continuing Legal Education. *Member:* Chicago, Illinois State and American Bar Associations. **PRACTICE AREAS:** Commercial Law; Mechanics Liens; Commercial and Real Estate Litigation; Bankruptcy; OSHA Law. **Email:** hturner@gould-ratner.com

---

BENJAMIN Z. GOULD (1913-1986)
HAROLD R. SCHRADZKE (1892-1949)
HENRY LITVAK (1920-1973)
FREDRICK G. GOULD (1943-1982)
KATHRYN SMITH MATKOV (1954-1998)
TERRENCE F. NETZKY (1942-1999)
SAMUEL SCHLESINGER (1913-2002)
HARRY M. COVEN (1926-2004)

ASSOCIATES

MARK E. ABRAHAM, born Chicago, Illinois, September 21, 1974; admitted to bar, 1999, Illinois. *Education:* Loyola University (B.A., magna cum laude, 1996); George Washington University Law School (J.D., 1999). Phi Beta Kappa. *Member:* Chicago and American Bar Associations. **PRACTICE AREAS:** Bankruptcy; Debtor and Creditor Rights; Commercial Litigation. **Email:** mabraham@gouldratner.com

JOHN B. BEERY, born Hinsdale, Illinois, February 18, 1974; admitted to bar, 1998, Illinois. *Education:* Dartmouth College (A.B., 1995); Northwestern University (J.D., 1998); New York University (LL.M. in Taxation, 1999). *Member:* Chicago and American Bar Associations. **PRACTICE AREAS:** Taxation. **Email:** jbeery@gouldratner.com

DAVID R. BROWN, admitted to bar, 2000, Illinois. *Education:* University of Illinois (B.A., 1997); Illinois Institute of Technology, Chicago-Kent College of Law (J.D., with honors, 2000). International Moot Court Honor Society. *Member:* Chicago, Illinois State and American Bar Associations. **PRACTICE AREAS:** Business Law; Corporate Law; Securities. **Email:** dbrown@gould-ratner.com

(This Listing Continued)

GOULD & RATNER, Chicago—Continued

SHANNON L. CLARK, born Honolulu, Hawaii, January 27, 1969; admitted to bar, 1995, Illinois; 1996, Indiana; 1998, Hawaii. *Education:* Indiana University (B.A., with honors, 1991; J.D., cum laude, 1995). Managing Editor, Indiana Journal of Global Legal Studies, 1994-1995. *Member:* Chicago, Hawaii State, and American Bar Associations. ***PRACTICE AREAS:*** Corporate Law; Litigation. ***Email:*** sclark@gould-ratner.com

CHRISTINA CONLIN, admitted to bar, 1998, Illinois. *Education:* University of Wisconsin (B.A., 1994); Loyola University-Chicago (J.D., cum laude, 1998). *Member:* Chicago and Illinois State Bar Associations. ***LANGUAGES:*** French. ***PRACTICE AREAS:*** Litigation. ***Email:*** cconlin@gould-ratner.com

SONAL P. DESAI, born Hoffman Estates, Illinois, November 9, 1979; admitted to bar, 2004, Illinois. *Education:* Benedictine College (B.A., magna cum laude, 2001); Northwestern University (J.D., 2004). *Member:* Chicago and American Bar Associations. ***PRACTICE AREAS:*** Real Estate; Environmental Law. ***Email:*** sdesai@gouldratner.com

ANNE E. DICKERSON, born Hinsdale, Illinois, July 23, 1958; admitted to bar, 1986, Illinois. *Education:* University of Wisconsin-Milwaukee (B.F.A., 1979); DePaul University (J.D., 1986). Member, Lawyers for the Creative Arts. *Member:* Chicago (Member, Federal Tax Section) and American Bar Associations. ***PRACTICE AREAS:*** Estate Planning Law; Charitable Organizations Law. ***Email:*** adickerson@gould-ratner.com

GERARD R. FELLOWS, born Grand Rapids, Michigan, June 24, 1972; admitted to bar, 1998, Illinois; 2000, Michigan. *Education:* Michigan State University (B.A., 1994); DePaul University (J.D., 1998). *Member:* Chicago and American Bar Associations. ***PRACTICE AREAS:*** Taxation Law. ***Email:*** gfellows@gould-ratner.com

HEATHER H. MANNING, born Warren, Michigan, June 20, 1976; admitted to bar, 2002, New York (Not admitted in Illinois). *Education:* University of Michigan (B.S., 1997); Georgetown University Law Center (J.D., cum laude, 2001). Executive Editor, The Tax Lawyer, 2000-2001. ***PRACTICE AREAS:*** Corporate Law; Securities.

JILL M. McNAMARA, born Chicago, Illinois, October 4, 1970; admitted to bar, 1995, Wisconsin; 1996, Illinois. *Education:* Northwestern University (B.S., 1992); Marquette University Law School (J.D., 1995). Certified Public Accountant, Illinois, 2002. *Member:* Chicago and American Bar Associations. ***PRACTICE AREAS:*** Taxation Law; Federal Income Tax Law; Estate Planning Law. ***Email:*** jmcnamara@gouldratner.com

KAREN OSIECKI MEEHAN, born Chicago, Illinois, September 8, 1949; admitted to bar, 1981, Illinois and U.S. District Court, Northern District of Illinois. *Education:* Loyola University; Northwestern University (B.S. G.Ed., 1977); Loyola University (J.D., 1981). Alpha Sigma Lambda. *Member:* Chicago, Illinois State and American Bar Associations. ***PRACTICE AREAS:*** Real Estate Law; Probate; Guardianships. ***Email:*** kmeehan@gould-ratner.com

JOHN J. SCHARKEY, born St. Louis, Missouri, June 1, 1972; admitted to bar, 1999, Illinois and U.S. District Court, Northern District of Illinois. *Education:* Washington University at St. Louis (B.A., with honors, 1999); Loyola University of Chicago School of Law (J.D., 2002). *Member:* Chicago and American Bar Associations. ***PRACTICE AREAS:*** Litigation. ***Email:*** jscharkey@gouldratner.com

MICHELLE L. SELIG, born Manhasset, New York, January 2, 1973; admitted to bar, 1999, New York; 2001, Illinois. *Education:* Cornell University (B.S., 1995); George Washington University (J.D., 1998). Member, Journal of International Law & Economics. ***PRACTICE AREAS:*** Real Estate; Land Use.

LAURA E. SMITH, born St. Louis, Missouri, April 27, 1976; admitted to bar, 2002, Illinois. *Education:* Duke University (A.B., cum laude, 1998); Northwestern University School of Law (J.D., cum laude, 2002). Order of the Coif. ***PRACTICE AREAS:*** Real Estate.

SHEA D. WELCH, born Jefferson City, Missouri, January 29, 1973; admitted to bar, 1998, Missouri; 1999, Illinois. *Education:* University of Missouri - Columbia (B.S., Accounting, cum laude, 1995); University of Missouri - Columbia School of Law (J.D., 1998). Order of the Coif. *Member:* Chicago and American Bar Associations. ***PRACTICE AREAS:*** Corporate Law; Business Law; Taxation. ***Email:*** swelch@gouldratner.com

REPRESENT: Henry Crown and Co.; CC Industries, Inc.; General Dynamics Corp. (Resources Group); Material Service Corp.; Freeman United Coal Mining Co.; Freeman Energy Corp.; Century-America LLC; Century Steel LLC; Tishman Speyer Crown Equities; Industrial Insurance Agency, Inc.; Aspen Skiing Co. (Colorado); Citation Oil & Gas Corp.; Crown Theatres, LP; Chicago Sweeteners, Inc.; Eltek, ASA; Great Dane Trailers L.P.; Van Vlissingen & Co.; V & V Food Products, Inc.; Lakewood Homes, Inc.; Concord Development Corp.; Crown Golf Properties; Wireless One Network; Active Screw & Fastener, L.P.; Plasco, Inc.; Crown Community Development; Ojai Resort Management (California); Bush Hog, LLC; Woodard, LLC.

GOZDECKI & DEL GIUDICE, LLP

221 NORTH LA SALLE STREET, SUITE 2200
CHICAGO, ILLINOIS 60601-1502
Telephone: 312-782-5010
Telecopier: 312-782-4324

Business Litigation and Counseling, Civil and Complex Litigation, Corporate, Shareholder, Partner and Business Ownership Disputes, Commercial, Distributorship, Franchise, Agency, Labor and Employment, Real Estate, Construction, Mechanic's Liens, Foreclosures, Securities, Antitrust and Trade Regulation, Health Care, Local State and Federal Liquor Regulation and Appeals.

MEMBERS OF FIRM

EUGENE E. GOZDECKI, born Chicago, Illinois, May 25, 1948; admitted to bar, 1976, Illinois, Indiana and U.S. District Court, Southern District of Indiana; 1979, U.S. District Court, Northern District of Illinois and U.S. Supreme Court. *Education:* University of Illinois (B.A., 1973); John Marshall Law School (J.D., magna cum laude, 1976). Executive Editor, John Marshall Journal of Practice and Procedure, 1975-1976. ***PRACTICE AREAS:*** Civil Litigation; Complex Litigation; Federal Criminal Practice; Business Counseling; Construction; Commercial; Securities; Antitrust. ***Email:*** g.gozdecki@gozdel.com

RICHARD A. DEL GIUDICE, born Chicago, Illinois, January 7, 1959; admitted to bar, 1985, Illinois and U.S. District Court, Northern District of Illinois; 1995, U.S. Court of Appeals, Seventh Circuit. *Education:* University of Miami, Florida (B.B.A., cum laude, 1980); DePaul University College of Law (J.D., 1985). Member, De Paul Law Review, 1983-1984. Certified Public Accountant, Illinois, 1981. (Managing Partner). ***PRACTICE AREAS:*** Business Litigation; Business Counseling; Civil Litigation; Complex Litigation; Corporate; Shareholder Disputes; Partnership Law; Business Law; Commercial; Franchise Law; Agency and Distributorships; Labor and Employment; Real Estate; Construction Law; Mechanics Liens; Foreclosures; Securities; Antitrust and Trade Regulation; Health Care; Appellate Practice; Liquor Law. ***Email:*** r.delgiudice@gozdel.com

DAVID S. AMERICUS, born Chicago, Illinois, April 17, 1962; admitted to bar, 1988, Illinois; 1990, U.S. District Court, Northern District of Illinois; 1995, U.S. Court of Appeals, Seventh Circuit; 1999, U.S. District Court, Central District of Illinois. *Education:* Northern Illinois University (B.S., 1984); John Marshall Law School (J.D., 1988). ***PRACTICE AREAS:*** Civil Litigation; Complex Litigation; Corporate Litigation; Business Litigation; Discrimination; Civil Appeals; Labor and Employment. ***Email:*** d.americus@gozdel.com

EARL E. FARKAS, born Chicago, Illinois, August 14, 1965; admitted to bar, 1994, Illinois and U.S. District Court, Northern District of Illinois. *Education:* Northern Illinois University (B.S., 1987); John Marshall Law School (J.D., magna cum laude, 1994). Staff Editor, John Marshall Law Review, 1992-1993. ***PRACTICE AREAS:*** Civil Litigation; Complex Litigation; Business Counseling; Labor and Employment; Appeals; Local, State and Federal Liquor Regulation. ***Email:*** e.farkas@gozdel.com

CAROLYN A. PYKOSZ, born Cleveland, Ohio, April 21, 1980; admitted to bar, 2005, Illinois. *Education:* Indiana University (B.A. with Honors, 2002); Loyola University (J.D., 2005). ***PRACTICE AREAS:*** Civil Litigation; Complex Litigation; Business Litigation; Labor and Employment; Health Care.

OF COUNSEL

JOSEPH P. MULHERN, born Evergreen Park, Illinois, September 29, 1949; admitted to bar, 1975, Illinois. *Education:* University of Notre Dame (B.A., 1971); Northwestern University School of Law (J.D., 1975).

CLIFFORD A. HARSTAD, born Covington, Kentucky, September 24, 1947; admitted to bar, 1973, Illinois and U.S. District Court, Northern District of Illinois; 1980, U.S. Court of Appeals, 7th Circuit and U.S. Supreme Court; 2002, U.S. Tax Court. *Education:* Michigan State University (B.A., 1969); University of Illinois, Urbana-Champaign (J.D., 1973). Chief Executive Officer, Beck Lease Services, 1991—; Vice President and General Counsel, JG Industries, 1980-1991. ***PRACTICE AREAS:*** Retail Leasing; Business Law; Real Estate; Small Business Corporations. ***Email:*** c.harstad@gozdel.com

REPRESENTATIVE CLIENTS: Wirtz Corporation; Chicago Blackhawk Hockey Team, Inc.; JMB Realty Corporation; United Center Joint Venture; Bismarck Enterprises, Inc.; Wirtz Realty Management Company; Louis Glunz Beer, Inc.; Wirtz Insurance Agency; Bradley Land Group, Inc.; Judge & Dolph, Ltd.; First Security Trust & Savings Bank; Monarch Beverage Company; DeLuca Liquor & Wine, Ltd.; Marketstaff, Inc.; Cloverhill Pastry - Vend Corporation.

GRAEFE & HANSEN, LTD.

55 WEST MONROE STREET, SUITE 3550
CHICAGO, ILLINOIS 60603
Telephone: 312-236-0177
Fax: 312-236-5517
Email: hansen@ghemployerlaw.com
Email: graefe@ghemployerlaw.com
URL: http://www.ghemployerlaw.com

Management Labor Law, Employment Law, Employment Litigation, Wrongful Termination Defense, Labor Arbitration, Collective Bargaining, Labor Relations.

ANTHONY S. GRAEFE, born Des Moines, Iowa, December 2, 1947; admitted to bar, 1981, Illinois; 1982, U.S. District Court, Northern District of Illinois; U.S. Court of Appeals, Seventh, Fourth and D.C. Circuits; 1984, U.S. Court of Appeals, Eleventh Circuit. *Education:* College of the Holy Cross (B.A., cum laude, 1970); University of Michigan (M.A., 1972); Northwestern University (J.D., 1981). *Member:* Chicago, Illinois State and American Bar Associations. ***PRACTICE AREAS:*** Management Labor Law; Employment Litigation; Wrongful Termination Defense; Labor Arbitration; Collective Bargaining; Labor Relations. ***Email:*** tonygatty@aol.com

MARK D. HANSEN, born Detroit, Michigan, May 16, 1956; admitted to bar, 1987, Illinois and U.S. District Court, Northern District of Illinois; U.S. Court of Appeals, 6th Circuit; U.S. Court of Appeals, 7th Circuit. *Education:* University of Illinois (B.A., 1981); John Marshall Law School (J.D., 1987). *Member:* Chicago and American Bar Associations. ***PRACTICE AREAS:*** Management Labor Law; Collective Bargaining; Wrongful Termination. ***Email:*** hansonattorney@sbcglobal.net

JEFFREY B. GRANICH

53 W. JACKSON BOULEVARD, SUITE 840
CHICAGO, ILLINOIS 60604
Telephone: 312-939-9009
Pager: 312-490-4636
Fax: 312-939-9669
Email: coffee@xsite.net
URL: http://www.granichlaw.com

Criminal Law, Civil Rights, DUI, Drug Crimes, Felonies, Homicides, Juvenile Law, Misdemeanors, Parole and Probation, Sexual Assault, Traffic Violations and Police Misconduct.

(This Listing Continued)

FIRM PROFILE: Jeffrey B. Granich is a Solo Practitioner in areas of criminal law and civil rights. Extensive trial work in both state and federal courts, including civil motion practice and trial as well as hundreds of bench and jury criminal trials. Also concentrating on murder cases including death penalty work.

JEFFREY B. GRANICH, born Chicago, Illinois, January 6, 1966; admitted to bar, 1991, Illinois. *Education:* Indiana University (B.A., Political Science, 1988); Case Western Reserve University (J.D., 1991). Recipient: American Jurisprudence Award, Torts; Academic Scholarship. Group Leader, 1988 and Tour Guide/Counselor, 1985-1987, Zionist Organization of America, Israel Summer Tours. Lecturer, Criminal Law, Bloomington High School South, Indiana, 1992-1996. Teacher, English, Beit Sepher Katz Nelson, Ashqelon, 1984. Member, Board of Governors, Public Interest Law Foundation (Member, Building and Grounds Committee). Volunteer Attorney, First Defense Legal Aid. *Member:* Chicago, Illinois State and American Bar Associations; The Association of Trial Lawyers of America; American Civil Liberties Union; National Association of Criminal Defense Lawyers.

GRANT AND GRANT

PROFESSIONAL CORPORATION

Established in 1943

30 NORTH LA SALLE STREET
29TH FLOOR
CHICAGO, ILLINOIS 60602
Telephone: 312-641-3600
Fax: 312-641-2723
Email: info@grantandgrant.com
URL: http://www.lawyers.com/grantandgrantlaw

Northbrook, Illinois Office: 707 Skokie Boulevard, Suite 600, 60062. Telephone: 847-291-4343. Fax: 312-641-2723.

Complex Family Law including Divorce, Dissolution of Marriage, Marital Property Distribution including Retirement Benefits, Spousal Support, Alimony, Maintenance, Child Custody, Visitation, Child Support, Domestic Violence, Paternity, all phases of Matrimonial Litigation, Post Divorce Modification, Premarital Agreements, Separation Agreements, Marital Settlement Agreements, Postmarital Agreements and Appeals.

FIRM PROFILE: Grant and Grant, established in 1943 by Louis Z. Grant, is considered one of the oldest matrimonial law firms in the State of Illinois. The firm has represented prominent men and women and is responsible for higher court decisions that have helped to shape Illinois matrimonial law. The principals, Burton F. Grant and Joan C. Grant, a unique and dynamic husband and wife team recognized as experts in matrimonial law, have extensive trial experience, and are frequently called upon to lecture for the major bar associations. Mr. Grant has been called upon as an expert witness in matrimonial litigation. Mrs. Grant is frequently appointed by the Court to represent children in highly contested custody matters, and appointed to bar association committees and special task forces.

LOUIS Z. GRANT (1907-1992)

BURTON F. GRANT, born Chicago, Illinois, March 16, 1938; admitted to bar, 1962, Illinois and U.S District Court, Northern District of Illinois. *Education:* DePaul University (B.A., 1959; J.D., 1962); John Marshall Law School (LL.M., 1965). Listed in Law and Leading Attorneys, 1996—. Author: "IICLE, Family Law-Motion Practice," DePaul Law Review. Instructor, Family Law, DePaul College of Law, 1978-1984. Listed as top 5% of attorneys by Best Attorneys Network in 2005; Selected by peers as Leading Lawyer in Family Law by Leading Lawyers Network; Top 20 Divorce Lawyers by Northshore Magazine. *Member:* Chicago (Chair, Fees and Ethics Sub-Committee of Matrimonial Committee, 1992-1994), North Suburban (Director, 1994—), Northwest Suburban, Illinois State, Lake County and American Bar Associations; Decalogue Society of Lawyers. American Academy of Matrimonial Lawyers (Member, Admissions Committee, 1993—). ***PRACTICE AREAS:*** Family Law (95%, 2000); Appellate Practice (5%, 20); Child Custody (1000); Premarital Agreements (100); Divorce (2000); Matrimonial Law. ***Email:*** bfg@grantandgrant.com

JOAN C. GRANT, born Chicago, Illinois, September 2, 1943; admitted to bar, 1980, Illinois and U.S. District Court, Northern District of Illinois; 1982, Florida. *Education:* University of Michigan (B.A., with distinction, 1965) DePaul University (J.D., 1980). Listed in Law and Leading Attorneys, 1998—. Voted, by Peers, as a "Super Lawyer," 2005. Author: "Family Law Litigation in Illinois," National Business Institute; Chapter, "College Education," ISBA Family Law Handbook. Certified Child Representative, Guardian ad Litem and Attorney for Child by the Circuit Court of Cook County, Domestic Relations Division. Approved Child Representative, 19th Judicial Circuit Court, Family Division, Lake County, Illinois. *Member:* Chicago (Board of Managers, 1994-1996; Vice-Chair, Court Liaison Committee, 1993-2000; Chair, 1992-1993; Vice-Chair, 1991-1992 and Secretary, 1990-1991, Matrimonial Law Committee; North Suburban, Lake County (Member, Family Law Committee) and Illinois State (Family Law Section Council, 1993-1999; Vice-Chair, 2003-2004; Chair, 2004-2005; Secretary, 2002-2003; Bench and Bar Section Council, 1999—; Domestic Violence Task Force) Bar Associations; The Florida Bar; Women's Bar; Association of Women Attorneys. ***PRACTICE AREAS:*** Family Law; Divorce; Matrimonial Law; Spousal Support; Child Custody; Child Support; Paternity; Tax Considerations; Retirement Benefits; Litigation; Premarital Agreements; Separation Agreements; Domestic Violence. ***Email:*** jcg@grantandgrant.com

LAW OFFICES OF GRAY & IDRIS, P.C.

CHICAGO, ILLINOIS

(See Joilet)

General Practice.

GREEN & KUCHEL, P.C.

CHICAGO, ILLINOIS

(See Hammond, Indiana)

Commercial Litigation, Negligence, Business, Business Planning, Contracts, Law Suits, Corporate, Real Estate, Wills and Probate, Trusts and Estates, Estate Planning, Estate Administration, Guardianships, Asset Protection, Personal Injury, Automobile Accidents, Slip and Fall, Wrongful Death, Taxation, Municipal Law, Employment Law, Wrongful Termination, Sexual Harassment, Discrimination, Disability Accommodation, Employee Benefits, Social Security Disability, Workers Compensation, Civil Rights, Family Medical Leave Act, ADEA, Litigation.

STEVEN A. GREENBERG

Established in 1987

820 WEST JACKSON, SUITE 310
CHICAGO, ILLINOIS 60607
Telephone: 312-879-9500
Fax: 312-993-1554
Email: greenberglaw@mac.com
URL: http://www.sgreenberglaw.com

The defense of serious Federal and State Criminal Matters, Civil Rights, Injury, Appellate.

STEVEN A. GREENBERG, born Oak Park, Illinois, May 4, 1960; admitted to bar, 1986, Illinois, U.S. Court of Appeals, Seventh Circuit and U.S. Supreme Court. *Education:* Indiana University (B.S., 1982); Northern Illinois University (J.D., 1986). Named Leading Illinois Defense Attorney. Legal Analyst, Fox News Channel. *Member:* Illinois State Bar Association; Illinois Association of Criminal Defense Lawyers (Past Amicus Chair); National Association of Criminal Defense Lawyers. ***PRACTICE AREAS:*** Criminal Defense; Federal Litigation; State Government Law; Appellate Practice; Litigation.

FREDDI L. GREENBERG

CHICAGO, ILLINOIS

(See Evanston)

Energy Law, Non-Utility Electric Generation and Power Marketing, Landfill Gas and Natural Gas, Public Utility Law, Municipal Electric Utilities, Business Law.

GREENBERG TRAURIG, LLP

Established in 1967

77 WEST WACKER DRIVE, SUITE 2500
CHICAGO, ILLINOIS 60601
Telephone: 312-456-8400
Facsimile: 312-456-8435
Email: info@gtlaw.com
URL: http://www.gtlaw.com

Miami, Florida Office: 1221 Brickell Avenue, 33131. Telephone: 305-579-0500. Facsimile: 305-579-0717.

Wilmington, Delaware Office: The Nemours Building, 1007 North Orange Street, Suite 1200, 19801. Telephone: 302-661-7000. Facsimile: 302-661-7360.

Albany, New York Office: 54 State Street, 6th Floor, 12207. Telephone: 518-449-7470. Facsimile: 518-689-3499.

New York, N.Y. Office: MetLife Building, 200 Park Avenue, 10166. Telephone: 212-801-9200. Facsimile: 212-801-6400.

Washington, D.C. Office: 800 Connecticut Avenue, N.W., Suite 500, 20006. Telephone: 202-331-3100. Facsimile: 202-331-3101.

Atlanta, Georgia Office: The Forum, 3290 Northside Parkway, Suite 400, 30327. Telephone: 678-553-2100. Facsimile: 678-553-2212.

Boston, Massachusetts Office: One International Place, 3rd Floor, 02110. Telephone: 617-310-6000. Facsimile: 617-310-6001.

McLean, Virginia Office: 1750 Tysons Boulevard, Suite 1200, 22102. Telephone: 703-749-1300. Facsimile: 703-749-1301.

Philadelphia, Pennsylvania Office: One Commerce Square, Suite 2700, 2001 Market Street, 19103. Telephone: 215-988-7800. Facsimile: 215-988-7801.

Phoenix, Arizona Office: 2375 East Camelback Road, Suite 700, 85016. Telephone: 602-445-8000. Facsimile: 602-445-8100.

Fort Lauderdale, Florida Office: 401 East Las Olas Boulevard, Suite 2000, 33301. Telephone: 954-765-0500. Facsimile: 954-765-1477.

West Palm Beach, Florida Office: 777 South Flagler Drive, Suite 300 East, 33401. Telephone: 561-650-7900. Facsimile: 561-655-6222.

Boca Raton, Florida Office: 5100 Town Center Circle, Suite 400, 33486. Telephone: 561-955-7600. Facsimile: 561-338-7099.

Other Boca Raton, Florida Office: 4800 North Federal Highway, Tower B, Suite 300, 33431. Telephone: 561-367-0430. Fax: 561-362-8803.

Orlando, Florida Office: 450 South Orange Avenue, Suite 650, 32801. Telephone: 407-420-1000. Facsimile: 407-420-5909.

Tallahassee, Florida Office: 101 East College Avenue, 32301. Telephone: 850-222-6891. Facsimile: 850-681-0207.

Denver, Colorado Office: The Tabor Center, 1200 17th Street, Suite 2400, 80202. Telephone: 303-572-6500. Facsimile: 303-572-6540.

East Palo Alto, California Office: 1900 University Avenue, 5th Floor, 94303. Telephone: 650-328-8500. Facsimile: 650-328-8508.

Costa Mesa, California Office: Center Tower, 650 Town Center Drive, Suite 1700, 92626. Telephone: 714-708-6500. Facsimile: 714-708-6501.

Sacramento, California Office: 1201 K Street, Suite 1100, 95814. Telephone: 916-442-1111. Facsimile: 916-448-1709.

(This Listing Continued)

GREENBERG TRAURIG, LLP, Chicago—Continued

Santa Monica, California Office: 2450 Colorado Avenue, Suite 400 East, 90404. Telephone: 310-586-7700. Facsimile: 310-586-7800.
Florham Park, New Jersey Office: 200 Campus Drive, P.O. Box 677, 07932. Telephone: 973-360-7900. Facsimile: 973-301-8410.
Dallas, Texas Office: 600 Three Galleria Tower, 13155 Noel Road, 75240. Telephone: 972-419-1250. Facsimile: 972-419-1251.
Other Dallas, Texas Office: 2200 Ross Avenue, Suite 4700E, 75201. Telephone: 972-419-9100. Facsimile: 972-419-9101.
Houston, Texas Office: 1000 Louisiana, Suite 1800, 77002. Telephone: 713-374-3500. Facsimile: 713-374-3505.
Las Vegas, Nevada Office: 3773 Howard Hughes Parkway, Suite 500 North, 89109. Telephone: 702-792-3773. Facsimile: 702-792-9002.
Zurich, Switzerland Office: Dufourstrasse 1, 8057. Telephone: +41 44 364 26 00. Facsimile: +41 44 364 27 13.
Amsterdam, Netherlands Office: Strawinskylaan 3127, 1077 ZX. Mailing Address: Post Office Box 75306, 1070 AH Amsterdam, Netherlands. Telephone: +31 20 30 17 300. Facsimile: +31 20 30 17 350.

Administrative Law, Admiralty Law, Agricultural Law, Aircraft Finance and Leasing, Alternative Dispute Resolution, Americans with Disabilities Act, Antitrust, Appellate Practice, Arbitration, Aviation Law, Bankruptcy, Banks and Banking, Biotechnology, Broadcasting Law, Brownfields Redevelopment, Business Immigration, Business Law, Class Action Defense, Commercial Litigation, Communications Law, Constitutional Law, Construction Law, Consumer Finance, Copyrights, Corporate Governance, Corporate Law, Customs and International Trade, Education Law, Employee Benefits, Executive Compensation, Energy, Entertainment Law, Environmental Law, ERISA, FCC Licensing, FCC Regulation, Federal Government Law, Federal Legislative Law, Finance, Financial Institutions Law, Franchises and Franchising, Gaming Law, Government Affairs, Government Contracts, Governmental Law, Health Care, Immigration Law, Indians and Native Populations, Information Technology, Insurance Coverage, Intellectual Property, International Business Law, International Trade, Joint Ventures, Labor and Employment, Land Use, Legislative Practice, Litigation, Lobbying, Maritime Law, Mediation, Mergers, Acquisitions and Divestitures, Mining Law, Motion Pictures and Television, Multimedia Law, Music Law, Nonprofit and Charitable Organizations, Oil and Gas Law, Partnership Law, Patents, Privatization, Probate, Public Finance, Public Infrastructure, Public Utility Law, Railroad Law, Real Estate, Regulatory Law, Resorts and Leisure, Securities, Sports Law, Strategic Alliances, Structured Finance, Sweepstakes, Taxation, Telecommunications Law, Trade Regulation, Trademarks, Transportation, Trusts and Estates, White Collar Criminal Defense, Wills, Workouts, Zoning Law.

FIRM PROFILE: For more than three decades, Greenberg Traurig has delivered practical, business-focused solutions for clients, from emerging companies to Fortune 500 corporations. Our international network of offices provides a multi-disciplinary team with the strategic business, legal, and political experience required to solve the increasingly complex needs of regional, national, and global companies.

RUTH A. BAHE-JACHNA, admitted to bar, 1989, Illinois; 1993, U.S. Court of Appeals, Seventh Circuit; 1989, U.S. District Court, Northern District of Illinois, including Trial Bar; U.S. District Court, Northern District of Indiana. *Education:* International Christian University, Tokyo, Japan; Wartburg College (B.A., summa cum laude, 1980); Northwestern University School of Law (J.D., 1989). Presidential Scholar, 1976. Notes and Comment Editor, Northwestern University Law Review, 1988-1989. Co-Author, "The Treatment of Children as Chattel in Recent Adoption Decisions," Human Rights, Section of Individual Rights and Responsibilities, American Bar Association Quarterly Magazine, Vol. 26, No. 2, Spring 1999. Faculty, Telecommunications Industry Bankruptcy and Workouts Forum, Washington, D.C., September 1999. Vice Chair, Wartburg College Board of Regents. Member, The Economic Club of Chicago. Editorial Board, Product Liability Law & Strategy, American Lawyer Media.*Member:* Chicago (Chair, Class Litigation Committee), Seventh Circuit, Federal Communications and American (Member and Co-Chair, Book Publishing Board, Litigation Section) Bar Associations. ***REPORTED CASES:*** Schmude v. Sheahan, 198 F. Supp. 2d 964 (N.D. Ill. 2002); Bergfeld v. Unimin Corp., 319 F.3d 350 (8th Cir. 2002); Anderson v. Romero, 72 F.3d 518 (7th Cir. 1995); In re Petition of Kirchner, 164 Ill. 2d 468, 649 N.E.2d 324 (1995); Anderson v. Romero, 42 F.3d 1121 (7th Cir. 1994). ***PRACTICE AREAS:*** Complex Commercial Litigation; Products Liability; Class Actions; Labor and Employment; Telecommunications Law; Appellate Practice. ***Email:*** baher@gtlaw.com

SEAN W. BEZARK, born Chicago, Illinois, August 4, 1965; admitted to bar, 1990, Illinois; U.S. District Court, Northern District of Illinois. *Education:* University of Michigan (B.S., with distinction, 1987); Loyola University of Chicago School of Law (J.D., 1990). Editor-at-Large, Loyola University of Chicago Law Journal. Student Editor, The Business Lawyer. Legal Writing Teaching Assistant, Loyola University of Chicago School of Law. *Member:* Chicago, Illinois State and American Bar Associations. ***PRACTICE AREAS:*** Environmental; Real Estate Development; Retail Industry. ***Email:*** bezarks@gtlaw.com

FRANCIS A. CITERA, born 1958; admitted to bar, 1983, Illinois and U.S. District Court, Northern District of Illinois; 1990, Trial Bar, U.S. District Court, Northern District of Illinois; 1993, U.S. Court of Appeals, Seventh Circuit; 2002, U.S. Court of Appeals, Eighth Circuit; 2003, U.S. Court of Appeals, Fourth Circuit. *Education:* Columbia College (B.A., 1980); University of Miami (J.D. cum laude, 1983). Member, Moot Court Board. Research and Writing Editor, University of Miami Law Review, 1982-1983. *Member:* Chicago Bar Association (Past Chair, Class Litigation Committee); American Bar Association. ***PRACTICE AREAS:*** Litigation; Civil Practice; Class Actions; Products Liability; Mass Torts. ***Email:*** citeraf@gtlaw.com

LAURENCE B. DOBKIN, born Chicago, Illinois, October 18, 1962; admitted to bar, 1987, Illinois. *Education:* University of Illinois (B.S., with highest honors, 1984; J.D., 1987). Beta Gamma Sigma; Delta Theta Phi. *Member:* Chicago, Illinois State and American Bar Associations. ***PRACTICE AREAS:*** Real Estate; Retail Industry. ***Email:*** dobkinl@gtlaw.com

(This Listing Continued)

THOMAS E. DUTTON, admitted to bar, 1987, Illinois and U.S. District Court, Northern District of Illinois. *Education:* University of Iowa (B.A., 1984); Columbia University School of Law (J.D., 1987). ***PRACTICE AREAS:*** Litigation. ***Email:*** duttont@gtlaw.com

ANDREW J. ENSCHEDÉ, admitted to bar, 1994, New York and U.S. District Court, Southern and Eastern Districts of New York; 1998, Illinois; 2002, Indiana and U.S. District Court, Northern District of Illinois; 2003, U.S. District Court, Southern District of Indiana. *Education:* Tufts University (B.A., 1990); Leiden University, The Netherlands, International Law Program; John Marshall Law School (J.D., 1994). ***LANGUAGES:*** Dutch, French. ***PRACTICE AREAS:*** Litigation. ***Email:*** enschedea@gtlaw.com

KEVIN D. FINGER, born 1963; admitted to bar, 1993, Illinois; U.S. District Court, Northern District of Illinois including Trial Bar; U.S. Court of Appeals, Sixth and Seventh Circuits. *Education:* University of Notre Dame (B.S.E.E., 1985); Loyola University (J.D., 1993). ***PRACTICE AREAS:*** Litigation; Corporate Integrity; White Collar Criminal Defense. ***Email:*** fingerk@gtlaw.com

HERBERT H. FINN, born Chicago, Illinois, May 2, 1965; admitted to bar, 1991, Illinois and U.S. District Court, Northern District of Illinois; U.S. District Court, District of Colorado; U.S. District Court, Western District of Michigan; U.S. Court of Appeals for the Federal Circuit; U.S. Court of Appeals, Seventh Circuit; registered to practice before U.S. Patent and Trademark Office. *Education:* University of Illinois at Urbana (B.S., 1987); DePaul University (M.B.A., 1991; J.D., 1991). Member, Decalogue Society of Lawyers; Listed Strathmore's Who's Who. *Member:* Chicago, Illinois State and American Bar Associations; Association of Trial Lawyers of America; International Trademark Association. ***PRACTICE AREAS:*** Patent, Trademark and Copyright; Unfair Competition; Administrative Agency. ***Email:*** finnh@gtlaw.com

MICHAEL T. FISHMAN, born Cleveland, Ohio, December 12, 1968; admitted to bar, 1995, Ohio; 2001, Illinois. *Education:* Ohio State University (B.A., 1991); Cleveland-Marshall College of Law (J.D., 1995). ***LANGUAGES:*** Spanish. ***PRACTICE AREAS:*** Real Estate. ***Email:*** fishmanm@gtlaw.com

PAUL T. FOX, born New York, New York, January 17, 1953; admitted to bar, 1978, Illinois; 1979, U.S. District Court, Northern District of Illinois and U.S. Court of Appeals, Seventh Circuit; 1984, U.S. District Court, Northern District of Illinois including Trial Bar; 1986, U.S. Supreme Court; 1987, U.S. Court of Appeals for the Federal Circuit; 1989, Wisconsin; 1990, U.S. District Court, Western District of Wisconsin; 1992, U.S. District Court, Eastern District of Wisconsin; 1993, U.S. District Court, Eastern District of Michigan; 1994, U.S. District Court, Central District of Illinois; 2001, U.S. District Court, Southern District of Illinois. *Education:* Northwestern University (B.A., 1975; J.D., cum laude, 1978). Founder and Co-Managing Shareholder, Greenberg Traurig LLP Chicago Office. Member, Order of the Coif. Faculty Member, National Institute for Trial Advocacy. Adjunct Faculty Member, Northwestern University School of Law. Trustee, New Trier High School Educational Foundation. Former Chair, Glencoe, Illinois Nominating Caucus. *Member:* Chicago and American (Member, Section on Litigation) Bar Associations; State Bar of Wisconsin. ***REPORTED CASES:*** Rendler v. Corus Bank, N.A., 272 F.3d 992 (7th Cir. 2001); Adreani v. First Colonial Bankshares Corp., 154 F.3d 389 (7th Cir. 1998); Bank Leumi Le Israel, B.M. v. Lee, 928 F.2d 232 (7th Cir. 1991); Dana Corp. v. American Precision Corp., 827 F.2d 755 (7th Cir. 1987); United States General, Inc. v. Albert, 792 F.2d 678 (7th Cir. 1986); Hill v. St. Paul Fed'l Bank for Savings, 329 Ill. App. 3d 705, 768 N.E.2d 322 (1st Dist. 2002); Bank of Chicago v. Park National Bank, 237 Ill. App. 3d 1085, 606 N.E.2d 72 (1st Dist. 1992). ***PRACTICE AREAS:*** Commercial Litigation; Class Action Defense; Banking Litigation; Employment Litigation. ***Email:*** foxp@gtlaw.com

MARK R. GALIS, born Pittsburgh, Pennsylvania, October 10, 1966; admitted to bar, 1991, Illinois; 1992, Pennsylvania; 1994, U.S. Court of Appeals for the Federal Circuit; registered to practice before U.S. Patent and Trademark Office. *Education:* University of Notre Dame (B.S.M.E., 1988); George Washington University (J.D., 1991). *Member:* Chicago and American Bar Associations. ***PRACTICE AREAS:*** Intellectual Property; Litigation; Software Licensing. ***Email:*** galism@gtlaw.com

MATTHEW T. GENSBURG, born Highland Park, Illinois, January 12, 1958; admitted to bar, 1984, Illinois and Georgia; 1985, U.S. District Court, Northern District of Illinois. *Education:* University of Michigan (B.B.A., 1980); Emory University School of Law (J.D., 1983). Law Clerk to the U.S. District Judge B. Avant Edenfield, Southern District of Georgia, 1983-1984. *Member:* State Bar of Georgia. ***PRACTICE AREAS:*** Corporate Reorganization; Bankruptcy; Commercial Litigation. ***Email:*** gensburgm@gtlaw.com

JOHN F. GIBBONS, born New York, New York, 1959; admitted to bar, 1985, Illinois; 1989, California. *Education:* University of Notre Dame (B.A., 1982; J.D., 1985). Member, University of Notre Dame Law Review. Assistant U.S. Attorney, 1988-1994. Assistant States Attorney, Chief Financial Crime Unit, 1994-1996. Member, Secretary of State Securities Advisory Committee. *Member:* Chicago and Illinois State Bar Associations. ***PRACTICE AREAS:*** Litigation; White Collar Criminal Defense; Retail Industry. ***Email:*** gibbonsj@gtlaw.com

DANIEL D. GORDON, admitted to bar, 1995, Illinois. *Education:* Yale University (B.A., magna cum laude, 1992); Yale Law School (J.D., 1995). ***PRACTICE AREAS:*** Corporate; Securities; Private Equity; Venture Capital; Fund Formation. ***Email:*** gordondd@gtlaw.com

RICHARD D. HARRIS, born Chicago, Illinois, September 26, 1948; admitted to bar, 1975, Illinois; 1978-1982, U.S. Court of Customs and Patent Appeals; 1984, U.S. Court of Appeals for the Federal Circuit and U.S. Court of Appeals, Seventh Circuit; 1986, U.S. Supreme Court; 1987, U.S. District Court, Eastern District of Michigan and U.S. Court of Appeals, Third Circuit; U.S. District Court, Northern District of Illinois; U.S. District Court, District of Colorado; registered to practice before U.S. Patent and Trademark Office. *Education:* University of Illinois (B.S., Eng., 1971; B.A, Econ., 1971); DePaul University (J.D., 1975). Co-Author: "The Entrepreneur's Trademark Guide," Chicago Bar Association, 1981. *Member:* Chicago (Board Member, Executive Committee, 1977-1978 and Chairman, Intellectual Property Law Committee, 1977-1978, Director, 1979-1981 and Vice Chairman, 1981-1983, Young Lawyers' Section), Illinois State and American (Member: Section of Patent, Trademark and Copyright Law; Committee on Patent, Trademark and Copyright Law, Young Lawyers Division, 1980; Chairman, Trademark Subcommittee, 1980) Bar Associations; Bar Association of the Seventh Federal Circuit; American Intellectual Property

(This Listing Continued)

Law Association; Patent Law Association of Chicago; Decalogue Society of Lawyers. ***PRACTICE AREAS:*** Patent, Trademark and Copyright; Unfair Competition; Administrative Agency. ***Email:*** harrisr@gtlaw.com

GARY R. JAROSIK, born New Haven, Connecticut; admitted to bar, 1991, Maryland; 1995, Illinois, U.S. Court of Appeals for the Federal Circuit and U.S. District Court, Northern District of Illinois; U.S. Supreme Court; registered to practice before U.S. Patent and Trademark Office. *Education:* Bucknell University (B.S.E.E., 1986); University of Maryland (J.D., 1991). ***PRACTICE AREAS:*** Intellectual Property; Intellectual Property Litigation. ***Email:*** jarosikg@gtlaw.com

DANIEL L. KRAUS, born Chicago, Illinois, January 23, 1958; admitted to bar, 1984, Illinois. *Education:* University of Minnesota (B.S., 1980; J.D., 1984; M.B.T., 1990). Certified Public Accountant, Minnesota, 1981. ***PRACTICE AREAS:*** Tax; Affordable Housing; Real Estate Development. ***Email:*** krausd@gtlaw.com

CHARLES B. LEUIN, born 1968; admitted to bar, 1994, Illinois and U.S. District Court, Northern District of Illinois; 1996, U.S. Court of Appeals, Sixth Circuit. *Education:* Duke University (A.B., 1990); University of Illinois (J.D., magna cum laude, 1994). *Member:* Chicago and American Bar Associations. ***PRACTICE AREAS:*** Complex Litigation. ***Email:*** leuinc@gtlaw.com

PETER H. LIEBERMAN, born Chicago, Illinois, May 17, 1962; admitted to bar, 1989, New York; 1992, Illinois. *Education:* University of Michigan (A.B., with high honors and high distinction, 1984); Harvard University (J.D., cum laude, M.P.P., 1988). Editor, Harvard Law Review, 1986-1988. ***PRACTICE AREAS:*** Corporate and International Transactions; Securities Regulation; Mergers and Acquisitions; Restructurings. ***Email:*** liebermanp@gtlaw.com

COREY E. LIGHT, born New York, N.Y., June 1, 1956; admitted to bar, 1982, Illinois and U.S. District Court, Northern District of Illinois. *Education:* University of Illinois (B.S., 1978); DePaul University (J.D., 1982). *Member:* Illinois State and American Bar Associations. ***PRACTICE AREAS:*** Real Estate; Retail Industry. ***Email:*** lightc@gtlaw.com

MARK J. McCOMBS, born Blue Island, Illinois, September 28, 1959; admitted to bar, 1984, Illinois and U.S. District Court, Northern District of Illinois. *Education:* The American University (B.S., magna cum laude, 1981); Northwestern University (J.D., 1984). Pi Alpha Alpha; Pi Sigma Alpha. Author: "Real Estate and Sales Tax Abatements" Illinois Land Use Law, IICLE, 2004; Co-Author: with Susan M. Vance, "AIDS and Employment," Employment Termination, IICLE, 1988; with Jerome H. Torshen, "Privileges," Illinois Civil Trial Evidence, IICLE, 1987. Special Economic Development Counsel, 1994—, Special Corporate Counsel (Investigations), 1998— and Administrative Hearings Officer, 1999—, Calumet Park, Illinois. Village Attorney, 1999—, Phoenix, Ilinois. Special Economic Development Counsel, 2002— and Administrative Hearings Officer, 2003—, Posen, Illinois; Special Economic Development Counsel, 2003—, Oak Forest, Illinois; Village Attorney, Sauk Village, Illinois, 1988-2002. Special Economic Development Counsel, Monee, Illinois, 1999-2001. Special Litigation Counsel, Tinley Park, Illinois, 1993-1995. Special Litigation Counsel, Lansing, Illinois, 1993-1995. Illinois State Treasurer, Transition Task Force, Local Government, 1990. Electoral Board Hearing Officer, Calumet Township, Illinois, 1989. General Attorney, Blue Island, Illinois, Park District, 1985-1987. General Attorney, Northlake, Illinois, Fire Protection District, 1985-1987. Honors: Designation of "Mark McCombs Drive" by Calumet Park, Illinois (recognizing economic development leadership), 2003. Listed, Who's Who in America, 2001—. *Member:* South Suburban Mayors and Managers Association (Chairman, Municipal Attorneys Committee, 2001—); Justinian Society of Lawyers. ***PRACTICE AREAS:*** Government; Municipal Law; Public Finance; Zoning, Planning and Land Use; Election, Campaign and Political Law; Government Contracts. ***Email:*** mccombsm@gtlaw.com

JANE B. McCULLOUGH, born Muroc, California, May 3, 1945; admitted to bar, 1981, Illinois. *Education:* University of Michigan; Elmhurst College (B.A., 1976); DePaul College of Law (J.D., cum laude, 1981). Member, De Paul Law Review, 1979-1981. *Member:* Chicago Bar Association. ***PRACTICE AREAS:*** Litigation. ***Email:*** mcculloughj@gtlaw.com

PAUL D. McGRADY, JR., born Huntington, West Virginia, July 30, 1971; admitted to bar, 1996, Ohio; 1997, Illinois, U.S. District Court, Northern District of Illinois and U.S. Court of Appeals, Seventh Circuit. *Education:* Cedarville College (B.A., 1993); DePaul University (J.D., 1996). Former In-House Counsel, True Value Hardware Company, Chicago; Adjunct Professor of Law, DePaul University College of Law, Center for Intellectual Property and Information Technology, 2001—. *Member:* Ohio State Bar Association (Intellectual Property Section); Chicago Bar Association (Co-Chair, Intellectual Property Commitee, Young Lawyers Section); International Trademark Association - Meetings Committee (Co-Chair, Trademark Administrator's Conference, 2006; Trademark Administrator's Conference Team, 2005; Trademarks Basics Conference Team, 2003); Intellectual Property Constituency of ICANN. ***REPORTED CASES:*** NAF Domain Name Decision No. 97849 TruServ Corporation v. CreativeV (8/17/2001); NAF Domain Name Decision No. 99703 G.D. Searle & Co. v. Celebrex Online (10/24/2001); NAF Domain Name Decision No. 99704 G.D. Searle & Co. v. Mark Johnson (10/24/2001); NAF Domain Name Decision No. 100572 G.D. Searle & Co. v. Access Rx, CR, S.A. (12/4/2001); NAF Domain Name Decision No. 100647 G.D. Searle & Co. v. Cory Christensen (12/4/2001); NAF Domain Name Decision No. 104979 G.D. Searle & Co. v. RaveClub Berlin (3/26/2002); NAF Domain Name Decision No. 105733 Delta Corporate Identity, Inc. v. Venta a/k/a Leonard Bogucki (4/15/2002); NAF Domain Name Decision No. 105750 Delta Corporate Identity, Inc. v. Dotsan (4/18/2002); NAF Domain Name Decision No. 105859 Delta Corporate Identity, Inc. v. Private (4/12/2002); NAF Domain Name Decision No. 106112 Delta Corporate Identity, Inc. v. Seventh Summit Ventures (5/6/2002); NAF Domain Name Decision No. 109375 Delta Corporate Identity, Inc. v. Patrick Ory (5/22/2002); NAF Domain Name Decision No. 109739 Hachette Filipacchi Presse v. Corporate Services (7/8/2002); NAF Domain Name Decision No. 110778 G.D. Searle & Co. v. Montgomery Byers (6/3/2002); NAF Domain Name Decision No. 110783 G.D. Searle & Co. v. Entertainment Hosting Services, Inc. (6/3/2002); NAF Domain Name Decision No. 110795 Monsanto Company v. Rowena Tollitt (6/4/2002); NAF Domain Name Decision No. 112559 G.D. Searle & Co. v. James Mahony (6/12/2002); NAF Domain Name Decision No. 112611 G.D. Searle & Co. v. John Barry (6/14/2002); NAF Domain Name Decision No. 114286 Manpower, Inc. v. P.G. Koenraadt (7/10/2002); NAF Domain Name Decision No. 114610 G. D. Searle & Co.

(This Listing Continued)

v. Buy This Domain aka John Barry (7/23/2002); NAF Domain Name Decision No. 114657 Delta Corporate Identity, Inc. v. Ameriasa (7/30/2002); NAF Domain Name Decision No. 114676 G.D. Searle & Co. v. Michael Kerr (8/1/2002); NAF Domain Name Decision No. 114677 G. D. Searle & Co. v. Northside Computers (9/8/2002); NAF Domain Name Decision No. 114707 G.D. Searle & Co. v. 24-7-Commerce.com (7/31/2002); NAF Domain Name Decision No. 114708 G. D. Searle & Co. (a wholly owned subsidiary of Pharmacia Corp.) v. Woodrow Bridges a/k/a Sales (8/9/2002); NAF Domain Name Decision No. 115043 Kohler Co. v. Chris Friedland dba Faucet Direct Inc. (8/8/2002); NAF Domain Name Decision No. 115044 Kohler Co. v. Daniel Auer (8/14/2002); NAF Domain Name Decision No. 115044 Kohler Co. v. Daniel Auer (8/14/2002); NAF Domain Name Decision No. 116736 G.D. Searle & Co. v. Red Light Entertainment (8/26/2002); NAF Domain Name Decision No. 116896 G.D. Searle & Co. v. Per Ronnlund (9/3/2002); NAF Domain Name Decision No. 117023 G.D. Searle & Co. v. Javier Benavides (9/5/2002); NAF Domain Name Decision No. 117024 G.D. Searle & Co. v. Javier Benavides aka None (9/6/2002); NAF Domain Name Decision No. 117905 G.D. Searle & Co. v. 24-dollars-for-3-pill-viagra-trial-pack.com (10/2/2002); NAF Domain Name Decision No. 117911 G.D. Searle & Co. v. Fred Pelham (9/19/2002); NAF Domain Name Decision No. 117914 G.D. Searle & Co. v. PNP Management (10/4/2002); NAF Domain Name Decision No. 118168 G.D. Searle & Co. v. Optimized Marketing Services (9/19/2002); NAF Domain Name Decision No. 118181 G.D. Searle & Co. v. Damien Wallace (10/7/2002); NAF Domain Name Decision No. 118276 G.D. Searle & Co. v. SD Domains aka Steve Dyke (10/11/2002); NAF Domain Name Decision No. 118277 G.D. Searle & Co. v. Martin Marketing (10/1/2002); NAF Domain Name Decision No. 118306 G.D. Searle & Co. v. NA (10/7/2002); NAF Domain Name Decision No. 118307 G.D. Searle & Co. v. Paramount Marketing (9/27/2002); NAF Domain Name Decision No. 123870 Europcar International v. Thomas Wilde (10/23/2002); NAF Domain Name Decision No. 123901 G.D. Searle & Co. v. Kevin Dunham (10/9/2002); NAF Domain Name Decision No. 123920 G.D. Searle & Co. v. [domain name holder] (11/8/2002); NAF Domain Name Decision No. 123927 G.D. Searle & Co. v. Innovative Solution Technologies aka Vedavyasa Alapati (10/23/2002); NAF Domain Name Decision No. 123931 G.D. Searle & Co. v. John Gergen (10/18/2002); NAF Domain Name Decision No. 123933 G.D. Searle & Co. v. Celebrex Drugstore (11/21/2002); NAF Domain Name Decision No. 124508 G.D. Searle & Co. v. Celebrex Cox-2 Vioxx.com (10/16/2002); NAF Domain Name Decision No. 124514 G.D. Searle & Co. v. Celebrex Conference Correspondent (10/21/2002); NAF Domain Name Decision No. 124518 G.D. Searle & Co. v. Interlocution, Inc. (10/28/2002); NAF Domain Name Decision No. 124537 G.D. Searle & Co. v. E.T. Corp (10/22/2002); NAF Domain Name Decision No. 124755 G.D. Searle & Co. v. Domain Manager (10/28/2002); NAF Domain Name Decision No. 125477 G. D. Searle & Co. v. Xenadrin-Source.com (11/7/2002); NAF Domain Name Decision No. 125477 G. D. Searle & Co. v. Xenadrin-Source.com (11/7/2002); NAF Domain Name Decision No. 125749 G.D. Searle & Co. v. Multimeds Inc. (11/20/2002); NAF Domain Name Decision No. 125755 G. D. Searle & Co. v. SHg d/b/a SHG Resources (11/18/2002); NAF Domain Name Decision No. 126632 G.D. Searle & Co. v. Universal Medical Alliance (11/15/2002); NAF Domain Name Decision No. 126643 G.D. Searle & Co. v. J. Roller Management (11/22/2002); NAF Domain Name Decision No. 126644 G.D. Searle & Co. v. Rick Brewer dba Strategical Networks LLC (11/22/2002); NAF Domain Name Decision No. 126654 G.D. Searle & Co. v. DMG Online (11/19/2002); NAF Domain Name Decision No. 126655 G.D. Searle & Co. v. Paul Vickery (11/29/2002); NAF Domain Name Decision No. 126657 G.D. Searle & Co. v. 24-7-Commerce.com (12/5/2002); NAF Domain Name Decision No. 126827 G.D. Searle & Co. v. Duece Strategies (11/26/2002); NAF Domain Name Decision No. 126828 G.D. Searle & Co. v. Timothy Brennan dba Chance Technologies, LLC (11/25/2002); NAF Domain Name Decision No. 126829 G.D. Searle & Co. v. Robin Cimock (11/13/2002); NAF Domain Name Decision No. 126830 G.D. Searle & Co. v. MedScripts, LLC aka Elizabeth Skinner (12/2/2002); NAF Domain Name Decision No. 126831 G.D. Searle & Co. v. Vioxx & Celebrex Arthritis Help (12/2/2002); NAF Domain Name Decision No. 126837 G.D. Searle & Co. v. Celebres Xenical Online (12/2/2002); NAF Domain Name Decision No. 126838 G.D. Searle & Co. v. Erica Amane (11/25/2002); NAF Domain Name Decision No. 126839 G.D. Searle & Co. v. Joann Hefelinger (11/25/2002); NAF Domain Name Decision No. 127640 G.D. Searle & Co. v. Via Real (11/21/2002); NAF Domain Name Decision No. 127704 G.D. Searle & Co. v. T. DeMaria c/o Boriqua Enterprizes (12/4/2002); NAF Domain Name Decision No. 128077 G.D. Searle & Co. v. David Gregg (12/4/2002); NAF Domain Name Decision No. 128144 G.D. Searle & Co. v. Balloon Junction Marketing (12/1/2002); NAF Domain Name Decision No. 128146 G.D. Searle & Co. v. dfrantum (12/9/2002); NAF Domain Name Decision No. 128644 G.D. Searle & Co. v. Mike Flynn (12/17/2002); NAF Domain Name Decision No. 128668 G.D. Searle & Co. v. Argo Wibowo (12/18/2002); NAF Domain Name Decision No. 129128 G.D. Searle & Co. v. Sean aka Sean Kim (12/27/2002); NAF Domain Name Decision No. 132450 Delta Corporate Identity, Inc. and Delta Air Lines, Inc. v. 1-800 Communications, Inc. (12/27/2002); NAF Domain Name Decision No. 132450 Delta Corporate Identity, Inc. and Delta Air Lines, Inc. v. 1-800 Communications, Inc. (12/27/2002); NAF Domain Name Decision No. 133619 Delta Corporate Identity, Inc. and Delta Air Lines, Inc. v. Tuna Orbay (12/30/2002); NAF Domain Name Decision No. 133621 Delta Corporate Identity, Inc. and Delta Air Lines, Inc. v. Seventh Summit Ventures (12/31/2002); NAF Domain Name Decision No. 137036 G.D. Searle & Co. v. Zyphen Marketing (1/13/2003); NAF Domain Name Decision No. 137673 CPFilms Inc. v. Markus Herbig (2/7/2003); NAF Domain Name Decision No. 146219 G.D. Searle & Co. v. Celebrex Medication (3/25/2003); NAF Domain Name Decision No. 148166 Diners Club International Ltd. v. Al Powell (4/14/2003); NAF Domain Name Decision No. 149414 Diners Club International Ltd. v. SPS aka DCS aka ADC (4/21/2003); NAF Domain Name Decision No. 151543 G.D. Searle & Co. v. Caroline Street Clinic (4/30/2003); NAF Domain Name Decision No. 155462 Diners Club International, Ltd. v. Havec Lis (6/2/2003); NAF Domain Name Decision No. 155892 Manpower, Inc. v. BigMart.com (6/12/2003); NAF Domain Name Decision No. 156839 Diners Club International Ltd. v. Domain Admin (6/23/2003); NAF Domain Name Decision No. 167968 Toastmasters International v. Bealo Group S.A. (8/25/2003); NAF Domain Name Decision No. 169085 Diners Club International, Ltd. v. Infotechnics Limited (8/20/2003); NAF Domain Name Decision No. 193692 Prema Toy Company v. Administration Local (10/27/2003); NAF Domain Name Decision No. 221172 Travelers Express Co. Inc. v. Craig Satinoff D.C. (2/10/2004); NAF Domain Name Decision No. 234378 Travelers Express Company. Inc. v. NJ Industrial Research Center Inc. (3/22/2004); NAF Domain Name Decision No. 237441 DBTEL Incorporated v. K Hsu (4/6/2004); NAF Domain Name Decision No. 237571 Travelers Express Company, Inc. v. Bahamas Connect Ltd. B-81 (4/7/2004); NAF

(This Listing Continued)

GREENBERG TRAURIG, LLP, Chicago—Continued

Domain Name Decision No. 244131 Diners Club International Ltd. v. Kim Brown a/k/a Miss K.J. Brown (4/29/2004); NAF Domain Name Decision No. 250823 Diners Club International Ltd. v Sajeda Ali (6/11/2004); NAF Domain Name Decision No. 273995 Project Management Institute, Inc. v. Dan Prather aka Bethlehem Temple aka The Alliance (7/21/2004); NAF Domain Name Decision No. 275511 Travelers Express Company, Inc. v. Henry Tsung (7/7/2004); NAF Domain Name Decision No. 282454 Hickory Farms, Inc. v. 1550507 Ontario Inc. (7/12/2004); NAF Domain Name Decision No. 293539 Travelers Express Co. Inc. v. Florin Dragnea (8/25/2004); NAF Domain Name Decision No. 304785 Manpower, Inc. v. Digital Pulsar, Proxy (9/16/2004); NAF Domain Name Decision No. 304785 Manpower, Inc. v. Digital Pulsar, Proxy (9/16/2004); NAF Domain Name Decision No. 338427 Diners Club International Ltd. v. Car In Won Australia pty Ltd (11/10/2004); NAF Domain Name Decision No. 387130 Citigroup Global Markets, Inc. d/b/a Smith Barney v. Superior Electrical Contractors c/o David Davidson (2/7/2005); NAF Domain Name Decision No. 404547 Citigroup Inc. v. LaPorte Holdings, Inc. (3/4/2005); NAF Domain Name Decision No. 409747 Diners Club International Ltd. v. LaPorte Holdings, Inc. (3/15/2005); NAF Domain Name Decision No. 422746 Asian and Western Classics B.V. v. New York Link, Inc. (3/30/2005); NAF Domain Name Decision No. 445224 Diners Club International Ltd. v. Jeffrey Demerly (5/3/2005); NAF Domain Name Decision No. 453926 Citigroup Inc. and Citigroup Global Markets, Inc. d/b/a Smith Barney v. Asia Ventures (5/19/2005); NAF Domain Name Decision No. 495538 Citigroup Inc. v. Gene Yarsky (7/22/2005); NAF Domain Name Decision No. 502782 Diners Club International Ltd. v. Cameron Jackson (8/4/2005); NAF Domain Name Decision No. 505498 Citigroup Inc. v. - aka Birgit Klostermann (8/11/2005); NAF Domain Name Decision No. 508460 Citigroup Inc. and Diners Club International Ltd. v. Citibank, N.A. (8/1/2005). ***PRACTICE AREAS:*** Intellectual Property; Information Technology. ***Email:*** mcgradyp@gtlaw.com

GRETCHEN N. MILLER, born 1971; admitted to bar, 1996, Arizona; 1999, District of Columbia; 2000, Illinois. *Education:* University of Arizona (B.A., 1993); George Washington University Law School (J.D., with honors, 1996). *Member:* Chicago and American Bar Associations; State Bar of Arizona; Defense Research Institute; District of Columbia Bar Organization. ***PRACTICE AREAS:*** Commercial Litigation; Products Liability. ***Email:*** millerg@gtlaw.com

NANCY A. MITCHELL, born February 9, 1962; admitted to bar, 1988, Illinois. *Education:* Indiana University (B.A., with honors, 1984); University of Michigan (J.D., cum laude, 1987). Contributing Editor, Michigan Law Review, 1985-1987. *Member:* Chicago, Illinois State and American Bar Assns. ***PRACTICE AREAS:*** Banks and Banking; Finance; Financial Restructuring; Municipal Finance; Insolvency. ***Email:*** mitchelln@gtlaw.com

DONNA B. MORE, admitted to bar, 1983, Illinois. *Education:* Tufts University (B.A., 1979); Northwestern University (M.A., Political Science, 1980); Georgetown University Law Center (J.D., 1983). ***PRACTICE AREAS:*** Government Affairs; Litigation; Gaming Law. ***Email:*** mored@gtlaw.com

PAUL K. MORTON, born Chicago, Illinois, January 25, 1962; admitted to bar, 1987, Illinois. *Education:* University of Michigan (B.A., with distinction, 1984); Northwestern University (J.D., 1987). *Member:* Chicago and American Bar Associations. ***PRACTICE AREAS:*** Mergers and Acquisitions; Corporate Law; Venture Capital; Restructurings. ***Email:*** mortonp@gtlaw.com

ROBERT E. NEIMAN, born April 18, 1941; admitted to bar, 1966, Illinois and U.S. District Court, Northern District of Illinois. *Education:* Indiana University (B.S., Business Administration, 1963); Indiana University School of Law (J.D., 1966). Mediator, Arbitrator. Past Director, United Way of Glencoe. Member: Wilmette Human Relations Committee, President, 1972; Wilmette Plan Commission. Trustee, Temple Am Shalom. Director: Anixter Center; Lambs Farm, Inc. Chairman, Wilmette Plan Commission, 1974-1975. Member, Panel of Arbitrators, American Arbitration Association. *Member:* Chicago, Illinois State and American Bar Associations. ***PRACTICE AREAS:*** Corporate Law; Securities Law; Mergers and Acquisitions; Finance; Joint Ventures; Real Estate Development; Workouts; Real Estate Sales; Leases and Leasing; Partnership Law; Real Estate; Zoning Law; Construction Law; Dealership Law; Radio Common Carrier. ***Email:*** neimanr@gtlaw.com

NANCY A. PETERMAN, admitted to bar, 1991, Illinois, U.S. District Court, Northern District of Illinois, U.S. Court of Appeals, Seventh Circuit and U.S. Supreme Court. *Education:* University of Michigan (B.A., with high distinction, 1988; J.D., cum laude, 1991). ***PRACTICE AREAS:*** Debtor/Creditor; Bankruptcy Law; Insolvency Law. ***Email:*** petermann@gtlaw.com

RITA ALLISS POWERS, born Hammond, Indiana, July 16, 1964; admitted to bar, 1990, Illinois and U.S. District Court, Northern District of Illinois; 1995, U.S. District Court, Southern District of Ohio; 1997, U.S. District Court, District of Minnesota and U.S. Court of Appeals, Sixth Circuit; 2000, U.S. District Court, District of Arizona; 2001, U.S. District Court, Eastern District of Misouri; 2002, U.S. District Court, Central District of Illinois; 2004, U.S. Court of Appeals, Seventh Circuit. *Education:* DePauw University (B.A., cum laude, 1986); Vanderbilt University (J.D., 1990). Phi Delta Phi. Member, 1988-1989, and Executive Editor, 1989-1990, Vanderbilt Journal of Transnational Law. *Member:* Chicago and American Bar Associations; Women's Bar Association; Chicago Council of Lawyers. ***REPORTED CASES:*** U.S. v. Neufeld, 949 F.Supp. 555 (S.D. Ohio 1996); People v. Wilkinson, 285 Ill.App.3d 727 (1996); Edward Gray Corp. v. National Union Fire Ins. Co. of Pittsburgh, PA, 94 F.3d 363 (1996); Budget Rent-A-Car Sys., Inc. v. Consolidated Equity, LLC, No. 04 C 1772, 2005 U.S. Dist. LEXIS 16070 (N. D. Ill. Aug. 3, 2005); Ferolie Corp. v. Advantage Sales & Mktg., LLC, No. 04 C 5425, 2004 U.S. Dist. Lexis 21738 (N. D. Ill. Oct. 25, 2004); Murray c. Citibank, N.A., No. 04 C 3294, 2004 U.S. Dist. LEXIS 20941 (N. D. Ill. Oct. 18, 2004). ***PRACTICE AREAS:*** Litigation. ***Email:*** powersr@gtlaw.com

E. PAUL QUINN, admitted to bar, 1991, Illinois. *Education:* University of Iowa (B.B.A., Accounting, 1986); University of Virginia (J.D., 1991). Certified Public Accountant, Iowa, 1986. ***LANGUAGES:*** German. ***PRACTICE AREAS:*** Corporate Law; Securities. ***Email:*** quinne@gtlaw.com.com

(This Listing Continued)

JAMES G. RICHMOND, born Sacramento, California, 1944; admitted to bar, 1969, Indiana; 1975, U.S Court of Appeals, Seventh Circuit; 1991, Illinois. *Education:* Indiana University (B.S., 1966) Indiana University School of Law (J.D., 1969). U.S Attorney, Northern District of Indiana, 1985-1991. Special Counsel to Deputy Attorney General William P. Barr for Financial Institution Fraud, 1990-1991. Chairman, Attorney General's Advisory Committee, 1989-1991. Assistant U.S. Attorney, Northern District of Indiana, 1976-1983. Special Agent, IRS-CID, 1974-1976. Special Agent, FBI, 1971-1973. Fellow, American College of Trial Lawyers. *Member:* Federal and American Bar Associations; National Association of Criminal Defense Lawyers; American College of Trial Lawyers. [U.S Army Reserves, 1969-1971]. ***PRACTICE AREAS:*** Commercial Litigation; Bank Fraud; Gaming Law; Corporate Investigations; Health Care Fraud; Federal Criminal Law. ***Email:*** richmondj@gtlaw.com

JULIA R. SARRON, born Peoria, Illinois, March 8, 1957; admitted to bar, 1981, Illinois. *Education:* Yale University (B.A., 1978); Columbia University (J.D., 1981). ***PRACTICE AREAS:*** Corporate and Securities. ***Email:*** sarronj@gtlaw.com

ROBERT I. SCHWIMMER, born Chicago, Illinois, 1948; admitted to bar, 1974, Illinois. *Education:* American University (B.S., with honors, 1971); DePaul University (J.D., 1974). *Member:* Chicago, Illinois State and American Bar Associations. ***PRACTICE AREAS:*** Mergers, Acquisitions and Divestitures; Corporate Law; Securities. ***Email:*** schwimmerr@gtlaw.com

KEITH J. SHAPIRO, born Chicago, Illinois, November 14, 1958; admitted to bar, 1983, Illinois; U.S. District Court, Eastern District of Wisconsin. *Education:* University of Illinois (B.S., 1980); Emory University (J.D., 1983). Fellow, American College of Bankruptcy. Member, R3. Co-Editor-in-Chief, Wiley's Annual Bankruptcy Law Update. Former Adjunct Professor of Law, McGeorge School of Law. Contributing Author: Norton Bankruptcy Law and Practice treatise and Advanced Chapter 11 Bankruptcy Practice treatise. Member, Advisory Board, Georgetown University Law Center and ABI's "Views from the Bench." Member, Advisory Board, St. John's University School of Law, Bankruptcy LL.M. Program. Member, Board of Editors and Board of Advisors, West's Annual Survey of Bankruptcy Law, 1984-2002. Founder and First Chairman, American Bankruptcy Board of Certification, 1992-1995. General Counsel, Association of Insolvency Accountants; 1993—. Chair, American Bankruptcy Institute Health Care Insolvency Manual, 1997. Alumni Advisor, Emory Bankruptcy Developments Journal. Founding Chair, Law and Justice Committee, United States Holocaust Memorial Museum, 1997—. Law Clerk to Hon. Richard N. DeGunther, U.S. Bankruptcy Judge, Northern District of Illinois, 1983-1984. Member, Emory Law School Council. Listed in the Best Lawyers in America. Listed in the K&A Restructuring Register of 100 Top Insolvency Professionals. Listed in Chambers & Partners USA Guide. *Member:* Chicago (Member, Bankruptcy and Reorganization Committee, 1999-2000); American Bar Associations; American Bankruptcy Institute (Chairman of the Board, 2002-2003; President, 2000-2001; Former Vice-President, Education; Former Corporate Secretary; Former Member of Executive Committee and Board of Directors; Founding Chair, Committee on Health Care Insolvency, 1994-1998; Founding Chair, Committee on Professional Compensation in Bankruptcy Cases); INSOL International (Former Member, Board of Directors). ***PRACTICE AREAS:*** Bankruptcy Law; Insolvency Law; Corporate Reorganization; International Law. ***Email:*** shapirok@gtlaw.com

HOWARD E. SILVERMAN, born Gary, Indiana, January 7, 1958; admitted to bar, 1984, Illinois and U.S. District Court, Northern District of Illinois; 1985, U.S. Court of Appeals for the Federal Circuit; 1987, U.S. Court of Appeals, Third Circuit; registered to practice before U.S. Patent and Trademark Office. *Education:* Purdue University (B.S.E.E., 1981); Washington University (J.D., 1984). *Member:* American Bar Association. ***PRACTICE AREAS:*** Patent, Trademark and Copyright; Intellectual Property Transactions and Litigation; Unfair Competition; Administrative Agency. ***Email:*** silvermanh@gtlaw.com

RICHARD A. SIRUS, born Oak Park, Illinois, June 17, 1958; admitted to bar, 1983, Illinois. *Education:* Loyola University (B.B.A., 1980; J.D., 1982). Certified Public Accountant, Illinois, 1986. *Member:* American Institute of Certified Public Accountants; Illinois Institute of Certified Public Accountants (Past President, North Shore Chapter). ***PRACTICE AREAS:*** ERISA. ***Email:*** sirusr@gtlaw.com

DOUGLAS B. TEANEY, born Granite City, Illinois, May 24, 1960; admitted to bar, 1987, Illinois; U.S. District Court, Northern District of Illinois; registered to practice before U.S. Patent and Trademark Office. *Education:* Illinois Institute of Technology (B.S.M.A.E., with honors, 1983); Northern Illinois University (J.D., cum laude, 1987). Pi Tau Sigma; Delta Theta Phi. Staff Member, 1985-1986 and Editor-in-Chief, 1986-1987, Northern Illinois University Law Review. ***LANGUAGES:*** German. ***PRACTICE AREAS:*** Patent, Trademark & Copyright; Unfair Competition; Administrative Agency. ***Email:*** teaneyd@gtlaw.com

JEFFREY S. TOROSIAN, born Valley Stream, N.Y., October 19, 1968; admitted to bar, 1993, Illinois; U.S. District Court, Northern District of Illinois; U.S. District Court, Eastern District of Wisconsin; U.S. District Court, Western District of Michigan; U.S. Court of Appeals, Seventh Circuit; U.S. Tax Court. *Education:* University of Chicago (B.A., 1990); Pepperdine University (J.D., 1993). Literary Editor, Pepperdine Law Review. Adjunct Professor, DePaul University College of Law. Member, Executives' Club of Chicago. Member, City Club of Chicago. Member, Chicago Cabinet, University of Chicago. Chair, Chicago Regional Annual Giving Committee, University of Chicago. Member, New York Regional Annual Giving Committee, University of Chicago. *Member:* American Bar Association (Member, Subcommittee on Securities Litigation); International Bar Association (Member, International Litigation Committee). ***PRACTICE AREAS:*** Litigation. ***Email:*** torosianj@gtlaw.com

RANDI L. VALERIOUS, admitted to bar, 1990, Illinois. *Education:* University of Michigan (B.A., with distinction, 1987); Harvard Law School (J.D., 1990). Member, Board of Directors, Anixter Center, 1996—. *Member:* Chicago, Illinois State and American Bar Associations. ***PRACTICE AREAS:*** Mergers and Acquisitions; Finance; Public Offerings; Strategic Alliances; Corporate Law; Technology Law. ***Email:*** valeriousr@gtlaw.com

OF COUNSEL

RICHARD E. DICK, born Chicago, Illinois, November 24, 1946; admitted to bar, 1973, Illinois; 1974, U.S. Court of Appeals, 3rd, 5th and 7th Circuits; 1976, U.S. Court of Appeals, 9th Circuit; 1984, U.S. Court of Appeals for the Federal Circuit; 1986, U.S. Su-

(This Listing Continued)

preme Court; registered to practice before U.S. Patent and Trademark Office and Canadian Patent and Trademark Office. *Education:* Illinois Institute of Technology (B.S.I.E., 1969); Loyola University (J.D., cum laude, 1973). *Member:* Chicago, Illinois State and American (Member, Patent, Trademark and Copyright Law Section) Bar Associations; Bar Association of the Seventh Federal Circuit; American Intellectual Property Law Association; Patent Law Association of Chicago. ***PRACTICE AREAS:*** Patent, Trademark and Copyright; Unfair Competition; Administrative Agency. ***Email:*** dickr@gtlaw.com

AMY C. KURSON, born July 14, 1968; admitted to bar, 1995, Illinois. *Education:* Bob Jones University (B.S., 1991); Chicago-Kent College of Law (J.D., 1994). *Member:* Chicago Bar Association. ***PRACTICE AREAS:*** Government Affairs; Land Development; Retail Collections. ***Email:*** kursona@gtlaw.com

MYRON LIEBERMAN, born Chicago, Illinois, February 14, 1931; admitted to bar, 1954, Illinois. *Education:* University of Illinois and Stanford University (B.S., 1952); Stanford University and Northwestern University (LL.B., 1954). Order of the Coif. Member, Board of Editors, Northwestern University Law Review, 1953-1954. *Member:* Chicago, Illinois State and American Bar Associations. ***PRACTICE AREAS:*** Corporate; Securities. ***Email:*** liebermanm@gtlaw.com

RAYMOND S. McGAUGH, born Omaha, Nebraska, September 1, 1954; admitted to bar, 1984, Nebraska; 1988, Illinois; U.S. District Court, Northern and Central Districts of Illinois; U.S. District Court, District of Nebraska. *Education:* Creighton University (B.A., 1976; J.D., cum laude, 1984, Alpha Sigma Nu); Georgia State University (M.H.A., 1978). Lamda Alpha International. Author: "The MLER Supplementary Bar Preparation Program," 10 Saint Louis University Law Review 271, 1991. Member, Board of Directors: The Edgar Lomax Company, an SEC Registered Investment Advisory Firm; First Personal Bank; Illinois State Chartered Commercial Bank. Member, Board of Arbitrators, NASD Regulations, Inc. *Member:* Chicago, Cook County, Nebraska State, American and National Bar Associations; Chicago Mortgage Attorneys Association (Past President); National Association of Bond Lawyers. ***PRACTICE AREAS:*** Real Estate; Banking; Commercial Lending; Corporate Finance; Financial Services; Creditors; Municipal Finance; General Corporate Practice. ***Email:*** mcgaughr@gtlaw.com

DAVID W. SCHOENBERG, born Chicago, Illinois, October 20, 1942; admitted to bar, 1966, Illinois; 1969, U.S. Court of Military Appeals; 1970, U.S. Supreme Court. *Education:* Indiana University (A.B., 1963); University of Illinois (J.D., 1966). Phi Beta Kappa; Order of the Coif; Phi Alpha Delta. Assistant Editor, University of Illinois Law Forum, 1965-1966. *Member:* Chicago, Illinois State and American Bar Associations. [Capt. U.S. Army, 1967-1970]. ***PRACTICE AREAS:*** Corporate; Mergers, Acquisitions and Divestitures. ***Email:*** schoenbergd@gtlaw.com

SAMUEL K. SKINNER, born 1938; admitted to bar, 1966, Illinois. *Education:* University of Illinois at Urbana-Champaign (B.S., 1960); DePaul University (J.D., 1966). De-Paul Law Review, 1964-1965. Lecturer, Trial Practice, John Marshall Law School, 1974-1977. Chairman, Illinois Capitol Development Board, 1979—. Special Assistant, Illinois Attorney General. Counsel, Illinois Judicial Inquiry Board. Assistant United States Attorney, 1968-1975 and United States Attorney, 1975-1977, Northern District of Illinois. Former Secretary of Transportation, 1989-1991. Former White House Chief of Staff, 1991-1992. *Member:* Chicago, Illinois State and American Bar Associations; Legal Club of Chicago; Law Club of Chicago. ***PRACTICE AREAS:*** Governmental Affairs; Litigation. ***Email:*** skinners@gtlaw.com

G. RAY WARNER, born Columbia, South Carolina, December 16, 1955; admitted to bar, 1980, Georgia; 1982, Illinois. *Education:* Emory University (B.A., 1977); Northwestern University (J.D., cum laude, 1980); New York University School of Law (LL.M., Corporation Law, 1985). Professor of Law & Director LL.M. in Bankruptcy at St. John's University School of Law; Faculty Advisor, American Bankruptcy Institute Law Review; Phi Beta Kappa; Phi Delta Epsilon. Listed: Who's Who Among Students in American Colleges and Universities; Who's Who in American Law. General Motors Scholar; John Henry Wigmore Scholar. Member: Mortar Board. Finalist, National Merit Scholarship. Participant, National Moot Cort Team, 1980. Recipient: 1997 Outstanding Professor Award, 1995 Best Friend Award, 1993 Outstanding Professor Award and Pierson Award, University of Missouri at Kansas City; W. Oliver Rasch Award, Journal of the Missouri Bar, 1987; Dean's Letter of Commendation for Outstanding Performance, New York University School of Law; Wigmore Key, Most Outstanding Senior Award, Northwestern University School of Law. Author: "The Anti-Bankruptcy Act: Revised Article 9 and Bankruptcy," 9 Am. Bankr. Inst. L. Rev. 3 (2001), "Repossession Titles and Turnover Under Revised Article 9," 23 Am. Bankr. Inst. J. 22 (March 2004), "Rethinking DIP Counsel's Fiduciary Duty," __ Daily Bankr. Rev. ___ (March 2004), "Revised Article 9 of the UCC: Attachment, Filing and Foreclosure Under Revised Article 9," 16 Com. L. Bull. 10 (March/April 2001). Lecturer: "Current Developments and Trends in Bankruptcy Practice," United States Trustee Program's Chapter 7 Trustee Training Conference, Columbia, South Carolina, May 20, 2004; "Wearing Too Many Hats: Can You Ethically Do What You Want in the Case?," New York City Bankruptcy Conference, American Bankruptcy Institute, May 17, 2004; "Fiduciary Duty and DIP Counsel's Role," Commercial and Bankruptcy Section Meeting, Connecticut State Bar, New Haven, Connecticut, March 23, 2004; "Current & Future Role of the Courts in the Turnaround Process," Turnaround Management & Corporate Restructuring Summit, New York, New York, February 26, 2004; "Changing the Lawyer's Role in Bankruptcy," Keynote Address, William J. O'Neill Bankruptcy Institute, Cleveland Bar Association, Cleveland, Ohio, December 11, 2003; "Conflicts Within the Bankruptcy System," Ninth Circuit Chief Bankruptcy Judges' Meeting, La Quinta, California, December 4, 2003; "Current Developments and Trends in Chapter 13 Practice," United States Trustee Program's Chapter 13 Trustee Training Conference, Columbia, South Carolina, June 26, 2003; "Creative Lawyering, Pushing the Envelope and Going Beyond?" 16th Annual Northwest Bankruptcy Institute, Seattle, Washington, April 23, 2003; "Revised Article 9: Attachment, Filing, and Foreclosure," 16th Annual Northwest Bankruptcy Institute, Seattle, Washington, April 23, 2003; "Chapter 11: The Land of Opportunity," 16th Annual Northwest Bankruptcy Institute, Seattle, Washington, April 23, 2003; "New Legislative Developments: Changing the Lawyer's Role," Annual Spring Meeting, American Bankruptcy Institute, Washington, D.C., April 13, 2003; "Supreme Court Ushers in the Nextwave of Bankruptcy Discrimination," Kansas City Kansas Bankruptcy Bar Association, Kansas City, Kansas, March 19, 2003; "Is Revised Article 9 an Anti-Bankruptcy Act? Yes," Bankruptcy and the UCC: Points of Intersection and Conflict, Oklahoma City University School of Law, Oklahoma City, Oklahoma, January 23, 2003. Member, American College of Bankruptcy, 1999-2000. *Member:* American Bankruptcy Institute (Member: Executive Committee, 1997-2003; Board of Directors, 1992-2004); American Board of Certification (Chair, 1999-2000; President, 1999; First Vice President and President-Elect, 1988; Member: Board of Directors, 1991-2003 and 2004—; Management Committee, 1998-2003; Executive Committee, 1991-2003; Dean and Charter Dean, 1991-1995; Faculty, 1991-1998; 2004—). ***REPORTED CASES:*** Fidelity Financial Services, Inc. v. Fink,—U.S.—, 118 S.Ct. 651, 139 L.Ed.2d 571 (S.Ct. 1/13/98)(9-0)(Souter, J.). ***PRACTICE AREAS:*** Bankruptcy Law; Commercial Law; Secured Transactions; Litigation. ***Email:*** warnerg@gtlaw.com

ASSOCIATES

DAVID W. BADDLEY, admitted to bar, 1998, Florida; 2004, Illinois. *Education:* Georgia Institute of Technology (B.S., magna cum laude, 1994); University of Florida College of Law (J.D., with honors, 1998). ***PRACTICE AREAS:*** Restructuring; Reorganization; Bankruptcy. ***Email:*** baddleyd@gtlaw.com

MICHAEL J. BAUM, born Chicago, Illinois; admitted to bar, 2002, Illinois. *Education:* University of Texas at Austin (B.B.A., 1999); Loyola University (J.D., 2002). ***LANGUAGES:*** Spanish. ***PRACTICE AREAS:*** Real Estate. ***Email:*** baumm@gtlaw.com

BRAD R. BERTOGLIO, born Arlington Heights, Illinois, October 2, 1973; admitted to bar, 2000, Illinois. *Education:* University of Illinois (B.S.E.E., with honors, 1995); Chicago-Kent College of Law (J.D., with high honors, 2000). Order of the Coif; Law Review, 1997-1999. National Semi-Finalist, Giles Sutherland Rich Moot Court Competition, 1999. *Member:* American Bar Association; American Intellectual Property Law Association. ***PRACTICE AREAS:*** Intellectual Property. ***Email:*** bertogliob@gtlaw.com

JAMES J. CASERIO, born Park Ridge, Illinois, February 17, 1971; admitted to bar, 1996, Illinois. *Education:* Northwestern University (B.A., with distinction, 1993); University of Michigan Law School (J.D., 1996). Phi Beta Kappa. Associate Editor and Contributing Editor, Michigan Journal of International Law, 1994-1996. ***PRACTICE AREAS:*** Real Estate; Finance. ***Email:*** caserioj@gtlaw.com

ABIGAIL A. CLAPP, born 1974; admitted to bar, 1999, Illinois. *Education:* Indiana University (B.A., 1996); Indiana University School of Law - Bloomington (J.D., cum laude, 1999). Law Clerk, U.S. District Court, Northern District of Indiana, 1999-2001. *Member:* Illinois State and American Bar Associations; Seventh Circuit Bar Association. ***PRACTICE AREAS:*** Litigation. ***Email:*** clappa@gtlaw.com

PAUL DEL AGUILA, born Lima, Peru, September 16, 1975; admitted to bar, 2001, Missouri and U.S. District Court, Western District of Missouri; 2003, Illinois. *Education:* University of California at Irvine (B.A., 1998); University of Illinois (J.D., 2001). ***PRACTICE AREAS:*** Litigation. ***Email:*** delaguilap@gtlaw.com

KIMBERLY M. DESHANO, born June 5, 1974; admitted to bar, 1999, Illinois. *Education:* Miami University (B.A., magna cum laude, 1996); Case Western Reserve University School of Law (J.D., magna cum laude, 1999). Order of the Coif, 1999. Articles Editor, Case Western Reserve Law Review.1999 National Moot Court Team. Miami University Honors in Economics, 1996. Co-Author: "Fungibility of Lottery Revenues and Support for Public Education," JOURNAL OF EDUCATION FINANCE, Fall 2002. Author: Educational Vouchers and the Religion Clauses under Agostini: Resurrection Insurrection and a New Direction, CWRU L. REV., Summer 1999. Studied Economics of Eastern European Integration at Miami University Dolibois European Center in Luxembourg, 1995. *Member:* Chicago, Illinois State and American Bar Associations. ***PRACTICE AREAS:*** Litigation. ***Email:*** deshanok@gtlaw.com

JEFFREY P. DUNNING, born Belleville, Illinois, April 20, 1974; admitted to bar, 1998, Missouri; 2000, Illinois; 2001, U.S. District Court, Northern District of Illinois; 2003, U.S. Court of Appeals, Federal Circuit. *Education:* University of Illinois at Urbana-Champaign (B.S., 1995; M.S., 2000); Washington University (J.D., 1998). Tau Beta Pi; University of Illinois James Scholar, 1991-1995. Author: "The Helms-Burton Act: A Step in the Wrong Direction for United States Policy Toward Cuba," Washington University Journal of Urban and Contemporary Law, Vol. 54, Summer 1998; "The Latest Threat to E-Commerce: The PanIP Patent Litigation," The Intellectual Property Strategist, Vol. 9, No. 7, April 2003. Member, American Institute of Aeronautics and Astronautics. *Member:* Chicago, Illinois State and American (Member, Intellectual Property Section) Bar Associations; American Intellectual Property Law Association. ***LANGUAGES:*** German. ***REPORTED CASES:*** National Diamond Syndicate, Inc. v. Flanders Diamond USA, Inc., et al., 264 F.Supp.2d 631 (N.D.Ill. 2003), 67 USPQ2d 1671 (N.D.Ill. 2003). ***PRACTICE AREAS:*** Trademark; Copyright; Unfair Competition; Administrative Agency Practice; Patents; Intellectual Property. ***Email:*** dunningj@gtlaw.com

DANIEL T. FAHNER, born July 14, 1975; admitted to bar, 2000, Illinois; 2001, U.S. District Court, Northern District of Illinois. *Education:* University of Michigan (B.A., 1997); Northwestern University (J.D., 2000). *Member:* Illinois State and American Bar Associations; Chicago Inn of Court. ***PRACTICE AREAS:*** Litigation; White Collar Crime. ***Email:*** fahnerd@gtlaw.com

PAUL J. FERAK, admitted to bar, 2000, Illinois and U.S. District Court, Northern District of Illinois; 2004, U.S. Court of Appeals, Sixth and Seventh Circuits. *Education:* Northern Illinois University (B.A., 1997); Chicago-Kent College of Law (J.D., 2000). ***PRACTICE AREAS:*** Litigation. ***Email:*** ferakp@gtlaw.com

GREGORY A. FISHMAN, admitted to bar, 1998, Illinois; 2004, New York. *Education:* The Ohio State University (B.A., 1993); Case Western Reserve University (J.D., 1998). ***PRACTICE AREAS:*** Real Estate. ***Email:*** fishmang@gtlaw.com

ERIC G. GREENFIELD, born Highland Park, Illinois, February 2, 1978; admitted to bar, 2003, Illinois. *Education:* University of Illinois (B.S., 2000); University of Illinois, College of Law (J.D., magna cum laude, 2003). ***PRACTICE AREAS:*** Real Estate; Real Estate Finance. ***Email:*** greenfielde@gtlaw.com

JORDAN HERZOG, born Chicago, Illinois, July 13, 1961; admitted to bar, 1993, Illinois and U.S. District Court, Northern District of Illinois; registered to practice before U.S. Patent and Trademark Office. *Education:* University of Illinois at Urbana (B.S.C.S., 1983); DePaul University (J.D., with honors, 1993). Order of the Coif. Recipient, American

(This Listing Continued)

GREENBERG TRAURIG, LLP, Chicago—Continued

Jurisprudence Awards in Constitutional Process, Civil Procedure, Remedies and Commercial Paper. Recipient, Dean's Scholarship. ***PRACTICE AREAS:*** Intellectual Property. ***Email:*** herzogj@gtlaw.com

HOWARD K. JERUCHIMOWITZ, born New York, New York, October 8, 1972; admitted to bar, 1997, Illinois and U.S. District Court, Northern District of Illinois; 1999, U.S. District Court, Western District of Michigan; 2000, U.S. Court of Appeals, Sixth Circuit; 2002, U.S. Court of Appeals, Seventh Circuit and U.S. Supreme Court. *Education:* Brandeis University (B.A., cum laude, 1994); Cornell Law School (J.D., cum laude, 1997). Phi Delta Phi. Champion, Cornell Law School Moot Court, 1997. Recipient: CALI Award; The Chicago Lawyers' Committee for Civil Rights Under Law Pro Bono Award. Editor, Cornell Law Review, 1997. Author, Note, "Tobacco Advertising," 82:2 Cornell Law Review 432, 1997. Panelist , Northwestern University School of Law, "The Importance of Legal Writing in Law Firms and Corporate Practice". *Member:* Chicago, Illinois State and American Bar Associations. ***REPORTED CASES:*** International Casings Group, Inc. v. Premium Standard Farms, Inc., 358 F. Supp. 2d 863 (W.D. Mo. 2005); Milwaukee Safeguard Insurance Co. v. Selcke, 324 Ill. App. 3d 344 (1st Dist. 2001). ***PRACTICE AREAS:*** Litigation; Commercial Litigation; White Collar Criminal Defense; Insurance Litigation; Real Estate Operations. ***Email:*** Jeruchimowitzh@gtlaw.com

ROBERT W. LANNAN, born October 15, 1969; admitted to bar, 1997, District of Columbia; 1998, Illinois. *Education:* Georgetown University (A.B., magna cum laude, 1992; J.D., 1995); George Washington University (LL.M., Environmental Law, with highest honors, 1999). [Capt., U.S. Army Judge Advocate General's Corps, 1995-1999]. ***PRACTICE AREAS:*** Bankruptcy. ***Email:*** lannanr@gtlaw.com

TODD A. MAZUR, born Buffalo, New York, August 20, 1975; admitted to bar, 2000, Illinois. *Education:* Indiana University - Bloomington (B.A., with high distinction, 1997); Indiana University School of Law - Bloomington (J.D., magna cum laude, 2000). Order of the Coif. Member, Indiana Law Journal, 1999-2000. ***PRACTICE AREAS:*** Mergers and Acquisitions; Corporate Law; Securities. ***Email:*** mazurt@gtlaw.com

MARY KATHRYN McCREERY, born June 29, 1974; admitted to bar, 1999, Illinois. *Education:* Marquette University (B.A., magna cum laude, 1996); University of Notre Dame (J.D., magna cum laude, 1999). ***PRACTICE AREAS:*** Real Estate. ***Email:*** walshm@gtlaw.com

RYAN H. McLENNAN, admitted to bar, 2002, Illinois. *Education:* Vanderbilt University (B.A., magna cum laude); Northwestern University (J.D.). Coordinating Note Editor, The Journal of Criminal Law and Criminology. *Member:* Chicago Bar Association. ***PRACTICE AREAS:*** Corporate; Securities. ***Email:*** mclennanr@gtlaw.com

AMIT MEHTA, admitted to bar, 2000, Illinois. *Education:* St. Louis University (B.S.B.A., Honors, 1997); Georgetown University Law Center (J.D., 2000). *Member:* American Bar Association. ***PRACTICE AREAS:*** Corporate; Securities; Private Equity. ***Email:*** mehtaa@gtlaw.com

SHERRI MORISSETTE, born Chicago, Illinois, 1970; admitted to bar, 1998, Illinois. *Education:* Western Illinois University (B.A., 1992; M.A., 1995); Northwestern University School of Law (J.D., 1998). Phi Alpha Delta. *Member:* Chicago and Illinois Bar Associations; American Bankruptcy Institute. ***PRACTICE AREAS:*** Bankruptcy; Reorganization; Creditors Rights. ***Email:*** morissettes@gtlaw.com

JEFFREY G. MOTE, born November 28, 1964; admitted to bar, 1997, Illinois; U.S. District Court, Northern and Central Districts of Illinois, Northern District of Texas and Eastern District of Wisconsin; U.S. Court of Appeals, Seventh and Federal Circuits; U.S. Supreme Court. *Education:* University of Illinois (B.S.I.E., 1986; J.D., magna cum laude, 1997). Law Clerk to the Hon. Harlington Wood, U.S. Court of Appeals, Seventh Circuit, 1997-1998. *Member:* Chicago (Member: Patent, Intellectual Property and Trial Sections) and American (Member: Intellectual Property and Litigation Sections) Bar Associations; American Intellectual Property Law Association. [Naval Aviator, U.S. Navy, 1987-1994]. ***PRACTICE AREAS:*** Intellectual Property; Trademark Litigation; Patent Litigation; Trademark Licensing; Patent Licensing; Copyrights; Trade Secrets; Unfair Competition. ***Email:*** motej@gtlaw.com

CAMERON M. NELSON, born Oriville, California, May 19, 1976; admitted to bar, 2001, Illinois; 2002, U.S. District Court, Northern District of Illinois. *Education:* University of Illinois at Urbana-Champaign (B.S.M.E., 1998; B.S., Psychology, 1998); Chicago-Kent School of Law (J.D., 2001). ***PRACTICE AREAS:*** Patents; Trademarks; Copyrights; Anti-Counterfeiting. ***Email:*** nelsonc@gtlaw.com

GREGORY E. OSTFELD, born Houston, Texas, July 5, 1973; admitted to bar, 1998, Illinois. *Education:* George Washington University (B.A., summa cum laude, 1995); University of Chicago (J.D., honors, 1998). *Member:* Chicago Bar Association; Lesbian and Gay Bar Association of Chicago. ***REPORTED CASES:*** Heller Financial, Inc. v. Prudential Ins. Co. of America, 371 F.3d 944 (7th Cir. 2004); REP MCR Realty, L.L.C. v. Lynch, 363 F.Supp.2d 984 (N.D. Ill. 2005). ***PRACTICE AREAS:*** Litigation; Shareholder Disputes; Construction Litigation; Antitrust; Products Liability Defense; Consumer Litigation; Class Action Defense. ***Email:*** ostfeldg@gtlaw.com

MATTHEW PREWITT, born Greenville, Mississippi, 1973; admitted to bar, 1996, Illinois. *Education:* Delta State University (B.A., 1993); University of Chicago Law School (J.D., 1996). ***PRACTICE AREAS:*** Litigation; Appellate Practice. ***Email:*** prewittm@gtlaw.com

EDWARD M. SHIN, born Detroit, Michigan, December 2, 1973; admitted to bar, 2001, Illinois. *Education:* University of Michigan (B.A., 1996); Washington University School of Law (J.D., 2001). Recipient: Judge Samuel M. Breckenridge Court Award, 2001 (awarded to one graduating student for excellence in appellate advocacy); Jessup International Moot Court, Regional Champion, 2000 and 2001. Member, Washington University Journal of Law & Policy, 1999-2001. Team Captain, Jessup International Moot Court, 2001. Co-Author, "A Pain in the Assets: Avoiding Successor Liability," Corporate Counsel, October 2003; "M & A Deals and Insurance Rights - Watch Out for Magic Words," Corporate Counsel, January 2004; "War Is Not Yet Won, but A Key Battle Ends In Victory," Chicago Daily Law Bulletin, October 21, 2003. *Member:* Chicago, American, Korean American and Asian American Bar Associations. ***LANGUAGES:*** Korean. ***PRACTICE AREAS:*** Litigation; Commercial Law; Complex and Multi-District Litigation; Products Liability; Class Actions. ***Email:*** shine@gtlaw.com

JEFFREY L. TERRY, admitted to bar, 2000, Illinois. *Education:* University of Illinois (B.S., 1991); Loyola University (J.D., 2000). Certified Public Accountant, Illinois, 1991. ***PRACTICE AREAS:*** Corporate and Securities. ***Email:*** terryj@gtlaw.com

JASON M. TOON, admitted to bar, 1999, Missouri; 2000, Illinois. *Education:* St. Louis University (B.A., magna cum laude, 1996); Creighton University (J.D., cum laude, 1999). Board of Editors and Research Editor, Creighton Law Review, 1997-1999. Member, Board of Directors, Association of Corporate Counsel (St. Louis Chapter), 2001-2004. Counsel, The May Department Stores Company, 1999-2004. Associate, Wildman, Harrold, Allen & Dixon LLP, 2004-2005. *Member:* Chicago Bar Association; The Missouri Bar; International Council of Shopping Centers. ***PRACTICE AREAS:*** Shopping Center Development; Commercial Real Estate; Retail. ***Email:*** toonj@gtlaw.com

ANDREW T. WHITE, born Wilmette, Illinois, May 31, 1978; admitted to bar, 2003, Illinois; U.S. District Court, Northern District of Illinois. *Education:* Fairfield University (B.S., 2000); Loyola University Chicago School of Law (J.D., 2003). *Member:* Chicago, Illinois State and American Bar Associations. ***PRACTICE AREAS:*** Real Estate. ***Email:*** whitea@gtlaw.com

COLLIN B. WILLIAMS, born Mission Viejo, California, 1976; admitted to bar, 2003, Mississippi; 2004, Illinois; U.S. Court of Appeals, Fifth Circuit; U.S. District Court, Northern and Southern Districts of Mississippi. *Education:* Middlebury College (B.A., 1998); Tulane University Law School (J.D., cum laude, 2003). Senior Managing Editor, Tulane Environmental Law Journal, 2002-2003. ***PRACTICE AREAS:*** Reorganization, Bankruptcy and Restructuring; Litigation. ***Email:*** williamsco@gtlaw.com

ANDRÉ L. ZAFRANI, born Chicago, Illinois, 1973; admitted to bar, 1998, Illinois. *Education:* University of Arizona (B.A., 1995); Northwestern University (J.D., 1998); University of Chicago (M.B.A., 2001). ***PRACTICE AREAS:*** Corporate Reorganization; Mergers and Acquisitions. ***Email:*** zafrania@gtlaw.com

ARIE BEN ZOLLER, admitted to bar, 2000, Illinois. *Education:* Loyola University (B.A., magna cum laude, 1997); Chicago-Kent College of Law (J.D., with high honors, 2000). Phi Beta Kappa; Order of the Coif. Member, Chicago-Kent College of Law, Law Review, 1998-2000. ***PRACTICE AREAS:*** Business Law. ***Email:*** zollera@gtlaw.com

(For biographical data on Wilmington, Delaware, Miami, Florida, New York, New York, Washington, D.C., Atlanta, Georgia, Boston, Massachusetts, McLean, Virginia, Las Vegas, Nevada, Philadelphia, Pennsylvania, Phoenix, Arizona, Fort Lauderdale, Florida, Boca Raton, Florida, West Palm Beach, Florida, Orlando, Florida, Tallahassee, Florida, East Palo Alto, California, Irvine, California, Sacramento, California, Santa Monica, California, Denver, Colorado, Florham Park, New Jersey, Dallas, Texas, Houston, Texas, Zurich, Switzerland and Amsterdam, Netherlands personnel, see Professional Biographies at those locations)

GREENBERGER, KRAUSS & TENENBAUM

CHICAGO, ILLINOIS

(See Schwartz Cooper Chartered)

J. CLIFFORD GREENE, JR.

77 WEST WACKER DRIVE, SUITE 3200
CHICAGO, ILLINOIS 60601
Telephone: 312-424-4002
Cell: 312-371-6501
Fax: 312-236-0336
Email: jcliffordgreene@msn.com
URL: http://www.lawyers.com/greene

Employment Discrimination, Wrongful Termination, Civil Litigation, White Collar Crime, Employment Law, Entertainment Law, Appellate Practice, Criminal Defense, Criminal Appeals, Driving While Intoxicated, Drug Crimes, Felonies, Homicide, Juvenile Law, Misdemeanors, Parole and Probation, Sexual Assault, Automobile Accidents and Injuries, Slip and Fall, and Divorce.

J. CLIFFORD GREENE, JR., born Chicago, Illinois, December 11, 1951; admitted to bar, 1994, Illinois, U.S. District Court, Northern District of Illinois including Trial Bar and U.S. Court of Appeals, Seventh Circuit. *Education:* Delaware State University (B.S., 1976); Hamline University (J.D., 1993). Member, Federal Defender Bar. President, Cooling Board Record Company, 1998—. Professional Actor. *Member:* Chicago Bar Association; National Association of Criminal Defense Lawyers; The Association of Trial Lawyers of America. [Major, U.S.M.C., Retired]

JAMES P. GREENE AND ASSOCIATES

Established in 1999

75 EAST WACKER DRIVE, SUITE 730
CHICAGO, ILLINOIS 60601
Telephone: 312-346-8077
Fax: 312-346-8066
Email: gglaweco@aol.com
URL: http://www.jamesgreenelaw.com

Tax Law, Estate Planning, Elder Law, Asset Protection, Business Planning.

FIRM PROFILE: Mr. Greene is both an experienced Economist and Attorney. He has practiced Tax Law since 1995. He graduated from the Georgetown University Law Center in Washington D.C.-J.D./LL.M. (Tax) and worked in the National Office of the Internal Revenue Service, in the Passthrough and Special Industries division. Mr. Greene concentrates his practice in Tax, Elder Law, Asset Protection, Estate Planning and Business Planning. Mr. Greene maintains a full service Law office in Chicago Illinois and a Tax Law office in Nevada. He is a faculty member

(This Listing Continued)

for the John Marshall Law School, in Chicago where he teaches Corporate Tax Law and International Tax Law. In 2000, Mr. Greene was elected the 1st president of the Nevada Chapter of The National Association of Tax Professionals, which has more than 100 Tax Practitioners available in Nevada. He lectures throughout the United States on Tax issues and Tax form preparation. When he is not teaching Tax Law, Mr. Greene teaches Micro and Macro Economics at the University of Nevada Las Vegas, and is a Former Member of the Board of Trustees for the Community Colleges of Southern Nevada. He is a frequent speaker on legal and economic issues facing small businesses for the Clark County Economic Opportunity Board Micro Business Program.

JAMES P. GREENE, born New York, New York; admitted to bar, 1995, Illinois; U.S. Court of Federal Claims. *Education:* State University of New York at Oswego (B.A., cum laude, 1976); University of Maryland (M.A., cum laude, 1978); Georgetown University (J.D., 1994; LL.M., Taxation, 1995). Economic Fellow, University of Chicago. Autonomous Teaching Assistant. Contributing Writer on Estate Planning, Wills and Trusts, Las Vegas Sentinel Voice Newspaper. Coordinator, Legal Support Program and Regular Speaker on Legal and Economic Issues Facing Small Businesses, Clark County Economic Board Micro Business Program. Former National Speaker, Tax Matters, National Association of Tax Professionals. Adjunct Faculty, LL.M. Tax Program, John Marshall Law School. Economics Instructor: Microeconomics, Macroeconomics, Law and Economics, University of Nevada Las Vegas. Instructor, Economics, Mathematics and Law, Community Colleges of Southern Nevada. Teaching Assistant, Corporate Finance, University of Chicago, School of Business. Economics Instructor: Roosevelt University; University of Maryland. *Member:* Chicago (Member, Trust and Estate Planning Sections), Illinois State and American Bar Associations. ***PRACTICE AREAS:*** Tax Law; Estate Planning; Elder Law; Asset Protection; Business Planning.

ASSOCIATE

MARTHE C. PURMAL, born Chicago, Illinois, July 9, 1942; admitted to bar, 1966, Illinois; U.S. District Court, Northern District of Illinois, including Trial Bar, U.S. Court of Appeals, Seventh Circuit and U.S. Supreme Court. *Education:* Northwestern University (B.A., 1963); Chicago-Kent College of Law (J.D., 1966). Managing Trial Attorney, CNA Insurance Company, 1992-1998. Managing Attorney, Great American Insurance Company, 1987-1992. Senior Trial Attorney, Travelers Insurance Company, 1979-1987. Trial Attorney, S. Paul Zumbakis & Associates, 1976-1979. Staff Attorney, Managing Attorney and Senior Litigator, Legal Assistance Foundation of Chicago, 1969-1976. Trial Attorney, Allstate Insurance Company, 1966-1969. *Member:* Illinois State Bar Association. ***PRACTICE AREAS:*** Insurance Defense; Probate; Nursing Home Abuse and Neglect; Elder Law; Litigation. ***Email:*** mpurmal@sbcglobal.net

GREENE AND LETTS

Established in 1990

111 WEST WASHINGTON STREET
SUITE 1650
CHICAGO, ILLINOIS 60602
Telephone: 312-346-1100
Telefax: 312-346-4571
URL: http://www.greeneandletts.com

Practice before Federal and State Courts. Civil Litigation including Personal Injury Defense, Insurance and General Liability, Product Liability Defense, Employment, Commercial and Contract, Municipal Law, Real Estate, Finance and General Business Law.

FIRM PROFILE: Greene and Letts was founded in January of 1990, by Martin P. Greene and Eileen M. Letts. The firm has the distinction of being listed among the best law firms in the country in a survey conducted by The American Lawyer magazine. Clients are primarily comprised of medium to large corporations along with sole proprietorships and public sector entities.

MEMBERS OF FIRM

MARTIN P. GREENE, born Chicago, Illinois, March 15, 1951; admitted to bar, 1977, Illinois and U.S. District Court, Northern District of Illinois; 1979, U.S. Court of Appeals, Seventh Circuit. *Education:* University of Illinois at Chicago (B.A., 1974); University of Chicago Law School (J.D., 1977). *Member:* Cook County, American and National Bar Associations. ***PRACTICE AREAS:*** Employment Law; Corporate Law; Civil Litigation; Commercial Litigation; Municipal. ***Email:*** mpgreene@greeneandletts.com

EILEEN M. LETTS, born Lansing, Michigan, October 14, 1954; admitted to bar, 1979, Illinois and U.S. District Court, Northern District of Illinois. *Education:* The Ohio State University (B.A., 1975); IIT/Chicago-Kent College of Law (J.D., 1978). *Member:* Chicago, Cook County, American and National Bar Associations. ***PRACTICE AREAS:*** Personal Injury Defense; Insurance Defense; Product Liability; Commercial Litigation; Municipal. ***Email:*** emletts@greeneandletts.com

ALLEN P. WALKER, born Chicago, Illinois, March 4, 1961; admitted to bar, 1987, Illinois and U.S. District Court, Northern District of Illinois. *Education:* DePaul University (B.S., 1983; J.D., 1986). *Member:* Chicago and Cook County Bar Associations. ***PRACTICE AREAS:*** Commercial; Contracts; Business Litigation; Municipal. ***Email:*** apwalker@greeneandletts.com

KEVIN T. LEE, born Chicago, Illinois, April 22, 1958; admitted to bar, 1983, Illinois. *Education:* Ripon College; Northwestern University (B.S., 1980); IIT/Chicago-Kent College of Law (J.D., 1983). *Member:* Cook County Bar Association. (Also Partner at Wilson, Lee and Davis). ***PRACTICE AREAS:*** Employment Defense; Tort Litigation; Product Liability. ***Email:*** ktlee@greeneandletts.com

ASSOCIATES

JOHN A. GOUDGE, born Louisville, Kentucky; admitted to bar, 1977, Illinois and U.S. District Court, Northern District of Illinois; 1979, U.S. District Court, Central District of Illinois. *Education:* United States Military Academy; University of Wisconsin (B.S., 1967); University of Chicago (J.D., 1977); United States Army Command and General Staff College (1983). Arbitrator Cook County Mandatory Arbitration. ***LANGUAGES:*** German. ***PRACTICE AREAS:*** Insurance Defense; Insurance Coverage; ERISA; Construction Litigation; Products Liability. ***Email:*** jagoudge@greeneandletts.com

CARL K. TURPIN, born Hamilton, Ohio, August 14, 1950; admitted to bar, 1988, Illinois; 1989, U.S. District Court, Northern District of Illinois; 1990, U.S. Court of Appeals, Seventh Circuit. *Education:* Howard University (B.A., cum laude, 1973); DePaul University Law School (J.D., 1987). *Member:* Cook County Bar Association. ***PRACTICE AREAS:*** Employment; Personal Injury. ***Email:*** ckturpin@greeneandletts.com

ALFRED M. SWANSON, JR., born Uniontown, Pennsylvania, June 19, 1946; admitted to bar, 1982, Illinois, U.S. District Court, Northern District of Illinois and U.S. Court of Appeals, Seventh Circuit; 1988, U.S. Supreme Court. *Education:* University of Illinois (B.S., 1968); Illinois Institute of Technology, Chicago-Kent College of Law (J.D., with honors, 1982). *Member:* Chicago, Illinois State Bar Association. ***PRACTICE AREAS:*** Personal Injury Law; Products Liability Law; Torts; Civil Litigation. ***Email:*** amswanson@greeneandletts.com

KATHRYN WOODWARD, admitted to bar, 2003, Illinois. *Education:* University of Wisconsin-Madison (B.A., Journalism and Mass Communications, 1999); Chicago-Kent College of Law, Illinois Institute of Technology (J.D., certificate in Litigation and Alternative Dispute Resolution, 2002). *Member:* Chicago and Illinois State Bar Associations; Justinian Society of Lawyers. ***PRACTICE AREAS:*** Employment Law.

LUCILLE A. BLACKBURN, born Chicago, Illinois, February 7, 1973; admitted to bar, 2003, Illinois. *Education:* University of Illinois at Chicago (B.A., Criminal Justice, 1995); John Marshall Law School (J.D., 2002). *Member:* Cook County Bar; Black Women Lawyers Association. ***PRACTICE AREAS:*** Tort Defense; Premises Liability; Workers Compensation.

TERRY MILLER, admitted to bar, 1998, Illinois. *Education:* University of Illinois (B.S., 1986; M.B.A., Finance and Marketing, 1991); DePaul University (J.D., 1998). ***PRACTICE AREAS:*** Tort Defense; Personal Injury; Civil Litigation; Business Litigation.

BYRON M. WARDLAW, born Chicago, Illinois, December 8, 1973; admitted to bar, 2004, Illinois. *Education:* Illinois State University (B.A., 1996); John Marshall Law School (J.D., 2002). ***PRACTICE AREAS:*** Corporate Law; Real Estate; Commercial Litigation. ***Email:*** bmwardlaw@greeneandletts.com

RIANA N. SHIPPS, admitted to bar, 2003, Illinois. *Education:* Washington University (B.A., 2000); University of Michigan (J.D., 2003). ***PRACTICE AREAS:*** Employment Law. ***Email:*** rshipps@greeneandletts.com

SPECIAL COUNSEL

CHRISTOPHER S. DAVIS, born Chicago, Illinois, March 29, 1950; admitted to bar, 1974, Ohio; 1986, Indiana; 1988, Illinois. *Education:* Southern Illinois University (B.A., 1971); University of Akron Law School (J.D., 1974). Arbitrator, Cook County Mandatory Arbitration. ***PRACTICE AREAS:*** Labor and Employment; Mediation. ***Email:*** csdavis@greeneandletts.com

REPRESENTATIVE CLIENTS: Advocate Health Care; Allied Tube & Conduit Corporation; City of Chicago; City Colleges of Chicago; Drimler Chrysler Financial; Eastman Kodak Company; The Boling Company; General Casualty; Illinois Tool Works; Metropolitan Pier and Exposition Authority; Northwestern Mimelin Hospital; Sara Lee Corporation; State Farm Insurance Company; Travelers Insurance Company; University of Chicago; University of Illinois; White Castle System, Inc.

GRIFFITH & JACOBSON, LLC

55 WEST MONROE STREET, SUITE 3550
CHICAGO, ILLINOIS 60603-5020
Telephone: 312-236-8110
Fax: 312-236-6724
URL: http://www.gjlaw.com

Business Formation and Structuring, Finance, Commercial Contracts and Transactions, Mergers and Acquisitions, Buy-outs, Regulatory Matters, Succession Planning for Closely Held Businesses, Income, Sales, Use, Excise and Other Tax Issues, Estate Planning.

JAMES D. JACOBSON, born Chicago, Illinois, October 24, 1956; admitted to bar, 1981, Illinois; U.S. District Court, Northern District of Illinois; 1982, U.S. Tax Court; U.S. Court of Appeals, 7th Circuit and U.S. Supreme Court. *Education:* Indiana University, Bloomington (B.S., Accounting and Finance, 1978); DePaul University (J.D., 1981). Sigma Alpha Epsilon. Certified Public Accountant, Illinois, 1980. Board Member: DePaul College of Law Dean's Advisory Committee; Chicago Legal Clinic, a non-profit organization providing legal services to the poor. Previous employment: Accountant, Abbott Laboratories, 1977-1978; Chicago Appeals Division, Internal Revenue Service, 1980-1981; Attorney, Schwartz & Freeman (now Michael, Best & Friedrich), 1981-1983. *Member:* Chicago, Illinois State (Member, Tax Law Committees) and American (Member, Federal Taxation, State and Local Taxes, Asset Protection and Corporate and Business Law Committees) Bar Associations; American Institute for Certified Public Accountants; Illinois State CPA Society. ***PRACTICE AREAS:*** Business Law; Mergers, Acquisitions and Divestitures; Commercial Loans; Letters of Credit; Loans; Secured Lending; Business Succession Planning; Buy-Sell Agreements; Buying and Selling of Businesses; Limited Liability Company Law; Business Litigation; Contracts; Leases and Leasing; Family Limited Partnerships; Partnership Organization; Partnership Formation; Family Wealth Transfer; Living Trusts; Estate Planning; Wills. ***Email:*** jdj@gjlaw.com

LOUIS MICHAEL BELL, admitted to bar, 1978, Illinois; U.S. District Court, Northern District of Illinois and U.S. Court of Appeals, 7th Circuit. *Education:* Princeton University (A.B., cum laude, 1966; Ph.D., cum laude, Comparative Literature, 1975); University of Chicago Law School (J.D., 1978). Phi Beta Kappa. Member, University of Chicago Law Review, 1976-1978. Instructor, John Marshall Law School, 1979. Previous employment, Brown and Platt. *Member:* Chicago and American (Member, Sections on: Business

(This Listing Continued)

GRIFFITH & JACOBSON, LLC, Chicago—Continued

Law; Practice Management) Bar Associations; National Association of Bond Lawyers. ***LANGUAGES:*** Hungarian, German, French, Latin. ***PRACTICE AREAS:*** Banking Law; Finance; Private Placement; Corporate Law.

LOUIS A. RASCIA, born 1961; admitted to bar, 1987, Illinois. *Education:* DePaul University (B.S., Accounting); Loyola University (J.D.). Previous employment: Price Waterhouse Tax Department. ***PRACTICE AREAS:*** Commercial Transactions; Labor and Employment; Corporate Successions; Estate Planning; Probate; Commercial Real Estate Contracts; Estate Administration; Family Limited Partnerships; Partnership Formation; Probate Taxation; Estate and Gift Taxation.

JAMES E. MAHONEY, born 1952; admitted to bar, 1978, Indiana; U.S. District Court, Southern District of Indiana; 1987, Illinois; U.S. Court of Appeals, 7th Circuit; 1988, U.S. District Court, Northern District of Illinois; 1989, U.S. Court of Appeals, 2nd Circuit; 1991, U.S. District Court, Eastern District of Wisconsin. *Education:* University of Chicago (B.A., with honors, 1974); Indiana University (J.D., magna cum laude, 1978). *Member:* Chicago, Illinois State, Indiana State and Seventh Circuit Bar Associations; Atticus Finch Inn of Court. ***PRACTICE AREAS:*** Litigation; Chancery and Equity; Federal Civil Practice; Civil Practice; Commercial Litigation; Commercial Mediation; Complex Commercial Litigation; Construction Liens; Construction Litigation; Construction Mediation; Materialmens Liens; Mechanics Liens; Breach of Contract; Commercial Contracts; Contract Litigation; Corporate Dissolutions; Civil Litigation; Complex Litigation; Federal Civil Litigation; Trial Practice; Trade Secrets; Trade Secret Misappropriation; Fiduciary Litigation; Unfair Competition. ***Email:*** jem@gjlaw.com

ASSOCIATE

ARIEH M. FLEMENBAUM, admitted to bar, 1996, Illinois; 1997, Florida. *Education:* Tulane University (B.A., International Relations and French Studies, 1993; J.D., 1996), University of Chicago Law School (Visiting Scholar, 1995). Founding Member, Tulane Honor Society, 1990-1992. Visiting Scholar, University of Chicago Law School. Seminar Instructor, Estate Planning, Merrill Lynch, 2001-2002. Editor, CBA YLS Probate Handbook, 2000. *Member:* Chicago and Illinois State Bar Associations. ***LANGUAGES:*** Spanish, French and Hebrew. ***PRACTICE AREAS:*** Business Transactions; Commercial Contracts; Commercial Lending; Finance; Secured Transactions; Mergers, Acquisitions and Divestitures; Commercial Real Estate Transactions; Commercial Real Estate Leasing; Estate Planning; Business Succession Planning. ***Email:*** amf@gjlaw.com

GRIPPO & ELDEN LLC

Established in 1988

111 SOUTH WACKER DRIVE
CHICAGO, ILLINOIS 60606
Telephone: 312-704-7700
Fax: 312-558-1195; 312-263-7356
Email: info@grippoelden.com
URL: http://www.grippoelden.com

General Practice.

MEMBERS OF FIRM

THEODORE W. GRIPPO, born Oak Park, Illinois, January 30, 1928; admitted to bar, 1953, Illinois; 1954, U.S. District Court, Northern District of Illinois. *Education:* Georgetown University (B.S., 1949); Northwestern University (J.D., 1953); DePaul College of Law (LL.M., Taxation, 1981). Phi Delta Phi. State of Illinois Securities Commissioner, 1956-1958. Superintendent, Corporation, Securities and Index Divisions, 1959-1962. Co-Author: "Going Private," Securities Law, Illinois Institute for CLE, 1991; "Registration of Securities in Business Combinations," Securities Law, Illinois Institute for CLE, 1991. Author: "In Defense of State Takeover Laws," 8 Northern Illinois University Law Journal, 1988; "MITE Made Right," 76 Illinois Bar Journal 844, 1987. "Use of Tax-Free Triangular Merger for the Acquisition of Two Corporations with Cross-Ownership," 14 John Marshall Law Review 33, 1980; "Rule 145, Securities Law," Illinois Institute for CLE, 1979; "How the New S.E.C. Rule 145 Affects Business Combinations," 55 Chicago Bar Record 11, 1973; "Exhaustion of Administrative Remedies: Need or Nuisance?" 50 Illinois Bar Journal 494, 1962. Adjunct Professor, Business Planning, Loyola University School of Law, Chicago, Illinois, 1978-1983. *Member:* Chicago and American Bar Associations. ***Email:*** tgrippo@grippoelden.com

GARY M. ELDEN, born Chicago, Illinois, December 11, 1944; admitted to bar, 1969, Illinois and U.S. District Court, Northern District of Illinois, Trial Bar, 1982; 1973, U.S. Supreme Court and U.S. Court of Appeals, Seventh Circuit; 1985, U.S. District Court, Eastern District of Michigan; 1988, U.S. Court of Appeals, Eighth Circuit; 1990, U.S. Court of Appeals, Sixth and Tenth Circuits; 1992, U.S. District Court, Eastern District of Wisconsin. *Education:* University of Illinois (B.A., summa cum laude, 1966); Harvard Law School (J.D., magna cum laude, 1969). Author: "Negligence is not Corruption: The Scienter Requirement of the Foreign Corrupt Practices Act," 49 George Washington Law Review 819, 1981; "How to be a Target Company," 23 New York Law Review 423, 1978; "Litigation under Illinois' Securities Laws," 60 Illinois Bar Journal 28, 1971; "The Constitutionality of Statutory Racial Classifications," 47 Journal of Urban Law 591, 1969. *Member:* Chicago (Secretary, Committee on Appellate Procedure, 1974-1975) and American Bar Associations; Appellate Lawyers Association (Director, 1975-1977); Chicago Council of Lawyers. Fellow, American College of Trial Lawyers. ***Email:*** gelden@grippoelden.com

PHILIP C. STAHL, born Baltimore, Maryland, February 4, 1948; admitted to bar, 1974, Illinois and U.S. District Court, Northern District of Illinois; 1975, U.S. Court of Appeals, Seventh Circuit; 1977, District of Columbia; 1978, U.S. Supreme Court; 1982, U.S. District Court Northern District of Illinois, Trial Bar; 1986, U.S. Court of Appeals, Sixth Circuit. *Education:* University of Maryland (B.A., with honors, 1970); George Washington University (J.D., with highest honors, 1974). Order of the Coif. Note and Topics Editor, George Washington Law Review, 1973-1974. Author: "Class Certification Orders: An Argument for the Defendant's Right to Appeal," 42 George Washington Law Review 621, 1974; "Application of the EEOC Guidelines to Employment Test Validation," 41 George Washington Law Review 505, 1973. *Member:* American Bar Association (Member, Litigation Section). ***Email:*** pstahl@grippoelden.com

JOHN R. McCAMBRIDGE, born Chicago, Illinois, January 4, 1952; admitted to bar, 1977, Illinois and U.S. District Court, Northern District of Illinois, Trial Bar, 1982; 1979, U.S. Court of Appeals, Seventh Circuit; 1980, U.S. Court of Appeals, Tenth Circuit; 1988, U.S. Court of Appeals, Eighth Circuit; 1989, U.S. Supreme Court. *Education:* Harvard College (A.B., cum laude, 1974); Harvard Law School (J.D., cum laude, 1977). *Member:* American Bar Association (Member, Litigation and Antitrust Sections). ***Email:*** jmccambridge@grippoelden.com

DONALD A. VOGELSANG, born Baltimore, Maryland, November 23, 1949; admitted to bar, 1979, Indiana; 1980, Illinois and U.S. District Court, Northern District of Illinois, Trial Bar, 1987; 1987, U.S. Court of Appeals, Seventh Circuit; 1989, U.S. Supreme Court. *Education:* Indiana University (B.A., 1975); John Marshall Law School (J.D., with highest distinction, 1979). Law Clerk to Justice David Linn, Illinois Appellate Court, First District, 1980-1982. *Member:* Chicago, Illinois State and American Bar Associations. ***Email:*** dvogelsang@grippoelden.com

CHARLES S. BERGEN, born St. Joseph, Michigan, March 17, 1955; admitted to bar, 1981, Washington; 1984, Illinois and U.S. District Court, Northern District of Illinois, Trial Bar; 1985, U.S. Court of Appeals, Seventh Circuit and U.S. District Court, Eastern District of Michigan. *Education:* Harvard College (A.B., 1977); Harvard Law School (J.D., 1981). ***Email:*** cbergen@grippoelden.com

IRVING C. FABER, born Buffalo, New York, August 9, 1945; admitted to bar, 1982, District of Columbia; 1983, U.S. District Court for the District of Columbia and U.S. Court of Appeals, District of Columbia Circuit; 1984, Illinois and U.S. District Court, Northern District of Illinois, Trial Bar, 1989; 1985, U.S. Court of Appeals, Seventh Circuit; 1990, U.S. Court of Appeals, Sixth Circuit; 1992, U.S. District Court, Eastern District of Wisconsin; 1996, U.S. District Court, Eastern District of Michigan. *Education:* Princeton University (A.B., summa cum laude, 1966); Harvard University (A.M., 1969); Cornell University (J.D., magna cum laude, 1982). Order of the Coif. *Member:* American Bar Association. ***Email:*** ifaber@grippoelden.com

GREGORY C. JONES, born Chicago, Illinois, April 2, 1942; admitted to bar, 1967, Illinois; 1981, U.S. District Court, Northern District of Illinois, Trial Bar; 1997, U.S. District Court, Eastern District of Wisconsin; 1998, U.S. District Court, Western District of Wisconsin. *Education:* Cornell University (B.A., 1964); University of Michigan (J.D., magna cum laude, 1967); Harvard Law School (LL.M., 1968). Order of the Coif. Author: "Organizing a Large U.S. Attorneys Office," Journal of the Section of Litigation, American Bar Association, Vol. 5, No. 4, Summer, 1979. Trial Attorney, Criminal Division, Department of Justice, Washington, D.C., 1968-1972. With United States Attorneys Office, Northern District of Illinois, Chicago, Illinois, 1972-1985. Assistant United States Attorney, 1972-1977. First Assistant United States Attorney, 1977-1985. Fellow, American College of Trial Lawyers. ***Email:*** gjones@grippoelden.com

LYNN HAGMAN MURRAY, born Indianapolis, Indiana, April 16, 1960; admitted to bar, 1985, Illinois and U.S. District Court, Northern District of Illinois, Trial Bar, 1993; 1993, U.S. Court of Appeals, Seventh Circuit. *Education:* University of Illinois (B.S., with high honors, 1982; J.D., magna cum laude, 1985). *Member:* American Bar Association. ***Email:*** lmurray@grippoelden.com

DAVID E. SCHOENFELD, born New York, N.Y., May 22, 1959; admitted to bar, 1985, Minnesota; 1987, Illinois and U.S. District Court, Northern District of Illinois, Trial Bar, 1996, and District of Minnesota; 1991, U.S. Court of Appeals, Seventh Circuit; 1997, U.S. District Court, District of Colorado and U.S. District Court, Eastern District of Michigan; 1998, U.S. Court of Appeals, Second Circuit. *Education:* Carleton College (B.A., cum laude, 1981); Washington University (J.D., 1985). Executive Notes and Comments Editor, Washington University Law Quarterly, 1984-1985. Law Clerk to Hon. Donald D. Alsop, Chief Judge, U.S. District Court, District of Minnesota, 1985-1987. Lecturer, University of Minnesota School of Law, 1986-1987. ***Email:*** dschoenfeld@grippoelden.com

MATTHEW I. HAFTER, born Ann Arbor, Michigan, March 21, 1961; admitted to bar, 1986, Illinois; 1991, U.S. District Court, Northern District of Illinois. *Education:* University of Michigan (B.Mus.A., with high distinction, 1983; J.D., 1986). Co-Author: "Going Private," Securities Law, Illinois Institute for CLE, 1991; "Registration of Securities in Business Combinations," Securities Law, Illinois Institute for CLE, 1991. *Member:* American Bar Association. ***Email:*** mhafter@grippoelden.com

GEORGE R. DOUGHERTY, born Philadelphia, Pennsylvania, July 22, 1960; admitted to bar, 1987, Illinois and U.S. District Court, Northern District of Illinois, 1998, Trial Bar; 1996, U.S. Court of Appeals, Seventh Circuit. *Education:* Swarthmore College (B.A., 1982); Northwestern University (J.D., 1987). ***Email:*** gdougherty@grippoelden.com

MARC S. LAUERMAN, born Racine, Wisconsin, May 4, 1958; admitted to bar, 1987, Wisconsin, Illinois and U.S. District Court, Western District of Wisconsin and Northern District of Illinois, Trial Bar; 1988, U.S. District Court, Western District of Arkansas; 1989, U.S. Court of Appeals, Tenth Circuit and U.S. District Court, Eastern District of Arkansas; 1990, U.S. Court of Appeals, Eighth Circuit and U.S. District Court, Eastern District of Michigan; 1991, U.S. Court of Appeals, Seventh Circuit. *Education:* Pitzer College (B.A., 1979); University of Wisconsin-Madison (J.D., cum laude, 1987). ***Email:*** mlauerman@grippoelden.com

MICHAEL P. CONWAY, born Perth Amboy, New Jersey, November 30, 1964; admitted to bar, 1989, Illinois; 1990, U.S. District Court, Northern District of Illinois including Trial Bar; 1991, U.S. Court of Appeals, Seventh and Sixth Circuits; 1995, U.S. District Court, Eastern District of Michigan. *Education:* University of Illinois (A.B., cum laude with high distinction, 1986); University of Chicago (J.D., cum laude, 1989). Phi Beta Kappa. Member, University of Chicago Law Review, 1987-1989. Law Clerk to Hon. Marvin E. Aspen, U.S. District Court, Northern District of Illinois, 1989-1990. *Member:* American Bar Association. ***Email:*** mconway@grippoelden.com

TODD C. JACOBS, born Cedar Rapids, Iowa, October 25, 1963; admitted to bar, 1989, Illinois and U.S. District Court, Northern District of Illinois including Trial Bar; 1997, U.S. Court of Appeals, Seventh Circuit and U.S. District Court, Eastern District of Michigan.

(This Listing Continued)

Education: University of Iowa (B.A., summa cum laude, 1986); University of Virginia (J.D., 1989). Phi Beta Kappa; Order of the Coif. *Member:* American Bar Association. ***Email:*** tjacobs@grippoelden.com

PATRICK T. NASH, born Akron, Ohio, June 24, 1966; admitted to bar, 1991, Illinois and U.S. District Court, Northern District of Illinois; 1995, U.S. Court of Appeals, Sixth Circuit; 1997, U.S. District Court, District of Arizona; 2004, U.S. District Court, Northern District of Illinois, including Trial Bar. *Education:* University of Akron (B.A., summa cum laude, 1988); Northwestern University (J.D., 1991). Member, Journal of International Law and Business. *Member:* Chicago and American Bar Associations. ***Email:*** pnash@grippoelden.com

MATTHEW O. SITZER, born St. Paul, Minnesota, August 25, 1966; admitted to bar, 1992, Illinois and U.S. District Court, Northern District of Illinois including Trial Bar; 1998, U.S. District Court, Eastern District of Michigan. *Education:* University of Notre Dame (B.A., magna cum laude, 1988); Northwestern University (J.D., 1992). Coordinating Note and Comment Editor, Journal of Criminal Law and Criminology, 1991-1992. *Member:* Chicago and American Bar Associations. ***Email:*** msitzer@grippoelden.com

GARY M. MILLER, born Rockford, Illinois, June 17, 1969; admitted to bar, 1995, Illinois; 1996, U.S. District Court, Northern District of Illinois; 1998, U.S. Court of Appeals, Eleventh Circuit; 1999, U.S. Court of Appeals, Seventh Circuit. *Education:* University of Illinois (B.A., 1991); University of North Carolina (J.D., with high honors, 1995). Phi Beta Kappa; Order of the Coif. Member, North Carolina Law Review, 1993-1994. Law Clerk, Hon. Rebecca Beach Smith, U.S. District Court, Eastern District of Virginia, 1995-1996. Author: "Balancing the Welfare of Children With The Rights of Parents: Peterson v. Rogers and the Role of Religion in Custody Disputes," 73 North Carolina Law Review 127, 1995. *Member:* American Bar Association. ***Email:*** gmiller@grippoelden.com

LAURA K. McNALLY, born Evanston, Illinois, October 16, 1969; admitted to bar, 1995, Illinois; 1996, Louisiana; 1997, District of Columbia. *Education:* Northwestern University (B.A., 1991); Tulane University (J.D., magna cum laude, 1994). Member: Order of the Coif; Moot Court Board. Member, Tulane Law Review. Law Clerk, Honorable F. A. Little, Jr., U.S. District Court, Western District of Louisiana, 1994-1995. ***Email:*** lmcnally@grippoelden.com

ASSOCIATES

JOHN E. BUCHEIT, born Decorah, Iowa, February 18, 1973; admitted to bar, 1998, Illinois. *Education:* Drake University (B.A., 1995); University of Iowa College of Law (J.D., 1998). Order of the Coif; Phi Beta Kappa. ***Email:*** jbucheit@grippoelden.com

MARK H. CARNOW, born Evanston, Illinois, April 23, 1974; admitted to bar, 2001, Illinois and U.S. District Court, Northern District of Illinois. *Education:* Northwestern University (B.A., 1996); University of Illinois (J.D., cum laude, 2001). ***Email:*** mcarnow@grippoelden.com

SHANNON J. CASSELL, (admission pending). *Education:* Texas Tech University (B.A., 1995); Northwestern University (J.D., 2005). ***Email:*** scassell@grippoelden.com

AMY J. COLLINS, born Palo Alto, California, May 13, 1976; admitted to bar, 2001, Illinois and U.S. District Court, Northern District of Illinois. *Education:* University of Virginia (B.A., 1998); University of Virginia School of Law (J.D., 2001). Raven Society. *Member:* Chicago, Illinois State and American Bar Associations. ***Email:*** acollins@grippoelden.com

KRISTEN A. DOLAN, admitted to bar, 2001, Maryland and District of Columbia; 2004, Illinois. *Education:* Colorado College (B.A., 1998); Georgetown University Law Center (J.D., 2001). Phi Beta Kappa. Former Legal Intern, Department of Justice, Antitrust Division, 1999. ***Email:*** kdolan@grippoelden.com

SELVYN W. FLETCHER, born Kingston, Jamaica, October 12, 1972; admitted to bar, 1997, Illinois; 1998, U.S. District Court, Northern District of Illinois. *Education:* Northwestern University (B.S., 1994); Columbia University (J.D., 1997). ***Email:*** wfletcher@grippoelden.com

MAGGIE M. HANEL, born St. Louis, Missouri, October 25, 1979; (admission pending). *Education:* Barnard College (B.A., cum laude, 2002); University of Notre Dame (J.D., 2005).

JACOB W. HARRELL, born 1976; admitted to bar, 2004, Illinois. *Education:* Northwestern University (B.A., 1998); University of Michigan (J.D., 2004). ***Email:*** jharrell@grippoelden.com

MICHAEL W. KAZAN, born Chicago, Illinois, September 29, 1969; admitted to bar, 1997, Illinois and U.S. Court of Appeals, 7th Circuit; 1999, U.S. District Court, Northern District of Illinois. *Education:* Elmhurst College (B.A., 1994); Washington University (J.D., 1997). Order of the Coif. ***Email:*** mkazan@grippoelden.com

ZUBAIR A. KHAN, born Chicago, Illinois, June 30, 1976; admitted to bar, 2001, Illinois. *Education:* Northwestern University (B.A., 1998); University of Michigan (J.D., 2001). *Member:* Chicago, Illinois State and American Bar Associations. ***LANGUAGES:*** Urdu. ***Email:*** zkhan@grippoelden.com

CLAUDIA M. LAURENS, born Chicago, Illinois, November 21, 1974; admitted to bar, 1999, Illinois; 2000, U.S. District Court, Northern District of Illinois. *Education:* University of Illinois at Urbana (B.A., 1996; J.D., 1999). ***Email:*** claurens@grippoelden.com

JEFFREY W. LUENZ, born Columbus, Indiana, October 15, 1973; admitted to bar, 2000, Illinois and Indiana. *Education:* Indiana University, Bloomington (B.A., 1995; J.D., cum laude, 1999). ***Email:*** jluenz@grippoelden.com

PATRICK R. MALONE, born Toledo, Ohio, July 20, 1977; admitted to bar, 2002, Illinois. *Education:* University of Notre Dame (B.A., 1999); Northwestern University (J.D., 2002). ***Email:*** pmalone@grippoelden.com

AMANDA H. McMURTRIE, born Greenville, Michigan, January 21, 1977; admitted to bar, 2003, Illinois and Wisconsin. *Education:* University of Michigan (B.A., 1999); University of Wisconsin-Madison (J.D., 2003). ***Email:*** amcmurtrie@grippoelden.com

(This Listing Continued)

SARAH D. McTURNAN, born Evanston, Illinois, November 27, 1973; admitted to bar, 2002, Illinois and U.S. District Court, Northern District of Illinois. *Education:* Northwestern University (B.A., 1995); University of Chicago (J.D., 2002). ***Email:*** smcturnan@grippoelden.com

BRIAN J. MOWBRAY, born Wilmington, North Carolina, July 29, 1978; admitted to bar, 2003, Illinois. *Education:* University of North Carolina at Chapel Hill (B.S., 2000); University of Michigan, Ann Arbor (J.D., 2003). ***Email:*** bmowbray@grippoelden.com

PETER S. ROESER, born Birmingham, Michigan, September 29, 1970; admitted to bar, 1998, Illinois and U.S. District Court, Northern District of Illinois; 1999, US. District Court, Northern District of Indiana. *Education:* University of Wisconsin (B.A., 1993); Loyola University, Chicago (J.D., cum laude, 1998). ***Email:*** proeser@grippoelden.com

JUDY A. SMITH, born Livonia, Michigan, March 1, 1970; admitted to bar, 1995, Illinois. *Education:* Michigan State University (B.A., with honors, 1991); University of Michigan (J.D., 1994). *Member:* Chicago and American Bar Associations. ***Email:*** jsmith@grippoelden.com

MAILE H. SOLIS-SZUKALA, born Urbana, Illinois, October 17, 1973; admitted to bar, 1998, Illinois and U.S. District Court, Northern District of Illinois. *Education:* University of Iowa (B.A., with honors and distinction, 1995); University of Chicago (J.D., 1998). ***LANGUAGES:*** Spanish. ***Email:*** msolis@grippoelden.com

ROBERT D. STONEBRAKER, born Davenport, Iowa, May 6, 1975; admitted to bar, 2002, Illinois; 2003, U.S. District Court, Northern District of Illinois. *Education:* Yale University (B.A., 1997); Northwestern University (J.D., cum laude, 2001). Order of the Coif. ***Email:*** rstonebraker@grippoelden.com

MARY L. SWIETNICKI, admitted to bar, 2002, Massachusetts; 2004, Illinois. *Education:* Brown University (A.B., magna cum laude, 1996); University of Chicago (J.D., 2001). Law Clerk to the Hon. Michael Moore, U.S. District Court, Southern District of Florida, 2001-2002. ***Email:*** mswietnicki@grippoelden.com

ANDREW SZOT, born Warren, Michigan, November 16, 1974; admitted to bar, 2001, Illinois. *Education:* University of Michigan (B.A., with distinction, 1997; J.D., 2000). ***Email:*** aszot@grippoelden.com

SENIOR COUNSEL

JAMES P. GITZLAFF, born Milwaukee, Wisconsin, January 8, 1969; admitted to bar, 1995, Illinois and U.S. District Court, Northern District of Illinois; 1996, U.S. District Court, Eastern District of Wisconsin. *Education:* Purdue University (B.A., 1991); University of Illinois, Urbana-Champaign (J.D., magna cum laude, 1995). National Merit Scholar, Purdue University. ***Email:*** jgitzlaff@grippoelden.com

PAUL A. SHELDON, born Wausau, Wisconsin, November 17, 1967; admitted to bar, 1992, Illinois and U.S. District Court, Northern District of Illinois; 1993, U.S. Court of Appeals, Seventh Circuit. *Education:* Illinois Benedictine College (B.A., 1988); Loyola University (J.D., cum laude, 1992). Alpha Sigma Nu. Member, Law Review, 1991-1992. *Member:* Chicago, Illinois State and American Bar Associations. ***Email:*** psheldon@grippoelden.com

GROTEFELD & DENENBERG, LLC

105 WEST ADAMS STREET, SUITE 2300
CHICAGO, ILLINOIS 60603
Telephone: 312-551-0200; 888-551-0700
Facsimile: 312-601-2402

Bingham Farms, Michigan Office: 30800 Telegraph Road, Suite 3858. Telephone: 248-727-7100. Facsimile: 248-593-5808.

San Francisco, California Office: 100 Spear Street, Suite 1850. Telephone: 415-344-9670. Facsimile: 415-989-2802.

Plantation, Florida Office: 8181 West Broward Boulevard, Suite 380, 33334. Telephone: 954-916-4780. Facsimile: 954-916-4785

Los Angeles, California Office: 199 Avenue of the Stars, Suite 1100 (Century Park), 90067. Telephone: 310-356-4683. Facsimile: 310-772-0631.

Insurance Litigation, Subrogation, First and Third Party Defense, Insurance Coverage and General Civil Litigation.

MARK S. GROTEFELD, born Chicago, Illinois, September 18, 1956; admitted to bar, 1981, Illinois and U.S. District Court, Northern District of Illinois including Trial Bar; 1982, Florida; 1987, U.S. Court of Appeals, Seventh Circuit; 1990, U.S. Supreme Court and U.S. District Court, Eastern District of Wisconsin. *Education:* University of Arizona (B.A., 1978); University of Strasbourg, Strasbourg, France; John Marshall Law School (J.D., 1981). *Member:* Illinois State and American Bar Associations; The Florida Bar; Association of Trial Lawyers of America. ***LANGUAGES:*** German and Spanish. ***PRACTICE AREAS:*** Litigation; Insurance; Commercial Law; Civil Rights; Professional Negligence; Personal Injury. ***Email:*** msg@gd-llc.com

STEVE C. SILVEY, born July 26, 1957; admitted to bar, 1988, Illinois; 1989, including Trial Bar, U.S. District Court, Northern and Central Districts of Illinois, U.S. District Court, Eastern District of Wisconsin, U.S. District Court, Northern District of Indiana, U.S. District Court, Northern and Southern Districts of Mississippi and U.S. Supreme Court. *Education:* Elmhurst College (B.S.); DePaul University (J.D., 1988). Editor, "Subrogation Manual" Property Loss Research Bureau. Founding Member and Executive Director, Executive Committee Member. Listed in the Millennium Edition of Who's Who in Executives and Business. Former Clerk, Chief Justice, Illinois Court of Claims. Certified in OSHA 501 Compliance, Illinois Safety Council. Author: "What's the Impact of Spoliation on your Product Claim? A 50 State Summary," National Association of Subrogation Professionals. Co-Author: "A Primer on Hazardous Materials Regulation," Trucking Industry Defense Association Newsletter; "Daubert and Kumho: Changes in Admissibility of Expert Opinion", American Law Journal, September 2001. Participant, "Unfunded Pension Liability Roundtable," Harris Bank, Chicago. *Member:* Chicago (Former Member, Judicial Evaluation Committee) and Illinois State Bar Associations; Association of Trial Lawyers of

(This Listing Continued)

GROTEFELD & DENENBERG, LLC, Chicago—Continued

America; TEC a National Organization of CEO's; National Association of Subrogation Professionals; The Eagle Institute and Eagle Summit. ***PRACTICE AREAS:*** Civil Litigation; Insurance Law; Subrogation; Commercial Litigation. ***Email:*** scs@gd-llc.com

DANIEL G. GALIVAN, born Chicago, Illinois, April 10, 1962; admitted to bar, 1989, Illinois. *Education:* Loyola University of Chicago (B.A., 1985); John Marshall Law School (J.D., 1989). Order of John Marshall Distinction. Adjunct Professor, Paralegal Studies, MacCormac College, 1996. Assistant Cook County State's Attorney, 1989-2000. *Member:* Fenwick and American Bar Associations. ***PRACTICE AREAS:*** Civil Litigation; Subrogation; Insurance Defense. ***Email:*** dgg@gd-llc.com

BRAD M. GORDON, born Elk Grove, Illinois, June 30, 1971; admitted to bar, 1997, Illinois, U.S. District Court, Northern and Southern Districts of Illinois and U.S. District Court, Northern and Southern Districts of Indiana. *Education:* University of Iowa (B.B.A., 1993); DePaul College of Law (J.D.). Phi Alpha Delta. ***PRACTICE AREAS:*** Subrogation; Insurance Defense; Civil Litigation. ***Email:*** bmg@gd-llc.com

LYNN K. WEAVER, born Chicago, Illinois, January 10, 1965; admitted to bar, 1990, Illinois and U.S. District Court, Northern, Central and Southern Districts of Illinois. *Education:* University of Illinois (B.A., 1987); DePaul University (J.D., 1990). Cook County States Attorney's Office, 1990-1999. ***PRACTICE AREAS:*** Civil Litigation; Insurance Law; Subrogation; Commercial Law. ***Email:*** lkw@gd-llc.com

PATRICK R. GAREIS, born Washington, D.C., June 29, 1965; admitted to bar, 1991, Illinois. *Education:* Eastern Illinois University (B.A., 1988); Illinois Institute of Technology, Chicago-Kent College of Law (J.D., 1991). Chicago Bar Association; Prosecutor's Bar Association. ***PRACTICE AREAS:*** Civil Litigation. ***Email:*** prg@gd-llc.com

DANIEL J. BIEDERMAN, born Cincinnati, Ohio, August 17, 1957; admitted to bar, 1986, Illinois; 1988, U.S. District Court, Northern District of Illinois and U.S. Court of Appeals, Seventh Circuit; 1996, U.S. Supreme Court. *Education:* DePaul University (B.A., 1979; M.A., 1983); John Marshall Law School (J.D., 1986). ***PRACTICE AREAS:*** Litigation; Environmental.

JULIE FOURNIER, admitted to bar, 1999, Illinois. *Education:* Michigan State University (B.S., 1996); DePaul University (J.D., 1999). *Member:* Chicago, Illinois State and American Bar Associations. ***PRACTICE AREAS:*** Commercial Litigation; Subrogation.

MEGAN E. RITENOUR, born Park Ridge, Illinois, April 10, 1977; admitted to bar, 2003, Illinois. *Education:* University of Illinois, Urbana-Champaign (B.A., 2000); DePaul University College of Law (J.D., 2003). Order of the Barrister. Member, National Moot Court Society, 2001-2003. ***PRACTICE AREAS:*** Civil Litigation; Subrogation. ***Email:*** mr@gd-llc.com

ANOOJ M. THAKRAR, born Bombay, India, November 23, 1977; admitted to bar, 2004, Illinois and U.S. District Court, Northern District of Illinois. *Education:* State University of New York at Geneseo (B.A., 1999); John Marshall Law School (J.D., 2003); University of Parma, Law Department (Comparative Law Studies). Law Student Advisor, 2001-2002. *Member:* Chicago, Illinois State and American Bar Associations. ***LANGUAGES:*** Gujarati and Hindi. ***PRACTICE AREAS:*** Subrogation; Insurance; Civil Litigation. ***Email:*** amt@gd-llc.com

MICHAEL P. SWISTAK, born Royal Oak, Michigan, January 22, 1979; admitted to bar, 2004, Illinois. *Education:* Michigan State University (B.A., 2001); DePaul University (J.D., 2004). Phi Beta Kappa. Member, National Moot Court Society. ***PRACTICE AREAS:*** Insurance Subrogation; Landlord and Tenant Law; Civil Litigation. ***Email:*** mpr@gd-llc.com

OF COUNSEL

WILLIAM S. GROTEFELD, born Chicago, Illinois, December 29, 1941; admitted to bar, 1971, Illinois, U.S. Court of Appeals, 7th Circuit and U.S. District Court, Northern District of Illinois. *Education:* Elmhurst College (A.B., 1965); John Marshall Law School (J.D., cum laude, 1971). Member, Order of John Marshall. ***PRACTICE AREAS:*** Subrogation; Third Party Defense. ***Email:*** wsg@gd-llc.com

REPRESENTATIVE CLIENTS: Available Upon Request.
REFERENCE: Northern Trust.

(For Complete Biographical Data on all Personnel, see Professional Biographies at Bingham Farms, Michigan, San Francisco, California and Plantation, Florida)

GRUND AND LEAVITT, P.C.

812 NORTH DEARBORN
CHICAGO, ILLINOIS 60610
Telephone: 312-640-0500
Fax: 312-640-8274
Email: info@grundlaw.com
URL: http://www.grundlaw.com

Matrimonial Law including Domestic Relations, Divorce, Distribution of Property, Child Custody, Spousal Support, Visitation Rights, Appellate Practice.

FIRM PROFILE: The firm of Grund Starkopf Leavitt, P.C., was formed in 1985. The firm's partners and associates have significant experience in such areas as valuation and disposition of business interests, custody, prenuptial agreements, appellate work and other significant matrimonial litigation. Mr. Grund is involved in the professional community through his active participation in bar activities, teaching, speaking, and writing for various publications.

DAVID I. GRUND, born February 5, 1947; admitted to bar, 1972, Illinois. *Education:* DePaul University (B.S., in Accounting, 1968; J.D., 1972). Who's Who in American Law. Lecturer for: I.I.C.L.E.; Chicago Bar Association, Young Lawyers Division; American Academy of Matrimonial Lawyers. *Member:* American Academy of Matrimonial Lawyers (Illinois Chapter Board of Governors, 1994—; Chairman of Admissions Committee, 1991-1993). ***REPORTED CASES:*** In re The Marriage of Duerr, 91 D 3295; In re The Marriage of Frederick, 90 D 0659; In re The Marriage of Winton, 90 D 0592; In re The Marriage of Gocal, 90 D 0303; In re The Marriage of Glickman, 89 D 2525; In re The Marriage of Silber, 87 D 2893; In re The Marriage of Kosterka, 87 D 1046; In re The Marriage of Foley, 86 D 1251; Hutchings v. Sternberg, 82 - 1661; In re The Marriage of Schmidt, 83 D 1106; In re The Marriage of Goldstein, 80 D 958; Hoffman v. Clark Street Roadhouse, 79-84; Farley v. Blackwood, 77-62; Avdich v. Kleinert, 76-531. ***PRACTICE AREAS:*** Family; Domestic Relations; Matrimonial; Divorce; Appellate Practice. ***Email:*** dgrund@grundlaw.com

(This Listing Continued)

LAWRENCE S. STARKOPF, born Chicago, Illinois, January 22, 1949; admitted to bar, 1975, Illinois. *Education:* University of Arizona (B.A., 1971); University of Baltimore (J.D., 1975). *Member:* Chicago, Illinois State and American Bar Associations; Decalogue Society of Lawyers; American Academy of Lawyers. ***PRACTICE AREAS:*** Family. ***Email:*** lstarkopf@grundlaw.com

MARVIN J. LEAVITT, born Rome, Italy; admitted to bar, 1976, Illinois, U.S. District Court, Northern District of Illinoisa nd U.S. Court of Appeals, Seventh Circuit. *Education:* Northern Illinois University (B.A., 1972); Chicago-Kent College of Law (J.D., 1976). Author, "The New DUI Law and Statutory Summary Suspension, YLS Journal Vol. 15, No. 4 (1986). Guest Faculty, Intensive Trial Workshop, University of Chicago, 1997-1999. Formerly: Judge, Circuit Court of Cook County, 1995-1996 and 1998-2000; Justice, Illinois Appellate Court, First District, 1996-1998 and Third Division, 1997-1998. *Member:* Chicago and Illinois State Bar Associations; Illinois Association of Criminal Defense Lawyers; Illinois Judges Association; Decalogue Society of Lawyers (Board Member, 1997-1999). ***PRACTICE AREAS:*** Appellate Practice; Criminal Law; Family Law. ***Email:*** mleavitt@grundlaw.com

ROBERT S. KIPNIS, born Chicago, Illinois, August 30, 1965; admitted to bar, 1990, Illinois. *Education:* University of Wisconsin (B.A., 1987); DePaul University (J.D., 1990). *Member:* Chicago and Illinois State (Member: Family Law and Young Lawyers Sections) Bar Associations. ***PRACTICE AREAS:*** Family Law. ***Email:*** rkipnis@grundlaw.com

MICHAEL KOENIGSBERGER, born LaGrange, Illinois, August 15, 1970; admitted to bar, 1995, Illinois. *Education:* University of Illinois (B.A., 1992); DePaul University (J.D., 1995). ***PRACTICE AREAS:*** Family Law. ***Email:*** mkoenigsberger@grundlaw.com

---

DAVID CHARLES ADAMS, born Park Ridge, Illinois, April 24, 1964; admitted to bar, 1991, Illinois; 1992, U.S. District Court, Northern District of Illinois; 1998, U.S. Court of Appeals, Seventh Circuit. *Education:* University of Illinois, Urbana-Champaign (B.A., with high honors, Political Science, 1987; J.D., 1991; M.B.A., 1991). Pi Sigma Alpha. Law Clerk, Honorable John P Tully, Illinois Appellate Court, First District, 1992-1997. Instructor, Business Law, University of Illinois, Urbana-Champaign, 1990-1991. *Member:* Chicago and Illinois State Bar Associations; Appellate Lawyers Association. ***LANGUAGES:*** Spanish and Italian. ***PRACTICE AREAS:*** Appellate Practice; Matrimonial Law. ***Email:*** dadams@grundlaw.com

ALYSSA MOGUL, born Chicago, Illinois, August 6, 1970; admitted to bar, 1998, Illinois. *Education:* Emory University (B.A., 1992); Chicago-Kent College of Law (J.D., 1998). ***PRACTICE AREAS:*** Matrimonial Law. ***Email:*** amogul@grundlaw.com

---

GUIBORD HOMSY, LLP

20 NORTH CLARK STREET
SUITE 3200
CHICAGO, ILLINOIS 60602
Telephone: 312-596-7777
Fax: 312-596-7788
URL: http://www.guibordhomsy.com

New York, New York Office: 1350 Avenue of the Americas, Suite 3100, 10019. Telephone: 212-479-5620. Facsimile: 212-479-5621.

Environmental Law and Litigation, Brownsfields and Legacy Liability Restructuring, Commercial Litigation, Construction Law and Litigation, Corporate Finance and Transactions, Fund/Tax Expertise/Islamic Banking, International Practice, Policyholder Insurance Coverage Advice and Litigation, Toxic and Mass Tort.

BARBARA B. GUIBORD, born White Plains, New York, June 14, 1951; admitted to bar, 1977, New York; 1979, U.S. District Court, Western District of New York; 1983, Illinois; 1995, U.S. District Court, Northern District of Illinois; 1996, U.S. Court of Appeals, Ninth and Second Circuits. *Education:* Connecticut College (B.A., cum laude, 1973); Fordham University (J.D., 1976). Writing and Research Editor, Fordham University Urban Law Journal, Vol. IV, 1975-1976. Author: Note, "The New Equal Protection: Substantive Due Process Resurrected Under a New Name?" 3 Fordham Law Journal 311, 1975. Adjunct Professor of Environmental Law, Rachel Carson College of Environmental Studies, State University of New York at Buffalo, September, 1983 to December, 1983. Presenter: "The New Hazardous Solid Waste Amendments of 1984," Hofstra Law School Environmental Symposium, 1985; "Title III SARA: Community Right to Know," 1987; "Lender Liability Under Environmental Law," Continuing Legal Education Satellite Network, Inc., Springfield, Illinois, 1988 and 1989; "Environmental Auditing," 1988; "Siting Issues Surrounding Medical Waste Treatment and Disposal Facilities," Environmental Symposium sponsored by Katten, Muchin & Zavis, Chicago, 1990; "Environmental Aspects of Doing a Deal," American Bar Association, 1990; "Managing Risk-Anticipating Liability-Structuring the Deal," Continuing Legal Education Satellite Network, Inc., Springfield, Illinois, 1990. Associate General Counsel, New York State Department of Environmental Conservation, 1980-1983. Founder, Division of Hazardous Waste Enforcement. Attorney, Environmental Protection Bureau of the New York State Attorney General's Office. *Member:* Illinois State, New York State (Member, Environmental Law Section) and American (Member, Committee on Land and Natural Resources, 1988-1992) Bar Associations. ***LANGUAGES:*** French. ***PRACTICE AREAS:*** Environmental Law; Environmental Litigation; Insurance Coverage Litigation. ***Email:*** bguibord@guibordhomsy.com

JOSEPH G. HOMSY, born New York, New York, February 27, 1945; admitted to bar, 1978, New York and U.S. District Court, Southern, Eastern and Northern Districts of New

(This Listing Continued)

York; 1988, Illinois, U.S. District Court, Northern and Southern Districts of Illinois and U.S. Court of Appeals, Second, Fourth and Seventh Circuits. *Education:* University of Pennsylvania (B.A., 1966); New England School of Law (J.D., 1977). Author: "The Scope of Private Cost-Recovery Actions under CERCLA §107 (a) (4) (B) And Allocation Among Potentially Responsible Parties," *Hazardous Waste Litigation,* Practicing Law Institute, 1988; "Environmental Reporting Required by the Securities and Exchange Commission," BNA Environment Report, 1991. *Member:* American Bar Association (Member, Sections on: Litigation and Environmental Law); American Association of Corporate Counsel; Environmental Law Institute (Associate Representative, 1984-1987). [Capt., USAF, 1967-1971]. ***REPORTED CASES:*** Pneumo Abex., et al. v. Bessemer and Lake Erie Railroad Co., Inc., et al, 921 F. Supp. 336, 936 F. Supp. 1250 (E.D. Va. 1996); Chemical Waste Management, Inc., et al. v. Armstrong World Industries, et al. 669 F. Supp. 1285 (E.D. Pa. 1987). ***PRACTICE AREAS:*** Litigation; Environmental Law; Environmental Litigation; Insurance Coverage Litigation. ***Email:*** jhomsy@guibordhomsy.com

ASSOCIATE

DOUGLAS W. MICHAUD, born Waterville, Maine, December 28, 1967; admitted to bar, 1994, Illinois; 1995, U.S. District Court, Northern District of Illinois and U.S. Court of Appeals, Seventh Circuit; 1999, California and U.S. District Court, Northern District of California; 2000, U.S. District Court, Eastern District of California. *Education:* Tufts University (B.Sc., cum laude, 1990); DePaul University (J.D., 1994). Recipient, American Jurisprudence Award for Legal Writing. Editor, Journal of Art & Entertainment Law. Executive Board Member, Moot Court Society. *Member:* Chicago, Illinois State and American Bar Associations. ***PRACTICE AREAS:*** Environmental Litigation; Commercial Litigation; Insurance Coverage Litigation. ***Email:*** dmichaud@guibordhomsy.com

GUNTY & McCARTHY

Established in 1991

150 SOUTH WACKER DRIVE, SUITE 1025
CHICAGO, ILLINOIS 60606
Telephone: 312-541-0022
Facsimile: 312-541-0033

Asbestos, Toxic Tort, Latex, Chemical Exposure, Repetitive Injury, Product Liability, Workers' Compensation, Insurance Coverage and Transportation Loss Litigation.

FIRM PROFILE: Gunty & McCarthy is a professional, service-oriented law firm which limits its practice to civil defense matters. Founded in 1991, Gunty & McCarthy has established a clientele which includes many of the nation's leading insurers and businesses. Gunty & McCarthy prides itself on providing quality legal services and unparalleled service to its clients.

SUSAN GUNTY, born Vallejo, California, May 18, 1953; admitted to bar, 1980, Illinois; 1986, U.S. District Court, Northern District of Illinois including Trial Bar; 1990, U.S. District Court, Central District of Illinois; 1995, Missouri, U.S. District Court, Western and Eastern Districts of Wisconsin, U.S. District Court, Southern District of Illinois, U.S. Court of Appeals, Seventh Circuit and U.S. Supreme Court; 1996, Indiana. *Education:* Loyola University (B.A., 1975; M.A., 1977; J.D., 1980). Recipient, Loyola Law School Service and Leadership Award. Author: "The Hyde Amendment and Medicaid Abortions," ABA Forum, Vol. XVI, No. 4, Spring 1981; "A Critical Look at Hedonic Damages," Illinois Bar Journal, Vol. 80, June 1992. *Member:* Chicago and Illinois State Bar Associations; Defense Research Institute; Illinois Association of Defense Counsel. ***REPORTED CASES:*** Bailey v. City of Chicago, 116 Ill.App.3d 862, 72 Ill.Dec. 427, 452 N.E.2d 680, 1983; Mudd v. Goldblatt, 118 Ill.App.3d 431, 73 Ill.Dec. 657, 454 N.E.2d 754, 1983; Froud v. Celotex Corp., 98 Ill.2d 324, 74 Ill.Dec. 629, 456 N.E.2d 131, 1983; Hengels v. Gilski, 127 Ill.App.3d 894, 83 Ill.Dec. 101, 469 N.E. 2d 708, 1984; Board of Education v. City of Chicago, 171 Ill.App.3d 737, 121 Ill.Dec. 643, 525 N.E.2d 950, 1988; Board of Education v. City of Chicago, 131 Ill.2d 428, 137 Ill.Dec. 635, 546 N.E. 2d 580, 1989; G.M. Sloan Mosaic v. Newman Lustig, 199 Ill.App. 3d 518, 145 Ill.Dec. 633, 557 N.E.2d 403, 1990; Bowden v. Public Building Commission of Chicago, 167 Ill.2d 550, 667 N.E.2d 1055, 1996. ***PRACTICE AREAS:*** Toxic Torts; Asbestos Litigation; Repetitive Trauma; Latex Allergy Litigation; Lead Poisoning Litigation; AIDS Litigation; Chemical Exposure; Products Liability; Major Claims; Personal Injury; Insurance Defense; Catastrophic Injury. ***Email:*** Susan.Gunty@GuntyMcCarthy.com

JAMES P. McCARTHY, born Chicago, Illinois, March 22, 1959; admitted to bar, 1984, Illinois; 1987, U.S. District Court, Northern District of Illinois. *Education:* University of Notre Dame (B.B.A., 1981); John Marshall Law School (J.D., 1984). Lecturer: Western Loss Association, October 1991; Workers' Compensation Claims Association, March 1994. Member: Illinois Firefighters Association, 1981—; Legislative Advisor to State Representative James R. Strange, 1986-1991. Republican Committeeman, 1990—. Chairman, Political Action Committee, DuPage County Young Republicans, 1994. *Member:* Chicago, Du Page County and Illinois State Bar Associations; Casualty Adjusters Association of Chicago; Western Loss Association; Illinois Self-Insureds Association; Blue Goose International (Member and Officer, Chicago Pond); Defense Research Institute; Workers' Compensation Claims Association; Workers' Compensation Lawyers Association. ***REPORTED CASES:*** Barrett Moving and Storage Company v. All States Air Cargo, Inc., 823 F. Supp. 498 (1993). ***PRACTICE AREAS:*** Products Liability; Medical Devices Litigation; Insurance Coverage; Toxic Torts; Repetitive Trauma; Transportation; Cargo Claims; Mold Litigation; Insurance Defense. ***Email:*** Jim.McCarthy@GuntyMcCarthy.com

PAUL D. VAN LYSEBETTENS, born Chicago, Illinois, May 28, 1961; admitted to bar, 1994, Illinois and U.S. District Court, Northern District of Illinois. *Education:* American Conservatory of Music (B.Mus., 1983); Chicago-Kent College of Law, Illinois Institute of Technology (J.D., 1994). *Member:* Illinois State and American Bar Associations; Illinois Association of Defense Trial Counsel; Defense Research Institute. ***PRACTICE AREAS:*** Asbestos Litigation; Toxic Torts; Products Liability; Lead Poisoning Litigation; Personal Injury; Insurance Defense. ***Email:*** Paul.VanLysebettens@GuntyMcCarthy.com

STEPHEN K. MILOTT, born Chicago, Illinois, February 20, 1950; admitted to bar, 1977, Illinois; 1978, U.S. District Court, Northern District of Illinois including Trial Bar; 1988, U.S. Court of Appeals, Seventh Circuit; 1995, U.S. Supreme Court; 2002, Indiana. *Education:* Northeastern Illinois University (B.A., 1971); John Marshall Law School (J.D., 1977). Recipient, West Company Prize for Scholastic Achievement. Member, National Institute for Trial Advocacy, 1980-1982. Cook County State's Attorney's Office, 1980-1985. ***PRACTICE AREAS:*** Asbestos Litigation; Toxic Torts; Insurance Defense; Family Law. ***Email:*** Stephen.Milott@GuntyMcCarthy.com

ROBERT G. FREYDER, born Oak Park, Illinois, December 21, 1954; admitted to bar, 1981, Illinois and U.S. District Court, Northern District of Illinois including Trial Bar. *Education:* Beloit College (B.A., 1978); Loyola University (J.D., 1981); DePaul University (LL.M., Taxation, 1988). Recipient, American Jurisprudence Award, Advanced Corp. Tax. *Member:* Chicago Bar Association. ***LANGUAGES:*** German. ***PRACTICE AREAS:*** Insurance Defense Litigation; Civil Litigation Defense; Insurance Coverage Litigation; Asbestos Litigation. ***Email:*** Bob.Freyder@GuntyMcCarthy.com

JEAN M. FRENCH, born Chicago, Illinois, December 31, 1959; admitted to bar, 1986, Illinois and U.S. District Court, Northern District of Illinois. *Education:* University of Illinois (B.S., 1982); John Marshall Law School (J.D., 1985). *Member:* Chicago (Member, Judicial Evaluation Committee) and Illinois State Bar Associations; Women's Bar Association of Illinois. ***PRACTICE AREAS:*** Personal Injury; Insurance Defense; Products Liability; Subrogation; Asbestos Litigation. ***Email:*** Jean.French@GuntyMcCarthy.com

MARY ANN O'REILLY, born Chicago, Illinois, September 8, 1954; admitted to bar, 1982, Illinois; 1982, U.S. District Court, Northern District of Illinois; 1983, New York. *Education:* University of Illinois (B.S.N., Nursing, 1977); DePaul University (J.D., 1982). Registered Nurse, 1977. ***PRACTICE AREAS:*** Litigation. ***Email:*** maryann.oreilly@guntymccarthy.com

CATHERINE L. CARLSON, born Ann Arbor, Michigan, August 7, 1978; admitted to bar, 2003, Illinois and U.S. District Court, Northern District of Illinois. *Education:* Stephens College (B.A., 1996); Chicago-Kent College of Law (J.D., 2003). ***Email:*** cathie.carlson@guntymccarthy.com

MARA E. COHEN, born July 22, 1974; admitted to bar, 2000, Illinois. *Education:* Indiana University (B.A., 1996); John Marshall Law School (J.D., 2000). ***PRACTICE AREAS:*** Litigation; Insurance Coverage. ***Email:*** mara.cohen@GuntyMcCarthy.com

JEREMY B. HARRIS, born Chicago, Illinois, April 9, 1974; admitted to bar, 2001, Illinois. *Education:* University of Arizona (B.A., 1997); DePaul University College of Law (J.D., 2000). Member, Tourette Syndrome Association. ***PRACTICE AREAS:*** Asbestos Defense; Criminal Defense. ***Email:*** jeremy.harris@guntymccarthy.com

JENNIFER B. GROSZEK, born St. Louis, Missouri, March 6, 1977; admitted to bar, 2002, Illinois; 2003, Missouri. *Education:* University of Wisconsin, Stevens Point (B.A., 1999); Valparaiso University (J.D., 2001). *Member:* Chicago, Illinois State and American Bar Associations; Bar Association of Metropolitan St. Louis; American Trial Lawyers Association. ***Email:*** jennifer.groszek@guntymccarthy.com

SHERYL E. HEALY, born Cedar Rapids, Iowa, January 25, 1950; admitted to bar, 1985, Illinois and U.S. District Court, Northern District of Illinois. *Education:* University of Iowa (B.A., 1973); University of Loyola School of Law (J.D., 1984). Recipient, Justice White Award. Author, "The Uniform Mediation Ack, Illinois Newest Privilege," Illinois Bar Journal, February, 2004. Cook County Circuit Court Mediator. *Member:* Chicago and Illinois State Bar Associations. ***PRACTICE AREAS:*** Civil Litigation; Commercial; Products Liability; Medical Malpractice; Appellate. ***Email:*** sheryl.healy@guntymccarthy.com

PATRICIA M. KELLY, born Brooklyn, New York, January 20, 1953; admitted to bar, 1980, Illinois and U.S. District Court, Northern District of Illinois. *Education:* College of William & Mary (B.A., 1975); DePaul University College of Law (J.D., 1980). ***REPORTED CASES:*** Production Stamping v. Maryland Casualty, 1999 Wis.2d 322, 541 N.W.2d 584 (Wis. App. 1996). ***PRACTICE AREAS:*** Insurance Coverage. ***Email:*** patricia.kelly@guntymccarthy.com

SCOTT D. PFEIFFER, born Mt. Vernon, Illinois, May 2, 1973; admitted to bar, 2000, Illinois and U.S. District Court, Northern District of Illinois; 2001, Northern District of Illinois Trial Bar and U.S. District Court, Northern District of Indiana. *Education:* Southern Illinois University (B.A., 1997); John Marshall Law School (J.D., 2000). ***PRACTICE AREAS:*** Commercial Litigation; ERISA. ***Email:*** scott/pfeiffer@guntymccarthy.com

STEPHANIE M. THILLENS, admitted to bar, 1999, Illinois. *Education:* St. Mary's College (B.A., 1995); Illinois Institute of Technology (J.D., 1999). *Member:* Chicago Bar Association. ***PRACTICE AREAS:*** Insurance Defense. ***Email:*** stephanie.thellens@guntymccarthy.com

JAMES P. KASPER, born Dubuque, Iowa, October 6, 1976; admitted to bar, 2004, Illinois; 2005, U.S. District Court, Northern District of Illinois. *Education:* Loras College (B.A., 1999); John Marshall Law School (J.D., 2004). ***PRACTICE AREAS:*** Insurance Defense; Toxic Torts. ***Email:*** jamie.kasper@guntymccarthy.com

TAMIKA D. MARSHALL, born Clark Air Force Base, August 30, 1977; admitted to bar, 2003, Illinois. *Education:* University of North Carolina at Charlotte (B.A., 1999); Thomas M. Cooley Law School (J.D., 2003). ***Email:*** tamika.marshall@guntymccarthy.com

OF COUNSEL

RICHARD L. McLENNAN, born Louisville, Kentucky, October 31, 1959; admitted to bar, 1983, Missouri; 1986, Illinois. *Education:* Wabash College (B.A., cum laude, 1980); Washington University (J.D., 1983). Order of the Coif. Staff Attorney, Missouri Court of Appeals, 1983-1986. *Member:* The Bar Association of Metropolitan St. Louis; The Missouri Bar; American Bar Association; American Judicature Society. (Resident, St. Louis, MO Office). ***PRACTICE AREAS:*** Asbestos Litigation. ***Email:*** richard.mclennan@guntymccarthy.com

REPRESENTATIVE CLIENTS: Ace Aetna Life & Casualty Co.; Agricultural Excess and Surplus Insurance Co. (AESIC); AIG Risk Management (AIGRM); AIG Technical Services (AIGTS); ALCOA, INC.; Allstate Insurance Co.; American Art Clay; American International Adjustment Company (AIAC); American International Group; Alexsis Risk Management; American Centennial Insurance Co.; Atlantic Mutual Companies; Aurora Pump Company; Bollinger Industries; Burger King; Cesal Products, Inc.; Chubb Group of Insurance Cos.; Cigna Insurance Cos.; CNA Insurance Cos.; Colonial Penn Insurance; Commercial Union Insurance Co.; Cooper Industries; Corhart Refractories; Crane Co.; Crawford & Co.; M.H. Detrick; Dossert Corporation; Federal Express; Fireman's Fund Insurance Co.; First Non-

(This Listing Continued)

GUNTY & McCARTHY, Chicago—Continued

Profit Companies; General Casualty Insurance Co.; General Medical; General Signal Technologies, Corp.; Grant Wilson, Inc.; GRE America Group; The Hartford; Highlands Insurance Company; Home Insurance Co.; Illinois Fibre Specialty Co.; Illinois Non-Profit Risk Management Association; Intercargo Insurance; KCG, Inc.; Kemper Insurance Co.; Kentile Floors, Inc.; Kentucky Fried Chicken; Lexington Insurance Company; Liberty Mutual Insurance Co.; Melrath Co.; National Indemnity Insurance Co.; National Liability and Fire Insurance Co.; National Union Fire Insurance; Ogden Allied Security Services; Okonite Co.; Pecora Corp.; Reynolds Metals Co.; Rex Roto; Ruco Drywall Products, Inc.; Safeco Insurance Co.; Schultz Fire & Safety Corp.; SEICO/Hartford Insurance Co.; SOS Products, Inc.; Strange & Coleman Sidener Supply Company; Successa by Murgerto KC Wall Products, Inc.; Sumitomo Marine Insurance Co.; Travelers Insurance Co.; United States Fire Insurance, Co.

SUSAN CHRISTINE HADDAD

SUITE 2100, THREE FIRST NATIONAL PLAZA
70 WEST MADISON STREET
CHICAGO, ILLINOIS 60602
Telephone: 312-236-2298
FAX: 312-236-0089

Domestic Relations, Matrimonial, Family Law, Divorce.

SUSAN CHRISTINE HADDAD, born Chicago, Illinois, December 26, 1942; admitted to bar, 1977, Illinois; 1978, U.S. District Court, Northern District of Illinois; 1980, District of Columbia. *Education:* Lake Forest College (B.A., 1964); University of Chicago (M.A., 1967); John Marshall Law School (J.D., 1977). *Member:* American Bar Association; Women's Bar Association of Illinois (President, 1986-1987).

HAGENS BERMAN SOBOL SHAPIRO, LLP

Established in 1993

60 WEST RANDOLPH STREET, SUITE 200
CHICAGO, ILLINOIS 60601
Telephone: 312-762-9235
Facsimile: 312-762-9286
Email: info@hbsslaw.com
URL: http://www.hbsslaw.com

Seattle, Washington Office: 1301 Fifth Avenue, Suite 2900, 98101. Telephone: 206-623-7292. Facsimile: 206-623-0594.
Phoenix, Arizona Office: 2425 East Camelback Road, Suite 620, 85016. Telephone: 602-840-5900. Facsimile: 602-840-3012.
Los Angeles, California Office: 700 South Flower Street, Suite 2940, 90017-4101. Telephone: 213-330-7150. Facsimile: 213-330-7152.
Cambridge, Massachusetts Office: One Main Street, 4th Floor, 02142. Telephone: 617-482-3700. Facsimile: 617-482-3003.

Exclusively Litigation including Securities, Antitrust, Consumer Fraud and Employment Discrimination, Environmental, Class and Derivative Actions in all State and Federal Courts, almost always for plaintiffs.

FIRM PROFILE: Hagens Berman Sobol Shapiro, LLP prosecutes class and private actions nationwide on behalf of individual and institutional clients. The firm's litigation practice is principally in the areas of securities and antitrust class actions in federal and state courts, corporate governance litigation including claims for breach of fiduciary duty, as well as in prosecuting complex consumer claims, violations of federal anti-discrimination law, toxic tort litigation and litigation on behalf of foreign citizens under the Alien Tort Claims Act. In those cases where we have served as either lead counsel or as a member of plaintiffs' executive committee, the firm has recovered sums in excess of two hundred billion dollars, often successfully advancing novel and socially beneficial principles. In this connection, we have developed important new law in the areas in which we litigate. We also handle, on behalf of major institutional clients, more general complex commercial litigation involving antitrust issues and allegations of breach of fiduciary duty, fraud and negligence. The firm also served as special counsel and lead national counsel to thirteen states in their litigation against the tobacco industry, and is representing various states in litigation against the pharmaceutical industry. .

ELIZABETH ANNE FEGAN, born Hinsdale, Illinois, April 6, 1971; admitted to bar, 1995, Illinois; U.S. District Court, Central and Northern Districts of Illinois; 1997, U.S. Court of Appeals, Seventh Circuit. *Education:* Michigan State University (B.A., 1992); Loyola University (J.D., 1995). *Member:* Chicago and American Bar Associations; National Employment Lawyers Association; American Trial Lawyers Association. ***PRACTICE AREAS:*** Commercial Litigation; Class Action; Civil Rights; Complex and Multi-District Litigation; Commercial Class Actions; Consumer Litigation; Antitrust Litigation; Municipal Litigation. ***Email:*** beth@hbsslaw.com

TIMOTHY A. SCOTT, born De Kalb, Illinois, February 3, 1970; admitted to bar, 1997, Illinois and U.S. District Court, Northern District of Illinois. *Education:* Knox College (B.A., 1992); Chicago-Kent College of Law (J.D., 1997). ***PRACTICE AREAS:*** Antitrust; Class Action Litigation; Complex and Multi-District Litigation; Complex Litigation; ERISA. ***Email:*** tims@hbsslaw.com

REPRESENTATIVE CLIENTS: Microsoft; Lucient; Chicago Teachers Retirement Fund; Alaska Electrical Workers Pension Fund; National Elevators Union Pension Fund; IBEW Pension Fund.

(For complete biographical data on other personnel, see Professional Biographies at, Seattle, Washington, Phoenix, Arizona, Los Angeles, California and Cambridge, Massachusetts)

HALLIHAN INTELLECTUAL PROPERTY LAW, LTD.

125 SOUTH WACKER DRIVE, SUITE 2080
CHICAGO, ILLINOIS 60606
Telephone: 312-223-0010
Fax: 312-873-4383
URL: http://www.hiplaw.net
Email: questions@hallihan.com
URL: http://www.hallihan.com

Litigation, Intellectual Property Law, Patents, Trademarks, Copyrights, Trade Secrets and Entertainment Law.

WILLIAM J. (HAL) HALLIHAN, admitted to bar, 1996, Illinois; registered to practice before U.S. Patent and Trademark Office; registered to practice before Canadian Intellectual Property Office. *Education:* University of Illinois (B.S., 1989); John Marshall Law School (J.D., 1995). ***PRACTICE AREAS:*** Litigation; Intellectual Property; Patents; Trademarks; Copyrights; Trade Secrets; Entertainment Law.

HAMMAN & BENN

CHICAGO, ILLINOIS

(See Much Shelist Freed Denenberg Ament & Rubenstein, P.C.)

ALAN H. HAMMERMAN

640 NORTH LA SALLE STREET
SUITE 670
CHICAGO, ILLINOIS 60610
Telephone: 312-642-1322
Fax: 312-642-9401
Email: LAWOFF@AMERITECH.NET

Federal Tax, Estate Planning and Probate Law.

ALAN H. HAMMERMAN, born Chicago, Illinois, May 16, 1933; admitted to bar, 1959, Illinois. *Education:* Harvard University (A.B., 1955); Cornell University; Northwestern University (J.D., 1958). Teaching Fellow, John Marshall Law School, 1961-1965. *Member:* Chicago, Illinois State and American (Member, Federal Tax Committee) Bar Associations.

OF COUNSEL

STEPHEN L. SEFTENBERG, born Oak Park, Illinois, February 24, 1935; admitted to bar, 1959, Illinois; 1962, U.S. District Court, Eastern and Northern Districts of Illinois; 1963, U.S. Court of Appeals, Seventh Circuit and U.S. Supreme Court; 1987, U.S. Tax Court; 1989, Florida. *Education:* Harvard University (A.B., magna cum laude, 1956; LL.B., 1959). Author: "Income Taxation of Trusts and Estates After The Tax Reform Act of 1986," American College of Trust and Estate Counsel Probate Notes, 1986 (reprinted in Trusts and Estates Magazine, 1986). *Member:* Palm Beach County and American Bar Associations; The Florida Bar; East Coast (Florida) Estate Planning Council. (Also Practicing Individually, West Palm Beach, Florida). ***PRACTICE AREAS:*** Estate Planning; Estate Administration; Closely Held Corporations; Charitable Trusts and Foundations; Probate; Wills; Real Estate; Taxation; International Taxation. ***Email:*** SLSeftenberg.law@bigfoot.com

CRAIG B. HAMMOND, LTD.

Established in 1979

77 WEST WASHINGTON, SUITE 1805
CHICAGO, ILLINOIS 60602
Telephone: 312-236-5006
Fax: 312-236-2103
Email: chammon2@ix.netcom.com
URL: http://www.lawyers.com/craigbhammondlaw

Child Custody, Visitation Rights, Family Law, Matrimonial Law, Divorce, Child Support, Domestic Violence, Premarital Agreements, Spousal Support, Mediation and Tax Law and Retirement Benefit Plans.

CRAIG B. HAMMOND, born Augusta, Georgia, October 11, 1942; admitted to bar, 1979, Illinois. *Education:* Newberry College (B.A., with honors, 1965); University of Chicago; IIT Chicago-Kent College of Law (J.D., with honors, 1979). *Member:* Chicago (Member, Matrimonial Committee), Illinois State and American (Member, Family Law and Litigation Sections) Bar Associations; The Association of Trial Lawyers of America; Illinois Trial Lawyers Association; Women's Bar Association of Illinois; Academy of Family Mediators; National Association of Women Lawyers. ***LANGUAGES:*** Polish.

JOEL F. HANDLER

55 WEST WACKER DRIVE, SUITE 950
CHICAGO, ILLINOIS 60601
Telephone: 312-621-0008
FAX: 312-629-2916
Email: jhandler@cogan-mcnabola.com

General Trial and Appellate Practice in State and Federal Courts. Administrative Law, General Business and Commercial Law, Personal Injury, Matrimonial Law, Chancery and Employment Law including State and Federal Discrimination Actions. Termination, Retaliatory Discharge and Breach of Employment Contracts, Torts, Wills, Premises Liability, Products Liability, Defamation and Trade Secrets.

(This Listing Continued)

JOEL F. HANDLER, born Chicago, Illinois, April 19, 1951; admitted to bar, 1975, Illinois. *Education:* University of Illinois (B.A., with highest honors, 1972); DePaul University College of Law (J.D., summa cum laude, 1975). Member. De Paul Law Review, 1975. *Member:* Chicago and Illinois State Bar Associations; National Employment Lawyers Association.

REPRESENTATIVE CLIENTS: Community & Economic Development Association of Cook County, Inc,; Rockford Systems, Inc.; American Equipment Leasing, Inc.; VMS Realty; Lincoln Technical Institute of Arizona; Barrett Design and Construction Co., Inc.; Mattison Technologies, Inc.; Kenard Construction Co.; Mass Polymers Co.; Manufacturers Technical Institute; Windy City Graphics; Advanced Data Design, Inc; Peak Therapeutics, Inc.; Cable America, Inc., Universal Technical Institute, Inc.; Bond Capital, Ltd.; Europaper, B.V.; Kings Arts & Craft Products Inc.; Fiber Corporation of America, Inc.; Premier International Enterprises, Inc.; Environ Corp.; Bauhs Dring Main; Temp-Masters Corp.; Scorpio Apparel, Inc.; MIC Capital, Inc.; Hale Lofts Condominium Ass'n; Hale Granace Condominium Ass'n.; Blondes Have More Fun, Inc.; Crown Jewels, Ltd.; American Chartered Bank; Advantage Freight Network.

HANDLER, THAYER & DUGGAN, LLC

191 N. WACKER DRIVE
23RD FLOOR
CHICAGO, ILLINOIS 60606
Telephone: 312-641-2100
Fax: 312-641-6866
URL: http://www.htdlaw.com

Transactional Practice, Business, Finance, Estate Planning, Tax, Real Estate, Sports and Entertainment.

PARTNERS

THOMAS J. HANDLER, born Chicago, Illinois, March 8, 1956; admitted to bar, 1983, Illinois; 1985, U.S. Tax Court. *Education:* University of Illinois (B.S., 1979); DePaul University (J.D., 1983). *Member:* Chicago, Illinois State and American Bar Associations. ***PRACTICE AREAS:*** Estate Planning; Taxation; Business Law. ***Email:*** thandler@htdlaw.com

STEVEN J. THAYER, born Cedar Rapids, Iowa, January 31, 1966; admitted to bar, 1991, Illinois; 2001, Iowa. *Education:* University of Illinois, Urbana-Champaign (B.A., 1988); DePaul University (M.B.A. and J.D., 1991). *Member:* Chicago, Illinois State, Iowa State and American Bar Associations. ***PRACTICE AREAS:*** Business Law; Estate Planning; Taxation; Real Estate. ***Email:*** sthayer@htdlaw.com

JAMES M. DUGGAN, born August 25, 1969; admitted to bar, 1994, Illinois. *Education:* University of Illinois, Urbana-Champaign (B.A., Marketing, 1991); DePaul University (M.B.A. and J.D., 1994). ***PRACTICE AREAS:*** Taxation; Trusts and Estates; Business Law. ***Email:*** jduggan@htdlaw.com

DOUGLAS S. ROBSON, born Baltimore, Maryland, January 25, 1967; admitted to bar, 1992, Illinois; 1993, U.S. District Court, Northern District of Illinois. *Education:* Indiana University, Bloomington (B.A., 1989); DePaul University (J.D., 1992). *Member:* Chicago and Illinois State Bar Associations. ***PRACTICE AREAS:*** Trusts and Estates; Business Law; Commercial Real Estate. ***Email:*** drobson@htdlaw.com

GREGORY J. BERTSCH, born Akron, Illinois, May 24, 1971; admitted to bar, 2000, Illinois. *Education:* Loyola University (B.B.A., Accounting, 1993); DePaul University College of Law (J.D., 2000). *Member:* Chicago and Illinois State Bar Associations. ***PRACTICE AREAS:*** Trusts and Estates; Business Law; Taxation. ***Email:*** gbertsch@htdlaw.com

ASSOCIATES

STEVEN M. BONNEAU, born Providence, Rhode Island, August 19, 1971; admitted to bar, 1998, Ohio; 1999, Illinois. *Education:* Boston College (B.A., 1993); University of Dayton (J.D., 1998). *Member:* Chicago, Illinois State and American Bar Associations. ***PRACTICE AREAS:*** Estate Planning; Estate Administration; Tax Law; Business Transactions. ***Email:*** sbonneau@htdlaw.com

SHARON A. HANNAFORD, admitted to bar, 1993, Illinois. ***PRACTICE AREAS:*** Family Law; Corporate Law; Business Law; Estate Planning. ***Email:*** shannaford@htdlaw.com

SUSAN F. LIFVENDAHL, born New York, New York, September 5, 1967; admitted to bar, 1993, Illinois and U.S. District Court, Northern District of Illinois. *Education:* Boston College (B.S., 1989); Loyola University of Chicago (J.D., 1993). Associate, Vedder Price Kaufman & Kammholz, 1998-2001; Ross & Hardies, 1993-1998. *Member:* Chicago and American Bar Associations. ***PRACTICE AREAS:*** Corporate Law. ***Email:*** slifvendahl@htdlaw.com

HEATHER A. NICHOLS, born January 29, 1971; admitted to bar, 1999, Illinois. *Education:* DePaul University (B.S., Accounting, 1993; J.D., 1999). *Member:* Chicago, Illinois State and American Bar Associations. ***PRACTICE AREAS:*** Estate Planning; Taxation. ***Email:*** hnichols@htdlaw.com

GISELLE C. PIRARO, born Chicago, Illinois; admitted to bar, 1999, Illinois. *Education:* DePaul University (B.A., 1996); John Marshall Law School (J.D., 1999). ***PRACTICE AREAS:*** Real Estate; Corporate Law. ***Email:*** gpiraro@htdlaw.com

CATHERINE A. BATTIN, born McHenry, Illinois, March 13, 1971; admitted to bar, 1999, Illinois. Formerly with Ernst & Young LLP. ***PRACTICE AREAS:*** Tax Law; Estate Planning. ***Email:*** cschultz@htdlaw.com

ANDREW M. STROTH, born Chicago, Illinois, November 28, 1967; admitted to bar, 2001, Illinois and U.S. District Court, Northern District of Illinois. *Education:* University of Illinois (B.A., Liberal Arts, 1990); Northwestern University School of Law (J.D., 2000). Adjunct Professor, Northwestern University School of Law. *Member:* Chicago, Cook County and American Bar Associations. ***PRACTICE AREAS:*** Contracts; Entertainment and the Arts; Sports Law. ***Email:*** astroth@htdlaw.com

ERIC E. KALNINS, born West Islip, New York, January 22, 1973; admitted to bar, 1999, Illinois. *Education:* Augustana College (B.A., Accounting); Thomas M. Cooley Law School (J.D.); DePaul University (LL.M., Taxation). ***PRACTICE AREAS:*** Estate Planning; Litigation; Tax Law; Corporate Law; Real Estate. ***Email:*** ekalnins@htdlaw.com

JEFFREY J. BUDZIK, admitted to bar, 2004, Florida; 2005, Illinois. *Education:* DePaul University (B.S., Accounting, 1998); University of Miami (J.D., 2002). *Member:* Illinois State Bar Association; The Florida Bar. ***PRACTICE AREAS:*** Taxation; International Taxation; Estate Planning; Asset Protection.

OF COUNSEL

RICHARD D. HART, born Chicago, Illinois, May 15, 1953; admitted to bar, 1978, Illinois; 1979, California; 1981, U.S. District Court, Northern District of Illinois; 1983, U.S. District Court, Central District of California. *Education:* Drake University (B.S., Business Administration, 1975); DePaul University (J.D., 1978). *Member:* Chicago, Illinois State and American (Vice Chairperson, International Tort and Insurance Law and Practice Committee, Tort and Insurance Practice Section, 1986-1987) Bar Associations; The State Bar of California. ***PRACTICE AREAS:*** Administrative Law; Contracts; Business Law; Commercial Litigation. ***Email:*** rhart@htdlaw.com

BARRY N. MORRELL, born Philadelphia, Pennsylvania, February 18, 1943; admitted to bar, 1975, Virginia; 1976, Louisiana; 1977, Illinois; 1979, Texas; 1986, Pennsylvania; 1987, New Jersey; 2004, U.S. District Court, Northern District of Illinois. *Education:* University of Pennsylvania, (B.A.); New York University, (M.B.A.); American University, (J.D.); Georgetown University, (L.L.M., Taxation). Former Associate: Pope, Ballard, Sherard & Fowle; Phelps Dunbar. ***PRACTICE AREAS:*** International Taxation; Domestic Taxation; Commercial Law of People's Republic of China. ***Email:*** bmorrell@htdlaw.com

MICHAEL T. HANNAFAN & ASSOCIATES, LTD.

Established in 1979
ONE EAST WACKER DRIVE, SUITE 1208
CHICAGO, ILLINOIS 60601
Telephone: (312) 527-0055
Fax: (312) 527-0220
URL: http://www.lawyers.com/hannafan
Email: mth@hannafanlaw.com
URL: http://www.hannafanlaw.com

General Trial and Appellate Practice in State and Federal Courts Including General Business, Commercial, Patent Infringement, Antitrust, Securities, Legal and Medical Malpractice, Employment Termination and Discrimination, Products Liability, Class Action, Estate and Probate Litigation, Personal Injury, Contract, White Collar Criminal Defense and Bankruptcy Trial Law.

FIRM PROFILE: The Firm was founded in 1979 by Michael T. Hannafan, formerly a litigation partner with Kirkland & Ellis, Chicago, Illinois. The firm has a national practice which concentrates on a wide variety of Plaintiffs' and Defendants' trial and arbitration matters. Mr. Hannafan is a Fellow of The American College of Trial Lawyers and is noted among the best lawyers in America by his peers. Mr. Hannafan has tried more than 45 cases (including 21 jury trials) to verdict, judgment or decision.

MICHAEL T. HANNAFAN, born Clinton, Iowa, March 5, 1942; admitted to bar, 1970, Illinois and U.S. District Court, Northern District of Illinois including Trial Bar; 1972, U.S. Court of Appeals, 7th Circuit; 1974, U.S. Court of Appeals, Eighth Circuit; 1975, U.S. Supreme Court; 1986, U.S. Court of Appeals for the Federal Circuit; 1987, U.S. District Court, Western District of Wisconsin. *Education:* University of Missouri (B.J., 1964); Washington University of St. Louis (J.D., 1970). Order of the Coif. Managing Editor, Washington University Law Quarterly, 1969-1970. Fellow, American College of Trial Lawyers. Listed in: "The Best Lawyers in America," 1995—; Bar Register of Preeminent Lawyers, 1995—. Named, 2005 Illinois Super Lawyer in General Litigation. Special Master Appointment. Adjunct Professor, Trial Advocacy, Northwestern University School of Law. Certified Mediator, Circuit Court of Cook County, Illinois. Associate, 1970-1977; Partner, 1977-1979, Kirkland & Ellis. Member, Illinois Leading Attorneys. *Member:* American Bar Association (Member, Section of Litigation); The Association of Trial Lawyers of America. Chicago Lincoln American Inn of Court. [1st. Lt., U.S. Army, 1964-1966]. ***REPORTED CASES:*** Michael Jordan v. Karla Knafel, 823 N.E.2d 1113 (Ill. App. 2005); The Society of Lloyd's v. Estate of John William McMurray and Harris Trust & Savings Bank, 274 F. 3d 1133, (7th Cir. 2001); The Society of Lloyd's v. Ashenden 233 F.3d 473 (7th Cir. 2000); Monsanto Co. v. Spray-Rite Service Corp., 465 U.S. 752 (1984); The Society of Lloyd's v. Ashenden, 1999 WL 2847745 (N.D. Ill, 1999); Ashenden v. Lloyd's of London, 934 F. Supp. 992 (N.D. Ill, 1996); Jackson Jordan, Inc. v. Leydig, Voit & Mayer, 158 Ill. 2d 240 (Sup. Ct. Ill., 1994); In Re: Estate of Hoover, 155 Ill. 2d 402 (Ill., 1993); Arachnid, Inc., v. Industrial Design Electronics Associates, Inc., 862 F. 2d 322 (Fed. Cir. 1988); Arachnid, Inc. v. Merit Industries, Inc., 939 F. 2d 1574 (Fed. Cir., 1991); In Re: Midway Airlines, Inc., 180 B.R. 1009 (N.D. Ill, 1995); AM International, Inc. v. Graphic Management Associates, Inc., 44 F. 3d 572 (7th Cir. 1995); Continental Grain Co. v. FMC Corp., 327 N.E. 2d 572 (Ill. App. 1975). ***PRACTICE AREAS:*** Trial Practice; General Litigation; Business; Appellate; Antitrust; White Collar Criminal Defense; Employment; Patent Litigation; Professional Liability; Products Liability; Securities; Personal Injury; Estate Litigation; Class Actions.

NICHOLAS A. PAVICH, born Detroit, Michigan, December 4, 1972; admitted to bar, 1999, Illinois and U.S. District Court, Northern District of Illinois including Trial Bar. *Education:* Rutgers University (B.A., Classical Languages and History, 1995); Washington University (J.D., 1998). *Member:* Chicago and Illinois State (Member, Trial Law Section) Bar Associations. ***LANGUAGES:*** Ancient Greek, Latin and Spanish. ***REPORTED CASES:*** In Re Sills, 260 BR 675 (Bankr. N.D. Ill. 2000). ***PRACTICE AREAS:*** Trial Practice; General Litigation; Business; Appellate; Antitrust; White Collar Criminal Defense; Employment Law; Patent; Professional Liability; Products Liability; Securities; Personal Injury; Estate Litigation; Class Actions.

(This Listing Continued)

MICHAEL T. HANNAFAN & ASSOCIATES, LTD., Chicago—Continued

BLAKE T. HANNAFAN, born Arlington Heights, Illinois, June 28, 1973; admitted to bar, 1998, Illinois and U.S. District Court, Northern District of Illinois including Trial Bar. *Education:* Vanderbilt University (B.A., Political Science, 1995); Washington University (J.D., 1998). Order of the Coif. Member, Washington University Law Quarterly, 1997-1998. *Member:* Chicago Bar Association. ***REPORTED CASES:*** Colleen Kramer v. Bank of America Securities, LLC, 355 F.3d 961 (7th Cir. 2004). ***PRACTICE AREAS:*** Trial Practice; Litigation; Business Law; Appellate Practice; Antitrust; White Collar Criminal Defense; Employment Law; Patents; Professional Liability; Products Liability; Securities; Personal Injury; Estate Litigation; Class Actions.

LEGAL SUPPORT PERSONNEL

DIANA MUCKER, born Chicago, Illinois, October 9, 1951. Formerly with, Winston & Strawn. (Office Manager, Legal Assistant). ***Email:*** dmm@hannafanlaw.com

REFERENCE: The Northern Trust Co.

LAW OFFICES OF RICHARD HANUS

Established in 1990

SUITE 2500
161 NORTH CLARK STREET
CHICAGO, ILLINOIS 60601
Telephone: 312-357-0033
Fax: 312-357-0286
URL: http://www.lawyers.com/usavisacounsel
Email: rhanus@usavisacounsel.com
URL: http://www.usavisacounsel.com

Immigration and Naturalization, Business Immigration, Citizenship, Consular Law, Deportation, Employment Authorizations, Employment Immigration, Employment Visas, Family Immigration Law, Immigration Law, Investor Vistas, Labor Certifications, Permanent Visas, Political Asylum, Refugee Law, Religious Visas, Visas.

FIRM PROFILE: Practice focuses exclusively in immigration law matters. Representing individuals, families and corporations since 1990.

RICHARD HANUS, born Chicago, Illinois, August 27, 1963; admitted to bar, 1988, Illinois; U.S. District Court, Northern District of Illinois; U.S. Court of Appeals, Sixth, Seventh and Eighth Circuits. *Education:* Northwestern University (B.S., Communication Studies/Philosophy, 1985); University of Illinois College of Law (J.D., 1988). Immigration Law Clinic Chair, Chicago Volunteer Legal Services. *Member:* Kane County Bar Association; West Suburban Bar Association; Northwest Suburban Bar Association; American Immigration Lawyers Association. ***LANGUAGES:*** Spanish, Polish, Russian, Lithuanian and Hebrew.

LAW OFFICES OF PATRICIA A. HARDIMAN, LTD.

77 W. WASHINGTON STREET, SUITE 600
CHICAGO, ILLINOIS 60602
Telephone: 312-782-3090
Facsimile: 312-782-0993
Email: PAHardiman@aol.com
URL: http://www.hardimanlawoffices.com

Worker's Compensation, Personal Injury, Negligence, Construction Defects, Medical Malpractice.

MEMBERS OF FIRM

PATRICIA A. HARDIMAN, born Rochester, New York, November, 29, 1954; admitted to bar, 1981, Illinois. *Education:* Boston College (B.S., 1976); John Marshall Law School (J.D., 1980). ***PRACTICE AREAS:*** Worker's Compensation (60%); Personal Injury (30%); Negligence (10%). ***Email:*** PAHardiman@aol.com

EUGENE C. HARDIMAN, born Boston, Massachusetts, 1952; admitted to bar, 1979, Illinois. *Education:* University of Massachusetts (B.A., 1975); John Marshall Law School (J.D., 1979). *Member:* Illinois State Bar Association; Association of Trial Lawyers of America. ***PRACTICE AREAS:*** Personal Injury; Workers Compensation.

DAVID G. HARDING

100 NORTH LASALLE STREET, SUITE 1610
CHICAGO, ILLINOIS 60602
Telephone: 312-782-3039
Fax: 312-236-0678
Email: hardlaw@netzero.com
URL: http://www.lawyers.com/harding

Bankruptcy, Lawsuits, Business Litigation, Contracts, Corporate Law, Limited Liability Company Law, Environmental Law, Estate Planning, Wills, Probate, Real Estate, Residential Real Estate.

DAVID G. HARDING, born Galesburg, Illinois, October 29, 1954; admitted to bar, 1981, Illinois and U.S. District Court, Northern District of Illinois; 1983, Trial Bar; 1996, U.S. Court of Appeals, Seventh Circuit. *Education:* Southern Illinois University (B.A., 1977); John Marshall Law School (J.D., 1981). Recipient: Pro Bono Service Award, Chicago Bar Association, 1998; Distinguished Service Award, Chicago Volunteer Legal Services Foundation, 1988, 1991, 1996. Arbitrator, Cook County Mandatory Court-Annexed

(This Listing Continued)

Arbitration Program, 1990-1992. Member, Board of Directors, Chicago Volunteer Legal Services Foundation, 1990-1992. ***REPORTED CASES:*** Matter of Lefkas General Partners, 112 F.3d 896; H & H Press, Inc. v. Axelrod, 265 Ill.App.3d 670. ***PRACTICE AREAS:*** Bankruptcy; Business Litigation; Contracts; Corporate Law; Environmental Law; Estate Planning; Wills; Probate; Trusts and Estates; Real Estate.

HARRINGTON, THOMPSON, ACKER & HARRINGTON, LTD.

Established in 1969

310 SOUTH MICHIGAN AVENUE, SUITE 2000
CHICAGO, ILLINOIS 60604
Telephone: 312-922-8833
Fax: 312-922-3044
URL: http://www.harringtonlaw.com

Civil Trial and Appellate Practice in all Courts. Plaintiff Personal Injury, Wrongful Death, Federal Employers Liability Act (FELA), Medical Malpractice, Products Liability, Civil Rights and Construction Related Torts.

FIRM PROFILE: The law firm of Harrington, Thompson, Acker & Harrington, Ltd., concentrates in civil trial and appellate practice and works exclusively in the areas of personal injury and wrongful death in federal and state courts throughout the States of Illinois, Indiana, Michigan, Ohio, Wisconsin and Pennsylvania. The firm was founded in 1969 by Robert E. Harrington, Sr. and James E. Harrington and was originally known as Harrington & Harrington, Ltd. The firm name was changed to its present name in 1992. The firm members collectively provide over 200 years of experience as trial and appellate lawyers working on behalf of plaintiffs in all areas of the personal injury field. The president of the firm, Robert E. Harrington, Jr. is a designated FELA legal counsel for the United Transportation Union. Our case load is deliberately restricted to give each client personal and careful attention, resulting in legal services of the highest quality.

ROBERT E. HARRINGTON, JR., born Chicago, Illinois, February 7, 1950; admitted to bar, 1976, Illinois; 1978, Florida. *Education:* John Carroll University (B.A., 1972); Chicago-Kent College of Law (J.D., 1976). Assistant Public Defender, Cook County Public Defender's Office, 1976-1977. *Member:* Chicago, Illinois State and American Bar Associations; The Association of Trial Lawyers of America; Illinois Trial Lawyers Association. ***PRACTICE AREAS:*** Personal Injury; Wrongful Death; Federal Employers Liability Act (FELA).

ROBERT B. THOMPSON, born Chicago, Illinois, May 25, 1950; admitted to bar, 1975, Illinois. *Education:* Millikin University (B.S., 1972); Chicago-Kent College of Law, Illinois Institute of Technology (J.D., cum laude, 1975). Lecturer, Appellate Advocacy, Loyola University Law School, 1977-1978. *Member:* Chicago Bar Association. ***PRACTICE AREAS:*** Personal Injury; Wrongful Death; Federal Employers Liability Act (FELA).

LAURENCE C. ACKER, born Chicago, Illinois, March 26, 1951; admitted to bar, 1976, Illinois. *Education:* University of Notre Dame (B.A., 1973); Loyola University (J.D., 1976). Assistant Public Defender, Cook County, 1976-1978. *Member:* Chicago (Member, Young Lawyers Committee, 1977-1979), Illinois State and American Bar Associations; Illinois Trial Lawyers Association. ***PRACTICE AREAS:*** Personal Injury; Wrongful Death; Federal Employers Liability Act (FELA).

PATRICK J. HARRINGTON, born Evergreen Park, Illinois, September 3, 1960; admitted to bar, 1985, Illinois. *Education:* John Carroll University (B.A., 1982); Loyola University (J.D., 1985). Phi Alpha Delta. Member, Loyola National Moot Team, 1984-1985. *Member:* Illinois State and American Bar Associations; Illinois Trial Lawyers Association; The Association of Trial Lawyers of America. ***PRACTICE AREAS:*** Personal Injury; Wrongful Death; Federal Employers Liability Act (FELA).

KENNETH J. SOPHIE, JR., born Milwaukee, Wisconsin, July 11, 1950; admitted to bar, 1977, Illinois. *Education:* John Carroll University (B.A., 1972); John Marshall Law School (J.D., cum laude, 1977). Alpha Sigma Nu. *Member:* Illinois State Bar Association (Member, Civil Practice and Procedure Section, 1987-1991); Illinois Trial Lawyers Association (Member, Amicus Curiae Committee, 1989-1991). ***PRACTICE AREAS:*** Personal Injury; Wrongful Death; Federal Employers Liability Act (FELA).

VINCENT B. BROWNE, born Cushing, Oklahoma, June 8, 1972; admitted to bar, 1997, Illinois and U.S. District Court, Northern District of Illinois. *Education:* Depauw University (B.A., Philosophy, 1994); Depaul College of Law (J.D., 1997). *Member:* Chicago and Illinois State Bar Associations; The Association of Trial Lawyers of America. ***PRACTICE AREAS:*** Personal Injury; Wrongful Death; Federal Employers Liability Act (FELA). ***Email:*** vbrowne@harringtonlaw.com

ROBERT E. HARRINGTON, III, born Evergreen Park, Illinois, April 2, 1977; admitted to bar, 2002, Illinois. *Education:* John Carroll University (B.A., 1999); Loyola University (J.D., 2002). *Member:* Chicago, Illinois State and American Bar Associations; The Association of Trial Lawyers of America; Illinois Trial Lawyers Association. ***PRACTICE AREAS:*** Personal Injury; Wrongful Death; Medical Malpractice; Federal Employers Liability Act (FELA). ***Email:*** bharrington@harringtonlaw.com

DANIEL W. PISANI, born Chicago, Illinois, March 7, 1967; admitted to bar, 1992, Illinois, U.S. District Court, Northern District of Illinois, U.S. Court of Appeals, Seventh Circuit and U.S. Supreme Court. *Education:* Marquette University (B.A., 1989); Chicago-Kent College of Law, Illinois Institute of Technology (J.D., 1992). *Member:* Chicago and Illinois State Bar Associations. ***PRACTICE AREAS:*** Plaintiffs Personal Injury; Federal Employers Liability Act (FELA). ***Email:*** dpisani@harringtonlaw.com

REFERENCE: American National Bank and Trust Co., Chicago, Illinois.

THE LAW OFFICES OF DANIEL HARRIS

150 NORTH WACKER DRIVE
SUITE 3000
CHICAGO, ILLINOIS 60606
Telephone: 312-960-1802
Fax: 312-960-1936
Email: lawofficedh@yahoo.com
URL: http://www.lawyers.com/danielharris

Class Actions, Consumer Protection.

DANIEL M. HARRIS, born Chicago, Illinois, May 23, 1951; admitted to bar, 1978, Illinois; 1981, U.S. District Court, Northern District of Illinois; 1982, U.S. Court of Appeals, Seventh Circuit, U.S. Supreme Court and U.S. District Court, Northern District of Illinois including Trial Bar. *Education:* Johns Hopkins University (B.A., 1972); Harvard University (J.D., magna cum laude, 1977). Phi Beta Kappa. Recipient, Sears Prize. Member, and Note Editor, Volume 90, Harvard Law Review. Author: "The Fourth Amendment: Past and Future," 68 Judicature 37 (1984); "The Return to Common Sense: A Response to 'The Incredible Shrinking Fourth Amendment'," 22 American Criminal Law Review 25 (1984); "The Politics of Statutory Construction," 4 Brigham Young Univ. L. Rev. 745 (1985). Co-Author: Herzel and Harris, "A Solution To All Problems," Financial Times (London version), p.32, March 17, 1988; Herzel and Harris, "Fighting Crime on the Street," Financial Times, September 15, 1988; Herzel and Harris, "A More Just and Contentious Society," London Financial Times, p.15, November 3, 1988. Law Clerk: Honorable James Browning, Chief Judge, U.S. Court of Appeals, Ninth Circuit, 1977-1978; Honorable Justice William Brennan, Associate Justice, U.S. Supreme Court, 1978-1979. ***PRACTICE AREAS:*** Class Actions; Consumer Protection. ***Email:*** lawofficedh@yahoo.com

HARRIS KESSLER & GOLDSTEIN LLC

A Limited Liability Company
640 NORTH LA SALLE STREET
SUITE 590
CHICAGO, ILLINOIS 60610-3731
Telephone: 312-280-0111
Fax: 312-280-8232
URL: http://www.hkgold.com

Waukegan, Illinois Office: 404 Water Street, 60085. Telephone: 847-263-1919. Fax: 847-244-8891.

General Business Practice including Litigation, Secured Lending, Real Estate, Health Care and Estate Planning.

STEVEN M. HARRIS, born Chicago, Illinois, May 30, 1956; admitted to bar, 1981, Illinois. *Education:* Northern Illinois University (B.S., Finance, magna cum laude, 1978); Illinois Institute of Technology, Chicago-Kent College of Law (J.D., with honors, 1981). Legal Editor, American Academy of Orthopedic Surgeons; Monthly Contributor, AM News contract language. Co-Author: "Medical Practice Divorce," AMA Press, July 2001. Professor, Practice Management Curriculum, Northwestern University Dental School, 1988-2001. Faculty, University of Illinois College of Dentistry, 1988-1995; Trustee, 1989-1999; Treasurer, 1991-1993; Chairman, 1993-1997, Deerfield Park District Foundation, Trustee, 1999-2001 and Mayor, 2001— Village of Deerfield, Illinois. ***PRACTICE AREAS:*** Business Law; Health Care; Contracts; Corporate Law. ***Email:*** sharris@hkgold.com

RICHARD N. KESSLER, born Harvey, Illinois, September 6, 1957; admitted to bar, 1982, Illinois, U.S. District Court, Northern District of Illinois and U.S. Court of Appeals, Seventh Circuit. *Education:* University of Illinois (B.A., 1979); Illinois Institute of Technology; Chicago-Kent College of Law (J.D., 1982). Teacher, Business Law, Barat College, 1987. Assistant State's Attorney, Lake County State's Attorney Office, 1982-1984. *Member:* Lake County and Illinois State Bar Associations; Jefferson Inns of Court. ***REPORTED CASES:*** Poeta v. Sheridan Point Shopping Plaza, 195 Ill.App.3d 852, 552 N.E.2d 1248 (2d Dist. 1990); Goldstein v. Mitchell, 144 Ill.App.3d 474, 494 N.E.2d 914 (2d Dist. 1986); Corwin v. Abbott Laboratories, 353 Ill. App.3d 848 (2nd Dist., 2004). ***PRACTICE AREAS:*** Trial Practice; Commercial Litigation; Health Care Litigation; Employment Litigation; Class Action; Shareholder Derivative Claims. ***Email:*** rkessler@hkgold.com

JOHN A. GOLDSTEIN, born Chicago, Illinois, July 27, 1959; admitted to bar, 1984, Illinois and U.S. District Court, Northern District of Illinois. *Education:* Washington University (A.B., magna cum laude, 1981); Northwestern University (J.D., 1984). Phi Beta Kappa. *Member:* Chicago Mortgage Attorneys Association (Past President). ***PRACTICE AREAS:*** Real Estate Law; Secured Lending; Land Acquisitions; Land Sales; Real Estate Acquisitions; Real Estate Contracts; Real Estate Leasing; Real Estate Sales; Commercial Leasing; Lease Terminations; Office Leasing; Retail Leasing. ***Email:*** jgold@hkgold.com

RICK L. HINDMAND, born Lincoln, Nebraska, March 23, 1959; admitted to bar, 1986, Illinois, 1993, Pennsylvania. *Education:* Northwestern University (B.A., with honors, 1981); University of Michigan (J.D., cum laude, 1986). *Member:* Chicago Bar Association (Chair, Healthcare Law Committee, 2002-2003; Vice-Chair, Health Law Committee, 2001-2002; Member, Corporation and Business Law Committee); American Health Lawyers Association; Illinois State (Member, Health Care Section Council, 2005-2006) Bar Association; Illinois Association of Healthcare Attorneys. ***PRACTICE AREAS:*** Health Care; Physician Practices; Physicians Contracts; Business Law; Corporate Law. ***Email:*** hindmand@hkgold.com

RYANN WHALEN, born Chicago, Illinois, February 16, 1969; admitted to bar, 1993, Wisconsin and U.S. District Court, Eastern District of Wisconsin; 1995, Illinois and U.S. District Court, Northern District of Illinois. *Education:* University of Wisconsin-Madison (B.A., 1990); Marquette University (J.D., 1993). *Member:* Chicago Bar Association (Member, Probate Practice, Asset Protection and Trust Law Committees); State Bar of Wisconsin. ***PRACTICE AREAS:*** Estate Planning; Wills; Trust Law; Transfer Tax; Asset Protection Planning; Estate Administration; Guardianship. ***Email:*** rwhalen@hkgold.com

JAMES W. MARKS, born Camp LeJeune, North Carolina, October 27, 1956; admitted to bar, 1984, Colorado; 1987, Illinois; U.S. District Court, Northern District of Illinois and U.S. Court of Appeals, Seventh Circuit. *Education:* University of Chicago (B.A., with honors, 1979); Tulane University (J.D., cum laude, 1984). Order of the Coif. Tulane Merit Scholar. Articles Editor, The Maritime Lawyer, 1983-1984. Recent Article: Conflicts Credentialing: Hospitals and the Use of Financial Considerations to Make Medical Staffing Decisions, William Mitchell Law Review, Volume 31, Number 3, 2005. *Member:* Chicago, Illinois State and American Bar Associations; American Health Lawyer Association; American Society of Medical Association Counsel. ***PRACTICE AREAS:*** Trial Practice; Commercial Litigation; Health Care Litigation; Employment Litigation. ***Email:*** jmarks@hkgold.com

JAYME R. MATCHINSKI, born Elgin, Illinois, December 15, 1966; admitted to bar, 1992, Illinois. *Education:* Northern Michigan University (B.S., 1989); Valparaiso University School of Law (J.D., 1992). Recent Article: Conflicts Credentialing: Hospitals and the Use of Financial Considerations to Make Medical Staffing Decisions, William Mitchell Law Review, Volume 31, Number 3, 2005. *Member:* American Health Lawyers Association; Illinois Association of Healthcare Attorneys; Illinois State Bar Association. ***PRACTICE AREAS:*** Health Care Law; Corporate Law. ***Email:*** jmatchinski@hkgold.com

PAMELA MITCHELL BELYN, admitted to bar, 1999, Illinois. *Education:* Howard University (B.B.A., Finance, 1990); Case Western Reserve University (J.D., 1999). *Member:* Chicago, Illinois State and American Bar Associations. ***PRACTICE AREAS:*** Corporate Law; Health Care Law; Taxation; Employment Law; Employer Representation; Business Law. ***Email:*** pbelyn@hkgold.com

JASMINE DE LA TORRE, born Chicago, Illinois, March 6, 1972; admitted to bar, 1998, Illinois. *Education:* University of Illinois at Chicago (B.A., 1994); University of Illinois at Champaign (J.D., magna cum laude, 1998). ***LANGUAGES:*** Serbian and Spanish. ***REPORTED CASES:*** Corwin v. Abbott, 353 11 App.3d 848, appeal denied 2005 Ill Lexis 609 (Mar 30, 2005); Lake County Riverboat v. Illinois Gaming Board, 332 811 App.3d 127 (1st Dist, 2002). ***PRACTICE AREAS:*** Commercial Litigation; Appellate Practice; Health Care Litigation; Restrictive Covenant Enforcement; Contract; Corporate Governance; Directors and Officers Liability. ***Email:*** jdelatorre@hkgold.com

TODD L. ERDMAN, born Kansas City, Missouri, May 29, 1973; admitted to bar, 1998, Illinois. *Education:* Bradley University (B.S., cum laude, Political Science, 1995); DePaul University (J.D., 1998). Pi Gamma Mu. Order of Omega. Recipient, CALI Excellence for the Future Award. Author: DePaul Journal of Art and Entertainment, Fall 1997, Volume III. Formerly with: Handler Trayer & Duggan, LLC, 1999-2003; Daniel M. Greenberg Chtd., 1998-1999. *Member:* Chicago and Illinois State Bar Associations. ***PRACTICE AREAS:*** Real Estate; Land Acquisitions; Land Sales; Real Estate Acquisitions; Real Estate Contracts; Real Estate Leasing; Real Estate Sales; Commercial Leasing; Office Leasing; Retail Leasing; Corporate Law. ***Email:*** terdman@hkgold.com

ALAN D. LEIB, born Chicago, Illinois, July 11, 1962; admitted to bar, 1987, Illinois. *Education:* University of Illinois (B.S., with high honors, 1984; J.D., 1987). Dean's List. Certified Public Accountant, Illinois, 1984. *Member:* American Bar Association. ***PRACTICE AREAS:*** Corporate Law; Corporate Finance; Estate Planning. ***Email:*** aleib@hkgold.com

BEATRIZ M. OLIVERA, born Chicago, Illinois, March 22, 1956; admitted to bar, 1980, California; 1987, Illinois; 1991, U.S. District Court, Northern District of Illinois and U.S. District Court, Northern, Central and Southern Districts of California. *Education:* Northwestern University (B.A., 1977); University of Michigan (J.D., 1980). Arbitrator: National Association of Securities Dealers; Cook County Mandatory Program. *Member:* Chicago (Member, 1980—; Chair, Entertainment Law Committee, 1995-1996), Illinois State and American Bar Associations. ***LANGUAGES:*** Spanish. ***PRACTICE AREAS:*** Business Litigation; Commercial Litigation; Insurance Coverage; Entertainment Law; Music Law; Employment Law; Probate Litigation; Trust Litigation. ***Email:*** bolivera@hkgold.com

HARRISON & HELD, LLP

Established in 2003
333 W. WACKER DRIVE, SUITE 950
CHICAGO, ILLINOIS 60606
Telephone: 312-332-1111
Fax: 312-332-1150
URL: http://www.harrisonheld.com

Trust Litigation, Estate Planning, Probate, Employment Discrimination, Commercial Dispute Litigation, General Litigation, Nonprofit Corporations, Guardianship, Premarital Agreements, Elder Law, Trusts and Estates.

LOUIS S. HARRISON, born Evanston, Illinois, March 9, 1959; admitted to bar, 1984, Illinois. *Education:* Colgate University (B.A., magna cum laude, in Mathematics, 1981); Duke University (J.D., with high honors, 1984); University of Chicago (M.B.A., with honors, in Finance, 2002). Senior Editor, Duke-Alaska Law Review, 1983-1984. Adjunct Professor of Law, DePaul University Law School, Illinois Kent School of Law and Northwestern University (Estate and Gift Taxation, Estate Planning, Fiduciary Income Tax Planning). Experience as Expert Witness. Contributing Editor, Tax Companion (Dearborn Publishing, 1990-1996). Author of over 100 Published Articles and Speeches, including in Estate and Financial Planning Reporter, Commerce Clearing House; Estate Planning Taxes-The Magazine; Boston University Journal of Tax Law 30; DePaul Law Review; Journal of Taxation for Accountants; Syracuse Law Review; Tax Lawyer Journal of Partnership Taxation; The Journal of Taxation; Estates, Gifts and Trusts Journal; Journal of Asset Protection; Journal of Asset Protection, Federal Estate and Gift Tax Anthology; Massachusetts Law Review; Illinois Bar Journal; Pepperdine Law Review; Taxation for Lawyers; Probate and

(This Listing Continued)

HARRISON & HELD, LLP, Chicago—Continued

Property; Florida Bar Journal; South Carolina Lawyer; Michigan Bar Journal; Illinois Institute of Continuing Legal Education, 1997. *Member:* Chicago (Member, Federal Taxation Committee; Past Chairperson, Estate and Gift Tax Division; Member, Trust Law Committee), Illinois State and American Bar Associations; Chicago Estate Planning Council. Fellow, American College of Trust and Estate Counsel. ***PRACTICE AREAS:*** Trust Litigation; Federal Tax Controversies; Estate Planning; Business Planning. ***Email:*** LHarrison@harrisonheld.com

ROBERT S. HELD, born Roslyn Heights, New York, March 15, 1957; admitted to bar, 1996, Illinois. *Education:* State University of New York at Buffalo (B.A., 1980); Eastern New Mexico University (M.B.A., 1987); DePaul University (J.D., 1995). Co-Author: with Charles F. Newlin, "Hedging Death and Taxes," Trusts & Estates, Jan. 2004. Co-Author: with Louis S. Harrison, "Sham Transaction Doctrine," Trusts & Estates, Feb. 2003. Co-Author: with John M. Hughes, 'Handling Family Limited Partnerships and LLCs," Illinois Estate Administration, IICLE, 2003. Instructor, Certificate Program in Financial Planning, DePaul University. *Member:* Chicago (Former Chairman, Federal Taxation Committee), Illinois State and American Bar Associations. ***PRACTICE AREAS:*** Estates; Probate. ***Email:*** rheld@harrisonheld.com

EDWARD O. PACER, born Oak Park Illinois, April 23, 1962; admitted to bar, 1988, Illinois and U.S. District Court, Northern District of Illinois; 1991, Northern District of Illinois Trial Bar. *Education:* University of Dallas; University of Illinois (B.A., 1984); Loyola University (J.D., 1988). Partner, Williams, Montgomery & John Ltd., 1998-2002. Associate, Williams & Montgomery Ltd., 1993-1997. Assistant States Attorney, Cook County, Illinois, 1988-1993. ***PRACTICE AREAS:*** Trust Litigation; Employment Discrimination; Commercial Litigation; General Litigation; Arbitration. ***Email:*** epacer@harrisonheld.com

CHARLES F. NEWLIN, born Palestine, Illinois, November 18, 1953; admitted to bar, 1978, Illinois and U.S. District Court, Northern District of Illinois; 1980, U.S. Tax Court. *Education:* Illinois Wesleyan University (B.A., summa cum laude, 1975); Harvard University (J.D., cum laude, 1978). Partner, Mayer, Brown & Platt, 1985-1994. Partner, Sonnenschein, Nath & Rosenthal, 1994-2000. Partner, McGuire Woods LLP, 2000-2003. *Member:* Chicago Bar Association (Probate Practice Committee); Chicago Estate Planning Council. Fellow, American College of Trust and Estate Counsel (Elder Law Committee; Fiduciary Income Tax Committee). ***PRACTICE AREAS:*** Nonprofit Corporations; Guardianship; Premarital Agreements; Elder Law; Nonprofit Tax Law; Trusts and Estates. ***Email:*** mnewlin@harrisonheld.com

EMILY J. KUO, born Worcester, Massachusetts, February 1, 1973; admitted to bar, 1997, Illinois. *Education:* University of North Carolina at Chapel Hill (B.S., summa cum laude, with highest distinction, 1994); University of Chicago (J.D., 1997). Phi Beta Kappa. Comment Editor, The University of Chicago Legal Forum. Intern, Labor and Employment Division, Civil Actions Bureau, Cook County State's Attorney. Law Clerk for the Honorable Gordon J. Quist, U.S. District Court, Western District of Michigan. Author: Comment, "The Enforceability Gap of Covenants Not to Compete in Telecommuting Employment Relationships," The University of Chicago Legal Forum 565, 1996. Co-Author: with Louis S. Harrison, "Attorneys' Fees: An Assessment of the Current Standards for Fee Awards," Estate, Trust, and Guardianship Litigation, IICLE, 2002; "United States Estate (and Generation-Skipping Transfer) and Gift (and Generation-Skipping Transfer) Tax Returns," Illinois Estate Administration, IICLE, 2003. Associate, Lord, Bisssell & Brook, LLP, 1998-2003. *Member:* Chicago, Illinois State and American Bar Associations. ***PRACTICE AREAS:*** Estate Planning; Probate. ***Email:*** ekuo@harrisonheld.com

MICHAEL J. DURKIN, born Chicago, Illinois, April 25, 1958; admitted to bar, 1983, Illinois. *Education:* University of Illinois (B.S., 1980); DePaul University (J.D., 1983). Certified Public Accountant, 1982. ***PRACTICE AREAS:*** Trusts and Estates; Probate. ***Email:*** mdurkin@harrisonheld.com

GREGORY A. FREZADOS, born St. Louis, Missouri, November 16, 1968; admitted to bar, 1994, Illinois and U.S. District Court, Northern District of Illinois. *Education:* Middlebury College (B.A., 1990); Tulane University (J.D., 1994). *Member:* Chicago Bar Association (Member, Trust Law Committee; Young Lawyers' Section, Estate Planning Committee). ***PRACTICE AREAS:*** Trust Litigation; Estate Planning; Probate; Nonprofit Corporations; Guardianship; Real Estate; Trusts and Estates.

WILLIAM J. HARTE, LTD.

Established in 1960

SUITE 1100, 111 WEST WASHINGTON STREET
CHICAGO, ILLINOIS 60602
Telephone: 312-726-5015
Fax: 312-641-2455

Negligence, Tort, Chancery, Antitrust and Securities Law. Trials and Appeals. State and Local Taxation.

WILLIAM J. HARTE, born Chicago, Illinois, September 26, 1931; admitted to bar, 1959, Illinois; 1971, U.S. Supreme Court. *Education:* Loyola University and Quincy College (B.A., 1954); University of Notre Dame (J.D., 1959). Phi Alpha Delta. *Member:* Chicago, South Suburban, West Suburban, Illinois State, Federal and American Bar Associations; Women's Bar Association of Illinois; Celtic Legal Society of Chicago; Appellate Lawyers Association of Illinois (President, 1972); Illinois Trial Lawyers Association (President, 1975); The Association of Trial Lawyers of America. Fellow: American College of Trial Lawyers; International Academy of Trial Lawyers; American Board of Trial Advocates; American Academy of Appellate Lawyers. ***PRACTICE AREAS:*** Negligence; Tort; Chancery; Securities; Trial; Appeals; Tax.

ERIK D. GRUBER, born Seattle, Washington, April 21, 1962; admitted to bar, 1988, Illinois. *Education:* Boston University (B.A., 1984); University of Illinois (J.D., 1988). Phi Alpha Delta. *Member:* Illinois State Bar Association; Illinois Trial Lawyers Association; The Association of Trial Lawyers of America. ***PRACTICE AREAS:*** Negligence; Tort; Chancery; Trial Practice; Appeals; Tax; Professional Discipline.

DANA M. PESHA, born Chicago, Illinois, August 4, 1978; admitted to bar, 2003, Illinois. *Education:* Bradley University (B.S., 2000); John Marshall Law School (J.D., 2003). ***PRACTICE AREAS:*** Negligence; Torts; Professional Discipline; Trial Practice; Appellate Practice.

OF COUNSEL

DAVID J. WALKER, born Evergreen Park, Illinois, December 5, 1939; admitted to bar, 1980, Illinois. *Education:* St. Mary of the Lake (M.A., 1964); Loyola University (LL.D., 1980). *Member:* Chicago, Illinois State and American Bar Associations; Illinois Trial Lawyers Association; Appellate Lawyers Association of Illinois; Association of Professional Responsibility Lawyers.

THE HEALY LAW FIRM

111 WEST WASHINGTON STREET, SUITE 1425
CHICAGO, ILLINOIS 60602
Telephone: 312-977-0100; 1-800-922-4500
Fax: 312-977-0795
URL: http://www.healylawfirm.com

Personal Injury, Wrongful Death, Products Liability, Bus Accidents, SUV Rollover, Crashworthiness, Automotive Defects, Defective Tires, Defective Airbags, Defective Seatbelts, Defective Restraints, Roof Crush, Quadriplegia, Paraplegia, Brain Injury, Brain Trauma, Spinal Injury, Traumatic Brain Injury, Medical Malpractice, Airplane Crashes, Automobile Accidents, Railroad, Trucking and Construction Injuries, Workers Compensation.

FIRM PROFILE: The Healy Law Firm is a dynamic, aggressive firm which has a record of getting exceptionally favorable results in difficult, complex cases.

MARTIN J. HEALY, JR., born Chicago, Illinois, March 2, 1944; admitted to bar, 1968, Illinois; U.S. District Court, Northern District of Illinois, including Trial Bar; U.S. Court of Appeals, Seventh Circuit; U.S. Supreme Court. *Education:* University of Notre Dame (B.A.); Loyola University (J.D.). Associate Editor, Law Review, Loyola University School of Law. Recipient: Law Alumni Scholar; Judge Geary Scholar. Law Clerk, Supreme Court of Illinois. Counsel, Democratic Leadership, Illinois House of Representatives. Associate, James A. Dooley Associates. Chief of General Counsel Division and First Assistant Corporation Counsel, Corporation Counsel's Office, City of Chicago. Chairperson, Illinois Supreme Court Rules Committee, 2004—. Member, Supreme Court Committee, Civil Pattern Jury Instructions. Commissioner, Illinois Supreme Court Committee on Character and Fitness. Author: "Scope of the Discovery of Documents is Significantly Enlarged," 55 Illinois Bar Journal 530; "Intersectional Collisions," Illinois Institute for Continuing Legal Education, 1983, 1985, 1987, 1994, 1997-2001; "Sunshine is Vital to Public Safety," Illinois Bar Journal, March 2004; "A Trial Lawyer's Introduction to SUV Rollover Claims," Illinois Bar Journal, December, 2001; "Silent Killer on the Highway," Trial ATLA, August, 2000; "A Voyage of Discovery," Trial Journal, ITLA, Spring 1999. Moderator: "Insurance Law: Insights and Update"; "Update and Review Seminar"; "More Than an Evidence Seminar"; "Persuasion at Trial"; "Point/Counterpoint," Illinois Trial Lawyers Association. Lecturer: Chicago Bar Association; Illinois State Bar Association; Illinois Trial Lawyers Association; Illinois Institute of Continuing Legal Education; National Institute of Municipal Law Officers. Board of Directors: Chicago National Bank, Chicago, Illinois; Edens Bank, Wilmette, Illinois; Plaza Bank, Norridge, Illinois. President Chairman of the Board, Irish Fellowship Club of Chicago. Director, St. Patrick's Day Parade Committee of Chicago. Vice President, Board of Governors, Loyola University School of Law. *Member:* Chicago Bar Association (Chair, Tort Litigation Committee; Chair and Moderator, Tort Litigation Annual Seminars; Lecturer, Young Members Section); and Illinois State Bar Association (Chair, Tort Law Section Council; Assembly Delegate; Chair, Young Members Speakers Committee); Illinois Trial Lawyers Association (President, 1998-1999; President-Elect, 1997-1998; 2nd Vice President, 1996-1997; Third Vice-President, 1995-1996; Parliamentarian, 1994-1995; Secretary, 1993-1994; Treasurer, 1992-1993; Chairman, Legislative Committee, 1992-1995; Member, Executive Committee, 1993—; Seminar Planning Chair); The Association of Trial Lawyers of America (Executive Committee, 2005—; Board of Governors, 2002—; President's Club, 2002—; Chair, Truck Underride Litigation Group); Society of Trial Lawyers; American Board of Trial Advocates (Board of Directors); Celtic Legal Society of Chicago (First Vice President, 2001-2002; President, 2002-2003). (Certified as a Civil Trial Advocacy Specialist by the National Board of Trial Advocacy). ***PRACTICE AREAS:*** Personal Injury; Wrongful Death; Products Liability; Medical Malpractice; Truck Accidents; Railroad Accidents and Injuries; Aviation Accidents.

DANIEL B. MALONE, born Chicago, Illinois, July 11, 1957; admitted to bar, 1986, Illinois; U.S. District Court, Northern District of Illinois. *Education:* University of Illinois (B.A., 1979); DePaul University (J.D., 1986). Author: "Workers Compensation Trial Notebook," Chapter on Settlement Estates, Callaghan's Trial Practice Series, Chapter 9 on plaintiffs opening statements. *Member:* Chicago (Chairman, Tort Litigation Committee, 1992) and Illinois State Bar Associations (Council Member, New Tort Law Section, 2003-2004; Association of Trial Lawyers of America; Illinois Trial Lawyers Association (Co-Chairman, Product Liability Committee, 2000-2001; (Guest Lecturer: "Case Law Update," Products Liability Litigation Seminar; "Settlement Contracts" Workers Compensation Seminar). ***PRACTICE AREAS:*** Personal Injury; Wrongful Death; Products Liability; Medical Malpractice; Truck Accidents; Railroad Accidents; Workers Compensation. ***Email:*** dmalone@healylawfirm.com

J.T. TERENCE GEOGHEGAN, born Galway, Ireland, August 14, 1955; admitted to bar, 1993, Illinois; Solicitor, Ireland. *Education:* University College Galway (B.A., 1976); John Marshall Law School (J.D., 1992). Guest Speaker: Illinois Institute for Continuing Legal Education; Irish Law, Irish American Heritage Center. *Member:* Chicago and Illinois State Bar Associations; Association of Trial Lawyers of America; Illinois Trial Lawyers Association. ***PRACTICE AREAS:*** Personal Injury; Medical Malpractice. ***Email:*** jtgeoghegan@healylawfirm.com

(This Listing Continued)

JOHN P. SCANLON, born Chicago, Illinois, March 29, 1962; admitted to bar, 1990, Illinois and U.S. District Court, Northern District of Illinois. *Education:* Illinois Benedictine College (B.A., Honors, 1986); DePaul University (J.D., 1990). Member, DePaul Law Review. Author: "Hearing Loss Cases," Workers Compensation Notebook; "Tort Immunity Act Once Again A Shield At Construction Sites," Tort Trends, Vol. 33, No. 3; "Silent Killer on the Highway," Trial Magazine August 2000. Moderator, Lecturer, Author: "Tort Immunity Act - What Every Practitioner Should Know," ISBA Publication, May 2001. Moderator, Lecturer: "When a Walkway Becomes a Structural Work Act Support," Tort Trends, Illinois State Bar Association, April 1998; "Illinois Supreme Court Holds One Year Tort Immunity Act Limitations Apply to Medical Malpractice Actions," Tort Trends, Illinois State Bar Association, Volume 35 #2, March 2000; "Intersectional Collisions," Illinois Institute of Continuing Legal Education, Spring 2000. *Member:* Illinois State Bar Association (Chair, Tort Law Section, 2001); Illinois Trial Lawyers Association (Chair, Products Liability Section, 2004-2005). ***REPORTED CASES:*** Kaufman v. Illinois Institute of Technology, 314 Ill.App.3d 149, 731 N.E.2d 795 (1st dist 2000). ***PRACTICE AREAS:*** Personal Injury; Wrongful Death; Products Liability; Workers' Compensation. ***Email:*** jpscanlon@healylawfirm.com

ASSOCIATES

DAVID P. HUBER, born Illinois, November 12, 1968; admitted to bar, 1993, Illinois. *Education:* University of Illinois Champaign-Urbana (B.A., 1990); Loyola University (J.D., 1993). Co-author, "Intersectional Collisions," chapter in Proving Fault in Automobile Accidents. *Member:* Chicago, Illinois State and American Bar Associations; Illinois Trial Lawyers Association (Guest Lecturer: "Accident Reconstruction"); Association of Trial Lawyers of America. ***PRACTICE AREAS:*** Personal Injury; Wrongful Death; Products Liability; Medical Malpractice; Truck Accidents; Railroad Accidents and Injuries; Automotive Crashworthiness; Tire/Rim Mismatch. ***Email:*** dhuber@healylawfirm.com

KEVIN T. VEUGELER, born Evergreen Park, Illinois, February 25, 1971; admitted to bar, 1996, Illinois and U.S. District Court, Northern District of Illinois. *Education:* Northern Illinois University (B.A., honors, cum laude, 1993); University of Illinois at Champaign-Urbana (J.D., 1996). Lecturer: "Trials in our Current Culture," "Liens,"; "Construction Cases," Illinois Trial Lawyers Association; "Settlement Strategies," Illinois Institute for Continuing Legal Education; "Rules and Procedures," Illinois Uninsured and Underinsured Motorist Benefits, Illinois State Bar Association. Publication, "The Health Care Services Lien Act," Tort Trends, December 2003. *Member:* Chicago and Illinois State (Tort Law Section Council) Bar Associations; Illinois Trial Lawyers Association; Association of Trial Lawyers of America; Workers Compensation Lawyers Association. ***PRACTICE AREAS:*** Personal Injury; Workers' Compensation; Wrongful Death; Medical Malpractice; Construction; Truck Accidents. ***Email:*** kveugeler@healylawfirm.com

DIANA M. JACOB, born London, England, December 31, 1970; admitted to bar, 1997, Illinois and U.S. District Court, Northern District of Illinois. *Education:* Loyola University Chicago (B.S., honors, magna cum laude, 1992); IIT-Chicago Kent College of Law (J.D., 1996). *Member:* Chicago (Member, Young Lawyers Section Trial Techniques Committee) and Illinois State Bar Associations; Illinois Trial Lawyers Association (Member, Medical Negligence Committee); The Association of Trial Lawyers of America. ***LANGUAGES:*** Arabic. ***PRACTICE AREAS:*** Medical Malpractice. ***Email:*** djacob@healylawfirm.com

JACK CANNON, born Chicago, Illinois, November 16, 1963; admitted to bar, 1993, Illinois. *Education:* Loyola University (B.A., 1987); John Marshall Law School (J.D., 1993). *Member:* Illinois State Bar Association; Illinois Trial Lawyers Association; Association of Trial Lawyers of America; Workers Compensation Lawyers Association. ***PRACTICE AREAS:*** Personal Injury; Workers Compensation; Products Liability. ***Email:*** jcannon@healylawfirm.com

OF COUNSEL

TERRY SULLIVAN, born 1943; admitted to bar, 1968, Illinois; 1986, New York. *Education:* St. Josephs College (B.S., 1965); Loyola University (J.D., 1968). (Also Member, The Sullivan Firm, Rolling Meadows)

LAW OFFICES OF
IRA N. HELFGOT

Established in 1992

THREE FIRST NATIONAL PLAZA
70 WEST MADISON STREET, SUITE 3700
CHICAGO, ILLINOIS 60602
Telephone: 312-558-3013
Fax: 312-263-9104
Email: iralaw@aol.com

Commercial Litigation, Business Law, Contracts, Creditor's Rights, Civil Trial and Plaintiff's Professional Liability, Legal Malpractice, Commodities, Securities, Investments.

IRA N. HELFGOT, born Chicago, Illinois, June 24, 1956; admitted to bar, 1982, Illinois and U.S. District Court, Northern District of Illinois; 1986, U.S. District Court, Northern District of Illinois including Trial Bar. *Education:* Northern Illinois University (B.A., in Political Science, 1978); DePaul University (J.D., 1981). Mortar Board Society. Member, DePaul Law Review, 1979-1980. Author: "Notification Trumps Excess Carrier's Right to Recover," Chicago Daily Law Bulletin, March 2, 2001; "When Proceeds of The Sale of Homestead Property Are Not Exempt," Illinois Creditor's Bar Association, Sept./Oct. 2000; "Rematch: Fee Disputes v. Malpractice Actions," Chicago Daily Law Bulletin, August 25, 2000; "Law Unsettled On Excess Carrier's Right to Sue Counsel," Chicago Daily Law Bulletin, June 5, 2000; "Suing an Expert Witness for Professional Malpractice," Chicago Daily Law Bulletin, November 24, 1999; "Decision Stretches to Outer Limits of Attorney's Duty," Chicago Daily Bulletin, June 25, 1999; "No Lien Attaches to Award Against Attorneys," Chicago Daily Bulletin, March 7, 1999; "Plaintiff Wins Rare Summary Judgment," Chicago Daily Bulletin, November 4, 1998; "Obtaining Defendant's Credit Reports," Du Page County Bar Association Brief, November, 1998; "Land Trusts and Homesteads," Illinois Creditor's Bar Association Newsletter, August/September 1998; Breaking Up a Law Firm is Hard to Do," Chicago Daily Bulletin, May 13, 1998; "This Legal Bill Could Prove Costly for Attorney," Chicago Daily Law Bulletin, October 1, 1997; "Aiding, Abetting a Breach of Fiduciary Duty," Chicago Daily Law Bulletin, March 27, 1997; "One Bad Turn Deserves Guarded Action," Chicago Daily Law Bulletin, November 19, 1996; "Fight Against Fees Precludes Malpractice Action," Chicago Daily Law Bulletin, August 16, 1996; "Fee Forfeitures Hit Right Where It Hurts Most," Chicago Daily Law Bulletin, July 25, 1996; "Land Trusts and Homesteads," Chicago Daily Law Bulletin, Jan. 8, 1996; "Lawyers May Lack Protection from Punitive Damage Claims," Chicago Daily Law Bulletin, Nov. 21, 1994. Co-Author: "Attorney's Legal Liability, Duties to the Client: Defining the Standards of Care," Chapter 2, Ill. Inst. for CLE, Supp. 2005; "Attorney's Legal Liability, Duties to the Client: Defining the Standards of Care," Chapter 2, Ill. Inst. for CLE; "Chancery and Special Remedies, Specific Performance," Chapter 3, Ill. Inst. for CLE, Supp. 1989; "Advising Illinois Financial Institutions, Overview of the RICO Act as Applied to Financial Institutions," Chapter 18, Ill. Inst. for CLE; "Legal Checklists, Mortgaging Real Estate," Part 18, Checklist 18-3, Supp. 1985, with B. Becker, B. Savin & D. Becker; "Chancery & Special Remedies, Maxims of Equity," Chapter 15, Ill. Inst. for CLE, Supp. 1985; "A Guide to Foreclosure," 65 Chicago Bar Record 8, July-August, 1983; "Wolston v. Reader's Digest Association, Inc., A Chilling Effect on the Media's Privilege," 26 Decalogue Journal 16, Summer 1980. Associate, Braun & Rivkin, Ltd., 1987-1992. Lecturer: "Real Estate Levies," Illinois Credit Union League, October 1, 2004; "Real Estate Levies," Illinois Creditor's Bar Association, November 11, 2003. Life Member, National Registry of Who's Who. Arbitrator, Chicago Mercantile Exchange. *Member:* Illinois State Bar Association (Member, Committee on Judicial Evaluation, 1999-2002); Illinois Creditor's Bar Association (Member, Board Member at Large, 1998-1999; Director at Large, 2003-2005; Vice President, Education, 2004—). ***REPORTED CASES:*** C.A.M. Affiliates, Inc. v. First American Title Insurance Company, (Ill. App. 1 Dist., August 6, 1999 (No. 98-2039); Matter of Lake States Commodities, Inc., 936 F.Supp. 1461, Fcd. Sec. L. Rep. P 99,349, Comm. Fut. L. Rep. P 26,815 (N.D.Ill., Jul 24, 1996) (NO. 96 C 0587); Apostolou v. Geldermann, Inc., 919 F.Supp. 289, Comm. Fut. L. Rep. P 26,699 (N.D.Ill., Jan 25, 1996) (NO. 94 C 3876); Import Sales, Inc. v. Continental Bearings Corp., 217 Ill.App.3d 893, 577 N.E.2d 1205, 160 Ill.Dec 634 (Ill.App. 1 Dist., May 17, 1991) (NO. 1-89-1312); Gerill Corp. v. Jack L. Hargrove Builders, Inc., 128 Ill.2d 179, 538 N.E.2d 530, 131 Ill.Dec. 155 (Ill., Mar 29, 1989) (NO. 66788, 67035); Federal Sav. and Loan Ins. Corp. v. Transamerica Ins. Co., 705 F.Supp. 1328 (N.D.Ill., Jan 25, 1989) (NO. 87 C 6996); Toyomenka (America), Inc. v. Combined Metals Corp., 139 Ill.App.3d 654, 487 N.E.2d 1172, 94 Ill.Dec. 295, 42 UCC Rep.Serv. 1267 (Ill.App. 1 Dist., Dec 31, 1985) (NO. 84-0569).

(This Listing Continued)

HELLER AND FRISONE, LTD.

Established in 1973

33 NORTH LASALLE STREET, SUITE 1200
CHICAGO, ILLINOIS 60602
Telephone: 312-236-3644
Fax: 312-236-3595
Email: nick@hellerfrisone.com
Email: paul@hellerfrisone.com
URL: http://www.hellerandfrisone.com

Commercial and Consumer Collection Litigation.

FIRM PROFILE: Heller and Frisone, Ltd. provides commercial and consumer collection litigation and other services to hundreds of clients throughout the United States. We are skilled in all phases of collection, business and construction litigation and have effectively prosecuted and defended our clients in the Appellate and Supreme Court of Illinois.

The clients served by the firm represent a diverse group of industries, including insurance, construction, manufacturing, banks, finance companies, credit unions, health care providers, law and accounting firms and service organizations.

PAUL M. HELLER, born Chicago, Illinois, March 22, 1943; admitted to bar, 1968, Illinois; 1982, U.S. District Court, Northern District of Illinois including Trial Bar. *Education:* DePaul University; IIT/Chicago-Kent College of Law (LL.B., 1968). Graduate of Advanced Trial Technique. Author/Lecturer, "Collecting a Judgment," a National Business Institute seminar. Editor, "Trial Technique Revised," by Irving Goldstein and Fred Lane. Participating Attorney, Chicago Volunteer Legal Services Agency. Member, Panel of Arbitrators, American Arbitration Association. *Member:* Chicago, Illinois State and American Bar Associations; Commercial Law League of America; Decalogue Society of Lawyers; Association of Trial Lawyers of America; Illinois Trial Lawyers Association. ***PRACTICE AREAS:*** Commercial Litigation; Consumer Collections; Appellate Practice; Business Litigation; Bankruptcy; Mortgage Foreclosure. ***Email:*** pheller@enteract.com

NICHOLAS J. FRISONE, born Poughkeepsie, New York, March 12, 1958; admitted to bar, 1984, Illinois and U.S. District Court, Northern District of Illinois including Trial Bar; 1990, Massachusetts. *Education:* University of Maryland (B.A., 1980); John Marshall Law School (J.D., 1983). The Gavel Society. Associate Justice, Moot Court Executive Board, John Marshall Law School. Publication: Author/Lecturer, "Prelitigation Collection Procedures," a Lorman Education Services Seminar. *Member:* Chicago, Illinois State and American Bar Associations. ***PRACTICE AREAS:*** Commercial Litigation; Consumer Collections; Construction Litigation; Appellate Practice; Business Litigation; Bankruptcy; Mortgage Foreclosure.

JASON R. ZIEMANN, born Elgin, Illinois, July 28, 1975; admitted to bar, 2002, Illinois. *Education:* Bradley University (B.S., 1998); John Marshall Law School (J.D., 2002). Associate Justice, Moot Court Executive Board. Tutor, Minority Legal Education Resources. *Member:* Chicago, Illinois State and American Bar Associations.

REPRESENTATIVE CLIENTS: Bank of America; Budget Rent-A-Car; City of Chicago; Great American Finance Co.; Hartford Fire Insurance Co.; Jewel Food Stores; Manufacturer's Bank; North Shore Gas Co.; Peoples Energy Corp.; SBC; State Farm Insurance Co.; TCF Bank; Temple Federal Credit Union; Wells Fargo Financial Corp.; Choice Hotels Inc.

HENDERSON & LYMAN

175 WEST JACKSON BOULEVARD
SUITE 240
CHICAGO, ILLINOIS 60604
Telephone: 312-986-6960
Fax: 312-986-6961
Email: administrator@Henderson-Lyman.com
URL: http://www.henderson-lyman.com

New York, N.Y. Office: 152 West 57th Street, 18th Floor, 10019. Telephone: 212-957-4600.

Practice concentrated in Commodities, Securities, Corporate Transactions, Commercial and Residential Real Estate Development, Commercial Litigation and Transaction, Environmental Law and Estate Planning.

FIRM PROFILE: The firm is nationally recognized in the representation of futures and securities industry participants. The firm's practice concentrates in the representation of Commodities and Securities industry registrants, providing counsel in the areas of Litigation, Compliance, Registration, Disclosure, Business Organization and Transactional issues, as well as General Commercial and Corporate Litigation. The firm has offices in Chicago and New York.

MEMBERS OF FIRM

JEFFRY M. HENDERSON, born 1958; admitted to bar, 1985, Illinois, U.S. District Court, Norther District of Illinois including Trial Bar and U.S. Court of Appeals, Second, Seventh and Ninth Circuit. *Education:* St. Norbert College (B.A., 1981); John Marshall Law School (J.D., 1984); Chicago-Kent College of Law (LL.M., in Financial Services Law, 1993). Member, Futures Regulation Committee. ***Email:*** jhenderson@henderson-lyman.com

MARK M. LYMAN, born 1959; admitted to bar, 1985, Illinois. *Education:* Providence College (B.A., 1981); John Marshall Law School (J.D., 1984). Delta Theta Phi. ***Email:*** mlyman@henderson-lyman.com

JOSEPH A. GIRARDI, born 1946; admitted to bar, 1972, Illinois and U.S. District Court, Northern District of Illinois including Trial Bar; 1988, U.S. District Court, Southern District of Illinois and U.S. Court of Appeals, Seventh Circuit. *Education:* University of Illinois (B.A., 1968); Chicago-Kent College of Law (J.D., with distinction, 1972). ***Email:*** jgirardi@henderson-lyman.com

DOUGLAS E. AREND, born 1958; admitted to bar, 1983, Illinois; 1984, U.S. Tax Court; 1991, New York and U.S. Seventh Circuit Court of Appeals; 1996, U.S. Supreme Court. *Education:* University of Michigan (A.B., 1980); University of Michigan Law School (J.D., 1983).

ROBERT CHRISTIE, born 1948; admitted to bar, 1995, Illinois and U.S. District Court, Northern District of Illinois; 1999, U.S. Tax Court; 2002, U.S. Court of Appeals, Fourth and Seventh Circuits; 2003, U.S. Court of Appeals, Ninth Circuit; 2004, U.S. District Court, Southern District of Texas; 2005, U.S. District Court, District of Colorado and U.S. District Court, Northern District of Texas. *Education:* Kansas State University (B.S.C.S., B.S.B.A., 1972); DePaul University School of Law (J.D., 1995). Editor-in-Chief, DePaul Business Law Journal. ***Email:*** rchristie@henderson-lyman.com

ASSOCIATES

ANTHONY A. CAVALLO
RYAN FOX
BRIAN E. LEWIS
KURT NEWSOM
MICHAEL D. SEFTON
SCOTT P. SLYKAS
ANDREA STULGIES-CLAUSS

HENNESSY & ROACH, P.C.

Established in 1996
MARQUETT BUILDING
140 S. DEARBORN STREET, SUITE 520
CHICAGO, ILLINOIS 60603
Telephone: 312-346-5310
Fax: 312-346-5330
Email: hennroach@hennessyroach.com
URL: http://www.hennessyroach.com

St. Louis, Missouri Office: 720 Olive Street, Suite 2222, 63101. Telephone: 314-231-0770. Fax: 314-231-0990.
Springfield, Illinois Office: 2501 Chatham Road, Suite 220, 62704. Telephone: 217-726-0037. Fax 217-726-0137.

Workers Compensation Defense, including litigation, mediation and arbitration; Liability Defense, including insurance defense, construction accidents, post-structured work act; Employer Liability, retaliatory discharge; Premises Liability, industrial machinery, auto and truck, consumer products; Insurance Coverage, Transportation, Property Damage, Fire Loss, Motor Vehicle Accidents, Industrial Accidents; Civil, State and Federal Appeals, Industrial Commission Appeals.

FIRM PROFILE: Hennessy & Roach, P.C. is Chicago based general practice law firm with additional offices in Springfield and St. Louis, Missouri. The firm handles matters throughout the State of Illinois and Missouri. Founded by Thomas G. Hennessy and James P. Roach on May 17, 1993, the firm continues to grow and flourish through its dedication to some core philosophies.

(This Listing Continued)

First, the firm concedes that the Chicago/Springfield/St. Louis legal market are very competitive. To thrive in these areas, we seek to provide the most efficient and cost-effective legal services in the industry by stressing service inclusive of regular and timely reporting and unparalleled accessibility. The era of the attorney on a pedestal making every decision necessary on a claim without regular and detailed consultation with the client is an anachronism. A law firm is only one of many vendors a client retains in defending its claims. Therefore, a law firm should be held to the same high standards of service demanded of other vendors. At Hennessy & Roach we strive for and attain that ideal.

Second, the firm does not follow a single defense philosophy. Nobody can know our client's business as well as our client. Therefore, it is impractical for a law firm with a diverse clientele such as Hennessy & Roach to dictate to a single philosophy to all clients in the defense of claims. Instead, we communicate extensively to ascertain each client's individual defense philosophy, and we strive to uncover the reasons behind that philosophy. In this way, we can work with each client to resolve each claim as consistently as possible within each client's expectations.

Third, the attorneys at Hennessy & Roach take the label "Counselors at Law" seriously. We do not dictate strategies and decisions on claims to our clients. Instead, we ensure that our clients are extensively informed of all relevant facts and law impacting any decisions which need to be made on a claim. Additionally, we ensure that our clients are aware of all their options when making decisions. The ultimate decision, however, is always left up to the client after extensive consultation with the firm.

Fourth, our firm advocates a relationship with our clients that goes beyond simply working on claims. Each attorney is available to discuss legal issues or to provide an initial evaluation by phone on any claim regardless of whether the claim has been referred to our office. We are available to provide seminars on a variety of issues to all of our clients.

Fifth, Hennessy & Roach stresses flexibility to meet the needs and demands of our clients. The size of our firm facilitates easy adaptation to those needs and demands. Our client's requests can be dealt with immediately since we do not have to take any client issues to committee. Our energies are expended in complying with client requests, not in meetings discussing those requests. Unlike some larger and older law firms, Hennessy & Roach is not mired in its own bureaucracy when serving the client's needs.

Sixth, the firm is committed to low file loads. If a defense attorney has an excessive amount of work to complete, he or she cannot provide the type of unsurpassed service that Hennessy & Roach strives to provide. The simple solution to this problem is manageable file counts for each attorney. Actions, however, speak louder than words, and our history speaks volumes-each time file loads have risen to a level where service to our clients could suffer, we have added a qualified attorney. This ensures that the level of unsurpassed legal services continues uninterrupted.

Lastly, a law firm is only as good as the people it employs. We have worked diligently since the firm's inception to assemble a team of smart, experienced and hardworking attorneys that share the philosophies discussed above. The firm is acutely aware that while we hope the name Hennessy & Roach evokes a positive image in the claims community, it is the attorneys behind the name that truly make the firm.

MANAGING PARTNERS

THOMAS G. HENNESSY, admitted to bar, 1988, Illinois; 1989, U.S. District Court, Northern District of Illinois. *Education:* Illinois State University (B.S., 1984); John Marshall Law School (J.D., 1988). ***PRACTICE AREAS:*** Workers Compensation; Insurance Defense; Labor and Employment; Construction Law. ***Email:*** thennessy@hennessyroach.com

JAMES P. ROACH, II, admitted to bar, 1990, Illinois and U.S. District Court, Northern District of Illinois. *Education:* University of Illinois (B.A., 1987; J.D., 1990). ***PRACTICE AREAS:*** Workers Compensation; Insurance Defense; Labor and Employment; Construction Law. ***Email:*** jroach@hennessyroach.com

GUY N. MARAS, admitted to bar, 1995, Illinois. *Education:* Marquette University (B.A., 1987); DePaul University (M.S., Public Policy, 1991); John Marshall Law School (J.D., 1995). ***PRACTICE AREAS:*** Workers Compensation; Insurance Defense; Labor and Employment; Construction Law. ***Email:*** gmaras@hennessyroach.com

PARTNERS

JOSEPH J. HIGGINS, admitted to bar, 1989, Illinois and U.S. District Court, Northern District of Illinois. *Education:* University of Florida (B.A., 1983); John Marshall Law School (J.D., 1989). ***PRACTICE AREAS:*** Workers Compensation; Insurance Defense; Labor and Employment; Construction Law. ***Email:*** jhiggins@hennessyroach.com

EDWARD L. HENNESSY, admitted to bar, 1994, Illinois and U.S. District Court, Northern District of Illinois. *Education:* Northern Illinois University (B.A., 1989; Graduate Degree in Management, 1991); Thomas M. Cooley Law School (J.D.; 1994). ***PRACTICE AREAS:*** Workers Compensation; Insurance Defense; Labor and Employment; Construction Law. ***Email:*** ehennessy@hennessyroach.com

MICHAEL P. GEARY, admitted to bar, 1995, Illinois and U.S. District Court, Northern District of Illinois. *Education:* Miami University (B.A., 1992); Wake Forest University (J.D., 1995). ***PRACTICE AREAS:*** Workers Compensation; Industrial Insurance; Labor and Employment; Construction Law. ***Email:*** geary@hennessyroach.com

JOSEPH A. ZWICK, admitted to bar, 1990, Illinois. *Education:* Loyola University (B.S., Psychology, 1987); John Marshall Law School (J.D., 1990). ***PRACTICE AREAS:*** Workers Compensation; Industrial Insurance; Insurance Defense; Labor and Employment; Construction Law. ***Email:*** jzwick@hennessyroach.com

MARY ANNE H. CAPRON, admitted to bar, 1982, Illinois; U.S. District Court, Northern District of Illinois including Trial Bar; d U.S. Court of Appeals, Seventh Circuit and U.S. Supreme Court. *Education:* University of Illinois at Champaign-Urbana (B.A., Political Science, summa cum laude, 1979); DePaul University College of Law (J.D., with

(This Listing Continued)

honors, 1982). ***PRACTICE AREAS:*** Civil Practice; Insurance Defense; Labor and Employment; Medical Malpractice; Transportation; Torts. ***Email:*** mcapron@hennessyroach.com

SHERYL R. LAPKA, admitted to bar, 1997, Illinois. *Education:* University of Illinois, Chicago (B.A., Criminal Justice, 1994); Chicago-Kent College of Law (J.D., 1997). ***PRACTICE AREAS:*** Workers Compensation; Insurance Defense; Labor and Employment; Construction Law. ***Email:*** slapka@hennessyroach.com

WILLIAM J. HAWKINS, admitted to bar, 1985, Illinois and U.S. District Court, Northern District of Illinois; 1987, U.S. Tax Court. *Education:* University of Illinois (B.S., 1982); John Marshall Law School (J.D., 1985). ***PRACTICE AREAS:*** Advertising and Marketing; Aged and Aging; Agency and Distributorships; Alternative Dispute Resolution; Antitrust and Trade Regulation; Asset Protection; Bankruptcy; Banks and Banking; Business Law; Chancery and Equity; Commercial Law; Commodities; Contracts; Corporate Law; Debtor and Creditor; Equipment Finance and Leasing; Fidelity and Surety; Finance; Franchises and Franchising; Internet Law; Investments; Leases and Leasing; Divestitures; Mortgages; Partnership Law; Probate; Property Law; Public Finance; Real Estate; Securities; Taxation; Trusts and Estates; Wills; Zoning, Planning and Land Use. ***Email:*** whawkins@hennessyroach.com

JAMES L. CLARKE, admitted to bar, 1988, Illinois. *Education:* Illinois State University (B.S., Political Science, 1982); John Marshall Law School (J.D., 1988). ***PRACTICE AREAS:*** Civil Practice; Insurance Defense; Labor and Employment; Medical Malpractice; Transportation; Torts. ***Email:*** jclarke@hennessyroach.com

---

JOHN C. WILSON, admitted to bar, 1978, Illinois. *Education:* Valparaiso University (B.A., 1973); John Marshall Law School (J.D., 1978). ***PRACTICE AREAS:*** Workers Compensation; Insurance Defense; Labor and Employment; Construction Law. ***Email:*** jwilson@hennessyroach.com

NATALIE J. ROMO, admitted to bar, 2000, Illinois. *Education:* University of Illinois (B.A., 1996; J.D., 1999). ***PRACTICE AREAS:*** Workers Compensation; Insurance Defense; Labor and Employment; Construction Law. ***Email:*** nromo@hennessyroach.com

THOMAS C. FLAHERTY, admitted to bar, 1999, Illinois. *Education:* University of Illinois (B.S., 1994); Valparaiso University (J.D., 1999). [With Illinois Army National Guard, 1988-1994]. ***PRACTICE AREAS:*** Workers Compensation; Insurance Defense; Labor and Employment; Construction Law. ***Email:*** tflaherty@hennessyroach.com

JASON D. KOLECKE, admitted to bar, 2001, Illinois. *Education:* Marquette University (B.S., Criminology and Sociology, 1996); John Marshall Law School (J.D., 2001). ***REPORTED CASES:*** John Carl v. J.W. Trenching (98 WC 30356); Thomas Rieck v. Professional Plumbing (01 WC 30356); John Klein v. Klein Construction (00 WC 58441); Mary Krzeckowski v. B-Way (04 WC 9959). ***PRACTICE AREAS:*** Workers Compensation; Insurance Defense; Labor and Employment; Construction Law. ***Email:*** jkolecke@hennessyroach.com

LAURA D. HRUBEC, admitted to bar, 2002, Illinois. *Education:* North Central College (B.S., Political Science, cum laude, 1998); DePaul University College of Law (J.D., 2002). ***REPORTED CASES:*** Renee Neely v. Caritas. ***PRACTICE AREAS:*** Workers Compensation; Insurance Defense; Labor and Employment; Construction Law. ***Email:*** lhrubec@hennessyroach.com

CHRISTOPHER S. CRAWFORD, admitted to bar, 1999, Illinois, U.S. District Court, Northern and Central Districts of Illinois, U.S. District Court, Northern District of Indiana and U.S. District Court, Western District of Michigan. *Education:* University of Illinois (B.S., Agriculture, 1995); Drake University Law School (J.D., 1998). ***REPORTED CASES:*** Hatton v. United Parcel Service, Victor McIntosh, Madison County, 01 LM 1310; Chaney v. Shiraki, Cook County, 03 L 001155. ***PRACTICE AREAS:*** Civil Practice; Insurance Defense; Labor and Employment; Medical Malpractice; Transportation; Torts. ***Email:*** ccrawford@hennessyroach.com

LISA R. ROZEN, admitted to bar, 2002, Illinois. *Education:* University of Wisconsin at Madison (B.A., Sociology, 1998); University of Florida (J.D., 2001). ***PRACTICE AREAS:*** Workers Compensation; Insurance Defense; Labor and Employment; Construction Law. ***Email:*** lrozen@hennessyroach.com

MARIA L. CAPPIELLO, admitted to bar, 2004, Illinois and U.S. District Court, Northern District of Illinois. *Education:* Hawaii Pacific University (B.A., Justice Administration, summa cum laude, 1999); Southern Illinois University School of Law (J.D., 2004). ***PRACTICE AREAS:*** Civil Practice; Insurance Defense; Labor and Employment; Medical Malpractice; Transportation; Torts. ***Email:*** mcappiello@hennessyroach.com

JAMES W. LOWRY, admitted to bar, 2004, Illinois; 2005, Wisconsin. *Education:* Texas Christian University (1999); Southern Illinois University School of Law (J.D., 2004). ***PRACTICE AREAS:*** Advertising and Marketing; Aged and Aging; Agency and Distributorships; Alternative Dispute Resolution; Antitrust and Trade Regulation; Asset Protection; Bankruptcy; Banks and Banking; Business Law; Chancery and Equity; Commercial Law; Commercial Real Estate; Commodities; Contracts; Corporate Law; Debtor and Creditor; Equipment Finance and Leasing; Fidelity and Surety; Finance; Franchises and Franchising; Internet Law; Investments; Leases and Leasing; Divestitures; Mortgages; Partnership Law; Probate; Property Law; Public Finance; Real Estate; Securities; Taxation; Trusts and Estates; Wills; Zoning, Planning and Land Use. ***Email:*** jlowry@hennessyroach.com

HEATHER L. BOYER, admitted to bar, 2003, Illinois and U.S. District Court, Northern District of Illinois. *Education:* Illinois State University (1999); The John Marshall Law School (J.D., 2003). ***PRACTICE AREAS:*** Workers Compensations; Insurance Defense; Labor and Employment; Construction Law. ***Email:*** hboyer@hennessyroach.com

OF COUNSEL

JOHN J. MURPHY, JR., admitted to bar, 1981, Illinois and U.S. District Court, Northern District of Illinois; 1991, U.S. Court of Appeals, Seventh Circuit; 1992, U.S. Supreme Court. *Education:* Loyola University (B.A., 1969; M.S.I.R., 1977); Illinois Institute of Technology/Chicago-Kent College of Law (J.D., with high honors, 1981). ***PRACTICE AREAS:*** Labor and Employment; Collective Bargaining; Unfair Labor Practices; Employment Discrimination. ***Email:*** jmurphy@hennessyroach.com

P. NEILL PETRONELLA, admitted to bar, 1964, Florida and U.S. District Court, Southern District of Florida; 1966, U.S. Court of Appeals, Fifth Circuit; 1968, Illinois; 1976, Massachusetts; 1979, U.S. District Court, Northern District of Indiana. *Education:* Indiana University (B.S., 1959); University of Miami School of Law (LL.B., 1964).

Languages: English, Spanish.

REPRESENTATIVE CLIENTS: Ace Hardware; Advance Transformer Company; Advantica/Denny's Restaurants; AmCOMP; American Home Products; Arkansas Best; Freightway, Inc.; Armstrong Tools; Autozone; Automobile Club of Southern California; Avis; Bank One; Borg Warner; Brach & Brock Confections; Brownyard Claims; Budget Rent A Car; Cambridge Integrated; Canteen Corporation; Cass Transport; Century Workers' Compensation; Chubb Insurance Company; Cherry Corporation; Celotex Corporation; City of Chicago - Department of Aviation; Clinton Electronics; CNA Insurance Company; Commonwealth Edison; Compass Group; Crawford & Company; Culligan; Cunningham Lindsey; Danville Metal Stamping; Dart Transit; Dominick's Finer Foods; Eagle Foods; Eagle Wings Industries, Inc.; ESIS; EMC Insurance Companies; Employer's Security Insurance; FCCI/Monroe Guaranty Insurance; Federal Mogul; Forest Preserve District of Cook County, Illinois; Frito-Lay, Inc.; GAB Robins; Gates McDonald; Great American Insurance; G&K Services, Inc.; Hendrickson Stamping; Interlake; Jewel Food Stores; Joslyn Corporation; Kelly Temporary Services; Kemper Insurance; Liberty International Canada; Liberty Mutual Insurance Co.; Lucent Technologies; Manufacturers Life Insurance; Company USA; Marshalls; Midwest Insurance Co.; Montgomery Ward; Nabisco; Nestle; USA, Norrell Temporary Services; Northrop Grumman; Omni Super Stores; OSI Corporation; Penske Truck Leasing; Plano Molding Corporation; Prime Trucking; Risk Enterprise; Rollins, Inc.; RSKCo.; Ryerson Tull, Inc.; SBC Ameritech; Schwan's Sales Corporation; Sedgwick CMS; Sentry Insurance; Southwest Airlines, Spartan Light Metal Products, Terminix, T.J. Maxx, Transport Corporation of America; Travelers Insurance Company; Unitrin Property & Casualty Ins.; Universal Underwriters; Walgreens; Ward North America, Inc.; Westfield Insurance Companies; White Way Sign; Witco Corporation; Yellow Freight Systems; Zenith Electronics; Zexel Corporation.

KENNETH A. HENRY

Established in 1987

120 WEST MADISON STREET, SUITE 600
CHICAGO, ILLINOIS 60602-4106
Telephone: 312-857-0100
Fax: 312-857-1157
URL: http://www.kahlaw.com
Email: khenry@kahlaw.com
URL: http://www.lawyers.com/kahlaw

Labor and Employment Law, OSHA, Wage and Hour Matters, Sexual Harassment, Employment Discrimination, Wrongful Termination, Union Management Relations, Real Estate, Commercial Real Estate, Residential Real Estate, Buying and Selling a House or Business, Bankruptcy, Chapter 7, Chapter 11, Corporate and Commercial Law, Litigation, Alternative Dispute Resolution, Mediation.

FIRM PROFILE: Mr. Henry has developed his practice to represent a wide range of clients. His clients base includes unions, Fortune 100 companies, small businesses and individuals. He is actively involved with arbitration and mediation.

KENNETH A. HENRY, born 1951; admitted to bar, 1976, Illinois; 1981, U.S. Supreme Court; 1982, Trial Bar, U.S. District Court, Northern District of Illinois, U.S. Court of Appeals, Seventh Circuit; 1984, U.S. Court of Appeals, Federal Circuit. *Education:* University of Wisconsin-Madison (B.S., 1972); Illinois Institute of Technology (J.D., 1976). Instructor: U.S. Department of Labor, Occupational Safety and Health Administration National Training Institute, 1978-1987; IIT/Chicago-Kent College of Law, 1983-1985. Trial Attorney, Office of the Solicitor, Region V, U.S. Department of Labor, Chicago, 1978-1985. Arbitrator, Labor, Employee Benefits and Commercial Panels, American Arbitration Association, 1982—. Arbitrator, Mandatory Arbitration Program, Circuit of Cook County, Illinois and Nineteenth Judicial Circuit, Lake County, Illinois, 1990—.

HICKEY, MELIA & ASSOCIATES

CHARTERED

Established in 1995

77 WEST WASHINGTON STREET, SUITE 800
CHICAGO, ILLINOIS 60602
Telephone: 312-422-9400
Fax: 312-422-9410
Email: Firm@hmklawfirm.com
URL: http://www.hmalawfirm.com

General, Civil Trial and Appellate Practice. Medical Malpractice, Commercial Litigation, Criminal, Casualty Litigation, Health Care and Hospital, Employment, Products Liability, Toxic Tort Law, Corporate Law and Estate Planning and Administration.

FIRM PROFILE: Hickey, Melia & Associates, Chartered practices primarily in the greater Chicago area, though it frequently represents clients in many jurisdictions. Each of the partners offers a diverse wealth of experience in negotiations, counseling and litigation. Practicing in a small "boutique" setting, the firm services large corporations, insurance companies, physician groups and family or individual businesses. The firm's trial and appellate practice spans the various state and federal courts and requires frequent appearances before administrative agencies, arbitration panels and ADR mediators. The firm also has extensive experience in the representation of individuals who have been the subject of criminal investigations or professional disciplinary proceedings.

RICHARD J. HICKEY, III, admitted to bar, 1980, Illinois; U.S. District Court Northern and Central Districts of Illinois including Trial Bar; U.S. Court of Appeals, Sixth and Seventh Circuits. *Education:* University of Illinois (B.A., Economics, magna cum laude, 1977); University of Illinois College of Law (J.D., cum laude, 1980). Phi Beta Kappa. Author: "Specific Defenses to Medical Malpractice Actions," IICLE, 1982 and subsequent

(This Listing Continued)

HICKEY, MELIA & ASSOCIATES, CHARTERED, Chicago—Continued

years; "Venue Motions and Strategies in Illinois State Courts," Lorman Business Publications, 1992, 1994; Global Instructor, Wildman, Harrold, Allen & Dixon, 1980-1995, Elected to Partnership, 1988, Chairman of Trial Practice Group, 1994-1995. *Member:* Chicago, Illinois State and American Bar Associations; Chicago Trial Lawyers Club; Society of Trial Lawyers. ***PRACTICE AREAS:*** Civil Litigation; Trial Practice; Employment Law; Business Transactions. ***Email:*** Hickey@hmklawfirm.com

EDWARD J. MELIA, admitted to bar, 1981, Illinois. *Education:* Northwestern University (B.S.J., with honors, 1976); Loyola University (J.D., 1981). Listed, Who's Who in American Law. Author: "Punitive Damages in Mass Tort Litigation: Can Overkill Be Avoided," 77 Ill. Bar J. 478, May, 1989. Contributing Editor: *Illinois Torts,* Matthew Bender; "Discovery in Medical Malpractice," Lorman Publications, 1993, 1994, 1995. Lecturer (CBA; ISBA; ABA; IICLE), in Trial Practice, Civil Procedure, Mass Tort Litigation, Medical Malpractice. Former Instructor, Loyola University School of Law. *Member:* Chicago, Illinois State (Member, Subcommittee to Review Constitutionality of the Illinois Judicial Reform Act, 1989; Elected Member, State Bar General Assembly, 1994) and American Bar Associations; Society of Trial Lawyers; American Board of Trial Advocates. ***PRACTICE AREAS:*** Medical Negligence; Health Care; Product Liability; Torts; Transportation. ***Email:*** Melia@hmklawfirm.com

---

CHRISTOPHER R. ZINK, admitted to bar, 1998, Illinois and U.S. District Court, Northern District of Illinois; 1999, U.S. Court of Appeals, Seventh Circuit; 2000, U.S. District Court, Central District of Illinois. *Education:* Carleton College (B.A., 1995); Loyola University (J.D., 1998). Recipient: The CALI Award for Outstanding Achievement in Corporations, Corporate Tax I, Legal Writing I and Legal Writing II. *Member:* Illinois State and American Bar Associations. ***PRACTICE AREAS:*** Medical Malpractice; Commercial Litigation. ***Email:*** zink@hmklawfirm.com

GABRIEL P. HARDY, admitted to bar, 1995, Illinois. *Education:* Bowling Green State University (1992); Case Western Reserve University (J.D., 1995). ***PRACTICE AREAS:*** Litigation; Medical Malpractice. ***Email:*** hardy@hmklawfirm.com

KELLY MAUREEN O'MALLEY, admitted to bar, 2000, Michigan; 2002, Illinois. *Education:* University of Michigan (B.A., 1995); Loyola University (J.D., 2000). Co-Editor, Children's Legal Rights Journal, 1999. *Member:* Illinois State and American Bar Associations. ***PRACTICE AREAS:*** Medical Malpractice; Commercial Litigation. ***Email:*** omalley@hmklawfirm.com

KRISTIN A. AHMADIAN, admitted to bar, 2004, Illinois and U.S. District Court, Northern District of Illinois. *Education:* Hope College, Holland, Michigan (B.A., 2001); John Marshall Law School (J.D., 2004). Staff Editor, The John Marshall Journal of Computer and Information Law, 2003-2004. Team Member, August A. Randigs Jr. National Products Liability Moot Court Competition, 2003. Author: "Is it Legal for a Physician to Receive Payment for Prescribing a Drug?," Virtual Mentor: Ethics Journal of the American Medical Association, Vol. 5, No.7 (July 2003). *Member:* Illinois State Bar Association, American Bar Associations. ***PRACTICE AREAS:*** Medical Malpractice; Insurance Defense; Litigation. ***Email:*** ahmadian@hmklawfirm.com

COUNSEL

DANIEL C. HOFERT, admitted to bar, 1985, Illinois; 1989, U.S. District Court, Northern, Central and Southern Districts of Illinois. *Education:* Elmhurst College (B.A., 1981); Chicago-Kent College of Law, Illinois Institute of Technology (J.D., 1985; LL.M., 2004). ***PRACTICE AREAS:*** Medical Malpractice; Health Care; Litigation.

HILFMAN, MARTIN & BARR, P.C.

Established in 1974

SUITE 1700
33 NORTH DEARBORN STREET
CHICAGO, ILLINOIS 60602
Telephone: 312-236-5207
Facsimile: 312-236-2321
URL: http://www.hfmblaw.com
URL: http://www.hfmb.com

Medical Malpractice, Legal Malpractice, Professional Negligence, Personal Injury, Airplane Crash Litigation, Automobile Accidents, Hospital Negligence, Automotive Products Liability, Wrongful Death, Railroad Accidents, Product Liability, Drug and Medical Device Litigation, Construction Injuries, General Negligence, Personal Injury, Workers Compensation and Commercial Litigation.

LOUIS HILFMAN, born Chicago, Illinois, October 24, 1943; admitted to bar, 1969, Illinois. *Education:* Michigan State University (B.S., 1965); John Marshall Law School (J.D., with high distinction, 1969). Member, Moot Court. Editor-in-Chief, John Marshall Journal of Practice and Procedure, 1968-1969. Instructor, Case Analysis and Introduction to the Study of Law, John Marshall Law School, 1970-1972. *Member:* Chicago (Member, Judicial Evaluation Committee, 1983-1990) and Illinois State Bar Associations; The Association of Trial Lawyers of America (Member, Birth Trauma Litigation Group); Illinois Trial Lawyers Association (Member, Board of Managers, 1988—; Executive Committee Member; Co-Chair, Medical Malpractice Committee, 1992-1995; Constitutional Challenge Committee, 1995—); Trial Lawyers for Public Justice. ***REPORTED CASES:*** Martinez v. Erickson (1989) 127 Ill. 2d. 112; Hernon v. Corrigan (1992) 149 Ill. 2d. 190; Dralle v. Ruder (1988) 124 Ill. 2d. 61. ***PRACTICE AREAS:*** Plaintiffs Personal Injury; Medical Negligence; Product Liability; Construction Accidents; Wrongful Death. ***Email:*** lhilfman@hfmb.com

WILLIAM F. MARTIN, born Evergreen Park, Illinois, August 6, 1958; admitted to bar, 1983, Illinois; 1984, U.S. District Court, Northern District of Illinois. *Education:* Marquette University (B.A., 1980); Loyola University (J.D., 1983). Author, "Trial Considerations: Burden of Proof, Motions in Living, Jury Instructions and Closing Arguments," Illinois Trial Lawyers Association, February 2000. Member, Illinois Attorney General Nursing Home Task Force, 1989. *Member:* Chicago and Illinois State Bar Associations; Illinois Trial Lawyers Association; The Association of Trial Lawyers of America. ***PRACTICE AREAS:*** Construction Accidents; Product Liability; Medical Negligence; Premises Liability; General Negligence. ***Email:*** wfmartin@hfmb.com

WILLIAM L. BARR, JR., born Indianapolis, Indiana, June 25, 1948; admitted to bar, 1976, Illinois and U.S. District Court, Northern District of Illinois including Trial Bar; 1987, U.S. Court of Appeals, Seventh Circuit; 1989, U.S. Supreme Court. *Education:* Brown University (A.B., 1970); John Marshall Law School (J.D., with distinction, 1976). Member, John Marshall Journal of Practice & Procedure Law Review, 1975-1976. *Member:* Chicago, Illinois State and American Bar Associations; Illinois Trial Lawyers Association; The Association of Trial Lawyers of America. ***PRACTICE AREAS:*** Plaintiffs Personal Injury; Litigation; Medical Negligence; Hospital Liability; Construction Accidents; Product Liability; Airplane Crash Litigation; Wrongful Death; Workers Compensation. ***Email:*** wlbarr@hfmb.com

PATRICK J. SULLIVAN, born Chicago, Illinois, October 8, 1943; admitted to bar, 1969, Illinois and U.S. District Court, Northern District of Illinois. *Education:* Villanova University (B.A., 1966); DePaul University (J.D., 1969). *Member:* Chicago Bar Association; Illinois Trial Lawyers Association; The Association of Trial Lawyers of America. ***PRACTICE AREAS:*** Personal Injury; Workers Compensation.

JAMES P. TUTAJ, born Milwaukee, Wisconsin, September 18, 1964; admitted to bar, 1993, Illinois. *Education:* Marquette University (B.A., 1987); John Marshall Law School (J.D., summa cum laude, 1993). *Member:* Illinois State Bar Association; Illinois Trial Lawyers Association. ***PRACTICE AREAS:*** Workers Compensation; Medical Malpractice; Personal Injury.

OF COUNSEL

PHILIP E. LANE, born Council Bluffs, Iowa, April 30, 1948; admitted to bar, 1997, Illinois. *Education:* University of Illinois (B.S., 1970); Northwestern University Medical School (M.D., 1974); Chicago-Kent College of Law (J.D., 1992). *Member:* Chicago, Illinois State and American Bar Associations. (Also Of Counsel, Hilfman, Fogel, Martin & Barr, P.C., Chicago, Illinois)

JERRY L. LAMBERT, admitted to bar, 1972, Illinois; 1980, Florida; 1983, District of Columbia. *Education:* Eastern Illinois University (B.S., 1962); Chicago-Kent College of Law (J.D., 1972). *Member:* The Florida Bar; The District of Columbia Bar. ***PRACTICE AREAS:*** Labor Law (50%); Personal Injury Law (20%); Real Estate (15%); Corporate Law (10%); Appellate Practice (5%).

HILL LAW OFFICES

211 EAST ONTARIO
SUITE 1225
CHICAGO, ILLINOIS 60611
Telephone: 312-640-6331
Fax: 312-640-6333
Email: deborahhill@msn.com

Commercial Real Estate Leasing and Transactions.

DEBORAH FISH HILL, born Joliet, Illinois, December 27, 1956; admitted to bar, 1981, Illinois. *Education:* University of Illinois (B.S., with high honors, 1978; J.D., 1981). Co-author: "Selecting and Effectively Using an Expert Witness," Business and Commercial Litigation, IICLE, 1988 Edition. Assistant Editor, Court of Appeals for the Federal Circuit Newsletter, 1983-1986. Editor-in-Chief, Illinois Bar Journal Recent Decisions, 1980-1981. Recipient, Rickert Award for Excellence in Writing, 1980-1981. Author: Casenote, "Constitutional Law/Parental Responsibility: Vanthour-nout v. Burge," Illinois Bar Journal, March, 1980. *Member:* Chicago, Illinois State and American Bar Associations. ***PRACTICE AREAS:*** Commercial Real Estate Leasing and Transactions. ***Email:*** deborahhill@msn.com

OF COUNSEL

GEORGE VERNON (Also Practicing Individually, Monroe, Wisconsin)

STANLEY L. HILL & ASSOCIATES, P.C.

10 SOUTH LA SALLE STREET, SUITE 1301
CHICAGO, ILLINOIS 60603
Telephone: 312-917-8888
Fax: 312-781-9401
Email: stanhill@megsinet.net
URL: http://www.stanleyhilllaw.com

Criminal Law, Felonies, Misdemeanors, Driving While Intoxicated, DUI, Assaults, Traffic Violations, Civil Litigation, Plaintiffs Personal Injury, Automobile Accidents, Truck Accidents, Wrongful Death, Municipal Law, School Law, Employment Law, Wrongful Termination, Harassment.

STANLEY L. HILL, admitted to bar, 1974, Illinois; 1975, U.S. District Court, Northern District of Illinois; 1979, U.S. Court of Appeals, Seventh Circuit. *Education:* Northwestern University (B.S. in Journalism, 1970); University of Michigan (J.D., 1973). Clinical Fellow, University of Chicago Law School, 1975-1977. Adjunct Professor/Lecturer, DePaul University College of Law, 1974-1985. General Counsel, Illinois School District 88, 1995-2003; Corporation Counsel, Village of Maywood, 1988-1997; Village Prosecutor, Village of Maywood, 1982-1997; Acting Director, University of Chicago Law School, Criminal Defense Consortium of Cook County, 1976-1977; Staff Attorney, University of

(This Listing Continued)

Chicago Law School, Woodlawn Criminal Defense Services, 1975-1976; Assistant State's Attorney, Office of Cook County State's Attorney, 1973-1975. President, Board of Directors, Ada S. McKinley Community Services, Inc., 2004— (Director, Board of Directors, 1996—). Commodore, Jackson Park Yacht Club, 2004— (Director, 1999—). Member, Maywood Chamber of Commerce, 1989—. Director, Board of Directors, Ancona School, 1990-1997. *Member:* Cook County and Illinois State Bar Associations. **Email:** stanhill@megsinet.net

HINSHAW & CULBERTSON LLP

Hinshaw & Culbertson LLP is an Illinois registered limited liability partnership that has elected to be governed by the Illinois Uniform Partnership Act (1997)

Established in 1934

222 NORTH LA SALLE STREET, SUITE 300
CHICAGO, ILLINOIS 60601-1081
Telephone: 312-704-3000
Facsimile: 312-704-3001
Telex: 880248
Email: kfox@hinshawlaw.com
URL: http://www.hinshawlaw.com

Other Office Locations: Appleton, Wisconsin; Belleville, Illinois; Boston, Massachusetts; Champaign, Illinois; Crystal Lake, Illinois; Edwardsville, Illinois; Fort Lauderdale, Florida; Jacksonville, Florida; Joliet, Illinois; Lisle, Illinois; Los Angeles, California; Miami, Florida; Milwaukee, Wisconsin; Minneapolis, Minnesota; New York, New York; Peoria, Illinois; Phoenix, Arizona; Portland, Oregon; Providence, Rhode Island; Rockford, Illinois; St. Louis, Missouri; San Francisco, California; Schererville, Indiana; Springfield, Illinois; Tampa, Florida; Waukegan, Illinois.

Appellate, Banking & Financing, Bankruptcy & Creditors' Rights, Class Action Litigation, Civil Rights Defense, Commercial Litigation, Corporate, Construction Law, Director & Officer Liability, Employee Benefits, Environmental, Fidelity & Surety, General Liability Litigation, Government, Health Care, Insurance Coverage, Insurance and Reinsurance, Labor & Employment, Legal Malpractice, Medical Malpractice, Mergers & Acquisitions, Municipal Liability, Personal Injury Defense, Public Law, Products Liability Litigation, Professional Liability, Regulatory, Real Estate, School Law, Securities, Taxation, Transportation, White Collar Crime and Workers' Compensation Defense.

FIRM PROFILE: Hinshaw & Culbertson LLP is a national AMLaw 200 firm with 425 lawyers in 27 offices coast-to-coast. The firm offers a full-service practice, with an emphasis in commercial and defense litigation, corporate, environmental, employment and construction law, as well as the representation of professionals in their liability and risk management matters.

Hinshaw provides services to a range of clients in financial services, construction, health care, not-for-profit, insurance, legal, manufacturing, real estate, transportation and other industries. Firm clients also include government agencies, municipalities and schools.

Hinshaw was founded in 1934. The firm is headquartered in Chicago, and maintains offices in 12 states: Arizona, California, Florida, Illinois, Indiana, Massachusetts, Minnesota, Missouri, New York, Oregon, Rhode Island and Wisconsin.

PARTNERS

LEO J. ATHAS, born Chicago, Illinois, August 18, 1943; admitted to bar, 1973, Illinois and U.S. District Court, Northern District of Illinois; 1978, U.S. Court of Appeals, Seventh Circuit. *Education:* University of Illinois (B.S., 1964); Illinois Institute of Technology, Chicago-Kent College of Law (J.D., 1969). General Counsel/Legal Advisor: Office of Superintendent of Public Education, 1973-1974; Illinois State Board of Education, 1974-1975. *Member:* Chicago and Illinois State (Chairman, School Law Committee, 1977-1978) Bar Associations. (Also at Lisle, Illinois Office). ***PRACTICE AREAS:*** School Law. **Email:** lathas@hinshawlaw.com

DAN L. BOHO, born Chicago, Illinois, September 18, 1952; admitted to bar, 1977, Illinois and U.S. District Court, Northern District of Illinois. *Education:* Loyola University (B.A., 1974; J.D., 1977). *Member:* Chicago, Illinois State (Past Assembly Member) and American Bar Associations; American Arbitration Association (Panel Member); Association of Defense Trial Attorneys; Federation of Insurance and Corporate Counsel; Defense Research Institute; Illinois Association of Defense Trial Counsel; Illinois Society of Trial Lawyers (Board Member); Trial Lawyers Club of Chicago (Past President); Polish American Association (Past Chairman of the Board); Japan America Society (Board Member); Travelers and Immigrants Aid (Board Member); Advocates Society. Fellow, American College of Trial Lawyers. ***PRACTICE AREAS:*** Commercial Litigation; Personal Injury Litigation; Construction Liability; Building Management Litigation; Products Liability Litigation; ADR/Mediation; National and Regional Litigation Programs. **Email:** dboho@hinshawlaw.com

STEVEN R. BONANNO, born Oswego, New York, September 21, 1966; admitted to bar, 1992, Illinois and U.S. District Court, Northern District of Illinois. *Education:* Alfred University (B.A., with honors, 1989); John Marshall Law School (J.D., with honors, 1992). Phi Kappa Phi; Alpha Lambda Delta. Executive Editor, John Marshall Law School Review, 1991-1992. *Member:* Illinois State Bar Association. ***PRACTICE AREAS:*** Transportation; Products Liability; Construction Litigation; Personal Injury; General Liability. **Email:** sbonanno@hinshawlaw.com

ROY M. BOSSEN, born Chicago, Illinois, July 28, 1951; admitted to bar, 1979, Illinois, Missouri and U.S. District Court, Western District of Missouri. *Education:* Boston University (B.L.S., magna cum laude, 1975); St. Louis University (M.H.A., 1979; J.D., 1979). Adjunct Professor, Legal Aspects of Health Administration, George Williams College, 1982-1985. Guest Lecturer, Illinois Institute of Technology/Kent College of Law, 1985. *Member:* Illinois State Bar Association; American Academy of Hospital Attorneys; Illinois Association of Health Care Attorneys (President, 2004). ***PRACTICE AREAS:*** Hospital Law; Health Care; Physician Groups; Managed Care; Corporate Law. **Email:** rbossen@hinshawlaw.com

(This Listing Continued)

THOMAS L. BROWNE, born Chicago, Illinois, May 13, 1949; admitted to bar, 1974, Illinois, including Trial Bar; U.S. District Court, Northern District of Illinois; U.S. Court of Appeals, Seventh Circuit. *Education:* Northwestern University (B.A., 1971); John Marshall Law School (J.D., with honors, 1974). Executive Editor, The John Marshall Journal of Practice and Procedure, 1973-1974. *Member:* Illinois State Bar Association; Defense Research Institute; Association of Professional Responsibility Lawyers. ***PRACTICE AREAS:*** Lawyers' civil liability, professional responsibility and risk management. **Email:** tbrowne@hinshawlaw.com

KEVIN JOSEPH BURKE, born Evanston, Illinois, September 5, 1956; admitted to bar, 1983, Illinois; 1985, U.S. District Court, Northern District of Illinois including Trial Bar. *Education:* Boston College (B.A., 1978); New England School of Law (J.D., 1982). Certified as a Mediator of Medical Legal Disputes through Loyola University Law School Health Law Center. *Member:* Illinois State Bar Association (Assembly Member, 1986-1995); Trial Lawyers Club of Chicago; Illinois Defense Counsel; Chicago Inn of Court; Defense Research Institute. Fellow: Illinois Bar Foundation; American Society of Law and Medicine. ***PRACTICE AREAS:*** General Litigation; Medical Malpractice; Commercial Litigation; ADR/Mediation. **Email:** kburke@hinshawlaw.com

LISA M. BURMAN, admitted to bar, 1989, Illinois. *Education:* Loyola University (B.S., 1986); Illinois Institute of Technology (J.D., 1989; LL.M. in Taxation, 1995). Recipient, American Jurisprudence Award in Personal Income Tax, Pension and Profit Sharing Plans and Securities Law. Certified Public Accountant, Illinois, 1986. *Member:* Chicago (Member, Employee Benefits Committee, 1992—; Chairman, 2003-2004) and American Bar Associations. ***PRACTICE AREAS:*** Employee Benefits; ERISA Litigation. **Email:** lburman@hinshawlaw.com

PETER H. CARLSON, born Chicago, Illinois, October 16, 1966; admitted to bar, 1991, Illinois; 1996, U.S. District Court, Northern District of Illinois. *Education:* Boston College (B.A., 1988); Illinois Institute of Technology-Chicago Kent College of Law (J.D., 1991). ***PRACTICE AREAS:*** Transportation; Construction Litigation; Personal Injury Litigation; General Liability Litigation; Commercial Litigation; Products Liability Litigation; Workers' Compensation Defense. **Email:** pcarlson@hinshawlaw.com

PAUL J. CHERNER, born Philadelphia, Pennsylvania, 1943; admitted to bar, 1968, Wisconsin; 1971, District of Columbia; 1972, U.S. Supreme Court; 1974, Illinois, including Trial Bar. *Education:* Temple University (B.S., 1965); University of Wisconsin-Madison (J.D., 1968). *Member:* Chicago, DuPage County and American Bar Associations; The District of Columbia Bar; State Bar of Wisconsin. [US Army Reserve, 1968-1974]. ***SPECIAL AGENCIES:*** National Labor Relations Board - former Trial Attorney and former Legal Assistant to NLRB Board Member John H. Fanning. ***PRACTICE AREAS:*** Labor and Employment. **Email:** pcherner@hinshawlaw.com

PAUL J. CLEMENTI, born Evanston, Illinois, April 3, 1966; admitted to bar, 1991, Wisconsin, Illinois, U.S. District Court, Northern District of Illinois, U.S. District Court, Eastern District of Wisconsin and U.S. Court of Appeals, Seventh Circuit. *Education:* University of Illinois (B.A., 1988); Marquette University School of Law (J.D., 1991). Recipient, Deans Award 1990, 1991. Recipient, University Leadership Award, 1991. Editor in Chief, Marquette University Law School Journal, 1990-1991. *Member:* American Bar Association (Member, Litigation Section); Justinian Society; Federal Trial Bar. ***PRACTICE AREAS:*** Commercial Litigation; Professional Liability Litigation; Products Liability Litigation; Employment Law. **Email:** pclementi@hinshawlaw.com

SHAWN P. CLIFFORD, born Evergreen Park, Illinois, May 27, 1958; admitted to bar, 1984, Illinois and U.S. District Court, Northern District of Illinois. *Education:* Boston College (B.A., magna cum laude, 1980); University of San Diego (J.D., 1984). Member, San Diego Law Review. *Member:* Illinois State Bar Association. ***PRACTICE AREAS:*** Civil Litigation; Medical Malpractice. **Email:** sclifford@hinshawlaw.com

WILLIAM J. CONNELLY, born Wilkes-Barre, Pennsylvania, May 25, 1954; admitted to bar, 1983, Illinois and U.S. District Court, Northern, Central and Eastern Districts of Illinois. *Education:* DePaul University (B.A., with highest honors, 1980; J.D., 1983). Phi Alpha Delta; Phi Alpha Theta. Intern, United States Environmental Protection Agency, Region V, Regional Counsel's Office, Chicago, Illinois, 1982. ***PRACTICE AREAS:*** Creditors Rights/Bankruptcy; Commercial Litigation. **Email:** wconnell@hinshawlaw.com

CLARE CONNOR RANALLI, born Danville, Illinois, July 23, 1960; admitted to bar, 1986, Illinois and U.S. District Court, Northern, Central and Eastern Districts of Illinois; U.S. District Court, Eastern District of Michigan; U.S. Court of Appeals, Seventh Circuit. *Education:* University of Illinois (B.A., with honors, 1982); DePaul University (J.D., with honors, 1986). Registered Lobbyist in the State of Illinois. Presentations: "Recoupment of Medicaid Payments by IDPA - What Doctors, Hospitals and Their Lawyers Need to Know," Illinois Association of Health Care Attorneys, 2002; "Finding the Right Person for the Right Job," Community Bankers Association of Illinois' Annual Convention, 2001; "Confidentiality of Medical Records in the Emergency Department," Emergency Nurses Association, 1998; "ERISA and Unique Claims," Hinshaw & Culbertson Insurance Symposium, 1997; "Confidentiality of Mental Health and HIV Treatment Records," multiple hospitals, 1996. *Member:* Illinois State and American Bar Associations; Illinois Association of Healthcare Attorneys; American Health Lawyers Association. ***PRACTICE AREAS:*** Corporate Health Care; Risk Management; Regulatory Counseling; Regulatory Litigation; Joint Ventures; Medicare Reimbursement; Privacy; Medical Staff Matters; Employment Law. **Email:** cranalli@hinshawlaw.com

DAVID R. CREAGH, born Chicago, Illinois, December 20, 1959; admitted to bar, 1985, Illinois and U.S. District Court, Northern District of Illinois. *Education:* University of Notre Dame (B.A., cum laude, 1982; J.D., cum laude, 1985). *Member:* Illinois State Bar Association; Illinois Association of Defense Trial Counsel; Trial Lawyers Club of Chicago. ***PRACTICE AREAS:*** Products Liability; Construction Law; Premises Liability. **Email:** dcreagh@hinshawlaw.com

ANDREW B. CRIPE, born Minneapolis, Minnesota, March 22, 1973; admitted to bar, 1997, Illinois and U.S. District Court, Northern District of Illinois. *Education:* University of Minnesota (B.A., 1994); Loyola University, Chicago (J.D., 1997). ***PRACTICE AREAS:*** Labor and Employment; Commercial Litigation. **Email:** acripe@hinshawlaw.com

JAMES G. CULBERTSON (1934-1969)

(This Listing Continued)

HINSHAW & CULBERTSON LLP, Chicago—Continued

KENT J. CUMMINGS, born Lake Charles, Louisiana, June 13, 1961; admitted to bar, 1993, Illinois and U.S. District Court, Northern District of Illinois; 1994, U.S. Court of Appeals, Seventh Circuit; 2000, U.S. District Court, Southern District of Illinois. *Education:* University of Maine (B.A., 1987); Loyola University (J.D., cum laude, 1993). ***PRACTICE AREAS:*** Insurance Services; Risk Management; Captive Insurance; Reinsurance Dispute Resolution; Insurance Coverage Litigation; Insurance Regulatory Representation and Compliance; Corporate Organization and Operation; Insurance Claim Administration and Excess Limits. ***Email:*** kcumming@hinshawlaw.com

MICHAEL J. CUNNINGHAM, born Pittsburgh, Pennsylvania, August 2, 1962; admitted to bar, 1990, Illinois. *Education:* Indiana University (B.S., 1984; J.D., cum laude, 1989). ***PRACTICE AREAS:*** Personal Injury Defense; Commercial Litigation. ***Email:*** mcunningham@hinshawlaw.com

STANLEY J. DAVIDSON, born Chicago, Illinois, October 22, 1946; admitted to bar, 1971, Illinois and U.S. District Court, Northern District of Illinois; 1973, U.S. Court of Appeals, Seventh Circuit; 1982, U.S. Supreme Court. *Education:* University of Illinois (B.A., with honors, 1968); Loyola University (J.D., 1971). Participant, National Moot Court Competition. Member, Loyola University Law Journal, 1969-1970. Associate Editor, Loyola University Law Journal, 1970-1971. Law Clerk to the Honorable Thomas J. Moran, Justice, Illinois Appellate Court, 2nd District, 1971-1973. *Member:* Illinois State Bar Association; Appellate Lawyers Association (Member, Board of Directors, 1978-1980; Treasurer, 1982-1983; Secretary, 1983-1984; Vice President, 1984-1985; President, 1985-1986); Decalogue Society of Lawyers; American Society of Hospital Attorneys; Defense Research Institute; Society of Trial Lawyers of Illinois; American Board of Trial Advocates. ***PRACTICE AREAS:*** Medical Malpractice; Health Care; Appeals. ***Email:*** sdavidson@hinshawlaw.com

AIMEE E. DELANEY, born Chicago Heights, Illinois, March 31, 1973; admitted to bar, 1998, Illinois; 2000, U.S. District Court, Northern District of Illinois; 2003, U.S. Court of Appeals, Seventh Circuit; 2005, U.S. District Court, Central District of Illinois. *Education:* University of Iowa (B.A., 1995); Loyola University (J.D., 1998). Senior Articles Editor, Consumer Law Review, 1997-1998. *Member:* American Bar Association; Illinois Defense Council. ***PRACTICE AREAS:*** Labor and Employment Litigation; Commercial Litigation. ***Email:*** adelaney@hinshawlaw.com

JOHN W. DUBBS, III, born Chicago, Illinois, July 2, 1951; admitted to bar, 1976, Illinois; 1977, Florida. *Education:* University of Illinois (B.S., with honors, 1973); Northwestern University (J.D., 1976); University of Chicago (M.B.A., 1981). Certified Public Accountant, Illinois, 1980. *Member:* The Florida Bar. ***PRACTICE AREAS:*** Mergers and Acquisitions; Taxation; Employee Benefits. ***Email:*** jdubbs@hinshawlaw.com

CARLTON D. FISHER, born Zanesville, Ohio, January 4, 1953; admitted to bar, 1978, Illinois; 1979, U.S. District Court, Northern District of Illinois including Trial Bar; 1981, U.S. Court of Military Appeals; 1991, U.S. Court of Appeals, Seventh Circuit. *Education:* University of Illinois (B.A., with high honors, 1975; J.D., 1978). Phi Beta Kappa; Omicron Delta Kappa; Phi Alpha Delta. Member: National Moot Court Team, 1977; Moot Court Board, 1977-1978. *Member:* American Bar Association; Defense Research Institute; Illinois Association of Defense Trial Counsel; Transportation Lawyers Association; Trucking Industry Defense Association. [Major, U.S. Marine Corps Reserve, J.A.D., 1979-1996]. ***PRACTICE AREAS:*** Transportation Law; Products Liability; Premises Liability; Commercial Litigation. ***Email:*** cfisher@hinshawlaw.com

LYNDON M. FLOSI, born Chicago, Illinois, July 25, 1960; admitted to bar, 1985, Illinois; 1990, U.S. District Court, Northern District of Illinois. *Education:* DePaul University (B.A., 1982); John Marshall Law School (J.D., 1985). *Member:* Illinois State Bar Association. ***LANGUAGES:*** Italian. ***PRACTICE AREAS:*** Personal Injury Law; Auto/Vehicular; Premises Liability; Products Liability. ***Email:*** lflosi@hinshawlaw.com

STEPHANIE R. GAINES, admitted to bar, 1995, Illinois and U.S. District Court, Northern District of Illinois. *Education:* Loyola University (B.S., Marketing); University of Iowa (M.B.A., J.D.). Adjunct Professor, Business Law, Governors State University. *Member:* American Bar Association (Member, Section on Labor & Employment); National Bar Association; Black Women Lawyers Association. ***PRACTICE AREAS:*** Employment Law; Commercial Litigation. ***Email:*** sgaines@hinshawlaw.com

THOMAS F. GING, born Pittsburgh, Pennsylvania, September 8, 1941; admitted to bar, 1966, Virginia and District of Columbia; 1970, Ohio, Illinois and U.S. District Court, Northern District of Illinois including Trial Bar, U.S. Court of Appeals, Seventh Circuit and U.S. Supreme Court; 1989, U.S. District Court, Eastern District of Wisconsin; 1990, U.S. Court of Appeals, Tenth Circuit; 1991, U.S. Federal Circuit Court of Appeals; 1997, U.S. Tax Court. *Education:* John Carroll University (A.B., magna cum laude, 1963); Georgetown University (J.D., 1966); George Washington University (LL.M., 1970). Speaker: "The Federal Trademark Dilution Act," Minnesota Institute of Legal Education, March 1998. *Member:* Chicago and American Bar Associations. [Capt., JAGC, U.S. Army, 1966-1970]. ***PRACTICE AREAS:*** Commercial Litigation; Intellectual Property Litigation and Counselling; Contracts; Hospital; Health Care Law; Transportation Law; Construction; Real Estate Litigation. ***Email:*** tging@hinshawlaw.com

ALAN I. GREENE, born Chicago, Illinois, February 20, 1945; admitted to bar, 1969, Illinois and U.S. District Court, Northern District of Illinois including Trial Bar; 1975, U.S. Court of Appeals, Ninth Circuit; 1981, U.S. Court of Appeals, Seventh Circuit; 1985, U.S. Court of Appeals, Second Circuit; 1996, U.S. District Court, Central District of Illinois; 1997, U.S. District Court, Eastern District of Wisconsin and U.S. Court of Appeals, Fifth Circuit; 2002, U.S. District Court, Western District of Michigan; 2003, U.S. Court of Appeals, Sixth Circuit; 2004, U.S. District Court, Western District of Wisconsin. *Education:* University of Wisconsin-Madison (B.B.A., with honors, 1966); Harvard Law School (J.D., 1969). Presenter on Damages and Expert Witnesses at Conferences for the National Association of Certified Valuation Analysts (NACVA), 1997, 1999, 2001, 2003 and 2004. *Member:* Chicago (Professional Responsibility and Judicial Evaluation Committees), Illinois State and American Bar Associations; National Association of Certified Valuation Analysts (Litigation Forensics Board). ***PRACTICE AREAS:*** Commercial Litigation; Employment Litigation; Antitrust and Trade Regulation; ADR/Mediation; Environmental Litigation; Insurance Coverage and ERISA Disputes. ***Email:*** agreene@hinshawlaw.com

(This Listing Continued)

EDMUND GRONKIEWICZ, born Chicago, Illinois, February 4, 1939; admitted to bar, 1965, Illinois and U.S. District Court, Northern District of Illinois; 1969, U.S. Court of Appeals, Seventh Circuit; 1971, U.S. Supreme Court. *Education:* Loyola University, Chicago (A.B., summa cum laude, 1961; M.A., magna cum laude, 1963; J.D., cum laude, 1965). Phi Alpha Delta; Blue Key; Phi Sigma Tau. Member: Advisory Board, St. Mary of Nazareth Hospital, 1969—; Legal Advisory Group, Central Administration, Orthodox Church in America, 1974-1990. Legal Consultant, Old Catholic Vicarate of Chicago, 1975-1990. Diocesan Counsel, Diocese of the Midwest, Orthodox Church in America, 1973-1990. Member: Catholic Archdiocese of Chicago, Archdiocesan Hospital Ethics Commission, 1985—; Equestrian Order of the Holy Sepulchre of Jerusalem; The Military and Hospitaller Order of St. Lazarus of Jerusalem; Knights of Malta, Federal Association; Constantinian Order of St. George. *Member:* West Suburban and Illinois State Bar Associations; Advocates Society; American Academy of Hospital Attorneys; American Society of Law and Medicine; American College of Legal Medicine (Associate in Law); Illinois Hospital Attorneys Association. ***PRACTICE AREAS:*** Health Care; Trusts and Estates. ***Email:*** egronkiewicz@hinshawlaw.com

THOMAS M. HAMILTON, JR., born Takoma Park, Maryland, February 26, 1944; admitted to bar, 1969, Indiana and U.S. District Court, Southern District of Indiana; 1971, Illinois and U.S. District Court, Northern District of Illinois including Trial Bar, 1982; 1993, U.S. District Court, Northern District of Illinois; U.S. Court of Appeals, Seventh Circuit. *Education:* Indiana University (B.A., 1966; J.D., 1969). Chairman, Illinois Institute for Continuing Legal Education. General editor, "Commercial and Professional Liability Insurance," IICLE 2005. *Member:* Illinois State and Indiana State Bar Associations; Defense Research Institute; Trial Lawyers Club of Chicago; Society of Trial Lawyers; International Association of Insurance Counsel; Illinois Defense Counsel (Director, 1983-1985). ***PRACTICE AREAS:*** Insurance Coverage Litigation; Bad Faith; Insurer Claim Administration and Excess Limits. ***Email:*** thamilton@hinshawlaw.com

JAMES HARBERT, born Aberdeen, Maryland, December 4, 1954; admitted to bar, 1979, District of Columbia; 1980, Illinois and U.S. Tax Court; 1983, U.S. Court of Appeals, Seventh Circuit and U.S. District Court, Northern District of Illinois, Trial Bar, 1992; 1993, U.S. Court of Federal Claims; 1997, U.S. District Court, Central District of Illinois. *Education:* College of William & Mary (A.B., 1976); University of Virginia (J.D., 1979). ***PRACTICE AREAS:*** Employee Benefits Litigation; Employee Benefits; Tax Litigation. ***Email:*** jharbert@hinshawlaw.com

MATTHEW R. HENDERSON, born Valparaiso, Indiana, July 9, 1966; admitted to bar, 1992, Illinois; 1993, U.S. District Court, Northern District of Illinois; 1996, U.S. District Court, Central District of Illinois. *Education:* University of Notre Dame (B.A. cum laude, 1989); University of Minnesota (J.D. cum laude, 1992). Author: "Breach of Fiduciary Duty," Attorney's Legal Liability, Illinois Institute for Continuing Legal Education, 2002, Supplement 2005; "Recovering Costs in Illinois Civil Actions," Illinois Bar Journal, September 2000; "Resolving Contractual Ambiguity: The Parol Evidence Rule and the Rules of Contract Construction," Illinois Bar Journal, April 1999; "Making the Most of Rule 216 Requests to Admit," Illinois Bar Journal, Aug 1995. Co-Author: "Arbitration and the New 'Public Policy' Doctrine," Minnesota Trial Lawyer, Fall 1995. Speaker: "Recent Developments in the Fair Debt Collection Practices Act," Annual Legal Malpractice and Risk Management Seminar, March 2005; "The Jurisdiction Jungle and New Developments in Insurance Coverage Law," Annual Legal Malpractice and Risk Management Seminar, March 2004; "Legal Ethics: Identifying and Preventing Conflicts of Interest," Illinois Association of Defense Trial Counsel, November 2002, 2003, 2004. *Member:* Chicago Bar Association (Member, Lawyer Regulation Committee); Illinois State Bar Association; Illinois Association of Defense Counsel. ***REPORTED CASES:*** Greco v. Trauner, Cohen & Thomas, L.L.P., 412 F.3d 360 (2nd Cir. 2005); Blair v. Supportkids, Inc., 222 F.Supp.2d 1038 (N.D.Ill. 2002); Pettit v. Retrieval Masters Creditors Bureau, Inc., 211 F.3d 1057 (7th Cir. 2000); Sanders v. Jackson, 209 F.3d 998 (7th Cir. 2000); Patterson v. North Shore Agency, Inc., 126 F.Supp.2d 1138 (N.D.Ill. 2000); DiRosa v. North Shore Agency, Inc., 56 F.Supp.2d 1039 (N.D.Ill. 1999); Wells v. McDonough, 188 F.R.D. 277 (N.D.Ill. 1999); Pettit v. Retrieval Masters Creditors Bureau, Inc., 42 F.Supp.2d 797 (N.D.Ill. 1999); Pikes v. Riddle, 38 F.Supp.2d 639 (N.D.Ill. 1999); Long v. Gray, 306 Ill.App.3d 445, 714 N.E.2d 1041 (1st Dist. 1999). ***PRACTICE AREAS:*** Legal Malpractice; Attorney Disciplinary Proceedings; Class Action Litigation; Commercial Litigation. ***Email:*** mhenderson@hinshawlaw.com

MARY J. HESS, born 1959; admitted to bar, 1991, Illinois and U.S. District Court, Northern District of Illinois. *Education:* Rosary College (B.A., 1981); DePaul University (J.D., 1991). ***PRACTICE AREAS:*** Commercial Litigation; Construction Litigation; Environmental Law; General Liability Litigation; Indoor Air Quality; Personal Injury Litigation; Products Liability Litigation; Toxic Torts. ***Email:*** mhess@hinshawlaw.com

TIMOTHY A. HICKEY, born Fort Wayne, Indiana, December 19, 1964; admitted to bar, 1990, Florida; 1994, Illinois and U.S. District Court, Northern, Central and Southern Districts of Illinois including Trial Bar. *Education:* DePauw University (B.A., 1987); University of Florida (J.D., 1990). *Member:* Chicago and American Bar Associations; Chicago Surety Claims Association. ***PRACTICE AREAS:*** Fidelity and Surety; Construction Litigation; Commercial Litigation. ***Email:*** thickey@hinshawlaw.com

SUSAN M. HICKMAN, born Hillsboro, Illinois, March 2, 1951; admitted to bar, 1979, Illinois, U.S. District Court, Central District of Illinois and U.S. Court of Appeals, Seventh Circuit; 1988, U.S. Supreme Court. *Education:* Northwestern University (B.S., 1972); Southern Illinois University (J.D., magna cum laude, 1979). Member, Law Review Staff, Southern Illinois University School of Law. *Member:* Illinois State Bar Association (Member, Sections on: Tort Law, Civil Practice and Procedure); Defense Research Institute; Illinois Defense Counsel. ***PRACTICE AREAS:*** Environmental Law; Toxic Tort Defense; Indoor Air Quality; Personal Injury Litigation; Class Action Litigation. ***Email:*** shickman@hinshawlaw.com

JOSEPH H. HINSHAW (1934-1973)

JAMES M. HOFERT, born Chicago, Illinois, July 5, 1954; admitted to bar, 1979, Illinois, U.S. District Court, Northern District of Illinois, including Trial Bar, 1982 and U.S. Court of Appeals, Seventh Circuit; 1997, U.S. Court of Appeals, Fifth Circuit; U.S. District Court, Central District of Illinois. *Education:* Grinnell College (B.A., 1976); Chicago-Kent College of Law (J.D., with honors, 1979). Semi Finalist, Moot Court Competition, 1978.

(This Listing Continued)

Member: Illinois State Bar Association; Society of Trial Lawyers. ***PRACTICE AREAS:*** Medical Malpractice; Products Liability; Construction Litigation; Toxic Tort. ***Email:*** jhofert@hinshawlaw.com

WILLIAM J. HOLLOWAY, born Chicago, Illinois, November 22, 1935; admitted to bar, 1965, Illinois and U.S. District Court, Northern District of Illinois; 1973, U.S. Court of Appeals, Federal Circuit; 1987, U.S. District Court, Eastern District of Wisconsin; 1988, Wisconsin. *Education:* Iowa State University (B.S., 1958); Northwestern University (J.D., 1965); DePaul University (M.S., Taxation, 1974). Co-Author: "Employment Termination: Rights and Remedies," BNA, 1st Ed. 1985, 2nd Ed. 1992. Fellow, American College of Trial Lawyers, 1985. Fellow, American College of Labor Employment Lawyers, 2000. *Member:* Illinois Society of Trial Lawyers. ***PRACTICE AREAS:*** Employment Law; Employment Litigation; Real Estate Litigation. **Email:** wholloway@hinshawlaw.com

CECILIA A. HORAN, born Chicago, Illinois, June 7, 1966; admitted to bar, 1997, Illinois and U.S. District Court, Northern District of Illinois. *Education:* Columbia College (B.A., 1989); The John Marshall Law School (J.D., 1997). *Member:* Chicago Bar Association; Illinois Association of Defense Trial Counsel. ***PRACTICE AREAS:*** Personal Injury Litigation; Product Liability Litigation; Intellectual Property Litigation. ***Email:*** choran@hinshawlaw.com

LINDA K. HORRAS, born Joliet, Illinois, December 4, 1961; admitted to bar, 1989, Illinois and U.S. District Court, Northern District of Illinois; 1991, U.S. Court of Appeals, Seventh Circuit; 1996, U.S. District Court, Central District of Illinois; 1997, U.S. District Court, Northern District of Indiana. *Education:* Loyola University (B.S., summa cum laude, 1985); John Marshall Law School (J.D., with distinction, 1989). Member, John Marshall Law Review, 1988-1989. *Member:* Illinois State Bar Association. ***PRACTICE AREAS:*** Labor and Employment Law; Employment Litigation; Employment Advice and Counseling; Employment Policies; Labor Relations. ***Email:*** lhorras@hinshawlaw.com

KURT L. HUDSON, born Chicago, Illinois, March 19, 1949; admitted to bar, 1977, Illinois; 1978, U.S. Tax Court and U.S. District Court, Northern District of Illinois. *Education:* Northern Illinois University (B.S., 1971); DePaul University (J.D., 1977; LL.M., 1988). ***PRACTICE AREAS:*** Medicare Reimbursement Litigation; Health Care Law. ***Email:*** khudson@hinshawlaw.com

FRITZ K. HUSZAGH, born Chicago, Illinois, May 20, 1953; admitted to bar, 1981, Illinois and U.S. District Court, Northern District of Illinois; 1982, Wisconsin; 1994, U.S. District Court, Eastern District of Wisconsin; 1996, U.S. Court of Appeals, Seventh Circuit; 1999, U.S. District Court, Southern District of Illinois. *Education:* St. Olaf College (B.A., 1975); Chicago-Kent College of Law (J.D., with honors, 1981). Recipient, American Jurisprudence Award in Torts. *Member:* Illinois State Bar Association (Member, Section on Civil Practice and Insurance); Trial Lawyers Club; Defense Research Institute; Illinois Defense Counsel. ***PRACTICE AREAS:*** Excess and Reinsurance; Insurance Coverage Litigation; General Liability; Errors and Omissions Litigation. ***Email:*** fhuszagh@hinshawlaw.com

ANTHONY J. JACOB, born Chicago, Illinois, March 19, 1972; admitted to bar, 1998, Illinois and U.S. District Court, Northern District of Illinois. *Education:* Northern Illinois University (B.A., 1994); The John Marshall Law School (J.D., 1998; LL.M., Taxation and Employee Benefits, 2003). Student Publications Editor, "The John Marshall Law Review"; Member, Moot Court Team. *Member:* Chicago Bar Association; Illinois State Bar Association; Illinois Council of School Law Attorneys; National School Boards Association Council of School Attorneys. ***PRACTICE AREAS:*** School Law; Corporate Banking Law; Corporate Finance; Mergers and Acquisitions; Corporate Governance; Corporate Organization; Corporate Real Estate; Real Estate; Taxation; Employee Benefits; Education Law; School Board Defense. ***Email:*** ajacob@hinshawlaw.com

ROBERT M. KONOP, born Two Rivers, Wisconsin, June 8, 1946; admitted to bar, 1973, Wisconsin and U.S. District Court, Western District of Wisconsin (Not admitted in Illinois). *Education:* University of Wisconsin-Madison (B.S., Nuclear Engineering, 1969; J.D., 1973). *Member:* State Bar of Wisconsin; American Bar Association (Member, Sections on: Tort and Insurance Practice; Labor and Employment Law); Defense Research Institute. ***PRACTICE AREAS:*** Fidelity and Surety; Director and Officer Liability; Casualty Insurance. ***Email:*** rkonop@hinshawlaw.com

KRISTY M. KELLY, born December 25, 1973; admitted to bar, 1999, Illinois. *Education:* University of Illinois at Urbana-Champaign (B.A., 1995); Loyola University (J.D., 1998). ***PRACTICE AREAS:*** Products Liability; Medical Malpractice; Municipal Liability. ***Email:*** kkelly@hinshawlaw.com

PHILIP REED KUJAWA, born Chicago, Illinois, September 29, 1963; admitted to bar, 1991, Illinois and U.S. District Court, Northern District of Illinois; 2005, U.S. Court of Appeals, Seventh Circuit. *Education:* Loyola University (B.S., 1986); Illinois Institute of Technology, Chicago-Kent College (J.D., 1991). *Member:* Illinois State Bar Association; Defense Research Institute; Illinois Association of Defense Trial Counsel; Trial Lawyers Club of Chicago. ***PRACTICE AREAS:*** Construction Litigation; Products Liability Defense; Environmental Law; Contract Litigation; Complex and Multi-District Litigation. ***Email:*** pkujawa@hinshawlaw.com

JOHN Y. LEE, born Seoul, Korea, February 15, 1960; admitted to bar, 1986, Illinois and U.S. District Court, Northern District of Illinois; 1993, U.S. Supreme Court; U.S. Court of Appeals, Seventh Circuit. *Education:* Dartmouth College (B.A., 1982); Northwestern University (J.D., 1986). Editor-in-Chief, Northwestern Journal of International Law and Business, 1985-1986. ***LANGUAGES:*** Korean. ***PRACTICE AREAS:*** Commercial Litigation; Employment Litigation; Insurance Coverage Litigation; Intellectual Property Litigation; International Business. ***Email:*** jlee@hinshawlaw.com

MICHAEL J. LEECH, born Cumberland, Maryland, December 3, 1951; admitted to bar, 1976, Illinois and U.S. District Court, Northern District of Illinois, including Trial Bar; 1991, U.S. Court of Appeals, Seventh Circuit. *Education:* University of Virginia (B.A., with distinction, 1973); Suffolk Law School and University of Virginia (J.D., 1976). Co-Author: "Employment Termination: Rights and Remedies," BNA, 1st Ed. 1985, 2nd Ed. 1992. Contributor: "Employment Discrimination Law," Lindermann & Grossman, 3d Ed. 1996, Chapter 11, National Origin Discrimination; "Sexual Harassment in Employment Law, 1992, Lindermann & Kadue; *Handbook on Employment Termination*, Illinois Institute for CLE, 1st, 2d & 3d Ed. (2002), Chapter 8, Partners and Minority Shareholders. Coll. of Lab. & Emplt. Lawyers Liaison to ALI Restatement of Employment Law Project (2004). *Member:* College of Labor and Employment Lawyers. ***PRACTICE AREAS:*** Mediation; Employment Law; Business Litigation. ***Email:*** mleech@hinshawlaw.com

(This Listing Continued)

SAMUEL G. LEVIN, born Chicago, Illinois, September 21, 1960; admitted to bar, 1985, Illinois, U.S. District Court, Northern District of Illinois and U.S. Court of Appeals, Seventh Circuit; 1987, U.S. District Court, Central District of Illinois. *Education:* Lawrence University (B.A., cum laude, Government, Economics, History, 1982); DePaul University College of Law (J.D., 1985). *Member:* DuPage County Bar Association; West Suburban Bar Association. ***PRACTICE AREAS:*** Commercial Litigation; Insurance Coverage Litigation; Products Liability Litigation; Professional Liability Litigation. ***Email:*** slevin@hinshawlaw.com

DAVID H. LEVITT, born Chicago, Illinois, August 30, 1954; admitted to bar, 1979, Illinois and U.S. District Court, Northern District of Illinois including Trial Bar. *Education:* University of Illinois (B.A., 1976); Loyola University of Chicago (J.D., 1979); John Marshall Law School (L.L.M., Intellectual Property, 2000). Member, National Moot Court Team. Author: "A Critical Look at the Right of Publicity: Proper Plaintiffs and Proper Damages," News Source of the Center for Intellectual Property Law of The John Marshall Law School, Summer 2000; "Legitimate Uses of Trademarks in Cyberspace," Chicago Bar Association Computer Law Committee, 2002; "The Red Herring of Negligent Hiring Claims," Trucking Industry Defense Association, 1997; "Declaratory Judgment Suits," Illinois Institute for Continuing Legal Education's Liability Insurance. Speaker: "Liability Beyond Tort and Contract: Copyright and False Designation," American Institute of Architects, 2003. *Member:* American Bar Association (Member, Sections on: Litigation; Intellectual Property; Torts and Insurance Practice); Illinois Association of Defense Trial Counsel (Board Member); Defense Research Institute; Trucking Industry Defense Association (Charter Member); American Intellectual Property Law Association; Professional Liability Underwriting Society. ***PRACTICE AREAS:*** Tort Defense; Intellectual Property Litigation; Insurance Coverage; Products Liability Litigation; Transportation; Risk Management. ***Email:*** dlevitt@hinshawlaw.com

CRAIG T. LILJESTRAND, born Milwaukee, Wisconsin, July 13, 1965; admitted to bar, 1990, Illinois and U.S. District Court, Northern District of Illinois; 1991, U.S. District Court, Western District of Michigan; 2003, U.S. District Court, Northern District of Indiana. *Education:* Eastern Illinois University (B.A., with honors, 1987); John Marshall School of Law (J.D., 1990). 2005, named one of "40 Illinois Attorneys Under Forty to Watch" by "Chicago Daily Law Bulletin" and "Chicago Lawyer" Magazine. Member, Law Review for the Software Law Journal; Member, Law Review Executive Editorial Board. Judicial Law Clerk to the Honorable Doyle A. Rowland, U.S. District Court, Western District of Michigan. *Member:* Chicago and Illinois State Bar Associations; Defense Research Institute. ***PRACTICE AREAS:*** Products Liability; Toxic Torts; Litigation. ***Email:*** cliljestrand@hinshawlaw.com

ALAN R. LIPTON, born Chicago, Illinois, January 8, 1950; admitted to bar, 1980, California, U.S. District Court, Northern District of California and U.S. Ninth Circuit Court of Appeals; 1993, U.S. District Court, Eastern District of California; 1994, Indiana and Illinois, U.S. District Court, Northern District of Illinois, including Trial Bar and U.S. District Court, Northern and Southern Districts of Indiana; 2000, U.S. Court of Appeals, Seventh Circuit; 2004, U.S. Tax Court. *Education:* University of Illinois, Champaign/Urbana (B.A., with distinction, 1971); University of Chicago; McGeorge School of Law, University of the Pacific (J.D. 1980). *Member:* State Bar of California; Indiana State Bar Association; American Bar Association (Member, Sections on: Intellectual Property Law; Litigation); Illinois Association of Defense Trial Counsel; Defense Research Institute. ***PRACTICE AREAS:*** Commercial Litigation; Civil Rights Defense Litigation; Intellectual Property Litigation; Personal Injury Litigation; Professional Liability Litigation; Insurance Coverage; Toxic Torts; Construction Litigation; Employment Litigation. ***Email:*** alipton@hinshawlaw.com

NANCY G. LISCHER, born Davenport, Iowa, May 16, 1952; admitted to bar, 1981, Illinois and U.S. District Court, Northern District of Illinois including Trial Bar, 1982; 1983, U.S. Court of Appeals, Seventh Circuit; 1985, U.S. Court of Appeals, Eleventh Circuit; 1987, U.S. Supreme Court and U.S. Court of Appeals for the Federal Circuit; 1990, U.S. Court of Appeals, Tenth Circuit and U.S. District Court, Central and Southern Districts of Illinois; 1996, U.S. Court of Appeals, Third Circuit; 1999, U.S. Court of Appeals, Eighth Circuit; 2003, U.S. Court of Appeals, Second Circuit; 2004, U.S. Court of Appeals, First Circuit. *Education:* Schiller College, Madrid, Spain; Valparaiso University (B.A., 1974); DePaul University College of Law (J.D., 1981). Assistant Attorney General, 1981-1984. *Member:* Seventh Circuit Bar Association; Appellate Lawyers Association; Women's Bar Association. ***LANGUAGES:*** Spanish. ***REPORTED CASES:*** Rodrigue v. Olin Employees Credit Union, 406 F.3d 434 (7th Cir. 2005) (UCC); Lo v. Provena Covenant Medical Center, 342 Ill.App.3d 975, 796 N.E.2d 607, 277 Ill.Dec. 521 (4th Dist. 2003), later proceeding, 356 Ill.App.3d 538, 826 N.E.2d 592, 292 Ill.Dec. 451 (4th Dist. 2005) (physician credentialing); Parks v. Wells Fargo Home Mortgage, Inc., 398 F.3d 937 (7th Cir. 2005) commercial litigation/punitive damages); Diaz v. Provena Hospitals, 352 Ill.App.3d 1165, 817 N.E.2d 206, 288 Ill.Dec. 81 (2d Dist. 2004) (National Practitioner Data Bank/federal preemption); Payton v. County of Kane, 308 F.3d 673 (7th Cir. 2002) (constitutional law/class action); Richard Marker Associates v. Pekin Ins. Co., 318 Ill.App.3d 1137, 743 N.E.2d 1078, 252 Ill.Dec. 922 (2d Dist. 2001) (insurance coverage); Garibaldi v. Applebaum, 194 Ill.2d 438, 742 N.E.2d 279, 252 Ill.Dec. 29, 16 IER Cases 1553 (Ill. 2000), reversing, 301 Ill.App.3d 849, 704 N.E.2d 698, 235 Ill.Dec. 125, 14 IER Cases 1008 (1st Dist. 1998) and 273 Ill.App.3d 536, 653 N.E.2d 42, 210 Ill.Dec. 455 (1st Dist. 1995) (physician credentialing); Hartford Ins. Co. of Illinois v. Kelly, 309 Ill.App.3d 800, 723 N.E.2d 288, 243 Ill.Dec. 256 (1st Dist. 1999) (insurance coverage); Bowden v. Cary Fire Protection Dist., 304 Ill.App.3d 274, 710 N.E.2d 548, 237 Ill.Dec. 918 (2d Dist. 1999) (municipal/EMT liability); People Who Care v. Rockford Bd. of Educ., School Dist. No. 205, 171 F.3d 1083, 133 Ed. Law Rep. 708 (7th Cir. 1999) (constitutional law/school desegregation); Brock v. Anderson Road Associates, 301 Ill.App.3d 168, 703 N.E.2d 568, 234 Ill.Dec. 707 (2d Dist. 1998) (municipal/EMT liability); Albiero v. City of Kankakee, 122 F.3d 417, 38 Fed.R.Serv.3d 1008 (7th Cir. 1997) (constitutional law); Stillman v. Travelers Ins. Co., 88 F.3d 911, 35 Fed.R.Serv.3d 1015 (11th Cir. 1996) (federal appellate procedure/insurance coverage); Jones by Jones v. Webb, 45 F.3d 178 (7th Cir. 1995) (constitutional law); Transcraft, Inc. v. Galvin, Stalmack, Kirschner & Clark, 39 F.3d 812, 41 Fed. R. Evid. Serv. 275 (7th Cir. 1994) (professional malpractice); Hartford Acc. & Indem. Co. v. Chicago Housing

(This Listing Continued)

HINSHAW & CULBERTSON LLP, Chicago—Continued

Authority, 12 F.3d 92 (7th Cir. 1993) (insurance coverage). ***PRACTICE AREAS:*** Civil Appellate Practice; Professional Liability; Constitutional Law; Insurance Coverage. ***Email:*** nlischer@hinshawlaw.com

TOM H. LUETKEMEYER, born Evanston, Illinois, December 19, 1956; admitted to bar, 1982, Illinois and U.S. District Court, Northern District of Illinois; 1998, U.S. District Court, Central District of Illinois; 2000, U.S. District Court, Northern District of Indiana. *Education:* Loyola University (B.A., B.S., magna cum laude, 1979; J.D., 1982). Adjunct Professor of Labor Law, Employment Discrimination and Employment Law, Loyola University School of Law, 1987—. *Member:* Illinois State Bar Association; American Academy of Hospital Attorneys; Illinois Association of Hospital Attorneys. ***PRACTICE AREAS:*** Corporate Health Care; Management Labor; Employment Law. ***Email:*** tluetkemeyer@hinshawlaw.com

STEPHEN H. MALATO, born Chicago, Illinois, September 25, 1953; admitted to bar, 1978, Illinois; 1981, U.S. District Court, Northern District of Illinois, including Trial Bar. *Education:* Western Illinois University (B.A., 1975); IIT/Chicago-Kent College of Law (J.D., with high honors, 1978). Member, Moot Court. Member, Legal Club of Chicago. *Member:* Chicago Bar Association; American College of Mortgage Attorneys. ***PRACTICE AREAS:*** Real Estate Law; Banking and Financing; Construction Litigation; Contracts and Agreements; Environmental Compliance; Corporate Organization and Governance; Limited Liability Company Law; Zoning Law. ***Email:*** smalato@hinshawlaw.com

THOMAS Y. MANDLER, born Chicago, Illinois, October 26, 1946; admitted to bar, 1972, Illinois, U.S. District Court, Northern District of Illinois and U.S. Court of Appeals, Seventh Circuit; 1976, U.S. Supreme Court; 1997, U.S. District Court, Eastern District of Wisconsin; 1981, U.S. District Court, Central District of Illinois; 2003, U.S. District Court, Southern District of Illinois. *Education:* University of Wisconsin-Madison (B.A., 1968); University of Illinois (J.D., 1971). Recipient, Addis E. Hull Award for Excellence in Continuing Legal Education, 2000. Associate Editor, University of Illinois Law Forum, 1970-1971. Author: "How An Employer Can Minimize Employment Discrimination Risks," IICLE, 1998; "How To Hire, Manage And Terminate Employees," IICLE, 1999. Member, Board of Directors, 1982-1995, Member, Executive Committee, 1988-1995 and Chairman, 1993-1994, Illinois Institute of Continuing Legal Education. Member, 1991— and President, 1996-1997, 2000—, Board of Education, Highland Park-Deerfield High School District 113. *Member:* American Bar Association (Member, Committee on Labor Arbitration and the Law of Collective Bargaining Agreements, Labor Relations Section, 1979—; Associate Editor and Chapter Editor, "Discipline and Discharge in Arbitration," 1998, 2001 Supplement). ***PRACTICE AREAS:*** Labor Relations; Collective Bargaining; Employment Advice and Counseling; Corporate and Business Law. ***Email:*** tmandler@hinshaw.com

PAUL M. MARKESE, born Elmhurst, Illinois, August 18, 1971; admitted to bar, 1999, Illinois and U.S. District Court, Northern District of Illinois. *Education:* Loyola University (B.A., 1994); John Marshall Law School (J.D., 1998). Pi Sigma Alpha, Political Science Honor Society; Golden Key National Honor Society. Team Member, Tulane National Sports Law Moot Court Competition. Co-Author: "The Asbestos Compensation Fairness Act," DRI For The Defense, June, 2003. *Member:* American Bar Association. ***PRACTICE AREAS:*** Environmental Litigation; Toxic Tort; Occupational Safety and Health; Personal Injury Litigation. ***Email:*** pmarkese@hinshawlaw.com

NEWTON C. MARSHALL, II, born Summit, New Jersey, September 13, 1964; admitted to bar, 1992, Illinois and U.S. District Court, Northern District of Illinois. *Education:* Denison University (B.A., 1986); Case Western Reserve University (J.D., 1992); DePaul University. *Member:* Illinois State Bar Association; Illinois Association of Defense Trial Counsel. ***PRACTICE AREAS:*** Commercial Litigation; Construction Litigation; Architects and Engineers Liability Litigation; Real Estate; Agents and Brokers Liability Litigation; Fraud Defense; Alternative Dispute Resolution; Mediation. ***Email:*** nmarshall@hinshawlaw.com

TERRENCE P. McAVOY, born Evergreen Park, Illinois, April 27, 1961; admitted to bar, 1987, Illinois and U.S. District Court, Northern District of Illinois; 1990, U.S. Court of Appeals, 7th Circuit. *Education:* University of Illinois (B.S., 1983); John Marshall Law School (J.D., with distinction, 1987). Member, John Marshall Law Review, 1986-1987. *Member:* Illinois State Bar Association (ISBA); Chicago Bar Association (CBA); Defense Research Institute (DRI); Professional Liability Underwriters Society (PLUS); Illinois Association of Defense Trial Counsel. ***PRACTICE AREAS:*** Professional Liability; Legal and Medical Malpractice Defense; Dental and Accountant Malpractice; General Liability; Insurance Coverage. ***Email:*** tmcavoy@hinshawlaw.com

THOMAS P. McGARRY, born Evanston, Illinois, June 4, 1951; admitted to bar, 1980, Illinois and U.S. District Court, Northern District of Illinois including Trial Bar; 1991, U.S. Court of Appeals, 7th Circuit. *Education:* Marquette University (B.A., 1973); DePaul University (J.D., 1980). Phi Sigma Alpha. Member, Writing Staff, De Paul Law Review, 1979-1980. General Editor and Chapter Co-Author, "Litigating the Legal Malpractice Case" and "The Limitation of Liability Through Business Forms," in "Illinois Attorney Legal Liability," Illinois Institute of Continuing Legal Education (IICLE), 2002. Co-Editor, "Attorney Discipline Proceedings: Illinois Practice and Procedure," Law Bulletin Publishing Co., 2002. Author: Chapter, "Attorney Communications," in "Defense Counsel Practice Management Manual," International Association of Defense Counsel, 2002; Chapter, "Limited Liability Entities," in "Legal Malpractice: The Law Office Guide to Purchasing Legal Malpractice Insurance," West Group, 2002. Co-Author, "Ethics" Column, in "Chicago Lawyer". *Member:* Chicago (Member, Legal Malpractice Committee), Illinois State and American (Member, Standing Committee, Lawyer's Professional Liability) Bar Associations; Defense Research Institute; Professional Liability Underwriters Society; Association of Professional Responsibility Lawyers; Illinois Association of Defense Trial Counsel; Trial Lawyers Club of Chicago. [U.S. Navy, 1973-1977, Lieut.]. ***PRACTICE AREAS:*** *Litigation; Professional Liability; Professional Responsibility; Insurance.* ***Email:*** tmcgarry@hinshawlaw.com

DANIEL W. McGRATH, born Evanston, Illinois, March 12, 1957; admitted to bar, 1982, Illinois and U.S. District Court, Northern District of Illinois including Trial Bar; 1999, U.S. District Court, Central and Southern Districts of Illinois. *Education:* Loyola

(This Listing Continued)

University of Chicago (B.A., magna cum laude, 1979; J.D., 1982). Alpha Sigma Nu; Blue Key. Member, National Moot Court Team. *Member:* Illinois State Bar Association; Illinois Association of Defense Trial Counsel; Society of Trial Lawyers; Defense Research Institute; Federation of Defense & Corporate Counsel. ***PRACTICE AREAS:*** Product Liability; Environmental Litigation; Commercial Litigation; Tort Litigation. ***Email:*** dmcgrath@hinshawlaw.com

CHRISTINE OLSON McTIGUE, born Minneapolis, Minnesota, May 23, 1960; admitted to bar, 1984, Illinois and U.S. District Court, Northern District of Illinois; 1987, U.S. Court of Appeals, 7th Circuit; 2005, U.S. Court of Appeals, 8th Circuit. *Education:* University of Minnesota (B.A., magna cum laude, 1981); Loyola University (J.D., 1984). Phi Beta Kappa. ***PRACTICE AREAS:*** Appellate; Insurance Coverage Litigation. ***Email:*** colson@hinshawlaw.com

GARY E. MEDLER, born St. Anne, Illinois, March 19, 1952; admitted to bar, 1980, Illinois; 1981, U.S. Court of Appeals, Seventh Circuit; 1982, U.S. District Court, Northern District of Illinois. *Education:* Michigan State University (B.A., 1974); DePaul University (J.D., 1980). *Member:* Illinois State and American Bar Associations. ***PRACTICE AREAS:*** Banking; Mergers and Acquisitions; Corporate Law; Securities; Corporate Governance and Organization. ***Email:*** gmedler@hinshawlaw.com

GREGG I. MINKOW, born Chicago, Illinois, July 6, 1957; admitted to bar, 1981, Illinois; 1984, U.S. District Court, Northern District of Illinois including Trial Bar; 1991, Texas. *Education:* Lake Forest College (B.A., Economics, 1978); University of Illinois School of Law (J.D., 1981). Former In-House Counsel: The Dun & Bradstreet Corporation; A.C. Nielsen Company. Former Vice-President and Lead Counsel, IMS America, Ltd. and Assistant General Counsel, IMS International (divisions of The Dun & Bradstreet Corporation). ***PRACTICE AREAS:*** Business Acquisitions; Real Estate; Joint Ventures; Franchise Law; Outsourcing; Leasing; Contracts; Litigation; Trademarks; Advertising; ERISA; Employment. ***Email:*** gminkow@hinshawlaw.com

LAWRENCE R. MOELMANN, born Oak Park, Illinois, October 13, 1947; admitted to bar, 1973, Illinois and U.S. District Court, Northern District of Illinois; 1975, U.S. Court of Appeals, Seventh Circuit. *Education:* Princeton University (A.B., magna cum laude, 1970); University of Michigan (J.D., cum laude, 1973). *Member:* Cook County, Illinois State and American (Fidelity and Surety Law Committee, Vice-Chair, 1992-1996, 1998—) Bar Associations; Defense Research Institute (Fidelity and Surety Committee, Chair, 1995-1998); International Association of Defense Counsel (Fidelity and Surety Committee; Chairman, 1992-1993, Vice Chairman, 1989-1992); Surety Claims Institute; National Bond Claims Association. ***PRACTICE AREAS:*** Fidelity and Surety; Construction Litigation; Commercial Litigation; Bankruptcy and Creditors Rights. ***Email:*** lmoelmann@hinshawlaw.com

CAROLINE A. MONDSCHEAN, born Chicago, Illinois, June 24, 1963; admitted to bar, 1989, Illinois and U.S. District Court, Northern District of Illinois. *Education:* St. Joseph's College (B.S., 1985); Drake University (J.D., 1989). Member, Drake University Law Review. *Member:* Chicago Bar Association. ***PRACTICE AREAS:*** Professional Liability. ***Email:*** cmondschean@hinshawlaw.com

RENEE J. MORTIMER, born Chicago, Illinois, February 1, 1967; admitted to bar, 1991, Illinois; 1992, U.S. District Court, Northern and Central Districts of Illinois; 1998, Indiana and U.S. District Court, Northern District of Indiana; 2000, U.S. District Court, Southern District of Indiana. *Education:* Indiana University (B.A., English, 1988); Loyola University of Chicago School of Law (J.D., 1991). *Member:* Lake County Bar Association; Illinois State Bar Association; Calumet American Inn of Court; Women's Bar Association of Illinois; Defense Research Institute. (Partner-in-Charge of Schererville, Indiana Office). ***PRACTICE AREAS:*** Medical Malpractice Defense; Transportation; Defense Litigation; Products Liability Defense; Municipal Defense; Municipal Liability; ERISA Litigation; National and Regional Litigation Programs; Risk Management. ***Email:*** rmortimer@hinshawlaw.com

DONALD L. MROZEK, born Chicago, Illinois, March 17, 1947; admitted to bar, 1973, Illinois; 1982, U.S. District Court, Northern District of Illinois, including Trial Bar and U.S. Court of Appeals, Seventh Circuit; 1993, U.S. District Court, Eastern District of Wisconsin; 1999, U.S. District Court, Eastern District of Michigan. *Education:* Northwestern University (B.S.E., 1969); DePaul University (J.D., with honor, 1973). *Member:* Illinois State Bar Association; International Association of Defense Counsel; Defense Research Institute; Trial Lawyers Club of Chicago; National Bond Claims Association; Surety Claims Institute; Illinois Bankers Association. ***PRACTICE AREAS:*** Commercial Litigation; Fidelity, Fiduciary and Surety Claims and Litigation; Corporate and Business Law; Design and Management of National Regional Litigation Programs. ***Email:*** dmrozek@hinshawlaw.com

THOMAS R. MULROY, III, born Chicago, Illinois, March 27, 1973; admitted to bar, 1998, Illinois; 1999, U.S. District Court, Northern District of Illinois. *Education:* University of Illinois (B.A., 1995); Loyola University (J.D., 1998). Law Clerk to the Honorable William D. Maddux and Honorable Donald J. O'Brien, Circuit Court of Cook County, 1997-1998. *Member:* Chicago Bar Association (YLS Co-Chairman, Professional Responsibility and Ethics Committee). ***LANGUAGES:*** Italian. ***REPORTED CASES:*** West Suburban Bank v. Attorneys' Title Insurance Fund, Inc, 761 N.E.2d 346 (2nd Dist. Ill. 2001); Gant v. L.U. Transport, Inc., 770 N.E.2d 1155 (1st Dist. Ill. 2002); Guardian Pipeline, L.L.C. v. 950.80 Acres of Land, 210 F.Supp.2d 976 (N.D.Ill.2002). ***PRACTICE AREAS:*** Medical Malpractice; Construction; School Law; Commercial Litigation; Products Liability. ***Email:*** tmulroy@hinshawlaw.com

BRENDAN A. O'BRIEN, born LaGrange, Illinois, April 21, 1969; admitted to bar, 1996, Illinois and U.S. District Court, Northern District of Illinois. *Education:* Illinois State University (B.S., 1991); John Marshall Law School (J.D., 1996). *Member:* Chicago and Illinois State Bar Associations. ***PRACTICE AREAS:*** Medical Malpractice Defense; General Tort Defense. ***Email:*** bobrien@hinshawlaw.com

DONALD A. O'BRIEN, born Oak Park, Illinois, March 1, 1948; admitted to bar, 1977, Illinois and U.S. District Court, Northern District of Illinois; 1979, U.S. Court of Appeals, Seventh Circuit; 1980, U.S. Supreme Court. *Education:* Loyola University (B.A., 1969); John Marshall Law School (J.D., with distinction, 1977). Order of John Marshall. *Member:*

(This Listing Continued)

Dupage and American Bar Associations; Illinois Association of Defense Trial Counsel; Defense Research Institute. [With U.S. Army, 1969-1973]. ***PRACTICE AREAS:*** Medical Law; Commercial Law; Construction law. ***Email:*** dobrien@hinshawlaw.com

YVONNE C. OCRANT, born Highland Park, Illinois, July 13, 1973; admitted to bar, 1999, Illinois; 2004, U.S. District Court, Northern District of Indiana. *Education:* Northern Illinois University (B.S., 1995); DePaul University (J.D., 1999). Author: De Paul Law Review, Member, 1997-1999 and Executive Editor, 1998-1999. Author: "A Constitutional Challenge to Encryption Export Regulations: Software is Speechless," De Paul Law Review, Winter 1998, Vol. 48; "HEADS UP!" Scribe, April, June-July, Sept.-Nov. 2003, Jan., Mar., July 2004; "Legal Bits," From the Horses Mouth, May-Oct. 2004. Speaker: American Bar Association, Employment Rights and Responsibility Committee Meeting, 2004; American Bar Association, Annual Meeting, 2004. Board Member, Cowboy Dreams of Illinois, Barrington, Illinois. Member, Advisory Council for Hooved Animal Humane Society, Woodstock, Illinois. *Member:* Chicago, Seventh Circuit, Illinois State and American Bar Associations. ***PRACTICE AREAS:*** Employment Litigation; Employment Advice and Counseling; Commercial Litigation; Equine Law. ***Email:*** yocrant@hinshawlaw.com

RENEE P. O'NEILL, born Chicago, Illinois, 1970; admitted to bar, 1995, Illinois; U.S. District Court, Northern District of Illinois. *Education:* Fairfield University (B.A., cum laude, 1992); DePaul University (J.D., 1995). ***PRACTICE AREAS:*** Commercial Litigation; Professional Liability Litigation; Accountant's Liability Litigation; Attorney Ethics and Discipline Matters; Appellate Law; Fidelity and Surety. ***Email:*** roneill@hinshawlaw.com

DEAN E. PARKER, born Duluth, Minnesota, May 14, 1954; admitted to bar, 1979, Wisconsin and Illinois; 1983, Minnesota. *Education:* University of Wisconsin (B.B.A., with distinction, 1976; J.D., 1979). Beta Gamma Sigma; Phi Kappa Phi; Beta Alpha Psi. *Member:* State Bar of Wisconsin; American Bar Association; International Council of Shopping Centers; Chicago Clean Cities Coalition. ***PRACTICE AREAS:*** Corporate; Real Estate; Banking and Financing; Corporate and Business Law. ***Email:*** dparker@hinshawlaw.com

RICHARD B. POLONY, born LaGrange, Illinois, April 7, 1964; admitted to bar, 1995, Illinois and U.S. District Court, Northern District of Illinois; 2001, U.S. District Court, Central District of Illinois. *Education:* Loyola University (B.B.A., 1987); Chicago-Kent College of Law (J.D., 1995). ***PRACTICE AREAS:*** Commercial Litigation; Fidelity and Surety; Director and Officer Liability; Construction; Real Estate; Banking and Financing; ARD/Mediation. ***Email:*** rpolony@hinshawlaw.com

CAROL PROCTOR, born Aurora, Illinois; admitted to bar, 1985, Illinois and U.S. District Court, Northern District of Illinois. *Education:* Aurora College (B.A., 1973); Northern Illinois University (M.S., 1979); DePaul University (J.D., 1985). Executive Editor, De Paul Law Review, 1984-1985. *Member:* Illinois State Bar Association; Trial Lawyers Club of Chicago; Illinois Association of Defense Trial Counsel; Defense Research Institute. ***PRACTICE AREAS:*** Insurance Coverage; Bad Faith; ERISA. ***Email:*** cproctor@hinshawlaw.com

STEVEN M. PUISZIS, born Chicago, Illinois, May 23, 1954; admitted to bar, 1979, Illinois and U.S. District Court, Northern District of Illinois; 1983, Trial Bar; 1991, U.S. Court of Appeals, 7th Circuit; 1999, U.S. Supreme Court. *Education:* DePaul University (B.S., 1976; Beta Alpha Psi); Loyola University (J.D., 1979). Author, "Illinois Municipal Tort Liability," 1st Ed. (Michie) 1993; 2d Ed. Lexis Publishing (formerly Mathew Bender) 2001, with yearly annual cummulative supplements. *Member:* Illinois State Bar Association; Illinois Association of Defense Trial Council (Member, Board of Directors, 1995—; President-elect, 2005); Defense Research Institute; Association of Defense Trial Attorneys; Society of Trial Lawyers. ***PRACTICE AREAS:*** Professional Liability; Municipal Liability; Government Defense; Public Officials Liability; Law Enforcement Liability. ***Email:*** spuiszis@hinshawlaw.com

DANIEL M. PURDOM, born Melrose Park, Illinois, August 21, 1952; admitted to bar, 1978, Illinois and U.S. District Court, Southern and Central Districts of Illinois; 1980, U.S. District Court, Northern District of Illinois and U.S. Court of Appeals, Seventh Circuit; 1990, U.S. Court of Appeals, Eleventh Circuit; U.S. District Court, Eastern District of Wisconsin. *Education:* Illinois State University (B.S., 1974); Southern Illinois University (J.D., with highest honors, 1978). Articles Editor, Southern Illinois University Law Journal, 1977-1978. Law Clerk, U.S. District Judge James L. Foreman, Southern District of Illinois, 1978-1980. Assistant U.S. Attorney, Northern District of Illinois 1980-1986. Trial Advocacy Institute Instructor, Department of Justice Advocacy Institute. National Trial Advocacy Institute Instructor, Loyola University and Northwestern University. Named "Leading Lawyers" 2004, 2005. Named "Illinois Super Lawyers" 2005. *Member:* DuPage County, Illinois State and American Bar Associations; Association of Defense Trial Attorneys; National Association of Criminal Defense; American Health Lawyers Association. ***PRACTICE AREAS:*** White Collar Crime; Health Care Fraud and Abuse; Corporate Compliance; Commercial Litigation. ***Email:*** dpurdom@hinshawlaw.com

BERNARD E. JUDE QUINN, born Bethlehem, Pennsylvania, August 12, 1960; admitted to bar, 1986, Pennsylvania and U.S. District Court, Eastern District of Pennsylvania; 1987, New Jersey and U.S. District Court, District of New Jersey; 1994, U.S. Court of Appeals, Third Circuit; 2001, U.S. District Court, Middle District of Pennsylvania; 2004, U.S. District Court, Northern District of Illinois; 2005, Illinois and U.S. District Court, Central District of Illinois. *Education:* University of Notre Dame (B.A., Government and International Relations, 1982); Villanova University School of Law (J.D., 1986). Author: "Pennsylvania Evidence," Packel & Poulin, West 1987 - Opinion Testimony by Lay Witnesses; "Impact of Amendments to Pennsylvania Workers' Compensation Act on the Motor Vehicle Financial Responsibility Law, the Pennsylvania Courts' interpretation of what constitutes maintenance or use of a motor vehicle and Damages recoverable in a Wrongful Death and Survival Action and "An Overview of Sexual Harassment Claims and Employer Defenses." Contributing Author: *Manual on Trying the Automobile Injury Case in New Jersey*; *Manual on Trying the Soft Tissue Injury Case.* Regional Editor, "American Law Firm Association compendium on Employment Law". *Member:* National Lawyers Association. ***PRACTICE AREAS:*** Civil Rights Defense; Medical Malpractice; Employment Litigation; General Liability Litigation; Products Liability Litigation. ***Email:*** jquinn@hinshawlaw.com

LAURIE S. RANDOLPH, born Chicago, Illinois, December 28, 1954; admitted to bar, 1979, Illinois and U.S. District Court, Northern District of Illinois including Trial Bar; 1985, California. *Education:* Northern Illinois University (B.S., magna cum laude, 1976); DePaul University (J.D., with honors, 1979). Lecturer, Illinois Institute for Continuing Legal Education; Chicago Bar Association Continuing Legal Education. Arbitrator, Cook County Circuit Court Mandatory Arbitration Program, 1990—. Member, Panel of Arbitrators, American Arbitration Association. *Member:* State Bar of California; American Bar Assocation (Member, Construction Forum); International Association of Defense Counsel; Society of Trial Lawyers (Past Director); American Institute of Architects (Affiliate Member); Defense Research Institute; Illinois Defense Counsel; Chicago Building Congress (Membership Chairman, 1991-1993); Women's Bar Association of Illinois. ***PRACTICE AREAS:*** Construction Law; Design Professionals Liability Litigation; Contracts and Agreements; Insurance Coverage Litigation; Products Liability; Architects and Engineers Liability Litigation. ***Email:*** lrandolph@hinshawlaw.com

MARCOS REILLY, born San Juan, Puerto Rico, January 28, 1962; admitted to bar, 1986, Illinois; 1987, U.S. District Court, Northern District of Illinois including Trial Bar; 1990, U.S. District Court, Eastern District of Wisconsin; 1993, U.S. Court of Appeals for the Federal Circuit; 1997, U.S. Court of Appeals, Seventh Circuit; 2003, U.S. District Court, Central District of Illinois. *Education:* Northwestern University (B.A., 1983); University of Michigan (J.D., 1986). *Member:* Illinois State Bar Association. ***LANGUAGES:*** Spanish. ***PRACTICE AREAS:*** Commercial Litigation; Intellectual Property; Construction; Indoor Air Quality; Employment. ***Email:*** mreilly@hinshawlaw.com

DAVID J. RICHARDS, born Chicago, Illinois, August 11, 1970; admitted to bar, 1995, Illinois and U.S. District Court, Northern District of Illinois. *Education:* Loyola University (B.A., cum laude, 1992); Valparaiso University (J.D., summa cum laude, 1995). Executive Managing Editor, Valparaiso University Law Review, 1994-1995. ***PRACTICE AREAS:*** Products Liability Litigation; General Liability Litigation; Commercial Litigation. ***Email:*** drichards@hinshawlaw.com

J. WILLIAM ROBERTS, admitted to bar, 1968, Illinois and U.S. District Court, Central District of Illinois; 1969, U.S. Court of Appeals, Seventh Circuit; 1978, U.S. Supreme Court; 2001, U.S. District Court, Northern and Southern Districts of Illinois. *Education:* Illinois Wesleyan University (B.A., 1964); Washington University (J.D., 1967). Managing Partner, Hinshaw & Culbertson LLP, 1997—. Chief Legal Counsel to Illinois Governor Jim Edgar, 1995-1997. U.S. Attorney, Central District of Illinois, 1986-1993. U.S. Attorney General's Advisory Committee of U.S. Attorneys (Chairman, 1991-1992. Senior Advisory to the Attorney General in Washington, D.C., 1991-1992. State's Attorney of Sangamon County, 1979-1986. Assistant U.S. Attorney, Central District of Illinois, 1968-1972. *Member:* Sangamon County (President, 1983) and Illinois State (Member, Board of Governors, 1994-2000; Chair, Criminal Justice Section Council, 1984-1985) Bar Associations; National District Attorneys Association (Board of Directors, 1982-1986). (Also at Springfield, Illinois Office). ***PRACTICE AREAS:*** Complex Civil and Criminal Litigation; Criminal Defense; Government Relations; Corporate Compliance Law. ***Email:*** broberts@hinshawlaw.com

DANIEL K. RYAN, born Chicago, Illinois, October 19, 1959; admitted to bar, 1985, Colorado and U.S. District Court, District of Colorado; 1987, Illinois and U.S. District Court, Northern District of Illinois; 1989, U.S. District Court, Northern District of Illinois including Federal Trial Bar; 1991, U.S. District Court, Southern District of Illinois; 1994, U.S. District Court, Central District of Illinois and U.S. District Court, Eastern District of Wisconsin; 1998, U.S. Court of Appeals, Seventh Circuit; 2001, U.S. District Court, Southern District of Indiana and U.S. District Court, Western District of Wisconsin; 2004, U.S. Court of Appeals, Eighth Circuit. *Education:* University of Notre Dame (B.A., 1981); Loyola University of Chicago School of Law (J.D., 1984). *Member:* Illinois State Bar Association; Defense Research Institute. ***PRACTICE AREAS:*** Commercial Litigation; Class Action Litigation; Health Care Litigation; ERISA Litigation; Employment Litigation; Fidelity and Surety; Director and Officer Liability. ***Email:*** dryan@hinshawlaw.com

ADAM L. SAPER, admitted to bar, 1998, Illinois and U.S. District Court, Northern District of Illinois. *Education:* DePaul University (B.A., Political Science, magna cum laude, 1995); John Marshall Law School (J.D., cum laude, 1998). Staff Editor, The John Marshall Law Review, 1998. ***PRACTICE AREAS:*** Commercial Litigation; Class-Action Litigation; Director and Officer Liability Litigation; Employment Litigation; Securities Litigation. ***Email:*** asaper@hinshawlaw.com

DAVID M. SCHULTZ, born Cook County, August 15, 1961; admitted to bar, 1988, Illinois; 1991, U.S. District Court, Northern District of Illinois; 1993, U.S. Court of Appeals, Seventh Circuit; 1994, U.S. Supreme Court; 1995, Trial Bar; 1997, U.S. District Court, Central District of Illinois; 2001, U.S. District Court, Southern District of Illinois and U.S. District Court, Southern District of Indiana; 2003, U.S. District Court, Northern District of Indiana; 2005, U.S. Court of Appeals, Second Circuit and U.S. District Court, Eastern and Western Districts of Wisconsin. *Education:* University of Illinois (B.S., 1984); John Marshall Law School (J.D., 1988). *Member:* Chicago, Seventh Circuit, Illinois State, Federal and American (Member, Section on: Professional Responsibility) Bar Associations; American Collectors Association (Member, Attorney Program). ***PRACTICE AREAS:*** Professional Liability; Civil Trial Litigation; Class Action Defense. ***Email:*** dschultz@hinshawlaw.com

JOHN E. SEBASTIAN, born Gary, Indiana, May 21, 1968; admitted to bar, 1995, Illinois, U.S. District Court, Northern and Central Districts of Illinois and U.S. Court of Appeals, Seventh Circuit. *Education:* Purdue University (B.S., Construction Engineering Technology, 1990); Northern Illinois University College of Law (J.D., 1995). Associate Editor, Construction Lawyer Quarterly, publication of the Construction Forum Subcommittee, American Bar Association. Co-author of Chapter 10, Surety Bonds, "Construction Law in Illinois," Illinois Institute for Continuing Legal Education (1997 and 1999). Presentations: "How to Conduct an Adversary Proceeding to Pursue a Contractor's Affirmative Claim," American Bar Association Annual Midwinter Meeting of the Construction Forum/Surety and Fidelity Subcommittee (January 2003); "The Illinois Payment Bond and Mechanics Lien Act," Chicago Surety Claims Association Meeting (2002); "A Primer on Assessing a Principal's Affirmative Claim," Chicago Surety Claims Association Meeting (2000). *Member:* Chicago and American (Member, Tips & Construction Forum, 1997—) Bar Associations; Defense Research Institute. ***PRACTICE AREAS:*** Surety Law; Construction Litigation; Commercial Litigation. ***Email:*** jsebastian@hinshawlaw.com

(This Listing Continued)

HINSHAW & CULBERTSON LLP, Chicago—Continued

JENNIFER M. SENDER, born Park Ridge, Illinois, May 10, 1966; admitted to bar, 1991, Illinois and U.S. District Court, Northern District of Illinois; 1992, U.S. District Court, Central District of Illinois; 1994, U.S. District Court, Eastern District of Michigan. *Education:* Northern Illinois University (B.A., cum laude, 1988); Loyola University (J.D., 1991). Recipient, American Jurisprudence Award in Alternative Dispute Resolution. Author: "Simple Strategies for Lowering Litigation Costs," Minority Corporate Counsel Association, 4th Annual CLE Expo, March 2005; "Resolving Ambiguities: A Case Study of Judicial Interpretations of Mold Exclusions," American Bar Association Tort Trial and Insurance Practice Seminar, 2003; "Construction Defect and Mold Litigation," National Business Institute, 2002; "CPR for your ADR: Alternative Dispute Resolution Primer," The Practical Lawyer, October 2005; "Remediation of Mold vs. Spoliation of Evidence: When and How to Preserve Evidence," HarrisMartin Columns, 2002; "Mold Allergy: Idiosyncratic Reaction or Cause of Action," HarrisMartin Columns, 2001. *Member:* American Bar Association (Member, Products Liability Section); Women's Bar Association of Illinois (First Vice President (President elect), 2005-2006; Founder, Corporate Counsel Committee); Society of Women Environmental Professionals (Founding Member, Chicago Chapter). ***REPORTED CASES:*** Kravcik v. Golub & Co., 676 N.E.2d 668 (1st Dist. 1996); Enaharo v. Abubakar, 408 F.3d 877 (N.D. Ill. 2005). ***PRACTICE AREAS:*** Commercial Litigation; Products Liability Litigation; Environmental Litigation; Class Action Litigation; Risk Management. ***Email:*** jsender@hinshawlaw.com

ROBERT T. SHANNON, born Chicago, Illinois, March 30, 1969; admitted to bar, 1995, Illinois and U.S. District Court, Northern District of Illinois. *Education:* Indiana University (B.A., 1991); Loyola University (J.D., 1995). Named to "40 Illinois Attorneys Under Forty to Watch," Law Bulletin Publishing Co., 2003. ***PRACTICE AREAS:*** Municipal Law; Administrative Law; Civil Rights; International Torts. ***Email:*** rshannon@hinshawlaw.com

HARVEY M. SHELDON, born December 7, 1942; admitted to bar, 1968, Illinois and U.S. District Court, Northern District of Illinois including Trial Bar; 1972, U.S. Court of Appeals, Seventh Circuit; 1978, U.S. Court of Appeals for the District of Columbia Circuit; 1980, U.S. Supreme Court. *Education:* Amherst College (B.A., cum laude, 1965); Harvard University (J.D., 1968); DePaul University (Certificate in Mediation). Recipient, Outstanding Service Award, Chemical Industry Council of Illinois, 2004. Author: "Environmental Concerns in Real Estate Transactions," The Environmental Counselor, September 1992. Co-Author: "Attorneys Guide to Environmental Liability," ABA General Practice Section, 1991; chapter, "Air Pollution," IICLE Handbook, 1993. Member, Board of Advisors, The Environmental Counselor; Contributing Editor, Environmental Compliance and Litigation Strategy. Special Prosecutor, State of Illinois, 1970-1971. Chief, Environmental Control Division, Office of the Illinois Attorney General, 1972-1973. Regional Counsel, Midwest Region, United States Environmental Protection Agency, 1973-1974. Special Counsel, Illinois Department of Mines and Minerals, 1979-1983. Senior Lecturer, Loyola University of Chicago, 1984-1990. *Member:* Illinois State, Federal and American (Member, Environmental Litigation Committee, 1987—; Environmental Energy and Natural Resources Committee) Bar Associations; Association for Conflict Resolution. ***PRACTICE AREAS:*** Environmental Law; Litigation; Admininistrative Law; Alternative Dispute Resolution; Appellate Practice. ***Email:*** hsheldon@hinshawlaw.com

TIMOTHY G. SHELTON, born Denver, Colorado, March 24, 1947; admitted to bar, 1992, Illinois and U.S. District Court, Northern District of Illinois; 1998, U.S. Court of Appeals, Seventh Circuit and U.S. Court of Appeals, Eighth Circuit. *Education:* Pomona College (B.A., 1969); Georgetown University (J.D., 1992). *Member:* American Bar Association; Appellate Lawyers Association of Illinois. ***PRACTICE AREAS:*** Appellate; Professional Liability Litigation; Insurance Coverage Litigation. ***Email:*** tshelton@hinshawlaw.com

KEVIN R. SIDO, born Edwardsville, Illinois, 1951; admitted to bar, 1975, Illinois and U.S. District Court, Northern District of Illinois including Trial Bar; 1976, U.S. Tax Court; 1977, U.S. Court of Appeals, Seventh Circuit; 1979, U.S. Supreme Court; 1984, U.S. District Court, Central District of Illinois; 1993, U.S. District Court, Southern District of Illinois; 1994, U.S. District Court, Western District of Michigan; 1995, U.S. District Court, Northern District of Indiana; 2003, U.S. District Court, Eastern District of Michigan. *Education:* University of Illinois (B.A., with high honors, 1972; J.D., 1975). Phi Beta Kappa; Phi Delta Phi. Lecturer and Author, Illinois Institute for Continuing Legal Education, 1979—. Arbitrator, Cook County Circuit Court Mandatory Arbitration Program, 1990-1997. Member, Panel of Arbitrators, American Arbitration Association. *Member:* Illinois State and American Bar Associations; Illinois Defense Counsel (Seminar Committee Chairman, 1981-1982; Director, 1982-1983, 1988-1994); Defense Research Institute (Chairman, Architects & Engineers Professional Liability Committee, 1982-1986; State Area Chairman, 1988-1994); International Association of Defense Counsel (Vice-chair, Construction Law Committee); American Board of Trial Advocates; Appellate Lawyers Association; Society of Trial Lawyers (Illinois); American Institute of Architects (Professional Affiliate); American Society of Civil Engineers (Associate); Society of Illinois Construction Attorneys. ***PRACTICE AREAS:*** Professional Liability Litigation; Architects and Engineers Liability; Design Professionals Liability; Construction Law; Products Liability Litigation; Insurance Coverage Litigation; ADR/Mediation. ***Email:*** ksido@hinshawlaw.com

DAVID A. SORENSEN, born Elmhurst, Illinois, December 22, 1965; admitted to bar, 1993, Illinois and U.S. District Court, Northern District of Illinois; 1995, Indiana and U.S. District Court, Northern and Southern Districts of Indiana. *Education:* University of Michigan (B.A., 1988); Indiana University (J.D., 1993). *Member:* Chicago and American Bar Associations; Defense Research Institute; Illinois Association of Defense Counsel. ***PRACTICE AREAS:*** Medical Malpractice; Insurance Coverage; Products Liability. ***Email:*** dsorensen@hinshawlaw.com

ELIZABETH F. STARUCK, born Kenosha, Wisconsin, April 16, 1970; admitted to bar, 1995, Illinois and U.S. District Court, Northern District of Illinois. *Education:* University of Iowa (B.A., 1992); Illinois Institute of Technology, Chicago-Kent School of Law (J.D., 1995). *Member:* American Bar Association. ***PRACTICE AREAS:*** Fidelity; Insurance Coverage Litigation; Professional Liability Litigation; White Collar Crime; Professional Responsibility and Ethics. ***Email:*** estaruck@hinshawlaw.com

(This Listing Continued)

THOMAS P. SUKOWICZ, born Chicago, Illinois, September 24, 1955; admitted to bar, 1985, Illinois; 1999, Florida. *Education:* Loyola University (B.A., 1977); University of Notre Dame (M.A., 1979); DePaul University (J.D., 1985). Co-author: *Attorney Disciplinary Proceedings: Illinois Practice and Procedure,* Law Bulletin Publishing Company (2002); chapter on "Attorney Liability Risk Management" in Attorney Legal Liability, Illinois Institute for Continuing Legal Education (2002); monthly Ethics Column in Chicago Lawyer magazine. Author: *Illinois Code of Paralegal Ethics* for the Paralegal Association (1997); numerous articles on professional responsibility and professional liability issues. Editor of Newsletters published by Hinshaw & Culbertson for lawyers and their brokers and insurers. Frequent speaker at seminars on topics of attorney ethics and risk management. Served as Faculty Member, Illinois Institute of Professional Responsibility at the request of the Illinois Attorney Registration and Disciplinary Commission. Former Adjunct Professor, Professional Responsibility, De Paul University College of Law in Chicago. *Member:* The Florida Bar; American Bar Association. (Also at Fort Lauderdale, Florida Office). ***PRACTICE AREAS:*** Legal Malpractice; Legal Ethics and Professional Responsibility; Risk Management. ***Email:*** tsukowicz@hinshawlaw.com

PETER D. SULLIVAN, born Evanston, Illinois, November 9, 1958; admitted to bar, 1983, Illinois and U.S. District Court, Northern District of Illinois, including Trial Bar; 1986, U.S. District Court, Eastern District of Michigan; 1989, U.S. District Court, Eastern District of Wisconsin; 1993, U.S. District Court, Western District of Michigan; 1994, U.S. District Court, Southern District of Illinois; 1996, U.S. District Court, Central District of Illinois; 2001, U.S. Court of Appeals, Seventh Circuit. *Education:* University of Notre Dame (B.A., 1980); Loyola University School of Law, Chicago (J.D., 1983). *Member:* Chicago, Illinois State and American Bar Associations; Defense Research Institute. ***PRACTICE AREAS:*** Professional Liability Litigation; Commercial Litigation; Accountant's Liability; Legal Malpractice; Director and Officer Liability; Class Action Litigation; Securities Litigation; Mediation and Arbitration. ***Email:*** psullivan@hinshawlaw.com

TIMOTHY M. SULLIVAN, born Chicago, Illinois, November 12, 1949; admitted to bar, 1975, Illinois. *Education:* Loyola University (B.S., 1971; J.D., with honors, 1975). Articles Editor, Loyola Law Journal, 1974-1975. *Member:* Illinois State Bar Association. ***PRACTICE AREAS:*** Corporate and Business Law; Mergers and Acquisitions; Securities. ***Email:*** tsullivan@hinshawlaw.com

ROBERT H. SUMMERS, JR., born Evergreen Park, Illinois, January 15, 1965; admitted to bar, 1991, Illinois and U.S. District Court, Northern District of Illinois; 1992, U.S. District Court, Eastern and Western Districts of Arkansas. *Education:* University of Illinois (B.A., 1987); John Marshall School of Law (J.D., 1991). *Member:* Illinois State Bar Association. ***PRACTICE AREAS:*** Medical Malpractice; Construction Litigation; Premises Litigation; Products Liability. ***Email:*** rsummers@hinshawlaw.com

STEPHEN R. SWOFFORD, born St. Louis, Missouri, October 24, 1947; admitted to bar, 1975, Illinois; 1976, U.S. Court of Appeals, Seventh Circuit; 1978, U.S. Supreme Court; 1987, U.S. Court of Appeals, Federal Circuit; 1997, U.S. Court of Appeals, Fifth Circuit; 2003, U.S. Court of Appeals, Eighth Circuit; 2004, U.S. Court of Appeals, First Circuit. *Education:* Northwestern University (B.S., 1969); The John Marshall Law School (J.D., with honors, 1975). *Member:* Illinois State Bar Association; Appellate Lawyers Association (President, 1993-1994); Defense Research Institute. Fellow, American Academy of Appellate Lawyers. ***PRACTICE AREAS:*** Appeals; Professional Liability. ***Email:*** sswofford@hinshawlaw.com

JEROME R. VAINISI, born Chicago, Illinois, October 7, 1941; admitted to bar, 1969, Illinois; 1987, Michigan. *Education:* Georgetown University (B.S.B.A., 1963); Chicago Kent College of Law (J.D., 1969). Moot Court Champion. Phi Delta Phi. ***PRACTICE AREAS:*** Sports and Entertainment Law; Professional Athlete Contract Negotiations in Football, Hockey, Basketball and Baseball; Corporate and Individual Sports Related Activity Negotiations; NCAA Compliance and Infraction Matters. ***Email:*** jvainisi@hinshawlaw.com

KATHRYN S. VANDER BROEK, born Royal Oak, Michigan, June 3, 1963; admitted to bar, 1994, Illinois and U.S. District Court, Northern District of Illinois 2003, U.S. Court of Appeals, Seventh Circuit. *Education:* Michigan State University (B.A., 1985); University of Chicago, School of Social Service Administration (M.A., 1986); Loyola University, Chicago School of Law (J.D., 1994). Lecturer: "Law & Social Work," University of Illinois, Jane Addams College of Social Work, 1997-2000; "Social Work & the Law," University of Chicago, School of Social Service Administration, 2002—. Licensed Clinical Social Worker. *Member:* Chicago Bar Association; National Association of Social Workers. ***PRACTICE AREAS:*** School Law; Special Education Law; Labor and Employment Law. ***Email:*** kvanderb@hinshawlaw.com

JAMES C. VLAHAKIS, born Lansing, Michigan, January 20, 1970; admitted to bar, 1995, Illinois; 1996, Michigan, U.S. District Court, Northern and Central Districts of Illinois and U.S. Court of Appeals, Seventh Circuit; 1999, U.S. District Court, Northern District of Indiana; 2005, U.S. District Court, Eastern District of Michigan. *Education:* Michigan State University (B.A., 1992); Loyola University (J.D., 1995). Visiting Scholar, Cambridge University, England, 2000. ***PRACTICE AREAS:*** Commercial Litigation; Class Action Litigation; Constitutional Law; Civil Rights Litigation; Municipal Law. ***Email:*** jvlahakis@hinshawlaw.com

JOSHUA G. VINCENT, born New York, New York, November 15, 1958; admitted to bar, 1983, Illinois and U.S. District Court, Northern District of Illinois; 1985, U.S. Court of Appeals, Seventh Circuit; 1986, U.S. Court of Appeals, Tenth Circuit; 1991, U.S. Court of Appeals, Federal Circuit; 1995, U.S. Court of Appeals, Ninth Circuit; 1998 Arizona and U.S. District Court, District of Arizona; 2002, U.S. Court of Appeals, Eighth Circuit; 2005, U.S. Supreme Court. *Education:* University of Michigan (B.A., 1980); DePaul University Law School (J.D., 1983). Adjunct Professor of Appellate Brief Writing, De Paul University, Fall, 1989-1994. Member, Leading Lawyers Network. Selected as Super Lawyer, "Super Lawyers" magazine, 2005. *Member:* American Bar Association; Illinois Appellate Lawyers Association (Member, Board of Directors, 1988-1990). ***PRACTICE AREAS:*** Professional Liability Litigation; Commercial Litigation; Employment Litigation; Products Liability Litigation; Appellate; Premises Liability Defense; Contract Litigation. ***Email:*** jvincent@hinshawlaw.com

MATTHEW P. WALSH, II, born Oaklawn, Illinois, August 3, 1967; admitted to bar, 1992, Illinois and U.S. District Court, Northern District of Illinois; 1993, U.S. Court of

(This Listing Continued)

Appeals, Seventh Circuit. *Education:* Bradley University (B.S., Business, 1989); Illinois Institute of Technology, Chicago-Kent College of Law (J.D., 1992). ***PRACTICE AREAS:*** Construction; Municipal Liability Litigation; Civil Rights Defense Litigation; Medical Malpractice; Risk Management; Workers' Compensation. ***Email:*** mwalsh@hinshawlaw.com

PETER A. WALSH, born Evergreen Park, Illinois, June 24, 1958; admitted to bar, 1983, Illinois. *Education:* University of Notre Dame (B.A., 1980; J.D., 1983). *Member:* Illinois State Bar Association; Trial Lawyers Club of Chicago; Defense Research Institute; National Association of Defense Trial Counsel; National Association of Railroad Trial Counsel; Trucking Industry Defense Association. ***PRACTICE AREAS:*** Construction Law; Municipal Liability Litigation; Civil Rights Defense Litigation; Medical Malpractice; Risk Management; Workers Compensation. ***Email:*** pwalsh@hinshawlaw.com

JENNIFER W. WELLER, born Deland, Florida, March 18, 1974; admitted to bar, 1999, Illinois and U.S. District Court, Northern District of Illinois. *Education:* University of Illinois (B.A., 1996); Loyola University (J.D., 1999). Member, Loyola University Chicago Law Journal, 1997-1999. Co-Author: with John J. Lynch, "Third Party Practice-Contribution and Indemnity," Illinois CML Practice, Illinois Institute for Continuing Legal Education, Supplement 2000. *Member:* Chicago, Illinois State and American Bar Associations. ***PRACTICE AREAS:*** Medical Malpractice; Professional Liability Litigation; Litigation. ***Email:*** jweller@hinshawlaw.com

TODD M. YOUNG, born Valparaiso, Indiana, May 2, 1958; admitted to bar, 1983, Illinois. *Education:* Dartmouth College (A.B., cum laude, 1980); University of Toulouse, Toulouse, France; University of Chicago (J.D., 1983). Member, 1981-1982 and Comment Editor, 1982-1983, University of Chicago Law Review. Adjunct Faculty Member: Mergers and Acquisitions, Northwestern University School of Law, 1999—; Canon Law, Seabury-Western Theological Seminary (Episcopal), 2000-2005. Author: "Corporate Operating and Maintenance Issues," Business Law Series (IL Institute for Continuing Legal Education, Ed., 2005 and two prior editions); "Organizing and Advising a Small Business," Starting Points: The Fundamentals of Practice in Illinois (IL Institute for Continuing Legal Education, Ed., 2005 and two prior editions). Chancellor, Episcopal Diocese of Chicago, 2003—; Assistant Chancellor, 1995-2002. *Member:* Chicago and American Bar Associations. ***LANGUAGES:*** French. ***PRACTICE AREAS:*** Corporate Law; Mergers, Acquisitions and Divestitures; Finance; Religious Institutions; Securities. ***Email:*** tyoung@hinshawlaw.com

CLIFFORD E. YUKNIS, born Chicago, Illinois, January 22, 1950; admitted to bar, 1974, Illinois and U.S. District Court, Northern District of Illinois; 1975, U.S. Court of Appeals, Seventh Circuit; 1977, U.S. Supreme Court; 1978, U.S. District Court, Eastern District of Wisconsin; 1983, U.S. Tax Court. *Education:* DePaul University of Chicago (B.A., summa cum laude, 1971); Harvard University Law School (J.D., 1974). Harvard Law School Society of Illinois. *Member:* Chicago Bar Association; The Lawyers Club of Chicago; Illinois Association of Defense Trial Counsel. ***PRACTICE AREAS:*** Litigation. ***Email:*** cyuknis@hinshawlaw.com

ASSOCIATES

DAVID J. ALFINI, born Chicago, Illinois, May 6, 1972; admitted to bar, 2000, Illinois and Indiana. *Education:* New York University (B.A., Political Science, 1993); Indiana University (M.A., Slavic Languages and Literatures); Indiana University School of Law (J.D., 2000). Moot Court. ***LANGUAGES:*** Czech. ***PRACTICE AREAS:*** Litigation; Products Liability; Transportation; Premises Liability. ***Email:*** dalfini@hinshawlaw.com

ANTHONY E. ANTOGNOLI, born Melrose Park, Illinois, May 15, 1975; admitted to bar, 2000, Illinois; 2004, U.S. Tax Court; 2005, U.S. District Court, Northern District of Illinois. *Education:* University of Illinois (B.S., Finance, 1997); Loyola University, Chicago (J.D., 2000; Certificate in Tax Law, 2000). Co-Author, Comments of the Chicago Bar Association's Employee Benefits Committee regarding the future of the Employee Plans determination letter program, August, 2003. Co-Author, "Fiduciary Responsibility Under the 'Serious Consideration' Standard," DC Plan Investing, November 30, 2000. Assisted in drafting "State Taxation of Business Trusts: Limits, Concerns and Opportunities," Journal of Multistate Taxation, February, 2000; reprinted, Business Entities, September/October, 2000. *Member:* Chicago Bar Association (Member, Employee Benefits Committee; Chairman, IRS Subcommittee). ***REPORTED CASES:*** DeGrave v. National Automatic Merchandising Association Pension Plan, 2005 WL 1204605, 35 Employee Benefits Cas. 2145. ***PRACTICE AREAS:*** Employee Benefits / ERISA; Federal Taxation; Executive Compensation. ***Email:*** aantognoli@hinshawlaw.com

V. BRETTE BENSINGER, born Washington, D.C., November 21, 1977; admitted to bar, 2005, Illinois. *Education:* Northwestern University (B.A., English, 2000); Illinois Institute of Technology, Chicago-Kent College of Law (J.D., 2005). Dean's List; Student Editor, Employment Policy Journal; Recipient, CALI Award, Highest Grade in Class. ***LANGUAGES:*** Spanish. ***PRACTICE AREAS:*** Labor and Employment; Employer Liability; Employment Defense; Employment Law; Municipal Defense; Municipal Liability; Medical Malpractice Defense.

JASON S. BENTLEY, born Kalamazoo, Michigan, April 18, 1973; admitted to bar, 2003, Illinois. *Education:* Valparaiso University (B.A., Political Science, Writing and Theatre, 1996); DePaul University (J.D., 2001). Author: "A Consular Experience: Assets and Concerns," DePaul International Law Journal, Winter, 2000. Vice-President, DePaul International Law Society, 1999-2000. *Member:* Illinois State Bar Association. ***PRACTICE AREAS:*** Environmental Litigation; Municipal Liability; Commercial Litigation; Transportation. ***Email:*** jbentley@hinshawlaw.com

MATTHEW J. CANNA, admitted to bar, 2003, Illinois. *Education:* University of Notre Dame (B.S., Mechanical Engineering, 2000); Chicago-Kent College of Law, Illinois Institute of Technology (J.D., 2003). *Member, Intellectual Property Law Society.* ***PRACTICE AREAS:*** General Liability Litigation. ***Email:*** mcanna@hinshawlaw.com

CLINT B. CHARNES, born Beech Grove, Indiana, December 13, 1972; admitted to bar, 2001, Illinois, U.S. District Court, Northern District of Illinois and U.S. Court of Appeals, Seventh Circuit. *Education:* Indiana University (B.A., cum laude, 1995); Valparaiso University (J.D., cum laude, 2001). Executive Board Member of Valparaiso Law Moot Court

(This Listing Continued)

Society, 1999-2001. *Member:* Illinois Association of Defense Trial Counsel. ***PRACTICE AREAS:*** Products Liability; Premises Liability; General Tort Defense; Insurance Coverage Litigation; Construction Law; Toxic Torts. ***Email:*** ccharnes@hinshawlaw.com

RENEE C. CHOY, born Chicago, Illinois, November 20, 1979; admitted to bar, 2005, Illinois. *Education:* Northwestern University (B.A., Sociology and Political Science, honors in Sociology, 2001); Chicago-Kent College of Law, Illinois Institute of Technology (J.D., 2005). 1999, Congressional Intern, Chicago office of the Honorable Richard J. Durbin, United State Senate (D-IL). President, Corporate Law Society, 2002-2004. *Member:* Asian-Pacific American Law Students Association. ***PRACTICE AREAS:*** Litigation; Professional Liability; Agents and Brokers Errors and Omissions; Agents and Brokers Liability; Architects and Engineers Errors and Omissions; Architects and Engineers Liability; Architects and Engineers Malpractice; Design Professionals Errors and Omissions; Design Professionals Liability; Design Professionals Malpractice; Professional Errors and Omissions; Professional Liability Defense; Professional Malpractice; Professional Negligence.

APRIL M. DAHL, born Missoula, Montana, December 14, 1977; admitted to bar, 2003, Illinois. *Education:* University of Notre Dame (B.A., English, 2000; J.D., 2003). *Member:* Chicago Bar Association. ***PRACTICE AREAS:*** General Liability Litigation; Products Liability Litigation; Toxic Tort Litigation. ***Email:*** adahl@hinshawlaw.com

KAREN M. EICHE, born Milwaukee, Wisconsin, November 18, 1969; admitted to bar, 1999, California and U.S. District Court, Southern District of California; 2003, U.S. District Court, Eastern and Central Districts of California; 2005, Illinois. *Education:* Cardinal Stritch College (B.S., cum laude, Business Management, 1994); California Western School of Law (J.D., 1998). *Member:* State Bar of California; American Bar Association; San Diego County Bar Association (Member, Construction Law and Business Law Sections); American General Contractor Association; American Subcontractor Association. ***PRACTICE AREAS:*** Fidelity and Surety; Construction Litigation. ***Email:*** keiche@hinshawlaw.com

SHARON M. FIGLIULO, born Tucson, Arizona; admitted to bar, 2001, Illinois and U.S. District Court, Northern District of Illinois. *Education:* St. Mary's University of Minnesota (B.A., 1997); Loyola University, Chicago (J.D., 2001). *Member:* Chicago Inn of Court. ***PRACTICE AREAS:*** Medical Malpractice; Professional Liability Litigation; Government and Municipal Litigation; Construction Litigation; Personal Injury Litigation. ***Email:*** sfigliulo@hinshawlaw.com

ROBERT J. FINLEY, born Fort Belvoir, Virginia, March 14, 1973; admitted to bar, 2001, Illinois and U.S. District Court, Northern District of Illinois. *Education:* Marquette University (B.A., 1995); DePaul University (J.D., 2001). *Member:* Chicago, Illinois State and American Bar Associations. ***PRACTICE AREAS:*** Workers' Compensation Defense; Personal Injury Defense Litigation; Real Estate Agents Errors and Omissions Liability; General Liability Litigation; National and Regional Litigation Programs. ***Email:*** rfinley@hinshawlaw.com

KATHERINE FOLEY, born Chicago, Illinois, March 26, 1966; admitted to bar, 1991, Illinois and U.S. District Court, Northern District of Illinois; 1994, U.S. Court of Appeals, Seventh Circuit. *Education:* University of Illinois, Urbana-Champaign (B.A., 1988); Loyola University, Chicago (J.D., 1991). *Member:* Illinois State Bar Association. ***PRACTICE AREAS:*** Workers Compensation; Personal Injury. ***Email:*** kfoley@hinshawlaw.com

BARBARA A. GALLANT, born Jackson, Michigan, August 24, 1971; admitted to bar, 2002, Illinois. *Education:* Northern Michigan University (B.S., Nursing, 1996); Thomas M. Cooley Law School (J.D., 2002). *Member:* Chicago and American Bar Associations. ***PRACTICE AREAS:*** Medical Malpractice; Health Care; Premises Liability. ***Email:*** bgallant@hinshawlaw.com

JENNIFER K. GUST, born 1971; admitted to bar, 2001, Illinois. *Education:* Indiana University (B.A., 1993); Loyola Unversity, Chicago (J.D., 2001). Hartigan Fellow, 1999. Participant, Niagara Moot Court Competition, 2000. Editor-in-Chief, 2000-2001 and Chief Articles Editor, 1999-2000, Loyola Consumer Law Review. Law Clerk to Hon. Thomas P. Quinn, Chancery Division, Cook County, Illinois, 2002. Author: "Proximate Cause and the Lost Chance Doctrine," Loyola Consumer Law Review, vol. 4, 1999. *Member:* Chicago and Illinois State Bar Associations. ***PRACTICE AREAS:*** Tort Coverage; Commercial Litigation. ***Email:*** jgust@hinshawlaw.com

JENNIFER L. GUTHRIE, born Mayfield Heights, Ohio, September 10, 1976; admitted to bar, 2001, Illinois and U.S. District Court, Northern District of Illinois. *Education:* Miami University (B.A., 1998) Loyola University, Chicago (J.D., 2001; LL.M., 2002; Certificate in Health Law). *Member:* Chicago Bar Association. ***PRACTICE AREAS:*** Products Liability; Toxic Torts; Indoor Air Quality; Mold Litigation; Health Care Privacy. ***Email:*** jguthrie@hinshawlaw.com

JENNIFER M. HANNA, admitted to bar, 2002, Illinois and U.S. District Court, Northern District of Illinois. *Education:* Loyola University, Chicago (B.S., Psychology, 1998); University of Illinois-College of Law (J.D., 2002). Phi Alpha Delta (President, Magruder Chapter). Captain, Trial Team. Member, Phillip C. Jessup International Moot Court. *Member:* Illinois State Bar Association; American Bar Association. ***PRACTICE AREAS:*** Professional Liability Litigation; Legal Malpractice; Consumer Litigation. ***Email:*** jhanna@hinshawlaw.com

ELIOTT M. HEDIN, born Tulsa, Oklahoma, July 28, 1974; admitted to bar, 2000, Missouri; 2001, Illinois; 2003, U.S. District Court, Southern and Central Districts of Illinois; 2004, U.S. Court of Appeals, Seventh Circuit; 2005, U.S. District Court, Northern District of Illinois. *Education:* University of Illinois (B.S., 1996); Washington University School of Law (J.D., 2000). Law Clerk to The Honorable Wiley Y. Daniel, U.S. District Court, District of Colorado, 2001 - 2003. *Member:* Illinois State and American Bar Associations. ***PRACTICE AREAS:*** Medical Malpractice Defense; General Liability Litigation; Commercial Litigation; Mineral Law. ***Email:*** ehedin@hinshawlaw.com

CORINNE CANTWELL HEGGIE, born Fort Hood, Texas, June 9, 1976; admitted to bar, 2002, Illinois and U.S. District Court, Northern District of Illinois; 2005, U.S. District Court, Northern and Southern Districts of Indiana. *Education:* University of Illinois, Urbana-Champaign (B.A., French, 1998); DePaul University (J.D., 2001). *Member:* Chicago

(This Listing Continued)

HINSHAW & CULBERTSON LLP, Chicago—Continued

and Illinois State Bar Associations. ***LANGUAGES:*** French and Spanish. ***PRACTICE AREAS:*** Civil Rights Defense Litigation; Municipal Liability; Professional Liability Litigation; Medical Malpractice. ***Email:*** cheggie@hinshawlaw.com

MELINA T. HIPSKIND, born Chicago, Illinois, August 29, 1979; admitted to bar, 2004, Illinois and U.S. District Court, Northern District of Illinois. *Education:* University of Illinois (B.A., Political Science, 2001); DePaul University College of Law (J.D., 2004; Certificate in Health Law, 2004). Co-Author, "Sarbanes-Oxley Refresher and Update," Declarations, Summer 2004. *Member:* Chicago Bar Association; Illinois State Bar Association; American Bar Association. ***LANGUAGES:*** French. ***PRACTICE AREAS:*** Products Liability; Premises Liability. ***Email:*** mhipskind@hinshawlaw.com

BETTY Y. JANG, born Chicago, Illinois; admitted to bar, 1994, Illinois; 1995, U.S. District Court, Northern District of Illinois; 2002, U.S. Supreme Court. *Education:* University of Illinois, Urbana-Champaign (B.A., 1991); Chicago-Kent College of Law (J.D., 1994). Recipient: American Jurisprudence Award, Medical Malpractice Seminar, 1994; Ernest A. Turk Book Award, 1993-94; Chicago-Kent Alumni Association Scholarship, 1993-1994. Adjunct Professor, Trial Advocacy Program, University of Illinois, College of Law, 2002—. Selected Facilitator and Forum Participant, Illinois Supreme Court Committee on Professionalism, August, November 2003. Guest Lecturer, University of Illinois, Political Science, "The Legal System", 2001—. Judge for University of Illinois, College of Law, Moot Court Competition, Legal Writing Oral Arguments, ABA Negotiation Competition, 2000—. Guest Speaker: University of Illinois, College of Law, Asian American Law Students Association, March 2002; University of Illinois, Pre-Law Club, March 2002. Member, Board of Directors, CU One to One Mentoring Scholarship Foundation, 2001. Member, Fundraising Committee, The United Way, 2001. Attorney, Office of the Cook County Public Defender, 1995-2001. Certified Arbitrator, Cook County Mandatory Arbitration. *Member:* Champaign County, Illinois State (Recipient, "Young Lawyer of the Year," 2004) and American Bar Associations; National Asian Pacific American Bar Association; Asian American Bar Association of Greater Chicago Area; East Central Illinois Women Attorneys' Association. ***LANGUAGES:*** French and Korean. ***PRACTICE AREAS:*** Labor and Employment Law; Workers Compensation; General Liability. ***Email:*** bjang@hinshawlaw.com

KIMBERLY A. JANSEN, born 1973; admitted to bar, 1999, Illinois and U.S. District Court, Northern District of Illinois; 2004, U.S. Court of Appeals, Seventh, Eighth and Ninth Circuits. *Education:* Knox College (B.A., magna cum laude, 1994); University of Illinois at Urbana-Champaign (M.Ed., 1999; J.D., magna cum laude, 1999). Phi Beta Kappa. Recipient, CALI Awards in International Litigation and Arbitration, Comparative International Civil Procedure, and Comparative International Copyright Principles, 1997-1999. Judicial Clerk to: The Honorable Thomas Homer, Third District Illinois Appellate Court, 1999-2001; The Honorable Judith Cohen, First District, Illinois Appellate Court, 2001-2002. *Member:* American Bar Association; Appellate Lawyers Association. ***LANGUAGES:*** German. ***PRACTICE AREAS:*** Appellate Practice; Commercial Litigation. ***Email:*** kjansen@hinshawlaw.com

VALERIE L. KAHN, born Lima, Ohio, October 28, 1975; admitted to bar, 2001, Illinois and U.S. District Court, Northern District of Illinois. *Education:* Boston University (B.A., with distinction, cum laude, 1998) Case Western Reserve University (J.D., 2001). Phi Alpha Delta, Vice Justice, Hay Chapter, 1998-1999. Author: "Fighting Sexual Harassment Abroad: The Extraterritorial Application of Tital VII." *Member:* Chicago Bar Association. ***PRACTICE AREAS:*** Labor and Employment; Workers Compensation Defense; Construction Litigation. ***Email:*** vkahn@hinshawlaw.com

MAX J. KANTER, born Elmhurst, Illinois, February 28, 1976; admitted to bar, 2005, Illinois. *Education:* University of Illinois (B.S., Biology, 1998); Loyola University Chicago (M.S. with distinction, Biology, 2001); Illinois Institute of Technology Chicago-Kent College of Law (J.D., 2005). ***PRACTICE AREAS:*** Litigation; Defense Litigation; Commercial Liability; Real Estate; Litigation; Intellectual Property Litigation.

CHADWEL D. KASDIN, born Chicago, Illinois, July 16, 1975; admitted to bar, 2000, Illinois. *Education:* Skidmore College (B.A., cum laude, 1997); Washington University School of Law (J.D., 2000). *Member:* Illinois State Bar Association. ***PRACTICE AREAS:*** Medical Malpractice Defense; Commercial Litigation; Premises Liability. ***Email:*** ckasdin@hinshawlaw.com

ANGELA S. KELVER, born South Bend, Indiana, August 9, 1975; admitted to bar, 2003, Illinois. *Education:* St. Mary's College (B.A., 1997); Indiana University School of Law - Bloomington (J.D., cum laude, 2003). ***PRACTICE AREAS:*** Products Liability; Commercial Litigation; Tort Defense. ***Email:*** akelver@hinshawlaw.com

PETER M. KING, born Elmhurst, Illinois, November 26, 1974; admitted to bar, 2003, Illinois and U.S. District Court, Northern and Central Districts of Illinois. *Education:* Eastern Illinois University (B.A., 1999); John Marshall Law School (J.D., 2003). *Member:* DuPage County and Illinois State Bar Associations. ***PRACTICE AREAS:*** Commercial Litigation; Employment Litigation; Labor Law; School Law and Litigation; Student Matters. ***Email:*** pking@hinshawlaw.com

STEVEN M. KLACZYNSKI, born July 4, 1965; admitted to bar, 1990, Illinois; 1991, Michigan; 2004, U.S. District Court, Northern District of Illinois. *Education:* University of Michigan (B.A., Political Science, 1987); University of Detroit-Mercy School of Law (J.D., 1990). Member, Editorial Staff, Michigan Business Law Journal. Adjunct Professor, Triton Community College, 1998-2000. Trial Advocacy Coach, Loyola University Law School, 1999-2000. ***PRACTICE AREAS:*** Medical Malpractice; Products Liability Litigation; Municipal Liability; Commercial Litigation; Professional Liability; Construction Litigation; Criminal Defense. ***Email:*** sklaczynski@hinshawlaw.com

DANIELLE R. LEBLANG, born Springfield, Illinois, December 4, 1978; admitted to bar, 2005, Illinois. *Education:* Illinois State University (B.S., Mass Communications, magna cum laude, 2001); John Marshall Law School (J.D., 2005). Recipient, Dean's Scholarship. *Member:* Chicago and Illinois State Bar Associations. ***PRACTICE AREAS:*** Workers Compensation Defense; General Liability Litigation; Transportation Litigation; Commercial Litigation; Personal Injury Defense. ***Email:*** dleblang@hinshawlaw.com

(This Listing Continued)

ABEL LEON, admitted to bar, 2003, Illinois; 2004, U.S. Court of Appeals, Seventh Circuit. *Education:* Carleton College (B.A., 1998); DePaul University College of Law (J.D., 2003). National Order of Barristers. Member, Moot Court Society. Best Oralist, Moot Court Competition, Hispanic National Bar Association. Member, Latino Law Student Association. Vice President, De Paul University School of Law. Author, "The Americans with Disabilities Act," The John Marshall Law Review (Summer 2003). *Member:* Chicago and American Bar Associations; Hispanic Lawyers Association of Illinois; National Order of Barristers. ***LANGUAGES:*** Spanish, French. ***PRACTICE AREAS:*** School Law; Employment Law; Real Estate. ***Email:*** aleon@hinshawlaw.com

JAMES M. LYDON, born Chicago, Illinois, 1966; admitted to bar, 1992, Illinois and U.S. District Court, Northern District of Illinois, including Trial Bar. *Education:* University of Michigan (B.A., 1988); Chicago-Kent College of Law (J.D., 1992). Cook County State's Attorney, 1992-1999. Member, Federal Defender Program, 2002—. *Member:* Chicago Bar Association; Chicago Inn of Court. ***PRACTICE AREAS:*** Litigation; Construction Litigation; Medical Malpractice; Products Liability; Municipal Litigation; Criminal Law. ***Email:*** jlydon@hinshawlaw.com

BARRY F. MACENTEE, born Oak Lawn, Illinois, June 6, 1976; admitted to bar, 2001, Illinois and U.S. District Court, Northern District of Illinois. *Education:* John Carroll University (B.A., Philosophy, cum laude, 1998); Loyola University, Chicago (J.D., 2001). Alpha Sigma Nu. Member, Jesuit Honor Society. Member, International Commercial Arbitration Moot Court Team, Loyola University of Chicago. Participant, Willem C. Vis Arbitral Moot in Vienna, Austria. *Member:* Chicago (Member: Federal Civil Procedure Committee; Commercial Litigation Committee) and Illinois State Bar Associations. ***PRACTICE AREAS:*** Accounting Malpractice Defense; Commercial Litigation; Legal Malpractice Defense; Directors and Officers Liability Defense. ***Email:*** bmacentee@hinshawlaw.com

CHRISTOPHER G. MARKEY, born July 29, 1950; admitted to bar, 1996, Illinois; 1997, U.S. District Court, Northern District of Illinois and U.S. Court of Appeals, Seventh Circuit. *Education:* Loyola University (B.A., cum laude, 1973); DePaul University (M.S., Business and Rehabilitation Administration, 1978); The John Marshall Law School (J.D., 1996). *Member:* Chicago and Illinois State Bar Associations; Chicago Inn of Court; Illinois Trial Lawyers Association; American Trial Lawyers Association; Illinois Association of Criminal Defense Lawyers. ***PRACTICE AREAS:*** Professional Liability Litigation; Legal Malpractice; Municipal Liability; White Collar Crime. ***Email:*** cmarkey@hinshawlaw.com

FRANK J. MARSICO, born Melrose Park, Illinois, December 14, 1969; admitted to bar, 1995, Illinois and U.S. District Court, Northern District of Illinois; 1999, U.S. District Court, Eastern District of Wisconsin. *Education:* Marquette University (B.A., 1992); DePaul University College of Law (J.D., 1995). Member, Executive Board, DePaul University College of Law Moot Court Society. Participant, National Moot Court Competitions. Externship, Cook County State's Attorney's Office, 1994-1995. *Member:* Illinois State Bar Association; American Bar Association. ***PRACTICE AREAS:*** Medical Malpractice; Litigation. ***Email:*** fmarsico@hinshawlaw.com

KOURTNEY A. MULCAHY, born Springfield, Illinois, April 2, 1975; admitted to bar, 2002, Illinois and U.S. District Court, Northern District of Illinois. *Education:* University of Illinois (B.A., 1997); The John Marshall Law School (J.D., 2001; LL.M., Intellectual Property Law, 2004). *Member:* Chicago and American Bar Associations. ***PRACTICE AREAS:*** Intellectual Property Transactions; Intellectual Property Litigation; Civil Rights Defense; Professional Liability Litigation. ***Email:*** kmulcahy@hinshawlaw.com

CONRAD C. NOWAK, born Chicago, Illinois, September 3, 1973; admitted to bar, 2003, Illinois; 2004, U.S. District Court, Northern District of Illinois. *Education:* DePaul Ulniversity (B.A., History, with honors, 1998); Loyola University Chicago School of Law (J.D., 2002). Member: Phi Kappa Phi; Phi Alpha Theta. Featured Articles Editor, Loyola University Chicago Forum of International Law, 2001-2002. Assistant Features Editor, Public Interest Law Reporter, 2001-2002. Dean's list. Student Representative, Loyola Business Law Advisory Board. Judicial Clerk to the Honorable William D. Maddux, Presiding Judge of the Law Division of the Circuit Court of Cook County, 2003-2005. ***LANGUAGES:*** Polish, Serbo-Croatian. ***PRACTICE AREAS:*** Medical Malpractice Defense; Defense Litigation; Personal Injury Defense.

TIMOTHY S. O'BRIEN, born Park Ridge, Illinois, August 28, 1974; admitted to bar, 2005, Illinois. *Education:* Marquette University (B.S., Business Administration, 1996); The John Marshall Law School (J.D., cum laude, 2005). Member, Moot Court Council. Class Representative, Student Bar Association. Recipient, John Marshall Alumni Association Scholarship, 2003. Lead Articles Editor, "The John Marshall Law Review". Extern to The Honorable Judge Samuel Der' - Yeghiayan, U.S. District Court, Northern District of Illinois. *Member:* Illinois State and New York State Bar Associations. ***PRACTICE AREAS:*** Defense Litigation; Construction Litigation; Employment Litigation; Employment Defense; Appellate Practice.

THOMAS L. O'CARROLL, born New York City, New York, March 10, 1972; admitted to bar, 1997, Illinois and U.S. District Court, Northern District of Illinois; 1999, U.S. Court of Appeals, Seventh Circuit. *Education:* Tulane University (B.A., History and Political Science, 1994); DePaul University College of Law (J.D., 1997). Member, Executive Board, DePaul Moot Court Society. Recipient: Best Brief, Intramural Moot Court Appellate Competition, 1995; Class of 1962 Scholarship Award for Academic Achievement in 1997. Member, DePaul Law Review. Editor, Journal of Health & Hospital Law. *Member:* Illinois State Bar Association. ***PRACTICE AREAS:*** Medical Malpractice Defense; Appellate Practice; Products Liability Litigation; Personal Injury Litigation. ***Email:*** tocarroll@hinshawlaw.com

PETER E. PEDERSON, born Litchfield, Illinois, November 9, 1974; admitted to bar, 1999, Illinois and U.S. District Court, Northern District of Illinois; 2000, U.S. District Court, Central District of Illinois; 2004, Washington and U.S. Court of Appeals, Seventh Circuit; 2005, U.S. District Court, Southern District of Illinois. *Education:* University of Illinois (B.A., Economics, cum laude, 1996); Boston University (J.D., cum laude, 1999). Phi Beta Kappa. *Member:* Illinois State and American Bar Associations. ***PRACTICE AREAS:*** ERISA Litigation; Class Actions; Commercial Litigation. ***Email:*** ppederson@hinshawlaw.com

JUSTIN M. PENN, born Peoria, Illinois, August 8, 1976; admitted to bar, 2004, Illinois. *Education:* University of Notre Dame (B.A., cum laude, Human Resource Manage-

(This Listing Continued)

ment and Theology, 1999); The John Marshall Law School (J.D., cum laude, 2004). ***PRACTICE AREAS:*** Litigation; Professional Liability Litigation; Legal Malpractice; Medical Malpractice. ***Email:*** jpenn@hinshawlaw.com

JENNIFER R. RICCOLO, born Cedar Rapids, Iowa, September 24, 1978; admitted to bar, 2004, Illinois. *Education:* University of Iowa (B.A., English and Italian, 2000); Loyola University Chicago, School of Law (J.D., Trial Advocacy Certificate, 2004). Member, Corboy Trial Team. Secretary, Student Bar Association. Recipient, Philip H. Corboy Fellowship. ***LANGUAGES:*** Italian. ***PRACTICE AREAS:*** Professional Liability Litigation; Medical Malpractice. ***Email:*** jriccolo@hinshawlaw.com

JOSEPH E. RUBAS, born Chicago, Illinois, May 5, 1973; admitted to bar, 1998, Illinois and U.S. District Court, Northern District of Illinois; 2000, U.S. District Court, Central District of Illinois. *Education:* University of Illinois (B.A., Political Science, 1995; B.S., Psychology, 1995); Loyola University (J.D., cum laude, 1998). *Member:* Chicago and Illinois State Bar Associations. ***PRACTICE AREAS:*** Professional Liability; Medical Malpractice; Construction Litigation; Transportation. ***Email:*** jrubas@hinshawlaw.com

LINNEA L. SCHRAMM, born Chicago Heights, Illinois, May 4, 1958; admitted to bar, 1996, Florida; 2003, Illinois. *Education:* University of Florida (B.S., 1980 and 1984; M.S., 1987; J.D., 1995). *Member:* Chicago, Illinois State and American Bar Associations; American Psychiatric Nurses Association; Chicago Area Nurse Attorney Association. ***PRACTICE AREAS:*** Medical Malpractice; Insurance Defense. ***Email:*** lschramm@hinshawlaw.com

MICHAEL P. SMITH, born Urbana, Illinois, December 26, 1974; admitted to bar, 2003, Illinois. *Education:* Millikin University (B.A., 1997); University of Illinois (J.D., 2003). Recipient, Rickert Award. Dean's List. *Member:* Illinois State and American Bar Associations. ***PRACTICE AREAS:*** Commercial Litigation; Legal Malpractice. ***Email:*** msmith@hinshawlaw.com

TODD P. STELTER, born Harvey, Illinois, May 15, 1976; admitted to bar, 2002, Illinois and U.S. District Court, Northern District of Illinois; 2004, U.S. District Court, Northern District of Indiana and U.S. District Court, Central and Southern Districts of Illinois. *Education:* University of Illinois at Urbana-Champaign (B.A., 1999); Loyola University, Chicago School of Law (J.D., 2002). *Member:* Chicago Bar Association. ***PRACTICE AREAS:*** Professional Liability Litigation; Legal Malpractice; Commercial Litigation; General Liability Litigation; Class Action Litigation. ***Email:*** tstelter@hinshawlaw.com

SHANNON K. STEVENS, born Peoria, Illinois, April 22, 1970; admitted to bar, 1999, Illinois. *Education:* University of Wisconsin-Milwaukee (B.A., 1993); DePaul University (J.D., 1999). *Member:* Chicago Bar Association. ***PRACTICE AREAS:*** Professional Malpractice Defense. ***Email:*** sstevens@hinshawlaw.com

DANIEL A. TREVINO, born 1975; admitted to bar, 1999, Illinois and U.S. District Court, Northern District of Illinois. *Education:* University of Illinois at Urbana-Champaign (B.A., 1996); DePaul University (J.D., 1999). *Member:* Chicago Bar Association; Hispanic Lawyers Association of Illinois. ***LANGUAGES:*** Spanish. ***PRACTICE AREAS:*** Transportation; General Liability Litigation; Personal Injury Litigation. ***Email:*** dtrevino@hinshawlaw.com

CLAY M. ULLRICK, admitted to bar, 1999, Illinois and U.S. District Court, Northern District of Illinois; 2000, U.S. Court of Appeals, Seventh Circuit. *Education:* Northern Illinois University (B.A., 1995); John Marshall Law School (J.D., 1999). *Member:* Illinois State and American Bar Associations. ***PRACTICE AREAS:*** Commercial Litigation; Employment Counseling and Litigation; Construction Law. ***Email:*** cullrick@hinshawlaw.com

RICHARD VELÁZQUEZ, born Chicago, Illinois, March 12, 1976; admitted to bar, 2003, Illinois. *Education:* Loyola University (B.A., 1998); DePaul University (J.D., 2002). Recipient of the CALI Award for Excellence in the Study of Civil Litigation Strategy, 2002. Legal Extern to the Hon. Joseph N. Casciato, 2002. White House Intern in the Office of Presidential Schedule and Advance, 1998. *Member:* American Bar Association; Chicago Bar Association; Hispanic Lawyers Association of Illinois. ***LANGUAGES:*** Spanish. ***PRACTICE AREAS:*** Professional Liability Litigation; Employment Litigation; Commercial Litigation; Medical Malpractice; Commercial Litigation. ***Email:*** rvelazquez@hinshawlaw.com

TERRY WAND, born Chicago, Illinois; admitted to bar, 2004, Illinois; 2005, U.S. District Court, Northern District of Illinois. *Education:* Xavier University of Louisiana (B.S., Biology, with honors in English); Indiana University - Bloomington School of Law (J.D., 2004). Editorial Staff, Federal Communications Law Journal. *Member:* Cook County Bar Association; Black Women Lawyers Association. ***PRACTICE AREAS:*** Legal Malpractice Litigation; Personal Injury Litigation; Commercial Litigation. ***Email:*** twand@hinshawlaw.com

DIANE E. WEBSTER, born Chicago, Illinois, September 6, 1979; admitted to bar, 2004, Illinois. *Education:* Arizona State University (B.A., Political Science, 2001); New England School of Law (J.D., 2004). Dean's List. New England Scholar. Recipient: Charles Hamilton Houston Scholarship; CALI Excellence of the Future Award - Negotiation. Associate Editor and Lead Articles Editor, "Journal of International and Comparative Law" (2002-2004). ***LANGUAGES:*** Spanish. ***PRACTICE AREAS:*** Medical Malpractice; Professional Liability Litigation; Real Estate; Municipal Law; Civil Rights. ***Email:*** dwebster@hinshawlaw.com

WILLIAM YU, born Chicago, Illinois, August 7, 1968; admitted to bar, 1996, Illinois and U.S. District Court, Northern District of Illinois. *Education:* Oberlin College (B.A., 1990); Charles University Prague, Czech Republic International Law Program (1994); The John Marshall Law School (J.D., 1996). Member, Chicago Commission on Human Relations, Advisory Council on Asian Affairs, 2003-2005. *Member:* Illinois State Bar Association; Asian American Bar Association (President, 2003-2004); Korean American Bar Association; National Asian Pacific American Bar Association (Midwest Regional Governor, 2004—). ***REPORTED CASES:*** Marthon v. Maple Grove Condominium Association, 101 F. Supp. 2d 1041 (N.D. Ill. 2000). ***PRACTICE AREAS:*** Commercial Litigation; Professional Liability Litigation; Civil Rights Defense; Real Estate Agent and Broker Errors and Omissions Liability; Products Liability Litigation. ***Email:*** wyu@hinshawlaw.com

JAVIER E. ZAMORA, born Los Gatos, California; admitted to bar, 2000, Illinois; 2002, District of Columbia. *Education:* University of California at Los Angeles (B.A., 1995); DePaul University (J.D., 2000). UCLA Army R.O.T.C., 1995. Recipient, Williams Foundation, Raymond Goldfarb Scholarship, 1997. Member, Jessup International Moot Court, International Finals, 1999. Member, Mexico City Committee, Chicago Sister Cities Program, 2001. Member, Board of Directors, Hispanic Lawyers Association of Illinois, 2003. Arbitrator, NASD Regulation, Inc. *Member:* Chicago, Illinois State, American and International Bar Associations; Hispanic National Bar Association; Hispanic Lawyers Association of Illinois; Chicago Council on Foreign Relations. [Captain, U.S. Army Reserve, 1988—]. ***LANGUAGES:*** Spanish. ***PRACTICE AREAS:*** Mergers, Acquisitions and Divestitures; Securities Law; Corporate Law; Debt and Equity Finance. ***Email:*** jzamora@hinshawlaw.com

OF COUNSEL

ROBERT E. ELLIS, born Chicago, Illinois, July 31, 1933; admitted to bar, 1957, Illinois. *Education:* University of Illinois (LL.B., 1957). Phi Delta Phi. *Member:* Illinois State Bar Association. ***PRACTICE AREAS:*** Title Insurance. ***Email:*** rellis@hinshawlaw.com

JAMES L. FLETCHER, born Washington, D.C., August 25, 1943; admitted to bar, 1968, Illinois. *Education:* Loyola University (B.S., in Hum., 1965); Northwestern University (J.D., 1968; Ph.D., 1971). Phi Alpha Delta; Alpha Sigma Nu. Instructor, John Marshall Law School, 1972-1977. Parliamentarian: Illinois House of Representatives, 1970: Illinois State Senate, 1973. Deputy Governor, State of Illinois, 1977-1979. *Member:* Illinois State Bar Association; American Judicature Society. ***PRACTICE AREAS:*** Governmental Relations; State Administrative Law. ***Email:*** jfletcher@ftoklaw.com

WILLIAM P. GROGAN, born Chicago, Illinois, May 22, 1949; admitted to bar, 1988, Illinois, U.S. District Court, Northern District of Illinois, U.S. Court of Appeals, Seventh Circuit and U.S. Court of Appeals for the Federal Circuit. *Education:* Loyola University (A.B., 1971; M.A., 1974; J.D., 1986); University of St. Mary of the Lake (M. Div.; S.T.B., cum laude; S.T.L., summa cum laude, 1976); Oxford University, St. Cross College, Oxford, England (M.St., 1987). *Member:* Illinois State Bar Association; Catholic Lawyers Guild. ***LANGUAGES:*** French and Spanish. ***PRACTICE AREAS:*** Medical Malpractice; Medical Ethics. ***Email:*** wgrogan@hinshawlaw.com

MICHAEL J. KASPER, born Evergreen Park, Illinois, September 2, 1964; admitted to bar, 1989, Illinois. *Education:* University of Notre Dame (B.A., cum laude, History, 1986); Northwestern University School of Law (J.D., 1989). ***REPORTED CASES:*** Campuzano v. Illinois State Board of Elections, et al., 200 F.Supp.2d 905 (N.D. Ill. 2002); Barnett v. U.S. Department of Commerce, et al., No. 02 C 2401 (N.D. Ill. 2002); Winters v. State Board of Elections, et al., 197 F. Supp.2d 1110 (N.D. Ill. 2001), aff'd ____ U.S. ____, ____ S.Ct. ____ (2001); Cole-Randazzo v. Ryan, et al., 762 N.E.2d 485 (Sup. Ct. Ill. 2001); Tully v. Orr, et al., No. 01 CH 00959 (Cir. Ct. Cook Cty. 2001); Granberg v. Didrickson, et al., 665 N.E.2d 398 (Ill. App. Ct., 1st Dist. 1996); Graham v. Illinois State Toll Highway Authority, 695 N.E.2d 360 (Ill. 1998); Johnson v. Edgar, 176 Ill.2d 499, 680 N.E.2d 1372 (Ill. 1997); Nader 2000 Primary Committee v. Illinois State Board of Elections, 00 C 4401 (N.D. Ill. 2000); Burny v. Clinton, 96 CO 00037 (Cir. Ct. Cook Cty. 1996); Anderson v. Graham, No. 77768 (Sup. Ct. Ill. 1994); Nolan v. Cook County Officers Electoral Board, 768 N.E.2d 216 (Ill. App. Ct., 1st Dist. 2002). ***PRACTICE AREAS:*** Legislative Law; Governmental Law. ***Email:*** mkasper@ftoklaw.com

COURTNEY C. NOTTAGE, born 1960; admitted to bar, 1990, Illinois and U.S. District Court, Northern District of Illinois; 1991, U.S. Court of Appeals, 7th Circuit; 1993, U.S. Supreme Court; 1996, U.S. Court of Appeals, District of Columbia Circuit and U.S. Court of Federal Claims. *Education:* Indiana State University (B.S., Sociology, 1982); Indiana University (J.D., 1987). Chief Legal Counsel, 1993-1998 and Chief of Staff, 1999-2005, to Illinois State Senate Minority Leader Emil Jones, Jr. ***PRACTICE AREAS:*** Government Affairs. ***Email:*** courtneynottage@aol.com

TIMOTHY J. O'BRIEN, born Evanston, Illinois, June 11, 1948; admitted to bar, 1981, Illinois, U.S. District Court, Northern District of Illinois and U.S. Court of Appeals, Seventh Circuit. *Education:* University of Illinois (B.A., cum laude, 1972); The John Marshall Law School (J.D., 1981). Deputy Director and General Counsel, Illinois Department of Public Aid, 1991-1994. General Counsel, Illinois Department of Public Health, 1986-1989. Deputy Inspector General, Office of Governor of Illinois, 1984-1986. Assist States Attorney, Cook County, 1981-1984. *Member:* Chicago and Illinois State Bar Associations; American Health Lawyers Association. [U.S. Army, 1967-1969, Vietnam]. ***PRACTICE AREAS:*** Health Care Law; Government; Administrative Law. ***Email:*** obrienfto@aol.com

WILLIAM O. SHANK, born Hamilton, Ohio, January 11, 1924; admitted to bar, 1951, Ohio; 1955, Illinois and U.S. District Court, Northern District of Illinois; 1954, U.S. Supreme Court. *Education:* Miami University (A.B., 1947); Yale University (J.D., 1950). Listed in: Who's Who in America; Who's Who in American Law. Class Secretary, Yale University. Member: Civic Federation of Chicago; Chicago Crime Commission; Library of International Relations; Council of Community Services, Chicago; Senior Citizens Committee of the City of Crystal Lake. Member, Advisory Committee, eLawForum, Washington, D.C. *Member:* Legal Club of Chicago (Past President); Law Club of Chicago; Lawyer's Club of the City of Chicago; Chicago Bar Association (Chairman, Coproate Law Departments Committee); Yale Law School Association of Illinois (Former President). Life Fellow, American Bar Foundation. (Also at Crystal Lake, Illinois Office). ***PRACTICE AREAS:*** Corporate Governance. ***Email:*** wshank@hinshawlaw.com

CLIVE M. TOPOL, born Chicago, Illinois, February 16, 1949; admitted to bar, 1975, Illinois; 1982, U.S. District Court, Northern District of Illinois. *Education:* University of Illinois (B.S., 1971); University of Illinois College of Law (J.D., 1975). Legal Counsel, Illinois House of Representatives, Republican Staff, 1975-1976. Assistant Counsel, 1976-1978, Associate Legislative Counsel, 1978-1980 and Member, Special Committee on Legislative Process, 1979, Illinois State Bar Association. Member, Governmental Affairs Committee, Illinois Manufacturers Association. *Member:* Illinois State Bar Association. ***PRACTICE AREAS:*** Legislative Representation; State Administrative Law. ***Email:*** ctopol@ftoklaw.com

REPRESENTATIVE CLIENTS: ServiceMaster; PPG; Hobart; Schindler; Westinghouse; Textron; Laidlaw; Menards; BMW; CNA Insurance Company; Chubb Insurance Group; Cigna Corp.; Continental Insurance; Farmers Insurance; Aetna Life & Casualty Co.; Allstate Insurance Co.; Facial, Plastic and Reconstructive Surgery, Inc.; Chicago Hospital Risk Pooling; Conco, Inc.; Duplex Group; Fireman's Fund American; General Accident Group; Hartford

(This Listing Continued)

HINSHAW & CULBERTSON LLP, Chicago—Continued

Insurance Group; Maryland Casualty Co.; Prudential Insurance Co.; St. Mary of Nazareth Hospital; St. Therese Hospital; INRYCO, Inc.; Switchcraft, Inc.; University of Illinois; Holy Cross Hospital; Northwestern Memorial Hospital; St. Bernards; Shand, Morahan & Co., Inc.; U.S.F.&G.; American Academy of Orthopaedic Surgeons; First Federal Savings Bank of Champaign-Urbana; Inland Steel Co.; Condell Memorial Hospital; Illinois State Medical Insurance Services.

HODES, KEATING & PILON

39 SOUTH LASALLE STREET, SUITE 1020
CHICAGO, ILLINOIS 60603-1731
Telephone: 312-553-1440
Fax: 312-553-1470
Email: hkp@hkp-customs.com
URL: http://www.hkp-customs.com

Customs Law, International Trade Regulation, Administrative Law, Commercial Litigation, International Transportation Law.

MICHAEL G. HODES, born Chicago, Illinois, February 13, 1952; admitted to bar, 1976, Illinois; 1977, U.S. District Court, Northern District of Illinois; 1980, U.S. Court of International Trade; 1982, U.S. Court of Appeals for the Federal Circuit; 1996, U.S. Supreme Court. *Education:* University of Illinois (B.A., 1973); Loyola University (J.D., 1976). *Member:* Chicago (Vice-Chair, 1982; Chair, 1983, Customs Law Committee) and Illinois State Bar Associations. ***PRACTICE AREAS:*** Customs Law; International Trade Regulation; Administrative Law. ***Email:*** mhodes@hkp-customs.com

THOMAS M. KEATING, born Chicago, Illinois, June 15, 1949; admitted to bar, 1983, Illinois, U.S. Court of Appeals for the Federal Circuit, U.S. Court of International Trade, U.S. Court of Appeals, Seventh Circuit and U.S. District Court, Northern District of Illinois. *Education:* Northwestern University (Ph.B., 1978) alpha sigma lambda; DePaul University (J.D., 1983). Recipient, American Jurisprudence Award in Constitutional Law. Author: Articles, "Detailed Billing and Attorney Client Privilege," Ill. Bar Jour., November 1996. Lecturer: Illinois State Bar Association: Trade Act of 1988, 1988; U.S.-Canada Free Trade Agreement, 1990; The GATT, 1994; Chicago Bar Association: Grey Market's Uncertain Future, 1986; Trade Remedy Laws After the Trade Act, 1988, 1989. International Trade Club: Country of Origin and Marking Requirements, 2001, 2004; Customs Tariff Classification Fundamentals, 1992; U.S. Customs Valuation, 1987; U.S. Customs 807 Treatment of Importations From Maquiladoras, 1988; Legal Rights and Remedies of Importers, 1989. *Member:* Chicago (Chair, Customs & International Trade Law Committee, 1988-1989 and 1989-1990), Illinois State Bar Association (Member, International and Immigration Law Section, Member of Section Council - Chair, Twinning Subcommittee, 1990-1992; Chair, International and Immigration Law Section, 1992-1993); International Trade Club of Chicago (President, 1994-1995; Member, Board of Directors, 1990—; Secretary, 1991-1993; Treasurer, 1993-1994 and 1995—2004; Chair, Import Committee, 1989-1990). ***PRACTICE AREAS:*** Customs and International Trade Law. ***Email:*** tkeating@hkp-customs.com

LAWRENCE R. PILON, born San Antonio, Texas, September 17, 1952; admitted to bar, 1984, Illinois and U.S. District Court, Northern District of Illinois including Trial Bar; U.S. Court of International Trade and U.S. Court of Appeals for the Federal Circuit; 1997, U.S. Supreme Court. *Education:* Illinois State University (B.M.E., 1975); Chicago-Kent College of Law (J.D., 1984). Member: National Trial Competition Team; Philip Jessup International Law Moot Court Competition Team. Member, Chicago-Kent Law Review. Instructor, William Rainey Harper College, 1988—. Member, Customs Brokers and Foreign Freight Forwarder's Association of Chicago. *Member:* Chicago (Member, 1984—; Vice-Chair, 1990; Chair, 1991; Legislative Liaison, 1991, Customs and U.S. International Trade Law Committee), Illinois and American (Member: Customs and Tariffs Committee, 1984-1986; Legal Technology Advisory Council, 1986-1988) Bar Associations; Customs and International Trade Bar Association (Member, Technology Committee, 1998). ***LANGUAGES:*** French. ***PRACTICE AREAS:*** Customs Law; International Trade Regulation; International Transportation; Commercial Litigation. ***Email:*** lpilon@hkp-customs.com

---

JESSICA T. DePINTO, born Chicago, Illinois, May 7, 1969; admitted to bar, 1996, Illinois and U.S. District Court, Northern District of Illinois; 1999, U.S. Court of International Trade. *Education:* University of Wisconsin-Madison (B.A., cum laude, 1991); Indiana University, Bloomington (M.A., 1993); Chicago-Kent College of Law, Illinois Institute of Technology (J.D., 1996). *Member:* Chicago (Chair, 2004-2005 and Vice Chair, 2003-2004, Customs Law Committee); Illinois State (Chair, Immigration and International Law Section Council, 2003-2004) and American Bar Associations; Justinian Society of Lawyers. ***LANGUAGES:*** Italian. ***PRACTICE AREAS:*** Customs Law; International Trade Regulation; Federal Regulatory Law. ***Email:*** jdepinto@hkp-customs.com

MICHELLE WELSH, born Lansing, Michigan, September 1, 1979; admitted to bar, 2004, Illinois and U.S. Court of International Trade. *Education:* University of Michigan, Ann Arbor (B.A., 2001); Loyola University, Chicago (J.D., 2004). Member, Willem C. Vis International Commercial Arbitration Moot Competition Team. Recipient, CALI Excellence for Future Award in European Union Law. *Member:* Chicago, Illinois State and American Bar Associations. ***PRACTICE AREAS:*** Customs Law; International Trade Regulation. ***Email:*** mwelsh@hkp-customs.com

HOEY & FARINA, P.C.

542 SOUTH DEARBORN, SUITE 200
CHICAGO, ILLINOIS 60605
Telephone: 312-939-1212
Toll Free: 888-425-1212
Fax: 312-939-7842
Email: info@hoeyfarina.com
URL: http://www.hoeyfarina.com

Federal Employers' Liability Act, Personal Injury.

(This Listing Continued)

FIRM PROFILE: Hoey & Farina, P.C. is an experienced, national law firm dedicated to representing seriously injured individuals and their families. We are available toll free 888-425-1212, 24 hours a day to discuss legal rights and potential legal action with regards to railroad accidents, construction or work accidents, medical malpractice, defective products, and other serious accidents. There is no charge or obligation for consulting one of our attorneys. Se Habla Español.

JAMES L. FARINA, born Chicago, Illinois, 1954; admitted to bar, 1979, Illinois; 1980, U.S. District Court, Northern District of Illinois; 1990, U.S. Court of Appeals, 7th Circuit; 1992, U.S. District Court, Central District of Illinois; 1999, U.S. Court of Appeals, 6th Circuit; 2000, U.S. District Court, Northern District of Indiana; 2002, U.S. District Court, Southern District of Indiana, Northern District of Ohio and Eastern District of Wisconsin. *Education:* Illinois State University (B.S., 1976); Chicago-Kent College of Law (J.D., 1979). Phi Eta Sigma Honorary Society; ; Justinian Society of Lawyers, 1979-2004. *Member:* American Bar Association; Academy of Rail Labor Attorneys; Illinois Trial Lawyers Association; American Trial Lawyers Association. ***REPORTED CASES:*** DeBiasio v. IL Central; Fenderson v. Lemont Engineering. ***PRACTICE AREAS:*** Federal Employers Liability Act (FELA); Personal Injury; Wrongful Death; Medical Malpractice; Products Liability. ***Email:*** farina@hoeyfarina.com

HOFELD AND SCHAFFNER

A Partnership including A Professional Corporation
SUITE 3120
30 NORTH LA SALLE STREET
CHICAGO, ILLINOIS 60602-2506
Telephone: 312-372-4250
Telecopier: 312-372-1766
Email: bmurphy@hofeldandschaffner.com
URL: http://www.hofeldandschaffner.com

Plaintiffs Personal Injury and Wrongful Death, Aviation, Medical Negligence, Professional Negligence, Product Liability, Premises Liability, Construction Accidents FELA and Automobile Accidents. Litigation Practice.

ALBERT F. HOFELD, (LTD.), born Chicago, Illinois, October 5, 1936; admitted to bar, 1964, Illinois. *Education:* Harvard University (B.A., 1958); University of Chicago (J.D., 1964). Author: "Strict Liability in Product Liability," Chapter 1 of the Products Liability Practice Handbook, IICLE, April, 1980; "Product Liability—1978," Vol. 1, No. 1, Fall of 1978, *ITLA JOURNAL;* "Strict Liability in Product Liability," Chapter 1 of the Product Liability Practice Handbook, IICLE, April, 1977; "Looking at a Decade of Products Liability Law in Illinois—Where We've Been and Where We're Going," Vol. 64, No. 6, February, 1976, *Illinois Bar Journal;* "How to Prove Pain and Suffering," Chapter 2, Proof of Damages Handbook, IICLE, 1977; "Allergic Drug Reaction—Manufacturer's Failure to Warn," November, 1967, *The Trial Lawyers' Guide;* "Value of Discovery in a Products Liability Case," May, 1970, *The Trial Lawyers' Guide;* "Athletes—Their Rights and Correlative Duties," Winter, 1976, *The Trial Lawyers' Guide;* "Toward Understanding, Analyzing and Improving 'No Fault' in a Products Liability Case," May, 1970, *The Trial Lawyers' Guide.* Member: Inquiry Board, Attorney Registration and Disciplinary Commission, 1978-1980; Board of Directors, Harvard Club of Chicago, 1977-1980. Director and Faculty Member, College of Trial Advocacy, Illinois Wesleyan University, 1980-1984. Member, Joint Legislative Committee of the Illinois State Bar Association-Chicago Bar Association. *Member:* Chicago (Member, Committees on: Legislative, 1973-1977; Evaluation of Candidates, 1975-1979; Tort Litigation, 1973-1977; Inquiry, 1972-1974; Negligence, 1969-1973; Civil Practice, 1967-1974; Professional Ethics, 1966-1969), Illinois State (Secretary, 1978-1980; Second Vice-President, 1981—; President, 1983-1984; Vice-President, 1980-1983; Member: Board of Governors, 1976-1980; Assembly, 1976-1980; Standing Committee on Legislation, 1977-1978; Ad Hoc Search Committee for Director of Legislative Affairs, 1978-1979; Board Liaison to Civil Practice and Procedure Section, 1978-1979; Public Relations Committee, 1968-1970; Civil Practice and Procedure Section Council; Tort Law Section Council; Ad Hoc Committee to Review Unification in Illinois, 1977-1978; Member, Special Committee: Review of Illinois Disciplinary Procedures, 1978; Judicial Merit Selection Implementation, 1977-1978; Automobile Accident Reparations, 1971; Member: Ad Hoc Committee to consider IBC Structural Problems; Ad Hoc Committee on Public Speaking Training for Officers; Standing Committee on Scope and Correlation of Work, 1978-1982; Special Committee to Investigate Membership) and American (Member, House of Delegates, 1982-1984) Bar Associations; Illinois Trial Lawyers Association (Member: Board of Managers, 1974—; Chairman: Legislative Committee, 1977-1980; Products Liability Committee, 1977-1980; Vice President, 1979-1982; President, 1982-1983); The Association of Trial Lawyers of America (Governor, 1984-1988; Member: Merit Award Committee; Education Committee); Illinois Bar Foundation (Charter Member); Inner Circle of Advocates. Fellow: American Bar Foundation; American College of Trial Lawyers. [1st Lt., U.S. Army Artillery, 1959-1961]. ***PRACTICE AREAS:*** Litigation; Personal Injury; Torts; Product Liability. ***Email:*** ahofeld@hofeldandschaffner.com

HOWARD SCHAFFNER, born Chicago, Illinois, November 2, 1943; admitted to bar, 1970, Illinois. *Education:* Roosevelt University (B.A., 1967); John Marshall Law School (J.D., 1970). Member, Gavel Society. Author: Chapter, "Proof of Pain and Suffering," Proof of Damages, Illinois Institute of Continuing Legal Education, 1985, 1987; Chapter, "Institutional Negligence," Medical Negligence, Illinois Institute of Continuing Legal Education, 1985, 1987; Chapter, "Update on the Law of Produce Liability," IICLE, 1984, 1986; Article, "Pleading Wilful and Wanton Misconduct," Illinois Trial Lawyers Association Journal, 1984. Instructor: Dram Shop Liability, IICLE, 1982; Trial Technique, National Institute of Trial Advocacy, 1988; Railroad Crossing Cases, National Institute of Highway Safety, 1984; Preparing and Trying the Product Liability Case, Young Lawyers Section, Chicago Bar Association, 1986; Proof of Damages, Illinois Trial Lawyers Association, 1986; Mock Trial Presentation, Illinois Trial Lawyers Association, 1984; Using an Economist at Trial, Lecture and Demonstration, IICLE, 1987. *Member:* Illinois State Bar Association (Member, Judicial Screening Committee); Illinois Trial Lawyers Association (Elected, Board of Governors, 1984-1988; Chairman, Seminar Committee, 1987-1988;

(This Listing Continued)

Vice Chairman, Civil Practice Committee, 1985-1986). ***PRACTICE AREAS:*** Personal Injury; Litigation; Torts; Products Liability. ***Email:*** hschaffner@hofeldandschaffner.com

BRIAN MURPHY, born Evanston, Illinois, October 20, 1964; admitted to bar, 1989, Illinois and U.S. District Court, Northern District of Illinois. *Education:* St. Mary's College (B.A., 1986); Loyola University of Chicago School of Law (J.D., 1989). Author: "The Art of Witness Examination: Direct and Cross: Albert Hofeld, Nat Ozmon, Brian Murphy, Mark Taxman," June 12, 1993; Medical Malpractice Trial Notebook: Chapter 2: Statute of Limitations (2000-2004 Editions), Illinois Trial Lawyers Association. Lecturer: Rule 213, Illinois Trial Lawyers Association, Young Lawyers Seminar, January 9, 1999; Rule 213: Chicago Bar Association, Young Lawyers Division, 1999; Medical Depositions, Illinois Institute of Continuing Legal Education, Jumers Hotel, Bloomington, Illinois, 2000; Medical Depositions, Illinois Institute of Continuing Legal Education, Standard Club, Chicago, Illinois, 2000; Hospital Liability, Illinois Trial Lawyers Association, Medical Malpractice Seminar, December 9, 2000; Maximizing Lost Wage Claims, Illinois Institute of Continuing Legal Education, University Club, Chicago, Illinois, December 13, 2000; OB/Gyn Cases, Illinois Trial Lawyers Association, Medical Malpractice Seminar, December 8, 2001. Seminar Planning Chair and Moderator, Illinois Trial Lawyers Association Update Seminar, Ritz Carlton Hotel, Chicago, Illinois, September 14, 2002; Proving Damages in Medical Cases, Illinois Trial Lawyers Association Medical Malpractice Seminar, December 6, 2003; Plaintiff's Opening Statement, Illinois Trial Lawyers Association Point-Counterpoint Seminar, April 3, 2004; Damages, Illinois Trial Lawyers Association Update & Review Seminar, October 11, 2004. *Member:* Illinois Trial Lawyers Association (Member, Board of Managers; Medical Malpractice Committee Co-Chair, 2005-2006; Legislative Committee, 1997-1999; Program Planning Chair for the Illinois Law Update Seminar, September 2002); Chicago and Illinois (Member, Judicial Evaluation Committee, 1996-1998) Bar Associations; Catholic Lawyers Guild of Chicago (Member, Executive Committee on Clerical Abuse, 2002). ***PRACTICE AREAS:*** Personal Injury; Wrongful Death; Medical Malpractice; Construction Litigation. ***Email:*** bmurphy@hofeldandschaffner.com

---

JOHN J. MACINERNEY, born New York, New York, April 27, 1960; admitted to bar, 1996, Illinois. *Education:* State University of New York at Oneonta (B.A., B.S., 1993); Loyola University Chicago School of Law (J.D., 1996). *Member:* Illinois State and American Bar Associations; Illinois Trial Lawyers Association (Member, Medical Negligence Committee, 2000—; Civil Practice and Rules Committee, 2000—); Association of Trial Lawyers of America. ***PRACTICE AREAS:*** Plaintiffs Personal Injury Litigation; Medical Negligence; Products Liability; Premises Liability; Wrongful Death; Motor Vehicle Accidents and Injuries. ***Email:*** jmacinerney@hofeldandschaffner.com

LYNNE PLUM DUFFEY, born Chicago, Illinois, June 10, 1959; admitted to bar, 1989, Illinois. *Education:* Mundelein College (B.A., 1984); Chicago-Kent College of Law (J.D., 1989). *Member:* Illinois State Bar Association; Illinois Trial Lawyers Association. ***PRACTICE AREAS:*** Personal Injury; Medical Malpractice. ***Email:*** lduffey@hofeldandschaffner.com

---

HOGAN MARREN, LTD.

Established in 1993
180 NORTH WACKER DRIVE
SUITE 600
CHICAGO, ILLINOIS 60606
Telephone: 312-946-1800
FAX: 312-946-9818
Email: hmadm@aol.com
URL: http://www.hmltd.com

Health Care, Labor, Corporate, Venture Capital and Business Litigation Law.

FIRM PROFILE: Hogan Marren, Ltd. offers health care clients solutions to strategic issues and guidance in structuring and documenting transactions. The legal professionals provide decades of expertise and experience in corporate law, tax, labor and employment law, ERISA, healthcare legislation and regulations, fraud and abuse, reimbursement and other areas of law that impact both the oversight of a business and the unique nature of health care and labor organizations, Taft-Hartley Trust and other For-Profit and Not-for-Profit entities.

EDWARD M. HOGAN, born Chicago, Illinois; admitted to bar, 1977, Illinois, U.S. District Court, Northern District of Illinois, U.S. District Court, Northern District of Indiana and U.S. Court of Appeals, Seventh Circuit. *Education:* University of Notre Dame (A.B., 1970); Loyola University (M.B.A., 1973); Chicago Kent College of Law (J.D., 1977). Special Assistant Attorney General, Illinois, 1983-1985. *Member:* Chicago, Illinois State and Federal (Chairman, Labor Law Committee, Chicago Chapter, 1979) Bar Associations. ***PRACTICE AREAS:*** Litigation; Administrative; Governmental; Labor; Health Care. ***Email:*** emh@hmltd.com

JOHN P. MARREN, born Chicago, Illinois; admitted to bar, 1983, Illinois and U.S. District Court, Northern District of Illinois. *Education:* St. Xavier College (B.A., 1978); Loyola University of Chicago (J.D., 1983). Adjunct Professor, J.L. Kellogg Graduate School of Management and Loyola University, College of Law. ***PRACTICE AREAS:*** Health Care Law. ***Email:*** jpm@hmltd.com

CAROL C. HOGAN, born Chicago, Illinois; admitted to bar, 1986, Illinois. *Education:* St. Mary's College (B.A., cum laude, 1972); University of Chicago (M.A., 1975); Loyola University of Chicago (J.D., magna cum laude, 1986). Editor, Loyola University Law Review, 1985-1986. ***PRACTICE AREAS:*** Health Care Law; Nonprofit Tax Law. ***Email:*** cch@hmltd.com

PATRICK E. DEADY, born Chicago, Illinois; admitted to bar, 1977, Illinois; 1980, District of Columbia; 1981, U.S. District Court, Northern District of Illinois including Trial Bar; 1983, U.S. District Court, District of Maryland; 1988, U.S. Court of Appeals, Seventh Circuit; 1989, U.S. Court of Appeals, Eleventh Circuit. *Education:* Marquette University (B.A., 1972); Loyola University (J.D., cum laude, 1977). Recipient: U.S. Department of Justice, Special Achievement Award, 1986; Special Commendation, 1980. Senior Instructor: Trial Advocacy Program, Loyola University School of Law, 1985—; Trial Advocacy Program, John Marshall Law School, 1985-1987; Attorney General's Advocacy Institute, U.S. Department of Justice, 1982-1987. Assistant U.S. Attorney, Northern District of Illinois, 1980-1983, 1984-1987; Assistant U.S. Attorney, District of Maryland, 1983-1984. Trial Attorney, U.S. Department of Justice, Civil Rights Division, 1977-1980. *Member:* Chicago and American (Member, Sections on: Criminal Justice; Litigation; Labor and Employment; Healthcare) Bar Associations. ***REPORTED CASES:*** AKW Construction & Environmental Services Co. v. John Galioto, et.al., 2000 WL 1809976 (N.D.Ill. Dex. 11, 2000); Glaziers Local Union No. 27 v. Joint Conference Board, et.al., 1999 WL 311698 (N.D. Ill., May 13, 1999); Alley Drywall Co., 333 NLRB 1005 (March 7, 2001); Advance Cast Stone v. Bridge, Structural and Reinforcing Iron Workers, Local Union No. 1, 2002 WL 31163757, 170 L.R.R.M. 3190 (N.D. Il. Sept 30, 2002); Weiland, et.al. v. Linear Construction Co., et.al., 2003 WL 1565846, 30 Emp. Ben. Cases 2399 (N.D. Ill. Mar. 24, 2003). ***PRACTICE AREAS:*** Commercial Litigation; White Collar Criminal Defense; Labor; ERISA Litigation; Employment Litigation; Health Care Litigation. ***Email:*** ped@hmltd.com

KELLY McCLOSKEY CHERF, born Arlington, Virginia, October 1, 1964; admitted to bar, 1990, Virginia and District of Columbia; 1994, Illinois. *Education:* University of Notre Dame (B.A., 1987); George Washington National Law Center (J.D., 1990). ***PRACTICE AREAS:*** Litigation. ***Email:*** kmc@hmltd.com

LIMO T. CHERIAN, born Alleppey Kerala, India, March 21, 1969; admitted to bar, 1992, Maryland; 1993, Illinois. *Education:* Marquette University (B.A., 1989); Georgetown University Law Center (J.D., 1992). Assistant Attorney General, Office of the Illinois Attorney General, 1994-1997. ***LANGUAGES:*** Malayalam. ***PRACTICE AREAS:*** Commercial Litigation; Corporate Litigation; Energy Conservation; Business Litigation; Securities Litigation. ***Email:*** ltc@hmltd.com

LAURA C. LIU, born Carbondale, Illinois; admitted to bar, 1991, Illinois and U.S. District Court, Northern District of Illinois. *Education:* Youngstown State University (B.S., Biology, Chemistry, 1987); University of Cincinnati (J.D., 1991). ***LANGUAGES:*** Mandarin Chinese. ***PRACTICE AREAS:*** Health Care Law; Litigation. ***Email:*** lcl@hmltd.com

CHERYL L. SEGAL, born Rochester, New York; admitted to bar, 1988, Illinois. *Education:* Northwestern University (B.A., 1985; J.D., 1988). *Member:* Chicago and American Bar Associations; American Academy of Hospital Attorneys. ***PRACTICE AREAS:*** Health Care Law. ***Email:*** cls@hmltd.com

JEFFREY M. TESKE, born Minneapolis, Minnesota, December 10, 1955; admitted to bar, 1982, Illinois. *Education:* Indiana University (B.A., with distinction, 1978; J.D., cum laude, 1982). Phi Beta Kappa. Co-Author: "Hospital Collaboration: The Need for an Appropriate Antitrust Policy," 29 Wake Forest Law Review 107, Spring 1999. Adjunct Professor, Loyola University - Chicago School of Law. *Member:* Chicago and American Bar Associations; American Health Lawyers Association; Illinois Association of Healthcare Attorneys. ***PRACTICE AREAS:*** Health Care; Trade and Professional Associations. ***Email:*** jmt@hmltd.com

---

TIMOTHY B. CAPREZ, born Milwaukee, Wisconsin, July 9, 1978; admitted to bar, 2003, Illinois. *Education:* University of Wisconsin-Madison (B.A., 2000); Loyola University School of Law (J.D., 2003). *Member:* Chicago, Illinois State and American Bar Associations. ***PRACTICE AREAS:*** Labor and Employment; Health Care; Corporate Law. ***Email:*** tbc@hmltd.com

MATTHEW J. CLEVELAND, born Denver, Colorado, September 14, 1972; admitted to bar, 1998, Illinois and U.S. District Court, Northern District of Illinois. *Education:* University of Puget Sound (B.A., 1994); John Marshall Law School (J.D., cum laude, 1998). Phi Alpha Phi. Leads Article Editor, John Marshall Law Review, 1997-1998. Author: Note, "Title VII and Negative Job References: Employees Find Safe Harbor in Robinson v. Shell Oil Company," 31 J. Marshall L. Rev. 521, 1998. Adjunct Professor, The John Marshall Law School. *Member:* Chicago and American Bar Associations; Illinois Association of Healthcare Attorneys; AFL-CIO Lawyers (Coordinating Committee). ***PRACTICE AREAS:*** Health Care; Corporate Law; Labor Law; Employment Law. ***Email:*** mjc@hmltd.com

JOHN MICHAEL TECSON, born Akron, Ohio, January 14, 1975; admitted to bar, 2001, Illinois. *Education:* University of Illinois (B.A., 1998); William Mitchell College of Law (J.D., 2001). *Member:* Chicago Bar Association. ***PRACTICE AREAS:*** Commercial Litigation; Employment Law; Creditors Rights. ***Email:*** m.tecson@hmltd.com

---

HOLLAND & KNIGHT LLP

131 SOUTH DEARBORN STREET, 30TH FLOOR
CHICAGO, ILLINOIS 60603
Telephone: 312-263-3600
Fax: 312-578-6666
URL: http://www.hklaw.com

Annapolis, Maryland Office: State Circle Building, 47 State Circle, Suite 400, 21401. Telephone: 410-263-7800. Fax: 410-263-3768.

Atlanta, Georgia Office: One Atlantic Center, 1201 West Peachtree Street, N.E., Suite 2000, 30309. Telephone: 404-817-8500. Fax: 404-881-0470.

Beijing, China Office: No. 33, 14th Floor, IBM Tower, Pacific Century Place, 2 A Workers Stadium Road North, Chaoyang District, 100027. Telephone: 86-10-653-91232. Fax: 86-10-653-91060.

Bethesda, Maryland Office: 3 Bethesda Metro Center, Suite 800, 20814. Telephone: 301-654-7800. Fax: 301-656-3978.

Boston, Massachusetts Office: 10 St. James Avenue, 11th Floor, 02116. Telephone: 617-523-2700. Fax: 617-523-6850.

Bradenton, Florida Office: Bradenton Financial Center, 1401 West Manatee Avenue, Suite 1200, 34205. Telephone: 941-748-7076. Fax: 941-747-9774.

Fort Lauderdale, Florida Office: One East Broward Boulevard, Suite 1300, 33301. Telephone: 954-525-1000. Fax: 954-463-2030.

(This Listing Continued)

HOLLAND & KNIGHT LLP, Chicago—Continued

Jacksonville, Florida Office: 50 North Laura Street, Suite 3900, 32202. Telephone: 904-353-2000. Fax: 904-358-1872.
Lakeland, Florida Office: 92 Lake Wire Drive, 33815. Telephone: 863-682-1161. Fax: 863-688-1186.
Los Angeles, California Office: 633 West Fifth Street, 21st Floor, 90071. Telephone: 213-896-2400. Fax: 213-896-2450.
Mexico City, Mexico Office: Holland & Knight - Gallastegui y Lozano, S.C., Edificio Arcos Bosques Corporativo, Paseo de los Tamarindos 400-B, Piso 2, Delegación Cuajimalpa, Bosques de las Lomas, 05120. Telephone: 525-55-261-1866. Fax: 525-55-261-1867.
Miami, Florida Office: 701 Brickell Avenue, Suite 3000, 33131. Telephone: 305-374-8500. Fax: 305-789-7799.
New York, New York Office: 195 Broadway, 24th Floor, 10007. Telephone: 212-513-3200. Fax: 212-385-9010.
Northern Virginia: 1600 Tysons Boulevard, Suite 700, McLean, Virginia, 22102. Telephone: 703-720-8600. Fax: 703-720-8610.
Oakbrook Terrace, Illinois Office: One Mid America Plaza, Suite 1000, 60181. Telephone: 630-954-2100. Fax: 630-954-2112.
Orlando, Florida Office: SunTrust Building, Suite 2600, 200 South Orange Avenue, 32801. Telephone: 407-425-8500. Fax: 407-244-5288.
Portland, Oregon Office: 2300 U.S. Bancorp Tower, 111 Southwest Fifth Avenue, 97204. Telephone: 503-243-2300. Fax: 503-241-8014.
Providence, Rhode Island Office: One Financial Plaza, Suite 1800, 02903. Telephone: 401-751-8500. Fax: 401-553-6850.
Rancho Santa Fe, California Office: 6050 El Tordo, 92067. Telephone: 858-756-4410. Fax: 858-756-4386.
Sacramento, California Office: 1215 K Street, 17th Floor, 95814. Telephone: 916-503-1695. Fax: 916-503-2401.
San Antonio, Texas Office: 112 East Pecan Street, Suite 2700, 78205. Telephone: 210-229-3000. Fax: 210-229-1194.
San Francisco, California Office: 50 California Street, Suite 2800, 94111. Telephone: 415-743-6900. Fax: 415-743-6910.
Seattle, Washington Office: 2600 Pike Tower, 520 Pike Street, 98101. Telephone: 206-340-1825. Fax: 206-623-4363.
St. Petersburg, Florida Office: 200 Central Avenue, Suite 1600, 33701. Telephone: 727-896-7171. Fax: 727-822-8048.
Tallahassee, Florida Office: 315 South Calhoun Street, Suite 600, 32301. Telephone: 850-224-7000. Fax: 850-224-8832.
Tampa, Florida Office: 100 North Tampa Street, Suite 4100, 33602. Telephone: 813-227-8500. Fax: 813-229-0134.
Tokyo, Japan Office: Akasaka Tokyu Building, 7th Floor, 2-14-3 Nagatacho, Chiyoda-Ku, Tokyo, 100-0014. Telephone: 03-3539-5881. Fax: 03-3503-1033.
Washington, D.C. Office: 2099 Pennsylvania Avenue, N.W., Suite 100, 20006. Telephone: 202-955-3000. Fax: 202-955-5564.
West Palm Beach, Florida Office: 222 Lakeview Avenue, Suite 1000, 33401. Telephone: 561-833-2000. Fax: 561-650-8399.
Representative Offices:
Caracas, Venezuela Office: Tinoco, Travieso, Planchart & Núñez, Avenida Francisco De Miranda, Torre Country Club, Pisos 1 y 2, Chacaito, 1050. Telephone: 582-12-952-9033 (Master). Fax: 582-12-953-1053/8365/7583.
Helsinki, Finland Office: Holland & Knight Oy, Pohjoisesplanadi 33, FIN-00100. Telephone: 358-9-684-1520. Fax: 358-9-6841-5252.
Tel Aviv, Israel Office: Haim Samet, Steinmetz, Haring & Co. Advocates, 23 Begin Road, 66814. Telephone: 972-3-567-0100. Fax: 972-3-567-01010.

Litigation, Government Law, Business Law, Real Estate Law and Private Wealth Services.

FIRM PROFILE: At Holland & Knight we leverage the talents and resources of our entire firm to provide effective advocacy and comprehensive, integrated solutions in virtually all areas of the law, across the U.S., and around the world. The firm's infrastructure, along with its collaborative approach, enables clients to benefit fully from the size of our team, the depth of our experience and our extensive geographic footprint.

Holland & Knight's "one firm" structure allows the firm to support the most complex matters at all levels. The firm is organized into five practice Sections—Litigation, Government, Business, Real Estate and Private Wealth Services. Through integrated practice groups and industry-based teams, we can provide efficient and responsive legal representation anywhere in the world. We serve clients on the basis of their needs, not merely location. Holland & Knight's interdisciplinary approach assures that clients have access to the lawyers with the most appropriate experience.

CHICAGO MEMBERS

BARBARA A. ADAMS, born Chicago, Illinois, September 12, 1958; admitted to bar, 1983, Illinois and U.S. District Court, Northern District of Illinois; 1985, U.S. Court of Appeals, Seventh Circuit. *Education:* Knox College (B.A., 1980); Northwestern University (J.D., 1983). Phi Beta Kappa. Executive Editor, Northwestern Journal of International Law and Business, 1982-1983. Member, Knox College Board of Trustees, 1998—. *Member:* Chicago (Member, Local Government Committee, Chair, 1993-1994) and American Bar Associations; Illinois Municipal League (Member, Home Rule Attorneys Committee; Chair, 1998-1999); International Municipal Lawyers' Association (Chair, Health and Environment Section, 2004-2005; Chair, Contracts, Frachises & Technology Section, 2001-2002). ***PRACTICE AREAS:*** Municipal Law; Water Law; Cable TV; Telecommunications; Alcoholic Beverages; Construction; Public Finance. ***Email:*** barbara.adams@hklaw.com

HENRY S. ALLEN, JR., born Bronxville, New York; admitted to bar, 1974, Illinois; 1983, U.S. Supreme Court. *Education:* Washington University (A.B., magna cum laude, 1969); Cornell University (M.P.A., 1973; J.D., 1974). Phi Beta Kappa; Omicron Delta Epsilon. Recipient: H.U.D. Fellowship, 1969-1971; National Center Health Services Research, HEW, Traineeship, 1973-1975. Adjunct Professor, Cornell University, 1996—. ***PRACTICE AREAS:*** Health Law; Antitrust Law; Civil Litigation. ***Email:*** henry.allen@hklaw.com

THOMAS P. ARDEN, admitted to bar, 1985, Illinois. *Education:* Cornell University (B.A., 1981); Yale University (J.D., 1985). Member, Board of Editors, Yale Law Journal, 1984-1985. Recipient, Nathan Burkan Award. Author: *Nontraditional Marks:* Trademark Rights in Sounds, Colors, Scents and Product Designs, (2001); "The Questionable Utility of Copyright Notice: Statutory and Nonlegal Incentives in the Post-Berne Era," 26 Intellectual Property Law Review 351 (1994); "The Conflicting Treatment of Compilations of Facts Under the United States and British Copyright Laws," 19 AIPLA Quarterly Journal 267 (1992). *Member:* Chicago, Illinois State and American Bar Associations; American Judicature Society; Copyright Society of the U.S.A. ***PRACTICE AREAS:*** Civil Litigation; Trademark Law; Copyright Law; Licensing; Information Technology. ***Email:*** thomas.arden@hklaw.com

MICHAEL J. BOLAND, admitted to bar, 1985, Illinois and U.S. District Court, Northern District of Illinois. *Education:* Niles College; Loyola University of Chicago (B.A., cum laude, 1978); Northwestern University (J.D., 1985). *Member:* Chicago (Member, Securities Law and Corporation Law Committees), Illinois State and American Bar Association (Member, Business Law Section and Committee on Federal Regulation of Securities). ***PRACTICE AREAS:*** Securities Law; Capital Formation; Mergers and Acquisitions; Corporate Governance. ***Email:*** michael.boland@hklaw.com

MALCOLM H. BROOKS, born April 24, 1955; admitted to bar, 1980, Illinois, U.S. District Courts, Northern District of Illinois, Eastern Districts of Michigan, U.S. District Court, Northern District of New York and U.S. District Court, District of Colorado; U.S. Court of Appeals, Sixth and Seventh Circuits. *Education:* Northern Michigan University (B.S., summa cum laude, 1977); University of Michigan (J.D., cum laude, 1979). *Member:* Chicago, Illinois State (Member, Committees on: Litigation; Intellectual Property Law) and American (Member, Committees on: Antitrust Law; Litigation; Intellectual Property Law) Bar Associations. ***PRACTICE AREAS:*** Civil Litigation; Travel Law; Intellectual Property Law. ***Email:*** chip.brooks@hklaw.com

MARK E. BURKLAND, born Rochelle, Illinois, June 20, 1957; admitted to bar, 1982, Illinois, U.S. District Court, Northern District of Illinois, U.S. Court of Appeals, Seventh Circuit, and U.S. Supreme Court. *Education:* University of Illinois (B.S., with honors, 1979; J.D., with honors, 1982). Articles Editor, University of Illinois Law Review, 1981-1982. Law Clerk, Hon. William J. Bauer, Judge, U.S. Court of Appeals for Seventh Circuit, 1982-1984. *Member:* Chicago, Illinois State, and American Bar Associations. Fellow, American Bar Association. ***PRACTICE AREAS:*** Environmental. ***Email:*** mark.burkland@hklaw.com

SCOTT F. BURNS, born Normal, Illinois, January 4, 1971; admitted to bar, 1996, Illinois; U.S. District Court, Northern District of Illinois. *Education:* University of Illinois (B.A., 1993); Loyola University, Chicago (J.D., 1996). *Member:* Illinois State and American Bar Associations; Illinois Association of Defense Trial Counsel; Defense Research Institute. ***PRACTICE AREAS:*** Product Liability; Commercial Litigation; Mass Torts; Alternative Dispute Resolution. ***Email:*** scott.burns@hklaw.com

MARTIN J. CAMPANELLA, born Chicago, Illinois; admitted to bar, 1971, Illinois. *Education:* University of Illinois (B.S., high honors, 1968); Harvard University (J.D., 1971). Phi Kappa Phi; Beta Gamma Sigma; Beta Alpha Psi. President, 1998-1999, Harvard Law Society of Illinois. *Member:* Chicago Bar Association (Chairman, Young Lawyers Section, 1979-1980; Member, Board of Managers, 1981-1983). ***PRACTICE AREAS:*** Corporate Law; Employee Benefits. ***Email:*** martin.campanella@hklaw.com

JAMES R. CARR, born Gary, Indiana, September 19, 1957; admitted to bar, 1985, Illinois, U.S. Court of Appeals, Seventh Circuit and U.S. District Court, Northern District of Illinois including Trial Bar. *Education:* University of Notre Dame (B.A., 1979; J.D., 1984). Assistant State's Attorney, 1992-2000 (Chief, Civil Trial Division, 1995-2000), Lake County, Illinois. *Member:* Lake County, Illinois State and American (Member, Sections on: Litigation and Construction Law) Bar Associations. ***PRACTICE AREAS:*** Government; Construction Law; Litigation. ***Email:*** james.carr@hklaw.com

MARTIN G. DURKIN, JR., born Washington, D.C., November 23, 1962; admitted to bar, 1988, Illinois, U.S. District Court, Northern and Central Districts of Illinois including Trial Bar and U.S. Court of Appeals, Seventh Circuit; 1993, U.S. Supreme Court; 1997, U.S. Court of Appeals, Eleventh Circuit. *Education:* Loyola University; University of Colorado at Boulder (B.A., summa cum laude, 1985); University of Illinois (J.D., cum laude, 1988). *Member:* American Bar Association (Member, Sections on: Litigation; Antitrust Law; Tort and Insurance Practice). ***Email:*** martin.durkin@hklaw.com

STEVEN M. ELROD, born Chicago, Illinois, July 12, 1957; admitted to bar, 1982, Illinois. *Education:* Tulane University (B.A., magna cum laude with special honors, 1979); Northwestern University (J.D., 1982). Author: "Illinois Eminent Domain Practice," Illinois Institute of Continuing Legal Education, 2002; "Illinois Land Use Law," Illinois Institute of Continuing Legal Education, 1999. Member, Holland & Knight LLP Directors Committee. Member, Board of Directors, Constitutional Rights Foundation, Chicago, 1988—. Faculty Member and Lecturer, National College of District Attorneys. Village Attorney, Northbrook, Illinois; Corporation Counsel, Highland Park, Illinois. *Member:* Chicago (Chairman, Local Government Committee, 1989-1990) and American (Member, State and Local Government Law Section) Bar Associations. ***PRACTICE AREAS:*** Land Use Law; Zoning Law; Real Estate Transactions; Retail Leasing; Local Government Law. ***Email:*** steven.elrod@hklaw.com

VICTOR P. FILIPPINI, JR., born Chicago, Illinois, October 20, 1958; admitted to bar, 1983, Illinois; 1984, Florida. *Education:* Harvard University (A. B., magna cum laude, 1980); University of Michigan (J.D., cum laude, 1983). 65rMember, 1981-1982 and Senior Editor, 1982-1983, University of Michigan Journal of Law Reform. Author: "A Year Later: Klaeren v. Lisle and the Troubles It Has Wrought," 9 Publ. Int. L. Rptr. _ (Spring 2004); "If It Ain't Broke, Fix It? Assessing the Impact of Klaeren v. Lisle on Illinois Zoning Law," 8 Publ. Int. L. Rptr. 12 (Spring 2003); "The Klaeren Case: Entering the Brave New World of Illinois Zoning Law - Part 2," Illinois Municipal Review (April 2003); "The Klaeren Case: Entering the Brave New World of Illinois Zoning Law - Part 1," Illinois Municipal Review (Jan. 2003); "Annexation Consolidation: Transfers of Territory," Ill. Jur. Municipal Law,

(This Listing Continued)

Ch. 11, 1995; "Public Improvements," Ill. Jur. Municipal Law, Ch. 16, 1995; "1987-1988 Illinois Law Survey: State and Local Government," 20 Loyola Law Journal 623, 1989; "1986-1987 Illinois Law Survey: State and Local Government," 19 Loyola Law Journal 691, 1988; Note, "Soliciting Sophisticates: A Modest Proposal for Attorney Solicitation," 16 University of Michigan Journal of Law Reform 585. Village Attorney: Bannockburn, Illinois; Glencoe, Illinois, 1993—; Grayslake, Illinois, 1994—; Long Grove, Illinois, 2003—. City Attorney, Lake Forest, Illinois, 2000—. Secretary, Board of Directors, Constitutional Rights Foundation of Chicago, 1997. Faculty, National Business Institute, 1998—. *Member:* The Florida Bar; American Bar Association. (Illinois Land Use and Government Practice Group Leader). ***PRACTICE AREAS:*** Local Government Law; Land Use; Real Estate; Litigation. ***Email:*** victor.filippini@hklaw.com

SHAYLE P. FOX, born Chicago, Illinois, July 20, 1934; admitted to bar, 1957, Illinois; 1958, U.S. District Court, Northern District of Illinois; 1963, U.S. Court of Appeals, Seventh Circuit; 1967, U.S. Supreme Court; 1970, U.S. Court of Appeals, Eighth Circuit; 1982, U.S. District Court, Northern District of California; U.S. Court of Appeals, Ninth Circuit; 1988, U.S. Court of Appeals for the District of Columbia Circuit. *Education:* Drake University and University of Illinois (B.S., with highest honors, 1954); DePaul University School of Law (J.D., 1957). Beta Gamma Sigma; Phi Kappa Phi; Beta Alpha Psi. Recipient: University of Illinois, University Honors, Bronze Tablet. Co-Author: "The Use of Civil RICO Against Corporate Employees," BNA Civil RICO Report, July 1988. Guest Lecturer, DePaul University and IIT-Kent School. Judge, Midwestern Regional Moot Court finals. Certified Public Accountant, Illinois, 1955. *Member:* Chicago (Member: Unauthorized Practice Committee, 1960-1964; Younger Members Committee, 1960-1962; Committee on Inquiry, 1971-1973; Committee on Corporations, 1971-1973; Committee on Legal Economics, 1981-1982), Illinois State and American Bar Associations. [U.S. Army, active duty, 1957-1958; Air Force Reserve, 1958-1963]. ***PRACTICE AREAS:*** Business Transactions (33%); Labor and Employment (33%); Commercial Litigation (33%). ***Email:*** sfox@hklaw.com

PETER M. FRIEDMAN, born Highland Park, Illinois, August 28, 1962; admitted to bar, 1990, Illinois; 1993, U.S. District Court, Northern District of Illinois. *Education:* Allegheny College (B.A., 1985); American University's Washington College of Law (J.D., 1989). Dean's List, Allegheny College. Federal Circuit Editor, American University Law Review. Co-Author: "Municipal Property," Chapter 23, Municipal Law and Practice in Illinois (Ill. Inst. for CLE, 1994). Legislative Director, Rep. John E. Porter (IL-10), Washington, D.C., 1986-1989. Judicial Clerk, Honorable Suzanne B. Conlon, U.S. District Court, Northern District of Illinois, 1990-1991. *Member:* Chicago and Illinois State Bar Associations. ***Email:*** peter.friedman@hklaw.com

ANTHONY L. FRINK, born Evanston, Illinois, January 26, 1955; admitted to bar, 1982, Illinois and U.S. District Court, Northern District of Illinois. *Education:* Yale University (B.A., 1977); Illinois Institute of Technology-Chicago Kent College of Law (J.D., with honors, 1982). Real Estate Broker, Illinois, 1988. Author: "Drafting for Due Diligence in Contracts of Sale," The Practical Real Estate Lawyer, Vol. 8, No. 5, September 1992. Member, Advisory Board, Roosevelt University, Chicago School of Real Estate, 2002. *Member:* Chicago, Illinois State and American (Member, Real Property, Probate and Trust Law Section, 1991) Bar Associations. (Illinois Real Estate Transactions Group Leader). ***PRACTICE AREAS:*** Real Estate; Construction; Financial Services; Litigation. ***Email:*** anthony.frink@hklaw.com

STEFFANIE N. GARRETT, admitted to bar, 1991, Illinois; 1998, U.S. District Court, Northern District of Illinois and Trial Bar; 2002, U.S. District Court, Central District of Illinois. *Education:* Smith College (A.B.,1988); College of William & Mary (J.D., 1991). ABA Moot Court Team (National Finalist, 1989-1990). Phi Delta Phi, (Vice-President, 1989-1990). Cook County Assistant State's Attorney, Criminal Trial Division (1991-1997). Cook County Court Watchers (Board Member, 1998-1999). Alumnae Association of Smith College (Board of Directors, 2000-2003). Special Assistant Attorney General, 1998—. *Member:* Illinois State and American Bar Associations. ***LANGUAGES:*** French. ***PRACTICE AREAS:*** Civil Litigation; Eminent Domain. ***Email:*** steffanie.garrett@hklaw.com

ANDREW R. GELMAN, admitted to bar, 1970, Virginia; 1971, Illinois. *Education:* University of Pennsylvania (B.A., 1967); University of Virginia (J.D., 1970). Author: Article, trustee liability, "Steer Carefully," *The Compleat Lawyer,* Vol. 2, No. 3, 1985 (American Bar Association); Chapter, "County Division," *Chicago Lawyers Court Handbook,* 1975-1996 editions. Member: Chicago Estate Planning Council, 1978—; Committee on Character and Fitness of the Illinois Supreme Court, 1979-1995. Member, Task Force of Special Commission on the Administration of Justice in Cook County, 1986-1987. *Member:* Chicago (Member: Probate Practice Committee, 1973—; Board of Managers, 1978-1980; Division Chairman, Probate Practice Committee, 1981-1982; Chairman, Young Lawyers Section, 1976-1977; Editor, Young Lawyers Journal, 1973-1974), Illinois State (Member, Assembly, 1981-1987) and American (Chair, Probate and Estate Planning Committee of General Practice Section, 1994-1997; Member: Commission on Mental and Physical Disability Law, 1995-1997; Commission on Public Understanding About the Law, 1987-1991; Standing Committee on Judicial Selection, Tenure and Compensation, 1982-1987) Bar Associations; Virginia State Bar; Chicago Council of Lawyers; American Judicature Society (Member, Board of Directors, 1978-1983). ***PRACTICE AREAS:*** Estate Planning Law; Probate Law; Taxation Law; Aged and Aging; Asset Protection; Contested Trusts and Estates. ***Email:*** andy.gelman@hklaw.com

ROBERT H. GERSTEIN, born June 10, 1935; admitted to bar, 1959, Illinois. *Education:* University of Illinois (A.B., 1956); University of Chicago (J.D., 1959). ***PRACTICE AREAS:*** Real Estate; Affordable Housing; Community Development. ***Email:*** robert.gerstein@hklaw.com

STEVEN L. GILLMAN, born New York, N.Y., July 30, 1954; admitted to bar, 1980, Illinois. *Education:* Cornell University (B.S., 1976); University of Michigan (J.D., 1980). Phi Kappa Phi. Member, Society of Barristers. Contributing Editor: Desk Manual, *Labor and Employment Law,* Labor and Employment Committee, American Bar Association. Co-Author: "The Common Law Contract and Tort Rights of Union Employees: What Effect After the Demise of the 'At Will' Doctrine?" Chicago-Kent Law Review, Winter 1983; "Reductions in Workforce and the Age Discrimination Dilemma: Procedures and Safeguards," Midwest Labor and Employment Law Journal, Vol. 1, No. 5, July/August 1984; "The Americans With Disabilities Act: Civil Rights for Handicapped Workers," The Brief (Tort & Insurance Practice Section ("TIPS") of the American Bar Association, Vol. 20, No. 4,

(This Listing Continued)

Summer 1991. Arbitrator, Commercial and Employment Panels, American Arbitration Association. *Member:* Chicago, Illinois State (Labor and Employment Law Section Council) and American (Section of Labor and Employment Law) Bar Associations; Industrial Relations Research Association. ***PRACTICE AREAS:*** Litigation. ***Email:*** steven.gillman@hklaw.com

VICTOR P. HENDERSON, born Queens, New York, June 7, 1961; admitted to bar, 1988, New York; 1990, Illinois; 1991, District of Columbia. *Education:* Wharton School, University of Pennsylvania (B.S.E., 1983); Georgetown University (J.D., 1988). Member, Georgetown Journal of Legal Ethics, 1986-1988. Certified Public Accountant, Commonwealth of Pennsylvania, 1985. Member, GLegislative Assistant, Office of the Honorable Edolphus Towns, 1988. Counsel, Committee on Standards of Official Conduct, U.S. House of Representatives, 1989. Chairman, Chicago Committee on Minorities In Large Law Firms, 1993-1995. Financial Secretary and Board Member - Cook County Bar Association, 1994-1996. Ethics Officer, Chicago Housing Authority, 1999—. Board Member, Public Interest Law Initiave, 2000-2002.*Member:* Chicago (Board Member, 1999-2001), Cook County and American Bar Associations. ***PRACTICE AREAS:*** Commercial Litigation; Product Liability Law. ***Email:*** Victorp.Henderson@hklaw.com

KENNETH A. JENERO, admitted to bar, 1980, Illinois and U.S. District Court, Northern District of Illinois including Trial Bar; 1987, U.S. District Court, Eastern District of Michigan; 1988, U.S. District Court, Central District of Illinois; 1992, U.S. Court of Appeals, Tenth Circuit; 1994, U.S. District Court, Eastern District of Pennsylvania and U.S. Court of Appeals, Sixth Circuit. *Education:* DePaul University (B.A., 1977; J.D., with highest honors, 1980). Author: "Hoffman Plastics v. NLRB: Changing the Scope of Remedial Discretion Afforded Regulatory Agencies," 28 Emp. Rel. L.J. 107 (Autumn, 2002); "The Evolving FMLA: Guidance From Some Recent Court Decisions, 27 Emp. Rel. L.J. 51 (Spring, 2002); "The Supreme Court's Latest Word on Retaliation," 27 Emp. Rel. L.J. 111 (Autumn, 2001); "Staying Competitive in the Twenty-First Century: Visa Alternatives for Global Employers," 27 Emp. Rel. L.J. 1058 (Summer, 2001); "The Next Generation of ADA Claims: The 'Regarded As' Prong of the Definition of Disability," 26 Emp. Rel. L.J. 99 (Summer, 2000); "Employers Beware: Unilateral Handbook Modifications May Not Be Binding," 25 Emp. Rel. L.J. 123 (Spring, 2000); "Weingarten Revisited: NonUnion Workers Have Right to Presence of Co-Worker During Disciplinary Interviews," 26 Emp. Rel. L.J. (Winter, 2000); "EEOC Issues Policy Guidance on Reasonable Accommodation and Undue Hardship Under the ADA," 25 Emp. Rel. L.J. (Autumn, 1999); "Drafting Enforceable Non-Competition Agreements," 25 Emp. Rel. L.J. 119 (Winter, 1999); "Revisiting the Legality of Employee Participation Programs Under the National Labor Relations Act," 25 Emp. Rel. L.J. 119 (Summer, 1999); "Supreme Court Adopts Stringent Standard for Employer Liability in Supervisor Harassment Cases," 24 Emp. Rel. L.J. 113 (Winter, 1998); "Revisiting Employer Sexual Harassment Policies in Light of Oncale," Emp. Rel. L.J. 129 (Autumn, 1998); "Drafting An Effective Independent Contractor Agreement," 23 Emp. Rel. L.J. 125 (Spring, 1998). *Member:* Chicago, Illinois State and American (Member: Section on Labor and Employment Law; Committee on Development of the Law of Individual Rights and Responsibilities in the Work Place, 1982—; Employee Relations Law Journal, Member, Editorial Advisory Board; Author, Labor - Management Relations Column) Bar Associations; Chicago Southland Chamber of Commerce (General Counsel and Director, 1995—; Chair, Human Resources Council, 2001—). ***PRACTICE AREAS:*** Labor and Employment Litigation and Counseling. ***Email:*** kenneth.jenero@hklaw.com

CHARLES E. JOERN, JR., born Oak Park, Illinois, April 27, 1951; admitted to bar, 1980, Illinois, U.S. District Court, Northern District of Illinois including Trial Bar, U.S. Court of Appeals, Seventh Circuit and U.S. Supreme Court. *Education:* Knox College (B.A., 1973); University of Colorado (M.A., 1976); DePaul University (J.D., 1980). Contributing Author: "Protecting the Record and Perfecting the Appeal"; "Federal Civil Practice," Illinois Institute/Continuing Legal Education, 1980—. Member, Chicago Volunteer Legal Services Foundation.—. *Member:* Chicago (Member, 1981-1986 and Chairman, 1985 and 1986, Child Abuse and Neglect Committee), Illinois State and American (Member, Litigation Section) Bar Associations; Defense Research Institute. ***REPORTED CASES:*** Loitz v. Remington Arms Co., Inc. 138 Ill.2d 404, 563 N.E.2d 397 (Ill.1990); American National Bank v. National Advertising Co. 149 Ill.2d 14, 594 N.E.2d 313 (Ill. 1992); Uniroyal Goodrich Tire Co. v. Mutual Trading Corp. 63 F3d 516 (7th Cir. 1995). ***Email:*** charles.joern@hklaw.com

MICHAEL J. KANUTE, born St. Charles, Illinois, April 1, 1965; admitted to bar, 1990, Illinois; 1993, U.S. District Court, Northern District of Illinois. *Education:* University of Notre Dame (B.A., 1987); Loyola University (J.D., cum laude, 1990). Executive Editor of Student Articles, Loyola University Law Journal, 1989-1990. Law Clerk to Justice Allen Hartman, Illinois Appellate Court, First District, 1990-1992. *Member:* Chicago, Illinois State and American Bar Associations. ***Email:*** mkanute@hklaw.com

NAOMI F. KATZ, born Los Angeles, California, July 10, 1970; admitted to bar, 1996, California; 1997, Illinois. *Education:* Washington University (B.A., magna cum laude, 1992); University of Michigan (J.D., 1996). Phi Beta Kappa. *Member:* Chicago, Illinois State and American Bar Associations. ***PRACTICE AREAS:*** Employment Law. ***Email:*** nkatz@hklaw.com

THOMAS J. KINASZ, admitted to bar, 1982, Illinois and U.S. District Court, Northern District of Illinois; 1984, U.S. Tax Court. *Education:* Niles College of Loyola University (B.S., summa cum laude, 1979); Northwestern University (J.D., 1982). Co-Author: "Tax Considerations in Organizing Closely Held Corporations," Chapter 2 of *Closely Held Corporations* (Illinois Institute for Continuing Legal Education, 1999). *Member:* Chicago and Illinois State Bar Associations. ***PRACTICE AREAS:*** Taxation Law; Corporate Law; Exempt Organizations Law; Pass Through Entities. ***Email:*** tom.kinasz@hklaw.com

CHARLES D. KNIGHT, born Aurora, Illinois, April 20, 1953; admitted to bar, 1978, Illinois and U.S. District Court, Northern District of Illinois; 1980, U.S. Court of Appeals, Seventh Circuit; 1984, U.S. Court of Appeals, Eighth Circuit; 1985, U.S. Court of Appeals, Ninth Circuit; 2000, U.S. Supreme Court. *Education:* University of Illinois (A.B., summa cum laude, 1975; J.D., magna cum laude, 1978). Phi Beta Kappa; Order of the Coif. Articles Editor, University of Illinois Law Review, 1977-1978. Law Clerk to Judge Harlington Wood, Jr., U.S. Court of Appeals, Seventh Circuit, 1978-1979. Staff Attorney, U.S. Court of Appeals, Seventh Circuit, 1979-1980. Special Assistant U.S. Attorney, 1992-1993. *Member:* Chicago, Illinois State and American Bar Associations. ***PRACTICE AREAS:*** Appellate Practice; Civil Litigation; Complex Litigation. ***Email:*** charles.knight@hklaw.com

(This Listing Continued)

HOLLAND & KNIGHT LLP, Chicago—Continued

JERRY KOKOLIS, born Oak Park, Illinois, November 18, 1965; admitted to bar, 1990, Illinois. *Education:* University of Chicago (B.A., with honors, 1987); Northwestern University (J.D., 1990). Executive Editor, Northwestern Journal of International Law and Business, 1989-1990. *Member:* Chicago and American (Member, Litigation Section) Bar Associations. ***PRACTICE AREAS:*** Litigation. ***Email:*** jerry.kokolis@hklaw.com

FRANCES H. KRASNOW, admitted to bar, 1978, Illinois. *Education:* University of Michigan (B.A., with high distinction, 1973); Northwestern University (J.D., 1978). Member, Northwestern University National Moot Court Team. Recipient: Lowden-Wigmore Prize; American College of Trial Lawyers Medal for Excellence in Advocacy. Phi Beta Kappa. James B. Angell Scholar. Lecturer, Minority Legal Education Resources, Northwestern University School of Law, 1979. ***PRACTICE AREAS:*** Family Law; Advertising and Promotion Law; Commercial Litigation; Health Club Law; Employment Litigation. ***Email:*** fran.krasnow@hklaw.com

ROBERT J. LABATE, admitted to bar, 1983, Illinois and U.S. District Court, Northern District of Illinois including Trial Bar; 1995, New Mexico. *Education:* Yale University (B.A., 1975); Case Western Reserve University (J.D., 1983). Associate Editor, Case Western Reserve Journal of International Law, 1982-1983. Writer of monthly, "Law and Entertainment," column in Chicago Entertainment Trade Paper "PerformInk." Co-creator and moderator of annual seminar series, "The Business of Independent Film Production." *Member:* Illinois State and American Bar Associations. ***PRACTICE AREAS:*** Entertainment Law; Debtor and Creditor; Corporate Law. ***Email:*** robert.labate@hklaw.com

DAVID M. LEFKOW, born Chicago, Illinois; admitted to bar, 1978, Illinois; 1979, U.S. District Court, Northern District of Illinois including Trial Bar; 1986, U.S. Court of Appeals, Seventh Circuit; 2003, Washington. *Education:* University of Illinois (B.A., with honors, 1973); Capital University (J.D., 1977); Loyola University (M.S.I.R., 1983). Lecturer, IIT-Chicago-Kent College of Law Public Sector Labor Relations Institute, 1986-2001. Board of Directors, Center for Conflict Resolution, 1980-1993. Permanent Arbitrator, National Mediation Board. *Member:* Washington State Bar Association; American Bar Association. ***PRACTICE AREAS:*** Labor and Employment. ***Email:*** david.lefkow@hklaw.com

BRUCE D. LORING, born June 5, 1948; admitted to bar, 1973, Wisconsin; 1978, Illinois. *Education:* University of Wisconsin (B.B.A., with honors, 1970; J.D., cum laude, 1973). Order of the Coif. *Member:* Chicago (Chairman, Land Trust Committee, 1991-1992) and American Bar Associations. ***PRACTICE AREAS:*** Mortgage Law; Real Estate (Property) Law; Real Estate Development Law.

DAVID S. MANN, born Chicago, Illinois, July 14, 1937; admitted to bar, 1962, Illinois. *Education:* University of Notre Dame (A.B., cum laude, 1959); Northwestern University (J.D., 1962). Northwestern University Law Review, 1961-1962. Adjunct Professor, Northwestern University School of Law, 2001—. Member, 1976-1992 and Chairman, 1981-1992, Evanston, Illinois, Zoning Amendment Committee. Chairman, Evanston, Illinois Zoning Commission, 1988-1991. Member, 1987-1994 and Vice-President, 1993-1994, Clients' Security Fund of the Bar of Illinois. Member, Attorney Registration and Disciplinary Commission Inquiry Board, 1997—. *Member:* Chicago (Member, 1974-1980 and Chairman, 1975-1976, House Committee; Member, 1965-1980 and Chairman, 1973-1974, Local Government Committee; Member, 1979-1985 and Chairman, 1983-1984, Professional Fees Committee; Member: Professional Responsibility Committee, 1979-1985; Board of Managers, 1992-1994), Illinois State and American Bar Associations; The Lawyers Club of Chicago. Fellow: Chicago Bar Foundation (Director, 1999—). ***PRACTICE AREAS:*** Commercial Transactions; Corporate and Real Estate Law; Advertising and Promotion Law. ***Email:*** david.mann@hklaw.com

ELIAS N. MATSAKIS, admitted to bar, 1974, Illinois. *Education:* University of Chicago (B.A., with honors, 1971); Harvard University (J.D., cum laude, 1974). Recipient, David C Hilliard Award, Young Lawyers Section, Chicago Bar Association. Staff Member, Harvard Civil Rights and Civil Liberties Law Review, 1972. *Member:* Chicago (Chairman, Pro Se Court Committee, Young Lawyers Section, 1977), Illinois State and American Bar Associations; Hellenic Bar Association of Illinois; Commercial Law League of America. ***PRACTICE AREAS:*** Health Care Law; Bankruptcy Law; Real Estate Corporate Finance; Commercial Transactions. ***Email:*** elias.matsakis@hklaw.com

JAMES T. MAYER, born December 24, 1958; admitted to bar, 1984, Illinois and U.S. District Court, Northern District of Illinois. *Education:* Emory University (B.A., with high honors in History, 1980; M.B.A., 1984; J.D., 1984); University of Chicago Law School. Phi Delta Phi. *Member:* Chicago, Illinois State and American Bar Associations; International Council of Shopping Centers. ***PRACTICE AREAS:*** Real Estate; Banking; Corporate. ***Email:*** james.mayer@hklaw.com

C. GRANT McCORKHILL, born Salem, Ohio, August 17, 1961; admitted to bar, 1988, Illinois and U.S. District Court, Northern District of Illinois. *Education:* College of Wooster (B.A., 1984); Case Western Reserve University School of Law (J.D., 1987). National Society of Barristers. Best Advocate, Jonathan Ault Moot Court Competition. Co-Author: "The Determinants of Income Inequality in Metropolitan Areas," Vol. 10, No. 2, Review of Business 17, Fall, 1988. *Member:* Chicago (Member, Sections on: Banking Law; Real Estate Law), Illinois State and American Bar Associations. ***PRACTICE AREAS:*** Real Estate Law; Corporate Law; Banking Law. ***Email:*** grant.mccorkhill@hklaw.com

CRAIG McCROHON, admitted to bar, 1989, Illinois. *Education:* Harvard University (B.A., 1984); London School of Economics, London, England; Wharton School of Business (M.B.A., 1989); University of Pennsylvania (J.D., 1989). Listed in: Who's Who in American Law, 1992—; Chicago Lawyer 40 Illinois Attorneys Under 40, 2001. President, Technology Executives Roundtable of the Northwestern/Evanston University Research Park, 1997-2001. ***PRACTICE AREAS:*** Corporate Law; Banking Law; Technology Law. ***Email:*** craig.mccrohon@hklaw.com

GREGORY R. MEEDER, *born Febuary 1, 1956; admitted to bar, 1983, Illinois. Education:* University of Illinois (B.A., 1978); Illinois Institute of Technology, Chicago-Kent College of Law (J.D., 1983). Author, "The Public Construction Contract Act," 30 I.L.C.S., 557/1. Commissioner, Village of Palos Park Municipal Board, 1995—. Special Assistant Attorney General, Illinois State Toll Highway Authority. *Member:* Chicago, DuPage County and Illinois State Bar Associations; Underground Contractors Association (Member, Board of Directors, 1996-2000; Counsel, 2000—). ***Email:*** gregory.meeder@hklaw.com

ROBERT M. MINTZ, born Hammond, Indiana, September 18, 1960; admitted to bar, 1987, Illinois and U.S. District Court, Northern District of Illinois; 1988, U.S. Tax Court. *Education:* Indiana University (B.S., 1982); Chicago-Kent College of Law (J.D., 1986). Recipient: American Jurisprudence Award in Investments Law; Florence and Lawrence West Scholarship. Certified Public Accountant, Illinois, 1982. Author: "A New Way to Do Business in Illinois: The Limited Liability Company," Illinois Bar Journal, Vol. 81, December 1993; "Are Discrimination Awards Tax Exempt? An Unsettled Question," ABA Tort and Insurance Practice Section Newsletter, Winter 1992; "Summary of Proposed Changes To CFTC's Minimum Financial Requirements For FCM's & IB's," Commodities Law Letter, Vol. VI, No. 3, May, 1986. Co-Author: "Hazardous Waste: Harmful to Your Health and to Your Wallet," ISBA Real Property Newsletter, January, 1989. *Member:* Chicago (Member, Corporate and Tax Sections), Illinois State and American Bar Associations. ***PRACTICE AREAS:*** Privately Held Business Law; Financial Institutions Law; Banking Law. ***Email:*** robert.mintz@hklaw.com

JAMES A. MOEHLING, admitted to bar, 1965, Illinois. *Education:* Northwestern University (B.A., with honors, 1962; J.D., 1965). Phi Alpha Delta. Member, Board of Editors, Northwestern Law Review, 1964-1965. *Member:* Chicago, Illinois State and American Bar Associations. ***PRACTICE AREAS:*** Business Law; Real Estate Law; Business Planning; Family Business Law; Business Estate Planning; Trusts and Estates; Business Acquisitions Law; Closely Held Business Law; Family Trusts; Contracts; Partnership Law. ***Email:*** jim.moehling@hklaw.com

DONALD G. MULACK, admitted to bar, 1966, Illinois; 1979, U.S. Supreme Court; U.S. Court of Appeals, 4th, 7th, 9th and 11th Circuits. *Education:* Northern Illinois University (B.S., 1963); Illinois Institute of Technology/Chicago-Kent College of Law (J.D., 1966). Phi Delta Phi. Author: "Government Regulation of Not-For-Profit Corporations," IICLE, 1994, 2000. Assistant Attorney General, State of Illinois, 1969-1978. Chief, Charitable Trust Division, 1973-1976; Chief, Litigation, 1974-1976; Chief, Consumer Fraud Division, 1976-1978. *Member:* Chicago Bar Association (Chairman, Trade and Professional Associations Committee, 1987-1988). ***REPORTED CASES:*** Qualitex v. Jacobson, 115 S.Ct. 1300(1995). (Landmark color trademark case). ***PRACTICE AREAS:*** Business Litigation; Trademark. ***Email:*** donald.mulack@hklaw.com

CHRISTOPHER J. MURDOCH, born Pittsburgh, Pennsylvania, September 21, 1962; admitted to bar, 1987, Illinois and U.S. District Court, Northern District of Illinois including Trial Bar; 1990, U.S. Court of Appeals, Eleventh Circuit; 1999, U.S. Court of Appeals, Seventh Circuit. *Education:* Georgetown University (B.A., 1984); University of Michigan (J.D., 1987). *Member:* American Bar Association. ***Email:*** cmurdoch@hklaw.com

MARTIN P. MURPHY, born Joliet, Illinois September, 19, 1963; admitted to bar, 1990, Illinois and U.S. District Court, Northern District of Illinois. *Education:* University of Notre Dame (B.B.A., 1985); Northwestern University (J.D., 1990). *Member:* Chicago, Illinois State and American Bar Associations. ***PRACTICE AREAS:*** Real Estate Law. ***Email:*** marty.murphy@hklaw.com

JOHN R. MUSSMAN, born Covington, Kentucky, March 9, 1952; admitted to bar, 1983, Illinois. *Education:* Kalamazoo College (B.A., 1974); University of Michigan (J.D., 1983). Research Assistant, Legislative Assistant to U.S. Senator Edward Zorinsky, Nebraska, 1977-1980. *Member:* Chicago and American Bar Associations. ***PRACTICE AREAS:*** Banking Law (40%); Commercial Law (30%); Consumer Credit Law (30%). ***Email:*** john.mussman@hklaw.com

CARL A. NEUMANN, admitted to bar, 1968, Wisconsin; 1974, Illinois. *Education:* University of Wisconsin-Milwaukee (B.A., 1964); Northwestern University (M.A., 1966); University of Wisconsin-Madison (J.D., 1968). Attorney, Chicago Regional Office, Securities and Exchange Commission, 1968-1969. *Member:* DuPage County Bar Association. (Also at Oakbrook Terrace Office). ***PRACTICE AREAS:*** Corporate Law; Mergers and Acquisitions; Banking Law; Family Business; Estate Planning; Employee Stock Ownership Plans. ***Email:*** carl.neumann@hklaw.com

MATTHEW E. NORTON, born Ottawa, Illinois, September 6, 1964; admitted to bar, 1989, Illinois. *Education:* St. Ambrose College (B.A., magna cum laude, 1986); University of Illinois (J.D., 1989). ***Email:*** mnorton@hklaw.com

JOHN R. NYWEIDE, admitted to bar, 1973, Illinois. *Education:* Miami University (B.A., 1969); Vanderbilt University (J.D., 1973). Omicron Delta Kappa; Phi Alpha Theta; Phi Delta Phi. *Member:* American Bar Association; Chicago Estate Planning Council. ***PRACTICE AREAS:*** Real Estate Law; Business Law; Estate Planning Law. ***Email:*** jack.nyweide@hklaw.com

JENNIFER S. OOSTERBAAN, born Chicago, Illinois, December 29, 1966; admitted to bar, 1995, Illinois and U.S. District Court, Northern District of Illinois including Trial Bar. *Education:* University of Illinois (B.S., 1990; J.D., cum laude, 1995). Litigation Counsel, Attorney Registration and Disciplinary Commission of the Supreme Court of Illinois, 1995-1997. Associate, Jenner & Block, 1997-2000. *Member:* Chicago and American Bar Associations; Defense Research Institute. ***PRACTICE AREAS:*** Commercial Litigation; Business Law; Class Actions; Complex and Multi-District Litigation; Fraud and Deceit; Contracts; Trade Secrets; Mass Torts; Products Liability; Toxic Torts; Environmental Law; Professional Liability; Apellate Practice. ***Email:*** joosterbaan@hklaw.com

MORGAN J. ORDMAN, admitted to bar, 1967, Illinois; U.S. District Court, Northern District of Illinois; U.S. Tax Court; U.S. Claims Court; U.S. Supreme Court. *Education:* DePauw University (B.A., 1963); University of Chicago (J.D., 1966). *Member:* Chicago, Illinois State and American Bar Associations. ***PRACTICE AREAS:*** Corporate Law; Federal Taxation; Estate Planning. ***Email:*** morgan.ordman@hklaw.com

TODD S. PARKHURST, born Evanston, Illinois, March 8, 1941; admitted to bar, 1968, Illinois; 1973, U.S. District Court, Northern District of Illinois including Trial Bar, U.S. Court of Military Appeals and U.S. Supreme Court; 1977, U.S. Court of Appeals, Seventh Circuit; 1978, U.S. Court of Appeals for the Federal Circuit; 1989, U.S. District Court, Eastern District of Wisconsin; registered to practice before U.S. Patent and Trademark Office. *Education:* University of Illinois (B.S. in Gen. Engr., 1963); University of Pennsylva-

(This Listing Continued)

nia (J.D., 1966). Phi Alpha Delta. Member, Sharswood Law Club. Author: "Q's and A's about the EPC and the PCT," Illinois Bar Journal, 1976; "The License Agreement," Illinois Bar Journal, 1991; "Piatt and Parkhurst, Trade Secrets: Cases and Materials," 2002. Captain, Contracting Officer, U.S. Army Electronics Command, 1966-1968. Hearing Officer, Illinois Pollution Control Board, 1972-1996. Adjunct Professor of Law, John Marshall Law School, 1980-1984. Adjunct Professor of Law, IIT/Chicago-Kent College of Law, 1989, 1992—. Director and President, 1990, Lifeline Pilots, 1988—. Listed in: Best Lawyers in America, 2005; Illinois Superlawyer, 2005. *Member:* Chicago Bar Association; Patent Law Association of Chicago (Chairman, Computer Law Committee, 1996-1997); International Trademark Association; Licensing Executives Society; Intellectual Property Law Association of Chicago; Law Club of Chicago. [Capt., U.S. Army, Corps Engr., 1966-1968]. ***SPECIAL AGENCIES:*** American Arbitration Panels, Certified Mediator. ***REPORTED CASES:*** Phillips Screw Co. v. Amtel, 965 F.Supp. 3 (D.Mass. 1978); Publications International Ltd. v. Bally, 215 USPQ 861 (N.D. Ill. 1982); Chore Time v. Cumberland Equipment: 217 USPQ 168 (E.D. Tenn. 1982), affirmed 218 USPQ 673 (F. Cir. 1983); Duo-Tint v. Moline Cumberland Equipment, 217 USPQ 168 (E.D. Tenn. 1982), affirmed 218 USPQ 673 (F. Cir. 1983); Duo-Tint v. Moline Supply Co., 200 USPQ 410 (Ill. App. 1977); Wurlitzer v. Electrokey, 380 F. Supp. 576 (N.D. Texas 1974). ***PRACTICE AREAS:*** Patent Law; Trademark Law; Copyright Law; Trade Secret Law; Computer Law; Litigation; International Intellectual Property Law. ***Email:*** todd.parkhurst@hklaw.com

GEORGE M. PEARCE, born Evergreen Park, Illinois, December 7, 1954; admitted to bar, 1979, Illinois; 1987, Wisconsin. *Education:* Knox College (B.A., 1976); DePaul University (J.D., 1979); John Marshall Law School (LL.M., in Taxation, 1984). Phi Beta Kappa; Phi Alpha Delta. Recipient, American Jurisprudence Award for Contracts. *Member:* Chicago, Illinois State and American Bar Associations; State Bar of Wisconsin. (Member, Family Business Section-Private Wealth Services Group). ***PRACTICE AREAS:*** Business Planning Law; Family Business Law; Employment Law; Minority Business Enterprise Law. ***Email:*** george.pearce@hklaw.com

SCOTT W. PETERSEN, born Chicago, Illinois, February 16, 1947; admitted to bar, 1973, Illinois; 1974, U.S. District Court, Northern District of Illinois including Trial Bar; U.S. Court of Appeals, Seventh Circuit; 1985, U.S. Supreme Court. *Education:* Augustana College (B.A., 1968); Illinois Institute of Technology/Chicago-Kent College of Law (J.D., 1973). Phi Alpha Delta. Moot Court Finalist. Assistant States Attorney of Cook County, Illinois, 1973-1978. President and General Counsel, The Chicago Paper Tube & Can Co., 1978-1985. President, The Manuscript Society, 2002-2004. ***LANGUAGES:*** Spanish. ***PRACTICE AREAS:*** Trademark Law; Copyright Law; Artistic Property; Literary Property; Latin American Trade. ***Email:*** scott.petersen@hklaw.com

CHARLES L. PHILBRICK, born Philadelphia, Pennsylvania; admitted to bar, 1988, Illinois and U.S. District Court, Northern District of Illinois; 1991, District of Columbia and U.S. Court of Appeals, First Circuit; 1995, U.S. District Court, Northern District of Texas; 1996, U.S. District Court, Southern District of Illinois and U.S. District Court, Southern District of California; 1997, U.S. Court of Appeals, Seventh Circuit and U.S. District Court, Eastern and Western Districts of Michigan. *Education:* Trinity University (B.A., 1985); New England School of Law (J.D., 1988). ***PRACTICE AREAS:*** Litigation. ***Email:*** charles.philbrick@hklaw.com

S. RICHARD PINCUS, born Washington, D.C., May 15, 1936; admitted to bar, 1961, Illinois. *Education:* George Washington University (B.A., 1958); University of Chicago (J.D., 1961). Phi Eta Sigma; Phi Beta Kappa; Phi Delta Phi. Attorney, National Labor Relations Board, Chicago, 1961-1967. Adjunct Professor of Law, Illinois Institute of Technology/Chicago-Kent College of Law, 1982. Author: "Labor Relations Considerations: Summary of the Taft-Hartley Act," Chap. 12, Organizing and Advising Illinois Businesses, 1975-Rev. 1978. Co-Author: "The Common Law Contract and Tort Rights of Union Employees: What Effect After the Demise of the 'At Will' Doctrine?" Chicago-Kent Law Review, Winter 1983; "Final and Binding Arbitration: A Sensible Alternative to Expensive Employment Litigation," Journal of Health and Hospital Law, Nov. 1989. Arbitrator, Special Employment Panel, American Arbitration Association. *Member:* Chicago (Member, Labor and Employment Law Committee, 1982—), Illinois State and American (Member, State and Local Labor Law Committee, Labor and Employment Law Section, 1979—; Chairman, 1979-1981) Bar Associations; American Judicature Society; Industrial Relations Research Association; American Academy of Hospital Attorneys. ***PRACTICE AREAS:*** Labor Law; Employment Relations. ***Email:*** richard.pincus@hklaw.com

FRANCES E. PRELL, born Decatur, Illinois, September 1, 1949; admitted to bar, 1978, Illinois; 1984, Florida. *Education:* Eastern Illinois University (B.A., magna cum laude, 1972); University of Illinois (J.D., 1978). *Member:* Chicago, Illinois State and American Bar Associations; The Florida Bar; Legal Club of Chicago. ***Email:*** fprell@hklaw.com

MICHAEL J. RANALLO, born Cleveland, Ohio, September 5, 1954; admitted to bar, 1980, Illinois and U.S. District Court, Northern District of Illinois; 1990, Ohio; U.S. District Court, Northern District of Ohio; U.S. Court of Appeals, Sixth Circuit; 1999, U.S. District Court, Eastern District of Michigan. *Education:* Kent State University (B.A., summa cum laude, 1976); Ohio State University (J.D., with honors, 1980). Phi Beta Kappa; Phi Alpha Delta (Chapter Justice, 1979). *Member:* American Bar Association (Member, Sections on: Labor and Employment; Litigation). ***Email:*** mranallo@hklaw.com

MICHAEL D. RECHTIN, born Chicago, Illinois, December 4, 1967; admitted to bar, 1988, Wisconsin; 1992, Michigan; 1994, Illinois. *Education:* Massachusetts Institute of Technology (B.S., 1989); University of Notre Dame (J.D., 1992). ***Email:*** michael.rechtin@hklaw.com

RICHARD A. REDMOND, born October 4, 1947; admitted to bar, 1972, Illinois and U.S. District Court, Northern District of Illinois; 1975, U.S. Court of Appeals, Seventh Circuit; 1976, U.S. Supreme Court. *Education:* University of Notre Dame (B.A., 1969); Cornell University (J.D., 1972). Author: "Valuation of Property In Eminent Domain," and "Environmental Law Issues in Eminent Domain Litigation," Illinois Eminent Domain Practice, Illinois Institute for Continuing Legal Education, 2002. Special Assistant to the Attorney General, 1974—. Member, 1983 and Chair, 1993-1997, Illinois Supreme Court Committee on Professional Responsibility. *Member:* Chicago (Chair, Eminent Domain Subcommittee, 1982-1987), Illinois State and American Bar Associations. ***PRACTICE AREAS:*** Civil Litigation; Eminent Domain Law; Legal Ethics. ***Email:*** richard.redmond@hklaw.com

(This Listing Continued)

EDWARD F. RYAN, born Chicago, Illinois, September 14, 1943; admitted to bar, 1968, Illinois; 1984, Florida; U.S. District Court, Northern District of Illinois; U.S. Court of Appeals, Seventh and Eleventh Circuits; U.S. Supreme Court. *Education:* University of St. Thomas (B.A., magna cum laude, 1965); Georgetown University (J.D., 1968). *Member:* Chicago and American Bar Associations; The Florida Bar. Fellow, American Bar Foundation. ***Email:*** eryan@hklaw.com

ANNE HAMBLIN SCHIAVE, admitted to bar, 1973, Illinois. *Education:* University of Chicago (A.B., 1970; J.D., 1973). Phi Beta Kappa. *Member:* Chicago and American (Member, Business Law Section) Bar Associations; Illinois Womens' Bar Association. ***PRACTICE AREAS:*** Business Law; Mergers and Acquisitions; Securities Law. ***Email:*** anne.schiave@hklaw.com

TODD J. SCHNEIDER, admitted to bar, 1995, Wisconsin, Illinois and U.S. District Court, Northern District of Illinois and Eastern District of Wisconsin. *Education:* Northwestern University (B.A., 1992); Marquette University (J.D., 1995). Associate Editor, Marquette Law Review, 1994-1995. *Member:* Chicago Bar Association; American Bar Association; State Bar of Wisconsin; Chicago Estate Planning Council. ***REPORTED CASES:*** WIGGINS v. SMITH, WARDEN, et al., U.S. Supreme Court Docket No. 02-311. ***PRACTICE AREAS:*** Estate Planning; Trust and Estate Administration; Fiduciary Income Taxation; Business Succession Planning. ***Email:*** todd.schneider@hklaw.com

ROBERT C. SCHNITZ, admitted to bar, 1975, Illinois. *Education:* Harvard University (B.A., magna cum laude, 1967); Harvard Law School (J.D., 1975). *Member:* Chicago and American Bar Associations. [1st Lieutenant, U.S. Army, 1969-1971]. (Section Operations Manager). ***PRACTICE AREAS:*** Legal Ethics. ***Email:*** robert.schnitz@hklaw.com

PHILLIP M. SCHREIBER, born Chicago, Illinois; admitted to bar, 1992, Illinois and U.S. District Court, Northern District of Illinois; 1998, U.S. Court of Appeals, Seventh Circuit; 2002, U.S. District Court, Northern District of Indiana. *Education:* University of Illinois (A.B., magna cum laude, 1989); Northwestern University (J.D., 1992). Phi Beta Kappa; Phi Kappa Phi. Co-Author: "National Railroad Passenger Corporation v. Morgan: The End of the Line for the Continuing Violation Doctrine or an Express Route for Plaintiffs?" 28 Emp. Rel. L.J., Winter 2003; "Hoffman Platics v. NLRB: Changing The Scope Of Remedial Discretion Afforded Regulatory Agencies," 28 Emp. Rel. L.J., Autumn 2002; "The Next Generation Of ADA Claims: The 'Regarded As' Prong Of The Definition Of Disability," 26 Emp. Rel. L.J., Summer, 2000; "Weingarten Revisited: Nonunion Workers Also Have Right To Presence Of Coworker During Investigatory Interviews," 26 Emp. Rel. L.J., Winter, 2000; "Employers Beware: Unilateral Handbook Modifications May Not Be Binding," 25 Emp. Rel. L.J., Spring 2000; "Drafting Enforceable Non-Competition Agreements," 25 Emp. Rel. L.J., Winter 1999; "Revisiting The Legality Of Employee Participation Programs Under the NLRA," 25 Emp. Rel. L.J., Summer 1999; "Revisiting Sexual Harassment Policies In Light Of Oncale," 24 Emp. Rel. L.J., Autumn 1998; "Drafting Effective Independent Contractor Agreements," 23 Emp. Rel. L.J., Spring 1998. *Member:* Chicago and American (Member, Labor and Employment Law Section) Bar Associations. ***PRACTICE AREAS:*** Labor and Employment. ***Email:*** phillip.schreiber@hklaw.com

MARK L. SHAPIRO, born Brookline, Massachusetts, February 18, 1949; admitted to bar, 1974, Illinois and U.S. District Court, Northern District of Illinois including Trial Bar; 1977, U.S. Court of Appeals, Seventh Circuit. *Education:* Wesleyan University (B.A., with honors, 1970); University of Chicago (J.D., 1974). Public Office: Attorney, Solicitor's Office, U.S. Department of Labor, 1974-1979. *Member:* Illinois State and American (Member, Sections on: Labor and Employment; Litigation) Bar Associations. ***PRACTICE AREAS:*** Labor Law; Employment Relations; Litigation; Class Actions; Disabled Access; Occupational Safety and Health; Trade Secrets. ***Email:*** mark.shapiro@hklaw.com

MICHELE E. SIBLEY GONZALES, admitted to bar, 1994, Illinois. *Education:* University of Chicago (B.A., 1987); Chicago-Kent College of Law (J.D., with honors, 1994). Co-Author: Chapter 13, "Environmental Law and Eminent Domain," Illinois Eminent Domain Practice (2002 Illinois Institute of Continuing Legal Education). *Member:* Chicago and Illinois State Bar Associations. ***LANGUAGES:*** French. ***PRACTICE AREAS:*** Commercial Litigation; Eminent Domain; Real Estate Litigation; Covenants Not to Compete. ***Email:*** michele.sibleygonzales@hklaw.com

COLIN SMITH, born DeKalb, Illinois, October 4, 1955; admitted to bar, 1980, Illinois; 1985, Florida. *Education:* DePauw University (B.A., 1977); Washington University (J.D., 1980). Phi Beta Kappa; Order of The Coif. Senior Editor, Washington University Law Quarterly, 1979-1980. Illinois Co-Editor, Product Liability Desk Reference (Aspen Law and Business). *Member:* Illinois State and American Bar Associations; The Florida Bar; Illinois Association of Defense Trial Counsel. ***Email:*** colin.smith@hklaw.com

MARK A. SPOGNARDI, admitted to bar, 1984, Illinois; 1986, U.S. District Court, Northern District of Illinois including Trial Bar; 1988, U.S. Court of Appeals, Seventh Circuit; 2000, U.S. District Court, Central District of Illinois including Trial Bar. *Education:* University of Iowa (B.A., with honors, 1980); DePaul University College of Law (J.D., 1984). Phi Beta Kappa. Mansfield Fellow. Author: "Having Your Waffle and Eating It Too: The EEOC's Right to Circumvent Arbitration Agreements," Emp. Rel. L.J., Vol. 28, No. 1 (Summer, 2002); "Bad Law and Bad Politics: OSHA's Ill-Fated Ergonomics Standard," Emp. Rel. L.J., Vol. 27, No. 1 (Summer, 2001); "The Sting: Testers May Sue Under Title VII Circuit Court Rules," Emp. Rel. L.J., Vol. 26, No. 4 (Spring, 2001); "In the Lion's Den: Religious Accommodation and Harassment in the Workplace," Employee Relations Law Journal, Vol. 25, No. 4 (Spring 2000); "Conducting a Successful Union-Free Campaign: A Primer (Part II)," Employee Relations Law Journal, Vol. 24, No. 3 (Winter 1998); "Conducting a Successful Union-Free Campaign: A Primer (Part I)," Employee Relations Law Journal, Vol. 24, No. 2 (Autumn 1998); "Allentown Mack v. NLRB: The Twilight of the Good Faith Reasonable Doubt Doctrine," Emp. Rel. L.J., Vol. 24, No. 1 (Summer 1998); "Organizing Through Cyberspace: Electronic Communications and the National Labor Relations Act," Emp. Rel. L.J., Vol. 23, No. 4 (Spring 1998); "Conducting a Human Resources Audit: A Primer," Emp. Rel. L.J., Vol. 23, No. 1 (Summer 1997); "Defending Against the Corporate Campaign: Selected Legal Responses to Common Union Tactics," Emp. Rel. L.J., Vol. 22, No. 2 (Autumn 1996); "Navigating the STAA: A Survey and Recent Developments Under the Anti-Retaliation Provisions of the Surface Transportation Assistance Act," Labor Law Journal (April 1996); "Temporary Employment Relationships: Review of the Joint Employer Doctrine Under the NLRA," Emp. Rel. L.J., Vol. 21, No. 2 (Autumn 1995). Staff Counsel to Board Member, NLRB, Washington, D.C., 1984-1986. Field At-

(This Listing Continued)

HOLLAND & KNIGHT LLP, Chicago—Continued

torney, NLRB, Region 13, 1986-1988. Member, Elk Grove Village Chamber of Commerce. *Member:* Chicago, Illinois State and American Bar Associations; National Tranportation Employee Relations Association (Board Member); Midwest Textile Service Association (General Counsel); Transportation Lawyers Association; Society for Human Resources Management. ***REPORTED CASES:*** Central States v. Hunt Truck Lines, Inc., 296 F. 3d 624 (7th Cir. 2002); 133 F. Supp 2d. 1076 (N.D. Il. 2000); 204 F. 3d 736 (7th Cir. 2000); 43 F. Supp 2d 942 (N.D. Il. 1999); NLRB v. Case Corporation 995 F. 2d 700 (7th Cir. 1993); Agretti, et al. v. ANR Freight Systems, Inc., 982 F. 2d 242 (7th Cir. 1992); Joe B. Foods, Inc. d/b/a Butera Finer Foods, 296 NLRB 950 (1988). ***PRACTICE AREAS:*** Management Labor Relations and Employment Law; Pension Litigation. ***Email:*** mark.spognardi@hklaw.com

LEWIS T. STEADMAN, JR., born Evanston, Illinois, June 21, 1956; admitted to bar, 1982, Illinois and U.S. District Court, Northern District of Illinois, including Trial Bar. *Education:* Northwestern University (B.A., 1978); John Marshall Law School (J.D., 1982). *Member:* Intellectual Property Law Association of Chicago; International Trademark Association; International Patent and Trademark Association. ***PRACTICE AREAS:*** Patent Law; Trademark Law; Copyright Law; Trade Dress; Litigation; International Trade Law; Unfair Competition Law. ***Email:*** lsteadma@hklaw.com

TODD D. STEENSON, born Minneapolis, Minnesota, October 1, 1966; admitted to bar, 1993, Minnesota and U.S. District Court, District of Minnesota; 1996, Illinois; 1997, U.S. District Court, Northern District of Illinois; 1998, U.S. Court of Appeals, Third, Seventh and Ninth Circuits; 2000, U.S. Court of Appeals, Eleventh Circuit. *Education:* Augsburg College (B.A., summa cum laude, 1989); University of Minnesota (J.D., summa cum laude, 1992). Order of the Coif. Note and Comment Editor, Minnesota Law Review, 1991-1992. Law Clerk, Hon. Frank J. Magill, U.S. Court of Appeals, Eighth Circuit, 1992-1993. Author: Note, "The Public Sector Compensatory Time Exception to the Fair Labor Standard Act: Trying to Compensate For Congress's Lack of Clarity," 75 Minnesota Law Review 1807, 1991; Chapter, "Retaliatory Discharge -- The Public Policy Doctrine," in Employment Termination (Illinois Institute of Continuing Legal Education, 2002). *Member:* American Bar Association (Member, Labor and Employent Section). ***REPORTED CASES:*** Rauen v. U.S. Tobacco Manufacturing Ltd. Pshp., 319 F.3d 891 (7th Cir. 2003); Stopka v. Alliance of American Insurers, 141 F.3d 681 (7th Cir. 1998). ***PRACTICE AREAS:*** Labor and Employment Law; Litigation. ***Email:*** todd.steenson@hklaw.com

MARK J. STEGER, born June 19, 1959; admitted to bar, 1985, Illinois and U.S. Court of Appeals, Seventh Circuit. *Education:* University of Illinois (B.S., Finance, 1981; M.S., Finance, 1982); Seattle University School of Law (J.D., 1985). *Member:* Illinois State and American Bar Associations. ***PRACTICE AREAS:*** Environmental Law; Employee Health and Safety Law. ***Email:*** mark.steger@hklaw.com

WILLIAM M. STEVENS, born Akron, Ohio, December 29, 1943; admitted to bar, 1969, Illinois; U.S. District Court, Northern and Central Districts of Illinois, including Trial Bar; U.S. District Court, Northern District of Indiana; U.S. Court of Appeals, Seventh and Ninth Circuits; U.S. Supreme Court. *Education:* Miami University (B.A., 1965); Northwestern University (J.D., 1968). *Member:* Chicago (Chairman: Environmental Law Committee, 1972-1973; Law School Liaison Committee, 1973-1974; Member: Executive Committee, 1972-1974; Environmental Law Committee, 1977-1978; Civil Procedure Committee, 1979-1980; Commodities Law Committee, 1979-1980), Illinois State and American (Chairman, Litigation Committee, 1985-1987 and TV Satellite Broadcasts Committee, 1986-1988; Member, Committees on: Program Board, 1986-1987; Substantive Law, 1985-1986; Advocacy, 1984-1985; Commodities Regulation, 1978-1981) Bar Associations; Chicago Lawyers Club. [Lt., USNR (ret.)]. ***REPORTED CASES:*** Stevens v. Rooks Pitts & Poust, 289 Ill.App.3d 991, 225 Ill.Dec. 48, 682 N.E.2d 1125 (1997). ***PRACTICE AREAS:*** Copyright; Employment Law; Insurance; Commercial Litigation. ***Email:*** william.stevens@hklaw.com

MAUREEN STRAUTS, born December 12, 1950; admitted to bar, 1976, Illinois. *Education:* Illinois Wesleyan University (B.A., magna cum laude, 1973); Northwestern University (J.D., 1976). Order of Coif. Member, Northwestern University Law Review, 1975-1976. City Council, Alderman-City of Park Ridge, 1993-2001. Member, Board of Directors, Economic Corporation, Park Ridge, 2002—. *Member:* Illinois State and American Bar Associations; DuPage County Estate Planning Council. ***PRACTICE AREAS:*** Land Use; Zoning; Estate Planning; Premarital Agreements; Probate; Elder Law; Trust Administration; Real Estate. ***Email:*** maureen.strauts@hklaw.com

JONATHAN E. STROUSE, born Whitefish Bay, Wisconsin; admitted to bar, 1986, Wisconsin, Illinois, U.S. District Court, Northern District of Illinois and U.S. Tax Court. *Education:* University of Wisconsin (B.B.A., with distinction, 1978; J.D., cum laude, 1986). Certified Public Accountant: Wisconsin, 1980. Contributing Author: *Online Law: The SPA's Legal Guide to Doing Business on the Internet,* Addison-Wesley (1996). *Member:* American Bar Association. ***PRACTICE AREAS:*** Commercial Litigation; Tax Controversies; Tax Litigation; Debtor and Creditor. ***Email:*** jonathan.strouse@hklaw.com

JULIE A. TAPPENDORF, born Dubuque, Iowa, August 18, 1964; admitted to bar, 1997, Illinois. *Education:* Illinois State University (B.A., 1985); William S. Richardson School of Law/University of Hawaii (J.D., 1997). University of Hawaii Law Review: Member, 1995-1997 and Executive Editor of Research, 1996-1997. Dean's Scholar, 1994. Michael P. Porter Scholar, 1996. West Publishing Scholar, 1997. Adjunct Professor, John Marshall School of Law. Co-Author: "Bargaining for Development," (Environmental Law Institute July, 2003); "From the Traditional to the More Creative: Incentives for Historic Preservations," published by the American Bar Association in a book titled Current Trends and Practical Strategies in Land Use Law and Zoning, (2004). Author: "A Practical Guide to Drafting Architectural Design Regulations," The Municipal Lawyer (March/April 2003); "Architectural Design Regulations: What Can a Municipality Do to Protect Against Unattractive, Inappropriate, and Just Plain Ugly Structures?" 34 Urban Lawyer 961 (Fall 2002); "Annexation Agreements and Development Agreements," Chapter 14, Trends in Land Use Law from A to Z, Adult Uses to Zoning (ABA 2001); "Unconstitutional Land Development Conditions and the Development Agreement Solution: Bargaining for Public Facilities After Nollan and Dolan," Case W. Res. L. Rev. 2001 (Euclid Symposium), republished in "The Land Use and Environmental Law Review"; "Vernonia Sch. Dist. v. Acton: Now Children Must Shed Their Constitutional Rights at the Schoolhouse Gate," 18 U. Haw. L. Rev. 869, (1996). Pro Bono Partner, Holland & Knight's Chicago Office. Member, Board of Directors, Public Interest Law Initiative (PILI). *Member:* Chicago and American Bar Associations; American Planning Association. [U.S. Army, Military Intelligence, 1988-1996 Active & Reserves]. ***REPORTED CASES:*** Graf et al. v. Village of Lake Bluff, No. 91715 (Illinois Supreme Court, June 19, 2003); Graf et al. v. Village of Lake Bluff, 321 Ill. App. 3d 897, 255 Ill. Dec. 97 748 N.E.2d 801, (2d Dist. 2001). ***PRACTICE AREAS:*** Local Government Law; Land Use; Zoning Law; Real Estate Development. ***Email:*** julie.tappendorf@hklaw.com

ROBERT E. TONN, born Morristown, New Jersey, January 21, 1968; admitted to bar, 1996, California; 2000, Illinois. *Education:* University of California, Los Angeles (B.A., 1990); University of San Francisco School of Law (J.D., 1996). Comments Editor, University of San Francisco Law Review. ***PRACTICE AREAS:*** Product Liability Litigation; Commercial Litigation. ***Email:*** robert.tonn@hklaw.com

STEVEN B. VARICK, admitted to bar, 1979, Illinois, U.S. District Court, Northern District of Illinois, including Trial Bar, U.S. Court of Appeals, Third and Seventh Circuits and U.S. Supreme Court. *Education:* Knox College (B.A., cum laude, 1976); University of Chicago (J.D., 1979). *Member:* Chicago and American (Member, Litigation, Antitrust and Labor and Employment Law Sections) Bar Associations; Chicago Council of Lawyers (Secretary, 1986-1987; Treasurer, 1987-1988). ***PRACTICE AREAS:*** Civil Litigation; Antitrust; Appellate Litigation; Employment Law; Environmental Litigation. ***Email:*** steven.varick@hklaw.com

ROBERT W. VYVERBERG, JR., born Rockford, Illinois, May 1, 1968; admitted to bar, 1993, Illinois and U.S. District Court, Northern District of Illinois; 1994, U.S. Court of Appeals, Seventh Circuit; 1996, U.S. District Court, Central District of Illinois; 1997, U.S. District Court, Southern District of Illinois; 1999, U.S. Court of Appeals, Eighth Circuit; 2005, U.S. Court of Appeals, Tenth Circuit. *Education:* University of Illinois (B.S., 1990; J.D., magna cum laude, 1993). Associate Editor, University of Illinois Law Review, 1991-1993. *Member:* Chicago, Illinois State and American Bar Associations. ***PRACTICE AREAS:*** Labor and Employment; Products Liability; Litigation. ***Email:*** robert.vyverberg@hklaw.com

RICHARD R. WINTER, born Chicago, Illinois; admitted to bar, 1987, Illinois and U.S. District Court, Northern District of Illinois; 1988, U.S. Court of Appeals, Fourth Circuit; 1989, U.S. Court of Appeals, Seventh and Ninth Circuits; 1995, U.S. Court of Appeals, Eighth and Eleventh Circuits; 1998, U.S. Supreme Court; 1999, U.S. Tax Court. *Education:* University of Illinois (B.S., 1976); DePaul University (M.B.A., 1983); Chicago-Kent College of Law (J.D., 1986). *Member:* American Bar Association (Member, Sections on: Antitrust Law; Intellectual Property; Litigation; TIPs). ***PRACTICE AREAS:*** Litigation; Antitrust; Intellectual Property; Securities; Insurance. ***Email:*** rich.winter@hklaw.com

THOMAS R. WOODROW, born Chicago, Illinois, August 4, 1960; admitted to bar, 1985, Illinois; 1986, Florida. *Education:* Georgetown University (A.B., cum laude, 1982); Loyola University (J.D., 1985). *Member:* Chicago, Illinois State and American Bar Associations; The Florida Bar. ***Email:*** twoodrow@hklaw.com

DAVID E. ZAJICEK, born June 27, 1939; admitted to bar, 1964, Illinois; 1977, California; U.S. District Court, Northern District of Illinois including Trial Bar. *Education:* Bradley University (B.S., with honors, 1961); Northwestern University School of Law (J.D., 1964). *Member:* Chicago, DuPage County Bar Associations; State Bar of California. [Capt., USAF, Judge Advocate Corps, 1964-1967]. ***PRACTICE AREAS:*** Corporate Law; Mergers, Acquisitions and Divestitures; International Trade; Zoning, Planning and Land Use; Litigation. ***Email:*** david.zajicek@hklaw.com

LARRY M. ZANGER, admitted to bar, 1970, Illinois, U.S. District Court, Northern District of Illinois, U.S. Court of Appeals, Seventh Circuit, U.S. Tax Court and U.S. Claims Court. *Education:* Northwestern University (B.S.B.A.; J.D.). Beta Alpha Psi. Elijah Watt Sells Award. Illinois CPA Examination. Monthly Columnist: "Computer Law," for The Chicago Computer Guide, 1989-2002; Illinois Bar Journal (two-time Lincoln Award winner); Course Books for the Illinois Institute for Continuing Legal Education. Chapter Author and Editor, Online Law, The Software Publisher's Association, 1996. Adjunct Professor, University of Illinois Chicago-College of Commerce and Benedictine University. Certified Public Accountant, Illinois. *Member:* Chicago (Past Chairman, Computer Law Committee) and DuPage County Bar Associations; Computer Law Association. ***PRACTICE AREAS:*** Electronic Commerce; Computers and Software; Corporate Law; Intellectual Property. ***Email:*** larry.zanger@hklaw.com

SENIOR COUNSEL

DANIEL ACOSTA, born Chicago, Illinois, September 19, 1966; admitted to bar, 1993, Illinois. *Education:* Princeton University (A.B., cum laude, 1988); Stanford University (J.D., 1993). ***LANGUAGES:*** Spanish. ***PRACTICE AREAS:*** Real Estate Acquisitions (15%); Real Estate Contracts (20%); Real Estate Exchanges (5%); Real Estate Finance (30%); Real Estate Sales (30%). ***Email:*** daniel.acosta@hklaw.com

LAWRENCE A. COLES, JR., born Milwaukee, Wisconsin, February 15, 1929; admitted to bar, 1957, Wisconsin and Illinois. *Education:* University of Wisconsin (B.S., 1952; J.D., 1957). Phi Delta Phi. Co-Author: Comment to Article 8, "Investment Securities," Illinois Uniform Commercial Code in *Smith-Hurd Illinois Annotated Statutes,* 1963. Co-author: Article, "Wall Street Trading Firms as Securities Insiders," 12 Cleveland Marshall Law Review, 1963. Author of the following Illinois Institute for Continuing Legal Education Handbook Chapters: "Financing the Illinois Business," in *Organizing and Advising Illinois Business,* 1972; "Financing the On-Going Business," in *Closely Held Corporations* 1990; "Federal and State Securities Law Considerations" in *Buying and Selling Business,* 1982. Co-Author, "Regulation A: Small Business Financing Exemption" in Securities Law, 1979; "Introduction to Exempt Financing" and "Private Offering Exemptions Under Federal Law," in Securities Law, 1991; "Introduction Organizational Procedure and Forms" in *Organizing and Advising Not For Profit Corporations,* 1981; "SEC Regulation D: New Federal Regulation for Exempt Transactions" in *Practical Application of Securities Law to Real Estate, Banking and Business Practice,* 1982; "Securities Registration and Exemptions," in Real Estate Syndications, 1983. Author: Article, "Indemnification of Officers and Directors of Illinois Corporations; The Need For Statutory Clarification," Chicago Bar Record, 1970; Article, "An Introduction to Regulation A: Small Business Financing Ex-

(This Listing Continued)

emption," Chicago Bar Record, 1974; Article, "Has Securities Law Regulation in the Private Capital Markets Become a Deterrent to Capital Growth: A Critical Review," 58 Marquette Law Review, No. 3, p. 395, 1975; Article, "Corporate Indemnification: Another Opportunity For Illinois to Come Into the Twentieth Century," Chicago Bar Record, 1975; Article, "Regulation D—New Rules for Raising Capital in Non Public Financings," 70 Illinois Bar Journal 612, 1982. Lecturer, Securities Regulation, Loyola University Law School, Chicago, 1978-1979. Seminar sponsored by the Illinois Institute for Continuing Legal Education and the Illinois State Bar Association, Topic: "Financing and Managing Closely Held Business, The Owner's Interest and Perspective - How to Raise Capital," Chicago, Illinois, September 1987. Seminar sponsored by IIT/Chicago-Kent College of Law, Topic: "Corporate Mergers and Acquisitions, a Securities Lawyer's View," Chicago, Illinois, December 1987. Seminar sponsored by the Chicago Bar Association, Topic: "Lawyers' Responsibilities in Securities Transactions - Observations of an Expert Witness for the Defense," Chicago, Illinois, February 1988. Seminar sponsored by the Illinois Institute for Continuing Education, Topic: "Buying and Selling Businesses," 1987. Seminar sponsored by the Illinois Institute for Continuing Legal Education, First Annual W. McNeil Kennedy Securities Law Seminar, Topic: "Exempt Securities Offerings," Chicago, Illinois, May 1988; Seminar sponsored by the Illinois Institute for Continuing Legal Education and the Illinois State Bar Association, Topic: "Enhancing the Effectiveness of the Business Attorney Advisor," Chicago, Illinois, June 1988. Seminar sponsored by the Illinois Institute for Continuing Legal Education, Second Annual W. McNeil Kennedy Securities Law Seminar, Topic: "Private Financial Alternatives," Chicago, Illinois, June 1989. Advanced Corporate and Securities Law Institute, University of Houston Law Center: Topic: "Raising Capital for Small/Medium Sized Businesses", Houston, Texas, November 1990; Third Annual W. McNeil Kennedy Securities Law Seminar: Securities Law Update, Moderator, Chicago, Illinois, October 1990; Seminar sponsored by The Business and Professional Institute, College of DuPage: Topic: "Selling Your Business - Your Attorney, Helper or Hindrance", Glen Ellyn, Illinois, May 1990. Seminar sponsored by Kellogg Graduate School of Management, Northwestern University, Topic: "Managing the Closely Held Company in Changing Times," Lawyers' Panel, January 1992. Member, Securities Advisory Committee to Illinois Secretary of State, 1982—. *Member:* Chicago (Member: Corporation Law Committee, 1964—; Member, 1964— and Chairman, 1966-1967, Commercial Code Committee; Member, 1964— and Chairman, 1972-1973; Securities Law Committee, 1983; Member, Computer Law Committee, Board of Managers, 1985—), Illinois State (Member of Council, Corporation and Securities Law Section, 1968—; Editor, Newsletter of Commercial, Banking and Bankruptcy Law Section, 1967; Co-Editor, Newsletter, 1969-1970 and Corporation and Securities Law Section Chairman, 1972-1973; Member of Council, Business Advice and Financial Planning Section), Federal (Member, Securities Committee, 1977—) and American (Member: Subcommittee on Investment Securities of Uniform Commercial Code Committee, 1964—; Subcommittee on Private Offering and Simplification of Capital Formation for Small Business of State Regulation of Securities Committee, 1976—; Subcommittee of Securities Regulation of Small Business Committee, 1979—; Subcommittee on High Technology Ventures of Small Business Committee, 1983—; Committee on Developments in Business Financing, 1985; Section on Corporation, Banking and Business Law) Bar Associations; State Bar of Wisconsin (Member, Corporation, Banking and Business Law Section). ***PRACTICE AREAS:*** Corporate Law; Securities Law; Business Law.

JAMES G. HAFT, admitted to bar, 1984, Illinois and U.S. District Court, Northern District of Illinois; 1988, U.S. Court of Appeals, Seventh Circuit; 1989, U.S. Supreme Court. *Education:* University of Wisconsin (B.B.A., 1980; M.S., Real Estate, 1982); Georgetown University (J.D., cum laude, 1984). Author: "The Americans with Disabilities Act: Concerns for Lenders, Owners, and Tenants," The Real Estate Finance Journal, 1992. Board Member, University of Wisconsin Center for Real Estate, 2004—. President, Wisconsin Real Estate Alumni Association, 1997-1999. Board Member, Dean's Advisory Board, University of Wisconsin, School of Business, 2000-2004. Member: Urban Land Institute; Central Michigan Avenue Association; National Association of Industry and Office Parks. ***PRACTICE AREAS:*** Real Estate; Construction Law. ***Email:*** james.haft@hklaw.com

IAIN JOHNSTON, born Chicago, Illinois, June 11, 1965; admitted to bar, 1990, Illinois; 1991, District of Columbia. *Education:* Rockford College (B.S.G.S., cum laude, 1987); John Marshall Law School (J.D., cum laude, 1990). Judicial Law Clerk to the Honorable Philip G. Reinhard, Illinois Appellate Court, Second District and U.S. District Court, Northern District of Illinois, 1990-1992. Assistant Attorney General and Unit Supervisor of Civil Prosecutions, Illinois, 1993-1998. Member, Advisory Board Member, Federal Discovery News, 1995-2005. Member, Scottish Law Society. *Member:* Illinois State Bar Association (Chair, Vice-Chair and Secretary, Individual Rights and Responsibilities Section, 1993-1999);. ***REPORTED CASES:*** Chavez v. Illinois State Police, 251 F.3d 612 (7th Cir. 2001); Nevel v. Schaumburg, 297 F.3d 673 (7th Cir. 2002); Milwaukee Safeguard v. Selke, 754 N.E.2d 349 (1st Dist. 2002); Nationwide v. Shapo, 767 N.E.2d 936 (4th Dist. 2002). ***PRACTICE AREAS:*** Government Law; Civil Litigation. ***Email:*** iain.johnston@hklaw.com

ADAM KINGSLEY, born Brooklyn, New York, May 25, 1965; admitted to bar, 1991, Illinois. *Education:* Cornell University (B.S., 1987); Duke University (J.D., 1991). ***PRACTICE AREAS:*** Land Use; Government. ***Email:*** adam.kingsley@hklaw.com

MARK J. NORA, born Chicago, Illinois, August 30, 1952; admitted to bar, 1981, Illinois and U.S. District Court, Northern District of Illinois. *Education:* University of Tennessee at Knoxville (B.A., 1974); John Marshall Law School (J.D., 1981). Phi Alpha Delta. *Member:* Chicago (Member, Real Estate Committee; Zoning and Land Use Planning Subcommittee) and American (Member, Committees on: Real Estate, Planning and Probate) Bar Associations. ***PRACTICE AREAS:*** Zoning Planning and Land Use; Real Estate; Real Estate Finance; Municipal Law; Alcoholic Beverage. ***Email:*** mark.nora@hklaw.com

SARAH E. PACE, born Iowa City, Iowa, April 27, 1962; admitted to bar, 1993, Illinois. *Education:* Beloit College (B.A., magna cum laude, 1984); Northwestern University (J.D., 1993). *Member:* American Bar Association. ***PRACTICE AREAS:*** Land Use; Government; Commercial Litigation. ***Email:*** sarah.pace@hklaw.com

CAROLE LAUDE PECHI, born Harvey, Illinois, October 22, 1962; admitted to bar, 1990, Illinois and U.S. District Court, Northern District of Illinois. *Education:* University of Illinois (A.B., 1984); IIT-Chicago-Kent College of Law (J.D., 1990). Recipient: Children of Disabled Veterans Scholarship; Shirley Schmidt Scholarship; American Jurisprudence Award, Labor Law. Member, International Council of Shopping Centers, 1992—. Author: "Drafting Shopping Center Leases Around Mitigation of Damages Requirements," Shopping Center Law Report, 2000; "Selected Issues in Build to Suit Leases," in Construction Issues, International Council of Shopping Centers, 1995. Published in Shopping Center Law Report, Commercial Lease Law Insider and Management Insider. *Member:* Chicago Bar Association; International Council of Shopping Centers. ***LANGUAGES:*** French. ***PRACTICE AREAS:*** Real Estate; Leasing; Small Business Law. ***Email:*** carole.pechi@hklaw.com

JOHN D. RYAN, admitted to bar, 1973, New York; 2001, Illinois. *Education:* Fordham University School Of Law (J.D., 1972). ***PRACTICE AREAS:*** Transactions; Commercial Real Estate; Contracts; Corporate Law; Equipment Finance and Leasing; Office Leasing; Retail Leasing; Industrial Leasing; Commercial Leasing. ***Email:*** jay.ryan@hklaw.com

PETER J. STRAND, admitted to bar, 1987, Wisconsin and Illinois, U.S. District Court, Northern District of Illinois and U.S. District Court, Western District of Wisconsin; 1991, U.S. Court of Appeals, 7th Circuit; 2001, U.S. District Court, Eastern District of Wisconsin. *Education:* University of Wisconsin-Madison (B.A., 1976; J.D., 1987). Adjunct Professor, Chicago-Kent College of Law, Marquette University Law School and DePaul University College of Law for Entertainment Law. Member: Board of Governors, Chicago Chapter, National Academy of the Recording Arts and Sciences; Board of Directors The Old Town School of Folk Music; Board of Directors/Honors Council Lawyers for the Creative Arts. *Member:* Chicago, Illinois State and American (Member, Forum on Entertainment and Sports Industries) Bar Associations; State Bar of Wisconsin. ***PRACTICE AREAS:*** Entertainment; Intellectual Property; Litigation. ***Email:*** peter.strand@hklaw.com

ASSOCIATES

ROBYN C. AXBERG, born Englewood, Colorado, August 10, 1976; (admission pending). *Education:* University of Texas (B.A., 1998); Loyola University (J.D., 2005). ***PRACTICE AREAS:*** Business Law. ***Email:*** robyn.axberg@hklaw.com

NASER BASEER, admitted to bar, 2003, Illinois. *Education:* Chicago-Kent College of Law (J.D., 2003). *Member:* Chicago, Illinois State and American Bar Associations. ***LANGUAGES:*** Hindi, Urdu and Spanish. ***PRACTICE AREAS:*** Intellectual Property. ***Email:*** naser.baseer@hklaw.com

STEVEN C. BAUER, born 1976; admitted to bar, 2004, Illinois. *Education:* University of Illinois (B.A., 1998); Chicago-Kent College of Law (J.D., 2004). ***PRACTICE AREAS:*** Land Use; Local Government. ***Email:*** steve.bauer@hklaw.com

TERRI L. BRIESKE, born February 21, 1966; admitted to bar, 1998, Illinois. *Education:* University of Illinois (B.A., University Honors, 1994) Phi Beta Kappa; Northwestern University (J.D., 1998). Phi Beta Kappa. ***PRACTICE AREAS:*** Family Law. ***Email:*** terri.brieske@hklaw.com

MARISSA CASHY BRINKLEY, born January 9, 1970; admitted to bar, 1996, Illinois; 1998, District of Columbia. *Education:* Loyola University (J.D., 1996). ***Email:*** marissa.brinkley@hklaw.com

TIMOTHY A. BRINKLEY, born November 30, 1967; admitted to bar, 1996, Illinois. *Education:* Western Illinois University (B.A., 1990); Loyola University Chicago School of Law (J.D., 1996). *Member:* Illinois State Bar Association. ***LANGUAGES:*** Russian. ***PRACTICE AREAS:*** Real Estate (100%). ***Email:*** timothy.brinkley@hklaw.com

ANDREA L. BRISKI, born Chicago, Illinois, November 20, 1973; admitted to bar, 2004, Illinois. *Education:* Valparaiso University (B.A., 1999); Chicago-Kent College of Law (J.D., with honors, 2003). *Member:* Chicago, Illinois and American Bar Associations. ***PRACTICE AREAS:*** Real Estate; Commercial Leasing. ***Email:*** andrea.briski@hklaw.com

MAUREEN ELIZABETH BROWNE, born October 18, 1974; admitted to bar, 2004, Illinois. *Education:* University of Notre Dame (B.A., Psychology, 1996); Georgetown University (M.P.P., 2000); Catholic University of America (J.D., 2004). *Member:* Chicago Bar and Illinois State Bar Associations. ***PRACTICE AREAS:*** Land Use and Local Government Law. ***Email:*** maureen.browne@hklaw.com

CHRISTOPHER W. CARMICHAEL, born August 28, 1974; admitted to bar, 2002, Massachusetts and Illinois; U.S. Court of Appeals, Seventh Circuit; U.S. District Court, Northern District of Illinois including Trial Bar; U.S. District Court, Central District of Illinois. *Education:* Loyola University (B.A., 1997); DePaul University (J.D., with highest honors, 2001). Law Clerk to Honorable William J. Bauer, Senior Circuit Judge, U.S. Court of Appeals, Seventh Circuit, 2001-2002. Order of the Coif and Phi Kappa Phi. Article and Note Editor, DePaul Law Review, Vol. 50. Author: "Encouraging Settlements Using Federal Rule 68: Why Non-Prevailing Defendants Should be Awarded Attorney's Fees, Even in Civil Rights Cases," 48 Wayne L. Rev. 1449 (2003); "Proposals for Reforming the American Electoral System After the 2000 Presidential Election: Universal Registration, Mandatory Voting and Negative Balloting" 23 Hamline J. Pub. L. & Pol'y 255 (2002); "An Argument on the Merits for More DePaul Law Graduates in Federal Circuit Judgeships" 50 De-Paul L. Rev. 1069 (2001). *Member:* Massachusetts and American Bar Associations; Seventh Circuit Bar Association. ***REPORTED CASES:*** Daniels v. Bursey, No. 04-4316 (7th Cir. 2005); In re Chicago Sun-Times Circulation Litigation, No. 04 CH 9757 (Chancery Div. Cook County, IL) (class action); Roper v. Simmons, No. 03-633 (U.S. S.Ct. 2004) (brief for amicus curiae the Consitution Project); Wiggins v. Smith, No. 02-311, 71 U.S.L.W. 4560, 123 S.Ct. 2527 (2003) (brief for amicus curiae the Consitution Project); Daniels, et al. v. Bursey, et al., No. 03 C 1550, 2003 WL 22053580 (N.D. Ill. Sept. 3, 2003) (class action); Chicago Printing Co. v. Heidelberg USA, Inc., No. 01 C 3251, 2003 WL 21501781 (N.D. Ill. June 27, 2003); MS Produce, Inc. v. Burger King Corp., 2003 WL 21087883 (N.D.Ill., May 12, 2003). ***PRACTICE AREAS:*** Commercial Litigation (85%); Appellate Practice (10%, 6); Intellectual Property Litigation (5%, 3). ***Email:*** christopher.carmichael@hklaw.com

JAMES P. CHIVILO, born Park Ridge, Illinois, February 10, 1975; admitted to bar, 2000, Illinois. *Education:* Illinois Benedictine College (B.A., 1997); John Marshall Law School (J.D., 2000). (Also at Oakbrook Terrace Office). ***PRACTICE AREAS:*** Litigation; Construction Law; Insurance Law; General Commerical Litigation. ***Email:*** james.chivilo@hklaw.com

(This Listing Continued)

(This Listing Continued)

HOLLAND & KNIGHT LLP, Chicago—Continued

LAURA A. DEROUIN, admitted to bar, 1995, Illinois and U.S. District Court, Northern District of Illinois; 1999, U.S. District Court, Central District of Illinois and U.S. Court of Appeals, 7th Circuit; 2000, U.S. District Court, Southern District of Illinois. *Education:* University of Illinois (B.S., cum laude, 1991); Georgetown University Law Center (J.D., 1995). ***PRACTICE AREAS:*** Commercial Litigation (50%); Employee Benefits Litigation (50%). ***Email:*** laura.derouin@hklaw.com

KELLY D. DEWITT, born St. Louis, Missouri, August 12, 1975; admitted to bar, 2000, Illinois and U.S. District Court for the Northern District of Illinois; 2002, Georgia. *Education:* University of Illinois (B.S., with high honors, 1997); University of Illinois College of Law (J.D., cum laude, 2000). *Member:* Chicago and American Bar Associations. ***PRACTICE AREAS:*** Labor and Employment. ***Email:*** kelly.dewitt@hklaw.com

ERIC DORKIN, admitted to bar, 1998, Illinois and U.S. District Court, Northern District of Illinois; 1999, U.S. Court of Appeals, Seventh Circuit; 2000, U.S. District Court, Northern District of Indiana. *Education:* State University of New York at Albany (B.A., 1988); University of Iowa College of Law (J.D., with high distinction, 1998). Order of the Coif. Articles Editor, Iowa Law Review. Author: Note, "Debunking Integrity's 'Equality Advantage': The Absence of Coordination in Ronald Dworkin's Law Empire," Iowa Law Review; "Development, The IMF, and Institutional Investors: The Mexican Financial Crisis," Transactional Law and Contemporary Problems; Chapman & Dorkin, "Federal Court Prison Litigation Project Revised Handbook (8th ed.), 1998. Member, Committee for the United States Northern District Court Prisoner Civil Rights Pattern Jury Instructions. *Member:* Illinois State and American Bar Associations. ***PRACTICE AREAS:*** Commercial Litigation. ***Email:*** eric.dorkin@hklaw.com

LISA A. ELLIS, born New Orleans, Louisiana, March 5, 1974; admitted to bar, 2001, Illinois. *Education:* Indiana University (B.A.J., 1996); Loyola University (J.D., 2001). *Member:* American Bar Association. ***PRACTICE AREAS:*** Product Liability. ***Email:*** lisa.ellis@hklaw.com

KRISTEN E. FLIGEL COCHRANE, admitted to bar, 1992, Illinois; 1999, U.S. Supreme Court. *Education:* Indiana University (B.A., cum laude, 1989); Southern Illinois University (J.D., 1992); Georgetown University Law Center (LL.M., 2003). Associate Editor, Southern Illinois University Law Journal, 1991-1992. Author: "Delay in 911 Emergency Medical Rescue: The Status of Liability for Municipalities and Government Employees," The Journal of Legal Medicine, December 1991. *Member:* Chicago and American Bar Associations. ***PRACTICE AREAS:*** Corporate Law; Entertainment and the Arts; Media Communications. ***Email:*** kristen.cochrane@hklaw.com

LAURA CHRISTINE GAROFALO, born Ann Arbor, Michigan, August 14, 1977; admitted to bar, 2005, Illinois. *Education:* Washington University (B.S.B.A., 1999); Loyola University (M.B.A., 2002; J.D., 2005). ***PRACTICE AREAS:*** Labor and Employment (100%). ***Email:*** laura.garofalo@hklaw.com

BARBARA A. GIMBEL, born March 23, 1973; admitted to bar, 1998, Illinois. *Education:* University of Illinois (B.A., 1995); DePaul University of Law (J.D., 1998). Author: "The Res Judicata Doctrine Under Illinois and Federal Law," Illinois Bar Journal, July 2000; "Partnership Dissolution and Accounting," Handbook of Chancery and Special Remedies, IICLE, 1999. *Member:* Chicago, American and Illinois State Bar Associations. ***Email:*** barbara.gimbel@hklaw.com

KAREN E. GOSSMAN, born Des Plaines, Illinois, October, 3, 1979; admitted to bar, 2003, Illinois. *Education:* Drake University (B.A., magna cum laude, 2000; J.D., with honors, 2003). ***PRACTICE AREAS:*** Commercial Litigation; Product Liability. ***Email:*** karen.gossman@hklaw.com

ROBERT E. HARIG, born December 6, 1964; admitted to bar, 1992, Illinois. *Education:* University of Notre Dame (B.B.A., 1987); DePaul University College of Law (J.D., 1992). Notre Dame Club of Chicago Scholar. Certified Public Accountant, Illinois, 1992. Legal Counsel, Addison Association of Industry and Commerce. *Member:* Chicago and Illinois State Bar Associations. ***Email:*** rharig@hklaw.com

MATTHEW DARREN HEINKE, born Marengo, Illinois, February 19, 1978; admitted to bar, 2003, Illinois. *Education:* Unversity of Illinois (B.S., 2000; J.D., 2003). ***PRACTICE AREAS:*** Municipal Law; Real Estate. ***Email:*** matthew.heinke@hklaw.com

JERALD HOLISKY, born Duluth, Minnesota, September 11, 1956; admitted to bar, 1989, Illinois. *Education:* University of Minnesota (B.A., 1978); John Marshall Law School (J.D., with high distinction, 1989). Executive Editor, John Marshall Law Review, 1988-1989. ***PRACTICE AREAS:*** Corporate; Business Law; Shareholder Disputes; Closely Held Business Law; Investment Adviser Regulation. ***Email:*** jerry.holisky@hklaw.com

TROY D. HOYT, born Provo, Utah; admitted to bar, 2002, Illinois; 2002, U.S. District Court, Northern District of Illinois; 2003, U.S. District Court, Central District of Illinois. *Education:* Arizona State University (B.S., magna cum laude, 1997); University of Chicago (J.D., 2002). Beta Gamma Sigma. Managing Editor, Roundtable Law Journal, 2001-2002. Semi-Finalist, Moot Court Competition, 2000. *Member:* Chicago and Illinois State Bar Associations. ***PRACTICE AREAS:*** Litigation; Products Liability. ***Email:*** troy.hoyt@hklaw.com

LISA JOHNSON, born March 19, 1976; admitted to bar, 2003, Illinois. *Education:* University of Chicago (B.A., 1999); Harvard Law School (J.D., 2003). ***Email:*** lisa.johnson@hklaw.com

STACI L. KETAY, admitted to bar, 1997, Illinois and U.S. District Court, Northern District of Illinois; 2003, U.S. District Court, Central District of Illinois. *Education:* University of Illinois (B.A., 1994); Chicago-Kent College of Law (J.D., with honors, 1997). Co-Author: "Having Your Waffle and Eating It Too: The EEOC's Right to Circumvent Arbitration Agreements," 28 Emp. Rel. L.J. Summer 2002; "The Evolving FMLA: Guidance from Some Recent Court Decisions," 27 Emp. Rel. L. J. Spring 2002; "Perspective - Bad Law and Bad Politics: OSHA's Ill-Fated Ergonomics Standard," 27 Emp. Rel. L.J. Summer 2001; "The Sting: 'Testers' May Sue Under Title VII, Circuit Court Rules," 26 Emp. Rel. L.J. Spring 2001; "In the Lion's Den: Religious Accommodation and Harassment in the Workplace," 25 Emp. Rel. L. J. Spring 2000; "EEOC Issues Policy Guidance on Reasonable Accommodation and Undue Hardship Under the ADA," 25 Emp. Rel. L. J., Autumn 1999. *Member:* Chicago and Illinois State Bar Associations. ***PRACTICE AREAS:*** Labor and Employment. ***Email:*** staci.ketay@hklaw.com

CHRISTINA LAROSA, born 1979; (admission pending). *Education:* Loyola University (J.D., 2005).

AMY E. MCSHANE, born October 10, 1972; admitted to bar, 1997, Florida; 1998, U.S. District Court, Middle District of Florida and U.S. District Court, Northern District of Illinois; 2002, Illinois. *Education:* St. Bonaventure University (B.A., magna cum laude, 1994); Boston University School of Law (J.D., 1997). *Member:* Chicago Bar Association and American Bar Association; The Florida Bar. ***PRACTICE AREAS:*** Real Estate; Land Use; Commercial Real Estate; Real Estate Acquisitions; Real Estate Dispositions; Real Estate Leasing; Commercial Leasing. ***Email:*** amy.mcshane@hklaw.com

JENNIFER E. MILLER, born Harbor City, California, April 6, 1976; admitted to bar, 2001, Illinois. *Education:* Miami University (B.A., 1997); University of Akron (J.D., 2001). ***PRACTICE AREAS:*** Product Liability; Commercial Law; Complex and Multi-District Litigation; Torts; Mass Torts; Tort Defense. ***Email:*** jennifer.miller@hklaw.com

JAMES T. MUELLER, born Winfield, Illinois, February 4, 1968; admitted to bar, 1995, Illinois and U.S. District Court, Northern District of Illinois; 2000, U.S. Court of Appeals, Seventh Circuit. *Education:* University of Illinois, Urbana-Champaign (B.A., 1990; J.D., magna cum laude, 1994). *Member:* Chicago Bar Associaiton; American Bar Association. ***PRACTICE AREAS:*** Commercial Litigation; Construction Law; Local Government Defense; Eminent Domain. ***Email:*** jim.mueller@hklaw.com

SEAN NASH, born Chicago, Illinois, June 22, 1971; admitted to bar, 1998, Illinois and U.S. District Court, Northern District of Illinois; 2000, U.S. District Court, Central District of Illinois; 2001, U.S. Court of Appeals, Seventh Circuit; 2002, U.S. Supreme Court. *Education:* Stanford University (B.A., 1993); Northwestern University (J.D., 1998). *Member:* Chicago, Illinois State and American Bar Associations. ***PRACTICE AREAS:*** Labor and Employment Law; Product Liability; General Litigation. ***Email:*** snash@hklaw.com

HART M. PASSMAN, born Chicago, Illinois, April 9, 1978; (admission pending). *Education:* Washington University (B.A., 2000); Northwestern University (J.D., 2005). ***PRACTICE AREAS:*** Land Use; Local Government Law. ***Email:*** hart.passman@hklaw.com

JAAFAR RIAZI, born September 29, 1978; (admission pending). *Education:* DePaul University (J.D., magna cum laude, 2005). ***LANGUAGES:*** Italian and Spanish. ***Email:*** jaafar.riazi@hklaw.com

ERIC ROBBEN, born St. Louis, Missouri; admitted to bar, 2002, Illinois; 2002, U.S. District Court, Northern District of Illinois. *Education:* University of Notre Dame (B.A., magna cum laude, 1999); Washington University in St. Louis (J.D., 2002). Order of the Coif. ***PRACTICE AREAS:*** Commercial Litigation. ***Email:*** eric.robben@hklaw.com

SUZANNE E. ROLLIER, born Westwood, New Jersey, 1970; admitted to bar, 2004, Illinois. *Education:* Northwestern University (B.A., 1992); Arizona State University College of Law (J.D., cum laude, 2004). ***PRACTICE AREAS:*** Litigation. ***Email:*** suzanne.rollier@hklaw.com

MATTHEW SINGER, born July 1, 1979; admitted to bar, 2004, Illinois. *Education:* Indiana University School of Law (J.D., 2004). ***Email:*** matthew.singer@hklaw.com

LEAH WARDAK, born September 11, 1977; admitted to bar, 2005, Illinois. *Education:* Loyola University Chicago School of Law (J.D., 2005). ***Email:*** leah.wardak@hklaw.com

DAVID SCOTT WARNER, born Milwaukee, Wisconsin, March 26, 1966; admitted to bar, 1995, California; 2000, Illinois; 2003, Nevada. *Education:* Northwestern University (B.A., Economics, 1988); University of Vermont; University of California, Los Angeles School of Law (J.D., 1995). Phi Eta Sigma. General Counsel Redevelopment Association of Nevada, 2004. *Member:* American Bar Association (State and Local Government Committee). ***PRACTICE AREAS:*** State and Local Government (33%); Land Use (33%); Real Estate (33%). ***Email:*** david.warner@hklaw.com

OF COUNSEL

ROBERT O. CASE, born January 26, 1922; admitted to bar, 1949, Illinois; 1954, U.S. District Court, Northern District of Illinois; 1956, U.S. Supreme Court; 1964, U.S. Claims Court; 1969, U.S. Tax Court; 1983, including Trial Bar. *Education:* Brown University (A.B., 1946); Columbia University (LL.B., 1949). *Member:* Chicago and American (Member, Sections on: Corporation, Banking and Business Law; Real Property, Probate and Trust Law) Bar Associations; Lawyer-Pilot Bar Association. ***PRACTICE AREAS:*** General Corporate; Securities Law; Estate Planning. ***Email:*** robert.case@hklaw.com

DAVID L. FARGO, born Chicago, Illinois, April 26, 1927; admitted to bar, 1954, Illinois and U.S. District Court, Northern and Eastern Districts of Illinois; 1975, U.S. Supreme Court. *Education:* Northwestern University (B.S., 1949; J.D., 1954). Foreign Service Staff Officer, U.S. Department of State, 1949-1951. Elected, American College of Probate Counsel ("ACPC"), now American College of Trust and Estate Counsel ("ACTEC") 1965. President, Illinois St. Andrew Society, 1981-1983. Honorary Governor, 1983-2001. Director, Chicago Estate Planning Council, 1983-1986. Fellow, and Member, 1965—, American College of Trust and Estate Counsel ("ACTEC"). Member, Chicago Estate Planning Council, 1962—. *Member:* Chicago (Chairman, Probate Practice Committee, 1971-1972), Illinois State and American Bar Associations; The Lawyers Club of Chicago. [USNR, WWII through end of Korean Emergency]. ***SPECIAL AGENCIES:*** Served in Office of Special Representative of Marshall Plan Paris, France, 1949-1951. ***PRACTICE AREAS:*** Trusts and Estates; Litigation; Tax; Dispute Resolution. ***Email:*** david.fargo@hklaw.com

DONALD A. GILLIES, born Evanston, Illinois, September 15, 1931; admitted to bar, 1956, Illinois. *Education:* Denison University (B.A., 1953); Northwestern University (J.D., 1956). Phi Delta Phi; Phi Beta Kappa; Omicron Delta Kappa. Associate Editor, Editorial Board, Northwestern University Law Review, 1955-1956. *Member:* Illinois State and American Bar Associations; Lawyers Club of Chicago. Fellow, American College of Trust and Estate Counsel (Member, Professional Standards and International Estate Planning Committees). ***PRACTICE AREAS:*** Taxation; Estate Planning. ***Email:*** donald.gillies@hklaw.com

(This Listing Continued)

ROBERT C. NEWMAN, born Amboy, Illinois, June 17, 1943; admitted to bar, 1972, Illinois. *Education:* University of Illinois (B.S., 1965; J.D., 1972). Notes and Comments Editor, University of Illinois Law Review, 1972. ***Email:*** robert.newman@hklaw.com

DAVID G. O'LEARY, born Pittsfield, Illinois, January 5, 1948; admitted to bar, 1978, Illinois; 1979, Florida; 1980, U.S. Tax Court. *Education:* University of Illinois (B.S., 1970); Loyola University (J.D., 1978). Certified Public Accountant, Illinois, 1976. *Member:* Chicago and American Bar Associations; The Florida Bar; American Institute of Certified Public Accountants. ***PRACTICE AREAS:*** Employee Benefits; Federal Taxation; State Taxation; Estate Planning; Business Planning. ***Email:*** david.oleary@hklaw.com

G. GALE ROBERSON, JR., born Chicago, Illinois; admitted to bar, 1960, Illinois; 1961, U.S. District Court, Northern District of Illinois including Trial Bar. *Education:* Dartmouth College (A.B., cum laude, 1955); Harvard University (LL.B., 1960). Lecturer, Illinois Institute for Continuing Legal Education, 1965—, and Chicago Bar Association, 1980—. Public Arbitrator and Mediator, National Association of Securities Dealers, Inc. *Member:* Chicago (Chairman, Securities Law Committee, 1980-1981), Illinois State (Member: Corporation, Securities and Business Law Sections) and American (Member, Business Law) Bar Associations. [U.S. Navy, Active, 1955-1957]. ***PRACTICE AREAS:*** Closely Held Corporations; Estate Planning. ***Email:*** gale.roberson@hklaw.com

DAVID SHAYNE, born Chicago, Illinois; admitted to bar, 1960, Illinois. *Education:* Yale University (B.A., 1956); Harvard University (LL.B., 1959). *Member:* Chicago (Member, Trust Law and Federal Taxation Committees), Illinois State (Member, Section on Estate Planning, Probate and Trust Law) and American (Member, Real Property, Probate and Trust Law Section) Bar Associations; Chicago Council of Lawyers; Chicago Estate Planning Council. ***PRACTICE AREAS:*** Estate Planning Law; Probate Law; Taxation Law. ***Email:*** david.shayne@hklaw.com

JACK M. SIEGEL, born Chicago, Illinois, June 20, 1926; admitted to bar, 1951, Illinois and Illinois Supreme Court; 1958, U.S. District Court, Northern District of Illinois; 1970, U.S. Supreme Court; 1974, U.S. Court of Appeals, Seventh Circuit. *Education:* University of Chicago (M.A., 1948; J.D., 1951). Lecturer, Illinois Institute for Continuing Legal Education, 1984, 1987 and 1989. Corporation Counsel of City of Evanston, Village Attorney: Village of Arlington Heights; Village of Schaumburg; Village of Riverwoods. *Member:* Chicago, Illinois State and American Bar Associations; Illinois Appellate Lawyers Association;. ***PRACTICE AREAS:*** Municipal Law. ***Email:*** jack.siegel@hklaw.com

MICHAEL L. WEISSMAN, born September 11, 1934; admitted to bar, 1958, District of Columbia; 1959, Illinois; 1960, U.S. District Court, Northern District of Illinois and U.S. Court of Appeals, Seventh Circuit; 1963, U.S. Court of Appeals, District of Columbia Circuit and Eighth Circuit and U.S. Supreme Court; 1983, U.S. District Court, Eastern District of Wisconsin. *Education:* University of Chicago; Northwestern University (B.S., 1954); University of Pennsylvania (M.B.A., 1956); Harvard University (LL.B., 1958). Beta Alpha Psi. Fulbright Scholar, Faculty of Law, University of Sydney, Australia, 1958-1959. Author: "Reinsurance Pools and the Federal Securities Laws," 9 Loyola University of Chicago Law Journal 313, 1978; "Litigation Risks Facing Lenders," Illinois Banker, April 1984; "The Changing Liability of Accountants for Negligent Audits," The Secured Lender, November/December 1987; "The Privity Issue: When Can a Lender Rely on an Audited Financial Statement," The Journal of Commercial Bank Lending, April 1989; "The Plant Closing Laws: A New Threat to Secured Lenders," The Secured Lender, May/June 1989; "Equitable Subordination: Alive But Not Very Well," 6 Commercial Lending Review 27, 1991; "The Consequences of a Fiduciary Relationship," The Journal of Commercial Lending, 1994; "Is a Faxed Document Enforceable?" The Secured Lender, July/August 1994; "The Law of Guaranty in the United States," Comparative Law Yearbook of International Business, 1996; "Lender Liability," Executive Enterprises Publication Co., 1988; Chap. 10, "Attorney's Fees and Costs: Shifting the Burden of Litigation, Commercial Damages," Matthew Bender & Co., 1985. Assistant Professor of Business Law and Accounting, Roosevelt University, 1959-1961. Lecturer in Economics, Lake Forest College, 1979-1980. Adjunct Professor, John Marshall Law School, 1999-2002. Director, 1990—, and Chairman, 2001—, Illinois Institute for Continuing Legal Education. Instructor, Illinois Bankers Association, Bank Administration Institute, Risk Management Association. *Member:* Chicago, Illinois State and American (Member, Section on Business Law, Committee on Commercial Financial Services, 1982—) Bar Associations; Association of Commercial Finance Attorneys (Director, 1988-1990). ***PRACTICE AREAS:*** Banking Law; Creditors Rights Law; Real Estate. ***Email:*** michael.weissman@hklaw.com

(For Biographical Data of other firm Personnel, see Professional Biographies at other offices indicated in the heading of this card).

SHERYL Y. HOLLOWAY

Established in 2003

70 W. MADISON, SUITE 1400
CHICAGO, ILLINOIS 60602
Telephone: 312-214-3144
Fax: 773-660-8686
Email: sherylholloway507@yahoo.com
URL: http://www.sherylholloway.com

Real Estate Closings, Evictions, Divorces, Wills, Personal Injury, Guardianships, Expungements.

FIRM PROFILE: This firm believes in providing high quality legal services at an affordable rate. We seek to achieve the best possible result for each and every client. We seek to service clients of diverse backgrounds.

SHERYL Y. HOLLOWAY, born 1951; admitted to bar, 1993, Michigan; 1995, Illinois. *Education:* University of Illinois (B.A., 1977); Howard University (J.D., 1982). ***LANGUAGES:*** English. ***PRACTICE AREAS:*** Real Estate Closings; Evictions; Divorces; Wills; Personal Injury; Guardianships; Expungements.

Language: English.

HOOGENDOORN & TALBOT

122 SOUTH MICHIGAN AVENUE
SUITE 1220
CHICAGO, ILLINOIS 60603-6107
Telephone: 312-786-2250
FAX: 312-786-0708
URL: http://www.hoogendoorntalbot.com

Estate Tax and Financial Planning, Business and Corporate Law, Commercial, Personal Injury, Insurance Disputes, Litigation, Real Estate Law and Charitable Tax Planning.

FIRM PROFILE: Hoogendoorn & Talbot was founded in 1985, when Messrs. Hoogendoorn and Talbot left their partnerships at Kirkland & Ellis to start a Firm centered on representing families with substantial assets and business concerns. As other partners from major Chicago firms joined the practice, the Firm's initial concentration in tax, estate and financial planning, real estate and trust and estate litigation expanded to include commercial and personal injury litigation, and corporate and business law. Today, the Firm serves individuals, owners of family businesses, public corporations, and major private and public charitable and religious institutions. The Firm encourages its personnel to engage in civic, charitable and religious activities, since the Firm is committed to serving the community through the use of law as an instrument of justice.

MEMBERS OF FIRM

CASE HOOGENDOORN, born Vinkeveen, Utrecht, The Netherlands, September 1, 1943; admitted to bar, 1969, Illinois; 1971, U.S. District Court, Northern District of Illinois. *Education:* Calvin College (A.B., 1966); University of Chicago (J.D., 1969). Author: "Transfers of Opportunities - an Opportunity to Avoid Transfer Tax," The Tax Magazine, December 1993. *Member:* Chicago (Member, Probate Practice Committee, 1971—; Division Chairman, 1975-1976; Executive and Legislative Committee, 1975-1977) and American Bar Associations; Chicago Estate Planning Counsel; Christian Legal Society. ***PRACTICE AREAS:*** Trusts and Estates; Tax Law; Business Planning; Charitable Trusts and Foundations. ***Email:*** choogendoorn@hoogendoorntalbot.com

EARL A. TALBOT, born Chicago, Illinois, January 23, 1939; admitted to bar, 1964, Illinois and U.S. District Court, Northern District of Illinois. *Education:* Wabash College (A.B., 1961); University of Illinois (J.D., 1964). Lamda Alpha. *Member:* Chicago, Illinois State and American (Chairman, Title Insurance Committee of the Real Property, Trust and Probate Section, 1982-1984) Bar Associations; American College of Real Estate Lawyers. ***PRACTICE AREAS:*** Real Estate Law. ***Email:*** etalbot631@earthlink.net

THOMAS J. GODFREY, JR., born Chicago, Illinois, June 7, 1934; admitted to bar, 1957, Colorado; 1959, Illinois. *Education:* University of Notre Dame (A.B., magna cum laude, 1954); Harvard University (J.D., cum laude, 1957). Adjunct Professor of Law, Loyola University Law School, 1978-1979. *Member:* Chicago (Member, Probate Practice Committee, 1968—) and Illinois State Bar Associations; American College of Trust and Estate Counsel; Chicago Estate Planning Council; Legal Club of Chicago. ***PRACTICE AREAS:*** Estate Planning Law; Trust; Probate; Business Law. ***Email:*** tgodfrey@hoogendoorntalbot.com

KATHRYN E. SKELTON, born Fairmont, Minnesota, May 17, 1949; admitted to bar, 1976, Illinois. *Education:* Michigan State University (B.A., with high honors, 1971); University of Illinois (J.D., with honors, 1976). Phi Beta Kappa; Order of the Coif. *Member:* Chicago (Member, Corporate Law Committee) and American Bar Associations. ***PRACTICE AREAS:*** Business Law; Corporate Law; Tax and Business Planning Law. ***Email:*** kskelton@hoogendoorntalbot.com

BRUCE J. VAN HEUKELEM, born Denver, Colorado, March 24, 1953; admitted to bar, 1979, Colorado; 1980, Michigan; 1982, Illinois. *Education:* Calvin College (B.A., 1975); Valparaiso University (J.D., 1979). Articles Editor, Valparaiso University Law Review, 1978-1979. Judicial Clerk, Justice James L. Ryan, Michigan Supreme Court, 1980-1982. ***PRACTICE AREAS:*** Civil Litigation. ***Email:*** bvanheukelem@hoogendoorntalbot.com

BRIAN L. DOBBEN, born Detroit, Michigan, June 26, 1959; admitted to bar, 1984, Michigan; 1985, Illinois. *Education:* Valparaiso University (B.A., with high distinction, 1981); Duke University (J.D., 1984); DePaul College of Law (LL.M., Taxation, 1991). James F. Bidlake Writing Award. Author: "Estate Planning: The Initial Client Interview," 81 Ill. B. J. 261 (May 1993). *Member:* Chicago (Chairman, YLS Estate Planning Committee, 1989-1990) and Illinois State (Member, Trust and Estate Section Council, 1991-1994) Bar Associations; State Bar of Michigan; Chicago Estate Planning Council. ***PRACTICE AREAS:*** Estate and Business Planning Law. ***Email:*** bdobben@hoogendoorntalbot.com

RICHARD D. BOONSTRA, born Argentina, January 3, 1957; admitted to bar, 1983, Illinois, including Trial Bar and U.S. District Court, Northern District of Illinois. *Education:* Trinity Christian College; Calvin College (B.A., 1979); John Marshall Law School (J.D., 1983). *Member:* Chicago (Member, Sections on, Family Law and Civil Practice) and Illinois State Bar Associations. ***PRACTICE AREAS:*** Domestic Relations; Commercial Litigation; Real Estate Law. ***Email:*** rboonstra@hoogendoorntalbot.com

RICHARD M. SAWDEY, born Buffalo, New York, January 8, 1943; admitted to bar, 1968, Illinois and U.S. District Court, Northern District of Illinois. *Education:* Michigan State University (B.S., cum laude, 1965); University of Michigan Law School (J.D., cum laude, 1968). Attorney, R.R. Donnelley & Sons Company, 1974-1988, Secretary, 1983-1985, Vice President and Secretary 1985-1988. Director, Lakeside Bank, 1981-1993. *Member:* Chicago (Chairman, Financial and Investment Services Committee, 1994-1995) and American Bar Associations; Chicago Estate Planning Council and National Association of Stock Plan Professionals. ***PRACTICE AREAS:*** Business and Corporate Law; Executive Compensation; Estate Planning. ***Email:*** rsawdey@hoogendoorntalbot.com

DAVID G. STROM, born Cleveland, Ohio, February 27, 1947; admitted to bar, 1974, Illinois and U.S. District Court, Northern District of Illinois; 1975, U.S. Tax Court. *Education:* University of Michigan (A.B., 1969; J.D., 1974). Phi Beta Kappa; Phi Sigma Alpha.

(This Listing Continued)

HOOGENDOORN & TALBOT, Chicago—Continued

Member: Chicago Bar Association. ***PRACTICE AREAS:*** Trusts and Estates; Probate; Contested Trusts and Estates; Family Wealth Transfer; Taxation. ***Email:*** dstrom@hoogendoorntalbot.com

KEVIN J. TODD, born Wabasha, Minnesota, March 5, 1963; admitted to bar, 1988, Minnesota; 1989, Illinois and U.S. District Court, Northern District of Illinois; 1991, U.S. Court of Appeals, Seventh Circuit; 1992, U.S. Supreme Court. *Education:* Cedarville College (B.A., cum laude, 1985); University of Minnesota (J.D., 1988). Author: Blaustein, Grant, Lohr & Todd, "The Role of Stare Decisis in the Reconsideration of Roe v. Wade," 15 Amer. J. L. & Med. 204 (1989); Linton & Todd, "Abortion Under the Illinois Constitution: The Framers Did Not Incorporate a Right to Abortion," 81 Ill. B.J. 31 (January 1993); Todd, ed., "Lex Vitae: A Reporter of Life and Death Issues in the Law," (quarterly, 1988-1992). Special Assistant Attorney General for the Territory of Guam, 1992. *Member:* Illinois State Bar Association; Christian Legal Society. ***PRACTICE AREAS:*** Civil Litigation; Medical Malpractice Defense. ***Email:*** ktodd@hoogendoorntalbot.com

TODD M. VAN BAREN, born Chicago Heights, Illinois, December 17, 1967; admitted to bar, 1993, Illinois and U.S. District Court, Northern District of Illinois. *Education:* Calvin College (B.A., 1990); University of Chicago (J.D., 1993). *Member:* Chicago and Illinois State Bar Associations. ***PRACTICE AREAS:*** Estate and Tax Planning; Real Estate. ***Email:*** tvanbaren@hoogendoorntalbot.com

LAURENCE J. KLINE, born Chicago, Illinois, August 10, 1946; admitted to bar, 1972, Illinois. *Education:* Northwestern University (B.S.B.A., 1968); University of Michigan (J.D., 1971). Frederick Austin Scholar. Author: "Disinheriting Uncle Sam: An Estate Planning Guide for Illinois Residents," Vireo Publishing, 1999; Chapter 1, "Creation of the Trust," Trust Administration in Illinois, 1976 IICLE, rev. 1979, 1983, 1987, 1992, 1995, 1999; "Jumping the Bandwagon of Probate Practice Automation," CBA Record, 1992. *Member:* Chicago Bar Association (Member, Trust Law Committee, 1976—; Section Chair, 1991-1992; Chair, 1996-1997). [Sergeant, U.S. Army Reserve, 1969-1975.]. ***PRACTICE AREAS:*** Estate Planning; Probate; Trust Administration. ***Email:*** lkline@hoogendoorntalbot.com

ASSOCIATES

MELISSA HOOGENDOORN DE VRIES, born Oak Lawn, Illinois, September 18, 1969; admitted to bar, 1994, Illinois and U.S. District Court, Northern District of Illinois. *Education:* Calvin College (B.A., 1991); University of Illinois (J.D., cum laude, 1994). *Member:* Chicago and American Bar Associations. ***PRACTICE AREAS:*** Estate Planning; Probate Law. ***Email:*** mdevries@hoogendoorntalbot.com

JOSEPH WRIGHT, born Cape May, New Jersey, November 19, 1964; admitted to bar, 1999, Illinois. *Education:* West Virginia University (B.S., 1987); DePaul University (J.D., 1998). Member: Moot Court Honor Society; Christian Legal Society. Author: "Skyrocketing Dollars and the Tax Reform Act of 1997: Estate Planning For Professional Athlete In A New Millenium," The Sports Lawyers Journal, Spring, 1999; "NFL Contract Negotiations In the Aftermath of *White v. National Football League IV* Depaul Journal of Art and Entertainment Law, Fall, 1997. *Member:* American Bar Association (Member, Sections on: Tax; Business; Entertainment and Sports). ***PRACTICE AREAS:*** Estate Planning; Business Planning; Sports Law. ***Email:*** jwright@hoogendoorntalbot.com

SALLY R. WAGENMAKER, born Toronto, Ontario, Canada, December 31, 1966; admitted to bar, 1990, Georgia; 1994, Illinois. *Education:* University of Mississippi (B.A., summa cum laude, 1987); Emory University (J.D., with distinction, 1990). Order of the Coif. Managing Editor, Emory Law Journal, 1989-1991. Law Clerk to Hon. William C. O'Kelley, U.S. District Court, Northern District of Georgia, 1990-1992. Author, "Trial by Certainty: Implications of DNA Fingerprinting," 39 Emory Law Journal, 309 (1990). *Member:* Chicago and American Bar Associations; State Bar of Georgia. ***PRACTICE AREAS:*** Employment; Labor; Family; Real Estate. ***Email:*** swagenmaker@hoogendoorntalbot.com

BRIAN D. YELEY, born Bloomington, Indiana, September 5, 1974; admitted to bar, 1999, Illinois; 2000, Indiana and U.S. District Court, Northern District of Illinois; U.S. District Court, Southern District of Indiana. *Education:* Indiana University (B.S., 1996); Indiana University School of Law (J.D., 1999). Beta Gamma Sigma, Golden Key National Honor Society. Recipient, Indiana Journal of Global Legal Studies, Scribes Award, 1999. *Member:* Chicago Bar Association; Christian Legal Society. ***LANGUAGES:*** Spanish. ***PRACTICE AREAS:*** Wills; Trusts; Estates; Planning. ***Email:*** byeley@hoogendoorntalbot.com

ROBERT A. JANOSKI, born Chicago, Illinois, August 9, 1937; admitted to bar, 1962, Illinois. *Education:* University of Notre Dame (A.B., cum laude, 1959); University of Chicago (J.D., 1962). Past President, Chicago Estate Planning Council. *Member:* Chicago and Illinois State Bar Associations. ***PRACTICE AREAS:*** Estate Planning; Probate; Trust; Taxation (Federal, Estate and Gift). ***Email:*** rjanoski@hoogendoorntalbot.com

SHARON M. BUCCINO, born Milwaukee, Wisconsin; admitted to bar, 1987, Illinois. *Education:* Marquette University (B.S., cum laude, 1984); Loyola University (J.D., cum laude, 1987). Beta Gamma Sigma. Certified Public Accountant, Illinois, 1984. ***PRACTICE AREAS:*** Estate Planning; Estate Administration; Premarital Agreements. ***Email:*** sbuccino@hoogendoorntalbot.com

LEGAL SUPPORT PERSONNEL

LEGAL ASSISTANTS

ANNE R. DECKER, C.P.A., C.F.P.

NANCY J. EPSTEIN

LINDA W. TOUHY

KRISTIN TOWNER (Legal Administrator)

HOOKS LAW OFFICES, P.C.

Established in 1990

29 S. LASALLE STREET, SUITE 333

CHICAGO, ILLINOIS 60603

Telephone: 312-553-5252

Telefax: 312-553-1510

International Cable Address: Chgolawyer

Email: chgolawyer@sbcglobal.net

URL: http://www.hookslaw.com

Federal and State Criminal Defense Trial and Appellate Practice (all Felony Crimes including: White Collar, Fraud, Sexual, Weapons, Homicide, Bribery, Conspiracy and Drug Offenses; all Misdemeanor Crimes, including D.U.I., D.W.I. and D.W.B., involving: professionals, doctors, lawyers, business owners/executives, clergy and law enforcement officials). Commercial Litigation, Contract Litigation, Corporate Internal Investigations, Major Incident Management, Civil Fraud, Class Action, Defamation, Election Law and Sexual Harassment Defense. Premises Liability Defense, serious Personal Injury, Wrongful Death, selective Police Misconduct Litigation (Plaintiff and Defense), selective Professional Liability and Governmental Liability. Representation before Military Criminal Courts Martial and Administrative Boards, Disciplinary Labor Arbitrations, Professional Disciplinary License Boards, Academic/Disciplinary hearing/appeals panels (undergraduate, graduate and professional schools); Liquor Licensing Boards and Zoning and Permit Boards.

FIRM PROFILE: Firm owner is a former U.S. Marine Officer (Lt. Col.) who was trained by the best to be one of the best. Tough, aggressive and informed criminal defense representation in white collar, blue collar and no collar cases. Federal, state and grand jury representation.

WILLIAM H. HOOKS, born Memphis, Tennessee; admitted to bar, 1981, Illinois, U.S. District Court, Northern District of Illinois, including Trial Bar, and U.S. Court of Appeals, Seventh Circuit; 1982, U.S. Tax Court and U.S. Court of Military Appeals, Seventh Circuit; 1995, U.S. Supreme Court; 2000, U.S. District Court, Southern District of Illinois; 2001, U.S. District Court, Central District of Illinois. *Education:* DePaul University (B.A., Sociology/Emphasis in Criminal Justice, 1975); Upper Division Scholar, College Entrance Examination Board, 1973-1975. Officer Student: U.S. Marine Corps (USMC) Officer Candidate School, Quantico, VA, 1972-1974; Officer Basic School & Communications Officer School, Quantico, VA, 1975; U.S. Army Intelligence School, Fort Devens, MA, 1976; Chicago-Kent College of Law (Chicago-Kent), Illinois Institute of Technology (IIT), (J.D., 1981). President, Chancellor Kent International Law Society, 1980-1981. Graduate: U.S. Army Electronic Warfare/Cryptologic Tactical Operations Officer Course, Fort Devens, MA, 1977; Judge Advocate Course, U.S. Naval Justice School, Newport, RI, 1982; Law of Warfare Course, Naval War College, Newport, RI, 1982; Criminal Defense Advocacy Course, Center for Trial and Appellate Advocacy, University of California at Hastings College of Law, Hastings, CA., 1983; Homicide Investigation course, University of Louisville, Southern Police Institute, Louisville, KY, 2001. Recipient: Cook County Bar Association's (CCBA) Vanguard Award, 2000, Presidential Award, 1994, Richard E. Westbrook Award for Legal Excellence, 1993, 2004, Ming Award, 2005 and Meritorious Service Award for Outstanding Service in the Investigation, Screening and Evaluation of State Trial and Appellate Justices and Judicial Applicants, 1989; National Black Expo President's Award for Leadership, 2000; Black Law Students Association (BLSA) Alumnus Award, 2000; Silver Beaver Award, Boy Scouts of America (BSA), 1996; Navy Commendation Medal for Meritorious Legal Performance, 1982-1985; Certificates of Commendation, Director of Intelligence (USMC), 1980-1982. Featured in: Illinois Leading Criminal Defense Lawyers, 2003—; Illinois Law and Leading Attorneys; Leading American Attorneys; Business and Consumer Guidebooks, highlighted in area of Criminal Law with mention listings in Personal Injury and Medical Malpractice, 1996-1999; Chicago-Kent Citations, Fall 1996. Adjunct Professor: Advanced Trial Advocacy, DePaul University, College of Law, Lawyering Skill Center, 1993-1999. Trial Advocacy, Chicago-Kent, IIT, 1997. Instructor, Mandel Legal Clinic Intensive Trial Practice Workshop, University of Chicago, 1993-1998; Trial Judge, University of Chicago Law School, Trial Advocacy Competition, 1993-1994. Member: Chicago (Judicial Investigations Committee; Judicial Hearings Committee; Vice Chairman, Appellate Review Committee, 1993-1994); Cook County (President, 1999-2000; Director, Board of Directors; General Counsel; Chairman, Committee on Continuing Legal Education and Trial Advocacy; ARDC Liaison Committee; Chairman and Chief Investigator, Subcommittee on Judicial Investigations; Co-Chair, Reparations Legal Defense Team); Federal (President, 1998-1999; Director, Board of Directors, U.S. Senate District Court Nominations Screening Committee, 2000; Member, National Council, 1995-1999; Chair, White Collar Crimes, Criminal Law Section, 2001—); American (Criminal Justice, Litigation); National (Criminal Law & Juvenile Justice; Military Law) Bar Associations; National Association of Criminal Defense Lawyers, Life Member; Illinois Association of Criminal Defense Lawyers (Vice President, Director, Board of Directors). Fellow, American Bar Foundation, 2002—; Million Dollar Advocates Forum; NAACP; National Eagles Scout Association. Life Member; Chairman, Scouting Against Drugs, BSA; Director, Board of Directors, Chicago Area Council, BSA, 1987-1997; Director, Board of Directors, Chicago-Kent Alumnae/ Association; Marine Corps League, Chicago Police Chapter, Life Member; Southern Police Institute Alumni Association, 2001—; Chairman, Drug Education, Drug Abuse and Youth Seminar, Department of Justice/IIT/BSA, 1988; Cook County State's Attorney's Task Force on Gangs and Task Force on Drugs, 1987-1989; Chicago Committee on Minorities in Large Firms; Advisory Committee on Circuit Rules, Seventh Circuit Court of Appeals, 2001—; U.S. Magistrate Judge Merit Selection Committee, 2001; U.S. District Court Civil Rights Pattern Jury Instruction Committee, 2001; Advisory Committee, Study of the Rules of Practice and Internal Operating Procedures of District and Bankruptcy Courts, U.S. District Courts, Northern District of Illinois, 1990-1999; U.S. District Court Committee, Race, Gender, Religious, Disabilities and Age Bias Task Force, 1997-1999; Chairman, U.S. District Court Magistrate Judge Merit Selection Subcommittee, 1994; Commissioner Chairman, Hearing Panel, Attorney Registration and Disciplinary Commission (ARDC), Illinois Supreme Court, 1994—; ARDC Hearing Panel, 1993—; U.S. District Court Advisory Panel to Review the Current Service of Certain U.S. Magistrate Judges, 1993; ARDC Inquiry Panel, 1991-1992. Special States Attorney, Cook County, Illinois, 2003—. Attorney: Hinshaw & Culbertson, 1986-1989; Pretzel & Stouffer Chartered, 1985-1986. Head Administrative Law Officer, Marine Corps Base, Quantico,

(This Listing Continued)

VA, 1984. Prosecutor/Trial Counsel, USMC, 1983-1984. Criminal Defense Counsel, USMC, 1982-1983. Platoon Commander, Officer, Signals Intelligence Electronic Warfare, USMC; Cryptologic Watch Officer, Naval Security Group/U.S. National Security Agency, 1976-1981. Book Reviewer: "Crime Scene," Chicago Daily Law Bulletin (CHIDLB), Feb. 1996; "Black Judges on Justice: Perspectives From The Bench," CHIDLB, September 25, 1995; "Hugo Black: A Biography," CHIDLB, July 1995; "Heavy Justice: The State of Indiana v. Michael G. Tyson," CHIDLB, March 1995; "Search & Seizure Checklist," CHIDLB; "Great American Trials," CHIDLB, May 1994. Contributing Author: Stein, Closing Arguments - "The Art and The Law," various sections including Specimens of Eloquence - Criminal Cases, Abstract Principles of Justice, Burden of Proof, Guilt by Association, Closing Appeal to the Jurors re: Jurors Responsibility, Lawyers-Defense View, Presumption of Innocence, Witness Credibility and Witness-Credibility Testimony of Money Launderer Smurfs, Witnesses-Expert, Conspiracy-Frontal Assault, 1997-2001. Cumulative Supplement, Clark-Boardman-Callaghan. Television Commentary and Panelist: "Prosecutorial Misconduct, Does it Exist?" Phil Ponce's Chicago Tonight, WTTW Channel 11, 1999; "California v. Damien Williams, et. al. (Reginald Denny beating case), Juror Behavior, Mistrial Law and Jury Nullification in High Visibility Criminal Trials," John Calloway's Chicago Tonight, WTTW Channel 11, 1993; "U.S. v. Former Congressman Mel Reynolds, Justice or Not," Phil Ponce's Chicago Tonight, WTTW Channel 11, 1997; "U.S. v. Miriam Santos, 7th Circuit Reverses Trial Court," 2000; "Superbowl Surveillance," 2001; "Ashcroft (Attorney General) Nomination," 2001; "Senator Fitzgerald's nomination of Patrick Fitzgerald to U.S. Attorney," 2001; "The Lone Holdout Black Juror," 2001. Radio Panelist: "Prosecutorial Misconduct, a Crime in Progress," WGCI radio, 1999; "Right to a Fair Trial, the Reynolds Case," WGCI radio, 1997: "Police Brutality, Real or Imaginary," Real Life, WSSD radio, Chicago, 1995; "Civil Law Implications of the Verdict in California v. O.J. Simpson," World Objective, WVON radio, 1995; "Lawyers Disciplinary Complaints, How to Make Them and Why," WJJD radio, 1994; "Black Injustice in the White System," WVON radio, 2000; "Use of Anonymous Juries in Criminal Cases," Mara Tapp Show, WBEZ radio, 1993. Featured in article entitled: "Attorney Bill Hooks fighting for civil rights in King fashion," N'DIGO magapaper, 2003; "Girl X settles with CHA for $3 million," Chicago Sun-Times, April 18, 2002; "30 Tough Lawyers," Chicago magazine, March 2002; "They've trod the same ground, share goals and cases," CHIDLB, September 26, 2001; "Influential African Americans in the Chicagoland Area," N'DIGO magapaper, 2001; "Black Lawyers Unite on Illegal FBI Raid," Chicago Defender, 2004; "Jail Chief Ordered Off Job by Days End," Chicago Tribune, 2004; "Jail Chief Ordered Gone by Today in Defeat for Sheriff," Chicago Sun Times, 2004; "Closure Order in E2 Case Debated," Chicago Tribune, 2004; "Judge Rule County Jail Director Appointment Illegal," Chicago Defender, 2004; "Hooks to be a demanding President for Cook County Bar," Chicago Lawyer, June 1999; "Ex-Marine Takes Command of Cook County Bar Group," CHIDLB, June 1997; "Northern Trust Hit by Teller Scam," Crain's Chicago Business, September 1998; "Pincham, Hooks, Share Views in Trial Practice," Bar News, Illinois State Bar Association, 1998; "Closing Argument," Chicago Bar Association, 1993; "His Wins May Be Routine But Aren't Orthodox," CHIDLB, 1993. Presentation & Trial Demonstration: Drug Prosecutions and Case Preparation, U.S. Army Trial (Prosecutor) Assistance Program, Fort Dix, NJ, 1984; Drug Prosecutions and Urine Testing, U.S. Naval Reserve Appellate Judge Advocate General, 1984; Demonstrative Evidence, USMC Judge Advocate General Training, Quantico, VA, 1984; Prosecution and Defense of a Military Homicide Case, University of Notre Dame Law School, 1989; Drug Education, Drug Abuse and Youth Seminar, Department of Justice/IIT/BSA, 1988. Guest Speaker: "Art of War - When Trial Goes to War: A Criminal Practitioner's Perspective," Office of Public Defender of Cook County, 2002; "Duty to do Right-Civil Rights & Human Rights," Illinois Department of Human Rights, 20th Anniversary; "Black on Black Crime," Center for Social Justice, Chicago Police Dept.; "Racial Profiling, A Crime in Action," Muslim Bar Association, February 2000; "A Black Prosecutor's Community Responsibility," National Black Prosecutor's Association, 2000; Illinois Department of Human Rights Annual EEOC/AA Conference, 2000; Martin Luther King Day Speaker, City of Urbana, 2001; "The Evolution of Affirmative Action - One Lawyer's Brief Perspective," Midwest Transportation Civil Rights Conference, Illinois Dept. of Transportation and Federal Highway Administration, 2001; "Trial Tactics and Dramatic Closing Arguments," Chicago Bar Association, Solo Practice Network, 1993; "The Fine Line Between Effective Advocacy and Criminal or ARDC Sanctions: The Practice of Criminal Law and Professional Responsibility," Illinois Institute For Continuing Legal Education, 1996; "Responsibility to Yourself and the Community," National Association of Black Narcotics Agents, Annual Meeting, 2000; "Police Accountability and Misconduct," Criminal Law Committee, Chicago Bar Association, 1998; "Fighting the Good Fight Against Hate Driven Arson," U.S. Department of Justice, National Church Burning Task Force Conference, Myrtle Beach, SC 1997; "The Black Prosecutors and the Community," National Black Prosecutors Association, 1997; "Playing to Win, Criminal and Civil Trial Views," Illinois State Bar Association (ISBA), 1997; U.S. District Court, Northern District of Illinois, Special Ceremonial Session in Dedication of the James B. Parsons Memorial Courtroom, 1996. Lecturer: "The Lawyers Moral and Legal Obligation to Locate and Attack Police and Prosecutorial Misconduct," Quinnipiac University School of Law, 2005; "Aggressive Closing Arguments, How to Win," Office of the Cook County Public Guardian. Speaker and Panelist: Rainbow/PUSH Day, 2000; "Truth In Action," Racial Profiling, Cable TV, Chicago Human Rights Commission; "Avoiding Litigation in Sexual Harassment and Drug Testing Disputes," Loyola University, Institute of Human Resources and Industrial Relations, 1994; "Future Legal and Public Policy Trends and Issues," Office of International Criminal Justice, University of Illinois and Chicago Police Department, 1994; "Hate Crime Legislation, a National Perspective," Operation PUSH, 1994; "Criminal Law & Federal Courts," 1995; "Is Racism on the Rise?" Black Expo 1996; "Racism and the Criminal Justice System," Black Expo 1999; "Black Youth Survival Rights Under the First Amendment and Fourth Amendments," LINKS-Chicago Chapter; "Are We Communicating? Discovery Beyond Brady v. Maryland," Federal Bar Association (FBA), Chicago Chapter, 1996; "The Bill of Rights and the War on Terrorism," Seventh U.S. Judicial Conference, 2003; "Chicago-Kent's Alumnae/i Roundtable For Litigators," Chicago-Kent College of Law, 2003; "Administrative Law Judges and Agencies Working to Enhance Public Confidence in Administrative Adjudication," Illinois Association of Administrative Law Judges, 2003; "Aggravated Felony in Immigration Law - Prior Convictions - Drug Offense," Immigration Law Program, 2003. Moderator: "Playing by the Local Rules of the U.S. District Court (N.D. Ill.) History and Comments by the Experts," Chicago Chapter, FBA, 2000; "Traveling While Black, the Violation of Black and Brown Peoples' Civil

(This Listing Continued)

Rights by Law Enforcement Authorities," National Bar Association (NBA)-Region VII Conference, Chicago, 1999; "Celebrate MLK Day As It Was Meant to Be, Racial Profiling What It Means," Illinois Lawyers in Criminal Justice/CCBA, John Marshall Law School/Federal Defender Program; "Fending Against the Tax Cops," CCBA, 1993; "Medical Malpractice Cases - The Basics," CCBA, 1993; "Enhancing Judicial Civility," FBA - Chicago, 1998; "Make No New Friends Entrapment Law: Proving Entrapment; Trial Procedures; How Much Can Due Process Stand," FBA, 1996; "Local Rules by the Experts," Chicago Chapter FBA, 2000; "Honorable James Benton Parsons Day," Law Day, 1999-2005, CCBA, U.S. District Court (N.D., Ill.); "Avoiding Lawyer Disciplinary Complaints," National Bar Association, Region VII Meeting, 1993; "Investigating Police Brutality, Is There Anyone Home?"; Cross Examination, Planning and Techniques," CBA, Committee on Minorities in the Profession, CBA, 1996; "Handling Major Drug Cases," CCBA, 1992. Co-Host and Speaker: "Cross Examination with Authority, Techniques and Methods," ISBA, Chicago; "Career Strategies for African-American Lawyers," BLSA Chicago-Kent, 1990; "Stop The Violence Gang Workshop," Office of the Cook County State's Attorney/University of Illinois (Chicago Campus), 1991. Keynote Speaker: "Salute to African-American Veterans," Montford Point Marine Association, 2003; "Gangs and Drugs in the Urban Environment," U.S. Department of Justice, Columbus Board of Education, Columbus Police Department, Community Workshop on Gangs and Drugs, Columbus, OH, 1989. [Lt.Col., U.S. Marine Corps Reserve, Retired]. ***PRACTICE AREAS:*** Federal Criminal Law; State Criminal Law; White Collar Crime; Murder; Rape; Crimes of Violence; Bribery and Entrapment Matters; Grand Jury Representation; State and Federal; Education Law; Administrative Law; College and University Law; Professional Licensing Regulation; Professional Discipline; Criminal Conspiracy; Criminal Defense; Criminal Fraud; Felonies; Misdemeanors; Military Criminal Law; Fourth Amendment Law; Corporate Internal Investigations; Major Incident Management; Contract Fraud; White Collar Fraud; Fire Loss; Insurance Investigations; Labor Arbitration; Civil Litigation; Judicial Discipline; Military Administrative Law; Military Courts Martial; Premises Security; Catastrophic Injury; White Collar Defense; Spinal Injury; Accidents; Head Injury. ***Email:*** chgolawyer@sbcglobal.net

GENERAL COUNSEL FOR: Midway Broadcasting Corporation d/b/a WVON Radio-1450 AM; N'Digo Magapaper; N'Digo Foundation.
REPRESENTATIVE CLIENTS: Justice R. Eugene Pincham (Ill. Appellate Court, retired); The Taylor Group, LLC; The Foster Group, Inc.; Buford Law Offices, LLC; Law Offices of Carl Anthony Walker; Albertsons (Jewel Food Stores); Ford Motor Credit Company; UOP, LLC; Village of Dolton; Chicago Transit Authority; Chicago Park District; Cook County Bar Association; The Cotton Club; Montford Point Marine Association; Chicago Police Marines; Christian Dream Builders; Community of St. Sabina Church; Father Michael Pfleger; Former Chicago Bull Marcus Fizer; Girl X.

DENNIS W. HOORNSTRA ATTORNEY

CHICAGO, ILLINOIS

(See Wheaton)

Real Estate, Dissolution of Marriage Law.

HORVATH & LIEBER, P.C.

Established in 1987

10 SOUTH LA SALLE, SUITE 1400
CHICAGO, ILLINOIS 60603
Telephone: 312-419-6600
Fax: 312-419-6666
URL: http://www.hlpc-law.com

Insurance Coverage Defense and Subrogation. Professional Liability Defense, Inland Marine, Warehouse Legal Liability and Cargo Legal Liability, Product Liability, Commercial Litigation, Environmental and Directors and Officers Liability. Appellate Practice.

ROSEMARIE J. GUADNOLO, born Chicago, Illinois, November 2, 1946; admitted to bar, 1973, Illinois and U.S. District Court, Northern District of Illinois; 1976, U.S. Court of Appeals, Seventh Circuit; 1981, U.S. Supreme Court. *Education:* Loyola University (B.A., 1968); Northwestern University (J.D., 1973). Member, Northwestern Law Review, 1971-1973. Arbitrator, American Arbitration Association. ***PRACTICE AREAS:*** Commercial Litigation; Appellate Practice; Professional Liability. ***Email:*** rguadnolo@hlpc-law.com

JOHN F. HORVATH, born Evergreen Park, Illinois, October 10, 1946; admitted to bar, 1974, Illinois. *Education:* DePaul University (B.S.C., 1968); John Marshall Law School (J.D., 1974). *Member:* Chicago, Illinois State and American Bar Associations; International Association of Defense Counsel; Defense Research Institute; Illinois Association of Defense Trial Counsel. ***PRACTICE AREAS:*** Insurance Coverage; Insurance Defense; Subrogation; Products Liability; Inland Marine Law; Warehouse Liability; Cargo Liability; Professional Liability; Commercial Litigation. ***Email:*** jhorvath@hlpc-law.com

HOWARD L. LIEBER, born Chicago, Illinois, June 8, 1957; admitted to bar, 1983, Illinois. *Education:* Loyola University (B.A., 1980; J.D., 1983). *Member:* Chicago, Illinois State and American Bar Associations; Defense Research Institute (Member, Tort and Insurance Practice Section); Western Loss Association. ***PRACTICE AREAS:*** Professional Liability; Medical Malpractice; Legal Malpractice; Insurance Defense; Insurance Coverage; Products Liability; Environmental Law; Warehousing; Commercial Litigation; Directors and Officers Liability. ***Email:*** hlieber@hlpc-law.com

DAVID L. POINDEXTER, born Urbana, Illinois, November 4, 1957; admitted to bar, 1982, Illinois, U.S. District Court, Northern District of Illinois including Trial Bar and U.S. Court of Appeals, Seventh Circuit. *Education:* University of Illinois (B.A., 1979; J.D., 1982). *Member:* Chicago, Illinois State and American Bar Associations. ***PRACTICE AREAS:*** Commercial Litigation; Professional Liability; Warehousing; Insurance Defense; Products Liability; Appellate Practice. ***Email:*** dpoindexter@hlpc-law.com

JOEL S. SIEGEL, born October 6, 1936; admitted to bar, 1960, Illinois. *Education:* University of Michigan (B.A., 1957); Harvard University (J.D., 1960). *Member:* Illinois State Bar Association. ***PRACTICE AREAS:*** Appellate Practice; Litigation; Probate. ***Email:*** jsiegel@hlpc-law.com

(This Listing Continued)

HORVATH & LIEBER, P.C., Chicago—Continued

DUANE C. WEAVER, born Chicago, Illinois, June 2, 1952; admitted to bar, 1987, Illinois and U.S. District Court, Northern District of Illinois; 1993, U.S. District Court, Central District of Illinois; 1995, U.S. Court of Appeals, Seventh Circuit. *Education:* California State University at Dominguez Hills; Loyola University (B.A., 1979; J.D., 1987). *Member:* Transportation Lawyers Association. ***PRACTICE AREAS:*** Inland Marine; Marine; Insurance Defense; Insurance Coverage; Warehousing; Cargo Claims; Professional Liability; Commercial Litigation; Subrogation. ***Email:*** dweaver@hlpc-law.com

OF COUNSEL

JOHN J. ENRIGHT, admitted to bar, 1951, Illinois and U.S. District Court, Northern District of Illinois; 1952, U.S. Court of Appeals, 7th Circuit; 1959, U.S. District Court, Eastern District of Wisconsin; 1960, U.S. Supreme Court; 1965, U.S. District Court, Southern District of Indiana. *Education:* University of Chicago (Ph.B., 1947; J.D., 1951). Attorney, 1954-1964 and Chief, Branch of Enforcement, Chicago Regional Office, 1959-1964, Securities and Exchange Commission.

REPRESENTATIVE CLIENTS: Chubb Group; One Beacon Ins. Co.; Continental Insurance Co.; Fireman's Fund; American International Group; St. Paul Insurance Co.; Zurich-American, Ins. Co.; Risk Enterprise Management, Ltd.; Tamarack American; Reliance Insurance Co.; Kemper Ins. Co.; Hartford Ins. Co.; Seneca Ins. Co.

HORWITZ, HORWITZ & ASSOCIATES

Established in 1924

25 E. WASHINGTON STREET, SUITE 900
CHICAGO, ILLINOIS 60602
Telephone: 312-372-8822
Fax: 312-372-1673
Email: office@horwitzlaw.com
URL: http://www.horwitzlaw.com

Work-Related Injuries, Auto Accidents, Personal Injury, Negligence, Railroad Injuries, Riverboat Injuries, Consumer Fraud, Defective Products, Malpractice.

CLIFFORD W. HORWITZ, born Chicago, Illinois, May 5, 1959; admitted to bar, 1984, Illinois. *Education:* University of Florida (B.A., 1981); Chicago-Kent College of Law, IIT (J.D., with high honors, 1984). *Member:* American Bar Association. ***PRACTICE AREAS:*** Personal Injury; Construction Negligence; Products Liability. ***Email:*** office@horwitzlaw.com

MITCHELL W. HORWITZ, born Chicago, Illinois, 1954; admitted to bar, 1979, Illinois and Florida. *Education:* Northern Illinois University (B.A., 1976); John Marshall Law School (J.D., with honors, 1979). *Member:* Illinois State and American Bar Associations; Illinois Trial Lawyers Association; The Association of Trial Lawyers of America; Illinois Workers Compensation Lawyers Association. ***PRACTICE AREAS:*** Workers Compensation. ***Email:*** mitch@horwitzlaw.com

MARC A. PERPER, born Chicago, Illinois, 1953; admitted to bar, 1984, Illinois and U.S. District Court, Northern District of Illinois; 1985, U.S. Court of Appeals, Seventh Circuit; 1987, U.S. Supreme Court. *Education:* University of Illinois (B.A., with honors, 1981; M.A., 1978); Chicago Kent College of Law (J.D., 1984). Phi Kappa Phi. *Member:* Chicago, Illinois State and American Bar Associations; Illinois Trial Lawyers Association; Workers' Compensation Lawyers Association. ***PRACTICE AREAS:*** Workers Compensation; Appellate Practice. ***Email:*** marc@horwitzlaw.com

O. RANDOLPH BRAGG, born Lock Haven, Pennsylvania, August 9, 1948; admitted to bar, 1973, West Virginia and U.S. District Court, Southern District of West Virginia; 1974, Pennsylvania and U.S. District Court, Middle District of Pennsylvania; 1979, U.S. Court of Appeals, Third Circuit; 1982, U.S. District Court, Eastern District of Pennsylvania; 1986, U.S. Court of Appeals, Second and Fourth Circuits; 1987, Delaware and U.S. District Court, District of Delaware and Western District of New York; 1988, U.S. Court of Appeals, Eleventh Circuit; 1989, U.S. District Court, Northern District of New York; 1991, U.S. Court of Appeals, Sixth Circuit; 1992, U.S. Supreme Court; 1994, Illinois, U.S. District Court, Northern District of Illinois and U.S. Court of Appeals, Seventh Circuit; 1996, U.S. District Court, Central District of Illinois and Western District of Michigan; 1997, U.S. Court of Appeals, Ninth and Tenth Circuits; 1998, U.S. Court of Appeals, Eighth Circuit and U.S. District Court, Western District of Wisconsin; 1999, U.S. Court of Appeals, Fifth Circuit; 2000, U.S. District Court, Eastern District of Wisconsin and Northern District of Texas; 2002, U.S. District Court, District of Colorado; 2005, U.S. District Court, Northern District of Indiana. *Education:* Fairmont State College (B.S., 1970); West Virginia University College of Law (J.D., 1973). Contributing Author: "Fair Debt Collection," National Consumer Law Center, 2nd ed. 1991 and supplements. *Member:* West Virginia State Bar. ***REPORTED CASES:*** Dutton v. Wolpoff & Abramson, 962 F.2d 459 (4th Cir. 1992); Hollis v. Roberts, 984 F.2d 1159 (11th Cir. 1993); Carroll v. Wolpoff & Abramson, 961 F.2d 459 (4th Cir. 1992); Graziano v. Harrison, 950 F.2d 107 (3d Cir. 1991); Miller v. Payco-General American Credits, Inc., 943 F.2d 482 (4th Cir. 1991); Pipiles v. Credit Bureau, Inc., 886 F.2d 22 (2d Cir. 1989); Emanuel v. American Credit Exchange, 870 F.2d 805 (2d Cir. 1989); Smith v. Law Offices of Mitchell N. Kay, 124 B.R. 182 (D.Del. 1991). ***PRACTICE AREAS:*** Consumer Law; Class Actions. ***Email:*** rand@horwitzlaw.com

JAY R. LUCHSINGER, born Chicago, Illinois, January 26, 1950; admitted to bar, 1989, Illinois; 1990, U.S. District Court, Northern District of Illinois; 1995, Wisconsin. *Education:* Western Illinois University (B.A., History, 1975); John Marshall Law School (J.D., 1989). *Member:* The Association of Trial Lawyers of America. ***PRACTICE AREAS:*** Personal Injury; Product Liability; Medical Malpractice; Workers Compensation.

WAYNE L. NEWMAN, *born Chicago, Illinois, March 20, 1961; admitted to bar, 1986,* Illinois. *Education:* University of Illinois (B.S., 1983; J.D., 1986). *Member:* Chicago, Will County, Illinois State and American Bar Associations; Workers' Compensation Lawyers Association. ***PRACTICE AREAS:*** Workers Compensation. ***Email:*** wayne@horwitzlaw.com

(This Listing Continued)

ASSOCIATES

VALERIE C. BARICH, admitted to bar, 2000, Illinois and U.S. District Court, Northern District of Illinois. *Education:* Illinois State University (B.S., 1992); Depaul University School of Law (J.D., 1998). *Member:* Will County and Illinois State Bar Associations. ***PRACTICE AREAS:*** Personal Injury. ***Email:*** valerie@horwitzlaw.com

MICHAEL D. CARTER, JR., born Effingham, Illinois; admitted to bar, 1997, Illinois. *Education:* Southern Illinois University (B.S., 1991); Chicago-Kent College of Law (J.D., 1997). Founding member, National College of DUI Defense. *Member:* Illinois State Bar Association; Illinois Trial Lawyers Association; Association of Trial Lawyers of America. ***PRACTICE AREAS:*** Personal Injury. ***Email:*** office@horwitzlaw.com

RICHARD J. DOHERTY, born Indianapolis, Indiana, January 12, 1962; admitted to bar, 1994, Illinois. *Education:* Northern Illinois University (B.A., 1986); John Marshall Law School (J.D., 1994). ***REPORTED CASES:*** Ventura v. Home Servicing of America, 1996 U.S. Dist. LEXIS 4583 (N.D. Ill. 1996); Keele v. Wexler, 1996 U.S. Dist. LEXIS 3253 (N.D. Ill. 1996). ***PRACTICE AREAS:*** Consumer Protection; Class Actions. ***Email:*** rich@horwitzlaw.com

DANIEL E. McKENZIE, born Denver, Colorado; admitted to bar, 2003, Illinois and U.S. District Court, Northern District of Illinois; 2005, U.S. District Court, Southern District of Illinois. *Education:* University of Michigan (B.A., 1997); Northwestern University School of Law (J.D., 2003). Phi Alpha Delta. *Member:* Illinois State Bar Association. ***PRACTICE AREAS:*** Consumer Fraud. ***Email:*** dan@horwitzlaw.com

RAY PODOBNIK, born 1943; admitted to bar, 1979, Illinois. *Education:* Northern Illinois University (B.S.); Lewis University (J.D.).

CRAIG M. SHAPIRO, born Highland Park, Illinois; admitted to bar, 2005, Illinois and U.S. District Court, Northern District of Illinois. ***PRACTICE AREAS:*** Consumer Protection; Class Actions. ***Email:*** craig@horwitzlaw.com

JAMES M. SMITH, born Chicago, Illinois; admitted to bar, 2005, Illinois, U.S. District Court, Northern and Southern Districts of Illinois. ***PRACTICE AREAS:*** Consumer Protection; Class Actions. ***Email:*** jsmith@horwitzlaw.com

MARK WEISSBURG, admitted to bar, 1995, Illinois and U.S. District Court, Northern District of Illinois. *Education:* University of Wisconsin, Madison (B.S., Communication Arts, 1987); John Marshall Law School (J.D., cum laude, 1995). Lead Articles Editor, John Marshall Law Review Board, 1994-1995. Lecturer: ISBA; IICLE. Adjunct Professor of Law, John Marshall Law School. *Member:* Chicago and American Bar Associations; Federal Trial Bar; Illinois Trial Lawyers Association. ***PRACTICE AREAS:*** Workers Compensation; Medicare.

Languages: Spanish and Polish.

HORWOOD MARCUS & BERK

CHARTERED

Established in 1975

180 NORTH LASALLE STREET, SUITE 3700
CHICAGO, ILLINOIS 60601
Telephone: 312-606-3200
Telecopier: 312-606-3232
URL: http://www.hmblaw.com

Corporate, Federal and State Taxation, Real Estate, Trust and Estate Planning and Probate Law. Commercial and Tax Litigation.

KEITH H. BERK, born Chicago, Illinois, May 26, 1958; admitted to bar, 1983, Illinois. *Education:* University of Illinois (B.S., with high honors, 1980; J.D., 1983). Certified Public Accountant, Illinois. ***PRACTICE AREAS:*** Business Planning. ***Email:*** kberk@hmblaw.com

KENNETH W. BOSWORTH, born Chicago, Illinois, July 30, 1950; admitted to bar, 1975, Illinois and U.S. District Court, Northern District of Illinois. *Education:* Northwestern University; Northern Illinois University (B.S., 1971); John Marshall Law School (J.D., 1975). ***PRACTICE AREAS:*** Real Estate; Financing; Business Planning. ***Email:*** kboswort@hmblaw.com

BRIAN L. BROWDY, born Chicago, Illinois, April 22, 1969; admitted to bar, 1996, Illinois. *Education:* Northwestern University (B.A., 1991); DePaul University College of Law (J.D., 1996). ***PRACTICE AREAS:*** State Taxation; Local Taxation. ***Email:*** bbrowdy@hmblaw.com

LAWRENCE J. FELLER, born Highland Park, Illinois, December 30, 1968; admitted to bar, 1994, Illinois. *Education:* University of Michigan (B.B.A., 1991); University of Illinois (J.D., magna cum laude, 1994). Certified Public Accountant, Illinois, 1991. ***PRACTICE AREAS:*** Business Planning; Real Estate. ***Email:*** lfeller@hmblaw.com

JOEL M. FRIEDMAN, born Chicago, Illinois, April 23, 1949; admitted to bar, 1975, Illinois. *Education:* University of Illinois (B.S., 1971); John Marshall Law School (J.D., 1975). Certified Public Accountant, Illinois, 1973. ***PRACTICE AREAS:*** Taxation; Estate Planning; Business Planning. ***Email:*** jfriedma@hmblaw.com

KENNETH A. GOLDSTEIN, born Chicago, Illinois, September 1, 1965; admitted to bar, 1990, Illinois; 1991, Florida. *Education:* University of Iowa (B.B.A., 1987); John Marshall Law School (J.D., cum laude, 1990). Phi Delta Phi. Certified Public Accountant, Illinois. ***PRACTICE AREAS:*** Estate Planning; Business Planning. ***Email:*** kgoldste@hmblaw.com

JORDAN M. GOODMAN, born Chicago, Illinois, January 8, 1960; admitted to bar, 1985, Illinois. *Education:* Indiana University (B.S., with high honors, 1982); University of Illinois (J.D., 1985). Certified Public Accountant, Illinois, 1982. ***PRACTICE AREAS:*** State Taxation; Local Taxation. ***Email:*** jgoodman@hmblaw.com

JEFFREY A. HECHTMAN, born Chicago, Illinois, March 24, 1964; admitted to bar, 1989, Illinois; 1990, U.S. District Court, Northern District of Illinois. *Education:* Univer-

(This Listing Continued)

sity of Pennsylvania-Wharton School (B.S.E., magna cum laude, 1986); University of Chicago (J.D., 1989). Certified, Public Accountant, Illinois, 1986. ***PRACTICE AREAS:*** Finance; Real Estate; Business Planning. ***Email:*** jhechtma@hmblaw.com

RICHARD M. HORWOOD, born East Cleveland, Ohio, April 7, 1940; admitted to bar, 1965, Ohio; 1970, Illinois. *Education:* Colgate University (A.B., 1962); American University (M.B.A., 1967); University of Pennsylvania (LL.B., 1965); George Washington University (LL.M. in Taxation, 1969). ***PRACTICE AREAS:*** Business Planning; Estate Planning. ***Email:*** rhorwood@hmblaw.com

DAVID A. HUGHES, born New York, N.Y., May 25, 1966; admitted to bar, 1991, Illinois. *Education:* University of Notre Dame (B.A., magna cum laude, 1988); Columbia University (J.D., 1991). Phi Beta Kappa. ***PRACTICE AREAS:*** State Taxation; Local Taxation. ***Email:*** dhughes@hmblaw.com

JAMES L. JERUE, born Fond Du Lac, Wisconsin, October 18, 1956; admitted to bar, 1982, Illinois. *Education:* Northwestern University (B.A., 1979); University of California at Los Angeles (J.D., 1982). ***PRACTICE AREAS:*** Venture Capital; Business Planning; Securities; Mergers and Acquisitions; Health Care. ***Email:*** jjerue@hmblaw.com

HOWARD D. LERMAN, born Chicago, Illinois, May 20, 1940; admitted to bar, 1965, Illinois and U.S. District Court, Northern District of Illinois; 1975, U.S. Tax Court. *Education:* University of Illinois (B.S., 1961); Northwestern University (J.D., 1965). Certified Public Accountant, Illinois. ***PRACTICE AREAS:*** Estate Planning; Probate; Business Planning; Taxation. ***Email:*** hlerman@hmblaw.com

FRED O. MARCUS, born Chicago, Illinois, March 8, 1948; admitted to bar, 1974, Illinois. *Education:* University of Illinois (B.S., in Accounting, 1970); DePaul University (J.D., 1974). ***PRACTICE AREAS:*** State Taxation; Local Taxation. ***Email:*** fmarcus@hmblaw.com

DAVID S. RUSKIN, born Chicago, Illinois, October 20, 1966; admitted to bar, 1991, Illinois and U.S. District Court, Northern District of Illinois. *Education:* University of Wisconsin (B.A., 1988); Loyola University (J.D., 1991). *Member:* Chicago, Illinois State and American Bar Associations. ***PRACTICE AREAS:*** Commercial Litigation; Business Law; Real Estate Law.

MARILYN A. WETHEKAM, born Chicago, Illinois, July 24, 1951; admitted to bar, 1977, Illinois; 1989, Texas. *Education:* Loyola University (B.A., 1973); Chicago-Kent College of Law, Illinois Institute of Technology (J.D., 1978); John Marshall Law School, Chicago (LL.M., 1983). ***PRACTICE AREAS:*** State Taxation; Local Taxation. ***Email:*** mwetheka@hmblaw.com

HAL J. WOOD, born Chicago, Illinois, February 19, 1968; admitted to bar, 1993, Illinois and U.S. District Court, Northern District of Illinois. *Education:* University of Illinois (B.A., 1990; J.D., cum laude, 1993). ***PRACTICE AREAS:*** Civil Litigation; Business Planning. ***Email:*** hwood@hmblaw.com

JEFFREY A. ZALUDA, born Bridgeport, Connecticut, June 1, 1960; admitted to bar, 1986, Illinois. *Education:* University of Massachusetts (B.A., magna cum laude, 1982); American University (J.D., cum laude, 1986). ***PRACTICE AREAS:*** Business Planning; Estate Planning; Tax; Family Business; Asset Protection. ***Email:*** jzaluda@hmblaw.com

---

BRENDA M. ALLISON, born Akron, Ohio, August 22, 1976; admitted to bar, 2002, Illinois. *Education:* University of North Carolina at Chapel Hill (B.A., 1998); DePaul University (J.D., magna cum laude, 2002). Order of the Coif. Member, DePaul University Law Review, 2000-2002. ***PRACTICE AREAS:*** Litigation. ***Email:*** ballison@hmblaw.com

J. DAVID BALLINGER, born Lynwood, California, August 5, 1970; admitted to bar, 1995, Illinois. *Education:* University of California, Santa Barbara (B.A., 1991); Depaul University (J.D., 1995). ***PRACTICE AREAS:*** Real Estate; Real Estate Taxation. ***Email:*** dballinger@hmblaw.com

C. ERIC FADER, born Darby, Pennsylvania, October 22, 1969; admitted to bar, 1998, Illinois. *Education:* Bradley University (B.S., 1991); DePaul University College of Law (J.D., 1998). Certified Public Accountant, Illinois. ***PRACTICE AREAS:*** State Taxation; Local Taxation. ***Email:*** efader@hmblaw.com

BENJAMIN N. FEDER, born Skokie, Illinois, September 16, 1976; admitted to bar, 2002, Illinois. *Education:* University of Illinois (A.B., summa cum laude, 1997); Northwestern University School of Law (J.D., 2002). Phi Beta Kappa. ***PRACTICE AREAS:*** Estate Planning. ***Email:*** bfeder@hmblaw.com

STAVROS S. GIANNOULIAS, born Chicago, Illinois, February 3, 1977; admitted to bar, 2002, Illinois. *Education:* Miami University (B.A., Psychology, 1999); Chicago-Kent College of Law (J.D., with honors, 2002). *Member:* Chicago, Illinois State and American Bar Associations. ***LANGUAGES:*** Modern Greek. ***PRACTICE AREAS:*** Commercial Litigation; Business Litigation. ***Email:*** sgiannoulias@hmblaw.com

CHADWICK A. HOYT, born Illinois, 1971; admitted to bar, 1996, Illinois. *Education:* University of Iowa (B.S., with highest distinction, 1993); University of Chicago (J.D., with honors, 1996). Phi Beta Kappa. *Member:* Illinois State and American Bar Associations. ***PRACTICE AREAS:*** Business Planning; Corporate Finance; Business Acquisitions. ***Email:*** choyt@hmblaw.com

JENNIFER A. JORS, born Milwaukee, Wisconsin, October 24, 1973; admitted to bar, 1998, Illinois. *Education:* University of Wisconsin-La Crosse (B.A., with honors, 1995); DePaul University College of Law (J.D., with honors, 1998). Order of the Coif. *Member:* Chicago Bar Association. ***PRACTICE AREAS:*** Estate Planning; Taxation. ***Email:*** jjors@hmblaw.com

SCOTT A. JOSEPHSON, born Skokie, Illinois, November 8, 1971; admitted to bar, 1998, Illinois. *Education:* University of Arizona (B.A., 1993); New England School of Law (J.D., cum laude, 1998). ***PRACTICE AREAS:*** Business Planning. ***Email:*** sjosephs@hmblaw.com

KATE KANABAY, born Hinsdale, Illinois, April 22, 1971; admitted to bar, 1996, Wisconsin; 2001, Illinois. *Education:* Marquette University (B.A., 1993; J.D., 1996). ***PRACTICE AREAS:*** Business Planning; Real Estate. ***Email:*** kkanabay@hmblaw.com

(This Listing Continued)

PETER J. KENNY, born Ft. Leavenworth, Kansas, June 16, 1972; admitted to bar, 1999, New York; 2002, Illinois. *Education:* Boston College (B.A., 1994); University of Virginia (J.D., 1998). ***PRACTICE AREAS:*** Business Planning; Securities. ***Email:*** pkenny@hmblaw.com

KENNETH KLASSMAN, born Cleveland, Ohio, April 1, 1978; admitted to bar, 2003, Illinois. *Education:* University of Wisconsin-Madison (B.A., 2000); Chicago-Kent College of Law, Illinois Institute of Technology (J.D., 2003). *Member:* Chicago, Illinois State and American Bar Associations. ***PRACTICE AREAS:*** Real Estate; Business Law; Tax Law.

SHELLEY H. KOREN, born Des Moines, Iowa, June 30, 1974; admitted to bar, 1998, Missouri; 2001, Illinois and California. *Education:* Washington University (A.B., with honors, 1995; J.D., 1998; M.A., 1999). *Member:* The Missouri Bar; State Bar of California. ***PRACTICE AREAS:*** Business Planning. ***Email:*** skoren@hmblaw.com

AARON D. RACHELSON, born Washington, D.C., December 11, 1973; admitted to bar, 1998, Illinois. *Education:* University of Michigan (B.A., 1995; J.D., 1998). *Member:* Chicago and American Bar Associations. ***Email:*** arachelson@hmblaw.com

ANGELA L. VITALE, born Montrose, Pennsylvania, February 27, 1977; admitted to bar, 2002, Virginia; 2003, District of Columbia; 2005, Illinois. *Education:* George Washington University (B.B.A., Finance, 1995); Vanderbilt University (J.D., 2002). ***PRACTICE AREAS:*** Corporate. ***Email:*** avitale@hmblaw.com

KRISTIN L. VUCINOVICH, born Duluth, Minnesota, July 8, 1975; admitted to bar, 2000, Illinois. *Education:* University of St. Thomas (B.A., magna cum laude, 1997); Loyola University, Chicago (J.D., 2000). ***PRACTICE AREAS:*** Real Estate; Finance; Condominium Law. ***Email:*** kvucinov@hmblaw.com

LAUREN J. WOLVEN, born Queens, New York, 1974; admitted to bar, 1999, Illinois. *Education:* Indiana University (B.A., magna cum laude, 1996); University of Illinois (J.D., magna cum laude, 1999). Phi Beta Kappa. ***LANGUAGES:*** Spanish. ***PRACTICE AREAS:*** Estate Planning; Business Planning; Probate. ***Email:*** lwolven@hmblaw.com

OF COUNSEL

JAMES H. RYAN, born Philadelphia, Pennsylvania, December 1, 1940; admitted to bar, 1966, Illinois. *Education:* Ursinus College (A.B., cum laude, 1963); Harvard University (J.D., 1966). ***PRACTICE AREAS:*** Litigation; Corporate Finance; Public Finance; Taxation. ***Email:*** jryan@hmblaw.com

---

HOWARD & NEMOY

Established in 1989

111 W. WASHINGTON STREET, SUITE 1023

CHICAGO, ILLINOIS 60602

Telephone: 312-782-7120
Fax: 312-782-7126
URL: http://www.howardandnemoylaw.com
Email: pnemoy@howardandnemoy.com
URL: http://www.howardandnemoy.com

Personal Injury, Wrongful Death, Automobile Accidents, Trucking Accidents, Professional Negligence, Nursing Home Abuse, Sexual Abuse, Dog Bites, Railroad Accidents, Slip and Fall, Automotive Products Liability, Aviation Accidents, Airplane Crashes, Boating Accidents, Workers' Compensation.

FIRM PROFILE: A highly experienced and respected plaintiff's personal injury firm that has been fighting for it's clients' rights and bringing them justice for fifteen years.

MEMBERS OF FIRM

PAUL I. NEMOY, born Chicago, Illinois, 1953; admitted to bar, 1978, Illinois; U.S. District Court, Northern District of Illinois. *Education:* University of Illinois, Chicago (B.A. with honors, 1975); Illinois Institute of Technology, Chicago-Kent College of Law, (J.D. with honors, 1978). *Member:* Illinois State and American Bar Associations. ***PRACTICE AREAS:*** Personal Injury. ***Email:*** pnemoy@howardandnemoy.com

JOSEPH PIEROTTI, born Chicago, Illinois, 1968; admitted to bar, 1994, Illinois; U.S. District Court, Northern District of Illinois. *Education:* DePaul University (B.S., Accounting, 1990); Illinois Institute of Technology, Chicago-Kent College of Law (J.D., 1994). ***PRACTICE AREAS:*** Personal Injury. ***Email:*** jpierotti@howardandnemoy.com

---

HOWE & HUTTON, LTD.

Established in 1985

20 NORTH WACKER DRIVE, SUITE 4200

CHICAGO, ILLINOIS 60606-9833

Telephone: 312-263-3001
Fax: 312-372-6685
Email: hh@howehutton.com
URL: http://www.howehutton.com

Washington, D.C. Office: 1901 Pennsylvania Avenue, N.W., Suite 1007, 20006. Telephone: 202-466-7252. Fax: 202-466-5829.
Ballwin (St. Louis), Missouri Office: 1421 Buckhurst Court, 63021. Telephone: 636-256-3351. Fax: 636-256-3727.

General Representation of Not for Profit Organizations, Associations and Related Entities, Antitrust, Corporate, Employment, Contract, Administrative, Tax, Travel, Transportation, Meetings, Expositions and Hospitality Industry, Intellectual Property Law, Arbitration, Alternative Dispute Resolution, Trial and Appellate Practice.

JONATHAN T. HOWE, born Evanston, Illinois, December 16, 1940; admitted to bar, 1966, Illinois; 1967, U.S. Court of Appeals, 7th Circuit and U.S. Tax Court; 1970, U.S. Supreme Court; 1976, District of Columbia; 1980, U.S. Court of Appeals, 9th Circuit; 1984, U.S. Court of Appeals, 5th, 6th and 11th Circuits; 1990, U.S. Claims Court; 1992, U.S. Dis-

(This Listing Continued)

HOWE & HUTTON, LTD., Chicago—Continued

trict Court, Northern District of Texas; 1998, U.S. District Court, District of Colorado and U.S. District Court, Eastern District of Michigan; 1999, U.S. Court of Appeals, 10th Circuit. *Education:* Northwestern University (B.A., with honors, 1963); Duke University (J.D., with highest distinction, 1966). Order of the Coif; Phi Alpha Delta. Recipient, Phi Alpha Delta Outstanding Scholastic Achievement Award. President, 1977-1979, Illinois Association of School Boards. President, 1987-1988, National School Boards Association. President, 1973-1983, Northbrook Illinois Board of Education. Chair and Trustee, National School Boards Foundation, 1994—. Vice Chairman, 1983-1985 and Charter Member, Legal Section, American Society of Association Executives Legal Committee. Member, Board of Directors, National Risk Retention Association, 1988-1989. Member, International Forum of Travel and Tourism Advocates, 1987—. Founding President, Academy of Hospitality Industry Attorneys, 1991—. Member, Special Subcommittee of the Secretary of State for Illinois on the Illinois Not for Profit Corporation Act, 1984-1987. Member, Board of Visitors, Duke University School of Law, 1984-1990; Life Member, Board of Visitors, Duke University School of Law, 1991—. Delegate, Convention Liaison Council, 1986-1989. *Member:* The District of Columbia Bar; Chicago (Founding Chairman, Trade Association and Professional Society Law Committee, 1984-1986), Illinois State (Co-Editor, Antitrust Newsletter, 1968-1970; Section Council Member, 1980-1981; Member, Sections on: Antitrust Law; Civil Practice and Procedure; Criminal Justice; Environmental Control Law; School Law) and American (State Membership Chairman, Young Lawyers' Section, 1968-1973; State Co-Chairman, 1970-1973; Regional Chairman, 1972, Environmental Quality Committee; Vice Chairman, Sports Law Committee, 1986-1999; Member, Committee on Meetings and Travel, 1988-1994; Special Advisor, Standing Committee on Meetings and Travel, 1994—; Member, Presidential Task Force on Membership Benefits for Disabled Lawyers, 1991-1994; Member, Sections on: Antitrust Law; Business Law; Litigation; International Law and Practice; Administrative Law and Regulatory Practice; Law Practice Management; Tort and Insurance Practice) Bar Associations; American Judicature Society; Legal Club of Chicago; The Law Club of Chicago; American Society of Medical Association Counsel. Life Fellow, Chicago Bar Foundation; Fellow, American Bar Foundation. ***LANGUAGES:*** German. ***SPECIAL AGENCIES:*** Illinois Secretary of State Task Force on Not for Profit Corporations. ***PRACTICE AREAS:*** Not For Profit Corporations; Antitrust; Travel, Tourism, Hotel and Meetings Liability; Arbitration; Alternative Dispute Resolution; Trial and Appellate. ***Email:*** jth@howehutton.com

TERRENCE HUTTON, born Detroit, Michigan, 1939; admitted to bar, 1972, Illinois, U.S. District Court, Northern District of Illinois and U.S. Court of Appeals, 7th Circuit; 1979, U.S. Supreme Court. *Education:* University of Notre Dame (B.B.A., 1961); Northwestern University (J.D., 1972). Order of the Coif. Member: Board of Editors, Northwestern University Law Review, 1971-1972. *Member:* Chicago, Illinois State (Member, Sections on: Administrative Law; Commercial, Banking and Bankruptcy Law; Corporation and Securities Law; Federal Taxation; Corporate Law Departments; Family Law; Tort Law; Intellectual Property; State and Local Law; Law Office Economics; Health Care Law; Business Advice and Financial Planning) and American (Member, Sections on: Administrative Law and Regulatory Practice; Intellectual Property; International Law; Taxation; Senior Lawyers) Bar Associations. [Lt., U.S. Navy, 1962-1966]. ***PRACTICE AREAS:*** Not for Profit Corporations; Corporate; Business; Antitrust; Employment; Contracts; Hotel and Meetings; Trial and Appellate. ***Email:*** th@howehutton.com

JOHN M. PETERSON, born Galesburg, Illinois, August 28, 1947; admitted to bar, 1974, Illinois and U.S. District Court, Northern District of Illinois; 1998, U.S. District Court, District of Colorado and U.S. District Court, Eastern District of Michigan; 1999, U.S. Court of Appeals, Tenth Circuit; 2003, U.S. Court of Appeals, Ninth Circuit. *Education:* Northern Illinois University (B.S., 1969); John Marshall Law School (J.D., with honors, 1974). Member, John Marshall Law Review, 1973-1974. Director, Chicago Office, Federal Trade Commission, 1986-1987. Member: American Society of Association Executives. Association Forum of Chicagoland. *Member:* Chicago (Chair, Trade and Professional Associations Law Committee, 1994-1995; Member, Antitrust Law Committee), Illinois State (Chair, Antitrust and Unfair Competition Section Council, 1993-1994) and American (Member, Sections on: Antitrust; Law Practice Management) Bar Associations; Legal Club of Chicago. ***PRACTICE AREAS:*** Nonprofit Organizations Law; Antitrust; Administrative; Trade Regulation Law; Litigation. ***Email:*** jmp@howehutton.com

BARBARA DUNN, born Detroit, Michigan, December 30, 1966; admitted to bar, 1992, Illinois and U.S. District Court, Northern District of Illinois; 1999, Missouri. *Education:* University of Michigan (B.A, 1989); John Marshall Law School (J.D., 1992). Executive Candidacy Editor and Member, Editorial Board, John Marshall Law Review, 1991-1992. *Member:* Bar Association of Metropolitan St. Louis; Chicago (Member, Trade and Professional Association Law Committee, Chair, 1998-1999; Legislative Liaison, 1993-1994) and American Bar Associations; The Missouri Bar; St. Louis Society of Association Executives; American Society of Association Executives (Member, Legal Sections Committee, 2003-2004); Association Forum of Chicagoland. ***PRACTICE AREAS:*** Not For Profit Corporations; Travel; Tourism; Hotel and Meeting Liability; Employment; Contracts; Copyrights and Trademarks; Internet Law. ***Email:*** bfd@howehutton.com

SAMUEL J. ERKONEN, born Princeton, Illinois, October 18, 1963; admitted to bar, 1989, Illinois and U.S. District Court, Northern District of Illinois; 1999, U.S. District Court, District of Columbia. *Education:* University of Iowa (B.B.A., 1986); Washington University (J.D., 1989); Kent College of Law (LL.M., 1996). *Member:* Chicago Bar Association. ***PRACTICE AREAS:*** Commercial Litigation; Commercial Contracts; Artistic Property; Tax Exempt Organizations. ***Email:*** sje@howehutton.com

C. MICHAEL DEESE, born Mobile, Alabama, October 6, 1951; admitted to bar, 1976, Ohio; 1978, District of Columbia; 1988, U.S. Supreme Court. *Education:* Phillips Universitat, Marburg, Germany and Davidson College (A.B., 1973); University of Pennsylvania (M.A., 1976; J.D., 1976). Phi Eta Sigma. *Member:* The District of Columbia Bar; American Bar Association. ***PRACTICE AREAS:*** Nonprofit and Charitable Organizations; Litigation; Advertising Law. ***Email:*** cmd@howehutton.com

---

LELAND J. BADGER, born Evanston, Illinois, May 15, 1948; admitted to bar, 1973, Illinois and U.S. District Court, Northern District of Illinois; 1975, U.S. Court of Claims, and U.S. Court of Appeals, District of Columbia Circuit; 1976, District of Columbia and U.S. Court of Appeals, Seventh Circuit; 1977, U.S. Supreme Court; 1983, U.S. District Court for the District of Columbia; 1982, U.S. Court of Appeals for the Federal Circuit; U.S. District Court Trial Bar. *Education:* Dartmouth College (A.B., summa cum laude with highest distinction, 1970); Harvard Law School (J.D., 1973). Phi Beta Kappa; Pi Lambda Phi. Member, Harvard Journal on Legislation, 1971-1972. Attorney Advisor to the General Counsel to the Secretary of the Air Force (Member, Honors Program, Office of Air Force General Counsel, The Pentagon, 1973-1975). National Institute of Trial Advocacy: Graduate, 1977; Assistant Teaching Team Leader, 1979. Assistant Adjunct Lecturer in Trial Practice, Northwestern University Law School, 1978. Partner: Jenner & Block, 1980-1992; Epstein Becker & Green, 1992-1993. *Member:* The District of Columbia Bar; Chicago, Illinois State (Member, Sections of: Civil Practice and Procedure; Tort Law; Antitrust Law; Health Law; Corporation Law), and American (Member, Sections of: Litigation; Antitrust Law; Health Forum; Business Law) Bar Associations. [Capt., U.S. Air Force, 1973-1975]. (Resident, Washington, D.C. Office). ***PRACTICE AREAS:*** Nonprofit Organizations Law; Association Law; Health Care Law; Litigation; Antitrust Law; Government Contracts Law; Arbitration; Mediation. ***Email:*** ljb@howehutton.com

(This Listing Continued)

DAVID WALTER NORRIS, born Chicago, Illinois, November 14, 1950; admitted to bar, 1987, Illinois. *Education:* Illinois Institute of Technology (B.S., 1973); Northwestern University (M.M., 1976); DePaul University (M.S.T., 1980); ITT Chicago-Kent College of Law (J.D., with honors, 1987). Certified Public Accountant, Illinois, 1976. *Member:* Chicago Bar Association. ***PRACTICE AREAS:*** Not for Profit Corporations; Taxation; Employee Benefits; Executive Compensation; Employment Agreements; Corporate; Estate Planning. ***Email:*** dwn@howehutton.com

NATHAN J. BREEN, born Colorado Springs, Colorado, March 3, 1974; admitted to bar, 1999, Illinois and U.S. District Court, Northern District of Illinois. *Education:* DePaul University (B.A., 1996); The John Marshall Law School (J.D., 1999). Executive Lead Articles Editor, The John Marshall Law Review, 1998-1999. *Member:* Chicago, Illinois State and American Bar Associations. ***PRACTICE AREAS:*** Trademarks; Internet Law; Copyright; Contracts; Litigation. ***Email:*** njb@howehutton.com

NAOMI R. ANGEL, born Wilkes-Barre, Pennsylvania, August 28, 1948; admitted to bar, 1987, Illinois and U.S. District Court, Northern District of Illinois; 1991, U.S. Court of Appeals, Seventh and Federal Circuits. *Education:* University of California at Los Angeles (B.A., 1970); DePaul University (J.D., 1987). Member, DePaul Law Review, 1985-1987. *Member:* Chicago Bar Association (Chair of Trade & Professional Associations Committee, 2001-2002); American Society of Association Executives; Association Forum of Chicagoland. ***PRACTICE AREAS:*** Trade Association Law; Nonprofit Organization Law; Antitrust; Hotel Liability; Internet Law; Mediation; Litigation. ***Email:*** nra@howehutton.com

OF COUNSEL

LAYTON E. OLSON, born Los Angeles, California, September 30, 1942; admitted to bar, 1968, California; 1969, Illinois. *Education:* Pomona College (B.A., 1964); Boalt Hall School of Law, University of California (J.D., 1967). Author: "Exempt 1-2-3," Self Published, 1994; "Do You Comply with Fund Raising Law," Chicago Area Technical Assistant Providers, Association of Consultants to Nonprofits, 1992; "Honorable Matters," National Society of Fund Raising Executives, Chicago Chapter, 1991. Legal Advisor, Starting a Nonprofit Organization in Illinois, Do It Right the First Time, Nonprofit Financial Center, 2000. Faculty Member: Law of Tax Exempt Organizations, DePaul University Graduate Public Services Program, 1993; Spertus College Graduate Human Services Program, 1994-1997. Member, Association of Fundraising Professionals, Midwest Technology Access Group, 1982— and Illinois Community Technology Consortium, 2001. *Member:* Chicago (Member: Committees on, Tax Exempt Organization, 1986—; Trade and Professional Associations, 1988—; Chair, 1996-1997) Bar Association; Association of Consultants to Nonprofits. ***PRACTICE AREAS:*** Nonprofit Corporations; Charitable Institutions; General Corporate; Real Estate. ***Email:*** leo@howehutton.com

GERARD P. PANARO, born Throop, Pennsylvania, July 5, 1949; admitted to bar, 1977, District of Columbia; 1978, Maryland. *Education:* University of Scranton (B.A., magna cum laude, 1971); Boston College (Ph.D., 1975); Georgetown University (J.D., 1977). Alpha Sigma Nu. Member, Employment Law Manual. *Member:* The District of Columbia Bar; Bar Association of the District of Columbia; Maryland State Bar Association. ***PRACTICE AREAS:*** Employment Law; Nonprofit Organizations. ***Email:*** gpp@howehutton.com

---

HOWREY LLP

321 NORTH CLARK STREET, SUITE 3400
CHICAGO, ILLINOIS 60610
Telephone: 312-595-1239
Fax: 312-595-2250
URL: http://www.howrey.com

Washington, D.C. Office: 1299 Pennsylvania Avenue, N.W., 20004-2402. Telephone: 202-783-0800. Fax: 202-383-6610.

Los Angeles, California Office: 550 South Hope Street, Suite 1100, 90071-2604. Telephone: 213-892-1800. Fax: 213-892-2300.

Menlo Park, California Office: 301 Ravenswood Avenue, 94025. Telephone: 650-463-8100. Fax: 650-463-8400.

Houston, Texas Office: 1111 Louisiana, 25th Floor, 77002. Telephone: 713-787-1400. Fax: 713-787-1440.

Other Houston, Texas Office: Wells Fargo Plaza, 1000 Louisiana Street, Suite 1800, 77002. Telephone: 713-654-7600. Fax: 713-654-7690.

Irvine, California Office: 2020 Main Street, Suite 1000. Telephone: 949-721-6900.

London Office: City Point, One Ropemaker Street, EC2Y 9HS. Telephone: 011 44 207 6283303. Fax: 011 44 207 065 6650.

San Francisco, California Office: 525 Market Street, Suite 3600. Telephone: 415-848-4900. Fax: 415-848-4999.

Brussels, Belgium Office: Avenue des Nerviens 9-31, 1040. Telephone: 011 322-741-1011. Fax: 011 322-741-1012.

(This Listing Continued)

Amsterdam, The Netherlands Office: The Rembrandt Tower, 31st Floor, One Amstelplein, 1096 HA. Telephone: +31 (0) 20 592 4411. Fax: +31 (0) 20 463 7296.

General and Trial Practice including Antitrust, Commercial Litigation, Complex Tort, Corporate Responsibility, Corporate and Transactional, Environmental, Government Contracts, Insurance Coverage, Intellectual Property, International Trade, Products Liability, Securities Litigation, Supreme Court and Appellate and White Collar Criminal Defense.

FIRM PROFILE: Howrey LLP is a world leader in intellectual property, antitrust/competition, and complex business litigation. Founded in 1956, Howrey LLP employs more than 550 attorneys, as well as over 50 economic, financial, environmental consultants, and economic research analysts in offices in Washington, D.C., Amsterdam, Brussels, Chicago, Houston, Irvine, London, Los Angeles, Menlo Park and San Francisco. Howrey is the second most-frequently mentioned firm in the National Law Journal's 2000 survey "Who Represents Corporate America," a listing of law firms preferred by Fortune 250 non-financial companies and ranked first in IP Worldwide's 1999 survey of "Who Represents the World's Most Valuable IP Rights?". Howrey is also the leading antitrust firm in the world according to the Global Competition Review (2003) and its attorneys include many former FTC and DOJ officials and current and former ABA officers, council members, and committee chairs. Unrivaled in our plaintiff and defense work in high-stakes cases, the firm has litigated in the federal courts of 49 states and represented clients in over 1,500 federal and state court cases since 1995 and handled 444 Supreme Court and appellate matters over the past 6 years. The firm is ranked in the top 25 firms nationally for its pro bono efforts.

RESIDENT PARTNERS

JOEL G. CHEFITZ, born Boston, Massachusetts, August 27, 1951; admitted to bar, 1976, Illinois; U.S. Supreme Court, U.S. Court of Appeals, Second, Third, Fourth, Fifth, Seventh, Ninth, District of Columbia and Federal Circuits, U.S. District Court, Northern District of Illinois including Trial Bar. *Education:* Boston University (A.B., cum laude, 1972; J.D., magna cum laude, 1976). Recipient, Faculty Prize, as graduate demonstrating greatest legal scholarship, Boston University. Note and Case Editor, Boston University Law Review, 1975-1976. Law Clerk to Judge Walter Jay Skinner, U.S. District Court for the District of Massachusetts, 1976-1977. *Member:* Chicago, Seventh Circuit and American Bar Associations. Fellow, American Bar Foundation. ***PRACTICE AREAS:*** Business Litigation; Antitrust; Securities; Mergers and Acquisitions. ***Email:*** chefitzj@howrey.com

DAVID W. CLOUGH, born 1952; admitted to bar, 1993, Illinois; registered to practice before U.S. Patent and Trademark Office. *Education:* University of Arizona (B.S., 1974); University of Wisconsin-Madison (Ph.D., Microbiology, 1979); Harvard University (Post Doctoral Fellowship); Chicago-Kent College of Law, Illinois Institute of Technology (J.D., 1993). Instructor, 1981-1984 and Research Assistant Professor, 1984-1988, Center for Genetics, University of Illinois College of Medicine, 1981-1984. Assistant Professor, Department of Cell Biology and Center for Endocrinology Metabolism and Nutrition, Northwestern University Medical School. Guest Lecturer, "Intellectual Property Law Program," John Marshall Law School, 1994-1997. *Member:* Chicago and American Bar Associations; Intellectual Property Law Association of Chicago. ***REPORTED CASES:*** Cambridge Antibody Technology Limited, Medical Research Council, The Scripps Research Institute, and Stratagene v. Morphosys AG and Morphosys USA, Inc., Case No. 1:01CV01980 (JR) (U.S. District Court, District of Columbia); E.L.I. v. Sacon Laboratories (U.S. District Court, Northern District of Illinois); Morphosys AG v. Cambridge Antibody Technology Limited, Case No. 1:01CV01384 (JR) (U.S. District Court, District of Columbia); Morphosys AG v. Cambridge Antibody Technology Limited, Case No. 1:99CV01012 (JR) (U.S. District Court, District of Columbia); Morphosys AG v. Cambridge Antibody Technology Limited, Case No. 1:00CV00146 (JR) (U.S. District Court, District of Columbia); Joany Chou v. The University of Chicago, Arch Development Corporation (now known as University of Chicago Technology and Intellectual Property), Bernard Roizman and Aviron, Civil Action No. 99 C 4495 (U.S. District Court, Northern District of Illinois, Eastern Division); Promega v. LifeCodes (U.S. District Court, District of Utah). ***PRACTICE AREAS:*** Intellectual Property. ***Email:*** cloughd@howrey.com

CHRISTINE A. DUDZIK, born Cleveland, Ohio, May 25, 1952; admitted to bar, 1988, Illinois; 1989, U.S. District Court, Northern District of Illinois; registered to practice before U.S. Patent and Trademark Office. *Education:* Northern Illinois University (B.S., Biology, 1976); Chicago-Kent College of Law, Illinois Institute of Technology (J.D., 1988). *Member:* Chicago and American Bar Associations; Intellectual Property Law Association of Chicago. ***PRACTICE AREAS:*** Patent Litigation; Biotechnology Patents; Pharmaceutical Patents; Patent Infringement. ***Email:*** dudzikc@howrey.com

JAMES E. HANLON, JR., born Chicago, Illinois, May 23, 1959; admitted to bar, 1984, Illinois and U.S. District Court, Northern District of Illinois including Trial Bar. *Education:* DePaul University (B.A., 1981; J.D., with honors, 1984). *Member:* Chicago, Seventh Circuit and American Bar Associations. ***PRACTICE AREAS:*** Commercial Litigation; Securities Litigation; Antitrust. ***Email:*** hanlonj@howrey.com

KENNETH M. KLIEBARD, born Suffern, New York, February 25, 1963; admitted to bar, 1989, Illinois; U.S. Court of Appeals, Seventh and Eleventh Circuits; U.S. District Court, Northern District of Illinois including Trial Bar, Southern District of Illinois and Eastern District of Wisconsin. *Education:* University of Wisconsin-Madison (B.A., 1986); University of California, Boalt Hall School of Law (J.D., 1989). *Member:* American Bar Association. ***PRACTICE AREAS:*** Commercial Litigation; Class Action Defense. ***Email:*** kliebardk@howrey.com

STEPHEN D. LIBOWSKY, born Atlanta, Georgia, December 3, 1957; admitted to bar, 1982, Georgia; 1984, Illinois. *Education:* Vanderbilt University (B.A., 1979); University of Georgia (J.D., 1982). Georgia Law Review. Law Clerk to U.S. District Court Judge G. Ernest Tidwell, Northern District of Georgia, 1982-1984. *Member:* State Bar of Georgia; American Bar Association. ***PRACTICE AREAS:*** Litigation; Antitrust; Professional Responsibility; ERISA Litigation. ***Email:*** libowskys@howrey.com

TODD L. McLAWHORN, born Kinston, North Carolina, August 21, 1967; admitted to bar, 1992, New York; 1997, Illinois. *Education:* East Carolina University (B.A., magna

(This Listing Continued)

cum laude, 1988); University of North Carolina (J.D., with honors, 1991). *Member:* Chicago and American Bar Associations. ***PRACTICE AREAS:*** Litigation; Class Action Defense; Antitrust and Trade Regulation. ***Email:*** mclawhornt@howrey.com

EDWARD M. O'TOOLE, born Harlowton, Montana, June 1, 1935; admitted to bar, 1962, Illinois; registered to practice before U.S. Patent and Trademark Office. *Education:* University of Notre Dame (B.S., 1958; J.D., 1961). Law Clerk, U.S. Court of Appeals, Seventh Circuit, 1961-1962. Author: "Amgen and Scripps: Decided and Undecided Issues," BLI, 1991; "How to Conduct Markman Hearing," PLI, 2001. *Member:* Federal Circuit and American Bar Associations; Lawyers Club; Barristers of the Patent Law. [Capt., JAGC, U.S. Army, 1963-1965]. ***REPORTED CASES:*** Amgen v. Chugai; Amgen v. Hoechst; Eltech v. PPG; Tenneco v. SC Johnson; ICI v. Henkel; CPG v. Mego. ***PRACTICE AREAS:*** Patent Infringement; Patents; Trade Secrets; Trademark Litigation; Patent Licensing. ***Email:*** otoolee@howrey.com

MICHAEL P. PADDEN, born Chicago, Illinois, August 17, 1956; admitted to bar, 1982, Illinois; 1983, U.S. District Court, Northern District of Illinois, U.S. District Court, Northern District of Indiana and U.S. Court of Appeals, Seventh Circuit; 1985, U.S. District Court, District of Wyoming; 1998, U.S. District Court, Middle District of Florida; 1999, United States Supreme Court. *Education:* University of Notre Dame (B.A., magna cum laude, 1978); Stanford University (J.D., 1981). Phi Beta Kappa. Associate Editor, Stanford Law Review, 1980-1981. Author: "FTC and DOJ Issue Revised Safety Zones," Health Care Antitrust Manual, Vol. 1, No. 9, Monthly Bulletin, November 1994; "New York Court Refuses to Block Merger of Long Island Hospitals," Healthcare Financial Management, March 1998; "Supreme Court Weighs In On Trade Dress Protection After Patent Expiration," Chicago 2001; "Hatch-Waxman Changes," National Law Journal, February 23, 2004. Speaker: "Applying Unilateral Effects Analysis To Hospital Consolidation," Health Care Antitrust Forum, Chicago, 1996; "Staying Ahead in e-Business Method Patenting," Chicago, 2000; "Exclusive Contracts, Market Share Discounts and Bundled Discounts," Chicago, 2001. Law Clerk to Honorable William C. Lee, United States District Court, Northern District of Indiana, 1981-1982. *Member:* American Bar Association (Member, Sections on: Litigation; Antitrust; Intellectual Property). ***REPORTED CASES:*** Arth Main Street Drugs, Inc. v. Beer Distributors of Indiana, Inc., et al., 1984 WL 19606; 1988-2 Trade Cases 68,313 Michigan Avenue National Bank, et al. v. Evan, Incorporated, 581 N.E.2d 872 (1st Dist. 1988); Colorado Interstate Gas Company, et al. v. Natural Gas Pipeline Company of America, et al., 661 F.Supp. 1448, aff'd in part; rev'd in part 885 F.2d 683 (10th Cir. 1989); Verson International Limited v. Allied Products Corp., 723 F.Supp. 1(N.D. Ill 1989); Compagnie Des Bauxites De Guinee v. Hammermills Inc., 1992 WL 122712 (D.D.C.); Calumet Breweries, Inc. v. G. Heileman Brewing Company, Case No. 951 F. Supp. 749 (N.D. Ind. 1994); Allied Products Corporation v. Verson International Group plc, et al., 899 F. Supp. 358 (N.D. Ill. 1995); Orlando Regional Healthcare System, Inc., et al. v. Columbia/HCA Healthcare Corporation, et al., 923 F. Supp. 1534 (M.D. Fla., 1996); Videojet Systems International, Inc. v. InkJet, Inc., 1997 WL 138008 (N.D. Ill.); Stroick, et al. v. Village of West Dundee, et al., 319 Ill. App. 3d 468, 744 N.E. 2d 1279 (2d Dist 2001); Village of Sleepy Hollow v. Pulte Home Corporation, 336 Ill. App. 3d 506; 783 N.E. 2d 1093 (2d Dist 2003); Oakwood Laboratories, L.L.C. et al. v. TAP Pharmaceutical Products, Inc., et al. (N.D. Ill.) 2003 WL 21011785 and 2003 WL 22400759. ***PRACTICE AREAS:*** Intellectual Property Litigation; Commercial Litigation; Antitrust and Trade Regulation. ***Email:*** paddenm@howrey.com

ERNEST SUMMERS III, born Hammond, Indiana, December 2, 1953; admitted to bar, 1980, Illinois. *Education:* Indiana University (A.B., 1976; M.B.A., 1980; J.D., 1980). ***PRACTICE AREAS:*** Insurance Coverage (50%); Commercial Litigation (30%); Alternative Dispute Resolution (10%); Antitrust (10%). ***Email:*** summerse@howrey.com

RESIDENT ASSOCIATES

LOUIS A. CRISOSTOMO, (admission pending). *Education:* University of Wisconsin-Madison (B.A., 2001); University of Notre Dame (J.D., 2005). ***PRACTICE AREAS:*** Litigation; Antitrust. ***Email:*** crisostomol@howrey.com

DANIEL A. DORFMAN, born Manhasset, New York, December 6, 1979; admitted to bar, 2005, Illinois. *Education:* University of Maryland (B.A., 2002); Northwestern University (J.D., cum laude, 2005). ***PRACTICE AREAS:*** International Litigation; Complex Litigation. ***Email:*** dorfmand@howrey.com

MICHAEL K. OBERNESSER, born Syracuse, New York, June 24, 1974; admitted to bar, 2001, Illinois. *Education:* Xavier University (B.A., 1998); Northwestern University School of Law (J.D., 2001). ***LANGUAGES:*** Spanish. ***PRACTICE AREAS:*** Litigation. ***Email:*** obernesserm@howrey.com

SALMAAN QUADER, admitted to bar, 2004, Illinois. *Education:* Michigan State University (B.A., 1995; B.S., 1995; M.S., 1999); Michigan State University College of Law (J.D., 2004). President, Biotechnology Law Society, 2002-2003. *Member:* American Intellectual Property Law Association. ***LANGUAGES:*** French, Urdu. ***PRACTICE AREAS:*** Patent Law; Intellectual Property. ***Email:*** quaders@howrey.com

THOMAS L. RUFFNER, born Wickliffe, Ohio, March 6, 1978; admitted to bar, 2003, Illinois and U.S. District Court, Northern District of Illinois. *Education:* Wake Forest University (B.S., 2000); DePaul University College of Law (J.D., 2003). Author: "The Failed GE/Honeywell Merger: The Return of Portfolio Effects Theory?" 52 De Paul Law Review 1285. *Member:* Chicago, Illinois and American Bar Associations. ***PRACTICE AREAS:*** Global Litigation (50%); Antitrust (50%). ***Email:*** ruffnert@howrey.com

JOSEPH J. SIPRUT, born Evanston, Illinois, December 1, 1977; admitted to bar, 2003, Illinois, U.S. District Court, Northern District of Illinois and U.S. Court of Appeals, Seventh Circuit. *Education:* Marquette University (B.A., 1999); Northwestern University (J.D., 2003). Member, Northwestern National Moot Court Team. Recipient, First Place, Andrew P. Vance Memorial Writing Competition, Customs and International Trade Bar Association. Managing Editor, Northwestern Law Review, 2002-2003. Author: "Taking Your First Deposition," Litigation 101 Project, American Bar Association, 2005, available at www.abanet.org/yld/litigation/secondchair; "Calling All Angels: How Outside Investors Can Finance a Demo Album," ABA, 2005, also available at www.starpolish.com; "Can a Stranger to a Contract Acquire the Rights of a Party Thereto? A Primer on Illinois Third-Party Beneficiary Law," Ill. B.J., 2005; "Defending Your First Deposition," Litigation 101 Project, American Bar Association, 2005, available at www.abanet.org/yld/litigation/

(This Listing Continued)

HOWREY LLP, Chicago—Continued

lit101pdf/Siprut.pdf; "The Disservice Performed by American Idol: Why Getting Signed to a Major Record Label is Harder Than It Looks on TV," Star Polish Newsletter, March 17, 2005, also available at www.starpolish.com, republished in Get Signed, available at www.getsigned.com; "Rational Irrationality: Why Playing the World Trade Organization as a Scapegoat Reduces the Social Costs of Armchair Economics," 29 Brook J. Int'l. L. 709, 2004; "Avoid the Smoking Gun: How In-House Counsel Can Preserve the Attorney-Client Privilege," 92 Ill. B.J. 586, 2004; "It Takes Two to Cooperate," Second Chair, American Bar Association, December 2004, available at www.abanet.org/litigation/secondchair/.org, republished in Committee on Pretrial Practice & Discovery Newsletter, Vol. 12, No. 2, at 12, Spring 2005; "Be Not Afraid: Why Lawyers' 'Fancy Contracts' Help Musicians, Not Hurt Them," Practicing Law Institute Newsletter, All-Star Toolbox, Vol. 2, Issue 16, 2004, also available at www.starpolish.com; "The Peppercorn Reconsidered: Why a Promise to Sell Blackacre for Nominal Consideration Should Be Binding," 97 N.W. L. Rev. 1809, 2003. *Member:* Chicago and American (Vice-Chairman, Litigation Committee, Young Lawyers Division) Bar Associations. ***PRACTICE AREAS:*** Trial Practice; Complex Litigation; Civil Litigation. ***Email:*** siprutj@howrey.com

LISA C. SULLIVAN, born Chicago, Illinois, September 24, 1972; admitted to bar, 1997, Illinois. *Education:* Illinois Wesleyan University (B.A., 1994); Harvard University (J.D., 1997). ***PRACTICE AREAS:*** Commercial Litigation; Antitrust. ***Email:*** sullivanl@howrey.com

RESIDENT SENIOR ASSOCIATES

THOMAS W. JENKINS, JR., born Latrobe, Pennsylvania, October 28, 1974; admitted to bar, 2000, Illinois. *Education:* Michigan State University (B.S., 1997); University of Michigan (J.D., 2000). *Member:* American Bar Association. ***PRACTICE AREAS:*** Intellectual Property. ***Email:*** jenkinst@howrey.com

TEDDY C. SCOTT, born Lubbock, Texas, June 3, 1966; admitted to bar, 2000, California; 2002, Illinois; registered to practice before U.S. Patent and Trademark Office. *Education:* Texas Tech University (B.S., 1990); University of Texas at Austin (Ph.D., 1997); Northwestern University School of Law (J.D., cum laude, 2000). ***PRACTICE AREAS:*** Patent Intellectual Property. ***Email:*** scottt@howrey.com

MICHAEL V. HUBBARD

200 WEST MADISON STREET, SUITE 710
CHICAGO, ILLINOIS 60606
Telephone: 312-345-9290
Fax: 312-372-8456
Email: advice@idolaw2.com
URL: http://www.idolaw2.com

Elder Law, Bankruptcy, Real Estate, Wills and Trusts, Probate, Chapter 7 and 11 Bankruptcy.

MICHAEL V. HUBBARD, admitted to bar, 2000, Illinois. *Education:* University of Illinois, Chicago (B.S.E.E., 1971); DePaul University College of Law (J.D., with honors, 1974). Court Appointed Attorney and Guardian Ad Litem, for Disabled Adults in Cook County. Member, Board of Directors, National Alliance for the Mentally Ill. *Member:* National Academy of Elder Law Attorneys; Center for Disability and Elder Law (Panel Member); Chicago (Member, College of Trial Lawyers) and American Bar Associations. ***PRACTICE AREAS:*** Elder Law; Guardianship; Bankruptcy; Real Estate; Wills; Trust Law; Probate; Litigation.

HUBBARD BUSINESS COUNSEL

222 N. LASALLE STREET, SUITE 300
CHICAGO, ILLINOIS 60601-1013
Telephone: 312-704-3624
Fax: 312-704-3001
Email: b.h@hbcounsel.com
URL: http://www.hbcounsel.com

Closely Held Businesses, Mergers and Acquisitions.

FIRM PROFILE: Outside General Counsel to Middle-Market Companies; Business and Corporate Law; Mergers and Acquisitions; Private Placements.

MEMBER OF FIRM

G. WILLIAM HUBBARD, II, born Elgin, Illinois, September 9, 1951; admitted to bar, 1978, Illinois. *Education:* U.S. Military Academy (B.S., 1973); IIT/Chicago-Kent College of Law (J.D., with high honors, 1978). Certified Public Accountant, Illinois, 1978. Recognized as one of Illinois' Closely Held Business and Mergers and Acquisitions "Super-Lawyers" by Law and Politics Magazine in connection with Chicago Magazine (www.superlawyers.com). Co-author: Chapter on Illinois/Delaware/Nevada corporations in an Illinois Institute for Continuing Legal Education Handbook. Author: Two chapters in Mergers and Acquisitions Handbook for Small and Midsize Companies, edited by West and Jones (New York: Wiley, 1997). Past President and Director, West Point Society of Chicago. Member, Mergers and Acquisitions Special Interest Group Task Force, Illinois CPA Society. *Member:* Chicago Bar Association (Member, Business Law Mergers and Acquisitions Sub-committee); Association for Corporate Growth, Midwest Business Brokers and Intermediaries Association. [Officer, U.S. Army, Berlin and Augsburg, Germany]. ***PRACTICE AREAS:*** Business Law; Mergers and Acquisitions. ***Email:*** b.h@hbcounsel.com

HUBBARD & O'CONNOR, LTD.

Established in 1981
900 WEST JACKSON BOULEVARD, SUITE 6W
CHICAGO, ILLINOIS 60607
Telephone: 312-421-5960
Fax: 312-421-5310
Email: ehubbard@hubbardoconnor.com
URL: http://www.lawyers.com/hubbardoconnorlaw

General Civil Trial Practice. Employment Related Litigation and Counsel. Domestic Relations and Family Law. Probate. Labor and Employment, Americans with Disabilities Act, Employment Discrimination, Family and Medical Leave Act, Sexual Harassment, Wrongful Termination, Executive Compensation.

FIRM PROFILE: Founded in October, 1981, by Elizabeth Hubbard, the firm has grown to include 2 members and an associate attorney. The firm is well known on both the local and national level for its active involvement in employment discrimination and civil rights issues. The firm's philosophy and reputation is to provide the highest quality legal representation to clients involved in employment and domestic relations litigation. The firm's extensive practice has resulted in litigation and negotiation with almost every major law firm in the city involved in both employment and domestic relations practices. Our firm provides personalized attention to the concerns and needs of each client. The greatest sources of client referral are from clients, opposing parties or their attorneys who are seeking qualified and knowledgeable trial attorneys, capable of negotiating aggressively for the clients referred.

ELIZABETH LOUISE HUBBARD, born Springfield, Illinois, March 10, 1949; admitted to bar, 1974, Illinois, U.S. District Court, Northern District of Illinois and U.S. Court of Appeals, Seventh Circuit; 1984, U.S. Supreme Court; 2000, U.S. District Court, Central District of Illinois. *Education:* Millikin University; University of Kentucky (B.A., 1971); Chicago-Kent College of Law, Illinois Institute of Technology (J.D., with honors, 1974). Articles Editor, IIT-Chicago-Kent Law Review, 1973-1974. Co-Author: "The Medical and Legal Aspects of Child Abuse," 50 Chicago-Kent Law Review 45, 1973. Supplement Author & Editor, "Litigating Sexual Harassment & Sex Discrimination Cases," James Publishing, 1998 Edition, 1999 Edition, 2000 Edition, 2001 Edition, 2002 Edition, 2003 Edition. Panel Speaker, Chicago Bar Association's "Attorney Fee Update Program," March 1, 1988. Panel Speaker, Chicago Bar Association's Federal Civil Procedure Recent Developments Seminar, April 26, 1989. Panel Speaker, "Sexual Harassment" Human Resources Management of Chicago Seminar, 1992; Panel Speaker, Intl. Brotherhood of Electrical Workers' Convention on "Sexual Harassment" October 1, 1992; Seminar Workshop Leader and Keynote Speaker, "Sexual Harassment - A Sensitive Workplace Issue," Women in Management, November 2, 1992. Panel Speaker (with written materials): "Family Law, Custody and Placement Issues," Workman Education Services, March 30, 1994; "Effective Techniques For Litigating Sexual Harassment Cases," Illinois Institute for Continuing Legal Education, April 25 and April 26, 1994; "Developing, Maintaining and Expanding A Plaintiff's Employment Law Practice," National Employment Lawyers Association Annual Convention, June 30, 1994, Seattle, Washington; "Americans with Disabilities Act Litigation," Illinois Institute for Continuing Legal Education, March 23, 24, 30, 31, 1995; Panel Speaker (with written materials): "Employment Termination Update, 1995," Illinois Institute for Continuing Legal Education, April 7 and 13, July 28, 1995; Panel Speaker (with written materials): "Worker's Compensation Update 1996," Council for Education on Management, Chicago, IL, June 7, 1996; "Punitive Damages," 1996 NELA National Conference, San Diego, California, June 27, 1996. Panel Speaker, Practising Law Institute, Age Discrimination, Chicago, 1998, 1999, 2001. Guest Speaker, National Public Radio "Talk of the Nation," March 25, 1998. Secretary, National Organization for Women, 1977-1978. *Member:* Chicago (Secretary, Federal Civil Procedure Committee, 1986-1987; Vice Chair, 1987-1988; Chair, 1988-1989) and Illinois State Bar Associations; National Employment Lawyers Association (Moderator, Annual Legal Seminar, Ill., 1992; Moderator and Speaker, NELA Seminar, November 21, 1994, Third Anniversary of 1991 Civil Rights Act; Chair, Illinois NELA, 1992-1995). ***REPORTED CASES:*** Byrne v. Avon Products, Inc., 328 F.3d 379 (7th Cir. 2003); Hennessy v. Penril Datacomm Networks, Inc., 69 F.3d 1344 (7th Cir. 1995); Hennessy v. Penril Datacomm Networks, et. al. 864 F. Supp. 759 (N.D. Ill. 1994); Marek v. Chesny 473 U.S. 1 (1985); Swanson v. Elmhurst Chrysler Plymouth 882 F. 2d 1235 (7th Circuit 1989); Macaluso v. Alsip Bank, Lexis 10043 (N.D. Ill 1995); Hoskins v. Drake, et al, Lexis 7090 (N.D. Ill. 1995); Moore v. Chicago Police Board (3d Dist. Ill.App. 1976). ***PRACTICE AREAS:*** Employment Rights Litigation; Domestic Relations; Civil Trials and Litigation. ***Email:*** ehubbard@hubbardoconnor.com

JOHN CAMPBELL O'CONNOR, born Evanston, Illinois, April 7, 1965; admitted to bar, 1990, Illinois; 1992, U.S. District Court, Northern District of Illinois; 1994, U.S. Court of Appeals, Seventh Circuit; 2000, U.S. District Court, Central District of Illinois. *Education:* University of Illinois (B.A., 1987); Indiana University (J.D., cum laude, 1990). Speaker: "Crossing The Line In Employment Litigation," Iowa State SHRM Conference, 1996; Iowa State SHRM Conference, 1999. Co-Author: "Basic Wage and Hour Law in Illinois," NBI, November, 2000; "School Law in Illinois," NBI, 2001. *Member:* Illinois State Bar Association; National Employment Lawyers Association. ***REPORTED CASES:*** Byrne v. Avon Products, Inc., 328 F.3d 379 (7th Cir. 2003); Hennessy v. Penril Datacom Networks, Inc., 69 F.3d 1344 (7th Cir. 1995); Leahr v. Metropolitan Pier, 1997 U.S. Dist. Lexis 10601; Hennessy v. Penril Datacomm Networks, et al, 864 F. Supp. 759 (N.D. Ill. 1994); Quiroz v. Hartgrove Hospital, 1999 U.S. Dist. LEXIS 4595 (N.D. Ill. 1999). ***PRACTICE AREAS:*** Employment Rights Litigation; Employment Contracts; Executive Compensation; Civil Trials; Civil Litigation. ***Email:*** joconnor@hubbardoconnor.com

---

BRIAN D. EKSTROM, born Cedar Rapids, Iowa, December 14, 1975; admitted to bar, 2002, Illinois. *Education:* University of Iowa College of Business (B.B.A., 1998); University of Iowa College of Law (J.D., 2001). ***PRACTICE AREAS:*** Employment Rights; Domestic Relations. ***Email:*** bekstrom@hubbardoconnor.com

HUBERT & FOWLER, P.C.

Established in 1981

188 WEST RANDOLPH STREET
SUITE 801
CHICAGO, ILLINOIS 60601
Telephone: 312-368-0213
Fax: 312-782-4811
URL: http://www.hubert-fowler.com
URL: http://www.hfqlaw.com
Email: info@Hubert-Fowler.com
URL: http://www.hubert-fowlerlaw.com

Administrative Law, Appellate Practice, Chancery and Equity, Civil Rights, Commercial Law, Complex Litigation, Constitutional Law, Construction Law, Contracts, Corporate Law, Criminal Defense, Employment Discrimination, Environmental Law, Government Law, Health Care, Insurance Defense, Libel and Slander, Defamation, Litigation, Products Liability, Professional Liability, Torts, Toxic Torts, Civil Litigation.

FIRM PROFILE: Hubert & Fowler is a minority owned firm founded in 1981 by Donald Hubert. Since its inception, the firm has been a full-service civil practice litigation boutique that has been saluted for its diversity and professionalism. The firm has performed legal services for diverse public and private sector clients and is routinely brought in to litigate highly-publicized, high-profile complex cases. The firm's commitment to each of its clients is to be a superb-quality legal service provider, sensitive to the issues of the public's perception of the client, cost containment, accountability and the client's unique business concerns. The firm has been awarded the highest rating from Martindale Hubbell.

MEMBERS OF FIRM

DONALD HUBERT, born Chicago, Illinois, April 12, 1948; admitted to bar, 1973, Illinois; 1976, U.S. Court of Appeals, Seventh Circuit; 1973, U.S. District Court, Northern District of Illinois. *Education:* Loyola University of Chicago (B.A., 1970); University of Michigan Law School (J.D., 1973). Selected, Leading Lawyer, Illinois Super Lawyers, Illinois publication surveys. Member, Editorial Board, "Lawyers Manual of Professional Conduct," American Bar Association, Bureau of National Affairs. Recipient: Person of the Year Award, Chicago Lawyer, 1992; Abraham Lincoln Award, Chicago Sun-Times, 1992. Assistant, Financial Crimes Unit, Illinois. Co-Chair, Cook County Courts' Committee on Courts for the 21st Century. Chairman, Illinois Supreme Court Committee on Professional Responsibility. Member: Civil Justice Reform Act Advisory Group, District Court, Northern District of Illinois, 1995; Society of Trial Lawyers, 1995—; Illinois Labor Relations Board; Governor's Commission on Capital Punishment; Mayor's Advisory Committee, Department of Administrative Hearings; Board of Directors, Chicago Public Library; Illinois Supreme Court Chief Justice Mary Ann McMorrow's Judicial Appointment Committee; Appointed Assistant Special Prosecutor; Illinois Appellate Lawyers Association, 1989-1990; Illinois Criminal Justice Information Council/Authority, 1977-1991. *Member:* Chicago (President, 1996-1997; Committees: Cook County, Illinois State and American Bar Associations; Society of Trial Lawyers; International Academy of Trial Lawyers (Fellow); The American College of Trial Lawyers (Fellow); Chicago Inn of Court (President, 2003-2004). **PRACTICE AREAS:** Civil Litigation; Appellate Practice; Complex Litigation; Torts; Professional Practices; Judicial Discipline; Criminal Defense; Government; Constitutional Law. **Email:** dhubert@Hubert-Fowler.com

PHILIP J. FOWLER, born Downey, California, November 6, 1961; admitted to bar, 1986, Illinois and U.S. District Court, Northern District of Illinois including Trial Bar; 1990, U.S. Court of Appeals, Seventh Circuit; 1999, U.S. District Court, Northern District of Indiana. *Education:* University of Notre Dame (B.A., 1983); Loyola University (J.D., 1986). Recipient: Leading Lawyers Network, 2003-2004. Co-Author: "Construction Safety Considerations for Building Owners and Managers, Skylines," October, 1995. Coach: Chicago Kent Moot Court Team, 1999; Loyola University School of Law Trial Practice Team, 2002. Instructor: "Voire Dire," The CBA College of Trial Lawyers Master Advocate Course, 2001; "Successful Strategies for Winning Commercial Cases in Federal Court - Summary Judgments;" "Trial Advocacy," Chicago Bar Association Young Lawyers' Section, 2000. *Member:* Chicago, Illinois State and American Bar Associations; Illinois Trial Lawyers Association. **PRACTICE AREAS:** Administrative Agency Practice; Torts; Employment Discrimination; Chancery Practice; Legal Malpractice; Commercial Liability; Business Law; Products Liability; Complex Litigation; Civil Litigation; Insurance Defense; Criminal Law. **Email:** pfowler@Hubert-Fowler.com

ASSOCIATES

MYRON F. MACKOFF, admitted to bar, 1994, Illinois and U.S. District Court, Northern District of Illinois including Trial Bar. *Education:* University of Michigan (B.A., cum laude, 1991); Northwestern University School of Law (J.D., 1994). Judicial Extern to, U.S. District Judge George W. Lindberg. Assistant Attorney General, Illinois, 1995-2002. Member, Constitutional Rights Foundation of Chicago. *Member:* Illinois State and Chicago Bar Associations; National Association of Attorneys General (Subcommittee, Energy Deregulation). **PRACTICE AREAS:** Litigation; Environmental Law; Civil Practice; Constitutional Law; Complex Litigation; Chancery and Equity; Administrative Law; Government; Torts. **Email:** mmackoff@Hubert-Fowler.com

STEPHANIE L. STEWART-PAGE, admitted to bar, 1994, Illinois, U.S. District Court, Northern District of Illinois. *Education:* Iowa State University (B.A., with honors, 1991); Northwestern University School of Law (J.D., 1994). Counsel, 1994-1999, Senior Counsel to the Administrator, 1999-2002, Attorney Registration and Disciplinary Commission of the Supreme Court of Illinois. Faculty Member: Northwestern University School of Law's Mock Trial Institute; National Institute of Trial Advocacy. *Member:* Chicago Bar Association (Chair, Professional Responsibility Committee, Young Lawyers Section, 1998-1999); Association of Certified Fraud Examiners. **PRACTICE AREAS:** Administrative Law; Complex Litigation; Chancery and Equity; Civil Litigation; Constitutional Law; Government; Professional Liability; Torts. **Email:** sstewartpage@Hubert-Fowler.com

(This Listing Continued)

TED S. LI, born Kunming, Yunnan, China, June 27, 1978; admitted to bar, 2003, Illinois. *Education:* State University of New York at Binghamton (B.A., 2000); University of Chicago (J.D., 2003). *Member:* Chicago Bar Association. **LANGUAGES:** Mandarin. **PRACTICE AREAS:** Litigation. **Email:** tli@Hubert-Fowler.com

GABRIEL A. CARAVELLO, born Houston, Texas, June 28, 1977; admitted to bar, 2003, Illinois. *Education:* Rice University (B.A., cum laude, 2000); University of Chicago (J.D., 2003). *Member:* Chicago Bar Association. **PRACTICE AREAS:** Civil Litigation; Complex Litigation. **Email:** gcaravello@Hubert-Fowler.com

ETHAN P. MANDZIARA, born Detroit, Michigan, December 25, 1971; admitted to bar, 2003, Illinois. *Education:* University of Illinois, Chicago (B.A., 1998); Loyola University (J.D., 2003). *Member:* Chicago and Illinois State Bar Associations. **PRACTICE AREAS:** Civil Litigation; Legal Ethics; Residential Real Estate. **Email:** emandziara@Hubert-Fowler.com

SHERRY J. DAUN, born Kiel, Wisconsin, May 12, 1977; admitted to bar, 2003, Illinois. *Education:* University of Wisconsin-Stevens Point (B.S., cum laude, 2000); University of Chicago (J.D., 2003). *Member:* Chicago Bar Association. **PRACTICE AREAS:** Civil Litigation. **Email:** sdaun@Hubert-Fowler.com

REPRESENTATIVE CLIENTS: Daimler Chrysler; Coca-Cola; ConAgra; McDonald's; SBC; City of Chicago; CHA; Metropolitan Pier and Exposition Authority, and Illinois Gaming Board.

JEFFREY M. HUCEK

CHICAGO, ILLINOIS

(See Oak Brook)

Estate Planning, Family Wealth Transfers, Wills, Trusts and Estates, Estate and Gift Taxation, Charitable Gift Planning, Contested Trusts and Estates, Premarital Agreements, Real Estate.

HUGHES SOCOL PIERS RESNICK & DYM, LTD.

Established in 1985

70 WEST MADISON, SUITE 4000
CHICAGO, ILLINOIS 60602
Telephone: 312-580-0100
Telecopy: 312-580-1994
URL: http://www.ghsltd.com

General Civil and Litigation Practice in all Courts. Insurance and Reinsurance. Personal Injury, Immigration, Civil Rights, Class Actions, Labor and Employment, Commercial, Professional Liability, Litigation.

ROBERT R. ANDERSON, born Elmhurst, Illinois, January 3, 1959; admitted to bar, 1984, Illinois. *Education:* Boston University (B.A., 1981); Northwestern University (J.D., 1984). *Member:* Chicago Bar Association; Federalist Society for Law and Public Policy Studies; Defense Research Institute. **PRACTICE AREAS:** Insurance Bad Faith; Insurance Coverage; Construction Law; Litigation; Environmental Law. **Email:** randerson@ghslaw.com

JOSÉ J. BEHAR, born La Habana, Cuba, December 7, 1965; admitted to bar, 1990, Illinois. *Education:* University of Michigan (A.B., 1987); Northwestern University (J.D., 1990). **LANGUAGES:** Spanish. **PRACTICE AREAS:** Employment Discrimination; Labor and Employment Law; Civil Rights. **Email:** jbehar@ghslaw.com

MARK S. DYM, born Lakewood, New Jersey, May 4, 1957; admitted to bar, 1982, Illinois. *Education:* The Hill School (1975); University of Virginia (B.A., in History, with high distinction, 1979); George Washington University National Law Center (J.D., with honors, 1982). *Member:* Chicago, Illinois State and American Bar Associations; Association of Trial Lawyers of America; Chicago Volunteer Legal Services (Volunteer Attorney and Guest Speaker, 1982—); Illinois Trial Lawyers Association. **PRACTICE AREAS:** Personal Injury; Commercial Litigation; International Business Law; Sports Law; Entertainment Law; Corporate Law. **Email:** mdym@ghslaw.com

JOHN K. HUGHES, born Evanston, Illinois, August 7, 1948; admitted to bar, 1974, Illinois; 1982, U.S. District Court, Northern District of Illinois including Trial Bar; 1980, U.S. Court of Appeals, Seventh Circuit; 1986, Wisconsin; 1991, U.S. District Court, Eastern District of Wisconsin; 1993, U.S. District Court, Central District of Illinois. *Education:* College of the Holy Cross (A.B., cum laude, 1970); University of Chicago (M.A., 1971; J.D., 1974). *Member:* Chicago, Illinois State and American Bar Associations; State Bar of Wisconsin; Society of Trial Lawyers; Defense Research Institute; American Board of Trial Advocates; American Inns of Court. **PRACTICE AREAS:** Medical Malpractice; Legal Malpractice; Professional Liability; Trial Practice; Insurance Law; Insurance Defense; Commercial Litigation; Personal Injury. **Email:** jhughes@ghslaw.com

BERNICE JACOBS, born Richmond, Indiana, September 9, 1946; admitted to bar, 1983, Illinois. *Education:* Indiana University (B.A., 1968; M.A., 1972); IIT/Chicago-Kent School of Law (J.D., 1982). **LANGUAGES:** French. **SPECIAL AGENCIES:** Arbitrator, Cook County Mandatory Arbitration Program. **PRACTICE AREAS:** Medical Malpractice; Litigation; Personal Injury; Insurance Litigation; Professional Liability. **Email:** bjacobs@ghslaw.com

RICHARD F. JOHNSON, born Chicago, Illinois, July 12, 1944; admitted to bar, 1969, Illinois and U.S. District Court, Northern District of Illinois; 1977, U.S. Court of Appeals, Seventh Circuit; 1978, U.S. Supreme Court; 1980, U.S. Court of Appeals, Second Circuit; 1991, U.S. Court of Appeals, Ninth Circuit; 1993, U.S. Court of Appeals, Fifth Circuit; 2000, U.S. District Court, Central District of Illinois. *Education:* Miami University (B.S., 1966); Northwestern University (J.D., cum laude, 1969). Law Clerk to Hon. Richard B. Austin, Judge, U.S. District Court, Northern District of Illinois, 1969-1970. Author: "Interjurisdictional Depositions," IICLE, Illinois Civil Discovery Practice, 1979, 1983, 1987, 1996, 2003. Member, Union League Club. *Member:* Chicago Bar Association; Illinois As-

(This Listing Continued)

HUGHES SOCOL PIERS RESNICK & DYM, LTD., Chicago—Continued

sociation of Defense Trial Counsel (Past Member, Board of Directors); National Association of Railroad Trial Counsel. ***PRACTICE AREAS:*** Insurance Law; Railroad Law; Admiralty and Maritime Law. ***Email:*** rjohnston@ghslaw.com

JOSHUA KARSH, born St. Louis, Missouri, March 30, 1963; admitted to bar, 1990, Illinois. *Education:* Yale University (B.A., 1986); University of Chicago (J.D., 1989). ***PRACTICE AREAS:*** Class Actions; Commercial Litigation; Civil Rights; Appellate Practice. ***Email:*** jkarsh@ghslaw.com

PETER M. KATSAROS, born Chicago, Illinois, November 28, 1950; admitted to bar, 1978, Illinois; 1982, U.S. District Court, Northern District of Illinois, 1982, Trial Bar, U.S. District Court, Northern District of Indiana and U.S. Court of Appeals, Seventh Circuit; 1992, U.S. District Court, District of Delaware. *Education:* Indiana University (B.A., summa cum laude, 1972); University of Illinois (J.D., 1978). Rhodes Scholarship Finalist, 1972. Faculty Member, National Institute of Trial Advocacy (NITA), 1984—. Adjunct Professor of Law, Trial Advocacy and Pre-Trial Litigation, Northwestern University Law School, 1990—. Administrative Assistant to Governor of Illinois, 1973-1975; Executive Director of the Governor's Commission on Mortgage Practices, 1973-1975. Public Member, Illinois Board of Banks and Trust Companies, 1975-1979. *Member:* Chicago, Illinois State and American (Member, Litigation, Labor and Employment and Torts Section) Bar Associations; The Association of Trial Lawyers of America; Illinois Trial Lawyers Association. ***PRACTICE AREAS:*** Commercial Litigation; Tort Litigation; Employment Litigation. ***Email:*** pkatsaros@ghslaw.com

BARRY LOCKE, born Philadelphia, Pennsylvania, November 26, 1947; admitted to bar, 1991, Illinois. *Education:* Temple University (M.B.A., 1975); John Marshall Law School (J.D., 1991). Arbitrator, Circuit Court, Cook County. *Member:* Chicago (Member, Judicial Evaluation Committee) and Illinois State (Member, Judicial Evaluation Committee) Bar Associations. (Also Member, Barry Locke and Associates, LTD., Chicago, Illinois). ***PRACTICE AREAS:*** Family Law; Divorce; Child Support; Parental Rights; Child Custody. ***Email:*** blocke@ghslaw.com

KIMBERLEY MARSH, born Boston, Massachusetts, April 13, 1957; admitted to bar, 1986, Illinois and U.S. District Court, Northern District of Illinois. *Education:* Wellesley College (B.A., 1979); Illinois Institute of Technology/Chicago-Kent College of Law (J.D., 1986). *Member:* Chicago and Illinois State Bar Associations; Illinois Trial Lawyers Association. ***PRACTICE AREAS:*** Trial Practice; Medical Malpractice. ***Email:*** kmarsh@ghslaw.com

TERENCE J. MORAN, born Chicago, Illinois, January 27, 1954; admitted to bar, 1983, Illinois; U.S. District Court, Northern District of Illinois, 1986, Trial Bar; 1986, U.S. Court of Appeals, Seventh Circuit. *Education:* University of Illinois (B.A., 1976); Loyola University (J.D., cum laude, 1983). Legal Writing Instructor, Loyola University of Chicago, 1984-1989. Adjunct Professor, Trial Advocacy, 1990—. Assistant Corporation Counsel, 1987-1993 and Chief of Labor Department, 1989-1993, City of Chicago Law Department. *Member:* Chicago, Illinois State, Federal and American Bar Associations. ***PRACTICE AREAS:*** Tort Litigation; Labor and Employment Law; Civil Rights. ***Email:*** tmoran@ghslaw.com

DONALD G. PETERSON, born Oak Park, Illinois; admitted to bar, 1966, Illinois; 1982, U.S. District Court, Northern District of Illinois including Trial Bar; 1983, U.S. Court of Appeals, Seventh Circuit; 1984, U.S. Supreme Court; 1999, U.S. District Court, Northern District of Indiana. *Education:* Miami University (B.A., 1962); Northwestern University (J.D., 1965). Member, Illinois Supreme Court Rules Committee. Editor, "Trial Briefs Newsletter," Illinois State Bar Association, 1980-1985. Editor-in-Chief, Illinois Bar Journal. Speaker: "Illinois Construction Defect Claims," "Improving the Jury Trial Process," "The Trial Lawyer and the Code of Professional Responsibility," "Jury Selection: Preparing and Conducting Voir Dire," "Comparative Negligence and the Contribution Act," "Civil Rights Attorney's Fees under §1988 and Rule 68," "Taking the Experts Deposition," "Opinion Evidence in Illinois Courts," "Trial Bar Skills for Practicing Attorneys," "Individual Immunities under §1983 Liability," "Everything You Need to Know About Settlements." *Member:* Chicago (Chair, Judiciary Committee) and Illinois State (Member, Board of Governors; Chair, Civil Practice and Procedure Council; General Chairman, Special Committee to Develop a Proposal for Mandatory Continuing Legal Education; Chair, Professional Quality in the Practice of Law) and American Bar Associations; Trial Lawyers Club of Chicago; Illinois Association Defense Trial Counsel; Defense Research Institute; Appellate Lawyers Association of Illinois; The Society of Trial Lawyers; Transportation Lawyers Association; American Institute of Architects, Northeast Illinois (Affiliate Member); Professional Liability Underwriting Society; American Collectors Association (Members' Attorney Program). ***REPORTED CASES:*** Marek v. Chesny, 473 U.S. (1985); Hernon v. Corrigan, 149 Ill. 2d 190 (1992); Richardson v. Chapman, 175 Ill. 2d 98 (1997). ***PRACTICE AREAS:*** Construction Litigation; Architects and Engineers Malpractice; Legal Malpractice; Insurance Coverage Litigation; Accounting Malpractice; Construction Defects; Professional Liability; Contracts. ***Email:*** dpeterson@ghslaw.com

MATTHEW J. PIERS, born Chicago, Illinois, May 1, 1951; admitted to bar, 1974, Illinois and U.S. District Court, Northern District of Illinois, 1982, Trial Bar; 1976, U.S. District Court, Southern District of Illinois; 1986, U.S. Supreme Court; 1989, U.S. Court of Appeals, Seventh Circuit. *Education:* Cornell University; University of Chicago (J.D., 1974). Member, National Institute of Trial Advocacy, 1976. Deputy Corporation Counsel, City of Chicago, 1984-1989. Recipient, Legal Eagle Award from Independent Voters of Illinois, 1981 (for civil rights litigation) and 1985 (for election law litigation). Board Co-Chair, National Safe Workplace Institute. Member, Public Policy Committee, Jewish Council on Urban Affairs. *Member:* Chicago and Illinois State Bar Associations; American College of Trial Lawyers; The Association of Trial Lawyers of America; Chicago Council of Lawyers. ***PRACTICE AREAS:*** Trial Practice; Appellate Practice; Civil Rights; Housing Law; Election Law. ***Email:*** mpiers@ghslaw.com

KALMAN D. RESNICK, born Chicago, Illinois, October 4, 1948; admitted to bar, 1973, Illinois, U.S. District Court, Northern and Central Districts of Illinois, U.S. Court of Appeals, Fifth, Sixth, Seventh and Ninth Circuits and U.S. Supreme Court. *Education:* Oberlin College (B.A., 1970); University of Michigan (J.D., 1973). *Member:* Chicago Council of Lawyers; American Immigration Lawyers Association. ***LANGUAGES:*** Spanish. ***PRACTICE AREAS:*** Immigration and Naturalization; Labor and Employment Law. ***Email:*** kresnick@ghslaw.com

FREDERICK S. RHINE, born Evanston, Illinois, August 6, 1960; admitted to bar, 1986, Illinois and U.S. District Court, Northern District of Illinois; 1987, U.S. Court of Appeals, Seventh Circuit; 1991, U.S. Supreme Court. *Education:* Illinois Institute of Technology (B.S., with high honors, 1982); Columbia University (J.D., 1986). Managing Editor, Columbia Journal of Law & Social Problems, 1985-1986. Author: "Waiver in the Federal Courts," Appellate Law Review, 1996. *Member:* Illinois and American Bar Associations; Appellate Lawyers Association. ***PRACTICE AREAS:*** Appellate Practice; Civil Litigation; Civil Rights; Labor and Employment Law. ***Email:*** frhine@ghslaw.com

MARY M. ROWLAND, born Akron, Ohio, October 8, 1961; admitted to bar, 1989, Illinois. *Education:* University of Michigan (B.A., 1984); University of Chicago (J.D., 1988). ***PRACTICE AREAS:*** Trial Practice; White Collar Crime. ***Email:*** mrowland@ghslaw.com

DONNA KANER SOCOL, born Chicago, Illinois, September 5, 1952; admitted to bar, 1976, Illinois; 1982, U.S. District Court, Northern District of Illinois including Trial Bar. *Education:* Northwestern University (B.A., cum laude, 1973); DePaul University (J.D., cum laude, 1976). Member, DePaul Law Review, 1974-1976. Member, Institutional Review Board, JFK Eye Institute. *Member:* Chicago, Illinois State and American Bar Associations; The Association of Trial Lawyers of America; Illinois Trial Lawyers Association; Lawyers Club of Chicago; American Academy of Hospital Attorneys; Illinois Association of Hospital Attorneys. ***PRACTICE AREAS:*** Tort; Medical Malpractice; Professional Liability. ***Email:*** dsocol@ghslaw.com

J. ERIC VANDER AREND, born Lancaster, South Carolina, July 17, 1958; admitted to bar, 1991, Illinois; 1992, U.S. District Court, Northern District of Illinois; 1995, U.S. Court of Appeals, Seventh Circuit. *Education:* Philadelphia College of Textiles & Science (B.F.A., 1980); Northwestern University (J.D., 1991). Member, The Lawyers' Committee For Civil Rights Under The Law, 1992. ***PRACTICE AREAS:*** Commercial Litigation; Employment and Labor Law; Personal Injury. ***Email:*** jvanderarend@ghslaw.com

MARK B. WEINER, born Kankakee, Illinois, June 19, 1963; admitted to bar, 1989, Illinois and U.S. District Court, Northern District of Illinois. *Education:* Phillips Exeter Academy (1981); University of Illinois (B.A., 1985); University of Denver (J.D., 1988). Associate Editor, University of Denver Transportation Law Journal. *Member:* Chicago, Illinois State and American Bar Associations. ***LANGUAGES:*** French. ***PRACTICE AREAS:*** Personal Injury. ***Email:*** mweiner@ghslaw.com

---

NATALIE A. BAUTISTA, born Elmhurst, Illinois, July 26, 1975; admitted to bar, 2002, Illinois. *Education:* Michigan State University (B.A., 1997); Chicago-Kent College of Law (J.D., 2001). ***PRACTICE AREAS:*** Immigration and Naturalization. ***Email:*** nbautista@ghslaw.com

JULIET V. BERGER-WHITE, born Chicago, Illinois, July 26, 1973; admitted to bar, 1999, Illinois. *Education:* University of Wisconsin-Madison (B.S., with distinction, 1995); Northwestern University (J.D., cum laude, 1999). Law Clerk to Chief Judge Barbara B. Crabb, U.S. District Court, Western District of Wisconsin, 1999-2001. ***PRACTICE AREAS:*** Litigation; Civil Rights. ***Email:*** jberger-white@ghslaw.com

SAMIR ZIA CHOWHAN, born South Bend, Indiana, December 20, 1973; admitted to bar, 2001, Illinois. *Education:* Indiana University (B.A., 1997); Chicago-Kent College of Law (J.D., 2000). *Member:* Chicago and Illinois State Bar Associations; American Immigration Lawyers Association. ***PRACTICE AREAS:*** Immigration and Naturalization. ***Email:*** schowhan@ghslaw.com

CARA ANN HENDRICKSON, admitted to bar, 2001, Illinois and U.S. District Court, Northern District of Illinois. *Education:* Northwestern University (B.A., cum laude, 1997); Harvard Law School (J.D., cum laude, 2001). Phi Beta Kappa. Law Clerk, Hon. Ann Williams, 7th Circuit Court of Appeals, 2002-20003. Author: "Racial De-segregation and Income Deconcentration in Public Housing-9," Geo J. on Poverty Law & Policy 35 (2002). ***PRACTICE AREAS:*** Litigation; Civil Rights; Housing Law. ***Email:*** chendrickson@ghslaw.com

CATHY L. HIGGENS, born Oak Park, Illinois, January 12, 1973; admitted to bar, 1999, Illinois. *Education:* DePaul University (B.A., 1995); Chicago-Kent College of Law, Illinois Institute of Technology (J.D., 1999). *Member:* Chicago Bar Association (Member, Immigration and Nationality Law Committee; Young Lawyers Section, Immigration Committee); American Immigration Lawyers Association. ***LANGUAGES:*** Spanish. ***PRACTICE AREAS:*** Immigration and Naturalization. ***Email:*** chiggens@ghslaw.com

ALLISON G. MARGOLIES, born Arlington Heights, Illinois, February 28, 1971; admitted to bar, 2000, Illinois. *Education:* University of Pennsylvania (B.A., 1993); George Washington University (J.D., with honors, 2000). ***PRACTICE AREAS:*** Civil Rights; Labor and Employment; Commercial Litigation. ***Email:*** amargolies@ghslaw.com

PETER C. McLEOD, born Flint, Michigan, January 10, 1970; admitted to bar, 2002, Illinois. *Education:* Purdue University (B.A. 1992); Chicago-Kent College of Law (J.D., 2002). Member, Moot Court Honor Society. *Member:* Chicago and Illinois State Bar Associations. ***PRACTICE AREAS:*** Commercial Litigation; Medical Malpractice Defense. ***Email:*** pmcleod@ghslaw.com

ALEX R. MONTGOMERY, born Evanston, Illinois, October 24, 1973; admitted to bar, 2002, Illinois. *Education:* Williams College (B.A., 1996); University of Chicago (J.D., 2002). Member, Lawyer's Club. Formerly with Life Span Center for Legal Services. *Member:* Illinois State Bar Association. ***LANGUAGES:*** Spanish. ***PRACTICE AREAS:*** Civil Rights. ***Email:*** amontgomery@ghslaw.com

FAZILA VAID, born Karachi, Pakistan, May 23, 1975; admitted to bar, 2000, Illinois. *Education:* University of Illinois at Chicago (B.A., 1996); Chicago-Kent College of Law (J.D., 2000). ***LANGUAGES:*** Urdu, Gujrati and Spanish. ***PRACTICE AREAS:*** Immigration Law. ***Email:*** fvaid@ghslaw.com

(This Listing Continued)

OF COUNSEL

GARY CHODOROW, born Albuquerque, New Mexico, May 3, 1967; admitted to bar, 1993, California; 1995 Illinois. *Education:* Duke University (B.A., 1989); University of California at Berkeley (J.D., 1993). Phi Beta Kappa. Author: How To Fight Immigration-Related Employment & Discrimination (ACLU, 1993), with Lucas Guttentag; Co-Author: Immigration Consequences of Criminal Activity, In Jailhouse Lawyers Manual (Columbia Human Rights L.Rev., 3d ed. 1992). Professor of Law, Beijing Waignoyu Daxne, Beijing, China. *Member:* American Immigration Lawyers Association; National Lawyers Guild. ***LANGUAGES:*** Spanish and Mandarin Chinese. ***PRACTICE AREAS:*** Immigration and Naturalization; Visas. ***Email:*** gchodorow@ghslaw.com

LAW OFFICES OF THADDEUS HUNT

53 WEST JACKSON BOULEVARD, SUITE 1620
CHICAGO, ILLINOIS 60604
Telephone: 312-834-0609
Fax: 312-834-0610
Email: huntlaw@innoport.com
URL: http://www.thaddeusjhunt.com

Bankruptcy, Consumer Bankruptcy, Commercial Bankruptcy, Foreclosures, Libel, Slander and Defamation, Consumer Fraud, Automobile Accidents, Dog Bites, Slip and Fall, Condominium Law, Homeowners Association Law, Landlord and Tenant Law, Residential Real Estate, Buying and Selling a Home, Business Law, Mechanics Liens, Breach of Contract, Identity Theft, Commercial Transactions, Civil Litigation, Federal Litigation, Trial Practice.

THADDEUS HUNT, born Middletown, Indiana, September 3, 1974; admitted to bar, 2002, Illinois; U.S. District Court, Central and Northern Districts of Illinois, U.S. Court of Federal Claims and U.S. Court of Appeals, Seventh Circuit. *Education:* Purdue University, Lafayette (B.A., 1997); John Marshall Law School (J.D., 2002). ***PRACTICE AREAS:*** Bankruptcy; Consumer Bankruptcy; Commercial Bankruptcy; Foreclosures; Libel, Slander and Defamation; Consumer Fraud; Condominium Law; Homeowners Association Law; Landlord and Tenant Law; Residential Real Estate; Real Estate Acquisitions; Real Estate Sales; Business Formation; Small Business Law; Mechanics Liens; Breach of Contract; Commercial Litigation; Identity Theft; Commercial Transactions; Civil Litigation; Federal Litigation; Trial Practice.

THE HUNT LAW GROUP, L.L.C.

101 NORTH WACKER DRIVE
SUITE 612
CHICAGO, ILLINOIS 60606
Telephone: 312-780-7481
Fax: 312-780-7587
Email: bhunt@hunt-lawgroup.com

Commercial Litigation, Professional Liability, Construction Litigation, Products Liability, Transportation Litigation, Premises Liability, Insurance Coverage, Appellate Practice.

BRIAN J. HUNT, born Chicago, Illinois, June 23, 1964; admitted to bar, 1991, Illinois; U.S. District Court, Northern and Central Districts of Illinois; U.S. District Court, Northern District of Indiana; U.S. Court of Appeals, Third Circuit. *Education:* University of Michigan (B.B.A., with high distinction, 1986); University of Illinois (J.D., magna cum laude, 1991). Beta Alpha Psi. Member, University of Illinois Law Review. Certified Public Accountant, Illinois, 1986. Member, Illinois CPA Society. *Member:* Illinois State and American Bar Associations; American Law Institute; Defense Research Institute. ***PRACTICE AREAS:*** Commercial Litigation; Professional Liability; Construction Litigation; Products Liability; Transportation Litigation; Insurance Coverage; Appellate Practice.

W. SCOTT TRENCH, born Naperville, Illinois, 1973; admitted to bar, 1999, Illinois. *Education:* Arizona State University (B.S., 1995); DePaul University (J.D., 1999). ***PRACTICE AREAS:*** Commercial Litigation; Construction Litigation; Premises Liability; Transportation Liability; Appeals.

C. MURRAY HARRIS, born Oxford, England, U.K., December 5, 1976; admitted to bar, 2003, Massachusetts; 2004, Rhode Island; 2005, Illinois. *Education:* Middlebury College (B.A., 1999); Boston University School of Law (J.D., cum laude, 2003). Editor-in-Chief, American Journal of Law & Medicine, 2002-2003. Paul J. Liacos Scholar, 2001-2002. ***PRACTICE AREAS:*** Commercial Litigation; Professional Liability; Construction Litigation; Products Liability. ***Email:*** mharris@hunt-lawgroup.com

OF COUNSEL

MARK R. MAYER, born Chicago, Illinois, October 14, 1954; admitted to bar, 1983, Illinois. *Education:* Loyola University (B.A., magna cum laude, 1976); Illinois Institute of Technology, Chicago-Kent College of Law (J.D., 1983). *Member:* Chicago Bar Association. ***PRACTICE AREAS:*** Construction Liability; Transportation Liability; Premises Liability; Products Liability. ***Email:*** mmayer@hunt-lawgroup.com

STEVEN R. HUNTER

Established in 1996
820 WEST JACKSON BOULEVARD, SUITE 310
CHICAGO, ILLINOIS 60607
Telephone: 312-466-9466
Fax: 312-993-1554
Email: srhunterlaw@sbcglobal.net
URL: http://www.lawyers.com/srhlaw

Criminal Trial and Appellate Practice. Drug Cases, Drugs and Narcotics, Drug Crimes, Cocaine, Heroin, Conspiracy, Fraud, Bank Fraud, Theft, Murder, Homicide, Guns, Weapons, Juvenile Criminal Law, Forgery, White Collar Crime, Felonies, Misdemeanors.

(This Listing Continued)

STEVEN R. HUNTER, born 1962; admitted to bar, 1987, Illinois; 1996, U.S. District Court, Northern District of Illinois; 2003, U.S. District Court, Central District of Illinois; U.S. Court of Appeals, Seventh Circuit. *Education:* University of Michigan (A.B., 1984; J.D., 1987). Recipient, Certificate of Merit, University of Michigan Law School. Author, "The Juvenile Court in Theory and in Operation," CBA Record, November 1990. Formerly with, Cook County Public Defender's Office. *Member:* Chicago Bar Association (Member, Criminal Committee, 1996—). ***PRACTICE AREAS:*** Criminal Trial; State and Federal; Appellate Law; Personal Injury; Drugs and Narcotics; Drug Crimes; Cocaine; Heroin; Conspiracy; Fraud; Bank Fraud; Theft; Murder; Homicide; Guns; Weapons; Juvenile Criminal Law; White Collar Crime; Felonies; Misdemeanors.

HURLEY, McKENNA & MERTZ

33 N. DEARBORN STREET
SUITE 1430
CHICAGO, ILLINOIS 60602
Telephone: 312-553-4900
Fax: 312-553-0964
URL: http://www.hurley-lawfirm.com
Email: cthurley@hurley-law.com
URL: http://www.hurley-law.com

Personal Injury, Plaintiff, Medical Negligence, Nursing Home Abuse.

FIRM PROFILE: Mr. Hurley limits his practice to the representation of injured people and their families. Mr. Hurley was first licensed to practice law in 1984 and since that time he has been a trial lawyer representing clients throughout Illinois and the midwest.

Mr. Hurley received his early training first as a trial lawyer at a small plaintiff's firm and then at Baker & McKenzie. During his years at Baker & McKenzie, Mr. Hurley represented major hospitals, corporations and insurance companies as well as severely injured individuals. This experience gave him invaluable insight into the inner workings of defense law firms and particularly insurance companies.

Mr. Hurley's practice was founded on the principle of service to his clients. All clients are treated courteously and honestly. All cases are pursued ethically and aggressively. Clients are regularly invited to telephone or meet with Mr. Hurley personally, anytime they have questions about their cases. Virtually, all of Mr. Hurley's cases are referred by attorneys with knowledge of Mr. Hurley's record as a trial lawyer and by prior clients.

CHRISTOPHER T. HURLEY, born Missoula, Montana, June 29, 1959; admitted to bar, 1984, Illinois and U.S. District Court, Northern District of Illinois; 1990, U.S. District Court, District of Utah; 1997, U.S. Court of Appeals, Seventh Circuit and U.S. District Court, Eastern District of Wisconsin. *Education:* Colgate University (B.A., honors, 1981); Loyola University (J.D., 1984). Alpha Tau Omega. Recipient, Leadership and Service Award, Loyola University School of Law, 1984. Lecturer: Federal Trial Bar Practice Course, Chicago Bar Association, 1995-1996; Damages, Illinois Trial Lawyers Association, 1996, 2002; Prior Similar Accidents, Illinois Trial Lawyers Association, 1997; Wrongful Death Damages, Illinois Trial Lawyers Association, 1998; Proof of Proximate Cause, Illinois Trial Lawyers Association, 1994; Impact of Impact, Illinois Trial Lawyers Association, 1995; Civility, Illinois Defense Council, 1995-1998. Author: Taking Control, Law Practice Management, May 2002; The Plaintiff's Lawyers Perspective on Contingency Fees, CBA Record, October 1994. *Member:* Chicago (Member: Legislative Committee; Tort Law Committee; Civil Practice Committee) and Illinois State Bar Associations; Illinois Trial Lawyers Association (Member: Board of Managers; Board of Advocates); American Trial Lawyers Association; Trial Lawyers Club of Chicago (Member, Board of Managers); Fellow, American College of Trial Lawyers. ***REPORTED CASES:*** Hernandez v. Woodbridge Nursing Home, 287 Ill.App.3d 641, 678 N.E.2d 788; Britton v. Soltes, 205 Ill.App.3d 943, 563 N.E.2d 910; Northern Trust Bank v. Carl, 200 Ill.App.3d 773, 558 N.E. 2d 451; Delgatto v. Brandon Associates, Ltd., 172 Ill.App.3d 424, 526 N.E.2d 384; Kasper v. Saint Mary of Nazareth Hosp., 135 F.3d 1170; Credo v. Zema Systems Corp., 944 F.Supp. 677; Sonnemaker v. U.S., 807 F.Supp. 483; Modelski v. Navistar International trade Corporation, 1999, 1st Dist. 302 Ill.App.3d 879, 707N.E.2d 239, 236 Ill. Dec 394; Johnson v. Zema Systems Inc., 1999, 7th Cir., 170 F.3d 734. ***PRACTICE AREAS:*** Medical Malpractice; Birth Trauma; Personal Injury; Wrongful Death; Product Liability; Product Defects; Brain Injury; Nursing Home Liability. ***Email:*** cthurley@hurley-law.com

MARK R. McKENNA, born Chicago, Illinois, July 23, 1968; admitted to bar, 1994, Illinois and U.S. District Court, Northern District of Illinois; U.S. Court of Appeals, Seventh Circuit; U.S. District Court, Central District of Illinois; U.S. District Court, Southern District of Illinois. *Education:* Northwestern University (B.A., History, 1989); University of Illinois College of Law (J.D., 1994). Lecturer: Certificates of Merit in Medical Negligence Cases, Chicago Bar Association, 2001; Oncology Malpractice, Illinois Trial Lawyers Association, 1999; Medical-Legal Work for Physicians, Marianjoy Rehabilitation Hospital, 2002. *Member:* Chicago Bar Association; Association of Trial Lawyers of America; Illinois Trial Lawyers Association. ***REPORTED CASES:*** Johnson v. Zema Systems Corp., 170 F.3d 734 (7thCir.1999); Credo v. Zema Systems Corp., 944 F.supp.677 (N.D. 111 1996); Kaspern. Saint Mary of Nazareth Hospital, 135 F.3d 1170 (7thCir.1999). ***PRACTICE AREAS:*** Medical Malpractice; Product Liability; Personal Injury; Construction Negligence; Employment Discrimination. ***Email:*** mark@hurley-law.com

MICHAEL T. MERTZ, born St. Paul, Minnesota, May 7, 1972; admitted to bar, 1997, Illinois; 1998, U.S. District Court, Northern District of Illinois; 1999, U.S. District Court, Eastern District of Wisconsin. *Education:* Gustavus Adolphus College (B.A., 1994); DePaul University (J.D., 1997). *Member:* Chicago and Illinois State Bar Associations; Illinois Trial Lawyers Association; Association of Trial Lawyers of America. ***LANGUAGES:*** Spanish. ***PRACTICE AREAS:*** Medical Malpractice; Product Liability; Person Injury; Wrongful Death; Birth Trauma; Brain Injury; Nursing Home Liability. ***Email:*** mike@hurley-law.com

(This Listing Continued)

HURLEY, McKENNA & MERTZ, Chicago—Continued

ASSOCIATES

LARA M. PALLES, born Chicago, Illinois, 1975; admitted to bar, 2002, Illinois and U.S. District Court, Northern District of Illinois. *Education:* Columbia College (B.A., Theater, Marketing-Film, with honors, 1998); DePaul University (J.D., 2001). ***Email:*** lmpalles@hurley-law.com

MICHAEL S. KEATING, born Melrose Park, Illinois, 1975; admitted to bar, 2002, Illinois and U.S. District Court, Northern District of Illinois. *Education:* Marquette University (B.S., Business Administration, 1997); DePaul University (J.D., 2002). Lecturer: Tort Reform in Illinois, Chicago Bar Association, 2005. *Member:* Chicago and Illinois State Bar Associations; The Association of Trial Lawyers of America; Illinois Trial Lawyers Association. ***Email:*** mskeating@hurley-law.com

HURLEY STANNERS, LIMITED

Established in 1994

30 SOUTH WACKER DRIVE, SUITE 2300
CHICAGO, ILLINOIS 60606-7410
Telephone: 312-236-6700
Fax: 312-236-6706
URL: http://www.lawyers.com/hurleystanners
Email: jhurley@komdr.com
URL: http://www.hurleystanners.com

International and Domestic Business, Commercial Transactions and Real Estate Practice, with Concentrations in the Marketing, Creative Arts and Entertainment Fields.

JOANNE F. HURLEY, born Minneapolis, Minnesota, August 28, 1950; admitted to bar, 1978, Illinois; 1982, U.S. District Court, Northern District of Illinois. *Education:* Michigan State University (B.A., 1972; B.S., 1975); DePaul University (J.D., 1978). Member, DePaul University Law Review. Law Clerk, Honorable Calvin C. Campbell, Illinois Appellate Court (1st District). Hearing Officer, Chicago Park District Disciplinary Hearings, 1983-1984. Certified Arbitrator, Cook County Arbitration Program, 1999-2002. Author: "The Treatment of Presumptions in Illinois: Adding Insult to Injury," The DePaul Law Review, Vol. 27, No. 3, 1978; "Confidentiality Plan Can Protect Corporate Assets," Chicago Industrial Bulletin, Vol. 13, No. 1, January/February 1994. Partner: Robbins, Rubinstein, Salomon & Greenblatt, Ltd., 1984-1989; Schwartz & Freeman, 1990-1994. U.S. Outside General Counsel, Tony Stone Images Group, 1988-1998; Of Counsel, Flamm & Teibloom, 1995—. *Member:* Chicago, Illinois State and American Bar Associations. (Also Member of Kelly, Olson, Michod, DeHaan & Richter, L.L.C.). ***PRACTICE AREAS:*** Business Formation; Business Law; Corporate Law; Limited Liability Company Law; Commercial Transactions; Contracts; Entertainment and the Arts; Artists Rights; Artistic Property; International Intellectual Property; Commercial Real Estate Contracts; Commercial Leasing; Business Sales; Construction Contracts; Employment Severance and Contracts; Noncompetition and Non-Solicitation Agreements; Business Acquisitions; Distribution Agreements. ***Email:*** jhurley@komdr.com

ICE MILLER

Established in 1910

200 WEST MADISON
SUITE 3500
CHICAGO, ILLINOIS 60606-3417
Telephone: 312-726-1567
Fax: 312-726-7102
Email: info@icemiller.com
URL: http://www.icemiller.com

REVISER OF THE INDIANA LAW DIGEST FOR THIS DIRECTORY.

Indianapolis, Indiana Office: One American Square, Box 82001. Telephone: 317-236-2100. Fax: 317-236-2219. Internet Email: info@icemiller.com. Web Site Address: http://www.icemiller.com.
Washington, D.C. Office: 1090 Vermont Avenue, N.W., Suite 920. Telephone: 202-824-8600. Fax: 202-824-8601. Email: info@icemiller.com. Web Site Address: http://www.icemiller.com

Administrative Law, Antitrust, Appellate Practice, Architectural Malpractice Law, Banking, Bankruptcy, Broadcasting and Communications, Cable TV, Cable TV Franchising, Civil and Criminal Litigation, Civil Rights, Coal Law, College and University Law, Commercial and Business Litigation, Complex Litigation, Computer Law, Contracting and Litigation, Construction Law, Corporate Law, Corporate Finance, Creditors Rights Law, Drug and Medical Device Litigation, Economic Development and Incentives, Education Law, Employee Benefits Law, Entrepreneurial Services, Environmental Law, Estate Development and Finance, Franchise Law, Gaming Law, Gift and Estate Tax, Governmental Affairs, Governmental Relations, Governmental Services and Lobbying, Government Law, Government (Public) Contract Law, Government Procurement, Guardianship, Health Care Law, Immigration Law, Insurance Law, Intellectual Property and Licensing, International Law, Labor and Employment Law (including Equal Employment Litigation, ERISA Practice and Occupational Safety and Health Matters), Liability Risk Management, Licensing, Management Labor Relations Law, Mergers and Acquisitions, Minerals and Mining, Municipal Finance (Bond) Law, Municipal Finance (Bond), Dispute Resolution and Litigation, Municipal Litigation, Municipal Solid Waste Resource Recovery, Municipal Utility Regulation, Occupational Hazards Law (Black Lung, Asbestosis, etc.), Patent, Trademark and Copyright, Plaintiff's Trial Practice, Probate Law, Product Liability Law, Public Agency, Public Authority Financing Law, Public Contract Law, Public Employment Relations, Public Entity Law, Public Finance, Public Health Law, Public Housing Law, Public Schools, Public Sector Collective Bargaining, Public Utility Law, Public Works, Professional Malpractice Law, Real Estate Law (including Sales, Development and Financing, Mortgage Banking, Secured Transactions, Sale/Leasebacks, Condominiums and Zoning), Regulation, Risk and Claims Management, Securities Regulation Law, Sports Law, Taxation (Federal, State and Local), Tax Exempt Organizations, Tort Law, Toxic Torts, Transportation Law, Utility Law, Venture Capital, Venture Finance Services, Workers' Compensation.

FIRM PROFILE: A full-service law firm that also offers professional business advice, with offices in Indianapolis, South Bend and Chicago, Ice Miller has provided counsel on a local, state and national level since 1910.

The Firm was founded in Indianapolis on April 28, 1910, when three general practitioners formed a partnership under the name of Henley Matson Gates. The Firm experienced continuous growth and acquired a national reputation and a national practice. The Firm presently consists of 220 lawyers and 41 paraprofessionals, and an additional 250 staff employees, making it the largest law firm in Indianapolis.

Ice Miller's core departments are Corporate Law, Litigation, Labor and Employment, Real Estate Development, and Municipal Finance. From these core disciplines, Ice Miller lawyers have developed in-depth experience and knowledge in a variety of highly refined areas of concentration which allows the Firm to put together teams of attorneys to satisfy the increasingly sophisticated and multi-faceted needs of its clients. These areas of concentration are set forth below.

Most notable growth areas include: Advanced Technology Law Banking Law, Construction Law, Drug and Device Law, Employee Benefits Dispute Resolution, Entrepreneurial Law, Environmental Law, Governmental Services, Health Law, Intellectual Property (including Patent Law), International Law, Merger and Acquisition Law, Municipal Law, Occupational Hazards Law, Professional Liability Law, and Sports and Entertainment Law.

Ice Miller also has the largest litigation practice in the state, representing national, regional and locally domiciled clients for which it has obtained numerous "landmark" decisions in areas which include corporate, probate, professional, drug and device, and contractual liability.

LAW FIRM ALLIANCES/ASSOCIATIONS: ***UNITED STATES LAW FIRM GROUP***

Henley Matson & Gates	1910-1912
Matson Gates & Ross	1912-1914
Matson Kane & Ross	1914-1922
Matson Carter Ross & McCord	1922-1930
Matson Ross McCord & Clifford	1930-1939
Matson Ross McCord & Ice	1939-1942
Ross McCord Ice & Miller	1942-1963
Ice Miller Donadio & Ryan	1963-2000.

PARTNERS

JOHN D. BURKE, born Evanston, Illinois, 1965; admitted to bar, 1990, Illinois; U.S. Court of Appeals, Seventh Circuit; U.S. District Court, Northern District of Illinois; U.S. District Court, Central District of Illinois; U.S. District Court, Eastern District of Illinois; U.S. District Court, Western District of Wisconsin. *Education:* Lake Forest College (B.A., cum laude, 1987); Chicago-Kent College of Law, Illinois Institute of Technology (J.D., with honors, 1990). *Member:* Chicago Bar Association (Member, Judicial Evaluation Committee). ***REPORTED CASES:*** Paul H. Schwendener v. Jupiter Elec. (Illinois App. 2005); Board of Ed. of Sunset School Dist. No. 29 v. Village of Northbrook, IL (Illinois App. 1998); Kurtz v. Solomon (Illinois App. 1995). ***PRACTICE AREAS:*** Litigation; Complex Litigation. ***Email:*** john.burke@icemiller.com

ANTHONY NIMMO, born Coventry, England, August 15, 1954; admitted to bar, 1983, Indiana; 1987, Illinois; U.S. District Court, Northern District of Illinois including Trial Bar; registered to practice before U.S. Patent and Trademark Office. *Education:* Purdue University (B.S., 1978); Indiana University (J.D., 1983). Associate Editor, Indiana University Law Review, 1982-1983. Lecturer, Purdue University, 2001—. *Member:* Chicago and American Bar Associations; Intellectual Property Law Association of Chicago. ***REPORTED CASES:*** National Gypsum Company v. USG; Hyseq, Inc. v. Affymetrix, Inc. ***Email:*** anthony.nimmo@icemiller.com

ROBERT J. SCHILLERSTROM, born Harvey, Illinois, March 2, 1952; admitted to bar, 1980, Illinois. *Education:* Illinois College (B.A., with honors, 1974); Chicago-Kent College of Law, Illinois Institute of Technology (J.D., with honors, 1980). DuPage County Republican Committeeman, 1983—. Commissioner and President, Naperville Park District, 1983-1985. Forest Reserve Commissioner, 1986-1992. Member: DuPage County Regional Planning Commission, 1988-1992; Board of Directors, Copley Hospital, 1993—; DuPage County Conservation Foundation, 1994-1998; DuPage County Water Commission, 1996-1998. Elected Member, DuPage County Board, 1998—. ***PRACTICE AREAS:*** Public Affairs. ***Email:*** robert.schillerstrom@icemiller.com

RICHARD A. SCHNURR, born Stoughton, Wisconsin, September 20, 1955; admitted to bar, 1981, Illinois and U.S. District Court, Northern District of Illinois; 1983, U.S. Court of Appeals, Seventh Circuit; U.S. Court of Appeals for the Federal Circuit; registered to practice before U.S. Patent and Trademark Office. *Education:* Indiana University (B.S., cum laude, 1978); University of Illinois (J.D., 1981). Phi Beta Kappa. *Member:* Illinois State and American (Member, Intellectual Property Section) Bar Associations; Intellectual Property Law Association of Chicago. ***REPORTED CASES:*** Abbott Laboratories, Inc. v. Sharma-Breach of research contract, blood analyzer technology; ADAHF v. Bisco, Inc.-Dental adhesives; American Optical Corp. v. Signet Armorlite, Inc.-Progressive ophthalmic lenses; Amersham International v. Baxter Travenol Laboratories-Immunoassay medical test systems; Amersham International v. Corning Glass Works-Immunoassay medical test systems; Amersham International v. Corning Glass Works-Immunoassay medical test systems; Amgen v. Chugai Genetics-Recombinant DNA technology; Amgen, Inc. v. Chugai Pharmaceutical Ltd.-Recombinant DNA technology; ATGF v. ATIF-Trademark opposition; Baird, et al. v. Bisco, Inc.-Product liability deceptive trade practices regarding dental adhesives; Chanell, et al. v. Cohen, et al.-Copyright infringement unfair competition; Dentalite, Inc. v. Bisco, Inc.-Breach of distribution contract unfair competition; Duchossois Communications Co. of California, Inc. v. Radio Ventura Radio station Service mark infringement; EMKG v. Bisco, Inc.-Glass ionomer technology; Essilor v. Signet Armorlite, Inc.-Abrasion-resistant coatings; Fritsch v. Linn-Patent interference; GroMaster v. King Systems, Inc.-Trade dress 43(a) unfair competition; GroMaster v. Riverside Manufactur-

(This Listing Continued)

ing-Feeder technology; GroMaster, Inc. v. King Systems, Inc.-Feeder technology; Grotnes Manufacturing v. Hess-Trade secret regarding auto wheel forming machine technology; Hyseq v. Affymetrix and Affymetrix v. Hyseq-DNA sequencing technology; IJR v. Colt Industries, Inc. & Fanuc-Electrical discharge machining; Illinois Masonic Medical Center v. Highland Park Hospital-Hospital service mark infringement; Industrie Cometto v. Cometto Corp.-Trademark opposition; Intel Corp. v. Thrall Car Manufacturing Co.-Railroad container car; Intertech Resources, Inc. v. Vital Signs, Inc.-Medical resuscitator technology; Invacare Corp. v. Everest & Jennings-Wheelchair technology; Ivoclar v. Bisco, Inc.-Dental light curing gun technology; Jackson, et al. v. Intertech Resources, Inc. v. Inspiron Corp.-Medical humidifier technology; King Systems, Inc. v. GroMaster, Inc.-Feeder technology declaratory judgement; Merrill Chase Galleries v. Kirschen-Breach of restrictive covenant unfair competition; Midgley, et al. v. Hertl, et al.-Patent interference; Mion Int'l v. Bisco, Inc.-Dental cement technology; Novo, et al. v. Pharmacia, et al.-Recombinant DNA technology - human growth hormone; ORC v. Signet Armorlite, Inc.-Reexamination proceeding; Schmidt v. First Security Bank, et al.-Unfair competition breach of contract; Signet Armorlite v. Dahi-Polyester Ophthalmic Lens Technology. Trade Secret/Patent Infringement/Breach of Employment Agreement; Signet Armorlite v. Transitions Optical-Ophthalmic Lenses. Antitrust/Unfair Competition; Signet Armorlite, Inc. v. American Optical Corp.-Progressive ophthalmic lenses; Signet Armorlite, Inc. v. BMC, Inc.-Abrasion-resistant lens coating; Signet Armorlite, Inc. v. ODC Corporation-Coated ophthalmic lens technology; Solaia v. Jefferson-Smurfit et al.-PLC software control technology; Steoan Company v. Oxid LP-aromatic polyols technology; Thrall Car Manufacturing Co. v. Gunderson Corp.-Railroad center beam lumber car; Thrall Car Manufacturing Co. v. Trinity Industries, Inc.-Railroad auto rack car; Trinity Industries, Inc. v. Thrall Car Manufacturing Co.-Railroad hopper car; Women's Health Resources v. St. Louis Hospital-Trademark concurrent use proceedings. ***PRACTICE AREAS:*** Intellectual Property; Antitrust; Unfair Competition. ***Email:*** richard.schnurr@icemiller.com

JAMES A. SHANAHAN, born Rushville, Indiana, October 27, 1951; admitted to bar, 1977, Indiana; 1997, Illinois. *Education:* University of Notre Dame (B.B.A., cum laude, 1973); Indiana University (J.D., magna cum laude, 1977). Order of the Coif. *Member:* National Association of Bond Lawyers; Indiana Municipal Lawyers Association. ***PRACTICE AREAS:*** Municipal Finance or Bond Law; Lease Law; Airport Law; School Law; Tax-Exempt Financing Law. ***Email:*** shanahan@icemiller.com

THOMAS C. SMITH, born Fort Wayne, Indiana, 1961; admitted to bar, 1988, Illinois; 1992, Indiana. *Education:* Indiana University (B.A., 1983; J.D., cum laude, 1988). Phi Beta Kappa. *Member:* National Association of Bond Lawyers; National Council of State Housing Agencies. ***PRACTICE AREAS:*** Public Finance; Securities. ***Email:*** tom.smith@icemiller.com

OF COUNSEL

PATRA S. GEROULIS, born Chicago, Illinois, October 8, 1975; admitted to bar, 2000, Illinois. *Education:* DePaul University (B.S., with highest honors, 1997); University of Notre Dame Law School (J.D., cum laude, 2000). *Member:* Chicago Bar Association; National Association of Bond Lawyers. ***LANGUAGES:*** Greek and French. ***PRACTICE AREAS:*** Municipal Finance; Public Finance. ***Email:*** patra.geroulis@icemiller.com

BRIAN J. LUM, born Chicago, Illinois, 1960; admitted to bar, 1998, Illinois; U.S. District Court, Northern District of Illinois; registered to practice before U.S. Patent and Trademark Office. *Education:* University of Chicago (B.A., 1982; Ph.D., 1990); Loyola University, Chicago (J.D., 1998). ***PRACTICE AREAS:*** Intellectual Property; Intellectual Property Litigation; Intellectual Property Prosecution. ***Email:*** brian.lum@icemiller.com

ASSOCIATE

JOAN G. RITCHEY, born Oak Ridge, Tennessee, 1972; admitted to bar, 2001, Illinois; U.S. District Court, Northern District of Illinois. *Education:* Boston University (B.A., 1994); New York University (M.A., 1997); Washington University (J.D., 2001). *Member:* Chicago, Illinois State and American Bar Associations. ***Email:*** joan.ritchey@icemiller.com

REVISER OF THE INDIANA LAW DIGEST FOR THIS DIRECTORY.

(For complete biographical data on all personnel, see Professional Biographies at Indianapolis, Indiana)

THE LAW OFFICES OF PHILIP A. IGOE

221 N. LA SALLE STREET, SUITE 655
CHICAGO, ILLINOIS 60601
Telephone: 312-372-4298
Fax: 312-372-5147

Bankruptcy Law, Criminal Law, DUI/DWI, Traffic Violations, Transportation Law, White Collar Crimes.

PHILIP A. IGOE, admitted to bar, 1977, Illinois; 1981, U.S. District Court, Northern District of Illinois. *Education:* University of Illinois (B.A., Chemistry); Chicago-Kent College of Law, Illinois Institute of Technology (J.D.). ***PRACTICE AREAS:*** Bankruptcy; Criminal Law; Driving While Intoxicated; Traffic Violations; Transportation; White Collar Crime.

IMMIGRATION LAW CENTER, P.C.

53 WEST JACKSON BOULEVARD, SUITE 860
CHICAGO, ILLINOIS 60604
Telephone: 312-461-1005
Fax: 312-461-1012
Email: immigrationlawcenter@att.net
URL: http://www.guycroteaulaw.com

Immigration Law, Visas, Work Permits, Employment Immigration, Citizenship, Business Law, Small Business Law, Family Businesses, Contracts, Civil Litigation, Consumer Bankruptcy.

(This Listing Continued)

GUY V. CROTEAU, born Evergreen Park, Illinois, April 6, 1952; admitted to bar, 1987, Illinois and U.S. District Court, Northern District of Illinois; 2001, U.S. Court of Appeals, Fourth Circuit; 2002, U.S. Court of Appeals, Eleventh Circuit; 2003, U.S Court of Appeals, Third and Seventh Circuits. *Education:* University of Illinois (B.A., 1981); The John Marshall Law School (J.D., 1987). Executive Editor, John Marshall Law Review, 1986. *Member:* Chicago and Illinois State Bar Associations; American Immigration Lawyers Association. [With U.S. Navy, 1973-1979]. ***PRACTICE AREAS:*** Immigration Law; Bankruptcy; Business Law. ***Email:*** immigrationlawcenter@att.net

LAW OFFICES OF SANDY N. ISAACSON

1000 NORTH HALSTED, SUITE 203
CHICAGO, ILLINOIS 60622
Telephone: 312-255-0007
Fax: 312-255-0009
Email: snilaw@comcast.net
URL: http://www.sandynisaacson.com

Family, Divorce, Child Custody, Child Support, Personal Injury, Medical Malpractice, Automobile Accidents, Workers Compensation, Wrongful Death, Probate, Real Estate, Corporate, Business, Contracts, Trusts and Estates, Business Litigation, General Practice.

SANDY N. ISAACSON, born Dallas, Texas, November 14, 1941; admitted to bar, 1967, Illinois and U.S. District Court, Northern District of Illinois. *Education:* DePaul University (J.D., 1967). *Member:* Chicago Bar Association. ***PRACTICE AREAS:*** Family Law; Real Estate; Corporate Law; Business Litigation; General Practice; Personal Injury; Probate; Medical Malpractice.

IWAN CRAY HUBER HORSTMAN & VANAUSDAL LLC

Established in 1999

303 WEST MADISON STREET, SUITE 2200
CHICAGO, ILLINOIS 60606
Telephone: 312-332-8450
Fax: 312-332-8451
Email: attorneys@iwancray.com
URL: http://www.iwancray.com

Clarendon Hills, Illinois Office: 115 W. 55th Street, Suite 400, 60514. Telephone: 630-789-8200.

Litigation Practice. Product Liability, Insurance Coverage, E-Commerce, Commercial, Professional Liability, Medical Malpractice, Transportation Liability, Premises Liability, Hospital Liability, Toxic Tort, Environmental Litigation and Civil Appeals in State and Federal Courts.

FIRM PROFILE: We recognize that purchasers of legal services today seek more resourceful, efficient and responsive lawyers than ever before. As a result, our litigation practice is designed to deliver the quality and value that our clients expect. The size, focus and technological commitment of our firm give us significant advantages over traditionally structured firms for achieving success in legal disputes. Although we are a litigation firm, we do not simply litigate; we work closely with our clients to provide individualized counseling, approaches and solutions to satisfy their unique legal and commercial needs.

LORI E. IWAN, born Chicago, Illinois, January 17, 1958; admitted to bar, 1983, Illinois. *Education:* University of Illinois (B.A., 1980; J.D., 1983). Co-Author: "E-Guide for the Legal Professional," 2003; "Enron and the D&O Aftermath: Tips and Traps for the Unwary," FDCC Quarterly, Vol. 53, No. 1, Fall 2002; "Expect the Unexpected: Managing the Jury's Expectations in Product Liability Cases," For the Defense, March 2001; Author: "TRO's and Preliminary Injunctions: The 24-Hour Trial, Defense Research Institute," Trial Techniques Master Trial Attorneys Speak, November 2000; "Sue Now Get Sick Later: An Analysis of Claims for Medical Monitoring and Fear of Cancer Damages," Defense Research Institute Trial Tactics Monograph, April, 1999; "Hey Litigator...Try This," For the Defense, March 1999; "Debunking the Neuropsychological Injury," Michigan Defense Trial Counsel Midwinter Meeting, December 3, 1999; "Lori's Links," a monthly Internet column regarding legal research sites on the World Wide Web, www. the federation.org. *Member:* American Bar Association (Member, Sections on: Litigation; Corporate Counsel); Defense Research Institute (Law Institute, 1998-2000; Co-Chair, CLE Committee for 1999 Annual Meeting; Member, Sections on: Technology; Products Liability; Trial Tactics); Illinois Association of Defense Trial Counsel; Legal Club of Chicago (President); Federal Defense and Corporate Counsel (Director 2002-2005; Vice-Chair, Technology; Dean of Litigation Management College, 2002-2004). ***PRACTICE AREAS:*** Commercial Litigation (50%); Products Liability (30%); Toxic Torts (20%). ***Email:*** lei@iwancray.com

DANIEL K. CRAY, born Quincy, Illinois, June 20, 1956; admitted to bar, 1981, Illinois. *Education:* Illinois State University (B.S., with high honors, 1978); University of Illinois (J.D., 1981). Co-Author: "Reimportation and It's Risks," For The Defense, June 2001. Author: "Motions to Remove," Defense Counsel Training Manual, International Association of Defense Counsel, 1995; "Federal Preemption Monograph," Illinois Association of Defense Trial Counsel Quarterly, Third Quarter, 1996; "Defending Product Liability Cases in Illinois After the *Best* Decision," Illinois Association of Defense Trial Counsel Quarterly, Fourth Quarter, 1998. Illinois Representative, National Jury Innovations Project. *Member:* DuPage County Bar Association (Judicial Evaluation Committee, 1998); International Association of Defense Counsel (IADC Trial Academy Faculty, 2000; Chair, Class Action and Multi-party Litigation, 2004-2005; Vice Chair, ADR Committee, 2003—; Vice Chair, Drug and Medical Devices Committee, 2004-2005); Defense Research Institute (Member: Products Liability Section; Steering Committee, Drug and Medical Devices); Illinois Association of Defense Trial Counsel (Member, Board of Directors, 2001—). ***PRACTICE AREAS:*** Commercial Litigation; Products Liability; Professional Liability; Toxic Torts. ***Email:*** dkc@iwancray.com

(This Listing Continued)

IWAN CRAY HUBER HORSTMAN & VANAUSDAL LLC, Chicago—Continued

MICHAEL D. HUBER, born Owensboro, Kentucky, March 23, 1960; admitted to bar, 1985, Illinois; 1996, Indiana. *Education:* Wabash College (A.B., cum laude, 1982); Indiana University (J.D., cum laude, 1985). Delta Theta Phi. Author: "Courtroom 2001," Defense Research Institute, Products Liability Conference, January 2000; "The Sins of the Fathers...Offensive Collateral Estoppel Revisited". Co-Author: "Expect the Unexpected: Managing Jury's Expectations in Product Liability Cases," For the Defense, March 2001; For the Defense, Defense Research Institute, October 1999; "COURTROOM 2000 - Mastering the Medium of the Millennium," presentation to Defense Research Institute, Mid-Year Meeting, September 1999; Study on Relative Jury Volatility of Illinois Counties, June 1999; Staffing under PPS: Practical Legal Considerations, Interviewee, Postacute Payment Report, Vol. 3, No. 5, May 1999; Defending First Party Fraud and Arson Claims, for Allstate Insurance Company, Special Claims Unit Seminar, Indianapolis, IN, 1997. *Member:* Chicago, Illinois and Indiana State Bar Associations; Defense Research Institute; International Association of Defense Counsel (Faculty Member of Trial Academy, 2003); Trucking Industry Defense Association. ***PRACTICE AREAS:*** Commercial Litigation; Computer Law; Construction Law; Litigation; Medical Malpractice; Products Liability; Professional Liability; Transportation Law; Insurance. ***Email:*** mdh@iwancray.com

JAMES K. HORSTMAN, born Chicago, Illinois, November 7, 1953; admitted to bar, 1980, Illinois. *Education:* DePauw University (B.A., 1975); Yale University (M.A.R., 1977); Washington University (J.D., 1980). Co-Author: "Peaceful Co-Existence in Complex Litigation: Defendants Can't We Just Get Along?" For The Defense, July 2000. Author: "Punitive and Other Damages for Emotional Distress in Third Party Bad Faith Actions," FICC Quarterly, Fall 1999; "Winding the Litigation Clock - Statutes of Limitations and the Year 2000," Mealey's Year 2000 Report, April 1999; "Ten Good Reasons to Worry About Tobacco Liability Exposure," For the Defense, August, 1997; "Federal Preemption: Still a Cure for Managed Care Liability Claims?," For the Defense, July, 1997; "Using Annuity Cost Evidence to Contain Awards for Future Damages," DRI Monograph: The Economic Expert in Litigation, 1993; "Parent-Child Tort Immunity in Illinois, "Illinois Bar Journal, 1990. *Member:* Illinois State and American (Member: Business Law and Litigation Sections) Bar Associations; Appellate Lawyers Association; Defense Research Institute (Member, Insurance Coverage Section); Federation of Defense and Corporate Counsel (Member: Insurance Coverage Committee; Technology Committee). ***PRACTICE AREAS:*** Appellate Practice; Commercial Litigation; Computer Law; Insurance; Reinsurance. ***Email:*** jkh@iwancray.com

RODNEY E. VANAUSDAL, born Wooster, Ohio, July 24, 1958; admitted to bar, 1983, Illinois. *Education:* Indiana University (B.S., 1980; J.D., 1982). Beta Gamma Sigma. Co-Author: "Reimportation and Its Risks," For The Defense, June 2001. Author: "How Does The Legal Community Determine Which Pressure Ulcers Are Avoidable?," National Pressure Ulcer Advisory Board, Chicago, Illinois, May 2000; "Legal Importance of Documentation," Cynthia Chow & Associates Annual Education Seminar, September 2000; "Health Care in the New Millennium," The Memphis Case Manager's Association, Memphis, Tennessee, May 1, 1997; "Managed Care and Malpractice: Issues to Consider," American Association of Health Plans, Dallas, Texas, November 21, 1996; "Defending the Gatekeepers and Providers," presented to Employers Reinsurance Corporation, Overland Park, Kansas, September 11, 1997; "Counseling and Negotiating: The Defense Perspective," Instructor, John Marshall Law School, Chicago, Illinois 1993-1997. *Member:* Illinois State and American Bar Associations; American Society for Healthcare Risk Management; Illinois Association of Healthcare Attorneys. ***PRACTICE AREAS:*** Litigation; Products Liability; Medical Malpractice; Professional Liability. ***Email:*** rev@iwancray.com

STEPHEN W. HEIL, born Joliet, Illinois, March 6, 1965; admitted to bar, 1990, Illinois and U.S. District Court, Northern District of Illinois; 1995, U.S. District Court, Central District of Illinois; 2003, U.S. District Court, Southern District of Indiana; 2005, U.S. District Court, Western District of Michigan. *Education:* Lewis University, Valedictorian (B.A., 1987); University of Illinois (J.D., cum laude, 1990). Author: "Ten Critical Steps to the Effective Defense of a Transportation Case," Continuing Legal Education for Private Industry. Arbitrator, NASD. *Member:* Illinois State Bar Association (Member, Tort Law Section); Defense Research Institute (Member, Construction Law, Trucking Law). ***PRACTICE AREAS:*** Commercial Litigation; Construction Law; Products Liability; Transportation. ***Email:*** swh@iwancray.com

---

BENJAMIN B. BELCHER, born Detroit, Michigan, September 27, 1972; admitted to bar, 2001, Illinois and U.S. District Court, Northern District of Illinois. *Education:* Central Michigan University (B.S., cum laude, 1994; M.A., 1997); University of Illinois College of Law (J.D., 2001). *Member:* American Bar Association; Defense Research Institute. ***PRACTICE AREAS:*** Insurance Coverage; Reinsurance; Appellate Practice; Commercial Litigation.

LADONNA L. BOECKMAN, born Stillwater, Oklahoma, August 29, 1973; admitted to bar, 1998, Iowa; 2000, Illinois and U.S. District Court, Northern District of Illinois; 2004, U.S. District Court, Southern District of Illinois; 2005, U.S. District Court, Southern District of Indiana. *Education:* Drake University (B.A., magna cum laude, 1995); Drake University Law School (J.D., with honors, 1998). Phi Alpha Delta (Member, Executive Board, 1997-1998). Notes Editor, Drake Law Review. Moot Court Board. Member, 1995-1998 and Vice President, 1997-1998, Drake Law Women. Author: Note, "Bestowing the Key to Public Education: The Effects of Judicial Determinations or the Individuals with Disabilities Education Act on Disabled and Non-Disabled Students," 46 Drake L. Rev. 855, 1998. *Member:* Illinois State, Iowa State and American Bar Associations. ***PRACTICE AREAS:*** Products Liability; Toxic Torts; Defense Litigation.

BRYAN T. BUTCHER, born Hammond, Indiana, April 4, 1975; admitted to bar, 2000, Illinois; 2002, U.S. District Court, Northern District of Illinois. *Education:* St. Joseph's College (B.S., 1997); John Marshall Law School (J.D., 2000). *Member:* Chicago Bar Association. ***PRACTICE AREAS:*** Transportation; Products Liability; Premises Liability; Medical Malpractice; Personal Injury. ***Email:*** btb@iwancray.com

(This Listing Continued)

ADAM C. CARTER, born Mendota, Illinois, February 4, 1976; admitted to bar, 2001, Illinois and U.S. District Court, Northern District of Illinois. *Education:* Augustana College (B.A., cum laude, 1998); University of Illinois (J.D., cum laude, 2001). Omicron Delta Kappa; Sigma Tau Delta. Member, Mortar Board National Honor Society. Presidential Scholar. Foundations Scholar. *Member:* Chicago, Illinois State and American (Member, Litigation Section) Bar Associations. ***PRACTICE AREAS:*** Commercial Litigation; Products Liability; Construction Litigation; Premises Liability; Transportation Litigation. ***Email:*** accl@iwancray.com

DOUGLAS M. DEWITT, born Columbus, Ohio, November 12, 1974; admitted to bar, 2001, Illinois. *Education:* The Ohio State University (B.S., magna cum laude, 1996); University of Illinois, Urbana-Champaign (J.D., cum laude, 2001). *Member:* Chicago and Illinois State Bar Associations. ***PRACTICE AREAS:*** Litigation; Commercial Litigation; Products Liability; Insurance. ***Email:*** dmd@iwancray.com

DAVID J. FARINA, born Schenectady, New York, January 16, 1968; admitted to bar, 1995, Illinois; 1997, U.S. District Court, Northern District of Illinois. *Education:* State University of New York at Plattsburgh (B.S., 1989); The John Marshall Law School (J.D., 1995). Alpha Sigma Phi. Recipient, Wojcik Award, 1990. *Member:* Chicago and Illinois State Bar Associations; Defense Research Institute. ***PRACTICE AREAS:*** Commercial Litigation; Medical Malpractice; Legal Malpractice; Products Liability; Commercial Transportation. ***Email:*** djf@iwancray.com

DAVID E. KRAVITZ, born Chicago, Illinois, July 17, 1968; admitted to bar, 1994, Illinois and U.S. District Court, Northern District of Illinois. *Education:* University of Wisconsin (B.A., 1990); Chicago-Kent College of Law (J.D., 1994). Dean's List. *Member:* Chicago, Illinois State and American Bar Associations. ***PRACTICE AREAS:*** Litigation; Real Estate. ***Email:*** dek@iwancray.com

TIMOTHY C. SAMUELSON, born Chicago, Illinois, October 12, 1972; admitted to bar, 1998, Illinois; 1999, Indiana and U.S. District Court, Northern District of Indiana; 2003, U.S. District Court, Northern District of Illinois. *Education:* Valparaiso University (B.A., 1995); Indiana University (J.D., 1998). *Member:* Chicago, Illinois and Indiana State Bar Associations. ***PRACTICE AREAS:*** Commercial Litigation; Products Liability; Civil Litigation. ***Email:*** tcs@iwancray.com

JENNIFER L. TWEETON, born Minneapolis, Minnesota; admitted to bar, 2005, Illinois. *Education:* University of Minnesota (B.A., 2000); William Mitchell College of Law (J.D., 2004). ***Email:*** jlt@iwancray.com

CHRISTOPHER D. WEHRMAN, born April 21, 1976; admitted to bar, 2002, Illinois. *Education:* Michigan State University (B.A., Political Science, Pre-Law, 1998); Michigan State University Detroit College of Law (J.D., 2002). ***PRACTICE AREAS:*** Tort Liability. ***Email:*** cwehrman@cypclaw.com

RONALD L. WISNIEWSKI, born Muskegon, Michigan, April 17, 1966; admitted to bar, 1992, California; 1994, Illinois. *Education:* University of Notre Dame (B.A., 1988); Valparaiso University (J.D., 1991). Delta Theta Phi. Member, Orange County Bar Association, 1992-1993. *Member:* Chicago, Illinois State and American Bar Associations; State Bar of California. ***PRACTICE AREAS:*** Commercial Litigation; Employment Litigation; Insurance Litigation. ***Email:*** rlw@iwancray.com

---

JACKSON LEWIS LLP

320 WEST OHIO STREET, SUITE 500
CHICAGO, ILLINOIS 60610
Telephone: 312-787-4949
Facsimile: 312-787-4995
URL: http://www.jacksonlewis.com

Other offices located in: Atlanta, GA; Boston, MA; Cary, NC; Dallas, TX; Greenville, SC; Hartford, CT; Long Island, NY; Los Angeles, CA; Miami, FL; Minneapolis, MN; Morristown, NJ; New York, NY; Orlando, FL; Pittsburgh, PA; Sacramento, CA; San Francisco, CA; Seattle, WA; Stamford, CT; Vienna, VA; White Plains, NY.

Satellite Offices: 127 Dorrance Street, Providence, Rhode Island 02903. Phone: 401-490-3444. Fax: 401-454-8855.

1225 Market Street, Wheeling, West Virginia 26003. Phone: 304-230-1461. Fax: 304-230-1462.

11 Federal Plaza, Suite 300, Youngstown, OH 44503. Phone: 330-746-2324. Fax: 330-746-7023.

Employment, Labor, Benefits, Immigration Law, and Other Related Litigation, On Behalf of Management Exclusively.

PARTNERS

CATHRYN E. ALBRECHT, born 1958; admitted to bar, 1990, Illinois. *Education:* University of Wisconsin (B.A., 1981); Loyola University (J.D., cum laude, 1990). ***Email:*** albrechc@jacksonlewis.com

ROBERT E. ARROYO, born 1948; admitted to bar, 1974, Illinois; 1987, U.S. Court of Appeals, Sixth and Seventh Circuits; 1990, U.S. Court of Appeals, Tenth and Eleventh Circuits; 1991, U.S. Court of Appeals, Eighth Circuit; 2005, U.S. Supreme Court. *Education:* Southern Illinois University (B.S., 1970); John Marshall Law School (J.D., 1974). *Member:* Hispanic Lawyers Association of Illinois. ***Email:*** arroyor@jacksonlewis.com

JAMES F. BOTANA, born 1963; admitted to bar, 1992, Illinois. *Education:* Chicago State University (B.S., magna cum laude, 1985); DePaul University (J.D., 1992). *Member:* Hispanic Lawyers Association of Illinois (Member, Judiciary Evaluation Section). ***LANGUAGES:*** Spanish. ***Email:*** botanaj@jacksonlewis.com

PETER R. BULMER, born 1959; admitted to bar, 1986, Illinois; 1987, U.S. Court of Appeals, Sixth Circuit; 1989, U.S. Court of Appeals, Seventh Circuit; 1992, U.S. Court of Appeals, Eighth Circuit; 1993, U.S. Supreme Court. *Education:* University of Notre Dame (B.A., 1981); Creighton Law School (J.D., cum laude, 1986). Member, 1984-1986 and Editor-in-Chief, 1985-1986, Creighton Law Review. (Managing Partner, Chicago Office). ***Email:*** bulmerp@jacksonlewis.com

(This Listing Continued)

MICHAEL R. FLAHERTY, born 1946; admitted to bar, 1977, Illinois; 1980, U.S. Court of Appeals, 6th, 7th and 9th Circuits; 1982, U.S. Supreme Court; 1996, New York; 1997, U.S. Court of Appeals, 2nd Circuit; 1999, U.S. Court of Appeals, 8th Circuit. *Education:* University of Notre Dame (A.B., cum laude, 1968); University of Chicago (M.B.A., 1972); University of Michigan (J.D., cum laude, 1976). ***Email:*** flahertm@jacksonlewis.com

JACOBSON & SORKIN, LTD.

77 WEST WASHINGTON STREET, SUITE 1500
CHICAGO, ILLINOIS 60602
Telephone: 312-236-8628
Fax: 312-236-6905
URL: http://www.JacobsonSorkin.com

Personal Injury, Construction Accidents, Workers Compensation, Nursing Home Litigation, Medical Malpractice, Automobile Accidents, Truck Accidents, Dog Bites, Railroad Accidents, Bus Accidents, Sexual Abuse, Slip and Fall, Pedestrian Injuries, Wrongful Death, Products Liability.

MEMBERS OF FIRM

MILTON C. JACOBSON, born 1936; admitted to bar, 1960, Illinois. *Education:* University of Illinois at Navy Pier; DePaul University (J.D., 1960). ***Email:*** Jacobson_Sorkin@yahoo.com

STEVEN W. JACOBSON, admitted to bar, 1989, Illinois. *Education:* University of Iowa (B.A., 1985); John Marshall Law School (J.D. with honors, 1988). ***Email:*** Jacobson_Sorkin@yahoo.com

LYNNE F. SHAPIRO, admitted to bar, 1991, Illinois. *Education:* Indiana University (B.A., 1988); Loyola University (J.D., 1991). ***Email:*** Jacobson_Sorkin@yahoo.com

MARIA J. JAFFE

8 SOUTH MICHIGAN AVENUE, SUITE 3200
CHICAGO, ILLINOIS 60603
Telephone: 312-641-1050
Fax: 312-641-1052
URL: http://www.mariajaffelawfirm.com

Northfield, Illinois Office: 1 Northfield Plaza, Suite 300, 60093. Telephone: 847-441-1814.

Adoption, Child Support, Criminal Law, Custody and Visitation, Debtor/Creditor, Divorce, Family Law, Immigration Law, Landlord/Tenant, Mediation, Medical Malpractice, Motor Vehicle Accidents, Plaintiff Personal Injury, Real Estate.

MARIA J. JAFFE, admitted to bar, 2002, Illinois. *Education:* Loyola University, Chicago (B.S., Nursing, 1978); John Marshall Law School (J.D., 2001). ***PRACTICE AREAS:*** Adoption Law; Child Support; Criminal Law; Child Custody; Visitation Rights; Debtor and Creditor; Divorce; Family Law; Immigration Law; Landlord and Tenant Law; Mediation; Medical Malpractice; Motor Vehicle Accidents and Injuries; Plaintiffs Personal Injury; Real Estate.

RICHARD JAFFE

Established in 1980
100 WEST MONROE STREET, SUITE 714
CHICAGO, ILLINOIS 60603
Telephone: 312-372-1245
Fax: 312-372-1247
Email: RICKYJAFFE@AOL.COM
URL: http://www.lawyers.com/jaffelaw

Business Law, Family Law, Commercial Litigation, Debtor and Creditor, Collections, Commercial Real Estate, Residential Real Estate, Personal Injury, Probate.

RICHARD JAFFE, born Chicago, Illinois, July 1, 1951; admitted to bar, 1976, Illinois, U.S. District Court, Northern District of Illinois. *Education:* University of Wisconsin-Madison (B.A., 1973); Illinois Institute of Technology, Chicago-Kent College of Law (J.D., 1976).

JANICH LAW GROUP

Established in 2001
222 NORTH LASALLE STREET, SUITE 2500
CHICAGO, ILLINOIS 60601
Telephone: 312-609-4528
Fax: 312-609-5005
Email: djanich@janichlawgroup.com
URL: http://www.janichlawgroup.com

Employee Benefits, Executive Compensation, Employee Benefits Litigation, Estate Litigation, Estate Planning and Administration, Business Successorship Planning.

FIRM PROFILE: Janich Law Group concentrates its practice in employee benefits, executive compensation, ERISA and employee benefits litigation, estate planning and administration, and business successorship planning. The firm provides general counsel services to its domestic and multinational corporate clients. In addition to corporations and other business entities, the firm represents business owners, executive and other professionals.

DANIEL N. JANICH, born Chicago, Illinois, August 8, 1952; admitted to bar, 1978, Illinois and U.S. District Court, Northern District of Illinois; 1980, U.S. Court of Appeals, Seventh Circuit; 1986, U.S. Tax Court; 1990, U.S. Supreme Court. *Education:* Marian College (B.A., History, cum laude, 1974); The John Marshall Law School (J.D., 1978); DePaul University (LL.M., in Taxation, 1986). Recipient, Teaching Fellowship, DePaul University College of Law, 1984-1985. Author: "Contingent Workers & Employee Benefits," Chapter of ERISA Litigation, 2003; "Underwater Stock Options and Repricing Strategy: Is Your Company Drowning in Confusion?" 13 The Journal of Employee Ownership Law and Finance 17, Fall 2001; "When Remarriage Muddies the Waters: QDROs and Surviving Spouse Protection," 24 A.B.A. Sec. Pub. Family Advocate 39, Fall 2001; "Recent Changes to the Minimum Distribution Rules for Tax-Qualified Retirement Plans," Profit Sharing, July/August 1998; "Some Health FSAs Are Exempt From HIPAA's Requirements, But Not All," Plan Horizons, Spring 1998. Contributing Author and Associate Senior Editor: Employee Benefits Law, BNA. Co-Author: "A Tiered Approach to Equity Design with Multiple Equity Compensation Vehicles," Chapter of Beyond Stock Options, 2004; "If Not Options, Then What? Equity Compensation in Today's Economy," Workspan, September 2003; "When Is An Activity 'Substantially Related' to a Health Care Institution's Tax-Exempt Purpose?" 20 Journal of Health & Hospital Law 145 and 193, 1987. *Member:* Chicago (Chair, Employee Benefits Committee, 2000-2001; Vice-Chair, 1999-2000; Chair, 401K Proposed Regulation Subcommittee, 2003) and American (Member, Employee Benefits Committee, Labor and Employment Law Section; Co-Chair, Reporting and Disclosure Subcommittee, 2003—) Bar Associations; National Association of Stock Plan Professionals; National Center for Employee Ownership. ***Email:*** djanich@janichlawgroup.com

(This Listing Continued)

JAROS, TITTLE & O'TOOLE, LIMITED

Established in 1916
20 NORTH CLARK STREET, SUITE 510
CHICAGO, ILLINOIS 60602
Telephone: 312-750-1000
Fax: 312-332-6136
Email: info@jtolaw.com
URL: http://www.jtolaw.com

Real Estate, Foreclosure, Probate, Corporate, Savings and Loan Law, Banking and Mortgage Banking. Litigation in State and Federal Courts. Estate Planning, Bankruptcy. Designated Counsel, Federal Home Loan Mortgage Corporation (Freddie Mac).

JOSEPH J. JAROS (1899-1975)

VERNON TITTLE (1906-1981)

JOSEPH J. JAROS, JR., born Chicago, Illinois, November 18, 1937; admitted to bar, 1962, Illinois. *Education:* Georgetown University (A.B., 1959); Northwestern University (J.D., 1962). *Member:* DuPage County and Illinois State Bar Associations. ***PRACTICE AREAS:*** Probate; Estate Planning; Corporate; Savings and Loan; Real Estate.

WILLIAM G. O'TOOLE, born Chicago, Illinois, October 25, 1934; admitted to bar, 1961, Illinois; 1962, U.S. District Court, Northern District of Illinois. *Education:* University of Detroit (B.S., 1956); DePaul University (J.D., 1961). Beta Alpha Psi. Listed in Who's Who in America, 1987—. Member, Lay Board of Trustees, De Paul University College of Law, 1971-1974. *Member:* Chicago, Southwest (President, 1969), Illinois State and American Bar Associations; Illinois Trial Lawyers Association; Illinois Mortgage Bankers Association (Member, Board of Directors, 1987-1991). ***PRACTICE AREAS:*** Banking; Mortgage Banking Law; Savings and Loan Law; Foreclosure; Corporate; Real Estate.

JAMES E. TRAUSCH, born Chicago, Illinois, November 5, 1957; admitted to bar, 1982, Illinois; 1986, U.S. District Court, Northern District of Illinois. *Education:* University of Notre Dame (B.A., 1979); Illinois Institute of Technology/Chicago-Kent College of Law (J.D., 1982). Chairman, Amate House, Young Adult Volunteer Program for Archdiocese of Chicago, 1995—. *Member:* Chicago Bar Association; Illinois Mortgage Bankers Association (Member, Board of Directors, 1992-1996; General Counsel, 1997—). ***PRACTICE AREAS:*** Foreclosure; Litigation; Banking; Mortgage Banking; Real Estate; Probate; Estate Planning. ***Email:*** jet@jtolaw.com

LINDA J. HERBER, born Chicago, Illinois, October 31, 1956; admitted to bar, 1981, Illinois; 1982, U.S. District Court, Northern District of Illinois. *Education:* St. Marys College (B.A., 1978); DePaul University (J.D., 1981).

MONIQUE N. O'TOOLE, born Chicago, Illinois, June 23, 1967; admitted to bar, 1992, Illinois. *Education:* University of Colorado at Boulder (B.A., 1989); John Marshall Law School (J.D., 1992); Loyola Law School (LL.M., Health Law, 1997). Assistant States Attorney, Criminal Division, DuPage County, Illinois, 1992-1995. Assistant Attorney General, Appeals Division and Healcare Bureau, 1995-2003. ***Email:*** motoole@jtolaw.com

REPRESENTATIVE CLIENTS: ABN AMRO Mortgage Corp.; Advance Bank; Advanta Mortgage Corporation; American Home Mortgage; Amcore Mortgage; APEX Mortgage; Atlantic Mortgage; Bank of America; Cendent Mortgage Corp.; Chas Mortgage; Delta Funding Corporation; Dovenmuehle Mortgage Inc.; Draper & Kramer Inc.; Fairbanks Capital Corp.; Fifth Third Bank; First Colonial Mortgage Corporation; First Horizon Home Loan Corp.; Ford Consumer Finance Company; GE Capital Corp.; GN Mortgage; Heartland Bank; Illinois Housing Development (IHDA); LaSalle Home Mortgage Corporation; Mountain States Mortgage Center Inc.; North American Mortgage Corp.; Standard Federal Savings; United Mortgage and Loan Investment Corporation of North Carolina; Washington Mutual; Wells Fargo Mortgage Corp.; Western Mortgage; WMC Mortgage Corporation.
DESIGNATED COUNSEL: Federal Home Loan Mortgage Corp. (Freddie Mac).

JENKENS & GILCHRIST

A PROFESSIONAL CORPORATION
Established in 1951
225 WEST WASHINGTON, SUITE 2600
CHICAGO, ILLINOIS 60606-3418
Telephone: 312-425-3900
Facsimile: 312-425-3909
Email: jenkens@jenkens.com
URL: http://www.jenkens.com

Austin, Texas Office: 401 Congress, Suite 2500. Telephone: 512-499-3800. Facsimile: 512-499-3810.

(This Listing Continued)

JENKENS & GILCHRIST, A PROFESSIONAL CORPORATION, Chicago—Continued

Dallas, Texas, Office: 1445 Ross Avenue, Suite 3700. Telephone: 214-855-4500. TWX: 910-861-4047. Telex: 73-2595. Facsimile: 214-855-4300. International Facsimile: 214-855-4300.
Los Angeles, California Office: Jenkens & Gilchrist, LLP, 12100 Wilshire Boulevard, 15th Floor. Telephone: 310-820-8800. Facsimile: 310-820-8859.
Houston, Texas Office: 1401 McKinney, Suite 2700. Telephone: 713-951-3300. Facsimile: 713-951-3314.
Washington, D.C. Office: 901 15th Street N.W. Telephone: 202-326-1500. Facsimile: 202-326-1555.
San Antonio, Texas Office: 112 East Pecan Street, Suite 900. Telephone: 210-246-5000. Facsimile: 210-246-5999.
Pasadena, California Office: Jenkins & Gilchrist, 55 South Lake Avenue, Suite 650. Telephone: 626-578-7400. Fax: 626-304-9711.

General Practice including Corporate and Securities Law, Estates and Trusts, Bankruptcy, Administrative Law, Antitrust, Aviation, Commercial Lending, Communications, Computer Law, Construction Law, Employee Benefits (ERISA), Energy, Environmental Law, Federal Practice, Financial Institutions, Finance, Franchise and Distribution Law, Governmental Affairs, Health Law, Hospitality (REIT), Immigration, Intellectual Property (Prosecution, Litigation and Transactional), International Law, Internet Law, Labor and Employment Law, Land Use, Litigation (Commercial, Tax and Fiduciary), Mergers and Acquisitions, Product Liability, Real Estate Services, Securities, Tax, Toxic Tort, Trade Regulation, Transportation, Venture Capital.

FIRM PROFILE: Jenkens & Gilchrist was founded in 1951 in Dallas, Texas. With nine strategic bases from which to operate - New York City and Washington, D.C. in the eastern United States, Chicago in the central, Austin, Dallas, Houston and San Antonio in the south, and Los Angeles and Pasadena on the west coast - the Jenkens team is able to provide clients with a unique combination of national resources with personalized service. Our goal is to act as a business partner with our clients, combining legal experience, business acumen, and the practiced art of listening, in order to identify challenges, seize opportunities, and deliver solutions.

Jenkens & Gilchrist provides legal counsel in more than twenty-five areas of practice to industries and business leaders around the world. The depth of experience and diversity of a national firm provides a stability that gives confidence, even in the midst of environments characterized by high-consequence change.

SHAREHOLDERS

DANIEL J. BURNHAM, born Belleville, Illinois, February 9, 1967; admitted to bar, 1995, Illinois; registered to practice before U.S. Patent and Trademark Office. *Education:* University of Illinois (B.S.M.E., with honors, 1989); Saint Louis University (J.D., cum laude, 1995). *Member:* Illinois State and Federal Circuit Bar Associations. ***PRACTICE AREAS:*** Intellectual Property. ***Email:*** dburnham@jenkens.com

JANET M. GARETTO, born Chicago, Illinois, June 16, 1972; admitted to bar, 1997, Illinois; registered to practice before U.S. Patent and Trademark Office. *Education:* Northwestern University (B.A., Chemistry, 1994); Loyola University (J.D., cum laude, 1997). *Member:* Chicago and American Bar Associations; Federal Circuit Bar Association (Member, Board of Managers); American Intellectual Property Law Association; Intellectual Property Law Association of Chicago. ***PRACTICE AREAS:*** Intellectual Property. ***Email:*** jgaretto@jenkens.com

JOHN C. GATZ, born Royal Oak, Michigan, July 31, 1968; admitted to bar, 1996, Illinois; registered to practice before U.S. Patent and Trademark Office. *Education:* Michigan Technological University (B.S.C.M., cum laude, 1990); University of Illinois (J.D., magna cum laude, 1996). *Member:* American Bar Association; American Intellectual Property Law Association; Intellectual Property Law Association of Chicago. ***PRACTICE AREAS:*** Intellectual Property. ***Email:*** jgatz@jenkens.com

DONNA ZAK GUERIN, born Chicago, Illinois, September 3, 1960; admitted to bar, 1984, Illinois, U.S. Tax Court, U.S. District Court, Northern District of Illinois and U.S. Court of Appeals, Seventh Circuit. *Education:* DePaul University (B.S.C., with high honors, 1981; J.D., with honors, 1984); Chicago-Kent College of Law, Illinois Institute of Technology (LL.M., Taxation, 1994). Certified Public Accountant, Illinois. *Member:* Chicago, Illinois State and American Bar Associations; National Association of Bond Lawyers. ***PRACTICE AREAS:*** Taxation; Municipal Finance. ***Email:*** dguerin@jenkens.com

KEITH C. HANNIGAN, born New York, N.Y., December 7, 1965; admitted to bar, 1991, Illinois. *Education:* University of Chicago (B.A., with honors, 1987); Stanford University (J.D., 1991). *Member:* Chicago and American Bar Associations. ***PRACTICE AREAS:*** Complex Commercial Litigation; Construction Litigation; International Arbitration. ***Email:*** khannigan@jenkens.com

PAUL R. KITCH, born Southfield, Michigan, April 1, 1966; admitted to bar, 1993, Illinois; registered to practice before U.S. Patent and Trademark Office. *Education:* University of Michigan (B.S.E.E., summa cum laude, 1989; J.D., 1993). *Member:* Chicago and American Bar Associations; American Intellectual Property Law Association; Intellectual Property Law Association of Chicago. ***PRACTICE AREAS:*** Intellectual Property. ***Email:*** pkitch@jenkens.com

CHARLES B. LEWIS, born Neenah, Wisconsin, 1950; admitted to bar, 1976, Illinois, U.S. District Court, Northern District of Illinois including Trial Bar and U.S. Court of Appeals, Seventh Circuit. *Education:* University of Michigan (B.A., 1972); University of San Francisco (J.D., 1976). Former President, Trial Lawyers Club of Chicago.*Member:* Chicago, Illinois State and American (Member, Construction Industry Forum) Bar Associations; American Arbitration Association; Society of Illinois Construction Attorneys; Illinois Road and Transportation Builders Association, Design/Build Task Force; Chicago Building Congress. ***PRACTICE AREAS:*** Construction Law; Litigation; Major Projects; Energy Law; Natural Resources Law; Real Estate Development Law. ***Email:*** clewis@jenkens.com

(This Listing Continued)

EDWARD F. McCORMACK, born Detroit, Michigan, July 19, 1962; admitted to bar, 1989, Illinois and U.S. District Court, Northern District of Illinois including Trial Bar; 1991, District of Columbia; 1992, U.S. District Court for the District of Columbia. *Education:* University of Michigan (B.A., with honors, 1984); University of Virginia (J.D., 1989). Evans Scholar. Editor, Virginia Journal of International Law. *Member:* Chicago, Illinois State and American (Member, Litigation Section) Bar Associations. ***PRACTICE AREAS:*** Civil Litigation; Products Liability Defense; Environmental Litigation; Intellectual Property. ***Email:*** emccormack@jenkens.com

MARGO WOLF O'DONNELL, born Kansas City, Missouri, May 19, 1968; admitted to bar, 1994, Illinois. *Education:* Yale University (B.A., magna cum laude, 1990); University of Michigan (J.D., 1994). *Member:* Chicago and American Bar Associations. ***PRACTICE AREAS:*** Litigation. ***Email:*** modonnell@jenkens.com

STEPHEN G. RUDISILL, admitted to bar, 1964, Illinois; 1987, Texas and U.S. Court of Appeals for the Federal Circuit; registered to practice before U.S. Patent and Trademark Office. *Education:* Duke University (B.S.E.E., with distinction, 1959); New York University (J.D., cum laude, 1963). Order of the Coif. *Member:* Chicago, Illinois State and American Bar Associations; State Bar of Texas; Federal Trial Bar, Northern District of Illinois; Seventh Circuit Bar Association; Federal Circuit Bar Association; Patent Law Association of Chicago; American Intellectual Property Law Association. ***PRACTICE AREAS:*** Intellectual Property. ***Email:*** srudisill@jenkens.com

JODI ROSEN WINE, born Cleveland, Ohio, August 18, 1960; admitted to bar, 1992, Illinois. *Education:* University of Colorado at Boulder (B.S., 1984); University of Chicago (J.D., 1992). *Member:* American Bar Association (Member, Litigation Section). ***PRACTICE AREAS:*** Commercial Litigation. ***Email:*** jwine@jenkens.com

OF COUNSEL

PAUL M. DAUGERDAS, born Chicago, Illinois, September 25, 1950; admitted to bar, 1974, Illinois; 1975, U.S. Tax Court, U.S. District Court, Northern District of Illinois and U.S. Court of Appeals, Seventh Circuit. *Education:* DePaul University College of Commerce (B.S., with honors, 1972); DePaul University School of Law (J.D., cum laude, 1974). *Member:* Chicago, Illinois State and American Bar Associations; Illinois CPA Society; American Institute of CPA's; Association for Corporate Growth; Equipment Leasing Association; Futures Industry Association; International Fiscal Association. ***PRACTICE AREAS:*** Taxation; Corporate Finance; Mergers and Acquisitions. ***Email:*** pdaugerdas@jenkens.com

ERWIN MAYER, born Chicago, Illinois, September 9, 1963; admitted to bar, 1987, Illinois. *Education:* University of Illinois (B.S., 1984); Loyola University (J.D., 1987). *Member:* Chicago, Illinois State and American Bar Associations. ***PRACTICE AREAS:*** Tax. ***Email:*** emayer@jenkens.com

HAROLD N. WELLS, born Bridgeton, New Jersey, May 25, 1930; admitted to bar, 1974, New Jersey; 1984, U.S. Court of Appeals for the Federal Circuit; registered to practice before U.S. Patent and Trademark Office (Not admitted in Illinois). *Education:* Lehigh University (B.S.Ch.E., 1951); Massachusetts Institute of Technology (M.S.Ch.E., 1954); Seton Hall University (J.D., 1974). ***PRACTICE AREAS:*** Intellectual Property. ***Email:*** hwells@jenkens.com

COUNSEL

JOHN P. LUTHER, born 1953; admitted to bar, 1985, Oklahoma; 1986, U.S. Court of Appeals, Federal Circuit; 1992, U.S. Court of International Trade and U.S. Court for Federal Claims; 2004, Washington and U.S. Supreme Court; registered to practice before U.S. Patent and Trademark Office (Not admitted in Illinois). *Education:* University of Massachusetts (B.S., Chemistry, 1977; M.S., Molecular Biochemistry, 1981); University of Oklahoma (J.D., 1985). Phi Delta Phi. Member, University of Oklahoma Law Review, 1984-1985. *Member:* Washington State, Oklahoma and International Bar Associations; American Intellectual Property Law Association; Association of Trial Lawyers of America; American Indian Bar Association. ***REPORTED CASES:*** Xechem v. University of Texas; M.D. Anderson Cancer Center and Dorr-Oliver v. Fluid Quip. ***PRACTICE AREAS:*** Intellectual Property. ***Email:*** jluther@jenkens.com

ASSOCIATES

MARK ANDERSON, born St. Charles, Illinois, April 1, 1977; admitted to bar, 2003, Illinois. *Education:* University of Illinois at Urbana-Champaign (B.S., Mechanical Engineering, with honors, 1999); University of Illinois College of Law (J.D., magna cum laude, 2003). ***PRACTICE AREAS:*** Intellectual Property. ***Email:*** manderson@jenkens.com

SORINEL CIMPOES, born Romania, January 22, 1970; admitted to bar, 2001, Illinois and U.S. District Court, Northern District of Illinois; registered to practice before U.S. Patent and Trademark Office. *Education:* Illinois Institute of Technology (B.S., 1991); Chicago-Kent College of Law, Illinois Institute of Technology (J.D., 2001). Member, Moot Court. *Member:* Chicago Bar Association. ***PRACTICE AREAS:*** Intellectual Property. ***Email:*** scimpoes@jenkens.com

NICHOLAS M. DUDZIAK, born Chicago, Illinois, 1979; (admission pending). *Education:* University of Illinois-Chicago (B.S.M.E., 2001); John Marshall Law School (J.D., cum laude, 2005). ***LANGUAGES:*** Ukrainian. ***PRACTICE AREAS:*** Intellectual Property. ***Email:*** ndudziak@jenkens.com

RUSSELL J. GENET, born Barberton, Ohio, November 15, 1971; admitted to bar, 1998, Illinois; registered to practice before U.S. Patent and Trademark Office. *Education:* Purdue University (B.S.E.E., 1995); Chicago-Kent College of Law, Illinois Institute of Technology (J.D., 1998). ***PRACTICE AREAS:*** Intellectual Property. ***Email:*** regenet@jenkens.com

JEFFREY L. HAMERA, born Berwyn, Illinois, October 20, 1964; admitted to bar, 1994, Illinois; 1997, U.S. Court of Appeals, Fourth Circuit. *Education:* University of Illinois (B.S., 1986; M.S., 1987); Northwestern University (J.D., cum laude, 1994). *Member:* Chicago and American (Member, Construction Industry Forum) Bar Associations; National Society of Professional Engineers. ***PRACTICE AREAS:*** Construction Law. ***Email:*** jhamera@jenkens.com

(This Listing Continued)

CRISTINA T. HAWILO, born Grosse Pointe Shores, Michigan; admitted to bar, 2004, Illinois. *Education:* University of Michigan (B.A., Economics, 2001); University of Michigan Law School (J.D., 2003). Recipient: Regents Alumni Scholarship; Scholarship Recognition Award. ***LANGUAGES:*** Spanish and Arabic. ***PRACTICE AREAS:*** Litigation. ***Email:*** chawilo@jenkens.com

NICK KAHLON, born Shelby, Ohio, September 1, 1975; admitted to bar, 2000, Texas; 2003, Illinois. *Education:* University of Delaware (B.Sc., 1997); University of Texas (J.D., 2000). *Member:* State Bar of Texas. ***PRACTICE AREAS:*** Intellectual Property. ***Email:*** nkahlon@jenkens.com

JEREMIE D. MOLL, born Freeport, Illinois, January 2, 1978; admitted to bar, 2003, Illinois. *Education:* Illinois Wesleyan University (B.A., Chemistry/Physics, 2000); The John Marshall Law School (J.D., cum laude, 2003). Member, The Order of John Marshall. Managing Editor, The John Marshall Review of Intellectual Property Law, 2003. Co-Author: "Willfulness Trends of the Federal Circuit and Recommendations to Avoid Willful Infringement," 14 Intellectual Property & Technology Law Journal, No. 11, at 7-15 (2002). ***PRACTICE AREAS:*** Intellectual Property. ***Email:*** jmoll@jenkens.com

WILLIAM D. PEGG, born July 25, 1967; admitted to bar, 1998, Maryland; 2001, District of Columbia; 2005, Illinois; registered to practice before U.S. Patent and Trademark Office. *Education:* Rutgers University (B.S.M.E., 1990); Chicago-Kent College of Law, Illinois Institute of Technology (J.D., 1998). Senior Associate, Chicago-Kent Law Review, 1996-1998. *Member:* Maryland State Bar Association; American Intellectual Property Law Association. ***Email:*** wpegg@jenkens.com

AMY L. SIEROCKI, admitted to bar, 2003, Illinois; registered to practice before U.S. Patent and Trademark Office. *Education:* University of Michigan (B.S., Chemistry, 1990); Illinois Institute of Technology (Ph.D., Environmental Engineering, 2000); Loyola University, Chicago (J.D., 2003). *Member:* Federal Circuit Bar Association. ***PRACTICE AREAS:*** Intellectual Property. ***Email:*** asierocki@jenkens.com

JUSTIN D. SWINDELLS, born South Korea, 1973; admitted to bar, 1998, Illinois; registered to practice before the U.S. Patent and Trademark Office. *Education:* Rensselaer Polytechnic Institute (B.S.E.E., summa cum laude, 1995); Chicago-Kent College of Law (J.D., 1998). Judicial Extern, Honorable Rebecca Pallmeyer. Law Clerk, Honorable Martin C. Ashman, U.S. Magistrate Judge, Northern District of Illinois. Author: "Make Money by Exposing Secrets," Illinois Technology, August/September 2002. *Member:* Chicago and Illinois State Bar Associations; Illinois Patent Law Association of Chicago. ***PRACTICE AREAS:*** Intellectual Property. ***Email:*** jswindells@jenkens.com

CYNTHIA THOMPSON, born Oak Lawn, Illinois, March 12, 1974; admitted to bar, 2000, Illinois. *Education:* Valparaiso University (B.S., 1996); Northwestern University (J.D., 2000). *Member:* Chicago and American Bar Associations; Intellectual Property Law Association of Chicago; American Intellectual Property Law Association. ***PRACTICE AREAS:*** Intellectual Property. ***Email:*** cthompson@jenkens.com

ELIZABETH WISZOWATY, born Chicago, Illinois; admitted to bar, 2004, Illinois. *Education:* University of Notre Dame (B.S., Chemical Engineering, 2001); Loyola University, Chicago School of Law (J.D., 2004). ***LANGUAGES:*** Polish. ***PRACTICE AREAS:*** Intellectual Property. ***Email:*** ewiszowaty@jenkens.com

(For biographical data on other personnel, See Professional Biographies at Austin, Dallas, San Antonio and Houston, Texas, Washington, D.C. and Los Angeles, California)

JENNER & BLOCK LLP

A Partnership including Professional Corporations

ONE IBM PLAZA

CHICAGO, ILLINOIS 60611

Telephone: 312-222-9350
FAX: 312-527-0484
Telex: 270469
TWX: 9102215409
Cable Address: "Jenblock"
URL: http://www.jenner.com

Washington, D.C. Office: 601 Thirteenth Street, N.W., Twelfth Floor. Telephone: 202-639-6000. FAX: 202-639-6066. Cable Address: "Jenblock."

Dallas, Texas Office: 1717 Main Street, Suite 3150. Telephone: 214-746-5700. FAX: 214-746-5757.

New York, N.Y. Office: 919 Third Avenue.

Administrative Law; Advertising and Marketing; Agency and Distributorships; Alternative Dispute Resolution; Antitrust and Trade Regulation; Appellate Practice; Aviation and Aerospace; Bankruptcy; Banks and Banking; Biotechnology; Business Law; Chancery and Equity; Civil Practice; Class Action; Commercial Law; Commercial Real Estate; Commodities; Communications and Media; Complex and Multi District Litigation; Computers and Software; Constitutional Law; Construction Law; Consumer Law; Contracts; Copyrights; Corporate Law; Debtor and Creditor; Disabilities; Employee Benefits; Energy; Environmental Law; Family Law; Finance; Franchises and Franchising; Government; Government Contracts; Health Care; Hospital Law; Intellectual Property; International Law; Labor and Employment; Libel, Slander and Defamation; Litigation; Mergers, Acquisitions and Divestitures; Occupational Safety and Health; Partnership Law; Patents; Privacy Law; Probate; Products Liability; Professional Liability; Real Estate; Regulatory Law; RICO; Securities; Taxation; Technology and Science; Torts; Toxic Torts; Trade and Professional Associations; Trade Secrets; Trademarks; Trusts and Estates; Unfair Competition; Utility Law; Wills.

CHAIRMAN OF THE FIRM

JEROLD S. SOLOVY, born Chicago, Illinois, April 10, 1930; admitted to bar, 1955, Illinois and District of Columbia. *Education:* University of Michigan (B.A., with honors and distinction, 1952); Harvard Law School (LL.B., cum laude, 1955). Phi Beta Kappa; Phi Kappa Phi; Pi Sigma Alpha; Phi Eta Sigma. Member, Board of Editors, Harvard Law Review, 1953-1955. Member, Harvard Law School Visiting Committee, 1986-1992. Member, Harvard Committee on University Resources, 1993-1998. Member, Editorial Board, Moore's Federal Practice. Author: Moore's Federal Practice, Chapter 11, Sanctions and Chapter 23, Class Actions. Chair, Illinois Supreme Court Special Commission on the Administration of Justice, 1992-1993. Chair, Special Commission on the Administration of Justice in Cook County, 1984-1991. Chair, Criminal Justice Project of Cook County, 1987-1991. Chair, Cook County Criminal Justice Coordinating Council, 1989-1991. Member: Board of Trustees, U.S. Supreme Court Historical Society, 1993—; American Judicature Society's Center for Judicial Independence, 1997—; Board of Directors, National Equal Justice Library, 1998—. Member, Third Circuit Rule 11 Task Force, 1987-1988. Member: Illinois Supreme Court Committee on Jury Instructions in Criminal Cases, 1961-1968, 1975-1977; Cook County Judicial Advisory Council, 1975-1977, 1982-1989, Chair, 1989-1991. *Member:* Chicago (Chair, Defense of Indigent Prisoners Committee, 1963-1964; Chair, Special Committee on Volunteer Defender Services, 1968-1971; Co-Chair, Commission on Administration of Criminal Justice in Cook County, 1971-1975; Chair, Continuing Commission on Administration of Criminal Justice in Cook County, 1975-1976), Illinois State and American (Chair, Litigation Section Discovery Committee, 1982-1985; Chair, Litigation Section Trial Practice Committee, 1985-1988; Co-Chair, Federal Procedure Committee, 1988-1989; Member: Task Force on Lawyers Ancillary Business Activities, 1989-1991; Special Review Committee on Federal Civil Rules, 1989-1992; Liaison to the ABA Post Conviction Death Penalty Representation Project, 1990-1994) Bar Associations; American Law Institute. American College of Trial Lawyers. ***PRACTICE AREAS:*** Civil and Appellate Litigation; Securities Litigation; Intellectual Property; Complex Litigation; Class Actions; Insurance Litigation. ***Email:*** jsolovy@jenner.com

PARTNERS

CATHERINE ABBOTT, born Bryan, Texas, June 30, 1969; admitted to bar, 1996, Illinois; 2003, District of Columbia. *Education:* Duke University (B.A., 1991); Washington University (J.D., 1996). Order of the Coif. Associate Editor, Washington University Law Quarterly. (Resident, Washington, D.C. Office). ***PRACTICE AREAS:*** Corporate; Defense and Aerospace; Mergers and Acquisitions; Securities; Corporate Law. ***Email:*** cabbott@jenner.com

AARON A. BARLOW, born Englewood, New Jersey, December 19, 1963; admitted to bar, 1989, Illinois, U.S. District Court, Northern District of Illinois and U.S. Court of Appeals, Federal Circuit; registered to practice before U.S. Patent and Trademark Office. *Education:* Massachusetts Institute of Technology (B.S. Ch.E., 1986); University of Chicago (J.D., 1989). *Member:* American Intellectual Property Law Association; Federal Circuit Bar Association. ***PRACTICE AREAS:*** Patent Litigation. ***Email:*** abarlow@jenner.com

TIMOTHY J. BARRON, born Berwyn, Illinois, December 11, 1962; admitted to bar, 1990, California; 1992, Illinois; U.S. District Court, Northern District of Illinois including Trial Bar; U.S. District Court, Northern, Central and Eastern Districts of California; U.S. Court of Appeals, Seventh and Ninth Circuits; registered to practice before U.S. Patent and Trademark Office, 1995. *Education:* Iowa State University (B.S.M.E., 1985); Santa Clara University (J.D., 1990). Technical Editor, Santa Clara Law Review. ***PRACTICE AREAS:*** Patent Litigation. ***Email:*** tbarron@jenner.com

MATT D. BASIL, born Monterey, California, March 11, 1973; admitted to bar, 1997, Illinois and U.S. District Court, Northern District of Illinois. *Education:* University of Illinois (B.S., with high honors, 1994); Loyola University School of Law (J.D., cum laude, 1997). Law Clerk to the Honorable Charles P. Kocoras, U.S. District Court, Northern District of Illinois, 1998-1999. ***PRACTICE AREAS:*** Litigation. ***Email:*** mbasil@jenner.com

DONALD E. BATTERSON, born Minneapolis, Minnesota, October 26, 1966; admitted to bar, 1994, Illinois. *Education:* Northern Illinois University (B.S., summa cum laude, 1989); Emory University School of Law (J.D., with distinction, 1993). Author: "A Trend Ephemeral, Eternal, Neither?: A Durational Look at the New Judicial Federalism," 42 Emory Law Journal 209, 1993. ***PRACTICE AREAS:*** General Corporate; Securities; Mergers and Acquisitions. ***Email:*** dbatterson@jenner.com

DAVID R. BENNETT, born Washington, D.C., September 20, 1971; admitted to bar, 1997, Illinois; 1998, U.S. District Court, Northern District of Illinois; U.S. Court of Appeals for the Federal Circuit; registered to practice before U.S. Patent and Trademark Office, 1999. *Education:* Virginia Polytechnic Institute and State University (B.S.M.E., cum laude, 1993); College of William & Mary School of Law (J.D., 1997). Student Note Editor, William & Mary Environmental Law and Policy Review. ***PRACTICE AREAS:*** Patent Litigation (95%); Trademark Prosecution (5%). ***Email:*** dbennett@jenner.com

DEBBIE L. BERMAN, born Springfield, Illinois, January 31, 1966; admitted to bar, 1990, Illinois and U.S. District Court, Northern District of Illinois, 1995, Trial Bar; 1992, U.S. Court of Appeals, Seventh Circuit; 1996, U.S. Tax Court; 2000, U.S. Court of Federal Claims. *Education:* Brandeis University (A.B., summa cum laude, with high honors in Economics, 1987); Harvard University (J.D., cum laude, 1990). Phi Beta Kappa. Author: "Social Desirability of Safety-Related Research Joint Ventures: Effect of Tort Liability on the Social Welfare Calculation," Loyola Consumer Law Reporter (Vol. 4, No. 1 Fall 1991). *Member:* Chicago, Illinois State and American Bar Associations; American Intellectual Property Law Association; Intellectual Property Law Association of Chicago. (Cross-reference with Debbie L. Moeckler). ***REPORTED CASES:*** Tutman v. CBS, 54F Supp. 2d 817 (Northern District of Illinois 1999); Tutman v. CBS, 209F 3d 1044 (7th Circuit 2000). ***PRACTICE AREAS:*** Complex Litigation; Trade Secrets and Unfair Competition; Media and First Amendment; Intellectual Property. ***Email:*** dberman@jenner.com

JOSEPH G. BISCEGLIA, born Chicago, Illinois, March 12, 1949; admitted to bar, 1973, Illinois; 1977, U.S. Court of Appeals, Ninth Circuit; 1979, U.S. Supreme Court; 1983, U.S. Court of Appeals, Second Circuit; 1984, U.S. Court of Appeals, Seventh Circuit; U.S. District Court, Northern District of Illinois, Trial Bar. *Education:* University of Illinois at Chicago (B.A., with honors, 1970); DePaul University (J.D., summa cum laude, 1973). Phi Eta Sigma; Phi Kappa Phi; Pi Gamma Mu. Edmund J. James Scholar, 1966-1970. Notes and Comments Editor, DePaul Law Review, 1972-1973. Author: Case Note, "Electronic Surveillance and the Supreme Court: A Move Back?" 21 DePaul Law Review 806, 1972; Comment, "Blockbusting—Judicial and Legislative Response to Real Estate Dealers' Excesses," 22 DePaul Law Review 818, 1973. Co-Author and Faculty Member: "Illinois Construction Claims," Lorman Education Services, 2001-2003; "Construction Claims Under Illinois Law," The Cambridge Institute, 1990-1991. Co-Author: "A Review of the Illinois Civil Justice Reform Act of 1995," 83 Ill. Bar Journal 282, June 1995. Author: "Summary of Recent Amendments to Federal Rules of Civil Procedure," Trial Briefs, Vol. 39, No. 2,

(This Listing Continued)

JENNER & BLOCK LLP, Chicago—Continued

Feb. 1994. Co-Author: "The Illinois Supreme Court's New Discovery Rules," Trial Briefs, Vol. 41, No. 2, Oct. 1995. Judicial Law Clerk to Justice Henry L. Burman, Illinois Appellate Court, First District, 1973-1975. Adjunct Professor of Law, The John Marshall Law School, Appellate Advocacy, 1974-1977 and Trial Advocacy, 1985—. Frequent Lecturer, "Developments in Civil Practice & Procedure," Ill. Bar Assn. 1989—. *Member:* Chicago, Illinois State (Third Vice President, 2004-2005; Member, Board of Governors, 2002—; Assembly Delegate, 1988-1994, 1995—; Chair, Assembly Committee on Hearings, 1989-1990; Member, Assembly Committee on Finance, 1995-1996; Chair, Assembly Committee on Agenda and Program, 1998—; Secretary, 1989-1990, Vice Chair, 1990-1991, Chair, 1991-1992, Civil Practice and Procedure Section Council; Editor and Frequent Contributor, "Trial Briefs" Newsletter, 1991—; Allerton House Conference Committee Member: "Appellate Courts," 1990, "Access To Civil Justice," 1992; "Expert Witnesses," 1994; Member, Committee on Supreme Court Rules, 1990—, Co-Chair, 1991-1993; Secretary, 1995-1996; Member, Special Committee on Certification of Attorney Specialization, 1992-1993, 1996-1997; Member, Task Force on Minorities and the Justice System, 1993-1998; Chair, Task Force on Governance for the Next Century, 1995-1997; Member, Committee on Judicial Evaluations, 1997—; Recipient, 1997 Board of Governors Award), American and Federal (Member, Board of Directors, Chicago Chapter, 1997—) Bar Associations; Justinian Society of Lawyers (Secretary, 1987-1988; Treasurer, 1988-1989; Third Vice President, 1989-1990; Second Vice President, 1990-1991, First Vice President, 1991-1992, President, 1992-1993). ***PRACTICE AREAS:*** Litigation; Construction Law. ***Email:*** jbisceglia@jenner.com

SAMUEL W. BLOCK (1911-1970)

BRIAN R. BOCH, born Evanston, Illinois, November 2, 1970; admitted to bar, 1995, Illinois. *Education:* University of Illinois (A.B., summa cum laude, 1992); Northwestern University (J.D., cum laude, 1995). Phi Beta Kappa. Order of the Coif. Recipient, University Honors (Bronze Tablet), University of Illinois. Note and Comment Editor, Journal of Criminal Law & Criminology. ***PRACTICE AREAS:*** Mergers and Acquisitions; Securities; Corporate. ***Email:*** bboch@jenner.com

GEORGE S. BOSY, born Chicago, Illinois, October 13, 1952; admitted to bar, 1977, Illinois, U.S. District Court, Northern District of Illinois including Trial Bar, U.S. Court of Appeals, Third, Seventh and Federal Circuits and U.S. Supreme Court; registered to practice before U.S. Patent and Trademark Office. *Education:* University of Illinois (B.S., Chemical Engineering, 1974); Northwestern University (J.D., 1977). *Member:* Chicago, Illinois State and American Bar Associations. ***PRACTICE AREAS:*** Patent Litigation; Trial Practice; Appellate Practice; Patent Licensing Law; Antitrust; Unfair Competition. ***Email:*** gbosy@jenner.com

GREGORY M. BOYLE, born Chicago, Illinois, June 9, 1971; admitted to bar, 1997, Illinois and U.S. District Court, Northern District of Illinois. *Education:* Carleton College (B.A., magna cum laude, 1993); Harvard University (J.D., cum laude, 1997). Phi Beta Kappa. *Member:* Illinois State and American Bar Associations; Chicago Council of Lawyers. ***PRACTICE AREAS:*** Litigation; Professional Liability Litigation; Construction Law; White Collar Criminal Defense. ***Email:*** gboyle@jenner.com

DAVID J. BRADFORD, born Chicago, Illinois, September 19, 1952; admitted to bar, 1976, Illinois; 1979, U.S. District Court, Northern District of Illinois and U.S. Court of Appeals, Seventh Circuit; 1985, U.S. Supreme Court. *Education:* Michigan State University (B.A., with highest honors, 1973); University of Chicago (J.D., cum laude, 1976). Phi Kappa Phi; Order of the Coif. Author: "Recent Developments in the Battle for D&O Coverage in the Wake of Bankruptcy," Insurance Coverage Law Bulletin, April 2002; "Corporate Litigation: An Inside-Out Economic Perspective," Corporate Legal Times, August, 1994; "Judge Rubin: A Legacy Unaccomplished," 52 Louisiana Law Review 1441, 1992. Lecturer, University of Chicago Law School, 1993-1995. ***SPECIAL AGENCIES:*** General Counsel and Director, MacArthur Justice Center and J. Roderick MacArthur Foundation, 1985—. ***REPORTED CASES:*** Gaines vs. Theriet, 665 F. Supp. 1342; Gaines vs. Theriet, 846 F. 2d 402; Bradford Exchange A.G. vs. Dept. of Revenue, 508 N.E. 2d 316; First Pacific Bank vs. Nation of Islam, 463 N.E. 2d 732. ***PRACTICE AREAS:*** Appellate and Supreme Court Practice; Domestic and International Arbitration; Corporate Bankruptcy Restructuring; Class Action Litigation; Insurance Litigation and Counseling; Litigation Practice; Media and First Amendment Practice; Professional Liability Litigation; Securities Litigation; Complex Litigation; Bankruptcy Litigation; Financial Transaction Litigation; Constitutional Law; Real Estate Litigation; Class Actions. ***Email:*** djbradford@jenner.com

TRACI M. BRAUN, born Madison, Wisconsin, October 16, 1970; admitted to bar, 1998, Wisconsin, Illinois and U.S. District Court, Northern District of Illinois. *Education:* University of Wisconsin, Madison (B.A., 1992); University of Wisconsin Law School (J.D., 1997). ***PRACTICE AREAS:*** Litigation; Product Liability and Mass Tort Defense; Insurance Litigation and Counseling. ***Email:*** tbraun@jenner.com

PETER J. BRENNAN, born Chicago, Illinois, December 1, 1959; admitted to bar, 1985, Illinois; 1987, New York. *Education:* Georgetown University (B.A., 1982); Georgetown University Law Center (J.D., 1985). *Member:* Chicago and American Bar Associations. ***PRACTICE AREAS:*** Litigation. ***Email:*** pbrennan@jenner.com

MICHAEL T. BRODY, born Milwaukee, Wisconsin, August 9, 1958; admitted to bar, 1983, Illinois; 1984, U.S. District Court, Northern District of Illinois. *Education:* University of Wisconsin-Madison (B.S., 1980); University of Chicago (J.D., cum laude, 1983). Order of the Coif. Comment Editor, University of Chicago Law Review, 1982-1983. Author: Comment, "Inflation, Productivity and the Total Offset Method of Calculating Damages for Lost Future Earnings," 49 University of Chicago Law Review, 1003, 1983. Co-Author: "Ketchum v. Bryne: the Hard Lessons of Discriminatory Redistricting in Chicago," 64 Chicago-Kent Law Review 497, 1988. Law Clerk, Judge Antonin Scalia, U.S. Court of Appeals for the District of Columbia Circuit, 1983-1984. *Member:* American Bar Association; Chicago Council of Lawyers; Seventh Circuit Bar Association. ***PRACTICE AREAS:*** Litigation; Appellate and Supreme Court Practice; Class Action Litigation; Insurance Litigation and Counseling; Securities Litigation; Media and First Amendment. ***Email:*** mbrody@jenner.com

(This Listing Continued)

PATRICIA A. BRONTE, born New Orleans, Louisiana, March 29, 1957; admitted to bar, 1988, Illinois, U.S. District Court, Northern and Central Districts of Illinois, Trial Bar, 1993 and U.S. Court of Appeals, Seventh Circuit. *Education:* University of Southern Mississippi (B.M., with honors, 1978); West Virginia University (M.M., with honors, 1980); Northwestern University (J.D., cum laude, 1987). Co-author, "Inheriting Insurance Coverage for Successor Liabilities," Mealey's Litigation Report: Insurance, January 25, 2005; "'Pay First' Provisions and the Insolvent Policyholder," Law Journal Newsletters: The Insurance Coverage Law Bulletin, Vol. 3, No. 5, June 2004; "Coverage Issues for the Insolvent Policyholder," Coverage, March/April 2004; Co-author, "American College of Trial Lawyers' Report on Military Commissinos for the Terrorist," March 2003. *Member:* American Bar Association; Chicago Council of Lawyers. ***PRACTICE AREAS:*** Litigation; Insurance Litigation and Counseling; Bankruptcy Litigation.

JERRY J. BURGDOERFER, born Jeffersonville, Indiana, May 3, 1958; admitted to bar, 1984, Illinois; U.S. District Court, Northern District of Illinois; U.S. Tax Court. *Education:* Indiana University (B.S., 1980; M.B.A., 1983; J.D., cum laude, 1983). Phi Eta Sigma; Phi Delta Phi. Program Faculty Member: Northwestern University Annual Ray Garrett, Jr. Corporate and Securities Law Institute, April 10-11, 2003 (Panel Chair); SEC Issues Update 2002, Glasser LegalWorks Seminar, April 30, 2002; Northwestern University Annual Ray Garrett, Jr. Corporate and Securities Law Institute, April 11-12, 2002; Negotiating and Drafting Major Business Agreements, Insight Information Seminar, December 5-7, 2001; Mergers and Acquisitions Institute, University of Chicago, October 29-30, 2001; Securities Law Seminar, Chicago Bar Association, May 22, 2001; SEC Issues Update 2001, Glasser LegalWorks Seminar, May 1, 2001; Buying and Selling Businesses - Negotiating, Structuring & Closing the Deal, Illinois Institute for Continuing Legal Education, March 16, 2001; Mergers & Acquisitions Institute, Fulcrum Seminars, June 22, 2000; SEC Issues Update 2000, Glasser LegalWorks Seminar, May 11, 2000; Conducting Due Diligence, Practising Law Institute Seminar, June 10, 1999; Chicago Bar Association Corporation Law Seminar, May 6, 1999; Annual Securities Law Institute, Chicago Bar Association, March 18, 1998; Publications: "Audit Committees and Auditor Independence: The Three-Pronged Regulatory Approach," Northwestern University Annual Ray Garrett, Jr. Corporate and Securities Law Institute, April 11, 2003; "Recent Developments—Proxy Statements and Disclosures," Glasser LegalWorks, April 30, 2002; "Material Adverse Change Clauses in Acquisition Agreements," Northwestern University Annual Ray Garrett, Jr. Corporate and Securities Law Institute, April 11, 2002; "International and Cross Border Agreements," Insight Information Inc., December 2001; "Communicating with Employees, Customers, Investors, Analysts and the Media," Executive Enterprises, October 2001; "Securities Law Issues in Raising Capital," Chicago Bar Association, May 2001; "Proxy Statements and Disclosure," Glasser LegalWorks, April 11, 2001; "Non-Tax Issues in Asset vs. Stock Transactions," Illinois Institute for Continuing Legal Education, March 2001; "Director's and Officer's Liability, Prevention, Insurance and Indemnification," Law Journal Press, 2000; "Achieving a Positive Outcome: The Friendly Deal," Fulcrum, June 2000; "Audit Committees," Glasser LegalWorks, May 2000; "Buying and Selling Businesses," Illinois Institute for Continuing Legal Education, 2000; "Proposed Regulations under the Securities Act of 1933 and Securities Exchange Act of 1934," Chicago Bar Association, May 1999; "Shareholder Proposals under Rule 14a-8 of the Securities Exchange Act of 1934," Chicago Bar Association Annual Securities Law Institute, Mar. 1998; "Protecting a Friendly Deal from a Hostile Offer," The Corporate Board, Vol. XVI, No. 95, Nov./Dec. 1995; "When East Meets West: Understanding Contract Laws Remedies in the People's Republic of China," 3 Willamette University Bulletin of International Law & Policy, No. 1, 1996. With Mori Sogo Law Offices, Tokyo, Japan, 1991-1993. Member, Executive and Planning Committee, Northwestern University School of Law Annual Ray Garrett, Jr. Corporate and Securities Law Institute. *Member:* Chicago (Chairman, 1999-2000, Vice Chairman, 1998-1999 and Reporter, 1997-1998, Securities Law Committee; Chairman, 1996-1998, Securities Exchange Act Sub-Committee; Member, Corporation and Securities Law Committees), Illinois State (Member, Section of Corporation, Securities and Business Law), American (Member, Business Law Section and Federal Regulation of Securities Sub-Committees on Disclosure and Continuous Reporting and Proxy Statements and Business Combinations), Inter-Pacific and International Bar Associations; The Economic Club of Chicago; The Executives Club of Chicago; The Japan-America Society of Chicago. ***LANGUAGES:*** Japanese. ***PRACTICE AREAS:*** Corporate Law; Securities; International Law. ***Email:*** jburgdoerfer@jenner.com

JENNIFER A. BURKE, born Chicago, Illinois, July 25, 1970; admitted to bar, 1995, Illinois. *Education:* Georgetown University (B.S., 1992); Chicago-Kent College of Law (J.D., 1995). *Member:* Chicago, Illinois State and American Bar Associations. ***PRACTICE AREAS:*** Litigation; Environmental; Insurance Litigation and Counseling; Products Liability and Mass Tort Defense. ***Email:*** jburke@jenner.com

JOHN J. BUTTITA, born Chicago, Illinois, January 24, 1954; admitted to bar, 1979, Illinois. *Education:* DePaul University (B.S., 1976); DePaul College of Law (J.D., 1979). ***PRACTICE AREAS:*** Tax; Estate Planning; Family Business Law; Family Partnerships. ***Email:*** jbuttita@jenner.com

ROBERT L. BYMAN, born Chicago, Illinois, November 25, 1945; admitted to bar, 1970, Illinois. *Education:* University of Illinois (B.A., 1967; J.D., 1970). Member, 1968-1970 and Notes and Comments Editor, 1969-1970, Illinois Law Forum. Author: "A New Boundary for Zone of Peril," 1969 Illinois Law Forum 125; "Handling Witnesses," Illinois Institute For Continuing Legal Education Handbook on Illinois Civil Trial Practice, 1979; "Initial Evaluation of the Case," Illinois Institute For Continuing Legal Education Handbook on Handling Business and Commercial Litigation, 1981, 1985, 1988 and 1990 supplement; "Presenting Testimony," Illinois Institute for Continuing Legal Education Handbook on Illinois Civil Trial Practice, 1982, 1986, 1991. Chapter Author: "Direct Examination," PLI Civil Practice Strategies and Techniques, 1986; "Circumstantial Evidence," Matthew Bender Federal Evidence Practice Guide, 1989; "Opening Statements," Matthew Bender Federal Evidence Practice Guide, 1990; "Expert Witnesses," PLI Winning Strategies and Techniques for Civil Litigators, 1992. Co-Author: *West Illinois Civil Practice Guide*, 1998, 1999. Columnist, *National Law Journal*, 1998—. Senior Instructor, Trial Bar Skills Seminar, IICLE, 1983-1986. Panelist, IIT/Chicago-Kent, Commodities Law Seminar, 1983, 1988, 1990 and 1991. Public Arbitrator: Chicago Board Options Exchange, 1985—; National Futures Association, 1988—; Chicago Mercantile Exchange, 1988—. Member, Panel of Commercial Arbitrators, American Arbitration Association, 1978—. Chairman, Federal Civil Procedure Committee, 2002-2005. *Member:* Chicago, Illinois State and

(This Listing Continued)

American Bar Associations. American College of Trial Lawyers. ***REPORTED CASES:*** Commodity Futures Trading Commission vs. Schor, et al, 478 U.S. 833, 106 S. Ct. 3245 (1986); Panara v. Liquid Carbonic Indus. Corp., 116 F.3d 1482 (7th Cir. 1997); Panaras v. Liquid Carbonic Indus. Corp., 94F.3d 338 (7th Cir. 1996); Panaras v. Liquid Carbonic Indus. Corp., 74 F.3d 786 (7th Cir. 1996); Abbott vs. Bristol-Myers, 971 F. 2d 6 (7th Cir. 1992); Woodall vs. Drake Hotel, Inc., 913 F.2d 477 (7th Cir. 1990); Schor vs. Commodity Futures Trading Commission, 740 F.2d 1262 (D.C. Cir. 1984); Black vs. Brown, 513 F.2d 652 (7th Cir. 1975); Mopex, Inc. v. Chicago Stock Exchange, 2003 U.S.Dist. LEXIS (N.D. Ill. 2003); Medline Industries, Inc. v. Maersk Medical Ltd., 230 F.Supp 2d 857 (N.D. Ill. 2003); GE Capital Corp. v. DirecTV, Inc., 94 F. Supp. 2d 190 (D.Ct. 1999); Carroll v. De-Tella, 1999 U.S. District Lexis 9056 (N.D. Illinois, 1999); Medic Alert v. Corel Corp., 43 F. Supp. 2d 933 (N.D. Illinois, 1999); Naguib v. Ill. Dept of Prof'l. Reg., 986 F. Supp. 1082 (N.D. Ill. 1997); Sara Lee Corp. v. Litton Indus., 1991 U.S. Dist. Lexis 12914; Baranski vs. Serhant, 603 F. Supp. 232 (N.D. Ill. 1985); Baranski vs. Serhant, 602 F. Supp. 33 (N.D. Ill. 1985); Black vs. Brown, 524 F. Supp. 856 (N.D. Ill. 1981); Prince v. Hanes Corp., 1980 U.S. Dist. Lexis 10353 (Northern District of Illinois 1980); Forty-Eight Insulations, Inc. vs. Johns Manville Products Corp., 472 F. Supp. 385 (N.D. Ill. 1979); Alliance to End Repression vs. Rochford, 75 F.R.D. 441 (N.D. Ill. 1977); Alliance to End Repression vs. Rochford, 75 F.R.D. 435 (N.D. Ill. 1976); Alliance to End Repression vs. Rochford, 75 F.R.D. 438 (N.D. Ill. 1976); Rush-Hampton Industries, Inc. vs. Home Ventilation Institute, 419 F. Supp. 19 (M.D. Fla. 1976); Jerry Etshokin vs. Commissioner of Internal Revenue, 59 T.C.M. (CCH) 753 (U.S. Tax Ct. 1990); In re Angelo, CFTC Lexis 87 (1993); BAS Investments, Inc. vs. Laken, 1991 CFTC Lexis (1991); In re Angelo, CCH Commodity Futures Law Reporter 24,943 (1990); Wall Street Establishment vs. Conti Commodity Services, CCH Commodity Futures Law Reporter 21,897 (1983); North Pier Terminal Co. vs. Tully, 62 Ill. 2d 540, 343 N.E.2d 507 (1976); People v. Sykes, 793 N.E. 2d 816 (1st Dist. Ill.App.Ct. 2003); McGarrity v. Berlin Metals, 744 N.E. 2d 71 (3d Dist. Ind. Ct. App. 2002); People v. Heaton, 266 Ill.App.3d 469, 640 N.E. 2d 630 (5th Dist. 1994); People vs. Dowaliby, 221 Ill. App. 3d 788, 582 N.E. 2d 1243 (1st Dist. 1991); Ill. App. 3d (October 30, 1991); Prassas vs. Prassas, 102 Ill. App. 3d 319, 430 N.E. 2d 28 (1st Dist. 1981); Prassas vs. Prassas, 94 Ill. App. 3d 311, 418 N.E.2d 904 (1st Dist. 1981); Van C. Argiris & Co. vs Anwest, 91 Ill. App. 3d 836, 414 N.E. 2d 1256 (1st Dist. 1981); People vs. Cox, 71 Ill. App. 3d 850, 389 N.E.2d 1238 (1st Dist. 1979); Mergenthaler Linotype Co. vs. Storch, 66 Ill. App. 3d 789, 383 N.E.2d 1379 (1st Dist. 1978); Lurie vs. Skokie, 64 Ill. App. 3d 217, 380 N.E.2d 1120 (1st Dist. 1978); People vs. Washington, 63 Ill. App. 3d 1037, 380 N.E.2d 1010 (1st Dist. 1978); Skokie Federal Savings & Loan vs. Illinois Savings & Loan Board, 61 Ill. App. 3d 977, 378 N.E.2d 1090 (1st Dist. 1978); Edgewater Construction Co. vs. Percy Wilson, 44 Ill. App. 3d 220, 357 N.E.2d 1307 (1st Dist. 1976). ***PRACTICE AREAS:*** Intellectual Property; Technology Law; Litigation; Arbitration. ***Email:*** rbyman@jenner.com

JULIA M. CARPENTER, born Hendersonville, North Carolina, September 3, 1961; admitted to bar, 1987, Illinois; 1989, District of Columbia and Virginia. *Education:* College of William & Mary (B.A., 1983); University of North Carolina (J.D., with honors, 1987). Note and Comment Editor, North Carolina Law Review, 1986-1987. Law Clerk to Judge Samuel Coleman, Virginia Court of Appeals, 1987-1988. *Member:* Virginia State Bar; District of Columbia Bar; American Bar Association. (Resident, Washington, D.C. Office). ***PRACTICE AREAS:*** Litigation; Appellate and Supreme Court Practice; Media and First Amendment. ***Email:*** jcarpenter@jenner.com

DONALD R. CASSLING, born Dallas, Texas, November 18, 1950; admitted to bar, 1977, Illinois, U.S. District Court, Northern District of Illinois and U.S. Courts of Appeals, Fifth and Seventh Circuits; 1983, U.S. District Court, Northern District of Illinois, Trial Bar; 1998, U.S. Court of Federal Claims; 2004, U.S. District Court, Eastern District of Wisconsin. *Education:* Duke University (A.B., cum laude, 1972); University of Chicago (J.D., 1976). Editor, University of Chicago Law Review, 1975-1976. Law Clerk, Chief Judge John R. Brown, United States Court of Appeals, Fifth Circuit, 1976-1977. Co-Author: "Uniform Commercial Code, with Illinois Code Comments," West 1997 & 2003; annual supplements to "Illinois Code Comments to Uniform Commercial Code," 1983-1987; "Illinois Practice—UCC Forms Annotated," and "Uniform Laws Annotated—UCC Forms and Materials," 1983—. Author: "Banking Briefs," Banking Law Journal, 2003—. Board of Editors, Banking Law Journal, 2003—. *Member:* Illinois State and American (Member: Business Law Section, Uniform Commercial Code Committee; Litigation Section) Bar Associations. ***PRACTICE AREAS:*** Commercial Law; Uniform Commercial Code; Intellectual Property; Technology Law. ***Email:*** dcassling@jenner.com

THERESA CHMARA, born Trenton, New Jersey, December 27, 1963; admitted to bar, 1988, New Jersey and Pennsylvania (inactive); 1990, District of Columbia. *Education:* Boston College (B.A., cum laude, 1985); Georgetown University (J.D., cum laude, 1988). Lead Articles Editor, Georgetown Immigration Law Journal, 1987-1988. (Resident, Washington, D.C. Office). ***LANGUAGES:*** Polish. ***PRACTICE AREAS:*** Media and First Amendment; Litigation; Civil Appeals; Advertising Law. ***Email:*** tchmara@jenner.com

TIMOTHY J. CHORVAT, born Chicago, Illinois, November 22, 1961; admitted to bar, 1986, Illinois; 1987, U.S. District Court, Northern District of Illinois including Trial Bar; 1992, U.S. Court of Appeals, Seventh Circuit; 1994, U.S. Supreme Court; 1997, U.S. District Court, District of Arizona. *Education:* Northwestern University (B.A., 1983); University of Michigan (J.D., magna cum laude, 1986). Phi Beta Kappa; Order of the Coif. Contributing Editor, Michigan Law Review, 1984-1986. Assistant Professor, IIT/Chicago-Kent College of Law, 1988-1989. *Member:* Seventh Circuit, Illinois State and American Bar Associations. ***PRACTICE AREAS:*** Litigation; Bankruptcy and Insolvency; Class Action Litigation; Securities Litigation. ***Email:*** tchorvat@jenner.com

DAVID A. CHURCHILL, born Fort Collins, Colorado, May 13, 1952; admitted to bar, 1979, District of Columbia; 1980, U.S. Claims Court and U.S. District Court for the District of Columbia Circuit; 1982, U.S. Court of Appeals for the Federal Circuit. *Education:* University of Colorado (B.A., magna cum laude, 1974); University of Vienna, Austria; Cornell University (J.D., cum laude, 1979). Editor-in-Chief, Cornell International Law Journal, 1978-1979. Law Clerk to the Hon. Louis Spector, Trial Judge, U.S. Court of Claims, 1979-1980. Member, Advisory Council, U.S. Court of Federal Claims, 1993-2003. *Member:* The District of Columbia Bar; Federal Circuit and American (Past Chair, Section of Public Contract Law, 1998-1999) Bar Associations; U.S. Court of Federal Claims Bar Association (President - 2004). (Resident, Washington, D.C. Office). ***PRACTICE AREAS:*** Government Contracts Litigation and Counseling; Arbitration; Bid Protests; Export Regulation. ***Email:*** dchurchill@jenner.com

(This Listing Continued)

ELIZABETH ABBENE COLEMAN, born Chicago, Illinois, April 13, 1967; admitted to bar, 1996, Illinois. *Education:* University of Illinois (B.S., 1990); Loyola University (J.D., cum laude, 1996). Senior Member, Loyola University Law Journal. ***PRACTICE AREAS:*** Litigation; Class Action Litigation; Products Liability and Mass Tort Defense. ***Email:*** ecoleman@jenner.com

JEFFREY D. COLMAN, born Milwaukee, Wisconsin, November 3, 1947; admitted to bar, 1973, California; 1975, Illinois. *Education:* University of Wisconsin (B.A., 1970); Stanford University (J.D., 1973). Fellow, American College of Trial Lawyers. Teaching Fellow, Clinical Legal Education Program, Stanford Law School, 1973-1974. Lecturer, Criminal Trial Practice (1980-1982) and Adjunct Professor (1983-1984), Northwestern University Law School. Member and Secretary-Treasurer, Illinois Supreme Court Committee on Pattern Jury Instructions In Criminal Cases, 1976-1984. Member and Chairman, Illinois Supreme Court Committee on Post-Conviction Review of Death Sentences, 1987-1991. Member, National Board of Directors, Mexican American Legal Defense and Educational Fund, 1984-1988; 1991-1995. Member, Board of Directors, Committee for Honest Elections, 1984-1988. Member, Board of Directors, John Howard Association, 1989-2000. President, 2003-2005 and Member, 1995—, Board of Directors, Chicago Bar Foundation; President, 2002-2004 and Member, 1999—, Board of Directors, Constitutional Rights Foundation of Illinois; Member, Board of Directors, Leadership Council on Metropolitan Open Committees, 1996-1997. Member, Board of Advisors, Georgetown University Corporate Counsel Institute, 1999—. *Member:* Chicago, Federal and American Bar Associations; Chicago Council of Lawyers. ***PRACTICE AREAS:*** Litigation; Appellate Practice; Class Action Litigation; Product Liability Litigation; Mass Tort Defense; Professional Liability Litigation; White Collar Criminal Defense. ***Email:*** jcolman@jenner.com

DEIRDRE E. CONNELL, born Chicago, Illinois, May 5, 1966; admitted to bar, 1990, Illinois and U.S. District Court, Northern District of Illinois; 1993, U.S. Court of Appeals, Seventh Circuit. *Education:* Cornell College (B.A., magna cum laude, 1987); University of Iowa (J.D., with high distinction, 1990). ***PRACTICE AREAS:*** Litigation; Class Action Litigation; Securities Litigation. ***Email:*** dconnell@jenner.com

JACOB I. CORRÉ, born Philadelphia, Pennsylvania, June 17, 1959; admitted to bar, 1986, Illinois and U.S. District Court, Northern District of Illinois; 1995, U.S. Court of Appeals, Seventh Circuit and U.S. Supreme Court. *Education:* University of Chicago (A.B., with honors, 1981); Yale University Law School (J.D., 1985). Phi Beta Kappa. ***PRACTICE AREAS:*** Litigation.

JOSEPH P. COVINGTON, born Luxembourg, December 18, 1946; admitted to bar, 1974, Arizona and U.S. District Court, District of Arizona and U.S. Court of Appeals, 9th Circuit; 1978, Supreme Court of Virginia, U.S. District Court, Eastern District of Virginia and U.S. Court of Appeals, 4th Circuit; 1986, District of Columbia. *Education:* University of Virginia (B.A., 1968; J.D., 1973). Assistant U.S. Attorney, Arizona, 1974 and 1982-1985, Litigation Supervisor, Criminal Fraud Division, Department of Justice. Purple Heart, U.S. Army Infantry, Vietnam, 1969. (Resident, Washington, D.C. Office). ***LANGUAGES:*** German. ***PRACTICE AREAS:*** Government Contracts; Litigation; Criminal Antitrust; White Collar Criminal Defense; FCPA and Export Regulation; Compliance Counseling; Ethics and Compliance Issues. ***Email:*** jcovington@jenner.com

JOHN F. COX, born Park Ridge, Illinois, June 4, 1970; admitted to bar, 1995, Illinois; 1996, Florida, Ohio and U.S. District Court, Northern District of Illinois. *Education:* Indiana University (B.A., with distinction, 1992); University of Chicago Law School (J.D., 1995). Recipient, Indiana University James Moffat Senior Award in Economics. Board Member, Guild Board, 2004— and Associate Board, 2003-2004, Boys & Girls Clubs of Chicago. Board Member, Young Professionals Advisory Board, Columbus Zoo, 2001-2002. Formerly with: Jenner & Block, Chicago, Illinois, 1995-1999; Vorys, Sater, Seymour and Pease LLP, Columbus, Ohio, 1999-2002. ***PRACTICE AREAS:*** Mergers, Acquisitions and Divestitures; Business Law; Corporate Law; Securities. ***Email:*** jcox@jenner.com

ELIZABETH A. DAVIDSON, born Springfield, Illinois, May 8, 1965; admitted to bar, 1997, Illinois. *Education:* University of Illinois (B.S., high honors, 1988); University of Kentucky (J.D., cum laude, 1997) Order of the Coif. ***PRACTICE AREAS:*** Corporate Finance; Bankruptcy; Corporate Reorganization. ***Email:*** edavidson@jenner.com

GEOFFREY M. DAVIS, born Madison, Wisconsin, June 6, 1964; admitted to bar, 1992, Illinois and U.S. District Court, Northern District of Illinois, U.S. Court of Appeals, Seventh Circuit and U.S. Tax Court. *Education:* University of Wisconsin-Madison (B.B.A., with honors, 1986); Boston University School of Law (J.D., cum laude, 1992). Staff Member, Law Review. Law Clerk to Hon. William T. Hart, U.S. District Court, Northern District of Illinois, 1992-1994. *Member:* Chicago Bar Association (Chair, Partnership Division, 2005, Corporate Tax Division, 2003). ***REPORTED CASES:*** RAR v. Turner Diesel, Ltd., 107 F.3d 1272 (7th Cir. 1997); Turner v. Bernstein, C.A. No. 16190 (Del. Ch. June 6, 2000). ***PRACTICE AREAS:*** Tax Practice; Tax Controversy Practice. ***Email:*** gdavis@jenner.com

DAVID W. DeBRUIN, born Hinsdale, Illinois, March 29, 1955; admitted to bar, 1980, District of Columbia. *Education:* Indiana University (B.A., with highest distinction, 1977); University of Michigan (J.D., summa cum laude, 1980). Law Clerk to: Hon. Harry T. Edwards, U.S. Court of Appeals, District of Columbia Circuit, 1980-1981; Justice John Paul Stevens, U.S. Supreme Court, 1981-1982. Staff Attorney, Public Defender Service for the District of Columbia, 1982-1986. Associate Special Counsel, Impeachment of Judge Harry E. Claiborne, Committee on the Judiciary, United States House of Representatives, 1986. (Resident, Washington, D.C. Office). ***PRACTICE AREAS:*** Civil, Criminal and Appellate Litigation. ***Email:*** ddebruin@jenner.com

MICHAEL B. DeSANCTIS, born Los Angeles, California, August 1, 1969; admitted to bar, 1998, New York, New Jersey, District of Columbia, U.S. Court of Appeals, Third Circuit and U.S. District Court, District of New Jersey; U.S. Court of Appeals, Sixth Circuit; 2001, U.S. Supreme Court, U.S. District Court, District of Maryland and U.S. Court of Appeals, Eleventh Circuit; 2002, U.S. Court of Appeals, District of Columbia Circuit, U.S. Court of Appeals, Ninth Circuit and U.S. District Court for the District of Columbia; 2003, U.S. Court of Appeals, Fourth Circuit. *Education:* Boston College (B.A., summa cum laude, 1991); New York University School of Law (J.D., cum laude, 1995). Phi Beta Kappa; Phi Alpha Theta. Editor-in-Chief, NYU School of Law Moot Court Casebook. Clerk: Hon. Dolores K. Sloviter, Chief Judge, U.S. Court of Appeals, Third Circuit, 1997-1998; Hon.

(This Listing Continued)

JENNER & BLOCK LLP, Chicago—Continued

Maryanne Trump Barry, U.S. District Court, District of New Jersey, 1995-1997. *Member:* The District of Columbia Bar (Member, Section on Communications and Computer Law); Bar Association of the District of Columbia (Member, Appellate Courts Committee); Federal Telecommunications Bar Association; American Bar Association (Member: Air and Space Law Forum; Section of Aviation Litigation). (Resident, Washington, D.C. Office). ***PRACTICE AREAS:*** Appellate Litigation; Litigation; Telecommunications Law; Administrative Law. ***Email:*** mdesanctis@jenner.com

CHRISTOPHER C. DICKINSON, born Slinger, Wisconsin, May 28, 1960; admitted to bar, 1988, Wisconsin and U.S. District Court, Western District of Wisconsin; 1989, Illinois and U.S. District Court, Eastern District of Wisconsin and Northern District of Illinois; 1992, U.S. Court of Appeals, Seventh Circuit; 2001, U.S. Court of Appeals, Third Circuit. *Education:* University of Wisconsin (B.A., with distinction, 1982; J.D., cum laude, 1988). Phi Beta Kappa; Phi Kappa Phi. *Member:* American Bar Association; State Bar of Wisconsin. ***PRACTICE AREAS:*** Insurance Litigation and Counseling. ***Email:*** cdickinson@jenner.com

MICHAEL A. DOORNWEERD, born Royal Oak, Michigan, April 10, 1970; admitted to bar, 1996, Illinois and U.S. District Court, Northern District of Illinois; 1997, U.S. Court of Appeals, Fifth Circuit; 2000, U.S. District Court, Southern District of Illinois and U.S. Court of Appeals, Third Circuit; 2001, U.S. Court of Federal Claims; 2003, U.S. Court of Appeals, Seventh Circuit. *Education:* Kalamazoo College (B.A., cum laude, 1992); Northwestern University (J.D., cum laude, 1995). Phi Beta Kappa. Coordinating Note and Comment Editor, Northwestern University Law Review. Law Clerk to Judge Cornelia G. Kennedy, U.S. Court of Appeals, Sixth Circuit, 1995-1996. *Member:* Illinois State and American Bar Associations. ***PRACTICE AREAS:*** Litigation; ERISA Litigation; Tax Controversy. ***Email:*** mdoornweerd@jenner.com

KEVIN B. DUCKWORTH, born Ypsilanti, Michigan, March 21, 1959; admitted to bar, 1985, Illinois. *Education:* Fisk University (B.A., 1981); North Carolina Central University School of Law (J.D., 1985). ***PRACTICE AREAS:*** Products Liability Defense; Mass Tort Defense; Commercial Litigation; Litigation; Corporate Finance. ***Email:*** kduckworth@jenner.com

KEVIN C. DWYER, born Baltimore, Maryland, September 12, 1958; admitted to bar, 1985, District of Columbia; 1987, U.S. Court of Appeals, Fourth Circuit; 1989, U.S. Court of Federal Claims; 1993, U.S. Court of Appeals, Federal Circuit. *Education:* University of Notre Dame (B.A., with honors, 1980); Yale University (M.A., 1981); Duke University (J.D., 1985). Executive Editor, Duke Law Journal, 1984-1985. *Member:* District of Columbia Bar; American Bar Association (Member, Public Contract Law Section). (Resident, Washington, D.C. Office). ***PRACTICE AREAS:*** Government Contract Law; Government Contract Cost Accounting; Health Care Contracting. ***Email:*** kdwyer@jenner.com

LARRY P. ELLSWORTH, born Ann Arbor, Michigan, January 7, 1947; admitted to bar, 1973, District of Columbia; 1991, Texas; 1992, New York. *Education:* Michigan State University (B.A., 1969); Harvard Law School (J.D., 1972). (Resident, Washington, D.C. Office). ***PRACTICE AREAS:*** Securities Litigation; Internal Investigations; Securities Advice. ***Email:*** lellsworth@jenner.com

JEROME L. EPSTEIN, born San Antonio, Texas, December 21, 1961; admitted to bar, 1986, Pennsylvania (inactive); 1988, District of Columbia; 1994, Maryland. *Education:* University of Pennsylvania (B.S., Econ., magna cum laude, 1983; J.D., cum laude, 1986). Comment Editor, University of Pennsylvania Law Review. Law Clerk to Hon. Thomas Penfield Jackson, U.S. District Court for the District of Columbia, 1986-1987. Trial Attorney, Honors Program, U.S. Department of Justice, Civil Division, 1987-1990. (Resident, Washington, D.C. Office). ***PRACTICE AREAS:*** Civil Litigation; Telecommunications Law; Intellectual Property and Technology Law; Products Liability and Mass Tort Defense. ***Email:*** jepstein@jenner.com

STEVEN B. FABRIZIO, born Plainview, New York, December 20, 1963; admitted to bar, 1989, New York; 1991, Pennsylvania; 1992, District of Columbia. *Education:* Georgetown University (B.S.B.A., 1985); Georgetown University Law Center (J.D., 1988). Co-Chair, Entertainment and New Media. (Resident, Washington, D.C. Office). ***PRACTICE AREAS:*** Intellectual Property Litigation (60%); Technology Litigation (30%); Litigation (10%). ***Email:*** sfabrizio@jenner.com

JILL SUGAR FACTOR, admitted to bar, 1986, Illinois. *Education:* Washington University (B.S.B.A., 1982; M.B.A., 1983); Northwestern University School of Law (J.D., 1986). ***PRACTICE AREAS:*** Mergers and Acquisitions; Corporate Finance; Securities. ***Email:*** jfactor@jenner.com

KATHERINE A. FALLOW, born Washington, D.C., June 10, 1969; admitted to bar, 1996, Massachusetts; 1999, District of Columbia. *Education:* University of California, Berkeley (B.A., with highest honors, 1991); Harvard University (J.D., magna cum laude, 1996). Phi Beta Kappa. Clerk: Hon. Robert E. Keeton, U.S. District Court, District of Massachusetts, 1996-1997; Hon. Rosemary Barkett, U.S. Court of Appeals, Eleventh Circuit, 1997-1998. (Resident, Washington, D.C. Office). ***PRACTICE AREAS:*** Litigation; Appellate Practice; Supreme Court; Media and First Amendment. ***Email:*** kfallow@jenner.com

JAMES H. FELDMAN, born Chicago, Illinois, August 30, 1943; admitted to bar, 1969, Illinois; 1971, California. *Education:* Tufts University (B.A., 1965); University of Illinois (J.D., 1968); New York University (LL.M., 1970). Listed in Best Lawyers in America in Domestic Relations Category, Naifeh & Smith, all editions, 1983-2006. Author: "Maintenance Review and Modification," Chapter for AAML Course, Family Law Seminar for Experienced Attorneys, October 2005; "Courts Assess Dissipation of Assets," Chicago Daily Law Bulletin, February 13, 2003; "Initial Interview and Client Relations," Chapter for ISBA Course, Law Ed Series, Family 101: Learn from the Experts, October 2002; "Beginning Strategies and Initial Considerations," Chapter in Handbook for First Annual Family Law Conference, Illinois Institute for Continuing Legal Education, April 2002; "The Shifting Venues of Marital Negotiations," FairShare, June 1996; "Clients: How to Take on Their Problems Without Making Them Your Own," ABA Family Advocate, Fall 1994; "Which Confidences are Protected," ABA Family Advocate, Fall 1991; "Blowing the Whistle on Another Lawyer," ABA Family Advocate, Spring 1990; "The Initial Interview"

(This Listing Continued)

and "Ethics," ABA Family Advocate, Winter 1990; "Dangerous Liaison: Dealing with the Press in Family Litigation," Annual Meeting Compendium at 19, American Bar Association, Family Law Section, 1989; "Historical and Practice Notes Supplement, Illinois Marriage and Dissolution Of Marriage Act and Husband and Wife Act, Smith-Hurd Illinois Annot. Statutes, West, 1983-1988; "Silences in the Storm: Testimonial Privileges in Matrimonial Disputes," XXI Family Law Quarterly 189, 1987, ABA; "Taming Transmutation—A Guide to Illinois' New Rules on Property Classification and Division Upon Dissolution of Marriage," Illinois Bar Journal, March, 1984; "Classification of Property Upon Dissolution of Marriage," Illinois Bar Journal, October, 1982. Faculty Member, Illinois Institute for Continuing Legal Education, 1975—. *Member:* Illinois State and American (Family Law Section: Chair, Ethical Practice and Procedures Committee, 1988-1992; Co-Chair, Federal Legislation/Congressional Relations Committees, 1995-2000; Litigation Section: Chair, Domestic Relations and Family Law Litigation Committee, 1988-1990) Bar Associations. Certified Fellow, American Academy of Matrimonial Lawyers. ***PRACTICE AREAS:*** Family Law. ***Email:*** jfeldman@jenner.com

JAMES P. FIEWEGER, born Moline, Illinois, December 22, 1963; admitted to bar, 1991, Illinois. *Education:* University of Notre Dame (B.A., 1986); DePaul University College of Law (J.D., 1991). Law Review. Order of the Coif. Adjunct Professor, Trial Advocacy, DePaul University College of Law, 2003-2005. Assistant United States Attorney, Northern District of Illinois, 2000-2005. ***PRACTICE AREAS:*** Commercial Litigation; White Collar Criminal Defense. ***Email:*** jfieweger@jenner.com

BILL S. FORCADE, born Lincoln, Nebraska, January 22, 1946; admitted to bar, 1976, Illinois and U.S. District Court, Northern District of Illinois; 1977, U.S. Court of Appeals, Seventh Circuit; 1982, U.S. Supreme Court. *Education:* University of Illinois (B.S., 1971); John Marshall Law School (J.D., 1976). Author: "The Expanding Scope of the NSR Program," Andrews Litigation Reporter-Environmental, Vol. 25, Issue 3, September 10, 2004, p.18; "On the Horizon: Top Issues in Air Quality Management in 2004," Environmental Protection, Vol. 15, No. 1, p. 22, January 2004; "Shifting Winds Ahead: Top Issues in Air Quality Management in 2003," Environmental Protection, Vol. 14, No. 1, p. 22, January/February 2003; "An Aerial View of 2002: Top Issues in Air Quality Management in 2002," Environmental Protection, Vol. 13, No. 1, p. 16, January 2002; "Responding to Terror Threat: The Environmental Component," Chicago Daily Law Bulletin, Lawyers' Forum, p. 5, October 26, 2001; "How to Minimize Civil Penalties in Environment," Environmental Law Reporter, 30 EL 11031, November 2000; "Illinois Environmental Civil Penalties 1990-1999," Air and Waste Management Association, Lake Michigan States Section Newsletter Vol. 38, No. 4, First Quarter 2000; "Define My Source, Please: Problems in the New Source Review Permitting Process" Environment Compliance and Litigation Strategy, Vol. 14, No. 9, February 1999; "Compliance Assurance Monitoring: Avoiding Pitfalls from the Costly New Rules," North Carolina Lawyers Weekly, December 1, 1997; "Lobbying Within The Law," The Neighborhood Works, Vol. 17, No. 5, October/November 1994; "Lobbying In Illinois: A Guide for Nonprofit Organizations," a Booklet Published by the Community Economic Development Law Project, 1994; "The Employee Commute Options Act: Are Illinoisans Being Taken for a Ride?" The CBA Record, Vol. 8, No. 4, May 1994. "Environmental Rule Making in Illinois," The John Marshall Law Review, Vol. 27, No. 3, Fall 1993; "Public Participation in Siting," Chapter 4, American Association for the Advancement of Science Selected Symposium, Hazardous Waste Management, 1988. Part Time Instructor, Northeastern Illinois University, Chicago, 1982 and 1984. Board Member: Illinois Pollution Control Board, Chicago, 1983-1993; Skokie Board of Health, 1995-2002. Research Chemist, 1971-1976. Commissioner, Illinois Environmental Regulatory Review Commission 2000—. Member, Board of Directors, Lake Michigan States Section, Air and Waste Management Association, 2001-2003. Member, Chicagoland Chamber of Commerce, Environmental Committee, 1996—. Member, University of Illinois at Chicago, School of Public Health, Dean's Advisory Committee, 2002—. President, 2000-2001, Director, 1997—, Illinois Association of Environmental Professionals. Member, Advisory Committee, Hazardous Waste Research and Information Council, Champaign, 1989-1990. Volunteer Deputy Registrar, Chicago Board of Election Commissioners, 1989-1993. Democratic Election Judge, 53rd Precinct, 42nd Ward, Chicago Board of Election Commissioners, 1982-1984. *Member:* Chicago (Chairman, Administrative Law Committee, 1993-1994; Chairman, Committee on Science Technology and the Law, 1991-1992) and American (Chairman, Water Quality Subcommittee, Committee on Environmental, Energy and Natural Resources Law, Business Law Section, 2004—) Bar Associations. [U.S. Army, Petroleum Products Analyst, 1968-1969]. ***PRACTICE AREAS:*** Environmental; Trade Association. ***Email:*** bforcade@jenner.com

RICHARD T. FRANCH, born Melrose Park, Illinois, September 23, 1942; admitted to bar, 1967, Illinois; U.S. Supreme Court; U.S. Court of Appeals, Second, Third, Fourth, Sixth, Seventh, Eighth and Ninth Circuits; 1995, U.S. Tax Court. *Education:* University of Notre Dame (B.A., cum laude, 1964); University of Chicago (J.D., 1967). Member, Illinois Supreme Court Rules Committee, 1978-1983. *Member:* American Law Institute. Fellow, American College of Trial Lawyers. ***PRACTICE AREAS:*** Commercial Litigation and Arbitration; Reinsurance; International Arbitration.

CHRIS C. GAIR, born Springfield, Illinois, January 25, 1959; admitted to bar, 1985, Illinois. *Education:* Duke University (A.B., 1981); University of Chicago Law School (J.D., 1985). Phi Beta Kappa; Order of the Coif. ***PRACTICE AREAS:*** White Collar Criminal Defense and Counseling; Antitrust; Complex Litigation. ***Email:*** cgair@jenner.com

GREGORY S. GALLOPOULOS, born Detroit, Michigan, October 8, 1959; admitted to bar, 1984, Illinois. *Education:* University of Michigan (A.B., with highest distinction, 1981; J.D., magna cum laude, 1984). Phi Beta Kappa. Order of the Coif. Author: "Preserving Error For Appeal In Illinois," Illinois Bar Journal, October, 1990. *Member:* Illinois State, Seventh Circuit and American Bar Associations. ***PRACTICE AREAS:*** Complex Litigation; Tax Litigation; Accounting Malpractice; Business Fraud. ***Email:*** ggallopoulos@jenner.com

IAN HEATH GERSHENGORN, born New York, N.Y., February 21, 1967; admitted to bar, 1994, Massachusetts; 1995, District of Columbia. *Education:* Harvard University (A.B., magna cum laude, 1988; J.D., magna cum laude, 1993). Phi Beta Kappa. Member, Harvard Law Review. Author: "Winship on Rough Waters: The Erosion of the Reasonable Doubt Standard," 106 Harvard Law Review 1093, 1993; "The Fall of the FCC's Personal Attack and Political Editorial Rules," Communications Lawyer, Spring 2001; "Telemarketing Restrictions and the First Amendment," Communications Lawyer, Summer 2002. Co-

(This Listing Continued)

Author: with Philip B. Heymann, "Pursuing Justice, Respecting the Law: The U.S. Experience with Extraterritorial Statutes," Criminal Law Forum, Autumn 1991; with Philip B. Heymann," A Comment on United States v. Alvarez-Machain," Criminal Law Forum, Spring 1993. Law Clerk to: Justice John Paul Stevens, U.S. Supreme Court, 1994-1995; Judge Amalya L. Kearse, U.S. Court of Appeals, Second Circuit, 1993-1994. Assistant to Attorney General Janet Reno, 1997 and Special Assistant and Counsel to Deputy Attorney General Jamie S. Gorelick, 1995-1997, U.S. Department of Justice. (Resident, Washington, D.C. Office). ***PRACTICE AREAS:*** Civil Litigation; Appellate Practice; Communications and Media. ***Email:*** igershengorn@jenner.com

ELAINE J. GOLDENBERG, born New York, New York, February 10, 1972; admitted to bar, 1998, Massachusetts; 2002, District of Columbia (Not admitted in Illinois). *Education:* Harvard University (A.B., 1993; J.D., 1997). (Resident, Washington, D.C. Office). ***PRACTICE AREAS:*** Litigation. ***Email:*** egoldenberg@jenner.com

MARC A. GOLDMAN, born Washington, D.C., May 12, 1966; admitted to bar, 1994, Pennsylvania; 1996, District of Columbia. *Education:* Harvard University (A.B., magna cum laude, 1988; J.D., magna cum laude, 1993). Supervising Editor, Harvard Law Review, 1992-1993. Law Clerk to Hon. Edward Becker, U.S. Court of Appeals, Third Circuit, 1993-1994. Visiting Professor of Constitutional Law, University of Iowa Law School, Spring 1999. (Resident, Washington, D.C. Office). ***PRACTICE AREAS:*** Civil Litigation; Appellate Practice; Telecommunications Law. ***Email:*** mgoldman@jenner.com

ROBERT L. GRAHAM, born Chicago, Illinois, January 9, 1948; admitted to bar, 1972, Illinois; 1973, California. *Education:* University of Michigan (B.A., with highest distinction, 1969); Harvard University (J.D., 1972). Phi Beta Kappa; Phi Eta Sigma; Angell Scholar. Member, Editorial Board: Harvard Civil Rights-Civil Liberties Law Review, 1972; Illinois Environmental Laws and Regulations, 1978; Shepard's Environmental Liability In Commercial Transactions Reporter, 1990-1992. Co-Author or Author: "Environmental Law and Policy: Nature, Law and Society," West Publishing Co., 2d Edition, 1998, Supplement 1999-2003, 3rd Edition (Aspen Publishers), 2004; "The Evolution of Equal Protection-Education, Municipal Services & Wealth," 7 Harvard Civil Rights-Civil Liberties Law Review 103, 1972; "Review by Means of Extraordinary Writs," Illinois Civil Practice After Trial, Illinois Institute For Continuing Legal Education, 1976, 1980, 1984, 1986; "Book Review, Balancing the Scales of Justice: Financing Public Interest Law in America," 8 Loyola of Chicago Law Journal 665, 1977; "Affirmative Action" and "Building Court," Tenants' Rights Handbook of the Illinois Institute for Continuing Legal Education, 1975, 1978; "Landlord's Duty to Maintain," Representing Residential Tenants, Illinois Institute For Continuing Legal Education, 1983; "The Legal Protection of Computer Software," Communications of the ACM, Volume 27, Number 5, May, 1984 at 422; "Disclosure and Due Diligence Obligations Arising From Business Statutes and Regulations Having Environmental Impacts," The Impact of Environmental Regulations on Business Transactions, Practicing Law Institute, 1988-1990, 153; "Environmental Risk Management Under The New FDIC Guidelines," The Review of Banking and Financial Services, Vol. 9, No. 22, at 221; The Brownfields Book, July 1997. Adjunct Professor of Environmental Law: Northwestern University School of Law, 1990-2001; Loyola University School of Law, 1973-1978. Member: Illinois Supreme Court Committee on Jury Instructions in Civil Cases (Associate Member, 1981-1986; Member, 1986-1995); The Fund for Justice (Member, Board of Directors, 1977-1988; 1990-2001; Chairman, 1987); Chicago Council of Lawyers (Member, Board of Governors, 1977-1979; 1982-1983; President, 1979-1981; Delegate to American Bar Association, 1988). Member, American Law Institute. Environmental Law and Policy Center (Chair, 2000-2003); Board Member, 1993-2000; 2003-2004). Fellow, American Bar Foundation. ***PRACTICE AREAS:*** Environmental; Civil Litigation; Class Actions; Appellate Practice; Supreme Court; Intellectual Property; Health Care; Intellectual Property and Technology Law; Insurance Litigation and Counseling; Products Liability and Mass Tort Defense. ***Email:*** rgraham@jenner.com

RICHARD J. GRAY, born Dearborn, Michigan, November 22, 1948; admitted to bar, 1974, Illinois; 1994, Colorado; U.S. District Court, Northern District of Illinois; U.S. District Court, Eastern District of Michigan; U.S. Court of Appeals, Sixth and Seventh Circuits; U.S. Supreme Court. *Education:* University of Michigan (A.B., magna cum laude, 1971; J.D., 1974). Phi Beta Kappa; Pi Sigma Alpha. Member, 1972-1973 and Staff Editor, 1973-1974, University of Michigan Journal of Law Reform. Author: Note, "A Proposal to Prevent the Stranding of Airline Passengers," 6 University of Michigan Journal of Law Reform 399, 1973. Co-Author: "Defense of Evictions" and "Affirmative Action," Tenants' Rights Handbook of the Illinois Institute for Continuing Legal Education, 1975; "Illinois Discovery Reform: A Rationale, Rules and Result," The Review of Litigation, University of Texas School of Law, Spring, 1997; "Contracting on the Net," Tech Law Group, Inc., Paris, France, September 28, 2001. Member, Board of Directors of the Tech Law Group, Inc. *Member:* American Bar Association (Member, Legal Opportunity Scholarship Committee 2003—; Presidential Advisory Council on Diversity in the Profession, 2002-2005; Section Officers' Conference, Member, Financial Affairs Comittee 2005—; Member, Financial Reorganization Committee, 2004-2005; Liaison to the Board of Governors' Finance Committee, 2002-2003; Corporate Sponsorship Committee, 2001-2002; Continuing Legal Education Committee, 1993-1994); Section of Litigation (Member Task Force on the Judiciary, 2005-2006; Co-Chair, Non-Dues Revenue Committee, 2004-2005; Co-Chair, Diversity Plan Implementation Committee, 2002-2004; Non-Dues Revenue Committee, 2000; Co-Chair, Minority Judicial Intern Program Committee, 2002-2003; Revenue Officer and Member, Executive Committee, 1998-2002; Co-Chair, Task Force on State Justice Initiatives, 1995-1998; Ad Hoc Committee on State Justice Initiatives, 1997-1998; Division Director, CLE Programs, 1994-1995; Committee on National Institutes, Vice Chair, 1990-1991, Co-Chair, 1991-1994); Federal Bar Association. Markey Wigmore Inn of Court. ***PRACTICE AREAS:*** Litigation; Intellectual Property; Technology Law; Telecommunications Law; Insurance Coverage; Class Actions. ***Email:*** rgray@jenner.com

E. LYNN GRAYSON, born Tampa, Florida, May 10, 1961; admitted to bar, 1986, Illinois; U.S. District Court, Central, Southern and Northern Districts of Illinois. *Education:* Franklin College of Indiana (B.A., with high honors, 1983); Indiana University (J.D., 1986). Delta Zeta. Phi Alpha Delta. Recipient, 2000 Alta May Hulett Award for Contributions to Women Attorneys. Author: "The Chicago Call to Action for Women Attorneys," Women Lawyers Journal, Winter 2005; "The Remarkable Life and Times of Alta May Hulett," The Catalyst, February 2004, Vol. 9., No. 3, Page 4; "Five Things Every Lawyer Should Know About the Alliance For Women," CBA Record, January 2004, Vol. 18, No. 1, page 39.

(This Listing Continued)

"NJDEP's Initiative to Recover Natural Resource Damages," Lake Michigan States Section, Air & Waste Management Association Newsletter, December 2003, Vol. 43, No. 4; "EPA Extends Deadline For New Rule On Oil Spills," Chicago Daily Law Bulletin, January 24, 2003. Co-Author: "The Business Dilemma: 21st Century Natural Resource Damage Liabilities for 20th Century Industrial Progress," The Environmental Law Reporter, November 2001; "EPCRA — Basics, Dos and Dont's," The Natural Resources and Environmental Journal, American Bar Association, Summer 2001; Co-Author: with Christine Picker, Steven Siros and Stacy Bettison, "The Business Dilemma: 21st Century Natural Resource Damage Liabilities for 20th Century Industrial Progress," The Environmental Law Reporter, November 2001; "Good News: A Year 2000 Update on Brownfields Development," Environmental Compliance and Litigation Strategy, September 2000; "Hot Topics in Region V," IL Association of Environmental Professionals, May 2000; "EPA's New Shotgun Approach: Multimedia Enforcement," Environmental Protection, January 1999; "EPA's Y2K Enforcement Policy," Chicago Daily Law Bulletin, March 1999; "Chemical Release Reporting: What Illinois Practitioners Need to Know," CBA Record, April 1998; "A Reality Check on Environmental Enforcement," Chicago Daily Law Bulletin, April 1998; "Release Reporting Issues in Commercial/Industrial Real Estate Transactions," BNA Due Diligence Guide, February 1997; "Brownfields, v. Environmental Justice Conflict or Consensus," ABA Sonreel Newsletter, January 1996; "Risk Plan Program Poses Liability Concerns," BNA's Environmental Compliance Bulletin, March, 1994; "Illinois Industry Benefits from Pollution Prevention," Illinois Legal Times, April, 1993; "Pollution Prevention Proves Costly for Business," ECON, September, 1992; "New D.O.T. Regulation Aims at Hazardous Waste Haulers," Chicago Daily Law Bulletin, September 11, 1992; "Companies File Revised Form R at Own Risk, Still Vulnerable to Citizens' Lawsuits," Environmental Protection News, June 22, 1992; "Deadline Dilemma: Tardy EPA Forms Put Industry in a Bind," Industry Week, June 15, 1992; "The Pollution Prevention Act of 1990: Emergence of a New Environmental Policy," Environmental Law Reporter, June, 1992; "Pollution Reports to Put Industry in Quagmire," Chicago Daily Law Bulletin, April 24, 1992; "Uncertainty over Toxics Reporting Hampers Compliance," BNA National Environmental Watch, April 6, 1992. Co-Author: with Seth D. Lamden, "Good News: 2000 Brownfields Review," The Environmental Counselor, January, 2001; with Christina Riewer, "EPA's Audit Policy and State Audit Privilege Laws: Moving Beyond Command and Control?" Environmental Law Reporter, May 1997; with Rebecca L. Raftery, "Realizing the Maximum Value in Real Estate Transactions by Minimizing Environmental Liberties," CBA Record, December 1996; with Stephen A.K. Palmer, "The Brownfield Phenomenon: An Analysis of Environmental Economic and Community Concerns," Environmental Law Institute, Environmental Law Reporter, July 1995. *Member:* Chicago (Chair, 2004-2005, Executive Committee 2005-2006; Vice Chair, 2003; Member, Alliance for Women, 1993-2006), Illinois State (Assembly Delegate, 1997-1999; Member, Illinois Bar Journal Editorial Board, 1997-2001; Past Chairperson, Environmental Law Committee, 1993-1994) and American (Member, Sections on: Natural Resources, Energy and Environmental Law; Business Law; Chair: Environmental Energy and Natural Resources Committee; Outreach Committee) Bar Associations; Air & Waste Management Association (Chairperson, 1998-1999). ***PRACTICE AREAS:*** Environmental Law. ***Email:*** lgrayson@jenner.com

DAVID M. GREENWALD, born Niles, Michigan, February 11, 1961; admitted to bar, 1986, Illinois; U.S. District Court, Northern District of Illinois including Trial Bar; U.S. Court of Appeals, Seventh Circuit; U.S. District Court, Eastern District of Michigan; U.S. Court of Federal Claims. *Education:* Georgetown University (A.B., cum laude, 1983); University of Michigan (J.D., cum laude, 1986). Alpha Sigma Nu; Pi Sigma Alpha. Author or Co-Author: Testimonial Privileges, 3d ed.(Thomson West 2005); "Tight spot: Corporations are finding that disclosing privileged information to the government means disclosing it to private litigants, too. They need to take several steps in advance," The Deal, April 5, 2004; "Protecting Confidential Legal Information: A Handbook for Analyzing Issues under the Attorney-Client Privilege and the Work Product Doctrine," Jenner & Block, 2004; "Selective Waiver of Privileges," For The Defense, December 2002; "The surprising viability of the self-critical analysis privilege in Illinois federal courts," ISBA Trial Briefs, Vol. 46, No. 5, April 2001; "Preserving The Confidentiality of Legal Audit Findings," The Corporate Litigator, ABA, 1989. *Member:* Illinois State and American Bar Associations. ***PRACTICE AREAS:*** Civil and Criminal Litigation; Government Contracting Litigation; Insurance Coverage Litigation; Reinsurance. ***Email:*** dgreenwald@jenner.com

JOSEPH P. GROMACKI, born Milwaukee, Wisconsin, May 17, 1965; admitted to bar, 1992, Illinois. *Education:* Yale University (B.A., 1987); University of Virginia School of Law (J.D., 1992). Articles Editor, Virginia Journal of International Law. Clerk: Honorable Hubert L. Will, U.S. District Court, Northern District of Illinois, 1992-1994. *Member:* American Bar Association. ***PRACTICE AREAS:*** Corporate; Mergers and Acquisitions; Securities. ***Email:*** jgromacki@jenner.com

DAVID K. HAASE, born Chicago, Illinois, March 29, 1963; admitted to bar, 1989, Illinois; 1990, U.S. District Court, Northern District of Illinois, including Trial Bar; U.S. District Court, Southern District of Illinois; U.S. District Court, District of Colorado; U.S. Court of Appeals, Seventh Circuit. *Education:* Carleton College (B.A., summa cum laude, 1985); Harvard Law School (J.D., cum laude, 1988). Phi Beta Kappa. Author: "Final Overtime Requirements," Natural Law Journal May 24, 2004," "Overtime Requirements," Natural Law Journal March 29, 2004, "Evaluating the Desirability of Federally Mandated Parental Leave," Family Law Quarterly, Fall, 1988, Contributing Editor to "Developing Labor Law," Third Edition. *Member:* Illinois State and American (Member, Labor and Employment Law Section, Employee Rights and Responsibilities Committee) Bar Associations. ***PRACTICE AREAS:*** Labor and Employment Law; Restrictive Covenants; Employee Benefits Litigation; Executive Compensation; Litigation; Class Action Litigation. ***Email:*** dhaase@jenner.com

JOHN J. HAMILL, born Rockville Centre, New York, August 2, 1968; admitted to bar, 1993, Illinois; 1994, U.S. District Court, Northern District of Illinois; 1995, U.S. Court of Appeals, Third Circuit; 1996, U.S. Court of Appeals, Sixth Circuit; 1998, U.S. Court of Appeals, Seventh Circuit; 1999, U.S. Court of Appeals, Fourth, Fifth, Tenth and District of Columbia Circuits; 2000, U.S. Supreme Court and U.S. Court of Appeals, Eleventh Circuit; 2001, U.S. Court of Appeals, Ninth Circuit, U.S. District Court, Western District of Michigan, U.S. District Court, Western District of Wisconsin, U.S. District Court, Eastern District of Arkansas and U.S. District Court, Central District of Illinois. *Education:* University of Notre Dame (B.A., summa cum laude, 1990); Harvard University (J.D., cum laude, 1993). Co-Author: Case Note, "State Oil v. Khan," 36 ISBA Antitrust & Unfair Competition Law,

(This Listing Continued)

JENNER & BLOCK LLP, Chicago—Continued

May 1998; "Discovery in Federal and State Courts in Illinois," 1996 Supplement (IICLE); "1995 Antitrust Guidelines for the Licensing of Intellectual Property," 33 ISBA Antitrust & Unfair Competition Law, June. 1995. *Member:* Seventh Circuit Bar Association; Illinois Appellate Lawyers Association. ***PRACTICE AREAS:*** Litigation; Antitrust; Trade Regulation; Appellate Practice; Supreme Court Practice; Telecommunications. ***Email:*** jhamill@jenner.com

DAVID A. HANDZO, born Colts Neck, New Jersey, April 20, 1954; admitted to bar, 1980, Illinois; 1984, District of Columbia. *Education:* Princeton University (B.A., magna cum laude, 1976); University of Michigan (J.D., magna cum laude, 1980). Order of the Coif. Staff Attorney, District of Columbia Public Defender Service, 1984-1988. (Resident, Washington, D.C. Office). ***PRACTICE AREAS:*** Civil Law; Criminal Law; Bankruptcy Litigation; Advertising Law. ***Email:*** dhandzo@jenner.com

JOHN R. HARRINGTON, born Normandy, Missouri, September 3, 1968; admitted to bar, 1995, Illinois; 1997, U.S. Court of Appeals, Seventh Circuit; 1998, U.S. District Court, Northern District of Illinois, U.S. District Court, District of Colorado and U.S. Court of Appeals, Sixth Circuit; 1999, U.S. Court of Appeals, Fourth and Tenth Circuits; 2001, U.S. District Court, Eastern District of Michigan; 2002, U.S. District Court, Western District of Wisconsin. *Education:* Northwestern University (B.A., 1990); Indiana University, Bloomington (J.D., magna cum laude, 1995). Order of the Coif. Author: "Up In Smoke: The FTC's Refusal to Apply the Unfairness Doctrine to Camel Cigarette Advertising," 47 Fed. Comm. L.J. 593, 1995. *Member:* Federal Communications Bar Association. ***PRACTICE AREAS:*** Litigation; Telecommunications Law. ***Email:*** jharrington@jenner.com

DONALD R. HARRIS, (LTD.), born Lake Preston, South Dakota, April 21, 1938; admitted to bar, 1963, Illinois, U.S. District Court, Northern District of Illinois, U.S. District Court, Western District of Texas, U.S. District Court, Eastern District of Wisconsin and U.S. Court of Appeals, Third, Fourth, Sixth, Seventh, Ninth and Federal Circuits; 1977, U.S. Supreme Court; 1995, U.S. Court of Federal Claims. *Education:* State University of Iowa (B.A., 1959; J.D., 1961). Order of the Coif; Phi Delta Phi. Notes Editor, Iowa Law Review, 1960-1961. Author: "Complying With U.S. Antitrust Laws," III-5 International Legal Strategy 42 (1994); "Recent U.S. Litigation Effecting Japanese Companies," III-6 International Legal Strategy 35 (1994). *Member:* Chicago, Illinois State, Seventh Federal Circuit, ITC Trial Lawyers and American Bar Associations; American College of Trial Lawyers; Chicago Council of Lawyers. ***PRACTICE AREAS:*** Litigation; Antitrust; Trade Regulation; White Collar Criminal Defense Counseling; Intellectual Property; Technology Law. ***Email:*** dharris@jenner.com

PHILIP L. HARRIS, born Cedar Rapids, Iowa, March 5, 1958; admitted to bar, 1983, Iowa; 1984, Illinois. *Education:* Northwestern University (B.A., 1980); University of Chicago Law School (J.D., 1983). *Member:* Chicago, Illinois State, Iowa State and American Bar Associations; American Law Institute; Defense Research Institute. ***PRACTICE AREAS:*** Product Liability Litigation; Mass Tort Litigation; Commercial Litigation. ***Email:*** pharris@jenner.com

ARNOLD HARRISON, born Chicago, Illinois March 31, 1945; admitted to bar, 1970, Illinois. *Education:* University of Illinois (B.S., Accounting, 1967); Northwestern University (J.D., cum laude, 1970). Beta Alpha Psi; Phi Eta Sigma. Recipient, Elijah Sells Medal -CPA exam. Instructor, DePaul School of Law, LL.M. in Taxation Program, 1979-1983; Practitioner Instructor, Northwestern School of Law L.L.M. Program, 2003 and 2004. Member, Tenant-in-Common Association. *Member:* Chicago (Past Chairman, Corporate Tax Committee) and American Bar Associations. Past Member: Illinois CPA Society; American Institute of CPAs. ***PRACTICE AREAS:*** Taxation. ***Email:*** aharrison@jenner.com

MARK R. HEILBRUN, born Iowa City, Iowa, March 12, 1963; admitted to bar, 1990, Georgia; 1991, District of Columbia. *Education:* Emory University (B.A., summa cum laude, 1986); University of Texas at Austin (J.D., with honors, 1990). Phi Beta Kappa; Executive Editor, Review of Litigation; Order of the Coif; Deputy Staff Director and General Counsel, U.S. Senate Committee on the Judiciary, 2001- 2005. Emory University Board of Governors. (Resident, Washington, D.C. Office). ***PRACTICE AREAS:*** Appellate Litigation; Public Policy; Unfair Competition. ***Email:*** mheilbrun@jenner.com

WILLIAM D. HEINZ, born Carlinville, Illinois, November 26, 1947; admitted to bar, 1973, Illinois. *Education:* Millikin University (B.S., 1969); University of Illinois (J.D., 1973). Order of the Coif. Member, 1971-1972 and Notes and Comments Editor, 1972-1973, University of Illinois Law Forum (now Law Review). Law Clerk, Hon. Walter P. Gewin, U.S. Court of Appeals, Fifth Circuit, 1973-1974. Adjunct Professor, Northwestern University School of Law. Faculty, National Institute for Trial Advocacy. Member: Board of Visitors, University of Illinois College of Law, 1990-1993; Named Distinguished Graduate of University of Illinois College of Law, 1995; President's Council University of Illinois. Chair, Board of Directors, Legal Aid Bureau of Chicago, 1999-2001. Member: Executive Committee, Board of Directors, Metropolitan Family Services of Chicago; Board of Directors, North American Company for Life and Health Insurance; Board of Directors, Partners Financial Holdings, Inc., a Bank Holding Co. *Member:* Chicago (Member, Committee on Judicial Evaluation, 1990-1993), Illinois State (Chairman, Standing Committee on Liaison with the Attorney Registration and Disciplinary Commission, 1991-1992; Member, Special Committee on Professionalism, 1992-1995; Member, Section Council on Civil Practice and Procedure) and American Bar Associations; The Legal Club of Chicago. American College of Trial Lawyers. ***PRACTICE AREAS:*** Litigation; Unfair Competition Law; Professional Liability; Intellectual Property; Technology Law. ***Email:*** wheinz@jenner.com

REGINALD J. HILL, born Birmingham, Alabama, December 5, 1962; admitted to bar, 1994, Illinois; 1995, U.S. District Court, Northern District of Illinois; 2001, U.S. Court of Appeals, Seventh Circuit; 2004, U.S. Court of Appeals, Ninth and Federal Circuits; registered to practice before U.S. Patent and Trademark Office. *Education:* Tuskegee University (B.S.E.E., with highest honors, 1984); Georgia Institute of Technology (M.S.E.E., 1985); John Marshall Law School (J.D., cum laude, 1994). Eta Kappa Nu; Kappa Alpha Psi; Order of John Marshall; Giles S. Rich Moot Court Competition, Semi-Finalist. Recipient: Kappa Alpha Psi Southern Province Achievement Award, 1984; AT&T Distinguished Member of Technical Staff Award; National Merit Achievement Scholarship; National Action Council for Minorities in Engineering (NACME) Scholarship; NCR Scholarship. Co-Author: "Inevitable Disclosure — No Noncompete Is Needed," Employment Law Strategist, Vol. 3, No. 8, December 1997; "Hilton Davis Preserves Doctrine of Equivalents With Clarifications?" Intellectual Property Litigation, Vol. VIII, No. 1, Spring 1997. Author: "Shrinkwrap Licenses Are Enforceable," Intellectual Property Litigation, Vol. VIII, No. 3, Fall 1996; "Supreme Court Unanimously Affirms Markman v. Westview Instrument," Intellectual Property Litigation, Vol. VIII, No. 2, Summer 1996; "Can You Copy A Device Disclosed In An Expired Utility Patent?" ISBA Intellectual Property, Vol. 37, No. 4, June 1998. *Member:* Cook County, Illinois State (Chair, 2001-2002, Intellectual Property Section Council), and American (Seventh Circuit Reporter, 1994-1998, Intellectual Property Litigation Newsletter) Bar Associations. ***PRACTICE AREAS:*** Intellectual Property; Trade Secrets and Unfair Competition. ***Email:*** rhill@jenner.com

NORMAN M. HIRSCH, born Waco, Texas, February 19, 1955; admitted to bar, 1981, Illinois. *Education:* University of Chicago (B.A., with honors, 1977); Stanford University (J.D., 1980). Phi Beta Kappa. Note Editor, Stanford Law Review, 1979-1980. Law Clerk: Hon. Fred J. Cassibry, U.S. District Court, Eastern District of Louisiana, 1980-1981; Hon. Cecil F. Poole, U.S. Court of Appeals for the Ninth Circuit, 1981-1982. *Member:* Illinois State and American Bar Associations; Chicago Council of Lawyers. ***PRACTICE AREAS:*** Litigation; Antitrust and Trade Regulation; Professional Liability Litigation; Appellate Practice. ***Email:*** nhirsch@jenner.com

SAM HIRSCH, born Washington, D.C., December 2, 1962; admitted to bar, 1995, Maryland; 1997, District of Columbia. *Education:* Rice University (B.A., 1984); Harvard University (J.D., 1993). Treasurer and Editor, Harvard Law Review, 1992-1993. (Resident, Washington, D.C. Office). ***PRACTICE AREAS:*** Litigation; Election Law. ***Email:*** shirsch@jenner.com

WILLIAM A. HOHENGARTEN, born St. Paul, Minnesota, August 27, 1960; admitted to bar, 1995, New York; 1998, District of Columbia. *Education:* Reed College (B.A., 1984); Northwestern University (Ph.D., 1991); Yale University (J.D., 1994). Notes Editor, Yale Law Journal. (Resident, Washington, D.C. Office). ***PRACTICE AREAS:*** Litigation. ***Email:*** whohengarten@jenner.com

RUSSELL J. HOOVER, born Evanston, Illinois, April 27, 1940; admitted to bar, 1965, Illinois. *Education:* University of Notre Dame (A.B., cum laude, 1962); Georgetown University (J.D., 1965). *Member:* Illinois State and American (Member, Sections on: Litigation; Civil Practice and Procedure; Bench and Bar) Bar Associations. ***PRACTICE AREAS:*** Civil Law; Criminal Litigation; Tort Defense Law; Professional Liability; Attorney Disciplinary Proceedings; Environmental Law. ***Email:*** rhoover@jenner.com

DONALD S. HORVATH, born Chicago, Illinois, August 21, 1958; admitted to bar, 1984, Illinois. *Education:* University of Illinois (B.S., 1980); IIT/Chicago-Kent College of Law (J.D., 1984). Certified Public Accountant, Illinois, 1980. *Member:* Chicago, Illinois State and American Bar Associations. ***PRACTICE AREAS:*** Real Estate Law; Construction Law; Real Estate Finance. ***Email:*** dhorvath@jenner.com

DANIEL J. HURTADO, born Detroit, Michigan, October 18, 1949; admitted to bar, 1993, Illinois. *Education:* University of Michigan (B.A., 1980); Northwestern University (M.A., 1981; J.D., cum laude, 1993). Angell Scholarship. Articles Editor, Journal of Criminal Law and Criminology. Author: "Native American Graves Protection and Repatriation Act: Does it Subject Museums to an Unconstitutional Taking?" 6 Hofstra Property Law Journal 1, 1993. *Member:* Chicago, Illinois State, American and Hispanic National Bar Associations; Hispanic Lawyers Association of Illinois; American Intellectual Property Law Association. ***PRACTICE AREAS:*** Litigation; Class Action Litigation; Intellectual Property; Technology Law. ***Email:*** dhurtado@jenner.com

ANDREW A. JACOBSON, born Peru, Illinois, January 4, 1964; admitted to bar, 1992, Illinois and U.S. District Court, Northern District of Illinois, including Trial Bar; 2000, U.S. Court of Appeals, Federal Circuit. *Education:* Loyola University of Chicago (B.A., summa cum laude, 1986); University of Illinois (J.D., summa cum laude, 1992). Order of the Coif. Topics Editor, University of Illinois Law Review. *Member:* Chicago and American Bar Associations; American Intellectual Property Law Association. ***PRACTICE AREAS:*** Litigation; Intellectual Property. ***Email:*** ajacobson@jenner.com

ALBERT E. JENNER, JR. (1907-1988)

DAVID JIMÉNEZ-EKMAN, born Chicago, Illinois, October 23, 1967; admitted to bar, 1992, Illinois; 1993, U.S. District Court, Northern District of Illinois; 1994, U.S. District Court, Southern District of Illinois and U.S. Court of Appeals, Seventh Circuit; 1996, U.S. Supreme Court. *Education:* University of Chicago (A.B., with honors, 1988); Boalt Hall School of Law, University of California at Berkeley (J.D., 1992). Order of the Coif. Law Clerk, Honorable Suzanne B. Conlon, U.S. District Court, Northern District of Illinois, 1992-1993. *Member:* Chicago and American Bar Associations. ***PRACTICE AREAS:*** Appellate Practice; Litigation; Media and First Amendment; Professional Liability; White Collar Crime. ***Email:*** djimenez-ekman@jenner.com

PAUL F. JOCK II, born Indianapolis, Indiana, January 25, 1943; admitted to bar, 1970, Illinois; 1990, New York. *Education:* University of Notre Dame (B.B.A., cum laude, 1965); University of Chicago Law School (J.D., 1970). Associate Editor, The University of Chicago Law Review. Associate Member, Indiana Association of Certified Public Accountants, 1966—. *Member:* American Bar Association; The Association of the Bar of the City of New York. [Lieutenant, U.S. Naval Reserve, 1965-1967]. (Resident, New York, N.Y. Office). ***PRACTICE AREAS:*** Corporate and Securities; Investment Management; Private Market Funds and Investments. ***Email:*** pjock@jenner.com

ELMER W. JOHNSON, born Denver, Colorado, May 2, 1932; admitted to bar, 1957, Illinois. *Education:* Yale College (B.A., 1954); University of Chicago Law School (J.D., 1957). Vice President and General Counsel of International Harvester Company, 1981-1982. Special Counsel to Chairman of Ameritech Corp., 1982-1983. Vice President and General Counsel (1983-1987) and Executive Vice President and Director (1987-1988) of General Motors Corporation. Member, Legal Advisory Committee of New York Stock Exchange, 1987-1989. President and CEO, Aspen Institute (1999-2002). ***PRACTICE AREAS:*** Corporate. ***Email:*** ejohnson@jenner.com

CHESTER T. KAMIN, born Chicago, Illinois, July 30, 1940; admitted to bar, 1965, Illinois; 1971, U.S. Supreme Court; 1982, District of Columbia. *Education:* Harvard University (A.B., magna cum laude, 1962); University of Chicago (J.D., 1965). Lecturer in Law, University of Chicago Law School, 2001—. Member, Executive Board, Chicago Vol-

(This Listing Continued)

unteer Legal Services, 1968-1970. Member, Advisory Committee, Chicago Volunteer Legal Services Foundation, 1988—. Special Counsel to the Governor of Illinois, 1973-1974. Commissioner, Illinois Law Enforcement Commission, 1975-1977. Member, Illinois Criminal Justice Information Systems Council, 1976-1977. *Member:* Chicago (Chairman, Committee on Constitutional Revision, 1971-1972), Illinois State (Assembly Representative, 1972-1973) and American Bar Associations; Chicago Council of Lawyers; Lawyers' Club of the City of Chicago; American College of Trial Lawyers; American Bar Foundation. ***REPORTED CASES:*** Lead counsel in: Blue Cross & Blue Shield Mutual of Ohio v. Blue Cross & Blue Shield Association, 110 F.3d 318 (6th Cir. 1997); MCI Communications Corporation v. American Telephone & Telegraph, 708 F.2d 1081 (7th Cir. 1983), cert. denied, 104 S.Ct. 234; Mite Corp. v. Dixon, No. 79 C 200 (N.D. Ill.), 633 F.2d 486 (7th Cir. 1980), aff'd, 102 S.Ct 2629 (1982); United States v. Western Electric Co., 993 F.2d 1572 (D.C. Cir. 1993); Walker v. State Board of Elections, 65 Ill.2d 543, 359 N.E.2d 113 (1977). ***PRACTICE AREAS:*** Litigation. ***Email:*** ckamin@jenner.com

KATHLEEN E. KARELIS, born Pittsburgh, Pennsylvania, October 14, 1960; admitted to bar, 1990, Florida; 1991, District of Columbia. *Education:* Rollins College (B.A., 1985); Florida Institute of Technology (M.B.A., 1987); University of Miami School of Law (J.D., 1990). Order of the Coif; Managing Editor, University of Miami Law Review. (Resident, Washington, D.C. Office). ***PRACTICE AREAS:*** Government Contracts; Health Care Law; White Collar Criminal Defense and Counseling. ***Email:*** kkarelis@jenner.com

BRENT E. KIDWELL, born Gas City, Indiana, August 8, 1967; admitted to bar, 1993, Illinois, Indiana, U.S. District Court, Southern and Northern Districts of Indiana, U.S. District Court, Northern District of Illinois, U.S. Court of Appeals, Fifth and Seventh Circuits. *Education:* Indiana University (B.A., 1990; J.D., summa cum laude, 1993). Articles Editor, Indiana Law Review, 1992-1993. Author: "A Nation Divided: By What Standard Should Fourth Amendment Seizure Findings be Reviewed on Appeal," 26 Ind. L. Rev. 117, 1992; "The Americans with Disabilities Act of 1990: Overview and Analysis," 26 Ind. L. Rev. 707, 1993. Clerk, Hon. John D. Tinder, U.S. District Court, Southern District of Indiana, 1993-1994. [U.S. Army Reserve, Indiana National Guard, Spec. 4, 1984-1991]. ***PRACTICE AREAS:*** Litigation; Intellectual Property; Technology. ***Email:*** bkidwell@jenner.com

CHRISTIAN E. KIMBALL, born Salt Lake City, Utah, June 22, 1955; admitted to bar, 1983, Illinois. *Education:* Harvard University (B.A., magna cum laude, 1979); University of Chicago Law School (J.D., 1983). Order of the Coif. Associate Professor, Boston University School of Law, 1993-1998. Author: "Convertible Debt: Conversion as a Bargain Purchase," December 1995, Taxes, 781, reprinted in The Monthly Digest of Tax Articles, August 1996; "Taxing Uncertainty: Warrants and Convertible Debt in Private Taxable Acquisitions," December 1991, Taxes, 866; "Organizing the Corporate Venture," with Jeffrey T. Sheffield (First published by Corporate Clearing House in 1987; 1995 Edition published by Little, Brown and Company in 1995. Reprinted by the Practicing Law Institute in 1997 and each year thereafter). ***PRACTICE AREAS:*** Federal Income Tax (100%). ***Email:*** ckimball@jenner.com

CARTER H. KLEIN, born Waukegan, Illinois, July 11, 1947; admitted to bar, 1972, Illinois and U.S. District Court, Northern District of Illinois. *Education:* University of Illinois (B.A., 1969; J.D., summa cum laude, 1972). Partner, Jenner & Block, LLC, 1974—. Clerk to Judge Glenn K. Seidenfeld, Illinois Appellate Court, Second District, 1972-1974. Adjunct Professor of Business Law, Kellogg Graduate School of Management, Northwestern University, 1985-1987. Chair, Letter of Credit Subcommittee, American Bar Association Business Law Section (2003-2005); Chair, Consumer Credit Committee, Chicago Bar Association, 1993-1994; Co-Chair, Commercial and Financial Transactions Committee, Chicago Bar Association (September 2003-2004); Chair, International Law Committee, Chicago Bar Association, 2000-2001; Member, Editorial Advisory Board, Documentary Credit World (Letter of Credit Survey, Inc.). Editor, Uniform Laws Annotated Uniform Commercial Code - Forms and Materials (West Publishing). Editor, Illinois Practice - Uniform Commercial Code Forms Annotated (West Publishing). Participated in drafting process of Revised Article 5 of Uniform Commercial Code and International Standby Practices (ISP98). *Articles:* "Letters of Credit in Financial Transactions," Advanced Commercial Finance and Creditors Rights in Illinois (Illinois Institute for Continuing Legal Education, 1993); "Preferences in Letter of Credit Transactions - Review and Update," 10 Letters of Credit Report (July/August 1995); "Subrogation Rights and Letters of Credit -- Get Ready," 10 Letters of Credit Report 1 (May/June 1995); "Ten Noteworthy Letter of Credit Cases from the Twentieth Century - A Commercial Lawyer's View," 3 Documentary Credit World 17 (Dec. 1999); "Transfers and Assignments of Proceeds of Letter of Credit Proceeds," 2001 Annual Letter of Credit Survey 92-116 (Institute for International Banking Law & Practice); "Preparing for Security Interests in Letter of Credit Proceeds under Revised Article 9 of the UCC," 12 International Financial Services Association Network (May 2001); "How to Structure a Lease to Protect Against the Risk of a Bankruptcy of the Tenant," 26 Real Estate Issues 35-45 (Fall 2001); "Letters of Credit in Lease Transactions -- Part I," 16 ABA Probate & Property 28-33 (July/August 2002); "Letters of Credit in Lease Transactions, Part II: Drafting Tips," 16 ABA Probate & Property 43-47 (Nov./Dec. 2002); "The Effect on Letters of Credit of Enron," 7 Documentary Credit World," 21-29 (May 2003); "Real World Revised Article 9: Practical Guidance for 2003 and Beyond—Perfection Issues," 3-1 — 3-66 & 4-1 — 4-26 (IICLE Sept. 2003). *Member:* Chicago, Illinois State and American Bar Associations. ***PRACTICE AREAS:*** Banking Law; Commercial Loans; Loan Workouts; Consumer Credit; Uniform Commercial Code; Franchises and Franchising; Distribution; International Business Transactions. ***Email:*** cklein@jenner.com

TOBIAS L. KNAPP, born Madison, Wisconsin, November 17, 1969; admitted to bar, 1998, Massachusetts; 2000, New York; 2004, District of Columbia. *Education:* Amherst College (B.A., cum laude, 1991); Boston University School of Law (J.D., cum laude, 1997). Editor, Boston University Law Review. *Member:* The District of Columbia Bar. (Resident, New York, N.Y. Office). ***PRACTICE AREAS:*** Corporate; Securities; Mergers and Acquisitions. ***Email:*** tknapp@jenner.com

C. JOHN KOCH, born Peoria, Illinois, May 26, 1956; admitted to bar, 1981, Illinois, U.S. District Court, Northern District of Illinois and U.S. Court of Appeals, Seventh Circuit; 1984, Colorado, U.S. District Court, District of Colorado and U.S. Court of Appeals, Tenth Circuit. *Education:* Washington University (A.B., summa cum laude, 1978); University of

(This Listing Continued)

Chicago (J.D., 1981). Phi Beta Kappa. Law Clerk to Judge David M. Ebel, U.S. Court of Appeals, Tenth Circuit, 1988. *Member:* American Bar Association. ***PRACTICE AREAS:*** Civil Law; Securities Litigation; Appellate Litigation. ***Email:*** jkoch@jenner.com

JEFFREY A. KOPPY, born Detroit, Michigan, September 30, 1969; admitted to bar, 1994, Illinois; 1996, U.S. District Court, Northern District of Illinois; 2001, U.S. District Court, Eastern District of Michigan. *Education:* University of Michigan (B.A., with distinction, 1991; J.D., magna cum laude, 1994). Order of the Coif. Member, 1991-1992 and Articles Editor, 1992-1993, University of Michigan Law Review. Law Clerk to Hon. Suzanne B. Conlon, U.S. District Court, Northern District of Illinois, 1994-1995. *Member:* Chicago and American Bar Associations. ***PRACTICE AREAS:*** Bankruptcy; Complex Civil Litigation; Intellectual Property; Telecommunications Law; Arbitration; Products Liability; Mass Torts. ***Email:*** jkoppy@jenner.com

DAVID M. KROEGER, born Quincy, Illinois, June 27, 1965; admitted to bar, 1992, New York; 1994, Illinois; 1995, U.S. Court of Appeals, Seventh Circuit and U.S. District Court, Central and Northern Districts of Illinois; 2001, U.S. Court of Appeals, Eighth Circuit; 2002, U.S. Court of Appeals, Second Circuit; 2003, U.S. District Court, Western District of Michigan. *Education:* University of Notre Dame (B.A., magna cum laude, 1987); University of Illinois (J.D., summa cum laude, 1990). Order of the Coif. Articles Editor, University of Illinois, 1989-1990. Law Clerk, Judge Harlington Wood, Jr., U.S. Court of Appeals, Seventh Circuit, 1990-1991. *Member:* Illinois State and American Bar Associations. ***PRACTICE AREAS:*** Litigation; Insurance Litigation and Counseling; Reinsurance Practice; Arbitration. ***Email:*** dkroeger@jenner.com

KENNETH A. KROOT, born Detroit, Michigan, October 1, 1956; admitted to bar, 1981, Illinois and U.S. District Court, Northern District of Illinois including Trial Bar; 1983, U.S. Court of Appeals, Seventh Circuit. *Education:* University of Erlangen-Nuremberg, Erlangen, West Germany; Kalamazoo College (B.A., magna cum laude, 1978); University of Michigan (J.D., cum laude, 1981). Phi Beta Kappa. Instructor, Legal Writing and Research, University of Michigan Law School, 1980-1981. *Member:* American Bar Association. ***PRACTICE AREAS:*** Intellectual Property and Technology Law; Products Liability; Mass Torts; Insurance Litigation; Class Action Litigation. ***Email:*** kkroot@jenner.com

DAVID C. LAYDEN, born Lafayette, Indiana, December 20, 1967; admitted to bar, 1993, Illinois and U.S. District Court, Northern District of Illinois; 1998, U.S. District Court, Western District of Michigan; 1999, U.S. District Court, Northern District of Indiana and U.S. Court of Appeals, Sixth Circuit; 2002, U.S. Supreme Court. *Education:* Washington University (B.A., magna cum laude, 1990); University of Michigan (J.D., cum laude, 1993). Phi Beta Kappa. *Member:* American Bar Association; Chicago Council of Lawyers. ***PRACTICE AREAS:*** Litigation; Bankruptcy; Corporate Reorganization; Insurance Litigation; Telecommunications Law. ***Email:*** dlayden@jenner.com

VINCENT E. LAZAR, born Chicago, Illinois, September 12, 1965; admitted to bar, 1990, Illinois and U.S. District Court, Northern District of Illinois; 1992, U.S. Court of Appeals, Seventh Circuit; 1998, U.S. Court of Appeals, Fifth Circuit; 2002, U.S. Court of Appeals, Second Circuit. *Education:* Northwestern University (B.A., 1987); University of Illinois College of Law (J.D., magna cum laude, 1990). Order of the Coif. Co-Author: Illinois Civil Litigation Guide, West Publishing, 2003. *Member:* Chicago and Illinois State Bar Associations; American Bankruptcy Institute; Turnaround Management Association. ***PRACTICE AREAS:*** Bankruptcy; Loan Restructuring; Commercial Litigation. ***Email:*** vlazar@jenner.com

LESLIE H. LEPOW, born New York, N.Y., September 16, 1949; admitted to bar, 1975, District of Columbia. *Education:* Columbia University (A.B., 1971); Georgetown University (J.D., 1974). (Resident, Washington, D.C. Office). ***PRACTICE AREAS:*** Government Contracts; Minority and Small Business Law; Government Investigations. ***Email:*** llepow@jenner.com

BARRY LEVENSTAM, born Chicago, Illinois, July 10, 1953; admitted to bar, 1978, Illinois and U.S. District Court, Northern District of Illinois; 1979, U.S. Court of Appeals, Seventh Circuit; 1981, U.S. Court of Appeals, District of Columbia Circuit; 1983, U.S. Supreme Court; 1987, U.S. Court of Appeals, Fifth and Ninth Circuits; 1988, U.S. Court of Appeals, Sixth Circuit; 1989, U.S. Court of Appeals for the Federal Circuit; 1991, U.S. District Court, Southern District of Illinois; 1993, U.S. Court of Appeals, Second Circuit; 1994, U.S. District Court, Central District of Illinois; 1999, U.S. Court of Appeals Eighth Circuit; 2000, U.S. Court of Appeals, Third Circuit; 2002, U.S. Court of Appeals, Tenth Circuit. *Education:* University of Illinois (B.S., summa cum laude, 1975; J.D., magna cum laude, 1978). Phi Beta Kappa; Order of the Coif. Member, Board of Editors, University of Illinois Law Forum, 1977-1978; Clerkships: Law Clerk: Hon. Robert J. Steigmann, 1977-1978; Hon. Philip W. Tone, U.S. Court of Appeals, Seventh Circuit, 1978-1979. Publications/Presentations: Co-Author: *Illinois Civil Litigation Guide*, West Publishing, 2002-2005; "The Attorney's Guide to the Seventh Circuit Court of Appeals," Seventh Circuit Bar Association, 1987-2005; "Preserving Error for Appeal in Illinois," 78 Illinois Bar Journal, 494, 1990; "Punitive Awards Against Successor Corporations: Deterrent of Malicious Torts or Legitimate Acquisitions?" 26 Tort & Insurance Law Journal 27, 1990; "The Role of Special Litigation Committees in Shareholder Derivative Litigation," Tort & Insurance Law Practice Journal, Vol. XXV, No. 4, Summer, 1990; "Plaintiff's Burden of Proving Enhanced Injury in Crashworthiness Cases: A Clash Worthy of Analysis," 38 De Paul Law Review 55, 1988; "Preserving Error in Civil Cases: Some Fundamental Principles," 1988 Trial Lawyer's Guide 1; "Special Litigation Committees," ALI-ABA Course Materials Journal, Vol. 9, No. 5, 1985. Author: Casenote, "Prohibition of Political Contributions by Illinois Liquor Licenses Constitutional," 1977 University of Illinois Law Forum 320. Member, University of Illinois College of Law Board of Visitors, 1997-2000. Lecturer: U.S. Court of Appeals, Seventh Circuit, Preservation of Error for Appeal, 2002; U.S. Court of Appeals, Seventh Circuit, Handling Appointed Appeals, 2000; U.S. Court of Appeals, Seventh Circuit, Persuasive Oral Argument, 1998; Federal Bar Association, Brief Writing for the Seventh Circuit, 1997; Seventh Circuit Judicial Conference, Civility in the Court of Appeals, 1996; Du Page County Bar Association, Preserving Error For Appeal, 1991; PLAC, Punitive Damages, 1990; IICLE, Handling an Appeal in the Seventh Circuit, 1987. Assistant to Chairman, Governor's Task Force on Crime and Corrections, 1992-1993. Recipient, The Walter J. Cummings Award for Pro Bono Advocacy in the Seventh Circuit for 1994. Co-Chair, Firm's Appellate and Supreme Court Practice Group; Co-Chair, Firm's Pro Bono Committee. *Member:* Illinois State, Seventh Circuit, Federal, and American Bar Associations; Appellate Lawyers Association; American Law Institute; American Academy of Appellate

(This Listing Continued)

JENNER & BLOCK LLP, Chicago—Continued

Lawyers. ***PRACTICE AREAS:*** Civil and Criminal Appellate Practice; Supreme Court Practice; Complex Court Litigation; Product Liability Law; Media and First Amendment Law. ***Email:*** blevenstam@jenner.com

RICHARD F. LEVY, born 1930; admitted to bar, 1954, New York; 1956, California; 1957, Illinois. *Education:* University of Pennsylvania (B.S., 1951); Columbia University (LL.B., 1954). (Also at New York, N.Y. Office). ***PRACTICE AREAS:*** Corporate Reorganization; Litigation; International Finance; Corporate Law; Bankruptcy. ***Email:*** rlevy@jenner.com

SUSAN C. LEVY, born Chicago, Illinois, October 10, 1957; admitted to bar, 1982, Illinois; U.S. District Court, Northern District of Illinois including Trial Bar; U.S. Court of Appeals, Seventh Circuit; 1994, U.S. Court of Appeals, Eighth Circuit. *Education:* Cornell University (A.B., magna cum laude, 1979); Harvard University (J.D., 1982). Phi Beta Kappa. *Member:* American Bar Association (Member, Litigation Section). ***PRACTICE AREAS:*** Civil Litigation; Insurance Litigation and Counseling; Products Liability and Mass Tort Defense; Government Contracts. ***Email:*** slevy@jenner.com

CHRISTOPHER D. LIGUORI, born New York, N.Y., August 17, 1962; admitted to bar, 1987, Illinois; 1988, U.S. District Court, Northern District of Illinois including Trial Bar; 1993, U.S. Court of Appeals, Fourth Circuit; 1996, U.S. Court of Appeals, Seventh and Ninth Circuits; 2000, U.S. Court of Federal Claims. *Education:* University of Michigan (B.A., 1984); American University, Washington College of Law (J.D., magna cum laude, 1987). Senior Topics Editor, American University Journal of International Law and Policy, 1986-1987. *Member:* American Bar Association (Member, Litigation Section). ***PRACTICE AREAS:*** Litigation; Products Liability and Mass Tort Defense; Domestic and International Arbitration; Shareholder Derivative Lawsuits. ***Email:*** cliguori@jenner.com

TERI A. LINDQUIST, born Clinton, Iowa, March 10, 1959; admitted to bar, 1986, Illinois and U.S. District Court, Northern District of Illinois; 2004, New York. *Education:* State University of New York at Plattsburgh (B.A., 1981); Northwestern University (J.D., 1986). *Member:* American Bar Association; New York State Bar Association. ***PRACTICE AREAS:*** Corporate Law; Commercial Law; Private Equity; Uniform Commercial Code; Finance; Bankruptcy Reorganization; Corporate Restructuring. ***Email:*** tlindquist@jenner.com

S. TONY LING, born Bloomington, Indiana, November 9, 1970; admitted to bar, 1996, Illinois and Indiana. *Education:* Northwestern University (B.A., 1993); Indiana University School of Law (J.D., cum laude, 1996). *Member:* Illinois State and American Bar Associations. ***PRACTICE AREAS:*** Employee Benefits; Executive Compensation. ***Email:*** tling@jenner.com

LINDA L. LISTROM, born Topeka, Kansas, March 17, 1952; admitted to bar, 1977, Illinois and U.S. District Court, Northern District of Illinois; 1978, U.S. Court of Appeals, Seventh Circuit. *Education:* University of Houston (B.A., magna cum laude, 1974); Harvard University (J.D., 1977). *Member:* American Bar Association, Section of Litigation (Co-Chair, Trial Practice Committee, 2002—; Member, Training the Trial Lawyer Task Force, 2002-2003; Member, Civil Trial Practice Standards Update Task Force, 2003—). American College of Trial Lawyers. ***PRACTICE AREAS:*** Civil Litigation. ***Email:*** llistrom@jenner.com

ERIC L. LOHRENZ, born Lincoln, Illinois, August 11, 1962; admitted to bar, 1987, Illinois and U.S. District Court, Northern District of Illinois; 1994, U.S. District Court, Eastern District of Wisconsin; 1998, U.S. District Court, Northern District of Indiana; 2003, U.S. Court of Appeals for the Federal Circuit; registered to practice before U.S. Patent and Trademark Office, 2000. *Education:* University of Illinois (B.S., with highest honors, 1984); Stanford Law School (J.D., with distinction, 1987). Tau Beta Pi; Phi Kappa Phi. Bronze Tablet. *Member:* American Bar Association; American Intellectual Property Law Association. ***PRACTICE AREAS:*** Patent Litigation. ***Email:*** elohrenz@jenner.com

DANIEL MACH, born Englewood, New Jersey, January 30, 1970; admitted to bar, 1998, New York; 1999, District of Columbia. *Education:* Princeton University (B.A., 1992); New York University (J.D., magna cum laude, 1996). Order of the Coif. Articles Editor, New York University Law Review. Author: "The Bold and the Beautiful: Art, Public Spaces and the First Amendment," 72 N.Y.U. L. Rev. 383, 1997. Law Clerk, The Hon. Barry T. Moskowitz, U.S. District Court, Southern District of California, 1996-1997. (Resident, Washington, D.C. Office). ***PRACTICE AREAS:*** Constitutional Law; First Amendment Law; Appellate Practice; Civil Litigation; Telecommunications Law. ***Email:*** dmach@jenner.com

THADDEUS J. MALIK, born Oak Park, Illinois, October 7, 1966; admitted to bar, 1991, Illinois. *Education:* Northwestern University (B.A., with distinction); Harvard Law School (J.D., cum laude, 1991). Phi Beta Kappa; Pi Sigma Alpha; Phi Alpha Delta; Phi Eta Sigma. *Member:* American Bar Association (Member, Business Law and Corporate Securities Sections). ***PRACTICE AREAS:*** Corporate; Mergers and Acquisitions; Securities. ***Email:*** tmalik@jenner.com

EDWARD F. MALONE, born Rockville Centre, New York, August 31, 1964; admitted to bar, 1991, Illinois; 1995, U.S. Court of Appeals, Seventh Circuit and U.S. District Court, Northern District of Illinois; 2000, Trial Bar; 2001, U.S. Supreme Court. *Education:* University of Chicago (A.B., with honors, 1986); University of California at Los Angeles (J.D., 1991). Order of the Coif. Chief Note and Comment Editor, UCLA Law Review. Author: "Legacy of the Reconstruction: The Vagueness of the Criminal Civil Rights Statutes," 38 UCLA Law Review 163, October 1990. Co-Author: "Testimonial Privileges," Thomson West, Third Edition, 2005; "Selected Issues Under the Federal Rules of Evidence," IICLE Federal Criminal Practice, 2005; "Who Goes to Jail? A Guide to Liability Under HIPAA," Compliance Today, January 2002; "Selected Issues Under the Federal Rules of Evidence," IICLE Federal Criminal Practice, 1997. Law Clerk to Judge Cynthia Holcomb Hall, U.S. Court of Appeals, Ninth Circuit. *Member:* American Bar Association; Chicago Council of Lawyers; Board of Governors. ***PRACTICE AREAS:*** Litigation; White Collar Criminal Defense; Appellate Practice; Health Care; Antitrust and Trade Regulation. ***Email:*** emalone@jenner.com

JULIE MONTZ MANDANAS, born Cedar Falls, Iowa, February 4, 1969; admitted to bar, 1997, Illinois and U.S. District Court, Northern District of Illinois. *Education:* Northwestern University (B.A., 1991); University of Illinois (J.D., magna cum laude, 1997). *Member:* Chicago and American Bar Associations. ***PRACTICE AREAS:*** Real Estate. ***Email:*** jmandanas@jenner.com

ROBERT T. MARKOWSKI, born Evergreen Park, Illinois, January 14, 1953; admitted to bar, 1978, Illinois and U.S. District Court, Northern District of Illinois including Trial Bar; U.S. Court of Appeals, Seventh Circuit; U.S. Court of Appeals, Ninth Circuit; U.S. District Court, Central District of Illinois; U.S. District Court, Eastern District of Michigan. *Education:* DePaul University (B.A., highest honors, 1975); University of Illinois (J.D., magna cum laude, 1978). Order of the Coif. Articles Editor, University of Illinois Law Forum, 1977-1978. Counsel to the Illinois Supreme Court Committee on Pattern Jury Instructions in Criminal Cases, 1981-1984. Co-Author: "Settlement and Comprimise," Class Actions, IICLE, 2001. Author: Note, "Compensability of the Elimination of Direct Access," University of Illinois Law Forum 463, 1977; Comment, "Remand Order Review After Thermtron Products," University of Illinois Law Forum 1086, 1977. *Member:* Federal and American Bar Associations. ***PRACTICE AREAS:*** Litigation; Professional Liability Litigation; Class Action Litigation; White Collar Criminal Defense; Counseling; Insurance Litigation Counseling. ***Email:*** rmarkowski@jenner.com

RONALD L. MARMER, born Miami, Florida, July 24, 1952; admitted to bar, 1977, Illinois; U.S. Supreme Court; U.S. Courts of Appeals, Second, Sixth, Seventh and Ninth Circuits; U.S. District Court, Northern District of Illinois, including Trial Bar and Eastern District of Michigan. *Education:* Northwestern University (B.S., with highest distinction, 1974; M.A., 1974); University of Virginia (J.D., 1977). Order of the Coif. Notes Editor, Virginia Law Review, 1976-1977. Author: "Opinion Polls and the Law of Evidence," 62 Virginia Law Review 1101, 1976. Co-Author: "Moore's Federal Practice, Vol. 5, Ch. 23 (3d ed.), 2004; "Class Actions, Notice to Members of the Class," IICLE, 2004; "Conducting Internal Investigations After Sarbanes-Oxley: Best Practices," American Law Institute-American Bar Association, 2004; "Operating In The New World Of Securities Reform," Insights, 1996; "Securities Law, Special Problems of Insiders," IICLE, 1996 Supplement; "Soft Information Litigation In The State Courts: The Next Frontier," Fulcrum Information Services, Inc., 1996; "Defending Director and Officer Liability Litigation," AIG Consultants, Inc., 1992; "Potential Liability of Attorneys In Securities Transactions," American Bar Association, 1991; "The Role of Litigation In Control Contests," The Corporate Analyst, 1989; "Developments In Insider Trading Under Rules 10b-5 and 14e-3," American Bar Association National Institute on Insider Trading, 1987; "The Use of Civil RICO in Securities Litigation," The Review of Securities and Commodities Regulation, Vol. 18, 1985; "Strategic Considerations for Civil Conspiracy Claims Under RICO," American Bar Association, 1983; "Waiver of the Attorney-Client Privilege by Disclosure to Government Agencies," American Bar Association, 1983; "Hostile Tender Offers: Offensive and Defensive Litigation Strategies," American Bar Association, 1983; "Preserving the Confidentiality of Legal Audits," American Bar Association, 1983; "Strategic Considerations for Civil RICO, Section 16(b), Special Litigation Committees and Settlements," American Law Institute-American Bar Association, 1983; "Private Rights of Action for Violation of Proxy and Tender Rules," Practicing Law Institute, 1983; "Developments Under Rules 10b-5 and 14e-3," Practicing Law Institute, 1982; "Fiduciary Duties of Board in Control Contests," Practicing Law Institute, 1982. Member, Third Circuit Task Force on the Selection of Class Counsel, 2001. *Member:* Chicago (Member, Council of Lawyers); Chicago Chairman, Securities Committee, 1995-1996; Vice Chairman, Securities Committee, 1993-1995; Chairman, Subcommittee on Professional Responsibility of Securities Lawyers, 1988-1990), Illinois State and American (Member, Sections on: Litigation, Co-Director, Division V, Substantive Areas of Litigation, 2002—; Co-Director, Division VI, The Profession, 2001-2002; Co-Chair, Securities Litigation Committee, 2000-2001, Member, Task Force on the Public Perception of the Litigation Process, 1999-2000; Co-Chair, Professional Liability Litigation Committee, 1995-1999; Business Law, Vice Chair, Securities Litigation Subcommittee, 1993-1999) Bar Associations; American Law Institute. ***PRACTICE AREAS:*** Litigation; Class Actions; Securities Litigation; Professional Liability. ***Email:*** rmarmer@jenner.com

SARAH R. MARMOR, born Minneapolis, Minnesota, September 7, 1965; admitted to bar, 1993, Illinois and U.S. Court of Appeals, Seventh Circuit; 1995, U.S. District Court, Northern District of Illinois. *Education:* Princeton University (B.A., magna cum laude, 1987); Northwestern University (J.D., magna cum laude, 1993). Order of the Coif. ***LANGUAGES:*** French. ***PRACTICE AREAS:*** Products Liability; Mass Tort Defense; Litigation; Insurance Litigation; Labor and Employment. ***Email:*** smarmor@jenner.com

ARTHUR MEAD MARTIN, born Cleveland Heights, Ohio, March 29, 1942; admitted to bar, 1966, Illinois; 1969, U.S. District Court, Northern District of Illinois; 1970, U.S. Court of Appeals, Seventh Circuit; 1980, U.S. Supreme Court; 2000, U.S. Court of Appeals, Federal Circuit. *Education:* Princeton University (A.B., 1963); Harvard University (LL.B., 1966). Instructor in Law, University of Wisconsin Law School, 1966-1968. Illinois Legislative Reference Bureau, 1969. Author: "Applicability of State Blue Sky Laws to Employee Benefit Plans," Chicago Bar Record, 1978. Co-Author: "Historical and Practice Notes" to the Illinois Civil Practice Act and Supreme Court Rules, Smith-Hurd Edition of the Illinois Revised Statutes, 1972-1988; "The Role of Litigation in Control Contests," Practicing Law Institute, 1988, The Corporate Analyst, 1989; "Directors' Obligations to Monitor for Law Compliance and Ethical Behavior," Prentice-Hall Law and Business, 1987. Member, Consultative Group on Restatement of Agency, Illinois, 1999—. *Member:* Chicago (Member, Board of Editors, Chicago Bar Record, 1970-1986), Illinois State and American Bar Associations; American Arbitration Association (Panel Member, 1991-1995); American Law Institute; Legal Club of Chicago; Law Club of Chicago. ***PRACTICE AREAS:*** Corporate Law; Securities Law; Mergers and Acquisitions Law; General Business Law; Licensing of Intellectual Property. ***Email:*** amartin@jenner.com

CRAIG C. MARTIN, born Newark, New Jersey, July 1, 1963; admitted to bar, 1988, Colorado and U.S. District Court, District of Colorado; 1989, Illinois, U.S. Court of Appeals, Tenth Circuit and U.S. District Court, Northern District of Illinois including Trial Bar; 1993, U.S. Court of Appeals, Second Circuit; 1996, U.S. District Court, District of Arizona; 1997, U.S. Court of Appeals, Fifth Circuit; 1998, U.S. Court of Appeals, Third and Ninth Circuits; 1999, U.S. Supreme Court, U.S. District Court, Eastern and Western Districts of Michigan; 2000, U.S. Court of Appeals, Sixth Circuit; 2001, U.S. Court of Appeals, Seventh Circuit. *Education:* University of Notre Dame (B.A., magna cum laude, 1985); Harvard Law School (J.D., 1988). Co-Author: "The Fiduciary Exception to the Attorney-Client Privilege," 34 Tort & Insurance Law Journal 827, Spring 1999. Vice-Chair, Board of

(This Listing Continued)

Directors, Boys & Girls Clubs of Chicago, 1996—. Member, Board of Directors, Chicago Foundation for Education, 1998—. *Member:* Colorado, Illinois State and American Bar Associations; Economic Club of Chicago. ***PRACTICE AREAS:*** Litigation; Complex Commercial Litigation; ERISA Litigation; Intellectual Property and Technology Litigation; Employment Litigation; Employee Benefits; Compensation; Business Counseling. ***Email:*** cmartin@jenner.com

JEFF J. MARWIL, born Huntington Woods, Michigan, October 10, 1961; admitted to bar, 1986, Illinois; 1988, U.S. District Court, Northern District of Illinois, Trial Bar. *Education:* University of Michigan (B.A., 1983); DePaul University (J.D., 1986). Member, De-Paul Law Review, 1985-1986. ***PRACTICE AREAS:*** Corporate Restructuring; Bankruptcy; Creditor's Rights; Healthcare Insolvency; Finance. ***Email:*** jmarwil@jenner.com

TERRI L. MASCHERIN, born Trenton, New Jersey, July 9, 1959; admitted to bar, 1984, Illinois and U.S. District Court, Northern District of Illinois including Trial Bar; 1987, U.S. Court of Appeals, Seventh Circuit; 1991, U.S. District Court, Northern District of California; 1995, U.S. Supreme Court; 1998, U.S. District Court, Eastern and Western Districts of Michigan and U.S. District Court, Eastern and Western Districts of Wisconsin; 1999, U.S. District Court, District of Arizona, U.S. District Court, District of Colorado and U.S. Court of Appeals, Sixth, Ninth and Tenth Circuits. *Education:* Duke University (A.B., magna cum laude, 1981); Northwestern University (J.D., cum laude, 1984). Phi Eta Sigma; Order of the Coif. President's Senior Leadership Award, 1981. Managing Editor, Journal of Criminal Law and Criminology, 1983-1984. Chairperson, Julius H. Miner Moot Court Board, 1983-1984. Member, Board of Directors, Chicago Lawyers' Committee for Civil Rights Under The Law, 1991-1997. *Member:* Chicago Bar Association (Chair, Strategic Planning Committee; Past Member, Board of Managers; Past Member, Executive Council, Young Lawyers Section, Past Chair, Professional Responsibility Committee; and Past Member, Judicial Evaluation Committee); American Bar Association (Member, Sections on: Litigation; Communications; Chair, Steering Committee of the Death Penalty Representation Project); Illinois State Bar Association; Women's Bar Association of Illinois. ***PRACTICE AREAS:*** Litigation; Telecommunications Law; Bankruptcy; Corporate Restructuring; Intellectual Property Litigation; Technology Law. ***Email:*** tmascherin@jenner.com

LORELIE S. MASTERS, born Fremont, Michigan, December 5, 1954; admitted to bar, 1981, District of Columbia; 1982, U.S. Court of Appeals for the District of Columbia Circuit and U.S. District Court for the District of Columbia; 1985, U.S. District Court, Eastern District of Michigan; 1986, U.S. Court of Appeals, Fourth Circuit; 1998, U.S. Supreme Court; 2000, New York. *Education:* Georgetown University (A.B., 1977); Notre Dame University Law School (J.D., 1981). Scholar, Thomas J. and Alberta White Center for Law and Public Policy. Editor-in-Chief, Journal of Legislation, 1980-1981. Books: Author: "Liability Insurance in International Arbitration: The Bermuda Form," Hart Publishing, Oxford, England, July 2004; "Insurance Coverage Litigation," Aspen Law & Business, 2d Edition, Jan. 2000. Representative Articles: "Dangers Lurk in Cyberspace: A Primer on Risks and Insurance," Business Law Today, July/August 2002, at 40; "Terrorism Insurance," Legal Times, April 15, 2002, at 31; "Coverage for 'Incorporation' of a Policyholder's Defective Products into Third Party Property," Coverage, Vol. 5, No. 6, Nov./Dec. 1995, at 20. Co-Author with J. Kazanjian, "Beware of 'Absolutes': 'Absolute' or 'Total' Pollution Exclusions Should Not Bar Insurance Coverage of Product Claims Against Pesticide Manufacturers," Pesticides, Chemical Regulation, and Right-to-Know Committee Newsletter, Newsletter of the American Bar Association, Section of Environment, Energy and Resources, Vol. 2, No. 2, May 2001, at 7. *Member:* District of Columbia Bar (Member, Judicial Evaluations Committee, 2000—; Steering Committee, Section of Litigation, 2003—); American Bar Association (Member, Section on Litigation; Co-Chair, Newsletters Committee; Insurance Coverage Litigation Committee, 2000-2003). (Resident, Washington, D.C. Office). ***REPORTED CASES:*** Central Me. Power Co. v. Ernest A. Moore, No. CV-93-489 (Me. Super. Ct. May 16, 1999 and Jury Verdict, Jan. 10, 2000); Hoechst Celanese Corp. v. North River Insurance Co., No. 89C-SE-35 (jury verdict, Del. Super. Ct. Sept. 26, 1997); Hoechst Celanese Corp. v. Certain Underwriters at Lloyd's, London, 673 A.2d 164 (Del. 1996); Hoechst Celanese Corp. v. Certain Underwriters at Lloyd's, London, 656 A.2d 1094 (Del. 1995); In re Hoechst Celanese Corp., 584 N.Y.S.2d 805 (1st Dep't 1992). ***PRACTICE AREAS:*** Litigation; Insurance Coverage; Arbitration. ***Email:*** lmasters@jenner.com

JOHN H. MATHIAS, JR., born Chicago, Illinois, March 7, 1947; admitted to bar, 1972, Illinois; 1976, California. *Education:* Dartmouth College (A.B., 1969); Harvard University (J.D., 1972). Phi Beta Kappa. Co-Author: "Insurance Coverage Disputes," Law Journal Seminars Press, 1996; "Directors and Officers Liability: Prevention Insurance and Indemnification," Law Journal Press, 2000. *Member:* Chicago, Illinois State and American (Co-Chair, Insurance Coverage Litigation Committee, Section of Litigation, 1992-1994; Council Member, 1998-2001) Bar Associations; Dartmouth Lawyers Association (President, 1984-1989). ***PRACTICE AREAS:*** Litigation; Insurance Coverage Litigation; Class Actions. ***Email:*** jmathias@jenner.com

J. KEVIN McCALL, born Evanston, Illinois, July 9, 1953; admitted to bar, 1979, Illinois and U.S. Court of Appeals, Third Circuit; 1980, U.S. Court of Appeals, Seventh Circuit and U.S. District Court, Northern District of Illinois; 1990, U.S. Court of Appeals, Ninth and District of Columbia Circuits and U.S. District Court, Eastern District of Michigan; 1996, U.S. District Court, Southern District of Texas; 1998, U.S. Supreme Court; 2001, U.S. District Court, Southern District of Illinois; 2002, U.S. Court of Appeals, Eleventh Circuit. *Education:* Loyola University of Chicago (A.B., 1976; J.D., cum laude, 1979). Author: "A New Combination to Davy Jones' Locker: Melee Over Marine Minerals," Loyola University of Chicago Law Journal Vol. 9, No. 4, 1978. Executive Editor, Loyola Law Journal, 1978-1979. Law Clerk to Hon. Warren H. Young, U.S. District Court, Virgin Islands, 1979-1980. Vice President, Board of Directors, Pro Bono Advocates, 1990-1991. *Member:* Illinois State and American Bar Associations. ***PRACTICE AREAS:*** Litigation; Class Actions; Securities Law; Insurance; Professional Liability Litigation; Commercial Law; Uniform Commercial Code; Labor and Employment. ***Email:*** jmccall@jenner.com

THOMAS J. McCARTHY, born Milwaukee, Wisconsin, December 11, 1955; admitted to bar, 1981, Illinois; 1982, U.S. District Court, Northern District of Illinois; 1984, U.S. Court of Appeals for the Seventh Circuit; 1988, U.S. District Court, Central District of Illinois; 1993, U.S. Court of Appeals for the Federal Circuit. *Education:* Cornell University (A.B., 1978); Georgetown University (J.D., magna cum laude, 1981). Phi Alpha Delta. Law

(This Listing Continued)

Clerk, District Judge Marvin E. Aspen, Northern District of Illinois, 1982. *Member:* American Bar Association (Member: Litigation Section; Individual Rights Section; Public Utility, Communications and Transportation Law Section); Chicago Council of Lawyers. ***PRACTICE AREAS:*** Litigation; Commercial Arbitration; Energy; Securities Litigation; Professional Liability Litigation; Class Action Litigation; Products Liability; Mass Tort Defense. ***Email:*** tmccarthy@jenner.com

JAMES A. McKENNA, born Chicago, Illinois, March 9, 1952; admitted to bar, 1977, Illinois. *Education:* University of Dayton (B.A., 1974); Northwestern University (J.D., 1977). Note and Comment Editor, Northwestern University Law Review, 1976-1977. Author: "Reverse Freedom of Information Acts Suits: Confidential Information in Search of Protection," 70 Northwestern University Law Review 996, 1976; "The Constitutional Protection of Private Papers: The Role of a Hierarchical Fourth Amendment," 53 Indiana Law Journal 55, 1977. *Member:* Illinois State and American Bar Associations. ***PRACTICE AREAS:*** Litigation; Intellectual Property; Antitrust; Class Actions; Reinsurance; Technology Law. ***Email:*** jmckenna@jenner.com

THOMAS A. MONSON, born Mason City, Iowa, April 2, 1960; admitted to bar, 1985, Illinois. *Education:* University of Illinois (B.S., Mechanical Engineering, 1982); Harvard Law School (J.D., cum laude, 1985). ***PRACTICE AREAS:*** Mergers and Acquisitions; Securities; General Corporate. ***Email:*** tmonson@jenner.com

SCOTT J. MOORE, born Framingham, Massachusetts, 1960; admitted to bar, 1988, Illinois; 2001, District of Columbia. *Education:* University of Illinois at Chicago (B.S., with highest honors, 1985); University of Illinois School of Law (J.D., magna cum laude, 1988). Phi Kappa Phi. *Member:* American Bar Association. ***PRACTICE AREAS:*** Corporate Finance; Asset Securitization; Corporate Law. ***Email:*** smoore@jenner.com

GAIL H. MORSE, born August 27, 1957; admitted to bar, 1982, California; 1985, District of Columbia; 1993, Illinois; 1994, Colorado. *Education:* University of San Diego (B.B.A., magna cum laude, 1979; J.D., cum laude, 1982); Georgetown University (M.L.T., 1986). Phi Alpha Delta. Member, San Diego Law Review, 1981-1982. Attorney-Advisor, Office of Chief Counsel, Legislation and Regulations Division, Internal Revenue Service, 1983-1987. *Member:* Chicago, San Diego and American Bar Associations. ***PRACTICE AREAS:*** Tax Law. ***Email:*** gmorse@jenner.com

DANIEL R. MURRAY, born Alexandria, Louisiana, March 23, 1946; admitted to bar, 1970, Illinois. *Education:* University of Notre Dame (A.B., maxima cum laude, 1967); Harvard University (J.D., 1970). Co-Author: "Uniform Laws Annotated—UCC Forms and Materials," 2001; "Illinois Practice: Uniform Commercial Code with Illinois Code Comments," 2003; "Secured Transactions," 1978; "Illinois Practice—UCC Forms Annotated," 2002; "Problems of Proof in a Paperless World: Electronic Information As Evidence in Commercial Litigation, 35 U.C.C.L.J. 1 (2002); "The Uniform Rules of Evidence: State Gladiators Go High Tech With Records—Will the Feds Follow?," 54 Okla. L. Rev. 573 (2001); and "Stepping Up to the Next Level from the UETA To the URE and Beyond," 37 Idaho Law Reviw 415 (2001). Contributing Editor, Norton Bankruptcy Law and Practice, 2nd Edition. Trustee, Chicago, Missouri and Western Railway Co., 1988-1997. Adjunct Professor, University of Notre Dame Law School. Member: American College of Commercial Finance Lawyers; American Bankruptcy College; American Law Institute; Board of Trustees, Catholic Theological Union, Chicago, Illinois; National Board of Advisors, Bernardin Center for Theology and Ministry; Board of Directors, Big Shoulders Fund; Board of Governors, Catholic Lawyers Guild. *Member:* Chicago, Illinois State and American (Member, Business Bankruptcy Committee, Uniform Commercial Code Committee, and Subcommittees on Secured Transactions, Litigation and Commercial Paper, and Payment Systems, Business Law Section) Bar Associations; American Bankruptcy Institute; Chicago Council of Lawyers; The Lawyers Club of Chicago; Transportation Lawyers Association; Association of Transportation Practitioners. ***PRACTICE AREAS:*** Commercial Law; Litigation; Reorganization Law; Bankruptcy Law; Transportation Law. ***Email:*** dmurray@jenner.com

MATTHEW M. NEUMEIER, born Racine, Wisconsin, September 13, 1954; admitted to bar, 1987, New York; 1988, Michigan and U.S. District Court, Eastern District of Michigan; 1991, Illinois and U.S. District Court, Northern District of Illinois including Trial Bar; 1992, U.S. Court of Appeals, Seventh Circuit and U.S. Supreme Court; 1998, U.S. Court of Appeals, Federal Circuit. *Education:* University of Michigan (B.G.S., with distinction, 1981); Harvard University (J.D., magna cum laude, 1984). Editor, Harvard Law Review, 1982-1984. Law Clerk: Hon. J. Clifford Wallace, U.S. Court of Appeals, 9th Circuit, 1984-1985; Hon. Warren E. Burger, Chief Justice of the U.S. Supreme Court, 1985-1986. Author: Note, "Class Certification in Mass Accident Cases Under Rule 23(b)(1)," 96 Harv. L. Rev. 1143, 1983. Author: "Legal Developments USA: The People v. Corporate America," Legal Week, 2004; "Preservation Orders: Navigating An Electronic Minefield," Mealey's Litigation Report: Discovery, 2004; "Electronic Dividends: Achieving Maximum Returns Through The Rule 26(f) Conference," Mealey's Litigation Report: Discovery, 2004; "Paper Or Plastic? — The Hunt For Electronic Treasure During Discovery," Mealey's Litigation Report: Discovery, 2003; "How The Supreme Court Decides To Review Intellectual Property Cases," The Review of Intellectual Property Law at The John Marshall Law School, Vol. 3, No. 1, 2003, 3 J. Marshall Rev. Intell. Prop. L. 19; "Avoiding The Pitfalls Of Electronic Discovery," Mealey's Litigation Report: Discovery, 2003; "Recent Trends in Federal Preemption of State Law Claims Under The Federal Home Owners' Loan Act of 1933," 2002. Co-Author: "Directors & Officers Liability: Prevention, Insurance and Indemnification," Law Journal Press Treatise, 2000; "Law Department Management," Successful Partnering Between Inside and Outside Counsel," R. Haig, ed., West Group, 2000; "Offensive and Defensive Strategy and Tactics for Electronic Discovery," Glasser Legal Works, new events 2000; "Advertising Liability on the Internet," Annual Meeting, American Bar Association, 2000 and The Practical Lawyer, July 2001; The Anticybersquatting Consumer Protection Act, Annual Meeting, American Bar Association, 2000; SEC and Internet Issues: SEC Issues Update 2000, Glasser Legal Works, 2000; "e-Commerce 'Storefront' Development and Hosting," Practicing Law Institute, 1999 and 2000; "Restatement (Third) of Torts: Products Liability-New Developments," Products Liability Committee, American Bar Association Litigation Section, 2000; "Defending the Class Action Lawsuit," National Business Institute, 2000; "Consumer Bankruptcy: The Reaffirmation Process," Rev. of Banking & Fin. Services, Vol. 15, No. 1, 1999; "Reaffirmation Agreement Litigation: The Defense Perspective," Practicing Law Institute, 1999. Speaker: Co-Chair, Mealey's Trial Preparation Skills for Paralegals Conference, 2003; 2003 John Marshall Law

(This Listing Continued)

JENNER & BLOCK LLP, Chicago—Continued

School Intellectual Property Law Conference; LegalTech (Chicago, IL and New York City), 2002; Executive Breakfast Briefing: Electronic Discovery in the Corporate Environment, 2002; Co-Chair, 5th, 6th and 7th Annual Online & Internet Commerce Law Institute, Glasser Legal Works and ABA Section of Science & Technology Law Seminar, 2000; "TROs & Injunctions: Domain Name and Trademark Battles," Intellectual Property Litigation Seminar, Loyola University Chicago School of Law, 2000 and 2004; SEC and the Internet, SEC Issues Update 2000, Glasser Legal Works Seminar, 2000; "e-Commerce: Strategies for Success in the Digital Economy," Practicing Law Institute, 1999 and 2000; "Business Torts on the Electronic Frontier," Tort & Insurance Practice Section Annual Meeting, American Bar Association, 2000; "Litigating the Class Action Lawsuit," National Business Institute, 2000; Third, Fourth, Fifth, Sixth and Seventh Annual Conferences on Electronic Discovery, Glasser Legal Works Seminar, 2000-2004; "Electronic Evidence: Discovery," Chicago Bar Association Seminar, 2000; Products Liability Committee Mid-Year Meeting, American Bar Association Litigation Section, 2000; "Intellectual Property Seminar on e-Commerce," Chicago Bar Association Young Lawyers Section, 2000; "Consumer Financial Services Litigation," Practicing Law Institute, 1999; "Year 2000 Legal Issues Overview," John Marshall Law School, LL.M. course on Contemporary Problems in Computer Law, 1999; "Prospects for Year 2000 Litigation," Computer Law Committee, Chicago Bar Association, 1999; "Dealing with Year 2000 Issues: New Mandatory SEC Disclosures," Pricewaterhouse Coopers General Counsel Forum, 1998. Special Assistant to Chairman, Commission on the Bicentennial of the U.S. Constitution, 1986. Adjunct Professor, Contemporary Problems in Computer Law, Computers and the Law, and High Technology Litigation, John Marshall Law School, 2000—. *Member:* The Association of the Bar of the City of New York; Chicago, Illinois State and American (Member, Sections on: Litigation, Product Liability Committee, Large Law Firm, Class Actions and Judicial Evaluation Hearing Committee; Business Law; Science and Technology; Tort and Insurance Practice) Bar Associations; State Bar of Michigan; Defense Research Institute. ***PRACTICE AREAS:*** Class Actions; Products Liability and Mass Tort Defense; Trademark Litigation; Intellectual Property; Technology Law. ***Email:*** mneumeier@jenner.com

EDWARD J. NEVERIL, born Chicago, Illinois, January 6, 1968; admitted to bar, 1996, Illinois and U.S. District Court, Northern District of Illinois; 1998, U.S. Court of Appeals, Fifth Circuit. *Education:* United States Military Academy (B.S., 1990); Northwestern University (J.D., cum laude, 1996). Law Clerk for Honorable E. Grady Jolly, U.S. Court of Appeals for Fifth Circuit, 1997-1998. ***PRACTICE AREAS:*** Corporate Transactional. ***Email:*** eneveril@jenner.com

JOHN W. NEWLIN, III, born Oswego, New York, July 17, 1969; admitted to bar, 1994, Illinois. *Education:* Pennsylvania State University (B.A., 1991); University of Illinois College of Law (J.D., 1994). ***PRACTICE AREAS:*** Estate Planning and Administration; Tax Practice. ***Email:*** jnewlin@jenner.com

RAYMOND N. NIMROD, born Evanston, Illinois, November 18, 1959; admitted to bar, 1984, Illinois, U.S. District Court, Northern District of Illinois including Trial Bar, U.S. Court of Appeals, Federal Circuit and U.S. Supreme Court; registered to practice before U.S. Patent and Trademark Office. *Education:* University of Notre Dame (B.S. Ch.E., 1981); Loyola University (J.D., with high honors, 1984). Tau Beta Pi. *Member:* Chicago, Federal Circuit and American Bar Associations; American Intellectual Property Law Association; Intellectual Property Law Association of Chicago. ***PRACTICE AREAS:*** Patent Litigation; Trial Practice; Appellate Practice; Patent Licensing; Trade Secrets. ***Email:*** rnimrod@jenner.com

CATHERINE R. NOLAN, born Plainfield, New Jersey, April 23, 1951; admitted to bar, 1988, Maryland; 1989, District of Columbia. *Education:* Cedar Crest College (B.A., 1973); Washington College of Law, American University (J.D., 1988). Senior Counsel, Energy and Commerce Committee, U.S. House of Representatives, 1991-1997. *Member:* The District of Columbia Bar; Federal Communications Bar Association. (Resident, Washington, D.C. Office). ***PRACTICE AREAS:*** Public Policy. ***Email:*** cnolan@jenner.com

MATTHEW J. OPPENHEIM, born Silver Spring, Maryland, February 8, 1967; admitted to bar, 1993, Maryland; 1994, District of Columbia. *Education:* University of Wisconsin (B.A., 1989); Cornell University Law School (J.D., 1993). Member, Copyright Society, 1999-2004. (Resident, Washington, D.C. Office). ***PRACTICE AREAS:*** Litigation; Copyrights; Intellectual Property; Technology Law; Entertainment; New Media Law. ***Email:*** moppenheimer@jenner.com

ROBERT S. OSBORNE, admitted to bar, 1979, Illinois. *Education:* Harvard University (A.B., magna cum laude, 1976); Harvard Law School (J.D., magna cum laude, 1979). ***PRACTICE AREAS:*** Corporate; Mergers & Acquisitions; Securities. ***Email:*** rosborne@jenner.com

DEAN N. PANOS, born Chicago, Illinois, August 19, 1965; admitted to bar, 1990, Illinois, Indiana and U.S. District Court, Northern District of Illinois and Northern and Southern Districts of Indiana; 1993, U.S. Court of Appeals, Seventh Circuit. *Education:* Miami University (B.S., Accounting, 1987); Valparaiso University (J.D., high distinction and senior honors, 1990). Instructor, Business Law, Valparaiso University, 1989-1990. *Member:* American Bar Association. ***PRACTICE AREAS:*** Commercial Litigation; Products Liability; Mass Torts Defense; Class Actions; White Collar Criminal Defense. ***Email:*** dpanos@jenner.com

PATRICK L. PATRAS, born Kankakee, Illinois, October 27, 1967; admitted to bar, 1992, Illinois; 1993, U.S. District Court, Northern District of Illinois; registered to practice before U.S. Patent and Trademark Office. *Education:* University of Illinois (B.S., with honors, 1989; J.D., magna cum laude, 1992). Tau Beta Pi. *Member:* American Bar Association; Intellectual Property Law Association of Chicago. ***PRACTICE AREAS:*** Intellectual Property; Technology Law. ***Email:*** ppatras@jenner.com

JOEL T. PELZ, born Peoria, Illinois, November 10, 1955; admitted to bar, 1980, Illinois; U.S. District Court, Northern District of Illinois including Trial Bar, U.S. District Court, Central District of Illinois; U.S. Court of Appeals, Sixth, Seventh and Eleventh Circuits; U.S. Supreme Court. *Education:* Valparaiso University (B.A., 1977); Harvard Law School (J.D., cum laude, 1980). Pi Sigma Alpha and Phi Alpha Theta, Harvard Law School. *Member:* Chicago, Illinois State, Seventh Circuit and American Bar Associations; Chicago Council of Lawyers. ***REPORTED CASES:*** Dunne v. County of Cook, 108 Ill. 2d 161

(This Listing Continued)

(1985); Curry v. Baker, 802 F.2d 1302 (11th Cir. 1986); PACI v. Daley, 976 F.2d 335 (7th Cir. 1994). ***PRACTICE AREAS:*** Litigation; Reinsurance Practice; Bankruptcy Litigation; Constitutional and Civil Rights; Redistricting Litigation. ***Email:*** jpelz@jenner.com

THOMAS J. PERRELLI, born Falls Church, Virginia, March 12, 1966; admitted to bar, 1991, Virginia; 1993, District of Columbia. *Education:* Brown University (A.B., magna cum laude, 1988); Harvard University (J.D., magna cum laude, 1991). (Resident, Washington, D.C. Office). ***PRACTICE AREAS:*** Litigation; Public Policy. ***Email:*** tperrelli@jenner.com

RONALD R. PETERSON, born Chicago, Illinois, July 27, 1948; admitted to bar, 1974, Illinois, U.S. District Court, Northern District of Illinois and U.S. Court of Appeals, Seventh Circuit; 1976, U.S. District Court, Eastern District of Wisconsin; 1978, U.S. District Court, Northern District of Indiana; 1980, U.S. District Court, Central District of Illinois; 1984, U.S. Court of Appeals, Eighth Circuit; 1991, Court of Appeals, Sixth Circuit; 1996, U.S. Court of Appeals, Ninth Circuit; 1998, U.S. District Court, Western District of Michigan; 2004, U.S. District Court, Eastern District of Michigan. *Education:* Ripon College (A.B., cum laude, 1970); University of Chicago (J.D., 1973). Author: "Bankruptcy Seventh Circuit Review," 52 Chicago-Kent Law Review, Winter 1976; "What's Worse Than Losing Money in Bankruptcy," 96 The Wholesaler, 1989. Co-Author: "The Fraudulent Conveyance Defense," CF&M Magazine, 1986; "Enforcing Judgments Against Property Held in Tenancy by the Entireties," Illinois Bar Journal, 1999. *Member:* Chicago, Illinois State and American (Member, Business Bankruptcy Committee and Commercial Financial Services Committee, 1980—) Bar Associations; American College of Bankruptcy; American Bankruptcy Institute; Commercial Law League of America; International Association of Insolvency Practitioners. ***PRACTICE AREAS:*** Commercial Law; Litigation; Reorganization Law; Bankruptcy Law; Sales, Use and Occupation Taxes. ***Email:*** rpeterson@jenner.com

ADAM V. PETRAVICIUS, admitted to bar, 1995, Illinois. *Education:* University of Michigan (B.S.E.E., magna cum laude, 1992); Harvard University (J.D., magna cum laude, 1995). *Member:* Chicago and American Bar Associations. ***PRACTICE AREAS:*** Intellectual Property; Technology Law; Corporate. ***Email:*** adamp@jenner.com

MEGAN B. POETZEL, born Milwaukee, Wisconsin, February 9, 1973; admitted to bar, 1997, Illinois; 1998, U.S. District Court, Northern District of Illinois and U.S. Court of Appeals, Seventh Circuit. *Education:* University of Michigan (B.S., with honors, 1994); Chicago-Kent College of Law (J.D., with high honors, 1997). Order of the Coif; Member, 1995-1997, and Executive Articles Editor, 1996-1997, Chicago-Kent Law Review. *Member:* Chicago and American Bar Associations. ***PRACTICE AREAS:*** Securities Litigation; Reinsurance; Insurance Litigation and Counseling. ***Email:*** mpoetzel@jenner.com

ANTHONY C. PORCELLI, born Oak Park, Illinois, September 14, 1969; admitted to bar, 1994, Illinois; 1995, U.S. District Court, Northern District of Illinois; 1997, Trial Bar. *Education:* University of Notre Dame (B.B.A., magna cum laude, 1991); Northwestern University (J.D., cum laude, 1994). Author: "Sixth Amendment—Right to Confront One's Accuser When The Victim Does Not Testify," Northwestern University School of Law Journal of Criminal Law and Criminology, Vol. 83, No. 4, Winter 1993. *Member:* Illinois State and American Bar Associations. ***PRACTICE AREAS:*** Litigation; Construction Law; Health Care. ***Email:*** aporcelli@jenner.com

ROBERT M. PORTMAN, born Chicago, Illinois, February 28, 1959; admitted to bar, 1986, Illinois and U.S. District Court, Northern District of Illinois; 1991, U.S. Supreme Court; 1995, District of Columbia; 2000, U.S. Court of Appeals, Seventh Circuit. *Education:* Northwestern University (B.A., summa cum laude, 1980), Phi Beta Kappa; Harvard University (J.D., magna cum laude, 1985); Harvard Kennedy School of Government (M.P.P., 1985). Law Clerk, Judge Mark Wolf, U.S. District Court, Massachusetts, 1985-1986. Special Assistant to the Secretary, U.S. Department of Labor, Jan.-Oct. 1993. Deputy Assistant Secretary, Office of the American Workplace, U.S. Department of Labor, 1993-1995. *Member:* District of Columbia Bar (Member, Health Law Section; Chair, Council on Sections); American Bar Association (Member, Health Law Section); American Health Lawyers Association; American Society of Medical Association Counsel; American Society of Association Executives (Legal Section Council). (Resident, Washington, D.C. Office). ***PRACTICE AREAS:*** Health Care Law; Litigation; Association Law; Antitrust; Legislative and Regulatory. ***Email:*** rportman@jenner.com

PAUL V. POSSINGER, born Oceanport, New Jersey, December 2, 1968; admitted to bar, 1993, Illinois; 1995, U.S. District Court, Northern District of Illinois. *Education:* La Salle University (B.A., with honors, 1990); College of William & Mary (J.D., 1993). Member, 1991-1992 and Executive Professional Articles Editor, 1992-1993, William and Mary Law Review. *Member:* Illinois State Bar Association; American Bankruptcy Institute. ***PRACTICE AREAS:*** Bankruptcy; Corporate Reorganization. ***Email:*** ppossinger@jenner.com

SUZANNE J. PRYSAK, born Dearborn, Michigan, October 18, 1971; admitted to bar, 1997, Illinois; 1998, U.S. District Court, Northern District of Illinois, U.S. District Court, Southern District of Illinois, and U.S. Court of Appeals, Seventh Circuit. *Education:* University of Michigan (B.A., with high honors, 1993; J.D., magna cum laude, 1997). Order of the Coif. *Member:* Chicago, Illinois State and American Bar Associations. ***PRACTICE AREAS:*** Litigation. ***Email:*** sprysak@jenner.com

R. DOUGLAS REES, born Provo, Utah, May 24, 1962; admitted to bar, 1989, Illinois and U.S. District Court, Northern District of Illinois; 1990, U.S. Court of Appeals, Seventh Circuit. *Education:* Brigham Young University (B.A., 1985); Northwestern University (J.D., 1989). Co-Author: RICO Business and Commercial Litigation in Federal Courts (West 2003). Co-Author: Enforcement of Employee Restrictive Covenants, CBA Seminar, January 21, 1999. ***PRACTICE AREAS:*** Litigation; RICO Litigation; Trade Secrets; Unfair Competition. ***Email:*** drees@jenner.com

RONALD IAN REICIN, born Chicago, Illinois, December 11, 1942; admitted to bar, 1967, Illinois. *Education:* University of Michigan (B.B.A., with high distinction, 1964; M.B.A., 1967; J.D., cum laude, 1967). Phi Kappa Phi; Beta Gamma Sigma; Beta Alpha Psi. Certified Public Accountant, Illinois, 1964. *Member:* Chicago (Member, Committees on: Federal Taxation, 1968-1983; Land Trusts, 1974-1976, 1980-1984; Real Property Law, 1979-2004), Illinois State and American (Member, Sections of Taxation and Real Property)

(This Listing Continued)

Bar Associations; Chicago Mortgage Attorneys' Association (Member, Executive Committee, 1985—); The Lawyers Club of Chicago. ***PRACTICE AREAS:*** Real Estate. ***Email:*** rreicin@jenner.com

MATTHEW J. RENAUD, born Washington, D.C., August 15, 1964; admitted to bar, 1992, Illinois; 1993, U.S. District Court, Northern District of Illinois. *Education:* University of Michigan (B.S.E., cum laude, 1989; J.D., cum laude, 1992). Associate and Contributing Editor, Michigan Law Review. Author: "Spink v. Lockheed Corporation: The Ninth Circuit Outlaws Pension Plan Window Waivers," Taxes, November 1995. [Spec. 4, U.S. Army, 1982-1985]. ***PRACTICE AREAS:*** Employee Benefits; Executive Compensation. ***Email:*** mrenaud@jenner.com

DONALD I. RESNICK, born Chicago, Illinois, July 19, 1950; admitted to bar, 1975, Illinois and U.S. District Court, District of Illinois. *Education:* University of Illinois (B.S., 1972); Harvard University (J.D., 1975). Phi Beta Kappa; Phi Kappa Phi. Member, 1986—and Director-at-Large, 1986—, Illinois Chapter of the Real Estate Investment Association. *Member:* American Bar Association (Member, Real Property, Probate and Trust Law Section). ***PRACTICE AREAS:*** Real Estate; Construction; Bankruptcy; Insolvency. ***Email:*** dresnick@jenner.com

HARRY J. ROPER, born Bridgeport, Connecticut, April 15, 1940; admitted to bar, 1966, Illinois, U.S. District Court, Northern District of Illinois including Trial Bar, U.S. Court of Appeals, Third, Seventh and Federal Circuits and U.S. Supreme Court; registered to practice before U.S. Patent and Trademark Office. *Education:* Rensselaer Polytechnic Institute (B.S., Electrical Engineering, 1962); New York University (LL.B., 1966). Phi Alpha Delta. Frequent participant in ALI-ABA Trial of a Patent Case. *Member:* Chicago and American (Chairman, Intellectual Properties Committee, Litigation Section, 1982-1986) Bar Associations; Bar Association of the Seventh and Federal Circuits; Intellectual Property Law Association of Chicago; American Intellectual Property Law Association; Chicago Council of Lawyers; Barristers of Patent Law. Fellow of the American Bar Foundation. ***PRACTICE AREAS:*** Patent Litigation; Trial Practice; Appellate Practice; Patent Licensing Law; Technology Litigation; Trade Secrets. ***Email:*** hroper@jenner.com

CARLA J. ROZYCKI, born Toronto, Ontario, Canada, June 9, 1952; admitted to bar, 1977, Illinois, U.S. District Court, Northern District of Illinois, including Trial Bar, U.S. District Court, Central and Southern Districts of Illinois, U.S. District Court, Eastern District of Michigan and U.S. Court of Appeals, Fourth, Sixth, Seventh and Ninth Circuits. *Education:* University of Illinois (B.S., 1974); Northwestern University (J.D., 1977). *Member:* Chicago, Illinois State, Seventh Circuit and American Bar Associations; National Association of College and University Attorneys. ***PRACTICE AREAS:*** Labor and Employment; Litigation. ***Email:*** crozcki@jenner.com

MICHAEL C. RUPE, born Richmond, Indiana; admitted to bar, 1998, Ohio (inactive); 2000, Illinois. *Education:* The Ohio State University (B.A.); University of Cincinnati (J.D.). ***PRACTICE AREAS:*** Corporate Reorganization; Bankruptcy. ***Email:*** mrupe@jenner.com

ROIBIN J. RYAN, born 1961; admitted to bar, 1988, Illinois. *Education:* University of Illinois (B.S.); Georgetown University Law Center (J.D.). ***PRACTICE AREAS:*** Litigation and Dispute Resolution. ***Email:*** rryan@jenner.com

ERIC A. SACKS, born Kankakee, Illinois, August 28, 1967; admitted to bar, 1992, Illinois and U.S. District Court, Northern District of Illinois; 1996, U.S. Court of Appeals, Sixth Circuit; 1998, U.S. District Court, Eastern District of Wisconsin; 1999, U.S. Court of Appeals, Eleventh Circuit; 2002, U.S. District Court, District of Colorado. *Education:* Carleton College (B.A., magna cum laude, 1989); Harvard University (J.D., magna cum laude, 1992). Phi Beta Kappa. Law Clerk to the Honorable John A. Nordberg, U.S. District Court, Northern District of Illinois, 1992-1994. *Member:* Chicago and American Bar Associations. ***PRACTICE AREAS:*** Commercial Litigation; Antitrust and Trade Regulation. ***Email:*** esacks@jenner.com

DAVID P. SANDERS, born Chicago, Illinois, September 24, 1949; admitted to bar, 1974, Illinois, U.S. Court of Appeals, Seventh and Fourth Circuits and U.S. District Court, Northern District of Illinois including Trial Bar. *Education:* University of Wisconsin (B.A., with distinction, 1971) Phi Kappa Phi; Georgetown University Law Center (J.D., 1974). Editor, American Criminal Law Review, 1973-1974. Listed in The Best Lawyers in America, First Amendment Law, Naifeh & Smith, 1995—; Listed in "Chambers USA America's Leading Business Lawyers 2003-2005, (Media and Entertainment category); Adjunct Professor of Trial Advocacy, Northwestern University Law School, 1981-1991. Co-Author, "Illinois Chapter of 50-State Survey of Privacy and Related Media Torts," Media Law Resource Center, 1995—. Member, Defense Counsel Section, Media Law Resource Center. *Member:* American Bar Association; Chicago Council of Lawyers (Chairman, Federal Judicial Evaluation Committee, 1989-2001). ***PRACTICE AREAS:*** Commercial Litigation; Media and First Amendment Law; Professional Liability Litigation; Class Action Litigation. ***Email:*** dsanders@jenner.com

LAWRENCE S. SCHANER, born Chicago, Illinois, March 29, 1960; admitted to bar, 1986, California; 1988, Illinois; U.S. Court of Appeals, Fourth, Fifth, Seventh, Eighth and Ninth Circuits; U.S. District Court, Northern District of Illinois; U.S. Court of Federal Claims; U.S. Tax Court. *Education:* Duke University (A.B., magna cum laude, 1982); Stanford University (J.D., 1986). Law Clerk to the Honorable Cecil F. Poole, U.S. Court of Appeals, Ninth Circuit, 1986-1987. *Member:* Illinois State and American Bar Associations. ***PRACTICE AREAS:*** Litigation; Arbitration; Insurance. ***Email:*** lschaner@jenner.com

STEPHANIE A. SCHARF, admitted to bar, 1985, Illinois; 1986, U.S. District Court, Northern District of Illinois including Trial Bar; U.S. District Court, Central and Southern Districts of Illinois, U.S. District Court, Northern District of Indiana and U.S. District Court, Western District of Michigan. *Education:* Stanford University (M.A., Communications, 1972); University of Chicago (Ph.D., Behavioral Sciences, 1978; J.D., 1985). Recipient, Outstanding Member Award, National Association of Women Lawyers, 2002. Editor, Book, "The Use of Epidemiology in Tort Litigation: A Survey of Federal and State Jurisdictions," American Bar Association, 2003. Articles: "Direct-to-Consumer Advertising of Prescription Pharmaceuticals and Medical Devices," TechLaw Group, Inc. International, April 30, 2004; "Through the Glass Ceiling: Best Practices for Women Lawyers and Their Firms," Women Lawyers Journal, Spring, 2004; "Benchmarking for Success: Introducing NAWL Assessment Questionnaire," Women Lawyers Journal, Spring, 2004; "After Kumho Tire: The Court as the Gatekeeper of Expert Testimony," August, 1999; "Preparing the Expert Case," May, 1999; "Communications Specialists Help with Damage Control," U.S. Business Litigation Magazine, February, 1997; "The Media and Products Litigation," For the Defense Magazine, Defense Research Institute, October, 1996; "Marketing Pharmaceutical Products on the Internet: Managing Risks and Limiting Liabilities in the World of E-Commerce," Products Liability Newsletter, January, 2001; "Marketing Products on the Internet: Managing Risks, Limiting Liabilities and Litigating Disputes," September, 2000; "Perceptions of Women Trial Lawyers," September, 2000; "Post-Sale Duties to Warn, Recall and Retrofit: A Midwest Survey: Manufacturers Face Differing Duties in the Midwest," American Bar Association, March, 2002. Sustaining Member, Product Liability Advisory Council. Chair, Best Interest of the Child Subcommittee, Child Protection Advisory Committee, Circuit Court of Cook County, 1995-1996. Senior Study Director, National Opinion Research Center (NORC), University of Chicago, 1976-1982. *Member:* Chicago, American (Member: Litigation Section, Product Liability Committee, Mass Torts Committee, Editor, Mass Torts Committee Newsletter, 2001—; Co-Editor, Product Liability National Newsletter, 1997-2000; Co-Chair, Subcommittee on Experts, 1997—) and International Bar Associations; National Association of Women Lawyers (President, 2004-2005); Defense Research Institute. ***LANGUAGES:*** French. ***PRACTICE AREAS:*** Products Liability and Mass Tort Defense; Class Action Defense; Insurance Litigation; Complex Business Litigation. ***Email:*** sscharf@jenner.com

(This Listing Continued)

STANLEY A. SCHLITTER, born Decorah, Iowa, January 27, 1950; admitted to bar, 1977, Illinois and U.S. District Court, Northern District of Illinois; 1982, U.S. Court of Appeals for the Federal Circuit; 1989, District of Columbia; registered to practice before U.S. Patent and Trademark Office. *Education:* Iowa State University (B.S.E.E., with distinction, 1972); University of Iowa (J.D., with honors, 1977). *Member:* American Bar Association; Institute of Electrical and Electronics Engineers; American Intellectual Property Law Association; Intellectual Property Law Association of Chicago. ***PRACTICE AREAS:*** Intellectual Property Law. ***Email:*** sschlitter@jenner.com

MARSHALL JOHN SCHMITT, born Milwaukee, Wisconsin, June 11, 1959; admitted to bar, 1983, Illinois; 1984, U.S. District Court, Northern District of Illinois, 1991, Trial Bar; 1986, U.S. Court of Appeals, Seventh Circuit; 1995, U.S. Court of Federal Claims; 2004, U.S. District Court, Eastern District of Michigan; registered to practice before U.S. Patent and Trademark Office. *Education:* University of Chicago (B.S., 1980); Harvard University (J.D., cum laude, 1983). Phi Beta Kappa. Law Clerk to the Hon. Bernard M. Decker, Senior District Judge, U.S. District Court for the Northern District of Illinois, 1983-1984. Co-Author: "Private Enforcement," Antitrust and Unfair Competition Handbook, Illinois Institute for Continuing Legal Education, 1996. *Member:* Chicago, DuPage County, Illinois State and American Bar Associations; American Intellectual Property Law Association; Intellectual Property Law Association of Chicago. ***PRACTICE AREAS:*** Civil Litigation; Intellectual Property; Technology Law. ***Email:*** mschmitt@jenner.com

MARK D. SCHNEIDER, born New York, N.Y., April 4, 1954; admitted to bar, 1984, New York; 1985, District of Columbia; 1996, Maryland. *Education:* Swarthmore College (B.A., with high honors, 1976); Oxford University, Oxford, England (M.Phil., 1979); Columbia University (J.D., 1983). Phi Beta Kappa. Leedom Fellow. Stone Scholar. Editor, Columbia Law Review, 1982-1983. Law Clerk to: Hon. James L. Oakes, Second Circuit, 1983-1984; Hon. Harry A. Blackmun, Associate Justice, U.S. Supreme Court, 1984-1985. Author, "Peaceful Labor Picketing and the First Amendment," 82 Columbia Law Review 1469 (1983). *Member:* District of Columbia Bar; New State York Bar Association; Maryland State Bar Association; U.S. Supreme Court Bar; American Bar Association; Federal Communications Bar Association. (Resident, Washington, D.C. Office). ***PRACTICE AREAS:*** Telecommunications; Appellate and Supreme Court Practice; Labor and Employment. ***Email:*** mschneider@jenner.com

SCOTT T. SCHUTTE, born Sigel, Illinois, August 16, 1966; admitted to bar, 1995, Illinois. *Education:* Illinois State University (B.S., 1988); Chicago-Kent College of Law, Illinois Institute of Technology (J.D., 1995) Valedictorian. Editor-in-Chief, Chicago Kent Law Review. Law Clerk to Hon. Milton J. Shadur, U.S. District Court, Northern District of Illinois, 1995-1996. ***PRACTICE AREAS:*** Litigation; Class Action Litigation; Insurance Litigation and Counseling. ***Email:*** sschutte@jenner.com

DANIEL J. SCHWARTZ, born Atlanta, Georgia, April 29, 1970; admitted to bar, 1995, Illinois and U.S. District Court, Northern District of Illinois. *Education:* Northwestern University (B.S.M.E., 1992; J.D., 1995). ***PRACTICE AREAS:*** Intellectual Property; Litigation; Technology and Science; Trademarks; Unfair Competition. ***Email:*** djschwartz@jenner.com

WILLIAM L. SCOGLAND, born Moline, Illinois, April 2, 1949; admitted to bar, 1975, Illinois and U.S. District Court, Northern District of Illinois; 1987, U.S. Tax Court. *Education:* Augustana College (B.A., magna cum laude, 1971); Harvard University (J.D., cum laude, 1975). Phi Beta Kappa; Omicron Delta Kappa. *Member:* American Bar Association. ***PRACTICE AREAS:*** Employee Benefits; Executive Compensation. ***Email:*** wscogland@jenner.com

JEFFREY T. SHAW, born Council Bluffs, Iowa, July 31, 1960; admitted to bar, 1986, Illinois. *Education:* Northwestern University (B.A., 1982); University of Iowa (J.D., with distinction, 1986). Senior Articles Editor, Iowa Law Review, 1985-1986. Recipient, Faculty Award for Legal Scholarship, 1986. Author: Comment, "New York v. Quarles: The 'Public Safety' Exception to Miranda," 70 Iowa Law Review 1075 (1985); Note, "Diversity Jurisdiction and the Limited Partnership: A 'Real Party' Rule as Federal Common Law," 71 Iowa Law Review 235 (1985). *Member:* Illinois State and American Bar Associations. ***PRACTICE AREAS:*** Litigation; Appellate Practice; Supreme Court Practice; Intellectual Property; Health Care. ***Email:*** jshaw@jenner.com

GABRIELLE SIGEL, born Baltimore, Maryland, June 15, 1957; admitted to bar, 1983, Illinois and U.S. District Court, Northern District of Illinois; 1985, U.S. Court of Appeals, Seventh Circuit; 1992, U.S. Court of Appeals, Fifth Circuit; 2002, Massachusetts. *Education:* Oberlin College (B.A., 1980); Boston University (J.D., cum laude, 1983). Note and Comment Editor, Annual Review of Banking Law, 1982-1983. Author: "Retail Repurchase Agreements Overcoming Insecurity Within the Securities Laws," 2 Annual Review of Banking Law, 1983. New York City Urban Fellow, 1978-1979. Law Clerk, Hon. Frank H. Easterbrook, U.S. Court of Appeals, Seventh Circuit, 1985. Adjunct Professor, Environmental Law, Northwestern University School of Law, 1990—. *Member:* Illinois State and

(This Listing Continued)

JENNER & BLOCK LLP, Chicago—Continued

American Bar Associations. ***PRACTICE AREAS:*** Environmental Law; Products Liability; Mass Torts; Torts; Construction Law; Labor and Employment; Insurance Litigation and Counseling; Litigation. ***Email:*** gsigel@jenner.com

JOHN B. SIMON, born Cleveland, Ohio, August 8, 1942; admitted to bar, 1967, Illinois; 1968, U.S. Court of Appeals, Seventh Circuit; 1967, U.S. District Court, Northern District of Illinois including Trial Bar. *Education:* University of Wisconsin-Madison (B.S., 1964); DePaul University (J.D., 1967). Member, DePaul Law Review, 1967. Assistant U.S. Attorney, Northern District of Illinois, 1967-1974 and Chief, Civil Division, 1971-1974, U.S. Department of Justice. Honors Program, 1968. Special Counsel to Director, Illinois Department of Public Aid, 1974-1975. Consultant, Commission on the Review of the National Policy Toward Gambling, 1975-1976. Chairman, Law Council, DePaul University, 1975-1979. President, DePaul University Law Alumni Board, 1984-1985. President, DePaul University Alumni Association, 1985-1987. Chairman, Special Gifts Committee, 1986-1990. Member, 1990—, Vice Chair, 1995—, and Chair, 2004—, DePaul University Board of Trustees. Chair, Plant and Physical Property Committee, 1992-1995. National Chair For Annual Giving, 1991-1994. Chair, Advancement Committee, 1995-1999. Chair, Simon Commission, 1990-1991. Special Consultant to Administrator, Drug Enforcement Administration, U.S. Department of Justice, 1976-1977. Counsel, Illinois Governor's Revenue Study Commission on Legalized Gambling, 1977. Special Counsel, Illinois Racing Board, 1979-1980. Commissioner, Illinois Racing Board, 1990—. General Trustee, 1993-1998, Regent, 1998—, Chancellor, 2001—, Lincoln Academy of Illinois. Member, Illinois Supreme Court Planning and Oversights Committee for a Judicial Performance Evaluation Program, 1997-1998, 2000—. Member, Illinois Supreme Court Rules Committee, 2004—. Member, 1998—, Treasurer, 2001-2002 and Vice President, 2002-2003, President, 2003—, Lawyer's Trust Fund of Illinois. Member, Village of Glencoe Zoning Board of Appeals, 1981-1986; Chairman, 1984-1986. President, Glencoe Historical Society, 1979-1982. Member, Glencoe School Board Nominating Committee, 1978-1981 and Chairman, Rules Committee, 1980-1981. Director, Chicago World's Fair—1992 Authority, Member Executive, Intergovernmental, (Vice Chairman) and By-Laws Committees, 1983-1985. Member, Special Commission on the Administration of Justice in Cook County, Chancery Division Task Force, 1985-1987. Lecturer: DePaul University College of Law, 1978, 1981; U.S. Attorney General's Advocacy Institute, Washington, D.C., 1974. Lecturer, National Conference on Organized Crime, Washington, D.C., 1975. Member of Faculty, Cornell Institute on Organized Crime, Ithaca, New York, 1976. Chicago Bar Association Antitrust Symposia, 1977, 1981. Faculty, Practising Law Institute, Chicago, Illinois, 1984. Recipient: Judge Learned Hand Human Relations Award, 1994; DePaul University College of Law Award for Outstanding Service to Legal Profession, 1996; American ORT Jurisprudence Award, 1999. *Member:* Chicago (Member, Board of Managers, 1987-1988; Chairman, House Committee, 1989-1990; Treasurer, 1990-1991; Second Vice President, 1991-1992; First Vice President, 1992-1993; President, 1993-1994. Member, Federal Civil Procedure Committee, 1979-1985; Secretary, 1983, 1984; Vice Chairman, 1984-1985, Chairman, 1985-1986; Committee on Evaluation of Candidates, 1982-1986; Special Committee on the Bicentennial of the U.S. Constitution, 1986-1987), Illinois State, Federal, Women's and American (Member, Committee on Liaison with Federal Judiciary, 1983-1985) Bar Associations. ***PRACTICE AREAS:*** Corporate Law; Government Relations Law; Civil Litigation; Insurance; Public Finance. ***Email:*** jsimon@jenner.com

STEVEN M. SIROS, born Mt. Vernon, Illinois, May 25, 1969; admitted to bar, 1994, Illinois and U.S. District Court, Northern District of Illinois; 1996, U.S. Court of Appeals, Seventh Circuit. *Education:* Illinois State University (B.A., 1991); Northern Illinois University (J.D., magna cum laude, 1994). Article Editor, Northern Illinois University Law Review. Author: "Borders, Barriers and Other Obstacles to a Holistic Environment," Vol. 13, p. 633-677, Northern Illinois University Law Review; "Transboundary Pollution in the Great Lakes," Vol. 20, p. 287-312, Southern Illinois University Law Review. *Member:* Chicago, Illinois State, Federal and American Bar Associations. ***LANGUAGES:*** French. ***PRACTICE AREAS:*** Environmental; Energy; Natural Resources; Insurance Litigation; Products Liability; Mass Torts. ***Email:*** ssiros@jenner.com

CHARLES B. SKLARSKY, born Chicago, Illinois, June 13, 1946; admitted to bar, 1973, Illinois, Wisconsin and U.S. District Court, Northern District of Illinois; 1978, U.S. Court of Appeals, Seventh Circuit; 1986, U.S. Court of Appeals, Second Circuit. *Education:* Harvard College (B.A., 1968); University of Wisconsin-Madison (J.D., 1973). Adjunct Professor of Law, Trial Advocacy, Chicago-Kent College of Law, 1982-1986. Assistant State's Attorney of Cook County, 1973-1978. Assistant United States Attorney for the Northern District of Illinois, Chief Criminal Receiving and Appellate Division, 1978-1986. *Member:* Chicago and American Bar Associations; American College of Trial Lawyers. ***PRACTICE AREAS:*** Complex Commercial Litigation; Antitrust; Class Action Litigation; Energy; Products Liability; Mass Torts; White Collar Criminal Defense; Compliance Counseling; Health Care Fraud. ***Email:*** csklarsky@jenner.com

ROBERT Z. SLAUGHTER, born Rockford, Illinois, August 19, 1954; admitted to bar, 1982, Illinois. *Education:* Princeton University (A.B., 1978); University of Chicago Law School (J.D., 1982). Fellow-Leadership Greater Chicago, 1985-1986. Director: Chicago Legal Clinic, 1985-2002; Community Mental Health Council, 1986-1990; NAACP Chicago Southside Branch, 1986-1989. Member, Community Economic Development Law Project Advisory Board, Chicago, 1985-1991. *Member:* Illinois State and American Bar Associations. ***PRACTICE AREAS:*** Business Law; Corporate Law; Mergers, Acquisitions and Divestitures. ***Email:*** rslaughter@jenner.com

DANIEL W. SMITH, born Aurora, Illinois, January 4, 1965; admitted to bar, 1992, Illinois; 1993, U.S. District Court, Northern District of Illinois; 1994, U.S. Court of Appeals, Seventh Circuit; 1996, U.S. District Court, Eastern District of Wisconsin; 2001, U.S. Court of Appeals, Sixth Circuit; 2004, U.S. Court of Appeals, Ninth Circuit. *Education:* University of Notre Dame (B.A., with Honors, 1987); University of Illinois College of Law (J.D., magna cum laude, 1992). Order of the Coif. University of Illinois Law Review. *Member:* Illinois State and Federal Bar Associations. ***PRACTICE AREAS:*** Litigation. ***Email:*** dsmith@jenner.com

PAUL M. SMITH, born Salt Lake City, Utah, March 9, 1955; admitted to bar, 1981, District of Columbia; 1988, Maryland. *Education:* Amherst College (B.A., summa cum laude, 1976); Yale Law School (J.D., 1979). Phi Beta Kappa. Editor-in-Chief, Yale Law Journal, 1978-1979. Law Clerk to: Hon. James L. Oakes, U.S. Court of Appeals, Second Circuit, 1979-1980; Justice Lewis F. Powell Jr., U.S. Supreme Court, 1980-1981. *Member:* American Bar Association; Washington Council of Lawyers (President, 1990-1991); The District of Columbia Bar (Board of Governors, 2002-2005). (Resident, Washington, D.C. Office). ***PRACTICE AREAS:*** Civil and Appellate Litigation; Media and First Amendment Law; Election Law; Antitrust. ***Email:*** psmith@jenner.com

SHELLEY SMITH, born Shirley, Massachusetts, October 8, 1961; admitted to bar, 1988, New York and U.S. District Court, Southern and Eastern Districts of New York; 1991, Illinois, U.S. District Court, Northern District of Illinois including Trial Bar and U.S. Court of Appeals, Seventh and Fifth Circuits. *Education:* State University of New York at Stony Brook (B.A., Valedictorian, summa cum laude, 1984) Phi Beta Kappa; Columbia University School of Law (J.D., 1988). Harlan Fiske Stone Scholar. Member, 1986-1987 and Managing Editor, 1987-1988, Columbia Journal of Law and Social Problems. *Member:* Chicago and American Bar Associations. ***PRACTICE AREAS:*** Litigation; Antitrust and Trade Regulation; Class Actions; Patents. ***Email:*** smalinowski@jenner.com

LISE T. SPACAPAN, born Coral Gables, Florida, November 4, 1957; admitted to bar, 1984, Illinois, U.S. District Court, Northern District of Illinois, U.S. District Court, Southern District of Illinois and U.S. Court of Appeals, Seventh, Tenth and Eleventh Circuits. *Education:* Vanderbilt University (B.S., 1979); DePaul University College of Law (J.D., 1984). Editor-in-Chief, De Paul Law Review. *Member:* American Bar Association. ***PRACTICE AREAS:*** Litigation. ***Email:*** lspacapan@jenner.com

TANYA J. STANISH, born Hammond, Indiana, June 10, 1969; admitted to bar, 1995, Illinois. *Education:* DePauw University (B.A., 1991); DePaul University (J.D., with honors, 1995). Order of the Coif. Author: "English Only Rules in the Workplace: Discrimination or Employer Prerogative," DePaul Business Law Journal. Speaker: Illinois Institute for Continuing Legal Education Family Law Conference, 2002 and 2003; National Business Institute, Inc., 2001, 2003, and 2005. Member: DePaul University Family Law Center Advisory Committee (Member, Board of Directors); Illinois Institute for Continuing Education Family Law Advisory Committee (Member, Board of Directors). *Member:* Chicago (Past Co-Chair, Young Lawyers Section, Family Law Committee, 1999-2002), Illinois State (Council Member, Family Law Section, 2001—) and American Bar Associations. ***PRACTICE AREAS:*** Family Law. ***Email:*** tstanish@jenner.com

ROBERT R. STAUFFER, born Lubbock, Texas, July 12, 1961; admitted to bar, 1986, Illinois and U.S. District Court, Northern District of Illinois. *Education:* University of Missouri at Columbia (B.A., summa cum laude, 1983); Harvard University (J.D., magna cum laude, 1986). Author: "Enforcement Actions in the Post-Enron World: Zero Tolerance In the White Collar Arena," 37 Rev. Sec. and Comm. Reg. 13, July 2004; Note, "Tenant Blacklisting: Tenant Screening Services and the Right to Privacy," Harvard Journal of Legislation, Winter, 1987; "Preventing, Investigating, and Addressing Criminal Conduct in the Corporate Environment," Corporate Counsel's Guide to Legal Audits & Investigations, Business Laws, Inc., November 1999. Law Clerk to Hon. Ilana S. Rovner, U.S. District Court, Northern District of Illinois, 1988-1990. Part Time Instructor, Legal Writing, Loyola University School of Law, 1990-1991. *Member:* American Bar Association; Illinois State Bar Association; Chicago Bar Association; American Health Lawyers Association. ***PRACTICE AREAS:*** Litigation; Health Care; Appellate Practice; White Collar Criminal Defense; Insurance Litigation. ***Email:*** rstauffer@jenner.com

CATHERINE L. STEEGE, born Chicago, Illinois, August 19, 1956; admitted to bar, 1982, Illinois, U.S. District Court, Northern District of Illinois and U.S. Court of Appeals, Third, Seventh, Eighth and Ninth Circuits. *Education:* Northwestern University (B.S.J., 1978); DePaul University (J.D., 1982). Managing Editor Lead Articles, DePaul University Law Review, 1981-1982. Author: Note, "Arrest Warrants Required for Arrests Within the Home—Payton v. New York," 30 DePaul Law Review 207, 1980. *Member:* Chicago, Illinois State and American Bar Associations; American College of Bankruptcy. Fellow, American College of Bankruptcy. ***PRACTICE AREAS:*** Bankruptcy; Insolvency; Litigation. ***Email:*** csteege@jenner.com

BARBARA S. STEINER, born Highland Park, Illinois, June 14, 1949; admitted to bar, 1974, Illinois; U.S. District Court, Northern District of Illinois including Trial Bar; U.S. District Court, Western District of Texas; U.S. Court of Appeals, Second, Sixth, Seventh, Ninth, Tenth and Federal Circuits; U.S. Supreme Court. *Education:* University of Michigan (B.A., with high honors, 1970; J.D., with honors, 1974). Angell's Scholar. *Member:* Illinois State (Member, Antitrust and Unfair Competition Council, 1984-1992; Secretary, 1989; Vice Chair, 1990; Chair, 1991) and American Bar Associations. ***PRACTICE AREAS:*** Trial and Appellate Litigation; Antitrust Law; Intellectual Property; Technology Law; Insurance Coverage Litigation. ***Email:*** bsteiner@jenner.com

RICHARD P. STEINKEN, born Chicago, Illinois, February 24, 1954; admitted to bar, 1980, Illinois; U.S. District Court, Northern District of Illinois, including Trial Bar; U.S. Court of Appeals, Fifth, Sixth and Seventh Circuits. *Education:* Northwestern University (B.S.J., 1976); University of Illinois (J.D., magna cum laude, 1980). Order of the Coif. Member, Board of Editors, University of Illinois Law Forum, 1979-1980. *Member:* Chicago and American Bar Associations; Chicago Council of Lawyers. ***PRACTICE AREAS:*** Trial and Appellate Litigation; Antitrust Law; Products Liability; Mass Tort Defense; Class Action Litigation. ***Email:*** rsteinken@jenner.com

AVIDAN J. STERN, born Washington, D.C., December 9, 1964; admitted to bar, 1989, Illinois; 1990, U.S. District Court, Northern District of Illinois, including Trial Bar; 1993, U.S. Court of Appeals, Seventh Circuit; 1995, U.S. Supreme Court; 1996, U.S. District Court, Central District of Illinois; 2003, U.S. District Court, Southern District of Illinois. *Education:* University of Pennsylvania (B.A., magna cum laude, 1986); University of Chicago (J.D., with honors, 1989). Editor: *The Reporter* (Federal Civil Procedure Newsletter available at www.fedcivpro.com). Co-Author: "The Illinois Supreme Court's New Discovery Rules," 41 ISBA Trial Briefs No. 2, 1995; Insider Trading Chapter of "Securities Regulation," Illinois Institute for Continuing Legal Education, 1997; "Private Litigation Under the Investment Company Act of 1940," in "Securities Regulation," Illinois Institute for Continuing Legal Education, 2003. Author: "Seventh Circuit Rejects Assuming the Truth of Plaintiffs Allegations When Considering Class Certification," 2001 Moore's Federal Practice Update 115, August 2001; "Seventh Circuit Rules Amended," 16 CBA Record 31, January 2002; "Forgoing Interlocutory Appeals: The New 'Law of the Case'," 90 Illinois Bar Journal 652 (2002). *Member:* Chicago (Chair, Federal Civil Procedure Committee,

(This Listing Continued)

1996-1998), Seventh Circuit and American Bar Associations. ***PRACTICE AREAS:*** Litigation Practice; Class Action Litigation; Securities Litigation. ***Email:*** astern@jenner.com

WILLIAM R. STOUGHTON, born Waterbury, Connecticut, November 2, 1958; admitted to bar, 1985, Virginia; 1988, District of Columbia; 1989, U.S. Court of Appeals for the Federal, District of Columbia and Eleventh Circuits and U.S. Court of Federal Claims; 1990, U.S. District Court, District of Connecticut and U.S. Court of Appeals, Fifth Circuit; 1993, Texas; 1994, U.S. District Court, Northern District of Texas; 1996, U.S. District Court, Southern District of Texas; 1997, U.S. District Court, Eastern District of Texas; 2000, U.S. District Court, Western District of Texas; registered to practice before U.S. Patent and Trademark Office. *Education:* Rensselaer Polytechnic Institute (B.S., cum laude, 1980); Georgetown University (J.D., cum laude, 1985). Author: "FASA's Contract Financing Provisions: More Glitter Than Gold?" Federal Contracts Report, BNA, 1997. Co-Author: "False Claims Actions Based on Alleged Underpayment of Oil Gas and Mineral Royalties: Managing the Risk," *Texas State Bar Oil, Gas and Mineral Law Section Newsletter,* 1999; "Kill the Sovereign Immunity Dinosaur," Texas Lawyer, 1995; "Procurement Review," Federal Publications, 1993-1995; Restrictions on Consultant Services," *Briefing Papers,* May, 1990. *Member:* Dallas and American (Member, Sections of: Public Contract Law; Litigation) Bar Associations; State Bar of Texas; National Contract Management Association. [Lieutenant, U.S. Navy, 1980-1985]. (Resident, Dallas, Texas Office). ***PRACTICE AREAS:*** Government Contracts; Litigation; Intellectual Property; Technology Law; Products Liability; Mass Tort Defense. ***Email:*** wstoughton@jenner.com

BARRY SULLIVAN, born Newburyport, Massachusetts, January 11, 1949; admitted to bar, 1975, Massachusetts and Illinois; 1976, U.S. District Court, Northern District of Illinois including Trial Bar and U.S. Court of Appeals, Seventh Circuit; 1977, U.S. Court of Appeals, Tenth Circuit; 1978, U.S. Supreme Court; 1986, U.S. Court of Appeals, Eleventh Circuit; 1987, U.S. Court of Appeals, Fifth and Ninth Circuits; 1993, U.S. Court of Appeals, Federal Circuit; 1994, U.S. Court of Appeals, District of Columbia Circuit; 1995, Virginia; 1997, U.S. Court of Appeals, Fourth Circuit; 2002, U.S. Court of Appeals, Second and Third Circuits; 2004, U.S. Court of Appeals, Sixth and Eighth Circuits. *Education:* Middlebury College (A.B., cum laude, high honors in Philosophy and Political Science, 1970); University of Chicago (J.D., 1974). Phi Beta Kappa. Yeats Society (Sligo, Ireland) Scholar, 1968. Woodrow Wilson Fellow, 1970. National Honor Scholar, University of Chicago, 1970-1974. Associate Editor, University of Chicago Law Review, 1973-1974. Author: Book Review, Vol. 27 Dublin University Law Journal 431, 2005; "Precedent and Constitutional Adjudication," Vol. 3(2) Warsaw University Law Review 141, 2004; ""Naked Fitzies and Iron Cages: Individual Values, Professional Virtues, and the Struggle for Public Space," Vol. 78 Tulane Law Review 1687, 2004; Book Review, Vol. 25 Dublin University Law Journal 300, 2003; "On the Borderlands of Chevron"s Empire: An Essay on Title VII, Agency Procedures and Priorities, and the Power of Judicial Review," Vol. 62 Louisiana Law Review 317, 2002; Book Review Essay, Vol. 5 Legal Ethics 179, 2002; "The Problem and Possibilities of Professionalism," Vol. 21 Dublin University Law Journal 108, 1999; "John Wisdom: Watchman of the Republic, Forester of the Soul," Vol. 69 Mississippi Law Journal 1, 1999; "A Tribute to Lewis F. Powell, Jr.," Vol. 56 Washington and Lee Law Review 16, 1999; Book Review, Vol. 115 (16) Christian Century 556 (May 20-27, 1998); Book Review, Vol. 25 (1) Human Rights 5, Winter 1998; "Professions of Law," Vol. 9 Georgetown Journal of Legal Ethics 1235, 1996; "To See Life Steadily and To See It Whole: For Judge Wisdom in His Ninety-first Year," Vol. 53 Washington and Lee Law Review 1, 1996; "Not Unmindful of the Future: Some Reflections on Stability and Change," Vol. 52 Washington and Lee Law Review 323, 1995; "Foreword: Civil Rights 1995," Vol. 1 Race & Ethnic Ancestry Law Digest iv, 1995; "When the Environment is Other People: An Essay on Science, Culture, and The Authoritative Allocation of Values," Vol. 69 Notre Dame Law Review 597, 1994; Review Essay, Vol. 89 Northwestern University Law Review 116, 1994; "AIDS: Law, Public Policy and the Continuing Work of the American Bar Association, Vol. 27 John Marshall Law Review 273, 1994; "Among School Children: AIDS, The Law and The Public Schools," in Child, Parent and State: Law and Policy Reader (S. Humm, et al., eds.) (Temple University Press 1994); "AIDS and the Medical Boards: Some Legal Issues," Vol. 78 Federation Bulletin 266, 1991; "Dedication: For Judge Wisdom on His Eighty-Fifth Birthday," Vol. 64 Tulane Law Review 1341, 1990; "Historical Reconstruction, Reconstruction History and The Proper Scope of Section 1981," Vol. 98 Yale Law Journal 541, 1989; "AIDS: Law, Public Policy and The Work of The American Bar Association," Vol. 21 University of Toledo Law Review 1, 1989; Book Review Essay, Vol. 32 American Journal of Legal History 173, 1988; Book Review, Vol. 4 Constitutional Commentary 452, 1987; "The Honest Muse: Judge Wisdom and The Uses of History," Vol. 60 Tulane Law Review 314, 1985; Book Review Essay, Vol. 29 American Journal of Legal History 349, 1985; Book Essay, Vol. 60 Notre Dame Law Review 237, 1984; "Some Thoughts on the Constitutionality of Good Samaritan Statutes," Vol. 8 American Journal of Law and Medicine 26, 1982; Book Review, Vol. 35 Southwestern Law Journal 1111, 1982; "Standards of Review," American Bar Association Appellate Advocacy Source Book, 1981; "Exhaustion of Administrative Remedies Under Section 1983," Vol. 41 University of Chicago Law Review 537, 1974. Co-Author: Coleman and Sullivan, "Foreword: Enduring and Empowering: The Bill of Rights in the Third Millennium," Vol. 65 Law and Contemporary Problems 1, Spring 2002; Kurczewski and Sullivan, "The Bill of Rights and The Emerging Democracies," Vol. 65 Law and Contemporary Problems 251, Spring 2002; Sullivan and Podgor, "Respect, Responsibility and The Virtue of Introspection: An Essay on Professionalism in the Law School Environment," Vol. 15 Notre Dame Journal of Law, Ethics & Public Policy 117, 2000; Sullivan, Levenstam and von Ebers, "Preserving Error in Civil Cases: Some Fundamental Principles," Vol. 32 Trial Lawyer"s Guide 1, 1988; Katz, Sullivan and Beach, "Legal Change and Legal Autonomy: Charitable Trusts in New York, 1777-1893," Vol. 3 Law and History Review 51, 1985. Law Clerk, Hon. John Minor Wisdom, U.S. Court of Appeals, Fifth Circuit, New Orleans, Louisiana, 1974-1975. Associate, Jenner & Block, 1975-1980. Lecturer in Law, Loyola University of Chicago Law School, 1978-1979. Assistant to the Solicitor General of the United States, March 1980-December 1981. Partner, Jenner & Block, 1981-1994. Special Assistant Attorney General, State of Illinois, 1989-1990; Special Assistant State"s Attorney, Cook County, Illinois 2002-2003. Lecturer, Illinois Institute for Continuing Legal Education, 1984 (Civil Rights Litigation); 1987 and 1990 (Federal Appellate Practice). Adjunct Professor of Law, Northwestern University School of Law, 1990-1992. Visiting Professor of Law, Northwestern University School of Law, 1992-1993. Dean, School of Law, Washington and Lee University, 1994-1999; Vice-President, Washington and Lee University, 1998-1999; Professor of Law, Washington and Lee University, 1994-

(This Listing Continued)

2001. Fulbright Professor, Faculty of Law and Administration, University of Warsaw, Poland, 2000. Visiting Professor, Center for American Law, Faculty of Law and Administration, University of Warsaw, Poland, 2002, 2003. Lecturer, University of Chicago Law School, 2001-2002. Senior Lecturer, Irving B. Harris Graduate School of Public Policy Studies, University of Chicago 2005—. Member: Visiting Committee, University of Chicago Divinity School, 1987-2001; Visiting Committee, Irving B. Harris Graduate School of Public Policy Studies, University of Chicago, 2001—; Board of Trustees, Catholic Theological Union, 1993-2003, Trustee Emeritus, 2003—. Member, National Advisory Council, Center for Religion, The Professions and The Public, University of Missouri, 2003—. Member, Advisory Board, International Human Rights Law Institute, DePaul University, 2003—. Member, Editorial Board, Dublin University Law Journal, 2004—. Visiting Fellow, Queen Mary and Westfield College, University of London, Engla. *Member:* Chicago, Virginia (Chair, Section on Education of Lawyers, 1998-1999), Illinois State and American (Chair, ABA Coordinating Committee on AIDS, 1988-1994; Member, ABA Standing Committee on Amicus Curiae Briefs, 1990-1994, 2004—. Member, Council of the Section of Individual Rights and Responsibilities, 1993-1998; Chair, Section of Legal Education Committee on Professionalism, 1999-2000; Member, Section of Legal Education Standards Review Committee, 2002-2005) Bar Associations; American Law Institute; Lawyers Club of Chicago; Bar Association of the Seventh Federal Circuit (Vice-Chairman, Committee on Administration of Justice, 1985-1986). ***PRACTICE AREAS:*** Supreme Court Litigation; Appellate Practice. ***Email:*** bsullivan@jenner.com

THOMAS P. SULLIVAN, (LTD.), born Evanston, Illinois, March 23, 1930; admitted to bar, 1952, Illinois; 1982, California; 1997, New Mexico. *Education:* Loras College; Loyola University (LL.B., cum laude, 1952). Delta Theta Phi; Alpha Sigma Nu. Awards: Loyola University Law School Medal of Excellence Award, 1965, and Damen Award, 2004; Illinois Public Defender Association Award for Contribution of Service to the Indigent Accused, 1972; The Civitas Award for exceptional service by The American Alliance for Rights & Responsibilities, 1994; Constitutional Rights Foundation Service Award, 1990, and Bill of Rights in Action Award, 1993; Justice John Paul Stevens Award, 2000; Albert E. Jenner, Jr. Award for exceptional legal services to the needy, 2003, and American Bar Association Section of Litigation John Minor Wisdom Public Service and Professionalism Award, 2003. Northwestern University Center on Wrongful Convictions Award, 2003; American Judicature Society Justice Award, 2004; Chicago Lawyer's Person of the Year Award, 2004; Legal Assistance Foundation of Metropolitan Chicago Lifetime Achievement Award, 2005; Editor, Student Law Review, 1952. Lecturer on Civil Procedure, Loyola University School of Law, 1966-1967. Lecturer and author on civil and criminal trial and appellate litigation, 1961—. Lecturer, National Institute of Trial Advocacy, 1973-1974, 1977, 1981, 1998-2001, 2004. Member, Illinois Judicial Conference Committee on Pattern Jury Instructions in Criminal Cases, 1961-1968. Member, Illinois Supreme Court Rules Committee, 1972-1977. Member, Committee on Federal Criminal Jury Instructions of the Seventh Circuit, 1976-1980, 1981-1985. United States Attorney for the Northern District of Illinois, July, 1977-April, 1981. Co-Chair, Illinois Governor Commission on Capital Punishment, 2000-2003. Chair, Advisory Board, Northwestern University School of Law Center on Wrongful Convictions, 2004—; Chair, Illinois Capital Punishment Reform Study Committee, 2005—. Laureate, ISBA Academy of Illinois Lawyers. Board of Directors, Housing Choice Partners of Illinois, 2005—; Board of Directors, Leadership Counsel for Metropolitan Open Committees, 2005—. *Member:* Chicago (Chairman, Defense of Indigent Prisoners Committee, 1958-1959; Chairman, Operation of Circuit Court Committee, 1968-1969), Illinois State (Chairman, Junior Bar Section, 1959-1960; Civil Practice and Procedure Section, 1966-1967; Member, Board of Governors, 1961-1962 and 1968-1972) and American (Chairman, Illinois Committee on Defense of Indigent Persons, 1963-1969; Member, Steering Committee, Death Penalty Moratorium Implementation Project, 2003—) Bar Associations; Federal Bar Association; Bar Association of the Seventh Federal Circuit; Chicago Council of Lawyers; National Association of Criminal Defense Lawyers; American Board of Criminal Lawyers; American Judicature Society; American Law Institute (Judicial Independence and Accountability Task Force, 2003—); CPS Institute for Dispute Resolution; American Arbitration Association Large Complex Case Panel; Lawyers Club of Chicago. Fellow, American College of Trial Lawyers. [U.S. Army, 1952-1954]. ***PRACTICE AREAS:*** Civil Practice; Criminal Law; Civil Appeals; Criminal Appeals; Arbitration; Mediation.

HOWARD S. SUSKIN, born Chicago, Illinois, August 9, 1959; admitted to bar, 1983, Illinois and U.S. District Court, Northern District of Illinois; 1984, U.S. Court of Appeals, Seventh Circuit; 1985, U.S. Court of Appeals, Sixth Circuit; 1987, U.S. Court of Appeals, Fourth Circuit. *Education:* Northwestern University (B.A., with distinction, 1980); University of Michigan (J.D., with honors, 1983). Phi Beta Kappa. Editor, Michigan Law Review, 1981-1983. Co-Author: *Illinois Civil Litigation Guide* (West 1998, 2000, 2003-2005); Editor, ABA Survey of State Class Action Law (2002-2005). Instructor, Legal Writing and Research, University of Michigan Law School, 1982-1983. Arbitrator, Circuit Court of Cook County, Illinois. *Member:* Chicago (Chairman, 1997-1998 and Vice-Chairman, 1996-1997, Securities Law Committee; Chairman, Subcommittee on Securities Litigation and Enforcement, 1994-1995; Legislative Liaison, 1995-1998; Chairman, 2005-2006 and Vice-Chairman, 2004-2005, Class Action Law Committee; Member, Judicial Evaluation Committee) and American (Co-Chair, Class and Derivative Actions Subcommittee, 2001—) Bar Associations; National Association of Securities Dealers, Inc. (Member, Board of Arbitrators); National Futures Association (Member, Board of Arbitrators); Chicago Board Options Exchange (Member, Board of Arbitrators); American Arbitration Association (Member, Board of Arbitrators); New York Stock Exchange (Member, Board of Arbitrators). ***PRACTICE AREAS:*** Litigation; Class Action Litigation; Professional Liability Litigation; Securities Litigation; Arbitration. ***Email:*** hsuskin@jenner.com

BRIAN I. SWETT, born Chicago, Illinois, September 7, 1970; admitted to bar, 1996, Illinois. *Education:* Johns Hopkins University (B.A., 1992); Johns Hopkins University School of Advanced International Studies (M.A., 1993); New York University School of Law (J.D., 1996). Phi Beta Kappa. ***PRACTICE AREAS:*** Loan Restructuring; Workouts; Bankruptcy; Commercial Law; Uniform Commercial Code. ***Email:*** bswett@jenner.com

JERRY L. SWITZER, JR., born Grinnell, Iowa, December 7, 1965; admitted to bar, 1992, Illinois; 1993, U.S. District Court, Northern District of Illinois; 1993, U.S. Court of Appeals, Seventh Circuit; 1997, U.S. District Court, Central District of Illinois; 2000, U.S. District Court, Northern District of Oklahoma; 2001, U.S. Court of Appeals, Tenth Circuit. *Education:* Knox College (B.A., 1988); University of Iowa (J.D., with high distinction,

(This Listing Continued)

JENNER & BLOCK LLP, Chicago—Continued

1992). Note and Comment Editor, Iowa Law Review. *Member:* Chicago and American Bar Associations; American Bankruptcy Institute. ***PRACTICE AREAS:*** Bankruptcy; Insolvency; Commercial Law; Uniform Commercial Code. ***Email:*** jswitzer@jenner.com

JEREMY M. TAYLOR, born Lafayette, Indiana, February 27, 1970; admitted to bar, 1997, Illinois and U.S. District Court, Northern District of Illinois; 2000, U.S. Court of Appeals, Seventh Circuit; 2004, U.S. Supreme Court. *Education:* University of Virginia (B.A., 1992); University of Mississippi (J.D., summa cum laude, 1997). Executive Articles Editor, Mississippi Law Journal, 1995-1997. Author: "The Ghost of Harlan: The Unfulfilled Search for Judicially Manageable Standards in Voting Rights Litigation," 65 Miss. L. J. 431, 1995. *Member:* American Bar Association; Christian Legal Society. ***PRACTICE AREAS:*** Litigation; Eminent Domain. ***Email:*** jmtaylor@jenner.com

MICHAEL S. TERRIEN, born Milwaukee, Wisconsin, April 1, 1964; admitted to bar, 1992, Illinois. *Education:* University of Minnesota (B.S., with high distinction, 1987); Northwestern University (J.D., magna cum laude, 1992). Order of the Coif. Law Clerk for Judge David R. Thompson, U.S. Court of Appeals, Ninth Circuit, 1992-1993. ***PRACTICE AREAS:*** Bankruptcy; Corporate Restructuring; Corporate Law; Finance. ***Email:*** mterrien@jenner.com

MARK K. THOMAS, born Chicago, Illinois, April 10, 1955; admitted to bar, 1981, California and Illinois. *Education:* Northwestern University (B.A., 1977); University of San Diego School of Law (J.D., 1980). Law Clerk to the Honorable Robert L. Eisen, Bankruptcy Judge, 1980-1982. ***PRACTICE AREAS:*** Corporate Restructuring; Workouts; Bankruptcy. ***Email:*** mthomas@jenner.com

MATTHEW J. THOMAS, born Livonia, Michigan, April 16, 1972; admitted to bar, 1997, Illinois and U.S. District Court, Northern District of Illinois; 1999, U.S. Court of Appeals, Seventh Circuit. *Education:* University of Michigan (B.B.A., with high distinction, 1994; J.D., cum laude, 1997). *Member:* Chicago and American Bar Associations. ***PRACTICE AREAS:*** Litigation. ***Email:*** mthomas@jenner.com

JAMES L. THOMPSON, born Madison, Wisconsin, May 31, 1963; admitted to bar, 1988, Illinois; 1989, U.S. Court of Appeals, Sixth and Seventh Circuits and U.S. District Court, Northern District of Illinois; 1995, Trial Bar. *Education:* Carleton College (B.A., magna cum laude, 1985); University of Michigan (J.D., cum laude, 1988). Phi Beta Kappa; Order of the Coif. Associate Editor, Michigan Law Review, 1986-1988. Law Clerk, Hon. Ralph B. Guy, Jr., U.S. Court of Appeals, Sixth Circuit, 1988-1989. Author: Note, "Citizen Suits & Civil Penalties Under the Clean Water Act," Michigan Law Review, Vol. 85, No. 7, June, 1987. Co-Author: "Sanctions in Federal Litigation," 1991; "Private Litigation Under the Investment Company Act of 1940," Securities Law (Illinois Institute for Continuing Legal Education), 2003. *Member:* Chicago and American Bar Associations. ***PRACTICE AREAS:*** Commercial Litigation; Securities Litigation; Intellectual Property; Technology Law; Litigation. ***Email:*** jthompson@jenner.com

JOHN E. TITUS, born Lawton, Oklahoma, February 27, 1966; admitted to bar, 1994, Illinois; 1995, U.S. District Court, Northern District of Illinois; 1997, U.S. Court of Appeals, Federal Circuit; 2000, U.S. Court of Appeals, Seventh Circuit. *Education:* North Carolina State University (B.S.E.E., 1988; M.S.E.E., 1991); University of North Carolina School of Law (J.D., with honors, 1994). Recipient, American Jurisprudence Award, Remedies. Articles Editor, North Carolina Journal of International Law and Commercial Regulation, 1993-1994. ***PRACTICE AREAS:*** Patent Litigation; Trial Practice; Appellate Practice. ***Email:*** jtitus@jenner.com

WILLIAM L. TOLBERT, JR., born 1963; admitted to bar, 1989, Ohio; 2004, District of Columbia. *Education:* The Ohio State University (B.S., cum laude, 1985); Case Western Reserve University School of Law (J.D., cum laude, 1988). Recipient, Byron Woodside Award, 2001 and Supervisory Excellence Award, 1998, U.S. Securities and Exchange Commission. (Resident, Washington, D.C. Office). ***PRACTICE AREAS:*** Corporate; Mergers and Acquisitions; Securities. ***Email:*** wtolbert@jenner.com

C. STEVEN TOMASHEFSKY, born New York, N.Y., November 8, 1950; admitted to bar, 1985, Illinois; 1986, U.S. District Court, Northern District of Illinois, 1996, Trial Bar; 1987, U.S. Court of Appeals, Seventh Circuit; 1992, U.S. Court of Appeals, Sixth Circuit; 1993, U.S. Court of Appeals, Second Circuit and U.S. District Court, Southern District of Illinois. *Education:* Harvard University (A.B., cum laude, 1972); University of Chicago (J.D., with honors, 1985). Order of the Coif. Articles Editor, University of Chicago Law Review, 1984-1985. Law Clerk, Hon. Milton I. Shadur, U.S. District Court, Northern District of Illinois, 1985-1986. Author: Comment, "Antipsychotic Drugs and Fitness to Stand Trial: The Right of the Unfit Accused to Refuse Treatment," 52 U. Chi. Law Rev. 773 (1985); "We Do Have An Adversary System, Don't We?" 18 Litigation 23 (Fall 1991). Lecturer: ALI-ABA course of study on Lender Liability and Other Complex Litigation Involving Financial Institutions, 1992; IICLE Federal Trial Practice Update, 1995; Chicago Bar Association Motion Practice Seminar, 2001; U.S. Attorney's Office, Western District of Michigan The Rules of Brief Writing, 2005; Board Chair, Sargent Shriver National Center on Poverty Law (formerly National Clearinghouse for Legal Services), 1998-2002; Board Chair, Chicago Area Project, 2000-2004. *Member:* American Bar Association; Chicago Council of Lawyers (President, 1994-1996; Member, Board of Governors, 1988-1990; Chairperson, Federal Courts Committee, 1990-1994). ***PRACTICE AREAS:*** Litigation; Technology Law; Intellectual Property; Bankruptcy Litigation. ***Email:*** stomashefsky@jenner.com

SETH A. TRAVIS, born Brooklyn, New York, July 20, 1972; admitted to bar, 1996, Illinois and U.S. District Court, Northern District of Illinois. *Education:* Bernard M. Baruch College, City University of New York (B.B.A., magna cum laude, 1993); Northwestern University School of Law (J.D., cum laude, 1996). Author: "Enforcement Actions in the Post-Enron World: Zero Tolerance in the White-Collar Arena," The Review of Securities & Commodities Regulation, Vol. 37, No. 13, July 2004; "Guiding the Courts Discretion—A Proposed Definition of The Phrase 'Non-Violent Offense' Under U.S.S.G. Sec. 5K2.13," 86 J. Crim. L. and Criminology 530, 1996. *Member:* Chicago and American Bar Association. ***PRACTICE AREAS:*** Litigation; White Collar Crime; Criminal Defense; Health Care. ***Email:*** stravis@jenner.com

(This Listing Continued)

TERRENCE J. TRUAX, born Miami, Florida, January 11, 1961; admitted to bar, 1988, Illinois; 1989, North Carolina (inactive) and U.S. District Court, Northern District of Illinois, 1994, Trial Bar. *Education:* Florida State University (B.A., 1983); University of North Carolina (J.D., 1988). Articles Editor, North Carolina Law Review, 1987-1988. Other work experience, Mori-Sogo Law Offices, Tokyo, Japan, 1995-1996. *Member:* Illinois State and American Bar Associations. ***PRACTICE AREAS:*** Complex Litigation; Intellectual Property Litigation. ***Email:*** ttruax@jenner.com

STEVEN R. TRYBUS, born Chicago, Illinois, November 3, 1960; admitted to bar, 1986, Illinois, U.S. District Court, Northern District of Illinois including Trial Bar; 1987, U.S. Court of Appeals, Federal Circuit; 1991, U.S. Court of Appeals, Seventh Circuit; 1992, U.S. Supreme Court; 2002, U.S. District Court, Eastern District of Michigan; 2004, U.S. District Court, Eastern District of Wisconsin; registered to practice before U.S. Patent and Trademark Office. *Education:* Illinois Institute of Technology (B.S.Ch.E., with high honors, 1982); Chicago-Kent College of Law, Illinois Institute of Technology (J.D., with high honors, 1986). Tau Beta Pi. Recipient: West Hornbook Award; American Jurisprudence Awards. Staff Member, 1984-1985 and Notes and Comments Editor, 1985-1986, Chicago-Kent Law Review. Author, "Federal Circuit Jurisdiction: This Court, That Law," 61 Chicago-Kent Law Review 731, 1985. Part-Time Professor, IIT/Chicago-Kent College of Law, 1991. *Member:* Chicago, Federal Circuit and American Bar Associations; American Intellectual Property Law Association; Intellectual Property Law Association of Chicago; The Association of Trial Lawyers of America; American Institute of Chemical Engineers. ***PRACTICE AREAS:*** Patent Litigation; Trial Practice; Appellate Practice; Patent Counseling; Patent Opinions; Trademark Litigation and Counseling; Copyright Litigation and Counseling; Unfair Competition Litigation. ***Email:*** strybus@jenner.com

ANTON R. VALUKAS, born Chicago, Illinois, June 21, 1943; admitted to bar, 1969, Illinois. *Education:* Lawrence University (B.A., 1965); Northwestern University (J.D., 1968). Author: "Internal Investigations of Corporate Misconduct," Prentice Hall Law & Business-Corporation, April 1992; "Criminal Liability of Corporations & Their Agents," The Review of Securities & Commodities Regulation, July 1992. Co-Author: with Robert R. Stauffer, Chapter 5, "Cooperation with Authorities; Acceptance of Responsibility; Obstruction of Justice; Interests of the Corporation and its Employees; Vagaries of Prosecutorial Discretion," BNA/ACCA Compliance Manual: Prevention of Corporate Liability, February 1993; with Robert R. Stauffer, Establishing an Effective Compliance Program: "Threshold Considerations," and Investigation and Disclosure of Violations," Compliance Programs and the Corporate Sentencing Guidelines, November 1993; with Robert R. Stauffer, "Corporate Internal Investigations," Corporate Counsel's Guide to Legal Audits & Investigations, February 1995; with William A. Von Hoene, Jr. and Liza M. Murphy, "Cameras in the Courtroom: An Overview," Communications Lawyer, Fall 1995; with William A. Von Hoene, Jr. and Thomas S. O'Neill, "Motions in Limine," Business and Commercial Litigation in Federal Courts, West Publications, 2001; "Crisis Management: The Economy, Security and Coping with the Unexpected," April 2002; with Robert Stauffer, "Preventing, Investigating and Addressing Misconduct in the Corporate Environment," Spring 2002. Instructor, Trial Practice, John Marshall School of Law, 1972-1976. Adjunct Professor, Trial Practice, Northwestern School of Law, 1980-1982. Assistant United States Attorney, 1970-1976. United States Attorney, Northern District of Illinois, 1985-1989. *Member:* Chicago and American Bar Associations; American College of Trial Lawyers; The Law Club of Chicago. ***PRACTICE AREAS:*** Civil Law; Criminal Litigation; Antitrust and Trade Regulation; Appellate and Supreme Court Practice; Class Action Litigation; Government Contracts; Health Care Law; Litigation Practice; Media and First Amendment Practice; Products Liability and Mass Tort Defense; Professional Liability Litigation; White Collar Criminal Defense and Counseling. ***Email:*** avalukas@jenner.com

MARC VAN ALLEN, born Battle Creek, Michigan, May 4, 1966; admitted to bar, 1992, Illinois; 1993, U.S. District Court, Northern District of Illinois. *Education:* University of Chicago (B.A., 1989); University of Michigan (J.D., 1992). *Member:* Chicago and American Bar Associations. ***PRACTICE AREAS:*** Litigation. ***Email:*** mvanallen@jenner.com

DONALD B. VERRILLI, JR., born New Rochelle, New York, June 29, 1957; admitted to bar, 1987, New York; 1989, District of Columbia. *Education:* Yale University (B.A., cum laude, 1979); Columbia University (J.D., 1983). Editor-in-Chief, Columbia Law Review, 1982-1983. Law Clerk to: Hon. J. Skelly Wright, U.S. Court of Appeals for the District of Columbia Circuit, 1983-1984; Justice William J. Brennan, Jr., U.S. Supreme Court, 1984-1985. Samuel Rubin Research Fellow, Columbia University, 1985-1986. Adjunct Professor of Law, Georgetown University Law Center, 1991-2001. Lecturer, Washington College of Law, American University, 1995. (Resident, Washington, D.C. Office). ***PRACTICE AREAS:*** Civil and Appellate Litigation; Telecommunications Law; Media and First Amendment Law; Election Law. ***Email:*** dverrilli@jenner.com

MARK P. VRLA, born Chicago, Illinois, May 8, 1959; admitted to bar, 1997, Illinois and U.S. District Court, Northern District of Illinois; registered to practice before U.S. Patent and Trademark Office. *Education:* University of Illinois (B.S.E., 1982; J.D., magna cum laude, 1997). Professional Engineer, Illinois, 1993. ***PRACTICE AREAS:*** Intellectual Property; Technology Law. ***Email:*** mvrla@jenner.com

JAMES A. VROMAN, born Hinsdale, Illinois, September 8, 1948; admitted to bar, 1977, Illinois and U.S. District Court, Northern District of Illinois including Trial Bar; U.S. District Court, Eastern District of Wisconsin; U.S. Court of Appeals, Seventh Circuit. *Education:* University of Illinois (B.S., 1970; J.D., magna cum laude, 1977). Order of the Coif. Author: "Burden of Coming Forward With Evidence Under the Affirmative Defense Statute;" "The Potential Liability of Private Police Under Section 1983 of the Civil Rights Act," University of Illinois Law Forum, 1976; "Fair Share Fees: The Balance Between Practicably and Constitutionality," The Illinois Public Employees Relations Report, Summer, 1987; "A Treble-Cost Recovery Right Under CERCLA For Private Citizens," Environmental Report, September 1, 1989 at 753. Co-Author: "The Availability of Stigma Damages in Claims Against Environmental Consultant for Negligent Misrepresentation," The Guarantor, Spring 1997; "Disposal and Remedial Options Under the PCB Mega Rule," ELR News & Analysis, August 1999; "The Voluntary Performance of Environmental Remediation and AICPA Statement of Position 96-1," Corporate Real Estate and the Law, AECRE Newsletter, Summer 2000; "Superfund Memoranda of Agreements: An Opportunity to Promote Development," BNA Environment Reporter, December 22, 2000. *Member:* Chicago (Member, Environmental Law Committee) and American (Member, Sections on: Litiga-

(This Listing Continued)

tion; Tort; Insurance; Product Liability; Environmental, Energy and Resources, Environmental Litigation Subcommittee) Bar Associations; Federal Bar Association. [U.S. Marine Corps, 1972-1974, Captain]. ***PRACTICE AREAS:*** Environmental; Construction Law; Toxic Torts; Real Estate; Litigation. ***Email:*** jvroman@jenner.com

CHARLOTTE L. WAGER, born London, England, November 16, 1964; admitted to bar, 1992, Illinois. *Education:* University of London, Queen Mary College (LL.B., 1988); College of William & Mary; University of Illinois (J.D., summa cum laude, 1992). Order of the Coif. President: University of London Inner Temple Students Society, 1984-1985; Queen Mary College of Law Society, 1984-1985. Instructor of Law, University of Illinois, College of Law, 1989-1991. *Member:* Chicago and American Bar Associations. ***LANGUAGES:*** French and Italian. ***PRACTICE AREAS:*** Litigation; Insurance Litigation and Counseling; Reinsurance Practice. ***Email:*** cwager@jenner.com

MICHAEL S. WALSH, born Chicago, Illinois, September 29, 1951; admitted to bar, 1978, Illinois and U.S. District Court, Northern District of Illinois; 1983, U.S. Court of Appeals, Federal Circuit; 1985, U.S. Court of Appeals, Ninth Circuit. *Education:* Colgate University (A.B., Physics, 1973); Cornell University (M.B.A., 1975); Southern Methodist University (J.D., 1978). Adjunct Professor, Loyola University School of Law, 2000-2003. Lecturer: Cornell Johnson Graduate School of Management; Northwestern Kellogg School of Management; The John Marshall Law School, 2000. *Member:* Chicago and American Bar Associations; Computer Law Association. ***PRACTICE AREAS:*** Intellectual Property Law; Technology Law. ***Email:*** mwalsh@jenner.com

RONALD L. WANKE, born Chicago, Illinois, June 22, 1941; admitted to bar, 1968, Illinois and U.S. District Court, Northern District of Illinois; 1983, U.S. Court of Appeals for the Federal Circuit; registered to practice before U.S. Patent and Trademark Office. *Education:* Northwestern University (B.S.E.E., 1964); DePaul University (J.D., 1968). Eta Kappa Nu. Member, De Paul Law Review, 1967-1968. Lecturer: "Computers and the Law," The John Marshall Law School, 1985-1994; Continuing Legal Education Seminars, "Computer Law," The Chicago Bar Association, 1985, 1986, 1987. Author: "Protection Against Failing Vendors," Software Law Journal, Vol. I, No. 4, Fall, 1987; "Changes In United States Patent Law As A Result Of The General Agreement On Tariffs And Trade," International Legal Strategy, Vol. IV-7, 1995. Co-Author: Chapter 4, "United States Patent Law and the General Agreement on Tariffs and Trade," International Intellectual Property Law 1997, John Wiley & Sons, 1998. ***PRACTICE AREAS:*** Intellectual Property Law; Technology Law. ***Email:*** rwanke@jenner.com

J. ALEX WARD, born Baltimore, Maryland, August 11, 1967; admitted to bar, 1992, Virginia; 1999, District of Columbia. *Education:* Duke University (B.A., magna cum laude, 1989); Harvard University (J.D., cum laude, 1992), Phi Beta Kappa. Law Clerk: Hon. Eugene Sullivan, U.S. Court of Appeals for the Armed Forces, 1991-1992; Hon. Karen L. Henderson, U.S. Court of Appeals, D.C. Circuit, 1996-1997. Assistant to the General Counsel of the Army and U.S. Army Captain, 1992-1996. *Member:* The District of Columbia Bar; American Bar Association. (Resident, Washington, D.C. Office). ***PRACTICE AREAS:*** Litigation; Government Contracts. ***Email:*** award@jenner.com

JOHN F. WARD, JR., born Detroit, Michigan, September 2, 1965; admitted to bar, 1991, Illinois and U.S. District Court, Northern District of Illinois; 1992, U.S. Court of Appeals, Seventh Circuit. *Education:* University of Michigan (B.A., 1987; J.D., 1990). Law Clerk, Hon. Terrence T. Evans, U.S. District Court, Eastern District of Wisconsin, 1990-1991. *Member:* American Bar Association. ***PRACTICE AREAS:*** Litigation. ***Email:*** jward@jenner.com

KATHY COLEMAN WEINBERG, born Birmingham, Alabama, April 4, 1953; admitted to bar, 1978, Texas; 1984, U.S. Claims Court. *Education:* Cornell University (B.A., 1974; J.D., with honors, 1977). Co-Author: "Procurement Review," Government Contract Briefing Papers, 1986-1990, 1995. *Member:* Dallas and American Bar Association (Member, Section of Public Contract Law); State Bar of Texas; National Contract Management Association. (Resident, Dallas, Texas Office). ***PRACTICE AREAS:*** Government Contracts. ***Email:*** kweinberg@jenner.com

JOHN E. WELCH, born Gothenburg, Nebraska, December 23, 1954; admitted to bar, 1982, California and U.S. District Court, Central District of California; 1987, District of Columbia; 2000, Florida. *Education:* University of Nebraska at Lincoln (B.A., with highest distinction, 1977); Harvard University (J.D., magna cum laude, 1982). Phi Beta Kappa. Member of Board of Editors, Harvard Law Review, 1980-1982. Author, Note, "Police Liability for Negligent Failure to Prevent Crime," 94 Harvard Law Review 821 (1981). *Member:* State Bar of California; The District of Columbia Bar; Federal Communications Bar Association (Member, Transactional Practice Committee, 1996). (Resident, Washington, D.C. Office). ***PRACTICE AREAS:*** Corporate Law; Mergers, Acquisitions and Divestitures; International Law; Telecommunications Law. ***Email:*** jwelch@jenner.com

DANIEL J. WINTERS, born Chicago, Illinois; admitted to bar, 1992, Illinois; 1993, U.S. District Court, Northern District of Illinois; Illinois Capitol Litigation Trial Bar. *Education:* Georgetown University (B.A., 1989); University of Illinois (J.D., 1992). Associate Editor and Business Manager, University of Illinois Law Review. ***PRACTICE AREAS:*** Litigation; Trade Secrets and Unfair Competition; Labor and Employment; Defense and Aerospace. ***Email:*** dwinters@jenner.com

ASSOCIATES

JONATHAN F. ALLEN, born Madison, Wisconsin, August 1, 1973; admitted to bar, 2002, Illinois and U.S. District Court, Northern District of Illinois. *Education:* University of Wisconsin-Madison (B.B.A., 1995; J.D., cum laude, 2002). Certified Public Accountant, 1999, inactive. *Member:* American Bar Association. ***PRACTICE AREAS:*** Corporate Law; Corporate Finance; Securities; Mergers and Acquisitions. ***Email:*** jallen@jenner.com

AMANDA S. AMERT, born Eugene, Oregon, June 21, 1975; admitted to bar, 2000, Illinois. *Education:* Williams College (B.A., cum laude, 1997); Duke University School of Law (J.D., cum laude, 2000). Law Clerk, Hon. Roger L. Wollman, U.S. Court of Appeals, Eighth Circuit, 2000-2001. ***PRACTICE AREAS:*** Litigation; ERISA Litigation. ***Email:*** aamert@jenner.com

(This Listing Continued)

GINGER D. ANDERS, born Washington, D.C., August 28, 1977; admitted to bar, 2003, New York; 2005, District of Columbia. *Education:* Yale University (B.A., 1999); Columbia University Law School (J.D., 2002). (Resident, Washington, D.C. Office). ***PRACTICE AREAS:*** Litigation and Dispute Resolution. ***Email:*** ganders@jenner.com

HOWARD W. ANDERSON III, born Norfolk, Virginia, February 16, 1980; (admission pending). *Education:* University of Virginia (B.A., 2002); Indiana University School of Law - Bloomington (J.D., 2005). Order of the Coif. ***PRACTICE AREAS:*** Litigation and Dispute Resolution. ***Email:*** handerson@jenner.com

JOSEPH F. ARIAS, born Aurora, Illinois, April 4, 1976; admitted to bar, 2002, Illinois and U.S. District Court, Northern District of Illinois; 2003, U.S. Court of Appeals, Seventh Circuit. *Education:* Cornell University (A.B., 1998); University of Illinois College of Law (J.D., magna cum laude, 2002). Order of the Coif. *Member:* Illinois State Bar Association. ***REPORTED CASES:*** Smith v. Winters, 2003 U.S. App. Lexis 14960. ***PRACTICE AREAS:*** Litigation Practice; Insurance Litigation and Counseling. ***Email:*** jarias@jenner.com

RICHARD W. ARNHOLT, born Lincoln, Nebraska, November 11, 1972; admitted to bar, 2003, New York; 2004, District of Columbia. *Education:* University of St. Andrews (M.A., with honors, 1997); Georgetown University Law Center (J.D., cum laude, 2002; LL.M., with distinction, 2003). *Member:* American Bar Association (Member, Section of Public Contract Law, 2003— and Young Lawyers Division Liaison to Section of Public Contract Law, 2004-2006). (Resident, Washington, D.C. Office). ***PRACTICE AREAS:*** Government Contracts. ***Email:*** rarnholt@jenner.com

DAVID W. AUSTIN, born Colorado Springs, Colorado, June 28, 1965; admitted to bar, 2001, Illinois. *Education:* University of Maryland/European Division (B.A., 1995); The John Marshall Law School (J.D., cum laude, 2001). Justinian Society of Lawyers. *Member:* American and Chicago Bar Associations; Lesbian and Gay Bar Association. ***LANGUAGES:*** Italian. ***PRACTICE AREAS:*** Litigation. ***Email:*** daustin@jenner.com

MAREK H. BADYNA, born Bialogard, Poland, June 17, 1962; admitted to bar, 2003, Illinois. *Education:* Adam Mickiewicz University Faculty of Law (LL.M., 1986); University of Chicago Law School (J.D., 2003). ***LANGUAGES:*** Polish. ***PRACTICE AREAS:*** Litigation. ***Email:*** mbadyna@jenner.com

TERENCE G. BANICH, II, born Chicago, Illinois, February 3, 1974; admitted to bar, 1999, Illinois and U.S. District Court, Northern District of Illinois; 2000, District of Columbia and U.S. Court of Appeals, Seventh Circuit; 2001, California; U.S. District Court, Central District of California; 2002, U.S. Court of Appeals, Tenth Circuit; 2003, U.S. District Court, Eastern District of Michigan and U.S. District Court, Southern District of California. *Education:* University of San Diego (B.A., magna cum laude, 1996); Loyola University, Chicago (J.D., cum laude, 1999). *Member:* Los Angeles County, Illinois State and Chicago Bar Associations; State Bar of California; District of Columbia Bar. ***PRACTICE AREAS:*** Litigation; Bankruptcy; White Collar Criminal Defense and Counseling; Construction Law; Commercial Law. ***Email:*** tbanich@jenner.com

ANGELA M. BARRY, admitted to bar, 2004, Illinois and U.S. District Court, Northern District of Illinois. *Education:* Wellesley College (B.A., 2000); Northwestern University School of Law (J.D., 2004). *Member:* American Bar Association. ***LANGUAGES:*** French. ***PRACTICE AREAS:*** Litigation and Dispute Resolution. ***Email:*** abarry@jenner.com

SHANNON P. BARTLETT, born Chicago, Illinois, December 1, 1977; admitted to bar, 2003, Illinois and U.S. District Court, Northern District of Illinois. *Education:* Washington University (B.A., 1998); DePaul University College of Law (J.D., summa cum laude, 2003). Order of the Coif. ***PRACTICE AREAS:*** Litigation and Dispute Resolution. ***Email:*** sbartlett@jenner.com

COURTNEY M. BEEMER, born Chicago, Illinois; admitted to bar, 2000, Illinois; 2001, U.S. District Court, Northern District of Illinois. *Education:* Georgetown University (B.S.F.S., magna cum laude, 1997); University of Chicago (J.D., 2000). Phi Beta Kappa. Law Clerk to Hon. Nathaniel M. Gorton, U.S. District Court, District of Massachusetts, 2000-2001. ***PRACTICE AREAS:*** Litigation. ***Email:*** cbeemer@jenner.com

IRIS BENNETT, born Spokane, Washington; admitted to bar, 2000, California. *Education:* Radcliffe College (A.B., 1989); New York University Law School (J.D., 1999). (Resident, Washington, D.C. Office). ***LANGUAGES:*** Spanish. ***PRACTICE AREAS:*** Litigation. ***Email:*** ibennett@jenner.com

ERIC BERGER, born New York, New York, January 19, 1973; admitted to bar, 2005, Maryland. *Education:* Brown University (B.A., 1995); Columbia University Law School (J.D., 2003). Articles Editor, Columbia Law Reveiw; Kent Scholar. (Resident, Washington, D.C. Office). ***PRACTICE AREAS:*** Litigation and Dispute Resolution Practice. ***Email:*** eberger@jenner.com

BETHANY KAYE BIESENTHAL, born Bedford, Indiana, March 4, 1979; admitted to bar, 2004, Illinois. *Education:* University of Wisconsin-Madison (B.A., 2000); John Marshall Law School (J.D., magna cum laude, 2004). Distinguished Scholar; Staff Editor, John Marshall Law Review (2003-2004). ***PRACTICE AREAS:*** Litigation (100%). ***Email:*** bbiesenthal@jenner.com

ROBERT J. BLAZEJOWSKI, born Chicago, Illinois, September 28, 1974; admitted to bar, 2001, Illinois. *Education:* University of Indiana, Bloomington (B.S., 1996); John Marshall Law School, Chicago (J.D., cum laude, 2001). *Member:* Chicago and American Bar Association. ***PRACTICE AREAS:*** Litigation; White Collar Criminal Defense and Counseling; Construction Law. ***Email:*** rblazejowski@jenner.com

JOELLE K. BLOMQUIST, born Coon Rapids, Minnesota, August 1, 1980; (admission pending). *Education:* Macalester College (B.A., 2002); University of Michigan Law School (J.D., 2005). Phi Beta Kappa. ***PRACTICE AREAS:*** Litigation and Dispute Resolution; General Litigation. ***Email:*** jblomquist@jenner.com

GREGORY D. BONIFIELD, born Houston, Texas, December 6, 1974; admitted to bar, 2000, Illinois. *Education:* Hendrix College (B.A., 1997); University of California, Berkeley (J.D., 2000). *Member:* Illinois State Bar Association. ***PRACTICE AREAS:*** Patent Litigation. ***Email:*** gbonifield@jenner.com

DENISE KIRKOWSKI BOWLER, born Troy, Pennsylvania, 1975; admitted to bar, 2000, Illinois and U.S. District Court, Northern District of Illinois. *Education:* University

(This Listing Continued)

JENNER & BLOCK LLP, Chicago—Continued

of Notre Dame (B.A., magna cum laude, 1997); University of Michigan (J.D., cum laude, 2000). *Member:* Illinois State and American Bar Associations. ***PRACTICE AREAS:*** Litigation; Securities Litigation; Trade Secrets. ***Email:*** dbowler@jenner.com

DONALD S. BOYCE, JR., born St. Louis, Missouri, August 7, 1972; admitted to bar, 2004, Illinois. *Education:* St. Louis University (B.A., 2001); University of Notre Dame (J.D., 2004). ***PRACTICE AREAS:*** Litigation Practice. ***Email:*** dboyce@jenner.com

PATRICIA BOYE-WILLIAMS, born Syracuse, New York, February 28, 1976; admitted to bar, 2003, Illinois. *Education:* Cornell University (B.S., 1998); Chicago-Kent College of Law, Illinois Institute of Technology (J.D., 2003). Order of the Coif. ***PRACTICE AREAS:*** Environmental Law; Energy; Natural Resources. ***Email:*** pboye-williams@jenner.com

KALI N. BRACEY, born Southfield, Michigan, August 10, 1971; admitted to bar, 1997, New York; 1998, District of Columbia. *Education:* Spelman College (B.A., 1993); Yale University (J.D., 1996). *Member:* District of Columbia Bar; American Bar Association. (Resident, Washington, D.C. Office). ***PRACTICE AREAS:*** Litigation; Insurance Coverage; White Collar Criminal Defense; Entertainment and New Media. ***Email:*** kbracey@jenner.com

AARON BRUHL, born San Bernardino, California, April 10, 1977; admitted to bar, 2004, New York; 2005, District of Columbia. *Education:* Pomona College (B.A., summa cum laude, 1999); University of Cambridge (M. Phil., 2001); Yale University (J.D., 2003). Author: "Using Statutes to Set Legislative Rules," Journal of Law and Politics, Vol. 19, Fall, 2003. Judicial Clerkship, Chief Judge Carolyn Dineen King, U.S. Court of Appeals, Fifth Circuit. *Member:* New York State Bar Association. (Resident, Washington, D.C. Office). ***PRACTICE AREAS:*** Litigation. ***Email:*** abruhl@jenner.com

EVAN JAY BUDIN, born Wilmington, Delaware, March 27, 1978; admitted to bar, 2004, Illinois. *Education:* Michigan State University (B.S., 2000); John Marshall Law School (J.D., 2004). ***PRACTICE AREAS:*** Intellectual Property.

ANA R. BUGAN, born Cleveland, Ohio, July 18, 1969; admitted to bar, 2002, Illinois. *Education:* Kenyon College (A.B., magna cum laude, 1991); Harvard Law School (J.D., 2002). Phi Beta Kappa. ***LANGUAGES:*** Spanish and French. ***PRACTICE AREAS:*** Litigation; White Collar Criminal Defense and Counseling. ***Email:*** abugan@jenner.com

MICHAEL L. CEBULA, born Wilmington, Ohio, October 30, 1978; (admission pending). *Education:* Xavier University (B.A., 2001); Harvard Law School (J.D., cum laude, 2005). ***PRACTICE AREAS:*** Litigation and Dispute Resolution. ***Email:*** mcebula@jenner.com

CHRISTINE L. CHILDERS, born Beech Grove, Indiana, November 4, 1970; admitted to bar, 2002, Illinois. *Education:* University of Nevada (B.S., cum laude, 1998); Valparaiso University (J.D., magna cum laude, 2002). Author, "Keep On Pleading: The Co-Existence of Notice Pleading and the New Scope of Discovery Standard of Federal Rule of Civil Procedure 26(b)(1)," 36 Valparaiso University Law Review 677 (2002). ***PRACTICE AREAS:*** Bankruptcy; Loan Restructuring; Securities. ***Email:*** cchilders@jenner.com

MARILYN J. CHIMES, born Detroit, Michigan, July 1, 1956; admitted to bar, 1999, Illinois and U.S. District Court, Northern District of Illinois; registered to practice before U.S. Patent and Trademark Office. *Education:* Michigan State University (B.S., 1977; D.V.M., 1979); Chicago-Kent College of Law (J.D., 1999). Order of the Coif. Kent Legal Scholar. Notes and Comments Editor, Chicago-Kent Law Review, 1997-1998. Licensed Veterinarian: Michigan, 1979; New York, 1980; Illinois, 1985. Diplomate, American College of Laboratory Animal Medicine, 1993. *Member:* Chicago, Illinois State and American Bar Associations; American Veterinary Medical Law Association; American Intellectual Property Law Association; American Veterinary Medical Association; American College of Laboratory Animal Medicine. ***PRACTICE AREAS:*** Intellectual Property; Technology Law; Biotechnology; Health Care. ***Email:*** mchimes@jenner.com

MARTEZ M. CLARK, born Chicago, Illinois; admitted to bar, 2003, Illinois. *Education:* Illinois Wesleyan University (B.A., 2000); Stanford University Law School (J.D., 2003). ***PRACTICE AREAS:*** Litigation. ***Email:*** mclark@jenner.com

ROBERT H. CLARKE, born Milwaukee, Wisconsin, February 1, 1977; admitted to bar, 2003, Wisconsin; 2004, Illinois. *Education:* University of Wisconsin-Madison (B.S., 1999; J.D., cum laude, 2003). Law Clerk to the Honorable David T. Prosser, Wisconson Supreme Court. Editor-in-Chief, Wisconsin Law Review, 2002-2003. *Member:* State Bar of Wisconsin. ***PRACTICE AREAS:*** Corporate; Mergers and Acquisitions; Securities; Corporate Finance; Private Equity and Emerging Companies. ***Email:*** rclarke@jenner.com

JOHN F. COSTELLO, JR., born Maywood, Illinois, August 13, 1975; admitted to bar, 2003, Illinois. *Education:* Quincy University (B.S., 1997); John Marshall Law School (J.D., 2003). ***PRACTICE AREAS:*** Litigation Practice; Trade Secrets and Unfair Competition; Labor and Employment. ***Email:*** jcostello@jenner.com

SUZANNE M. COURTHEOUX, born Chicago, Illinois; admitted to bar, 2004, Illinois. *Education:* Yale University (B.A., 2000); University of Chicago Law School (J.D., 2004). *Member:* Chicago Bar Association; Chicago Council of Lawyers. ***PRACTICE AREAS:*** Litigation; Labor and Employment. ***Email:*** scourtheoux@jenner.com

CRAIG A. COWIE, admitted to bar, 2001, California; 2005, District of Columbia. *Education:* Bowling Green State University (B.S., summa cum laude with honors, 1998); University of Michigan (M.A., 1993); University of California, Berkeley - Boalt Hall School of Law (J.D., 2000). Order of the Coif; Dragonette Award for Civil Litigation Trial Practice; Co-Chair, Appellate Advocacy Program; Books & Research Editor, Ecology Law Quarterly. Law Clerk, Hon. Sidney R. Thomas, United States Court of Appeals, Ninth Circuit. (Resident, Washington, D.C. Office). ***PRACTICE AREAS:*** Litigation and Dispute Resolution; Appellate Practice; Constitutional Law; First Amendment Law; Telecommunications. ***Email:*** ccowie@jenner.com

ROBERT J. DART, born Atlanta, Georgia, July 17, 1979; admitted to bar, 2004, Illinois and U.S. District Court, Northern District of Illinois. *Education:* Duke University (A.B., 2001); University of Chicago Law School (J.D., 2004). *Member:* Illinois State Bar Association; Chicago Bar Association. ***PRACTICE AREAS:*** Litigation and Dispute Resolution; Complex Commercial Litigation. ***Email:*** rdart@jenner.com

(This Listing Continued)

MERCEDES M. DAVIS, born Los Angeles, California, May 23, 1980; (admission pending). *Education:* The Ohio State University (B.S.B.A., 2002); Harvard Law School (J.D., 2005). Executive Director and Student Attorney, Harvard Legal Aid Bureau. ***PRACTICE AREAS:*** Corporate. ***Email:*** mdavis@jenner.com

DAMIEN P. DELANEY, born Lexington, Virginia, April 28, 1977; admitted to bar, 2003, Illinois. *Education:* College of William & Mary (B.A., 1999); Washington & Lee University (J.D., cum laude, 2003). Law Clerk to the Hon. John M. Rogers, U.S. Court of Appeals, Sixth Circuit, 2003-2004. Author, "Better to Let Ten Guilty Men Live: The Presumption of Life - A Principle to Govern Capital Sentencing," 14 Capital Defense Journal 283 (2002). ***PRACTICE AREAS:*** Litigation. ***Email:*** ddelaney@jenner.com

MATTHEW R. DEVINE, born Evanston, Illinois, August 7, 1967; admitted to bar, 2004, Illinois. *Education:* University of Iowa (B.A., 1996); Loyola University Chicago (J.D., cum laude, 2004). ***PRACTICE AREAS:*** Litigation and Dispute Resolution. ***Email:*** mdevine@jenner.com

ALISON A. DIETERICHS, born Denton, Texas, December 4, 1974; admitted to bar, 2003, Illinois; 2004, U.S. District Court, Northern District of Illinois. *Education:* University of Wisconsin-Madison (B.A., 1997); Chicago-Kent College of Law, Illinois Institute of Technology (J.D., 2003). Phi Beta Kappa. *Member:* Chicago and American Bar Associations. ***LANGUAGES:*** Spanish. ***PRACTICE AREAS:*** Litigation (100%). ***Email:*** adieterichs@jenner.com

MATTHEW R. DiPENTIMA, born Oklahoma City, Oklahoma, August 31, 1975; admitted to bar, 2003, Illinois; 2004, U.S. District Court for the District of Columbia, U.S. District Court, Northern District of Illinois; and U.S. Court of Appeals, Seventh Circuit. *Education:* Boston College (B.A., 1997); Northwestern University (J.D., 2003). Phi Beta Kappa. ***PRACTICE AREAS:*** Litigation (75%); Appellate Practice (25%). ***Email:*** mdepentima@jenner.com

NADA DJORDJEVIC, born Chicago, Illinois, June 25, 1970; admitted to bar, 2002, Illinois. *Education:* Grinnell College (B.A., 1996); University of Illinois (J.D., summa cum laude, 2002). Order of the Coif. ***PRACTICE AREAS:*** Class Actions; Litigation; Commercial Litigation; Products Liability; Commercial Law. ***Email:*** ndjordjevic@jenner.com

IRINA Y. DMITRIEVA, born Moscow, Russia, May 26, 1973; admitted to bar, 2003, Illinois. *Education:* Moscow State University (Bachelors in Journalism, 1995); University of Minnesota, Twin Cities (M.A., Art and Mass Communications, 1998); University of Florida (J.D., 2003; Ph.D., Art and Mass Communications, 2003). Order of the Coif. Member, Florida Law Review, 2002-2003. ***LANGUAGES:*** Russian. ***PRACTICE AREAS:*** First Amendment Law.

CHRIS-TIA DONALDSON, born Detroit, Michigan; admitted to bar, 2003, Illinois. *Education:* Harvard University (A.B., 2000); Harvard Law School (J.D., 2003). ***PRACTICE AREAS:*** Corporate; Mergers and Acquisitions; Corporate Finance; Securities. ***Email:*** cdonaldson@jenner.com

DANIEL S. DOOLEY, born Houston, Texas, September 23, 1973; admitted to bar, 2001, Illinois. *Education:* University of Minnesota (B.A., 1996); Indiana University School of Law (J.D., cum laude, 2001). ***PRACTICE AREAS:*** Litigation. ***Email:*** ddooley@jenner.com

DEBRA M. DOYLE, born New Haven, Connecticut; admitted to bar, 2000, Illinois. *Education:* Southern Methodist University (B.S., 1997); University of Notre Dame (J.D., 2000). ***PRACTICE AREAS:*** Trusts and Estates; Probate; Taxation. ***Email:*** ddoyle@jenner.com

DAVID S. DRACHLER, born Chicago, Illinois, October 24, 1977; admitted to bar, 2002, Illinois. *Education:* Northwestern University (B.A., 1999); University of Pennsylvania (J.D., 2002). ***PRACTICE AREAS:*** Corporate Law; Mergers and Acquisitions; Securities. ***Email:*** ddrachler@jenner.com

JOHN WESLEY DRURY, born Platteville, Wisconsin, September 29, 1978; admitted to bar, 2004, Illinois. *Education:* Marquette University (B.A., 2001); Northwestern University School of Law (J.D., cum laude, 2004). ***PRACTICE AREAS:*** Litigation; Labor and Employment. ***Email:*** jdrury@jenner.com

DAWN M. DUFFY, born Woodhaven, New York, May 14, 1978; (admission pending). *Education:* New York University (B.A., 1999); University of Chicago Law School (J.D., 2005). ***PRACTICE AREAS:*** Tax. ***Email:*** dduffy@jenner.com

JEFFREY S. EBERHARD, born Houston, Texas, April 15, 1974; admitted to bar, 2002, Illinois. *Education:* Colgate University (B.A., cum laude, 1996); Northwestern University School of Law (J.D., cum laude, 2001). Order of the Coif. ***PRACTICE AREAS:*** Litigation; Intellectual Property. ***Email:*** jeberhard@jenner.com

LISA M. EDDINGTON, born South Holland, Illinois, July 30, 1974; admitted to bar, 1999, Illinois. *Education:* University of Illinois (B.S., 1996); Northwestern University (J.D., 1999). Order of the Coif. ***PRACTICE AREAS:*** Commercial Litigation; White Collar Criminal Defense. ***Email:*** lwhitlock@jenner.com

FRANK J. EICHENLAUB IV, admitted to bar, 2002, Illinois. *Education:* Indiana University (B.A., 1993); University of North Carolina at Chapel Hill (J.D., honors, 2002). "Carnivore: Taking A Bit Out Of The Fourth Amendment?," 80 North Carolina Law Review (2002). ***PRACTICE AREAS:*** Real Estate. ***Email:*** feichenlaub@jenner.com

ELIZABETH L. FINE, born Chicago, Illinois, July 11, 1976; admitted to bar, 2004, Illinois. *Education:* SUNY Binghamton (B.A., 1998); University of Michigan Law School (J.D., cum laude, 2004). ***PRACTICE AREAS:*** Litigation Practice. ***Email:*** efine@jenner.com

MELISSA C. FOGERTY, born New Haven, Connecticut, October 21, 1980; (admission pending). *Education:* Boston College (B.A., 2002); Harvard Law School (J.D., 2005). ***LANGUAGES:*** French. ***PRACTICE AREAS:*** Corporate. ***Email:*** mfogerty@jenner.com

EMILY M. FRANK, born St. Louis, Missouri, March 10, 1976; admitted to bar, 2002, Illinois. *Education:* St. Louis University (B.S., Biology, 1998); Washington University School of Law (J.D., 2002). ***PRACTICE AREAS:*** Patent Litigation. ***Email:*** efrank@jenner.com

(This Listing Continued)

JARED O. FREEDMAN, born Philadelphia, Pennsylvania, November 2, 1969; admitted to bar, 1999, New York; 2000, District of Columbia. *Education:* Harvard University (A.B., magna cum laude, 1991); Yale University (J.D., 1997). Law Clerk: Hon. Dana Fabe, Alaska Supreme Court, 1997-1998; Hon. Michael Ponsor, U.S. District Court, District of Massachusetts, 1998-1999. (Resident, Washington, D.C. Office). ***PRACTICE AREAS:*** Litigation; Appellate Practice; Supreme Court; Media and First Amendment. ***Email:*** jfreedman@jenner.com

WENDY L. FRITZ, born Seoul, South Korea, February 24, 1971; admitted to bar, 2003, Illinois. *Education:* University of Chicago (B.A., 1994); Boston University School of Law (J.D., magna cum laude, 2003). Distinguished Military Graduate, University of Chicago. [Captain, U.S. Army, 1988-1999]. ***PRACTICE AREAS:*** Litigation. ***Email:*** wfritz@jenner.com

ANTHONY S. GABRIELSON, born Salt Lake City, Utah, October 26, 1975; admitted to bar, 2001, Minnesota; 2004, Illinois. *Education:* University of Iowa (B.A., highest distinction with honors, 1998); Harvard Law School (J.D., 2001). Phi Beta Kappa (President, 1998); Mortar Board; Omicron Delta Kappa. Phi Alpha Delta Law Fraternity (President, 1996-1998). Law Clerk to the Hon. Ann D. Montgomery, U.S. District Court, District of Minnesota. ***PRACTICE AREAS:*** Litigation; Litigation and Dispute Resolution Practice; Intellectual Property. ***Email:*** agabrielson@jenner.com

AMI J. GALANI, born Skokie, Illinois; admitted to bar, 2004, Illinois. *Education:* Denison University (B.A., 2000); Washington University (J.D., 2004). Order of the Coif. ***PRACTICE AREAS:*** Corporate. ***Email:*** agalani@jenner.com

CLAUDIA GALLO, born Charleston, South Carolina, August 26, 1974; admitted to bar, 1999, Illinois and U.S. District Court, Northern District of Illinois; 2005, New York. *Education:* Loyola University of Chicago (B.A., with honors, cum laude, 1996); Illinois Institute of Technology, Chicago-Kent College of Law (J.D., high honors, 1999). Order of the Coif. Member, Chicago-Kent Law Review, 1997-1999. Notes and Comment Editor, 1998-1999. ***PRACTICE AREAS:*** Family Law; Litigation. ***Email:*** cgallo@jenner.com

JESSICA A. GARASCIA, born Fairfax County, Virginia, June 8, 1979; (admission pending). *Education:* Oberlin College (B.A., 2001); Indiana University School of Law - Bloomington (J.D., magna cum laude, 2005). Order of the Coif. Author: "The Price We Are Willing to Pay for Juvenile Justice: Mentally Ill Children and Their Disproportionate Share of the Burden," 80 Indiana Law Journal 489 (2005). ***PRACTICE AREAS:*** Corporate. ***Email:*** jgarascia@jenner.com

STEPHEN M. GEISSLER, born Cary, Illinois, November 25, 1974; admitted to bar, 2000, Illinois. *Education:* University of Illinois (B.S., Electrical Engineering, 1997; J.D., cum laude, 2000). ***PRACTICE AREAS:*** Patent Litigation; Patent Prosecution; Intellectual Property. ***Email:*** sgeissler@jenner.com

RICK Y. GELBOIM, born New York, New York, March 11, 1979; admitted to bar, 2004, Illinois. *Education:* Syracuse University (B.S., magna cum laude, 2001); Washington University (J.D., 2004). ***PRACTICE AREAS:*** Estate Planning. ***Email:*** rgelboim@jenner.com

REENA R. GOKANI, born Winfield, Illinois, July 5, 1979; (admission pending). *Education:* University of Illinois, Urbana-Champaign (B.A., 2001); University of Michigan Law School (J.D., cum laude, 2005). ***PRACTICE AREAS:*** Litigation and Dispute Resolution. ***Email:*** rgokani@jenner.com

JASON J. GREEN, born Oak Park, Illinois, March 2, 1976; admitted to bar, 2002, Illinois. *Education:* University of Illinois (B.S., 1999); John Marshall Law School (J.D., cum laude, 2002). Author, "Is Zippo's Sliding Scale a Slippery Slope of Uncertainty? A Case for Abolishing Web Site Interactivity as a Conclusive Factor in Assessing Minimum Contacts in Cyberspace," 34 John Marshall Law Review 1051. ***PRACTICE AREAS:*** Litigation. ***Email:*** jgreen@jenner.com

ANTHONY J. GRZYB, born Chicago, Illinois, March 22, 1960; admitted to bar, 1999, Illinois. *Education:* Illinois Institute of Technology (B.B.A., 1983); University of Illinois (J.D., 1999). Harno Scholar. [Major, U.S. Marine Corps, 1984-1996]. ***PRACTICE AREAS:*** Corporate; Securities; Mergers and Acquisitions; Corporate Finance; Private Equity. ***Email:*** agrzyb@jenner.com

MICHAEL S. GULLAND, born Washington, D.C., October 27, 1978; admitted to bar, 2004, Illinois. *Education:* University of Virginia (B.A., 2001); Northwestern University School of Law (J.D., cum laude, 2004). ***PRACTICE AREAS:*** Litigation Practice. ***Email:*** mgulland@jenner.com

JOHN HAARLOW, JR., born Hinsdale, Illinois, August 4, 1977; admitted to bar, 2004, Illinois. *Education:* Princeton University (A.B., 1999); University of Illinois School of Law (J.D., summa cum laude, 2004). Order of the Coif. Co-author: "Attorney Client Privileges In Testimonial Privileges," West Publishing (forthcoming, 2005). ***PRACTICE AREAS:*** Intellectual Property; Litigation and Dispute Resolution Practice. ***Email:*** jhaarlow@jenner.com

ADAM A. HACHIKIAN, born Boston, Massachusetts, January 20, 1979; admitted to bar, 2004, Illinois. *Education:* Harvard College (A.B., 2001); University of Michigan Law School (J.D., 2004). ***PRACTICE AREAS:*** Litigation and Dispute Resolution Practice. ***Email:*** ahachikian@jenner.com

BRIAN D. HANSEN, born Sioux City, Iowa, March 6, 1975; admitted to bar, 2000, Illinois. *Education:* University of Iowa (B.A., Psychology, 1996; J.D., 2000). Order of the Coif. ***PRACTICE AREAS:*** Litigation; Class Actions. ***Email:*** bhansen@jenner.com

CHRISTINA TOMARAS HANSEN, born Oak Park, Illinois, March 17, 1975; admitted to bar, 2000, Illinois and U.S. District Court, Northern District of Illinois. *Education:* University of Notre Dame (B.A., cum laude, 1997); Washington University (J.D., 2000). *Member:* Chicago and American Bar Associations. ***PRACTICE AREAS:*** Litigation. ***Email:*** chansen@jenner.com

SHAHID U. HAQUE, born Augusta, Georgia, July 2, 1979; (admission pending). *Education:* University of Southern Indiana (B.S., 2001); Chicago-Kent College of Law (J.D., high honors, 2005). Order of the Coif; Bar and Gavel Award. Author: Chicago-Kent Law Review, Vol. 79, Page 1357. Teaching Assistant, Chicago-Kent, 2003-2004. ***LANGUAGES:*** Pashto. ***PRACTICE AREAS:*** Litigation and Dispute Resolution. ***Email:*** shaque@jenner.com

(This Listing Continued)

SARAH HARDGROVE-KOLENO, born Peoria, Illinois, September 30, 1971; admitted to bar, 1996, Illinois. *Education:* University of Illinois (B.S., magna cum laude, 1993; J.D., magna cum laude, 1996). *Member:* Chicago, Illinois State and American Bar Associations. ***PRACTICE AREAS:*** Complex Civil Litigation; White Collar Criminal Defense and Counseling; Construction Law. ***Email:*** shardgrove-koleno@jenner.com

KATHLEEN HARTNETT, born Bronx, New York, June 24, 1974; admitted to bar, 2003, District of Columbia and New York. *Education:* Harvard College (A.B., magna cum laude, 1996); Harvard Law School (J.D., magna cum laude, 2000). (Resident, Washington, D.C. Office). ***LANGUAGES:*** Proficient in written and oral French. ***PRACTICE AREAS:*** Litigation. ***Email:*** khartnett@jenner.com

JENNIFER A. HASCH, born September 30, 1974; admitted to bar, 2000, Illinois. *Education:* Vanderbilt University (B.A., 1997); University of California, Berkeley, Boalt Hall School of Law (J.D., 2000). ***PRACTICE AREAS:*** Litigation. ***Email:*** jhasch@jenner.com

BRIAN HAUCK, born St. Louis, Missouri, February 27, 1976; admitted to bar, 2001, Wisconsin; 2003, District of Columbia. *Education:* DePauw University (B.A., summa cum laude, 1998); Harvard Law School (J.D., cum laude, 2001). Phi Beta Kappa. Harvard Law Review. (Resident, Washington, D.C. Office). ***PRACTICE AREAS:*** Litigation; Entertainment and New Media. ***Email:*** bhauck@jenner.com

BRIAN C. HAUSSMANN, born Hammond, Indiana, January 26, 1979; admitted to bar, 2004, Illinois. *Education:* Indiana University-Bloomington (B.A., with high distinction, 2001); Cornell Law School (J.D., cum laude, 2004). ***PRACTICE AREAS:*** General Litigation. ***Email:*** bhaussmann@jenner.com

SEAN C. HERRING, born Chicago, Illinois, August 28, 1979; (admission pending). *Education:* University of Michigan (B.A., 2001); Loyola University Chicago Law School (J.D., 2005). ***PRACTICE AREAS:*** Commercial Law. ***Email:*** sherring@jenner.com

MATTHEW HERSH, born Washington, D.C., October 31, 1967; admitted to bar, 1999, District of Columbia. *Education:* Columbia University (B.A., 1990); Georgetown University (J.D., cum laude, 1999). (Resident, Washington, D.C. Office). ***PRACTICE AREAS:*** Litigation. ***Email:*** mhersh@jenner.com

CLIFTON J. HEYDA, born Berwyn, Illinois, December 24, 1974; admitted to bar, 2002, Illinois. *Education:* University of Illinois (B.A., 1997); University of Texas at Austin (J.D., 2002). ***PRACTICE AREAS:*** Litigation. ***Email:*** cheyda@jenner.com

JONATHAN HILL, born Leesburg, Virginia, August 2, 1972; admitted to bar, 1998, Illinois. *Education:* Virginia Polytechnic Institute and State University (B.S.M.E., 1993; M.S., Mechanical Engineering, 1995); College of William & Mary School of Law (J.D., 1998). ***PRACTICE AREAS:*** Patent Litigation; Intellectual Property Licensing; Intellectual Property. ***Email:*** jhill@jenner.com

MELISSA M. HINDS, born Marion, Ohio, July 27, 1978; admitted to bar, 2003, Indiana (Not admitted in Illinois). *Education:* Bowling Green State University (B.S., magna cum laude, 2000); University of Michigan Law School (J.D., cum laude, 2003). ***PRACTICE AREAS:*** Bankruptcy, Workout and Corporate Reorganization. ***Email:*** mhinds@jenner.com

LI-CHUNG DANIEL HO, born Taiwan, August 17, 1965; admitted to bar, 1997, Illinois and U.S. District Court, Northern District of Illinois; registered to practice before U.S. Patent and Trademark Office. *Education:* University of Michigan, Dearborn (B.S.M.E., 1987; M.S.M.E., 1988); University of Illinois (M.B.A., 1992); Case Western Reserve University (J.D., 1997). Licensed Professional Engineer, Michigan, 1994. Arbitrator, National Association of Securities Dealers. ***PRACTICE AREAS:*** Intellectual Property Litigation; Technology Litigation; Intellectual Property Counseling; Licensing; Transactional Practice; Trademarks; Patent Prosecution; Arbitration. ***Email:*** dho@jenner.com

KERI L. HOLLEB HOTALING, born Honolulu, Hawaii, August 21, 1973; admitted to bar, 2000, Illinois. *Education:* Allegheny College (B.A., 1995); University of Virginia School of Law (J.D., 2000). Phi Beta Kappa. *Member:* Chicago and American Bar Associations. ***PRACTICE AREAS:*** Environmental, Energy and Natural Resources Law; Litigation and Dispute Resolution. ***Email:*** khotaling@jenner.com

BOBBY J. HOLLIS II, born Homestead AFB, Florida, March 24, 1974; admitted to bar, 2000, Illinois, District of Columbia, U.S. Court of Appeals for the District of Columbia Circuit and U.S. District Court, Northern District of Illinois. *Education:* University of Florida (B.A., 1996); University of Iowa College of Law (J.D., 1999). Phi Beta Kappa; Golden Key; CPS Juris Secundum. Journal of Corporate Law, Fall 1999. *Member:* American Bar Association. ***LANGUAGES:*** French. ***PRACTICE AREAS:*** Corporate. ***Email:*** bhollis@jenner.com

DARRICK J. HOOKER, born Chicago, Illinois, August 6, 1974; admitted to bar, 2001, Illinois. *Education:* University of Illinois (B.S.B.A., 1997); Indiana University School of Law-Bloomington (J.D., 2000). Order of the Barristers. *Member:* Chicago, Cook County and American Bar Associations. ***PRACTICE AREAS:*** Intellectual Property; Patent Litigation. ***Email:*** dhooker@jenner.com

TIMOTHY A. HUDSON, born New Albany, Indiana, June 13, 1974; admitted to bar, 2000, Illinois and U.S. District Court, Northern District of Illinois. *Education:* University of Wisconsin-Madison (B.A., 1996); University of Michigan (J.D., 2000). Phi Beta Kappa; Phi Kappa Phi; Golden Key National Honor Society. *Member:* Chicago and Illinois State Bar Associations. ***PRACTICE AREAS:*** Litigation; Bankruptcy; Insurance Defense. ***Email:*** thudson@jenner.com

RACHEL A. JERIS, born July 14, 1978; admitted to bar, 2003, Illinois; 2004, U.S. Court of Appeals, Sixth Circuit. *Education:* Vanderbilt University (B.A., magna cum laude, 2000); University of Illinois College of Law (J.D., summa cum laude, 2003). Order of the Coif. Law Clerk: Honorable Karen Nelson Moore, 2003-2004. *Member:* American Bar Association. ***PRACTICE AREAS:*** Litigation. ***Email:*** rjeris@jenner.com

TODD K. JOHNSTON, born Phoenix, Arizona, August 29, 1972; (admission pending). *Education:* Brigham Young University (B.S., 2000); Arizona State University (M.B.A., 2002); University of Iowa College of Law (J.D., with distinction, 2005). ***PRACTICE AREAS:*** Corporate. ***Email:*** tjohnston@jenner.com

(This Listing Continued)

JENNER & BLOCK LLP, Chicago—Continued

ELIZABETH A. KALISZ, born Anderson, Indiana, November 5, 1979; (admission pending). *Education:* Purdue University (B.A., with distinction and honors, 2002); Indiana University School of Law (J.D., summa cum laude, 2005). Phi Beta Kappa. Executive Articles Editor, Indiana Law Review, 2003-2005. ***PRACTICE AREAS:*** Bankruptcy, Workout and Corporate Reorganization. ***Email:*** ekalisz@jenner.com

KATHY A. KARCHER, admitted to bar, 2001, Illinois. *Education:* University of Illinois, Urbana-Champaign (B.A.); University of Illinois Law School (J.D., 2001). ***PRACTICE AREAS:*** Civil Litigation; Class Actions. ***Email:*** kkarcher@jenner.com

DAVID M. KAVANAUGH, born Beatrice, Nebraska, June 8, 1978; admitted to bar, 2004, Illinois. *Education:* University of Nebraska-Lincoln (B.S.B.A., with highest distinction, 2001); University of Texas at Austin (J.D., with honors, 2004). ***PRACTICE AREAS:*** Corporate (100%). ***Email:*** dkavanaugh@jenner.com

BENJAMIN J. KEITH, born Logan, Utah, March 22, 1976; admitted to bar, 2004, Illinois. *Education:* Yale University (B.A., magna cum laude, 1998); Harvard Law School (J.D., cum laude, 2002). Phi Beta Kappa. Harvard Law Review. ***PRACTICE AREAS:*** Litigation Practice; Appellate and Supreme Court Practice; Tax Controversy Practice. ***Email:*** bkeith@jenner.com

FAZAL R. KHAN, admitted to bar, 2001, Illinois. *Education:* University of Chicago (B.A., with honors, 1995); University of Illinois College of Law (J.D., magna cum laude, 2000); University of Illinois College of Medicine (M.D., 2003). Sigma Xi Science Society. ***PRACTICE AREAS:*** Litigation; Health Care; Biotechnology; Intellectual Property. ***Email:*** fkhan@jenner.com

KRISTOPHER R. KIEL, admitted to bar, 2002, Illinois. *Education:* Northwestern University (B.S.I.E., cum laude, 1999); University of Michigan Law School (J.D., 2001). Registered to practice before U.S. Patent and Trademark Office, 2000. ***PRACTICE AREAS:*** Intellectual Property; Technology Law. ***Email:*** kkiel@jenner.com

BRYAN D. KING, born Huntington, New York, January 5, 1973; admitted to bar, 1998, California; 2003, Illinois. *Education:* Stanford University (B.A., 1995); Columbia University (J.D., 1998). ***PRACTICE AREAS:*** Litigation. ***Email:*** bking@jenner.com

REBECCA J. KRASAEATH, born St. Louis, Missouri, May 28, 1977; admitted to bar, 2004, Illinois. *Education:* Emory University (B.S., 1999); Northwestern University School of Law (J.D., 2004). ***PRACTICE AREAS:*** Intellectual Property (100%). ***Email:*** rkrasaeath@jenner.com

JAYNE LAIPRASERT, born Chicago, Illinois, July 22, 1980; admitted to bar, 2004, Illinois. *Education:* University of Chicago (B.A., 2000); Columbia Law School (J.D., 2004). ***PRACTICE AREAS:*** Bankruptcy (40%); Corporate Restructuring (20%); Commercial Law (20%). ***Email:*** jlaiprasert@jenner.com

JANICE H. LAM, born Baltimore, Maryland, March 30, 1978; (admission pending). *Education:* Yale University (B.A., 2000); George Washington University Law School (J.D., 2005). ***PRACTICE AREAS:*** Litigation and Dispute Resolution. ***Email:*** jlam@jenner.com

OLIVER LARSON, born Battle Creek, Michigan, August 21, 1975; admitted to bar, 1999, Illinois and U.S. District Court, Northern District of Illinois. *Education:* University of Michigan (B.A., 1996; J.D., 1999). ***PRACTICE AREAS:*** Litigation. ***Email:*** olarson@jenner.com

LISA S. LAUER, born Detroit, Michigan, November 19, 1977; admitted to bar, 2004, Illinois. *Education:* Wayne State University (B.S., summa cum laude, 1999); University of Michigan Law School (J.D., 2004). ***PRACTICE AREAS:*** Corporate (100%). ***Email:*** llauer@jenner.com

WILLIAM R. LEE, born Silver Spring, Maryland, October 9, 1979; admitted to bar, 2003, Illinois. *Education:* Northwestern University (B.S.J., 2000); University of Chicago Law School (J.D., 2003). ***PRACTICE AREAS:*** Litigation. ***Email:*** wlee@jenner.com

JORGE M. LEON, born Los Angeles, California, December 1972; admitted to bar, 1998, Illinois. *Education:* University of Illinois (B.S., 1995); University of Illinois College of Law (J.D., magna cum laude, 1998). Notes and Comments Editor, University of Illinois Law Review. Author: "Two Hats One Head: Reconciling Disability Benefits and the ADA," U. Ill. L. Rev. 1139, 1997. ***LANGUAGES:*** Spanish. ***PRACTICE AREAS:*** Employee Benefits; Executive Compensation. ***Email:*** jleon@jenner.com

JENNIFER S. LEVIN, born Hinsdale, Illinois, June 6, 1977; admitted to bar, 2002, Illinois. *Education:* Emory University (B.A., 1998); Northwestern University School of Law (J.D., 2002). Associate Editor, Law Review. ***PRACTICE AREAS:*** Real Estate; Real Estate Finance; Real Estate Development. ***Email:*** jlevin@jenner.com

ERIN N. LINDER, born South Bend, Indiana, December 22, 1979; (admission pending). *Education:* Northwestern University (B.A., magna cum laude, 2002); University of Illinois College of Law (J.D., 2005). Rickert Award Harno Scholar, Northwestern University. Author: "Punishing Prenatal Alcohol Abuse: The Problems Inherent in Utilizing Civil Commitment to Address Addiction," University of Illinois Law Review 873 (2005). ***PRACTICE AREAS:*** Litigation and Dispute Resolution. ***Email:*** elinder@jenner.com

DARREN H. LUBETZKY, born May 4, 1972; admitted to bar, 1998, Illinois. *Education:* Duke University (B.A., cum laude, 1994); University of Michigan (J.D., cum laude, 1998). (Resident, Washington, D.C. Office). ***PRACTICE AREAS:*** Litigation. ***Email:*** dlubetzky@jenner.com

PAUL D. MARGOLIS, born Portsmouth, Virginia, November 25, 1976; admitted to bar, 2001, Illinois; 2001, U.S. District Court, Northern District of Illinois; 2003, U.S. Court of Appeals for the Federal Circuit. *Education:* University of Illinois at Urbana/Champaign (B.S., High Honors, 1998); University of Illinois College of Law (J.D., 2001). ***PRACTICE AREAS:*** Intellectual Property Litigation. ***Email:*** pmargolis@jenner.com

JOSEPH F. MARINELLI, born Milwaukee, Wisconsin, December 15, 1972; admitted to bar, 1999, Wisconsin and Illinois; U.S. District Court, Northern District of Illinois; U.S. District Court, Western District of Wisconsin; U.S. Court of Appeals, Federal Circuit. *Education:* Purdue University (B.S.M.E., 1996); University of Wisconsin (J.D., 1999). ***PRACTICE AREAS:*** Litigation; Intellectual Property. ***Email:*** jmarinelli@jenner.com

(This Listing Continued)

GALEN R. MASON, born San Francisco, California, April 24, 1976; admitted to bar, 2002, Illinois. *Education:* St. Olaf College (B.A., 1998); University of Missouri (J.D., 2002). Staff Member, University of Missouri Law Review. ***PRACTICE AREAS:*** Employee Benefits; Executive Compensation. ***Email:*** gmason@jenner.com

MICHELLE M. McATEE, born Davenport, Iowa, January 19, 1973; admitted to bar, 1999, Massachusetts; 2003, Illinois. *Education:* Marquette University (B.S., Speech Pathology, cum laude, 1995); University of Iowa (J.D., 1998). Alpha Sigma Nu. Equal Justice Foundation Class Representative, University of Iowa College of Law. Recipient, Marquette University Student Leadership Award. Volunteer Lawyer's Project Housing Court Volunteer, 1999-2003. Member, Boston Bar Association, 1999-2003. *Member:* Chicago, Illinois State and American Bar Associations. ***PRACTICE AREAS:*** Real Estate (100%). ***Email:*** mmcatee@jenner.com

EDWARD P. McKENNA, born New York, New York, June 17, 1975; admitted to bar, 2004, Illinois; 2005, U.S. District Court, Northern District of Illinois. *Education:* University of Texas at Austin (B.A., 1997); Northwestern University School of Law (J.D., 2003). ***PRACTICE AREAS:*** Litigation (100%). ***Email:*** emckenna@jenner.com

DANIEL P. McLAUGHLIN, born Orange, California, June 2, 1977; admitted to bar, 2004, Illinois. *Education:* Marquette University (B.A., 1999); University of Illinois College of Law (J.D., 2004). ***PRACTICE AREAS:*** Litigation Practice. ***Email:*** dmclaughlin@jenner.com

DANIEL C. McMURTRIE, born Ann Arbor, Michigan, October 4, 1977; admitted to bar, 2003, Illinois and Wisconsin. *Education:* University of Michigan (B.A., 2000); University of Wisconsin Law School (J.D., cum laude, 2003). ***PRACTICE AREAS:*** Litigation. ***Email:*** dmcmurtrie@jenner.com

STEVEN R. MEIER, born Merrill, Wisconsin; admitted to bar, 1998, New York; 2002, U.S. Tax Court; 2003, Illinois. *Education:* University of Wisconsin (B.A., 1988); Harvard University (A.M., 1991); Columbia University (J.D., 1998). Harlan Fiske Stone Scholar. Moot Court Student Editor. Managing Editor, Parker School Journal of East European Law. *Member:* Chicago (Member, Federal Taxation Committee, 2003—), New York State (Member, Tax Section, 1998—) and American (Member, Section of Taxation, 1998—) Bar Associations. ***LANGUAGES:*** Russian. ***PRACTICE AREAS:*** Tax Law. ***Email:*** smeier@jenner.com

BRIAN H. MELDRUM, born Mt. Clemens, Michigan, December 22, 1974; admitted to bar, 2000, Illinois and U.S. District Court, Northern District of Illinois. *Education:* University of Michigan (A.B., 1997; J.D., 1999). *Member:* Chicago and American Bar Associations; American Bankruptcy Institute. ***PRACTICE AREAS:*** Commercial Litigation; Bankruptcy. ***Email:*** bmeldrum@jenner.com

ROBIN M. MERIWEATHER, born Detroit, Michigan, April 17, 1974; admitted to bar, 1998, Illinois. *Education:* University of Michigan (B.A., 1995); Yale University (J.D., 1998). Phi Beta Kappa. Law Clerk, The Hon. Merrick B. Garland, U.S. Court of Appeals, D.C. Circuit, 1998-1999. *Member:* American Bar Association. (Resident, Washington, D.C. Office). ***PRACTICE AREAS:*** Litigation. ***Email:*** rmeriweather@jenner.com

ZACHARY V. MOEN, born Eau Claire, Wisconsin, March 2, 1978; admitted to bar, 2003, Illinois and U.S. District Court, Northern District of Illinois; 2004, District of Columbia. *Education:* Wheaton College (B.A., cum laude, 2000); Loyola University Chicago School of Law (J.D., magna cum laude, 2003). ***PRACTICE AREAS:*** Litigation. ***Email:*** zmoen@jenner.com

THOMAS P. MONROE, born Peoria, Illinois, September 6, 1973; admitted to bar, 2001, Illinois. *Education:* Monmouth College (B.A., 1995); Loyola University of Chicago (J.D., 2001). ***PRACTICE AREAS:*** Complex Business Litigation; Construction Law; Products Liability and Mass Tort Defense; Trial Practice; White Collar Criminal Defense and Counseling. ***Email:*** tmonroe@jenner.com

DANIEL I. MORALES, born Washington, D.C., January 24, 1980; (admission pending). *Education:* Williams College (B.A., magna cum laude, 2002); Yale University Law School (J.D., 2005). Phi Beta Kappa. ***LANGUAGES:*** Spanish. ***PRACTICE AREAS:*** Litigation and Dispute Resolution. ***Email:*** dmorales@jenner.com

MOLLY J. MORAN, born Hammond, Indiana, September 26, 1968; admitted to bar, 1998, Illinois; U.S. District Court, Northern District of Illinois. *Education:* Indiana University (B.A., 1990); Indiana University School of Law (J.D., 1998). *Member:* Chicago and American Bar Associations. ***PRACTICE AREAS:*** Litigation. ***Email:*** mmoran@jenner.com

MEGHAN C. MORRISSEY, born Oak Lawn, Illinois, November 10, 1978; admitted to bar, 2004, Illinois. *Education:* University of Illinois (B.A., 2000); University of Chicago Law School (J.D., 2004). ***PRACTICE AREAS:*** Litigation Practice. ***Email:*** mmorrissey@jenner.com

DARREN M. MUNGERSON, born Geneseo, Illinois, November 30, 1972; admitted to bar, 1998, Illinois and U.S. District Court, Northern District of Illinois; 2000, U.S. District Court, Southern and Central Districts of Illinois. *Education:* University of Illinois, Urbana-Champaign (B.S., 1995), Bronze Tablet; Harvard Law School (J.D., cum laude, 1998). ***PRACTICE AREAS:*** Labor and Employment. ***Email:*** dmungerson@jenner.com

THALIA L. MYRIANTHOPOULOS, born Chicago, Illinois, April 15, 1973; admitted to bar, 2001, Illinois; 2002, U.S. Court of Appeals, Seventh Circuit; 2003, U.S. District Court, Northern District of Illinois. *Education:* Haverford College (B.A., 1995); Harvard Law School (J.D., 2001). ***PRACTICE AREAS:*** Litigation. ***Email:*** tmyrianthopoulos@jenner.com

MAYA D. NATH, born Redhill, United Kingdom, July 10, 1979; admitted to bar, 2005, Massachusetts and New York (Not admitted in Illinois). *Education:* Columbia College (B.A., 2001); New York University School of Law (J.D., 2004). ***PRACTICE AREAS:*** Litigation and Dispute Resolution; General Commercial Litigation. ***Email:*** mnath@jenner.com

PHILLIP W. NELSON, born East Chicago, Indiana, October 9, 1978; admitted to bar, 2004, Illinois. *Education:* Wabash College (A.B., 2001); Duke University (J.D., 2004). Phi Beta Kappa. ***PRACTICE AREAS:*** Bankruptcy; Workout; Corporate Reorganization. ***Email:*** pnelson@jenner.com

(This Listing Continued)

KATHRYN C. NEWMAN, born Minot, North Dakota, June 3, 1973; admitted to bar, 1999, Arizona; 2002, Illinois. *Education:* Georgetown University (B.A., 1995); Georgetown University Law Center (J.D., 1999). ***PRACTICE AREAS:*** Litigation and Dispute Resolution; Securities Litigation. ***Email:*** knewman@jenner.com

ANDREW S. NICOLL, born Salt Lake City, Utah, January 26, 1977; admitted to bar, 2004, Illinois. *Education:* Brigham Young University (B.S., 2004; M.Acc., 2004; J.D., magna cum laude, 2004). ***PRACTICE AREAS:*** Bankruptcy; Workout; Corporate Reorganization. ***Email:*** anicoll@jenner.com

ERIN M. O'CONNELL, born Kenosha, Wisconsin, December 28, 1978; admitted to bar, 2004, Illinois; 2005, California. *Education:* Cornell University (B.A., 2000); Stanford Law School (J.D., with distinction, 2004). ***PRACTICE AREAS:*** Litigation Practice (100%). ***Email:*** eoconnell@jenner.com

CHRISTOPHER M. O'CONNOR, born Port Huron, Michigan, June 5, 1975; admitted to bar, 2000, Illinois. *Education:* Albion College (B.A., magna cum laude, 1997); Case Western Reserve University (J.D., magna cum laude, 2000). Phi Beta Kappa. Order of the Coif. Editor in Chief, Case Western Reserve Law Review, 1999-2000. Author: "Problems of Proof in a Paperless World: Electronic Evidence in Commercial Litigation," 35 Uniform Commercial Code Law Journal 1 (2002) (with D. Murray and T. Chorvat); "Stop Harassing Her or We'll Both Sue: Bystander Injury Sexual Harassment," 50 Case Western Reserve Law Review 501 (1999). *Member:* Illinois and American (Member, Litigation Section, 1999—) Bar Associations. ***PRACTICE AREAS:*** Litigation. ***Email:*** coconnor@jenner.com

BRIAN P. O'DONNELL, born Landstuhl, Germany, March 31, 1971; admitted to bar, 2001, Illinois and U.S. District Court, Northern District of Illinois. *Education:* Ruprecht-Karls Universitaet Heidelberg (Kzz., 1993); University of Illinois, Champaign-Urbana (B.A., 1994); The London School of Economics (M.Sc., 1995); Loyola University, Chicago (J.D., 2001). ***PRACTICE AREAS:*** Intellectual Property; Litigation. ***Email:*** bodonnell@jenner.com

ANDREW J. OLEJNIK, born DeKalb, Illinois, April 11, 1979; admitted to bar, 2004, Illinois. *Education:* University of Notre Dame (B.A., summa cum laude, 2001); Stanford Law School (J.D., 2004). Phi Beta Kappa. ***PRACTICE AREAS:*** Bankruptcy; Commercial Law; Alternative Dispute Resolution. ***Email:*** aolejnik@jenner.com

VERA OVADIA, born Berkeley, California, December 14, 1964; admitted to bar, 1991, Arizona; 1993, District of Columbia; 1995, New York; 2002, Illinois. *Education:* University of Virginia (B.A., 1987; J.D., 1991). *Member:* Chicago and American Bar Associations. ***PRACTICE AREAS:*** Employment Law; Litigation. ***Email:*** vovadia@jenner.com

VITO M. PACIONE, born Elgin, Illinois, July 19, 1978; admitted to bar, 2003, Illinois. *Education:* University of Illinois, Urbana-Champaign (B.A., 2000); University of Illinois School of Law (J.D., summa cum laude, 2003). *Member:* Chicago, Illinois State and American Bar Associations. ***PRACTICE AREAS:*** Real Estate. ***Email:*** vpacione@jenner.com

EMILY S. PALMER, born Toledo, Ohio, June 11, 1977; admitted to bar, 2004, Illinois. *Education:* Williams College (B.A., 1999); University of Michigan Law School (J.D., 2003). ***PRACTICE AREAS:*** Litigation (100%). ***Email:*** epalmer@jenner.com

CHRISTOPHER V. PARENTE, born Scranton, Pennsylvania, June 10, 1979; admitted to bar, 2004, Illinois. *Education:* University of Scranton (B.S., 2001); Notre Dame Law School (J.D., 2004). Notre Dame Law Review. ***PRACTICE AREAS:*** Litigation Practice. ***Email:*** cparente@jenner.com

SEJAL PARIKH, born Warren, Michigan, May 2, 1980; (admission pending). *Education:* University of Michigan (B.S.M.E., 2001); University of Michigan Law School (J.D., 2004). ***PRACTICE AREAS:*** Litigation and Dispute Resolution. ***Email:*** sparikh@jenner.com

CHRISTINE A. PARKER, born Palos Heights, Illinois, August 17, 1974; admitted to bar, 2002, Illinois. *Education:* Trinity Christian College (B.S., 1996); College of William & Mary (M.B.A., 2002; J.D., 2002). Beta Gamma Sigma. Editor, William & Mary Law Review, 2001-2002. *Member:* Chicago and American Bar Associations; Christian Legal Society. ***PRACTICE AREAS:*** Corporate Law; Securities; Mergers and Acquisitions. ***Email:*** cparker@jenner.com

IORDAN A. PEEV, born Plovdiv, Bulgaria, October 19, 1965; admitted to bar, 2000, Illinois. *Education:* Southern Illinois University, Carbondale (B.S., cum laude, 1997; J.D., 2000; M.Acct./Taxation, 2000). Certified Public Accountant: Illinois, 2002 and Missouri, 2004. Certified Management Accountant, 2001. Member: Illinois Certified Public Accountant Society, 1997—; American Institute of Certified Public Accountants, 1997—; Tax Law Society, 1999-2000. *Member:* Illinois State, Chicago and American Bar Associations; Institute of Management Accountants. ***LANGUAGES:*** Bulgarian. ***PRACTICE AREAS:*** Mergers and Acquisitions; Tax Practice; Tax Controversies. ***Email:*** ipeev@jenner.com

LAURA E. PELANEK, born Milwaukee, Wisconsin, February 8, 1979; admitted to bar, 2004, Illinois. *Education:* University of Virginia (B.A., 2001); University of Texas (J.D., with honors, 2004). Order of the Coif. ***PRACTICE AREAS:*** Litigation and Dispute Resolution. ***Email:*** lpelanek@jenner.com

DAMON D. PERRY, born Chicago, Illinois, December 6, 1978; admitted to bar, 2003, Illinois. *Education:* University of Michigan (B.A., 1999; J.D., 2002). Contributing Editor, Michigan Law Review, 2001-2002. ***PRACTICE AREAS:*** Commercial Litigation (100%). ***Email:*** dperry@jenner.com

ELAYNA T. PHAM, admitted to bar, 1999, Illinois. *Education:* American University (B.A., 1996); Chicago-Kent College of Law (J.D., 1999). ***PRACTICE AREAS:*** Intellectual Property; Trademark; Copyright; Trade Secrets and Unfair Competition. ***Email:*** epham@jenner.com

MONICA R. PINCIAK, born Evergreen Park, Illinois, July 18, 1974; admitted to bar, 1999, Illinois. *Education:* DePaul University (B.S., 1996); Chicago-Kent College of Law (J.D., 1999). ***PRACTICE AREAS:*** Litigation; White Collar Criminal Defense and Counseling; Appellate and Supreme Court Practice. ***Email:*** mpinciak@jenner.com

LUKE C. PLATZER, born Cambridge, Massachusetts, August 30, 1978; admitted to bar, 2005, New York. *Education:* Harvard College (A.B., 2000); Stanford University Law School (J.D., 2003). Order of the Coif. (Resident, Washington, D.C. Office). ***PRACTICE AREAS:*** Litigation and Dispute Resolution; Civil Litigation. ***Email:*** lplatzer@jenner.com

ELIZABETH G. PORTER, born Boston, Massachusetts; admitted to bar, 2003, District of Columbia. *Education:* Brown University (B.A., 1991); Columbia University Law School (J.D., 2000). (Resident, Washington, D.C. Office). ***PRACTICE AREAS:*** Appellate Litigation; Regulatory. ***Email:*** eporter@jenner.com

DUANE POZZA, born San Antonio, Texas, April 7, 1976; admitted to bar, 2003, California (Not admitted in Illinois). *Education:* University of Texas at Austin (B.A., 1998); Stanford University (J.D., with distinction, 2002). (Resident, Washington, D.C. Office). ***PRACTICE AREAS:*** Litigation. ***Email:*** dpozza@jenner.com

EDWARD G. QUINLISK, born Evergreen Park, Illinois, April 27, 1972; admitted to bar, 2000, Illinois. *Education:* Roosevelt University (B.A., 1996); DePaul University (J.D., with honors, 1999); New York University (LL.M., Taxation, 2000). Order of the Coif. ***PRACTICE AREAS:*** Corporate Law; Securities. ***Email:*** equinlisk@jenner.com

KATHERINE RAHILL, born Washington, D.C., January 3, 1977; admitted to bar, 2002, Colorado (Not admitted in Illinois). *Education:* Northwestern University (B.A., 1999); University of Michigan Law School (J.D., 2002). Phi Beta Kappa. Order of the Coif. ***PRACTICE AREAS:*** Environmental, Energy and Natural Resources Law. ***Email:*** krahill@jenner.com

GAYLE A. RANA, born San Jose, Costa Rica, March 31, 1977; admitted to bar, 2002, Illinois. *Education:* Northwestern University (B.A., summa cum laude, 1999); Harvard Law School (J.D., 2002). ***LANGUAGES:*** Spanish. ***PRACTICE AREAS:*** Litigation Practice. ***Email:*** grana@jenner.com

JAY S. READEY, born Columbus, Ohio, January 24, 1972; admitted to bar, 2004, Illinois. *Education:* Yale University (B.A., 1994); Yale Law School (J.D., 2004); Yale School of Management (M.B.A., 2004). ***PRACTICE AREAS:*** Mergers and Acquisitions; Securities; Corporate and Municipal Finance. ***Email:*** jreadey@jenner.com

STEPHANIE L. REINHART, born Tuscola, Illinois, April 11, 1980; (admission pending). *Education:* Illinois Wesleyan University (B.A., 2002); University of Illinois College of Law (J.D., summa cum laude, 2005). Order of the Coif; Harno Scholar. Author: "Dirty words you cannot say on TV: Does the First Amendment prohibit Congress from banning certain words?" University of Illinois Law Review (2005). *Member:* American Bar Association; Illinois State Bar Association. ***PRACTICE AREAS:*** Litigation and Dispute Resolution. ***Email:*** sreinhart@jenner.com

MATTHEW H. RICE, born Olympia, Washington, November 30, 1975; admitted to bar, 2003, Illinois. *Education:* University of Michigan (B.A., with high honors and high distinction, 1998); Stanford University Law School (J.D., 2003). ***PRACTICE AREAS:*** Litigation. ***Email:*** mrice@jenner.com

DAVID B. ROBBINS, born 1975; admitted to bar, 2003, Maryland; 2005, Illinois. *Education:* Yale University (B.A., 1997); University of Maryland Law School (J.D., 2003); University of Maryland (M.B.A., 2003). (Resident, Washington, D.C. Office). ***PRACTICE AREAS:*** Government Contracts. ***Email:*** drobbins@jenner.com

CYNTHIA J. ROBERTSON, born West Lafayette, Indiana, April 27, 1968; admitted to bar, 1998, Illinois and U.S. District Court, Northern District of Illinois; 2001, District of Columbia. *Education:* Vanderbilt University (B.A., 1990); University of Illinois (J.D., 1998). Order of the Coif. (Resident, Washington, D.C. Office). ***PRACTICE AREAS:*** General Litigation; Government Contracts Litigation; White Collar Criminal Defense and Counseling. ***Email:*** crobertson@jenner.com

PETER H. ROSENBAUM, born Lansing, Michigan, September 21, 1971; (admission pending). *Education:* University of Michigan (B.A., 1994); Loyola University Chicago School of Law (J.D., magna cum laude, 2005). ***PRACTICE AREAS:*** Corporate. ***Email:*** prosenbaum@jenner.com

ROSS M. ROSENBERG, born Cincinnati, Ohio, January 25, 1970; admitted to bar, 2002, New York; 2003, Illinois. *Education:* University of Pennsylvania (B.A., 1992); Northwestern University Law School (J.D., cum laude, 1999). Recipient, Raoul Berger Essay Prize. ***PRACTICE AREAS:*** Antitrust; Commercial Litigation; Products Liability. ***Email:*** rrosenberg@jenner.com

ALEXANDER ROZENBLAT, born June 10, 1978; admitted to bar, 2003, Illinois; registered to practice before U.S. Patent and Trademark Office. *Education:* Northwestern University (B.A., 2000); DePaul University College of Law (J.D., magna cum laude, 2003). Phi Alpha Delta (Clerk, 1999-2000). Order of the Coif. ***LANGUAGES:*** Russian. ***PRACTICE AREAS:*** Intellectual Property; Technology Law; Patent Prosecution; Trademark Prosecution. ***Email:*** arozenblat@jenner.com

LAURA A. SAKULICH, born Rochester, Michigan, May 19, 1976; admitted to bar, 2004, Illinois. *Education:* Western Michigan University (B.M., 1999); Brigham Young University (J.D., 2004). ***PRACTICE AREAS:*** Corporate (100%). ***Email:*** lsakulich@jenner.com

HEINZ J. SALMEN, born Skokie, Illinois, February 28, 1976; (admission pending). *Education:* North Park University (B.S., 1998); Loyola University Chicago School of Law (J.D., 2005). ***PRACTICE AREAS:*** Intellectual Property. ***Email:*** hsalmen@jenner.com

JOSEPH A. SALTIEL, admitted to bar, 2001, Illinois; registered to practice before U.S. Patent and Trademark Office. *Education:* University of Illinois (B.S., 1996; M.S., 1998; J.D., magna cum laude, 2001). Chancellor Scholar; Lincoln Scholar. Member, Law Review. ***LANGUAGES:*** Spanish. ***PRACTICE AREAS:*** Intellectual Property and Technology; Litigation; Trade Secrets; Unfair Competition. ***Email:*** jsaltiel@jenner.com

BRIAN S. SCARBROUGH, born Lancaster, Ohio, February 1, 1979; admitted to bar, 2004, Illinois. *Education:* Duke University (B.A., magna cum laude, 2001); Harvard Law School (J.D., 2004). Phi Beta Kappa. *Member:* Chicago, Illinois State and American Bar Associations. ***PRACTICE AREAS:*** Litigation and Dispute Resolution Practice. ***Email:*** bscarbrough@jenner.com

(This Listing Continued)

JENNER & BLOCK LLP, Chicago—Continued

RINA L. SCATES, born West Long Branch, New Jersey, June 16, 1979; (admission pending). *Education:* University of Utah (B.S., 2001); Brigham Young University Law School (J.D., magna cum laude, 2005). ***PRACTICE AREAS:*** Litigation and Dispute Resolution. ***Email:*** rscates@jenner.com

JOHN R. SCHLEPPENBACH, born Quincy, Illinois (Adams), February 4, 1978; admitted to bar, 2003, Illinois. *Education:* Millikin University (B.A./B.S., 2000); University of Illinois College of Law (J.D., 2003). Order of the Coif. ***PRACTICE AREAS:*** Litigation and Dispute Resolution. ***Email:*** jschleppenbach@jenner.com

DARREN J. SCHMIDT, born Petaluma, California, 1974; admitted to bar, 2001, New York; 2002, Illinois. *Education:* Indiana University (B.A., 1996); Columbia University (J.D., 2000). Phi Beta Kappa. Harlan Fiske Stone Scholar. Recipient, Senior Achievement Award, Indiana University. Law Clerk to the Hon. Marvin Aspen, U.S. District Court, Northern District of Illinois. ***PRACTICE AREAS:*** Litigation; Entertainment and New Media; Intellectual Property. ***Email:*** dschmidt@jenner.com

RUTH A. SCHOENMEYER, born Royal Oak, Michigan, October 18, 1970; admitted to bar, 1995, Colorado; 1996, Illinois. *Education:* University of Michigan (A.B., with highest distinction, 1992; J.D., 1995). Phi Beta Kappa. James B. Angell Scholar. *Member:* Chicago and American Bar Associations. ***PRACTICE AREAS:*** Real Estate. ***Email:*** rschoenmeyer@jenner.com

JOSEPH A. SCHOUTEN, born Appleton, Wisconsin, September 28, 1978; admitted to bar, 2004, Illinois. *Education:* University of Dayton (B.A., 2001); College of William & Mary (J.D., 2004). ***PRACTICE AREAS:*** Litigation and Dispute Resolution. ***Email:*** jschouten@jenner.com

ERIN R. SCHRANTZ, born Arlington Heights, Illinois, February 1, 1975; admitted to bar, 2000, Illinois and U.S. District Court, Northern District of Illinois; 2001, U.S. District Court, Central District of Illinois. *Education:* University of Illinois, Urbana-Champaign (B.A., 1997); Indiana University School of Law - Bloomington (J.D., cum laude, 2000). Member, Indiana Law Journal, 1998-2000. Author: Indiana Law Journal, Volume 75 Spring 2000. ***PRACTICE AREAS:*** Litigation; White Collar Criminal Defense; Class Action Litigation. ***Email:*** eschrantz@jenner.com

KRISTEN GARVEY SCHULZ, born New York, N.Y., December 5, 1970; admitted to bar, 1996, Texas and U.S. District Court, Northern District of Texas; 1997, U.S. District Court, Eastern District of Texas; 2000, U.S. District Court, Southern and Western Districts of Texas; 2001, U.S. Court of Federal Claims. *Education:* Trinity University (B.A., 1993); University of Texas (J.D., with honors, 1996). (Resident, Dallas, Texas Office). ***PRACTICE AREAS:*** Government Contracts Claims Disputes; Commercial Litigation; Government Ethics and Compliance; Intellectual Property; Technology Law. ***Email:*** kschulz@jenner.com

LISA T. SCRUGGS, born Elgin, Illinois, January 10, 1971; admitted to bar, 1998, Illinois and U.S. District Court, Northern District of Illinois; 1999, U.S. Court of Appeals, Seventh Circuit. *Education:* Georgetown University (B.A., cum laude, 1993); University of Chicago (M.A., 1994; J.D., 1998). Articles Editor, University of Chicago Roundtable, 1997-1998. Law Clerk to the Hon. Ann C. Williams, U.S. Court of Appeals, Seventh Circuit. ***PRACTICE AREAS:*** Litigation. ***Email:*** lscruggs@jenner.com

SALLY K. SEARS CODER, born Dearborn, Michigan, September 15, 1974; admitted to bar, 1999, Illinois and U.S. District Court, Northern District of Illinois; 2000, U.S. Court of Appeals, Eleventh Circuit. *Education:* Michigan State University (B.A., 1996); University of Michigan (J.D., cum laude, 1999). Order of the Coif. Managing Editor, Journal of Law Reform. *Member:* Chicago and American Bar Associations. ***PRACTICE AREAS:*** Commercial Litigation; Arbitration; International Arbitration; Intellectual Property. ***Email:*** ssears_coder@jenner.com

JASON A. SELVEY, born Oak Lawn, Illinois, May 8, 1980; (admission pending). *Education:* Northwestern University (B.A., 2002); University of Illinois College of Law (J.D., summa cum laude, 2005). ***PRACTICE AREAS:*** Litigation and Dispute Resolution. ***Email:*** jselvey@jenner.com

JILL R. SHEIMAN, born Philadelphia, Pennsylvania, December 21, 1975; admitted to bar, 2000, Connecticut and Illinois; 2001, District of Columbia, U.S. District Court, Northern District of Illinois and U.S. Tax Court. *Education:* University of Michigan (B.A., with distinction, 1997); Northwestern University (J.D., 2000); New York University (LL.M. in Taxation, 2001). *Member:* Chicago and American (Member, Sections on: Business Law; Taxation) Bar Associations. ***PRACTICE AREAS:*** Mergers, Acquisitions and Divestitures; Corporate Law; Securities. ***Email:*** jsheiman@jenner.com

SHANA A. SHIFRIN, born Park Ridge, Illinois, March 8, 1978; admitted to bar, 2003, Illinois. *Education:* University of Pennsylvania (B.A., cum laude, 2000); Northwestern University School of Law (J.D., 2003). Senior Editor, Journal of International Law and Business. ***PRACTICE AREAS:*** Litigation. ***Email:*** sshifrin@jenner.com

JEFFREY R. SHUMAN, born Panorama City, California, August 1, 1978; admitted to bar, 2003, Illinois. *Education:* University of Illinois, Urbana-Champaign (B.A., summa cum laude, with distinction, 2000; B.S., with highest honors, 2000); Harvard Law School (J.D., 2003). ***LANGUAGES:*** Portuguese. ***PRACTICE AREAS:*** Corporate Law; Mergers, Acquisitions and Divestitures; Securities. ***Email:*** jshuman@jenner.com

PETER A. SIDDIQUI, born Chicago, Illinois, June 20, 1976; admitted to bar, 2002, Illinois. *Education:* DePauw University (B.A., 1998); Indiana University School of Law - Indianapolis (J.D., magna cum laude, 2002). Member, Indiana Law Review. ***PRACTICE AREAS:*** Bankruptcy. ***Email:*** psiddiqui@jenner.com

MARGARET J. SIMPSON, born Aitkin, Minnesota, October 19, 1961; admitted to bar, 1997, Illinois. *Education:* St. Olaf College (B.A., summa cum laude, 1983); University of Wisconsin, Madison (M.S., Economics, 1985; Ph.D., Economics, 1991); University of Chicago (J.D., with honors, 1997). Phi Beta Kappa. *Member:* Illinois State and American Bar Associations; American Economic Association. ***PRACTICE AREAS:*** Antitrust; Litigation. ***Email:*** msimpson@jenner.com

RAYMOND D. SINNAPPAN, born Chicago, Illinois, September 30, 1972; admitted to bar, 1997, Illinois. *Education:* University of Illinois, Urbana-Champaign (B.S., 1994); Northwestern University (J.D., 1997). ***PRACTICE AREAS:*** Employee Benefits; ERISA Counseling; Benefit Issues in Transactions; Executive Compensation. ***Email:*** rsinnappan@jenner.com

MARC D. SOKOL, born Hammond, Indiana, October 12, 1970; admitted to bar, 2001, Illinois. *Education:* Northwestern University (B.A., 1992); Indiana University School of Law (J.D., summa cum laude, 2001); Duke University Fuqua School of Business (M.B.A., 2003). ***PRACTICE AREAS:*** Commercial Litigation. ***Email:*** msokol@jenner.com

DOUGLAS A. SONDGEROTH, born Mendota, Illinois, October 21, 1976; admitted to bar, 2002, Illinois. *Education:* Augustana College (B.A., 1999); Boston College (J.D., 2002). Phi Beta Kappa; Order of the Coif. ***PRACTICE AREAS:*** Litigation; Class Action Litigation; ERISA Litigation; Defense and Aerospace. ***Email:*** dsondgeroth@jenner.com

MICHELLE SPELLER-THURMAN, born Columbia, Missouri, November 13, 1968; admitted to bar, 1999, Illinois. *Education:* University of Illinois, Urbana-Champaign (B.S., 1991); Northwestern University (J.D., 1999). ***PRACTICE AREAS:*** Corporate; Corporate Finance. ***Email:*** mspeller-thurman@jenner.com

SCOTT A. SPENCER, born Brazoria, Texas, October 13, 1972; admitted to bar, 2003, Illinois. *Education:* Texas Tech University (B.S., 1997); University of Illinois College of Law (J.D., 2003). ***PRACTICE AREAS:*** Intellectual Property; Litigation. ***Email:*** sspencer@jenner.com

COURTNEY A. STEVENS, born Murphysboro, Illinois, May 6, 1979; admitted to bar, 2004, Illinois. *Education:* Southeast Missouri State University (B.S., summa cum laude, 2001); University of Illinois College of Law (J.D., magna cum laude, 2004). ***PRACTICE AREAS:*** Corporate (100%). ***Email:*** cstevens@jenner.com

CLAY STIFFLER, born Grand Rapids, Michigan, February 9, 1971; admitted to bar, 1999, Illinois and U.S. District Court, Northern District of Illinois; U.S. Court of Appeals, Sixth Circuit. *Education:* Michigan State University (B.A., 1993); Loyola University of Chicago (J.D., magna cum laude, 1999). *Member:* Chicago, Illinois State and American Bar Associations. [Sergeant, U.S. Army, 1993-1996]. ***PRACTICE AREAS:*** Litigation. ***Email:*** rstiffler@jenner.com

JEREMY T. STILLINGS, born Detroit, Michigan, December 21, 1977; admitted to bar, 2003, Illinois and U.S. District Court, Northern District of Illinois. *Education:* Tulane University (B.S.M., 2000); University of Texas School of Law (J.D., 2003). ***PRACTICE AREAS:*** Bankruptcy; Commercial Law; Corporate Restructuring. ***Email:*** jstillings@jenner.com

JOHN R. STORINO, born Maywood, Illinois, August 23, 1974; admitted to bar, 2000, Illinois and U.S. District Court, Northern District of Illinois; 2001, U.S. Court of Appeals, Seventh Circuit. *Education:* University of Notre Dame (B.A., 1997; J.D., cum laude, 2000). Contributing Author: *Insurance Coverage Disputes,* Law Journal Press, 2001. *Member:* Illinois State and American Bar Associations; Chicago Inn of Court. ***PRACTICE AREAS:*** Litigation. ***Email:*** jstorino@jenner.com

EMMA J. SULLIVAN, born Evanston, Illinois, April 29, 1975; admitted to bar, 1999, Illinois. *Education:* University of Illinois (B.S., 1996; J.D., magna cum laude, 1999). Order of the Coif. Member, University of Illinois Law Review. ***PRACTICE AREAS:*** Labor and Employment. ***Email:*** esullivan@jenner.com

JOANNE H. SWEENEY, born Princeton, New Jersey, June 30, 1973; admitted to bar, 1999, Illinois and U.S. District Court, Northern District of Illinois; 2000, Massachusetts. *Education:* Miami University (Ohio) (B.S., cum laude, 1995); Loyola University of Chicago School of Law (J.D., magna cum laude, 1999). Executive Editor, Loyola Law Review, 1998-1999. Philip H. Cabby Fellowship in Trial Advisory; National Mock Team. ***PRACTICE AREAS:*** Litigation; White Collar Criminal Defense and Counseling; Product Liability. ***Email:*** jsweeney@jenner.com

SHEHLA F. SYED, born Toronto, Ontario, Canada, February 23, 1977; admitted to bar, 2001, Maryland; 2002, Illinois; registered to practice before U.S. Patent and Trademark Office. *Education:* Johns Hopkins University (B.A., Biology and Economics, 1998); University of Pennsylvania Law School (J.D., 2001). *Member:* Federal Circuit Bar Association; Intellectual Property Law Association of Chicago. ***PRACTICE AREAS:*** Patent Litigation; Prosecution and Counseling. ***Email:*** ssyed@jenner.com

MARY C. TALARICO, born Owosso, Michigan, September 28, 1965; admitted to bar, 1995, Illinois and U.S. District Court, Northern District of Illinois. *Education:* Albion College (B.A., 1987); John Marshall Law School (J.D., 1995). Phi Delta Phi. Seminars: Claims Against the Estate, Illinois Institute for Continuing Legal Education, Illinois Estate Administration: Process and Practice (June 2, 2004); Claims Against the Estate, Illinois Institute for Continuing Legal Education, Illinois Estate Administration: Process and Practice (June 20, 2003); Planned Giving, American Medical Association Foundation, AMA House of Delegates Annual Meeting (June 16, 2003); Valuation: Challenges and Opportunities, Chicago Bar Association, Federal Tax Committee, Estate and Gift Tax Division (September 5, 2002); Valuation: Challenges and Opportunities, Illinois Institute for Continuing Legal Education, Illinois Probate: the Essentials & More for Administering Estates of All Sizes (June 20, 2002); New Developments in the Tax Law With a Focus On Estate Planning, Chicago Bar Association, Young Lawyers Section Tax Law Committee (November 6, 2001); Planning Considerations Under The Economic Growth and Tax Relief Reconciliation Act of 2001, Chicago Bar Association, Estate and Gift Tax Division of the Federal Taxation Committee (September 6, 2001); Fundamentals Of Estate Planning, Asset Ownership and Estate and Gift Taxation, Professional National Title Network, Inc. (March, 2001); Current Events: Legislative and Judicial Developments, National Business Institute (April, 1999); Fundamentals Of Estate Planning, American College of Surgeons (May, 1999); Fundamentals Of Estate Planning, College of DuPage (November, 1998). Publications: Co-Author, "Claims Against the Estate," Handling the Probate Maze Illinois Estate Administration, Illinois Institute for Continuing Legal Education (June 2005); Co-Author, "Claims Against the Estate," Illinois Estate Administration, Illinois Institute for Continuing Legal Education (June 2003); Co-Author, "The New Estate and Gift Tax Law: Estate Planning Pointers," Vol. 90, No. 2, Illinois Bar Journal, Pages 80-87 (February 2002); Co-Author, "Estate and Gift Tax Changes: What's New in the New Law?," Vol. 90, No. 1, Illinois Bar Journal, Pages 24-31 (January 2002); Co-Author, "Lifetime Gifts After EGTRRA 2001 - Is There Anything Left To Do?," Illinois State Bar Association Law Ed Seminar Primer on New Tax Law and Other Developments (presented in Chicago, Illinois - September 13,

(This Listing Continued)

2001, Bloomington, Illinois - September 28, 2001); Co-Author, "Valuation: Challenges and Opportunities," Illinois Institute for Continuing Legal Education (presented in June, 2000); Co-Author, "Estate Planning for Mid-Sized Business Owners," McGladry Pullen National Tax Specialists Conference (presented in October, 1999); "A Brief Summary of the IRS Restructuring and Reform Act of 1998," Illinois State Bar Association, The Corporate Lawyer (Vol. 36, No. 2, December, 1998); "A Brief Summary of the IRS Restructuring and Reform Act of 1998," Illinois State Bar Association, Trusts and Estates Newsletter (Vol. 45, No. 1, September 1998); "Recent Tax Cases And Rulings," Illinois State Bar Association, Trusts and Estates Newsleter (Vol. 44, No. 5, June 1998). *Member:* Chicago (Member, 1995—; Executive Subcommittee of the Federal Taxation Committee, 2000—; Federal Taxation Committee, 1999—; Estate and Gift Tax Division of the Federal Taxation Committee, 1999—; Chair, Estate and Gift Tax Division of the Federal Taxation Committee, 2001-2002; Secretary, Estate and Gift Tax Division of the Federal Taxation Committee, 1999-2000), Illinois State (Member, 1995—; Trusts and Estates Section, 1998—) and American (Member, 1995—; Real Property, Probate and Trust Law Section, 1998—) Bar Associations; Chicago Estate Planning Council (Member, 2000—). ***PRACTICE AREAS:*** Estate Planning; Trusts and Estates. ***Email:*** mtalarico@jenner.com

AMY L. TENNEY, admitted to bar, 2000, Virginia; U.S. Court of Appeals, Fourth Circuit; U.S. District Court, Eastern District of Virginia; 2002, U.S. Court of Appeals, First Circuit. *Education:* University of Maryland (B.A., High Honors, 1996); New York Law School (J.D., magna cum laude, 2000). Supervising Editor, New York Law School Law Review (1998-1999). Law Clerk: Honorable Leonie M. Brinkema, U.S. District Court, Eastern District of Virginia (2000-2001); Honorable Frank M. Coffin, U.S. Court of Appeals, First Circuit (2001-2002). (Resident, Washington, D.C. Office). ***PRACTICE AREAS:*** Litigation. ***Email:*** atenney@jenner.com

ANGELA M. TERRY, born Hinsdale, Illinois, December 11, 1971; admitted to bar, 2004, Illinois. *Education:* St. Norbert College (B.A., 1994); Loyola University, Chicago (J.D., 2004). ***PRACTICE AREAS:*** Intellectual Property. ***Email:*** aterry@jenner.com

WADE A. THOMSON, born Chicago, Illinois, February 29, 1976; admitted to bar, 2004, Illinois. *Education:* Kalamazoo College (B.A., cum laude, 1998); University of Illinois College of Law (J.D., magna cum laude, 2003). Assistant Editor, University of Illinois Law Review. ***LANGUAGES:*** Spanish. ***PRACTICE AREAS:*** Litigation. ***Email:*** wthomson@jenner.com

JESSICA TILLIPMAN, born Sioux City, Iowa, June 30, 1978; admitted to bar, 2003, Virginia; 2004, U.S. Court of Federal Claims. *Education:* Miami University (Ohio) (B.A., cum laude, 2000); George Washington University Law School (J.D., with honors, 2003). Clerkship: Honorable Lawrence Margolis, U.S. Court of Federal Claims. *Member:* American Bar Association. (Resident, Washington, D.C. Office). ***PRACTICE AREAS:*** Government Contracts; Litigation. ***Email:*** jtillipman@jenner.com

SANDI J. TOLL, born Albany, New York, November 24, 1975; admitted to bar, 2002, Illinois and U.S. District Court, Northern District of Illinois; 2004, U.S. Court of Appeals, Seventh Circuit. *Education:* Cornell University (B.S., 1997); Loyola University (J.D., magna cum laude, 2002). Childlaw Fellow. Member, Editorial Staff, Loyola University Chicago Law Review, 2001-2002. ***PRACTICE AREAS:*** Litigation; Family Law. ***Email:*** stoll@jenner.com

CHRISTOPHER TOMPKINS, born Boston, Massachusetts, February 19, 1975; admitted to bar, 2000, Illinois and U.S. District Court, Northern District of Illinois; U.S. Court of Federal Claims. *Education:* Catholic University of America (B.A., cum laude, 1997); Loyola University Chicago School of Law (J.D., magna cum laude, 2000). ***PRACTICE AREAS:*** Litigation; Commercial Law; Uniform Commercial Code; Securities Litigation; Intellectual Property; Technology Law. ***Email:*** ctompkins@jenner.com

SARA E. TONNIES, born Dearborn, Michigan, January 27, 1980; (admission pending). *Education:* University of Notre Dame (B.S., 2002); DePaul University College of Law (J.D., with honors, 2005). ***Email:*** stonnies@jenner.com

HEATHER M. TREW, admitted to bar, 2001, New York and District of Columbia. *Education:* Stanford University (A.B., 1997); University of Michigan Law School (J.D., 2000). (Resident, Washington, D.C. Office). ***PRACTICE AREAS:*** Government Contracts; Litigation. ***Email:*** htrew@jenner.com

JILL M. TROXEL, born Urbana, Illinois, October 28, 1980; (admission pending). *Education:* University of Illinois (B.A., 2001); The University of Texas School of Law (J.D., with honors, 2005). Order of the Barristers; Order of the Coif. Phi Alpha Delta. Author: "The Review of Litigation," Vol. 24, No. 3. ***PRACTICE AREAS:*** Litigation and Dispute Resolution. ***Email:*** jtroxel@jenner.com

AMY K. TRUEBLOOD, born Portsmouth, Virginia, April 1, 1978; admitted to bar, 2002, Virginia; 2003, Illinois. *Education:* Harvard University (A.B., magna cum laude, 1999); University of Virginia School of Law (J.D., 2002). ***PRACTICE AREAS:*** Litigation. ***Email:*** atrueblood@jenner.com

ANDREW W. VAIL, born Des Plaines, Illinois, December 12, 1976; admitted to bar, 2003, Illinois. *Education:* University of North Carolina (B.A., 1999); University of Illinois College of Law (J.D., cum laude, 2003). Harno Scholar. Member, Moot Court Bench, 2001-2003. Stuart Greenberger Research Assistant in Legal Ethics.l. *Member:* Chicago, Illinois State, (Member, Young Lawyers Division Counsel, 2005-2006), Seventh Circuit and American Bar Associations. ***PRACTICE AREAS:*** Litigation. ***Email:*** avail@jenner.com

MARTINA E. VANDENBERG, born Raleigh, North Carolina, November 19, 1968; admitted to bar, 2002, New York; 2004, District of Columbia and U.S. District Court for the District of Columbia. *Education:* Pomona College (B.A., cum laude, 1990); Oxford University (M.Phil., 1992); Columbia University (J.D., 2000). Rhodes Scholar; Truman Scholar. Formerly with Human Rights Watch. *Member:* New York State Bar Association. (Resident, Washington, D.C. Office). ***LANGUAGES:*** Russian. ***PRACTICE AREAS:*** Litigation; White Collar Criminal Defense and Counseling. ***Email:*** mvandenberg@jenner.com

SHYNI R. VARGHESE, born Bombay, India, April 23, 1974; admitted to bar, 2002, Illinois. *Education:* University of Chicago (A.B., 1996); University of Illinois (J.D., magna cum laude, 2002). *Member:* Chicago, Illinois State and American Bar Associations. ***PRACTICE AREAS:*** Litigation; Securities Litigation. ***Email:*** svarghese@jenner.com

(This Listing Continued)

HILLARY A. VICTOR, born Chicago, Illinois, May 24, 1976; admitted to bar, 2001, Illinois and U.S. District Court, Northern District of Illinois. *Education:* North Central College (B.A., 1998); The John Marshall Law School (J.D., cum laude, 2001). Order of John Marshall. Author: "Big Brother Is At Your Back Door: An Examination Of The Effect Of Encryption Regulation On Privacy and Crime," Vol. 18, J. Marshall J. Computer & Info. L. *Member:* Chicago, DuPage County, Illinois State and American Bar Associations; Association of Trial Lawyers of America. ***PRACTICE AREAS:*** Litigation; Securities Litigation. ***Email:*** hvictor@jenner.com

DAVID E. WALTERS, born Hinsdale, Illinois, August 30, 1972; admitted to bar, 1998, Illinois; 2003, U.S. District Court, Northern District of Indiana. *Education:* University of Notre Dame (B.S., 1994; J.D., 1998). *Member:* Chicago and American Bar Associations; Constitutional Rights Foundation; Chicago Inn of Court; Youth Innovation Foundation. ***LANGUAGES:*** Spanish. ***PRACTICE AREAS:*** Litigation; Health Care; White Collar Crime; Fraud and Abuse. ***Email:*** dwalters@jenner.com

ERINN L. WEHRMAN, born Ann Arbor, Michigan, 1978; admitted to bar, 2003, Illinois and U.S. District Court, Northern District of Illinois; 2004, U.S. Court of Appeals, Seventh Circuit and U.S. District Court, Central District of Illinois; 2005, U.S. District Court, Southern District of Illinois. *Education:* Michigan State University (B.A., with high honors, 2000); Loyola University, Chicago School of Law (J.D., cum laude, 2003). ***PRACTICE AREAS:*** Litigation. ***Email:*** ewehrman@jenner.com

DANIEL J. WEISS, born St. Louis, Missouri, January 3, 1973; admitted to bar, 1998, Illinois. *Education:* American University (B.A., magna cum laude, 1995); University of Chicago (J.D., with honors, 1998). ***PRACTICE AREAS:*** Litigation; Telecommunications. ***Email:*** dweiss@jenner.com

ANDERS C. WICK, born Chicago Heights, Illinois, January 10, 1974; admitted to bar, 2001, Illinois. *Education:* University of Chicago (A.B., 1996); University of Michigan, Ann Arbor (J.D., cum laude, 2001). Member, University of Michigan Law Review, 1999-2001. ***PRACTICE AREAS:*** Antitrust and Trade Regulation; Litigation; Tax Controversies. ***Email:*** awick@jenner.com

SCOTT WILKENS, born St. Louis, Missouri, March 25, 1971; admitted to bar, 2003, California; 2004, District of Columbia. *Education:* University of North Carolina at Chapel Hill (B.A., 1993); Harvard Law School (J.D., 2002). Fulbright Scholar. Henry Luce Scholar. Morehead Scholar. Truman Scholar. (Resident, Washington, D.C. Office). ***LANGUAGES:*** German, French. ***PRACTICE AREAS:*** Appellate Practice; Supreme Court Practice; Litigation. ***Email:*** swilkens@jenner.com

JOHN P. WOLFSMITH, born Chicago, Illinois, May 9, 1973; admitted to bar, 1998, Illinois and U.S. District Court, Northern District of Illinois; 2000, U.S. Court of Appeals, Seventh Circuit. *Education:* Bradley University (B.A., cum laude, 1995); University of Illinois (J.D., magna cum laude, 1998). ***PRACTICE AREAS:*** Litigation. ***Email:*** jwolfsmith@jenner.com

CAROLINE LEWIS WOLVERTON, born Waterbury, Connecticut, April 5, 1969; admitted to bar, 1995, Colorado. *Education:* Harvard University (A.B., 1991); Harvard Law School (J.D., 1995). (Resident, Washington, D.C. Office). ***PRACTICE AREAS:*** Litigation. ***Email:*** cwolverton@jenner.com

ELTON Y. WONG, born Tuscaloosa, Alabama, May 28, 1979; (admission pending). *Education:* Iowa State University (B.S., 2001); University of Iowa College of Law (J.D., with distinction, 2005). ***PRACTICE AREAS:*** Litigation and Dispute Resolution. ***Email:*** ewong@jenner.com

GREGORY M. WU, admitted to bar, 2003, Illinois. *Education:* Duke University (A.B., 2000); Harvard Law School (J.D., 2003). Phi Beta Kappa; Phi Eta Sigma. ***PRACTICE AREAS:*** Employee Benefits; Executive Compensation. ***Email:*** gwu@jenner.com

JASON E. YEAROUT, born Winfield, Kansas, October 18, 1976; admitted to bar, 2002, Illinois. *Education:* Washburn University of Topeka (B.A., 1999); College of William & Mary (J.D., 2002). Author, "Individualized School Searches and the Fourth Amendment: Whats A School District To Do?" 10 William & Mary Bill of Rights journal 489 (2002); Co-author, "Jury still out on "innocent landouner" defense"," Chicago Daily Law Bulletin, June 2002. ***PRACTICE AREAS:*** Environmental Law. ***Email:*** jyearout@jenner.com

PETER J. YOUNG, admitted to bar, 2002, Illinois. *Education:* Central Michigan University (B.A.A., 1993); Ball State University (M.A., 1995); Indiana University School of Law (J.D., summa cum laude, 2002). Top Advocate, Intramural Moot Court Competition. Editor-in-Chief, Indiana Law Review, 2001-2002. Author, "The Case Against Carnivore: Preventing Law Enforcement From Devouring Privacy," 35 Indiana Law Review 303 (2001). ***PRACTICE AREAS:*** Commercial Law; Litigation. ***Email:*** pyoung@jenner.com

BRADLEY M. YUSIM, born Skokie, Illinois, February 22, 1976; admitted to bar, 2002, Illinois. *Education:* University of Texas at Austin (B.S.E.E., 1998); University of Illinois (J.D., magna cum laude, 2002). Author, "Satellite: Like a Diamond in the Sky," Journal of Law, Technology and Policy, Vol. 2001, Issue 2. ***PRACTICE AREAS:*** Litigation; Intellectual Property and Technology Law. ***Email:*** byusim@jenner.com

BLAIR R. ZANZIG, born Woodstock, Illinois, September 15, 1973; admitted to bar, 2000, Illinois and U.S. District Court, Northern District of Illinois. *Education:* University of Florida (B.S.B.A., with honors, 1995; M.S., 1997); University of Michigan (J.D., cum laude, 2000). ***PRACTICE AREAS:*** Litigation. ***Email:*** bzanzig@jenner.com

STEVEN McMAHON ZELLER, born Sioux City, Iowa, February 28, 1967; admitted to bar, 1996, Illinois and U.S. District Court, Northern District of Illinois; 2003, U.S. District Court, Central District of Illinois; registered to practice before the U.S. Patent and Trademark Office. *Education:* Iowa State University (B.S.M.E., 1989); Northwestern University School of Law (J.D., 1996). Note and Comment Editor, Northwestern University Law Review. *Member:* American Bar Association; American Intellectual Property Law Association. ***PRACTICE AREAS:*** Intellectual Property and Technology Law; Patent Litigation. ***Email:*** szeller@jenner.com

OF COUNSEL

RONALD DeKOVEN, admitted to bar, 1968, Illinois; 1981, New York. *Education:* Stanford University (B.A., 1965); University of Chicago (J.D., 1968). (Also Associate Member of 3/4 South Square, London, England). ***PRACTICE AREAS:*** Bankruptcy; Workout; Corporate Reorganization. ***Email:*** rdekoven@jenner.com

(This Listing Continued)

JENNER & BLOCK LLP, Chicago—Continued

EDWARD JACKSON, born Havre de Grace, Maryland, February 21, 1953; admitted to bar, 1988, Maryland; 1989, District of Columbia. *Education:* Southern Adventist University (B.S., 1975); University of Maryland School of Law (J.D., 1988). (Resident, Washington, D.C. Office). ***PRACTICE AREAS:*** Government Contracts (50%); Defense and Aerospace (30%); Health Care Law (20%). ***Email:*** ejackson@jenner.com

ROBERT V. JAMBOR, born Chicago, Illinois, August 29, 1936; admitted to bar, 1963, Illinois; 1974, U.S. Supreme Court; 1963, U.S. District Court, Northern District of Illinois; 1982, Trial Bar. *Education:* Kettering University, General Motors Institute (B.M.E., 1959); John Marshall Law School (J.D., 1963). *Member:* American Bar Association; Intellectual Property Association of Chicago. ***PRACTICE AREAS:*** Patents; Trademarks; Copyrights; Unfair Competition Causes.

CHARLES J. McCARTHY, (LTD.), born Taos, New Mexico, June 26, 1937; admitted to bar, 1962, Illinois and U.S. District Court, Northern District of Illinois; 1964, U.S. Court of Appeals, Seventh Circuit. *Education:* Regis University (B.S., cum laude, 1959); Georgetown University (J.D., 1962). Member, Board of Editors, Georgetown Law Journal, 1961-1962. *Member:* Chicago, Illinois State and American Bar Associations; National Association of Bond Lawyers; Illinois Secretary of State Business Corporation Acts Advisory Committee. ***PRACTICE AREAS:*** Corporate Law; Securities Law; Mergers and Acquisitions Law; Business Law; Financial Institutions Law; Trade Association Law. ***Email:*** cmccarthy@jenner.com

BENJAMIN K. MILLER, born Springfield, Illinois, November 5, 1936; admitted to bar, 1961, Illinois and U.S. District Court, Central and Northern Districts of Illinois; U.S. Supreme Court. *Education:* Southern Illinois University (B.A., 1958); Vanderbilt University School of Law (J.D., 1961). Moot Court. Justice, Supreme Court of Illinois, 1984-2001 (Chief Justice, 1991-1994); Justice, Appellate Court of Illinois, 1982-1984; Judge of the Circuit Court, Seventh Judicial Circuit of Illinois, 1976-1982 (Chief Judge, Criminal Division, 1976-1982; Chief Judge of Circuit, 1980-1982). Author of 487 Illinois Supreme Court and numerous Illinois Appellate Court opinions. Honorary Doctor of Law, John Marshall Law School, 1991. Member, National Conference of Chief Justices, 1991-1994 (Vice Chair of Conference, 1993). First recipient of Illinois Family Violence Coordinating Council Annual "Justice Benjamin K. Miller Recognition Award," 2001. Adjunct Professor, Southern Illinois School of Medicine, 1974 —. *Member:* American, Illinois State (Member, Board of Governors, 1970-1976; Treasurer, 1974-1976) and Sangamon County Bar Associations. [U.S. Army Reserves, 1961-1965; Lieutenant, U.S. Navy Reserves, 1965-1970]. ***PRACTICE AREAS:*** Appellate Practice; Supreme Court Practice; Products Liability; Mass Tort Defense. ***Email:*** bmiller@jenner.com

HENRY M. SCHAFFER, born Brooklyn, New York, August 22, 1943; admitted to bar, 1973, Illinois; 1974, U.S. District Court, Northern District of Illinois; 1979, Ohio; 1980, U.S. District Court, Northern District of Ohio and U.S. Supreme Court; 1985, U.S. Court of Appeals, Sixth Circuit. *Education:* Columbia University (A.B., 1964); Washington University (M.A., 1969); University of California at Berkeley (J.D., 1973). Co-Author: "Keeping In Step With Music Licensing," Meeting Planners International, 1992; "Involuntary Non-Servitude: The Current Judicial Enforcement of Employee Covenants not to Compete, A Proposal for Reform," 57 Southern California Law Review 531, 1984. Associate Professor of Law, University of Toledo College of Law (Contracts, Trial Advocacy, Civil Procedure, Remedies), 1979-1983; 1987-1989. Assistant Professor, Washington University (History), 1968-1969. Assistant Professor, Monticello College (History), 1969-1970. ***PRACTICE AREAS:*** Trade and Professional Associations; Travel; Tourism; Hotel and Meeting Liability; Employment; Copyright. ***Email:*** hschaffer@jenner.com

---

JESTER, KENWORTHY & EAGLE LLC

53 W. JACKSON BOULEVARD, SUITE 1324
CHICAGO, ILLINOIS 60604
Telephone: 312-435-9901
Fax: 312-435-9903
URL: http://www.jkelaw.com

Criminal Law, Federal Criminal Law, Drug Crimes, DUI, Traffic Violations, Juvenile Law, Criminal Appeals.

MEMBERS OF FIRM

ANDREW T. JESTER, born 1969; admitted to bar, 1995, Illinois and U.S. District Court, Northern District of Illinois. *Education:* Bowling Green State University (B.A., 1991); John Marshall Law School (J.D., 1995). *Member:* Chicago Bar Association; National Association of Criminal Defense Lawyers. ***PRACTICE AREAS:*** Criminal Law; Drug Crimes; Driving While Intoxicated; Traffic Violations; Federal Criminal Law. ***Email:*** atjester@jkelaw.com

DIANA L. KENWORTHY, born 1968; admitted to bar, 1995, Illinois and U.S. District Court, Northern District of Illinois. *Education:* The Ohio State University (B.A., summa cum laude, 1991; J.D., 1995). Phi Beta Kappa. *Member:* Chicago Bar Association (Member, Judicial Evaluation Committee, 1999—); Women's Bar Association of Illinois; Decalogue Society of Lawyers. ***PRACTICE AREAS:*** Drug Crimes; Driving While Intoxicated; Traffic Violations; Criminal Law; Juvenile Law. ***Email:*** dkenworthy@jkelaw.com

ROSS M. EAGLE, born 1966; admitted to bar, 1993, Illinois and U.S. District Court, Northern District of Illinois; 2003, U.S. District Court, Central District of Illinois. *Education:* University of Wisconsin-Madison (B.A., 1988); John Marshall Law School (J.D., 1993). *Member:* Chicago Bar Association (Member, Criminal Law Committee and Criminal Justice Committee, 1998—); National Association of Criminal Defense Attorneys. ***REPORTED CASES:*** People v. Arna, 168 Ill 2d 107 (1995). ***PRACTICE AREAS:*** Criminal Law; Federal Criminal Law; Drug Crimes; Driving While Intoxicated; Traffic Violations; Juvenile Law; Criminal Appeals. ***Email:*** rmeagle@jkelaw.com

DONALD L. JOHNSON

SUITE 1401, 33 NORTH DEARBORN STREET
CHICAGO, ILLINOIS 60602
Telephone: 312-263-7000
Fax: 312-263-3051

Civil and Trial Practice, Business, Real Estate and Partnership Litigation, Professional Malpractice.

DONALD L. JOHNSON, born Iowa; admitted to bar, 1962, Iowa and Wisconsin; 1966, Illinois. *Education:* Luther College (B.A.); State University of Iowa (J.D., with distinction, 1962). Author: "Mortgage Commitment Litigation," Illinois Institute of Continuing Legal Education, 1980-1988; "Real Estate Brokers Litigation," Illinois Institute of Continuing Legal Education, 1981-1988; "Mortgage Commitment Litigation," Illinois Institute of Continuing Legal Education, 1981-1988. *Member:* Chicago and Illinois State Bar Association.

JOHNSON & ASSOCIATES, P.C.

887 NORTH LA SALLE STREET
CHICAGO, ILLINOIS 60610-3219
Telephone: 312-236-1616
Facsimile: 312-642-3609
Email: japc@ix.netcom.com
URL: http://www.lawyers.com/johnson&assoc

Family Law, Probate and Estate Planning, Criminal, Appellate, Real Estate Transactions and Commercial Litigation.

DOROTHY BERTRAM JOHNSON, born Chicago, Illinois, March 15, 1947; admitted to bar, 1973, Illinois and U.S. District Court, Northern District of Illinois; 1976, U.S. Supreme Court; 1979, U.S. Court of Appeals, 7th Circuit. *Education:* Miami University (B.A., 1968); Salmon P. Chase College of Law (1968-1971); IIT-Chicago-Kent College of Law (J.D., 1973). Delta Theta Phi. Recipient, American Jurisprudence Award, 1969. Assistant States Attorney for Cook County, Criminal Division, 1973-1975. Member, Cook County Divorce Education Project for Parents. Instructor, Walton Division of Industrial College of Engineering, 1981-1985. Circuit Court of Cook County Attorney for Child Program, 1987—. Bar Association Coordinator, Cook County Expedited Child Support Enforcement Pilot Project. Foundation President, 1997-1999, Chair and Board of Directors, 1999-2002, St. Paul's House and Health Care Center. *Member:* Chicago (Chair, 1991-1992, Vice-Chair, 1990-1991 and Secretary, 1989-1990, Matrimonial Law Committee; Member: Probate Committee; Judicial Evaluation Committee; Court Liaison Committee for Circuit Court of Cook County) and Illinois State Bar Associations. ***REPORTED CASES:*** Matter of Estate of Friedman, (Ill. App. 1 Dist.) 1984, 78 Ill. Dec. 573, 462 N.E.2d 692, 123 Ill. App. 3d 82; Estate of Shedrick, Ill. App. 1 Dist. 1984, 78 Ill. Dec. 462, 462 N.E.2d 581; DeFoggio v. U.S. 484 F.Supp. 233 (N.D.IL 1975), affirmed DiFoggio v. DeLisa, 618 F2d 111 (7th Cir. 1980); Schieb v. Grant et al 814 F.Supp. 736 (N.D.IL 1993), affirmed .22 F3d 149 (7th Cir. 1994), rehg denied 1994 U.S. App. Lexis 13371, Cert denied US, 115 S.Ct. 320 (1994). ***PRACTICE AREAS:*** Matrimonial Law; Family; Probate; Criminal Law; Real Estate.

COLEEN A. BLAKE, born Burlington, Iowa, December 11, 1954; admitted to bar, 1992, Illinois. *Education:* University of Illinois (B.S.E.E., 1978); Loyola University (J.D., 1992). Member, Institute of Electrical and Electronics Engineers. ***PRACTICE AREAS:*** Matrimonial; Family; Probate.

LEGAL SUPPORT PERSONNEL

ROSARIO V. CABRERA, born Chicago, Illinois, April 21, 1964. *Education:* Roosevelt University (Paralegal Certificate). Licensed Real Estate Sales Agent. *Member:* Illinois Paralegal Association. (Paralegal - Legal Secretary). ***LANGUAGES:*** Spanish. ***PRACTICE AREAS:*** Client Contact; Pleadings; Discovery; Clerking; Real Estate. ***Email:*** rmccabrera@aol.com

---

JOHNSON & BELL, LTD.

Established in 1975
55 EAST MONROE STREET
SUITE 4100
CHICAGO, ILLINOIS 60603-5896
Telephone: 312-372-0770
Facsimile: 312-372-9818
Email: info@johnsonandbell.com
URL: http://www.johnsonandbell.com

Waukegan, Illinois Office: 325 Washington Street, Suite 200, 60085. Telephone: 847-662-7458. Facsimile: 847-662-7366.
Highland, Indiana Office: 9000 Indianapolis Boulevard, Suite A, 46322. Telephone: 219-923-5250. Facsimile: 219-923-6170.

Trial practice in state and federal courts, including national coordinating counsel. Appellate Law, Asbestos Litigation, Automotive Product Liability Litigation, Aviation Litigation, Benefits, Business Litigation and Practice, Complex Plaintiff Litigation, Construction Litigation, Corporate Health Care, Criminal Litigation, Employment Law, ERISA, Environmental Law, Financial Crimes, Financial Institution Representation, General Negligence and Premises Liability, Gun Litigation, Hospital Law and Medical Liability, Insurance Coverage, Intellectual Property, Long Term Care/Nursing Home Liability, Mass Tort, Medical Device Liability, Mold Litigation, Municipal Liability, National Coordinating Counsel, Probate, Product Liability, Professional Liability, Railroad Litigation, Toxic Tort and Trucking and Transportation.

(This Listing Continued)

FIRM PROFILE: Johnson & Bell, Ltd. began in 1975 with a handful of lawyers operating out of a small LaSalle Street, Chicago, office. It has grown since into a 110-attorney firm with offices in Chicago, Waukegan, Illinois, and Highland, Indiana. Founders William V. Johnson and John W. Bell have seen their law firm develop into one of the Midwest's premier litigation firms with expertise in complex cases of all types. The firm's initial client base of insurance companies has expanded to include international corporations in industries as varied as drug-store chains and heavy equipment manufacturers. Led by a strong corps of trial attorneys who have tried hundreds of cases to verdict, the firm has garnered a reputation for taking on matters that have drawn national attention.

For more information about our firm, areas of practice, and attorneys, please visit our Web site at www.johnsonandbell.com.

LAW FIRM ALLIANCES/ASSOCIATIONS: **AMERICAN LAW FIRM ASSOCIATION (ALFA):** *Johnson & Bell, Ltd. is the exclusive Chicago area law firm of ALFA, an international association of independent law firms dedicated to improving the quality, efficiency, and affordability of legal services.*

SHAREHOLDERS

WILLIAM V. JOHNSON, born Owensboro, Kentucky, January 7, 1940; admitted to bar, 1966, Illinois. *Education:* Marquette University (B.A., 1962); University of Kentucky and Chicago-Kent College of Law, Illinois Institute of Technology (J.D., 1966). *Member:* Illinois State and American Bar Associations; Association of Chicago Trial Lawyers; International Academy of Trial Lawyers; International Society of Trial Lawyers; American College of Trial Lawyers; American Board of Trial Advocates; Society of Trial Lawyers; Federation of Defense & Corporate Counsel; Defense Research Institute. ***PRACTICE AREAS:*** Civil Trial; Catastrophic Injury; Class Actions; Medical Malpractice; Personal Injury; Products Liability. ***Email:*** johnsonw@jbltd.com

JOHN W. BELL, born Chicago, Illinois, May 3, 1946; admitted to bar, 1971, Illinois and U.S. District Court, Northern District of Illinois. *Education:* University of Southern California and Northwestern University (B.A., 1968); Loyola University (J.D., cum laude, 1971). *Member:* Chicago (Chairman, Medical-Legal Relations Committee, 1994-1995; Member, Nominating Committee, 1995, Best Lawyers in America, 1995-1996, Who's Who in American Law, 1996-1997), Hellenic, Illinois State (Member: Tort Liability Section; Aviation Committee, 1982-1986) and American (Member, Torts and Insurance Practice Section) Bar Associations; Illinois Defense Counsel; Defense Research Institute; Society of Trial Lawyers; International Association of Insurance Defense Counsel; Federal Trial Bar. American College of Trial Lawyers. ***PRACTICE AREAS:*** Products Liability; Casualty Insurance; Public Utility Law; Commercial Litigation; Environmental Litigation. ***Email:*** bellj@jbltd.com

JACK T. RILEY, JR., born Dayton, Ohio, February 17, 1946; admitted to bar, 1973, Illinois and U.S. District Court, Northern District of Illinois. *Education:* Denison University (B.A., 1968); Georgetown University (J.D., cum laude, 1973). *Member:* Chicago, Illinois State, Federal and American Bar Associations; Defense Research Institute; Trial Lawyers Club; Society of Trial Lawyers; Federation of Defense & Corporate Counsel (President); Illinois Association of Defense Trial Counsel (President). ***LANGUAGES:*** French. ***PRACTICE AREAS:*** Commercial Litigation; Construction Litigation; Medical Malpractice; Toxic Torts; Asbestos; Premises Liability; Products Liability. ***Email:*** rileyj@jbltd.com

BRIAN C. FETZER, born Chicago, Illinois, December 27, 1950; admitted to bar, 1975, Illinois and U.S. District Court, Northern District of Illinois. *Education:* Xavier University (B.S.B.A., magna cum laude, 1972); Northwestern University (J.D., cum laude, 1975). *Member:* Chicago (Member, Committee on Evaluation of Candidates, 1983-1987), Illinois State and American Bar Associations; Society of Trial Lawyers; Defense Research Institute; International Association of Defense Counsel; Illinois Association of Hospital Attorneys; American Society of Healthcare Risk Management; Illinois Defense Counsel (Member, Board of Directors, 1983-1989); Trial Lawyers Club of Chicago (President, 1990); Federal Trial Bar; American College of Trial Lawyers. ***PRACTICE AREAS:*** Medical Malpractice; Medical Device and Drug Law; Products Liability. ***Email:*** fetzerb@jbltd.com

THOMAS J. ANDREWS, born New York, N.Y., November 19, 1952; admitted to bar, 1977, Illinois; 1980, U.S. District Court, Northern District of Illinois including Trial Bar. *Education:* Eastern Washington University (B.A., magna cum laude, 1973); University of Michigan (J.D., 1977). ***PRACTICE AREAS:*** Construction Law; Insurance; Pharmacy Law; Personal Injury; Torts; Products Liability; Professional Liability. ***Email:*** andrewst@jbltd.com

WILLIAM G. BEATTY, born Moline, Illinois, July 13, 1953; admitted to bar, 1978, Illinois; 1979, U.S. District Court, Northern District of Illinois including Trial Bar, U.S. Court of Appeals, Seventh Circuit and U.S. Claims Court; 1990, Arizona, Colorado, U.S. Supreme Court, U.S. District Court, Central and Southern Districts of Illinois, U.S. District Court, District of Arizona, U.S. District Court, Eastern and Western Districts of Arkansas and U.S. District Court, District of Colorado; 1992, U.S. Court of Appeals, Eighth Circuit; 1994, U.S. District Court, Northern District of Indiana; 1996, U.S. Court of Appeals, Federal Circuit. *Education:* Augustana College (B.A., cum laude, 1975); Creighton University and Chicago-Kent College of Law, Illinois Institute of Technology (J.D., with honors, 1978). *Member:* Chicago and Illinois State Bar Associations; State Bar of Arizona; Defense Research Institute; Illinois Association of Defense Trial Counsel (Member, Board of Directors). ***PRACTICE AREAS:*** Products Liability; Employee Benefits; Employment Law; Asbestos Litigation. ***Email:*** beattyw@jbltd.com

JOHN A. CHILDERS, born Chicago, Illinois, June 9, 1955; admitted to bar, 1980, Illinois and U.S. District Court, Northern District of Illinois. *Education:* Northwestern University (B.A., 1977); Northwestern University (J.D., 1980). *Member:* Cook County, Illinois State and American Bar Associations; Defense Research Institute. ***PRACTICE AREAS:*** Pharmacy Litigation; Products Liability; Premises Liability; Litigation; Construction Litigation. ***Email:*** childersj@jbltd.com

MARGARET A. UNGER, born Chicago, Illinois, April 12, 1953; admitted to bar, 1979, Illinois and U.S. District Court, Northern District of Illinois. *Education:* University of Dayton and Loyola University (B.A., 1975); John Marshall Law School (J.D., 1979). *Member:* Chicago, Illinois State and American Bar Associations; Trial Lawyers Club of Chicago; Illinois Society of Trial Lawyers. ***PRACTICE AREAS:*** Medical Malpractice Defense Litigation; Premises Liability; Violent Crimes; Defense Litigation. ***Email:*** ungerm@jbltd.com

H. PATRICK MORRIS, born Chicago, Illinois, September 6, 1956; admitted to bar, 1984, Illinois, U.S. District Court, Northern, Central and Southern Districts of Illinois including Trial Bar, U.S. District Court, Northern and Southern Distrcits of Indiana, U.S. District Court, Western District of Michigan and U.S. District Court, District of Puerto Rico. *Education:* Tulane University; University of Illinois (B.A., 1979); Illinois Institute of Technology/Chicago-Kent College of Law (J.D., 1983). *Member:* Defense Research Institute (Member, Board of Directors, 2000—; Chair, Toxic Tort and Environmental Law Committee, 1998-2000; Chair, Diversity Committee, 2004—). ***PRACTICE AREAS:*** Toxic Torts; Products Liability; Mass Torts; Pharmaceutical. ***Email:*** morrisp@jbltd.com

SCOTT W. HOYNE, born Evanston, Illinois, February 16, 1950; admitted to bar, 1975, Illinois, U.S. District Court, Northern District of Illinois including Trial Bar and U.S. Court of Appeals, Seventh Circuit. *Education:* Northwestern University (B.A., with distinction, 1972; J.D., 1975). *Member:* Illinois State and American Bar Associations; American Arbitration Association (Member, Commercial Panel); Defense Research Institute. ***PRACTICE AREAS:*** First and Third Party Casualty Losses/Trials; Insurance Coverage. ***Email:*** hoynes@jbltd.com

FREDERICK S. MUELLER, born Westfield, New Jersey, February 10, 1951; admitted to bar, 1976, Illinois and U.S. District Court, Northern District of Illinois. *Education:* Indiana University (B.S., cum laude, 1973); University of Sheffield, England and Indiana University (J.D., 1976). *Member:* Chicago (Member, Environmental Law Committee), Illinois State (Member, Environmental Law Section) and American (Member, Natural Resources and Environment Section) Bar Associations; Defense Research Institute Trial Lawyers Association. ***PRACTICE AREAS:*** Environmental Law; Natural Resources; Administrative Law; Personal Injury; Torts; Products Liability. ***Email:*** muellerf@jbltd.com

JOSEPH R. MARCONI, born Chicago Heights, Illinois, November 3, 1949; admitted to bar, 1976, Illinois and U.S. District Court, Northern District of Illinois; 1977, U.S. Court of Appeals, Seventh Circuit; 1995 U.S. Supreme Court. *Education:* Iowa State University (B.S., 1972); John Marshall Law School (J.D., 1976). *Member:* Chicago, Illinois State and American Bar Associations. ***PRACTICE AREAS:*** Complex Business Litigation; Professional Liability; Litigation; Intellectual Property. ***Email:*** marconij@jbltd.com

ROBERT M. BURKE, born Chicago, Illinois, December 29, 1958; admitted to bar, 1984, Illinois; 1985, U.S. District Court, Northern District of Illinois including Trial Bar; 1992, U.S. Court of Appeals, Seventh Circuit; 1997, U.S. District Court, Northern District of Indiana; 1998, U.S. District Court, Central District of Illinois. *Education:* University of Illinois (B.S., cum laude, 1981; J.D., 1984). *Member:* Chicago and Illinois State Bar Associations; Illinois Defense Counsel. ***PRACTICE AREAS:*** Litigation; Insurance; Personal Injury; Torts; Premises Liability; Railroad Liability; Transportation. ***Email:*** burker@jbltd.com

GLENN F. FENCL, born Elmhurst, Illinois, October 9, 1952; admitted to bar, 1980, Illinois and U.S. District Court, Northern and Southern Districts of Illinois and including Trial Bar. *Education:* University of Illinois (B.A., History, 1974); IIT Chicago-Kent College of Law (J.D., with honors, 1980). *Member:* Illinois State Bar Association; International Association of Defense Counsel (IADC); Illinois Defense Counsel (IDC); Illinois Society of Trial Lawyers; Defense Research Institute (DRI). ***PRACTICE AREAS:*** Product Liability; Insurance Coverage Litigation; Construction Litigation; Professional Liability; Transportation. ***Email:*** fenclg@jbltd.com

DAVID J. LOUGHNANE, born Chicago, Illinois, September 3, 1947; admitted to bar, 1972, Illinois and U.S. District Court, Northern District of Illinois including Trial Bar. *Education:* University of Wisconsin (B.A., 1969); Loyola University (J.D., 1972). ***PRACTICE AREAS:*** Litigation; Health Care Law; Drug and Medical Device Litigation. ***Email:*** loughnaned@jbltd.com

JOSEPH F. SPITZZERI, born Chicago, Illinois, September 3, 1957; admitted to bar, 1983, Illinois and U.S. District Court, Northern District of Illinois including Trial Bar; 1984, U.S. Court of Appeals, Seventh Circuit; 1987, U.S. Supreme Court. *Education:* University of Illinois (B.S., Criminal Justice and Political Science, 1981); John Marshall Law School (J.D., 1983). *Member:* Chicago, Kane County, Illinois State and American Bar Associations; Trial Lawyers Club of Chicago; Illinois Association of Defense Trial Counsel; Kane County Justinian Society of Lawyers (Secretary, 1995). ***PRACTICE AREAS:*** Civil Rights; Construction Litigation; Employment Law; Municipal Liability; Products Liability; Transportation. ***Email:*** spitzzerij@jbltd.com

DENNIS C. CUSACK, born Chicago, Illinois, December 29, 1958; admitted to bar, 1985, Illinois, and U.S. District Court, Northern District of Illinois including Trial Bar, 1999. *Education:* St. John's University (B.A., 1981); Hamline University; University of Notre Dame (J.D., 1985). ***PRACTICE AREAS:*** Litigation; Products Liability; Environmental Law; Construction Law; Medical Malpractice. ***Email:*** cusackd@jbltd.com

STEVEN B. NOVY, born Manitowoc, Wisconsin, December 23, 1947; admitted to bar, 1973, Illinois; 1974, U.S. District Court, Northern District of Illinois including Trial Bar; 1984, Wisconsin; 1986, U.S. District Court, Eastern District of Wisconsin; 1996, U.S. District Court, Western District of Wisconsin. *Education:* University of Illinois (B.A., 1970); University of Notre Dame (J.D., 1973). ***PRACTICE AREAS:*** Transportation (55%); Tort Defense (40%); Cargo Claims (5%). ***Email:*** novys@jbltd.com

JOSEPH B. CARINI, III, born Chicago, Illinois, February 18, 1963; admitted to bar, 1988, Illinois and U.S. District Court, Northern District of Illinois. *Education:* Marquette University (B.A., 1985); John Marshall Law School (J.D., with distinction, 1988). ***PRACTICE AREAS:*** Construction Litigation; Litigation; Insurance Coverage; Premises Liability. ***Email:*** carinij@jbltd.com

RICK L. HAMMOND, born Chicago, Illinois, October 11, 1951; admitted to bar, 1988, Illinois; 1996, Indiana. *Education:* Southern Illinois University (B.A., 1975); American College (Chartered Life Underwriter, 1980); John Marshall Law School (J.D., 1988). *Member:* Chicago Bar Association (Insurance Law Committee); Illinois State Bar Association (Chairman, Insurance Law Section Council, 1993-1994); American Bar Association

(This Listing Continued)

JOHNSON & BELL, LTD., Chicago—Continued

(Member, Tort and Insurance Practice Section; Vice-Chair, Property Insurance Law Committee); Federation of Defense and Corporate Counsel; Illinois Association of Defense Trial Counsel (Board of Directors and Editorial Staff). ***LANGUAGES:*** Spanish. ***PRACTICE AREAS:*** Insurance Coverage; Insurance Bad Faith Litigation. ***Email:*** hammondr@jbltd.com

JAMES K. TOOHEY, born Evanston, Illinois, 1944; admitted to bar, 1969, Illinois; 1971, U.S. District Court, Northern District of Illinois; 1972, U.S. Court of Appeals, Seventh Circuit; 1975, U.S. Court of Appeals, Eighth Circuit; 1988, U.S. Supreme Court; 1991, U.S. District Court, Central District of Illinois. *Education:* University of Notre Dame (B.B.A., 1966); Northwestern University School of Law (J.D., 1969). *Member:* Illinois State Bar Association (Member, Civil Practice and Procedure Section Council, 1995-1998); Illinois Society of Trial Lawyers; Illinois Association of Trial Defense Counsel; Defense Research Institure; Association for Advancement of Automotive Medicine. ***REPORTED CASES:*** Graves v. North Shore Gas (2nd Dist. IL); Barsanti v. The Peoples Gas Light and Coke Company (1st Dist. IL); Boddie v. Litton Industries (1st Dist. IL); Ralston v. Casanova (1st Dist. IL); Stein v. Volkswagen (USDC IL); Curry v. Louis Allis (1st Dist. IL); Belfour v. Volkswagen (2nd Dist. IL); Soper v. Volkswagen (USDC IL); Schlunk v. Volkswagen (1st Dist. IL / U.S. Sup. Ct.); McNamee v. Federated (1st Dist. IL / IL Sup. Ct.); Jenkins v. Dr. Wu (IL Sup. Ct.); Hartman v. Pittsburgh Corning (5th Dist. IL); Griggs v. Firestone (8th Cir.). ***PRACTICE AREAS:*** Products Liability; Toxic Torts; Commercial Litigation; Recreational Products Liability. ***Email:*** tooheyj@jbltd.com

MICHAEL P. SIAVELIS, born Chicago, Illinois; admitted to bar, 1967, Illinois, U.S. District Court, Northern District of Illinois including Trial Bar and U.S. Court of Appeals, Seventh Circuit. *Education:* Lake Forest College; DePaul University (B.S.; J.D.). [U.S. Army; U.S. Army Reserves]. ***SPECIAL AGENCIES:*** Assistant United States Attorney Northern District of Illinois; Deputy Chief Criminal Division. ***PRACTICE AREAS:*** Civil Trial; Commercial Litigation; Employment Litigation. ***Email:*** siavelism@jbltd.com

WILLIAM A. GEISER, born Chicago, Illinois, September 30, 1956; admitted to bar, 1983, Illinois and U.S. District Court, Northern District of Illinois. *Education:* University of Wisconsin (B.A., 1980); Illinois Institute of Technology/Chicago-Kent College of Law (J.D., with honors, 1983). *Member:* Chicago, Illinois State and American Bar Associations. ***PRACTICE AREAS:*** Personal Injury; Torts; Toxic Torts; Transportation; Railroad Liability; Elder Law; Medical Malpractice; Construction Litigation; Commercial Litigation. ***Email:*** geiserw@jbltd.com

KEVIN G. OWENS, born Evergreen Park, Illinois, June 8, 1958; admitted to bar, 1983, Illinois and U.S. District Court, Northern District of Illinois; 1990, U.S. District Court, Western District of Michigan. *Education:* Marquette University (B.A., 1980); DePaul University (J.D., 1983). *Member:* Chicago, Illinois State and American Bar Associations; Defense Research Institute; Illinois Association of Defense Trial Counsel. ***PRACTICE AREAS:*** Civil Litigation; Commercial Litigation; Products Liability; Construction Litigation; Real Estate. ***Email:*** owensk@jbltd.com

CHARLES P. RANTIS, born Chicago, Illinois, April 16, 1960; admitted to bar, 1985, Illinois and U.S. District Court, Northern District of Illinois; 1996, U.S. District Court, Northern District of Indiana; 1997, U.S District Court, Central District of Illinois; 2000, U.S. District Court, Southern District of Illinois. *Education:* DePaul University (B.S., 1982); Chicago-Kent College of Law (J.D., 1985). ***PRACTICE AREAS:*** Products Liability; Construction Negligence; Premises Liability; General Negligence. ***Email:*** rantisc@jbltd.com

ROBERT J. COMFORT, born Joliet, Illinois, December 9, 1960; admitted to bar, 1986, Illinois and U.S. Court of Appeals, Seventh Circuit. *Education:* University of Santa Clara (B.A., cum laude, 1983); University of Notre Dame (J.D., 1986). *Member:* Chicago, Illinois State and American Bar Associations; Illinois Association of Defense Trial Counsel. ***PRACTICE AREAS:*** Hotel and Hospitality Law; Medical Malpractice; Products Liability; Automobile and Transportation Liability; Manufacturers Liability; Sports Law; Health Care. ***Email:*** comfortr@jbltd.com

DANIEL C. MURRAY, born Evanston, Illinois; admitted to bar, 1976, Illinois; 1979, U.S. Court of Appeals, Seventh Circuit; 1980, U.S. District Court, Northern District of Illinois including Trial Bar; 1992, U.S. District Court, Eastern District of Michigan; 1994, U.S. District Court, Eastern District of Wisconsin; 2003, U.S. District Court, Central and Southern Districts of Illinois. *Education:* Marquette University (B.A. Economics); Loyola University of Chicago (J.D. 1976). *Member:* Federal (Board of Directors, Chicago Chapter) and Seventh Federal Circuit Bar Associations; Chicago Legal Advocacy To Incarcerated Mothers. ***PRACTICE AREAS:*** Complex Federal Civil Litigation; Federal Criminal Litigation; Federal Grand Jury Matters; Municipal Liability; Environmental Law. ***Email:*** murrayd@jbltd.com

WILLIAM K. McVISK, born Chicago, Illinois, October 8, 1953; admitted to bar, 1977, Illinois and U.S. District Court, Northern District of Illinois, 1986, Trial Bar; 1978, U.S. Court of Appeals, Seventh Circuit; 1999, Indiana and U.S. District Court, Northern and Southern Districts of Indiana; 2001, U.S. Court of Appeals, Tenth Circuit. *Education:* University of Illinois (B.A., History, 1974); Northwestern University (J.D., cum laude, 1977). *Member:* Illinois Association of Hospital Attorneys (President, 2001-2002); Illinois Association of Trial Defense Attorneys; Chicagoland Healthcare Risk Management Society. ***PRACTICE AREAS:*** Insurance; Health Care; Medical Malpractice; Litigation; Personal Injury; Torts. ***Email:*** mcviskw@jbltd.com

KATHRYN K. LOFT, born Wisconsin, February 29, 1952; admitted to bar, 1987, Illinois and U.S. District Court, Northern District of Illinois. *Education:* University of Wisconsin (B.S., 1974); IIT/Chicago-Kent College of Law (J.D., 1987). ***PRACTICE AREAS:*** Medical Malpractice Defense; Products Liability Defense. ***Email:*** loftk@jbltd.com

GREGORY D. CONFORTI, born Aurora, Illinois, August 9, 1963; admitted to bar, 1988, Illinois and U.S. District Court, Northern District of Illinois; 1990, U.S. Court of Appeals, Seventh Circuit; 1994, U.S. District Court, Northern District of Illinois including Trial Bar. *Education:* Coe College (B.A., 1985); Wake Forest University (J.D., 1988). *Member:* Illinois State Bar Association; American Law Firm Association; Defense Research Institute; Justinian Society of Lawyers. ***PRACTICE AREAS:*** Transportation; Products Liability; Construction Law; Premises Liability; Torts; Litigation; Employment Claims; Employment Discrimination. ***Email:*** confortig@jbltd.com

FRANK P. NOWICKI, born Chicago, Illinois, November 25, 1954; admitted to bar, 1979, Illinois and U.S. District Court, Northern District of Illinois; 1980, U.S. Court of Appeals, Seventh Circuit; 1990, U.S. Supreme Court. *Education:* DePaul University (B.A., summa cum laude, 1976); Loyola University (J.D., 1979). ***PRACTICE AREAS:*** Litigation; Transportation; Mass Torts; Class Actions. ***Email:*** nowickif@jbltd.com

GREGORY E. SCHILLER, born Chicago, Illinois, August 13, 1960; admitted to bar, 1985, Illinois. *Education:* University of Michigan (B.A., 1982); Indiana University (J.D., 1985). ***PRACTICE AREAS:*** Hospital Liability; Medical Liability. ***Email:*** schillerg@jbltd.com

HOWARD W. FOSTER, born Boston Massachusetts, November 4, 1962; admitted to bar, 1989, Illinois and U.S. District Court, Northern District of Illinois; 1993, Trial Bar; U.S. Court of Appeals, Second, Third, Sixth, Seventh, Ninth and Eleventh Circuits; U.S. Supreme Court. *Education:* Brandeis University (B.A., with honors, 1984); Boston University (J.D., 1988). ***REPORTED CASES:*** Commercial Cleaning Services v. Colin Service Systems, 271 F.3d 374 (2d Cir. 2001); Mendoza v. Zirkle Fruit Co., 301 F.3d 1163 (9th Cir. 2002); Lengle v. Attorney's Title Guaranty Fund, Inc., 2202 WL 31163672 (N.D. Ill. 2002); Trollinger v. Tyson foods, Inc., 370 f.3d 602 (6th Cir. 2004); Williams v. Mohawk Industries, Inc., 411 F.3d 1252 (11th Cir. 2005). ***PRACTICE AREAS:*** RICO; Consumer Fraud; Class Actions. ***Email:*** fosterh@jbltd.com

ROBERT R. McNAMARA, born Oak Park, Illinois, January 7, 1962; admitted to bar, 1987, Illinois. *Education:* University of Notre Dame (B.A., 1984); Loyola University (J.D., 1987). ***PRACTICE AREAS:*** Toxic Torts; Products Liability; Construction Law; Premises Liability. ***Email:*** mcnamarar@jbltd.com

MARILYN McCABE REIDY, born Evergreen Park, Illinois, February 28, 1952; admitted to bar, 1991, Illinois and U.S. District Court, Northern and Central Districts of Illinois; U.S. Court of Appeals, Seventh Circuit. *Education:* Northern Illinois University (B.S., 1972); Chicago State University (M.S., 1978); Illinois Institute of Technology, Chicago-Kent College of Law (J.D., with honors, 1991). ***PRACTICE AREAS:*** Hospital Liability; Medical Liability; Litigation. ***Email:*** reidym@jbltd.com

DAVID M. MACKSEY, born Oskaloosa, Iowa, August 25, 1963; admitted to bar, 1990, Illinois and U.S. District Court, Northern District of Illinois. *Education:* University of Iowa (B.A., 1987; J.D., with distinction, 1990). *Member:* Chicago, Illinois State and American Bar Associations; Defense Research Institute; Illinois Association of Defense Trial Counsel (Member, Professional Liability Committee). ***PRACTICE AREAS:*** Appellate Practice; Civil Appeals; Complex Business Litigation; Professional Liability. ***Email:*** mackseyd@jbltd.com

TERRY A. TAKASH, born Chicago, Illinois, January 22, 1960; admitted to bar, 1986, Illinois. *Education:* Western Illinois University (B.S., 1982); John Marshall Law School (J.D., 1986). *Member:* Chicago and Illinois State Bar Associations. ***PRACTICE AREAS:*** Professional Licensing; Litigation; Insurance Coverage; Medical Malpractice. ***Email:*** takasht@jbltd.com

PATRICK T. GARVEY, born Des Moines, Iowa, February 19, 1963; admitted to bar, 1993, Illinois and U.S. District Court, Northern District of Illinois. *Education:* Eastern Illinois University (B.A., 1985); IIT-Chicago Kent College of Law (J.D., 1993). *Member:* Chicago and Illinois State Bar Associations. ***PRACTICE AREAS:*** Insurance; Toxic Torts; Personal Injury; Torts; Products Liability. ***Email:*** garveyp@jbltd.com

MARK D. JOHNSON, born Evanston, Illinois, May 21, 1965; admitted to bar, 1993, Illinois. *Education:* Marquette University (B.A., 1988); John Marshall Law School (J.D., 1993). ***PRACTICE AREAS:*** Premises Liability; Products Liability; Professional Liability. ***Email:*** johnsonmd@jdltd.com

ANDREW J. KOVARIK, born Chicago, Illinois, June 17, 1960; admitted to bar, 1992, Illinois and U.S. District Court, Northern District of Illinois. *Education:* Loyola University (B.A., 1983); John Marshall Law School (J.D., cum laude, 1992). *Member:* Chicago and American Bar Associations. ***PRACTICE AREAS:*** Hospital Liability; Medical Liability; General Negligence. ***Email:*** kovarika@jbltd.com

LYNN M. REID, born Park Ridge, Illinois, March 5, 1961; admitted to bar, 1990, Illinois and U.S. District Court, Northern District of Illinois. *Education:* Valparaiso University (B.S., 1983); DePaul University (J.D., 1990). Registered Nurse, Illinois, 1984. *Member:* Chicago, Illinois State and American Bar Associations. ***PRACTICE AREAS:*** Medical Malpractice; Hospital Law; Civil Litigation; Nonprofit Corporations. ***Email:*** reidl@jbltd.com

ROBERT SPITKOVSKY, JR., born Chicago, Illinois, March 12, 1962; admitted to bar, 1988, Illinois. *Education:* Drake University (B.A., 1984; J.D., 1987). *Member:* Illinois State Bar Associations. ***PRACTICE AREAS:*** Asbestos Litigation; Toxic Torts; Premises Liability. ***Email:*** spitkovsky@jbltd.com

STEVE C. CANTY, admitted to bar, 1996, Illinois. *Education:* University of Illinois (B.A., 1993); DePaul University (J.D., with honors, 1996). *Member:* Lake County, McHenry County and Illinois State Bar Associations; Defense Research Institute. ***PRACTICE AREAS:*** General and Civil Litigation; Tort Litigation; Personal Injury; Premises Liability; Transportation. ***Email:*** cantys@jbltd.com

MATTHEW L. JOHNSON, born Chicago, Illinois, March 22, 1970; admitted to bar, 1996, Illinois. *Education:* Wittenberg University (B.A., 1992); John Marshall Law School (J.D., 1996). *Member:* American Bar Association. ***PRACTICE AREAS:*** Premises Liability; Products Liability; Medical Malpractice. ***Email:*** johnsonm@jbltd.com

JULIE M. KENNEDY, born Youngstown, Ohio, November 15, 1970; admitted to bar, 1996, Illinois and U.S. District Court, Northern District of Illinois. *Education:* University of Wisconsin at Milwaukee (B.A., Political Science, 1993); John Marshall Law School, Chicago (J.D., 1996). *Member:* Chicago, Illinois State and American Bar Associations. ***PRACTICE AREAS:*** Professional Negligence; Products Liability; Premises Liability. ***Email:*** kennedyj@jbltd.com

CHARLENE S. MITCHELL, born Chicago, Illinois, November 28, 1968; admitted to bar, 1995, Illinois. *Education:* University of Notre Dame (B.A., 1990); John Marshall Law

(This Listing Continued)

School (J.D., cum laude, 1995). *Member:* Illinois State Bar Association. ***PRACTICE AREAS:*** Medical Malpractice; Hospital Law; Insurance Defense. ***Email:*** mitchellc@jbltd.com

EDWARD W. HEARN, born Goshen, Indiana, July 30, 1969; admitted to bar, 1995, Indiana and U.S. District Court, Northern and Southern Districts of Indiana; 2003, U.S. District Court, District of Colorado (Not admitted in Illinois). *Education:* Purdue University (B.S., 1992); Valparaiso University School of Law (J.D., cum laude, 1995). *Member:* Defense Research Institute of Indiana; Defense Trial Counsel of Indiana. ***REPORTED CASES:*** Lovings v. Cleary, 799 N.E.2d 76 (Ind.Ct.App.2003); Thomas v. Dyer Construction Co., 698 N.E.2d 320 (Ind.Ct.App.1998); AT&T Wireless v. Town Porter, 203 F.Supp.2d 985 (N.D.Ind.2003). ***PRACTICE AREAS:*** Product Liability; Business Litigation; Transportation Law; Sports Law; Entertainment Law; Insurance Coverage. ***Email:*** hearnw@jbltd.com

KEITH L. GIBSON, born Indianapolis, Indiana, November 8, 1970; admitted to bar, 1996, Illinois Supreme Court and Ohio Supreme Court. *Education:* Indiana University (B.A., 1993); DePaul University College of Law (J.D., 1996). *Member:* Chicago Bar Association. ***PRACTICE AREAS:*** Construction Negligence; Product Liability; Trucking and Transportation. ***Email:*** gibsonk@jbltd.com

MICHAEL A. LATONA, born Erie, Pennsylvania, September 12, 1956; admitted to bar, 1981, Illinois, U.S. District Court, Northern District of Illinois and U.S. Court of Appeals, Seventh District. *Education:* DePaul University (B.A., 1978; M.B.A., 1984); Loyola University (J.D., 1981). *Member:* Chicago and American (Member: Real Property, Probate and Trust Section; Business Law Section) Bar Associations. ***LANGUAGES:*** Italian. ***PRACTICE AREAS:*** Corporate Law; Real Estate; Probate Administration. ***Email:*** latonam@jbltd.com

ASSOCIATES

Julie E. Benes
Garrett L. Boehm, Jr.
Paul E. Brady
Christopher J. Carlos
Steven G. Carlson
Jeffery G. Chrones
Tracie V. Coleman
Timothy R. Couture
Mary K. Cryar
David A. Cyr
David F. Fanning
Cecilio L. Franco, IV
Brian P. Gainer (admission pending)
Matthew A. Galin
Eydie R. Glassman
Jonathon W. Goken
Richard R. Gordon
Katie E. Gorrie
Sean J. Hardy
Haley A. Harris (admission pending)
Thomas J. Hayes
Michael C. Holy
Kathryn R. Hoying
Meanith Huon
Sean P. Hussey
Michael H. Israel
Kurt E. Keagle (Not admitted in IL)
Angela M. Kotsalieff
Michael J. Laux
William J. Leeder, III
Christopher W. Loweth
Nicholas R. Lykins
Paige C. Manley
Rory L. Margulis
Eric W. Moch
Cristina Mungai
Meiko L. Ogura
Jason Orleans
Henry A. Parkhurst
Michael A. Pauletto
James E. Phelan
Victor Pioli
Deborah G. Relihan
Justin A. Relihan
Sammi L. Renken
Juanita B. Rodriguez (admission pending)
Jennifer Tomsak Rose
Peter R. Ryndak
Justin D. Scheid
Carl M. Schultz
Meghan M. Sciortino (admission pending)
Jared M. Scott
Ronald E. Scott
Joshua S. Singewald
Martha C. Szatkowski
Lauren Ann Wieland
Matthew K. Wollin
William T. Young
Daniel J. Zlatic

REPRESENTATIVE CLIENTS: Advocate Health Care Systems; AIG Technical Services, Inc.; Assurant Health; Atlantic Mutual Insurance Co.; Certain Underwriters at Lloyds, London; City of Harvey; CNH America, LLC; Elliott Turbomachinery Co., Inc.; Emerson Electric Company; Essex Insurance Company; Exxon Mobil; Hilton Hotels Corporation; Illinois Provider Trust; ISBA Mutual Insurance Co.; Lynch Ford, Inc.; Provena Health; Rockville Risk Management Associates; St. Paul Travelers Companies; Volkswagen of America; Walgreen Company; Waste Management, Inc.; Western General Management, Inc.

JOHNSON AND COLMAR

300 SOUTH WACKER DRIVE
SUITE 1000
CHICAGO, ILLINOIS 60606
Telephone: 312-922-1980
Fax: 312-922-9283
URL: http://www.jocolaw.com

Business Planning, Acquisitions, Securities, Business and Governmental Litigation, Employee Benefits, State and Local Government Law, Real Estate and Estate Planning and Probate.

RUSSELL E. Q. JOHNSON (1938-1980)

CRAIG P. COLMAR, born Evanston, Illinois, November 7, 1952; admitted to bar, 1977, Illinois and U.S. District Court, Northern District of Illinois. *Education:* Northwestern University (B.A., 1974); Rheinische Friedrich-Wilhelms-Universitat, Bonn, West Germany; Northwestern University (J.D., 1977). *Member:* Chicago and American Bar Associations. ***PRACTICE AREAS:*** Business Planning; Business Acquisitions; Securities. ***Email:*** cpcolmar@jocolaw.com

MICHAEL BONN, born New York, N.Y., October 31, 1945; admitted to bar, 1973, Wisconsin; 1977, Illinois. *Education:* Yale College (B.A., 1967); St. Catherine's College, University of Oxford, Oxford, England; Harvard Law School (J.D., 1973). *Member:* American Bar Association; State Bar of Wisconsin. ***PRACTICE AREAS:*** Business Acquisitions; Securities; Tax. ***Email:*** mbonn@jocolaw.com

MARK V. CHESTER, born Chicago, Illinois, April 22, 1952; admitted to bar, 1977, Illinois and U.S. District Court, Northern District of Illinois including Trial Bar; 1979, Georgia; 1980, U.S. Court of Appeals, Seventh Circuit; 1981, U.S. Supreme Court and U.S. Court of Appeals, Fifth and Eleventh Circuits; 1991, U.S. Court of International Trade. *Education:* Emory University (B.A., and M.A., 1974); Victoria University of Manchester, Manchester, England; Northwestern University (J.D., cum laude, 1977). Assistant State's Attorney, Cook County, 1977-1981. Special Assistant State's Attorney, 1981-1994. *Member:* Chicago and Illinois State Bar Associations; State Bar of Georgia. ***PRACTICE AREAS:*** State and Local Government Law; Business Litigation; Governmental Litigation; Business Planning. ***Email:*** mvchester@jocolaw.com

JOAN S. CHERRY, born Chicago, Illinois, January 26, 1949; admitted to bar, 1974, Illinois and U.S. District Court, Northern District of Illinois; 1978, U.S. Court of Appeals, Seventh Circuit; 1979, U.S. Supreme Court. *Education:* Lake Forest College (B.A., 1971); Loyola University, Chicago, Illinois (J.D., 1974). Lecturer, Appellate Advocacy, Adjunct Faculty, Loyola University School of Law, 1976-1988. Assistant State's Attorney, Cook County, 1975-1991, (Chief, Civil Actions Bureau, 1986-1991). *Member:* Chicago and American Bar Associations; Appellate Lawyers Association (Director, 1981-1983 and 1985-1987). ***PRACTICE AREAS:*** State and Local Government Law; Business Litigation; Governmental Litigation; Employment Law. ***Email:*** jscherry@jocolaw.com

ROBIN C. FRIEDMAN, born Elizabeth, New Jersey, August 18, 1957; admitted to bar, 1984, Illinois and U.S. District Court, Northern District of Illinois. *Education:* University of Chicago (B.A., 1978; J.D., 1984). Phi Beta Kappa. ***PRACTICE AREAS:*** Business Planning; Employee Benefits; Health Care Law. ***Email:*** rcfriedman@jocolaw.com

JOAN M. MEYERS, born Erie, Pennsylvania, August 26, 1962; admitted to bar, 1990, Connecticut and U.S. District Court, District of Connecticut; 1991, Illinois. *Education:* Allegheny College (B.S., 1984); New York Law School (J.D., 1990). *Member:* Chicago and American Bar Associations. ***PRACTICE AREAS:*** Business Litigation; Government Litigation; Real Estate. ***Email:*** jmmeyers@jocolaw.com

PETER J. DAANE, born Sheboygan, Wisconsin, September 9, 1964; admitted to bar, 1996, Illinois. *Education:* University of Wisconsin-Oshkosh (B.S., 1988); DePaul University (J.D., 1996). Recipient, CALI Award: Mediation; Business Transactions. ***PRACTICE AREAS:*** Corporate Law; Business Acquisitions; Securities; Corporate Finance. ***Email:*** pdaane@jocolaw.com

MURRAY J. LEWISON, born Chicago, Illinois, May 24, 1952; admitted to bar, 1997, Illinois, U.S. District Court, Northern District of Illinois. *Education:* Indiana University (B.S., 1974); Drake University (J.D., 1976). Beta Gamma Sigma. ***PRACTICE AREAS:*** Real Estate; Business Planning; Estate Planning. ***Email:*** mlewison@jocolaw.com

OF COUNSEL

JOHN L. COLMAR, born Wheeling, West Virginia, August 6, 1916. (1916-2004)

JOHNSON & NEWBY, LLC

Established in 2005

39 S. LASALLE STREET
SUITE 820
CHICAGO, ILLINOIS 60603
Telephone: 312-345-1306
Fax: 312-345-1308
URL: http://www.lawyers.com/johnsonnewby

Bankruptcy, Business Litigation and Commercial Collections.

MEMBERS OF FIRM

CINDY M. JOHNSON, born Oak Park, Illinois, November 6, 1963; admitted to bar, 1988, Illinois; 1989, U.S. District Court, Northern District of Illinois; 1992, U.S. Court of Appeals, Seventh Circuit; 1995, U.S. Supreme Court. *Education:* University of Chicago (B.A., with honors, 1985); Illinois Institute of Technology Chicago-Kent College of Law (J.D., 1988). Author: "A Creditor's Lawyers Guide to Assignments for the Benefit of Creditors," Illinois Bar Journal, December, 1997; Article, "Bankruptcy Practice: It's a Jungle Out There," Chicago Bar Association, Record, February/March 1995. Co-Author: Chapter, "Enforcement of Judgments," Illinois Institute for Continuing Legal Education Publication, Creditors Rights in Illinois, 1995; "Creditors' Rights in Bankruptcy Chapter," Illinois Institute for Continuing Legal Education Publication Creditors Rights in Illinois, 2004. Lecturer: "Representing Creditors in Bankruptcy Proceedings," Illinois State Bar Association Annual Meeting, 2002; "Post-Judgment Collections," Yearly, 1997-2001 and 2004, Illinois State Bar Association mid-year meeting; "Collecting from a Defendant Who has Filed Bankruptcy," Yearly at Collection of Judgments Seminar, Chicago Bar Association; Judgement Enforcement in Illinois Seminar, Lorman Education Services, 2002, 2003; "Automatic Stay," and "Discharge and Dischargeability," Illinois Institute of Continuing Legal Education Seminar, entitled Consumer Bankruptcy Essentials of Chapter 7 and Chapter 13, 2003. Panel Member: General Practice, Small and Solo Committee's Seminar entitled Bankruptcy for the Rest of Us, ABA Annual Meeting, 2003; "Creditors Rights in Bankruptcy" 27th Annual Attorneys Conference for Attorneys Representing Financial Institutions, Illinois Credit Union League, 2004; American Bankruptcy Institute's Chicago Consumer Bankruptcy Conference, 2004. *Member:* Illinois State and American Bar Associations; Illinois Creditors Bar Association (President, 2003-2005; Executive Vice-President, 2002-2003; Board Member, 2000-2001; Secretary, 1999-2000); American Bankruptcy Institute. (Managing Partner). ***REPORTED CASES:*** Logemann Holding, Inc. v Lieber, 341 Ill.App.3d 689, 793 N.E.2d 135 (1st Dist. 2003); In re Dobek, 278 B.R. 496 (Bankr. N.D. Ill. 2002). ***PRACTICE AREAS:*** Business Litigation; Collections; Debtor and Creditor; Bankruptcy Law. ***Email:*** CJohnson@JNLegal.net

DAVID A. NEWBY, born Indianapolis, Indiana, December 20, 1959; admitted to bar, 1985, Illinois and U.S. District Court, Northern District of Illinois including Trial Bar. *Edu-*

(This Listing Continued)

JOHNSON & NEWBY, LLC, Chicago—Continued

cation: Institute of European Studies, Vienna, Austria; Wabash College (A.B., magna cum laude, 1982); Columbia University (J.D., 1985). Phi Beta Kappa. Member, Board of Directors, Chicago Chapter, Turnaround Management Association, 1998-2000. Mediator, Circuit Court, Cook County, Illinois. *Member:* Chicago (Chair, 1992-1993 and Director, 1993-1994, Bankruptcy Committee, Young Lawyers Section); American Bankruptcy Institute. (Certified in Business Bankruptcy Law by the American Board of Certification). ***PRACTICE AREAS:*** Bankruptcy Law; Commercial Litigation. ***Email:*** DNewby@JNLegal.net

ASSOCIATES

BETH ANNE ALCANTAR, born Park Ridge, Illinois, July 19, 1971; admitted to bar, 1995, Illinois. *Education:* University of Illinois, Urbana-Champaign (B.A., 1992; J.D., 1995). Author: "Franchisor Liability for the Criminal Acts of Others," Franchise Law Journal, Summer 1999; "Dangers in Disclosure" (relating to social security numbers on pleadings), Illinois Creditors Bar Association Newsletter, July 2004. *Member:* American Bar Association; Illinois Creditors Bar Association. ***PRACTICE AREAS:*** Business Litigation; Collections; Debtor and Creditor; Bankruptcy Law. ***Email:*** Beth@JNLegal.net

REBECCA M. SHANAMAN, born York, Pennsylvania, December 9, 1976; admitted to bar, 2004, Pennsylvania; 2005, Illinois. *Education:* LaSalle University (B.A., 1999); Loyola University (J.D., 2004). *Member:* Chicago Bar Association (Member, Bankruptcy Committee, Young Lawyers Section). ***PRACTICE AREAS:*** Commercial Litigation; Bankruptcy Law. ***Email:*** Rebecca@JNLegal.net

LAW OFFICE OF THERESA V. JOHNSON

CHICAGO, ILLINOIS

(See Westmont)

Foreign and Domestic Intellectual Property (IP) including Patents, Trademarks, Trade Secrets, Copyrights, Unfair Competition, Licensing, International IP Arbitration and Mediation, IP Litigation, Madrid Protocol Trademark Filing and Consultation, Patent Cooperation Treaty and Paris Convention Filing, International Law, Immigration, Entertainment Law, Defamation, Title VII Discrimination/Retaliation, Family Medical Leave Act (FMLA), Americans with Disabilities Act (ADA), Personal Injury, Mechanics Liens, Replevin/Recovery of Engagement Ring, Probate, Estates.

JOLIVETTE & TEMPLER, P.C.

Established in 1988

10 SOUTH LA SALLE STREET
SUITE 1017
CHICAGO, ILLINOIS 60603
Telephone: 312-419-8800
Facsimile: 312-419-0705
Email: jolidave@juno.com

General Civil Trial and Commercial Law. Corporate, Real Property, Mortgage Law, Appellate Practice, Professional Conduct of Attorneys.

DAVID J. JOLIVETTE, born Madison, Wisconsin, December 11, 1942; admitted to bar, 1970, Wisconsin and Illinois. *Education:* University of Wisconsin-Madison (B.S., 1965; J.D., 1970). Phi Alpha Delta. Note Editor, University of Wisconsin Law Review, 1969-1970. *Member:* Chicago, Illinois State and American Bar Associations; State Bar of Wisconsin. ***PRACTICE AREAS:*** Commercial; Corporate; Real Property; Estate Planning. ***Email:*** jolidave@juno.com

LAWRENCE M. TEMPLER, born Chicago, Illinois, October 26, 1946; admitted to bar, 1971, Illinois and U.S. District Court, Northern District of Illinois including Trial Bar. *Education:* University of Illinois (B.S., 1968); Northwestern University (J.D., cum laude, 1971). Law Clerk, Chief Justice Glenn K. Seidenfeld, Illinois Appellate Court, Second District, 1971-1973. Author of Monthly Column on Legal Ethics, Chicago Daily Law Bulletin; Member: Illinois Supreme Court Committee on Professional Responsibility, 1985-1997; Illinois Supreme Court Committee on Attorney Civility, 2001—. Co-Chair, Illinois State and Chicago Bar Association Joint Committee on drafting present Illinois Rules of Professional Conduct. Member Illinois State And Chicago Bar Association Committee on Certification and Specialization of Lawyers. Member, Committee re ethics opinions for judges, Illinois State, Chicago Bar Association and Illinois Judges Association. Member, Panel of Arbitrators, American Arbitration Association. *Member:* Chicago (Member, Committee on Alternative Dispute Resolution) and Illinois State (Member, Former Chairman on Committee on Professional Conduct; Member, 1982—; Chairman, 1984-1986; Committee on Ethics, 2000) Bar Associations. ***PRACTICE AREAS:*** Commercial Litigation; Appellate Practice; Legal Professional Responsibility; Alternative Dispute Resolution. ***Email:*** templerlm@aol.com

JONES DAY

77 WEST WACKER
CHICAGO, ILLINOIS 60601-1692
Telephone: 312-782-3939
Telecopier: 312-782-8585
Email: counsel@jonesday.com
URL: http://www.jonesday.com

In Atlanta, Georgia: 1420 Peachtree Street, N.E., Suite 800. Telephone: 404-521-3939. Telecopier: 404-581-8330.
In Beijing, China: 3201 China World Tower 1, No. 1 Jianguomenwai Avenue. Telephone: 86-10-5866-1111. Telecopier: 86-10-5866-1122.

(This Listing Continued)

In Brussels, Belgium: Boulevard Brand Whitlocklaan 165, 1200 Brussels. Telephone: 32-2-645-14-11. Telecopier: 32-2-645-14-45.
In Cleveland, Ohio: North Point, 901 Lakeside Avenue. Telephone: 216-586-3939. Telecopier: 216-579-0212.
In Columbus, Ohio: 325 John H. McConnell Boulevard, Suite 600. Telephone: 614-469-3939. Telecopier: 614-461-4198.
In Dallas, Texas: 2727 North Harwood Street. Telephone: 214-220-3939. Telecopier: 214-969-5100.
In Frankfurt, Germany: Hochhaus am Park, Grüneburgweg 102, 60323 Frankfurt am Main. Telephone: 49-69-9726-3939. Telecopier: 49-69-9726-3993.
In Hong Kong, China: 31st Floor, Edinburgh Tower, The Landmark, 15 Queen's Road, Central. Telephone: 852-2526-6895. Telecopier: 852-2868-5871.
In Houston, Texas: 717 Texas, Suite 3300. Telephone: 832-239-3939. Telecopier: 832-239-3600.
In Irvine, California: 3 Park Plaza, Suite 1100. Telephone: 949-851-3939. Telecopier: 949-553-7539.
In London, England: 21 Tudor Street. Telephone: 44-20-7039-5959. Telecopier: 44-20-7039-5999.
In Los Angeles, California: 555 South Flower Street, Fiftieth Floor. Telephone: 213-489-3939. Telecopier: 213-243-2539.
In Madrid, Spain: Velázquez 51, 4th Floor. Telephone: 34-91-520-39-39. Telecopier: 34-91-520-39-38.
In Menlo Park, California: 2882 Sand Hill Road, Suite 240. Telephone: 650-739-3939. Telecopier: 650-739-3900.
In Milan, Italy: Via Turati, 16/18. Telephone: 39-02-7645-4001. Telecopier: 39-02-7645-4400.
In Moscow, Russia: Smolenskaya Square 3, 9th Floor, 121099 Moscow. Telephone: 7-095-980-6769. Telecopier: 7-095-980-6765.
In Munich, Germany: Prinzregentenstr. 11, 80538 Munich. Telephone: 089-20 60 42-200. Telecopier: 089-20 60 42-293.
In New York, New York: 222 East 41st Street. Telephone: 212-326-3939. Telecopier: 212-755-7306.
In Paris, France: 120, rue du Faubourg Saint-Honoré. Telephone: 33-1-56-59-39-39. Telecopier: 33-1-56-59-39-38.
In Pittsburgh, Pennsylvania: 500 Grant Street, One Mellon Bank Center, 31st Floor. Telephone: 412-391-3939. Telecopier: 412-394-7959.
In San Diego, California: 12750 High Bluff Drive, Suite 300. Telephone: 858-314-1200. Telecopier: 858-314-1150.
In San Francisco, California: 555 California Street, 26th Floor. Telephone: 415-626-3939. Telecopier: 415-875-5700.
In Shanghai, China: 30th Floor, Shanghai Kerry Centre, 1515 Nanjing Road West. Telephone: 86-21-2201-8000. Telecopier: 86-21-5298-6569.
In Singapore, Singapore: 30 Cecil Street, #29-01 Prudential Tower. Telephone: 65 6 538 3939. Telecopier: 65 6 536 3939.
In Sydney, Australia: Australia Square, Level 38, 264-278 George Street. Telephone: 61-2-8272-0500. Telecopier: 61-2-8272-0599.
In Taipei, Taiwan: 6th Floor, 2 Tun Hwa South Road, Section 2. Telephone: (886-2) 2704-6808 or (886-2) 7712-3399. Telecopier: (886-2) 2704-6791.
In Tokyo, Japan: Shiroyama MT Building, 6th Floor, 1-17 Toranomon 4-chome, Minato-ku, Tokyo 105-0001. Telephone: 81-3-3433-3939. Telecopier: 81-3-5401-2725.
In Washington, D.C.: 51 Louisiana Avenue, N.W. Telephone: 202-879-3939. Telecopier: 202-626-1700.

Full-Service Civil Practice, Antitrust and Competition Law, Business Restructuring and Reorganization, Capital Markets, Complex Commercial and Multrijurisdictional Litigation, Corporate Criminal Investigations, Employee Benefits and Executive Compensation, Energy Delivery and Power, Government Regulation, Health Care, Intellectual Property and Technology, International Litigation and Arbitration, Issues and Appeals, Labor and Employment, Lending/Structured Finance and Derivatives, Life Sciences, Mergers and Acquisitions, Oil and Gas, Private Equity, Products Liability, Personal Injury Torts and Health Litigation, Real Estate and Environment, Securities and Shareholder Litigation, Tax.

MEMBERS OF FIRM IN CHICAGO

JONI L. ANDRIOFF, born Massillon, Ohio; admitted to bar, 1987, Illinois. *Education:* Northwestern University (B.A., 1980); IIT Chicago-Kent College of Law (J.D., 1986). Law Clerk to Judge Wilkinson, U.S. Court of Appeals, Fourth Circuit, 1986-1987. ***PRACTICE AREAS:*** Employee Benefits; Executive Compensation. ***Email:*** jlandrioff@jonesday.com

ROBERT DEAN AVERY, born Youngstown, Ohio; admitted to bar, 1971, Ohio; 1973, California; 2001, Illinois. *Education:* Northwestern University (B.A., 1966); Columbia University (J.D., 1969). Law Clerk to Judge Anderson, U.S. Court of Appeals, Second Circuit, 1969-1970. ***PRACTICE AREAS:*** Corporate Law; Corporate Governance; Mergers and Acquisitions; Securities. ***Email:*** rdavery@jonesday.com

ERIC P. BERLIN, born Livingston, New Jersey; admitted to bar, 1993, Illinois. *Education:* Dartmouth College (B.A., 1989); University of Wisconsin (J.D., 1993). Order of the Coif. ***Email:*** epberlin@jonesday.com

JOHN F. BIBBY, JR., born Milwaukee, Wisconsin; admitted to bar, 1989, Wisconsin and Illinois. *Education:* University of Wisconsin (B.A., 1985; J.D., 1989). ***PRACTICE AREAS:*** Health Care Finance; Tax Exempt Bonds. ***Email:*** jfbibby@jonesday.com

SCOTT W. BURT, born Denver, Colorado; admitted to bar, 1991, Texas; 2003, Illinois. *Education:* University of Colorado (B.A., 1985); University of Denver (J.D., 1989). ***PRACTICE AREAS:*** Intellectual Property Litigation; Patent Litigation; Trademark Litigation; Intellectual Property Rights; Intellectual Property Licensing. ***Email:*** swburt@jonesday.com

STEVEN T. CATLETT, born Moline, Illinois; admitted to bar, 1986, Ohio; 1999, Illinois. *Education:* University of Pennsylvania (B.S., 1982); Columbia University (J.D., 1985). Special Assistant to the Legal Adviser, U.S. Department of State, 1985-1986. Law Clerk to: Judge Starr, U.S. Court of Appeals, District of Columbia Circuit, 1986-1987; Jus-

(This Listing Continued)

tice O'Connor, U.S. Supreme Court, 1987-1988. ***PRACTICE AREAS:*** Employment Discrimination; Executive Employment Law; Employee Benefits Litigation; Employment Litigation. ***Email:*** stcatlett@jonesday.com

RICHARD A. CHESLEY, born Cincinnati, Ohio; admitted to bar, 1985, Ohio; 1997, Illinois. *Education:* Northwestern University (B.A., 1982); University of Cincinnati (J.D., 1985). ***LANGUAGES:*** Spanish. ***Email:*** rchesley@jonesday.com

PETER D. CLARKE, born Worcester, Massachusetts; admitted to bar, 1975, Illinois. *Education:* University of Michigan (B.B.A., 1972); Indiana University (J.D., 1975). Order of the Coif. ***PRACTICE AREAS:*** Utility Law; Utility Acquisitions; Public Utility Finance; Securities; Corporate Law. ***Email:*** pdclarke@jonesday.com

LYNN LELAND COE, born Springfield, Illinois; admitted to bar, 1976, Illinois. *Education:* Wesleyan University (B.A., 1969); Harvard University (J.D., 1972). ***PRACTICE AREAS:*** Health Care Finance; Tax Exempt Bonds. ***Email:*** llcoe@jonesday.com

JAMES R. DALY, born Lynn, Massachusetts; admitted to bar, 1982, Illinois. *Education:* The Ohio State University (B.A., 1977); Case Western Reserve University (J.D., 1980). Law Clerk to Judge Weick, U.S. Court of Appeals, Sixth Circuit, 1980-1981. ***PRACTICE AREAS:*** Complex Commercial Litigation; Class Action Defense. ***Email:*** jrdaly@jonesday.com

LAWRENCE C. DiNARDO, born Brooklyn, New York; admitted to bar, 1974, Indiana; 1981, Illinois. *Education:* University of Notre Dame (B.A., 1971; J.D., 1974). ***PRACTICE AREAS:*** Labor and Employment; Employment Discrimination. ***Email:*** lcdinardo@jonesday.com

MICHAEL F. DOLAN, born Dougherty, Iowa; admitted to bar, 1982, Illinois. *Education:* Loras College (B.S., 1971); Southern Illinois University (M.S., 1973); University of Iowa (M.B.A., 1981; J.D., 1981). Order of the Coif. ***PRACTICE AREAS:*** Environmental Due Diligence; Environmental Health and Safety; Environmental Litigation; Groundwater Contamination; OSHA. ***Email:*** mfdolan@jonesday.com

BRIAN W. EASLEY, born Omaha, Nebraska; admitted to bar, 1990, Texas; 2000, Illinois. *Education:* University of Dallas (B.A., 1987); University of Michigan (J.D., 1990). ***PRACTICE AREAS:*** Labor and Employment; Labor Relations; Collective Bargaining. ***Email:*** beasley@jonesday.com

SUSAN ELLIOTT, born Cleveland, Ohio; admitted to bar, 1983, Ohio; 1991, Illinois. *Education:* Kent State University (B.A., 1976); Cleveland State University (J.D., 1983). Law Clerk to Judge Markus, Ohio Court of Appeals, Eighth District, 1983-1985. ***PRACTICE AREAS:*** Real Estate Secured Lending; Corporate Real Estate; Commercial Leasing. ***Email:*** selliott@jonesday.com

BRAD B. ERENS, born Chicago, Illinois; admitted to bar, 1991, Illinois. *Education:* Yale University (B.A., 1988); University of Chicago (J.D., 1991). Phi Beta Kappa; Order of the Coif. ***Email:*** bberens@jonesday.com

IRENE S. FIORENTINOS, born Corfu, Greece; admitted to bar, 1984, Illinois. *Education:* Ohio University (B.S., 1981); Northwestern University (J.D., 1984). ***PRACTICE AREAS:*** Complex Commercial Litigation; Employment Litigation. ***Email:*** ifiorentinos@jonesday.com

CHRISTOPHER W. FLYNN, born Frankfurt, Germany; admitted to bar, 1984, Illinois. *Education:* Kalamazoo College (B.A., 1981); Boston University (J.D., 1984). ***LANGUAGES:*** Spanish. ***PRACTICE AREAS:*** Public Utility Regulation; Utility Rates; Energy Acquisitions; Energy Deregulation; Energy Marketing. ***Email:*** cflynn@jonesday.com

THOMAS F. GARDNER, born New York, New York; admitted to bar, 1969, Illinois. *Education:* Illinois Wesleyan University (B.S., 1966); University of Illinois (J.D., 1969). Order of the Coif. ***PRACTICE AREAS:*** Antitrust; Dealership Law; Contract Litigation. ***Email:*** tfgardner@jonesday.com

JUNE K. GHEZZI, born Albany, New York; admitted to bar, 1983, Illinois. *Education:* State University of New York, Albany (B.A., 1974); University of Chicago (M.A., 1977); Loyola University, Chicago (J.D., 1983). Phi Beta Kappa. ***PRACTICE AREAS:*** Complex Commercial Litigation; Drug and Medical Device Litigation; Alternative Dispute Resolution. ***Email:*** jkghezzi@jonesday.com

ROBERT J. GRAVES, born Hinsdale, Illinois; admitted to bar, 1984, Illinois. *Education:* Illinois Wesleyan University (B.A., 1980); University of Illinois (J.D., 1984). Order of the Coif. Law Clerk to Judge Gee, U.S. Court of Appeals, Fifth Circuit, 1984-1985. ***LANGUAGES:*** German. ***PRACTICE AREAS:*** Commercial Finance; Structured Finance; Workouts; Uniform Commercial Code. ***Email:*** rjgraves@jonesday.com

MICHAEL J. GRAY, born Skokie, Illinois; admitted to bar, 1992, Illinois. *Education:* University of Michigan (B.A., 1989); Northwestern University (J.D., 1992). ***PRACTICE AREAS:*** Management Labor Law; Labor Litigation. ***Email:*** mjgray@jonesday.com

JAMES C. HAGY, born Cleveland, Ohio; admitted to bar, 1978, Ohio; 1988, Illinois. *Education:* Case Western Reserve University (B.A., 1975; J.D., 1978). Phi Beta Kappa; Order of the Coif. ***PRACTICE AREAS:*** Corporate Real Estate; Real Estate Finance; Real Estate Leasing. ***Email:*** jchagy@jonesday.com

STEPHEN E. HALL, born Ann Arbor, Michigan; admitted to bar, 1994, Illinois. *Education:* Northwestern University (B.A., 1991); University of Illinois (J.D., 1994). Order of the Coif. ***Email:*** sehall@jonesday.com

MICHELLE MORGAN HARNER, born Canton, Ohio; admitted to bar, 1995, Ohio; 2002, Illinois. *Education:* Boston College (B.A., 1992); The Ohio State University (J.D., 1995). Order of the Coif. Law Clerk to Judge Bodoh, U.S. Bankruptcy Court, Northern District of Ohio, 1995-1996. ***PRACTICE AREAS:*** Bankruptcy; Bankruptcy Chapter 11; Bankruptcy Litigation; Insolvency; Out of Court Debt Restructuring. ***Email:*** mmharner@jonesday.com

PAUL E. HARNER, born Albuquerque, New Mexico; admitted to bar, 1990, Ohio; 2002, Illinois. *Education:* Duke University (B.A., 1985; J.D., 1988). Phi Beta Kappa; Order of the Coif. Law Clerk to Judge Phillips, Jr., U.S. Court of Appeals, Fourth Circuit, 1988-1989. ***PRACTICE AREAS:*** Bankruptcy; Bankruptcy Chapter 11; Insolvency; Bankruptcy Litigation. ***Email:*** peharner@jonesday.com

(This Listing Continued)

CAROL A. HOGAN, born Oak Park, Illinois; admitted to bar, 1989, Illinois. *Education:* University of Illinois (B.A., 1986); Loyola University, Chicago (J.D., 1989). ***PRACTICE AREAS:*** Complex Commercial Litigation; Drug and Medical Device Litigation; Toxic Tort Defense. ***Email:*** chogan@jonesday.com

ROBERT J. JOSEPH, born New York, New York; admitted to bar, 1988, Illinois. *Education:* Indiana University (B.A., 1985); Harvard University (J.D., 1988). Phi Beta Kappa. ***PRACTICE AREAS:*** Public Utility Finance; Corporate Finance; Securities. ***Email:*** rjjoseph@jonesday.com

DAVID J. KATES, born Chicago, Illinois; admitted to bar, 1995, Illinois. *Education:* Brandeis University (B.A., 1992); Washington University (J.D., 1995). Order of the Coif. ***PRACTICE AREAS:*** Health Care Finance; Tax-Exempt Finance; Debt Finance. ***Email:*** djkates@jonesday.com

ELIZABETH CLOUGH KITSLAAR, born Beverly, Massachusetts; admitted to bar, 1988, Illinois. *Education:* Mount Holyoke College (A.B., 1979); Case Western Reserve University (J.D., 1982). Order of the Coif. ***LANGUAGES:*** French. ***PRACTICE AREAS:*** Mergers and Acquisitions; Securities; Business Law. ***Email:*** ekitslaar@jonesday.com

ROBERT C. LEE, born New York, New York; admitted to bar, 1985, Illinois. *Education:* University of Virginia (B. Plan., 1982); University of Michigan (J.D., 1985). ***LANGUAGES:*** Spanish. ***PRACTICE AREAS:*** International Real Estate; Real Estate Finance; Real Estate Investment Trusts; Private Equity. ***Email:*** rclee@jonesday.com

JOHN A. MARLOTT, born Peoria, Illinois; admitted to bar, 1995, Illinois; 1996, District of Columbia; registered to practice before U.S. Patent and Trademark Office. *Education:* University of Illinois (B.S., 1990); George Washington University (J.D., 1995). Order of the Coif. Patent Examiner, U.S. Patent and Trademark Office, 1990-1993. ***PRACTICE AREAS:*** Intellectual Property Litigation; Intellectual Property Rights; Intellectual Property Licensing; Computer and Software Patents; Internet Patents. ***Email:*** jamarlott@jonesday.com

THOMAS P. McNULTY, born Indianapolis, Indiana; admitted to bar, 1989, Illinois. *Education:* Indiana University (B.A., 1980; J.D., 1983). Deputy Prosecuting Attorney, Owen County, Indiana, 1983-1984. Deputy Counsel, President's Commission on Organized Crime, 1984-1986. Trial Attorney, U.S. Department of Justice, 1986-1989. ***LANGUAGES:*** Spanish. ***PRACTICE AREAS:*** Complex Business Litigation; White Collar Criminal Defense; Commercial Litigation. ***Email:*** tpmcnulty@jonesday.com

TIMOTHY J. MELTON, born Urbana, Illinois; admitted to bar, 1989, Illinois. *Education:* Gordon College (B.A., 1983); Wayne State University (J.D., 1987). Order of the Coif. Law Clerk to Judge Suhrheinrich, U.S. District Court, Eastern District of Michigan, 1987-1989. ***PRACTICE AREAS:*** Securities; Technology Law; Mergers, Acquisitions and Divestitures. ***Email:*** tjmelton@jonesday.com

MICHAEL J. MITCHELL, born Milwaukee, Wisconsin; admitted to bar, 1980, Illinois. *Education:* University of Illinois (B.S., 1977; J.D., 1980). Certified Public Accountant, Illinois, 1977. ***PRACTICE AREAS:*** Health Care Finance; Tax Exempt Bonds. ***Email:*** mmitchel@jonesday.com

EDWARD A. PURNELL, born Cleveland, Ohio; admitted to bar, 1990, Ohio; 2002, Illinois. *Education:* Princeton University (B.A., 1976); American Graduate School of International Management (M.I.M., 1979); Harvard University (J.D., 1990). ***LANGUAGES:*** Korean. ***PRACTICE AREAS:*** Corporate Taxation; Tax Controversies; Securitization. ***Email:*** epurnell@jonesday.com

DANIEL E. REIDY, born Chicago, Illinois; admitted to bar, 1974, Illinois. *Education:* Loyola University, Chicago (B.A., 1971); University of Michigan (J.D., 1974). Order of the Coif. Law Clerk to Judge Cummings, U.S. Court of Appeals, Seventh Circuit, 1974-1975. Assistant U.S. Attorney, 1975-1985, First Assistant U.S. Attorney, 1985-1987, U.S. Attorney's Office, Northern District of Illinois. Fellow, American College of Trial Lawyers. ***PRACTICE AREAS:*** Corporate Criminal Law; Corporate Investigations; Complex Commercial Litigation; Patent Litigation. ***Email:*** dereidy@jonesday.com

WILLIAM P. RITCHIE, born Columbus, Ohio; admitted to bar, 1971, Ohio; 1987, Illinois. *Education:* The Ohio State University (B.S., 1968); University of Virginia (J.D., 1971). ***PRACTICE AREAS:*** Mergers and Acquisitions; Corporate Finance; Takeovers; Corporate Governance. ***Email:*** wpritchie@jonesday.com

MARK P. ROTATORI, born Waterbury, Connecticut; admitted to bar, 1994, Illinois. *Education:* University of Notre Dame (B.A., 1991); Case Western Reserve University (J.D., 1994). ***Email:*** mprotatori@jonesday.com

LEE ANN RUSSO, born Norfolk, Virginia; admitted to bar, 1982, Illinois. *Education:* University of Notre Dame (B.A., 1977); University of Virginia (J.D., 1980). Law Clerk to Judge Kellam, U.S. District Court, Eastern District of Virginia, 1980-1981. ***PRACTICE AREAS:*** Class Action Defense; Complex Business Litigation; Securities Litigation; Commercial Arbitration. ***Email:*** larusso@jonesday.com

PAUL T. RUXIN, born Cleveland, Ohio; admitted to bar, 1968, Illinois; 1977, Ohio. *Education:* Amherst College (B.A., 1965); University of Virginia (LL.B., 1968). Order of the Coif. ***PRACTICE AREAS:*** Public Utility Regulation; Public Utility Rates; Independent Power. ***Email:*** paultruxin@jonesday.com

RONALD A. SANDLER, born Chicago, Illinois; admitted to bar, 1966, Illinois; registered to practice before U.S. Patent and Trademark Office. *Education:* University of Illinois (B.S., 1962); George Washington University (J.D., 1965). Order of the Coif. Patent Examiner, U.S. Patent and Trademark Office, 1963-1965. ***PRACTICE AREAS:*** Patent Litigation; Copyright Litigation; Trademarks; Intellectual Property Licensing; Intellectual Property Portfolio Management. ***Email:*** ronaldasandler@jonesday.com

DEBRA J. SCHNEBEL, born Newark, New Jersey; admitted to bar, 1975, Illinois. *Education:* Allegheny College (B.A., 1972); Northwestern University (J.D., 1975); University of Chicago (M.B.A., 1981). Phi Beta Kappa. Staff Attorney, U.S. Securities and Exchange Commission, 1975-1980. ***PRACTICE AREAS:*** Structured Finance; Commercial Finance; Utility Finance. ***Email:*** dschnebel@jonesday.com

(This Listing Continued)

JONES DAY, Chicago—Continued

PAUL W. SCHROEDER, born Chicago, Illinois; admitted to bar, 1972, Illinois. *Education:* University of Illinois (B.A., 1969; J.D., 1972). Phi Beta Kappa; Order of the Coif. ***PRACTICE AREAS:*** Complex Commercial Litigation; Environmental Litigation; Insurance Litigation. ***Email:*** pwschroeder@jonesday.com

BRIAN L. SEDLAK, born Chicago, Illinois; admitted to bar, 1993, Illinois. *Education:* Northeastern Illinois University (B.S., 1990); Chicago-Kent College of Law, Illinois Institute of Technology (J.D., 1993). Order of the Coif. Certified Public Accountant, Illinois, 1993. ***Email:*** brianlsedlak@jonesday.com

TINA M. TABACCHI, born San Jose, Costa Rica; admitted to bar, 1992, Illinois. *Education:* Miami University (A.B., 1988); The Ohio State University (J.D., 1991). Phi Beta Kappa; Order of the Coif. Law Clerk to Judge Bivins, New Mexico Court of Appeals, 1991-1992. ***PRACTICE AREAS:*** Complex Business Litigation; Pharmaceutical Intellectual Property; Drug and Medical Device Defense; Class Action Defense. ***Email:*** tmtabacchi@jonesday.com

RICHARD K. TOMEI, born Benton, Illinois; admitted to bar, 1987, Indiana; 1990, Illinois. *Education:* University of Illinois (B.S., 1984; J.D., 1987). ***PRACTICE AREAS:*** Health Care Finance; Tax Exempt Bonds. ***Email:*** rktomei@jonesday.com

CHARLES T. WEHLAND, born Baltimore, Maryland; admitted to bar, 1986, Texas; 1993, Illinois. *Education:* University of Virginia (B.A., 1983); New York University (J.D., 1986). Order of the Coif. ***PRACTICE AREAS:*** Environmental Law; Environmental Litigation; Clean Air Act; Clean Water Act. ***Email:*** ctwehland@jonesday.com

JAMES A. WHITE, born New York, New York; admitted to bar, 1985, Illinois. *Education:* University of Chicago (A.B., 1980); University of Wisconsin (J.D., 1985). Order of the Coif. ***PRACTICE AREAS:*** Complex Commercial Litigation; Antitrust; Bankruptcy Litigation; Patent Litigation. ***Email:*** jawhite@jonesday.com

EDWARD B. WINSLOW, born Chicago, Illinois; admitted to bar, 1995, Illinois. *Education:* Boston College (B.A., 1992); University of Virginia (J.D., 1995). Phi Beta Kappa. ***Email:*** ebwinslow@jonesday.com

DAVID L. WITCOFF, born Chicago, Illinois; admitted to bar, 1982, Illinois; registered to practice before U.S. Patent and Trademark Office. *Education:* Stanford University (B.S.E.E., 1979); University of California, Boalt Hall School of Law, Berkeley (J.D., 1982). Tau Beta Pi. ***PRACTICE AREAS:*** Intellectual Property Litigation; Intellectual Property Licensing; Intellectual Property Rights. ***Email:*** dlwitcoff@jonesday.com

OF COUNSEL

DANIEL J. BACASTOW, born Evergreen Park, Illinois; admitted to bar, 1982, Illinois. *Education:* Pomona College (B.A., 1979); Northwestern University (J.D., 1982). ***Email:*** djbacastow@jonesday.com

JOSEPH H. GOLANT, born Chicago, Illinois; admitted to bar, 1966, California; 1999, Illinois; registered to practice before U.S. Patent and Trademark Office. *Education:* University of Illinois (B.S., 1962); University of Chicago (J.D., 1965). Assistant U.S. Attorney, U.S. Attorney's Office, 1971-1973. Lecturer on Law, University of California, Los Angeles and University of Southern California, 1973-1995. ***Email:*** jhgolant@jonesday.com

WILLIAM J. HARMON, born Ottawa, Illinois; admitted to bar, 1979, Illinois. *Education:* Bradley University (B.A., 1972); University of Illinois (J.D., 1979). Order of the Coif. ***Email:*** wjharmon@jonesday.com

WILLIAM S. McKAY, JR., born New Castle, Pennsylvania; admitted to bar, 1972, Illinois. *Education:* Allegheny College (B.A., 1969); Northwestern University (J.D., 1972). ***Email:*** wsmckay@jonesday.com

DAN B. MILLER, born Kansas City, Missouri; admitted to bar, 1994, Illinois. *Education:* University of Kansas (B.S., 1959); University of Texas (LL.B., 1965). *Member:* American College of Real Estate Lawyers. ***PRACTICE AREAS:*** Real Estate Investment; Real Estate Finance. ***Email:*** dbmiller@jonesday.com

JAMES B. RADEN, born Chicago, Illinois; admitted to bar, 1966, Illinois; 1989, Michigan; registered to practice before U.S. Patent and Trademark Office. *Education:* University of Illinois (B.S., 1962); University of Chicago (J.D., 1965). ***Email:*** jbraden@jonesday.com

RONALD S. RIZZO, born Kenosha, Wisconsin; admitted to bar, 1965, Wisconsin; 1967, California; 1999, Illinois. *Education:* St. Norbert College (B.S., 1963); Georgetown University (LL.B., 1965; LL.M., 1966). Co-Chair, Employee Benefits Committee, Section of Taxation, The State Bar of California, 1979-1981. Chair, Employee Benefits Committee, Tax Section, American Bar Association, 1988-1989. Fellow, American College of Tax Counsel. ***PRACTICE AREAS:*** Employee Benefits; Employee Stock Ownership Plans; Executive Compensation. ***Email:*** rsrizzo@jonesday.com

BOYD J. SPRINGER, born East Orange, New Jersey; admitted to bar, 1978, Illinois. *Education:* University of Illinois (A.B., 1975; J.D., 1978). Order of the Coif. ***PRACTICE AREAS:*** Energy Regulation; Energy Acquisitions; Utility Mergers; Energy Project Development; Energy Contracts. ***Email:*** bjspringer@jonesday.com

ROBERT A. YOLLES, born Milwaukee, Wisconsin; admitted to bar, 1965, Illinois. *Education:* Northwestern University (B.A., 1962; J.D., 1965). ***PRACTICE AREAS:*** Debt and Equity Finance; Energy Acquisitions; Mergers and Acquisitions Finance. ***Email:*** rayolles@jonesday.com

COUNSEL

JOHN B. CAROTHERS III, born Cincinnati, Ohio; admitted to bar, 1975, Missouri; 1979, Illinois. *Education:* Denison University (B.A., 1968); Washington University (J.D., 1975). ***Email:*** jbcarothers@jonesday.com

JAMES C. DUNLOP, born West Bend, Wisconsin; admitted to bar, 1991, Illinois. *Education:* Georgetown University (B.S., 1986); University of Virginia (J.D., 1991). Law Clerk to Judge Crigler, U.S. District Court, Western District of Virginia, 1991-1992. Special Assistant Attorney General, Office of the Attorney General, Commonwealth of Virginia, 1997-1998. ***Email:*** jcdunlop@jonesday.com

SUSAN I. MATEJCAK, born St. Paul, Minnesota; admitted to bar, 1986, Illinois. *Education:* Northern Illinois University (B.A., 1983); Loyola University, Chicago (J.D., 1986). ***Email:*** simatejcak@jonesday.com

JANE K. MURPHY, born Western Springs, Illinois; admitted to bar, 1990, Illinois. *Education:* University of Notre Dame (B.A., 1987); George Washington University (J.D., 1990). Order of the Coif. ***Email:*** jkmurphy@jonesday.com

SANDRA BYSTER WEISS, born Chicago, Illinois; admitted to bar, 1984, Illinois; registered to practice before U.S. Patent and Trademark Office. *Education:* University of Illinois (B.S., 1976; M.S., 1977); DePaul University (J.D., 1984). ***Email:*** sbweiss@jonesday.com

DANIEL E. WHITE, born Barre, Vermont; admitted to bar, 1995, Illinois. *Education:* Michigan State University (B.S., 1975; B.A., 1978); University of Akron (J.D., 1987). ***Email:*** dewhite@jonesday.com

ASSOCIATES

STACY A. BAIM, born Detroit, Michigan; admitted to bar, 1998, Illinois; registered to practice before U.S. Patent and Trademark Office. *Education:* University of Michigan (B.S.E., 1995; J.D., 1998). Law Clerk to Judge Carr, U.S. District Court, Northern District of Ohio, 1998-1999. ***Email:*** sabaim@jonesday.com

CARRIE E. BASSI, born Highland Park, Illinois; admitted to bar, 2003, Illinois. *Education:* Georgetown University (B.S., 1997); University of Virginia (J.D., 2002). Law Clerk to Judge Carter, U.S. District Court, District of Maine, 2002-2003. ***LANGUAGES:*** French and Spanish. ***Email:*** cbassi@jonesday.com

MELISSA R. BEITING, born Lexington, Kentucky; admitted to bar, 2004, Illinois. *Education:* University of Notre Dame (B.A., 2001); Georgetown University (J.D., 2004). ***LANGUAGES:*** French. ***Email:*** mrbeiting@jonesday.com

CHARLES N. BENSINGER, III, born Louisville, Kentucky; admitted to bar, 1997, Illinois. *Education:* Bradley University (B.S., 1992); Washington University (J.D., 1996). Order of the Coif. Law Clerk to Judge Brorby, U.S. Court of Appeals, Tenth Circuit, 1996-1997. ***Email:*** cnbensingeriii@jonesday.com

MARC S. BLACKMAN, born Detroit, Michigan; admitted to bar, 1996, Illinois; registered to practice before U.S. Patent and Trademark Office. *Education:* University of Michigan (B.S., 1993); George Washington University (J.D., 1996). ***Email:*** msblackman@jonesday.com

JON-THOMAS BLOCH, born Alexandria, Virginia; admitted to bar, 2004, Illinois. *Education:* University of Virginia (B.S., 1998); University of Chicago (J.D., 2004). ***Email:*** jtbloch@jonesday.com

CASSANDRA L. BOYLE, born Manchester, Connecticut; admitted to bar, 1997, Illinois. *Education:* Texas A & M University (B.B.A., 1994); Harvard University (J.D., 1997). ***Email:*** cboyle@jonesday.com

BRADLEY C. BRASSER, born Grand Rapids, Michigan; admitted to bar, 2000, Illinois. *Education:* Northwestern University (B.A., 1997); Indiana University (J.D., 2000). Order of the Coif. ***Email:*** bcbrasser@jonesday.com

AMY L. COBB, born Duncan, Oklahoma; admitted to bar, 2001, Illinois. *Education:* University of Oklahoma (B.A., 1998); Chicago-Kent College of Law, Illinois Institute of Technology (J.D., 2001). ***Email:*** acobb@jonesday.com

MARK A. CODY, born New York, New York; admitted to bar, 1996, Illinois. *Education:* Dartmouth College (B.A., 1992); St. John's University (J.D., 1996). ***Email:*** macody@jonesday.com

EMILY A. COLANTINO, born Springfield, Illinois; admitted to bar, 2003, Illinois. *Education:* Northwestern University (B.A., 2000); University of Texas (J.D., 2003). Phi Beta Kappa. ***LANGUAGES:*** Spanish. ***Email:*** ecolantino@jonesday.com

LINDSEY D. DATES, born Blue Island, Illinois; admitted to bar, 2003, Illinois. *Education:* University of Illinois (B.A., B.A., 2000; J.D., 2003). ***Email:*** ldates@jonesday.com

RACHAEL E. DEHNER, born St. Louis, Missouri; admitted to bar, 2004, New York (Not admitted in Illinois). *Education:* University of Wisconsin-Madison (B.A., 1999); Yeshiva University, Benjamin N. Cardozo School of Law (J.D., 2002). ***Email:*** redehner@jonesday.com

CATHERINE M. DIETZ, born Warwick, Rhode Island; admitted to bar, 2004, Illinois. *Education:* University of Notre Dame (B.A., 1997); Northwestern University (J.D., 2004). ***LANGUAGES:*** Spanish. ***Email:*** cmdietz@jonesday.com

PATRICK M. D'ONOFRIO, born Elmhurst, Illinois; admitted to bar, 2002, Illinois. *Education:* University of Notre Dame (B.B.A., 1999); Loyola University, Chicago (J.D., 2002). ***Email:*** pdonofrio@jonesday.com

LAURA M. EARL, born Indianapolis, Indiana; admitted to bar, 2002, Illinois. *Education:* Indiana University (B.A., 1991); Northwestern University (J.D., 2002). ***Email:*** learl@jonesday.com

MICHAEL P. EARLEY, born Bremerton, Washington; admitted to bar, 2003, Illinois. *Education:* University of Notre Dame (B.A., 1997; J.D., 2003). ***Email:*** mearley@jonesday.com

SARAH H. EBERHARD, born Chicago, Illinois; admitted to bar, 2001, Illinois. *Education:* Colgate University (B.A., 1994); Northwestern University (J.D., 2001). ***Email:*** sheberhard@jonesday.com

KEVIN P. FERGUSON, born Hammond, Indiana; admitted to bar, 1999, Illinois; registered to practice before U.S. Patent and Trademark Office. *Education:* Wabash College (A.B., 1996); University of Michigan (J.D., 1999). ***Email:*** kpferguson@jonesday.com

MICHAEL S. FERRELL, born Richmond, Virginia; admitted to bar, 2002, Illinois. *Education:* Texas A & M University (B.B.A., 1994); Vanderbilt University (M.Ed., 1997); Loyola University, Chicago (J.D., 2002). ***Email:*** mferrell@jonesday.com

(This Listing Continued)

YELENA FERTMAN, born Kherson, Ukraine; admitted to bar, 1998, Indiana; 2002, Illinois. *Education:* Kherson Pedagogical Institute (B.A., 1983); Indiana University, Indianapolis (J.D., 1998). ***LANGUAGES:*** Russian, Ukrainian. ***Email:*** yfertman@jonesday.com

MINDY A. FINNIGAN, born Independence, Iowa; admitted to bar, 2002, Illinois. *Education:* University of Iowa (B.A., 1999); Indiana University, Bloomington (J.D., 2002). Phi Beta Kappa; Order of the Coif. Law Clerk to Judge Richard L. Young, U.S. District Court, Southern District of Indiana, 2002-2004. ***Email:*** mfinnigan@jonesday.com

JAMES A. FRANCQUE, born Geneseo, Illinois; admitted to bar, 1996, Illinois. *Education:* Northern Illinois University (B.S., 1991); Loyola University, Chicago (J.D., 1996). ***Email:*** jafrancque@jonesday.com

TARA A. FUMERTON, born Iowa City, Iowa; admitted to bar, 2003, Illinois. *Education:* University of Iowa (B.S., 2000; J.D., 2002). ***Email:*** tfumerton@jonesday.com

GREGORY J. GALLAGHER, born Gary, Indiana; admitted to bar, 2004, Illinois. *Education:* University of Notre Dame (B.S.C.E., 1994); University of North Carolina (J.D., 2004). ***Email:*** ggallagher@jonesday.com

CAROL P. GEISLER, born Evergreen Park, Illinois; admitted to bar, 2003, Illinois. *Education:* Valparaiso University (B.A.); John Marshall Law School (J.D., 2003). ***Email:*** cgeisler@jonesday.com

KELLY P. GLAUBERMAN, born Neptune, New Jersey; admitted to bar, 1998, Illinois. *Education:* Harvard University (A.B., 1995); Northwestern University (J.D., 1998). Law Clerk to Justice Coleman, Jr., New Jersey Supreme Court, 1998-1999. ***Email:*** kpglauberman@jonesday.com

ILANA GLAZIER, born Detroit, Michigan; admitted to bar, 2000, Illinois. *Education:* University of Michigan (B.A., 1997); University of Chicago (J.D., 2000). Phi Beta Kappa. ***Email:*** iglazier@jonesday.com

REBECCA L. GRAINES, born Chicago, Illinois; admitted to bar, 2002, Illinois. *Education:* University of Michigan (B.A., 1999); Chicago-Kent College of Law (J.D., 2002). Order of the Coif. ***Email:*** rgraines@jonesday.com

ROBERT C. GRIFFITH, born Philadelphia, Pennsylvania; admitted to bar, 2002, Illinois. *Education:* Carleton College (B.A., 1990); Indiana University (J.D., 2002). Order of the Coif. ***Email:*** rgriffith@jonesday.com

ALICIA M. HAWLEY, born Freeport, Illinois; admitted to bar, 2002, Illinois. *Education:* Miami University (B.A., 1998); Northwestern University (J.D., 2002). ***LANGUAGES:*** French. ***Email:*** ahawley@jonesday.com

TIMOTHY J. HEVERIN, born Bergenfield, New Jersey; admitted to bar, 1997, Illinois. *Education:* University of Notre Dame (B.S., 1991; J.D., 1997). ***Email:*** tjheverin@jonesday.com

MORGAN R. HIRST, born Pontiac, Illinois; admitted to bar, 2001, Illinois. *Education:* Indiana University (B.A., 1998); University of Illinois (J.D., 2001). ***Email:*** mhirst@jonesday.com

CHARLES E. JUISTER, born Elgin, Illinois; admitted to bar, 2001, Illinois. *Education:* University of Illinois (B.S.M.E., 1990); Northwestern University (J.D., 2001). Tau Beta Pi; Order of the Coif. ***Email:*** cejuister@jonesday.com

MATTHEW D. KELLAM, born Winamac, Indiana; admitted to bar, 2001, Illinois; registered to practice before U.S. Patent and Trademark Office. *Education:* University of Notre Dame (B.S., 1997); Indiana University (J.D., 2001). Order of the Coif. ***Email:*** mkellam@jonesday.com

MARY M. KIMURA, born Honolulu, Hawaii; admitted to bar, 2000, Illinois. *Education:* Georgetown University (B.S.F.S., 1997); University of Chicago (J.D., 2000). Phi Beta Kappa. ***Email:*** mmkimura@jonesday.com

BRENT D. KNIGHT, born Mount Clemens, Michigan; admitted to bar, 1998, Illinois. *Education:* University of Michigan (B.A., 1994; J.D., 1998). Order of the Coif. ***Email:*** bdknight@jonesday.com

ROBERT E. KREBS, born Silver Spring, Maryland; admitted to bar, 2002, Illinois. *Education:* Trinity College (B.A., 1993); University of California, Davis (J.D., 2002). Order of the Coif. ***Email:*** rkrebs@jonesday.com

KRISTAN Q. LADEN, born South Bend, Indiana; admitted to bar, 1996, Illinois. *Education:* Boston College (B.A., 1991); Chicago-Kent College of Law, Illinois Institute of Technology (J.D., 1996). ***Email:*** kqladen@jonesday.com

PHUONG T. LAM, born Saigon, Vietnam; admitted to bar, 1998, Illinois. *Education:* University of Illinois (B.S., 1995); University of Notre Dame (J.D., 1998). ***Email:*** ptlam@jonesday.com

JOEL T. MAY, born Fort Wayne, Indiana; admitted to bar, 2000, Illinois. *Education:* Valparaiso University (B.A., 1997); Indiana University (J.D., 2000). ***Email:*** jtmay@jonesday.com

ELIZABETH B. McREE, born Jackson, Mississippi; admitted to bar, 2001, Illinois. *Education:* Davidson College (B.A., 1995); Universite de Lille III, France (Licence Histoire de l'Art, 1998); University of Chicago (J.D., 2001). Phi Beta Kappa. ***LANGUAGES:*** French. ***Email:*** emcree@jonesday.com

AMANDA E. MEYERS, born Buffalo, New York; admitted to bar, 1999, Illinois. *Education:* Georgetown University (B.A., 1995; M.A., 1996; J.D., 1999). Law Clerk to Judge Leinenweber, U.S. District Court, Northern District of Illinois, 1999-2000. ***LANGUAGES:*** Spanish. ***Email:*** ameyers@jonesday.com

NENAD M. MILENKOVICH, born Cleveland, Ohio; admitted to bar, 2000, Illinois. *Education:* The Ohio State University (B.S., 1992); University of Illinois (Doctor of Pharmacy, 1997); John Marshall Law School (J.D., 2000). ***LANGUAGES:*** Serbo-Croatian, Spanish. ***Email:*** nmmilenkovich@jonesday.com

MICHELLE L. MILLER, born Crawford, Wisconsin; admitted to bar, 2002, Wisconsin and Illinois. *Education:* University of Wisconsin, Madison (B.S., 1999; J.D., 2002). Order of the Coif. ***Email:*** michellemiller@jonesday.com

(This Listing Continued)

JOHN K. MIN, born Seoul, Republic of Korea; admitted to bar, 2004, Illinois. *Education:* University of Chicago (B.A., 2001; J.D., 2004). ***LANGUAGES:*** Korean. ***Email:*** jmin@jonesday.com

J. RYAN MITCHELL, born Santa Monica, California; admitted to bar, 1999, Illinois. *Education:* University of Utah (B.S., 1996); University of Nebraska (J.D., 1999). ***Email:*** jrmitchell@jonesday.com

THOMAS N. MOLINS, born Chicago, Illinois; admitted to bar, 1993, Illinois; 1994, New York; 1995, Massachusetts. *Education:* Georgetown University (B.A., 1989; LL.M., 1994); University of San Diego (J.D., 1993). Attorney Advisor to Judge Fay, U.S. Tax Court, February-June, 1995. ***LANGUAGES:*** Spanish. ***Email:*** tnmolins@jonesday.com

KENDRA L. MORRILL, born Stamford, Connecticut; admitted to bar, 1994, Illinois. *Education:* University of Notre Dame (B.A., 1989); Chicago-Kent College of Law, Illinois Institute of Technology (J.D., 1994). Law Clerk: to Judge O'Connell and Judge Trafelet, Circuit Court of Cook County, 1994-1995; to Judge Alesia, U.S. District Court, Northern District of Illinois, 1995-1997. ***Email:*** klmorrill@jonesday.com

TRISHA L. MOWBRAY, born Buffalo, New York; admitted to bar, 2004, Illinois. *Education:* University of North Carolina (B.A., B.A., 2000); University of Michigan (J.D., 2004). ***Email:*** tlmowbray@jonesday.com

BRIAN S. MULCAHY, born Royal Oak, Michigan; admitted to bar, 2002, Illinois. *Education:* University of Michigan (B.B.A., 1999; J.D., 2001). ***Email:*** bmulcahy@jonesday.com

BRIAN J. MURRAY, born Akron, Ohio; admitted to bar, 2000, Illinois; 2002, District of Columbia; registered to practice before U.S. Patent and Trademark Office. *Education:* University of Notre Dame (B.S., 1997; J.D., 2000). Tau Beta Pi. Law Clerk to: Judge O'Scannlain, U.S. Court of Appeals, Ninth Circuit, 2001-2002; Justice Scalia, U.S. Supreme Court, 2002-2003. ***Email:*** bjmurray@jonesday.com

KELLY M. NEFF, born Daegu, Korea; admitted to bar, 2003, Illinois. *Education:* DePaul University (B.A., 2000); Chicago-Kent College of Law (J.D., 2003). Order of the Coif. ***Email:*** kneff@jonesday.com

JOHN D. NEUMANN, born Hinsdale, Illinois; admitted to bar, 1999, Illinois and Wisconsin. *Education:* Washington and Lee University (B.A., 1993); University of Wisconsin (J.D., 1999). ***Email:*** jdneumann@jonesday.com

BETH A. O'CONNOR, born Detroit, Michigan; admitted to bar, 1998, Illinois. *Education:* University of Michigan (A.B., 1993; J.D., 1998). ***Email:*** baoconnor@jonesday.com

HEATHER M. O'SHEA, born Garden City, Michigan; admitted to bar, 1995, Texas; 1999, District of Columbia (Not admitted in Illinois). *Education:* Texas Christian University (B.S., 1992); Loyola University, Chicago (J.D., 1995; LL.M., 1999). ***Email:*** hoshea@jonesday.com

GREGORY S. OTSUKA, born Dallas, Texas; admitted to bar, 1999, Illinois. *Education:* University of Illinois (B.S., 1995); Northwestern University (J.D., 1999). ***Email:*** gsotsuka@jonesday.com

NIKKI J. PALMER, born Highland Park, Illinois; admitted to bar, 2000, Illinois. *Education:* Tulane University of Louisiana (B.A., 1997); Northwestern University (J.D., 2000). ***LANGUAGES:*** Spanish. ***Email:*** njpalmer@jonesday.com

KRISTIN L. PARKER, born Adrian, Michigan; admitted to bar, 1999, Illinois. *Education:* The Ohio State University (B.A., 1996); Northwestern University (J.D., 1999). ***Email:*** kristinparker@jonesday.com

JENNIFER PELIC, born Youngstown, Ohio; admitted to bar, 2004, Illinois. *Education:* Saint Mary's College (B.B.A., 1999); Northwestern University (J.D., 2004). ***Email:*** jpelic@jonesday.com

GISELLE M. PÉREZ, born Miami, Florida; admitted to bar, 2004, Illinois. *Education:* Boston University (B.A., 2000); Northwestern University (J.D., 2004). Phi Beta Kappa. ***LANGUAGES:*** Spanish. ***Email:*** gperez@jonesday.com

JOHN T. PERUGINI, born Hartford, Connecticut; admitted to bar, 1996, Illinois. *Education:* University of Notre Dame (B.B.A., 1991; J.D., 1996). Certified Public Accountant, Illinois, 1993. ***Email:*** jtperugini@jonesday.com

MICHELLE S. QUINTOS, born Quincy, Illinois; admitted to bar, 2002, Illinois. *Education:* University of Illinois (B.S., 1999; J.D., 2002). ***Email:*** mquintos@jonesday.com

PAULA S. QUIST, born Genoa, Nebraska; admitted to bar, 2002, Illinois. *Education:* Nebraska Wesleyan University (B.A., 1998); University of Nebraska (J.D., 2002). Order of the Coif. ***Email:*** pquist@jonesday.com

MICHAEL J. RAUSCH, born Madison, Wisconsin; admitted to bar, 2004, Illinois. *Education:* University of Wisconsin (B.S., 2001); Northwestern University (J.D., 2004). ***Email:*** mjrausch@jonesday.com

SHEILA SAEGH, born Cleveland, Ohio; admitted to bar, 1998, New York; 2004, Illinois. *Education:* University of Pennsylvania (B.S., 1993); Case Western Reserve University (J.D., 1997). ***LANGUAGES:*** Spanish. ***Email:*** ssaegh@jonesday.com

ERICKA K. SCARPACE, born Milwaukee, Wisconsin; admitted to bar, 2004, Wisconsin (Not admitted in Illinois). *Education:* University of Wisconsin, Madison (B.S., 2000; J.D., 2004). ***Email:*** escarpace@jonesday.com

LESLIE E. SCHAFER, born Terre Haute, Indiana; admitted to bar, 2000, Illinois. *Education:* St. Louis University (B.A., 1995); Indiana University (J.D., Master of Public Affairs, 2000). Phi Beta Kappa. ***Email:*** lschafer@jonesday.com

EFRAT R. SCHULMAN, born Iaifa, Israel; admitted to bar, 2003, Illinois. *Education:* University of Michigan (B.B.A., 2000; J.D., 2003). ***LANGUAGES:*** Hebrew. ***Email:*** eschulman@jonesday.com

KRISTA S. SCHWARTZ, born Naperville, Illinois; admitted to bar, 1996, Illinois; registered to practice before U.S. Patent and Trademark Office. *Education:* University of Illinois (B.S., 1989); Northwestern University (M.S., 1991); Chicago-Kent College of Law, Illinois Institute of Technology (J.D., 1996). Order of the Coif. ***Email:*** ksschwartz@jonesday.com

(This Listing Continued)

JONES DAY, Chicago—Continued

MARGARET M. SEURYNCK, born Chicago, Illinois; admitted to bar, 2001, Illinois. *Education:* University of Notre Dame (B.B.A., 1995); Northwestern University (J.D., 2001). Certified Public Accountant, 1995, Illinois. ***Email:*** mseurynck@jonesday.com

JOSEPH P. SHEREDA, born Detroit, Michigan; admitted to bar, 1998, Illinois. *Education:* University of Michigan (B.A., 1995); George Washington University (J.D., 1998). ***Email:*** jpshereda@jonesday.com

KAREY V. SKIERMONT, born New Orleans, Louisiana; admitted to bar, 2002, Illinois. *Education:* University of Nebraska (B.A., 1998; J.D., 2001). Phi Beta Kappa; Order of the Coif. Law Clerk to Justice Gerrard, Nebraska Supreme Court, 2001- 2002. ***Email:*** kskiermont@jonesday.com

TATJANA STOLJAROVA, born Kohtla-Jarue, Estonia; admitted to bar, 2003, Illinois. *Education:* Saint-Petersburg State University (B.A., 1996); Vanderbilt University (J.D., 2003). ***LANGUAGES:*** Russian. ***Email:*** tstoljarova@jonesday.com

MICHAEL G. STROHMEIER, born Frankfurt am Main, Germany; admitted to bar, 1999, Illinois; 2000, New York. *Education:* University of Bayreuth, Germany (First State Examination, 1994); State of Bavaria, Germany (Second State Examination, 1996); University of Illinois (LL.M., 1997; J.D., 1999). ***LANGUAGES:*** German and Spanish. ***Email:*** mgstrohmeier@jonesday.com

ALBERT D. STURTEVANT, III, born Washington, D.C.; admitted to bar, 2002, Illinois. *Education:* Stanford University (B.A., 1994); New York University (J.D., 2002). ***Email:*** adsturtevant@jonesday.com

TAMARA IRWIN TRAVIS, born Muncie, Indiana; admitted to bar, 1998, Illinois. *Education:* Indiana University (B.A., 1994); Stanford University (J.D., 1998). Phi Beta Kappa. Law Clerk to: Chief Judge Barker, U.S. District Court, Southern District of Indiana, 1999-2000; Chief Judge Aspen and Judge Gottschall, U.S. District Court, Northern District of Illinois, 2001. ***Email:*** ttravis@jonesday.com

HEATHER A. VARON, born Columbus, Ohio; admitted to bar, 2003, Illinois. *Education:* Duke University (B.S., 2000); Harvard University (J.D., 2003). ***LANGUAGES:*** Spanish. ***Email:*** hvaron@jonesday.com

JILL S. VOROBIEV, born Oak Lawn, Illinois; admitted to bar, 1996, Illinois. *Education:* Amherst College (B.A., 1993); University of Notre Dame (J.D., 1996). ***LANGUAGES:*** Spanish. ***Email:*** jvorobiev@jonesday.com

ADAM W. WIERS, born Oaklawn, Illinois; admitted to bar, 2002, Pennsylvania (Not admitted in Illinois). *Education:* Calvin College (B.A., 1999); University of Michigan (J.D., 2002). ***Email:*** awwiers@jonesday.com

JASON G. WINCHESTER, born Canton, Illinois; admitted to bar, 1996, Illinois. *Education:* University of Illinois (B.A., 1993; J.D., 1996). Order of the Coif. ***Email:*** jgwinchester@jonesday.com

MEGAN M. WOLFINGER, born Buffalo, New York; admitted to bar, 2000, Illinois. *Education:* State University of New York at Geneseo (B.A., 1997); State University of New York at Buffalo (J.D., 2000). ***Email:*** mwolfinger@jonesday.com

JOHN M. WRIGHT, born Yankton, South Dakota; admitted to bar, 2002, Illinois. *Education:* Duke University (B.A., 1998); University of Virginia (J.D., 2002). ***Email:*** jwright@jonesday.com

MICHELLE YOKOYAMA, born Munich, Germany; admitted to bar, 2003, Illinois. *Education:* Northwestern University (B.A., 1999); Loyola University, Chicago (J.D., 2003). ***Email:*** myokoyama@jonesday.com

KATE L. ZARCZYNSKI, born Dallas, Texas; admitted to bar, 2002, Illinois. *Education:* Northwestern University (B.A., 1997); University of Texas (J.D., 2002). ***Email:*** kzarczynski@jonesday.com

GRAZIA M. ZORUB, born Durham, North Carolina; admitted to bar, 2003, New York (Not admitted in Illinois). *Education:* Duke University (B.A., 1998); Georgetown University (J.D., 2001). Phi Beta Kappa. ***LANGUAGES:*** French and Italian. ***Email:*** gmzorub@jonesday.com

STAFF ATTORNEYS

Wendy A. Aeschlimann
Laura A. Dahl

Languages: French, German, Hebrew, Hindi, Korean, Marathi, Russian, Serbo-Croatian, Spanish, and Ukrainian.

JONES LAW OFFICES

Established in 1997

25 EAST WASHINGTON STREET, SUITE 906
CHICAGO, ILLINOIS 60602
Telephone: 312-236-2112
Facsimile: 312-236-2634
Email: mej@joneslaw.org
URL: http://www.lawyers.com/joneslaw

All Aspects of General Business, Corporate, Partnership and Limited Liability Law with emphasis on Business, Financial and Legal Consulting, Commercial Mediation, Dispute Resolution, Business and Commercial Litigation, Public and Private Bond Finance, Mergers, Acquisitions, and Divestitures, Business Turnaround, Financial Restructuring and Workouts, Commercial Bankruptcy and Reorganizations, Creditors Rights, Contracts, Secured Transactions, Commercial Real Estate including Construction and Mortgage Foreclosure Litigation, Business Succession and Estate Planning, Elder Law.

MITCHELL E. JONES, born New York, NY., July 19, 1952; admitted to bar, 1980, Illinois and U.S. District Court, Northern District of Illinois including Trial Bar; 1982, U.S. Court of Appeals, Seventh Circuit; 1992, California; 2001, U.S. District Court, Eastern District of Wisconsin. *Education:* Long Island University (B.A., 1974); John Marshall Law School (J.D., 1980). Author: "Can a Bankruptcy Court Enjoin the IRS From Accessing the 100% Penalty Against Responsible Officers & Directors of a Corporation that has Filed for Protection Under Chapter 11 of the Bankruptcy Code," Commercial Law Journal, 1985; "Suits Against a State Under the Bankruptcy Code for Retrospective Monetary Relief," Commercial Law Journal, 1986; "Confirmation of Chapter 11 Plans of Reorganization by 'Cramdown' of Unsecured Creditors Despite Retention of Equity Ownership," Commercial Law Journal, 1988. Chairman Arbitrator, Cook County Mandatory Arbitration Program. Partner: Rooks, Pitts and Poust, 1994-1997; Vedder, Price, Kaufman & Kammholz, 1988-1994; Epton, Mullin & Druth, 1985-1988. *Member:* Chicago Bar Association (Member: Bankruptcy and Reorganization Committee, 1982—; Chapter 11 Subcommittee, 1982—); State Bar of California; American Bar Association (Member, Alternative Dispute Resolution Section); Bankruptcy Mediation Panel for The U.S. Bankruptcy Court Northern District of Illinois. ***PRACTICE AREAS:*** Business Law; Private Bond Finance; Public Bond Finance; Commercial Bankruptcy; Insolvency; Financial Restructuring. ***Email:*** mej@joneslaw.org

(This Listing Continued)

LINDA S. KAGAN

MONADNOCK BUILDING
53 WEST JACKSON BOULEVARD, SUITE 1108
CHICAGO, ILLINOIS 60604
Telephone: 312-362-1500
Fax: 312-362-0052
Email: lskagan@speakeasy.net
URL: http://www.lawyers.com/lindaskaganlaw

Appellate and Civil Practice, Family, Domestic Relations and Real Estate Law. Immigration and Naturalization Law.

LINDA S. KAGAN, born Chicago, Illinois, December 25, 1952; admitted to bar, 1980, Illinois and U.S. District Court, Northern District of Illinois Including Trial Bar; 1986, U.S. Court of Appeals, Seventh Circuit. *Education:* Beloit College and Loyola University (B.A., magna cum laude, 1975; J.D., 1980). Co-author with Errol Zavett: "Appeals," Illinois Institute for Continuing Legal Education, Family Law, 1984—. Director, Women's Bar Association of Illinois, 1987-1989. *Member:* Illinois State Bar Association; Appellate Lawyers Association (Editor, The Brief, 1989-1994; Director, 1988-1990; 1996-1998); American Immigration Lawyers Association. ***LANGUAGES:*** Spanish.

PENNY NATHAN KAHAN & ASSOCIATES, LTD.

208 SOUTH LASALLE STREET
SUITE 1660
CHICAGO, ILLINOIS 60604
Telephone: 312-855-1660
Fax: 312-855-1431
URL: http://www.lawyers.com/pennykahanlaw
Email: pnkahan@pnkahan.com
URL: http://www.pnkahan.com

Employment Contracts, Employment Litigation, Severance Agreements, Executive Employment Agreements, Alternative Dispute Resolution, Expatriate Employment Issues, Counseling on Employment-Related Problems, Disability Accommodation, Discrimination, Sexual Harassment and Wrongful Termination, Family and Medical Leave Act, Americans with Disabilities Act.

FIRM PROFILE: Represents individuals in resolving workplace problems; negotiating and drafting executive and professionals' employment contracts and separation packages; alternative dispute resolution and mediation; litigation and trial of all employment related cases including; statutory discrimination, common law contract claims, restrictive covenants and employment-based torts.

In 2002, Ms. Kahan completed the Employment Law Mediator training program sponsored by the Alliance for Education in Dispute Resolution and the Cornell/Perc Institute on Conflict Resolution.

PENNY NATHAN KAHAN, born Chicago, Illinois; admitted to bar, 1979, Illinois, U.S. District Court, Northern District of Illinois including Trial Bar and U.S. Court of Appeals, Seventh Circuit. *Education:* Roosevelt University (B.A., 1966); University of Chicago; Boalt Hall School of Law, University of California (J.D., 1978). Selected as an Illinois Super Lawyer and one of the top 50 female lawyers in Illinois, May 2005. Recognized as a "Leading American Attorney" in employment law since 2002. Fellow of the College of Labor and Employment Lawyers, 2000. Fellow, American Bar Foundation, 2002. Author: "Summary Judgment in Employment Cases: When and Why?", American Law Institute American Bar Association Continuing Legal Education Course of Study (Sept. 2005); "Harassment Law Update," American Law Institute American Bar Association Continuing Legal Education Course of Study (Sept. 2005); "Mediation as a Model for Resolving Employment Disputes in the New Millennium," 1*Employee Rights Quarterly*4 (Spring 2001); "Jury Science: Focus Groups and Mock Jury Trials in Trial Preparation" Chapter in *Litigating the Sexual Harassment Case*, Second Edition, (ABA 2000); "Evaluation and Investigation of Discharge Claims: Employee's Perspective," Employment Termination Handbook, Illinois Institute for Continuing Legal Education, 1994; "Privacy Issues," *Employment Discrimination and Employment Termination*, Illinois Institute for Continuing Legal Education (1990); "Evaluating the Plaintiff's Employment Case," *Employment Termination and Related Workplace Issues Handbook*, Illinois Institute for Continuing Legal Education, Supplement (May 1998); Employment Litigation: *Forms and Publications*, Mathew Bender, 1991; Civil Rights Litigation and Attorney Fees Annual Handbook, Volume VI, Clark Boardman Co., Ltd., 1990. Editorial Advisory Board, 1997-Present, *Estimating and Proving Damages in Employment Cases*, James Publishing. Recent Speeches: *Employee Rights and Employment Policy Law Journal*, Chicago Kent College of Law. NELA

(This Listing Continued)

14th Annual Convention, "Taking a Deep Breath, Stress Management for the Plaintiff's Employment Lawyer," June 2003, Vail, Colorado; PLI-31st Annual Institute on Employment Law, "How to Win a Motion for Summary Judgment in Discrimination or Harassment Retaliation Cases," September 30, 2002, Chicago, Illinois; PLI-32nd Annual Institute on Employment Law, "Discovery Issues in Employment Discrimination Cases," October 2003, Chicago, Illinois; ABA Annual Meeting, "The 'Rambo' Adversary: How to Deal with Difficult or Unethical Opposing Counsel," August 2001, Chicago, Illinois; "Sexual Harassment Law Update" American Psychiatric Association Annual Meeting, Chicago, Illinois, May 17, 2000; "Successful Negotiation Techniques for Employment Cases" National Employment Lawyers Association Annual Convention, Washington D.C., June 23, 2000; The Twelfth Annual EEO Conference, "Effectively Handling and Resolving EEO Disagreements," May 13, 1999; Panelist, "Current Developments in Employment Law," ALI-ABA, July 23-25, 1998, 1999, 2001, Sante Fe, New Mexico; "Accommodations of Religious Beliefs and Practices in the Workplace," Decalogue Society, June 10, 1998; EEO Mediation Conference, Loyola University, Institute of Human Resources and Industrial Relations; Workshop in "Case Selection and Preparation for Mediation," Chicago, Illinois, April 24, 1997; "How to Win a Motion for Summary Judgment in Discrimination or Harassment Retaliation Cases," Practicing Law Institute 31st Annual Institute on Employment Law, Chicago, Illinois, November 7, 2002; "Discovery Issues in Employment Discriminatioin Cases - Including Views from the Bench," Practicing Law Institute 32nd Annual Institute on Employment Law, Chicago, Illinois, October 20, 2003; "Deposition of Adverse Party Witness in Sexual Harassment and Hostile Work Environment," Chicago Bar Association Young Lawyers Section, Chicago, Illinois, March 5, 2004; Panelist, "Training on Breast Cancer and Legal Advocacy," ABA Commission on Women and The Women's Bar Association of Illinois, Chicago, Illinois, October 29, 2004; "Settling the Case: Strategies for Negotiating the Best Outcome for Your Client," National Employment Lawyers Association Litigating Harassment Claims, Chicago, Illinois, March 12, 2005; "Selecting a Case for Mediation: A Plaintiff's Attorney's Perspective," Nation Employment Lawyers Association Indiana, Indianapolis, Indiana, June 9, 2005. *Member:* Illinois State Bar Association (Member, Labor and Employment Law Section Council, 1990-1992); National Employment Lawyers Association (Member, Executive Board, 1985-1995; Treasurer, 1993-1995; Founder and Chair, Illinois Chapter, 1985-1992); National Employee Rights Institute/Workplace Fairness (Executive Board, 1996-2001); Leading American Attorneys Bar Association. ***REPORTED CASES:*** Dinkins v. Varsity Contractors, Inc., 2005 WL599979 (N.D. Ill. 2005) (denying defendant's partial motion for summary judgment on FMLA claim); Bowers v. Radiological Society of North America, 2000 WL 716036 (N.D. Ill. March 18, 2000)(denial of defendant's motion for summary judgement); Hall v. Carlson, 1987 WL 6298 (N.D. III. Jan, 30, 1987) and 1985 WL 2412 (N.D. III. Aug. 28, 1985); Hall v. Board of Education, 639 F. Supp. 501 (N.D III 1986); Alexa Belda v. Morse-Diesel, Inc., 1990 WL 207441 (N.D. III. Dec, 1990)(denial of defendant's summary judgment motion); Kirstein and Cook Spring Co., Ch. No. 1984CF699150, 1991 WL 699150, 1991 WL 698581, 1991 WL 698594, and 1991 WL 698150 (Ill. HRC July 22, 1991, May 24, 1991 and Mar. 28, 1991); Kingsbury and Rogers Engineering Corp., Ch. No. 1991 Ca 3706, 1993 WL 818060 (Ill. HRC May 7, 1993); Albert M. Vajda v. Arthur Andersen & Company, 253 III. App. 3d, 345 (1st Dist. 1993); Bristow v. Drake Street Inc., 41 F.3d 345 (7th Cir. 1995); Lynn v. Acme Metals, Inc., No. 94 C 5633, 1995 WL 472747, 1995 WL 370230 (N.D. Ill. Aug. 8, 1995 and June 20, 1995); Verdict; Linda Place v. Abbot Laboratories, Jury Verdict of $500, 000 December 1998, Sexual Harrassment/Retaliation, Northern District of Illinois. ***PRACTICE AREAS:*** Executive Employment Law. ***Email:*** pnkahan@pnkahan.com

---

KRISTIN M. CASE, born Kansas City, Missouri, March 24, 1975; admitted to bar, 2000, Missouri; 2001, Illinois. *Education:* Central Missouri State University (B.S., 1997); University of Missouri School of Law (J.D., 2000). Co-Chair, YLS Labor and Employment Committee. *Member:* Co-Chair of the YLS Labor and Employment Committee; Chicago and Illinois State Bar Associations; National Employment Lawyers Association (Member, Illinois Chapter). ***PRACTICE AREAS:*** Employment Law. ***Email:*** kcase@pnkahan.com

LEGAL SUPPORT PERSONNEL

DEBI AGOSTINELLI. Email: dra@pnkahan.com

YLDA KOPKA, born 1979. *Education:* University of Illinois (B.A., 2002); Chicago-Kent College of Law. (Law Clerk). ***Email:*** yk@pnkahan.com

KALCHEIM HABER & KUZNIAR

134 N. LA SALLE, 21ST FLOOR
CHICAGO, ILLINOIS 60601
Telephone: 312-236-9445; 773-782-3456
Fax: 312-236-7932
URL: http://www.khk-law.com

Family Law, Divorce, Child Custody, Child Support, Modifications.

MEMBERS OF FIRM

MICHAEL W. KALCHEIM, born Chicago, Illinois, February 9, 1943; admitted to bar, 1967, Illinois and U.S. District Court, Northern District of Illinois. *Education:* University of Wisconsin-Madison (B.S., 1965); DePaul University (J.D., 1967). *Member:* Chicago (Member, Matrimonial Law Committee), Illinois State and American Bar Associations; American Academy of Matrimonial Lawyers (Former Vice President, Board of Managers, Illinois Chapter). ***PRACTICE AREAS:*** Family Law; Divorce; Child Custody; Child Support.

MICHAEL A. HABER, born 1952; admitted to bar, 1976, Illinois. *Education:* Roosevelt University (B.A., 1974); DePaul University, College of Law (J.D., 1976). ***PRACTICE AREAS:*** Family Law; Real Estate Law; Corporate Law; Divorce.

PAMELA J. KUZNIAR, born Chicago, Illinois, December 12, 1957; admitted to bar, 1991, Illinois. *Education:* Loyola University (B.S., 1980; J.D., 1991). ***PRACTICE AREAS:*** Family Law; Child Custody; Child Support; Divorce.

KAMENEAR KADISON SHAPIRO & CRAIG

Established in 1931
20 NORTH CLARK STREET, SUITE 2200
CHICAGO, ILLINOIS 60602
Telephone: 312-332-0490
FAX: 312-332-6163

General Civil and Criminal Trial Practice. Bankruptcy and Reorganization, Commercial and Creditors Rights, Probate, Estate Planning, Real Estate, Mechanics Lien, Corporation Law and Federal Practice.

MEMBERS OF FIRM

MAURICE KAMENEAR (1904-1975)

JOSEPH L. KADISON (1907-2003)

STEVEN J. KADISON, born Chicago, Illinois, June 14, 1944; admitted to bar, 1969, Illinois. *Education:* Brown University (B.S., 1966); John Marshall Law School (J.D., 1969). Recipient, Department of Justice Outstanding Service Award from Attorney General, 1975. Instructor, Trial Practice, John Marshall Law School, Chicago, Illinois, 1975-1976. Assistant U.S. Attorney, 1970-1977; Deputy Chief, Special Prosecutions Division, Financial Crimes Section, 1974; Chief, Criminal, Receiving and Appellate Division, 1975; Deputy U.S. Attorney and Chief of Special Prosecutions Division, 1976-1977, Office of the U.S. Attorney, Northern District of Illinois. *Member:* Chicago Bar Association; The Association of Trial Lawyers of America; National Association of Criminal Defense Attorneys. ***PRACTICE AREAS:*** Litigation; Business Law; Commercial Litigation; Personal Injury Law; Civil Law; Criminal Law. ***Email:*** skadison@flamm.com

JOEL H. SHAPIRO, born Chicago, Illinois, February 18, 1949; admitted to bar, 1975, Illinois. *Education:* University of Illinois (B.A., 1971); DePaul University (J.D., cum laude, 1975). *Member:* Chicago (Member, Committee on Bankruptcy and Reorganization, 1977—) and Illinois State Bar Associations. ***PRACTICE AREAS:*** Bankruptcy Law; Litigation; Civil Law. ***Email:*** jshapiro@flamm.com

THOMAS M. CRAIG, born Streator, Illinois, May 25, 1955; admitted to bar, 1983, Illinois. *Education:* Southern Illinois University (B.A., 1977); University of San Francisco (J.D., 1983). *Member:* Chicago Bar Association. ***PRACTICE AREAS:*** Commercial Litigation; Business Litigation; Construction Law; Mechanics Lien Law; Collection Law. ***Email:*** tcraig@flamm.com

REPRESENTATIVE CLIENTS: GE Supply Company, a division of General Electric Company; Revere Electric Supply Co.; Fifth Third Bank; Travelers Express Company, Inc.; York International Corporation.

LAW OFFICES OF SCOTT T. KAMIN

Established in 1995
20 EAST JACKSON BOULEVARD, SUITE 600
CHICAGO, ILLINOIS 60604
Telephone: 312-322-0077
Cell Phone: 312-307-8848
Fax: 312-322-1041
Email: ScottTKamin@aol.com
URL: http://www.chicagodefenseattorney.net

Criminal Defense, Felonies, Homicide, Misdemeanors, Sexual Assault and Wrongful Convictions.

FIRM PROFILE: Respected for his innovative strategies, Mr. Kamin practices criminal law both at the trial and appellate levels. He tries cases at 2650 S. California and the Dirksen Federal Building; he appeals cases before the Seventh Circuit and the Illinois Appellate Courts. In addition to helping people accused of crimes, Mr. Kamin also handles cases involving police brutality and wrongful convictions. Coexisting with his private practice is Mr. Kamin's pro bono activities. He serves on the Board of Directors of First Defense Legal Aid (FDLA), the Young Professional's Board of the Coordinated Advice and Referral Program for Legal Services (CARPLS), The Seventh Circuit Panel of Appointed Attorneys, and the Comite Exigemos Justicia.

SCOTT T. KAMIN, born Chicago, Illinois, June 10, 1966; admitted to bar, 1995, Illinois and U.S. District Court, Northern District of Illinois; 1996, U.S. Court of Appeals, Seventh Circuit; 1999, U.S. Supreme Court. *Education:* Occidental College (B.A., History, 1989); Drake University School of Law (J.D., 1994).

REPRESENTATIVE CLIENTS: Larry Ollins; Omar Saunders; Angel Rodriguez; William Kapp; John Rhoads.

KANE, CARBONARA & MENDOZA, LTD.

ONE NORTH FRANKLIN, SUITE 2700
CHICAGO, ILLINOIS 60606
Telephone: 312-726-2322
Telecopier: 312-726-2425
Email: info@kcmfirm.com
URL: http://www.kcmfirm.com

Commercial Litigation and Business Advice, Government Controversy and Investigations, Administrative Law, Employment Law, Constitutional Law and Civil Rights, Government Contracting, Negligence and Insurance Coverage Litigation.

FIRM PROFILE: Kane, Carbonara & Mendoza, Ltd., was founded in 2000 by attorneys with a depth of experience in representing clients in disputes in both state and federal court and before government boards and agencies. The firm's practice includes litigation and business advice. Clients include public and private corporations, partnerships and individuals.

(This Listing Continued)

KANE, CARBONARA & MENDOZA, LTD., Chicago—Continued

WILLIAM K. KANE, born Gary, Indiana, July 22, 1960; admitted to bar, 1986, Illinois; 1987, U.S. District Court, Northern and Central Districts of Illinois including Trial Bar; 1991, U.S. District Court, Eastern District of Michigan and U.S. Court of Appeals, Seventh Circuit; 1997, U.S. Tax Court. *Education:* Miami University (B.S. in Finance, 1982); John Marshall Law School (J.D., 1986). Assistant, Illinois Attorney General, 1986-1991. *Member:* Chicago, Illinois State, American (Member, Sections on Litigation and Antitrust) and Seventh Circuit Bar Associations. ***REPORTED CASES:*** Chicago School Reform Board v. Martin, 723 NE2d 731 (1st Dist. 1999); Zych v. Seabird, 941 F.2d 525 (7th Cir.1993); Zych v. Lady Elgin, 960 F.2d 665 (7th Cir. 1992); Zapata v. Hartigan, 749 F.Supp 864 (N.D. Ill 1990); Easterhouse v. Dept. of Children and Family Services, 204 Ill.App.3d 312 (1st Dist.1990); Schmerhorn v., Illinois Dept. of Registration and Education, 185 Ill.App.3d 312 (1st Dist.1990); Thillens v. Fryzel, 712 F.Supp. 1319 (N.D.Ill. 1988). ***PRACTICE AREAS:*** Complex Commercial Litigation; Unfair Trade Practice; Anti-Trust; Trade Secrets; Corporate Law; Government Controversy. ***Email:*** wkane@kcmfirm.com

RICHARD M. CARBONARA, born Evanston, Illinois, February 24, 1957; admitted to bar, 1985, Illinois and U.S. District Court, Northern District of Illinois; 1987, Trial Bar; 1990, U.S. District Court, Central and Southern Districts of Illinois. *Education:* Loyola University (B.S., cum laude, 1979; J.D., 1984). Psi Chi. Assistant Illinois Attorney General, 1985-1991. Faculty Member, National Business Institute Seminar, "How To Litigate Your First Civil Trial." Board of Directors, Italian American Political Coalition. *Member:* Chicago and Illinois State Bar Associations; The Association of Trial Lawyers of America; Justinian Society of Lawyers. ***PRACTICE AREAS:*** Civil Litigation; Government; Complex Commercial Litigation. ***Email:*** rcarbonara@kcmfirm.com

ADRIAN MENDOZA, born Chicago, Illinois, August 28, 1968; admitted to bar, 1994, Illinois and U.S. District Court, Northern District of Illinois; 1997, Indiana and U.S. District Court, Northern and Southern Districts of Indiana. *Education:* DePaul University (B.S., 1990); The John Marshall Law School (J.D., 1994). Publications: Defense of Food Contamination Claims (IDC Quarterly Journal, March 2003); The Merry-Go-Round Isn't So Merry: Defending a Playground Equipment Claim (IDC Quarterly Journal, 1997); Product Liability - The Effect Of The Presumption, E. Ruff, A. Mendoza (ISBA Legal Education Series 1996). *Member:* Illinois State and American Bar Associations; Defense Research Institute; Illinois Association of Defense Trial Counsel. ***REPORTED CASES:*** Johnson v. Apna Ghar, Inc., No. 00 C 7752, U.S. District Court for the Northern District of Illinois, Eastern Division, Reversed by, Remanded by Johnson v. Apna Ghar, Inc., 330 F.3d 999, 2003 U.S. App. Lexis 11096 (7th Cir. Ill., 2003); Prevue Pet Prods. v. Avian Adventures, No. 99 C 8317, U.S. District Court for the Northern District of Illinois, Eastern Division; Comcourt Inc. v. Coconut Code, Ins. 2002 WL 1349913 (S.D. Ind. 2002); Swarn v. Pizza King, 2001 WL 1712507 (S.D. Ind 2302); Prevue Pet Products, Inc. v. Avian Adventures, 200 F.R.D. 413 (N.D. Ill. 2001); Johnson v. Apna Ghar, 2001 WL 293134 (N.D. Ill. 2000); Tucker v. Division Sales. Inc. 315 Ill. App.3d 472 (3rd Dist. 2000). ***PRACTICE AREAS:*** Employment Litigation; Commercial Litigation; Product Liability. ***Email:*** amendoza@kcmfirm.com

MARINA POPOVIC, born Belgrade, Yugoslavia, August 31, 1966; admitted to bar, 1992, Illinois and U.S. District Court, Northern District of Illinois; 1994, U.S. District Court, Central District of Illinois. *Education:* DePaul University (B.A., Political Science, 1988); Loyola University (J.D., 1991). Member, Pi Sigma Alpha. Dean's List. Illinois Bar Review Instructor, 1993. Certified Mediator, 2000—. ***LANGUAGES:*** Serbo-Croatian. ***REPORTED CASES:*** Washington v. State of Ill. DCFS 919 F.Supp. U8Z-1996; Oak Park & River Forest A.S. Dist. No. 200 v. Ill. State Board of Education 886 F.Supp. 1417-1995; Lasley v. Godinez 833 F. Supp. 714-1993; Kelly ex rell. Kelly v. State 50 Ill.Ct.Cl. 146-1998; American Janitorial Services, Inc., v. State 50 Ill.Ct.Cl. 208-1998; Charles Robinson v. State 47 Ill. Ct. Cl. 364-1994. ***PRACTICE AREAS:*** Employment Litigation; Commercial Litigation; Construction Law; Labor Law. ***Email:*** mpopovic@kcmfirm.com

---

BEN CAPRARO, born Chicago, Illinois, March 25, 1975; admitted to bar, 2002, Illinois. *Education:* DePaul University (J.D., 2001). Moot Court Trial Team. ***PRACTICE AREAS:*** Commercial Litigation; Government Controversy. ***Email:*** bcapraro@kcmfirm.com

ALLISON SEGER NOBACK, born Chicago, Illinois, July 30, 1977; admitted to bar, 2003, Illinois. *Education:* University of Illinois (B.A., 1999); Loyola University (J.D., 2002). ***PRACTICE AREAS:*** Commercial Litigation; Employment Litigation. ***Email:*** asnoback@kcmfirm.com

BRIAN M. WISHNOW, born Royal Oak, Michigan, March 18, 1978; admitted to bar, 2003, Illinois; registered to practice before U.S. Patent and Trademark Office. *Education:* Johns Hopkins University (B.A., 2000); Vanderbilt University (J.D., 2003). ***PRACTICE AREAS:*** Commercial Litigation; Intellectual Property Litigation. ***Email:*** bwishnow@kcmfirm.com

ERIN B. HINES, born Evanston, Illinois, February 8, 1969; admitted to bar, 1998, Illinois and U.S. District Court, Northern District of Illinois; 1999, U.S. Court of Appeals, Seventh Circuit. *Education:* University of Wisconsin-Madison (B.A., 1991); Loyola University (J.D., 1998). Articles Editor, Consumer Law Review. *Member:* Chicago and American Bar Associations. ***PRACTICE AREAS:*** Commercial Litigation. ***Email:*** ehines@kcmfirm.com

OF COUNSEL

DON H. REUBEN, born Chicago, Illinois, September 13, 1928; admitted to bar, 1952, Illinois; 1957, U.S. Supreme Court; 1996, California. *Education:* Northwestern University (B.S., 1949; J.D., 1952). Order of the Coif. Recipient, NU Law Alumni Award for Worthy Achievement in Profession, April 2002. Author: "Our Judicial Election Laws, or How to Have a Lawsuit Without Really Trying," Chicago Bar Record, February 1969; "The Trial of a Condemnation Case-Verdict for $4,825,000 Affirmed," The Trial Lawyers Guide, November, 1970. Co-Author: "Structural Work Act," The Art of Discovery, Illinois Institute for Continuing Legal Education, Library of Congress Card Number 75-2756, 1975. Guest Lecturer on Law, College of the Desert, 2003. Lecturer, Discovery and Practical Legal Ethics in California for the National Business Institute. Member: Illinois Supreme Court Committee on Rules, 1963-1973; Illinois Supreme Court Committee on Jury Instructions, 1963-1968. Special Assistant Attorney General, State of Illinois, 1963-1964, 1969-1972. Counsel for Illinois Treasurer for Congressional, State Legislative and Judicial Reapportionment, 1963. Counsel, Special Session, Illinois House of Representatives, 1964. Counsel to Speaker, Illinois House of Representatives, 1965. Special Counsel to Illinois Legislature, 1965-1967. Member: Visiting Committee of University of Chicago Law School, 1976-1979; Citizens Board of the University of Chicago, 1976-1979; Northwestern University Board of Trustees, 1977—; Pitzer College Board of Trustees, 1979-1983; Committee to study Caseflow Management in the Law Division of the Circuit Court of Cook County, 1979-1988; Advisory Implementation Committee of the U.S. District Court, Northern District of Illinois (to implement Devitt Committee Report, a Committee to Consider Standards for Admission to practice in Federal Courts), 1981-1983. *Member:* Chicago, Illinois State and Desert Bar Associations; State Bar of California. Fellow: American Bar Foundation; American College of Trial Lawyers (Member, American College of Trial Rule 23 Committee, 1975-1982); International College of Trial Lawyers; American Bar Association (Member: Standing Committee of Federal Judiciary, 1973-1979; Standing Committee on Judicial Selection, Tenure and Compensation, 1982-1985); American Law Institute. (Also Practicing Individually in Indian Wells, California). ***REPORTED CASES:*** NLRB v. Catholic Bishop of Chicago, 440 U.S. 490 (1979); New York Times v. Sullivan, 376 U.S. 967 (1964); Pape v. Time Magazine, 402 U.S. 970 (1971), 401 U.S. 279 (1971), 397 U.S. 1062 (1970), 384 U.S. 909 (1966), 375 U.S. 902 (1963). ***PRACTICE AREAS:*** Commercial Litigation; Corporate Governance; First Amendment Law; Professional Responsibility. ***Email:*** dreuben456@aol.com

CHARLES A. BRIZZOLARA, born Chicago, Illinois, November 20, 1929; admitted to bar, 1959, Illinois. *Education:* Lake Forest College (B.A., 1951); Illinois Institute of Technology/Chicago-Kent College of Law (J.D., 1957). Editor-in-Chief, Chicago-Kent Law Review, 1956-1957. Senior Vice President, Secretary and General Counsel, Walter E. Heller, International Corporation, 1972-1985. Member, International Business Law Committee, American Bar Association, 1982—. ***PRACTICE AREAS:*** Corporate Law; Commercial Finance. ***Email:*** cbrizzolara@kcmfirm.com

---

KANE & FISCHER, LTD.

208 SOUTH LA SALLE STREET, SUITE 1800
CHICAGO, ILLINOIS 60604
Telephone: 312-422-7200
Fax: 312-422-7217

Securities, Securities Litigation, Securities Arbitration, Business Litigation, Banking Litigation, Broker Dealer Arbitration, SEC Enforcement.

RONALD P. KANE, born Chicago, Illinois, June 3, 1947; admitted to bar, 1972, Illinois and U.S. District Court, Northern District of Illinois, including Trial Bar; U.S. Court of Appeals, Seventh Circuit; 2004, U.S. District Court, Northern District of Indiana. *Education:* Northern Illinois University (B.S., 1969); Loyola University (J.D., 1972). Associate Editor, Loyola Law Review, 1971-1972. Author: "Section 5 of The Federal Trade Commission Act: An Antitrust Supplement," 2 Loyola Law Journal 306 (1972); "Improper Corporate Payments: The Second Half of Watergate," 9 Securities Law Rev. 703 (1977). Adjunct Professor, Loyola University, 1974-1986. Assistant Regional Administrator (Enforcement), Chicago Regional Office-U.S. Securities and Exchange Commission, 1977-1984. Special Assistant U.S. Attorney for the Eastern District of Missouri and the Southern District of Illinois. Recipient: Frank J. McGarr Award, Chicago Chapter of the Federal Bar Association, 1978-1979; Irving M. Pollack Award, Securities and Exchange Commission, 1982. Member, U.S. Securities and Exchange Commission Alumni Association. *Member:* Chicago, Illinois State, and American Bar Associations. ***PRACTICE AREAS:*** Securities Litigation; Securities Arbitration; Banking Litigation; Business Litigation; SEC Enforcement. ***Email:*** rkane@kfltd.com

DIANE C. FISCHER, born Chicago, Illinois, November 26, 1953; admitted to bar, 1985, Illinois and U.S. District Court, Northern District of Illinois, including Trial Bar; U.S. Court of Appeals, Seventh Circuit. *Education:* Southern Illinois University (B.S., 1975); DePaul University Law School (J.D., 1985). Certified Public Accountant, Illinois, 1980. Branch Chief, Enforcement, Chicago Regional Office, U.S. Securities and Exchange Commission, 1987-1990. Member, U.S. Securities and Exchange Commission Alumni Association. *Member:* Chicago and American Bar Associations. ***PRACTICE AREAS:*** Securities Litigation; Securities Arbitration; Business Litigation; SEC Enforcement. ***Email:*** dfischer@kfltd.com

---

THOMAS A. VOLZ, born Washington, DC, 1969; admitted to bar, 1996, Illinois and U.S. District Court, Northern District of Illinois. *Education:* College of William & Mary (B.A., 1991); Washington University (J.D., 1996). Articles Editor, Journal of Urban & Contemporary Law, 1995-1996. *Member:* Chicago, Illinois State and American Bar Associations. ***PRACTICE AREAS:*** Securities Litigation; Securities Arbitration; Commercial Litigation. ***Email:*** tvolz@kfltd.com

ROBERT C. SCREMIN, born Dubuque, Iowa, October 20, 1964; admitted to bar, 1998, California; 1999, South Dakota; 2003, Florida; 2004, Illinois. *Education:* University of South Florida (B.A., 1994); University of South Dakota (J.D., 1998). Formerly with: Gunderson Palmer Goodsell & Nelson; Law Office of Michael Stepanian. *Member:* American Bar Association; National Association of Criminal Defense Lawyers. ***PRACTICE AREAS:*** Securities Arbitration; Business Litigation; Federal Criminal Law. ***Email:*** rscremin@kfltd.com

JENNIFER L. KLEBES, born New Jersey, 1973; admitted to bar, 1999, Pennsylvania; 2000, U.S. District Court, Northern District of Illinois; 2004, Illinois. *Education:* Rowan University (B.A., 1996); University of Pittsburgh School of Law (J.D., cum laude, 1999). Recipient, Health Law Certificate, 1999. Staff, University of Pittsburgh Law Review, 1998-1999. Senior Attorney, Enforcement, Midwest Regional Office, U.S. Securities and Ex-

(This Listing Continued)

change Commission, 1999-2004. *Member:* Illinois State Bar Association; Hispanic National Bar Association. ***PRACTICE AREAS:*** SEC Enforcement; Securities Litigation; Securities Arbitration. ***Email:*** jklebes@kfltd.com

REPRESENTATIVE CLIENTS: Charles Schwab & Company, Inc.; Wachovia Securities, LLC; H&R Block Financial Advisors, Inc.; Morgan Stanley; RBC Dain Rauscher; Mesirow Financial, Inc.; Bamc of America Investment Services, Inc.; Wells Fargo Investments, LLC.

THE KAPLAN GROUP LTD.

Established in 1967

180 NORTH LA SALLE STREET

CHICAGO, ILLINOIS 60601

Telephone: 312-641-2555

Facsimile: 312-641-6265

URL: http://www.lawyers.com/kaplangroup

General Civil and Corporate Law, Real Estate and Real Estate Taxes, Federal and State Tax Matters, Construction and Mechanics Liens, Merger and Acquisitions, Banking, Non-Profit Organizations, Immigration, Insurance Law, Probate, Personal Planning, Estate Planning, Estate and Trust Administration, Mediation, Estate and Gift Taxes, Employment Law, Employee Benefits, Pension Plans, Profit Sharing Plans, 401(K) Plans, Litigation, International Corporate, Transactional Law. Internal Investigations, White Collar Criminal Process, Securities Litigation, Tax Controversies.

FIRM PROFILE: Our firm provides a broad range of comprehensive legal services that are carefully tailored to each client's individual needs. We pride ourselves on our relationships with our clients--on our thorough understanding of their business operations and on helping each client fully understand and realize their personal and business goals. It is through this understanding that we are able to provide the creative, sophisticated and practical legal solutions that have become our hallmark. Each member of our firm is committed to civic involvement.

HOWARD GORDON KAPLAN, born Chicago, Illinois, June 1, 1941; admitted to bar, 1967, Illinois and U.S. District Court, Northern District of Illinois; 1971, U.S. Supreme Court; 1980, District of Columbia; 1982, New York; 1983, Wisconsin. *Education:* University of Illinois (B.S., with high honors, 1962); John Marshall Law School (J.D., 1967). Certified Public Accountant, Illinois, 1963. Treasurer, Illinois Development Finance Authority. Chairman, Governor's Commission on Discrimination and Hate Crimes. *Member:* Chicago, Illinois State, New York State and American Bar Associations; The District of Columbia Bar; State Bar of Wisconsin. ***Email:*** hkaplan@kp-kg.com

RHONDA D. KAPLAN-KATZ, born Park Ridge, Illinois, May 9, 1963; admitted to bar, 1989, Illinois. *Education:* University of Wisconsin at Madison (B.S., 1985); John Marshall Law School (J.D., 1989). *Member:* Illinois and American Bar Associations. ***LANGUAGES:*** Hebrew. ***Email:*** rkatz@kp-kg.com

BENNETT E. KAPLAN, born Chicago, Illinois, April 13, 1965; admitted to bar, 1990, Illinois; U.S. District Court, Northern District of Illinois including Trial Bar; U.S. Court of Appeals, Seventh Circuit. *Education:* University of Michigan (B.B.A., 1987); Northwestern University Law School (J.D., 1990). Assistant U.S. Attorney, Northern District of Illinois, Chicago, 1992-1999. Staff Attorney, U.S. States Court of Appeals, Second Judicial Circuit, 1990-1991. Commissioner, Governor's Commission on Discrimination and Hate Crimes. Member, Cook County Hate Crime Prosecution Council. Certified Public Accountant, 1992. *Member:* Illinois State Bar Association (Member, Criminal Justice Section Council). ***PRACTICE AREAS:*** Complex Business Litigation; White Collar Crime; Grand Jury Practice; Regulatory Law; Securities Litigation; Internal Investigations; Tax Controversies; Election Law. ***Email:*** bkaplan@kp-kg.com

ASSOCIATE

MERCY T. TANG-TELLEZ, born Taiwan, Republic of China; admitted to bar, 1996, Illinois. *Education:* Northeastern Illinois University (B.S., 1993); Thomas M. Cooley Law School (J.D., 1996); DePaul University (LL.M., 1998). *Member:* Illinois State, Asian American and American Bar Associations. ***LANGUAGES:*** Mandarin and Taiwanese. ***PRACTICE AREAS:*** Taxation; Corporate Law.

OF COUNSEL

KARNIG KERKONIAN, born Chicago, Illinois, May 20, 1972; admitted to bar, 1999, Illinois. *Education:* Harvard University (A.B., magna cum laude, 1994); Cambridge University (International Law, 1997); University of Chicago Law School (J.D., 1999). ***PRACTICE AREAS:*** Corporate Law; Litigation; First Amendment Litigation; Insurance Coverage.

KAPLAN PAPADAKIS & GOURNIS, LLP

180 NORTH LA SALLE STREET, SUITE 2108

CHICAGO, ILLINOIS 60601

Telephone: 312-726-0531

Fax: 312-726-4928

Email: dpapadakis@kpglaw.com

URL: http://www.lawyers.com/kaplanpapadakisandgournis

Professional Liability Defense; Errors and Omissions, Insurance Defense; Civil Litigation; Construction Law; Employment Law; Real Estate Transactions; Business Law.

FIRM PROFILE: KP&G concentrates in civil litigation with an emphasis on professional liability defense cases. KP&G has defended business professionals in errors and omissions cases including mortgage brokers, credit reporting services, insurance agencies, builders, lawyers, auctioneers, appraisers, premium finance companies, trade publications, public adjusters, lenders, market research companies and real estate brokers. KP&G has also defended general liability insurance claims as well as employment practices liability claims. In addition, KP&G serves the needs of individuals, institutions, and insurers on a variety of matters including coverage cases, contractual and business disputes, real estate transactions and municipal matters.

ERIC D. KAPLAN, born Waukegan, Illinois, May 18, 1966; admitted to bar, 1992, Illinois and U.S. District Court, Northern District of Illinois. *Education:* Knox College (B.A., cum laude, 1988); Washington University (J.D., 1992). Executive Articles Editor, Washington University Journal of Urban and Contemporary Law. Author: Note, "Attorney Fee Recovery Pursuant to CERCLA 107 (a) (4) (B)," 42 Wash. U.J. Urb. & Contemp. L. 251 (1992). ***PRACTICE AREAS:*** Civil Litigation; Professional Liability. ***Email:*** EKaplan@kpglaw.com

DEAN J. PAPADAKIS, born Oak Park, Illinois, May 13, 1969; admitted to bar, 1994, Illinois and U.S. District Court, Northern District of Illinois. *Education:* University of Illinois (B.A., 1991); Chicago-Kent College of Law (J.D., 1994). Visiting Student, University of Illinois College of Law, 1993-1994. Member, University of Illinois Law Review, 1993-1994. *Member:* Chicago Bar Association. ***LANGUAGES:*** Greek. ***PRACTICE AREAS:*** Civil Litigation; Commercial Real Estate Transactions. ***Email:*** DPapadakis@KPGlaw.com

DEAN GOURNIS, born Oak Park, Illinois, November 23, 1970; admitted to bar, 1995, Illinois and U.S. District Court, Northern District of Illinois. *Education:* Lake Forest College (B.A., magna cum laude, 1992); University of Illinois (J.D., 1995). ***LANGUAGES:*** Greek. ***PRACTICE AREAS:*** Civil Litigation; Insurance Defense; Intellectual Property; Corporate. ***Email:*** DGournis@kpglaw.com

SPIRO G. ZARKOS, born Oak Park, Illinois, March 18, 1971; admitted to bar, 1997, Illinois. *Education:* University of Wisconsin-Madison (B.S., 1993); Chicago-Kent College of Law (J.D., with honors, 1997). *Member:* Chicago, Illinois State and American Bar Associations. ***LANGUAGES:*** Greek. ***PRACTICE AREAS:*** Civil Litigation. ***Email:*** SZarkos@KPGlaw.com

OF COUNSEL

MICHAEL H. BERMAN, born Brooklyn, New York, March 28, 1945; admitted to bar, 1969, Illinois. *Education:* Loyola University (B.S., 1966); John Marshall Law School (J.D., 1969). Partner, Berman and Trachtman, 1979-1995. *Member:* The Association of Trial Lawyers of America. [Capt., U.S. Army, 1969-1971]. (Also Practicing Individually). ***PRACTICE AREAS:*** Torts; Medical Malpractice; Civil Litigation; Professional Liability.

REPRESENTATIVE CLIENTS: Media Professional Insurance; Euclid Insurance Services, Inc.; Scottsdale Insurance Company; National Casualty Company; AIG; Travelers Property and Casualty; State Farm Insurance Company; Aon Technical Resources; Smurfit-Stone Container Corporation; Box USA Group, Inc.; Oxford Bank & Trust; Associated Underwriters of America; Pacific Construction Services, Inc.; Whirly Centers of Chicago, Inc.; The Scotts Company; Abbott Laboratories; Bax Global; Trader Publishing; La Bamba West, Inc.; Jimmy Johns Enterprises, Inc.; Ozark Motor Lines; Thompson Coburn; DoveBid, Inc.; AccuVal Ltd.; Marlin Energy, Inc. and Daniel J. Edelman, Inc.

KAPLAN, VON OHLEN & MASSAMILLO, LLC

Established in 1988

120 NORTH LA SALLE STREET

24TH FLOOR

CHICAGO, ILLINOIS 60602-2421

Telephone: 312-345-3000

Fax: 312-345-3119

URL: http://www.kvolaw.com

New York, New York Office: 90 Park Avenue, 18th Floor, 10016.

Civil Litigation, Trial and Appellate Practice in all Courts. Aviation, Employment and Labor, Environmental, Commercial, Construction, Insurance and Reinsurance, Mass Disaster, Outer Space, Products Liability, Professional Liability, Toxic Torts and Transportation.

MEMBERS OF FIRM

LARRY S. KAPLAN, born Chicago, Illinois, January 8, 1950; admitted to bar, 1975, Illinois; 1976, U.S. District Court, Northern District of Illinois including Trial Bar and U.S. Court of Appeals, Seventh and Ninth Circuits. *Education:* University of Southern California (B.A., magna cum laude, 1972) Phi Beta Kappa; University of Chicago (J.D., 1975). Author: *Complex Federal Litigation: An Attorney's Guide to Management and Trial,* a book published by Shepards/McGraw Hill. "Space-Specific Remedies for Torts in Outer Space: What Path Will U.S. Law Follow?," International Law Reporter, Winter, 1988; "Allocation of Risk Based on Fault: Is It Feasible for Satellite Losses?" International Bar Association, 1985; "Contribution Among Defendants: How & When to Get It," Journal of Air Law & Commerce, 1983; "Predicting the Application of Vicarious Liability to Fixed Base Operators: Still Guess Work After All These Years," Journal of Air Law and Commerce, Fall, 1981; "Malfunction and Loss of Space Craft," Am Jur Trials, 1991. Co-Author: "Dark Clouds in the Sunny Skies of First-Party Property Insurance: Punitive Damages for Breach of Contract," Trial Lawyer's Guide, Fall, 1979. *Member:* Illinois State, American and International (Vice Chairman, Outer Space Committee, 1987-1989) Bar Associations. ***PRACTICE AREAS:*** Aviation Law; Aerospace Law. ***Email:*** lkaplan@kvolaw.com

ROBERT C. VON OHLEN, JR., born New York, New York, August 7, 1959; admitted to bar, 1984, Illinois, U.S. District Court, Northern District of Illinois and U.S. Court of Appeals, 7th Circuit; 1990, U.S. District Court, Northern District of Indiana and U.S. District Court, Northern District of California; 1991, U.S. Supreme Court; 1994, U.S. District Court, Eastern District of Wisconsin and U.S. Court of Appeals, 4th Circuit; 1997, U.S. District Court, District of Arizona and U.S. Court of Appeals, 3rd and 5th Circuits; 1998, U.S. Court of Appeals, 9th Circuit; 1999, U.S. District Court, Eastern and Western District of Arkansas. *Education:* University of Notre Dame (B.A., magna cum laude, 1981; J.D., 1984). Phi Beta Kappa. Licensed Private Pilot. *Member:* Illinois State and American (Member, Aviation and Space Law Committee; Chairman, Warsaw Convention Subcommittee,

(This Listing Continued)

KAPLAN, VON OHLEN & MASSAMILLO, LLC, Chicago—Continued

Aviation Litigation Section, 1997-1998) Bar Associations. ***PRACTICE AREAS:*** Aviation Law; Commercial Litigation; Insurance Law; Products Liability; Employment Law. ***Email:*** rvonohlen@kvolaw.com

EUGENE MASSAMILLO, born Brooklyn, New York, December 18, 1955; admitted to bar, 1981, New York; 1983, U.S. District Court, Southern and Eastern Districts of New York and U.S. Court of Appeals, Third Circuit; 1988, U.S. Court of Appeals, Second Circuit; 1990, U.S. Court of Appeals, Ninth Circuit (Not admitted in Illinois). *Education:* New York University (B.A., 1977); Fordham University (J.D., 1980). Guide To World's Leading Aviation Lawyers (Euromoney 2004). Assistant District Attorney: Office of the Special Narcotics Prosecutor, New York City, 1982-1983; Richmond County, New York, 1980-1982. Private Pilot's License, SEL, 1993. Instrument Rating, 1995. Vice Chair, Aviation and Space Law Committee, American Bar Association, 1996—. *Member:* The Association of the Bar of the City of New York (Member, Aeronautics Committee, 1988-1992); Aviation Insurance Association; Lawyer-Pilot Bar Association. (Resident, New York, NY Office). ***LANGUAGES:*** Spanish. ***Email:*** emassamillo@bhmr.com

RICHARD A. WALKER, born Tulsa, Oklahoma, July 20, 1955; admitted to bar, 1987, Illinois and U.S. District Court, Northern District of Illinois; 1989, U.S. District Court, Eastern District of Michigan and U.S. Court of Appeals, 6th Circuit; 1991, U.S. Court of Appeals, 7th Circuit; 2000, U.S. Court of Appeals, 9th Circuit. *Education:* University of Oklahoma (B.A., 1977; J.D., 1987). Recipient, Eugene Kuntz-Oxford Scholarship. Member, American Indian Law Review, 1985-1986. Intern, Hon. Alma Wilson, Supreme Court of Oklahoma, 1986-1987. *Member:* Chicago and American Bar Associations. ***LANGUAGES:*** French, Spanish, Italian and German. ***REPORTED CASES:*** In re Air Crash Disaster at Sioux City, Iowa, 734 F.Supp. 1425; In re Air Crash Disaster at Detroit Metropolitan Airport, 791 F.Supp. 1204; Allendale Tulual Ins., Co. vs. Excess Ins. Co. LTD., 992 F. Supp. 270. ***PRACTICE AREAS:*** Aviation; Reinsurance; Litigation. ***Email:*** rwalker@kvolaw.com

JAMES S. STICKLES, JR., born Briston, Connecticut, September 27, 1951; admitted to bar, 1979, Illinois and U.S. District Court, Northern District of Illinois; 1985, U.S. Court of Appeals, Seventh and Eighth Circuits; U.S. Court of Federal Claims. *Education:* University of Illinois; MacMurray College (B.S., 1974); John Marshall Law School (J.D., 1979). *Member:* Chicago, Illinois State and American Bar Associations. ***PRACTICE AREAS:*** Commercial Insurance Coverage; Environmental; Construction; Products Liability; First Parts Property; Warehouse Legal Liability. ***Email:*** jstickles@kvolaw.com

KEITH S. YAMAGUCHI, born Chicago, Illinois, December 15, 1961; admitted to bar, 1995, Illinois, U.S. District Court, Northern District of Illinois and U.S. Court of Appeals, Seventh Circuit. *Education:* Brown University (B.S., 1984); University of Connecticut (J.D., 1994). ***PRACTICE AREAS:*** Aviation Law; Insurance Defense. ***Email:*** kyamaguchi@kvolaw.com

THOMAS C. SOKOL, born Fort Monroe, Virginia, October 4, 1944; admitted to bar, 1995, Indiana; 1996, Illinois, U.S. District Court, Northern and Southern Districts of Indiana and U.S. District Court, Northern and Central Districts of Illinois. *Education:* St. Louis University (B.S., Aeronautics, 1966); Golden Gate University (M.B.A., 1974); Industrial College of the Armed Forces (1987); Indiana University (J.D., 1995). [Commercial Pilot, U.S. Air Force, 1966-1992]. ***PRACTICE AREAS:*** Aviation Litigation; Products Liability Defense; Insurance Defense; Mass Disaster Litigation. ***Email:*** tsokol@kvolaw.com

TELLY ANDREWS, born Chicago, Illinois, November 27, 1972; admitted to bar, 1997, Illinois, U.S. District Court, Northern and Southern Districts of Illinois; U.S. District Court, Eastern and Western Districts of Arkansas; U.S. District Court, Middle District of Florida; U.S. District Court, Eastern District of Texas; U.S. Court of Appeals, Seventh Circuit and U.S. Supreme Court. *Education:* University of Illinois, Urbana (B.A., 1994); Loyola University, Chicago (J.D., 1997). Phi Alpha Delta. Judicial Extern to Honorable George M. Marovich, U.S. District Court. *Member:* Chicago and American Bar Associations. ***LANGUAGES:*** Greek. ***REPORTED CASES:*** In re Estate of Elfayer v. City of Chicago, 325 Ill. App. 3d. 1076 (Ill. App. 1st Dist. 2001); Lie v. Boeing Co., 311 F. Supp. 2d. 725 (N.D. Ill. 2004); MAC Funding Corp. v. Northeast Impressions, Inc., 215 F. Supp. 2d. 978 (N.D. Ill. 2002). ***PRACTICE AREAS:*** Aviation Law; Products Liability; Commercial Litigation. ***Email:*** tandrews@kvolaw.com

NICHOLAS E. PANTELOPOULOS, born Athens, Greece, October 21, 1964; admitted to bar, 1990, Connecticut; 1991, New York, District of Columbia and U.S. District Court, Northern District of New York; 1995, U.S. District Court, Southern and Eastern District of New York; 1996, U.S. Court of Appeals, Second Circuit; 2000, U.S. Supreme Court and U.S. Court of International Trade (Not admitted in Illinois). *Education:* U.S. Merchant Marine Academy (B.S., 1986); Albany Law School at Union College (J.D., 1990); Fordham University (LL.M., Intl. Trade, with honors, 1991). Licensed: U.S. Coast Guard Merchant Marine Licenses, Third Mate; Unlimited Tonnage upon Oceans, 1986; Third Assistant Engineer Unlimited Horsepower, 1986. Proctor in Admiralty, Maritime Law Association of the United States, 1995—. *Member:* American Bar Association (Section on Torts and Insurance Practice). (Resident, New York, NY Office). ***LANGUAGES:*** Greek. ***Email:*** nep@bhmr.com

LAWRENCE MENTZ, born New York, New York, November 5, 1946; admitted to bar, 1973, New York, U.S. District Court, Southern and Eastern Districts of New York; 1974, District of Columbia and U.S. Court of Appeals, Second Circuit; 1977, U.S. Supreme Court; 1980, U.S. Court of Appeals for the District of Columbia Circuit and U.S. Court of Appeals, Fifth and Eleventh Circuits; 1986, U.S. District Court, Northern District of Texas and U.S. District Court, Northern District of California; 1990, U.S. Court of Appeals, Ninth Circuit; 1992, U.S. Court of Appeals, Seventh Circuit; U.S. District Court, Northern District of Illinois (Not admitted in Illinois). *Education:* Rensselaer Polytechnic Institute (B.S., Physics, 1968); University of Notre Dame (J.D., 1973). Author: "Pre-trial and Post-trial Motions," Ch. 23, Federal Civil Practice (Albany 1989); 2000 Air Courier Access Act and Foreign Air Carriers: "Handicapping Regulators," *Air & Space Lawyer (Winter, 2000)*. Member, Task Force, New York State Constitutional Convention, 1996-1997. *Member:* The Association of the Bar of the City of New York (Member, Aeronautics Committee, 1988-1990, 1992-1994); New York State (Member: Committee on Federal Courts; Committee on Supreme Courts, 1986-1990; Member, Executive Committee, 1989—, Commercial and Federal Litigation Sections; Environmental Law Section), Federal and American (Member, Sections on: Antitrust; Litigation; Member, Aviation Law Committee, 1977—) Bar Associations; The District of Columbia Bar. [Ensign, USNR, 1969-1970]. (Resident, New York, NY Office)

OF COUNSEL

ANTHONY W. ECKERT, III, born Montclair, New Jersey, August 14, 1964; admitted to bar, 1989, New Jersey and U.S. District Court, District of New Jersey; 1990, New York and U.S. District Court, Southern and Eastern Districts of New York; 1995, U.S. District Court, Northern District of New York (Not admitted in Illinois). *Education:* St. Lawrence University (B.A., magna cum laude, 1986, Phi Beta Kappa); Boston University (J.D., 1989). *Member:* The Association of the Bar of the City of New York; New York State and American (Member, Litigation Section) Bar Associations. (Resident, New York, NY Office). ***PRACTICE AREAS:*** Aviation Law; Admiralty and Maritime Law; Commercial Litigation. ***Email:*** aeckert@bhmr.com

ASSOCIATES

WALTER L. BUZANOWSKI, born Westwood, New Jersey, September 1, 1978; admitted to bar, 2004, Illinois and U.S. District Court, Northern District of Illinois. *Education:* University of Michigan (B.A., 2001); DePaul University College of Law (J.D., summa cum laude, 2004). Order of the Coif. ***PRACTICE AREAS:*** Aviation Law; Commercial Litigation. ***Email:*** wbuzanowski@kvolaw.com

CHRISTOPHER T. CONRAD, born Villa Park, Illinois, May 20, 1973; admitted to bar, 1998, Illinois and U.S. District Court, Northern District of Illinois. *Education:* Michigan State University (B.A., 1995); DePaul University (J.D., 1998). *Member:* Chicago Bar Association. ***PRACTICE AREAS:*** Commercial Litigation; Aviation; Insurance Coverage; Products Liability. ***Email:*** cconrad@kvolaw.com

PAUL H. KUZNETSKY, born Chicago, Illinois, March 20, 1956; admitted to bar, 1981, Illinois. *Education:* University of Illinois (B.A., 1978); De Paul University College of Law (J.D., 1981). ***PRACTICE AREAS:*** Commercial Litigation. ***Email:*** pkuznetsky@kvolaw.com

LUKE C. McHENRY, born Wichita, Kansas, March 15, 1976; admitted to bar, 2003, Illinois and U.S. District Court, Northern District of Illinois. *Education:* Washington University (B.A., 1998); Northwestern University (J.D., 2003). ***PRACTICE AREAS:*** Commercial Litigation; Products Liability.

DANIEL V. SANTIAGO, born St. Louis, Missouri, December, 16, 1970; admitted to bar, 1996, Illinois; 2000, California. *Education:* Northwestern University (B.A., 1993); University of Michigan (J.D., 1996). ***PRACTICE AREAS:*** Commercial Litigation.

TODD M. SARANECKI, born Chicago, Illinois, January 17, 1970; admitted to bar, 1996, Illinois. *Education:* University of Iowa (B.A., 1993); Chicago-Kent College of Law, Illinois Institute of Technology (J.D., 1996). ***PRACTICE AREAS:*** Commercial Litigation; Insurance Litigation; Health Care Litigation; Managed Care Litigation; Aviation Litigation; Complex Litigation; ERISA. ***Email:*** tsaranecki@kvolaw.com

CATHERINE N. TETZLAFF, born Evanston, Illinois, March 25, 1974; admitted to bar, 2002, Illinois. *Education:* Marquette University (B.A., cum laude, 1996); DePaul University College of Law (J.D., magna cum laude, 2002). *Member:* Chicago and Illinois State Bar Associations. ***PRACTICE AREAS:*** Commercial Litigation; Products Liability.

JOHN R. ZILLMER, born Chicago, Illinois, September 12, 1960; admitted to bar, 2003, Illinois and U.S. District Court, Northern District of Illinois. *Education:* University of Illinois, Urbana-Champaign (B.A., 1982); Chicago-Kent College of Law, Illinois Institute of Technology (J.D., 2003). *Member:* Lake County and American Bar Associations. ***PRACTICE AREAS:*** Commercial Litigation. ***Email:*** jzillmer@kvolaw.com

(This Listing Continued)

KARBAL, COHEN, ECONOMOU, SILK & DUNNE, LLC

200 SOUTH MICHIGAN, 20TH FLOOR
CHICAGO, ILLINOIS 60604
Telephone: 312-431-3700
Fax: 312-431-3670
URL: http://www.karballaw.com

Insurance, Reinsurance, Civil Litigation, Commercial Litigation, Insurance Coverage, Environmental Law, Environmental Coverage, Toxic Torts, Products Liability, Directors and Officers Liability Insurance, Fidelity and Surety Bonds, Employment Practices Liability, Labor and Employment, Professional Liability, Legal Malpractice, Accountant Malpractice, Agents and Brokers Errors and Omissions, Design Professional Liability, Architect's Liability, Engineers' Liability, Casualty Insurance, Bankers' Bond, Insurance Defense, Excess Liability Coverage, Bad Faith, Property Insurance.

STEVEN R. APEL, admitted to bar, 1988, Illinois, U.S. District Court, Northern District of Illinois and U.S. District Court, Western District of Michigan; 1989, U.S. Court of Appeals, Sixth Circuit. *Education:* Loyola University of Chicago (B.B.A., 1984); John Marshall Law School (J.D., 1987). Phi Delta Phi. Co-Author: "Managing Risk: An Environmental Engineering Perspective," Proceedings of the National Conference of Environmental Engineers, 1998; "Shop Drawing Review Practices and Procedures, and Available Insurance Coverages," Proceedings of the National Society of Professional Engineers Annual Convention, 1999. ***PRACTICE AREAS:*** Insurance Coverage; Complex Litigation; Environmental Insurance Coverage; Professional Liability Insurance Coverage; Toxic Torts. ***Email:*** sapel@karballaw.com

EDWARD A. COHEN, admitted to bar, 1981, Illinois and U.S. District Court, Northern District of Illinois including Trial Bar; 1985, U.S. Court of Appeals, Seventh Circuit. *Education:* State University of New York at Binghamton (B.S., 1978); John Marshall Law School (J.D., 1981). Associate Research Editor, John Marshall Law Review, 1981. *Member:* Chicago, Illinois State and American Bar Associations. ***PRACTICE AREAS:*** Commercial Litigation; Insurance; Contracts; Business Law. ***Email:*** ecohen@karballaw.com

(This Listing Continued)

RODERICK T. DUNNE, admitted to bar, 1985, Illinois, U.S. District Court, Northern, Central and Southern Districts of Illinois including Trial Bar, U.S. Court of Appeals, Third, Seventh and Ninth Circuits and U.S. Supreme Court. *Education:* Williams College (B.A., 1982); Northwestern University (J.D., 1985). Arbitrator, Cook County Circuit Court Mandatory Arbitration Program. ***PRACTICE AREAS:*** Litigation; Insurance Coverage; Toxic Torts; Products Liability; Construction Litigation. ***Email:*** rdunne@karballaw.com

DENA ECONOMOU, admitted to bar, 1991, Illinois and U.S. District Court, Northern District of Illinois. *Education:* Loyola University (B.B.A., 1988); IIT/Chicago-Kent College of Law (M.B.A., 1991; J.D., 1991). Moot Court Society. Adjunct Professor, Business Law, Illinois Institute of Technology, 1991-1993. ***PRACTICE AREAS:*** Insurance Coverage Litigation. ***Email:*** deconomou@karballaw.com

STACY S. FREEL, admitted to bar, 1993, Illinois and U.S. District Court, Northern District of Illinois. *Education:* Emory University (B.A., 1990); Loyola University (J.D., 1993). Member, Loyola Law Journal. *Member:* Chicago Bar Association. ***PRACTICE AREAS:*** Insurance Coverage; Complex Litigation. ***Email:*** sfreel@karballaw.com

SAMUEL M. GREENBERG, admitted to bar, 1993, Illinois and U.S. District Court, Northern District of Illinois. *Education:* Arizona State University (B.S., 1988); John Marshall Law School (J.D., 1993). Lead Articles Editor, Software Law Journal. Speaker, Seminars for the University of Chicago Hospitals, Cook County Chiropractic Society and Chicago Bar Association Committees. *Member:* Chicago and Illinois State Bar Associations. ***PRACTICE AREAS:*** Employment Practices Liability; Professional Liability; Fidelity and Surety; Directors and Officers Liability Insurance Coverage. ***Email:*** sgreenberg@karballaw.com

LARRY A. HOELLWARTH, admitted to bar, 1983, Illinois and U.S. District Courts, Northern and Central Districts of Illinois; 1999, U.S. Court of Appeals, Seventh Circuit. *Education:* Albion College (B.A., summa cum laude, 1970); Northwestern University (J.D., 1983). Phi Beta Kappa. Member, National Moot Court Team. *Member:* Chicago and American (Member: Insurance Coverage Litigation Committee; Tort and Insurance Practice Section, Professional Liability Committee; Standing Committee on Lawyers' Professional Liability) Bar Associations; Professional Liability Underwriting Society. ***REPORTED CASES:*** Smith v. Newman, 682 N.E.2d 1245 (2nd Dist.Ill 1997). ***PRACTICE AREAS:*** Insurance Coverage; Professional Liability Defense; Professional Liability Insurance Coverage; Attorneys Liability; Accountants Liability; Agents and Brokers Errors and Omissions; Design Professionals Errors and Omissions. ***Email:*** lhoellwarth@karballaw.com

WAYNE S. KARBAL, admitted to bar, 1991, Illinois and U.S. District Court, Northern District of Illinois. *Education:* University of Michigan (B.A., 1983); Northwestern University (D.D.S., 1988); DePaul University (J.D., 1991). Assistant Casenotes Editor, Journal of Health and Hospital Law, 1990-1991. Licensed Dentist, Illinois and Michigan, 1988. *Member:* Chicago and American Bar Associations; American Dental Association. ***PRACTICE AREAS:*** Complex Litigation; Environmental Insurance Coverage; Employment Discrimination; Commercial Litigation. ***Email:*** wkarbal@karballaw.com

MICHELE T. OSHMAN, born Baltimore, Maryland, February 16, 1958; admitted to bar, 1986, Maryland; 1987, Illinois and U.S. District Court, Northern District of Illinois; 2001, District of Columbia. *Education:* Towson University (B.A., 1981); University of Baltimore School of Law (J.D., 1986). *Member:* The District of Columbia Bar; Defense Research Institute. ***PRACTICE AREAS:*** Insurance Coverage; Litigation; Complex Litigation; Mass Torts. ***Email:*** moshman@karballaw.com

JOHN K. SILK, admitted to bar, 1979, Indiana and U.S. District Court, Southern District of Indiana; 1980, U.S. Court of Appeals, Seventh Circuit; 1981, Illinois and U.S. District Court, Northern District of Illinois. *Education:* Yale University (B.A., 1976); Indiana University School of Law (J.D., 1979). Member, Indiana Law Journal, 1978-1979. *Member:* American Bar Association (Member: Torts and Insurance Practice Section; Fidelity and Surety Law Committee; Employer-Employee Relations Committee; Professionals, Officers and Directors Liability Law Committee); Professional Liability Underwriting Society. ***PRACTICE AREAS:*** Commercial Insurance; Fidelity and Surety; Employment Practices Liability Insurance; Directors and Officers Liability Insurance; Professional Liability; Insurance Coverage. ***Email:*** jsilk@karballaw.com

ASSOCIATES

ADAM R. BUNGE, born St. Paul, Minnesota, December 22, 1977; admitted to bar, 2003, Illinois. *Education:* University of North Dakota (B.A., 1999); Northern Illinois University (J.D., cum laude, 2003). Moot Court, 2002-2003. ***LANGUAGES:*** Spanish. ***PRACTICE AREAS:*** Insurance Defense. ***Email:*** abunge@karballaw.com

PATRICIA M.B. CARACCI, admitted to bar, 1996, Illinois and U.S. District Court, Northern District of Illinois. *Education:* John Carroll University (B.A., 1991); DePaul University (J.D., 1996). Member, DePaul Law Review, 1994-1995. Recipient, American Jurisprudence Award. Listed in Who's Who of American Law Students, 1994. Arbitrator, Cook County Mandatory Arbitration Program. Governing Board Member, Field Museum's Field Associates. *Member:* Chicago Bar Association (Member and Investigator, Judicial Evaluation Committee); National Society of Professional Insurance Investigators. ***PRACTICE AREAS:*** Employment Law; Professional Liability Defense; Insurance Coverage; Employment Practices Liability Insurance; Fidelity and Surety. ***Email:*** pbradtke@karballaw.com

LINDA J. CARWILE, admitted to bar, 2002, Illinois and U.S. District Court, Northern District of Illinois. *Education:* University of Louisville (B.S., 1992; M.P.A., 1996); Indiana University School of Law - Indianapolis (J.D., 2001). *Member:* Chicago Bar Association. ***PRACTICE AREAS:*** Insurance Coverage; Litigation; Professional Liability.

DENNIS B. CONDON, admitted to bar, 1991, Illinois and U.S. District Court, Northern District of Illinois; 1997, U.S. District Court, Southern District of Illinois. *Education:* Loyola University (B.A., 1977); ITT/Chicago-Kent College of Law (J.D., with high honors, 1991). Order of the Coif. Notes and Comment Editor, Chicago-Kent Law Review, 1990-1991. ***PRACTICE AREAS:*** Employment Practices Liability Insurance; Insurance Coverage. ***Email:*** dcondon@karballaw.com

(This Listing Continued)

CATHLEEN G. CROWLEY, admitted to bar, 2003, Illinois and U.S. District Court, Northern District of Illinois. *Education:* Regis University (B.A.); John Marshall Law School (J.D.). *Member:* Chicago and American Bar Associations. ***PRACTICE AREAS:*** Insurance Coverage; Toxic Torts.

ALAN P. JACOBUS, born Princeton, New Jersey, December 14, 1968; admitted to bar, 1993, Louisiana; 1996, Illinois; 2000, California. *Education:* Tulane University (B.A., 1990; J.D., 1993). *Member:* Defense Research Institute. ***PRACTICE AREAS:*** Civil Litigation; Insurance Coverage; Bond Coverage. ***Email:*** ajacobus@karballaw.com

CHARLES F. MORRISSEY, admitted to bar, 1997, Illinois and U.S. District Court, Northern District of Illinois including Trial Bar. *Education:* St. Ambrose College (1991); John Marshall Law School (J.D., 1997). Assistant State's Attorney, Cook County, 1997-2001. *Member:* Illinois State and American Bar Associations. ***PRACTICE AREAS:*** Insurance Coverage; Complex Commercial Litigation; Environmental Coverage; Toxic Tort Litigation. ***Email:*** cmorrissey@karballaw.com

PAUL PARKER, admitted to bar, 1981, Illinois; 1982, U.S. District Court, Northern District of Illinois including Trial Bar; 1988, U.S. Court of Appeals, Seventh Circuit. *Education:* Southern Illinois University (B.S., 1978); John Marshall Law School (J.D., 1981). Member, John Marshall Law Review. *Member:* Illinois State Bar Association (Member, Insurance Law Section). ***PRACTICE AREAS:*** Insurance Litigation; Toxic Torts. ***Email:*** pparker@karballaw.com

SUVERNA PATEL, admitted to bar, 2001, Illinois. *Education:* Loyola University (B.B.A., 1998); DePaul University (J.D., M.B.A., 2001). Phi Alpha Delta. Order of the Coif. Dean's List Scholar. *Member:* Chicago and American Bar Associations; Asian Pacific American Law Student Association (Vice-President, 1999-2000). ***PRACTICE AREAS:*** Insurance Coverage Litigation; Environmental Litigation; Professional Liability.

GERALD E. ZIEBELL, admitted to bar, 1996, Illinois and U.S. District Court, Northern District of Illinois; 1997, U.S. Court of Appeals, Eighth Circuit; U.S. District Court, Eastern District of Michigan. *Education:* University of Chicago (B.A., 1981); IIT/Chicago Kent College of Law (J.D., with highest honors, 1996). Order of the Coif. ***PRACTICE AREAS:*** Insurance Coverage; Asbestos Litigation; Commercial Litigation. ***Email:*** gziebell@karballaw.com

REPRESENTATIVE CLIENTS: Certain Underwriters at Lloyds, London; The Hartford Financial Services Group, Inc.; Ace Global Markets, Ltd.; Allianz Underwriters Ins. Co.; Benchmark Professional Ins. Services, Inc.; CNA Credit; Equitas Ltd.; Glaxo Wellcome Insurance (Bermuda) Ltd; SmithKline Beecham Insurance Limited, London; QBE International Ins. Ltd.; Shand Morahan & Co., Inc.; State Farm Mutual Automobile Ins. Co.; The St. Paul Companies.

KARLIN & FLEISHER, L.L.C.

SUITE 1505
111 WEST WASHINGTON STREET
CHICAGO, ILLINOIS 60602-2703
Telephone: 312-346-8620
Fax: 312-346-8743

General Negligence, Trials and Appeals, Medical Malpractice and other Professional Liability, Products Liability, Railroad, Maritime and Aviation Negligence Law and Workers Compensation Law.

FIRM PROFILE: KARLIN AND FLEISHER was founded over 40 years ago and concentrates exclusively in injury litigation on behalf of plaintiffs. The firm has 9 attorneys with substantial support by in-house investigators, paralegals, law clerks and clerical staff. Over 90% of the firm's files are referrals from attorneys who recognize the professional skills and responsiveness of the members of KARLIN AND FLEISHER.

LEO S. KARLIN (1908-1974)

RICHARD S. FLEISHER, born Chicago, Illinois, November 19, 1937; admitted to bar, 1962, Illinois and U.S. District Court, Northern District of Illinois; 1979, U.S. Supreme Court. *Education:* University of Illinois (B.A., 1959); DePaul University (J.D., 1962). Nu Beta Epsilon. *Member:* Chicago (Member: Committee on Medical-Legal Law, 1968-1970; Committee of Unauthorized Practice, 1968-1970; Committee on Negligence Law, 1971; Plaintiff's Committee of MDL 391, 1995) and Illinois State Bar Associations; Illinois Trial Lawyers Association (Member, Board of Managers, 1975—); The Association of Trial Lawyers of America (State Committeeman, 1966-1971); Trial Lawyers Club; Decalogue Society of Lawyers; Maritime Law Association of the United States. ***REPORTED CASES:*** Liepelt vs. Norfolk and Western Railway Co., 444, U.S. 490; Gray vs. American Standard Radiator, 22 Il. 2d 432; Robak vs. U.S.A., 658 F2d 471. ***PRACTICE AREAS:*** Negligence Litigation.

CHARLES V. FALKENBERG, III, born Evanston, Illinois, October 9, 1961; admitted to bar, 1986, Illinois and U.S. District Court, Northern and Central Districts of Illinois. *Education:* University of Notre Dame (B.B.A., 1983); Loyola University (J.D., 1986). Phi Alpha Delta. *Member:* Chicago and Illinois State Bar Associations; Illinois Trial Lawyers Association; The Association of Trial Lawyers of America. ***PRACTICE AREAS:*** Personal Injury Litigation; Negligence; Products Liability; Professional Liability; Worker's Compensation Law. ***Email:*** userND83@aol.com

JONATHAN B. FLEISHER, born Chicago, Illinois, June 8, 1970; admitted to bar, 1995, Illinois and U.S. District Court, Northern District of Illinois. *Education:* Syracuse University (B.S., cum laude, 1992); De Paul University (J.D., 1995). *Member:* Illinois State Bar Association; Illinois Trial Lawyers Association; Association of Trial Lawyers of America. ***PRACTICE AREAS:*** Personal Injury Litigation; Medical Malpractice.

RONALD G. FLEISHER, born Chicago, Illinois, December 25, 1939; admitted to bar, 1966, Illinois and U.S. District Court, Northern District of Illinois; 1979, U.S. Supreme Court. *Education:* University of Illinois (B.S., 1961); De Paul University (J.D., 1966). Certified Public Accountant, Illinois, 1961. *Member:* Chicago and Illinois State Bar Associa-

(This Listing Continued)

KARLIN & FLEISHER, L.L.C., Chicago—Continued

tions; Illinois Trial Lawyers Association; The Association of Trial Lawyers of America; Illinois Society of Certified Public Accountants. **REPORTED CASES:** Campen vs. Executive House, 105 Ill. App. 3d 576. **PRACTICE AREAS:** Negligence Litigation.

JOEL M. KAPLAN, born Chicago, Illinois, June 5, 1947; admitted to bar, 1973, Illinois, U.S. District Court, Northern District of Illinois and U.S. Tax Court. *Education:* University of Illinois (B.A., 1969); De Paul University (J.D., 1973). *Member:* Chicago and Illinois State Bar Associations; Illinois Trial Lawyers Association; The Association of Trial Lawyers of America. **PRACTICE AREAS:** Medical Negligence; Tort Litigation. **Email:** jimbral@aol.com

CHARLES E. TANNEN, born Chicago, Illinois, October 24, 1933; admitted to bar, 1960, Illinois; 1961, U.S. District Court, Northern District of Illinois; 1982, U.S. District Court, Southern District of Wisconsin. *Education:* Wright Jr. College; DePaul University (LL.B., 1959). President, Moot Court Board, 1958. *Member:* Illinois Trial Lawyers Association; American Board of Trial Advocates. **PRACTICE AREAS:** Construction Litigation; Product Liability; Medical Malpractice; Railroad; Common Carriers.

REFERENCE: The La Salle National Bank, Chicago, Illinois.

MARK L. KARNO & ASSOCIATES

Established in 1994

33 NORTH LA SALLE STREET, SUITE 3200
CHICAGO, ILLINOIS 60602
Telephone: 312-701-0090
Fax: 312-701-0600
Email: mlkarno@sbcglobal.net
URL: http://www.karnolaw.com

Wrongful Death, Personal Injury, Premises Liability, Products Liability, Medical Malpractice, Automobile Accidents, Real Estate Transactions, Insurance and Worker's Compensation, Spinal Injury, Head Injury, Pedestrian Injuries.

FIRM PROFILE: The Law Office of Mark L. Karno & Associates includes on staff a Spanish speaking employee.

MARK L. KARNO, born Chicago, Illinois, May 18, 1957; admitted to bar, 1982, Illinois and U.S. District Court, Northern District of Illinois including Trial Bar; 1984, U.S. Court of Appeals, Seventh Circuit. *Education:* University of Illinois-Urbana (B.S., high honors, 1979); Illinois Institute of Technology, Chicago-Kent College of Law (J.D., 1982). Phi Kappa Phi. Author: "Statute of Limitations on Injured Minors' Medical Claims, the Solution," 28 ISBA Tort Trends 3 (July, 1992); "Written Exculpatory Clauses as a Defense to Tort Claims: A Survey of Illinois Case Law and Pointers to the Practitioner," 28 ISBA Tort Trends 4 (March, 1993); "Legal Malpractice Issues Facing the Tort Law Practitioner," 29 ISBA Tort Trends 4 (April, 1994); "House Bill 20 Turns the Petrillo Doctrine Upside Down," 30 ISBA Tort Trends 8 (June, 1995) "Section 143A of the Insurance Code: A proposed amendment," 32 ISBA Tort Trends I (August, 1996). *Member:* Chicago (Chairperson: Civil Practice Committee, Division 1, 1995-1996; Civil Practice Committee, Division IV, 1997-1998) and Illinois State (Member: Tort Law 1989—; Chairperson, 2002-2003; Insurance Law Section Council, 1995—; Standing Committee on Judicial Evaluations, 1998-2000; Co- Editor, Tort Trends) Bar Associations. Fellow, Illinois Bar Foundation. **LANGUAGES:** Spanish. **REPORTED CASES:** Wilson v. Teloptic Cable Construction Co., 314 Ill.App.3d 107, 731 N.E.2d 899, 247 Ill.Dec. 126 (1st Dist., 5th Div., 2000); Walters v. Walters, 238 Ill. App.3d 1086, 178 Ill.Dec. 176, 605 N.E.2d 432; Szymakowski v. Szymakowski, 185 Ill. App. 3d 746, 134 Ill. Dec. 193, 542 N.E. 2d 372 (1st Dist., 4th Div., 1989).

ASSOCIATE

SCOTT DAVID DESALVO, born Chicago, Illinois, January 27, 1969; admitted to bar, 1998, Illinois; U.S. District Court, Northern District of Illinois. *Education:* DePaul University (B.A., 1993; J.D., 1997). Member, Phi Alpha Delta; Evening Law Student Society. *Member:* Chicago, Illinois State and American Bar Associations; Association of Trial Lawyers of America. **LANGUAGES:** Spanish. **REPORTED CASES:** Sal Desalvo v. The Industrial Commission, 307 Ill. App. 3d 628; 718 N.E.2d 572; 1999 Ill.App.LEXIS 611; 241 Ill. Dec.1. **PRACTICE AREAS:** Plaintiffs Personal Injury; Civil Litigation; Workers Compensation; Wrongful Death; Medical Malpractice; Products Liability. **Email:** sdesalvo@att.net

Language: Spanish.

PETER D. KASDIN, LTD.

Established in 1982

120 NORTH LA SALLE STREET, SUITE 1000
CHICAGO, ILLINOIS 60602
Telephone: 312-630-1990
Facsimile: 312-630-1103
Email: pdkltd@kasdinlaw.com
URL: http://www.lawyers.com/peterdkasdin

General Civil Trial and Appellate Practice. Personal Injury, Negligence, Medical Negligence, Professional Negligence, Product Liability, Premises Liability, Construction Injury, Wrongful Death Law, Vehicular Injury Law, Railroad Litigation and Injury, and General Commercial Litigation.

PETER D. KASDIN, born Newark, New Jersey, July 15, 1942; admitted to bar, 1967, Tennessee; 1968, Illinois, U.S. District Court, Northern District of Illinois and U.S. Court of Appeals, 7th Circuit; 1974, U.S. Court of Appeals, 5th Circuit; 1976, U.S. Court of Appeals, 9th Circuit; 1978, U.S. Supreme Court. *Education:* Rutgers University (A.B., cum laude, 1964); Vanderbilt University, University of Tennessee, College of Law (J.D., cum laude, 1967). Order of the Coif; Phi Delta Phi. Member of Staff, University of Tennessee, College of Law Review, 1966-1967. Instructor of Law, University of Illinois, College of Law, 1967-1968. Member, Graduate Teaching Fellowships Appointments Committee, University of Illinois College of Law, 1967-1968. Arnstein, Gluck, Weitzenfeld & Minow, 1968-1981. Senior Partner, Arnstein, Gluck, Weitzenfeld & Minow, 1973-1981. Speaker, Seminar on Trial Techniques, Chicago Bar Association, 1981. Faculty, Illinois Institute for Continuing Legal Education, 1989. Faculty, Trial Techniques, Chicago Bar Association, 1980-1981. Faculty, The Program of Continuing Medical Education, University of Maryland School of Medicine, 1995. *Member:* Illinois State and American Bar Associations; The Association of Trial Lawyers of America; Illinois Trial Lawyers Association; American Society of Law & Medicine. **REPORTED CASES:** Granados v. Harney, 82 L 206; Roberts v. Sears, Roebuck and Co., 573 F.2d 976 (7th Cir. 1978), cert. den. 439 U.S. 860 (1978), on remand 471 F.Supp. 372 (N.D. Ill., 1979), vacated 617 F.2d 460 (7th Cir. 1980), cert. den. 449 U.S. 975 (1980); Von Brimer v. Whirlpool Corporation, 536 F.2d 838 (9th Cir. 1976), 367 F.Supp. 740 (N.D. Cal. 1973), 362 F.Supp. 1182 (N.D. Cal. 1973); Edwards v. Sears, Roebuck and Co., 512 F.2d 276 (5th Cir. 1974); Johnson v. Sears, Roebuck and Co., 303 N.E.2d 627 (Ill. 1973), leave to appeal den.; Rose v. Sears, Roebuck and Co., 299 N.E.2d 95 (Ill. 1973), leave to appeal den.; Smith v. Sears, Roebuck and Co., 95 Ill.App.3d 174 (2d Dist. 1981); Dugan v. Sears, Roebuck and Co., 113 Ill.App.3d 740 (1st Dist. 1983), 73 Ill.Dec.320, 454 N.E.2d 64 (1983), leave to appeal den.; Woolems v. Kastil, 461 So.2d 954 (Fla. 1984); Dillie v. Bisby, 459 N.E.2d 1097, 77 Ill.Dec. 1 (3d Dist. 1984), 121 Ill.App.3d 559 (3d Dist. 1984), 106 Ill.2d 487 (1985), 136 Ill.App.3d 170 (3d Dist. 1985); Hresil v. Sears, Roebuck and Co., 403 N.E.2d 678 (Ill. 1980); Chatham v. Chatham, 370 N.E.2d 50 (Ill. 1977); Sarafin v. Sears, Roebuck and Co., 446 F.Supp. 611 (N.D. Ill. 1978), 73 F.R.D. 585 (N.D. Ill. 1977); Fetta v. Sears, Roebuck and Co., 77 F.R.D. 411 (D.R.I. 1977); Van Jacobs v. Roper Corporation, 97 Ill.App.3d 610 (1st Dist. 1981); Nash v. Sears, Roebuck and Co., 163 N.W.2d 471 (Mich. 1970); Seder v. Arlington Park, 134 Ill.App. 3d 512 (1st Dist. 1985), leave to appeal den. 107 Ill.2d ; Brown v. Tenney, 155 Ill.App.3d 605, 508 N.E. 2d 347 (1st Dist. 1987); Zakarian v. Prudential Ins. Co. of America, 652 F.Supp. 1126 (N.D. Ill. 1987); lead Amicus Curiae Counsel in Hoover v. The May Department Stores, 378 N.E.2d 762 (Ill. 1978). **PRACTICE AREAS:** Civil Practice; Appellate Practice; Personal Injury; Negligence Law; Medical Negligence; Professional Negligence; Products Liability; Premises Liability; Construction Accidents; Wrongful Death; Vehicular Injury; Railroad Litigation; Railroad Accidents and Injuries; Commercial Litigation.

DAVID W. HEPPLEWHITE, born Cleveland, Ohio, September 10, 1951; admitted to bar, 1981, Illinois, U.S. District Court, Northern District of Illinois and U.S. Court of Appeals, 7th Circuit. *Education:* Colorado College (B.A., Pi Gamma Mu, 1973); Drake University (M.A., Beta Beta Beta, 1978; J.D., 1981). Member of Staff, Drake University Law Review, 1980-1981. Law Clerk, Hon. Harold Leventhal, District of Columbia Circuit Court of Appeals, Selected, 1979. Guest Lecturer, University of Illinois. Speaker, "The Evolving Pharmacy Jurisprudence: Changing the Law for a Changing Profession," Drake University Law School and College of Pharmacy and Health Science, 1994. Faculty, American Society of Plastic and Reconstructive Surgery/Plastic Surgery Educational Foundation, Spring Institute, 1996. **PRACTICE AREAS:** Civil Practice; Appellate Practice; Personal Injury; Negligence Law; Medical Negligence; Professional Negligence; Products Liability; Premises Liability; Construction Accidents; Wrongful Death; Vehicular Injury; Railroad Litigation; Railroad Accidents and Injuries; Commercial Litigation.

KATTEN MUCHIN ROSENMAN LLP

A Partnership including Professional Corporations

525 WEST MONROE STREET, SUITE 1600
CHICAGO, ILLINOIS 60661-3693
Telephone: 312-902-5200
Fax: 312-902-1061
URL: http://www.kattenlaw.com

Charlotte, North Carolina Office: 401 South Tryon Street, Suite 2600, 28202-1935. Telephone: 704-444-2000. Fax: 704-444-2050.

Los Angeles, California Office: 2029 Century Park East, Suite 2600, 90067-3012. Telephone: 310-788-4400. Fax: 310-788-4471.

New York, New York Office: 575 Madison Avenue, 10022-2585. Telephone: 212-940-8800. Fax: 212-940-8776.

Palo Alto, California Office: 260 Sheridan Avenue, Suite 450, 94306-2047. Telephone: 650-330-3652. Fax: 650-321-4746.

Washington, D.C. Office: 1025 Thomas Jefferson Street, N.W., East Lobby, Suite 700, 20007-5201. Telephone: 202-625-3500. Fax: 202-298-7570.

Irving, Texas Office: 5215 N. O'Connor Boulevard, Suite 200, 75039-3732. Telephone: 972-868-9058. Fax: 972-868-9068.

Advertising, Anti-Fraud Counseling and Litigation, Antitrust, Apparel and Fashion, Aviation, Bankruptcy, Reorganization and Creditors' Rights, Corporate and Securities, Corporate Governance, Customs and International Trade, Employee Benefits and Executive Compensation, Entertainment and Media, Entertainment and Media Finance, Entertainment and Media Litigation, Environmental, FCC and Telecommunications, Finance and Structured Finance, Financial Institutions, Financial Markets and Products, Financial Services, Health Care, Health Care Compliance, Health Care Insolvency, Health Information and HIPAA Compliance, Hotel and Hospitality, Intellectual Property, Intellectual Property Litigation, Investment Management, Labor and Employment, Licensing and Distribution, Life Sciences, Litigation and Dispute Resolution, Matrimonial and Family Law, Mergers and Acquisitions, Music Law, Private Client Services, Private Equity, Public Finance, Publishing, Real Estate, Real Estate Development, Real Estate Finance, Real Estate Litigation, Real Estate Taxation, Securities, Securities Litigation, Shopping Center and Retail Law, Sports Law and Sports Facilities, Tax Planning and Litigation, Taxation of Financial Products, Technology, Trusts and Estates, White Collar Criminal and Civil Litigation.

FIRM PROFILE: Katten Muchin Rosenman LLP is a national, full-service law firm with offices in the nation's largest centers of business, government, finance and technology. Our 600 attorneys in more than 50 practice areas provide timely and cost-effective counsel to clients in

(This Listing Continued)

numerous industries. We are business advisors and advocates for a wide range of public and private companies, from entrepreneurial, emerging-growth, and middle market firms to global Fortune 100 corporations, as well as government entities and major universities, museums and other charitable and cultural organizations.

Based on a survey of corporate counsel at Fortune 1000 companies, we have been placed on BTI Consulting Client Service A Team. Our leading practices and attorneys have been recognized in Chambers & Partners Guides, Who's Who Legal, Leading Lawyers Network, Corporate Counsel, and the Expert Guides published by Euromoney Institutional Investor PLC. In addition, Corporate Board Member has recognized the Firm based on its survey of CEOs and directors of major public companies.

Katten Muchin Zavis
Rosenman & Colin

PARTNERS

KRISTIN J. ACHTERHOF, born Duluth, Minnesota, October 1, 1965; admitted to bar, 1991, Illinois; U.S. District Court, Northern District of Illinois. *Education:* Macalester College (B.A., Phi Beta Kappa, magna cum laude, 1988); Northwestern University Law School (J.D., 1991). Member, Board of Directors, Northwestern University School of Law Alumni. *Member:* Chicago and American Bar Associations; International Trademark Association. ***LANGUAGES:*** German. ***PRACTICE AREAS:*** Litigation and Dispute Resolution; Intellectual Property Law; Trademarks and Trade Secrets; Technology and New Media; Copyright Protection; Internet and E-Commerce; Music Law; Entertainment and Media. **Email:** kristin.achterhof@kattenlaw.com

JAMES CRAIG ANDERSON, born Detroit, Michigan, December 20, 1961; admitted to bar, 1993, Illinois and U.S. District Court, Northern District of Illinois. *Education:* Michigan State University (B.A., with high honors, 1984); University of Michigan (M.B.A., with distinction, 1989); Northwestern University (J.D., 1993). Phi Kappa Phi; Beta Gamma Sigma. *Member:* Chicago and American Bar Associations. ***PRACTICE AREAS:*** Finance; Reorganization. **Email:** james.anderson@kattenlaw.com

BRIAN D. ANNULIS, born Baltimore, Maryland, December 30, 1966; admitted to bar, 1992, Missouri and Maryland; 1996, District of Columbia; 1997, Illinois. *Education:* Loyola College (B.A., magna cum laude, 1988); St. Louis University (J.D., cum laude, 1992; M.H.A., with honors, 1992). *Member:* Chicago, Illinois State and American Bar Associations; American Health Lawyers Association. ***PRACTICE AREAS:*** Health Care (80%); Corporate (20%). **Email:** brian.annulis@kattenlaw.com

NICOLE NEHAMA AUERBACH, born Bethesda, Maryland, May 14, 1966; admitted to bar, 1993, Illinois and U.S. District Court, Northern District of Illinois; 1994, U.S. Court of Appeals, 7th Circuit; 1997, U.S. Court of Appeals, Eleventh Circuit and U.S. Tax Court. *Education:* University of Wisconsin at Madison (B.A., 1988); DePaul University (J.D., with honors, 1993). Order of the Coif. Moot Court Society. Recipient, Illinois Women's Bar Association Scholarship. Editor, Law Review. *Member:* Chicago Bar Association (Member, Judicial Evaluation Committee); DePaul College of Law Alumni Association; Women's Bar Association. ***PRACTICE AREAS:*** Litigation and Dispute Resolution; Intellectual Property Litigation; Advertising; Promotion Law. **Email:** nicole.auerbach@kattenlaw.com

STEVEN F. BANGHART, born Ann Arbor, Michigan, February 18, 1952; admitted to bar, 1983, Michigan; 1984, Illinois. *Education:* Michigan State University (B.A., 1974); University of Michigan (M.H.S.A., 1976); Thomas M. Cooley Law School (J.D., cum laude, 1983). Member, Thomas M. Cooley Law Review, 1982-1983. *Member:* Illinois State Bar Association (Chairman, Health Care Section Council); American Health Lawyers Association. ***PRACTICE AREAS:*** Health Care Law; Mergers and Acquisitions. **Email:** steven.banghart@kattenlaw.com

SHELDON I. BANOFF, (P.C.), born Chicago, Illinois, July 10, 1949; admitted to bar, 1974, Illinois and U.S. Tax Court. *Education:* University of Illinois (B.S., 1971); University of Chicago (J.D., 1974). Associate Editor, University of Chicago Law Review, 1973-1974. Co-Editor, "Shop Talk" Department, Journal of Taxation, 1984—. Lecturer in Law, University of Chicago Law School, 1989-1992. Chair, University of Chicago Law School Tax Conference, 1993-1994. *Member:* Chicago (Chairman: Federal Taxation Committee, 1985-1986; Chairman, Large Law Firm Committee, 1999-2000) and American Bar Associations. ***PRACTICE AREAS:*** Federal Taxation; Business Planning; Corporate and Securities; Real Estate. **Email:** sheldon.banoff@kattenlaw.com

STEVEN L. BASHWINER, (P.C.), born Cincinnati, Ohio, August 3, 1941; admitted to bar, 1966, Illinois; 1967, U.S. District Court, Northern District of Illinois; Trial Bar, 1982; 1968, U.S. Court of Appeals, Seventh Circuit; 1970, U.S. Supreme Court; 1988, U.S. District Court, Eastern District of Wisconsin; 1990, U.S. Court of Appeals, Fourth Circuit. *Education:* Holy Cross College (A.B., with honors, 1963); University of Chicago (J.D., 1966). *Member:* Chicago and American Bar Associations; Chicago Inns of Court; Lawyers Club of Chicago. ***PRACTICE AREAS:*** Litigation; Business Litigation; Securities Litigation; Employee Benefits and Executive Compensation. **Email:** steven.bashwiner@kattenlaw.com

JONATHAN K. BAUM, born Chicago, Illinois, January 27, 1957; admitted to bar, 1982, Illinois; U.S. District Court, Northern District of Illinois; Trial Bar, 1983; 1988, U.S. Supreme Court; 1983, U.S. Court of Appeals, Seventh Circuit; 1995, U.S. Court of Appeals, Fifth and Ninth Circuits. *Education:* Harvard University (A.B., magna cum laude, 1978); University of Chicago (J.D., cum laude, 1982). Order of the Coif. Law Clerk to Judge Bernard M. Decker, U.S. District Court, Northern District of Illinois, 1982-1983. Member: Law Firm Pro Bono Project; Pro Bono Students America; Youth Organizations Umbrella, Inc. *Member:* American Bar Association. ***PRACTICE AREAS:*** Constitutional and Civil Rights Litigation; Pro Bono Administration; Litigation and Dispute Resolution. **Email:** jonathan.baum@kattenlaw.com

ALAN M. BERRY, (P.C.), born Chicago, Illinois, July 6, 1944; admitted to bar, 1969, Illinois. *Education:* University of Wisconsin (B.S., 1966); Boston University (J.D., 1969). *Member:* Chicago, Illinois State and American Bar Associations. ***PRACTICE AREAS:*** Estate Planning; Business Planning; Investment Management; Corporate and Securities; Private Equity. **Email:** alan.berry@kattenlaw.com

(This Listing Continued)

VICTOR H. BEZMAN, (P.C.), born Chicago, Illinois, December 24, 1941; admitted to bar, 1967, Illinois. *Education:* University of Illinois (B.S., 1963); Northwestern University (J.D., cum laude, 1966); New York University (LL.M. in Taxation, 1967). Certified Public Accountant, Illinois, 1963. Graduate Editor, Tax Law Review, New York University, 1966-1967. *Member:* Chicago and American Bar Associations. ***PRACTICE AREAS:*** Tax Law; Trusts and Estates; Corporate and Securities. **Email:** victor.bezman@kattenlaw.com

CRAIG C. BRADLEY, born September 22, 1958; admitted to bar, 1983, Illinois. *Education:* Elmhurst College (B.S., summa cum laude, 1980); Indiana University (J.D., cum laude, 1983). Adjunct Assistant Professor, Business Law, Kellogg Graduate School of Management, Northwestern University, 1999-2001. *Member:* Chicago Software Association (Board of Directors). ***PRACTICE AREAS:*** Corporate; Mergers and Acquisitions; Securities; Joint Ventures; Strategic Alliances; Partnerships; Intellectual Property Law; Life Sciences; Internet and E-Commerce; Private Equity; Technology and New Media. **Email:** craig.bradley@kattenlaw.com

MATTHEW S. BROWN, born Chicago, Ill., January 29, 1955; admitted to bar, 1978, Illinois. *Education:* Eastbourne College, Sussex, U.K. and Connecticut College (B.A., magna cum laude, 1975, Phi Beta Kappa); Georgetown University (J.D., 1978). Editor, American Criminal Law Review, 1977-1978. *Member:* Chicago and American (Member, Law and Accounting Subcommittee of the Section of Business Law, 1986—) Bar Associations. ***PRACTICE AREAS:*** Corporate and Securities; Corporate Governance; Mergers and Acquisitions; Life Sciences; Private Equity. **Email:** matthew.brown@kattenlaw.com

DAVID J. BRYANT, born Fostoria, Ohio, December 17, 1961; admitted to bar, 1987, Illinois. *Education:* University of Illinois (B.S., 1984); Northwestern University (J.D., 1987). *Member:* Chicago and American Bar Associations. ***PRACTICE AREAS:*** Real Estate Law; Finance. **Email:** david.bryant@kattenlaw.com

DENISE S. BURN, born October 13; admitted to bar, 1984, Illinois. *Education:* Northwestern University (B.A., with honors, 1972); Northwestern University School of Law (J.D., 1984). *Member:* American Bar Association. ***PRACTICE AREAS:*** Bankruptcy; Bankruptcy Reorganization; Creditors Rights; Finance; Financial Services Law. **Email:** denise.burn@kattenlaw.com

JAMES A. BURNS, JR., born Ann Arbor, Michigan, November 24, 1955; admitted to bar, 1980, Illinois; 1981, U.S. District Court, Northern District of Illinois; 1982, U.S. Court of Appeals, Seventh Circuit; 1986, U.S. District Court, Eastern District of Michigan and U.S. Court of Appeals, Sixth Circuit; 1989, U.S. Supreme Court; 1997, U.S. Court of Appeals, Fifth Circuit; 1999, U.S. Court of Appeals, Eighth Circuit. *Education:* University of Michigan (A.B., with high distinction, 1977; J.D., cum laude, 1980). Member: Editorial Advisory Board, Employee Relations Law Journal, 1991—. *Member:* American Bar Association (Member, Employee Rights and Responsibilities Committee of the Section of Labor and Employment Law, 1994—). ***PRACTICE AREAS:*** Labor Law; Employment Litigation; Employee Benefits; Executive Compensation. **Email:** jim.burns@kattenlaw.com

MICHAEL R. CALLAHAN, born New York, N. Y., April 11, 1953; admitted to bar, 1979, Illinois. *Education:* Northern Illinois University (B.A., 1975); DePaul University (J.D., 1979). Note and Comment Editor, DePaul Law Review, 1978-1979. Law Clerk, Justice Daniel P. Ward, Illinois Supreme Court, 1979-1981. *Member:* Chicago and American Bar Associations; Illinois Association of Hospital Attorneys; American Health Lawyers Association. ***PRACTICE AREAS:*** Health Care Law; Corporate; Antitrust; Credentialing; Managed Care; Mergers; Integrated Delivery Systems; Health Care Compliance. **Email:** michael.callahan@kattenlaw.com

DAWN M. CANTY, born Chicago, Illinois, June 21, 1964; admitted to bar, 1989, Illinois; U.S. District Court, Northern District of Illinois; U.S. Court of Appeals, 7th Circuit. *Education:* University of Chicago (A.B., with honors, 1986); University of Michigan (J.D., 1989). *Member:* Chicago and American (Co-Chair, Membership subcommittee of ABA Class Action and Derivative Suits) Bar Associations. ***PRACTICE AREAS:*** Litigation and Dispute Resolution; Insolvency Proceedings; Securities; Technology; Commercial Litigation; Consumer Fraud; Product Liability; Labor and Employment. **Email:** dawn.canty@kattenlaw.com

STUART J. CHANEN, born Evanston, Illinois, September 26, 1959; admitted to bar, 1986, Illinois; 1987, U.S. District Court, Northern District of Illinois, including Trial Bar and U.S. Court of Appeals, Seventh and Ninth Circuits. *Education:* Brandeis University (B.A., cum laude, 1981); Northwestern University (J.D., 1985). Member and Notes and Comments Editor, Northwestern Law Review, 1983-1985. Law Clerk to Hon. John F. Grady, Chief Judge, U.S. District Court, Northern District of Illinois, 1986. Adjunct Professor, Northwestern University School of Law, 1993—. Chairman, Subcommittee on Professional Responsibility, 1995-1998 and Member, Board of Governors, 1992-1995, Chicago Council of Lawyers. ***PRACTICE AREAS:*** Litigation; Alternative Dispute Resolution; White Collar Criminal Defense; Civil Litigation; Media Law; Legal Malpractice; Attorney Discipline. **Email:** stuart.chanen@kattenlaw.com

CHARLES CHEJFEC, admitted to bar, 1996, Illinois; U.S. Court of Appeals, Seventh Circuit; U.S. District Court, Northern District of Illinois. *Education:* University of Wisconsin, Madison (B.A., 1990); John Marshall Law School (J.D., 1996). *Member:* Illinois State and American Bar Associations; American Inns of Court. ***PRACTICE AREAS:*** Litigation; Alternative Dispute Resolution; Intellectual Property; Intellectual Property Litigation; Health Care; White Collar Crime; Civil Litigation. **Email:** charles.chejfec@kattenlaw.com

ERIC C. COHEN, born Toronto, Ontario, Canada, March 27, 1948; admitted to bar, 1974, Florida and Ohio; 1977, Illinois and U.S. District Court, Northern District of Illinois including Trial Bar; U.S. Court of Appeals, Seventh and Federal Circuits; registered to practice before U.S. Patent and Trademark Office. *Education:* Case Institute of Technology (B.S., Physics, 1971); University of Miami (J.D., cum laude, 1973). Member, 1973-1974 and Case Note Editor, 1974, University of Miami Law Review. Frequent Lecturer and Presenter at the Patent Resources Group, the 60 Practicing Law Institute, and the International Anticounterfeiting Coalition. *Member:* Chicago, Seventh Circuit, Federal Circuit and American Bar Associations; Intellectual Property Law Association of Chicago; Licensing Executives Society. ***REPORTED CASES:*** Notable Appellate Court decisions: Hard Rock Cafe Licensing Corp. v. Parvez, 955 F.2d 1143 (7th Cir. 1992); General Electric Company v. Speicher, 877 F.2d 531 (7th Cir. 1989); Midway Mfg. Co. v. Artic International, Inc., 704 F.2d 1009 (7th Cir. 1983). Notable District Court decisions: General Electric Company v.

(This Listing Continued)

KATTEN MUCHIN ROSENMAN LLP, Chicago—Continued

Souris; General Electric v. R Squared Scan Systems, Inc.; John Crane v. Durametallic Corporation, No. 95 C 2840 (N. D. Ill., filed 1995); Jason, Inc. v. Youhan Electronics, Co. Ltd.; Long-Airdox Co. v. Stamler Corporation; North American Philips v. Konami (America) Inc. et al.; Konami(America) Inc. v. Hartford Insurance; Satyan G. Pitroda v. Casio, Inc. et al.; Hard Rock Cafe Licensing Corp. v. Pacific Graphics, 776 F. Supp. 1454 (W.D. Wash. 1991). Representative Litigation Matters: Biovail Labs., Inc. v. TorPharm, Inc., No. 01-9008 (N.D. Ill.); Biovail Labs., Inc. v. TorPharm, Inc., No. 02-7119 (E.D. Pa.); Bayer AG, Bayer Corp. & Pfizer, Inc. v. Biovail Corp., Nos. 98-1282, 98-1340, 98-1492, 98-1768, 01-1205, 01-1206 (D.P.R.); Biovail Labs. Inc. v. Bayer AG, Bayer Corp. & Pfizer, Inc., No. 98-731 (W.D. Pa.); Bayer AG v. Biovail Corp., 279 F.3d 1340, 1345 (Fed. Cir. 2002); Biovail Corp. v. Andrx Pharmaceuticals, Inc., 239 F.3d 1297, 1301 (Fed. Cir. 2001); Novartis Corp. v. Biovail Laboratories, Inc., No. 01-1442 (D.P.R.); General Electric v. R. Squared Scan Systems, Inc., No. 87-249-WS (M.D.N.C. 1987); General Electric Company v. Souris, (E.D. Mich. 1987); General Electric Company v. Speicher, 877 F.2d 531 (7th Cir. 1989); General Electric Company v. Sannet, (C.D. Cal. 1984); General Electric Company v. Hercules Air Products, (D. Kentucky 1984); Finnsugar BioProducts, Inc. v. Amalgamated Sugar Company, No. 97-8746 (N.D. Ill.); Finnsugar BioProducts, Inc. v. Monitor Sugar Corp., No. 00-10381 (E.D. Mich.); Implant Innovations, Inc., v. Nobelpharma AB, 1998 U.S. Dist. LEXIS 15794, No. 93 C 7489 (N.D. Ill., 1998); SPI Lighting, Inc. v. Visa Lighting Corp., No. 96-CV-0585 (E.D. Wis., filed 1996); Jason, Inc. v. Youhan Electronics, Co. Ltd., No. 95-C-0345 (E.D. Wis., filed 1995); Long-Airdox Co. v. Stamler Corporation, No. 2:97 CV 66 (E.D. Tenn., filed 1996); John Crane v. Durametallic Corporation, No. 95 C 2840 (N. D. Ill., filed 1995); Louisville Bedding Company v. Perfect Fit Industries, Inc., No. C-94-0244L(S) (W.D. Kentucky, filed April 12, 1994); Louisville Bedding Company v. Hollander Home Fashions Corp., No. 3:94-CV-0703-D (N.D. Texas, filed April 12, 1994); North American Philips Corp. v. Konami (America) Inc. et al., 93 C 3261 (N.D. Ill., filed 1993); Pitroda v. Casio, Inc. et al., No. 93 C 4991 (N.D. Ill., filed 1993); Fisher & Paykel, Ltd. v. Saratoga Medical, (N.D.N.Y. 1985); Itofca, Inc. v. MegaTrans Logistics, Inc., 322 F.3d 928 (7th Cir. 2003); Mitel, Inc. v. Iqtel, Inc., 124 F.3d 1366 (10th Cir. 1997); Midway Mfg. Co. v. Artic International, Inc. 704 F.2d 1009 (7th Cir. 1983); Conan Properties, Inc. v. Mattel, Inc., 712 F. Supp. 353 (S.D.N.Y. 1989), motion for reconsideration granted in part, 1990 U.S. Dist. LEXIS 16481 (1990); Williams Elects. Inc. v. Bally Mfg. Corp., U.S. Dist. LEXIS 15569 (N.D. Ill. 1983); Midway Mfg. Co. v. Strohon, 564 F.Supp. 741 (N.D. Ill. 1983); 3M Company v. Manufacturers 3M S.A. de C.V., No. 01-8417 (S.D. Fla.); Starbucks Corp. v. Necta Sweet, Inc., 00-1977 (W.D. Wash.); Aliant Communications Inc. v. Interstate Energy, Inc., 4-98-CV-80345 (S. D. Iowa); Hard Rock Cafe Licensing Corp. v. Parvez, 955 F.2d 1143 (7th Cir. 1992); Hard Rock Cafe Licensing Corporation v. Pacific Graphics, 776 F. Supp. 1454 (W.D. Wash. 1991); Hard Rock Cafe v. Hite, No. 91-00101 ACK (D. Hawaii 1991); Cardtoons, L.C. v. Major League Baseball Players Ass'n, 95 F.3d 959 (10th Cir. 1996); Foley Medical v. Fisher & Paykel Medical et al., (S.D. Ohio 1985). ***PRACTICE AREAS:*** Intellectual Property; Intellectual Property Litigation; Litigation and Dispute Resolution; Biotechnology; Manufacturing; Technology. ***Email:*** eric.cohen@kattenlaw.com

TANYA L. CURTIS, born Lexington, Kentucky, November 2, 1965; admitted to bar, 1991, Illinois. *Education:* Indiana University (B.A., 1987); University of Virginia (J.D., 1991). *Member:* Intellectual Trademark Association; Chicago Software Association. ***PRACTICE AREAS:*** Intellectual Property; Electronic Business; Technology and Internet; Corporate and Securities. ***Email:*** tanya.curtis@kattenlaw.com

THERESA L. DAVIS, born Milwaukee, Wisconsin, September 2, 1966; admitted to bar, 1994, Illinois. *Education:* University of Wisconsin-Madison (B.A., with honors and distinction, 1990); IIT Chicago-Kent College of Law, Illinois Institute of Technology (J.D., with honors, 1994). ***PRACTICE AREAS:*** Securities Litigation; Directors and Officers Liability; Employment Litigation; Commercial Litigation; Anti-Fraud Counseling and Litigation. ***Email:*** theresa.davis@kattenlaw.com

W. KENNETH DAVIS, JR., born Cleveland, Mississippi, April 10, 1961; admitted to bar, 1990, Illinois. *Education:* University of Chicago (A.B., 1983); DePaul University (J.D., with honor, 1990). Order of the Coif. Managing Editor, Journal of Health and Hospital Law, 1989-1990. *Member:* American Health Lawyers Association; Illinois Association of Healthcare Attorneys; California Society of Healthcare Attorneys; American Society of Medical Association Counsel. ***PRACTICE AREAS:*** Health Care Law; Corporate Law. ***Email:*** ken.davis@kattenlaw.com

DENISE M. DEVINE, born Evergreen Park, Illinois, October 2, 1967; admitted to bar, 1994, Illinois. *Education:* Colorado State University (B.S., 1989); DePaul University College of Law (J.D., 1994). Member, DePaul University Law Review, 1992-1994. Certified Public Accountant, 1991—. *Member:* Illinois State Bar Association. ***PRACTICE AREAS:*** Corporate and Securities; Mergers and Acquisitions; Private Equity; Securities. ***Email:*** denise.orlinski@kattenlaw.com

DAVID R. DLUGIE, born Chicago, Illinois, November 23, 1960; admitted to bar, 1986, Illinois. *Education:* University of Illinois (B.S., with highest honors, 1981; M.A.S., 1982; J.D., 1986). Certified Public Accountant, Illinois, 1981. *Member:* Chicago, Illinois State and American Bar Associations. ***PRACTICE AREAS:*** Real Estate Law; Real Estate Finance; Securitization. ***Email:*** david.dlugie@kattenlaw.com

LEAH J. DOMITROVIC, born Pittsburgh, Pennsylvania, July 16, 1966; admitted to bar, 1991, Illinois and U.S. District Court, Northern District of Illinois; 1994, District of Columbia; 2000, U.S. Court of Appeals, Seventh Circuit. *Education:* University of Notre Dame (B.A., cum laude, 1988); University of Chicago (J.D., 1991). *Member:* The District of Columbia Bar. ***PRACTICE AREAS:*** Securities; Directors and Officers Liability. ***Email:*** leah.domitrovic@kattenlaw.com

DAVID M. DUNBAR, born Binghamton, New York, July 9, 1960; admitted to bar, 1989, Illinois; 1991, U.S. Court of International Trade and U.S. Court of Appeals for the Federal Circuit. *Education:* College of the Holy Cross (B.A., cum laude, 1983); University of Illinois (J.D., 1989). Phi Alpha Theta. Recipient: Harno Memorial Scholarship; Rickert Award for Excellence, International Moot Court. Co-Author: Walsh and Dunbar, "Deemed Exports of Technology," CBA Record, Feb.-March 1997, 46. With U.S. Peace Corps, Botswana, Africa, 1984-1986. *Member:* Chicago (Member: Customs and U.S. International Trade Law Committee; International and Foreign Law Committee) and Customs and International Trade Bar Associations. ***LANGUAGES:*** Portuguese. ***PRACTICE AREAS:*** Customs Law; International Trade; Export Controls. ***Email:*** david.dunbar@kattenlaw.com

JEFFREY L. ELEGANT, born Chicago, Illinois, December 20, 1954; admitted to bar, 1979, Illinois. *Education:* Knox College (B.A., cum laude, 1976); Washington University (J.D., 1979). Phi Beta Kappa; Pi Sigma Alpha. Instructor, American Institute of Banking, 1983—. *Member:* Chicago and American (Member: Section on Commercial, Banking and Corporate; Subcommittee on Commercial Financial Services 1986—) Bar Associations. ***PRACTICE AREAS:*** Banking Law; Corporate Law; Creditors Rights Law; Finance and Reorganization. ***Email:*** jeffrey.elegant@kattenlaw.com

JONATHAN S. FELD, born Detroit, Michigan, August 10, 1952; admitted to bar, 1980, New York; 1988, District of Columbia; 1999, Illinois. *Education:* Reed College (B.A., 1974, Phi Beta Kappa); Harvard University (MCRP, 1979); Boston University (J.D., 1979). American Judicature Society. Member, Board of Editor, Business Crimes Bulletin. Assistant U.S. Attorney, District of New Jersey, 1982-1987. Associate Deputy Attorney General, U.S. Department of Justice, 1990-1991. Associate Independent Counsel, U.S. Department of Housing and Urban Development (HUD), 1995-1996. *Member:* Illinois and American Bar Association. ***PRACTICE AREAS:*** White Collar Criminal Defense; Complex Civil Litigation; Complex Business Litigation; Corporate Governance; Securities. ***Email:*** jonathan.feld@kattenlaw.com

LEONARD A. FERBER, born Albany, New York, July 19, 1957; admitted to bar, 1983, Illinois. *Education:* University of Michigan (A.B., with high distinction, 1979); University of Pennsylvania (J.D., 1983). Phi Beta Kappa. *Member:* Chicago and American Bar Associations; Internet Executives Club (Board of Advisors). ***PRACTICE AREAS:*** Technology and Computer Law; General Corporate Law; Mergers and Acquisitions; Licensing and Distribution. ***Email:*** leonard.ferber@kattenlaw.com

KURT W. FLORIAN, JR., born Melrose Park, Illinois, April 14, 1959; admitted to bar, 1984, Illinois. *Education:* University of Chicago (A.B., 1981); Duke University (J.D., 1984). Phi Beta Kappa. Author: "How much Security is in an Annuity" - Insights; "Through Management's Looking Glass," Best's Review. Faculty Member, University of Illinois, Chicago, 1990. *Member:* Chicago and American Bar Associations. ***LANGUAGES:*** Spanish. ***PRACTICE AREAS:*** Financial Services; Financial Institutions; Mergers and Acquisitions; Corporate and Securities; Investment Management. ***Email:*** kurt.florian@kattenlaw.com

GARY J. FOX, born Chicago, Illinois, January 10, 1957; admitted to bar, 1984, Illinois. *Education:* Roosevelt University (B.A., with honors, 1980); DePaul University (J.D., with honors, 1984). *Member:* Chicago and American Bar Associations. ***PRACTICE AREAS:*** Real Estate; Finance. ***Email:*** gary.fox@kattenlaw.com

RENÉE M. FRIEDMAN, born Chicago, Illinois, April 27, 1956; admitted to bar, 1980, Illinois. *Education:* Northwestern University (B.A., 1977); Washington University (J.D., 1980). Editor-in-Chief, Urban Law Annual, 1979-1980. *Member:* Chicago Bar Association; National Association of Bond Lawyers. ***PRACTICE AREAS:*** Public Finance; Health Care Finance; Utilities; Financial Products. ***Email:*** renee.friedman@kattenlaw.com

JAMES M. GECKER, born Milwaukee, Wisconsin, July 1, 1947; admitted to bar, 1974, Georgia; 1976, Illinois and U.S. District Court, Northern District of Illinois; 1977, Wisconsin; 1978, Ohio; 1984, U.S. Court of Appeals, Seventh Circuit; 1985, U.S. District Court, Eastern District of Michigan; 1987, U.S. Court of Appeals, Fifth and Sixth Circuits; 1989, U.S. Court of Appeals, Federal Circuit. *Education:* University of California at Berkeley (A.B., 1971); Loyola University (M.S.I.R., 1984); University of Wisconsin (J.D., cum laude, 1974). Phi Beta Kappa. Adjunct Professor, 1996—; Instructor, Loyola University of Chicago, Institute of Industrial Relations, 1987-1995. Member, Board of Advisors, Center for Employment Dispute Resolution. *Member:* American Bar Association (Member, Section on Labor and Employment Law and Litigation). ***PRACTICE AREAS:*** Labor and Employment Law; Litigation and Dispute Resolution. ***Email:*** james.gecker@kattenlaw.com

SCOTT M. GETTLESON, born Detroit, Michigan, January 1, 1967; admitted to bar, 1992, Illinois; registered to practice before U.S. Patent and Trademark Office. *Education:* University of Michigan (B.S.E., Computer Engineering, magna cum laude, 1989); University of Illinois (J.D., 1992). Tau Beta Pi; Eta Kappa Nu; Phi Alpha Delta. *Member:* Chicago and Illinois State Bar Associations; Intellectual Property Law Association of Chicago. ***LANGUAGES:*** Spanish. ***PRACTICE AREAS:*** Intellectual Property Litigation; Electrical, Computer and Mechanical Patent Law; E-Commerce; Business Method Patents; Litigation and Dispute Resolution. ***Email:*** scott.gettleson@kattenlaw.com

RENÉ GHADIMI, admitted to bar, 1992, Illinois; 1993, U.S. District Court, Northern District of Illinois. *Education:* State University of New York at Stony Brook (B.A., 1978); Hofstra University (M.B.A, with distinction, 1987); University of Chicago (J.D., 1992). Beta Gamma Sigma. Author: "Distinguishing Between Securities Accounts and Deposit Accounts Under the UCC," Illinois Bar Journal, December, 2000. *Member:* Chicago and American Bar Associations. ***PRACTICE AREAS:*** Structured Real Estate Finance; Secured and Cash Flow Lending; Commercial Finance; Structured Finance; Finance and Reorganization. ***Email:*** rene.ghadimi@kattenlaw.com

SUSAN L. GOLDENBERG, born Hempstead, New York, November 27, 1962; admitted to bar, 1987, Illinois, U.S. District Court, Northern District of Illinois. *Education:* University of Michigan (B.A., cum laude, 1984); University of Chicago (J.D., 1987). *Member:* Chicago and American Bar Associations. ***PRACTICE AREAS:*** Estate Planning; Corporate and Securities. ***Email:*** susan.goldenberg@kattenlaw.com

JULIE L. GOTTSHALL, born Buffalo, New York, July 7, 1966; admitted to bar, 1991, Illinois; 1994, District of Columbia; U.S. District Court, Northern District of Illinois; U.S. Court of Appeals, Eleventh Circuit; U.S. Court of Appeals, Seventh Circuit; U.S. District Court, Northern District of Indiana; U.S. District Court, Eastern District of Michigan; U.S. District Court, District of Arizona; U.S. District Court, Western District of Michigan. *Education:* Cornell University (B.S., Industrial and Labor Relations, 1988); George Washington University (J.D., with honors, 1991). Member, George Washington Law Review, 1990-1991. *Member:* American Bar Association; Chicago Bar Association; Cook County Circuit Court Arbitration. ***PRACTICE AREAS:*** Employment Law; Labor; Litigation and Dispute Resolution. ***Email:*** julie.gottshall@kattenlaw.com

(This Listing Continued)

STUART E. GRASS, born Detroit, Michigan, October 13, 1946; admitted to bar, 1971, Michigan; 1972, New York; 1973, California; 1977, Illinois. *Education:* University of Michigan (B.A., 1968; J.D., cum laude, 1971); New York University (LL.M. in Taxation, 1976). *Member:* Chicago and American (Member, Section of Taxation) Bar Associations. ***PRACTICE AREAS:*** Corporate and Securities; Trusts and Estates. ***Email:*** stuart.grass@kattenlaw.com

BRYAN J. GREEN, born New Orleans, Louisiana, December 4, 1959; admitted to bar, 1989, Illinois; U.S. District Court, Northern District of Illinois. *Education:* Northwestern University (B.A., Chemistry, 1982); University of Akron (J.D., 1988). *Member:* Chicago and American Bar Associations. ***PRACTICE AREAS:*** Corporate; Environmental Law. ***Email:*** bryan.green@kattenlaw.com

LEWIS GREENBAUM, born New York, N.Y., July 29, 1948; admitted to bar, 1974, New York; 1978, Illinois. *Education:* New York University (B.A., with honors, 1970); Georgetown University (J.D., 1973). ***PRACTICE AREAS:*** Public Finance; Local Government; Financial Services; Securities. ***Email:*** lewis.greenbaum@kattenlaw.com

RUSSELL E. GREENBLATT, (P.C.), born Chicago, Illinois, January 7, 1952; admitted to bar, 1978, Illinois; 1983, California; 1992, U.S. Tax Court. *Education:* Indiana University (B.S., magna cum laude, 1973); Northwestern University (J.D., cum laude, 1978). Certified Public Accountant, Illinois and Georgia, 1973. Office of Chief Counsel, Internal Revenue Service, 1978-1980. *Member:* American Bar Association; American College of Employee Benefits Counsel; Self Insurance Association of Illinois; Self Insurance Institute of America, Inc.; WEB Network of Benefits Professionals. ***PRACTICE AREAS:*** Employee Benefits and Executive Compensation; Tax Planning and Litigation; Health Information and HIPAA Compliance; Corporate and Securities. ***Email:*** russell.greenblatt@kattenlaw.com

ARTHUR W. HAHN, born Chicago, Illinois, July 30, 1944; admitted to bar, 1969, Illinois. *Education:* Miami University (B.A., 1966); London School of Economics and Political Science; Northwestern University (J.D., 1969). Law Clerk to Federal District Judge Alexander J. Napoli, 1969-1971. Faculty Chairman, Chicago-Kent College of Law Graduate School of Financial Services Law, 1989-1998. Trustee and member of Executive Committee, Futures Industry Institute. Director and Board of Directors, Teach for America. Trustee, Ravinia Festival. *Member:* Chicago Bar Association; American Arbitration Association; Economic Club Futures and Options Association (FOA); Futures Industry Association; International Swaps and Derivatives Association; Legal Club of Chicago; Illinois Council on Economic Education (Chairman, Institute for Financial Markets). ***PRACTICE AREAS:*** Litigation and Dispute Resolution; Investment Management; Mergers and Acquisitions; Securities; Technology; Financial Markets and Products; Financial Services. ***Email:*** arthur.hahn@kattenlaw.com

MEGAN HARDIMAN, born Urbana, Illinois, April 16, 1968; admitted to bar, 1993, Wisconsin; 1995, Illinois. *Education:* Institute for European Studies, Vienna, Austria; University of Illinois (B.S., Journalism, with high honors, 1990; J.D., cum laude, 1993). *Member:* Chicago and American Bar Associations; State Bar of Wisconsin. ***PRACTICE AREAS:*** Health and Hospital Law; Corporate; Tax Exempt Organizations. ***Email:*** megan.hardiman@kattenlaw.com

CHARLES HARRIS, born Chicago, Illinois, June 15, 1961; admitted to bar, 1989, Illinois. *Education:* DePaul University (B.S., 1983); Illinois Institute of Technology, Chicago-Kent College of Law (J.D., with high honors, 1989). Order of the Coif. Law Review Editor. *Member:* Chicago and Illinois State Bar Associations. ***PRACTICE AREAS:*** Corporate and Securities; Trusts and Estates. ***Email:*** charles.harris@kattenlaw.com

MICHAEL O. HARTZ, born Flint, Michigan, July 24, 1953; admitted to bar, 1978, Michigan; 1979, Florida; 1980, Illinois. *Education:* Kalamazoo College (B.A., 1975); University of Detroit (J.D., 1978); University of Florida (LL.M. in Taxation, 1979). Author: "Sales of Property: Will Self-Cancelling Installment Notes Make Private Annuities Obsolete?" TAXES The Tax Magazine, August 1981. Adjunct Professor of Law, John Marshall Law School, 1984-1991. ***PRACTICE AREAS:*** Corporate and Securities; Trusts and Estates. ***Email:*** michael.hartz@kattenlaw.com

TED S. HELWIG, born Galesburg, Illinois, July 26, 1954; admitted to bar, 1980, Illinois. *Education:* North Park College (B.A., 1977); Loyola University of Chicago (J.D., 1980). Law Clerk to Judges Crowley and Flaum, N.D.Ill., 1980-1983. Assistant U.S. Attorney, 1983-1989. Member: Futures International Law Letter; North Park Friendship Center. *Member:* Chicago and American Bar Associations; Futures Industry Association; Securities Industry Association. ***PRACTICE AREAS:*** Securities Enforcement; Financial Services Enforcement Litigation; White Collar Criminal and Civil Litigation; RICO Litigation; Consumer Fraud Class Action Litigation. ***Email:*** ted.helwig@kattenlaw.com

MARY ELLEN HENNESSY, born Rockville Center, New York, June 26, 1950; admitted to bar, 1979, Illinois. *Education:* Manhattanville College (B.A., magna cum laude, 1972); Georgetown University (J.D., 1979). *Member:* Seventh Circuit Bar Association (Board of Governors); Orwood Condominium Association. ***PRACTICE AREAS:*** Securities Litigation; Complex and Class Action Litigation; Litigation and Dispute Resolution. ***Email:*** maryellen.hennessy@kattenlaw.com

JANET GOELZ HOFFMAN, born Pittsburgh, Pennsylvania, August 25, 1949; admitted to bar, 1979, Illinois; 1980, U.S. Tax Court. *Education:* Lake Forest College (B.A., cum laude, 1973); Northwestern University (J.D., cum laude, 1978). Managing Editor, Northwestern University Law Review, 1977-1978. *Member:* American Bar Association; National Association of Bond Lawyers; Swedish Retirement Association (Board of Directors). ***PRACTICE AREAS:*** Public Finance; Financial Services Law; Non-Profit Organizations. ***Email:*** janet.hoffman@kattenlaw.com

JAMES WELLINGTON HUTCHISON, born Cincinnati, Ohio, November 30, 1969; admitted to bar, 1995, Illinois; U.S. District Court, Northern District of Illinois; U.S. District Court, Central District of Illinois. *Education:* Northwestern University (B.A., 1991); New York University (J.D., 1995). *Member:* American Bar Association; Chicago Bar Association; Center for Disability & Elder Law. ***LANGUAGES:*** Spanish. ***PRACTICE AREAS:*** Litigation and Dispute Resolution; Bankruptcy, Reorganization and Creditors' Rights. ***Email:*** james.hutchison@kattenlaw.com

KENNETH M. JACOBSON, born Chicago, Illinois, May 24, 1954; admitted to bar, 1979, Illinois. *Education:* University of Illinois (B.A., 1976); Stanford University (J.D., 1979). *Member:* Chicago and American Bar Associations; Chicago Mortgage Attorneys Association; American College of Real Estate Lawyers. ***PRACTICE AREAS:*** Real Estate Law. ***Email:*** kenneth.jacobson@kattenlaw.com

MICHAEL A. JACOBSON, born Chicago, Illinois, September 28, 1969; admitted to bar, 1994, Illinois. *Education:* University of Iowa (B.B.A., 1991); DePaul University (J.D., 1994). Phi Eta Sigma; Order of the Coif. Recipient, American Jurisprudence Award, Contracts. DePaul Law Review, 1992-1994. Author, "Claims and Remedies Against Defunct Corporations, Partnerships, and Unincorporated Associations," *Creditor's Rights in Illinois,* 1995 edition, Chapter 7, IICLE. ***PRACTICE AREAS:*** Corporate Finance; Bankruptcy; Finance and Reorganization. ***Email:*** michael.jacobson@kattenlaw.com

TARA GOFF KAMRADT, born Paterson, New Jersey, November 20, 1967; admitted to bar, 1992, New Jersey and U.S. District Court, District of New Jersey; 1993, New York; 1995, Illinois. *Education:* Pennsylvania State University (B.S., 1989); New York Law School (J.D., 1992). Member, Law Review, New York Law School. *Member:* American Bar Association (Business Law Section). ***PRACTICE AREAS:*** Corporate and Securities; Health Information and HIPAA Compliance; Mergers and Acquisitions; Private Equity. ***Email:*** tara.kamradt@kattenlaw.com

CHRISTIAN T. KEMNITZ, born June 10, 1970; admitted to bar, 1995, Michigan; 1996, Illinois, U.S. District Court, Northern District of Illinois and U.S. Court of Appeals, Fifth Circuit. *Education:* Michigan State University (B.A., 1992); University of Chicago (J.D., 1995). *Member:* Chicago and Illinois State Bar Association; State Bar of Michigan. ***LANGUAGES:*** German. ***PRACTICE AREAS:*** Antitrust; Financial Services; Litigation and Dispute Resolution; White Collar Criminal and Civil Litigation. ***Email:*** christian.kemnitz@kattenlaw.com

DAVID H. KISTENBROKER, admitted to bar, 1980, Illinois and Wisconsin. *Education:* University of Wisconsin-Whitewater (B.S., magna cum laude, 1975); Marquette University (M.A., Foreign Policy, magna cum laude, 1977; J.D., 1980). Special Assistant to the Illinois Attorney General. Member, Executive's Club of Chicago. ***PRACTICE AREAS:*** Corporate Governance; Business Litigation; Securities Litigation; Litigation and Dispute Resolution. ***Email:*** david.kistenbroker@kattenlaw.com

ADAM R. KLEIN, born Newburgh, New York, January 2, 1971; admitted to bar, 1995, Illinois. *Education:* Cornell University (B.S., 1992); Harvard University (J.D., 1995). Golden Key. *Member:* American Bar Association. ***PRACTICE AREAS:*** Corporate and Securities; Corporate Governance; Mergers and Acquisitions; Sports Law; Sports Facilities; Advertising. ***Email:*** adam.klein@kattenlaw.com

CHARLES R. KRIKORIAN, born Waukegan, Illinois, May 18, 1961; admitted to bar, 1995, Illinois and U.S. District Court, Northern District of Illinois; 1998, U.S. Court of Appeals for the Federal Circuit; registered to practice before U.S. Patent and Trademark Office. *Education:* University of Illinois (B.S., Microbiology, 1983); Loyola University of Chicago (Ph.D., Molecular Biology, 1992); DePaul University (J.D., with honors, 1995). Order of the Coif; Sigma Xi. Recipient: Congressional Scholarship, University of Illinois; Loyola University President's Medallion; Schmidt Dissertation Fellowship. Research Staff, DePaul Law Review. Lecturer and Presenter at the American Bar Association and American Chemical Society meetings on infringement of intellectual property rights and on Hatch-Waxman litigation. Author of various journal articles and abstracts summarizing research in virology and molecular biology. *Member:* Licensing Executives Society; Association of University Technology Managers. ***LANGUAGES:*** French and Armenian. ***PRACTICE AREAS:*** Intellectual Property; Intellectual Property Litigation; Life Sciences; Litigation; Litigation and Dispute Resolution; Biotechnology. ***Email:*** charles.krikorian@kattenlaw.com

STEWART T. KUSPER, born Chicago, Illinois, October 25, 1964; admitted to bar, 1991, Illinois. *Education:* University of Notre Dame (B.A., 1987); Illinois Institute of Technology, Chicago-Kent College of Law (J.D., 1991). Order of the Coif. Staff Member, Chicago-Kent Law Review, 1990-1991. Member, Chicago-Kent Moot Court Society, 1991-1992. ***PRACTICE AREAS:*** Financial Services; Litigation and Dispute Resolution; Real Estate Litigation; Securities. ***Email:*** stewart.kusper@kattenlaw.com

HOWARD S. LANZNAR, born Champaign, Illinois, August 15, 1955; admitted to bar, 1983, Illinois. *Education:* Amherst College (B.A., magna cum laude, 1977); University of Chicago (J.D., cum laude, 1983). Phi Beta Kappa; Order of the Coif. Member, The University of Chicago Law Review, 1981-1983. *Member:* Chicago and American Bar Associations. ***PRACTICE AREAS:*** Corporate; Mergers and Acquisitions; Securities. ***Email:*** howard.lanznar@kattenlaw.com

MARK E. LAUGHMAN, born South Bend, Indiana, August 25, 1967; admitted to bar, 1994, Illinois; 1996, Indiana. *Education:* San Francisco State University (B.A., 1989); University of Notre Dame (J.D., 1994). Managing Editor, Notre Dame Law Review, 1993-1994. Author: "The Leaning Tower: Do the Proposed Amendments to SEC Rule 15c2-12 Violate the Securities Acts Amendments of 1975?" 69 Notre Dame L. Rev. 1167, 1994, reprinted in The Bondbuyer, April 25, 1994, p.25. *Member:* Chicago and Illinois State Bar Associations; Eugene Field Neighborhood Association; National Association of Bond Lawyers. ***PRACTICE AREAS:*** Financial Services; Public Finance. ***Email:*** mark.laughman@kattenlaw.com

LAWRENCE D. LEVIN, born Chicago, Illinois, May 10, 1959; admitted to bar, 1985, Illinois and U.S. District Court, Northern District of Illinois. *Education:* University of Illinois (B.S., with honors, 1981; J.D., 1985). Certified Public Accountant, Illinois, 1981. *Member:* Chicago and American Bar Associations. ***PRACTICE AREAS:*** Corporate Mergers and Acquisitions; Securities Law. ***Email:*** lawrence.levin@kattenlaw.com

KEVIN S. MACKINNON, born San Jose, California, June 29, 1958; admitted to bar, 1983, California, U.S. District Court, Northern District of California and U.S. Court of Appeals, 9th Circuit; 1984, Illinois and U.S. Court of Appeals, 7th Circuit. *Education:* University of California at Santa Barbara (B.A., English Literature, with honors, 1980); University of Santa Clara (J.D., 1983). Phi Alpha Delta. Editor-in-Chief, Santa Clara Law Review, 1982-1983. Author: Comment, "Computer Malpractice: Are Computer Manufacturers, Service Bureaus and Programmers Really the Professionals They Claim to Be?" 23 Santa Clara Law Review 1065, 1983. *Member:* Chicago and American Bar Associations;

(This Listing Continued)

KATTEN MUCHIN ROSENMAN LLP, Chicago—Continued

International Trademark Association. ***LANGUAGES:*** French. ***PRACTICE AREAS:*** Intellectual Property Litigation; Advertising; Corporate and Securities; Intellectual Property; Licensing and Distribution; Technology. ***Email:*** kevin.mackinnon@kattenlaw.com

SETH R. MADORSKY, born Cleveland, Ohio, August 29, 1961; admitted to bar, 1986, Illinois. *Education:* University of Michigan (B.A., with honors, 1983); Cornell University (J.D., 1986). *Member:* Chicago, Illinois State and American Bar Associations; Pension Real Estate Association (PREA). ***PRACTICE AREAS:*** Real Estate. ***Email:*** seth.madorsky@kattenlaw.com

REID A. MANDEL, born Minneapolis, Minnesota, March 31, 1954; admitted to bar, 1981, Minnesota and Illinois. *Education:* Yale University (B.A., 1977); New York University (J.D., 1980). Law Clerk, Supreme Court of Minnesota, 1980-1981. Adjunct Professor, John Marshall Law School, 1995-1999. *Member:* Chicago and American Bar Associations. ***PRACTICE AREAS:*** Asset-Backed Securities; Taxation; Finance and Reorganization; Litigation. ***Email:*** reid.mandel@kattenlaw.com

FLOYD A. MANDELL, (P.C.), born Chicago, Illinois, June 17, 1948; admitted to bar, 1973, Illinois and Florida. *Education:* Northern Illinois University (B.A., magna cum laude, 1970); University of Illinois (J.D., 1973). Member, Editorial Board, Illinois Bar Journal, 1972-1973. Adjunct Professor, Chicago-Kent Law School, 1994-1995. *Member:* American Bar Association; Chicago Bar Association; Illinois Institute of Technology Kent College of Law Intellectual Property Law Association of Chicago; International Anti-counterfeiting Coalition, Inc.; International Trademark Association; Patent Law Association of Chicago. ***PRACTICE AREAS:*** Litigation and Intellectual Property Law; Trademarks; Trade Secrets; Copyright Protection; Technology; Entertainment and Media Litigation; Music Law; Advertising; Life Sciences. ***Email:*** floyd.mandell@kattenlaw.com

JONATHAN L. MARKS, born Chicago, Illinois, January 19, 1964; admitted to bar, 1989, Illinois. *Education:* Yale University (B.A., 1986); University of Michigan Law School (J.D., 1989). ***PRACTICE AREAS:*** Litigation and Dispute Resolution; White Collar Criminal and Civil Litigation; Business Litigation. ***Email:*** jonathan.marks@kattenlaw.com

LAURA KEIDAN MARTIN, born Detroit, Michigan, October 8, 1964; admitted to bar, 1989, Illinois, U.S. District Court, Northern District of Illinois. *Education:* University of Michigan (B.A., with high honors, 1986); Harvard University (J.D., cum laude, 1989). *Member:* American Bar Association; Chicago Bar Association; Illinois Association of Healthcare Attorneys (Board Member and Vice President); National Health Lawyers Association. ***PRACTICE AREAS:*** Antitrust; Health Care; Health Care Compliance; Health Information and HIPAA Compliance. ***Email:*** laura.martin@kattenlaw.com

NINA B. MATIS, (P.C.), born New York, N.Y., June 23, 1947; admitted to bar, 1973, Illinois. *Education:* Smith College (A.B., cum laude, 1969); New York University (J.D., 1972). Adjunct Professor, Northwestern University, 1984-1987. General Counsel, Starwood Financial Trust; Board Member, Burnham Pacific. *Member:* American Bar Association; American College of Real Estate Lawyers; Chicago Finance Exchange; Chicago Real Estate Executive Women; Chicago Real Estate Women; Economic Club of Chicago; Lambda Alpha International (Ely Chapter); International Council of Shopping Centers; Lakefront SRO; Pension Real Estate Association (PREA); Real Estate Finance Forum; The Chicago Network Urban Land Institute. ***PRACTICE AREAS:*** Real Estate Law (Development; Leasing; Financing; Partnership); Hotel and Hospitality; Mergers and Acquisitions. ***Email:*** nina.matis@kattenlaw.com

WILLIAM E. MATTINGLY, (P.C.), born Decatur, Illinois, March 6, 1948; admitted to bar, 1975, Indiana; 1978, Illinois. *Education:* Purdue University (B.S.I.E., 1971; M.S.E., 1972); Indiana University (J.D., cum laude, 1975). *Member:* American Bar Association; Chicagoland Chamber of Commerce; Illinois State Chamber of Commerce; Chicago Business Group on Health; Midwest Business Group on Health. ***PRACTICE AREAS:*** ERISA; Employee Benefits; Managed Care; Health Information and HIPAA Compliance. ***Email:*** william.mattingly@kattenlaw.com

THOMAS J. McFADDEN, born South Bend, Indiana, March 21, 1954; admitted to bar, 1979, Indiana; 1989, Illinois. *Education:* University of Notre Dame (B.A., with honors, 1976; J.D., 1979); Loyola University of Chicago (LL.M., with highest honors, 1989). Trustee of Holy Cross College, Notre Dame, Indiana. Congregation of the Sisters of the Holy Cross, Holy Cross College, Notre Dame Indiana. *Member:* American Health Lawyers Association. ***PRACTICE AREAS:*** Health Care; Health Care Compliance; Mergers and Acquisitions. ***Email:*** tthomas.mcfadden@kattenlaw.com

ADAM M. MEEK, born Chicago, Illinois, April 3, 1965; admitted to bar, 1991, Illinois and U.S. District Court, Northern District of Illinois. *Education:* University of Michigan (A.B., with high distinction, 1988); Northwestern University (J.D., 1991). James B. Angell Scholar. *Member:* American Bar Association; Chicago Bar Association; Illinois State Bar Association. ***PRACTICE AREAS:*** Environmental Services; Litigation; Real Estate. ***Email:*** adam.meek@kattenlaw.com

KENNETH W. MILLER, born Chicago, Illinois, October 25, 1960; admitted to bar, 1985, Illinois and U.S. District Court, Northern District of Illinois; 1986, U.S. Tax Court. *Education:* University of Illinois (B.S., with highest honors, 1982); Northwestern University (J.D., magna cum laude, 1985). Order of the Coif. Northwestern University Law Review, 1983-1985. Certified Public Accountant, Illinois, 1982. *Member:* American Bar Association. ***PRACTICE AREAS:*** Corporate; Mergers and Acquisitions; Venture Capital Law. ***Email:*** ken.miller@kattenlaw.com

LESLIE DAWN MINIER, born Los Angeles, California, October 19, 1965; admitted to bar, 1994, Illinois. *Education:* Tuskegee University (B.S.E.E., 1987); Georgia Institute of Technology (M.S.E.E., 1988); Northwestern University (M.B.A., 1994; J.D., 1994). *Member:* American Bar Association. ***PRACTICE AREAS:*** Corporate and Securities; Mergers and Acquisitions; Private Equity. ***Email:*** leslie.minier@kattenlaw.com

WARREN Y. NAKATANI, born Westfield, New Jersey, January 26, 1970; admitted to bar, 1995, Missouri; 1996, Illinois. *Education:* Washington University (B.A., 1992); University of Pittsburgh (J.D., magna cum laude, 1995). Order of the Coif. Articles Editor, University of Pittsburgh Law Review. *Member:* Chicago and American Bar Associations.

(This Listing Continued)

PRACTICE AREAS: Commercial Litigation; White Collar Crime; Tort Defense; Intellectual Property; Civil Litigation; Litigation and Dispute Resolution; Bankruptcy, Reorganization and Creditors Rights. ***Email:*** warren.nakatani@kattenlaw.com

TERRY E. NEWMAN, (P.C.), born Chicago, Illinois, January 15, 1947; admitted to bar, 1977, Illinois; 1991, District of Columbia. *Education:* Loyola University (B.A., 1969); DePaul University (J.D., 1977). Assistant States Attorney, Cook County, 1977-1979. Secretary of the Board of Trustees, City Colleges of Chicago, 1989. *Member:* The District of Columbia Bar; Chicago (Member, Real Estate Tax Section), Illinois State and American Bar Associations. ***PRACTICE AREAS:*** Ad Valorem Taxation. ***Email:*** terry.newman@kattenlaw.com

DOUGLAS L. NOREN, born Chicago, Illinois, June 22, 1967; admitted to bar, 1992, Illinois and U.S. District Court, Northern District of Illinois; 1998, New York. *Education:* Washington University (B.A., magna cum laude, 1989); Northwestern University (J.D., 1992). Phi Beta Kappa. ***PRACTICE AREAS:*** Real Estate Development; Real Estate Finance; Real Estate. ***Email:*** douglas.noren@kattenlaw.com

J. PHILLIP O'BRIEN, born Monmouth, Illinois, January 6, 1949; admitted to bar, 1974, Illinois. *Education:* Western Illinois University (B.A., 1971); University of Illinois (J.D., 1974). Corporate Counsel, American Hospital Association, 1981-1984. *Member:* National Health Lawyers Association. ***PRACTICE AREAS:*** Health Care Law. ***Email:*** phillip.obrien@kattenlaw.com

STEVEN R. OLSON, born Baraboo, Wisconsin, July 10, 1955; admitted to bar, 1982, Illinois. *Education:* Andrews University (B.S., 1978); The John Marshall Law School (J.D., 1982). Psi Chi. Co-Author: "Health Care Construction Projects," Construction Joint Ventures, Wiley Law Publication, 1992. *Member:* American Health Lawyers Association. ***PRACTICE AREAS:*** Health Care Law. ***Email:*** steven.olson@kattenlaw.com

KENNETH J. OTTAVIANO, born Chicago, Illinois, January 1, 1970; admitted to bar, 1996, Illinois and U.S. District Court, Northern District of Illinois. *Education:* Lake Forest College (B.A., 1992); Thomas M. Cooley Law School (J.D., cum laude, 1996). *Member:* Illinois State Bar Association; American Bankruptcy Institute. ***PRACTICE AREAS:*** Bankruptcy; Reorganization; Creditors Rights. ***Email:*** kenneth.ottaviano@kattenlaw.com

JOHN S. PANIAGUAS, born Gary, Indiana, September 7, 1951; admitted to bar, 1982, Illinois and U.S. District Court, Northern District of Illinois; 1983, U.S. Court of Appeals, Seventh Circuit; 1984, U.S. Court of Appeals for the Federal Circuit; 1986, U.S. Supreme Court; 1987, Indiana; 1995, U.S. District Court, District of Nebraska; registered to practice before U.S. Patent and Trademark Office. *Education:* Purdue University (B.S.E., 1973); DePaul University (J.D., 1982). Tau Beta Pi. Professional Engineer: Indiana, 1978; Illinois, 1984. Adjunct Professor of Law, Intellectual Property Law, DePaul University College of Law, 1999—. *Member:* Lake County (Indiana), Indiana State, Chicago, Illinois State and American (Member, Patent, Trademark and Copyright Section) Bar Associations; Intellectual Property Law Association of Chicago; American Intellectual Property Law Association. ***PRACTICE AREAS:*** Intellectual Property; Patents, Trademarks, Copyrights; Trade Secrets; Unfair Competition; Computers and Software; Technology and Science; Patent Law. ***Email:*** johnp@kattenlaw.com

KEITH D. PASCUS, born Chicago, Illinois, October 23, 1956; admitted to bar, 1982, Illinois. *Education:* University of Illinois (B.S., 1978; M.A.S., 1982; J.D., cum laude, 1982). Certified Public Accountant, Illinois, 1981. *Member:* Chicago and American Bar Associations. ***PRACTICE AREAS:*** Commercial Real Estate Law. ***Email:*** keith.pascus@kattenlaw.com

TIMOTHY J. PATENODE, born Ft. Leonard Wood, Missouri, April 18, 1956; admitted to bar, 1981, Illinois. *Education:* Northwestern University (B.A., 1977; J.D., cum laude, 1981). Member, 1979-1980, and Executive Editor, 1980-1981, Northwestern Journal of International Law and Business. *Member:* Chicago and American Bar Associations. ***PRACTICE AREAS:*** General Commercial Litigation. ***Email:*** timothy.patenode@kattenlaw.com

JEFFREY R. PATT, born Chicago, Illinois, April 28, 1962; admitted to bar, 1987, Illinois. *Education:* University of Illinois (B.S., 1984); Chicago-Kent College of Law (J.D., with high honors, 1987). Member of Order of the Coif and A Lead Articles Editor of the IIT Chicago-Kent Law Review. ***PRACTICE AREAS:*** Corporate Governance; Corporate and Securities; Health Care Compliance; Mergers and Acquisitions; Private Equity; Securities. ***Email:*** jeffrey.patt@kattenlaw.com

DANIEL J. PERLMAN, born Highland Park, Illinois, October 13, 1960; admitted to bar, 1985, Illinois and New York. *Education:* University of Michigan (B.A., with high distinction, 1982); Northwestern University (J.D., 1985). Chairman, American Cancer Society Greater Chicago Downtown Board. *Member:* Chicago Bar Association; International Council of Shopping Centers. ***PRACTICE AREAS:*** Fund Formation; Hotel and Hospitality; Real Estate; Real Estate Development; Joint Ventures; Strategic Alliances; Partnerships; Financial Institutions. ***Email:*** daniel.perlman@kattenlaw.com

MICHAEL M. PHILIPP, born Winfield, Kansas, March 5, 1959; admitted to bar, 1992, Illinois and U.S. District Court, Northern District of Illinois. *Education:* University of Chicago (B.A., 1981); DePaul College of Law (J.D., 1992). Attorney, Chicago Mercantile Exchange. *Member:* Chicago Bar Association (Futures Regulation); Futures Industry Association (Law and Compliance Division). ***PRACTICE AREAS:*** Financial Services; Investment Management; Securities. ***Email:*** michael.philipp@kattenlaw.com

GREGORY P. L. PIERCE, born Detroit, Michigan, December 16, 1957; admitted to bar, 1984, Illinois and U.S. District Court, Northern District of Illinois. *Education:* University of Illinois (B.A., 1980; M.B.A., J.D., 1984). *Member:* Chicago and American Bar Associations; American College of Real Estate Lawyers; Legal Club of Chicago. ***PRACTICE AREAS:*** Joint Ventures; Strategic Alliances; Partnerships; Real Estate. ***Email:*** greg.pierce@kattenlaw.com

DEBRA S. RADE, born 1953; admitted to bar, 1980, Illinois, U.S. District Court, Northern District of Illinois and U.S. Court of Appeals, Seventh Circuit; 1986, U.S. Court of Appeals, Sixth Circuit. *Education:* University of Illinois, Champaign-Urbana (B.A., 1975); DePaul University College of Law (J.D., 1980). Adjunct Professor, Ethics Course, Northwestern University School of Law. Commissioner, Design Review Commission, City of Highland Park. General Counsel, Katten Muchin Zavis Rosenman. *Member:* Chicago and American Bar Associations; American Israel Chamber of Commerce Chicago (Mem-

(This Listing Continued)

ber, Executive Committee of the Board). ***PRACTICE AREAS:*** Corporate; Securities; Corporate Governance; Joint Ventures; Strategic Alliances; Partnerships; Mergers and Acquisitions; Product Liability. ***Email:*** debra.rade@kattenlaw.com

NANCY J. RICH, born Chicago, Illinois, June 11, 1959; admitted to bar, 1984, Illinois and U.S. District Court, Northern District of Illinois including Trial Bar. *Education:* Loyola University (Honors A.B., magna cum laude, 1981; J.D., 1984). Author: "The Clean Air Act Amendments of 1990: Clean Air At What Cost," Loyola Consumer Law Reporter, Winter, 1991. Assistant Illinois Attorney General, Environmental Control Division, 1984-1987. *Member:* Chicago and American Bar Associations. ***PRACTICE AREAS:*** Environmental; Complex Litigation. ***Email:*** nancy.rich@kattenlaw.com

HOWARD M. RICHARD, (P.C.), born Oak Park, Illinois, September 20, 1944; admitted to bar, 1968, Illinois. *Education:* Cornell University (B.A., 1965); Harvard University (LL.B., 1968). Member, Board of Editors, Harvard Law Review, 1967-1968. Co-Author, "Illinois Limited Liability Company -- Forms and Practice Manual," Data Trace Legal Publishers, Inc., Copyright 1994. *Member:* Chicago and American (Member, Section on Real Property, Probate and Trust Law) Bar Associations. ***PRACTICE AREAS:*** Real Estate Law. ***Email:*** howard.richard@kattenlaw.com

BRIAN F. RICHARDS, born Oaklawn, Illinois, January 23, 1967; admitted to bar, 1992, Illinois. *Education:* University of Illinois (B.S., with highest honors, 1989); University of Virginia (J.D., 1992). Order of the Coif. ***PRACTICE AREAS:*** Mergers and Acquisitions; Corporate Law; Private Equity; Technology and New Media. ***Email:*** brian.richards@kattenlaw.com

SAUL E. RUDO, born Baltimore, Maryland, August 2, 1958; admitted to bar, 1983, Illinois; 1985, Florida. *Education:* University of Illinois (B.S., with highest honors, 1980); Harvard University (J.D., 1983). Member, Bronze Tablet. Certified Public Accountant, Illinois, 1980. Member: Bernard Weigner Jewish Community Center; University of Illinois Commerce Department Alumni Association. *Member:* Chicago Bar Association; Association for Corporate Growth. ***PRACTICE AREAS:*** Tax Planning and Litigation; Private Equity; Mergers and Acquisitions; Taxation of Financial Products; Corporate and Securities; Employee Benefits and Executive Compensation; Private Investment Funds. ***Email:*** saul.rudo@kattenlaw.com

RUSSELL B. SELMAN, born Brooklyn, New York, May 30, 1954; admitted to bar, 1980, Missouri; 1981, District of Columbia; 1987, Illinois. *Education:* New College (B.A., 1975); Syracuse University (M.P.A., 1978); Washington University (J.D., 1979). *Member:* The District of Columbia Bar; The Missouri Bar; Illinois State Bar Association. ***PRACTICE AREAS:*** Environmental. ***Email:*** russell.selman@kattenlaw.com

VINCENT A. F. SERGI, (P.C.), born Kew Gardens, New York, June 13, 1946; admitted to bar, 1974, Illinois. *Education:* Beloit College (B.A., 1968); Northwestern University (J.D., cum laude, 1974). ***PRACTICE AREAS:*** Finance and Reorganization; Real Estate Finance; Corporate. ***Email:*** vincent.sergi@kattenlaw.com

STEVEN A. SHAPIRO, (P.C.), born Chicago, Illinois, October 22, 1950; admitted to bar, 1975, Illinois; 1983, Florida. *Education:* University of Illinois (B.S., 1971); Illinois Institute of Technology, Chicago-Kent College of Law (J.D., with high honors, 1975). Editor, Chicago-Kent Law Review, 1974-1975. *Member:* American Bar Association. ***PRACTICE AREAS:*** Finance and Reorganization; Financial Institutions; Financial Services; Corporate Law. ***Email:*** steven.shapiro@kattenlaw.com

DAVID R. SHEVITZ, (P.C.), born Syracuse, New York, June 3, 1941; admitted to bar, 1966, Illinois. *Education:* Kenyon College (B.A., cum laude, 1963); University of Michigan (J.D., with honors, 1966). Co-Author: "Sale of Restricted Securities: Rule 144," Securities Law Practice (Ill. Inst. for CLE, 1973); "Rule 146 Adopted," 7 Rev. Sec. Reg. 911, 1974; "The Private Offering Exemption," Securities Law, Ill. Inst. for CLE, 1979. *Member:* Chicago and American Bar Associations. ***PRACTICE AREAS:*** Corporate and Securities; Internet and E-Commerce; Joint Ventures; Strategic Alliances; Partnerships; Mergers and Acquisitions; Private Equity; Securities. ***Email:*** dave.shevitz@kattenlaw.com

STUART P. SHULRUFF, born Chicago, Illinois, April 28, 1959; admitted to bar, 1984, Illinois. *Education:* University of Illinois (B.S., high honors, 1981); Loyola University of Chicago (J.D., cum laude, 1984). Certified Public Accountant, Illinois, 1981. *Member:* Chicago and Illinois State Bar Associations. ***PRACTICE AREAS:*** Corporate Finance; Finance and Reorganization; Financial Services. ***Email:*** stuart.shulruff@kattenlaw.com

JOHN SIEGER, born Minneapolis, Minnesota, May 13, 1969; admitted to bar, 1994, Indiana, U.S. District Court, Northern and Southern Districts of Indiana, U.S. District Court, Northern and Central Districts of Illinois and U.S. District Court, Eastern and Western Districts of Wisconsin; 1997, Illinois. *Education:* University of Illinois (B.S., 1991); University of Michigan Law School (J.D., 1994). *Member:* American Bankruptcy Institute. ***PRACTICE AREAS:*** Bankruptcy; Reorganization; Creditors Rights; Commercial Litigation. ***Email:*** john.sieger@kattenlaw.com

HARVEY M. SILETS, born Chicago; admitted to bar, 1955, Illinois; 1956, New York. *Education:* DePaul U. (B.S.C., cum laude, 1952); U. of Michigan (J.D., 1955). Adj. Prof. of Taxation, Chicago-Kent College of Law, 1985—. Chief Tax Atty., U. S. Atty's. Off., N.D. of Ill., 1960-1962. *Member:* Federal Bar Association (Chicago Chap., Pres., 1977-1978); 7th Circuit Bar Association (Pres., 1990-1991). Fellow: American Board of Criminal Lawyers; American College of Trial Lawyers; American College of Tax Counsel; International Academy of Trial Lawyers. Fellow, The Society for Advance Legal Studies, London. ***PRACTICE AREAS:*** Federal Criminal Defense Law; Federal Civil Law; Tax Litigation. ***Email:*** harvey.silets@kattenlaw.com

ROSS O. SILVERMAN, born Toledo, Ohio, August 3, 1960; admitted to bar, 1986, Georgia; 1989, District of Columbia; 1995, Illinois; U.S. District Court, Northern District of Illinois, including Trial Bar; U.S. Court of Appeals, Seventh Circuit. *Education:* Ohio State University (B.A., 1982); University of Toledo (J.D., cum laude, 1985). Order of the Coif. Trial Attorney, Criminal Section of Tax Division, U.S. Department of Justice, 1988-1990. Assistant U.S. Attorney, Northern District of Illinois, 1990-1994. *Member:* Chicago and Illinois State Bar Associations; State Bar of Georgia; District of Columbia Bar. ***PRACTICE AREAS:*** Anti-Fraud Counseling and Litigation; Health Care Compliance; Health Information and HIPAA Compliance; Litigation and Dispute Resolution; White Collar Criminal and Civil Litigation. ***Email:*** ross.silverman@kattenlaw.com

(This Listing Continued)

MARK C. SIMON, born Ann Arbor, Michigan, April 28, 1954; admitted to bar, 1979, Illinois. *Education:* Carleton College (B.A., magna cum laude, 1976); University of Michigan (J.D., with honors, 1979). Phi Beta Kappa. Board Member, Community Economic Development Law Project. Co-Author: "Legal Opinions in Illinois Real Estate Secured Loan Transactions," *Member:* Chicago (Chairman, Real Estate Finance Subcommittee, 1993-1995) and American Bar Associations. ***PRACTICE AREAS:*** Real Estate; Commercial. ***Email:*** mark.simon@kattenlaw.com

ANN MARIE SINK, born Evergreen Park, Illinois, November 2, 1953; admitted to bar, 1982, Illinois and U.S. District Court, Northern District of Illinois. *Education:* Loyola University of Chicago (B.A., 1974; M.A., 1976); DePaul University (J .D., 1981). Assistant Corporation Counsel, City of Chicago, Illinois, 1984-1987. *Member:* Chicago, Illinois State and American Bar Associations. ***PRACTICE AREAS:*** Real Estate; Commercial Finance; Corporate Finance. ***Email:*** annmarie.sink@kattenlaw.com

NINA MOMTAZEE SITZER, born St. Louis, Missouri, October 13, 1967; admitted to bar, 1992, Missouri and U.S. District Court, Eastern District of Illinois; 1993, Illinois. *Education:* London School of Economics and Political Science, London, England; Emory University (B.A., 1989); Northwestern University (J.D., 1992). *Member:* Illinois State and American Bar Associations; The Missouri Bar. ***PRACTICE AREAS:*** Real Estate. ***Email:*** nina.sitzer@kattenlaw.com

ANDREW D. SMALL, born Chicago, Illinois, December 31, 1964; admitted to bar, 1989, Illinois. *Education:* University of Michigan (B.B.A., 1986); University of Chicago (J.D., 1989). *Member:* Chicago and American Bar Associations. ***PRACTICE AREAS:*** Real Estate Development and Finance; Real Estate Acquisition and Disposition; Real Estate Leasing. ***Email:*** andrew.small@kattenlaw.com

PAMELA G. SMITH, born Chicago, Illinois, June 4, 1962; admitted to bar, 1990, Illinois and U.S. District Court, Northern District of Illinois; 1996, U.S. Court of Appeals, Fourth Circuit; 2000, U.S. Court of Appeals, Seventh Circuit. *Education:* Northwestern University (B.S., 1984); Loyola University of Chicago (J.D., cum laude, 1990). Recipient, AmJur Award, Evidence, Loyola University of Chicago. Executive Editor, Publications, Loyola University of Chicago Law Journal, 1989-1990. ***PRACTICE AREAS:*** Business Litigation; Litigation and Dispute Resolution; Complex Commercial Litigation; Securities Litigation. ***Email:*** pamela.smith@kattenlaw.com

ZIEMOWIT T. SMULKOWSKI, born Gdansk, Poland, October 24, 1970; admitted to bar, 1996, Illinois. *Education:* Loyola University (B.A., 1993); Northwestern University (J.D., 1996). ***PRACTICE AREAS:*** Corporate and Securities; Tax Planning and Litigation. ***Email:*** ziemowit.smulkowski@kattenlaw.com

GIL M. SOFFER, born Chicago, Illinois, September 11, 1964; admitted to bar, 1989, Illinois; 1992, California. *Education:* Brown University (A.B., magna cum laude, 1986); Harvard University (J.D., cum laude, 1989). Phi Beta Kappa. Instructor, Loyola Law School, 2000. Assistant U.S. Attorney, U.S. District Court, Northern District of Illinois, 1994-2000. *Member:* American Bar Association. ***LANGUAGES:*** French, Hebrew. ***PRACTICE AREAS:*** Anti-Fraud Counseling and Litigation; Litigation and Dispute Resolution; White Collar Criminal and Civil Litigation. ***Email:*** gil.soffer@kattenlaw.com

BONITA L. STONE, born Chicago, Illinois, January 30, 1955; admitted to bar, 1979, Illinois. *Education:* University of Illinois (B.A., 1976); Northwestern University (J.D., cum laude, 1979). Staff Member and Editorial Board, Northwestern Journal of Criminal Law and Criminology, 1977-1979. Member, North Suburban Jewish Community Center. *Member:* American Bar Association (Former Chair, State Law Subcommittee of ABA, Class Action and Derivative Suit Committee). ***PRACTICE AREAS:*** Corporate and Securities; Labor and Employment; Litigation and Dispute Resolution. ***Email:*** bonita.stone@kattenlaw.com

MARCIA W. SULLIVAN, (P.C.), born Chicago, Illinois, November 30, 1950; admitted to bar, 1975, Illinois. *Education:* DePauw University (B.A., 1972); Indiana University (J.D., 1975). Phi Beta Kappa. Adjunct Professor, IIT Chicago-Kent College of Law, 1991-1993. *Member:* Chicago, Illinois State and American Bar Associations; American Land Title Association. ***PRACTICE AREAS:*** Real Estate Law; Financing Law. ***Email:*** marcia.sullivan@kattenlaw.com

IRA J. SWIDLER, born Chicago, Illinois, September 27, 1954; admitted to bar, 1979, Illinois. *Education:* University of Illinois (B.S., 1976; J.D., summa cum laude, 1979). Certified Public Accountant, Illinois, 1976. *Member:* Chicago and American Bar Associations. ***PRACTICE AREAS:*** Real Estate Development, Financing, Acquisitions and Dispositions, and Leasing. ***Email:*** ira.swidler@kattenlaw.com

MARTIN T. TULLY, born June 10; admitted to bar, 1990, Illinois; U.S. District Court, Northern District of Illinois; U.S. Court of Appeals, Seventh Circuit. *Education:* University of Illinois (B.A., 1987); DePaul University College of Law (J.D., cum laude, 1990). Order of the Coif. ***PRACTICE AREAS:*** Litigation and Dispute Resolution; Labor and Employment; Intellectual Property Litigation. ***Email:*** martin.tully@kattenlaw.com

JAMES D. VAN DE GRAAFF, born Evanston, Illinois, April 18, 1960; admitted to bar, 1987, Illinois. *Education:* Brigham Young University (B.A., 1983); Georgetown Law Center (J.D., 1987). *Member:* Securities Industry Association. ***LANGUAGES:*** Spanish. ***PRACTICE AREAS:*** Financial Institutions; Financial Markets and Products; Financial Services; Securities. ***Email:*** james.vandegraaff@kattenlaw.com

ALEXANDER S. VESSELINOVITCH, born May 11; admitted to bar, 1978, Illinois; U.S. District Court, Northern District of Illinois including Trial Bar; U.S. Court of Appeals, Seventh Circuit; U.S. Supreme Court. *Education:* Leningrad State University (Certificate, 1974); University of Chicago (B.A., 1975); Columbia University School of Law (J.D., 1978). Approved Neutral, CPR Institute for Dispute Resolution, New York, N.Y. Member, London Court of International Arbitration. ***LANGUAGES:*** Russian and Serbo-Croatian. ***PRACTICE AREAS:*** Litigation and Dispute Resolution; White Collar Criminal and Civil Litigation; White Collar Crime; Civil Litigation. ***Email:*** alexander.vesselinovitch@kattenlaw.com

TIMOTHY J. VEZEAU, born Detroit, Michigan, August 16, 1944; admitted to bar, 1972, Illinois. *Education:* St. Louis University (B.S.E.E., cum laude, 1966); Georgetown University (J.D., 1971). Pi Mu Epsilon; Eta Kappa Nu. Patent Examiner, United States Patent Office, 1968-1970. Patent Advisor, United States Office of Naval Research, 1971. Selected as "Leading Illinois Attorney in Intellectual Property Law." *Member:* Chicago,

(This Listing Continued)

KATTEN MUCHIN ROSENMAN LLP, Chicago—Continued

Illinois State and American Bar Associations; Intellectual Property Law Association of Chicago; Legal Club of Chicago. ***PRACTICE AREAS:*** Intellectual Property Infringement; Intellectual Property Licensing; Intellectual Property Litigation; Patent Infringement; Patent Litigation; Life Sciences. ***Email:*** timothy.vezeau@kattenlaw.com

CARL E. VOLZ, born Chicago, Illinois, January 7, 1970; admitted to bar, 1995, Illinois; 2000, U.S. District Court, Northern District of Illinois. *Education:* Ohio University (B.A., Political Science, 1992; B.S.J., 1992); Chicago-Kent College of Law, Illinois Institute of Technology (J.D., 1995). ***LANGUAGES:*** Spanish. ***PRACTICE AREAS:*** Business Litigation; Litigation and Dispute Resolution; Securities Litigation. ***Email:*** carl.volz@kattenlaw.com

ZACHARY D. WAGMAN, born Chicago, Illinois, July 23, 1964; admitted to bar, 1989, Illinois. *Education:* University of Wisconsin at Madison (B.A., 1986); University of Illinois (J.D., magna cum laude, 1989). Member, University of Illinois Law Review. ***PRACTICE AREAS:*** Finance and Reorganization; Financial Services; International Transactions and Litigation. ***Email:*** zack.wagman@kattenlaw.com

MILTON S. WAKSCHLAG, born Omaha, Nebraska, July 4, 1955; admitted to bar, 1980, Illinois. *Education:* University of Chicago (J.D., 1980); DePaul University (LL.M. Taxation, 1987). *Member:* American Bar Association (Last Retiring Chair, Tax-Exempt Financing Committee, Tax Section); National Association of Bond Lawyers. ***PRACTICE AREAS:*** Financial Services; Public Finance; Sports Law; Sports Facilities; Tax Planning and Litigation; Hotel and Hospitality; Real Estate. ***Email:*** milton.wakschlag@kattenlaw.com

HERBERT S. WANDER, (P.C.), born Cincinnati, Ohio, March 17, 1935; admitted to bar, 1960, Ohio and Illinois. *Education:* University of Michigan (A.B., 1957); Yale University (LL.B., 1960). Phi Beta Kappa. Member: Board of Editors, Yale Law Journal; Legal Advisory Committee to the Board of Governors of the New York Stock Exchange; NASD Legal Advisory Board; Editor, Vol. 49 of the Business Lawyer, 1993-1994. *Member:* American Bar Association (Chair, Business Law Section, 1995-1996; Executive Committee, Federal Regulation of Securities Committee, 1983-2000). ***PRACTICE AREAS:*** Corporate and Securities Law. ***Email:*** herbert.wander@kattenlaw.com

MARYANN A. WARYJAS, born Chicago, Illinois; admitted to bar, 1983, Illinois. *Education:* Loyola University (B.S., magna cum laude); Northwestern University (J.D., cum laude, 1983). President and Member, Board of Directors, Chicago Finance Exchange. Member, Business Women's Network. *Member:* Chicago and American Bar Associations. ***PRACTICE AREAS:*** Corporate Law; Securities Law; Venture Capital; Mergers and Acquisitions; Executive Compensation; Corporate Investigations; Internet Law; Financial Law; Workouts; Restructurings; Employment Matters; Independent Investigations. ***Email:*** maryann.waryjas@kattenlaw.com

ELIZABETH FLEMING WEBER, born Watseka, Illinois, November 16, 1949; admitted to bar, 1974, Massachusetts; 1978, Illinois; 1984, New York. *Education:* University of Illinois (B.A., 1971); Boston University (J.D., 1974). Phi Beta Kappa. Assistant Staff Counsel, Supreme Judicial Court of Massachusetts, 1976-1977. *Member:* National Association of Bond Lawyers. ***PRACTICE AREAS:*** Financial Services; Health Care; Public Finance; Securities. ***Email:*** elizabeth.weber@kattenlaw.com

NEIL H. WEINBERG, born Louisville, Kentucky, July 11, 1964; admitted to bar, 1991, Illinois. *Education:* University of Illinois (B.S., 1986); Washington University, St. Louis (J.D., 1991). *Member:* Chicago Bar Association (Member, Trust Law and Probate Practices Committees); Chicago Estate Planning Council; Greater North Shore Estate Planning Council. ***PRACTICE AREAS:*** Trusts and Estates; Tax. ***Email:*** neil.weinberg@kattenlaw.com

WALTER S. WEINBERG, born Chicago, Illinois, September 12, 1956; admitted to bar, 1981, Illinois. *Education:* University of Chicago (B.A., 1978); Northwestern University (J.D., cum laude, 1981). Phi Beta Kappa; Order of the Coif. Member, Editorial Board, Northwestern Journal of International Law and Business, 1980-1981. Author: Note, "Mannington Mills, Inc. v. Congoleum Corporation: A Further Step Toward a Complete Subject Matter Jurisdiction Test," 2 Northwestern Journal of International Law and Business 241, 1980. *Member:* National Association of Small Business Investment Companies. ***PRACTICE AREAS:*** Corporate and Securities; Mergers and Acquisitions; General Corporate Law; Private Equity. ***Email:*** walter.weinberg@kattenlaw.com

JOHN ROBERT WEISS, born May 7, 1961; admitted to bar, 1985, Illinois; 1987, U.S. District Court, Northern District of Illinois and U.S. Court of Appeals, Seventh Circuit; 1989, U.S. Supreme Court; U.S. Court of Appeals, Eighth Circuit; U.S. District Court, Central District of Illinois. *Education:* Northwestern University (B.A., 1982; J.D., 1985). *Member:* American Bar Association; American Bankruptcy Institute; Turnaround Management Association. ***PRACTICE AREAS:*** Bankruptcy, Reorganization and Creditors' Rights; Finance and Reorganization; Real Estate Litigation. ***Email:*** john.weiss@kattenlaw.com

PETER R. WILSON, born Chicago, Illinois, August 12, 1968; admitted to bar, 1995, Illinois. *Education:* Colgate University (B.A., 1990); University of Illinois (J.D., 1995). Editor, University of Illinois Law Review. *Member:* Chicago Bar Association. ***PRACTICE AREAS:*** Anti-Fraud Counseling and Litigation; Business Litigation; Litigation and Dispute Resolution; White Collar Criminal and Civil Litigation. ***Email:*** peter.wilson@kattenlaw.com

JANET H. WINNINGHAM, admitted to bar, 1982, Illinois; U.S. District Court, Northern District of Illinois. *Education:* DePauw University (B.A., with distinction, 1973); Rosary College (M.A.L.S., 1977); Loyola University of Chicago (J.D., 1982). Recipient, Hugh L. Dick Memorial Award. Member, Editorial Board, Loyola Law Journal, 1981-1982. Author: "Solely for Investment Purposes: Evolution of a Statutory Exemption Under Clayton Section 7," Loyola University of Chicago Law Journal Vol. 12, No. 3, 1982. Member, Board of Education, School District 167, 1978—. *Member:* American Bar Association; International Council on Shopping Centers. ***PRACTICE AREAS:*** Real Estate; Real Estate Development; Real Estate Finance. ***Email:*** janet.winningham@kattenlaw.com

MARK D. WOOD, born Chicago, Illinois, January 8, 1966; admitted to bar, 1990, Illinois and U.S. District Court, Northern District of Illinois. *Education:* University of Illinois (B.S., with high honors, 1987); University of Michigan (J.D., cum laude, 1990). Certified Public Accountant, Illinois, 1987. *Member:* Chicago and American Bar Associations. ***PRACTICE AREAS:*** Corporate and Securities; Corporate Governance; Mergers and Acquisitions; Private Equity; Securities. ***Email:*** mark.wood@kattenlaw.com

SHELDON T. ZENNER, born Chicago, Illinois, January 11, 1953; admitted to bar, 1978, Illinois; U.S. Court of Appeals, Seventh and Ninth Circuits; U.S. District Court, Northern District of Illinois including Trial Bar; U.S. District Court, Central District of Illinois. *Education:* Northwestern University (B.A., cum laude, 1974; J.D., cum laude, 1978). Journal of Criminal Law and Criminology, 1977-1978. Member, Starlight Foundation. *Member:* American Bar Association; Seventh Circuit Bar Association; Chicago Council of Lawyers; National Institute of Trial Attorneys. ***PRACTICE AREAS:*** Anti-Fraud Counseling and Litigation; Health Care Compliance; White Collar Criminal and Civil Litigation. ***Email:*** sheldon.zenner@kattenlaw.com

MARK S. ZOLNO, born Chicago, Illinois, May 10, 1943; admitted to bar, 1978, Illinois; 1979, U.S. Court of International Trade and U.S. Court of Appeals for the Federal Circuit; 1996, U.S. Supreme Court. *Education:* Northern Illinois University (B.S., 1965); Universidad de las Americas, Puebla, Mexico (M.A., International Relations, cum laude, 1974); The John Marshall Law School (J.D., 1978). Member, The John Marshall Law Review, 1977-1978. *Member:* American Association of Exporters and Importers; Canadian Club of Chicago; Custom Brokers and Foreign Freight Forwarders Association of Chicago, Inc.; Japan America Society of Chicago, Inc.; Joint Industry Group (JIG); The International Trade Association of Greater Chicago; United States of America-China Chamber of Commerce; United States-Mexico Chamber of Commerce. ***PRACTICE AREAS:*** Customs and International Trade. ***Email:*** mark.zolno@kattenlaw.com

RETIRED FOUNDING PARTNER

MICHAEL WM. ZAVIS, (P.C.), born Chicago, Illinois, April 19, 1937; admitted to bar, 1961, Illinois. *Education:* Wharton School, University of Pennsylvania (B.S., 1958); University of Chicago (J.D., 1961). University of Chicago Law Review, 1960-1961. *Member:* Seventh Federal Circuit, Chicago and Illinois State Bar Associations. ***Email:*** michael.zavis@kattenlaw.com

ASSOCIATES

SETH M. AIGNER, admitted to bar, 2002, Illinois. *Education:* Wittenberg University (B.A., 1997); Boston College School of Law (J.D., 2002). ***PRACTICE AREAS:*** Finance and Reorganization; Business Reorganization. ***Email:*** seth.aigner@kattenlaw.com

GEOFF AUYEUNG, admitted to bar, 2001 Illinois. *Education:* University of Illinois (J.D., cum laude, 2001). ***LANGUAGES:*** Chinese. ***PRACTICE AREAS:*** Lending and Secured Transactioins. ***Email:*** manchit.auyeung@kattenlaw.com

WILLIAM F. BAARSMA, born Tacoma, Washington, October 18, 1970; admitted to bar, 2003, Illinois. *Education:* University of Puget Sound (B.A., 1993); Northwestern University School of Law (J.D., 2003). *Member:* American Bar Association. ***PRACTICE AREAS:*** Real Estate; Real Estate Finance. ***Email:*** william.baarsma@kattenlaw.com

KARL R. BARNICKOL, born Evanston, Illinois, October 13, 1971; admitted to bar, 1997, Illinois and U.S. District Court, Northern District of Illinois; 1998, Missouri. *Education:* Georgetown University (A.B., 1994); Washington University (J.D., 1997). Order of the Coif. *Member:* Chicago and American Bar Associations. ***LANGUAGES:*** Spanish. ***PRACTICE AREAS:*** Litigation and Dispute Resolution; Mergers and Acquisitions; Securities Litigation; White Collar Criminal and Civil Litigation. ***Email:*** karl.barnickol@kattenlaw.com

DAVID F. BENSON, admitted to bar, 2003, Illinois and U.S. District Court, Northern District of Illinois. *Education:* Vanderbilt University (B.S., cum laude, 1999); Chicago-Kent College of Law, Illinois Institute of Technology (J.D., with honors, 2003). *Member:* Chicago, Illinois State and American Bar Associations. ***PRACTICE AREAS:*** Litigation; Alternative Dispute Resolution. ***Email:*** david.benson@kattenlaw.com

FRITZ E. BERCKMUELLER, born Tiffin, Ohio, July 17, 1975; admitted to bar, 2000, Illinois; U.S. District Court, Northern District of Illinois. *Education:* Washington & Lee University (B.A., 1997); University of Chicago (J.D., 2000). Phi Beta Kappa. ***PRACTICE AREAS:*** Securities Litigation; Litigation and Dispute Resolution; Antitrust. ***Email:*** fritz.berckmueller@kattenlaw.com

BETHANY N. BONNER, admitted to bar, 2003, Illinois. *Education:* Michigan State University (B.A., with high honors, 1998); Georgetown University (J.D., 2003). ***PRACTICE AREAS:*** Real Estate. ***Email:*** bethany.bonner@kattenlaw.com

CATHLEEN A. BOOTH, born Toledo, Ohio, July 2, 1974; admitted to bar, 2000, Illinois. *Education:* Ohio Northern University (B.S., with high distinction, 1996); University of Toledo (J.D., magna cum laude, 2000). Associate Member, 1998-1999 and Editor-in-Chief, University of Toledo Law Review. Author: "Civil Protection Orders: Effective Legislation or Protectionist Attitude?," University of Toledo Law review, 30:4 (2000). ***PRACTICE AREAS:*** Corporate and Securities; Mergers and Acquisitions. ***Email:*** cathleen.booth@kattenlaw.com

KELLYE BOWERS, admitted to bar, 1998, Ohio (Not admitted in Illinois). *Education:* University of Kentucky (B.A., 1993); Indiana University School of Law (J.D., 1998). ***PRACTICE AREAS:*** Real Estate. ***Email:*** kellye.bowers@kattenlaw.com

RACHEL S. BROWN, born Detroit, Michigan, May 19, 1974; admitted to bar, 2000, Illinois. *Education:* University of Michigan (B.A., 1996); Loyola University (J.D., cum laude, 2000). Moot Court Team. Legal Writing Tutor, 1998-1999. *Member:* American Bar Association. ***PRACTICE AREAS:*** Real Estate. ***Email:*** rachel.brown@kattenlaw.com

DAVID J. CALICCHIA, admitted to bar, 1999, Illinois. *Education:* University of Chicago (B.A., 1992; M.A., 1995); New York University (J.D., 1999). *Member:* Chicago and American Bar Associations. ***PRACTICE AREAS:*** Corporate Law; Securities; Internet Law; E-Commerce; Joint Ventures; Strategic Alliances; Partnership Law; Mergers and Acquisitions; Tax Planning; Tax Litigation. ***Email:*** david.calicchia@kattenlaw.com

JEFFREY A. CHADWICK, admitted to bar, 2001, Illinois and U.S. District Court, Northern District of Illinois. *Education:* Wabash College (B.A., summa cum laude, 1998); Indiana University School of Law, Bloomington (J.D., cum laude, 2001). Phi Beta Kappa. Managing Editor, Indiana Law Journal. *Member:* American Bar Association; American

(This Listing Continued)

Bankruptcy Institute. ***LANGUAGES:*** Spanish. ***PRACTICE AREAS:*** Bankruptcy; Reorganization; Creditors Rights; Finance; Business Litigation. ***Email:*** jeffrey.chadwick@kattenlaw.com

SONJA K. CLAYTON-PEDERSEN, born Milwaukee, Wisconsin, September 30, 1976; admitted to bar, 2001, California; 2002, District of Columbia and U.S. District Court for the District of Columbia; 2003, Illinois. *Education:* Rhodes College (B.A., 1998); Vanderbilt University (J.D., 2001). ***PRACTICE AREAS:*** Litigation; Alternative Dispute Resolution. ***Email:*** sonja.clayton-pedersen@kattenlaw.com

DAVID P. COHEN, born Chicago, Illinois; admitted to bar, 1998, Illinois and Massachusetts; 2002, California. *Education:* University of Illinois, Urbana-Champaign (B.A. in Finance, with distinction, summa cum laude, 1992); Boalt Hall School of Law, University of California, Berkeley (J.D., 1997; M.P.P., 1997). Phi Beta Kappa. Member, Bronze Tablet. Author: "Improving the Supply of Affordable Housing: The Role of the Low-Income Housing Tax Credit," Journal of Law and Policy, 1998; "Congress Grapples with Expiring Section 8 Contraction," Housing Law Bulletin, 1994. Member, Forum on Affordable Housing and Community Development Law. *Member:* State Bar of California; American Bar Association (Member, Forum on Affordable Housing and Community Development Law). ***PRACTICE AREAS:*** Real Estate; Real Estate Development; Real Estate Finance; Affordable Housing; Tax Credits; Government. ***Email:*** david.cohen@kattenlaw.com

GENEVIEVE M. DANIELS, born Chicago, Illinois, March 30, 1968; admitted to bar, 1993, Illinois and U.S. District Court, Northern District of Illinois; 2001, U.S. District Court, Central District of Illinois and U.S. District Court, Northern District of Indiana. *Education:* Loyola University (B.A., magna cum laude, 1993); Northwestern University (J.D., 1993). Member, Board of Directors, Plasticene Physical Theater Company. *Member:* Chicago Bar Association. ***PRACTICE AREAS:*** Litigation; Alternative Dispute Resolution; Commercial Litigation; Labor and Employment; Appellate Practice. ***Email:*** genevieve.daniels@kattenlaw.com

KRISTEN M. DANYLUK, admitted to bar, 2004, Illinois. *Education:* Cornell University (B.A., 1999); University of Michigan Law School (J.D., 2004). ***PRACTICE AREAS:*** Corporate; Securities; Technology. ***Email:*** kristen.danyluk@kattenlaw.com

SAMPREETI DE, born Calcutta, India, September 12, 1972; admitted to bar, 2000, Illinois. *Education:* University of Illinois (B.S., 1994); Loyola University (J.D., 2000). *Member:* Chicago and American Bar Associations. ***PRACTICE AREAS:*** Corporate and Securities; Mergers and Acquisitions. ***Email:*** sampreeti.de@kattenlaw.com

ANGELA J. DELPH, born Muncie, Indiana, September 29, 1972; admitted to bar, 2003, Illinois. *Education:* University of Illinois (B.A., 1995); University of Illinois, College of Law (J.D., 2003). ***PRACTICE AREAS:*** Finance and Reorganization. ***Email:*** angela.delph@kattenlaw.com

LAURA M. DREZNES, born Chicago, Illinois, November 14, 1979; admitted to bar, 2004, Illinois. *Education:* University of Dayton (B.A., 2001); University of Illinois (J.D., 2004). ***PRACTICE AREAS:*** Labor and Employment; Litigation; Dispute Resolution. ***Email:*** laura.dreznes@kattenlaw.com

CHAD A. DIEHL, admitted to bar, 2003, Illinois; U.S. District Court, Northern District of Illinois. *Education:* University of Iowa (Phar.D., 2000); Loyola University Chicago School of Law (J.D., 2003). ***PRACTICE AREAS:*** Litigation; Alternative Dispute Resolution. ***Email:*** chad.diehl@kattenlaw.com

JOSEPH B. DiRAGO, admitted to bar, 2004, Illinois. *Education:* Drake University (B.A., magna cum laude, 2001); University of Illinois (J.D., magna cum laude 2004). Associate Editor, Elder Law Journal. *Member:* American Bankruptcy Institute. ***PRACTICE AREAS:*** Bankruptcy; Reorganization; Creditor Rights; Financial Services. ***Email:*** joseph.dirago@kattenlaw.com

MICHAEL J. DIVER, born Oak Park, Illinois, October 15, 1969; admitted to bar, 1996, Illinois and U.S. District Court, Northern District of Illinois. *Education:* Bucknell University (B.A., 1991); Northwestern School of Law of Lewis & Clark College (J.D., cum laude, 1996). ***PRACTICE AREAS:*** Corporate Securities; Mergers and Acquisitions; Venture Capital; Private Equity; Securities. ***Email:*** michael.diver@kattenlaw.com

ADAM M. DOCKS, born Royal Oak, Michigan, March 7, 1979; admitted to bar, 2004, Illinois. *Education:* University of Michigan at Ann Arbor (B.A., with distinction, 2001); Emory University School of Law (J.D., 2004). Notes and Comments Editor, Emory Bankruptcy Developments Journal. ***PRACTICE AREAS:*** Real Estate. ***Email:*** adam.docks@kattenlaw.com

STEVE J. DOLLEAR, born 1974; admitted to bar, 2002, Illinois. *Education:* Marquette University (B.S., 1996); Loyola University School of Law (J.D., 2002). ***PRACTICE AREAS:*** Litigation; Alternative Dispute Resolution. ***Email:*** steven.dollear@kattenlaw.com

KIMBERLY F. DOMBROW, born March 29, 1976; admitted to bar, 2001, Illinois and U.S. District Court, Northern District of Illinois. *Education:* Northwestern University (B.A., cum laude, 1998; J.D., cum laude, 2001). *Member:* Chicago, Illinois State and American Bar Associations. ***PRACTICE AREAS:*** Real Estate. ***Email:*** kimberly.fuldauer@kattenlaw.com

MICHAEL A. DORFMAN, born Chicago, Illinois, March 30, 1973; admitted to bar, 1998, Illinois and U.S. District Court, Northern District of Illinois; registered to practice before U.S. Patent and Trademark Office. *Education:* University of Illinois (B.S.E.E., 1995); DePaul University (J.D., 1998). *Member:* Chicago, Illinois State and American Bar Associations. ***PRACTICE AREAS:*** Intellectual Property; Intellectual Property Litigation. ***Email:*** michael.dorfman@kattenlaw.com

WILLIAM J. DORSEY, born Kansas City, Missouri, March 31, 1973; admitted to bar, 1998, Missouri and U.S. District Court, Western District of Missouri; 1999, Kansas; 2000, Illinois and U.S. District Court, Northern and Central Districts of Illinois. *Education:* Claremont McKenna College (B.A., 1995); University of Michigan Law School (J.D., 1998). *Member:* Chicago Bar Association; Kansas City Metropolitan Bar Association. ***PRACTICE AREAS:*** Labor and Employment; Trade Secret; Fiduciary Duty Law; Commercial Litigation. ***Email:*** william.dorsey@kattenlaw.com

(This Listing Continued)

DANIEL M. ENTSMINGER, admitted to bar, 2002, Illinois. *Education:* Wittenberg University (B.A., 1999); Northwestern University School of Law (J.D., 2002). ***PRACTICE AREAS:*** Finance; Business Reorganization. ***Email:*** daniel.entsminger@kattenlaw.com

PHILLIP M. ESTAVER, born Jackson, Michigan, March 28, 1949; admitted to bar, 1974, Missouri; 1997, Illinois. *Education:* Michigan State University (B.S., with honors, 1971); University of Kansas (J.D., 1974). Phi Delta Phi; Pi Gamma Mu. *Member:* The Missouri Bar. ***PRACTICE AREAS:*** Corporate; Banking; Real Estate. ***Email:*** phillip.estaver@kattenlaw.com

VALENTINA FAMPARSKA, born Botevgrad, Bulgaria, January 25, 1964; admitted to bar, 1987, Bulgaria; 1999, Illinois. *Education:* Sofia University (J.D., 1986); Loyola University (J.D., 1999). ***LANGUAGES:*** Bulgarian and Russian. ***PRACTICE AREAS:*** Corporate and Securities; Tax Planning and Litigation. ***Email:*** valentina.famparska@kattenlaw.com

MEGAN A. FLAHERTY, born Evergreen Park, Illinois, June 18, 1967; admitted to bar, 2003, Illinois. *Education:* Miami University (B.S., 1989); Chicago-Kent College of Law (J.D., 2002). ***PRACTICE AREAS:*** Financial Services. ***Email:*** megan.flaherty@kattenlaw.com

MICHAEL T. FOLEY, born Oak Lawn, Illinois, August 14, 1967; admitted to bar, 1995, Illinois. *Education:* Knox College; DePaul University (B.S., 1991); Chicago-Kent College of Law, Illinois Institute of Technology (J.D., 1995). Beta Gamma Sigma; Order of the Coif. Member, Chicago-Kent College Law Review, 1993-1994. *Member:* Chicago and American Bar Associations. ***PRACTICE AREAS:*** Financial Markets and Products; Financial Services; Securities Litigation. ***Email:*** michael.foley@kattenlaw.com

BARRIE M. FRIEND, born Chicago, Illinois, November 9, 1979; admitted to bar, 2004, Illinois. *Education:* University of Michigan (B.A., 2001); Georgetown University Law Center (J.D., 2004). ***PRACTICE AREAS:*** Finance and Reorganization; Financial Services. ***Email:*** barrie.friend@kattenlaw.com

AMY MOOR GAYLORD, born New Hyde Park, New York, August 2, 1972; admitted to bar, 1997, Illinois; 1998, U.S. District Court, Northern and Central Districts of Illinois. *Education:* Cornell University (B.S., 1994); University of Illinois (J.D., 1997, Dean's List). *Member:* Chicago, Illinois State and American Bar Associations. ***PRACTICE AREAS:*** Labor and Employment Law; Litigation and Dispute Resolution; Employee Benefits and Executive Compensation; Business Litigation. ***Email:*** amy.moorgaylord@kattenlaw.com

LAUREN GEOFFREY, admitted to bar, 2004, Illinois. *Education:* University of Michigan (B.A., with high distinction, 2001); Harvard Law School (J.D., 2004). ***PRACTICE AREAS:*** Trusts and Estates. ***Email:*** lauren.geoffrey@kattenlaw.com

BROOKS GILES, admitted to bar, 1999, Illinois. *Education:* University of Chicago (B.A., 1996); Duke University (J.D.; 1999; LL.M., 1999). *Member:* Chicago, Illinois State and American Bar Associations. ***PRACTICE AREAS:*** Corporate Governance; Private Placement; Public Offerings; Mergers, Acquisitions and Divestitures; Leveraged Acquisitions; Leveraged Buyouts. ***Email:*** brooks.giles@kattenlaw.com

JONATHAN GRABER, admitted to bar, 2002, Illinois. *Education:* Western Michigan University (B.B.A., summa cum laude, 1999); Loyola University Chicago School of Law (J.D., cum laude, 2002). ***PRACTICE AREAS:*** Trusts and Estates; Private Client Services. ***Email:*** jonathan.graber@kattenlaw.com

ADAM M. GRANT, admitted to bar, 2003, Illinois. *Education:* Pitzer College (B.A., 1999); Northwestern University (J.D., 2003). ***PRACTICE AREAS:*** Real Estate. ***Email:*** adam.grant@kattenlaw.com

GREGORY S. GROSSMAN, admitted to bar, 2003, Illinois. *Education:* University of Illinois (B.S., with high honors, 2000); George Washington University Law School (J.D., with high honors, 2003). *Member:* Chicago and American Bar Associations. ***PRACTICE AREAS:*** Corporate and Securities; Corporate Governance; Mergers and Acquisitions; Private Equity. ***Email:*** gregory.grossman@kattenlaw.com

MARK RICHARD GROSSMANN, born Chicago, Illinois, April 14, 1972; admitted to bar, 1997, Illinois and U.S. District Court, Northern District of Illinois. *Education:* University of Wisconsin, Madison (B.B.A., 1994); Loyola University (J.D., magna cum laude, 1997). Member, Lynn Sage Cancer Research Foundation. *Member:* Chicago and American Bar Associations. ***PRACTICE AREAS:*** Mergers and Acquisitions; Corporate and Securities; Venture Capital; Private Equity; Securities. ***Email:*** mark.grossmann@kattenlaw.com

MARK D. GUIDUBALDI, born Cleveland, Ohio, September 16, 1972; admitted to bar, 1997, Ohio; 2001, Illinois. *Education:* Miami University, Ohio (B.S.B.A., 1994); Boston College Law School (J.D., cum laude, 1997). ***PRACTICE AREAS:*** Corporate and Securities; Mergers and Acquisitions; Private Equity; Securities. ***Email:*** mark.guidubaldi@kattenlaw.com

ALLEN B. GUTTERMAN, born Nashville, Tennessee, September 8, 1973; admitted to bar, 1998, Illinois. *Education:* University of Wisconsin-Madison (B.A., 1995); John Marshall Law School (J.D., 1998). *Member:* Chicago and Illinois State Bar Associations; Decalogue Society. ***PRACTICE AREAS:*** White Collar Crime; Civil Litigation. ***Email:*** allen.gutterman@kattenlaw.com

ERIC P. HALVERSON, admitted to bar, 2001, Illinois. *Education:* Lawrence University (B.A., 1997); University of Wisconsin Law School (J.D., cum laude, 2001). ***PRACTICE AREAS:*** Corporate; Securities. ***Email:*** eric.halverson@kattenlaw.com

MARIA L. HAMILTON, born Minot, North Dakota, April 16, 1976; admitted to bar, 2002, Illinois. *Education:* University of North Dakota (B.A., 1998); Harvard Law School (J.D., 2002). ***PRACTICE AREAS:*** Finance; Business Reorganization. ***Email:*** maria.hamilton@kattenlaw.com

EMILY J. HENSON, born Springfield, Ohio, February 2, 1974; admitted to bar, 2002, Illinois and U.S. District Court, Northern District of Illinois. *Education:* University of Dayton (B.A., 1996); DePaul University School of Law (J.D., 2002). ***PRACTICE AREAS:*** Litigation; Alternative Dispute Resolution. ***Email:*** emily.henson@kattenlaw.com

(This Listing Continued)

KATTEN MUCHIN ROSENMAN LLP, Chicago—Continued

ANGELITA E. HERNANDEZ, admitted to bar, 2004, Illinois. *Education:* Iowa State University (B.A, 1998); DePaul University (J.D., 2004). ***PRACTICE AREAS:*** Real Estate. ***Email:*** angelita.hernandez@kattenlaw.com

MATTHEW M. HINDERMAN, admitted to bar, 2004, Illinois. *Education:* University of Notre Dame (B.B.A., 1997); Loyola University Chicago (J.D., 2004). ***PRACTICE AREAS:*** Tax Planning; Litigation. ***Email:*** matthew.hinderman@kattenlaw.com

JUSTIN M. HINES, born Chicago, Illinois, July 6, 1969; admitted to bar, 1999, Illinois and U.S. District Court, Northern District of Illinois. *Education:* Fairfield University (B.A., 1993); Emory University (J.D., 1999). *Member:* Chicago and Illinois State Bar Associations. ***PRACTICE AREAS:*** Health Care Insolvency; Financial Services; Bankruptcy; Reorganization; Creditors Rights. ***Email:*** justin.hines@kattenlaw.com

ANDREW D. HOEG, admitted to bar, 2003, Illinois and U.S. District Court, Northern District of Illinois. *Education:* University of Iowa (B.B.A., 1997); University of Illinois, College of Law (J.D., 2003). ***PRACTICE AREAS:*** Litigation and Dispute Resolution. ***Email:*** andrew.hoeg@kattenlaw.com

DEAN V. HOFFMAN, admitted to bar, 2003, Illinois and U.S. District Court, Northern District of Illinois. *Education:* University of California, Berkeley (B.A., 1994); George Mason University (M.A., 1999); University of Virginia (J.D., 2003). ***PRACTICE AREAS:*** Litigation; Alternative Dispute Resolution. ***Email:*** dean.hoffman@kattenlaw.com

FERRIS J. HUSSEIN, born Chicago, Illinois, March 1, 1977; admitted to bar, 2003, Illinois and U.S. District Court, Northern District of Illinois. *Education:* University of Michigan (B.A., 1999); University of Virginia School of Law (J.D., 2003). *Member:* Chicago, Illinois State and American Bar Associations; Fenwick Bar Association; Cabrini Green Legal Aid. ***PRACTICE AREAS:*** Anti-Fraud Counseling; Anti-Fraud Litigation; White Collar Criminal Litigation; Civil Litigation; Litigation; Dispute Resolution. ***Email:*** ferris.hussein@kattenlaw.com

JONI S. JACOBSEN, born Salt Lake City, Utah, December 4, 1967; admitted to bar, 1997, Illinois and U.S. District Court, Northern District of Illinois. *Education:* University of Utah (B.A., History, 1991); University of Chicago (J.D., 1997). *Member:* Chicago and American Bar Associations. ***PRACTICE AREAS:*** Business Litigation; Intellectual Property Litigation; Intellectual Property; Internet and E-Commerce; Litigation and Dispute Resolution. ***Email:*** joni.jacobsen@kattenlaw.com

GREG E. JANSEN, admitted to bar, 1999, Illinois. *Education:* Illinois Wesleyan University (B.A., 1996); University of Minnesota (J.D., 1999). *Member:* Illinois Bar Association; American Institute of Certified Public Accountants; Illinois Certified Public Accountants Society. ***PRACTICE AREAS:*** Corporate Law; Securities; Mergers and Acquisitions; Private Equity; Securities Litigation. ***Email:*** greg.jansen@kattenlaw.com

ADAM JOHNSON, admitted to bar, 2001, Illinois. *Education:* University of Illinois, Urbana-Champaign (B.A., 1998); Indiana University (J.D., 2001). ***PRACTICE AREAS:*** Real Estate. ***Email:*** adam.johnson@kattenlaw.com

JENNY L. JOHNSON, born Oak Lawn, Illinois, June 16, 1974; admitted to bar, 1998, Illinois and U.S. District Court, Northern District of Illinois. *Education:* University of the South (B.A., 1995); Harvard University (J.D., 1998). Phi Beta Kappa; Omicron Delta Kappa. Member: Harvard Club of Chicago; Harvard Law Society of Chicago. ***PRACTICE AREAS:*** Anti-Fraud Counseling and Litigation; Litigation and Dispute Resolution; White Collar Criminal and Civil Litigation. ***Email:*** jenny.johnson@kattenlaw.com

KATHY P. JOSEPHSON, admitted to bar, 2002, Illinois. *Education:* Northwestern University (B.A., 1999; J.D., 2002). ***PRACTICE AREAS:*** Litigation; Alternative Dispute Resolution. ***Email:*** kathy.josephson@kattenlaw.com

TYE J. KLOOSTER, admitted to bar, 2003, Florida; 2004, Illinois. *Education:* University of Iowa (B.B.A., 2000); Drake University Law School (J.D., 2003); New York University School of Law (LL.M. in Taxation, 2004). *Member:* Chicago, Illinois State and American Bar Associations. ***PRACTICE AREAS:*** Trusts and Estates; Taxation. ***Email:*** tye.klooster@kattenlaw.com

JOHN KROL, born Chicago, Illinois, January 4, 1972; admitted to bar, 1997, Illinois. *Education:* University of Illinois (B.A., 1994); DePaul University (J.D., 1997). *Member:* Chicago Bar Association. ***PRACTICE AREAS:*** Finance and Reorganization; Public Administration; Financial Services. ***Email:*** john.krol@kattenlaw.com

DAVID M. KUSHNIR, born Evanston, Illinois, April 11, 1972; admitted to bar, 1997, Illinois. *Education:* University of Michigan (B.A., magna cum laude, 1994); Loyola University (J.D., 1997). *Member:* Chicago and American Bar Associations. ***PRACTICE AREAS:*** Estate Planning. ***Email:*** david.kushnir@kattenlaw.com

DEREK F. LADGENSKI, admitted to bar, 1999, Illinois. *Education:* University of Illinois (B.A. and B.S., 1996); University of Illinois College of Law (J.D., 1999). Member, Community Economic Develpment Law Project. *Member:* Illinois State and American Bar Associations. ***PRACTICE AREAS:*** Finance; Bankruptcy Reorganization. ***Email:*** derek.ladgenski@kattenlaw.com

SHARRON C. LAMOREAUX, born Chandler, Arizona, September 11, 1963; admitted to bar, 1993, Illinois. *Education:* Brigham Young University (B.A., 1986); Washington and Lee University (J.D., 1993). *Member:* Chicago, Illinois State and American Bar Associations. ***PRACTICE AREAS:*** Corporate Insurance; Financial Services. ***Email:*** sharron.lamoreaux@kattenlaw.com

CHRISTIAN J. LANE, admitted to bar, 1998, Illinois. *Education:* Stanford University (A.B., 1993); University of Minnesota Law School (J.D., 1998). ***PRACTICE AREAS:*** Real Estate. ***Email:*** christian.lane@kattenlaw.com

DANIEL B. LANGE, admitted to bar, 2001, Illinois. *Education:* Jewish Theological Seminary of America (B.A., 1997); Washington University School of Law (J.D., 2001). ***PRACTICE AREAS:*** Employee Benefits; Executive Compensation. ***Email:*** daniel.lange@kattenlaw.com

(This Listing Continued)

MELISSA F. LANGSDORF, born Philadelphia, Pennsylvania, October 23, 1976; admitted to bar, 2003, Illinois. *Education:* Cornell University (B.A., 1998); Northwestern University School of Law (J.D., cum laude, 2003). ***PRACTICE AREAS:*** Finance and Reorganization. ***Email:*** melissa.langsdorf@kattenlaw.com

JEANNIE LEE, born Bronx, New York, July 12, 1972; admitted to bar, 2004, New York; U.S. District Court, Eastern and Southern Districts of New York (Not admitted in Illinois). *Education:* Smith College (B.A., English, 1994); American University (M.F.A., 1998); Washington College of Law of American University (J.D., 2002). Co-Author, "Fourth Circuit Strengthens In Rem Jurisdiction in Domain Name Cases," IP TODAY (January 2003). *Member:* American Bar Association. ***PRACTICE AREAS:*** Corporate Law; Securities; Intellectual Property; Technology Law. ***Email:*** jeannie.lee@kattenlaw.com

RYAN J. LIEBL, born Great Bend, Kansas, 1975; admitted to bar, 2004, Illinois. *Education:* University of Notre Dame (B.A., magna cum laude, 1997); Chicago-Kent College of Law (J.D., high honors, 2004). Executive Notes and Comments Editor, Chicago-Kent Law Review. Judicial Extern to: Honorable Ann Claire Williams, U.S. Court of Appeals, Seventh Circuit; Honorable Arlander Keys, U.S. District Court, Northern District of Illinois. Author, "Rule of Law in Postwar Iraq: From Saddam Hussein to the American Soldiers Involved in the Abu Ghraib Prison Scandal, What Law Governs Whose Actions?," 28 Hamline Law Rewiew, 2004; "State Unclaimed Property Statutes and Employee Benefit Plans: Will ERISA Preemption Excuse Compliance of Benefits Plans with State Unclaimed Property Statutes?," 2004 Aspen Employment Law Update 187, 2004. *Member:* Chicago and American Bar Associations. ***PRACTICE AREAS:*** Employee Benefits; Executive Compensation. ***Email:*** ryan.liebl@kattenlaw.com

ALEX LIKER, admitted to bar, 2001, Illinois. *Education:* Loyola University (B.S., 1998); Chicago-Kent College of Law (J.D., 2001). ***LANGUAGES:*** Russian and Ukranian. ***PRACTICE AREAS:*** Corporate; Finance; Mergers and Acquisitions; Private Equity. ***Email:*** alex.liker@kattenlaw.com

MICHAEL J. LOHNES, born Decatur, Illinois, October 21, 1977; admitted to bar, 2004, Illinois. *Education:* University of Southern California (B.A., 2000); George Washington University (J.D., with highest honor, 2004). ***PRACTICE AREAS:*** Litigation; Dispute Resolution. ***Email:*** michael.lohnes@kattenlaw.com

STEPHEN J. LOMBARDO, III, admitted to bar, 1999, Illinois. *Education:* Georgetown University (B.S.B.A., 1996; J.D., 1999). ***PRACTICE AREAS:*** Corporate Law; Securities; Mergers and Acquisitions; Securities Litigation. ***Email:*** stephen.lombardo@kattenlaw.com

AMY E. LUM, admitted to bar, 1996, Illinois; 1998, U.S. District Court, Northern District of Illinois. *Education:* Michigan State University (B.A., 1993); Loyola University, Chicago (J.D., 1996). Senior Attorney, Enforcement Division, U.S. Securities and Exchange Commission in Chicago. ***PRACTICE AREAS:*** Litigation; Dispute Resolution. ***Email:*** amy.lum@kattenlaw.com

SCOTT E. LYONS, born Boston, Massachusetts, December 28, 1970; admitted to bar, 1996, Illinois. *Education:* University of Illinois (B.S., Finance, 1993; J.D., 1996). ***PRACTICE AREAS:*** Finance and Reorganization; Corporate and Securities; Internet and E-Commerce; Mergers and Acquisitions; Private Equity. ***Email:*** scott.lyons@kattenlaw.com

KATHERINE A. MAJEWSKI, admitted to bar, 2003, Illinois. *Education:* Claremont McKenna College (B.A., 2000); University of Michigan (J.D., 2003). ***PRACTICE AREAS:*** Corporate and Securities. ***Email:*** katherine.majewski@kattenlaw.com

JASON M. MARKS, born New Haven, Connecticut, January 26, 1976; admitted to bar, 2001, Illinois. *Education:* University of Chicago (A.B., 1998); The George Washington University Law School (J.D., with honors, 2001). ***LANGUAGES:*** Hebrew and Latin. ***PRACTICE AREAS:*** Litigation; Alternative Dispute Resolution. ***Email:*** jason.marks@kattenlaw.com

BELINDA I. MATHIE, admitted to bar, 2001, Illinois; 2002, U.S. District Court, Northern District of Illinois and U.S. Court of Appeals, Eighth Circuit. *Education:* University of Michigan (B.A., 1998); University of Chicago (J.D., 2001). ***PRACTICE AREAS:*** Litigation; Alternative Dispute Resolution. ***Email:*** belinda.mathie@kattenlaw.com

MICHELLE McGUINESS, born Chicago, Illinois, January 3, 1970; admitted to bar, 2001, Illinois and U.S. District Court, Northern District of Illinois. *Education:* University of Illinois (B.A., 1993); University of Chicago (J.D., 2001). *Member:* Chicago Bar Association; Women's Bar Association of Illinois. ***PRACTICE AREAS:*** Business Litigation; Litigation and Dispute Resolution; Securities Litigation. ***Email:*** michelle.mcguiness@kattenlaw.com

MEGAN P. McKNIGHT, admitted to bar, 2003, Illinois and U.S. District Court, Northern District of Illinois. *Education:* Kalamazoo College (B.A., cum laude, 1999); University of Michigan (J.D., cum laude, 2003). *Member:* Chicago and American Bar Associations. ***LANGUAGES:*** Spanish. ***PRACTICE AREAS:*** Litigation; Alternative Dispute Resolution. ***Email:*** megan.mcknight@kattenlaw.com

CAROLYN E. MILLER, born Evanston, Illinois, February 15, 1979; admitted to bar, 2004, Illinois. *Education:* Miami University (B.A., cum laude, 2001); DePaul University (J.D., cum laude, 2004). Editor, DePaul University Law Review. ***PRACTICE AREAS:*** Intellectual Property; Technology and Science. ***Email:*** carolyn.miller@kattenlaw.com

JAMES E. MITCHELL, born Indianapolis, Indiana, October 12, 1966; admitted to bar, 1997, Illinois and U.S. District Court, Northern District of Illinois. *Education:* DePauw University (B.A., 1989); Indiana University (M.A., 1991); DePaul University (J.D., 1997). Beta Kappa. ***PRACTICE AREAS:*** Environmental Services. ***Email:*** james.mitchell@kattenlaw.com

MONICA J. MOSBY, born Chicago, Illinois, April 23, 1973; admitted to bar, 2004, Illinois. *Education:* DePaul University (B.S., 1996; J.D., cum laude, 2004). Judicial Extern to Honorable Ronald A. Guzman, U.S. District Court, Northern District of Illinois. Fellow Representative, PILI Board of Directors as the 2004-2006. *Member:* Chicago, Cook County and American Bar Associations; Black Women Lawyers' Association of Greater Chicago. ***PRACTICE AREAS:*** Litigation; Dispute Resolution. ***Email:*** monica.mosby@kattenlaw.com

(This Listing Continued)

MATTHEW A. OLINS, admitted to bar, 2001, Illinois and U.S. District Court, Northern District of Illinois. *Education:* Kenyon College (B.A., 1996); Washington University (J.D., 2001). *Member:* Chicago and American Bar Associations; American Bankruptcy Institute. ***PRACTICE AREAS:*** Bankruptcy; Reorganization; Creditors Rights; Finance. ***Email:*** mathew.olins@kattenlaw.com

HEATHER KUHN O'TOOLE, admitted to bar, 2002, Illinois. *Education:* University of Illinois (B.S., 1998); Loyola University Chicago School of Law (J.D., 2002). ***PRACTICE AREAS:*** Litigation; Alternative Dispute Resolution. ***Email:*** heather.otoole@kattenlaw.com

RAM PADMANABHAN, born Vancouver, British Columbia, November 7, 1968; admitted to bar, 1993, Illinois, U.S. Court of Appeals, 7th Circuit and U.S. District Court, Northern and Central Districts of Illinois. *Education:* McGill University (B.A., with distinction, 1990); Northwestern University School of Law (J.D., cum laude, 1993). Executive Editor, Northwestern University Law Review. Law Clerk to the Honorable William J. Bauer, U.S. Court of Appeals for the Seventh Circuit, 1993-1995. Adjunct Professor, Northwestern University School of Law, 2000-2001. *Member:* Chicago and American Bar Associations. ***PRACTICE AREAS:*** Corporate; Securities; Mergers and Acquisitions; Sports Law; Sports Facilities Development; Technology; Advertising. ***Email:*** rp@kattenlaw.com

ALYX S. PATTISON, born Salt Lake City, Utah, July 8, 1974; admitted to bar, 2003, Illinois. *Education:* University of Utah (B.A., 1997); Northwestern University School of Law (J.D., 2003). ***PRACTICE AREAS:*** Litigation and Dispute Resolution. ***Email:*** alyx.pattison@kattenlaw.com

KYLE A. PETERSEN, born New Haven, Connecticut, July 27, 1973; admitted to bar, 2001, Illinois. *Education:* Indiana University at Bloomington (B.A., 1995); Chicago-Kent College of Law (J.D., 2001). Order of the Coif. Member, Chicago-Kent Law Review, 2000-2001. *Member:* Chicago and American Bar Associations; Women's Bar Association of Illinois. ***PRACTICE AREAS:*** Labor and Employment. ***Email:*** kyle.peterson@kattenlaw.com

CAROLYNN PFAFF, born Woodford Green, Essex, England, May 5, 1968; admitted to bar, 1999, Illinois. *Education:* Miami University (B.S., 1990); Indiana University (J.D., 1999). ***PRACTICE AREAS:*** Trusts and Estates. ***Email:*** carolynn.pfaff@kattenlaw.com

DANIEL J. POLATSEK, born Abington, Pennsylvania, October 26, 1970; admitted to bar, 1997, Illinois, U.S. District Court, Northern District of Illinois and U.S. Court of Appeals, Seventh Circuit. *Education:* Tulane University (B.A., 1992); John Marshall Law School (J.D, 1996). Pi Sigma Alpha. Member, National Criminal Procedure Moot Court Team, 1995 and 1996. Staff Editor, John Marshall Journal of Computer and Information Law, 1995-1996. Judicial Law Clerk, Honorable Margaret Stanton McBride, Illinois Appellate Court, 1998-2000. Author: "Preserving the Attorney-Client Privilege: *Ex Parte* Interviews of Former Corporate Employees," For the Defense, Vol. 44, No. 12 (December 2002); "Attorney-Client Privilege, Corporate Clients and the Control-Group Test," IL Bar Jnr., Vol. 91, February 2003; "Thermal Imaging and the Fourth Amendment: Pushing the Katz Test Towards Terminal Velocity," 13 J. Marshall J. Computer & Info. L. 453 (1995). Office of the State Appellate Defender, 1997-1998. *Member:* Chicago, Illinois State and American Bar Associations. ***REPORTED CASES:*** People v. Hilt, 698 N.E.2d 233, 298 Ill.App.3d 121 (1998). ***PRACTICE AREAS:*** Litigation and Dispute Resolution; Anti-Fraud Counseling and Litigation; White Collar Criminal and Civil Litigation. ***Email:*** daniel.polatsek@kattenlaw.com

ANGELA C. RAMEY, admitted to bar, 2004, Illinois. *Education:* University of Illinois at Chicago (B.A., 1994); University of Illinois at Chicago (M.A, 1997); Chicago Law School (J.D., 2004). ***PRACTICE AREAS:*** Finance and Reorganization; Financial Services. ***Email:*** angela.ramey@kattenlaw.com

BRADLEY S. ROCHLEN, born Royal Oak, Michigan, October 7, 1973; admitted to bar, 1998, Illinois. *Education:* University of Michigan (B.A., 1995; J.D., 1997). ***PRACTICE AREAS:*** Environmental Services; Intellectual Property Litigation; Intellectual Property; Litigation and Dispute Resolution. ***Email:*** bradley.rochlen@kattenlaw.com

ERIC R. ROCK, admitted to bar, 2004, Illinois; U.S. Court of International Trade; U.S. Court of Appeals, Federal Circuit. *Education:* Loyola University (B.A., magna cum laude, 2000; J.D. 2004). Recipient, National Customs Brokers Association Scholarship Award, 1998. Brokers License, Illinois, 1990. Author, "The Future Impact of Technology on the Broker and Forwarder," 1998. Member, Former Vice-President and Customs Committee Chairman, Customs Brokers and Foreign Freight Forwarder's Association of Chicago. *Member:* Chicago Bar Association. ***SPECIAL AGENCIES:*** Customs and Border Protection; Food and Drug Administration; Department of Agriculture; Fish & Widlife Service; Bureau of Alcohol, Tobacco and Firearms. ***PRACTICE AREAS:*** Customs Trade (50%); International Trade (50%). ***Email:*** eric.rock@kattenlaw.com

KIRK ROSS, born Grand Rapids, Michigan, December 1, 1974; admitted to bar, 2004, Illinois. *Education:* Berry College (B.S.B.A., cum laude,1997); Bowling Green State University (M.A., 2001); Northwestern University School of Law (J.D., 2004). ***LANGUAGES:*** German. ***PRACTICE AREAS:*** Corporate; Securities; Technology. ***Email:*** kirk.ross@kattenlaw.com

JEFFREY L. RUDD, born San Antonio, Texas, September 5, 1975; admitted to bar, 2000, Illinois. *Education:* University of Illinois (B.A., 1997); Georgetown University (J.D., cum laude, 2000). ***PRACTICE AREAS:*** Labor and Employment. ***Email:*** jeffrey.rudd@kattenlaw.com

JENNIFER C. RYAN, born February 12, 1975; admitted to bar, 2001, Illinois. *Education:* Northern Illinois University (B.A., 1997); University of Illinois (J.D., 2001; M.B.A., 2001). *Member:* American Bar Association. ***PRACTICE AREAS:*** Litigation; Dispute Resolution. ***Email:*** jennifer.ryan@kattenlaw.com

BLAKE EVAN SCHULMAN, born Philadelphia, Pennsylvania, February 13, 1977; admitted to bar, 2002, Illinois. *Education:* University of Michigan (B.B.A., with high distinction, 1999; J.D., cum laude, 2001). *Member:* Chicago and American Bar Associations. ***PRACTICE AREAS:*** Corporate and Securities; Mergers and Acquisitions; Private Equity. ***Email:*** blake.schulman@kattenlaw.com

STEVEN A. SCHWAB, born Cincinnati, Ohio, September 22, 1977; admitted to bar, 2002, Illinois. *Education:* Miami University of Ohio (B.A., 1999); Loyola University Chicago School of Law (J.D., cum laude, 2002). *Member:* American Bar Association. ***PRACTICE AREAS:*** Financial Services; Commodities. ***Email:*** steven.schwab@kattenlaw.com

JULIE P. SETREN, born Baltimore, Maryland, November 10, 1978; admitted to bar, 2003, Illinois and U.S. District Court, Northern District of Illinois. *Education:* George Washington University (B.A., summa cum laude, 2000); Northwestern University School of Law (J.D., cum laude, 2003). *Member:* Chicago and American Bar Associations. ***PRACTICE AREAS:*** Intellectual Property; Intellectual Property Litigation; Internet and E-Commerce; Music Law; Entertainment and Media. ***Email:*** julie.setren@kattenlaw.com

JASON P. SHAFFER, born 1975; admitted to bar, 2000, Illinois, U.S. District Court, Northern District of Illinois and U.S. Court of Appeals, Seventh Circuit; 2002, U.S. District Court, Northern District of Indiana. *Education:* Cedarville University (B.A., 1997); Chicago-Kent College of Law, Illinois Institute of Technology (J.D., with honors, 2000). *Member:* Chicago (Member, Trial Techniques Committee), Illinois State and American Bar Associations. ***PRACTICE AREAS:*** Litigation; Alternative Dispute Resolution; Business Litigation; Intellectual Property; Intellectual Property Litigation. ***Email:*** jason.shaffer@kattenlaw.com

BRIAN T. SHEEDY, admitted to bar, 2001, Georgia (Not admitted in Illinois). *Education:* University of Notre Dame (B.A., 1999); Duke University (J.D., 2001). ***PRACTICE AREAS:*** Real Estate. ***Email:*** brian.sheedy@kattenlaw.com

VICTORIA SHUSTERMAN, born September 13, 1973; admitted to bar, 1998, Illinois. *Education:* Northwestern University (B.A., 1995); Washington University (J.D., 1998). *Member:* Chicago and American Bar Associations. ***LANGUAGES:*** Russian. ***PRACTICE AREAS:*** Real Estate; Real Estate Finance. ***Email:*** victoria.shusterman@kattenlaw.com

DAVID S. SLOVICK, born Wisconsin, August 9, 1972; admitted to bar, 1998, Illinois; 2000, U.S. District Court, Northern District of Illinois; 2004, U.S. District Court, Eastern District of Wisconsin. *Education:* University of Wisconsin-Madison (B.A., 1994); Chicago-Kent College of Law (J.D., 1998). *Chicago and Illinois State Bar Associations.* ***PRACTICE AREAS:*** Securities Litigation. ***Email:*** david.slovick@kattenlaw.com

ERIC ANTHONY SMITH, admitted to bar, 1999, Illinois. *Education:* University of Illinois (B.A., 1995; M.B.A., 1999; J.D., 1999). ***PRACTICE AREAS:*** Corporate Law; Securities; Mergers and Acquisitions; Private Equity; Securities Litigation. ***Email:*** eric.smith@kattenlaw.com

KIMBERLY THOMPSON SMITH, born Bloomington, Illinois, November 16, 1972; admitted to bar, 1998, Illinois. *Education:* University of Illinois (B.A., summa cum laude, 1995); Georgetown University (J.D., 1998). Author: "Cell Phone Snooping: Why Electronic Eavesdropping Goes Unpublished," Vol. 35, American Criminal Law Review, 1997. *Member:* Chicago and American Bar Associations. ***PRACTICE AREAS:*** Mergers and Acquisitions; Securities Regulation; Venture Capital; Private Equity; Securities. ***Email:*** kimberly.smith@kattenlaw.com

JENNIFER A. SMULIN, admitted to bar, 2003, Illinois. *Education:* University of Illinois (B.S., 2000); DePaul University (J.D., summa cum laude, 2003). ***PRACTICE AREAS:*** Litigation; Alternative Dispute Resolution. ***Email:*** jennifer.smulin@kattenlaw.com

DAVID J. STAGMAN, admitted to bar, 1993, Illinois. *Education:* Princeton University (B.A., 1986); University of Chicago (M.A., 1989); Northwestern University (J.D., 1993). Associate Note and Comment Editor, Northwestern University Law Review. *Member:* Chicago Bar Association. ***PRACTICE AREAS:*** Anti-Fraud Counseling and Litigation; Antitrust; Litigation; Dispute Resolution; White Collar Criminal and Civil Litigation. ***Email:*** david.stagman@kattenlaw.com

CHRISTOPHER J. STETLER, admitted to bar, 2004, Illinois. *Education:* Washington University (B.A., with honors 2001); University of Illinois (J.D., magna cum laude, 2004). ***PRACTICE AREAS:*** Litigation; Dispute Resolution. ***Email:*** christopher.stetler@kattenlaw.com

JOANNA R. STEVANSON, admitted to bar, 2004, Illinois. *Education:* Williams College (B.A., 1998); University of Virginia (J.D., 2004). ***LANGUAGES:*** Spanish. ***PRACTICE AREAS:*** Litigation; Dispute Resolution. ***Email:*** joanna.stevason@kattenlaw.com

BRYAN F. STROH, admitted to bar, 2002, Illinois and U.S. District Court, Northern District of Illinois. *Education:* Princeton University (A.B., 1998); University of Virginia School of Law (J.D., 2002). ***PRACTICE AREAS:*** Litigation and Dispute Resolution; Alternative Dispute Resolution. ***Email:*** bryan.stroh@kattenlaw.com

MICHAEL J. SUMMERHILL, admitted to bar, 1998, Ohio; 1999, U.S. District Court, Northern District of Ohio; 2000, U.S. Court of Appeals, 7th Circuit; 2001, Illinois and U.S. District Court, Northern District of Illinois. *Education:* The Ohio State University (B.A., 1994); John Marshall Law School (J.D., cum laude, 1998). Editor-in-Chief, The John Marshall Law Review. *Member:* American Bar Association; Chicago Volunteer Legal Services; Defense Research Institute. ***LANGUAGES:*** Spanish. ***PRACTICE AREAS:*** Business Litigation; Litigation; Dispute Resolution; Products Liability; Securities Litigation. ***Email:*** michael.summerhill@kattenlaw.com

PHILIP TORTORICH, born Melrose Park, Illinois, August 17, 1974; admitted to bar, 1999, Illinois and U.S. District Court, Northern District of Illinois. *Education:* Loyola University (B.A., 1996; J.D., cum laude, 1999). Phi Alpha Delta (Founding Member, Undergraduate Chapter, 1996.) *Member:* Chicago and Illinois State Bar Associations. ***PRACTICE AREAS:*** Trusts and Estates; Probate; Corporate Law. ***Email:*** philip.tortorich@kattenlaw.com

DAVID J. VALECK, born Mount Clemens, Michigan, March 14, 1972; admitted to bar, 1999, New York; 2000, Illinois. *Education:* Michigan State University (B.A., 1994); University of Michigan (M.B.A./J.D., 1998). *Member:* New York State Bar Association. ***PRACTICE AREAS:*** Finance and Reorganization; Structured Finance. ***Email:*** david.valeck@kattenlaw.com

AARON J. VANGETSON, admitted to bar, 2003, Illinois. *Education:* University of Illinois (B.S., with high honors, 1999; J.D., magna cum laude, 2003). *Member:* Chicago and American Bar Associations. ***PRACTICE AREAS:*** Corporate Law; Securities; Corporate Governance; Mergers and Acquisitions; Private Equity. ***Email:*** aaron.vangetson@kattenlaw.com

(This Listing Continued)

KATTEN MUCHIN ROSENMAN LLP, Chicago—Continued

JOSEPH A. VENZON, admitted to bar, 1997, Illinois. *Education:* Harvard University (A.B., 1994); Northwestern University (J.D., 1997). *Member:* Chicago and American Bar Associations. ***LANGUAGES:*** Spanish. ***PRACTICE AREAS:*** Real Estate. ***Email:*** joseph.venzon@kattenlaw.com

RITU VIG, admitted to bar, 2002, Michigan (Not admitted in Illinois). *Education:* University of Illinois at Urbana-Champaign (B.S., Finance, 1999; J.D., 2002). ***LANGUAGES:*** Hindi and Spanish. ***Email:*** ritu.vig@kattenlaw.com

RACHEL M. VORBECK, born Kansas City, Missouri, June 15, 1971; admitted to bar, 1996, Illinois. *Education:* University of Missouri (B.A., 1993); Northwestern University School of Law (J.D., 1996). ***PRACTICE AREAS:*** Litigation and Dispute Resolution. ***Email:*** rachel.vorbeck@kattenlaw.com

MICHAEL S. WEISMAN, born Chicago, Illinois, December 27, 1958; admitted to bar, 1999, Illinois and U.S. District Court, Northern District of Illinois. *Education:* University of Illinois (B.A., 1981); Chicago-Kent College of Law, Illinois Institute of Technology (J.D., 1998). ***PRACTICE AREAS:*** Litigation and Dispute Resolution; White Collar Criminal and Civil Litigation; Securities; Financial Services. ***Email:*** michael.weisman@kattenlaw.com

BECKY A. WILLIAMS, born Oak Lawn, Illinois, June 5, 1973; admitted to bar, 2000, Illinois. *Education:* Marquette University (B.A., 1995); DePaul University (J.D., 2000). ***PRACTICE AREAS:*** Intellectual Property. ***Email:*** becky.williams@kattenlaw.com

JENNIFER I. WOLFE, born Skokie, Illinois, July 29, 1974; admitted to bar, 2000, Illinois. *Education:* Indiana University (B.S., 1996); DePaul University College of Law (J.D., 2000). Business Manager, Editor, De Paul Law Review, 1999-2000. ***LANGUAGES:*** Spanish. ***PRACTICE AREAS:*** Finance and Reorganization. ***Email:*** jennifer.wolfe@kattenlaw.com

TODD D. YAROSS, born Cincinnati, Ohio, March 4, 1978; admitted to bar, 2004, Ohio; 2005, Illinois. *Education:* The Ohio State University (B.A., 2000); Northwestern University (J.D., 2004). *Member:* American Bar Association. ***LANGUAGES:*** Spanish. ***PRACTICE AREAS:*** Corporate Law; Mergers and Acquisitions; Private Equity. ***Email:*** todd.yaross@kattenlaw.com

LANCE A. ZINMAN, born Manhasset, New York, January 14, 1973; admitted to bar, 1998, Illinois. *Education:* Michigan State University (B.A., summa cum laude, honors, 1995); Northwestern University (J.D., cum laude, 1998). Phi Kappa Phi; Beta Gamma Sigma. Journal of International Law and Business - Note and Comment Editor, Northwestern University. *Member:* Chicago and American Bar Associations. ***PRACTICE AREAS:*** Corporate; Securities; Mergers and Acquisitions; Music Law; Sports Law; Sports Facilities Development; Advertising; Financial Services. ***Email:*** lance.zinman@kattenlaw.com

JOHN E. ZUMMO, born Chicago, Illinois, October 25, 1969; admitted to bar, 1997, Illinois; 1999, District of Columbia. *Education:* Marquette University (B.A., cum laude, 1992); John Marshall Law School (J.D., cum laude, 1997). *Member:* Illinois State Bar Association. [Lt., U.S. Navy, 1997-2000]. ***PRACTICE AREAS:*** Litigation; Alternative Dispute Resolution; White Collar Crime; Civil Litigation; Commercial Litigation. ***Email:*** john.zummo@kattenlaw.com

STAFF ATTORNEYS

ERICA TINA HELFER, born New York, N.Y., January 5, 1956; admitted to bar, 1980, Missouri; 1981, Illinois; U.S. District Court, Northern District of Illinois. *Education:* Washington University (A.B., 1976); St. Louis University (J.D., cum laude, 1980). Law Clerk to Senior Judge William H. Becker, U.S. District Court, Western District of Missouri, 1980-1981. Author: "Search and Seizure in Public Schools: Are Our Children's Rights Going to the Dogs?" 24 St. Louis University Law Journal, 1979. *Member:* Chicago and Illinois State Bar Associations. ***LANGUAGES:*** French. ***PRACTICE AREAS:*** Environmental Law; Family Law; Corporate Insurance; Financial Services. ***Email:*** ericatina.helfer@kattenlaw.com

REBECCA JANOVSKY, born Gary, Indiana, November 21, 1962; admitted to bar, 1988, Indiana; 1999, Illinois. *Education:* Miami University (B.A., 1985); Indiana University School of Law (J.D., 1988). ***PRACTICE AREAS:*** Real Estate. ***Email:*** rebecca.janovsky@kattenlaw.com

KELLI CHASE PLOTZ, born Spring Valley, Illinois, June 3, 1961; admitted to bar, 1986, Illinois. *Education:* University of Illinois, Champaign-Urbana (B.S., 1983); DePaul University College of Law (J.D., 1986). *Member:* Chicago and Illinois State Bar Associations; Women's Bar Association. ***PRACTICE AREAS:*** Corporate and Securities; Trusts and Estates. ***Email:*** kelli.plotz@kattenlaw.com

OF COUNSEL

LIZABETH F. HORN, born Muncie, Indiana, April 9, 1947; admitted to bar, 1974, Illinois. *Education:* DePauw University (B.A., 1969); Loyola University of Chicago (J.D., 1974). *Member:* Chicago (Member, Committee on Probate Practice, 1976; Chairman, Div. V, 1979-1980; Executive Committee, 1978-1981) and Illinois State (Member, Trusts and Estates Subcommittee, 1979) Bar Associations. ***PRACTICE AREAS:*** Trusts and Estates; Corporate; Securities. ***Email:*** lizabeth.horn@kattenlaw.com

KATHLEEN A. JAREMA, born Harvey, Illinois, December 10, 1946; admitted to bar, 1987, Michigan (inactive); 1988, District of Columbia (inactive); 1990, Illinois; U.S. District Court, Northern District of Illinois. *Education:* Southern Illinois University (B.A., 1972); National College of Education (M.S., 1976); Detroit College of Law at Michigan State University (J.D., cum laude, 1987). ***PRACTICE AREAS:*** Corporate and Securities; Securities. ***Email:*** kathleen.jarema@kattenlaw.com

MELVIN L. KATTEN, (P.C.), born Chicago, Illinois, September 5, 1936; admitted to bar, 1963, Illinois. *Education:* University of Illinois (B.S., 1958); The John Marshall Law School (J.D., 1963). Certified Public Accountant, Illinois, 1960. Vice Chairman, Roosevelt University. Past President, Better Government Association. Chairman: Auditorium Theater

(This Listing Continued)

of Roosevelt University, Inc.; Greater Chicago/Wisconsin Regional Board of the Anti-Defamation League. *Member:* Chicago, Illinois State and American Bar Associations. ***PRACTICE AREAS:*** Tax; Corporate. ***Email:*** melvin.katten@kattenlaw.com

ALLAN B. MUCHIN, (P.C.), born Manitowoc, Wisconsin, January 10, 1936; admitted to bar, 1961, Wisconsin and Illinois. *Education:* University of Wisconsin (B.B.A., 1958; LL.B., 1961). Attorney, Regional Counsel's Office, Internal Revenue Service, Chicago, 1961-1965. *Member:* Chicago, Illinois State and American Bar Associations. ***PRACTICE AREAS:*** Corporate and Taxation. ***Email:*** allan.muchin@kattenlaw.com

STEPHEN M. NEUMER, born Grand Rapids, Michigan, July 27, 1940; admitted to bar, 1966, Illinois. *Education:* University of Michigan (B.B.A., magna cum laude, 1962); Stanford University (J.D., 1965). Beta Alpha Psi; Beta Gamma Sigma; Phi Kappa Phi. Member, Board of Editors, Stanford Law Review. *Member:* Chicago, American and International Bar Associations. ***PRACTICE AREAS:*** Corporate; Securities; Mergers and Acquisitions. ***Email:*** stephen.neumer@kattenlaw.com

MELVIN E. PEARL, (P.C.), born Chicago, Illinois, February 25, 1936; admitted to bar, 1960, Illinois; U.S. Tax Court. *Education:* University of Wisconsin (B.B.A., 1957); Northwestern University (J.D., 1960). Special Trial Attorney, Office of the Chief Counsel, Internal Revenue Service, Washington, D.C., 1960-1965. Member: Alzheimer's Foundation; Better Boys Foundation; Film School of the Art Institute; RKO Pictures; Taylor Capital Group. ***PRACTICE AREAS:*** Corporate Finance Law; Entertainment and Media; Finance and Reorganization; Mergers and Acquisitions. ***Email:*** melvin.pearl@kattenlaw.com

SPECIAL COUNSEL

MARGARET P. GRIFFITHS, born Evergreen Park, Illinois, May 18, 1966; admitted to bar, 1991, Illinois and U.S. District Court, Northern District of Illinois. *Education:* Purdue University (B.A., 1988); DePaul University (J.D., 1991). Member, 1989-1990, Editor of Notes and Comments, 1990-1991, DePaul Business Law Journal. *Member:* Chicago (Member, Tort Litigation Committee), Illinois State and American Bar Associations; Women's Bar Association of Illinois (Member, Tort Committee). ***PRACTICE AREAS:*** Health Care. ***Email:*** margaret.griffiths@kattenlaw.com

STACEY KOMON, admitted to bar, 1994, Illinois; 2000, California. *Education:* University of Illinois at Urbana-Champaign (B.S., 1991); Loyola University of Chicago School of Law (J.D., 1994). ***PRACTICE AREAS:*** Venture Capital; Mergers and Acquisitions; Private Equity; Corporate. ***Email:*** stacey.komon@kattenlaw.com

PATRICIA LEVY, born Cincinnati, Ohio, May 11, 1959; admitted to bar, 1985, Illinois. *Education:* Miami University (B.Phil., cum laude, 1981); University of Virginia (J.D., 1985). Vice President and General Counsel, Chicago Stock Exchange, 1997-1999. Executive Director, SBC Warburg Dillon Reed, 1992-1997. Associate, Schiff Hardin & Waite, 1985-1992. ***PRACTICE AREAS:*** Financial Services Law. ***Email:*** pat.levy@kattenlaw.com

LISA K. SHEBAR, admitted to bar, 1993, Texas; 1995, Illinois and U.S. District Court, Northern District of Illinois. *Education:* Wheaton College (B.A., Mathematics and Economics, cum laude, 1990); University of Illinois College of Law (J.D., 1993). *Member:* Chicago and American Bar Associations; International Trademark Association. ***PRACTICE AREAS:*** Intellectual Property Litigation; Intellectual Property; Litigation; Alternative Dispute Resolution.

LINDA K. SHORE, born Detroit, Michigan, April 28, 1959; admitted to bar, 1984, Florida; 1989, District of Columbia (Not admitted in Illinois). *Education:* Boston University (B.A., summa cum laude, 1980); University of Michigan (J.D., 1983); Georgetown University (LL.M., Labor, 1989). Phi Beta Kappa. Author: "Rethinking Fiduciary Structures in the Post-Enron Era," Tax Management Compensation Planning Journal, November 2003; "Fallout from the Enron Debacle: How Will ESOPs Be Affected? A Legislative Overview," Beyster Institute Ezine, June 2002; "Charging Expenses to an ERISA Plan: The New Rules," Tax Management Compensation Planning Journal, September 2001; "DOL's Final Rule on Insurance Company General Accounts: How Much Does It Resolve?" Tax Management Compensation Planning Journal, June 2000; "One Good Deed May Go Unpunished: Do Plan Sponsors Really Increase Fiduciary Risk by Offering Third-Party Investment Advice to Participants?" Tax Management Compensation Planning Journal, August 1999; "SEC and DOL Developments in Executive Compensation: The Plot Thickens," Tax Executives Institutte 52nd Annual Conference, October 1997; "Law vs. Technology: 'Paperless' Participant Loans," Employee Benefits Quarterly, August 1997; Chapter, "Insurance Companies as Fiduciaries," Life Insurance Answer Book, Aspen Publishers, Inc., 1997—. Adjunct Professor, Georgetown University Law Center, 1994—. Attorney, Office of Regulations and Interpretations, Pension and Welfare Benefits Administration, U.S. Department of Labor, Washington, D.C., 1984-1988. *Member:* District of Columbia Bar; The Florida Bar; American Bar Association (Section on Taxation). ***PRACTICE AREAS:*** Employee Benefits Law; Executive Compensation. ***Email:*** linda.shore@kattenlaw.com

THOMAS E. SWEENEY, born Evergreen Park, Illinois, March 10, 1957; admitted to bar, 1988, Illinois. *Education:* Southern Illinois University (B.S., 1980; M.A., 1981); Loyola University (J.D., 1988). ***PRACTICE AREAS:*** Real Estate; Real Estate Taxation. ***Email:*** thomas.sweeney@kattenlaw.com

MELISSA L. WESTBROOK, born Perth Amboy, New Jersey, May 6, 1969; admitted to bar, 1994, New York (Not admitted in Illinois). *Education:* University of Missouri at Columbia (B.A., with honors, Political Science, cum laude, 1991) Phi Beta Kappa; New York University School of Law (J.D., 1994). Phi Kappa Phi. Named University Scholar, University of Missouri. Member, Honors College. Staff Editor, New York University Review of Law and Social Change, 1993-1994. *Member:* American Bar Association. ***PRACTICE AREAS:*** Corporate Law; Securities; Capital Markets; Private Equity. ***Email:*** melissa.westbrook@kattenlaw.com

KAYE SCHOLER LLP

A New York Limited Liability Partnership

3 FIRST NATIONAL PLAZA
SUITE 4100
70 WEST MADISON STREET
CHICAGO, ILLINOIS 60602
Telephone: 312-583-2300
Facsimile: 312-583-2360
URL: http://www.kayescholer.com

New York, N.Y.: 425 Park Avenue, 10022-3598. Telephone: 212-836-8000. Telex: 234860 KAY UR. Facsimile: 212-836-8689.
Washington, D.C.: McPherson Building, 901 Fifteenth Street, N.W., Suite 1100, 20005-2327. Telephone: 202-682-3500. Facsimile: 202-682-3580.
Los Angeles, California: 1999 Avenue of the Stars, Suite 1600, 90067-6048. Telephone: 310-788-1000. Facsimile: 310-788-1200.
West Palm Beach, Florida Office: Phillips Point, West Tower 900, 777 South Flagler Drive, 33401-6163. Telephone: 561-802-3230. Facsimile: 561-802-3217.
Shanghai, Peoples Republic of China: Suite 1504-1506 CITIC Square, 1168 Nanjing Xi Lu, 200041. Telephone: 011 86-21 5298-4266. Facsimile: 011 86-21 5298-4277.
London, England Office: 5th Floor, 120 Aldersgate Street, EC 1A 4JQ. Telephone: 011-020-8528-1006, Fax: 011-020-8528-1174.
Frankfurt, Germany Office: Bockenheimer Landstr. 61, 60325. Telephone: 011-49-69-25494-0. Fax: 011-49-69-25494-4444.

General and Administrative Practice. Banking Law, Bankruptcy, Finance, Securitization.

RESIDENT PARTNERS

STEPHEN E. GARCIA, born April 1962; admitted to bar, 1987, Illinois and U.S. District Court, Northern District of Illinois; 1988, U.S. Court of Appeals, 7th Circuit. *Education:* Michigan State University (B.A., 1984); University of Michigan (J.D., 1987).

DANIEL HARTNETT, born September 1957; admitted to bar, 1986, Illinois; 1987, Texas. *Education:* Northwestern University (B.A., 1979; M.M., 1983; J.D., 1986). ***Email:*** dhartnett@kayescholer.com

GARY R. SILVERMAN, born 1961; admitted to bar, 1986, Illinois; 1987, Colorado; 1988, District of Columbia; 1994, New York. *Education:* Brandeis University (B.A., 1983); Northwestern University (J.D., 1986); University of Chicago Graduate School of Business (M.B.A., 1990). (Partner, Corporate/Finance). ***PRACTICE AREAS:*** Corporate Law; Finance. ***Email:*** gsilverman@kayescholer.com

MICHAEL B. SOLOW, born January 1959; admitted to bar, 1984, Illinois, U.S. District Courts, Northern District of Illinois including Trial Bar, U.S. District Court, Northern District of Texas, Arizona and U.S. Court of Appeals, 4th, 6th, 7th and 8th Circuits; U.S. Supreme Court. *Education:* University of Illinois (A.B., summa cum laude, 1981); Harvard Law School (J.D., 1984).

SHELDON L. SOLOW, born September 1950; admitted to bar, 1975, Illinois. *Education:* University of Illinois (B.A., with highest honors, 1972); Harvard University (J.D., 1975).

ANTHONY G. STAMATO, admitted to bar, 1991, Illinois; U.S. District Court, Northern District of Illinois. *Education:* Stanford University (A.B., 1988); University of Chicago (J.D., 1991).

COUNSEL

JEFFREY E. ALTSHUL, born October 1956; admitted to bar, 1981, Wisconsin and U.S. District Court, Western District of Wisconsin; 1982, U.S. District Court, Eastern District of Wisconsin; 1988, Illinois. *Education:* University of Wisconsin-Milwaukee (B.A., with honors, 1978); Drake University (J.D., 1981). ***Email:*** jaltshul@kayescholer.com

HAROLD D. ISRAEL, admitted to bar, 1993, Illinois. *Education:* University of Michigan (B.B.A., 1987); University of Illinois (J.D., magna cum laude, 1993). Certified Public Accountant, Michigan, 1987. Law Clerk to Hon. John D. Schwartz, Chief Bankruptcy Judge, Northern District of Illinois, 1994-1995. ***PRACTICE AREAS:*** Business Reorganization. ***Email:*** hisrael@kayescholer.com

JOEL L. MILLER, born September 1935; admitted to bar, 1961, Illinois. *Education:* University of Illinois (B.S., 1957); Northwestern University (J.D., 1961).

LAURETTA J. MORAN, born October 1947; admitted to bar, 1983, Illinois. *Education:* University of Chicago (M.A., 1974; J.D., 1983). ***Email:*** lmoran@kayescholer.com

(For complete biographical data on other personnel, see Professional Biographies at New York, New York, Los Angeles, California, Washington, D.C., West Palm Beach, Florida, Shanghai, China and London, England)

GEORGE MICHAEL KEANE, JR.

Established in 1981

225 W. WASHINGTON STREET, SUITE 1701
CHICAGO, ILLINOIS 60606
Telephone: 312-726-4548
Fax: 312-726-1591
Email: keaneandkeane@sbcglobal.net

Ad Velorem Tax Law, Real Estate Law, Probate, Property Tax Appeals.

FIRM PROFILE: Working to solve your Real Estate Tax Problems. In 1981, Keane and Keane was established with George Michael Keane, Jr., George M. Keane (1914-1994) and Thomas E. Keane (1905-1996), Of Counsel. Since 1977 practice has been concentrated in all types of real estate assessment and tax matters in Cook County and collar counties dealing with assessors, Boards of Review, Property Tax Appeal Board, Department of Revenue, Circuit and Appellate Courts, concerning all types of property from vacant land to high rise office buildings.

GEORGE MICHAEL KEANE, JR., born Chicago, Illinois, November 6, 1947; admitted to bar, 1972, Illinois; 1974, Florida. *Education:* University of Notre Dame (A.B., 1969); Northwestern University (J.D., 1972). Assistant State's Attorney, Cook County, 1972. Assistant Corporation Counsel, City of Chicago, 1972-1977. Administrative Assistant, Legal Department, Office of the Cook County Treasurer, 1978-1992. Elected Member, 1993-1997 and President, 1995-1997, Board of Education, Lyons Township High School District #204. *Member:* Chicago, Illinois State and American Bar Associations. ***LANGUAGES:*** English. ***REPORTED CASES:*** Mill Creek Development v. PTAB, 345 Ill App 3rd 790 (3rd Dist, 2004). ***PRACTICE AREAS:*** Ad Valorem Tax Law; Real Estate Assessment; Real Estate Tax Law; Real Estate Law; Probate Law; Property Tax Appeals.

REPRESENTATIVE CLIENTS: Care Centers, Inc.; Radio Flyer, Inc.; OGI Partners, Inc.; Chicago Powdered Metal Products Co., Inc.; Bays Hospitality LLC.

KEATING & SHURE, LTD.

Established in 1993

SUITE 1550
150 NORTH WACKER DRIVE
CHICAGO, ILLINOIS 60606
Telephone: 312-201-8585
Fax: 312-201-9368
Email: ksltd@flash.net
URL: http://www.keatingandshure.com

Commercial Litigation, Bankruptcy, Creditors' Rights and Employment Litigation.

KEVIN T. KEATING, born Chicago, Illinois, July 17, 1950; admitted to bar, 1982, Illinois, U.S. District Court, Northern District of Illinois and U.S. Court of Appeals, Seventh Circuit. *Education:* Loyola University (B.A., magna cum laude, 1972; J.D., cum laude, 1982); Graduate Theological Union (M.A., 1975). Member, 1980-1981 and Editor-in-Chief, 1981-1982, Loyola University Law Journal. Instructor, Loyola University, Chicago School of Law, 1988-1992. Associate, 1982-1987 and Partner, 1988-1992, McDermott, Will & Emery. *Member:* Chicago and Illinois State Bar Associations. ***PRACTICE AREAS:*** Bankruptcy; Creditors' Rights; Commercial Litigation; Employment Litigation.

MARK E. SHURE, born Evergreen Park, Illinois, July 15, 1958; admitted to bar, 1984, Illinois, U.S. District Court, Northern District of Illinois and U.S. Court of Appeals, Seventh and District of Columbia Circuits. *Education:* Northern Illinois University (B.S., summa cum laude, 1980); Loyola University (J.D., cum laude, 1984). Member, 1982-1983 and Managing Editor, 1983-1984, Loyola Law Journal. Associate, 1984-1989 and Partner, 1990-1992, McDermott, Will & Emery. ***PRACTICE AREAS:*** Commercial Litigation; Creditors' Rights; Bankruptcy; Employment Litigation.

JUDITH M. SEGLER, born Evergreen Park, Illinois, January 16, 1958; admitted to bar, 1983, Illinois. *Education:* Illinois State University (B.S., 1980); Indiana University School of Law (J.D., 1983). ***PRACTICE AREAS:*** Commercial Litigation; Creditors' Rights; Insurance.

KELLY JEANNE McCLINTIC, born Edina, Minnesota, October 10, 1973; admitted to bar, 1998, Illinois. *Education:* Northern Illinois University (B.A., 1995); Illinois Institute of Technology, Chicago-Kent College of Law (J.D., 1998). *Member:* Illinois Bar Association; Womens Bar Association of Illinois.

KEEFE & ASSOCIATES, LLC

Established in 2003

118 NORTH CLINTON, SUITE 300
CHICAGO, ILLINOIS 60661
Telephone: 312-756-1800
Fax: 312-756-1901
URL: http://www.keefe-law.com
Email: ekeefe@keefelaw.com
URL: http://www.keefe-lawfirm.com

Workers Compensation, Employment Litigation, Liability.

EUGENE F. KEEFE, born Norman, Oklahoma, January 17, 1954; admitted to bar, 1980, Illinois and U.S. District Court, Northern District of Illinois including Trial Bar; 1988, U.S. Court of Appeals, Seventh Circuit. *Education:* Loyola University, Chicago (B.A., 1977); John Marshall Law School (J.D., 1980). Staff Member, John Marshall Law Review, 1979. Arbitrator, Cook County Mandatory Court Annexed Arbitration. Editor, Workers' Compensation Law Update, July, 1992—. Co-Author: with George Klauke, Jr., The Road To Understanding Worker's Compensation, Journal of Workers' Compensation, Vol. 4 No. 2, Winter, 1995, Standard Press, Boston, MA. Lecturer and Presenter: LRP Publications Annual National Workers' Compensation and Disability Conference, 1992 to 1995, 1997—. Presentation Materials, 1997, Organizing Claims Programs for Effective Defense. Presentation Materials, 1995, Selected Topics in Controlling Litigation Costs in Workers' Compensation. Lecturer and Presenter: Mechanical Contractors Association 1996 Annual Meeting, Workers' Compensation in the Mechanical Industry. Annual Construction Safety Conference 1994—. North Dakota Workers' Compensation Bureau Annual Seminar, Bismarck, N.D., 1995, Developing Trend's in Workers' Compensation. National Erectors Association, 1998, Joint Labor-Safety Forum, Current Trends in Workers' Compensation; Build Safe '98, 1998 Chicagoland Construction Safety Seminar, Lunch workshop on Workers' Compensation in the Construction Industry. Lorman Educational Services Seminars, Workers Compensation in Illinois; Safety Prevention, Cost Control, ADA, FMLA and Workers' Compensation 1999—. Tenth Annual Road Builders Confer-

(This Listing Continued)

KEEFE & ASSOCIATES, LLC, Chicago—Continued

ence, Managing Workers' Compensation Claims, February 2000. Downstate Illinois Occupational Safety & Health Day, Understanding Workers Comp; Myth or Management?, March 2000; Workers' Compensation Update 2002, June 2002; Fundamentals of Workers' Compensation, August 2002. ASSE Northeastern Illinois Chapter Meeting, August 2002. SEAK, Inc., Managing Difficult and Challenging Employees, March 2002. Council on Education in Management, Proactive Steps for Lawfully Handling Pre-Existing Injuries and Repeat Claimants, March 2000. Southwest Suburban Chicago Illinois Association of Occupational Nurses, September 2000. *Member:* Chicago Bar Association; Illinois Workers' Compensation Lawyers Association; Workers' Claims Association. ***PRACTICE AREAS:*** Workers Compensation; Employment Litigation; General Liability. ***Email:*** ekeefe@keefe-law.com

---

MICHAEL J. DANIELEWICZ, born Chicago, Illinois, July 5, 1967; admitted to bar, 1993, Illinois. *Education:* Villanova University (B.A., 1989); Thomas M. Cooley Law School (J.D., 1992). ***PRACTICE AREAS:*** Workers Compensation; Employment Litigation; General Liability. ***Email:*** mdanielewicz@keefe-law.com

JOHN P. CAMPBELL, JR., born Evergreen Park, Illinois, December 11, 1972; admitted to bar, 1999, Illinois. *Education:* University of Illinois, Urbana-Champaign (B.A., 1995); Chicago Kent College of Law (J.D., 1999). *Member:* Chicago and Illinois State Bar Associations. ***PRACTICE AREAS:*** Workers Compensation; Employment Litigation; General Liability. ***Email:*** jcampbell@keefe-law.com

JOSEPH NEEDHAM, born Oak Lawn, Illinois, August 13, 1972; admitted to bar, 1999, Illinois. *Education:* Loyola University, Chicago (B.S., 1995); John Marshall Law School (J.D., 1999). ***PRACTICE AREAS:*** Workers Compensation; Employment Litigation; General Liability. ***Email:*** jneedham@keefe-law.com

SHAWN R. BIERY, born Hardin, Montana, May 12, 1971; admitted to bar, 2001, Illinois. *Education:* Montana State University (B.S., 1997); Thomas Jefferson School of Law (J.D., 2001). [With, U.S. Marine Corps, June 1989-April 1993]. ***PRACTICE AREAS:*** Workers Compensation; Employment Litigation; General Liability. ***Email:*** sbiery@keefe-law.com

JAMES F. EGAN, born Evergreen Park, Illinois, October 10, 1957; admitted to bar, 1988, Illinois; 1993, U.S. District Court, Northern District of Indiana. *Education:* University of Illinois, Chicago Circle (B.A., 1979); John Marshall Law School (J.D., 1988). ***PRACTICE AREAS:*** Workers Compensation. ***Email:*** jegan@keefe-law.com

KEGAN & KEGAN, LTD.

Established in 1941

79 WEST MONROE STREET, SUITE 1320
CHICAGO, ILLINOIS 60603-4969
Telephone: 312-782-6495
Fax: 312-782-6494
Email: info@KeganLaw.com
URL: http://www.KeganLaw.com

U.S. and International Patents, Trademarks, Copyrights, Computers, Internet, Information Technology, Licensing, Unfair Trade Practices, Advertising Matters, Federal Litigation, Counsel to Counsel.

FIRM PROFILE: Since 1941, Kegan & Kegan, Ltd. has provided its select clients personalized strategic advice, preventative guidance, and when needed crisis counseling and defense. We focus our legal practice on United States and international trademark, copyright, patent, and computer law. Domestic and foreign clients seek our counsel for their new business ventures, general contract issues, licensing, negotiations, and litigation. Our clients range from individual inventors and business people, to small businesses, to large national and international corporations. We represent clients throughout the United States and in foreign countries. We take pride both in our long term representation of established clients and in our quality representation of new clients.

ALBERT I. KEGAN (1908-1963)
ESTHER O. KEGAN (1913-2000)

DANIEL L. KEGAN, born Chicago, Illinois, March 3, 1944; admitted to bar, 1984, Illinois and U.S. District Court, Northern District of Illinois; 1995, U.S. Supreme Court. *Education:* Swarthmore College (B.S., 1965); Northwestern University (Ph.D., 1971; J.D., 1984). Co-Author, "FDA May Consume Food Trademarks", Trademark Reporter, 1997. Author: "Survey Evidence in Copyright Litigation", J Copyright Society, 1985; "Polital Trademarks," 15BA IP, 2004. Walter P. Murphy Fellow. Recipient, First Prize, ASCAP Nathan Burkan Competition, Northwestern University. Registered Psychologist. Qualified Expert Witness, Forensic Survey Research. *Member:* Chicago (Organizer, Computer User Groups, 1986—), Illinois State (Member of Council, Intellectual Property Section, 1987—) and American (Member of Council, Economics of Law Practice Section, 1983-1984; Chair, Survey Committee, 1984) Bar Associations; Copyright Society of USA; American Psychological Association; Association Media Psychology; Organization Development Network. ***REPORTED CASES:*** Architemps Inc. v. Architemps Ltd., 9 U.S.P.Q. 1826 (S.D.N.Y., Nov. 1988), 11 U.S.P.Q. 1885 (S.D.N.Y., Apr. 1989). Artmark vs. E. Mishan, 26 U.S.P.Q, 2d 1201 (N.D. IL 1992); Computer Program Written in On-Screen Icons Copyrighted. Guide to Computer Law 60,011 (June 9, 1989); Ory v. McDonald, 68 U.S.P.Q. 1812 (C.D. CA 2003). ***PRACTICE AREAS:*** Computer Law; Intellectual Property; Business; Litigation; Trademarks; Copyrights. ***Email:*** daniel@keganlaw.com

---

CYNTHIA L. SCOTT, born Troy, Ohio, January 7, 1947; admitted to bar, 1982, Illinois; 1983, U.S. District Court, Northern District of Illinois. *Education:* Ohio Wesleyan University (B.A., 1969); University of Pennsylvania (M.S., 1971); Chicago-Kent School of Law (J.D., 1982).

(This Listing Continued)

MARC E. FINEMAN, born Trenton, New Jersey, December 13, 1970; admitted to bar, 1996, Illinois and U.S. District Court, Northern District of Illinois; registered to practice before the U.S. Patent and Trademark Office. *Education:* Rutgers University, College of Engineering (B.S., Ceramic Engineering, 1993); The John Marshall Law School (J.D., 1996). Author: "The Nuts and Bolts of Insignia Recordation Under the Fastener Quality Act," ISBA Intellectual Property Newsletter, January 1998. Member: The John Marshall Law Review; American Ceramics Society, 1991-1994; The National Institute of Ceramic Engineers, 1991-1993; The Optical Society of America, 1993-1994. *Member:* Chicago, Illinois State and American Bar Associations; American Intellectual Property Law Association; Intellectual Property Law Association of Chicago; Keramos, The National Ceramic Engineering Honor Society. ***PRACTICE AREAS:*** Patents; Computer Law; Trademarks; Copyrights; Inventions; Internet; Information Technology. ***Email:*** marc@keganlaw.com

OF COUNSEL

JAY R. GIUSTI, born Harvey, Illinois, August 2, 1956; admitted to bar, 1981, Illinois and U.S. District Court, Northern District of Illinois including Trial Bar; 1990, U.S. Court of Appeals, Seventh Circuit; 1998, U.S. Supreme Court. *Education:* Georgetown University (B.A., 1978; J.D., 1981). *Member:* Illinois State Bar Association (Member, Legal Technology Committee, 1997-2000). ***PRACTICE AREAS:*** Litigation; Appellate Practice; Arbitration; Computer Law.

KELLEY DRYE & WARREN LLP

333 WEST WACKER DRIVE
CHICAGO, ILLINOIS 60606
Telephone: 312-857-7070
Fax: 312-857-7095
Email: info@kelleydrye.com
URL: http://www.kelleydrye.com

New York, N.Y. Office: 101 Park Avenue. Telephone: 212-808-7800. Fax: 212-808-7897.
Stamford, Connecticut Office: Two Stamford Plaza, 281 Tresser Boulevard. Telephone: 203-324-1400. Fax: 203-327-2669; 203-964-3188.
Washington, D.C. Office: 1200 19th Street, N.W., Suite 500. Telephone: 202-955-9600. Fax: 202-955-9792.
Parsippany, New Jersey Office: 200 Kimball Drive. Telephone: 973-503-5900. Fax: 973-503-5950.
Vienna, Virginia Office: 8000 Towers Crescent Drive, Suite 1200. Telephone: 703-918-2300. Fax: 703-918-2450.
Brussels, Belgium Office: 106 Avenue Louise, 1050. Telephone: 011-32-2-646-1110. Fax: 011-32-2-640-0589.
Affiliated Offices:
Jakarta, Indonesia: Soebagjo, Jatim, Djarot, Plaza DM, 17th Floor, Jalan Jend. Sudirman Kav. 25, Jakarta 12920, Indonesia. Telephone: 011-62-21-5229765. Fax: 011-62-21-5229752.
Mumbai (Bombay) India: Wakhariya & Wakhariya, 41 Bajaj Bhawan, 226 Nariman Point, Mumbai 400021. Telephone: 91-22-281-0336; 91-22-285-9820. Fax: 91-22-281-0337. Email: shabbirw@counsellor.com.

Litigation, Commercial Litigation, Emerging Growth Companies, Employee Benefits, Executive Compensation, Environmental Law, Financial Institutions, Health Care, Immigration, Insurance, Intellectual Property, Technology Litigation, International Law, Labor and Employment Law, Mergers and Acquisitions, Private Clients, Products Liability, Project Finance, Infrastructure, Real Estate Law, Restructuring, Creditors Rights, Securities, Broker-Dealer, Securities Litigation, Telecommunications, Trade Regulation, Antitrust, White Collar Crime, Corporate Investigations.

PARTNERS

MARY JO BOLDINGH, born Columbus, OH, 1957; admitted to bar, 1991, IL; registered to practice before U.S. Patent and Trademark Office. *Education:* Loyola University (A.B., 1980); Northwestern University (M.S., 1985); Chicago-Kent College of Law, Illinois Institute of Technology (J.D., with honors, 1991). ***PRACTICE AREAS:*** Intellectual Property. ***Email:*** mboldingh@kelleydrye.com

SUSAN J. GREENSPON, admitted to bar, 1989, IL. *Education:* University of Wisconsin-Madison (B.A., 1986); Loyola University (J.D., 1989). *Member:* Chicago, Illinois State and American Bar Associations; Northwest Suburban Bar Association; American Women's Association. ***PRACTICE AREAS:*** Venture Capital Financing; Business Transactions; Technology; E-Commerce. ***Email:*** sgreenspon@kelleydrye.com

HENRY T. KELLY, born Chicago, IL, 1961; admitted to bar, 1987, IL and U.S. District Court, Northern District of Illinois, including Trial Bar; 1993, U.S. Court of Appeals, Seventh Circuit; 1996, U.S. Supreme Court. *Education:* University of Illinois (B.A., 1984); John Marshall Law School (J.D., 1987). ***PRACTICE AREAS:*** Commercial Litigation; Telecommunications. ***Email:*** hkelly@kelleydrye.com

TIMOTHY R. LAVENDER, born 1960; admitted to bar, 1987, KY; 1988, IL and U.S. Tax Court. *Education:* University of Notre Dame (B.B.A., 1982); University of Louisville (J.D., 1987). Certified Public Accountant, Illinois, 1984. *Member:* Chicago and American Bar Associations. ***PRACTICE AREAS:*** Mergers and Acquisitions; Private Finance; Venture Capital; Technology. ***Email:*** tlavender@kelleydrye.com

DAVID A. RAMMELT, admitted to bar, 1990, IL, WI, U.S. Supreme Court, U.S. Court of Appeals, Seventh Circuit, U.S. District Court, Northern and Central Districts of Illinois, U.S. District Court, Eastern District of Michigan and U.S. District Court, District of Arizona including Federal Trial Bar. *Education:* Hamilton College (B.A., 1986); Indiana University (J.D., cum laude, 1990). ***PRACTICE AREAS:*** Information Technology; Intellectual Property; Antitrust and Trade Regulation; Business Litigation. ***Email:*** drammelt@kelleydrye.com

M. DAVID SHORT, admitted to bar, 1995, IL and U.S. District Court, Northern District of Illinois; 1998, U.S. District Court, District of Arizona; 2001, U.S. District Court, Central District of Illinois. *Education:* University of Notre Dame (B.A., with honors, Gov-

(This Listing Continued)

ernment, 1992); University of Illinois, College of Law (J.D., cum laude, 1995). ***PRACTICE AREAS:*** Products Liability; Commercial Litigation. ***Email:*** mshort@kelleydrye.com

JULIAN SOLOTOROVSKY, born Plainfield, NJ, October, 1951; admitted to bar, 1978, IL, U.S. District Court, Northern District of Illinois and U.S. Court of Appeals, Seventh Circuit. *Education:* University of Virginia (B.A., 1973); John Marshall Law School (J.D., 1978). Assistant U.S. Attorney, U.S. District Court, Northern District of Illinois, 1978-1987. Deputy Chief, Special Prosecutions Division, 1985-1987. ***PRACTICE AREAS:*** White Collar Criminal; Toxic Torts; Complex and Multi-District Litigation. ***Email:*** jsolotorovsky@kelleydrye.com

SLAWOMIR (STEVE) Z. SZCZEPANSKI, born Lodz, Poland, 1948; admitted to bar, 1976, NY and DC; 1977, IL; registered to practice before U.S. Patent and Trademark Office. *Education:* Rensselaer Polytechnic Institute (B.S.Ch.E., 1971; M.S.Ch.E., 1972); Albany Law School of Union University (J.D., 1975). ***PRACTICE AREAS:*** Intellectual Property Litigation; Intellectual Property Licensing; Intellectual Property Counseling; Intellectual Property Related Antitrust. ***Email:*** sszczepanski@kelleydrye.com

STEPHEN A. WOOD, born USNS Sangley Point, Republic of the Philippines, July, 1957; admitted to bar, 1992, IL and U.S. District Court, Northern District of Illinois; 1993, U.S. District Court, Central District of Illinois; 1996, U.S. Court of Appeals, Seventh Circuit. *Education:* George Washington University (B.A., cum laude, 1980); Loyola University (J.D., cum laude, 1992). ***PRACTICE AREAS:*** Litigation. ***Email:*** swood@kelleydrye.com

SPECIAL COUNSEL

KATHERINE L. TABOR, born South Bend, IN, July, 1965; admitted to bar, 1990, IL, IN and U.S. District Court, Northern District of Illinois; registered to practice before U.S. Patent and Trademark Office. *Education:* University of Southern California (B.S., 1987); Valparaiso University School of Law (J.D., with high distinction, 1990). ***PRACTICE AREAS:*** Intellectual Property; Technology. ***Email:*** ktabor@kelleydrye.com

ASSOCIATES

DAWN M. BEERY, born Chicago, IL, 1972; admitted to bar, 1998, IL and U.S. District Court, Northern District of Illinois. *Education:* Indiana University (B.A., with highest honors, 1995); Northwestern University (J.D., cum laude, 1998). ***PRACTICE AREAS:*** Commercial Litigation; Products Liability; Construction Law. ***Email:*** dbeery@kelleydrye.com

KENN BROTMAN, born Manhasset, NY, June, 1970; admitted to bar, 1995, FL; 1996, IL. *Education:* University of Miami (B.S., 1992); Northern Illinois University (J.D., 1995). ***PRACTICE AREAS:*** Products Liability; Commercial Litigation. ***Email:*** kbrotman@kelleydrye.com

STEPHANIE E. CARTER, born Chicago, IL, November, 1964; admitted to bar, 1994, IL. *Education:* University of Illinois, Urbana-Champaign (B.S.E.E., 1988); DePaul University College of Law (J.D., 1994). ***PRACTICE AREAS:*** Intellectual Property; Information Technology; Corporate. ***Email:*** scarter@kelleydrye.com

JOSEPH E. DONOVAN, born Kansas City, KS, 1969; admitted to bar, 1997, CO and IL. *Education:* Washburn University of Topeka (B.A., 1991; J.D., 1995); University of San Francisco Law School, Dublin, Ireland. ***PRACTICE AREAS:*** Telecommunications. ***Email:*** jdonovan@kelleydrye.com

THOMAS H. FERGUSON, born Granite City, IL, October, 1971; admitted to bar, 1997, IL. *Education:* Old Dominion University (B.S.B.A., Financial Management, 1994); University of Dayton (J.D., 1997). ***PRACTICE AREAS:*** Mergers and Acquisitions; Venture Capital; Corporate. ***Email:*** tferguson@kelleydyre.com

GLEN J. GESICKI, born Chicago, IL, November, 1970; admitted to bar, 2004, IL; registered to practice before U.S. Patent and Trademark Office. *Education:* University of Illinois (M.S., 1995); DePaul University College of Law (J.D., summa cum laude, 2004). Phi Kappa Phi. American Chemical Society, 1992—. ***PRACTICE AREAS:*** Intellectual Property. ***Email:*** ggesicki@kelleydrye.com

SCOTT R. KASPAR, born Hinsdale, IL, October, 1975; admitted to bar, 2003, IA and U.S. District Court, Southern District of Iowa; 2005, IL and U.S. District Court, Northern District of Illinois; registered to practice before U.S. Patent and Trademark Office. *Education:* University of Illinois, Urbana-Champaign (B.S.M.E., 1998); Drake University Law School (J.D., 2003). ***PRACTICE AREAS:*** Intellectual Property; Technology Law; Litigation. ***Email:*** skaspar@kelleydrye.com

MATTHEW C. LUZADDER, admitted to bar, 2004, Illinois; 2005, FL. *Education:* Indiana University (B.A., 2001; J.D., 2004). ***PRACTICE AREAS:*** Telecommunications; Litigation. ***Email:*** mluzadder@kelleydrye.com

ANDREW P. PILLSBURY, admitted to bar, 1996, MI; 1999, IL. *Education:* University of Michigan (B.B.A., 1992; J.D., 1996). ***PRACTICE AREAS:*** Mergers and Acquisitions; Corporate; Emerging Companies. ***Email:*** apillsbury@kelleydrye.com

CAROLINE C. PLATER, born Milwaukee, WI, May, 1971; admitted to bar, 1998, IL. *Education:* Marquette University (B.A., cum laude, 1993); DePaul University (J.D., 1998). ***PRACTICE AREAS:*** Commercial Litigation; Business Litigation; Products Liability Litigation; Medical Malpractice Litigation. ***Email:*** cheon@kelleydrye.com

JAMES M. REILAND, born Edina, MN, 1976; admitted to bar, 2003, NY; 2005, IL. *Education:* Washington University (B.A., 1998); Northwestern University (J.D., 2002). ***PRACTICE AREAS:*** Commercial Litigation. ***Email:*** jreiland@kelleydrye.com

(For Biographical Data on all Personnel, see Professional Biographies at New York, N.Y.).

LAW OFFICES OF JOHN G. KELLY, P.C.

100 W. MONROE, SUITE 1900
CHICAGO, ILLINOIS 60603
Telephone: 312-346-3390
Fax: 312-346-6549
Email: jklawoffices@aol.com
URL: http://www.kellylawchicago.com

Medical Malpractice, Personal Injury, Premises Liability, Products Liability.

(This Listing Continued)

JOHN G. KELLY, born Oak Park, Illinois, April 22, 1961; admitted to bar, 1986, Illinois. *Education:* Spring Hill College (B.S., 1983); John Marshall Law School (J.D., 1986). Director: Chicago Volunteer Legal Services Corporation; John Marshall Law School Alumni Association; Catholic Charities of Chicago; Chicago Volunteer Legal Services Corp. Associate, Cassidy, Schade & Gloor, 1986-1990. Assistant Corporation Counsel, City of Chicago, 1990-1995. *Member:* Illinois Trial Lawyers Association; The Association of Trial Lawyers of America.

GREGORY R. IGNOFFO, born May 30, 1979; admitted to bar, 2004, Illinois. *Education:* Dominican University (B.A., 2001); John Marshall Law School (J.D., 2004). ***PRACTICE AREAS:*** Plaintiffs Personal Injury; Medical Malpractice; Products Liability. ***Email:*** gignoffo@aol.com

---

KELLY, OLSON, MICHOD, DeHAAN & RICHTER, L.L.C.

Established in 1872

30 SOUTH WACKER DRIVE, SUITE 2300
CHICAGO, ILLINOIS 60606
Telephone: 312-236-6700
Facsimile: 312-236-6706

Munster, Indiana Office: Cohen, Kelly, Olson, DeHaan & Richter, L.L.C., 9337 Calumet Avenue, Suite A-1, 46321. Telephone: 219-836-1171. Facsimile: 312-836-2003.

Estate Planning, Probate, Banking Litigation, Transactions, Finance, Construction Law, Creditors Rights, General Civil Practice, Personal Injury Law, Mechanics Lien Litigation, Corporate Law, Mediation and Arbitration, Family Law, Divorce.

MEMBERS OF FIRM

JOHN A. KELLY, JR., born Chicago, Illinois, August 25, 1931; admitted to bar, 1956, Illinois. *Education:* University of Michigan (B.B.A., 1953; M.B.A., 1956; J.D., 1956). ***PRACTICE AREAS:*** Corporate Law; Business Law; Estate and Business Planning. ***Email:*** jkelly@komdr.com

RAYMOND OLSON, JR. (1933-2004)

CHARLES L. MICHOD, JR., born Champaign, Illinois, July 19, 1943; admitted to bar, 1968, Illinois; 1969, New York. *Education:* Princeton University (A.B., 1965); University of Michigan (J.D., 1968). ***PRACTICE AREAS:*** Corporate/Business Law; Estate Planning; State and Local Taxation. ***Email:*** cmichod@komdr.com

RONALD M. DeHAAN, born Evergreen Park, Illinois, April 29, 1942; admitted to bar, 1967, Illinois, U.S. District Court, Northern District of Illinois, including Trial Bar and U.S. Court of Appeals, 7th Circuit. *Education:* Northwestern University (B.A., 1964); University of Illinois (J.D., 1967). ***REPORTED CASES:*** Armstrong v. RTC, 234 Ill. App. 3d 162, 599 N.E, 2d 1209; Vinci v. Bass, 39 Ill. App. 3d 1016, 352 N.E. 2d 369; Barnwell v. First Midwest Bank N.A., 296 Ill. App. 3d 1079, 726 N.E. 2d 1194. ***TRANSACTIONS:*** $10, 000, 000 Term Credit Facility from Northwest Bank to Becker Beeper, Inc. (1994). ***PRACTICE AREAS:*** Litigation; Construction Law; Banks and Banking; Business Law; Commercial Collections; Employment Law. ***Email:*** rdehaan@komdr.com

PAUL J. RICHTER, born Chicago, Illinois, March 25, 1946; admitted to bar, 1971, Illinois, U.S. District Court, Northern District of Illinois, including Trial Bar and U.S. Court of Appeals, 7th Circuit. *Education:* Roosevelt University; John Marshall Law School (J.D., 1971). ***PRACTICE AREAS:*** Banks and Banking; Litigation; Finance; Commercial Real Estate; Manufacturers Liability; Commercial Law; Bankruptcy. ***Email:*** prichter@komdr.com

FRANK G. SIEPKER, born Quincy, Illinois, May 19, 1939; admitted to bar, 1968, Missouri and Illinois. *Education:* Purdue University (B.S., Eng. Sciences, 1961); University of Illinois (J.D., 1968). *Member:* Illinois State Bar Association. [Lt., U.S. Navy, 1961-1965]. ***PRACTICE AREAS:*** Banking; Corporate; Business Law. ***Email:*** fsiepker@komdr.com

STEPHEN B. COHEN, born East Chicago, Indiana, March 14, 1939; admitted to bar, 1965, Indiana and Illinois. *Education:* Harvard University (A.B., 1961); Vanderbilt University (J.D., 1964); University of Cambridge, Downing College, England (LL.M., International Law, with honors, 1966); Diploma in International Law, 1972. ISBA ADR Section Council (Secretary). Certified for Court Ordered mediation, Indiana. Included on Official List of Mediators, Cook County Circuit Court Major Case Court Annexed Civil Mediation. ***PRACTICE AREAS:*** Real Estate; Litigation; Civil Practice; Estate Planning; Business Transactions; OWI; Traffic Citations; Civil Mediation; Arbitration. ***Email:*** scohen@komdr.com

MARK A. COSTA, born Chicago, Illinois, November 29, 1956; admitted to bar, 1982, Illinois; 1990, Wisconsin. *Education:* Georgetown University (B.S., 1979); University of Illinois (J.D., cum laude, 1982). Certified Public Accountant, Illinois, 1982. *Member:* Illinois State Bar Association; State Bar of Wisconsin. ***Email:*** mcosta@komdr.com

STEVEN A. KOGA, born Chicago, Illinois, May 11, 1950; admitted to bar, 1977, Illinois, U.S. District Court, Northern District of Illinois and U.S. Tax Court. *Education:* DePaul University (B.S., 1972); John Marshall Law School (J.D., 1977). ***PRACTICE AREAS:*** Estate and Business Planning; Federal Income, Estate and Gift Taxation; Probate; Trust Administration; Corporate; Real Estate. ***Email:*** skoga@komdr.com

DAVID S. ADDUCE, born Oak Lawn, Illinois, January 24, 1965; admitted to bar, 1990, Illinois and U.S. District Court, Northern District of Illinois, including Trial Bar; U.S. Court of Appeals for the Seventh Circuit. *Education:* University of Illinois (B.A., 1987); DePaul University College of Law (J.D., 1990). ***PRACTICE AREAS:*** Civil Litigation; Construction Litigation; Banking Litigation; Commercial Collections; Creditor Bankruptcy; Trial Practice; Appellate Practice; Consumer Collections; Real Estate Foreclosure; Personal Injury. ***Email:*** dadduce@komdr.com

(This Listing Continued)

KELLY, OLSON, MICHOD, DEHAAN & RICHTER, L.L.C., Chicago—Continued

KENNETH L. COUGHLAN, born Chicago, Illinois, July 8, 1940; admitted to bar, 1967, Illinois and U.S. District Court, Northern District of Illinois. *Education:* University of Notre Dame (B.A., 1962); Northwestern University School of Law (J.D., 1966). ***PRACTICE AREAS:*** Banking; Finance; Corporate Law; Intellectual Property Licensing; Mergers and Acquisitions; Commercial Law; Commercial Real Estate. ***Email:*** kcoughlan@komdr.com

MICHAEL G. SWIATEK, born Chicago, Illinois, 1947; admitted to bar, 1980, Illinois and U.S. District Court, Northern District of Illinois including Trial Bar. *Education:* University of Notre Dame (B.S.C.E., 1969); John Marshall Law School (J.D., 1980). ***PRACTICE AREAS:*** Construction Litigation; Commercial Litigation; Litigation; General Practice. ***Email:*** mswiatek@komdr.com

JOANNE F. HURLEY, born Minneapolis, Minnesota, August 28, 1950; admitted to bar, 1978, Illinois; 1982, U.S. District Court, Northern District of Illinois. *Education:* Michigan State University (B.A., 1972; B.S., 1975); DePaul University (J.D., 1978). Member, DePaul University Law Review. Law Clerk, Honorable Calvin C. Campbell, Illinois Appellate Court (1st District). Hearing Officer, Chicago Park District Disciplinary Hearings, 1983-1984. Certified Arbitrator, Cook County Arbitration Program, 1999-2002. Author: "The Treatment of Presumptions in Illinois: Adding Insult to Injury," The DePaul Law Review, Vol. 27, No. 3, 1978; "Confidentiality Plan Can Protect Corporate Assets," Chicago Industrial Bulletin, Vol. 13, No. 1, January/February 1994. Partner: Robbins, Rubinstein, Salomon & Greenblatt, Ltd., 1984-1989; Schwartz & Freeman, 1990-1994. U.S. Outside General Counsel, Tony Stone Images Group, 1988-1998; Of Counsel, Flamm & Teibloom, 1995—. *Member:* Chicago, Illinois State and American Bar Associations. (Also Practicing Individually). ***PRACTICE AREAS:*** Business Formation; Business Law; Corporate Law; Limited Liability Company Law; Commercial Transactions; Contracts; Entertainment and the Arts; Artists Rights; Artistic Property; International Intellectual Property; Commercial Real Estate Contracts; Commercial Leasing; Business Sales; Construction Contracts; Employment Severance and Contracts; Noncompetition and Non-Solicitation Agreements; Business Acquisitions; Distribution Agreements. ***Email:*** jfhurley@hurleystanners.com

ASSOCIATES

MARC J. CHALFEN, born Chicago, Illinois, June 3, 1951; admitted to bar, 1976, Illinois; U.S. District Court, Northern and Central Districts of Illinois; U.S. Court of Appeals, Seventh Circuit; U.S. Supreme Court. *Education:* University of Illinois (B.A., with high honors and distinction in Economics, 1973); Washington University (J.D., 1976). Associate Editor, Urban Law Annual, 1974-1975. ***PRACTICE AREAS:*** Civil And Business Litigation; Banks and Banking; Commercial Real Estate Foreclosure; Creditors Rights. ***Email:*** mchalfen@komdr.com

MELISSA L. COVER, born Peoria, Illinois, March 19, 1978; admitted to bar, 2003, Illinois. *Education:* University of Illinois (B.A., Economics, 2000); Washington University (J.D., 2003). ***PRACTICE AREAS:*** Probate; Estate Planning; Trusts; Trust Administration; Taxation; Corporate Law. ***Email:*** mcover@komdr.com

JEREMIAH C. VAN HECKE, born Milwaukee, Wisconsin, July 30, 1974; admitted to bar, 1999, Florida; 2005, Illinois, U.S. District Court, Northern District of Illinois; including Trial Bar. *Education:* Northwestern University (B.A., 1996); Tulane University School of Law (J.D., 1999). ***PRACTICE AREAS:*** Commercial Litigation; Construction Litigation; Employment Litigation; Business Law; Real Estate Litigation; Trademark Litigation; Trial Practice. ***Email:*** jvanhecke@komdr.com

ROBERT BRADLEY JOHNSON, born Okmulgee, Oklahoma, May 2, 1971; admitted to bar, 2002, Illinois and U.S. District Court, Northern District of Illinois. *Education:* Northwestern University (B.A., 1993); Loyola University, Chicago, School of Law (J.D., 2002). *Member Illinois State and Chicago Bar Associations.* ***PRACTICE AREAS:*** Real Estate; Business Law; Corporate Law; Banks and Banking. ***Email:*** bjohnson@komdr.com

OF COUNSEL

ALVIN L. KAPLAN, born Chicago, Illinois, January 25, 1924; admitted to bar, 1951, Illinois, U.S. District Court, Northern District of Illinois and U.S. Tax Court. *Education:* University of Illinois (B.S., cum laude, 1949; J.D., 1951). ***PRACTICE AREAS:*** Corporate Law; Business Law; Trusts; Taxation. ***Email:*** akapalan@komdr.com

CHARLES L. MICHOD, born Chicago, Illinois, September 10, 1917; admitted to bar, 1942, Illinois. *Education:* University of Illinois (A.B., 1939); Harvard Law School (L.L.B., 1942). ***PRACTICE AREAS:*** Probate; Trust and Estate Planning.

TIMOTHY F. KELLY AND ASSOCIATES

CHICAGO, ILLINOIS

(See Dyer, Indiana)

General Practice, Commercial, Business Law, Business Planning, Contracts, Business Litigation, Business Enterprises, Wills and Probate, Trusts and Estates, Asset Protection, Guardianships, Estate Planning, Corporation, Real Estate, Labor and Employment, Trials and Appeals in all Courts, Insurance Defense, Automobile Accidents, Slip and Fall, Wrongful Death, Products Liability, Professional Liability and Medical Malpractice.

LAW OFFICES GERHARD E. W. KELTER, JR.

A PROFESSIONAL CORPORATION

Established in the United States in 1974

120 SOUTH LA SALLE STREET, SUITE 1450

CHICAGO, ILLINOIS 60603-4105

Telephone: 312-853-0900
Telex: 256274 Scanlex Cgo
Telefax: 312-853-3176
Email: lawgekcgo@aol.com
URL: http://www.lawgek.com

Affiliated Offices: Berlin, Bonn, Frankfurt, Hamburg, Munich, Schwerin, Stockholm, Sydney

International and Domestic Corporate and Commercial Law. Mergers and Acquisitions, Commercial Litigation, Immigration and Naturalization, Products Liability, Labor and Employment Law, Insurance Defense, Disabilities Law, Real Estate, Trust and Estate Planning, and Food and Drug Regulation.

FIRM PROFILE: The Firm was established by Dr. Gerhard Kelter in 1974. In addition to our established U.S. practice, we represent numerous well-known European companies. The Firm's size is particularly well-suited to the European tradition of excellence in service and accessibility to the professionals who are working on projects.

As lawyers to business, we take pride in addressing our clients' problems with solutions that are not only legally correct, but that are also grounded in business reality. Our daily dealings with our clients in Europe also make us sensitive to the cultural differences in the way business is conducted in different parts of the world.

We have represented many of our present clients since the Firm was founded; such long-standing relationships are another example of our European heritage and tradition.

Over the years we have developed a network of professionals in other areas-insurance, accounting, banking, real estate-who can provide all of the services a business would require. We welcome the opportunity to share those relationships with you. The Firm is fluent in German, French, Swedish, Danish and Norwegian. The Firm is a member of the American Society of International Law, the German-American Chamber of Commerce, the Swedish-American Chamber of Commerce, the Scottish Business Forum and the German American Lawyers Association (Deutsch Amerikanische Juristen-Vereinigung E.V.).

GERHARD KELTER, JR., born Stockholm, Sweden, January 10, 1941; admitted to bar, 1968, Sweden; 1972, Illinois; 1979, U.S. District Court, Northern District of Illinois. *Education:* Hoegre Allmaenna Laeroverket foer Gossar paa Norrmalm, Stockholm, Sweden (B.A., 1960); University of Stockholm, Stockholm, Sweden (M.A., 1963; J.D., 1968); Chicago-Kent College of Law, Illinois Institute of Technology (J.D., 1971). Instructor, Business Administration, Business Law, Osteraker Handelsskola, Stockholm, Sweden, 1964-1967. *Member:* Chicago, Illinois State and American (Member, Sections on: International Law; Antitrust Law) Bar Associations; American Society of International Law. ***LANGUAGES:*** Swedish, Danish, Norwegian, German and French. ***PRACTICE AREAS:*** International Corporate Law; Commercial Law; Trade Regulation; Tax Law.

PATRICK J. KRONENWETTER, born Saint Marys, Pennsylvania, January 7, 1954; admitted to bar, 1978, Pennsylvania; 1981, Illinois; U.S. Court of Appeals, 7th Circuit; U.S. District Court, Northern District of Illinois including Trial Bar and U.S. District Court, Western District of Pennsylvania. *Education:* University of Notre Dame (B.A., with high honors, 1975); University of Pittsburgh (J.D., 1978). Note Editor, University of Pittsburgh Law Review, 1977-1978. Author, "Wrongful Birth and Emotional Distress Damages," 39 University of Pittsburgh Law Review, Spring 1977. Member, Spinal Cord Injury Association of Illinois. *Member:* Du Page County, Illinois State (Member, Standing Committee on Professional Conduct; Chair, Standing Committee on Insurance Programs, 2000-2001, 2005-2006; Member, Standing Committee on Lawyers with Disabilities, 1991-1995) and Pennsylvania Bar Associations. ***REPORTED CASES:*** Branson v. West, 1999 U.S. Dist. LEXIS 19173. ***PRACTICE AREAS:*** Corporate Law; Employment Law; Commercial Law; Disabilities; Litigation.

JOSEPH G. DI CAMILLO, born Fairview Park, Ohio, September 8, 1965; admitted to bar, 1990, Illinois and U.S. District Court, Northern District of Illinois. *Education:* Northwestern University (B.A., 1987); Loyola University (J.D., 1990). Phi Sigma Alpha. Recipient: Academic Achievement Award in Environmental Law; Political Science Concentration Certificate in International Politics. Author, "Recent Developments in Lender Liability," IBA LAW Watch, Vol. 2, No. 4, 1988. Law Clerk to the Hon. Elaine E. Bucklo, U.S. District Judge, 1990-1991. *Member:* Chicago, American and International Bar Associations; American Immigration Lawyers Association, American Trial Lawyers Association (Defense Member). ***LANGUAGES:*** French. ***TRANSACTIONS:*** United States Counsel to Arjo AB Global Offering of 14,554,997 Shares. ***PRACTICE AREAS:*** Commercial Law; Corporate Law; Products Liability; Immigration Law; Food and Drug Regulation.

JENNIFER I. GAZ, born Goettingen, Germany, March 2, 1972; admitted to bar, 1997, Illinois; 1998, U.S. District Court, Northern District of Illinois. *Education:* University of Illinois, Urbana-Champaign (B.A., 1994); DePaul University College of Law (J.D., 1997). ***LANGUAGES:*** German. ***PRACTICE AREAS:*** Immigration Law; Commercial Law; Litigation. ***Email:*** lawgekcgo@aol.com

THE LAW OFFICES OF CHRISTOPHER C. KENDALL, P.C.

77 W. WACKER DRIVE, SUITE 4800
CHICAGO, ILLINOIS 60601-1664
Telephone: 312-606-8642
Fax: 312-444-1028
Email: ckendall@ckendall.com
URL: http://www.ckendall.com

Commercial Litigation, ARDC Defense, Land Use, Business Disputes, Breach of Contract and Warranty, Fraud, Conspiracy, Theft of Trade Secrets, Breach of Fiduciary Duty, Covenants Not to Compete, Mechanics Lien Litigation, Negotiation and Alternate Dispute Resolution.

CHRISTOPHER C. KENDALL, born Alexandria, Virginia, September 26, 1966; admitted to bar, 1992, Illinois and U.S. District Court, Northern District of Illinois. *Education:* University of Illinois (B.A., 1988); John Marshall Law School (J.D., summa cum laude, 1992). Moot Court. Staff Editor, The John Marshall Law Review. *Member:* Chicago, Illinois State and American Bar Associations. ***PRACTICE AREAS:*** Commercial Litigation; ARDC Defense; Land Use; Business Disputes; Breach of Contract; Warranty Fraud; Conspiracy; Theft of Trade Secrets; Breach of Fiduciary Duty; Covenants Not To Compete; Mechanics Liens Litigation; Negotiation; Alternative Dispute Resolution. ***Email:*** ckendall@ckendall.com

---

SUSAN A. FINNEGAN, admitted to bar, 1999, Illinois; U.S District Court, Northern District of Illinois and U.S. Court of Appeals, 7th Circuit. *Education:* Albion College (B.A., cum laude, 1996); Chicago-Kent College of Law (J.D., with honors, 1999). Dean's List; International Law Moot Court, Judicial Intern, Hon. George W. Lindberg, U.S., District Court, Northern District of Illinois. ***PRACTICE AREAS:*** Commercial Litigation; Mechanics Liens Litigation. ***Email:*** sfinnegan@ckendall.com

PAUL WOJCIECHOWKSI, born Chicago, Illinois, September 19, 1978; admitted to bar, 2003, Illinois and U.S. District Court, Northern District of Illinois. *Education:* University of Chicago (A.B., 2000); Loyola University Chicago (J.D., 2003). ***PRACTICE AREAS:*** Commercial Litigation; Real Estate; Land Use. ***Email:*** pw@ckendall.com

PATRICK J. KENNEALLY, LTD.

30 NORTH LASALLE STREET, SUITE 4030
CHICAGO, ILLINOIS 60602
Telephone: 312-236-2522
Fax: 312-236-6188
Email: bhk@kenneallylaw.com
URL: http://www.kenneally-law.com

Catastrophic Personal Injury, Wrongful Death, Medical Malpractice including Birth Injuries, Obstetrics, Cancer, Failure to diagnose/misdiagnosis; Personal Injury including Product Injuries, Unsafe Products, Dangerous and Defective Products, Tire Failure, Industrial Machinery, Home Products and Tools, Manufacturing and Design Defects; Personal Injury including Automobile Accidents and Injuries, Trucking Accidents, Motorcycle Accidents, Dangerous Construction Sites, Construction Accidents and Injuries, Premises Liability, Slip/Trip and Falls, Animal Attack Injuries, Dog Bites.

PATRICK J. KENNEALLY, born Chicago, Illinois, October 17, 1942; admitted to bar, 1971, Illinois; 1975, California; U.S. District Court, Northern District of Illinois including Trial Bar. *Education:* University of Illinois (B.A., 1964); Loyola University (M.S., 1967; J.D., 1971). *Member:* Illinois Trial Lawyers Association (Board of Managers, 1976—); American Trial Lawyers Association (Board Member, Professional Negligence Section, 1980—); Birth Trauma Litigation Group. [Captain, U.S. Army, Artillery, 1964-1966]. ***PRACTICE AREAS:*** Personal Injury; Litigation; Products Liability; Aviation Law; Construction Law; Negligence; Medical Malpractice; Business Litigation; Corporate Litigation. ***Email:*** pjk@kenneallylaw.com

ROBERT F. GEIMER, born Chicago, Illinois, July 16, 1965; admitted to bar, 1991, Illinois and U.S. District Court, Northern District of Illinois. *Education:* Loyola University (B.A., 1988); University of Illinois (J.D., 1991). Associate Editor, University of Illinois Law Review, 1990-1991. ***PRACTICE AREAS:*** Medical Malpractice; Products Liability; Accidents. ***Email:*** contact@kenneallylaw.com

BRENDAN H. KEVENIDES, born Glen Ridge, New Jersey, January 30, 1969; admitted to bar, 1996, Illinois and U.S. District Court, Northern District of Illinois including Trial Bar. *Education:* University of Pittsburgh (B.A., 1991); DePaul University (J.D., 1996). Golden Key. Recipient, CALI Award for Excellence in Advanced Trial Advocacy. ***PRACTICE AREAS:*** Medical Malpractice; Wrongful Death; Products Liability; Motor Vehicle Accidents and Injuries; Premises Liability. ***Email:*** contact@kenneallylaw.com

HARSHA S. NARAYAN, born East Lansing, Michigan, September 17, 1968; admitted to bar, 2000, Illinois; 2001, U.S. District Court, Northern District of Illinois. *Education:* Loyola University (B.A., 1995); John Marshall Law School (J.D., 2000). ***PRACTICE AREAS:*** Medical Malpractice; Wrongful Death; Products Liability; Personal Injury. ***Email:*** contact@kenneallylaw.com

LAW OFFICES OF JAMES P. KENNY

11 SOUTH LASALLE STREET, SUITE 1600
CHICAGO, ILLINOIS 60603
Telephone: 312-641-0700
Fax: 312-896-1474
Email: james@kennylawfirm.com
URL: http://www.kennylawfirm.com

Insurance Litigation, Legal Malpractice, Professional Liability, Civil Litigation, Commercial Law.

JAMES P. KENNY, admitted to bar, 1997, Illinois; U.S. District Court, Northern District of Illinois. *Education:* Loyola University (B.A., cum laude, 1992); John Marshall Law School (J.D., 1997). Executive Production Editor, The John Marshall Journal of Computer and Information Law, 1997. *Member:* Chicago, Illinois State and American (Committee Member, Insurance Coverage Litigation and Professional Liability Litigation) Bar Associations. ***PRACTICE AREAS:*** Insurance Litigation; Legal Malpractice; Professional Liability; Civil Litigation; Commercial Law.

KERNS, PITROF, FROST & PEARLMAN, L.L.C.

THREE FIRST NATIONAL PLAZA, SUITE 5350
70 WEST MADISON
CHICAGO, ILLINOIS 60602
Telephone: 312-261-4550
Fax: 312-261-4565
URL: http://www.kpfplaw.com

General Civil Litigation and Trial Practice. Appellate, Business Litigation, Directors and Officers Liability, Employment and Labor, Fidelity and Surety, Health Care, Insurance and Reinsurance Coverage, Maritime.

MEMBERS OF FIRM

CHRISTOPHER KERNS, born Chicago, Illinois, August 26, 1954; admitted to bar, 1981, Illinois. *Education:* Fairfield University (B.A., English, 1976); John Marshall Law School (J.D., 1981). Assistant State's Attorney, Cook County, 1981-1984. ***PRACTICE AREAS:*** Health Care; Insurance Coverage; Reinsurance. ***Email:*** ckerns@kpfplaw.com

ELIZABETH A. PITROF, born Mobile, Alabama, November 24, 1946; admitted to bar, 1985, Illinois; 1992, District of Columbia. *Education:* Mount St. Agnes College; DePaul University (B.A., cum laude, 1969); Loyola University (J.D., cum laude, 1985). *Member:* American Bar Association; Professional Liability Underwriting Society. ***PRACTICE AREAS:*** Insurance Coverage; Professional Liability; Insurance Agents and Brokers Errors and Omissions; Directors and Officers Liability; Toxic Torts; Reinsurance. ***Email:*** epitrof@kpfplaw.com

CIARA RYAN FROST, born Chicago, Illinois, November 2, 1964; admitted to bar, 1989, Illinois. *Education:* Santa Clara University (B.A., 1986); Loyola University (J.D., 1989). ***PRACTICE AREAS:*** Insurance Coverage; Health Care. ***Email:*** cfrost@kpfplaw.com

MARC J. PEARLMAN, born Highland Park, Illinois, December 5, 1965; admitted to bar, 1991, Illinois. *Education:* Cornell University (B.A., 1988); University of Michigan (J.D., 1991). ***PRACTICE AREAS:*** Civil Litigation; Business Litigation; Insurance Coverage; Insurance Defense; Reinsurance; Arbitration; Products Liability. ***Email:*** mpearlman@kpfplaw.com

GREGORY J. SIMON, born Chicago, Illinois, June 8, 1963; admitted to bar, 1988, Illinois. *Education:* Harvard College (B.A., cum laude, 1985); University of Michigan (J.D., cum laude, 1988). Adjunct Professor, DePaul College of Law, 1993-1997. *Member:* Chicago (Member, Judicial Evaluation Committee, 1995-2001) and Illinois State Bar Associations. ***LANGUAGES:*** Spanish and German. ***PRACTICE AREAS:*** Commercial Litigation; Reinsurance; Governmental Regulation. ***Email:*** gsimon@kpfplaw.com

MARK E. WILSON, born 1963; admitted to bar, 1989, Illinois; 1990, U.S. Court of Appeals, Seventh Circuit and U.S. District Court, Northern District of Illinois; 1992, U.S. District Court, Central District of Illinois; 1993, U.S. Supreme Court. *Education:* Kalamazoo College (B.A., 1985); Université de Strasbourg (1983-1984); University of Minnesota (J.D., cum laude, 1988). *Member:* American Bar Association (Member, Sections on: Business Law; Litigation; Torts; Insurance Practice). ***LANGUAGES:*** French. ***PRACTICE AREAS:*** Commercial Litigation; Uniform Commercial Code; Banking Litigation; Check Fraud; Wire Fraud; Insurance Coverage. ***Email:*** mwilson@kpfplaw.com

ASSOCIATES

JOAN E. BRADY, born Cleveland, Ohio, August 12, 1967; admitted to bar, 1992, Illinois. *Education:* Michigan State University (B.A., 1989); Ohio State University (J.D., 1992). Order of the Coif. Recipient, American Jurisprudence Award for Evidence and Estates. ***PRACTICE AREAS:*** Insurance Law. ***Email:*** jbrady@kpfplaw.com

JASON P. MINKIN, born Chicago, Illinois, March 7, 1971; admitted to bar, 1998, Illinois; 1999, U.S. District Court, Northern District of Illinois; 2000, U.S. District Court, Northern District of Iowa. *Education:* University of Minnesota (B.A., 1994); DePaul University College of Law (J.D., 1998); Tulane Law School (LL.M. in Admiralty, 1999). *Member:* Chicago and Illinois State Bar Associations; Maritime Law Association of the United States; Propeller Club of the United States, Port of Chicago. ***PRACTICE AREAS:*** Insurance Coverage; Reinsurance; Commercial Litigation; Maritime Litigation; Products Liability. ***Email:*** jminkin@kpfplaw.com

JODI R. MARVET, born Highland Park, Illinois, January 21, 1962; admitted to bar, 1988, Florida; 2000, Illinois. *Education:* University of Florida (B.A., 1984; J.D., 1987). Phi Beta Kappa. *Member:* The Florida Bar; Illinois State Bar Association. ***PRACTICE AREAS:*** Insurance Coverage; Commercial Litigation; Bankruptcy. ***Email:*** jmarvet@kpfplaw.com

(This Listing Continued)

KERNS, PITROF, FROST & PEARLMAN, L.L.C., Chicago—Continued

MEGHAN A. WELCH, born Hackensack, New Jersey, March 27, 1974; admitted to bar, 2002, Illinois. *Education:* Dartmouth College (A.B., 1996); Tulane Law School (J.D., 2001). *Member:* Chicago, Illinois State and American Bar Associations. ***Email:*** msherlock@kpfplaw.com

MICHAELA RYAN, born Lexington, Kentucky, July 12, 1963; admitted to bar, 1991, Illinois. *Education:* Georgetown University (B.A., 1986); Chicago-Kent College of Law (J.D., 1991). ***PRACTICE AREAS:*** Insurance Defense. ***Email:*** mryan@kpfplaw.com

DEBRA B. GOLDBERG, born Philadelphia, Pennsylvania, June 16, 1975; admitted to bar, 2000, Illinois. *Education:* Washington University (B.A., 1997); George Washington University (J.D., M.P.H., 2000). *Member:* Illinois State Bar Association. ***PRACTICE AREAS:*** Insurance Coverage; Civil Litigation. ***Email:*** dgoldberg@kpfplaw.com

LOUISE M. GOODWIN, born Evanston, Illinois, January 7, 1965; admitted to bar, 1993, Connecticut; 1995, Illinois, U.S. District Court, Northern District of Illinois and Northern District of Indiana. *Education:* College of the Holy Cross (B.A., 1987); Emory University (J.D., 1992). ***PRACTICE AREAS:*** Insurance Coverage; Environmental Litigation. ***Email:*** lgoodwin@kpfplaw.com

SCOTT A. HANFLING, born Elgin, Illinois, November 17, 1973; admitted to bar, 1998, Illinois and U.S. District Court, Middle District of Illinois; 1999, U.S. District Court, Central District of Illinois; 2000, U.S. Court of Appeals, Seventh Circuit; 2002, U.S. Court of Appeals, Fourth Circuit; 2003, U.S. District Court, District of Colorado. *Education:* Northwestern University (B.A., 1995); Chicago-Kent College of Law (J.D., 1998). Chicago Kent Moot Court Honor Society. ***PRACTICE AREAS:*** Commercial Litigation; Employment Law; Insurance Coverage; Toxic Tort; Products Liability. ***Email:*** shanfling@kpfplaw.com

ELLEN O'LAUGHLIN, born Chicago, Illinois, July 7, 1963; admitted to bar, 1991, Illinois; 1992, U.S. District Court, Northern District of Illinois. *Education:* Lawrence University (B.A., 1985); Loyola University (J.D., 1991). ***Email:*** eolaughlin@kpfplaw.com

OF COUNSEL

MICHAEL L. BROOKS, born Detroit, Michigan, December 26, 1962; admitted to bar, 1988, Illinois. *Education:* Kalamazoo College (B.A., 1985); University of Michigan (J.D., cum laude, 1988). Order of the Coif. ***PRACTICE AREAS:*** Commercial Litigation; Civil Litigation. ***Email:*** mbrooks@kpfplaw.com

KRISTIN DODGE McMAHON, born Lowell, Massachusetts, December 18, 1965; admitted to bar, 1990, Connecticut; 1991, New York; 1995, Illinois and Massachusetts. *Education:* Fairfield University (B.S., with honors, 1987); Boston University (J.D., 1990). ***PRACTICE AREAS:*** Insurance Coverage; Professional Liability; Reinsurance. ***Email:*** kdmcmahon@kpfplaw.com

SPECIAL COUNSEL

ROBERT C. THURSTON, born Darby, Pennsylvania, October 13, 1962; admitted to bar, 1987, Pennsylvania; 1988, New Jersey; 1992, Illinois. *Education:* University of Michigan (A.B., 1984); The Ohio State University College of Law (J.D., 1987). ***LANGUAGES:*** German. ***PRACTICE AREAS:*** Insurance Litigation; Reinsurance; Commercial Litigation. ***Email:*** tjthurston@kpfplaw.com

KEVIN EDWARD WHITE & ASSOCIATES

Established in 2003

77 WEST WACKER DRIVE, SUITE 4800
CHICAGO, ILLINOIS 60601
Telephone: 312-606-8602
Fax: 312-606-8603
Email: kwhite@kevinedwardwhiteassociates.com
URL: http://www.kevinedwardwhiteassociates.com

Complex Litigation, Civil Litigation, Commercial Law, Corporate Law, Franchises.

FIRM PROFILE: Providing risk management for the entrepreneur.

KEVIN E. WHITE, born Evanston, Illinois, 1954; admitted to bar, 1981, Wisconsin, Illinois and U.S. District Court, Northern District of Illinois; 1982, U.S. Court of Appeals, Seventh Circuit; 1986, U.S. Court of Appeals, Ninth Circuit; 2003, U.S. District Court, Western District of Wisconsin. *Education:* Knox College (B.A., cum laude, 1978); University of Wisconsin-Madison (J.D., 1981). Elected, Lincoln Academy, 1986. *Member:* Chicago, Illinois, Seventh Circuit, Federal and American (Member, Section on Antitrust, Business Law and Individual Rights, Responsibilities) Bar Associations. ***PRACTICE AREAS:*** Civil Appeals; Alternative Dispute Resolution; Complex and Multi-District Litigation; Fraud and Deceit; Civil RICO. ***Email:*** kwhite@kevinedwardwhiteassociates.com

KIESLER & BERMAN

70 WEST MADISON, SUITE 4200
CHICAGO, ILLINOIS 60602
Telephone: 312-332-2840
FAX: 312-332-4547
Email: info@thekillerbees.com
URL: http://www.kieslerberman.com

Joliet Office: 57 North Ottawa Street, Suite 210. Telephone: 815-723-2755. Fax: 815-723-2763.

(This Listing Continued)

General Civil Trial and Appellate Practice, Insurance, Workers Compensation, Trucking Law, Construction Litigation, Corporation, Real Estate and Probate Law. Asbestos Litigation, Civil Rights Law, Estate Planning, Insurance Coverage, Insurance Defense Law, Medical Malpractice Law, Police Misconduct, RICO, Surety and Fidelity Bond Law, Tort Law, Toxic Substances Law and Toxic Torts, Lanham Act Litigation, Condemnation Litigation, Arbitrations.

FIRM PROFILE: Kiesler & Berman was founded April 16, 1963 by Robert L. Kielser and Marvin D. Berman, former classmates and graduates of the University of Illinois College of Law. The practice was started primarily as an insurance defense and subrogation firm with a sub-emphasis on corporate and real estate. The firm now services the entire Cook County area, as well as the collar counties of Lake, McHenry, Boone, Winnebago, Kane, DeKalb, LaSalle, DuPage, Will, Kendall, Grundy and Kankakee through its office located in Joliet, Illinois. The firm specializes in all phases of insurance defense, Workers' Compensation and coverage work and continues its practice in corporate, real estate and probate.

FOUNDERS

MARVIN D. BERMAN, born Chicago, Illinois, May 25, 1931; admitted to bar, 1955, Illinois; 1959, U.S. District Court, Northern District of Illinois; 1964, U.S. Court of Appeals, 7th Circuit; 1974, U.S. Supreme Court. *Education:* University of Illinois (B.S., 1953; J. D., 1955). Member, Moot Court Team. *Member:* Chicago (Chairman, Insurance Law Committee, 1983-1984), Illinois State and American Bar Associations; Society of Trial Lawyers; Illinois Association of Defense Trial Counsel; Defense Research and Trial Lawyers Association. ***LANGUAGES:*** Spanish. ***TRANSACTIONS:*** Attorney for Crown Drug Co. merger with Vitarene, Inc. ***PRACTICE AREAS:*** Insurance Coverage Interpretation and Litigation; Probate; Estate Planning; Corporate; Real Estate. ***Email:*** mdb@thekillerbees.com

ROBERT L. KIESLER, born Chicago, Illinois, August 25, 1932; admitted to bar, 1956, Illinois; 1959, U.S. District Court, Northern District of Illinois; 1962, U.S. Court of Appeals, 7th Circuit; 1974, U.S. Supreme Court. *Education:* University of Illinois (B.S., 1954; J.D., 1956). Lecturer, Illinois Institute for Continuing Legal Education on Declaratory Actions and Insurance Law, 1979—. Police and Fire Commissioner, Winnetka, Illinois, 1979-1986. *Member:* Chicago (Member, Bench and Bar Section; Chairman, Insurance Law Committee, 1981-1982), Illinois State (Chairman, Insurance Law Section, 1982-1983; Vice Chairman, Tort Law Section Council, 1988-1989) and American Bar Associations; Society of Trial Lawyers; Illinois Association of Defense Trial Counsel (Board of Directors, 1986-1996); Defense Research and Trial Lawyers Association. ***PRACTICE AREAS:*** Insurance Coverage; Insurance Defense Law; Tort. ***Email:*** rlk@thekillerbees.com

PARTNERS

STEPHEN B. FREW, born Painesville, Ohio, March 8, 1951; admitted to bar, 1976, Illinois and U.S. District, Northern District of Illinois; 1978, U.S. Court of Appeals, 7th Circuit. *Education:* Indiana University (A.B., 1973); Case Western Reserve University (J.D., 1976). Member, Case Western Law Review, 1975-1976. *Member:* Chicago (Chair of Circuit Court Committee, 1996-1997; Member, Insurance Law Committee), Illinois State (Delegate to General Assembly, 1996-1997; Member Sections on: Tort Law, Civil Practice and Procedure and Insurance) and American Bar Associations; Illinois Association of Defense Trial Counsel; Society of Trial Lawyers (Board of Directors, 2002-2003; Nominating Committee, 2005). (Managing Partner). ***REPORTED CASES:*** Kempes v. Dunlop Tire & Rubber Co., 192 Ill. App 3d 209 (1989); Davis v. Pakmor, 284 Ill.App.3d 214 (1996); USF&G v. Specialty Coatings, 180 Ill.App.3d 378, 535 N.E.2d 1071 (1st Dist. 1989); Kelly v. Northwest Community Hospital, 66 Ill.App.3d 679 (1978); Martin v. Hertz, 104 Ill.App.3d 592 (1982); Clay v. Pepper Construction Co., 205 Ill.App.3d 1018 (1990); Adami v. Green Giant, 849 F.Supp. 615 (N.D.Ill 1994); Knoblauch v. DEF Express Corp., 86 F.2d 684 (7th Cir. 1996). ***PRACTICE AREAS:*** Civil Trials and Appeals; Insurance Defense; Professional Malpractice; Product Liability; Construction Litigation; Insurance Coverage. ***Email:*** sbf@thekillerbees.com

CLINTON J. FEIL, born Chicago, Illinois, September 3, 1946; admitted to bar, 1971, Illinois and U.S. District Court, Northern District of Illinois including Trial Bar; 1976, U.S. Court of Appeals, 7th Circuit. *Education:* Northwestern University (B.S., 1968; J.D., cum laude, 1971). Phi Alpha Delta. *Member:* Chicago, Illinois State and American Bar Associations; Illinois Association of Defense Trial Counsel. ***REPORTED CASES:*** Aetna v. Globe Co., 60 Ill. App 3d 957 (1978); Zielinski v. A. Epstein & Sons Int'l, 179 Ill. App 3d 340 (1989); Farley v. Barber Coleman Co., 269 Ill. App 3d 104 (1994) app. den.; Duncan v. Church of the Living God, 278 Ill. App 3d 588 (1996) app. den. ***PRACTICE AREAS:*** Civil Trials and Appeals; Insurance Defense; Tort; Construction Litigation; Employer Liability; Libel and Slander; Products Liability. ***Email:*** cjf@thekillerbees.com

ALAN P. MILLER, born Detroit, Michigan, January 17, 1938; admitted to bar, 1965, Illinois and U.S. District Court, Northern District of Illinois including Trial Bar; 1974, U.S. Court of Appeals, 7th Circuit; 2004, U.S. District Court, Central District of Illinois. *Education:* Brown University (A.B., 1959); University of Michigan (J.D., 1963). Recipient, Campbell Competition Award (Moot Court), University of Michigan Law School. Past Chairman, American Cancer Society Annual Drive, Kenilworth. Independent Arbitrator, Three Person Arbitrations. Chair Qualified Circuit Court, Cook County Mandatory Arbitration Program. *Member:* Chicago (Past Chair, Circuit Court Committee, 2000-2001) and Illinois State Bar Associations; Defense Research Institute; Illinois Association of Defense Trial Counsel; Society of Trial Lawyers (Member; Board of Directors, 1991-1993; President, 2000-2001). ***REPORTED CASES:*** Gulley vs. Fountalas, 153 Ill. App 3d 100 (1987); Claudy vs. Commonwealth Edison, 169 Ill.2d 39 (1995); Peterson v. Ress Enterprises, Inc., 292 Ill. App 3d 566 (1997). ***PRACTICE AREAS:*** Insurance Defense; Trucking Law; Construction Litigation; Tort; Arbitrations and Mediations; Condemnation; Civil Trials and Appeals. ***Email:*** apm@thekillerbees.com

JOHN R. GAROFALO, born Chicago, Illinois, April 27, 1940; admitted to bar, 1967, Illinois and U.S. District Court, Northern District of Illinois. *Education:* University of Notre Dame (B.B.A., 1962); John Marshall Law School (J.D., 1966). Township Attorney, Oak Park Township, Oak Park, Illinois, 1969—. Chair Qualified Arbitrator, Cook County Mandatory Arbitration Program. Member of Panel, American Arbitration Association. *Member:* Chicago (Vice Chair of Circuit Court Committee, 1997-1998; Chairman, Circuit

(This Listing Continued)

Court Committee, 1998-1999; Member, Tort Litigation Committee) and Illinois State Bar Associations; Illinois Association of Defense Trial Counsel; Society of Trial Lawyers (Member, Board of Directors, 1993-1995); Justinian Society of Lawyers. ***REPORTED CASES:*** Dick vs. Gursoy, 124 Ill. App.3d 185; 471 N.E.2d 195 Dowen vs. Hall, 191 Ill. App.3d 903; 548 N.E.2d 346 Arnold vs. Chicago Ridge, 181 Ill. App.3d 778; 537 N.E.2d 823; Schoch v. U. of Chicago 87 Ill. App. 3d 856; Moricoli v. P & S Managerment Co., 104 Ill. App. 2d 234. ***PRACTICE AREAS:*** Personal Injury; Insurance; Local Government. ***Email:*** jrg@thekillerbees.com

DALE L. SCHLAFER, born Detroit, Michigan, April 22, 1938; admitted to bar, 1962, Illinois and U.S. District Court, Northern District of Illinois. *Education:* Amherst College (A.B., 1959); University of Chicago (J.D., 1962). Arbitrator, American Arbitration Association. Chair Qualified Arbitrator, Cook County Mandatory Arbitration Program. *Member:* Chicago (Past Chairman, Insurance Law Committee), Illinois State and American (Past Chairman, Automobile Committee; Past Vice-Chairman, Excess, Surplus Lines and Reinsurance Committee, Torts and Insurance Practice Section) Bar Associations; Illinois Association of Defense Trial Counsel (Board of Directors, 1997-2000; Chairman, Insurance Committee); Trucking Industry Defense Association; Defense Research Institute. ***PRACTICE AREAS:*** Medical Negligence Defense; Chiropractic Malpractice Defense; Podiatric Malpractice Defense; Insurance Coverage; Automotive Dealership Law; Trucking Law; Civil Trials and Appeals. ***Email:*** dls@thekillerbees.com

PATTI OLSON DEUEL, born Chicago, Illinois, May 3, 1959; admitted to bar, 1985, Illinois and U.S. District Court, Northern District of Illinois; U.S. Court of Appeals, 7th Circuit. *Education:* Northern Illinois University (B.A., 1981); John Marshall Law School (J.D., 1985). Executive Editor, John Marshall Law Review, 1984-1985. *Member:* Illinois State Bar Association (Member, Insurance Law Section); Illinois Association of Defense Trial Counsel. ***REPORTED CASES:*** USF&G vs. Wilkin Insulation Co., 144 Ill.2d 64 (1991); St. Paul vs. Smith, 337 Ill. App.3d 1054(2003); United States Fire Insurance Co. vs. Hartford, 312 Ill. App 3d 153 (2000); USF&G vs. Jiffy Cab Co., 265 Ill. App.3d 533 (1994). ***PRACTICE AREAS:*** Insurance Coverage; Appellate Practice; Insurance Defense Law. ***Email:*** pmd@thekillerbees.com

WILLIAM P. McELLIGOTT, born Chicago, Illinois, June 11, 1963; admitted to bar, 1989, Illinois. *Education:* University of Illinois (B.A., 1985); Chicago-Kent College of Law, Illinois Institute of Technology (J.D., 1988). Member, Knights of Columbus. *Member:* Chicago Bar Association (Member, Young Lawyers Section). ***PRACTICE AREAS:*** Civil Trials; Construction Litigation; Premises Liability; Tort. ***Email:*** wpm@thekillerbees.com

SENIOR TRIAL COUNSEL

EDWARD L. COOPER, born Chicago, Illinois, March 22, 1931; admitted to bar, 1955, Illinois; 1963, U.S. District Court, Northern District of Illinois and U.S. Supreme Court. *Education:* University of Illinois; Roosevelt University; Chicago-Kent College of Law, Illinois Institute of Technology (J.D., 1954). Member, Chicago Kent Law Review, 1952. ***PRACTICE AREAS:*** General Civil Trial; Appellate; Insurance Defense; Tort. ***Email:*** elc@thekillerbees.com

ASSOCIATES

BRYAN W. LUCE, born Louisville, Kentucky, September 2, 1961; admitted to bar, 1986, Illinois; 1988, U.S. District Court, Northern District of Illinois; 1989, U.S. District Court, Central District of Illinois. *Education:* University of Illinois (B.A., 1983; J.D., 1986). Phi Beta Kappa. *Member:* Chicago Bar Association (Member, Appellate Section). ***LANGUAGES:*** Russian and German. ***REPORTED CASES:*** Delaney vs. McDonald's Corp., 158 Ill2d 465 (1994); McGee vs. Kerr-Hickman Chrysler-Plymouth, Inc., 93 F3d 380 (7th Cir. 1996). ***PRACTICE AREAS:*** Civil Trial and Appeals; Insurance Defense; Consumer Law; Construction Litigation. ***Email:*** bwl@thekillerbees.com

DONNA D. CIANCIO, born Highland Park, Illinois, January 1, 1966; admitted to bar, 1992, Illinois and U.S. District Court, Northern District of Illinois. *Education:* Purdue University (B.A., 1988); Chicago-Kent College of Law, Illinois Institute of Technology (J.D., 1992). *Member:* Chicago and Illinois State Bar Associations; Justinian Society of Lawyers. ***PRACTICE AREAS:*** Insurance Defense. ***Email:*** ddc@thekillerbees.com

VICTORIA P. KARASIK, born New Orleans, Louisiana, October 23, 1949; admitted to bar, 1983, Illinois; 1996, Arizona. *Education:* Louisiana State University (B.A., 1973); DePaul University College of Law (J.D., 1983). *Member:* Illinois State Bar Association. ***PRACTICE AREAS:*** Insurance Defense Litigation; Insurance Arbitration; General Liability; Automobile Liability Defense. ***Email:*** vpk@thekillerbees.com

ALAN E. NEUMANN, born Chicago, Illinois, September 9, 1943; admitted to bar, 1977, Illinois and U.S. District Court, Northern District of Illinois. *Education:* Michigan State University (B.A., with honors, 1966); Chicago-Kent College of Law, Illinois Institute of Technology (J.D., 1976). *Member:* Chicago and Illinois State Bar Associations; Workers Compensation Lawyers Association. ***LANGUAGES:*** French. ***PRACTICE AREAS:*** Workers Compensation. ***Email:*** aen@thekillerbees.com

JEANNE M. ZEIGER, born Waterloo, Iowa, December 25, 1952; admitted to bar, 1979, Illinois; 1982, U.S. District Court, Northern District of Illinois; 2001, U.S. District Court, Central District of Illinois. *Education:* University of Iowa (B.S., 1975); Washington University School of Law (J.D., 1979). Associate Editor, Urban Law Annual. *Member:* Chicago and Illinois State Bar Associations. ***REPORTED CASES:*** Institute of London Underwriters vs Hartford Fire Insilo, 234 Ill. App. 3d 70, 599 N.E 2d 1311 (1992); Motor Vehicle Casualty Company vs 65F Energy, Inc., 193 Ill. App 3d 1, 549 N.E 2d 884 (1989). ***PRACTICE AREAS:*** Civil Litigation; Insurance Coverage Litigation; Appellate Practice. ***Email:*** jmz@thekillerbees.com

RICHARD L. ELSLIGER, born Toronto, Ontario, Canada, June 14, 1963; admitted to bar, 1989, Minnesota; 1991, Illinois and District of Columbia; U.S. District Court, Northern District of Illinois. *Education:* University of Toronto (B.A., 1986); Southern Illinois University School of Law (J.D., 1989). ***PRACTICE AREAS:*** Trial Practice; General Liability; Insurance Defense; Contracts; Transportation Law; Insurance Coverage Matters. ***Email:*** rle@thekillerbees.com

THOMAS E. GONZALES, born Dallas, Texas, June 7, 1972; admitted to bar, 1999, Illinois; U.S. District Court, Northern District of Illinois. *Education:* University of Texas at Austin (B.B.A., 1994); University of Chicago (M.L.A., 1999); DePaul University College of Law (J.D., 2002). *Member:* Chicago, Illinois State and American Bar Associations. ***PRACTICE AREAS:*** Labor Law; Insurance Defense. ***Email:*** teg@thekillerbees.com

LINGZHI ZHAO, born Hebei, China, October 30, 1972; admitted to bar, 2003, Illinois. *Education:* Peking University (M.A., 1997); Michigan State University, Detroit College of Law (J.D., 2003). Dean's List, 2003. Associate, Journal of International Law, Michigan State University. *Member:* Chicago and Illinois State Bar Association. ***LANGUAGES:*** Chinese, Japanese and French. ***PRACTICE AREAS:*** Family Law; Insurance Defense; Consumer Law. ***Email:*** lxz@thekillerbees.com

SENIOR COUNSEL

WILLIAM M. STROUD, born Chicago, Illinois, March 12, 1935; admitted to bar, 1983, Illinois; 1994, U.S. Court of Federal Claims; 1996, U.S. Tax Court. *Education:* Roosevelt University (B.S.C., 1957); Chicago-Kent College of Law, Illinois Institute of Technology (J.D., 1983). Certified Public Accountant, Illinois, 1957. Controller, Town of Camillus, N.Y., 1970-1975. Illinois Certified Public Account Society, 1959-1967 and 1980—. *Member:* Chicago, Illinois State and American (Chairman, Committees on: Taxation Law; Torts) Bar Associations. ***PRACTICE AREAS:*** Taxation Law; Business Law; Corporate Law; Estate Planning; Trusts; Probate. ***Email:*** wms@thekillerbees.com

FRANK N. RAGO, born Chicago, Illinois, August 24, 1919; admitted to bar, 1946, Illinois and U.S. District Court, Northern District of Illinois. *Education:* Herzl College; DePaul University (LL.B., 1945). *Member:* Illinois State Bar Association; Society of Trial Lawyers. ***Email:*** fnr@thekillerbees.com

LAW PRACTICE OF
PATRICIA D. KING

211 EAST ONTARIO STREET, SUITE 1800
CHICAGO, ILLINOIS 60611
Telephone: 312-283-5350
Fax: 312-283-5005
Email: patking@patkinglaw.com
URL: http://www.patkinglaw.com

Health Care Law, Hospital Law, Computers and Software Law.

PATRICIA D. KING, born Milwaukee, Wisconsin, January 5, 1952; admitted to bar, 1977, Wisconsin, Illinois, U.S. District Court, District of Wisconsin and U.S. District Court, Northern District of Illinois. *Education:* University of Wisconsin (B.A., with honors, 1974; J.D., 1977); University of Chicago (M.B.A., 1982). Author: "The Illinois Living Will Act: What It Could Mean to Physician and Patient," Illinois Bar, April, 1984. *Member:* Chicago (Member, Health Law Committee; Member, 1981—, and Chairman, 1987-1988, Health and Hospital Law Committee, Young Lawyers Section) and Illinois State Bar Associations; American Health Lawyers Association; Illinois Association of Hospital Attorneys. ***PRACTICE AREAS:*** Health Care.

KINZY & ASSOCIATES, P.C.

3053 WEST ARMITAGE, SUITE 1F
CHICAGO, ILLINOIS 60647
Telephone: 773-486-9529
Fax: 773-486-9344
Email: kapconline@ameritech.net
URL: http://www.kinzyandassociates.com

Immigration, Deportation, Real Estate, Business Law, Asset Protection, Estate Planning.

KYLE M. KINZY, born Columbia, Missouri, March 27, 1970; admitted to bar, 1996, Illinois; 1997, Texas. *Education:* Baylor University (B.A., Economics, 1992); South Texas College of Law (J.D., 1995). *Member:* Chicago Bar Association; State Bar of Texas. ***PRACTICE AREAS:*** Business Law; Commercial Litigation; Intellectual Property Litigation; Alternative Dispute Resolution; Immigration and Naturalization; Real Estate; Internet Law; General Practice. ***Email:*** kapconline@ameritech.net

KIPNIS & KAHN, LTD.

Established in 1971
30 NORTH LA SALLE STREET, SUITE 2024
CHICAGO, ILLINOIS 60602
Telephone: 312-726-3700
Fax: 312-726-4644
Email: kipniskahnlaw@aol.com
URL: http://www.kipniskahnlaw.com

Joliet, Illinois Office: 54 N. Ottawa, Suite 305, 60432. Telephone: 815-726-7370.

Civil Litigation, Family Law, Corporate Litigation, Church Law, Personal Injury, Worker's Compensation, Auto Accidents, Medical Malpractice, Slip and Fall, Airplane Crashes, Train Crashes, Wrongful Death.

CLAUDE B. KAHN, born 1936; admitted to bar, 1960, Maryland; 1961, District of Columbia; 1966, Illinois; 1993, Colorado. *Education:* American University (LL.B., 1960). ***PRACTICE AREAS:*** Civil Litigation; Family Law; Corporate Litigation; Church Law; Personal Injury.

GLENN J. KAHN, born Highland Park, Illinois, April 27, 1965; admitted to bar, 1991, Illinois. *Education:* Lake Forest College (B.A., 1987); Chicago-Kent College of Law, Illinois Institute of Technology (J.D., 1991). *Member:* Chicago and American Bar Associations. ***PRACTICE AREAS:*** Personal Injury; Workers Compensation; Corporate Litiga-

(This Listing Continued)

KIPNIS & KAHN, LTD., Chicago—Continued

tion; Automobile Accidents; Medical Malpractice; Airplane Crash Litigation; Train Crash Litigation; Wrongful Death.

KIRKLAND & ELLIS LLP

And Affiliated Partnerships
200 EAST RANDOLPH DRIVE
CHICAGO, ILLINOIS 60601
Telephone: 312-861-2000
Facsimile: 312-861-2200
URL: http://www.kirkland.com

Los Angeles, California Office: 777 South Figueroa Street. Telephone: 213-680-8400. Facsimile: 213-680-8500.
San Francisco, California Office: 555 California Street. Telephone: 415-439-1400. Facsimile: 415-439-1500.
Washington, D.C. Office: 655 Fifteenth Street, N.W. Telephone: 202-879-5000. Facsimile: 202-879-5200.
New York, New York Office: Citigroup Center, 153 East 53rd Street. Telephone: 212-446-4800. Facsimile: 212-446-4900.
London, England Office: Kirkland & Ellis International LLP, Tower 42, 25 Old Broad Street. Telephone: 011-44-20-7816-8700. Facsimile: 011-44-20-7816-8800.
Munich, Germany Office: Kirkland & Ellis International LLP, Maximilianstrasse 11. Telephone: +49 89 2030 6000. Facsimile: +49 89 2030 6100.

Advertising, Advertising and Marketing, Alternative Dispute Resolution, Antitrust Litigation, Antitrust and Trade Regulation, Appellate, Arbitration, Asset-Backed Securities, Asset-Backed Finance, Banking, Bankruptcy and Workouts, Bankruptcy Reorganization, Biotechnology, Business Law, Civil Litigation, Class Action, Commercial Litigation, Competition and Antitrust Law, Computer Law, Computer and Technology, Computers and Software, Contested Tax Matters, Contract, Copyrights, Corporate, Counseling, Creditor's Rights, Debtor-Creditor Law, Digital Commerce, Distribution Litigation, Divestitures, Employee Benefits, Employment Litigation, Employment Law, Environmental Litigation, ERISA, Estate Planning, Executive Compensation, Finance, Financial Services, Foreign Tax Planning, Franchise Law, Franchise and Distribution, Fund Formation, Futures Law, Health Care, Institutional Investment, Insurance Coverage, Intellectual Property, Intercompany Transfer-Pricing, International Law, Joint Ventures, Labor and Employment, Legislative, Leveraged Acquisitions, Leveraged Buyouts, Licensing, Litigation, Marketing, Mass Torts, Mergers and Acquisitions, Patent Litigation, Planning and Administration, Private Equity, Product Liability, Real Estate, Restructuring, Secured Lending, Securities, Strategic Alliances, Tax, Taxation, Technology and Science, Technology Licensing, Technology Transactions, Telecommunications, Torts, Trade Secrets and Intellectual Property, Trademarks, Trusts and Estates, Unfair Competition, Venture Capital, White Collar Crime, Workout and Bankruptcy, Workouts, Reorganizations and Bankruptcy, Worldwide Litigation and Arbitration.

PARTNERS OF FIRM

WEYMOUTH KIRKLAND (1877-1965)

HOWARD ELLIS (1892-1968)

ELLEN THERESE AHERN, admitted to bar, 1992, Illinois. *Education:* Georgetown University (A.B., 1989); University of Michigan (J.D., 1991). ***PRACTICE AREAS:*** Litigation; Products Liability; Environmental Law. ***Email:*** eahern@kirkland.com

CINDY S. AHN, admitted to bar, 1998, Illinois; registered to practice before U.S. Patent and Trademark Office. *Education:* University of Illinois at Urbana-Champaign (B.S., Biology, 1994); The American University, Washington College of Law (J.D., cum laude, 1998). ***PRACTICE AREAS:*** Intellectual Property; Biotechnology; Pharmaceutical; Life Science; Patent Infringement Litigation. ***Email:*** cahn@kirkland.com

IMRON T. ALY, admitted to bar, 1999, Illinois; 2000, Missouri; registered to practice before U.S. Patent and Trademark Office. *Education:* Duke University (B.S.E., cum laude, 1996); Georgetown University Law Center (J.D., magna cum laude, 1999). ***LANGUAGES:*** Spanish, Urdu. ***PRACTICE AREAS:*** Intellectual Property; Patent Litigation. ***Email:*** ialy@kirkland.com

JOHN J. AMBERG, admitted to bar, 1999, Illinois. *Education:* University of Illinois at Urbana-Champaign (B.S., with highest honors, 1996); University of Chicago (J.D., with honors, 1999). ***PRACTICE AREAS:*** Litigation; Class Actions. ***Email:*** jamberg@kirkland.com

AMY CURTNER ANDREWS, admitted to bar, 1995, Illinois. *Education:* Kenyon College (B.A., 1989); University of Michigan (J.D., 1994). ***PRACTICE AREAS:*** Litigation. ***Email:*** aandrews@kirkland.com

GARY E. AXELROD, admitted to bar, 1997, Illinois. *Education:* University of Illinois (B.S., with high honors, 1994; J.D., magna cum laude, 1997). ***PRACTICE AREAS:*** Real Estate. ***Email:*** gaxelrod@kirkland.com

JANET S. BAER, admitted to bar, 1982, Illinois. *Education:* University of Wisconsin (B.A., 1979); DePaul University (J.D., 1982). ***PRACTICE AREAS:*** Bankruptcy; Commercial Litigation. ***Email:*** jbaer@kirkland.com

GABOR BALASSA, admitted to bar, 1997, Illinois. *Education:* Columbia University (B.A., 1994; J.D., 1997). ***PRACTICE AREAS:*** Litigation. ***Email:*** gbalassa@kirkland.com

JON A. BALLIS, admitted to bar, 1994, Illinois. *Education:* Lehigh University (B.A., magna cum laude, 1991); Harvard Law School (J.D., cum laude, 1994). ***PRACTICE AREAS:*** Leveraged Acquisitions; Mergers and Acquisitions; Venture Capital; Private Equity.

(This Listing Continued)

MICHAEL D. BELSLEY, admitted to bar, 1996, Illinois. *Education:* Northwestern University (B.A., 1992; J.D., 1996). ***PRACTICE AREAS:*** Corporate; Mergers, Acquisitions and Divestitures; Venture Capital; Private Equity; Securities. ***Email:*** mbelsley@kirkland.com

DAVID M. BERNICK, (P.C.), admitted to bar, 1978, Illinois. *Education:* University of Chicago (B.A., 1974; J.D., 1978). ***PRACTICE AREAS:*** Commercial Litigation. ***Email:*** dbernick@kirkland.com

JACK N. BERNSTEIN, admitted to bar, 1995, Illinois. *Education:* Emory University (B.A., 1986); John Marshall Law School (J.D., 1995; LL.M., 1998). ***PRACTICE AREAS:*** Employee Benefits. ***Email:*** jbernstein@kirkland.com

WENDY L. BLOOM, admitted to bar, 1993, Illinois. *Education:* University of Pennsylvania (B.A., summa cum laude, 1988); Harvard University (J.D., magna cum laude, 1992). ***PRACTICE AREAS:*** Commercial Litigation. ***Email:*** wbloom@kirkland.com

ANDREW B. BLOOMER, admitted to bar, 1992, Wisconsin and Illinois. *Education:* Harvard University (A.B., magna cum laude, 1988); University of Wisconsin-Madison (J.D., cum laude, 1992). ***PRACTICE AREAS:*** Commercial Litigation. ***Email:*** abloomer@kirkland.com

JAMES J. BOLAND, admitted to bar, 1995, Illinois. *Education:* University of Chicago (B.A., 1987); Northwestern University (J.D., cum laude, 1995). ***PRACTICE AREAS:*** Litigation. ***Email:*** jboland@kirkland.com

NADER R. BOULOS, admitted to bar, 1994, Illinois. *Education:* Stanford University (A.B., 1991); University of Michigan (J.D., 1994). ***PRACTICE AREAS:*** Litigation. ***Email:*** nboulos@kirkland.com

MICHAEL P. BREGENZER, admitted to bar, 1994, Illinois; 2004, Nevada. *Education:* University of Notre Dame (B.A., 1991); University of Illinois (J.D., cum laude, 1994). ***PRACTICE AREAS:*** Intellectual Property Litigation; Patent Litigation; Trademark Litigation; Trade Secrets; Commercial Litigation. ***Email:*** mbregenzer@kirkland.com

MICHELLE H. BROWDY, admitted to bar, 1990, Illinois. *Education:* Princeton University (B.S.E., 1986); Harvard University (S.M., 1987); Yale Law School (J.D., 1990). ***PRACTICE AREAS:*** Commercial Litigation; Products Liability. ***Email:*** mbrowdy@kirkland.com

ROBERT T. BUDAY, admitted to bar, 1991, Indiana; 1999, Illinois. *Education:* Indiana University (B.S., 1988; J.D., 1991). ***PRACTICE AREAS:*** Real Estate. ***Email:*** rbuday@kirkland.com

JONATHAN BUNGE, admitted to bar, 1990, Illinois. *Education:* Princeton University (A.B., cum laude, 1984); University of Chicago (J.D., with honors, 1988). ***PRACTICE AREAS:*** Litigation. ***Email:*** jbunge@kirkland.com

CHRISTOPHER BUTLER, admitted to bar, 1989, New York; 1998, Illinois. *Education:* University of Pennsylvania (B.A., 1984); Fordham University (J.D., 1988). ***PRACTICE AREAS:*** Corporate Law; Finance; Secured Lending. ***Email:*** cbutler@kirkland.com

DAVID K. CALLAHAN, admitted to bar, 1991, Illinois. *Education:* Campbell University (A.A., 1984); University of Chicago (A.B., 1987); University of Michigan (J.D., 1991). ***PRACTICE AREAS:*** Intellectual Property; Litigation; Counseling. ***Email:*** dcallahan@kirkland.com

RICHARD J. CAMPBELL, JR., admitted to bar, 1996, Pennsylvania; 1997, Illinois. *Education:* Stanford University (A.B., 1993); Northwestern University (J.D., 1996). ***PRACTICE AREAS:*** Corporate Law. ***Email:*** rcampbell@kirkland.com

THOMAS L. CAMPBELL, admitted to bar, 1995, Illinois. *Education:* University of Chicago (B.A., 1992); IIT/Chicago-Kent College of Law (J.D., 1995). ***PRACTICE AREAS:*** Litigation; Insurance; Environmental Law. ***Email:*** tcampbell@kirkland.com

CAROLE A. CHENEY, admitted to bar, 1991, Illinois. *Education:* University of Illinois at Urbana-Champaign (B.S., 1983); University of Illinois at Springfield (M.A., 1984); Northwestern University School of Law (J.D., 1991). ***PRACTICE AREAS:*** Litigation. ***Email:*** ccheney@kirkland.com

FRANK CICERO, JR., (P.C.), admitted to bar, 1965, Illinois; 1987, Colorado. *Education:* Wheaton College (A.B., 1957); Princeton University (M.P.A., 1962); University of Chicago (J.D., 1965). ***PRACTICE AREAS:*** Commercial Litigation. ***Email:*** fcicero@kirkland.com

KEVIN J. COENEN, admitted to bar, 1997, Illinois. *Education:* University of Missouri (B.S.B.A., summa cum laude, 1991); Ohio State University (J.D., summa cum laude, 1997). ***PRACTICE AREAS:*** Taxation. ***Email:*** kcoenen@kirkland.com

PAUL DAVID COLLIER, admitted to bar, 1999, Illinois. *Education:* University of Illinois (B.S., 1993; J.D., 1999). ***PRACTICE AREAS:*** Patents; Trademarks; Copyrights. ***Email:*** pcollier@kirkland.com

JAMES B. COUGHLAN, admitted to bar, 1989, Illinois; 2004, District of Columbia. *Education:* Bradley University (B.S., 1986); DePaul University College of Law (J.D., 1989); John Marshall Law School (LL.M., 1991). ***PRACTICE AREAS:*** Intellectual Property; Patent Infringement Litigation. ***Email:*** jcoughlan@kirkland.com

KEITH S. CROW, (P.C.), admitted to bar, 1986, Illinois. *Education:* Yale College (B.S., 1983); University of Chicago (J.D., 1986). ***PRACTICE AREAS:*** Corporate; Venture Capital and Leveraged Acquisitions; International Law; International Acquisitions and Investments. ***Email:*** kcrow@kirkland.com

LUKE L. DAUCHOT, admitted to bar, 1986, Illinois; 1988, Ohio; 1998, Brussels (Associated Member). *Education:* Case Western Reserve University (B.A., magna cum laude, 1983; J.D., 1986). ***LANGUAGES:*** Dutch, French. ***PRACTICE AREAS:*** Intellectual Property; Litigation. ***Email:*** ldauchot@kirkland.com

BRIAN E. DAVIS, admitted to bar, 1998, Pennsylvania; 2000, Illinois. *Education:* Ball State University (B.U.P.D./B.S., 1995); University of Pittsburgh (J.D., 1998). ***PRACTICE AREAS:*** Real Estate.

(This Listing Continued)

ROBERT C. DAVIS III, admitted to bar, 1999, Illinois. *Education:* Duke University (A.B., 1994); University of Georgia (J.D., 1999; M.B.A., 1999). ***PRACTICE AREAS:*** Corporate Law. ***Email:*** rdavis@kirkland.com

TERRENCE J. DEE, admitted to bar, 1992, Missouri; 1993, Illinois. *Education:* Wesleyan University (B.A., 1987); Washington University (J.D., 1992). ***PRACTICE AREAS:*** Litigation; Products Liability; Securities. ***Email:*** tdee@kirkland.com

WILLIAM E. DEVITT, admitted to bar, 1995, Illinois; 1996, District of Columbia. *Education:* University of Notre Dame (B.S.E.E., 1986); The Catholic University of America (J.D., magna cum laude, 1995). ***PRACTICE AREAS:*** Intellectual Property; Technology Law. ***Email:*** wdevitt@kirkland.com

NICK DiCRESCENZO, admitted to bar, 1997, Illinois. *Education:* University of Chicago (B.A., 1990; J.D., 1997). ***PRACTICE AREAS:*** Corporate Law; Securities; Mergers and Acquisitions; Venture Capital. ***Email:*** ndicrescenzo@kirkland.com

MARTIN A. DiLORETO, JR., admitted to bar, 1997, Illinois. *Education:* Michigan State University (B.A., 1991); University of Michigan (J.D., 1997). ***PRACTICE AREAS:*** Mergers and Acquisitions; Private Equity. ***Email:*** mdiloreto@kirkland.com

ALEX DIMITRIEF, admitted to bar, 1985, Illinois; 1987, District of Columbia; 2002, New York. *Education:* Yale College (B.A., 1981); Harvard Law School (J.D., 1985). ***PRACTICE AREAS:*** Products Liability; Commercial Litigation. ***Email:*** alex.dimitrief@kirkland.com

JOHN DONLEY, admitted to bar, 1985, Illinois. *Education:* Harvard College (B.A., 1979); University of Chicago (J.D., 1985). ***PRACTICE AREAS:*** Commercial Litigation; Products Liability. ***Email:*** jdonley@kirkland.com

TIMOTHY A. DUFFY, admitted to bar, 1994, Illinois. *Education:* University of Colorado, Colorado Springs (B.A., 1991); University of Chicago (J.D., 1994). ***PRACTICE AREAS:*** Litigation. ***Email:*** tduffy@kirkland.com

DEBORAH DUNN, admitted to bar, 1995, Illinois. *Education:* University of Utah (B.A., 1988); Brigham Young University (M.A., 1991; J.D., 1995). ***PRACTICE AREAS:*** Trusts and Estates. ***Email:*** ddunn@kirkland.com

DAVID L. EATON, admitted to bar, 1978, Illinois. *Education:* University of Michigan (B.A., 1974); University of Illinois (J.D., 1978). ***PRACTICE AREAS:*** Restructuring; Insolvency; Workouts; Bankruptcy. ***Email:*** deaton@kirkland.com

BARACK S. ECHOLS, admitted to bar, 1999, Illinois. *Education:* University of Chicago (B.A./M.A., 1994; J.D., with honors, 1999). ***PRACTICE AREAS:*** Litigation. ***Email:*** bechols@kirkland.com

ROBERT B. ELLIS, (P.C.), admitted to bar, 1991, Illinois. *Education:* University of Illinois at Champaign/Urbana (B.S., 1988; J.D., 1991). ***PRACTICE AREAS:*** Commercial Litigation; Environmental Law. ***Email:*** rellis@kirkland.com

CARTER W. EMERSON, admitted to bar, 1972, Illinois. *Education:* Miami University (B.S., 1969); Northwestern University (J.D., 1972). ***PRACTICE AREAS:*** Corporate; Securities; Mergers and Acquisitions; Venture Capital. ***Email:*** cemerson@kirkland.com

DAVID T. ERIE, admitted to bar, 1984, Illinois. *Education:* Duke University (A.B., 1981); University of Chicago, (J.D., 1984). ***PRACTICE AREAS:*** Legal Ethics; Professional Responsibility; Commercial Litigation; Insurance Coverage; Products Liability; Antitrust. ***Email:*** derie@kirkland.com

LISA G. ESAYIAN, admitted to bar, 1991, Illinois. *Education:* Princeton University (A.B., 1986); Northwestern University (J.D., 1991). ***PRACTICE AREAS:*** Commercial Litigation; Environmental; Insurance Coverage. ***Email:*** lesayian@kirkland.com

BRUCE I. ETTELSON, admitted to bar, 1989, Illinois. *Education:* University of Pennsylvania (B.S.E., 1986); University of Chicago (J.D., 1989). ***PRACTICE AREAS:*** Corporate; Mergers and Acquisitions; Venture Capital. ***Email:*** bettelson@kirkland.com

KEVIN R. EVANICH, admitted to bar, 1980, Illinois. *Education:* University of Wisconsin, Milwaukee (B.A., 1976); Northwestern University (J.D., 1980). ***PRACTICE AREAS:*** Corporate; Mergers and Acquisitions; Private Equity and Leveraged Acquisitions; Private Equity Fund Formation. ***Email:*** kevanich@kirkland.com

JAMES P. FALEY, JR., admitted to bar, 1998, Illinois. *Education:* Brown University (A.B., 1992); Northwestern University School of Law (J.D., cum laude, 1998). ***PRACTICE AREAS:*** Corporate Law. ***Email:*** jfaley@kirkland.com

R. SCOTT FALK, P.C., admitted to bar, 1989, Illinois. *Education:* Harvard University (A.B., 1985; J.D., 1989). ***PRACTICE AREAS:*** Corporate; Mergers, Acquisitions and Divestitures; Securities. ***Email:*** sfalk@kirkland.com

MICHAEL G. FATALL, admitted to bar, 1997, Illinois. *Education:* University of Kansas (B.A., 1991); Northwestern University (J.D., 1997). ***PRACTICE AREAS:*** Intellectual Property. ***Email:*** mfatall@kirkland.com

CATHERINE E. FAZIO, admitted to bar, 1993, California; 1996, Massachusetts; 2002, Illinois. *Education:* University of California, Berkeley (B.A., with highest distinction, 1990); Stanford University (J.D., 1993). ***Email:*** cfazio@kirkland.com

MARK A. FENNELL, admitted to bar, 1998, Illinois. *Education:* University of Rochester (B.A., magna cum laude, 1992); University of Chicago (J.D., with honors, 1998). ***PRACTICE AREAS:*** Private Equity; Venture Capital; Mergers and Acquisitions. ***Email:*** mfennell@kirkland.com

BARRY E. FIELDS, admitted to bar, 1991, Illinois. *Education:* Bellarmine College (B.A., 1988); University of Chicago (J.D., 1991). ***PRACTICE AREAS:*** Products Liability; Commercial Litigation. ***Email:*** bfields@kirkland.com

JEFFREY A. FINE, admitted to bar, 1995, New York; 1996, Illinois. *Education:* Indiana University (B.S., Accounting, 1991); Columbia University (J.D., 1994). ***PRACTICE AREAS:*** Securities; Mergers and Acquisitions; Corporate Law. ***Email:*** jfine@kirkland.com

KAREN M. FINE, admitted to bar, 1995, New York; 1996, Illinois. *Education:* Yale University (B.A., summa cum laude, 1991); Columbia University School of Law (J.D., 1994). ***PRACTICE AREAS:*** Litigation. ***Email:*** kfine@kirkland.com

(This Listing Continued)

CATHERINE L. FITZPATRICK, admitted to bar, 1996, Illinois and U.S. District Court, Northern District of Illinois; 2000, U.S. Court of Appeals, Seventh Circuit. *Education:* Northern Illinois University (B.S., 1984); University of Chicago (J.D., with honors, 1995). ***PRACTICE AREAS:*** Commercial Litigation; Appellate Practice. ***Email:*** cfitzpatrick@kirkland.com

MICHAEL P. FORADAS, admitted to bar, 1981, Illinois. *Education:* College of William & Mary (A.B., Philosophy, with high honors, 1978); Northwestern University (J.D., cum laude, 1981). Order of the Coif. ***PRACTICE AREAS:*** Commercial Litigation; Insurance Coverage; Products Liability; Mass Torts. ***Email:*** mforadas@kirkland.com

MICHAEL D. FOSTER, admitted to bar, 1998, Illinois. *Education:* Miami University (B.A., 1994); Loyola University (J.D., 1998). ***PRACTICE AREAS:*** Litigation. ***Email:*** mfoster@kirkland.com

SCOTT W. FOWKES, admitted to bar, 1988, Illinois. *Education:* Cornell University (B.A., 1985); University of Michigan (J.D., cum laude, 1988). ***PRACTICE AREAS:*** Commercial Litigation; Products Liability; Antitrust; Class Actions. ***Email:*** sfowkes@kirkland.com

ARIEL A. FOX, admitted to bar, 1998, New York; 2003, Illinois. *Education:* University of Michigan (A.B., in Philosophy, with highest distinction, 1991); Yale Law School (J.D., 1995). ***PRACTICE AREAS:*** Transactional; Secured Transactions; Leveraged Acquisitions; Mezzanine Finance; Secured Lending; Corporate Contracts; Corporate Formation; Venture Capital; Investment Partnerships. ***Email:*** afox@kirkland.com

MICHELLE A.H. FRANCIS, admitted to bar, 1998, Illinois. *Education:* University of Illinois (B.S., 1991); University of Chicago (J.D., with honors, 1998). ***PRACTICE AREAS:*** Intellectual Property; Patents; Copyrights; Trademarks; Computer and Software Patents. ***Email:*** mfrancis@kirkland.com

WILLARD G. FRAUMANN, (P.C.), admitted to bar, 1973, Illinois. *Education:* University of Michigan (A.B., 1970); Harvard Law School (J.D., 1973). ***PRACTICE AREAS:*** Corporate; Mergers and Acquisitions; Venture Capital; Securities; International Transactions. ***Email:*** wfraumann@kirkland.com

JONATHAN P. FRIEDLAND, admitted to bar, 1994, New Jersey; 1995, Arizona; 1996, New York; 1999, Illinois. *Education:* State University of New York at Albany (B.S., magna cum laude, 1991); University of Pennsylvania (J.D., 1994). ***PRACTICE AREAS:*** Bankruptcy. ***Email:*** jfriedland@kirkland.com

ANGELA BONFIELD FRYE, admitted to bar, 1997, Illinois. *Education:* Northwestern University (B.A., 1994); Chicago-Kent College of Law (J.D., with high honors, 1997). ***PRACTICE AREAS:*** Litigation. ***Email:*** afrye@kirkland.com

JODY S. GALE, admitted to bar, 1999, Illinois. *Education:* Albion College (B.A., summa cum laude, 1995); Case Western Reserve School of Law (J.D., cum laude, 1999); Weatherhead School of Management, Case Western Reserve University (M.B.A., 1999). ***PRACTICE AREAS:*** Mergers and Acquisitions; Securities Law; Private Equity. ***Email:*** jgale@kirkland.com

TODD A. GALE, admitted to bar, 1987, Michigan; 1989, District of Columbia; 1990, California; 1995, Illinois. *Education:* Michigan State University (B.A., 1984); University of Notre Dame (J.D., 1987). ***PRACTICE AREAS:*** Intellectual Property; Litigation. ***Email:*** todd.gale@kirkland.com

GREGORY W. GALLAGHER, admitted to bar, 1997, Illinois. *Education:* University of Illinois (B.S., 1994; J.D., 1997). ***PRACTICE AREAS:*** Taxation. ***Email:*** ggallagher@kirkland.com

PAUL R. GARCIA, admitted to bar, 1992, Illinois. *Education:* Vassar College (A.B., 1987); University of Chicago (J.D., 1992). ***LANGUAGES:*** Spanish. ***PRACTICE AREAS:*** Intellectual Property Litigation. ***Email:*** pgarcia@kirkland.com

C. GRAHAM GERST, admitted to bar, 1998, Illinois. *Education:* Williams College (B.A., cum laude, 1993); University of Chicago (J.D., with honors, 1998). ***PRACTICE AREAS:*** Intellectual Property; Litigation. ***Email:*** ggerst@kirkland.com

DOUGLAS C. GESSNER, admitted to bar, 1989, Illinois. *Education:* University of Michigan (B.A., 1986); Harvard University (J.D., 1989). ***PRACTICE AREAS:*** Mergers and Acquisitions; Corporate Law; Venture Capital. ***Email:*** dgessner@kirkland.com

MARGARET A. GIBSON, P.C., admitted to bar, 1989, New York; 1990, Illinois. *Education:* University of Michigan (B.A., 1984); Northwestern University (J.D., 1987). ***PRACTICE AREAS:*** Corporate Law; Venture Capital; Leveraged Acquisitions; Private Equity. ***Email:*** mgibson@kirkland.com

RICHARD C. GODFREY, admitted to bar, 1979, Illinois. *Education:* Augustana College (B.A., 1976); Boston University (J.D., 1979). ***PRACTICE AREAS:*** Commercial Litigation. ***Email:*** rgodfrey@kirkland.com

ROBERT B. GOLDBERG, admitted to bar, 1997, Illinois. *Education:* University of Illinois (B.A., 1994); New York University (J.D., 1997). ***PRACTICE AREAS:*** Corporate. ***Email:*** rgoldberg@kirkland.com

CHRISTOPHER J. GREENO, admitted to bar, 1998, Illinois. *Education:* Southwest Missouri State University (B.S., magna cum laude, 1995); Northwestern University (J.D., cum laude, 1998). ***PRACTICE AREAS:*** Mergers, Acquisitions and Divestitures; Venture Capital Investments; Business Formations; Investment Partnership Formations; Corporate Law. ***Email:*** cgreeno@kirkland.com

STEPHEN C. HACKNEY, admitted to bar, 1997, Illinois. *Education:* Rice University (B.A., cum laude, 1994); University of Chicago (J.D., with honors, 1997). ***PRACTICE AREAS:*** Commercial Litigation; Federal Securities Law; Alternative Dispute Resolution; Criminal Appeals. ***Email:*** shackney@kirkland.com

JOHN F. HAGAN JR., admitted to bar, 1996, Illinois. *Education:* University of Chicago (B.A., 1993); New York University (J.D., 1996). ***PRACTICE AREAS:*** Litigation. ***Email:*** jhagan@kirkland.com

BRYAN S. HALES, admitted to bar, 1996, Texas; 1997, Illinois. *Education:* Rose-Hulman Institute of Technology (B.S., magna cum laude, 1993); University of Michigan (J.D., cum laude, 1996). (Also at San Francisco, California Office). ***PRACTICE AREAS:*** Intellectual Property. ***Email:*** bhales@kirkland.com

(This Listing Continued)

KIRKLAND & ELLIS LLP, Chicago—Continued

JEFFREY C. HAMMES, (P.C.), admitted to bar, 1985, Illinois; 2003, California. *Education:* University of Wisconsin (B.B.A., 1980); Northwestern University (J.D., 1985). ***PRACTICE AREAS:*** Mergers and Acquisitions; Private Equity; Corporate. ***Email:*** jhammes@kirkland.com

DAVID A. HANDLER, admitted to bar, 1992, Illinois. *Education:* University of Illinois College of Commerce (B.S., in Finance with highest honors, 1989); Northwestern University School of Law (J.D., 1992). ***PRACTICE AREAS:*** Trust and Estate; Trust Planning; Trust Administration; Estate Administration; Private Foundations; Tax Exempt Organizations; Estate & Gift Tax Planning. ***Email:*** dhandler@kirkland.com

STEVEN J. HARPER, (P.C.), admitted to bar, 1979, Illinois. *Education:* Northwestern University (B.A., 1976; M.A., 1976); Harvard Law School (J.D., 1979). ***PRACTICE AREAS:*** Commercial Litigation; Antitrust and Trade Regulation; Insurance Coverage; Litigation; Products Liability; Construction Tort. ***Email:*** sharper@kirkland.com

JOHN F. HARTMANN, P.C., admitted to bar, 1987, Illinois. *Education:* University of Minnesota (B.S., 1984; J.D., 1987). ***PRACTICE AREAS:*** Antitrust and Trade Regulation; Commercial Litigation; Securities; Shareholder Litigation; White Collar Crime. ***Email:*** jhartmann@kirkland.com

ROBERT M. HAYWARD, admitted to bar, 1997, Arizona; 1998, Illinois. *Education:* Northwestern University (B.S., 1994; J.D., cum laude, 1997). ***PRACTICE AREAS:*** Corporate Law; Securities Law; Initial Public Offerings; Leveraged Acquisitions; Mergers and Acquisitions; Private Equity; Venture Capital. ***Email:*** rhayward@kirkland.com

LAURA A. HEPBURN, admitted to bar, 1995, Illinois. *Education:* University of Illinois (B.S., 1992); Northwestern University (J.D., cum laude, 1995). ***PRACTICE AREAS:*** Intellectual Property; Litigation. ***Email:*** ltenbroeck@kirkland.com

LOUIS R. HERNANDEZ, admitted to bar, 1996, Illinois. *Education:* University of Illinois at Urbana-Champaign (B.S., with highest honors, 1993); Stanford University Law School (J.D., 1996). ***PRACTICE AREAS:*** Corporate; Financing and Secured Transactions; Mezzanine Finance; Corporate Finance. ***Email:*** lhernandez@kirkland.com

GLEN E. HESS, admitted to bar, 1967, Illinois; 1990, New York. *Education:* Cornell University (A.B., summan cum laude, 1964); Harvard Law School (LL.B., magna cum laude, 1967). ***PRACTICE AREAS:*** Corporate Law. ***Email:*** ghess@kirkland.com

JOHN T. HICKEY, JR. (P.C.), admitted to bar, 1977, Illinois. *Education:* Georgetown University (A.B., 1974); University of Chicago (J.D., 1977). ***PRACTICE AREAS:*** Commercial Litigation. ***Email:*** jhickey@kirkland.com

ROGER J. HIGGINS, admitted to bar, 1997, California; 1999, District of Columbia and Illinois. *Education:* San Diego State University (B.A., 1978); Naval Postgraduate School (M.S., 1984); University of San Diego School of Law (J.D., cum laude, 1996). ***PRACTICE AREAS:*** Bankruptcy; Restructuring. ***Email:*** rhiggins@kirkland.com

JONATHAN E. HINKEMEYER, admitted to bar, 1998, Illinois. *Education:* Northwestern University (B.A., 1995); Chicago-Kent College of Law (J.D., 1998). ***PRACTICE AREAS:*** Litigation. ***Email:*** jhinkemeyer@kirkland.com

JOCELYN A. HIRSCH, admitted to bar, 1995, Wisconsin and Illinois. *Education:* University of Wisconsin, Madison (B.A., 1991; J.D., cum laude, 1995). ***PRACTICE AREAS:*** Corporate; Secured Lending; Commercial Law. ***Email:*** jhirsch@kirkland.com

SHELLY MATTHEW HIRSCHTRITT, admitted to bar, 1998, Illinois. *Education:* University of Michigan (A.B., 1995); Harvard University (J.D., 1998). ***PRACTICE AREAS:*** Corporate Law. ***Email:*** shirschtritt@kirkland.com

NEIL S. HIRSHMAN, admitted to bar, 1990, Illinois; registered to practice before U.S. Patent and Trademark Office. *Education:* University of Illinois (B.S.E.E., 1987); Harvard University (J.D., 1990). ***PRACTICE AREAS:*** Intellectual Property; Technology Transactions; Transactions; Counseling; Outsourcing; Internet Law; E-Commerce. ***Email:*** nhirshman@kirkland.com

GARY M. HOLIHAN, admitted to bar, 1993, Illinois. *Education:* University of Notre Dame (B.B.A., 1981); Chicago-Kent College of Law (J.D., 1993). ***PRACTICE AREAS:*** Corporate Law; Mutual Funds; Leveraged Acquisitions; Mergers and Acquisitions; Private Business Law; Corporate Finance; Venture Capital; Private Equity. ***Email:*** gholihan@kirkland.com

G. COURTNEY HOLOHAN, admitted to bar, 1998, Illinois. *Education:* Northwestern University (B.S., with distinction, 1995); Duke University (J.D., with high honors, 1998). ***PRACTICE AREAS:*** Intellectual Property. ***Email:*** cholohan@kirkland.com

LISA M. HOLUBAR, admitted to bar, 1999, Illinois. *Education:* Miami University (B.S., 1996); DePaul University (J.D., 1999). ***PRACTICE AREAS:*** Intellectual Property; Trademark Law; Advertising Law. ***Email:*** lholubar@kirkland.com

VICKI VALLEN HOOD, admitted to bar, 1977, Illinois; 1991, New York. *Education:* Northwestern University (B.A., 1974; M.M., 1977; J.D., 1977). ***PRACTICE AREAS:*** Employee Benefits; ERISA. ***Email:*** vhood@kirkland.com

ANNE MARRS HUBER, admitted to bar, 1992, Minnesota; 1995, Illinois. *Education:* Marquette University (B.A., magna cum laude, 1989); University of Minnesota at Minneapolis (J.D., cum laude, 1992). ***LANGUAGES:*** Spanish. ***PRACTICE AREAS:*** Bankruptcy and Workouts; Creditors' Rights. ***Email:*** ahuber@kirkland.com

CAROL ANNE HUFF, admitted to bar, 1996, Illinois. *Education:* University of Maryland (B.A., Valedictorian, 1993); Duke University School of Law (J.D., magna cum laude, 1996). ***PRACTICE AREAS:*** Securities; Mergers and Acquisitions; Corporate Law. ***Email:*** chuff@kirkland.com

BARRY F. IRWIN, admitted to bar, 1992, Illinois; 1993, District of Columbia; registered to practice before U.S. Patent and Trademark Office. *Education:* University of Notre Dame (B.S.A.E., 1988; J.D., magna cum laude, 1992). ***PRACTICE AREAS:*** Intellectual Property Litigation. ***Email:*** birwin@kirkland.com

JOSEPH J. JACOBI, admitted to bar, 1997, Indiana and U.S. District Court, Northern and Southern Districts of Indiana; 2000, U.S. Court of Appeals, Federal Circuit; 2001, Illinois; 2002, U.S. District Court, Central District of Illinois; 2003, U.S. District Court, Northern District of Illinois. *Education:* State University of New York at Buffalo (B.A., magna cum laude, 1994); Harvard Law School (J.D., cum laude, 1997). ***PRACTICE AREAS:*** Intellectual Property. ***Email:*** jjacobi@kirkland.com

GARRY W. JAUNAL, admitted to bar, 1999, Illinois. *Education:* Purdue University (M.S., 1994); Northwestern University (J.D., cum laude, 1999). ***LANGUAGES:*** Russian and Spanish. ***PRACTICE AREAS:*** Banking and Secured Lending; Debtor and Creditor; Mergers and Acquisitions; Private Equity; Corporate Law. ***Email:*** gjaunal@kirkland.com

JOHN M. JENNINGS, admitted to bar, 1997, Illinois. *Education:* University of Virginia (B.A., 1988); Northwestern University (J.D., magna cum laude, 1997; M.B.A., with distinction, 1997). ***PRACTICE AREAS:*** Corporate; Securities; Mergers and Acquisitions. ***Email:*** jjennings@kirkland.com

GARRETT B. JOHNSON, admitted to bar, 1973, Illinois. *Education:* Princeton University (A.B., 1968); University of Michigan (J.D., 1971); Max Planck Institute for Foreign and International Criminal Law, Freiburg, Germany (1971-1972). ***PRACTICE AREAS:*** Litigation. ***Email:*** gjohnson@kirkland.com

GEORGE A. JOSEPH, admitted to bar, 1976, Illinois. *Education:* Loyola University, Rome, Italy and University of Michigan (B.A., 1973); Boston University (J.D., 1976). ***PRACTICE AREAS:*** Commercial Litigation. ***Email:*** gjoseph@kirkland.com

JAMES C. JOSLIN, admitted to bar, 1996, Illinois. *Education:* Illinois Wesleyan University (B.A., 1993); The Ohio State University (J.D., summa cum laude, 1996). ***PRACTICE AREAS:*** Litigation. ***Email:*** jjoslin@kirkland.com

GARY A. JUNGELS, admitted to bar, 1997, Illinois. *Education:* University of Notre Dame (B.B.A., highest honors, 1992); University of Illinois (J.D., magna cum laude, 1997). ***PRACTICE AREAS:*** Corporate Law; Fund Formation; Investment Company Law. ***Email:*** gjungels@kirkland.com

CHRIS P. KALLOS, admitted to bar, 1994, Illinois. *Education:* University of Virginia (B.S., 1989); Harvard University (J.D., 1994). ***PRACTICE AREAS:*** Corporate Law; Mergers, Acquisitions and Divestitures; Venture Capital. ***Email:*** ckallos@kirkland.com

JAMES W. KAPP, III, admitted to bar, 1994, Missouri; 1995, Kansas; 1997, Illinois. *Education:* Northwestern University (B.S., 1991); University of Minnesota (J.D., magna cum laude, 1994). ***PRACTICE AREAS:*** Bankruptcy. ***Email:*** jkapp@kirkland.com

HARIKLIA KARIS, admitted to bar, 1995, Illinois. *Education:* Loyola University of Chicago (B.B.A., 1990); DePaul College of Law (J.D., 1995). ***LANGUAGES:*** Greek. ***PRACTICE AREAS:*** Litigation. ***Email:*** hkaris@kirkland.com

ANDREW A. KASSOF, admitted to bar, 1998, New York; 2000, Illinois. *Education:* University of Virginia (B.A., magna cum laude, 1994); George Washington University (J.D., high honors, 1997). ***PRACTICE AREAS:*** Commercial Litigation. ***Email:*** andrew_kassof@chicago.kirkland.com

ANDREW M. KAUFMAN, admitted to bar, 1974, Texas; 1976, Georgia; 1993, Illinois. *Education:* Yale University (B.A., 1971); Vanderbilt University (J.D., 1974). ***PRACTICE AREAS:*** Lending and Secured Transactions; Finance; Mergers, Acquisitions and Divestitures; Workouts, Reorganizations and Bankruptcy; Corporate Law and Counseling. ***Email:*** akaufman@kirkland.com

BRIAN P. KAVANAUGH, admitted to bar, 1999, Illinois. *Education:* Northwestern University (B.A., 1996); University of Illinois (J.D., magna cum laude, 1999). ***PRACTICE AREAS:*** Litigation. ***Email:*** bkavanaugh@kirkland.com

NATALIE HOYER KELLER, admitted to bar, 1997, Illinois. *Education:* University of Montana (B.S., 1992); University of Utah (J.D., 1997). ***PRACTICE AREAS:*** Taxation. ***Email:*** nkeller@kirkland.com

STACEY TOBIN KERN, admitted to bar, 1996, Illinois. *Education:* Duke Univ. (A.B., magna cum laude, 1992); Cornell Univ. (J.D., cum laude, 1996). ***PRACTICE AREAS:*** Corporate; Securities; Mergers and Acquisitions. ***Email:*** skern@kirkland.com

MICHAEL H. KERR (P.C.), admitted to bar, 1972, Illinois. *Education:* Duke University (B.A., 1969); Columbia University (J.D., 1972). ***PRACTICE AREAS:*** Corporate; Mergers and Acquisitions; Venture Capital; Securities. ***Email:*** mkerr@kirkland.com

MARC KIESELSTEIN, (P.C.), admitted to bar, 1988, Illinois. *Education:* Queens College of the City University of New York (B.A., magna cum laude, 1985); University of Chicago (J.D., 1988). ***PRACTICE AREAS:*** Corporate Reorganization; Workouts; Asset Based Finance. ***Email:*** mkieselstein@kirkland.com

GREGG KIRCHHOEFER, admitted to bar, 1982, Illinois. *Education:* St. Louis University (B.S.C., 1972; J.D., cum laude, 1982). ***PRACTICE AREAS:*** Outsourcing; Strategic Alliances; Corporate; Computer and Technology; Technology Transactions; Intellectual Property Procurement; Mergers and Acquisitions. ***Email:*** gkirchhoefer@kirkland.com

SARAH E. KIRSON, admitted to bar, 1994, Illinois. *Education:* University of Illinois (B.S., with highest honors, Bronze Tablet, 1991); Harvard University (J.D., cum laude, 1994). ***PRACTICE AREAS:*** Mergers and Acquisitions; Venture Capital; Private Equity; Fund Formation; General Corporate. ***Email:*** skirson@kirkland.com

MATTHEW N. KLEIMAN, admitted to bar, 1992, Illinois. *Education:* University of Pennsylvania (B.A., 1989); Northwestern University (J.D., 1992). ***PRACTICE AREAS:*** Bankruptcy/Workout; Secured Lending. ***Email:*** mkleiman@kirkland.com

NORBERT B. KNAPKE, II, admitted to bar, 1992, Illinois. *Education:* University of Notre Dame (B.A., magna cum laude, 1987); Duke University (J.D., magna cum laude, 1992). ***PRACTICE AREAS:*** Corporate Law; Leveraged Buyouts. ***Email:*** nknapke@kirkland.com

ROBERT J. KOPECKY, admitted to bar, 1979, Illinois. *Education:* Kalamazoo College (B.A., 1972); University of Chicago (J.D., 1979). ***PRACTICE AREAS:*** Commercial Litigation; Securities and Derivative Litigation; Appellate Practice. ***Email:*** rkopecky@kirkland.com

(This Listing Continued)

HOWARD G. KRANE (P.C.), admitted to bar, 1957, Illinois. *Education:* Grinnell College (A.B., 1954); University of Chicago (J.D., 1957). ***PRACTICE AREAS:*** Tax; Tax Structuring Matters; Contested Tax Matters; Tax Planning. ***Email:*** hkrane@kirkland.com

ROBERT G. KRUPKA (P.C.), admitted to bar, 1974, Illinois; 1991, Colorado and District of Columbia; 1998, California; registered to practice before U.S. Patent and Trademark Office. *Education:* Georgetown University (B.S., 1971); University of Chicago (J.D., 1974). (Also at Los Angeles, California and Washington, D.C. Offices). ***PRACTICE AREAS:*** Intellectual Property; Litigation; Advertising and Marketing; Antitrust and Trade Regulation; Biotechnology; International Trade; Appellate Practice. ***Email:*** bkrupka@kirkland.com

THOMAS OTMAN KUHNS, admitted to bar, 1980, Illinois. *Education:* Lafayette College (B.A., 1977); Northwestern University (J.D., 1980). ***PRACTICE AREAS:*** Commercial Litigation; Environmental Litigation. ***Email:*** tkuhns@kirkland.com

DOUGLAS J. KURTENBACH, (P.C.), admitted to bar, 1986, Illinois. *Education:* Rockhurst College (B.A., 1983); Columbia University (J.D., 1986). ***PRACTICE AREAS:*** Mass Torts; Class Actions; Antitrust; Patents; Commercial Litigation. ***Email:*** dkurtenbach@kirkland.com

WALTER R. LANCASTER, admitted to bar, 1987, Illinois. *Education:* University of Illinois (B.A., 1984); Harvard Law School (J.D., 1987). ***PRACTICE AREAS:*** Commercial Litigation; Corporate; Contract; Products Liability. ***Email:*** wlancaster@kirkland.com

JAMES ANDREW LANGAN, admitted to bar, 1982, Illinois. *Education:* University of Illinois (A.B., 1979); Harvard Law School (J.D., 1982). ***PRACTICE AREAS:*** Antitrust; Commercial Litigation; Products Liability; Class Actions. ***Email:*** alangan@kirkland.com

DANIEL EDWARD LAYTIN, admitted to bar, 1998, Illinois. *Education:* University of Michigan (A,B., 1995; J.D., 1998). ***PRACTICE AREAS:*** Litigation; Antitrust; Trade Regulation. ***Email:*** dlaytin@kirkland.com

GARRET LEACH, admitted to bar, 1996, Illinois; registered to practice before U.S. Patent and Trademark Office. *Education:* University of Illinois (B.S., 1990); Loyola University (J.D., 1996). ***PRACTICE AREAS:*** Patents; Copyrights; Trademarks; Unfair Competition. ***Email:*** gleach@kirkland.com

CRAIG D. LEAVELL, admitted to bar, 1998, Illinois. *Education:* University of Illinois (B.S., 1995; J.D., 1998). ***PRACTICE AREAS:*** Intellectual Property. ***Email:*** cleavell@kirkland.com

ELLI LEIBENSTEIN, admitted to bar, 1992, Illinois. *Education:* Northeastern Illinois University (B.A., 1983); University of Chicago (J.D., 1992). ***PRACTICE AREAS:*** Commercial Litigation. ***Email:*** eleibenstein@kirkland.com

JACK S. LEVIN (P.C.), admitted to bar, 1961, Illinois. *Education:* Northwestern University (B.S., 1958); Harvard Law School (LL.B., 1961). ***PRACTICE AREAS:*** Corporate Law; Finance; Venture Capital; Mergers, Acquisitions and Divestitures; Taxation. ***Email:*** jlevin@kirkland.com

ADAM J. LEVINE, admitted to bar, 1995, Illinois. *Education:* University of Pennsylvania (B.S., 1992); University of Chicago (J.D., 1995). ***PRACTICE AREAS:*** Corporate Law; Mergers and Acquisitions; Venture Capital. ***Email:*** alevine@kirkland.com

RUSSELL E. LEVINE, P.C., born June 6, 1960; admitted to bar, 1986, Illinois; 1993, New York; 2005, District of Columbia; registered to practice before U.S. Patent and Trademark Office. *Education:* University of Michigan (B.S., Interdisciplinary Engineering, 1982; B.S., Economics, 1982); University of Chicago (J.D., 1986). ***PRACTICE AREAS:*** Intellectual Property. ***Email:*** rlevine@kirkland.com

MARK S. LILLIE, admitted to bar, 1984, Colorado; 1995, Illinois. *Education:* Northwestern University (B.S., 1981); University of Denver (J.D., 1984). ***PRACTICE AREAS:*** Commercial Litigation. ***Email:*** mlillie@kirkland.com

JEREMY SETH LISS, admitted to bar, 1999, Michigan and Illinois. *Education:* University of Michigan (B.B.A., 1995; J.D., 1998). ***PRACTICE AREAS:*** Corporate Law; Mergers and Acquisitions; Securities; Private Equity. ***Email:*** jliss@kirkland.com

OLGA A. LOY, admitted to bar, 1998, Illinois. *Education:* Illinois State University (B.A., 1995); University of Illinois (J.D., magna cum laude, 1998). ***LANGUAGES:*** Russian. ***PRACTICE AREAS:*** Federal Taxation; Corporate; Fund Formation. ***Email:*** oloy@kirkland.com

NATHANIEL M. MARRS, admitted to bar, 1996, Illinois. *Education:* University of Michigan (A.B., summa cum laude, Phi Beta Kappa, 1993; J.D., 1996). ***PRACTICE AREAS:*** Corporate Law; Real Estate. ***Email:*** nmarrs@kirkland.com

DARYLL V. MARSHALL, admitted to bar, 1999, Illinois. *Education:* Temple University (B.B.A., Finance, 1996); Boston University (J.D., 1999). ***PRACTICE AREAS:*** Finance; Secured Transactions; Leveraged Acquisitions; Mezzanine Finance; Restructuring & Workout. ***Email:*** dmarshall@kirkland.com

MARIANO ELÍ MARTÍNEZ, admitted to bar, 1999, Illinois. *Education:* Boston College (B.S., 1996); University of Chicago (J.D., 1999). ***LANGUAGES:*** Spanish. ***PRACTICE AREAS:*** Corporate Law. ***Email:*** mariano_martinez@chicago.kirkland.com

TODD F. MAYNES, P.C., admitted to bar, 1988, Illinois. *Education:* Brigham Young University (B.A., 1984; J.D., 1987). ***PRACTICE AREAS:*** Tax. ***Email:*** tmaynes@kirkland.com

STEVEN D. McCORMICK, P.C., admitted to bar, 1972, Illinois. *Education:* St. Louis University and University of Notre Dame (A.B., 1968); Northwestern University (J.D., 1971). ***PRACTICE AREAS:*** Commercial Litigation; Antitrust; Intellectual Property; Products Liability. ***Email:*** smccormick@kirkland.com

JAMIE H. McDOLE, admitted to bar, 1999, Illinois. *Education:* University of Iowa (B.S.E., Chemical Engineering, 1996); Chicago-Kent College of Law (J.D., 1999). ***PRACTICE AREAS:*** Intellectual Property Litigation and Counseling. ***Email:*** jmcdole@kirkland.com

(This Listing Continued)

ANDREW R. McGAAN, (P.C.), admitted to bar, 1986, Connecticut; 1991, Illinois. *Education:* Cornell University (A.B., with honors, 1983; J.D., magna cum laude, 1986). ***PRACTICE AREAS:*** Product Liability; Mass Tort; Securities; Antitrust. ***Email:*** amcgaan@kirkland.com

JANETTE A. McMAHAN, admitted to bar, 1998, Illinois. *Education:* Dartmouth College (B.A., Government, with honors, 1992); Northwestern University (J.D., 1998). ***PRACTICE AREAS:*** Corporate; Transactional; Asset Securitization; Capital Markets; Fund Formation; Initial Public Offerings; Leveraged Acquisitions; Mergers and Acquisitions; Mezzanine Finance; Private Company; Public Company; Venture Capital/Private Equity. ***Email:*** jmcmahan@kirkland.com

SCOTT McMILLIN, admitted to bar, 1996, Illinois. *Education:* Williams College (B.A., magna cum laude, 1993); Harvard Law School (J.D., magna cum laude, 1996). ***PRACTICE AREAS:*** Litigation; Environmental. ***Email:*** smcmillin@kirkland.com

TONI B. MERRICK, admitted to bar, 1975, Oklahoma; 1988, Illinois. *Education:* Wellesley College (B.A., 1966); Oklahoma City University (J.D., 1975). ***PRACTICE AREAS:*** ERISA; Fiduciary Law; Employee Benefits. ***Email:*** tmerrick@kirkland.com

GREGORY R. METZ, admitted to bar, 1999, Illinois. *Education:* Washington University, St. Louis (B.A., summa cum laude, 1996); Northwestern University School of Law (J.D., cum laude, 1999). ***PRACTICE AREAS:*** Corporate Law. ***Email:*** gmetz@kirkland.com

ROBERTO S. MICELI, admitted to bar, 1996, Wisconsin; 2000, Illinois. *Education:* University of Wisconsin, Madison (B.B.A., 1991); University of Minnesota (J.D., cum laude, 1995); New York University (LL.M., Taxation, 1996). ***PRACTICE AREAS:*** Real Estate; Tax; Corporate Law. ***Email:*** rmiceli@kirkland.com

ALEXANDRA MIHALAS, admitted to bar, 1991, Illinois; 1994, District of Columbia; 2000, New York. *Education:* Haverford College (B.S., 1987); Harvard University (J.D., 1991). ***PRACTICE AREAS:*** Employee Benefits. ***Email:*** amihalas@kirkland.com

TODD A. MILLER, admitted to bar, 1997, Michigan; 2000, Illinois. *Education:* University of Illinois at Urbana-Champaign (B.A., 1993); University of Notre Dame Law School (J.D., cum laude, 1997). ***PRACTICE AREAS:*** Corporate; Asset Finance; Securitization; Financing and Secured Transactions. ***Email:*** tamiller@kirkland.com

J. CHAD MITCHELL, admitted to bar, 1998, Illinois and U.S. District Court, Northern District of Illinois; 1999, U.S. District Court, Western District of Michigan and U.S. Court of Appeals, Third Circuit; 2000, U.S. District Court, District of Nevada; 2001, U.S. District Court, Eastern District of Wisconsin; 2004, U.S. District Court, District Court of Colorado. *Education:* Eastern Oregon University (B.S., 1995); Brigham Young University (J.D., 1998). ***PRACTICE AREAS:*** Litigation. ***Email:*** jcmitchell@kirkland.com

SCOTT A. MOEHRKE, admitted to bar, 1989, Wisconsin (Not admitted in Illinois). *Education:* Marquette University (B.A., cum laude, 1985); Duke University (J.D., with high honors, 1989). ***PRACTICE AREAS:*** Securities; Investment Management; Corporate Law. ***Email:*** smoehrke@kirkland.com

GABRIELA I. MONAHAN, admitted to bar, 1993, Illinois. *Education:* Baylor University (B.A., 1988); Loyola University of Chicago (J.D., 1992). ***LANGUAGES:*** Spanish. ***PRACTICE AREAS:*** Commercial Litigation; Products Liability; International Arbitration; Alternative Dispute Resolution. ***Email:*** gmonahan@kirkland.com

KENNETH P. MORRISON, P.C., admitted to bar, 1983, Illinois. *Education:* Yale College (B.A., 1977); Massachusetts Institute of Technology (M.B.A., 1983); Boston University (J.D., 1983). ***PRACTICE AREAS:*** Asset-Backed Securities; Securities; Finance. ***Email:*** kmorrison@kirkland.com

JAMES C. MUNSON, admitted to bar, 1970, Wisconsin; 1971, Illinois. *Education:* Yale College (B.A., 1966); University of Wisconsin (J.D., 1969). ***PRACTICE AREAS:*** Energy; Litigation; Commercial Litigation; Arbitration; Mass Torts; Securities Litigation; Shareholder Litigation. ***Email:*** jmunson@kirkland.com

JAMES H. MUTCHNIK, admitted to bar, 1989, Illinois. *Education:* University of Pennsylvania, Wharton School (B.S., 1986); Northwestern University (J.D., 1989). ***PRACTICE AREAS:*** Antitrust and Trade Regulation; White Collar Crime. ***Email:*** jmutchnik@kirkland.com

DENNIS M. MYERS, P.C., admitted to bar, 1990, Ohio; 1996, Illinois. *Education:* Case Western Reserve University (B.A., 1987); Harvard University (J.D., 1990). ***PRACTICE AREAS:*** Corporate Law (Securities). ***Email:*** dmyers@kirkland.com

LINDA K. MYERS, P.C., admitted to bar, 1990, New York; 1993, Illinois. *Education:* University of Wisconsin-Madison (B.A., 1986); Georgetown University (J.D., 1989). ***PRACTICE AREAS:*** Commercial Finance; Corporate Law; Bankruptcy and Workout. ***Email:*** lmyers@kirkland.com

MICHAEL NEWMAN, admitted to bar, 1998, Illinois; registered to practice before U.S. Patent and Trademark Office, 1998. *Education:* University of Iowa (B.S.I.E., 1990); Chicago-Kent College of Law (J.D., 1998). ***PRACTICE AREAS:*** Intellectual Property Transactions; Intellectual Property Outsourcing; Intellectual Property Litigation. ***Email:*** mnewman@kirkland.com

EMILY NICKLIN, admitted to bar, 1977, Illinois. *Education:* University of Chicago (B.A., 1975; J.D., 1977). ***PRACTICE AREAS:*** Commercial Litigation. ***Email:*** enicklin@kirkland.com

MARK NOMELLINI, admitted to bar, 1997, Illinois. *Education:* Harvard University (A.B., summa cum laude, 1994); Yale University (J.D., 1997). ***PRACTICE AREAS:*** Litigation. ***Email:*** mnomellini@kirkland.com

JEFFERY S. NORMAN, admitted to bar, 1992, Illinois. *Education:* Washington University (A.B., 1989; J.D., 1992). ***PRACTICE AREAS:*** Intellectual Property; Private Equity. ***Email:*** jnorman@kirkland.com

JAMES N. NOWACKI, (P.C.), admitted to bar, 1973, Illinois; 1982, New York. *Education:* Princeton University (A.B., 1969); Yale Law School (J.D., 1973). ***PRACTICE AREAS:*** Commercial Litigation; Construction Law; Contract Disputes; Insurance Coverage; Products Liability; Professional Liability Defense. ***Email:*** jnowacki@kirkland.com

(This Listing Continued)

KIRKLAND & ELLIS LLP, Chicago—Continued

GERALD T. NOWAK, admitted to bar, 1993, Illinois. *Education:* Michigan State University (B.A., 1986); Auburn University (M.B.A., 1990); University of Michigan (J.D., 1993). ***PRACTICE AREAS:*** Corporate; Mergers and Acquisitions; Securities. ***Email:*** gnowack@kirkland.com

MAUREEN O'BRIEN, admitted to bar, 1998, Illinois. *Education:* University of California at Los Angeles (B.A., 1995); Chicago-Kent College of Law (J.D., with high honors, 1998). ***PRACTICE AREAS:*** Employee Benefits. ***Email:*** mo'brien@kirkland.com

JEFFREY S. O'CONNOR, admitted to bar, 1991, California; 1996, Illinois. *Education:* Marquette University (B.S., 1982); University of Wisconsin (M.D., 1986); University of Southern California (J.D., 1990). ***PRACTICE AREAS:*** Securities; Corporate; Asset Based Finance. ***Email:*** joconnor@kirkland.com

JOHN R. O'NEIL, admitted to bar, 1998, Illinois. *Education:* University of Wisconsin (B.B.A., 1991); Northwestern University (J.D., cum laude, 1998). ***PRACTICE AREAS:*** Corporate. ***Email:*** jo'oneil@kirkland.com

REED S. OSLAN, admitted to bar, 1987, Indiana; 1990, Illinois. *Education:* University of Colorado (B.A., 1984); Indiana University (J.D., 1987). ***PRACTICE AREAS:*** Litigation; Bankruptcy Litigation; Commercial Litigation; Environmental Litigation. ***Email:*** roslan@kirkland.com

STACEY GARBIS PAGONIS, admitted to bar, 1999, Illinois. *Education:* University of Wisconsin-Madison (B.A., 1995); Northwestern University School of Law (J.D., 1999). ***LANGUAGES:*** Greek. ***PRACTICE AREAS:*** Commercial Litigation. ***Email:*** spagonis@kirkland.com

MICHAEL D. PALEY, admitted to bar, 1995, Illinois. *Education:* University of Colorado at Boulder (B.A., 1991); Washington University (J.D., 1995). ***PRACTICE AREAS:*** Corporate; Leveraged Acquisitions; Mergers and Acquisitions; Venture Capital; Private Equity. ***Email:*** mpaley@kirkland.com

MARK A. PALS, PH.D., admitted to bar, 1989, Illinois. *Education:* Dartmouth College (A.B., 1982); University of Illinois (Ph.D., 1988); Northwestern University (J.D., 1989). (Also at San Francisco, California Office). ***PRACTICE AREAS:*** Litigation; Intellectual Property; Biotechnology; Pharmaceutical. ***Email:*** mpals@kirkland.com

JANE S. PARK, admitted to bar, 1998, New York; 2000, Illinois. *Education:* Harvard University (B.A., magna cum laude, 1994); Harvard Law School (J.D., cum laude, 1997). ***PRACTICE AREAS:*** Commercial Litigation; Employment Discrimination; Products Liability; Class Action Defense; Securities Class Actions; Federal Civil Litigation. ***Email:*** jpark@kirkland.com

THOMAS G. PASTERNAK, admitted to bar, 1991, Illinois; 1996, Michigan; registered to practice before U.S. Patent and Trademark Office. *Education:* United States Naval Academy (B.S.M.E., with distinction, 1982); University of Michigan (J.D., cum laude, 1991). ***PRACTICE AREAS:*** Intellectual Property Litigation. ***Email:*** tpasternak@kirkland.com

STEPHEN R. PATTON, P.C., admitted to bar, 1978, Illinois. *Education:* Indiana University (A.B., 1975); Georgetown University (J.D., 1978). ***PRACTICE AREAS:*** Commercial Litigation; Antitrust; Contract; Products Liability. ***Email:*** spatton@kirkland.com

ADAM PAUL, admitted to bar, 1997, Virginia; 1998, Maryland; 1999, District of Columbia; 2005, Illinois. *Education:* James Madison University (B.A., cum laude, 1994); Catholic University of America (J.D., cum laude, 1997). ***PRACTICE AREAS:*** Restructuring; Insolvency; Workout; Bankruptcy; Litigation. ***Email:*** apaul@kirkland.com

DREW G. A. PEEL, admitted to bar, 1992, Illinois. *Education:* Davidson College (A.B., Political Science, cum laude, Phi Beta Kappa, 1989); University of Chicago Law School (J.D., 1992). ***PRACTICE AREAS:*** Antitrust; Competition; Labor and Employment; Franchise Law; Distribution; Intellectual Property; Patent Infringement; Litigation; Appellate Practice; Commercial Litigation; Commercial Arbitration; Construction Litigation; ERISA Litigation; International Arbitration; Alternative Dispute Resolution; Products Liability; Securities Litigation; Shareholders Law. ***Email:*** dpeel@kirkland.com

FRANCESCO PENATI, admitted to bar, 1993, Pennsylvania; 1998, Illinois. *Education:* Georgetown University (B.S.F.S., 1984); Notre Dame Law School (J.D., magna cum laude, 1993). ***LANGUAGES:*** Italian. ***PRACTICE AREAS:*** Banking; Secured Lending; Mergers and Acquisitions; Divestitures; Corporate Law. ***Email:*** fpenati@kirkland.com

SANFORD E. PERL, P.C., admitted to bar, 1990, Illinois. *Education:* University of Illinois (B.S., 1987); University of Michigan (J.D., 1990). ***PRACTICE AREAS:*** Corporate; Mergers and Acquisitions; Securities; Venture Capital and Leveraged Acquisitions. ***Email:*** sperl@kirkland.com

RICHARD W. PORTER, (P.C.), admitted to bar, 1987, Illinois. *Education:* Middlebury College (B.A., 1981); University of Chicago (J.D., 1986). ***PRACTICE AREAS:*** Corporate; Venture Capital; Mergers and Acquisitions; Securities; Corporate Counseling. ***Email:*** rporter@kirkland.com

JEFFREY S. QUINN, admitted to bar, 1998, Illinois. *Education:* Eastern Michigan University (B.A., 1989); DePaul University (J.D., 1998). ***PRACTICE AREAS:*** Employee Benefits. ***Email:*** jquinn@kirkland.com

ROBIN A. RADEMACHER, admitted to bar, 1998, Illinois. *Education:* University of Michigan (B.A., 1995); DePaul University (J.D., 1998). ***PRACTICE AREAS:*** Intellectual Property. ***Email:*** rrademacher@kirkland.com

JAMES W. RANKIN, admitted to bar, 1968, Illinois; 1986, California. *Education:* Oberlin College (A.B., 1965); University of Chicago (J.D., 1968). ***PRACTICE AREAS:*** Health Care; Litigation; Antitrust; Corporate. ***Email:*** jrankin@kirkland.com

MATTHEW T. REGAN, admitted to bar, 1995, Illinois. *Education:* Georgetown University (B.S., 1992); Harvard University (J.D., 1995). ***PRACTICE AREAS:*** Litigation. ***Email:*** mregan@kirkland.com

TRACY L. REILLY, admitted to bar, 1996, Illinois; 1998, Colorado. *Education:* Northern Illinois University (B.A., summa cum laude, 1990); Valparaiso University (J.D., summa cum laude, 1995). ***PRACTICE AREAS:*** Internet Law; Intellectual Property; Entertainment Law; Promotion Law; Advertising and Marketing; Media. ***Email:*** treilly@kirkland.com

LINDA S. RESH, admitted to bar, 1989, Illinois; registered to practice before U.S. Patent and Trademark Office. *Education:* University of Wisconsin-Milwaukee (B.S., 1980; M.S., 1981); Loyola University of Chicago (J.D., 1989). ***PRACTICE AREAS:*** Intellectual Property. ***Email:*** lresh@kirkland.com

GEOFFREY A. RICHARDS, admitted to bar, 1995, Illinois. *Education:* University of Wisconsin (B.A., 1992); Northwestern University School of Law; Brooklyn Law School (J.D., 1995). ***Email:*** grichards@kirkland.com

JEFFREY W. RICHARDS, admitted to bar, 1995, Illinois. *Education:* Bradley University (B.S., Finance, magna cum laude, 1992); University of Chicago (J.D., with honors, 1995). ***PRACTICE AREAS:*** Corporate; Mergers and Acquisitions; Venture Capital; Securities. ***Email:*** jrichards@kirkland.com

STEPHEN L. RITCHIE, P.C., admitted to bar, 1989, Illinois. *Education:* University of Virginia (B.A., 1985); University of Chicago (J.D., 1988). ***PRACTICE AREAS:*** Corporate; Mergers and Acquisitions; Securities; Venture Capital. ***Email:*** sritchie@kirkland.com

BRADLEY V. RITTER, admitted to bar, 1991, Illinois. *Education:* Northwestern University (B.A., 1987); University of Illinois College of Law (J.D., 1991). ***PRACTICE AREAS:*** Real Estate; Private Equity; Loan Restructuring. ***Email:*** britter@kirkland.com

MARIA PELLEGRINO RIVERA, admitted to bar, 1995, Illinois; 1997, Arizona. *Education:* Northwestern University (B.A., with distinction, 1991); University of Chicago (J.D., with honors, 1995). ***PRACTICE AREAS:*** Litigation. ***Email:*** mrivera@kirkland.com

J. ROBERT ROBERTSON, (P.C.), admitted to bar, 1990, Illinois; 1992, Texas and U.S. District Court, Northern District of Illinois including Trial Bar; U.S. Court of Appeals, Fourth, Seventh, Eighth and Ninth Circuits; U.S. District Court, District of Columbia. *Education:* Virginia Military Institute (B.A., with distinction, 1977); University of Chicago (J.D., with honors, 1990). ***PRACTICE AREAS:*** Antitrust; Litigation; Franchise and Distribution; Mergers and Acquisitions. ***Email:*** rrobertson@kirkland.com

DONALD E. ROCAP, admitted to bar, 1980, Pennsylvania; 1990, Illinois. *Education:* Duke University (B.A., 1977); University of Virginia (J.D., 1980). ***PRACTICE AREAS:*** Tax. ***Email:*** drocap@kirkland.com

JAMES S. ROWE, admitted to bar, 1991, Illinois. *Education:* University of Illinois (B.A., 1988); Duke University (J.D., 1991). ***PRACTICE AREAS:*** Corporate. ***Email:*** jrowe@kirkland.com

DAVID S. ROYAL, admitted to bar, 1997, Illinois. *Education:* Yale University (B.A., summa cum laude, 1993; J.D., 1997). ***PRACTICE AREAS:*** Transactional; Capital Markets; Public Mergers and Acquisitions; Venture Capital; Private Equity. ***Email:*** droyal@kirkland.com

ANDREW R. RUNNING, admitted to bar, 1982, Illinois. *Education:* University of Chicago (A.B., 1979); Yale Law School (J.D., 1982). ***PRACTICE AREAS:*** Commercial Litigation; Bankruptcy Litigation; Environmental Law; Insurance Law. ***Email:*** arunning@kirkland.com

ANUP SATHY, admitted to bar, 1995, Illinois. *Education:* University of Illinois (B.S., highest honors, 1992); Northwestern University (J.D., cum laude, 1995). ***PRACTICE AREAS:*** Debtor-Creditor Law; Corporate Restructuring. ***Email:*** asathy@kirkland.com

JAMES H. SCHINK (P.C.), admitted to bar, 1968, Illinois. *Education:* Yale University (B.A., 1965; J.D., 1968). ***PRACTICE AREAS:*** Environmental Law & Hazardous Waste Liability & Compliance; Commercial Litigation; International Law; Worldwide Litigation and Arbitration; Competition; Antitrust. ***Email:*** jschink@kirkland.com

JOHN A. SCHOENFELD, (P.C.), admitted to bar, 1991, Illinois. *Education:* Lawrence University (B.A., 1986); Harvard University (J.D., 1990). ***PRACTICE AREAS:*** Corporate; Venture Capital; Finance; Mergers, Acquisitions and Divestitures. ***Email:*** jschoenfeld@kirkland.com

RAY C. SCHROCK, admitted to bar, 1998, Illinois. *Education:* Western Michigan University (B.B.A., magna cum laude, 1994); Chicago-Kent College of Law, Illinois Institute of Technology (J.D., high honors, 1998). ***PRACTICE AREAS:*** Restructuring. ***Email:*** rschrock@kirkland.com

STEVEN C. SEEGER, admitted to bar, 1997, Illinois. *Education:* Wheaton College (B.A., summa cum laude, 1993); University of Michigan (J.D., magna cum laude, 1997). ***PRACTICE AREAS:*** Litigation. ***Email:*** sseeger@kirkland.com

JEFFREY SEIFMAN, (P.C.), admitted to bar, 1992, Illinois. *Education:* University of Michigan (B.A., magna cum laude, 1989; J.D., 1992). ***PRACTICE AREAS:*** Corporate; Venture Capital; Finance. ***Email:*** jseifman@kirkland.com

DAVID R. SELIGMAN, admitted to bar, 1996, Illinois; 1998, Florida. *Education:* Dartmouth College (A.B., cum laude, 1993); University of Miami (J.D., summa cum laude, 1996). ***LANGUAGES:*** Spanish. ***PRACTICE AREAS:*** Bankruptcy Reorganization; Workouts; Commercial Litigation. ***Email:*** dseligman@kirkland.com

MARCUS E. SERNEL, admitted to bar, 1997, Illinois. *Education:* University of Illinois - Urbana-Champaign (B.S.Ch.E., 1992); Loyola University (J.D., 1997). ***PRACTICE AREAS:*** Patent Litigation; Antitrust. ***Email:*** msernel@kirkland.com

JEFFREY T. SHEFFIELD, (P.C.), admitted to bar, 1980, Illinois. *Education:* University of Chicago (B.A., 1976); Harvard Law School (J.D., 1979). ***PRACTICE AREAS:*** Tax; Tax Structuring Matters; Contested Tax Matters; Tax Planning; Venture Capital and Leveraged Acquisitions. ***Email:*** jsheffield@kirkland.com

JAMES A. SHIMOTA, admitted to bar, 1999, Illinois. *Education:* University of Michigan (B.S.E., 1996; J.D., 1999). ***PRACTICE AREAS:*** Intellectual Property. ***Email:*** jshimota@kirkland.com

ANNE M. SIDRYS, admitted to bar, 1992, Illinois. *Education:* University of Iowa (B.B.A., 1984); Georgetown University (J.D., 1992). ***PRACTICE AREAS:*** Securities; Commercial Litigation. ***Email:*** asidrys@kirkland.com

(This Listing Continued)

BRIAN D. SIEVE, P.C., admitted to bar, 1988, Illinois. *Education:* Wittenberg University (B.A., 1985); University of Chicago (J.D., 1988). ***PRACTICE AREAS:*** Intellectual Property; Patent Infringement; Trademark Infringement; Trade Secrets; Noncompetition and Non-Solicitation Agreements; Commercial Litigation; Products Liability. ***Email:*** bsieve@kirkland.com

MICHAEL SLADE, admitted to bar, 1999, Texas; 2001, Illinois. *Education:* Emory University (B.A., 1996); Harvard University (J.D., 1999). ***PRACTICE AREAS:*** Litigation. ***Email:*** mslade@kirkland.com

DOUGLAS G. SMITH, admitted to bar, 1996, Illinois; 1999, District of Columbia; registered to practice before U.S. Patent and Trademark Office. *Education:* State University of New York at Buffalo (B.S./B.A., 1993); Northwestern University (J.D., 1996); University of Chicago (M.B.A., 1999). ***PRACTICE AREAS:*** Litigation. ***Email:*** dsmith@kirkland.com

LESLIE M. SMITH, (P.C.), admitted to bar, 1987, Illinois. *Education:* Georgetown University (B.A., 1984; J.D., 1987). ***PRACTICE AREAS:*** Commercial Litigation. ***Email:*** lsmith@kirkland.com

RENEE D. SMITH, admitted to bar, 1995, Illinois. *Education:* Miami University (B.A., 1992); Harvard University (J.D., 1995). ***PRACTICE AREAS:*** Litigation. ***Email:*** rdsmith@kirkland.com

TEFFT W. SMITH, admitted to bar, 1971, Illinois; 1998, District of Columbia. *Education:* Brown University (B.A., 1968); University of Chicago (J.D., 1971). (Also at Chicago, Illinois Office). ***PRACTICE AREAS:*** Competition and Antitrust Law; Sales of Business Disputes; Commercial Litigation. ***Email:*** tsmith@kirkland.com

SALLIE G. SMYLIE, (P.C.), admitted to bar, 1989, Illinois. *Education:* Salem College (B.A., 1977); DePaul College of Law (J.D., 1989). ***PRACTICE AREAS:*** Litigation; Products Liability. ***Email:*** ssmylie@kirkland.com

KAREN G. SODKE, admitted to bar, 1998, Illinois. *Education:* Northwestern University (B.S., 1991); Northwestern University School of Law (J.D., cum laude, 1998). ***PRACTICE AREAS:*** Corporate; Capital Markets; Mergers and Acquisitions; Venture Capital; Private Equity. ***Email:*** ksodke@kirkland.com

GREGORY E. SPITZER, admitted to bar, 1989, Illinois. *Education:* University of Illinois (B.S., 1985); Northwestern University (J.D., 1989). ***PRACTICE AREAS:*** Real Estate (Property) Law; Finance. ***Email:*** gspitzer@kirkland.com

JAMES H. M. SPRAYREGEN, admitted to bar, 1985, Illinois and New York. *Education:* University of Michigan (B.A., 1982); University of Illinois (J.D., 1985). ***PRACTICE AREAS:*** Workout and Bankruptcy; Commercial Litigation; Corporate. ***Email:*** jsprayregen@kirkland.com

JOHN H. STASSEN, (P.C.), admitted to bar, 1968, Illinois. *Education:* Northwestern University (B.S., 1965); Harvard Law School (J.D., 1968). ***PRACTICE AREAS:*** Futures Law; Financial Services; Legislative; Corporate. ***Email:*** jstassen@kirkland.com

PAUL R. STEADMAN, admitted to bar, 1996, Illinois; 1998, District of Columbia; registered to practice before U.S. Patent and Trademark Office. *Education:* Rice University (B.S., 1991); University of Chicago (J.D., 1996). ***PRACTICE AREAS:*** Intellectual Property; Litigation; International Trade Commission. ***Email:*** psteadman@kirkland.com

MATTHEW E. STEINMETZ, admitted to bar, 1988, New York; 1989, Illinois. *Education:* Alma College (B.S., 1984); University of Notre Dame (J.D., 1987); University of Chicago (M.B.A., 1989). ***PRACTICE AREAS:*** Venture Capital and Leveraged Acquisitions; Corporate. ***Email:*** msteinmetz@kirkland.com

JAMES A. STEMPEL, admitted to bar, 1989, Illinois. *Education:* University of Michigan (B.G.S., 1985); IIT/Chicago Kent College of Law (J.D., 1989). ***PRACTICE AREAS:*** Workout and Bankruptcy; Mergers and Acquisitions. ***Email:*** jstempel@kirkland.com

WILLIAM A. STREFF, JR., P.C., admitted to bar, 1974, Illinois; registered to practice before U.S. Patent and Trademark Office. *Education:* Northwestern University (B.S.M.E., 1971; J.D., 1974). ***PRACTICE AREAS:*** Intellectual Property; Computer Law; Antitrust and Trade Regulation; Litigation; Alternative Dispute Resolution. ***Email:*** wstreff@kirkland.com

EDWARD T. SWAN, admitted to bar, 1977, Illinois. *Education:* Dartmouth College (A.B., 1972); Northwestern University (M.B.A., 1977); Northwestern University (J.D., 1977). ***PRACTICE AREAS:*** Corporate; Mergers and Acquisitions; Venture Capital and Leveraged Acquisitions; Private Equity Fund Formation. ***Email:*** eswan@kirkland.com

MAUREEN E. SWEENEY, admitted to bar, 1996, Illinois. *Education:* University of Michigan (B.S., 1993; J.D., 1996). ***PRACTICE AREAS:*** Corporate. ***Email:*** msweeney@kirkland.com

CHRISTIAN CHADD TAYLOR, admitted to bar, 1994, Illinois. *Education:* Rose-Hulman Institute of Technology (B.S.E.E., cum laude, 1991); Indiana University at Bloomington (J.D., magna cum laude, 1994). ***PRACTICE AREAS:*** Intellectual Property; Litigation. ***Email:*** ctaylor@kirkland.com

ANDREW J. TERRY, admitted to bar, 1998, Illinois. *Education:* Indiana University (B.A., 1994; M.B.A., 1998; J.D., magna cum laude, 1998). ***PRACTICE AREAS:*** Corporate Law. ***Email:*** aterry@kirkland.com

ANGELO F. TIESI, admitted to bar, 1987, Illinois. *Education:* University of Illinois (B.S., 1984); Loyola University, Chicago (J.D., 1987). ***PRACTICE AREAS:*** Trusts and Estates. ***Email:*** atiesi@kirkland.com

DOUGLAS D. TIMMER, admitted to bar, 1995, Wisconsin; 1998, Illinois. *Education:* Cornell College (B.A., summa cum laude, 1992); University of Virginia (J.D., 1995). ***PRACTICE AREAS:*** Private Equity; Fund Formation; Mergers and Acquisitions; Securities; Corporate. ***Email:*** dtimmer@kirkland.com

MICHAEL G. TIMMERS, P.C., admitted to bar, 1982, Illinois. *Education:* University of Chicago (B.A./M.A., 1979); Northwestern University (J.D., 1982). ***PRACTICE AREAS:*** Corporate; Venture Capital and Leveraged Acquisitions. ***Email:*** mtimmers@kirkland.com

(This Listing Continued)

STEPHEN G. TOMLINSON, P.C., admitted to bar, 1984, Illinois; 2003, New York. *Education:* University of Michigan (A.B., 1981; J.D., 1984). ***PRACTICE AREAS:*** Real Estate; Corporate; Finance. ***Email:*** stomlinson@kirkland.com

THOMAS A. TOZER, admitted to bar, 1991, Illinois. *Education:* University of Chicago (B.A., 1982; M.A., 1985); Indiana University (J.D., 1991). ***PRACTICE AREAS:*** Commercial Litigation; Product Liability; Construction Law; Environmental Litigation; Class Actions. ***Email:*** ttozer@kirkland.com

SETH TRAXLER, admitted to bar, 1997, Illinois. *Education:* University of Kansas (B.A., cum laude, 1993, Phi Beta Kappa); Northwestern University (J.D., cum laude, 1997). ***PRACTICE AREAS:*** Intellectual Property; Technology Transactions; Litigation. ***Email:*** straxler@kirkland.com

CHRISTOPHER M.R. TURNER, admitted to bar, 1996, Illinois. *Education:* Wesleyan University (B.A., 1989); Stanford Law School (J.D., with distinction, 1995). ***PRACTICE AREAS:*** Litigation. ***Email:*** cmturner@kirkland.com

WILLIAM E. TYMM, admitted to bar, 1970, Illinois. *Education:* DePaul University (B.S., 1967; J.D., 1970). ***PRACTICE AREAS:*** Corporate; Securities. ***Email:*** wtymm@kirkland.com

BRIAN C. VAN KLOMPENBERG, admitted to bar, 1998, Illinois. *Education:* Michigan State University (B.A., 1995); University of Chicago (J.D., 1998). ***PRACTICE AREAS:*** Venture Capital; Debt Finance; Equity Finance; Corporate Law. ***Email:*** bvanklompenberg@kirkland.com

KEVIN T. VAN WART, (P.C.), admitted to bar, 1982, Illinois. *Education:* Ohio Wesleyan University (B.A., 1976); Boston University (J.D., 1982). ***PRACTICE AREAS:*** Litigation; Products Liability; Torts. ***Email:*** kvanwart@kirkland.com

KEITH E. VILLMOW, admitted to bar, 1993, Illinois. *Education:* Swarthmore College (B.A., 1979); Stanford University (J.D., 1993). ***PRACTICE AREAS:*** Taxation. ***Email:*** kvillmow@kirkland.com

GREGORY VOGELSPERGER, admitted to bar, 2000, New York; 2003, Illinois. *Education:* College of the Holy Cross (B.A., 1992); University of Chicago (J.D., 1999). ***Email:*** gvogelsperger@kirkland.com

H. KURT VON MOLTKE, admitted to bar, 1986, New York; 1990, Illinois. *Education:* Northwestern University (B.A., 1982); University of Michigan (J.D., 1985). ***PRACTICE AREAS:*** Corporate; Securities; Venture Capital; Private Equity; Mergers and Acquisitions. ***Email:*** kvonmoltke@kirkland.com

MICHAEL H. WEED, admitted to bar, 1996, Illinois. *Education:* University of Iowa (B.S., 1991; M.B.A., 1992); Columbia University (J.D., 1996). ***PRACTICE AREAS:*** Corporate; Mergers, Acquisitions and Divestitures; Private Equity; Venture Capital; Securities. ***Email:*** mweed@kirkland.com

ROSS M. WEISMAN, admitted to bar, 1993, New Hampshire; 1994, Illinois. *Education:* Northwestern University (B.A., 1988); Boston University School of Law (J.D., cum laude, 1993). ***PRACTICE AREAS:*** Advertising; Marketing; Intellectual Property. ***Email:*** rweisman@kirkland.com

JOHN A. WEISSENBACH, admitted to bar, 1980, Illinois. *Education:* Princeton University (A.B., 1977); Harvard University (J.D., 1980). ***PRACTICE AREAS:*** Mergers, Acquisitions and Divestitures; Venture Capital; Mezzanine Finance; Corporate; Finance; Securities; Private Equity Transactions. ***Email:*** jweissenbach@kirkland.com

DONNA M. WELCH, admitted to bar, 1994, Illinois. *Education:* University of Chicago (B.A., 1988); DePaul University (J.D., 1994). ***PRACTICE AREAS:*** Commercial Litigation; Labor and Employment. ***Email:*** dwelch@kirkland.com

WILLIAM R. WELKE, admitted to bar, 1983, Illinois. *Education:* Massachusetts Institute of Technology (S.B., 1980); University of Michigan (J.D., 1983). ***PRACTICE AREAS:*** Taxation; Venture Capital; Mergers and Acquisitions; Joint Ventures; International. ***Email:*** wwelke@kirkland.com

RAYMOND P. WEXLER, (P.C.), admitted to bar, 1967, Missouri; 1973, Illinois. *Education:* Washington University (B.A., 1964; J.D., 1967); New York University (LL.M., Taxation, 1972). ***PRACTICE AREAS:*** Tax. ***Email:*** rwexler@kirkland.com

JEFFREY L. WILLIAN, (P.C.), admitted to bar, 1986, Illinois. *Education:* Miami University (B.S., 1983); American University (J.D., 1986). ***PRACTICE AREAS:*** Commercial Litigation; Antitrust; Corporate; Contract; Environmental; Intellectual Property; Products Liability. ***Email:*** jwillian@kirkland.com

ROBERT A. WILSON, admitted to bar, 1999, Minnesota; 2000, Illinois. *Education:* University of Wisconsin, Madison (B.A., 1992); Northwestern University (J.D., 1999). ***PRACTICE AREAS:*** Corporate. ***Email:*** rwilson@kirkland.com

HELEN E. WITT, admitted to bar, 1982, Illinois. *Education:* Yale College (B.A., 1979); University of Chicago (J.D., 1982). ***PRACTICE AREAS:*** Litigation. ***Email:*** hwitt@kirkland.com

W. ALLEN WOOLLEY, admitted to bar, 1991, Colorado; 1995, Illinois. *Education:* Dartmouth College (A.B., 1987); Duke University (M.A., J.D., 1991). ***PRACTICE AREAS:*** Commercial Litigation; Employment Litigation; Environmental Litigation. ***Email:*** awoolley@kirkland.com

MICHAEL D. WRIGHT, admitted to bar, 1988, Illinois; 1993, California. *Education:* Purdue University (B.S., 1985); Indiana University School of Law (J.D., cum laude, 1988). ***PRACTICE AREAS:*** Corporate; Mezzanine Finance; Financing; Secured Transactions; Restructuring; Insolvency; Workout; Bankruptcy; Asset Finance; Securitization.

MARY E. ZAUG, admitted to bar, 1996, Illinois. *Education:* University of Wisconsin, Madison (B.S.Ch.E., 1989); Loyola University Chicago (J.D., magna cum laude, 1996). ***PRACTICE AREAS:*** Intellectual Property. ***Email:*** mzaug@kirkland.com

ROBERT R. ZITKO, admitted to bar, 1994, Illinois. *Education:* University of Illinois (B.S., 1988; J.D., magna cum laude, 1994). ***PRACTICE AREAS:*** Employee Benefits. ***Email:*** rzitko@kirkland.com

(This Listing Continued)

KIRKLAND & ELLIS LLP, Chicago—Continued

TED H. ZOOK, admitted to bar, 1988, Illinois. *Education:* Illinois Wesleyan University (B.A., 1985); University of Virginia (J.D., 1988). ***PRACTICE AREAS:*** Corporate; Mergers, Acquisitions and Divestitures; Venture Capital. ***Email:*** tzook@kirkland.com

DAVID J. ZOTT, admitted to bar, 1986, Illinois. *Education:* Virginia Military Institute; Northwestern University (B.A., 1983); University of Michigan (J.D., 1986). ***PRACTICE AREAS:*** Commercial Litigation. ***Email:*** dzott@kirkland.com

ASSOCIATES

DAVID A. AGAY, admitted to bar, 1998, Illinois. *Education:* Pomona College (B.A., 1994); University of Michigan (J.D., 1997). ***PRACTICE AREAS:*** Banking Reorganization; Corporate Reorganization; Workouts; Litigation; Corporate Law. ***Email:*** dagay@kirkland.com

AMEER I. AHMAD, admitted to bar, 2001, Illinois. *Education:* University of Illinois - Urbana (B.S., 1997); University of Illinois (J.D., 2001). ***PRACTICE AREAS:*** Corporate Law. ***Email:*** aahmad@kirkland.com

GEORGE P. ALEXANDER, admitted to bar, 2002, Illinois. *Education:* Northwestern University (B.A., 1999); New York University (J.D., 2002). ***PRACTICE AREAS:*** Corporate Law. ***Email:*** galexander@kirkland.com

SUZANNE MILNE ALEXANDER, admitted to bar, 2004, Illinois. *Education:* Northwestern University (B.S. in Education, 1996); DePaul University (J.D., summa cum laude, 2004). ***PRACTICE AREAS:*** Intellectual Property; Litigation. ***Email:*** salexander@kirkland.com

JAMES ALLEN, admitted to bar, 2000, Michigan (Not admitted in Illinois). *Education:* Reed College (B.A., in History, 1992); University of Michigan (J.D., cum laude, 2000). ***PRACTICE AREAS:*** Transactional; Real Estate. ***Email:*** jallen@kirkland.com

KRISTEN J. ALLEN, admitted to bar, 2002, Illinois. *Education:* University of Missouri-Columbia (B.J., summa cum laude, 1999); University of Illinois College of Law (J.D., magna cum laude, 2002). ***PRACTICE AREAS:*** Intellectual Property. ***Email:*** kallen@kirkland.com

JOHN A. AMASH, born May 3, 1976; admitted to bar, 2001, Illinois. *Education:* Harvard University (A.B., 1998); University of Michigan Law School (J.D., 2001). ***PRACTICE AREAS:*** Litigation. ***Email:*** jamash@kirkland.com

GEOFFREY L. ANDERMAN, (admission pending). *Education:* Washington University (B.A., 2002); University of Southern California (J.D., 2005). ***PRACTICE AREAS:*** Corporate Law. ***Email:*** ganderman@kirkland.com

MATTHEW ANTINOSSI, admitted to bar, 1999, Illinois. *Education:* Asbury College (B.A., 1995); The Ohio State University (J.D., 1999). ***PRACTICE AREAS:*** Employee Benefits. ***Email:*** mantinossi@kirkland.com

JAMES J. ANTONOPOULOS, admitted to bar, 2003, Illinois. *Education:* University of Illinois (B.S., Accounting, 2000; J.D., 2003). ***PRACTICE AREAS:*** Corporate; Venture Capital; Workouts; Bankruptcy. ***Email:*** jantonopoulos@kirkland.com

SHUAIB A. ATIQUE, admitted to bar, 2003, California; 2004, Massachusetts (Not admitted in Illinois). *Education:* University of Illinois, Urbana-Champaign (B.S., 2000); University of Michigan (J.D., 2003). ***LANGUAGES:*** Urdu. ***PRACTICE AREAS:*** Intellectual Property; Biotechnology; Pharmaceuticals; Life Sciences; Patent Infringement. ***Email:*** satique@kirkland.com

ALISON R. AUBRY, admitted to bar, 2003, Massachusetts (Not admitted in Illinois). *Education:* University of Illinois at Urbana-Champaign (B.S., 1999); Harvard Law School (J.D., 2003). ***PRACTICE AREAS:*** Litigation. ***Email:*** aubrya@kirkland.com

CEYLAN A. AYASLI, (admission pending). *Education:* Massachusetts Institute of Technology (B.S., 2000); University of Chicago (J.D., 2005). ***LANGUAGES:*** Turkish. ***PRACTICE AREAS:*** Litigation. ***Email:*** cayasli@kirkland.com

DEAN C. BACHUS, admitted to bar, 2004, Illinois. *Education:* University of Iowa (B.A., B.M., 1995); Western Illinois University (M.A. 1997); University of Chicago (J.D., 2004). ***PRACTICE AREAS:*** Tax Law. ***Email:*** dbachus@kirkland.com

JUSTIN A. BARKER, admitted to bar, 2001, Illinois. *Education:* Brigham Young University (B.A., 1998); Brigham Young University, J. Reuben Clark Law School (J.D., magna cum laude, 2001). ***PRACTICE AREAS:*** Antitrust; Competition; Litigation; Commercial Litigation; Commercial Arbitration; Franchise and Distribution. ***Email:*** jbarker@kirkland.com

JAMES P. BARTLEY, admitted to bar, 2005, Illinois. *Education:* Illinois Wesleyan University (B.A., 1995); John Marshall Law School (J.D., magna cum laude, 2005). ***PRACTICE AREAS:*** Real Estate. ***Email:*** jbartley@kirkland.com

BENJAMIN WILL BATES, admitted to bar, 2002, Illinois. *Education:* University of Utah (B.A., Linguistics, 1999); University of Utah, S. J. Quinney College of Law (J.D., 2002), Order of the Coif. ***PRACTICE AREAS:*** Corporate Law. ***Email:*** bbates@kirkland.com

ANDREW BAUTISTA, admitted to bar, 2003, Illinois. *Education:* Columbia University (B.A., 2000); Stanford University (J.D., 2003). ***LANGUAGES:*** Russian. ***PRACTICE AREAS:*** Antitrust; Competition; Litigation; White Collar Criminal Defense. ***Email:*** abautista@kirkland.com

HEATHER BAWDEN, admitted to bar, 2002, Illinois. *Education:* University of Illinois (B.A., 1999); Harvard Law School (J.D., 2002). ***Email:*** hbawden@kirkland.com

ERIC BENNETT, admitted to bar, 2001, Illinois. *Education:* Northern Illinois University (B.S., 1996; M.P.A., 1998); Northwestern University (J.D., cum laude, 2001). ***PRACTICE AREAS:*** Real Estate. ***Email:*** ebennett@kirkland.com

RYAN BLAINE BENNETT, admitted to bar, 2000, Illinois. *Education:* Michigan State University (B.A., 1996); University of Notre Dame (J.D., 2000). ***PRACTICE AREAS:*** Bankruptcy Reorganization; Corporate Restructuring; Commercial Litigation. ***Email:*** rbennett@kirkland.com

(This Listing Continued)

SALVATORE BIANCA, admitted to bar, 2003, Illinois and New York. *Education:* University of Texas (B.A., 1998); University of Chicago Law School (J.D., 2001). ***PRACTICE AREAS:*** Restructuring; Insolvency; Workouts; Bankruptcy. ***Email:*** sbianca@kirkland.com

JESSICA L. BINA, admitted to bar, 2004, Illinois. *Education:* University of Michigan (B.A., 2001); Northwestern University School of Law (J.D., 2004). ***PRACTICE AREAS:*** Real Estate. ***Email:*** jbina@kirkland.com

FRED W. BLAKESLEE, II, (admission pending). *Education:* The Ohio State University (B.S.B.A., 1999); Northwestern University (J.D., 2002). ***Email:*** fblakeslee@kirkland.com

THOMAS N. BLANCHARD, admitted to bar, 2001, Illinois. *Education:* Northwestern University (B.A., 1995); University of Michigan (J.D., 2001). ***PRACTICE AREAS:*** Corporate Law; Private Equity. ***Email:*** tblanchard@kirkland.com

SAMUEL BLATNICK, admitted to bar, 2003, New York; 2004, Illinois. *Education:* Georgetown University (B.S., 1998); University of Chicago (J.D., 2002). ***PRACTICE AREAS:*** Litigation. ***Email:*** sblatnick@kirkland.com

TANYA BRADY, admitted to bar, 1999, Illinois and Georgia. *Education:* National University of Ireland, Dublin, Ireland (B.C.L., 1988); DePaul University (J.D., 1998). ***PRACTICE AREAS:*** Real Estate Acquisitions; Real Estate Development; Real Estate Leasing; Real Estate Sales. ***Email:*** tbrady@kirkland.com

STEPHANIE A. BRENNAN, admitted to bar, 2003, Illinois. *Education:* Dartmouth College (B.A., 1999); Yale University (J.D., 2002). ***PRACTICE AREAS:*** Litigation. ***Email:*** sbrennan@kirkland.com

TODD BROBERG, (admission pending). *Education:* Wheaton College (B.A., magna cum laude, 1998); University of Chicago (J.D., 2005). ***PRACTICE AREAS:*** Intellectual Property. ***Email:*** tbroberg@kirkland.com

PAUL S. BROWN, admitted to bar, 2001, California (Not admitted in Illinois). *Education:* University of Illinois (B.S., 1998); Northwestern University (J.D., 2001). ***PRACTICE AREAS:*** Intellectual Property; Commercial Litigation. ***Email:*** pbrown@kirkland.com

MATTHEW S. BRYANT, admitted to bar, 2005, Illinois. *Education:* University of Pennsylvania (B.A., 2002); Northwestern University (J.D., 2005). ***Email:*** mbryant@kirkland.com

MATTHEW BUCKLEY, (admission pending). *Education:* University of Michigan (B.A., 1999); Stanford Law School (J.D., with distinction, 2005). ***PRACTICE AREAS:*** Litigation. ***Email:*** mbuckley@kirkland.com

LACEY J. BUNDY, (admission pending). *Education:* University of Washington (B.A., cum laude, 1999); Northwestern University (J.D., cum laude, 2005). ***PRACTICE AREAS:*** Corporate Law. ***Email:*** lbundy@kirkland.com

ASHLEY J. BURDEN, (admission pending). *Education:* Loyola University (B.A., summa cum laude, 2002); University of Illinois (J.D., magna cum laude, 2005). ***PRACTICE AREAS:*** Litigation. ***Email:*** aburden@kirkland.com

WILLIAM R. BURKE, admitted to bar, 2003, New York; 2005, Illinois. *Education:* University of Illinois (B.A., 1995); Columbia University (J.D., 2002). ***PRACTICE AREAS:*** Corporate Law. ***Email:*** wburke@kirkland.com

KATHARINE K. BURNS, (admission pending). *Education:* Ohio Wesleyan University (B.A., summa cum laude, 1998); University of Chicago (M.A., 2001); University of Vermont (M.S., 2002); Cornell University Law School (J.D., cum laude, 2005). ***PRACTICE AREAS:*** Litigation. ***Email:*** kburns@kirkland.com

JASON W. CALLEN, admitted to bar, 2003, Illinois; U.S. Court of Appeals, Seventh Circuit. *Education:* Washington & Lee University (B.A., magna cum laude, 1998); University of Chicago (J.D., 2003). ***PRACTICE AREAS:*** Litigation. ***Email:*** jcallen@kirkland.com

RACHEL CANTOR, admitted to bar, 2003, New York and District of Columbia (Not admitted in Illinois). *Education:* Yale University (B.S., cum laude, 1995); University of Chicago (J.D., with honors, 2000). ***PRACTICE AREAS:*** Tax Law. ***Email:*** rcantor@kirkland.com

MICHAEL CAREW, (admission pending). *Education:* University of Rochester (B.S., B.A., magna cum laude, 2000); Harvard Law School (J.D., cum laude, 2004). ***PRACTICE AREAS:*** Tax Law; Tax Planning. ***Email:*** mcarew@kirkland.com

MARC J. CARMEL, admitted to bar, 2000, Illinois. *Education:* University of Michigan (B.B.A., 1994; M.Acctg., 1994); Harvard Law School (J.D., 2000). ***PRACTICE AREAS:*** Bankruptcy; Workouts. ***Email:*** mcarmel@kirkland.com

SUSAN CAMPBELL CAUDELL, admitted to bar, 2005, New York (Not admitted in Illinois). *Education:* Bryn Mawr College (A.B., cum laude, 2000); University of Chicago (J.D., 2004). ***PRACTICE AREAS:*** Litigation. ***Email:*** scampbell@kirkland.com

ERIK W. CHALUT, admitted to bar, 1999, Illinois. *Education:* Michigan State University (B.A., 1996); University of Michigan Law School (J.D., 1999). ***PRACTICE AREAS:*** Bankruptcy. ***Email:*** echalut@kirkland.com

TARUN J. CHANDRAN, admitted to bar, 2003, Illinois. *Education:* University of Michigan (B.A., cum laude, 2000; J.D., 2003). ***PRACTICE AREAS:*** Real Estate. ***Email:*** tchandran@kirkland.com

AARON D. CHARFOOS, admitted to bar, 2002, Illinois and U.S. District Court, Northern District of Illinois. *Education:* Northwestern University (B.A., 1997; J.D., 2002). ***PRACTICE AREAS:*** Intellectual Property. ***Email:*** acharfoos@kirkland.com

BRANDI L. CHUDOBA, admitted to bar, 2004, Illinois. *Education:* Northwestern University (B.S., 2001); University of Illinois College of Law (J.D., magna cum laude, 2004). ***PRACTICE AREAS:*** Litigation. ***Email:*** bchudoba@kirkland.com

SCOTT CLAIR, admitted to bar, 2003, Illinois. *Education:* Marquette University (B.A., English and Philosophy, cum laude, 1994); University of Michigan (M.A., Journalism, 1996); University of Illinois (J.D., summa cum laude, 2003). ***PRACTICE AREAS:*** Litigation. ***Email:*** sclair@kirkland.com

(This Listing Continued)

MICHAEL I. COHEN, (admission pending); admitted to bar, registered to practice before U.S. Patent and Trademark Office. *Education:* Bradley University (B.S., 1997; M.S., 1999); University of Illinois (J.D., summa cum laude, 2005). ***PRACTICE AREAS:*** Intellectual Property. ***Email:*** micohen@kirkland.com

KHARA COLEMAN, admitted to bar, 2003, Illinois. *Education:* Washington University (A.B., 1999; J.D., 2003). ***LANGUAGES:*** French and Spanish. ***PRACTICE AREAS:*** Litigation. ***Email:*** kcoleman@kirkland.com

LISA H. COX, admitted to bar, 2000, Illinois. *Education:* University of Illinois (B.S., summa cum laude, 1997; J.D., cum laude, 2000). ***PRACTICE AREAS:*** Real Estate. ***Email:*** lcox@kirkland.com

AMY E. CRAWFORD, (admission pending). *Education:* University of Notre Dame (B.A., magna cum laude, 1998); University of Chicago (J.D., 2004). ***PRACTICE AREAS:*** Litigation. ***Email:*** aecrawford@kirkland.com

KATHERINE M. CUNNINGHAM, admitted to bar, 1999, Wisconsin; 2003, Illinois. *Education:* Williams College (B.A., cum laude, 1995); Northwestern University (J.D., 1999). ***PRACTICE AREAS:*** Trusts and Estates; Tax Planning. ***Email:*** kcunningham@kirkland.com

TIFFANY P. CUNNINGHAM, admitted to bar, 2002, Illinois. *Education:* Massachusetts Institute of Technology (S.B., 1998); Harvard Law School (J.D., 2001). ***LANGUAGES:*** French. ***PRACTICE AREAS:*** Intellectual Property. ***Email:*** tcunningham@kirkland.com

GIANNI L. CUTRI, admitted to bar, 2000, Illinois. *Education:* University of Illinois (B.S.M.E., 1997); University of Illinois (J.D., 2000). ***PRACTICE AREAS:*** Intellectual Property. ***Email:*** gcutri@kirkland.com

MICHAEL B. DANIEL, admitted to bar, 2005, Pennsylvania (Not admitted in Illinois). *Education:* University of Michigan (B.B.A., with distinction, 2001; J.D., cum laude, 2004). ***PRACTICE AREAS:*** Corporate Law; Venture Capital; Private Equity. ***Email:*** mdaniel@kirkland.com

THAD DAVIS, (admission pending). *Education:* University of Chicago (B.A., 1991; J.D., 2005); University of Southern California (M.F.A., 1999). ***PRACTICE AREAS:*** Tax Law. ***Email:*** tdavis@kirkland.com

DAWN H. DAWSON, admitted to bar, 2001, Illinois. *Education:* University of Memphis (B.S., Biology, summa cum laude, 1994); University of Illinois (J.D., summa cum laude, 2001). ***PRACTICE AREAS:*** Intellectual Property; Biotechnology; Pharmaceutical Intellectual Property; Life Sciences; Information Technology; Internet Law; E-Commerce; Patent Infringement. ***Email:*** ddawson@kirkland.com

DAVID H. DeCELLES, admitted to bar, 2005, Illinois. *Education:* Northwestern University (B.A., cum laude, 1999); University of Chicago (J.D., 2004). ***PRACTICE AREAS:*** Litigation. ***Email:*** ddecelles@kirkland.com

JASON P. DESAI, admitted to bar, 2001, Illinois. *Education:* Stanford University (A.B., with distinction, 1998); Harvard Law School (J.D., 2001). ***PRACTICE AREAS:*** Corporate Law. ***Email:*** jdesai@kirkland.com

MICHAEL T. DIERKES, admitted to bar, 2001, Illinois. *Education:* University of Chicago (A.B., 1998); University of Illinois College of Law (J.D., 2001). ***PRACTICE AREAS:*** Litigation. ***Email:*** mdierkes@kirkland.com

MOLLY DiRAGO, (admission pending); admitted to bar, 2004, Illinois and U.S. District Court, Northern District of Illinois. *Education:* Illinois State University (B.S., magna cum laude, 1998); Boalt Hall School of Law, University of California (J.D., 2004). ***PRACTICE AREAS:*** Litigation. ***Email:*** mdirago@kirkland.com

EDWARD A. DONOVAN, admitted to bar, 2004, Illinois. *Education:* United States Military Academy, West Point (B.S., 1996); University of Virginia (J.D., 2004). ***PRACTICE AREAS:*** Corporate Law. ***Email:*** eadonovan@kirkland.com

MELODY DRUMMOND, (admission pending). *Education:* Georgetown University (B.A., 2000); Oxford University, Oxford, England (M.Sc., 2002); University of Chicago (J.D., 2005). ***PRACTICE AREAS:*** Intellectual Property. ***Email:*** mdrummond@kirkland.com

MICHAEL A. DUFFY, admitted to bar, 2000, Illinois. *Education:* Boston College (A.B., 1996); Northwestern University School of Law (J.D., 2000). ***LANGUAGES:*** Spanish. ***PRACTICE AREAS:*** Litigation. ***Email:*** maduffy@kirkland.com

ANDREW DUSTIN, admitted to bar, 2003, Illinois. *Education:* University of Chicago (B.A., Political Science, with honors, 1999); University of Michigan Law School (J.D., cum laude, 2003). ***PRACTICE AREAS:*** Litigation. ***Email:*** adustin@kirkland.com

STEPHANIE R. DYKEMAN, admitted to bar, 2004, Illinois. *Education:* University of Wisconsin-Madison (B.A., 2001); University of California, Boalt Hall School of Law (J.D., 2004). ***PRACTICE AREAS:*** Litigation. ***Email:*** sdykeman@kirkland.com

SCOTT M. EDENFIELD, admitted to bar, 2002, Illinois, U.S. District Court, Northern District of Illinois and U.S. Court of Appeals, Seventh Circuit. *Education:* University of Georgia (A.B., 1999); University of Chicago (J.D., 2002). ***PRACTICE AREAS:*** Litigation. ***Email:*** sedenfield@kirkland.com

JAMAL M. EDWARDS, admitted to bar, 2002, Illinois; 2003, Michigan and U.S. District Court, Eastern District of Michigan; 2004, U.S. Court of Appeals, Fourth Circuit. *Education:* Morehouse College (B.A., 1998); University of Michigan Law School (J.D., 2002). ***LANGUAGES:*** Spanish. ***PRACTICE AREAS:*** Intellectual Property; Litigation; Real Estate. ***Email:*** jedwards@kirkland.com

KATHELEEN A. EHRHART, admitted to bar, 2000, Illinois. *Education:* University of Illinois (B.S., 1997); University of Chicago (J.D., with honors, 2000). ***PRACTICE AREAS:*** Commercial Litigation. ***Email:*** kehrhart@kirkland.com

ISRAEL J. ENCINOSA, admitted to bar, 2003, Illinois. *Education:* Boston College (B.A., 2000); University of Chicago (J.D., 2003). ***LANGUAGES:*** Spanish. ***PRACTICE AREAS:*** Litigation; Antitrust; Competition Litigation. ***Email:*** iencinosa@kirkland.com

(This Listing Continued)

WENDY NETTER EPSTEIN, admitted to bar, 2003, Illinois and U.S. District Court, Northern District of Illinois; 2004, U.S. Court of Appeals, Ninth Circuit. *Education:* University of Illinois (B.A., summa cum laude, 1999); Harvard Law School (J.D., cum laude, 2003). ***PRACTICE AREAS:*** Litigation. ***Email:*** wepstein@kirkland.com

CHRISTOPHER J. ESBROOK, admitted to bar, 2004, Illinois. *Education:* Loyola University (B.B.A., magna cum laude, 2001); University of Illinois (J.D., magna cum laude, 2004). ***PRACTICE AREAS:*** Litigation. ***Email:*** cesbrook@kirkland.com

LEONID FELLER, admitted to bar, 2001, Illinois. *Education:* University of Michigan (A.B., 1996); Harvard Law School (J.D., 2000). ***LANGUAGES:*** Russian. ***PRACTICE AREAS:*** Litigation. ***Email:*** lfeller@kirkland.com

AMANDA N. FELTMAN, (admission pending). *Education:* Indiana University (B.A., magna cum laude, 2002); Indiana University School of Law (J.D., magna cum laude, 2005). ***PRACTICE AREAS:*** Litigation. ***Email:*** afeltman@kirkland.com

WENDY A. FLESKE, admitted to bar, 2004, Illinois; 2005, U.S. District Court, Northern District of Illinois. *Education:* Dartmouth College (A.B., 1998); Oxford University (M.St., 1999); University of California, Boalt Hall School of Law (J.D., 2004). ***PRACTICE AREAS:*** Real Estate. ***Email:*** wfleske@kirkland.com

PAUL S. FONDAHN, admitted to bar, 2004, Illinois. *Education:* Vanderbilt University (B.A., magna cum laude, 2001); Columbia University Law School (J.D., 2004). ***PRACTICE AREAS:*** Corporate. ***Email:*** pfondahn@kirkland.com

COREY D. FOX, admitted to bar, 2004, Illinois. *Education:* University of Michigan (B.A., cum laude, 1999); Northwestern University (J.D., cum laude, 2004). ***PRACTICE AREAS:*** Corporate Law. ***Email:*** cfox@kirkland.com

TED M. FRANKEL, admitted to bar, 2003, Illinois. *Education:* Princeton University (A.B., 2000); Northwestern University (J.D., 2003). ***PRACTICE AREAS:*** Corporate; Mergers and Acquisitions; Venture Capital; Private Equity. ***Email:*** tfrankel@kirkland.com

SARAH J. FREY, (admission pending). *Education:* Washington University (B.A., 1997); St. Louis University (E.M.I.B., 2000); University of Illinois (J.D., magna cum laude, 2004). ***PRACTICE AREAS:*** Intellectual Property. ***Email:*** sfrey@kirkland.com

COLLEEN M. GARLINGTON, (admission pending). *Education:* University of Notre Dame (B.S., 1987); DePaul University (J.D., summa cum laude, 2005). ***PRACTICE AREAS:*** Intellectual Property. ***Email:*** cgarlington@kirkland.com

JOHN C. GEKAS, admitted to bar, 2003, Illinois. *Education:* University of Michigan (B.A., Classical Civilization, 2000); University of Virginia Law School (J.D., 2003). ***PRACTICE AREAS:*** Litigation. ***Email:*** jgekas@kirkland.com

JEFFREY W. GETTLEMAN, admitted to bar, 1974, Illinois and U.S. District Court, Northern District of Illinois; 1984, Maine. *Education:* University of Wisconsin-Madison (B.A., 1968); University of Chicago (J.D., 1974). ***PRACTICE AREAS:*** Bankruptcy. ***Email:*** jgettleman@kirkland.com

ADAM GILL, admitted to bar, 2003, California and U.S. District Court, Northern District of California; U.S. Court of Appeals, Ninth Circuit; 2004, Illinois. *Education:* University of South Carolina (B.A., with honors, 1994); University of California, Hastings College of Law (J.D., 2002). ***PRACTICE AREAS:*** Intellectual Property; Patent Infringement Litigation; Trademark Litigation; Copyright Litigation; Antitrust Litigation; Competition Litigation. ***Email:*** agill@kirkland.com

JOHN A. GLASSGOW, admitted to bar, 1998, Illinois. *Education:* University of Notre Dame (B.A., magna cum laude, 1992); Princeton University (M.P.A., 1998); Northwestern University (J.D., 1998). ***PRACTICE AREAS:*** Corporate Law. ***Email:*** jglassgow@kirkland.com

SERENA JEAN GONDEK, admitted to bar, 2004, Illinois; registered to practice before U.S. Patent and Trademark Office, 2003. *Education:* Johns Hopkins University (B.S., 1999); Syracuse University (M.S., 2001); DePaul University College of Law (J.D., magna cum laude, 2004). ***PRACTICE AREAS:*** Intellectual Property; Patent Infringement Litigation; Biotechnology; Pharmaceutical; Life Science; Trademark Litigation; Copyright Litigation. ***Email:*** sgondek@kirkland.com

WARREN R. GOODWORTH, admitted to bar, 2002, Massachusetts (Not admitted in Illinois). *Education:* Utah State University (B.A., 1998); Syracuse University (J.D., cum laude, 2001). ***LANGUAGES:*** Spanish. ***PRACTICE AREAS:*** Corporate; Venture Capital; Private Equity. ***Email:*** wgoodworth@kirkland.com

UDAY GORREPATI, admitted to bar, 2005, Illinois. *Education:* Yale University (B.A., 1999); Harvard Law School (J.D., 2004). ***PRACTICE AREAS:*** Corporate Law. ***Email:*** ugorrepati@kirkland.com

DAVID GRASSMICK, admitted to bar, 2002, Illinois. *Education:* University of Virginia (B.A., 1983); University of Illinois (J.D., 2002). ***PRACTICE AREAS:*** Commercial Litigation. ***Email:*** dgrassmick@kirkland.com

JOANNA B. GUNDERSON, (admission pending). *Education:* University of Illinois (B.S., 2002); John Marshall Law School (J.D., 2005). ***PRACTICE AREAS:*** Intellectual Property.

CHRISTOPHER A. HACKER, (admission pending). *Education:* University of Wisconsin (B.S., 2000); Northwestern University (J.D., 2005). ***LANGUAGES:*** Spanish. ***PRACTICE AREAS:*** Litigation. ***Email:*** chacker@kirkland.com

STEVEN S. HALL, admitted to bar, 2004, Illinois. *Education:* Kansas State University (B.S., summa cum laude, 2001); Cornell University Law School (J.D., magna cum laude, 2004). ***PRACTICE AREAS:*** Corporate Law. ***Email:*** shall@kirkland.com

MARK S. HAMILL, admitted to bar, 2001, Illinois. *Education:* Washington & Jefferson College (B.A., 1989); Northwestern University (J.D., 2001). ***PRACTICE AREAS:*** Antitrust; Competition; Securities Litigation; Shareholders Law; Commercial Litigation. ***Email:*** mhamill@kirkland.com

BRAD HANNA, admitted to bar, 2001, Wisconsin and Illinois. *Education:* Southern Illinois University (B.A., 1995); University of Wisconsin at Madison (J.D., 2001). ***PRACTICE AREAS:*** Corporate Law. ***Email:*** bhanna@kirkland.com

(This Listing Continued)

KIRKLAND & ELLIS LLP, Chicago—Continued

ERIC D. HAYES, (admission pending). ***PRACTICE AREAS:*** Intellectual Property; Patent Infringement; Trademark Litigation; Copyright Litigation. ***Email:*** ehayes@kirkland.com

AMY C. HAYWOOD, admitted to bar, 2003, Virginia; 2004, District of Columbia (Not admitted in Illinois). *Education:* University of Missouri, Columbia (B.A., magna cum laude, 1997); Georgetown University (J.D., 2003). ***PRACTICE AREAS:*** Class Actions; Toxic Torts; Mass Torts; Litigation. ***Email:*** ahaywood@kirkland.com

R. CHRIS HECK, admitted to bar, 2001, Illinois. *Education:* Amherst College (B.A., 1997); University of Chicago (J.D., 2000). ***PRACTICE AREAS:*** Litigation. ***Email:*** rcheck@kirkland.com

JARED E. HEDMAN, admitted to bar, 2002, Illinois. *Education:* Northern Illinois University (B.S., 1989); Loyola University (J.D., 2002). ***PRACTICE AREAS:*** Intellectual Property Litigation. ***Email:*** jhedman@kirkland.com

MATTHEW J. HERTKO, (admission pending). *Education:* Northwestern University (B.S., 2002); University of Illinois (J.D., summa cum laude, 2005). ***PRACTICE AREAS:*** Patent Infringement. ***Email:*** mhertko@kirkland.com

ELIZABETH S. HESS, admitted to bar, 2004, Illinois. *Education:* University of Chicago (A.B., with honors, 2001); University of Chicago Law School (J.D., 2004). ***PRACTICE AREAS:*** Litigation. ***Email:*** ehess@kirkland.com

SCOTT F. HESSELL, admitted to bar, 2001, Illinois. *Education:* University of Michigan (B.A., 1997); University of Chicago (J.D., with honors, 2001). ***PRACTICE AREAS:*** Litigation. ***Email:*** shessell@kirkland.com

DAVID W. HIGER, admitted to bar, 2004, Idaho (Not admitted in Illinois). *Education:* University of Washington (B.S., 1995); Gonzaga University (J.D., summa cum laude, 2004). ***PRACTICE AREAS:*** Intellectual Property. ***Email:*** dhiger@kirkland.com

MARGARET LEE HUDGINS, admitted to bar, 2004, Illinois. *Education:* University of Chicago (A.B., 1995); IIT/Chicago-Kent College of Law (J.D., with high honors, 2004). ***PRACTICE AREAS:*** Tax; Tax Planning; Trusts and Estates. ***Email:*** mhudgins@kirkland.com

BENJAMIN W. HULSE, admitted to bar, 2002, Illinois; 2003, U.S. Court of Appeals, Eighth Circuit. *Education:* Harvard University (A.B., Social Studies, magna cum laude, 1999); University of Chicago Law School (J.D., with honors, 2002). ***PRACTICE AREAS:*** Litigation. ***Email:*** bhulse@kirkland.com

CHAD J. HUSNICK, admitted to bar, 2004, Illinois. *Education:* University of Wisconsin-Madison (B.S., with distinction, 2001); University of Chicago (J.D., with honors, 2004). ***PRACTICE AREAS:*** Restructuring; Insolvency; Workouts; Bankruptcy. ***Email:*** chusnick@kirkland.com

CAMDEN HUTCHISON, (admission pending). *Education:* University of Rochester (B.A., 2002); Columbia University (J.D., 2005). ***PRACTICE AREAS:*** Corporate Law. ***Email:*** chutchison@kirkland.com

JUSTIN R. ISHBIA, admitted to bar, 2004, Illinois. *Education:* Michigan State University (B.A., Accounting, high honors, 2000); Vanderbilt University Law School (J.D., 2004). ***PRACTICE AREAS:*** Corporate; Venture Capital; Private Equity. ***Email:*** jishbia@kirkland.com

TOMOKO ITOGA, admitted to bar, 2000, California; 2002, District of Columbia; 2005, Illinois; registered to practice before U.S. Patent and Trademark Office. *Education:* Brown University (B.S., 1994); Northwestern University (J.D., 1999). ***LANGUAGES:*** Japanese. ***PRACTICE AREAS:*** Intellectual Property. ***Email:*** titoga@kirkland.com

TAMARA G. JAIN, admitted to bar, 2002, Illinois. *Education:* Cornell University (B.A., 1998); University of Michigan (J.D., cum laude, 2002). ***PRACTICE AREAS:*** Corporate; Real Estate. ***Email:*** tjain@kirkland.com

ADRIANNE K. JAKOLA, admitted to bar, 2001, Illinois. *Education:* Northwestern University (B.A., 1998); University of Chicago (J.D., 2001). ***PRACTICE AREAS:*** Litigation. ***Email:*** kwiechens@kirkland.com

JAMI A. JAROSCH, admitted to bar, 2001, Illinois. *Education:* Emory University (B.A., 1998); University of Michigan (J.D., 2001). ***PRACTICE AREAS:*** Intellectual Property. ***Email:*** jjarosch@kirkland.com

RYAN L. JENSEN, admitted to bar, 2001, Illinois; 2003, Utah; U.S. District Court, Northern District of Illinois and U.S. District Court, District of Utah. *Education:* Utah State University (B.A., magna cum laude, 1997); Brigham Young University (J.D., magna cum laude, 2001). ***LANGUAGES:*** Russian. ***PRACTICE AREAS:*** Corporate Law. ***Email:*** rjensen@kirkland.com

JOSHUA D. JEWKES, admitted to bar, 2002, Illinois. *Education:* Brigham Young University (B.A., 1999); J. Reuben Clark Law School, Brigham Young University (J.D., 2002). ***LANGUAGES:*** Swedish, Dutch and German. ***PRACTICE AREAS:*** Commercial Litigation. ***Email:*** jjewkes@kirkland.com

DAVID E. JOHANSON, (admission pending). *Education:* Northwestern University (B.A., 1998); Northwestern University School of Law (J.D., cum laude, 2004). ***PRACTICE AREAS:*** Corporate. ***Email:*** djohanson@kirkland.com

ANDREA L. JOHNSON, admitted to bar, 2004, Illinois. *Education:* Wartburg College (B.A., summa cum laude, 2001); Tulane University (J.D., magna cum laude, 2004). ***PRACTICE AREAS:*** Bankruptcy. ***Email:*** ajohnson@kirkland.com

JULIE M. JOHNSON, (admission pending). *Education:* Niagara University (B.A., summa cum laude, 2000); The Ohio State University College of Law (J.D., with honors, 2004). ***PRACTICE AREAS:*** Corporate. ***Email:*** jmjohnson@kirkland.com

JORDAN L. JONAS, (admission pending). *Education:* University of Michigan (B.S.E., 1999); University of Illinois (J.D., 2005). ***PRACTICE AREAS:*** Intellectual Property. ***Email:*** jjonas@kirkland.com

(This Listing Continued)

MICHELLE W. JORDAN, admitted to bar, 2002, Illinois. *Education:* Ohio State University (B.S.M.E., 1988); University of Cincinnati (M.B.A., 1994); Northwestern University School of Law (J.D., 2002). ***PRACTICE AREAS:*** Intellectual Property. ***Email:*** mjordan@kirkland.com

MARY L. KACZMAREK, admitted to bar, 2001, California; 2002, Illinois. *Education:* Pomona College (B.A., cum laude, 1998); University of Chicago Law School (J.D., with honors, 2001). ***PRACTICE AREAS:*** Tax and Planning; Trusts and Estates. ***Email:*** mkaczmarek@kirkland.com

CHRISTOPHER M. KAISER, (admission pending). ***PRACTICE AREAS:*** Intellectual Property. ***Email:*** ckaiser@kirkland.com

JEFFREY B. KAPLAN, admitted to bar, 2002, Illinois. *Education:* University of Wisconsin-Madison (B.B.A., 1999); Harvard Law School (J.D., 2002). ***PRACTICE AREAS:*** Corporate. ***Email:*** jkaplan@kirkland.com

SHIRA J. KAPPLIN, admitted to bar, 2003, Illinois. *Education:* Georgia Institute of Technology (B.S., with honors, 1995; M.S., 2000); University of Chicago (J.D., with honors, 2003). ***PRACTICE AREAS:*** Intellectual Property; Patent Infringement Litigation; Trademark Litigation; Copyright Litigation. ***Email:*** skapplin@kirkland.com

ALEXANDER L. KARAN, admitted to bar, 2000, Illinois. *Education:* University of Chicago (A.B., with honors, 1994); University of Virginia (J.D., 2000). ***LANGUAGES:*** Russian. ***PRACTICE AREAS:*** Litigation. ***Email:*** akaran@kirkland.com

CHAD A. KEETCH, (admission pending). *Education:* Brigham Young University (B.A., 2001); The Ohio State University (M.B.A., 2005; J.D., 2005). ***LANGUAGES:*** Spanish. ***PRACTICE AREAS:*** Corporate Law. ***Email:*** ckeetch@kirkland.com

ROBERT KIBURZ, admitted to bar, 2004, Illinois. *Education:* DePauw University (B.A., magna cum laude, 1998); University of Michigan Law School (J.D., magna cum laude, 2003). ***PRACTICE AREAS:*** Transactional. ***Email:*** rkiburz@kirkland.com

KEVIN M. KILEEN, admitted to bar, 2004, Illinois. *Education:* University of Notre Dame (B.B.A., 1999); University of Illinois (J.D., summa cum laude, 2004). ***PRACTICE AREAS:*** Litigation. ***Email:*** kkileen@kirkland.com

RYAN KILKENNEY, admitted to bar, 2003, Illinois. *Education:* Case Western Reserve University (B.A., English, summa cum laude, 1999); The Ohio State University (J.D., summa cum laude, 2003). ***PRACTICE AREAS:*** Corporate; Litigation. ***Email:*** rkilkenney@kirkland.com

COLBY ANNE KINGSBURY, admitted to bar, 2000, Illinois. *Education:* Otterbein College (B.F.A., with honors, 1991); DePaul School of Law (J.D., with honors, 2000). ***PRACTICE AREAS:*** Litigation; Intellectual Property. ***Email:*** ckingsbury@kirkland.com

NANCY L. KOWALCZYK, (admission pending). *Education:* University of Notre Dame (B.A., 1995); University of Minnesota Law School (J.D., magna cum laude, 2004). ***PRACTICE AREAS:*** Corporate. ***Email:*** nkowalczyk@kirkland.com

S. RAJA KRISHNAMOORTHI, admitted to bar, 2000, Illinois. *Education:* Princeton University (B.S.E., Mechanical Engineering, summa cum laude, 1995); Harvard Law School (J.D., cum laude, 2000). ***LANGUAGES:*** Tamil. ***PRACTICE AREAS:*** Litigation; Commercial Litigation; Commercial Arbitration. ***Email:*** rkrishnamoorthi@kirkland.com

JOHN C. KROCAK, (admission pending). *Education:* University of Minnesota-Minneapolis and St. Paul (B.S.B., 2001); University of Chicago (J.D., 2005). ***PRACTICE AREAS:*** Corporate Law. ***Email:*** jkrocak@kirkland.com

ROSS KWASTENIET, admitted to bar, 2002, Illinois. *Education:* Calvin College (B.A., 1999); University of Michigan (J.D., 2001). ***PRACTICE AREAS:*** Bankruptcy; Restructuring. ***Email:*** rkwasteniet@kirkland.com

BENJAMIN F. LANGNER, (admission pending). *Education:* Northwestern University (B.A., 1999); Tulane University Law School (J.D., magna cum laude, 2002). Order of the Coif. ***Email:*** blangner@kirkland.com

ELIZABETH A. LARSEN, admitted to bar, 2002, Illinois. *Education:* Princeton University (A.B., History, magna cum laude, 1998); Universitaet Muenster (Fulbright Scholar, 1998-1999); University of Chicago Law School (J.D., with honors, 2002). ***PRACTICE AREAS:*** Litigation. ***Email:*** blarsen@kirkland.com

ANDREW B. LEHMAN, (admission pending). *Education:* Vanderbilt University (B.A., magna cum laude, 1999); University of Chicago (M.A., 2001); University of Texas (J.D., 2005). ***PRACTICE AREAS:*** Corporate Law. ***Email:*** alehman@kirkland.com

DENEESE WALIA LEVIN, admitted to bar, 2003, Illinois. *Education:* Northwestern University (B.A., Political Science and American Culture, 1997); University of Chicago Law School (J.D., 2003). ***PRACTICE AREAS:*** Corporate. ***Email:*** dwalialevin@kirkland.com

ALEX C. LEVINE, admitted to bar, 2002, Illinois. *Education:* Oberlin College (B.A., 1999); Stanford University Law School (J.D., 2002). ***PRACTICE AREAS:*** Litigation. ***Email:*** aclevine@kirkland.com

NICHOLAS J. LEZAK, (admission pending). *Education:* University of Chicago (A.B., 2002); University of Michigan (J.D., 2005). ***PRACTICE AREAS:*** Employee Benefits. ***Email:*** nlezak@kirkland.com

CHUAN LI, admitted to bar, 1999, New York; 2001, Illinois. *Education:* University of International Business & Economics (LL.B., 1994); University of Iowa (J.D., 2001). ***LANGUAGES:*** Chinese. ***PRACTICE AREAS:*** Corporate Law. ***Email:*** cli@kirkland.com

STEPHANIE S. LIANG, admitted to bar, 2002, Illinois. *Education:* Georgetown University (B.S.F.S., 1998); The University of Chicago Law School (J.D., 2002). ***PRACTICE AREAS:*** Corporate. ***Email:*** sliang@kirkland.com

RUSSELL S. LIGHT, admitted to bar, 2001, Illinois; 2002, District of Columbia. *Education:* Massachusetts Institute of Technology (B.S., 1998; M.Eng., 1998); University of Chicago (J.D., with high honors, 2001). ***PRACTICE AREAS:*** Tax Law; Corporate Law. ***Email:*** rlight@kirkland.com

(This Listing Continued)

CHRISTOPHER R. LIRO, admitted to bar, 2001, Illinois. *Education:* Massachusetts Institute of Technology (S.B., 1990); University of Michigan Law School (J.D., 2000). ***PRACTICE AREAS:*** Intellectual Property. ***Email:*** cliro@kirkland.com

EVA LO, admitted to bar, 1998, New York; 2003, California; 2005, Illinois. *Education:* University of Pennsylvania (B.A., 1990); St. John's University School of Law (J.D., 1997). ***LANGUAGES:*** Mandarin Chinese. ***PRACTICE AREAS:*** Real Estate. ***Email:*** elo@kirkland.com

JEFFREY M. LOEB, admitted to bar, 2004, Illinois. *Education:* Dartmouth College (A.B., summa cum laude, 1999); Harvard Law School (J.D., cum laude, 2004). ***PRACTICE AREAS:*** Corporate Law. ***Email:*** jloeb@kirkland.com

MATTHEW S. LOVELL, admitted to bar, 2002, Illinois. *Education:* Wheaton College (B.A., magna cum laude, 1998); Harvard Law School (J.D., magna cum laude, 2002). ***PRACTICE AREAS:*** Intellectual Property; Transactional. ***Email:*** mlovell@kirkland.com

SAMANTHA M. MANN, admitted to bar, 2000, Illinois. *Education:* University of Illinois (B.A., 1997; J.D., 2000). ***PRACTICE AREAS:*** Corporate. ***Email:*** smann@kirkland.com

MICHAEL J. MANO, (admission pending). *Education:* St. Michael's College (B.A., 1999); Washington University (J.D., 2004). ***PRACTICE AREAS:*** Corporate Law. ***Email:*** mmano@kirkland.com

MICAH E. MARCUS, admitted to bar, 1999, Illinois. *Education:* University of Arizona (B.A., 1995); DePaul University (J.D., with honors, 1999). ***PRACTICE AREAS:*** Bankruptcy; Reorganization. ***Email:*** mmarcus@kirkland.com

ELISABETH M. MARTIN, admitted to bar, 2002, New York; 2003, Illinois. *Education:* Harvard University (A.B., 1996); Columbia University Law School (J.D., 2001). ***Email:*** emmartin@kirkland.com

RACHEL MASORY, admitted to bar, 2003, Illinois. *Education:* Northwestern University (B.S.J., Journalism and Economics, magna cum laude, 2000); Harvard Law School (J.D., 2003). ***PRACTICE AREAS:*** Corporate. ***Email:*** rmasory@kirkland.com

BRYCE A. MAUTNER, admitted to bar, 2005, Illinois. *Education:* University of Michigan (B.S.E., 2002); University of Illinois College of Law (J.D., magna cum laude, 2005). ***PRACTICE AREAS:*** Intellectual Property. ***Email:*** bmautner@kirkland.com

JAMES J. MAZZA, JR., admitted to bar, 2001, Illinois. *Education:* Vanderbilt University (B.A., cum laude, 1997); University of Illinois College of Law (J.D., magna cum laude, 2001). ***LANGUAGES:*** Spanish. ***PRACTICE AREAS:*** Bankruptcy. ***Email:*** jmazza@kirkland.com

JAMENDA A. McCOY, admitted to bar, 2003, Illinois. *Education:* University of Missouri, Columbia (B.A., 1998); Northwestern University (J.D., 2003). ***LANGUAGES:*** Spanish. ***PRACTICE AREAS:*** Litigation. ***Email:*** jmccoy@kirkland.com

RYAN J. McCRATE, admitted to bar, 2003, Illinois. *Education:* Case Western Reserve University (B.S., 1998); Yale University (J.D., 2003). ***PRACTICE AREAS:*** Real Estate. ***Email:*** rmccrate@kirkland.com

CLINTON S. McHUGH, (admission pending). *Education:* Duke University (B.A., 2002); University of Virginia (J.D., 2005). ***PRACTICE AREAS:*** Corporate Law. ***Email:*** cmchugh@kirkland.com

JAMES T. McLAUGHLIN, JR., admitted to bar, 2005, Illinois. *Education:* University of Florida (B.A., 2000); Northwestern University (J.D., cum laude, 2004). ***LANGUAGES:*** Spanish. ***Email:*** jmclaughlin@kirkland.com

ANDREW H. McWHIRTER, admitted to bar, 2000, Illinois; 2002, Michigan. *Education:* University of Pennsylvania (B.A., 1989); University of Southern California School of Cinema-Television (M.A., 1994); University of Michigan Law School (J.D., 2000). ***PRACTICE AREAS:*** Transactional; Real Estate. ***Email:*** amcwhirter@kirkland.com

MARIA A. MEGINNES, admitted to bar, 2004, Illinois. *Education:* University of Chicago (A.B., with honors, 2001); Harvard Law School (J.D., cum laude, 2004). ***PRACTICE AREAS:*** Litigation; Intellectual Property. ***Email:*** mmeginnes@kirkland.com

DREW MEYER, (admission pending). *Education:* Johns Hopkins University (B.A., 2000); Northwestern University (J.D., 2005). ***PRACTICE AREAS:*** Litigation. ***Email:*** dmeyer@kirkland.com

JAMIE L. MIGNON, admitted to bar, 2001, Illinois. *Education:* Northern Michigan University (B.S., 1997); DePaul University (J.D., 2001). ***PRACTICE AREAS:*** Corporate Law. ***Email:*** jmignon@kirkland.com

JEFFREY RICHARD MILLER, admitted to bar, 2002, Illinois. *Education:* University of Michigan (B.A., 1999); University of Chicago Law School (J.D., 2002). ***PRACTICE AREAS:*** Litigation. ***Email:*** jmiller@kirkland.com

DAVID P. MILLIGAN, (admission pending). *Education:* Florida Institute of Technology (B.S., 1988); University of Houston (M.B.A., 1990); University of Michigan (J.D., magna cum laude, 2005). ***PRACTICE AREAS:*** Corporate Law. ***Email:*** dmilligan@kirkland.com

CHRISTINA D. MITAKIS, admitted to bar, 2004, Illinois. *Education:* Northwestern University (B.A., 1998); Vanderbilt University (J.D., 2004). ***PRACTICE AREAS:*** Litigation. ***Email:*** cmitakis@kirkland.com

TOM MONAGAN, admitted to bar, 2002, Illinois. *Education:* Northwestern University (B.S.J., 1993); The Ohio State University (J.D., 2002). ***PRACTICE AREAS:*** Intellectual Property. ***Email:*** tmonagan@kirkland.com

DANIEL C. MOORE, admitted to bar, 2005, Illinois. *Education:* Princeton University (B.A., 1997); University of Minnesota (J.D., magna cum laude, 2005). ***PRACTICE AREAS:*** Intellectual Property; Litigation. ***Email:*** dmoore@kirkland.com

JONATHAN MOORE, admitted to bar, 2002, Illinois. *Education:* Wheaton College (B.A., 1997); University of Virginia (J.D., 2002). ***LANGUAGES:*** French. ***PRACTICE AREAS:*** Litigation. ***Email:*** jmoore@kirkland.com

(This Listing Continued)

THOMAS J. MOREL, admitted to bar, 2000, Illinois. *Education:* Yale University (B.A., 1990); University of Chicago (J.D., with honors, 2000). ***PRACTICE AREAS:*** Litigation. ***Email:*** tmorel@kirkland.com

KEVIN L. MORRIS, admitted to bar, 2002, Illinois. *Education:* Butler University (B.S., 1995; M.B.A., Finance, 1996); University of Chicago (J.D., 2002). ***PRACTICE AREAS:*** Corporate; Private Equity; Mergers and Acquisitions. ***Email:*** kmorris@kirkland.com

MICHELLE MULKERN, (admission pending). *Education:* Ohio Wesleyan University (B.A., 1999); The Ohio State University (J.D., 2002). ***PRACTICE AREAS:*** Corporate. ***Email:*** mmulkern@kirkland.com

JOHN M. MUNO, admitted to bar, 2004, Illinois. *Education:* University of Illinois (B.S., 1992; B.S., 1993); DePaul University (M.B.A., with distinction, 2000); Northwestern University (J.D., cum laude, 2004). ***PRACTICE AREAS:*** Corporate Law. ***Email:*** jmuno@kirkland.com

NADIA MURAD, (admission pending). *Education:* Northwestern University (B.A., magna cum laude, 2002); University of Michigan (J.D., cum laude, 2005). ***PRACTICE AREAS:*** Corporate Law. ***Email:*** nmurad@kirkland.com

MARISA MURILLO, admitted to bar, 2003, North Carolina; 2005, Illinois. *Education:* Yale University (B.A., 1998); University of Southern California Law School (J.D., 2002). ***LANGUAGES:*** Spanish. ***PRACTICE AREAS:*** Corporate; Financing; Secured Transactions. ***Email:*** mmurillo@kirkland.com

KAREN NELSON, admitted to bar, 2000, Illinois. *Education:* Cornell University (B.S., 1993); Northwestern University School of Law (J.D., 2000). ***PRACTICE AREAS:*** Intellectual Property. ***Email:*** knelson@kirkland.com

ERIK S. NEWTON, (admission pending). *Education:* Hillsdale College (B.A., 2002); Vanderbilt University (J.D., 2005). ***LANGUAGES:*** German. ***PRACTICE AREAS:*** Litigation.

ALEXANDER T. NGUYEN, admitted to bar, 2003, Illinois. *Education:* Harvard University (A.B., Social Sciences, magna cum laude, 1999); Yale University (J.D., 2003). ***PRACTICE AREAS:*** Litigation. ***Email:*** anguyen@kirkland.com

HOWARD S. NORBER, admitted to bar, 2001, New York (Not admitted in Illinois). *Education:* Michigan State University (B.A., cum laude, 1993); University of Chicago (J.D., cum laude, 2000). ***PRACTICE AREAS:*** Corporate Law. ***Email:*** hnorber@kirkland.com

KRISTA L. NUNEMAKER, admitted to bar, 2000, Illinois. *Education:* University of Michigan (B.B.A., 1997; J.D., 2000). ***PRACTICE AREAS:*** Intellectual Property. ***Email:*** knunemaker@kirkland.com

SVEN NYLEN, admitted to bar, 2002, Illinois. *Education:* Northwestern University (B.A., 1999); University of Illinois (J.D., magna cum laude, 2002). ***PRACTICE AREAS:*** Corporate Restructuring; Bankruptcy. ***Email:*** snylen@kirkland.com

LARRY J. OBHOF, admitted to bar, 2004, Illinois. *Education:* Ohio State University (B.A., summa cum laude, 2000); Yale University Law School (J.D., 2003). ***PRACTICE AREAS:*** Litigation; Antitrust; Competition. ***Email:*** lobhof@kirkland.com

SEAN P. O'BRIEN, admitted to bar, 1998, Indiana; 2000, Illinois. *Education:* University of Notre Dame (B.A., 1990); Indiana University School of Law - Indianapolis (J.D., summa cum laude, 1997). ***PRACTICE AREAS:*** Corporate; Financing; Secured Transactions. ***Email:*** sobrien@kirkland.com

REBECCA OLDROYD, (admission pending). *Education:* Brigham Young University (B.S., magna cum laude, 2001; J.D., cum laude, 2005). ***PRACTICE AREAS:*** Employee Benefits. ***Email:*** roldroyd@kirkland.com

JASON OSBORN, admitted to bar, 2003, New York; 2004, Illinois. *Education:* New York University (B.A., 1999); Univeristy of Michigan (J.D., cum laude, 2002). ***PRACTICE AREAS:*** Corporate. ***Email:*** josborn@kirkland.com

ERICK S. OTTOSON, admitted to bar, 1999, Minnesota; 2004, Illinois. *Education:* University of North Carolina at Chapel Hill (B.S., 1996); University of Minnesota Law School (J.D., magna cum laude, 1999). ***PRACTICE AREAS:*** Intellectual Property. ***Email:*** eottoson@kirkland.com

LUCY K. PARK, admitted to bar, 2000, Illinois. *Education:* Smith College (B.A., 1990); University of Chicago (M.A., 1994); Chicago-Kent College of Law, Illinois Institute of Technology (J.D., 2000). ***LANGUAGES:*** Korean. ***PRACTICE AREAS:*** Trusts and Estates. ***Email:*** lpark@kirkland.com

RACHEL L. PERNIC, admitted to bar, 2001, Illinois. *Education:* Indiana University (B.S., Chemistry, 1995); Northwestern University School of Law (J.D., 2001). ***PRACTICE AREAS:*** Intellectual Property. ***Email:*** rpernic@kirkland.com

RACHEL PERRIER, admitted to bar, 2000, Illinois. *Education:* Concordia College (B.A., magna cum laude, 1991); University of Chicago (J.D., with honors, 2000). ***PRACTICE AREAS:*** Litigation. ***Email:*** rperrier@kirkland.com

AMY R. PETERS, admitted to bar, 2002, Illinois. *Education:* Vanderbilt University (B.A., cum laude, 1999); University of Leeds, Leeds, England (1998); Georgetown University Law Center (J.D., 2002). ***PRACTICE AREAS:*** Corporate; Secured Lending. ***Email:*** apeters@kirkland.com

THEODORE A. PETO, admitted to bar, 2002, Illinois. *Education:* University of Illinois (B.S., 1997; J.D., 2002). ***Email:*** tpeto@kirkland.com

D. JOSEPH PIECH, admitted to bar, 2004, Illinois. *Education:* University of Michigan (B.S.E., summa cum laude, 2000); Harvard Law School (J.D., 2004); Oxford University, Oxford, England (B.C.L., 2005). ***PRACTICE AREAS:*** Litigation. ***Email:*** dpiech@kirkland.com

DEANNA N. PIHOS, (admission pending). *Education:* Northwestern University (B.S., cum laude, 2001); Cornell University Law School (J.D., magna cum laude, 2005). ***PRACTICE AREAS:*** Litigation. ***Email:*** dpihos@kirkland.com

(This Listing Continued)

KIRKLAND & ELLIS LLP, Chicago—Continued

CLARE M. PINKERT, admitted to bar, 2004, Illinois. *Education:* Dartmouth College (A.B., cum laude, 1997); University of Chicago (J.D., with honors, 2003). ***PRACTICE AREAS:*** Litigation. ***Email:*** cpinkert@kirkland.com

ELEFTHERIA TERRY PLATIS, admitted to bar, 2003, Illinois. *Education:* Northwestern University (B.A., History and Political Science, magna cum laude, 1999); New York University (J.D., 2003). ***LANGUAGES:*** Greek and Spanish. ***PRACTICE AREAS:*** Corporate. ***Email:*** tplatis@kirkland.com

KARIN WRAY PREUSSE, admitted to bar, 2004, Illinois. *Education:* University of Illinois at Urbana-Champaign (B.S., with honors, 1999); University of Chicago Law School (J.D., 2004). ***PRACTICE AREAS:*** Intellectual Property. ***Email:*** kpreusse@kirkland.com

WILLIAM T. PRUITT, (admission pending). *Education:* Michigan State University (B.A., with high honors, 2001); Vanderbilt University Law School (J.D., 2004). ***PRACTICE AREAS:*** Litigation. ***Email:*** wpruitt@kirkland.com

TRAVIS QUICK, admitted to bar, 2003, Illinois. *Education:* Illinois State University (B.A., summa cum laude, 2000); University of Illinois (J.D., magna cum laude, 2003). ***LANGUAGES:*** Spanish. ***PRACTICE AREAS:*** Litigation. ***Email:*** tquick@kirkland.com

JOSHUA Z. RABINOVITZ, admitted to bar, 2000, Illinois. *Education:* Northwestern University (B.A., History, cum laude, 1997); University of Chicago Law School (J.D., 2000). ***PRACTICE AREAS:*** Litigation. ***Email:*** jrabinovitz@kirkland.com

RICHARD S. RADNAY, admitted to bar, 2000, Illinois. *Education:* Cornell University (B.S., 1994); Northwestern University (J.D., 2000). ***PRACTICE AREAS:*** Corporate. ***Email:*** rradnay@kirkland.com

SARA K. RANKIN, admitted to bar, 2000, Illinois. *Education:* University of Oregon (B.A., magna cum laude, 1992); Harvard University (M.Ed., 1994); New York University (J.D., 2000). ***PRACTICE AREAS:*** Litigation. ***Email:*** srankin@kirkland.com

RAMYA RAVINDRAN, admitted to bar, 2004, Illinois. *Education:* Rice University (B.S., magna cum laude, 2001); Harvard Law School (J.D., magna cum laude, 2004). ***PRACTICE AREAS:*** Intellectual Property. ***Email:*** rravindran@kirkland.com

JOHN W. REALE, admitted to bar, 2002, Massachusetts; 2004, Illinois. *Education:* Saint Anselm College (B.A., 1995); University of Massachusetts (B.A., cum laude, 1999); Indiana University School of Law (J.D., magna cum laude, 2002). ***PRACTICE AREAS:*** Litigation; Commercial Litigation; Commercial Arbitration; Securities; Shareholder Litigation. ***Email:*** jreale@kirkland.com

NEAL J. REENAN, admitted to bar, 2003, Illinois. *Education:* Harvard University (A.B., Government, cum laude, 1993); Northeastern University (M.B.A., M.S., Accounting, 1994); University of Michigan Law School (J.D., magna cum laude, 2003). ***PRACTICE AREAS:*** Transactional. ***Email:*** nreenan@kirkland.com

JENNIFER M. RHODES, admitted to bar, 2004, Illinois. *Education:* University of Illinois (B.S., cum laude, 1997; A.M., 2000); University of Chicago (J.D., 2003). ***LANGUAGES:*** Spanish. ***PRACTICE AREAS:*** Litigation. ***Email:*** jrhodes@kirkland.com

ROGER D. RHOTEN, (admission pending). *Education:* Indiana University (B.S., 1996); Harvard Law School (J.D., 2002). ***Email:*** rrhoten@kirkland.com

JILLIAN RICE, admitted to bar, 2003, Illinois. *Education:* University of Illinois at Urbana-Champaign (B.A., Political Science and History, with highest distinction, 2000); Northwestern University School of Law (J.D., 2003). ***PRACTICE AREAS:*** Tax and Planning. ***Email:*** jrice@kirkland.com

MATTHEW RICHARDS, admitted to bar, 2000, Illinois. *Education:* Johns Hopkins University (B.A., 1995); Columbia University (M.A., 1998); University of Chicago (J.D., 2000). ***PRACTICE AREAS:*** Corporate Law. ***Email:*** mrichards@kirkland.com

ANN MARIE T. RIZZO, admitted to bar, 2001, Illinois. *Education:* DePaul University (B.S., 1997; J.D., 2001). ***PRACTICE AREAS:*** Intellectual Property. ***Email:*** arizzo@kirkland.com

SARA A. ROBINSON, admitted to bar, 2000, Illinois; 2001, District of Columbia. *Education:* University of Notre Dame (B.A., Philosophy, summa cum laude, Phi Beta Kappa, 1997); University of Chicago (J.D., 2000). ***PRACTICE AREAS:*** Corporate; Fund Formation; Investment Management. ***Email:*** srobinson@kirkland.com

DAVID ROKACH, admitted to bar, 2003, Illinois. *Education:* Brisk Rabbinical College (B.H.L., Talmud, 1999); University of Chicago Law School (J.D., with honors, Order of the Coif, 2003). ***PRACTICE AREAS:*** Intellectual Property. ***Email:*** drokach@kirkland.com

C.W. ROSS, admitted to bar, 2004, Illinois. *Education:* Brigham Young University (B.A., cum laude, 2001); Harvard Law School (J.D., cum laude, 2004). ***LANGUAGES:*** Spanish. ***PRACTICE AREAS:*** Corporate Law. ***Email:*** cwross@kirkland.com

EDWARD K. RUNYAN, admitted to bar, 2000, Illinois; registered to practice before U.S. Patent and Trademark Office. *Education:* Purdue University (B.S., 1982); DePaul University (J.D., 2000). ***PRACTICE AREAS:*** Patent Law; Intellectual Property. ***Email:*** erunyan@kirkland.com

JOSEPH MICHAEL RUSSELL, admitted to bar, 2003, Illinois. *Education:* Georgetown University (B.A., English, magna cum laude, 1993); Trinity College, Dublin (M. Phil., Anglo-Irish Literature, 1996); University of Wisconsin-Madison (M.A., English Literature, 1997); Northwestern University (J.D., 2003). ***PRACTICE AREAS:*** Litigation. ***Email:*** jrussell@kirkland.com

ANGELA ROHMAN RUSSO, (admission pending). *Education:* Dartmouth College (B.S., magna cum laude, 2001); University of Chicago (J.D., 2005). ***PRACTICE AREAS:*** Taxation. ***Email:*** arusso@kirkland.com

(This Listing Continued)

BRYAN C. RUTSCH, admitted to bar, 2005, Illinois and Wisconsin; registered to practice before U.S. Patent and Trademark Office. *Education:* University of Wisconsin (B.S., 1999; J.D., cum laude, 2005). ***PRACTICE AREAS:*** Patent Infringement; Biotechnology; Pharmaceutical Patents; Life Sciences. ***Email:*** brutsch@kirkland.com

COLLEEN RYAN, admitted to bar, 2003, Illinois. *Education:* University of Wisconsin (B.A., 1996); Northwestern University (J.D., 2003). ***PRACTICE AREAS:*** Corporate. ***Email:*** cryan@kirkland.com

PETER J. RYAN, admitted to bar, 2004, Illinois. *Education:* University of Notre Dame (B.A., 2001); Washington University (J.D., 2004). ***PRACTICE AREAS:*** Employee Benefits. ***Email:*** pryan@kirkland.com

TANA M. RYAN, admitted to bar, 2003, Illinois. *Education:* University of California, Los Angeles (B.A., Business Economics and History, cum laude, 2000); University of Chicago Law School (J.D., 2003). ***PRACTICE AREAS:*** Transactional. ***Email:*** tryan@kirkland.com

NABIL SABKI, admitted to bar, 1999, Illinois. *Education:* University of Michigan (B.A., 1996); University of Minnesota Law School (J.D., 1999). ***LANGUAGES:*** Arabic. ***PRACTICE AREAS:*** Investment Management; Corporate; Securities. ***Email:*** nsabki@kirkland.com

SARA B. SAGER, (admission pending). *Education:* University of Iowa (B.A., 2002; J.D., 2005). ***PRACTICE AREAS:*** Corporate Law. ***Email:*** ssager@kirkland.com

KATHRYN B. SANDERSON, admitted to bar, 2004, Illinois. *Education:* Northwestern University (B.A., cum laude, 2001); University of Virginia Law School (J.D., 2004). ***PRACTICE AREAS:*** Litigation; Intellectual Property; Patent Infringement Litigation. ***Email:*** ksanderson@kirkland.com

NARIA K. SANTA LUCIA, (admission pending). *Education:* University of Chicago (A.B., 2002; J.D., 2005). ***LANGUAGES:*** Korean. ***PRACTICE AREAS:*** Litigation. ***Email:*** nsantalucia@kirkland.com

AMANDA COCHRAN SARAFA, admitted to bar, 2002, Illinois. *Education:* University of Michigan (B.B.A., Accounting and Finance, with highest distinction, 1997); Northwestern University School of Law (J.D., cum laude, 2002). ***PRACTICE AREAS:*** Corporate; Capital Markets; Venture Capital; Private Equity; Mergers and Acquisitions; Initial Public Offerings. ***Email:*** asarafa@kirkland.com

GEORGE D. SAX, admitted to bar, 2003, Illinois. *Education:* Northwestern University (B.S.J., 2000); Stanford University (J.D., 2003). ***PRACTICE AREAS:*** Litigation. ***Email:*** gsax@kirkland.com

RENEE M. SCHREIBER, admitted to bar, 2002, Illinois. *Education:* Loyola University, Chicago (B.A., magna cum laude, 1998); Northwestern University School of Law (J.D., 2002). ***PRACTICE AREAS:*** Transactional. ***Email:*** rschreiber@kirkland.com

JUSTIN K. SCHWARTZ, admitted to bar, 1999, Illinois. *Education:* Princeton University (A.B., cum laude, 1979); Cambridge University, Cambridge, England (M.Phil., 1982); University of Michigan (Ph.D., 1989); Ohio State University (J.D., summa cum laude, 1998). ***PRACTICE AREAS:*** Litigation. ***Email:*** jschwartz@kirkland.com

KAREN SCHWEICKART, (admission pending). *Education:* University of California, Berkeley (B.A., History, 1995); University of Chicago Law School (J.D., with honors, 2003). ***PRACTICE AREAS:*** Intellectual Property. ***Email:*** kschweickart@kirkland.com

NICHOLAS JOSEPH SECCO, admitted to bar, 2001, Illinois. *Education:* Louisiana State University (B.A., Philosophy and Film, 1998); Northwestern University (J.D., cum laude, 2001). ***PRACTICE AREAS:*** Litigation. ***Email:*** nsecco@kirkland.com

KYLE P. SEELBACH, admitted to bar, 2004, Illinois. *Education:* University of Illinois at Urbana-Champaign (B.A., cum laude, 2001; J.D., summa cum laude, 2004). ***PRACTICE AREAS:*** Litigation. ***Email:*** kseelbach@kirkland.com

KAL K. SHAH, admitted to bar, 2001, Illinois; registered to practice before U.S. Patent and Trademark Office. *Education:* University of Illinois (B.S., Bioengineering, 1995); Loyola University (J.D., cum laude, 2001). ***LANGUAGES:*** Hindi and Gujurati. ***PRACTICE AREAS:*** Intellectual Property; Patent Litigation. ***Email:*** kshah@kirkland.com

PALAK V. SHAH, admitted to bar, 2002, Illinois. *Education:* Cornell University (B.S., 1999); University of Chicago (J.D., 2002). ***PRACTICE AREAS:*** Intellectual Property. ***Email:*** pshah@kirkland.com

CHRISTOPHER T. SHANNON, admitted to bar, 2001, Illinois. *Education:* Salve Regina University (B.S., 1995); University of Chicago Law School (J.D., 2001). ***Email:*** cshannon@kirkland.com

JESSE SHELEY, admitted to bar, 2003, Illinois. *Education:* Indiana University (B.A., Political Science, with high distinction, 1999); Indiana University School of Public and Environmental Affairs (M.P.A., International Affairs, 2003); Indiana University School of Law (J.D., cum laude, 2003). ***LANGUAGES:*** Chinese. ***PRACTICE AREAS:*** Corporate. ***Email:*** jsheley@kirkland.com

YAMAN SHUKAIRY, (admission pending). *Education:* University of Michigan (B.B.A., 2000; J.D., magna cum laude, 2005). ***LANGUAGES:*** Arabic. ***PRACTICE AREAS:*** Corporate Law. ***Email:*** yshukairy@kirkland.com

JESSICA HELENA SICSU, admitted to bar, 1996, Venezuela; 2002, Illinois. *Education:* Universidad Catolica Andres Bello (Attorney, cum laude, 1996); University of Illinois, Urbana-Champaign (LL.M., 1998; J.D., 2002). ***LANGUAGES:*** Spanish and French. ***PRACTICE AREAS:*** Corporate; Mergers and Acquisitions. ***Email:*** jsicsu@kirkland.com

BRANDON B. SMITH, (admission pending). *Education:* Hiram College (B.A., magna cum laude, 2002); Cornell University Law School (J.D., magna cum laude, 2005). ***PRACTICE AREAS:*** Corporate Law. ***Email:*** smithb@kirkland.com

LESLEY GAYLE SMITH, (admission pending). *Education:* Washington University (B.S., 1998); Ohio State University College of Law (J.D., summa cum laude, 2004). ***PRACTICE AREAS:*** Intellectual Property. ***Email:*** lgsmith@kirkland.com

(This Listing Continued)

ROBERT D. SNOW, JR., admitted to bar, 2001, Illinois. *Education:* Western Illinois University (B.A., 1984); The John Marshall Law School (J.D., 2001). ***PRACTICE AREAS:*** Litigation. ***Email:*** rsnow@kirkland.com

JOHN SOAVE, III, admitted to bar, 2001, Illinois. *Education:* University of Michigan (B.S.E., 1998; J.D., magna cum laude, 2001). ***PRACTICE AREAS:*** Tax. ***Email:*** jsoave@kirkland.com

AARON D. SPIRA, admitted to bar, 2004, Illinois. *Education:* Earlham College (B.A., PAGS, 1996); Northwestern University (J.D., 2004). ***PRACTICE AREAS:*** Litigation. ***Email:*** aspira@kirkland.com

LINNEA C. STACK, admitted to bar, 2003, Illinois. *Education:* University of Michigan (B.A., 1998); Chicago-Kent College of Law (J.D., 2003). ***PRACTICE AREAS:*** Transactional. ***Email:*** lstack@kirkland.com

MATT T. STAMPS, (admission pending). *Education:* Indiana University (B.A., with distinction, 2001); University of Chicago Law School (J.D., 2004). ***PRACTICE AREAS:*** Litigation. ***Email:*** mstamps@kirkland.com

BENJAMIN D. STANLEY, admitted to bar, 2003, Illinois. *Education:* Brigham Young University (B.S., Psychology and Philosophy, minor in Symbolic Logic, 2000; J.D., magna cum laude, 2003). ***PRACTICE AREAS:*** Environmental; Intellectual Property; Litigation. ***Email:*** bstanley@kirkland.com

NYIKA O. STRICKLAND, admitted to bar, 2001, Illinois. *Education:* Massachusetts Institute of Technology (B.S., Electrical Engineering, 1998); Northwestern University (J.D., 2001). ***PRACTICE AREAS:*** Intellectual Property; Internet Law; E-Commerce; Patent Infringement Litigation. ***Email:*** nstrickland@kirkland.com

DAVID E. SUCHAR, admitted to bar, 2002, Illinois. *Education:* DePaul University (B.A., high honors, 1998); Georgetown University Law Center (J.D., cum laude, 2002). ***PRACTICE AREAS:*** Litigation; White Collar Criminal Defense; Trademark and Copyright Litigation; Commercial Litigation; Securities and Shareholder Litigation. ***Email:*** dsuchar@kirkland.com

SCOTT D. SUGINO, admitted to bar, 2003, Illinois. *Education:* Harvard University (A.B., cum laude, 1996); Hitotsubashi University (M.A., 2001); University of Chicago Law School (J.D., with honors, 2003). ***LANGUAGES:*** Japanese. ***PRACTICE AREAS:*** Tax; European Law; Pacific Rim Law. ***Email:*** ssugino@kirkland.com

MICHAEL E. SULLIVAN, admitted to bar, 1999, Illinois. *Education:* University of Wisconsin - Madison (B.A., 1992); Northwestern University (J.D., 1999). ***PRACTICE AREAS:*** Corporate Law. ***Email:*** msullivan@kirkland.com

DEANNA R. SWITS, (admission pending). *Education:* University of Notre Dame (B.A., magna cum laude, 2002); Vanderbilt University (J.D., 2005). ***PRACTICE AREAS:*** Intellectual Property. ***Email:*** dswits@kirkland.com

AREK SYCZ, admitted to bar, 2003, Illinois. *Education:* Warsaw University (B.A., 2000; M.A., 2000); Northwestern University (J.D., 2003). ***PRACTICE AREAS:*** Corporate. ***Email:*** asycz@kirkland.com

WENDY L. TAMBLYN, admitted to bar, 1999, Illinois. *Education:* Cornell College (B.A., 1995); Loyola University Chicago School of Law (J.D., 1999). ***PRACTICE AREAS:*** Real Estate. ***Email:*** wtamblyn@kirkland.com

JOHN E. TANGREN, admitted to bar, 2003, Illinois. *Education:* University of Chicago (B.A., 2000; J.D., with honors, 2003). ***PRACTICE AREAS:*** Litigation. ***Email:*** jtangren@kirkland.com

BERNARD TAYLOR, admitted to bar, 2002, Illinois. *Education:* Harvard University (B.A., 1992); University of Michigan (J.D., 2002). ***PRACTICE AREAS:*** Litigation. ***Email:*** btaylor@kirkland.com

KATHRYN F. TAYLOR, admitted to bar, 2001, Illinois. *Education:* Westminster College (B.A., 1995); Washington University (J.D., 2001). ***PRACTICE AREAS:*** Commercial Litigation. ***Email:*** kftaylor@kirkland.com

JOHN C. THURMOND, admitted to bar, 2002, Illinois. *Education:* University of Notre Dame (B.A., 1994); University of Notre Dame Law School (J.D., 2002). ***PRACTICE AREAS:*** Real Estate. ***Email:*** jthurmond@kirkland.com

STEVEN M. TOTH, (admission pending). *Education:* The Ohio State University (B.S., 1998; B.S. Ch.E., 1999; J.D., 2005). ***PRACTICE AREAS:*** Corporate Law. ***Email:*** stoth@kirkland.com

DANIEL M. TREVINO, admitted to bar, 2002, Illinois. *Education:* Northern Illinois University (B.S., 1994); University of Illinois College of Law (J.D., magna cum laude, 2002). ***PRACTICE AREAS:*** Real Estate. ***Email:*** dtrevino@kirkland.com

KEVIN S. UELAND, admitted to bar, 2002, Illinois. *Education:* Miami University (B.A., English Lit., 1999); DePaul University College of Law (J.D., 2002). ***PRACTICE AREAS:*** Litigation; Antitrust; Competition. ***Email:*** kueland@kirkland.com

KARLA P. VALENTI, (admission pending). *Education:* University of Notre Dame (B.A., magna cum laude, 1997); Columbia University (J.D., 2005). Harlan Fiske Stone Scholar. ***LANGUAGES:*** Spanish. ***PRACTICE AREAS:*** Corporate Law. ***Email:*** kvalenti@kirkland.com

MARK VARBONCOUER, admitted to bar, 2000, Illinois. *Education:* University of Illinois, Urbana-Champaign (B.S., 1988; J.D., 2000). ***PRACTICE AREAS:*** Intellectual Property. ***Email:*** mvarboncouer@kirkland.com

LYDIA E. WAHLKE, (admission pending). *Education:* University of Southern California (B.S., magna cum laude, 1999; J.D., 2005). ***PRACTICE AREAS:*** Litigation; Intellectual Property. ***Email:*** lwahlke@kirkland.com

REBECCA D. WALKER, admitted to bar, 2003, New Mexico; 2005, Illinois; registered to practice before U.S. Patent and Trademark Office, 2003. *Education:* University of Illinois at Urbana-Champaign (B.S., 1999; M.S., 2000); Pepperdine University School of Law (J.D., cum laude, 2003). ***PRACTICE AREAS:*** Patent Infringement Litigation; Biotechnology; Pharmaceuticals; Life Sciences. ***Email:*** rwalker@kirkland.com

(This Listing Continued)

MIN WANG, (admission pending). *Education:* California Institute of Technology (Ph.D., 2000); University of Illinois (J.D., 2003). ***LANGUAGES:*** Chinese. ***Email:*** mwang@kirkland.com

YONG WANG, (admission pending). *Education:* Peking University (B.A., 1997; LL.B., 1998); Columbia University (J.D., 2003). ***LANGUAGES:*** Chinese, German, French. ***PRACTICE AREAS:*** Mergers and Acquisitions; Private Equity; Venture Capital; Leveraged Buyouts; Capital Markets; Asset Securitization. ***Email:*** ywang@kirkland.com

NOAH F. WEBSTER, admitted to bar, 2004, Illinois and American Samoa; U.S. District Court, Eastern District of Michigan and U.S. Court of Appeals, Sixth Circuit. *Education:* United States Military Academy (B.S., 1995); University of Illinois (J.D., magna cum laude, 2003). ***PRACTICE AREAS:*** Intellectual Property. ***Email:*** nwebster@kirkland.com

SUSAN L. WELSH, admitted to bar, 2001, Illinois. *Education:* University of Michigan (B.A., Political Science, with distinction, 1995); University of Illinois College of Law (J.D., magna cum laude, 2001). ***PRACTICE AREAS:*** Corporate; Financing and Secured Transactions. ***Email:*** swelsh@kirkland.com

PAUL WIERBICKI, (admission pending). *Education:* Vanderbilt University (B.A., 2002); New York University (J.D., 2005; Advance Certificate in Business, 2005). ***PRACTICE AREAS:*** Loan Restructuring. ***Email:*** pwierbicki@kirkland.com

CHARLA ANN WILLIAN, admitted to bar, 2004, Illinois. *Education:* Miami University (B.S., summa cum laude, 2001); Indiana University School of Law - Bloomington (J.D., magna cum laude, 2004). ***PRACTICE AREAS:*** Corporate Law. ***Email:*** cwillian@kirkland.com

RAYMOND C. WOODRING, (admission pending). *Education:* University of Chicago (B.A., 1999); Yale University Law School (J.D., 2004). ***LANGUAGES:*** French. ***PRACTICE AREAS:*** Intellectual Property. ***Email:*** rwoodring@kirkland.com

JOHN R. WORTH, (admission pending). *Education:* Wabash College (B.A., magna cum laude, 1997); University of Chicago, The Divinity School (M.A., 2001); Indiana University School of Law (J.D., magna cum laude, 2004). ***PRACTICE AREAS:*** Litigation. ***Email:*** jworth@kirkland.com

GUOHUA WU, admitted to bar, 1995, China; 2002, New York (Not admitted in Illinois). *Education:* Ji Lin University, China (B.A., 1992); Cornell University (J.D., 2001). ***LANGUAGES:*** Mandarin Chinese. ***PRACTICE AREAS:*** Corporate Finance; Private Equity; Securitization; Joint Ventures. ***Email:*** awu@kirkland.com

QI (ALEXANDER) YANG, admitted to bar, 2004, Ohio (Not admitted in Illinois). *Education:* Beijing University Law School (LL.B., 2000); University of Minnesota Law School (J.D., cum laude, 2003). ***LANGUAGES:*** Mandarin Chinese (Native), English. ***PRACTICE AREAS:*** Corporate Finance; Venture Capital; Private Equity; Mergers and Acquisitions; Fund Formation; Capital Markets; Initial Public Offerings; Investement Management. ***Email:*** qyang@kirkland.com

SETH R. YOHALEM, admitted to bar, 2004, Illinois. *Education:* Amherst College (B.A., magna cum laude, 2001); Columbia University (J.D., 2004). Harlan Fiske Stone Scholar. ***PRACTICE AREAS:*** Litigation. ***Email:*** syohalem@kirkland.com

THOMAS H. YOUNG, admitted to bar, 2003, Illinois. *Education:* Kenyon College (B.A., cum laude, History, 1999); University of Michigan (J.D., cum laude, 2002). ***Email:*** tyoung@kirkland.com

JEFFREY J. ZEIGER, admitted to bar, 2001, Illinois. *Education:* Washington & Lee University (B.A., 1996); University of Michigan School of Law (J.D., 2001). ***PRACTICE AREAS:*** Litigation. ***Email:*** jzeiger@kirkland.com

SCOTT R. ZEMNICK, admitted to bar, 2001, Illinois. *Education:* University of Michigan (B.A., 1998); Chicago-Kent College of Law (J.D., 2001). ***PRACTICE AREAS:*** Bankruptcy. ***Email:*** szemnick@kirkland.com

CHRISTOPHER A. ZIEBARTH, admitted to bar, 2000, Illinois. *Education:* Middlebury College (B.A., 1994); Duke University (J.D., 2000). ***PRACTICE AREAS:*** Corporate Law. ***Email:*** cziebarth@kirkland.com

MEREDITH ZINANNI, admitted to bar, 2003, Illinois. *Education:* Washington University (B.A., Physics, with honors, 2000); Duke University (J.D., 2003). ***PRACTICE AREAS:*** Intellectual Property. ***Email:*** mzinanni@kirkland.com

ERICA B. ZOLNER, admitted to bar, 2002, Illinois. *Education:* Oklahoma State University (B.A., 1998); Northwestern University (J.D., 2002). ***PRACTICE AREAS:*** Litigation. ***Email:*** ezolner@kirkland.com

OF COUNSEL

JAMES M. AMEND, (P.C.), admitted to bar, 1968, Illinois; registered to practice before U.S. Patent and Trademark Office. *Education:* University of Michigan (B.S.E., 1964; J.D., 1967). ***PRACTICE AREAS:*** Intellectual Property Law; Counseling; Commercial Litigation. ***Email:*** jamend@kirkland.com

KRISTINE L. ANDERSON, admitted to bar, 1991, Illinois. *Education:* Oral Roberts University (B.A., 1981); ITT-Chicago Kent College of Law (J.D., 1991). ***PRACTICE AREAS:*** Commercial Litigation. ***Email:*** kanderson@kirkland.com

DEBRA BEINSTEIN, admitted to bar, 1991, Illinois. *Education:* University of Michigan (B.A., 1988); University of Chicago (J.D., 1991). ***PRACTICE AREAS:*** Litigation. ***Email:*** dbeinstein@kirkland.com

HOLDEN BIXLER, admitted to bar, 2002, Illinois. *Education:* University of Illinois (B.A., 1998); Indiana University School of Law - Bloomington (J.D., 2001). ***PRACTICE AREAS:*** Financial Restructuring. ***Email:*** hbixler@kirkland.com

ERICA BEUTLER, admitted to bar, 2000, Illinois. *Education:* Yale University (B.A., 1993); Northwestern School of Law (J.D., 1999). ***PRACTICE AREAS:*** Litigation. ***Email:*** ebeutler@kirkland.com

(This Listing Continued)

KIRKLAND & ELLIS LLP, Chicago—Continued

LAUREN HENNESSEY BREIT, admitted to bar, 2000, Illinois; registered to practice before U.S. Patent and Trademark Office. *Education:* Cornell University (B.A., 1995); Northwestern University (J.D., 2000). ***PRACTICE AREAS:*** Intellectual Property; Patent Litigation. ***Email:*** lbreit@kirkland.com

HOLLY W. BULL, admitted to bar, 1997, Illinois and New York (inactive). *Education:* University of Delaware (B.S., Economics and English, with high honors, 1987); University of Iowa College of Law (J.D., with honors, 1996). ***PRACTICE AREAS:*** Restructuring; Insolvency; Workouts; Bankruptcy. ***Email:*** hbull@kirkland.com

JENNIFER CLARKE-SMITH, admitted to bar, 2003, Illinois. *Education:* Purdue University (B.A., 1996); Catholic University of America (J.D., cum laude, 2003). ***PRACTICE AREAS:*** Antitrust; Competition. ***Email:*** jclarkesmith@kirkland.com

REBECCA O'NEAL FRUCHTMAN, admitted to bar, 1987, California; 1990, District of Columbia; 2000, Illinois. *Education:* Georgetown University (B.S.F.S., 1982); University of Texas (M.A.I.S., summa cum laude, 1984); Georgetown University Law Center (J.D., 1987). ***PRACTICE AREAS:*** Bankruptcy, Reorganization and Workouts. ***Email:*** rfruchtman@kirkland.com

FRANCIS J. GERLITS, (P.C.), admitted to bar, 1958, Illinois. *Education:* University of Notre Dame (Ph.B., 1953); University of Chicago (J.D., 1958). ***PRACTICE AREAS:*** Corporate; Commercial Litigation. ***Email:*** fgerlits@kirkland.com

EMILE KARAFIOL, admitted to bar, 1979, Illinois. *Education:* Princeton University (A.B., 1956); Cornell University (Ph.D., 1965); University of Chicago (J.D., 1979). ***LANGUAGES:*** German, French, Polish. ***PRACTICE AREAS:*** Private Equity; Fund Formation; Venture Capital Investments; Leveraged Acquisitions; Mergers and Acquisitions; Government Regulations. ***Email:*** ekarafiol@kirkland.com

JOHN E. KIRKPATRICK, (P.C.), admitted to bar, 1955, Ohio; 1962, Illinois. *Education:* Amherst College (A.B., 1951); Harvard Law School (J.D., 1954). ***PRACTICE AREAS:*** Corporate; Tax; Estate Planning; Trusts and Estates. ***Email:*** jkirkpatrick@kirkland.com

LORI A. LENARD, admitted to bar, 1992, Illinois. *Education:* Western Illinois University (B.A., 1988); Chicago-Kent College of Law, Illinois Institute of Technology (J.D., with honors, 1992). ***PRACTICE AREAS:*** Employee Benefits; ERISA; Executive Compensation. ***Email:*** llenard@kirkland.com

KEVIN M. McKENNA, admitted to bar, 1990, Massachusetts; 2002, Colorado; 2004, Illinois. *Education:* University of Notre Dame (B.A., Anthropology, magna cum laude, 1986); University of Michigan Law School (J.D., cum laude, 1989). ***LANGUAGES:*** French. ***PRACTICE AREAS:*** Real Estate; Financing and Secured Transactions. ***Email:*** kmckenna@kirkland.com

CHERYL L. MEIER, admitted to bar, 1996, Illinois. *Education:* University of Illinois (B.S., summa cum laude, 1989); Illinois State University (M.B.A., summa cum laude, 1994); University of Illinois (J.D., summa cum laude, 1996). ***PRACTICE AREAS:*** Intellectual Property Transactions; Technology Transfers; Computer Law; Internet Law. ***Email:*** cmeier@kirkland.com

KELLY A. SCHELL, admitted to bar, 1995, Illinois. *Education:* DePaul University (B.S., 1990); John Marshall Law School (J.D., 1995). ***PRACTICE AREAS:*** Corporate. ***Email:*** kschell@kirkland.com

JOSEPH U. SCHORER, admitted to bar, 1978, California; 1981, Illinois. *Education:* Northwestern University (B.A., with highest distinction, 1975); Harvard Law School (J.D., cum laude, 1978). ***PRACTICE AREAS:*** Corporate Law; Employment Law; Securities; Consumer Finance; Corporate Finance; Mergers and Acquisitions. ***Email:*** jschorer@kirkland.com

RACHEL REAGLER SCHULMAN, admitted to bar, 1989, Illinois. *Education:* Indiana University (B.S., 1986); University of Illinois (J.D., 1989). ***PRACTICE AREAS:*** Bankruptcy. ***Email:*** rschulman@kirkland.com

WILLIAM S. SINGER, admitted to bar, 1965, Illinois. *Education:* Brandeis University (B.A., 1962); Columbia University (LL.B., 1965). ***PRACTICE AREAS:*** Corporate; Legislative. ***Email:*** wsinger@kirkland.com

STEPHANIE STERN, admitted to bar, 2001, District of Columbia; 2003, Illinois. *Education:* Brown University (B.A., 1996); Yale University Law School (J.D., 1999). ***PRACTICE AREAS:*** Litigation; Environmental. ***Email:*** sstern@kirkland.com

JEFFREY W. STEVENSON, admitted to bar, 1989, Illinois. *Education:* Drake University (B.S., 1980); IIT/Chicago Kent College of Law (J.D., 1989). ***PRACTICE AREAS:*** ERISA. ***Email:*** jstevenson@kirkland.com

KRISTAL S. STIPPICH, admitted to bar, 1998, Illinois; 2000, District of Columbia. *Education:* Wheaton College (B.A., 1991; M.A., 1992); University of Chicago Law School (J.D., 1998). ***PRACTICE AREAS:*** Litigation. ***Email:*** kstippich@kirkland.com

ROGER L. TAYLOR, admitted to bar, 1971, Illinois. *Education:* Knox College (B.A., 1963); Northwestern University (J.D., 1971). ***PRACTICE AREAS:*** Labor and Employment; Litigation. ***Email:*** rtaylor@kirkland.com

P. RENÉE WICKLUND, admitted to bar, 1998, California; 1999, Illinois. *Education:* Syracuse University (B.A., summa cum laude, 1994); University of Chicago (A.M., 1995); Yale University (J.D., 1998). ***LANGUAGES:*** German. ***PRACTICE AREAS:*** Labor and Employment; Litigation; Commercial Litigation and Arbitration; ERISA Litigation. ***Email:*** rwicklund@kirkland.com

VISITING ATTORNEYS

CHRISTIANE ALBRECHT, admitted to bar, 2004, Germany (Not admitted in the United States). *Education:* University for Public Management of the Federation, Germany (Diploma in Public Management, 1995); University of Potsdam School of Law, Potsdam, Germany (First State Board Examination of the State of Brandenburg, 2001); Court of Appeals of the State of Brandenburg, Germany (Second State Board Examination of the State of Brandenburg, 2003); Northwestern University (LL.M., 2005). ***LANGUAGES:*** German. ***PRACTICE AREAS:*** Corporate Law.

OSCAR STEPHENS C., admitted to bar, 2002, Chile (Not admitted in the United States). *Education:* Pontificia Universidad Católica de Chile, Escuela de Derecho, Santiago, Chile (LL.B., 2001); Northwestern University (LL.M., 2005). ***LANGUAGES:*** Spanish. ***Email:*** ostephens@kirkland.com

(For Biographical Data on Washington, D.C., New York, N.Y., Los Angeles, California and London, England, see Professional Biographies at those points respectively)

KLEIN DUB & HOLLEB, LTD.

303 WEST MADISON STREET, 23RD FLOOR
CHICAGO, ILLINOIS 60606-3308
Telephone: 312-464-9400
Email: info@labor-law.com
URL: http://www.labor-law.com

Lake County Office: 660 La Salle Place, Suite 100, Highland Park, Illinois, 60035. Telephone: 847-681-9100. Fax: 847-681-1600.

Private and Public Sector Labor Law, Employment Law, Employment Discrimination and Affirmative Action. Litigation in State and Federal Courts and before Administrative Agencies in all listed practice areas.

FIRM PROFILE: Klein Dub & Holleb, Ltd. offers full-service, prevention-focused labor and employment law counseling for management clients located throughout the United States. Our experience enables us to emphasize early case evaluation and the delivery of cost-effective representation. When defending employers before administrative agencies or in court, we are pro-active and forceful, consistent with the client's business philosophy. We approach all matters with thorough preparation, diligent follow-through, creativity and unparalleled personal service.

ROBERT M. KLEIN, born Chicago, Illinois, March 21, 1957; admitted to bar, 1982, Wisconsin, Illinois, U.S. District Court, Western District of Wisconsin, U.S. District Court, Northern District of Illinois, U.S. Court of Appeals, Seventh Circuit and U.S. Supreme Court. *Education:* University of Wisconsin (B.B.A., 1979; J.D., 1982). Recipient, American Jurisprudence Award, Excellence in Labor Relations Law. Commissioner, Illinois Supreme Court Disciplinary Commission, 1986-1994; Chairman, Inquiry Panels, 1989-1992; Hearing Board, 1992-1994. Member, International Foundation of Employee Benefit Plans, 1989-1994. Member, Japanese Chamber of Commerce Chicago, 1989—. *Member:* Chicago (Vice-Chairman, YLS Labor Law Committee, 1984-1985; Task Force on Youth Justice, 1991-1992; Lawyers Regulation Committee, 1991—), Illinois State (Secretary, Employee Benefits Section Council, 1991-1992; Vice Chair, 1992-1993; Chair, 1993-1994) and Wisconsin State Bar Associations. ***PRACTICE AREAS:*** Labor and Employment; Public Sector Labor Relations; Employment Discrimination; Affirmative Action; Management Labor Law.

ALLEN W. DUB, born Cleveland, Ohio, February 20, 1953; admitted to bar, 1978, Ohio and U.S. District Court, Northern District of Ohio; 1984, Illinois; 1985, U.S. District Court, Northern District of Illinois; U.S. Court of Appeals, Seventh Circuit. *Education:* George Washington University (B.A., with distinction, 1975); Cleveland Marshall College of Law (J.D., 1978). Member, Franchise Oversight and Development Committee, Evanston Cable Commission, Evanston, Illinois, 1984-1987. Commissioner, Evanston Cable Commission, Evanston, Illinois, 1987-1988. Field Attorney, National Labor Relations Board, 1978-1981. *Member:* Chicago (Member, Labor and Employment Law Section; Chairperson, NLRB Subcommittee, 1985-1986; Young Lawyers Section Chairperson of Labor and Employment Law Division, 1985-1986; Young Lawyers Section Chairperson of Labor and Employment Law Division, 1986-1987) and American (Member, Labor and Employment Law Section) Bar Associations. ***PRACTICE AREAS:*** Labor and Employment; Public Sector Labor Relations; Employment Discrimination; Affirmative Action; Management Labor Law. ***Email:*** awd@labor-law.com

JOSHUA D. HOLLEB, born Chicago, Illinois, May 18, 1957; admitted to bar, 1983, Illinois; 1984, U.S. Court of Appeals, Seventh Circuit; 1985, U.S. District Court, Northern District of Illinois including Trial Bar. *Education:* Middlebury College (B.A., 1979); IIT/Chicago-Kent College of Law (J.D., with high honors, 1983). *Member:* Chicago (Member, Labor and Employment Section) and American (Member, Sections on: Labor and Employment and Litigation) Bar Associations; Industrial Relations Research Association (Chicago Chapter). ***PRACTICE AREAS:*** Labor and Employment; Public Sector Labor Relations; Employment Discrimination; Affirmative Action; Management Labor Law. ***Email:*** jdh@labor-law.com

MICHAEL PAULL, born Evanston, Illinois, January 30, 1961; admitted to bar, 1986, Illinois, U.S. District Court, Northern District Illinois including Trial Bar and U.S. Court of Appeals, Fifth, Seventh and Eighth Circuits; U.S. District Court, Western District of Michigan. *Education:* University of Illinois (B.S., with honors, 1983); Northwestern University (J.D., 1986). Gold Key; Phi Eta Sigma; Alpha Lambda Delta. *Member:* Chicago, Illinois State and American Bar Associations. ***PRACTICE AREAS:*** Labor and Employment; Public Sector Labor Relations; Employment Discrimination; Affirmative Action; Management Labor Law. ***Email:*** map@labor-law.com

OF COUNSEL

LAWRENCE A. REICH, born Chicago, Illinois, April 6, 1937; admitted to bar, 1974, Illinois and U.S. District Court, Northern District of Illinois; U.S. Court of Appeals, Fourth, Seventh and Eleventh Circuits. *Education:* Stanford University (A.B., 1959); John Marshall Law School (J.D., 1974). *Member:* Chicago (Member, Labor and Employment Law Committee) and American (Member, Labor and Employment Law Section) Bar Associations. ***PRACTICE AREAS:*** Labor and Employment; Employment Discrimination; Management Labor Law. ***Email:*** lar@labor-law.com

DAVI L. HIRSCH, born Chicago, Illinois, February 24, 1957; admitted to bar, 1982, Illinois. *Education:* University of Illinois (B.S.W., 1979); DePaul University (J.D., 1982).

(This Listing Continued)

Phi Alpha Delta. Phi Kappa Phi. Member: Moot Court, 1981-1982; National Moot Court Competition, 1981; Illini Top 100 Club. Note and Comments Editor, DePaul Law Review, 1981-1982. Judicial Clerkship, U.S. Court of Appeals for the Seventh Circuit, 1982-1984. Adjunct Faculty Member, DePaul University College of Law, 1982-1984. Teaching Assistant, Chicago-Kent College of Law, Illinois Institute of Technology, 1994. *Member:* Federal Trial Bar. ***PRACTICE AREAS:*** Employment Discrimination; Management Labor Law; Commercial Litigation. ***Email:*** dhirsch@labor-law.com

SIDNEY C. KLEINMAN

Established in 1958

14 NORTH PEORIA STREET - 5H
CHICAGO, ILLINOIS 60607
Telephone: 312-850-8050
FAX: 312-850-8053
Email: sidc@kleinmansnet.com
URL: http://www.lawyers.com/sckleinman

Business Law, Corporate Law, Estate Planning, Financial Law and Real Estate.

FIRM PROFILE: For over 40 years, Sidney C. Kleinman has provided personalized legal problem solving services on behalf of business entities and individuals for a wide range of business, financial, estate planning, probate and real estate projects, including the analysis of multiple dimensions of existing legal issues and the creation of preventive legal solutions. As required by the specific needs of each project, Mr. Kleinman, as appropriate, under his direction and control utilizes the specialized skills of others to efficiently and successfully resolve the legal problem at hand.

SIDNEY C. KLEINMAN, born Detroit, Michigan, May 11, 1932; admitted to bar, 1957, Michigan; 1958, Illinois. *Education:* University of Michigan (B.A., 1954; J.D., with distinction, 1957). Phi Beta Kappa; Phi Kappa Phi. Principal, Sidney C. Kleinman Ltd., 1972-1985. Partner, McBride Baker & Coles, 1985-1994. *Member:* Chicago, Illinois State and American Bar Associations.

LAW OFFICE OF MITCHELL A. KLINE

Established in 1999

203 N. LASALLE STREET
SUITE 2100
CHICAGO, ILLINOIS 60601
Telephone: 312-558-1454
Fax: 312-346-9603
URL: http://www.klinelawfirm.com
Email: mitchellakline@aol.com
URL: http://www.mitchellkline.com

Sexual Harassment, Discrimination, Age Discrimination, Sex Discrimination, Disability Discrimination, Race Discrimination, Religious Discrimination, Workers' Compensation.

FIRM PROFILE: Mitchell Kline has represented employees and employers in sexual harassment, discrimination, and worker's compensation cases since 1999. Mr. Kline has been an attorney in Illinois since 1978. For a more complete profile see my website: http://www.mitchellkline.com.

MITCHELL A. KLINE, born Harvey, Illinois, July 30, 1953; admitted to bar, 1978, Illinois. *Education:* Harvard University (B.A., with honors, 1975); Indiana University School of Law (J.D., 1978). Administrative Law Judge, Illinois Human Rights Commission, 1996-1998. Staff Attorney, Illinois Industrial Commission, 1995-1996. Owner, Kline's Department Store, Chicago Heights, 1983-1995. Assistant State's Attorney, Cook County, 1978-1983. *Member:* Chicago Bar Association; Decalogue Society of Lawyers. ***PRACTICE AREAS:*** Workers Compensation; Labor and Employment; Employment Discrimination.

KLISE & BIEL, LTD.

1478 WEST WEBSTER AVENUE
CHICAGO, ILLINOIS 60614
Telephone: 773-871-6446
Fax: 773-871-6902
URL: http://www.kliseandbiel.com
Email: zoe@kliseandbiel.com
URL: http://www.lawyers.com/kliseandbiel

Business Formation, Limited Liability Company Law, Chancery Practice, Commercial Real Estate Acquisitions, Commercial Real Estate Contracts, Commercial Real Estate Sales, Construction Contracts, Breach of Contract, Commercial Contracts, Contract Litigation, Corporate Formation, Nonprofit Corporations, Small Business Corporations, Commercial Landlord and Tenant Law, Commercial Leasing, Evictions, Landlord and Tenant Law, Lease Terminations, Leasing, Office Leasing, Civil Litigation, Limited Partnerships, Partnership Dissolution, Partnership Formation, Partnership Organization, Condominium Association Law, Condominium Conversions, Condominium Development, Condominium Law, Real Estate Acquisitions, Real Estate Brokers and Agents Liability, Real Estate Contracts, Real Estate Development, Real Estate Leasing, Real Estate Litigation, Residential Real Estate, Residential Real Estate Development, Residential Real Estate Sales.

JOHN D. KLISE, born LaGrange, Illinois, September 15, 1967; admitted to bar, 1997, Illinois. *Education:* University of Michigan (B.A., 1989); John Marshall Law School (J.D., cum laude, 1997). *Member:* Chicago, Illinois State and American Bar Associations. ***Email:*** john@kliseandbiel.com

ZOE G. BIEL, born Chicago, Illinois, 1970; admitted to bar, 1999, Illinois. *Education:* University of Wisconsin-Madison (B.A., 1992); John Marshall Law School (J.D., 1997).

(This Listing Continued)

Semi-Finalist, Dean Fred F. Herzog Moot Court Competition, 1995. International Human Rights Work with Professors Ruebner and Wojcik, 1997-2000. *Member:* Chicago, Illinois State and American Bar Associations; Chicago Council of Lawyers (Judicial Evaluation, 2000—). ***Email:*** zoe@kliseandbiel.com

KNELL & POULOS

A PROFESSIONAL CORPORATION
555 WEST JACKSON BOULEVARD
SUITE 700
CHICAGO, ILLINOIS 60661-5700
Telephone: 312-277-3000
Fax: 312-277-3008
Email: home@knellpoulos.com
URL: http://www.knellpoulos.com

Wheaton, Illinois Office: 511 West Wesley, 60187. Telephone: 630-681-1512.

Workers Compensation Defense, Insurance Defense, Employment Defense.

BRADLEY C. KNELL, born Joliet, Illinois, July 14, 1962; admitted to bar, 1988, Illinois and U.S. District Court, Northern District of Illinois. *Education:* Eastern Illinois University (B.A., 1984); Ohio Northern University (J.D., 1987). *Member:* Chicago, DuPage County, Illinois State and American Bar Associations; Illinois Workers' Compensation Trial Attorneys' Association; Workers' Compensation Claims Association. (Also at Wheaton Office). ***PRACTICE AREAS:*** Workers' Compensation. ***Email:*** bknell1@knellpoulos.com

DAVID T. POULOS, born Elmhurst, Illinois, March 22, 1967; admitted to bar, 1992, Illinois and U.S. District Court, Northern District of Illinois. *Education:* Southern Methodist University; University of Illinois (B.A., 1989); Illinois Institute of Technology (J.D., 1992). *Member:* Chicago, Illinois State and American Bar Associations. (Also at Wheaton Office). ***PRACTICE AREAS:*** Workers Compensation; Labor and Employment. ***Email:*** dpoulos@knellpoulos.com

JOHN J. O'CONNOR, admitted to bar, 1986, Illinois and U.S. District Court, Northern District of Illinois. *Education:* Illinois State University (B.A., 1982); John Marshall Law School (J.D., 1986). Former Illinois Defense Counsel Member. *Member:* Kane, DuPage County, Illinois State and American Bar Associations. (Also at Wheaton Office). ***PRACTICE AREAS:*** Civil litigation; Premises Liability; Construction Litigation; Institutional Neglect; Product Liability. ***Email:*** joconnor@knellpoulos.com

---

TINA R. SWANSON, born Park Ridge, Illinois, October 1, 1970; admitted to bar, 1998, Illinois. *Education:* Loyola University (B.A., magna cum laude, 1994); Chicago-Kent College of Law (J.D., 1997). Formerly with Desveaux, Tobin and Flynn. *Member:* Workers Compensation Lawyers Association. ***PRACTICE AREAS:*** Workers Compensation. ***Email:*** tswanson@knellpoulos.com

PAUL-ERIC SEAL, born Kankakee, Illinois, April 10, 1962; admitted to bar, 1988, Illinois; 1995, Indiana. *Education:* Loyola University (A.B., Honors, 1985; J.D., 1988). *Member:* Workers Compensation Lawyers Association. ***PRACTICE AREAS:*** Workers Compensation.

ROBERT M. HARRIS, born Chicago, Illinois, March 6, 1963; admitted to bar, 1988, Illinois. *Education:* University of Illinois (B.A., 1985); John Marshall Law School (J.D., 1988); Loyola University (M.S.I.R., 1991). *Member:* Workers Compensation Lawyers Association. ***PRACTICE AREAS:*** Workers Compensation. ***Email:*** rharris@knellpoulos.com

RYAN M. MAHONEY, born Park Ridge, Illinois, July 10, 1971; admitted to bar, 2000, Illinois. *Education:* Taylor University (B.S., 1993); John Marshall Law School (J.D., 2000). *Member:* Workers Compensation Lawyers Association. ***PRACTICE AREAS:*** Workers Compensation. ***Email:*** rmahoney@knellpoulos.com

OF COUNSEL

ROBERT J. KARTHOLL, JR., born Illinois, May 2, 1948; admitted to bar, 1973, Illinois and U.S. District Court, Northern District of Illinois; 1995, including Trial Bar. *Education:* Benedictine University (B.A., 1970); DePaul University (J.D., 1973). Chairman, DuPage County Zoning Board of Appeals, 1993—. *Member:* Illinois State and American Bar Associations. ***PRACTICE AREAS:*** Labor and Employment; Age Discrimination in Employment; Sexual Harassment; Equal Employment Opportunity Law; Wrongful Termination.

KNEPPER & GLADNEY

150 NORTH WACKER DRIVE, SUITE 3050
CHICAGO, ILLINOIS 60606
Telephone: 312-957-1300
Fax: 312-957-1070
URL: http://www.kg-legal.com
URL: http://www.lawyers.com/knepper&gladney

Commercial Litigation and Appellate Practice, Securities and Commodities Law, Labor and Employment Law.

MEMBERS OF FIRM

THOMAS M. KNEPPER, born Evanston, Illinois, October 3, 1945; admitted to bar, 1972, Illinois; U.S. Courts of Appeals, Seventh, Eighth, Tenth and Eleventh Circuits; U.S. District Court, Northern District of Illinois; U.S. District Court, Eastern District of Wisconsin; U.S. District Court, District of Nebraska; U.S. District Court, Northern District of Texas; U.S. Supreme Court. *Education:* University of Notre Dame (B.A., 1967); Chicago-Kent College of Law (J.D., 1972). Contributing Author and Faculty Member, Illinois Insti-

(This Listing Continued)

KNEPPER & GLADNEY, Chicago—Continued

tute for Continuing Legal Education, 1974-1979. ***PRACTICE AREAS:*** Commercial Litigation; Appellate Practice; Commodities Law; Securities Law. ***Email:*** tk@kg-legal.com

JILL J. GLADNEY, born Centralia, Missouri, May 10, 1967; admitted to bar, 1991, Illinois; U.S. Court of Appeals, Seventh Circuit; U.S. District Court, Northern District of Illinois; U.S. District Court, Eastern District of Wisconsin. *Education:* University of Missouri (B.S., cum laude, 1988); University of Chicago (J.D., 1991). *Member:* Chicago (Vice-Chair, 1999-2000; Chair, 2000-2001, Solo and Small Firm Practice Committee), Illinois State and American (Member, Labor and Employment Law Section) Bar Associations. ***PRACTICE AREAS:*** Labor Law; Employment Law; Commercial Litigation; Appellate Practice. ***Email:*** jill@kg-legal.com

WILLIAM R. KNOX

3376 NORTH CENTRAL
CHICAGO, ILLINOIS 60634
Telephone: 773-383-7748
Fax: 312-873-4699

Civil Litigation, Criminal Law, Drug Crimes, Driving While Intoxicated, Traffic Violations, Evictions, Family Law, Divorce, Child Custody, Child Support, Domestic Relations, Personal Injury, Automobile Accidents, Trucking Accidents, Slip and Fall, Wrongful Death.

WILLIAM R. KNOX, admitted to bar, 2002, Illinois. *Education:* Dominican University (B.A., 1994); DePaul University (J.D., 2001). *Member:* Chicago, Illinois State, Dupage County and American Bar Associations.

LAW OFFICE OF KURT J. KOLAR

Established in 2000

123 WEST MADISON, SUITE 1800
CHICAGO, ILLINOIS 60602
Telephone: 312-641-3230
Fax: 312-641-3225
Email: kjkolar@kjkolarlaw.com
URL: http://www.kjkolarlaw.com

Business Organization/Advising; Contract Law, Contract Drafting/Revision/Negotiation; Breach of Contract Litigation, Economic Torts, Interference with Prospective Economic Advantage, Defamation, Patent/Trademark/Copyright Infringement, Deceptive Business Practices, Fraud; Commercial Bankruptcy/Reorganization; Entertainment Law, Civil Litigation; Condominium Law; Recording Artist, Independent Record Label Representation, Real Estate Transactions, Litigation, and Consumer and Creditors Rights.

KURT J. KOLAR, born Lakewood, Ohio, September 1, 1968; admitted to bar, 1996, Illinois and U.S. District Court, Northern District of Illinois; 1997, U.S. District Court, Central District of Illinois. *Education:* Marquette University (B.A., 1990); Pepperdine University (J.D., 1996). *Member:* Chicago Bar Association. ***PRACTICE AREAS:*** Business Law; Business Organization; Contracts; Breach of Contract; Economic Torts; Defamation; Trademark Infringement; Copyright Infringement; Deceptive Trade Practices; Civil Fraud; Commercial Bankruptcy; Small Business Reorganization; Entertainment Law; Real Estate Litigation.

LAW OFFICES OF KOMIE AND ASSOCIATES

Established in 1976

ONE NORTH LA SALLE STREET
SUITE 4200
CHICAGO, ILLINOIS 60602-4005
Telephone: 312-263-2800
Fax: 312-263-2803
URL: http://www.komie-and-associates.com
URL: http://www.lawyers.com/komielaw

Civil and Criminal Litigation. Federal, State, International, Trial and Appellate Practice. Complex Litigation, Criminal Defense, Divorce, Family Law, Probate, Taxation, Immigration Law, International Criminal Law, Real Estate Law.

FIRM PROFILE: In 1976, Komie and Associates was founded by Stephen Komie and has grown over 26 years into a full service domestic and international litigation firm. The Firm represents clients in the courts of Illinois, Europe, England, Ireland, Canada, Hong Kong and New Zealand.

STEPHEN M. KOMIE, born Chicago, Illinois, 1949; admitted to bar, 1976, Illinois, U.S. Supreme Court, U.S. Court of Appeals, Sixth, Seventh and Eighth Circuits, U.S. District Court, Central, Northern and Southern Districts of Illinois, U.S. District Court, Northern District of Indiana, U.S. District Court, Eastern District of Michigan, U.S. District Court, Eastern District of Missouri, U.S. Tax Court and Illinois Supreme Court. *Education:* University of Arizona (B.A., M.A.); DePaul College of Law (J.D., 1976); National College of Criminal Defense Lawyers and Public Defenders (1977). Recipient: Public Service Award for Pro Bono Service, American Trial Lawyers Association, 1994; Illinois State Bar Association Board of Governors Award, 1991; Illinois State Bar Association Certificate of Appreciation, June 1986, September, 1990, October 1990; Chicago Bar Certificate of Appreciation, June, 1984, February, 1987. *Author:* "Attorney's Bill of Rights," Adopted by the State Bar, June, 1990; "Illinois State Bar Association Legislation Proposed to Protect Attorney/Client Relationship," Chicago Law Bulletin, March 12, 1987; "Little RICO Bill Should Not Be Passed," The Bar News, June 1984; "Little RICO in Illinois, The Case Against It," Chicago Law Bulletin, April, 1984. Founding Member, Illinois Attorney's for Criminal Justice, 1984. Member: American Bar Association Elected Member, Criminal Justice Section Council, Small Firm and Solo Practice Task Force, 1990-1992; Illinois State Bar Association, Judicial Compensation Committee, 1990. *Member:* Chicago Bar Association (Chairperson: Criminal Law Committee; Defense of Prisoner Committee; Liaison, American Bar Association Criminal Justice Section Counsel), Illinois State Bar Association (Secretary, 1996—; Member: Board of Governors, 1992-1998; 1999—; Assembly, 1985-1998; By-Laws Assembly Committee; Mandatory Continuing Legal Education Committee; Chairman: Credentials Committee, 1985; Criminal Justice Section, 1989; Professionalism Committee, 1991-1992; Traffic Courts and The Law Committee); International Bar Association (1998, Chairman, Family Law); Illinois Bar Foundation (Director). (Also Principal, Drunken Driving Defense Lawyers of Illinois, Ltd.). ***PRACTICE AREAS:*** Family; Civil Litigation; International Law; Criminal Law; Probate; Real Estate. ***Email:*** stephen_m_komie@komie-and-associates.com

ASSOCIATES

DARIUS R. DIRMANTAS, born Chicago, Illinois, 1968; admitted to bar, 2000, Illinois and U.S. District Court, Northern District of Illinois. *Education:* Massachusetts Maritime Academy (B.S., 1992); Loyola University School of Law, Chicago (J.D., 2000). U.S. Coast Guard Chief Engineers License, 1995 . *Member:* Chicago, Illinois State and American Bar Associations. (Also Associate to Drunken Driving Defense Lawyers of Illinois Ltd.). ***LANGUAGES:*** Lithuanian. ***PRACTICE AREAS:*** Criminal Law; Internet Crimes; Drug Crimes; Felonies; Driving While Intoxicated. ***Email:*** darius_r_dirmantas@komie-and-associates.com

ELISABETH A. RITTER, born Evanston, 1969; admitted to bar, 1994, Illinois; 1995, Missouri. *Education:* Northwestern University (B.A., 1991); Washington University (J.D., 1994). *Member:* Illinois State Bar Association; The Missouri Bar. (Also Associate, Drunken Driving Defense Lawyers of Illinois, Ltd.). ***PRACTICE AREAS:*** Family Law; Civil Litigation; Probate. ***Email:*** elisabeth_a_ritter@komie-and-associates.com

BRIAN E. KING, born Chicago, Illinois, July 17, 1970; admitted to bar, 1996, Illinois, U.S. Court of Appeals, Seventh Circuit, U.S. District Court, Northern District of Illinois and U.S. District Court, Eastern District of Michigan. *Education:* Michigan State University (B.S., 1993); DePaul University (J.D., 1996). Phi Alpha Delta. Graduate, National College of DUI Defense, Harvard Law School, 1997. *Member:* Chicago, Illinois and American Bar Associations. ***LANGUAGES:*** German. ***PRACTICE AREAS:*** Driving While Intoxicated; Appellate Practice; Criminal Law.

SARAH E. TONEY, born Illinois, 1978; admitted to bar, 2004, Illinois and U.S. District Court, Northern District of Illinois. *Education:* Miami University (B.S., 2000); Loyola University of Chicago School of Law (J.D., 2003). *Member:* Chicago, Illinois State and American Bar Associations; National College for DUI Defense. ***PRACTICE AREAS:*** Criminal Defense; Driving While Intoxicated; Child Abuse and Neglect; Drug Crimes; Internet Crimes. ***Email:*** stoney@komie-and-associates.com

OF COUNSEL

MARC D. WOLFE, born Los Angeles, California, 1951; admitted to bar, 1976, Illinois and U.S. Court of Appeals, Seventh Circuit. *Education:* University of Denver (B.A.B.S., 1973); John Marshall Law School (J.D., 1976). *Member:* Du Page County and Illinois State Bar Associations. (Also Of Counsel to Drunken Driving Defense Lawyers of Illinois, Ltd.). ***PRACTICE AREAS:*** Divorce; Commercial; Criminal; Real Estate.

LEGAL SUPPORT PERSONNEL

PAUL J. CIOLINO, born Chicago, Illinois, 1956. *Education:* Wichita State University (1980). Recipient: Award for Excellence in Child Sexual Abuse Investigations; Dante Award, 1999; Advocate for Justice Award (presented by Illinois Attorneys for Criminal Justice); 1999 Investigator of the Year by the Louisiana Association of Private Investigators. Author: Article on: "Fundamental Seduction," Voyle A. Glover, Published by Brevia Publishing Co., 1990. Co-author, "Advanced Forensic Civil Investigations", Lawyers and Judges Publishing Company. Adjunct Lecturer, Medill School of Journalism, Northwestern University. Senior Investigator, Illinois Department of Children and Family Services, 1983-1987. In Charge of Homicide and Mass Molestation Investigations for 6 Counties. *Member:* Illinois State Bar Association; National Association of Criminal Defense Lawyers; Association of Certified Fraud Examiners; American College of Forensic Examiners. (Staff Investigator) (Also Staff Investigator, Drunken Driving Defense Lawyers of Illinois, Ltd.)

JAMES L. KOPECKY, P.C.

321 N. CLARK STREET, SUITE 2200
CHICAGO, ILLINOIS 60610
Telephone: 312-527-3966
Fax: 312-527-3968
URL: http://www.jlkopecky.com
Email: info@jlkopecky.com
URL: http://www.jlkopeckylaaw.com

Securities, Securities Fraud, Securities Arbitration and Litigation, Shareholder Disputes, Business and Contract Litigation, General Civil Litigation and Personal Injury.

JAMES L. KOPECKY, born Chicago, Illinois, February 13, 1968; admitted to bar, 1994, Illinois and U.S. District Court, Northern District of Illinois. *Education:* University of Illinois (B.A., 1990); Loyola University (J.D., 1994). Branch Chief, Division of Enforcement, U.S. Securities and Exchange Commission, 1999-2002. *Member:* Chicago and Illinois State Bar Associations. ***Email:*** info@jlkopecky.com

KOREIN TILLERY

CHICAGO, ILLINOIS

(See St. Louis, Missouri)

Class Action, Securities Law, Environmental Law, Commercial Litigation, Pension and Profit Sharing, Railroad, Maritime, Medical Malpractice, Product Liability, Toxic Tort, General Negligence, Trial Practice.

(This Listing Continued)

KOZACKY & WEITZEL, P.C.

ONE NORTH LASALLE, SUITE 3150
CHICAGO, ILLINOIS 60602
Telephone: 312-696-0900
Fax: 312-696-0905
Email: pkozacky@kozacky.com
URL: http://www.kozacky.com

Admiralty and Maritime Law, Commercial Law, Business Litigation, Construction, Contract Litigation, Litigation, Real Estate Litigation, Business Fraud, Business Arbitration, Chancery Practice, Federal Civil Practice, Contracts, Insurance Coverage, Commercial Landlord and Tenant Law, Long-Arm Litigation, Transportation Law.

FIRM PROFILE: Founded in 1997 as Paul J. Kozacky & Associates, P.C., Kozacky & Weitzel, P.C. is a trial practice boutique specializing in admiralty and general commercial litigation. The firm acts as Chicago correspondent for club's maritime protection and indemnity and regularly represents vessel owners in commercial disputes. Since its founding, Kozacky & Weitzel, P.C. has grown to represent small, medium and large companies in several areas of business litigation.

PAUL J. KOZACKY, born January 8, 1959; admitted to bar, 1984, Illinois; 1994, U.S. Supreme Court. *Education:* University of Illinois (A.B., cum laude, 1981) James Scholar; Georgetown University (J.D., cum laude, 1984). Phi Beta Kappa. Member, American Criminal Law Review, 1982-1984. Author: "Narrow Venue Statutes and Third Party Practice: Some Third Party Defendants Get to Go Home," 39 DePaul Law Review 389, 1990. *Member:* Chicago Bar Assn.; Maritime Law Assn. of the United States. ***LANGUAGES:*** Ukrainian. ***PRACTICE AREAS:*** Admiralty and Maritime Law; Commercial Law; Litigation. ***Email:*** pkozacky@kozacky.com

JEROME R. WEITZEL, born New York, N.Y., February 12, 1969; admitted to bar, 1993, Illinois. *Education:* Loyola University (B.A., 1990); DePaul University (J.D., 1993). *Member:* Chicago Bar Association. ***PRACTICE AREAS:*** Commercial Litigation; Construction Litigation; Admiralty Litigation; Real Estate Litigation. ***Email:*** jweitzel@kozacky.com

---

JEFFREY S. BECKER, born Skokie, Illinois; admitted to bar, 2004, Illinois, U.S. District Court, Northern District of Illinois and U.S. Court of Appeals, Seventh Circuit. *Education:* Illinois Wesleyan University (B.A., 2001); DePaul University (J.D., magna cum laude, 2004). Psi Chi; Order of the Coif; Phi Kappa Phi. Member, DePaul University Law Review, 2002-2004. Licensed Real Estate Broker, Illinois, 2005. Author: "A Legal War on Terrorism: Extending New York v. Quarles and the Departure from Enemy Combatant Designations," 53 DePaul L. Rev. 831, 2003. *Member:* Chicago, Illinois State and American Bar Associations. ***PRACTICE AREAS:*** Commercial Litigation; Real Estate Litigation; Employment Litigation; Admiralty and Maritime Law; Construction Litigation. ***Email:*** jbecker@kozacky.com

THE KRAFSUR LAW GROUP LLC

Established in 2000
30 NORTH LASALLE STREET, SUITE 4300
CHICAGO, ILLINOIS 60602
Telephone: 312-899-0911
Fax: 312-899-0220
URL: http://www.krafsurlaw.com

Captive Insurance Formation and Management, Insurance Coverage Counseling, Enterprise Risk Management and Alternative Risk Financing Advice, Alternative Dispute Resolution, Emergency Services and Emergency Products Counseling, All Litigation Relating to These Specialties.

JAY V. KRAFSUR, born Highland Park, Illinois, July 11, 1956; admitted to bar, 1984, Illinois and U.S. District Court, Northern and Central Districts of Illinois; 1985, Colorado; 1995, U.S. Court of Appeals, Seventh Circuit; 1997, U.S. Supreme Court. *Education:* University of Colorado (B.A., 1978); Chicago-Kent College of Law (J.D., with honors, 1984). Member, Editorial Board of Moot Court Society, 1983-1984. Winner: 1st Annual Chicago Bar Association Moot Court Competition Award; Finalist: 1983 American Bar Associations Moot Court Competition. Member, Mayoral Commission Investigating Chicago Paramedic System, 1986. Instructor, Chicago-Kent College of Law, 1988-1990. *Member:* Chicago, Illinois State and American Bar Associations; American Ambulance Association; National Emergency Number Association; Association of Public-Safety Communications International; American Society for Testing and Materials. ***PRACTICE AREAS:*** Captive Insurance; Emergency Services Law; Insurance Coverage; Insurance Litigation; Alternative Dispute Resolution; Risk Management. ***Email:*** jkrafsur@krafsurlaw.com

ERIC L. ROUTMAN, admitted to bar, 1980, Illinois and U.S. District Court, Northern District of Illinois; U.S. Court of Appeals, Seventh Circuit. *Education:* George Washington University (B.B.A., 1976); John Marshall Law School (J.D., 1980). Member, Moot Court Competition. Author: "Investigating the Feasibility of a New Off-Shore Captive Domicile: An American Indian Reservation," CPCU Journal, Fall, 1999; "The Insured Filed for Bankruptcy: What's Next for the Insurer," Journal of Reinsurance, Spring, 1999; "Back to the Future: Coverage Claims Under Corporate Predecessor Liability Policies for CERCLA Liability," CPCU; "Declaratory Judgment Expense: Who Pays?," Global Reinsurance, Fall, 1994; "Cleaning Up America: Superfund and its Impact on the Insurance Industry," CPCU Journal, Sept., 1988. Board Member and Instructor, Insurance School of Chicago. Chartered Property and Casualty Underwriter, since 1985. National Governor of CPCU Society, 2000-2003. CPCU Society Executive Committee, 2002-2003. National CPCU Chair, Consulting, Litigation and Expert Witness Section, 1996-1999. President, Chicago CPCU Chapter 1998-2000. *Member:* Chicago, Illinois State and American (Member, Tort and Insurance Practice Section; Vice-Chair, International Dispute Resolution Committee; Liaison, TIPS Alternative Dispute Resolution Committee) Bar Associations. ***PRACTICE AREAS:*** Captive Insurance; Insurance Coverage; Risk Management; Alternative Dispute Resolution; Professional Liability; Employment Practices Liability Insurance. ***Email:*** eroutman@krafsurlaw.com

(This Listing Continued)

KRALOVEC, JAMBOIS & SCHWARTZ

GOODMAN THEATRE BUILDING
60 WEST RANDOLPH STREET, 4TH FLOOR
CHICAGO, ILLINOIS 60601
Telephone: 312-782-2525
Fax: 312-855-0068
URL: http://www.kjs-law.com

Representing Plaintiff's Medical Malpractice, Personal Injury and Products Liability Law.

MEMBERS OF FIRM

JOHN B. KRALOVEC, born Hinsdale, Illinois, August 29, 1956; admitted to bar, 1981, Illinois and U.S. District Court, Northern District of Illinois. *Education:* University of Illinois (B.S., 1978); Loyola University (J.D., 1981). Instructor, Trial Demonstration: Loyola University School of Nursing; Evangelical Hospital Association. Masters in Trial "The Closing Argument." Lecturer: Railroad Crossing Collisions, Illinois Institute for Continuing Legal Education; University of Illinois College of Medicine, 1981-1987; Civil Trial Practice, Illinois Trial Lawyers Association. Member, Ad Hoc Advisory Committee to Circuit Court of Cook County Law Division. Appointed to Illinois Supreme Court Committee on Civil Jury Instructions, 1996-1998. *Member:* Chicago (Member, Chicago Trial Techniques Committee, 1982; Judicial Evaluation Committee Investigator; Judicial Evaluation Committee Hearing Officer; Illinois Supreme Court Committee on Personal Injury Subsections, 1996—), Illinois State and American Bar Associations; Illinois Trial Lawyers Association (Board of Managers; Board of Advocate's). ***PRACTICE AREAS:*** Medical Malpractice; Personal Injury; Products Liability. ***Email:*** jkralovec@kjs-law.com

STEVEN K. JAMBOIS, born Champaign-Urbana, Illinois, April 22, 1957; admitted to bar, 1982, Illinois and U.S. District Court, Northern District of Illinois. *Education:* Indiana University at Bloomington (B.S., 1979); Chicago-Kent College of Law (J.D., with honors, 1982). *Member:* Chicago, Illinois State and American Bar Associations; Illinois Trial Lawyers Association; The Association of Trial Lawyers of America. ***PRACTICE AREAS:*** Medical Malpractice; Personal Injury; Products Liability. ***Email:*** sjambois@kjs-law.com

ALLEN N. SCHWARTZ, born Austin, Texas, January 21, 1959; admitted to bar, 1984, Illinois. *Education:* University of Illinois (B.A., 1981); Illinois Institute of Technology/Chicago-Kent College of Law (J.D., with high honors, 1984). *Member:* Chicago and Illinois State Bar Associations; Illinois Trial Lawyers Association; The Association of Trial Lawyers of America. ***PRACTICE AREAS:*** Medical Malpractice; Personal Injury; Products Liability. ***Email:*** aschwartz@kjs-law.com

DAVID E. SCHWARTZ, born Austin, Texas, January 4, 1958; admitted to bar, 1983, Illinois; U.S. District Court, Federal Trial Bar; U.S. Court of Appeals, Seventh Circuit. *Education:* Illinois Wesleyan University (B.A., 1980); DePaul College of Law (J.D., 1983). *Member:* DuPage County and Illinois State Bar Associations; Illinois Trial Lawyer's Association; The Association of Trial Lawyers of America. ***PRACTICE AREAS:*** Medical Malpractice; Personal Injury; Products Liability. ***Email:*** dschwartz@kjs-law.com

ASSOCIATES

ROBERT J. KELLEHER, born Chicago, Illinois, September 24, 1965; admitted to bar, 1991, Illinois and U.S. District Court, Federal Trial Bar. *Education:* University of Iowa (B.A., 1987); Northern Illinois University (J.D., cum laude, 1990). Phi Alpha Delta. Notes and Comments Editor, Northern Illinois University Law Review. Lecturer and Contributing Author: Illinois Trial Lawyers Association. *Member:* DuPage, DuPage County, Chicago, Illinois State and American Bar Associations; Illinois Trial Lawyers Association; Association of Trial Lawyers of America. ***PRACTICE AREAS:*** Plaintiff's Personal Injury Law; Medical Malpractice; Products Liability Law. ***Email:*** rkelleher@kjs-law.com

CRAIG P. MANNARINO, born Bristol, Connecticut, August 31, 1969; admitted to bar, 1996, Illinois, U.S. District Court, Northern, Central and Southern Districts of Illinois including Trial Bar and U.S. Court of Appeals, Seventh Circuit. *Education:* Wesleyan University (B.A., 1991); DePaul College of Law (J.D., with honors, 1996). Phi Alpha Delta. Order of the Coif. DePaul Law Review. Author, "Jury Instructions" (Chapter in Medical Malpractice Notebook - Illinois Trial Lawyers Association). *Member:* Chicago and Illinois State Bar Associations; Illinois Trial Lawyers Association; Association of Trial Lawyers of America. ***PRACTICE AREAS:*** Civil Litigation; Medical Malpractice; Products Liability. ***Email:*** cmannarino@kjs-law.com

NATHAN J. MIROCHA, born Rock Island, Illinois, September 25, 1974; admitted to bar, 1999, Illinois and U.S. District Court, Northern District of Illinois. *Education:* University of Illinois (B.A., 1996); DePaul University College of Law (J.D., 1999). Member, Moot Court Society. *Member:* Chicago, Illinois State and American Bar Associations; Illinois Trial Lawyers Association; The Association of Trial Lawyers of America. ***PRACTICE AREAS:*** Personal Injury; Medical Malpractice; Products Liability. ***Email:*** nmirocha@kjs-law.com

ALEXANDER SUKHMAN, born Minsk, Belarns, June 18, 1973; admitted to bar, 1999, Illinois and U.S. District Court, Northern District of Illinois. *Education:* University of Illinois Urbana-Champaign (B.A., 1996); Chicago-Kent College of Law, Illinois Institute of Technology (J.D., 1999). ***PRACTICE AREAS:*** Medical Malpractice; Personal Injury; Products Liability. ***Email:*** asukhman@kjs-law.com

RYAN E. YAGODA, born Skokie, Illinois, October 9, 1974; admitted to bar, 1999, Illinois and U.S. District Court, Northern District of Illinois; 2001, Minnesota and U.S. Court of Appeals, 7th Circuit. *Education:* University of Illinois (B.A., 1996); Chicago-Kent College of Law, Illinois Institute of Technology (J.D., with high honors, 1999). Order of the Coif. Notes and Comments Editor, Law Review. Adjunct Professor, Legal Drafting - Trial Preparation, Chicago-Kent College of Law, 2002-2003. Member: Illinois State Bar Association; Association of Trial Lawyers of America. ***PRACTICE AREAS:*** Medical Malpractice; Personal Injury; Products Liability. ***Email:*** ryagoda@kjs-law.com

(This Listing Continued)

KRALOVEC, JAMBOIS & SCHWARTZ, Chicago—Continued

MICHAEL S. SHINSKY, born Skokie, Illinois, August 3, 1976; admitted to bar, 2001, Illinois. *Education:* University of Illinois (B.S., 1998); Chicago-Kent College of Law, Illinois Institute of Technology (J.D., 2001). Member and Coach, Trial Advocacy Team. Recipient, First Annual Warren Wolfson Award. Assistant State's Attorney, 2001-2004. *Member:* Chicago and Illinois State Bar Associations; Prosecutors Bar Association. ***PRACTICE AREAS:*** Medical Malpractice; Personal Injury; Products Liability. ***Email:*** mshinsky@kjs-law.com

KRASNOW SAUNDERS CORNBLATH, LLP

THE BOYCE BUILDING
500 NORTH DEARBORN STREET, SECOND FLOOR
CHICAGO, ILLINOIS 60610
Telephone: 312-755-5700
Fax: 312-755-5720
Email: bizlaw@ksc-law.com
URL: http://www.ksc-law.com

Business Law, Real Estate Development, Leasing and Lending, Land Use, Corporate, Commercial and Municipal Finance, Mergers and Acquisitions, Municipal Law, State and Federal Civil Litigation, Intellectual Property, Intellectual Property Infringement and Trademark Litigation, Wills, Trusts and Estates, Estate Planning for Unmarried Couples, Disability Law.

FIRM PROFILE: Krasnow Saunders Cornblath, LLP, represents a broad range of clients in both the private and public sectors. The Firm specializes in business transactions of all types, real estate transactions, estate planning and in providing solutions to business problems of entrepreneurial and family businesses. It's litigation practice involves resolving complex business disputes for both plaintiffs and defendants.

FRANCIS A. BENINATI, born London, England, November 23, 1947; admitted to bar, 1972, Illinois and U.S. Tax Court. *Education:* Duke University (A.B., 1969); University of Richmond; University of Virginia (J.D., 1972). Co-Author: Supplements to Chapters, "Claims Against the Estate and Marshalling Assets," Illinois Estate Administration, 1977 and 1979; "Creditors Rights Against Decedents Estates," Creditors Rights in Illinois, 1977: Chapters, "Creditors Rights Against Decedents Estates," Creditors Rights in Illinois, 1980; "Claims Against the Estate and Marshalling Assets," Illinois Estate Administration, 1981 and "Sample Estate Plans," Basic Estate Planning, 1980, 1983, 1985, 1986 and 1990, all published by the Illinois Institute for Continuing Legal Education. Author, Chapter, "Probate Division," Court Handbook for Young Lawyers, published by Young Lawyers Section of the Chicago Bar Association, 1979, 1981, 1984, 1987 and 1989. *Member:* Chicago (Member, 1977— and Chairman, 1981-1982, Probate Practice Committee, Division IV), Illinois State and American Bar Associations; Chicago Estate Planning Council. ***LANGUAGES:*** Italian. ***PRACTICE AREAS:*** Estate Planning; Wills; Probate; Taxation. ***Email:*** fbeninati@ksc-law.com

DINA A. BRADFORD, born Chicago, Illinois, October 19, 1975; admitted to bar, 2000, Illinois. *Education:* Northwestern University (B.A., magna cum laude, 1997); Loyola University Chicago School of Law (J.D., magna cum laude, 2000). ***LANGUAGES:*** Greek. ***PRACTICE AREAS:*** Real Estate. ***Email:*** dbradford@ksc-law.com

GLEN R. CORNBLATH, born St. Louis, Missouri, April 18, 1958; admitted to bar, 1983, Illinois. *Education:* Hebrew University, Jerusalem, Israel; Northwestern University (B.A., with distinction, 1980); University of Pennsylvania (J.D., cum laude, 1983). Phi Beta Kappa; Order of the Coif. Member, Board of Editors and Columnist, "Retail Law Strategist," 2001—. Adjunct Faculty, IIT Chicago Kent Law School, 1994-1999. Instructor, Legal Writing, University of Pennsylvania, 1982-1983. ***PRACTICE AREAS:*** Real Estate Development; Leases and Leasing. ***Email:*** gcornblath@ksc-law.com

SUE ANN FISHBEIN, born Chicago, Illinois, November 17, 1950; admitted to bar, 1974, Illinois; 1977, U.S. District Court, Northern District of Illinois; 1991, Florida. *Education:* University of Michigan (B.A., with honors, 1970); University of Illinois (M.A., 1972; J.D., 1974). *Member:* Chicago Bar Association. ***PRACTICE AREAS:*** Real Estate. ***Email:*** sfishbein@ksc-law.com

FREDERICK M. KAPLAN, born Chicago, Illinois, December 6, 1954; admitted to bar, 1980, Illinois and U.S. District Court, Northern District of Illinois. *Education:* Universite de Montpellier, Montpellier, France (1972-1973); George Washington University (B.A., 1977); Illinois Institute of Technology/Chicago-Kent College of Law (J.D., 1980). Member, Lead Articles Editor, Chicago-Kent Law Review. Member, Editorial Board, Shopping Center Law Report. Lead Instructor, BOMI Commercial Real Estate Law Course. ***LANGUAGES:*** French. ***PRACTICE AREAS:*** Real Estate; Construction Law; Business Transactions; Disability law. ***Email:*** fkaplan@ksc-law.com

HENRY C. KRASNOW, born Chicago, Illinois, September 20, 1942; admitted to bar, 1967, Illinois and U.S. District Court, Northern District of Illinois and U.S. Court of Appeals, Seventh Circuit; 1982, U.S. Supreme Court. *Education:* University of Michigan (A.B., 1963); University of Chicago (J.D., 1966). Editorial Board, University of Chicago Law Review, 1964-1966. Certified Public Accountant, Illinois, 1966. Adjunct Professor: IIT Kent College of Law, Business Practice, 1981-1982; Real Estate Transactions, 1981; Corporations, 1981-1982; Adjunct Professor: IIT Stuart School of Business, Law, Business and Society, 1992-1994. Law Clerk to U.S. District Judge James B. Parsons, 1966-1967. Member, Editorial Board, Chicago Lawyer, 1980-1982. Member, 1985-1990, First Vice President, 1985, Treasurer, 1986 and President, 1987, Playground and Recreation Board, City of Evanston, Illinois. *Member:* Chicago, Illinois State and American Bar Associations; Chicago Council of Lawyers (Vice President, 1979-1980; Member, Board of Trustees, 1980-1983; 1985-1986). ***PRACTICE AREAS:*** Business Litigation; Real Estate Development; Intellectual Property; Mergers and Acquisitions; Business Law. ***Email:*** hkrasnow@ksc-law.com

LORA K. SANBERG, born New York, N.Y., November 16, 1943; admitted to bar, 1980, Illinois. *Education:* Barry College (B.A., 1977); Northwestern University (J.D., cum laude, 1980). Order of the Coif. Member, Editorial Board, Journal of Criminal Law and Criminology, 1978-1979. *Member:* Chicago and American Bar Associations. ***PRACTICE AREAS:*** Real Estate; Corporate Law; Retail and Office Leasing. ***Email:*** lsanberg@ksc-law.com

(This Listing Continued)

DAVID A. SAUNDERS, born Chicago, Illinois, June 3, 1939; admitted to bar, 1964, Illinois and U.S. District Court, Northern District of Illinois. *Education:* Oberlin College (A.B., 1961); University of Chicago (J.D., 1964). Member, 1986-1992 and Chair, 1990-1992, Board of Ethics, City of Evanston, Illinois. *Member:* Chicago and American Bar Associations, Chicago Council of Lawyers. ***PRACTICE AREAS:*** Business Law; Commercial Finance; Mergers and Acquisitions; Municipal Finance. ***Email:*** dsaunders@ksc-law.com

CHARLES A. VALENTE, born Brooklyn, New York, July 13, 1962; admitted to bar, 1988, Illinois; 1989, U.S. District Court, Northern District of Illinois including Trial Bar and U.S. Court of Appeals, Seventh Circuit; 1992, U.S. District Court, Central District of Illinois; 1993, U.S. Court of Appeals, Eighth Circuit; 1995, Florida, U.S. Supreme Court, and U.S. Court of Appeals, Sixth Circuit; 2003, U.S. Court of Appeals, Ninth Circuit. *Education:* State University of New York at Stony Brook (B.A., 1984); Washington University (J.D., 1988). Washington University Journal of Urban and Contemporary Law, 1986-1988. Trial Advocacy Program, National Institute of Trial Advocacy, March 1994. *Member:* American Bar Association; National Association of Securities Dealers (Member, Board of Arbitrators, 1992—). ***PRACTICE AREAS:*** Civil Litigation; Federal Civil Litigation; ADA Litigation. ***Email:*** cvalente@ksc-law.com

RICHARD DEMAREST YANT, born East Chicago, Indiana, September 10, 1955; admitted to bar, 1982, Illinois. *Education:* Purdue University (B.S., 1977; M.S., 1979); University of Illinois College of Law (J.D., cum laude, 1982). *Member:* Illinois State, Chicago and American Bar Associations. ***PRACTICE AREAS:*** Real Estate; Commercial Finance; Corporate. ***Email:*** ryant@ksc-law.com

SENIOR COUNSEL

ROBERT M. BERGER, born Chicago, Illinois, January 29, 1942; admitted to bar, 1966, Illinois. *Education:* University of Michigan (A.B., 1963) Phi Beta Kappa; University of Chicago (J.D., 1966). Order of the Coif. Comments Editor, University of Chicago Law Review, 1965-1966. Author: "Construction Financing, Banking and Loans," in 4-volume treatise Construction Law (Matthew Bender Co., 1991 and annual supps.). Adjunct Professor: Northwestern University Law School, 1997-; Graduate (LL.M.) Program in Real Estate Law, The John Marshall Law School, 1995-1997. Reporter, Revised Uniform Limited Partnership Act.*Member:* Chicago (Board of Managers, 1970-1972; Real Property Committee Chair, 1984-1988) and American (Partnership Law Committee Chair, 1981-1988) Bar Associations; American College of Real Estate Lawyers (Member, Board of Governors, 1995-1998); American Law Institute (Advisory Committee, Restatement of the Law, (Third) Property Mortgages); Chicago Council of Lawyers (Co-Founder and Board Member, 1969-1972). ***LANGUAGES:*** Hebrew. ***PRACTICE AREAS:*** Real Estate; Finance; Business Organizations; Business Transactions. ***Email:*** rberger@ksc-law.com

RICHARD A. JANNEY, born Omaha, Nebraska, May 27, 1972; admitted to bar, 2000, Illinois and U.S. District Court, Northern District of Illinois. *Education:* Butler University (B.S., 1994); Chicago-Kent College of Law (J.D., 2000). Member, Moot Court Honor Society. *Member:* Chicago Bar Association; Intellectual Property Law Association of Chicago. ***PRACTICE AREAS:*** Litigation; Intellectual Property. ***Email:*** rjanney@ksc-law.com

GREGORY KANE, admitted to bar, 2002, Illinois. *Education:* Grinnell College (B.A., 1996); University of Chicago Law School (J.D., 2002). ***PRACTICE AREAS:*** General Corporate; Commercial Real Estate.

MARGARET A. LAVANISH, born Akron, Ohio, August 24, 1969; admitted to bar, 2001, Illinois and U.S. District Court, Northern District of Illinois. *Education:* Duke University (A.B., cum laude, 1991); University of Chicago (J.D., 2001). ***PRACTICE AREAS:*** Commercial Litigation. ***Email:*** mlavanish@ksc-law.com

STANLEY F. WRUBLE, III, born South Bend, Indiana; admitted to bar, 1997, Indiana; 1998, Michigan; 2003, Illinois. *Education:* Valparaiso University (B.A., magna cum laude, 1994); University of Notre Dame (J.D., with distinction, 1997). Pi Sigma Alpha; Sigma Tau Delta; Alpha Lambda Delta. Lecturer, Legal Writing, Notre Dame , 1996-1997. Trial Advocacy, Northwestern School of Law, 2005—. ***PRACTICE AREAS:*** Employment Law; Employment Litigation; Litigation. ***Email:*** swruble@kcs-law.com

THE LAW OFFICES OF STUART P. KRAUSKOPF

2 NORTH LASALLE STREET, SUITE 1200
CHICAGO, ILLINOIS 60602
Telephone: 312-377-9592
Fax: 312-264-5618
Email: stu@stuklaw.com

Litigation, Business Litigation, Business Law, Insurance.

STUART P. KRAUSKOPF, born Chicago, Illinois, December 4, 1959; admitted to bar, 1985, Illinois and U.S. District Court, Northern District of Illinois. *Education:* University of Illinois (B.A., 1982); IIT/Chicago-Kent College of Law (J.D., with distinction, cum laude, 1985). Phi Eta Sigma. *Member:* Chicago (Founder and Chairman, Attorney Malpractice — Prevention and Case Handling Committee), Illinois State and American Bar Associations. ***PRACTICE AREAS:*** Litigation; Business Litigation; Business Law; Insurance.

KREISMAN LAW OFFICES

A Professional Corporation

Established in 1979

55 WEST MONROE STREET
SUITE 3720
CHICAGO, ILLINOIS 60603-5011
Telephone: 312-346-0045
Fax: 312-346-2380
Email: bob@robertkreisman.com
URL: http://www.robertkreisman.com

Practice in all State and Federal Courts. Plaintiff's Personal Injury Litigation, Medical Negligence, Health Care, Wrongful Death Litigation, Premises Liability, Vehicular Accidents, Construction Accidents, Employment Litigation, Product Liability, Commercial Litigation.

FIRM PROFILE: Robert D. Kreisman founded this law firm in 1979. It is the goal of Kreisman Law Offices to uphold the highest principles while representing the rights of its clients. Kreisman Law Offices is committed to seeking justice for its clients.

ROBERT D. KREISMAN, born St. Louis, Missouri, March 1, 1950; admitted to bar, 1976, Illinois, Missouri, U.S. District Court, Northern District of Illinois including Trial Bar and U.S. Court of Appeals, Seventh Circuit. *Education:* University of Missouri (B.A., 1972); John Marshall Law School (J.D., with honors, 1976); DePaul University (LL.M., Taxation, 1981). Author: "The UCC Judicial Admissions Exception to the Statute of Frauds," Illinois Bar Journal, January 1989; "Jury Selection: Who Chooses Whom?" Trial, January, 2000; "The Deposition Gift," ATLA Annual Meeting, July 2000; "My Fair Witness-The Metamorphosis-The Critics Rave," ATLA Case Workshop, 2001; "Out of Order: The Unpredicted Story Order," Illinois Trial Lawyers Association, January Seminar, 2003; "Where's the Surprise? For Practice or for Keeps; Focus Groups Compared to Trial," Trial Journal, Winter 2004. Lecturer: Chicago Bar Association Seminar on "Close Corporation Act," 1978; National College of Advocacy's "Trial Advocacy College," Knoxville, TN, 1999; Voir Dire College, Phoenix, AZ, 1999' ATLA Annual Meeting, Chicago, IL, 2000; ATLA Deposition College, Denver, CO, 2001. Case Workshop Program, San Diego, 2001; Case Workshop Program, Chicago, 2001. ATLA Teleconference, "Juries After September 11," 2001; ATLA Case Workshop Program, Phoenix, AZ, 2002; Illinois Trial Lawyers Association, moderator/faculty, "Identifying and Overcoming Jury Bias," Chicago, IL, January 18, 2003; The Association of Trial Lawyers of America/National College of Advocacy, ATLA Case Workshop Program, faculty, Atlanta, GA. February 27, 2003-March 2, 2003 and Phoenix, Arizona, February 2004. IPE Faculty/Lecturer, "Mastering the Trial Notebook," February 2004. Regional Coordinator, ATLA National Student Trial Advocacy Competition, 2004; IPE Faculty/Lecture, "Trying Civil Cases," August 2004. ATLA Case Workshop Program, Faculty, Atlanta, GA., April 14-17, 2005. *Member:* Chicago, Illinois State (Member, Section on Tort Law) and American (Member, Section on Litigation) Bar Associations; Bar Association of Metropolitan St. Louis; The Missouri Bar; The Association of Trial Lawyers of America; Illinois Trial Lawyers Association; Trial Lawyers for Public Justice; Trial Lawyers Care; Decalogue Society of Lawyers. ***LANGUAGES:*** Spanish. ***REPORTED CASES:*** Moricoli v. Schwartz (1977), 46 Ill.App.3d 481; Jablonski v. Multack (1978), 63 Ill.App.3d 908; Bebee v. Fields (1979), 79 Ill.App.3d 1009; Goldstein Oil Company v. Illinois Property Tax Appeal Board (1987), 156 Ill.App.3d 180; DF Activities Corporation v. Brown (7th Cir. 1988), 851 F.2d 920; Acme Propane v. Tenexco (7th Cir. 1988), 844 F.2d 1317; Carollo v. Financial Federal Savings & Loan Assoc. (1989), 182 Ill.App.3d 996; United Bank of Crete-Steger v. Gainer Bank, N.A. (7th Cir. 1989); 4300 Marine Drive Condominium Association v. Tenenblatt (1991), 221 Ill.App.3d 877. ***PRACTICE AREAS:*** Personal Injury Litigation; Medical Negligence; Products Liability; Wrongful Death; Birth Trauma; Brain Injury; Commercial Litigation; Employment Litigation; State and Federal Litigation. ***Email:*** bob@robertkreisman.com

LEGAL SUPPORT PERSONNEL

YOLANDA FLORES

MAAREN JOHNSON

Language: Spanish.

DAVID K. KREMIN & ASSOCIATES, P.C.

221 N. LASALLE STREET, SUITE 1900
CHICAGO, ILLINOIS 60601
Telephone: 312-456-9000
Toll Free: 1-800-ASK-A-LAWYER (1-800-275-2529)
Fax: 312-456-9900
Email: ASKALAWYER@aol.com
URL: http://www.1800askalawyer.com

Personal Injury, Litigation, Automobile Accidents, Work Accidents, Premises Liability, Product Liability, Fire and Casualty Cases, Medical Malpractice, Birth Defects, Dram Shop, Workers Compensation, Catastrophic Injuries, Spinal Cord, Airplane Crash and Slip and Fall, Wrongful Death.

DAVID K. KREMIN, born Chicago, Illinois, August 26, 1955; admitted to bar, 1983, Illinois, U.S. District Court, Northern District of Illinois and U.S. Federal Court. *Education:* University of Illinois (B.S., 1977; M.B.A., 1980); Illinois Institute of Technology, Chicago-Kent College of Law (J.D., highest honors, 1983). Law Clerk to Hon. Irving R. Norman, Circuit Court of Cook County, Illinois, 1982. Listed in: "Who's Who in American Law"; "Who's Who in Executives and Professionals"; " Million Dollar Plus List Published Chicago Lawyer Magazine Survey". Recent Recovery Clients' Awarded over $50 million. Awarded Leading Personal Injury Attorney Distinction 3 consecutive years. Admitted in the Million Dollar Advocates Forum. *Member:* Chicago, Illinois State and American Bar Associations; Decalogue Society of Lawyers; Illinois Trial Lawyers Association; The Association of Trial Lawyers of America; National Lawyers Association (Chairperson, Tort Division). (Also Member, 1-800-Ask-A-Lawyer & Associates). ***PRACTICE AREAS:*** Plaintiffs Personal Injury; Wrongful Death.

(This Listing Continued)

S. RANDOLPH KRETCHMAR

CHICAGO, ILLINOIS

(See Wilmette)

Mental Health Law, Right to Refuse Psychiatry.

KRISLOV & ASSOCIATES, LTD.

20 NORTH WACKER DRIVE, SUITE 1350
CHICAGO, ILLINOIS 60606
Telephone: 312-606-0500
Telecopier: 312-606-0207
Email: mail@krislovlaw.com
URL: http://www.krislovlaw.com

Trials and Appeals. Class and Derivative Actions in Pension, Municipal, Securities Law, Tax Litigation and Consumer Law, Public Interest and Whistleblower Cases.

CLINTON A. KRISLOV, born Cleveland, Ohio, May 7, 1949; admitted to bar, 1974, Illinois, U.S. District Court, Northern District of Illinois including Trial Bar, U.S. Claims Court and U.S. Tax Court; 1976, U.S. Court of Appeals, Seventh Circuit; 1979, U.S. Supreme Court; 1981, U.S. Court of Appeals, Fifth Circuit; 1982, Michigan and U.S. Court of Appeals for the Federal Circuit; 1984, U.S. Court of Appeals, Third and Eleventh Circuits; 2005, U.S. Court of Appeals, Sixth Circuit and U.S. District Court, Southern District of Illinois. *Education:* Northwestern University (B.A., with distinction, 1971); Cornell Law School (J.D., 1974). Phi Beta Kappa. Moot Court Board. Author: "Scrutiny of the Bounty: Incentive Awards for Plaintiffs in Class Actions," 78 Illinois Bar Journal 286, June, 1990; "Incentive Awards to Named Plaintiffs," Chicago Bar Association Class Action Committee Newsletter, 1989; "Tax Considerations in Buying, Selling and Dissolving the Professional Practice," in Professional Practices, IICLE, 1986; "Civil and Criminal Tax Litigation," in 1981 Federal Tax Skills Course, IICLE, 1981; "Evaluating Publicly Syndicated Investments," in Basic Tax Shelters, IICLE, 1984. Co-Author: "Impact of Code Secs. 6103, 6110 and 7609 upon IRS Audits," 54 Taxes 846, 1976, with Harnack. Adjunct Professor, Federal Income Taxation, IIT/Chicago-Kent College of Law, 1976-1977. Chairman, Federal Tax Skills Program, IICLE, 1981. Member, Board of Editors, Class Action Reports, 1992—. *Member:* Chicago (Vice-Chair, 1995-1997 and Chair, 1997-2000, Class Litigation Committee; Vice Chair, Federal Civil Practice Committee, 2005-2006), Illinois State and American (Member, Sections on: Litigation; Tax, Corporation, Banking and Business Law; Chairman, Special Study of Fifth Amendment Protection of Sole Proprietor Business Records, 1982) Bar Associations; The Association of Trial Lawyers of America; Chicago Counsel of Lawyers; Illinois Trial Lawyers Association; National Association of Securities and Commercial Attorneys (NASCAT). ***REPORTED CASES:*** People ex rel. Sklowdowski v. State, 162 Ill.2d 117, 642 N.E.2d 1180, 205 Ill.Dec. 63 (Ill., June 16, 1994); Georgine v. Amchem Products, Inc., 1994 WL 201184 (E.D.Pa., Apr. 05, 1994); Ryan v. City of Chicago, 148 Ill.App.3d 638, 499 N.E.2d 517, 101 Ill.Dec. 929 (Ill.App. 1 Dist., Sept. 23, 1986); Matter of Grand Jury Subpoena Duces Tecum, 725 F.2d 1110 (7th Cir. (Ill.), Jan. 16, 1984); In re Bank America Securities Lit., 210 FRD 694 (ED Mo. 2002); In re DVI Securities Lit., 2005 WL 13079 (ED Pa. 2005); In re Mercury Finance Co., 249 B.R.4; Krislov v. Rednour, 226 F.3d 851 (7th Cir. 2000) cert. den.; McGuffage v. Irislov, 53145 1147 (2000); County of Cook ex rel. Rifkin v. Bear Stearns, Co., Inc., 215 Ill. 2d 466 (2005); Schachitti v. Prudential Sec., Inc., 1999 U.S. Dist. LEXIS 19391 (1999); Zazove v. Pelikan, Inc., 326 Ill. App.3d 798 (1st Dist. 2000); Commercial Cleaning Services, Inc. L.L.C. v. Colin Service Systems, Inc., 271 F.3d 374 (2d Cir. 2001); Montgomery v. Aetha Plywood Inc., 231 F.3d 399 (7th Cir. 2000). ***Email:*** clint@krislovlaw.com

KENNETH T. GOLDSTEIN, born Chicago, Illinois, August 6, 1968; admitted to bar, 1997, Illinois; 1998, U.S. District Court, Northern District of Illinois and U.S. Court of Appeals, Seventh Circuit. *Education:* University of Wisconsin at Madison (B.A., 1990); John Marshall Law School (J.D., 1996). *Member:* Chicago and Illinois State Bar Association; American Trial Lawyers Association. ***PRACTICE AREAS:*** Class Action; Consumer Fraud; Antitrust. ***Email:*** ken@krislovlaw.com

MICHAEL R. KARNUTH, born Chicago, Illinois, September 8, 1965; admitted to bar, 1999, Illinois and U.S. District Court, Northern District of Illinois; 2003, U.S. Court of Appeals, Seventh Circuit. *Education:* Loyola University (B.B.A., 1988); Chicago-Kent College of Law (J.D., with honors, 1999). Recipient, CALI award, Advanced Research; Securities. Certified Public Accountant, Illinois, 1991. *Member:* Chicago, Illinois State and American Bar Associations; Illinois and American Society of Certified Public Accountants. ***REPORTED CASES:*** Primax Recoveries, Inc. v. Sevilla, 324 F.3d 544 (7th Cir. Apr. 1, 2003); In re DVI, Inc. Sec. Litig., 2005 WL 1307959 (E.D. P.2d May 31, 2005); Doyle v. Blue Cross Blue Shield of Illinois, 149 F.Supp. 2d 427 (N.D. Ill. June 5, 2001). ***PRACTICE AREAS:*** Class Action Litigation; Securities Litigation; Consumer Fraud. ***Email:*** mike@krislovlaw.com

JESSICA J. MEAD, born Iowa City, Iowa, September 25, 1977; admitted to bar, 2003, Illinois and U.S. District Court, Northern District of Illinois. *Education:* Coe College (B.A., cum laude, 2000); Drake University (J.D., with honors, 2003). Recipient: CALI Award, Consumer Protection Practice. *Member:* Chicago and Illinois State Bar Associations. ***PRACTICE AREAS:*** Class Actions; Consumer Fraud; Securities Litigation. ***Email:*** jessica@krislovlaw.com

JASON P. STIEHL, born Belleville, Illinois, May 18, 1976; admitted to bar, 2001, Illinois and U.S. District Court, Northern District of Illinois. *Education:* Trinity University (B.S.B.A., 1997); Chicago-Kent College of Law, Illinois Institute of Technology (J.D., with honors, 2001). Recipient: CALI Award, Seminar in Capital Punishment. *Member:* Chicago and Illinois Bar Associations. ***PRACTICE AREAS:*** Class Actions; Consumer Fraud; Mass Torts; Securities Litigation. ***Email:*** jason@krislovlaw.com

(This Listing Continued)

KRISLOV & ASSOCIATES, LTD., Chicago—Continued

W. JOEL VANDER VLIET, born Grand Rapids Michigan, November 27, 1977; admitted to bar, 2005, Illinois. *Education:* Hope College (B.A., 2000); University of Michigan (J.D., 2004). ***PRACTICE AREAS:*** Class Action Litigation; Consumer Fraud; Securities Litigation. ***Email:*** joel@krislovlaw.com

ELIZABETH NEUGENT-DIXON, born Des Moines, Iowa, November 4, 1977; admitted to bar, 2003, Illinois. *Education:* Marquette University (B.A., 2000); Drake University (J.D., 2003). ***PRACTICE AREAS:*** Class Action Litigation; Consumer Fraud; Securities Litigation. ***Email:*** liz@krislovlaw.com

REPRESENTATIVE CLIENT: Retired Chicago Police Assn.

KUBASIAK, FYLSTRA, REIZEN & ROTUNNO

PROFESSIONAL CORPORATION
TWO FIRST NATIONAL PLAZA
20 SOUTH CLARK STREET, SUITE 2900
CHICAGO, ILLINOIS 60603
Telephone: 312-630-9600
Fax: 312-630-7939
URL: http://www.kfrrlaw.com

General Practice including representation of Business Entities (Formation, Operation, Acquisition and Merger), Commercial Litigation (Ownership Disputes, Contract, Trust and Estate, Construction, Securities and Financial Litigation), Taxation (Federal, State, Local and International), and Commercial Real Estate (Finance, Construction, Defaults and Workouts and Environmental Matters), Municipal Law (Development Agreements, Land Use Planning and Governmental Relations).

GERALD E. KUBASIAK, born Coldwater, Michigan, April 11, 1940; admitted to bar, 1968, Illinois; 1969, New York. *Education:* Western Michigan University (B.B.A., 1962); Loyola University (J.D., 1967); New York University (LL.M., in Taxation, 1968). Author: "Income Tax Considerations in Administering A Settlement Fund," 62 Chicago Bar Record 212, 1980; "U.S. Income Tax Planning for a Nonresident's Personal Service Income," 16 The International Lawyer 397, 1981; "Tax Break Available to Class Action Defendants, But Ambiguities Remain," 70 Journal of Taxation 5, 1989. Co-author: "Federal Income Taxes Affecting Real Estate," Real Estate Syndication, Illinois Institute for Continuing Legal Education, 1983. *Member:* Chicago (Member, Federal Taxation Committee), New York State and American (Member, Section of Taxation) Bar Associations. ***Email:*** gkubasiak@kfrrlaw.com

RAYMOND A. FYLSTRA, born Grand Rapids, Michigan, October 12, 1947; admitted to bar, 1972, Illinois. *Education:* Hope College (B.A., cum laude, 1969); Northwestern University School of Law (J.D., 1972). Author: "Settlement of Class Action Cases Prior to Class Certification," 69 Illinois Bar Journal 24, 1980. *Member:* Chicago (Member: Civil Practice Committee, Division I, Chairman, 1993-1994; Civil Practice Executive Committee, Chairman, 1996-1997), DuPage County, Illinois State and American Bar Associations. ***PRACTICE AREAS:*** Complex Commercial Litigation; Construction Insurance; Construction Litigation; Fiduciary Litigation; Trial Practice. ***Email:*** rfylstra@kfrrlaw.com

DANIEL J. KUBASIAK, born Sturgis, Michigan, February 19, 1949; admitted to bar, 1981, Illinois. *Education:* Xavier University (B.A., 1971); Northwestern University (M.M., 1974); Loyola University (J.D., 1981). Chief Administrative Officer, Committee on Finance, Chicago City Council, 1983-1987. *Member:* Chicago, Illinois State and American Bar Associations. ***PRACTICE AREAS:*** Administrative Law; Corporate Law; Municipal Law. ***Email:*** dkubasiak@kfrrlaw.com

RICHARD S. REIZEN, born Chicago, Illinois, June 17, 1954; admitted to bar, 1980, Illinois; U.S. District Court, Northern District of Illinois including Trial Bar. *Education:* Clark University (B.A., 1976); Loyola University (J.D., 1980). Member, Loyola University Law Journal, 1979-1980. Author: "Davis v. Passman: Implied Constitutional Remedies for Congressional Employees," 11 Loy. Chi. L. J., 179 (1979). Co-Author: "New Limits on Accountant's Liability: Lenders Beware," Illinois Banker, Vol. 71 (1991). Arbitrator, National Futures Association, 1987—. Faculty Member: Advanced Investigator Training Schools for both the Federal Deposit Insurance Corporation and the Resolution Trust Corporation. *Member:* Chicago, Illinois State, Federal and American (Member, Construction Litigation Committee) Bar Associations. ***Email:*** rreizen@kfrrlaw.com

STEVEN J. ROTUNNO, born Chicago, Illinois, August 22, 1953; admitted to bar, 1978, Illinois; U.S. District Court, Northern and Central Districts of Illinois including Trial Bar; U.S. Court of Appeals, Seventh Circuit. *Education:* University of Illinois (B.A., 1975); Loyola University (J.D., 1978). Phi Beta Kappa; Evans Scholar. Author: "Standard of Liability For Directors and Officers In Suits Brought By FDIC," IBA Law Watch," Fall 1992. Co-Author: "Commercial Liability Issues," chapter of the *Healthcare Liability Desk Book*, 1995. Author: "Making Healthcare Business Decisions Without Being Sued," published and presented at the seminar: Health Care Liability Issues in the 90's (January 1995); "Risk Managers Must Now Worry About Corporate Liability Claims" for the Chicagoland Healthcare Risk Management Society (Fall 1996). *Member:* Chicago (President, Young Lawyers Section, 1989-1990; Board of Managers, 1991-1993) and American Bar Associations. ***PRACTICE AREAS:*** Securities; Construction Law; Professional Liability; Complex Litigation. ***Email:*** srotunno@kfrrlaw.com

GREGORY A. THORPE, born Oak Park, Illinois, April 20, 1950; admitted to bar, 1978, Illinois. *Education:* University of Illinois (B.A., with honors, 1974); Illinois Institute of Technology/Chicago-Kent College of Law (J.D., with high honors, 1978). Notes and Comments Editor, Chicago-Kent Law Review, 1977-1978. *Member:* Illinois Mortgage Bankers Association (President, 2003). Fellow, American College of Mortgage Attorneys. ***PRACTICE AREAS:*** Commercial Real Estate; Finance. ***Email:*** gthorpe@kfrrlaw.com

JOHN A. DIENNER, III, born Evanston, Illinois, May 22, 1945; admitted to bar, 1972, Illinois and U.S. District Court, Northern District of Illinois; 1973, U.S. Court of Appeals, Seventh Circuit; 1975, U.S. Supreme Court; 1983, U.S. Tax Court. *Education:* DePauw University (B.A., 1969); John Marshall Law School (J.D., 1972). Assistant State's Attorney, Cook County, 1973-1981. Chief of Federal Litigation Division, 1975-1979. General Counsel, Cook County Hospital System, 1979-1981. *Member:* Chicago Bar Association (Member, Sections on: Securities Law; Business Law). ***PRACTICE AREAS:*** Civil Litigation; Commercial Litigation; Civil Appeals; Securities Arbitration; Securities Fraud; Attorney Discipline. ***Email:*** jdienner@kfrrlaw.com

DANIEL C. McCABE, born Aurora, Illinois, November 23, 1968; admitted to bar, 1994, Illinois; U.S. District Court, Northern District of Illinois. *Education:* Northwestern University (B.A., 1991); Chicago-Kent College of Law (J.D., 1994). Moot Court Honor Society. Recipient: Jessup Award, 1991. Formerly with Peterson & Ross. ***PRACTICE AREAS:*** Complex Commercial Litigation; Contract Litigation; Construction Litigation; Insurance Litigation. ***Email:*** dmccabe@kfrrlaw.com

JOHN C. ANDERSON, born Joliet, Illinois, December 27, 1970; admitted to bar, 1999, Illinois. *Education:* Illinois State University (B.S., 1995); John Marshall Law School (J.D., 1999). Staff Editor, The John Marshall Law Review, 1997-1998. Law Clerk: Justice Thomas L. Kilbride, Illinois Supreme Court; Justice Robert Chapman Buckley, Illinois Appellate Court. Author: "Transmitting Legal Documents Over the Internet: How to Protect Your Client and Yourself," 27 Rutgers Computer & Tech. L. J. 1, 2001; "Respecting Human Rights: Multinational Corporations Strike Out," 2 U. PA. J. Lab. & Employment L. 463, 2000; "A Proposed Code of Ethics for Employers and Customers of Notaries: A Companion to the Notary Public Code of Professional Responsibility," 32 J. Marshall L. Rev. 887, 1999 (with M. Closen); "Document Authentication in Electronic Commerce: The Misleading Notary Public Analog for the Digital Signature Certification Authority," 17 J. Marshall J. Computer & Info. L. 833, 1999 (with M. Closen); "Three Generations Later and Still No Class: Protecting Americans With Disabilities Under 42 U.S.C. Section 1985 (3), the Ku Klux Klan Act," 47 Drake L. Rev. 537, 1999. ***PRACTICE AREAS:*** Appellate Practice; Commercial Litigation. ***Email:*** janderson@kfrrlaw.com

CLARKE M. GILLESPIE, III, born Auburn, Alabama, December 20, 1961; admitted to bar, 1995, Illinois. *Education:* University of Chicago (B.A., 1992); IIT Chicago - Kent College of Law (J.D. with honors, 1995). Recipient: University of Chicago Howell-Murray Alumni Award, Maroon Key Society; American Jurisprudence Award in Trial Advocacy. ***PRACTICE AREAS:*** Commercial Litigation; Construction Litigation; Estate Litigation; Trust Litigation. ***Email:*** mgillespie@kfrrlaw.com

NOËL P. GOUDREAU, born LaSalle, Illinois, September 25, 1969; admitted to bar, 1996, Illinois, U.S. District Court, Northern and Central Districts of Illinois and U.S. Court of Appeals, Seventh Circuit. *Education:* University of Illinois (B.S., with honors, 1991); Loyola University at Chicago (J.D., cum laude, 1996). Phi Kappa Phi. *Member:* Chicago, Illinois State and American Bar Associations. ***PRACTICE AREAS:*** Business Law; Employee Benefits; Labor and Employment; Taxation; Trusts and Estates. ***Email:*** ngoudreau@kfrrlaw.com

BARRY P. KALTENBACH, born Oak Park, Illinois, October 8, 1972; admitted to bar, 1999, Illinois; 2000, U.S. District Court, Northern District of Illinois. *Education:* Northern Illinois University (B.S., 1995); John Marshall Law School (J.D., magna cum laude, 1999). Phi Alpha Delta (Member, 1996-1999; Treasurer, and Recruitment Chair, 1996-1997). Member, Editorial Board, The John Marshall Law Review. *Member:* Chicago and Illinois State Bar Associations; Defense Research Institute. ***PRACTICE AREAS:*** Commercial Litigation; Construction Law; Insurance Litigation. ***Email:*** bkaltenbach@kfrrlaw.com

ROBERT C. KIMMETH, JR., born Park Ridge, Illinois; admitted to bar, 1996, Illinois and U.S. District Court, Northern District of Illinois. *Education:* Cornell University (B.A., magna cum laude, 1988); University of Michigan (M.P.P., 1990; J.D., 1996). *Member:* Chicago and American Bar Associations. ***PRACTICE AREAS:*** Complex Commercial Litigation; Securities Arbitration; Insurance Coverage; Professional Malpractice. ***Email:*** rkimmeth@kfrrlaw.com

MANUEL J. PLACENCIA, JR., born East Chicago, Indiana, September 27, 1972; admitted to bar, 1998, Illinois and U.S. District Court, Northern District of Illinois. *Education:* Dartmouth College (B.A., Philosophy, 1994); University of Illinois (J.D., 1997). *Member:* Illinois State Bar Association. ***PRACTICE AREAS:*** Commercial Litigation. ***Email:*** mplacencia@kfrrlaw.com

JEANNIE M. RIDINGS, born Illinois; admitted to bar, 2005, Illinois. *Education:* Mount Mary College (B.A., Philosophy, 1992); The George Washington University (M.A., Philosophy, Social Policy, 2001; Ph.D., Human Sciences, 2004); Northwestern University School of Law (J.D., 2004). ***PRACTICE AREAS:*** Commercial Litigation; Construction Litigation; Commercial Contracts. ***Email:*** jridings@kfrrlaw.com

ERIC P. SPARKS, born Bloomington, Illinois, May 2, 1970; admitted to bar, 2003, Illinois and U.S. District Court, Northern District of Illinois. *Education:* University of Illinois (B.S., summa cum laude, 1992); Northwestern University (Ph.D., 2001); University of Chicago Law School (J.D., 2003). Phi Beta Kappa. *Member:* Chicago and Illinois State Bar Associations. ***PRACTICE AREAS:*** Commercial Litigation; Trusts and Estates; Construction Litigation. ***Email:*** esparks@kfrrlaw.com

OF COUNSEL

ELLEN CHAPELLE, born Ann Arbor, Michigan, August 30, 1966; admitted to bar, 1991, Illinois; 1992, U.S. District Court, Northern District of Illinois. *Education:* University of Michigan (B.A., with high honors, 1988; J.D., cum laude, 1991). ***PRACTICE AREAS:*** Commercial Litigation; Construction Litigation. ***Email:*** echapelle@kfrrlaw.com

(This Listing Continued)

STEVEN H. KUH, P.C.

ONE NORTH FRANKLIN STREET, SUITE 650
CHICAGO, ILLINOIS 60606-3420
Telephone: 312-236-5500
Facsimile: 312-236-3462
Email: stevenkuh@hotmail.com

Commercial Litigation. Employment Litigation. General Practice.

(This Listing Continued)

FIRM PROFILE: In 20 years of practice, Steven H. Kuh has represented corporate, insurance, and individual clients before the state and federal trial and appellate courts in various jurisdictions. He has litigated cases for business fraud, breach of contract, breach of fiduciary duty, misappropriation of trade secrets, unfair competition, and discrimination in employment.

STEVEN H. KUH, born Oceanside, New York, September 8, 1959; admitted to bar, 1984, District of Columbia; 1988, Maryland and Illinois. *Education:* University of Barcelona, Barcelona, Spain; Tufts University (B.A., summa cum laude, 1981); Georgetown University (J.D., 1984), Phi Beta Kappa. Case & Notes Editor, Law & Policy in International Business, 1983-1984. Author: Casenote, "R. v. Banville: An Extraterritorial Application of Canada's Fair Trial Law," 8 ASILS Intl. L.J. 103 (1984). *Member:* Illinois State Bar Association; The District of Columbia Bar; Maryland State Bar Association. ***PRACTICE AREAS:*** Business Litigation; Commercial Litigation; Business Law; Employment Law; Employment Discrimination; Business Piracy; Wrongful Termination. ***Email:*** stevenkuh@hotmail.com

MARK J. KUPIEC

77 WEST WASHINGTON, SUITE 519
CHICAGO, ILLINOIS 60602
Telephone: 312-541-1878
Fax: 312-641-1745
URL: http://www.chicago-zoning.com

Zoning, Planning and Land Use, Eminent Domain, Condemnation, Real Estate, Building Code Compliance, Business Licensing.

FIRM PROFILE: Mark Kupiec has concentrated his practice in Zoning Law and related issues in Chicago, Illinois for over 20 years.

MARK J. KUPIEC, born Chicago, Illinois; admitted to bar, 1975, Illinois. *Education:* Northwestern University (B.A., 1971); John Marshall Law School (J.D., 1975). *Member:* Chicago (Member, Real Estate Committee), Illinois and American (Member, Real Estate and Trusts and Estates Committees) Bar Associations. [U.S. Army Reserves, 1971-1977]

KURASCH & KLEIN

188 WEST RANDOLPH STREET, SUITE 1201
CHICAGO, ILLINOIS 60601
Telephone: 312-372-7250
Fax: 312-372-7254
Email: dkurasch@chicagopilaw.com
URL: http://www.chicagopilaw.com

Milwaukee, Wisconsin Office: 1640 North Jackson Street, 53202. Telephone: 414-313-5677. Fax: 414-277-0907.

Personal Injury; Accidents, Automobile Accidents and Injuries; Wrongful Death, Workers Compensation, Medical Malpractice, Nursing Home Accidents, Catastrophic Injury, Trusts Accidents, Motorcycle Accidents, Boating Accidents.

FIRM PROFILE: For more than thirty years, our firm has established expertise in successfully and aggressively pursuing every type of personal injury litigation. The firm of Kurasch & Klein is fluent in the foreign languages of Polish and Spanish.

MEMBERS OF FIRM

DONALD A. KURASCH, born Oklahoma City, Oklahoma, May 22, 1945; admitted to bar, 1972, Illinois. *Education:* Grinnell College (B.A., 1967); University of Illinois (J.D., 1972). *Member:* Chicago, Illinois State and American Bar Associations. ***PRACTICE AREAS:*** Personal Injury; Workers Compensation; Medical Malpractice; Accidents; Automobile Accidents and Injuries; Wrongful Death; Premises Liability; Products Liability; FELA Occupational Hearing Loss. ***Email:*** dkurasch@chicagopilaw.com

DANIEL KLEIN, born Dayton, Ohio; admitted to bar, 1990, Illinois; 1994, Florida. *Education:* Ohio State University (B.A., 1987; J.D., 1990). *Member:* Chicago Bar Association; The Florida Bar; Illinois Trial Lawyers Association. ***PRACTICE AREAS:*** Personal Injury; Medical Malpractice; Wrongful Death; Products Liability; Accidents; Automobile Accidents and Injuries; Nursing Home Negligence; Construction Accidents. ***Email:*** dklein@chicagopilaw.com

ASSOCIATE

ELISSA A. TISDAHL, admitted to bar, 2004, Illinois; registered to practice before U.S. Patent and Trademark Office. *Education:* Bates College (B.S., 2000); Chicago Kent College of Law (J.D., 2003). ***LANGUAGES:*** Spanish. ***PRACTICE AREAS:*** Plaintiffs Personal Injury; Medical Malpractice; Wrongful Death; Products Liability; Automobile Accidents and Injuries. ***Email:*** etisdahl@chicagopilaw.com

KURLANDER & GRIPPO, LLP

155 NORTH MICHIGAN AVENUE, SUITE 620
CHICAGO, ILLINOIS 60601
Telephone: 312-616-4246
Facsimile: 312-239-9343
URL: http://www.kurlanderandgrippo.com

General Civil Practice, Antitrust and Trade Regulation, Civil Litigation, Commercial Litigation, Corporate Law, Business Law, Bankruptcy, Employee Benefits, Family Law, Divorce, Taxation, Insurance, Labor Law, Mergers and Acquisitions, Product Liability, Real Estate, Commercial Real Estate, Trusts and Estates, Trademarks, Copyrights.

MICHELE S. KURLANDER, born St. Louis, Missouri, July 20, 1944; admitted to bar, 1969, Illinois. *Education:* University of Michigan (B.A., 1966); Northwestern University (J.D., 1969). *Member:* Chicago (Member, Real Estate Section), Illinois State (Member, Real Estate, Probate and Trust Law Section) and American (Member, Real Estate, Probate and Trust Law Section) Bar Associations. ***PRACTICE AREAS:*** Commercial Real Estate; Business Law; Trusts and Estates. ***Email:*** lawmichele@aol.com

THEODORE W. GRIPPO, JR., born Chicago, Illinois, February 6, 1953; admitted to bar, 1980, Illinois and U.S. District Court, Northern District of Illinois including Trial Bar; U.S. Court of Appeals, Seventh Circuit; U.S. Supreme Court. *Education:* Grinnell College (B.A., 1977); Northwestern University (J.D., 1980); DePaul University (LL.M., Taxation, 1986). Member: Staff, 1978-1979 and Editorial Board, 1979-1980, Journal of Criminal Law & Criminology. *Member:* Chicago and Illinois State Bar Associations. ***LANGUAGES:*** French and Italian. ***PRACTICE AREAS:*** Commercial Litigation; Family Law; Divorce; Real Estate. ***Email:*** tgrippo@lckb-law.com

OF COUNSEL

WILLIAM F. COALE (1921-1989)

AMOS J. COFFMAN, JR., born New York, N.Y., August 16, 1940; admitted to bar, 1965, Illinois. *Education:* Harvard University (A.B., 1962); University of Michigan (J.D., 1965). Editor, Michigan Law Review, 1964-1965. *Member:* Chicago and American (Member, Sections on Business Law and Real Estate, Probate and Trust Law) Bar Associations. ***PRACTICE AREAS:*** Business Law; Corporate Law; Trusts and Estates; Probate. ***Email:*** acoffman@lckb-law.com

LEON E. LINDENBAUM, born Chicago, Illinois, May 20, 1937; admitted to bar, 1961, Illinois; U.S. District Court, Northern District of Illinois including Trial Bar; U.S. Court of Appeals, Seventh Circuit. *Education:* University of Wisconsin (B.B.A., 1958; J.D., 1961). Trial Attorney, Antitrust Division, U.S. Department of Justice, 1961-1966. *Member:* Illinois State and American Bar Associations. ***PRACTICE AREAS:*** Civil Litigation. ***Email:*** llindenbaum@lckb-law.com

KUTAK ROCK LLP

Established in 1965

ONE SOUTH WACKER DRIVE
CHICAGO, ILLINOIS 60606-4614
Telephone: 312-602-4100
Facsimile: 312-602-4101
URL: http://www.kutakrock.com

Atlanta, Georgia Office: Suite 2100, 225 Peachtree Street, NE, 30303-1731. Telephone: 404-222-4600. Facsimile: 404-222-4654.
Denver, Colorado Office: Suite 3100, 1801 California Street, 80202-2658. Telephone: 303-297-2400. Facsimile: 303-292-7799.
Des Moines, Iowa Office: Suite 124, Highland Building, 4201 Westown Parkway, Des Moines, 50266-6720. Telephone: 515-224-1266. Facsimile: 515-457-7669.
Fayetteville, Arkansas Office: The Three Sisters Building, 214 West Dickson Street, 72701-5221. Telephone: 501-973-4200. Facsimile: 501-973-0007.
Kansas City, Missouri Office: Valencia Place, Suite 200, 444 West 47th Street, 64112-1914. Telephone: 816-960-0090. Telefax: 816-960-0041.
Little Rock, Arkansas Office: Suite 1100, 425 West Capitol Avenue, 72201-3409. Telephone: 501-975-3000. Facsimile: 501-975-3001.
Los Angeles, California Office: Suite 3000, 555 West Fifth Street, 90013-1010. Telephone: 213-996-8478. Facsimile: 213-996-8479.
Oklahoma City, Oklahoma Office: Suite 475, 6305 Waterford Boulevard, 73118-1116. Telephone: 405-848-2475. Facsimile: 405-842-5748.
Omaha, Nebraska Office: The Omaha Building, 1650 Farnam Street, 68102-2186. Telephone: 402-346-6000. Facsimile: 402-346-1148.
Scottsdale, Arizona Office: Suite 300, 8601 N. Scottsdale Road, 85253-2742. Telephone: 480-429-5000. Facsimile: 480-429-5001.
Washington, D.C. Office: Suite 1000, 1101 Connecticut Avenue, NW, 20036-4374. Telephone: 202-828-2400. Facsimile: 202-828-2488.
Irvine, California Office: Suite 1100, 18201 Von Karman Avenue, 92612-1077. Telephone: 949-417-0999. Facsimile: 949-417-5394.
Pasadena, California Office: Suite 308, 201 South Lake Avenue, 91101-3004. Telephone: 626-432-1630. Facsimile: 626-432-1614.
Richmond, Virginia Office: Bank of America Center, Suite 800, 1111 East Main Street, 23219-3103. Telephone: 804-644-0313. Facsimile: 804-783-6192.
Wichita, Kansas Office: Suite 370, 8301 East 21st Street North, 67206-2935. Telephone: 316-609-7900. Facsimile: 316-630-8021.

Civil Litigation and Bankruptcy, Public Finance, Corporate and Structured Finance, Banking and Commercial Lending, Real Estate Law, Taxation Law, Health Care and Hospital Law.

FIRM PROFILE: Founded in Omaha in 1965, Kutak Rock conducts a full-service, multidisciplinary practice. While the firm has long had a nationally recognized public and corporate finance practice, we have also developed a sophisticated business and litigation practice representing clients across the country in complex transactions and major litigation. Kutak Rock has represented every major investment banking firm in the United States; major European, Asian and domestic money-center banks; savings and loan associations; insurance companies; national real estate syndicators and developers; major national franchising enterprises; and numerous other financial institutions, businesses and state and local governmental units. The firm's litigation practice group represents corporate and individual clients in federal and state courts nationwide in complex civil litigation matters and represents clients in arbitration and mediation proceedings. The firm's Healthcare/hospital law group represents hospitals and physician organizations in numerous states.

PARTNERS

JERRY B. WALLACK, born New York, N.Y., April 15, 1952; admitted to bar, 1978, Illinois and U.S. District Court, Northern District of Illinois; 1980, U.S. Tax Court. *Education:* Oberlin College (A.B., 1974); University of Chicago (A.M., Public Policy Studies,

(This Listing Continued)

KUTAK ROCK LLP, Chicago—Continued

1977; J.D., 1978). Co-author: with Mark A. Hall, "Intergovernmental Cooperation and the Transfer of Powers," University of Illinois Law Review 775, 1981. *Member:* Chicago Bar Association. ***PRACTICE AREAS:*** Public Finance; Structured Finance. ***Email:*** jerry.wallack@kutakrock.com

ROBERT M. STAR, born Chicago, Illinois, October 24, 1945; admitted to bar, 1973, Illinois. *Education:* Miami University; University of California at Berkeley (A.B., 1967); University of Chicago (J.D., 1973). *Member:* National Association of Bond Lawyers. ***PRACTICE AREAS:*** Municipal Finance; Public Authority Finance. ***Email:*** robert.star@kutakrock.com

DENNIS L. HOLSAPPLE, born Corona, California, March 10, 1953; admitted to bar, 1978, Nebraska and U.S. District Court, District of Nebraska; 1987, New York; 1991, Illinois. *Education:* University of Iowa (B.A., with high distinction, 1975); University of Michigan (J.D., magna cum laude, 1978). ***PRACTICE AREAS:*** Securities Law and Municipal Finance; Municipal Debt. ***Email:*** dennis.holsapple@kutakrock.com

JAY GILBERT, born Chicago, Illinois, July 20, 1949; admitted to bar, 1975, Illinois; 1996, Wisconsin. *Education:* Indiana University (B.A., 1971; J.D., 1975). *Member:* Chicago and Illinois State Bar Associations. ***Email:*** jay.gilbert@kutakrock.com

KEVIN L. BARNEY, born Logan, Utah, September 1, 1958; admitted to bar, 1985, Illinois. *Education:* Brigham Young University (B.A., 1982); University of Illinois (J.D., 1985); DePaul University (LL.M., Taxation, 1990). *Member:* Chicago and American Bar Associations. ***PRACTICE AREAS:*** Public Finance. ***Email:*** kevin.barney@kutakrock.com

(For biographical data of Atlanta Lawyers, see Professional Biographies at Atlanta, Georgia).
(For biographical data of Denver Lawyers, see Professional Biographies at Denver, Colorado).
(For biographical data of Des Moines Lawyers, See Professional Biographies at West Des Moines, Iowa).
(For biographical data of Fayetteville Lawyers, see Professional Biographies at Fayetteville, Arkansas).
(For biographical data of Kansas City Lawyers, see Professional Biographies at Kansas City, Missouri)
(For biographical data of Little Rock Lawyers, see Professional Biographies at Little Rock, Arkansas).
(For biographical data of Irvine, see Professional Biographies at Irvine, California).
(For biographical data of New York Lawyers, see Professional Biographies at New York, N.Y.).
(For biographical data of Oklahoma City Lawyers, see Professional Biographies at Oklahoma City, Oklahoma).
(For biographical data of Omaha Lawyers, see Professional Biographies at Omaha, Nebraska).
(For biographical data of Pasadena Lawyers, see Professional Biographies at Pasadena, California).
(For biographical data of Pittsburgh Lawyers, see Professional Biographies at Pittsburgh, Pennsylvania).
(For biographical data of Richmond Lawyers, see Professional Biographies at Richmond, Virginia).
(For biographical data of Scottsdale Lawyers, see Professional Biographies at Scottsdale, Arizona).
(For biographical data of Washington Lawyers, see Professional Biographies at Washington D.C.).

LaBARGE, CAMPBELL & LYON, L.L.C.

200 WEST JACKSON BOULEVARD
SUITE 2050
CHICAGO, ILLINOIS 60606
Telephone: 312-580-9010
Fax: 312-580-9011
Email: kcampbell@lcllaw.com
URL: http://www.lcllaw.com

General Civil and Trial Practice in all Courts, with Emphasis in Transportation Liability Law, Building Construction Liability Law, Products Liability Law, Medical Malpractice Law, Asbestos Litigation, Commercial Litigation, Insurance Coverage and Appellate Practice.

FIRM PROFILE: LaBarge, Campbell & Lyon, L.L.C. was founded in 1997 by Michael R. LaBarge, Kevin Campbell and Bruce W. Lyon. The firm is dedicated to representing insurance carriers, their insureds, self-insured corporations and individuals in all aspects of civil litigation and insurance related matters and has an unwavering commitment to providing the highest quality legal services to our clients at a reasonable cost. This includes not only being ready, willing and able to try any case, but also working with our clients to thoroughly evaluate cases at an early stage so that a determination can be made as to whether settlement should be explored. The principals also have extensive experience in various forms of alternative dispute resolution, including mediation and arbitration. The firm has state-of-the-art computer technology including legal research, e-mail, voice mail and billing systems that can accommodate a client's specific billing requirements.

MICHAEL R. LaBARGE, born La Grange, Illinois, December 14, 1956; admitted to bar, 1982, Illinois and U.S. District Court, Northern District of Illinois, 1988, Trial Bar. *Education:* University of Notre Dame (B.A., 1979); University of Illinois (J.D., 1982). Selected as a Leading Illinois Attorney in Law and Leading Attorneys. *Member:* Chicago and Illinois State Bar Associations; Defense Research Institute. ***PRACTICE AREAS:*** Transportation Liability; Construction Liability; Premises Liability; Insurance Coverage. ***Email:*** mlabarge@lcllaw.com

KEVIN CAMPBELL, born Detroit, Michigan, November 6, 1956; admitted to bar, 1982, Illinois and U.S. District Court, Northern District of Illinois. *Education:* Denison University (B.A., 1979); Boston University (J.D., 1982). Omicron Delta Kappa; Omicron Delta Epsilon; Mortar Board. *Member:* Chicago and Illinois State Bar Associations; The Society of Trial Lawyers; Defense Research Institute; Illinois Association of Healthcare Attorneys. ***PRACTICE AREAS:*** Medical Malpractice; Nursing Home Liability; Construction Liability; Products Liability; Transportation Liability; Insurance Bad Faith Defense. ***Email:*** kcampbell@lcllaw.com

BRUCE W. LYON, born Evanston, Illinois, December 31, 1959; admitted to bar, 1984, Illinois and U.S. District Court, Northern, Central and Southern Districts of Illinois, Western District of Wisconsin and Northern District of Indiana. *Education:* St. Olaf College (B.A., cum laude, 1981); DePaul University (J.D., with honors, 1984). *Member:* Chicago and Illinois State Bar Associations; Illinois Association of Defense Trial Counsel. ***PRACTICE AREAS:*** Products Liability; Construction Liability; Asbestos Litigation; Commercial Litigation; Transportation Liability; Insurance Coverage. ***Email:*** blyon@lcllaw.com

---

DEBORAH J. KLEIN, born Chicago, Illinois, July 14, 1970; admitted to bar, 1994, Illinois, U.S. District Court, Northern and Central Districts of Illinois, U.S. Court of Appeals, Seventh Circuit and U.S. Supreme Court; 2001, Indiana; U.S. District Court, Northern and Southern Districts of Indiana. *Education:* University of Illinois (B.A., 1991); DePaul University (J.D., with honors, 1994). Order of the Coif. Editor, DePaul-LCA Journal of Art and Entertainment Law. *Member:* Lake County, Chicago, Illinois State and Indiana State Bar Associations. ***PRACTICE AREAS:*** Transportation Liability; Construction Liability; Premises Liability; Appellate Practice; Insurance Coverage. ***Email:*** dklein@lcllaw.com

MELANIE A. STRUBBE, born Los Angeles, California, September 11, 1970; admitted to bar, 1995, California and U.S. District, Southern District of California; 1996, Nevada; 1997, Illinois. *Education:* Northwestern University (B.A., 1992); Houston University Law Center (J.D., cum laude, 1995). Order of the Barons. Member, American Concrete Institute. *Member:* Orange County Bar Association; Chicago and Illinois State Bar Associations. ***PRACTICE AREAS:*** Insurance Defense; Construction Litigation. ***Email:*** mstrubbe@lcllaw.com

ANGIE M. GROVE, born Bowling Green, Ohio, September 30, 1976; admitted to bar, 2001, Illinois. *Education:* Miami University (B.A., 1998); DePaul University (J.D., 2001). ***PRACTICE AREAS:*** Insurance Defense; Construction Law; Personal Injury. ***Email:*** agrove@lcllaw.com

BROOKE H. MATTEUCCI, born LaGrange, Illinois; admitted to bar, 2002, Illinois. *Education:* University of Iowa (B.A., 1998); DePaul University (J.D., 2002). ***PRACTICE AREAS:*** Transportation Liability; Premises Liability; Construction Litigation. ***Email:*** bmatteucci@lcllaw.com

LISA L. LANTERO, born Chicago, Illinois, September 29, 1958; admitted to bar, 1983, Illinois and U.S. District Court, Northern District of Illinois. *Education:* University of Colorado at Boulder (B.A., with honors, 1980); DePaul University (J.D., 1983). Member, DePaul University Law Review, 1980-1983. *Member:* Chicago and Illinois State Bar Associations. ***LANGUAGES:*** French. ***PRACTICE AREAS:*** Construction Liability; Transportation Liability; Premises Liability; Commercial Litigation; Insurance Coverage. ***Email:*** llantero@lcllaw.com

DIANA D. McCALL, born Olney, Illinois; admitted to bar, 2002, Illinois. *Education:* Southern Illinois University, Edwardsville (B.S., with honors, 1984); University of Illinois (J.D., cum laude, 2002). Author: "Stating the Obvious: Patents and Biological Material," Journal of Law, Technology and Policy, University of Illinois, Spring, 2003. *Member:* Chicago and Illinois State Bar Associations. ***PRACTICE AREAS:*** Insurance Defense; Construction Litigation. ***Email:*** dmccall@lcllaw.com

KATHERINE M. BENSON, born Milwaukee, Wisconsin; admitted to bar, 2003, Illinois. *Education:* University of Dayton (B.A., in History, cum laude, 1999); DePaul University (J.D., 2003). ***PRACTICE AREAS:*** Insurance Defense. ***Email:*** kbenson@lcllaw.com

CINDY DOBBINS, born Evanston, Illinois, August 24, 1972; admitted to bar, 2004, Illinois. *Education:* Purdue University (B.A., 1994); John Marshall Law School (J.D., 2004). Dean's List. Editor, The Journal of Computer and Information Law, 2002-2004. *Member:* Chicago, Illinois State and American Bar Associations; Womens Bar Association. ***PRACTICE AREAS:*** Insurance Defense; Construction Law. ***Email:*** cdobbins@lcllaw.com

MICHAEL J. MacFARLANE, born Blue Island, Illinois, June 15, 1975; admitted to bar, 2001, Illinois. *Education:* Eastern Illinois University (B.A., summa cum laude, 1997); DePaul University (J.D., 2001). *Member:* Chicago, Illinois State and American Bar Associations. ***PRACTICE AREAS:*** Civil Litigation. ***Email:*** mmacfarlane@lcllaw.com

REPRESENTATIVE CLIENTS: A list of representative clients will be made available upon request.

LADAS & PARRY LLP

224 SOUTH MICHIGAN AVENUE
CHICAGO, ILLINOIS 60604
Telephone: 312-427-1300
Telecopy: 312-427-6663; 312-427-6668
Email: chmail@ladasparry.com
URL: http://www.ladas.com

New York, N.Y. Office: 26 West 61st Street. Telephone: 212-708-1800. Telecopy: 212-246-8959; 212-246-8925.
Los Angeles, California Office: 5670 Wilshire Boulevard. Telephone: 323-934-2300. Telecopier: 323-934-0202.
London, England Office: High Holborn House, 52-54 High Holborn, WC1V 6RR. Telephone: 44-71-242-5566. Telex: 262433 MONREF G. Telecopy: 44-207-405-1908.
Munich, Germany Office: Dachauerstrasse 37, 80335 Munich, Germany. Telephone: (089) 269077. Fax: 49-89-269040.

Patent, Trademark, Copyright, Unfair Competition, Licensing, Entertainment and Litigation.

(This Listing Continued)

MEMBERS OF FIRM

RICHARD J. STREIT, born Chicago, Illinois, December 21, 1935; admitted to bar, 1965, Illinois; 1968, U.S. District Court, Northern District of Illinois; registered to practice before U.S. Patent and Trademark Office. *Education:* University of Notre Dame (B.S.M.E., 1957); John Marshall Law School (LL.B., 1965). *Member:* Illinois State Bar Association; Intellectual Property Law Association of Chicago; American Intellectual Property Law Association.

FREDERICK W. MEYERS, born South Bend, Indiana, February 24, 1955; admitted to bar, 1981, Ohio; 1983, U.S. Court of Appeals for the Federal Circuit; 1985, Illinois and U.S. District Court, Northern District of Illinois. *Education:* University of Arkansas (B.A., 1978); Case Western Reserve University (J.D., 1981). *Member:* Chicago (Chairman, Patent, Trademark and Copyright Committee, 1996-1997) and Illinois State Bar Associations; Patent Law Association of Chicago; International Trademark Association (Chairman, Regulatory Analysis Committee, Latin American Subcommittee, 1996-1997).

JOHN E. McKIE, born Washington, D.C., December 28, 1956; admitted to bar, 1982, District of Columbia; 1991, U.S. Court of Appeals for the Federal Circuit (Not admitted in Illinois). *Education:* University of Notre Dame (A.B., 1979); George Washington University (J.D., cum laude, 1982). Attorney-Adviser, U.S. International Trade Commission, 1987-1990. *Member:* District of Columbia Bar; American Bar Association (Member, Patent, Trademark and Copyright Section and Franchising Forum); American Intellectual Property Law Association.

ASSOCIATES

EDWARD J. CHALFIE, born Chicago, Illinois, July 6, 1948; admitted to bar, 1978, Illinois and U.S. Court of Appeals, Seventh Circuit; 1979, U.S. District Court, Northern District of Illinois and U.S. Court of Appeals for the Federal Circuit; 1988, U.S. District Court, Eastern District of Michigan; registered to practice before U.S. Patent and Trademark Office. *Education:* Massachusetts Institute of Technology (B.S., 1970); Loyola University (J.D., 1978). **REPORTED CASES:** Qualitex Co. v. Jacobson Products Co., Inc., 514 U.S. 159 (1995). **PRACTICE AREAS:** Intellectual Property; Patent Prosecution; Trademark Prosecution; Licensing; Patents; Copyrights; Trademarks. **Email:** ejchalfie@arnstein.com

W. DENNIS DREHKOFF, born St. Louis, Missouri, July 20, 1946; admitted to bar, 1972, Missouri and U.S. District Court, Western and Eastern Districts of Missouri; 1982, Illinois; registered to practice before U.S. Patent and Trademark Office. *Education:* St. Louis College of Pharmacy (B.S., 1969); University of Missouri (J.D., 1972). Associate Editor, The Urban Lawyer. Registered Pharmacist, State of Missouri, 1969. Adjunct Professor, John Marshall Law School, 1988—. Patent Counsel, Kraft Inc., 1982-1985; Patent Counsel, Fujisawa USA, Inc., 1990-1995. *Member:* Licensing Executive Society; National Plant Patent Owners Association; Association of University Technology Managers; Intellectual Property Law Association of Chicago; American Intellectual Property Law Association.

BURTON S. EHRLICH, born Chicago, Illinois, July 21, 1953; admitted to bar, 1978, Illinois; U.S. District Court, Northern District of Illinois and U.S. Court of Appeals, 7th Circuit. *Education:* Northeastern Illinois University (B.A., 1974); DePaul University (M.B.A., 1975); Chicago Kent College of Law, Illinois Institute of Technology (J.D., 1978); John Marshall School of Law (LL.M., in Intellectual Property Law, 1988).

BRIAN W. HAMEDER, born Park Ridge, Illinois, May 28, 1975; admitted to bar, 2000, Illinois and U.S. District Court, Northern District of Illinois; registered to practice before the Patent and Trademark Office. *Education:* Rose-Hulman Institute of Technology (B.S.M.E., 1997); John Marshall Law School (J.D., 2000). *Member:* American Bar Association (Member, Intellectual Property Section); American Intellectual Property Law Association; Intellectual Property Law Association of Chicago.

PATRICIA M. HOYLE, born London, England; admitted to bar, 2000, Wisconsin; registered to practice before U.S. Patent and Trademark Office (Not admitted in Illinois). *Education:* University of London (B.Sc., Chemistry, 1974; Ph.D., Chemistry, 1978); University of Wisconsin Law School (J.D., 2000). *Member:* American Bar Association (Member, Intellectual Property Section); American Intellectual Property Law Association; Royal Society of Chemistry, England; Royal Society of Medicine, England. **LANGUAGES:** French.

RYAN M. KAATZ, born Detroit Lakes, Minnesota, June 11, 1975; admitted to bar, 2004, Minnesota (Not admitted in Illinois). *Education:* University of Minnesota (B.A., 1998); Hamline University School of Law (J.D., 2004).

JOSEPH P. KRAUSE, born Chicago, Illinois, March 10, 1955; admitted to bar, 1983, Illinois; 1998, U.S. District Court, Northern District of Illinois; registered to practice before U.S. Patent and Trademark Office, 1985. *Education:* Illinois Institute of Technology (B.S.E.E., 1977); John Marshall Law School (J.D., 1983).

VALERIE R. NEYMEYER-TYNKOV, born Clinton, Iowa, November 24, 1969; admitted to bar, 2001, Illinois; registered to practice before the U.S. Patent and Trademark Office. *Education:* University of Iowa (B.A., Lit., 1991; M.S., Pharmacology, 1996); Chicago-Kent College of Law (J.D., 2001). *Member:* American Bar Association; American Intellectual Property Law Association; American Association for the Advancement of Science.

W. WILLIAM PARK, born Geumsan, South Korea, 1967; admitted to bar, 2001, Colorado (Not admitted in Illinois). *Education:* University of Illinois, Urbana-Champaign (B.S.E.E., 1991); DePaul University (J.D., 2001). *Member:* Colorado Bar Association. **LANGUAGES:** Korean.

OF COUNSEL

DONALD P. REYNOLDS, born Plattsburgh, New York, 1929; admitted to bar, 1961, New York; 1972, Illinois; registered to practice before U.S. Patent and Trademark Office. *Education:* Cornell University (B.E.E., 1953; J.D., 1955); Syracuse University (M.E.E., 1964). Tau Beta Pi; Eta Kappa Nu; Sigma Xi. Formerly, Director of the Center for Intellectual Property Law, John Marshall Law School. [U.S. Navy, 1946-1948]

(For biographical data of the New York personnel, see Professional Biographies at New York, N.Y.)

(For biographical data of the Los Angeles personnel, see Professional Biographies at Los Angeles, California)

(For biographical data of the London personnel, see Professional Biographies at London, England)

(For biographical data of the Munich personnel, see Professional Biographies at Munich, Germany)

LADDEN & ALLEN, CHARTERED

55 WEST MONROE STREET, SUITE 3950
CHICAGO, ILLINOIS 60603
Telephone: 312-853-3000
Fax: 312-201-1436
URL: http://www.lawyers.com/l&alaw

Family Law, Complex Matrimonial Litigation, Premarital Agreements, Postnuptial Agreements, Child Custody, Paternity, Divorce and the interrelationship of Corporate Law and Estate Planning.

RONALD S. LADDEN, born Chicago, Illinois, June 12, 1931; admitted to bar, 1956, Illinois. *Education:* Drake University (B.A., 1953); DePaul University (J.D., 1956). Associate Editor, Illinois Journal of Family Law, 1985-1986. Author: "Irrationally Held Truths: A Mildly Iconoclastic Look at the Illinois Marriage and Dissolution of Marriage Act," Illinois Bar Journal, Vol. 70, No. 10, June, 1982; "The Uniform Premarital Agreement Act: An Ill-Reasoned Retreat from the Unconscionability Analysis," American Journal for Family Law, Vol. 4, No. 3, Fall, 1990. Reviewed, 8 Journal of American Academy of Matrimonial Lawyers 145, Spring, 1992; "Enforceability of Jewish Marriage Contracts in Civil Courts," American Journal of Family Law, Fall, 1992; "Preparing Clients for Custody Litigation," FAIRSHARE, Vol. 14, No. 6, June 1994. Lecturer: "Preparing Clients for Custody Litigation," American Bar Association, San Diego, California, 1993; "Enterprise vs. Personal Good Will: Where Are We?" American Academy of Matrimonial Lawyers, Koloa, Hawaii, March 1996. Presenter: "Implications of Baby Richard Case," International Academy of Matrimonial Lawyers, Paris, France, November 1995; paper on removal of children to sister states, Illinois State Bar Association, June 1996 and Graduate Mediation Institute of America, Inc., May 1996; "Illinois Parentage Act: The High Cost of Sex," to the Chicago Bears Football Team, Rookie Class, August 1999. President, Illinois Chapter, American Academy of Matrimonial Lawyers, 1989-1990. Listed in Best Lawyers in America, Seaview/Putnam, 1983. Lecturer and Demonstrator, Illinois Institute of Continuing Legal Education. Member, Management Advisory Committee to the Presiding Judge, Domestic Relations Division, Circuit Court, Cook County, 1986—. *Member:* Illinois State (Member, Family Law Section Council) and American (Member, Section on Family Law; Executive Council, Custody Committee, 1985-1986) Bar Associations; American Academy of Matrimonial Lawyers (Illinois Chapter Vice-President; Illinois Chapter Sub-board of Examiners, 1984-1986; Senior Committee, 1986—); Graduate Mediation Institute of America. Fellow, American Academy of Matrimonial Lawyers. Fellow, International Academy of Matrimonial Lawyers.

GEMMA B. ALLEN, born Chicago, Illinois, June 28, 1948; admitted to bar, 1970, Florida; 1972, Illinois. *Education:* Loyola University (B.S., magna cum laude, 1966); University of Michigan (J.D., 1969). Author: Survey of Family Law, Southern Illinois University Law Journal, 1995. Lecturer and Author on Family Law, Chicago Bar Association, Illinois State Bar Association and Illinois Institute of Continuing Legal Education. Guest Speaker and Panel Moderator, ISBA annual meetings and seminar. Appointed Member, Governor's Task Force on Child Support. Appointed Member, Task Force on Attorneys for Children (1997-1998). Founder and Chair, Think-Tank Seminar on Marriage, Divorce and Custody Reform. *Member:* Illinois State (Past-Chairman, Family Law Committee on Mediation and Alternative Dispute Resolution; Appointed Member, Family Law Section Council, 1996-1997, 1997-1998, 1998-1999; Co-Chair, Model Mediation Act Subcommittee) and American (Member, Family Law Section) Bar Associations. **PRACTICE AREAS:** Family Law.

LAKE, TOBACK & D'ARCO

A Partnership including a Professional Corporation
33 NORTH DEARBORN, SUITE 900
CHICAGO, ILLINOIS 60602
Telephone: 312-726-7111
Fax: 312-726-2385
URL: http://www.ltddivorce.com
URL: http://www.lawyers.com/ltddivorce

Family Law including Complex Matrimonial Litigation, Domestic Relations, Financial Discovery and Analysis, Tax Considerations and Retirement Benefits, Divorce Mediation and Negotiation, Custody, Visitation Rights, Adoptions and Appeals, Parentage and Paternity Proceedings.

MEMBERS OF FIRM

STEVEN R. LAKE, born Chicago, Illinois, June 15, 1948; admitted to bar, 1974, Illinois. *Education:* University of Illinois (B.A., 1970); University of Colorado School of Law (J.D., 1973). Author: Domestic Relations Chapter, IICLE Handbook; "Trying Contested Custody Cases", IICLE, 1997, 1998. Instructor: Matrimonial Law Skills, IICLE, June, 1986 and April, 1987; Northwestern University, Spring, 1984; John Marshall Law School, Fall, 1984, 1986; Winning Crucial Preliminary Motions, IICLE AND AAML, September, 1990. *Member:* Chicago (Member, Family Law Section), Illinois State and American Bar Associations; American Academy of Matrimonial Lawyers (Member, Board of Managers,

(This Listing Continued)

LAKE, TOBACK & D'ARCO, Chicago—Continued

Illinois Chapter; Chairman, Bench and Bar Committee, 1995-1996); Association of Trial Lawyers of America. **PRACTICE AREAS:** Family Law; Divorce; Domestic Relations; Mediation; Matrimonial. **Email:** srlake@ltddivorce.com

ALAN J. TOBACK, born Bronx, New York, February 7, 1958; admitted to bar, 1982, Illinois. *Education:* State University of New York at Albany (B.A., 1979); John Marshall Law School (J.D., 1982). Author: "Refusal to Submit to Paternity Blood - Testing A Legal Quagmire," 1 Illinois, Journal Family Law at 1 (November/December 1984); "Paternity Proceedings," Chapter 63, Family Law & Practice, Matthew Bender 1986; "Domestic Relations - Quick Guide for the Legal Assistant, IICLE, 1989; "Dissipation of Marital Assets: A Review and Criticism," Illinois Bar Journal, April 1991; "Changes to IMDMA May Make It Easier for Spouses to Obtain Maintenance," The Chicago Daily Law Bulletin, October 1992; "Removal: A Historical and Practical Perspective," Illinois Family Law Report, November 1992; "Maintenance" -- Illinois State Bar Association, Family Law Handbook, Fall 1994; Lecturer: Illinois State Bar Association Annual and Mid-Year Meetings 1993, 1994 and 1995. Member, Board of Managers, 1992; Vice President, 1994-1997, Illinois Chapter, American Academy of Matrimonial Lawyers. Chairperson Continuing Legal Education Committee, Family law Section Council, Illinois State Bar Association, 1993. President, Illinois Chapter, American Academy of Matrimonial Lawyers, 1998-2000. Secretary, Family Law Counsel, Illinois State Bar Association, 1999-2000. *Member:* Chicago (Member, Matrimonial Law Committee), Illinois State (Member, Family Law Section Council; Chair, Family Law Section, 2000-2001) and American (Member, Family Law Section) Bar Associations. **PRACTICE AREAS:** Family Law; Divorce; Domestic Relations; Matrimonial; Paternity; Adoption Law. **Email:** ajtoback@ltddivorce.com

JOHN M. D'ARCO, born Chicago, Illinois, January 2, 1970; admitted to bar, 1995, Illinois; 1998, Florida. *Education:* University of Illinois (B.A., 1991); John Marshall Law School, Chicago (J.D., 1995). Former Attorney, Cook County, Illinois Public Defender's Office. *Member:* Chicago, Illinois State and American Bar Associations. **PRACTICE AREAS:** Family Law; Criminal Law; Real Estate. **Email:** jdarco@ltddivorce.com

ASSOCIATES

LAURA N. ASHMORE, born Fort Lee, Virginia, April 1, 1969; admitted to bar, 1994, Illinois and U.S. District Court, Northern District of Illinois. *Education:* DePaul University Theatre School (B.F.A., 1991); DePaul University (J.D., 1994). *Member:* Chicago and Illinois State Bar Associations. **PRACTICE AREAS:** Matrimonial Law; Family Law; Domestic Relations. **Email:** ashmore@ltddivorce.com

HOLLY ANN BENCIVENGA, born Massapequa, New York, November 30, 1974; admitted to bar, 1999, Illinois. *Education:* University of North Carolina at Chapel Hill (A.B., Sociology, with distinction, 1996); American University (J.D., 1999). *Member:* Chicago and Illinois State Bar Associations. **PRACTICE AREAS:** Family Law; Domestic Relations. **Email:** hollyb@ltddivorce.com

MICHAEL G. DI DOMENICO, born Evanston, Illinois, May 30, 1977; admitted to bar, 2003, Illinois. *Education:* DePaul University (B.A., 1999); John Marshall Law School (J.D., 2003; LL.M., 2003). **PRACTICE AREAS:** Family Law. **Email:** mdidomenico@ltddivorce.com

ERIN J. BOGNAR, born Elkhart, Indiana, July 4, 1971; admitted to bar, 1999, Illinois. *Education:* Indiana University (B.A., 1993); St. Louis University (J.D., 1999). Former Member: Illinois Appellate Court; Madison County State's Attorney's Office. *Member:* Chicago and Illinois State Bar Associations. **PRACTICE AREAS:** Matrimonial Law; Family Law; Domestic Relations; Criminal Law. **Email:** ebognar@ltddivorce.com

ANDREW M. ENGLE, born Chicago, Illinois, November 5, 1978; admitted to bar, 2004, Illinois. *Education:* University of Illinois (B.S., 2000); DePaul University (J.D., 2004). **PRACTICE AREAS:** Family Law; Divorce; Adoption. **Email:** aengle@ltddivorce.com

BERNADETTE I. ROSSMOORE, born Budapest, Hungary, July 7, 1974; admitted to bar, 1999, Illinois. *Education:* University of Michigan (B.A., 1996); Washington College of Law of American University (J.D., 1999). **PRACTICE AREAS:** Family. **Email:** brossmoore@ltddivorce.com

OF COUNSEL

REBECCA B. FEINBERG, born Chicago, Illinois, December 20, 1971; admitted to bar, 1998, Illinois. *Education:* Lake Forest College (B.A., 1994); Loyola University of Chicago Law School (J.D., 1997). Formerly with: Rosenfeld, Rotenberg, Hafron & Shapiro; Ralla, Klepak & Associates. Co-Author: Illinois Institute Continuing Legal Education 2000 Family Section Parentage Chapter, 1995, 1996, 1997. Teaching Assistant, Legal Writing, Loyola Law School, Chicago, Illinois. *Member:* Chicago (Member, Family Law Section) and Illinois State Bar Associations. **PRACTICE AREAS:** Matrimonial Law; Family Law; Domestic Relations.

LANDON & WICKERSTY, LTD.

SUITE 1119, 77 WEST WASHINGTON STREET
CHICAGO, ILLINOIS 60602
Telephone: 312-782-4780
Fax: 312-372-9399
Email: lwltd@ameritech.net

Wills and Probate, Trusts and Estate Planning Law. Corporate Law, Business Law, Real Estate and Drainage Law, General Civil and Trial Practice.

J. HERBERT LANDON, born Jerseyville, Illinois, August 26, 1931; admitted to bar, 1960, Illinois and Missouri. *Education:* University of Illinois (B.S., 1953); Washington University (J.D., 1960). *Member:* Chicago and Illinois State Bar Associations. **PRACTICE AREAS:** Probate; Wills; Trust and Estate Planning; Civil Litigation; Real Estate; Drainage Law.

WILLIAM J. WICKERSTY, born Suffern, New York, April 26, 1965; admitted to bar, 1990, Illinois. *Education:* Wabash College (B.A., 1987); University of Kansas (J.D., 1990). Phi Delta Phi. *Member:* Chicago and Illinois State Bar Associations. **PRACTICE AREAS:** Probate; Real Estate; Business Law; Taxation.

JENNIFER A. ATKIN, born Grand Rapids, Michigan, April 21, 1977; admitted to bar, 2004, Illinois. *Education:* University of Colorado (B.A., 1999); University of Denver (J.D., 2003). *Chicago and Illinois State Bar Associations.* **PRACTICE AREAS:** Probate; Wills; Trusts; Estate Planning; Real Estate. **Email:** lwltd@ameritech.net

REPRESENTATIVE CLIENTS: Alpha Motor Ways, Inc.; A & M Tool Co., Inc.; Chicago Tract Society; Evergreen Park Ministry, Inc.; Maxicrop USA, Inc.; The Methodist Home; P.B. Ohrstrom & Sons, Inc.; Terp Meyers Architects, Inc.; West Skokie Drainage District; W.J. Tighe Trucking, Inc.

(This Listing Continued)

LANE & LANE

33 NORTH DEARBORN STREET, SUITE 2300
CHICAGO, ILLINOIS 60602-3199
Telephone: 312-332-1400
Fax: 312-899-8003
Email: lanelaw@lane-lane.com
URL: http://www.lane-lane.com

Trial Practice in all areas involving Serious Personal Injury and Wrongful Death. Emphasis in Medical and Professional Negligence, Products Liability, Premises Liability and Vehicular Negligence, Medical Malpractice, Automobile Accidents, Slip and Fall, Animal Bites, Railroad Accidents, Toxic Torts, Class Actions, Jones Act, OSHA.

MEMBERS OF FIRM

FRED LANE, born April 1, 1925; admitted to bar, 1950, Illinois. *Education:* Loyola University (J.D., 1950). Editor, Medical Trial Technique Quarterly. Former Assistant State's Attorney of Cook County. Author: Lane's Goldstein Trial Technique (3 volumes); Lane Medical Litigation Guide (4 volumes); Lane's Goldstein Trial Technique Quarterly; Lane's Goldstein Litigation Forms (3 volumes). Instructor: Trial Practice, Trial Technique Institute for the Illinois State Bar Association. *Member:* Chicago and Illinois State (President, 1986-1987) Bar Associations; Society of Trial Lawyers; American Trial Lawyers Association; Illinois Trial Lawyers Association (Past President); Decalogue Society of Lawyers; American Board of Trial Advocates (Diplomat and Past President). Fellow, International Academy of Trail Lawyers. **PRACTICE AREAS:** Personal Injury; Medical Negligence; Products Liability; Premises Liability; Vehicular Negligence; Litigation; Professional Negligence. **Email:** fredinill@aol.com

STEPHEN I. LANE, born Chicago, Illinois, May 1, 1953; admitted to bar, 1978, Illinois and U.S. District Court, Northern District of Illinois; 1995, U.S. Supreme Court. *Education:* University of Illinois (B.A., 1975); Illinois Institute of Technology/Chicago-Kent College of Law (J.D., 1978). Phi Alpha Delta. Justinian Society. Author: "Illinois Civil Trial Practice," 1979—; "Causes of Action," 2002 both published by Illinois Institute for Continuing Legal Education. Research Coordinator, *Goldstein Trial Technique,* 1978—, Callaghan and Company. Member, Board of Directors, The Center for Disability and Elder Law. *Member:* Chicago (Member, Committees: Civil Practice; Hospital & Health Care; Medico-Legal Relations; Sports Law; Trial Techniques; Tort Litigation; Circuit Court; Entertainment; Judicial Evaluation; Chair, Subcommittee to Investigate Use of Mail, Fax and Teleconferencing in Courts; Member, Committee to study the Legal Needs Assessment of the State of Illinois), DuPage County, Kane County, Lake County, Northwest Suburban, Illinois State (Member, Board of Governors, 1989-1991, 1993-1999, 2000—; Secretary, 1995; Member: Tort Law Section Council and Special Committee on Professionalism, 1985—; Task Force on Professionalism, First Joint Committee of the Board of Governors, 1987—; Member, ISBA Assembly, 1989-1991, 1991—; Committee to study the Lawyer Referral Service; Board Subcommittees on Insurance Programs; Committee to Review Mock Trial Programs, 1989-1990; Amicus Curiae Study Committee; Member, Assembly: Budget and Audit, Legislation, Personnel, Professionalism (Standing Committee), Scope and Correlation Committees; Special Committee to Review the Client's Security Fund; Liaison to the Attorneys Registration and Disciplinary Commission Committee; Committee on the Mentally Disabled, Delivery of Legal Services, Law Education, Admission and Competence Committee; Lawyers With Disabilities; Standing Committee on Legal Technology and Professionalism Committees; Commercial and Bankruptcy Law, Law Office Economics and Tort Law Section Councils; Chair of the Standing Committee on Community Involvement, 1994-1996; Education Law Section Council), and American Bar Associations; Illinois Trial Lawyers Association (Member, Committees: Amicus Curiae; Rules; Publications; Membership; Medical Negligence; Legislative Law; Civil Procedures); The Association of Trial Lawyers of America; American College of Legal Medicine (Associate in Law); Decalogue Society of Lawyers (Member, Board of Directors); Bohemian Lawyers' Association of Chicago; American Association of Legal Nurse Consultants; Association of Womens' Health, Obstetric and Neonatal Nurses. Fellow, Illinois Bar Foundation. **PRACTICE AREAS:** Personal Injury; Medical Negligence; Products Liability; Premises Liability; Vehicular Negligence; Litigation; Professional Negligence; Medical Malpractice; Automobile Accidents and Injuries. **Email:** stevelane@lane-lane.com

SCOTT D. LANE, born Chicago, Illinois, July 31, 1962; admitted to bar, 1988, Illinois; 1989, U.S. District Court, Northern District of Illinois; 1995, U.S. Supreme Court. *Education:* Southern Methodist University (B.A., cum laude, 1984); Loyola University of Chicago (J.D., 1988). Law Review, Loyola University. Recipient of the American College of Trial Lawyers Medal for Excellence in Advocacy. Selected as one of the "40 Attorneys Under 40 in Illinois to Watch." Member, Loyola Circle of Advocates. Life Member, National Register of Who's Who in America. Former Cook County Assistant State's Attorney. Instructor and Coach of Trial Team, Loyola University of Chicago. Instructor, Illinois State Bar Association Trial Technique Institute. Lecturer, numerous bar association seminars on various topics pertaining to Civil Litigation. Contributing Editor, Lane's Goldstein Trial Technique and Lane Medical Litigation Guide. Author: "Illinois Law Survey: Torts, (1985-1986)," Loyola University Law Journal; "Proof of Facts," Illinois Civil Practice, Volume II

(This Listing Continued)

IICLE; "Opinion Evidence," Illinois Civil Trial Evidence, IICLE; Supplements to Actions and Remedies: Intentional Torts (1989-1990) and Professional Malpractice (1989) (Callaghan & Co.); "Employment Discrimination," Loyola Quarterly, Summer, 1988 Edition; "Should Our Roads Be Safe For Intoxicated Drivers?," ISBA Tort Trends, Vol. 29, No. 4, April 1994; "Disability and Aggravation of a Pre-existing Condition: No Longer Separate Categories of Damages," ISBA Tort Trends, Vol. 31, No. 1, October 1995; "The Admissibility and Use of Habit Evidence in Medical Malpractice Actions," ISBA Tort Trends, Vol. 31, No. 6, May 1996; "Burrell v. Southern Truss: Total of Health Care Provider Liens May Not Exceed One-Third of Plaintiff's Settlement—Will This Holding Facilitate Settlement of Personal Injury Cases?", ISBA Tort Trends, Vol. 32, No. 4, January, 1997; "Motions to Transfer Venue Based Upon Forum Nonconveniens: To Be Successful, Defendants Must Meet a Heavy Burden," ISBA Tort Trends, Vol. 33, No. 3, February 1998; "Questioning Your First Witness," School's Out: A Practice Primer for New Attorneys, IICLE, 1999; "Cammon v. West Suburban Hospital Medical Center: The First District Addresses the Relation Back Doctrine, the Requirements of § 2-622, and the Statute of Limitations in Spoliation of Evidence Cases," ISBA Tort Trends, Vol. 35, No.2, March 2000; "Voir Dire: Do Lawyers Have a Right to Question Directly?", Illinois Bar Journal Vol. 89, No.10, October 2001 and ISBA Trial Briefs, Vol. 47, No.1, September 2001; "Spoliation of Evidence," Illinois Causes of Action, IICLE. *Member:* Chicago (Moot Court Committee), Illinois State (Assembly for the First Judicial District; Tort Law Section Council; Civil Practice and Procedure Section Council) and American Bar Associations; The Association of Trial Lawyers of America; Illinois Trial Lawyers Association (Member, Committees on: Amicus Curiae; Medical Negligence; Product Liability; Civil Practice and Rules); American College of Legal Medicine. Fellow, Illinois Bar Foundation; Decalogue Society of Lawyers. **PRACTICE AREAS:** Personal Injury; Medical Negligence; Products Liability; Premises Liability; Vehicular Negligence; Litigation; Professional Negligence. **Email:** scottlane@lane-lane.com

ASSOCIATE

MARK A. BROWN, born Chicago, Illinois, June 22, 1967; admitted to bar, 1994, Illinois. *Education:* University of Illinois at Urbana-Champaign (B.A., 1990); Chicago-Kent College of Law, Illinois Institute of Technology (J.D., 1993). Member: Judicial Screening Committee, 1991—; Civil Litigation Committee, 1997—. Author: "Civil Litigation Practice Reminder: Worker's Compensation Lien and Proceeds from Uninsured/Underinsured Policies," Illinois State Bar Association's Young Lawyers Journal, May, 1999. Seminar Organizer and Moderator: "Meet the Judges of the 3rd Judicial District to Discuss Supreme Court Rule 213," November, 1999. *Member:* Chicago and Illinois State Bar Associations; Northwest Suburban Bar Association (Chairman, Young Lawyers Committee, 1998-2000); Illinois Trial Lawyers Association (Member, Civil Practice and Rules Committee, 1998—). **PRACTICE AREAS:** Personal Injury; Products Liability; Medical Malpractice; Wrongful Death. **Email:** markbrown@lane-lane.com

OF COUNSEL

John F. Sandner
Daniel M. Cullan (Not admitted in IL)
Eugene K. Hollander (Also practicing individually)

MEDICAL STAFF

Cathleen Lazo-Miller, R.N., M.S. (R.N.)

THE LAW OFFICES OF MARC J. LANE

A PROFESSIONAL CORPORATION

Established in 1971

SUITE 2100
180 NORTH LA SALLE STREET
CHICAGO, ILLINOIS 60601-2701
Telephone: 312-372-1040
800-372-1040
Fax: 312-346-1040
URL: http://www.marcjlane.com
Email: success@marcjlane.com
URL: http://www.lawyers.com/marcjlane

Federal and International Taxation, Trust and Estate Planning, Probate, Elder Law, Real Estate, Nonprofit, Internet Law, Corporation, Securities and Banking Law.

FIRM PROFILE: The Law Offices of Marc J. Lane and its financial-services affiliates are uniquely structured to create and implement business, tax, retirement, investment, estate, and succession planning strategies for individual, corporate, and nonprofit clients.

Protecting Today's Wealth. Building Tomorrow's.

MARC J. LANE, born Chicago, Illinois, August 30, 1946; admitted to bar, 1971, Illinois and U.S. District Court, Northern District of Illinois; 1974, U.S. Tax Court. *Education:* University of Illinois (B.A. in Political Science, with honors and high distinction, 1967); Northwestern University (J.D., 1971); The Lawyers' Institute, John Marshall Law School. Master Registered Financial Planner, The International Association of Registered Financial Planners, Inc., 1987. Certified Investment Specialist, The International Association of Registered Financial Planners, Inc., 1993—. Northern Illinois University College of Law, Certificate in Mediation, 1995. General Securities Principal, National Association of Securities Dealers, Inc., 1996—. Registered Options Principal, National Association of Securities Dealers, Inc., 1997—. Recipient: One of "Best Financial Advisors," Worth Magazine, 1999. Adjunct Professor of Law, Northwestern University School of Law. Adjunct Professor of Business, College of Business Administration, University of Illinois. Author of 30 books and numerous articles on corporate organization, personal finance and investments.

(This Listing Continued)

PRACTICE AREAS: Individual Taxation; Corporate Tax Planning; Business Tax Planning; Estate Planning; Investments; Retirement Planning; Elder Law; International Trade; Business Law; Taxation; Trusts and Estates; Wills; Probate. **Email:** mlane@marcjlane.com

OF COUNSEL

ROSALYN S. WATSON, born Chicago, Illinois, January 4, 1965; admitted to bar, 1998, Illinois. *Education:* University of Michigan (B.A., 1986; J.D., 1995). **Email:** rwatson@marcjlane.com

---

JOSHUA S. KREITZER, born New York, N.Y., September 19, 1972; admitted to bar, 1997, Illinois. *Education:* Harvard University (B.A., 1993); University of South Florida (M.A., 1994); Northwestern University (J.D., 1997). **PRACTICE AREAS:** Taxation; Estate Planning; Corporate Law; Business Law; Tax Exempt Organizations. **Email:** jkreitzer@marcjlane.com

JOHN J. LAPINSKI, born Melrose Park, Illinois, April 27, 1961; admitted to bar, 1988, Illinois. *Education:* Elmhurst College (B.S., 1983); Illinois Institute of Technology, Chicago-Kent College of Law (J.D., 1987). **Email:** jlapinski@marcilane.com

REFERENCE: Bank of America.

LANER, MUCHIN, DOMBROW, BECKER, LEVIN AND TOMINBERG, LTD.

Established in 1945

515 NORTH STATE STREET, SUITE 2800
CHICAGO, ILLINOIS 60610
Telephone: 312-467-9800
Fax: 312-467-9479
URL: http://www.lmdblt.com

Labor and Employment Relations Law, Employee Benefits Law and Related Litigation.

FIRM PROFILE: Laner, Muchin, Dombrow, Becker, Levin and Tominberg, Ltd. was established in 1945. Since its inception, the Firm has exclusively practiced labor and employment relations law. The Firm currently provides a full range of services in labor and employment relations, in employee benefits, and in litigation in all of these areas to more than 400 Companies/Employers in almost every state in the U.S. and in Canada. The Firm also serves as business advisor to many of its clients. The Firm's clients employ from several employees to 20,000 employees, represent an expansive cross-section of private and public employers and are non-union or union organized. For example, the Firm represents such diverse clients as manufacturing companies, banks, insurance companies, professional sports teams, hospitals and health care facilities, educational institutions, computer and data processing services firms, communications companies, hotels, construction firms, distribution firms, mines and real estate investment companies.

LAWRENCE F. DOPPELT (1935-1979)

ARTHUR B. MUCHIN, born Manitowoc, Wisconsin, June 15, 1943; admitted to bar, 1967, Wisconsin; 1968, Illinois and U.S. District Court, Northern District of Illinois including Trial Bar; 1976, U.S. Court of Appeals, Seventh Circuit; 1987, U.S. Supreme Court and U.S. Court of Appeals, Ninth Circuit; 1992, U.S. Court of Appeals, District of Columbia Circuit; 1997, U.S. Court of Appeals, Fourth Circuit. *Education:* University of Wisconsin (B.S., 1965; J.D., 1967). Attorney, National Labor Relations Board, 13th Region, Chicago, Illinois, 1967-1970. Named: one of the Leading Lawyers in Illinois, 2004-2005; Illinois Super Lawyer, 2005. *Member:* Chicago Bar Association (Member, Labor Law Committee, 1972-1976). **PRACTICE AREAS:** Labor and Employment. **Email:** amuchin@lanermuchin.com

ANTHONY E. DOMBROW, born New York, N.Y., April 6, 1945; admitted to bar, 1969, Wisconsin; 1973, Illinois; 1974, U.S. Court of Appeals, Eighth Circuit; 1976, U.S. Court of Appeals, Seventh Circuit and U.S. Supreme Court; 1978, U.S. District Court, Northern District of Illinois; 1986, U.S. Court of Appeals, Tenth Circuit. *Education:* University of Wisconsin (B.A., with honors, 1966; J.D., with honors, 1969). Listed in: "The Best Lawyers in America" and "Who's Who in American Law." Member, Integrated Liberal Studies Honors Program, 1962-1964. Author: "Review of the Law of the United States Court of Appeals for the Seventh Circuit: Labor Law," 50 Chicago-Kent Law Review 309, 1973. Guest Lecturer, Labor and Employment Relations, American Management Association, 1984— and American Arbitration Association, 1990—. Attorney, National Labor Relations Board, 13th Region, Chicago, Illinois, 1969-1972. Special Labor and Employment Law Counsel, University of Illinois, 1992—. Member, The College of Labor and Employment Lawyers, 2003—. Named one of the Leading Lawyers in Illinois, 2004. Named Illinois Super Lawyer, 2005. *Member:* Chicago Bar Association (Member, Labor Law Committee, 1973—); State Bar of Wisconsin (Member, Labor Law Committee, 1976—). **PRACTICE AREAS:** Labor and Employment. **Email:** adombrow@lanermuchin.com

ALAN M. LEVIN, born New York, N.Y., December 8, 1947; admitted to bar, 1974, Illinois and U.S. District Court, Northern District of Illinois; 1975, U.S. Court of Appeals, Seventh Circuit; 1978, U.S. Supreme Court. *Education:* Yale University (B.A., cum laude, 1971); University of Chicago (J.D., 1974). Author: "Seventh Circuit Review: Labor Law," 51 Chicago-Kent Law Review 509, 1974; "The Dilemma of the Small Plan Fiduciary under ERISA," 56 Chicago-Kent Law Review 589, 1980; "Privatization: A Management Perspective," The Illinois Public Relations Report, Spring, 1989. Faculty, Institute for Applied Management and Law, 1986-1994. Past-Lecturer, Illinois Institute For Continuing Legal Education. Past-President, Executives Guild, Ltd. Named one of the Leading Lawyers in Illinois, 2004. *Member:* Chicago Bar Association (Member, Committee on Labor Law, 1976—). [with U.S. Army, 1967-1969]. **PRACTICE AREAS:** Labor and Employment. **Email:** alevin@lanermuchin.com

(This Listing Continued)

LANER, MUCHIN, DOMBROW, BECKER, LEVIN AND TOMINBERG, LTD., Chicago—Continued

CARL S. TOMINBERG, born Wurzburg, Germany, March 20, 1949; admitted to bar, 1974, Illinois; 1975, U.S. District Court, Northern District of Illinois including Trial Bar and U.S. Court of Appeals, Seventh Circuit; 1982, U.S. Court of Appeals, Eleventh Circuit; 1986, U.S. Supreme Court. *Education:* Roosevelt University (B.S.B.A., in Finanee, 1971); DePaul University (J.D., magna cum laude, 1974). Beta Gamma Sigma. Recipient, Three American Jurisprudence Awards. Member, De Paul Law Review, 1973-1974. Author: "Secret Land Trusts," 23 De Paul Law Review 509, 1973; "Construction Law in Illinois," IICLE Chapter, 1997, 2004. Faculty, Institute for Applied Management and Law, 1986-1997. Advisory Council for Loyola University Institute for Industrial Relations, 1987-1995. Special Corporation Counsel, City of Chicago, 1984-1989. Special Assistant States Attorney, Kane County, 1991—. Special Labor Counsel: State of Illinois, 1991—; Chicago Housing Authority, 1999—; Chicago City Colleges, 1992—; City of Palos Hills, 1985—; City of Highland Park, 1997-2005; Kane County, 1991—. Chief Judge: Sixteenth Judicial Circuit, 1993—; City of Thornton, 1996—; City of Bensenville, 2003—; Village of Homewood, 2000—; Village of Lake Bluff, 2000—; DeKalb County, 1996—; State Fire Marshal's Office, 1999—. Guest Lecturer, The John Marshall Law School and Chicago Kent College of Law Public Sector Labor Relations Conference, 1986-2000. Attorney: U.S. Department of Justice, Washington, D.C. and Chicago, Illinois, 1974-1975; Immigration and Naturalization Service, 1974-1975; National Labor Relations Board, Region 13, Chicago, Illinois, 1975-1979. Member: Institute for Law and the Workplace; Public Sector Advisory Board, Kent College of Law. Named: one of the Leading Lawyers in Illinois, 2004; Illinois Super Lawyer, 2005-2006. Listed in the 2006 Edition of "The Best Lawyers in America". *Member:* Chicago Bar Association (Member, Labor Law Section; Alternative Dispute Resolutions Committee and Local Government Committee); Northwest Suburban Bar Association (Past Co-Vice Chairman, Employment Law Committee); International Foundation of Employee Benefit Plans. ***PRACTICE AREAS:*** Labor and Employment. ***Email:*** ctominberg@lanermuchin.com

MARK L. JUSTER, born Chicago, Illinois, June 26, 1950; admitted to bar, 1976, Illinois; 1980, U.S. District Court, Northern District of Illinois; 1981, U.S. Court of Appeals, Seventh Circuit; 1992, U.S. Court of Appeals, District of Columbia Circuit. *Education:* Miami University (B.A., with honors, 1972); Washington University (J.D., 1975). Member, Urban Law Annual, 1973-1975. Author: "Creditor Remedies and Due Process: Comparing Mitchell and Fuentes," 10 Urban Law Annual 243, 1975; Chapter, "The Labor Law Handbook, 1984," IICLE, 1984, 1988, 1991, 1996, 1998, 1999, 2002. Contributing Author: "The Developing Labor Law, Supplements," and Third Edition, ABA Section of Labor Law, 1982—. Attorney-Advisor, Section of Rates, Interstate Commerce Commission, 1976-1977 and Attorney, National Labor Relations Board, Region 14, 1977-1980. Named one of the Leading Lawyers in Illinois, 2004-2005. Named Illinois Super Lawyer, 2005-2006. *Member:* American Bar Association (Member, Labor Law Section). ***PRACTICE AREAS:*** Labor and Employment. ***Email:*** mjuster@lanermuchin.com

GARY ALAN WINCEK, born Oak Park, Illinois, October 8, 1957; admitted to bar, 1982, Illinois, U.S. District Court, Northern District of Illinois and U.S. District Court, Eastern District of Michigan; 1991, U.S. Court of Appeals, Seventh Circuit. *Education:* Loyola University (B.S., 1979); Illinois Institute of Technology-Chicago Kent College of Law (J.D., 1982). Member, Who's Who in Executives and Professionals. *Member:* Chicago (Member, Labor Law Section), DuPage County (Member, Employment Law/Labor Law Committee) and Illinois State Bar Associations. ***PRACTICE AREAS:*** Labor and Employment. ***Email:*** gwincek@lanermuchin.com

MICHAEL KLUPCHAK, born Chicago, Illinois, June 27, 1951; admitted to bar, 1982, Illinois, U.S. District Court, Northern District of Illinois and U.S. Court of Appeals, Seventh and District of Columbia Circuits. *Education:* Dartmouth College (A.B., cum laude, 1973) Rufus Choate Scholar; Northwestern University (J.D., cum laude, 1982). Law Clerk, New Hampshire Legal Assistance, Manchester, New Hampshire, 1975-1977. Field Examiner, National Labor Relations Board, Region 10, Atlanta, Georgia, 1977-1980. Research Assistant, Arbitrator Stephen Goldberg, 1981-1982. Named: one of the Leading Lawyers in Illinois, 2004; Super Lawyer, 2005. *Member:* Chicago (Member, Labor Law Section) and Illinois State Bar Associations; Dartmouth Lawyers Association. ***PRACTICE AREAS:*** Labor and Employment. ***Email:*** mklupchak@lanermuchin.com

JOSEPH H. YASTROW, born Chicago, Illinois, February 23, 1954; admitted to bar, 1978, Illinois and U.S. District Court, Northern District of Illinois. *Education:* Dartmouth College (A.B., cum laude, 1975); Southern Methodist University (J.D., 1978). Member, The Barristers. Rufus Choate Scholar. Member, Board of Editors, Southwestern Law Journal, 1977-1978. Selected as one of Illinois Leading Illinois Attorneys (Labor and Employment Law). Named as one of America's Leading Business Lawyers, by Chambers & Partners, 2003-2004, 2004-2005. Listed in International Who's Who of Labour and Employment Lawyers, 2005-2006. Member: Dartmouth Lawyers Association; American Employment Law Council; College of Labor and Employment Lawyers. *Member:* Chicago (Vice-Chairman, 1991-1992 and Chairman, 1992-1993, Labor and Employment Law Committee; Chair, Employment Torts Subcommittee, 1996-1998 and National Labor Relations Board Subcommittee, 1994-1995) and American (Member, Labor and Employment Law Section and Employee Rights and Responsibilities Subcommittee; Management Co-Chair, Employment Practices Liability Insurance Committee) Bar Associations. ***PRACTICE AREAS:*** Labor and Employment. ***Email:*** jyastrow@lanermuchin.com

JOSEPH M. GAGLIARDO, born Chicago, Illinois, November 21, 1952; admitted to bar, 1977, Illinois, U.S. District Court, Northern District of Illinois including Trial Bar, U.S. Court of Appeals, Seventh Circuit and U.S. Supreme Court. *Education:* DePaul University (B.S., with high honors, 1974); John Marshall Law School (J.D., 1977). Recipient, John Marshall Law School Distinguished Service Award, 1988. Recipient: Edward T. Lee Scholarship and Bobbs-Merrill Company Prize. Elected Member, Board of Trustees, The John Marshall Law School, 1996—. Member, The Order of John Marshall. Recipient. Named one of the Leading Lawyers in Illinois, 2004. Arbitrator in employment and commercial disputes. *Member:* Chicago (Member, Labor and Employment Committee, 1986—), Illinois State (Assembly Member, 1986-1992, 1997-2001, 2004—; Chairperson, Assembly Rules and Bylaws Committee, 1998-1999; Assembly Member, Finance Committee, 1989; Member, Standing Committee on Judicial Evaluations, 1998-2003; Member, Special Committee on Judicial Redistricting, 1989-1990, Standing Committee on Alternative Dispute Resolution, 1990-1991 and Civil Procedure Section Council, 1991-1996; Chair of the Labor Section Council, 1989-1990; Member, Sections of: Labor and Employment; Administrative; Local Government), Federal (President, Chicago Chapter, 1997-1998 and National Council Member, 1999-2000) and American (Member, Section of: Labor and Employment; Local Government; Litigation) Bar Associations; National Institute of Municipal Law Officers; Illinois Municipal League; Illinois Public Employer Labor Relations Association; Justinian Society of Lawyers (Member, 1977—; President, 1994-1995); Chicago Council of Lawyers. ***PRACTICE AREAS:*** Labor and Employment. ***Email:*** jgagliardo@lanermuchin.com

ROBERT H. BROWN, born Chicago, Illinois, February 18, 1947; admitted to bar, 1972, Illinois and U.S. District Court, Northern District of Illinois including Trial Bar; 1977, Connecticut; 1980, U.S. Court of Appeals, Ninth Circuit and U.S. Supreme Court; 1981, U.S. Court of Appeals, Tenth Circuit; 1983, U.S. Court of Appeals, Seventh Circuit; 1986, Florida; 1988, U.S. District Court, Eastern District of Wisconsin; 1990, U.S. Court of Appeals, Fourth Circuit; 1996, U.S. Court of Appeals, Fifth Circuit; 1998, U.S. District Court, District of Colorado and U.S. Court of Appeals, Sixth Circuit. *Education:* Northwestern University (B.S.J., 1969); University of Michigan (J.D., 1972). United Air Lines, Inc., Chicago, Illinois, 1979-1985; Trial Attorney: U.S. Department of Labor, Chicago, Illinois, 1972-1979. Named one of the Leading Lawyers in Illinois, 2004-2005; Chicago Super Lawyer, 2005; Who's Who in American Law, 2005-2006. *Member:* American Bar Association. ***REPORTED CASES:*** Union Tank Car v. OSHA, 192 F.3d. 701 (7th. Cir., 1999); Gleason v. Mesirow Financial, 118 F.3d. 1134 (7th Cir., 1997); Tobey v. Extel/JWP, 985 F.2d. 330 (7th Cir., 1993); McGrady v. Eastfield, 914 F.2d 1491 (4th Cir., 1990); Barnett v. United Air Lines, 738 F.2d. 358, 729 F.2d 693 (10th Cir., 1984); Jones v. Centurion, 268 F.Supp 2d 1004 (ND IL. 2003); Baudin v. Courtesy Litho, 24 F.Supp 2d. 887 (ND IL 1998); Union Tank Car, 2001 OSHD (CCH) 32,315 (OSHRC 2001). ***PRACTICE AREAS:*** Labor and Employment; Safety and Health. ***Email:*** rbrown@lanermuchin.com

JAMES J. CONVERY, born Chicago, Illinois, April 9, 1956; admitted to bar, 1981, Illinois and U.S. District Court, Northern District of Illinois, Trial Bar; 1989, U.S. Court of Appeals, Seventh Circuit; 1990, U.S. District Court, Central District of Illinois; 1991, U.S. District Court, District of Colorado; 1995, U.S. Court of Appeals, Tenth Circuit and U.S. District Court, Eastern District of Michigan; 1996, U.S. Court of Appeals, Sixth Circuit; 1999, U.S. District Court, Southern District of Illinois; 2000, U.S. District Court, Western District of Michigan; 2005, U.S. Court of Appeals, Eleventh Circuit. *Education:* DePaul University (B.S.C., 1978; J.D., 1981). Author: "Attorney's Fees: The Mushrooming Cloud of Litigation," Fioretti and Convery, 34 De Paul Law Review 943, 1985; "Attorney's Fees Under the Civil Rights Act-A Time for Change," Fioretti and Convery, 16 John Marshall Law Review 261, 1983; "A Primer on the New Work Force Law: The Americans with Disabilities Act," Devience and Convery, 16 Journal of Rehabilitative Administration 40, 1992; "Restrictive Covenants & Confidentiality Restrictions under Illinois Law," Convery and Bradley, CBA Record, 1999. *Member:* Chicago, Illinois State and Federal Bar Associations. ***REPORTED CASES:*** Woolner v. Flair Communications, 2004 U.S. Dist. LEXIS 746 (N.D. Ill. 2004); Warren v. Hotel Inter-Continental Chicago, 2003 U.S. Dist. LEXIS 109 (N.D. Ill. 2003); Quinn v. Ultimo, 2001 U.S. Dist. LEXIS 2064 (N.D. Ill. 2001); Hawkins v. MAXIMUS, Inc. 2000 U.S. Dist. LEXIS 18884, 84 Fair Emp. Prac. Cas. 1217 (N.D. Ill 2000); Schultz v. Sallie Mae, Inc. 1999 U.S. Dist. LEXIS 16870 (N.D. Ill 1999). ***PRACTICE AREAS:*** Labor and Employment. ***Email:*** jconvery@lanermuchin.com

ROBERT S. LETCHINGER, born May 15, 1955; admitted to bar, 1982, Illinois; U.S. District Court, Northern District of Illinois; 1991, U.S. Court of Appeals, Seventh Circuit; 1992, U.S. Supreme Court. *Education:* Carleton College (B.A., magna cum laude, 1978); Northwestern University (J.D., 1982). Phi Beta Kappa. Author: "AIDS: An Employer's Dilemma," Personnel, Vol. 63, No. 2, p. 58, 1986, reprinted in Chicago Bar Record, Vol. 67 No. 2, p. 86, 1986. Co-Author: "Reduction in Work Force and the Age Discrimination Dilemma: Procedures and Safeguards," Midwest Labor and Employment Law Journal, Vol. 1, No. 5, p. 83, 1984. Named one of the Leading Lawyers in Illinois, 2004. Named Illinois Super Lawyer, 2005. ***PRACTICE AREAS:*** Labor and Employment. ***Email:*** rletchinger@lanermuchin.com

VIOLET M. CLARK, born New Bern, North Carolina, February 6, 1957; admitted to bar, 1983, Illinois and U.S. District Court, Northern District of Illinois. *Education:* Brown University (B.A., 1979); University of Chicago; Cornell University (J.D., 1982). Hearing Officer: Chicago Commission on Human Relations; Cook County Commission on Human Rights. Named one of the Leading Lawyers in Illinois, 2004. *Member:* Cook County and National Bar Associations; Black Women Lawyers' Association. ***PRACTICE AREAS:*** Labor and Employment. ***Email:*** vclark@lanermuchin.com

JAMES F. VANEK, born Wareham, Massachusetts, September 23, 1959; admitted to bar, 1985, Illinois. *Education:* St. Louis University (B.S., 1982); John Marshall Law School (J.D., 1985). Co-Author: "Employee Benefits and Collective Bargaining," IICLE Supplement. Member, International Foundation of Employee Benefits. *Member:* Chicago Bar Association (Member, Employee Benefits Committee). ***PRACTICE AREAS:*** Employee Benefits; Executive Compensation. ***Email:*** jvanek@lanermuchin.com

JEFFREY P. CARREN, born Chicago, Illinois, October 8, 1946; admitted to bar, 1973, Illinois and U.S. District Court, Northern District of Illinois; 1976, U.S. Court of Appeals, Seventh Circuit; 1980, U.S. Supreme Court. *Education:* University of Illinois (A.B., with high honors, 1968); Northwestern University Law School (J.D., 1972). Phi Eta Sigma. Edmund James Scholar. Member, Panel of Arbitrators, American Arbitration Association. Note and Comment Editor, Northwestern University Law Review, 1971-1972. Named one of the Leading Lawyers in Illinois, 2004. *Member:* Chicago (Member, Employee Benefits Committee), Illinois State (Member, Employee Benefits Section) and American (Member, Employee Benefits Committee, Tax Section and Employee Benefits and Executive Compensation Committee, Business Law Section) Bar Associations. ***PRACTICE AREAS:*** Employee Benefits; Executive Compensation. ***Email:*** jcarren@lanermuchin.com

JILL P. O'BRIEN, born Elmhurst, Illinois, September 6, 1964; admitted to bar, 1989, Illinois; 1990, U.S. District Court, Northern District of Illinois; 2005, U.S. Supreme Court. *Education:* Western Illinois University (B.S., Law Enforcement Administration, 1986); John Marshall Law School (J.D., 1989). Phi Delta Phi. Executive Editor, John Marshall Law Review, 1988-1989. Author: "Duldulao v. St. Mary of Nazareth Hospital Center: Illinois

(This Listing Continued)

Recognizes Handbook Exception to At-Will Employment Doctrine," 21:3 John Marshall Law Review. Member, Board of Directors, John Marshall Law School Alumni Association. Member, Board of Directors, Chicago Center for Conflict Resolution.Chair, Labor Advisory Committee, American Arbitration Association, Labor Advisory Committee (Chair, 2000-2003). Recognized in 2002 as one of the "40 Illinois Attorneys Under Age 40 to Watch". Recipient of Distinguished Service Award from The John Marshall Law School Alumni Association, 2004. Named Illinois Super Lawyer, 2005-2006. *Member:* Chicago (Co-Chair of Alliance for Women, 2002-2003; Member, Executive Board, 2002-2005), and Illinois State (Chair, Labor and Employment Law Section Council, 2003-2004; Member, Women in the Law Committee; Member, Standing Committee on Judicial Evaluations) Bar Associations; Catholic Lawyers Guild (Member, Board of Governors); Women's Bar Association of Illinois; Northwest Bar Association; Children's Oncology Services, Inc. (Advisory Board). ***PRACTICE AREAS:*** Labor and Employment. ***Email:*** jobrien@lanermuchin.com

NEIL P. STERN, born Cleveland, Ohio, October 8, 1958; admitted to bar, 1984, Illinois and U.S. District Court, Northern District of Illinois; 1986, U.S. District Court, Eastern District of Wisconsin; 2003, U.S. Court of Appeals, Sixth Circuit. *Education:* Oberlin College (A.B., 1981); Ohio State University (J.D., with honors, 1984). Order of the Coif. Managing Editor, Ohio State Law Journal, 1983-1984. Author: "Practice and Procedure Before the United States Equal Employment Opportunity Commission," Employment Discrimination, Chapter IV, 1986, Illinois Committee on Continuing Legal Education; "Death or Disability of Judges in Civil Litigation: Substitution under Federal Rule 63," 44 Ohio State Law Journal 1125, 1984. Member, Illinois Governor's Grievance Panel, 1987-1989. *Member:* Chicago (Co-Chairman, Employment and Labor Law Committee on Alternative Dispute Resolution, 1996-1998) Bar Association. ***LANGUAGES:*** Spanish. ***REPORTED CASES:*** Coronet Foods v. NLRB, 158 F.3d 782 (4th Cir. 1998); Dept. of Central Management Services v. Illinois State Labor Relations Board, 278 Ill. App. 3d 79, 662 N.E.2d 131 (1996). ***PRACTICE AREAS:*** Labor and Employment; Business Immigration. ***Email:*** nstern@lanermuchin.com

THOMAS BRADLEY, born Chicago, Illinois, March 16, 1957; admitted to bar, 1988, Illinois, U.S. District Court, Northern District of Illinois including Trial Bar and U.S. District Court, Eastern District of Wisconsin. *Education:* University of Chicago (B.A., 1979); John Marshall Law School (J.D., with highest distinction, 1988). Member: Cardozo Moot Court Competition, 1987; National Moot Court Competition, 1988. Recipient, Corpus Juris Secundum Award for outstanding legal scholarship. Executive Editor, John Marshall Law Review, 1987-1988. Law Clerk to the Honorable Harry D. Leinenweber, U.S. District Court, Northern District of Illinois, 1989-1990. Author: "Prohibiting Payments to Surrogate Mothers: Love's Labor Lost and the Constitutional Right of Privacy," 20 J. Marshall L. Rev., 715, 1987. Co-Author: "Restrictive Covenants & Confidentiality Restrictions Under Illinois Law," CBA Record, January 1999, 58-62. *Member:* American Immigration Lawyers Association; American Health Lawyers Association. ***PRACTICE AREAS:*** Labor and Employment; Immigration. ***Email:*** tbradley@lanermuchin.com

SCOTT A. GORE, born Memphis, Tennessee, June 19, 1964; admitted to bar, 1989, Illinois. *Education:* Indiana University (B.S., 1986); Case Western Reserve University (J.D., cum laude, 1989). Recipient, American Jurisprudence Award, Contracts; Commendation Awards, 1991-1992. Trial Attorney, National Labor Relations Board, Region 13, 1989-1993. *Member:* Chicago and American Bar Associations. ***PRACTICE AREAS:*** Labor and Employment. ***Email:*** sgore@lanermuchin.com

JEFFREY S. FOWLER, born Vicksburg, Michigan, September 27, 1959; admitted to bar, 1991, Illinois and U.S. District Court, Northern District of Illinois; 1992, U.S. District Court, Southern District of Illinois; 1993, U.S. Court of Appeals, Sixth, Seventh and Tenth Circuits; U.S. District Court Trial Bar, Northern District of Illinois; 1995, U.S. District Court, Eastern District of Michigan; 1997, U.S. District Court, Central and Southern Districts of Illinois and U.S. District Court, Eastern and Western Districts of Arkansas. *Education:* University of Houston at Clear Lake (B.S., in Government, summa cum laude, 1988); The John Marshall Law School (J.D., summa cum laude, 1991). Member, The John Marshall Law Review. Author: "Employee Benefits and Collective Bargaining," Employee Benefits Law, IICLE 1993 and 1997; "Rowe v. State Bank of Lombard: The Key to Unlocking a Landlord's Duty to Provide Security," 23 J. Marshall Law Review 131, 1989; "Insurance Coverage of Employee Claims," I Employment Law Strategist 7, 1994; "Holiday Season a Special Time (for Legal Concerns)," Chicago Daily Law Bulletin, December 15, 1995; "Plaintiff's Emotional Damages Sword has Two Edges," Chicago Daily Law Bulletin, 1995; "Right of Prevailing Defendants to Recover Attorneys Fees Under Section 706 (II) of the Civil Rights Act of 1964," 134 A.L.R. Fed. 161, 1997; "What Constitutes Racial Harassment in Employment Violation of Title VII of the Civil Rights Act of 1964, A.L.R. Fed., Spring, 1998. *Member:* DuPage County, Chicago and American Bar Associations; Christian Legal Society. [U.S. Army, 1977-1980]. ***REPORTED CASES:*** Homeyer v. Stanley Tulchin & Assoc., 91 F.3d 959 (7th Cir. 1996); Conn v. GATX Terminals Corp., 18 F.3d 419 (7th Cir. 1994); HLMF Local No. 667 v. Wells Lamont Corp., 170 F. Supp. 2d 796 (W.D. Tn. 2001); Oliva v. Pride Container, 81 F. Supp. 2d 907 (N.D. Ill. 2000); Freemon v. Foley, 911 F. Supp. 326 (N.D. Ill. 1995); EEOC v. Chicago Club, 881 F. Supp. 350 (N.D. Ill. 1995); Hartlein v. Illinois Power Co., 151 Ill. 2d 142, 601 N.E.2d 720 (1992). ***PRACTICE AREAS:*** Labor and Employment. ***Email:*** jfowler@lanermuchin.com

CLIFFORD R. PERRY III, born New York, N.Y., May 29, 1965; admitted to bar, 1990, Illinois; U.S. District Court, Northern District of Illinois; 1997, U.S. District Court, Central District of Illinois and U.S. Court of Appeals, Seventh Circuit; 2000, Trial Bar; 2001, U.S. Supreme Court; 2002, U.S. District Court, Northern District of Indiana; 2004, U.S. District Court, Eastern and Western Districts of Michigan. *Education:* Northwestern University (B.S.I.E., 1987); Washington University (J.D., 1990). Listed in, International Who's Who. Primary Notes and Comments Editor, 1989-1990, Staff Member, 1988-1989, Washington University Law Quarterly. Author: Note, "State Administrative Preclusion in ADEA Federal Court Suits-Answering Elliot's Call," 67 Washington University Law Quarterly 1331, 1989; Case Note: "Fidelity Financial Services, Inc. v. Joseph Hicks, et al.," (Ill. App. 1st Dist. 1994), ISBA Trial Briefs, Vol. 40, No. 2, December, 1994. *Member:* Chicago, Illinois State and American Bar Associations. ***PRACTICE AREAS:*** Labor and Employment. ***Email:*** cperry@lanermuchin.com

GREGORY R. JAMES, JR., born Chicago, Illinois, March 28, 1959; admitted to bar, 1988, Illinois; 1990, U.S. District Court, Northern and Central Districts of Illinois and U.S. District Court, Western District of Wisconsin; 1999, U.S. District Court, Southern District of Illinois; 2003, U.S. District Court, Northern District of Indiana; 2004, U.S. District Court, Northern District of New York. *Education:* Rutgers University (B.A., 1982); John Marshall Law School (J.D., with highest distinction, 1988). Lead Articles Editor, Software Law Journal. Executive Lead Articles Editor and Staff Member, The John Marshall Law Review. Author: Casenote, *California v Ciraolo:* Are The Protections of the Fourth Amendment Earthbound?" 20 John Marshall Law Review 343, 1986. Judicial Law Clerk to Judge John A. Terry, District of Columbia Court of Appeals, 1988-1989. Member, The Order of John Marshall. [Captain, U.S. Army, 1980-1986]. ***PRACTICE AREAS:*** Labor and Employment; Civil Rights. ***Email:*** gjames@lanermuchin.com

JENNIFER A. NABER, born Chicago, Illinois, October 31, 1962; admitted to bar, 1988, Illinois and U.S. District Court, Northern District of Illinois; 1997, U.S. District Court, Central District of Illinois; 1998, U.S. District Court, Western District of Michigan; 2000, U.S. District Court, Eastern District of Michigan; 2002, U.S. District Court, Northern District of Indiana. *Education:* DePaul University (B.A., 1984); Loyola University (J.D., 1988). Board Member, Youth Guidance. *Member:* Chicago and Illinois State Bar Associations. ***PRACTICE AREAS:*** Labor and Employment. ***Email:*** jnaber@lanermuchin.com

JANICE M. RAUEN, born Chicago, Illinois, August 19, 1964; admitted to bar, 1990, Illinois and U.S. District Court, Northern District of Illinois; 1995, U.S. Court of Appeals, Seventh Circuit. *Education:* University of Illinois (B.A., 1987); Chicago-Kent College of Law (J.D., 1990). Instructor, Labor and Employment Law, Roosevelt University Lawyer's Assistant Program, 1997. *Member:* Chicago and American Bar Associations. ***PRACTICE AREAS:*** Labor and Employment. ***Email:*** jrauen@lanermuchin.com

ANDREW S. GOLDBERG, born Park Ridge, Illinois, March 1, 1970; admitted to bar, 1996, Illinois. *Education:* Illinois State University (B.S., Business and Communications, cum laude, 1993); University of California School of Law, Los Angeles (J.D., 1996). Order of the Coif. Phi Delta Phi. Red Tassel/Mortar Board Honorary Society, 1992. Co-Author: "Employee Benefits and Collective Bargaining Chapter Supplement," and Author: "State Laws Chapter," of the Labor Law Handbook, Illinois Institute for Continuing Legal Education and Employee Benefits Law Manual, 2003. *Member:* Chicago, Illinois State and American (Member, Equal Employment Opportunity Committee, Labor Law Section) Bar Associations. ***PRACTICE AREAS:*** Labor and Employment. ***Email:*** agoldberg@lanermuchin.com

MARK W. BENNETT, born Bloomington, Indiana, June 16, 1964; admitted to bar, 1992, Illinois. *Education:* DePaul University (B.A., 1987; J.D., 1992). ***PRACTICE AREAS:*** Labor and Employment. ***Email:*** mbennett@lanermuchin.com

ROBERT T. BERNSTEIN, born Rochester, New York, July 5, 1969; admitted to bar, 1995, Illinois, Wisconsin and U.S. District Court, Northern District of Illinois; 1998, U.S. Court of Appeals, Fourth Circuit; 1999, District of Columbia. *Education:* Cornell University (B.S., 1991); University of Wisconsin (J.D., 1995). Member, Moot Court Board. Managing Editor, Wisconsin Law Review. *Member:* American Bar Association (Member, Labor and Employment and Equal Employment Opportunity Sections); Management Co-Chair for the Chicago District EEOC's Liaison Program and for the ABA's annual Equal Employment Opportunity publication; Labor and Employment Planning Committee for the Illinois Institute of Continuing Legal Education; Contributing Editor to the Fourth Edition of Barbara Lindemann's and Paul Grossman's "Employment Discrimination" treatise; Chicago Chapter Chair for Cornell School of Industrial and Labor Relations and Member of the national Cornell ILR Board of Directors. ***PRACTICE AREAS:*** Labor and Employment; Litigation. ***Email:*** rbernstein@lanermuchin.com

---

JOSHUA A. DOMBROW, born Evanston, Illinois; admitted to bar, 1998, Illinois and U.S. District Court, Northern District of Illinois; 2003, U.S. Court of Appeals, Seventh Circuit. *Education:* Northwestern University (B.A., 1995); Loyola University Chicago School of Law (J.D., cum laude, 1998); Georgetown University Law Center (LL.M., with distinction, International and Comparative Law, 2000). Golden Key National Honor Society. Recipient, Loyola University Chicago School of Law, Center for Computer-Assisted Legal Instruction (CALI) Awards for excellent achievement in Environmental Law, Estates and Federal Jurisdiction. Executive Editor and Contributing Writer, The Forum, The International Law Journal of Loyola University Chicago School of Law, 1997-1998. Co-Author: "Alternative Dispute Resolution of Employment Law Claims," Practising Law Institute's 30th Annual Institute on Employment Law, 2001. *Member:* American Bar Association (Labor and Employment Section). ***PRACTICE AREAS:*** Labor and Employment; Litigation. ***Email:*** jdombrow@lanermuchin.com

DEBRAI G. HAILE, born Addis Ababa, Ethiopia, August 25, 1971; admitted to bar, 1997, Illinois and U.S. District Court, Northern District of Illinois. *Education:* American University (B.A., 1994); University of Illinois (J.D., 1997). Recipient: Rickerts Award for Excellence in Lawyering, 1997; Just the Beginning Foundation Scholarship, 1996. Notes Editor, Recent Decisions Section, Illinois Bar Journal. Member, Elder Law Journal. Faculty Speaker, Lorman Education Services, 1999—. *Member:* Chicago and American Bar Associations. ***Email:*** dhaile@lanermuchin.com

MONICA B. LASKY, born Chicago, Illinois, May 15, 1966; admitted to bar, 1992, Illinois. *Education:* Amherst College (B.A., 1988); Harvard University (J.D., cum laude, 1992). Phi Beta Kappa. Law Clerk to: Honorable Stephen F. Eilperin, D.C. Superior Court, 1992-1993; Honorable John F. Grady, Northern District of Illinois, 1993-1994. ***PRACTICE AREAS:*** Employee Benefits. ***Email:*** mlasky@lanermuchin.com

ALLISON M. LYNN, born Chicago, Illinois, June 22, 1973; admitted to bar, 2003, Wisconsin and Illinois. *Education:* Universite de Paris, Sorbonne (Certificate in French, 1994); University of Oklahoma (B.A., 1996); University of Chicago (M.A., 1997); University of Wisconsin-Madison (J.D., 2003). Recipient: Bruce F. Beilfuss Memorial Award, 2002 and Ruth B. Doyle Award, 2003, University of Wisconsin-Madison. *Member:* Chicago, Illinois and American Bar Associations; State Bar of Wisconsin. ***LANGUAGES:*** French and Russian. ***PRACTICE AREAS:*** Labor and Employment; Litigation. ***Email:*** alynn@lanermuchin.com

MARGARET C. McGRATH, born Toronto, Canada, April 8, 1958; admitted to bar, 2004, Illinois; 2005, U.S. District Court, Northern District of Illinois. *Education:* Loyola University (B.A., cum laude, 1995; B.S., cum laude 1995); John Marshall Law School (J.D.,

(This Listing Continued)

LANER, MUCHIN, DOMBROW, BECKER, LEVIN AND TOMINBERG, LTD., Chicago—Continued

summa cum laude, 2004; LL.M. with honors, 2004). Alpha Sigma Lambda; Omricron Delta Epsilon; Order of John Marshall, 2004. Author: "Insulin-Dependent Diabetes and Access to Treatment in the Workplace: The Failure of the Americans with Disabilities Act to Provide Protection," 37 J. Marshall Law Rev. 957 (2004). *Member:* Chicago, Illinois State and American Bar Associations. ***Email:*** mmcgrath@lanermuchin.com

LAURA R. MEEHAN, born Newport News, Virginia, October 28, 1974; admitted to bar, 1999, Illinois. *Education:* Miami University (B.A., 1996); Chicago-Kent College of Law (J.D., 1999). *Member:* Chicago and American Bar Associations. ***PRACTICE AREAS:*** Employee Benefits. ***Email:*** lmeehan@lanermuchin.com

DEVLIN J. SCHOOP, born Chicago, Illinois, September 17, 1971; admitted to bar, 1997, Illinois; 1998, U.S. District Court, Northern and Central Districts of Illinois and U.S. Court of Appeals, Seventh Circuit; 2000, U.S. Court of Appeals, Fourth, Sixth, Eighth and Eleventh Circuits and U.S. District Court for the District of Columbia; 2001, U.S. Court of Appeals for the Federal Circuit and U.S. Supreme Court; 2002, U.S. District Court, Eastern District of Wisconsin. *Education:* University of Illinois (B.A., 1994); University of Illinois (J.D., 1997). Member, University of Illinois Law Review. Law Clerk to the Hon. Blanche M. Manning, U.S. District Court, Northern District of Illinois, 1997-1999. *Member:* Cook County, Chicago, Illinois State and Federal Bar Associations; Seventh Circuit Bar Association. ***REPORTED CASES:*** Lake County Riverboat L.P. v. Gaming Board, 730 N.E. 2d 524, 313 Ill. App. 3d 943 (2d Dist. 2000). ***PRACTICE AREAS:*** Labor Law; Employment Litigation. ***Email:*** dschoop@lanermuchin.com

SONYA OLDS SOM, born Pittsburgh, Pennsylvania, August 14, 1972; admitted to bar, 1997, Georgia; 2005, Illinois. *Education:* Kalamazoo College (B.A., 1994); Cornell University (J.D., International Legal Affairs and Business Law, 1997). *Member:* Chicago and American Bar Associations; AILA. ***LANGUAGES:*** Spanish, French and Italian. ***PRACTICE AREAS:*** Immigration Law. ***Email:*** ssom@lanermuchin.com

MARK L. STOLZENBURG, born Buffalo, New York, August 12, 1978; admitted to bar, 2003, Illinois; 2004, U.S. District Court, Central District of Illinois; 2005, U.S. District Court, Northern District of Illinois. *Education:* Cornell University, School of Industrial and Labor Relations (B.S., 2000); Washington University (J.D., 2003). Executive Articles Editor, Washington University Law Quarterly, 2002-2003. Author: Note, "Blind Faith or Efficiency? The Difference Between the Fifth Circuit and all Others on the Topic of Private Sector Impasse Bargaining", 80 Wash. U. L. Q. 1341 (2002). *Member:* Chicago, Illinois State and American Bar Associations. ***Email:*** mstolzenburg@lanermuchin.com

WILLIAM P. SWEENEY, born Bloomington, Illinois, October 4, 1976; admitted to bar, 2002, Illinois. *Education:* Millikin University (B.S., 1999); John Marshall Law School (J.D., 2002). Member, The John Marshall Law Review, 2001. ***PRACTICE AREAS:*** Employee Benefits. ***Email:*** wsweeney@lanermuchin.com

OF COUNSEL

ISAIAH S. DORFMAN, born Kiev, Russia, March 17, 1907; admitted to bar, 1931, Illinois; 1936, U.S. Supreme Court; 1937, U.S. District Court, Northern District of Illinois; 1939, U.S. Court of Appeals, Seventh Circuit. *Education:* University of Chicago (Ph.B., 1927; J.D., 1931). Lecturer on Labor Law, National University Law School, 1942-1943. Regional Attorney, Region 13, 1937-1942 and Chief, Special Litigation Unit, Washington, D.C., 1942-1943, National Labor Relations Board. *Member:* Chicago (Member, Committees on: Unauthorized Practice of Law, 1961-1964; Labor and Employment Law, 1979-1980; Administrative Law, 1979-1980, Chairman, 1966-1967), Illinois State and American Bar Associations.

DANIEL J. ASHLEY, born Chicago, Illinois, March 20, 1952; admitted to bar, 1977, Illinois. *Education:* University of Illinois (A.B., 1974; J.D. 1977). International Moot Court Competition. Member, Profit Sharing Council of America. Author: "Plan Terminations - Practical Considerations After Government Approval Has Been Received," Journal of Pension Benefits, Winter, 1994; "Schoonejongen v. Curtis-Wright Corp.," The Law Works, May, 1994; "Pension Benefits and Divorce - Dealing With QDROs," Profit Sharing Magazine, April 1988. Co-Author: "A Guide to Successful Early Retirement Windows," Research Institute of America, October 1992. *Member:* Chicago (Member, Employee Benefit Committee, 1977—; Chair, Determination Letter Task Force, 2001-2003; Secretary, 1990-1991; Vice-Chair, 1991-1992; Chair, 1992-1993; Chair, Plan Qualification Subcommittee, 1986; Chair, Distributions Subcommittee, 1989; Member, Task Force on State Wage Deductions and Cafeteria Plans) Illinois State and American Bar Associations. ***LANGUAGES:*** German. ***PRACTICE AREAS:*** Employee Benefits; ERISA Compliance; Qualified Retirement Plans; Tax Exempt Organizations. ***Email:*** dashley@lanermuchin.com

HERMAN J. DE KOVEN, born Chicago, Illinois, November 3, 1912; admitted to bar, 1936, Illinois. *Education:* University of Chicago (B.A., 1934; J.D., 1936). Order of the Coif; Phi Beta Kappa. Attorney, Supervising Attorney and General Attorney, National Labor Relations Board, Washington, D.C. and Chicago, Illinois, 1941-1953.

SEYMOUR COHEN, born Chicago, Illinois, September 27, 1917; admitted to bar, 1941, Indiana; 1948, Illinois; 1949, U.S. District Court, Northern District of Illinois; 1971, U.S. Supreme Court; 1977, U.S. Court of Appeals, Seventh Circuit. *Education:* Indiana University (B.S., 1939; J.D., 1941). Author: "The Minority Union's Right to Strike," 16 Indiana Law Journal, 377, 1941; "N.L.R.B.: Poacher on the Arbitral Domain," 55 American Bar Association Journal 437, 1969. Attorney, National Labor Relations Board, Washington, D.C., 1946-1947. *Member:* Chicago (Vice Chairman, 1959-1961 and Chairman, 1961-1963, Labor Law Committee) and American Bar Associations.

RICHARD W. LANER, born Chicago, Illinois, July 12, 1933; admitted to bar, 1956, Illinois; 1957, U.S. District Court, Northern District of Illinois; 1971, U.S. Court of Appeals, Sixth Circuit. *Education:* Northwestern University (B.S.L., 1955; LL.B., 1956). Order of the Coif. Member, The College of Labor and Employment Lawyers. *Listed in:* "The Best Lawyers in America" and "Who's Who in American Law." Author: "A Buyer Views the Purchase of a Unionized Business," 47 Chicago Bar Record 93, December 1965; "Future for School Labor Relations," Chicago Sun Times, September 26, 1971; "Review of the Law of the United States Court of Appeals for the Seventh Circuit: Labor Law," 50 Chicago-Kent Law Review 309, 1973; "Employer-Employee Relations: Unions and Hospitals," 46 Radiologic Technology, 10, July/August, 1974; "Five Obstacles to Labor Peace in the Schools," 43 Illinois School Board Journal 21, January/February 1975; "The Unions Are Coming," 4 Hospital Housekeeping 15, April/May, 1975; "Collective Bargaining—How Are Your School Board Policies," 43 Illinois School Board Journal 10, May/June, 1975; "Increasing Productivity in the Schools," Chicago Principals Reporter 10, 1975; "Pre-Election Pointers," 22 Executive Housekeeper 18, 1975; "Unions—Now is the Time to Review Your Labor Relations Policies," 24 Building Operating Management 34, August, 1977; "Why Employees Join Unions?" 7 Management World 8, Vol. 20, July and August, 1978; "The Dilemma of the Small Plan Fiduciary Under ERISA," 56 Chicago-Kent Law Review 589, 1980; "Interest Arbitration: A New Terminal Impasse Resolution Procedure for Illinois Public Sector Employees," 60 Chicago-Kent Law Review 839, 1984; "Will Your Employees Join a Union?" Hotel and Management 6, November 12, 1985. Named one of the Leading Lawyers in Illinois, 2004. *Member:* Chicago (Member, 1961—; Vice Chairman, 1971-1972 and Chairman, 1972-1973, Labor Law Committee) and American Bar Associations. ***PRACTICE AREAS:*** Labor and Employment. ***Email:*** rlaner@lanermuchin.com

LAWRENCE JAY WEINER, born March 9, 1941; admitted to bar, 1964, Illinois and Florida (inactive); 1969, U.S. Court of Appeals, Seventh Circuit and U.S. District Court, Northern District of Illinois; 1974, U.S. Supreme Court. *Education:* University of Miami (B.B.A., summa cum laude, 1961); Harvard Law School (LL.B., 1964). Beta Gamma Sigma. Asst. U.S. Attorney/U.S. Dept. of Justice, 1964-1967; Attorney, Asher, Greenfield, Gubbins & Segall, 1967-1971; Former equity partner at: Weiner, Wexler & Spak, P.C., Schwartz & Freeman, and Scariano, Himes & Petrarca, Ltd.; ISBA Journal, "Arbitration - Practice & Procedure," 1971; Banking Law Journal, "Regulations G T & U and Their Effect on Foreign Transactions," 1972; IICLE, School Law, "Teacher Rights & Responsibilities," 1978, 1980, 1985; IICLE, Employment Terminations and Issues in the Workplace, "Legal Arguments With Respect to Drug Testing of Public Employees: Who Has What Leg to Stand On," 1987. Elected Trustee for Barrington Area Library District, 1999 —;. *Member:* Chicago (Committee on Inquiry, 1967-1973; Federal Civil Practice Committee, 2001-present, former Vice Chair), Illinois State (School Law Section Council 1984, 1987, 1994-2002, Newsletter Editor, 1990—, Chair 2001-2002; Elected General Assembly Representative 1987-1993, 1994-2003; Section Council on Alternative Dispute Resolution 1992-1996, Chair 1993-1994; ADR Section Council Liaison to ADR Committees of the Illinois Supreme Court, U.S. Dist. Court and U.S. Bankruptcy Court for the Northern District off Illinois, 1994-1996; Judicial Evaluations Committee, 2001—); Elected Trustee for Village of North Barrington, Board of Directors 1997-1999; Chicago Lincoln Inn of Court (2001-2004); Illinois Appellate Lawyers' Association; Decalogue Society. ***PRACTICE AREAS:*** Employment Litigation; Discrimination Litigation; Labor Arbitration; Administrative Proceedings; Management Labor and Employment Law; Federal and State Appeals. ***Email:*** lweiner@lanermuchin.com

WILLIAM L. BECKER, born Long Island City, New York, January 29, 1943; admitted to bar, 1969, Missouri; 1973, Illinois; 1974, U.S. District Court, Northern District of Illinois; 1975, U.S. Court of Appeals, Fourth Circuit; 1976, U.S. Court of Appeals, Seventh Circuit and U.S. Supreme Court; 1977, U.S. Court of Appeals, Fifth Circuit; 1979, U.S. District Court, Eastern District of Kentucky; 1983, U.S. District Court, Eastern District of Michigan. *Education:* Haverford College (B.A., 1965); Washington University (J.D., 1969). Delta Theta Phi. Attorney, National Labor Relations Board, 14th Region, 1969-1972. Contributing Author: "The Developing Labor Law," and its Supplements, ABA Section of Labor Law, 1972-2005. "Human Resource Director's Handbook," Mary Cook, Editor, Prentice-Hall, 1984. Of Counsel, 2005—, Managing Partner, 1988-2004, Member, 1976-2004 and Associate, 1972-1976, Laner, Muchin, Dombrow, Becker, Levin and Tominberg, Ltd. Named one of the Leading Lawyers in Illinois, 2004. General Counsel, Harpo, Inc., 2005—. *Member:* Chicago and American (Member, Sections on: Labor and Employment; Entertainment Law) Bar Associations; The Missouri Bar. ***PRACTICE AREAS:*** Labor and Employment; Entertainment Law. ***Email:*** wbecker@lanermuchin.com

REFERENCE: NBD Bank Chicago.

KEIL M. LARSON

Established in 1990

800 N. CLARK STREET, SUITE 222
CHICAGO, ILLINOIS 60610
Telephone: 312-664-9300
Fax: 312-664-5363
Email: keil@keillarson.com
URL: http://www.keillarson.com

Real Estate Litigation, Condominium Disputes, Real Estate Transactions, Probate Litigation, Partition Suits, Foreclosures, Lien Litigation, Specific Performance, Contract Litigation, Appraisal Litigation, Builder Litigation, Construction Defects, Landlord Tenant Law, Fraud Litigation, Immigration.

KEIL M. LARSON, born Peoria, Illinois, September 30, 1960; admitted to bar, 1985, Illinois; U.S. Supreme Court; U.S. Court of Appeals, Seventh Circuit; U.S. District Court, Northern and Eastern Districts of Illinois; U.S. District Court Western District of Michigan. *Education:* University of Illinois (B.A. in Political Science, 1982); John Marshall Law School (J.D., 1985). *Member:* Chicago, Illinois State and America Bar Associations; American Immigration Lawyers Association.

LASKY & RIFKIND, LTD.

351 W. HUBBARD STREET
CHICAGO, ILLINOIS 60610
Telephone: 312-634-0057
Fax: 312-634-0059
Email: Lasky@Laskyrifkind.com
URL: http://www.laskyrifkind.com

New York, New York Office: 100 Park Avenue, 10017. Telephone: 212-907-0800.

(This Listing Continued)

(This Listing Continued)

Litigation Practice including Securities, Business, Commercial, Class Actions, Professional Malpractice and Appellate Practice.

LEIGH R. LASKY, born Chicago, Illinois, June 12, 1960; admitted to bar, 1985, Illinois; U.S. District Court, Northern District of Illinois, including Trial Bar; U.S. Court of Appeals, Seventh Circuit. *Education:* University of Illinois (B.A., 1982); John Marshall Law School (J.D., 1985). *Member:* Chicago and American Bar Associations. (Resident, New York, N.Y. Office). ***PRACTICE AREAS:*** Securities Litigation; Business; Commercial Litigation; General; Franchise Litigation. **Email:** lasky@laskyrifkind.com

NORMAN RIFKIND, born Chicago, Illinois, June 20, 1960; admitted to bar, 1985, Illinois and U.S. District Court, Northern District of Illinois including Trial Bar; 1987, U.S. Court of Appeals, Seventh Circuit; 1990, U.S. Court of Appeals, Sixth Circuit and U.S. District Court, Eastern District of Michigan; 1991, U.S. Court of Appeals, Fourth and Eighth Circuits; 1992, U.S. District Court, Central District of Illinois; 1993, U.S. Court of Appeals, Eleventh Circuit. *Education:* Indiana University (B.S., 1982); Loyola University (J.D., 1985). Phi Alpha Delta. Recipient, American Jurisprudence Award in Evidence and Labor Law. Author: Negligent Misrepresentation in Illinois: The Third Party (Non) requirement," 82 Illinois Bar Journal 668 (1994). Arbitrator for Cook County Mandatory Arbitration, Member Pro Bono Advocates. *Member:* Chicago, Illinois State and American Bar Associations. ***PRACTICE AREAS:*** Securities, Business and Commercial Litigation; Securities Arbitration; Professional Malpractice; Appellate Practice. **Email:** rifkind@laskyrifkind.com

LATHAM & WATKINS LLP

SEARS TOWER
SUITE 5800
CHICAGO, ILLINOIS 60606
Telephone: 312-876-7700
Telecopier: 312-993-9767
URL: http://www.lw.com

Brussels, Belgium; Costa Mesa, California; Frankfurt, Germany; Hamburg, Germany; Hong Kong, China; London, England; Los Angeles, California; Menlo Park, California; Milan, Italy; Moscow, Russia; Newark, New Jersey; New York, N.Y.; Paris, France; Reston, Virginia; San Diego, California; San Francisco, California; Shanghai, China; Singapore; Tokyo, Japan; Washington, D.C.

Complex Commercial Litigation, Distributor Termination, Franchise Arbitration and Litigation, Antitrust, General Corporate, Corporate Governance, Public Corporations, Corporate Workouts, Securitization, Corporate Reorganization, Corporate Finance, Corporate Contracts, Takeovers, Tender Offers, Securities, Mergers, Acquisitions and Divestitures, Corporate Tax Controversies, Federal and State Tax Controversies, Federal Taxation, Illinois Taxation, Corporate Control Contests, Employee Benefits, Environmental Law, Environmental Insurance Coverage, Toxic Tort Defense, Commercial Finance, Debt and Equity Finance, Structured Finance, Financial Restructuring, Secured Finance, Unsecured Finance Insolvency, Fraudulent Conveyance, Pre-Bankruptcy Workouts, Information Technology Contracts, Information Technology Licensing, Intellectual Property Infringement, Intellectual Property Litigation, Intellectual Property Licensing, Information and Privacy, Trademarks, Real Estate Development, Real Estate Finance.

PARTNERS

MARY ROSE ALEXANDER, admitted to bar, 1989, California; 1990, Illinois; 1991, District of Columbia. *Education:* University of California at San Diego (B.A., 1986); Columbia University (J.D., 1989). ***PRACTICE AREAS:*** Commercial Litigation; Environmental Litigation; Tort Litigation; Employment Litigation; Environmental Insurance Coverage; Insurance Litigation.

JOSEF S. ATHANAS, admitted to bar, 1991, Illinois. *Education:* Indiana University (B.S., 1988); University of Chicago (J.D., 1991). ***PRACTICE AREAS:*** Bankruptcy; Debtor and Creditor; Finance.

J. DOUGLAS BACON, admitted to bar, 1983, Texas; 1989, Illinois. *Education:* University of Texas (B.B.A., 1980); University of Texas (J.D., 1983). ***PRACTICE AREAS:*** Creditors Rights; Bankruptcy Reorganization; Insolvency; Secured Finance.

STEPHEN S. BOWEN, admitted to bar, 1972, Illinois. *Education:* Wabash College (B.A., 1968); University of Chicago (J.D., 1972).

JAMES A. CHERNEY, admitted to bar, 1973, Illinois. *Education:* Tufts University (B.A., 1969); Columbia University (J.D., 1973). ***PRACTICE AREAS:*** Antitrust Litigation; Commercial Litigation; Bankruptcy Litigation; Consumer Class Actions; Health Care Litigation.

DAVID G. CRUMBAUGH, admitted to bar, 1976, Illinois. *Education:* Illinois State University (B.S., 1973); University of Illinois (J.D., 1976). ***PRACTICE AREAS:*** Secured Lending; Out of Court Debt Restructuring; Leveraged Buyouts; Mergers, Acquisitions and Divestitures.

JAMES W. DORAN, admitted to bar, 1981, Illinois. *Education:* University of Iowa (B.B.A., 1978); Stanford University (J.D., 1981). ***PRACTICE AREAS:*** Finance; Banks and Banking; Commercial Law.

DIANA SLYFIELD DOYLE, admitted to bar, 1996, Illinois. *Education:* Northwestern University (B.S.J., 1988); University of Chicago (J.D., 1996). ***PRACTICE AREAS:*** Taxation; Corporate Taxation; Corporate Reorganizations; Mergers, Acquisitions and Divestitures; Federal Tax Controversies.

DAVID S. FOSTER, admitted to bar, 1985, Illinois. *Education:* Princeton University (A.B., 1979); Yale Law School (J.D., 1983). ***PRACTICE AREAS:*** Intellectual Property Litigation; Commercial Litigation.

DOUGLAS A. FREEDMAN, admitted to bar, 1985, Illinois. *Education:* Western Michigan University (B.S., 1981); Northwestern University (J.D., 1985). ***PRACTICE AREAS:*** Litigation.

(This Listing Continued)

MARK D. GERSTEIN, admitted to bar, 1984, Illinois. *Education:* University of Michigan (B.A., 1981); University of Chicago (J.D., 1984). ***PRACTICE AREAS:*** Mergers and Acquisitions; Takeovers; Corporate Governance; Securities.

WILLIAM J. GIBBONS, admitted to bar, 1972, Illinois. *Education:* Northwestern University (B.A., 1968; J.D., 1972). ***PRACTICE AREAS:*** Securities Litigation; Commercial Litigation; Consumer Class Actions; Class Action Defense; Antitrust Litigation; Franchise Litigation.

ROBERT G. GOLDMAN, admitted to bar, 1984, California; 1994, Illinois. *Education:* University of Wisconsin (B.B.A., 1979); University of California School of Law (J.D., 1984). ***PRACTICE AREAS:*** Taxation; Partnership Law.

MARCELO HALPERN, admitted to bar, 1992, Illinois; 1993, U.S. Tax Court. *Education:* Wesleyan University (B.A., 1985); Columbia University (M.B.A., 1992; J.D., 1992). ***PRACTICE AREAS:*** Computers and Software; Internet Law; Technology Joint Ventures; Intellectual Property; Technology Law; Technology Licensing.

RONALD W. HANSON, admitted to bar, 1975, Illinois. *Education:* St. Olaf College (B.A., 1972); University of Chicago (J.D., 1975). ***PRACTICE AREAS:*** Commercial Bankruptcy; Commercial Workouts; Bankruptcy Litigation; Lender Liability; Banking Regulation; Creditors Rights.

TIM HARDWICKE, admitted to bar, 1989, Illinois. *Education:* Vanderbilt University (B.A., 1986); University of Chicago (J.D., 1989). ***PRACTICE AREAS:*** Litigation; Class Actions; Antitrust; Securities.

THOMAS J. HEIDEN, admitted to bar, 1971, Michigan; 2004, Illinois. *Education:* University of Notre Dame (B.A., 1967); Cornell University (J.D., 1971). ***PRACTICE AREAS:*** Civil Litigation; Trial Practice.

DAVID S. HELLER, admitted to bar, 1978, Illinois. *Education:* Northwestern University (B.A., 1974); Georgetown University (J.D., 1978). ***LANGUAGES:*** Spanish. ***PRACTICE AREAS:*** Business Reorganization; Bankruptcy.

ROBIN M. HULSHIZER, admitted to bar, 1992, California; 1996, Illinois. *Education:* Northwestern University (B.S., 1986); University of Iowa (J.D., 1991). ***PRACTICE AREAS:*** Environmental Law; Litigation.

JAMES G. HUNTER, JR., admitted to bar, 1967, Illinois; 1980, California. *Education:* Case Institute of Technology (B.S., 1965); University of Chicago (J.D., 1967). ***PRACTICE AREAS:*** Antitrust; Business Litigation; Complex Litigation; Federal Civil Practice; Patent Litigation; Securities Litigation.

ROGER J. JONES, admitted to bar, 1987, Illinois. *Education:* State University of New York at Buffalo (B.A., 1973; M.A., 1975; Ph.D., 1979; J.D., 1984). ***PRACTICE AREAS:*** Federal Tax Controversies; Appellate Practice; International Taxation; Federal Income Tax; State Tax Controversies.

THOMAS E. KEIM, JR., admitted to bar, 1993, Illinois. *Education:* Yale University (B.A., 1989); Cambridge University, Cambridge, England (M.Phil., 1990); University of Chicago (J.D., 1993). ***PRACTICE AREAS:*** Corporate Law; Mergers, Acquisitions and Divestitures; Securities Law; Investments.

BRADLEY E. KOTLER, admitted to bar, 1995, Illinois. *Education:* Emory University (B.B.A., 1992); Georgetown University (J.D., 1995). ***PRACTICE AREAS:*** Commercial Finance; Corporate Finance; Corporate Law; Commercial Real Estate.

JOSEPH M. KRONSNOBLE, admitted to bar, 1991, Illinois. *Education:* University of Wisconsin at Madison (B.B.A., 1985; M.S., 1986); University of Chicago (J.D., 1991). ***PRACTICE AREAS:*** Tax Law.

MICHAEL D. LEVIN, admitted to bar, 1967, Illinois. *Education:* University of Michigan (A.B., 1964; J.D., 1967). ***PRACTICE AREAS:*** Corporate Finance; Corporate Organization; Mergers and Acquisitions; Public Companies; Securitization.

LAURENCE H. LEVINE, admitted to bar, 1971, Illinois. *Education:* Case Western Reserve University (B.A., 1968); Northwestern University (J.D., 1971). ***PRACTICE AREAS:*** Commercial Litigation; Environmental Litigation; Government Contract Fraud.

RICHARD A. LEVY, admitted to bar, 1983, Illinois. *Education:* Amherst College (B.A., 1977); Yale University (J.D., 1982). ***PRACTICE AREAS:*** Bankruptcy; Financial Restructuring; Secured Finance; Asset Based Finance; International Insolvency.

JANET MALLOY LINK, admitted to bar, 1995, California; 1998, Illinois. *Education:* Yale University (B.A., 1992); Columbia University (J.D., 1995). ***PRACTICE AREAS:*** Litigation.

CHRISTOPHER D. LUEKING, admitted to bar, 1987, Illinois. *Education:* St. Olaf College (B.A., 1984); University of Michigan (J.D., 1987). ***PRACTICE AREAS:*** Corporate Law; Securities.

JOHN P. LYNCH, admitted to bar, 1967, Illinois. *Education:* Marquette University (B.A., 1964); Northwestern University (J.D., 1967). (Also at Paris Office). ***PRACTICE AREAS:*** Antitrust; Competition; Employment Law; Intellectual Property; Technology Law; Public Company Representation.

ELLEN L. MARKS, admitted to bar, 1991, Illinois. *Education:* Northwestern University (B.A., 1988); University of Michigan (J.D., 1991); Vermont College (M.F.A., 2002). ***PRACTICE AREAS:*** Corporate Finance; Securitization; Public Offerings; Securities Regulation; Derivative Products; International Capital Markets.

JULI WILSON MARSHALL, admitted to bar, 1984, California; 1995, Illinois. *Education:* Michigan State University (B.A., 1981); University of Michigan (J.D., 1984). ***PRACTICE AREAS:*** Complex Litigation; Class Actions; Intellectual Property; Insurance; Products Liability; Torts.

RICHARD S. MELLER, admitted to bar, 1982, Illinois. *Education:* Brown University (A.B., 1979); University of Michigan (J.D., 1982). ***PRACTICE AREAS:*** Business Planning; Corporate Law; Partnership Law.

MARK S. MESTER, admitted to bar, 1987, Illinois. *Education:* Yale University (B.A., 1982; J.D., 1986). ***LANGUAGES:*** Latin.

JEFFREY G. MORAN, admitted to bar, 1988, Illinois. *Education:* Bradley University (B.S., 1985); University of Michigan (J.D., 1988).

(This Listing Continued)

LATHAM & WATKINS LLP, Chicago—Continued

KEVIN M. MURPHY, admitted to bar, 1981, Illinois. *Education:* Wheaton College (B.A., 1978); University of Chicago (J.D., 1981). ***PRACTICE AREAS:*** Civil Litigation; Bankruptcy; Environmental Litigation; Insurance Litigation.

DAVID A. NELSON, admitted to bar, 1992, Illinois. *Education:* Stanford University (B.S.E.E., 1987); Northwestern University (J.D., 1992). ***PRACTICE AREAS:*** Intellectual Property Litigation; Intellectual Property Licensing; Intellectual Property Infringement.

CARY R. PERLMAN, admitted to bar, 1988, Illinois. *Education:* University of Michigan (A.B., 1984); Harvard University (J.D., 1987). ***PRACTICE AREAS:*** Environmental Litigation; Complex Litigation.

PHILIP J. PERZEK, admitted to bar, 1986, Illinois. *Education:* Northern Illinois University (B.S., 1982); Northwestern University (J.D., 1986). ***PRACTICE AREAS:*** Banking Law; Finance; Creditors Rights; Bankruptcy.

MICHAEL A. PUCKER, admitted to bar, 1989, Massachusetts; 1992, Illinois. *Education:* Columbia University (B.A., 1983; J.D., 1988). ***PRACTICE AREAS:*** Corporate Law; Business Planning; Mergers, Acquisitions and Divestitures.

VIK PURI, admitted to bar, 1993, Illinois. *Education:* University of Illinois (B.A., 1990); Boston University (J.D., 1993). ***PRACTICE AREAS:*** Finance.

DAVID K. RATHGEBER, admitted to bar, 1985, Illinois. *Education:* College of St. Thomas; University of Notre Dame (B.A., 1982); Northwestern University (J.D., 1985). ***PRACTICE AREAS:*** Mergers, Acquisitions and Divestitures; Commercial Law; Banks and Banking.

KEVIN A. RUSSELL, admitted to bar, 1980, Illinois. *Education:* Albion College (A.B., 1977); University of Michigan (J.D., 1980). ***PRACTICE AREAS:*** Franchise Litigation; Commercial Litigation; Intellectual Property Litigation.

NANCY L. SCHIMMEL, admitted to bar, 1981, Illinois; 1995, New York. *Education:* Williams College (B.A., 1978); Georgetown University (J.D., 1981); Northwestern University, J. L. Kellogg Graduate School of Management (M.M., 1987). ***PRACTICE AREAS:*** Banks and Banking; Finance; Securitization; Secured Transactions; Debtor and Creditor.

KENNETH G. SCHULER, admitted to bar, 1994, Illinois. *Education:* University of Northern Iowa (B.A., 1990); University of Michigan (J.D., 1993). ***PRACTICE AREAS:*** Intellectual Property Litigation; Commercial Litigation; Securities Litigation.

DONALD L. SCHWARTZ, admitted to bar, 1974, Illinois. *Education:* Macalester College (B.A., 1971); University of Chicago (J.D., 1974). ***PRACTICE AREAS:*** Banks and Banking; Finance; Bankruptcy.

ROBIN L. STRUVE, admitted to bar, 1987, Illinois. *Education:* University of Colorado at Boulder (B.A., 1984); Harvard University (J.D., 1987). ***PRACTICE AREAS:*** Employee Benefits.

ROBERT W. TARUN, admitted to bar, 1974, Illinois. *Education:* Stanford University (A.B., 1971); University of Chicago (M.B.A., 1982); DePaul University (J.D., 1974). ***PRACTICE AREAS:*** Business Litigation; Antitrust; White Collar Criminal Defense; Corporate Investigations.

MATTHEW W. WALCH, admitted to bar, 1994, Illinois. *Education:* Miami University (B.A., 1991); Georgetown University (J.D., 1994). ***PRACTICE AREAS:*** Commercial Litigation; Intellectual Property Litigation; Trademark Prosecution; Trademark Licensing; Information Technology Transactions.

OF COUNSEL

SANDHYA C. BUDINGER, admitted to bar, 1990, Illinois. *Education:* Northwestern University (B.A., 1986; J.D., 1990). ***PRACTICE AREAS:*** Employee Benefits.

NANCY SCHEURWATER HUNTER, admitted to bar, 1983, California; 1993, Illinois. *Education:* Wellesley College (B.A., 1979); Harvard University (J.D., 1983). ***PRACTICE AREAS:*** Securities Litigation; Professional Liability.

ASSOCIATES

KRISTINE A. ACKERMAN, admitted to bar, 1998, Wisconsin; 1999, Illinois. *Education:* University of Wisconsin-Madison (B.A., 1992; J.D., 1998). ***PRACTICE AREAS:*** Asset Based Finance; Commercial Finance; Securitization; Corporate Law.

MANCHIT AUYEUNG, admitted to bar, 2001, Illinois. *Education:* Rush University (B.S., 1996); University of Illinois (J.D., 2001). ***LANGUAGES:*** Mandarin.

JULIE D. BAILEY, admitted to bar, 1998, Illinois. *Education:* Truman State University (B.S., 1994); Drake University Law School (J.D., 1998). ***PRACTICE AREAS:*** Litigation.

JENNY C. BAKER, admitted to bar, 2001, Illinois. *Education:* University of Memphis (B.A., 1998); University of Michigan Law School (J.D., 2001). ***PRACTICE AREAS:*** Employee Benefits.

STEPHANIE BARKER, admitted to bar, 2004, Illinois. *Education:* Dartmouth College (A.B., 2001); University of Michigan (J.D., 2004). ***LANGUAGES:*** French.

BRENDAN S. BEASLEY, admitted to bar, 2002, Illinois. *Education:* University of Findlay (B.A., 1998); University of Pennsylvania (J.D., 2002). ***LANGUAGES:*** Spanish. ***PRACTICE AREAS:*** Business Acquisitions; Insolvency.

CHRISTOPHER P. BENNETT, admitted to bar, 1999, Illinois. *Education:* University of Missouri (B.A., 1994; J.D., 1999). ***PRACTICE AREAS:*** Corporate.

CATHY A. BIRKELAND, admitted to bar, 1997, Illinois. *Education:* Dartmouth College (B.A., 1994); Northwestern University (J.D., 1997). ***PRACTICE AREAS:*** Corporate Finance; Mergers and Acquisitions.

CARRIE BORDEWICK, admitted to bar, 2000, Illinois. *Education:* Northwestern University (B.S.J., 1997); Duke University (J.D., 2000). ***PRACTICE AREAS:*** Corporate Law.

(This Listing Continued)

RODERICK O. BRANCH, admitted to bar, 2003, New York (Not admitted in Illinois). *Education:* Texas Christian University (B.A., 1998); Harvard Law School (J.D., 2001). ***LANGUAGES:*** Spanish, French and Italian. ***PRACTICE AREAS:*** Corporate Finance; International Corporate Finance.

DAVID M. BUCHANAN, admitted to bar, 2000, California; 2004, Illinois. *Education:* Brigham Young University (B.A., 1996; J.D., 1999). ***LANGUAGES:*** Spanish. ***PRACTICE AREAS:*** Commercial Banking; Mergers and Acquisitions; Leveraged Buyouts; Bankruptcy.

B. JOHN CASEY, admitted to bar, 2000, Illinois. *Education:* Georgetown University (B.A., 1996); University of Chicago Law School (J.D., 2000). ***PRACTICE AREAS:*** Commercial Litigation; Class Action Defense; Securities Litigation.

YAEL M. CITRO, admitted to bar, 2001, Illinois. *Education:* University of Michigan (B.A., 1994); University of Pennsylvania (J.D., 2001). ***LANGUAGES:*** Hebrew. ***PRACTICE AREAS:*** Finance; Taxation.

LISA PLUNKETT CONLON, admitted to bar, 1998, Illinois. *Education:* Northwestern University (B.A., 1988); University of Michigan (J.D., 1998). ***PRACTICE AREAS:*** Litigation.

ALICE E. DECKER, admitted to bar, 2004, Illinois. *Education:* Swarthmore College (B.A., 1998); Northwestern University (J.D., 2004).

JOSHUA P. DEHNKE, admitted to bar, 2004, Illinois. *Education:* University of Missouri (B.A., 2001); University of Texas at Austin (J.D., 2004).

MIA GRACE DIBELLA, admitted to bar, 2001, New York; 2002, Illinois. *Education:* Colgate University (B.A., 1994); Northwestern University (J.D., 2001). ***PRACTICE AREAS:*** Corporate Finance; Mergers and Acquisitions.

ROBERT A. DROBNAK, admitted to bar, 2000, Illinois. *Education:* Bradley University (B.S., 1997); University of Pennsylvania (J.D., 2000). ***PRACTICE AREAS:*** Commercial Finance; Asset Based Finance; Corporate Law; Workouts; Out of Court Debt Restructuring.

JACOB B. DROUILLARD, admitted to bar, 2004, Illinois. *Education:* University of Dayton (B.S., 1997); University of Michigan (J.D., 2004).

KERRY DUCEY, admitted to bar, 2001, Illinois. *Education:* University of Notre Dame (B.A., 1998); Vanderbilt University (J.D., 2001). ***LANGUAGES:*** Spanish. ***PRACTICE AREAS:*** Corporate Finance; Corporate Governance; Mergers and Acquisitions.

BRADLEY C. FARIS, admitted to bar, 2000, Illinois. *Education:* Miami University (B.A., 1996); Harvard University (J.D., 2000). ***PRACTICE AREAS:*** Public Corporations; Takeovers; Tender Offers.

MICHAEL J. FARIS, admitted to bar, 1990, Illinois. *Education:* Harvard University (A.B., 1986); University of Chicago (J.D., 1989). ***PRACTICE AREAS:*** Civil Litigation; Complex Litigation.

FRED C. FISHER, admitted to bar, 2002, Illinois. *Education:* Miami University (B.S., 1998); Northwestern University (J.D., 2002). ***PRACTICE AREAS:*** Commercial Finance; Cross Border Finance; Asset Based Finance.

TIMOTHY P. FITZSIMONS, admitted to bar, 2002, Illinois. *Education:* University of Notre Dame (B.A.,1999); Northwestern University School of Law (J.D., 2002).

ARTHUR F. FOERSTER, admitted to bar, 2000, Illinois. *Education:* Bradley University (B.S., 1996); University of California at Lost Angeles (J.D., 1999). ***PRACTICE AREAS:*** Environmental Law; Litigation.

ANDRÉ M. GEVEROLA, admitted to bar, 2003, Illinois. *Education:* University of California, San Diego (B.S., 2000); University of Chicago (J.D., 2003).

TASNEEM K. GOODMAN, admitted to bar, 2002, Illinois. *Education:* University of Chicago (A.B., 1997; J.D., 2002). ***LANGUAGES:*** Gujrati, French, Arabic and Hindi. ***PRACTICE AREAS:*** Corporate Law.

NICHOLAS B. GORGA, admitted to bar, 2002, Illinois. *Education:* Princeton University (A.B., 1999); University of Michigan (J.D., 2002). ***PRACTICE AREAS:*** Litigation.

SCOTT W. HAIRSTON, admitted to bar, 2002, Illinois. *Education:* Duke University (B.A., 1998); University of Michigan (J.D., 2001).

JULIE S. B. HAMMOND, admitted to bar, 1999, Illinois. *Education:* Brigham Young University (B.A., 1995; J.D., 1999). ***LANGUAGES:*** Portuguese and Spanish. ***PRACTICE AREAS:*** Corporate Law; Mergers and Acquisitions.

MICHAEL F. HARTE, admitted to bar, 2000, Illinois. *Education:* University of Notre Dame (B.S., 1995; J.D., 2000); New York Medical College (M.S., 1998). ***PRACTICE AREAS:*** Litigation; Civil Litigation; Intellectual Property Litigation; Patent Litigation.

ADAM HERZOG, admitted to bar, 2004, Illinois. *Education:* Wharton School of Business (B.S., 2000); University of Chicago (J.D., 2004).

AMANDA J. HOLLIS, admitted to bar, 2003, Illinois. *Education:* University of Illinois (B.S., 2000); University of North Carolina (J.D., 2003). ***PRACTICE AREAS:*** Patent Litigation; Pharmaceutical Patents; Biotechnology Patents; Intellectual Property Licensing; Federal Civil Litigation.

MAAIKE S. HUDSON, admitted to bar, 1999, Illinois. *Education:* University of Wisconsin (B.A., 1996); University of Michigan (J.D., 1999). ***PRACTICE AREAS:*** Commercial Litigation; White Collar Criminal Defense.

NICHOLAS O. ISAACSON, admitted to bar, 1998, Illinois. *Education:* Harvard University (A.B., 1994); Columbia University Law School (J.D., 1998); University of Chicago (M.B.A., 2004). ***PRACTICE AREAS:*** Corporate Finance; Mergers and Acquisitions; Corporate Reorganization.

JENNIFER R. JAFFE, admitted to bar, 2002, Illinois. *Education:* Washington University (B.A., 1999); Northwestern University (J.D., 2002).

(This Listing Continued)

ILDIKO JONA, admitted to bar, 1998, Hungary; 2000, New York; 2003, Illinois. *Education:* Jozsef Attila University (J.D., 1995; M.B.A., 1999); Northwestern University (LL.M., 1997); Loyola University, Chicago (J.D., 2003). ***LANGUAGES:*** Hungarian. ***PRACTICE AREAS:*** Commercial Loans; Loan Restructuring.

ZACHARY A. JUDD, admitted to bar, 2002, Illinois. *Education:* Wabash College (B.A., 1999); University of Illinois (J.D., 2002).

AMY J. KAPPELER, admitted to bar, 1998, Illinois. *Education:* Northwestern University (B.A., 1995; J.D., 1998). ***PRACTICE AREAS:*** Litigation; Environmental Law.

KARL A. KARG, IV, admitted to bar, 1994, Illinois. *Education:* Arizona State University (B.S., 1989); Vermont Law School (J.D., 1994). ***PRACTICE AREAS:*** Environmental Law.

DANIELLE SUSAN KEMP, admitted to bar, 2000, Illinois; 2001, Florida. *Education:* University of Florida (B.A.E., 1994; M.Ed., 1995); University of Chicago (J.D., 2000). ***PRACTICE AREAS:*** Bankruptcy; Insolvency; Workouts.

MISHEL KETA, admitted to bar, 1998, Illinois. *Education:* Benedictine University (B.S., 1987); DePaul University (M.A., 1989); Northwestern University (J.D., 1998). ***PRACTICE AREAS:*** Finance.

LIVIA M. KISER, admitted to bar, 2001, Illinois. *Education:* University of Illinois (B.A., 1986); Northwestern University (J.D., 2001). ***PRACTICE AREAS:*** Litigation; Professional Liability; Regulatory Law; Commercial Law; Securities; Torts.

PETER P. KNIGHT, admitted to bar, 1999, Illinois. *Education:* Kalamazoo College (B.A., 1995); New York University (J.D., 1999). ***PRACTICE AREAS:*** Creditors Rights; Bankruptcy; Insolvency.

ELIZABETH OPPER KRAEMER, admitted to bar, 1998, Illinois. *Education:* Northwestern University (B.S.J., 1992); Ohio State University (MLHR, 1993); University of California School of Law, Los Angeles (J.D., 1998). ***PRACTICE AREAS:*** Commercial Litigation; Employment Litigation.

ERIK A. LOPEZ, SR., admitted to bar, 2000, New York; 2005, Illinois. *Education:* University of Chicago (B.A., 1995); New York University (J.D., 1999). ***PRACTICE AREAS:*** Mergers and Acquisitions; International Mergers and Acquisitions; Takeovers; Tender Offers; Corporate Governance; Securities.

JOHN J. MARHOEFER, admitted to bar, 2003, Illinois. *Education:* Ball State University (B.S., 1980); Chicago-Kent College of Law (J.D., 2003).

JULIE M. MARION, admitted to bar, 2001, Illinois. *Education:* University of Illinois (B.S., 1995); University of North Carolina (J.D., 2001). ***PRACTICE AREAS:*** Federal Income Tax; Tax Controversies.

KEVIN C. MAY, admitted to bar, 1996, Illinois. *Education:* University of Iowa (B.A., 1993); University of Pennsylvania (J.D., 1996).

SASHA MAYERGOYZ, admitted to bar, 2000, Illinois. *Education:* Cornell University (B.S.E.E., 1996); Northwestern University (J.D., 1999). ***LANGUAGES:*** Russian. ***PRACTICE AREAS:*** Litigation.

DAVID McKONE, admitted to bar, 2002, Virginia; 2003, District of Columbia; 2005, Illinois. *Education:* Michigan State University (B.S., 1997); University of Michigan (J.D., 2002). ***PRACTICE AREAS:*** Intellectual Property Litigation.

MATTHEW B. MOCK, admitted to bar, 2000, Illinois. *Education:* State University of New York at Binghamton (B.A., 1994); University of Michigan (J.D., 2000). ***PRACTICE AREAS:*** Antitrust; Class Action Defense; Complex Litigation; White Collar Crime.

PETER MOORE, admitted to bar, 2003, Illinois. *Education:* Northwestern University (B.S., 2000; J.D., 2003). ***PRACTICE AREAS:*** Civil Litigation; Computer and Software Patents; Criminal Appeals; Software Copyright.

JOANN P. MURPHY, admitted to bar, 2003, Illinois. *Education:* Indiana University (B.S., 1998); Northwestern University School of Law (J.D., 2003). ***PRACTICE AREAS:*** Corporate Law.

JOEL STEVEN NECKERS, admitted to bar, 2004, Illinois. *Education:* Hope College (B.A., 2001); University of Michigan (J.D., 2004).

ALLISON O'NEILL, admitted to bar, 2004, Illinois. *Education:* Hobart and William Smith Colleges (B.A., 2001); Cornell University Law School (J.D., 2004).

PAIGE S. ORMOND, admitted to bar, 2002, Illinois. *Education:* Syracuse University (B.F.A., 1997); Suffolk University School of Law (J.D., 2002).

LOPA PATEL, admitted to bar, 2004, Illinois. *Education:* Duke University (B.A., 2000); Northwestern University (J.D., 2004).

MARK PAUL RAMSEY, admitted to bar, 1998, Illinois; 2003, District of Columbia. *Education:* Indiana University (B.A., 1993; J.D., 1998); Georgetown University (M.S., 1995). ***LANGUAGES:*** Spanish, Catalan and Italian. ***PRACTICE AREAS:*** Asset Based Finance; Commercial Finance; Cross Border Finance; International Finance; Structured Finance; Secured Finance.

CAROLINE A. RECKLER, admitted to bar, 2001, Illinois. *Education:* Duke University (B.A., 1997); University of Michigan (J.D., 2001). ***PRACTICE AREAS:*** Bankruptcy; Debtor and Creditor; Finance.

ANDREW R. ROBERSON, admitted to bar, 2000, California; 2002, District of Columbia; 2004, Illinois. *Education:* University of Washington (B.A., 1996); Pepperdine University School of Law (J.D., 1999); New York University (LL.M., 2000). ***PRACTICE AREAS:*** Federal Tax Controversies; Tax Litigation; Federal Income Tax.

LESLIE N. ROSEN, admitted to bar, 2002, Illinois. *Education:* Cornell University (B.A., 1999); University of Chicago (J.D., 2002).

SCOTT SCHOETTES, admitted to bar, 2004, Illinois. *Education:* University of Southern California (B.F.A., 1989); Georgetown University (J.D., 2002).

ERIN S. SHAW, admitted to bar, 1998, Illinois. *Education:* University of Notre Dame (B.A., 1995); University of Michigan (J.D., 1998). ***PRACTICE AREAS:*** Litigation; SEC Enforcement; Securities Litigation.

(This Listing Continued)

VERONICA A. SILVA-MININ, admitted to bar, 2003, Illinois. *Education:* Universidad Nacional de Tucumañ (Abogado, 1999); University of Pennsylvania (LL.M., 2001; J.D., 2003). ***LANGUAGES:*** Spanish and Portuguese. ***PRACTICE AREAS:*** Employee Benefits.

KEITH A. SIMON, admitted to bar, 1999, Illinois. *Education:* University of Illinois (B.S., 1996); Northwestern University (J.D., 1999). ***PRACTICE AREAS:*** Insolvency; Bankruptcy Reorganization.

ADAM R. SKILKEN, admitted to bar, 2001, Illinois. *Education:* Dartmouth College (B.A., 1995); Northwestern University (M.B.A., 2000; J.D., 2001). ***LANGUAGES:*** Spanish. ***PRACTICE AREAS:*** Corporate Law.

AMANDA J. SMITH, admitted to bar, 2003, Illinois. *Education:* University of Illinois (B.S., 2000); University of North Carolina School of Law (J.D., 2003).

CINDY SOBEL, admitted to bar, 2004, Illinois. *Education:* Washington University (B.A., 1999); Northwestern University (J.D., 2004).

DEBORAH L. STEINER, admitted to bar, 1998, Illinois. *Education:* Manchester College (B.A., 1993); Cornell University (J.D., 1998). ***PRACTICE AREAS:*** Litigation.

DANIEL B. STOLARSKY, admitted to bar, 2000, Illinois. *Education:* University of California at Los Angeles (B.A., 1996); University of Michigan (J.D., 2000). ***PRACTICE AREAS:*** Corporate Law; Finance.

R. BRIAN TANNER, admitted to bar, 2003, Illinois. *Education:* Georgia Institute of Technology (B.S., 1998); Emory University School of Law (J.D., 2001). ***PRACTICE AREAS:*** Commercial Litigation.

STEPHEN R. TETRO, II, admitted to bar, 1995, Illinois. *Education:* Cornell University (B.S., 1992); University of Chicago (J.D., 1995). ***PRACTICE AREAS:*** Bankruptcy; Insolvency.

KAITLIN REIDY VERBER, admitted to bar, 2004, Illinois. *Education:* Dartmouth College (B.A., 1999); Northwestern University (J.D., 2004).

PETER N. WITTY, admitted to bar, 1997, Illinois. *Education:* University of Notre Dame (B.S., 1989; J.D., 1997). ***PRACTICE AREAS:*** Litigation; Patent Litigation.

FAN ZHANG, admitted to bar, 2004, Illinois. *Education:* China University of Political Science and Law (LL.B., 2001); University of Chicago (LL.M., 2002); Columbia University (J.D., 2004). ***LANGUAGES:*** Mandarin Chinese.

LATIMER LEVAY JURASEK LLC

55 WEST MONROE STREET, SUITE 1100
CHICAGO, ILLINOIS 60603
Telephone: 312-422-8000
Fax: 312-422-8001
Email: info@lljlaw.com
URL: http://www.lljlaw.com

Corporate Law, Mergers and Acquisitions, Commercial Finance, Securities, Real Estate, Estate Planning, Commercial Litigation, Business Law, Tax.

CARY R. LATIMER, born Chicago, Illinois; admitted to bar, 1997, Illinois and U.S. District Court, Northern District of Illinois. *Education:* University of Michigan (B.A., 1994); Loyola University (J.D., 1997). *Member:* Chicago Bar Association. ***PRACTICE AREAS:*** Corporate Law; Mergers and Acquisitions; Commercial Finance; Securities; Real Estate; Estate Planning. ***Email:*** clatimer@lljlaw.com

BRIAN D. LEVAY, born New York, N.Y.; admitted to bar, 1988, Illinois and U.S. District Court, Northern District of Illinois. *Education:* Tufts University (B.A., 1985); Washington University School of Law (J.D., 1988). Associate Editor, Washington University Journal of Urban and Contemporary Law. ***PRACTICE AREAS:*** Real Estate; Commercial Litigation; Business Law. ***Email:*** blevay@lljlaw.com

MICHAEL C. JURASEK, born Aurora, Illinois, 1973; admitted to bar, 1998, Illinois and U.S. District Court, Northern District of Illinois. *Education:* Michigan State University (B.A., 1995); Loyola University of Chicago (J.D., 1998); DePaul University College of Law (LL.M., Taxation, 2003). Certified Public Account, Illinois. ***PRACTICE AREAS:*** Business Law; Mergers and Acquisitions; Taxation; Estate Planning. ***Email:*** mjurasek@iljlaw.com

SHERYL A. FYOCK, born Kansas City, Missouri, August 26, 1964; admitted to bar, 1990, Illinois and U.S. District Court, Northern District of Illinois; 1992, U.S. Court of Appeals, Seventh Circuit. *Education:* Drake University (B.A., 1985); University of Kansas (J.D. and M.A., 1990). ***PRACTICE AREAS:*** Commercial Litigation; Lenders Rights; Bankruptcy.

DONALD B. LEVINE, born Chicago, Illinois, June 11, 1945; admitted to bar, 1969, Illinois and U.S. District Court, Northern District of Illinois, including Trial Bar; 1972, U.S. Court of Appeals, Seventh Circuit. *Education:* University of Wisconsin (B.A., 1966); DePaul University College of Law (J.D., 1969). Mediation Certification, Northwestern University, 2004. *Member:* Chicago and American Bar Associations; Association for Conflict Resolution. ***PRACTICE AREAS:*** Business Litigation; Employment Law; Business Transactions; Real Estate. ***Email:*** dlevine@lljlaw.com

---

VANESSA E. SEILER, born Kenosha, Wisconsin, January 16, 1974; admitted to bar, 1999, Illinois. *Education:* Drake University (B.A., 1995); Chicago-Kent College of Law, Illinois Institute of Technology (J.D., 1999). *Member:* Illinois State Bar Association; Women's Bar Association. ***LANGUAGES:*** French. ***PRACTICE AREAS:*** Civil Litigation; Commercial Litigation; Real Estate Litigation.

LAVIN & WALDON, P.C.

444 NORTH MICHIGAN AVENUE
SUITE 2600
CHICAGO, ILLINOIS 60611
Telephone: 312-670-4260
Fax: 312-670-4275

Corporate, Finance, Real Estate Transactions, and Commercial Litigation.

FIRM PROFILE: Since its establishment as a business law firm in 1993, Lavin & Waldon, P.C. has consistently provided sophisticated and efficient legal representation of corporate and individual interests, with an emphasis on personalized attention and timely results. The attorneys in the firm have broad-based experience in a wide variety of commercial and financial transactions and settings, as well as extensive accomplishments in resolving commercial litigation disputes through negotiations, at trial, and in appellate courts, arbitration, mediation and administrative hearings. In order to meet client needs, the firm, on an ongoing basis, coordinates a network of other firms in specialized areas including zoning, real estate tax law and intellectual property. Our clients are engaged in a wide array of businesses, industries and professions. Clients range in size and complexity from large corporations engaged in national and international trade, to small businesses, individual proprietors and professionals. Commercial clients include both publicly-held and privately-owned businesses.

Lavin & Waldon, P.C. brings to its clients' problems and opportunities an entrepreneurial spirit, an aggressive attitude designed to achieve practical solutions, and an unrelenting commitment to excellence, integrity and professionalism.

STEVEN H. LAVIN, born Chicago, Illinois, July 27, 1955; admitted to bar, 1980, Illinois. *Education:* University of Illinois (B.A., in Accounting, 1977); Loyola University School of Law (J.D., 1980). *Member:* Chicago, Illinois State and American Bar Associations. ***PRACTICE AREAS:*** Corporate Law; Real Estate; Tax Law; International Transactions; Finance. ***Email:*** shlavin@lwblaw.com

DENNIS C. WALDON, born Berwyn, Illinois, December 23, 1946; admitted to bar, 1973, Illinois. *Education:* University of Chicago (B.A., 1969); Harvard University (J.D., 1973). Recipient, 2003 Award for Excellence in Pro Bono Service from the United States District Court for the Northern District of Illinois and Chicago Chapter of the Federal Bar Association. *Member:* Chicago, Illinois State and American Bar Associations; The Lawyers Club of Chicago; The Executives' Club of Chicago. ***REPORTED CASES:*** Occidental Fire and Casualty Co. v. Continental Illinois National Bank, 918 F.2d 1312 (1990); Wilk v. AMA, 719 F.2d 207 (1983); Havoco of America, Ltd. v. Hollobow, 702 F.2d 643 (1983); Fulton-Carroll Center, Inc. v. ICNC, 628 N.E.2d 1121 (1993); Devick v. Platinum Technology, Inc., 735 N.E.2d 153 (2000); Scott v. York Woods Community Association, 768 N.E.2d 847 (2002); Midwest Canvas Corp. v. Cantar/Polyair Corp., 2003 WL 22053582 (N.D. Ill). ***PRACTICE AREAS:*** General Civil Trial; Appellate Practice; Commercial Litigation; Securities Litigation; Intellectual Property Litigation. ***Email:*** dwaldon@lwblaw.com

JEROLD R. LAVIN, born Chicago, Illinois, March 10, 1960; admitted to bar, 1986, Illinois. *Education:* University of Illinois (B.A., 1982); Harvard University (J.D., 1985). Former Visiting Associate Professor and Managing Director, Graduate Program in Financial Services Law, Chicago-Kent College of Law. ***LANGUAGES:*** Russian and Spanish. ***PRACTICE AREAS:*** Commercial Litigation; International Transactions. ***Email:*** jlavin@lwblaw.com

JENNIFER J. GEDVILLE, born Danville, Illinois, May 12, 1971; admitted to bar, 1999, Illinois. *Education:* Millikin University (B.A., 1991); DePaul University (J.D., 1999). *Member:* Chicago, Illinois State and American Bar Associations. ***PRACTICE AREAS:*** Corporate Law; Commercial Litigation. ***Email:*** jgedville@lwblaw.com

LAWRENCE, KAMIN, SAUNDERS & UHLENHOP, L.L.C.

Established in 1932

208 SOUTH LA SALLE STREET, SUITE 1750
CHICAGO, ILLINOIS 60604-1188
Telephone: 312-372-1947
Telecopier: 312-372-2389
Email: LKSU@LKSU.com

General Civil Practice. Securities, Commodities, Futures and Securities Regulation. Corporate, Business and Closely Held Businesses. Acquisitions, Divestitures and Mergers, Products Liability, Construction, Commercial and General Litigation, Arbitration and Mediation. Federal Taxation, Estate Planning, Probate, Trust, Real Estate and Employment Law.

FIRM PROFILE: For over 70 years, our law firm, now known as Lawrence, Kamin, Saunders & Uhlenhop, L.L.C., has been dedicated to serving the legal needs of business clients. We know and understand our clients' business demands and as a result our firm has grown on its own strengths and merits. Our client base is one that is reflected throughout the country, although our practice is primarily concentrated in the Chicago area. Furthermore, our commitment to time and cost effective case management is demonstrated by our active involvement in the areas of arbitration, mediation and case management.

MEMBERS OF FIRM

RAYMOND E. SAUNDERS, born Chicago, Illinois, July 3, 1932; admitted to bar, 1956, Illinois. *Education:* University of Illinois; Northwestern University (B.S., cum laude, 1953; J.D., 1956). Order of the Coif; Beta Gamma Sigma; Phi Alpha Delta. Member, Editorial Board, Northwestern University Law Review, 1955-1956. Illinois Silver Medal and Elijah Watt Sells Award, 1954. Certified Public Accountant, Illinois, 1955. *Member:* Chicago Bar Association. ***PRACTICE AREAS:*** Acquisitions, Divestitures and Mergers; Federal Income Taxation; Estate and Gift Taxation. ***Email:*** rsaunders@lksu.com

(This Listing Continued)

PAUL B. UHLENHOP, born Litchfield, Illinois, October 22, 1936; admitted to bar, 1961, Illinois; 1962, New York. *Education:* University of Illinois (B.A., with honors, 1958; J.D., 1961). Phi Delta Phi. Public Member, Business Conduct Committee, Chicago Mercantile Exchange, 1992—. Author: "Personal Trading Policies and Procedures Including Insider Trading Rules," NSCP 2003 National Membership Meeting, October 29-31, 2003; "Key Points for Introducing Broker-Dealers to Understand in Connection with Clearing Arrangements," NRS Fall Compliance Conference, September 7-10, 2003; "Research Analyst Conflicts," NSCP Midwest Regional Meeting, June 2, 2003; "Security Futures Two Years After the CFMA: An Assessment," Futures & Derivatives Law Report, Vol. 23, No. 2, April 2003; "SEC Proposed Rule 13b2-2: Improper Influence on Conduct of Audits," ABA Section of Business Law Regulation of Futures and Derivatives Instruments Committee Meeting, February 6-8, 2003; "Conflicts Regarding Research Recommendations," NRS Fall Compliance Conference, September 9-12, 2002; "The Sarbanes-Oxley Act of 2002 Impact on Broker-Dealers," NSCP Currents, September/October 2002; "A Pool Too Big for a FCM or a Broker-Dealer," Futures & Derivatives Law Report, Vol. 22, No.5, July/August 2002; "Security Futures-A New Frontier," The Review of Securities and Commodities Regulation, Vol. 35, No.10, May 29, 2002; "Capital, Customer Funds and Margin After the Commodity Futures Modernization Act of 2000," Futures & Derivatives Law Report, Vol. 21, No.7, October 2001; Securities Law, Chapter 6-Regulation of Broker-Dealers, Co-Author, IICLE, 2001; "Who is a Proprietary Trader? A Changing and Rocky Landscape," Futures & Derivatives Law Report, Vol. 20, No. 8, November 2000; "Securities Sites and Online Trading Become Regulatory Priorities," Journal of Taxation of Investments, Autumn, 2000; "When Broker-Dealer Activities Require Investment Advisor Registration: SEC Grants Interim Relief and Proposes Changes," NSCP Currents, 2000; "When is an FCM, CTA or Pool a Securities Broker-Dealer, an Investment Advisor or an Investment Company Under the Securities Laws," Futures and Derivatives Law Report, 1999. "What Every Compliance Professional Should Know About Derivatives," National Society of Compliance Professionals Annual Meeting, October 24, 1996; "FCM's: Guarantors of Customers' Funds?," 16 Futures & Derivatives Law Report 10, p. 1 (Dec. 1996); "Swaps are Nothing But Contracts...Right Now," Securities News, Fall, 1996; Member, Board of Visitors, College of Law, University of Illinois, 1981-1987; President, 1984-1986. Adjunct Professor, University of Illinois College of Law, 1993—. Adjunct Professor, IIT/Chicago-Kent College of Law, 1986—. Attorney, Securities and Exchange Commission, 1962-1963. Member, Board of Editors, Futures & Derivatives Law Report. Planning Committee Member, Ray Garrett, Jr. Corporate & Securities Institute, 1983—. Director, National Society of Compliance Professionals, 2002—. *Member:* Chicago (Member, 1966—, Committee on Securities Law; Chairman, 1977-1978, Chairman, Broker Dealer Sub-Committee, 1974-1976, 1983-1996; Member, Committee on Antitrust, 1968—; Chairman, Committee on Futures and Derivatives, 1998-1999), Illinois State and American (Member, Sections on: Antitrust Law; Business Law; Litigation; Member, Broker Dealer Sub-Committee; Chairman, Sub-Committee on Futures Litigation, 1986—) Bar Associations. ***LANGUAGES:*** French. ***PRACTICE AREAS:*** Securities and Commodities; Securities Regulation; Securities Litigation; International Law. ***Email:*** puhlenhop@lksu.com

KENT LAWRENCE, born Chicago, Illinois, September 15, 1944; admitted to bar, 1969, Illinois. *Education:* Brandeis University (B.A., 1966); Northwestern University (J.D., cum laude, 1969). Order of the Coif. Member, Editorial Board, Northwestern University Law Review, 1968-1969. Adjunct Professor, Northwestern University School of Law, 1982-1993. Member, Illinois Supreme Court Alternative Dispute Resolution Coordinating Committee, 1992-1993; Advisor, Judicial Conference of Illinois ADR Coordinating Committee, 1994—; Member Board of Visitors, College of Law, Northern Illinois University, 1992—. Member, Panel of Arbitrators, 1974—, American Arbitration Association. Member, Board of Arbitrators, 1977—, National Association of Securities Dealers. *Member:* Chicago Bar Association (Member, Committees on: Securities Law, 1971—; Arbitration and Alternative Dispute Resolutions, 1977— and Vice Chairman, 1985-1987 and 1997-1998; Chair, 1987-1988 and 1998-1999). ***PRACTICE AREAS:*** Arbitration; Mediation; Securities Litigation. ***Email:*** klawrence@lksu.com

ROBERT L. SCHLOSSBERG, born 1940; admitted to bar, 1964, Illinois. *Education:* DePaul University (B.S., 1961); Northwestern University (J.D., cum laude, 1964). Order of the Coif; Beta Gamma Sigma. Member, Board of Editors, Northwestern University Law Review, 1963-1964. Illinois Silver Medal and Elijah Watt Sells Award, 1961. Certified Public Accountant, Illinois, 1961. ***PRACTICE AREAS:*** Mergers and Acquisitions; Corporate Law. ***Email:*** rschlossberg@lksu.com

CHARLES J. RISCH, born Milwaukee, Wisconsin, May 9, 1949; admitted to bar, 1982, Wisconsin, Illinois, U.S. District Court, Northern District of Illinois including Trial Bar and U.S. District Court, Eastern District of Wisconsin; 1990, U.S. Court of Appeals, Seventh Circuit;1993, U.S. Supreme Court. *Education:* University of Wisconsin (B.A., 1979; J.D., cum laude, 1982). Order of the Coif. American Jurisprudence Award (Business Torts). *Member:* Chicago and American Bar Associations; State Bar of Wisconsin; Defense Research Institute. ***PRACTICE AREAS:*** Products Liability; Securities Litigation; Commercial Litigation; Arbitration; Mediation. ***Email:*** crisch@lksu.com

MICHAEL WISE, born Omaha, Nebraska, September 3, 1954; admitted to bar, 1979, Illinois and U.S. District Court, Northern District of Illinois including Trial Bar. *Education:* Columbia University (B.A., 1976); Washington University (J.D., 1979). Order of the Coif. Co-Author "Managing Regulatory Investigations and Examinations for Cause," Securities & Commodities Regulation, 2001. Author: "Self Regulatory Organizations and Tender Offers," chapter in *Mergers and Acquisitions Handbook,* McGraw-Hill, 1986. Adjunct Professor, University of Illinois, College of Law; IIT/Chicago-Kent College of Law. *Member:* Chicago Bar Association. ***PRACTICE AREAS:*** Securities Regulation; Securities Litigation; Commodities Regulation; Corporate. ***Email:*** mwise@lksu.com

PETER E. COOPER, born Washington, D.C., March 28, 1959; admitted to bar, 1985, New York; 1986, U.S. District Court, Southern and Eastern Districts of New York; 1994, Illinois and U.S. District Court, Northern District of Illinois; 1995, U.S. Court of Appeals, Seventh Circuit. *Education:* Cornell University (B.A., 1980); Georgetown University; New York University (J.D., 1984). *Member:* Chicago (Chairman, Securities Litigation and Enforcement Subcommittee, Securities Law committee) and American (Member, Securities Arbitration Subcommittee, Litigation Section) Bar Associations. ***PRACTICE AREAS:*** Securities and Commodities Litigation; Commercial Litigation; Arbitration. ***Email:*** pcooper@lksu.com

(This Listing Continued)

DAVID L. REICH, born Chicago, Illinois, January 11, 1963; admitted to bar, 1991, Illinois. *Education:* Indiana University (B.S., finance, 1985); Northwestern University (J.D., 1991). ***PRACTICE AREAS:*** Corporate Law; Business Law; Real Estate; Corporate Finance; Estate Planning. ***Email:*** dreich@lksu.com

JOHN S. MONICAL, born Pontiac, Illinois, January 25, 1968; admitted to bar, 1994, Illinois and U.S. District Court, Northern District of Illinois; 2002, U.S. District Court, Eastern District of Wisconsin. *Education:* University of Illinois (B.S., 1991); Northern Illinois Law School (J.D., 1994). Member, 1992-1994 and Editorial Board, 1993-1994, Northern Illinois University Law Review. Author and Presenter: "Document Retention Requirements of the CPSC/NHTA and their Discovery Protections," Defense Research Institute Product Liability Conference, Juvenile Products Breakout Session (2003); "The Post-Sale Duty to Warn and Recall: Are they Preempted When NHTSA or the CPSC Oversees the Manufacturer's Conduct?" Defense Research Institute Product Liability Conference, Juvenile Products Breakout Session (February 2001); "State Child Product Safety Acts-The Good News and the Bad," Defense Research Institute Product Liability Conference, Juvenile Products Breakout Session (February 2000). Co-Author, "Computer Litigation Support Systems," Chapter 6, Business Litigation Handbook, Illinois Institute for Continuing Legal Education (1996). *Member:* Chicago and Illinois State Bar Associations; Defense Research Institute. ***PRACTICE AREAS:*** Commercial Litigation; Products Liability; Securities. ***Email:*** jmonical@lksu.com

JOHN D. RUARK, born Chicago, Illinois, August 10, 1964; admitted to bar, 1992, Illinois. *Education:* Yale University (B.A., 1986); John Marshall Law School (J.D., cum laude, 1992); Chicago-Kent College of Law (LL.M., with high honors, Financial Services Law, 2000). *Member:* Chicago Bar Association. ***PRACTICE AREAS:*** Commodities; Securities. ***Email:*** jruark@lksu.com

ASSOCIATES

PAUL M. WELTLICH, born Chicago, Illinois, October 6, 1964; admitted to bar, 1995, Illinois; U.S. District Court, Northern District of Illinois; 1996, U.S. Court of Appeals, Seventh Circuit. *Education:* University of Illinois (B.A., 1986); The John Marshall Law School (J.D., 1995). Phi Delta Phi. Staff Editor, Software Law Journal, 1993. Business Managing Editor, The John Marshall Journal of Computer and Information Law, 1994. Editor/Publisher of the Chicago Bar Associations Young Lawyers Section Labor and Employment Law Committee Newsletter, monthly, 1996-1999. *Member:* Chicago (Member: Core Committee; Young Lawyers Section of the Labor and Employment Law Committee, 1995— and Co-Chair, 1997-1998 and 1998-1999), American and Illinois State Bar Associations. ***PRACTICE AREAS:*** Employment Discrimination; Products Liability; General Litigation. ***Email:*** pweltlich@lksu.com

MITCHELL B. GOLDBERG, born Chicago, Illinois, April 20, 1974; admitted to bar, 1999, Illinois. *Education:* DePaul University (B.A., with highest honors, 1996; J.D., with honors, 1999). Golden Key. Member, Order of the Coif. *Member:* Chicago, Illinois State and American Bar Associations. ***PRACTICE AREAS:*** Securities; Commodities Futures; General Practice; Products Liability. ***Email:*** mgoldberg@lksu.com

RHONDA V. TURNER, admitted to bar, 2004, Illinois. *Education:* Alabama State University (B.A., summa cum laude, 2000); Harvard Law School (J.D., 2003). ***Email:*** rturner@lksu.com

MEMBERS

A. CHARLES LAWRENCE (1907-1990)
JAMES J. LAWRENCE (1910-1992)
MAX FREDERICK GOLDBERG (1899-1996)
HOWARD P. KAMIN (1929-1997)

OF COUNSEL

ROBERT J. LAWRENCE, born Chicago, Illinois, February 15, 1944; admitted to bar, 1969, Illinois. *Education:* University of Michigan (B.S.E., 1965); Northwestern University (J.D., 1969). *Member:* Chicago and American Bar Associations. ***PRACTICE AREAS:*** Estate Planning; Real Estate; Pension and Profit Sharing; Corporate; Business. ***Email:*** rlawrence@lksu.com

REPRESENTATIVE CLIENTS: Alberto-Culver Co.; Altschuler, Melvoin & Glasser LLP; Beacon Investment Company; Cadillac Machinery Company, Inc.; Capital Securities Investment Corporation; Carr Futures Inc.; Delta Industries, Ltd.; Evenflo Company, Inc.; Feldman, Ingardona & Co.; Fimat USA Inc.; Gelber Group, LLC; Gofen & Glossberg, L.L.C.; Goldenberg, Hehmeyer & Co.; Howe Barnes Investments, Inc.; Kempler Industries, Inc.; Kolcraft Enterprises, Inc.; Landquist & Son, Inc.; Lemley, Yarling & Co.; Lyons Electric Company; Melvin Securities LLC; Merrill Lynch, Pierce, Fenner & Smith Incorporated; M.R. Bauer Foundation; Shatkin, Arbor, Karlov & Co.; Silicon Valley Bank; Steiner Electric Company; Trans Market Group, L.L.C.; Westwood Management Corporation; Zurich Kemper Group entities.

LEBOEUF, LAMB, GREENE & MACRAE L.L.P.

A Limited Liability Partnership including Professional Corporations

Established in 2005

TWO PRUDENTIAL PLAZA
180 NORTH STETSON AVENUE, SUITE 1175
CHICAGO, ILLINOIS 60601
Telephone: 312-794-8000
Fax: 312-794-8100
URL: http://www.llgm.com

Eastern United States:
New York, N.Y. Office: 125 West 55th Street. Telephone: 212-424-8000. Facsimile: 212-424-8500. Telex: 423416 or 1561363.
Washington, D.C. Office: 1875 Connecticut Avenue, N.W. Telephone: 202-986-8000. Facsimile: 202-986-8102. Telex: 440274.
Albany, New York Office: One Commerce Plaza, 99 Washington Avenue, Suite 2020. Telephone: 518-626-9000. Facsimile: 518-626-9010.
Boston, Massachusetts Office: 260 Franklin Street. Telephone: 617-439-9500. Facsimile: 617-439-0341; 439-0342.
Harrisburg, Pennsylvania Office: 200 North Third Street, Suite 300, P.O. Box 12105. Telephone: 717-232-8199. Facsimile: 717-232-8720.
Hartford, Connecticut Office: Goodwin Square, 225 Asylum Street, 13th Floor. Telephone: 860-293-3500. Facsimile: 860-293-3555.
Pittsburgh, Pennsylvania Office: One Gateway Center, Fort Duquesne Boulevard, Suite 1600. Telephone: 412-594-2300. Facsimile: 412-594-5237.
Western United States:
Los Angeles, California Office: 725 South Figueroa Street, Suite 3100. Telephone: 213-955-7300. Facsimile: 213-955-7399. Telex: 678982.
San Francisco, California Office: One Embarcadero Center, Suite 400. Telephone: 415-951-1100. Facsimile: 415-951-1180; 951-1181. Telex: 470167.
Southern United States:
Houston, Texas Office: 1000 Main Street, Suite 2550. Telephone: 713-287-2000. Facsimile: 713-287-2100.
Jacksonville, Florida Office: 50 North Laura Street, Suite 2800. Telephone: 904-354-8000. Facsimile: 904-353-1673.
European Offices:
Brussels, Belgium Office: Rue de Luxemburgstr 14A, B-1000 Brussels, Belgium. Telephone: 011-32-2-227-0900. Facsimile: 011-32-2-227-0909.
London, England Office: LeBoeuf, Lamb, Greene & MacRae (A London Based Multinational Partnership); One Minster Court, Mincing Lane, 6th Floor, London EC3R 7AA England. Telephone: 011-44-20-7-459-5000. Facsimile: 011-44-20-7-459-5099.
Moscow, Russian Federation Office: Nikitsky Pereulok, 5 (formerly Ulitsa Belinskogo) 103473 Moscow, Russian Federation. Telephone: 011-7-095-737-5000. Facsimile: 011-7-095-737-5050.
Paris, France Office: 130 rue du Faubourg Saint-Honoré 75008 Paris, France. Telephone: 011-33-1-53-93-77-00. Facsimile: 011-33-1-42-56-08-06.
Asian Offices:
Almaty, Kazakhstan Office: Prospect Seyfullin, 531, 5th Floor, 480083, Almaty, Republic of Kazakhstan. Telephone: 011-7-3272-50-7575. Facsimile: 011-7-3272-50-7576.
Beijing, China Office: Room B8, 21st Floor, Hanwei Plaza, No. 7 Guanghau Road, Chaoyang District, Beijing 10004, China. Telephone: 011-8610-6561-0422. Facsimile: 011-8610-6561-0425.
Bishkek, Kyrgyz Office: Ulitsa Panfilova, 205 Bishkek, Kyrgyz Republic. Telephone: 011-996-3312-22-2994. Facsimile: 011-996-3312-66-2233.
Tashkent, Uzbekistan Office: Ulitsa Turab Tula, 1 700003 Tashkent, Republic of Uzbekistan. Telephone: 011-7-3712-40-6050. Facsimile: 011-7-3712-40-6052.
African Office:
Johannesburg, South Africa Office: 11 Alice Lane, 2nd Floor, West Wing, Standard Bank Building, Sandton 2196, Johannesburg, South Africa. Telephone: 27-011-784-0233. Fax: 27-11-784-2855.

General Practice including Banking, Bankruptcy, Copyrights, Corporate, Corporate Finance, Energy, Health Care, Insurance, Intellectual Property, Interactive Media, Internet and Telecommunications, International (Corporate, M&A, Energy), Life Insurance, Litigation, Mergers and Acquisitions, Municipal Bonds, Patents, Project Finance, Public Finance, Privatization, Real Estate, Taxation, Trademarks, Trusts and Estates, Utilities and Venture Capital.

PARTNERS

ELIZABETH M. BRADSHAW, born 1966; admitted to bar, 1994, Illinois. *Education:* College of the Holy Cross (B.A., cum laude, 1988); University of Chicago (J.D., 1994). Phi Beta Kappa. ***PRACTICE AREAS:*** Litigation; Intellectual Property; Antitrust. ***Email:*** ebradshaw@llgm.com

JAMES R. DWYER, admitted to bar, 1980, Illinois; 1981, California. *Education:* University of Notre Dame (B.A., with high honors, 1977); University of California at Los Angeles (J.D., 1980). Co-Author: "An Analysis of the Insurance Regulatory Aspects of Demutualization," *Demutualization and Other New Opportunities for Insurance Companies,* p. 126, New York: Law & Business, Inc./Harcourt Brace Jovanovich, 1984; *Analysis of Standard Mortgage Clause and Selected Provisions of the New York Standard Fire Policy,* XIX THE FORUM 639, No. 4, Summer 1984. *Member:* State Bar of California; American Bar Association (Member, Tort and Insurance Practice Section). ***PRACTICE AREAS:*** Insurance Mergers and Acquisitions. ***Email:*** jdwyer@llgm.com

MICHAEL H. KING, P.C., born 1943; admitted to bar, 1970, Illinois and U.S. District Court, Northern District of Illinois; 1972, U.S. District Court, Eastern District of Wisconsin; U.S. District Court, Northern District of California; 1974, U.S. Court of Appeals, Seventh Circuit; 1975, U.S. Supreme Court; 1979, U.S. Court of Appeals, Fifth Circuit; 1983, U.S. Court of Appeals, Third Circuit; 1987, U.S. Court of Appeals, Tenth Circuit; 1987, U.S. Tax Court; 1988, U.S. District Court, District of Nebraska; 1992, U.S. District Court, Central District of Illinois; 1994, U.S. Court of Appeals, Second Circuit; 1998, U.S. Court of Appeals, Federal Circuit. *Education:* University of Chicago and Washington University (B.S., 1967); Washington University (J.D., 1970). Who's Who in America, 1995—. Member, Washington University Urban Law Annual, 1969-1970. Co-Author: "Model Jury Instructions in Criminal Antitrust Cases," ABA Press, 1982; "Effective Dispute Resolution for the International Commercial Lawyer," 1989 KLUWER. Co-author: Handbook on Antitrust Grand Jury Investigations, 1988 ABA Press; "Fair is Fair: Implied Covenants in Commercial Leases."; with Peter N. Witty,"Know Thyself As You Know Thy Enemy: Setting Goals and Keeping Focus When Mediating IP Disputes," 37 Akron Law Review, 2004. Author: "Selecting an Appropriate Damage Expert in a Patent Case: An Examination of the Current Status of Daubert," The University of Akron School of Law Sixth Annual Richard C. Sughrue Symposium on Intellectual Property Law and Policy. Special Attorney, U.S. Department of Justice, Organized Crime and Racketeering Section, 1970-1973. Assistant U.S. Attorney, Northern District of Illinois, 1973-1975. Delegate, Antitrust Section, American Bar Association to United States Sentencing Commission, 1986. Chairman of the Board of Commissioners, State Appellate Defender Program, 1989-1996. Member, Board of Governors, Mid-America Club.

(This Listing Continued)

(This Listing Continued)

LEBOEUF, LAMB, GREENE & MACRAE L.L.P., Chicago—Continued

KEITH P. SCHOENEBERGER, born 1948; admitted to bar, 1974, Illinois; U.S. Supreme Court. *Education:* Georgetown University (B.A., cum laude, 1970); Northwestern University (J.D., 1974). ***PRACTICE AREAS:*** Litigation; Intellectual Property; Antitrust. ***Email:*** kschoene@llgm.com

NEAL L. WOLF, born 1949; admitted to bar, 1974, Arizona; 1983, Illinois; 1999, California. *Education:* Princeton University (B.A., magna cum laude, 1970); University of Chicago (J.D., 1974). Fellow, American College of Bankruptcy, 1997—. ***PRACTICE AREAS:*** Bankruptcy; Insolvency; Business Reorganizations; Business Litigation. ***Email:*** nwolf@llgm.com

COUNSEL

TIMOTHY A. BARNES, born 1967; admitted to bar, 1996, Ohio; 1999, Illinois. *Education:* Miami University (B.A., 1989); The Ohio State University (M.A., 1992; J.D. 1995). Phi Kappa Phi. ***LANGUAGES:*** Japanese, French and German. ***PRACTICE AREAS:*** Bankruptcy; Corporate Reorganization. ***Email:*** tabarnes@llgm.com

DARREN J. HUNTER, admitted to bar, 1988, Illinois. *Education:* University of Illinois (B.A., 1984); Chicago-Kent College of Law, Illinois Institute of Technology (J.D., with high honors, 1988). Order of the Coif. ***PRACTICE AREAS:*** Litigation; Energy; Environmental Law. ***Email:*** dhunter@llgm.com

SPENCER R. WOOD, born 1971; admitted to bar, 1996, Illinois. *Education:* University of Wisconsin (B.S., 1993); University of Oklahoma (J.D., 1996). ***PRACTICE AREAS:*** Litigation; Intellectual Property; Fiduciary Litigation; Patents. ***Email:*** swood@llgm.com

(Biographical data on Members of the Firm, Counsel, Of Counsel and Special Counsel in Washington, D.C., New York, New York, Albany, New York, Boston, Massachusetts, Harrisburg, Pennsylvania, Hartford, Connecticut, Salt Lake City, Utah, Los Angeles, California, San Francisco, California, Jacksonville, Florida, Houston, Texas, Pittsburgh, Pennsylvania, Chicago, Illinois, London, England, Brussels, Belgium, Almaty, Kazakhstan, Moscow, Russian Federation, Paris, France, Johannesburg, South Africa and Beijing, China are listed in the respective Biographical Sections)

LAW OFFICES OF DAVID L. LEE

Established in 1993

SUITE 660, 53 WEST JACKSON BOULEVARD
CHICAGO, ILLINOIS 60604
Telephone: 312-347-4400
Facsimile: 312-347-3272
Email: d-lee@davidleelaw.com
URL: http://www.davidleelaw.com

Civil Rights, Employment Law, Employment Discrimination, Employment Contracts, Employee Benefits, Retaliation, Unpaid Wages, Unpaid Overtime, Unpaid Commissions, Executive Employment Contracts and Executive Severance Negotiations.

DAVID L. LEE, born Chicago, Illinois, October 30, 1952; admitted to bar, 1977, Illinois and U.S. District Court, Northern District of Illinois; 1980, U.S. Court of Appeals, 7th Circuit; 1981, U.S. Supreme Court; 1982, U.S. District Court, Northern District of Illinois, Trial Bar; 1994, U.S. Court of Appeals, First Circuit; 1995, U.S. District Court, Central District of Illinois; 1998, U.S. District Court, Eastern District of Wisconsin; 2000, U.S. District Court, Southern District of Illinois. *Education:* Northwestern University (B.A., 1974; J.D., magna cum laude, 1977). Order of the Coif. Author: "Handling Wage, Hour and Unpaid-Wage Claims on the Employee Side," Chapter 1, 8th Annual Employment Law Update and Workshop course book, Illinois Institute of Continuing Legal Education (2005); "Creative Uses of Requests for Admissions for Plaintiffs Employment Lawyers," *The Employee Advocate,* Fall 2002; "Summary Judgment: The Intersection of Legal Writing and Trial Practice," April 1998 CBA Record 16; "Emphasis and De-emphasis," *The Compleat Legal Writer,* May 1997 CBA Record 68; "Requests for Admissions," *The Compleat Legal Writer,* April 1997 CBA Record 42; "Why Plaintiff's Lawyers Love the FLSA," Council on Education in Management HR Strategies, (1996); "A Few Words on Choosing Words Well," 7 Practical Litigator 71 (1996); "Kinder, Gentler Confirming Letters," *The Compleat Legal Writer,* January 1996 CBA Record 36; "Responding to Arguments," *The Compleat Legal Writer,* June/July 1995 CBA Record 58; "Best of Both Worlds: Computerized and Manual Legal Research," *The Compleat Legal Writer,* May 1995 CBA Record 50; "Red Flags," *The Compleat Legal Writer,* January 1995 CBA Record 46; "High-Tech Traps," *The Compleat Legal Writer,* November 1994 CBA Record 52; "Beating Writer's Block," *The Compleat Legal Writer,* October 1994 CBA Record 50; "The Proper Level of Ignorance," *The Compleat Legal Writer,* September 1994 CBA Record 50; "Analogizing Your Case to a Precedent," *The Compleat Legal Writer,* June 1994 CBA Record 42; "Writing the Statement of Facts," *The Compleat Legal Writer,* May 1994 CBA Record 42. Co-Author: "A View from the Other Side," Council on Education in Management Personnel Law Update (1999) (with Sarah R. Masarachia); "Kiss My Grits and Other Eloquent Retorts: Incivility in Legal Writing," April 1999 CBA Record 28 (with Sarah R. Masarachia); "The Top Eleven Mistakes Employers Make in Firing and/or Disciplining Employees," Council on Education in Management Discipline & Termination Law (1999) (with Sarah R. Masarachia); "How to Protect a Client from Misappropriation of Computer Software—A Frontier without a Direction," Chapter 12, in Patent, Trademark and Trade Secret, Illinois Institute of Continuing Legal Education (1980), (with Ellen C. Newcomer); "Judges in an Age of Mistrust: Morial and the Policy of Required Registration," 54 Tulane L. Rev. 382 (1980) (with Allan Ashman and Judith Rosenbaum); "Protecting the Record and Perfecting the Appeal," Chapter 11 in Federal Civil Practice, Illinois Institute of Continuing Education (1978) (with Richard J. Brennan and Duane M. Kelly); "A Constitutional Perspective on Judicial Tenure," 62 Judicature 465 (1978) (with Judith Rosenbaum); "Non-Lawyer Judges: The Long Road North," 53 Chicago-Kent Law Review 565 (1977) (with Allan Ashman). Hearing Officer, Cook County Commission on Human Rights. Arbitrator: Circuit Court of Cook County, Illinois; National Assn. of Securities Dealers; National Futures Assn. *Member:* Chicago and American (Member, Sections on: Labor and Employment Law; Law Practice Management; Litigation) Bar Associations; National Employment Lawyers Association (Member, Board of Directors, Illinois Chapter, 2000—; Vice President, Illinois Chapter, 2004—).

(This Listing Continued)

LEE, MANN, SMITH, McWILLIAMS, SWEENEY & OHLSON

CHICAGO, ILLINOIS

(See Barnes & Thornburg)

LEFF, COHEN & WINKLER, LTD.

Established in 1967

303 WEST MADISON STREET, SUITE 1700
CHICAGO, ILLINOIS 60606
Telephone: 312-782-2700
Fax: 312-782-9300
Email: lcwchicago.com
URL: http://www.lcwchicago.com

General Commercial, Federal and State Taxation, Property Tax and Assessment Law, Estate Planning, Probate and Real Estate Law.

SHERWIN H. LEFF, born 1941; admitted to bar, 1967, Illinois. *Education:* University of Wisconsin-Madison (B.S., accounting, 1962); John Marshall Law School (J.D., 1967). Certified Public Accountant. ***PRACTICE AREAS:*** Closely Held Business Law; Closely Held Business Taxation; Real Estate Tax Assessment; Estate Planning; Mergers and Acquisitions. ***Email:*** sleff@lcwchicago.com

AARON COHEN, born 1928; admitted to bar, 1956, Illinois. *Education:* University of Illinois (B.S., 1951; J.D., 1956). Certified Public Accountant. Adjunct Lecturer of Law: Kent College; John Marshall Law School; Roosevelt University; University of Illinois. ***PRACTICE AREAS:*** Commercial Law; Commercial Transactions; Business Law; Income Tax; Estate Taxation; Estate Planning. ***Email:*** acohen@lcwchicago.com

THOMAS W. WINKLER, born 1956; admitted to bar, 1982, Illinois. *Education:* University of Illinois (B.S., accounting, 1979; J.D., 1982). Certified Public Accountant. *Member:* Chicago and Illinois State Bar Associations. ***PRACTICE AREAS:*** Business Planning; Commercial Transactions; Real Estate; Trusts and Estates; Real Estate Tax Appeals. ***Email:*** twinkler@lcwchicago.com

RONALD G. GLOSNIAK, born Chicago, Illinois, 1950; admitted to bar, 1975, Illinois. *Education:* Loyola University (B.A., cum laude, 1972; J.D., 1975). ***PRACTICE AREAS:*** Real Estate Tax Assessment; Real Estate Tax Appeals. ***Email:*** rglosniak@lcwchicago.com

ROBERT S. McCARTY, born Naperville, Illinois, 1962; admitted to bar, 1989, Illinois. *Education:* University of Illinois (B.S., accounting, 1984); Loyola University (J.D., cum laude, 1989). Certified Public Accountant. ***PRACTICE AREAS:*** Trusts and Estates; Probate; Business Law; Real Estate; Taxation. ***Email:*** rmccarty@lcwchicago.com

RICHARD M. COHEN, born Chicago, Illinois, February 16, 1964; admitted to bar, 1991, Illinois. *Education:* Northwestern University (B.S.J., 1986); Chicago-Kent College of Law (J.D., 1991). Certified Financial Planner (CFP) and Licensed Life Insurance Producer, Illinois. *Member:* Chicago, Illinois State and American Bar Associations. ***PRACTICE AREAS:*** Closely Held Business Law; Trusts and Estates; Wills; Probate; Real Estate; Securities. ***Email:*** rcohen@lcwchicago.com

ROBERT C. ANSANI, born Melrose Park, Illinois, 1956; admitted to bar, 1999, Illinois. *Education:* University of Arizona (B.A., 1979); John Marshall Law School (J.D., 1999; LL.M., Taxation, 2001). *Member:* Chicago Bar Association. ***PRACTICE AREAS:*** Estate Planning; Estate Administration; Trusts and Estates; Business Law; Tax Law. ***Email:*** ransani@lcwchicago.com

DAVID LEHMAN LAW OFFICES

SUITE 520
55 WEST VAN BUREN STREET
CHICAGO, ILLINOIS 60605-1110
Telephone: 312-360-0050
Fax: 312-360-0725
Email: davidlehmanlaw@davidlehmanlaw.com
URL: http://www.davidlehmanlaw.com

Immigration Law, Investor, Entertainer and International Business Personnel Transfers. All Immigrant, Non-Immigrant and Business Visas, Immigration Court Proceedings. Sarbanes-Oxley, Employment, State and Federal Civil Litigation.

DAVID O. LEHMAN, born Decatur, Illinois; admitted to bar, 1973, Illinois; 1978, U.S. District Court, Northern District of Illinois including Trial Bar. *Education:* Harvard University (A.B., 1969); University of Pennsylvania (J.D., 1973). Recipient: Honorary National Merit Scholarship; English Speaking Union Scholarship, University College London, 1970. Article & Book Review Editor, University of Pennsylvania Law Review, 1972-1973. Law Clerk to: Mr. Justice Schaefer, Supreme Court of Illinois, 1973-1974; Judge John Minor Wisdom, U.S. Court of Appeals, 5th Circuit, 1974-1975. *Member:* Chicago Bar Association; American Immigration Lawyers Association. ***SPECIAL AGENCIES:*** Department of Homeland Security; Board of Immigration Appeals. ***PRACTICE AREAS:*** Immigration and Naturalization; Litigation.

LAW OFFICES
ROBERT E. LEHRER

Established in 1996

36 SOUTH WABASH STREET, SUITE 1310
CHICAGO, ILLINOIS 60603
Telephone: 312-332-2121
Fax: 312-422-0708
Email: relehrer@aol.com
Email: lehrerlawoffice@aol.com
URL: http://www.lawyers.com/relehrer

Civil Litigation, Civil Rights, Constitutional Law, Family Law, Children.

FIRM PROFILE: The Law Offices of Robert E. Lehrer is the successor firm of Lehrer & Redleaf, established in 1996. Mr. Lehrer has extensive trial and appellate experience in the conduct of civil litigation generally, but, most particularly, in plaintiffs' civil rights litigation (including class actions and institutional reform cases) and family law cases. Because of Mr. Lehrer's expertise in federal and Illinois state practice, other law offices frequently have retained him to assist them on cases presenting complex questions in these areas.

ROBERT E. LEHRER, born Hartford, Connecticut, May 1, 1945; admitted to bar, 1971, Massachusetts; 1972, Vermont; 1973, District of Columbia, Illinois, and U.S. District Court, Northern, Central, Southern Districts of Illinois, including Trial Bar; U.S. Court of Appeals, Third, Sixth and Seventh Circuits and U.S. Supreme Court. *Education:* Yale College (B.A., cum laude, 1967); Harvard Law School (J.D., cum laude, 1970). Deputy Director and Litigation Director, Legal Assistance Foundation of Chicago, 1983-1996. Lecturer: Remedies, Loyola University of Chicago School of Law, 2004—; Illinois Civil Procedure, DePaul University College of Law, 2005—. Hearing Officer, Illinois State Board of Education (special education cases under IDEA), 2005—. *Member:* Chicago and American Bar Associations; Chicago Council of Lawyers; Association of Trial Lawyers of America.

LEO & WEBER, P.C.

ONE N. LASALLE STREET
SUITE 3600
CHICAGO, ILLINOIS 60602
Telephone: 312-857-0910
Fax: 312-857-1240
URL: http://www.leoweber.com

Bankruptcy, Fidelity and Surety Bonds, Commercial Litigation, Construction Law and General Litigation.

T. SCOTT LEO, born Chicago, Illinois, May 24, 1954; admitted to bar, 1980, Illinois. *Education:* University of Illinois (B.A., 1976); Washington University (J.D., 1980). Author: "Subrogation Rights of Surety on a Fidelity Bond Against the Officers' and Directors' of the Insured, XVIII The Forum 2, (Summer 1983); Completion By the Surety: Assessing the Risk and Limiting the Loss," Bond Default Manual, (R. Wisner ed., 1987); "Application of Statutes of Limitation Governing Construction Activity to Construction Bond Sureties," 10 The Construction Lawyer 1, (January 1990); "Surety's Right to Salvage," Handling Fidelity, Surety, and Financial Risk Claims, (Cushman, Blick & Mekder ed., 1990); "The Financing Surety and The Chapter 11 Principal," XXVI Tort & Ins. L.J. 7, (1990); Co-Author: "The 50 Most Important Questions a Surety Can Ask About Bankruptcy," ABA 1992; Author: "The Contract Surety and Some Suretyship Defenses," William and Mary L. Rev. (Summer 1993); "Bankruptcy Considerations and Bond Defaults," Bond Default Manual 2nd Edition (D. Clore ed 1995); Adviser to the American Law Institute Restatement (Third) Suretyship "New Restatement of Suretyship and Guaranting Raises some Practical Problems," 65 Def. Couns. J.1 (April 1998). Co-Editor, "The Restatement of Suretyship and Guaranty: A Translation for the Practitioner," (ABA 2005). Adviser to the Restatement of the Law Third, Suretyship and Guaranty, 1996. *Member:* American Bar Association (Chair, Fidelity and Surety Law Committee, 2002-2003, Tort and Insurance Practice Section). ***Email:*** sleo@leoweber.com

MICHAEL J. WEBER, born Chicago, Illinois, July 1, 1958; admitted to bar, 1983, Illinois and U.S. District Court, Northern and Central Districts of Illinois and Eastern District of Wisconsin. *Education:* Indiana University (B.S., 1980; J.D., 1983). Speaker: "A Day Late and a Dollar Short-Failure to Notify the Surety of Default and Termination," presented to the National Bond Claims Association, Kiawah Island, S.C., Oct. 1999. Author: "Check Please? The 'Check 21' Act and Its Impact on Check Fraud Claims," Fidelity & Surety Law Committee, Tort and Insurance Practice Section, American Bar Association Mid-Winter Meeting, New York, NY, January 2005; "Surety Bonds," Construction Law in Illinois, Illinois Institute for Continuing Legal Education (1997, Supp. 2003); "ATMs and Check Fraud: Who's Watching the Store?", Fidelity Law Association, Philadelphia, PA, October 2003; "Who's Watching the Store-The Impact of a Professional's Neglect on the Probate Bond Surety," Fidelity & Surety Law Committee, Tort and Insurance Practice Section, American Bar Association Annual Meeting, Chicago IL, August 2001; "The Mysterious Beyond-Jurisdictional Issues in Cyberspace," Fidelity & Surety Law Committee, Tort and Insurance Practice Section, American Bar Association Mid-Winter Meeting, New York, NY, January 2001; "Construction Law in Illinois Surety Bonds," Illinois Institute for CCE 1997; "Illinois State Statute and Commentary," Payment Bond Manual, Tort and Insurance Practice Section, American Bar Association, 1991 and 1995; "Motions for Summary Judgment and the Financial Institution Bond--Throwing Caution to the Wind," American Bar Association, *The Brief,* Vol. 24, No. 1, Fall 1994; "Protecting the Project: The Role of the Surety," Troubled Construction Loans: Law and Practice, Chapter 4, Wiley Law Publications, 1991. *Member:* American Bar Association (Member, Tort and Insurance Practice Section; Vice-Chair, Fidelity and Surety Law Committee). ***PRACTICE AREAS:*** Fidelity and Surety Bonds; Commercial Litigation; Construction Law; General Litigation; Litigation. ***Email:*** mweber@leoweber.com

GRACE WINKLER CRANLEY, born Marshall, Missouri, May 8, 1964; admitted to bar, 1993, Illinois and U.S. District Court, Northern District of Illinois; 1996, U.S. Court of Appeals, Seventh Circuit; 2000, U.S. District Court, Central District of Illinois and Eastern District of Wisconsin. *Education:* University of Illinois (B.A., 1987); Chicago-Kent College of Law (J.D., 1993). Co-Author: "Proper Disclosure of Employees as Experts," 1994; "Legal Malpractice: Recent Developments and Trends in the Law," 1996. *Member:* Illinois State and American (Member, Fidelity and Surety Law Committee, Tort and Insurance Practice Section) Bar Associations. ***PRACTICE AREAS:*** Fidelity and Surety; Bonds; General Litigation; Commercial Litigation. ***Email:*** gcranley@leoweber.com

(This Listing Continued)

ASSOCIATES

NEIL A. KRAETSCH, born Belleville, Illinois, October 24, 1973; admitted to bar, 1999, Illinois and U.S. District Court, Northern District of Illinois. *Education:* University of Illinois (B.A., 1996); Washington University (J.D., 1999). Phi Delta Phi. *Member:* American Bar Association. ***PRACTICE AREAS:*** Fidelity and Surety; Commercial Litigation; Construction Law; Litigation. ***Email:*** nkraetsch@leoweber.com

JENNIFER SUSNJARA, born Santa Claus, Indiana, July 28, 1977; admitted to bar, 2003, Illinois; 2004, Indiana, U.S. District Court, Northern and Southern Districts of Indiana and Northern District of Illinois; 2005, Minnesota. *Education:* Indiana University (B.S., Business, 1999); Chicago-Kent College of Law, Illinois Institute of Technology (J.D., 2003). Member, Chicago Surety Claims. *Member:* American Bar Association. ***PRACTICE AREAS:*** Fidelity and Surety; Commercial Litigation. ***Email:*** jsusnjara@leoweber.com

BRYAN M. SEIFERT, born Buffalo, New York, November 22, 1975; admitted to bar, 2003, Illinois and U.S. District Court, Northern District of Illinois. *Education:* Illinois Institute of Technology (B.Arch., 1999); Chicago-Kent College of Law, Illinois Institute of Technology (J.D., 2003). License, Insurance Practice, Delaware, 2003—. Author, "International Construction Dispute Adjudication Under the FIDIC Conditions of Contract and the Dispute Adjudication Board," Journal of Protection Issues in Engineering Education and Practice, American Society of Civil Engineers, April 2005. Member, American Institute of Architects, 2003—. *Member:* Chicago, Illinois State and American Bar Associations. ***PRACTICE AREAS:*** Fidelity and Surety; Construction Law; Commercial Litigation; Litigation. ***Email:*** bseifert@leoweber.com

OF COUNSEL

JOEL R. PAGE, JR., born Gary, Indiana, May 14, 1958; admitted to bar, 1983, Indiana; U.S. Court of Appeals, Seventh and District of Columbia Circuits; U.S. District Court, Northern and Southern Districts of Indiana; 1991, Illinois and U.S. District Court, Northern District of Illinois. *Education:* Wabash College (A.B., cum laude, 1980); Indiana University (J.D., 1983). Associate Attorney, Eichhorn, Eichhorn & Link, Hammond, Indiana, 1983-1989. Assistant General Counsel, Acme Metals, Inc., 1989-2002; General Counsel, Acme Steel Company, 1998-2002; Chairman, 1989-1990. *Member:* Indiana State Bar Association (Member, Corporate Counsel Section). ***PRACTICE AREAS:*** Fidelity and Surety; Construction Law; Commercial Litigation. ***Email:*** jpage@leoweber.com

---

LEOPOLD & ASSOCIATES, L.L.C.

Established in 2005

150 NORTH MICHIGAN AVENUE
SUITE 2700
CHICAGO, ILLINOIS 60601
Telephone: 312-781-6212
Fax: 312-781-6213
Email: leopoldlaw@sbcglobal.net
URL: http://www.valerieleopold.com

Medical Malpractice, Birth Injury, Hospital Negligence, Obstetric Malpractice, Orthopedic Malpractice, Emergency Room Errors, Pregnancy Problems, Brain Damage, Cerebral Palsy, Surgical Mistakes, Nursing Errors, Cancer Misdiagnosis, Wrongful Death, Amputations, Nursing Home Negligence, Paralysis Cases, Motorcycle, Truck, Car and Pedestrian Accidents, Burn Injury, Drug and Medical Device Litigation, Sports Injury, Railroad Accidents and Injuries, Torts, Defective Products Liability, Toxic Torts and Class Action Litigation.

FIRM PROFILE: Leopold & Associates, L.L.C. is a Chicago law firm committed to providing the best representation possible for people injured by doctors, hospitals, products and accidents. This law firm is dedicated to obtaining both justice and substantial sums of money for clients in complex injury and medical malpractice cases. We will review your medical records with our expert medical-legal analytical skills and handle your case from inception to verdict or settlement.

VALERIE A. LEOPOLD, born Chicago, Illinois, February 13, 1953; admitted to bar, 1977, Illinois. *Education:* Iowa State University (B.A., with honors, 1974); Harvard University (J.D., summa cum laude, 1977). Instructor, National Institute for Trial Advocacy, 1985—. Trial Advocacy Professor, DePaul University School of Law, 1986—. *Member:* Chicago, Illinois State and American (Member, Litigation Section) Bar Associations; Illinois Trial Lawyers Association (Member, Board of Managers); The Association of Trial Lawyers of America. ***LANGUAGES:*** Spanish and English. ***PRACTICE AREAS:*** Medical Malpractice; Wrongful Death; Personal Injury; Automobile Accidents and Injuries; Construction Accidents; Class Action Litigation; Products Liability. ***Email:*** leopoldlaw@sbcglobal.net

Languages: English and Spanish.

NORMAN J. LERUM, P.C.

Established in 1986

SUITE 2100
100 WEST MONROE STREET
CHICAGO, ILLINOIS 60603
Telephone: 312-782-1087
Facsimile: 312-782-3773
Email: njlerum@msn.com
URL: http://www.normanjlerum.com

Trial and Appellate Practice in all State and Federal Courts concentrating in the following areas: Business Litigation, Contract Litigation, Chancery Practice, Plaintiff's Personal Injury (with emphasis on brain and spinal cord injuries), Construction Litigation, Aviation Law, Wrongful Death Law, Professional Negligence, Railroad Accidents and Injuries, Employment Litigation, Arbitration and Mediation.

FIRM PROFILE: Norman J. Lerum, P.C. is a trial lawyer with 30 years experience in handling and staffing significant litigation. He has been listed for several years in Martindale-Hubbell's Bar Register of Preeminent Lawyers and has achieved the highest legal ability rating from Martindale-Hubbell. Mr. Lerum is associated with Michael J. Samis, an experienced transactional lawyer, to better serve clients in need of counsel in real estate, general contract and corporate matters.

NORMAN J. LERUM, born South Bend, Indiana, 1949; admitted to bar, 1975, Illinois, Indiana, U.S. District Court, Northern District of Illinois including Trial Bar, U.S. Court of Appeals, Seventh Circuit, U.S. Claims Court and U.S. Court of Appeals, Federal Circuit. *Education:* University of Notre Dame (B.A., cum laude, 1971; J.D., 1974). Recipient, Dean's Award, Notre Dame Law School, 1974. Member, National Moot Court Team. Instructor: Legal Research and Writing, Loyola University Law School, 1976-1977; Trial Practice Course, Chicago Bar Association, 1983-1988; Insurance School of Chicago, 1985-1987; Illinois Institute for Continuing Legal Education, "Winning In Chancery and Special Remedies Practice" October 18, 1990. Law Clerk, Hon. Joseph Burke, Illinois Appellate Court, 1974-1976. Legal Advisor, Tangley Oaks Homeowner Association, 1985-2002. Board Member, Catholic Charities of the Archdiocese of Chicago, 1999-2002. Treasurer, Loyola Academy Hockey Club, 1999-2002. *Member:* Chicago Bar Association (Member, Executive Committee, 1980-1985; Chair, National Moot Court Committee, 1980; Chair, Committee on Evaluating Devitt Recommendations regarding Trial Practice Requirements in Federal Court, 1981; Chair, Trial Practice Course Committee, 1981-1985; Member, Judicial Evaluation Committee, 1985-1990); Illinois State Bar Association; Illinois Appellate Lawyers Association; Illinois Trial Lawyers Association; The Association of Trial Lawyers of America. ***REPORTED CASES:*** Bruce Allen Palmer v. Avco Distributing Corporation, 82 Ill.2d 211, 412 N.E.2d 959 (1980); Delux Ice Cream Corp. v. RCH Tool Corp. and Semner H. Bates, N.V., 726 F.2d 1209 (7th Cir. 1984); F. Lee Griffith, et al. v. Mitsubishi Aircraft International, et al., 136 Ill.2d 101, 554 N.E.2d 209 (1990); George Szczerbaniuk v. Memorial Hospital for McHenry County, 180 Ill.App.3d 706, 536 N.E.2d 138 (1989); Malatesta v. Mitsubishi Aircraft International, 275 Ill.App. 3d 370, 655 N.E.2d 1093 (1995); Perry R. Pennington Co. v. T. R. Miller Co., Inc., 994 F.2d 390 (7th Cir. 1993); United States of America ex rel. Rev. Frank Robert Cordee Hahn v. Vernon Revis and U.S. Board of Paroles and Pardons, 520 F.2d 632 (7th Cir. 1975) and 560 F.2d 264 (7th Cir. 1977); Genevieve Bakos v. Adrian G. Russell, et al., 49 Ill.App. 3d 539, 364 N.E.2d 581 (1977); Peggy J. Faust v. Michael Reese Hospital, et al., Illinois, 79 Ill.App.3d 69, 398 N.E.2d 287, (1979); Delta Oil Company v. Lloyd Arnold, 66 Ill.App.3d 375, 384 N.E.2d 25 (1978); David Claiborne v. Carell Hutchinson, Jr., 67 Ill.App.3d 374, 385 N.E.2d 29 (1978); Phyllisa A. Farnor v. IRMCO Corporation, et al., 73 Ill.App.3d 851, 392 N.E.2d 591 (1979); Albert Barron v. Kane & Roach, et al., Four States Machinery Company v. Berdsboro Corporation, 79 Ill.App.3d 44, 398 N.E.2d 244 (1979); Melvin VanDygriff v. Commonwealth Edison Company, 68 Ill.App.3d 396, 386 N.E.2d 318 (1979); Helen T. Novak v. Michael Reese Hospital and Medical Center and Robert Buchanan, 71 Ill.App.3d 1112, 392 N.E.2d 1386 (1979); Albert Brucar and Ruth Brucar v. Ira Rubin, Marvin Juron and Harry Weisberg, 638 F.2d 987 (7th Cir. 1980); C.R. Mohan Rao, M.D., S.C. v. M. Hari Kishan Rao, M.D., 718 F.2d 219 (7th Cir. 1983); Mary Lou Fox v. Sheldon Cohen, M.D., Alexian Brothers Medical Center, et al., 84 Ill.App.3d 744, 406 N.E.2d 178 (1980); Carol Elaine Williams, et al. v. St. Joseph Hospital, et al., 629 F.2d 448 (7th Cir. 1980); Jacqueline M. Przybylski, et al. v. Perkins & Will Architects, Inc., et al., 95 Ill.App.3d 620, 420 N.E.2d 524 (1981); Eileen Burns Lerum, Executrix of the Estate of Hortense Burns v. Margaret Heckler, Secretary of the Department of Health and Human Services, 774 F.2d 210 (7th Cir. 1985); Oakleaf of Illinois, et al. v. Oakleaf & Associates, Inc., 173 Ill.App.3d 637, 527 N.E.2d 926 (1988); Amanda Beck v. Secretary of the Department of Health and Human Services, 924 F.2d 1029 (Fed. Cir. 1991); James Shannon Long v. Georgetown College, Ky. Court of Appeals, No. 91 CA 1819, unpublished opinion issued September 2, 1992; M.J. Oldensteadt Plumbing v. K-Mart, 195 Ill.Dec. 906, 629 N.E.2d 214 (1994); Palda v. General Dynamics Corp., 47 F.3d 872 (7th Cir. 1995); Jean Lindquist v. Chicago and Northwestern Transportation Company, et. al., Appellate Court of Illinois, Second District, 722 N.E. 2d 270, 242 Ill.Dec. 781 (1999). ***Email:*** njlerum@msn.com

OF COUNSEL

MICHAEL J. SAMIS, born 1948; admitted to bar, 1973, Illinois; U.S. District Court, Northern District of Illinois. *Education:* Xavier University (B.A., cum laude, 1970); Loyola University, Chicago, School of Law (J.D., 1973). Instructor, Real Estate Law, Triton College, 1975-1980. *Member:* Illinois State Bar Association; Lake Forest Symphony Association, Inc. (Legal Counsel; Member, Board of Directors, 1993-2005); Onwentsia Gardens Homeowners' Association, Inc. (Legal Counsel; Member, Board of Directors, 1986-1990, 1998-2002). ***PRACTICE AREAS:*** General Practice; Business Law; Corporate Law; Nonprofit Corporations; Religious Organizations; Business Transactions; Real Estate; Real Estate Transfers; Contracts; Employment Law; Probate; Commercial Law; Construction Contracts; Litigation. ***Email:*** mjsamis4@aol.com

REPRESENTATIVE CLIENTS: Barrett Construction Company; Executive Home Mortgage Corporation; The Greeby Companies, Inc.; The Taubman Company; The Redemptorists/Denver Province; The Redemptorist Society of California; Mount Sinai Hospital; Radio Maryja; M&R Precision Machining, Inc.; Holy Redeemer Center; Liguori Publications.

LESAVICH HIGH-TECH LAW GROUP, PC

39 S. LASALLE STREET
CHICAGO, ILLINOIS 60603
Telephone: 312-332-3751
Fax: 312-332-3752
URL: http://www.hightech-iplaw.com
Email: stephen.lesavich@lhtlg.com
URL: http://www.lhtlg.com

Software Patents, High-Tech Patents, Patent, Trademark Copyright Law, Licensing, Litigation, Internet Law, E-Commerce Law, Business Method Patents.

FIRM PROFILE: The Lesavich High-Tech Law Group, PC counsels high-tech start-up, emerging and established clients in all areas of intellectual property law and Internet law. The Firm serves a wide range of clients in the computer, Internet and telecommunications industries. The Lesavich High-Tech Law Group, PC uses its specialized high-tech experience to assist clients in procuring, managing, protecting, leveraging, licensing and asserting intellectual property. The Lesavich High-Tech Law Group, PC prepares and prosecutes patent, trademark and copyright applications in the United States and around the world. The Lesavich High-Tech Law Group, PC also opposes and defends trademarks and provides litigation and litigation consulting for complex, high-tech intellectual property disputes.

STEPHEN LESAVICH, born Kenosha, Wisconsin, April 17, 1959; admitted to bar, 1996, Wisconsin and U.S. District Court, Eastern and Western Districts of Wisconsin; 1997, Oregon; 1999, Illinois and U.S. District Court, Northern District of Illinois; registered to practice before the U.S. Patent and Trademark Office. *Education:* University of Wisconsin at Madison (B.S., with distinction, 1981; J.D., 1995); University of Wisconsin at Milwaukee (M.S., Computer Science, 1986); Illinois Institute of Technology (Ph.D., Computer Science, 1991). Alpha Zeta; Gamma Sigma Delta. Founder, Lesavich High-Tech Law Group, P.C., 2002. Partner, 2000-2002 and Associate, 1997-1999, McDonnell Boehnen Hulbert & Berghoff, Chicago, Illinois. Associate, 1996-1997 and Technical Consultant for Computer-related Intellectual Property Issues, 1995, Klarquist Sparkman Campbell Leigh & Winston LLP, Portland, Oregon. Senior Engineer, U.S. Robotics, Skokie, Illinois, 1992-1993. Member, Technical Staff, AT&T Bell Laboratories, Naperville, Illinois, 1986-1992. Author: "It may now take Robotic Vision to Determine When a Software Invention is Actually Ready for Patenting," IP & Tech. L.J., Nov. 2001, at 1; "Protecting Digital Content in a Peer-to-Peer World," IP & Tech. L.J., Nov. 2000, at 12; "Keystroke Spies: Conflicting Privacy Rights," Nat. L.J., May 22, 2000, at A23; "Case Adds Uncertainty to Web Copyright Laws," Nat. L.J., Jan 31, 2000, at C9; "The New Japan-U.S. Patent Agreements: Will They Really Protect U.S. Patent Interests in Japan?" 14 Wis. Int'l L.J. 155 (1995). Listed in: *Who's Who in American Law*, 1998—; *Who's Who:* American Law Students, 1994 and 1995. Member, Wisconsin International Law Journal, 1994-1995. Recipient: American Jurisprudence Award in Telecommunications Law, 1995; AT&T Network Architecture Award, 1992; AT&T Bell Labs Software Quality Awards, 1990 and 1991. Adjunct Instructor, Computer Science, University of Wisconsin-Parkside, Kenosha, Wisconsin, 1985-1986. Adjunct Professor: Portland State University, Portland, Oregon, 1996-1999; Oregon Center for Advanced Technology Education, Beaverton, Oregon, 1996-1997. Legal Advisor, Board of Directors, Assisi Software Corporation, Troutdale, Oregon, 1997-1998. *Member:* Chicago, Kenosha, Illinois State and American Bar Associations; State Bar of Wisconsin; Oregon State Bar; Association for Computing Machinery (Member, 1984—); Institute of Electronic and Electrical Engineers (Member, 1984-2000; Senior Member, 2000—; Member, IEEE Committee on Multimedia Computing, 1997—). ***PRACTICE AREAS:*** Software Patents; Trademarks; Copyright law; Patent Licensing; Litigation; Internet Law; Internet Patents; Computer Patents. ***Email:*** stephen.lesavich@lhtlg.com

ANDREW W. LEVENFELD & ASSOCIATES, LTD.

221 N. LASALLE STREET, SUITE 2800
CHICAGO, ILLINOIS 60601-1206
Telephone: 312-782-5858
Fax: 312-419-9876
Email: levenfeld@yahoo.com
URL: http://www.levenfeldlaw.com

Civil Litigation, Trial Practice, Commercial and Residential Real Estate, Buying and Selling a Home, Condominium Law, Cooperative Housing Law, Homeowners Association Law, Land Acquisitions, Sales, Trusts, Real Estate Arbitration, Real Estate Development, Real Estate Development, Real Estate Leasing, Real Estate Mediation, Real Estate Tax Liens, Construction Law, Trusts and Estates, Elder Law, Estate Administration, Estate Planning, Estate Litigation, Family Trust, Powers of Attorney, Trust Litigation, Wealth Preservation, Probate Litigation, Asset Protection, Guardianship, Tax Litigation, Wills, Probate, Employment Discrimination, Sex Discrimination, Age Discrimination, Conservatorship, Corporate Law, Nonprofit Organization Law, Corporate Litigation, S Corporations, Small Business Corporations, Litigation, Consumer Fraud.

ANDREW W. LEVENFELD, born 1948; admitted to bar, 1973, Illinois, Florida, Indiana, U.S. District Court, Northern District of Illinois, U.S. District Court, Northern District of Indiana, U.S. Court of Appeals, Seventh Circuit and U.S. Tax Court. *Education:* Michigan State University (B.S., 1970); Rutgers University Law School (J.D., 1973). *Member:* Illinois State Bar Association. ***Email:*** levenfeld@yahoo.com

ASSOCIATE

JEFFREY SCOTT SELL, born Peoria, Illinois, May 6, 1969; admitted to bar, 1995, Illinois and Supreme Court of the State of Illinois; U.S. District Court, Northern District of Illinois. *Education:* Bradley University (B.A., 1991); University of Illinois (J.D., 1994). *Member:* Chicago and Illinois State Bar Associations; Illinois Real Estate Lawyers Association. ***Email:*** jsell@levenfeldlaw.com

LEVENFELD PEARLSTEIN, LLC

Established in 1999

2 NORTH LASALLE STREET, SUITE 1300
CHICAGO, ILLINOIS 60602
Telephone: 312-346-8380
Facsimile: 312-346-8434
Email: lplegal@lplegal.com
URL: http://www.lplegal.com

Northfield Office: 211 Waukegan Road, Suite 300, 60093. Telephone: 847-441-7676. Facsimile: 847-441-9976.

Business Law, Corporate Law, Technology Law, Mergers, Acquisitions and Divestitures, Litigation, Real Estate, Banks and Banking, Financial Institutions Law, Finance, Secured Lending, Federal Taxation, State Taxation, Securities, Bankruptcy, Workouts, Homeowners Association Law, Condominium Law, Intellectual Property, Employee Benefits, Wealth Preservation, Estate Planning, Trust Law, Probate, International Asset Protection, Commercial Law, Franchise Law, Employment Law, Executive Employment Law, Environmental Litigation.

MEMBERS OF FIRM

DAVID B. BERZON, born Akron, Ohio, 1959; admitted to bar, 1984, Illinois. *Education:* Tulane University (B.S., cum laude, 1981); American University Washington College of Law (J.D., cum laude, 1984). *Member:* Chicago Bar Association. ***PRACTICE AREAS:*** Real Estate Development Law; Leasing; Real Estate Sales and Acquisitions; Finance and Workouts. ***Email:*** dberzon@lplegal.com

GARY I. BLACKMAN, born Chicago, Illinois, 1959; admitted to bar, 1984, Illinois; U.S. District Court, Northern District of Illinois including Trial Bar and U.S. Court of Appeals, Seventh Circuit. *Education:* University of Illinois (B.S., 1981); DePaul University (J.D., 1984). *Member:* Illinois State Bar Association. ***PRACTICE AREAS:*** Commercial Litigation; Banking Litigation; Real Estate; Bankruptcy; Condominium Law; Partnership Law; Appellate Practice. ***Email:*** gblackman@lplegal.com

STEVEN BRIGHT, born Chicago, Illinois, 1955; admitted to bar, 1980, Illinois. *Education:* Northwestern University (B.S., 1976); DePaul University (J.D., 1980). *Member:* Leading Lawyer Network. ***PRACTICE AREAS:*** Banks and Banking; Workouts; Financial Restructuring; Corporate Law; Real Estate. ***Email:*** sbright@lplegal.com

MITCHELL BRYAN, born Chicago, Illinois, 1956; admitted to bar, 1982, Illinois and U.S. District Court, Northern District of Illinois; 1996, Trial Bar and U.S. Court of Appeals, Seventh Circuit. *Education:* University of Illinois (B.A., 1979); Washington University (J.D., 1982). *Member:* Chicago and American Bar Associations. ***REPORTED CASES:*** Latigo Ventures v. Laventhal & Horwath, 876 F.2d 1322 (7th Cir. 1989); Hernandez v. Childers, 736 F.Supp. 903 (N.D.Ill. 1990). ***PRACTICE AREAS:*** Commercial Litigation; Intellectual Property Litigation; Real Estate Litigation; Insurance Litigation; Corporate Law. ***Email:*** mbryan@lplegal.com

JORDAN M. CRAMER, born Chicago, Illinois, 1968; admitted to bar, 1993, Illinois, U.S. District Court, Northern District of Illinois and U.S. Court of Appeals, Seventh Circuit. *Education:* University of Illinois (B.S., 1990); Chicago-Kent College of Law, Illinois Institute of Technology (J.D., with honors, 1993). *Member:* Chicago and Illinois State Bar Associations; Federal Trial Bar. ***PRACTICE AREAS:*** Commercial Litigation; Real Estate Litigation; Banking Litigation; Condominium Law. ***Email:*** jcramer@lplegal.com

HOWARD S. DAKOFF, born Chicago, Illinois, 1970; admitted to bar, 1996, Illinois and U.S. District Court, Northern District of Illinois. *Education:* University of Wisconsin-Madison (B.S., 1992); John Marshall Law School (J.D., 1996). *Member:* Chicago and Illinois State Bar Associations. ***PRACTICE AREAS:*** Homeowners Association Law; Litigation; Real Estate. ***Email:*** hdakoff@lplegal.com

KATHERINE SMITH DEDRICK, born LaGrange, Illinois, 1957; admitted to bar, 1983, Illinois and U.S. District Court, Northern District of Illinois; 1992, U.S. District Court, Central District of Illinois; 1995, U.S. Court of Appeals, Seventh and Ninth Circuits; 1996, California. *Education:* Arizona State University (B.S., Business, 1979); Chicago-Kent College of Law, Illinois Institute of Technology (J.D., with high honors, 1983). ***PRACTICE AREAS:*** Litigation. ***Email:*** kdedrick@lplegal.com

PETER F. DONATI, born Bloomfield Hills, Michigan, 1967; admitted to bar, 1992, Illinois. *Education:* Cornell University (B.S., 1989); Oxford University, Oxford, England; University of Michigan (J.D., cum laude, 1992). Phi Kappa Phi. Law Clerk to the Hon. Frank J. Battisti, U.S. District Court, Northern District of Ohio, 1992-1993. *Member:* Chicago and Illinois State Bar Associations. ***PRACTICE AREAS:*** Labor and Employment (100%). ***Email:*** pdonati@lplegal.com

LEON I. EDELSON, born Chicago, Illinois, 1954; admitted to bar, 1988, Illinois. *Education:* Indiana University (B.A., 1980); Georgetown University (J.D., 1988); John Marshall Law School (LL.M., 1994). *Member:* American Bar Associations; American Intellectual Property Law Association; Intellectual Property Law Association of Chicago. ***PRACTICE AREAS:*** Intellectual Property. ***Email:*** ledelson@lplegal.com

STEVEN "SONNY" F. GINSBERG, born Bronx, New York, 1965; admitted to bar, 1991, California; 1992, Illinois. *Education:* Cornell University (B.A., 1987); University of Michigan (J.D., 1991). Co-Author: "Title Insurance Needed in Portfolio Acquisitions," The National Law Journal, 1995. Member, Board of Director, Near Northwest Chamber of Commerce. *Member:* Chicago, Illinois State and American Bar Associations. ***PRACTICE AREAS:*** Commercial Real Estate; Development; Lending; Land Use. ***Email:*** sginsberg@lplegal.com

DONALD A. GLASSBERG, born Chicago, Illinois, 1937; admitted to bar, 1968, Illinois. *Education:* University of Michigan (B.B.A., 1959); DePaul University (J.D., 1968). Author: "The Estate Planner." *Member:* Chicago, Illinois State and American Bar Associations; Leading Lawyer Network. ***PRACTICE AREAS:*** Wealth Preservation; Family Wealth Transfer; Estate Planning; Trust Planning; Probate; Federal Taxation; State Taxation; International Asset Protection; International Taxation; Business Law; Corporate Law. ***Email:*** dglassberg@lplegal.com

(This Listing Continued)

STEVEN P. GOMBERG, born Chicago, IL, 1947; admitted to bar, 1973, Illinois and U.S. District Court, Northern District of Illinois including Trial Bar; 1976, U.S. Court of Appeals, Seventh Circuit; 1981, U.S. Tax Court. *Education:* Bradley University (B.S., 1969); DePaul University (J.D., 1973). *Member:* American Bar Association; The Securities Industry Association. ***PRACTICE AREAS:*** Securities and Broker-Dealer Litigation; Arbitration; Mediation; Securities Regulation and Enforcement; Business Litigation; Commercial Litigation. ***Email:*** sgomberg@lplegal.com

BEAU T. GREIMAN, born Britt, Iowa, 1969; admitted to bar, 1994, Illinois; 1999, Iowa. *Education:* University of Iowa (B.B.A., with honors, 1991; J.D., with high distinction, 1994). *Member:* Chicago, Illinois State and American Bar Associations. ***REPORTED CASES:*** Estate of Dickens v. Haag, 2001 WL 23100 (Iowa App., 2001). ***PRACTICE AREAS:*** Commercial Litigation. ***Email:*** bgreiman@lplegal.com

DARRYL P. JACOBS, born Chicago, Illinois, 1963; admitted to bar, 1988, Illinois. *Education:* University of Illinois (B.S., 1985); Harvard University (J.D., 1988). *Member:* American Bar Association. ***PRACTICE AREAS:*** Taxation; Corporate; Real Estate.

THOMAS G. JAROS, born Chicago, Illinois, 1967; admitted to bar, 1992, Illinois; 1994, U.S. District Court, Eastern District of Wisconsin. *Education:* Knox College (B.A., cum laude, 1989); Chicago-Kent College of Law, Illinois Institute of Technology (J.D., with high honors, 1992). Order of the Coif. ***PRACTICE AREAS:*** Real Estate; Secured Finance; Banking Law; Bankruptcy. ***Email:*** tjaros@lplegal.com

MARC S. JOSEPH, born Chicago, Illinois, 1956; admitted to bar, 1981, Illinois. *Education:* University of Illinois (B.S., magna cum laude, 1978; J.D., magna cum laude, 1981). *Member:* Chicago Bar Association; Leading Lawyer Network. ***PRACTICE AREAS:*** Real Estate; Finance; Banking Law; Corporate Law; Securities. ***Email:*** mjoseph@lplegal.com

AARON S. KASE, born Mt. Home, Idaho, 1968; admitted to bar, 1995, Illinois. *Education:* University of Wisconsin at Madison (B.A., with highest honors, 1990); University of Chicago (J.D., 1995). ***PRACTICE AREAS:*** Corporate Law; Securities Law. ***Email:*** akase@lplegal.com

BRIAN K. KOZMINSKI, born Brookfield, Wisconsin, 1970; admitted to bar, 1995, Illinois. *Education:* University of Illinois at Urbana/Champaign (B.A., 1992); DePaul University College of Law (J.D., 1995). *Member:* Chicago and Illinois State Bar Associations. ***PRACTICE AREAS:*** Real Estate. ***Email:*** bkozminski@lplegal.com

SCOTT A. MEYERS, born St. Louis, Missouri, 1966; admitted to bar, 1992, New York; 1993, Illinois. *Education:* University of Pennsylvania (B.S., cum laude, 1988); Georgetown University (J.D., cum laude, 1991). Recipient, John M. Olin Law and Economic Fellowship. Managing Editor, American Criminal Law Review.

MARK D. PEARLSTEIN, born Bakersfield, California, 1948; admitted to bar, 1975, Illinois. *Education:* University of Illinois (B.A., 1970); DePaul University (J.D., 1974). Chairman, Community Associations Institute, Legislative Action Committee, 1995—. Inductee, CAI College of Community Association Lawyers. *Member:* Chicago Bar Association; Leading Lawyer Network. ***REPORTED CASES:*** Hilton v. Darien Homes Condominium Ass'n., No. 1-88-2604 (Ill.App.Ct. 1st Dist. 1989). ***PRACTICE AREAS:*** Homeowners Association Law; Corporate Law; Real Estate; Probate. ***Email:*** mpearlstein@lplegal.com

SCOTT H. REYNOLDS, born Chicago, Illinois, 1951; admitted to bar, 1976, Illinois, U.S. District Court, Northern District of Illinois including Trial Bar and U.S. Court of Appeals, Seventh Circuit. *Education:* University of Illinois (B.A., 1972; M.A., 1973); Northwestern University (J.D., 1976). *Member:* Chicago Bar Association. ***PRACTICE AREAS:*** Corporate Law; Real Estate; Litigation; Bankruptcy. ***Email:*** sreynolds@lplegal.com

ROBERT ALAN ROMANOFF, born Park Ridge, Illinois, 1963; admitted to bar, 1989, Illinois. *Education:* University of Iowa (B.A., cum laude, 1986); University of Michigan (J.D., 1989). Phi Beta Kappa. Associate Articles Editor, Michigan Journal of International Law, 1987-1989. Instructor, University of Michigan Law School, 1988-1989. *Member:* Chicago and Illinois State Bar Associations. Fellow, The American College of Trust and Estate Counsel. ***PRACTICE AREAS:*** Estate Planning; Trust Administration; Estate Administration; Business Succession Planning.

KEITH A. ROSS, born Skokie, Illinois, 1967; admitted to bar, 1992, Illinois. *Education:* University of Illinois (B.S., Finance, 1989); Chicago-Kent College of Law, Illinois Institute of Technology (J.D., 1992). *Member:* Chicago and Illinois State Bar Associations. ***PRACTICE AREAS:*** Real Estate; Corporate Law; Business Law. ***Email:*** kross@lplegal.com

PHILIP E. RUBEN, born Chicago, Illinois, 1958; admitted to bar, 1983, Illinois. *Education:* University of Illinois (B.S., 1980); Chicago-Kent College of Law, Illinois Institute of Technology (J.D., 1983). *Member:* Chicago and Illinois State Bar Associations. ***PRACTICE AREAS:*** Corporate Law; Securities; Wealth Preservation. ***Email:*** pruben@lplegal.com

BRYAN I. SCHWARTZ, born Hawthorne, California, 1960; admitted to bar, 1986, Illinois. *Education:* University of Florida (B.A., 1982); John Marshall Law School (J.D., 1986). *Member:* Chicago, Illinois State and American Bar Associations; Leading Lawyer Network. ***PRACTICE AREAS:*** Bankruptcy; Financial Institutions Law; Banks and Banking; Creditors Rights; Corporate Law; Technology Law. ***Email:*** bschwartz@lplegal.com

WILLIAM S. SCHWARTZ, born Chicago, Illinois, 1965; admitted to bar, 1990, Illinois. *Education:* University of Illinois (B.A., 1987); Chicago-Kent College of Law, Illinois Institute of Technology (J.D., with honors, 1990). (Resident, Northfield, Illinois). ***PRACTICE AREAS:*** Commercial Litigation; Bankruptcy; Banking Law; Financial Institutions Law; Real Estate. ***Email:*** wschwartz@lplegal.com

RUSSELL I. SHAPIRO, born Chicago, Illinois, 1964; admitted to bar, 1989, Illinois. *Education:* University of Illinois (B.S., with highest honors, 1986); University of Pennsylvania (J.D., 1989). Certified Public Accountant, Illinois, 1986. *Member:* Chicago and American Bar Associations. ***PRACTICE AREAS:*** Corporate Law; Mergers, Acquisitions and Divestitures; Technology Law. ***Email:*** rshapiro@lplegal.com

ABRAHAM TRIEGER, born Munich, Germany, 1951; admitted to bar, 1975, Illinois and U.S. District Court, Northern District of Illinois. *Education:* Northwestern University

(This Listing Continued)

LEVENFELD PEARLSTEIN, LLC, Chicago—Continued

(B.A., with honors, 1972); Loyola University (J.D., 1975). *Member:* Chicago Bar Association; Leading Lawyer Network. ***PRACTICE AREAS:*** Real Estate. ***Email:*** atrieger@lplegal.com

MICHAEL J. TUCHMAN, born Chicago, Illinois, 1958; admitted to bar, 1984, Illinois. *Education:* Northern Illinois University (B.S., summa cum laude, 1980); University of Illinois (J.D., 1984). Certified Public Accountant, Illinois, 1982. Adjunct Faculty Member: John Marshall Law School, 1992—. *Member:* Leading Lawyer Network. ***PRACTICE AREAS:*** Corporate Law; Mergers, Acquisitions and Divestitures; Federal Taxation; International Taxation; Tax Deferred Exchanges; Real Estate; Executive Employment Law. ***Email:*** mtuchman@lplegal.com

MARY K. WASIK, born Chicago, Illinois, 1956; admitted to bar, 1981, Illinois. *Education:* Loyola University (B.B.A., magna cum laude, 1978); University of Illinois (J.D., 1981). *Member:* Chicago, Illinois State and American Bar Associations. ***PRACTICE AREAS:*** Corporate; Business Law; Intellectual Property. ***Email:*** mwasik@lplegal.com

ASSOCIATES

MARK A. BIESIADA, born Illinois, 1973; admitted to bar, 2000, Illinois. *Education:* Illinois State University (B.S., 1995); John Marshall Law School (J.D., 1998). ***Email:*** mbiesiada@lplegal.com

REBECCA EDWARDS, born Ann Arbor, Michigan, 1976; admitted to bar, 2003, Louisiana (Not admitted in Illinois). *Education:* Tulane University (B.S., Criminal Justice, with departmental honors, 1998; J.D., 2003). *Member:* Louisiana State Bar Association. ***PRACTICE AREAS:*** Corporate Law; Securities (100%). ***Email:*** redwards@lplegal.com

JEFFREY C. FRIEDMAN, born Highland Park, Illinois, 1972; admitted to bar, 1999, Illinois. *Education:* University of Illinois (B.A., 1995); Chicago-Kent College of Law, Illinois Institute of Technology (J.D., 1999). *Member:* Chicago and American Bar Associations. ***PRACTICE AREAS:*** Real Estate. ***Email:*** jfriedman@lplegal.com

LINDA A. GALLAGHER, born Chicago, Illinois, 1952; admitted to bar, 1995, Illinois; 1996, U.S. District Court, Northern District of Illinois. *Education:* DePaul University (B.S., Commerce, 1991); Chicago-Kent College of Law, Illinois Institute of Technology (J.D., with honors, 1995). ***PRACTICE AREAS:*** Litigation; Securities. ***Email:*** lgallagher@lplegal.com

ERIC J. GENIN, born Chicago, Illinois, 1971; admitted to bar, 1996, Illinois. *Education:* University of Illinois (B.A., 1993); University of Michigan (J.D., 1996). *Member:* Chicago and Illinois State Bar Associations. ***PRACTICE AREAS:*** Real Estate. ***Email:*** egenin@lplegal.com

CHARLES J. GOETZ, born Buffalo, New York, 1968; admitted to bar, 1996, Illinois. *Education:* State University of New York at Buffalo (B.A., 1991; M.A., 1993); Chicago-Kent College of Law, Illinois Institute of Technology (J.D., 1996). ***Email:*** cgoetz@lplegal.com

CHRISTOPHER S. GRIESMEYER, born Boulder, Colorado, 1973; admitted to bar, 1999, Illinois. *Education:* Northwestern University (B.A., 1996); University of Virginia (J.D., 1999). *Member:* Chicago and Illinois State Bar Associations. ***PRACTICE AREAS:*** Commercial Litigation; Tort Defense; Labor and Employment. ***Email:*** cgriesmeyer@lplegal.com

VALLI V. GUPTA, born Milwaukee, Wisconsin, 1969; admitted to bar, 1997, Wisconsin; 2005, Illinois. *Education:* University of Notre Dame (B.A., 1991); Marquette University (J.D., 1997). *Member:* Chicago and American Bar Associations. ***Email:*** vgupta@lplegal.com

CHRISTOPHER M. HEINTSKILL, born Bay City, Michigan, 1974; admitted to bar, 2000, Illinois. *Education:* Loyola University, Chicago (B.A., 1996); Illinois Institute of Technology, Kent College of Law (J.D., 2000). *Member:* Chicago, Illinois State and American Bar Associations. ***PRACTICE AREAS:*** Commercial Litigation. ***Email:*** cheintskill@lplegal.com

MICHELE L. KRAUSE, born Hartford, Connecticut, 1969; admitted to bar, 1994, Illinois and U.S. District Court, Northern District of Illinois. *Education:* Illinois State University (B.S., 1991); Chicago-Kent College of Law, Illinois Institute of Technology (J.D., 1994). Co-Author: with Jennifer C. Jackson, "Avoiding Purchase Option Pitfalls"; with Jennifer C. Jackson, "Filling the Purchase Option Gap". Member, Professional Women's Network, 2004—. *Member:* Chicago, Illinois State and American Bar Associations; International Council of Shopping Centers. ***PRACTICE AREAS:*** Real Estate (100%). ***Email:*** mkrause@lplegal.com

NICK S. LEGATOS, born Chicago, Illinois, 1973; admitted to bar, 1998, Illinois and U.S. District Court, Northern District of Illinois. *Education:* Northwestern University (B.A., with honors, 1995); University of Illinois (J.D., magna cum laude, 1998). *Member:* Chicago and American Bar Associations. ***PRACTICE AREAS:*** Real Estate. ***Email:*** nlegatos@lplegal.com

JAMIE E. LEVINE, born New York, N.Y., 1970; admitted to bar, 2003, Illinois. *Education:* Johns Hopkins University (B.A., 1992); Northwestern University (J.D., 2003). *Member:* Chicago, Ilinois State and American Bar Associations. ***PRACTICE AREAS:*** Real Estate. ***Email:*** jlevine@lplegal.com

AMY W. MAHONE, born Lakeland, Florida, 1974; admitted to bar, 1999, Washington; 2005, Illinois. *Education:* Belmont University (B.A., cum laude, 1996); University of Tennessee (J.D., 1999). *Member:* Washington State Bar Association; American Health Lawyers Association. ***Email:*** amahone@lplegal.com

JAMES G. MARTIGNON, born St. Louis, Missouri, 1968; admitted to bar, 2002, Illinois and U.S. District Court, Northern District of Illinois. *Education:* Georgetown University, School of Foreign Service (B.S.F.S., 1991); Washington University School of Law (J.D., 2002). ***PRACTICE AREAS:*** Commercial Litigation; Bankruptcy. ***Email:*** jmartignon@lplegal.com

(This Listing Continued)

HEATHER L. MOORE, born Normal, Illinois, 1970; admitted to bar, 2001, Illinois. *Education:* DePaul University (B.A., with honors, 1996); DePaul University College of Law (J.D., 2000). ***Email:*** hmoore@lplegal.com

JASON P. NEUMARK, born Chicago, Illinois, 1970; admitted to bar, 1995, Illinois. *Education:* Princeton University (A.B., Economics, cum laude, 1992); Northwestern University (J.D., 1995). Member, Northwestern University Law Review. ***PRACTICE AREAS:*** Real Estate. ***Email:*** jneumark@lplegal.com

PATRICIA A. O'CONNOR, born Chicago, Illinois, 1959; admitted to bar, 1985, Illinois. *Education:* University of Illinois (B.A., 1981); John Marshall Law School (J.D., 1985). *Member:* Chicago and Illinois State Bar Associations. ***PRACTICE AREAS:*** Condominium Law; Real Estate; Commercial Litigation. ***Email:*** poconnor@lplegal.com

NEHA A. PARIKH, born Daytona Beach, Florida, 1975; admitted to bar, 2000, Illinois. *Education:* University of Florida (B.S., magna cum laude, 1997; J.D., 2000). *Member:* Chicago, Illinois State and American Bar Associations. ***PRACTICE AREAS:*** Commercial Litigation; Insurance Defense. ***Email:*** nparikh@lplegal.com

NATALIE M. PERRY, born Milwaukee, Wisconsin, 1967; admitted to bar, 1995, Illinois. *Education:* Indiana University (B.S., 1989); DePaul University (J.D., 1995). Certified Public Accountant, Illinois, 1990. *Member:* Chicago Bar Association (Vice-Chairman, Federal Estate and Gift Tax Committee, 2001—). ***PRACTICE AREAS:*** Estate Planning; Trust Administration; Estate Administration; Federal Taxation. ***Email:*** nperry@lplegal.com

BRIAN J. PLEVIAK, born January 31, 1975; admitted to bar, 2000, Illinois; 2001, Wisconsin. *Education:* University of Wisconsin-Madison (B.A., 1997); Chicago-Kent College of Law, Illinois Institute of Technology (J.D., 2000). *Member:* Wisconsin Bar Association; Inernational Bar Association. ***Email:*** bpleviak@lplegal.com

KEARA M. ROETHKE, born Milwaukee, Wisconsin, 1978; admitted to bar, 2003, Illinois and U.S. District Court, Northern District of Illinois. *Education:* Marquette University (B.A., 2000); John Marshall Law School (J.D., 2003). ***PRACTICE AREAS:*** Litigation; Homeowners Association Law. ***Email:*** kroethke@lplegal.com

ADAM B. ROME, born Skokie, Illinois, 1976; admitted to bar, 2002, Illinois. *Education:* Indiana University (B.A., 1999); Chicago-Kent College of Law, Illinois Institute of Technology (J.D., 2002). ***PRACTICE AREAS:*** Commercial Litigation. ***Email:*** arome@lplegal.com

JASON M. ROMICK, born Los Angeles, California, 1971; admitted to bar, 1997, Illinois and U.S. Court of Appeals, Seventh Circuit; 1998, U.S. District Court, Northern District of Illinois. *Education:* Washington University, St. Louis (B.S.B.A., with honors, 1994); University of Illinois, Champaign (J.D., summa cum laude, 1997). Order of the Coif. Member, University of Illinois Law Review. *Member:* Chicago and American Bar Associations. ***LANGUAGES:*** Spanish. ***PRACTICE AREAS:*** Corporate; Securities; Mergers and Acquisitions; Venture Capital.

STEVEN M. WEISS, born Park Ridge, Illinois, 1973; admitted to bar, 2002, Illinois. *Education:* University of Texas at Austin (B.A., History, Certificate of Completion for Business Foundations Program, 1995); Chicago-Kent College of Law (J.D., with honors, 2002). ***Email:*** sweiss@lplegal.com

MATTHEW R. ZAKARAS, born Harvey, Illinois, 1976; admitted to bar, 2001, Illinois. *Education:* Marquette University (B.A., 1998); DePaul University (J.D., 2001). *Member:* Chicago, Illinois and American Bar Associations. ***PRACTICE AREAS:*** Corporate Law; Securities. ***Email:*** mzakaras@lplegal.com

OF COUNSEL

JAMES D. BRUSSLAN, born Chicago, Illinois, 1957; admitted to bar, 1982, Illinois; 1983, U.S. District Court, Northern District of Illinois. *Education:* Tufts University (B.S., cum laude, 1979); University of California at Los Angeles (J.D., 1982). *Member:* Chicago, Illinois State and American Bar Associations. ***PRACTICE AREAS:*** Environmental Litigation; Counseling. ***Email:*** jbrusslan@lplegal.com

WILLIAM CASE CLARKE, admitted to bar, 1974, Illinois. *Education:* DePaul University (B.A.); University of Chicago (M.B.A.); DePaul University (J.D., 1974; LL.M, 1980). *Member:* Chicago Bar Association; Intellectual Property Law Association of Chicago; Leading Lawyer Network. ***PRACTICE AREAS:*** Intellectual Property. ***Email:*** wclarke@lplegal.com

JOSEPH S. FARRELL, born Chicago, Illinois, 1970; admitted to bar, 1995, Illinois. *Education:* Marquette University (B.S., 1992); John Marshall Law School (J.D., 1995). *Member:* Chicago Bar Association. ***PRACTICE AREAS:*** Corporate Law; Mergers and Acquisitions; Real Estate. ***Email:*** jfarrell@lplegal.com

MILTON A. LEVENFELD, born Chicago, Illinois, 1927; admitted to bar, 1950, Illinois. *Education:* University of Chicago (Ph.B., 1947; J.D., 1950). Certified Public Accountant, Illinois, 1951. *Member:* Chicago, Illinois State and American Bar Associations. ***PRACTICE AREAS:*** Federal Taxation; International Taxation; Business Planning; Wealth Preservation; Trusts and Estates; Probate. ***Email:*** mlevenfeld@lplegal.com

COUNSEL

G. JOHN BLUMBERG, born Riga, Latvia, May 21, 1937; admitted to bar, 1964, Illinois; 1996, Wisconsin; registered to practice before U.S. Patent and Trademark Office. *Education:* Harvard University (B.A., 1959); Rutgers University (LL.B., 1964). *Member:* State Bar of Wisconsin; American Bar Association; American Intellectual Property Law Association; Chicago Intellectual Property Law Association. (Senior Patent Attorney). ***LANGUAGES:*** Latin and German. ***PRACTICE AREAS:*** Intellectual Property. ***Email:*** jblumberg@lplegal.com

WILLIAM E. LEVIN & ASSOCIATES

200 WEST MADISON STREET, SUITE 710
CHICAGO, ILLINOIS 60606-3412
Telephone: 312-372-6544
Facsimile: 312-372-8456
URL: http://www.lawyers.com/levin&associates
Email: WmELevinChgo@cs.com
URL: http://www.williamelevinlawoffice.com

Federal Taxation, Corporate, Partnerships, Real Estate, Estate Planning, Trusts and Estates, Trials and Appeals.

FIRM PROFILE: William E. Levin has 38 years of experience in his own firm or as an associate or a partner/shareholder of large firms. He has great expertise in representing large and small businesses in sophisticated transactions and dealing with business problems and also in counseling individuals and families in their financial and personal affairs. When multiple lawyers are needed for a project, they are readily available to the firm.

WILLIAM E. LEVIN, born Chicago, Illinois, November 28, 1940; admitted to bar, 1966, Illinois; 1982, U.S. Tax Court. *Education:* Northwestern University (Ph.B., 1965); DePaul University (J.D., 1966); Columbia University (LL.M., 1967). Associate Editor, De Paul Law Review, 1965-1966. Instructor, Business Law, College of Liberal Arts, Jewish University of America, 1965-1966 and 1967-1968. Speaker, Estate Planning Seminars. *Member:* Illinois State and American Bar Associations. ***LANGUAGES:*** Hebrew. ***PRACTICE AREAS:*** Business; Federal Taxation; Corporate; Estate Planning; Probate; Mergers and Acquisitions; Real Estate.

REPRESENTATIVE CLIENTS: Advantage Marketing Associates, Inc.; Bar-Ilan University in Israel; Compus System, S.A.; Chicago Estimating Co., LLC; D. Drew Development, Ltd.; GlobalCom Solutions, Inc.; JRE Management Co.; James Reese Custom Homes, LLC; Miami Free Zone Corp.; North Suburban Cardiology Group, Ltd.; ORIX Real Estate Equities, Inc.; Quantum Cable, Inc.; Reese Development Company; Sluggers World Class Sports Bar, Inc.; TMK Development Ltd.
REFERENCES: Harris Trust and Savings Bank; The Northern Trust Company.

LEVIN & BREND, P.C.

20 N. WACKER DRIVE, SUITE 2920
CHICAGO, ILLINOIS 60606
Telephone: 312-726-4440
Fax: 312-726-0029
URL: http://www.levinbrend.com

Family Law, Complex Domestic Relations Issues, Divorce/Dissolution of Marriage, Financial Discovery, Forensic Accounting and Analysis related to Divorce, Business Valuation as related to Divorce, Tax Considerations related to Divorce, Property Rights, Prenuptial Agreements/ Premarital Agreements, Postnuptial Agreements, Administration, Child Custody and Visitation, Spousal Support/Alimony/Maintenance, Matrimonial Law and Litigation, Marital Settlement Agreements, Separation Agreements, Appeals; Commodities, Real Estate Ventures, Corporate Law.

FIRM PROFILE: Levin & Brend, P.C. is one of a select few matrimonial law firms in Chicago with an emphasis on business valuation and accounting as related to divorce. All partners are attorney/CPA's. In addition, Mr. Brend is the only lawyer in the country affiliated with both the American Academy of Matrimonial Lawyers and the American Society of Appraisers. The firm is listed in the Family Law section of the Bar Register of Preeminent Lawyers.

SANDER D. LEVIN, admitted to bar, 1974, Illinois and U.S. District Court, Northern District of Illinois; 1986, U.S. Tax Court; 1997, U.S. Court of Federal Claims. *Education:* Roosevelt University (B.S.B.A.); Loyola University (J.D.). Certified Public Accountant, Illinois, 1971. *Member:* Chicago and Illinois State Bar Associations; Decalogue Society; Illinois Certified Public Accountant Society; American Association of Attorneys Certified Public Accountants; Business Valuation Association. ***PRACTICE AREAS:*** Taxation; Commodities; Divorce Law; Family Law; Estate Planning. ***Email:*** s.levin@levinbrend.com

JEFFREY W. BREND, born Chicago, Illinois, June 16, 1957; admitted to bar, 1984, Illinois and U.S. District Court, Northern District of Illinois; 1985, U.S. Court of Appeals, Seventh Circuit; 1986, U.S. Tax Court; 1996, U.S. Court of Appeals for the Federal Circuit; 1998, U.S. Supreme Court. *Education:* Northern Illinois University (B.S., 1980); John Marshall Law School (J.D., 1984). Certified Public Accountant, 1985. Adjunct Professor of Law, Chicago-Kent School of Law. *Member:* Chicago (Past President, Matrimonial Law Committee), DuPage County, Illinois State and American Bar Associations; American Society of Appraisers; Illinois Certified Public Accountant Society; Association of Certified Fraud Examiners; American Association of Attorney Certified Public Accountants; Business Valuation Association. Fellow, Academy of Matrimonial Lawyers, 2001. ***PRACTICE AREAS:*** Divorce Law; Taxation Law; Business Litigation; Family Law; Business Valuation; Forensic Accounting. ***Email:*** j.brend@levinbrend.com

GREGORY A. PAPIERNIK, born Chicago, Illinois, May 18, 1958; admitted to bar, 1983, Illinois and U.S. District Court Northern District of Illinois; 1985, U.S. Tax Court. *Education:* University of Notre Dame (B.B.A., 1980); Chicago-Kent College of Law (J.D., with honors, 1983). Beta Alpha Psi. Certified Public Accountant, Indiana, 1982. Adjunct Professor, Lewis University, Romeoville, Illinois. Instructor, Convisor-Duffy CPA Review, Chicago, Illinois. *Member:* Chicago, Illinois State and American Bar Associations; National Academy of Elder Law Attorneys; American Society of Appraisers; Illinois Certified Public Accountant Society; American Association of Attorney Certified Public Accountants. ***PRACTICE AREAS:*** Individual Taxation; Corporate Tax Planning; Business Tax Planning; Estate Planning; Probate Administration; Retirement Planning; Elder Law; Nonprofit Organizations Law. ***Email:*** g.papiernik@levinbrend.com

JENNIFER M. FLETCHALL, born Chicago, Illinois, May 3, 1978; admitted to bar, 2004, Illinois. *Education:* University of Illinois, Champaign (B.S., 2000); John Marshall Law School (J.D., 2004). Moot Court Counsel, Dean's List. Recipient, Deans Scholarship. Co-Author: "Textbook Entitled Accounting for Divorce: Taxes, Business Valuation and Forensic Accounting," 2005; "Trial Issues: National Business Institute Manual Entitled Child Custody and Shared Parenting in Illinois," 2005. *Member:* Chicago, DuPage County, Illinois State and American Bar Associations; American Society of Appraisers; Certified Public Accountant Society; Business Valuation Association. ***PRACTICE AREAS:*** Family Law; Domestic Relations; Tax Law; Business Valuation; Forensic Accounting. ***Email:*** j.fletchall@levinbrend.com

J. DENISE NIEMCZYK, born Springfield, Illinois, October 11, 1976; admitted to bar, 2002, Illinois. *Education:* Bradley University (Psychology, 1998); John Marshall Law School (J.D., 2002). Dean's Scholarship, John Marshall Law School. Co-Author: "The Pro's Guide to Courtroom Presentation," National Certified Fraud Examiners Seminar, July, 2005; "Rights, Roles and Responsibilities of Child Advocates, Published in the DuPage County Brief, July, 2005. *Member:* Chicago, DuPage County and Illinois State Bar Associations. ***PRACTICE AREAS:*** Family Law; Domestic Relations. ***Email:*** j.d.niemczyk@levinandbrend.com

LEGAL SUPPORT PERSONNEL

JOHN M. CHRISTENSEN, born Mason City, Iowa, December 25, 1971. *Education:* University of Iowa (B.B.A., 1994). Certified Public Accountant, Illinois, 1997. *Member:* American Society of Appraisers; Association of Certified Fraud Examiners; Illinois Certified Public Accountant Society; American Institute of Certified Public Accountants; Ohio Society of Certified Public Accountants. (Certified Public Accountant). ***PRACTICE AREAS:*** Business Valuation; Forensic Accounting. ***Email:*** j.christensen@levinbrend.com

TRACY PATTERSON, born Chicago, Illinois, June 9, 1978. *Education:* DePaul University (Early Childhood Education, 2002). Assistant to Jeffery W. Bend, J. Denise Niemczyk and Jennifer M. Fletchall. Court Appointed Special Advocate, Cook County, 2004—. Assistant Kindergarten Teacher, 2002-2003. (Legal Assistant). ***LANGUAGES:*** Spanish. ***Email:*** t.patterson@levinbrend.com

LYDIA L. ROSSI, born Chicago, Illinois. *Education:* Rosevelt University (B.S., Computer, Science, 2004; M.S., Business Administration, Information Systems). Dean's List, 2002-2003. Youth Speaker, Mercy Home for Boys and Girls, Chicago, Illinois, 1999—. Assistant to Sander D. Levin, Jeffery W. Brend, Gregory A. Papiernik and John Christensen, CPA. Accounting Clerk, Lord, Bissell & Brook, LLP, 2001-2004. (IT/Financial Analyst). ***Email:*** l.rossi@levinbrend.com

LEVIN & FUNKHOUSER, LTD.

CHICAGO, ILLINOIS

(See Funkhouser Vegosen Liebman & Dunn Ltd.)

LEVIN GINSBURG

Established in 1979
180 NORTH LASALLE STREET, SUITE 3200
CHICAGO, ILLINOIS 60601-2800
Telephone: 312-368-0100
Fax: 312-368-0111
Email: lg@lgattorneys.com
URL: http://www.lgattorneys.com

Mergers and Acquisitions, Business Litigation, Commercial Litigation, Employment Litigation, Real Estate Litigation, Corporate, Closely Held Business Estate Planning, Closely Held Business Law, Closely Held Corporations, Commercial Real Estate, Construction Contracts, Divestitures, Employment Law, Entrepreneurial Business Law, Estate Planning, Family Business Law, Family Corporations, International Business Law, Landlord and Tenant Law, Probate, Taxation, Transportation, Trusts and Estates and Wills, Tobacco Master Settlement Agreement Expertise, Internet Law, Trademarks, Ownership and Management Succession Planning.

JOSEPH A. GINSBURG, admitted to bar, 1969, Illinois and U.S. District Court, Northern District of Illinois; 1976, Florida; 1986, U.S. Tax Court. *Education:* Roosevelt University (B.S., 1966); DePaul University College of Law (J.D., 1969). Pi Gamma Mu. Member, Board of Directors, Make-A-Wish Foundation of Northern Illinois, 1989—. Member, Union Internationale Des Avocats, 1996—. ***PRACTICE AREAS:*** International Business Law; Business Succession Planning; Business Law; Mergers and Acquisitions; Real Estate; Finance; Litigation; Tobacco Master Settlement Agreement Expertise. ***Email:*** jginsburg@lgattorneys.com

ANNE C. KEAYS, admitted to bar, 1985, Illinois; 1996, U.S. District Court, Northern District of Illinois. *Education:* Clarke College (B.A., 1966); Kellogg Graduate School of Management, Northwestern University (M.M., 1976); IIT/Chicago-Kent College of Law (J.D., 1984). Member, Board of Directors, Heartland International. ***PRACTICE AREAS:*** Computer Law; Information Technology; Internet Law. ***Email:*** ackeays@lgattorneys.com

ROBERT S. LEVIN, admitted to bar, 1966, Illinois; 1971, U.S. Supreme Court; 1986, U.S. Tax Court; U.S. District Court, Northern District of Illinois. *Education:* University of Illinois; DePaul University College of Law (J.D., 1966). ***PRACTICE AREAS:*** Business Law; Mergers and Acquisitions; Real Estate; Finance; Trust Law. ***Email:*** rlevin@lgattorneys.com

LISA ARLYN LOWE, admitted to bar, 1979, Colorado and U.S. District Court, District of Colorado; 1981, New York and U.S. District Court, Southern and Eastern Districts of New York; 1983, U.S. Court of Appeals, Second Circuit; 1985, Illinois and U.S. District Court, Northern District of Illinois; 1994, U.S. Supreme Court. *Education:* University of Florida (B.A., with high honors, 1976); University of Denver (J.D., 1979; M.S.J.A., 1979). Member, Board of Directors and Vice President, Metro Chicago Information Center. Member, Chicago Finance Exchange. ***PRACTICE AREAS:*** Banking; Community Development; Real Estate; Nonprofit and Charitable Organizations; Corporate. ***Email:*** llowe@lgattorneys.com

(This Listing Continued)

LEVIN GINSBURG, Chicago—Continued

MORRIS R. SAUNDERS, admitted to bar, 1979, Illinois and U.S. District Court, Northern District of Illinois; 1979, U.S. Court of Appeals, Seventh Circuit; 1980, U.S. Tax Court. *Education:* University of Virginia (B.A., 1971); John Marshall Law School (J.D., 1979); DePaul University College of Law (LL.M., 1985). ***PRACTICE AREAS:*** Trusts and Estates; Business Law; Corporate Law; Taxation; Real Estate; Closely Held Business Law; Wills; Probate; Mergers and Acquisitions. ***Email:*** msaunders@lgattorneys.com

JONATHAN M. WEIS, admitted to bar, 1996, Illinois and U.S. District Court, Northern District of Illinois; 2000, Trial Bar, U.S. District Court, Northern District of Illinois. *Education:* Cornell University (B.A., 1992); University of Illinois (J.D., cum laude, 1996). Member, Cornell University Tower Club Committee. *Member:* Chicago Bar Association (Chair, Civil Practice and Procedure Section). ***PRACTICE AREAS:*** Commercial Litigation; Business Torts; Employment Litigation; Real Estate Litigation; Construction Litigation; Landlord and Tenant Law; Debtor and Creditor Workouts; Telecommunications Competition; Tobacco Master Settlement Agreement Expertise. ***Email:*** jweis@lgattorneys.com

---

KEITH SHAYLAN BALDWIN, born Watseka, Illinois, June 4, 1973; admitted to bar, 2001, Illinois. *Education:* DePaul University (B.A., with honors, 1997); Loyola University Chicago School of Law (J.D., 2000). ***PRACTICE AREAS:*** Commercial Real Estate; Corporate Law; Business Law.

SASKIA NORA BRYAN, admitted to bar, 1998, Illinois and U.S. District Court, Northern District of Illinois. *Education:* University of North Carolina at Asheville (B.A., 1995); Northwestern University (J.D., 1998). ***LANGUAGES:*** Dutch. ***PRACTICE AREAS:*** Commercial Litigation; Employment Litigation. ***Email:*** sbryan@lgattorneys.com

JOSH S. KAPLAN, born Edina, Minnesota, February 21, 1976; admitted to bar, 2002, Illinois. *Education:* University of Wisconsin-Madison (B.A., History and Political Science, 1998); Chicago-Kent College of Law (J.D., 2002). Intellectual Property Certificate. *Member:* Chicago (Chair, Athletic Committee; Member, Judicial Evaluation Committee, 2004—) Bar Associations. ***PRACTICE AREAS:*** Commercial Litigation; Corporate; Transactional. ***Email:*** jkaplan@lgattorneys.com

ROBERT S. STRAUSS, born Chicago, Illinois, January 31, 1972; admitted to bar, 2000, Illinois and U.S. District Court, Northern District of Illinois. *Education:* University of Illinois (B.S., 1997); Chicago-Kent College of Law (J.D., with honors, 2000). Recipient, Chicago Kent Academic Excellence Scholarship. Judicial Clerk to, Hon. Robert V. Boharic, 2000-2002. Teaching Assistant, Civil Practice, for Professor Molly Lienart, Chicago Kent College of Law. *Member:* Chicago, Illinois State and American Bar Associations. ***PRACTICE AREAS:*** Commercial Litigation; Real Estate Litigation; Covenants Not To Compete; Employment Litigation. ***Email:*** rstrauss@lgattorneys.com

---

LEVIN & PERCONTI

325 NORTH LASALLE STREET
SUITE 450
CHICAGO, ILLINOIS 60610
Telephone: 312-332-2872
Fax: 312-332-3112
URL: http://www.levinperconti.com

Catastrophic personal injury, wrongful death, personal injury, medical malpractice including birth injuries, cancer, AIDS, failure to diagnose or misdiagnosis, obstetric, surgical, cardiac, orthopedic and nursing malpractice. Nursing home abuse and neglect including bedsores, malnutrition, dehydration, wandering, falls, fractures, physical, verbal and sexual abuse and assault, restraints, medication errors and burns. Aviation, defective products, defective drugs, attorney malpractice, airplane crashes, automobile, construction, workplace, commercial litigation, Federal Tort Claims Act and insurance.

FIRM PROFILE: Steven M. Levin and John J. Perconti founded the personal injury firm of Levin & Perconti in 1992. For over 10 years, the firm has worked to establish a national reputation for its representation of catastrophically injured clients and the families of those wrongfully killed. Levin & Perconti has grown to 8 attorneys, who combined represent over 125 years of experience as trial lawyers. In addition to its lawyers, the firm has a veteran staff of secretaries, paralegals and case support personnel skilled in serving the needs of the firm's clients. In addition to our lawyers and support staff, the firm has an established network of investigators, physicians, nurses, and experts to help us investigate and prosecute cases.

The firm has achieved numerous multi-million dollar verdicts and settlements for its clients and for the families of its clients. The firm has handled virtually every type of catastrophic personal injury or wrongful death type action. A significant portion of the firm's clients are referred by other lawyers who choose our firm to represent its clients because of our record of success.

In the area of medical malpractice, the firm has achieved notable victories in cases involving shoulder dystocia, cerebral palsy, cancer, prenatal HIV screening, improper postpartum care, defective drugs and pharmaceutical products, obstetric, surgical, cardiac, orthopedic, nursing and failure to diagnose or misdiagnose malpractice.

The firm is nationally recognized as a pioneer in litigating nursing home abuse, neglect and fraud. The firm is committed to improving the quality of nursing home care through litigation and this has resulted in the firm achieving substantial verdicts and settlements as well as in the implementation of significant remedial measures designed to protect nursing home residents form future harm. The firm understands that protecting one's rights is one of a families' most important responsibilities. Just as significant, the firm also understands the law. The firm is highly experienced in nursing home abuse and neglect litigation, working with outside consultants and industry insiders. The firm has mastered the intricacies of this extremely important and relatively new area of law and has the knowledge, experience and passion to hold nursing homes accountable for substandard care and conduct.

MEMBERS OF FIRM

STEVEN M. LEVIN, born Chicago, Illinois, February 9, 1951; admitted to bar, 1976, Illinois and U.S. District Court, Northern District of Illinois; U.S. Court of Appeals, Seventh Circuit. *Education:* University of Wisconsin-Madison (B.A., cum laude, 1973); Loyola University, Chicago Law School (J.D., cum laude, 1976). Recipient, Thomas Owens Award for Highest GPA. Lead Article Editor, Loyola University Law Review, 1976. *Member:* Chicago, Illinois State and American (Vice Chair, Medicine and Law Committee, Tort and Insurance Practice Section) Bar Associations; The Association of Trial Lawyers of America (Co-Chair, Nursing Home Litigation Group; Member, Birth Injury Litigation Group); Illinois Trial Lawyers Association: Decalogue Society; National Citizens Coalition for Nursing Home Reform and its "Committee of 20"; Advisory Committee of Illinois Citizens for Better Care: National Association of Elder Law Attorneys; City of Chicago Committee on Nursing Homes; Chicago Department of Aging Ombudsman Advisory Counsel; Board of Advisors for the Nursing Home Litigation Reporter; American Trial Lawyers Association Birth Injury Litigation Group; Member and Chairman Highland Park Zoning Board of Appeals; Ad Hoc Committee on Amusement Tax and Ravinia Park. ***PRACTICE AREAS:*** Catastrophic Personal Injury; Wrongful Death; Personal Injury; Medical Malpractice; Birth Injuries; Cancer; AIDS; Failure to diagnose or misdiagnosis; Obstetric; Surgical; Cardiac; Orthopedic and nursing malpractice; Nursing Home Abuse and Neglect including bedsores; Malnutrition; Dehydration; Wandering; Falls; Fractures; Physical, verbal and sexual abuse and assault; Restraints; Medication errors and burns; Aviation; Defective products; Defective drugs; Attorney malpractice; Airplane Crashes; Automobile; Construction; Work place; Commercial Litigation; Federal Tort Claims Act and insurance. ***Email:*** Sml@levinperconti.com

JOHN J. PERCONTI, born Chicago, Illinois, June 28, 1957; admitted to bar, 1982, Illinois and U.S. District Court, Northern District of Illinois. *Education:* University of Illinois (B.A., 1979); John Marshall Law School (J.D., 1982). *Member:* Chicago (Member, Federal Expert Witness Practice, November 1, 2000) and Illinois State Bar Associations; Illinois Trial Lawyers Association (Member, Medical Negligence Committee); American Trial Lawyers Association (Member, National College of Advocacy, Litigating Rezulin Cases); Society of Trial Lawyers; Justinian Society of Lawyers (Member, DuPage and Cook County Chapters). ***PRACTICE AREAS:*** Catastrophic Injury; Personal Injury; Wrongful Death; Medical Malpractice; Birth Injuries; Cancer; AIDS Litigation; Failure to Diagnose; Misdiagnosis; Obstetric Malpractice; Surgical; Cardiac; Orthopedic Malpractice; Nursing Malpractice; Nursing Home Abuse and Neglect; Bedsores; Malnutrition; Dehydration; Slip and Fall; Wandering; Fractures; Physical Abuse; Verbal Abuse; Sexual Abuse; Sexual Assault; Restraints; Medication Errors; Burns; Aviation Law; Product Defects; Defective Drugs; Attorney Malpractice; Airplane Crash Litigation; Automobile Accidents and Injuries; Construction Law; Work Place; Commercial Litigation; Federal Tort Claims; Insurance. ***Email:*** Jjp@levinperconti.com

SUSAN LEVIN NOVOSAD, born Chicago, Illinois, October 31, 1956; admitted to bar, 1986, Illinois and U.S. District Court, Northern District of Illinois; U.S. Supreme Court. *Education:* University of Illinois (B.S., 1978); John Marshall Law School (J.D., with distinction, 1986). Partner: Levin & Perconti, Chicago, Illinois. ***PRACTICE AREAS:*** Medical Malpractice; Legal Malpractice; Nursing Home Abuse and Neglect; Automobile Accidents; Truck Accidents; Airplane Accidents; Defective Products and Drugs; Slip and Fall. ***Email:*** Sln@levinperconti.com

MARY ELLEN CAGNEY, admitted to bar, 1976, Illinois and U.S. District Court, Northern District of Illinois; 1995, U.S. Supreme Court. *Education:* Newton College of the Sacred Heart, now Boston College (B.A., cum laude, 1972); DePaul University (J.D., cum laude, 1976). Recipient: Midwest Women's Center Tribute to Chicago Women, 1992; DePaul University Outstanding Service to the Legal Profession, 2002. Member: Children's Home and Aid Society of Illinois, Woman's Board, 2000— and Third Vice President, 2001-2003; DePaul Alumni Board, 1996— and President, 1997-1998. Cook County State's Attorney's Office, 1977-1996, Chief Deputy State's Attorney, 1991-1996. *Member:* Chicago (Elected Member, Board of Managers, 1995-1997; Chair: Judicial Evaluation Committee, (JEC) 1995, Hearing Division of JEC, 1994 and Investigation Division of JEC, 1993); Illinois State and American Bar Associations; Illinois Trial Lawyers Association; Women's Bar Association of Illinois. ***PRACTICE AREAS:*** Medical Malpractice; Legal Malpractice; Nursing Home Abuse and Neglect; Automobile Accidents; Truck Accidents; Airplane Crash Litigation; Defective Products and Drugs; Slip and Fall. ***Email:*** Mec@levinperconti.com

ASSOCIATES

JEFFREY E. MARTIN, born Chicago, Illinois, September 25, 1956; admitted to bar, 1982, Illinois and U.S. District Court, Northern District of Illinois. *Education:* North Park College (B.A., magna cum laude, 1978); Loyola University (J.D., 1982). Delta Mu Delta. Recipient, Louis Kokoris Memorial Scholarship in Political Science and Law, 1977. Member: Village of Arlington Heights, Illinois Plan Commission, 1989-1995; Chairman, Ordinance Review Subcommittee, 1992-1995; Institutional Review Board, Children's Memorial Hospital, 1995-1997. *Member:* Chicago, Illinois State and American Bar Associations; Illinois Trial Lawyers Association; The Association of Trial Lawyers of America. ***PRACTICE AREAS:*** Medical Malpractice; Legal Malpractice; Nursing Home Abuse and Neglect; Automobile Accidents; Truck Accidents; Airplane Crash Litigation; Defective Products and Drugs; Slip and Fall. ***Email:*** Jem@levinperconti.com

LAWRENCE B. FINN, born Miami Beach, Florida, October 25, 1961; admitted to bar, 1987, New Jersey; U.S. District Court, District of New Jersey; 1988, U.S. Court of Appeals, Third Circuit; 1989, Illinois and U.S. District Court, Northern District of Illinois including Trial Bar; 1990, U.S. Court of Appeals, Seventh Circuit; 1997, Michigan and U.S. District Court, Eastern District of Michigan; U.S. District Court, Central District of Illinois; 2000, U.S. Court of Appeals, Sixth Circuit. *Education:* Drew University (B.A., cum laude, 1983); Washington University (J.D., 1986). Law Clerk: to the Honorable Theodore J. McMillan, U.S. Court of Appeals, Eighth Circuit, 1985; the Honorable Roy W. Harper. *Member:* State

(This Listing Continued)

Bar of Michigan; American (Member, Sections on: Health Law; Tort Trial; Insurance; Member, Toxic and Hazardous Substances and Environmental Committee (Vice Chair, 1992-1994); Medicine and Law Committee, Litigation Committee) Bar Association; Defense Research Institute; International Association of Defense Counsel; Professional Liability Underwriter's Association; American College of Legal Medicine; American Health Lawyers Association; American Trial Lawyers Association (Member, Sections on: Product Liability; Toxic, Environmental and Pharmaceutical Torts). ***PRACTICE AREAS:*** Medical Malpractice; Legal Malpractice; Nursing Home Abuse and Neglect; Automobile Accidents; Truck Accidents; Airplane Crash Litigation; Product Defects; Slip and Fall. ***Email:*** lbf@levinperconti.com

ANNA POLYAK, born Belorussia, November 14, 1975; admitted to bar, 2004, Illinois. *Education:* Loyola University (B.S., 1999; J.D., 2003). *Member:* Illinois Womens Bar Association; Decalogue Society of Lawyers. ***LANGUAGES:*** Russian. ***PRACTICE AREAS:*** Medical Malpractice; Legal Malpractice; Nursing Home Abuse and Neglect; Automobile Accidents; Truck Accidents; Airplane Crash Litigation; Product Defects; Slip and Fall. ***Email:*** abp@levinperconti.com

STEPHEN J. COUKOS, born Indianapolis, April 24, 1970; admitted to bar, 1995, Florida; 1998, Illinois; 2001, U.S. District Court, Northern District of Indiana 2004, U.S. District Court, Northern District of Illinois. *Education:* Brown University (B.A., 1992); Indiana University School of Law (J.D., 1995). Former Associate, Maurides & Foley, LLC. Assistant State Attorney, Fort Meyers, Florida, 1995-2000. *Member:* Chicago, Hellenic and Illinois State Bar Associations; Illinois Trial Lawyers Association; Hellenic Bar Association. ***PRACTICE AREAS:*** Medical Malpractice; Legal Malpractice; Nursing Home Abuse and Neglect; Automobile Accidents; Truck Accidents; Airplane Crash Litigation; Product Defects; Drugs and Narcotics; Slip and Fall. ***Email:*** sjc@levinperconti.com

LEVIN, RIBACK LAW GROUP P.C.

Established in 1953

(Formerly Pekin & Levin & Associates)

200 NORTH LASALLE STREET, SUITE 2300
CHICAGO, ILLINOIS 60601
Telephone: 312-782-6717
Fax: 312-782-5128
URL: http://www.levinriback.com
Email: info@levinriback.com
URL: http://www.personalinjurylawyer1.com

Personal Injury, Catastrophic Injuries, Construction Accidents, Brain Injury, Spinal Cord Injury, Mild Head Injury, Premises Liability, Product Liability, Lasik Surgery, Medical Malpractice, Obstetric Malpractice, Reflex Sympathetic Dystrophy, Neurological Injuries, Automobile Accidents, Truck Accidents, Wrongful Death, Construction Site Safety, OSHA, Unsafe Job Conditions, Workers Compensation, Disability, Dog Bites, FELA, Railroad Accidents, Psychological Injury, Sever Burns and Birth Trauma.

FIRM PROFILE: Levin, Riback Law Group has a family history in Chicago dating back to 1953. The original firm, Pekin, Levin & Associates, was established in 1953 by Ralph L. Levin. As this family-run firm commemorates 50 years of service in the Chicago area, it continues to provide quality legal support and counsel to its clients. The reputation of attorneys at the Levin, Riback Law Group for thorough preparation is widely recognized and respected in the community. Founded on the belief that the team approach is the best, Levin. Riback Law Group successfully conducts investigation, research, discovery and trial - working together to achieve the most advantageous client outcome. Today, partners Rick and Steve Levin and Adam Riback bring diligence and dedication to the firm's tradition and experience, with record-setting results.

The Firm's practice is focused entirely on plaintiff personal injury and medical malpractice, including catastrophic accidents, automobile accidents, trucking accidents and medical and surgical malpractice.

RICHARD I. LEVIN, born Chicago, Illinois, December 3, 1960; admitted to bar, 1986, Illinois. *Education:* University of Wisconsin-Madison (B.B.A., Insurance and Real Estate, 1983); Illinois Institute of Technology, Chicago-Kent College of Law (J.D., 1986). Author: Contributed to *Chicago Bar Association Journal*; *Chicago Daily Law Bulletin*; *Chicago Bar Association Record*; chapter, "Uninsured and Underinsured Motorist Coverage in Illinois," *Automobile Handbook,* Illinois Trial Lawyers Association. Speaker, "Illinois Supreme Court Rule 213," Illinois Trial Lawyers Association, September 2001. Adjunct Professor, Northwestern University School of Law (Voted Northwestern University's Most Outstanding Adjunct, 1999-2000, 2000-2001, 2001-2002, 2002-2003); Instructor, National Institute for Trial Advocacy (NITA), Northwestern University Law School, Indiana University Law School and Colorado University Law School; Instructor, Northwestern's Undergraduate Mock Trial Institute; Instructor, Federal Trial Bar, 1998-1999; Adjunct Lecturer, Evidence and Trial Advocacy, De Paul University School of Law. Selected one of "40 Illinois Attorneys Under 40 to Watch," Chicago Daily Law Bulletin, 2000. Illinois Super Lawyer, Loyola NITA 2003, 2004, 2005. Leading Lawyers, NITA Boston, 2003, 2004, 2005. Listed, Top 5% of Illinois Lawyers, Leading Lawyers Network, 2003. NITA Team Leader: Trial Program for Midwest Regional, Loyola University Law School, 2002; Deposition Program for Midwest Regional, Loyola University Law School, 2003, 2004; Deposition Program for Eastern Regional, Rutgers Law School, 2001; *Member:* Chicago (Co-Chairman, Trial Techniques Division, 1995-1996 and 1996-1997) and Illinois State Bar Associations; The Association of Trial Lawyers of America; Illinois Trial Lawyers Association. ***PRACTICE AREAS:*** Personal Injury; Construction Accidents; Product Liability; Premises Liability; Medical Malpractice; Workers Compensation; Automobile Accidents; Catastrophic Injuries; Wrongful Death. ***Email:*** rlevin@levinriback.com

STEVEN R. LEVIN, born Chicago, Illinois, April 1, 1957; admitted to bar, 1981, Illinois; 1982, Florida and U.S. Court of Appeals, Seventh Circuit; U.S. District Court, Northern District of Illinois including Trial Bar. *Education:* Tulane University (B.A., 1979; J.D., 1981). *Member:* Illinois State Bar Association; The Florida Bar; Illinois Trial Lawyers Association (Member, Committee on Membership). ***PRACTICE AREAS:*** Personal Injury; Construction Accidents; Product Liability; Premises Liability; Medical Malpractice; Workers Compensation; Automobile Accidents; Catastrophic Injuries. ***Email:*** slevin@levinriback.com

ADAM RIBACK, admitted to bar, 1994, Illinois. *Education:* University of Illinois (B.A., 1990); Illinois Kent College of Law (J.D., 1994). Member, Moot Court Society, 1992-1994. Semi-Finalist, Jerome Prince Evidence Moot Court Competition, 1993. DePaul University Moot Court Coach, 1999. Instructor, Northwestern Undergraduate Mock Trial Institute. Selected: "40 Illinois Attorneys Under 40 to Watch," 2005. Adjunct Professor, Northwestern University. ***PRACTICE AREAS:*** Personal Injury; Construction Accidents; Product Liability; Premises Liability; Medical Malpractice; Workers Compensation; Automobile Accidents; Catastrophic Injuries. ***Email:*** ariback@levinriback.com

AMY R. PERLMAN, born Chicago, Illinois, September 1, 1958; admitted to bar, 1983, Illinois, U.S. District Court, Northern District of Illinois and U.S. Court of Appeals, Seventh Circuit. *Education:* Indiana University (B.A., 1980); DePaul University (J.D., 1983). Co-Author: "Transportation Negligence, Ch. 12. Comparative Negligence and Third Party Actions," IICLE, 1984, 1985. *Member:* Chicago, Illinois State and American Bar Associations; Illinois Trial Lawyers Association; The Association of Trial Lawyers of America. ***PRACTICE AREAS:*** Personal Injury; Construction Accidents; Product Liability; Premises Liability; Medical Malpractice; Workers Compensation; Automobile Accidents; Catastrophic Injuries. ***Email:*** aperlman@levinriback.com

ROBERT J. ADELMAN, admitted to bar, 1999, Illinois and U.S. District Court, Northern District of Illinois. *Education:* University of Wisconsin-Madison (B.A., 1996); DePaul University College of Law (J.D., 1999). Member, Moot Court Society. Editor, DePaul Art and Entertainment Journal. National Champion and Best Brief, Saul Lefkowitz Brand Names Intellectual Property Moor Court Competition, 1998. Best Oralist, Saul Lefkowitz Competition. Author: "Has Time Run Out for the NCAA? An Analysis of the NCAA as a Place of Public Accommodation." Coach, DePaul Moot Court Team, 2000. ***PRACTICE AREAS:*** Personal Injury; Construction Accidents; Product Liability; Premises Liability; Workers Compensation; Automobile Accidents; Catastrophic Injuries. ***Email:*** radelman@levinriback.com

ROBERT J. DOMOL, born June 7, 1979; admitted to bar, 2004, Illinois. *Education:* Michigan State University (B.A., 2001); DePaul University College of Law (J.D., 2004). ***PRACTICE AREAS:*** Automobile Negligence; Premises Liability; Products Liability; Personal Injury; Automobile Accidents; Wrongful Death.

OF COUNSEL

ARAM A. HARTUNIAN, born Chicago, Illinois, December 29, 1932; admitted to bar, 1955, Illinois; 1958, U.S. District Court, Northern District of Illinois; 1974, U.S. Court of Appeals, Seventh Circuit; 1976, California, U.S. Supreme Court and U.S. Court of Appeals for the District of Columbia and Tenth Circuits; 1978, U.S. Court of Appeals, Eighth Circuit; 1980, U.S. Court of Appeals, Fifth Circuit. *Education:* University of Illinois; DePaul University (LL.B., 1954). Instructor, Loyola University College of Law, 1982-1983. *Member:* Chicago and American (Member, Litigation, Antitrust Section) Bar Associations; Chicago Council of Lawyers; American Judicature Society. (Also practicing individually). ***LANGUAGES:*** Italian. ***REPORTED CASES:*** Amer. Natl. Bk. & Trust Co. vs. Haroco, Inc., 473 U.S. 606 (1985); Zipes vs. Trans World Airlines, 455 U.S. 385 (1982); Metropolitan Sanitary District vs. Ingram Corp. 85 Ill. 2d 458 (1981). ***Email:*** argo@enteract.com

RALPH L. LEVIN, born 1930; admitted to bar, 1953, Illinois. *Education:* University of Illinois; DePaul University.

LEVIN & SCHREDER, LTD

120 NORTH LA SALLE STREET, SUITE 3800
CHICAGO, ILLINOIS 60602
Telephone: 312-332-6300
Fax: 312-332-6393
Email: taxes@levinschreder.com
URL: http://www.levinschreder.com

Evanston, Illinois Office: 500 Davis Street, Suite 812, 60612-4269. Telephone: 847-492-5200. Fax: 847-492-9650.

Federal and International Income Tax Matters, Estate Planning, Family Wealth Counseling, Probate, Trust Administration, Probate and Trust Litigation and Contested Tax Matters.

ROBERT M. LEVIN, admitted to bar, 1967, Illinois. *Education:* Massachusetts Institute of Technology (B.S., 1963); Northwestern University (M.A., 1965); University of Chicago (J.D., 1967). ***PRACTICE AREAS:*** Federal Income Tax; International Taxation; Estate Planning; Estate Administration; Family Wealth Counseling. ***Email:*** bob@levinschreder.com

CARLEEN L. SCHREDER, admitted to bar, 1982, Illinois. *Education:* Lake Forest College (B.A., with honors, 1979); University of Chicago (J.D., 1982). Phi Beta Kappa. ***PRACTICE AREAS:*** Estate Planning; Estate Administration; Federal Income Tax; International Taxation; Family Wealth Counseling. ***Email:*** carleen@levinschreder.com

JAMES R. CAREY, admitted to bar, 1989, Illinois. *Education:* Marquette University (B.A., 1986); Loyola University of Chicago (J.D, 1989). ***PRACTICE AREAS:*** Contested Trusts and Estates; Guardianship; Estate Planning; Estate Administration; Probate. ***Email:*** jim@levinschreder.com

STUART J. KOHN, admitted to bar, 1987, Illinois. *Education:* University of Michigan (B.B.A., 1984); Loyola University of Chicago (J.D., 1987). ***PRACTICE AREAS:*** Estate Planning; Estate Administration; Family Wealth Counseling; Federal Income Tax. ***Email:*** stuart@levinschreder.com

MARGOT GORDON, admitted to bar, 1989, Illinois. *Education:* University of California at San Diego (B.A., 1985); University of Chicago (J.D., 1988). ***PRACTICE AREAS:*** Estate Planning; Estate Administration; Contested Trusts and Estates. ***Email:*** margot@levinschreder.com

(This Listing Continued)

(This Listing Continued)

LEVIN & SCHREDER, LTD, Chicago—Continued

THEODORE E. FROUM, admitted to bar, 1998, Illinois; 1999, Michigan and Florida. *Education:* Brandeis University (B.A., cum laude, 1994); Benjamin N. Cardozo School of Law (J.D., 1998); New York University (LL.M., Taxation, 1998). ***PRACTICE AREAS:*** Federal Income Tax; Estate Planning; Estate Administration; Contested Trusts and Estates. ***Email:*** ted@levinschreder.com

JULIE J. OLENN, admitted to bar, 2002, Illinois. *Education:* St. John's College (B.A., 1994); State University of New York College at Buffalo (J.D., magna cum laude, 2002). ***PRACTICE AREAS:*** Estate Planning; Estate Administration; Federal Income Tax. ***Email:*** julie@levinschreder.com

OF COUNSEL

DANIEL G. CEDARBAUM, admitted to bar, 1984, Illinois. *Education:* Harvard University (A.B., 1980; J.D., 1983). Law Clerk to Hon. Paul E. Plunkett, U.S. District Court, Northern District of Illinois, 1983-1985. *Member:* Chicago Bar Association. (Resident, Evanston Office). ***PRACTICE AREAS:*** Estate Planning; International Taxation; International Estate Planning. ***Email:*** dan@levinschreder.com

LAW OFFICES OF JEFFERY M. LEVING, LTD.

A PROFESSIONAL CORPORATION

19 SOUTH LA SALLE STREET, SUITE 450
CHICAGO, ILLINOIS 60603
Telephone: 312-807-3990
Fax: 312-807-4782
URL: http://www.dadsrights.com
Email: pr@dadsrights.com
URL: http://www.lawyers.com/Jeffery_Leving

Family Law, Matrimonial Litigation, Sophisticated Financial Discovery and Analysis, Tax Considerations and Retirement Benefits, Negotiation and Mediation, Father's Custody and Visitation Trials and Appeals. Interstate and Intrastate Litigation, International Child Abduction Cases.

FIRM PROFILE: The Law Offices of Jeffery M. Leving, Ltd., devotes its practice to matrimonial, paternity and custody law representing primarily fathers. The firm was founded in 1981 by Jeffery M. Leving who is a national litigator/consultant and co-author of the Illinois Joint Custody Law. All firm members are also expert litigators. ¶Leving was the Chicago attorney from the Elian Gonzalez case. He represented Manuel Gonzalez at Juan Miguel's request, to be designated as Elian's care giver in the early stages of the federal case. Leving was invited as an expert on CNN, CNBC, MSNBC, Fox National News and Court TV to analyze the Elian Gonzalez case.

JEFFERY M. LEVING, born Chicago, Illinois, July 2, 1951; admitted to bar, 1979, Illinois and U.S. District Court, Northern District of Illinois; 1980, U.S. Court of Appeals, Seventh Circuit and U.S. Supreme Court. *Education:* Southern Illinois University (B.S., 1974); Illinois Institute of Technology (J.D., 1979). Author: "Men Also Victims of Domestic Violence," Chicago Tribune, Nov. 2, 1993; Ground Breaking Book: "Fathers' Rights," (Basics Books), 1997. Co-Author: "The Father's Custody Case," Trial Magazine, January, 1999. Lecturer, Association of Trial Lawyers of America, July 18, 1995 and August 2, 2000. Testified before U.S. Commission on Child & Family Welfare (1995); Illinois Senate Committee on Divorce Law & Procedure (1996). *Member:* Chicago (Member, Matrimonial Law Committee) and Illinois State Bar Associations; The Association of Trial Lawyers of America; The Decalogue Society of Lawyers; Congressional Task Force on Fathers, Families and Public Policy. ***PRACTICE AREAS:*** Fathers' Custody Rights; Matrimonial Law; Family Law; Paternity Law; Divorce; Child Custody; Child Sexual Abuse; Visitation Rights; International Child Abduction. ***Email:*** pr@dadsrights.com

LEVUN, GOODMAN & COHEN, LLP

Comprised of Professional Corporations

ONE NORTH LA SALLE STREET
SUITE 1920
CHICAGO, ILLINOIS 60602
Telephone: 312-263-4661
Email: lgc@lgclaw.com
URL: http://www.lgclaw.com

Northbrook, Illinois Office: 500 Skokie Boulevard, Suite 650. Telephone: 847-509-7700. Fax: 847-509-7709.

General Business and Tax Practice including Federal and State Taxation, Corporate Law, Partnership Law, Employee Benefits and Executive Compensation, Real Estate, Estate Planning, Trust Administration, and Commercial Litigation.

(For complete biographical data on all personnel, see Professional Biographies at Northbrook, Illinois)

S. JEROME LEVY & ASSOCIATES, P.C.

Established in 1980

ONE EAST WACKER DRIVE, SUITE 2500
CHICAGO, ILLINOIS 60601
Telephone: 312-832-1616
FAX: 312-832-0270
URL: http://www.jeromelevylaw.com

Practice limited to Litigation including Plaintiff's Personal Injury, Wrongful Death, Medical and Dental Malpractice, Products Liability, Premises Liability, Commercial and Private Aviation Litigation, Chemical Exposure, Torts, Injuries, Insurance, Income Tax, Tax Planning.

(This Listing Continued)

S. JEROME LEVY, born Chicago, Illinois, May 14, 1930; admitted to bar, 1954, Illinois. *Education:* Grinnell College and Northwestern University (B.S.L., 1952); Northwestern University (B.L., 1954). Member, Board of Editors, Northwestern University Law Review, 1953-1954. Law Clerk to Judge Luther Swygert, U.S. Court of Appeals, 7th Circuit, 1954-1955. *Member:* Chicago, Illinois State and American Bar Associations. ***PRACTICE AREAS:*** Plaintiffs Personal Injury; Wrongful Death; Medical Malpractice; Medical Liability; Birth Trauma; Dental Malpractice; Products Liability; Chemical Exposure; Toxic Exposure; Automobile Accidents and Injuries; Airplane Crash Litigation; Aviation Accidents; Aviation Litigation; Torts. ***Email:*** sjlevy@jeromelevylaw.com

KARIN A. OLSON, born Chicago, Illinois, April 9, 1960; admitted to bar, 1990, Illinois and U.S. District Court, Northern District of Illinois. *Education:* DePaul University (B.A., 1982; J.D., 1990); Columbia College (M.A., 1987). Case Editor and Contributing Editor, Journal of Health and Hospital Law, 1989-1990. *Member:* Chicago, Illinois State and American Bar Associations; Association of Trial Lawyers of America; Illinois Trial Lawyers Association. ***PRACTICE AREAS:*** Plaintiffs Personal Injury; Wrongful Death; Medical Malpractice; Birth Trauma; Obstetric Malpractice; Dental Malpractice; Health Care; Accidents; Bodily Injury; Brain Injury; Products Liability; Premises Liability; Automobile Accidents and Injuries; Automobile Liability; Bicycle Accidents; Insurance Litigation; Slip and Fall; Torts. ***Email:*** kaolson@jeromelevylaw.com

OF COUNSEL

LESLIE A. STULBERG, born Kalamazoo, Michigan; admitted to bar, 1978, Illinois. *Education:* University of Michigan (B.A., 1966; M.A., 1967) Phi Beta Kappa; University of Chicago (J.D., 1978). Candidate in Philosophy, University of Michigan, 1970. *Member:* Chicago, Illinois State and American Bar Associations. ***LANGUAGES:*** French. ***PRACTICE AREAS:*** Income Tax; Federal Income Tax; Tax Planning. ***Email:*** lastulberg@jeromelevylaw.com

BARRY MICHAEL LEWIS

211 EAST ONTARIO STREET
SUITE 1800
CHICAGO, ILLINOIS 60611
Telephone: 312-372-2221
Fax: 312-377-1771
Email: blewislaw@aol.com
URL: http://www.barrylewislaw.com

Personal Injury, Medical Malpractice, Product Liability, Criminal, DUI, DWI, Traffic Violations, Felonies, Serious Misdemeanors, Drug Cases.

BARRY MICHAEL LEWIS, born Chicago, Illinois, 1950; admitted to bar, 1975, Illinois. *Education:* Northwestern University (B.A., 1972); John Marshall Law School (J.D., 1975). *Member:* Chicago Bar Association. ***PRACTICE AREAS:*** Criminal Law; Driving While Intoxicated; Drug Crimes; Felonies; Homicide; Murder; Manslaughter; Juvenile Law; Misdemeanors; Parole and Probation; Sexual Assault; Traffic Violations; Personal Injury; Airplane Crash Litigation; Automobile Accidents; Railroad Accidents; Truck Accidents; Sexual Abuse; Wrongful Death; Automotive Products Liability.

LEWIS, OVERBECK & FURMAN, LLP

Established in 1944

135 SOUTH LA SALLE STREET, SUITE 2300
CHICAGO, ILLINOIS 60603-4274
Telephone: 312-580-1200
Fax: 312-580-1201
Email: Firm@LEWISOVERBECK.COM
URL: http://www.lewisoverbeck.com

ERISA, Employee Benefits, Pension and Profit Sharing Plans, Apprenticeship Programs, Labor, State and Federal Courts Trials and Appeals, ERISA Litigation, Corporate, Federal and State Taxation, Business, Estate Planning, Real Estate, Trusts, Probate.

FIRM PROFILE: Since our establishment in 1944, our client base has grown to include privately-owned businesses and publicly-traded corporations, proprietorships and partnerships, trade associations and other not-for-profit organizations, pension and profit sharing plans, Taft-Hartley pension, welfare, apprenticeship and legal service trust funds and other types of trusts. Additionally, the firm represents many clients in service industries such as public relations, insurance, health care providers, real estate, energy and transportation.

MEMBERS OF FIRM

DAVID J. CREAGAN, JR., born Buffalo, New York, October 25, 1928; admitted to bar, 1953, Illinois. *Education:* Loyola University, Chicago (LL.B., 1953). Phi Alpha Delta. *Member:* Chicago (Member, Committee on Federal Taxation, 1966-1974) and American Bar Associations. [J.A.G. Army, 1954-1956]. ***Email:*** DCreagan@lewisoverbeck.com

TIM J. EMMITT, born Goshen, Indiana, May 13, 1940; admitted to bar, 1965, Illinois. *Education:* Wabash College (B.A., summa cum laude, 1962); University of Chicago (J.D., 1965). Phi Beta Kappa. *Member:* Chicago (Member, 1966— and Chair, 1989-1990, Probate Practice Committee; Member, 1987— and Chair, 1996-1997, Financial and Investment Services Committee), Illinois State and American Bar Associations; American College of Trust and Estate Counsel. ***Email:*** TEmmitt@lewisoverbeck.com

JAMES R. GANNON, born Detroit, Michigan, February 20, 1928; admitted to bar, 1958, Michigan; 1967, Illinois. *Education:* University of Detroit (Ph.B., 1955; M.B.A., 1968; LL.B., 1957). Delta Theta Phi. Member, Panel of Arbitrators, American Arbitration Association. *Member:* Chicago (Member, Civil Practice Committee, 1972-1984; Member, 1972-1998 and Chair, 1976-1977, Circuit Court Committee), Illinois State and American

(This Listing Continued)

Bar Associations; State Bar of Michigan; Illinois Defense Counsel; National Association of Railroad Trial Counsel; Conference of Freight Counsel; The Society of Trial Lawyers. **Email:** JGannon@lewisoverbeck.com

ROBERT A. SUBKOWSKY, born Troy, New York, November 16, 1949; admitted to bar, 1974, Illinois. *Education:* University of Connecticut (B.A. with honors, 1971); Northwestern University (J.D., cum laude, 1974). Phi Beta Kappa; Order of the Coif. *Member:* Chicago (Member, Corporation Law Committee, 1978—) and American Bar Associations; International Foundation of Employee Benefit Plans. **Email:** RSubkowsky@lewisoverbeck.com

DOUGLAS A. LINDSAY, born Coldwater, Michigan, October 21, 1951; admitted to bar, 1976, Illinois. *Education:* Kalamazoo College (B.A., 1973); John Marshall Law School (J.D. with highest distinction, 1976). Member, Order of John Marshall. *Member:* Chicago and American (Member, Litigation) Bar Associations; Defense Research Institute; Illinois Association of Defense Trial Counsel; National Association of Railroad Trial Counsel; International Foundation of Employee Benefit Plans. **Email:** DLindsay@lewisoverbeck.com

JOHN W. LOSEMAN, born St. Louis, Missouri, March 10, 1964; admitted to bar, 1989, Illinois and U.S. District Court, Northern District of Illinois; U.S. District Court, Northern District of Indiana, U.S. District Court, Central District of Illinois, U.S. Court of Appeals, Seventh Circuit and U.S. Supreme Court. *Education:* University of Illinois (B.A., 1986; J.D., 1989). Topics Editor, Illinois Law Review, 1988-1989. Author: "Unraveling the Illinois Retaliatory Discharge Tort," Illinois L. Rev. 517, 1989. *Member:* Chicago and Illinois State Bar Associations; International Foundation of Employee Benefit Plans. **Email:** JLoseman@lewisoverbeck.com

F. RICHARD SKWERES, born LaGrange, Illinois, October 27, 1970; admitted to bar, 1995, Illinois. *Education:* Loyola University, Chicago (B.A., 1992; J.D., 1995); John Marshall Law School (LL.M., in Employee Benefits, 2003). *Member:* Chicago and Illinois State Bar Associations; International Foundation of Employee Benefit Plans. ***PRACTICE AREAS:*** Employee Benefit. **Email:** rskweres@lewisoverbeck.com

ASSOCIATES

CHRISTINE S. LEE, born Skokie, Illinois, June 17, 1972; admitted to bar, 2000, Illinois. *Education:* University of Illinois, Urbana-Champaign (B.A., 1994); Loyola University, Chicago, School of Law (J.D., 1999). **Email:** clee@lewisoverbeck.com

SAGE FATTAHIAN, born Tehran, Iran, June 9, 1974; admitted to bar, 2002, Illinois. *Education:* University of Illinois (B.A., 1998); John Marshall Law School (J.D., 2002; LL.M., 2004). Formerly with: Employee Benefits Security Administration, U.S. Department of Labor. *Member:* American Bar Association. ***LANGUAGES:*** Farsi. ***PRACTICE AREAS:*** Employee Benefits. **Email:** sfattahian@lewisoverbeck.com

LISA M. SIMIONI, born 1971; admitted to bar, 2003, Illinois. *Education:* John Marshall Law School.

OF COUNSEL

PERRY H. LEWIS (1908-1995)
JOHN H. OVERBECK, JR. (1918-2003)
VICTOR E. FURMAN (1906-1992)
JOHN M. TEEVAN (1918-2000)
O. KEITH STOUTNER (1913-1995)

PAUL L. FRETER, born Chicago, Illinois, May 16, 1917; admitted to bar, 1948, Illinois. *Education:* University of Illinois (B.S., 1947; J.D., 1949). Phi Alpha Delta. Certified Public Accountant, Illinois, 1942. *Member:* Chicago (Member, Committee on Federal Taxation, 1955-1956 and 1976-1985; Member, 1969-1970 and Vice-Chairman, 1971-1972, Chairman, 1972-1973, Committee on the Legal Economics of the Legal Profession) and Illinois State (Member, Committee on Bar Economics, 1967) Bar Associations.

GEORGE W. PHILLIPS, born Hebron, Indiana, March 7, 1934; admitted to bar, 1959, Illinois. *Education:* DePauw University (B.A., 1956); Northwestern University (J.D., 1959). Phi Delta Phi. *Member:* Chicago (Member, 1960-1999 and Chair, 1969-1970, Probate Practice Committee: Member, Continuing Legal Education Committee, 1971-1975) and Illinois State Bar Associations; American College of Trust and Estate Counsel. **Email:** GPhillips@lewisoverbeck.com

THOMAS H. VARNER, born Marshalltown, Iowa, November 14, 1934; admitted to bar, 1961, Iowa; 1972, New York; 1973, Illinois. *Education:* University of Illinois (B.S., 1959); Northwestern University (J.D., 1961); New York University (LL.M., 1966). *Member:* Chicago Bar Association (Member, Committee on Employee Benefits, 1975—).

REFERENCES: LaSalle National Bank; The Northern Trust Co.; Harris Trust & Savings Bank; Bank of America; First National Bank of Chicago.

LEYDIG, VOIT & MAYER, LTD.

Established in 1893

TWO PRUDENTIAL PLAZA
180 NORTH STETSON AVENUE, SUITE 4900
CHICAGO, ILLINOIS 60601-6780

Telephone: 312-616-5600
Telecopier: 312-616-5700
Email: mail@leydig.com
URL: http://www.leydig.com

Rockford, Illinois Office: 6815 Weaver Road, Suite 300. Telephone: 815-963-7661. Telecopier: 815-963-7664.
Washington, D.C. Office: Leydig, Voit & Mayer, 700 Thirteenth Street, N.W., Suite 300. Telephone: 202-737-6770. Telecopier: 202-737-6776.
Seattle, Washington Office: 1420 Fifth Avenue, Suite 2200. Telephone: 206-521-5985. Telecopier: 206-224-3557.

(This Listing Continued)

Patent, Trademark, Copyright, Unfair Competition, Licensing and Related Antitrust and International Trade Law. Trials and Appeals.

FIRM PROFILE: Leydig, Voit & Mayer, Ltd. is among the oldest intellectual property law firms in the nation, with a history dating back to 1893. The firm provides a full range of intellectual property law services for domestic and international clients, and litigates on behalf of its clients in all areas of intellectual property law. The firm's technical expertise encompasses all technologies, from mechanics, electronics and chemistry to computer software and genetics. Leydig, Voit & Mayer prides itself on its ability to meet the most demanding intellectual property needs of it's clients.

JAMES B. MUSKAL, born Chicago, Illinois, 1938; admitted to bar, 1963, Illinois; U.S. Supreme Court; U.S. Court of Appeals for the Federal Circuit; U.S. District Court, Northern District of Illinois including Trial Bar; registered to practice before U.S. Patent and Trademark Office. *Education:* University of Illinois (B.S.M.E., 1960); DePaul University (J.D., 1963). **Email:** jmuskal@leydig.com

DENNIS R. SCHLEMMER, born Kankakee, Illinois, 1939; admitted to bar, 1964, Illinois; U.S. Court of Appeals for the Federal Circuit; U.S. District Court, Northern District of Illinois including Trial Bar; registered to practice before U.S. Patent and Trademark Office. *Education:* University of Illinois (B.S. Gen. Eng., 1961; J.D., 1964). **Email:** dschlemmer@leydig.com

GORDON R. COONS, born Omaha, Nebraska, 1939; admitted to bar, 1965, Illinois; U.S. Supreme Court; U.S. Court of Appeals for the Federal Circuit; U.S. District Court, Northern District of Illinois, including Trial Bar; registered to practice before U.S. Patent and Trademark Office. *Education:* Iowa State University (B.S. Ch.E., 1961); Georgetown University (J.D., 1965). **Email:** gcoons@leydig.com

JOHN W. KOZAK, born Chicago, Illinois, 1943; admitted to bar, 1968, Illinois and District of Columbia; U.S. Supreme Court; U.S. Court of Appeals for the Federal Circuit; U.S. District Court, Northern District of Illinois, including Trial Bar; registered to practice before U.S. Patent and Trademark Office. *Education:* University of Notre Dame (B.S.E.E., 1965); Georgetown University (J.D., 1968). **Email:** jkozak@leydig.com

MARK E. PHELPS, born Warren, Ohio, 1948; admitted to bar, 1975, Illinois; U.S. Supreme Court; U.S. Court of Appeals for the Federal Circuit; U.S. District Court, Northern District of Illinois, including Trial Bar; registered to practice before U.S. Patent and Trademark Office. *Education:* Massachusetts Institute of Technology (B.S.M.E., 1970); Northwestern University (J.D., 1975). **Email:** mphelps@leydig.com

H. MICHAEL HARTMANN, born Frankfurt/Main, Germany, 1948; admitted to bar, 1976, Illinois; 1991, Wisconsin; U.S. Supreme Court; U.S. Court of Appeals for the Federal Circuit; U.S. District Court, Northern District of Illinois, including Trial Bar; registered to practice before U.S. Patent and Trademark Office. *Education:* Colorado School of Mines (B.S. Petro. Eng., 1970); DePaul University (J.D., 1976). ***LANGUAGES:*** German. **Email:** mhartmann@leydig.com

BRUCE M. GAGALA, born Chicago, Illinois, 1952; admitted to bar, 1977, Illinois; U.S. Court of Appeals for the Federal Circuit; U.S. District Court, Northern District of Illinois, including Trial Bar; registered to practice before U.S. Patent and Trademark Office. *Education:* Drake University (B.A. Chem., 1973); Illinois Institute of Technology/Chicago-Kent College of Law (J.D., 1977). **Email:** bgagala@leydig.com

CHARLES H. MOTTIER, born Chicago, Illinois, 1955; admitted to bar, 1981, Illinois; U.S. Supreme Court; U.S. Court of Appeals for the Federal Circuit; U.S District Court, Northern District of Illinois, including Trial Bar; registered to practice before U.S. Patent and Trademark Office. *Education:* University of Illinois (B.S.G.E., 1978); Magdalen College, Oxford University; University of Illinois (J.D., 1981). ***LANGUAGES:*** French. **Email:** cmottier@leydig.com

JOHN KILYK, JR., born Reading, Pennsylvania, 1959; admitted to bar, 1983, Illinois; U.S. Supreme Court; U.S. Court of Appeals for the Federal Circuit; U.S. District Court, Northern District of Illinois; registered to practice before U.S. Patent and Trademark Office. *Education:* Kenyon College (B.A. Chem., 1980); Georgetown University (J.D., 1983). **Email:** jkilyk@leydig.com

ROBERT F. GREEN, born Champaign, Illinois, 1949; admitted to bar, 1974, Illinois; U.S. Supreme Court; U.S. Court of Appeals for the Federal Circuit; U.S. District Court, Northern District of Illinois; registered to practice before U.S. Patent and Trademark Office. *Education:* University of Illinois (B.S. Chem., 1971); John Marshall Law School (J.D., 1974). **Email:** rgreen@leydig.com

JOHN B. CONKLIN, born Omaha, Nebraska, 1952; admitted to bar, 1978, Ohio; 1983, Illinois; U.S. Court of Appeals for the Federal Circuit; U.S. District Court, Northern District of Illinois; registered to practice before U.S. Patent and Trademark Office. *Education:* Case Western Reserve University (B.S.E.E., 1974; J.D., 1978). **Email:** jconklin@leydig.com

JAMES D. ZALEWA, born Chicago, Illinois, 1947; admitted to bar, 1974, Illinois; U.S. Supreme Court; U.S. Court of Appeals, Federal and Seventh Circuits; U.S. District Court, Northern District of Illinois, including Trail Bar; registered to practice before U.S. Patent and Trademark Office. *Education:* University of Illinois (B.S. Eng. Physics, 1969); University of Chicago (J.D., 1974). **Email:** jzalewa@leydig.com

MARK J. LISS, born Chicago, Illinois, 1956; admitted to bar, 1981, Illinois; U.S. Court of Appeals, Federal and Seventh Circuits; U.S. District Court, Northern District of Illinois, including Trial Bar. *Education:* University of Illinois (B.A., 1978); Chicago-Kent College of Law (J.D., 1981). **Email:** mliss@leydig.com

JOHN M. BELZ, born East St. Louis, Illinois, 1948; admitted to bar, 1980, Texas; 1981, Illinois; 1985, District of Columbia; U.S. Court of Appeals for the Federal Circuit; U.S. District Court, District of Columbia; registered to practice before U.S. Patent and Trademark Office. *Education:* University of Missouri (B.S.E.E., 1975; M.S. Nuclear Eng., 1976); University of Texas (J.D., 1980). (Resident, Washington, D.C. Office). **Email:** jbelz@leydig.com

BRETT A. HESTERBERG, born Red Bud, Illinois, 1959; admitted to bar, 1984, Illinois; U.S. Court of Appeals for the Federal Circuit; U.S. District Court, Northern District

(This Listing Continued)

LEYDIG, VOIT & MAYER, LTD., Chicago—Continued

of Illinois, including Trial Bar; registered to practice before U.S. Patent and Trademark Office. *Education:* University of Illinois (B.S.E.E., 1981; J.D., 1984). ***Email:*** bhesterberg@leydig.com

JEFFREY A. WYAND, born Hagerstown, Maryland, 1942; admitted to bar, 1977, Maryland; 1988, District of Columbia; U.S. Court of Appeals for the Federal Circuit; registered to practice before U.S. Patent and Trademark Office. *Education:* Lehigh University (B.S.E.E., 1964; B.S. Eng. Physics, 1965); Carnegie-Mellon University (M.S.E.E., 1966); University of Maryland (J.D., 1977). (Resident, Washington, D.C. Office). ***Email:*** jwyand@leydig.com

PAUL J. KORNICZKY, born New York, N.Y., 1961; admitted to bar, 1986, Illinois; U.S. Court of Appeals for the Federal Circuit; U.S. District Court, Northern District of Illinois, including Trial Bar; registered to practice before U.S. Patent and Trademark Office. *Education:* The Cooper Union School of Engineering (B.E., 1982; M.E., 1985); State University of New York at Buffalo (J.D., 1986). ***Email:*** pkorniczky@leydig.com

PAMELA J. RUSCHAU, born Dayton, Ohio, 1959; admitted to bar, 1987, Illinois; U.S. Court of Appeals for the Federal Circuit; U.S. District Court, Northern District of Illinois; registered to practice before U.S. Patent and Trademark Office. *Education:* General Motors Institute (B.M.E., 1983); Ohio State University College of Law (J.D., 1987). ***Email:*** pruschau@leydig.com

STEVEN P. PETERSEN, born Park Ridge, Illinois, 1962; admitted to bar, 1987, Illinois; U.S. Supreme Court; U.S. Court of Appeals for the Federal Circuit; U.S. District Court, Northern District of Illinois, including Trial Bar; registered to practice before U.S. Patent and Trademark Office. *Education:* Northwestern University (B.S.E.E., 1984); University of Michigan (J.D., 1987). ***Email:*** spetersen@leydig.com

JOHN M. AUGUSTYN, born Chicago, Illinois, 1959; admitted to bar, 1987, Illinois; U.S. Supreme Court; U.S. Court of Appeals for the Federal Circuit; U.S. District Court, Northern District of Illinois; registered to practice before U.S. Patent and Trademark Office. *Education:* Illinois Institute of Technology (B.S. Engineering, 1981); Loyola University, Chicago (J.D., 1987). ***Email:*** jaugustyn@leydig.com

CHRISTOPHER T. GRIFFITH, born Lansing, Michigan, 1959; admitted to bar, 1988, Illinois; 1989, District of Columbia; U.S. Court of Appeals for the Federal Circuit; U.S. District Court, Northern District of Illinois, including Trial Bar; registered to practice before U.S. Patent and Trademark Office. *Education:* Michigan State University (B.S. Ch.E., emphasis in Biomedical Eng., 1983); University of Houston (J.D., 1987). ***Email:*** cgriffith@leydig.com

WESLEY O. MUELLER, born Mansfield, Ohio, 1961; admitted to bar, 1988, Illinois; U.S. Court of Appeals for the Federal Circuit; U.S. District Court, Northern District of Illinois; registered to practice before U.S. Patent and Trademark Office. *Education:* University of Cincinnati (B.S.E.E., 1985); Ohio State University (J.D., 1988). ***Email:*** wmueller@leydig.com

JEREMY M. JAY, born Hackensack, New Jersey, 1953; admitted to bar, 1990, Virginia; 1991, District of Columbia; U.S. Supreme Court; U.S. Court of Appeals for the Federal Circuit; U.S. District Court, Eastern District of Virginia; U.S. District Court, District of Columbia; registered to practice before U.S. Patent and Trademark Office. *Education:* University of Connecticut (B.S., Pre-Veterinary Technology, 1976; M.S., Zoology, 1978); Texas A&M University (Ph.D., Biology, 1985); George Mason University (J.D., 1990). (Resident, Washington, D.C. Office). ***Email:*** jjay@leydig.com

LYNN A. SULLIVAN, born Evanston, Illinois, 1950; admitted to bar, 1990, Illinois; U.S. District Court, Northern District of Illinois; U.S. Court of Appeals, Seventh Circuit. *Education:* University of Hawaii (B.A., 1976); University of LaVerne (M.S., 1978); DePaul University (J.D., 1990). ***Email:*** lsullivan@leydig.com

JEFFREY B. BURGAN, born Great Lakes, Illinois, 1955; admitted to bar, 1990, Louisiana and Illinois; U.S. Court of Appeals for the Federal Circuit; U.S. District Court, Northern District of Illinois, including Trial Bar; registered to practice before U.S. Patent and Trademark Office. *Education:* Rose-Hulman Institute of Technology (B.S.Ch.E., 1977); Loyola University of New Orleans (J.D., 1989). ***Email:*** jburgan@leydig.com

ELEY O. THOMPSON, born Washington, D.C., 1964; admitted to bar, 1990, Illinois; 1993, District of Columbia; U.S. Court of Appeals for the Federal Circuit; U.S. District Court, Northern District of Illinois; registered to practice before U.S. Patent and Trademark Office. *Education:* Virginia Polytechnic Institute and State University (B.S.E.E., 1987); George Mason University (J.D., 1990). ***Email:*** ethompson@leydig.com

MARK JOY, born Albuquerque, New Mexico, 1965; admitted to bar, 1990, Illinois; U.S. Court of Appeals for the Federal Circuit; U.S. District Court, Northern District of Illinois; registered to practice before U.S. Patent and Trademark Office. *Education:* University of Illinois (B.S., Computer Engineering, 1987); University of Michigan (J.D., 1990). ***Email:*** mjoy@leydig.com

DAVID M. AIRAN, born Chicago, Illinois, 1967; admitted to bar, 1993, Illinois; U.S. Court of Appeals for the Federal Circuit; U.S. District Court, Northern District of Illinois; registered to practice before U.S. Patent and Trademark Office. *Education:* Marquette University (B.S.E.E., 1989); Northwestern University (J.D., 1993). ***Email:*** dairan@leydig.com

XAVIER PILLAI, born Budhalur, Tamil Nadu, India, 1952; admitted to bar, 1994, Illinois and U.S. District Court, Northern District of Illinois; registered to practice before U.S. Patent and Trademark Office. *Education:* Case Western Reserve University (Ph.D., 1984); Chicago-Kent College of Law, Illinois Institute of Technology (J.D., 1994). ***LANGUAGES:*** Tamil and Hindi. ***Email:*** xpillai@leydig.com

Y. KURT CHANG, born Taipei, Taiwan, 1957; admitted to bar, 1995, Illinois; registered to practice before U.S. Patent and Trademark Office. *Education:* University of Wisconsin-Madison (Ph.D., 1989); Northwestern University School of Law (J.D., 1995). ***LANGUAGES:*** Chinese. ***Email:*** kchang@leydig.com

(This Listing Continued)

GREGORY C. BAYS, born Detroit, Michigan, 1967; admitted to bar, 1995, Illinois; U.S. District Court, Northern District of Illinois; registered to practice before U.S. Patent and Trademark Office. *Education:* University of Michigan (B.S.M.E., 1989); Case Western Reserve University (J.D., 1995). ***Email:*** gbays@leydig.com

STEVEN H. SKLAR, born Chicago, Illinois, 1969; admitted to bar, 1996, Illinois; U.S. District Court, Northern District of Illinois; registered to practice before U.S. Patent and Trademark Office. *Education:* Washington University (B.S.Ch.E., 1991); Northwestern University (J.D., 1996). ***Email:*** ssklar@leydig.com

TAMARA A. MILLER, born Milwaukee, Wisconsin, 1970; admitted to bar, 1996, Illinois; U.S. District Court, Northern District of Illinois. *Education:* Indiana University (B.A., 1993); Loyola University (J.D., 1996). ***Email:*** tmiller@leydig.com

M. DANIEL HEFNER, born Evanston, Illinois, 1967; admitted to bar, 1996, Illinois; U.S. District Court, Northern District of Illinois; registered to practice before U.S. Patent and Trademark Office. *Education:* Illinois Wesleyan University (B.A., 1990); Yale University (M.S., 1993; M.Phil., 1994); University of Illinois (J.D., magna cum laude, 1996). ***Email:*** mdhefner@leydig.com

SALIM A. HASAN, born Kanpur, India, 1967; admitted to bar, 1993, Illinois and Indiana; U.S. District Court, Northern District of Illinois; registered to practice before U.S. Patent and Trademark Office. *Education:* Indiana University (B.A., Chemistry and History, 1989; J.D., 1992); George Washington University (LL.M., 1994). ***LANGUAGES:*** Urdu, Hindi. ***Email:*** shasan@leydig.com

ROGER D. WYLIE, born Kansas City, Missouri, 1966; admitted to bar, 1991, Georgia; 1997, Washington; U.S. District Court, Northern District of Georgia; registered to practice before the U.S. Patent and Trademark Office. *Education:* Auburn University (B.S., Materials Eng., cum laude, 1988); Vanderbilt University (J.D., 1991). (Resident, Seattle, Washington Office). ***Email:*** rwylie@leydig.com

KENNETH P. SPINA, born Chicago, Illinois, 1962; admitted to bar, 1996, Illinois; U.S. District Court, Northern District of Illinois; registered to practice before U.S. Patent and Trademark Office. *Education:* Loyola University (M.S., 1988); DePaul College of Law (J.D., 1996). ***Email:*** kspina@leydig.com

---

PHILLIP M. PIPPENGER, born Midland, Michigan, 1969; admitted to bar, 1998, Illinois; U.S. District Court, Northern District of Illinois; registered to practice before U.S. Patent and Trademark Office. *Education:* California Institute of Technology (B.S.E.E., 1992); Wesleyan University, Connecticut (B.A., Physics, 1993); Rice University (M.S.E.E., 1995); Cornell Law School (J.D., 1998). ***Email:*** ppippenger@leydig.com

ANNE E. NAFFZIGER, born New Jersey, 1967; admitted to bar, 1998, Illinois; U.S. District Court, Northern District of Illinois; 2004, Washington. *Education:* DePaul University (B.A., Business, 1995; J.D., 1998). (Resident, Seattle, Washington Office). ***Email:*** anaffziger@leydig.com

VLADAN M. VASILJEVIC, born Waukegan, Illinois, 1974; admitted to bar, 1998, Illinois; U.S. District Court, Northern District of Illinois; registered to practice before U.S. Patent and Trademark Office. *Education:* University of Illinois (B.S.E.E., 1995; J.D., 1998). ***Email:*** vvasiljevic@leydig.com

CLAUDIA W. STANGLE, born Chicago, Illinois, 1970; admitted to bar, 1997, Illinois; U.S. District Court, Northern District of Illinois. *Education:* University of Michigan (B.A., Fine Arts, 1992); DePaul University (J.D., 1997). ***LANGUAGES:*** German. ***Email:*** cwerner@leydig.com

PAUL J. FILBIN, born Oak Park, Illinois, 1971; admitted to bar, 1999, Illinois; U.S. District Court, Northern District of Illinois. *Education:* University of Notre Dame (B.S.M.E.; B.A., English, 1994); Loyola University (J.D., 1999). ***Email:*** pfilbin@leydig.com

JOHN L. GASE, born Southfield, Michigan, 1973; admitted to bar, 1999, Illinois; U.S. District Court, Northern District of Illinois. *Education:* Michigan State University (B.S. Biochem., 1995); George Washington University (J.D., 1999). ***Email:*** jgase@leydig.com

JEREMY C. LOWE, born Belboir, Virginia, 1974; admitted to bar, 2000, Illinois; U.S. District Court, Northern District of Illinois. *Education:* University of Missouri-Columbia (B.S.Ch.E., 1996); Washington University (J.D., 1999). ***Email:*** jlowe@leydig.com

JOHN T. BRETSCHER, born Valparaiso, Indiana, 1958; admitted to bar, 1999, Illinois; U.S. District Court, Northern District of Illinois. *Education:* University of Chicago (B.A., Physics, 1981); Chicago-Kent College of Law, Illinois Institute of Technology (J.D., 1999). ***LANGUAGES:*** German. ***Email:*** jbretscher@leydig.com

ROBERT T. WITTMANN, born Milwaukee, Wisconsin, 1967; admitted to bar, 2000, Illinois; registered to practice before U.S. Patent and Trademark Office. *Education:* Marquette University (B.S.E.E., 1990); DePaul University (J.D., 2000). ***Email:*** rwittmann@leydig.com

J. KARL GROSS, born Chicago, Illinois, 1972; admitted to bar, 2001, Illinois; U.S. District Court, Northern District of Illinois. *Education:* Marquette University (B.S.M.E., 1994); Boston University (J.D., 2001). ***Email:*** kgross@leydig.com

SETH A. ROSE, born Falls Church, Virginia, 1977; admitted to bar, 2002, Illinois and U.S. District Court, Northern District of Illinois. *Education:* University of Virginia (B.A., American Government and Sociology, 1999); The Ohio State University (J.D., 2002). ***Email:*** srose@leydig.com

SAUMIL S. MEHTA, born Waukesha, Wisconsin, 1967; admitted to bar, 2002, Illinois; U.S. District Court, Northern District of Illinois. *Education:* University of Wisconsin-Madison (B.S., 1997); University of Virginia (M.S., 2000); University of Minnesota (J.D., 2002). ***Email:*** smehta@leydig.com

JASON T. MURATA, born Scarborough, Ontario, 1978; admitted to bar, 2003, Illinois and U.S. District Court, Northern District of Illinois. *Education:* McMaster University (B.S., Biochemistry, 1999); Washington University (M.A., Biology, 2002; J.D., 2002). ***Email:*** jmurata@leydig.com

(This Listing Continued)

SCOTT H. SCHULHOF, born Pittsburgh, Pennsylvania, 1971; admitted to bar, 2003, Illinois and U.S. District Court, Northern District of Illinois; registered to practice before U.S. Patent and Trademark Office. *Education:* Northwestern University (B.A., Computer Studies, 1994); Chicago-Kent College of Law, Illinois Institute of Technology (J.D., 2002). ***Email:*** sschulhof@leydig.com

AARON R. FEIGELSON, born Ann Arbor, Michigan, 1969; admitted to bar, 2002, Massachusetts; 2003, Illinois; registered to practice before U.S. Patent and Trademark Office. *Education:* University of Michigan (A.B., Mathematics, 1991); Northwestern University (Ph.D., Computer Science, 1995); University of Chicago (J.D., 2002). ***Email:*** afeigelson@leydig.com

L. SCOTT BEALL, born Elmhurst, Illinois, 1967; admitted to bar, 2003, Illinois; U.S. District Court, Northern District of Illinois; registered to practice before U.S. Patent and Trademark Office. *Education:* University of Illinois (B.S., Chemistry, 1991); Imperial College of Science, Technology and Medicine (Ph.D., Organic Chemistry, 1996); Rutgers University (J.D., 2003). ***Email:*** sbeall@leydig.com

LISA K. KELLY, born Seoul, South Korea, 1970; admitted to bar, 2004, Illinois; U.S. District Court, Northern District of Illinois. *Education:* Texas Woman's University (B.S. Biology and Psychology, 1993; M.S. Biology 1996); University of Texas (J.D., 2003). ***Email:*** lkelly@leydig.com

STEPHEN R. AUTEN, born Indiana, 1971; admitted to bar, 1997, Illinois; U.S. District Court, Northern District of Illinois, including the Trial Bar; registered to practice before U.S. Patent and Trademark Office. *Education:* University of Illinois (B.S., 1994); Chicago-Kent College of Law (J.D., 1997). ***Email:*** sauten@leydig.com

MARK A. NIEDS, born Chicago, Illinois, 1965; admitted to bar, 1994, Illinois. *Education:* Miami University (B.A., 1987); Chicago-Kent College of Law (J.D., 1994). ***Email:*** mnieds@leydig.com

CAROLINE L. STEVENS, born Evanston, Illinois, 1974; admitted to bar, 2001, Illinois. *Education:* Cornell University (B.F.A., 1996); University of Michigan (J.D., 2000). ***Email:*** cstevens@leydig.com

DOUGLAS A. ROBINSON, born Jefferson City, Missouri, 1978; admitted to bar, 2004, Illinois. *Education:* University of Missouri (B.S., 2000); Washington University (J.D., 2004). ***Email:*** drobinson@leydig.com

NANCY J. GETTEL, born Cass City, Michigan, 1976; admitted to bar, 2004, Illinois. *Education:* Alma College (B.S., 1998); Duke University (M.A., 2001); University of Michigan (J.D., 2004). ***Email:*** ngettel@leydig.com

PETER H. DOMER, born Chicago, Illinois, 1959; admitted to bar, 2004, Illinois. *Education:* Rice University (B.A., Biochemistry, 1981); Northwestern University (M.D., 1986; J.D., 2004). ***Email:*** pdomer@leydig.com

JEFFREY N. TURNER, born Joliet, Illinois, 1978; admitted to bar, 2004, Illinois. *Education:* University of Illinois (B.S.G.E., 2001); University of Houston (J.D., 2004). ***Email:*** jturner@leydig.com

SUSAN L. STEELE, born Grand Rapids, Michigan, 1970; admitted to bar, 2004, Illinois. *Education:* Hope College (B.S., 1992); Harvard University (M.A., 1995); University of Michigan (J.D., 2004). ***Email:*** ssteele@leydig.com

STEPHANIE M. LAWLEY, born Norfolk, Virginia, 1977; admitted to bar, 2004, Virginia; registered to practice before U.S. Patent and Trademark Office. *Education:* Mary Baldwin College (B.S., Biochemistry, magna cum laude, 1999); College of William & Mary (M.A., Biology, 2001); George Mason University (J.D., 2004). Phi Beta Kappa. (Resident, Washington, D.C. Office). ***Email:*** slawley@leydig.com

KURT T. BUECHLE, born Bryn Mawr, Pennsylvania, 1974; admitted to bar, 2002, Illinois; U.S. District Court, Northern District of Illinois; registered to practice before U.S. Patent and Trademark Office. *Education:* Haverford College (B.S., Chemistry, 1996); University of Michigan (M.S., Biological Chemistry, 1997); Indiana University School of Law - Bloomington (J.D., 2001). ***Email:*** kbuechle@leydig.com

THOMAS K. McBRIDE, JR., born Chicago, Illinois, 1967; admitted to bar, 2004, Illinois; registered to practice before U.S. Patent and Trademark Office. *Education:* University of Illinois (B.S., Chemical Engineering, 1989); University of Notre Dame (M.S., Chemical Engineering, 1991); Loyola University, Chicago (J.D., 2004). ***Email:*** tmcbride@leydig.com

JENNIFER M. DUK, born Cleveland, Ohio, 1972; admitted to bar, 2002, Illinois; U.S. District Court, Northern District of Illinois; registered to practice before U.S. Patent and Trademark Office. *Education:* Walsh University (B.S., Biology, 1995); Loyola University, Chicago (J.D., 2002). ***Email:*** jduk@leydig.com

MARCOS P. RIVAS, born Guatemala City, Guatemala, 1969; admitted to bar, 2003, Massachusetts; registered to practice before U.S. Patent and Trademark Office (Not admitted in Illinois). *Education:* University of Chicago (B.A., Philosophy, 1991); University of Alabama at Birmingham (Ph.D., Cell Biology, 2000); University of Pennsylvania Law School (J.D., 2003). ***Email:*** mrivas@leydig.com

CHRISTINE M. COCHRAN, born Hackettstown, New Jersey, April 24, 1977; admitted to bar, 2003, Illinois and U.S. District Court, Northern District of Illinois; registered to practice before U.S. Patent and Trademark Office. *Education:* University of Chicago (A.B., Biological Sciences, 1998); Washington University (J.D., 2003). ***Email:*** ccochran@leydig.com

ROB R. COTTLE, born Riverside, California, 1966; (admission pending). *Education:* California State University, Fresno (B.S., Computer Science, 1992); Gonzaga University (J.D., 2005). (Resident, Seattle, Washington Office). ***Email:*** rcottle@leydig.com

JOHN P. SNOW, born Southfield, Michigan, 1975; (admission pending). *Education:* University of Michigan (B.S., Biological Chemistry, 1998; J.D., 2005). ***Email:*** jsnow@leydig.com

JEFFREY S. DAVID, born Huntsville, Texas, 1980; (admission pending). *Education:* University of Texas at Austin (B.S., Electrical and Computer Engineering, 2002); Cornell University Law School (J.D., 2005). ***Email:*** jdavid@leydig.com

(This Listing Continued)

DIMITRY KAPMAR, born Odessa, Ukraine, 1973; (admission pending). *Education:* Illinois Institute of Technology (B.S., Electrical Engineering, 1996); John Marshall Law School (J.D., 2005). ***Email:*** dkapmar@leydig.com

EDWARD M. SIEGEL, born Glen Cove, New York, 1973; (admission pending). *Education:* University of Maryland (B.A., Government and Politics, 1995); University of Illinois (M.S., Chemistry, 2005; J.D., 2005). ***Email:*** esiegel@leydig.com

BRYAN D. MURPHY, born Milwaukee, Wisconsin, 1977; (admission pending). *Education:* University of Wisconsin-Madison (B.S., Mechanical Engineering, 2000; J.D., 2005). ***LANGUAGES:*** Spanish and Portuguese. ***Email:*** bmurphy@leydig.com

KEVIN C. PARKS, born Ames, Iowa, 1959; admitted to bar, 1985, New York, U.S. District Court, Southern and Eastern Districts of New York and New York Supreme Court; 1988, Illinois and U.S. District Court, Northern District of Illinois; State of Illinois Supreme Court; 2005, U.S. District Court, Western District of Michigan. *Education:* University of Iowa (B.A., English, 1981; J.D., with distinction, 1984). ***Email:*** kparks@leydig.com

OF COUNSEL

C. FREDERICK LEYDIG, born Denver, Colorado, 1925; admitted to bar, 1950, Illinois; U.S. Supreme Court; U.S. Court of Appeals for the Federal Circuit; U.S. District Court, Northern District of Illinois; registered to practice before U.S. Patent and Trademark Office. *Education:* Illinois Institute of Technology (B.S. Ch.E., 1945); DePaul University (J.D., 1950).

THEODORE W. ANDERSON, born Chicago, Illinois, 1926; admitted to bar, 1953, Illinois; U.S. Supreme Court; U.S. Court of Appeals for the Federal Circuit; U.S. District Court, Northern District of Illinois, including Trial Bar; registered to practice before U.S. Patent and Trademark Office. *Education:* University of Illinois (B.S.E.E., 1948); DePaul University (J.D., 1953). ***Email:*** tanderson@leydig.com

JOHN P. BUNDOCK, JR., born Floral Park, New York, 1926; admitted to bar, 1951, District of Columbia; 1954, Illinois; U.S. Court of Appeals for the Federal Circuit; U.S. District Court, District of Columbia; registered to practice before U.S. Patent and Trademark Office. *Education:* Tufts University (B.S.E.E., 1948); George Washington University (LL.B., 1950). (Resident, Washington, D.C. Office)

BERTON SCOTT SHEPPARD, born Zanesville, Ohio, 1936; admitted to bar, 1962, Illinois; U.S. Supreme Court; U.S. Court of Appeals for the Federal Circuit; U.S. District Court, Northern District of Illinois, including Trial Bar; registered to practice before U.S. Patent and Trademark Office. *Education:* Michigan State University (B.S. Agr. Eng., 1958); Northwestern University (J.D., 1961). ***Email:*** bsheppard@leydig.com

JOHN E. ROSENQUIST, born Chicago, Illinois, 1940; admitted to bar, 1968, Illinois; U.S. Supreme Court; U.S. Court of Appeals for the Federal Circuit; U.S. District Court, Northern District of Illinois, including Trial Bar; registered to practice before U.S. Patent and Trademark Office. *Education:* St. Marys College (B.A. Chem., 1961); Creighton University (M.S. Chem., 1962); John Marshall Law School (J.D., 1968). ***LANGUAGES:*** German. ***Email:*** jrosenquist@leydig.com

CHARLES S. OSLAKOVIC, born Chicago, Illinois, 1941; admitted to bar, 1973, Illinois; U.S. Court of Appeals for the Federal Circuit; U.S. District Court, Northern District of Illinois, including Trial Bar; registered to practice before U.S. Patent and Trademark Office. *Education:* Illinois Institute of Technology (B.S.E.E., 1966); DePaul University (J.D., 1973). (Resident, Rockford, Illinois Office). ***Email:*** coslakovic@leydig.com

JOHN D. FOSTER, born Moline, Illinois, 1943; admitted to bar, 1970, District of Columbia; U.S. Court of Appeals for the Federal Circuit; registered to practice before U.S. Patent and Trademark Office. *Education:* Iowa State University (B.S.Ch.E., 1965); Georgetown University (J.D., 1969). (Resident, Washington, D.C. Office)

LEYHANE & ASSOCIATES, LTD.

11 EAST ADAMS STREET, SUITE 1600
CHICAGO, ILLINOIS 60603
Telephone: 312-922-2996
Fax: 312-922-0323
Email: Leyhane329@aol.com
URL: http://www.lawyers.com/leyhanelaw

Other Chicago Office: 9924 S. Walden Parkway, 60643. Telephone: 773-238-5881. Fax: 312-922-0323.

Insurance Litigation, Insurance Coverage, Appellate Practice, General Practice, Commodities.

FRANCIS J. (JACK) LEYHANE, III, born Chicago, Illinois, 1957; admitted to bar, 1980, Illinois and U.S. District Court, Northern District of Illinois; 1986, U.S. Court of Appeals, Seventh Circuit. *Education:* Loyola University (A.B., 1977; J.D., 1980). Blue Key. Author: Column, "Civil Policy", Chicago Daily Law Bulletin, 1998—; "Substantial Compliance: Substantially Erroneous Doctrine," 9 Loy. Consumer L. Rep. 353, 1997; "It's No Lie: Civil Perjury Prosecutions Possible in Illinois," *CBA Record,* January 1999, Vol. 13, No. 1; "A Practitioner's Guide to Motion Practice in Chancery," *CBA Record,* Vol. 10, No. 8, November 1996; "Why Tenants Can Seldom Be Sued for Causing a Fire," Illinois Bar Journal, Vol. 79, p. 284, June, 1991. Co-Author: "Feeling at Home with Homeowners' Insurance," *Illinois Bar Journal,* Vol. 82, p. 383 (*Practice Tips,* July 1994); monthly column ("Insurance Issues"), *Chicago Daily Bulletin* (1992-1998); "Defenses & Contemporary Legal Issues," materials for seminars presented at ICAC National Arson Investigation Training Seminars (1993-1998). Speaker: Chicago Bar Association Continuing Legal Education Seminar, March 2000, "Insurance and Real Estate Transactions"; City of Chicago -- Department of Law, Enforcement Group Training Program (November 1997), "Motion Practice in Chancery Court"; National Arson Investigation Training Seminar, sponsored by the Insurance Committee for Arson Control (Houston, Texas, January 1997), "Defenses & Contemporary Legal Issues"; National Business Institute, Inc., CLE Seminar (September 1996), "Effective Discovery Procedures in Illinois"; CBA YLS CLE Seminar (April 1996), "The Uninsured/Underinsured Motorist Case"; CBA CLE Seminar (January 1996), "Chan-

(This Listing Continued)

LEYHANE & ASSOCIATES, LTD., Chicago—Continued

cery and Special Remedies"; CBA CLE Seminar (September 1993), "How to Effectively Present Your Case at a Mandatory Arbitration Hearing"; Western Loss Association 1992 Meeting, Delevan, Wisconsin, "Recent Developments in Property Law"; Casualty Adjusters Association of Chicago, 1989 Spring Seminar, "Selected Topics Re: CGL Policies, Workers Compensation and Employers' Liability Policies." *Member:* Chicago (Member: Board of Editors, CBA Record, 1998—; Insurance and Civil Practice Committees), Illinois State (Assembly, 1987-1990; Member, Sections on: Insurance Law; Civil Practice; Torts) and American Bar Associations; Appellate Lawyers Association of Illinois. Charter Life Fellow, Illinois Bar Foundation. ***PRACTICE AREAS:*** Appellate Practice; Chancery Practice; Civil Practice; Insurance Coverage; First and Third Party Insurance; Property Insurance; Personal Injury. ***Email:*** Leyhane329@aol.com

OF COUNSEL

EUGENE P. SULLIVAN, born Chicago, Illinois, January 2, 1958; admitted to bar, 1991, Illinois; 1992, U.S. District Court, Northern District of Illinois and U.S. Court of Appeals, Seventh Circuit. *Education:* Elmhurst College (B.S., 1981); Northern Illinois University (J.D., 1991). *Member:* DuPage County Bar Association. [Naval Flight Officer, 1981—, CAPT, U.S. Navy Reserves]. ***PRACTICE AREAS:*** Insurance; School Law; Military Operations. ***Email:*** genepsullivan@cs.com

JEFFREY G. LISS, P.C.

130 SOUTH JEFFERSON STREET, SUITE 501
CHICAGO, ILLINOIS 60661
Telephone: 312-876-0600
Fax: 312-782-7789
Email: JGLJGL@aol.com

Business and Real Estate Law, Estate Planning, Wills and Trusts.

JEFFREY G. LISS, born Chicago, Illinois, April 30, 1943; admitted to bar, 1968, Illinois and U.S. District Court, Northern District of Illinois; 1969, U.S. Court of Appeals, Seventh Circuit; 1978, U.S. Supreme Court; 1984, U.S. Tax Court. *Education:* Brown University (A.B., 1965); Harvard University (J.D., 1968); DePaul College of Law (LL.M., in Taxation, 1981). Author: "Drafting Around the Mortgage 'Due on Sale' Clause in the Installment Sale of Real Estate," 62 Chicago Bar Record 312, 1981; "Beware the New Transfer Tax Declarations," ISBA Real Property, October 1982; "Using Not-for-Profit Corporations for Tax-Exempt Financing: Revenue Ruling 63-20 Revisited," 31 De Paul Law Review 533, 1982; "Introduction to Proposed Illinois Mortgage Foreclosure Act," Chicago Law Bulletin, April 15-19, 1985; "Selected Comments About the Illinois Mortgage Foreclosure Law," IICLE, March, 1987; "Notices of Foreclosure Sales Under The New Law," Chicago Law Bulletin, October 7, 1987; "A Robot in Every Job," Analog, September, 1990; "Orbituary," Science Fiction Age, March 1994. Director, 1990-1993, 1996—, Board of Advisers, 1993-1996, Editor of Inside NSS, 1994-1997, Vice President, 1996-2000, Sr. Vice President, 2000-2005, National Space Society. Chair, 8th International Space Development Conference, 1989. *Member:* Chicago (Member: Real Property Law Committee, 1973—; Development of the Law Committee, 1981-2000 and Chairman, 1987-1988; Federal Taxation Committee, 1981-1990; Member: Committee on Evaluation of Judicial Candidates, 1969-1980; Younger Members Committee, 1968-1971 and Bar Association Structure Subcommittee Chairman, 1970-1971; Member, Executive Committee; Young Lawyers Section, 1971-1972), Illinois State (Member: Assembly, 1978-1984, 1985-1991, 1992-1998, 1999-2005 Real Estate Law Section Council, 1980-1987, 1993-1999, 2000-2005 and Chair, 1985-1986, 1997-1998; Vice Chair, Illinois Mortgage Foreclosure Law Drafting Committee, 1983-1987; Commercial, Banking and Bankruptcy Law Section Council, 1987-1991 and Chair, 1989-1990; Public Service Committee, 1977-1978; International Law Section Model Negotiations Project, 1970-1971) Bar Association.

LITCHFIELD CAVO LLP

Established in 1988

SUITE 300
303 WEST MADISON STREET
CHICAGO, ILLINOIS 60606-3300
Telephone: 312-781-6677
Fax: 312-781-6630
Email: firm@litchfieldcavo.com
URL: http://www.litchfieldcavo.com

Avon: 40 Tower Lane, Suite 200, Avon CT 06001-4222. Telephone: (860) 255-5577. Fax: (860) 255-5566.
Boston: 6 Kimball Lane, Suite 100, Lynnfield, MA 01940-2682. Telephone: (781) 309-1500. Fax: (781) 245-0167.
New Jersey: Commerce Center, 1800 Chapel Avenue West, Suite 140, Cherry Hill, NJ 08002. Telephone: (856) 854-3636. Fax: (856) 751-1230.
New York: 420 Lexington Avenue, Suite 1750, New York, NY 10170. Telephone: (212) 434-0100. Fax: (212) 434-0105.
Tampa: 5201 West Kennedy Boulevard, Suite 450, Tampa, FL 33609. Telephone: (813) 289-0690. Fax: (813) 289-0692.
Wisconsin: 13555 Bishop's Court, Suite 230, Brookfield, WI 53005-6224. Telephone: (262) 784-8800. Fax: (262) 784-8812.

General Liability, Business Litigation, Bad Faith/Extra Contractual Liability, Environmental/Toxic Tort Defense, Product Liability, Insurance Coverage Litigation, Construction, Executive Liability, Reinsurance, Professional Liability-Non Medical, Professional Liability - Medical, Truckers' Liability, Appellate Practice, Employment Liability, Intellectual Property, Workers' Compensation, First Party Property.

(This Listing Continued)

FIRM PROFILE: Litchfield Cavo LLP is a litigation firm with a national practice in state and federal trial and appellate courts. From its offices in Chicago, Wisconsin, Connecticut, Massachusetts, New Jersey, New York and Tampa, Litchfield Cavo represents insurers, their insureds, and other business clients in insurance coverage and defense, product liability, professional liability, tort, employment and commercial litigation. The success of our firm is founded upon the values we bring to our practice of law: hard work, responsiveness, litigation focus, creativity, civility, and the desire to build long-term relationships with our clients.

PARTNERS

KENNETH J. BARRISH, born Chicago, Illinois; admitted to bar, 1990, Illinois, U.S. District Court, Northern District of Illinois, 2000, U.S. Court of Appeals, Seventh Circuit; 2001, U.S. District Court, Northern District of Indiana. *Education:* University of Illinois, Urbana-Champaign (B.A., 1985); DePaul University College of Law (J.D., 1988). Co-Author, Case Supplement, "Employee Leave Rights Under State/Federal Law, What Every Illinois Employer Needs to Know," Seminar, National Business Institute, Spring, 1998; Seminar Handbook, "Mold and Silicosis Litigation in Illinois: A Defense Perspective," Winter 2003. Seminar Speaker: "Construction Litigation in Illinois," Lorman Education Services, Spring 2001; "Mold and Silicosis Litigation in Illinois: A Defense Perspective," Travelers Insurance Company, Winter 2003. ***REPORTED CASES:*** Henderson v. Jones Brothers Construction Corporation, 234 Ill.App. 3d 871, 602 N.E.2d 16 (1st Dist. 1992); American States Insurance Company v. Marshall Bailey, et al., 285 Ill. App. 3d 687, 675 N.E. 2d 939 (1st Dist. 1996). ***Email:*** barrish@litchfieldcavo.com

JONATHAN E. BARRISH, born Skokie, Illinois; admitted to bar, 1992, Illinois. *Education:* Northwestern University (B.A., with honors, 1989); Loyola University (J.D., 1992). ***LANGUAGES:*** Hebrew. ***REPORTED CASES:*** Jose Garcia v. Four Seasons Hotel Inc. 97 IIC 1046. ***Email:*** barrishj@litchfieldcavo.com

ALAN I. BECKER, born Kew Gardens, New York, June 18, 1946; admitted to bar, 1970, Illinois and U.S. District Court, Northern District of Illinois; 1971, U.S. Court of Appeals, Seventh Circuit; 1976, U.S. Supreme Court; 1982, U.S. District Court, Northern District of Illinois including Trial Bar; 1989, U.S. District Court, Northern District of California; 1990, U.S. Court of Appeals, Ninth Circuit; 1994, U.S. Court of Appeals, Fifth Circuit; 1996, U.S. Court of Appeals, Federal Circuit. *Education:* Cornell University (A.B., cum laude, 1967, Phi Beta Kappa, Phi Kappa Phi); Yale University (LL.B., 1970). Contributor: "Monograph, The Robinson-Patman Act: Policy and Law," Vol. 1 (American Bar Association, Antitrust Law Section, 1980). Certified Chairperson-Arbitrator, Mandatory Arbitration Program, Circuit Court of Cook County, Illinois. ***REPORTED CASES:*** Prime Leasing, Inc. v. Aetna Life Ins. Co., 1994 WL 698517 (N.D. Ill.), vacated, 65 F.3d 170 (7th Cir. 1995); White Industries, Inc. v. Cessna Aircraft Co., 657 F.Supp. 687 (W.D. Mo. 1986), aff'd, 845 F.2d 1497 (8th Cir. 1988); Chemetron Corp. v. McLouth Steel Co., 381 F.Supp. 245 (N.D. Ill. 1974), aff'd, 522 F.2d 469 (7th Cir. 1975). ***Email:*** becker@litchfieldcavo.com

TRACY C. BEGGS, born Fort Dix, New Jersey; admitted to bar, 1980, Illinois; U.S. District Court, Northern District of Illinois, including Trial Bar; Central District of Illinois; U.S. Court of Appeals, Seventh Circuit. *Education:* University of Michigan (B.A., 1976; J.D., 1980). ***REPORTED CASES:*** Smith v. American Motors Sales Corp., 215 Ill.App.3d 951 (1st Dist. 1991). ***Email:*** beggs@litchfieldcavo.com

JOHN R. CATIZONE (Resident, Tampa, Florida Office)

RICHARD C. CAVO (Resident, Avon, Connecticut Office)

ELIZABETH M. CHRISTOFARO (Resident, Avon, Connecticut Office)

ROBERT L. CIOCIOLA (Not admitted in Illinois; Resident, Lynnfield, Massachusetts Office)

THOMAS C. CLARK (Not admitted in Illinois; Resident, Avon, Connecticut Office)

BRADFORD COOKE (Resident, New York, N.Y. Office)

THOMAS M. CRAWFORD, born Seoul, South Korea; admitted to bar, 1992, Iowa and Illinois; 1995 Maryland; 2000, U.S. District Court, Northern District of Illinois. *Education:* University of Iowa (B.S., 1989); Thomas M. Cooley Law School (J.D., cum laude, 1992); Georgetown University (LL.M, 1993). ***Email:*** crawford@litchfieldcavo.com

MARK A. DARLING (Resident, Lynnfield, Massachusetts Office)

MICHAEL J. DUGAN (Resident, Cherry Hill, New Jersey Office/Avon, Connecticut Office)

CARRIE A. DURKIN, born Washington, D.C.; admitted to bar, 1979, Illinois, U.S. District Court, Northern District of Illinois and U.S. District Court of Appeals, Seventh Circuit; 1994, U.S. District Court, Eastern District of Wisconsin; 1995, U.S. Court of Appeals, Eighth Circuit; 1996, U.S. District Court, Eastern District of Michigan; 2000, U.S. District Court, Western District of Wisconsin. *Education:* Colby College (B.A., 1971); Chicago-Kent College of Law, Illinois Institute of Technology (J.D., with highest honors, 1979). *Member:* American Bar Association; Women's Bar Association. ***Email:*** durkin@litchfieldcavo.com

MARC S. EDRICH (Not admitted in Illinois; Resident, Avon, Connecticut Office)

EDWARD M. FOGARTY, JR. (Resident, New York, N.Y. Office)

MITCHELL H. FRAZEN, born Great Lakes, Illinois; admitted to bar, 1980, Illinois; U.S. District Court, Northern District of Illinois including Trial Bar; 1987, U.S. Court of Appeals, Seventh Circuit; 1994, U.S. District Court, Eastern District of Wisconsin; 1994, U.S. District Court, Eastern District of Michigan; 1995, U.S. Court of Appeals, Eighth Circuit. *Education:* University of Illinois (B.A., magna cum laude, 1977, Phi Beta Kappa); University of Michigan (J.D., magna cum laude, 1980). Order of the Coif. Certified Chairperson-Arbitrator, Mandatory Arbitration Program, Circuit Court of Cook County, Illinois. Author: "The Challenge of Insured-Insurer Conflicts of Interest for Illinois Defense Counsel," Lorman Business Centers, Illinois Insurance Law Seminars, 1994-1995. Member, Advisory Panel on Reappointment of U.S. Magistrate Judges, U.S. District Court for the Northern District of Illinois, 1993. ***REPORTED CASES:*** Wildrick v. North River Insur-

(This Listing Continued)

ance Co., 75 F.3d 432 (8th Cir. 1996); International Insurance Co. v. Guaranty National Insurance Co., 994 F2d 1280 (7th Cir. 1993); In re Salmonella Litigation, 198 Ill.App.3d 809, (1st Dist. 1990). ***Email:*** frazen@litchfieldcavo.com

DAWN M. GONZALEZ, born Detroit, Michigan, January 14, 1969; admitted to bar, 1994, Illinois; 1998, U.S. District Court, Northern District of Illinois. *Education:* University of Michigan (B.A., 1991); DePaul University (J.D., 1994). Co-Author: "A Primer on Contemporary Umbrella & Excess Insurance Issues," Glasser Legal Works 8th Annual Institute, 1998. ***Email:*** gonzalezd@litchfieldcavo.com

DANIEL T. HUGHES (Resident, New York, N.Y. Office)

MATTHEW J. IVERSON, born Milwaukee, Wisconsin; admitted to bar, 1964, Wisconsin and Illinois; U.S. District Court, Northern District of Illinois and U.S. Court of Appeals, Seventh, Eighth and Tenth Circuits. *Education:* University of Wisconsin (B.B.A., 1960, Phi Beta Kappa; LL.B., 1964). Order of the Coif. Co-Author: "Officers and Directors Liability Exposure Under Civil and Criminal Law," Washington Legal Foundation, 1999; "The New Discovery Rules in Illinois: What You Don't Know Can Hurt You," *Insight,* Illinois CPA Society, May 1996. Author: "Saving for a Rainy Day: What Do You Really Know About Your Professional Liability Policy?" *CBA Record,* Chicago Bar Association, November 1994; "Product Liability Litigation Creates Biomaterials Availability Crisis," Washington Legal Foundation, April 12, 1996; "Court Decisions Favor Preemption in Medical Device Litigation," Washington Legal Foundation, March 31, 1995; "Federal Preemption is Powerful Antidote to Product Liability Explosion Against Medical Device Manufacturers," Washington Legal Foundation, June 17, 1994; Continuing Professional Education Videocassette, "Accountants on Trial" (showing portions of a mock accounting malpractice trial distributed by the AICPA); AICPA Videocassette, "We've Got a Problem" (a training film prepared for tax accountants to illustrate professional liability exposures); AICPA Videocassette, "Litigation Services Video Course". ***REPORTED CASES:*** Behagen v. USA Basketball, 884 F.2d 524 (10th Cir. 1989), cert. denied, 471 U.S. 1010 (1990); Dockter v. Rudolph Wolff Futures, Inc., 913 F.2d 456 (7th Cir. 1990); Central Wisconsin Bankshares, Inc. v. Board of Governors of the Federal Reserve System, 583 F.2d 294 (7th Cir. 1978). ***Email:*** iverson@litchfieldcavo.com

JOHN J. JAROSAK (Not admitted in Illinois; Resident, Lynnfield, Massachusetts Office)

EILEEN P. KAVANAGH (Not admitted in Illinois; Resident, Lynnfield, Massachusetts Office)

KEARNEY W. KILENS, born Boston, Massachusetts; admitted to bar, 1985, Illinois and U.S. District Court, Northern and Central Districts of Illinois; 1991, U.S. Court of Appeals, Seventh Circuit. *Education:* Denison University (B.A., 1982); DePaul University (J.D., 1985). Omicron Delta Kappa. Member, Mortar Board. Author, "Employer Insurance Coverage for Employment Litigation," Illinois Bar Journal, January 1991 and PLI 1996, 1997. Co-Author: "In-House Counsel as Whistleblower: At-Will Employment on Trial," Employee Relations Law Journal, Summer, 1993; "Lawyers as Employees: Rights and Remedies," in Employment Termination Handbook, Illinois Institute for Continuing Legal Education, 1988, Supplement, 1990. Contributor, "Employee Termination Rights and Remedies," 2d edition, BNA Books, 1993 and 1998 Cum. Supplement. ***Email:*** kilens@litchfieldcavo.com

PETER C. KOBER (Resident, Lynnfield, Massachusetts Office)

DANIEL G. LITCHFIELD, born Hays, Kansas; admitted to bar, 1983, Illinois and U.S. District Court, Northern District of Illinois; 1984, U.S. Court of Appeals for the Seventh Circuit, U.S. Court of Appeals for the Federal Circuit and U.S. Court of International Trade; 1992, U.S. District Court, Central District of Illinois; 1994, U.S. District Court, Eastern District of Wisconsin; 1995, Pennsylvania; 1998, Trial Bar. *Education:* Drake University (B.A., summa cum laude, 1980, Phi Beta Kappa); University of Chicago (J.D., 1983). Co-Author: "The Polluter's Web: The Pollution Exclusion and the Question of Deception," CPCU Journal, June 1994; "Litigation Management Strategies Heading Toward the Trial of an Insurance Coverage Case," Litigation and Technology Management Report; "Corporate Relationships and Coverage," Coverage Section of Litigation, American Bar Association, Volume 8, Number 6, November/December 1998; "Property Damage Update: Pollution Exclusion," Coverage, Volume 9, Number 2, March/April 1999. ***REPORTED CASES:*** Goodyear Tire & Rubber Co. v. Aetna Casualty and Surety Co., 1995 WL 422733 (Ohio App.); A. Y. McDonald Industries, Inc. v. Employers Insurance of Wausau, et. al., 842 F.Supp. 1166 (N.D. Iowa 1993). ***Email:*** litchfield@litchfieldcavo.com

LYNNE M. MUELLER (Resident, Brookfield, Wisconsin Office)

MARK W. MURPHY (Resident, Lynnfield, Massachusetts Office)

HOPE G. NIGHTINGALE, born Montclair, New Jersey; admitted to bar, 1981, Illinois and U.S. District, Northern District of Illinois; U.S. Court of Appeals, Seventh Circuit. *Education:* Grinnell College (B.A., with honors, 1976, Phi Beta Kappa); University of Chicago (J.D., 1981). Author: "Liability of Insurance Agents and Brokers," *Coverage,* ABA Litigation Section, Fall 1997. ***REPORTED CASES:*** Brown & Williamson Tobacco Co. v. Jacobson, 827 F.2d 1119 (7th Cir. 1987); New Castle County v. Hartford Accident & Indemnity Co., 8 F.R. Serv. 3d 506 (S.D.N.Y. 1987). ***Email:*** nightingale@litchfieldcavo.com

LISA A. OONK (Resident, Tampa, Florida Office)

NICHOLAS J. PAROLISI, JR., born Lawrence, Massachusetts; admitted to bar, 1989, Illinois and U.S. District Court, Northern District of Illinois; 1998, Indiana; 1999, U.S. District Court, Central District of Illinois. *Education:* University of Massachusetts, Amherst (B.A., 1984); DePaul University (J.D., with honors, 1989). ***Email:*** parolisi@litchfieldcavo.com

PETER J. PONZIANI (Not admitted in Illinois; Resident, Avon, Connecticut Office)

MARK W. RATTAN (Resident, Brookfield, Wisconsin Office)

PAUL G. ROCHE (Resident, Avon, Connecticut Office)

JOSEPH B. ROYSTER, born St. Louis, Missouri; admitted to bar, 1990, California and U.S. District Court, Southern District of California; 1994, Illinois and U.S. District Court, Northern District of Illinois; 1996, U.S. Court of Appeals, Seventh Circuit; 1999, U.S. District Court, Northern and Central Districts of California; 2000, U.S. District Court, Western District of Wisconsin and U.S. Court of Appeals, Ninth Circuit. *Education:* Whittier College (B.A., 1987); Emory University (J.D., 1990). ***Email:*** royster@litchfieldcavo.com

J. RODNEY RUNYONS (Resident, Tampa, Florida Office)

GEORGE P. SMYRNIOTIS, born Evanston, Illinois; admitted to bar, 1989, Illinois. *Education:* Northeastern Illinois University (B.A., 1983); Chicago-Kent College of Law, Illinois Institute of Technology (J.D., 1989). ***REPORTED CASES:*** K.F. v. River Bend Community Unit School District No. 2, 2002 U.S. Dist. Lexis 12468 (2002); Smith v. Guide, 2002 U.S. Dist. Lexis 1193; Bell v. Marseilles Elementary School District No. 150, 2001 U.S. Distr. Lexis 2367 (2001); Trout v. Frega, 926 F. Supp. 117 (N.D.Ill.1996); West Bend Insurance v. Mulligan Masonry, 337 Ill.App.3d, 786 N.E.2d 1078 (2003). ***Email:*** smyrniotis@litchfieldcavo.com

SCOTT D. STEPHENSON, born St. Louis, Missouri; admitted to bar, 1987, Illinois; 1989, U.S. District Court, Northern District of Illinois. *Education:* University of Missouri, Columbia (B.A., 1983); John Marshall Law School (J.D., 1986). ***Email:*** stephenson@litchfieldcavo.com

PATRICK J. SULLIVAN, born Evergreen Park, Illinois; admitted to bar, 1990, New York and U.S. District Court, Southern and Eastern Districts of New York; 1992, District of Columbia; 1993, Illinois; U.S. District Court, Northern District of Illinois. *Education:* Northern Illinois University (B.A., cum laude, 1986); University of Iowa (J.D., with distinction, 1989). Co-Author: "Analysis and Update of 'Expected/Intended' Issues" and "Analysis and Update of 'Known Loss' Issues," papers prepared for Midwest Environmental Claims Association Annual Meeting, 1998. Author: "Bootstrapping of Hearsay Under Fed. R. Evid. 801(d)(2)(E): Further Erosion of the Co-Conspirator Exception," 74 Iowa L. Rev. 467 (1989). ***REPORTED CASES:*** Reliance Group Holdings, Inc. v. National Union Fire Ins. Co., 594 N.Y.S.2d 20 (1st Dept. 1993); Borg-Warner, Inc. v. Ins. Co. of North America, 577 N.Y.S.2d 953 (3rd Dept.), appeal denied, 600 N.E.2d 632 (1992); Ins. Corp. of Ireland v. J.L. Kelley, 570 N.Y.S.2d 569 (1st Dept. 1991). ***Email:*** sullivan@litchfieldcavo.com

CHARLES E. VERMETTE, JR. (Not admitted in Illinois; Resident, Avon, Connecticut Office)

ASSOCIATES

ALAN M. BERNOVER, born Chicago, Illinois; admitted to bar, 2001, Florida; 2002, Illinois and U.S. District Court, Northern District of Illinois. *Education:* University of Missouri (B.A., 1997); University of Miami (J.D., cum laude, 2001). ***Email:*** bernover@litchfieldcavo.com

JAMES M. BONALSKY (Resident, New York, N.Y. Office)

KATHLEEN J. COLLINS, born Philadelphia, Pennsylvania; admitted to bar, 1991, Pennsylvania and New Jersey; 1993, U.S. District Court, Eastern and Middle Districts of Pennsylvania; 2000, Illinois. *Education:* Rutgers University (B.A., 1987); Widener University (J.D., 1991). (Resident, Cherry Hill, New Jersey Office). ***Email:*** collins@litchfieldcavo.com

DAVID A. CORBETT (Not admitted in Illinois; Resident, Avon, Connecticut Office)

PETER CUSICK (Resident, New York, N.Y. Office)

LUANA DiSARRA (Resident, Lynnfield, Massachusetts Office)

DENNIS DOLAN, born Southfield, Michigan; admitted to bar, 1995, Illinois. *Education:* University of Notre Dame (B.S., 1989); Wayne State University (J.D., cum laude, 1995). ***Email:*** dolan@litchfieldcavo.com

STEPHANIE L. DYKEMAN (Resident, Brookfield, Wisconsin Office)

JODI ZILS GAGNE (Resident, Avon, Connecticut Office)

KATHLEEN M. HANSBERRY (Resident, Cherry Hill, New Jersey Office)

MICHAEL J. HEINLE, admitted to bar, 2002, Illinois. *Education:* Loyola University (B.A., 1999); Chicago-Kent College of Law (J.D., 2002). ***Email:*** heinle@litchfieldcavo.com

TIMOTHY S. JAJLIARDO (Not admitted in Illinois; Resident, Avon, Connecticut Office)

DANIEL P. JOHNSTON, born Evergreen Park, Illinois; admitted to bar, 1997, Illinois and U.S. District Court, Northern District of Illinois. *Education:* University of Illinois, Urbana-Champaign (B.A., 1993); Drake University (J.D., 1996). ***Email:*** johnston@litchfieldcavo.com

SAMANTHA A. LEVINSON, admitted to bar, 2001, Illinois. *Education:* Georgetown University (B.S., 1996); John Marshall Law School (J.D., 2001). RN Firefighter III, OSHA Hazmat, EMT-D, PSIA Ski Instructor. ***PRACTICE AREAS:*** Litigation. ***Email:*** levinson@litchfieldcavo.com

RICHARD A. LORD, JR. (Resident, Avon, Connecticut Office)

MARK S. NAZAROF, born Chicago, Illinois; admitted to bar, 2003, Illinois. *Education:* Illinois State University (B.S. in Political Science and History, 1999); Chicago-Kent College of Law (J.D., 2003). ***Email:*** nazarof@litchfieldcavo.com

JAMES P. ODDA (Resident, Brookfield, Wisconsin Office)

DANIEL S. ORENSTEIN, admitted to bar, 2000, Illinois. *Education:* University of Iowa (B.A., 1997); Chicago-Kent College of Law (J.D., 2000). ***Email:*** orenstein@litchfieldcavo.com

JACOB W. OSHER (Resident, Cherry Hill, New Jersey Office)

OHN PARK, born Seoul, Korea; admitted to bar, 1996, Illinois; 1997, U.S. District Court, Northern District of Illinois. *Education:* Dartmouth College (B.A., 1991); University of Illinois (J.D., 1996). ***Email:*** park@litchfieldcavo.com

WILLIAM J. PERRY, born Evanston, Illinois; admitted to bar, 1995, Illinois; 1999, Wisconsin. *Education:* University of Wisconsin at Madison (B.A., 1991); University of Illinois (J.D., 1995). ***Email:*** perry@litchfieldcavo.com

(This Listing Continued)

LITCHFIELD CAVO LLP, Chicago—Continued

BRIAN M. REID, born Columbus, Ohio; admitted to bar, 1993, Illinois. *Education:* University of Richmond (B.S., 1989); Chicago-Kent College of Law (J.D., 1993). ***Email:*** reid@litchfieldcavo.com

DEBORAH E. ROSER (Not admitted in Illinois; Resident, Avon, Connecticut Office)

JAMES W. SEXTON (Resident, Lynnfield, Massachusetts Office)

CHRISTOPHER J. SOCHACKI (Resident, Avon, Connecticut Office)

KEVIN J. SPAGNOLI (Resident, New York, N.Y. Office)

MELICENT B. THOMPSON (Not admitted in Illinois; Resident, Avon, Connecticut Office)

STEPHANIE WING TIPTON, born Brunswick, Maine; admitted to bar, 1999, Illinois and U.S. District Court, Northern District of Illinois. *Education:* University of Southern Maine, (B.A., magna cum laude, 1990); Chicago-Kent College of Law (J.D., 1999). ***Email:*** tipton@litchfieldcavo.com

MATTHEW D. WALKER, born Markham, Illinois; admitted to bar, 1997, Illinois. *Education:* University of Illinois (B.A., 1994); University of Illinois (J.D., 1997). ***Email:*** walker@litchfieldcavo.com

RENEE H. WISZOWATY, admitted to bar, 2002, Illinois. *Education:* Illinois Wesleyan University (B.A., cum laude, 1999); Drake University (J.D., 2002). ***Email:*** wiszowaty@litchfieldcavo.com

REPRESENTATIVE CLIENTS: AIG Technical Services, Inc.; Astrazeneca Pharmaceuticals; Bay View Bank; BDO Siedman; Bechtel Corp.; Certain Underwriters at Lloyd's, London; Chubb Group Insurance; Cincinnati Insurance Co.; Essex Insurance Co.; Farmers Insurance Group; Glaxo Smithkline Beecham; Hartford Insurance Co.; Kroger Cos.; Liberty International Underwriters; Lincoln General Insurance Co.; Mori Seiki Co., Ltd.; Old Dominion Freight Lines, Inc.; Rimkus Consulting Group, Inc.; Robert Morris College; Schindler Elevator Co.; Scottsdale Insurance Company; Shell Oil/Jiffy Lube International; Simon Property Group; St. Paul Travelers; U.S. Foodservice, Inc.; Vanguard Car Rental; W. L. Gore & Associates; Wells Fargo Mortgage Co.

LITTLER MENDELSON

A PROFESSIONAL CORPORATION

Established in 1942

200 NORTH LASALLE STREET, SUITE 2900

CHICAGO, ILLINOIS 60601-1014

Telephone: 312-372-5520
Facsimile: 312-372-7880
Email: info@littler.com
URL: http://www.littler.com

Offices located in: Phoenix, Arizona; California -- Fresno, Los Angeles, Sacramento, San Diego, San Francisco, San Jose, Santa Maria, Stockton and Walnut Creek; Denver, Colorado; Washington, D.C.; Miami, Florida; Atlanta, Georgia; Boston, Massachusetts; Minneapolis, Minnesota; Reno and Las Vegas, Nevada; Newark, New Jersey; New York, New York; Charlotte, North Carolina; Columbus, Ohio; Philadelphia and Pittsburgh, Pennsylvania; Dallas and Houston, Texas; Seattle, Washington.

Employment and Labor Law; Affirmative Action; Age Discrimination in Employment Civil Service; Collective Bargaining; Confidentiality Agreements; Covenants Not To Compete; Employee Drug Testing; Employee Privacy; Employer Liability; Employment Arbitration; Employment Breach of Contract; Employment Civil Rights; Employment Class Actions; Employment Discrimination; Employment Litigation; Equal Employment Opportunity Law; Fair Labor Standards; Family and Medical Leave Act; Harassment; Labor Relations; Labor Strikes; National Labor Relations Act; Noncompete Litigation; Noncompetition and Non-Solicitation Agreements; Personnel Policies; Prevailing Wage Litigation; Reductions in Force; Restrictive Covenants; Sexual Harassment; Title VII Discrimination; Unfair Labor Practices; Union Contract Negotiations; Union Elections; Union Organization; Wage and Hour Law; WARN Act; Whistleblower Litigation; Workplace Violence; Wrongful Termination; Wrongful Termination Defense.

FIRM PROFILE: Littler Mendelson, a Professional Corporation, is the largest law firm in the United States engaged exclusively in the practice of employment and labor law. The firm has 400 attorneys in 28 offices nationwide who represent and advise management in all major subspecialties of employment and labor law including wrongful termination; sex, race, and age discrimination; wage and hour law; NLRB cases and collective bargaining; workers' compensation; unemployment benefits; workplace violence; substance abuse; employee privacy rights; occupational safety and health; the ADA; FMLA; ERISA; employee benefits; tax issues and immigration.

JODY A. BALLMER, born Janesville, Wisconsin, April 15, 1965; admitted to bar, 1992, Illinois and U.S. District Court, Northern District of Illinois including Trial Bar; 1993, Wisconsin; U.S. Court of Appeals, Seventh and Eleventh Circuits; U.S. District Court, Central and Southern Districts of Illinois; U.S. District Court, Eastern District of Michigan; U.S. District Court, Northern and Southern Districts of Indiana. *Education:* University of Wisconsin at Platteville (B.S., summa cum laude, 1987); University of Minnesota (J.D., cum laude, 1992). ***PRACTICE AREAS:*** Labor and Employment. ***Email:*** jballmer@littler.com

PAUL E. BATEMAN, born Highland Park, Illinois, February 28, 1956; admitted to bar, 1980, District of Columbia; 1981, U.S. Court of Appeals, First, Fourth, Eighth, Ninth, Tenth and Eleventh Circuits and U.S. Court of Appeals, District of Columbia Circuit; 1984, Illinois; 1985, U.S. District Court, Northern District of Illinois, including Trial Bar; 1988, U.S. District Court, Eastern District of Michigan; U.S. Supreme Court. *Education:* Illinois State University (B.S., 1976); University of Michigan (J.D., 1980). Attorney, National Labor Relations Board, Appellate Court Branch, 1980-1984. *Member:* National and American (Member, Labor and Employment Law Section) Bar Associations; The District of Columbia Bar. ***PRACTICE AREAS:*** Labor and Employment. ***Email:*** pbateman@littler.com

(This Listing Continued)

DANA S. CONNELL, born Charleston, West Virginia, December 16, 1956; admitted to bar, 1982, Illinois; U.S. District Court, Northern District of Illinois including Trial Bar; U.S. District Court, Central District of Illinois; U.S. District Court, Western District of Arkansas; U.S. Court of Appeals, Sixth, Seventh, Eighth and Eleventh Circuits; U.S. Supreme Court. *Education:* Denison University (B.A., 1979); Phi Beta Kappa; Omicron Delta Kappa; Mortar Board; Washington & Lee School of Law (J.D., cum laude, 1982). ***PRACTICE AREAS:*** Labor and Employment. ***Email:*** dconnell@littler.com

SHANTHI V. GAUR, born Chicago, Illinois, August 6, 1970; admitted to bar, 1994, Illinois and U.S. District Court, Northern District of Illinois; U.S. District Court, Eastern and Western Districts of Arkansas; U.S. District Court, Western District of Michigan and Northern District of Ohio; U.S. District Court, Southern District of Indiana; U.S. Court of Appeals, Seventh and Eighth Circuits. *Education:* University of Chicago (B.A., 1991; J.D., 1994). ***PRACTICE AREAS:*** Labor and Employment. ***Email:*** sgaur@littler.com

KEITH C. HULT, born Evergreen Park, Illinois, September 9, 1950; admitted to bar, 1976, Illinois; U.S. District Court, Central and Northern Districts of Illinois including Trial Bar; 1986, U.S. Supreme Court; U.S. Court of Appeals, Fourth, Sixth, Seventh and Eighth Circuits; 2002, U.S. District Court, District of Colorado. *Education:* University of Illinois (A.B., with honors, 1972); The Ohio State University (J.D., cum laude, 1976). ***PRACTICE AREAS:*** Labor and Employment. ***Email:*** khult@littler.com

STEFANIE W. KOHEN, born Suffern, New York, July 16, 1967; admitted to bar, 1994, Illinois; 1997, New Jersey; U.S. District Court, Northern District of Illinois; U.S. District Court, District of New Jersey; U.S. District Court, Northern and Southern Districts of Indiana; U.S. Court of Appeals, Third and Seventh Circuits. *Education:* Rutgers University, Douglass College (B.A., 1989); The John Marshall Law School (J.D., 1994). ***PRACTICE AREAS:*** Labor and Employment. ***Email:*** skohen@littler.com

ROBERT C. LONG, born 1953; admitted to bar, 1979, Illinois. *Education:* Knox College (B.A., magna cum laude, 1975); Harvard University (J.D., 1979). (Also at Columbus, Ohio). ***PRACTICE AREAS:*** Labor and Employment. ***Email:*** rlong@littler.com

JAMES J. OH, born St. Paul, Minnesota, May 2, 1963; admitted to bar, 1987, Illinois; U.S. District Court, Northern and Central Districts of Illinois; U.S. District Court, District of Arizona; U.S. District Court, District of Nebraska; U.S. Court of Appeals, Second, Seventh, Eighth, Ninth and Eleventh Circuits. *Education:* Northwestern University (B.A., with honors, 1984; J.D., 1987). ***PRACTICE AREAS:*** Labor and Employment; Litigation. ***Email:*** joh@littler.com

DAVID J. PARSONS, born Berwyn, Illinois, May 15, 1946; admitted to bar, 1972, Illinois and District of Columbia; U.S. District Court, Northern District of Illinois including Trial Bar; U.S. District Court, Northern and Southern Districts of Indiana; 1978, U.S. Supreme Court; U.S. District Court, Central District of Illinois; U.S. Court of Appeals, Fourth, Fifth, Sixth, Seventh, Eighth and Eleventh Circuits; U.S. District Court, District of Arizona, U.S. District Court, Eastern District of Wisconsin and U.S. District Court, Western District of Michigan. *Education:* Denison University (B.A., 1968); University of Illinois (J.D., 1971). ***PRACTICE AREAS:*** Labor and Employment. ***Email:*** dparsons@littler.com

GARRISON L. PHILLIPS, born 1971; admitted to bar, 1996, Illinois. *Education:* University of Michigan (B.A., 1993); University of Illinois (J.D., 1996).

FREDERICK L. SCHWARTZ, born Madison, Wisconsin, January 7, 1963; admitted to bar, 1990, Illinois, U.S. District Court, Northern District of Illinois; U.S. District Court, Eastern District of Wisconsin and U.S. Court of Appeals, Fourth, Sixth and Seventh Circuits. *Education:* Cornell University (B.S., Industrial and Labor Relations, 1985); University of Minnesota (J.D., cum laude, 1990). ***PRACTICE AREAS:*** Labor and Employment. ***Email:*** fschwartz@littler.com

ADAM C. WIT, born Massapequa, New York, July 13, 1970; admitted to bar, 1995, Illinois and U.S. District Court for the Northern District of Illinois, including Trial Bar; U.S. District Court, Central District of Illinois; U.S. Court of Appeals, Fourth, Sixth and Seventh Circuits; U.S. District Court, Northern District of Indiana; U.S. District Court, District of Colorado. *Education:* George Washington University (B.A., summa cum laude, 1992); Boston College Law School (J.D., cum laude, 1995). Phi Beta Kappa. ***PRACTICE AREAS:*** Labor and Employment. ***Email:*** awit@littler.com

JOHN A. YBARRA, born Chicago, Illinois, October 29, 1961; admitted to bar, 1987, Illinois and U.S. District Court, Northern District of Illinois; U.S. District Court, Eastern District of Wisconsin; U.S. District Court, Western District of Michigan; U.S. District Court, Central District of Illinois; U.S. Court of Appeals, Seventh Circuit; U.S. District Court, Southern District of Indiana. *Education:* DePaul University (B.A., 1984); University of Michigan (J.D., 1987). ***PRACTICE AREAS:*** Employment Law; Unfair Competition; Wage and Hour Law; Class Actions; Litigation; Restrictive Covenants; Discrimination. ***Email:*** jaybarra@littler.com

D. Chad Anderton; Asilia S. Backus; Rachel F. Barner; David L. Christlieb; Terese Connolly; Melodie K. Craft; John Dijohn; Erin Dougherty Foley; Puamuh T. Ghogomu, II; Margaret Parnell Hogan; Stephanie Seay Kelly; Paul Krause; Mary C. O'Neil; Marissa Ross; Alan Satyr; Amy R. Schaefer; Amy Toepper; Amanda Helm Wright.

(For biographical data on personnel at other locations, see Professional Biographies at those cities).

LEONARD D. LITWIN

205 WEST RANDOLPH STREET
SUITE 1410
CHICAGO, ILLINOIS 60606-1894
Telephone: 312-346-9733
Fax: 312-704-4323
Email: leonardlitwin@sbcglobal.net
URL: http://www.lawyers.com/ldlitwinlaw

Personal Injury, Workers Compensation, Family Law, Divorce, Real Estate, Landlord and Tenant Law, Medical Malpractice, Wrongful Death, Social Security Disability, Trusts and Estates, Guardianship and Conservatorship, Consumer Bankruptcy, Adoption Law, Child Custody, Child Support, Premarital Agreements, Spousal Support, Automobile Accidents and Injuries, Dog Bites, Slip and Fall.

LEONARD D. LITWIN, born Chicago, Illinois, July 17, 1957; admitted to bar, 1982, Illinois and U.S. District Court, Northern District of Illinois. *Education:* University of Illinois (A.B., 1979); DePaul University (J.D., 1982). *Member:* Chicago and Illinois State Bar Associations; Illinois Trial Lawyers Association. ***LANGUAGES:*** Spanish. ***PRACTICE AREAS:*** Personal Injury; Divorce; Real Estate; Probate.

LAW OFFICE OF JOHN C. LIVENSPARGER

4753 NORTH BROADWAY
SUITE 620
CHICAGO, ILLINOIS 60640
Telephone: 773-784-2102
Fax: 773-784-2281
Email: livensparger@ameritech.net

Estate Administration, Probate, Real Estate, Corporate, Federal Taxation and Banking Law.

JOHN C. LIVENSPARGER, born Phoenix, Arizona, November 16, 1945; admitted to bar, 1976, Illinois; 1983, U.S. District Court, Northern District of Illinois. *Education:* University of Arizona (B.A., 1967); John Marshall Law School (J.D., with distinction, 1976; LL.M., Taxation, 1983). Phi Alpha Delta. Member, Order of John Marshall. *Member:* Chicago and Illinois State Bar Associations. ***PRACTICE AREAS:*** Estate Administration; Probate; Real Estate; Corporate Law; Federal Taxation; Banking.

LLOYD & CAVANAGH

SUITE 2050
200 WEST MADISON STREET
CHICAGO, ILLINOIS 60606
Telephone: 312-425-1900
Facsimile: 312-425-1904
Email: law@lloydcavanagh.com
URL: http://www.lloydcavanagh.com

Plaintiff's Personal Injury, Motor Vehicle Accidents and Injuries, Catastrophic Injury, Birth Trauma, Automotive Products Liability, Product Defects, Medical Negligence, Drug and Medical Device Litigation, Railroad Accidents and Injuries, Aviation Liability, Construction Accidents, Government Tort Liability, Health Care Liability, Nursing Home Negligence, Managed Care Liability, Wrongful Death.

FIRM PROFILE: Mr. Lloyd and Mr. Cavanagh regularly handle major personal injury and catastrophic loss cases. Mr. Lloyd has obtained numerous million dollar verdicts and settlements including a 9.7 million dollar verdict against a physician in a medical malpractice case and an 8.0 million dollar settlement in a hospital liability case. Mr. Cavanagh also has obtained numerous million dollar verdicts and settlements including a 21.3 million dollar verdict in a train-auto collision case and 9.1 million in a train auto crash.

MEMBERS OF FIRM

KURT D. LLOYD, born Chicago, Illinois, September 10, 1959; admitted to bar, 1985, Illinois; 1986, Florida; 1988, U.S. District Court, Northern District of Illinois including Trial Bar. *Education:* DePaul University (B.A., with honors, English, 1981); IIT/Chicago-Kent College of Law (J.D., 1985). Author: "Closing Argument," *Medical Malpractice Trial Notebook,* 2nd Edition, 1999; "Closing Argument," *Trial Notebook,* 1996. Guest Lecturer: "Use of Experts in Medical Malpractice cases," presented at Illinois Trial Lawyers Association, Point/Counterpoint Seminar, April 2004; Lawyer-Physician Debate: "Medical Malpractice and Tort Reform," presented at Loyola University Medical Center, Maywood, IL, Fall, 2003; "Deposing Defense Witnesses," presented to National Business Institute, Chicago, IL, Fall, 2003; "Governmental Immunity: The Current Case Law," Illinois State Bar Association, Update for Tort and Insurance Litigators, Seminar, April, 2000; "ACOG 163 and Related Defenses," presented at Illinois Trial Lawyers Association, Medical Negligence Seminar, December, 1999; "Jury Instructions," presented at Illinois Trial Lawyers Association, Medical Negligence Seminar, December, 1997; "Gatekeeper Liability: The Plaintiff Lawyer's Perspective," presented at the Chicago Bar Association HMO Liability Seminar, April, 1997; "Deposition Preparation, Strategy and Techniques," presented at the Illinois Trial Lawyers Association Negligence Seminar, February, 1997; "Obstetrics: Overcoming The Proximate Cause Defenses," presented at the Illinois Trial Lawyers Association Annual Medical Malpractice Seminar, December, 1996; Primary Care Physician Liability: New Responsibility Under Managed Care Plans," presented to the Chicago Bar Association Insurance Committee, April, 1996; "Medical Negligence Trials: The Opening Statement and Closing Argument," presented at the Illinois Trial Lawyers Association Annual Medical Malpractice Seminar, December, 1995; "Evidence: Proof in The Medical Negligence Case," presented at the Illinois Trial Lawyers Association Annual Trial Practice Seminar, April, 1994. Co-Chair, Illinois Trial Lawyers Association Continuing Education Programs, 1996-1997. *Member:* Illinois State and American Bar Associations; Illinois Trial Lawyers Association; The Association of Trial Lawyers of America (Member, Leader's Forum); American Board of Trial Advocates (Invited); Trial Lawyers for Public Justice. ***PRACTICE AREAS:*** Plaintiffs Personal Injury; Wrongful Death; Motor Vehicle Accidents and Injuries; Product Defects; Birth Trauma; Gynecology Malpractice; Medical Malpractice; Obstetric Malpractice; Nursing Malpractice; Drug and Medical Device Litigation; Aviation Liability. ***Email:*** kdl@lloydcavanagh.com

(This Listing Continued)

TIMOTHY J. CAVANAGH, born Chicago, Illinois, July 7, 1962; admitted to bar, 1987, Illinois and U.S. District Court, Northern District of Illinois including Trial Bar; 1991, U.S. Court of Appeals, Seventh Circuit. *Education:* John Carroll University (B.A., 1984); IIT Chicago-Kent College of Law (J.D., 1987). Recipient: Excellence in Community Award; Service Award; John Carroll University, December, 1999. Lecturer: "Proper Parties to Lawsuit" Illinois State Bar Association, Chicago, Illinois, January 9, 2004; "Damages Evidence" Lorman Education Services, Oak Brook, Illinois, December 17, 2003; "Railroad Evidence" Illinois Trial Lawyers Association, Chicago, Illinois, October 13, 2003; "Presenting the Expert for Deposition" Chicago Bar Association, Chicago, Illinois, October 3, 2002; "Opening and Closing Statements" Chicago Bar Association, Chicago, Illinois, May 8, 2001; "Evidence Seminar" Moderator, Illinois Trial Lawyers Association, Chicago, Illinois, May 5, 2001; "The Art of Maximizing Damages" Illinois Institute for Continuing Legal Education (IICLE), Chicago, Illinois, December 13, 2000; "Litigating a Civil Case in Cook County," Illinois State Bar Association, December 9, 1999; "The Plaintiffs' Attorney's View of Current Medical Malpractice Issues", Hospital Insurance Risk Managers (CHRMS), May 5, 1999; "Illinois Issues in Review," Television Program Panelist, Chicago, Illinois, February 19, 1999; "Trial Techniques," Moderator, Illinois Trial Lawyers Association, January 9, 1999; "Litigating a Civil Case in Cook County," Illinois State Bar Association, December 10, 1998; "Aggravation of a Pre-Existing Condition-Plaintiff's View," Illinois Trial Lawyers Association, May 9, 1998; "Arbitration", Chicago Bar Association, January 22, 1998; "Litigating a Civil Case in Cook County," Illinois State Bar Association, December 11, 1997; "Trial Objections and Effectively Responding to Objections," Chicago Bar Association, December 4, 1997; "Uninsured/Underinsured Motorist Claims," Illinois Trial Lawyers Association, September 6, 1997; "Jury Deliberations and After the Verdict," Illinois Trial Lawyers Association, May 3, 1997; "Litigating a Civil Case in Cook County," Illinois State Bar Association, December 12, 1996; "Trial Techniques," Program Planning Chair, Illinois Trial Lawyers Association, October 14, 1996; Litigating a Civil Case in Cook county," Illinois State Bar Association, May 31, 1996; "Slimming Down," Civil Pre Trial Practice Seminar, Illinois Trial Lawyers Association, February 3, 1996; Litigating a Civil Case in Cook County," Illinois State Bar Association, November 30, 1995; "Life Before and After House Bill 20 - Premises Liability Reforms," Illinois Trial Lawyers Association, May 6, 1995; "A Plaintiff's Counsel's Perspective on Joint & Several Liability and Section 2-1117" Chicago Bar Association, January 25, 1995; "Litigating a Civil Case in Cook County," Illinois State Bar Association, December 1994; "Litigating a Civil Case in Cook County," Illinois State Bar Association, November 11, 1993; "Public Service," Illinois State Bar Association, November 5, 1992. Author: "Supreme Court Hands Victory to Railroad Industry in Crossing Case," Illinois State Bar Association, Tort Trends, June, 2000; "Section 2-1117: Modified joint and several liability in Illinois," Illinois State Bar Association - Trial Briefs, 1995. Director, 1989-1992, Young Irish Fellowship Club of Chicago. Founder, Director, President, 1989—, Michael Begg Foundation. *Member:* Chicago (Tort Litigation Committee), Illinois State (Member, Elected Assembly Member, 1999-2000) and American Bar Associations; Illinois Trial Lawyers Association (Board of Advocates Member); Leading American Attorneys; Catholic Lawyers Guild of Chicago; The Trial Lawyers for Public Justice Foundation (TLPJ); The Million Dollar Advocates Forum. ***PRACTICE AREAS:*** Plaintiffs Personal Injury; Wrongful Death; Railroad Accidents and Injuries; Product Defects. ***Email:*** tjc@lloydcavanagh.com

ASSOCIATES

MATTHEW M. RUNDIO, born Evanston, Illinois, January 15, 1975; admitted to bar, 2000, Illinois and U.S. District Court, Northern District of Illinois. *Education:* University of Illinois at Urbana-Champaign (B.S., 1997); Loyola University (J.D., 2000). *Member:* Chicago, Illinois State and American Bar Associations; Illinois Trial Lawyers Association (Member, Amicus Curiae Committee, 2000—); Association of Trial Lawyers of America. ***PRACTICE AREAS:*** Plaintiffs Personal Injury; Wrongful Death; Medical Negligence. ***Email:*** mmr@lloydcavanagh.com

BRYAN C. LARSEN, born Des Moines, Iowa, April 1, 1977; admitted to bar, 2004, Illinois. *Education:* University of Texas (B.A., 1999); Illinois Institute of Technology, Chicago-Kent College of Law (J.D., 2003). *Member:* Illinois State Bar Association; Illinois Trial Lawyers Association. ***PRACTICE AREAS:*** Plaintiffs Personal Injury; Medical Negligence; Wrongful Death. ***Email:*** bel@lloydcavanagh.com

ROBERT K. LOCK, JR.

7144 NORTH HARLEM AVENUE, SUITE 323
CHICAGO, ILLINOIS 60631
Telephone: 773-631-0064
Fax: 206-338-6036
Email: debtlawyer@sbcglobal.net
URL: http://www.rklockandassociates.com

Complex Corporate Litigation and Negotiation, Credit Collection, Complex Class Action Litigation.

ROBERT K. LOCK, JR., born Chicago, Illinois, October 9, 1958; admitted to bar, 1989, Illinois. *Education:* University of Arizona (1978); University of San Francisco (B.A., English, 1980); John Marshall Law School (J.D., 1989). Assistant State's Attorney, Cook County, Illinois, 1985-1993. Executive Assistant, Illinois Commerce Commission, 1993-1996. Member, Mayor Daley's Council of Technology Advisors, 2003—. President and General Counsel, Competitive Strategies Group, 1996-2000. Contributing Author, International Engineering Consortium. Published Articles on Legal and Policy Issues. *Member:* Chicago (Chair, Public Utilities Committee, 1997-1998), Illinois State and American Bar Associations. ***LANGUAGES:*** Spanish and German. ***PRACTICE AREAS:*** Telecommu-

(This Listing Continued)

ROBERT K. LOCK, JR., Chicago—Continued

nications Law; Public Utilities Regulatory Law; Complex Corporate Litigation; Complex Class Action Litigation.

BARRY LOCKE & ASSOCIATES, LTD.

205 WEST WACKER DRIVE, SUITE 2333
CHICAGO, ILLINOIS 60606
Telephone: 312-553-1911
Fax: 312-251-0021
Email: blocke@205wacker.com
URL: http://www.barrylockechicagolaw.com

Family Law, Divorce, Child Custody, Child Support, Paternity, Parentage, Visitation Rights.

FIRM PROFILE: The firm was founded, "To preserve the best in trusts of the family and of society, improve the practice, elevate the standards and advance the cause of Matrimonial Law." Mr. Locke has extensive experience as a divorce mediator and as an attorney representing parties in matrimonial matters. The firm has handled many significant matters, especially in Chicago, Northbrook and Glenview.

BARRY LOCKE, born 1947; admitted to bar, 1991, Illinois. *Education:* Temple University (M.B.A., 1975); John Marshall Law School (J.D., 1991). (Also Member, Gessler Hughes Socol Piers Resnick & Dym, LTD., Chicago, Illinois). ***PRACTICE AREAS:*** Family Law.

LAW OFFICES OF DAVID H. LOCKS

5901 NORTH CICERO, SUITE 406
CHICAGO, ILLINOIS 60646-5711
Telephone: 773-736-5700
Fax: 773-736-5444
Email: lockslaw@aol.com
URL: http://www.lockslawfirm.com

Contested Wills, Trusts and Estates, Real Estate Transactions and Litigation, Mechanics Liens, Encroachments, Business and Commercial Transactions and Litigation and Insurance Coverage.

FIRM PROFILE: Convenient location off I-94 with free parking and free initial consultation.

Sole practitioner with 30 years of experience in varied general practice. Clients receive personal attention and round the clock availability.

DAVID H. LOCKS, born 1945; admitted to bar, 1971, Illinois. *Education:* University of Illinois (B.A., 1967); Northwestern University (J.D., 1971). ***PRACTICE AREAS:*** Contested Wills; Contested Trusts and Estates; Business Law; Civil Litigation.

ROBERT A. LOEB

221 N. LASALLE STREET
CHICAGO, ILLINOIS 60601
Telephone: 312-368-0611
Fax: 312-606-9133
URL: http://www.robertloeblaw.com
Email: robertloeb@att.net
URL: http://www.lawyers.com/robertaloeblaw

State and Federal Criminal Defense, Felonies, Misdemeanors, Criminal Law, DUI, Traffic Violations, Drug Crimes, White Collar Crime, Murder, Fraud, Wire Fraud, Mail Fraud, Mortgage Fraud, Social Security Fraud, Forfeiture, Gambling Law.

ROBERT A. LOEB, born Chicago, Illinois, 1951; admitted to bar, 1976, Illinois; U.S. Court of Appeals, Fifth and Seventh Circuits; U.S Supreme Court. *Education:* Bowdoin College (B.A., government, 1973); DePaul University (J.D., 1976). *Member:* Chicago, Illinois State and American Bar Associations; Chicago Council of Lawyers; National Association of Criminal Defense Lawyers. ***PRACTICE AREAS:*** Criminal Law; Federal Criminal Law.

LOEB & LOEB LLP

A Limited Liability Partnership including Professional Corporations
Established in 1909
SUITE 2300
321 NORTH CLARK STREET
CHICAGO, ILLINOIS 60610-4714
Telephone: 312-464-3100
Facsimile: 312-464-3111
URL: http://www.loeb.com

Los Angeles, California Office: Suite 2200, 10100 Santa Monica Boulevard, Los Angeles, 90067-4164. Telephone: 310-282-2000. Facsimile: 310-282-2200.
New York, New York Office: 345 Park Avenue, 10154-0037. Telephone: 212-407-4000. Facsimile: 212-407-4990.
Nashville, Tennessee Office: 1906 Acklen Avenue, 37212-3700. Telephone: 615-749-8300. Facsimile: 615-749-8308.

Advertising Law; Antitrust Law; Appellate Practice; Banking Law; Bankruptcy Law; Civil Litigation; Corporate Securities Law; Entertainment Law; Entertainment Finance; Environmental Law; General Corporate Law; Healthcare Law; Intellectual Property Law; International Law; Labor and Employment Law; Real Estate Law; Tax Law; Tax Exempt Organizations Law; Patent, Trademark, Copyright and Unfair Competition; Trusts and Estates, Wills and Probates; White Collar Criminal Investigation.

FIRM PROFILE: Loeb & Loeb LLP is a multiservice national law firm with more than 200 attorneys and offices in New York, Los Angeles, Chicago, and Nashville. The firm is recognized as a leading law firm in the areas of corporate and securities; litigation; entertainment and media; finance; real estate; intellectual property; private equity; employment; advertising and promotions and tax and wealth services. Our clients include some of the world's largest financial institutions, major media and entertainment companies, advertising groups, real estate companies, and Big Four accounting firms, as well as many high-net-worth individuals.

MEMBERS OF FIRM

DANIEL D. FROHLING, born Pompton Plains, New Jersey, May 16, 1957; admitted to bar, 1985, Illinois. *Education:* University of Freiburg; University of Michigan (A.B., 1980; J.D., cum laude, 1985). *Member:* Chicago, Illinois State and American Bar Associations; Intellectual Property Law Association of Chicago; International Trademark Association; American Intellectual Property Law Association. ***LANGUAGES:*** German. ***PRACTICE AREAS:*** Litigation; Intellectual Property; Trademark Law; Unfair Competition Law; Copyright Law. ***Email:*** dfrohling@loeb.com

MARY E. INNIS, born Springfield, Illinois, March 3, 1962; admitted to bar, 1987, Illinois. *Education:* Augustana College (B.A., cum laude, 1984); Boston University (J.D., 1987). Recipient, American Jurisprudence Award in Secured Transactions. Edward F. Hennessey Scholar. *Member:* Chicago (Member, Executive Council, Young Lawyers Section, 1992-1994; Chair, Intellectual Property Law Committee, Young Lawyers Section, 1992-1994), Illinois State and American Bar Associations; Intellectual Property Law Association of Chicago; International Trademark Association; Promotional Marketing Association. ***PRACTICE AREAS:*** Litigation; Intellectual Property; Advertising Law; Promotion Law. ***Email:*** minnis@loeb.com

DOUGLAS N. MASTERS, born Chicago, Illinois, April 19, 1963; admitted to bar, 1988, Illinois. *Education:* Cornell University (B.A., with distinction, 1985); Harvard Law School (J.D., cum laude, 1988). Phi Beta Kappa; Phi Delta Phi. Member, Mortar Board. Adjunct Professor, Trial Advocacy, Northwestern University School of Law, 2004—. Lecturer, Intellectual Property Litigation, University of Chicago Law School, 2004—. Editorial Board, Trademark Reporter, 1997—. *Member:* Chicago, Illinois State, Federal and American Bar Associations; Intellectual Property Law Association of Chicago; Chicago Council of Lawyers. ***PRACTICE AREAS:*** Litigation; Intellectual Property; Trademark Law; Copyright Law; Unfair Competition Law. ***Email:*** dmasters@loeb.com

EDWARD G. WIERZBICKI, born Chicago, Illinois, September 3, 1949; admitted to bar, 1975, Illinois. *Education:* Bradley University (B.A., magna cum laude, 1971); University of Chicago (J.D., 1975). Pi Sigma Alpha. Author: "The Right of Publicity and the Look Alike and Sound Alike Controversy," AIPLA Vol. IX No. 2 (February 1992). Member, Editorial Board, Trademark Reporter, 1983-1986; 1991-1994. Chairman, Saul Lefkowitz Moot Court Competition, Brand Names Education Foundation, 2000-2001. *Member:* Chicago, Illinois State and American Bar Associations; American Intellectual Property Law Association; Intellectual Property Law Association of Chicago; Lawyers for the Creative Arts; National Academy of Recording Arts and Sciences. ***PRACTICE AREAS:*** Litigation; Intellectual Property; Trademark Law; Copyright Law; Unfair Competition Law. ***Email:*** ewierzbicki@loeb.com

ASSOCIATES

NATHAN J. HOLE, born Lansing, Michigan, July 26, 1979; admitted to bar, 2004, Illinois. *Education:* Tulane University (B.A., cum laude, 2001); University of Michigan (J.D., 2004). ***PRACTICE AREAS:*** Intellectual Property; Litigation. ***Email:*** nhole@loeb.com

NERISSA COYLE McGINN, born Flemington, New Jersey, July 10, 1972; admitted to bar, 1997, Illinois. *Education:* University of Illinois (B.S., magna cum laude, 1994); Harvard University (J.D., cum laude, 1997). Adjunct Professor, The John Marshall Law School. ***PRACTICE AREAS:*** Litigation; Intellectual Property. ***Email:*** nmcginn@loeb.com

SUSAN E. LOGGANS & ASSOCIATES, P.C.

33 NORTH LASALLE STREET, SUITE 1910
CHICAGO, ILLINOIS 60602-2604
Telephone: 312-201-8600
Telecopier: 312-201-1180
URL: http://www.logganslaw.com

Plaintiffs Personal Injury Litigation, General Civil Trial Practice, Negligence Aviation, Product Liability, Wrongful Death, Medical Negligence and Tort Law, Commercial Litigation.

FIRM PROFILE: Susan E. Loggans & Associates, P.C., is a personal injury law firm whose name is synonymous with tough, no nonsense litigation resulting in appropriate compensation for victims injured or killed as a result of negligence or other improper conduct. "We will fight for you!" is the firm's promise. The firm was founded in Chicago in 1977 by Susan E. Loggans.

Ms. Loggans has represented hundreds of children with cerebral palsy in medical malpractice cases. She has recovered many millions of dollars to provide these children with needed care, equipment, educational computers and the means to sustain life. Reflecting a commitment to aid victims with cerebral palsy that is above and beyond just legal representation, Ms. Loggans herself has been active in many charitable organizations dealing with this devastating condition. One such organization is United Cerebral Palsy in Chicago where she has served as a member of the Board of Directors for the past fifteen years.

The firm handles cases involving aviation tragedies (Ms. Loggans is a multi-engine rated pilot), all types of medical negligence, product liability cases, motor vehicle collisions, construction injuries, and premises liability matters.

(This Listing Continued)

Holding national and state records such as a 16 million dollar cash recovery against an HMO and a 6.5 million dollar verdict in a malpractice case in a county just outside of Chicago, Ms. Loggans is an active trial attorney.

Named as one of the country's "Top 15 Trial Attorneys" by the National Law Journal in 1985, Ms. Loggans' career is remarkable. She is a multi-published writer and a popular lecturer and teacher, quick to donate her time as requested by many universities, law schools and organizations both in medicine and in the law nationally and internationally. She has been chosen to lead innumerable bar association sections, committees and programs. You may have seen her on Oprah, NBC's Today Show, or Montel Williams, where she has been asked to provide her expertise. For several years she hosted her own nationally syndicated radio talk show, and currently you can see her weekly TV show in Chicago and on FOX News.

Despite her active trial schedule, Susan personally supervises an office staff of thirty persons and directs a cadre of attorneys in the many aspects of tort law. The title of one of her publications, "...Nothing Left to Chance," could well describe her dedication to the law profession.

Susan E. Loggans & Associates, P.C., includes a number of other experienced trial lawyers, some of whom are also in demand as authors and lecturers on legal subjects related to the compensation of people injured through the fault of others.

SUSAN E. LOGGANS, born Clinton, Illinois, December 31, 1949; admitted to bar, 1974, Illinois; 1975, Florida. *Education:* University of Arkansas and University of Illinois (A.B., 1971); John Marshall Law School and DePaul University (J.D., 1974). Phi Alpha Delta (Vice Justice, 1972 and Justice, 1973). Recipient, Spirit of Love Award, Little City Foundation, 1986. Multi-Engine Rated Pilot, Illinois, 1976. Author: "Aviation Discovery: The Herculean Task," Trial Magazine, August, 1978; "A Demonstration of Demonstrative Evidence," Trial Diplomacy Journal, 1980; "Personal Injury Damages in International Aviation Litigation: The Plaintiff's Perspective," John Marshall Law Review, May, 1980; "Prejudgment Interest," Trial Magazine, January, 1981; "Psychiatrists and Hospitals: Liability for Patients' Self-Inflicted Injuries," The American Journal of Trial Advocacy, Vol. 5, No. 1, Summer, 1981; "Presumptions, Basic Burden of Proof Considerations," Illinois Trial Lawyers Journal, Vol. 3, November 4, 1981; "Practical Distinctions Between Litigation of Commercial and General Aviation Cases," Personal Injury Annual, Matthew Bender, 1981; "Psychiatric Malpractice Tips," The Malpractice Reporter, Summer, 1982; "Montreal Protocol Three - A Proposal Whose Time Has Passed," The Journal of Air Law and Commerce, March, 1983; "Effective Use of Discovery at Trial," Trial Diplomacy Journal, Spring, 1983; "Landing the Aviation Case," The Complete Lawyer, Fall, 1984; "Rape as an Intentional Tort," Trial Magazine, October, 1985; "Products Liability Litigation: Case Evaluation," Callaghan & Co., November, 1988; "Motions in Limine," *ATLA Litigating Tort Cases,* Chapter 19, Volume 2, 2003. Lecturer: "Aviation Discovery Methods," Association of Trial Lawyers of America, 1978; "The Law of Damages in Aviation Litigation," Association of Trial Lawyers of America, 1978; "Gathering the Evidence, Preparation of Damages, Source Materials, Proofs," Association of Trial Lawyers of America, 1978; "Sources of Experts in Aviation Products Cases," Association of Trial Lawyers of America, 1979; "Liability of Psychiatrists and Hospitals for Patient Suicide," Melvin Belli Seminars, July, 1980; "Client Interview, Investigation and Gathering Facts," Illinois Trial Lawyers Association, 1980; "Effective Use of Aviation Experts," Association of Trial Lawyers of America, 1980; "Initial Client Interview," Association of Trial Lawyers of America, National College of Advocacy, 1980; "Prejudgment Interest," Association of Trial Lawyers of America, 1980; "Federal Tort Claims Based on Negligence in Certification," Academy of Florida Trial Lawyers, 1981; "Settlement Techniques in Aviation Litigation," Association of Trial Lawyers of America, 1981; "Investigation of Aviation Accidents," Association of Trial Lawyers of America, 1982; "Effective Use of Discovery At Trial: Nothing Left to Chance," Association of Trial Lawyers of America, National College of Advocacy, 1982; "Proving Damages with an Economist," Association of Trial Lawyers of America, 1982; "Proving the Intangibles," Academy of Florida Trial Lawyer's, October, 1983; "Circumventing the Personal Injury and Wrongful Death Damages Limitation of the Warsaw Convention," Association of Trial Lawyers of America, 1984; "Avoiding Warsaw Limitations In Third-Party Products Claims," Products Liability Law and Techniques SMV Air Law Symposium, 1984; "Dynamic Closing Arguments," ABA Institute on Advanced Trial Techniques and Tactics, February, 1985; "Rape as an Intentional Tort," Trial Magazine, October, 1985; "Aviation Disaster Cases, New and Creative Concepts in Investigation and Discovery," Florida Trial Lawyers, December, 1986; The Profoundly Injured Child - Recognizing a Cause of Action Exists," Association of Trial Lawyers of America, 1986; "Voir Dire: Seeking the Open-Minded Peer," Legal-Medical Seminars, Inc., 1987; "Products Liability," The Mormon Group-Law Conference, 1987; "Products Liability-Voir Dire," Nevada Trial Lawyers Association, 1987; "Informed Consent," American Medical Writers Association, 1987; "Interspousal Tort Immunity," Chicago Bar Association, 1988. Member: The Women's Board, 1985— and Board of Directors, 1987, United Cerebral Palsy of Greater Chicago; "Cross-Ups in Cross-Examination, Trial Diplomacy Journal," Volume 15, Number 4, July/August, 1992. *Member:* Chicago (Member, Baker Task Force on Specialization and Certification, 1979; Chairman, Aviation Law Section, 1979 and 1980; Vice Chairman, 1978 and 1979; Member, Subcommittee on Medical Malpractice, 1977), Illinois State (Member: Board of Governors, 1980 and 1982; Assembly, First Judicial District, 1979 and 1981; Civil Practice and Procedure Section Council, 1978 and 1980; Tort Law Section Council, 1978 and 1980) and American (Vice Chairman, Committee on Aviation and Space Law, Section of Tort and Insurance Practice, 1979—; Vice Chairman, Special Committee on Uniform State Laws, Section of Tort and Insurance Practice, 1979 and 1980; Member: Standing and Advisory Committees, Aeronautical Law, 1980—; Section of Tort and Insurance Practice, 1974—; Litigation Section, 1978—) Bar Associations; The Florida Bar; The Association of Trial Lawyers of America (Chairman, 1982 and 1984, Vice Chairman, 1980 and 1982 and Secretary, 1978-1980, Aviation Law Section; Chairman, 1986-1987, Vice Chairman, 1985-1986 and Second Vice Chairman, 1984-1985, Tort Law Section; Vice Chair of Research and Legal Department, 1982 and 1983; Secretary, Young Lawyers Section, 1987 and 1980; Member, M Club, Political Action Committee, 1982—); Illinois Trial Lawyers Association (Member, Board of Managers, 1977-1982; Chairman, Special Committee on Organization, 1978; Vice Chairman, Membership Committee, 1977 and 1980); Florida Trial Lawyers Association; Florida Association of Women Lawyers; Lawyer-Pilots Bar Association; American Judicature Society; Roscoe Pound Foundation. Fellow, American Bar Foundation. Certified as a Civil Trial Advocate by the National Board of Trial Advocacy. ***PRACTICE AREAS:*** Plaintiffs Personal Injury Litigation. ***Email:*** loggans@logganslaw.com

(This Listing Continued)

MATTHEW R. BASINGER, born July 17, 1978; admitted to bar, 2003, Ohio and U.S. District Court, Northern District of Ohio; 2005, Illinois. *Education:* Ohio University (B.S., 2000); Cleveland-Marshall College of Law (J.D., 2003). ***PRACTICE AREAS:*** Plaintiffs Personal Injury. ***Email:*** mbasinger@logganslaw.com

---

LONGWELL ASSOCIATES

CHARTERED

111 WEST WASHINGTON STREET, SUITE 1625
CHICAGO, ILLINOIS 60602-2703
Telephone: 312-263-4730
Fax: 312-263-2055
Email: longwell@interaccess.com
URL: http://www.longwell-law.com

Oak Brook, Illinois Office: 1301 West 22nd Street, Suite 914, 60523. Telephone: 630-954-1480.

Family Law including Divorce/Dissolution of Marriage, Child Custody, Child Support, Visitation Rights, Spousal Support/Maintenance/Alimony, Pre-Marital/Post-Marital Agreements, Separation Agreements, QDROS, Marital Property Distribution, Guardianship, School Law including Special Education and Teacher, Dismissal.

FIRM PROFILE: Longwell Associates is different from most Family Law firms in that we work in partnership with our clients. We provide the legal know-how and support to enable clients to reach their desired goals, whether the issue is divorce, custody, support, parentage or something else. We want the results to be tailored to the client's unique situation, not based upon false assumptions or a cookie cutter model.

MARILYN F. LONGWELL, born Columbus, Ohio, June 15, 1943; admitted to bar, 1973, Illinois and U.S. District Court, Northern District of Illinois. *Education:* Muskingum College; The Ohio State University (B.A., 1965); DePaul University (J.D., 1973). Adjunct Professor: School Law, Kent - IIT College of Law, 1979-1981; Graduate School of Education, University of Illinois, 1979-1981. Court-Appointed Child Representative, 1991—. Finalist for Associate Judge, 1999 and 2001. *Member:* Chicago and Illinois State Bar Associations; Women's Bar Association; West Suburban Bar Association. ***PRACTICE AREAS:*** Family Law; School Law. ***Email:*** mlongwell@longwell-law.com

---

DEANNA R. BLAIR, born Boulder, Colorado, 1972; admitted to bar, 2001, Oregon; 2002, U.S. District Court, District of Oregon and U.S. Court of Appeals, Ninth Circuit; 2003, Illinois. *Education:* The Evergreen State College (B.A., 1996); Lewis and Clark College (J.D., cum laude, 2001). Dean's List. Phi Delta Phi. Formerly with Legal Aid Services of Oregon. *Member:* Chicago, DuPage and Illinois State Bar Associations. ***PRACTICE AREAS:*** Family Law. ***Email:*** dblair@longwell-law.com

DIANA T. EPSTEIN, born Boston, Massachusetts; admitted to bar, 1992, Illinois; U.S. District Court, Northern District of Illinois and U.S. Court of Appeals, Seventh Circuit. *Education:* Hartwick College (B.A.); St. John's University (M.A.); University of Wisconsin, Madison (Ph.D.); Chicago-Kent College of Law (J.D., 1992). Director, Blackman Kallick Bartelstein, LLP, 1997-2004. Founder and President, DTE Enterprises, 2002-2003. Associate Attorney, Longwell Associates, Chtd., 1992-1997. Law Clerk for Richard J. Prendergast Ltd., 1990-1992. Data Support Consultant, AON Corporation, 1988-1989. Planning Analyst, Systems Supervisor and Director of Corporate Planning, Chicago Board Options Exchange, 1983-1988. Program Evaluator, Systems Analyst, Applications Manager, Wisconsin Department of Health and Social Services, 1975-1983. Research Assistant and Teaching Assistant, University of Wisconsin-Madison, 1972-1975. Psychologist I, Southern Wisconsin Center, 1972. *Member:* Chicago Bar Association. ***PRACTICE AREAS:*** Family Law. ***Email:*** dtepstein@longwell-law.com

---

PETER B. LOUGHMAN

155 NORTH MICHIGAN AVENUE
SUITE 600
CHICAGO, ILLINOIS 60601
Telephone: 312-616-4250
Fax: 312-616-4252

Real Estate Transaction Law.

PETER B. LOUGHMAN, born Chicago, Illinois, October 29, 1948; admitted to bar, 1973, Illinois. *Education:* Kenyon College (A.B., 1970); Northwestern University (J.D., 1973). Executive Editor, Northwestern University Law Review, 1972-1973. *Member:* Chicago, Illinois State and American Bar Associations.

LAW OFFICE OF EMILY LOVE, P.C.

CHICAGO, ILLINOIS

(See Evanston)

Immigration and Naturalization.

LOVELLS

ONE IBM PLAZA
330 NORTH WABASH AVENUE, SUITE 1900
CHICAGO, ILLINOIS 60611
Telephone: 312-832-4400
Fax: 312-832-4444
Email: information@lovells.com
URL: http://www.lovells.com

REVISER OF THE GERMANY LAW DIGEST FOR THIS DIRECTORY.

Other Offices:
Alicante, Spain
Amsterdam, Netherlands
Beijing, Republic of China
Berlin, Germany
Brussels, Belgium
Budapest, Hungary Associated Office
Dusseldorf, Germany
Frankfurt, Germany
Hamburg, Germany
Ho Chi Minh City, Vietnam
Hong Kong
London, England
Madrid, Spain
Milan, Italy
Moscow, Russia
Munich, Germany
New York, N.Y.
Paris, France
Prague, Czech Republic
Rome, Italy
Shanghai, China
Singapore
Tokyo, Japan
Vienna, Austria Associated Office
Warsaw, Poland
Zagreb, Croatia Associated Office

Alternative Risk Transfer, Arbitration, Aviation, Banking, Banking Litigation, Capital Markets, Commercial and Trading Law, Commodities, Competition Trade and European Law, Computers Communications and Media, Construction, Consumer Financial Services, Corporate, Employees' Share Incentives, Employment, Energy, Environmental Law, Financial Service and Investment Funds, Fraud and Asset Recovery, Insolvency and Business Restructuring, Insurance and Reinsurance, International Arbitration, Intellectual Property, Litigation, Pensions, Private Equity, Product Liability, Project Finance, Property and Planning, Public Policy, Retail Finance, Tax.

PARTNERS

THOMAS F. BUSH, JR., born 1954; admitted to bar, 1979, Illinois. *Education:* Dartmouth College (A.B., magna cum laude, 1976); University of Chicago (J.D., 1979). Law Clerk to the Hon. Collins J. Seitz, Chief Judge, United States Court of Appeals for the Third Circuit, 1979-1980. *Member:* Chicago and American Bar Associations. ***SPECIAL AGENCIES:*** Federal Trade Commission; International Trade Commission; International Trade Administration. ***PRACTICE AREAS:*** Litigation. ***Email:*** tom.bush@lovells.com

GAIL M. GOERING, born 1964; admitted to bar, 1990, Illinois;1999, New York. *Education:* Bethel College (B.A., B.S., summa cum laude, 1987); University of Chicago (J.D., 1990). ***PRACTICE AREAS:*** Litigation; Trial Practice; Reinsurance; Insurance Insolvency; International Arbitration. ***Email:*** gail.goering@lovells.com

ERIC A. HAAB, born 1964; admitted to bar, 1989, Illinois. *Education:* University of Michigan (A.B., with high distinction, 1986); Harvard University (J.D., 1989). ***PRACTICE AREAS:*** Commercial Litigation; Reinsurance; Insurance Insolvency; International Arbitration; Consumer Financial Services. ***Email:*** eric.haab@lovells.com

DAVID C. LINDER, born Hutchinson, Minnesota, March 11, 1964; admitted to bar, 1990, Missouri and U.S. District Court, Western District of Missouri; 1991, Kansas and U.S. District Court, District of Kansas; 1992, U.S. Court of Appeals, Eighth Circuit; 1994, Minnesota and U.S. District Court, Eastern District of Wisconsin; 1995, U.S. Supreme Court; 1997, U.S. District Court, Eastern District of Michigan; 2003, U.S. District Court, District of Minnesota (Not admitted in Illinois). *Education:* University of Minnesota (B.A., summa cum laude, 1986; J.D., magna cum laude, 1990). Phi Beta Kappa. Order of the Coif. Recipient, Harry S. Truman Scholarship. Member, Minnesota Law Review, 1987-1988. Legal Writing Instructor, University of Minnesota Law School, 1987-1988. *Member:* American Bar Association. ***REPORTED CASES:*** Ormet Primary Aluminum Corp. v. Employers Ins. of Wausau, 725 N.E.2d 646 (Ohio 2000); Employers Ins. of Wausau v. Recticel Foam Corp., 716 N.E.2d 1015 (Ind. Ct. App. 1999), transfer denied, 735 N.E.2d 235 (Ind. 2000); Employers Ins. of Wausau v. Ehlco Liquidating Trust, 723 N.E.2d 687 (Ill. App. Ct. 1999), appeal denied, 729 N.E.2d 495 (Ill. 2000); Employers Ins. of Wausau v. Ehlco Liquidating Trust, 687 N.E.2d 82 (Ill. App. Ct. 1997), aff'd in part and rev'd in part, 708 N.E.2d 1122 (Ill. 1999); Employers Ins. of Wausau v. Browner, 52 F.3d 656 (7th Cir. 1995), cert. denied, 516 U.S. 1042 (1996); Interstate Power Co. v. Kansas City Power & Light Co., 992 F.2d 804 (8th Cir. 1993); United States v. Hardage, 982 F.2d 1436 (10th Cir. 1992), cert. denied, 510 U.S. 913 (1993). ***PRACTICE AREAS:*** Insurance; Litigation; Environmental Law. ***Email:*** david.linder@lovells.com

JOSEPH T. McCULLOUGH IV, born 1956; admitted to bar, 1985, Illinois. *Education:* Georgetown University (B.A., magna cum laude, 1979); Rijksuniversiteit te Gent, Belgium (Licentie in het Europees Recht, high honors, 1982); Northwestern University (J.D., cum laude, 1985; Order of the Coif); University of Exeter, England. ***LANGUAGES:*** Flemish, Dutch and German. ***PRACTICE AREAS:*** Reinsurance; Insurance Coverage; International Commercial Litigation; International Arbitration; Insurance Insolvency. ***Email:*** joe.mccullough@lovells.com

NEAL J. MOGLIN, born 1963; admitted to bar, 1988, Illinois. *Education:* Vanderbilt University (B.A., 1985; J.D., 1988). *Member:* Chicago, Illinois State and American Bar Associations. ***PRACTICE AREAS:*** Insurance; Reinsurance; Commercial Litigation. ***Email:*** neal.moglin@lovells.com

KAY E. WILDE, born 1964; admitted to bar, 1989, Illinois. *Education:* University of Wisconsin-Eau Claire (B.A., summa cum laude, 1986); University of Michigan (J.D., 1989). ***PRACTICE AREAS:*** Reinsurance. ***Email:*** kay.wilde@lovells.com

OF COUNSEL

ADAM B. GOODMAN, born Chicago, Illinois, August 13, 1970; admitted to bar, 1995, Illinois, U.S. District Court, Northern District of Illinois; 1996, U.S. Court of Appeals, Seventh Circuit; 1997, U.S. District Court, District of Colorado; 1998, U.S. District Court, Western District of Michigan, U.S. Court of Appeals, Tenth Circuit; 1999, Trial Bar; 2000, U.S. District Court, Eastern District of Wisconsin, U.S. Court of Appeals, Eighth Circuit; 2002, U.S. District Court, Central and Southern Districts of Illinois, U.S. District Court, Northern and Southern Districts of Indiana, U.S. Court of Appeals, Ninth Circuit; 2003, U.S. Supreme Court. *Education:* Rice University (B.A., 1992); University of Chicago (J.D., 1995). Arbitrator, Cook County, Illinois Mandatory Arbitration Program (chair qualified). President, Villa Improvement League, 2003-2004. *Member:* Seventh Circuit Bar Association; Chicago Council of Lawyers (Board of Governors and Chair, Federal Courts Committee 1999-2003). ***PRACTICE AREAS:*** Litigation; Bankruptcy; Insurance; Reinsurance. ***Email:*** adam.goodman@lovells.com

JOHN M. O'BRYAN, born Plainfield, New Jersey, June 4, 1968; admitted to bar, 1997, Illinois; 2001, U.S. Court of Appeals, Seventh Circuit; U.S. District Court, Northern District of Illinois. *Education:* Cornell University (A.B., 1990); Northwestern University (J.D., 1997). Associate Editor, Northwestern University Law Review, 1995-1997. *Member:* American and International Bar Associations. ***PRACTICE AREAS:*** Litigation. ***Email:*** john.obryan@lovells.com

BRAD OCKENE, born Santiago, Chile; admitted to bar, 1989, New York; 2003, Ohio; 2004, Illinois. *Education:* Yale University (B.A., 1984); Emory University (J.D., 1988). ***LANGUAGES:*** Spanish and French.

FRANK B. SLEPICKA, born 1967; admitted to bar, 1992, Illinois. *Education:* Northwestern University (B.A., 1989); University of Illinois College of Law (J.D., 1992). ***PRACTICE AREAS:*** Reinsurance; Arbitration; Insurance Coverage; Commercial Litigation. ***Email:*** frank.slepicka@lovells.com

MARYBETH WILKINSON, born Saint Joseph, Michigan, February 19, 1972; admitted to bar, 1997, Illinois and U.S. District Court, Northern District of Illinois. *Education:* Saint Mary's College (B.A., 1994); Northwestern University (J.D., 1997). *Member:* Chicago Bar Association. ***PRACTICE AREAS:*** Commercial Litigation; Reinsurance Disputes; Trademarks; Securities Litigation. ***Email:*** marybeth.wilkinson@lovells.com

ASSOCIATES

DARROW ABRAHAMS, born Chicago, Illinois, 1973; admitted to bar, 2002, Illinois. *Education:* University of Illinois at Champaign-Urbana (B.A., 1995; J.D., 2002); London School of Economics (M.S., 1996). ***PRACTICE AREAS:*** Litigation. ***Email:*** darrow.abrahams@lovells.com

JODI L. AHLMAN, born Des Moines, Iowa, May 3, 1975; admitted to bar, 2000, Iowa, U.S. District Court, Northern and Southern Districts of Iowa and U.S. Court of Appeals, Eighth Circuit (Not admitted in Illinois). *Education:* University of Iowa (B.A.,with highest distinction, 1997; J.D., with high distinction, 2000). Phi Delta Phi. Finalist, Moot Court Competition. Recipient: University Scholarship; Justice Ullenhopp Scholarship. High School Mock Trial Coach, 2000-2002. *Member:* Polk County and Iowa State Bar Associations; Defense Research Institute. ***PRACTICE AREAS:*** Insurance; Commercial Law. ***Email:*** jodi.ahlman@lovells.com

RACHAEL BLACKBURN, born Winfield, Illinois; admitted to bar, 2002, Wisconsin; 2003, Illinois. *Education:* University of Illinois (B.A.); University of Wisconsin (J.D.). ***PRACTICE AREAS:*** Commercial Litigation; Reinsurance. ***Email:*** rachael.blackburn@lovells.com

ED DIFFIN, born Drexel Hill, Pennsylvania, May 7, 1978; admitted to bar, 2003, Illinois and U.S. District Court, Northern District of Illinois. *Education:* Taylor University (B.A., magna cum laude, 2000); University of Chicago (J.D., 2003). *Member:* Chicago and Illinois State Bar Associations. ***PRACTICE AREAS:*** Litigation; Insurance; Reinsurance. ***Email:*** ed.diffin@lovells.com

ROBIN C. DUSEK, born August 1, 1973; admitted to bar, 1998, Illinois; 1999, U.S. District Court, Northern District of Illinois. *Education:* University of Notre Dame (B.A., 1995); College of William and Mary (J.D., 1998). *Member:* Women's Bar Association of Illinois. ***PRACTICE AREAS:*** Reinsurance; Insurance Coverage; Commercial Litigation. ***Email:*** robin.dusek@lovells.com

JONATHAN R. GLUSMAN, born New Haven, Connecticut, 1968; admitted to bar, 2004, Illinois and U.S. Court of Appeals, Seventh Circuit. *Education:* Beloit College (B.A., 1990); Washington University (J.D., 2004). *Member:* Illinois State Bar Association. ***Email:*** jonathan.glusman@lovells.com

ALEXIS A. HAWKER, born Englewood, Colorado, 1975; admitted to bar, 2000, Illinois and Washington. *Education:* DePauw University (B.A., cum laude, 1997); University of Michigan (J.D., cum laude, 2000). ***PRACTICE AREAS:*** Litigation. ***Email:*** alexis.hawker@lovells.com

MICHELE LYNN HORNISH, born Fort Wayne, Indiana, 1975; admitted to bar, 2001, Missouri; 2002, Illinois. *Education:* University of Missouri (B.A., summa cum laude, 1998; J.D., 2001). Order of the Coif; Order of the Barristers. ***PRACTICE AREAS:*** Commercial Litigation; Reinsurance. ***Email:*** michele.hornish@lovells.com

(This Listing Continued)

KRIS L. McCOY, born Mt. Vernon, Illinois, June 23, 1973; admitted to bar, 1999, Illinois. *Education:* University of Illinois (B.A., summa cum laude, Bronze Tablet, 1994; J.D., cum laude, 1999). Phi Beta Kappa. Contributor: "@ Risk: Internet and E-Commerce Insurance and Reinsurance Legal Issues," a Reactions Publishing, 2000. Co-author: "The Year 2000 Employment Practices Liability Insurance Update." *Member:* Chicago, Illinois and American Bar Associations. ***PRACTICE AREAS:*** Insurance Coverage; Reinsurance Litigation. **Email:** kris.mccoy@lovells.com

R. CHAD McCRACKEN, born Asheville, North Carolina, February 26, 1967; admitted to bar, 1999, Illinois and U.S. District Court, Northern District of Illinois. *Education:* Yale University (B.A., 1988); University of Texas at Austin (M.A., 1994; Ph.D., 1996; J.D., 1999). Book Review Editor, Texas Law Review, 1998-1999. ***PRACTICE AREAS:*** Commercial Litigation; Reinsurance. **Email:** chad.mccracken@lovells.com

RICHARD ALEXANDER NELSON, born Minnesota; admitted to bar, 2003, Illinois. *Education:* Duke University (B.A., 1998); Northwestern University (J.D., 2003). *Member:* Illinois State Bar Association. **Email:** alex.nelson@lovells.com

ERIN O'BRIEN, born Chicago, Illinois, 1975; admitted to bar, 2000, Illinois. *Education:* University of Illinois (B.A., 1997; J.D., 2000). *Member:* Illinois State and American Bar Associations. ***PRACTICE AREAS:*** Reinsurance; International Litigation; International Arbitration. **Email:** erin.obrien@lovells.com

PETER B. STEFFEN, born New Hampton, Iowa, February 8, 1977; admitted to bar, 2001, Illinois and U.S. District Court, Northern District of Illinois. *Education:* Washington University (A.B., cum laude, 1998); University of Chicago (J.D., 2001). ***PRACTICE AREAS:*** Reinsurance; Commercial Litigation. **Email:** pete.steffen@lovells.com

MITCHELL B. WEISS, born Chicago, Illinois, December 17, 1969; admitted to bar, 2000, Illinois. *Education:* Southern Illinois University (B.S., 1992; M. Acct., 1993); University of Chicago (J.D., 2000). Certified Public Accountant, Illinois, 1992. *Member:* Chicago, Illinois and American Bar Associations. ***PRACTICE AREAS:*** Commercial Litigation; Commercial Arbitration. **Email:** mitch.weiss@lovells.com

REVISER OF THE GERMANY LAW DIGEST FOR THIS DIRECTORY.

LOWERY & ASSOCIATES, LLC

333 WEST WACKER DRIVE
SUITE 420
CHICAGO, ILLINOIS 60606-1225
Telephone: 312-460-8788
Facsimile: 312-460-8790
Email: loweryllc@loweryllc.com
URL: http://www.loweryandassociatesllc.com

Insurance Defense, Transportation Law, Truck Accidents, Motor Carrier Defense, Motor Vehicle/Automobile Accidents, Subrogation, Cargo Claims, Commercial Litigation, Wrongful Death, Automobile Accidents and Injuries, Collections, General Business.

FIRM PROFILE: Our firm consists of experienced civil trial attorneys. We strive to provide the highest quality of legal representation and service. We look for proactive, creative and cost-effective solutions for our clients. Our focus is on service to the transportation industry.

TIMOTHY J. LOWERY, born Chicago, Illinois, December 17, 1959; admitted to bar, 1986, Illinois and U.S. District Court, Northern District of Illinois; 1995, U.S. District Court, Northern District of Illinois, Trial Bar; 1996, U.S. Court of Appeals, Seventh Circuit. *Education:* University of Illinois (B.A., English Literature, 1982); Chicago-Kent College of Law, Illinois Institute of Technology (J.D., 1985). Member, Moot Court Society. Member, American Bar Association Team, 1984. *Member:* Illinois State and American (Member, Transportation Section) Bar Associations; Defense Research Institute (Member, Trucking Law Subcommittee); Illinois Association of Defense Trial Counsel; Trucking Industry Defense Association. ***REPORTED CASES:*** Williams v. Bolsten, 184 Ill App. 3d 832, 540 N.E. 2d 966 (1989); Forrester v. Patrick, 167 Ill. App.3d 105, 520 N.E. 2d 1188 (1988); Burton v. Autumn Grain Transport, Inc., 222 Ill. App.3d 755, 584 N.E. 2d 377 (1991); Nieman Marcus Group, Inc. v. Quast Transfer, Inc., 1999 U.S. Dist. Lexis 9564. ***PRACTICE AREAS:*** Insurance Defense; Transportation Law; Truck Accidents; Motor Carrier Defense; Motor Vehicle Accidents and Injuries; Subrogation; Cargo Claims; Commercial Litigation; Wrongful Death; Automobile Accidents and Injuries; Collections; Business Law. **Email:** loweryllc@loweryllc.com

OF COUNSEL

MARTIN B. LOWERY, born Chicago, Illinois, 1926; admitted to bar, 1952, Illinois. *Education:* DePaul University (J.D., 1952). ***PRACTICE AREAS:*** Civil Rights; Employment Discrimination; Administrative Law; Appellate Practice; Litigation; Trial Law; Torts.

KATHLEEN A. SMITH-HASZTO, born Chicago, Illinois; admitted to bar, 1984, Illinois. *Education:* DePaul University (B.S., 1980); Illinois Institute of Technology (J.D., 1984). Arbitrator, Cook County Circuit Court (Chair-Qualified). Formerly with, U.S. General Counsel's Office Dept. of Agriculture. ***PRACTICE AREAS:*** Transportation; Motor Carrier Defense; Cargo Claims; Truck Accidents; Civil Appeals.

ASSOCIATES

JOHN R. WITHALL, born Chicago, Illinois January 22, 1947; admitted to bar, 1976, Illinois. *Education:* Aurora University (B.A., 1973); Chicago-Kent College of Law, Illinois Institute of Technology (J.D., 1976). ***PRACTICE AREAS:*** Torts; Truck Accidents; Motor Carrier Defense; Transportation.

MARIE T. LAPRES, admitted to bar, 1994, Illinois and U.S. District Court, Northern District of Illinois; 1998, Wisconsin. *Education:* University of Michigan (B.S.N., 1989); DePaul University (J.D., 1994). Registered Nurse, 1989—. *Member:* State Bar of Wisconsin; American Bar Association; The American Association of Nurse Attorneys. ***PRACTICE AREAS:*** Insurance; Torts. **Email:** loweryllc@loweryllc.com

BARBARA E. LUSKY

CHICAGO, ILLINOIS

(See Skokie)

Concentration in Family Law, Divorce, Child Custody, Child Support. Also available to practice in Probate, Estate Planning, Civil Litigation.

THOMAS W. LYNCH, P.C.

CHICAGO, ILLINOIS

(See Oak Lawn)

Federal Taxation, IRS and State Representation including Collections Division, Audits, Appeals, Tax Court and State or US District Court, State Taxation, Tax Appeals and Real Estate.

MACCABE & MCGUIRE

SUITE 3333, 77 WEST WACKER DRIVE
CHICAGO, ILLINOIS 60601
Telephone: 312-357-2600
Fax: 312-357-0317
Email: thefirm@maccabe-mcguire.com

Civil Litigation, Transportation, Railroad, Trucking, Premises Liability, Security, Hospitality, Products Liability, Asbestos Defense, Commercial Transactions and Litigation, Employment Law and General Practice.

MEMBERS OF FIRM

EDWARD H. MACCABE, born New York, N.Y., July 18, 1948; admitted to bar, 1978, Illinois, U.S. District Court, Northern District of Illinois including Trial Bar, Southern and Central Districts of Illinois, Northern District of Indiana and Court of Appeals, Seventh Circuit. *Education:* University of Illinois (B.S., 1973); Northern Illinois University (J.D., with honors, 1978). Member, Editorial Board, Northern Illinois University Law Review. *Member:* Chicago and Illinois State Bar Associations; National Association of Railroad Trial Counsel (President, 2003-2004); Academy of Hospitality Industry Attorneys; Trucking Industry Defense Association; Defense Research Institute. [U.S. Army, 1969-1971]. ***PRACTICE AREAS:*** Railroad Defense; Transportation Law; Premises Liability; Asbestos Litigation.

MAUREEN A. McGUIRE, born Chicago, Illinois, June 7, 1956; admitted to bar, 1981, Illinois, U.S. District Court, Northern District of Illinois including Trial Bar, Central District of Illinois and Court of Appeals, Seventh Circuit. *Education:* Loyola University (B.S., 1978); DePaul University (J.D., 1981). Member, De Paul Law Review (Casenote published). *Member:* Illinois State and American Bar Associations; Defense Research Institute; National Association of Railroad Trial Counsel; Women's Bar Association of Illinois; Academy of Hospitality Industry Attorneys; Trucking Industry Defense Association. ***PRACTICE AREAS:*** Civil Litigation; Railroad Defense; Premises Liability; Commercial Transactions.

ANTHONY R. RUTKOWSKI, born Cleveland, Ohio, September 3, 1966; admitted to bar, 1991, Illinois; U.S. District Court, Northern District of Illinois; U.S. Court of Appeals, Seventh Circuit. *Education:* Georgetown University (B.S., 1988); Loyola University School of Law (J.D., 1991). *Member:* Illinois State Bar Associations; Defense Research Institute; American Society for Industrial Security. ***PRACTICE AREAS:*** Civil Litigation; Commercial Litigation; Insurance Defense Litigation.

ASSOCIATES

TIMOTHY J. MURPHY, born Chicago, Illinois, December 3, 1954; admitted to bar, 1979, Illinois and U.S. District Court, Northern and Central Districts of Illinois including Trial Bar. *Education:* Northwestern University (B.S.S., 1976); DePaul University (J.D., 1979).

MICHAEL O. VATES, born Chicago, Illinois, January 21, 1975; admitted to bar, 2000, Illinois and U.S. District Court, Northern District of Illinois, including Trial Bar. *Education:* Northwestern University (B.A., 1997); DePaul University (J.D., 2000).

TIMOTHY J. DEFFET, born Portsmouth, Rhode Island, June 15, 1973; admitted to bar, 1998, Illinois; 2003, U.S. District Court, Northern District of Illinois, including Trial Bar. *Education:* University of Connecticut, Storrs (B.A., 1995); John Marshall Law School (J.D., 1998).

OF COUNSEL

BRIAN J. MULHERN, born Evergreen Park, Illinois, February 14, 1956; admitted to bar, 1981, Illinois and U.S. District Court, Northern District of Illinois. *Education:* University of Notre Dame (B.A., 1978); Northwestern University (J.D., 1981).

MACIOROWSKI, SACKMANN & ULRICH

221 NORTH LASALLE STREET, SUITE 3600
CHICAGO, ILLINOIS 60601
Telephone: 312-236-4600
Fax: 312-236-8459
URL: http://www.msulaw.com

Worker's Compensation Defense Law, including Hospital, Corporations and Business Defense and Labor and Employment Law.

FIRM PROFILE: Maciorowski, Sackmann & Ulrich is an aggressive defense firm, specializing in handling the defense of Workers' Compensation claims for employers, including hospitals, corporations and businesses. Each of the firm's partners has over twenty years of experience in managing and defending workers' compensation claims, and workers' compensation related issues.

(This Listing Continued)

MACIOROWSKI, SACKMANN & ULRICH, Chicago—Continued

The firm practices before the Illinois Industrial Commission, at each site, throughout the entire state. Our practice is exclusively the defense of employers. We take no claims on behalf of injured employees.

MEMBERS OF FIRM

ROBERT E. MACIOROWSKI, born Chicago, Illinois, July 26, 1949; admitted to bar, 1974, Illinois. *Education:* Illinois Benedictine College (B.A., 1971); DePaul University (J.D., 1974). Pi Gamma Mu. DePaul Law Review. Author: "Military Law—Pre-Induction Review," Section 10 (b) 5 of the Military Selective Service Act of 1967, The De Paul Law Review, 1974, Vol. XXII, No. 3. ***PRACTICE AREAS:*** Workers' Compensation Defense; The Americans with Disabilities Act; Third Party Liability; Products Liability; Retaliatory Discharge. ***Email:*** rmacior@msulaw.com

JEREMY P. SACKMANN, born Le Mars, Iowa, June 2, 1951; admitted to bar, 1977, Illinois. *Education:* Michigan State University (B.S., with highest honors, 1973); University of Illinois (J.D., 1977). Phi Beta Kappa; Phi Kappa Phi. *Member:* Chicago, Illinois State and American Bar Associations; Illinois Trial Lawyers Association. ***PRACTICE AREAS:*** Workers' Compensation Defense. ***Email:*** jsackmann@msulaw.com

ROBERT B. ULRICH, born Elmhurst, Illinois, January 8, 1951; admitted to bar, 1980, Illinois; U.S. District Court, Northern District of Illinois and U.S. Court of Appeals, 7th Circuit. *Education:* DePaul University (B.S., 1974; J.D., with honors, 1980). *Member:* Chicago and American (Management Chairman, Workers' Compensation, Labor and Employment Law Sections, 1992-1995) Bar Associations. ***PRACTICE AREAS:*** Workers' Compensation Defense; Labor and Employment Defense Litigation; Products Liability. ***Email:*** rulrich@msulaw.com

ASSOCIATES

GERALDINE M. BALOW, born Chicago, Illinois, June 24, 1955; admitted to bar, 1985, Illinois. *Education:* Mundelein College (1978); Chicago-Kent College of Law (J.D., 1985). *Member:* Chicago, Illinois State and American Bar Associations. ***PRACTICE AREAS:*** Workers Compensation. ***Email:*** gbalow@msulaw.com

TINA L. DePAUL, born Joliet, Illinois, March 4, 1978; admitted to bar, 2003, Illinois and U.S. District Court, Northern District of Illinois. *Education:* Bradley University (B.S., 2000); John Marshall Law School (J.D., 2003). *Member:* Will County, Illinois State and American Bar Associations; Joliet Area Young Professionals Association. ***PRACTICE AREAS:*** Workers Compensation. ***Email:*** tdepaul@msulaw.com

GARY K. GALE, born Chicago, Illinois; admitted to bar, 1980, Illinois. *Education:* Case Western Reserve University (B.A., 1973); University of Missouri (M.A., 1976); Illinois Institute of Technology; Chicago-Kent College of Law (J.D., 1980). *Member:* Illinois State Bar Association (Member, Workers Compensation Section); Workers Compensation Lawyers Association. ***PRACTICE AREAS:*** Workers Compensation. ***Email:*** ggale@msulaw.com

JULIE A. GARRISON, born Chicago, Illinois, June 16, 1958; admitted to bar, 1982, Illinois and U.S. District Court, Northern District of Illinois. *Education:* Valparaiso University (B.A., 1979); DePaul University (J.D., 1982). Phi Alpha Epsilon. *Member:* American Bar Association; Workers Compensation Lawyers Association. ***PRACTICE AREAS:*** Workers' Compensation. ***Email:*** jgarrison@msulaw.com

ERIC S. GRODSKY, born Milwaukee, Wisconsin, 1976; admitted to bar, 2002, Ohio and Wisconsin; 2003, Illinois. *Education:* University of Wisconsin-Madison (B.B.A.,1998); University of Wisconsin-Madison (J.D., 2002). *Member:* Illinois State, Ohio State and American Bar Associations; State Bar of Wisconsin. ***PRACTICE AREAS:*** Civil Litigation; Workers Compensation. ***Email:*** egrodsky@msulaw.com

ROBERT T. NEWMAN, born Urbana, Illinois, November 12, 1951; admitted to bar, 1976, Maryland; 1978, Illinois and U.S. District Court, Northern District of Illinois. *Education:* Johns Hopkins University (B.A., 1973); University of Maryland (J.D., 1976). Co-author: "Advanced Workers' Compensation in Illinois, 1995," copyright 1995, Presented to the 1995 National Business Institute Seminar on Workers; Compensation; "Advanced Workers' Compensation in Illinois, 1996," copyright 1996, Presented in the 1996 National Business Institute Seminar on Workers' Compensation. *Member:* Chicago Bar Association; Workers' Compensation Lawyers Association. ***PRACTICE AREAS:*** Workers Compensation Law. ***Email:*** rnewman@msulaw.com

LAW OFFICES OF MACKEY & KRAMER, P.C.

77 W. WASHINGTON STREET, SUITE 1300
CHICAGO, ILLINOIS 60602
Telephone: 312-263-2000
Fax: 312-263-3484
Email: info@mackey-kramer.com
URL: http://www.mklawoffices.com

Personal Injury, Medical Malpractice, Workers Compensation, Auto Accidents, Wrongful Death, Trucking Accidents, Boating Accidents, Bicycle Accidents, Tractor Accidents, Lawnmower Accidents, Products Liability, Railroad Accidents.

MONTGOMERY WILLIAM MACKEY, born Ann Arbor, Michigan, May 6, 1947; admitted to bar, 1985, Illinois and U.S. District Court, Northern District of Illinois; 1992, Trial Bar for the U.S. District Court, Northern District of Illinois. *Education:* University of Michigan (B.A., 1969); University of Wisconsin (M.S., 1971); Loyola University (J.D., cum laude, 1985). Phi Alpha Delta. Member, *Trial Lawyers for Public Justice, 1998*—. Board of Trustee, Ripon College, 1988-2002. Arbitrator, Circuit Court of Cook County Arbitration Program. *Member:* Illinois State Bar Association (Member Sections on: Tort Law; Civil Practice and Procedure; Workers Compensation); Illinois Trial Lawyers Association; American Trial Lawyers Associations. ***Email:*** monty@mackey-kramer.com

(This Listing Continued)

JACK L. KRAMER, born Chicago, Illinois, March 15,1956; admitted to bar, 1981, Illinois; 1982, U.S. District Court, Northern District of Illinois. *Education:* University of Illinois (B.A., 1978); Illinois Institute of Technology Kent College of Law (J.D., 1981). Illinois State Scholar. Arbitrator, Circuit Court of Cook County, Illinois Mandatory Arbitration Program. *Member:* Chicago and Illinois State Bar Associations. ***Email:*** jack@mackey-kramer.com

MADDEN, JIGANTI, MOORE & SINARS LLP

SUITE 1700
190 SOUTH LA SALLE STREET
CHICAGO, ILLINOIS 60603
Telephone: 312-346-4101
Fax: 312-346-4885
Email: mjms@mjms.com
URL: http://www.mjms.com

Tax and General Business.

MEMBERS OF FIRM

JOHN J. JIGANTI, born Chicago, Illinois, January 25, 1941; admitted to bar, 1964, Illinois; 1972, U.S. Tax Court; 1983, U.S. District Court, Northern District of Illinois including Trial Bar. *Education:* University of Notre Dame (A.B., 1963; LL.B., 1964). Author: "Tax Fraud Defenses" and "I.R.S. Prosecution Strategies," Illinois Institute for Continuing Legal Education, 1975, 1978, 1980, 1982 and 1985. "Tax Court Practice," 1983 and 1985. Coordinator: Illinois Institute for Continuing Legal Education Program. Author: "Federal Civil Tax Practice," 1983, 1985, 1987, 1989 and 1991. Member Board of Directors, Illinois Institute for Continuing Legal Education, 1981-1983; 1985-1987. *Member:* Chicago (Member: Board of Managers, 1978-1982; Candidates Committee, 1973-1978; Treasurer, 1982-1985; Second Vice-President, 1985-1986; First Vice-President, 1986-1987; President, 1987-1988) and Illinois State (Secretary-Treasurer, Lawyers Trust Fund of Illinois, 1992-1994; President, 1994-1997) Bar Associations; Illinois Bar Foundation. Fellow, International Academy of Trial Lawyers; Life Fellow: American Bar Foundation; Illinois Bar Foundation; Chicago Bar Foundation. ***PRACTICE AREAS:*** Tax; Estate Planning and Administration; Business Transactions. ***Email:*** jjiganti@mjms.com

JOHN G. MOORE, born Oak Park, Illinois, October 4, 1953; admitted to bar, 1979, Illinois and U.S. Court of Appeals, Seventh Circuit; 1980, U.S. Tax Court and U.S. District Court, Northern District of Illinois. *Education:* University of Notre Dame (B.B.A., 1975); DePaul University (J.D., 1979; LL.M., 1984). Certified Public Accountant, Illinois, 1975. *Member:* Chicago, Illinois State and American Bar Associations; Illinois Society of Certified Public Accountants; American Institute of Certified Public Accountants; Business Valuation Association. ***PRACTICE AREAS:*** Tax; Estate Planning and Administration; Business Transactions. ***Email:*** jgmoore@mjms.com

THEODORE A. SINARS, born Chicago, Illinois, October 8, 1943; admitted to bar, 1967, Illinois; 1972, U.S. Tax Court; 1982, U.S. Supreme Court and U.S. District Court, Northern District of Illinois including Trial Bar. *Education:* University of Notre Dame (B.B.A., cum laude, 1966; J.D., 1967). Beta Gamma Sigma; Beta Alpha Psi. Member, Notre Dame Law Review. Author: "Tax Fraud Defenses and Trial" and "I.R.S. Prosecution Strategies," Illinois Institute for Continuing Legal Education, 1975, 1978, 1980, 1982 and 1985 and "Tax Court Practice," 1983, 1985, 1987, 1989, 1990 and 1991; "Tax Fraud-The Defense Lawyer's Role," Chicago Bar Record, 1989; "Tax Fraud-A Primer For General Tax Practitioners" Tax Seminars Institute, 1990; "The Enrolled Agent's Role in Criminal Tax Investigations"; "Outer Limits of Tax Practice," EA Journal, Sept.-Oct., 1997; Jan.-Feb., 1998 and Mar.-Apr., 1999); "The Confidentiality Privilege Extended to Nonlawyers-How Limited Is It?", CCH-Journal of Tax Practice and Procedure, Apr.-May, 1999; "Criminal Tax Offenses and Procedure," *Mertens Law of Federal Income Taxation*, West Publishing, 2000. Adjunct Professor, Masters Tax Program, De Paul University Graduate School of Law, 1981—. Instructor, National Tax Practice Institute, National Association of Enrolled Agents, 1993—. Chairman and Practitioners' Representative, IRS Chicago District Director's Liaison Committee, 1984—. *Member:* Chicago (Member: Committee on Federal Taxation, 1979—, Chairman, 1988-1989; Chairman, Committee on Federal Civil and Criminal Tax Procedure, 1985-1986), Federal (Member: Board of Directors, 1983; Chairman, Committee on Federal Taxation, 1982; Treasurer, 1985; Secretary, 1986; Vice-President, 1987-1988; President, 1989) and American (Member, Committee on Civil and Criminal Tax Penalties, 1979) Bar Associations. ***PRACTICE AREAS:*** Tax; Estate Planning and Administration; Business Transactions; Tax Litigation; Civil and Criminal Tax Matters. ***Email:*** tasinars@mjms.com

PAUL M. SHERIDAN, III, born Evergreen Park, Illinois, July 4, 1963; admitted to bar, 1988, Illinois; 1989, U.S. District Court, Northern District of Illinois and U.S. Tax Court. *Education:* University of Notre Dame (B.B.A., 1985); Loyola University (J.D., 1988). Certified Public Accountant, Illinois, 1986. American Institute of Certified Public Accountants. *Member:* Chicago, Illinois State and American Bar Associations. ***PRACTICE AREAS:*** Tax; Estate Planning and Administration; Business Transactions. ***Email:*** sheridan@mjms.com

JOSEPH S. CAPITANI, born Chicago, Illinois, July 21, 1961; admitted to bar, 1987, Illinois; 1990, U.S. Tax Court; 1991, U.S. District Court, Northern District of Illinois and U.S. Court of Appeals, Seventh Circuit. *Education:* Northwestern University (B.A., 1983); Loyola University (J.D., 1987); DePaul University (LL.M., 1994). *Member:* Chicago, Illinois State and American Bar Associations. ***PRACTICE AREAS:*** Tax; Estate Planning and Administration; Business Transactions. ***Email:*** capitani@mjms.com

---

LEILA T. FRANCIS, born Chicago, Illinois, October 14, 1971; admitted to bar, 1997, Illinois. *Education:* University of Illinois (B.S., 1992); DePaul University (J.D., 1997); Chicago-Kent College of Law (LL.M., 1998). *Member:* Chicago (Co-Chairman, YLS Tax Law Committee, 1999-2000), Illinois State and American Bar Associations. ***PRACTICE AREAS:*** Tax Law; Estate Planning and Administration; Business Transactions. ***Email:*** ltfrancis@mjms.com

(This Listing Continued)

HOLLY A. BAILEY, born Adrian, Michigan, March 3, 1976; admitted to bar, 2002, Illinois. *Education:* Alma College (B.A., 1998); Chicago-Kent College of Law (J.D., 2002). *Member:* Chicago (Co-Chairman, Young Lawyers Section Social Committee, 2002-2004) and Illinois State Bar Associations. ***PRACTICE AREAS:*** Tax Law; Estate Planning; Estate Administration; Business Transactions. **Email:** hbailey@mjms.com

LEGAL SUPPORT PERSONNEL

JOHN D. SECKER, born Freeport, Illinois, November 19, 1947. *Education:* University of Notre Dame (B.B.A., 1969); DePaul University (M.S.T., 1977). Certified Public Accountant, Illinois, 1971—. Insurance Producer, Illinois, 1989—. Illinois CPA Society. *Member:* American Institute of Certified Public Accountants. (Director of Taxes). ***PRACTICE AREAS:*** Tax and Financial Planning and Compliance. **Email:** jdsecker@mjms.com

KATHERINE L. BRONKE, born Oak Lawn, Illinois, November 10, 1962. *Education:* DePaul University (B.S., 1984; M.S.T., 1989). Certified Public Accountant, Illinois, 1984. *Member:* Illinois Certified Public Accountant Society; American Institute of Certified Public Accountants. ***PRACTICE AREAS:*** Tax and Financial Planning and Compliance. **Email:** klbronke@mjms.com

SHEILA M. HANSEN, born Chicago, Illinois, August 6, 1963. *Education:* Loyola University (B.B.A., 1987); DePaul University (M.S.T., 1992). Certified Public Accountant, Illinois, 1988. *Member:* Illinois Certified Public Accountant Society; American Institute of Certified Public Accountants. ***PRACTICE AREAS:*** Tax, Financial Planning and Compliance; Estate Planning and Administration. **Email:** smhansen@mjms.com

WILLIAM F. MADDEN (1945-1992)

JOSEPH J. MADONIA & ASSOCIATES

5757 NORTH SHERIDAN, SUITE 10A
CHICAGO, ILLINOIS 60660
Telephone: 773-654-5065
Fax: 773-654-5066
Email: joemadonia@aol.com

Entertainment and Sports Law, including Multimedia, Intellectual Property, Copyright and Trademark Law, Music Law, Motion Pictures, Television, Publishing, Radio Stations and Labeling, Commercial and Contract Litigation.

FIRM PROFILE: Joseph J. Madonia is an attorney in Chicago, Illinois, with an international legal practice focusing on entertainment and sports, multi-media, corporate, intellectual property law and litigation. His practice has included the representation of a wide range of music, motion picture, television, publishing, multimedia and entertainment industry clients from Chicago to New York, Los Angeles, Nashville, Seattle, Miami, Toronto, Tokyo, Barcelona, Vienna, Paris and London. Mr. Madonia had done deals with and/or represented musical artists ranging from opera tenor Jose Carreras to Elton John, Buddy Guy, members of Fleetwood Mac, Guns N' Roses, the Smashing Pumpkins, Nine Inch Nails, Filter, the Stone Temple Pilots, the Staple Singers, the Cult, Third Eye Blind and the Libertines. He has represented gold and platinum selling musical groups, record labels, radio stations, label, publishing and radio executives, radio program and music directors, disc jockeys, managers, independent promoters and music producers, film producers, directors, actors, comedians, national talk show hosts, newscasters, as well as professional sports teams, athletes, artists, photographers, models and modeling and talent agencies. He has represented authors, screenwriters and playwrights and has secured and negotiated a wide range of literary and publishing deals, including joint venture arrangements and book deals with major international publishers. Mr. Madonia has represented clients in film and television deals ranging from independent films and television pilots to major motion picture, network and public television productions.

Over the past year Mr. Madonia has turned his attention towards social causes in acting as co-counsel to the female cadet victims of the sexual assault scandal at the United States Air Force Academy in Colorado Springs, Colorado. The case has been the subject of worldwide media attention and in-depth feature articles in magazines ranging from Vanity Fair (December, 2003) to the American Lawyer (February, 2004). In connection with the case, Mr. Madonia has been quoted in those articles, as well as in national newspapers and global media, ranging from articles in the Chicago Tribune to the New York Times, to appearances on the BBC, CNN, Fox News, and the Oprah Winfrey Show. Mr. Madonia has also engaged in extensive lobbying efforts before the United States Congress, which have resulted in the grant of upcoming hearings before the United States Senate Armed Services Committee for the victims of the scandal.

JOSEPH J. MADONIA, born Springfield, Illinois, August 12, 1962; admitted to bar, 1990, Illinois and U.S. District Court, Northern District of Illinois. *Education:* University of Illinois (B.S., 1986); Loyola University of Chicago (J.D., 1990). Co-Author: "The Sound Remains the Same: Protection of Voice from Commercial Misappropriation," *The National Academy of Recording Arts & Sciences Journal*, Vol. 3, No. 1, Spring 1992; "Using Sound-Alikes in Ads is Risky Business," The Corporate Legal Times, Vol. 2, No. 4, March 1992. Member: National Academy of Recording Arts and Sciences; The Independent Feature Project. Featured Panel Speaker, "The Road Less Traveled: Independent Filmmaking," 1999 seminar presented by the American Federation of Television and Radio Artists/Screen Actors Guild. Featured Speaker on the areas of artist management, publishing and record deals, "National Academy of Recording Arts and Sciences," 1995 National Academy of Recording Arts and Sciences. Panel Speaker on the areas of music, film and advertising law, "The Recording Academy Law Panel," 1995 seminar presented by the National Academy of Recording Arts and Sciences. Panel Speaker on the area of Entertainment Law, "The Singer's Conference," 1995 conference presented by What a Voice! Productions, Inc. Moderator and Speaker, "The Law of the Theatre," 1994 seminar presented by the Chicago Bar Association Creative Arts Committee. Featured Speaker, "Who to Know and How to Do It: Finding Career Building Resources in the Music Industry," 1994 workshop seminar presented by the National Academy of Recording Arts and Sciences. Moderator and Speaker, "The Anatomy of a Record Deal," 1993 seminar presented by the Chicago Bar Association Creative Arts Committee. Moderator and Speaker, "The Anatomy of the Film Deal," 1993 seminar presented by the Chicago Bar Association Creative Arts Committee. Moderator and Speaker, "Representing Clients in the Entertainment Industry," 1992 seminar presented by the Chicago Bar Association Creative Arts Committee. Member: The Independent Feature Project; National Academy of Recording Arts and Sciences/Grammy Awards. *Member:* Chicago and American (Member, Forum on the Entertainment and Sports Industry) Bar Associations; Intellectual Property Law Association of Chicago; Lawyers for the Creative Arts.

LAW OFFICES OF MARY CARMEN R. MADRID-CROST

10 S. LASALLE STREET
SUITE 3320
CHICAGO, ILLINOIS 60603
Telephone: 312-857-0857
Fax: 312-857-0858
URL: http://www.madridcrostlaw.com

Immigration.

MARY CARMEN R. MADRID-CROST, born Laoag City, Philippines, June 22, 1957; admitted to bar, 1994, New York (Not admitted in Illinois). *Education:* University of Philippines (A.B., 1978; LL.B., 1985); George Washington University (LL.M., 1992). *Member:* Chicago, Illinois State, New York State, FilipinoAmerican and American Bar Associations; American Immigration Lawyers Association. ***LANGUAGES:*** Tagalog.

ASSOCIATE

MICHAEL R. JARECKI, born Maywood, Illinois, January 31, 1979; admitted to bar, 2004, Illinois. *Education:* Loyola University, Chicago (B.A., magna cum laude, 2001); University of Illinois (J.D., 2004). Phi Beta Kappa. *Member:* American Bar Association; American Immigration Lawyers Association. ***LANGUAGES:*** Spanish. ***PRACTICE AREAS:*** Immigration Law.

MAGNANI & BUCK LTD.

321 SOUTH PLYMOUTH COURT
SUITE 1700
CHICAGO, ILLINOIS 60604
Telephone: 312-294-4800
Facsimile: 312-294-4815
Email: law@magnanibuck.com

Civil Trial and Appellate Practice in State and Federal Courts. Civil Rights Defense, Construction Liability, Insurance Coverage, Insurance Defense, Medical Malpractice, Professional Liability, Municipal Liability, Premises Liability, Products Liability and Transportation Liability.

FIRM PROFILE: Founded in 1987, the firm concentrates in insurance defense law. Peter J. Magnani, the firm's founder, had been a partner in the firm of Jacobs, Williams and Montgomery Ltd., now Williams, Montgomery & John Ltd., in Chicago. Thomas L. Buck, formerly of Williams, Montgomery & John Ltd., joined the firm in 1992. The firm places particular emphasis on the preparation and trial or settlement of civil lawsuits in state and federal courts. Representation includes both insurers and self-insurers. The firm is prepared to handle legal matters in any jurisdiction throughout Illinois, and to try cases anywhere in the country.

PETER J. MAGNANI, born Mason City, Iowa, March 20, 1946; admitted to bar, 1974, Illinois; U.S. District Court, Northern District of Illinois; U.S. Court of Appeals, Seventh Circuit. *Education:* Indiana University (B.E., 1971; J.D., 1974). *Member:* Chicago, Illinois State (Member, Standing Committee on Judicial Evaluations, 2003-2004) and American (Vice-Chair, Committee on International Tort and Insurance Practice, 1991-1992) Bar Associations; Illinois Association of Defense Trial Counsel; Defense Research Institute. ***REPORTED CASES:*** West v. Deere & Co., 145 Ill. 2d 177, 582 N.E. 2d 685 (1991). ***PRACTICE AREAS:*** Products Liability; Professional Liability; Transportation Liability. **Email:** pjm@magnanibuck.com

THOMAS L. BUCK, born Chicago, Illinois, September 9, 1957; admitted to bar, 1983, Illinois; U.S. District Court, Northern District of Illinois; U.S. Court of Appeals, Seventh Circuit. *Education:* Vanderbilt University (B.A., 1979); DePaul University (J.D., 1983). *Member:* Chicago and Illinois State Bar Associations; Trial Lawyers Club of Chicago; Illinois Association of Defense Trial Counsel; Defense Research Institute. ***PRACTICE AREAS:*** Insurance Coverage; Insurance Defense; Appellate Practice. **Email:** tlb@magnanibuck.com

---

XIMEN J. JANUSZYK, born Arlington Heights, Illinois, September 29, 1974; admitted to bar, 1999, Illinois and U.S. District Court, Northern District of Illinois; 2000, Indiana and U.S. District Court, Northern and Southern Districts of Indiana. *Education:* Northwestern University (B.A., 1996); Indiana University (J.D., cum laude, 1999). *Member:* Chicago Bar Association. ***PRACTICE AREAS:*** Insurance Defense. **Email:** xjj@magnanibuck.com

ALLISON A. BATT, born Sioux Falls, South Dakota, November 4, 1974; admitted to bar, 2000, Illinois and U.S District Court, Northern District of Illinois. *Education:* Drake University (B.A., cum laude, 1997); DePaul University College of Law (J.D., 2000). *Member:* Chicago Bar Association. ***PRACTICE AREAS:*** Insurance Defense. **Email:** aab@magnanibuck.com

MATTHEW T. VOLK, born Caro, Michigan, August 17, 1972; admitted to bar, 2002, Illinois and U.S. District Court, Northern District of Illinois. *Education:* Michigan State

(This Listing Continued)

MAGNANI & BUCK LTD., Chicago—Continued

University (B.A., with honors, 1998); University of Iowa College of Law (J.D., 2002). Member, Iowa Law Review. *Member:* Chicago Bar Association. ***PRACTICE AREAS:*** Insurance Defense; Appellate Practice. ***Email:*** mtv@magnanibuck.com

JENNIFER K. RAWE, born Sioux City, Iowa, February 18, 1978; admitted to bar, 2003, Iowa; 2004, Illinois. *Education:* University of Northern Iowa (B.A., summa cum laude, 2000); University of Iowa (J.D., with distinction, 2003). Member, Iowa Law Review. *Member:* Chicago and Illinois State Bar Associations. ***PRACTICE AREAS:*** Insurance Defense. ***Email:*** jkr@magnanibuck.com

REPRESENTATIVE CLIENTS: American Claims Service, Ltd.; Ariens Company/Gravely International; Associated Claims Enterprise, Inc.; Budget Rent a Car Corporation; Cambridge Integrated Services Group, Inc.; Dart Transit Company; DBG Claims; Deere & Company; Discover Re; Dollar Rent A Car Systems, Inc.; ELCO Administrative Services; Encompass Insurance (formerly CNA Personal Insurance); Enterprise Rent A Car; Lancer Claims Service; National Interstate Insurance; Progressive Casualty Insurance Company; Roper Industries, Inc.; Smurfit-Stone Container Corporation; Stevens Transport; Thrifty Rent-a-Car System, Inc.; York Claims Service, Inc.

MALLON & JOHNSON, P.C.

Established in 1996

19 SOUTH LA SALLE STREET, SUITE 1202
CHICAGO, ILLINOIS 60603
Telephone: 312-346-8890
Fax: 312-346-8896
Email: bmallon@mallonandjohnson.com
Email: djohnson@mallonandjohnson.com
URL: http://www.mallonandjohnson.com

Securities Regulation and Compliance.

BARBARA A. MALLON, born Evergreen Park, Illinois, October 6, 1958; admitted to bar, 1986, Illinois. *Education:* Northwestern University (B.A., 1980); John Marshall Law School (J.D., 1986). Member, National Registry of Who's Who. Senior Attorney, U.S. Securities and Exchange Commission, Office of Regulation and Division of Enforcement, 1986-1996. Author: "Investment Adviser Regulation," ICLE Securities Law Practice Handbook, 2003; "Limited Safe Harbor for Soft Dollar Payments," Compliance Checks, May 2002; "Supervising Sub-Advisers: The Legg-Mason Case," Currents, April/May 2002; "Supervising Register Representatives Who are Independent Investment Advisers," Compliance Checks, September 2001; "Impact of the 1996 Reform Act on Investment Advisers," Charles W. Schwab Newsletter December 1996; "Insider Trading in Non-Equity Securities," Review of Securities and Commodities Regulation, September, 1993; "SEC Enforcement," ICLE Securities Law Practice Handbook, (1991, 1996, 2003). *Member:* Chicago (Past Chair, Securities Law Committee) and Illinois State Bar Associations. ***SPECIAL AGENCIES:*** U.S. Securities and Exchange Commission. ***PRACTICE AREAS:*** Securities and Commodities Regulation and Litigation.

DEXTER JOHNSON, born Miami, Florida, September 16, 1958; admitted to bar, 1984, Florida; 1987, Illinois, including Federal Trial Bar. *Education:* University of Miami (B.B.A., 1980); Georgetown University Law Center (J.D., 1983). Phi Delta Phi. Member Editorial Board, American Criminal Law Review. Author: "Key Considerations in the Private Placement of Securities," Chapter 12, Securities Law, 2003 Edition, IICLE, Securities Law Practice Handbook; "The Role of Institutional Investors After the Securities Reform Act: Will Institutional Investors Act as Lead Plaintiff?" 25 Securities Regulation Law Journal 387, Winter 1998; "Staying Out of Trouble with the SEC: Tips for the Brokerage Firm," 44 The Practical Lawyer 47, January 1998; "No One Escapes: Why managers are liable for the wrongdoing of subordinates," Registered Representative, Vol. 21, No. 10, October 1997; "Insider Trading in Non-Equity Securities," Review of Securities and Commodities Regulation, September, 1993; "SEC Enforcement," ICLE Securities Law Practice Handbook, (1991), (1996). Co-author: "White-Collar Crime: Survey of Law," 20 American Criminal Law Review, 291-336, Fall, 1982. Attorney, U.S. Securities and Exchange Commission, Division of Enforcement, 1990-1996. Judicial Law Clerk, R. F. Collins, U.S. District Court Judge, Eastern District of Louisiana, 1984-1986. *Member:* Chicago (Co-Chair, Securities Litigation and Enforcement Committee, 2002-2003; Co-Vice Chair, Securities Law Committee, 2003-2004; Co-Chair, Securities Law Committee, 2004-2005) and Illinois State Bar Associations. ***SPECIAL AGENCIES:*** U.S. Securities and Exchange Commission. ***PRACTICE AREAS:*** Securities and Commodities Regulation and Litigation.

MANDEL, LIPTON AND STEVENSON LIMITED

SUITE 2210, 203 NORTH LA SALLE STREET
CHICAGO, ILLINOIS 60601
Telephone: 312-236-7080
Facsimile: 312-236-0781
URL: http://www.mandellipton.com

General Civil Practice. Corporation, Retirement Plans, Banking, Labor and Employment Relations, Family, Adoption and Child Custody, Mental Health and Developmental Disabilities, Probate, Estate and Tax Planning, Real Estate, Personal Injury, Bankruptcy, State and Federal Civil Trials and Appeals, Intellectual Property, Immigration and Nationality Law, College and University, International Trade.

FIRM PROFILE: Mandel, Lipton and Stevenson Limited is a general practice law firm founded in the 1960's. The firm's primary focus is the representation of individuals, professional and personal service corporations, partnerships, private and small and medium-size publicly held corporations, banks and not-for-profit entities, and their principals, in a full range of business and personal matters.

ALFRED R. LIPTON, born Chicago, Illinois, February 1, 1942; admitted to bar, 1966, Illinois; 1967, U.S. District Court, Northern District of Illinois; 1968, U.S. Court of Appeals, Seventh Circuit; 1973, U.S. Supreme Court. *Education:* University of Wisconsin-

(This Listing Continued)

Madison (B.S., 1963); University of Chicago (J.D., 1966). Member: Chicago Bar Association; Chicago Council of Lawyers. ***PRACTICE AREAS:*** Corporate Law; Business Law; Taxation; Trust and Estates; Probate. ***Email:*** alipton@mandellipton.com

LEONARD M. MALKIN, born Chicago, Illinois, January 27, 1941; admitted to bar, 1965, Illinois. *Education:* University of Wisconsin-Madison (B.B.A., 1962); University of Illinois (LL.B., 1965). *Member:* Chicago and Illinois State Bar Associations; Chicago Council of Lawyers; Decalogue Society of Lawyers. ***PRACTICE AREAS:*** Probate; Guardianship; Conservatorship; Family Law; Personal Injury. ***Email:*** lmalkin@mandellipton.com

R. PETER CAREY, born Rockville Centre, New York, September 4, 1948; admitted to bar, 1973, Illinois; 1983, U.S. District Court, Northern District of Illinois, Trial Bar. *Education:* Emory University and University of Illinois (B.A., 1970); University of Illinois (J.D., 1973). *Member:* Illinois State and American Bar Associations; Chicago Council of Lawyers. ***PRACTICE AREAS:*** Construction Litigation; Commercial Litigation; Labor and Employment; Labor Relations; Litigation; College and University Law. ***Email:*** pcarey@mandellipton.com

HENRY A. WALLER, born Chicago, Illinois, September 21, 1940; admitted to bar, 1966, Illinois. *Education:* University of Wisconsin (B.S., 1962); University of Chicago (J.D., 1966). *Member:* Chicago and Illinois State Bar Associations. ***PRACTICE AREAS:*** Real Estate; Trusts and Estates; Surrogacy Law. ***Email:*** hwaller@mandellipton.com

KATHLEEN ROSEBOROUGH, born Brookline, Massachusetts, July 14, 1944; admitted to bar, 1977, Illinois. *Education:* Georgetown University (B.S.F.S., 1965); University of Chicago (M.A., 1972); DePaul University (LL.B., 1977). Phi Beta Kappa. Member: Mediation Council of Illinois, 1985—; Divorce Mediation Institute, 1983—; Endispute, 1986-1989. ***PRACTICE AREAS:*** Family Law; Child Custody; Litigation; Family Mediation. ***Email:*** kroseborough@mandellipton.com

RICHARD A. LIFSHITZ, born Chicago, Illinois, July 26, 1951; admitted to bar, 1976, Illinois. *Education:* Washington University (B.A., cum laude, 1973; J.D., 1976). *Member:* Chicago Bar Association (Chair, Child Abuse Committee); American Academy of Adoption Attorneys. ***PRACTICE AREAS:*** Adoption Law; Family Law; Child Welfare; Child Custody; Corporate Law; Trust and Estates. ***Email:*** rlifshitz@mandellipton.com

TERRY YALE FEIERTAG, born Newark, New Jersey, July 7, 1941; admitted to bar, 1967, Illinois; 1969, U.S. District Court, Northern District of Illinois including Trial Bar; 1971, U.S. Court of Appeals, Seventh Circuit; 1977, U.S. Supreme Court; 1987, U.S. District Court, Eastern District of Wisconsin. *Education:* Bowdoin College (B.A., 1963); University of Chicago Law School (J.D., 1966). Founding Member, IMMLAW, the National Consortium of Immigration Lawyers. *Member:* American Immigration Lawyers Association. ***LANGUAGES:*** Spanish. ***SPECIAL AGENCIES:*** U.S. Dept. of Labor; U.S. Dept. of State; Department of Homeland Security; Bureau of Citizenship and Immigration Services; Bureau of Immigration and Customs Enforcement; Bureau of Customs and Border Protection; Executive Office of Immigration Review. ***PRACTICE AREAS:*** Immigration and Naturalization. ***Email:*** tfeiertag@mandellipton.com

CAROLYN E. WINTER, born Chicago, Illinois, April 23, 1944; admitted to bar, 1985, Illinois and U.S. District Court, Northern District of Illinois; 1994, U.S. Supreme Court. *Education:* Roosevelt University (B.S., with honors, 1966; Franklin Honor Society); Loyola University (J.D., 1985). *Member:* Chicago and Illinois State Bar Associations. ***PRACTICE AREAS:*** Family Law; Adoption Law; Mental Health Confidentiality. ***Email:*** cwinter@mandellipton.com

ANDRÉS J. GALLEGOS, born Caracas, Venezuela, December 3, 1960; admitted to bar, 1993, Illinois. *Education:* University of Southern Mississippi (B.S., 1989); St. Louis Law School (J.D., 1993). *Member:* Chicago (Member, Customs and International Trade Law Section), Illinois State (Member, International Law Section) and American (Member, Sections on: International Law, Business Law and Health Law) Bar Associations. [USAF, 1978-1991]. ***LANGUAGES:*** Spanish. ***PRACTICE AREAS:*** International Trade; Business Law; Corporate Law. ***Email:*** agallegos@mandellipton.com

REUBEN A. BERNICK, born Chicago, Illinois, January 27, 1951; admitted to bar, 1977, Illinois and U.S. District Court, Northern District of Illinois, Trial Bar, 1983; 1979, U.S. Court of Appeals, Seventh Circuit; 1987, U.S. Supreme Court. *Education:* University of Chicago (B.A., with honors, 1972); Harvard University (J.D., cum laude, 1977). Phi Beta Kappa. *Member:* Chicago and American Bar Associations. ***REPORTED CASES:*** Rudell v. Comprehensive Accounting, 802 F.2d 926 (7th Cir. 1986), cert. denied, 480 US 907 (1987). ***PRACTICE AREAS:*** Family Law; Litigation. ***Email:*** rbernick@mandellipton.com

JOAN E. COMISKEY, born Chicago, Illinois, March 24, 1954; admitted to bar, 1997, Illinois. *Education:* DePaul University (B.S., with highest honor, 1979; M.B.A., 1981); Illinois Institute of Technology, Chicago-Kent College of Law (J.D., 1997). ***PRACTICE AREAS:*** Family Law. ***Email:*** jcomiskey@mandellipton.com

---

TRACEY A. SALINSKI, born Dearborn, Michigan, July 7, 1966; admitted to bar, 1992, Illinois and Michigan. *Education:* University of Michigan (A.B., Economics, 1988); Detroit College of Law (J.D., 1991); John Marshall Law School (LL.M., Taxation, magna cum laude, 1993). *Member:* Chicago, Illinois State and American Bar Associations; State Bar of Michigan; Illinois Association of Healthcare Attorneys; American Health Lawyers Association. ***PRACTICE AREAS:*** Estate Planning; Business Law; Corporate Law; Health Care Law; Taxation. ***Email:*** tsalinski@mandellipton.com

AMANDA PETERSEN, born Edinburgh, Scotland, May 27, 1967; admitted to bar, 1993, British Columbia; 1998, Maine (Not admitted in Illinois). *Education:* University of Alberta (B.A., 1989); University of British Columbia (LL.B., 1991). Co-Author: "Business Immigration Law: Strategies for Employing Foreign Nationals," Law Journal Press, 2000; "Immigration Law-H-1B Visas for Specialty Workers," The National Law Journal, 1999; "Exhaustion of H-1B Visa Quota is Imminent," Dallas Human Resources Management Association, 1999. *Member:* American Immigration Lawyers Association. ***Email:*** apetersen@mandellipton.com

KIMBERLY R. LUSK, born Northampton, Massachusetts, March 5, 1970; admitted to bar, 2003, Illinois. *Education:* Arizona State University (B.A., Theater, 1994); Loyola

(This Listing Continued)

University (J.D., 2003). *Member:* Illinois State Bar Association (Member, Young Lawyer Division Council); Chicago Bar Association; American Bar Association; Women's Bar Association of Illinois. ***PRACTICE AREAS:*** Family Law; Child Custody; Estate Planning; Domestic Violence. ***Email:*** klusk@mandellipton.com

REFERENCES: Northern Trust Co.; Bank One; La Salle Bank FSB.

MANDELL MENKES LLC

333 WEST WACKER DRIVE, SUITE 300
CHICAGO, ILLINOIS 60606
Telephone: 312-251-1000
Fax: 312-251-1010
URL: http://www.mandellmenkes.com

General Civil Practice, Class Action Defense, Consumer Finance and Banking, Corporate, Commercial Litigation, Employment, Media, Entertainment and Intellectual Property Law including Copyright and Trademark Law, Computer and Technology Law, Health Care, Captive Insurance and Purchasing and Risk Retention Groups and Insurance Coverage, Directors and Officers Liability, Professional Liability, Casualty, Life, Health and Disability.

FIRM PROFILE: Mandell Menkes LLC brings together lawyers with extensive litigation and transactional experience. The firm represents business clients around the country in complex litigation, including class actions, contract drafting and negotiation, media, entertainment, intellectual property, and directors and officers liability and other matters. The firm was founded with a recognition that while some large firms provide a high level of service, clients are too often unable to obtain the responsiveness and personal attention that a smaller firm can offer. The firm is dedicated to providing a high quality of legal work and cost-effective legal results on a timely basis.

STEVEN L. BARON, born Ottawa, Ontario, Canada, February 24, 1962; admitted to bar, 1988, Minnesota; 1989, Illinois. *Education:* University of Wisconsin-Madison (B.A., with distinction, 1984); University of Minnesota (J.D., 1988). Member, 1986 and Developments Editor, 1987-1988, Minnesota Law Review. Law Clerk to Hon. Lawrence E. Agerter and Hon. Ancy L. Morse, Minnesota District Court, 1988-1989. Instructor, New Media Theory - Intellectual Property, Bradley University. Member, Lawyers Club. *Member:* Illinois State and American (Member, Litigation Section; Forum on Communications Law) Bar Associations. ***PRACTICE AREAS:*** Complex Commercial Litigation; Intellectual Property; Media; Entertainment. ***Email:*** sbaron@mandellmenkes.com

JOAN S. CALLAN, born Milwaukee, Wisconsin, July 23, 1961; admitted to bar, 1987, Wisconsin and U.S. District Court, Western District of Wisconsin; 1989, Illinois and U.S. District Court, Northern District of Illinois including Trial Bar; 2001, U.S. District Court, Eastern District of Wisconsin. *Education:* St. Mary's College (B.A., cum laude, 1984); University of Wisconsin (J.D., 1987). Phi Alpha Theta. *Member:* Illinois State Bar Association; State Bar of Wisconsin; Defense Research Institute; American Society for Healthcare Risk Management. ***PRACTICE AREAS:*** Commercial Litigation; Insurance Defense Litigation; Insurance Law. ***Email:*** jcallan@mandellmenkes.com

BRUCE E. DE'MEDICI, born Great Lakes, Illinois, December 14, 1954; admitted to bar, 1980, Michigan; 1983, Illinois. *Education:* University of Michigan (B.A., with distinction, 1977); Wayne State University (J.D., 1980). Author: "Recent Developments in Preference Law: A Look at In Re Lease-A-Fleet, Inc." The Transportation Lawyer, June, 1993, Vol. 2 No. 3; "Disciplines of Students with Disabilities, D.C.B.A. Brief, Vol. 12, Issue 4, Dec. 1999. Attorney, Office of the U.S. Trustee for the Northern District of Illinois, 1986-1988. Member, Bankruptcy Trustee Panel for the Northern District of Illinois, 1990-2000. *Member:* Chicago, DuPage County and Illinois State Bar Associations. ***PRACTICE AREAS:*** School Law; Bankruptcy; Commercial Litigation; Education Law. ***Email:*** bdemedici@mandellmenkes.com

J. DAVID DUFFY, born Tulsa, Oklahoma, January 29, 1969; admitted to bar, 1994, Georgia; 1997, Illinois; 2000, U.S. District Court, Northern District of Illinois. *Education:* University of Tulsa (B.A., cum laude, 1991); Emory University (J.D., 1994). Member, 1992 and Articles Editor, 1993-1994, Bankruptcy Developments Journal. Special Teams Member, Emory Moot Court Society, 1992-1994. *Member:* Member: Illinois State (Associate Member, Civil Practice & Procedure Council) and American (Member, Litigation and Tort, Trial and Insurance Practice Section) Bar Associations. ***PRACTICE AREAS:*** Commercial Law; Employment Litigation; Products Liability; Insurance Litigation. ***Email:*** dduffy@mandellmenkes.com

STEVEN P. MANDELL, born Rockford, Illinois, April 3, 1957; admitted to bar, 1982, Illinois and U.S. District Court, Northern District of Illinois including Trial Bar; 1991, U.S. District Court, Central District of Illinois; 1992, U.S. Court of Appeals, 7th Circuit; 2000, U.S. Court of Appeals, 6th Circuit. *Education:* University of Wisconsin (B.B.A., with honors, 1979); Georgetown University Law Center (J.D., 1982). Panelist, "Representing Your Client in Software Performance & System Failure Claims", PLI Information Technology Litigation, New York, NY, May, 2002; Moderator, "Recent Developments in Advertising Law, International Trademark Association Annual Meeting" San Francisco, Ca., May, 2001. Lecturer: "Intellectual Property Risks Associated with Internet Publishing," Loyola University Medical Center Symposium, Chicago, Il., March, 2001; Co-Chair, Licensing Intellectual Property, American Conference Institute, New York, NY, November 2000; San Francisco, Ca., October 2000. Lecturer, "Licensing Trademarks: Checklist and Practice Tips," American Conference Institute, Licensing Intellectual Property, New York, NY, November 2000; San Francisco, Ca., 2000. Lecturer, Liability For Online Content-What Are The Risks?, American Conference Institute Online Liability, Chicago, Il., October 2000. Lecturer, Issues Arising Out of Celebrity Licensing, PLI Understanding The Intellectual Property License, Chicago, Il., November 2000. Lecturer, "Pitfalls Associated with Licensing Characters, Celebrities and Other Intellectual Property," PLI Understanding The Intellectual Property License, Chicago, Il., 1999. Lecturer, "Celebrity and Character Licensing," PLI Understanding Property License, Chicago, Il., 1998. Co-Author: "Defamation Solely On Tone Of Voice," Communications Lawyer, Vol. 16, No. 4, Winter 1999. Co-Lecturer, "The Internet-A Superhighway of Information or Liability," Risk and Insurance Management Society Annual Conference, Atlanta, Ga., April 1997; Lecturer, "Jurisdictional Issues Raised By Infringement On the Web-Where Can Infringers Be Sued?," ABA, Section of Intellectual Property Law Summer Conference, San Diego, CA., June 1997; "Pitfalls In Licensing," PLI Understanding The Intellectual Property License, Chicago, Il., November 1997. Co-Lecturer, "The Risk of Being Wired and Protecting Your Techno Business," April 1998. Lecturer, "Common Pitfalls In Licensing," ABA Section of Intellectual Property Law Summer Conference, Williamsburg, Va., June 1998. Instructor, Legal Research and Writing, Georgetown University Law Center, 1981-1982. Member, Board of Directors, Medical Institute Research Council, Childrens Memorial Hospital. *Member:* Chicago and American (Member, Litigation; Intellectual Property; Communications Law Forum; Tort and Insurance Practice; Sports and Entertainment Sections) Bar Associations; International Trademark Association and Libel Defense Resource Center (Firm Liaison); ABA Forum on Communications Law (Governing Board, Central Division Co-Chair). ***PRACTICE AREAS:*** Commercial Litigation; Copyright Law; Trademark Law; Technology Law; Communications and Media; First Amendment Law; Insurance. ***Email:*** smandell@mandellmenkes.com

BRUCE N. MENKES, born Vicenza, Italy, August 7, 1959; admitted to bar, 1984, Illinois, U.S. District Court, Northern District of Illinois including Trial Bar, U.S. Court of Appeals, Seventh Circuit and U.S. Supreme Court. *Education:* College of William & Mary (B.A., with highest honors, 1981); University of Chicago (J.D., 1984). Author: "Complying with the Fair Debt Collection Practices Act," NBI, 1991; "Commercial Lending in Illinois - - Lender Liability," NBI, 2003. Lecturer: NBI ("Complying with the Fair Debt Collection Practices Act," 2001 and "Commercial Lending in Illinois," 2003) and Lorman Education Services ("Illinois Collection Law," 2000). *Member:* American Bar Association (Business Law Section; Consumer Financial Services Committee; Vice Chair Subcommittee on Debt Collection Practices and Bankruptcy, 2002—; Vice Chair, Subcommittee on Access to Services, 2001-2002) and Chicago Bar Association. ***PRACTICE AREAS:*** Business Law; Consumer Finance; Commercial Lending; Class Action Defense; Payment Systems; Credit Card Law. ***Email:*** bmenkes@mandellmenkes.com

DANIEL V. O'LEARY, JR., born Brooklyn, New York, May 26, 1942; admitted to bar, 1967, Illinois; U.S. District Court, Northern District of Illinois. *Education:* Georgetown University (A.B., cum laude, 1963); Yale University (LL.B., 1966). Moot Court Finalist. *Member:* Illinois State and American Bar Associations. [LCDR, U.S. Navy Reserve (Ret.)]. ***LANGUAGES:*** French and Spanish. ***REPORTED CASES:*** Dowlatshahi v. Motorola, Inc., 970 F.2d 289 (7th Cir., 1992). ***TRANSACTIONS:*** Sale of Shellmar Embalagem Moderna Ltda., Sao Paulo, Brazil. ***PRACTICE AREAS:*** Insurance; Reinsurance; Captive Insurance Companies. ***Email:*** doleary@mandellmenkes.com

NED S. OTHMAN, born Chicago, Illinois; admitted to bar, 1977, Illinois, U.S. District Court, Northern District of Illinois; 2001, New York. *Education:* University of Michigan (B.A., Economics, 1974; J.D., 1977). Member, Economics Honors Program, Highest Distinction, The University of Michigan. ***PRACTICE AREAS:*** Finance (50%); Corporate Law (30%); Securities (20%). ***Email:*** nothman@mandellmenkes.com

STEPHEN J. ROSENFELD, born Chicago, Illinois, July 11, 1968; admitted to bar, 1993, Illinois and U.S. District Court, Northern District of Illinois; 2000, U.S. District Court, District of Colorado and Eastern District of Michigan; 2002, U.S. Court of Appeals, Seventh Circuit. *Education:* University of Michigan (B.A., 1990); University of Illinois (J.D., cum laude, 1993). Phi Alpha Delta. Recipient, American Jurisprudence Award in Contract/Sales II. *Member:* American Bar Association (Member, Sections on: Litigation; Science and Technology Law; Tort Trial; Insurance Practice). ***PRACTICE AREAS:*** Information Technology; Complex Commercial Litigation; Computer Law; Intellectual Property Litigation; Insurance Litigation. ***Email:*** srosenfeld@mandellmenkes.com

ASSOCIATES

KEITH E. ALLEN, born October 29, 1974; admitted to bar, 2000, Illinois and U.S. District Court, Northern District of Illinois. *Education:* Morehouse College (B.A., 1996); University of Michigan (J.D., 2000). ***Email:*** kallen@mandellmenkes.com

RYAN T. BROWN, admitted to bar, 1999, Illinois. *Education:* University of Illinois at Urbana-Champaign (B.A., with honors, 1996); University of Illinois College of Law (J.D., 1999). ***Email:*** rbrown@mandellmenkes.com

NATALIE A. HARRIS, admitted to bar, 2000, Illinois, Wisconsin and U.S. District Court, Western District of Wisconsin and Northern District of Illinois. *Education:* University of Michigan (B.A., 1996); University of Wisconsin-Madison (J.D., 2000). ***Email:*** nharris@mandellmenkes.com

BRENDAN J. HEALEY, admitted to bar, 1997, Illinois; U.S. District Court, Northern District of Illinois; U.S. Court of Appeals, Sixth Circuit. *Education:* Stanford University (A.B., with honors and distinction, American Studies, 1988; A.M., English, 1989); New York University School of Law (J.D., 1997). ***Email:*** bhealey@mandellmenkes.com

KRISTIN L. LINGREN, admitted to bar, 1996, Illinois and Wisconsin; 1997, U.S. District Court, Northern District of Illinois; 2002, England and Wales as a solicitor; 2003, U.S. District Court, Central District of Illinois; 2004, U.S. District Court, Eastern District of Michigan; 2005, U.S. Supreme Court. *Education:* University of Wisconsin-Madison (B.A., with distinction, 1990; J.D.), London School of Economics and Political Science (LL.M., with honors, 2001). ***Email:*** klingren@mandellmenkes.com

ALEXIS E. PAYNE, admitted to bar, 1999, Illinois and U.S. District Court, Northern District of Illinois. *Education:* University of Michigan (B.A., with distinction, 1996); Ohio State University (J.D., 1999). ***Email:*** apayne@mandellmenkes.com

ELIZABETH N. PENDLETON, admitted to bar, 2001, Missouri and U.S. District Court, Western District of Missouri; 2002, Kansas and U.S. District Court, District of Kansas, 2004, Illinois and U.S. District Court, Northern District of Illinois, 2005; U.S. District Court, Central District of Illinois. *Education:* Kenyon College (B.A., 1998,cum laude); Boston College(J.D., 2001);. ***Email:*** ependleton@mandellmenkes.com

MICHAEL A. RAKOV, admitted to bar, 1995, Missouri; 1996, Illinois and U.S. District Court, Eastern District of Missouri. *Education:* Harvard University (B.A., magna cum laude, government, 1990); Washington University Law School (J.D., 1995). ***Email:*** mrakov@mandellmenkes.com

SUZANNE M. SCHEUING, admitted to bar, 1999, Illinois and U.S. District Court, Northern District of Illinois; 2001, U.S. District Court, District of Colorado; 2002, U.S.

(This Listing Continued)

MANDELL MENKES LLC, Chicago—Continued

District Court, Central District of Illinois; 2003, U.S. District Court, Southern District of Illinois. *Education:* Duke University (A.B., 1994); University of Texas (J.D., 1999). ***Email:*** sscheuing@mandellmenkes.com

PATRICK G. SOMERS, admitted to bar, 2005, Illinois, U.S. District Court, Federal District of Illinois, U.S. District Court, Northern District of Illinois. *Education:* Concordia University (B.A., 2000); DePaul University (J.D., 2004). ***Email:*** psomers@mandellmenkes.com

JOSHUA J. WALLAR, admitted to bar, 2002, Illinois and Wisconsin. *Education:* University of Wisconsin-Eau Claire (B.A., magna cum laude, 1997); University of Wisconsin-Madison (J.D., cum laude, 2002). ***Email:*** jwaller@mandellmenkes.com

OF COUNSEL

SUSAN S. O'BYRNE, admitted to bar, 2000, Illinois. *Education:* Lawrence University (B.A., cum laude, 1988); University of Notre Dame (M.A., English, 1993; Ph.D., English, 1995); DePaul University (J.D., 2000).

JENNIFER A. WIDMER, born Cleveland, Ohio, July 2, 1965; admitted to bar, 1990, Illinois; 1993, District of Columbia; U.S. Supreme Court. *Education:* Monmouth College (B.A., summa cum laude, 1987); Georgetown University (J.D., 1990). Editorial Board Member/Administrative Editor, The Tax Lawyer, 1988-1990. Member: Inns of Court Program, 1989-1990; Sex Discrimination Clinical Program, 1989-1990. *Member:* Chicago Bar Association. ***PRACTICE AREAS:*** Corporate; Trademark Licensing; Consumer Finance; Real Estate Leasing; Telecommunications Licensing. ***Email:*** jwidmer@mandellmenkes.com

MANGAN, LANGHENRY, GILLEN & LUNDQUIST

29 SOUTH LA SALLE STREET, SUITE 720
CHICAGO, ILLINOIS 60603
Telephone: 312-704-6700
Fax: 312-704-6777
Email: mlgl@mlgllaw.com

Joliet, Illinois Office: 18 West Cass Street, Suite 200, 60432. Telephone: 815-726-3600. Fax: 815-726-3676.
Rockford, Illinois Office: 6785 Weaver Road, Suite 2E, 61114. Telephone: 815-636-1800. Fax: 815-636-2860.
Wheaton, Illinois Office: 311 South County Farm Road, Suite K, 60187. Telephone: 630-653-5775. Fax: 630-653-5980.

General Liability Defense, Medical Malpractice Defense, Insurance Coverage, Class Action Defense and Insurance Defense.

MEMBERS

JERALD M. MANGAN, born Evergreen Park, Illinois, June 28, 1957; admitted to bar, 1982, Illinois; U.S. District Court, Northern District of Illinois including Trial Bar and U.S. Court of Appeals, 7th Circuit. *Education:* University of Kansas (B.A., 1978); DePaul University (J.D., 1982). DuPage Certified Arbitration Chairman, DuPage County. *Member:* DuPage County and Illinois State Bar Associations; Defense Research Institute. ***PRACTICE AREAS:*** General Liability Defense; Medical Malpractice Defense; Class Action Defense; Insurance Coverage. ***Email:*** jmangan@mlgllaw.com

JOHN G. LANGHENRY III, born Tokyo, Japan, August 10, 1958; admitted to bar, 1985, Illinois and U.S. District Court, Northern District of Illinois including Trial Bar. *Education:* University of Notre Dame (A.B., 1980); Loyola University (J.D., 1984). Seminar Speaker, Psychiatric Malpractice Defense. DuPage County Certified Arbitration Chairman. Mediator, Chicago Neighborhood Justice Center. *Member:* DuPage County and Illinois State Bar Associations; Defense Research Institute. ***PRACTICE AREAS:*** General Liability Defense; Medical Malpractice Defense; Psychiatric Malpractice Defense; Mental Health Professionals Malpractice Defense; Premises Liability Defense. ***Email:*** jlanghenry@mlgllaw.com

SUZANNE FAVIA GILLEN, born Chicago, Illinois, December 12, 1961; admitted to bar, 1987, Illinois and U.S. District Court, Northern District of Illinois. *Education:* Lake Forest College (B.A., 1984); Chicago-Kent College of Law (J.D., 1987). *Member:* DuPage County and Illinois State Bar Associations. ***PRACTICE AREAS:*** General Liability Defense; Products Liability Defense; Medical Malpractice; Insurance Coverage. ***Email:*** sgillen@mlgllaw.com

TROY A. LUNDQUIST, born Princeton, Illinois, January 3, 1967; admitted to bar, 1992, Illinois and U.S. District Court, Northern District of Illinois including Trial Bar. *Education:* University of Illinois (B.A., 1989); John Marshall Law School (J.D., 1992). National Champion, Civil Rights Moot Court, 1992. *Member:* Will County and Illinois State Bar Associations. ***PRACTICE AREAS:*** Medical Malpractice; Products Liability Defense; General Liability Defense; Public Officials Liability; Governmental Defense. ***Email:*** tlundquist@mlgllaw.com

ASSOCIATES

MELISSA J. GORDON, born Chicago, Illinois, July 8, 1969; admitted to bar, 1994, Illinois. *Education:* University of Texas (B.S., 1991); Illinois Institute of Technology-Chicago Kent College of Law (J.D., 1994). ***Email:*** mgordon@mlgllaw.com

JOHN P. PALUMBO, born Rochester, Minnesota, January 28, 1967; admitted to bar, 1994, Minnesota; 1996, Illinois. *Education:* College of the Holy Cross (B.A., 1989); DePaul University (J.D., 1994). *Member:* Chicago, Illinois State and American Bar Associations. ***PRACTICE AREAS:*** Litigation. ***Email:*** jpalumbo@mlgllaw.com

ADAM M. BERGER, born Chicago, Illinois, March 15, 1971; admitted to bar, 1999, Illinois and U.S. District Court, Northern District of Illinois; 2000, U.S. District Court, Northern District of Indiana; 2001, U.S. District Court, Southern District of Indiana; U.S. District Court, Southern and Central Districts of Illinois and U.S. Court of Appeals, Seventh Circuit. *Education:* Washington University (B.A., 1993); Loyola University at Chicago (J.D., 1999). ***PRACTICE AREAS:*** Civil Litigation; Insurance Defense; Consumer Fraud Defense. ***Email:*** aberger@mlgllaw.com

PEDRO CERVANTES, born Chicago, Illinois, October 15, 1978; admitted to bar, 2003, Illinois. *Education:* Augustana College (B.A., magna cum laude, 2000); University of Illinois College of Law (J.D., cum laude, 2003). *Member:* Chicago and Illinois State Bar Association. ***LANGUAGES:*** Spanish. ***PRACTICE AREAS:*** Defense Litigation; Medical Malpractice; Negligence Defense. ***Email:*** pcervantes@mlgllaw.com

LAWRENCE A. MANSON

CHICAGO, ILLINOIS

(See Highland Park)

Health Care Law, Litigation, Corporate Law.

MARAMBA & ASSOCIATES, LLC

CHICAGO, ILLINOIS

(See Arlington Heights)

Business Law, Chancery Practice, Corporate Litigation, Civil Litigation, Complex Litigation, Defense Litigation, Federal Litigation, Administrative Litigation, Business Enterprises, Business Litigation, Closely Held Business Law, Real Estate Litigation, Veterans Rights, Military Law, Wills, Commercial Collections, Post Judgment Collections, Closely Held Corporations.

SIDNEY MARGOLIS

Established in 1992
123 WEST MADISON STREET
SUITE 606
CHICAGO, ILLINOIS 60602
Telephone: 312-578-9382
Facsimile: 312-578-9384
Email: sidsume@sbcglobal.net

Litigation and Environmental Law.

FIRM PROFILE: Sidney Margolis founded his law firm in 1992. The firm services individuals and business clients in areas of litigation and environmental law. He has practiced in these areas since 1980. He is a member of the Federal Trial Bar and a certified mediator of the Circuit Court of Cook County, Illinois, Civil Mediation Program. Mr. Margolis was given the Chicago Volunteer Legal Services Foundation's Distinguished Service Award in 2002.

SIDNEY MARGOLIS, born Harare, Zimbabwe, December 9, 1946; admitted to bar, 1974, High Court of Zimbabwe; 1980, Illinois, U.S. District Court, Northern District of Illinois including Trial Bar and U.S. Court of Appeals, 7th Circuit; 1985, U.S. Court of Appeals, 6th Circuit. *Education:* University of London (LL.B., with honors, 1969); Northwestern University (J.D., 1979). Recipient, Chicago Volunteer Legal Services Foundation's Distinguished Services Award, 2002. Certified Mediator, Civil Mediation Program, Circuit Court, Cook County, Illinois.*Member:* Chicago, Illinois State, Federal and American (Member, Litigation and Environmental Sections) Bar Associations.

MARKS, MARKS AND KAPLAN, LTD.

55 WEST MONROE STREET, SUITE 3300
CHICAGO, ILLINOIS 60603
Telephone: 312-332-5200
Fax: 312-332-2952
URL: http://www.mmklawoffice.com
URL: http://www.mmk-ltd.com

General Civil, Corporate and Partnership. Business, Real Estate, Trial and Appellate Practice, Zoning, Environmental, Estate Planning, Trust, Probate and Negligence Law, Medical Malpractice, Professional Sports Injuries, Employment Law, Corporate Law, Business Law, Litigation.

FIRM PROFILE: The firm was founded by Kenneth J. Marks, Robert Marks and William S. Kaplan in 1946.

ARNEE J. EISENBERG, born 1949; admitted to bar, 1974, Illinois; 1981, U.S. District Court, Northern District of Illinois; 1994, U.S. Supreme Court. *Education:* University of Illinois (B.S., 1971; J.D., 1974). ***Email:*** aje@mmk-ltd.com

GILBERT W. GORDON, born 1949; admitted to bar, 1974, Illinois and U.S. District Court, Northern District of Illinois including Trial Bar; 1980, U.S. Supreme Court. *Education:* Bradley University (B.S., 1971); Loyola University (J.D., 1974). Arbitrator, Circuit Court of Cook County. Lecturer: Aviation and Space Law Section, American Bar Assn. Meeting, Washington, D.C., August 1999; NFLPA Agents Seminar, Chicago, Ill., June 1997; American Trial Lawyers Assn., "Representing Professional Athletes," Chicago National Convention, August 2000; Profile: *Chicago Lawyer Magazine,* April 1999. *Chicago, Illinois State and American Bar Associations; The Association of Trial Lawyers of America; Illinois Appellate Lawyers; Illinois Trial Lawyers Association; National Panel of Attorneys; NFL Players Association.* ***REPORTED CASES:*** Lead Counsel, United States Supreme Court, Wolens v. American Airlines, Inc., 115 S.Ct. 817 (1995). ***Email:*** gwg@mmk-ltd.com

SPENCER J. MARKS, born 1947; admitted to bar, 1974, Illinois and U.S. District Court, Northern District of Illinois, including Trial Bar; U.S. Court of Appeals, Seventh and Fifth Circuits; 1986, U.S. District Court, Eastern District of Wisconsin; 1994, U.S. Supreme Court. *Education:* Northern Michigan University (B.A., 1970); John Marshall Law School (J.D., 1973). ***Email:*** SJM@MMK-LTD.COM

(This Listing Continued)

RICHARD W. RAPPOLD, born 1953; admitted to bar, 1978, Illinois and U.S. District Court, Northern District of Illinois; 1987, U.S. Court of Appeals, Seventh Circuit. *Education:* Bradley University (B.A., cum laude, 1975); Loyola University (J.D., 1978). ***Email:*** RWR@MMK-LTD.COM

GERALD M. TENNER, born 1945; admitted to bar, 1969, Illinois. *Education:* University of Illinois (B.S., with honors, 1966; J.D., 1969). ***Email:*** GMT@MMK-LTD.COM

STEPHEN A. COHEN, born 1948; admitted to bar, 1973, Illinois and U.S. District Court, Northern District of Illinois, including Trial Bar; 1978, U.S. Court of Appeals, Seventh Circuit. *Education:* Yale University (B.A., cum laude, 1970); University of Chicago (J.D., 1973). ***Email:*** sac@mmk-ltd.com

SUSAN L. DAWSON, born 1972; admitted to bar, 2000, Illinois. *Education:* Ohio University (B.S.C., 1994); Loyola University School of Law (J.D., 2000). *Member:* Chicago, Illinois State and American Bar Associations. ***Email:*** sld@mmk-ltd.com

ROBERT E. HANEY, born 1959; admitted to bar, 1985, Illinois and U.S. District Court, Northern District of Illinois including Trial Bar; 1993, California and U.S. Court of Federal Claims. *Education:* Northwestern University (B.A., 1981); University of San Francisco (J.D., 1984). ***Email:*** REH@MMK-LTD.COM

IVY D. ISRAEL, born 1974; admitted to bar, 1999, Illinois. *Education:* University of Wisconsin-Madison (B.A., with honors, 1996); Chicago-Kent College of Law, Illinois Institute of Technology (J.D., 1999). ***Email:*** IDI@MMK-LTD.COM

OF COUNSEL

HOWARD D. GALPER, born 1931; admitted to bar, 1955, Illinois; 1959, U.S. Supreme Court. *Education:* Yale College (A.B., cum laude, 1952); Yale Law School (LL.B., 1955). ***Email:*** hdg@mmk-ltd.com

RONALD R. RASSIN, born 1943; admitted to bar, 1967, Illinois and U.S. District Court, Northern District of Illinois including Trial Bar. *Education:* DePaul University (B.S., with honors, 1965; J.D., 1967). Blue Key. ***PRACTICE AREAS:*** Commercial Litigation; Business Law; Real Estate Law. ***Email:*** rrr@mmk-ltd.com

---

MARSHALL, GERSTEIN & BORUN LLP

SEARS TOWER 6300
233 SOUTH WACKER DRIVE
CHICAGO, ILLINOIS 60606-6357
Telephone: 312-474-6300
Fax: 312-474-0448
Email: info@marshallip.com
URL: http://www.marshallip.com

Patent, Trademark, Copyright Litigation and Prosecution; Intellectual Property, Antitrust Law and Related Litigation.

FIRM PROFILE: Marshall, Gerstein & Borun LLP was founded over 50 years ago and continues to provide a full range of intellectual property law services for domestic and international clients. The firm specializes in worldwide acquisition, protection, and enforcement of patents, trademarks, copyrights, and trade secrets. Firm attorneys have acquired extensive litigation experience in United States courts and before the International Trade Commission. Clients are counseled in foreign litigation and related proceedings throughout Europe and Asia, and in Canada, Mexico, South Africa and Australia. Patent prosecution and litigation encompasses all areas of technology, with a strong orientation to the electronic, mechanical, chemical and biological sciences, including protein chemistry, molecular biology, immunology, pharmaceuticals, and all recombinant technologies.

PARTNERS

RICHARD H. ANDERSON, admitted to bar, 1973, Illinois; U.S. Supreme Court; U.S. Court of Appeals for the Federal Circuit; U.S. Court of Appeals, Seventh Circuit; U.S. District Court, Northern District of Illinois. *Education:* University of Kentucky (B.S. Ch.E., 1968); George Washington University (J.D., 1972). ***PRACTICE AREAS:*** Chemical Patents; Chemical Patent Prosecution. ***Email:*** randerson@marshallip.com

SCOTT E. BAXENDALE, admitted to bar, 1996, Illinois; U.S. Court of Appeals, Federal Circuit; U.S. District Court, Eastern District of Michigan; U.S. District Court, Northern District of Illinois; registered to practice before U.S. Patent and Trademark Office. *Education:* Case Western Reserve University (B.S.M.E., 1988); John Marshall Law School (J.D., 1996). ***PRACTICE AREAS:*** Mechanical, Electro-Mechanical and Process Control Systems; Patent Prosecution; Computer Software; Intellectual Property Portfolio Management. ***Email:*** sbaxendale@marshallip.com

MICHAEL F. BORUN, admitted to bar, 1970, Illinois; U.S. Supreme Court; registered to practice before the U.S. Patent and Trademark Office. *Education:* University of Chicago (B.S., Biology, 1964); Loyola University (J.D., 1970). ***PRACTICE AREAS:*** International Intellectual Property; Biotechnology Patent Prosecution; Molecular Biology Patents; Patent Interference Practice; Patent Litigation. ***Email:*** mborun@marshallip.com

PAUL C. CRAANE, admitted to bar, 1993, Illinois; U.S. District Court, Northern District of Illinois; U.S. Court of Appeals, Seventh Circuit; U.S. Court of Appeals for the Federal Circuit; registered to practice before U.S. Patent and Trademark Office. *Education:* University of Illinois Urbana-Champaign (B.S.M.E., with highest honors, 1990); Northern Illinois University College of Law (J.D., magna cum laude, 1993). ***PRACTICE AREAS:*** Intellectual Property Counseling; Intellectual Property Licensing; Intellectual Property Litigation; Patent Prosecution; Trademark Prosecution; Computer and Software Patents; Electrical Patents; Mechanical Patents; Trademark Registrations. ***Email:*** pcraane@marshallip.com

JEFFREY H. DEAN, admitted to bar, 1992, Illinois; U.S. District Court, Northern District of Illinois including Trial Bar; U.S. Court of Appeals for the Federal Circuit; U.S. Court of Appeals, Seventh Circuit; U.S. Court of Appeals, Third Circuit; U.S. District Court, Eastern District of Wisconsin. *Education:* University of Chicago (A.B., with honors, 1989); Harvard Law School (J.D., cum laude, 1992). ***PRACTICE AREAS:*** Litigation; Patent; Copyright; Trade Secrets; Biotechnology; Mechanical Arts. ***Email:*** jdean@marshallip.com

THOMAS L. DUSTON, admitted to bar, 1987, Illinois; U.S. District Court, Northern District of Illinois including Trial Bar; U.S. Court of Appeals, Federal Circuit; U.S. Court of Appeals, Third and Fifth Circuits; U.S. District Court, Eastern District of Michigan. *Education:* Columbia University (B.A., 1984); Hastings College of the Law, University of California (J.D., 1987). ***PRACTICE AREAS:*** Intellectual Property Litigation; Patent Litigation; Theft of Trade Secrets; Trademark Litigation. ***Email:*** tduston@marshallip.com

PATRICK D. ERTEL, admitted to bar, 1973, Minnesota; 1974, Illinois; 1980, U.S. Supreme Court; U.S. Court of Appeals for the Federal Circuit; registered to practice before U.S. Patent and Trademark Office. *Education:* University of Notre Dame (B.S., cum laude, 1970); Northwestern University (J.D., cum laude, 1973). ***PRACTICE AREAS:*** Intellectual Property Licensing; Intellectual Property Litigation; Intellectual Property Counseling; Electro-Mechanical Patents; Mechanical Patents. ***Email:*** pertel@marshallip.com

KEVIN M. FLOWERS, admitted to bar, 1997, Illinois; U.S. Court of Appeals for the Federal Circuit; U.S. District Court, Northern District of Illinois including Trial Bar; registered to practice before U.S. Patent and Trademark Office. *Education:* Ohio State University (B.S., Biology, 1986; M.A., Exercise Physiology, 1991; J.D., with honors, 1997); Pennsylvania State University (Ph.D., Cellular and Molecular Physiology, 1994). ***PRACTICE AREAS:*** Intellectual Property Litigation; Biotechnology Patents; Patent Litigation. ***Email:*** kflowers@marshallip.com

DAVID A. GASS, admitted to bar, 1992, Illinois; U.S. District Court, Northern District of Illinois; registered to practice before U.S. Patent and Trademark Office. *Education:* University of Michigan (B.S., Cellular and Molecular Biology, with highest honors and highest distinction, 1988); Boalt Hall School of Law, University of California - Berkeley (J.D., 1992). ***PRACTICE AREAS:*** Medical Intellectual Property; Biotechnology Patent Prosecution; Biotechnology Patents; Medical Patents; Molecular Biology Patents; International Intellectual Property; Patent Interference Practice. ***Email:*** dgass@marshallip.com

ROBERT M. GERSTEIN, admitted to bar, 1988, Illinois; U.S. District Court, Northern District of Illinois; registered to practice before U.S. Patent and Trademark Office. *Education:* University of Michigan (B.S.E., with honors, 1985; J.D., cum laude, 1988). ***PRACTICE AREAS:*** Licensing; Intellectual Property Counseling and Opinions; Intellectual Property Litigation; Computer and Software Patents; Electro-Mechanical Patents; Mechanical Patents; Patent Litigation. ***Email:*** rgerstein@marshallip.com

MICHAEL R. GRAHAM, admitted to bar, 1986, Illinois; U.S. District Court, Central and Northern Districts of Illinois. *Education:* Miami University (B.S.Ed., 1974); Ohio University (M.A., 1978); Fordham University (J.D., 1986). ***PRACTICE AREAS:*** Internet Law; International Trademarks; Trademark Litigation; Trademark Protection; Trademark Registration; Copyrights. ***Email:*** mgraham@marshallip.com

ROGER A. HEPPERMANN, admitted to bar, 1992, Illinois; U.S. District Court, Northern District of Illinois; registered to practice before U.S. Patent and Trademark Office. *Education:* University of Missouri (B.S., in Electrical Engineering, summa cum laude, 1986); Northwestern University (J.D., cum laude, 1992). ***PRACTICE AREAS:*** Intellectual Property Licensing; Intellectual Property Litigation; Computer and Software Patents; Electrical Patent Prosecution; Patent Infringement. ***Email:*** rheppermann@marshallip.com

MARTIN J. HIRSCH, admitted to bar, 1985, California; 1988, Illinois; registered to practice before U.S. Patent and Trademark Office. *Education:* University of Illinois, Champaign-Urbana (B.S., Computer Engineering, 1982; J.D., 1985). ***PRACTICE AREAS:*** Internet Law; Electronic Commerce; Computer Software Law; Computer Law; Software Protection. ***Email:*** mhirsch@marshallip.com

RICHARD B. HOFFMAN, admitted to bar, 1973, Illinois and U.S. District Court, Northern District of Illinois; U.S. Court of Appeals, Seventh and Ninth Circuits; U.S. Court of Appeals for the Federal Circuit; registered to practice before U.S. Patent and Trademark Office. *Education:* University of Illinois (B.S.G.E., 1970); DePaul University (J.D., 1973); John Marshall Law School (LL.M., 1981). ***PRACTICE AREAS:*** Intellectual Property Litigation; Patent Infringement; Patent Prosecution; Mechanical Patents; Licensing; Trade Secrets; Trademarks; International Intellectual Property. ***Email:*** rhoffman@marshallip.com

KEVIN D. HOGG, admitted to bar, 1984, Illinois; 1999, Ohio; U.S. District Court, Northern District of Illinois; U.S. District Court, District of Colorado; U.S. District Court, Eastern District of Michigan; U.S. Court of Appeals for the Federal Circuit; registered to practice before U.S. Patent and Trademark Office. *Education:* University of Cincinnati (B.S.M.E., magna cum laude, 1979; J.D., with honors, 1984). ***PRACTICE AREAS:*** Intellectual Property Litigation. ***Email:*** khogg@marshallip.com

WILLIAM J. KRAMER, admitted to bar, 1992, Illinois; U.S. District Court, Northern District of Illinois; registered to practice before U.S. Patent and Trademark Office. *Education:* University of Illinois (B.S., Finance, with high honors, 1989); Northwestern University (J.D., 1992). ***PRACTICE AREAS:*** Electrical Patents; Computer and Software Patents; Intellectual Property Litigation; Patent Licensing; Business Method Patents. ***Email:*** wkramer@marshallip.com

JEREMY R. KRIEGEL, admitted to bar, 1995, Michigan; 1996, Illinois; registered to practice before U.S. Patent and Trademark Office. *Education:* University of Rochester (B.S.M.E., with distinction, 1992); Washington University (J.D., 1995). ***PRACTICE AREAS:*** Intellectual Property; Litigation; Patent and Trademark Prosecution; Counseling. ***Email:*** jkriegel@marshallip.com

RICHARD M. LaBARGE, admitted to bar, 1985, Illinois; U.S. Court of Appeals, Second and Seventh Circuits; U.S. Court of Appeals for the Federal Circuit; U.S. District Court, Central and Northern Districts of Illinois; U.S. District Court, District of Colorado; registered to practice before U.S. Patent and Trademark Office. *Education:* University of Illinois (B.S.C.E., 1982); Wake Forest University (J.D., 1985). ***PRACTICE AREAS:*** Mechanical Patents; Trademark Protection. ***Email:*** rlabarge@marshallip.com

(This Listing Continued)

MARSHALL, GERSTEIN & BORUN LLP, Chicago—Continued

BRYAN J. LEMPIA, admitted to bar, 1993, Michigan; 1994, Illinois; 1996, Minnesota; registered to practice before U.S. Patent and Trademark Office. *Education:* Pennsylvania State University (B.S.M.E., 1985); University of Detroit (J.D., 1993). ***PRACTICE AREAS:*** Patent Prosecution. ***Email:*** blempia@marshallip.com

BRADFORD P. LYERLA, admitted to bar, 1980, Illinois, U.S. District Court, Northern and Central Districts of Illinois, U.S. District Court, Northern District of Indiana, U.S. District Court, Northern District of California, U.S. District Court, District of Nebraska, U.S. District Court, Eastern District of Wisconsin, U.S. Court of Appeals, Second Circuit, U.S. Court of Appeals, Seventh Circuit, U.S. Court of Appeals, Federal Circuit and U.S. Supreme Court. *Education:* University of Illinois (A.B., 1976; J.D., 1980). Phi Beta Kappa. Member, University of Illinois Law Review, 1978-1980. ***PRACTICE AREAS:*** Litigation. ***Email:*** blyerla@marshallip.com

GREGORY C. MAYER, admitted to bar, 1993, Illinois; U.S. District Court, Northern District of Illinois; registered to practice before U.S. Patent and Trademark Office. *Education:* University of Illinois (B.S.A.A.E., 1987); Stanford University (M.S., 1988); University of Chicago (J.D., 1993). ***PRACTICE AREAS:*** Electro-Mechanical Patents; Mechanical Patents; Patent Licensing; Patent Litigation; Copyright Litigation; Trademark Litigation. ***Email:*** gmayer@marshallip.com

WILLIAM K. MERKEL, admitted to bar, 1994, Illinois; registered to practice before U.S. Patent and Trademark Office. *Education:* Knox College (B.A., Psychology and Economics); University of Illinois (Ph.D., Biological Sciences, 1991); New York University (J.D., 1994). ***PRACTICE AREAS:*** Biotechnology Patents; Patent Infringement; Patent Licensing; Patent Litigation; Pharmaceutical Patents. ***Email:*** wmerkel@marshallip.com

CARL E. MOORE, JR., admitted to bar, 1969, Illinois; U.S. Supreme Court; U.S. Court of Appeals, Sixth and Seventh Circuits; U.S. Court of Appeals for the Federal Circuit; registered to practice before U.S. Patent and Trademark Office. *Education:* Loyola University (B.S.(N.S.), 1965; J.D., 1969). ***PRACTICE AREAS:*** Patent Litigation; Patent Prosecution. ***Email:*** cmoore@marshallip.com

MICHAEL MUCZYNSKI, admitted to bar, 1998, New York; 1999, Illinois; U.S. District Court, Northern District of Illinois; registered to practice before U.S. Patent and Trademark Office. *Education:* Michigan State University (B.S., Chemical Engineering, 1993); University of Michigan (J.D., 1997). ***PRACTICE AREAS:*** Intellectual Property. ***Email:*** mmuczynski@marshallip.com

JAMES J. NAPOLI, admitted to bar, 1991, Illinois; registered to practice before U.S. Patent and Trademark Office. *Education:* Ohio State University (B.S., cum laude, 1968); Northwestern University (M.S., 1970; Ph.D., 1973); DePaul University (J.D., with honors, 1991). ***PRACTICE AREAS:*** Chemical Intellectual Property; Pharmaceutical Intellectual Property; Chemical Patent Prosecution; Chemical Patents; Patent Prosecution. ***Email:*** jnapoli@marshallip.com

SANDIP H. PATEL, admitted to bar, 1996, Illinois; U.S. District Court, Northern District of Illinois; U.S. Court of Appeals for the Federal Circuit; registered to practice before U.S. Patent and Trademark Office. *Education:* Michigan State University (B.S., Chemical Engineering, with honors, 1993); Indiana University School of Law - Bloomington (J.D., 1996). ***PRACTICE AREAS:*** Patent Prosecution; Patent Litigation; Patent Interference Proceedings. ***Email:*** spatel@marshallip.com

DAVID C. READ, admitted to bar, 1992, Indiana; 1998, Illinois; U.S. Court of Appeals for the Federal Circuit; registered to practice before U.S. Patent and Trademark Office. *Education:* Purdue University (B.S.C.E., 1986); Valparaiso University School of Law (J.D., 1992). ***PRACTICE AREAS:*** Patent Prosecution; Intellectual Property Litigation; Mechanical Patents; Electro-Mechanical Patents; Patent Infringement. ***Email:*** dread@marshallip.com

LI-HSEIN (LILY) RIN-LAURES, M.D., admitted to bar, 1993, Illinois; U.S. Court of Appeals for the Federal Circuit; registered to practice before the U.S. Patent and Trademark Office. *Education:* Johns Hopkins University (B.A., with honors, Chemistry, 1984); Northwestern University Medical School (M.D., 1988); Harvard Law School (J.D., cum laude, 1992). ***PRACTICE AREAS:*** Biotechnology; Pharmaceutical; Litigation; Patent Prosecution; Patent Interference Proceedings; Chemistry/Chemical Engineering; Intellectual Property Licensing; International Intellectual Property. ***Email:*** lrinlaures@marshallip.com

THOMAS I. ROSS, admitted to bar, 1979, Illinois; U.S. District Court, Northern District of Illinois including Trial Bar; U.S. Court of Appeals for the Federal Circuit; U.S. Court of Appeals, Sixth and Seventh Circuits; U.S. District Court, Eastern District of Wisconsin; U.S. District Court, District of Connecticut; registered to practice before U.S. Patent and Trademark Office. *Education:* Purdue University (B.S.M.E., 1974); Georgetown University (J.D., 1979). ***PRACTICE AREAS:*** Intellectual Property Litigation. ***Email:*** tross@marshallip.com

JEFFREY S. SHARP, admitted to bar, 1984, Georgia and Illinois; U.S. District Court, Northern District of Illinois; registered to practice before U.S. Patent and Trademark Office. *Education:* Princeton University (B.S.E., 1980); University of Georgia (J.D., 1984). ***PRACTICE AREAS:*** Biotechnology Patents; Chemical Patents. ***Email:*** jsharp@marshallip.com

ANTHONY G. SITKO, admitted to bar, 1993, Michigan; 1995, Illinois; 1996, Wisconsin; registered to practice before U.S. Patent and Trademark Office. *Education:* University of Michigan (B.S.M.E., magna cum laude, 1986; M.S.M.E., 1988); Wayne State University (J.D., cum laude, 1992). ***PRACTICE AREAS:*** Electrical Intellectual Property; Intellectual Property Licensing; Mechanical Intellectual Property; Computer and Software Patents; Trademark Prosecution. ***Email:*** asitko@marshallip.com

PAUL B. STEPHENS, admitted to bar, 1998, Illinois. *Education:* University of Michigan (B.S.E., magna cum laude, 1993; M.S.E., 1995; J.D., 1998). Eta Kappa Mu; Tau Beta Pi. *Member:* Chicago and American Bar Associations. ***PRACTICE AREAS:*** Intellectual Property Law. ***Email:*** pstephens@marshallip.com

THOMAS K. STINE, admitted to bar, 1984, Illinois and U.S. District Court, Northern District of Illinois, Trial Bar; U.S. Court of Appeals for the Federal Circuit and U.S. Court of Appeals, Seventh Circuit; registered to practice before U.S. Patent and Trademark Office. *Education:* Purdue University (B.S.E.E., 1978); DePaul University (J.D., 1984). Adjunct Professor of Law, DePaul University. *Member:* Chicago (Chairman, Intellectual Property Law Committee, Young Lawyers Section, 1987-1989) and American Bar Associations; Intellectual Property Law Association of Chicago; American Intellectual Property Law Association. ***PRACTICE AREAS:*** Electronics; Computer Software Law; Litigation; Patent Prosecution. ***Email:*** tstine@marshallip.com

MICHAEL R. WEINER, admitted to bar, 1993, Illinois; U.S. Court of Appeals for the Federal Circuit; registered to practice before U.S. Patent and Trademark Office. *Education:* University of Illinois (B.S., Chemistry, 1984; J.D., summa cum laude, 1993). ***PRACTICE AREAS:*** Patent Litigation; Patent Interference Practice; Patent Prosecution; Chemical Patents. ***Email:*** mweiner@marshallip.com

JOSEPH A. WILLIAMS, JR., admitted to bar, 2000, Illinois; U.S. Court of Appeals, Federal Circuit; registered to practice before U.S. Patent and Trademark Office. *Education:* North Carolina State University (B.S., Chem., 1980); University of Tennessee, Knoxville (Ph.D., Biochem., 1988); DePaul University (J.D., 1999). ***Email:*** jwilliams@marshallip.com

JAMES P. ZELLER, admitted to bar, 1976, Illinois; U.S. Supreme Court; U.S. District Court, Northern District of Illinois; U.S. Court of Appeals for the Seventh Circuit; U.S. Court of Appeals for the Federal Circuit; registered to practice before U.S. Patent and Trademark Office. *Education:* University of Notre Dame (B.S.Ch.E., 1971); Indiana University, Bloomington (M.B.A., 1975); Indiana University School of Law - Bloomington (J.D., 1976). ***PRACTICE AREAS:*** Biotechnology Patents; Chemical Patents; Mechanical Patents; Patent Prosecution; Trademark Protection. ***Email:*** jzeller@marshallip.com

OF COUNSEL

ALLEN H. GERSTEIN, admitted to bar, 1963, Illinois; U.S. Supreme Court; registered to practice before U.S. Patent and Trademark Office. *Education:* University of Illinois (B.S., 1959); Northwestern University (J.D., 1962). ***PRACTICE AREAS:*** Intellectual Property Infringement; Intellectual Property Litigation; Proprietary Rights; Trademark Licensing; Trademark Litigation. ***Email:*** agerstein@marshallip.com

SPECIAL COUNSEL

MEGGAN F. DUFFY, born 1973; admitted to bar, 1998, Illinois; U.S. District Court, Northern District of Illinois; registered to practice before U.S. Patent and Trademark Office. *Education:* University of Illinois (B.S., General Engineering, 1995); Loyola University (J.D., 1998). ***PRACTICE AREAS:*** Intellectual Property. ***Email:*** mfd@marshallip.com

JOHN B. LUNGMUS, admitted to bar, 1954, Wisconsin; 1955, Illinois; registered to practice before U.S. Patent and Trademark Office. *Education:* Northwestern University (B.S., 1951; J.D., 1954). ***PRACTICE AREAS:*** Intellectual Property; Litigation; Patent and Trademark Prosecution; Counseling. ***Email:*** jlungmus@marshallip.com

ASSOCIATES

Matthias Abrell
Jill Anderfuren
George Christopher Braidwood
Gregory J. Chinlund
Pamela L. Cox
Jennifer J.E. Flory (admission pending)
Rashmi V. Gupta
Julianne Hartzell
Anthony S. Hind
Benjamin T. Horton (admission pending)
Mark H. Izraelewicz
Adam G. Kelly
Andrew M. Lawrence
Nabeela R. McMillian
Matthew C. Nielsen
Oliver T. Ong
Steven M. Parks (admission pending)
Chirag B. Patel
Cullen N. Pendleton
Aaron M. Peters
Russell C. Petersen
Jeremy D. Protas (admission pending)
Andrew D. Raymond
Randall G. Rueth
Alisa C. Simmons
Sharon M. Sintich
Andrew R. Smith (admission pending)
Gregory E. Stanton

LEGAL SUPPORT PERSONNEL

PATENT AGENTS

Jeffrey K. Berger
Jeanne M. Brashear
Eric M. Brusca
Michael A. Chinlund
Lynn Janulis
Katherine L. Neville
Greta E. Noland

(This Listing Continued)

JOHN E. MARSZALEK

Established in 1984

29 SOUTH LA SALLE STREET, SUITE 830
CHICAGO, ILLINOIS 60603
Telephone: 312-263-4570
Fax: 312-263-5939
Email: jmarszalek@aol.com
URL: http://www.johnmarszaleklaw.com

Plaintiff Personal Injury including Automobile Accidents, Trucking Accidents, Motorcycle Accidents, Catastrophic Accidents, Wrongful Death, Medical Malpractice, Workers Compensation, Workplace Injuries.

JOHN E. MARSZALEK, born Chicago, Illinois, October 24, 1951; admitted to bar, 1976, Illinois; U.S. District Court, Northern District of Illinois; 1979, Florida; 1986, U.S. District Court, Central District of Illinois; U.S. Court of Appeals, 7th Circuit and U.S. Supreme Court. *Education:* Rollins College (B.A., 1972); John Marshall Law School (J.D.,

(This Listing Continued)

1976). *Member:* Chicago and American Bar Associations; The Florida Bar; Illinois Trial Lawyers Association; The Association of Trial Lawyers of America. ***PRACTICE AREAS:*** Personal Injury; Construction Accidents; Automobile Accidents and Injuries; Truck Accidents; Products Liability; Workers Compensation.

PATRICK W. MARTIN

203 NORTH LASALLE STREET, SUITE 2100
CHICAGO, ILLINOIS 60601
Telephone: 312-332-3343
Fax: 312-346-9603

Workers Compensation, Third Party Liability, Insurance Defense.

PATRICK W. MARTIN, born Müenchweiler, Germany, October 26, 1957; admitted to bar, 1983, Illinois and U.S. District Court, Central District of Illinois. *Education:* Allegheny College (B.A., 1979); Chicago-Kent School of Law, Illinois Institute of Technology (J.D., 1983). *Member:* Illinois State and American Bar Associations. ***PRACTICE AREAS:*** Workers Compensation; Third Party Liability; Insurance Defense.

MARTIN, BROWN & SULLIVAN, LTD.

Established in 1992
321 SOUTH PLYMOUTH COURT
10TH FLOOR
CHICAGO, ILLINOIS 60604
Telephone: 312-360-5000
Fax: 312-360-5026
Email: FIRM@MBSLAW.COM
URL: http://WWW.MBSLAW.COM

Federal and State Trial and Appellate Practice, both Criminal and Civil. Federal and State Taxation.

FIRM PROFILE: Martin, Brown & Sullivan, Ltd. was founded in 1992. The firm practices with an emphasis in white-collar criminal defense; criminal securities, health care, tax and antitrust defense; commercial litigation and advice; federal and state civil tax administrative practice, litigation and advice; state and federal government disputes; administrative law; employment law; commodity disputes and litigation; and estate planning. The firm also provides general legal advice to individuals, partnerships, estates and corporations of all sizes.

ROYAL B. MARTIN, born Seattle, Washington, July 3, 1945; admitted to bar, 1970, Washington, Illinois and U.S. District Court, Northern and Central Districts of Illinois, U.S. District Court, Eastern District of Wisconsin; 1972, U.S. Court of Appeals, Seventh Circuit; 1976, U.S. Tax Court; 1977, U.S. Court of Appeals, Second, Fifth, Eighth and Eleventh Circuits; 1986, U.S. Court of Federal Claims; 2000, U.S. District Court, Western District of Michigan; 2004, U.S. Supreme Court. *Education:* University of San Francisco (B.A., 1967); University of Washington (J.D., 1970). Phi Alpha Delta. Contributing Author, Chicago-Kent Law Review, IICLE, 1977. Recipient, Special Commendation for Outstanding Service, Department of Justice, 1974. Author: "Trial of the Criminal Tax Fraud Case," 1975, 1978, 1982, 1985. Lecturer in Tax Fraud, Whiteside County Bar Association, 1981. Assistant U.S. Attorney, Northern District of Illinois, 1970-1975. Associate, Harris, Burman and Silets, 1975-1979. Partner, Silets & Martin, Ltd., 1979-1992. Chairman, Illinois State Appellate Defender Commission, 1977-1983. *Member:* Chicago, Illinois State, Washington State, Federal (Member: Committee on Criminal Law and Procedure, 1977—; Committee on Federal Taxation, 1977—), American (Former Chairman, Midwest Region, White Collar Crime Committee of the Criminal Justice Section) and Seventh Circuit (Former General Chair, Criminal Law and Procedure Committee) Bar Associations; Illinois Society of Trial Lawyers; National Association of Criminal Defense Lawyers. Fellow, American College of Trial Lawyers. ***PRACTICE AREAS:*** Tax Fraud Defense; White Collar Crime; Criminal Antitrust; Health Care Fraud Defense; Securities Fraud Defense; Federal Tax Administrative Practice. ***Email:*** MARTIN@MBSLAW.COM

STEVEN S. BROWN, born Manhattan, Kansas, February 26, 1948; admitted to bar, 1973, Missouri; 1974, U.S. Tax Court; 1977, Illinois; 1979, U.S. District Court, Northern District of Illinois including Trial Bar; 1983, U.S. Court of Appeals, Seventh Circuit; 1986, U.S. Court of Federal Claims; 1989, California and U.S. Court of Appeals, Eleventh Circuit; 2000, U.S. Court of Appeals, Fifth Circuit; 2003, U.S. Supreme Court. *Education:* University of Missouri (B.S.B.A., 1970; J.D., 1973). Phi Delta Phi. Author: "Grand Jury Secrecy Violations," Barrister, 1981; "Handling Criminal Tax Cases: A Lawyer's Guide, Closing the Civil Case After Criminal Investigation or Prosecution," Illinois Institute for Continuing Legal Education, 1985; "Appealing IRS Findings in Tax Audits," Illinois Manufacturers' Association Law Digest, 1989. Contributing Practitioner: "IRS Practice & Policy," Tax Management, Inc., 1990. "The Fallout After Ballard," Journal of Tax Practice & Procedure, 2005; "Secrecy and the Tax Court," Chicago Bar Association Record, 2005. Lecturer: "Trial Techniques in Tax Court," 29th Annual Tax Institute, Alabama State Bar, 1989; "Federal Tax Controversies - Practice Before the IRS, the District Court and the U.S. Tax Court," ABA & Federal Bar Association, 1992; "There's a CID Agent at the Door; Practical Considerations for the Accounting Professional," Illinois CPA Society, 38th Annual Tax Conference, 1992; "Evidence in the Tax Court," Midwest Regional IRS Appeals Office, 1992; "How The Budget Reconciliation Act of 1993 Affects You and Your Business," National Business Institute, 1994; "An Overview of IRS Examinations, Administrative Appeals and Tax Court Litigation," Chicago Bar Association, 2000. "IRS Practice & Procedures," 2005 Tax Conference, Illinois CPA Foundation. Panelist: "Representation of Promoters and Preparers in Tax Shelter Investigations," ABA Tax Section, 2003; "Privilege and Work Product in the Context of Tax Litigation, Lessons from the Trenches, " ABA Tax Section-CLE, 2004; "What Remains of the Attorney-Client and Accountant-Client Privileges in Tax Planning?" Arizona Bar Association Annual Meeting, 2004. Adjunct Professor, The John Marshall Law School —Graduate Tax Program, Civil Tax Procedure and Administrative Practice, 1985—. Member, Advisory Board, Center for Tax Law and Employee Benefits, The John Marshall Law School, 1997—. Trial Attorney, Office of Regional Counsel, 1973-1978

(This Listing Continued)

and Senior Trial Attorney, Office of District Counsel, 1978-1979, Internal Revenue Service, Chicago, Illinois. Associate, 1979-1985; Partner, 1985-1992, Silets & Martin, Ltd.; Partner, 1992—, Martin, Brown & Sullivan, Ltd. *Member:* Chicago (Member, 1980—, Subcommittee Chairman 1984-1985 and Member, Executive Council, 1983-1985, Federal Taxation Committee), Illinois State (Member, Section on Federal Taxation, 1979—), Federal (Member, Committee on Federal Taxation, 1977—) and American (Member: Taxation Section, 1973—; Court Procedure Committee) Bar Associations; The Missouri Bar; State Bar of California (Member, Taxation Section, 1989—). ***PRACTICE AREAS:*** Federal Tax Litigation; Federal Tax Administrative Practice. ***Email:*** BROWN@MBSLAW.COM

WILLIAM G. SULLIVAN, born Evanston, Illinois, July 1, 1949; admitted to bar, 1978, Illinois; U.S. District Court, Northern District of Illinois, including Trial Bar, U.S. Court of Appeals, Seventh, Fifth and Eleventh Circuits and U.S. Tax Court; 2004, U.S. Supreme Court. *Education:* Northern Illinois University (B.S., 1971); Chicago-Kent College of Law, Illinois Institute of Technology (J.D., with honors, 1978). Author, Illinois Statutes: Travel Promotion Consumer Protection Act, Ill. Rev. Stat. 1989, 720 ILCS 350/1; Illinois Burial Rights Act, Ill. Rev. Stat. 1989, 820 ILCS 135/1; Aggravated Stalking Law, Ill. Rev. Stat. 1989, 720 IL CS 5/12-74. Assistant Attorney General, Illinois Attorney General's Office, 1979-1989. Chief of Consumer Enforcement Bureau (including Antitrust, Consumer Protection & Public Utilities Divisions), 1986-1989. Chief of Toxic Waste Strike Force, 1984-1986. Chief of General Law Division, 1983-1986. Counsel to Illinois State Medical Center Commission, 1985-1989. Special Assistant Attorney General For: The Department of Transportation; Illinois Savings and Residential Finance Commission; Illinois Department of Mental Health; Illinois Department of Children and Family Services; Illinois Department of Public Aid. Lecturer, ABA Conference, Washington, D.C., 1987 (Banking Section), Conference on Consumer's Rights. Partner, Silets & Martin, 1989-1992. *Member:* Chicago, Illinois State, American and Seventh Circuit Bar Associations. ***PRACTICE AREAS:*** Federal and State Litigation; Commercial Litigation; Appellate Practice; Administrative Law. ***Email:*** SULLIVAN@MBSLAW.COM

LEIGH D. ROADMAN, born Richmond Heights, Missouri, February 5, 1959; admitted to bar, 1986, Illinois, U.S. District Court, Northern District of Illinois, including Trial Bar, U.S. Tax Court, U.S. Court of Appeals, Seventh and Eleventh Circuits and U.S. Court of Federal Claims. *Education:* University of Illinois (B.S., 1981); DePaul University (J.D., with honors, 1986). Member, DePaul University Law Review, 1985-1986. Author: "RICO Forfeiture: Can the Adversary be Removed from the Adversary Process?" DePaul University Law Review, 1986. Certified Public Accountant, Illinois, 1981. Member, Federal Defender Panel for the U.S. District Court, Northern District of Illinois, 1991—. Associate, Silets & Martin, Ltd., 1986-1992. Adjunct Professor, Civil Tax Procedure and Administrative Practice, The John Marshall Law School Graduate Tax Program, 1991-2000. *Member:* Chicago, Illinois State, Federal and American Bar Associations; Illinois Certified Public Accountants Society. ***PRACTICE AREAS:*** White Collar Crime; Securities Fraud Defense; Health Care Fraud Defense; Tax Fraud Defense; Federal Tax Administrative Practice; Commercial Litigation. ***Email:*** ROADMAN@MBSLAW.COM

DANIEL T. HARTNETT, born Chicago, Illinois, September 29, 1952; admitted to bar, 1977, Illinois and U.S. District Court, Northern District of Illinois; 1978, U.S. Court of Military Appeals; 1986, U.S. Supreme Court and U.S. Tax Court; U.S. Court of Appeals, Fifth, Seventh, Eighth and Eleventh Circuits. *Education:* University of Notre Dame (B.A., 1974); Loyola University (J.D., 1977). Author: "Tax and Money Laundering Offenses Under the Sentencing Guidelines," Practice Under the Federal Sentencing Guidelines; "Punitive Damages and The Illinois Survival Act," 7 Loyola University-Chicago Law Journal 811, 1976. Trial Attorney, Tax Division, United States Department of Justice, Criminal Section, 1982-1984 and Office of Special Litigation, 1984-1986. Associate, Silets & Martin, Ltd., 1986-1992. Adjunct Professor, The John Marshall Law School Graduate Tax Program. Lecturer: Federal Tax Institute, Chicago-Kent College of Law, 1988, 1989; "Federal Tax Controversies - Practice Before the IRS, the District Court and the U.S. Tax Court," ABA & Federal Bar Association, 1992; "There's a CID Agent at the Door; Practical Considerations for the Accounting Profession," Illinois CPA Society, 38th Annual Tax Conference, 1992. Member, Federal Defender Panel for the U.S. District Court, Northern District of Illinois, 1991—. *Member:* Chicago, Illinois State and American Bar Associations. [Capt., JAGC, U.S. Army, 1978-1982]. ***LANGUAGES:*** German. ***REPORTED CASES:*** U.S. v. Heffernan, 43 F.3d 1144 (7th Cir. 1994); Windy City Meat Co. v. U.S.D.A., 926 F.2d 672 (7th Cir. 1991); Resolution Trust Corp. v. Gallagher, et al., 800 F.Supp. 595 (N.D. III 1992); U.S. v. Duncan, 704 F. Supp. 830 (N.D. III 1989); Universal Manufacturing Inc. v. Commissioner, T.C. Memo. 1994-367, 68 T.C.M. (CCH) 305 (1994). ***PRACTICE AREAS:*** Federal Tax Litigation; Federal Tax Administrative Practice; Federal Criminal Defense Law. ***Email:*** HARTNETT@MBSLAW.COM

ROBERT S. GRABEMANN, born Evanston, Illinois, April 12, 1961; admitted to bar, 1986, Illinois and U.S. District Court, Northern District of Illinois, U.S. Court of Appeals, Seventh Circuit; U.S. Tax Court. *Education:* Harvard University (B.A., cum laude, 1983); Northwestern University (J.D., 1986). Associate, Winston & Strawn, 1986-1992. Arbitrator, Cook County Mandatory Arbitration Program. Author: Defense of Medical Malpractice Litigation, 1986, Illinois Institute of Continuing Legal Education. *Member:* Chicago Bar Association. ***PRACTICE AREAS:*** Commercial Litigation; Criminal Law (White Collar); Personal Injury. ***Email:*** GRABEMANN@MBSLAW.COM

VICTOR S. KOSTRO, born Chicago, Illinois, October 5, 1959; admitted to bar, 1993, Illinois; 1994, Florida; U.S. Tax Court. *Education:* University of Illinois (B.S., Accounting, 1987); Thomas M. Cooley Law School (J.D., 1993); University of Florida (LL.M., Taxation, 1994). *Member:* Chicago and Brevard County Bar Associations. ***PRACTICE AREAS:*** Corporate Transactional; Probate; Estate Planning; Real Estate. ***Email:*** KOSTRO@MBSLAW.COM

MASON N. FLOYD, born Indiana, Indianapolis, January 21, 1979; admitted to bar, 2004, Illinois; 2005, U.S. District Court, Northern District of Illinois, U.S. Court of Appeals, Seventh Circuit and U.S. Tax Court. *Education:* Depauw University (B.A., 2001); Indiana University (J.D., 2004). *Member:* Chicago and American Bar Associations. ***PRACTICE AREAS:*** Commercial Litigation; Federal Litigation; White Collar Criminal Defense. ***Email:*** FLOYD@MBSLAW.COM

(This Listing Continued)

MARTIN, BROWN & SULLIVAN, LTD., Chicago—Continued

OF COUNSEL

DENIS J. CONLON, born Springfield, Illinois, April 21, 1935; admitted to bar, 1961, Illinois; 1967, Wisconsin and U.S. District Court, Eastern and Western Districts of Wisconsin; U.S. District Court, Eastern District of Illinois; U.S. Tax Court; U.S. Court of Federal Claims. *Education:* Loyola University (B.S.C., 1958; J.D., 1961); DePaul University (LL.M., Tax, 1985). Phi Alpha Delta. Co-Author: "Federal Tax Practice," Chapter 7, IICLE; "The Tax Court From the IRS Register Perspective". Adjunct Professor: Tax Practice and Procedure, Chicago Kent College of Law, 1990-2003. IRS District Counsel, Chicago, 1978-1986; IRS Regional Counsel, Midwest, 1986-1992. Principal, Ernst & Young, LLP, 1992-2003. *Member:* Chicago, American (Member, Section on Taxation) and State Bar of Wisconsin. ***REPORTED CASES:*** Schroder v. Commissioner, 40 T.C. 30 (1963); Burr Oaks Corp. v. Commissioner, 43 T.C. 635 (1965); Roob v. Commissioner, 50 T.C. 891 (1968); Swiss Colony, Inc. v. Commissioner, 52 T.C. 25 (1969); Marc's Big Boy... Prospect, Inc. v. Commissioner, 52 T.C. 1073 (1969); Fisher v. Commissioner, 54 T.C. 905 (1970); Prudowsky's Estate v. Commissioner, 55 T.C. 890 (1971); Seay v. Commissioner, 58 T.C. 32 (1972); Ross Glove Co. v. Commissioner 60 T.C. 569 (1073); S.C. Johnson & Son, inc. v. Commissioner, 63 T.C. 778 (1975); Otto Kerner, Jr. v. Commissioner, 35 TCM 36, TC Memo 1976-12 (1976); Kansas City Southern Railway Co. v. Commissioner, 76 T.C. 1067 (1981); Midwest Generator Co. v. Commissioner, 55 TCM 90, TC Memo 1988-50 (1988). ***PRACTICE AREAS:*** Federal Tax. ***Email:*** CONLON@MBSLAW.COM

MARTIN, CRAIG, CHESTER & SONNENSCHEIN

CHICAGO, ILLINOIS

(See Oak Brook)

General Practice including: business organization and operations, acquisitions and divestitures, federal, state and local taxation, real estate and real estate finance, employee benefits, employment law, labor relations, not-for-profit and charitable organizations, municipal law, administrative proceedings, estate planning, probate and trust, family foundations and environmental law.

MARWEDEL, MINICHELLO & REEB, P.C.

10 SOUTH RIVERSIDE PLAZA, SUITE 720
CHICAGO, ILLINOIS 60606
Telephone: 312-902-1600
Fax: 312-902-9900
URL: http://www.mmr-law.com

General Civil Trial and Appellate Practice including Complex Litigation, Administrative Hearings, Alternate Dispute Resolution, Transportation Law, Admiralty and Maritime Law, Commercial Law, Technology Law, Personal Injury, Professional Liability and Insurance.

FIRM PROFILE: A unique firm for challenging times, we dedicate our efforts to finding creative and cost effective solutions to our clients' legal problems. The firm's shareholders have practiced together for many years, tried numerous, difficult cases and successfully prosecuted appeals in various state and federal courts and before administrative agencies resulting in many published opinions. In addition, we serve with distinction as officers or committee chairs in various professional and business organizations and have authored books and articles on a variety of subjects. Individually and collectively, we bring this wealth of knowledge, experience and common sense to each and every matter we handle.

SHAREHOLDERS

WARREN J. MARWEDEL, admitted to bar, 1972, Illinois and U.S. District Court, Northern District of Illinois; 1977, U.S. Supreme Court; 1979, U.S. Court of Appeals, Seventh Circuit; 1983, U.S. Court of Appeals, Eighth and Eleventh Circuits; 1985, U.S. Court of Appeals, Second Circuit; 1993, U.S. Court of Appeals, Sixth Circuit. *Education:* U.S. Merchant Marine Academy (B.S., 1966); University of Notre Dame (University of London Campus) and Loyola University (J.D., 1972). ***Email:*** wmarwedel@mmr-law.com

DENNIS MINICHELLO, admitted to bar, 1978, Illinois; 1979, U.S. District Court, Northern District of Illinois and U.S. Court of Appeals, Seventh Circuit; 1982, U.S. District Court, Central District of Illinois; 1990, U.S. Supreme Court; 2001, U.S. District Court, Northern District of Indiana. *Education:* Ohio University (B.A., 1974; M.A., 1974); Northwestern University (J.D., 1978). Fulbright Scholar, Italy, 1974-1975. ***Email:*** dminichello@mmr-law.com

ROBERT L. REEB, born Stockton, California; admitted to bar, 1988, Illinois and U.S. District Court, Northern District of Illinois; 1991, U.S. Court of Military Appeals; 1995, U.S. Court of Appeals, Seventh Circuit; 2001, U.S. District Court, Northern District of Indiana. *Education:* University of Dallas (B.A., Political Philosophy, cum laude, 1985); Loyola University of Chicago (M.A., Political Theory, cum laude, 1988; J.D., cum laude, 1988). ***Email:*** rreeb@mmr-law.com

LIMITED SHAREHOLDERS

SHARI L. FRIEDMAN, admitted to bar, 1986, Illinois and U.S. District Court, Northern District of Illinois; 1993, U.S. Court of Appeals, Seventh Circuit. *Education:* University of Illinois (B.S.W., 1983); DePaul University (J.D., with honors, 1986). Phi Alpha Delta. ***Email:*** sfriedman@mmr-law.com

WILLIAM P. RYAN, admitted to bar, 1982, Illinois and U.S. District Court, Northern District of Illinois; 1992, U.S. Court of Appeals, Seventh and Tenth Circuits and U.S. District Court, Northern District of Indiana; U.S. District Court, Southern District of Illinois. *Education:* Southern Illinois University (B.A., Economics, 1978); DePaul University (J.D. with Honors, 1982). ***Email:*** bryan@mmr-law.com

MASUDA, FUNAI, EIFERT & MITCHELL, LTD.

Established in 1961
SUITE 2500, 203 NORTH LASALLE STREET
CHICAGO, ILLINOIS 60601-1262
Telephone: 312-245-7500
Fax: 312-245-7467
Email: lawfirm@masudafunai.com
URL: http://www.masudafunai.com

Schaumburg, Illinois Office: Suite 800, 1475 East Woodfield Road, 60173-5485. Telephone: 847-734-8811. Fax: 847-734-1089.

Torrance, California Office: Suite 420, 19191 South Vermont Avenue, 90502-1051. Telephone: 310-630-5900. Fax: 310-630-5909.

International Business, Corporations, Corporate Financing and Reorganizations, Mergers and Acquisitions, Joint Ventures, Real Estate, Environmental Law, Banking, Finance and Lending, Antitrust and Trade Regulations, Unfair Competition, Commercial Transactions, Employment and Labor Relations, Immigration, Technology Licensing, Intellectual Property, Multistate and Local Taxation, Probate, Insurance Defense, Product and Professional Liability, Arbitration, Corporate and Commercial Litigation and Trials in all Courts, and General Civil Practice.

FIRM PROFILE: Full-service law firm advising clients in all aspects of corporate and commercial law, with special emphasis on international companies operating and investing in the U.S.

PRINCIPALS

ANTHONY J. BRUOZAS, admitted to bar, 1990, Illinois and U.S. District Court, Northern District of Illinois; 1995, U.S. Court of Appeals, Sixth and Seventh Circuits. *Education:* University of Illinois (B.S., 1987); Loyola University (J.D., 1990). ***PRACTICE AREAS:*** Commercial Litigation; Trade Secret Litigation; Distribution Counseling. ***Email:*** abruozas@masudafunai.com

JAMES M. COONAN, admitted to bar, 1973, Wisconsin; 1976, Illinois. *Education:* University of Wisconsin-Madison (J.D., 1972); University of Minnesota (M.B.A., 1983). ***PRACTICE AREAS:*** Business Law; Corporate Law; Mergers, Acquisitions and Divestitures; Securities. ***Email:*** jcoonan@masudafunai.com

LAURA TALLROTH EDMONDS, admitted to bar, 1996, Wisconsin, Illinois and U.S. District Court, Northern District of Illinois. *Education:* University of Wisconsin-Madison (B.A., 1990; J.D., 1996); Sophia University, Tokyo, Japan (1988-1989). ***LANGUAGES:*** Japanese. ***PRACTICE AREAS:*** Business Law; Commercial Finance; Corporate Organization; Mergers and Acquisitions. ***Email:*** ltallroth@masudafunai.com

HELMUT EIFERT (1929-1995)

JERROLD E. FINK, admitted to bar, 1971, Illinois and U.S. District Court, Northern District of Illinois including Trial Bar; 1974, U.S. Court of Appeals, 7th Circuit; 1976, U.S. Supreme Court. *Education:* University of California at Los Angeles (B.A., magna cum laude, 1968); Harvard University (J.D., cum laude, 1971). ***PRACTICE AREAS:*** Trade Regulation; Distribution; Antitrust; Litigation; Intellectual Property. ***Email:*** jfink@masudafunai.com

BRYAN Y. FUNAI, admitted to bar, 1981, Illinois; 1987, U.S. District Court, Northern District of Illinois; 1998, Ohio. *Education:* Northern Illinois University (B.S., 1978); Thomas M. Cooley Law School (J.D., 1981). (Also at Schaumburg Office). ***LANGUAGES:*** Japanese. ***PRACTICE AREAS:*** Business Immigration; Corporate; Mergers and Acquisitions; Contracts. ***Email:*** bfunai@masudafunai.com

MASARU FUNAI, admitted to bar, 1957, Illinois. *Education:* University of Hawaii (B.A., 1952); Northwestern University (J.D., 1957). (Also at Schaumburg Office). ***LANGUAGES:*** Japanese. ***PRACTICE AREAS:*** Business Development; Business Formation; Business Acquisitions and Sales; Joint Ventures. ***Email:*** mfunai@masudafunai.com

KATHLEEN M. GABER, admitted to bar, 1985, Georgia; 1986, Illinois; 1989, U.S. District Court, Northern District of Illinois. *Education:* University of Michigan at Ann Arbor (B.B.A., 1981; B.A., 1982); Emory University (J.D., 1985). (Also at Schaumburg Office). ***LANGUAGES:*** Croatian. ***PRACTICE AREAS:*** Business Immigration. ***Email:*** kgaber@masudafunai.com

KEITH WALTER GROEBE, admitted to bar, 1979, Illinois and U.S. District Court, Northern District of Illinois; 1980, U.S. Court of Appeals, 7th Circuit and U.S. Tax Court. *Education:* University of Illinois (B.A., 1975; M.A., 1976); DePaul University (J.D., 1979). ***PRACTICE AREAS:*** Real Estate; Industrial Real Estate; Commercial Real Estate; Business Law; Eminent Domain; Construction Law; Contracts. ***Email:*** kgroebe@masudafunai.com

TIMOTHY J. HAMMERSMITH, admitted to bar, 1993, Illinois; 1994, Florida. *Education:* University of South Florida (B.S., 1987); The John Marshall Law School (J.D., 1993). ***PRACTICE AREAS:*** Real Estate Taxation; Real Estate Transactions. ***Email:*** thammersmith@masudafunai.com

COLIN HARA, admitted to bar, 1978, Illinois and U.S. District Court, Northern District of Illinois; 1982, U.S. Court of Appeals, 7th Circuit; 1998, Ohio. *Education:* Loyola University (A.B., 1973); DePaul University (J.D., 1978). ***LANGUAGES:*** Japanese. ***PRACTICE AREAS:*** Corporate Law; Commercial Law; Employment Law; Contracts; Business Immigration. ***Email:*** chara@masudafunai.com

ELDON H. KAKUDA, admitted to bar, 1986, Pennsylvania; 1987, Illinois; 1998, Ohio. *Education:* University of Nebraska at Lincoln; Georgetown University, School of Foreign Service (B.S.F.S., 1982); Georgetown University (J.D., 1986). (Also at Schaumburg Office). ***LANGUAGES:*** Japanese. ***PRACTICE AREAS:*** Business Immigration; Contracts; Corporate Law; Employment Law. ***Email:*** ekakuda@masudafunai.com

ALAN M. KAPLAN, admitted to bar, 1980, Illinois; 1999, Ohio and Kentucky. *Education:* Northwestern University (B.S.E., 1973; M.A., 1975); DePaul University (J.D., 1980). (Also at Schaumburg Office). ***SPECIAL AGENCIES:*** National Labor Relations Board (NLRB); Equal opportunity Commission (EEOC); Occupational Safety & Health

(This Listing Continued)

Administration (OSHA). *PRACTICE AREAS:* Labor and Employment; Management Labor Law; Employment Discrimination; Collective Bargaining. ***Email:*** akaplan@masudafunai.com

STEVEN L. KATZ, admitted to bar, 1992, Illinois and U.S. District Court, Northern District of Illinois including Trial Bar; 1995, U.S. District Court, District of Arizona; 2002, U.S. Court of Appeals, Eighth Circuit. *Education:* University of Michigan (B.A., 1989); Northern Illinois University (J.D., magna cum laude, 1992). ***PRACTICE AREAS:*** Civil Litigation; Antitrust Law; Commercial Law; Distribution; Distribution and Sales; Unfair Trade. ***Email:*** skatz@masudafunai.com

DAYNE KONO, admitted to bar, 1982, Illinois; 1983, U.S. District Court, Northern District of Illinois; 1998, Kentucky and Ohio. *Education:* University of Michigan (A.B., 1978); Fordham University (J.D., 1982). ***LANGUAGES:*** Japanese. ***PRACTICE AREAS:*** Corporate Law; Commercial Law; Labor and Employment; Business Immigration; Intellectual Property. ***Email:*** dkono@masudafunai.com

REINHOLD F. KRAMMER, admitted to bar, 1993, Illinois and U.S. District Court, Northern District of Illinois. *Education:* University of Illinois (B.S., 1988); DePaul University (J.D., 1993). ***PRACTICE AREAS:*** Commercial Litigation; Civil Litigation; Creditor Rights; Commercial Law. ***Email:*** rkrammer@masudafunai.com

THOMAS MASUDA (1905-1986)

THOMAS P. McMENAMIN, admitted to bar, 1980, District of Columbia; 1990, Illinois. *Education:* University of Notre Dame (B.A., high honors, 1975); Georgetown University Law Center (J.D., 1980). ***LANGUAGES:*** French. ***PRACTICE AREAS:*** Finance; Mergers and Acquisitions; Divestitures. ***Email:*** tmcmenamin@masudafunai.com

GERALD L. MOREL, admitted to bar, 1972, Illinois, U.S. District Court, Northern and Central Districts of Illinois including Trial Bar, U.S. Court of Appeals, 7th Circuit and U.S. Supreme Court. *Education:* Northern Illinois University (B.S., 1969); Loyola University of Chicago (J.D., 1972). ***PRACTICE AREAS:*** Litigation; Commercial Law; Agency and Distributorships; Contracts. ***Email:*** gmorel@masudafunai.com

JOSEPH S. PARISI, admitted to bar, 1975, Illinois and U.S. District Court, Northern District of Illinois including Trial Bar; 1982, U.S. Court of Appeals, 7th Circuit. *Education:* University of Illinois (B.S., 1972); Loyola University of Chicago (J.D., 1975). (Also at Schaumburg Office). ***PRACTICE AREAS:*** Commercial Business Counseling; Distribution Law; Joint Ventures; Mergers and Acquisitions. ***Email:*** jparisi@masudafunai.com

STEPHEN M. PROCTOR, admitted to bar, 1982, Illinois; 1983, U.S. District Court, Northern District of Illinois; 1998, Ohio; 1999, Kentucky. *Education:* Indiana University (B.A., with high distinction, 1977; J.D., cum laude, 1982). (Also at Schaumburg Office). ***LANGUAGES:*** Japanese. ***PRACTICE AREAS:*** Agency and Distributorships; Labor and Employment; Commercial Law. ***Email:*** sproctor@masudafunai.com

GARY D. SANTELLA, admitted to bar, 1979, Illinois; 1980, U.S. District Court, Northern District of Illinois. *Education:* Loyola University of Chicago (B.A., 1976; J.D., 1979). ***PRACTICE AREAS:*** Litigation; Commercial Law; Agency and Distributorships; Contracts. ***Email:*** gsantella@masudafunai.com

NANCY E. SASAMOTO, admitted to bar, 1980, Illinois, U.S. District Court, Northern District of Illinois including Trial Bar, U.S. Court of Appeals, 7th Circuit and U.S. Supreme Court. *Education:* University of Illinois (B.S., 1977); Washington University (J.D., 1980). ***PRACTICE AREAS:*** Labor and Employment; Litigation; Trademarks; Commercial Law; Distribution. ***Email:*** nsasamoto@masudafunai.com

MARY W. SHELLENBERG, admitted to bar, 1974, Illinois and U.S. District Court, Northern District of Illinois. *Education:* Mundelein College (B.A., 1971); Loyola University of Chicago (J.D., 1974). ***PRACTICE AREAS:*** Mergers, Acquisitions and Divestitures; Business Entity Planning; Entity Formation; Employee Benefits. ***Email:*** mshellenberg@masudafunai.com

JOHN B. STANIS, admitted to bar, 1988, Illinois. *Education:* Illinois State University (B.S., 1985); University of Illinois (J.D., 1988). (Also at Schaumburg Office). ***LANGUAGES:*** Japanese. ***PRACTICE AREAS:*** Litigation; Labor and Employment; Commercial Law; Distribution; Distribution and Sales. ***Email:*** jstanis@masudafunai.com

EDWARD J. UNDERHILL, admitted to bar, 1984, Illinois, U.S. District Court, Northern District of Illinois including Trial Bar, U.S. Court of Appeals, 7th Circuit and U.S. Supreme Court. *Education:* Northern Illinois University (B.A., 1981; J.D., 1984). ***PRACTICE AREAS:*** Litigation; Arbitration; Commercial Law; Appellate Practice. ***Email:*** eunderhill@masudafunai.com

ROBERT S. WHITE, admitted to bar, 1993, Illinois. *Education:* University of Notre Dame (B.A., 1990); Illinois Institute of Technology Chicago-Kent (J.D., 1993). (Also at Schaumburg Office). ***PRACTICE AREAS:*** Business Immigration. ***Email:*** rwhite@masudafunai.com

ASSOCIATES

LAURENCE P. BECKER, admitted to bar, 1997, Illinois. *Education:* Syracuse University (B.S., 1985); John Marshall Law School (J.D., 1997); S.I. Newhouse School of Communications. ***PRACTICE AREAS:*** Commercial Law; Litigation; Distribution; Intellectual Property; Employment; Distribution and Sales. ***Email:*** lbecker@masudafunai.com

DAVID S. HWANG, admitted to bar, 1998, Illinois. *Education:* University of Illinois (B.A., 1994); Washington University (J.D., 1998). (Also at Schaumburg Office). ***PRACTICE AREAS:*** Business Immigration. ***Email:*** dhwang@masuafunai.com

JENNIFER A. JOYCE, born Park Ridge, Illinois, 1973; admitted to bar, 2000, Wisconsin; 2002, U.S. District Court, Eastern District of Wisconsin; 2003, Illinois. *Education:* University of Wisconsin, Oshkosh (B.A., magna cum laude, 1997); Marquette University Law School (J.D., 2000). ***LANGUAGES:*** German. ***PRACTICE AREAS:*** Real Estate. ***Email:*** jjoyce@masudafunai.com

GEORGE H. KOBAYASHI, admitted to bar, 2001, Illinois. *Education:* Creighton University (B.S.B.A., 1995); The John Marshall Law School (J.D., 2000). ***LANGUAGES:*** Japanese. ***PRACTICE AREAS:*** Intellectual Property; Internet Law; Corporate Law; Agency and Distribution; Commercial Law. ***Email:*** gkobayashi@masudafunai.com

(This Listing Continued)

JASON M. METNICK, admitted to bar, 2003, Illinois. *Education:* University of Michigan, Ann Arbor (B.A., 2000); DePaul University College of Law (J.D., 2003). ***LANGUAGES:*** Spanish, French and German. ***PRACTICE AREAS:*** Agency and Distributorships; Commercial Law; Civil Litigation; Business Law. ***Email:*** jmetnick@masudafunai.com

SHINOBU NISHIDA, admitted to bar, 2003, Illinois. *Education:* Indiana University - Bloomington (B.A., 1996); Indiana University School of Law - Bloomington (J.D., 2003). ***LANGUAGES:*** Japanese. ***PRACTICE AREAS:*** Labor and Employment; Business. ***Email:*** snishida@masudafunai.com

REYNARD L. TANIG, born Quezon City, Philippines, 1968; admitted to bar, 1993, Illinois and U.S. District Court, Northern District of Illinois. *Education:* University of Illinois at Urbana-Champaign (B.A., 1990); DePaul University College of Law (J.D., 1993). ***PRACTICE AREAS:*** Trusts and Estates; Probate; Estate and Gift Taxation; Business Law. ***Email:*** rtanig@masudafunai.com

GARY VIST, admitted to bar, 1999, Illinois and U.S. District Court, District of Illinois. *Education:* Loyola University, Chicago (B.S., 1996); Northwestern University (J.D., 1999). ***LANGUAGES:*** Russian, Ukrainian. ***PRACTICE AREAS:*** Employment Litigation; Franchise Litigation; Bankruptcy; Debtor and Creditor Collections; Commercial Litigation. ***Email:*** gvist@masudafunai.com

JENNIFER R.M.C. WATSON, admitted to bar, 2001, Illinois. *Education:* North Central College (B.A., 1997); Northwestern University School of Law (J.D., 2001). ***PRACTICE AREAS:*** Corporate Law; Mergers, Acquisitions and Divestitures; Employee Benefits; Taxation. ***Email:*** jwatson@masudafunai.com

SHINYA YAMAMOTO, admitted to bar, 1998, Illinois and U.S. District Court, Northern District of Illinois. *Education:* Michigan State University (B.A., Marketing, 1993); Illinois Institute of Technology Chicago-Kent College of Law (J.D., 1997). ***LANGUAGES:*** Japanese. ***PRACTICE AREAS:*** Real Estate. ***Email:*** syamamoto@masudafunai.com

OF COUNSEL

JEREMY A. GIBSON, admitted to bar, 1987, Illinois; 1998, Kentucky; 1999, Ohio. *Education:* Indiana University (B.A., 1984); University of Michigan (J.D., 1987). ***PRACTICE AREAS:*** Corporate Law; Commercial Law; Intellectual Property; Products Liability; Environmental Law. ***Email:*** jgibson@masudafunai.com

JEFFREY M. HUCEK, admitted to bar, 1983, Minnesota; 1984, U.S. Tax Court; 1989, Illinois; 1999, Colorado. *Education:* University of Virginia (B.S.C., Accounting, with distinction, 1977); University of Minnesota (J.D., cum laude, 1983). (Also practicing individually in Oak Brook). ***Email:*** jhucek@masudafunai.com

JAMES C. SHANLEY, (P.C.), admitted to bar, 1974, Illinois, U.S. Tax Court and U.S. Court of Federal Claims; 1990, California. *Education:* DePaul University (B.S.C., 1966; J.D., 1974). ***PRACTICE AREAS:*** Taxation Law; Corporate Law. ***Email:*** jshanley@masudafunai.com

MATEK LAW OFFICES, P.C.

77 WEST WASHINGTON STREET
SUITE 1313
CHICAGO, ILLINOIS 60602-3236
Telephone: 312-372-5800
Fax: 312-372-1276
URL: http://www.mateklaw.com
Email: mmatek@mateklaw.com
URL: http://www.michaelmateklawoffices.com

Subrogation, Collections, Commercial Litigation, Bankruptcy, Commercial Law.

MICHAEL S. MATEK, born Evanston, Illinois, July 9, 1957; admitted to bar, 1983, Illinois and U.S. District Court, Northern District of Illinois; 1990, New York. *Education:* Brandeis University (B.A., 1979); Chicago-Kent College of Law(J.D., 1983). Member, Jessup Cup International Moot Court Team Chicago-Kent, 1982-1983. Author: "Limiting Liability in Personal Computer Equipment Contracts," 88 Commercial Law Journal, p. 562, 1983. *Member:* Illinois State and American Bar Associations; Computer Law Association. ***PRACTICE AREAS:*** Subrogation; Collections; Commercial Litigation; Bankruptcy; Commercial Law. ***Email:*** mmatek@mateklaw.com

MATKOV, SALZMAN, MADOFF & GUNN

Established in 1983
SUITE 2900
55 EAST MONROE STREET
CHICAGO, ILLINOIS 60603-5709
Telephone: 312-332-0777
Telecopier: 312-332-6130
URL: http://www.matkovsalzman.com

Representing Management in Labor Relations, Employment Discrimination, Employee Benefits, Administrative Law and Civil and Administrative Litigation.

MEMBERS OF FIRM

GEORGE J. MATKOV, JR., born East St. Louis, Illinois, May 21, 1942; admitted to bar, 1966, Iowa and Illinois; U.S. District Court, Northern District of Illinois; U.S. Court of Appeals, Seventh and Eighth Circuits. *Education:* Knox College; University of Iowa (LL.B., 1966). Phi Delta Phi; Order of the Coif. *Member:* Illinois State, Iowa State and American (Member, Labor and Employment Law Section) Bar Associations. ***PRACTICE AREAS:*** Labor; Employment Discrimination; Employee Benefit Law; Administrative Law; Civil Trial. ***Email:*** matkov@matkovsalzman.com

(This Listing Continued)

MATKOV, SALZMAN, MADOFF & GUNN, Chicago—Continued

JAMES JOHN SALZMAN, born Wausau, Wisconsin, February 10, 1943; admitted to bar, 1973, Illinois; U.S. District Court, Northern District of Illinois including Trial Bar; U.S. Court of Appeals, Sixth and Eighth Circuits. *Education:* Georgetown University (B.S.F.S., 1965); University of Chicago (M.B.A., 1967); DePaul University (J.D., 1973). *Member:* Illinois State Bar Association. ***PRACTICE AREAS:*** Labor; Employment Discrimination Law; Administrative Law; Civil Trial. ***Email:*** salzman@matkovsalzman.com

JEFFREY L. MADOFF, born Detroit, Michigan, November 11, 1945; admitted to bar, 1974, Illinois; U.S. District Court, Northern District of Illinois including Trial Bar; U.S. Court of Appeals, Fourth, Sixth, Seventh, Ninth, Tenth and District of Columbia Circuits. *Education:* University of Western Ontario and Wayne State University (A.B., with high honors, 1967); University of Chicago (J.D., 1974). Phi Beta Kappa. ***PRACTICE AREAS:*** Labor; Employment Discrimination Law; Administrative Law; Civil Trial. ***Email:*** madoff@matkovsalzman.com

LARRY G. HALL, born Detroit, Michigan, March 11, 1954; admitted to bar, 1979, Illinois; U.S. District Court, Northern District of Illinois including Trial Bar; U.S. Court of Appeals, Second, Third, Fifth, Seventh and District of Columbia Circuits. *Education:* Ferris State University (B.S., high distinction, 1975); University of Michigan (J.D., cum laude, 1979). ***PRACTICE AREAS:*** Labor; Employment Discrimination; Administrative Law; Civil Trial. ***Email:*** hall@matkovsalzman.com

MICHAEL W. DUFFEE, born Mishawaka, Indiana, June 17, 1952; admitted to bar, 1977, Illinois and U.S. District Court, Northern District of Illinois including Trial Bar; 1979, U.S. Court of Appeals, Seventh Circuit; 1981, U.S. Supreme Court; 1987, U.S. Court of Appeals, Ninth Circuit; 2000, U.S. Court of Appeals for the District of Columbia Circuit. *Education:* DePaul University (B.A., with highest honors, 1974); Northwestern University (J.D., magna cum laude, 1977). Order of the Coif. ***PRACTICE AREAS:*** Labor and Employment Law. ***Email:*** duffee@matkovsalzman.com

STEVEN L. BRENNEMAN, born Washington, Iowa, October 6, 1959; admitted to bar, 1985, Illinois and U.S. District Court, Northern District of Illinois; 1991, U.S. Court of Appeals, Seventh Circuit; 1992, U.S. District Court, Central District of Illinois; 1995, U.S. Court of Appeals, Fifth Circuit; 2000, U.S. District Court, District of Colorado and U.S. District Court, Eastern District of Wisconsin; 2001, U.S. District Court, Northern District of Indiana, U.S. Court of Appeals, Eighth Circuit; 2003, U.S. District Court, Eastern District of Michigan; 2004, U.S. Court of Appeals, Tenth Circuit. *Education:* Goshen College (B.A., 1982); University of Michigan (J.D., magna cum laude, 1985). Trial Attorney, U.S. Equal Employment Opportunity Commission, Chicago District Office, 1987-1992. *Member:* Chicago Bar Association. ***PRACTICE AREAS:*** Labor and Employment Law; Administrative Law; Civil Litigation. ***Email:*** brenneman@matkovsalzman.com

CHRISTOPHER A. JOHLIE, born Evanston, Illinois, January 2, 1961; admitted to bar, 1988, Illinois; U.S. District Courts, Northern District of Illinois; Eastern District of Wisconsin; U.S. Court of Appeals, Fourth, Sixth, Seventh, Eighth and District of Columbia Circuits. *Education:* Indiana University (B.S., with high distinction, 1983); DePaul University (J.D., 1988). Recipient, American Jurisprudence Award in Labor Law II. Field Examiner, National Labor Relations Board, 1983-1984. ***PRACTICE AREAS:*** Labor and Employment Law. ***Email:*** johlie@matkovsalzman.com

CRAIG R. THORSTENSON, born Peoria, Illinois, November 21, 1961; admitted to bar, 1988, Illinois, U.S. District Court, Northern and Central Districts of Illinois, Eastern and Western Districts of Wisconsin and Western District of Michigan; U.S. Court of Appeals, Sixth and Seventh Circuits. *Education:* University of Colorado (B.S., 1984); University of Illinois (J.D., magna cum laude, 1988). Order of the Coif. *Member:* American Bar Association (Member, Sections on: Labor, Employment and Litigation). ***PRACTICE AREAS:*** Employment Litigation; Employment Counseling; Civil Trial. ***Email:*** thorstenson@matkovsalzman.com

THOMAS M. DUGARD, born Peoria, Illinois, 1966; admitted to bar, 1991, Illinois; 1992, District of Columbia (inactive). *Education:* University of Notre Dame (B.B.A., with highest honors, 1988); Stanford University (J.D., with distinction, 1991). Beta Gamma Sigma (President). Associate Editor, Stanford University Law Review, 1989-1991. ***PRACTICE AREAS:*** Labor Law; Employment Discrimination; Civil Litigation. ***Email:*** dugard@matkovsalzman.com

MELISSA CRAWFORD MAZZEO, born Vicksburg, Michigan, February 14, 1967; admitted to bar, 1995, Illinois and U.S. District Court, Northern and Central Districts of Illinois; 1998, U.S. Court of Appeals, Seventh Circuit; 2000, U.S. District Court, Eastern District of Wisconsin; U.S. District Court, Western District of New York. *Education:* University of Michigan (B.A., 1989); Vermont Law School (J.D., magna cum laude, 1995). *Member:* Chicago Bar Association (Member, Labor and Employment Section). ***PRACTICE AREAS:*** Labor and Employment; Civil Litigation. ***Email:*** mazzeo@matkovsalzman.com

ASSOCIATES

BRIAN J. KURTZ, born Cincinnati, Ohio, February 5, 1972; admitted to bar, 1997, Tennessee; 2000, Illinois; U.S. District Court, Northern District of Illinois. *Education:* Washington University (B.A., with honors, 1994); George Washington University Law School (J.D., with honors, 1997). ***PRACTICE AREAS:*** Labor Law; Employment Law. ***Email:*** kurtz@matkovsalzman.com

ANGELA MARIE HUBBELL, born Lima, Ohio, August 1, 1969; admitted to bar, 1995, Michigan; 1997, U.S. Court of Appeals, Sixth Circuit; 1998, Tennessee; U.S. District Court, Middle and Eastern Districts of Tennessee; 2004, U.S. District Court, Northern District of Illinois (Not admitted in Illinois). *Education:* Michigan State University (B.S., 1992); Ohio Northern University (J.D., with distinction, 1995); Northwestern University (LL.M., Taxation, with honors, 2003). Phi Kappa Phi. Contributing Editor: Ohio Northern University Law Review. Law Clerk, Hon. David W. McKeague, U.S. District Court for the Western District of Michigan, 1995-1996. Law Clerk, Hon. Pierce Lively, U.S. Court of Appeals for the Sixth Circuit, 1996-1997. Attorney Advisor, Hon. Stephen J. Swift, U.S. Tax Court, 2003. [U.S. Navy Reserve, 1989-1997]. ***PRACTICE AREAS:*** Employee Benefits; Executive Compensation; Multi-Employer Pensions; ERISA; Employment Law. ***Email:*** hubbell@matkovsalzman.com

KARIN ANDERSON, born Berwyn, Illinois, March 24, 1966; admitted to bar, 2002, Illinois; 2002, U.S. District Court, Northern District of Illinois. *Education:* Harvard University (B.A., cum laude, 1989); DePaul University College of Law (J.D., summa cum laude, 2003). Dean's List. Order of the Coif. Board Member, Community Mental Health, 1994-1996.*Member:* Chicago, Illinois State and American Bar Associations; Workers Compensation Lawyers Association. ***LANGUAGES:*** Swedish and Arabic. ***PRACTICE AREAS:*** Employment Law; Labor Law; Workers Compensation. ***Email:*** anderson@matkovsalzman.com

ELIZABETH A. WARD, born Chicago, Illinois, 1968; admitted to bar, 1994, Illinois and U.S. District Court, Northern District of Illinois. *Education:* Iowa Wesleyan College (B.A., Business Administration, summa cum laude, 1990); John Marshall Law School (J.D., 1994; LL.M., Employee Benefits, with honors, 2001). Phi Beta Kappa. *Member:* Chicago (Member, Employee Benefits, Young Lawyers Section) and Illinois State Bar Associations. ***PRACTICE AREAS:*** ERISA; Employee Benefits. ***Email:*** ward@matkovsalzman.com

BECKY L. KALAS, born Chariton, Iowa; admitted to bar, 2003, Illinois and U.S. District Court, Northern District of Illinois. *Education:* University of Iowa (B.A., 1994); Illinois Institute of Technology, Chicago-Kent College of Law (J.D., with honors, 2003). ***PRACTICE AREAS:*** Labor Law; Employment Litigation; Employment Counseling. ***Email:*** kalas@matkovsalzman.com

OF COUNSEL

ALLAN GUNN, born Chicago Heights, Illinois, June 2, 1936; admitted to bar, 1961, Illinois, U.S. District Court, Northern District of Illinois, U.S. Court of Appeals, Third and Seventh Circuits, and U.S. Supreme Court. *Education:* Carleton College (B.A., magna cum laude, 1958); University of Chicago (M.B.A., 1973); New York University (J.D., 1961). Phi Beta Kappa; Phi Delta Phi. Member, Board of Editors, New York University Law Review, 1960-1961. ***PRACTICE AREAS:*** Employee Benefits Law; Employment Law. ***Email:*** gunn@matkovsalzman.com

JAY G. SWARDENSKI, born Peoria, Illinois, September 16, 1939; admitted to bar, 1964, Illinois; 1980, New York; U.S. District Court, Northern District of Illinois including Trial Bar; U.S. District Court, Central District of Illinois; U.S. District Court, Southern, Eastern and Northern Districts of New York; U.S. Court of Appeals, Second, Third, Sixth and Seventh Circuits. *Education:* University of Wisconsin (B.A., with honors, 1961); Harvard Law School (LL.B., cum laude, 1964). *Member:* Association of the Bar of the City of New York; New York State and American (Member, Labor and Employment Law Section) Bar Associations. ***Email:*** swardenski@matkovsalzman.com

DEBORAH LEE SMITH, born Highland Park, Michigan, February 18, 1955; admitted to bar, 1988, Illinois. *Education:* University of Michigan (B.A., high distinction, 1978); Northwestern University (J.D., cum laude, 1987). Phi Beta Kappa; Order of the Coif. Angell Scholar. Wigmore Scholar. *Member:* Chicago and American Bar Associations. ***PRACTICE AREAS:*** Labor; Employment Discrimination Law; Administrative Law. ***Email:*** deb@matkovsalzman.com

TERI FIRMISS THOMPSON, born Chicago, Illinois, April 17, 1963; admitted to bar, 1992, Illinois; 1993, U.S. District Court, Northern District of Illinois; 1996, U.S. Court of Appeals, Seventh Circuit; 1999, U.S. District Court, Eastern District of Wisconsin; 2001, U.S. District Court, Central District of Illinois; 2004, U.S. Court of Appeals, Tenth Circuit. *Education:* University of Wisconsin (B.A., with honors, 1985); University of Pennsylvania (J.D., 1992). Phi Beta Kappa. Editor, University of Pennsylvania Law Review. *Member:* Chicago Bar Association; Chicago Council of Lawyers. ***PRACTICE AREAS:*** Employment Litigation; Employment Counseling. ***Email:*** thompson@matkovsalzman.com

LESLIE V. MATLAW, P.C.

P.O. BOX 4426
CHICAGO, ILLINOIS 60680-4426
Telephone: 312-804-3527
Fax: 312-896-9412
Email: send_2_leslie@hotmail.com

Housing Discrimination, Fair Housing Law.

LESLIE V. MATLAW, born Champaign, Illinois, June 3, 1961; admitted to bar, 1992, Illinois and U.S. District Court, Northern District of Illinois; 2000, Trial Bar; 2005, U.S. Court of Appeals, Seventh Circuit. *Education:* DePaul University (B.A., cum laude, 1987); Illinois Institute of Technology (J.D., 1991); Harvard University, Kennedy School of Government (Certificate, Executive Training Program, Housing and Community Development, 1998). Peer Tutor: DePaul University Writing Program, 1985-1987. Recipient: Departmental Award for Outstanding Senior English Major, 1987. Summer Associate: City of Chicago Law Department, 1989. Judicial Extern: U.S. District Court, Northern District of Illinois, 1989. Law Clerk: James D. Montgomery & Associates (former City of Chicago Corporation Counsel, Municipal and Civil Rights practice), 1990. Recipient: IIT Chicago-Kent Class Award (formerly American Jurisprudence Award) for Advanced Research/Labor Law, 1990. Teaching Assistant: IIT Chicago-Kent Legal Writing Program, 1990-1991. Investigator: U.S. Department of HUD, Office of Fair Housing & Equal Opportunity for the Midwest Region, 1991 and 1993-1995. Law Clerk (half time): Stanley L. Hill & Associates (Village of Maywood Corporation Counsel; Municipal and General Civil Law practice), 1991-1992. Law Clerk (half time): Levit & Lipshutz (Plaintiff's' Personal Injury and Real Estate Transactional practice), 1991-1992. Project Attorney: Futterman & Howard, Chartered (Plaintiffs' counsel in system-wide School Desegregation lawsuit), 1992-1993. Adjunct Instructor of Legal Writing: Loyola School of Law Master of Jurisprudence Program, 1996. Panel Attorney: Office of Illinois State Appellate Defender, 1996-1998. Staff Attorney: Interfaith Housing Center for the Northern Suburbs, 1998. Community Builder Fellow: U.S. Department of HUD, 1998-2000. Staff Attorney: Leadership Council for Metro-

(This Listing Continued)

politan Open Communities, Inc., 2000-2003. Attorney in private practice focused on Fair Housing matters, 2004 to present. **Email:** send_2_leslie@hotmail.com

MATUSHEK, NILLES & SINARS, L.L.C.

ONE NORTH LASALLE STREET, SUITE 2100
CHICAGO, ILLINOIS 60602
Telephone: 312-750-1215
Fax: 312-750-1273
Email: ejmatushek@matushek.com
URL: http://www.matushek.com

Complex Litigation including Asbestos, Toxic Torts, Benzene, Mold, Construction Law, Transportation Law, Aviation, Insurance Coverage, Products Liability Defense and Professional Malpractice, Civil Trials and Appeals.

EDWARD J. MATUSHEK III, born Chicago, Illinois, February 2, 1954; admitted to bar, 1982, Illinois and U.S. District Court, Northern District of Illinois including Trial Bar; 1996, U.S. District Court, District of Arizona; 2000, U.S. District Court, Northern District of Indiana. *Education:* Illinois Wesleyan University (B.A., 1975); The John Marshall Law School (J.D., 1982). *Member:* Chicago (Board of Managers, 1992-1994; Chair, Young Lawyers Section, 1990-1991), Illinois State and American Bar Associations; Illinois Association of Defense Trial Counsel; Defense Research Institute. **PRACTICE AREAS:** Asbestos Litigation; Toxic Torts; Transportation Law; Products Liability Defense; Construction Liability; Insurance Coverage. **Email:** ejmatushek@matushek.com

DAVID A. NILLES, born Blue Island, Illinois, December 12, 1962; admitted to bar, 1989, Illinois and U.S. District Court, Northern District of Illinois; 2000, U.S. District Court, Northern District of Indiana. *Education:* University of Illinois (B.S., 1985); The John Marshall Law School (J.D., 1989). Phi Delta Phi. Author: "New Parties," Illinois Civil Practice Handbook, Illinois Institute of Continuing Legal Education, 1997. *Member:* Chicago and Illinois State Bar Associations. **PRACTICE AREAS:** Asbestos Defense; Toxic Torts; Medical Malpractice Defense; Products Liability; Professional Liability. **Email:** danilles@matushek.com

DOUGLAS M. SINARS, born Chicago, Illinois, February 1, 1968; admitted to bar, 1993, Illinois; 2000, U.S. District Court, Northern District of Indiana. *Education:* University of Notre Dame (B.A., 1990); DePaul University (J.D., 1993). Author, "No Vested Right to Nursing Home Act Treble Damages," IDC Quarterly, 1999. *Member:* Chicago and Illinois State Bar Associations; Illinois Association of Defense Trial Counsel. **PRACTICE AREAS:** Asbestos Defense; Toxic Torts; Products Liability; Professional Liability; Commercial Litigation. **Email:** dmsinars@matushek.com

GARY W. KLAGES, admitted to bar, 1982, Illinois; U.S. District Court, Northern and Central Districts of Illinois and U.S. Supreme Court. *Education:* University of Nebraska (B.S.); John Marshall Law School (J.D., 1982). Author: "Medical Malpractice Liability from a Hospital's Prospective", Illinois Bar Journal, September, 1988; "Illinois Parentage Act of 1984, The Continuing Shift Towards Civil Enforcement", Illinois Bar Journal, June, 1985; "Outline of the Law Under Domestic Violence Act of 1986", Illinois Family Law Reports, August, 1987. *Member:* Illinois State and American Bar Associations; Illinois Association of Trial Defense Counsel. **REPORTED CASES:** Mikeal Ashpole et al. v. Brunswick Bowling and Billiards Corp., et al., 297 Ill.App.3d 725, 697 N.E.2d 1238 (1998); Robert W. Lempa et al. v. Gordon Finkel el al., 663 N.E.2d 158 (1996); Eloy Salazar et al. v. Wiley SandersTrucking Co., Inc., 216 Ill.App.2d 863, 576 N.E.2d 552 (1991); Brite Lights, Inc. V. Thomas W. Gooch III et al., 713 N.E.2d 155 (1999); Gary M. Kopier Sr., et al. v. Mark E. Harlow, et al., 2-96-1935 (1997); Kenneth Hedberg v. Joseph Mendino, 579 N.E.2d 398 (1991); Stanislaw Truzewski v. Outboard Motor Marine Corp., et al v. Mutual Maintenance Co. (Third-Party Defendant-Appellant), 272 Ill.App.3d 558, 685 N.E.2d 992 (1997). **PRACTICE AREAS:** Civil Litigation; Transportation Law; Asbestos Defense; Insurance Coverage; Commercial Litigation. **Email:** gwklages@matushek.com

ASSOCIATES

KRISTEN M. STREEPEY, born Ft. Wayne, Indiana, November 14, 1973; admitted to bar, 2000, Illinois; 2001, Indiana. *Education:* Taylor University (B.A., 1996); Indiana University (J.D., 2000). **PRACTICE AREAS:** Products Liability Defense; Asbestos and Toxic Torts; Toxic Torts; Insurance Coverage. **Email:** kmstreepey@matushek.com

MELISSA M. FALLAH, born Blue Island, Illinois, August 15, 1976; admitted to bar, 2001, Illinois. *Education:* University of Illinois (B.A.S., 1998); Washington University School of Law (J.D. 2001). **LANGUAGES:** Spanish and Farsi. **PRACTICE AREAS:** Asbestos Defense; Toxic Torts. **Email:** mmfallah@matushek.com

MEGAN S. MARZEC, born 1979; admitted to bar, 2004, Illinois; U.S. District Court, Northern District of Illinois. *Education:* University of Illinois, Urbana-Champaign (B.A., 2001); Chicago-Kent College of Law, Illinois Institute of Technology (J.D.). Dean's List scholar, Chicago-Kent School of Law. **PRACTICE AREAS:** Products Liability; Toxic Tort Defense; Asbestos; Occupational Injuries; Workers Compensation. **Email:** msmarzec@matushek.com

JENNY M. NORENBERG, born May 10, 1979; admitted to bar, 2004, Illinois. *Education:* University of Wisconsin-Madison (B.A., summa cum laude, 2001); University of Minnesota (J.D., cum laude, 2004). **PRACTICE AREAS:** Asbestos Defense; Litigation; Toxic Torts. **Email:** jmnorenberg@matushek.com

MAYER, BROWN, ROWE & MAW LLP

Established in 1881
71 S. WACKER
CHICAGO, ILLINOIS 60606-4637
Telephone: 312-782-0600
Facsimile: 312-701-7711
Telex: 190404
Cable: LEMAY
URL: http://www.mayerbrownrowe.com

Brussels, Belgium Office: Square de Meeûs 35, B-1000. Telephone: +011-32 2 502 55 17. Facsimile: + 011-32 2 502 54 21.

(This Listing Continued)

Charlotte, North Carolina Office: 214 N. Tryon Street, Suite 3800. Telephone: (704) 444-3500. Fax: (704) 377-2033.

Cologne, Germany Office: Kaiser-Wilhelm-Ring 27-29, 50672. Telephone: +49-221-5771-100. Facsimile: +49-221-5771-199.

Frankfurt am Main, Germany Office: Bockenheimer Landstraße 98-100, D-60323. Telephone: 011-49-69 79 41-0. Facsimile: 011-49-69 79 41-100.

Houston, Texas Office: 700 Louisiana Street, Suite 3600, 77002-2730. Telephone: (713) 221-1651. Facsimile: (713) 224-6410. Telex: 775809. Cable: LEMAYHOU.

London, England Office: 11 Pilgrim Street, London EC4V 6RW. Telephone: 011-44-207-248-4282. Facsimile: 011-44-207-248-2009.

Los Angeles, California Office: 350 South Grand Avenue, 25th Floor, 90071-1503. Telephone: (213) 229-9500. Facsimile: (213) 625-0248. Telex: 188089. Cable: LEMAYLA.

New York, New York Office: 1675 Broadway, 10019-5820. Telephone: (212) 506-2500. Facsimile: (212) 262-1910. Telex: 701842. Cable: LEMAYEN.

Palo Alto, California Office: Two Palo Alto Square, Suite 300, 94306. Telephone: (650) 331-2000. Facsimile: (650) 331-2060.

Paris, France Office: 41 Avenue Hoche, 75008. Telephone: 011-33-1-53-53-43-43. Facsimile: 011-33-1-53-96-03-83.

Washington, D.C. Office: 1909 K Street, N.W., 20006-1101. Telephone: (202) 263-3000. Facsimile: (202) 263-3300. Telex: 892603. Cable: LEMAYDC.

Representative Offices:

Beijing, People's Republic of China: 7-1-31, Qijayuanr, 9 Jianguomen Wai Avenue, Chaoyang District, 100600. Telephone: 011-86-10-85322221. Facsimile: 011-86-10-85322156.

Shanghai, People's Republic of China: 2805 Plaza 66, 1266 Nanjing Road West. Telephone: 011-86-21-6288-1250. Facsimile: 011-86-21-6288-1255.

Mexico City, Mexico, D.F., Independent Mexico Correspondent: Jáuregui, Navarrete, Nader y Rojas, S.C., Abogados Torre Arcos, Paseo de los Tamarindos No. 400-B. Col. Bosques de las Lomas, 05120. Telephone: 011-5255-5-267-45-00. Facsimile: 011-5255-5-267-45-98.

Antitrust, Appellate, Asia, Bankruptcy, Biotech, Pharma & Life Science, Chemicals, Collateralized Debt Obligation, Company Secretarial, Construction & Engineering, Corporate & Securities, Corporate Governance, Derivatives, E-commerce, Emerging Companies, Employee Benefits & Executive Compensation, Employee Share Incentives, Employment & Labour, Energy, Environment, Finance, Financial Services, Global Trade, Government, Government Contracts, Health Care, Information Technology, Insurance & Reinsurance, Intellectual Property, International Arbitration, Investment Management, Latin America, Legislative, Litigation & Dispute Resolution, Natural Resources, Outsourcing, Pensions, PPP/PFI & Infrastructure, Private Equity, Private Investment Fund, Pro Bono, Professional Practices, Project Finance, Property Rights, Public Law, Rail, Real Estate, Regulated Industries, Restructuring & Insolvency, Securitisation, Tax Controversy & Transfer Pricing, Tax Transactions & Consulting, Telecommunications & Media, Venture & Technology, Wealth Management.

RETIRED PARTNER

FRANK D. MAYER, JR., born Chicago, Illinois, December 23, 1933; admitted to bar, 1959, Illinois. *Education:* Amherst College (B.A., with honors, 1955); Corpus Christi College of Cambridge University, Cambridge, England; University of Chicago Law School (J.D., with honors, 1959). *Member:* American Bar Association (Co-Chair, Business Law Conflict of Interest Committee, 1997—). **Email:** fmayer@mayerbrownrowe.com

PARTNERS

DAVID F. ABBOTT, born Washington, D.C., April 26, 1953; admitted to bar, 1980, Illinois and U.S. District Court, Northern District of Illinois; 1981, U.S. Tax Court. *Education:* University of Denver; University of Illinois (B.A., 1975); State University of New York at Buffalo (J.D., magna cum laude, 1980). (New York, N.Y. Office). **Email:** dabbott@mayerbrownrowe.com

KAREN HEATHER HOLLAND ABBOTT, born 1963; admitted to bar, 1987, England. *Education:* Bristol University. (London, England Office). **PRACTICE AREAS:** Insurance Law; Reinsurance Law; Commercial Litigation. **Email:** kabbott@mayerbrownrowe.com

LEE N. ABRAMS, born Chicago, Illinois, February 28, 1935; admitted to bar, 1957, Illinois. *Education:* University of Michigan (A.B., 1955; J.D., 1957). Winner, Elijah Watt Sells Gold Medal, Highest Grade in the United States on the Uniform C.P.A. Examination. *Member:* American Bar Association (Chair, Franchising Forum, 1982-1985; Vice-Chair, Section of Antitrust Law, 1991-1992; Finance Officer, Section of Antitrust Law, 1979-1980). Fellow, American College of Trial Lawyers. **PRACTICE AREAS:** Antitrust; Franchises and Franchising; Litigation. **Email:** labrams@mayerbrownrowe.com

FIONA ADAMS, admitted to bar, 1993, England and Wales. Seconded to: HMV Media Group plc, 2000, General Counsel. (London, England Office). **PRACTICE AREAS:** Corporate. **Email:** fadams@mayerbrownrowe.com

RODNEY E. ALEXANDER, born Atlanta, Georgia, March 21, 1960; admitted to bar, 1988, Texas; 1996, North Carolina. *Education:* Sam Houston State University (B.S.P.S., cum laude, 1984); University of Houston (J.D., cum laude, 1988). Order of the Coif; Order of the Barons. Associate Editor, Houston Law Review, 1988; Assistant District Attorney, Mecklenburg County, North Carolina, 1998-2000. (Charlotte, North Carolina Office). **REPORTED CASES:** United States v. Pennington, 20 F.3d 593 (5th Cir. 1994). **PRACTICE AREAS:** Complex Commercial Litigation; Insurance and Reinsurance; Trade Secrets; Intellectual Property Litigation. **Email:** ralexander@mayerbrownrowe.com

ROBERT ALLAN, admitted to bar, 1967, England and Wales. Editor, "Digital Cable Radio - The Tensions Between The Music Industry and The Broadcasting Industry," IAEL. Regular Contributor to Trade and Legal Journals. (London, England Office). **LANGUAGES:** French. **PRACTICE AREAS:** Intellectual Property.

DAVID MARTIN ALLEN, born 1959; admitted to bar, 1984, England. *Education:* Bristol University. Licensed Insolvency Practitioner. *Member:* Insolvency Lawyers Association. (London, England Office). **PRACTICE AREAS:** Insolvency Law. **Email:** dallen@mayerbrownrowe.com

(This Listing Continued)

MAYER, BROWN, ROWE & MAW LLP, Chicago—Continued

J. TRENT ANDERSON, born Indianapolis, Indiana, July 22, 1939; admitted to bar, 1965, Indiana and Illinois. *Education:* Purdue University (B.S., 1961); University of Virginia (LL.B., 1964). Order of the Coif. Teaching Assistant, University of California Law School (Boalt Hall), 1964-1965. Adjunct Professor, Loyola University of Chicago Law School, 1985. ***PRACTICE AREAS:*** Corporate Law; Finance. ***Email:*** janderson@mayerbrownrowe.com

BRADLEY J. ANDREOZZI, born New York, N.Y., October 9, 1958; admitted to bar, 1984, New York; 1985, U.S. District Court, Southern and Eastern Districts of New York; 1986, U.S. Court of Appeals, First Circuit; 1990, U.S . Court of Appeals, Second Circuit; 1991, U.S. Supreme Court; 1999, Illinois, U.S. District Court, Northern District of Illinois and U.S. Court of Appeals, Seventh Circuit. *Education:* Yale University (B.A., 1980); University of Chicago (J.D., 1983). Co-Author: "Lender's Right to be Wrong on Material Adverse Change Affirmed," *Lender Liability News,* August 11, 1995. ***REPORTED CASES:*** AUSA Life Ins. Co. v. Ernst & Young, 206 F.3d 202 (2d Cir. 1998) and 991 F.Supp. 234 (S.D.N.Y. 1997); Kronfeld v. Trans World Airlines, 832 F.2d 726 (2d Cir. 1987) and 631 F.Supp. 1259 (S.D.N.Y. 1986); In re Corporacion de Servicios Medicos, 805 F.2d 440 (1st Cir. 1986); Kolbeck v. LIT America, 939 F.Supp. 240 and 923 F.Supp. 557 (S.D.N.Y. 1996); Avery v. State Farm Mutual Automobile Ins. Co., 746 N.E.2d 1242 (Ill. App., 5th Dist. 2001). ***PRACTICE AREAS:*** Trial Practice; Appellate Practice; Alternative Dispute Resolution. ***Email:*** bandreozzi@mayerbrown.com

BRIAN ARONSON, born Port Elizabeth, South Africa, November 22, 1966; admitted to bar, 1991, California. *Education:* American University (B.A., cum laude, 1988); Georgetown University (J.D., cum laude, 1991). (Los Angeles, California Office). ***LANGUAGES:*** Afrikaans. ***Email:*** baronson@mayerbrownrowe.com

JEAN-MARIE L. ATAMIAN, born New York, N.Y., March 8, 1960; admitted to bar, 1986, New York; 1991, U.S. District Court, Southern and Eastern Districts of New York; 1996, U.S. District Court, District of Colorado and U.S. Court of Appeals, Second Circuit. *Education:* Columbia College (B.A., summa cum laude, Phi Beta Kappa, 1981); Columbia University School of Law (J.D., 1984). *Member:* American Bar Association. (New York, N.Y. Office). ***LANGUAGES:*** French. ***PRACTICE AREAS:*** Securities Litigation; Financial Services Litigation; Complex Commercial Litigation. ***Email:*** jatamian@mayerbrownrowe.com

LAURA E. BADER, born San Francisco, California, September 6, 1966; admitted to bar, 1997, Illinois. *Education:* University of Chicago (B.A., with honors, 1988); University of Texas (J.D., with honors, 1996); University of Edinburgh, Scotland (LL.M., 1996). Order of the Coif. ***Email:*** lbader@mayerbrownrowe.com

MARY BAGNALL, admitted to bar, 1997, England and Wales. *Education:* College of Law, London; Wadhurst College, University of Westminster. Qualified as Fellow of the Institute of Legal Executives, 1992. (London, England Office). ***Email:*** mbagnall@mayerbrownrowe.com

ROBERT C. BAPTISTA, JR., born Buffalo, New York, September 14, 1948; admitted to bar, 1982, Illinois. *Education:* Wheaton College (B.A., 1970); Northern Illinois University (M.A., magna cum laude, 1976); University of Illinois (J.D., summa cum laude, 1982). ***PRACTICE AREAS:*** Finance; Corporate. ***Email:*** rbaptista@mayerbrownrowe.com

ROBERT N. BARNARD, born Madison, Wisconsin, December 15, 1947; admitted to bar, 1975, Illinois and U.S. District Court, Northern District of Illinois. *Education:* Harvard College (A.B., cum laude, 1969); Stanford Law School (J.D., 1975). [U.S. Army, 1969-1972, 1st Lieutenant]. (New York, N.Y. Office). ***Email:*** rbarnard@mayerbrownrowe.com

JONATHAN A. BARRETT, born Durham, North Carolina, September 14, 1949; admitted to bar, 1978, North Carolina. *Education:* University of North Carolina at Chapel Hill (B.A., 1972; J.D., with honors, 1978). Phi Beta Kappa. Business Manager, North Carolina Law Review, 1977-1978. [Lt., USNR, 1972-1975]. (Charlotte, North Carolina Office). ***PRACTICE AREAS:*** Business Law; Corporate Law; Mergers, Acquisitions and Divestitures. ***Email:*** jbarrett@mayerbrownrowe.com

JAMES R. BARRY, born Normal, Illinois, July 24, 1960; admitted to bar, 1985, Illinois and U.S. District Court, Northern District of Illinois; 1986, U.S. Tax Court. *Education:* DePaul University (B.S.C., with high honors, 1982; J.D., with honors, 1985). Certified Public Accountant, 1982. ***PRACTICE AREAS:*** Federal Income Tax; International Taxation. ***Email:*** jbarry@mayerbrownrowe.com

MARY R. BARRY, born Springfield, Illinois, March 1, 1965; admitted to bar, 1994, Illinois. *Education:* University of Illinois (B.A., 1987; J.D., summa cum laude, 1994). ***Email:*** mbarry@mayerbrownrowe.com

GREGORY L. BARTON, born Owensboro, Kentucky, 1959; admitted to bar, 1987, Illinois; 1988, U.S. Tax Court; 1990, U.S. Court of Federal Claims and U.S. District Court, Northern District of Illinois. *Education:* University of Notre Dame (B.S., magna cum laude, 1980); University of Southern California (M.S., 1981); University of Chicago (J.D., with honors, 1985). Order of the Coif; Law Review. Clerkship with Judge Richard A. Posner (U.S. Court of Appeals, Seventh Circuit), White House Office of Management and Budget. ***REPORTED CASES:*** Nissei Sangyo America, Ltd. v. IRS, 98-1 U.S. Tax Cas. (CCH) ¶ 50,288 (D.D.C. 1997), modified, 98-1 U.S. Tax Cas. (CCH) ¶ 50,289 (D.D.C. 1998); National Semiconductor Corp. v. Comm'r, 67 T.C.M. (CCH) 2849 (1994), acq. in result, 1995-2 C.B. 1; Hitachi America, Ltd. v. Comm'r, T.C. Docket No. 21553-90 (stipulated decision) (October 29, 1991); Nestle Holdings, Inc. v. Comm'r, 94 T.C. 803 (1990). ***PRACTICE AREAS:*** Federal Tax Controversies; Transfer Pricing; International Taxation. ***Email:*** gbarton@mayerbrownrowe.com

STEPHANIE BATES, born 1960; admitted to bar, 1985, England. *Education:* Southampton University. (London, England Office). ***PRACTICE AREAS:*** Corporate Finance Law; Mergers and Acquisitions Law; General Corporate Law. ***Email:*** sbates@mayerbrownrowe.com

SCOTT BAUGH, born Redding, California, 1962; admitted to bar, 1987, California. *Education:* Liberty University (B.A., summa cum laude, 1984); University of the Pacific, McGeorge School of Law (J.D., 1987). (Los Angeles, California Office). ***PRACTICE AREAS:*** Government. ***Email:*** srbaugh@mayerbrownrowe.com

(This Listing Continued)

BRANDON D. BAUM, born 1960; admitted to bar, 1985, California; U.S. Court of Appeals, Ninth and Federal Circuits and U.S. Supreme Court. *Education:* University of California, Berkeley (B.A., 1982); Hastings College of the Law, University of California (J.D., 1985). (Palo Alto, California Office). ***PRACTICE AREAS:*** Intellectual Property; Civil Litigation. ***Email:*** bbaum@mayerbrownrowe.com

TERESA A. BEAUDET, born Los Angeles, California, February 7, 1953; admitted to bar, 1980, California and U.S. District Court, Central District of California; 1991, U.S. Court of Appeals, Ninth Circuit; 1992, U.S. District Court, Eastern, Southern and Northern Districts of California; 1996, U.S. Supreme Court. *Education:* Loyola Marymount University of Los Angeles (B.A., magna cum laude, 1974; M.A., 1976); Loyola Law School (J.D., cum laude, 1980). Temporary Judge, Municipal Court of California, Los Angeles Judicial District, 1990—. Mediator, Joint Association Settlement Program, 1989-1997. Member, California State Bar Conference of Delegates, 1987-1997. *Member:* Los Angeles County Bar Association (Executive Committee, Litigation Section, 1985-1996, Chair, 1993-1994, Legislative Review Committee, Chair, 1986-1988; Judicial Resources Committee, Chair, 1990-1992); Los Angeles County Bar Association Foundation (Board Member, 1996—). (Los Angeles, California Office). ***REPORTED CASES:*** Hall v. American National Red Cross, 83 F. 3rd 919 (9th Cir. 1996); Prilliman v. United Air Lines, Inc., 53 Cal. App. 4th 935 (1997); EMA v. SCAQMD, 158 F. Supp. 2d 1107 (C.D. Cal. 2001), aff'd 309 F. 3rd 550 (9th Cir. 2002), 541 U.S. 246 (2004). ***PRACTICE AREAS:*** Complex and Multi-District Litigation; Labor and Employment; Class Actions; Real Estate Litigation. ***Email:*** tbeaudet@mayerbrownrowe.com

KENNETH D. BELL, admitted to bar, 1983, North Carolina. *Education:* Wake Forest University (B.A., 1980; J.D., 1983). First Assistant United States Attorney, 1993-2003 and Assistant United States Attorney, 1983-1988 and 1990-2003, U.S District Court, Western District of North Carolina. Republican Nominee, United States House of Representatives, 5th Congressional District of North Carolina, 1990. (Charlotte, North Carolina Office). ***REPORTED CASES:*** U.S. v. Bowe, 309 F.3d 234 (4th Cir. 2002); U.S. v. Bowe, 257 F.3d 336 (4th Cir. 2001); U.S. v. Brown, 155 F.3d 431 (4th Cir. 1998); U.S. v. McHan, 101 F.3d 1027 (4th Cir. 1996); U.S. v. Cheek, 94 F.3d 136 (4th Cir. 1996); U.S. v. Mackins, 32 F.3d 134 (4th Cir. 1994); U.S. v. McManus, 23 F.3d 878 (4th Cir. 1994); U.S. v. Brown, 856 F.2d 710 (4th Cir. 1988). ***PRACTICE AREAS:*** Litigation; Criminal Law. ***Email:*** kbell@mayerbrownrowe.com

RICHARD BEN-VENISTE, admitted to bar, 1968, New York; 1975, District of Columbia. *Education:* Muhlenberg College (A.B., magna cum laude, 1964); Columbia University (J.D., 1967); Northwestern University (LL.M., 1968). Co-Author: *Stonewall: The Real Story of the Watergate Prosecution,* Simon & Schuster, 1977. Chairman, D.C. Advisory Committee on Prison Education Reform, 1984-1986. Presidential Appointment to Nazi War Crimes and Japanese Imperial Government Records Interagency Working Group, 2000—. Commissioner, National Commission On Terrorist Attackes Upon The United States (9-11 Commission), 2002—. (Washington, D.C. Office). ***PRACTICE AREAS:*** Civil Litigation; White Collar Criminal Litigation; Congressional Investigations. ***Email:*** rben-veniste@mayerbrownrowe.com

JOHN C. BERGHOFF, JR., born Chicago, Illinois, July 1, 1941; admitted to bar, 1966, Illinois and U.S. District Court, Northern District of Illinois including Trial Bar; 1968, U.S. Court of Appeals, Seventh Circuit; 1974, U.S. Court of Appeals, District of Columbia Circuit and U.S. Supreme Court. *Education:* Northwestern University (B.S., with honors, 1963; J.D., 1966). ***Email:*** jberghoff@mayerbrownrowe.com

JOEL D. BERTOCCHI, born New York, N.Y., August 29, 1957; admitted to bar, 1983, Wisconsin; 1995, Illinois. *Education:* University of Wisconsin-Madison (B.A., with honors, 1979; J.D., cum laude, 1983). Solicitor General, State of Illinois, 1999-2002. Assistant U.S. Attorney, Northern District of Illinois (Chicago), Criminal Division, 1987-1999; Senior Appellate Counsel, 1989-1994. Staff Attorney, U.S. Court of Appeals, Seventh Circuit, 1985-1987. Law Clerk to The Honorable Aaron E. Goodstein, U.S. Magistrate Judge, U.S. District Court, Eastern District of Wisconsin, 1983-1985. Member, Seventh Circuit Committees on Criminal and Civil Jury Instructions. Vice Chairman, Illinois Criminal Code Rewrite and Reform Commission, 2000-2002. *Member:* Seventh Circuit Bar Association (Illinois Chair, Committee on Rules and Practice); Chicago Inn of Court. ***REPORTED CASES:*** Mathias v. WorldCom Technologies., Inc., 535 U.S. 682 (2002); Illinois v. McArthur, 531 U.S. 326 (2001); Hope Clinic v. Ryan, 195 F.3d 857 (7th Cir. 1999) (en banc); United States v. Krilich, 159 F.3d 1020 (7th cir. 1998); De Silva v. DiLeonardi, 125 F.3d 1110 (1997); United States v. Ashman, 979 F.2d 469 (7th Cir. 1992); United States v. Sanders, 962 F.2d 660 (7th Cir. 1992). ***PRACTICE AREAS:*** Litigation; Civil Appeals; Criminal Appeals. ***Email:*** jbertocchi@mayerbrownrowe.com

EDWARD S. BEST, born Chicago, Illinois, November 18, 1961; admitted to bar, 1986, Illinois and U.S. District Court, Northern District of Illinois. *Education:* University of Illinois (A.B., 1983); Loyola University, Chicago (J.D., cum laude, 1986). ***Email:*** ebest@mayerbrownrowe.com

BRUCE M. BETTIGOLE, admitted to bar, 1981, District of Columbia. *Education:* Yale University (B.A., 1978); Columbia University (J.D., 1981). (Washington, D.C. Office). ***PRACTICE AREAS:*** Litigation. ***Email:*** bbettigole@mayerbrownrowe.com

MICHAEL E. BIENIEK, born Chicago, Illinois, November 30, 1958; admitted to bar, 1989, Illinois. *Education:* Northwestern University (B.A., 1980); Washington & Lee Law School; University of Chicago (J.D., with honors, 1989). ***Email:*** mbieniek@mayerbrownrowe.com

DR. ULRIKE BINDER, born 1969; admitted to bar, 1998, Frankfurt. *Education:* University of Freiburg im Breisgau (Ph.D. in law, 1997); Berlin (Second Law Examination, 1998). (Frankfurt/Main, Germany Office). ***LANGUAGES:*** English, French, Spanish. ***PRACTICE AREAS:*** Corporate. ***Email:*** ubinder@mayerbrownrowe.com

CHRISTIAN F. BINNIG, born New Haven, Connecticut, November 10, 1961; admitted to bar, 1986, Georgia, Illinois and U.S. District Court, Northern District of Illinois; 2001, U.S. Court of Appeals, Eleventh Circuit. *Education:* University of Virginia (B.A., with high distinction, 1982); University of Michigan (J.D., cum laude, 1985). ***PRACTICE AREAS:*** Telecommunications and Media; Regulated Industries; Litigation. ***Email:*** cbinnig@mayerbrown.com

(This Listing Continued)

GILLIAN MARY BIRKBY, born 1948; admitted to bar, 1981, England. *Education:* Dundee University. *Member:* Institute of Arbitrators (Associate Member); Society of Construction Law. (London, England Office). ***LANGUAGES:*** French and Spanish. ***PRACTICE AREAS:*** Construction Law; Litigation; Arbitration. ***Email:*** gbirkby@mayerbrownrowe.com

TIMOTHY S. BISHOP, born Peterborough, England, March 6, 1958; admitted to bar, 1988, Illinois; 1992, U.S. Court of Appeals, Fifth and Seventh Circuits, U.S. Court of Appeals for the District of Columbia Circuit and U.S. Supreme Court; 1993, U.S. Court of Appeals, Ninth Circuit; 1994, U.S. Court of Appeals, Fourth Circuit; 1996, U.S. Court of Appeals, Second and Third Circuits; 1997, District of Columbia, U.S. Court of Appeals, Sixth Circuit and Federal Circuit and U.S. Tax Court; 1998, U.S. Court of Appeals, Eighth Circuit; 1999, U.S. Court of Appeals, Tenth Circuit; U.S. Court of Federal Claims. *Education:* Oxford University, England (B.A., first class honors, 1979; M.A., 1983; Dip. Law, 1986); Northwestern University (J.D., magna cum laude, 1985). Author: "Opposing Certiorai," ABA Litigation Manual (1999); "How to Petition the United States Supreme Court for Certiorari," Chicago Bar Association Record (Feb. 1997); "Recent Developments in Standing," ABA Section of Natural Resources, Energy and Environmental Law (March 1997). Law Clerk to: Justice Wm. Brennan, U.S. Supreme Court, 1988-1989; Judge James Oakes, U.S. Court of Appeals, Second Circuit, 1986-1987. ***PRACTICE AREAS:*** Appellate Practice; Litigation; Environmental Law. ***Email:*** tbishop@mayerbrownrowe.com

JAMES ARTHUR BLACK, born 1953; admitted to bar, 1977, England. *Education:* College of Law, London. (London, England Office). ***PRACTICE AREAS:*** Commercial Property Law; Property Development Law; Agricultural Property Law. ***Email:*** jblack@mayerbrownrowe.com

MICHAEL T. BLAIR, born 1962; admitted to bar, 1990, Illinois. *Education:* Colorado State University (B.S.); John Marshall Law School (J.D., 1990). ***PRACTICE AREAS:*** Corporate Law; Securities. ***Email:*** mblair@mayerbrownrowe.com

FRANCIS J. BLANCHFIELD, JR., born Chicago, Illinois, September 19, 1945; admitted to bar, 1970, New Jersey; 1974, New York; 1976, Georgia; 1981, North Carolina. *Education:* College of the Holy Cross (A.B., 1967); New York University (J.D., 1970; LL.M., in Taxation, 1974). Recipient: Vanderbilt Medal; Root-Tilden Scholarship. Law Secretary to Judge Samuel Allcorn, Jr., Chancery Division, New Jersey Superior Court, 1970-1971. Special Assistant to Assistant Attorney General, 1977-1979, Deputy Assistant Attorney General, Tax Division, U.S. Department of Justice, 1979-1980. Recipient, The Attorney General's Medal, 1980. Fellow, American College of Tax Counsel. [1st Lt., U.S. Army, 1971-1973]. (Charlotte, North Carolina Office). ***Email:*** fblanchfield@mayerbrownrowe.com

ROBERT E. BLOCH, born Irvington, New Jersey, March 22, 1947; admitted to bar, 1973, District of Columbia; 1975, U.S. Court of Appeals for the District of Columbia Circuit; 1977, U.S. Supreme Court. *Education:* Franklin & Marshall College (B.A., 1969); George Washington University (J.D., with honors, 1973). Antitrust Division, U.S. Department of Justice: Chief Professions and Intellectual Property Section, 1988-1993; Assistant Chief, Litigation I, 1985-1988; Assistant Chief, Trial Section, 1981- 1985; Trial Attorney, 1975-1981. Office of the Attorney General of Ohio, Assistant Attorney General, Antitrust Section, Columbus, 1973-1975. Author: "Responding to Criminal Antitrust Investigations," published by the American Bar Association Section of Antitrust Law(February 2001, revised January 2002); "The Antitrust Division's Amnesty Program," American Bar Association Section on Antitrust Law (February 1995); "State Action Immunity as a Defense in an Antitrust Health Care Context: What Works and What Doesn't," American Bar Association Antitrust Section and Forum on Health Care (October 1994); "Corporate Compliance Programs and Corporate Amnesty: The Perilous Pursuit of Virtue," Antitrust Report, Matthew Bender & Co. (June 1994); "Antitrust Competition and Health Care Reform," Health Affairs (Spring I February 1994); "The Antitrust Division's Corporate Amnesty Program," Antitrust Magazine (American Bar Association, December 1993); "Antitrust Enforcement and Health Care Reform," The National Law Journal (October 11, 1993); "Corporate Compliance Programs, Antitrust Enforcement and the New Organizational Sentencing Guidelines," Antitrust Report. Matthew Bender & Co. (April 1993). "Analyzing Provider Joint Ventures Outside the Safety Zones: Provider Integration, the Rule of Reason and Messenger Models Under the Health Care Antitrust Policy Statements," National Health Lawyers Association (February 1997); "Responding to Antitrust Criminal Investigations," The American Bar Association Section of Antitrust Law (February 1997); "U.S. Antitrust Law and Its Effect on Copyright Protections for the Music Industry," The Impact of Competitive Law on the Music Industry, MAKLU Publishers (January 1997; "Defending Provider Networks Before the Antitrust Enforcement Agencies," Health Care M & A, Practicing Law Institute (1997); "Most Favored Nation Clauses in Contracts Between Health Care Networks and Providers: The Search for Practical Antitrust Guidance," Antitrust Report, Matthew Bender & Co. (September 1996); "Defending Provider Networks and Hospital Mergers before the Antitrust Enforcement Agencies," National Health Lawyers Association (February 1996); "Innovation Policy and Antitrust Enforcement: The 1995 Antitrust Guidelines for Licensing of Intellectual property," Antitrust Report (Matthew Bender & Co. June 1995). Co-author of "An Analysis of Group Purchasing Organizations' Contracting Practices Under the Antitrust Laws," submitted for the Joint FTC/DOJ Hearings on Health Care and Competition Law and Policy(September 26, 2003); Co-author of "Analysis of Antitrust Issues Raised by B2B Exchanges: Practical Guidelines and Insights From the FTC B2B Workshop," published in Antitrust Report(Matthew Bender & Co. September 2000); Co-author of "Antitrust Analysis of Recent Provider Consolidations and Collaborations," (American Association of Health Plans and the American Bar Association Health Law Section April 1999); Co-author of "Analyzing and Defending Managed Care Mergers Under the Antitrust Laws," (American Bar Association/American Association of Health Plans April 1998); Co-Author of "Product Market Definition in Pharmaceutical Mergers," published in Antitrust Report, Matthew Bender & Co. (Sept. 1997). Co-author of "A New and Uncertain Future for Managed Care Mergers: An Antitrust Analysis of the Aetna/Prudential Merger, published in Antitrust Report, Matthew Bender & Co. (Oct. 1999); Co-author and Co-editor: Compendium of Informal Antitrust Enforcement Agency Advice in Health Care (American Bar Association, 1997); Handbook on Antitrust Grand Jury Investigations (American Bar Association, 1988); Sample Jury Instructions in Civil Antitrust Cases (American Bar Association, 1987); Criminal Antitrust Litigation Manual (American Bar Association, 1984); Sample Jury Instructions in Criminal

(This Listing Continued)

Antitrust Cases (American Bar Association, 1984).*Member:* The District of Columbia Bar (Member, Steering Committee, Antitrust and Consumer Law Section); American Bar Association (Member, Antitrust Section; Co-Chair, Federal Sentencing Guidelines Task Force, 1995-1997; Chair, 1994-1995 and Co-Chair, 1993-1994, Annual Meeting Committee; Section Vice Chair, 1992-1993; Council Member, 1989-1993; Chairman, 1986-1989 and Vice Chair, 1985-1986, Criminal Practice and Procedure Committee); American Health Lawyers Association (Vice Chair, Antitrust Substantive Law Committee, 1999-2001); Federal Bar Association (Chairman, Criminal Enforcement and Antitrust Law Committee, 1983-1985). (Washington, D.C. Office). ***PRACTICE AREAS:*** Antitrust Law; Health Care Law; Criminal Law. ***Email:*** rbloch@mayerbrownrowe.com

DAVID I. BLOOM, born Washington, D.C., March 27, 1954; admitted to bar, 1978, District of Columbia and U.S. District Court, District of Columbia; 1979, U.S. Court of Appeals, District of Columbia Circuit and Temporary Emergency Court of Appeals; 1983, U.S. Court of Appeals, Fifth Circuit; 1984, U.S. Court of Appeals, Seventh Circuit. *Education:* Brown University (A.B., magna cum laude, 1975); Yale University (J.D., 1978). (Washington, D.C. Office). ***PRACTICE AREAS:*** Federal Energy Regulation; Energy Finance. ***Email:*** dbloom@mayerbrownrowe.com

BRUCE C. BLOOMINGDALE, born 1968; admitted to bar, 1997, Illinois. *Education:* Michigan State University (B.S., 1991); Loyola University, Chicago School of Law (J.D., magna cum laude, 1997). (London, England Office). ***PRACTICE AREAS:*** Finance. ***Email:*** bbloomingdale@mayerbrownrowe.com

DAVID C. BOLSTAD, born Inglewood, California, November 2, 1958; admitted to bar, 1992, California. *Education:* California State University, Long Beach (B.S., 1985); Loyola Marymount University (M.B.A., 1987); Loyola Law School, Los Angeles (J.D., 1991). Order of the Coif. (Los Angeles, California Office). ***Email:*** dbolstad@mayerbrownrowe.com

FERN C. BOMCHILL, born Chicago, Illinois, February 25, 1948; admitted to bar, 1972, Illinois; U.S. District Court, Northern District of Illinois including Trial Bar, U.S. District Court, Eastern District of Michigan and U.S. Court of Appeals, Seventh Circuit. *Education:* University of Michigan (B.A., 1969); University of Chicago (J.D., 1972). *Member:* Federal Bar Association (President, Chicago Chapter). ***PRACTICE AREAS:*** Litigation; Class Actions; Consumer Law. ***Email:*** fbomchill@mayerbrownrowe.com

THOMAS W. BOTTOMLEE, born Gary, Indiana, July 31, 1962; admitted to bar, 1995, Illinois; 1998, Arizona. *Education:* Indiana University/Northwest (B.S.B.A., with distinction, 1984); Northwestern University School of Law (J.D., 1995). ***PRACTICE AREAS:*** Tax Law. ***Email:*** tbottomlee@mayerbrownrowe.com

STEPHEN JOHN BOTTOMLEY, born 1954; admitted to bar, 1980, England. *Education:* University of East Anglia. (London, England Office). ***PRACTICE AREAS:*** Corporate Finance Law; Venture Capital Law. ***Email:*** sbottomley@mayerbrownrowe.com

DAVID N. BOWEN, born University Park, Maryland, February 12, 1958; admitted to bar, 1983, Florida; 1988, U.S. Tax Court; 1996, District of Columbia. *Education:* University of Maryland (B.S., summa cum laude, 1980); College of William & Mary (J.D., 1983); University of Florida (LL.M., Taxation, 1987); George Washington University (LL.M., Litigation and Alternative Dispute Resolution, with highest honors, 2001). (Board Certified Tax Lawyer, Florida Bar Board of Legal Specialization) (Washington, D.C. Office). ***PRACTICE AREAS:*** Tax Controversies. ***Email:*** dbowen@mayerbrownrowe.com

GARY BOWNES, born 1962; admitted to bar, 1987, England. *Education:* Reading University. (London, England Office). ***PRACTICE AREAS:*** Commercial Property. ***Email:*** gbownes@mayerbrownrowe.com

FRANCIS R. BRADLEY, III, born Upper Darby, Pennsylvania, 1968; admitted to bar, 1992, Texas. *Education:* University of Texas (B.B.A., with honors, 1989); University of Houston (J.D., cum laude, 1992). (Houston, Texas Office). ***PRACTICE AREAS:*** Finance; Natural Resources; Banks and Banking. ***Email:*** fbradley@mayerbrown.com

CHRISTOPHER J. BRADY, born Asheville, North Carolina, June 16, 1961; admitted to bar, 1993, North Carolina. *Education:* University of North Carolina at Charlotte (B.S., cum laude, 1983); University of North Carolina at Chapel Hill (J.D., with high honors, 1993). Member, Order of the Coif. Recipient, Chief Justice Walter Clark Award. (Charlotte, North Carolina Office). ***Email:*** cbrady@mayerbrownrowe.com

ADDISON D. BRAENDEL, born Cuyahoga County, Ohio, January 15, 1964; admitted to bar, 1992, Illinois. *Education:* New School for Social Research; Temple University (B.A., summa cum laude, 1987); University of Chicago (J.D., 1992). ***PRACTICE AREAS:*** Corporate Law; Private Equity. ***Email:*** abraendel@mayerbrownrowe.com

PHILIP O. BRANDES, born Exeter, New Hampshire, March 27, 1968; admitted to bar, 1995, New York. *Education:* Amherst College (B.A., magna cum laude, 1990); Fordham University (J.D., 1994). (New York, N.Y. Office). ***LANGUAGES:*** German. ***PRACTICE AREAS:*** Corporate Law; Mergers and Acquisitions. ***Email:*** pbrandes@mayerbrownrowe.com

RICHARD S. BRENNAN, born St. Louis, Missouri, March 18, 1938; admitted to bar, 1965, Illinois. *Education:* Princeton University (A.B., 1960); University of Michigan (J.D., 1963). Member, Barristers. Executive Vice President, General Counsel and Secretary, Continental Bank Corporation, 1982-1994; General Counsel and Secretary, Case Corporation, 1995-1999. ***LANGUAGES:*** French. ***Email:*** rbrennan@mayerbrownrowe.com

ROBERT I. BRESSMAN, born Newark, New Jersey, January 18, 1954; admitted to bar, 1981, New York. *Education:* Columbia University (B.A., cum laude, 1976); Rutgers University Law School, Newark (J.D., 1980). (New York, N.Y. Office). ***Email:*** rbressman@mayerbrownrowe.com

SUSAN BRICE, born Dallas, Texas, February 28, 1970; admitted to bar, 1995, Illinois. *Education:* Northwestern University (B.S.J., 1992); Georgetown University (J.D., 1995). Board of Directors, Federal Bar Association, Chicago Chapter, 1997-1999. ***Email:*** sbrice@mayerbrownrowe.com

ANDREW BRIGGS, admitted to bar, 1992, England. (London, England Office). ***PRACTICE AREAS:*** Litigation; Alternative Dispute Resolution; Product Liability. ***Email:*** abriggs@mayerbrownrowe.com

(This Listing Continued)

MAYER, BROWN, ROWE & MAW LLP, Chicago—Continued

RONALD S. BRODY, born Waterville, Maine, April 1, 1961; admitted to bar, 1987, New York. *Education:* Dartmouth College (B.A., cum laude, 1983); University of Chicago (J.D., 1987). (New York, N.Y. Office). ***PRACTICE AREAS:*** Corporate Finance; High Yield Securities; Mergers and Acquisitions. ***Email:*** rbrody@mayerbrownrowe.com

HAYDEN D. BROWN, born Cleveland, Ohio, June 30, 1958; admitted to bar, 1984, Colorado; 1988, North Carolina. *Education:* University of Colorado at Boulder (B.A., cum laude, 1980); Northwestern School of Law of Lewis and Clark College (J.D., 1984); University of Denver (LL.M., in Taxation, 1986). *Member:* American Bar Association (Member: Section of Taxation; Committee on Banking and Savings Institutions; Chairman, 2001-2003). (Charlotte, North Carolina Office). ***Email:*** haydenbrown@mayerbrownrowe.com

MICHAEL BROWN, admitted to bar, 1993, England and Wales. *Education:* Selwyn College, Cambridge; College of Law London. (London, England Office). ***PRACTICE AREAS:*** Litigation. ***Email:*** mbrown@mayerbrownrowe.com

RACHEL BROWN, admitted to bar, 1992, England. *Education:* Oxford University (B.A., Hons., Chemistry, 1988). (London, England Office). ***PRACTICE AREAS:*** Insolvency; Professional Liability. ***Email:*** rbrown@mayerbrownrowe.com

STEPHEN BARNETT BROWN, born England, October 4, 1963; admitted to bar, 1991, England. *Education:* University of England (B.S., with honors, 1986; L.S.F., 1989). (London, England Office). ***PRACTICE AREAS:*** Pension and Financial Services Litigation; General Commercial Litigation; Shareholder Actions. ***Email:*** sbrown@mayerbrownrowe.com

ULRICH BRÜCKMANN, born 1951; admitted to bar, 1979, Germany. *Education:* University of Giessen; University of Paris I. (Frankfurt/Main, Germany Office). ***LANGUAGES:*** English, French. ***PRACTICE AREAS:*** Commercial Law; Distributorships; Trademarks. ***Email:*** ubrueckmann@mayerbrownrowe.com

RICHARD F. BULGER, born Sacramento, California, April 5, 1968; admitted to bar, 1993, Oregon; 1994, Illinois; 1997, U.S. District Court, Southern District of Illinois; 2001, U.S. Court of Appeals, Seventh Circuit. *Education:* DePauw University (B.A., 1990); Indiana University (J.D., 1993). Assistant Counsel, Illinois Environmental Protection Agency, 1994-1997. ***Email:*** rbulger@mayerbrownrowe.com

AMY MARLYSE BURGERT, born Watonga, Oklahoma, June 3, 1969; admitted to bar, 1995, Texas; 1996, U.S. District Court, Southern District of Texas; U.S. Court of Appeals, Fifth, Eighth and Federal Circuits; 2001, U.S. District Court, Western District of Texas; 2003, U.S. District Court, Eastern District of Texas. *Education:* Dartmouth College (B.A., 1991); University of Texas (J.D., 1995). Contributing Author: "Asset Protection: Domestic and International Law and Tactics," Clark Boardman Callaghan, 1995. (Houston, Texas Office). ***PRACTICE AREAS:*** Complex Litigation. ***Email:*** aburgert@mayerbrownrowe.com

J. KEITH BURT, born Chapel Hill, North Carolina, June 30, 1960; admitted to bar, 1985, Maryland; 1986, District of Columbia. *Education:* University of Maryland (B.S., 1982); George Washington University (J.D., with honors, 1985). Member, George Washington University Law Review, 1984-1985. Trial Attorney, U.S. Department of Justice, Civil Division, 1987-1989. (Washington, D.C. Office). ***PRACTICE AREAS:*** Complex Litigation; Energy; Government Contracts. ***Email:*** kburt@mayerbrownrowe.com

MICHAEL R. BUTOWSKY, admitted to bar, 1984, New York. *Education:* Boston University (B.A., 1981; J.D., 1984). (New York, N.Y. Office). ***PRACTICE AREAS:*** Banking and Finance; Corporate and Securities. ***Email:*** mbutowsky@mayerbrownrowe.com

SARAH BYRT, born 1963; admitted to bar, 1988, England. *Education:* Birmingham University; University of Limoges. United Kingdom Law Contributor to: "Les Dessins et Modèles"; "La Publicité et la Loi." Lecturer, Designs Law, Centre d'Etudes Internationales de la Propriété Industrielle. (Partner, Intellectual Property and Information Technology Group, London) (London, England Office). ***LANGUAGES:*** French. ***PRACTICE AREAS:*** Intellectual Property; Trademark Infringement; Patent Licensing; Information Technology. ***Email:*** sbyrt@mayerbrownrowe.com

TIMOTHY P. CALLAHAN, born Oak Park, Illinois, September 12, 1963; admitted to bar, 1988, Illinois. *Education:* University of Michigan (B.A., with high distinction, 1985; J.D., 1988). Co-author: "Construction Loans: Financing the Developer," Financing Real Estate Transactions, Illinois Institute for Continuing Legal Education, 1992. Contributor: White & Summers, "Uniform Commercial Code 3rd Edition", 1988. Delegate, Hindsdale Caucus. ***PRACTICE AREAS:*** Energy; Construction Law; Commercial Real Estate. ***Email:*** tcallahan@mayerbrownrowe.com

RICHARD A. CAMPBELL, born Harvey, Illinois, December 2, 1956; admitted to bar, 1983, Illinois; 1985, U.S. Tax Court. *Education:* University of Illinois (B.S., 1978; J.D., 1983). *Member:* Illinois State Bar Association (Past President, Trusts and Estates Section Council). ***PRACTICE AREAS:*** Estate Planning; Contested Trusts and Estates; Estate Administration. ***Email:*** rcampbell@mayerbrownrowe.com

WILLIAM CANDELARIA, born Albuquerque, New Mexico, May 10, 1970; admitted to bar, 1996, California; 1998, New York. *Education:* Stanford University (A.B., 1992; A.M., 1993); Harvard Law School (J.D., cum laude, 1995). Supervising Editor, Harvard Law Review, 1993-1995. Law Clerk to Hon. Harry Pregerson, U.S. Court of Appeals, Ninth Circuit, 1995-1996. Author, "Liberalismo Contra Democracia - Recent Judicial Reform in Mexico," Harvard L. Review, June 1995. Speaker, Conference on Latin American Legal Scholarship, European Law Research Center, Harvard Law School, March 2000. Member, Board of Directors, Lambda Legal Defense & Education Fund, 2004—. (New York, N.Y. Office). ***LANGUAGES:*** Spanish and Portuguese. ***PRACTICE AREAS:*** Finance; Securities; Corporate Governance. ***Email:*** wcandelaria@mayerbrown.com

JEFFREY P. CANTRELL, born August 11, 1961; admitted to bar, 1988, Georgia; *1989, New York; 1999, North Carolina. Education: Florida State University (B.A., magna* cum laude, 1983); University of Florida College of Law (J.D., with honors, 1988); New York University (LL.M. in Taxation, 1989). (Charlotte, North Carolina Office). ***PRACTICE AREAS:*** Taxation. ***Email:*** jcantrell@mayerbrownrowe.com

(This Listing Continued)

JAMES B. CARLSON, born Evanston, Illinois, February 23, 1955; admitted to bar, 1981, Illinois; 1993, New York. *Education:* Princeton University (B.A., magna cum laude, 1977); Northwestern University (J.D., cum laude, 1981). (New York, N.Y. Office). ***Email:*** jcarlson@mayerbrownrowe.com

DAVID A. CARPENTER, born Chicago, Illinois, October 5, 1962; admitted to bar, 1988, Illinois. *Education:* University of Illinois (B.A., 1984); DePaul University (J.D., 1987). Executive Vice President, Administration, Legal & Regulatory Affairs. ***LANGUAGES:*** French. ***TRANSACTIONS:*** Represented Fresenius AG, a global pharmaceutical concern, in the negotiation of US marketing and distribution rights with Abbott Laboratories for its Glycophos product (January 2002). Represented Nestle USA Inc. in the $2.6 billion acquisition of Chef America, the manker of Hot Pockets, Lean Pockets and Croissant Pockets (August, 2002). Represented Nestle S.A. (Switzerland) in the formation of a worldwide portable oral care joint venture with Colgate-Palmolive Company (June 2003). Represented Nestle S.A. (Switzerland) in the formation of a milk products joint venture throughout the Americas with Fonterra Co-operative Group Limited (New Zealand) (January 2003). Represented Nestle USA Inc. in the sale of its Ortega Mexican food division (August 2003). ***PRACTICE AREAS:*** Corporate Law; Securities; International Law. ***Email:*** dacarpenter@mayerbrownrowe.com

ANDREW JAMES CARRUTHERS, born 1949; admitted to bar, 1975, England. *Education:* Oxford University. *Member:* Company of City of London Solicitors International Litigation Practitioners Forum; Association of Pension Lawyers; London Solicitors Litigation Association; UIA. (London, England Office). ***PRACTICE AREAS:*** Commercial Litigation; Corporate Litigation; Arbitration; Pension Law. ***Email:*** acarruthers@mayerbrownrowe.com

JAMES A. CASEY, born Kalamazoo, Michigan; admitted to bar, 1995, Illinois; 1996, Michigan. *Education:* Western Michigan University (B.B.A., 1989); John Marshall Law School (J.D., cum laude, 1995). The Florida National Tax Law Moot Court Competition, 1995. Executive Editor, The John Marshall Law Review. Certified Public Accountant, Illinois, 1989. Law Clerk, Justice Anne M. Burke, Illinois Appellate Court, 1995-1996. ***Email:*** jcasey@mayerbrownrowe.com

DAVID CHADWICK, admitted to bar, 1991, England. *Education:* Newcastle University (Law degree). (London, England Office). ***PRACTICE AREAS:*** Insurance; Reinsurance; Political Risk Insurance. ***Email:*** dchadwick@mayerbrownrowe.com

TONY CHILD, born 1947; admitted to bar, 1971, England. *Education:* University College, London. (London, England Office). ***PRACTICE AREAS:*** Local Government; Public Law; Administrative Law; Health Law. ***Email:*** tchild@mayerbrownrowe.com

JEAN S. CHIN, admitted to bar, 1984, New York. *Education:* Barnard College (B.A., magna cum laude, 1978); Columbia University School of Law (J.D., 1983). Contributing Author to Capatides, A Guide to the Capital Markets Activities of Banks and Bank Holding Companies (1993); and Kravitt, ed., Securitization of Financial Assets. (New York, N.Y. Office). ***PRACTICE AREAS:*** Banking. ***Email:*** jchin@mayerbrownrowe.com

C. CABELL CHINNIS, JR., born Washington, D.C., May 28, 1958; admitted to bar, 1986, Pennsylvania; 1988, District of Columbia and U.S. Tax Court; 2002, California. *Education:* Princeton University (A.B., magna cum laude, 1980); Harvard University (K.S.G., 1981); Yale University (J.D., 1984). Phi Beta Kappa. Managing Editor, Yale Law Review. Law Clerk to The Hon. John Minor Wisdom, United States Court of Appeals for the Fifth Circuit (New Orleans, LA), 1984. Law Clerk to The Hon. Lewis F. Powell, Jr., United States Supreme Court (Washington, DC), 1985. (Palo Alto, California Office). ***PRACTICE AREAS:*** Federal Tax Controversies. ***Email:*** cchinnis@mayerbrownrowe.com

IAN CHRISTIE, born 1951; admitted to bar, 1978, England. *Education:* Leeds University. (London, England Office). ***PRACTICE AREAS:*** Commercial Property Law; Retail Law; Landlord and Tenant Law. ***Email:*** ichristie@mayerbrownrowe.com

DAVID A. CIANCUILLO, born Port Chester, New York, April 14, 1971; admitted to bar, 1997, Illinois. *Education:* Arizona State University (B.S., 1994); Loyola University (J.D., magna cum laude, 1997). Member, Loyola Law Journal. ***PRACTICE AREAS:*** Banking Law; Finance; Securitization. ***Email:*** dciancuillo@mayerbrownrowe.com

KATHERINE M. CLARK, born Chicago, Illinois, October 23, 1970; admitted to bar, 1997, Illinois. *Education:* University of Notre Dame (B.A., with honors, 1992); University of Chicago (J.D., with honors, 1997). ***LANGUAGES:*** Spanish. ***Email:*** kclark@mayerbrownrowe.com

JEREMY CLAY, born 1961; admitted to bar, 1985, England. *Education:* Oxford University. (London, England Office). ***PRACTICE AREAS:*** Commercial Property Law; Property Finance Law. ***Email:*** jclay@mayerbrownrowe.com

PAUL B. CLEMENCEAU, born Bordeaux, France, August 8, 1940; admitted to bar, 1965, Louisiana; 1969, U.S. District Court, Eastern District of Louisiana; 1971, Conseil Juridique, Paris, France; 1982, Texas and U.S. District Court, Southern District of Texas; 1992, Avocat, Paris, France. *Education:* Washington & Lee University (B.A., 1962); Tulane University (LL.B., 1965). Member, Board of Editors, Tulane Law Review, 1963-1964. Advisory Board, Houston Journal of International Law. Chairman, International Law Section, State Bar of Texas, 1985-1986. Member, Supervisory Board, Houston Journal of International Law. [Capt., U.S. Army Signal Corps., 1965-1969]. (Houston, Texas Office). ***LANGUAGES:*** French. ***PRACTICE AREAS:*** Mergers and Acquisitions; Corporate. ***Email:*** pclemenceau@mayerbrownrowe.com

IAN R. COLES, born Mexborough, England, September 12, 1956; admitted to bar, 1979, England; 1983, New York. *Education:* Cambridge University, England (B.A., 1978); Harvard University (LL.M., 1981). (Partner in Charge, London, England Office). ***Email:*** icoles@mayerbrownrowe.com

JOSEPH P. COLLINS, born Chicago, Illinois, April 9, 1950; admitted to bar, 1975, Illinois. *Education:* College of the Holy Cross (A.B., magna cum laude, 1972); New York University (J.D., 1975). Former Chair, ABA Derivatives Law Committee. ***PRACTICE AREAS:*** Securities; Mergers, Acquisitions and Divestitures; Commodities Regulation. ***Email:*** jcollins@mayerbrownrowe.com

GARY S. COLTON, JR., born Cleveland, Ohio, March 18, 1954; admitted to bar, 1980, Texas; 1981, U.S. Tax Court; 1998, Illinois. *Education:* Centre College of Kentucky (B.A., 1976); The Ohio State University (J.D., 1 978); University of Houston (LL.M., Taxa-

(This Listing Continued)

tion, 1995). Co-Author: "Compensating Fact Witnesses," 184 F.R.D. 425. Attorney-Advisor to the Honorable Juan F. Vasquez, United States Tax Court, 1995-1997. **Email:** gcolton@mayerbrownrowe.com

JOHN M. CONLON, born New York, N.Y., November 23, 1963; admitted to bar, 1991, New York. *Education:* Williams College (B.A., 1985); Universität Tübingen, Germany; Fordham University (J.D., 1990). (New York, N.Y. Office). **Email:** jconlon@mayerbrownrowe.com

VINCENT J. CONNELLY, born Chicago, Illinois, June 25, 1950; admitted to bar, 1975, Illinois, U.S. District Court, Northern District of Illinois and U.S. Court of Appeals, Seventh Circuit; 1978, U.S. Supreme Court. *Education:* University of Notre Dame (B.A., summa cum laude, 1972); University of Chicago (J.D., 1975). Board of Directors, Constitutional Rights Foundation Chicago. Former President, Chicago Inn of Court. Co-Founder, Wong Sun Society. *Member:* Chicago Bar Association (Board of Managers); American College of Trial Lawyers. **Email:** vconnelly@mayerbrownrowe.com

SEAN MICHAEL CONNOLLY, born 1960; admitted to bar, 1984, England. *Education:* University of London. *Member:* International Bar Association. (London, England Office). ***PRACTICE AREAS:*** Insurance Law; Reinsurance Law; International Litigation; Arbitration Law. **Email:** sconnolly@mayerbrownrowe.com

PAT S. CONTI, admitted to bar, 1986, New York; 1999, District of Columbia. *Education:* New York University (B.A., 1982); Brooklyn Law School (J.D., 1985). (Washington, D.C. Office). ***PRACTICE AREAS:*** Litigation. **Email:** pconti@mayerbrownrowe.com

GARY COOPER, admitted to bar, 1995, England and Wales. *Education:* Manchester University. (London, England Office). ***PRACTICE AREAS:*** Corporate; Securities. **Email:** gcooper@mayerbrownrowe.com

ANDREW COPLEY, born 1964; admitted to bar, 1989, England. *Education:* University of Bristol. *Member:* Law Society of England and Wales; British Venture Capital Association. (London, England Office). ***PRACTICE AREAS:*** Corporate Finance; Company Law; Commercial Law; Venture Capital. **Email:** acopley@mayerbrownrowe.com

ROBERT B. CORDLE, born Apex, North Carolina, March 14, 1941; admitted to bar, 1966, North Carolina. *Education:* Davidson College (A.B., with honors, 1963); New York University (LL.B., cum laude, 1966). Omicron Delta Kappa. Order of the Coif. Root-Tilden Scholar. Member, New York University Law Review, 1964-1965. Advocate, American Board of Trial Advocates (President, North Carolina Chapter, 1991-1995). Fellow, American College of Trial Lawyers. Member, Fourth Circuit Judicial Conference. [Captain, U.S. Army, Active Duty, 1966-1968]. (Charlotte, North Carolina Office). **Email:** rcordle@mayerbrownrowe.com

J. TYSON COVEY, born Peoria, Illinois, September 7, 1965; admitted to bar, 1991, Illinois and U.S. Court of Appeals, Seventh Circuit; 1992, U.S. District Court, Northern District of Illinois. *Education:* Augustana College (A.B., magna cum laude, 1987); University of Illinois (J. D., magna cum laude, 1991). Phi Beta Kappa; Order of the Coif. Knut Erikson Scholar. Harno Scholarship. Staff Member, 1989-1991 and Administrative Editor, 1990-1991, University of Illinois Law Review. Instructor, The Legal Environment of Business, University of Illinois, 1990-1991. Staff Attorney, U.S. Court of Appeals, Seventh Circuit, 1991-1993. **Email:** jcovey@mayerbrownrowe.com

GEORGE W. CRAVEN, born Louisville, Kentucky, March 11, 1951; admitted to bar, 1976, Illinois; 1980, Kentucky. *Education:* University of Notre Dame (B.A., with highest honors, 1973); Harvard Law School (J.D., cum laude, 1976). Author: Chapter 9, "Tax Issues," Securitization of Financial Assets, Prentice Hall Law and Business, 1991; "'Money' and 'Property' (Other than Money): An Exploration of 'Amount Realized' Under Section 1001(b)," delivered at the Annual Federal Tax Conference, of the University of Chicago Law School, 1992, reprinted in 70 Taxes—The Tax Magazine, 912, December, 1992. Secretary, United Way/Crusade of Mercy, Inc., 1998—. ***LANGUAGES:*** Japanese. ***PRACTICE AREAS:*** Federal Income Tax; Insurance; International Law. **Email:** gcraven@mayerbrownrowe.com

PAUL M. CRIMMINS, born Chicago, Illinois, June 6, 1963; admitted to bar, 1989, Illinois. *Education:* Niles College of Loyola University (B.S., 1985); Loyola University of Chicago (J.D., cum laude, 1989). Alpha Sigma Nu. American Jurisprudence Award. Author: "Tax Treatment of Contingent Liabilities on the Sale of a Business," De Paul Law Review, Volume 40, Issue 3, Spring 1991. *Member:* Chicago Bar Association (Co-Chair, Corporate Practice Section, Young Lawyer's Division). **Email:** pcrimmins@mayerbrownrowe.com

ROBERT E. CURLEY, born Chicago, Illinois, January 22, 1935; admitted to bar, 1959, Illinois. *Education:* Northwestern University (B.S., 1956); University of Notre Dame (LL.B., 1959); Georgetown University (LL.M., in Taxation, 1964). Attorney-Advisor, Division of Corporation Finance, U.S. Securities and Exchange Commission, Washington, D.C., 1961-1965. ***PRACTICE AREAS:*** Securities; Corporate Law. **Email:** rcurley@mayerbrownrowe.com

DAVID S. CURRY, born Bloomington, Indiana, April 9, 1951; admitted to bar, 1983, Illinois. *Education:* Emory University; Indiana University (B.A., 1973); Indiana University School of Law, Indianapolis (J.D., summa cum laude, 1979). **Email:** dcurry@mayerbrownrowe.com

PETER V. DARROW, born Ann Arbor, Michigan, September 7, 1950; admitted to bar, 1979, New York. *Education:* Columbia University (B.A., 1972); Trinity College, Oxford University (B. Phil., 1974); University of Michigan (J.D., 1978). Member, Michigan Law Review. Author, "Restructuring Corporate Debt in Latin America," International Financial Law Review (September/October 2003). Co-Author: "Restructuring Strategies for Mexican Eurobond Debt," Northwestern Journal of International Law & Business (Fall 1991). Co-Author: "Private Equity Investment in Latin America, *Latin American Law and Business Report* (Jan. 2000); "Financing Infrastructure Projects in the International Capital Markets: The Tribasa Toll Road Trust," The Financier (August 1994); "Establishing a US Commercial Paper Program," International Financial Law Review (April 1985). (New York, N.Y. Office). **Email:** pdarrow@mayerbrownrowe.com

RANIERO D'AVERSA, JR., born 1965; admitted to bar, 1991, New York and District of Columbia; U.S. District Court, Southern and Eastern Districts of New York and Western District of Michigan. *Education:* Adelphia University (B.B.A., summa cum laude); New York University (J.D., 1990). Journal of International Law and Politics. (New York, N.Y. Office). ***PRACTICE AREAS:*** Bankruptcy; Creditors Rights; Structured Finance. **Email:** rdaversa@mayerbrown.com

SALLY ALEXANDRA DAVIES, born Shrewsbury, Shropshire, August 10, 1969; admitted to bar, 1994, England and Wales; 2001, Solicitor Advocate with Higher Rights of Audience (Civil). *Education:* University of London, England (LL.B., with honors, 1991); The College of Law, London, England (J.D., 1992). (London, England Office). ***LANGUAGES:*** Spanish. **Email:** sdavies@eu.mayerbrownrowe.com

ROBERT P. DAVIS, born Syracuse, New York, April 12, 1949; admitted to bar, 1980, District of Columbia. *Education:* Brown University (A.B., 1971); Boston University (M.A., 1972); Syracuse University (M.P.A., 1973); Georgetown University (J.D., magna cum laude, 1980). Solicitor of the U.S. Department of Labor, 1989-1991. Chief of Staff to the Secretary of Transportation, 1983-1985. Publications: National Employment Law Institute, Litigation under the Fair Labor Standards Act (2003); "A Clearer View of the Exempt Status of Financial Services Employees," The Review of Banking and Financial Services (2004). (Washington, D.C. Office). ***LANGUAGES:*** French. **Email:** rdavis@mayerbrownrowe.com

SCOTT J. DAVIS, born Chicago, Illinois, January 8, 1952; admitted to bar, 1976, Illinois and U.S. District Court, Northern District of Illinois; 1977, U.S. Court of Appeals, Seventh Circuit; 1986, U.S. Court of Appeals, Eighth Circuit. *Education:* Yale University (B.A., cum laude, 1972); Harvard University (J.D., cum laude, 1976). Member, Board of Editors, Harvard Law Review, 1974-1976. Author/Co-Author: "Deal Protection After Omnicare," 14 International Company & Commercial Law Review 311 (2003); "Liability Under Sections 10, 18 and 20 of the Securities Exchange Act of 1934," printed in Understanding the Securities Laws 2000, PLI Corp. Law & Practice Handbook Series, No. BO-00P4, 2000; "Merger and Acquisition Agreements in Competitive Bidding Situations: Rights and Obligations Created by Corporation and Contract Law," 17 Securities Regulation Law Journal 3, 1989. Law Clerk to Hon. Luther M. Swygert, U.S. Court of Appeals, Seventh Circuit, 1976-1977. ***SPECIAL AGENCIES:*** Member, 1989— and Vice President, 1996—, Chicago Police Board. ***PRACTICE AREAS:*** Mergers and Acquisitions; Corporate Law; Securities; Litigation. **Email:** sdavis@mayerbrown.com

DEBORA DE HOYOS, born Monticello, New York, August 10, 1953; admitted to bar, 1978, Illinois; 1980, U.S. District Court, Northern District of Illinois. *Education:* Wellesley College (B.A., honors in political science, 1975); Harvard Law School (J.D., 1978). ***LANGUAGES:*** Spanish. **Email:** ddehoyos@mayerbrownrowe.com

DANIEL J. DELANEY, born Elmhurst, Illinois, August 17, 1964; admitted to bar, 1989, Illinois. *Education:* University of Illinois (B.A., magna cum laude, 1986); University of Chicago (J.D., with honors, 1989). Phi Beta Kappa. **Email:** ddelaney@mayerbrownrowe.com

KIRAN SIMON DESAI, born 1964; admitted to bar, 1990, England. *Education:* Keele University. (London, England Office). ***PRACTICE AREAS:*** EC Law; Competition Law. **Email:** kdesai@mayerbrownrowe.com

JOSEPH DeSIMONE, born New York, July 24, 1966; admitted to bar, 1996, New York and U.S. District Court, Eastern District of New York. *Education:* Princeton University (A.B., Political Science, 1988); Fordham Law School (J.D., 1994). Associate Editor, Law Review. Author, Note, "Expansion of Fraud-on-the-Market Theory to the Context of Newly Issued Securities," 61 Fordham Law Review 5151, 1993. A Supervising Attorney for the Columbia University School of Law Political Asylum Clinic, 1998, 1999. Law Clerk to Hon. Joseph McLaughlin, 2nd Circuit Court of Appeals, 1994-1995. (New York, N.Y. Office). **Email:** jdesimone@mayerbrownrowe.com

JULIAN C. D'ESPOSITO, JR., born New York, N.Y., August 6, 1944; admitted to bar, 1969, Illinois and U.S. District Court, Northern District of Illinois. *Education:* Loyola University (B.S., 1966); Northwestern University (J.D., cum laude, 1969). Counsel to the Governor of Illinois, 1977-1981. Chairman, Illinois State Toll Highway Authority, 1995-1999. Member: Illinois Capital Development Board, 1994-1995; Illinois Medical Center Commission, 1988-1994; Governor's Tax Reform Commission, 1982-1983; University of Illinois, Institute of Government and Public Affairs, National Advisory Committee. ***PRACTICE AREAS:*** Government. **Email:** jdesposito@mayerbrownrowe.com

JULIE MELLINDA DICKINS, born 1958; admitted to bar, 1982, England. *Education:* Bristol University. (London, England Office). ***LANGUAGES:*** French, German and Russian. ***PRACTICE AREAS:*** Property Litigation. **Email:** jdickins@mayerbrownrowe.com

PETER J.G. DICKINSON, born 1962; admitted to bar, 1988, England. *Education:* Southampton University; Bristol Polytechnic. *Member:* Law Society. (London, England Office). ***PRACTICE AREAS:*** Company Law; Commercial Law; Corporate Finance; Mergers and Acquisitions; Takeovers; Telecommunications Law. **Email:** pdickinson@mayerbrownrowe.com

THOMAS W. DIMOND, born 1958; admitted to bar, 1990, Illinois; U.S. Court of Appeals, Sixth Circuit; U.S. District Court, Northern and Central Districts of Illinois; U.S. District Court, Western District of Michigan; U.S. District Court, District of Utah. *Education:* University of Illinois (B.S., 1981); University of Chicago (J.D., 1990). Certified Public Accountant, 1982. ***PRACTICE AREAS:*** Environmental Law; Litigation. **Email:** tdimond@mayerbrownrowe.com

DOUGLAS A. DOETSCH, born Lake Charles, Louisiana, November 6, 1957; admitted to bar, 1987, New York; 1989, Illinois. *Education:* Kalamazoo College (B.A., magna cum laude, 1979); University De Dakar, Dakar, Senegal; Columbia University (J.D., 1986). Phi Bata Kappa. Author: "Securing Liquidity," Trade & Forfeiting, Sept. 1999; "Emerging Markets Cash Flow Securitizations Take Off," International Financial Law Review, November 1996; "Restructuring Strategies for Mexican Eurobond Debt," Northwestern Journal of International Law & Business, Fall 1995; "Developing Country Debt: A Summary of the Recent Impact on Commercial Banks," 1 The Financier 63, 1994. Contributing Author: *A Guide to the Capital Markets Activities of Banks and Bank Holding Companies,* Browne 1993; *Securitization of Financial Assets,* Prentice Hall Law & Business, 1993. ***LANGUAGES:*** French and Spanish. **Email:** ddoetsch@mayerbrownrowe.com

ROBERT M. DOW, JR., born Madison, Wisconsin, September 6, 1965; admitted to bar, 1993, Illinois and U.S. District Court, Northern District of Illinois; U.S. Court of Ap-

(This Listing Continued)

MAYER, BROWN, ROWE & MAW LLP, Chicago—Continued

peals, Fourth, Fifth, Sixth, Seventh, Ninth and Eleventh Circuits; U.S. Supreme Court. *Education:* Yale University (B.A., summa cum laude, 1987); Oxford University, England (M.Phil., International Relations, 1990; D.Phil., International Relations, 1997); Harvard University (J.D., cum laude, 1993). Phi Beta Kappa; Rhodes Scholar. Law Clerk, Hon. Joel M. Flaum, U.S. Court of Appeals, Seventh Circuit, 1993-1994. Co-author: with J.E. Muench, "Invalidation of Ohio Tort Reform Legislation," [2000] International Journal of Insurance Law 85 (January 2000). Co-Author: with J.C. Schroeder, "Arguing for Changes in the Law," 25(2) *Litigation* 37 (Winter 1999); with J.E. Muench, *When Judicial Activism Trumps Tort Reform: The Illinois Experience,* Washington Legal Foundation, Critical Legal Issues, Working Paper Series, No. 85 (June 1998). *Member:* Appellate Lawyers Association of Illinois (Director, 2000-2002; Officer, 2002-2005; President, 2005-2006). ***PRACTICE AREAS:*** Litigation; Appellate Practice. ***Email:*** rdow@mayerbrownrowe.com

DAVID F. DOWD, born Worcester, Massachusetts, August 25, 1966; admitted to bar, 1992, Virginia; 1994, District of Columbia. *Education:* Georgetown University (A.B., summa cum laude, 1989; J.D., magna cum laude, 1992). (Washington, D.C. Office). ***PRACTICE AREAS:*** Government Contracts; Litigation. ***Email:*** ddowd@mayerbrownrowe.com

JOSEPH E. DOYLE, born Elgin, Illinois, August 9, 1959; admitted to bar, 1985, Illinois. *Education:* University of Illinois (B.A., 1982); University of Minnesota (J.D., 1985). Phi Beta Kappa. Order of the Coif. Articles Editor, Minnesota Law Review, 1984-1985. ***PRACTICE AREAS:*** Corporate Law; Securities. ***Email:*** jdoyle@mayerbrownrowe.com

RALPH P. DUDZIAK, born Chicago, Illinois, January 5, 1961; admitted to bar, 1986, Illinois. *Education:* Augustana College (B.A., 1983); Vanderbilt University (J.D., 1986). ***Email:*** rdudziak@mayerbrownrowe.com

DAVID K. DUFFEE, born Minneapolis, Minnesota, April 8, 1959; admitted to bar, 1985, New York. *Education:* St. Olaf College (B.A., 1981); Columbia University (J.D., 1984). (New York, N.Y. Office). ***Email:*** dduffee@mayerbrownrowe.com

ROBERT T. DUFFY, born Columbus, Ohio, December 12, 1945; admitted to bar, 1971, Ohio (inactive); 1972, U.S. District Court, Southern District of Ohio; 1975, U.S. Court of Appeals, Second and Eighth Circuits; 1976, U.S. Court of Appeals, Ninth Circuit; 1977, U.S. Court of Appeals, Seventh Circuit; 1978, U.S. Supreme Court, U.S. Court of Appeals, Fourth and Tenth Circuits and U.S. Court of Appeals for the District of Columbia Circuit; 1979, U.S. Court of Appeals, First Circuit; 1981, U.S. Court of Appeals, Fifth and Eleventh Circuits; 1983, U.S. Tax Court and U.S. Court of Federal Claims; 1990, North Carolina and U.S. District Court, Middle District of North Carolina; 1993, U.S. District Court, Western District of North Carolina. *Education:* Education: Wright State University (B.A., 1968); Harvard Law School (J.D., 1971). Author: "Awards of Costs to Taxpayers: A Reform Proposal for Section 7430," 48 Tax Lawyer 937 (1995). Attorney, U.S. Department of Justice, Tax Division, 1974-1983. Recipient, Tax Division's Outstanding Attorney Award, 1977 and 1982. *Member:* Mecklenburg County (Trustee, 1999-2002) and American (Vice Chair, Committee on Court Procedure and Practice, Tax Section, 1999-2001) Bar Associations. (Charlotte, North Carolina Office). ***PRACTICE AREAS:*** Tax Controversies. ***Email:*** robertduffy@mayerbrownrowe.com

DANIEL DUMEZICH, born 1959; admitted to bar, 1989, Illinois; 1995, Indiana. *Education:* Western Michigan University (B.A, 1982); DePaul University (M.S.T., 1985); John Marshall Law School (J.D., 1989). Certified Public Accountant, Indiana, 1983. Public Service: Indiana Municipal Judge, 1995-1999. Member of the Indiana General Assembly, 1999-2000 State Representative. ***Email:*** ddumezich@mayerbrownrowe.com

THOMAS C. DURHAM, born Texarkana, Texas, April 27, 1955; admitted to bar, 1980, Illinois and U.S. District Court, Northern District of Illinois; 1981, U.S. Tax Court. *Education:* Cornell College (B.A., magna cum laude, 1977); New York University (J.D., 1980). ***Email:*** tdurham@mayerbrownrowe.com

THOMAS M. DURKIN, born Chicago, Illinois, December 26, 1953; admitted to bar, 1978, Illinois, U.S. District Court, Northern District of Illinois and U.S. Court of Appeals, Seventh Circuit; 2000, U.S. Court of Appeals, Federal Circuit. *Education:* University of Illinois (B.S., with honors, 1975); DePaul University (J.D., with honors, 1978). Certified Public Accountant, Illinois, 1975. Assistant U.S. Attorney, Northern District of Illinois, 1980-1993. First Assistant U.S. Attorney, 1990-1993. Chief, Special Prosecutions Division, 1990. Chief, Criminal Receiving and Appellate Division, 1989. Chairman Pro Bono Committee - Mayer, Brown, Rowe & Maw. Fellow, American College of Trial Lawyers. ***PRACTICE AREAS:*** White Collar Crime (50%); Litigation (50%). ***Email:*** tdurkin@mayerbrownrowe.com

LOUIS P. EATMAN, born Montgomery, Alabama, November 16, 1948; admitted to bar, 1974, California. *Education:* Georgetown University (B.S.F.S., cum laude, 1970); Stanford University (J.D., 1974; M.B.A., 1974). President, Constitutional Rights Foundation. (Los Angeles, California Office). ***PRACTICE AREAS:*** Banks and Banking; Commercial Real Estate. ***Email:*** leatman@mayerbrownrowe.com

DR. CHRISTOFER EGGERS, born 1960; admitted to bar, 1989, Germany. *Education:* University of Freiburg. (Frankfurt/Main, Germany Office). ***LANGUAGES:*** English. ***PRACTICE AREAS:*** Antitrust; Unfair Competition; Food, Drug and Cosmetics. ***Email:*** ceggers@mayerbrownrowe.com

RUSSELL R. EGGERT, born Chicago, Illinois, July 28, 1948; admitted to bar, 1973, Illinois; 1974, U.S. District Court, Northern District of Illinois; 1976, U.S. District Court, Central District of Illinois, U.S. Court of Appeals, First, Third, Fourth, Seventh, Ninth and District of Columbia Circuits; 1979, U.S. Supreme Court; 2001, U.S. District Court, Southern District of Illinois. *Education:* University of Illinois (A.B., 1970; J.D., 1973). ***PRACTICE AREAS:*** Administrative Law; Environmental Law; Complex Litigation. ***Email:*** reggert@mayerbrownrowe.com

REBECCA S. EISNER, born 1962; admitted to bar, 1989, Illinois; 1993, Georgia. *Education:* The Ohio State University (B.A. cum laude); University of Michigan (J.D., cum laude, 1989). Associate Group Counsel, Equifax, Inc., 1993-1995. ***Email:*** reisner@mayerbrownrowe.com

(This Listing Continued)

TIMOTHY B. ELLWOOD, born Beeville, Texas, July 27, 1961; admitted to bar, 1986, Texas. *Education:* Texas A & M University (B.B.A., cum laude, 1983); University of Houston (J.D., magna cum laude, 1986). (Houston, Texas Office). ***Email:*** tellwood@mayerbrownrowe.com

ALLEN ERENBAUM, born Pittsburgh, Pennsylvania, September 25, 1962; admitted to bar, 1987, Illinois; 2001, California. *Education:* Brandeis University (B.A., magna cum laude, 1984); Harvard Law School (J.D., cum laude, 1987). Director of Congressional Relations, US Immigration and Naturalization Service, 1997-2000. Counselor to the Commissioner, US Immigration and Naturalization Service, 1995-1997. Counsel, Committee on the Judiciary, US House of Representatives, 1991-1995. Associate, Preston Gates Ellis & Rouvelas Meeds, 1987-1991. (Los Angeles, California Office). ***PRACTICE AREAS:*** Government; Immigration. ***Email:*** aerenbaum@mayerbrownrowe.com

GRANT J. ESPOSITO, born New York, N.Y., March 9, 1967; admitted to bar, 1993, New York and U.S. District Court, Eastern and Southern Districts of New York; 1998, U.S. Court of Appeals, Eleventh Circuit; 2000, U.S. Court of Appeals, Tenth Circuit. *Education:* Cornell University (B.A., 1989); Fordham University (J.D., 1992). (New York, N.Y. Office). ***REPORTED CASES:*** Hollander v. Sandoz Pharmaceuticals Corporation et. al, 289 F.3d 1193 (10th Cir. 2002). ***PRACTICE AREAS:*** Complex Commercial Litigation; Products Liability; Professional Liability. ***Email:*** gesposito@mayerbrownrowe.com

RICHARD MARSHALL EVANS, born Liverpool, England, April 27, 1967; admitted to bar, 1992, United Kingdom. *Education:* Brasenose College (B.A., 1988); The College of Law, London, England (J.D., 1990). Assistant Editor, Occupational Pensions Law Reports. Has written articles for Pensions World and the Journal of Pensions Management. Drafted the National Association of Pension Funds' "Made Simple" guides to the Regulations under the Pensions Act. Contributing Author, Encyclopedia of Employment Law (Sweet & Maxwell). (London, England Office). ***PRACTICE AREAS:*** Pension Plans. ***Email:*** revans@mayerbrownrowe.com

TYRONE C. FAHNER, born Detroit, Michigan, November 18, 1942; admitted to bar, 1968, Michigan; 1969, Illinois. *Education:* University of Michigan (B.A., 1965); Wayne State University (J.D., 1968); Northwestern University (LL.M., 1971). Criminal Defense Litigation Unit, Northwestern University Law School, Ford Foundation Fellowship, 1969-1971. Assistant to the Dean, Wayne State University Law School, 1968-1969. Attorney General of Illinois, 1980-1983. Director, Illinois Department of Law Enforcement, 1977-1979. Assistant U.S. Attorney, Northern District of Illinois, 1971-1975. Chief, Special Prosecution Section, 1974-1975. Deputy Chief, Consumer Fraud and Civil Rights Section, 1973-1974. Member, Metropolis 2020 Project and Former Chairman, Governance Committee, Commercial Club of Chicago. Former Chairman, John Henry Wigmore Club, Northwestern University School of Law. *Member:* American College of Trial Lawyers; Chicago Inn of Court (Former President). ***PRACTICE AREAS:*** Civil Antitrust; Criminal Antitrust; Securities Litigation; Class Action Litigation; Corporate Governance. ***Email:*** tfahner@mayerbrownrowe.com

DONALD M. FALK, born San Francisco, California, February 6, 1957; admitted to bar, 1990, California; 1993, District of Columbia; U.S. Court of Appeals for the District of Columbia, Federal, Third, Fourth, Fifth, Sixth, Seventh, Eighth, Ninth and Tenth Circuits; U.S. District Court, Northern, Central and Eastern Districts of California; U.S. District Court for the District of Columbia; U.S. Supreme Court. *Education:* University of California at Berkeley (B.A., 1976); University of Chicago (M.A., 1977); Boalt Hall School of Law, University of California (J.D., 1990). Order of the Coif. Law Clerk to Hon. Douglas H. Ginsburg, U.S. Court of Appeals for the District of Columbia Circuit. Author: "Antitrust & Refusals to Deal after Nynex v. Discon," Practical Lawyer, April 2000, at 25. Co-Author: with Hon. Douglas H. Ginsburg, "The Court En Banc: 1981-1990," 59 Geo. Wash. L.Rev. 1008 (1991); with Robert E. Bloch, Robert L. Bronston and Jay S. Brown, "Settlement of Patent Disputes: Antitrust and Intellectual Property at the Crossroads' Antitrust Report (Nov. 2001); with Craig Isenberg, "Plus Ça Change? Anti-Trust Enforcement Under the Bush Administration," International Merger Focus (UK)(2002). (Palo Alto, California Office). ***PRACTICE AREAS:*** Appellate Practice; Antitrust and Trade Regulation; Intellectual Property. ***Email:*** dfalk@mayerbrownrowe.com

RICHARD J. FAVRETTO, born New York, N. Y., May 16, 1941; admitted to bar, 1966, New York; 1972, District of Columbia. *Education:* Iona College (B.A., cum laude, 1963); Catholic University of America (LL.B., 1966). Student Material Editor, Catholic University Law Review, 1965-1966. Trial Attorney, 1966-1973, Assistant Chief, Trial Section, 1973-1976, Deputy Director of Operations, 1976-1979, Deputy Assistant Attorney General, 1979-1981, Antitrust Division, U.S. Department of Justice. (Washington, D.C. Office). ***Email:*** rfavretto@mayerbrownrowe.com

JOHN A. FAYLOR, born 1945; admitted to bar, 1980, Germany; 1983, Pennsylvania. *Education:* Bard College (B.A.); University of Heidelberg; University of Michigan Law School (LL.M.). (Frankfurt/Main, Germany Office). ***LANGUAGES:*** English. ***PRACTICE AREAS:*** Corporate; Mergers and Acquisitions; Competition. ***Email:*** jfaylor@mayerbrownrowe.com

MICHAEL R. FEAGLEY, born Exeter, New Hampshire, February 1, 1945; admitted to bar, 1973, Illinois and Massachusetts; U.S. District Court, Northern and Central Districts of Illinois; U.S. district Court, Eastern District of Wisconsin; U.S. Court of Appeals, Sixth, Seventh, Eighth, Tenth and Federal Circuits; U.S. Supreme Court. *Education:* Wesleyan University (B.A., 1967); Harvard University (J.D., 1973). Author: "A Successful Binding Summary Jury Trial," Judicature, Vol. 79, No. 4; "Using ADR in Jury Trials to Create A Win-Win Result," Corporate Legal Times, Vol. 5, No. 44; "Summary Jury Trial," International Legal Strategy, Vol. V-8. *Member:* American Bar Association; Chicago Council of Lawyers. Fellow, American College of Trial Lawyers. [U.S. Army (ILT), 1969-1971, Vietnam 1970-1971]. ***PRACTICE AREAS:*** Litigation; Complex and Multi-District Litigation; Torts. ***Email:*** mfeagley@mayerbrownrowe.com

RONALD M. FEIMAN, born New York, N.Y., February 28, 1951; admitted to bar, 1978, New York. *Education:* Yale College (B.A., cum laude, 1972); New York University Law School (J.D., M.B.A., 1977). Recent Lectures Include: Mutual Fund Directors Forum, 2003; Mutual Fund Regulation in the Twenty-First Century, 2001, Publications include: Co-Author (with Merrill Magnus), "A Practical Guide to the Investment Company Act," 1996. Certified Public Accountant. Advisory Board Member, Mutual Fund Directors Forum. Appointed Member, RIC/REIT/REMIC Subcommittee, AICPA Tax Division, 1983-1985.

(This Listing Continued)

Member: Association of the Bar of the City of New York (Member, Committee on Investment Management Regulation); American Bar Association (Member: Business Law Section; Committee on Federal Regulation of Securities; Subcommittee on Investment Companies and Investment Advisers). (New York, N.Y. Office). ***PRACTICE AREAS:*** Investments; Securities; Banks and Banking. ***Email:*** rfeiman@mayerbrownrowe.com

IAN N. FEINBERG, born San Francisco, California, September 17, 1954; admitted to bar, 1979, California. *Education:* Stanford University (A.B., 1976); Stanford University School of Law (J.D., 1979). (Palo Alto, California Office). ***PRACTICE AREAS:*** Silicon Valley Practice; Intellectual Property. ***Email:*** infeinberg@mayerbrownrowe.com

JAMES R. FERGUSON, admitted to bar, 1976, Illinois; 1979, U.S. District Court, Northern District of Illinois including Trial Bar and U.S. Court of Appeals, Seventh Circuit; 1984, U.S. District Court, District of Connecticut and U.S. Court of Appeals, Second Circuit; 2001, U.S. Court of Appeals for the Federal Circuit. *Education:* Indiana University (B.A., M.A., 1972); Northwestern University School of Law (J.D., 1976). Author: "Strengthening Pharmaceutical and Biotechnology Patents," Genetic Engineering News (March 1, 2005); "Clinical Trials As Inside Information," New York Times, Oct. 19, 1997; "Biomedical Research and Insider Trading," New England Journal of Medicine, Aug. 28, 1997; "Overcoming Graymail: The Trial of Oliver North," Legal Times, May 15, 1989; "Public Officials and the Fifth Amendment," Wall Street Journal, Jan. 23, 1987; "Scientific Freedom, National Security and the First Amendment," Science, Aug. 12, 1983. ***PRACTICE AREAS:*** Intellectual Property; Commercial Litigation; White Collar Criminal Litigation. ***Email:*** jferguson@mayerbrownrowe.com

ROBERT F. FINKE, born Chicago, Illinois, March 11, 1941; admitted to bar, 1966, Illinois, U.S. District Court, Northern District of Illinois and U.S. Court of Appeals, Seventh Circuit; 1972, U.S. Supreme Court; 197 8, U.S. Court of Appeals, Sixth Circuit; 1982, U.S. Court of Appeals, Ninth Circuit; U.S. Court of Appeals, Eighth Circuit. *Education:* University of Michigan (A.B., 1963); Harvard University (J.D., 1966). *Member:* American Bar Association (Member, Sections on: Antitrust Law; Business Law; Legal Education and Admissions to the Bar; Vice Chair, 1982). ***Email:*** rfinke@mayerbrownrowe.com

SHEILA M. FINNEGAN, born Chicago, Illinois, January 1, 1960; admitted to bar, 1986, Illinois; 1987, U.S. Court of Appeals, Seventh Circuit. *Education:* Georgetown University School of Foreign Service (B.S.F.S., magna cum laude, 1982); University of Chicago (J.D., cum laude, 1986). Order of the Coif. Law Review. Law Clerk, Honorable Milton I. Shadur, U.S. District Court, Northern District of Illinois, 1986-1987. Criminal Division Chief, U.S. Attorneys Office, Northern District of Illinois. ***PRACTICE AREAS:*** White Collar Criminal Defense; Health Care Fraud; Products Liability. ***Email:*** sfinnegan@mayerbrownrowe.com

CHRISTOPHER FISHER, admitted to bar, 1995, England and Wales. *Education:* Reading University (LL.B., Hons., 1992); College of Law, London, 1993. (London, England Office). ***LANGUAGES:*** French and Spanish. ***PRACTICE AREAS:*** Labor and Employment. ***Email:*** cfisher@mayerbrownrowe.com

ROBERT V. FITZSIMMONS, born Bloomington, Indiana, November 18, 1959; admitted to bar, 1986, Illinois. *Education:* Northwestern University (B.A., 1982); John F. Kennedy School of Government, Harvard University (M.P.P., 1986); Harvard Law School (J.D., 1986). ***PRACTICE AREAS:*** Real Estate; Finance; Government. ***Email:*** rfitzsimmons@mayerbrownrowe.com

DELILAH B. FLAUM, born Columbia, Missouri, November 12, 1953; admitted to bar, 1980, Illinois and U.S. District Court, Northern District of Illinois and U.S. Court of Appeals, Seventh Circuit. *Education:* Georgetown University (B.S.F.S., with honors, 1976); Illinois Institute of Technology/Chicago Kent College of Law (J.D., with honors, 1980). Regional Director, U.S. Department of Health and Human Services, 1990-1993. ***PRACTICE AREAS:*** Health Care; Information Technology; Government; Regulatory Law. ***Email:*** dflaum@mayerbrownrowe.com

IAN FLOWERS, born 1959; admitted to bar, 1983, England. *Education:* Manchester University. (London, England Office). ***PRACTICE AREAS:*** Pensions. ***Email:*** iflowers@mayerbrownrowe.com

MARY C. FONTAINE, born Chicopee, Massachusetts, May 18, 1956; admitted to bar, 1981, Illinois and U.S. District Court, Northern District of Illinois; 1996, New York. *Education:* Syracuse University (B.A., summa cum laude, 1978); University of Chicago (J.D., 1981). ***Email:*** mfontaine@mayerbrownrowe.com

MICHAEL K. FORDE, born Evergreen Park, Illinois, February 27, 1972; admitted to bar, 1996, Illinois; 1997, District of Columbia. *Education:* Georgetown University (A.B., cum laude, 1993; J.D., 1996); University of Chicago Graduate School of Business (M.B.A., 1998). Law Clerk for The Honorable Mary Ann G. McMorrow, The Supreme Court of Illinois, 1997-1998; Law Clerk to The Honorable Charles P. Kocoras, U.S. District Court for the Northern District of Illinois, 1996-1997. Author: "The White House Counsel and Whitewater: Government Lawyers and the Scope of Privileged Communications," 16 Yale Law and Policy Review 109 (1998); Note, "The Exclusionary Rule at Sentencing: New Life Under the Federal Sentencing Guidelines?," 33 American Criminal Law Review 379 (1996). Chief Legal Counsel to the Illinois Comptroller, 1999. Chief Counsel to the Transition Team for the Illinois Comptroller-Elect, 1998-1999. ***PRACTICE AREAS:*** Civil Litigation; Government Relations; Securities Litigation. ***Email:*** mforde@mayerbrownrowe.com

ANNA FORGE, admitted to bar, 1982, England. *Education:* University of Kent at Canterbury (B.A., with honours, Law); College of Law (Law Society's Qualifying Examination). Co-Author: Butterworth's Local Government Finance. *Member:* Administrative Law Bar Association. (London, England Office). ***PRACTICE AREAS:*** Local Government Law; Public Sector Law; Public Law; Property Law; Private Finance Initiative; Public-Private Partnerships. ***Email:*** aforge@mayerbrownrowe.com

J. PAUL FORRESTER, born Sydney, Australia, December 6, 1953; admitted to bar, 1978, New South Wales, Australia; 1984, New York; 1988, Illinois. *Education:* University of Sydney (B.A., 1975; LL.B., 1977); Illinois Institute of Technology/Chicago-Kent College of Law (J.D., 1985). ***PRACTICE AREAS:*** Banking Law; Corporate Law; Energy. ***Email:*** jforrester@mayerbrownrowe.com

(This Listing Continued)

DOUGLAS B. FRANK, born Los Angeles, California, June 8, 1962; admitted to bar, 1989, California. *Education:* Northwestern University (B.A., 1984); Loyola Law School of Los Angeles (J.D., 1989). Member: St. Thomas More Honor Society; Scott Moot Court. (Los Angeles, California Office). ***Email:*** dfrank@mayerbrownrowe.com

RON D. FRANKLIN, born New York, N.Y., June 26, 1965; admitted to bar, 1994, New York and New Jersey. *Education:* Occidental College (A.B., cum laude, 1987); Columbia Business School (M.B.A., 1990); University of Michigan Law School (J.D., 1993). (Charlotte, North Carolina Office). ***LANGUAGES:*** Russian. ***PRACTICE AREAS:*** Finance; Corporate. ***Email:*** rfranklin@mayerbrownrowe.com

ANDREW L. FREY, born New York, N.Y., August 11, 1938; admitted to bar, 1962, New York; 1966, District of Columbia; 1972, U.S. Supreme Court. *Education:* Swarthmore College (B.A., with high honors, 1959); Columbia University (LL.B., 1962). Notes and Comments Editor, Columbia Law Review. Author: "Punitive Damages," Business and Commercial Litigation in Federal Courts (ABA 1998); "How to Write a Good Appellate Brief," Litigation Magazine. Deputy Solicitor General of the United States, 1974-1986. *Member:* American Law Institute; American Academy of Appellate Lawyers. (New York, N.Y., & Washington, D.C. Offices). ***PRACTICE AREAS:*** Civil Appeals; Criminal Appeals; Constitutional Law. ***Email:*** afrey@mayerbrownrowe.com

MICHELE-ANNE MARY FREYNE, born 1950; admitted to bar, 1978, England. *Education:* Trinity College, Dublin. (London, England Office). ***PRACTICE AREAS:*** Property Litigation; Matrimonial Law. ***Email:*** mfreyne@mayerbrownrowe.com

DENNIS G. FRIEDMAN, born Cleveland, Ohio, October 16, 1947; admitted to bar, 1982, Illinois; U.S. Court of Appeals, Seventh Circuit; U. S. District Court, Northern District of Illinois. *Education:* Amherst College (B.A., cum laude, 1969); Duke University (J.D., 1981). ***PRACTICE AREAS:*** Litigation; Telecommunications Law. ***Email:*** dfriedman@mayerbrownrowe.com

GARY D. FRIEDMAN, born New York, N.Y., June, 1961; admitted to bar, 1989, New York and U.S. District Court, Southern and Eastern Districts of New York; 1990, District of Columbia; 1995, U.S. Supreme Court; 1996, U.S. Court of Appeals, Second Circuit; 1997, U.S. District Court, Western District of New York; 1998, U.S. Court of Appeals, First Circuit; 2000, U.S. District Court, Northern District of New York. *Education:* Duke University (B.A., magna cum laude, 1983); Georgetown University (J.D., 1987). Author: "Summary Judgment After 'Desert Palace'," The New York Law Journal, August 28, 2003; "When Pretext is Enough in Discrimination Claims," The New York Law Journal, June 29, 2000; "Younger Workers May Be a New 'Protected Class', " The National Law Journal, July 5, 1999; "The Impact of 'Oubre'on Employers and Employees," The New York Law Journal, Feb. 19, 1998; "Disability - Related Questions and Medical Exams," The New York Law Journal, March 18, 1996. (New York, N.Y. Office). ***Email:*** gfriedman@mayerbrownrowe.com

CLAUDIA W. FROST, born Houston, Texas, February 17, 1954; admitted to bar, 1982, Texas. *Education:* University of Texas at Austin (B.A., 1975); University of Houston (M.A., 1979; B.A., 1979); University of Houston Law Center (J.D., magna cum laude, 1982). (Houston, Texas Office). ***PRACTICE AREAS:*** Appellate Litigation; Trial Litigation. ***Email:*** cfrost@mayerbrownrowe.com

ALFRED-CARL GAEDERTZ, born 1922; admitted to bar, 1953, Germany. *Education:* University of Mainz; University of Chicago, School of Law. (Frankfurt/Main, Germany Office). ***LANGUAGES:*** English. ***PRACTICE AREAS:*** Company Law; EU Antitrust; Unfair Trade; Trademarks.

DR. JOHANN-CHRISTOPH GAEDERTZ, born 1959; admitted to bar, 1987, Germany. *Education:* Universities of Freiburg, Mainz and Konstanz; University of the Pacific, McGeorge School of Law, Sacramento (LL.M.). (Frankfurt/Main, Germany Office). ***LANGUAGES:*** English, French. ***PRACTICE AREAS:*** Intellectual Property; Commercial Litigation; Antitrust. ***Email:*** hgaedertz@mayerbrownrowe.com

STEPHEN DAVID GARE, born 1950; admitted to bar, 1976, England. *Education:* Cambridge University. *Member:* City of London Solicitors Company Intellectual Property Sub-Committee; Member: INTA Anti-Counterfeiting and Enforcement Committee; AIPPI. Associate, Chartered Institute of Patent Agents. Co-editor, Blackstones Statutes on Intellectual Property. (London, England Office). ***PRACTICE AREAS:*** Intellectual Property Law; Information Technology Law; Litigation. ***Email:*** sgare@mayerbrownrowe.com

BARRY GASSMAN, born Bronx, New York, September 6, 1946; admitted to bar, 1972, New York, U.S. Court of Appeals, Second Circuit and U.S. District Court, Southern District of New York; 1977, Colorado, U.S. Court of Appeals, Tenth Circuit and U.S. District Court, District of Colorado; U.S. Tax Court; 1991, California (Not admitted in Illinois). *Education:* Clark University (A.B., 1968); State University of New York at Buffalo (J.D., cum laude, 1971); New York University (LL.M. in Taxation, 1974). (New York, New York Office). ***PRACTICE AREAS:*** Leveraged Leasing. ***Email:*** bgassman@mayerbrownrowe.com

CHRISTOF GAUDIG, born 1964; admitted to bar, 1994, Germany. *Education:* University of Freiburg; University of Cologne (First State Examination, 1989). (Cologne, Germany Office). ***LANGUAGES:*** English, German and Portuguese. ***PRACTICE AREAS:*** Mergers and Acquisitions; Corporate Law; Restructuring. ***Email:*** cgaudig@mayerbrownrowe.com

JOHN J. GEAREN, born Wareham, Massachusetts, September 1, 1943; admitted to bar, 1972, Illinois. *Education:* University of Notre Dame (B.A., 1965); Oxford University, Oxford, England (M.A., 1967); Yale University (J.D., 1970). Rhodes Scholar. ***PRACTICE AREAS:*** Real Estate; Corporate Law. ***Email:*** jgearen@mayerbrownrowe.com

DR. MARKUS GEISLER, born 1964; admitted to bar, 1996, Germany. *Education:* University of Applied Sciences Hildesheim (Master of Administrative Law, 1984); University of Osnabrück (First State Examination, 1992); University of of Wisconsin-Madison (LL.M., 1993); University of Osnabrück (Dr. iur., 1997). (Cologne, Germany Office). ***LANGUAGES:*** English, German. ***PRACTICE AREAS:*** Project Finance; Environmental; Aviation. ***Email:*** mgeisler@mayerbrownrowe.com

KENNETH S. GELLER, born New York, N.Y., September 22, 1947; admitted to bar, 1972, New York; 1986, District of Columbia. *Education:* City College of New York (B.A., magna cum laude, 1968); Harvard University (J.D., magna cum laude, 1971). Co-author:

(This Listing Continued)

MAYER, BROWN, ROWE & MAW LLP, Chicago—Continued

"Supreme Court Practice," (BNA 8th ed., 2002). Contributing Author: "Business and Commercial Litigation in Federal Courts" (Robert L. Haig ed., West Group & ABA 1998). Assistant Special Prosecutor, Watergate Special Prosecution Force, 1973-1975. Assistant to the Solicitor General, U.S. Department of Justice, 1975-1979. Deputy Solicitor General, 1979-1986. (Washington, D.C. Office). ***Email:*** kgeller@mayerbrownrowe.com

BRUCE L. GELMAN, born 1968; admitted to bar, 1993, Illinois. *Education:* Boston College (B.A., 1990); University of Detroit (J.D., 1992). ***Email:*** bgelman@mayerbrownrowe.com

BETTINA GETZ, born Davenport, Iowa; admitted to bar, 1982, Illinois; 1983, U.S. District Court, Northern District of Illinois; 1990, Trial Bar; 1992, U.S. Court of Appeals, Seventh Circuit; 1994, U.S. District Court, Western District of Michigan; 1998, U.S. Court of Appeals, Fifth Circuit; 1999, U.S. District Court, Eastern District of Wisconsin. *Education:* Michigan State University (B.A., with honors, 1976); DePaul University (J.D., with honors, 1982). Member, De Paul Law Review, 1981-1982. Judicial Law Clerk to Hon. Mel R. Jiganti, Illinois Appellate Court, 1982-1984. ***PRACTICE AREAS:*** Commercial Litigation; Commercial Arbitration; Health Care Litigation. ***Email:*** bgetz@mayerbrownrowe.com

RANDALL R. GIBEAU, born Atlanta, Georgia, February 9, 1971; admitted to bar, 1996, Georgia. *Education:* Duke University (A.B., 1993); Washington University School of Law (J.D., 1996). (New York, N.Y. Office). ***PRACTICE AREAS:*** Corporate Law; Securities; Information Technology. ***Email:*** rgibeau@mayerbrownrowe.com

STEVEN R. GILFORD, born Chicago, Illinois, December 2, 1952; admitted to bar, 1978, Illinois and U.S. District Court, Northern District of Illinois; 1981, U.S. Court of Appeals, Seventh Circuit; 1983, District of Columbia; 1989, U.S. Court of Appeals, Fifth Circuit; 1995, U.S. District Court, Eastern District of Michigan. *Education:* Dartmouth College (A.B., summa cum laude, 1974); Duke University (M.A., 1978; J.D., with distinction, 1978). Author: "Insurance Coverage Actions: Who, Where, and When to Sue," The Brief, Fall 1996, Vol. 26, No. 1, ABA Tort and Insurance Practice Section; "Prior Attention to Arbitration Clauses Help Ensure Fairness," Legal Update, The Review Worldwide Reinsurance, March 1995; "Alternatives to Insurance Liquidation: A U.S. Perspective," International Journal of Insurance Law, October 1994; 7th International Reinsurance Congress, October 1993; "The Responsibilities and Liabilities of Accountants and Actuaries to Life Insurers and in Life Insurance Insolvencies," ABA National Institute on Life Insurer Insolvency, June, 1993; Coordinator and Panelist, "The Uses and Abuses of Policy-Holders Litigation," RIMS Annual Meeting, March, 1992. ***PRACTICE AREAS:*** Litigation; Insurance; Reinsurance; Class Actions. ***Email:*** sgilford@mayerbrownrowe.com

MICHAEL J. GILL, born Springfield, Illinois, September 15, 1952; admitted to bar, 1977, Illinois and U.S. District Court, Northern District of Illinois; U.S. Court of Appeals, Seventh Circuit. *Education:* Northwestern University (B.A., 1974; J.D., magna cum laude, 1977). Adjunct Professor, Trial Practice, Northwestern University, 1987—. ***PRACTICE AREAS:*** Litigation. ***Email:*** mgill@mayerbrownrowe.com

JULIE A. GILLESPIE, admitted to bar, 1996, Illinois. *Education:* University of Maryland (B.A., 1993); Duke University (J.D., magna cum laude, 1996). ***Email:*** jsennello@mayerbrownrowe.com

MARK H. GITENSTEIN, born Montgomery, Alabama, March 7, 1946; admitted to bar, 1972, District of Columbia. *Education:* Duke University (A.B., 1968); Georgetown University (J.D., 1972). (Washington, D.C. Office). ***PRACTICE AREAS:*** Government; Administrative; Antitrust and Trade Regulation. ***Email:*** mgitenstein@mayerbrownrowe.com

RONALD B. GIVEN, born Indianapolis, Indiana, January 31, 1952; admitted to bar, 1978, Illinois; 1979, Indiana; 2004, New York. *Education:* St. Francis College (B.A., 1974); Florida Tech. University (M.B.A., 1975); Indiana University (J.D., 1978). ***PRACTICE AREAS:*** Business Law; Finance; International Trade. ***Email:*** rgiven@mayerbrownrowe.com

ROBERT E. GLENNON, JR., born Decatur, Illinois, April 23, 1948; admitted to bar, 1974, Florida; 1975, U.S. Tax Court; 1977, District of Columbia. *Education:* University of Illinois (B.S., 1971); University of Florida Law School (J.D., 1974; LL.M. in Taxation, 1975). (Washington, D.C. Office). ***PRACTICE AREAS:*** Government. ***Email:*** reglennon@mayerbrownrowe.com

DAVID M. GOLDMAN, born Phoenix, Arizona, July 14, 1962; admitted to bar, 1992, New York. *Education:* University of Pennsylvania (B.A., 1984); Columbia University (J.D., 1991); New York University (LL.M., Taxation, 1998). (New York, N.Y. Office). ***LANGUAGES:*** French. ***PRACTICE AREAS:*** Taxation. ***Email:*** dgoldman@mayerbrownrowe.com

ROBERT D. GOLDSCHEIN, born Los Angeles, California, September 28, 1954; admitted to bar, 1980, California, U.S. District Court, Central, Eastern, Northern and Southern Districts of California. *Education:* University of California at Berkeley (B.A., 1977); University of California at Los Angeles (J.D., 1980). (Los Angeles, California Office). ***PRACTICE AREAS:*** Commercial Finance; Trade Finance; Insolvency; Bankruptcy Reorganization. ***Email:*** rdgoldschein@mayerbrownrowe.com

JOSEPH I. GOLDSTEIN, admitted to bar, 1973, Pennsylvania; 1987, District of Columbia. *Education:* Rutgers University (B.A., 1964); University of Michigan (J.D., cum laude, 1972). (Washington, D.C. Office). ***PRACTICE AREAS:*** Litigation. ***Email:*** jgoldstein@mayerbrownrowe.com

HECTOR GONZALEZ, born Havana, Cuba, July 22, 1964; admitted to bar, 1988, New Jersey, New York and U.S. District Court, District of New Jersey; 1989, U.S. District Court, Eastern and Southern Districts of New York; 1991, U.S. Court of Appeals, Second Circuit; 1992, U.S. Court of Appeals for the Armed Forces. *Education:* Manhattan College (B.S., 1985); University of Pennsylvania (J.D., 1988). Assistant District Attorney, New York County District Attorney's Office, 1990-1993. Assistant U.S. Attorney, U.S. Attorney's Office, Southern District of New York, 1994-1999. Chief/Deputy Chief, Narcotics Unit, 1997-1999. Chair, 2002— and Member, 2000—, New York City Civilian Complaint Review Board. Member, Board of Directors, Puerto Rican Legal Defense and Education Fund, 2002—. Member, Board of Directors, New York Lawyers for the Public Interest, 2003—. Member, Board of Trustees, Manhattan College, 2004—. Fulbright Scholar, 1998. *Member:* The Association of the Bar of the City of New York (Member, Committee on Criminal Advocacy); Federal Bar Council; Hispanic National Bar Association. [Honorable Discharge, U.S. Army, 1983]. (New York, N.Y. Office). ***LANGUAGES:*** Spanish. ***PRACTICE AREAS:*** Litigation; Criminal Law; Securities. ***Email:*** hgonzalez@mayerbrownrowe.com

MARCIA E. GOODMAN, born Washington, D. C., December 21, 1953; admitted to bar, 1980, District of Columbia; 1985, Illinois; U.S. Court of Appeals, Sixth and Seventh Circuits; U.S. District Court, Northern District of Illinois including Trial Bar. *Education:* University of Michigan (B.A., with high honors, 1974; M.A., Japanese Studies); Harvard University (J.D., cum laude, 1980); Tokyo University, Faculty of Law, Tokyo, Japan. Author: "Testing, Testing A-D-A," Corporate Counsel Magazine (1999); "The Exercise and Control of Prosecutorial Discretion in Japan," 5 UCLA Pacific Basin Law Journal Nos. 1 and 2 (1986). Regular Contributor to International Legal Strategy, a Japanese language publication for Japanese business, on employment law and international litigation. Attorney: Akin, Gump, Strauss, Hauer & Feld, Washington, D.C., 1982-1984; Kovar, Nelson, Brittain & Sledz, 1984- 1992. ***LANGUAGES:*** Japanese. ***PRACTICE AREAS:*** Labor and Employment; International Commercial Law; ERISA Litigation. ***Email:*** mgoodman@mayerbrownrowe.com

JEFFREY I. GORDON, born Chicago, Illinois, December 13, 1948; admitted to bar, 1972, Illinois; 1974, District of Columbia. *Education:* Princeton University (B.A., cum laude, 1969); Harvard University (J.D., cum laude, 1972). Author: "FIRREA Real Estate Appraisal Regulations: New Exemptions and Simplifications," Journal of International Banking Law, Vol. 9, Issue 8, August 1994; "New Appraisal Requirements for Loan Amendments, Restructurings and Workouts," Butterworths Journal of International Banking and Financial Law, March 1992. Lecturer, Chicago Bar Association, Real Estate Securitization Conferences, 1994. (London, England Office). ***PRACTICE AREAS:*** Corporate Law; Securities. ***Email:*** jgordon@mayerbrownrowe.com

ROBERT E. GORDON, born Chicago, Illinois, September 15, 1954; admitted to bar, 1979, Illinois, U.S. District Court, Northern District of Illinois and U.S. Court of Appeals, Seventh Circuit. *Education:* University of Michigan (B.S., with high distinction, 1976); Northwestern University (J.D., cum laude, 1979). Order of the Coif. Author: Real Estate Chapter and co-author, Structuring chapter, *Securitization of Financial Assets,* Second Edition, Aspen Law & Business, 1997 (updated semi-annually); "FIRREA Real Estate Appraisal Regulations: New Exemptions and Simplification," Journal of International Banking Law, August 1994; "New Appraisal Requirements for Loan Amendments, Restructurings and Work-outs," Butterworths Journal of International Banking and Financial Law, March 1992. Contributing Author: *Construction Financing, Banking and Loans,* Chapter on Construction Law, Matthew Bender, 1986. Adjunct Professor, The John Marshall Law School, Real Estate Law Center (LL.M. Program in Real Estate Law), "Securitization of Real Estate," 1995—. Panelist, Roundtable on Synthetic Leasing, Annual Convention of the American Bar Association, 1998. ***PRACTICE AREAS:*** Real Estate; Lease Finance; Securitization. ***Email:*** rgordon@mayerbrownrowe.com

MAUREEN J. GORMAN, born Rockford, Illinois, December 17, 1955; admitted to bar, 1983, District of Columbia; 1986, Illinois. *Education:* College of William & Mary (B.A., Philosophy, 1978); Yale University (J.D., 1981). (Palo Alto, California Office). ***Email:*** mgorman@mayerbrownrowe.com

DAVID M. GOSSETT, born Chicago, Illinois, July 8, 1969; admitted to bar, 1997, Illinois and U.S. Court of Appeals, Seventh Circuit; 1999, U.S. Court of Appeals for the District of Columbia and Ninth Circuits; 2000, District of Columbia and U.S. District Court, District of Maryland; 2001, U.S. Supreme Court, U.S. Court of Appeals, Sixth Circuit and U.S. District Court for the District of Columbia; 2003, U.S. Court of Appeals, Fifth and Tenth Circuits; 2004, U.S. Court of Appeals, Second Circuit. *Education:* Reed College (B.A., 1991); University of Pennsylvania (M.A., 1993); University of Chicago (J.D., with high honors, 1997) Order of the Coif. National Science Foundation Fellow, University of Pennsylvania. Law Clerk, the Honorable Diane P. Wood, U.S. Court of Appeals for the Seventh Circuit, 1997-1998; Attorney, U.S. Department of Justice, Civil Division, 1998-2000. Author: Comment: "Chevron, Take Two: Deference to Revised Agency Interpretations of Statutes," 64 U. Chi. L. Rev. 681 (1997); "Dialogue with Archibald Cox: The Case for Campaign Finance Reform," 1 Green Bag 2d 289 (1998); "Dialogue with John Sexton: Legal Education Today and Tomorrow," 3 Green Bag 2d 417 (2000). Co-founder and Executive Editor, The Green Bag, 1997—. Reed College Alumni Board, 2003—; Executive Counsel of the Lawyers Committee for the Shakespeare Theatre, 2004—. (Washington, D.C. Office). ***REPORTED CASES:*** Central Laborers' Pension Fund v. Heinz, 124 S. Ct. 2230 (2004) (briefed and argued). ***PRACTICE AREAS:*** Appellate Practice; Litigation. ***Email:*** dgossett@mayerbrownrowe.com

ROBERT F. GRAY, JR., born Michigan, January 2, 1951; admitted to bar, 1977, California; 1978, Texas; 1979, District of Columbia. *Education:* University of Michigan (B.B.A., 1972; M.B.A., 1974); University of San Diego (J.D., 1977); New York University (LL.M., 1978). *Member:* Houston Bar Association; State Bar of California; State Bar of Texas; The District of Columbia Bar. Fellow, Houston Bar Foundation. (Houston, Texas Office). ***PRACTICE AREAS:*** Corporate; Securities. ***Email:*** rgray@mayerbrownrowe.com

DIANE GREEN-KELLY, born Chicago, Illinois, March 9, 1954; admitted to bar, 1993, Illinois and U.S. District Court, Northern District of Illinois, including Trial Bar; 1998, U.S. Court of Appeals, Seventh Circuit. *Education:* University of Illinois (B.S., 1975); DePaul University (M.S.T., 1978); John Marshall Law School (J.D., magna cum laude, 1993). Certified Public Accountant, 1976. Author: "Direct to Consumer Prescription Drug Advertising in the United States" (2002); "Arbitration Clauses as a Bar to Class Action Litigation," chapter in *Antitrust Class Actions: The Remedy of Choice for Resolving Systemwide Disputes Among Franchisees and Dealers,* ABA Section of Antitrust Law, Vol. II (Spring 1999); "Gift Certificate and Gift Card Programs: The State Law Quagmire," Franchise Law Journal, Vol. 23, No. 4 (Spring 2004); "FTC, Split Circuit Courts Raise Questions About Legality of Pharmaceutical Patent Suite Settlement," Antitrust Quarterly, Issue 5, Q4 (2004); "Jaws: Traps For The Unwary in Discounts and Disparate Pricing," Forum on Franchise, W8 (Oct. 2003). Articles Editor, Franchise Law Journal. *Member:* American Bar Association (Member: Sections on Antitrust; Forum on Franchising); American Health Lawyers Association. ***REPORTED CASES:*** B. Sanfield, Inc. v. Finlay Fine

(This Listing Continued)

Jewelry Corp., 258 F.3d 578 (7th Cir. 2001); B. Sanfield, Inc. v. Finlay Fine Jewelry Corp., 168 F.3d 967 (7th Cir. 1999); In re Synthroid Marketing Litigation, 110 F. Supp. 2d 676 (N.D. Ill. 2000); Collins v. International Dairy Queen, 980 F. Supp. 1469 (1998); Collins v. International Dairy Queen, 939 F. Supp. 875 (1996). ***PRACTICE AREAS:*** Antitrust and Trade Regulation Litigation; Health Care Regulation and Litigation; Products Liability; Franchise and Distribution Law. ***Email:*** dgreenkelly@mayerbrownrowe.com

RICHARD GREGORIAN, admitted to bar, 1993, England and Wales. *Education:* University of Westminister, Upper Second (LLB, Honors); London College of Law (First Class in Society Finals). Author of many articles in leading journals in the restructuring/insolvency and insurance fields. Authored the chapter on Schemes of Arrangement in Tolley's Insolvency looseleaf. Involved in drafting the Insurers' (Reorganisation and Winding Up) Regulations alongside the UK Treasury. (London, England Office). ***PRACTICE AREAS:*** Bankruptcy; Workout; Reorganization. ***Email:*** rgregorian@mayerbrownrowe.com

TERRI TRUITT GRIFFITHS, born Monterey, California, March 2, 1959; admitted to bar, 1988, Texas; 1989, U.S. District Court, Southern and Northern Districts of Texas; 1990, U.S. Court of Appeals, 5th Circuit; 1994, U.S. District Court, Western District of Texas. *Education:* West Texas State University (B.S., 1981); University of Houston (J.D., 1988). Phi Delta Phi (Life Member). Author: "Drafting Seismic Licenses to Avoid Litigation," 7th Annual Oil & Gas Law Institute, 1994. Co-Author: "Arbitrating International Oil and Gas Disputes: Practical Considerations," *International Exploration and Production Ventures,* American Association of Petroleum Geologists, 2000. Vice President, Board of Directors, University of Houston Law Center Alumni Association, 2000-2001. (Houston, Texas Office). ***REPORTED CASES:*** F.D.I.C. v. Brants, 2 F. 3d 147 (5th Cir. TEX 1993); Wilfred Academy of Hair and Beauty Culture, Houston, Tex. v. Southern Ass'n of Colleges and Schools, 957 F.2d 210 (5th Cir. TEX 1992). ***PRACTICE AREAS:*** Commercial Litigation; International Arbitration. ***Email:*** tgriffiths@mayerbrownrowe.com

ULF H. GRUNDMANN, born 1965; admitted to bar, 1995, Germany. *Education:* University of Bonn; University of Munich. Lecturer at Technische Universität Darmstadt. (Frankfurt/Main, Germany Office). ***LANGUAGES:*** English, French. ***PRACTICE AREAS:*** Pharmaceutical and Food Law; Unfair Competition; Intellectual Property. ***Email:*** ugrundmann@mayerbrownrowe.com

SALVATORE GUERRERA, born Bridgeport, Connecticut, August 2, 1962; admitted to bar, 1988, New York. *Education:* Fairfield University (B.A., 1984); University of Pennsylvania (J.D., 1987). (New York, N.Y. Office). ***Email:*** sguerrera@mayerbrownrowe.com

PAUL R. GUPTA, admitted to bar, 1975, New York; 1983, Massachusetts (Not admitted in Illinois). *Education:* Yale University (B.A., magna cum laude, 1971); Harvard Law School (J.D., 1974). Author: "Implementing the Recent Developments in Information Security, Business Continuity and Corporate Governance," Electronic Banking Law and Commerce Report; "Strategic Alliances," The Deal; "The Festo Opinion," European Intellectual Property Review (London); "Lessons Learned from Three Generations of Technology Contracts," Electronic Banking Law & Commerce Report; "Settlement Agreements and IP Disputes," E-Commerce Law & Strategy. (New York, N.Y. Office). ***PRACTICE AREAS:*** Litigation; Information Technology. ***Email:*** pgupta@mayerbrownrowe.com

FREDERIC L. HAHN, born Chicago, Illinois, April 28, 1941; admitted to bar, 1966, Illinois. *Education:* Cornell University (A.B., with distinction in all subjects, 1962; M.B.A., with distinction, 1963); Harvard University (J.D., magna cum laude, 1966). Certified Public Accountant, Illinois (Gold Medal), 1963. ***PRACTICE AREAS:*** Financial Law; Accountants Malpractice; Tax Controversies. ***Email:*** fhahn@mayerbrownrowe.com

C. WELLS HALL III, born 1947; admitted to bar, 1973, North Carolina; 1987, South Carolina. *Education:* North Carolina State University (B.S., with honors, 1970); Duke University (J.D., 1973). *Member:* North Carolina Bar Association (Chairman, Young Lawyers Division, 1984-1985; Chairman, Taxation Section, 1986-1988; Member, Board of Governors, 1989-1992). Fellow, American College of Trust and Estate Counsel (Regent, 2000-2005). Fellow, American College of Tax Counsel. (Charlotte, North Carolina Office). ***PRACTICE AREAS:*** Tax Transactions; Corporate and Business Planning; Estate Planning. ***Email:*** whall@mayerbrownrowe.com

ROBERT HAMILL, admitted to bar, 1986, England and Wales. *Education:* Sheffield University, (with honors, LL.B); Chester College of Law. (London, England Office). ***PRACTICE AREAS:*** Corporate; Securities. ***Email:*** rhamill@mayerbrownrowe.com

LAWRENCE R. HAMILTON, born Chicago, Illinois, April 9, 1957; admitted to bar, 1996, Illinois and U.S. District Court, Northern District of Illinois. *Education:* Harvard University (A.B., summa cum laude, 1977); University of Chicago (J.D., with honors, 1996). ***LANGUAGES:*** French. ***PRACTICE AREAS:*** Securities; Mergers, Acquisitions and Divestitures; Insurance Regulation. ***Email:*** lhamilton@mayerbrownrowe.com

SAMANTHA HAMPSHIRE, admitted to bar, 1990, England. *Education:* University of Birmingham (LL.B., 1987); Lancaster Gate College of Law (1989). (London, England Office). ***PRACTICE AREAS:*** Banking Law; Finance. ***Email:*** shampshire@mayerbrownrowe.com

CAMERON STREET HAMRICK, born Charlotte, North Carolina, November 4, 1958; admitted to bar, 1985, District of Columbia. *Education:* Duke University (B.A., magna cum laude, 1981; J.D., 1985). Co-Author: "The Civil False Claims Act," West Group Briefing Papers, Sept. 2001; "The Contract Disputes Act: Solid Foundation, Magnificent System," Public Contract Law Journal, Summer 1999; "Proving Federal Equitable Adjustment Claims," Federal Publications Inc. Construction Briefings, May 1993. *Member:* American Bar Association (Co-Chair, Access To Information Committee, Public Contract Law Section, 2002-2003). (Washington, D.C., Office). ***PRACTICE AREAS:*** Government Contracts; Civil Fraud; Federal Litigation. ***Email:*** chamrick@mayerbrownrowe.com

MARSHALL E. HANBURY, born Jackson, Mississippi, October 19, 1944; admitted to bar, 1969, Mississippi; 1977, U.S. Supreme Court and U.S.Court of Appeals, Fifth Circuit; 1981, District of Columbia; 1988, U.S.Court of Appeals, Fourth and Eleventh Circuits; 1997, U.S.Court of Appeals, Seventh Circuit; 1998, U.S. District Court, Southern District of Illinois (Not admitted in Illinois). *Education:* University of Mississippi (A.B., 1967); Mississippi College (Jackson) School of Law (LL.B., 1969). General Counsel, Commodity Futures Trading Commission, 1987-1989. ***PRACTICE AREAS:*** Commodities; Securities; Litigation. ***Email:*** mhanbury@mayerbrownrowe.com

KEVIN P. HAWKEN, born Tinley Park, Illinois, February 29, 1956; admitted to bar, 1984, New York; 1990, Illinois. *Education:* University of Illinois at Urbana-Champaign (B.A., 1978); Georgetown University (J.D., cum laude, 1983). Attorney: Shearman & Sterling, 1983-1986; Marks Murase & White, 1986-1989. (London, England Office). ***PRACTICE AREAS:*** Finance. ***Email:*** khawken@mayerbrownrowe.com

DR. MANFRED HEEMANN, born 1963; admitted to bar, 1993, Germany; 1994, New York. *Education:* University of Münster; University of Chicago Law School (LL.M.). (Frankfurt/Main, Germany Office). ***LANGUAGES:*** English. ***PRACTICE AREAS:*** Acquisition Finance; Banks and Banking; Capital Markets. ***Email:*** mheemann@mayerbrownrowe.com

WERNER J. HEIN, born 1942; admitted to bar, 1973, Germany; 1986, New York; 1999, District of Columbia. *Education:* Universities at Berlin, Bonn and Nice; Columbia University (LL.M., 1975). Wilkinson, Barker, Knauer & Quinn, Washington, D.C., 1987-1994. (Washington, D.C. Office). ***LANGUAGES:*** English, German and French. ***PRACTICE AREAS:*** Trade Regulations; Corporate; Information Technology. ***Email:*** whein@mayerbrownrowe.com

ROBERT A. HELMAN, born Chicago, Illinois, January 27, 1934; admitted to bar, 1956, Illinois. *Education:* University of Illinois and Northwestern University (B.S.L., 1954); Northwestern University (LL.B., 1956). Order of the Coif. Associate Editor, Northwestern University Law Review, 1955-1956. ***Email:*** rhelman@mayerbrownrowe.com

NICHOLAS HENCHIE, admitted to bar, 1995, England and Wales. *Education:* University College London (LL.B. with honors, 1991); Guildford College of Law (1992). (London, England Office). ***PRACTICE AREAS:*** Litigation. ***Email:*** nhenchie@mayerbrownrowe.com

FRANK H. HENNEBURG, born 1949; admitted to bar, 1975, Illinois; 1978, District of Columbia. *Education:* Georgetown University (A.B., magna cum laude, 1971); University of Chicago (J.D., 1975). Phi Beta Kappa. *Member:* The District of Columbia Bar. (Washington, D.C. Office). ***PRACTICE AREAS:*** Real Estate. ***Email:*** fhenneburg@mayerbrownrowe.com

MICHAEL L. HERMSEN, born Green Bay, Wisconsin, August 29, 1957; admitted to bar, 1986, Wisconsin; 1995, Illinois. *Education:* Marquette University (B.S., 1980; M.B.A., 1982); University of Wisconsin (J.D., 1986). Assistant Director, 1992-1994, Special Counsel, 1990-1992 and Staff Attorney, 1986-1990, United States Securities and Exchange Commission. ***PRACTICE AREAS:*** Securities; Corporate Law; Mergers, Acquisitions and Divestitures. ***Email:*** mhermsen@mayerbrownrowe.com

DR. RÜDIGER HERRMANN, born 1966; admitted to bar, 1996, Germany. *Education:* Universities of Freiburg im Breisgau, Lausanne, Mainz and Hagen. (Frankfurt/Main, Germany Office). ***LANGUAGES:*** English, French. ***PRACTICE AREAS:*** Unfair Competition; International Law; Biotechnology. ***Email:*** rherrmann@mayerbrownrowe.com

ROBERT M. HERTZBERG, admitted to bar, 1979, California and U.S. District Court, Southern District of California; 1983, U.S. Tax Court and U.S. Supreme Court. *Education:* University of Redlands (B.A., magna cum laude, 1976); Hastings College of Law, University of California (J.D., 1979). (Los Angeles, California Office). ***PRACTICE AREAS:*** Government. ***Email:*** rhertzberg@mayerbrownrowe.com

DR. RALF HESDAHL, born 1957; admitted to bar, 1988, Germany. *Education:* University of Gießen. (Frankfurt/Main, Germany Office). ***LANGUAGES:*** English. ***PRACTICE AREAS:*** Securitization; Banks and Banking; Commercial Law. ***Email:*** rhesdahl@mayerbrownrowe.com

JOHN T. HILDY, born Morris, Illinois, February 19, 1971; admitted to bar, 1996, Illinois, U.S. District Court, Northern District of Illinois and U.S. Tax Court. *Education:* University of Illinois (A.B., 1993); Northwestern University School of Law (J.D., 1996). Certified Public Accountant, Illinois, 1993. ***PRACTICE AREAS:*** Tax Controversies. ***Email:*** jhildy@mayerbrownrowe.com

ANDREAS HILFRICH, born 1960; admitted to bar, 1990, Germany. *Education:* University of Frankfurt am Main. (Frankfurt/Main, Germany Office). ***LANGUAGES:*** English. ***PRACTICE AREAS:*** Zoning, Planning and Land Use; Construction Law; Standard Terms and Conditions. ***Email:*** ahilfrich@mayerbrownrowe.com

DR. MARK C. HILGARD, born 1956; admitted to bar, 1984, Germany. *Education:* University of Freiburg im Breisgau. (Frankfurt/Main, Germany Office). ***LANGUAGES:*** English. ***PRACTICE AREAS:*** Corporate Law; Business Law; Mergers and Acquisitions. ***Email:*** mhilgard@mayerbrownrowe.com

CAROL A. HITSELBERGER, born Washington, D.C., January 7, 1964; admitted to bar, 1989, Illinois. *Education:* Bryn Mawr College (B.A., 1986); University of Pennsylvania (J.D., 1989). ***PRACTICE AREAS:*** Securitization; Structured Finance; Securities. ***Email:*** chitselberger@mayerbrownrowe.com

INGRID HOBBS, admitted to bar, 1994, England and Wales. *Education:* Queens University, Belfast (LL.B. with honors, 1991). (London, England Office). ***Email:*** ihobbs@mayerbrownrowe.com

LOUISE HOBBS, admitted to bar, 1995, England and Wales. *Education:* Cambridge University (New Hall, 1992); Chester College of Law (1993); Hamilton College (1998). (London, England Office). ***LANGUAGES:*** French. ***Email:*** lhobbs@mayerbrownrowe.com

DEBRA B. HOFFMAN, born Kenosha, Wisconsin, December 16, 1955; admitted to bar, 1986, Illinois. *Education:* Ripon College (B.A., with honors, 1978); DePaul University (J.D., with honors, 1986). Author: "Securities Law Aspects of Employee Benefit Plans," ICLE, 1992 and Supplement, 1997; "Pensions and Employee Benefits, How to Buy a U.S. Business," 1999, 2001 and 2002. ***PRACTICE AREAS:*** ERISA; Executive Compensation; Employee Benefits. ***Email:*** dhoffman@mayerbrownrowe.com

DR. HANS HOFMANN, born 1946; admitted to bar, 1974, Germany. *Education:* University of Frankfurt am Main. Notary Public, 1989. (Frankfurt/Main, Germany Office).

(This Listing Continued)

MAYER, BROWN, ROWE & MAW LLP, Chicago—Continued

LANGUAGES: English, French. ***PRACTICE AREAS:*** Commercial Real Estate; Corporate and Commercial Law; Mergers and Acquisitions. ***Email:*** hhofmann@mayerbrownrowe.com

FIONA HOLLAND, born Glasgow, United Kingdom, November 21, 1969; admitted to bar, 1994, Scotland, United Kingdom; 1997, England. *Education:* Edinburgh University, Scotland (LLB., with honors, 1991; DIPLP, 1992). (London, England Office). ***PRACTICE AREAS:*** Corporate. ***Email:*** fholland@eu.mayerbrownrowe.com

JAMES D. HOLZHAUER, born New York, N.Y., May 18, 1948; admitted to bar, 1980, Washington; 1984, District of Columbia; 1990, Illinois. *Education:* New York University (B.A., 1970); University of Michigan (J.D., magna cum laude, 1980). Law Professor, University of Chicago Law School, 1985-1988. Law Clerk to: Hon. Robert A. Ainsworth, U.S. Court of Appeals, Fifth Circuit, 1980-1981; Chief Justice Warren E. Burger, U.S. Supreme Court, 1981-1982. ***PRACTICE AREAS:*** Appellate Practice; Employment Law; Professional Liability. ***Email:*** jholzhauer@mayerbrownrowe.com

THOMAS R. HOOD, born Omaha, Nebraska, August 27, 1947; admitted to bar, 1973, Minnesota; 1975, New York and District of Columbia; 1978, Nebraska. *Education:* Yale University (B.A., 1969); University of Minnesota (J.D., cum laude, 1973); New York University (LL.M., 1974). (New York, N.Y. Office). ***SPECIAL AGENCIES:*** Counselor to the IRS Commissioner, 1990-1993. ***PRACTICE AREAS:*** Taxation. ***Email:*** thood@mayerbrownrowe.com

DIANA L. HOOVER, born El Campo, TX, December 18, 1958; admitted to bar, 1993, Texas; 1994, U.S. District Court, Southern District of Texas; 1995, U.S. District Court, Northern District of Texas; 1996, U.S. District Court, Eastern District of Texas; 2002, U.S. District Court, District of Colorado. *Education:* Southwest Texas State University (B.S., 1980); University of Houston (J.D., magna cum laude, 1993). Chief Note and Comment Editor, University of Houston Law Review, 1992-1993. (Houston, Texas Office). ***PRACTICE AREAS:*** Litigation; Employment Law; Class Action Defense. ***Email:*** ddavis@mayerbrownrowe.com

CHARLES M. HORN, born Boston, Massachusetts, September 28, 1951; admitted to bar, 1976, District of Columbia; 1977, U.S. District Court for the District of Columbia; U.S. Court of Appeals for the District of Columbia Circuit; 1980, U.S. Supreme Court. *Education:* Stanford University; Harvard University (A.B., magna cum laude, 1973); Cornell University (J.D., 1976). (Washington, D.C. Office). ***PRACTICE AREAS:*** Banks and Banking; Finance; Securities. ***Email:*** chorn@mayerbrownrowe.com

JOANNA K. HORSNAIL, born Vancouver, British Columbia, Canada, March 17, 1971; admitted to bar, 1996, Illinois. *Education:* University of Colorado at Boulder (B.S., 1993); Chicago-Kent College of Law (J.D., 1996). Order of the Coif. Chicago-Kent Law Review. *Member:* Women in Public Finance (President). ***PRACTICE AREAS:*** Public Finance; State Government Law; Local Government Law. ***Email:*** jhorsnail@mayerbrownrowe.com

JONATHAN HOSIE, admitted to bar, 1984, England and Wales. *Education:* University of Wales, Cardiff (LL.B., Hons., 1980); University of London, King's College (M.Sc., 1993). (London, England Office). ***LANGUAGES:*** French. ***PRACTICE AREAS:*** Construction and Engineering. ***Email:*** jhosie@mayerbrownrowe.com

NIGEL L. HOWARD, born Slough, Britain, 1965; admitted to bar, 1990, England and Wales (Solicitor); 1993, New York. *Education:* Lancaster University, Lancaster, Britain (B.A., with honors, 1987), University of London (LL.M., Intellectual Property Law, 1991). Author: "Outsourcing and ASP Arrangements," PLI Publications, 2002; "New Developments in Outsourced Manufacturing Arrangements," University of Texas, 2002; "Comparison of US and European Patent Law on the Protection of Software," Patent World 2002; "How to Use Patent Law to the Advantage of Open Source Software Developers," Intellectual Property Strategist, June 2001; "E-Commerce in Europe," New York Law Journal - Special Feature, Summer 1999. (New York, N.Y. Office). ***PRACTICE AREAS:*** Corporate Law; Securities. ***Email:*** nhoward@mayerbrownrowe.com

DAVID M. HUDANISH, born Perth Amboy, New Jersey, 1965; admitted to bar, 1991, New Jersey; 1992, New York and District of Columbia. *Education:* Georgetown University (B.A., magna cum laude, 1987; J.D., cum laude, 1991). (New York, N.Y. Office). ***PRACTICE AREAS:*** Technology; Intellectual Property; Corporate Law. ***Email:*** dhudanish@mayerbrownrowe.com

CARRIE KIGER HUFF, born McKeesport, Pennsylvania, June 12, 1949; admitted to bar, 1985, Illinois and U.S. District Court, Northern District of Illinois. *Education:* Pennsylvania State University (B.A., with high distinction, 1971); University of Chicago (M.A., with honors, 1972; J.D., 1985). *Member:* Chicago Council of Lawyers (President, 2005—). ***PRACTICE AREAS:*** Civil Litigation; Religious Institutions; Religious Institutions Liability. ***Email:*** chuff@mayerbrownrowe.com

ROBERT F. HUGI, born Kansas City, Missouri, March 2, 1958; admitted to bar, 1986, Illinois. *Education:* Northwestern University (B.S., 1980); University of Chicago (J.D., 1986). ***Email:*** rhugi@mayerbrownrowe.com

CHARLES P. HURLEY, born Cleveland, Ohio, June 24, 1955; admitted to bar, 1982, Ohio. *Education:* Kent State University (B.A., 1979); Case Western Reserve University (J.D., 1982). Law Clerk to The Honorable Alvin I. Krenzler, U.S. District Court for the Northern District of Ohio. (Washington, D.C. Office). ***PRACTICE AREAS:*** Taxation; Litigation. ***Email:*** churley@mayerbrownrowe.com

MICHAEL HUTCHINSON, born Durham, England, September 22, 1966; admitted to bar, 1991, United Kingdom. *Education:* University of Durham, England (B.A., 1988); The College of Law, Chester, England (LSF, 1989). Leading Individual for Environment in the Chambers Legal Directory 2001-2002. Senior Lecturer, Law University of North London, 1994-1996. (London, England Office). ***Email:*** mhutchinson@eu.mayerbrownrowe.com

FREDERICK D. HYMAN, born Brooklyn, New York; admitted to bar, 1993, New York and U.S. District Court, Southern District of New York. *Education:* University of Vermont (B.A., cum laude, 1989); Hofstra University (J.D., with distinction, 1992). Member, Hofstra Law Review. (New York, N.Y. Office). ***PRACTICE AREAS:*** Business Reorganization; Bankruptcy. ***Email:*** fhyman@mayerbrownrowe.com

SHARON A. ISRAEL, admitted to bar, 1994, Texas; registered to practice before U.S. Patent and Trademark Office. *Education:* Massachusetts Institute of Technology (B.S., Electrical Engineering, 1986); Emory University School of Business Administration (M.B.A., 1991); Emory University School of Law (J.D., 1991). (Houston, Texas Office). ***PRACTICE AREAS:*** Intellectual Property; Patent; Litigation. ***Email:*** sisrael@mayerbrownrowe.com

DAVID IVE, born 1950; admitted to bar, 1974, England. *Education:* Birmingham University. *Member:* British Branch of the International Fiscal Association. (London, England Office). ***PRACTICE AREAS:*** Tax Law. ***Email:*** dive@mayerbrownrowe.com

REBECCA L. JACKSON, born September 16, 1951; admitted to bar, 1978, District of Columbia; U.S. District Court, District of Columbia; U.S. Court of Appeals for the District of Columbia; U.S. Court of Federal Claims. *Education:* University of Missouri (B.S., with honors, 1972); Georgetown University (J.D., cum laude, 1978). *Member:* Bar Association of the District of Columbia (Chair, Young Lawyers Section, 1987-1988; Board Member, 1987-1991). (Washington, D.C. Office). ***PRACTICE AREAS:*** Health Care; Technology Outsourcing. ***Email:*** rljackson@mayerbrownrowe.com

CARYN L. JACOBS, born Chicago, Illinois, March 3, 1958; admitted to bar, 1984, Illinois and U.S. District Court, Northern District of Illinois; 1986, U.S. Court of Appeals, Eighth Circuit; 1987, U.S. Court of Appeals, Seventh Circuit. *Education:* Stanford University (A.B., with distinction, honors in Humanities, 1980), Phi Beta Kappa; Harvard University (J.D., cum laude, 1983). ***Email:*** cjacobs@mayerbrownrowe.com

PHILIPPA SUSAN JAMES, born 1956; admitted to bar, 1980, England. *Education:* University of Wales. (London, England Office). ***PRACTICE AREAS:*** Pensions Law. ***Email:*** pjames@mayerbrownrowe.com

JOHN A. JANICIK, born East St. Louis, Illinois, May 2, 1957; admitted to bar, 1986, Illinois and U.S. District Court, Northern District of Illinois. *Education:* Knox College (B.A., 1979); Loyola University of Chicago (J.D., 1986). Legislative Liaison, Illinois Department of Commerce and Community Affairs, 1982-1983. Assistant to Governor James R. Thompson, Chicago and Springfield, Illinois, 1981-1982. Member, Board of Directors, Better Business Bureau of Chicago and Northern Illinois, Inc., 1995—. Member, State Mandates Board of Review, State of Illinois, 1994—. Member, Capital Development Board, State of Illinois, 1990-1992. Chairman, Board of Ethics, State of Illinois, 1988-1989. ***Email:*** jjanicik@mayerbrownrowe.com

ROBERT M. JENKINS, III, born Fort Lauderdale, Florida, January 14, 1947; admitted to bar, 1974, California; 1975, District of Columbia and U.S. District Court, District of Columbia; Court of Appeals, Second, Third, Sixth and District of Columbia Circuits; 1980, Supreme Court; 1981, U.S. Court of Federal Claims. *Education:* Harvard College (B.A., 1969); University of California at Berkeley (J.D., with honors, 1974). Order of the Coif. Chief Note and Comment Editor, California Law Review, 1972-1974. Law Clerk to Hon. Malcolm R. Wilkey, U.S. Court of Appeals for the District of Columbia Circuit, 1974-1975. (Washington, D.C. Office). ***LANGUAGES:*** Spanish. ***PRACTICE AREAS:*** Regulated Industries; Government Contracts; Health Care. ***Email:*** rmjenkins@mayerbrownrowe.com

WILLIAM EDWARD JEWITT, born London, England, May 6, 1966; admitted to bar, 1991, England. *Education:* University of Bristol, England (LL.B., 1988); The College of Law, London, England (J.D., 1989). Author, Pensions Bulletin, Practical Law Magazine. (London, England Office). ***PRACTICE AREAS:*** Pension Fund Investments. ***Email:*** ejewitt@mayerbrownrowe.com

JAMES J. JOCHUM, born Dubuque, Iowa, June 16, 1965; admitted to bar, 1990, Wisconsin and U.S. District Court, Eastern and Western Districts of Wisconsin. *Education:* University of Iowa (B.A., with distinction, 1987); University of Iowa College of Law (J.D., with high honors, 1990). Co-Author: with Senator Grassley, "Reflections on the 1996 Farm Bill," Drake Journal of Agricultural Law, Volume 1, No. 1, Spring 1996. (Washington, D.C. Office). ***PRACTICE AREAS:*** Government and Global Trade. ***Email:*** jjochum@mayerbrownrowe.com

TREFOR MORGAN JOHN, born Stanmore, Middlesex, England, August 19, 1954; admitted to bar, 1978, England & Wales. *Education:* University of Sheffield, England (B.A., with honors, 1975); The College of Law, London, England (J.D., 1978). (London, England Office). ***LANGUAGES:*** English and French. ***PRACTICE AREAS:*** Corporate Tax Planning; Tax Shelters. ***Email:*** tjohn@eu.mayerbrownrowe.com

EDWARD D. JOHNSON, admitted to bar, 1989, New York; 1997, California; U.S. District Court, Southern and Eastern Districts of New York; U.S. Court of Appeals, Second Circuit. *Education:* University of Virginia (B.A., with highest distinction, 1983); Yale Law School (J.D., 1986). (Palo Alto, California Office). ***PRACTICE AREAS:*** Litigation. ***Email:*** wjohnson@mayerbrownrowe.com

ANITA JONES, born Epsom, Surrey, United Kingdom, June 15, 1966; admitted to bar, 1991, London, United Kingdom. *Education:* University College Cardiff (LLB., 1988); Guildford College of Law (J.D., 1991). (London, England Office). ***Email:*** anita.jones@eu.mayerbrownrowe.com

ERIKA Z. JONES, born Washington, D.C., June 10, 1955; admitted to bar, 1980, District of Columbia; 1987, U.S. Court of Appeals, District of Columbia Circuit and U.S. Supreme Court; 1992, U.S. Court of Appeals, Fourth Circuit; 1997, U.S. Court of Appeals, Ninth and Seventh Circuits; 2003, U.S. Court of Appeals, Second Circuit. *Education:* Georgetown University (A.B., magna cum laude, 1976; J.D., 1980). Chief Counsel, 1985-1989 and Special Counsel, 1981-1985, National Highway Traffic Safety Administration, Department of Transportation. (Washington, D.C. Office). ***Email:*** ejones@mayerbrownrowe.com

PAUL A. JORISSEN, born Detroit, Michigan, March 29, 1962; admitted to bar, 1991, Illinois. *Education:* University of Michigan (B.B.A., with distinction, 1987); Walsh College (M.S.T., with honors, 1991); Loyola University of Chicago (J.D., magna cum laude, 1991). Certified Public Accountant, Michigan, 1985. Author: "Challenge to Nonprofit Hos-

(This Listing Continued)

pital Mergers Under Section 7 of the Clayton Act," Loyola U. of Chicago Law Journal, Volume 22, Issue 2. (New York, N.Y. Office). **Email:** pjorissen@mayerbrownrowe.com

JAMES J. JUNEWICZ, born Erie, Pennsylvania, October 1, 1950; admitted to bar, 1977, Pennsylvania; 1978, District of Columbia; 1984, Illinois. *Education:* Georgetown University (B.S.F.S., 1972); Duquesne University (J.D., 1976); New York University (LL.M., 1978). Author: "Regulation FD: The SEC Raises the Stakes in Issuer-Analyst Communications," Securities & Commodities Regulation, Vol. 33, No. 20, November 28, 2000; "Tender Offers for Debt Securities," Insights, January 1996. Director, Pacific Gateway Exchange, Inc. (NASDAQ); "Handling Wall Street Analysts," Insights, January 1995. **Email:** jjunewicz@mayerbrownrowe.com

DR. HANS-GEORG KAMANN, born 1968; admitted to bar, 1998, Germany. *Education:* Universities of Passau and Bonn. (Frankfurt/Main, Germany Office). ***LANGUAGES:*** English and French. ***PRACTICE AREAS:*** European Union Law and Litigation; International Trade Law and Regulation; Antitrust. **Email:** hgkamann@mayerbrownrowe.com

IVAN P. KANE, born Detroit, Michigan, August 19, 1956; admitted to bar, 1981, Illinois. *Education:* University of Chicago (B.A., 1978; J.D., 1981). ***PRACTICE AREAS:*** Real Estate; Finance; Land Use. **Email:** ikane@mayerbrownrowe.com

MICHAEL ("MICKEY") KANTOR, born Nashville, Tennessee, August 7, 1939; admitted to bar, 1968, Florida; 1975, California; 1978, District of Columbia. *Education:* Vanderbilt University (B.A., 1961); Georgetown University (LL.B., 1968). United States Secretary of Commerce, 1996-1997. United States Trade Representative, 1993-1996. Member, Board of Directors: Pharmacia Corporation, Monsanto Company; Korea First Bank; National Association of Public Interest Lawyers. Member, Board of Visitors, Georgetown Law School. Trustee, International Commercial Diplomacy Project. Partner, Manatt, Phelps & Phillips; South Florida Migrant Legal Services; Migrant Legal Action Program. [U.S. Naval Officer, 1961-1965]. (Washington, D.C. Office). ***PRACTICE AREAS:*** Financial Services Law; E-Commerce. **Email:** mkantor@mayerbrownrowe.com

ALVIN CHARLES KATZ, born Chicago, Illinois, January 18, 1952; admitted to bar, 1977, Illinois. *Education:* University of Michigan (B.A., magna cum laude, honors in Economics, 1974); Stanford University (J.D., 1977). ***PRACTICE AREAS:*** Real Estate; Partnership Law; Joint Ventures. **Email:** akatz@mayerbrownrowe.com

J. BRADLEY KECK, born New York, N.Y., April 17, 1971; admitted to bar, 1996, Illinois. *Education:* University of Notre Dame (B.A., 1993); The Ohio State University (J.D., with honors, 1996) Order of the Coif. ***PRACTICE AREAS:*** Banking and Finance; Securitization. **Email:** jkeck@mayerbrownrowe.com

CHARLES S. KELLEY, born Tulsa, Oklahoma, January 16, 1963; admitted to bar, 1991, Texas; 1992, U.S. District Court, Southern District of Texas. *Education:* University of Texas (B.S.M.E., 1985; J.D., with high honors, 1991). Tau Beta Pi; Order of the Coif. Executive Editor, Texas Law Review. (Houston, Texas Office). **Email:** ckelley@mayerbrownrowe.com

CHRISTOPHER J. KELLY, admitted to bar, 1983, Illinois; 1990, U.S. Court of Appeals, Fourth Circuit; 2001, District of Columbia; 2003, U.S. Court of Appeals, Federal Circuit. *Education:* Harvard University (A.B., magna cum laude, 1980); Columbia University (J.D., 1983). Law Clerk to Judge John A. Terry, District of Columbia Court of Appeals, 1983-1984. Antitrust Division, U.S. Department of Justice, 1984-2001 (Trial Attorney, Chicago Field Office, 1984-1988; Trial Attorney, AT&T Decree Enforcement Task Force, 1988; Special Assistant, Office of Operations, 1988-1990; Trial Attorney, Communications & Finance Section, 1990-1993; Assistant Chief, Civil Task Force I, 1994-1995; Acting Chief, Civil Task Force I, 1995; Senior Counsel for Intellectual Property to the Assistant Attorney General, 1996-2001). Special Counsel, Kaye Scholer LLP, Washington, DC, 2001-2003. *Member:* American Bar Association (Member, Sections on: Antitrust; Intellectual Property); American Intellectual Property Law Association; Intellectual Property Owners Association. (Washington, D.C. Office). ***LANGUAGES:*** German, Italian. ***PRACTICE AREAS:*** Litigation; Antitrust and Trade Regulation; Intellectual Property. **Email:** cjkelly@mayerbrownrowe.com

ROBERT A. KELMAN, born New York, N.Y., October 30, 1945; admitted to bar, 1971, Illinois. *Education:* Middlebury College (A.B., 1968); University of Chicago (J.D., 1971). **Email:** rkelman@mayerbrownrowe.com

TERRY D. KERNELL, born Oklahoma City, Oklahoma, October 1, 1966; admitted to bar, 1991, Texas. *Education:* University of Oklahoma (B.A., 1988); Baylor University (J.D., with honors, 1991). (Houston, Texas Office). **Email:** tkernell@mayerbrownrowe.com

MICHAEL F. KERR, born Cleveland, Ohio, February 28, 1953; admitted to bar, 1982, Illinois and U.S. District Court, Northern District of Illinois; 1995, California and U.S. District Court, Central District of California; 1996, U.S. District Court, Northern District of California; 1997, U.S. District Court, Southern and Eastern Districts of California and U.S. Court of Appeals, Ninth Circuit. *Education:* Boston College (A.B, summa cum laude, 1974); University of Chicago (A.M., 1975; J.D., 1982). (Los Angeles, California Office). ***PRACTICE AREAS:*** Litigation. **Email:** mkerr@mayerbrown.com

WILLIAM H. KIEKHOFER, III, born Madison, Wisconsin, June 19, 1952; admitted to bar, 1980, California and U.S. District Court, Central District of California; 1982, U.S. District Court, Northern and Southern Districts of California; 1983, U.S. District Court, Eastern District of California; 1994, U.S. Court of Appeal, Ninth Circuit. *Education:* University of Wisconsin-Madison (B.A., with distinction, 1976); University of Southern California Law Center (J.D., 1980). Order of the Coif. Recipient: American Jurisprudence Awards: Bankruptcy & Constitutional Law. Author: "Bank of America National Trust and Savings Association v. 203 North LaSalle Street Partnership: The New Value Exception to the Absolute Priority Rule Is Alive, But Not Well," The Metropolitan Corporate Counsel, June 1999 and Century City Lawyer, Volume 8, Number 6 July/August 1999. Co-Author of chapter entitled "Bankruptcy and Licensing". Patent & High Technology Licensing, Practicing Law Institute, 2001. (Los Angeles, California Office). **Email:** wkiekhofer@mayerbrownrowe.com

ROGER J. KILEY, JR., born Chicago, Illinois, February 9, 1937; admitted to bar, 1966, Illinois, U.S. District Court, Northern District of Illinois and U.S. Court of Appeals, Seventh Circuit. *Education:* University of Notre Dame (B.A., 1958); Loyola University School of Law (J.D., cum laude, 1966). General Counsel, City Colleges of Chicago, 1969-1971; Private law practice, 1971-1976; Judge, Circuit Court Cook County, 1976-1989; Partner, Mayer Brown 1989-1995, 1997—; Chief of Staff, Mayor Richard M. Daley, 1995-1996; Senior Vice Present, General Counsel, SBC-midwest, 2001—. [Pilot, U.C.M.C., 1958-1962; Pilot, U.S.M.C.R., 1962-1967]. (Also Senior Vice President, General Counsel and Secretary, SBC-midwest). ***PRACTICE AREAS:*** Government (75%); Telecommunications (25%). **Email:** rkiley@mayerbrownrowe.com

JIN K. KIM, born Seoul, Korea, May 19, 1969; admitted to bar, 1995, New York. *Education:* Dartmouth College (A.B., 1991); University of Chicago (J.D., 1994). (New York, N.Y. Office). ***PRACTICE AREAS:*** Corporate Law; Securities; Finance. **Email:** jkkim@mayerbrownrowe.com

THOMAS S. KIRIAKOS, born Marshalltown, Iowa, October, 13, 1956; admitted to bar, 1981, Iowa (Certificate of Exemption, Iowa Admission); 1983, Illinois; 1984, U.S. District Court for the Northern District of Illinois; 1988, U.S. District Court for the Eastern District of Wisconsin; 1996, U.S. Court of Appeals, Seventh Circuit; 1996, U.S. Court of Appeals, Fourth Circuit; 1998, U.S. Supreme Court. *Education:* Grinnell College (B.A., 1978); University of Iowa (J.D., 1981). Principal author of "Chapter S: Bankruptcy," Securitization of Financial Assets, Aspen Law & Bus. (2d ed. 1996); co-author of "Has David Bowie Started a New Era of Celebrity Securitization?" Vol. 4, No. 5 of The Financier (Dec. 1997). ***PRACTICE AREAS:*** Bankruptcy; Loan Restructuring; Workouts; Securitization. **Email:** tkiriakos@mayerbrownrowe.com

THOMAS L. KITTLE-KAMP, born Milwaukee, Wisconsin, October 29, 1960; admitted to bar, 1988, Illinois; 1989, U.S. District Court, Northern District of Illinois; 1991, U.S. Tax Court; 1994, U.S. Court of Appeals, Ninth Circuit; 1995, U.S. Court of Appeals, Seventh and Tenth Circuits; 1998, U.S. Court of Federal Claims. *Education:* Bradley University (B.A., 1982); Northwestern University (J.D., 1988). Order of the Coif. Member, Northwestern Law Review. Co-Author: *Federal Income Taxation of Intellectual Properties and Intangible Assets,* Warren, Gorham & Lamont, 1997. ***PRACTICE AREAS:*** Tax Controversies; Tax Litigation. **Email:** tkittlekamp@mayerbrownrowe.com

DR. INGO KLEUTGENS, born 1965; admitted to bar, 1995. *Education:* University of Cologne. Tax Consultant, 2001. (Frankfurt/Main, Germany Office). ***LANGUAGES:*** English. ***PRACTICE AREAS:*** Taxation; Securitization; Structured Finance. **Email:** ikleutgens@mayerbrownrowe.com

MARC L. KLYMAN, born Detroit, Michigan, May 1, 1963; admitted to bar, 1988, Illinois. *Education:* University of Michigan (B.A., with highest distinction, 1985); Harvard University (J.D., cum laude, 1988). Co-author: "Credit and Liquidity Enhancement," Chapter 8 of Securitization of Financial Assets (Aspen Law & Business); "Investment by Insurance Companies," Chapter 17.03 of Securitization of Financial Assets (Aspen Law & Business). Moderator: "The Benefits of Third Party Guarantees, Wraps and Insurance in Structuring and Selling Deals," 3rd Annual Forum on Equipment/Auto Finance and Lease Securitization (Strategic Research Institute, 2002). Panelist: "Sleeping Easier at Night: Monoline Wraps, Residual Value Insurance and Other Insurance Guarantees," Seminar on Equipment Finance and Lease Securitization (Strategic Research Institute, 2001); "Follow the Yellow Brick Road - The Expert's Guide to Successfully Completing Your First Lease Securitization," Seminar on Equipment Lease Securitization (Strategic Research Institute, 2000). ***LANGUAGES:*** Spanish. ***PRACTICE AREAS:*** Securitization; Secured Lending. **Email:** mklyman@mayerbrownrowe.com

ELIZABETH M. KNOBLOCK, born February 2, 1955; admitted to bar, 1979, District of Columbia; 1988, New York. *Education:* Stetson University (B.A., magna cum laude, 1976); Georgetown University (J.D., 1979; LL.M., 1989); Nova University of Florida (M.B.A., 1993). (Washington, D.C. Office). ***PRACTICE AREAS:*** Corporate Law; Securities. **Email:** eknoblock@mayerbrownrowe.com

WILLIAM H. KNULL, III, born Coronado, California, April 14, 1948; admitted to bar, 1978, New York; 1987, Texas; U.S. District Court, Southern, Northern, Western and Eastern Districts of Texas and Southern, Eastern and Northern Districts of New York; U.S. Court of Appeals, Second and Fifth Circuits. *Education:* Yale University (B.A., magna cum laude, departmental honors in Political Science, 1970); University of Virginia (J.D., 1977). Member, Advisory Board, Institute of Transnational Arbitration. [Lieut., U.S. Navy, 1970-1974]. (Houston, Texas Office). ***PRACTICE AREAS:*** Complex Civil Litigation; Arbitration. **Email:** wknull@mayerbrownrowe.com

KENNETH E. KOHLER, born Auburn, California, May 28, 1953; admitted to bar, 1981, California. *Education:* University of California, Berkeley (B.S., with highest honors, 1977); Yale University (J.D., 1980). (Los Angeles, California Office). **Email:** kkohler@mayerbrownrowe.com

ANNE MARIE KONOPACK, born Joliet, Illinois, September 22, 1969; admitted to bar, 1994, Illinois. *Education:* Loyola University (B.B.A., magna cum laude, 1991; J.D., magna cum laude, 1994). ***PRACTICE AREAS:*** Tax. **Email:** akonopack@mayerbrownrowe.com

DAVID S. KRAKOFF, born Columbus, Ohio, March 16, 1949; admitted to bar, 1976, District of Columbia; 1977, U. S. District Court for the District of Columbia and U.S. Court of Appeals for the District of Columbia Circuit; 1979, U. S. Supreme Court; 2002, U. S. Court of Appeals, Fifth Circuit. *Education:* Dartmouth College (A.B., 1971); Antioch School of Law (J.D., 1975). Author: "For Client's Sake: Under Assault From Government And The ABA, The Privilege Needs Defenders," Legal Times, October 1, 2001; " Environmental Crimes Case, From Pretrial Proceedings to Sentencing Guidelines," American Bar Association, July 1999; " Environmental Crimes: Recent Trends," 1999 Wiley Environmental Law Update, June 1999; "The Hidden Cost to Corporate Settlements of Environmental Prosecutions" Is It Worth the Price?," The Environmental Corporate Counsel Report, January 10, 1999; "Environmental Reporting: New Criminal Exposure," The Metropolitan Corporate Counsel, March 1998. (Washington, D.C. Office). ***PRACTICE AREAS:*** Litigation. **Email:** dkrakoff@mayerbrownrowe.com

JASON H. P. KRAVITT, born Chicago, Illinois, January 19, 1948; admitted to bar, 1974, Illinois; 2002, New York. *Education:* Johns Hopkins University (A.B., 1969); Harvard University (J.D., cum laude, 1972); Cambridge University (Diploma, Comp. Law, 1973), Cambridge, England. Author: Securitization of Financial Assets, 2nd Ed. 1996. (New York, N.Y. Office). ***LANGUAGES:*** French. ***PRACTICE AREAS:*** Securitization; Structured Finance; Banking Regulation. **Email:** jkravitt@mayerbrownrowe.com

(This Listing Continued)

MAYER, BROWN, ROWE & MAW LLP, Chicago—Continued

SIMEON M. KRIESBERG, born Washington, D.C., June 4, 1951; admitted to bar, 1977, District of Columbia; 1978, U.S. District Court, District of Columbia and U.S. Court of Appeals, District of Columbia Circuit; 1979, U.S. Court of International Trade; 1981, U.S. Court of Appeals for the Federal Circuit; 1982, U.S. Supreme Court. *Education:* Harvard College (A.B., magna cum laude, 1973); Woodrow Wilson School of Public and International Affairs, Princeton University (M.P.A., 1977); Yale Law School (J.D., 1977). Author: "Toward the Twenty-First Century: Trends in U.S. Trade Remedies," in Private Investment Abroad, Matthew Bender, 1993. Guest Scholar, Brookings Institution, 1992-1993. Professorial Lecturer, Nitze School of Advanced International Studies, Johns Hopkins University, 1991-1993. Vice President and General Counsel, 1985-1987, Senior Counsel for International Trade, 1983-1985, Sears World Trade, Inc. Associate, Leva, Hawes, Symington, Martin & Oppenheimer, 1977-1983. Member: Roster of Dispute Resolution Panelists Under NAFTA (by appointment of U.S. Government), 1996-2004; Roster of Dispute Resolution Panelists under U.S.-Canada Free-Trade Agreement (by appointment of U.S. Government), 1990-1992. (Washington, D.C. Office). ***PRACTICE AREAS:*** International Trade Regulation; International Business Transactions; International Investment. ***Email:*** skriesberg@mayerbrownrowe.com

ROBERT J. KRISS, born Cleveland, Ohio, December 15, 1953; admitted to bar, 1978, Illinois and U.S. District Court, Northern District of Illinois; 1982, U.S. Court of Appeals, 7th Circuit; 1983, U.S. District Court, Northern District of Illinois including Trial Bar; 1984, U.S. Court of Appeals, 5th Circuit; 2000, U.S. Court of Appeals, 11th Circuit; 2001, U.S. Court of Appeals, 8th Circuit. *Education:* Cornell University (B.A., summa cum laude, 1975); Harvard Law School (J.D., cum laude, 1978). ***PRACTICE AREAS:*** Commercial Litigation; Information Technology; Securities; Consumer Class Action Defense. ***Email:*** rkriss@mayerbrown.com

JONATHAN D. KRON, born August 4, 1960; admitted to bar, 1985, Illinois; 1991, Wisconsin. *Education:* University of Illinois (B.S., with high honors, 1982; J.D., 1985). Phi Kappa Phi. ***PRACTICE AREAS:*** Leveraged Leasing; Secured Lending; Workouts. ***Email:*** jkron@mayerbrownrowe.com

HERBERT W. KRUEGER, born Milwaukee, Wisconsin, April 20, 1948; admitted to bar, 1974, Florida; 1975, Illinois and U.S. District Court, Northern District of Illinois. *Education:* University of Wisconsin (B.A., 1970); University of Chicago (J.D., 1974). ***Email:*** hkrueger@mayerbrownrowe.com

WILLIAM R. KUCERA, born Evanston, Illinois, May 11, 1972; admitted to bar, 1997, Illinois. *Education:* Colgate University (B.A., magna cum laude, 1994); Northwestern University (J.D., cum laude, 1997). Order of the Coif. ***Email:*** wkucera@mayerbrownrowe.com

KATHRYN A. KUSSKE, born St. Paul, Minnesota, June 16, 1958; admitted to bar, 1986, Maryland; 1987, District of Columbia. *Education:* Georgetown University (B.S.F.S., magna cum laude, 1980); American University (J.D., magna cum laude, 1985). Law Clerk, U.S. Court of Appeals for the District of Columbia Circuit, 1985-1986. Attorney, Clifford & Warnke, 1986-1991. (Washington, D.C. Office). ***Email:*** kkusske@mayerbrownrowe.com

MICHAEL E. LACKEY, JR., born Hopkinsville, Kentucky, May 3, 1961; admitted to bar, 1993, Florida; 1994, District of Columbia; 1999, U.S. Supreme Court. *Education:* Massachusetts Institute of Technology (B.S., 1983); George Washington University (J.D., with high honors, 1993). Order of the Coif. Articles Editor, The George Washington University Law Review, 1992-93. Law Clerk to Hon. Jacques L. Wiener, U.S. Court of Appeals Fifth Circuit, 1994-95. Listed in: Who's Who in American Law; Who's Who in the World. Adjunct Professor, Advanced Appellate Advocacy, The George Washington University Law School, 1995—. Associate Independent Counsel, 1997-1998. *Member:* Federal (Chair, Antitrust and Trade Regulation Section, 2003—) and American Bar Associations. [Lieutenant, U.S. Navy, 1983-1990; "Top Gun," 1987]. (Washington, D.C. Office). ***PRACTICE AREAS:*** Complex Civil Litigation; Criminal Defense Litigation; Appellate Litigation; Antitrust; Government Contracts. ***Email:*** mlackey@mayerbrownrowe.com

DOUGLAS J. LANDY, born New York, N.Y., September 22, 1967; admitted to bar, 1994, New York; 1995, U.S. District Court, Southern and Eastern Districts of New York. *Education:* University of Pennsylvania (B.A., 1989); Boston College Law School (J.D., with honors, 1993). (New York, N.Y. Office). ***PRACTICE AREAS:*** Banking and Finance. ***Email:*** dlandy@mayerbrownrowe.com

ANGELA R. LANG, born Olney, Illinois, July 2, 1971; admitted to bar, 1995, Indiana; 1999, Illinois. *Education:* Indiana University (B.S., highest distinction, 1992; J.D., summa cum laude, 1995). Order of the Coif. Associate, 1993-1994 and Managing Editor, 1994-1995, Indiana Law Journal. Author: Note, Mandatory Disclosure Can Improve the Discovery System," 70 Indiana Law Journal 657, 1995. Co-Author: "Skyrocketing Penalties Imposed for Noncompliance with Premerger Notification," Indiana Journal of Commerce & Industry, June 15-July 14, 1997. ***Email:*** arlang@mayerbrownrowe.com

DR. JÖRG MICHAEL LANG, born 1957; admitted to bar, 1988, Germany. *Education:* Business Apprenticeship Diploma, 1978; University of Frankfurt am Main. (Frankfurt/Main, Germany Office). ***LANGUAGES:*** German and English. ***PRACTICE AREAS:*** Commercial Real Estate; Corporate Law; Mergers and Acquisitions. ***Email:*** jlang@mayerbrownrowe.com

LARRY R. LANGDON, admitted to bar, 1961, California. *Education:* Ohio State University (B.A., 1959); Ohio State University College of Law (J.D., 1961); New York University School of Law (LL.M., Taxation, 1963). (Palo Alto, California Office). ***PRACTICE AREAS:*** Tax Controversies. ***Email:*** lrlangdon@mayerbrownrowe.com

REINHART LANGE, born 1957; admitted to bar, 1989, Germany. *Education:* University of Mainz. (Frankfurt/Main, Germany Office). ***LANGUAGES:*** English. ***PRACTICE AREAS:*** Unfair Competition; Trademarks; Patent Licensing. ***Email:*** rlange@mayerbrownrowe.com

PAUL L. LANGER, born March 29, 1959; admitted to bar, 1985, Illinois and U.S. District Court, Northern District of Illinois including Trial Bar; 1988, U.S. Court of Appeals, Seventh and Ninth Circuits; U.S. Supreme Court; 1999, U.S. District Court, Eastern District of Michigan. *Education:* University of Illinois (B.S., 1982); Loyola University of Chicago (J.D., 1985). James Scholar. Member, Loyola Law Journal, 1984-1985. Author: "Notice and the Duty to Defend: Back to the Basics," 39 For the Defense 6 (1997); "The Absolute Pollution Exclusion: Not Quite Absolute," 99 The Environmental Counselor 2, November 1996; "Trigger of Coverage for Environmental Claims," 7 Environmental Claims Journal 3, March 1995; "Environmental Insurance Coverage Issues in Illinois: Moving Toward Resolution," 82 Ill. Bar Journal 90, February 1994; "Section 2-621 Dismissal in Product Liability Actions," 77 Ill. Bar Journal, 704, September 1989. *Member:* Chicago Bar Association (Member, YLS Insurance Law Committee, Co-Chairman, 1992-1994). ***Email:*** planger@mayerbrownrowe.com

CHRISTOPHER PETER LANGFORD, born 1961; admitted to bar, 1985, England. *Education:* Oxford University. (London, England Office). ***PRACTICE AREAS:*** Insurance Law; Commercial Litigation. ***Email:*** clangford@eu.mayerbrownrowe.com

BENNETT W. LASKO, born Chicago, Illinois, September 3, 1961; admitted to bar, 1987, Illinois; 1988, U.S. District Court, Northern District of Illinois; 1990, U.S. Court of Appeals, Seventh Circuit; 1999, U.S. District Court, Eastern District of Wisconsin. *Education:* Grinnell College (B.A., with honors, 1983); Harvard University (J.D., cum laude, 1987). Law Clerk, Massachusetts Supreme Judicial Court, 1987-1988. Assistant Corporation Counsel, City of Chicago Department of Law, 1988-1991. ***REPORTED CASES:*** Isquith v. Caremark International, 136 F.3d 531 (7th Cir. 1998); Magma Power Co. v. Dow Chemical Co., 136 F.3d 316 (2d Cir. 1998); In re Cendant Corp. Sec. Litig., 81 F.Supp.2d 550 (D.N.J. 2000); In re Silicone Gel Breast Implants Prod. Liab. Litig., 887 F.Supp. 1455 (N.D. Ala. 1995); Chrysler Corp. v. Blackmon, 841 S.W.2d 844 (Tex. 1992). ***PRACTICE AREAS:*** Securities Litigation; Auditors Malpractice; Complex Litigation; Civil Litigation. ***Email:*** blasko@mayerbrownrowe.com

JOHN F. LAWLOR, born Evanston, Illinois, May 22, 1963; admitted to bar, 1988, Illinois. *Education:* Georgetown University (A.B., 1985); University of Notre Dame (J.D., cum laude, 1988). ***Email:*** jlawlor@mayerbrownrowe.com

LORIE SOARES LAZARUS, born San Jose, California, October 14, 1962; admitted to bar, 1988, California, U.S. District Court, Central District of California and U.S. Court of Appeals, Ninth Circuit. *Education:* University of Santa Clara (B.S.C., 1984); University of Southern California (M.B.A., 1988; J.D.,1988). (Los Angeles, California Office). ***LANGUAGES:*** Spanish and Portuguese. ***Email:*** llazarus@mayerbrownrowe.com

CHARLES J.E. LEACH, born May 26, 1951; admitted to bar, 1978, England and Wales. *Education:* University of East Anglia (B.A., 1973); The College of Law, London, England (J.D., 1977). Member, Court of St. Bride, 2001-2002. *Member:* City of London Solicitors Company. (London, England Office). ***LANGUAGES:*** German. ***PRACTICE AREAS:*** Commercial Property; Commercial Property Development; Leasing; Private Finance. ***Email:*** cleach@eu.mayerbrownrowe.com

ANDREW R. LEGG, admitted to bar, 1982, England and Wales. *Education:* Leeds University (LL.B., 1979); Chester Law School (Law Society Part II, 1980). (London, England Office). ***PRACTICE AREAS:*** Litigation. ***Email:*** alegg@mayerbrownrowe.com

WOLFGANG LEIP, born 1951; admitted to bar, 1982, Germany. *Education:* Universities of Heidelberg and Berlin; University of Arts, Berlin (Degree in Advertising and Communication, 1976); University of the Pacific, McGeorge School of Law, Sacramento (LL.M.). (Frankfurt/Main, Germany Office). ***LANGUAGES:*** English, Portuguese, Spanish. ***PRACTICE AREAS:*** International Litigation; Patents; Corporate Law. ***Email:*** wleip@mayerbrownrowe.com

MARY B. LEMUTH, born Sioux Falls, South Dakota; admitted to bar, 1992, Texas. *Education:* Rice University (B.A., 1970); University of Houston (J.D., magna cum laude, 1992). Order of the Barons; Order of the Coif. Houston Law Review (Administrative Editor), Southside Place City Council, 1988-1992. (Houston, Texas Office). ***PRACTICE AREAS:*** Real Estate; Energy; Finance. ***Email:*** mlemuth@mayerbrownrowe.com

FREDRICK S. LEVIN, born 1963; admitted to bar, 1988, Michigan; 1989, Illinois. *Education:* Princeton University (A.B.); University of Michigan (J.D., 1988). (Los Angeles, California Office). ***Email:*** flevin@mayerbrownrowe.com

WILLIAM A. LEVY, born Evanston, Illinois, November 19, 1963; admitted to bar, 1988, Illinois; 1989, U.S. District Court, Northern District of Illinois. *Education:* University of Pennsylvania (B.A., magna cum laude, 1985); University of Chicago (J.D., 1988). Member, University of Chicago Law Review. ***PRACTICE AREAS:*** Taxation (100%). ***Email:*** wlevy@mayerbrownrowe.com

PETER S. LIASKOS, born New York, N.Y., September 27, 1967; admitted to bar, 1993, New York; 1995, U.S. District Court, Southern and Eastern Districts of New York. *Education:* State University of New York at Albany (B.S., cum laude, 1989); William & Mary Law School (J.D., 1992). Member, A.B.A. Administrative Law Review. Co-Editor, Amicus Curiae. Co-Author: "The Role of Preemption in Administrative Law," A.B.A. Administrative Law Review, Spring, 1992. Member, Products Liability Committee, Association of the Bar of the City of New York, 1996-1998. (New York, N.Y. Office). ***Email:*** pliaskos@mayerbrownrowe.com

JAMES T. LIDBURY, born Chicago, Illinois, June 2, 1965; admitted to bar, 1990, Illinois; 1992, District of Columbia. *Education:* Universite Laval; Northwestern University (B.A., 1987); Northwestern University School of Law (J.D., 1990). Attorney, U.S. Securities and Exchange Commission, Division of Corporation Finance, 1992-1994. Chairman, Public Companies Subcommittee, Illinois Secretary of State's Business Law Advisory Committee. ***PRACTICE AREAS:*** Mergers and Acquisitions. ***Email:*** jlidbury@mayerbrownrowe.com

RICHARD DUNCAN LINSELL, born 1947; admitted to bar, 1973, England. *Education:* Cambridge University. *Member:* International Bar Association. (London, England Office). ***PRACTICE AREAS:*** Partnership Law; Company Law. ***Email:*** rlinsell@mayerbrownrowe.com

STUART M. LITWIN, born Skokie, Illinois, June 17, 1959; admitted to bar, 1985, Illinois. *Education:* University of Illinois (B.S., 1981); University of Chicago (J.D., 1985; M.B.A., cum laude, 1985). ***Email:*** slitwin@mayerbrownrowe.com

THEODORE A. LIVINGSTON, JR., born Cleveland, Ohio, July 21, 1946; admitted to bar, 1973, Illinois. *Education:* McPherson College (B.A., summa cum laude, 1969); University of Kansas (J.D., 1973). ***Email:*** tlivingston@mayerbrownrowe.com

(This Listing Continued)

ALVIN J. LORMAN, born Brooklyn, New York, October 8, 1945; admitted to bar, 1975, Virginia; 1976, District of Columbia. *Education:* Long Island University (B.A., cum laude, 1966); Ohio State University (M.A., 1968); University of Virginia School of Law (J.D., 1975). Member, Editorial Board, Virginia Law Review, 1973-1975. Law Clerk to the Hon. Leonard Braman, Superior Court of the District of Columbia, 1975-1976. Author: "Debate over 'Generic Biologics' Poses Unique Challenges for Policy Makers," (Washington Legal Foundation Legal Backgrounder, 2004); "FDA/Patent Law Intersection: What's New With Hatch-Waxman in Biotechnology Law: Biotechnology Patents & Business Strategies in the New Millennium," (Practicing Law Institute, 2001); "Clinical Trials Face Heightened Scrutiny as Science and Commerce Appear to Merge," 4 J Biolaw & Business No. 4 (2001); "The Chemical Weapons Convention," The National Law Journal (June 27, 1994); "Food Standards and the Quest for Healthier Foods, in Nutrition Labeling: Issues and Directions for the 1990's," Porter and Earl, eds. (National Academy Press, 1990). Co-author: "The Drug Wars: Generics and Pioneers Once Again Make Their Case to Congress," Boston Bar Association Health Law Section Newsletter (Summer 2001). Member, Editorial Advisory Board, Food and Drug Law Journal, 2004—. Member, Committee on Radiopharmaceuticals, United States Pharmacopoeia, 2000—. *Member:* American Bar Association (Vice Chairman, 1988-1991 and Member, Food, Drug & Cosmetic Law Committee). (Washington, D.C. Office). ***SPECIAL AGENCIES:*** Food and Drug Administration. ***PRACTICE AREAS:*** Food and Drug Regulation; Health Care; Biotechnology. ***Email:*** ajlorman@mayerbrownrowe.com

WARREN R. LOUI, admitted to bar, 1982, New York; 1987, California. *Education:* Massachusetts Institute of Technology (B.S., 1977); Stanford University (M.B.A., 1981; J.D., 1981). (Los Angeles, California Office). ***PRACTICE AREAS:*** Finance. ***Email:*** wloui@mayerbrownrowe.com

WAYNE R. LUEPKER, born Evergreen Park, Illinois, May 16, 1949; admitted to bar, 1979, Illinois. *Education:* Grinnell College (B.A., 1971); University of Chicago (J.D., 1979). Author: "Applying the Property-Services Distinction in Corporate Transactions: The New Economy Tests the Limits," 29 Taxes 3 (March 2001); "Change in Control Arrangements for Executives in Business Transactions," Out of the Vortex-Finding Order in Merger and Acquisitions Chaos, American Compensation Association (Autumn 1998); "Deferred Delivery of Option Stock," 25 Tax Management Compensation Planning Journal 5 (May 1997); "Design and Implementation of a Transferable Stock Option Program," LXVII Aspen Law & Business Corporation Reporter Service 3 (February 3, 1997); "Executive Severance Agreements," Executive Compensation (2002). *Member:* American Bar Association (Chair, Executive Compensation Subcommittee, Employee Benefits Committee, Taxation Section). ***PRACTICE AREAS:*** Employee Benefits. ***Email:*** wluepker@mayerbrownrowe.com

ROBIN R. LUNN, born Indiana, Pennsylvania, September 19, 1950; admitted to bar, 1975, Illinois and U.S. District Court, Northern District of Illinois. *Education:* University of Pittsburgh (B.A., 1972; J.D., 1975). Editorial Board, University of Pittsburgh Law Review, 1973-1975. ***PRACTICE AREAS:*** Environmental; Litigation; Insurance Coverage. ***Email:*** rlunn@mayerbrownrowe.com

GEORGE A. LUSCOMBE, II, born Jefferson, Iowa, October 22, 1944; admitted to bar, 1969, Illinois; 1972, District of Columbia, U.S. Supreme Court, U.S. Claims Court and U.S. Tax Court. *Education:* University of Illinois (B.S., 1966; J.D., 1969); George Washington University (LL.M. in Taxation, 1972). Order of the Coif. Certified Public Accountant, Illinois. Adjunct Professor of Taxation, Illinois Institute of Technology-Chicago-Kent College of Law, 1987-1993. Assistant Branch Chief, Legislation and Regulations Division, Office of Chief Counsel, Internal Revenue Service, 1972-1973. *Member:* Illinois State (Chair, Federal Taxation Section, 1991-1992) and American (Chair, Committee on Depreciation, Tax Section, 1980-1982) Bar Associations. ***PRACTICE AREAS:*** Taxation. ***Email:*** gluscombe@mayerbrownrowe.com

DANIEL W. LUTHER, born New Brunswick, New Jersey, May 3, 1961; admitted to bar, 1986, Illinois. *Education:* Georgetown University (A.B., magna cum laude, 1983; J.D., magna cum laude, 1986). General Counsel, Indianapolis Colts, Inc., 2001—. ***PRACTICE AREAS:*** Wealth Preservation; Sports Law; Entertainment Law. ***Email:*** dluther@mayerbrownrowe.com

KEITH LYON, admitted to bar, 1992, England. *Education:* Downing College, Cambridge University (B.A., Hons., 1988). (London, England Office). ***PRACTICE AREAS:*** Insurance; Reinsurance; Professional Indemnity; Financial Institutions Litigation. ***Email:*** klyon@mayerbrownrowe.com

BARRY N. MACHLIN, born Boston, Massachusetts, July 14, 1959; admitted to bar, 1985, Massachusetts; 1987, District of Columbia; 2000, Illinois and New York. *Education:* Brandeis University (B.A., summa cum laude, 1982); Harvard University (J.D., 1985). Phi Beta Kappa. ***PRACTICE AREAS:*** Project Finance; International Finance; Cross Border Investment. ***Email:*** bmachlin@mayerbrownrowe.com

MARCIA G. MADSEN, admitted to bar, 1979, District of Columbia; U.S. Court of Appeals for the District of Columbia Circuit; U.S. Court of Appeals for the Federal Circuit; U.S. Court of Appeals, Fourth and Sixth Circuits; U.S. Court of Federal Claims; U.S. District Court for the District of Columbia. *Education:* University of Utah (B.A., with honors, 1972); Washington College of Law of American University (J.D., 1976); Georgetown University Law Center (LL.M., 1980). Member, U.S. Court of Federal Claims Advisory Council. Member, Editorial Advisory Board, BNA Federal Contracts Reports. *Member:* American Bar Association (Chair, Section of Public Contract Law, 1997-1998); Board of Contract Appeals Bar Association (President, 1994); Federalist Society (Chair, Government Contracts Committee). (Washington, D.C. Office). ***PRACTICE AREAS:*** Government Contracts and Litigation. ***Email:*** mgmadsen@mayerbrownrowe.com

PAUL JOSEPH MAHER, born 1959; admitted to bar, 1984, England. *Education:* Bristol University. (London, England Office). ***PRACTICE AREAS:*** Corporate Law; Mergers and Acquisitions Law. ***Email:*** pmaher@mayerbrownrowe.com

JOSEPH A. MAHONEY, born 1963; admitted to bar, 1993, Missouri; 1995, U.S. District Court, Western District of Missouri and U.S. Court of Appeals for the Federal Circuit; 1999, Illinois and U.S.District Court, Northern District of Illinois; registered to practice before U.S. Patent and Trademark Office. *Education:* University of Nebraska Medical Center (Pharm.D., 1988); St. Louis University (J.D., cum laude, 1993). Editor-in-Chief, Saint Louis University Law Journal. Author: "A Case Study on Intellectual Property Aspects of

(This Listing Continued)

Biochips," Biotech Law and Litigation Summit, Tysons Corner, VA. and Palo Alto, Ca., Fulcrum Information Services, May 2001. Intellectual Property Protection and Technology Transfer: National Health Research Institutes, Taipei, Taiwan, April 2000; Battelle Memorial Institute, Columbus, OH., February, 2000; University of Kansas, Lawrence Kansas, April, 1998. Expert Panel Member, Attracting Venture Capital for Biotech Start-Ups, Chicago Biotechnology Network, Chicago, IL., February, 2000. ***PRACTICE AREAS:*** Patent Litigation; Pharmaceutical Patent Protection; Pharmaceutical Strategy; Biotechnology Patent Protection; Biotechnology Strategy; Licensing. ***Email:*** jamahoney@mayerbrownrowe.com

CARY J. MALKIN, born Chicago, Illinois, October 6, 1949; admitted to bar, 1974, Illinois and U.S. District Court, Northern District of Illinois; 2001, New York. *Education:* George Washington University (B.A., 1971); Northwestern University (J.D., 1974). Phi Beta Kappa; Order of the Coif. ***PRACTICE AREAS:*** Lease Finance; Cross Border Finance; Finance. ***Email:*** cmalkin@mayerbrownrowe.com

A. JOHN P. MANCINI, born 1964; admitted to bar, 1989, Connecticut; 1990, New York and U.S. District Court, Southern District of New York; U.S. District Court, Eastern District of New York; U.S. Court of Appeals, Second Circuit; U.S. District Court, District of Connecticut; U.S. District Court, Eastern District of Wisconsin; U.S. Tax Court. *Education:* Fairfield University (B.A., 1986); Georgetown University Law Center (J.D., 1989). Co-Author: "Implementing the Recent Development in Security, Business Continuity & Corporate Governance: Critical IT Issues for Financial Institutions," Electronic Banking Law and Commerce Report, January 2004; "Now More Than Ever, Cybersecurity Audits are Key," The National Law Journal, March 11, 2002; "Federal Court Makes Infringement Suits Based on Hyperlinking Difficult to Prove," Start-Up and Emerging Company Strategist, January 2002; "Third-Party Beneficiaries," Commercial Contracts: Strategies for Drafting and Negotiating, Aspen Publishers, Inc. (2002); "What's in a Name? How the Selection of a Domain Name Can Lead to U.S. Jurisdiction," November 20, 2001. (New York, N.Y. Office). ***LANGUAGES:*** Italian, French. ***PRACTICE AREAS:*** Litigation; Intellectual Property; Information Technology.

MARY K. MANDEVILLE, born St. Paul, Minnesota, February 6, 1963; admitted to bar, 1988, North Carolina. *Education:* University of South Carolina (B.S., magna cum laude, 1985); Duke University (J.D., with honors, 1988). Phi Beta Kappa. (Charlotte, North Carolina Office). ***PRACTICE AREAS:*** Commercial Litigation. ***Email:*** mmandeville@mayerbrownrowe.com

MARK D. MANELA, born Dallas, Texas, April 17, 1959; admitted to bar, 1984, Texas and U.S. Tax Court; 1986, U.S. Court of Appeals, Fifth Circuit; 1988, U.S. Court of Appeals for the District of Columbia; U.S. District Court, Southern, Northern and Eastern Districts of Texas. *Education:* University of Texas (B.B.A., with honors, 1981); University of Houston (J.D., 1984). (Houston, Texas Office). ***PRACTICE AREAS:*** Litigation. ***Email:*** mmanela@mayerbrown.com

KRISTIN PERNOLL MANZANO, born Honolulu, Hawaii, December 6, 1965; admitted to bar, 1992, Georgia; 1993, New York; 1995, U.S. District Court, Southern and Eastern Districts of New York; 1998, North Carolina. *Education:* Southern Methodist University (B.A., 1988); Tulane University Law School (J.D., cum laude, 1992). (Charlotte, North Carolina Office). ***LANGUAGES:*** French. ***Email:*** kmanzano@mayerbrownrowe.com

ANDREW S. MAROVITZ, born Chicago, Illinois, July 21, 1964; admitted to bar, 1989, Illinois and U.S. District Court, Northern District of Illinois; 1990, U.S. Court of Appeals, Seventh Circuit; 1994, U.S. Court of Appeals, Fourth Circuit; 1995, U.S. District Court, Central District of Illinois; 1999, U.S. Court of Appeals, Eighth Circuit; 2000, U.S. Court of Appeals, District of Columbia Circuit; 2004, U.S. Supreme Court. *Education:* Amherst College (B.A., 1986); Yale University (J.D., 1989). Phi Beta Kappa. Author: "Empagran and the Globalization of the Sherman Act," *Business Law International*, September 2003; "Snapshots After Kodak: Early Developments Following the Supreme Court's Recent Pronouncements on Tying and the Role of Summary Judgment in Antitrust Cases," *Of Interest,* March 1993; "Out of the 1980s and Into the 1990s: Lender Liability Lawsuits—Their Common Law Bases and Their Application to Failed LBOs," ALI-ABA Course of Study Materials, Lender Liability and Other Complex Litigation Involving Financial Institutions, October 1991; "Casting a Meaningful Ballot: Applying One-Person, One-Vote to Judicial Elections Involving Racial Discrimination," 98 Yale L.J. 1193, 1989. ***PRACTICE AREAS:*** Complex Litigation; Antitrust; Appellate Practice. ***Email:*** amarovitz@mayerbrownrowe.com

DANIEL R. MARSCHOLLEK, born 1972; admitted to bar, 1999. *Education:* Universities of Frankfurt am Main and Giessen; University of St. Gallen (M.B.L.-HSG). (Frankfurt/Main, Germany Office). ***LANGUAGES:*** English, French and Polish. ***PRACTICE AREAS:*** Intellectual Property; Trademarks; Copyrights. ***Email:*** dmarschollek@mayerbrownrowe.com

JOHN D. MARSHALL, born Chicago, Illinois, May 19, 1940; admitted to bar, 1965, Illinois; 1968, U.S. Tax Court; 1971, U.S. District Court, Northern District of Illinois. *Education:* University of Illinois (B.A., 1961); Illinois Institute of Technology/Chicago-Kent College of Law (J.D., with honors, 1965). ***Email:*** jmarshall@mayerbrownrowe.com

ALAN J. MARTIN, born Berwyn, Illinois, December 9, 1959; admitted to bar, 1985, Illinois and U.S. District Court, Northern District of Illinois including Trial Bar; 1997, U.S. Court of Appeals, Seventh Circuit; 1999, U.S. Court of Appeals, Third Circuit; 2002, U.S. Court of Appeals, Second Circuit and U.S. Supreme Court. *Education:* University of Illinois (B.A., summa cum laude, with highest distinction in Political Science, 1982); University of Virginia (J.D., 1985). Merriam Scholar. Author: "Putting Your Attorney on the Witness Stand and His Advice at Issue: The Perils of Selective Waiver of Privilege," Attorney-Client Privilege in Civil Litigation, American Bar Association, 1997. U.S. Department of State, Bureau of Intelligence Research, Office of Politico Military Analysis, 1981. *Member:* American Bar Association (Vice-Chair, Tort and Insurance Practice Section, 1996). ***PRACTICE AREAS:*** Commercial Litigation; Insurance Law; Reinsurance. ***Email:*** amartin@mayerbrownrowe.com

BRIAN J. MASSENGILL, born Washington, D.C., February 1, 1962; admitted to bar, 1995, Illinois. *Education:* Indiana University (B.S., 1984); University of Chicago (J.D., 1995). ***PRACTICE AREAS:*** Securities Fraud; Accountants Liability. ***Email:*** bmassengill@mayerbrownrowe.com

(This Listing Continued)

MAYER, BROWN, ROWE & MAW LLP, Chicago—Continued

GEOFREY L. MASTER, born Fort Worth, Texas, July 10, 1954; admitted to bar, 1980, New York and Texas; 2002, District of Columbia. *Education:* The University of Texas at Austin (B.A., with high honors, 1975; J.D., with honors, 1979; M.P.A., 1979); New York University (LL.M. in Taxation, 1983). Adjunct Professor, Texas Law School, 1985-1989. (Washington, D.C. Office). ***PRACTICE AREAS:*** Corporate; Technology; Information Technology Contracts; Computer Law. ***Email:*** gmaster@mayerbrownrowe.com

DANIEL A. MASUR, born Jacksonville, Florida, June 9, 1952; admitted to bar, 1977, District of Columbia. *Education:* Marquette University (B.A., cum laude, 1974); Georgetown University (J.D., 1977). Editor, Georgetown Law Journal. Vice President and General Counsel, Net Inc., 1994-1997; Partner, Reed, Smith, Shaw & McClay, 1977-1994. (Washington, D.C. Office). ***Email:*** dmasur@mayerbrownrowe.com

ANDREW MATTEI, born Brooklyn, New York, November 15, 1957; admitted to bar, 1988, New York. *Education:* State University of New York at Cortland (B.S., 1979); Fordham University (J.D., 1987). Co-Author, Proposed Rule 144A and Related Concerns, Journal of International Banking Law (1989). Co-Author, Reproposed Rule 144A and Related Concerns, Butterworth's Journal of International Banking and Financial Law (1989). Contributing Author: "Advising Illinois Financial Institutions," Illinois Institute of Continuing Legal Education, I.I.C.L.E. (1997). Contributing Author: "How to Buy a U.S. Business - A Guide to Negotiated and Hostile Acquisitions" (1999). (New York, N.Y. Office). ***Email:*** amattei@mayerbrownrowe.com

WAYNE C. MATUS, born 1950; admitted to bar, 1976, New York; 1979, District of Columbia and U.S. Supreme Court; U.S. Court of Appeals, Second Circuit; U.S. Court of Appeals, Ninth Circuit; U.S. Court of Appeals for the Federal Circuit; U.S. District Court, Southern and Eastern Districts of New York; U.S. District Court, District of Columbia; U.S. Tax Court. *Education:* The Johns Hopkins University (B.A., 1972); New York University School of Law (J.D., 1975). (New York, N.Y. Office). ***PRACTICE AREAS:*** Litigation; Intellectual Property; Information Technology. ***Email:*** wmatus@mayerbrownrowe.com

TERRI A. MAZUR, born Somers Point, New Jersey, October 8, 1959; admitted to bar, 1984, New Mexico and U.S. District Court, District of New Mexico; 1985, U.S. Court of Appeals, Tenth Circuit; 1987, Illinois and U.S. District Court, Northern District of Illinois including Trial Bar; 1988, U.S. Court of Appeals, Ninth Circuit; 1993, U.S. Court of Appeals, Seventh Circuit; 1997, U.S. Court of Appeals, Third Circuit. *Education:* Cornell University (B.A., magna cum laude, 1981); Northwestern University (J.D., cum laude, 1984). Contributing author: *ABA Antitrust Developments Handbook* (3d Ed. 1993). *Member:* Federal Bar Association (Member, Board of Directors). (New York, N.Y. Office). ***PRACTICE AREAS:*** Litigation. ***Email:*** tmazur@mayerbrownrowe.com

GREGORY R. McCLINTOCK, born Glendale, California, August 8, 1943; admitted to bar, 1969, California; 1972, U.S. Supreme Court. *Education:* Loma Linda University (B.A., 1965); University of Southern California (J.D., 1968). Member, Southern California Law Review, 1967-1968. Assistant to Director of Operations, Antitrust Division, United States Department of Justice, 1970-1972. Chairman, Institute for Business Law's Annual Conference on California Environmental Regulation, 1978-1994. General Counsel, Western States Petroleum Association, 1992—. (Los Angeles, California Office). ***Email:*** gmcclintock@mayerbrownrowe.com

HUGH R. McCOMBS, born Flint, Michigan, July 30, 1946; admitted to bar, 1975, Illinois and U.S. District Court, Northern District of Illinois including Trial Bar; 1979, U.S. Court of Appeals, Seventh Circuit; 1980, U.S. Supreme Court. *Education:* Yale University (B.A., 1968); Boston University (J.D., cum laude, 1973). ***PRACTICE AREAS:*** Trials and Arbitration of civil cases both in the U.S. and overseas; Construction; Toxic Torts; Mass Torts. ***Email:*** hmccombs@mayerbrownrowe.com

HOWARD M. McCUE, III, born Sumter, South Carolina, January 4, 1946; admitted to bar, 1971, Massachusetts; 1975, Illinois; 1977, U.S. Tax Court. *Education:* Princeton University (A.B., with honors, 1968); Harvard University (J.D., with honors, 1971). Phi Beta Kappa. Fellow, American College of Trust and Estate Counsel, Regent, Chair Charitable Planning and Exempt Organizations Committee. Fellow, American College of Tax Counsel. Academician, International Academy of Estate and Trust Law. Recipient, Chicago Estate Planning Council's Austin Fleming Award for lifetime achievement. Author: "Charitable Trust Administration: Enforcing Donor Intent When the Ties That Bind Become Frayed," University of Miami 38th Annual Heckerling Institute on Estate Planning (2004); "A Profession Under Siege - Ethical Decision Solutions To the Estate Planner's Dilemma," University of Miami 36th Annual Heckerling Institute on Estate Planning (2002); "Planning and Drafting to Influence Behavior," University of Miami 34th Annual Heckerling Institute on Estate Planning (2000); co-Author: "Trust Administration," IICLE (2002). Author, co-author and presenter of numerous other articles, speeches and books on charitable organizations, fiduciary litigation and estate planning topics. *Member:* Chicago Bar Association (Former Chair, Federal Taxation Committee); Chicago Bar Foundation (Former President); Lloyd A. Fry Foundation (Board Chair). [U.S. Navy, Active Duty, 1972-1975]. ***PRACTICE AREAS:*** Tax Exempt Organizations; Trusts and Estates. ***Email:*** hmccue@mayerbrownrowe.com

IAN JAMES McDONALD, born Romford, November 8, 1966; admitted to bar, 1992, England. *Education:* Cambridge University (B.A., 1988); Guilford University. (London, England Office). ***PRACTICE AREAS:*** Insolvency; Litigation. ***Email:*** imcdonald@mayerbrownrowe.com

KATHLEEN A. McGILL, admitted to bar, 1986, New York and District of Columbia; 1996, North Carolina. *Education:* University of Colorado (B.A., 1978); Georgetown University Law Center (J.D., 1985); The Edmund Walsh School of Foreign Service, Georgetown University (M.S.F.S., 1985). (Charlotte, North Carolina Office). ***LANGUAGES:*** Spanish. ***PRACTICE AREAS:*** Banking Law; Finance. ***Email:*** mmcgill@mayerbrownrowe.com

KATHRYN B. McGRATH, *born September 2, 1944; admitted to bar, 1969, District* of Columbia. *Education:* Mount Holyoke College (A.B., 1966); Georgetown University (J.D., 1969). (Washington, D.C. Office). ***PRACTICE AREAS:*** Corporate Law; Securities. ***Email:*** kmcgrath@mayerbrownrowe.com

(This Listing Continued)

DAVID MARTIN McINTOSH, II, born Oakland, California, June 8, 1958; admitted to bar, 1983, California; 1987, U.S. Supreme Court; 1989, Indiana. *Education:* Yale University (B.A., cum laude, 1980), University of Chicago (J.D., 1983). Visiting Professor, Ball State University School of Business, 2001—. Special Assistant to President Regan for Domestic Affairs, 1987-1988. U.S. Representative, 1995-2001. Executive Director Presidents Council on Competitiveness, 1990-1992. Member, U.S. Congress, 1995-2001. Sidley & Austin, Los Angeles, 1983-1986. *Member:* The Federalist Society (National Co-Chairman). (Washington, D.C. Office). ***LANGUAGES:*** German. ***PRACTICE AREAS:*** Government; Telecommunications; Health Care; Regulatory Law. ***Email:*** dmcintosh@mayerbrownrowe.com

IAN McKENNA, admitted to bar, 1991, England and Wales. *Education:* University of Limoges, France (Diploma in French Law, 1984); University of Birmingham (LL.B. Law with French, 1985); Chester College of Law (1989). (London, England Office). ***LANGUAGES:*** French. ***PRACTICE AREAS:*** Reinsurance. ***Email:*** jmckenna@mayerbrownrowe.com

T. MARK McLAUGHLIN, born Salem, Massachusetts, April 20, 1953; admitted to bar, 1978, Illinois and U.S. District Court, Northern District of Illinois; 1982, U.S. Court of Appeals, Seventh and Eleventh Circuits; 1992, U.S. District Court, Central District of Illinois and Eastern District of Wisconsin; 1999, U.S. Court of Appeals, Eighth Circuit; 2004, U.S. Court of Appeals, Tenth Circuit. *Education:* University of Notre Dame (B.A., 1975; J.D., 1978). ***PRACTICE AREAS:*** Litigation; Antitrust; Franchise Distribution. ***Email:*** mmclaughlin@mayerbrownrowe.com

PATRICK J. McNERNEY, born Oak Park, Illinois, July 24, 1957; admitted to bar, 1982, Illinois. *Education:* Loyola University (B.S., 1979); John Marshall Law School (J.D., 1982). Assistant States Attorney, Cook County States Attorney's Office, 1982-1989. ***PRACTICE AREAS:*** Real Property Tax Litigation; Personal Property Tax Litigation; Commercial Lease Litigation. ***Email:*** pmcnerney@mayerbrownrowe.com

JONATHAN C. MEDOW, born Chicago, Illinois, April 17, 1957; admitted to bar, 1981, Illinois and U.S. District Court, Northern District of Illinois; 1988, U.S. Court of Appeals, Seventh Circuit; 1997, U.S. Court of Appeals, Second Circuit; 2001, U.S. Court of Appeals, Third Circuit. *Education:* Stanford University (B.A., with distinction, 1978); Harvard University (J.D., magna cum laude, 1981). Member, Board of Editors, Harvard Law Review. Adjunct Professor of Trial Advocacy, Northwestern University. ***PRACTICE AREAS:*** Accountants Liability; Securities Litigation; Class Action Defense. ***Email:*** jmedow@mayerbrown.com

DAVID R. MELTON, born Milwaukee, Wisconsin, April 4, 1952; admitted to bar, 1977, Illinois and U.S. District Court, Northern District of Illinois; 1981, U.S. Court of Appeals, Seventh Circuit; 1982, U.S. Supreme Court; 1985, Trial Bar, U.S. District Court, Northern District of Illinois; 1991, U.S. Court of Appeals for the Federal Circuit. *Education:* University of Wisconsin (B.A., with distinction in History, 1974); University of Chicago (J.D., 1977). Board Member, 1996— and President, 2002-2003, Chicago Council of Lawyers. Board Member, Federal Bar Association, 1995—. ***PRACTICE AREAS:*** Patents; Trademarks; Trade Secrets; Copyright Litigation. ***Email:*** dmelton@mayerbrownrowe.com

ROBERT L. MENDENHALL, born Greensboro, North Carolina, July 15, 1954; admitted to bar, 1983, North Carolina; 1993, U.S. Tax Court. *Education:* Davidson College (A.B., 1976); University of North Carolina at Chapel Hill (J.D., 1983; M.B.A., 1983). Member, 1981-1983, Business Manager, 1982-1983, North Carolina Law Review. (Charlotte, North Carolina Office). ***Email:*** rmendenhall@mayerbrownrowe.com

DEMETRIOS G. METROPOULOS, born Saginaw, Michigan, May 30, 1963; admitted to bar, 1993, Illinois; 1995, U.S. District Court, Northern District of Illinois and U.S. Court of Appeals, Seventh Circuit; 2000, U.S. Court of Appeals, Sixth Circuit. *Education:* University of Michigan (B.B.A., 1985); Stanford University (J.D., 1995). Author: "Constitutional Dimensions of the North American Free Trade Agreement," 27 Cornell Int'l L.J. 141 (1994); Note, "Human Rights, Incorporated: The European Community's New Line of Business," 29 Stan. J. Int'l Law 131 (1993); Note, "Son of COBRA: The Evolution of a Federal Malpractice Law," 45 Stan. L.Rev. 263 (1992). Co-author, "Putting Your Attorney on the Witness Stand and His Advice At Issue," in Attorney-Client Privilege in Civil Litigation 139 (Vincent S. Walkowiak ed., 1997). ***LANGUAGES:*** Greek. ***REPORTED CASES:*** Michigan Bell Tel. Co. v. Strand, 305 F.3d 580 (6th Cir. 2002)(briefed and argued). ***PRACTICE AREAS:*** Litigation; Telecommunications Law; Appellate Practice. ***Email:*** demetro@mayerbrown.com

PAUL MEYER, born Chicago, Illinois, July 5, 1962; admitted to bar, 1987, Illinois. *Education:* Creighton University (B.A., 1984); University of Notre Dame (J.D., 1987). ***Email:*** pmeyer@mayerbrownrowe.com

JAMES R. MOGLE, born Niles, Michigan, September 9, 1944; admitted to bar, 1974, Virginia; 1979, District of Columbia, U.S. Tax Court and U.S. Supreme Court; 1982, Illinois; 1984, Michigan. *Education:* Northwestern University (B.S., 1966); Stanford University (M.B.A., 1968); American University (J.D., 1974); George Washington University National Law Center (LL.M., 1978). International Tax Counsel, Treasury Department, 1991-1992. Member: Advisory Board for IRS/George Washington University Institute on International Taxation, 1989-1991; IRS Commissioner's Advisory Group, 1990-1991; Board of Advisors, The Journal of International Taxation. *Member:* American Bar Association (Member, Section of Taxation, Foreign Activities of U.S. Taxpayers Committee, Section 482 Subcommittee); American Institute of Certified Public Accountants (Member: Advisory Task Force on IRS Quality Improvement Project for Coordinated Examination Program, 1989; International Tax Committee, 1991); National Council of the International Fiscal Association-U.S.A. Branch. (Washington, D.C. Office). ***PRACTICE AREAS:*** Taxation. ***Email:*** jmogle@mayerbrownrowe.com

MICHAEL A. MOLANO, born Bogota, Colombia, February 10, 1968; admitted to bar, 1994, California, U.S. District Court, Northern District of California and U.S. Court of Appeals, Ninth and Federal Circuits; registered to practice before U.S. Patent and Trademark Office. *Education:* Northwestern University (B.S.E.E., 1990); St. Louis University (J.D., 1993). Chairman and Faculty Member, "Fundamentals of Patent Prosecution," Practising Law Institute, December 2002, December 2003; Author: "Business Method and Software Patents," eBusiness and Insurance, CCH, Inc., Volume I, Chapter 9, 2001; "Litigating Assignor Estoppel Issues in Patent Cases," Fundamentals of Patent Prosecution, Winter

(This Listing Continued)

2002; "A Boot Camp for Claim Drafting and Amendment Writing," Practising Law Institute, December 2002. San Francisco Bay Area Intellectual Property Inn of Court, Treasurer, 2001—, Assistant Secretary, 2000-2001. *Member:* San Francisco Bay Area Intellectual Property Inn of Court (President, 2004—; Treasurer, 2001-2004; Assistant Secretary, 2000-2001). (Palo Alto, California Office). ***LANGUAGES:*** Spanish. ***PRACTICE AREAS:*** Intellectual Property. ***Email:*** mamolano@mayerbrownrowe.com

STEPHANIE M. MONACO, born September 13, 1957; admitted to bar, 1982, Maryland; 1992, District of Columbia. *Education:* University of Maryland (B.A., 1979); University of Baltimore (J.D., 1982). (Washington, D.C. Office). ***PRACTICE AREAS:*** Corporate Law; Securities. ***Email:*** smonaco@mayerbrownrowe.com

JAY PARRY MONGE, born New York, N.Y., March 15, 1943; admitted to bar, 1969, Illinois; 1981, New York; 2003, North Carolina. *Education:* Harvard University (A.B., cum laude, 1966); University of Virginia (LL.B., 1969). Contributing Author: "Advising Illinois Financial Institutions," Illinois Institute of Continuing Legal Education, I.I.C.L.E., 1974, 1978, 1981, 1984, 1987, 1993, 1997, 2002. (Charlotte, North Carolina Office). ***PRACTICE AREAS:*** Finance and Investments; Mergers and Acquisitions; Divestitures. ***Email:*** jmonge@mayerbrownrowe.com

JONATHAN MOODY, admitted to bar, 1995, England and Wales. *Education:* Winchester College (1973-1978); Williams College, Massachusetts (1978); Cambridge University (1979-1982); Ealing College, Common Professional Examination (1990-1991); City of London Polytechnic, Law Society Finals (1991-1992). (London, England Office). ***LANGUAGES:*** French. ***PRACTICE AREAS:*** Pensions; Business Planning. ***Email:*** jmoody@mayerbrownrowe.com

DONNA EVENSEN MORGAN, born Brooklyn, New York, February 28, 1957; admitted to bar, 1985, Illinois. *Education:* Colgate University (B.A., 1979); University of Michigan (J.D., cum laude, 1984). Co-author: "Illinois Estate Planning Forms and Commentary," I.I.C.L.E., 2002. *Member:* American College of Trust and Estate Counsel. ***PRACTICE AREAS:*** Estate Planning; Estate Administration; Federal Estate and Gift Taxation. ***Email:*** dmorgan@mayerbrownrowe.com

LOUIS P. MORITZ, born Chicago, Illinois, January 16, 1964; admitted to bar, 1990, Illinois; 1996, Florida. *Education:* University of Chicago (A.B., 1986; J.D., with honors, 1989). ***PRACTICE AREAS:*** Real Estate; Corporate. ***Email:*** lmoritz@mayerbrownrowe.com

ANDREW J. MORRIS, born Newport News, Virginia, July 29, 1958; admitted to bar, 1986, Maryland and U.S. Court of Appeals, Third Circuit; 1987, District of Columbia; U.S. Supreme Court; U.S. Court of Appeals for the District of Columbia, First, Third, Fourth and Eleventh Circuits. *Education:* University of Virginia (B.S., with distinction, 1980; J.D., 1985, Order of the Coif); University of Oxford, England (B.C.L., with honors, 1993). Certified Public Accountant. Author: "Clarifying the Imputation Doctrine: Charging Audit Clients With Responsibility for Unauthorized Audit Interference," Colum. Bus. L. Rev. 339, 2001; Jurisdiction in Cyberspace (Book Chapter), in E-Commerce, Law Journal Seminars Press (2000); Avoiding & Defending Against Securities Class Actions, 3 Journal of Internet Law (May 1999). Co-author: "Class Actions," in Federal Practice Manual (Seventh Circuit), Lwyrs Coop. (1998); "Federal Rule of Evidence 404 (b): The Fictitious Ban on Character Reasoning from Other Crimes Evidence," 17 Review of Litigation 181 (1998). Law Clerk to the Honorable Max Rosenn, U.S. Court of Appeals for the Third Circuit, 1985-1986. (Washington, D.C. Office). ***Email:*** amorris@mayerbrownrowe.com

NEIL MORRISON, born Wales, December, 1946; admitted to bar, 1973, Scotland; 1976, Hong Kong; 1986, England. *Education:* Edinburgh University (LL.B., 1969). (London, England Office). ***PRACTICE AREAS:*** Banking Law; Project Finance. ***Email:*** nmorrison@mayerbrownrowe.com

RICHARD J. MORVILLO, admitted to bar, 1975, New York and District of Columbia. *Education:* Colgate University (A.B., 1970); Fordham University (J.D., 1974). (Washington, D.C. Office). ***PRACTICE AREAS:*** Litigation. ***Email:*** rmorvillo@mayerbrownrowe.com

BEVERLEY MOSS, born 1967; admitted to bar, 1993, England. *Education:* Manchester University. (London, England Office). ***PRACTICE AREAS:*** Corporate Law; Corporate Finance. ***Email:*** bmoss@mayerbrownrowe.com

WILLIAM S. MOSS III, born Houston, Texas, October 15, 1969; admitted to bar, 1996, Texas. *Education:* Dartmouth College (B.A., 1992); Cambridge University (M.Phil., 1993); University of Texas School of Law (J.D., with honors, 1996). Member, Texas Law Review, 1994-1996. Law Clerk to the Honorable Royal Furgeson, U.S. District Court, Western District of Texas, 1996-1997. (Houston, Texas Office). ***LANGUAGES:*** German. ***PRACTICE AREAS:*** Corporate Law; Securities. ***Email:*** bmoss@mayerbrownrowe.com

DR. KLAUS J. MÜELLER, born 1965; admitted to bar, 1996, Germany. *Education:* Universities of Freiburg im Breisgau, Lausanne, Marburg/Lahn and Hamburg. (Frankfurt/Main, Germany Office). ***LANGUAGES:*** English, French. ***PRACTICE AREAS:*** Corporate Law; Mergers and Acquisitions; Corporate Restructuring. ***Email:*** kmueller@mayerbrownrowe.com

THOMAS M. MUELLER, born Mühlheim, Germany, January 1, 1961; admitted to bar, 1987, New York and U.S. District Court, Southern District of New York; 1991, U.S. District Court, District of Arizona; 1998, U.S. District Court, Eastern District of New York; 1999, U.S. Court of Appeals for the District of Columbia Circuit and U.S. District Court for the District of Columbia; 2000, U.S. Court of Appeals, Second Circuit; 2004, U.S. Supreme Court and U.S. Court of Appeals, Third Circuit. *Education:* Lehigh University (B.A., magna cum laude, 1983); University of Michigan (J.D., cum laude, 1986). (New York, N.Y. Office). ***LANGUAGES:*** German. ***PRACTICE AREAS:*** Antitrust; Class Actions; International Litigation and Arbitration. ***Email:*** tmueller@mayerbrownrowe.com

JOHN E. MUENCH, born Evanston, Illinois, July 21, 1948; admitted to bar, 1976, Illinois; U.S. Supreme Court; U.S. Court of Appeals, Sixth, Seventh, Eighth, Ninth, District of Columbia and Federal Circuits. *Education:* College of the Holy Cross (A.B., honors, magna cum laude, 1970); Northwestern University (J.D., magna cum laude, 1976). Order of the Coif. Editor-in-Chief, Northwestern University Law Review, 1975. Law Clerk to: Hon. Robert A. Spreobes, U.S. Court of Appeals, Seventh Circuit, 1976-1977; Justice John Paul Stevens, U.S. Supreme Court, 1977-1978. *Member:* Appellate Lawyers Association (Director, 1999-2000). ***Email:*** jmuench@mayerbrownrowe.com

(This Listing Continued)

J. THOMAS MULLEN, born Evanston, Illinois, August 27, 1940; admitted to bar, 1967, Illinois. *Education:* Princeton University (B.S.E., 1963); University of California (1964); University of Michigan (J.D., cum laude, 1967). ***PRACTICE AREAS:*** Finance; Project Finance; International Transactions. ***Email:*** tmullen@mayerbrownrowe.com

D. MICHAEL MURRAY, born Freeport, Illinois, December 5, 1971; admitted to bar, 1997, Illinois. *Education:* Northern Illinois University (B.S., 1994); DePaul University (J.D., 1997). Order of the Coif. Certified Public Accountant, Illinois, 1994. ***PRACTICE AREAS:*** Mergers, Acquisitions and Divestitures; Securities; Corporate Law. ***Email:*** mmurray@mayerbrownrowe.com

JOHN NADOLENCO, born Los Angeles, California, August 16, 1970; admitted to bar, 1995, California and U.S. District Court, Central and Northern Districts of California. *Education:* University of Arizona (B.A., summa cum laude, 1992); American University (J.D., summa cum laude, 1995). (Los Angeles, California Office). ***PRACTICE AREAS:*** Business Law; Securities; Real Property Litigation; Class Action Defense. ***Email:*** jnadolenco@mayerbrownrowe.com

PETER NÄGELE, born 1957; admitted to bar, 1987, Germany; 1988, New York. *Education:* University of Frankfurt, Germany. Co-Author, "Immobilien - Recht und Steuern; Handbuch für die Immobilienwirtschaft," 1996. Lecturer, Institute for Electronic Data Processing and Business Administration, Frankfurt/Main, 1982-1987. Assistant to the Max Planck Society, Institute for European Legal History, Frankfurt, 1984-1985. *Member:* German Bar Association; International Bar Association. (Frankfurt/Main, Germany Office). ***LANGUAGES:*** German and English. ***PRACTICE AREAS:*** Banking Law; Finance; Corporate Law; Securities. ***Email:*** pnaegele@mayerbrownrowe.com

LUCIA NALE, born 1964; admitted to bar, 1989, Illinois. *Education:* Loyola University (B.A.; J.D., 1989). ***Email:*** lnale@mayerbrownrowe.com

DAVID NAREFSKY, born Brooklyn, New York, April 12, 1955; admitted to bar, 1979, Illinois. *Education:* State University of New York at Binghamton (B.A., with honors, 1976); University of Michigan (J.D., cum laude, 1979). ***Email:*** dnarefsky@mayerbrownrowe.com

MIRIAM R. NEMETZ, born August 26, 1963; admitted to bar, 1990, Pennsylvania; 1992, District of Columbia. *Education:* Harvard University (B.A., 1985; J.D., 1989). Clerk to Judge Edward N. Cahn, E. D. Pennsylvania. (Washington, D.C. Office). ***REPORTED CASES:*** Sutton v. United Air Lines, Inc., 527 U.S. 471 (1999); Waste Management Holdings, Inc. v. Gilmore, 252 F.3d 316 (4th Cir. 2001); GTE New Media Services, Inc. v. BellSouth Corp., 199 F.3d 1343 (D.C. Cir. 2000); MIC Life Ins. Co. v. Hicks, 825 So. 2d 616 (Miss. 2002); General Motors Acceptance Corp. v. Baymon, 732 So. 2d 262 (Miss. 1999). ***PRACTICE AREAS:*** Civil Appeals; Civil Litigation. ***Email:*** mnemetz@mayerbrownrowe.com

BRIAN E. NEWHOUSE, born Galion, Ohio, February 22, 1953; admitted to bar, 1978, Connecticut; 1984, Illinois; 1985, California. *Education:* Denison University (B.A., with honors, 1975); University of Michigan (J.D., cum laude, 1978). (Los Angeles, California Office). ***PRACTICE AREAS:*** Finance. ***Email:*** bnewhouse@mayerbrownrowe.com

ANDREW A. NICELY, born Rochester, New York, December 11, 1967; admitted to bar, 1997, Virginia; 1998, District of Columbia, Illinois, U.S. District Court, Eastern District of Virginia and District of Columbia; 1999, U.S. Bankruptcy Court, Eastern District of Virginia; 2000, U.S. District Court, District of Maryland; 2001, U.S. Supreme Court. *Education:* Bates College (B.A., cum laude, with high honors, 1990); State University of New York at Buffalo (M.A., 1994); University of Pennsylvania (J.D., cum laude, 1997). Order of the Coif. Recipient, W. Foster Reeves Faculty Award. (Washington, D.C. Office). ***PRACTICE AREAS:*** Commercial Litigation; Labor and Employment; Appellate Practice. ***Email:*** anicely@mayerbrownrowe.com

TREVOR ANTHONY NICHOLLS, born 1950; admitted to bar, 1985, Solicitor, England. *Education:* Polytechnic of Central London. Qualified as a Civil Engineer, 1973. (London, England Office). ***PRACTICE AREAS:*** Construction Law. ***Email:*** tnicholls@mayerbrownrowe.com

C. MARK NICOLAIDES, born Detroit, Michigan, February 11, 1954; admitted to bar, 1981, New York and U.S. District Court, Southern and Eastern Districts of New York; 1983, U.S. Court of Appeals, Second Circuit. *Education:* Cornell University (B.A., 1976); University of Virginia (J.D., 1980). Phi Beta Kappa; Phi Kappa Phi. Lyle Moot Court Winner. (London, England Office). ***LANGUAGES:*** German and French. ***Email:*** mnicolaides@mayerbrownrowe.com

MICHAEL E. NIEBRUEGGE, born Alton, Illinois, April 21, 1952; admitted to bar, 1977, Illinois and U.S. District Court, Northern District of Illinois; 1982, Texas; 1988, U.S. District Court, Southern District of Texas. *Education:* Harvard University (B.A., 1974); Cornell University (J.D., 1977). (Houston, Texas Office). ***Email:*** mniebruegge@mayerbrownrowe.com

PHILIP J. NIEHOFF, born Beaver Dam, Wisconsin, December 31, 1959; admitted to bar, 1985, Wisconsin; 1991, Illinois. *Education:* University of Wisconsin-Madison (B.B.A., 1982; J.D., 1985); Georgetown University Law Center (LL.M., Securities Regulation, 1988). Contributing Author: Securities Law (Chapter on Public Securities Offerings), Illinois Institute for Continuing Legal Education; Securitization of Financial Assets (Chapter on Investment Companies), Jason Kravitt, Editor. ***PRACTICE AREAS:*** Securities; Corporate Law. ***Email:*** pniehoff@mayerbrownrowe.com

KENNETH E. NOBLE, born Amboy, Illinois; admitted to bar, 1991, Illinois and U.S. District Court, Northern District of Illinois; 1993, U.S. District Court, Eastern District of Michigan; 1995, U.S. Court of Appeals, Sixth Circuit; 1997, U.S. Court of Appeals, Seventh Circuit and U.S. Supreme Court; 1998, U.S. District Court, Western District of Wisconsin and U.S. District Court, Northern District of Indiana; 1999, U.S. District Court, Northern District of Ohio; 2002, New York; U.S. District Court, Southern District of New York. *Education:* Northern Illinois University (B.S., 1985); University of Chicago Law School, 1990-1991; University of Illinois College of Law (J.D., summa cum laude, 1991). Order of the Coif. Law Review. Rickert Award for Academic Excellence. Harno Scholar. American Jurisprudence Award. Certified Public Accountant, Illinois, 1985. Certified Management Accountant, 1986. (New York, N.Y. Office). ***PRACTICE AREAS:*** Bankruptcy. ***Email:*** knoble@mayerbrownrowe.com

(This Listing Continued)

MAYER, BROWN, ROWE & MAW LLP, Chicago—Continued

JOHN W. NOELL, born St. Louis, Missouri, August 4, 1956; admitted to bar, 1985, Illinois. *Education:* University of Notre Dame (B.B.A., cum laude, 1978); Loyola University (J.D., cum laude, 1985). Beta Alpha Psi; Beta Gamma Sigma; Alpha Sigma Nu. Recipient, Chief Justice White Scholarship Award. Editor-in-Chief, Loyola University of Chicago Law Journal. ***Email:*** jnoell@mayerbrownrowe.com

TIM NOSWORTHY, admitted to bar, 1995, England and Wales. *Education:* St. Anne's College, Oxford; Chester College of Law. (London, England Office). ***PRACTICE AREAS:*** Corporate. ***Email:*** tim.nosworthy@mayerbrownrowe.com

JONATHAN EDWARD NUGENT, admitted to bar, 1994, England and Wales. *Education:* Trinity College, Cambridge University, Cambridge, England (B.A., in Natural Sciences, 1990); The College of Law, London, England (J.D., 1991). (London, England Office). ***Email:*** jnugetn@eu.mayerbrownrowe.com

KEITH F. OBERKFELL, born St. Louis, Missouri, March 19, 1968; admitted to bar, 1993, Illinois. *Education:* University of Virginia (B.A., with highest distinction, 1990); Harvard Law School (J.D., cum laude, 1993). Phi Beta Kappa. (Charlotte, North Carolina Office). ***PRACTICE AREAS:*** Structured Finance. ***Email:*** koberkfell@mayerbrownrowe.com

LENNINE OCCHINO, born Green Bay, Wisconsin, October 29, 1956; admitted to bar, 1982, Illinois, U.S. District Court, Northern District of Illinois and U.S. Court of Appeals, Seventh Circuit. *Education:* University of Wisconsin-Madison (B.A., with honors, 1978); DePaul University (J.D., with honors, 1982); Yale University (LL.M., 1987). ***PRACTICE AREAS:*** Private Investment Funds; ERISA. ***Email:*** locchino@mayerbrownrowe.com

GER P. O'DONNELL, born Evanston, Illinois, May 23, 1967; admitted to bar, 1992, Illinois and U.S. District Court, Northern District of Illinois. *Education:* University of Illinois (B.S., Finance, highest honors, 1989; B.S. Accounting, highest honors, 1989); University of Michigan (J.D., cum laude, 1992). Bronze Tablet. Certified Public Accountant, Illinois. ***Email:*** godonnell@mayerbrownrowe.com

MICHELE L. ODORIZZI, born Chicago, Illinois, July 12, 1952; admitted to bar, 1976, Illinois; 1977, U.S. Court of Appeals, Seventh Circuit and U.S. District Court, Northern District of Illinois; 1980, U.S. Supreme Court; U.S. Court of Appeals, Second, Third, Fourth, Sixth, Eighth, Ninth and Tenth Circuits. *Education:* Northwestern University (B.A, 1973); University of Chicago (J.D., cum laude, 1976). Law Clerk to: Hon. Philip W. Tone, U.S. Court of Appeals, Seventh Circuit, 1976-1977; Justice John Paul Stevens, U.S. Supreme Court, 1979-1980. ***PRACTICE AREAS:*** Appellate Practice; Class Action Defense; Securities Class Actions; Shareholder Derivative Actions. ***Email:*** modorizzi@mayerbrownrowe.com

MICHAEL A. OLSEN, born Hindsdale, Illinois, August 20, 1971; admitted to bar, 1996, Illinois. *Education:* University of Michigan (B.A., 1993); DePaul University (J.D., 1996). ***Email:*** molsen@mayerbrownrowe.com

ANNA M. O'MEARA, born Chicago, Illinois, August 11, 1947; admitted to bar, 1984, Illinois and U.S. District Court, Northern District of Illinois. *Education:* Loyola University (B.S., cum laude, 1969; J.D., cum laude, 1984). Contributing Author: "Employee Benefits Law," Ill. Inst. for CLE, 1987, Supp. 1990. ***Email:*** aomeara@mayerbrownrowe.com

JOSEPH B. ORGAN, born Oak Park, Illinois, October 28, 1951; admitted to bar, 1977, Illinois. *Education:* Rollins College (B.A., 1973); Northwestern University (J.D., 1977); New York University (LL.M., Tax, 1983). ***Email:*** jorgan@mayerbrownrowe.com

DENNIS P. ORR, born New York, N.Y., December 29, 1952; admitted to bar, 1979, New York; 1996, District of Columbia. *Education:* Boston College (B.A., 1975); St. John's University (J.D., 1978). Author: "A Retreat From Absolute Immunity for Federal Officials," 51 St. John's Law Review 269 (1977); "New Light on an Old Debate: Negligence v. Scienter in an SEC Fraud Injunctive Suit," 51 St. John's Law Review 759 (1977). (New York, N.Y. Office). ***Email:*** dorr@mayerbrownrowe.com

CAROLYN P. OSOLINIK, born Brooklyn, New York, May 18, 1952; admitted to bar, 1977, District of Columbia; 1979, U.S. District Court for the District of Columbia and U.S. Court of Appeals for the District of Columbia Circuit; 1982, U.S. Supreme Court. *Education:* Lindenwood College (B.S., 1973); George Washington University (J.D., 1977). Attorney: Office of the Solicitor, U.S. Department of Interior, 1977-1979; Land and Natural Resources Division, U.S. Department of Justice, 1979-1981. Majority Counsel, Senate Judiciary Committee, 1981-1986. Chief Counsel to Senator Edward M. Kennedy, Senate Judiciary Committee, 1987-1992. (Washington, D.C. Office). ***Email:*** cosolinik@mayerbrownrowe.com

JONATHAN MICHAEL OULTON, born 1963; admitted to bar, 1989, England. *Education:* Leeds University. (London, England Office). ***PRACTICE AREAS:*** Litigation; Alternative Dispute Resolution; Insurance Law. ***Email:*** joulton@mayerbrownrowe.com

MICHAEL PABST, born Melbourne, Australia, August 9, 1969; admitted to bar, 1992, Australia. *Education:* Taylors College (B.A., 1987); Bond University (J.D., 1991). (London, England Office). ***Email:*** mpabst@mayerbrownrowe.com

RICHARD PAGE, born London, England, February 3, 1967; admitted to bar, 1993, England. *Education:* University of Birmingham, England (LL.B., 1990); The College of Law, London, England (Law Society Final Examination, 1991). (London, England Office). ***LANGUAGES:*** French (conversational). ***PRACTICE AREAS:*** Corporate Finance; Commercial Law; Telecommunications Law; Broadcasting Law. ***Email:*** rpage@mayerbrownrowe.com

DANUTA BEMBENISTA PANICH, born East Chicago, Indiana, April 9, 1954; admitted to bar, 1978, Illinois and U.S. District Court, Northern District of Illinois including Trial Bar; 1987, U.S. District Court, Central District of Illinois and U.S. Court of Appeals, Seventh Circuit; 2001, U.S. District Court, Northern District of Indiana. *Education:* Indiana University (A.B., cum laude, 1975; J.D., summa cum laude, 1978). ***Email:*** dpanich@mayerbrownrowe.com

(This Listing Continued)

DEAN CONSTANTINE PAPPAS, born Los Angeles, California, August 19, 1966; admitted to bar, 1991, California. *Education:* University of Southern California (B.S., 1988; J.D., 1991). Order of the Coif. Recipient, American Jurisprudence Awards in Legal Writing, Torts, Evidence, Bankruptcy Law. Staff, 1989-1990 and Notes Editor, 1990-1991, Southern California Law Review. (Los Angeles, California Office). ***LANGUAGES:*** Greek. ***PRACTICE AREAS:*** Real Estate. ***Email:*** dpappas@mayerbrownrowe.com

STANLEY J. PARZEN, born New York, N.Y., February 6, 1952; admitted to bar, 1978, Illinois and U.S. District Court, Northern District of Illinois; 1981, U.S. Court of Appeals, Seventh Circuit; 1983, U.S. Court of Appeals, Eighth Circuit; 1989, U.S. District Court, Northern District of California; 1990, U.S. Court of Appeals, Second Circuit; 1992, U.S. Court of Appeals for the District of Columbia Circuit and U.S. Court of Appeals, Fifth Circuit; 1994, U.S. Court of Appeals, Tenth Circuit; 1996, U.S. Court of Appeals, Ninth Circuit; U.S. District Court, District of Arizona and Western and Eastern Districts of Michigan; 2002, U.S. Court of Appeals, Sixth Circuit; 2003, U.S. Court of Appeals, Fourth Circuit. *Education:* Earlham College (B.A., 1973); Harvard Law School (LL.B., cum laude, 1976). Law Clerk to Hon. Harrison L. Winter, U.S. Court of Appeals, Fourth Circuit, 1976-1977. ***PRACTICE AREAS:*** Accountants Liability; Securities; Commercial Litigation. ***Email:*** sparzen@mayerbrownrowe.com

JAMES P. PATTI, born 1967; admitted to bar, 1994, Illinois. *Education:* Georgetown University (B.S.B.A., 1989); University of Chicago (J.D., 1994). ***LANGUAGES:*** Spanish. ***PRACTICE AREAS:*** Emerging Markets; Project Finance; Secured Lending. ***Email:*** jpatti@mayerbrownrowe.com

MARK G. PAULSON, born Pittsburgh, Pennsylvania, August 31, 1955; admitted to bar, 1988, Pennsylvania; 2000, District of Columbia; registered to practice before U.S. Patent and Trademark Office. *Education:* Western Connecticut University (B.A., 1981); Temple University Law School (J.D., 1987). (Washington, D.C. Office). ***PRACTICE AREAS:*** Intellectual Property; Litigation. ***Email:*** mpaulson@mayerbrownrowe.com

GEORGE A. PECOULAS, born Chicago, Illinois, October 30, 1949; admitted to bar, 1987, Illinois. *Education:* Southern Illinois University (B.A., 1971); John Marshall Law School (J.D., with highest distinction, 1987). ***LANGUAGES:*** Greek. ***Email:*** gpecoulas@mayerbrownrowe.com

EILEEN PENNER, born Northridge, California, March 24, 1963; admitted to bar, 1989, California and U.S. Court of Appeals, Ninth Circuit; 1994, U.S. Court of Appeals, Fifth Circuit and U.S. Supreme Court; 1995, U.S. Court of Appeals, First and Tenth Circuits; 1996, District of Columbia and U.S. Court of Appeals, Fourth Circuit; 1997, U.S. Court of Appeals, Sixth Circuit; 1998, U.S. Court of Appeals, Seventh Circuit; 1999, U.S. Court of Appeals, Second, Third and Eleventh Circuits. *Education:* University of California at Berkeley (B.A., 1984, Phi Beta Kappa); Harvard University (J.D., magna cum laude, 1988). Executive Editor, *Harvard Law Review; Harvard Civil Rights-Civil Liberties Law Review.* Adjunct lecturer in *Remedies,* American University, Washington College of Law, 1996; Instructor, Appellate Advocacy, Attorney General's Advocacy Institute, 1996; U.S. Department of Justice, Washington, D.C., 1989-1996; Appellate Section, Civil Rights Division, Appellate Attorney, 1994-1996; Housing and Civil Enforcement Section, Civil Rights Division, Trial Attorney, 1989-1994; Law Clerk to The Honorable Dorothy W. Nelson, U.S. Court of Appeals for the Ninth Circuit, 1988-1989. (Washington, D.C. Office). ***Email:*** epenner@mayerbrownrowe.com

BRUCE F. PERCE, born Chicago, Illinois, September 8, 1964; admitted to bar, 1990, Wisconsin and Illinois. *Education:* Colgate University (A.B., 1987); University of Wisconsin-Madison (J.D., cum laude, 1990); Georgetown University Law Center (LL.M., with distinction, 1993). ***PRACTICE AREAS:*** Securities; Mergers and Acquisitions; Corporate Law. ***Email:*** bperce@mayerbrownrowe.com

STUART P. PERGAMENT, born New York, N.Y., March 24, 1942; admitted to bar, 1980, New York; 1983, Colorado; 1987, District of Columbia. *Education:* State University of New York at Stony Brook (B.S.E., 1963; Ph.D., 1970); Princeton University (M.S.E, 1966); Fordham University (J.D., 1979). (Washington, D.C. Office). ***Email:*** spergament@mayerbrownrowe.com

SCOTT P. PERLMAN, born Brooklyn, New York, September 15, 1960; admitted to bar, 1987, New York; 1988, District of Columbia; 1991, U.S. District Court for the District of Columbia; 1992, U.S. Court of Appeals for the District of Columbia Circuit. *Education:* University of Pennsylvania (B.A., summa cum laude, 1982); Harvard University (J.D., magna cum laude, 1986). Co-author: Article, "Innovation Policy and Antitrust Enforcement: The 1995 Antitrust Guidelines for the Licensing of Intellectual Property," published in Mathew Bender & Co., Antitrust Report, June 1995; Article, "Most Favored Nation Clauses in Contracts Between Health Care Networks and Providers," published in Mathew, Bender & Co., Antitrust Report, September 1996; Article, "A New and Uncertain Future for Managed Care Mergers: An Antitrust Analysis of the Aetna/Prudential Merger," published in *Antitrust Report,* Matthew Bender & Co. (Oct. 1999); "Analysis of Antitrust Issues Raised by B2B Exchanges: Practical Guidelines and Insights from the FTC B2B Workshop," published in Antitrust Report, Matthew Bender & Co., September 2000; "United States v. Microsoft Corporation: Striking a Balance Between Antitrust Enforcement and Intellectual Property Rights in the New Economy," published by Texas Institute of Continuing Legal Education, October 2001; "Balancing Antitrust Issues and Intellectual Property Rights: A Practical Guide for Biotech/Pharma Companies Managing their IP Portfolios," Mayer, Brown, Rowe & Maw, June 2002; "FTC Targets Patent Settlement Agreements," National Law Journal, November 11, 2002. *Member:* Federal Bar Association (Chair, Antitrust & Trade Regulation Section, 1997—). (Washington, D.C. Office). ***TRANSACTIONS:*** Aetna's acquisitions of US Healthcare, NYLCare and Prudential; Dow Chemical's sales of Marion Merrell Dow to Hoescht and DowBrands to S.C. Johnson; the merger of Strong Memorial and Highland Hospitals in Rochester, New York; the merger of St. Joseph's and Candler Hospitals in Savannah, Georgia; formation of a joint venture between Cargill and Monsanto for the development of transgenic seed; formation of a joint venture between Bertelsmann's Doubleday Direct Book Club and Time Warner's Book of the Month Club. ***PRACTICE AREAS:*** Antitrust; Hart-Scott-Rodino; Litigation. ***Email:*** sperlman@mayerbrownrowe.com

ROBERT (BOB) PETERS, born Stanmore, Middx, United Kingdom, February 5, 1948; admitted to bar, 1971, England. *Education:* University of Durham, England (B.A., 1969); The College of Law, London, England (J.D., 1971). (London, England Office). ***Email:*** bpeters@eu.mayerbrownrowe.com

(This Listing Continued)

BRAD L. PETERSON, born Minneapolis, Minnesota, May 29, 1959; admitted to bar, 1988, Illinois. *Education:* Northwestern University; University of Chicago (M.B.A., 1982); Harvard Law School (J.D., 1988). Author: "The Smart Way to Buy Information Technology: How to Maximize Value and Avoid Costly Pitfalls," (AMACOM Books 1998). ***PRACTICE AREAS:*** Information Technology Contracts; Outsourcing; Strategic Alliances. ***Email:*** bpeterson@mayerbrownrowe.com

ANTONY DOUGLAS PHILLIPS, born Little Chalfont, Bucks, November 8, 1963; admitted to bar, 1991 England and Wales. *Education:* University College Cardiff (B.S.C., 1983); College of Law Guildford and Chester (C.P.E., 1984; L.S.F., 1985). Member, Law Society. (London, England Office). ***PRACTICE AREAS:*** Property Litigation. ***Email:*** aphillips@mayerbrownrowe.com

JEFFREY S. PIELL, born Detroit, Michigan, August 24, 1966; admitted to bar, 1991, Illinois and U.S. District Court, Northern District of Illinois; 1994, U.S. Court of Appeals, Sixth Circuit; 1999, U.S. Court of Appeals, District of Columbia Circuit; 2000, U.S.Court of Appeals, Seventh Circuit. *Education:* University of Michigan (B.A., with highest distinction, 1988); Harvard University (J.D., cum laude, 1991). Phi Beta Kappa. Co-Author: with Marcia E. Goodman, "Testing, Testing, A-D-A," Corporate Counsel, p. 48, Feb. 2000. ***PRACTICE AREAS:*** Employment Law; Employment Litigation; Class Actions. ***Email:*** jpiell@mayerbrownrowe.com

SCOTT N. PIERPONT, admitted to bar, 1990, Illinois; 1997, New York; 2001, Illinois. *Education:* Duke University (B.A., 1986); Kellogg Graduate School of Management (M.A., 1990); Northwestern University School of Law (J.D., 1990). (New York, N.Y. Office). ***PRACTICE AREAS:*** Finance. ***Email:*** spierpont@mayerbrownrowe.com

ANDREW J. PINCUS, born Hempstead, New York, April 17, 1957; admitted to bar, 1982, New York; 1983, District of Columbia and U.S. District Court, District of Columbia and U.S. Court of Appeals, District of Columbia Circuit; 1985, U.S. Supreme Court. *Education:* Yale University (B.A., cum laude, 1977); Columbia University School of Law (J.D., 1981). Stone Scholar. Kent Scholar. Notes and Comments Editor, Columbia Law Review, 1980-1981. Law Clerk to Hon. Harold H. Greene, U.S. District Court, District of Columbia, 1981-1982. Assistant to the Solicitor General, United States Department of Justice, 1984-1988. General Counsel, United States Department of Commerce, 1997-2000. Member, Advisory Commission on Electronic Commerce, 1999-2000. General Counsel, Andersen Worldwide, 2001-2003. (Washington, D.C. Office). ***PRACTICE AREAS:*** Appellate Litigation; Public Policy. ***Email:*** apincus@mayerbrownrowe.com

MATTHEW A. POSTHUMA, born Columbus, Ohio, June 13, 1969; admitted to bar, 1994, Illinois. *Education:* University of Michigan (A.B., summa cum laude, 1991); Harvard Law School (J.D., cum laude, 1994). Executive Editor, Harvard Journal of Law and Public Policy. ***LANGUAGES:*** Spanish. ***PRACTICE AREAS:*** Corporate and Securities Law; Commercial Law; Finance. ***Email:*** mposthuma@mayerbrownrowe.com

ASHISH S. PRASAD, born Detroit, Michigan, September 21, 1967; admitted to bar, 1994, Illinois. *Education:* University of Michigan (A.B., 1989); University of Chicago (J.D., 1993). Member, Law Review. ***Email:*** aprasad@mayerbrownrowe.com

MARK ADAM PRINSLEY, born 1956; admitted to bar, 1981, England. *Education:* Oxford University. *Member:* Institute ofTrade Mark Agents (Associate Member). (London, England Office). ***PRACTICE AREAS:*** Intellectual Property Law; Information Technology Law. ***Email:*** mprinsley@mayerbrownrowe.com

KEVIN A. RANG, born Mt. Clemens, Michigan, May 27, 1968; admitted to bar, 1995, Michigan; 2001, Illinois. *Education:* Michigan State University (B.A., 1990); University of Michigan (J.D., cum laude, 1995). Author: "E-Filing is Becoming a Virtual Reality," March 2000, Number 410. ***PRACTICE AREAS:*** Corporate Law (10%); Information Technology (30%); Outsourcing (60%). ***Email:*** krang@mayerbrownrowe.com

GEORGE A. RANNEY, JR., born Chicago, Illinois, April 11, 1940; admitted to bar, 1966, Illinois. *Education:* Harvard University (B.A., magna cum laude, 1962); University of Chicago (J.D., 1966). ***Email:*** granney@mayerbrownrowe.com

MITCHELL D. RAUP, born Baltimore, Maryland, May 25, 1959; admitted to bar, 1983, Illinois and U.S. District Court, Northern District of Illinois; 1991, U.S. Court of Appeals, Seventh Circuit; 1997, U.S. Court of Appeals, Sixth Circuit; 1998, District of Columbia; 1999, U.S. Court of Appeals, Third Circuit; 2000, U.S. Supreme Court. *Education:* University of Chicago (B.A., with honors, 1980); Duke University (J.D., with honors, 1983). Author: "Medical Boycotts by Health Care Providers: A Noett Pennington Defense," 69 Iowa l. Review 1393 (1984). Adjunct Professor of Antitrust Law, DePaul Law School, 1993-1996. (Washington, D.C. Office). ***PRACTICE AREAS:*** Antitrust and Trade Regulation; Litigation. ***Email:*** mraup@mayerbrownrowe.com

ELIZABETH A. RAYMOND, born Evanston, Illinois, July 30, 1957; admitted to bar, 1984, New York; 1988, Illinois. *Education:* Princeton University (A.B., summa cum laude, 1978); Clare College, Cambridge University, England (M.A., with honors, 1980); New York University (J.D., 1983). ***PRACTICE AREAS:*** Mergers and Acquisitions; Securities; Securitization. ***Email:*** eraymond@mayerbrownrowe.com

PHILIP R. RECHT, born Pittsburgh, Pennsylvania, June 10, 1953; admitted to bar, 1981, California. *Education:* Yale University (B.A., cum laude, with distinction in major, 1975); University of Pennsylvania (J.D., cum laude, 1981). Chief Counsel, 1994-1995 and Deputy Administrator, 1995-1999, National Highway Traffic Safety Administration, U.S. Department of Transportation. President, Century City Bar Association, 1992. President, California Political Attorneys Association, 1993, 1994. (Los Angeles, California Office). ***Email:*** precht@mayerbrownrowe.com

PHILLIP S. REED, born St. Louis, Missouri, December 25, 1956; admitted to bar, 1984, Illinois and U.S. District Court, Northern District of Illinois. *Education:* University of Cincinnati (B.A., with honors, 1980); Northwestern University (J.D., cum laude, 1984). ***Email:*** preed@mayerbrownrowe.com

CHRISTOPHER F. REGAN, admitted to bar, 1991, New York; 1992, District of Columbia. *Education:* State University of New York at Brockport (B.S., magna cum laude, 1987); University of Michigan Law School(J.D., 1990). ***PRACTICE AREAS:*** Litigation. ***Email:*** cregan2@mayerbrownrowe.com

(This Listing Continued)

MICHAEL REGAN, born 1955; admitted to bar, 1980, England. *Education:* Oxford University. (London, England Office). ***PRACTICE AREAS:*** Construction and Engineering Law; Insurance Law; Litigation; International Arbitration. ***Email:*** mregan@mayerbrownrowe.com

N. NEVILLE REID, born Milwaukee, Wisconsin, March 15, 1961; admitted to bar, 1987, Illinois; 1991, U.S. District Court, Northern District of Illinois; 1993, U.S. Court of Appeals, Seventh Circuit; 1997, U.S. Court of Appeals, Sixth Circuit. *Education:* Harvard University (B.A., Social Studies, magna cum laude, 1984; J.D., 1987). Publications: "Overview of Successor Liability For Tort Claims," printed in Seminar Materials for American Bankruptcy Institute's Winter Leadership Conference, December 5-7, 1996; "Will a Work-Out Work? Issues From the Lender's Perspective," printed in Seminar Materials for the Twenty-Fourth Annual Southeastern Bankruptcy Law Institute Seminar, Atlanta, GA, March 26-28, 1998; "Claims Trading," printed in Seminar Materials for the Twenty-Fourth Annual Southeastern Bankruptcy Law Institute Seminar, Atlanta, GA, March 26-28, 1998; "The Nature and Scope of a Trustee's Duties in a Potentially Solvent Estate," printed in Seminar Materials for the 1999 United States Trustee Seminar, Chicago, Illinois, March 6, 1999; "Fiduciary and Ethics Questions for Consideration at U.S. Trustee Seminar," printed in Seminar Materials for the 1999 United States Trustee Seminar, Chicago, Illinois, March 6, 1999 "The Basics of Substantive Consolidation," printed in Seminar Materials for the Chicago Bar Association Seminar, Chicago, Illinois, March 10, 1999; "Bankruptcy Treatment of Loans From Retirement Plans: Employer Strategies in Bankruptcy Cases", Benefits Law Journal, Vol. 13., No. 2, Summer 2000. ***PRACTICE AREAS:*** Bankruptcy; Creditors Rights; Litigation. ***Email:*** nreid@mayerbrownrowe.com

PETER W. RICHARDS-CARPENTER, born 1950; admitted to bar, 1974, England; 1986, as a Solicitor. *Education:* Haberdasher' Asla Hatcham; St. Catherine's College, Oxford (M.A., |974). (London, England Office). ***LANGUAGES:*** English, German and French. ***PRACTICE AREAS:*** Financial Markets; Banking and Financial Services. ***Email:*** prichardscarpenter@mayerbrownrowe.com

MARY B. RICHARDSON-LOWRY, born June 26, 1957; admitted to bar, 1986, Illinois. *Education:* University of San Francisco State (B.A., 1981); Texas Southern University (J.D., 1984). Building Commissioner City of Chicago, 1998-2002. Chairperson, Chicago Community Development Commission, 2003—. ***PRACTICE AREAS:*** Government Practice; Construction; Commercial Transactions; Contracts. ***Email:*** mrichardson-lowry@mayerbrownrowe.com

LAURA D. RICHMAN, born New York, N.Y., February 23, 1956; admitted to bar, 1981, Illinois and U.S. District Court, Northern District of Illinois. *Education:* Yale College (B.A., magna cum laude, 1977); University of Chicago (J.D., 1981). ***PRACTICE AREAS:*** Corporate Law; Securities; Limited Liability Company Law. ***Email:*** lrichman@mayerbrownrowe.com

MICHAEL P. RICHMAN, born New Rochelle, New York, March 12, 1953; admitted to bar, 1979, District of Columbia; 1980, U.S. District Court, District of Columbia and U.S. Court of Appeals, District of Columbia Circuit; 1982, U.S. Court of Appeals, Ninth Circuit; 1985, New York and U.S. District Court, Southern and Eastern Districts of New York; 1989, U.S. Court of Appeals, Second Circuit; 1996, U.S. District Court, Northern District of Illinois; 1998, U.S. District Court, Western District of Michigan; 2003, U.S. Court of Appeals, Third Circuit. *Education:* London School of Economics and Political Science, London, United Kingdom; Vassar College (A.B., cum laude, with honors in Political Science, 1975); Columbia University (J.D., 1979). Contributing Editor, "Straight and Narrow" Column, American Bankruptcy Institute Journal. *Member:* American Bankruptcy Institute (President, 2004-2005; Member, Executive Committee, 2001—; Director, Board of Directors, 1996—). (New York, N.Y. Office). ***TRANSACTIONS:*** National Bankruptcy Counsel to Center for Claims Resolution in Chapter 11 cases of asbestos producers and suppliers; National Bankruptcy Counsel to Ernst & Young Corporate Finance; Counsel to Bondholders' Committee in international restructuring of Uneximbank and Official Committee of Unsecured Creditors of Pegasus Gold Corporation. ***PRACTICE AREAS:*** Bankruptcy; Bankruptcy Litigation; Creditors' Rights. ***Email:*** mrichman@mayerbrownrowe.com

ROBERT S. RIGG, born Aberdeen, Maryland, July 25, 1964; admitted to bar, 1990, Illinois; registered to practice before the U.S. Patent and Trademark Office. *Education:* Purdue University (B.S., 1987); Valparaiso University (J.D., with honors, 1990). ***PRACTICE AREAS:*** Intellectual Property; Intellectual Property Litigation; Intellectual Property Licensing. ***Email:*** rrigg@mayerbrownrowe.com

DANIEL L. RING, born Cincinnati, Ohio, December 12, 1967; admitted to bar, 1993, Illinois. *Education:* Northwestern University (B.A., 1990); Loyola University (J.D., 1993). ***Email:*** dring@mayerbrownrowe.com

MICHAEL P. RISSMAN, born Chicago, Illinois, June 10, 1960; admitted to bar, 1986, Illinois; 1988, District of Columbia; 1989, U.S. District Court for the District of Columbia; 1990, U.S. District Court, Northern District of Illinois; 1992, U.S. District Court, Eastern District of Michigan; 1995, U.S. District Court, Central District of Illinois; 1992, U.S. Court of Appeals, Seventh and Fifth Circuits; 2003, U.S. Court of Appeals, Sixth Circuit. *Education:* Harvard University (A.B., magna cum laude, 1982); University of Chicago (J.D., cum laude, 1986). ***PRACTICE AREAS:*** Environmental Law; Litigation. ***Email:*** mrissman@mayerbrownrowe.com

JEFFREY F. ROBERTSON, admitted to bar, 1996, New York; 1997, District of Columbia. *Education:* University of Tennessee (B.A., 1990); Columbia University (J.D., 1994). (Washington, D.C. Office). ***PRACTICE AREAS:*** Litigation. ***Email:*** jfrobertson@mayerbrownrowe.com

NICHOLAS ROBERTSON, born 1964; admitted to bar, 1988, England. *Education:* Leicester University. (London, England Office). ***PRACTICE AREAS:*** Employment Litigation. ***Email:*** nrobertson@mayerbrownrowe.com

MELVILLE RODRIGUES, born March 26, 1958; admitted to bar, 1979, England. *Education:* Cambridge University, England (M.A., 1979); Open University (M.B.A., 2000). (London, England Office). ***Email:*** mrodrigues@mayerbrownrowe.com

ANNA ROGERS, born 1961; admitted to bar, 1985, England. *Education:* Oxford University. (London, England Office). ***LANGUAGES:*** French, German and Italian. ***PRACTICE AREAS:*** Pensions Law. ***Email:*** arogers@eu.mayerbrownrowe.com

(This Listing Continued)

MAYER, BROWN, ROWE & MAW LLP, Chicago—Continued

HOWARD J. ROIN, born Chicago, Illinois, August 28, 1953; admitted to bar, 1978, Illinois; 1979, U.S. Court of Appeals, District of Columbia Circuit; 1981, U.S. District Court, Northern District of Illinois; 1982, U.S. Court of Appeals, Seventh Circuit. *Education:* Amherst College (B.A., magna cum laude, 1975); University of Chicago (J.D., honors, 1978). ***Email:*** hroin@mayerbrownrowe.com

DAVID L. RONN, born Westwood, New Jersey, December 31, 1961; admitted to bar, 1990, Texas. *Education:* Rice University (B.A., 1983); Tulane University (M.B.A., 1985); University of Houston (J.D., 1990). (Houston, Texas Office). ***PRACTICE AREAS:*** Corporate Law; Securities. ***Email:*** dronn@mayerbrownrowe.com

MATTHEW A. ROONEY, born Jersey City, New Jersey, May 19, 1949; admitted to bar, 1975, Illinois and U.S. District Court, Northern District of Illinois; 1983, Trial Bar; 1990, U.S. Court of Appeals, Seventh Circuit. *Education:* Georgetown University (A.B., magna cum laude, 1971); University of Chicago (J.D., honors, 1974). Law Clerk to the Hon. Philip W. Tone, U.S. Circuit Court of Appeals, Seventh Circuit, 1974-1975. Fellow, American College of Trial Lawyers. ***PRACTICE AREAS:*** Trial Advocacy; Civil Litigation; Antitrust. ***Email:*** mrooney@mayerbrownrowe.com

LEONARD X ROSENBERG, born Chicago, Illinois, 1967; admitted to bar, 1992, Illinois. *Education:* Brandeis University (B.A., cum laude, 1989); Northwestern University (J.D., 1992). ***PRACTICE AREAS:*** Real Estate; Corporate Law; Finance. ***Email:*** lrosenberg@mayerbrownrowe.com

ANDREW S. ROSENMAN, born Chicago, Illinois, April 12, 1969; admitted to bar, 1995, Illinois, U.S. District Court, Northern District of Illinois and U.S. Court of Appeals, Seventh Circuit; 1996, Michigan, U.S. District Court, Eastern District of Michigan and U.S. Court of Appeals, Sixth Circuit; 2002, U.S. District Court, Western District of Michigan. *Education:* University of Michigan (B.A., 1991); Chicago-Kent College of Law (J.D., with high honors, 1995). Order of the Coif. Note and Comment Editor, Chicago-Kent Law Review, 1994-1995. Author: Note, "Babies Jessica, Richard and Emily: The Need for Legislative Reform of Adoption Laws," 70 Chi.-Kent L. Rev. 1851, 1995. Law Clerk to the Honorable Steven D. Pepe, Magistrate Judge, U.S. District Court, 1995-1996. ***PRACTICE AREAS:*** Labor and Employment; Litigation. ***Email:*** arosenman@mayerbrownrowe.com

MARTIN G. ROSENSTEIN, born Chicago, Illinois, August 21, 1953; admitted to bar, 1979, Illinois and U.S. District Court, Northern District of Illinois. *Education:* University of Illinois (B.S., highest honors, 1975); Loyola University (J.D., cum laude, 1979). ***Email:*** mrosenstein@mayerbrownrowe.com

MARC E. ROSENTHAL, born Evanston, Illinois, 1963; admitted to bar, 1990, Illinois. *Education:* Kenyon College (B.A.); John Marshall Law School (J.D., 1990). ***PRACTICE AREAS:*** Insurance; Litigation. ***Email:*** mrosenthal@mayerbrownrowe.com

JULIAN WENTWORTH ROSKILL, born 1950; admitted to bar, 1974, England. *Education:* Winchester College. *Member:* City of London Solicitors Company; Employment Lawyers Association. (London, England Office). ***LANGUAGES:*** French. ***PRACTICE AREAS:*** Contentious and Non-Contentious Employment Law; Industrial Relations Law. ***Email:*** jroskill@mayerbrownrowe.com

PHILIP R. ROTNER, admitted to bar, 1972, Illinois (inactive); 1973, Massachusetts; 1975, California; 1996, New York. *Education:* University of California at Berkeley (A.B., English, 1969); Harvard Law School (J.D., 1972). ***PRACTICE AREAS:*** Litigation. ***Email:*** protner@mayerbrownrowe.com

PAUL ROWELL, admitted to bar, 1993, England and Wales. Co-author of a tuition manual of the Pensions Management Institute. (London, England Office). ***PRACTICE AREAS:*** Pensions Law. ***Email:*** prowell@mayerbrownrowe.com

PAUL J.N. ROY, born Biddeford, Maine, April 16, 1955; admitted to bar, 1985, Illinois. *Education:* Colby College (B.A., 1978); Northwestern University (M.B.A., 1981); Loyola University (J.D., 1985). ***Email:*** proy@mayerbrownrowe.com

STUART M. ROZEN, born Chicago, Illinois, May 15, 1956; admitted to bar, 1981, Illinois. *Education:* University of Illinois (B.A., 1978; J.D., 1981). ***PRACTICE AREAS:*** Corporate Reorganization; Bankruptcy. ***Email:*** srozen@mayerbrownrowe.com

LEE H. RUBIN, born Peoria, Illinois, June 8, 1963; admitted to bar, 1989, California; 1991, District of Columbia. *Education:* Duke University (B.A., summa cum laude, 1985); Stanford University (J.D., with distinction, 1988). Phi Beta Kappa. Law Clerk to the Honorable Warren J. Ferguson, United States Court of Appeals for the Ninth Circuit, 1988-1989. Trial Attorney, U.S. Department of Justice, Civil Rights Division, 1989-1995. Assistant U.S. Attorney, District of Columbia, 1995-1997. (Palo Alto, California Office). ***Email:*** lrubin@mayerbrownrowe.com

JAVIER H. RUBINSTEIN, born Buenos Aires, Argentina, 1963; admitted to bar, 1989, Illinois and U.S. District Court, Northern District of Illinois; 1991, U.S. Court of Appeals, Seventh Circuit; 1992, U.S. District Court, Eastern District of Wisconsin; 1993, U.S. Supreme Court and U.S. Court of Appeals, Sixth Circuit; 1996, U.S. Court of Appeals, Ninth Circuit; 1997, U.S. Court of Appeals, Fifth Circuit and U.S. District Court, District of Arizona. *Education:* University of Michigan (B.A., high honors, 1984); Harvard University, John F. Kennedy School of Government (M.P.P., 1986); Georgetown University (J.D., cum laude, 1989). Named one of "40 Illinois Attorneys Under 40 to Watch," Chicago Lawyer Magazine (2001) and Chicago Daily Law Bulletin (2001). Author: "The Attorney-Client Privilege and International Arbitration," 18 Journal of International Arbitration 587 (December 2001); "Negotiating Arbitration Agreements for the Effective Resolution of Disputes Arising Out of International Commercial Transactions," X-7 International Legal Strategy (2001); "Handbook of Model International Arbitration Clauses & Comparison of Rules of Major International Arbitral Institutions" (1999); "The Federal Reserve Board's 'Liberalization' of Restrictions on LDC Debt-Equity Swaps," 20 Law & Policy in Int'l Business 163 (1988); "Addressing the Threat of Punitive Damages Claims in Franchise and Dealer Litigation," 15 Franchise Law Journal (Summer 1995); "Privilege Under Fire," 10 ACCA Docket (Summer 1995) also reprinted in Law Department Management Adviser, May 1994. Lecturer in Law, University of Chicago Law School, 1997—. Chair, Midwest Subcommittee on Arbitration, United States Council for International Business. Member, London Court of International Arbitration. Midwest Co-Chair, Business Torts Litigation

(This Listing Continued)

Committee, American Bar Association. (Board Certified Foreign Service Officer). ***LANGUAGES:*** Spanish. ***REPORTED CASES:*** Neder v. United States, 119 S. Ct. 1827 (1999); Uchumi Supermarkets v. Diners Club Int'l, 729 N.E.2d 505 (Ill.App. 1999); Zapata Hermanos Sucesores, S.A. v. Hearthside Banking Co., 155 F.Supp.2d 969 (2001); U.S. ex rel. Luckey v. Baxter Healthcare Corporation, 183 F.3d 730 (7th Cir. 1999). ***PRACTICE AREAS:*** International Commercial Arbitration; International Litigation; Supreme Court. ***Email:*** jrubinstein@mayerbrownrowe.com

DEBORAH SCHAVEY RUFF, born Gary, Indiana, February 24, 1959; admitted to bar, 1986, Illinois; registered to practice before U.S. Patent and Trademark Office. *Education:* Purdue University (B.S., Microbiology, 1981; Graduate Research Molecular Genetics, 1981-1982); Valparaiso University (J.D., 1986). Author: "Navigating Uncharted Waters - Taking Security Interests in U.S. Trademarks," International Financial Law Review Securitization Yearbook, 1999; "A Guide to Taking Security," Managing Intellectual Property Trademark Yearbook, 1998. Contributing Author: "How To Buy A U.S. Business --A Guide To Negotiated and Hostile Acquisitions", 1999 ;U.S. Correspondent for Intellectual Property Forum. U.S. Correspondent for the Intellectual Property Forum (periodical of the Intellectual Property Society of Australia and New Zealand). Attorney: Newman Williams Anderson & Olson, 1986-1991; Keck, Mahin & Cate, 1991-1996. Member, Regulatory Analysis Committee, 1993-1997, Public Relations Committee, 1998-2000, International Trademark Association. ***Email:*** druff@mayerbrownrowe.com

GEORGE RUHLEN, born Kyoto, Japan, March 3, 1950; admitted to bar, 1975, Texas; 1995, Illinois; 1999, New Mexico. *Education:* Rice University (B.A., 1972); University of Texas (J.D., 1975). ***Email:*** gruhlen@mayerbrownrowe.com

DONALD W. RUPERT, born Clearfield, Pennsylvania, October 15, 1946; admitted to bar, 1976, Texas; 1978, Illinois; 1979, U.S. District Court, Northern District of Illinois including Trial Bar; 1981, U.S. Court of Appeals, Seventh Circuit; 1982, U.S. Court of Appeals for the Federal Circuit; 1992, U.S. Supreme Court; 2000, U.S. District Court, Central District of Illinois; registered to practice before U.S. Patent and Trademark Office and the Canadian Patent Office. *Education:* Miami University (B.S., Chemistry, 1968); Washburn University (J.D., cum laude, 1976). [Capt., USAF, 1968-1974]. ***PRACTICE AREAS:*** Intellectual Property; Civil Litigation. ***Email:*** drupert@mayerbrownrowe.com

JOHN RUSHTON, born 1950; admitted to bar, 1975, England. *Education:* Cambridge University. (London, England Office). ***PRACTICE AREAS:*** Construction Law; Commercial Litigation; Arbitration Law. ***Email:*** jrushton@mayerbrownrowe.com

MARK W. RYAN, born Batavia, New York, October 6, 1955; admitted to bar, 1981, District of Columbia; 1982, U.S. Court of Appeals, District of Columbia Circuit and U.S. District Court, District of Columbia; 1989, U.S. Supreme Court; 1993, Maryland. *Education:* Syracuse University (B.A., magna cum laude, 1977; Phi Beta Kappa); Duke University (J.D., 1981). (Washington, D.C. Office). ***Email:*** mryan@mayerbrownrowe.com

JOHN R. SAGAN, born Champaign, Illinois, July 25, 1950; admitted to bar, 1983, Wisconsin; 1984, New York; 1988, Illinois. *Education:* Lawrence University (B.A., 1972); University of Wisconsin-Madison (J.D., cum laude, 1983). Attorney, Milbank, Tweed, Hadley & McCloy, 1983-1986. ***Email:*** jsagan@mayerbrownrowe.com

ALAN N. SALPETER, born Philadelphia, Pennsylvania, October 7, 1947; admitted to bar, 1972, Illinois. *Education:* American University (B.A., with honors, 1969, Omicron Delta Kappa); Villanova University (J.D., 1972). Managing Editor, Villanova Law Review. ***Email:*** asalpeter@mayerbrownrowe.com

DREW DANA SALVEST, born Perth Amboy, New Jersey, September 29, 1957; admitted to bar, 1988, New York. *Education:* Amherst College (B.A., cum laude, 1978); New York University (J.D., 1987). Dewey Ballantine (London), 1997-2001. Brown & Wood, 1987-1997. (London, England Office). ***LANGUAGES:*** English. ***PRACTICE AREAS:*** Banking; Finance; Securitization. ***Email:*** dsalvest@mayerbrownrowe.com

GAIL C. SARACCO, born October 19, 1966; admitted to bar, 1991, Illinois; 1992, District of Columbia. *Education:* Yale University (B.A., 1987); University of Michigan (J.D., cum laude, 1990). Associate Editor, 1988-1989 and Contributing Editor, 1989-1990, Michigan Law Review. ***PRACTICE AREAS:*** Corporate Law; Securities; Finance. ***Email:*** gsaracco@mayerbrownrowe.com

JEFFREY W. SARLES, born Buffalo, New York, May 30, 1948; admitted to bar, 1994, Illinois; U.S. Court of Appeals, Second, Third, Fourth, Fifth, Sixth, Seventh, Ninth, Tenth, Eleventh, District of Columbia and Federal Circuits; U.S. Supreme Court. *Education:* Wesleyan University (B.A., 1970); University of Chicago (M.A., 1971); Northwestern University (J.D., 1994). Adjunct Professor of Commercial Arbitration Law, Northwestern University, 1996—. Seventh Circuit Editor, American Bar Association's Appellate Practice Journal, 2001—. Editor-in-Chief, Northwestern University Law Review 1993-1994. Author: "The Confidentiality Conundrum in International Arbitration," ADR and the Law (2002); "U.S. Courts Divided Over Enforceability of Arbitral Subpoenas to Non-Parties," Mealey's International Arbitration Report, January 2001; "International Business Disputes are Increasingly Resolved by Arbitration," BNA's Corporate Counsel Weekly, May 10, 2000; "Defamation Law," National Law Journal, September 8, 1997; "Court Decisions Alter the Arbitration Landscape," National Law Journal, August 19, 1996; "Supersedeas Bonds: A Crushing Burden," National Law Journal, November 13, 1995. ***PRACTICE AREAS:*** Appellate Practice (50%, 50); Arbitration (30%, 40); Antitrust (20%, 20). ***Email:*** jsarles@mayerbrownrowe.com

JOHN M. SATALIC, born Chicago, Illinois, March 24, 1959; admitted to bar, 1986, Illinois. *Education:* Harvard University (B.A., 1981; J.D., cum laude, 1986). ***PRACTICE AREAS:*** Government; Regulatory Law; Administrative Law. ***Email:*** jsatalic@mayerbrownrowe.com

EDMUND MARK SAUTTER, born 1958; admitted to bar, 1983, England. *Education:* Cambridge University. (London, England Office). ***PRACTICE AREAS:*** Commercial Litigation. ***Email:*** esautter@mayerbrownrowe.com

ANDREW H. SCHAPIRO, born Chicago, Illinois, April 25, 1963; admitted to bar, 1992, Illinois; 1996, New York, U.S. Court of Appeals, Second Circuit and U.S. District Court, Southern District of New York. *Education:* Yale University (B.A., magna cum laude, 1985); Oxford University (B.A., First Class Honours, 1987); Harvard Law School (J.D., magna cum laude, 1990). Phi Beta Kappa. Articles Office Co-Chair, Harvard Law Review. Law Clerk, Hon. Richard A. Posner, U.S. Court of Appeals for the Seventh Circuit, 1991-

(This Listing Continued)

1992; Law Clerk, Hon. Harry A. Blackmun, U.S. Supreme Court, 1992-1993. Trial Attorney, Office of the Federal Defender for the Southern District of New York, 1993-1998. (New York, N.Y. Office). **Email:** aschapiro@mayerbrownrowe.com

PETER L. SCHER, born New York, N.Y., April 12, 1961; admitted to bar, 1988, New York; 1989, District of Columbia. *Education:* American University (B.A., 1983); Washington College of Law (J.D., 1987). U.S. Special Trade Negotiator (Rank of Ambassador), 1997-2000. Chief of Staff, USTR and Department of Commerce, 1995-1997. Staff Director, U.S. Senate Committee on Environmental and Public Works, 1993-1995. Chief of Staff, U.S. Senator Max Baucus, 1991-1993. (Washington, D.C. Office). **Email:** pscher@mayerbrownrowe.com

WILLIAM A. SCHMALZL, born Pittsburgh, Pennsylvania, July 16, 1953; admitted to bar, 1979, Illinois and U.S. District Court, Northern District of Illinois and U.S. Tax Court; 1982, U.S. Court of Appeals, Seventh Circuit; 1984, U.S. Court of Appeals, Eighth Circuit; 1985, U.S. Court of Appeals, Tenth Circuit; 1991, U.S. Supreme Court. *Education:* University of Pittsburgh (B.A., summa cum laude, 1974); Harvard University (J.D., magna cum laude, 1977). ***PRACTICE AREAS:*** Tax Controversies. **Email:** wschmalzl@mayerbrownrowe.com

JOHN R. SCHMIDT, born Chicago, Ill., 1943; admitted to bar, 1967, Illinois. *Education:* Harvard University (B.A., magna cum laude, 1964; J.D., cum laude, 1967). Editor, Harvard Law Review, 1965-1967. Visiting Scholar, Northwestern Law School, 1997. Associate Attorney General of the United States, 1994-1997, Ambassador and Chief U.S. Negotiator for the Uruguay Round under the General Agreement on Tariffs and Trade, 1993-1994. Chairman, Metropolitan Pier and Exposition Authority, 1989-1994. Chief of Staff for Mayor Richard M. Daley, 1989. Chairman, Illinois Guardianship & Advocacy Commission, 1979-1981. President, Chicago Council of Lawyers, 1974-1976. **Email:** jschmidt@mayerbrownrowe.com

JOHN P. SCHMITZ, born 1955; admitted to bar, 1985, Pennsylvania; 1994, District of Columbia. *Education:* Georgetown University (B.A., magna cum laude, 1976); California Institute of Technology (M.A., Economics, 1978); Stanford University (J.D., 1981). (Washington, D.C., Cologne and Frankfurt, Germany Offices). ***LANGUAGES:*** English and German. **Email:** jschmitz@mayerbrownrowe.com

EDWARD J. SCHNEIDMAN, born Quincy, Illinois, September 20, 1955; admitted to bar, 1980, Illinois and U.S. District Court, Northern District of Illinois. *Education:* University of Pennsylvania (B.S., 1977); Duke University (J.D., with honors, 1980). **Email:** eschneidman@mayerbrownrowe.com

JAMES C. SCHROEDER, born Madison, Wisconsin, July 5, 1956; admitted to bar, 1981, Wisconsin and U.S. District Court, Eastern District of Wisconsin; 1983, U.S. Court of Appeals, Seventh Circuit; 1988, Illinois and U.S. District Court, Northern District of Illinois; 1992, U.S. Court of Appeals, Fifth Circuit and U.S. Supreme Court; 1993, U.S. Court of Appeals, Ninth Circuit; 1994, U.S. Court of Appeals, Sixth and Tenth Circuits; 1997, U.S. Court of Appeals, Fourth Circuit; 1999, U.S. Court of Appeals, Eleventh Circuit. *Education:* Beloit College (B.A., summa cum laude, 1978); University of Wisconsin-Madison (J.D., cum laude, 1981). Co-Author: "Arguing for Changes in the Law," 25 Litigation 37, Winter 1999; "The Attorney's Guide to the Seventh Circuit Court of Appeals," State Bar of Wisconsin, 1996. Senior Staff Attorney, U.S. Court of Appeals, Seventh Circuit, 1985-1988. ***PRACTICE AREAS:*** Appellate Practice. **Email:** jschroeder@mayerbrownrowe.com

DAVID A. SCHUETTE, born Oak Park, Illinois, October 11, 1960; admitted to bar, 1985, Illinois. *Education:* Georgetown University (A.B., cum laude, 1982); University of Michigan (J.D., cum laude, 1985). Author: "Revised Insider Reporting and Short-Swing Liability Rules," International Company and Commercial Law Review, August 1991. **Email:** dschuette@mayerbrownrowe.com

ANDREA J. SCHWARTZMAN, born Montreal, Quebec, Canada, June 10, 1970; admitted to bar, 1996, Massachusetts; 1997, New York. *Education:* Harvard University (A.B., 1992); Columbia University (J.D., 1996). (New York, N.Y. Office). ***LANGUAGES:*** French. ***PRACTICE AREAS:*** Corporate Law; Securities. **Email:** aschwartzman@mayerbrownrowe.com

AMI G. SCOTT, admitted to bar, 1999, Illinois. *Education:* The Ohio State University (B.S.B.A., 1994; M.B.A., 1994); University of Michigan (J.D., 1997). **Email:** agscott@mayerbrownrowe.com

ZALDWAYNAKA L. SCOTT, born Shreveport, Louisiana, August 5, 1958; admitted to bar, 1983, Illinois. *Education:* University of Illinois, Urbana-Champaign (B.S., 1980); Indiana University School of Law (J.D., 1983). ***PRACTICE AREAS:*** Litigation. **Email:** zscott@mayerbrownrowe.com

STEVEN R. SELSBERG, born Baltimore, Maryland, 1961; admitted to bar, 1986, Texas; 1988, U.S. District Court, Southern, Northern, Eastern and Western Districts of Texas; U.S. Court of Appeals, Fifth and Eighth Circuits. *Education:* Georgetown University (A.B., cum laude, 1983); Washington University (J.D., 1986). Executive Articles Editor, Journal of Urban and Contemporary Law. Author: "My Dog Ate It! Spoliation of Evidence and the Texas Supreme Court's Ortega Decision," 62 Texas Bar J. 1014 1999; "Depositions: Should Courts End the Nonsense," 32 Houston Lawyer 29, 1995; "Judicial Activism and the DTPA," 31 Houston Lawyer, 1993. *Member:* Houston and American Bar Associations. (Houston, Texas Office). ***PRACTICE AREAS:*** Litigation; Dispute Resolution. **Email:** srselsberg@mayerbrownrowe.com

DEVI SHAH, admitted to bar, 1995, England and Wales. *Education:* Pembroke College, Oxford (B.C.L.); University College London (LL.B.). (London, England Office). ***PRACTICE AREAS:*** Litigation. **Email:** dshah@mayerbrownrowe.com

STEPHEN M. SHAPIRO, born Chicago, Illinois, May 3, 1946; admitted to bar, 1971, Illinois; 1972, California; 1991, District of Columbia; 1975, U.S. Supreme Court. *Education:* Yale University (B.A., magna cum laude, 1968; J.D., 1971). Phi Beta Kappa. Member, Board of Editors, Yale Law Journal, 1970-1971. Law Clerk, U.S. Court of Appeals, Ninth Circuit, 1971. Assistant to the Solicitor General, 1978-1980. Deputy Solicitor General of the United States, 1981-1983. Co-author with Robert L. Stern, Eugene Gressman and Kenneth S. Geller, "Supreme Court Practice," Bureau of National Affairs, 8th Ed., 2002; "Analysis of the 1997 Revisions of the Supreme Court Rules," Bureau of National Affairs, 1997; "Supreme Court Rules: the 1995 Revisions," Bureau of National Affairs, 1995; "Epitaph for Mandatory Jurisdiction," ABA Journal, December 1, 1988; "Supreme Court Rules: The 1990 Revisions," 58 U.S.L.W. 3555, 1990. Contributing Author: ABA "Appellate Practice Manual," 1992; "Litigation Manual: Special Problems and Appeals" (1999). Author: "Oral Argument in the Supreme Court of the United States," 33 Catholic U. L. Rev. 525 (1984). "Amicus Briefs in the Supreme Court," Litigation, Vol. 10, No. 3 (1984); "Oral Argument in The Supreme Court: The Felt Necessities Of the Time," Supreme Court Historical Society Yearbook (1985); "William Pinkney: The Supreme Court's Greatest Advocate," Litigation, May, 1987. "Rebels at the Supreme Court," Litigation, Winter, 1989; "Interview with Steve Shapiro," Litigation, Winter, 1997; with Wade H. McCree, "The Solicitor General and His Client," 59 Wash. U.L.Q. 337 (1981); "Questions, Answers and Prepared Remarks," Litigation, Spring 1989; "Significant Judicial Developments," 24th Annual Institute on Securities Regulation, 1992; "The Lawgiver's Faltering Hand," September, 1986, Legal Bulletin 213. "Judicial Restraint on Bank Regulatory Issues," Rev. Financial Services Regulation, Vol. 3, No. 6, 1987; "Certiorari Practice: The Supreme Court's Shrinking Docket," Litigation, Spring 1998; "Interstate Banking In the 1980's," 17th Annual Institute on Securities Regulation, 1985; "Breathing New Life into State Takeover Statutes," 19th PLI Annual Institute on Securities Regulation, 1987. Preface Author: "Collection of In-Chambers Opinions by The Justices of The Supreme Court of The United States" (2004). *Member:* American Law Institute (Life Member); American Academy of Appellate Lawyers; Institute of Judicial Administration (Member, Board of Directors). ***REPORTED CASES:*** Representative cases argued in the Supreme Court: F. Hoffmann-LaRoche, Ltd. v. Empagran, S.A. 124 S. Ct. 2359 (2004). Sprietsma v. Mercury Marine 537 U.S. 51 (2003). Chevron v. Echazabal 536 U.S. 73 (2002). Amchem v. George Windsor 521 U.S. 591 (1997). Hartford Ins. v. State of Calif. 509 U.S. 764 (1993). Va. Bankshares v. Sandberg 501 U.S. 1083 (1991). Amer. Trucking Assn v. Scheiner 483 U.S. 266 (1987). Northeast Bancorp v. Bd of Governors of Fed. Res. System 472 U.S. 159 (1985). Keeton v. Hustler 465 U.S. 770 (1984). Falls City Ind. v. Vanco Beverages 460 U.S. 428 (1983). Fidelity Fed. Savings v. De La Cuesta 458 U.S. 141 (1982). Edgar v. MITE Corp. 457 U.S. 624 (1982). Arizona v. Maricopa Cty. Medical Society 457 U.S. 332 (1982). Amer. Society of Mech. Engrs v. Hydrolevel 456 U.S. 556 (1982). NBC, ABC and CBS v. FCC and Carter-Mondale Pres. Committee 453 U.S. 367 (1981). Bd. of Governors of Fed. Res. v. Investment Co. Institute 450 U.S. 46 (1981). Rubin v. U.S. 449 U.S. 424 (1981). Calif. v. U.S. 447 U.S. 1 (1980). Chiarella v. U.S. 445 U.S. 222 (1980). Roberts v. U.S. 445 U.S. 552 (1980). Perrin v. U.S. 444 U.S. 37 (1979). U.S. v. Naftalin 441 U.S. 768 (1979). Bd. of Governors of Fed. Res. System v. First Lincolnwood Corp. 439 U.S. 234 (1978). ***PRACTICE AREAS:*** Supreme Court Practice; Appellate Practice; Trial Practice; Telecommunications Law; Antitrust; Federal Securities; Tort Litigation; Constitutional Law; RICO Litigation; Regulatory Law; Products Liability; Employment Law; Intellectual Property. **Email:** sshapiro@mayerbrownrowe.com

PAUL L. SHARER, born Sellersville, Pennsylvania, September 29, 1961; admitted to bar, 1991, Pennsylvania; 1992, District of Columbia; registered to practice before U.S. Patent and Trademark Office (Not admitted in Illinois). *Education:* Drexel University (B.S.Ch.E., 1985); Widener University School of Law (J.D., 1991). Member, American Chemical Society. ***PRACTICE AREAS:*** Intellectual Property; Patent Interference/Patent Litigation/Licensing; Medical Device Counseling. **Email:** psharer@mayerbrownrowe.com

CATE SHARP, born Tadcaster Yorkshire, England, September 5, 1966; admitted to bar, 1993, England. *Education:* University of London, England (B.Sc., 1988); The College of Law, England (J.D., 1991). (London, England Office). ***PRACTICE AREAS:*** Environmental. **Email:** csharp@eu.mayerbrownrowe.com

ANDREW SHARPLES, born 1959; admitted to bar, 1985, England. *Education:* Durham University. (London, England Office). ***PRACTICE AREAS:*** Corporate Finance Law; Company Law. **Email:** asharples@mayerbrownrowe.com

KEVIN L. SHAW, born Gibson City, Illinois, May 28, 1955; admitted to bar, 1980, Texas; 1982, Colorado; 1989, California. *Education:* University of Texas (B.A., with honors, 1976); University of Houston (J.D., cum laude, 1980). (Houston, Texas Office). ***PRACTICE AREAS:*** Real Estate; Environmental Law; Joint Ventures. **Email:** kshaw@mayerbrownrowe.com

RICHARD W. SHEPRO, born Berwyn, Illinois, May 9, 1953; admitted to bar, 1979, Illinois; 1981, California and U.S. Court of Appeals, 9th Circuit; 1982, U.S. District Court, Northern District of Illinois. *Education:* Harvard University (A.B., magna cum laude, 1975; J.D., cum laude, 1979); The London School of Economics (M.Sc., 1976). Author: *Bidders and Targets:* Mergers and Acquisitions in the U.S. (Oxford, England and Cambridge, Massachusetts: Basil Blackwell 1990) with Leo Herzel. Author or Co-author: "Corporate Law Affecting Changes in Control and Recapitalizations," I.I.C.L.E., 1996; "Next-to-last Word on Endangered Directors," 65 Harvard Business Review 38, 1987; "Negotiated Acquisitions: The Impact of Competition in the United States," The Business Lawyer, February 1989; "Setting the Boundaries for Disclosure," Securities Regulation Law Journal, Summer 1988; "Foreign Direct Investment in the United States: A Legal Analysis," IV Wisconsin International Law Journal 46, 1986. Lecturer: University of Chicago Law School; London Business School; The Ecole des Hautes Etudes Commerciales in Paris. Teaching Fellow, Harvard University, 1978-1979. Law Clerk to the Honorable James R. Browning, Chief Judge, U.S. Court of Appeals, Ninth Circuit, 1979-1981. Correspondent on Business Law to the Financial Times, 1986-1991. Special Assistant Attorney General, State of Illinois, 1981-1982. *Member:* American Law Institute. **Email:** rshepro@mayerbrownrowe.com

TIMOTHY C. SHERCK, born Hamilton, Ohio, February 27, 1949; admitted to bar, 1975, Illinois and U.S. District Court, Northern District of Illinois; 1977, U.S. Tax Court and U.S. District Court, Eastern District of Wisconsin; 1979, U.S. Court of Appeals, Seventh Circuit. *Education:* Northwestern University (B.A., with honors, 1971); Harvard University (J.D., cum laude, 1974). ***PRACTICE AREAS:*** Taxation (100%). **Email:** tsherck@mayerbrownrowe.com

RONALD M. SHOSS, born Houston, Texas, August 17, 1965; admitted to bar, 1990, Texas. *Education:* London School of Economics, London, England; Tulane University (B.A., summa cum laude, 1987); University of Texas at Austin (J.D., with honors, 1990). Phi Beta Kappa. (Houston, Texas Office). **Email:** rshoss@mayerbrownrowe.com

(This Listing Continued)

MAYER, BROWN, ROWE & MAW LLP, Chicago—Continued

JODI ANN SIMALA, born Chicago, Illinois, August 28, 1968; admitted to bar, 1993, Illinois. *Education:* Boston University (B.A., with distinction, Economics, summa cum laude, 1990; M.A., 1990); Harvard University (J.D., cum laude, 1993). Phi Beta Kappa. ***PRACTICE AREAS:*** Mergers, Acquisitions and Divestitures; Corporate Law; Securities. ***Email:*** jsimala@mayerbrownrowe.com

MICHAEL N. SLOYER, born New York, N.Y., March 31, 1961; admitted to bar, 1988, Pennsylvania (inactive); 1991, New York. *Education:* Columbia University (B.A., 1983; J.D., 1986). Phi Beta Kappa. Law Clerk to Judge William C. Conner, U.S. District Judge, Southern District of New York, 1986-1988. (New York, N.Y. Office). ***Email:*** msloyer@mayerbrownrowe.com

RICHARD SMITH, admitted to bar, 1995, England and Wales. *Education:* University of Sheffield; College of Law, Chester. (London, England Office). ***PRACTICE AREAS:*** Corporate. ***Email:*** rsmith@mayerbrownrowe.com

NEIL M. SOLTMAN, born Philadelphia, Pennsylvania, July 20, 1949; admitted to bar, 1975, California. *Education:* Temple University (B.A., magna cum laude, 1971); Catholic University of America (J.D., 1975). (Los Angeles, California Office). ***Email:*** nsoltman@mayerbrownrowe.com

RICHARD A. SPEHR, born Westfield, New Jersey, July 27, 1961; admitted to bar, 1987, New York, U.S. District Court, Southern and Eastern Districts of New York and U.S. Court of Appeals, Second Circuit. *Education:* State University of New York at Binghamton (B.A., 1983); St. John's University (J.D., 1986). Editor, Law Review. (New York, N.Y. Office). ***Email:*** rspehr@mayerbrownrowe.com

DOMINIC PAUL SPENSER UNDERHILL, born Winchester, England, February 22, 1962; admitted to bar, 1989, England and Wales. *Education:* Durham University, Oxford University; College of Law, London. *Member:* Associate of the Chartered Institute of Arbitrators; Law Society of England and Wales. (London, England Office). ***PRACTICE AREAS:*** Commercial Litigation; Property Litigation; Commercial Arbitration; Commercial Mediation. ***Email:*** dspenser@mayerbrownrowe.com

MARC F. SPERBER, born New York, NY., January 10, 1964; admitted to bar, 1992, Illinois. *Education:* University of Rochester (B.A. cum laude, 1986); Georgetown University (J.D. cum laude, 1992); The Robert Emmet McDonough School of Business, Georgetown University (M.B.A., 1992). Dean's List. Member, The Tax Lawyer, Georgetown University Law Center. Mayer, Brown & Platt, Chicago, 1992-1998 and 1999—. Credit Suisse First Boston Corporation, Chicago, 1998-1999. ***Email:*** msperber@mayerbrownrowe.com

GILLIAN SPROUL, admitted to bar, 1990, England and Wales. (London, England Office). ***PRACTICE AREAS:*** Antitrust and Trade Regulation. ***Email:*** gsproul@mayerbrownrowe.com

ANDREW STANGER, admitted to bar, 1997, England (not admitted in the U.S.) (Not admitted in Illinois). *Education:* Cambridge University (1981). (London, England Office) (not admitted in the U.S.). ***PRACTICE AREAS:*** Tax Controversies. ***Email:*** astanger@mayerbrownrowe.com

JAMES S. STANHAUS, born Evergreen Park, Illinois, October 22, 1945; admitted to bar, 1970, Illinois. *Education:* Georgetown University (A.B., magna cum laude, 1966); Harvard University (J.D., magna cum laude, 1970). Phi Beta Kappa. Member, Harvard Law Review, 1968-1970. ***Email:*** jstanhaus@mayerbrownrowe.com

ADRIAN L. STEEL, JR., born St. Louis, Missouri, January 2, 1950; admitted to bar, 1975, Missouri; 1976, Illinois; 1979, U.S. Supreme Court; 1981, District of Columbia. *Education:* University of Missouri at Columbia (A.B., 1972); University of Michigan (J.D., magna cum laude, 1975). Phi Beta Kappa; Order of the Coif. Law Clerk, Honorable William H. Webster, U.S. Court of Appeals, Eighth Circuit, 1975-1976. Special Assistant to Director of the FBI, 1978-1981. (Washington, D.C. Office). ***PRACTICE AREAS:*** Transportation Law; Administrative Law; Litigation. ***Email:*** asteel@mayerbrownrowe.com

PETER ALAN STEINER, born 1950; admitted to bar, 1988, England. *Education:* Cambridge University. (London, England Office). ***LANGUAGES:*** German. ***PRACTICE AREAS:*** Tax Law. ***Email:*** psteiner@mayerbrownrowe.com

RICHARD M. STEUER, born June 19, 1948; admitted to bar, 1974, New York; U.S. Supreme Court, U.S. Court of Appeals, Second, Third, Fifth Tenth and Federal Circuits, U.S. District Court, Northern, Southern, Eastern and Western District of New York. *Education:* Hofstra University (B.A., 1970); Columbia University (J.D., 1973). Phi Delta Phi. Author: "Customer-Instigated Exclusive Dealing," 68 Antitrust L.J. 239 (2000); "Retailing on the Internet," 12 Antitrust No. 3, pg. 50, 1998; "Counseling Without Case Law," 63 Antitrust L.J. 823 (1995); "A Guide to Marketing Law" (1986); "Exlusive Dealing in Distribution," 69 Cornell L. Rev. 101 (1983); (with Milton Handler) "Attempts to Monopolize and No-Fault Monopolization," 129 U. Pa. L. Rev. 125 (1980); "Employee Representation on the Board," Colum. J. of Transnational L. 225 (1977). Adjunct Associate Professor, New York University School of Law, 1985. Adjunct Professor, St. John's University School of Law, 2003. Member, Advisory Board, BNA Antitrust and Trade Regulation Report. *Member:* The Association of the Bar of the City of New York (Chair, Committee on Antitrust and Trade Regulation, 1995-1998); American Bar Association (Member, Section of Antitrust Law, Secretary and Communications Officer, 2004—, Council Member, 1993-1996, 2001-2004; Editorial Chair, Antitrust Magazine, 1998-2001; Chair, Publications Committee, 1996-1998; Chair, Sherman Act Section 1 Committee, 1992-1993). Fellow, American Bar Foundation. (New York, N.Y. Office). ***PRACTICE AREAS:*** Antitrust and Trade Regulation; Intellectual Property; Litigation. ***Email:*** rsteuer@mayerbrownrowe.com

ANDREW KENNETH STEWART, born 1962; admitted to bar, 1986, England. *Education:* Bristol University. (London, England Office). ***PRACTICE AREAS:*** Corporate Law; Commercial Law. ***Email:*** astewart@mayerbrownrowe.com

SCOTT M. STEWART, born Minneapolis, Minnesota, June 5, 1961; admitted to bar, 1989, Illinois; 1990, U.S. Tax Court. *Education:* Creighton University (B.S., 1983); Cornell University (M.B.A., 1986); Harvard University (J.D., 1989). ***PRACTICE AREAS:*** Tax Controversies; International Taxation. ***Email:*** sstewart@mayerbrownrowe.com

MARSHALL C. STODDARD, JR., born Rochester, New York, 1951; admitted to bar, 1976, Connecticut and U.S. District Court, District of Connecticut; 1981, California, U.S. District Court, Central District of California and U.S. Court of Appeals, Ninth Circuit. *Education:* Hobart College (B.A., 1973); Western England College School of Law (J.D., 1976). Author: "Financing Leveraged Buyouts—The Risk Grows," California Banker, Fall, 1987. Co-Author: "Advanced Chapter 11 Bankruptcy Practice," Professional Education Systems, Inc., 1987 • "Lender Liability, Theory and Practice," Professional Education Systems, Inc., 1988 &#8226. General Counsel, California Commercial Finance Conference of California, Inc., 1997—. *Member:* Los Angeles County (Member, Section on Commercial Law and Bankruptcy; Financial Lawyers Conference) and American (Member, Section on Commercial Law and Bankruptcy) Bar Associations. (Los Angeles, California Office). ***Email:*** mstoddard@mayerbrownrowe.com

J. ROBERT STOLL, born Philadelphia, Pennsylvania, November 19, 1950; admitted to bar, 1975, Indiana and U.S. District Court, Northern and Southern Districts of Indiana; 1981, Illinois and U.S. District Court, Northern District of Illinois; 1990, New York. *Education:* Haverford College (B.A., magna cum laude, 1972); Columbia University (J.D., 1975). ***Email:*** jstoll@mayerbrownrowe.com

JEFFREY M. STRAUSS, born Buffalo, New York, October 15, 1955; admitted to bar, 1981, Illinois and U.S. District Court, Northern District of Illinois, Trial Bar, 1986; 1984, U.S. Court of Appeals, Ninth Circuit. *Education:* University of Chicago (A.B., with honors, 1977) Phi Beta Kappa; University of Chicago School of Law (J.D., 1981). ***Email:*** jstrauss@mayerbrownrowe.com

MARKUS STRELOW, born 1961; admitted to bar, 1993, Cologne. *Education:* University of Bonn; First State Law Examination, Düsseldorf (1988); Second State Law Examination, Düsseldorf (1993). Law Clerk (Referendariat), Cologne and New York, 1991-1993. *Member:* German Bar Association; BVK. (Frankfurt/Main, Germany Office). ***LANGUAGES:*** English, French and German. ***PRACTICE AREAS:*** Corporate Law; Securities; Banking Law; Finance. ***Email:*** mstrelow@mayerbrownrowe.com

EVAN M. TAGER, born Columbia, South Carolina, May 27, 1960; admitted to bar, 1986, New York and U.S. District Court for the District of Maryland; 1987, District of Columbia and U.S. Court of Appeals, Eleventh Circuit; 1988, U.S. District Court for the District of Columbia; 1989, U.S. Court of Appeals for the District of Columbia Circuit and U.S. Court of Appeals, Fourth Circuit; 1990, U.S. Supreme Court; 1993, U.S. Court of Appeals for the Federal Circuit; 1995, U.S. Court of Appeals, Second Circuit; 1996, U.S. Court of Appeals, Seventh Circuit; 2001, U.S. Court of Appeals, Fifth Circuit; 2002, U.S. Court of Appeals, Ninth Circuit; 2003, U.S. Court of Appeals, Eighth Circuit; 2004, U.S. Court of Appeals, Sixth Circuit. *Education:* Princeton University (A.B., magna cum laude, 1982); Stanford University (J.D., 1985). Author: "Reading Between the Lines of Cooper Industries, Inc. v. Leatherman Tool Group, Inc., 121 S. Ct. 1678 (2001)," Mealey's Litigation Report: Insurance Bad Faith, Aug. 8, 2001, at 22; "The Constitutional Limitations on Class Actions," Mealey's Litigation Report: Class Actions, Jan. 2000, at 34; "Tips on Preserving Arguments for Appeal," Mealey's Insurance Law Weekly (Dec. 1, 1997). Co-author: with Frey, "Punitive Damages," in Business and Commercial Litigation in Federal Courts (West 1998). Law Clerk, Honorable Mary M. Schroeder, U.S. Court of Appeals, Ninth Circuit, Phoenix, Arizona, 1985-1986. (Washington, D.C. Office). ***PRACTICE AREAS:*** Appellate Litigation; Constitutional Law. ***Email:*** etager@mayerbrownrowe.com

JAMES E. TANCULA, born Oak Park, Illinois, August 31, 1957; admitted to bar, 1982, Illinois and U.S. District Court, Northern District of Illinois; 1992, Texas; 1993, U.S. District Court, Southern District of Texas; 1996, U.S. Court of Appeals, Fifth Circuit; 1999, U.S. District Court, Northern District of Texas. *Education:* Marquette University (A.B., magna cum laude, 1979); University of Chicago (J.D., 1982). (Houston, Texas Office). ***Email:*** jtancula@mayerbrownrowe.com

JOHN D. TAYLOR, born Inglewood, California, December 6, 1966; admitted to bar, 1994, Illinois; 1996, District of Columbia. *Education:* Georgetown University (B.S.F.S., 1989); University of Virginia (J.D., 1994). ***PRACTICE AREAS:*** Structured Finance; International Finance. ***Email:*** jdtaylor@mayerbrownrowe.com

MARK R. TAYLOR, born 1957; admitted to bar, 1990, Illinois. *Education:* Illinois State University (B.S.); Loyola University (J.D., 1990). ***PRACTICE AREAS:*** Government. ***Email:*** mtaylor@mayerbrownrowe.com

CHRISTOPH M. TEGEL, born 1966; admitted to bar, 1996, Germany. *Education:* University of Frankfurt am Main. (Frankfurt/Main, Germany Office). ***LANGUAGES:*** English. ***PRACTICE AREAS:*** Commercial Real Estate; Commercial Leases and Leasing; Environmental Law. ***Email:*** ctegel@mayerbrownrowe.com

JOEL S. TELPNER, admitted to bar, 1984, New York. *Education:* University of Iowa (B.B.A., 1978; J.D., with distinction, 1983); The Wharton School of the University of Pennsylvania (M.B.A., 1999). (New York, N.Y. Office). ***LANGUAGES:*** French. ***PRACTICE AREAS:*** Banking; Finance. ***Email:*** jtelpner@mayerbrownrowe.com

MARK R. TER MOLEN, born Ann Arbor, Michigan, February 27, 1962; admitted to bar, 1988, Illinois; 1989, U.S. District Court, Northern District of Illinois. *Education:* Cornell University (A.B., magna cum laude, 1984); University of Chicago (J.D., 1987). ***PRACTICE AREAS:*** Litigation; Toxic Torts; Complex Environmental Litigation; Environmental Regulation. ***Email:*** mtermolen@mayerbrownrowe.com

BERND THALMANN, born 1959; admitted to bar, 1989, Germany. *Education:* Universities of Hamburg and Giessen; University of Georgia, Athens, U.S.A. (LL.M.). (Frankfurt/Main, Germany Office). ***LANGUAGES:*** English, French. ***PRACTICE AREAS:*** Mergers and Acquisitions; Corporate. ***Email:*** bthalmann@mayerbrownrowe.com

JOHN J. THARP, JR., born Camp Lejeune, North Carolina, September 18, 1960; admitted to bar, 1990, Illinois; 1991, U.S. Court of Appeals, 7th Circuit; 1995, U.S. District Court, Northern District of Illinois; 1997, U.S. District Court, District of Colorado; 2004, U.S. Supreme Court. *Education:* Duke University (B.A., summa cum laude, 1982); Northwestern University (J.D., magna cum laude, 1990). Phi Beta Kappa; Order of the Coif. Law Clerk to the Honorable Joel M. Flaum, U.S. Court of Appeals, Seventh Circuit, 1990-1991. Assistant U.S. Attorney, Northern District of Illinois, 1992- 1997. Author: Northwestern University Law Review, Vol. 84, 1990; March 2000: "Don't Abandon Hope, All Ye Who Enter Here: Thoughts on the Successful Defense of a Healthcare Fraud Prosecution," Health Law Digest. [Captain, USMC (1982-1987)]. ***PRACTICE AREAS:*** Litigation; Complex and Multi-District Litigation; Criminal Law. ***Email:*** jtharp@mayerbrownrowe.com

(This Listing Continued)

PAUL W. THEISS, born Evanston, Illinois, April 11, 1960; admitted to bar, 1985, Illinois. *Education:* Amherst College (B.A., 1982); University of Chicago (J.D., 1985). ***PRACTICE AREAS:*** Corporate Law; Mergers, Acquisitions and Divestitures. ***Email:*** ptheiss@mayerbrownrowe.com

FREDERICK B. THOMAS, born Evanston, Illinois, August 13, 1949; admitted to bar, 1974, Illinois. *Education:* Dartmouth College (A.B., magna cum laude, 1971); University of Chicago (J.D., 1974). Law Clerk to Hon. John C. Godbold, U.S. Court of Appeals, Fifth Circuit, 1974-1975. ***PRACTICE AREAS:*** Mergers, Acquisitions and Divestitures; Corporate Law; Corporate Governance. ***Email:*** fthomas@mayerbrownrowe.com

IAIN VICTOR THOMAS, born Beckenham Kent, August 4, 1965; admitted to bar, 1990, England. *Education:* College of Law Lancaster Gate (1988); Bristol University (LL.B., with honors, 1987). (London, England Office). ***LANGUAGES:*** French. ***PRACTICE AREAS:*** Commercial Property. ***Email:*** ithomas@mayerbrownrowe.com

WILLIAM C. TOMPSETT, born New York, N. Y., December 22, 1948; admitted to bar, 1974, Pennsylvania; 1978, Illinois. *Education:* Haverford College (B.A., 1970); Cornell University (J.D., 1974). ***Email:*** wtompsett@mayerbrownrowe.com

JOHN M. TOUHY, born Chicago, Illinois, April 30, 1955; admitted to bar, 1980, Illinois and U.S. District Court, Northern District of Illinois; 1984, U.S. Court of Appeals, Seventh Circuit. *Education:* University of Chicago (B.A., with honors and special honors, 1977); New York University (J.D., 1980). ***Email:*** jtouhy@mayerbrownrowe.com

CHARLES S. TRIPLETT, born Kansas City, Missouri, 1948; admitted to bar, 1975, Missouri; 1993, District of Columbia; U.S. Tax Court. *Education:* Rockhurst College (B.S., 1970); University of Missouri at Kansas City (J.D., 1974; LL.M., 1977). Internal Revenue Service: Deputy Associate Chief Counsel, 1986-1992; Special Assistant to the Chief Counsel, 1992-1993. Member, Business and Industry Advisory Committee, OECD. *Member:* American Bar Association (Chair, Transfer Pricing Committee, 2002—); International Fiscal Association. (Washington, D.C. Office). ***PRACTICE AREAS:*** International Taxation; Tax Controversies. ***Email:*** ctriplett@mayerbrownrowe.com

BRIAN TRUST, born Brooklyn, New York, 1956; admitted to bar, 1987, New York; 1991, U.S. District of New York; 1997, U.S. District Court, Eastern District of Michigan. *Education:* Brooklyn College of the City University of New York (B.A., 1977); New York Law School (J.D., 1986). Articles Editor, Law Review. Assistant Editor, *Norton Bankruptcy Law and Practice,* 2nd edition. (New York, N.Y. Office). ***PRACTICE AREAS:*** Bankruptcy Chapter 11; Bankruptcy Reorganization; Commercial Workouts. ***Email:*** btrust@mayerbrownrowe.com

GEORGE J. TZANETOPOULOS, born Chicago, Illinois, March 30, 1960; admitted to bar, 1985, Illinois; 1986, U.S. District Court, Northern District of Illinois. *Education:* University of Chicago (B.A., with honors, 1982); University of Michigan (J.D., with honors, 1985). ***Email:*** gtzanetopoulos@mayerbrownrowe.com

MARK R. UHRYNUK, born Kenora, Ontario, Canada, December 20, 1958; admitted to bar, 1987, New York; 1995, England and Wales. *Education:* Dartmouth College (A.B., 1981); University of Western Ontario (M.B.A., with distinction, 1986; LL.B., with distinction, 1986). (London, England Office). ***PRACTICE AREAS:*** Mergers, Acquisitions and Divestitures; Securities; Business Law. ***Email:*** muhrynuk@mayerbrownrowe.com

ANGELA M. ULUM, born Wyandotte, Michigan, March 10, 1973; admitted to bar, 1997, Illinois. *Education:* University of Michigan (B.A., 1994; J.D., 1996). ***Email:*** aulum@mayerbrownrowe.com

ROBERT W. UNIKEL, born Chicago, Illinois, January 5, 1969; admitted to bar, 1993, Illinois; U.S. District Court, Northern District of Illinois including Trial Bar. *Education:* Dartmouth College (B.A., cum laude, 1990); Northwestern University (J.D., cum laude, 1993). Note and Comment Editor, Northwestern University Law Review, 1993. Finalist, Julius H. Miner Moot Court Competition, 1993. Author, "Bridging the Trade Secret Gap: Protecting 'Confidential Information' Not Rising to the Level Of Trade Secrets," 29 Loy. U. Chi. L.J. 841, 1998; "Better by Design: The Availability of Trade Dress Protection for Product Design and the Demise of Aesthetic Functionality," 85 Trademark Rep. 312, 1996. ***PRACTICE AREAS:*** Intellectual Property; Litigation. ***Email:*** runikel@mayerbrownrowe.com

JEFFREY A. USOW, born Milwaukee, Wisconsin, October 2, 1952; admitted to bar, 1977, Illinois. *Education:* University of Wisconsin (B.A., 1974); Harvard University (J.D., cum laude, 1977). ***Email:*** jusow@mayerbrownrowe.com

LANE W. VANDERSLICE, born Ann Arbor, Michigan, March 12, 1965; admitted to bar, 1993, Illinois. *Education:* Columbia University (B.A., 1986; J.D., 1993). Managing Editor, Columbia Law Review, 1992-1993. Kent Scholar. Judicial Clerk, Judge Walter Cummings, U.S. Court of Appeals, Seventh Circuit, 1993-1994. ***PRACTICE AREAS:*** Real Estate (5%); Associate Professional Development and Recruiting (95%). ***Email:*** lvanderslice@mayerbrownrowe.com

BARRY ALAN VAN DYKE, born Bellingham, Washington, September 9, 1954; admitted to bar, 1984, Illinois. *Education:* Dordt College (B.A., 1981); University of Chicago (J.D., cum laude, 1984). ***PRACTICE AREAS:*** Taxation. ***Email:*** avandyke@mayerbrownrowe.com

JON D. VAN GORP, born Denver, Colorado, June 12, 1969; admitted to bar, 1994, Texas; 1998, Illinois; 2004, New York. *Education:* Calvin College (B.A., 1991); Southern Methodist University (J.D., cum laude, 1994). Publications: "Impact of Regulation AB on Auto Loan and Lease Securitization," Journal of Structured Finance, Spring 2005; "Funding Mortgage Loans with Extendible Note Funding Facilities," Journal of Structured Finance, Fall 2004; "Collateral in Eastern Europe: Problems and Solutions," 29 International Lawyer 83 (1994). ***PRACTICE AREAS:*** Banks and Banking; Securities. ***Email:*** jvangorp@mayerbrownrowe.com

TERRY OTERO VILARDO, born Hato Rey, Puerto Rico, September 11, 1957; admitted to bar, 1984, Texas. *Education:* Georgetown University (B.S.F.S., 1979); University of Houston (J.D., 1984). (Houston, Texas Office). ***LANGUAGES:*** Spanish, Italian, French. ***Email:*** tvilardo@mayerbrownrowe.com

JOHN S. VISHNESKI III, born Virginia Beach, Virginia, August 27, 1963; admitted to bar, 1988, Illinois; 1989, District of Columbia and U.S. District Court, Northern District of Illinois. *Education:* University of Virginia (B.A., with honors, 1985; J.D., 1988). ***PRACTICE AREAS:*** Complex Insurance Litigation. ***Email:*** jvishneski@mayerbrownrowe.com

THOMAS M. VITALE, born New York, N.Y., 1956; admitted to bar, 1981, New York and U.S. District Court, Southern District of New York. *Education:* Princeton (A.B., magna cum laude, 1977); Stanford (J.D., 1980). (New York, N.Y. Office). ***Email:*** tvitale@mayerbrownrowe.com

PIERRE VOGELENZANG, born Noordwijk, The Netherlands; admitted to bar, 1972, Netherlands; 1981, California. *Education:* Harvard University; University of Leiden Law School (LL.M., 1969); Tulane University of Louisiana (LL.M., 1970); Stanford University (J.D., 1980). Recipient, Hilman Oehlman Jr. Award. Member, Stanford Law Review, 1979-1980. Author: "Intercompany Transactions in California Combined Reports," 52 Tax Notes 343 (1991); "Second-Stage Apportionment of Unitary Income," 49 Tax Notes 335 (1990); "The Resequencing Aspect of Rev. Rul. 87-66: Applying Kimbell-Diamond to Reorganizations," Parts 1 & 2, 15 Intl. Tax J. 197, 335 (1989), published in revised form in 18 J. Real Est. Tax., 219, 332 (1991); "Notice 88-89: The Impact of the Uniform Capitalization Rules on the Foreign Investor's Interest Deduction," 18 Tax Mgt. Intl. J. 24 (1989); "Two Aspects of Article 115 E.C.C. Treaty," 18 Common Mkt. L. Rev. 169 (1981). Member, Executive Committee, Tax Section, 1992-1993, Chair, Subcommittee on Passthrough Entities, Tax Section, 1992-1993, Los Angeles County Bar Association. (Los Angeles, California Office). ***Email:*** pvogelenzang@mayerbrownrowe.com

HOANG QUAN VU, born Saigon, Vietnam, November 6, 1969; admitted to bar, 1996, Texas. *Education:* Harvard College (A.B., magna cum laude, 1992); Harvard Law School (J.D., 1995). *Member:* State Bar of Texas; Asian American Bar Association of Houston (President, 2005); National Asian Pacific American Bar Association (Named 2004 NAPABA Best Lawyers Under 40 List). (Houston, Texas Office). ***LANGUAGES:*** Conversational Vietnamese. ***PRACTICE AREAS:*** General Banking and Finance; Project and Energy Finance; General Secured and Unsecured Lending; Workouts and Restructuring; Oil and Gas Lending; Leasing. ***Email:*** hvu@mayerbrownrowe.com

ARTHUR C. WALKER, JR., born Glen Ridge, New Jersey, March 3, 1971; admitted to bar, 1997, California; 1998, District of Columbia. *Education:* Georgetown University School of Business (B.S.B.A., magna cum laude, 1993); Georgetown University Law Center (J.D., cum laude, 1996; LL.M., Taxation, 1999). Author: "Tax Planning Opportunities Using QSSSs as Pass-Through Entities," Taxes, 1998. (Washington, D.C. Office). ***PRACTICE AREAS:*** Federal Income Tax; Federal Taxation; International Income Tax. ***Email:*** awalker@mayerbrownrowe.com

RICHARD MARK WALKER, born 1962; admitted to bar, 1988, England. *Education:* Cambridge University; College of Law, Guildford. (London, England and Frankfurt/Main, Germany Offices). ***LANGUAGES:*** French and German. ***PRACTICE AREAS:*** Corporate Finance; Commercial Law. ***Email:*** mwalker@mayerbrownrowe.com

MICHAEL A. WALLIN, admitted to bar, 1994, Australia. *Education:* Monash University (Bachelor of Economics, 1990; Bachelor of Laws, 1993); Royal Melbourne Institute of Technology (M Corporate Law, 1996). (London, England Office). ***PRACTICE AREAS:*** Corporate. ***Email:*** mwallin@mayerbrownrowe.com

KATHLEEN ANNE WALSH, born March 27, 1963; admitted to bar, 1990, New York and New Jersey. *Education:* Fordham University (B.A., 1984); Fordham University School of Law (J.D., 1989). Member, Fordham Law Review. (New York, N.Y. Office). ***PRACTICE AREAS:*** Corporate Law; Securities. ***Email:*** kwalsh@mayerbrown.com

STEPHEN JOSEPH WALSH, born 1958; admitted to bar, 1985, England. *Education:* Oxford University. (London, England Office). ***PRACTICE AREAS:*** Banking Law; Property Finance Law; Consumer Credit Law. ***Email:*** swalsh@mayerbrownrowe.com

JAMES R. WALTHER, born San Francisco, California, August 10, 1945; admitted to bar, 1972, California. *Education:* Stanford University (A.B., 1967); University of California, Los Angeles (J.D., 1972). (Los Angeles, California Office). ***Email:*** jwalther@mayerbrownrowe.com

ROBERT J. WARD, born Bethlehem, Pennsylvania, November 29, 1951; admitted to bar, 1978, New York, U.S. District Court, Southern and Eastern Districts of New York and U.S. Court of Appeals, Second Circuit; U.S. Claims Court. *Education:* Tufts University (B.A., 1973); New York University (J.D., 1977). (New York, N.Y. Office). ***Email:*** rward@mayerbrownrowe.com

MICHAEL O. WARNECKE, born Chicago, Illinois, June 28, 1941; admitted to bar, 1967, Illinois and U.S. District Court, Northern District of Illinois; U.S. Court of Appeals, Second, Fifth, Seventh, Ninth and Federal Circuits; U.S. Supreme Court. *Education:* Purdue University (B.S., M.E., 1963); George Washington University (J.D., 1967). Fellow, American College of Trial Lawyers. ***PRACTICE AREAS:*** Intellectual Property Litigation. ***Email:*** mwarnecke@mayerbrownrowe.com

STEVEN L. WASHINGTON, born Chicago, Illinois October 19, 1971; admitted to bar, 1999, Illinois. *Education:* University of Illinois (B.A., 1994); Northwestern University (J.D., 1997). ***Email:*** swashington@mayerbrownrowe.com

NEIL A. WASSERSTROM, born Cleveland, Ohio, October 25, 1959; admitted to bar, 1984, Texas, U.S. District Court, Southern District of Texas, U.S. Court of Appeals, Fifth Circuit. *Education:* Tulane University (B.A., cum laude, 1981); Tulane University School of Law (J.D., 1984). (Houston, Texas Office). ***Email:*** nwasserstrom@mayerbrownrowe.com

DON L. WEAVER, born Inglewood, California, December 1, 1951; admitted to bar, 1977, California. *Education:* University of California at Santa Barbara (B.A., with highest honors, 1973); University of Southern California (J.D., 1977). (Los Angeles, California Office). ***Email:*** dweaver@mayerbrownrowe.com

SETH J. WEINBERGER, born Jersey City, New Jersey, March 8, 1955; admitted to bar, 1980, New Jersey; 1982, Illinois. *Education:* University of Michigan (A.B., with high honors, 1977; J.D., cum laude, 1979). ***PRACTICE AREAS:*** Corporate Law; Information Technology; Venture Capital. ***Email:*** sweinberger@mayerbrownrowe.com

HARRY "HAP" WEITZEL, born Beaumont, Texas, March 10, 1964; admitted to bar, 1990, California; 1994, Texas; U.S. District Court, Central and Eastern Districts of California; U.S. District Court, Southern, Northern, Eastern and Western Districts of Texas;

(This Listing Continued)

MAYER, BROWN, ROWE & MAW LLP, Chicago—Continued

U.S. Court of Appeals, Fifth Circuit. *Education:* Texas Christian University (B.A., summa cum laude, 1987); Harvard University (J.D., cum laude, 1990). Phi Beta Kappa; National Registry of Who's Who; American Inns of Court, Garland Walker Inn; Texas Association of Defense Counsel; Greater Houston Partnership, Economic Development Advisory Committee; Houston World Affairs Council; Recognized as Texas "Super Lawyer" in 2004; Recognized as Texas "Rising Star" in 2004. *Member:* Houston (Administration of Justice Committee), Fifth Circuit and American Bar Associations. Fellow: American Bar Foundation; Texas Bar Foundation; Houston Bar Foundation. (Houston, Texas Office). ***PRACTICE AREAS:*** Litigation. ***Email:*** hpweitzel@mayerbrownrowe.com

ANDREW GEORGE WHITE, born 1950; admitted to bar, 1974, England. *Education:* Oxford University. *Member:* Association of Pension Lawyers. (London, England Office). ***PRACTICE AREAS:*** Pensions Law; Life Insurance Law; Financial Services Law. ***Email:*** awhite@mayerbrownrowe.com

NIGEL JULIAN WHITE, born 1964; admitted to bar, 1989, England. *Education:* Leicester University; College of Law, Guildford. (London, England Office). ***PRACTICE AREAS:*** Banking Law. ***Email:*** nwhite@mayerbrownrowe.com

PETER H. WHITE, born July 13, 1963; admitted to bar, 1991, Virginia; 2000, District of Columbia. *Education:* University of Notre Dame (B.A., with high honors, 1985); University of Virginia (J.D., 1989). Author: "Let's Make a Deal: Negotiating and Defending Immunity for Targets and Subjects,'" The Journal of the ABA Section of Litigation (Fall 2002); "The Virginia Birth-Related Neurological Injury Compensation Act: Tort Reform for an Endangered Specialty," 74 Virginia Law Review 1487 (1988). (Washington, D.C. Office). ***PRACTICE AREAS:*** Litigation. ***Email:*** pwhite@mayerbrownrowe.com

JEFFREY R. WHYTE, born New Britian, Connecticut, May 3, 1969; admitted to bar, 1996, Connecticut; 1997, New York. *Education:* University of Connecticut (B.A., magna cum laude, 1991; M.A., 1993); University of Connecticut School of Law (J.D., highest honors, 1996). Author: "Review of Economic Regulations Results in Corporate Law Changes," BNA's World Securities Law Report, Volume 4, Number 4, April 1998, co-authored with Jeffrey F. Browne; "Australia to Overhaul Financial System, Establish New Regulatory Bodies," BNA's Asia-Pacific Report, Volume 1, Number 3, October 1997, co-authored with Jeffrey F. Browne; "Legal Implications of Plain English," Practicing Law Institute's Understanding Plain English, Preparing for the SEC's Enactment, July 1997, co-authored with Robert B. Hiden, Jr. [U.S. Army Reserve, 1987-1990; Connecticut Army National Guard, 1990-1995]. (New York, N.Y. Office). ***PRACTICE AREAS:*** Corporate Finance; Securities. ***Email:*** jwhyte@mayerbrownrowe.com

ROBERT J. WILD, born Chicago, Illinois, September 6, 1961; admitted to bar, 1989, Illinois. *Education:* Loyola University of Chicago (B.B.A., 1983; J.D., 1989); DePaul University (M.S.T., 1987). Beta Alpha Psi. Executive Editor, Loyola Consumer Law Reporter, 1988-1989. Certified Public Accountant, Illinois, 1983. *Member:* Illinois State Bar Association (Appointed Officer and Seminar Speaker, Corporation, Securities and Business Law Section Council). ***PRACTICE AREAS:*** Mergers, Acquisitions and Divestitures; Securities; Corporate Law. ***Email:*** rwild@mayerbrownrowe.com

EDWARD H. WILLIAMS, born Evanston, Illinois, July 20, 1967; admitted to bar, 1993, Illinois and U.S. District Court, Northern District of Illinois; 2000, U.S. District Court, Northern District of Illinois Trial Bar. *Education:* Grinnell College (B.A., with honors, 1989); University of Michigan (J.D., cum laude, 1993). ***PRACTICE AREAS:*** Litigation; Professional Malpractice; Commercial Transactions. ***Email:*** ewilliams@mayerbrownrowe.com

SPENCER HOWARD KERVEN WILLIAMS, born 1946; admitted to bar, 1971, England. (London, England Office). ***PRACTICE AREAS:*** Commercial Property Law. ***Email:*** swilliams@eu.mayerbrownrowe.com

JOEL V. WILLIAMSON, born Akron, Ohio, May 26, 1945; admitted to bar, 1970, Kentucky; 1972, U.S. Tax Court; 1986, Illinois and State of Illinois Supreme Court; 1987, U.S. District Court, Northern District of Illinois; 1989, U.S. Court of Appeals, Eleventh Circuit; 1992, U.S. Court of Appeals, Seventh Circuit; 1993, U.S. Court of Appeals, Sixth Circuit; 1994, U.S. Court of Appeals, Ninth Circuit; 1998, U.S. Court of Appeals, District of Columbia Circuit; U.S. Court of Federal Claims; U.S. Court of Appeals, Eighth Circuit. *Education:* Davidson College (B.A., 1967); University of Kentucky School of Law (J.D., 1970). ***PRACTICE AREAS:*** Tax Controversies. ***Email:*** jwilliamson@mayerbrownrowe.com

RICHARD S. WILLIAMSON, born Evanston, Illinois, May 9, 1949; admitted to bar, 1974, Illinois; 1976, District of Columbia and U.S. Court of Appeals, District of Columbia Circuit; 1978, U.S. Supreme Court and U.S. District Court, District of Columbia. *Education:* Princeton University (A.B., cum laude, 1971); University of Virginia School of Law (J.D., 1974). Executive Editor, Virginia Journal of International Law, 1972-1974. Author: "The Appropriate Jurisdiction for Telecommunications Policy Making: The FCC or Federal District Court," Critical Legal Issues, The Washington Legal Foundation, No. 10, 1987; "Judicial Activism: Section 1983 and Antitrust Liability Chill Decision Making by State and Local Officials," Harvard Journal of Law and Public Policy, Vol. 6, p. 149, 1983; "Block Grants: One Year Late," Notre Dame Law School Journal of Legislation, Vol. 10, No. 2, 1983. Assistant to President Reagan for Intergovernmental Affairs, 1981-1983. Vice Chairman, Administrative Conference of the United States, 1981-1983. United States Ambassador to the United Nations Offices in Vienna, Austria, 1983-1985. Assistant Secretary of State, 1988-1989. ***PRACTICE AREAS:*** Government. ***Email:*** rswilliamson@mayerbrownrowe.com

KEITH J. WILLNER, born Topeka, Kansas, December 10, 1959; admitted to bar, 1984, California; 1988, District of Columbia. *Education:* University of Virginia (B.A., magna cum laude, 1981); University of Virginia School of Law (J.D., 1984). Listed in Chambers' Leading Real Estate Lawyers in Washington, DC. Member, Steering Committee of Real Estate, Housing and Land Use Section, District of Columbia Bar, 1997-2000, Financial Officer, 1998-2000. Chairman, Real Property Transactions Committee, Real Estate, Housing and Land Use Section, District of Columbia Bar, 1996-1997. Chairman, Commercial Transactions Committee, Real Estate, Housing and Land Use Section, District of Columbia Bar, 1995-1996. (Washington, D.C. Office). ***PRACTICE AREAS:*** Real Estate. ***Email:*** kwillner@mayerbrownrowe.com

GARY A. WINTERS, born Baltimore, Maryland, 1963; admitted to bar, 1992, Maryland; 1993, District of Columbia. *Education:* Northwestern University (B.A., 1985); Georgetown University (J.D., 1991). Author: "Unconstitutional Conditions as Nonsubsidies: When is Deference Inappropriate," 80 Geo. L.J. 161 (1991). Law clerk to Judge Carolyn D. King, U.S. Court of Appeals, Fifth Circuit, 1991-1992. (Washington, D.C. Office). ***PRACTICE AREAS:*** Antitrust; Commercial Litigation. ***Email:*** gwinters@mayerbrownrowe.com

DOUGLAS L. WISNER, born Chicago, Illinois, August 26, 1953; admitted to bar, 1978, New York. *Education:* University of Illinois (B.A., 1975); Boston College (J.D., 1978). Phi Beta Kappa. (New York, N.Y. Office). ***PRACTICE AREAS:*** Real Estate Finance; Real Estate Workouts; Real Estate Restructuring; Native American Financing; Casino Financing. ***Email:*** dwisner@mayerbrownrowe.com

MARK S. WOJCIECHOWSKI, born Southfield, Michigan, May 4, 1954; admitted to bar, 1982, New York. *Education:* Columbia University (A.B., 1976); Indiana University (J.D., cum laude, 1981). *Member:* Association of the Bar of the City of New York (Chairman, Committee on Corporation Law). (New York, N.Y. Office). ***PRACTICE AREAS:*** Corporate Law; Corporate Finance; Corporate Banking Law. ***Email:*** mwojciechowski@mayerbrownrowe.com

STEVEN WOLOWITZ, born Chicago, Illinois, June 27, 1952; admitted to bar, 1978, New York; 1979, U.S. District Court, Southern and Eastern Districts of New York; 1984, U.S. Court of Appeals, Second and Seventh Circuits; 1988, U.S. Court of Appeals, Fifth Circuit and U.S. Supreme Court. *Education:* George Washington University (B.A., with distinction, 1974; J.D., with honors, 1977). Author: "Contesting Price-Fixing Class Action Claims in Commodities Futures Markets," The Journal of Investment Compliance, Summer 2001; "Rogue Traders & Futures Brokers: Who Bears the Legal Responsibility for Unauthorized Trading?," 6 Secs. Litig. & Reg. Rep., No. 11, 2001; "Unexpected SEC Issues are Arising Online," *The National Law Journal,* February 9, 1998; "Shareholders, Stakeholders and the Law," *Directorship's Significant Issues Facing Directors: 1997,* February, 1997; "SEC Studies Disclosure in Securitizing," *The National Law Journal,* February 10, 1997. (New York, N.Y. Office). ***PRACTICE AREAS:*** Financial Services Litigation; Securities; Commodities. ***Email:*** swolowitz@mayerbrownrowe.com

IAN CHARLES WOOD, born Sheffield, Yorkshire, United Kingdom, March 31, 1950; admitted to bar, 1977, England and Wales. *Education:* Durham University (B.Sc., 1971; Nuclear Physics and M.Sc., 1974). Member, Union of European Practitioners in Industrial Property. Associate: The Chartered Institute of Patent Agents; Institute of Trade Mark Agents. (London, England Office). ***Email:*** iwood@eu.mayerbrownrowe.com

CRAIG A. WOODS, born Bartlesville, Oklahoma, March 13, 1969; admitted to bar, 1994, Illinois. *Education:* University of Kansas (B.S.E.E., 1991); Georgetown University (J.D., 1994). ***Email:*** cwoods@mayerbrownrowe.com

STEPHEN WOODWARD, admitted to bar, 1993, England and Wales. *Education:* University of Birmingham (LL.B., Honors, 1989); College of Law, Guildford. (London, England Office). ***LANGUAGES:*** French. ***PRACTICE AREAS:*** Litigation. ***Email:*** swoodward@mayerbrownrowe.com

NIGEL A. WRIGHT, born Christchurch, March 26, 1962; admitted to bar, 1987, England. *Education:* London School of Economics, London University (LL.B., 1984). *Member:* Law Society of England and Wales. (London, England Office). ***PRACTICE AREAS:*** Structured Finance; Acquisition Finance; International Banking Law. ***Email:*** nwright@mayerbrownrowe.com

DR. JÖRG WULFKEN, born 1960; admitted to bar, 1990. *Education:* University of Hamburg. (Frankfurt/Main, Germany Office). ***LANGUAGES:*** English. ***PRACTICE AREAS:*** Acquisition Finance; Banks and Banking; Capital Market Transactions. ***Email:*** jwulfken@mayerbrownrowe.com

RUSSELL R. YOUNG, born Detroit, Michigan, March 22, 1971; admitted to bar, 1996, Illinois and U.S. District Court for the Northern District of Illinois; 1997, U.S. Tax Court; 1999, U.S. Courts of Appeals for the Federal and Sixth Circuits; 2000, U.S. Courts of Appeals, Tenth Circuit; 2001, U.S. Courts of Appeals, Seventh and District of Columbia Circuits; 2002, U.S. District Court, District of Colorado and U.S. Supreme Court. *Education:* Washington University (A.B., 1993); Harvard Law School (J.D., cum laude, 1996). ***REPORTED CASES:*** Commissioner v. Banks, 543 U.S. __, 2005 WL 123825 (Jan. 24, 2005); Illinois Tool Works Inc. v. Commissioner of Internal Revenue, 355 F.3d 997 (7th Cir. 2004); Banks v. Commisioner, 345 F.3d 373 (6th Cir. 2003); Riggs Natl. Corp. v. Commissioner, 295 F.3d 16 (D.C. Cir. 2002); The Limited, Inc. v. Commissioner, 286 F.3d 324 (6th Cir. 2002), rev'g, 113 T.C. 169 (1999) (Subpart F, I.R.C. 956 "banking exception"). ***PRACTICE AREAS:*** Federal Tax Controversies (85%); Appellate Practice (15%). ***Email:*** ryoung@mayerbrownrowe.com

PATRICIA ANNE YURCHAK, born Boston, Massachusetts, July 18, 1967; admitted to bar, 1993, Illinois; U.S. Tax Court; U.S. District Court, Northern District of Illinois; U.S. Court of Appeals, Ninth Circuit; U.S. Supreme Court. *Education:* Harvard University (B.A., cum laude, 1989); University of Chicago (J.D., with honors, 1993). ***LANGUAGES:*** Spanish. ***REPORTED CASES:*** Riggs National Corp. v. Commissioner, _F.3d_, No. 01-1121 (D.C. Cir. 2002), rev'g and remanding T.C. Memo. 2001-12, 81 T.C.M. (CCH) 1023 (2001) ("Riggs II"), on remand from 163 F.3d 1363 (D.C. Cir. 1999), rev'g and remanding 107 T.C. 301 (1996) ("Riggs I"); The Limited, Inc. v. Commissioner of Internal Revenue, 286 F.3d 324 (6th Cir. 2002), rev'g, 113 T.C. 169 (1999); The Boeing Company and Consolidated Subsidiaries v. United States of America, Supreme Court of the United States, No. 01-1209; Intel Corporation v. Commissioner of Internal Revenue, 76 F.3d 976 (9th Cir. 1995); Nissei Sangyo America, Ltd. v. United States, 95-2 U.S. Tax Cas. (CCH) ¶ 50,327 (N.D. Ill. 1995). ***PRACTICE AREAS:*** Tax Controversies. ***Email:*** pyurchak@mayerbrownrowe.com

HERBERT L. ZAROV, born Chicago, Illinois, June 7, 1945; admitted to bar, 1979, Illinois and U.S. District Court, Northern District of Illinois; 1981, U.S. Court of Appeals, Seventh Circuit; 1984, U.S. Tax Court; 1985, U.S. Court of Federal Claims; 1990, U.S. Court of Appeals, Ninth Circuit; 1993, U.S. Court of Appeals, Third Circuit. *Education:*

(This Listing Continued)

Columbia University (B.A., 1967); University of Chicago (M.A., 1968; LL.B., 1979). ***PRACTICE AREAS:*** Mass Torts; Securities Fraud; Class Actions. ***Email:*** hzarov@mayerbrownrowe.com

DR. GUIDO ZEPPENFELD, born 1967; admitted to bar, 1997, Germany. *Education:* University of Frankfurt am Main, Cambridge/U.K. and Essex/U.K. (LL.M.). (Frankfurt/Main, Germany Office). ***LANGUAGES:*** English. ***PRACTICE AREAS:*** Labor and Employment; Employee Benefits; Commercial Law. ***Email:*** gzeppenfeld@mayerbrownrowe.com

NAZIM ZILKHA, born Rio de Janeiro, Brazil, July 10, 1964; admitted to bar, 1991, New York, New Jersey and U.S. District Court, Southern and Eastern Districts of New York and District of New Jersey; 1992, District of Columbia. *Education:* Duke University (B.S., Computer Science, B.A., French, cum laude, 1987; J.D., 1990). Phi Eta Sigma National Honor Society. (New York, N.Y. Office). ***LANGUAGES:*** Portuguese and French. ***PRACTICE AREAS:*** Securities; Mergers and Acquisitions; Corporate Finance. ***Email:*** nzilkha@mayerbrownrowe.com

SENIOR COUNSEL

THOMAS YOUNG ALLMAN, born Canton, Ohio, October 21, 1939; admitted to bar, 1965, Ohio (Not admitted in Illinois). *Education:* University of Cincinnati (B.S.I.M., 1962); Yale Law School (J.D., 1965). Author: "The Case for an E-Discovery Safe Habor," 70 Def. Couns. J. 417 (2003); "Electronic Evidence Discovery: A Primer," Monograph, National Center for the Public Interest (2002); "The Need for Federal Standards Regarding Electronic Discovery," 68 Def. Couns. J 206 (2001). ***PRACTICE AREAS:*** Litigation. ***Email:*** tyallman@mayerbrownrowe.com

ROGER W. BARRETT, born Kenilworth, Illinois, June 26, 1915; admitted to bar, 1940, Illinois. *Education:* Princeton University (A.B., 1937); Northwestern University (J.D., 1940). ***Email:*** rbarrett@mayerbrownrowe.com

STUART BERNSTEIN, born Chicago, Illinois, November 23, 1919; admitted to bar, 1947, Illinois. *Education:* University of Chicago (A.B., 1942; J.D., 1947). ***Email:*** sbernstein@mayerbrownrowe.com

JEROME F. DONOHOE, born Yankton, South Dakota, March 17, 1939; admitted to bar, 1964, Illinois; 1967, U.S. District Court, Northern District of Illinois. *Education:* St. John's University (B.A., 1961); University of South Dakota; University of Minnesota (J.D., cum laude, 1964). Vice President - Law, Santa Fe Pacific Corporation, 1984-1994. Chair, Public Utility, Communications and Transportation Law Section, American Bar Association. [Capt., U.S. Army JAGC, 1964-1967]. ***Email:*** jdonohoe@mayerbrownrowe.com

DAVID B. FINNEGAN, born New York, N.Y., July 17, 1933; admitted to bar, 1961, District of Columbia and Massachusetts; 1993, U.S. Supreme Court. *Education:* Boston College (B.S., 1956; J.D., 1960). U.S. House of Representatives, Washington, D.C., 1969-1995. Senior Counsel, Committee on Energy and Commerce (formerly the Committee on Interstate Foreign Commerce), 1976-1995. Counsel, Committee on Science and Technology, 1975-1976. Associate General Counsel, Committee on Government Operations, 1969-1975. Staff of Congressman Ken Heckler (D-WVA), Washington, D.C., 1969. U.S. Department of the Interior, Washington, D.C., 1960-1969. Assistant Legislative Counsel, 1968-1969. General Attorney, Office of the Legislative Counsel, 1963-1968. General Attorney, Office of the Solicitor, 1961-1963. Law Clerk, Office of the Solicitor, 1960-1961. (Washington, D.C. Office). ***Email:*** dfinnegan@mayerbrownrowe.com

JAMES W. GLADDEN, JR., born Pittsburgh, Pennsylvania, February 23, 1940; admitted to bar, 1964, Illinois; U.S. Supreme Court; U.S. Court of Appeals, Fourth, Fifth, Seventh, Eighth and Tenth Circuits; U.S. District Court, Northern and Southern Districts of Illinois; U.S. District Court, Eastern District of Michigan; U.S. District Court, Southern District of New York; U.S. District Court, Northern District of California. *Education:* DePauw University (A.B., with high distinction, 1961); Harvard University (J.D., cum laude, 1964). ***PRACTICE AREAS:*** Labor and Employment. ***Email:*** jgladden@mayerbrownrowe.com

LEO HERZEL, born New York, N.Y., September 10, 1923; admitted to bar, 1952, Illinois. *Education:* University of Iowa (A.B., 1947); University of Illinois (A.M., 1949); University of Chicago (J.D., 1952). ***Email:*** lherzel@mayerbrownrowe.com

THOMAS N. JERSILD, born Chicago, Illinois, December 12, 1936; admitted to bar, 1962, Illinois. *Education:* University of Chicago (B.A., 1957; J.D., 1961). ***Email:*** tjersild@mayerbrownrowe.com

WAYNE S. KAPLAN, born Chicago, Illinois, July 13, 1946; admitted to bar, 1975, U.S. Tax Court; 1976, U.S. Court of Federal Claims; 1979, U.S. Supreme Court; 1989, Illinois; 1991, U.S. Court of Appeals, Eleventh Circuit; 1994, U.S. Court of Appeals, Ninth Circuit. *Education:* Wharton School of Finance and Commerce, University of Pennsylvania (B.S., 1968); Harvard University (J.D., 1971). ***PRACTICE AREAS:*** Taxation. ***Email:*** wkaplan@mayerbrownrowe.com

M. MARVIN KATZ, born Laredo, Texas, May 12, 1935; admitted to bar, 1958, Texas; 1959, U.S. District Court, Southern District of Texas; 1961, U.S. Court of Appeals, Fifth Circuit; 1972, U.S. Supreme Court. *Education:* Texas A & M College (B.A., 1954); University of Texas (LL.B., with honors, 1959). Member, City of Houston Planning Commission, 1980— (Chairman, 1991—; Vice Chairman, 1984-1991). [United States Air Force, 1955-1957]. (Houston, Texas Office) (Board Certified, Commercial Real Estate Law, Texas Board of Legal Specialization). ***LANGUAGES:*** Spanish. ***Email:*** mkatz@mayerbrownrowe.com

KENNETH KLEIN, born July 26, 1951; admitted to bar, 1977, District of Columbia; 1979, U.S. Court of Federal Claims and U.S. District Court for the District of Columbia; 1996, U.S. Tax Court; 1997, U.S. Court of Appeals, Fourth Circuit; 1998, U.S. Supreme Court. *Education:* University of Delaware (B.A., magna cum laude, 1973); University of Georgia School of Law (J.D., cum laude, 1976); Georgetown University Law Center (M.L.T., 1980). Chair, 1999-2001 and Member, 1994-2001, Board of Trustees, The Langley School, McLean, VA. Past Member, Board of Visitors, University of Georgia School of Law. *Member:* American Bar Association (Taxation Section); American Society of International Law (Fellow, 1976-1977; Member: Executive Council, 1982-1984; Budget Committee, 1983-1993; Chairman, Budget Committee, 1990-1993; International Taxation Correspondent-International Legal Materials, 1985—); International Fiscal Association. (Washington, D.C. Office). ***PRACTICE AREAS:*** Tax Law; International Taxation. ***Email:*** kklein@mayerbrownrowe.com

PHILIP ALLEN LACOVARA, born New York, N.Y., July 11, 1943; admitted to bar, 1967, New York; 1974, District of Columbia; 1970, U.S. Supreme Court. *Education:* Georgetown University (A.B., magna cum laude, 1963); Columbia University Law School (J.D., summa cum laude, 1966). Deputy Solicitor General of the United States, 1972-1973. Counsel to Watergate Special Prosecutor (1973-1974). Managing Partner, Washington, D.C. office, Hughes Hubbard & Reed, 1974-1988. Vice President and Senior Counsel for Litigation and Legal Policy, General Electric Co., 1988-1990. Managing Director and General Counsel, Morgan Stanley & Co., 1990-1993. President, District of Columbia Bar, 1988-1989. (New York, N.Y. Office). ***PRACTICE AREAS:*** Appellate Practice; Constitutional Law; Corporate Law. ***Email:*** placovara@mayerbrown.com

HARVEY NIXON, born Chicago, Illinois, November 22, 1931; admitted to bar, 1960, Illinois. *Education:* Grinnell College (B.A., 1953); Harvard University (LL.B., 1960). Adjunct Professor of Law: Legal Ethics, Northwestern University Law School. ***PRACTICE AREAS:*** Professional Responsibility. ***Email:*** hnixon@mayerbrownrowe.com

PATRICK W. O'BRIEN, born Chicago, Illinois, December 5, 1927; admitted to bar, 1951, Illinois. *Education:* Northwestern University (B.S., 1947; J.D., 1950). ***Email:*** pobrien@mayerbrownrowe.com

SPECIAL COUNSEL

STANTON A. KESSLER, born Chicago, Illinois, March 27, 1934; admitted to bar, 1958, Illinois; 1964, District of Columbia. *Education:* Amherst College (B.A., 1955); Harvard University (LL.B., 1958). ***PRACTICE AREAS:*** International Taxation; Tax Law; International Corporate Law. ***Email:*** skessler@mayerbrownrowe.com

CHARLES A. ROTHFELD, born New York, N.Y., November 17, 1956; admitted to bar, 1982, New York and District of Columbia. *Education:* Cornell University (A.B., cum laude, 1977); University of Chicago (J.D., cum laude, 1980). Articles Editor, University of Chicago Law Review. Author: "Securities Litigation Reform — Early Signs of Success," Securities Litigation and Deregulation Reports (2ed); "The Surprising Case Against Punitive Damages in Libel Suits Against Public Figures," 19 Yale L. & Pol. Rev. 165 (2000); "Scheiner's Next Wave: Distinguishing Taxes From Fees Under the Commerce Clause," 17 State Tax Notes 1681 (1999);"From Japan Line to Barclays: The Rise and Fall of the Foreign Commerce Clause," 7 State Tax Notes 379 (1994); "Section 1983: The Civil Rights Alternative to Constitutional Challenges," 6 State Tax Notes 751 (1994). Law Clerk to: Justice Harry A. Blackmun, U.S. Supreme Court, 1981-1982; Judge Spottswood Robinson, III, U.S. Court of Appeals for the District of Columbia Circuit, 1980-1981. Assistant to the Solicitor General, U.S. Department of Justice, 1984-1988. Deputy Minority Counsel, U.S. House of Representatives Select Committee on the U.S. Role in Iranian Arms Transfers to Croatia and Bosnia. Consultant, HUD Independent Counsel inquiry, 1991-1996. Special Associate Independent Counsel, Iran-Contra inquiry, 1990-1992. Counsel, Democratic National Committee, 1988, 1992. Faculty, National Association of Attorneys General Supreme Court Advocacy Seminar, 1992. Consultant to Federal Courts Study Committee, 1989-1990. Board of Advisors, Georgetown University Law Center's Supreme Court Institute, 1999—. Advisory Board, State and Local Legal Center, 1991—. Regular lecturer on Supreme Court issues to state and local officials. (Washington, D.C. Office). ***PRACTICE AREAS:*** Appellate Litigation; Securities Litigation; Government and Legislative Affairs. ***Email:*** crothfeld@mayerbrownrowe.com

COUNSEL

FRANK E. ARADO, born Franklin Park, Illinois, July 9, 1970; admitted to bar, 1996, Illinois. *Education:* University of Chicago (B.A., 1992); University of Illinois (J.D./M.B.A., 1996). ***PRACTICE AREAS:*** Real Estate; Finance; Corporate Law.

DEBRA RAE BERNARD, born Chicago, Illinois, September 23, 1958; admitted to bar, 1985, Illinois; 1986, U.S. District Court, Northern District of Illinois; 1988, U.S. Court of Appeals, Seventh Circuit; 1989, U.S. District Court, Northern District of Illinois, Trial Bar; 1996 U.S. Court of Appelas, Federal Circuit. *Education:* University of Illinois (B.S., 1981); Chicago-Kent College of Law (J.D., with honors, 1985). ***LANGUAGES:*** Italian. ***PRACTICE AREAS:*** Intellectual Property Litigation. ***Email:*** dbernard@mayerbrownrowe.com

CAROL J. BILZI, born Huntington, New York, August 6, 1954; admitted to bar, 1986, Pennsylvania; 1987, District of Columbia. *Education:* New York State University at Albany (B.A., magna cum laude, 1976); Georgetown University (J.D., cum laude, 1986). (Washington, D.C. Office). ***Email:*** cbilzi@mayerbrownrowe.com

ALEXANDER B. BLADES, born Wellington, New Zealand, 1970; admitted to bar, 1994, New Zealand; 1998, New York. *Education:* Victoria University of Wellington (B.A., first class honors, 1993; LL.B. honors, 1994); University of Chicago (LL.M., 1997). (New York, N.Y. Office). ***PRACTICE AREAS:*** Banking; Finance. ***Email:*** abblades@mayerbrownrowe.com

ROBERT A. BLOOM, born Philadelphia, Pennsylvania, March 12, 1938; admitted to bar, 1963, Pennsylvania; 1970, Michigan; 1993, Illinois. *Education:* University of Pennsylvania (B.S., 1960); Villanova University School of Law (LL.B., 1963). Trustee, Highland Park Library, 1999—. President, Highland Park Public Library, 2002—. Board Of Managers, Equal Employment Advisory Council, 1986-1992. Chairman-Case Selection Committee, Equal Employment Advisory Council, 1988-1992. Fellow, The College of Labor and Employment Lawyers, 2001. ***PRACTICE AREAS:*** Labor and Employment.

SUSAN J. BOOTH, born Pasadena, California, July 7, 1964; admitted to bar, 1991, California. *Education:* Stanford University (B.A., 1985); University of California, Los Angeles (M.B.A./J.D., 1991). Managing Editor, UCLA Law Review. (Los Angeles, California Office). ***Email:*** sbooth@mayerbrownrowe.com

DANIEL T. BROWN, born Wilmington, Delaware, September 16, 1967; admitted to bar, 1994, Illinois; 2001, District of Columbia. *Education:* University of Delaware (B.A., 1991); Chicago-Kent College of Law, Illinois Institute of Technology (J.D., high honors, 1994). (Washington, D.C. Office). ***PRACTICE AREAS:*** Litigation. ***Email:*** dtbrown@mayerbrownrowe.com

(This Listing Continued)

MAYER, BROWN, ROWE & MAW LLP, Chicago—Continued

SUSAN T. BROWN, born Oakland, California, November 25, 1944; admitted to bar, 1975, District of Columbia. *Education:* Randolph-Macon Woman's College (A.B., 1966); Washington College of Law of American University (J.D., 1974). *Member:* The District of Columbia Bar; American Bar Association; Federal Circuit Bar Association; International Trademark Association; American Intellectual Law Association. (Washington, D.C. Office). ***PRACTICE AREAS:*** Intellectual Property. ***Email:*** stbrown@mayerbrownrowe.com

DR. GÜNTER BURGHARDT, admitted to bar, 1970, Germany (Not admitted in Illinois). *Education:* University of Hambrug (Ph.D., 1969). (Brussels, Belgium Office). ***PRACTICE AREAS:*** Regulatory Law; Trade Law; Government Relations; International Corporate Law; Financial Transactions. ***Email:*** gburghardt@mayerbrownrowe.com

PAUL CHANDLER, born Detroit, Michigan, July 1, 1965; admitted to bar, 1995, Illinois; registered to practice before U.S. Patent and Trademark Office. *Education:* University of Michigan (B.S.E.E., magna cum laude, 1987; J.D., cum laude, 1995); University of Illinois (M.S.E.E., 1989). ***PRACTICE AREAS:*** Information Technology Outsourcing; Intellectual Property. ***Email:*** pchandler@mayerbrownrowe.com

TIMOTHY J. CHOPPIN, born Washington, D.C., 1963; admitted to bar, 1994, District of Columbia; 1995, Maryland. *Education:* Haverford College (B.A., 1985); University of Pennsylvania (M.C.P., with distinction, 1989); Georgetown University Law Center (J.D., cum laude, 1994). (Washington, D.C. Office)

VICTORIA R. COLLADO, born 1964; admitted to bar, 1990, Illinois. *Education:* Duke University (A.B.); University of Texas (J.D., 1990). ***Email:*** vcollado@mayerbrownrowe.com

LESLIE S. CRUZ, admitted to bar, 1996, Maryland; 1997, District of Columbia. *Education:* University of Maryland (B.A., 1991); University of Maryland School of Law (J.D., 1995). (Washington, D.C. Office). ***PRACTICE AREAS:*** Corporate Law; Securities. ***Email:*** lcruz@mayerbrownrowe.com

RICHARD C. CUMMINGS, JR., born Evanston, Illinois, May 28, 1953; admitted to bar, 1978, Illinois; 1979, U.S. District Court, Northern District of Illinois. *Education:* Tulane University of Louisiana (B.A., 1975); Illinois Institute of Technology (J.D., 1978). Senior Attorney in Corporate and Regulatory Division of Law Department, Continental Bank. ***LANGUAGES:*** Spanish. ***Email:*** rcummings@mayerbrownrowe.com

KEVIN G. DESHARNAIS, born Baldwin, New York, March 11, 1966; admitted to bar, 1993, Illinois, New York and New Jersey. *Education:* Cornell University (B.S., 1988); Pace University (J.D., 1992). Attorney, Illinois Pollution Control Board, 1994-1997. ***Email:*** kdesharnais@mayerbrownrowe.com

SHARON L. DE VAULT, born Blue Island, Illinois, June 18, 1963; admitted to bar, 1990, Illinois. *Education:* University of Chicago (B.A., 1984); IIT Chicago-Kent College of Law (J.D., 1990). Co-Author: Investments Chapter of IICLE Trust Administration. ***PRACTICE AREAS:*** Trusts and Estates (70%); Taxation (25%); Nonprofit and Charitable Organizations (5%). ***Email:*** sdevault@mayerbrownrowe.com

RONALD R. DIETRICH, born Chicago, Illinois, December 30, 1957; admitted to bar, 1982, Illinois and U.S. District Court, Northern District of Illinois. *Education:* Northwestern University (B.A., 1979); Loyola University Law School (J.D., cum laude, 1982). ***PRACTICE AREAS:*** Real Estate (50%); Real Estate Finance (50%). ***Email:*** rdietrich@mayerbrownrowe.com

BOISE A. DING, born Orange, California, August 30, 1967; admitted to bar, 1994, New York; 1996, California. *Education:* Brown University (A.B., magna cum laude, 1990); Harvard University. Phi Beta Kappa. Associate, Simpson Thacher & Bartlett, New York, NY, 1993-1995. (Los Angeles, California Office). ***Email:*** bding@mayerbrownrowe.com

LISA A. DUNSKY, born Dayton, Ohio, October 10, 1963; admitted to bar, 1993, Illinois and U.S. District Court, Northern District of Illinois; 1998, U.S. District Court, Northern District of Indiana; 2003, U.S. District Court, Southern District of Texas, U.S. District Court, Eastern District of Michigan and U.S. Court of Appeals, Seventh and Ninth Circuits; 2004, U.S. Court of Appeals, Sixth Circuit. *Education:* University of Dayton (B.A., magna cum laude, 1986); University of Cincinnati (M.A., magna cum laude, 1990); University of Michigan (J.D., cum laude, 1993). ***PRACTICE AREAS:*** SEC Enforcement; Commodities Regulation; Commodities Futures. ***Email:*** ldunsky@mayerbrownrowe.com

LINDA H. EARLE, born Houston, Texas, June 13, 1952; admitted to bar, 1978, Texas. *Education:* Vanderbilt University (B.A., cum laude, 1974); University of Texas (J.D., with honors, 1978). (Houston, Texas Office). ***PRACTICE AREAS:*** Real Estate. ***Email:*** learle@mayerbrownrowe.com

JACK EDELBROCK, born Evergreen Park, Illinois, October 7, 1951; admitted to bar, 1989, Illinois; 1995, Colorado. *Education:* University of Illinois (B.S., Mathematics, high honors, 1973); Northwestern University (M.A., Economics, University Fellowship, 1974); Chicago-Kent College of Law (J.D., high honors, 1989). Order of the Coif. ***LANGUAGES:*** German. ***PRACTICE AREAS:*** Real Estate; Finance. ***Email:*** jedelbrock@mayerbrownrowe.com

JULIAN P. GEHMAN, born December 11, 1955; admitted to bar, 1992, Maryland. *Education:* University of Southern California (B.A., 1980); Georgetown University Law Center (J.D., cum laude, 1992). Phi Beta Kappa. (Washington, D.C. Office). ***Email:*** jgehman@mayerbrownrowe.com

PATRICIA V. GENTRY, born Butler, Missouri, July 16, 1955; admitted to bar, 1980, Oklahoma; 1990, Illinois. *Education:* University of Missouri-Columbia (B.S., cum laude, 1976); University of Denver (J.D., 1980). ***Email:*** pgentry@mayerbrownrowe.com

KARA K. GIBNEY, born Cedar Rapids, Iowa, March 2, 1970; admitted to bar, 1995, Iowa; 1999, Illinois. *Education:* Coe College (B.A., 1992); Drake University (J.D., 1995). ***Email:*** kgibney@mayerbrownrowe.com

JEFFREY A. GOLDMAN, born Milwaukee, Wisconsin, April 22, 1961; admitted to bar, 1992, New York and U.S. District Court, Southern District of New York; 1997, U.S. Tax Court; 1999, Illinois. *Education:* University of Wisconsin (B.A., 1987); Boston College; University of Chicago (J.D., with honors, 1990). Order of the Coif. Law Clerk to Justice

(This Listing Continued)

Charles Levin, Michigan Supreme Court, 1990-1991. ***PRACTICE AREAS:*** Federal Tax Controversies; International Tax Controversies; Insurance. ***Email:*** jgoldman@mayerbrownrowe.com

KAREN F. R. GROTBERG, born Ridgewood, New Jersey, August 16, 1955; admitted to bar, 1985, Illinois. *Education:* Kalamazoo College (B.A., magna cum laude, 1977); Northwestern University (J.D., cum laude, 1985). ***PRACTICE AREAS:*** Employee Benefits. ***Email:*** kgrotberg@mayerbrownrowe.com

MARIAN C. HANEY, born Chicago, Illinois, September 20, 1940; admitted to bar, 1974, Illinois and U.S. District Court, Northern District of Illinois Trial Bar, 1982; 1976, U.S. Court of Appeals, 7th Circuit; 1979, U. S. Supreme Court; 1984, U.S. Court of Appeals, 8th Circuit; 1985, U.S. Court of Appeals, 10th Circuit; 1987, U.S. Court of Appeals, 11th Circuit; 1991, U.S. Court of Appeals, 9th Circuit. *Education:* Loyola University of Chicago (B.S., 1966; M.B.A., 1971; J.D., 1974). Executive Editor, Loyola Law Journal, 1973-1974. Law Clerk to Honorable Edwin A. Robson, Northern District of Illinois, 1974-1976. ***PRACTICE AREAS:*** Labor and Employment.

WILLIAM J. HEALEY, born Scranton, Pennsylvania, November 23, 1961; admitted to bar, 1992, District of Columbia; 2002, California. *Education:* Pennsylvania State University (B.S., 1983); California Institute of Technology (Ph.D., 1989); University of California School of Law, Los Angeles (J.D., 1992). (Washington, D.C. Office). ***PRACTICE AREAS:*** Intellectual Property. ***Email:*** whealey@mayerbrownrowe.com

JOHN R. HEWITT, born Pittsburgh, Pennsylvania, July 13, 1944; admitted to bar, 1974, Ohio; 1982, U.S. District Court, Southern District of Ohio and U.S. District Court for the District of Columbia. *Education:* John Carroll University (B.A., 1966); Cleveland State University (J.D., 1974); Georgetown University Law Center (LL.M., 1984). Co-Editor and Author: Securities Practice and Electronic Technology, Law Journal Seminars-Press. Author: "SRO Rules on Review of Electronic Communications," The New York Law Journal, February 5, 1998; "The ABCs of Cybercompliance," The New York Law Journal, January 23, 1997; "SEC Takes Control of Cyberspace," The New York Law Journal, August 1, 1996. Financial NetNews Internet Compliance Man of the Year, 1998. (New York, N.Y. Office). ***Email:*** jhewitt@mayerbrownrowe.com

DANIEL G. HILDEBRAND, born New York, N.Y., June 20, 1966; admitted to bar, 1993, Illinois; 1994, U.S. Court of Appeals, Seventh Circuit and U.S. District Court, Northern District of Illinois; 2000, U.S. District Court, Southern District of Illinois. *Education:* Brown University (A.B., magna cum laude, 1988); Yale University (J.D., 1992). ***PRACTICE AREAS:*** Civil Litigation; Libel Defense; Federal Indian Law. ***Email:*** dhildebrand@mayerbrownrowe.com

ADAM K. HOLLANDER, born Chicago, Illinois, May 30, 1967; admitted to bar, 1992, Illinois and U.S. District Court, Northern District of Illinois; 1998, U.S. District Court, Eastern District of Michigan and U.S. Court of Appeals, Fifth Circuit. *Education:* Indiana University (B.A., 1989); DePaul University (J.D., with honors, 1992). Order of the Coif. Member, DePaul Law Review. Extern, Hon. Kenneth F. Ripple, U.S. Court of Appeals, Seventh Circuit. ***PRACTICE AREAS:*** Insurance. ***Email:*** ahollander@mayerbrownrowe.com

DIANE M. HUFF, born Greenville, Mississippi, July 29, 1959; admitted to bar, 1984, Illinois. *Education:* Augustana College (B.A., magna cum laude, 1981); University of Illinois (J.D., 1984). ***PRACTICE AREAS:*** Real Estate. ***Email:*** dhuff@mayerbrownrowe.com

JOHN CHAFER HUFF, born Sioux Falls, South Dakota, April 10, 1957; admitted to bar, 1984, Oregon; 1985, Washington; 1988, Illinois. *Education:* University of Michigan (B.S., with high distinction, 1979; J.D., cum laude, 1984). ***PRACTICE AREAS:*** Real Estate. ***Email:*** jhuff@mayerbrownrowe.com

GARY A. ISAAC, born Brooklyn, New York, June 15, 1960; admitted to bar, 1985, Connecticut; 1986, Illinois. *Education:* Columbia College (B.A., summa cum laude, 1982); Yale University (J.D., 1985). ***Email:*** gisaac@mayerbrownrowe.com

DEAN ALAN ISAACS, born Chicago, Illinois, April 7, 1961; admitted to bar, 1986, Illinois. *Education:* University of Illinois (B.A., summa cum laude, 1983; J.D., magna cum laude, 1986). ***Email:*** disaacs@mayerbrownrowe.com

NICOLA JACKSON, born Reading, England; admitted to bar, 1996, Illinois and U.S. District Court, Northern District of Illinois; 2001, U.S. Court of Appeals, Seventh Circuit; 2003, U.S. Court of Appeals, Sixth Circuit; 2002, U.S. Supreme Court. *Education:* Cornell University (B.A., 1991); Harvard University (J.D., 1996). ***PRACTICE AREAS:*** Appellate Practice; Litigation. ***Email:*** njackson@mayerbrownrowe.com

CHRISTINE JAGDE, admitted to bar, 1995, New York and U.S. District Court, Southern and Eastern Districts of New York; 2002, U.S. District Court, District of Colorado. *Education:* St. John's University (B.A., 1990; J.D., 1994). Author: "Creditor Can Recover Attorney's Fees Incurred in Making Substantial Contribution to a Bankruptcy Case; Its Intent is Irrelevant," The Banking Law Journal, September 2001; "Percentage of the Recovery Method-A Solvent Response for Bankruptcy Proceedings?" American Bankruptcy Institute Law Review, Winter 1994; "The Misuse of Prescription Drugs by the Elderly: When the Cure Becomes the Problem," New York State Assembly Subcommittee on Seniors Centers Legislative Report, November 1991. Notes and Comments Editor, American Bankruptcy Institute Law Review, 1993-1994. Legislative Aide to the Honorable Morton C. Hillman, New York State Assembly, 1990-1991. (New York, N.Y. Office). ***REPORTED CASES:*** Mendelsohn v. Gordon (In re Who's Who Worldwide Registry, Inc.), 197 B.R. 193 (Bkrptcy.E.D.N.Y., 1996). ***PRACTICE AREAS:*** Bankruptcy; Reorganization. ***Email:*** cjagde@mayerbrownrowe.com

SULTANA KALDIS, born Houston, Texas, June 17, 1948; admitted to bar, 1975, Texas. *Education:* Randolph-Macon Woman's College (A.B., cum laude, 1970); University of Houston (J.D., 1975). Member, Houston Law Review, 1974-1975. (Houston, Texas Office). ***PRACTICE AREAS:*** Real Estate. ***Email:*** skaldis@mayerbrownrowe.com

MARITONI D. KANE, born Urbana, Illinois, December 25, 1964; admitted to bar, 1993, Illinois and U.S. District Court, Northern District of Illinois; 1996, U.S. Court of Appeals, Seventh, Fourth and Sixth Circuits; 1998, U.S. District Court, Central District of Illinois. *Education:* Northwestern University (B.A., 1986); DePaul University (J.D., 1993). Article and Note Editor, DePaul Law Review. Editor, Mayer Brown Rowe & Maw LLP

(This Listing Continued)

Labor & Employment Newsletter. ***REPORTED CASES:*** Dunn v. United Airlines, Inc. 1998 WL 142400 (N.D.Ill. 1998); Pinkston v. University of Chicago, 2001 WL 1609395 (N.D.Ill. 2001); Woods and McGee v. Ernst & Young, LLP, 2002 WL 475182 (N.D.Ill. 2002); Wright and Martin v. Sears Roebuck and Co., 81 Fed.Appx. 37 (6th Cir. 2003); Nowak v. Oce-USA, Inc., 2004 WL 2967432 (N.D.Ill. 2004). ***PRACTICE AREAS:*** Labor and Employment; Occupational Safety and Health; Litigation. ***Email:*** mkane@mayerbrownrowe.com

BEVERLEY J. KLEIN, born Chicago, Illinois, February 22, 1949; admitted to bar, 1975, Illinois and U.S. District Court, Northern District of Illinois; 1988, U.S. Court of Appeals, Ninth Circuit; 1991, U.S. Court of Appeals, Sixth Circuit. *Education:* University of Illinois, Champaign-Urbana (B.A., cum laude, 1970) Phi Beta Kappa, Kappa Delta Pi, Phi Kappa Phi; Loyola University of Chicago School of Law (J.D., cum laude, 1975). Member, Editorial Board, Loyola Law Journal, 1974-1975. Law Clerk to The Honorable Frank J. McGarr, U.S. District Court, Northern District of Illinois, 1975-1977. Partner, Mayer Brown & Platt 1983-1992. General Counsel, Illinois Department of Children and Family Services, May, 1992-December, 1994. ***PRACTICE AREAS:*** Litigation (100%). ***Email:*** bklein@mayerbrownrowe.com

LAWRENCE M. KNOWLES, born Minneapolis, Minnesota, June 14, 1956; admitted to bar, 1983, Illinois; 2001, District of Columbia. *Education:* University of Minnesota (B.A., 1978); University of Chicago Law School (J.D., cum laude, 1983). ***PRACTICE AREAS:*** Real Estate. ***Email:*** lknowles@mayerbrownrowe.com

ANDREW M. KOFSKY, born Brooklyn, New York, September 14, 1969; admitted to bar, 1994, Florida and U.S. District Court, Southern and Middle Districts of Florida; 1995, U.S. Court of Appeals, Eleventh Circuit; 1997, U.S. District Court, Middle District of New Jersey; 2000, New York. *Education:* Cornell University, School of Industrial and Labor Relations (B.S., 1990); Columbia University School of Law (J.D., 1993). (New York, N.Y. Office). ***PRACTICE AREAS:*** Labor and Employment. ***Email:*** akofsky@mayerbrownrowe.com

PAUL J. KUNKEL, born Cincinnati, Ohio, August 4, 1956; admitted to bar, 1992, Illinois. *Education:* Princeton University (B.A., 1976); Northwestern University (Ph.D., 1984; J.D., 1992). ***PRACTICE AREAS:*** Tax Law. ***Email:*** pjkunkel@mayerbrownrowe.com

LAURENCE DUMURE LAMBERT, admitted to bar, 1989, Paris. *Education:* University of Paris II-Assas (Maîtrise Droit des Affaires, 1987; Magistère de Juriste d'Affaires, 1988). (Paris, France Office). ***LANGUAGES:*** French and English. ***PRACTICE AREAS:*** Employment Law. ***Email:*** ldumurelambert@mayerbrownrowe.com

BENJAMIN W. LAU, admitted to bar, 1991, New York. *Education:* California State University (B.S., magna cum laude, 1987); Fordham University (J.D., 1990). (New York, N.Y. Office). ***PRACTICE AREAS:*** Corporate; Securities. ***Email:*** blau@mayerbrownrowe.com

KIM A. LEFFERT, born Rochester, New York, May 25, 1961; admitted to bar, 1986, Illinois; 1995, U.S. Court of Appeals, Sixth Circuit; 1998, U.S. Court of Appeals, Seventh Circuit; 1999, U.S. Court of Appeals, Fourth Circuit; U.S. District Court, Northern District of Illinois (Trial Bar); U.S. District Court, Central District of Illinois; U.S. District Court, Southern District of Illinois; U.S. District Court, District of Colorado. *Education:* Cornell University (A.B., 1983); University of Chicago (J.D., 1986). *Member:* Chicago Bar Association (Co-Chair, Labor and Employment Committee, Young Lawyers Section, 1990-1991). ***PRACTICE AREAS:*** Labor and Employment; Litigation. ***Email:*** kleffert@mayerbrownrowe.com

THOMAS A. LIDBURY, born Chicago, Illinois, June 22, 1967; admitted to bar, 1992, Illinois; U.S. District Court, Northern District of Illinois and U.S. Court of Appeals, Seventh Circuit; U.S. District Court, District of Arizona; U.S. District Court, Eastern District of Michigan. *Education:* University of Chicago (B.A., 1989); Washington University (J.D., 1992) Order of the Coif. ***REPORTED CASES:*** Dow Chemical v. Fireman's Fund Ins., 217 F.Supp.2d 816 (E.D.Mich. 2002); Palos Community Hospital v. Illinois Health Facilities Planning Board, 328 Ill.App.3d 336 (2002), appeal denied, 199 Ill.2d 558; Zapata Hermanos Sucesores v. Heartside Baking, 155 F.Supp.2d 969 (N.D.Ill. 2001); In re Syntrhoid Marketing Litigation, 110 F.Supp.2d 676 (N.D.Ill. 2000), aff'd in part, vacated in part, 264 F.3d 712 (7th Cir. 2001); Malnove v. Hearthside Baking, 944 F.Supp. 657 (N.D.Ill. 1996) and 951 F.Supp. 151 (N.D.Ill. 1997). ***PRACTICE AREAS:*** Litigation; Insurance. ***Email:*** tlidbury@mayerbrownrowe.com

SERGE A. LOMAKO, born Ukraine, 1958; admitted to bar, 1988, USSR; 1995, Russia. *Education:* The Higher Marine and Engineering College, Novorossiisk, Russia (B.S., Navigation and Marine Sciences, 1982); The Academy of Sciences, Institute of State and Law, Kiev, Ukraine (Ph.D., International Law, 1988); The Academy of Foreign Trade of the Ministry of Foreign Economic Affairs of the USSR, Moscow, USSR (International Economist, FEM, 1991); The University of Houston Law School (Master of Laws, 1995). (Houston, Texas Office). ***LANGUAGES:*** English, Russian, Ukrainian, Spanish, French. ***PRACTICE AREAS:*** International Transactions; International Arbitration; Energy. ***Email:*** slomako@mayerbrownrowe.com

JOAN L. LONG, born Dixon, Illinois, September 8, 1956; admitted to bar, 1992, Illinois. *Education:* Illinois State University (B.S., 1978); Loyola University (J.D., 1992). Alpha Sigma Nu. Student Articles Editor, Loyola University Chicago Law Journal, 1992. ***PRACTICE AREAS:*** Intellectual Property; Internet Law; Litigation. ***Email:*** jlong@mayerbrownrowe.com

WILLIAM M. MANN, admitted to bar, 1999, Virginia; 2000, District of Columbia. *Education:* University of Richmond (B.A., 1993); University of Virginia (J.D., 1999). Co-Author: "New Anti-Money Laundering Rules To Have Impact on Broker-Dealers and Investment Companies," Crowell & Moring Securities Law Bulletin, March 2002; "Big Brother is Watching: The regulators are snooping more than ever for evidence of market manipulation by traders," with Pat S. Conti, as appeared in the January 2002 issue of Traders Magazine (Volume 15, Number 191); "SEC Report Suggests Possibility of Leniency Through Cooperation," Crowell & Moring Securities Law Bulletin, November 2001. (Washington, D.C. Office). ***PRACTICE AREAS:*** Litigation. ***Email:*** wmann@mayerbrownrowe.com

(This Listing Continued)

MARJORIE M. MARGOLIES, born Milwaukee, Wisconsin, November 30, 1962; admitted to bar, 1988, Illinois; 1989, U.S. District Court, Northern District of Illinois; 1990, U.S. Tax Court; 1992, U.S. Court of Federal Claims; 1994, U.S. Court of Appeals, Ninth Circuit; 2002, U.S. Supreme Court. *Education:* Brown University (B.A., magna cum laude, 1985); University of Michigan (J.D., 1988). ***LANGUAGES:*** French, Spanish, Hebrew. ***Email:*** mmargolies@mayerbrownrowe.com

KEVIN C. McDONALD, born New York, N.Y., November 11, 1955; admitted to bar, 1980, Illinois. *Education:* University of Chicago (A.B., 1977); Harvard Law School (J.D., 1980). ***PRACTICE AREAS:*** Finance; Leases and Leasing. ***Email:*** kmcdonald@mayerbrownrowe.com

VIRGINIA A. MELVIN, admitted to bar, 1987, New York; 1998, Connecticut. *Education:* Wellesley College (B.A., 1979); University of Minnesota (J.D., cum laude, 1986). Articles Editor, Minnesota Law Review, 1985-1986. Author, "Tel-Oren v. Libyan Arab Republic: Redefining the Alien Tort Claims Act" 70 Minn L. Rev. 211 (1986). (New York, N.Y. Office). ***PRACTICE AREAS:*** Finance. ***Email:*** vmelvin@mayerbrownrowe.com

CLIFFORD R. MICHEL, admitted to bar, 1997, New York; 1998, U.S. District Court, Southern and Eastern Districts of New York. *Education:* Beloit College (B.A., magna cum laude, 1974); University of Hawaii (M.A., 1976); New York University School of Law (J.D., 1996). Member, East-West Center Fellowship. (New York, N.Y. Office). ***PRACTICE AREAS:*** Litigation. ***Email:*** cmichel@mayerbrownrowe.com

DR. JOACHIM J. MODLICH, born Frankfurt/Main, 1966; admitted to bar, 1996, Germany. *Education:* Westfaelische Wilhelms-University Muenster (First State Examination 1993; Dr.jur., 1996). Publications: "Nationale Infrastrukturmaßnahmen und Art. 92 I EGV (National Infrastructures and Art. 92 EU-Treaty), Heymanns, Cologne, 1996; "Das Zivilprozeßrecht in Übersichten," (The Civil Procedure Law in Schedules), Vol. 1, 140 pages, 1996; Vol. 2, 70 pages, 1997; "M&A Real Estate Transaction," joint publication with Joachim Schloesser, M&A Review (in preparation); "Die Übertragung von Aktien," (The Transfer of Shares), joint publication with Dr. Dieter Leuering (in preparation); "Der zwischenstaatliche Handel in Art 92 I EGV," (The Inster-state Trade in Art, 92 EU-Treaty), Europäisches Wirtschafts-und Steuerrecht, September, 1996. *Member:* Cologne Bar. (Cologne, Germany Office). ***LANGUAGES:*** German, English. ***Email:*** jmodlich@mayerbrownrowe.com

JUDITH A. MONDELLO, born Detroit, Michigan; admitted to bar, 1985, Illinois; 1996, U.S. District Court, Northern District of Illinois. *Education:* University of Wisconsin-Madison (B.A., 1976); Illinois Institute of Technology, Chicago-Kent College of Law (J.D., 1995). Adjunct Professor, John Marshall Law School, Spring, 2001. *Member:* Federal Bar Association. ***LANGUAGES:*** Spanish. ***PRACTICE AREAS:*** Health Law; Medical Malpractice Defense. ***Email:*** jwick@mayerbrownrowe.com

DEBORAH ALFRED MONSON, born Boston, Massachusetts, February 20, 1959; admitted to bar, 1985, Illinois. *Education:* Princeton University (A.B., 1980); University of Michigan (J.D., 1985). ***PRACTICE AREAS:*** Investment Management; Derivative Products; Securities. ***Email:*** dmonson@mayerbrownrowe.com

ROBERT L. MORGAN, born Hot Springs, Arkansas, August 8, 1948; admitted to bar, 1979, Texas. *Education:* University of Houston (B.S., summa cum laude, 1976); University of Texas (J.D., with honors, 1979). Note Editor, Texas Law Review, 1978-1979. (Houston, Texas Office). ***Email:*** rmorgan@mayerbrownrowe.com

DONALD C. MORRIS, born Chicago, Illinois, December 7, 1949; admitted to bar, 1978, Illinois. *Education:* University of Illinois (B.A., with honors, 1971); DePaul University (J.D., 1978). ***PRACTICE AREAS:*** Trusts and Estates; Taxation. ***Email:*** dmorris@mayerbrownrowe.com

ADRIAEN M. MORSE, JR., admitted to bar, 1995, Virginia; 1997, California; 2003, District of Columbia. *Education:* United States Naval Academy (B.S., 1988); University of Richmond School of Law (J.D., 1995); Georgetown University Law Center (LL.M., 2003). (Washington, D.C. Office). ***PRACTICE AREAS:*** Litigation. ***Email:*** amorse@mayerbrownrowe.com

CHRISTOPHER P. MURPHY, born Sydney, Australia, May 28, 1949; admitted to bar, 1985, California and U.S. District Court, Central District of California; 1987, U.S. District Court, Eastern District of California; 1991, U.S. District Court, Northern and Southern Districts of California; 1992, U.S. Court of Appeals, Ninth Circuit; 1997, U.S. District Court District of Arizona. *Education:* University of Sydney, Sydney, Australia (B.A., 1970); LaTrobe University (Ph.D., 1982); University of California at Los Angeles School of Law (J.D., 1985). Order of the Coif. Recipient: American Jurisprudence Prize for Contracts, 1983; Federal Bar Association Award for Federal Procedure, 1984. Member, UCLA Law Review, 1983-1985. (Los Angeles, California Office). ***PRACTICE AREAS:*** Securities Litigation; Business Litigation. ***Email:*** cmurphy@mayerbrownrowe.com

STANLEY C. NARDONI, admitted to bar, 1981, Illinois; U.S. Supreme Court; U.S. Court of Appeals, Seventh and Federal Circuits; U.S. District Court, Northern District of Illinois. *Education:* DePaul University (B.A., summa cum laude, 1977; J.D., with honors, 1981). ***PRACTICE AREAS:*** Litigation. ***Email:*** scnardoni@mayerbrownrowe.com

DANIEL B. NELSON, born 1968; admitted to bar, 2000, New York. *Education:* Johns Hopkins University (B.A., 1989); Columbia University (M.A., 1993); New York University School of Law (J.D., 1996). (New York, N.Y. Office). ***PRACTICE AREAS:*** Structured Finance; Private Equity; Joint Ventures. ***Email:*** dnelson@mayerbrownrowe.com

RICHARD M. NEWMAN, born Brooklyn, New York, December 21, 1943; admitted to bar, 1968, Illinois. *Education:* Columbia College, Columbia University (A.B., 1965); Columbia University Law School (J.D., 1968). ***PRACTICE AREAS:*** Secured Finance (80%); Unsecured Finance (20%). ***Email:*** rnewman@mayerbrownrowe.com

LISA O'KEEFE, admitted to bar, 1991, Illinois. *Education:* Illinois State University (B.A., 1981); Loyola University (J.D., 1991). ***PRACTICE AREAS:*** Real Estate. ***Email:*** lokeefe@mayerbrownrowe.com

ROSARIA VIVO OWEN, born Naples, Italy, August 8, 1963; admitted to bar, 1991, Illinois. *Education:* University of Illinois, Urbana-Champaign (B.S., 1985); Loyola University, Chicago (J.D., 1991). ***LANGUAGES:*** Italian. ***PRACTICE AREAS:*** Complex Litigation; Defense Litigation; Insurance Coverage; Mediation. ***Email:*** rowen@mayerbrownrowe.com

(This Listing Continued)

MAYER, BROWN, ROWE & MAW LLP, Chicago—Continued

DENA PALERMO, admitted to bar, 1984, New York; 1985, Texas (Not admitted in Illinois). *Education:* State University of New York at Binghamton (B.S. Accounting, 1980), Boston University (J.D. magna cum laude, 1983). Note & Case Editor Boston University Law Review 1982-1983; Staff Member, Boston University Law Review 1981-82. Recipient, American Jurisprudence Award in Professional Responsibility 1983; Recipient, Book Award in Land Use 1983. Law Clerk to the Honorable Chief Judge John V. Singleton, Jr., 1983-1985. Author, Comment, "Ascertaining Undefined State Law Under the Erie Doctrine," Factors Etc., Inv. v. Pro Arts, Inc., 62 B.U.L. Rev. 817 (1982). Speaker, "Sanctions Under Tex. R. Civ. P.13," University of Houston Advanced Civil Litigation Seminar, March 1991. Speaker, American Bar Association Section of Litigation, 17th Annual Fall Meeting, "Junk Science as Today's Jewel: Should the Rules be Amended?", Phoenix, Arizona, November 4-7, 1992. Speaker, State Bar of Texas, 9th Annual Advanced Personal Injury Law Course, "Jury Charge," July 1993. Speaker, University of Houston Law Center Advanced Civil Discovery, "How to Invoke the Court's Power to Control Discovery: A Demonstration," Houston, Texas, June 1994. Speaker, American Bar Association Leadership Summit Meeting the Needs of Solo and Small Firm Lawyers, Topic: "Ending Isolation-Keys to Effective Programs," Chicago, Illinois, July 14-15, 1995. *Member:* Houston Bar Association (Director, 1992-1994; Fellow); State Bar of Texas (Life Fellow); Association of Women Attorneys (Director, 1993-1995); Association of Womens Attorneys Foundation (Trustee, 1993-1995; Charter Founder). ***REPORTED CASES:*** Ex Parte Tucci, 859 S.W.2d 1 (Tex. 1993); King v. Graham Holding Co., Inc., 762 S.W.2d 296 (Tex. App.--Houston (14th Dist.) 1988, no writ). ***PRACTICE AREAS:*** Litigation; Appellate. ***Email:*** dpalermo@mayerbrownrowe.com

REX A. PALMER, born Iowa City, Iowa, December 12, 1952; admitted to bar, 1981, Illinois. *Education:* Stanford University (A.B., 1978; J.D., 1981). ***PRACTICE AREAS:*** Real Estate. ***Email:*** rpalmer@mayerbrownrowe.com

JAMES A. PARKER, born Brooklyn, New York, May 14, 1946; admitted to bar, 1977, Illinois and U.S. District Court, Northern District of Illinois. *Education:* Midwestern University (B.A., cum laude, 1972); Illinois Institute of Technology (J.D., with honors, 1977). Member, IIT/Chicago-Kent Law Review, 1975-1977. ***Email:*** jparker@mayerbrownrowe.com

ROGER W. PATRICK, born Youngstown, Ohio, November 26, 1959; admitted to bar, 1984, District of Columbia. *Education:* Carnegie Mellon University (B.S., Chemistry, with University Honors, 1981); Yale University (J.D., 1984). (Washington, D.C. Office). ***PRACTICE AREAS:*** Environmental Law. ***Email:*** rpatrick@mayerbrownrowe.com

ROSS PAZZOL, born Chicago, Illinois, November 20, 1959; admitted to bar, 1987, Illinois. *Education:* University of Illinois (B.A., 1982); Loyola University (J.D., 1987). ***Email:*** rpazzol@mayerbrownrowe.com

KATHLEEN H. PENDER, born Chicago, Illinois, December 8, 1966; admitted to bar, 1992, Illinois. *Education:* University of Illinois (A.B., 1989; J.D., 1992). Order of the Coif. ***Email:*** kpender@mayerbrownrowe.com

GEORGE N. POLYDOROS, JR., born Houston, Texas, May 21, 1963; admitted to bar, 1989, Texas. *Education:* University of Texas (B.B.A., 1985); University of Houston (J.D., 1989). Beta Gamma Sigma; Order of the Barons. (Houston, Texas Office). ***Email:*** gpolydoros@mayerbrownrowe.com

KAREN L. PRENA, born Oak Park, Illinois, January 29, 1960; admitted to bar, 1989, Illinois; 1992, Washington. *Education:* University of Notre Dame (B.A., 1983); New York University (J.D., 1989). ***Email:*** kprena@mayerbrownrowe.com

SUSAN R. PROFFITT, born Evanston, Illinois, December 5, 1960; admitted to bar, 1993, Illinois. *Education:* Indiana University (B.S., 1988); Loyola University (J.D., 1993). ***Email:*** sproffitt@mayerbrownrowe.com

DENNIS M. QUINN, admitted to bar, 1979, Illinois. *Education:* University of Notre Dame (B.A., magna cum laude, 1972); University of Kansas (M.A., 1974); University of Kansas School of Law (J.D., 1979). ***PRACTICE AREAS:*** Corporate and Securities. ***Email:*** dquinn@mayerbrownrowe.com

CHARLES F. REGAN, JR., born Pittsburgh, Pennsylvania, June 12, 1959; admitted to bar, 1988, Illinois; 1989, U.S. District Court, Northern District of Illinois and U.S. Court of Appeals, Seventh Circuit. *Education:* University of Chicago (A.B., 1981); Northwestern University (J.D., cum laude, 1988). Managing Editor, Northwestern University Law Review. Law Clerk to Hon. Marvin E. Aspen, U.S. District Court, Northern District of Illinois, 1988-1989. ***REPORTED CASES:*** In re Sears Retiree Life Insurance Litigation, 90 F. Supp. 2d 940 (N.D. Ill. 2000); Bosco v. Chicago Transit Authority, 164 F. Supp. 2d 1040 (N.D. Ill 2001). ***PRACTICE AREAS:*** Civil Litigation; ERISA Class Actions. ***Email:*** cregan@mayerbrownrowe.com

LAURI BLUM REGAN, born Baltimore, Maryland, October 23, 1963; admitted to bar, 1989, New York. *Education:* Emory University (B.A., 1985); University of Maryland (J.D., with honors, 1988). (New York, N.Y. Office). ***PRACTICE AREAS:*** Finance.

CRAIG E. REIMER, born 1967; admitted to bar, 1992, Illinois. *Education:* Tufts University (B.A., magna cum laude, 1988); Loyola University (J.D., cum laude, 1992). ***PRACTICE AREAS:*** Bankruptcy; Commercial Workouts and Bankruptcies; International Insolvencies. ***Email:*** creimer@mayerbrownrowe.com

LINDA L. RHODES, born Washington, D.C., August 13, 1962; admitted to bar, 1987, Virginia; 1988, District of Columbia. *Education:* College of William & Mary (B.B.A., 1984); University of Virginia (J.D., 1987). (Washington, D.C. Office). ***PRACTICE AREAS:*** Corporate Law; Technology; Finance. ***Email:*** lrhodes@mayerbrownrowe.com

CECILIA A. ROTH, born Chicago, Illinois, March 3, 1954; admitted to bar, 1984, Illinois. *Education:* University of Chicago (A.B., 1976); University of Michigan (J.D., 1983). ***Email:*** croth@mayerbrownrowe.com

ABIGAIL L. RUDOFF, born Schenectady, New York, March 6, 1957; admitted to bar, 1994, Illinois. *Education:* Northern Illinois University (B.S., summa cum laude, University Honors, 1978); University of Pennsylvania (M.B.A., 1980); University of Chicago (J.D., 1994). Phi Kappa Phi; Beta Gamma Sigma. ***Email:*** arudoff@mayerbrownrowe.com

(This Listing Continued)

PAMELA J. SACKMANN, born Aurora, Illinois; admitted to bar, 1992, New York. *Education:* University of Illinois (B.S., summa cum laude, 1987); Stanford University (J.D., 1991). (New York, N.Y. Office). ***PRACTICE AREAS:*** Derivatives; Finance; Synthetic Securitizations. ***Email:*** psackmann@mayerbrownrowe.com

PATRICIA F. SHARKEY, born Evanston, Illinois, July 6, 1952; admitted to bar, 1980, Oregon; 1981, Illinois; 1989, U.S. District Court, Northern District of Illinois; 1990, U.S. Court of Appeals, Seventh Circuit. *Education:* University of Chicago (B.A., 1974); University of Oregon (J.D., 1980). Mayer, Brown & Platt, 1988— (Environmental Practice Area). Attorney and Regulatory and Legislative Liaison, Illinois Pollution Control Board, 1980-1985. Clerkship: Illinois Attorney General's Environmental Control Division, 1978; Clerkship, U.S. Attorneys office, District of Oregon, 1978-1980. ***PRACTICE AREAS:*** Environmental Law. ***Email:*** psharkey@mayerbrownrowe.com

MARK T. SHIPLEY, born Berkeley, California, August 16, 1944; admitted to bar, 1974, California; 1988, District of Columbia; 1989, Colorado. *Education:* Pomona College (B.A., 1966); University of California at Berkeley (M.A., 1968; C. Phil., 1971); University of Southern California (J.D., 1974). Co-Panelist, CEB Programs on: Financing Real Property Transactions, 1984; Introduction to Secured Real Property Transactions, 1985; and The Changing Climate in Real Property Financing, 1991. Panelist, Benjamin Crocker Symposium, 1987. (Los Angeles, California Office). ***Email:*** mshipley@mayerbrownrowe.com

SHIRA A. SILVER, born Forest Hills, New York, January 16, 1957; admitted to bar, 1984, New York. *Education:* University of Pennsylvania (B.A., 1978); Fordham University (J.D., 1981). (New York, N.Y. Office). ***PRACTICE AREAS:*** Real Estate Finance. ***Email:*** ssilver@mayerbrownrowe.com

ADAM C. SLOANE, born Glen Cove, New York, July 24, 1958; admitted to bar, 1993, Pennsylvania; 1994, District of Columbia and U.S. Court of Appeals, Eleventh Circuit; 1998, U.S. Court of Appeals, Ninth Circuit; 1999 U.S. Court of Appeals for the District of Columbia Circuit and U.S. District Court for the District of Columbia. *Education:* Haverford College (B.A., 1980); Princeton University (M.A., 1984); University of Michigan (J.D., magna cum laude, 1991). Order of the Coif. Book Review Editor, Michigan Law Review, 1990-1991. Law Clerk, Hon. Bruce Selya, U.S. Court of Appeals for the First Circuit, 1991-1992. Panelist, "Hours of Service," 37th Transportation Law Institute, 2004. (Washington, D.C. Office). ***PRACTICE AREAS:*** Regulatory Law; Appellate Practice; Litigation. ***Email:*** asloane@mayerbrownrowe.com

RICHARD A. SPEER, born Springfield, Ohio, November 7, 1928; admitted to bar, 1956, Virginia; 1957, Ohio; registered to practice before U.S. Patent and Trademark Office (Not admitted in Illinois). *Education:* Ohio State University (B. Met.E., 1953); George Washington University (LL.B., 1956). ***Email:*** rspeer@mayerbrownrowe.com

RICHARD A. STEINBERG, born New York, N.Y., May 22, 1946; admitted to bar, 1974, Virginia and U.S. District Court, Eastern District of Virginia; 1976, District of Columbia; 1980, U.S. Court of Appeals for the Federal Circuit; registered to practice before U.S. Patent and Trademark Office. *Education:* Cooper Union (B.Ch.E., 1967); George Washington University (J.D., 1974). (Washington, D.C. Office). ***PRACTICE AREAS:*** Intellectual Property. ***Email:*** rsteinberg@mayerbrownrowe.com

CATHERINE ANN STEVENS, admitted to bar, 1969, Alaska and U.S. District Court, District of Alaska; 1970, California and U.S. District Court, Southern District of California; 1971, U.S. Court of Appeals, Ninth Circuit; 1990, District of Columbia, U.S. Supreme Court and U.S. Court of Appeals for the District of Columbia Circuit. *Education:* Georgetown University (B.S.F.S., cum laude, 1966); George Washington University Law School (1967-1968); University of San Diego School of Law (J.D., cum laude, 1969). (Washington, D.C. Office). ***PRACTICE AREAS:*** Government (50%); Criminal Trial; Non-Profit (50%). ***Email:*** cstevens@mayerbrownrowe.com

DOREEN A. SULLIVAN, born Brooklyn, New York, 1963; admitted to bar, 1988, New Jersey; 1989, New York. *Education:* Lafayette College (A.B., 1985); New York Law School (J.D., summa cum laude, 1988). (New York, N.Y. Office). ***PRACTICE AREAS:*** Corporate Law; Securities. ***Email:*** dsullivan@mayerbrownrowe.com

MICHAEL T. SULLIVAN, born New London, Connecticut, October, 1968; admitted to bar, 1993, Illinois and U.S. District Court, Northern District of Illinois; 2000, U.S. Court of Appeals, Seventh Circuit. *Education:* Duke University (A.B., summa cum laude, 1990); Harvard University (J.D., cum laude, 1993). ***PRACTICE AREAS:*** Litigation; Telecommunications Regulation; Communications Law. ***Email:*** msullivan@mayerbrownrowe.com

ILANA Z. SULTAN, admitted to bar, 1994, Illinois; 1996, Georgia; 2000, District of Columbia. *Education:* Columbia University (B.A., 1990); University of Chicago Law School (J.D., 1994). Law Clerk, U.S. Court of Appeals for the Eleventh Circuit. Assistant State's Attorney for Cook County, Chicago, IL, 1994-1996. (Washington, D.C. Office). ***PRACTICE AREAS:*** Litigation. ***Email:*** isultan@mayerbrownrowe.com

WAYNE L. TANG, born Dearborn, Michigan, July 7, 1966; admitted to bar, 1991, Illinois and U.S. District Court, Northern District of Illinois. *Education:* University of Michigan (B.A., with distinction, 1988; B.S.E., magna cum laude, 1988); Michigan Law School (J.D., 1991). ***Email:*** wtang@mayerbrownrowe.com

DAVID M. THIMMIG, born Lansing, Michigan, December 10, 1962; admitted to bar, 1991, Illinois and U.S. District Court, Northern District of Illinois; 1996, U.S. District Court, Eastern District of Wisconsin; 1997, U.S. Court of Appeals for the Federal Circuit; registered to practice before U.S. Patent and Trademark Office. *Education:* General Motors Institute (B.S.M.E., 1986); University of Michigan (J.D., 1991). ***PRACTICE AREAS:*** Intellectual Property Litigation; Intellectual Property Prosecution; Intellectual Property Counseling. ***Email:*** dthimmig@mayerbrownrowe.com

RICHARD J. TIMMEL, born Milwaukee, Wisconsin, September 25, 1955; admitted to bar, 1990, Illinois. *Education:* University of Wisconsin-Milwaukee (D.S.M., 1980); Harvard University (J.D., cum laude, 1990). ***Email:*** rtimmel@mayerbrownrowe.com

JEFFREY G. TOUGAS, born Providence, Rhode Island, January 19, 1960; admitted to bar, 1991, Connecticut and U.S. District Court, District of Connecticut; 2004, Massachusetts. *Education:* Nichols College (B.S.B.A., 1982); Western New England College (M.B.A., 1986); Western New England College School of Law (J.D., 1990). *Member:* As-

(This Listing Continued)

sociation of Commercial Finance Attorneys. (New York, N.Y. Office). ***PRACTICE AREAS:*** Commercial Law; Bankruptcy; Workouts. ***Email:*** jgtougas@mayerbrownrowe.com

MARGUERITE E. TROSSEVIN, born Washington, D.C., May 12, 1949; admitted to bar, 1985, District of Columbia; 2003, Maryland. *Education:* Villanova University (B.A., summa cum laude, 1982; J.D., cum laude, 1985). (Washington, D.C. Office). ***PRACTICE AREAS:*** Government and Global Trade. ***Email:*** mtrossevin@mayerbrownrowe.com

TIMOTHY J. TYLER, born Houston, Texas, September 19, 1963; admitted to bar, 1994, Texas; 2003, U.S. Court of Appeals, Fifth Circuit. *Education:* Yale University (B.A., with honors, 1986); University of Texas (J.D., with honors, 1994). (Houston, Texas Office). ***LANGUAGES:*** German, French. ***PRACTICE AREAS:*** Commercial Litigation; International Arbitration. ***Email:*** ttyler@mayerbrownrowe.com

STEPHEN VAN DOLSEN, born Philadelphia, Pennsylvania, April 5, 1956; admitted to bar, 1989, New York; 1993, Illinois. *Education:* Penn State University (B.A., 1985); Fordham University (J.D., 1989). (New York, N.Y. Office). ***Email:*** svandolsen@mayerbrownrowe.com

ROBERT C. VARNELL, admitted to bar, 1997, Illinois. *Education:* University of Michigan (B.A., with highest distinction, 1993; J.D., cum laude, 1996). (Washington, D.C. Office). ***PRACTICE AREAS:*** Litigation.

JOHN J. VOORHEES, JR., born 1966; admitted to bar, 1992, Illinois and U.S. District Court, Northern District of Illinois; 1993, U.S. District Court, Eastern District of Michigan; 1996, U.S. Court of Appeals, Fourth Circuit; 1997, U.S. District Court, Eastern District of Wisconsin and U.S. Court of Appeals, Seventh Circuit. *Education:* Duke University (B.A., 1988); Washington University School of Law (J.D., 1991). Law Clerk to Chief Judge John D. Schwartz, U.S. Bankruptcy Court, Northern District of Illinois, 1991-1992. ***REPORTED CASES:*** In re: Handy Andy Home Improvement Centers, Inc., 144 F.3d 1125 (7th Cir. 1998); Spartan Mills v. Bank of America Illinois, 112 F.3d 1251 (4th Cir. 1997). ***PRACTICE AREAS:*** Bankruptcy; Workouts; Bankruptcy Reorganization.

KENNETH N. WEINSTEIN, born New York, New York, September 29, 1946; admitted to bar, 1974, Connecticut; 1980, District of Columbia; U.S. Court of Appeals, District of Columbia, Fourth and Eleventh Circuits. *Education:* Yale University (B.A., cum laude, 1968); Yale University Law School (J.D., 1974). Deputy Assistant General Counsel for Litigation, U.S. Department of Transportation, 1981-1988. Assistant Chief Counsel for Litigation, 1988-1997 and Associate Administrator for Enforcement, 1997-2005, National Highway Traffic Safety Administration. (Washington, D.C. Office). ***PRACTICE AREAS:*** Litigation; Automobile Regulation; Consumer Products Regulation. ***Email:*** kweinstein@mayerbrownrowe.com

KIMBERLY S. WINICK, born Hartford, Connecticut, 1958; admitted to bar, 1985, California; 1986, U.S. District Court, Central and Eastern Districts of California and U.S. Court of Appeals, Ninth Circuit; 1987, U.S. District Court, Northern District of California; 1992, U.S. District Court, Southern District of California; 1995, U.S. District Court, District of Arizona. *Education:* Middlebury College (B.A., cum laude, 1980); University of Texas, Austin (J.D., with honors, 1985). Author: "Severing and Combining Contracts," 19 Business Law News 10 (California State Bar) Fall, 1998; "Severable and Nonexecutory Contracts—Strategies Regarding Partial Assumption or Rejection," Maricopa County Bar Association, May, 1998. Co-author: "Waiving the Red Flag: Update on the Enforceability of Certain Waivers in Bankruptcy," Maricopa County Bar Association, May, 1998; "Securitized Mortgage Lending," Los Angeles County Bar Association, April, 1998; "Chapter 9 Municipal Bankruptcies: Treatment of Bondholders and Other Lenders," 26 Bankruptcy Court Decisions A-5, December 27, 1995. State Bar of California, Business Law Section, Education Committee (Co-Chair, 1997-1998). *Member:* State Bar of California; American Bar Association; Los Angeles Bankruptcy Forum (Vice President); Financial Lawyers Conference (Governor). (Los Angeles, California Office). ***LANGUAGES:*** Spanish. ***PRACTICE AREAS:*** Bankruptcy; Insolvency; Workouts. ***Email:*** kwinick@mayerbrownrowe.com

RICHARD G. ZIEGLER, born Rockville Centre, New York, March 15, 1959; admitted to bar, 1988, Michigan; 1989, U.S. District Court, Eastern District of Michigan; 1991, U.S. District Court, Western District of Michigan; 1992, Illinois and U.S. District Court, Northern District of Illinois; 1993, U.S. Court of Appeals, Third Circuit; 2005, U.S. Court of Appeals, Seventh Circuit. *Education:* University of Notre Dame (B.A., 1981); University of Illinois (M.A., 1983); University of Michigan (J.D., cum laude, 1988). ***PRACTICE AREAS:*** Bankruptcy; Creditors Rights; Financial Restructuring; Structured Finance. ***Email:*** rziegler@mayerbrownrowe.com

SENIOR ASSOCIATE

JASON K. SCHMITZ, born Chicago, Illinois, July 12, 1974; admitted to bar, 1999, Illinois. *Education:* Michigan State University (B.A., 1996); DePaul University College of Law (J.D., 1999). ATLA Wolfe Scholarship Recipient. Articles and Notes Editor, DePaul Business Law Journal. ***LANGUAGES:*** Spanish. ***PRACTICE AREAS:*** Intellectual Property. ***Email:*** jkschmitz@mayerbrownrowe.com

ASSOCIATES

K. ROBIN ABRAHAM, admitted to bar, 2001, Wisconsin and Illinois; 2002, District of Columbia. *Education:* University of Wisconsin-Madison (B.A., 1997; M.S., 2000; J.D., 2001). ***PRACTICE AREAS:*** Banking Law; Finance. ***Email:*** kabraham@mayerbrownrowe.com

PRITI SEKSARIA AGRAWAL, born February 10, 1976; admitted to bar, 2002, New York; 2003, District of Columbia. *Education:* Georgetown University (B.S.F.S., summa cum laude, 1998); Harvard Law School (J.D., 2001). (Resident, Washington D.C. Office). ***PRACTICE AREAS:*** Government; Global Trade. ***Email:*** psagrawal@mayerbrownrowe.com

ANDRES E. AGUILA, born Caracas, Venezuela, September 14, 1970; admitted to bar, 1997, Florida; 2002, New York. *Education:* Colgate University (B.A., 1992); University of Miami (J.D., cum laude, 1997). (New York, N.Y. Office). ***LANGUAGES:*** Spanish and French. ***PRACTICE AREAS:*** Derivatives; Securities; Corporate. ***Email:*** aaguila@mayerbrownrowe.com

(This Listing Continued)

MOHAMMED G. AHMED, (admission pending). *Education:* University of Illinois at Chicago (B.A., 2001); DePaul University College of Law (J.D., 2005). ***PRACTICE AREAS:*** Banking and Finance. ***Email:*** mahmed@mayerbrownrowe.com

THAIS M. ALEXANDER, born Worcester, Massachusetts, August 22, 1974; admitted to bar, 2002, New York. *Education:* Canisius College (B.A., magna cum laude, 1996); State University of New York at Buffalo (M.B.A., 2001; J.D., 2001). (Charlotte, North Carolina Office). ***PRACTICE AREAS:*** Banking and Finance. ***Email:*** talexander@mayerbrownrowe.com

SUZANNE V. ALWAN, born Laguna Beach, California, 1965; admitted to bar, 1999, New York; 2004, Georgia. *Education:* Arizona State University (B.A., summa cum laude, 1993); Duke University School of Law (J.D., 1998). (Charlotte, North Carolina Office). ***PRACTICE AREAS:*** Banking; Finance. ***Email:*** salwan@mayerbrownrowe.com

LISA M. AN, born Leyden, Illinois, October 27, 1970; admitted to bar, 1997, Illinois. *Education:* University of Illinois (B.A., 1992); The American University (J.D., summa cum laude, 1997). ***LANGUAGES:*** French. ***PRACTICE AREAS:*** Asset Based Finance; Secured Finance; Structured Finance. ***Email:*** lan@mayerbrownrowe.com

COURTNEY L. ANDERSON, born Cleveland, Ohio, October 28, 1977; admitted to bar, 2002, Illinois. *Education:* University of Pennsylvania (B.A., 1999; J.D., 2002). ***Email:*** clbreen@mayerbrownrowe.com

MACK D. ANDERSON, admitted to bar, 2003, California. *Education:* Occidental College (B.A., magna cum laude, 2000); University of Southern California (J.D., 2003). (Los Angeles, California Office). ***PRACTICE AREAS:*** Litigation. ***Email:*** maanderson@mayerbrownrowe.com

JEFFREY B. ANDREWS, born San Bernardino, California, August 26, 1971; admitted to bar, 1997, Texas; 2004, New York. *Education:* Trinity University (B.A., cum laude, 1994); University of Texas at Austin (J.D., 1997). (New York, N.Y. Office). ***PRACTICE AREAS:*** Corporate Law; Computers and Software; Intellectual Property. ***Email:*** jandrews@mayerbrownrowe.com

MICHELLE J. ANNUNZIATA, admitted to bar, 2004, New York. *Education:* University of Notre Dame (B.A., 1998); Fordham University School of Law (J.D., 2003). (New York, N.Y. Office). ***PRACTICE AREAS:*** Litigation. ***Email:*** mannunziata@mayerbrownrowe.com

MELISSA A. ANYETEI, (admission pending). *Education:* Northwestern University (B.A., 2002); Columbia University School of Law (J.D., 2005). ***PRACTICE AREAS:*** Intellectual Property. ***Email:*** manyetei@mayerbrownrowe.com

MONICA A. AQUINO, born Lakeland, Florida, May 17, 1974; admitted to bar, 1999, Florida; 2000, District of Columbia; 2001, U.S. District Court, District of Columbia; 2002, U.S. Court of Federal Claims. *Education:* University of Miami (B.A., magna cum laude, 1996; J.D., 1999). Recipient, Harvey T. Reid Full Merit Law Scholarship. Undergraduates Student Body President, 1995-1996. (Washington, D.C. Office). ***PRACTICE AREAS:*** Complex and Civil Litigation; Government Contracts (False Claims Act); White Collar Crime. ***Email:*** maaquino@mayerbrownrowe.com

MICHAEL ROBERT ARBOGAST, born March 3, 1976; admitted to bar, 2002, Massachusetts (Not admitted in Illinois). *Education:* DePaul University (B.S., summa cum laude, 1998); Harvard University (J.D., cum laude, 2002). ***LANGUAGES:*** Japanese. ***PRACTICE AREAS:*** Finance. ***Email:*** marbogast@mayerbrownrowe.com

RICHARD M. ASSMUS, born Bethlehem, Pennsylvania, 1973; admitted to bar, 1998, Illinois; 1998, U.S. District Court, Northern District of Illinois; 1999, U.S. Court of Appeals, Seventh Circuit; 2000, U.S. Court of Appeals, Federal Circuit; 2004, District of Columbia. *Education:* University of Chicago (B.S., Mathematics, 1995); University of Michigan (J.D., 1998). ***PRACTICE AREAS:*** Intellectual Property. ***Email:*** rassmus@mayerbrownrowe.com

GRACE K. AVEDISSIAN. *Education:* Rutgers University, Rutgers College (B.A., magna cum laude, 1997); American University, Washington College of Law (J.D., 2003). (New York, N.Y. Office). ***PRACTICE AREAS:*** Banking; Finance. ***Email:*** gkavedissian@mayerbrownrowe.com

GIANLUCA G. BACCHIOCCHI, born Rome, Italy, December 16, 1971; admitted to bar, 1999, New York; 2001, Illinois. *Education:* University of Michigan (B.A., with high distinction, 1994); New York University (J.D., 1998). ***LANGUAGES:*** Italian, Spanish. ***PRACTICE AREAS:*** Finance; Securitization; Corporate Law. ***Email:*** gbacchiocchi@mayerbrownrowe.com

ANDREW C. BAEK, born April 25, 1969; admitted to bar, 1995, New York; 2001, District of Columbia. *Education:* New York University, Leonard N. Stern School of Business (B.A., 1991); Brooklyn Law School (J.D., 1994). (Resident, Washington D.C. Office). ***PRACTICE AREAS:*** Banking; Finance. ***Email:*** abaek@mayerbrownrowe.com

JOSEPH R. BAKER, admitted to bar, 2004, New York. *Education:* Yale University (B.A., 1992); Columbia University Law School (J.D., 2002). (Washington, D.C. Office). ***PRACTICE AREAS:*** Appellate Practice; Litigation. ***Email:*** jbaker@mayerbrownrowe.com

VIOLETA I. BALAN, born Romania; admitted to bar, 2004, Illinois and U.S. District Court, Northern District of Illinois; 2005, U.S. Court of Appeals, Seventh Circuit. *Education:* Lake Forest College (B.A., magna cum laude, 1998); John Marshall Law School (J.D., summa cum laude, 2004). Author, Comment, "Recognition and Enforcement of Foreign Judgments in the United States and the Need for Federal Legislation," 37 J. Marshall L. Rev. 299 (2003). ***LANGUAGES:*** French, Romanian. ***PRACTICE AREAS:*** Litigation; International Arbitration; Electronic Discovery and Records Management. ***Email:*** vbalan@mayerbrownrowe.com

SONIA BALDIA, admitted to bar, 1992, India; 2000, New York; 2002, U.S. Court of Appeals for the Federal Circuit; registered to practice before U.S. Patent and Trademark Office. *Education:* Punjabi University (B.Sc., 1987); University of Delhi Faculty of Law (LL.B., 1991); University of Georgia School of Law (LL.M., 1992); George Washington University Law School (S.J.D., 1998). Registered Patent Attorney, Indian Patent Office, 1996. Consultant, USDOC and USAID on IT, Telecom and E-Commerce related international development projects 1998-2001. Steptoe & Johnson (Washington, DC), 1998-2000.

(This Listing Continued)

MAYER, BROWN, ROWE & MAW LLP, Chicago—Continued

Brobeck, Phleger & Harrison (New York), 1997-1998. Adjunct Faculty, George Washington University Law School, 1995-1998. (Washington, D.C. Office). ***LANGUAGES:*** Hindi and Punjabi. ***PRACTICE AREAS:*** Intellectual Property; Technology Transactions; Outsourcing. ***Email:*** sbaldia@mayerbrownrowe.com

MARCELLA J. BARGANZ, born Eau Claire, Wisconsin, September 3, 1972; admitted to bar, 1997, Wisconsin and Texas; 2001, Illinois; 2004, New York. *Education:* St. Mary's University (M.A., 1994); University of Wisconsin-Madison (J.D., 1997). Co-Editor-in-Chief, Women's Law Journal, 1996-1997. Co-author: "Hungary and Offshore Planning for Canadian Multinationals: A Second Look," International Tax Planning. (New York, N.Y. Office). ***PRACTICE AREAS:*** International Project Finance; Cross Border Leasing. ***Email:*** mbarganz@mayerbrownrowe.com

ZACHARY K. BARNETT, born Murphysboro, Illinois, June 12, 1976; admitted to bar, 2002, Illinois. *Education:* Elmhurst College (B.S., 1998); Northwestern University (J.D., 2002). ***PRACTICE AREAS:*** Banking Law; Finance. ***Email:*** zkbarnett@mayerbrownrowe.com

RAFIC H. BARRAGE, born Beirut, Lebanon, April 1, 1974; admitted to bar, 1999, Georgia; 2002, New York and U.S. District Court for the District of Columbia, U.S. Tax Court. *Education:* London Guildhall University (LL.B., with honors, Bachelor of Laws, 1995); Georgetown University Law Center (LL.M., in International and Comparative Law, with distinction, 1999); Georgetown University Law Center (LL.M. in Taxation, with distinction, 2000); Mercer University, Walter F. George School of Law (J.D., 1998). Co-author: "Breaking Down Barriers to Trade and Investment: U.S.-Germany Income Tax Treaty Revisited," (American Institute for Contemporary German Studies, Policy Report #15, 2004); "Reno v. American Civil Liberties Union: First Amendment Free Speech Guarantee Extended to the Internet," 49 Mercer L. Review 625 (1998). (New York, N.Y Office). ***LANGUAGES:*** Arabic, French, Spanish. ***PRACTICE AREAS:*** Tax Transactions. ***Email:*** rhbarrage@mayerbrownrowe.com

AMANDA T. BARRY, born 1974; admitted to bar, 2001, Illinois and U.S. District Court, Northern District of Illinois; registered to practice before U.S. Patent and Trademark Office. *Education:* University of Michigan (B.S., 1996; J.D., 2001); University of Cincinnati (M.S., 1998). ***PRACTICE AREAS:*** Patent Prosecution; Patent Litigation; Pharmaceutical Patent Prosecution. ***Email:*** abarry@mayerbrownrowe.com

BRENT A. BATZER, born Elmhurst, Illinois, 1978; (admission pending); admitted to bar, Admission Pending. *Education:* Case Western Reserve University (B.S.Eng., magna cum laude, 2001); University of Michigan (J.D., cum laude, 2004). ***PRACTICE AREAS:*** Intellectual Property (100%). ***Email:*** bbatzer@mayerbrownrowe.com

JASON S. BAZAR, born Norfolk, Virginia, March 17, 1971; admitted to bar, 1997, New York; 1998, Georgia. *Education:* James Madison University (B.A., 1993); California Western School of Law (J.D., magna cum laude, 1996); New York University School of Law (LL.M. in Taxation, 1997). Managing Editor, California Western Law Review and California Western International Law Journal, 1995-1996. *Member:* American Bar Association (Tax Section: Chairman, U.S. Activities of Foreigners & Tax Treaties Subcommittee on FDAP Withholding). (New York, N.Y. Office). ***PRACTICE AREAS:*** Tax. ***Email:*** jbazar@mayerbrownrowe.com

EMILIE M. BEAVERS, admitted to bar, 2004, Illinois. *Education:* Grinnell College (B.A., with honors, 2001); Columbia University Law School (J.D., 2004). ***LANGUAGES:*** Spanish. ***PRACTICE AREAS:*** Banks and Banking; Finance. ***Email:*** ebeavers@mayerbrownrowe.com

PATRICIA H. BECKER, born Feburuary 9, 1970; admitted to bar, 1994, Pennsylvania; 1995, U.S. Court of the Armed Forces. *Education:* University of Notre Dame (B.A., 1991); Washington & Lee University School of Law (J.D., 1994). [Major, U.S. Air Force, 1995-2002; Commissioned, 1991]. (Washington, D.C. Office). ***LANGUAGES:*** Spanish and French. ***PRACTICE AREAS:*** Government Contracts. ***Email:*** pbecker@mayerbrownrowe.com

NINA BEHRING, admitted to bar, 2005, Germany. *Education:* Ruprecht-Karls University, Heidelberg; University of New South Wales (LL.M., 2002). (Frankfurt/Main, Germany Office). ***LANGUAGES:*** English. ***PRACTICE AREAS:*** Banking and Finance. ***Email:*** nbehring@mayerbrownrowe.com

WENDY WATKINS BERA, admitted to bar, 1999, Texas. *Education:* University of Texas (B.A., 1991); University of Houston Law Center (J.D., magna cum laude, 1999). (Houston, Texas Office). ***PRACTICE AREAS:*** Litigation. ***Email:*** wbera@mayerbrownrowe.com

JEFFREY A. BERGER, (admission pending). *Education:* Brown University (B.A., with honors, magna cum laude, 1999); Northwestern University (J.D., 2003). ***PRACTICE AREAS:*** Litigation. ***Email:*** jberger@mayerbrownrowe.com

WILLIAM T. BERGIN, born 1968; admitted to bar, 1993, New York (Not admitted in Illinois). *Education:* Yale University (B.A., cum laude, 1990); Georgetown University Law Center (J.D., cum laude, 1993). Associate Editor, Georgetown Law Journal. (New York, N.Y. Office). ***PRACTICE AREAS:*** Corporate; Securities. ***Email:*** wbergin@mayerbrownrowe.com

ELLEN BERGMANN, born 1974; admitted to bar, 2001. *Education:* Universities of Konstanz, Heidelberg and Mainz. (Frankfurt/Main, Germany Office). ***LANGUAGES:*** English and French. ***PRACTICE AREAS:*** Antitrust. ***Email:*** ebergmann@mayerbrownrowe.com

CATHERINE A. BERNARD, born New York, April 23, 1971; admitted to bar, 2002, California; 2004, District of Columbia; 2005, Illinois. *Education:* Stanford University (B.A., 1995); New York University School of Law (J.D., 2002). Law Clerk to Hon. John P. Wiese, United States Court of Federal Claims, 2002-2003. ***PRACTICE AREAS:*** Litigation; Appellate Practice. ***Email:*** cbernard@mayerbrownrowe.com

CHRISTY-ANNE V. BETLER, admitted to bar, 2001, Massachusetts; 2003, North Carolina. *Education:* University of Virginia (B.A., 1997), University of North Carolina at Chapel Hill (J.D., 2001). *Member:* North Carolina State Bar; North Carolina Bar Association. (Charlotte, North Carolina Office). ***PRACTICE AREAS:*** Banking; Finance. ***Email:*** cbetler@mayerbrownrowe.com

ANDREW J. BETTWY, born January 25, 1972; admitted to bar, 1998, New York. *Education:* University of Arizona (B.A., summa cum laude, 1994); University of Notre Dame (J.D., magna cum laude, 1997). (New York, N.Y. Office). ***Email:*** abettwy@mayerbrownrowe.com

THORSTEN BEYERLEIN, admitted to bar, 2003, Germany (Not admitted in Illinois). *Education:* University of Passau. (Frankfurt/Main, Germany Office). ***LANGUAGES:*** English. ***PRACTICE AREAS:*** International Practice. ***Email:*** tbeyerlein@mayerbrownrowe.com

VIVEK G. BHATT, born Chicago, Illinois, August 5, 1974; admitted to bar, 2000, Illinois. *Education:* University of Illinois, Urbana-Champaign (B.S., 1997); Whittier Law School (J.D., 2000). Valedictorian, Whittier Law Review, 2000. ***Email:*** vbhatt@mayerbrownrowe.com

VANESSA M. BIONDO, born Teaneck, New Jersey, August 4, 1977; (admission pending). *Education:* Princeton University (A.B., magna cum laude, 1999); Georgetown University (J.D., cum laude, 2004). ***LANGUAGES:*** Italian and Spanish. ***PRACTICE AREAS:*** Litigation. ***Email:*** vbiondo@mayerbrownrowe.com

MARK S. BISKAMP, born Tyler, Texas, May 31, 1957; admitted to bar, 1982, Texas. *Education:* University of Texas at Austin (B.A., 1979); Southern Methodist University School of Law (J.D., 1982); University of Virginia (M.Ed., 1994; Ph.D., 1998). Notes & Comments Editor, Journal of Air Law and Commerce (1981-1982). Author: Biskamp, M. (2004), Drafting Real Estate Contracts for Sale: Income Producing Properties, Real Estate Documents, Workouts and Closings, University of Houston Law Foundation (Conference Faculty). Panelist, Sports Television Agreements, Houston Bar Association Sports & Entertainment Law Section, 2004. *Member:* Houston Bar Association; State Bar of Texas. (Houston, Texas Office). ***PRACTICE AREAS:*** Real Estate; Business; Sports. ***Email:*** mbiskamp@mayerbrownrowe.com

BARRY R. BLANKFIELD, born Rockford, Illinois, July 6, 1964; admitted to bar, 1990, Illinois and U.S. District Court, District of Northern Illinois; 1991, U.S. Court of Appeals for the Armed Forces; 2001, U.S. Supreme Court. *Education:* Drake University (B.S.B.A., cum laude, 1986); Washington University School of Law (J.D., 1990); Kellogg School of Management, Northwestern University (M.B.A., with distinction, 2003). [Commander, U.S. Navy Reserve, 2004—; U.S. Navy Judge Advocate General's Corps, 1990-2002; U.S. Navy Reserve, 2002—]. ***PRACTICE AREAS:*** Banking; Finance. ***Email:*** bblankfield@mayerbrownrowe.com

MICHAEL P. BODOSKY, admitted to bar, 1999, Pennsylvania. *Education:* The Pennsylvania State University (B.A., 1992); Duquesne University School of Law (J.D., 1998). United States Department of Justice, Antitrust Division, 1998-2003. Judicial Intern to the Honorable Carol Los Mansmann, U.S. Court of Appeals for the Third Circuit, 1998. *Member:* Federal (Vice Chair, Antitrust and Trade Regulation Section) and American (Member, Antitrust Law Section) Bar Associations. (Washington, D.C. Office). ***PRACTICE AREAS:*** Antitrust and Trade Regulation; Litigation. ***Email:*** mbodosky@mayerbrownrowe.com

JOHN P. BOELTER, admitted to bar, 2002, Illinois. *Education:* University of Minnesota (B.A., 1998; J.D., cum laude, 2002). ***LANGUAGES:*** Spanish. ***PRACTICE AREAS:*** Corporate; Securities. ***Email:*** jboelter@mayerbrownrowe.com

DR. MARIUS A. BOEWE, admitted to bar, 2002, Cologne. *Education:* University of Freiburg (1999). (Cologne, Germany Office). ***LANGUAGES:*** English. ***PRACTICE AREAS:*** Environmental. ***Email:*** mboewe@mayerbrownrowe.com

DEBRA L. BOGO-ERNST, admitted to bar, 2000, Illinois and U.S. District Court, Northern District of Illinois. *Education:* University of Illinois, Urbana-Champaign (B.A., cum laude, 1997); University of Illinois College of Law (J.D., magna cum laude, 2000). Author: "Can Parents Vicariously Consent to Recording a Telephone Conversation on Behalf of a Minor Child?: An Examination of the Vicarious Consent Exception Under Title III of the Omnibus Crime Control & Safe Streets Act of 1968," 2000 U. ILL. L. Rev. 321 (2000). ***PRACTICE AREAS:*** Litigation; Health Care; Biotechnology. ***Email:*** dernst@mayerbrownrowe.com

RYAN W. BORHO. *Education:* University of Illinois (B.A., 1999); American University, Washington College of Law (J.D., 2003). (New York, N.Y. Office). ***PRACTICE AREAS:*** Litigation. ***Email:*** rborho@mayerbrownrowe.com

JENNIFER L. BOUGHANEM, born 1977; (admission pending). *Education:* Marquette University (B.A., 1999; M.B.A., 2001); Loyola University Chicago School of Law (J.D., cum laude, 2005). ***PRACTICE AREAS:*** Derivatives. ***Email:*** jboughanem@mayerbrownrowe.com

TODD E. BOWEN, admitted to bar, 2001, New York. *Education:* Duke University (B.A., magna cum laude, 1997); New York University School of Law (J.D., 2000). (New York, N.Y. Office). ***PRACTICE AREAS:*** Corporate; Securities. ***Email:*** tebowen@mayerbrownrowe.com

PATRICK BRADY, admitted to bar, 2001, Illinois. *Education:* University of Wisconsin-Madison (B.A., 1991); Loyola University Chicago School of Law (J.D., 2001); Kellogg School of Management, Northwestern University (M.B.A., 2003). ***PRACTICE AREAS:*** Government. ***Email:*** pbrady@mayerbrownrowe.com

DR. MARTIN BRAUN, born 1970; admitted to bar, 2001. *Education:* University of Heidelberg, University of Aix-en-Provence (Maitrise en droit). (Frankfurt/Main, Germany Office). ***LANGUAGES:*** English and French. ***PRACTICE AREAS:*** Internet Law; Information Technology; Biotechnology. ***Email:*** mbraun@mayerbrownrowe.com

JEANNINE BRAUNE. *Education:* University of Munich; University of Pennsylvania (LL.M., 2000). (Frankfurt/Main, Germany Office). ***PRACTICE AREAS:*** Corporate and Securities. ***Email:*** jbraune@mayerbrownrowe.com

(This Listing Continued)

SARAH ELIZABETH BRESLIN, born Pittsburgh, Pennsylvania, 1977; admitted to bar, 2002, New Jersey, 2004, New York. *Education:* Boston College (B.A., 1999); St. John's University School of Law (J.D., 2002). (New York, N.Y. Office). ***PRACTICE AREAS:*** Litigation. ***Email:*** serooney@mayerbrownrowe.com

MARIA A. BRIES, born Rochester, Minnesota, May 24, 1973; admitted to bar, 1998, Illinois. *Education:* University of Iowa (B.B.A., with honors and high distinction, 1995); New York University (J.D., 1998). Certified Public Accountant, Iowa, 1995. Contributing Author: Chapter 8 "Investment Company Act in Securities Practice & Electronic Technology," Law Journals Seminar-Press, 1998. ***PRACTICE AREAS:*** Banking Law; Finance; Project Finance. ***Email:*** mbries@mayerbrownrowe.com

PATRICIA ANN BRITO, born San Antonio, Texas, March 4, 1945; admitted to bar, 1989, Texas. *Education:* Rice University (B.A., 1967; M.Acc., 1979); University of Houston (J.D., 1989). (Houston, Texas Office). ***Email:*** pbrito@mayerbrownrowe.com

MICHAEL E. BROGAN, admitted to bar, 2000, Illinois. *Education:* University of Iowa (B.A., 1996); Loyola University Chicago School of Law (J.D., 2000). ***PRACTICE AREAS:*** Banking and Finance. ***Email:*** mbrogan@mayerbrownrowe.com

ROBERT L. BRONSTON, born Mather AFB, California, May 24, 1969; admitted to bar, 1996, Virginia, U.S. District Court, Eastern District of Virginia and U.S. Court of Appeals, Fourth Circuit; 1997, U.S. Court of Appeals, Third Circuit; 1998, District of Columbia and U.S. Court of Appeals, Eighth and Ninth Circuits; 2000, U.S. Supreme Court; 2001, U.S. Court of Appeals for the Federal Circuit; 2003, U.S Court of Appeals, Fifth Circuit. *Education:* University of Pennsylvania (B.S. & B.A., 1991); University of Michigan (J.D., magna cum laude, 1995). (Washington, D.C. Office). ***PRACTICE AREAS:*** Appellate and Trial Litigation; Antitrust. ***Email:*** rbronston@mayerbrownrowe.com

MARK D. BROOKSTEIN, admitted to bar, 2001, Illinois. *Education:* University of Wisconsin-Madison (B.A., 1992); Chicago-Kent College of Law, Illinois Institute of Technology (J.D., with high honors, 2001). Author: Comment, "Why Should Gang Membership be a 'Status' Symbol: Status Crimes and City of Chicago v. Youkhana," 76 Chi.-Kent L. Rev. 703 (1999) (high score, 1999 Law Review Summer Write-On Competition); Note, "When History is History: Maxwell Street, 'Integrity' and the Failure of Historical Preservation Law," 76 Chi.-Kent L. Rev. 1847 (1999). ***PRACTICE AREAS:*** Litigation. ***Email:*** mbrookstein@mayerbrownrowe.com

CAROLINE E. BROWN, born Greensboro, North Carolina; admitted to bar, 2003, New York. *Education:* Duke University (B.A., 1998); University of Michigan Law School (J.D., 2002). (Washington, D.C. Office). ***PRACTICE AREAS:*** Litigation. ***Email:*** cebrown@mayerbrownrowe.com

GABRIELA RIVERO BROWN, born Mexico City, Mexico D.F., 1974; admitted to bar, 2000, Texas and U.S. District Court, Southern District of Texas; 2003, U.S. District Court, Eastern District of Texas. *Education:* Rice University (B.A., 1997); Yale University (J.D., 2000). (Houston, Texas Office). ***LANGUAGES:*** Spanish. ***PRACTICE AREAS:*** Litigation; International Arbitration. ***Email:*** grbrown@mayerbrownrowe.com

GERALD F. BROWN, admitted to bar, 1997, Illinois. *Education:* Harvard College (A.B., magna cum laude, 1992); University of Chicago Law School (J.D., cum laude, 1997). ***PRACTICE AREAS:*** Corporate Law. ***Email:*** gbrown@mayerbrownrowe.com

JAY S. BROWN, born Cleveland, Ohio, June 22, 1970; admitted to bar, 1995, Maryland; 1998, District of Columbia. *Education:* Santa Clara University (B.S., 1992); Syracuse University (J.D., magna cum laude, 1995). (Washington, D.C. Office). ***Email:*** jsbrown@mayerbrownrowe.com

JESSICA E. BROWN, born Philadelphia, Pennsylvania, June 28, 1974; admitted to bar, 1999, Illinois. *Education:* Oberlin College (B.A., 1996); University of Michigan (J.D., magna cum laude, 1999). Order of the Coif. ***Email:*** jesmith@mayerbrownrowe.com

JEFFREY M. BRUNS, born Madison, Wisconsin September 20, 1974; admitted to bar, 1999, Illinois; 2000, Wisconsin. *Education:* University of Wisconsin-Madison (B.B.A., 1996; J.D., cum laude, 1999). Order of the Coif. ***PRACTICE AREAS:*** Tax Law. ***Email:*** jbruns@mayerbrownrowe.com

TRICIA RENZE BUHRFIEND, (admission pending). *Education:* University of Notre Dame (B.B.A., magna cum laude, 1998); University of Iowa College of Law (J.D., 2005). ***PRACTICE AREAS:*** Tax Transactions. ***Email:*** tbuhrfiend@mayerbrownrowe.com

HENNINGER S. BULLOCK, admitted to bar, 2002, New York and U.S. District Court, Southern District of New York. *Education:* Northwestern University (B.A., 1998); Boston College Law School (J.D., 2001). (New York, N.Y. Office). ***PRACTICE AREAS:*** Litigation. ***Email:*** hbullock@mayerbrownrowe.com

MATTHEW B. BURKE, admitted to bar, 2003, Illinois. *Education:* University of Virginia (B.A., 1998); Northwestern University School of Law (J.D., cum laude, 2003). ***PRACTICE AREAS:*** Litigation. ***Email:*** mburke@mayerbrownrowe.com

J. BRETT BUSBY, born Austin, Texas, April 12, 1973; admitted to bar, 1999, New York; 2000, U.S. Court of Appeals, Fifth and Eleventh Circuits; 2001, Texas and U.S. District Court, Southern District of Texas; 2003, U.S Supreme Court. *Education:* Duke University (A.B., summa cum laude, 1995); Columbia University School of Law (J.D., 1998). Head Articles Editor, Columbia Journal of Transnational Law, 1997-1998; James Kent Scholar, 1998; Harlan Fiske Stone Scholar, 1996 and 1997; Young B. Smith Torts Prize. Law Clerk: Hon. Byron R. White, Associate Justice (Ret.) and Hon. John Paul Stevens, Associate Justice, U.S. Supreme Court, 1999-2000; Hon. Gerald Bard Tjoflat, U.S. Court of Appeals, Eleventh Circuit, 1998-1999. Author/Speaker: "Doing the Right Thing: Ethics and Professionalism in the Appellate Practice," University of Texas, 2001; "Jurisdiction to Limit Third-Country Interaction with Sanctioned States: the Iran and Libya Sanctions and Helms-Burton Acts," 36 Colum. J. Transnat'l L. 621 (1998). (Houston, Texas Office). ***PRACTICE AREAS:*** Civil Appeals.

ALISON M. BUTLER, born Evanston, Illinois, July 17, 1972; admitted to bar, 1998, Illinois. *Education:* University of Rochester (B.A., 1994); University of Michigan (J.D., 1998). ***Email:*** abutler@mayerbrownrowe.com

JOHN T. BYCRAFT, born Evanston, Illinois, October 5, 1966; admitted to bar, 1992, Illinois and U.S. District Court, Northern District of Illinois; 1995, U.S. District Court, Central District of Illinois; 1996, U.S. District Court, Southern District of Illinois. *Education:* Santa Clara University (B.S., cum laude, 1989); University of Notre Dame (J.D., 1992). ***PRACTICE AREAS:*** Aircraft Finance and Leasing (50%); Structured Finance (50%). ***Email:*** jbycraft@mayerbrownrowe.com

NICOLE R. BYRD, born South Bend, Indiana, May 21, 1970; admitted to bar, 1998, Illinois. *Education:* Purdue University (B.A., 1993); University of Notre Dame (J.D., 1998). ***Email:*** nbyrd@mayerbrownrowe.com

CHRISTINE D. CAGNINA, admitted to bar, 1995, Illinois. *Education:* University of Arizona (B.S., 1992); Northwestern University School of Law (J.D., 1995); DePaul University College of Law (LL.M., 2001). (Charlotte, North Carolina Office). ***PRACTICE AREAS:*** Tax Law. ***Email:*** ccagnina@mayerbrownrowe.com

EILEEN M. CANDIA, born Perth Amboy, New Jersey, June 30, 1969; admitted to bar, 2001, Pennsylvania and New Jersey; 2005, Illinois. *Education:* Point Park College (B.A., 1991); University of Pittsburgh (M.L.S., 1996); Temple University School of Law (J.D., 2001). Law Clerk to Hon. Ronald Buckwalter, U.S. Dist. Court for the E. D. Pa., 2001-2002. ***PRACTICE AREAS:*** Finance (100%). ***Email:*** ecandia@mayerbrownrowe.com

CRAIG W. CANETTI, born Queens, New York, April 15, 1968; admitted to bar, 1996, District of Columbia; 2002, U.S. Court of Appeals, Fifth Circuit; 2003, U.S. Court of Federal Claims. *Education:* Yale University (B.A., magna cum laude, 1990); Georgetown University (J.D., cum laude, 1995). Author: "Fifty Years After the Chicago Conference: A Proposal for Dispute Settlement Under the Auspices of the International Civil Aviation Organization," 26 Law & Policy Int'l Bus. 497, 1995. (Washington, D.C. Office). ***PRACTICE AREAS:*** Supreme Court Litigation; Federal and State Appellate Litigation; Federal and State Litigation. ***Email:*** ccanetti@mayerbrownrowe.com

LOURDES M. CANO, born Chicago, Illinois, August 25, 1976; admitted to bar, 2001, Pennsylvania and U.S. District Court, Western District of Pennsylvania; 2003, Illinois and U.S. District Court, Northern District of Illinois. *Education:* University of Illinois (B.S., 1998); University of Pittsburgh School of Law (J.D., 2001). ***PRACTICE AREAS:*** Bankruptcy; Workout; Reorganization. ***Email:*** lcano@mayerbrownrowe.com

NATHANIEL CARDEN, born Rhinebeck, New York, March 2, 1974; admitted to bar, 1999, Illinois. *Education:* Georgetown University (B.S., 1996); University of Chicago (J.D., 1999). Member, Vol. 65, No. 3, The University of Chicago Law Review. ***PRACTICE AREAS:*** Tax Controversies. ***Email:*** ncarden@mayerbrownrowe.com

MATTHEW S. CARRICO, (admission pending). *Education:* University of Michigan (B.A., 1999); Emory University School of Law (J.D., 2003). (New York, N.Y. Office). ***PRACTICE AREAS:*** Litigation. ***Email:*** mscarrico@mayerbrownrowe.com

ZACHARY A. CARRIER, (admission pending). *Education:* Colorado State University (B.S., 1999); University of Michigan Law School (J.D., 2005). ***PRACTICE AREAS:*** Banking and Finance. ***Email:*** zcarrier@mayerbrownrowe.com

STEPHEN A. CHAN, born Dallas, Texas, February 11, 1957; admitted to bar, 1989, Texas; 1990, Illinois. *Education:* University of Texas at Austin (B.S., 1978); University of Houston (M.B.A., 1981); DePaul University (J.D., 1989). Phi Eta Sigma. Member, Moot Court Board, 1987-1989. Member, Editorial Staff, De Paul Business Law Journal, 1988-1989. Registered Professional Engineer, Texas, 1979. Member, Committee on Reserves, American Petroleum Institute, 1978-1981. *Member:* Houston and American (Member, Corporation, Banking and Business Law Section) Bar Associations; State Bar of Texas; Texas Association of Bank Counsel; Asian American Bar Association; Society of Petroleum Engineers; American Institute of Banking. (Houston, Texas Office). ***PRACTICE AREAS:*** Real Estate. ***Email:*** sachan@mayerbrownrowe.com

SUSAN CHARLES, admitted to bar, 2000, Illinois. *Education:* Boston University (B.A., cum laude, 1993), Indiana University School of Law - Indianapolis (J.D., magna cum laude, 1997). Note Development Editor and First Editor, Indiana Law Review. Author: "Geoffrey Glanders et al., New EPA CAM Rule Affects Thousands of Facilities," Facilities Engineering, May/June 1998. ***PRACTICE AREAS:*** Environmental Law. ***Email:*** scharles@mayerbrownrowe.com

LESLIE CHEBLI, born Staten Island, New York, July 17, 1974; admitted to bar, 1999, New York; 2000, U.S. District Court, Eastern and Southern Districts of New York; 2004, U.S. Supreme Court. *Education:* Fordham University (B.A., 1995; J.D., 1998). (New York, N.Y. Office). ***Email:*** lchebli@mayerbrownrowe.com

DAVID K. CHENG, born 1973; admitted to bar, 1999, Nebraska; 2000, District of Columbia; 2003, U.S. Supreme Court and U.S. Tax Court; 2004, California. *Education:* University of California at Davis (B.A./B.S., 1996); Golden Gate University School of Law (J.D., magna cum laude, 1999); Georgetown University School of Law (LL.M., Taxation, with distinction, 2003). (Palo Alto, California Office). ***LANGUAGES:*** Cantonese. ***PRACTICE AREAS:*** Tax Controversy. ***Email:*** dkcheng@mayerbrownrowe.com

SCOTT A. CHESIN, admitted to bar, 2003, New York and Massachusetts. *Education:* Harvard University (A.B., cum laude, 1998); Columbia University School of Law (J.D., 2002). Law Clerk to the Honorable Pierre N. Leval, U.S. Court of Appeals, Second Circuit, 2002-2003. (New York, N.Y. Office). ***PRACTICE AREAS:*** Litigation. ***Email:*** sachesin@mayerbrownrowe.com

LANA CHIARIELLO, born Dover, New Jersey, January 9, 1970; admitted to bar, 1998, Florida. *Education:* University of South Florida (B.A., 1993); Boston University (J.D., magna cum laude, 1998). Executive Editor, Boston University Law Review. Law Clerk to Honorable Anne C. Conway, U.S. District Judge, Middle District of Florida, 1999-2000. Law Clerk to Honorable Melvin Brunetti, Sr.Circuit Judge, Ninth Circuit Court of Appeals, 2000-2001. (Los Angeles, California Office). ***Email:*** lchiariello@mayerbrownrowe.com

RENA S. CHNG, admitted to bar, 2000, California; U.S. District Court, Northern, Central, Eastern and Southern Districts of California. *Education:* University of Pennsylvania (B.A., 1994); Vanderbilt University (J.D., 2000). (Palo Alto, California Office). ***PRACTICE AREAS:*** Litigation. ***Email:*** rchng@mayerbrownrowe.com

ELIZABETH CHOI, admitted to bar, 2004, California. *Education:* University of California, Riverside (B.A., 1998); University of Southern California Law School (J.D., 2003). (Los Angeles, California Office). ***PRACTICE AREAS:*** Banking; Finance. ***Email:*** echoi@mayerbrownrowe.com

(This Listing Continued)

(This Listing Continued)

MAYER, BROWN, ROWE & MAW LLP, Chicago—Continued

CASARINE H. CHONG, admitted to bar, 2003, Illinois. *Education:* Pomona College (B.A., cum laude, 1997); Kellogg School of Management (M.B.A., 2003); Northwestern University School of Law (J.D., 2003). ***PRACTICE AREAS:*** Corporate and Securities. ***Email:*** cchong@mayerbrownrowe.com

MICHAEL W. CHRISTOPHERSON, admitted to bar, 2003, California. *Education:* University of Utah (B.A., 1997); Cornell University (J.D., magna cum laude, 2002). Law Clerk to the Honorable C. Arlen Beam, U.S. Court of Appeals, Eighth Circuit, 2002-2003. (Los Angeles, California Office). ***PRACTICE AREAS:*** Real Estate. ***Email:*** mchristopherson@mayerbrownrowe.com

SUJATA BARAI CHUGH, admitted to bar, 2003, Illinois. *Education:* Princeton University (B.A., summa cum laude, 1998); London School of Economics (M.Sc., 1999); Harvard University (J.D., 2003). ***LANGUAGES:*** Gujarati. ***PRACTICE AREAS:*** Banking Law; Finance. ***Email:*** sbaraichugh@mayerbrownrowe.com

ALLISON D. CITRON, born Brooklyn, New York, July 26, 1976; admitted to bar, 2002, New York. *Education:* Cornell University (B.S., 1998); Fordham Law School (J.D., 2001). (New York, N.Y. Office). ***PRACTICE AREAS:*** Bankruptcy; Workout; Bankruptcy Reorganization. ***Email:*** acitron@mayerbrownrowe.com

ANGELA L. CLARK, admitted to bar, 2001, New York. *Education:* American University (B.A., 1988); Loyola University Chicago School of Law (J.D., 2000). Lead Articles Editor, Loyola University Chicago Law Journal. Note, "City of Chicago v. Morales: Sacrificing Individual Liberty Interests for Community Safety," 31 Loy. U. Chi. L.J. 113 (1999). (New York, N.Y. Office). ***PRACTICE AREAS:*** Securitization; Banking; Finance. ***Email:*** aclark@mayerbrownrowe.com

BERWIN COHEN, admitted to bar, 1999, New Jersey; 2000, New York. *Education:* Ramapo College (B.A., College Honors, summa cum laude, 1996); New York Law School (J.D., cum laude, 1999); New York University (LL.M., 2002). Sigma Tau Delta; Phi Theta Kappa; Phi Sigma Omiron.; Editor, Journal of International and Comparative Law. (Palo Alto, California Office). ***LANGUAGES:*** Hebrew and Spanish. ***PRACTICE AREAS:*** Tax Controversy.

DANIEL A. COOK, born 1978; admitted to bar, 2004, Illinois. *Education:* Carleton College (B.A., 2000); University of Iowa College of Law (J.D., with distinction, 2004); Northwestern University School of Law (LL.M., 2005). ***PRACTICE AREAS:*** Tax Controversies. ***Email:*** dcook@mayerbrownrowe.com

MICHAEL D. COPPIN, born Mt. Pleasant, Iowa, September 26, 1964; admitted to bar, 1997, Illinois. *Education:* University of Illinois (B.A., 1986; M.B.A., 1988); Chicago-Kent College of Law (J.D., 1997). ***PRACTICE AREAS:*** Corporate Law; Securities. ***Email:*** mcoppin@mayerbrownrowe.com

DENNIS S. CORGILL, born San Bernardino, California, November 21, 1951; admitted to bar, 1982, California; 1983, District of Columbia. *Education:* Stanford University (B.A., 1973); University of Chicago (M.A., 1977); Yale University (J.D., 1982). Attorney, Office of Policy and Planning, Antitrust Division, U.S. Department of Justice, 1982-1984. *Member:* State Bar of California; The District of Columbia Bar; American Bar Association. (Palo Alto, California Office). ***PRACTICE AREAS:*** Litigation. ***Email:*** dcorgill@mayerbrownrowe.com

ERIC H. COTTRELL, born Frankfort, Kentucky, September 20, 1970; admitted to bar, 1995, North Carolina; 2001, U.S. District Court, Western District of North Carolina; 2003, U.S. District Court, Eastern and Middle Districts of North Carolina. *Education:* Wake Forest University (B.A., History, cum laude, 1992); University of North Carolina at Chapel Hill School of Law (J.D., with honors, 1995). Law Clerk to The Honorable Judge William T. Prince, U.S. Magistrate, Norfolk, VA., 1995-1996. Author: Casenote: "Civil Rights Plaintiffs, Clogged Courts, and the Federal Rules of Civil Procedure: The Supreme Court Takes a Look at Heightened Pleading Standards in Leatherman v. Tarrant County," 72 North Carolina Law Review, No. 4, May 1994; "There's Too Much Confusion Here, and I Can't Get No Relief: Alcoholic Employees and the Federal Rehabilitation Act in Little v. F.B.I.," 72 North Carolina Law Review, No. 6, October 1994. Assistant District Attorney, Charlotte, N.C., 1996-2000. (Charlotte, North Carolina Office). ***PRACTICE AREAS:*** Litigation. ***Email:*** ecottrell@mayerbrownrowe.com

SUSAN E. COWELL, admitted to bar, 2000, Illinois. *Education:* University of Wisconsin-Eau Claire (B.S., 1988); University of Wisconsin-Madison (M.S., 1992; M.S., 1995), Chicago-Kent College of Law (J.D., 2000). Judicial Extern to The Honorable Ann C. Williams, U.S. Court of Appeals, Seventh Circuit, Spring 2000. Author: Author: "Law at the Air/Water Interface: Is There a Gap Between the Regulation of Toxic Pollutants Under the Clean Air Act and the Clean Water Act?" 8 Wis. Envtl. L.J. 51 (2002); "Pretrial Mediation of Complex Scientific Cases: A Proposal to Reduce Jury and Judicial Confusion," 75 Chi.-Kent L. Rev. 981 (2000). Co-Author: "Partitioning and Transport of Total and Methyl Mercury in the Fox River, Wisconsin (USA)," 32 Environ. Sci. Technol. 1424 (1998); "Tributary Loading of Mercury to Lake Michigan: Importance of Seasonal Events and Phase Partitioning," 213 Science of the Total Environment 129 (1998); "Trace Metal Assessment of Lake Michigan Tributaries Using Low-Level Techniques," 30 Environ. Sci. Technol. 2093 (1996). ***PRACTICE AREAS:*** Environmental Law. ***Email:*** scowell@mayerbrownrowe.com

THERESE CRAPARO, born June 4, 1975. *Education:* Georgetown University (B.A., magna cum laude, 1997); New York University School of Law (J.D., 2002). (New York, N.Y. Office). ***PRACTICE AREAS:*** Litigation. ***Email:*** tcraparo@mayerbrownrowe.com

MARIEL CREO, admitted to bar, 1996, Mexico; 2004, New York. *Education:* Instituto Tecnologico y de Estudios Superiores de Monterrey (ITESM) (J.D., 1995); Georgetown University Law Center (LL.M., 1999). (New York, N.Y. Office). ***PRACTICE AREAS:*** Banking and Finance. ***Email:*** mcreo@mayerbrownrowe.com

EVAN A. CREUTZ, born Lambertville, Michigan; admitted to bar, 2003, New York. *Education:* Cornell University (B.A., 1998), Fordham University School of Law (J.D., 2001). Notes and Articles Editor: "Two Sides to Every Story: Measuring the Jurisdictional Amount in Federal Courts," 68 Fordham L. Rev. 1719. (New York, N.Y. Office). ***PRACTICE AREAS:*** Litigation. ***Email:*** ecreutz@mayerbrownrowe.com

(This Listing Continued)

BRIAN S. CROMWELL, born Bronx, New York, June 21, 1964; admitted to bar, 1996, North Carolina; 2000, U.S. District Court, Western District of North Carolina. *Education:* Fairleigh Dickinson University (B.S., 1987); Fordham University School of Law (J.D., 1995). (Charlotte, North Carolina Office). ***PRACTICE AREAS:*** Litigation. ***Email:*** bcromwell@mayerbrownrowe.com

THERESA M. CUMMINGS, admitted to bar, 2001, California. *Education:* Loyola Marymount University (B.A., magna cum laude, 1998); Loyola Law School (J.D., cum laude, Order of the Coif, 2001). St. Thomas More Law Honor Society. (Los Angeles, California Office). ***PRACTICE AREAS:*** Litigation. ***Email:*** tcummings@mayerbrownrowe.com

SHERI DRUCKER DAVIS, born Richland, Washington; admitted to bar, 2001, Illinois. *Education:* Northwestern University, Medill School of Journalism (B.S.J., 1997); Northwestern University School of Law (J.D., 2001). ***LANGUAGES:*** French. ***PRACTICE AREAS:*** Litigation. ***Email:*** sdruckerdavis@mayerbrownrowe.com

SEAN P. DAILEY, born California, 1974; admitted to bar, 2002, Illinois and U.S. District Court, Northern District of Illinois. *Education:* Georgetown University (B.S., 1996); Vanderbilt University (J.D., 2002). ***PRACTICE AREAS:*** Health Care; Litigation. ***Email:*** spdailey@mayerbrownrowe.com

REBECCA C. DAVENPORT, born 1971; admitted to bar, 2004, Illinois. *Education:* Northern Illinois University (B.S., with Honors, 2000; JD., summa cum laude, 2004). ***PRACTICE AREAS:*** ERISA. ***Email:*** rdaveport@mayerbrownrowe.com

H. RON DAVIDSON, (admission pending). *Education:* Cornell University (B.S., with honors, 1999; Master of Public Administration, 2000); University of Chicago (J.D., 2004). (Washington, D.C. Office). ***PRACTICE AREAS:*** Appellate Practice; Litigation; Criminal Defense. ***Email:*** hrondavidson@mayerbrownrowe.com

EDWARD A. DAVIS, born Ramapo, New York, 1969; admitted to bar, 1997, New York. *Education:* University of North Carolina at Chapel Hill (B.A., 1991); American University (J.D., 1995). (New York, N.Y. Office). ***Email:*** edavis@mayerbrownrowe.com

JOHN P. DAVIS, born Brooklyn, New York, February 3, 1967; admitted to bar, 1999, New York. *Education:* Manhattan College (B.S., 1989); New York Law School (J.D., 1998). Notes and Comments Editor, Law Review, New York Law School. (New York, N.Y. Office). ***LANGUAGES:*** French. ***Email:*** jodavis@mayerbrownrowe.com

MARGARET N. DAVIS, admitted to bar, 2002, Texas. *Education:* Emory University (B.A., 1980); Virginia Polytechnic Institute and State University (M.A., 1982); George Mason University (Ph.D., 1985); University of Houston Law Center (J.D., summa cum laude, 2002). (Houston, Texas Office). ***PRACTICE AREAS:*** Banking and Finance. ***Email:*** mndavis@mayerbrownrowe.com

SHANE D. DEATON, admitted to bar, 2005, New York. *Education:* Indiana University Kelley School of Business (B.S., with honors, 2001); Indiana University School of Law (J.D., cum laude, 2004). (New York, N.Y. Office). ***PRACTICE AREAS:*** Banking And Finance. ***Email:*** sdeaton@mayerbrownrowe.com

KATHERINE DEIBERT, born Sioux Falls, South Dakota, April 26, 1979; admitted to bar, 2004, Illinois. *Education:* University of Iowa (B.A., with high distinction, 2001); University of Minnesota (J.D., magna cum laude, 2004). Phi Beta Kappa; Order of the Coif. Member, Minnesota Law Review, 2002-2004. ***LANGUAGES:*** German. ***PRACTICE AREAS:*** Banking; Finance. ***Email:*** kdeibert@mayerbrownrowe.com

J. GREGORY DEIS, born Dayton, Ohio, April 27, 1975; admitted to bar, 2003, Illinois. *Education:* Marquette University (B.S., 1998); University of Illinois (J.D., 2002). ***PRACTICE AREAS:*** Litigation. ***Email:*** jgdeis@mayerbrownrowe.com

LAUREN A. DeKOVEN, born Chicago, Illinois, February 11, 1972; admitted to bar, 2000, New York; 2003, Illinois. *Education:* Stanford University (B.A., 1995); University of Pennsylvania Law School (J.D., 1998). (New York, N.Y. Office). ***PRACTICE AREAS:*** Banking and Finance. ***Email:*** ldekoven@mayerbrownrowe.com

MARK C. DEMPSEY, (admission pending). *Education:* University of Illinois (B.S., 1993); University of Illinois College of Law (J.D., 2005). ***PRACTICE AREAS:*** Banking and Finance. ***Email:*** mdempsey@mayerbrownrowe.com

FRANCO DESTRO, admitted to bar, 2003, New York. *Education:* Institue for Diplomatic Studies of the Ministry of Foreign Affairs (Master in International Affairs, 1999); University of Padova (J.D., 1999); Columbia University School of Law (LL.M., 2001). (New York, N.Y. Office). ***PRACTICE AREAS:*** Banking; Finance. ***Email:*** fdestro@mayerbrownrowe.com

RICHARD D. DEUTSCH, admitted to bar, 2003, Texas. *Education:* University of Texas (B.A., 1992; B.J., 1992); Southern Methodist University (J.D., 2002). (Houston, Texas Office). ***PRACTICE AREAS:*** Litigation; International Arbitration. ***Email:*** rdeutsch@mayerbrownrowe.com

KIMBERLY E. DIAMOND, born Heidelberg, Germany, August, 1967; admitted to bar, 1998, New Jersey; 1999, New York. *Education:* University of Michigan (A.B., with honors, 1989); Cornell Law School (J.D., 1998). (New York, N.Y. Office). ***PRACTICE AREAS:*** Banking; Finance; Securitization. ***Email:*** kdiamond@mayerbrownrowe.com

ANTHONY J. DIANA, born Philadelphia, Pennsylvania, February 17, 1968; admitted to bar, 1994, Pennsylvania; 1995, New York. *Education:* University of Pennsylvania (B.S./B.A., cum laude, 1990); Columbia Law School (J.D., 1993). Member, Columbia Law Review, 1991-1993. Law Clerk for Judge Jay C. Waldman, Eastern District of Pennsylvania, 1993-1994. (New York, N.Y. Office). ***Email:*** adiana@mayerbrownrowe.com

GINA M. DIOMEDI, born Ypsilanti, Michigan, January 25, 1969; admitted to bar, 2001, Illinois. *Education:* University of Michigan (B.A., with distinction, 1991); Loyola University (J.D., cum laude, 2001). ***PRACTICE AREAS:*** Litigation. ***Email:*** gdiomedi@mayerbrownrowe.com

PAUL A. DiSANGRO, born Boston, Massachusetts; admitted to bar, 1995, Florida; 1996, District of Columbia; 1999, California. *Education:* Georgetown University (B.A., magna cum laude, 1991; LL.M., Taxation, with distinction, 1997); University of Miami (J.D., magna cum laude, 1995). Harvey T. Reid Scholar. Order of the Coif. Member, University of Miami Law Review, 1993-1995. Author, "Editorial Explanation of the Proposed 1996 U.S.-Thailand Income Tax Treaty," 3 Tax Treaties 84,013-84,030 (Warren, Gorham &

(This Listing Continued)

Lamont eds., 1996). Co-Author, "United States Tax Policy on Electronic Commerce," 12 Intertax 429-444 (Dec. 1997). Adjunct Professor, International Tax, Tax LL.M. Program, Golden Gate University School of Law, 2001-2003. Speaker: "Transfer Pricing," Annual Meeting of the California Tax Bar, November 2004; "IRS Settlement Initiatives," San Jose State University Contemporary Issues Series on High Tech Taxation, May 2004; "Taxation of Forward and Futures Contracts," American Petroleum Institute's 64th Annual Federal Tax Forum, April 1998. (Palo Alto, California Office). ***PRACTICE AREAS:*** Tax Controversy; International Taxation. ***Email:*** pdisangro@mayerbrownrowe.com

MICHELLE V. DOHRA, born Rota, Spain, June 24, 1970; admitted to bar, 1995, California; 1996, Illinois and U.S. District Court, Northern District of Illinois. *Education:* University of California at Los Angeles (B.A., 1992); University of California School of Law, Davis (J.D., 1995). ***PRACTICE AREAS:*** Litigation; Real Estate Taxation. ***Email:*** mdohra@mayerbrownrowe.com

DANA S. DOUGLAS, born Hinsdale, Illinois, March 28, 1976; admitted to bar, 2002, Illinois and U.S. Court of Appeals, Third Circuit; 2003, U.S. District Court, Northern District of Illinois. *Education:* Northwestern University (B.A., 1998); University of Pennsylvania (J.D., 2001). Law Clerk to the Hon. Samuel A. Alito, Jr., U.S. Court of Appeals, Third Circuit, 2001-2002. ***Email:*** dsdouglas@mayerbrownrowe.com

PAUL M. DRUCKER, born Skokie, Illinois, August 7, 1973; admitted to bar, 1999, Illinois, U.S. District Court, Northern District of Illinois and U.S. Court of Appeals, Seventh Circuit; 2003, U.S. District Court, District of Colorado. *Education:* University of Kansas (B.A., 1995); DePaul University College of Law (J.D., 1999); Georgetown University Law Center (LL.M., Concentration in Environmental Law, with distinction, 2002). Author, "Wisconsin v. EPA: Tribal Empowerment and State Powerlessness Under Section 518(e) of the Clean Water Act," 5 U. Denv. Water L. Rev. 323 (Spring 2002). ***PRACTICE AREAS:*** Environmental Law; Litigation. ***Email:*** pdrucker@mayerbrownrowe.com

JOHN R. DUFF, admitted to bar, 2002, New Jersey; 2003, New York. *Education:* University of Notre Dame (B.A., 1994); St. John's University School of Law (J.D., 2001). (New York, N.Y. Office). ***PRACTICE AREAS:*** Litigation. ***Email:*** jduff@mayerbrownrowe.com

BRIAN J. DUNN, admitted to bar, 2003, Illinois. *Education:* University of Michigan (B.A., 1996); Northwestern University School of Law (J.D., cum laude, 2003). ***PRACTICE AREAS:*** Litigation. ***Email:*** bdunn@mayerbrownrowe.com

JEAN-JACQUES B. DUPRÉ, born New Orleans, Louisiana, 1973; admitted to bar, 1999, California. *Education:* University of Southern California (B.S., 1995); Loyola Marymount University (M.B.A., 1999); Loyola Law School, Los Angeles (J.D., 1999). (Los Angeles, California Office). ***PRACTICE AREAS:*** Real Estate.

ARIEL M. DYBNER, born New York, N.Y., January 28, 1969; admitted to bar, 1999, New York. *Education:* Amherst College (B.A., 1990); Georgetown University (M.S.F.S., 1992); Columbia University (J.D., 1997). (New York, N.Y. Office). ***LANGUAGES:*** Spanish. ***PRACTICE AREAS:*** Real Estate. ***Email:*** adybner@mayerbrownrowe.com

J. BENJAMIN EARTHMAN, born March 28, 1976; admitted to bar, 2002, New York; 2004, Tennessee. *Education:* Christian Brothers University (B.A., cum laude, 1998); University of Memphis, Cecil C. Humphreys School of Law (J.D., cum laude, 2001). *Member:* American Bar Association; New York State Bar Association; Tennessee Bar Association. (Charlotte, North Carolina Office). ***PRACTICE AREAS:*** Banking and Finance. ***Email:*** bearthman@mayerbrownrowe.com

WESTON T. EGUCHI, born Yokota AFB, Japan; (admission pending). *Education:* Harvard University (B.A., cum laude, 1999); New York University (J.D., 2004). (New York, N.Y. Office). ***PRACTICE AREAS:*** Bankruptcy; Loan Workouts; Bankruptcy Reorganization. ***Email:*** weguchi@mayerbrownrowe.com

DIRK EHLE, born Cologne, Germany, May 26, 1969; admitted to bar, 1998, Germany. *Education:* Universities of Freiburg, Aix-en-Provence, New York, Wuerzburg (1994; Dr.jur., 1996). Author: Thesis, "Consideration on environmental aspects in the EU antitrust law," Cologne 1996; Articles: "State regulation under the U.S. antitrust state action doctrine and under E.C. competition law - a comparative analysis," ECLR 1998, 380; "Vertical restraints and the rule of reason: new impacts by State Oil Co. v. Khan," DAJV-Newsletter 1998, 48; Various notes on: "environment and competition law," Natur und Recht 1997, 175, WuW 1999, 1196; EU competition law, in particular essential facilities doctrine: RIW 1999, 140 and EuZW 1999, 89; Various articles and notes on procedural aspects of administrative law: BayVBl, 1997, 344 and JuS 1999, 166. *Member:* German-American Lawyers Association; Association of International Young Lawyers. (Cologne, Germany Office). ***LANGUAGES:*** German, English and French. ***Email:*** dehle@mayerbrownrowe.com

JOCHEN EIMER, born 1972; admitted to bar, 2001. *Education:* University of Mainz. (Frankfurt/Main, Germany Office). ***LANGUAGES:*** English. ***PRACTICE AREAS:*** Unfair Competition; Corporate Law; Biotechnology. ***Email:*** jeimer@mayerbrownrowe.com

FRANK DAVID ENDEBROCK, admitted to bar, 1998, Cologne, Germany. *Education:* Albertus Magnus; University of Cologne. (Frankfurt/Main, Germany Office). ***LANGUAGES:*** English. ***PRACTICE AREAS:*** Real Estate. ***Email:*** fendebrock@mayerbrownrowe.com

STEFAN W. ENGELHARDT, born West Islip, New York, December 11, 1963; admitted to bar, 1990, New York and U.S. District Court, Southern and Eastern District of New York; 1997, U.S. Court of Appeals, Second Circuit. *Education:* Hamilton College (B.A., magna cum laude, 1986); Harvard University (J.D., 1989). Phi Beta Kappa. (New York, N.Y. Office). ***Email:*** sengelhardt@mayerbrownrowe.com

MAURICIO A. ESPANA. *Education:* New York University, College of Arts and Sciences (B.A., cum laude, 2000); Fordham University School of Law (J.D., 2003). (New York, N.Y. Office). ***PRACTICE AREAS:*** Litigation. ***Email:*** maespana@mayerbrownrowe.com

ERIC B. EVANS, born August 28, 1971; admitted to bar, 2004, California. *Education:* Harvard University (B.A., summa cum laude, 1993; M.A., 1997); University of Michigan Law School (J.D., magna cum laude, 2004). (Palo Alto, California Office). ***PRACTICE AREAS:*** Litigation. ***Email:*** eevans@mayerbrownrowe.com

DOUGLAS M. EVELEIGH, born Stamford, Connecticut, March 29, 1973; admitted to bar, 1998, Illinois; registered to practice before U.S. Patent and Trademark Office. *Education:* Boston University (B.S., 1995); John Marshall Law School (J.D., summa cum laude, 1998). CoAuthor: "Patenting Computer Software and Methods of Doing Business: The U.S. vs. the World, April 2000, International Trade & Business Law Annual. ***PRACTICE AREAS:*** Intellectual Property. ***Email:*** develeigh@mayerbrownrowe.com

CHRISTOPHER L. EXBERGER, admitted to bar, 2001, California. *Education:* University of California at Los Angeles (B.S., cum laude, 1998); New York University School of Law (J.D., 2001). (Los Angeles, California Office). ***PRACTICE AREAS:*** Banking Law; Finance. ***Email:*** cexberger@mayerbrownrowe.com

CHRISTIAN W. FABIAN, born Warren, Michigan, March 21, 1968; admitted to bar, 1994, Michigan; 1999, Illinois. *Education:* Oakland University (B.S.E., 1990); University of Detroit School of Law (J.D., cum laude, 1994). ***PRACTICE AREAS:*** Corporate; Securities. ***Email:*** cfabian@mayerbrownrowe.com

M. C. GEORGINA FABIAN, born México, D.F., 1970; admitted to bar, 1995, México; 2001, New York (Not admitted in Illinois). *Education:* Escuela Libre de Derecho (J.D., 1995); New York University School of Law (LL.M., 1997). Author: "Choosing an Effective Mediator: Qualifications that Should be Required by the Working Skills Examination Established by the Rules of Performance of the Centre for Alternative Justice for the Federal District," Eighth National Congress of the Mexican Bar, Mexico City Mexico, 2004. ***LANGUAGES:*** Spanish. ***PRACTICE AREAS:*** Litigation; Alternative Dispute Resolution. ***Email:*** gfabian@mayerbrownrowe.com

CLAIRE A. L. FALLONE, born October 23, 1977; admitted to bar, 2002, England and Wales; 2004, New York. *Education:* University of Durham, Durham, England (L.L.B. with honors, 1998); College of Law, Guildford, England (1999). (New York, N.Y. Office). ***PRACTICE AREAS:*** Corporate Law; Securities. ***Email:*** cfallone@mayerbrownrowe.com

MARIAM A. FARAH, admitted to bar, 2000, Illinois and U.S. District Court, Northern District of Illinois. *Education:* University of Utah (B.A., 1997); University of Chicago Law School (J.D., 2000). ***PRACTICE AREAS:*** Litigation. ***Email:*** mfarah@mayerbrownrowe.com

RYAN P. FARLEY, born Fort Lauderdale, Florida, June 9, 1973; admitted to bar, 1999, New York. *Education:* Georgetown University (B.S.F.S., 1995); Emory University (J.D., 1998). Author: "Ireland and Divorce: Is a Little Rebellion Now and Then a Good Thing?" Emory Int'l L.Rev. 515 (1997). (New York, N.Y. Office). ***PRACTICE AREAS:*** Government Contracts; Administrative Law; Litigation. ***Email:*** rfarley@mayerbrownrowe.com

GREGORY S. FEDER, admitted to bar, 1997, Virginia and U.S. Court of Appeals, Fourth Circuit; 1998, District of Columbia, U.S. District Court for the District of Columbia, U.S. Court of Appeals for the District of Columbia and Seventh Circuits and U.S. District Court, Eastern District of Virginia; 1999, U.S. Court of Appeals, Eleventh Circuit and U.S. Court of Appeals, Federal Circuit. *Education:* University of Virginia (B.A., 1992; J.D., 1997). Executive Editor, Virginia Journal of International Law, 1996-1997. Author: Note, "Enforcement of Intellectual Property Rights in China: You Can Lead a Horse to Water, But You Can't Make it Drink," 37 Va. J. Int'l L. 223 (1996). Co-author: "Management Responsibility After Sarbanes-Oxley," American Banker, June 11, 2003, at 10A; "Bank-Owned Life Insurance: Pre-Purchase Analysis & Post-Purchase Compliance," 118 Banking Law Journal 208 (Mar. 2001); "Challenging the Federal Driver's Privacy Protection Act: The Next Step in Developing a Jurisprudence of Process-Oriented Federalism under the Tenth Amendment," 53 U. Miami L. Rev. 71 (1998). Contributor: E-Commerce: Financial Products and Services (2001/Supp. 2002) (Chapter 4: Data Protection and Privacy in E-Commerce). (Washington, D.C. Office). ***PRACTICE AREAS:*** Financial Services Law; Banks and Banking; Regulatory Law. ***Email:*** gfeder@mayerbrownrowe.com

PETRA FENDT, admitted to bar, 2004, Germany. *Education:* University of Heidelberg. (Frankfurt/Main, Germany Office). ***LANGUAGES:*** English, French. ***PRACTICE AREAS:*** Banking and Finance. ***Email:*** pfendt@mayerbrownrowe.com

LISA J. FINE, born Chicago, Illinois, June 11, 1976; admitted to bar, 2001, Illinois; 2005, District of Columbia. *Education:* Tulane University (B.S., cum laude, 1998); Georgetown University Law Center (J.D., cum laude, 2001). Phi Beta Kappa. ***PRACTICE AREAS:*** Real Estate. ***Email:*** lfine@mayerbrownrowe.com

RYAN J. FITTS, born St. Louis, Missouri, April 16, 1974; admitted to bar, 2001, Illinois. *Education:* Marquette University (B.A., magna cum laude, 1996); University of Michigan Law School (J.D., cum laude, 2001). ***PRACTICE AREAS:*** Government Practice. ***Email:*** rfitts@mayerbrownrowe.com

NINA L. FLAX, (admission pending). *Education:* Duke University (B.A., 2002); Harvard Law School (J.D., 2005). ***PRACTICE AREAS:*** Corporate and Securities. ***Email:*** nflax@mayerbrownrowe.com

JASON B. FLIEGEL, born New York, N.Y., July 23, 1974; admitted to bar, 1999, Illinois. *Education:* University of Virginia (B.A., 1996); University of Chicago (J.D., 1999). ***Email:*** jfliegel@mayerbrownrowe.com

DIRK-PETER FLOR, admitted to bar, 1999, Germany. *Education:* University of Frankfurt. (Frankfurt/Main, Germany Office). ***LANGUAGES:*** English. ***PRACTICE AREAS:*** Corporate and Securities. ***Email:*** dflor@mayerbrownrowe.com

MONICA C. FLORES, born San Antonio, Texas, September 18, 1974; admitted to bar, 2000, Texas. *Education:* Princeton University (A.B., 1996); Columbia University (J.D., 2000). (Houston, Texas Office). ***PRACTICE AREAS:*** Litigation. ***Email:*** mflores@mayerbrownrowe.com

DAVID B. FOURNIER, admitted to bar, 2003, Illinois; registered to practice before the U.S. Patent and Trademark Office, 2002. *Education:* Lake Forest College (B.A., cum laude, 1997); Northwestern University (M.S., Biotechnology, 1999); DePaul University (J.D., 2003). ***PRACTICE AREAS:*** Intellectual Property. ***Email:*** dfournier@mayerbrownrowe.com

GREGORY A. FRANTZ, born Brooklyn, New York, 1974; admitted to bar, 2001, New York and U.S. District Court, Southern and Eastern Districts of New York. *Education:* Dartmouth College (A.B., summa cum laude, 1996) Phi Beta Kappa; Harvard Law School (J.D., cum laude, 2000). (Resident, New York Office). ***PRACTICE AREAS:*** Litigation; Intellectual Property. ***Email:*** gfrantz@mayerbrownrowe.com

(This Listing Continued)

MAYER, BROWN, ROWE & MAW LLP, Chicago—Continued

SHAUNA L. FULBRIGHT, admitted to bar, 2003, Illinois. *Education:* University of Michigan (B.A., with distinction, 2000); University of Michigan Law School (J.D., 2003). ***PRACTICE AREAS:*** Litigation. ***Email:*** slfulbright@mayerbrownrowe.com

DAVID W. FULLER, born Hilo, Hawaii, October 7, 1971; admitted to bar, 2000, Illinois, U.S. Court of Appeals, Eighth, Seventh, Ninth and Tenth Circuits; U.S. District Court, Northern District of Illinois. *Education:* St. Olaf College (B.A., magna cum laude, 1995); University of Minnesota Law School (J.D., cum laude, 1999). Law Clerk to the Honorable Roger L. Wollman, Chief Judge, U.S. Court of Appeals, Eighth Circuit, 1999-2000. Author: "Public School Access: The Constitutional Right of Home-Schoolers to 'Opt In' to Public Education on a Part-Time Basis," 82 Minnesota Law Review 1599 (1998). ***LANGUAGES:*** German, Spanish. ***PRACTICE AREAS:*** Litigation; Appellate. ***Email:*** dfuller@mayerbrownrowe.com

PAUL A. GALANTE, admitted to bar, 2002, New York (Not admitted in Illinois). *Education:* Rice University (B.A., 1997), St. John's University School of Law (J.D., 2000). ***PRACTICE AREAS:*** Litigation. ***Email:*** pgalante@mayerbrownrowe.com

MICHELLE A. GALE, admitted to bar, 2002, Illinois. *Education:* Calumet College of Saint Joseph (B.S., summa cum laude, 1999); The John Marshall Law School (J.D., magna cum laude, 2002). President's List; Dean's List. Order of John Marshall. Lead Articles Editor, The John Marshall Law Review. ***PRACTICE AREAS:*** Environmental Law; Toxic Tort Defense (60%); Environmental Due Diligence (40%). ***Email:*** magale@mayerbrownrowe.com

NATHAN B. GALER, (admission pending). *Education:* Georgetown University (B.S., magna cum laude, 2002); Harvard Law School (J.D., cum laude, 2005). ***LANGUAGES:*** German, Spanish. ***PRACTICE AREAS:*** Banking and Finance. ***Email:*** ngaler@mayerbrownrowe.com

WENDY DODSON GALLEGOS, born 1971; admitted to bar, 2001, Illinois. *Education:* Duke University (B.A., 1993); University of Illinois (J.D., summa cum laude, 2001). ***PRACTICE AREAS:*** Corporate Law; Securities. ***Email:*** wgallegos@mayerbrownrowe.com

F. TERESA GARCIA-REYES, (admission pending). *Education:* Texas A&M University (B.B.A., cum laude, 2001); Tulane University (J.D., summa cum laude, 2004). (Houston, Texas Office). ***PRACTICE AREAS:*** Litigation. ***Email:*** tgarciareyes@mayerbrownrowe.com

WILLIAM GARDNER, born Los Angeles, California, February 4, 1969; admitted to bar, 1998, New York and U.S. District Court, Southern and Eastern Districts of New York; 1999, New Jersey and U.S. District Court, District of New Jersey. *Education:* University of California at Los Angeles (B.S., Biochemistry, 1992); Brooklyn Law School (J.D., 1997). (New York, N.Y. Office). ***PRACTICE AREAS:*** Business Reorganization. ***Email:*** wgardner@mayerbrownrowe.com

JEREMY J. GASTON, born Carbondale, Illinois, July 16, 1971; admitted to bar, 1999, Texas. *Education:* Stanford University (B.S., Symbolic Systems, with academic distinction, 1993); University of Texas School of Law (J.D., with high honors, 1999). Author, Note, "Standing on Its Head: The Problem of Future Claimants in Mass Tort Class Actions," 77 Tex. L. Rev. 215, 1998. Law Clerk to: Honorable Sandra Day O'Connor, U.S. Supreme Court, 2001-2002; Honorable Patrick E. Higginbotham, U.S. Court of Appeals, Fifth Circuit, 1999-2000. (Houston, Texas Office). ***PRACTICE AREAS:*** Appellate Practice; Intellectual Property; Commercial Litigation. ***Email:*** jjgaston@mayerbrownrowe.com

CHRISTOPHER MICHAEL GAVIN, born Dubuque, Iowa, November 26, 1971; admitted to bar, 1999, Illinois. *Education:* University of Iowa (B.A., 1994); DePaul University (J.D., 1999). Editorial Board, De Paul University Law Review, 1998-1999. ***Email:*** cgavin@mayerbrownrowe.com

CAROLYN R. GEORGIADE, born Durham, North Carolina, August 29, 1975; admitted to bar, 2003, North Carolina. *Education:* Rhodes College (B.A., 1998); Duke University (J.D., 2003). (Charlotte, North Carolina Office). ***PRACTICE AREAS:*** Litigation. ***Email:*** crgeorgiade@mayerbrownrowe.com

THOMAS GERAGHTY, born Brooklyn, New York, May 10, 1970; admitted to bar, 1997, New York; 1999, Colorado; 2000, Illinois. *Education:* St. John's University (B.A., 1992); Yale University (J.D., 1995). ***Email:*** tgeraghty@mayerbrownrowe.com

HANS J. GERMANN, born Chatham, Illinois, October 2, 1975; admitted to bar, 2001, Illinois. *Education:* Carleton College (1995); University of Illinois (1998); Tulane Law School (J.D., 2001). Order of the Coif. Member, Tulane Law Review. ***PRACTICE AREAS:*** Regulated Industries. ***Email:*** hgermann@mayerbrownrowe.com

PETER GEY. *Education:* Technische Universität Dresden; Technicshce Universität Dresden and Johann Wolfgang von Goethe-Universität, Frankfurt; University of Chicago (LL.M., 2001). (Frankfurt/Main, Germany Office). ***PRACTICE AREAS:*** Antitrust and Trade Regulation. ***Email:*** pgey@mayerbrownrowe.com

MICHELE LEW GIBBONS, admitted to bar, 1999, New York. *Education:* Trinity University (B.A., with honors, 1993); Harvard University, John F. Kennedy School of Government, (M.P.P., 1995); New York University School of Law (J.D., 1998). (New York, N.Y. Office). ***PRACTICE AREAS:*** Corporate; Securities. ***Email:*** mgibbons@mayerbrownrowe.com

CLAIRE K. GIBSON, born Winona, Minnesota, July 30, 1974; admitted to bar, 2000, Illinois and U.S. District Court, Northern District of Illinois; 2003, Minnesota. *Education:* St. Mary's College of Indiana (B.A., magna cum laude, 1996); Washington University, St. Louis (J.D., 2000). Law Clerk to the Honorable Jean C. Hamilton, U.S. District Court for the Eastern District of Missouri, 2004-2005. ***PRACTICE AREAS:*** Corporate Law; Securities. ***Email:*** cgibson@mayerbrownrowe.com

JAMES P. GIGNAC, admitted to bar, 2005, Illinois. *Education:* Albion College (B.A., summa cum laude, 2001); Harvard Law School (J.D., 2004). ***Email:*** jgignac@mayerbrownrowe.com

(This Listing Continued)

EDITH G. GIMM, (admission pending). *Education:* Wellesley College (B.A., cum laude, 1994); Stanford University (M.A., 2000); Boston College (J.D., 2004). (New York, N.Y. Office). ***PRACTICE AREAS:*** Real Estate. ***Email:*** egimm@mayerbrownrowe.com

ANDREW GLANZMAN, (admission pending). *Education:* Indiana University (B.A., with high distinction, 2000); Harvard Law School (J.D., 2004). ***PRACTICE AREAS:*** Corporate Law. ***Email:*** aglanzman@mayerbrownrowe.com

REGINALD R. GOEKE, admitted to bar, 1995, New York and District of Columbia; 1996 U.S. District Court for the District of Columbia, U.S. District Court, District of Maryland and U.S. Court of Appeals, Fourth Circuit; 1997 U.S. Court of Appeals, Federal Circuit. *Education:* University of Michigan (B.A., magna cum laude, 1991); Harvard Law School (J.D., cum laude, 1994). (Washington, D.C. Office). ***PRACTICE AREAS:*** Litigation; Intellectual Property; Communications and Media. ***Email:*** rgoeke@mayerbrownrowe.com

JASON J. GOITIA, born 1978; admitted to bar, 2003, Florida; 2004, Illinois. *Education:* University of Florida (B.A., with honors, 2000); University of Chicago Law School (J.D., 2003). ***PRACTICE AREAS:*** Banking and Finance. ***Email:*** jgoitia@mayerbrownrowe.com

LAUREN ROSENBLUM GOLDMAN, born Great Neck, New York; admitted to bar, 1999, New York. *Education:* Cornell University (A.B., 1991); New York University (J.D., magna cum laude, 1997). Order of the Coif. Law Clerk to the Honorable Dennis Jacobs, U.S. Court of Appeals for the Second Circuit, 1997-1998. (New York, N.Y. Office). ***PRACTICE AREAS:*** Litigation. ***Email:*** lrgoldman@mayerbrownrowe.com

ANTONIA GOLIANOPOULOS, admitted to bar, 2001, New York. *Education:* Dartmouth College (B.A., 1997); Boston College Law School (J.D., cum laude, 2001). (New York, N.Y. Office). ***LANGUAGES:*** Greek. ***PRACTICE AREAS:*** Bankruptcy. ***Email:*** agolianopoulos@mayerbrownrowe.com

ERIKA GOSKER, admitted to bar, 1999, Illinois. *Education:* University of Illinois, Urbana-Champaign (B.S., magna cum laude, 1990; M.B.A., 1999; J.D., magna cum laude, 1999). Harno Fellow. Author: "The Marketing of Gambling to the Elderly," Elder L.J. 185, 1999. ***PRACTICE AREAS:*** ERISA; Corporate Law. ***Email:*** egosker@mayerbrownrowe.com

MICHAEL GOTTSCHALK, born 1972; admitted to bar, 2001, Düsseldorf, Germany. *Education:* University of Augsburg; University of Lausanne; University of Munich (J.D., 1999); Second State Law Examination, Munich (2001). (Frankfurt/Main, Germany Office). ***LANGUAGES:*** German and English. ***PRACTICE AREAS:*** Corporate Law; Securities. ***Email:*** mgottschalk@mayerbrownrowe.com

JONATHAN M. GRANDON, born Detroit, Michigan; admitted to bar, 2000, New York; 2004, Illinois. *Education:* Columbia University (B.A., 1997); University of Michigan Law School (J.D., 1999). ***PRACTICE AREAS:*** Corporate. ***Email:*** jgrandon@mayerbrownrowe.com

GERAMI A. GRANELLO, (admission pending). *Education:* University of Texas at Austin (B.A., with high honors, 1999); University of Texas School of Law (J.D., with honors, 2003). (Houston, Texas Office). ***LANGUAGES:*** Italian and Spanish. ***PRACTICE AREAS:*** Real Estate. ***Email:*** ggranello@mayerbrownrowe.com

BARBARA GRAYSON, admitted to bar, 2001, Illinois. *Education:* University of Missouri-Kansas City (B.A., with honors and distinction, 1998); Harvard Law School (J.D. magna cum laude, 2001). Honors College Scholar. ***PRACTICE AREAS:*** Trusts and Estates; Probate; Nonprofit and Charitable Organizations. ***Email:*** bgrayson@mayerbrownrowe.com

BRIAN F. GREDDER, admitted to bar, 2000, New York. *Education:* Princeton University (A.B., 1996); Fordham University School of Law (J.D., 1999). (New York, N.Y. Office). ***PRACTICE AREAS:*** Mergers, Acquisitions and Divestitures; Securities. ***Email:*** bgredder@mayerbrownrowe.com

SIMON G. GRIESER, born 1972; admitted to bar, 2001. *Education:* Joh. Wolfgang-Goethe-University of Frankfurt. (Frankfurt/Main, Germany Office). ***LANGUAGES:*** English. ***PRACTICE AREAS:*** Banking Law; Finance. ***Email:*** sgrieser@mayerbrownrowe.com

DAVID A. GROSSMAN, born Evanston, Illinois, September 30, 1975; admitted to bar, 2000, Illinois. *Education:* Rice University (B.A., 1997); New York University (J.D., 2000). ***PRACTICE AREAS:*** Litigation. ***Email:*** dagrossman@mayerbrownrowe.com

MASCHA JULIA GRUNDMANN, born 1971; admitted to bar, 1999. *Education:* Universities of Würzburg and Düsseldorf. (Frankfurt/Main, Germany Office). ***LANGUAGES:*** English and French. ***PRACTICE AREAS:*** Unfair Competition; Intellectual Property; Trademarks. ***Email:*** mgrundmann@mayerbrownrowe.com

PETER T. GRUSZKA, admitted to bar, 2000, Illinois. *Education:* Duke University (B.A.); Washington University School of Law (J.D., 1999). ***PRACTICE AREAS:*** Banking Law; Finance; Asset Securitization. ***Email:*** pgruszka@mayerbrownrowe.com

LOIC ERICK GUERIN, born Dole, France, September 27, 1972; admitted to bar, 1999, Paris, France (Not admitted in United States). *Education:* Paris I, Sorbonne (DEA in private law, 1995); Northwestern (LL.M./M, with honors, 2001). ***LANGUAGES:*** French. ***PRACTICE AREAS:*** Corporate Law. ***Email:*** lguerin@mayerbrownrowe.com

BRITTON B. GUERRINA, born Big Spring, Texas, September 7, 1968; admitted to bar, 1999, Illinois; 2002, District of Columbia. *Education:* University of Chicago (B.A., 1990; M.A., 1990; J.D., 1999). Order of the Coif. Editor-in-Chief, University of Chicago Law Review, 1998-1999. ***LANGUAGES:*** French. ***PRACTICE AREAS:*** Litigation; Appellate Practice; International Arbitration. ***Email:*** bguerrina@mayerbrownrowe.com

SHIRISH GUPTA, admitted to bar, 1999, California. *Education:* University of California at Berkeley (B.A., magna cum laude, 1995); University of Chicago Law School (J.D., 1999). (Palo Alto, California Office). ***LANGUAGES:*** Hindi. ***PRACTICE AREAS:*** Litigation. ***Email:*** sgupta@mayerbrownrowe.com

JENNIFER T. HA, admitted to bar, 2002, New York. *Education:* University of California, Los Angeles (B.S., cum laude, 1994); California State University, Los Angeles

(This Listing Continued)

(M.S., 1997); University of California, Berkeley School of Law (J.D., 2000). (Charlotte, North Carolina Office). ***PRACTICE AREAS:*** Finance. ***Email:*** jha@mayerbrownrowe.com

A. DAVID HAKIM, admitted to bar, 2003, England and Wales (Not admitted in the United States). *Education:* University of Leeds (B.A., Economics, with honors, 1998); Boston University School of Law (LL.M. in American Law, 2004). (New York, N.Y. Office). ***PRACTICE AREAS:*** Banking; Finance. ***Email:*** dhakim@mayerbrownrowe.com

JAIMY LEVINE HAMBURG, born Minneapolis, Minnesota, August 6, 1969; admitted to bar, 1995, Minnesota; 1996, District of Columbia; 1998, U.S. District Court, Northern District of Illinois; 1999, Illinois. *Education:* Washington University (B.A., 1991); University of Pennsylvania (J.D., magna cum laude, 1995). Order of the Coif. Comment Editor & Associate Editor, University of Pennsylvania Law Review, 1993-1995. Author, "Join The Sierra Club!": Imposition of Ideology as a Condition of Probation, 142 University of Pennsylvania Law Review 1841 (1994). ***PRACTICE AREAS:*** Environmental Law; Litigation. ***Email:*** jhamburg@mayerbrownrowe.com

NATHANIEL HAMSTRA, (admission pending). *Education:* University of Illinois at Urbana-Champaign (B.S., 2001); University of Michigan Law School (J.D., 2005). ***Email:*** nhamstra@mayerbrownrowe.com

JUDY SONG HAN, born Brooklyn, New York; admitted to bar, 2002, New York and New Jersey. *Education:* Rutgers University (B.A., summa cum laude, 1997); Northwestern University School of Law (J.D., 2001). (New York, N.Y. Office). ***PRACTICE AREAS:*** Real Estate. ***Email:*** jhan@mayerbrownrowe.com

ANDREW L. HANANEL, born New York, New York, June 3, 1979; (admission pending). *Education:* Duke University (B.S., 2001); Georgetown University (J.D., magna cum laude, 2005). Order of the Coif. Recipient, CALI Excellence for the Future Award in Tax I, 2004. ***PRACTICE AREAS:*** Real Estate. ***Email:*** ahananel@mayerbrownrowe.com

EMILY R. HANKS, admitted to bar, 2004, California; 2005, District of Columbia. *Education:* University of California, Berkeley (B.A., 2000); University of Virginia School of Law (J.D., 2003). Law Clerk to the Honorable Jeffrey T. Miller, United States District Court for the Southern District of California, 2003-2004. (Washington, D.C. Office). ***PRACTICE AREAS:*** Litigation. ***Email:*** ehanks@mayerbrownrowe.com

JOSHUA P. HANNA, born Napoleon, Ohio, June 28, 1975; admitted to bar, 1999, Illinois. *Education:* Ohio State University (B.A., summa cum laude, 1996); Northwestern University (J.D., 1999). Licensed Real Estate Broker, Illinois. ***PRACTICE AREAS:*** Real Estate. ***Email:*** jhanna@mayerbrownrowe.com

STACEY J. HANNA, born Elmira, New York, December 6, 1974; admitted to bar, 2002, New York. *Education:* Hamilton College (B.A., 1997); Cornell Law School (J.D., 2001). Recipient, CALI Awards in: Mergers and Acquisitions; Public Law. (New York, N.Y. Office). ***PRACTICE AREAS:*** Finance; Corporate; Securities. ***Email:*** shanna@mayerbrownrowe.com

GAYLE C. HANZ, admitted to bar, 1995, Texas. *Education:* University of Texas, Austin (B.A., with highest honors, 1992; J.D., with honors, 1995). (Houston, Texas Office). ***PRACTICE AREAS:*** Litigation. ***Email:*** gchanz@mayerbrownrowe.com

KARA E. HARCHUCK, born Pittsburgh, Pennsylvania, January 21, 1978; admitted to bar, 2003, Illinois. *Education:* Allegheny College (B.A., 2000); Northwestern University (J.D., 2003). Northwestern University Law Review, 2002. ***PRACTICE AREAS:*** Real Estate. ***Email:*** keharchuck@mayerbrownrowe.com

HEATHER A. HARLAN, admitted to bar, 1997, New York; 2000, California (Not admitted in Illinois). *Education:* University of Chicago (B.A., 1987); Columbia University (M.A., 1992); University of Notre Dame Law School (J.D., cum laude, 1995). ***PRACTICE AREAS:*** Corporate Law; Securities. ***Email:*** hharlan@mayerbrownrowe.com

CHARLES E. HARRIS, II, admitted to bar, 2003, Illinois; registered to practice before U.S. Patent and Trademark Office. *Education:* University of North Carolina at Chapel Hill (B.S., 1996); North Carolina Central University (M.S., summa cum laude, 2000); Cleveland-Marshall College of Law (J.D., summa cum laude, 2003). ***PRACTICE AREAS:*** Litigation. ***Email:*** charris@mayerbrownerowe.com

ERICK STEVEN HARRIS, born Madison, Wisconsin, November 5, 1975; admitted to bar, 2002, Illinois. *Education:* University of Wisconsin-Madison (B.A., 1998); Harvard University (J.D., 2002). ***Email:*** esharris@mayerbrownrowe.com

SARAH L. HARRIS, born Eugene, Oregon, May 15, 1974; admitted to bar, 2001, Illinois; 2003, Wisconsin. *Education:* Scripps College (B.A., 1996); Northwestern University (J.D., 2001). *Member:* State Bar of Wisconsin. ***LANGUAGES:*** French. ***PRACTICE AREAS:*** Corporate Law; Securities. ***Email:*** sharris2@mayerbrownrowe.com

DARA M. HARTMAN, born Plainview, New York, August 15, 1977; admitted to bar, 2003, New York; U.S. District Court, Southern and Eastern Districts of New York. *Education:* State University of New York at Binghamton (B.S., 1999); Fordham University School of Law (J.D., 2002). (New York, N.Y. Office). ***PRACTICE AREAS:*** Litigation. ***Email:*** dhartman@mayerbrownrowe.com

FRED W. HARTMAN, born Lewistown, Pennsylvania, December 22, 1973; admitted to bar, 1999, Pennsylvania. *Education:* Pennsylvania State University (B.A., 1996); University of Pittsburgh School of Law (J.D., 1999); Georgetown University (LL.M., with distinction, 2002). (Charlotte, North Carolina Office). ***PRACTICE AREAS:*** Tax Transactions. ***Email:*** fhartman@mayerbrownrowe.com

STEPHANIE G. HARTUNG, born 1967; admitted to bar, 1997, Germany. *Education:* Universities of Frankfurt am Main and Geneva; University of Pennsylvania Law School (LL.M.). (Frankfurt/Main, Germany Office). ***LANGUAGES:*** English, French. ***PRACTICE AREAS:*** Internet Law; Unfair Competition; Conflict of Laws. ***Email:*** shartung@mayerbrownrowe.com

ANDREW E. HARWEL, (admission pending). *Education:* University of Michigan (B.A., high honors, 2002); University of Michigan Law School (J.D., 2005). ***Email:*** aharwel@mayerbrownrwoe.com

ETHAN A. HASTERT, (admission pending). *Education:* University of Illinois at Urbana-Champaign (B.S., 2000); Northwestern University School of Law (J.D., 2005). ***PRACTICE AREAS:*** Litigation. ***Email:*** ehastert@mayerbrownrowe.com

(This Listing Continued)

JEANNY HAW, born Nashville, Tennessee; admitted to bar, 2001, Illinois and U.S. District Court, Northern District of Illinois; 2002, U.S. Court of Appeals, Seventh Circuit; registered to practice before U.S. Patent and Trademark Office. *Education:* Dartmouth College (B.A., 1994); Northwestern University (J.D., 2001). ***LANGUAGES:*** Korean. ***PRACTICE AREAS:*** Information Technology; Intellectual Property; Corporate. ***Email:*** jhaw@mayerbrownrowe.com

W.C. TURNER HERBERT, born Dallas, Texas, June 25, 1976; admitted to bar, 2004, North Carolina, U.S. Court of Appeals, Seventh Circuit and U.S. District Court, Western District of North Carolina; 2005, U.S. District Court, Eastern District of North Carolina. *Education:* Davidson College (B.A., Honors in Classics, 1998); University of St. Andrews (M.Litt., Classical Greek Language, 2000); University of North Carolina (J.D., 2004). Author: "Let's Be Reasonable: Rethinking the Prohibition Against Noncompete Clauses in Employment Contracts Between Attorneys in North Carolina," 82 N.C.L. Rev. 249 (2003); "Off the Beaten Path: An Analysis of the Supreme Court's Surprising Decision in Mickens v. Taylor," 81 N.C.L. Rev. 1268 (2003). (Charlotte, North Carolina Office). ***PRACTICE AREAS:*** Litigation. ***Email:*** therbert@mayerbrownrowe.com

DR. CAROLINE HERKSTRÖTER, admitted to bar, 2001, Frankfurt. *Education:* Johann-Wolfgang-Goethe University. (Frankfurt/Main, Germany Office). ***LANGUAGES:*** English. ***PRACTICE AREAS:*** Banking and Finance; Corporate and Securities. ***Email:*** cherkstroeter@mayerbrownrowe.com

KRISTINA K. HERRMANN, born Carson City, Nevada; admitted to bar, 2004, Illinois. *Education:* Bellarmine University (B.A., magna cum laude, 1999); Indiana University (M.B.A., 2004); Indiana University School of Law (J.D., magna cum laude, 2004). ***LANGUAGES:*** German. ***PRACTICE AREAS:*** Corporate; Information Technology. ***Email:*** kherrmann@mayerbrownrowe.com

THOMAS J. HERSHENSON, admitted to bar, 2004, New York. *Education:* Harvard University (B.A., cum laude, 1991); Georgetown University Law Center (J.D., 2002). (Washington, D.C. Office). ***PRACTICE AREAS:*** Litigation. ***Email:*** tjhershenson@mayerbrownrowe.com

MICHAEL-BRYANT HICKS, born Winston-Salem, North Carolina, August 9, 1974; admitted to bar, 1999, Texas. *Education:* University of North Carolina at Chapel Hill (B.A., 1996); Yale Law School (J.D., 1999). (Houston, Texas Office). ***LANGUAGES:*** Spanish. ***PRACTICE AREAS:*** Corporate Law; Securities. ***Email:*** mhicks@mayerbrownrowe.com

GESINE K. HILD, born 1974; admitted to bar, 2002. *Education:* University of Frankfurt. (Frankfurt/Main, Germany Office). ***LANGUAGES:*** English and French. ***PRACTICE AREAS:*** Intellectual Property; Unfair Competition; Trademarks. ***Email:*** gdrewitz@mayerbrownrowe.com

KAREN M. HILKE, born Mahwah, New Jersey, March 5, 1977; admitted to bar, 2003, Illinois. *Education:* University of Notre Dame (B.A., 1999); Northwestern University (J.D., 2003). ***Email:*** kmhilke@mayerbrownrowe.com

JANILE S. HILL, born Brooklyn, New York, October 4, 1973; admitted to bar, 1998, Illinois. *Education:* Rutgers University, Douglass College (B.A., 1995); Yale Law School (J.D., 1998). ***PRACTICE AREAS:*** Securitization; Structured Finance. ***Email:*** jhill@mayerbrownrowe.com

NATALIE M. HIOTT-LEVINE, born Bayonne, New Jersey, September 11, 1970; admitted to bar, 1995, New Jersey and U.S. District Court, District of New Jersey; 1998, New York and U.S. District Court, Eastern and Southern Districts of New York; 1999, U.S. District Court, District of Colorado. *Education:* Douglass College, Rutgers University (B.A., cum laude, with high honors in Political Science, 1992); New York University (J.D., 1995). Phi Beta Kappa. Douglass Scholar. Developments Editor, Journal of International Law and Politics, 1994-1995. Member, Executive Board, New York University School of Law Black, Latino, Asian Pacific American Law Alumni Association, 2004-2006. *Member:* New York State Bar Association (Committee on Women in the Law, Chairperson, 2005 Annual Program Subcommittee; Co-Chair of Programming Subcommittee, 2004—). (New York, N.Y. Office). ***PRACTICE AREAS:*** Litigation. ***Email:*** nhiottlevine@mayerbrownrowe.com

KATHRYN J. HOLAHAN, born 1974; admitted to bar, 2002, California; 2003, Illinois. *Education:* University of Georgia (B.B.A., summa cum laude, 1996); Northwestern University (J.D., cum laude, 2002). ***PRACTICE AREAS:*** Corporate Law; Securities. ***Email:*** kholahan@mayerbrownrowe.com

MICHELLE R. HOLL, born Parkersburg, West Virginia, 1972; admitted to bar, 1999, North Carolina; 2002, New York. *Education:* Queens College (B.A., cum laude, 1994); Wake Forest University School of Law (J.D., 1999). Law Clerk to The Honorable Catharine R. Carruthers, U.S. Bankruptcy Court for the Middle District of North Carolina, 1999-2000. (New York, N.Y. Office). ***LANGUAGES:*** German. ***PRACTICE AREAS:*** Bankruptcy; Workouts. ***Email:*** mholl@mayerbrownrowe.com

ANDREW D. HOLLENBECK, born Valparaiso, Indiana, March 31, 1979; admitted to bar, 2004, Indiana; 2005, Illinois. *Education:* Indiana University (B.S., 2001); Indiana University School of Law (J.D., 2003). ***PRACTICE AREAS:*** Banks and Banking; Finance. ***Email:*** ahollenbeck@mayerbrownrowe.com

HOUDIN HONARVAR, born May 8, 1976; admitted to bar, 2002, New York. *Education:* University of California, Los Angeles (B.A., 1998); Fordham University School of Law (J.D., 2001). (New York, N.Y. Office). ***PRACTICE AREAS:*** Corporate; Securities. ***Email:*** hhonarvar@mayerbrownrowe.com

RACHEL A. HOPF, born Jasper, Indiana, 1978; admitted to bar, 2004, Illinois. *Education:* University of Notre Dame (B.A., summa cum laude, 2001); University of Chicago Law School (J.D., 2004). ***PRACTICE AREAS:*** Corporate. ***Email:*** rhopf@mayerbrownrowe.com

CHRISTOPHER B. HORN, born Kansas City, Missouri, August 22, 1970; admitted to bar, 1996, Illinois. *Education:* Northwestern University (B.A., 1992); University of Illinois (J.D., cum laude, 1996). Associate Editor, University of Illinois Law Review. Author: "Capital Asset Pricing Theory and the Risk of Government Regulation: Who Needs the Takings Clause Anyway?" U.Ill.L.Rev. 945 (1995). (New York, N.Y. Office). ***Email:*** cbhorn@mayerbrownrowe.com

(This Listing Continued)

MAYER, BROWN, ROWE & MAW LLP, Chicago—Continued

DANIEL L. HORWOOD, admitted to bar, 1999, Illinois. *Education:* Connecticut College (B.A., 1996); University of Pennsylvania Law School (J.D., 1999). ***LANGUAGES:*** French. ***PRACTICE AREAS:*** Corporate and Securities. ***Email:*** dhorwood@mayerbrownrowe.com

MATTHEW C. HOUCHENS, born Champaign, Illinois, March 18, 1971; admitted to bar, 1997, Illinois and U.S. District Court, Northern District of Illinois; 1998, U.S. Tax Court. *Education:* University of Illinois (B.S.E., 1994); John Marshall Law School (J.D., summa cum laude, 1997). ***Email:*** mhouchens@mayerbrownrowe.com

SHOUFEN HU, born Taipei, Taiwan, August 18, 1973; admitted to bar, 1997, New York; 1999, District of Columbia; 2003, Illinois. *Education:* National Taiwan University (LL.B., 1995); Tulane Law School (LL.M., 1996; J.D., cum laude, 1998). Author: "WTO and New Opportunities in Ghina - Financial Services Industries," MBP Financial Services Regulatory Report; "WTO and New Opportunities in China - Telecommunications and Internet Industries," MBP Financial Services Regulatory Report. Contributor: Investment Product Deskbook: Banking Rules and Regulations (1995/Supp. 2001) (Chapter 13 - Ancillary Issues). ***LANGUAGES:*** Mandarin Chinese. ***PRACTICE AREAS:*** Finance; Securitization. ***Email:*** shu@mayerbrownrowe.com

WILLIAM H. J. HUBBARD, born Seattle, Washington, September 5, 1976; admitted to bar, 2002, Illinois, U.S. District Court, Northern District of Illinois and U.S. Court of Appeals, Fifth and Seventh Circuits. *Education:* University of Southern California (M.A., summa cum laude, 1997); University of Chicago (J.D., 2000). Clerk to Patrick E. Higginbotham, U.S. Court of Appeals for the Fifth Circuit. ***REPORTED CASES:*** Schultz v. Page, 313 F.3d 1010 (7th Cir. 2002). ***PRACTICE AREAS:*** Litigation (100%). ***Email:*** whubbard@mayerbrownrowe.com

BRIAN P. HUDAK, (admission pending). *Education:* University of Virginia (B.S., 2000); Washington & Lee University School of Law (J.D., 2003). (New York, N.Y. Office). ***PRACTICE AREAS:*** Litigation. ***Email:*** bphudak@mayerbrownrowe.com

DAVID G. HUME, born Washington, D.C., May 23, 1947; admitted to bar, 1973, New York; 1975, U.S. Court of Appeals, Second Circuit and U.S. District Court, Southern District of New York; 1986, U.S. District Court, Eastern District of New York. *Education:* Holy Cross College (A.B., 1969); Columbia Law School (J.D., 1972). (New York, N.Y. Office). ***PRACTICE AREAS:*** Banking. ***Email:*** dhume@mayerbrownrowe.com

DORESSIA L. HUTTON, born Jackson, Mississippi, January 26, 1975; admitted to bar, 2001, Illinois. *Education:* Tougaloo College (B.A., 1997); Northern Illinois University College of Law (J.D., summa cum laude, 2001). Member, Northern Illinois University Law Review. ***PRACTICE AREAS:*** Litigation. ***Email:*** doressiahutton@mayerbrownrowe.com

MATTHEW D. INGBER, born Newburgh, New York, July 4, 1973; admitted to bar, 1999, New York; 2000, U.S. District Court, Southern and Eastern Districts of New York. *Education:* University of Pennsylvania (B.A., magna cum laude, 1995); George Washington University (J.D., with honors, 1998). Articles Editor, International Journal of Law and Economics. (New York, N.Y. Office). ***Email:*** mingber@mayerbrownrowe.com

NANCY S. JACOBSON, admitted to bar, 1985, New York; 1988, Illinois. *Education:* University of Colorado (B.A., 1976); Georgetown University Law Center (J.D., 1984). ***PRACTICE AREAS:*** Real Estate. ***Email:*** nsjacobson@mayerbrownrowe.com

WILLIAM V. JACOBSEN, JR., born Jackson, Michigan, October 25, 1972; admitted to bar, 1997, Illinois. *Education:* Michigan State University (B.A., with honors, 1994); DePaul University (J.D., with honors, 1997). Order of the Coif. DePaul Law Review. ***Email:*** wjacobsen@mayerbrownrowe.com

ARIC S. JACOVER, born Evanston, Illinois, August 8, 1974; admitted to bar, 2002, Illinois. *Education:* University of Michigan (B.Mus., 1997); Georgetown University Law Center (J.D., cum laude, 2002). ***Email:*** asjacover@mayerbrownrowe.com

NEILL P. JAKOBE, admitted to bar, 2002, Illinois. *Education:* University of Notre Dame (B.A., cum laude, 1998); University of Michigan (J.D., cum laude, 2002). ***PRACTICE AREAS:*** General Litigation; Antitrust; Corporate. ***Email:*** npjakobe@mayerbrownrowe.com

CHRISTOPHER J. JANDACEK, born Austin, Texas, January 1, 1968; admitted to bar, 2001, Illinois. *Education:* Rice University (B.S.E.E., 1990); University of Cincinnati (M.S.E.E., 1996); University of Michigan (J.D., 2001). ***PRACTICE AREAS:*** Mergers and Acquisitions; Securities. ***Email:*** cjandacek@mayerbrownrowe.com

JOHN W. JARRELL, JR., born Woodbury, New Jersey, January 19, 1969; admitted to bar, 1995, Virginia; 1998, District of Columbia. *Education:* Rutgers University (B.A., 1991); George Washington University (J.D., high honors, 1995). Order of the Coif. (Washington, D.C. Office). ***Email:*** jjarrell@mayerbrownrowe.com

JEROME M.J.F. JAUFFRET, born Paris, France, September 25, 1954; admitted to bar, 1992, California and U.S. District Court, Central District of California; 1993, U.S. District Court, Southern, Northern and Eastern Districts of California; 1996, U.S. Supreme Court. *Education:* University of Dundee, Scotland, U.K. (M.A., 1976); Loyola Law School, Los Angeles (J.D., 1991). (Los Angeles, California Office). ***LANGUAGES:*** French. ***PRACTICE AREAS:*** Labor and Employment. ***Email:*** jjauffret@mayerbrownrowe.com

TILOMA JAYASINGHE, born December 18, 1976. *Education:* New York University (B.A., 1998); The George Washington University Law School (J.D., 2002). (New York, N.Y. Office). ***PRACTICE AREAS:*** Bankruptcy; Workout; Reorganization. ***Email:*** tjayasinghe@mayerbrownrowe.com

BRADFORD JEALOUS, III. *Education:* University of Virginia (B.A., 1995); University of Notre Dame Law School (J.D., 2003). (New York, N.Y. Office). ***PRACTICE AREAS:*** Litigation. ***Email:*** bjealous@mayerbrownrowe.com

DAVID A. JENSEN, admitted to bar, 2000, Illinois and Wisconsin. *Education:* Miami University (B.S./B.A., 1996); University of Wisconsin Law School (J.D. magna cum laude, 2000). ***PRACTICE AREAS:*** Litigation. ***Email:*** dajensen@mayerbrownrowe.com

JAY C. JOHNSON, admitted to bar, 2001, Virginia; 2002, U.S. Court of Appeals, Sixth Circuit. *Education:* Vanderbilt University (B.A., summa cum laude, 1998); University of Virginia School of Law (J.D., 2001). Order of the Coif. Law Clerk to The Honorable David A. Nelson, U.S. Court of Appeals for the Sixth Circuit, 2001. Virginia Law Review. Articles Development Editor, Journal of Law & Politics. (Washington, D.C. Office). ***PRACTICE AREAS:*** Litigation. ***Email:*** jcjohnson@mayerbrownrowe.com

LEETA JORDAN, born Chicago, Illinois, September 25, 1968; admitted to bar, 2000, New York and Massachusetts. *Education:* Smith College (A.B., 1989); Cornell University (J.D., 1999). (New York, N.Y. Office). ***Email:*** ljordan@mayerbrownrowe.com

SARAH E. JOSEPHSON, admitted to bar, 2004, Minnesota, District of Columbia and U.S. Court of Appeals, Eighth Circuit. *Education:* Georgetown University (B.A., magna cum laude, 1998; J.D., cum laude, 2001). (Washington, D.C. Office). ***PRACTICE AREAS:*** Litigation. ***Email:*** sejosephson@mayerbrownrowe.com

JON M. JUENGER, born Pittsfield, Illinois, July 30, 1966; admitted to bar, 2002, Illinois and U.S. District Court, Northern District of Illinois; 2003, U.S. Court of Appeals, Seventh Circuit. *Education:* University of Illinois (B.A., 1988; M.Ed., 1998); University of Minnesota (J.D., magna cum laude, 2002). Order of the Coif. Associate Editor, Minnesota Law Review. ***PRACTICE AREAS:*** Environmental Litigation; Toxic Torts. ***Email:*** jmjuenger@mayerbrownrowe.com

MOHIT KALRA, born Waseca, Minnesota, January 20, 1977; admitted to bar, 2002, Illinois. *Education:* University of Michigan (B.A., with high distinction, 1999); Harvard Law School (J.D., 2002). ***PRACTICE AREAS:*** Corporate Law; Securities. ***Email:*** mkalra@mayerbrownrowe.com

STEPHEN J. KANE, born Washington, D.C., March 5, 1973; admitted to bar, 2000, Illinois; 2001, U.S. Court of Appeals, Seventh and Eighth Circuits. *Education:* Trinity College (B.A., 1995); Georgetown University Law Center (J.D., magna cum laude, 2000). Order of the Coif. Law Clerk to Judge Frank J. Magill, U.S. Court of Appeals, Eighth Circuit. Author, "Competency to Stand Trial," 87 Geo. L.J. 1463, 1999. ***PRACTICE AREAS:*** Litigation; Appellate Practice. ***Email:*** skane@mayerbrownrowe.com

FLORE KANMACHER, admitted to bar, 2004, California. *Education:* St. Louis University (B.A., summa cum laude, 2000); University of California at Los Angeles School of Law (J.D., 2004). (Los Angeles, California Office). ***LANGUAGES:*** French. ***PRACTICE AREAS:*** Corporate; Securities. ***Email:*** fkanmacher@mayerbrownrowe.com

JASON KANNER, born Killeen, Texas, August 24, 1972; admitted to bar, 1998, New York. *Education:* American University (B.A., 1994; J.D., 1997). (New York, N.Y. Office). ***Email:*** jkanner@mayerbrownrowe.com

LOAN ANH TRAN KAO, born Binh Duong, Vietnam, July 23, 1972; admitted to bar, 1997, Texas. *Education:* Rice University (B.A., summa cum laude, 1994); Harvard University (J.D., 1997). Phi Beta Kappa; Omicron Delta Kappa. (Houston, Texas Office). ***Email:*** lkao@mayerbrownrowe.com

PATRICK J. KASSEN, born Detroit, Michigan, January 31, 1975; admitted to bar, 2002, New York (Not admitted in Illinois). *Education:* Princeton University (A.B., 1997); Harvard Law School (J.D., 2001). ***LANGUAGES:*** Spanish, French. ***PRACTICE AREAS:*** Real Estate. ***Email:*** pkassen@mayerbrownrowe.com

JENNIFER KEATING, born Wilmington, Delaware, August 19, 1973; admitted to bar, 1998, Illinois. *Education:* Cornell University (B.A., 1995); University of Chicago (J.D., 1998). ***Email:*** jkeating@mayerbrownrowe.com

JENNIFER L. KEEGAN, born Beverly, Massachusetts, January 11, 1969; admitted to bar, 1998, Illinois. *Education:* Wellesley College (B.A., 1991); University of Notre Dame Law School (J.D., cum laude, 1998). ***Email:*** jkeegan@mayerbrownrowe.com

ASIEH KEHYARI, admitted to bar, 2000, New York; 2004, District of Columbia. *Education:* George Mason University (B.A., 1992); American University, Washington College of Law (J.D., cum laude, 1999). (Washington, D.C. Office). ***PRACTICE AREAS:*** Real Estate. ***Email:*** akehyari@mayerbrownrowe.com

HYUN-JUNG A. KIM, born Seoul, South Korea, January 9, 1973; admitted to bar, 2004, New York (Not admitted in Illinois). *Education:* Oberlin College (B.A., 1996); Cornell University Law School (J.D., 2003). ***PRACTICE AREAS:*** Finance; Banks and Banking. ***Email:*** hkim@mayerbrownrowe.com

JOO HYANG KIM, admitted to bar, 2000, Illinois. *Education:* Ewha Women's University, Korea (B.A., 1995); Indiana University (B.A., 1997); University of Minnesota Law School (J.D. magna cum laude, 2000). ***LANGUAGES:*** Korean. ***PRACTICE AREAS:*** Banking Law; Finance. ***Email:*** jkim@mayerbrownrowe.com

SUZY KIM, born Seoul, Korea; admitted to bar, 2002, New York. *Education:* Columbia College, Columbia University (A.B., 1996); Fordham Law School (J.D., 2001). (New York, N.Y. Office). ***PRACTICE AREAS:*** Bankruptcy; Workout; Reorganization. ***Email:*** skim2@mayerbrownrowe.com

YALE K. KIM, born Los Angeles, California, January 22, 1969; admitted to bar, 1997, California. *Education:* University of California, Berkeley (B.A., 1991); Santa Clara University School of Law (J.D., 1995). Law Clerk to The Honorable Barry Russell, U.S. Bankruptcy Court, Central District of California, Los Angeles Division, and Bankruptcy Appellate Panel of the Ninth Circuit, 1996-1997. (Los Angeles, California Office). ***PRACTICE AREAS:*** Bankruptcy; Creditor's Rights; Commercial Litigation. ***Email:*** ykim@mayerbrownrowe.com

THERESE C. KING, born Oak Park, Illinois, March 31, 1975; admitted to bar, 2000, Illinois and U.S. District Court, Northern District of Illinois; 2001, U.S. Court of Appeals, Seventh Circuit. *Education:* Illinois Benedictine College (B.S., Biology, 1997); Chicago-Kent College of Law, Illinois Institute of Technology (J.D., with honors, 2000). ***PRACTICE AREAS:*** Commercial Litigation; Appellate Practice. ***Email:*** tking@mayerbrownrowe.com

DR. GABRIELE KIRCHHOFF, admitted to bar, 2004, Germany. *Education:* Duesseldorf (Second State Law Examination, 1999). (Cologne, Germany Office). ***PRACTICE AREAS:*** Corporate. ***Email:*** gkirchhoff@mayerbrownrowe.com

JOHN C. KLOOSTERMAN, admitted to bar, 1995, Wisconsin; 1996, California. *Education:* Loyola University of Chicago (A.B., with honors, 1991); University of Wisconsin Law School (J.D., 1995). Alpha Sigma Nu. Contributing Editor, "The Developing Labor Law," BNA Books. Teaching Assistant, Legal Writing, 1995, University of Wisconsin Law

(This Listing Continued)

School. Trial Attorney, National Labor Relations Board, 1996-1999. *Member:* State Bar of Wisconsin; State Bar of California; American Bar Association (Member, Labor and Employment Law and Litigation Sections; Member, Committee on the Development of the Law Under the NLRB). (Palo Alto, California Office). ***PRACTICE AREAS:*** Litigation; Labor and Employment; Intellectual Property. ***Email:*** jckloosterman@mayerbrownrowe.com

TROY B. KLYBER, born Peoria, Illinois, December 7, 1975; admitted to bar, 2001, Illinois. *Education:* University of Illinois (B.S., 1998); Georgetown University Law Center (J.D., 2001). ***PRACTICE AREAS:*** Intellectual Property; Internet Law; Patents; Copyrights; Litigation. ***Email:*** tklyber@mayerbrownrowe.com

JACK M. KNIGHT, JR., admitted to bar, 1994, North Carolina, U.S. District Court, Western, Middle and Eastern Districts of North Carolina and U.S. Court of Appeals, Fourth Circuit. *Education:* University of North Carolina at Chapel Hill (B.A., 1990); Washington College of Law, American University (J.D., cum laude, 1994). Jody Akers Scholar. (Charlotte, North Carolina Office). ***PRACTICE AREAS:*** Litigation; White Collar Fraud; Internal Investigations. ***Email:*** jknight@mayerbrownrowe.com

ANNETTE KNOTH, born 1970; admitted to bar, 1999. *Education:* University of Frankfurt am Main; University of Paris (Maitrise en droit). (Frankfurt/Main, Germany Office). ***LANGUAGES:*** English and French. ***PRACTICE AREAS:*** Labor and Employment; Social Security. ***Email:*** aknoth@mayerbrownrowe.com

MOLLIE S. KNOX, admitted to bar, 2000, Wisconsin. *Education:* Middlebury College (B.A. magna cum laude, 1995); University of Wisconsin Law School (J.D., 2000). (New York, N.Y. Office). ***LANGUAGES:*** Spanish and Portuguese. ***PRACTICE AREAS:*** Banking; Finance. ***Email:*** mknox@mayerbrownrowe.com

MATTHEW T. KOENDERS, admitted to bar, 2003, Illinois. *Education:* Wayne State University (B.S., summa cum laude, 2000); Harvard University (J.D., 2003). ***PRACTICE AREAS:*** Tax Transactions. ***Email:*** mkoenders@mayerbrownrowe.com

KERRY E. KOLODZIEJ, (admission pending). *Education:* Northwestern University (B.A., with honors, 2002); Georgetown University Law Center (J.D., 2005). ***PRACTICE AREAS:*** Environmental Law. ***Email:*** kkolodziej@mayerbrownrowe.com

HOLLY C. KOPACK WILLOBEE, (admission pending). *Education:* University of Michigan (B.S., 1999); Northwestern University (J.D., 2004). ***PRACTICE AREAS:*** ERISA. ***Email:*** hkopack@mayerbrownrowe.com

AMY S. KORTE, born St. Louis, Missouri, October 5, 1971; admitted to bar, 1999, Illinois and U.S. District Court, Northern District of Illinois. *Education:* College of William & Mary (B.A., cum laude, 1994); Washington University (J.D., 1999). Co-Author: "Bankruptcy Treatment of Loans from Retirement Plans: Employer Strategies in Employee Bankruptcy Cases," 13 Benefits Law Journal 63 (2000). Contributor, 2000 Wiley Bankruptcy Law Update. Author: "The Model Health Care Information and Accountability Act: Managed Care and Medical Malpractice Liability under an Amended ERISA," 55 Journal of Urban & Contemporary Law 161, 1999. ***Email:*** akorte@mayerbrownrowe.com

DR. DR. ADEM KOYUNCU, admitted to bar, 2004, Germany. *Education:* University of Cologne (First State Law Exam, 2001); University of Wuerzburg (Dr. med., magna cum laude, 2000); University of Mannheim (Ph.D. in law, summa cum laude, 2004). (Cologne, Germany Office). ***LANGUAGES:*** German, Turkish, English, Spanish. ***PRACTICE AREAS:*** Medical; Health Care; Pharmaceutical. ***Email:*** akoyuncu@mayerbrownrowe.com

JAN KRAAYVANGER, admitted to bar, 2002, Frankfurt am Main. *Education:* University of Mannheim. (Frankfurt/Main, Germany Office). ***LANGUAGES:*** English. ***PRACTICE AREAS:*** Litigation; Corporate Law; Commercial Law. ***Email:*** jkraayvanger@mayerbrownrowe.com

ANDREW T. KUGLER, born Santa Monica, California, November 6, 1972; admitted to bar, 1997, California. *Education:* University of California, Santa Barbara (B.A., with distinction, 1994); Columbia University School of Law (J.D., 1997). (Los Angeles, California Office). ***PRACTICE AREAS:*** Government. ***Email:*** akugler@mayerbrownrowe.com

JAMES M. KUNICK, born Marshfield, Wisconsin, September 13, 1963; admitted to bar, 1993, Florida and U.S. District Court, Middle District of Florida; 1996, Illinois; U.S. Court of Federal Claims; U.S. District Court, Southern District of Florida and Northern District of Illinois; U.S. Court of Appeals for the Federal Circuit; registered to practice before the U.S. Patent and Trademark Office. *Education:* University of Wisconsin (B.S.I.E., 1986); University of Miami (J.D., 1993). Author: "Trade Secret: A Forgotten Means of Protecting Your Intellectual Property," U.S. Patent Rights Association, 1994. Senior Systems Analyst, Andersen Consulting, 1986-1990. (Frankfurt/Main, Germany Office). ***PRACTICE AREAS:*** Information Technology; Business Process Outsourcing Transactions; Technology; Consulting Services Contracts; Technology Licensing; Technology Protection; HIPAA. ***Email:*** jkunick@mayerbrownrowe.com

GERMAIN D. LABAT, III, born Santa Monica, California, December 18, 1972; admitted to bar, 1999, California; 2000, U.S. District Court, Northern and Southern Districts of California and U.S. Court of Appeals, Ninth Circuit. *Education:* University of California at Santa Barbara (B.A., with honors, 1995); Boston College (J.D., cum laude, 1999). Notes Editor, Boston College Law Review, 1998-1999. (Los Angeles, California Office). ***LANGUAGES:*** Spanish. ***PRACTICE AREAS:*** Litigation. ***Email:*** glabat@mayerbrownrowe.com

RICHARD A. LAFONT, born New York, N.Y., November 10, 1964; admitted to bar, 1991, New York and U.S. District Court, Southern and Eastern Districts of New York; 1996, U.S. District Court, Northern District of New York; 1998, New Jersey and U.S. District Court, District of New Jersey; 2003, U.S. Court of Appeals, Second Circuit. *Education:* Harvard University (A.B., 1986); University of Pennsylvania (J.D., 1990). (New York, N.Y. Office). ***PRACTICE AREAS:*** Commercial Litigation. ***Email:*** rlafont@mayerbrownrowe.com

TIMOTHY C. LAMBERT, admitted to bar, 2001, New York; 2004, District of Columbia. *Education:* Boston University (B.A.); Georgetown University Law Center (J.D., magna cum laude, 2000). (Washington, D.C. Office). ***PRACTICE AREAS:*** Litigation. ***Email:*** tlambert@mayerbrownrowe.com

(This Listing Continued)

CRISTINA LANE, born 1979; admitted to bar, 2004, Illinois. *Education:* University of Michigan (B.A., with distinction, 2001); Northwestern University (J.D., 2004). ***PRACTICE AREAS:*** Finance. ***Email:*** clane@mayerbrownrowe.com

DR. ANDREAS LANGE, admitted to bar, 2002, Frankfurt. *Education:* First Exam, Cologne (1998). (Frankfurt/Main, Germany Office). ***LANGUAGES:*** English and French. ***PRACTICE AREAS:*** Banking Law; Finance. ***Email:*** alange@mayerbrownrowe.com

DEANN KAY LANZ, born South Bend, Indiana, January 15, 1971; admitted to bar, 1998, Texas. *Education:* Valparaiso University (B.A., 1995); Tulane University Law School (J.D., 1998). (Houston, Texas Office). ***LANGUAGES:*** Spanish. ***Email:*** dlanz@mayerbrownrowe.com

ADAM D. LARSON, (admission pending). *Education:* University of Illinois (B.S., highest honors, 2002); Harvard Law School (J.D., 2005). ***PRACTICE AREAS:*** Corporate and Securities. ***Email:*** alarson@mayerbrownrowe.com

SAUL R. LAURELES, born Seguin, Texas, November 7, 1965; admitted to bar, 1998, Texas. *Education:* University of Chicago (B.A., 1994); University of Michigan (J.D., 1998). [Journalist, Photographer, U.S. Army, 1984-1988]. (Houston, Texas Office). ***LANGUAGES:*** Spanish. ***PRACTICE AREAS:*** Corporate Finance; Securities; Banking; Finance. ***Email:*** slaureles@mayerbrownrowe.com

NICHOLAS A. LAVERIS, born Stamford, Connecticut, August 30, 1961; admitted to bar, 1989, New York, Massachusetts and U.S. District Court, Southern and Eastern Districts of New York; 1989, U.S. District Court, District of Massachusetts; 1990, U.S. Tax Court. *Education:* Southern Connecticut State University (B.S., 1983); New England School of Law (J.D., 1988). (New York, N.Y. Office). ***Email:*** nlaveris@mayerbrownrowe.com

JENNIFER D. LAWRENCE, born July 7, 1974; admitted to bar, 2003, New York. *Education:* Boston College (B.A., 1996); New York University School of Law (J.D., 2002). (Charlotte, North Carolina Office). ***PRACTICE AREAS:*** Corporate and Securities. ***Email:*** jlawrence@mayerbrownrowe.com

GRACE SOYON LEE, born Auburn, Alabama, 1974; admitted to bar, 2003, Illinois; 2004, U.S. Tax Court. *Education:* Williams College (B.A., cum laude, 1996); University of Chicago (M.A., 1999); Northwestern University (J.D., cum laude, 2003). ***LANGUAGES:*** Korean. ***PRACTICE AREAS:*** Tax Controversies. ***Email:*** gslee@mayerbrownrowe.com

IAN B. LEONG, admitted to bar, 2001, Texas. *Education:* University of North Carolina (B.A., with highest honors, 1993); University of Michigan (M.A., 1994; Ph.D., 1999); University of Virginia School of Law (J.D., 2001). (Los Angeles, California Office). ***PRACTICE AREAS:*** Banking and Finance; Mergers and Acquisitions. ***Email:*** ileong@mayerbrownrowe.com

NICKOLAI G. LEVIN, born Arlington Heights, Illinois, July 12, 1977; admitted to bar, 2004, Virginia; 2004, U.S. Court of Appeals, Fourth Circuit. *Education:* Dartmouth College (B.A. summa cum laude, 1999); Yale Law School (J.D., 2002). Author: The Nomos and Narrative of Matsushita, 73 Fordham L. Rev. (forthcoming 2005); "Age Discrimination in Employment Act" for the Oxford Companion to the Supreme Court (2d ed. 2004) (forthcoming); Constitutional Statutory Syntheses, 54 Ala. L. Rev. 1281 (2003); Case Note, The Kabuki Mask of Bush v. Gore, 111 Yale L.J. 223 (2001). (Washington, D.C. Office). ***PRACTICE AREAS:*** Litigation; Appellate Practice; Antitrust and Trade Regulation. ***Email:*** nlevin@mayerbrownrowe.com

HEATHER M. LEWIS, (admission pending). *Education:* Wheaton College (B.A., magna cum laude, 1995); Yale Divinity School (M. Div., 2001); Yale University Law School (J.D., 2004). ***PRACTICE AREAS:*** Litigation. ***Email:*** hlewis@mayerbrownrowe.com

JEFFREY H. LEWIS, admitted to bar, 2002, District of Columbia. *Education:* Louisiana State University (B.A., 1993); Catholic University, Columbus School of Law (J.D., 2000). Legislative Assistant to U.S. Senator John Breaux, 1995-1999. Executive Assistant to Congressman W.J. "Billy" Tauzin, 1993-1995. (Washington, D.C. Office). ***PRACTICE AREAS:*** Government Practice. ***Email:*** jhlewis@mayerbrownrowe.com

JONATHAN L. LEWIS, born Birmingham, Alabama, January 3, 1970; admitted to bar, 1999, Illinois and U.S. District Court, Northern District of Illinois. *Education:* University of Maryland (B.A., with honors in Economics, 1992; M.P.M., 1993); University of Michigan (J.D., cum laude, 1999). ***Email:*** jlewis@mayerbrownrowe.com

KAI LIEBRICH, admitted to bar, 2005, Germany. *Education:* Justus Liebig University of Giessen. (Frankfurt/Main, Germany Office). ***LANGUAGES:*** English. ***PRACTICE AREAS:*** Banking and Finance. ***Email:*** kliebrich@mayerbrownrowe.com

DAVID A.K. LINLEY, born Melbourne, Australia, November 17, 1972; admitted to bar, 1997, Victoria, Australia; 2001, England and Wales, U.K.; 2003, New York. *Education:* University of Melbourne (B.A., 1996; LL.B. with honors, 1996). (Resident, New York Office). ***PRACTICE AREAS:*** Finance. ***Email:*** dlinley@mayerbrownrowe.com

DENISE LOPEZ, born San Antonio, Texas; admitted to bar, 2004, Illinois. *Education:* University of Texas at Austin (B.B.A., with honors, 1999; M.P.A., with honors, 1999); Cornell University Law School (J.D., cum laude, 2004). Certified Public Accountant. ***PRACTICE AREAS:*** Tax Law (100%). ***Email:*** dlopez@mayerbrownrowe.com

SIMON LOPEZ, born London, England; admitted to bar, 2003, Texas. *Education:* University of Sussex, England (B.A., 2000); University of Houston Law Center (J.D., magna cum laude, 2003). (Houston, Texas Office). ***LANGUAGES:*** Spanish. ***PRACTICE AREAS:*** Corporate; Securities.

AGOSTINO LORENZINI, born Chicago, Illinois, February 6, 1963; admitted to bar, 1998, Illinois and U.S. District Court, Northern District of Illinois. *Education:* Loyola University Chicago (B.A., 1985); DePaul University (M.A., 1994); Loyola University Chicago School of Law (J.D., cum laude, 1998). Contributing Author, "Directors and Officers Liability Insurance Handbook" (Law Journal Press, 2000). ***LANGUAGES:*** Italian. ***PRACTICE AREAS:*** Litigation. ***Email:*** alorenzini@mayerbrownrowe.com

ZACHARY A. LUBER, born Evanston, Illinois, September 5, 1975; admitted to bar, 2000, Illinois. *Education:* Georgetown University (B.S.F.S., Magna Cum Laude, 1997); Northwestern University (J.D., Cum Laude, 2000). ***PRACTICE AREAS:*** Corporate; Securities. ***Email:*** zluber@mayerbrownrowe.com

(This Listing Continued)

MAYER, BROWN, ROWE & MAW LLP, Chicago—Continued

PHILIP LUCREZIA, born Avellino, Italy, September 27, 1979; (admission pending). *Education:* St. Thomas Aquinas College (B.S., summa cum laude, 2001); St. John's University School of Law (J.D., 2004). (Resident, New York Office). ***PRACTICE AREAS:*** Real Estate. ***Email:*** plucrezia@mayerbrownrowe.com

SUSANNE LÜHRMANN, born 1973; admitted to bar, 2001. *Education:* University of Würzburg. (Frankfurt/Main, Germany Office). ***LANGUAGES:*** English and French. ***PRACTICE AREAS:*** Intellectual Property; Trademarks; Unfair Competition. ***Email:*** sluehrmann@mayerbrownrowe.com

DAVID M. LUNDEEN, born Grand Rapids, Michigan, June 27, 1976; admitted to bar, 2004, Illinois. *Education:* University of Michigan (B.A., Classical Studies and Philosophy, with honors, 1999); Indiana University School of Law - Bloomington (J.D., magna cum laude, 2004). Order of the Coif. Executive Articles Editor, Indiana Journal of Global Legal Studies, 2003-2004. ***PRACTICE AREAS:*** Banking and Finance. ***Email:*** dlundeen@mayerbrownrowe.com

TODD E. LUNDELL. *Education:* Brigham Young University (B.A., 1999); Columbia University School of Law (J.D., 2002). (New York, N.Y. Office). ***PRACTICE AREAS:*** Litigation. ***Email:*** tlundell@mayerbrownrowe.com

JAMISON LYNCH, born 1970; admitted to bar, 1998, Illinois, Wisconsin, U.S. District Court, Northern District of Illinois and Western District of Wisconsin and U.S. Court of Appeals, Federal Circuit; registered to practice before U.S. Patent and Trademark Office. *Education:* University of Wisconsin (B.S.M.E., 1993; J.D., cum laude, 1998). ***PRACTICE AREAS:*** Intellectual Property; Pharmaceutical Intellectual Property; Intellectual Property Litigation. ***Email:*** jlynch@mayerbrownrowe.com

SAJIDA MAHDI ALI, born Chicago, Illinois, August 5, 1977; admitted to bar, 2002, Illinois. *Education:* Northwestern University (B.A., 1999; J.D., 2002). Senior Manuscript Editor, Northwestern Law Review, 2000-2001. Author, "Gateway to Arbitration: Issues of Contract Formation in Standard Form Contracts Shipped With Goods," Northwestern University Law Review, Fall 2000. ***Email:*** samahdi@mayerbrownrowe.com

JOHN N. MAHER, born Chicago, Illinois, September 10, 1970; admitted to bar, 1996, Illinois; 2000, U.S. Court of Appeals for the Armed Forces and U.S. Army Court of Criminal Appeals; 2001, U.S. Supreme Court, U.S. Court of Appeals, Federal Circuit and U.S. Court of International Trade; 2004, District of Columbia, U.S. Court of Appeals, Seventh Circuit and U.S. District Court, Northern and Central Districts of Illinois. *Education:* Bradley University (B.S., cum laude, 1992); Northern Illinois University (J.D., magna cum laude, 1996). Author, "Audio Properties Inc. v. Kovach: Illinois Covenants Not to Compete," The Counselor, Illinois State Bar Association, March 1996. Research Assistant, "Police Interrogations of Children & State Constitutions: Why Not Videotape the MTV Generation?" 25 U. Toledo L.Rev. 901 (1995). [United States Army Judge Advocate General's Corps, Germany, Macedonia, and Washington D.C., 1997-2001 Captain; United States Army Reserve, Andrews Air Force Base and Fort Sheridan, Illinois, 2001— Major]. ***PRACTICE AREAS:*** Government Contracts; Bid Protests. ***Email:*** jmaher@mayerbrownrowe.com

MARK J. MAIER, admitted to bar, 2000, Massachusetts; 2001, District of Columbia. *Education:* Pennsylvania State University (B.S.E.E., 1987; Distinguished Military Graduate); Suffolk University Law School (J.D., magna cum laude, 2000). Microsoft Certified Systems Engineer, 1994. [Capt., U.S. Army, Active Duty and Reserves.]. (Washington, D.C. Office). ***LANGUAGES:*** Danish. ***PRACTICE AREAS:*** Information Technology; Corporate. ***Email:*** mmaier@mayerbrownrowe.com

ELDAD Z. MALAMUTH, admitted to bar, 2001, Illinois; 2002, District of Columbia; 2003, U.S. Court of Federal Claims. *Education:* University of Michigan (B.S., 1997); University of Chicago (J.D.,with honors, 2001). (Washington, D.C. Office). ***PRACTICE AREAS:*** General and Appellate Litigation; Employment. ***Email:*** emalamuth@mayerbrownrowe.com

DAVID N. MALINGER, born Evergreen Park, Illinois, March 6, 1973; admitted to bar, 1998, Illinois. *Education:* University of Illinois (B.S., 1995); Drake University (J.D., 1998). Order of the Coif. Editor-in-Chief, Drake Law Review. ***Email:*** dmalinger@mayerbrownrowe.com

JENNIFER C. MALONEY, born Madrid, Spain, December 13, 1966; admitted to bar, 1992, Connecticut; 1995, District of Columbia. *Education:* New England Conservatory of Music (B.M., 1988); Western New England School of Law (J.D., magna cum laude, 1992). (Washington, D.C. Office). ***PRACTICE AREAS:*** Tax Controversies. ***Email:*** jmaloney@mayerbrownrowe.com

WILLIAM MALPICA, born N.Y., N.Y., April 12, 1968; admitted to bar, 2001, New York. *Education:* State University of New York at Albany (B.A., 1990); Fordham University (J.D., 2000). Member, New York City Commission on Human Rights (appointed by the Mayor of New York). Co-Author, "Expanding Latino Participation in the Legal Profession: Strategies for Increasing Latino Law School Enrollments," Fordham Urban Law Journal, May 2003 (with Mauricio España). Member, Board of Directors, Committee for Hispanic Children & Families. Member, Board of Trustees, Bronx Charter School for the Arts. (New York, N.Y. Office). ***LANGUAGES:*** Spanish. ***PRACTICE AREAS:*** Banking; Finance; Securitization. ***Email:*** wmalpica@mayerbrown.com

GREGORY A. MANTER, born May 12, 1978; admitted to bar, 2004, New York (Not admitted in Illinois). *Education:* University of Virginia (B.A., with distinction, 2000); Duke University School of Law (J.D., 2003; LL.M., International Law, 2003). ***PRACTICE AREAS:*** Corporate; Information Technology; Outsourcing. ***Email:*** gmanter@mayerbrownrowe.com

MICHAEL K. MARION, admitted to bar, 2005, New York. *Education:* The University of Michigan (B.A., 2001); The George Washington University Law School (J.D., 2004); New York University School of Law (LL.M., 2005). (Washington, D.C. Office). ***PRACTICE AREAS:*** Tax Transactions. ***Email:*** mmarion@mayerbrownrowe.com

MILOS MARKOVIC, admitted to bar, 1999, Illinois. *Education:* University of Illinois, Chicago (B.S., 1993); DePaul University (J.D., 1999). ***PRACTICE AREAS:*** Real Estate. ***Email:*** mmarkovic@mayerbrownrowe.com

(This Listing Continued)

HEATHER H. MARTIN, admitted to bar, 2003, Virginia; 2004, District of Columbia. *Education:* Utah State University (B.A., cum laude, 1997); The George Washington University Law School (J.D., with honors, 2003). (Washington, D.C. Office). ***PRACTICE AREAS:*** Litigation. ***Email:*** hhmartin@mayerbrownrowe.com

MICHAEL C. MASCIA, born Terrytown, New York, December 24, 1971; admitted to bar, 1998, North Carolina; 2003, Massachusetts. *Education:* University of North Carolina (B.A., 1994; J.D., 1998); Massachusetts Institute of Technology, Sloan School of Management (M.B.A., 2003). (Charlotte, North Carolina Office). ***PRACTICE AREAS:*** Banking; Finance. ***Email:*** mmascia@mayerbrownrowe.com

JOSHUA M. MASUR, admitted to bar, 1999, California and U.S. District Court, Northern District of California and U.S. District of Appeals, Ninth Circuit; 2002, U.S. Court of Appeals for the Federal Circuit; 2004, U.S. District Court, Central District of California. *Education:* Columbia University (A.B., 1990; J.D., 1999). Author: "A Most Uncommon Carrier: Online Service Provider Immunity Against Defamation Claims in Blumenthal v. Drudge," 40 Jurimetrics J. 217 (2000); "Safety in Numbers: Revisiting the Risks to Client Confidences and Attorney-Client Privilege Posed by Internet Electronic Mail," 14 Berkeley Tech. L.J. 1117 (1999); "Links, Liability and the Law: The Strange Case of Ticketmaster v. Microsoft," 23 Colum.-VLA J. Law & Arts 405 (1999). *Member:* San Francisco Bay Area Intellectual Property American Inn of Court (Secretary/Treasurer, 2004—). ***PRACTICE AREAS:*** Intellectual Property; Litigation. ***Email:*** jmasur@mayerbrownrowe.com

JOHN E. MAUK, admitted to bar, 2002, Virginia; registered to practice before U.S. Patent and Trademark Office. *Education:* Pennsylvania State University (B.S., 1991); John Hopkins University (M.A., 1998); College of William & Mary (J.D., 2002). (Washington, D.C. Office). ***PRACTICE AREAS:*** Intellectual Property. ***Email:*** jmauk@mayerbrownrowe.com

BRIAN T. MAY, born Portland, Oregon, February 26, 1974; admitted to bar, 1998, California; 2001, Illinois; registered to practice before U.S. Patent and Trademark Office. *Education:* University of Nevada, Reno (B.S., summa cum laude, 1995); University of Michigan (J.D., magna cum laude, 1998). Order of the Coif. ***Email:*** bmay@mayerbrownrowe.com

PETER M. McCAMMAN, (admission pending). *Education:* Cornell University (B.A., 1998); The Catholic University of America, Columbus School of Law (J.D., cum laude, 2005). (Washington, D.C. Office). ***PRACTICE AREAS:*** Corporate Law; Securities. ***Email:*** pmccamman@mayerbrownrowe.com

DOUGLAS E. McCORMACK, born New York, N.Y., October 28, 1972; admitted to bar, 1999, New York. *Education:* Princeton University (A.B., 1995); Harvard Law School (J.D., 1998). (New York, N.Y. Office). ***PRACTICE AREAS:*** Investment Company Law. ***Email:*** dmccormack@mayerbrownrowe.com

JILL K. McDOWELL, admitted to bar, 1998, Florida; 1999, District of Columbia; 2000, U.S. District Court for the District of Columbia. *Education:* University of Florida (B.S., with honors, 1990); Catholic University (J.D., magna cum laude, 1998). Author: "Congress Errs in Deregulating Broadcast Ownership Caps: More Monopolies Less Localism, Decreased Diversity and Violations of Equal Protection," 5 Comm. Law Conspectus 269, 1997. (Resident, Washington D.C. Office). ***PRACTICE AREAS:*** Regulated Industries. ***Email:*** jmcdowell@mayerbrownrowe.com

MARK A. MEARS, born Dhahran, Saudi Arabia, August 9, 1958; admitted to bar, 1985, California. *Education:* University of New Hampshire (B.S., magna cum laude, 1981); University of California at Los Angeles (J.D., 1985). Order of the Coif. (Los Angeles, California Office). ***Email:*** mmears@mayerbrownrowe.com

MATTHIAS J. MECKERT, admitted to bar, 2000, Darmstadt, Germany. *Education:* Joh. Gutenberg, Mainz. (Frankfurt/Main, Germany Office). ***LANGUAGES:*** English and French. ***Email:*** mjmeckert@mayerbrownrowe.com

ERIN E. MEEK, born Mansfield, Ohio, March 23, 1976; (admission pending). *Education:* University of Pennsylvania (B.A., magna cum laude, 1998); University of Michigan (J.D., 2004). (New York, N.Y. Office). ***LANGUAGES:*** French. ***PRACTICE AREAS:*** Banking Law; Finance. ***Email:*** emeek@mayerbrownrowe.com

STEVEN J. MEINER, born Brooklyn, New York, June 16, 1971; admitted to bar, 1996, New Jersey; 1997, New York; 1998, U.S. District Court, Southern and Eastern Districts of New York. *Education:* Brooklyn College (B.A., summa cum laude, 1993); Brooklyn Law School (J.D., cum laude, 1996). (New York, N.Y. Office). ***PRACTICE AREAS:*** Litigation. ***Email:*** smeiner@mayerbrownrowe.com

MIRJA MERTIN, LLM, MAÎTRISE EN DROIT, admitted to bar, 2005, Cologne. *Education:* Université d'Angers/France (1994); University of Cologne (1995-1997; 1999-2002); Université de Paris I, Panthéon- Sorbonne/France (1997-1999). Cologne, First State Law Examination, 2002. Legal Clerkship, Referendariat, Cologne and Washington, D.C., 2003-2005. (Cologne, Germany Office). ***LANGUAGES:*** German (native), Swedish (native), English and French. ***PRACTICE AREAS:*** Corporate; Finance. ***Email:*** mmertin@mayerbrownrowe.com

TOBIAS MESSER. *Education:* Universities of Frankfurt and Mainz. (Frankfurt/Main, Germany Office). ***PRACTICE AREAS:*** Corporate; Securities. ***Email:*** tmesser@mayerbrownrowe.com

TIFFANY L. METZ, born Tucson, Arizona, March 31, 1969; admitted to bar, 1998, Michigan (Not admitted in Illinois). *Education:* Siena Heights College (B.A., 1993); University of Michigan Law School (J.D., 1997). 1997 National Mock Trial Team. Co-Author, "Assignments for the Benefit of Creditors" and "Receiverships," both published in *The Michigan Business Law Journal,* Volume XIX, Number 3, 1999. Editorial Board of the Federal Bar Association's periodical), *The Federal Lawyer,* 1999—. ***Email:*** tmetz@mayerbrownrowe.com

LAURA DAWN METZGER. *Education:* Barnard College; Columbia University (B.A., magna cum laude, 1999); Benjamin N. Cardozo Law School (J.D., magna cum laude, Order of the Coif, 2002). (New York, N.Y. Office). ***PRACTICE AREAS:*** Bankruptcy; Workout; Reorganization. ***Email:*** lmetzger@mayerbrownrowe.com

(This Listing Continued)

VAZANTHA MEYERS, born Seattle, Washington, September 14, 1971; admitted to bar, 2004, Illinois. *Education:* Purdue University (B.A., 2000); Valparaiso University School of Law (J.D., magna cum laude, 2004). ***PRACTICE AREAS:*** Litigation (100%). ***Email:*** vmeyers@mayerbrownrowe.com

ADAM B. MILLER, born April 14, 1974; admitted to bar, 2000, Illinois. *Education:* American University (B.A., cum laude, 1996); Duke Law School (J.D., magna cum laude, 2000). (Resident, Washington D.C. Office). ***PRACTICE AREAS:*** Litigation. ***Email:*** abmiller@mayerbrownrowe.com

BRITT M. MILLER, born San Diego, California, September 29, 1973; admitted to bar, 1998, Illinois and U.S. District Court, Northern District of Illinois; U.S. Court of Appeals, Seventh Circuit; 2002, U.S. Supreme Court. *Education:* Auburn University (B.A., 1995); Northwestern University (J.D., 1998). Dean's List. Order of the Coif. Member, Northwestern University Law Review. Author: "Requests to Admit," *Illinois Practice - Civil Discovery,* West Publishing, 2000. ***PRACTICE AREAS:*** Litigation. ***Email:*** bmiller@mayerbrownrowe.com

CHARLES A. (VAN) MILLER, admitted to bar, 2002, Texas. *Education:* University of Mississippi (B.S., cum laude, 1993; M.S., 1993); Tulane University School of Law (J.D., cum laude, 2002). (Washington, D.C. Office). ***PRACTICE AREAS:*** Outsourcing. ***Email:*** camiller@mayerbrownrowe.com

ANSHUMAN MISHRA, admitted to bar, 2002, Illinois. *Education:* Gorakhpur University, India (B.A., 1995); Allahabad University, India (LL.B., 1998); University of San Diego School of Law (LL.M., 2002). ***LANGUAGES:*** Hindi, Punjabi, Ukranian. ***PRACTICE AREAS:*** Banking and Finance. ***Email:*** amishra@mayerbrownrowe.com

CHRISTOPHER A. MONSOUR, admitted to bar, 2005, Illinois. *Education:* The Florida State University (B.A., 2001); Harvard Law School (J.D., magna cum laude, 2004). ***LANGUAGES:*** Italian, French. ***PRACTICE AREAS:*** Litigation.

ISELA MORALES, born Chicago, Illinois, October 15, 1976; admitted to bar, 2002, Illinois. *Education:* Harvard and Radcliffe Colleges (A.B., cum laude, 1998); University of Michigan (J.D., cum laude, 2002). ***LANGUAGES:*** Spanish. ***PRACTICE AREAS:*** Corporate Law; Securities. ***Email:*** imorales@mayerbrownrowe.com

MICHAEL V. MORELLI, born Bronx, New York, May 2, 1972; admitted to bar, 1997, Connecticut; 1998, New York. *Education:* Georgetown University (B.S.B.A., 1994); Fordham University School of Law (J.D., 1997). (New York, N.Y. Office). ***PRACTICE AREAS:*** Real Estate. ***Email:*** mmorelli@mayerbrownrowe.com

LEE MORLOCK, admitted to bar, 2004, Illinois. *Education:* McGill University (B.Com., 2001); Harvard Law School (J.D., 2004). ***PRACTICE AREAS:*** Tax Transactions. ***Email:*** lmorlock@mayerbrownrowe.com

CAROL A. MORRISON, admitted to bar, 1998, New York; U.S. District Court, Southern and Eastern Districts of New York. *Education:* Queens College of the City University of New York (B.A., 1993); Columbia Law School (J.D., 1997). (New York, N.Y. Office). ***PRACTICE AREAS:*** Bankruptcy; Finance. ***Email:*** cmorrison@mayerbrownrowe.com

MATTHEW MOZIAN, born Bronx, New York, February 2, 1976; admitted to bar, 2002, New York. *Education:* State University of New York College at Geneseo (B.A., 1998); Albany Law School of Union University (J.D., 2001). Note and Comment Editor, Albany Law Review, 2000-2001. Author: "Reining in Interim Reliefs Cottage Industry: A Call to Resolve Jiggetts," 64 Albany Law Review 397 (2000). (New York, N.Y. Office). ***PRACTICE AREAS:*** Corporate Law; Securities; Finance. ***Email:*** mmozian@mayerbrownrowe.com

MONIQUE J. MULCARE, admitted to bar, 1992, New York and Connecticut; 1993, U.S. District Court, Eastern and Southern Districts of New York; 1996, U.S. Court of Appeals, Second Circuit. *Education:* Hunter College of the City University of New York (B.A., magna cum laude, 1988); New York University School of Law (J.D., 1991). Author: Article III, The Federal Magistrate, and the Power of Consent, Annual Survey of American Law, 1992/1993 Volume, Issue 2. Co-Author: Pahlavi: The Exception Not the Rule, New York Law Journal, May 19, 1997 (with Carol H. Arber); Treatment of Prior Bad Acts in Criminal and Civil Cases, New York Law Journal, August 8, 1995 (with Carol H. Arber). (New York, N.Y. Office). ***PRACTICE AREAS:*** Bankruptcy; Workout; Reorganization. ***Email:*** mmulcare@mayerbrownrowe.com

MELISSA MULROONEY, born Bronx, New York, July 22, 1973; admitted to bar, 2001, New York. *Education:* Boston College (B.A., cum laude, 1995); Fordham Law School (J.D., 2001). Notes and Articles Editor, Fordham Intellectual Property, Media & Entertainment Law Journal, 2000-2001. (New York, N.Y. Office). ***PRACTICE AREAS:*** Bankruptcy; Workouts; Business Reorganization. ***Email:*** mmulrooney@mayerbrownrowe.com

TRENT M. MURCH, born Normal, Illinois, November 15, 1971; admitted to bar, 1998, Illinois. *Education:* Bradley University (B.S., magna cum laude, 1995); University of Illinois (J.D., magna cum laude, 1998). ***PRACTICE AREAS:*** Banking Law; Finance; Securitization. ***Email:*** tmurch@mayerbrownrowe.com

CHRISTOPHER CHARLES MURRAY, born Fort Wayne, Indiana, March 30, 1971; admitted to bar, 2002, Illinois. *Education:* Case Western Reserve University (B.A., 1993); University of Pennsylvania (J.D., 2001). ***Email:*** ccmurray@mayerbrownrowe.com

DR. ARIANE MUSIL, born 1968; admitted to bar, 2000, Frankfurt am Main, Germany. *Education:* Universities of Munich, Speyer and Jena; University of Sydney (LL.M.). (Frankfurt/Main, Germany Office). ***LANGUAGES:*** English. ***PRACTICE AREAS:*** Mergers and Acquisitions; Corporate; Commercial. ***Email:*** amusil@mayerbrownrowe.com

VERA A. NACKOVIC, admitted to bar, 2003, Illinois. *Education:* St. Mary's College (B.S., 2000); Valparaiso University (J.D., 2003). ***PRACTICE AREAS:*** Intellectual Property. ***Email:*** vnackovic@mayerbrownrowe.com

ANTHONY J. NAPOLITANO, born Brooklyn, New York, January 22, 1975; admitted to bar, 2003, California; U.S. District Court for the Central District of California. *Education:* Loyola Marymount University (B.S. Accounting, 1997; B.S. Economics, 1997); Loyola Law School (J.D., cum laude, 2003). Order of the Coif; Articles Editor, Loyola Law Review, 2002-2003. Certified Public Accountant, Illinois, 1999. Author: "Web Site Annotation: The Intersection of New Communication Technologies and the Rights of Web Site Owners," 36 Loy. L.A. L. Rev. 493 (2002). (Los Angeles, California Office). ***PRACTICE AREAS:*** Bankruptcy; Financial Restructuring. ***Email:*** anapolitano@mayerbrownrowe.com

MICHAEL T. NEIDIGH, admitted to bar, 1998, Illinois and U.S. District Court, Northern District of Illinois. *Education:* Northwestern University (B.S., 1991); Loyola University Chicago School of Law (J.D. cum laude, 1998). ***PRACTICE AREAS:*** Securitization; Finance. ***Email:*** mneidigh@mayerbrownrowe.com

PETER T. NELSON, admitted to bar, 2002, Texas. *Education:* Carleton College (B.A., 1995); University of Houston Law Center (J.D., magna cum laude, 2002). (Houston, Texas Office). ***PRACTICE AREAS:*** Banking and Finance. ***Email:*** ptnelson@mayerbrownrowe.com

JADE EARL NEWBURN, born Sioux City, Iowa, September 18, 1974; admitted to bar, 2005, Illinois. *Education:* Brown University (A.B., magna cum laude, 1997); Balliol College, University of Oxford (B.A., 2000); Harvard Law School (J.D., cum laude, 2004). ***PRACTICE AREAS:*** Trusts and Estates. ***Email:*** jnewburn@mayerbrownrowe.com

CARA L. NEWMAN, born La Grange, Illinois, December 3, 1978; admitted to bar, 2004, Illinois. *Education:* Loyola University (B.A., summa cum laude, 2001); DePaul University (J.D., magna cum laude, 2004). (New York, N.Y. Office). ***PRACTICE AREAS:*** Banking and Finance; Securitization. ***Email:*** cnewman@mayerbrownrowe.com

MARK A. NICHOLSON, born Southfield, Michigan, May 6, 1975; admitted to bar, 2002, California (Not admitted in Illinois). *Education:* University of Notre Dame (B.A., 1997); University of Virginia (J.D., 2001). *Member:* State Bar of California. ***PRACTICE AREAS:*** Corporate Law; Securities. ***Email:*** mnicholson@mayerbrownrowe.com

ANDRZEJ R. NIEKRASZ, (admission pending). *Education:* St. Louis University (B.A., 1998); Northwestern University (M.A., 2002); The John Marshall Law School (J.D., 2005). ***LANGUAGES:*** Polish, Russian, Slovene. ***PRACTICE AREAS:*** Banking and Finance. ***Email:*** aniekrasz@mayerbrownrowe.com

NANCY V. NIETO, born Boston, Massachusetts, November 17, 1950; admitted to bar, 1995, California; 1997, New Mexico (Not admitted in Illinois). *Education:* San Diego State University (B.S., 1976); University of San Diego (J.D., cum laude, 1995). Order of the Coif. ***Email:*** nnieto@mayerbrownrowe.com

HANA NITKIN, (admission pending). *Education:* Stern School of Business, New York University (B.S., 2000); Fordham University School of Law (J.D., 2003). (New York, N.Y. Office). ***PRACTICE AREAS:*** Banking and Finance. ***Email:*** hnitkin@mayerbrownrowe.com

LAUREN F. NOLL, admitted to bar, 2000, Illinois; 2001, U.S. District Court, Northern District of Illinois and U.S. Court of Appeals, Seventh Circuit. *Education:* Miami University (B.A., summa cum laude, 1997); University of Illinois (J.D., magna cum laude, 2000). Law Clerk to: Hon. Kenneth F. Ripple, U.S. Court of Appeals for the Seventh Circuit, 2000-2001; Hon. Robin E. Hudson, North Carolina Court of Appeals, 2002-2003. Author, "Ethical Responsibilities and the International Lawyer: Mind the Gaps," 2000 University of Illinois Law Review Rev. 957. Adjunct Professor, Appellate Advocacy, Loyola University Chicago School of Law, 2003—. ***PRACTICE AREAS:*** Litigation. ***Email:*** lfnoll@mayerbrownrowe.com

ANGELA D. O'BRIEN, born Ft. Rucker, Alabama; admitted to bar, 1998, Indiana; 2000, Illinois. *Education:* University of Houston (B.A., 1994); Indiana University School of Law - Indianapolis (J.D., 1998). ***PRACTICE AREAS:*** Telecommunications Regulation; Regulated Industries. ***Email:*** aobrien@mayerbrownrowe.com

MARGARET A. O'CONNOR, born Evanston, Illinois, January 20, 1973; admitted to bar, 2001, Illinois; 2003, U.S. District Court, Northern District of Illinois. *Education:* University of Notre Dame (B.S., 1994); Loyola University (J.D., cum laude, 2001). [Navy ROTC 1990-1994; US Navy active 1994-1998; US Navy reserve 1998—]. ***PRACTICE AREAS:*** Intellectual Property. ***Email:*** moconnor@mayerbrownrowe.com

THOMAS O'DONNELL, admitted to bar, 2001, New York and Massachusetts. *Education:* Rhode Island College (B.A., 1997); St. John's University School of Law (J.D., 2000). (New York, N.Y. Office). ***PRACTICE AREAS:*** Litigation. ***Email:*** todonnell@mayerbrownrowe.com

CRISTIN OBSITNIK, admitted to bar, 1997, Illinois. *Education:* Amherst College (B.A., 1993); Loyola University Chicago School of Law (J.D., cum laude, 1997); Northwestern University School of Law (LL.M., 2005). ***PRACTICE AREAS:*** ERISA; Employee Benefits; Executive Compensation. ***Email:*** cobsitnik@mayerbrownrowe.com

FRANCISCO OCHOA, born Sacramento, California, August 7, 1978; admitted to bar, 2002, California; 2003, U.S. District Court, Northern, Southern, Central and Eastern Districts of California. *Education:* University of California at Davis (B.A., with honors, 1999); Stanford University School of Law (J.D., 2002). (Los Angeles, California Office). ***PRACTICE AREAS:*** Commercial Litigation; Labor and Employment. ***Email:*** fochoa@mayerbrownrowe.com

JASON M. OSBORN, born Troy, New York, January 26, 1976; admitted to bar, 2002, New York. *Education:* Hamilton College (B.A., 1998); University of Notre Dame Law School (J.D., magna cum laude, 2001). (Washington, D.C. Office). ***PRACTICE AREAS:*** Tax Controversy. ***Email:*** jmosborn@mayerbrownrowe.com

ROCHELLE D. OUTLAW, born Indianapolis, Indiana, 1974; (admission pending). *Education:* Rice University (B.A., 1997); Ohio Northern University, Pettit College of Law (J.D., with distinction, 2005). ***LANGUAGES:*** French. ***PRACTICE AREAS:*** Litigation. ***Email:*** routlaw@mayerbrownrowe.com

ARCHIS A. PARASHARAMI, admitted to bar, 2002, New York and District of Columbia; 2003, U.S. Court of Appeals, Third Circuit. *Education:* Princeton University (A.B., summa cum laude, 1997); Harvard Law School (J.D., cum laude, 2001). Law Clerk, Honorable Leonard I. Garth, U.S. Court of Appeals for the Third Circuit, 2002-2003. Co-Executive Editor for Student Authors, Harvard Civil Rights-Civil Liberties Law Review. (Washington, D.C. Office). ***PRACTICE AREAS:*** Appellate Litigation; General Litigation. ***Email:*** aparasharami@mayerbrownrowe.com

(This Listing Continued)

MAYER, BROWN, ROWE & MAW LLP, Chicago—Continued

DIANE PARK. *Education:* University of California at Los Angeles (B.A., cum laude, 1998); University of California Law School (J.D., 2002). (Los Angeles, California Office). ***LANGUAGES:*** Korean. ***PRACTICE AREAS:*** Litigation. ***Email:*** dpark@mayerbrownrowe.com

JAMES T. PARKINSON, born New York, N.Y., August 1, 1968; admitted to bar, 1999, California; 2003, District of Columbia. *Education:* Gettysburg College (B.A., 1990); University of Pennsylvania (M.S., 1994); Washington College of Law of American University (J.D., magna cum laude, 1999). (Washington, D.C. Office). ***PRACTICE AREAS:*** Litigation. ***Email:*** jtparkinson@mayerbrownrowe.com

MELISSA PASTRANA, admitted to bar, 2001, Illinois and U.S. District Court, Northern District of Illinois. *Education:* Harvard University (A.B., 1996); University of Chicago Law School (J.D., 2001). ***Email:*** mpastrana@mayerbrownrowe.com

HEIKE PAUL, born 1974; admitted to bar, 2001. *Education:* Universities of Mannheim and Lausanne. (Frankfurt/Main, Germany Office). ***LANGUAGES:*** English and French. ***PRACTICE AREAS:*** Pharmaceutical and Food Law; Intellectual Property. ***Email:*** hpaul@mayerbrownrowe.com

WILLIAM PAXTON, admitted to bar, 2002, Massachusetts and District of Columbia. *Education:* Colgate University (A.B., 1993); Harvard University (M.Div., 1997); Duke University (J.D., cum laude, 2000). Managing Editor, Duke Journal of Comparative & International Law. Editor, Duke Journal of Gender Law & Policy. Law Clerk to the Honorable Myron H. Bright, United States Court for the Court of Appeals for the Eighth Circuit. Vice-chairperson, Duke Moot Court Board. (Washington, D.C. Office). ***REPORTED CASES:*** Walton v. Briley, 361 F.3d 431 (7th Cir. 2004). ***PRACTICE AREAS:*** Appellate; Litigation. ***Email:*** wpaxton@mayerbrownrowe.com

DENNIS F. PENEPACKER, born Chicago, Illinois, April 28, 1969; admitted to bar, 1999, Illinois. *Education:* United States Naval Academy (B.S., Systems Engineering, 1991); Northwestern University (J.D., 1999). Author: Articles, "Outsourcing Contract Management" July 2005; "IP Ownership and Transferability" April 2003. [United States Navy, Active duty, 1991-1996; Qualified surface warfare officer and naval nuclear propulsion officer]. ***PRACTICE AREAS:*** Corporate Law; Information Technology Contracts and Licensing; Outsourcing. ***Email:*** dpenepacker@mayerbrownrowe.com

HEIKO PENNDORF, born 1968; admitted to bar, 2000, Germany. *Education:* Frankfurt/Main (Second State Law Examination, 1999). (Frankfurt/Main, Germany Office). ***LANGUAGES:*** German, English. ***PRACTICE AREAS:*** Tax Transactions; Securitization; Structured Finance. ***Email:*** hpenndorf@mayerbrownrowe.com

ERIN C. PERKINS, born Ashland, Ohio, 1969; admitted to bar, 1998, Illinois and U.S. District Court, Northern District of Illinois; 1999, U.S. Court of Appeals, Seventh Circuit. *Education:* Yale University (B.A., summa cum laude, 1990); Northwestern University (J.D., cum laude, 1998). Phi Beta Kappa. Member, Northwestern University Law Review, 1996-1998. Author, Comment, "Migratory Birds & Multiple Use Management: Using the Migratory Bird Treaty Act to Rejuvenate America's National Environmental Policy," 92 N.W.U.I. Rev. 817 (Winter 1998). ***PRACTICE AREAS:*** Commercial Litigation; International Dispute Resolution; Bankruptcy Litigation. ***Email:*** ecperkins@mayerbrownrowe.com

MARIE-ANNE PERLIA, (admission pending). *Education:* University of Illinois (B.A., 1986; M.A., 1994); Northwestern University (M.A., 1990); Loyola University (J.D., cum laude, 2004). Symposium Articles Editor and Associate Editor, Loyola University Chicago International Law Review, 2002-2004. ***LANGUAGES:*** French. ***PRACTICE AREAS:*** Banking Law; Finance. ***Email:*** mperlia@mayerbrownrowe.com

AMY WARD PERSHKOW, born November 14, 1973; admitted to bar, 1999, Virginia; 2000, District of Columbia. *Education:* Trinity College (B.A., cum laude, 1996); The Catholic University of America School of Law (J.D., 1999). (Washington, D.C. Office). ***PRACTICE AREAS:*** Corporate Law; Securities. ***Email:*** apershkow@mayerbrownrowe.com

JENNIFER M. PETERS, (admission pending). *Education:* University of Illinois, College of Commerce and Business Administration (B.S., with honors, 2002); Loyola University Chicago School of Law (J.D., magna cum laude, 2005). ***PRACTICE AREAS:*** Corporate and Securities. ***Email:*** jpeters@mayerbrownrowe.com

EMILY S. PETROVIC, born Covington, Kentucky, March 29, 1977; admitted to bar, 2003, Illinois. *Education:* University of Kentucky (B.S., 1999); Harvard Law School (J.D., 2003). ***PRACTICE AREAS:*** Wealth Management (100%). ***Email:*** epetrovic@mayerbrownrowe.com

MARK A. PETRY, admitted to bar, 2002, District of Columbia and New York. *Education:* College of Wooster (B.A., 1994); The George Washington University Law School (J.D., 2001). (Washington, D.C. Office). ***PRACTICE AREAS:*** Corporate and Securities. ***Email:*** mpetry@mayerbrownrowe.com

ANTHONY R. PFLUM, born Indianapolis, Indiana, December 1, 1970; admitted to bar, 2000, Texas. *Education:* Lawrence University (B.A., Anthropology, 1994); University of Texas School of Law, Austin (J.D., 2000). (Houston, Texas Office). ***PRACTICE AREAS:*** Securities; Corporate Law; Banks and Banking. ***Email:*** apflum@mayerbrownrowe.com

LORI PHILIPSON, born Utica, New York, April 26, 1954; admitted to bar, 1989, New York (Not admitted in Illinois). *Education:* Brown University (A.B., 1975); Harvard Law School (J.D., cum laude, 1988). (New York, N.Y. Office). ***PRACTICE AREAS:*** Real Estate. ***Email:*** lphilipson@mayerbrownrowe.com

MACKENZIE K. PHILLIPS, *born Chicago, Illinois; admitted to bar, 2004, Illinois.* *Education:* Cornell University (A.B., 1999) Dean's List; The University of Michigan Law School (J.D., 2004). Executive Editor, Michigan Law Review (Vol. 102). ***LANGUAGES:*** French. ***PRACTICE AREAS:*** Corporate and Securities. ***Email:*** mzphillips@mayerbrownrowe.com

MARCUS PICKEL, admitted to bar, 2002, Frankfurt am Main, Germany. *Education:* University of Mainz (2002). (Frankfurt/Main, Germany Office). ***PRACTICE AREAS:*** Corporate; Private Equity. ***Email:*** mpickel@mayerbrownrowe.com

EDWARD A. PIONKE, admitted to bar, 1999, Illinois. *Education:* University of Illinois, Urbana-Champaign (B.S., 1988); DePaul University (J.D., 1999). ***PRACTICE AREAS:*** ERISA. ***Email:*** epionke@mayerbrownrowe.com

KIRSTEN PIRZKALL, born Frankfurt, 1974; admitted to bar, 2003, Germany. *Education:* Johann-Wolfgang-Goethe University, Frankfurt. (Frankfurt/Main, Germany Office). ***LANGUAGES:*** English. ***PRACTICE AREAS:*** Banking and Finance. ***Email:*** kpirzkall@mayerbrownrowe.com

BRONWYN F. POLLOCK, born Los Angeles, 1977; admitted to bar, 2000, California and U.S. District Court, Central and Southern Districts of California. *Education:* University of Southern California (B.A., cum laude, 1996); Georgetown University Law Center (J.D., 2000). Senior Editor, Georgetown Journal of Poverty Law & Policy. (Los Angeles, California Office). ***PRACTICE AREAS:*** Litigation. ***Email:*** bpollock@mayerbrownrowe.com

DAVID D. POPE, born Evanston, Illinois, December 20, 1975; admitted to bar, 2001, Illinois and U.S. District Court, Northern District of Illinois; 2002, U.S. Court of Appeals, Seventh Circuit. *Education:* Colorado College (B.A., magna cum laude, 1998); University of Chicago (J.D., 2001). ***PRACTICE AREAS:*** Litigation. ***Email:*** dpope@mayerbrownrowe.com

CHRISTINE POULON, born February 16, 1968; admitted to bar, 1999, Maryland; 2002, District of Columbia and Florida. *Education:* Vassar College (B.A., 1989); University of Reading, Graduate School of European and International Studies (M.A., 1991); Washington College of Law of American University (J.D., 1999). (Washington, D.C. Office). ***LANGUAGES:*** Greek. ***PRACTICE AREAS:*** Banking Law; Finance. ***Email:*** cpoulon@mayerbrownrowe.com

MATTHEW R. POWERS, admitted to bar, 2003, Pennsylvania. *Education:* University of Colorado at Denver (B.A., summa cum laude, 1998); University of Chicago Law School (J.D., 2003). (Houston, Texas Office). ***PRACTICE AREAS:*** Real Estate. ***Email:*** mpowers@mayerbrownrowe.com

JASON L. PORTNOY, admitted to bar, 2003, Massachusetts; 2004, New York. *Education:* Rutgers College (B.S., 2000); Boston University (J.D., cum laude, 2003). (New York, N.Y. Office). ***PRACTICE AREAS:*** Corporate; Securities. ***Email:*** jportnoy@mayerbrownrowe.com

PEARL H. PROKOSH, born August 6, 1976; admitted to bar, 2003, Massachusetts. *Education:* McGill University (B.A., 1998); McGill University, Law School (LL.B, with Distinction, 2002; B.C.L., 2002). (Los Angeles, California Office). ***PRACTICE AREAS:*** Real Estate. ***Email:*** pprokosh@mayerbrownrowe.com

TRISTAN E. PROPST, born Cambridge, Massachusetts, December 26, 1968; admitted to bar, 1998, Texas. *Education:* Princeton University (A.B., magna cum laude, 1991); Tulane University (J.D./M.B.A., 1998). Beta Gamma Sigma; Order of the Coif; Tulane Law Review, Notes and Comments Editor. (Houston, Texas Office). ***PRACTICE AREAS:*** Commercial Banking; Secured Lending; Business Law. ***Email:*** tpropst@mayerbrownrowe.com

SHARON N. PURCELL. *Education:* Harvard University (B.A., 1998); Fordham University School of Law (J.D., 2003). (New York, N.Y. Office). ***PRACTICE AREAS:*** Corporate; Securities. ***Email:*** spurcell@mayerbrownrowe.com

DAVID H. PYUN, born Seoul, Korea, 1977. *Education:* Cornell University (B.A., with honors, 1999); New York University School of Law (J.D., 2000). (Los Angeles, California Office). ***PRACTICE AREAS:*** Banking; Finance. ***Email:*** dhpyun@mayerbrownrowe.com

MARIA M. RABASSA, born Mazatlan, Mexico, September 17, 1964; admitted to bar, 1990, California. *Education:* Harvard University (B.A., 1987); University of California at Berkeley (J.D., 1990). Moot Court Board Director. Associate Editor, California Law Review. (Los Angeles, California Office). ***LANGUAGES:*** Spanish. ***Email:*** mrabassa@mayerbrownrowe.com

JENNIFER L. RAKSTAD, admitted to bar, 1998, Illinois, U.S. District Court, Northern District of Illinois; 1999, U.S. District Court, District of Puerto Rico and U.S. Court of Appeals, First Circuit. *Education:* Augustana College (B.A. summa cum laude, 1992); New York University School of Law (J.D., 1998). ***LANGUAGES:*** Spanish. ***PRACTICE AREAS:*** Litigation. ***Email:*** jrakstad@mayerbrownrowe.com

DANIEL R. READ, born Hollywood, Florida, December 29, 1971; admitted to bar, 2003, Massachusetts; 2004, New York, Florida and District of Columbia. *Education:* The Florida State University (B.S., cum laude, 1994); New York University (LL.M., Taxation, 2004); Duke University (J.D., with high honors, 2003). Order of the Coif. (New York, N.Y. Office). ***PRACTICE AREAS:*** Tax Transactions. ***Email:*** dread@mayerbrownrowe.com

CONSTANTIN REHAAG, admitted to bar, 2005, Germany. *Education:* Universities of Passau and Freiburg. (Frankfurt/Main, Germany Office). ***PRACTICE AREAS:*** Intellectual Property. ***Email:*** crehaag@mayerbrownrowe.com

LAURA A. REILLY, born Smithtown, New York, 1970; admitted to bar, 1995, Virginia; 1996, District of Columbia; 1997, Maryland; 1999, New York. *Education:* Lafayette College (B.A., cum laude, 1992); George Washington University (J.D., with honors, 1995). (Washington, D.C. Office). ***PRACTICE AREAS:*** Real Estate. ***Email:*** lreilly@mayerbrownrowe.com

LIANNE S. REILLY, born United Kingdom; admitted to bar, 1996, England and Wales; 1998, California; 2002, New York. *Education:* University of Sussex, U.K. (B.A., honors, 1991); College of Law, York, U.K. (CPE and Diploma in Law, (Commendation), 1993-1994); Fordham University School of Law (LL.M., cum laude, 2001). (Washington, D.C. Office). ***LANGUAGES:*** French, Dutch. ***PRACTICE AREAS:*** Real Estate. ***Email:*** lsreilly@mayerbrownrowe.com

(This Listing Continued)

SARAH E. REYNOLDS, (admission pending). *Education:* University of Colorado-Boulder (B.A., 1998); University of Illinois at Chicago (M.A., 2000); University of Chicago, The Law School (J.D., 2005). ***PRACTICE AREAS:*** Litigation. ***Email:*** sreynolds@mayerbrownrowe.com

STEVEN E. RICH, born Los Angeles, California, August 11, 1971; admitted to bar, 1998, California and U.S. District Court, Central District of California; 2000, U.S. District Court, Southern District of California; 2001, U.S. Court of Appeals, Ninth Circuit. *Education:* University of California, Los Angeles (B.A., 1993); Loyola Law School (J.D., 1998). Extern to Honorable Kathleen P. March, U.S. Bankruptcy Court, Central District of California. Co-Author, "Ben Lee v. Sherman Block: Who Needs Congress To Amend The Bankruptcy Code When We Have The California Court of Appeals?" Bankr., Ct. Decisions Weekly News and Comment, Oct. 19, 1999, at A5. (Los Angeles, California Office). ***PRACTICE AREAS:*** Bankruptcy; Commercial Litigation. ***Email:*** srich@mayerbrownrowe.com

CHRISTOPHER JENE RICHART, admitted to bar, 2001, Texas. *Education:* University of Texas at Austin (B.A., 1998); University of Texas School of Law (J.D., high honors, 2001). (Houston, Texas Office). ***PRACTICE AREAS:*** Litigation. ***Email:*** cjrichart@mayerbrownrowe.com

LUKE S. RICHBOURG, born May 24, 1968; admitted to bar, 1997, New York. *Education:* Dartmouth College (B.A., cum laude, 1991); Cornell University Law School (J.D., 1995). (New York, N.Y. Office). ***LANGUAGES:*** Portuguese and Spanish. ***PRACTICE AREAS:*** Banking and Finance. ***Email:*** lrichbourg@mayerbrownrowe.com

THOMAS D. RICKS, admitted to bar, 2002, North Carolina. *Education:* Wake Forest University (B.S., 1996; J.D., magna cum laude, 2002). (Charlotte, North Carolina Office). ***PRACTICE AREAS:*** Corporate; Securities. ***Email:*** tdricks@mayerbrownrowe.com

CURTIS DEAN RIPLEY, born Alexandria, Minnesota, October 14, 1975; admitted to bar, 2001, Illinois; U.S. District Court, Northern District of Illinois; 2002, U.S. Court of Appeals, Seventh Circuit. *Education:* St. Cloud State University (B.A., summa cum laude, 1998); University of Minnesota (J.D., magna cum laude, 2001). ***PRACTICE AREAS:*** Litigation. ***Email:*** cripley@mayerbrownrowe.com

SANDRA RODRIGUEZ, admitted to bar, 2003, New York. *Education:* New York University (B.S., 1998); Columbia University (M.S.W., 1999); New York University School of Law (J.D., 2002). (New York, N.Y. Office). ***LANGUAGES:*** Spanish. ***PRACTICE AREAS:*** Litigation. ***Email:*** srodriguez@mayerbrownrowe.com

NICOLAS ROESSLER, born 1973; (admission pending). *Education:* University of Notre Dame and University of Mainz. (Frankfurt/Main, Germany Office). ***PRACTICE AREAS:*** Litigation; Labor. ***Email:*** nroessler@mayerbrownrowe.com

JAMIE L. ROMICK, born Chicago, Illinois, December 8, 1978; admitted to bar, 2004, Illinois. *Education:* Duke University (B.A., cum laude, 2001); Georgetown University Law Center (J.D., 2004). ***PRACTICE AREAS:*** Real Estate. ***Email:*** jlromick@mayerbrownrowe.com

BRAD P. ROSENBERG, born Philadelphia, Pennsylvania, January 8, 1972; admitted to bar, 1999, Virginia and U.S. Court of Appeals, Fourth Circuit; 2000, District of Columbia, U.S. District Courts, Eastern and Western Districts of Virginia; 2003, U.S. Court of Appeals, Seventh Circuit; 2004, U.S. Court of Appeals, Eighth and Eleventh Circuits. *Education:* University of Pennsylvania (B.A., magna cum laude, 1994); University of Virginia (J.D., 1999). Judicial Clerk, Honorable Norman K. Moon, U.S. District Court, Western District of Virginia, 1999-2000. Articles Editor, Virginia Tax Review, 1998-1999. State Party Counsel, Democratic Party of Virginia, 2004—. (Washington, D.C. Office). ***REPORTED CASES:*** Schumacher v. Tyson Fresh Meats, Inc., 221 F.R.D. 605 (D.S.D. 2004); AT&T Communications, Inc. v. Consolidated Rail Corp., 285 F. Supp. 2d 649 (E.D. Pa. 2003). ***PRACTICE AREAS:*** Litigation; Class Actions; Administrative Law. ***Email:*** brosenberg@mayerbrownrowe.com

JORDAN H. ROSENFELD, born New York, September 19, 1979; admitted to bar, 2005, New York. *Education:* University of Michigan (B.A., 2001); Boston University School of Law (J.D., cum laude, 2004). (New York, N.Y. Office). ***PRACTICE AREAS:*** Litigation. ***Email:*** jrosenfeld@mayerbrownrowe.com

EVE B. ROSS, admitted to bar, 1995, Illinois. *Education:* Sweet Briar College (A.B., 1978); DePaul College of Law (J.D., 1995). Director, Prarie Institute for Economic Growth & Freedom, 1993—. ***Email:*** ebaskowitz@mayerbrownrowe.com

ARACELI RUANO PINEDA, admitted to bar, 2003, California. *Education:* Claremont McKenna College (B.A., cum laude, 1992); University of California School of Law (J.D., 2001). (Los Angeles, California Office). ***PRACTICE AREAS:*** Government. ***Email:*** arpineda@mayerbrownrowe.com

GREGORY D. RUBACK, born New York, N.Y., September 8, 1967; admitted to bar, 2000, New York. *Education:* Babson College (B.S., 1989); Fordham University School of Law (J.D., 1999). (New York, N.Y. Office). ***PRACTICE AREAS:*** Finance. ***Email:*** gruback@mayerbrownrowe.com

DR. ISABELLA V. RUDES, born 1968; admitted to bar, 2000. *Education:* University of Giessen; Northwestern University School of Law, Chicago (LL.M.). (Frankfurt/Main, Germany Office). ***LANGUAGES:*** English, Italian and French. ***PRACTICE AREAS:*** Intellectual Property; Information Technology; Unfair Competition. ***Email:*** irudes@mayerbrownrowe.com

JORDAN M. RUDNICK, born Park Ridge, Illinois, July 27, 1967; admitted to bar, 1995, Illinois; 1997, District of Columbia; 1999, New York. *Education:* University of Chicago (B.A., 1990); The John Marshall Law School (J.D., cum laude, 1995). Law Review. Moot Court. Judicial Law Clerk to the Honorable Justice Joseph Gordon, Illinois Appellate Court, 1996-1997. ***Email:*** jrudnick@mayerbrownrowe.com

RICHARD T. RUZICH, born May 8, 1969; admitted to bar, 1996, Illinois and U.S. District Court, Northern District of Illinois; 1997, Indiana and U.S. District Court, Northern District of Indiana; 1998, U.S. Court of Federal Claims; 2001, U.S. Supreme Court; registered to practice before U.S. Patent and Trademark Office. *Education:* Bradley University (B.S.E.E.T., 1991); Southern Illinois University (J.D., cum laude, 1996); The John Marshall Law School (LL.M., with honors, 2002). United States Department of Justice, 1998-2002. ***PRACTICE AREAS:*** Intellectual Property. ***Email:*** rtruzich@mayerbrownrowe.com

(This Listing Continued)

ALLAN C. ("KELLY") RYAN, IV, born Chicago, Illinois, 1973; admitted to bar, 1998, Illinois. *Education:* College of the Holy Cross (B.A., 1995); Northwestern University (J.D., 1998). ***Email:*** akryan@mayerbrownrowe.com

KRISTIN M. RYLKO, (admission pending). *Education:* University of Illinois, Chicago (B.A., with highest distinction, 2002); Chicago-Kent College of Law, Illinois Institute of Technology (J.D., 2005). ***PRACTICE AREAS:*** Banking and Finance. ***Email:*** krylko@mayerbrownrowe.com

DIANE RENAE SABOL, born Cleveland, Ohio, June 28, 1977; admitted to bar, 2002, Illinois. *Education:* University of Notre Dame (B.A., 1999); Vanderbilt University (J.D., 2002). ***Email:*** drsabol@mayerbrownrowe.com

JONATHAN A. SAMBUR, born Bronx, New York, February 21, 1975; admitted to bar, 2001, Massachusetts and New York; 2002, U.S. Tax Court. *Education:* Brandeis University (B.A., 1997); Hofstra University School of Law (J.D., with distinction, 2000); New York University School of Law (LL.M, Taxation, 2001). Note, "Are Consensual Relationship Agreements a Solution to Sexual Harassment in the Workplace?" 17 Hofstra Lab. & Emp. L.J. 165 (co-author Alison Chen) (1999). (Washington, D.C. Office). ***PRACTICE AREAS:*** Tax Transactions. ***Email:*** jsambur@mayerbrownrowe.com

MARCELA D. SANCHEZ, admitted to bar, 2001, Illinois; 2003, U.S. District Court, Northern District of Illinois; 2004, U.S. Court of Appeals, Seventh Circuit. *Education:* New Mexico State University (B.A., 1997); University of Michigan (J.D., cum laude, 2001). ***PRACTICE AREAS:*** Litigation. ***Email:*** mdsanchez@mayerbrownrowe.com

DOUGLAS LAWRENCE SAWYER, born Livingston, New Jersey, February 9, 1973; admitted to bar, 2001, Illinois and U.S. District Court, Northern District of Illinois. *Education:* University of Illinois (B.S., 1996); DePaul College of Law (J.D., 2001). ***PRACTICE AREAS:*** Intellectual Property; Litigation. ***Email:*** dsawyer@mayerbrownrowe.com

ANDREW JOHN SCHAEFER, born Melbourne, Australia, December 16, 1970; admitted to bar, 1997, Illinois and U.S. District Court, Northern District of Illinois. *Education:* University of Chicago (A.B., 1992); Georgetown University (J.D., 1997). Author: The Canberra City-State: A Model for District Self-Government, 30 Urb. Law. 251 (1998); 1995 Canada-Spain Fishing Dispute (The Turbot War), 8 Geo. Int'l Envtl. L. Rev. 437 (1996). ***LANGUAGES:*** Spanish. ***PRACTICE AREAS:*** Litigation. ***Email:*** ajschaefer@mayerbrownrowe.com

SETH A. SCHAEFFER, (admission pending). *Education:* Colgate University (B.A., 1998); Fordham University (J.D., 2004). (New York, N.Y. Office). ***PRACTICE AREAS:*** Litigation. ***Email:*** sschaeffer@mayerbrownrowe.com

EVA SCHALAST, born 1966; admitted to bar, 1998, Germany. *Education:* University of Frankfurt. (Frankfurt/Main, Germany Office). ***LANGUAGES:*** English, French. ***PRACTICE AREAS:*** Unfair Competition; Intellectual Property; Commercial Law. ***Email:*** eschalast@mayerbrownrowe.com

TERRY SCHIFF, born Cornwall, New York, May 4, 1971; admitted to bar, 1997, Illinois; 2002, New York. *Education:* Syracuse University (B.A., 1993); DePaul University College of Law (J.D., 1997). Order of the Coif. (New York, N.Y. Office). ***PRACTICE AREAS:*** Mortgage Backed Securitization. ***Email:*** tschiff@mayerbrownrowe.com

VINCENT PAUL (TRACE) SCHMELTZ III, born Kansas City, Missouri, December 18, 1969; admitted to bar, 1997, Kansas; 1998, Missouri; 2000, Illinois; U.S. District Court, Northern District of Illinois including Trial Bar. *Education:* Principia College (B.A., 1992); University of Kansas School of Law (J.D., 1997). ***REPORTED CASES:*** In re IBP, Inc. Shareholders Litigation, 789 A.2d 14 (Del. Ch. 2001); Affiliated FM Insurance Company v. Neosho Construction Company, 192 F.R.D. 662 (D. Kan. 2000); Affiliated FM Insurance Company v. Neosho Construction Company, 1999 WL 445704 (D. Kan. June 24, 1999). ***PRACTICE AREAS:*** Litigation. ***Email:*** vschmeltz@mayerbrownrowe.com

DR. JENS PETER SCHMIDT, born 1969; admitted to bar, 1998, Germany. *Education:* University of Bonn (First Law Examination, 1993); University of Bonn (Dr. jur., 2000). (Brussels, Belgium Office). ***LANGUAGES:*** German and English. ***PRACTICE AREAS:*** Antitrust; Telecommunications. ***Email:*** jpschmidt@mayerbrownrowe.com

DR. BURKHARD SCHMITT, born 1972; admitted to bar, 2001, Germany (Not admitted in Illinois). *Education:* University of Münster (1991-1993 and 1995-1997)University of Liverpool (1993-1994); Münster, First State Law Examination (1997); University of Nottingham (1997-1998); Münster, doctor's degree (Ph.D. in law, in European competition law, 1999); Düsseldorf, legal clerkship (Referendariat, 1999-2001); Düsseldorf, Second State Law Examination (bar exam, 2001). (Frankfurt/Main, Germany Office). ***LANGUAGES:*** English and French. ***PRACTICE AREAS:*** Corporate; Mergers and Acquisitions; Antitrust. ***Email:*** bschmitt@mayerbrownrowe.com

MAGGIE J. SCHNEIDER, born Villa Park, Illinois, September 7, 1976; admitted to bar, 2001, Illinois; 2002, U.S. District Court, District of Maryland and U.S. Court of Appeals, Fourth and Seventh Circuits. *Education:* University of Illinois (B.A., 1998); University of Michigan (J.D., 2001). ***PRACTICE AREAS:*** Litigation (100%). ***Email:*** mschneider@mayerbrownrowe.com

STEVEN E. SCHRAIBMAN, admitted to bar, 1999, Illinois. *Education:* University of Texas (B.A., 1990); Northwestern University (J.D., 1999). (New York, N.Y. Office). ***PRACTICE AREAS:*** Banking; Finance. ***Email:*** sschraibman@mayerbrownrowe.com

GERO F. SCHREIBER, born 1972; admitted to bar, 2001, Germany. *Education:* University of Rennes/France (Licence en Droit, 1994); University of Saarbrücken/Germany (Erstes Juristisches Staatsexamen, 1997); University of London/U.K. (LL.M., 1998). (Cologne, Germany Office). ***LANGUAGES:*** German, English, French. ***PRACTICE AREAS:*** Mergers and Acquisitions; Corporate; Finance. ***Email:*** gschreiber@mayerbrownrowe.com

BETH ANN SCHULTZ, born Queens, New York, December 2, 1974; admitted to bar, 1999, Connecticut; 2000, New York and U.S. District Court, Southern and Eastern Districts of New York. *Education:* Fairfield University (B.A., magna cum laude, 1996); Boston College Law School (J.D., cum laude, 1999). Phi Beta Kappa; Alpha Sigma Nu; Sigma Tau Delta. (New York, N.Y. Office). ***PRACTICE AREAS:*** Litigation. ***Email:*** baschultz@mayerbrownrowe.com

(This Listing Continued)

MAYER, BROWN, ROWE & MAW LLP, Chicago—Continued

EVAN P. SCHULTZ, born New York, N.Y., October 29, 1969; admitted to bar, 1997, Alaska; 1998, District of Columbia. *Education:* Columbia College, Columbia University (B.A., 1991); University of Virginia, Graduate School of Arts and Sciences (M.A., 1995); University of Virginia School of Law (J.D., 1995). (Washington, D.C. Office). ***PRACTICE AREAS:*** Litigation. ***Email:*** eschultz@mayerbrownrowe.com

PETER SCHULTZ, born Watseka, Illinois, April 19, 1966; admitted to bar, 1994, Illinois. *Education:* University of Illinois (B.A., 1990); Harvard University (J.D., 1994). ***Email:*** pschultz@mayerbrownrowe.com

DIETMER SCHULZ, admitted to bar, 2000, Germany. *Education:* University of Heidelberg, First State Law Examination (1997); Heidelberg, Second State Law Examination (1999); University of Edinburgh (LL.M., 2002). (Frankfurt/Main, Germany Office). ***LANGUAGES:*** English and French. ***PRACTICE AREAS:*** Mergers and Acquisitions. ***Email:*** dschultz@mayerbrownrowe.com

SEAN T. SCOTT, admitted to bar, 2000, Illinois and U.S. District Court, Northern District of Illinois; 2005, U.S. Court of Appeals, Seventh Circuit. *Education:* Washington University (B.A. with College honors, 1997); University of Notre Dame Law School (J.D. magna cum laude, 2000). Articles Editor, Notre Dame Law Review. ***PRACTICE AREAS:*** Bankruptcy Litigation; Bankruptcy Reorganization; Commercial Workouts. ***Email:*** stscott@mayerbrownrowe.com

RUBY G. SEKHON, admitted to bar, 2002, New York and U.S. District Court, Southern and Eastern Districts of New York. *Education:* McGill University, Montreal, Canada (B.A., with honors, 1996; M.A., 1997); Osgoode Hall Law School, Toronto, Canada (LL.B., with honors, 2001). (New York, N.Y. Office). ***Email:*** rsekhon@mayerbrownrowe.com

JOSEPH SELIGA, born Oak Lawn, Illinois, May 1, 1972; admitted to bar, 2000, Illinois; 2001, U.S. Court of Appeals, Sixth Circuit. *Education:* Georgetown University (A.B., magna cum laude, 1994); University of Leicester, England (M.A., with distinction, 1996); Northwestern University (J.D., cum laude, 2000). Phi Beta Kappa; Marshall Scholar. Law Clerk, Hon. Danny J. Boggs, U.S. Court of Appeals, Sixth Circuit, 2000-2001; Author, "Democratic Solutions to Urban Problems," 25 Hamline L. Rev. 1 (2001); "Gautreaux: A Generation Later," 94 N.W. U.L. Rev. 1049 (2000). ***PRACTICE AREAS:*** State Government Law; Local Government Law; Election Law. ***Email:*** jseliga@mayerbrownrowe.com

MICHAEL A. SERAFINI, admitted to bar, 2001, Illinois. *Education:* University of Dayton (B.S., 1996); University of Michigan (J.D., 2001). ***PRACTICE AREAS:*** Corporate; Securities. ***Email:*** mserafini@mayerbrownrowe.com

SUMANA SETTY, admitted to bar, 2002, Illinois. *Education:* University of Michigan (B.A., 1996); Boston University-School of Management (M.B.A., 1999); Loyola University Chicago School of Law (J.D., 2002). (New York, N.Y. Office). ***PRACTICE AREAS:*** Banking and Finance. ***Email:*** ssetty@mayerbrownrowe.com

NATHAN H. SEVILLA, born Mexico, D.F., Mexico; admitted to bar, 2002, New York. *Education:* American University (B.A., magna cum laude, 1998); New York University School of Law (J.D., 2001). (New York, N.Y. Office). ***PRACTICE AREAS:*** Real Estate. ***Email:*** nsevilla@mayerbrownrowe.com

MATTHEW A. SHABAT, born Chicago, Illinois, July 22, 1975; admitted to bar, 2000, Illinois. *Education:* Stanford University (B.A., with honors, 1997); University of Pennsylvania (J.D., 2000). Author: "SEC Regulation of Attorneys Under the Foreign Corrupt Practices Act: Decisions on Efficiency and Their Role in International Anti-bribery Efforts," University of Pennsylvania Journal of International Economic Law, Volume 20, p.4 (1999). ***PRACTICE AREAS:*** Corporate Law; Securities. ***Email:*** mshabat@mayerbrownrowe.com

ANDREW D. SHAFFER, born Detroit, Michigan, April 19, 1972; admitted to bar, 1998, Michigan and U.S. District Court, Eastern District of Michigan; 2001, New York; 2002, U.S. District Court, Eastern and Southern Districts of New York. *Education:* Adrian College (B.A., 1994); University of Dayton School of Law (J.D., 1998); St. John's University School of Law (LL.M., 2000). Author: "Corporate Fiduciary Insolvent: The Fiduciary Relationship Your Corporate Law Professor (Should Have) Warned You About," 8 ABI L. Rev. 479 (2000); "Bankruptcy Update: Ninth Circuit Approves Retroactive Consolidation," 118 Bank. L.J. 778 (2001). (New York, N.Y. Office). ***PRACTICE AREAS:*** Commercial Bankruptcy; Finance; Litigation. ***Email:*** ashaffer@mayerbrownrowe.com

JACOB P. SHEEHAN, (admission pending). *Education:* Macalester College (B.A., 1997); Indiana University School of Law - Bloomington (J.D., cum laude, 2004). ***PRACTICE AREAS:*** Banking Law; Finance. ***Email:*** jsheehan@mayerbrownrowe.com

SHARI A. SHEPARD, born February 23, 1972; admitted to bar, 1999, New York; 2001, California. *Education:* University of Notre Dame (B.B.A., 1994); University of Michigan (J.D., 1997). Associate Editor, Michigan Journal of International Law. (New York, N.Y. Office). ***Email:*** sshepard@mayerbrownrowe.com

JONATHAN A. SHIFFMAN, born Boston, Massachusetts, September 3, 1969; admitted to bar, 2000, New York and U.S. District Court, Southern District of New York. *Education:* University of Chicago (A.B., 1991); New York University (J.D., cum laude, 1997). (New York, N.Y. Office). ***PRACTICE AREAS:*** Labor and Employment; Litigation. ***Email:*** jshiffman@mayerbrownrowe.com

DAVID T. SHIN, admitted to bar, 2003, North Carolina; 2005, Illinois. *Education:* Occidental College (B.A., cum laude, with distinction, 1998, Phi Beta Kappa); Vanderbilt University (J.D., 2003). Member, Vanderbilt Law Review. Articles Editor, Vanderbilt Journal of Transnational Law. Recipient, Raymonde I. Paul Scholarship. ***PRACTICE AREAS:*** Banking; Finance. ***Email:*** dtshin@mayerbrownrowe.com

DANIEL H. SHULMAN, born Park Ridge, Illinois, July 27, 1974; admitted to bar, 1999, Illinois and U.S. District Court, Northern District of Illinois; 2000, U.S. Court of Appeals, Federal Circuit; registered to practice before U.S. Patent and Trademark Office. *Education:* Northwestern University (B.A., Physics, 1996; B.A., Mathematics, 1996; B.A., Integrated Science Program, 1996); Loyola University Chicago (J.D., 1999). Student Articles Editor, Loyola University Chicago Law Journal. ***Email:*** dshulman@mayerbrownrowe.com

(This Listing Continued)

SCOTT JACOB SIEGLER, born Cleveland, Ohio, November 12, 1975; admitted to bar, 2002, New York. *Education:* Miami University (B.A., 1998); Weatherhead School of Management (M.B.A., 2001); Case Western Reserve University School of Law (J.D., cum laude, 2001). Articles Editor, Case Western Reserve Law Review. (New York, N.Y. Office). ***PRACTICE AREAS:*** Corporate Law; Securities. ***Email:*** ssiegler@mayerbrownrowe.com

DR. PATRICK SINEWE, born 1972; admitted to bar, 2001. *Education:* University of Mainz. (Frankfurt/Main, Germany Office). ***LANGUAGES:*** English. ***PRACTICE AREAS:*** Corporate Law; Taxation; Commercial Law. ***Email:*** psinewe@mayerbrownrowe.com

PARITA SINGLA, admitted to bar, 1998, Supreme Court of England and Wales; 2003, Illinois and U.S. District Court, Northern District of Illinois. *Education:* London Guildhall University (B.A., Hons., Law and Psychology, 1995); BPP Law School (Attorney Finals, LPC, 1997); College of Law (Professional Skills Course, November 1997). *Member:* United Kingdom Law Society. ***PRACTICE AREAS:*** Banking; Finance. ***Email:*** psingla@mayerbrownrowe.com

JULIA H. IRICK SKUBIS, (admission pending). *Education:* University of California, Los Angeles (B.A., 2001); University of Michigan Law School (J.D., 2005). ***PRACTICE AREAS:*** Tax Transactions. ***Email:*** jskubis@mayerbrownrowe.com

JOHN A. SLOAT, born Ann Arbor, Michigan, September 26, 1970; admitted to bar, 2002, Illinois. *Education:* Oberlin College (B.A., 1992); University of Michigan (J.D., cum laude, 2001). ***Email:*** jasloat@mayerbrownrowe.com

GILDA M. SMART, born Montreal, Quebec, Canada, June 9, 1971; admitted to bar, 1999, New York. *Education:* Middlebury College (B.A., cum laude, 1992); Osgoode Hall Law School, Canada (LL.B., 1998). (New York, N.Y. Office). ***LANGUAGES:*** French. ***Email:*** gsmart@mayerbrownrowe.com

HUTSON SMELLEY, admitted to bar, 1999, Texas. *Education:* University of Houston (B.S. magna cum laude, 1993); University of Houston Law Center (J.D., 1999); Texas A&M University (M.A., 1994). (Houston, Texas Office). ***PRACTICE AREAS:*** Litigation. ***Email:*** hsmelley@mayerbrownrowe.com

SHANNON SMITH, born Rochester, New York, 1978; (admission pending). *Education:* Boston College (B.S., 2001); Duke University (J.D., 2004). (New York, N.Y. Office). ***PRACTICE AREAS:*** Banking Law; Finance. ***Email:*** shsmith@mayerbrownrowe.com

CLAUDIUS O. SOKENU, born London, England; admitted to bar, 1997, New York; 2002, U.S. District Court, Eastern and Southern Districts of New York; 2003, U.S. Court of Appeals for the Third Circuit; 2004, District of Columbia. *Education:* South Bank University, London (LL.B., Upper Second Class Honors, 1994); London School of Economics and King's College London (LL.M., Corporations, 1995); Georgetown University Law School (LL.M., Securities and Financial Regulations, 1998). Author: "No Longer Kinder and Gentler: SEC Raises Stakes in Settled Enforcement Actions," Washington Legal Foundation, Legal Backgrounder, Vol. 18, No. 51, Dec. 5, 2003; "SEC Expands Foreign Corruption Law Beyond Congressional Intent," 8 Secs. Lit. & Reg. Rep. 5, Aug. 14, 2002, 8 Derivatives Lit. Rep. 19, Aug. 14, 2002, Washington Legal Foundation, Legal Backrounder, Vol 17 No. 28, Jul. 26, 2002; "Web Portals Rouse SEC: Who is a Trader, after all," National Law Journal, Mar. 11, 2002; "SEC Self-Policing Policy Presents Benefits and Pitfalls," 7 Secs. Lit. & Reg. Rep. 17, Feb. 27, 2002, Washington Legal Foundation, Legal Backrounder, Vol 17 No. 6, Jan. 25, 2002; "Avoiding Civil Monetary Penalties in SEC Enforcement Actions," NY Business Law Journal, Spring 2002, New Jersey Law Journal, Dec. 24, 2001. *Member:* The Association of the Bar of the City of New York (Secretary, Corporation Law Committee).*Member:* The Association of the Bar of the City of New York (Secretary, Corporation Law Committee). (New York, N.Y. Office). ***REPORTED CASES:*** Goldstein v. CIBC World Mkts. Corp., 776 N.Y.S. 2d 12 (1st Dep't 2004); PHP Liquidating, LLC v. Robbins, 291 B.R. 592 (D. Del. 2003); In re Initial Public Offering Sec. Litig., 241 F. Supp. 2d 281 (S.D.N.Y. 2003); In re Global Crossing Ltd. Sec. Litig ., 02 Civ. 910 (S.D.N.Y.) (GEL); In the Matter of Baker Hughes Inc., Exch. Act Rel. No. 44784 (Sept. 12, 2001); Securities and Exchange Commission v. Eric L. Mattson and James W. Harris, No. H-01-3106 (S.D. Tex. filed Sept. 11, 2001). ***PRACTICE AREAS:*** State and Federal Securities Litigation; Securities Enforcement Defense; Civil Litigation. ***Email:*** csokenu@mayerbrownrowe.com

JONATHAN SOKOTCH. *Education:* Amherst College (B.A., cum laude, 1998); New York University School of Law (J.D., 2003). (New York, N.Y. Office). ***PRACTICE AREAS:*** Litigation. ***Email:*** jsokotch@mayerbrownrowe.com

MATTHEW C. SOSTRIN, born Park Ridge, Illinois, September 29, 1978; admitted to bar, 2003, Illinois. *Education:* University of Illinois (B.A., 2000); University of Illinois College of Law (J.D., summa cum laude, 2003). Order of the Coif. ***PRACTICE AREAS:*** Environmental Law. ***Email:*** msostrin@mayerbrownrowe.com

TODD ROBERT SOUTHWELL, born Flint, Michigan, October 2, 1971; admitted to bar, 1997, Illinois; 1998, U.S. District Court, Northern District of Illinois. *Education:* University of Dayton (B.S.B.A., 1993); George Washington University Law School (LL.M., 1999); John Marshall Law School (J.D. 1997). Moot Court; Dean's List. Member: Environmental Lawyer Law Review; Corporate Law Review. ***PRACTICE AREAS:*** Corporate Law; Litigation; Environmental Law. ***Email:*** tsouthwell@mayerbrownrowe.com

VERONICA L. SPICER, born 1974; admitted to bar, 2001, Illinois and Kansas. *Education:* University of Missouri at Kansas City (B.A., with distinction and honors, 1997); University of Chicago (J.D., with honors, 2000). ***PRACTICE AREAS:*** Litigation. ***Email:*** vspicer@mayerbrownrowe.com

WILLIAM R. SPRINGER, admitted to bar, 2003, Minnesota and Illinois. *Education:* University of Michigan (B.A., 1995); University of Oxford, Saïd Business School, Keble College (M.B.A., 2001); Northwestern University (J.D., 2002). (New York, N.Y. Office). ***PRACTICE AREAS:*** Banking; Finance. ***Email:*** wspringer@mayerbrownrowe.com

SHANNON L. STEEGE, admitted to bar, 2001, New York. *Education:* Cornell University (B.A., 1997; J.D., 2000). (Houston, Texas Office). ***PRACTICE AREAS:*** Litigation. ***Email:*** ssteege@mayerbrownrowe.com

HEIDI L. STEIBER, born Bakersfield, California, February 20, 1974; admitted to bar, 2003, Massachusetts; 2004, District of Columbia. *Education:* Boston University (B.A., ma-

(This Listing Continued)

gna cum laude, 1995); Harvard Graduate School of Education (Ed.M., 1997); Cornell University Law School (J.D., cum laude, 2002). (Washington, D.C. Office). **Email:** hlsteiber@mayerbrownrowe.com

ANDREW W. STEIGLEDER, born Omaha, Nebraska, November 7, 1973; admitted to bar, 2002, Illinois. *Education:* Loyola University, New Orleans (B.B.A., 1997); Creighton University (J.D., 2002; M.B.A. cum laude, 2002); Northwestern University (LL.M. in Taxation, 2003). **Email:** asteigleder@mayerbrownrowe.com

JEFFREY T. STEINER, born Long Island, New York, May 24, 1977; admitted to bar, 2003, New York. *Education:* Deerfield Academy, 1995; Tufts University (B.A., cum laude, 1999); George Washington University Law School (J.D., with honors, 2002). (New York, N.Y. Office). ***PRACTICE AREAS:*** Real Estate. **Email:** jtsteiner@mayerbrownrowe.com

MICHAEL STEINGO, born October 13, 1972; admitted to bar, 1999, New York (Not admitted in Illinois). *Education:* University of Pennsylvania (B.A., cum laude, 1995); Columbia University School of Law (J.D., 1998). ***PRACTICE AREAS:*** Real Estate. **Email:** msteingo@mayerbrownrowe.com

ADRIAN R. STEWART, born 1970; admitted to bar, 2002, New York. *Education:* University of Arizona (B.A., 1995); University of Houston (M.F.A., 2000); University of Texas School of Law (J.D., 2000). Co-Author: with Basil Markesinis, "Tortious Liability for Negligent Misdiagnosis of Learning Disabilities: A Comparative Study of English and American Law," 36 Texas International Law Journal 427 (2001). (New York, N.Y. Office). ***PRACTICE AREAS:*** Corporate and Securities. **Email:** astewart2@mayerbrownrowe.com

REBECCA K. STEWART, born Florence, Alabama, December 5, 1975; admitted to bar, 2001, Texas. *Education:* University of Texas (B.A., 1998); Harvard Law School (J.D., 2001). (Houston, Texas Office). **Email:** rstewart@mayerbrownrowe.com

JAIME LYNN STILSON, (admission pending). *Education:* University of Michigan (B.A., 2000); University of Virginia School of Law (J.D., 2005). ***PRACTICE AREAS:*** Litigation. **Email:** jstilson@mayerbrownrowe.com

DANIEL K. STORINO, admitted to bar, 2004, Illinois. *Education:* University of Notre Dame (B.A., summa cum laude, 2001); University of Notre Dame Law School (J.D., magna cum laude, 2004). ***PRACTICE AREAS:*** Litigation. **Email:** dstorino@mayerbrownrowe.com

MARY M. STREETT, born Russellville, Arkansas, 1969; admitted to bar, 1998, Arkansas, 2000, New York; 2002, Illinois. *Education:* University of Tulsa (B.S.B.A., 1991); Georgetown University Law Center (1995-1996); University of Arkansas (J.D., 1996). Special Assistant, International Trade Administration, U.S. Department of Commerce, 1993-1994; Agency Representative, NAFTA Office, The White House, 1993-1994; Special Counsel, U.S. Department of Commerce, 1998-2000; Deputy General Counsel, U.S. Department of Commerce 2000-2001. ***PRACTICE AREAS:*** Litigation; Government. **Email:** mstreett@mayerbrownrowe.com

SARAH E. STREICKER, admitted to bar, 2004, Illinois. *Education:* University of Michigan (B.A., highest distinction, 2001); Harvard Law School (J.D., 2005). ***PRACTICE AREAS:*** Litigation. **Email:** sstreiker@mayerbrownrowe.com

MS. REIKO E. SUBER, admitted to bar, 2003, Illinois. *Education:* Hampton University (B.A., cum laude, 2000); Howard University (J.D., 2003). ***PRACTICE AREAS:*** Bankruptcy; Loan Workouts; Bankruptcy Reorganization. **Email:** resuber@mayerbrownrowe.com

KENNETH SUH, born St. Croix, U.S. Virgin Islands, 1966; admitted to bar, 1998, New York. *Education:* Columbia University (A.B., 1989); Fordham University (J.D., 1994). (New York, N.Y. Office). ***LANGUAGES:*** Spanish. **Email:** ksuh@mayerbrownrowe.com

CARL J. SUMMERS, admitted to bar, 2002, New York. *Education:* Illinois Wesleyan University (B.A., summa cum laude, 1996); University of Michigan (M.A., 1999); Yale Law School (J.D., 2001). Author: "Defeating Class Certification in Single-Building / Multiple-Occupant Mold Exposure Cases," Mealey's Litig. Rep.: Class Actions, July 17, 2003, at 36; Book Review, "Distorting Reason," 11 Yale J.L. & Human. 529 (2000). Co-Author: "Jurisdiction and Choice of Law in E-Commerce" (book chapter), in E-Commerce: Financial Products and Services (Law Journal Press, 2002); "Reconsidering Epistemology and Ontology in Status Identity Discourse," 17 Harv. Blackletter L.J. 113 (2001). (Washington, D.C. Office). ***PRACTICE AREAS:*** Appellate Practice; Litigation; Airline Regulation. **Email:** csummers@mayerbrownrowe.com

JOSEPH RONALD SUSTER, born Cleveland, Ohio, October 5, 1976; admitted to bar, 2001, Illinois. *Education:* John Carroll University (B.S.B.A., 1998); The Ohio State University (J.D., 2001). Order of the Coif. Certified Public Accountant, 2001. ***PRACTICE AREAS:*** Finance. **Email:** jsuster@mayerbrownrowe.com

MO TAHERZADEH, admitted to bar, 2000, Texas. *Education:* University of Texas at Dallas (B.A., cum laude, 1997); University of Houston (J.D., cum laude, 2000). Co-Author: "Proposed Rule 8a, Referral Fees: An Evolutionary Process," 66 Tex. Bar J. 982 (2003); Texas Legal Malpractice Update 2004, Advanced Civil Trial CLE. (Houston, Texas Office). ***PRACTICE AREAS:*** Litigation; Appellate Practice. **Email:** tmaherzadeh@mayerbrownrowe.com

SAGI TAMIR, admitted to bar, 1998, Israel. *Education:* Tel Aviv University, Israel (LL.B., 1997); New York University (LL.M. in Corporations Law, 2004). (New York, N.Y. Office). ***PRACTICE AREAS:*** Banking and Finance. **Email:** stamir@mayerbrownrowe.com

JAMES ALEXANDER TANAKA, born Lima, Peru, 1974; admitted to bar, 2003, New York. *Education:* Columbia College of Columbia University (B.A., 1996); The University of Chicago (M.A., 1999); Northwestern University School of Law (J.D., 2002). (New York, N.Y. Office). ***LANGUAGES:*** Spanish, Portuguese. ***PRACTICE AREAS:*** Corporate; Securities; International Finance. **Email:** jtanaka@mayerbrownrowe.com

KAREN H. TANG, admitted to bar, 1996, California. *Education:* University of California at Berkeley (B.S., 1992); University of Southern California Law Center (J.D., 1996). (Los Angeles, California Office). ***PRACTICE AREAS:*** Corporate Law; Securities.

(This Listing Continued)

ASHLEY E. TATMAN, admitted to bar, 2005, Indiana (Not admitted in Illinois). *Education:* Indiana University (B.A., with highest distinction, 2001); Indiana University School of Law (J.D., magna cum laude, 2004). ***PRACTICE AREAS:*** Corporate and Securities. **Email:** atatman@mayerbrownrowe.com

ANDREW E. TAUBER, born 1962; admitted to bar, 2000, New York. *Education:* Wesleyan University (B.A., 1984); Massachusetts Institute of Technology (S.M., 1992; Ph.D., 1997); Yale University Law School (J.D., 1999). (Washington, D.C. Office). ***LANGUAGES:*** German. ***PRACTICE AREAS:*** Litigation. **Email:** atauber@mayerbrownrowe.com

DANIEL L. TEDRICK, born Atlanta, Georgia, July 15, 1975; admitted to bar, 2000, North Carolina. *Education:* Davidson College (B.A., 1997); Wake Forest University (J.D., 2000). Member, Editorial Staff, Wake Forest Law Review, 1999-2000. (Charlotte, North Carolina Office). ***PRACTICE AREAS:*** Litigation. **Email:** dltedrick@mayerbrownrowe.com

HUGO A. TESTÉ, (admission pending). *Education:* University of Texas at Austin (B.S., 2000; B.A., with highest honors, 2000; J.D., 2004). (Houston, Texas Office). ***PRACTICE AREAS:*** Litigation. **Email:** hteste@mayerbrownrowe.com

AMY G. THOMPSON, born Terre Haute, Indiana, February 10, 1973; admitted to bar, 2000, New York. *Education:* Indiana University (B.A., 1994; J.D., 1999). Phi Beta Kappa. Editor-in-Chief, Indiana Journal of Global Legal Studies, 1998-1999. (New York, N.Y. Office). ***PRACTICE AREAS:*** Corporate Law; Finance.

MARGARET J. THOMPSON ANDERSON, admitted to bar, 2002, Illinois; 2005, North Carolina. *Education:* Duke University (B.A., magna cum laude, 1999); Vanderbilt University Law School (J.D., 2002). (Charlotte, North Carolina Office). ***LANGUAGES:*** Spanish, Italian. ***PRACTICE AREAS:*** Banking and Finance. **Email:** mjthompson@mayerbrownrowe.com

TARA E. THOMPSON, admitted to bar, 2003, Illinois and U.S. District Court, Northern District of Illinois. *Education:* University of Utah (B.A., cum laude, 2000); University of Chicago (J.D., 2003). ***LANGUAGES:*** Spanish. ***PRACTICE AREAS:*** Litigation.

HEATHER O'FARRELL TOWNSEND, born New Jersey, January 1, 1971; admitted to bar, 1998, Illinois; 1999, U.S. District Court, Northern District of Illinois. *Education:* Columbia University (A.B., 1993); University of Chicago (J.D., 1998). **Email:** htownsend@mayerbrownrowe.com

BRIAN KELLY TRACHTENBERG, born Lakewood, New Jersey, 1973; admitted to bar, 2002, Texas. *Education:* University of Massachusetts-Boston (B.A., Philosophy & Sociology, summa cum laude, 1998); University of Chicago Law School (J.D., 2002). (Houston, Texas Office). ***PRACTICE AREAS:*** Commercial Litigation; Commercial and International Arbitration. **Email:** BrianT@mayerbrownrowe.com

BRIAN P. TRAUMAN, admitted to bar, 1999, Florida; 2000, U.S. Tax Court; 2002, District of Columbia. *Education:* University of Florida (B.S.B.A., 1995; J.D., 1999); New York University (LL.M., 2000); Georgetown University Law Center (International Tax Classes, 2002-2003). Law Clerk to the Hon. L. Paige Marvel, U.S. Tax Court, 2000-2002. Co-Author: "The IRS's Proposed Cost-Sharing Regulations—Same Position, Different Venue," Tax Planning International, Bureau of National Affairs, 2002; "United States," The International Guide to Advance Rulings, International Bureau of Fiscal Documentation, 2002, 2003. Author: "2002 Tax Tips," The Young Lawyer, American Bar Association, 2003; "Home Office Deduction," The Young Lawyer, American Bar Association, 2003. *Member:* American Bar Association (John S. Nolan Fellowship, 2004-2005; Chair, 2003-2004 and Liaison to Tax Section, 2004—; Tax Law Committee, Young Lawyers Division; Vice-Chair, 2004—and Chair of VITA Subcommittee, 2003—; Tax Section Pro Bono Committee; Secretary, 2002-2004; Transfer Pricing Committee). (New York, N.Y. Office). ***PRACTICE AREAS:*** Federal Tax Controversies; Transfer Pricing; Tax Legislation. **Email:** bptrauman@mayerbrownrowe.com

CHRISTOPHER N. TRAVERS, born London, England, February 26, 1969; admitted to bar, 1998, New York. *Education:* Hamilton College (B.A., 1991); University of Virginia School of Law (J.D., 1997). (New York, N.Y. Office). **Email:** ctravers@mayerbrownrowe.com

AMIT K. TREHAN, admitted to bar, 2004, New York (Not admitted in Illinois). *Education:* Brown University (A.B., 2000); University of Michigan Law School (J.D., 2003). ***PRACTICE AREAS:*** Bankruptcy; Workout; Reorganization.

JOHN-DAVID TREUMANN, born Chicago, Illinois; (admission pending). *Education:* Brandeis University (B.A., 1992); Loyola University Chicago School of Law (J.D., cum laude, 2004). ***LANGUAGES:*** German. ***PRACTICE AREAS:*** Finance. **Email:** jdtreumann@mayerbrownrowe.com

BENJAMIN C. TSCHANN, admitted to bar, 2004, California. *Education:* Creighton University (B.A., magna cum laude, 1999); University of Notre Dame (J.D., 2004). (Los Angeles, California Office). ***PRACTICE AREAS:*** Real Estate. **Email:** btschann@mayerbrownrowe.com

LORRAINE M. TYSON, admitted to bar, 1999, Illinois. *Education:* Northwestern University (B.A.); University of Illinois College of Law (J.D., 1999). **Email:** ltyson@mayerbrownrowe.com

ISABELLE VAN SAMBECK, born August 21, 1971; admitted to bar, 2001, Germany. *Education:* University of Münster, University of Bonn, University of Cologne (First State Examination of Law, 1997); University of Edinburgh (LL.M., 1998). (Cologne, Germany Office). ***LANGUAGES:*** German and English. ***PRACTICE AREAS:*** Mergers and Acquisitions; Corporate Law; Employment Law. **Email:** ivsambeck@mayerbrownrowe.com

CARLOS A. VAZQUEZ, admitted to bar, 2004, Illinois. *Education:* University of Illinois at Urbana-Champaign (B.A., cum laude, 1999); Stanford University Law School (J.D., 2004). ***PRACTICE AREAS:*** Banking and Finance. **Email:** cvazquez@mayerbrownrowe.com

ELEFTERIS VELESIOTIS, born San Antonio, Texas, March 15, 1973; admitted to bar, 2000, Texas. *Education:* Yale College (B.A., 1995); University of Michigan Law School (J.D., 2000). (Houston, Texas Office). ***PRACTICE AREAS:*** Corporate. **Email:** evelesiotis@mayerbrownrowe.com

(This Listing Continued)

MAYER, BROWN, ROWE & MAW LLP, Chicago—Continued

NEERAJ VERMA, born Plainfield, New Jersey, January 17, 1975; admitted to bar, 2000, Texas; 2001, District of Columbia and U.S. District Court, Southern District of Texas. *Education:* George Washington University (B.A., 1997); University of Michigan Law School (J.D., 2000). (Houston, Texas Office). ***PRACTICE AREAS:*** Litigation. ***Email:*** nverma@mayerbrownrowe.com

DANI L. VOGT, admitted to bar, 1999, California. *Education:* University of California (B.A., 1993); Texas A&M University (M.A., 1995); University of California School of Law, Los Angeles (J.D., 1999). (Los Angeles, California Office). ***PRACTICE AREAS:*** Real Estate. ***Email:*** dlvogt@mayerbrownrowe.com

HEINRICH VON BÜNAU, born 1970; admitted to bar, 2000. *Education:* Universities of Heidelberg and Dresden. (Frankfurt/Main, Germany Office). ***LANGUAGES:*** German and English. ***PRACTICE AREAS:*** Corporate; Corporate Restructuring; Mergers and Acquisitions. ***Email:*** hvbuenau@mayerbrownrowe.com

GARY K. WACHTEL, born New York, N.Y., May 26, 1973; admitted to bar, 2003, Illinois. *Education:* Muhlenberg College (B.A., 1995); The John Marshall Law School (J.D., 2003). Order of John Marshall. Morrissey Scholar. Managing Editor, The John Marshall Law Review (2002-2003). Author: "Managing Partners Beware: Not all Malpractice Investigation Communications Are Privileged," 18 CBA Record 62, April 2004; "Reciprocal Discipline Meets Due Process," 14 No. 2 The Professional Lawyer 8, Winter 2003. ***PRACTICE AREAS:*** Banking Law; Finance. ***Email:*** gwachtel@mayerbrownrowe.com

JEREMIAH WAGNER, (admission pending). *Education:* University of Minnesota (B.A., 1999); Carlson School of Management (M.B.A., 2004); University of Minnesota Law School (J.D., 2005). ***PRACTICE AREAS:*** Banking Law; Finance. ***Email:*** jwagner2@mayerbrownrowe.com

JONATHAN C. WAGNER, born 1977; admitted to bar, 2002, Illinois. *Education:* University of Illinois (B.A., B.A., 1999); University of Minnesota (J.D., 2002). ***LANGUAGES:*** German. ***PRACTICE AREAS:*** Information Technology; Corporate; Securities. ***Email:*** jcwagner@mayerbrownrowe.com

LISA A. WALGENBACH, admitted to bar, 2004, California (Not admitted in Illinois). *Education:* Purdue University (B.S., 2001); Loyola Law School (J.D., 2004). (Los Angeles, California Office). ***PRACTICE AREAS:*** Litigation. ***Email:*** lwalgenbach@mayerbrownrowe.com

INGO WALLENBORN, admitted to bar, 2000, Germany. *Education:* University of Freiburg, Germany; Temple University, Philadelphia, (LL.M., 2000). (Frankfurt/Main, Germany Office). ***LANGUAGES:*** English. ***PRACTICE AREAS:*** Financial Services. ***Email:*** iwallenborn@mayerbrownrowe.com

MICHAEL O. WARE, born New York, N.Y., October 8, 1965; admitted to bar, 1996, New York; 1997, U.S. Court of Appeals, Second Circuit, U.S. District Court, Southern District of New York and U.S. District Court, Northern District of Texas; 1998, U.S. District Court, Eastern District of New York; 2000, U.S. Court of Appeals, Eighth Circuit and U.S. District Court for the District of Columbia; 2001, U.S. Court of Appeals, Sixth and District of Columbia Circuits; 2003, U.S. Court of Appeals, Seventh Circuit; 2004, U.S. Court of Appeals, Third Circuit. *Education:* Yale University (B.A., 1990); Fordham University (J.D., 1995). (New York, N.Y. Office). ***PRACTICE AREAS:*** International and Commercial Litigation; Antitrust; Securities and Derivatives Litigation. ***Email:*** mware@mayerbrownrowe.com

BONNIE SARAH WEINSTEIN, admitted to bar, 1998, California; 2005, New York. *Education:* Bryn Mawr College (B.A., cum laude, 1993); Hastings College of the Law, University of California (J.D., magna cum laude, 1998). (Palo Alto, California Office). ***PRACTICE AREAS:*** Litigation. ***Email:*** sweinstein@mayerbrownrowe.com

LYMAN C. WELCH, admitted to bar, 1993, Illinois; 2000, California. *Education:* Colgate University (A.B., 1990); Northwestern University (J.D., 1993). ***Email:*** lwelch@mayerbrownrowe.com

ROBERTA M. WERTMAN, (admission pending). *Education:* Bryn Mawr College (B.A., 1999); New York University School of Law (J.D., 2005). ***PRACTICE AREAS:*** Environmental Law. ***Email:*** rwertman@mayerbrownrowe.com

REB D. WHEELER, born Omaha, Nebraska; admitted to bar, 2000, New York. *Education:* Stanford University (B.A., with honors, 1996); George Washington University (J.D., 1999). Articles Editor, George Washington Law Review. (New York, N.Y. Office). ***Email:*** rwheeler@mayerbrownrowe.com

SAMANTHA B. WHITEHOUSE, born Southfield, Michigan, December 15, 1972; admitted to bar, 1998, Illinois; 2000, District of Columbia. *Education:* University of Michigan (B.A., 1994); Georgetown University Law Center (J.D., 1998). ***LANGUAGES:*** German, French. ***PRACTICE AREAS:*** Mergers and Acquisitions; Securities; Corporate Law. ***Email:*** swhitehouse@mayerbrownrowe.com

DANIEL P. WHITMORE, born Los Angeles, California, June 23, 1955; admitted to bar, 1996, Illinois. *Education:* University of Redlands (B.A., 1977), Phi Beta Kappa; University of Chicago (Ph.D., 1984); DePaul University (J.D., 1996). ***Email:*** dwhitmore@mayerbrownrowe.com

DR. MARCO WILHELM, born 1970; admitted to bar, 2002. *Education:* Universities of Bochum (VWA), Düsseldorf and Frankfurt/Main. (Frankfurt/Main, Germany Office). ***LANGUAGES:*** English. ***PRACTICE AREAS:*** Corporate Law; Mergers and Acquisitions. ***Email:*** mwilhelm@mayerbrownrowe.com

BRENT E. WILLIAMS, admitted to bar, 2003, Illinois. *Education:* University of Dayton (B.S., magna cum laude, 2000); The Ohio State University (J.D., 2003). ***PRACTICE AREAS:*** Corporate Law; Securities. ***Email:*** bewilliams@mayerbrownrowe.com

NICK S. WILLIAMS, born Maisons-Laffitte, France; admitted to bar, 1999, New York and U.S. District Court, Southern District of New York; 2000, U.S. District Court, Eastern District of New York; 2002, District of Columbia and U.S. Court of Federal Claims. *Education:* George Mason University (B.A., with highest distinction, 1994); University of Virginia School of Law (J.D., 1998). Member, Articles Review Board, Virginia Journal of International Law. (New York, N.Y. Office). ***PRACTICE AREAS:*** Commercial Litigation; Securities Litigation. ***Email:*** nickwilliams@mayerbrownrowe.com

MAYA Y. WILSON, born Pasadena, California, May 24, 1974; admitted to bar, 2001, New York. *Education:* Vassar College (A.B., 1996); Howard University (J.D., cum laude, 2000). (Washington, D.C. Office). ***PRACTICE AREAS:*** Financial Regulatory. ***Email:*** mwilson@mayerbrownrowe.com

DEBORAH L. WOLMARK, born Washington, D.C., March 5, 1977; (admission pending). *Education:* Northwestern University (B.A., 1998); Washington College of Law of American University (J.D., 2004). (New York, N.Y. Office). ***PRACTICE AREAS:*** Litigation. ***Email:*** dwolmark@mayerbrownrowe.com

TAMELA M. WOODS, admitted to bar, 2005, Illinois. *Education:* Spelman College (B.A., magna cum laude, 2001); University of Minnesota Law School (J.D., cum laude, 2004). ***PRACTICE AREAS:*** Corporate and Securities. ***Email:*** twoods@mayerbrownrowe.com

CATHERINE F. WONG, born Queens, New York; admitted to bar, 2003, New York. *Education:* UC-Berkeley (B.A., 1996); St. John's University School of Law (J.D., 2000). Executive Publications Editor, St. John's Law Review, 1999-2000. Author, Note, "St. Thomas on Deprogramming: Is it Justifiable?" 39 Catholic Lawyer 81 (1999). (New York, N.Y. Office). ***PRACTICE AREAS:*** Corporate; Securities. ***Email:*** cwong@mayerbrownrowe.com

MITCHELL M. WONG, born August 7, 1972; admitted to bar, 1999, New York; registered to practice before U.S. Patent and Trademark Office. *Education:* Columbia University (B.A., Economics, 1994); Cornell University (J.D., 1998). Managing Editor, Cornell Law Review, 1997-1998. Law Clerk to the Honorable Andrew J. Kleinfeld, U.S. Court of Appeals for the Ninth Circuit, 1998-1999. Author, Note, "The Aesthetic Functionality Doctrine and the Law of Trade Dress Infringement," 83 Cornell L. Rev. 1116 (1998), reprinted in NYIPLA Intellectual Property Law Annual—1998 (1999). U.S. Pegasus Scholar to the United Kingdom, The Honourable Societies of the Inns of Court, 2002. *Member:* NYCLA Inn of Court (Programming Chair, 2004—). (New York, N.Y. Office). ***PRACTICE AREAS:*** Litigation; Intellectual Property. ***Email:*** mwong@mayerbrownrowe.com

JAMIE E. WRAGE, born September 18, 1967; admitted to bar, 1997, California. *Education:* University of South Florida (B.A., 1989); University of Southern California (Master of Public Administration, 1990); Loyola Law School of Los Angeles (J.D., 1996). (Los Angeles, California Office). ***REPORTED CASES:*** Wilson v. Parker, Covert & Chidester (2002), 28 Cal.4th 811; Rivas v. Safety-Kleen Corp. (2002). ***PRACTICE AREAS:*** Litigation. ***Email:*** jwrage@mayerbrownrowe.com

CHARLES QIONG WU, born Shenyang, People's Republic of China, April 9, 1972; admitted to bar, 2003, Illinois. *Education:* University of Illinois at Urbana Champaign (M.U.P., 2000); Univesity of Chicago (J.D., 2003). ***LANGUAGES:*** Chinese. ***PRACTICE AREAS:*** Corporate. ***Email:*** cwu@mayerbrownrowe.com

TIM WYBITUL, admitted to bar, 2002, Germany. *Education:* University of Frankfurt am Main (State Law Examination, 1998). (Frankfurt/Main, Germany Office). ***LANGUAGES:*** English. ***PRACTICE AREAS:*** Employment Law. ***Email:*** twybitul@mayerbrownrowe.com

YASMIN YAVAR, admitted to bar, 2004, Texas. *Education:* University of Texas at Austin (B.J., 2000; B.A., Broadcast Journalism, with high honors, 2000; J.D., 2004). (Houston, Texas Office). ***LANGUAGES:*** Spanish and Portuguese. ***PRACTICE AREAS:*** Litigation. ***Email:*** yyavar@mayerbrownrowe.com

DANIEL I. YEH, admitted to bar, 2003, Pennsylvania. *Education:* University of Illinois (B.A., 1997); Northwestern University School of Law (J.D., 2002). (New York, N.Y. Office). ***PRACTICE AREAS:*** Corporate and Securities. ***Email:*** dyeh@mayerbrownrowe.com

CHAE UK YI, born Seoul, South Korea, October 17, 1969; admitted to bar, 2002, Illinois. *Education:* Tufts University (B.A., 1991); Loyola University of Chicago (J.D., 2002). ***PRACTICE AREAS:*** Banking and Finance (100%). ***Email:*** cuyi@mayerbrownrowe.com

JOSHUA D. YOUNT, born Bloomington, Illinois, October 8, 1972; admitted to bar, 1998, Illinois and U.S. Court of Appeals, Seventh Circuit; 2000, U.S. District Court, Northern District of Illinois; 2002, U.S. Court of Appeals, Sixth Circuit. *Education:* Illinois Wesleyan University (B.A., 1995); University of Chicago (J.D., 1998). Law Clerk to Hon. Ann C. Williams, U.S. Court of Appeals for the Seventh Circuit, 2000; Staff Attorney, U.S. Court of Appeals for the Seventh Circuit, 1998-1999; Executive Editor, U. Chicago Legal F. 1997-1998; Author: "The Rule of Lenity and Environmental Crime," U. Chicago Legal F. 607, 1997. ***PRACTICE AREAS:*** Appellate Practice; Litigation. ***Email:*** jdyount@mayerbrownrowe.com

LORI A. ZAHALKA, (admission pending). *Education:* DePaul University (B.A., summa cum laude, 1999); Harvard Law School (J.D., 2005). ***PRACTICE AREAS:*** Litigation. ***Email:*** lzahalka@mayerbrownrowe.com

KIMBERLY M. ZIELINSKI, born Jacksonville, Florida, May 31, 1975; admitted to bar, 2004, Illinois. *Education:* Lake Forest College (B.A., summa cum laude, 1997); Chicago-Kent College of Law, Illinois Institute of Technology (J.D., with high honors, 2004). Phi Beta Kappa. Valedictorian, Chicago-Kent College of Law, 2004. Executive Articles Editor, Chicago-Kent Law Review, 2003-2004. ***PRACTICE AREAS:*** ERISA; Employee Benefits; Executive Compensation. ***Email:*** kzielinski@mayerbrownrowe.com

CONSULTANT

ARANTZAZU GOLDEROS, admitted to bar, 2002, Spain. *Education:* College of Europe, Bruges (LL.M., 2000); University of Deusto, Bilbao (Law Degree & Diploma on Economics, 1999). (Brussels, Belgium Office). ***LANGUAGES:*** Spanish (native), English and French. ***PRACTICE AREAS:*** EU Antitrust; Spanish Antitrust Law. ***Email:*** agolderos@mayerbrownrowe.com

(This Listing Continued)

MAYER, FRIEDLICH, SPIESS, TIERNEY, BROWN & PLATT

CHICAGO, ILLINOIS

(See Mayer, Brown, Rowe & Maw)

McANDREWS, HELD & MALLOY, LTD.

34TH FLOOR
500 WEST MADISON STREET
CHICAGO, ILLINOIS 60661
Telephone: 312-775-8000
Fax: 312-775-8100
URL: http://www.mhmlaw.com

Federal and State Trial, Appellate and Agency Practice, Dispute Resolution and Licensing Involving Patents, Trademarks and Copyrights, Environmental Law, Trade Association, Warranty, Complex Technology and Antitrust Matters.

FIRM PROFILE: McAndrews, Held & Malloy, Ltd. is one of the nation's preeminent legal resources for intellectual property and technology matters. Our attorneys serve as counsel of choice for companies and institutions ranging from major multinationals and start-ups to world-class colleges and universities.

Our reputation, founded upon an unparalleled record of litigation successes before juries, as well as in bench trials and ADR proceedings, encompasses a full range of legal services. Our attorneys are known for their clear and effective communication skills, expertise and training in engineering and science, their passion for technology law, their command of winning business strategy and their tenacity - both inside and outside of the courtroom.

GEORGE P. McANDREWS, born Clinton, Iowa, July 29, 1935; admitted to bar, 1962, Illinois; U.S. District Court, Northern District of Illinois; U.S. Court of Appeals for the Federal Circuit; U.S. Supreme Court; registered to practice before U.S. Patent and Trademark Office. *Education:* University of Notre Dame (B.S. in M.E., cum laude, 1959; J.D., 1962). Editor-in-Chief, Notre Dame Law Review, 1961-1962. Chairman, National Conference of Law Review Editors, 1961-1962. Law Clerk, U.S. Court of Appeals, 7th Circuit, 1962-1963. Member, Advisory Council, College of Law, University of Notre Dame. Member, International Who's Who of Patent Lawyers. *Member:* Intellectual Property Law Association of Chicago; Abraham Lincoln Marovitz Inn of Court. (Managing Partner). ***Email:*** gmcandrews@mhmlaw.com

JOHN J. HELD, born Lansdale, Pennsylvania, May 3, 1938; admitted to bar, 1965, District of Columbia and Minnesota; 1970, Illinois; U.S. District Court, Northern District of Illinois; U.S. Court of Appeals, Seventh Circuit and Federal Circuit; U.S. Supreme Court; registered to practice before U.S. Patent and Trademark Office. *Education:* Purdue University (B.S.M.E., 1960); Georgetown University (J.D., 1964). Phi Delta Phi. Law Clerk, Hon. Joseph R. Jackson, U.S. District Court, District of Columbia, 1964-1965. *Member:* Chicago and American Bar Associations; The Lawyers Club of Chicago; American Intellectual Property Law Association; Intellectual Property Law Association of Chicago. Fellow, American Bar Association. ***PRACTICE AREAS:*** Patents; Trademarks; Copyrights; Trade Secrets; Unfair Competition. ***Email:*** jheld@mhmlaw.com

TIMOTHY J. MALLOY, born Hattiesburg, Mississippi, April 7, 1944; admitted to bar, 1969, Illinois; U.S. District Court, Northern District of Illinois; U.S. Court of Appeals for the Federal Circuit; U.S. Supreme Court; registered to practice before U.S. Patent and Trademark Office. *Education:* University of Notre Dame (B.S. in E.E., 1966; J.D., 1969). Eta Kappa Nu. Author: "Courtroom Design," Intellectual Property Today, Jan., 2000; "Patent Litigation," Chapter 6; "Organization, Vendor Support and Cost Control" Practising Law Institute, 2002; "Alternative for Righting the Wrong of an Arbitration Panel in IP Disputes" Metropolitan Corporate Counsel, June 2002 Vol. 10, No. 6. Adjunct Professor, University of Notre Dame. Chairperson, National Symposium on Patent Protection for Medical Devices, John Marshall Law School. *Member:* Chicago, Federal Circuit and American Bar Associations; Bar Association of the Seventh Federal Circuit; Intellectual Property Law Association of Chicago; American Intellectual Property Law Association; Barrister of the Patent Law. ***PRACTICE AREAS:*** Intellectual Property; Patents; Trademarks; Copyrights; Unfair Competition; Contracts; Litigation. ***Email:*** tmalloy@mhmlaw.com

WILLIAM M. WESLEY, born Green Bay, Wisconsin, December 19, 1943; admitted to bar, 1971, Illinois; U.S. District Court, Northern District of Illinois; U.S. Court of Appeals, Seventh Circuit and Federal Circuit; U.S. Supreme Court; registered to practice before U.S. Patent and Trademark Office. *Education:* Marquette University (B.E.E., 1966); Loyola University (J.D., cum laude, 1971). Tau Beta Pi; Eta Kappa Nu; Alpha Sigma Nu. Lecturer: American Bar Association; American Intellectual Property Law Association; International Trade Commission and Licensing Executive Society. Listed in: Who's Who Among American Lawyers, Euromoney Guide to the World's Leading Patent Law Experts. Hearing Officer, Illinois Pollution Control Board, 1972—. Member, Licensing Executive Society (L.E.S.). *Member:* Chicago and American Bar Associations; American Intellectual Property Law Association; Federal Circuit Bar Association; Intellectual Property Law Association of Chicago; International Trade Commission Trial Lawyers Association (Member, Executive Committee, 1991—). ***Email:*** bwesley@mhmlaw.com

LAWRENCE M. JARVIS, born Peoria, Illinois, January 17, 1950; admitted to bar, 1977, Illinois; U.S. District Court, Northern District of Illinois; U.S. Court of Appeals, Seventh Circuit and Federal Circuit; U.S. Supreme Court; registered to practice before U.S. Patent and Trademark Office. *Education:* University of Illinois (B.S.E.E., with honors, 1973); Catholic University of America (J.D., 1977). Eta Kappa Nu. Lecturer in Laws, Northwestern University Technological Institute, 1986. ***Email:*** ljarvis@mhmlaw.com

GREGORY J. VOGLER, born Jasper, Indiana, March 15, 1954; admitted to bar, 1984, Illinois, U.S. District Court, Northern District of Illinois; U.S. Court of Appeals, Federal Circuit; U.S. Supreme Court; registered to practice before U.S. Patent and Trademark Office. *Education:* Purdue University (B.S., with distinction in Engineering, 1977); DePaul University (J.D., with honors, 1984). Commissioner of Downers Grove, Illinois, 1991-1995. *Member:* Illinois State and American Bar Associations; American Intellectual Property Law Association; Federal Circuit Bar Association. ***PRACTICE AREAS:*** Patent Litigation. ***Email:*** gvogler@mhmlaw.com

JEAN DUDEK KUELPER, born Chicago, Illinois, December 2, 1954; admitted to bar, 1980, Illinois; U.S. District Court, Northern District of Illinois; U.S. Court of Appeals, Federal Circuit; U.S. Supreme Court; registered to practice before U.S. Patent and Trademark Office. *Education:* University of Notre Dame (B.S.E.E., 1976); Loyola University (J.D., 1980). Tau Beta Pi. Eta Kappa Nu. *Member:* Chicago and American Bar Associations; Intellectual Property Law Association of Chicago. ***PRACTICE AREAS:*** Electrical and Electronic Intellectual Property; Intellectual Property Arbitration; Intellectual Property Infringement; Intellectual Property Licensing; Intellectual Property Litigation; Medical Intellectual Property; Computer and Software Patents; Electrical and Electronic Patents; Patent Infringement; Patent Licensing; Patent Litigation; Patent Prosecution. ***Email:*** jkuelper@mhmlaw.com

HERBERT D. HART III, born Philadelphia, Pennsylvania, July 24, 1952; admitted to bar, 1977, Indiana; 1980, Illinois; registered to practice before U.S. Patent and Trademark Office. *Education:* Indiana University (B.A., Chemistry, 1974; J.D., 1977). Phi Eta Sigma. Law Clerk to: Judge Charles S. White, 1977-1978; Judge George B. Hoffman, Jr., 1978-1980, Court of Appeals of Indiana. Listed in: Euromoney's Guide to the World's Leading Trade Mark Law Practitioners; Euromoney's Guide to the World's Leading Patent Law Experts; Guide to Leading American Attorneys Practicing In Intellectual Property & Computer Law; Best Attorneys Network. Author: "No Prize For Being Second," Modern Drug Discovery, Vol. 5, No. 12 (Dec. 2002); "Demystifying The "I" Word," Intellectual Property Today, Vol. 10, No. 2 (Feb. 2003); "They're Infringing Our Patent! How You Can Help Your Attorney Prove It," BioProcess International, January 2004; "Patent or Parish: How a Delay in Applying Can Seriously Hurt Your Chance of Getting a Patent," Andrews Litigation Reporter, Vol. 11, Issue 4 (June 8, 2004); "Facing the Wolves: How to Develop a Survival Strategy for Intellectual Property," BioExecutive International, January 2005. Speaker: "A Primer On Patent Interferences," American Chemical Society National Meeting, Chicago, August 2001; "You And Your Lawyer," American Chemical Society National Meeting, New Orleans, March 2003. *Member:* Federal Circuit and American (Vice-Chair, Committee 104 - Patent Inter Partes Proceedings) Bar Associations; American Intellectual Property Law Association; Intellectual Property Law Association of Chicago; International Trademark Association (Firm Representative); International Trade Commission Trial Lawyers Association; American Chemical Society; Marques (Firm Representative). ***PRACTICE AREAS:*** Patent Interference Practice; Patent Infringement; Litigation; Licensing; Chemical Patents; Biotechnology Patents; Medical Intellectual Property; Biomedical Technology; Mechanical Patents; Design Patents; Organic Chemistry; Polymers; Trademark Litigation and Prosecution; Trademark Infringement; Trademark Licensing; International Trademarks; Trade Names; Trade Dress; Deceptive Trade Practices; Counterfeiting; Prosecution and Protection; Covenants Not To Compete; Technology Contracts; Trade Secrets. ***Email:*** hhart@mhmlaw.com

ROBERT W. FIESELER, born New York, N.Y., June 1, 1955; admitted to bar, 1984, Illinois, U.S. District Court, Northern District of Illinois and U.S. Court of Appeals for the Federal Circuit; registered to practice before U.S. Patent and Trademark Office. *Education:* Rensselaer Polytechnic Institute (B.S., Biomed. E. with honors, 1977; M.S., Statistics, 1978); Loyola University (J.D., 1984). Tau Beta Pi; Sigma Xi. Member and Lead Articles Editor, Loyola Law Review, 1983-1984. Licensed Professional Engineer, Illinois, 1982. *Member:* Chicago, Federal Circuit and American Bar Associations; American Intellectual Property Law Association; Intellectual Property Law Association of Chicago. ***LANGUAGES:*** Spanish. ***Email:*** rfieseler@mhmlaw.com

THOMAS J. WIMBISCUS, born LaSalle, Illinois, August 15, 1960; admitted to bar, 1985, Illinois; U.S. District Court, Central and Northern Districts of Illinois; U.S. Court of Appeals for the Federal Circuit; U.S. Supreme Court; registered to practice before U.S. Patent and Trademark Office. *Education:* University of Illinois (B.S. in Chemistry with honors, 1982; J.D., magna cum laude, 1985). Delta Theta Phi. Recipient: American Jurisprudence Award. Dean Harno Scholar. *Member:* Federal Circuit Bar Association; American Intellectual Property Law Association; Intellectual Property Law Association of Chicago; Chicago Bar Association; American Bar Association; Licensing Executive Society. ***Email:*** twimbiscus@mhmlaw.com

STEVEN J. HAMPTON, born Chicago, Illinois, December 7, 1951; admitted to bar, 1986, Illinois; U.S. District Court, Northern District of Illinois and U.S. Court of Appeals for the Federal Circuit; U.S. Supreme Court; registered to practice before U.S. Patent and Trademark Office. *Education:* University of Illinois (B.S.M.E., 1974; PhD. ME, 1981); Chicago-Kent College of Law (J.D., 1986). National Institutes of Health Post Doctoral-Fellowship, 1982-1983. *Member:* Illinois State Bar Association (Member, Patent, Trademark and Copyright Law Section); American Society of Mechanical Engineers; Intellectual Property Law Association of Chicago. ***Email:*** shampton@mhmlaw.com

PRISCILLA F. GALLAGHER, born Highland Park, Illinois, February 10, 1958; admitted to bar, 1984, Illinois, U.S. District Court, Northern District of Illinois, U.S. Court of Appeals for the Federal Circuit and U.S. Supreme Court; registered to practice before U.S. Patent and Trademark Office. *Education:* North Central College (B.A., in Chemistry and Biology, magna cum laude, 1980); Loyola University (J.D., 1984). Member, Loyola University Law Review. *Member:* Intellectual Property Law Association of Chicago. ***PRACTICE AREAS:*** Intellectual Property. ***Email:*** pgallagher@mhmlaw.com

STEPHEN F. SHERRY, born New York, N.Y., June 17, 1956; admitted to bar, 1982, Illinois, U.S. District Court, Northern District of Illinois and U.S. Court of Appeals, Seventh and Federal Circuits; U.S. District Court, Northern District of Illinois; registered to practice before U.S. Patent and Trademark Office. *Education:* Virginia Polytechnic Institute and State University (B.S. in Chem., cum laude, 1979); DePaul University (J.D., 1982). Editor, De Paul Law Review, 1981-1982. *Member:* Chicago and American Bar Associations; American Intellectual Property Law Association. ***PRACTICE AREAS:*** Patent Infringement; Intellectual Property Litigation.

PATRICK J. ARNOLD, JR., born Chicago, Illinois, May 2, 1966; admitted to bar, 1990, Illinois and U.S. District Court, Northern District of Illinois; registered to practice

(This Listing Continued)

McANDREWS, HELD & MALLOY, LTD., Chicago—Continued

before U.S. Patent and Trademark Office. *Education:* University of Illinois (B.A., 1987); Loyola University (J.D., 1990). *Member:* Chicago and American Bar Associations; Intellectual Property Law Association of Chicago. ***Email:*** parnold@mhmlaw.com

GEORGE F. WHEELER, born Milwaukee, Wisconsin, September 13, 1953; admitted to bar, 1977, Wisconsin; 1978, Ohio; 1984, Illinois; 1993, U.S. Court of Appeals for the Federal Circuit; 1996, U.S. District Court, Northern District of Illinois; U.S. District Court, Eastern and Western Districts of Wisconsin; registered to practice before U.S. Patent and Trademark Office. *Education:* University of Wisconsin (B.S., in Chemistry, 1974; J.D., 1977); John Marshall Law School (LL.M., Intellectual Property Law, 1991). Recipient, American Jurisprudence Award, Bankruptcy Law. Author: Thesis, "The History and Current Status of the Intent Requirement for Liability Under 35 USC 271(b)," John Marshall Law School, 1991. Publications: "Drafting Chemical Patent Claims in View of Recent Federal Circuit Cases," AIPLA Bulletin, July-August-September 1996, pp. 817-828; "How 18-Month Publication Affects Litigation," Recent Patent Rules— Implementation, Litigation and More," DePaul College of Law Center for Intellectual Property Law, February 15, 2001; "Recent Case Developments," American Chemical Society Annual Meeting, August 27, 2001; "Patent Term Adjustment Provisions of the American Inventors' Protection Act," AIPLA Annual Meeting, October, 2001, and News Source, Vol. III, No. 4, Winter 2002; "Ten Tips and Tricks for Patent Preparation and Prosecution," 2002 Intellectual Property Spring Seminar, Institute of Continuing Legal Education; "Creative Claim Drafting — Claim Drafting Strategies, Specification Preparation, Prosecution Tactics," Seminar on Practical Tips On Intellectual Property Law, American Bar Association Section of Intellectual Property Law, April 2, 2003; "Reissue Applications and Reexaminations," Seminar on Practical Tips On Enforcing and Defending Patents, American Bar Association Section of Intellectual Property Law, September 19, 2003. Frequent speaking engagements with the American Intellectual Property Law Association, American Bar Association, Intellectual Property Owners, Inc., Chicago Bar Association, and other legal organizations. *Member:* American Intellectual Property Law Association (Secretary, 2003-2004; Chair, Chemical Practice Committee, 2001-2003); Chicago Bar Association; Intellectual Property Law Association of Chicago; Intellectual Property Owners (Vice Chair, Patent Law U.S. Committee; Vice Chair, American Inventors Protection Act Committee, 2000-2001). ***PRACTICE AREAS:*** Chemical Patent Prosecution; Chemical Patents; Design Patents; Mechanical Patent Prosecution; Mechanical Patents; Medical Patents; Patent Applications; Patent Infringement; Patent Licensing; Patent Prosecution; Patent Protection; Pharmaceutical Patents. ***Email:*** gwheeler@mhmlaw.com

JANET M. McNICHOLAS, born Chicago, Illinois, September 13, 1951; admitted to bar, 1986, Illinois; U.S. District Court, Northern District of Illinois; registered to practice before U.S. Patent and Trademark Office. *Education:* Rosary College (B.A., 1973); University of Illinois (M.S., 1976; Ph.D., 1980); University of Chicago (J.D., cum laude, 1986). *Member:* American Bar Association; American Intellectual Property Law Association; Intellectual Property Law Association of Chicago; San Francisco Intellectual Property Law Association. ***PRACTICE AREAS:*** Intellectual Property; Biotechnology; Patents. ***Email:*** jmcnicholas@mhmlaw.com

CHRISTOPHER C. WINSLADE, born Pittsburgh, Pennsylvania, December 28, 1965; admitted to bar, 1992, Illinois and U.S. District Court, Northern District of Illinois; U.S. Court of Appeals for the Federal Circuit; U.S. Supreme Court; registered to practice before U.S. Patent and Trademark Office. *Education:* University of Notre Dame (B.S.E.E., B.A. Econ., 1989); The Ohio State University (J.D., 1992). *Member:* Chicago, Illinois State and Federal Bar Associations; American Intellectual Property Law Association. ***Email:*** cwinslade@mhmlaw.com

EDWARD A. MAS, II, born Chicago, Illinois, December 9, 1965; admitted to bar, 1992, Illinois, U.S. District Court, Northern District of Illinois and U.S. Court of Appeals for the Federal Circuit; registered to practice before U.S. Patent and Trademark Office. *Education:* Northwestern University (B.S.M.E., with distinction, 1987); University of Pennsylvania (J.D., cum laude, 1992). Tau Beta Pi; Pi Tau Sigma; Order of the Coif. Member, University of Pennsylvania National Moot Court Team. Recipient: The Wapner Newman & Associates Award for Civil Trial Advocacy; The Gordon A. Block Award for Wills and Future Interests. *Member:* Chicago, Illinois State and American Bar Associations; Chicago and American Intellectual Property Law Associations. ***Email:*** emas@mhmlaw.com

GREGORY C. SCHODDE, born New Brunswick, New Jersey, July 5, 1964; admitted to bar, 1992, Illinois, U.S. District Court, Northern District of Illinois including Trial Bar and U.S. Court of Appeals, Seventh and Federal Circuits; registered to practice before U.S. Patent and Trademark Office. *Education:* University of Pennsylvania (B.S.E.E., B.S., Econ., 1987); Drake University (J.D., with honors, 1992). Order of the Coif; Order of the Barristers. Managing Editor, Drake Law Review. Member, National Moot Court Team, Regional Champions, 1991. *Member:* American Bar Association; Intellectual Property Law Association of Chicago. ***Email:*** gschodde@mhmlaw.com

EDWARD W. REMUS, born Virginia, Minnesota, November 11, 1942; admitted to bar, 1970, Illinois; 1993, Montana; U.S. Supreme Court; U.S. Court of Appeals for the Federal Circuit; U.S. Court of Appeals, 7th Circuit; U.S. District Court, Northern District of Illinois including Trial Bar; registered to practice before U.S. Patent and Trademark Office. *Education:* University of Minnesota (B.Ch.E., 1965); DePaul University (J.D., 1970). Listed in Euromoney Guide to the World's Leading Patent Law Experts; Listed in Who's Who. *Member:* Federal Circuit and American Bar Associations; American Intellectual Property Law Association; American Institute of Chemical Engineers; Intellectual Property Law Association of Chicago. ***PRACTICE AREAS:*** Patent Litigation. ***Email:*** eremus@mhmlaw.com

DONALD J. POCHOPIEN, born Harvey, Illinois, November 28, 1946; admitted to bar, 1988, Illinois; U.S. District Court, Northern District of Illinois; 1989, U.S. Court of Appeals, Federal Circuit; registered to practice before U.S. Patent and Trademark Office. *Education:* Loyola University (B.S., in Chemistry, 1968); Illinois Institute of Technology (Ph.D., in Organic Chemistry, minors in Clin. Chemistry and Env. Chemistry, 1972); Michael Reese Hosp. (Post Doc. Fellowship in Clin. Biochem., 1972-1973); John Marshall Law School (J.D., with high distinction, 1988). Member, 1972— and Chairman, 1978-1979, American Association for Clinical Chemistry. Diplomate, American Board of Clinical Chemistry, 1976. Secretary, Planning Commission, Village of Long Grove, 1993-1994. Clerk, Village of Long Grove, 1994-1995. Trustee, Village of Long Grove, 1995-2002. *Member:* Intellectual Property Law Association of Chicago. ***REPORTED CASES:*** Spalding v. Acushnet, 718 F. Supp. 1023 (D. Mass 1989). ***PRACTICE AREAS:*** Chemical Patent Prosecution; Biochemical Patent Prosecution; Pharmaceutical Patent Prosecution; Biotechnology Patent Prosecution; Licensing; Patent Opinions. ***Email:*** dpochopien@mhmlaw.com

(This Listing Continued)

SHARON A. HWANG, born Naperville, Illinois, April 4, 1968; admitted to bar, 1993, Illinois, U.S. District Court, Northern District of Illinois, U.S. Court of Appeals, Federal Circuit and U.S. Supreme Court; registered to practice before U.S. Patent and Trademark Office. *Education:* University of Illinois (B.S., Elec. Eng., 1989); Boston College (J.D., 1993). Phi Alpha Delta (Marshall, 1992). Managing Editor, UCC Reporter Digest, 1992-1993. *Member:* Chicago, Illinois State, Federal Circuit and American Bar Associations; Asian-American Bar Association; Intellectual Property Law Association of Chicago. ***LANGUAGES:*** Chinese. ***REPORTED CASES:*** Amsted Industries v. ABC-NACO, Inc., 2001 U.S. Dist. LEXIS 13016 (N.D.Ill. 2001); Amsted Industries v. ABC-NACO, Inc., 2001 U.S. Dist. LEXIS 10245 (N.D.Ill. 2001); Stryker Corp. v. Davol Inc., 234 F.3d 1252 (Fed. Cir. 2000); Motorola, Inc. v. InterDigital Technology Corp., 121 F.3d 1461 (Fed. Cir. 1997); Laitram Corp. v. NEC Corp., 62 F.3d 1388 (Fed. Cir. 1995); In re Laitram Machinery, 34 U.S.P.Q.2d 1725 (Fed. Cir. 1995). ***PRACTICE AREAS:*** Patent Litigation; Electrical Patents; Mechanical Patents; Medical Patents; Patent Prosecution; Trademark Litigation; Trademark Prosecution. ***Email:*** shwang@mhmlaw.com

DAVID D. HEADRICK, born Chicago, Illinois, October 16, 1966; admitted to bar, 1993, Illinois, U.S. District Court, Northern District of Illinois and U.S. Court of Appeals, Federal Circuit; registered to practice before U.S. Patent and Trademark Office. *Education:* Marquette University (B.S.E.E., 1989); University of Minnesota (J.D., magna cum laude, 1993). Tau Beta Pi. Editor, University of Minnesota Law Review, 1991-1993. *Member:* Chicago, Illinois State and American Bar Associations; Intellectual Property Law Association of Chicago. ***Email:*** dheadrick@mhmlaw.com

ALEJANDRO MENCHACA, born Chicago, Illinois, August 19, 1963; admitted to bar, 1989, Illinois; registered to practice before U.S. Patent and Trademark Office. *Education:* Massachusetts Institute of Technology (B.S., Ch.E., 1985); Loyola University of Chicago (J.D., 1989). Adjunct Professor: Patent and Trade Secrets Law, International Intellectual Property Law, Unfair Competition, The John Marshall Law School, 1994—; Licensing Intellectual Property, Loyola University of Chicago School of Law, Fall 2001. Assistant U.S. Attorney, Northern District of Illinois, 1996-1997. ***LANGUAGES:*** Spanish. ***Email:*** amenchaca@mhmlaw.com

KIRK A. VANDERLEEST, born Pella, Iowa, December 6, 1964; admitted to bar, 1994, Illinois and U.S. District Court, Northern District of Illinois; registered to practice before the U.S. Patent and Trademark Office. *Education:* Iowa State University (B.S.I.E., 1987); Chicago-Kent College of Law (J.D., with high honors, 1994). Order of the Coif. *Member:* American Bar Association; American Intellectual Property Law Association. ***Email:*** kvanderleest@mhmlaw.com

RICHARD T. McCAULLEY, JR., born West Hartford, Connecticut, September 27, 1965; admitted to bar, 1994, Illinois and U.S. District Court, Northern District of Illinois; 1995, U.S. District Court, Western District of Wisconsin; U.S. Court of Appeals, Federal Circuit; registered to practice before U.S. Patent and Trademark Office. *Education:* Trinity College (B.S., Biomedical Engineering, 1987); University of Notre Dame (J.D., magna cum laude, 1994). ***Email:*** rmccaulley@mhmlaw.com

PETER J. McANDREWS, born Evergreen Park, Illinois, January 3, 1968; admitted to bar, 1995, Illinois; U.S. District Court, Northern District of Illinois and U.S. Court of Appeals for the Federal Circuit; registered to practice before the U.S. Patent and Trademark Office. *Education:* Marquette University (B.S.E.E., 1991); The John Marshall Law School (J.D., cum laude, 1995). Phi Delta Phi. Recipient: Order of John Marshall. ***Email:*** pmcandrews@mhmlaw.com

LELAND G. HANSEN, born Holbrook, Arizona, January 25, 1965; admitted to bar, 1995, Illinois and U.S. District Court, Northern District of Illinois; U.S. District Court, Western District of Michigan. *Education:* Brigham Young University (B.S., with highest university honors, 1992); University of Chicago (J.D., 1995). *Member:* Chicago, Illinois State and American Bar Associations; Intellectual Property Law Association of Chicago; J. Reuben Clark Law Society. ***LANGUAGES:*** Spanish. ***Email:*** lhansen@mhmlaw.com

JAMES M. HAFERTEPE, born Des Plaines, Illinois, November 17, 1969; admitted to bar, 1995, Illinois and U.S. District Court, Northern District of Illinois; 1996, U.S. Court of Appeals, Sixth Circuit; 2001, U.S. Court of Appeals for the Federal Circuit; registered to practice before U.S. Patent and Trademark Office. *Education:* University of Illinois (B.S.A.A.E., with honors, 1992); University of Chicago (J.D., with honors, 1995). Sigma Gamma Tau; Golden Key. Mandel Legal Aid Clinic. *Member:* Chicago, Illinois State and American Bar Associations; Intellectual Property Law Association of Chicago; American Intellectual Property Law Association. ***Email:*** jhafertepe@mhmlaw.com

JONATHAN R. SICK, born Hinsdale, Illinois, September 24, 1969; admitted to bar, 1995, Illinois and U.S. District Court, Northern District of Illinois; 2000, U.S. Court of Appeals for the Federal Circuit; registered to practice before U.S. Patent and Trademark Office. *Education:* University of Illinois (Ch.E., with distinction, 1992); Chicago Kent College of Law (J.D., with high honors, 1995). Notes and Comments Editor, Chicago Kent Law Review. *Member:* Chicago Bar Association. ***Email:*** jsick@mhmlaw.com

ELIGIO C. PIMENTEL, born Exeter, California, 1966; admitted to bar, 1995, Illinois and U.S. District Court, Northern District of Illinois; registered to practice before U.S. Patent and Trademark Office. *Education:* Stanford University (B.S., 1988); University of Minnesota (J.D., cum laude, 1995). *Member:* Chicago and American Bar Associations; Hispanic National Bar Association. ***LANGUAGES:*** Spanish. ***PRACTICE AREAS:*** Intellectual Property; Litigation. ***Email:*** eligio@mhmlaw.com

JAMES P. MURPHY, born October 17, 1965; admitted to bar, 1992, Illinois; 1993, U.S. District Court, Northern District of Illinois; 1995, Minnesota; registered to practice before U.S. Patent and Trademark Office. *Education:* Michigan State University (B.S., Engineering, 1987); DePaul University (J.D., with honors, 1992). Order of the Coif. Member, Editorial Staff, DePaul University Law Review, 1991-1992. Law Clerk to the Honorable

(This Listing Continued)

James H. Alesia, U.S. District Court, Northern District of Illinois, 1992-1994. Co-Author: "Trial of Inequitable Conduct, Laches and Prosecution History Estoppel Issues," Patent Litigation 1992, Vol. 1, p.727. *Member:* Chicago, Illinois State and American Bar Associations. ***PRACTICE AREAS:*** Intellectual Property; Patent Litigation; Trademark Litigation; Copyright Litigation; Patent Procurement; Intellectual Property Counseling; Intellectual Property Transfers; Intellectual Property Due Diligence; Commercial Litigation. ***Email:*** jmurphy@mhmlaw.com

DEAN A. PELLETIER, born Webster, Massachusetts, January 27, 1969; admitted to bar, 1995, Illinois; U.S. District Court, Northern District of Illinois, including Trial Bar; U.S. District Court, Central District of Illinois; U.S. Court of Appeals for the Federal Circuit; registered to practice before U.S. Patent and Trademark Office. *Education:* Northwestern University (B.S., 1991); Washington University (J.D., 1995). *Member:* Chicago, Illinois State and American Bar Associations; American Intellectual Property Law Association; Intellectual Property Owners Association. ***PRACTICE AREAS:*** Intellectual Property; Intellectual Property Litigation; Trademark Litigation; Patent Litigation. ***Email:*** dpelletier@mhmlaw.com

MICHAEL B. HARLIN, born Blue Island, Illinois, September 28, 1968; admitted to bar, 1996, Illinois and U.S. District Court, Northern District of Illinois; registered to practice before U.S. Patent and Trademark Office. *Education:* Yale University (B.S., Chemistry, 1990); Chicago-Kent College of Law (J.D., with high honors, 1996). ***PRACTICE AREAS:*** Chemical Intellectual Property; Intellectual Property Licensing; Pharmaceutical Intellectual Property; Biotechnology Patents; Chemical Patents; Patent Licensing; Patent Prosecution; Pharmaceutical Patents. ***Email:*** mharlin@mhmlaw.com

JAMES R. NUTTALL, born Cleveland, Mississippi, October 19, 1972; admitted to bar, 1997, Illinois and U.S. District Court, Northern District of Illinois; 1999, U.S. Court of Appeals for the Federal Circuit; 2000, U.S. District Court, Central District of Illinois; registered to practice before U.S. Patent and Trademark Office. *Education:* University of Illinois (B.S.I.E., 1994); Loyola University of Chicago (J.D., 1997). ***PRACTICE AREAS:*** Intellectual Property; Litigation. ***Email:*** jnuttall@mhmlaw.com

ROBERT A. SURRETTE, born Boston, Massachusetts, July 10, 1966; admitted to bar, 1997, Illinois. *Education:* University of Massachusetts (B.S.M.E., 1989); Rensselaer Polytechnic Institute (Master of Business Administration, 1992; Master of Science, Mechanical Engineering, 1994); Chicago-Kent College of Law (J.D., with high honors, 1997). ***PRACTICE AREAS:*** Intellectual Property; Litigation. ***Email:*** bsurrette@mhmlaw.com

JOSEPH M. BARICH, born Chicago, Illinois, April 10, 1972; admitted to bar, 1998, Illinois and U.S. District Court, Northern District of Illinois; registered to practice before U.S. Patent and Trademark Office. *Education:* University of Illinois, Urbana-Champaign (B.S.E.E., 1994; M.S.E.E., 1996); Boston College Law School (J.D., 1998). ***PRACTICE AREAS:*** Electrical Intellectual Property; Electronic Intellectual Property; Intellectual Property Licensing; International Intellectual Property; International Licensing; Computer Patents; Design Patents; Electrical Patents; Electronic Patents; Patent Licensing; Patent Prosecution; Patent Protection. ***Email:*** jbarich@mhmlaw.com

SCOTT P. McBRIDE, born Edina, Minnesota, July 10, 1973; admitted to bar, 1998, Illinois; 1999, U.S. Court of Appeals for the Federal Circuit; registered to practice before U.S. Patent and Trademark Office. *Education:* University of Wisconsin-Madison (B.S., Astrophysics, 1995); University of Dayton (J.D., magna cum laude, 1998). ***PRACTICE AREAS:*** Intellectual Property; Litigation; Patent Litigation; Intellectual Property Arbitration; Trademark Prosecution; Patent Prosecution; Mechanical Patents; Electrical Patents. ***Email:*** smcbride@mhmlaw.com

PATRICIA J. McGRATH, born Evergreen Park, Illinois; admitted to bar, 1998, Illinois; and U.S. District Court, Northern District of Illinois and U.S. Court of Appeals for the Federal Circuit; registered to practice before U.S. Patent and Trademark Office. *Education:* St. Xavier College (B.S., Biology); Elmhurst College (B.S., Chemistry, 1983); Chicago-Kent College of Law (J.D., with honors, 1998). ***PRACTICE AREAS:*** Intellectual Property Law; Litigation. ***Email:*** pmcgrath@mhmlaw.com

TROY A. GROETKEN, born Sioux City, Iowa, July 26, 1970; admitted to bar, 1997, Iowa; 2000, Illinois; U.S. District Court, Northern District of Illinois; U.S. District Court, Southern District of Iowa; U.S. Court of Appeals for the Federal Circuit; U.S. Supreme Court; registered to practice before U.S. Patent and Trademark Office. *Education:* Drake University (B.S., Pharmacy, cum laude, 1994; J.D., cum laude, 1997); John Marshall Law School (LL.M., Intellectual Property Law, with honors, 1998). ***PRACTICE AREAS:*** Patents; Trademarks; Copyrights; Intellectual Property Litigation. ***Email:*** tgroetken@mhmlaw.com

GERALD C. WILLIS, JR., born Camden, New Jersey, January 18, 1968; admitted to bar, 1996, Illinois and U.S. District Court, Northern District of Illinois; 2002, U.S. Court of Appeals, Ninth Circuit. *Education:* Illinois State University (B.S., 1991); The John Marshall Law School (J.D., cum laude, 1996). ***PRACTICE AREAS:*** Patent Litigation; Trademark Litigation; Antitrust Litigation. ***Email:*** gwillis@mhmlaw.com

JOHN A. WIBERG, born Wisconsin Rapids, Wisconsin, February 5, 1968; admitted to bar, 1998, Minnesota; 2001, Illinois; registered to practice before U.S. Patent and Trademark Office. *Education:* University of Wisconsin at Milwaukee (B.S.E.E. with honors, 1992); Chicago-Kent College of Law, Illinois Institute of Technology (J.D., 1998). ***PRACTICE AREAS:*** Patent Prosecution; Electrical Patents; Computer Patents; Trademark Law. ***Email:*** jwiberg@mhmlaw.com

WILHELM L. RAO, born St. Louis, Missouri; admitted to bar, 1999, Illinois; U.S. District Court, Northern District of Illinois and U.S. Court of Appeals for the Federal Circuit. *Education:* Washington University (B.S., cum laude, 1995; M.S.E., 1995); Chicago-Kent College of Law, Illinois Institute of Technology (J.D., with honors, 1999). ***PRACTICE AREAS:*** Intellectual Property Litigation; Transactional Practice. ***Email:*** wrao@mhmlaw.com

SANDRA A. FRANTZEN, born Beirut, Lebanon, August 4, 1974; admitted to bar, 1999, Illinois; U.S. District Court, Northern District of Illinois; U.S. Court of Appeals for the Federal Circuit; registered to practice before U.S. Patent and Trademark Office. *Education:* Iowa State University (B.S., Chemistry and Environmental Studies, with highest distinction); University of Chicago (J.D., with honors). ***LANGUAGES:*** Arabic. ***PRACTICE AREAS:*** Intellectual Property. ***Email:*** sfrantzen@mhmlaw.com

RONALD SPUHLER, born Fort Wayne, Indiana, April 6, 1973; admitted to bar, 1999, Illinois. *Education:* Purdue University (B.S., 1995); Chicago-Kent College of Law, Illinois Institute of Technology (J.D., with honors, 1999). ***PRACTICE AREAS:*** Intellectual Property Law. ***Email:*** rspuhler@mhmlaw.com

CHRISTOPHER V. CARANI, born Oak Park, Illinois, September 14, 1973; admitted to bar, 1999, Illinois and U.S. District Court, Northern District of Illinois; 2001, U.S. Court of Appeals for the Federal Circuit; registered to practice before the U.S. Patent and Trademark Office. *Education:* Marquette University (B.S.I.E., 1995); University of Chicago (J.D., 1999). ***LANGUAGES:*** Italian and Spanish. ***PRACTICE AREAS:*** Intellectual Property Litigation; Intellectual Property Licensing; Intellectual Property Prosecution. ***Email:*** ccarani@mhmlaw.com

MIRUT P. DALAL, born Houston, Texas, September 30, 1969; admitted to bar, 1997, Texas; 2003, Illinois; registered to practice before U.S. Patent and Trademark Office. *Education:* University of Texas (B.S., Electrical Engineering, 1991); University of Houston (M.S., Computer Engineering, 1994); University of Texas (J.D., 1997). ***PRACTICE AREAS:*** Intellectual Property. ***Email:*** mpdalal@sbcglobal.net

RONALD A. DICERBO, born Schenectady, New York, April 18, 1968; admitted to bar, 2000, Illinois. *Education:* State University of New York at Buffalo (B.S., 1992); John Marshall Law School (J.D., 1999). ***PRACTICE AREAS:*** Intellectual Property; Antitrust. ***Email:*** rdicerbo@mhmlaw.com

JENNIFER E. LACROIX, born Knoxville, Tennessee; admitted to bar, 2000, Illinois and U.S. District Court, Northern District of Illinois. *Education:* Worcester Polytechnic Institute (B.S., Civil Engineering and Society, Technology & Policy, 1997); Northwestern University School of Law (J.D., 2000). ***PRACTICE AREAS:*** Intellectual Property; Patent Law. ***Email:*** jlacroix@mhmlaw.com

JOSEPH F. HARDING, born Hammond, Indiana, February 5, 1969; admitted to bar, 2000, Illinois, U.S. District Court, Northern District of Illinois and U.S. Court of Appeals for the Federal Circuit; registered to practice before U.S. Patent and Trademark Office. *Education:* Purdue University (B.S.M.E., 1991); University of Michigan (J.D., cum laude, 2000). ***PRACTICE AREAS:*** Intellectual Property; Patent Litigation; Patent Prosecution. ***Email:*** jharding@mhmlaw.com

JOSEPH M. BUTSCHER, born Joliet, Illinois, October 28, 1975; admitted to bar, 2000, Illinois and U.S. District Court, Northern District of Illinois. *Education:* Lewis University (B.S., 1997); University of Notre Dame (J.D., 2000). ***PRACTICE AREAS:*** Intellectual Property. ***Email:*** jbutscher@mhmlaw.com

Sara Bartos
John L. Abramic
Michael J. Fitzpatrick
David Z. Petty
Michael T. Cruz (Not admitted in IL)
Christopher N. George
Matthew A. Anderson
Yufeng Ma
Dennis H. Jaskoviak, Jr.
Deborah A. Laughton
William B. Gont
Dennis P. Hackett
Hopeton Walker
Shawn L. Peterson
Ognyan (Oggie) Beremski
Philip H. Sheridan
Christopher R. Carroll
Christopher M. Scharff
Consuelo G. Erwin
Peter J. Prommer
Merle Elliott
Brian C. Bianco
Paul W. McAndrews (admission pending)
Andrew B. Karp (admission pending)
Laura M. Personick
Jonathan M. Rushman
Jeremy N. Gayed
Christopher J. Buchko
Leonard D. Conapinski
Michael J. Krautner (admission pending)
Adam J. Faier (admission pending)
James H. Williams (admission pending)
Sarah A. Kofflin (admission pending)
Ali H. Shah (admission pending)
Patrick V. Bradley (admission pending)
Christina F. Polyn (admission pending)

OF COUNSEL

S. JACK SAUER, born Chicago, Illinois, December 11, 1934; admitted to bar, 1963, Illinois. *Education:* Northwestern University (B.A., Economics, 1956; J.D., 1963). *Member:* Chicago Bar Association.

(This Listing Continued)

McBREEN & KOPKO

SUITE 2520, 20 NORTH WACKER DRIVE
CHICAGO, ILLINOIS 60606
Telephone: 312-332-6405
Fax: 312-332-2657
Email: counsel@mmklaw.com

Irvine, California Office: 2 Venture Avenue, Suite 240. Telephone: 949-453-8900. Fax: 949-453-8989.

(This Listing Continued)

McBREEN & KOPKO, Chicago—Continued

Philadelphia, Pennsylvania Office: Eight Penn Center, 1628 John F. Kennedy Boulevard, Suite 1400. Telephone: 215-864-2600. Fax: 215-864-2610.

Montvale, New Jersey Office: 110 Summit Avenue. Telephone: 201-476-5400. Fax: 201-573-0574.

Jericho, New York Office: 500 North Broadway. Telephone: 516-364-1095. Fax: 516-364-0612.

General Practice, Corporate, Mergers and Acquisitions, Securities, Commodities, Real Estate, Aviation, General and Commercial Litigation, Appellate Practice, Toxic Torts, Products Liability, Medical Malpractice and Environmental Law.

MEMBERS OF FIRM

FREDERICK H. KOPKO, JR., born Norwich, Connecticut, July 11, 1955; admitted to bar, 1980, Illinois. *Education:* University of Connecticut (B.A., magna cum laude, 1977); University of Notre Dame (J.D., 1980); University of Chicago (M.B.A., with high honors, 1995). Phi Beta Kappa; Beta Gamma Sigma. Staff Member, 1978-1979 and Associate Editor, 1979-1980, Notre Dame Law Review. Author: Comment, Notre Dame Law, 1979; "Leveraged Leasing After ERTA," Commercial Law Journal, February 1982; "Investment Limited Partnerships -- Blue Sky Regulation," ABA National Institute, 1984. Co-author: "Commodity Pools -- The Financial Planner's Vehicle to Commodity Trading," The Financial Planner 63, 1982; "Marketing Issues, Investment Limited Partnerships," ABA National Institute, 1984. Member, Active Panel of Arbitrators, National Futures Association, 1983—. *Member:* Chicago Bar Association (Member, Futures Regulation Law Committee, 1986-1988). ***PRACTICE AREAS:*** Mergers and Acquisitions; Securities; Commodities; Corporate. ***Email:*** fkopko@mmklaw.com

HUGH G. McBREEN, born Chicago, Illinois, April 18, 1955; admitted to bar, 1980, Illinois; 1982, U.S. District Court, Northern and Central Districts of Illinois including Trial Bar; 1995, U.S. Court of Appeals, Seventh Circuit. *Education:* Dartmouth College, Hanover, New Hampshire (A.B., cum laude, distinction in History, 1977); University of Notre Dame (J.D., 1980). *Member:* Illinois State and American Bar Associations. ***PRACTICE AREAS:*** Commercial and General Litigation; Appellate Practice; Aviation; Products Liability. ***Email:*** hmcbreen@mmklaw.com

BRIAN J. HOGAN, born Fort Dodge, Iowa, February 27, 1957; admitted to bar, 1982, Illinois; 1986, U.S. District Court, Northern District of Illinois and U.S. Court of Appeals, Seventh Circuit; 1993, California; 1996, U.S. District Court, Central District of California. *Education:* University of Notre Dame (B.A., summa cum laude, 1979); University of Chicago (J.D., 1982); Northwestern University, Kellogg Graduate School of Management (M.M., 1988). *Member:* State Bar of California; Illinois State Bar Association. (Resident, Irvine, California Office). ***LANGUAGES:*** Spanish, French and Italian. ***PRACTICE AREAS:*** Corporate Law; Commercial Real Estate; Bankruptcy; Employment Litigation.

JAMES RUSSELL STERN, born Evanston, Illinois, August 8, 1956; admitted to bar, 1981, Illinois. *Education:* University of Michigan (B.A., with high honors, high distinction, 1978); Boalt Hall School of Law, University of California at Berkeley (J.D., 1981). Phi Beta Kappa. Certified Public Accountant, Illinois, 1981. *Member:* Chicago Bar Association. ***PRACTICE AREAS:*** Mergers and Acquisitions; Securities; Commodities; Corporate. ***Email:*** jstern@mmklaw.com

THOMAS J. BRADLEY, born Springfield, Pennsylvania, July 29, 1954; admitted to bar, 1980, Pennsylvania; 1986, New Jersey. *Education:* St. Joseph's College (B.A., 1976); University of Notre Dame Law School (J.D., 1980). Member, Journal of Legislation, 1979-1980. Author: "The All Volunteer Army, Conscription and Other Alternatives," Note, 7 Journal of Legislation 125, 1980; "Medical-Legal Issues in HIV Treatment: Part 1," The AIDS Reader, April, 2001; "Medical-Legal Issues in HIV Treatment: Part 2," The AIDS Reader, September 2001. Judge Pro Tem, Philadelphia Court of Common Pleas. *Member:* Pennsylvania Bar Association; Defense Research Institute. [Capt., JAGC, U.S. Army, 1981-1984]. (Resident, Philadelphia, Pennsylvania Office). ***PRACTICE AREAS:*** Products Liability; Medical Malpractice; Employment Law. ***Email:*** tjbradley@mcbreenkopko.com

LEONARD D. KIRSCH, born Brooklyn, New York, July 10, 1955; admitted to bar, 1981, New York; 1983, U.S. District Court, Eastern and Southern Districts of New York. *Education:* Queens College (B.A., 1976); State University of New York at Buffalo (J.D., 1980); New York University School of Law (LL.M., 1985). Author: Ground Handling International Magazine Legal Column and Ground Handling Monthly Newsletter. Presenter: Cargo Security, Amsterdam, 2005; War Risk Insurance Needs, U.S. Equitime Organizational Meeting, 2002. Speaker: Airport Relations from U.S. Perspective, Prague, 2003; U.S. and European Antitrust Policy, Rome, 2002; Doing Business at New York Airports, 2001. Seminar Speaker: Airport Managers Professional Development Program. Panel Chairperson and Speaker: Airports International Executive Environmental Conference (1993). Assistant General Counsel, Hudson General Corporation, 1987-1995. (Resident, Jericho, N.Y. Office). ***PRACTICE AREAS:*** Aviation Law; Commercial Law; Litigation. ***Email:*** lkirsch@mklawnyc.com

RICHARD A. AUERBACH, born Queens, New York, January 16, 1954; admitted to bar, 1981, New York; 1983, U.S. District Court, Southern and Eastern Districts of New York. *Education:* Queens College of the City of New York (B.A., magna cum laude, 1977); DePaul University Law School (J.D., 1980). Seminar Presenter, Non-Profit Round Table 2005, "Big Ideas for Small Businesses," La Guardia Community College, 1984-1995. Member, Vice President Joining Everyone to Share (JETS), Semantics. (Resident, Jericho, N.Y. Office). ***PRACTICE AREAS:*** Commercial Litigation; Trusts and Estates; Corporate; Non-profit Law; Matrimonial; Real Estate. ***Email:*** rauerbach@mklawnyc.com

MARY ELIZABETH KOPKO, born Moline, Illinois, October 29, 1958; admitted to bar, 1983, Illinois; 1985, U.S. Court of Appeals, Seventh Circuit; 1992, U.S. Supreme Court. *Education:* St. Mary's College, Notre Dame (B.A., with high honors, 1980); Loyola University of Chicago (J.D., 1983). Staff Member, Loyola Law Journal, 1982-1983. *Member:* Chicago Bar Association. ***PRACTICE AREAS:*** Social Security; Employment Law; Criminal Appeals.

ROBERT S. MORAN, JR., born Brooklyn, New York, September 6, 1953; admitted to bar, 1979, New York and U.S. District Court, Southern and Eastern Districts of New York; 1982, New Jersey and U.S. District Court, District of New Jersey. *Education:* St. John's University (B.A., summa cum laude, 1975); St. John's University School of Law (J.D., 1978). Associate Editor, Federal Casenote Review, St. John's University School of Law, 1977-1978. *Member:* New York County Lawyer's Association. (Resident, Montvale, New Jersey Office). ***PRACTICE AREAS:*** Corporate; Commercial Litigation; General Practice.

PAUL J. McBREEN, born Chicago, Illinois, January 13, 1960; admitted to bar, 1986, Illinois. *Education:* University of Denver (B.A., 1983); DePaul University College of Law, Chicago (J.D., 1986). Recipient, Hornbeck Scholar Award. *Member:* Chicago and American Bar Associations. ***PRACTICE AREAS:*** Commercial and General Litigation; Appellate Practice; Aviation; Products Liability. ***Email:*** pmcbreen@mmklaw.com

ANJALI DAYAL, born Montreal, Canada, April 1, 1965; admitted to bar, 1992, Illinois; U.S. District Court, Northern District of Illinois. *Education:* University of Chicago (B.A., 1988); Syracuse University College of Law (J.D., 1992). ***LANGUAGES:*** Hindi and French. ***PRACTICE AREAS:*** Medical Malpractice Defense. ***Email:*** adayal@mmklaw.com

HELENE GORMAN BRADLEY, born Philadelphia, Pennsylvania, February 16, 1957; admitted to bar, 1982, Pennsylvania; 1983, U.S. Court of Appeals, Eleventh Circuit. *Education:* University of Notre Dame (B.A., cum laude, 1979; J.D., summa cum laude, 1982). Associate Editor, Notre Dame Law Review, 1981-1982. *Member:* Philadelphia, Pennsylvania and American (Member, Taxation Section) Bar Associations. (Resident, Philadelphia, Pennsylvania Office). ***PRACTICE AREAS:*** Tax Law.

MICHELE TATE McBREEN, born Detroit, Michigan, November 23, 1954; admitted to bar, 1981, Illinois; 1983, U.S. District Court, Northern District of Illinois; 1984, U.S. Court of Appeals, Fourth Circuit. *Education:* University of Notre Dame (A.B., cum laude, 1976; J.D., 1980). *Member:* Chicago Bar Associations. ***PRACTICE AREAS:*** Employment Law; ERISA; Corporate Law; Appellate Practice.

ANNIE K. STROBL, born Chicago, Illinois, May 10, 1960; admitted to bar, 1986, Illinois. *Education:* Loyola University of Chicago (B.S., cum laude, 1982); Illinois Institute of Technology, Chicago Kent College of Law (J.D., 1985). *Member:* Chicago Bar Association. ***PRACTICE AREAS:*** Commercial and General Litigation; Appellate Practice. ***Email:*** astrobl@mmklaw.com

YURI F. PETOUKHOV, born Irkutsk, Russia, April 12, 1968; (admission pending). *Education:* Tomsk State University (B.A. with high honors, 1994). Author: Dissertation, "Status and the System of Electoral Commissions in Russia"; "Classification of Electoral Commissions in Russia," Novosibirsk, Science, 1997; "Some Aspects of the Legal Status of Electoral Associations as Subjects of Electorial Process," Barnaul, 1997. Senior Lecturer, "Status and the System of Electoral Commissions in Russia." Member and Senior Lecturer, Tomsk State University, Department of Law. ***LANGUAGES:*** Russian. ***PRACTICE AREAS:*** International Law; Corporate Law; Bankruptcy; Commercial Law.

DON L. HOCHLER, born New York, N.Y., May 25, 1957; admitted to bar, 1982, New York and U.S. District Court, Southern and Eastern Districts of New York (Not admitted in Illinois). *Education:* Queens College (B.A., cum laude, 1978); St. John's University School of Law (J.D., 1981). Phi Alpha Delta. Village Prosecutor, Village of Roslyn, 1987—. *Member:* Nassau County Bar Association. ***PRACTICE AREAS:*** Commercial Litigation; Health Care; Real Estate.

NORMAN N. BLUTH, born Queens, New York, August 18, 1966; admitted to bar, 1993, New York; 2002, U.S. District Court, Eastern and Southern Districts of New York. *Education:* Hamilton College (B.A., 1988); Jacob D. Fuchsberg Law Center at Touro College (J.D., 1992). Member, Moot Court Board. *Member:* American Bar Association; Wings Club of New York and JFK Airport Rotary Club (President). (Resident, Jericho, N.Y. Office). ***PRACTICE AREAS:*** Aviation Law; Mergers and Acquisitions; Commercial Litigation; Corporate Litigation. ***Email:*** nbluth@mklawnyc.com

ASSOCIATES

REGINA MOVSESYAN, born Moscow, Russia, July 8, 1972; admitted to bar, 1998, New York and U.S. District Court, Southern and Eastern Districts of New York. *Education:* Moscow State Law Academy (J.D.); Touro Law, Center (LL.M.). Member, Rotary Russian Gift of Life. Member, New York Russian Club, Air Cargo Association. *Member:* New York State Bar Association. (Resident, Jericho, N.Y. Office). ***LANGUAGES:*** Russian. ***PRACTICE AREAS:*** Matrimonial; Real Estate; Commercial Litigation; International Commercial Law; Contract Law.

T. BRENT COSTELLO, admitted to bar, 1978, New York; 1997, California (Not admitted in Illinois). *Education:* Yale University (B.A., 1974); Georgetown University (J.D., 1977). ***PRACTICE AREAS:*** Corporate Law.

NANCY J. LEDDY, born Philadelphia, Pennsylvania, November 4, 1946; admitted to bar, 1985, Pennsylvania; 1987, New Jersey. *Education:* Temple University (B.A., 1971; M.A., 1973); Widener University (J.D., 1985). Judge Pro Tem, Philadelphia Court of Common Pleas. (Resident, Philadelphia, Pennsylvania Office). ***PRACTICE AREAS:*** Products Liability; Premises Liability. ***Email:*** nleddy@mcbreenkopko.com

CHRISTOPHER J. BOYLE, born Darby, Pennsylvania, December 20, 1969; admitted to bar, 2001, Pennsylvania and New Jersey. *Education:* St. Joseph's University (B.S., 1993); Temple University (J.D., 2001). *Member:* Philadelphia and Pennsylvania Bar Associations. (Resident, Philadelphia, Pennsylvania Office). ***PRACTICE AREAS:*** Premises Liability; Products Liability; Subrogation and Recovery. ***Email:*** cjboyle@mcbreenkopko.com

ANDREA MAIER, born Philadelphia, Pennsylvania, October 3, 1963; admitted to bar, 1988, Pennsylvania and New Jersey. *Education:* LaSalle University (B.S., cum laude, 1985); Widener University (J.D., 1988; M.A., 1989). *Member:* Pennsylvania and American Bar Associations. (Resident, Philadelphia, Pennsylvania Office). ***PRACTICE AREAS:*** Premises Liability; Products Liability. ***Email:*** amaier@mcbreenkopko.com

SPENCER R. HORN, born Suffern, New York, December 4, 1981; (admission pending). *Education:* University of Miami (B.A., 2002); Jacob D. Fuchsberg Law Center at Touro College (J.D., 2005). Phi Alpha Delta. President, Student Bar Association. Licensed Glider and Powered Pilot. *Member:* American Bar Association. [Civil Air Patrol, United

(This Listing Continued)

States Air Force Auxiliary]. (Resident, Jericho, N.Y. Office). **PRACTICE AREAS:** Commercial Law; Commercial Litigation; Corporate Law; Aviation (focus on corporate and general aviation). **Email:** shorn@mklawnyc.com

OF COUNSEL

RALPH T. VERRILL, born New York, New York, March 8, 1937; admitted to bar, 1965, New York, U.S. District Court, Southern and Eastern Districts of New York and U.S. Court of Appeals, Second Circuit (Not admitted in Illinois). *Education:* Columbia University (A.B., 1958); New York University School of Law (LL.B., 1964). *Member:* New York State and American (Member: Section on Real Property, Probate and Trust Law; Forum Committee on Air and Space Law) Bar Associations. [Comisat Quartermaster Corps, U.S. Army, 1959-1961]. **PRACTICE AREAS:** Aviation; Real Estate; Commercial Transactions.

GERARD TERRY, born New York, N.Y., May 15, 1954; admitted to bar, 1986, New York (Not admitted in Illinois). *Education:* Queens College, C.U.N.Y. (B.A., 1981); St. John's University (J.D., 1985). Village Attorney, Inc. Village of Manorhaven, 2000—; Counsel, Town of North Hempstead Board of Zoning Appeals; Counsel, Nassau County Board of Elections; Member, N.Y. State Democratic Committee, 1998—; Counsel, Judicial Screening Committee, Nassau Democratic Committee, 1987—; Assistant Counsel, N.Y. State Assembly Speaker, 1988; Legislative Counsel, N.Y. State Governor, 1985-1988. *Member:* Nassau County and New York State Bar Associations. **PRACTICE AREAS:** Municipal Law (50%); Commercial Law (25%); Labor Law (25%).

McBRIDE BAKER & COLES

CHICAGO, ILLINOIS

(See Holland & Knight LLC)

JOSEPH P. McCAFFERY ATTORNEY AT LAW

CHICAGO, ILLINOIS

(See Aurora)

Criminal Litigation, White Collar, Felonies, Misdemeanors, Civil Defense, Legal Malpractice Defense, Insurance Defense, Medical Malpractice, Personal Injury, Divorce, Wills and Trusts, Real Estate Transactions, Banking, Securities, Corporate and Commercial Litigation.

GARY D. McCALLISTER & ASSOCIATES, LTD.

Established in 1996

120 NORTH LA SALLE STREET
CHICAGO, ILLINOIS 60602
Telephone: 312-345-0611
Fax: 312-345-0612
Email: gdm@gdmlawfirm.com
URL: http://www.lawyers.com/gdmlawfirm

Plaintiff's Personal Injury, Products Liability, Medical, Legal Malpractice, Wrongful Death, Insurance, Pharmaceutical, Antitrust, Business, Commercial, Complex and Multi-District Litigation and Class Actions in all State and Federal Trial and Appellate Courts.

FIRM PROFILE: Gary D. McCallister & Associates, Ltd. is most often called upon to handle complex lawyer referred cases where responsiveness and professional expertise are required. The firm's team approach to litigation provides the resources and personal attention which referring counsel and our clients desire.

GARY D. McCALLISTER, born Chicago, Illinois, October 30, 1950; admitted to bar, 1975, Kansas; 1988, Colorado; 1994, Illinois and U.S. Supreme Court; U.S. Court of Appeals, Seventh, Ninth and Tenth Circuits; U.S. District Court, Northern and Central Districts of Illinois; U.S. District Court, District of Kansas; U.S. District Court, District of Colorado; U.S. District Court, Northern District of California. *Education:* Kansas State University (B.S., 1972); Washburn University School of Law (J.D., 1975). Phi Delta Phi. Business Editor, Washburn Law Journal, 1974-1975. Author: "Survey of Tort Damage Law," 14 Washburn Law Journal, Spring, 1975; "Insurance Medical Payment Struck By Provisions Physical Contact Requirement," 13 Washburn Law Journal, Winter 1994. Adjunct Assistant Professor, Trial Techniques, Washburn University School of Law, 1980-1985, 1990-1991. Faculty Member, Kansas College of Advocacy, Annual Trial Tactics and Techniques, 1984-1989. Member, Panel of Arbitrators, American Arbitration Association; Panel of Mediators, Kansas Federal District Court. *Member:* Chicago and Kansas Bar Associations; Illinois Trial Lawyers Association; Kansas Trial Lawyers Association (Member, Board of Governors, 1980—, President, 1988, Legislative Vice President, 1983; Vice President, Continuing Legal Education, 1985-1986); Colorado Trial Lawyers Association; Trial Lawyers for Public Justice; The Association of Trial Lawyers of America. (Also Partner, Davis, Unrein, McCallister, Biggs & Head, LLP, Topeka, Kansas). **PRACTICE AREAS:** Complex Commercial Litigation; Antitrust; Business Torts; Personal Injury; Products Liability; Professional Liability; Pharmacy Law; Multi-District and Class Action Litigation. **Email:** gdm@gdmlawfirm.com

ERIC I. UNREIN, born Topeka, Kansas, March 20, 1968; admitted to bar, 1993, Kansas; 1997, Illinois; U.S. District Court, District of Kansas; U.S. District Court, Northern District of Illinois; U.S. Court of Appeals, Seventh and Tenth Circuits. *Education:* University of Kansas (B.A., with highest honors, 1990); University of Texas School of Law (J.D., with honors, 1993). Phi Beta Kappa; Phi Kappa Phi; Omicron Delta Kappa; Pi Sigma Alpha. Member: Mortar Board; Owl Society; Order of the Coif. Member, 1991-1992 and Associated Editor, 1993, The Review of Litigation. Recipient, Undergraduate Scholarship and Awards: Solon Summerfield, Hall Family Foundation, Phi Gamma Delta Educational Foundation, Lee J. Phillips, June Ritchie, Pusitz, College of Liberal Arts & Sciences (Paul B. Lawson Award), College Honors Program (Martha C. Clarke & Veta B. Lear Awards), Department of Economics (Domenico Gagliardo & A.J. Boynton Awards), Department of Political Science (Pi Sigma Alpha Faculty Award). Recipient, Law School Scholarships and Awards: Israel Dreeben Scholarship, Dean's Achievement Awards (Antitrust & Payment Systems), Wilson Herndon Award. Law Clerk: U.S. District Judge Dale E. Saffels, Senior Judge, District of Kansas, 1993-1995; U.S. Circuit Judge for the Tenth Circuit Court of Appeals, Judge Mary Beck Briscoe, 1995-1996. *Member:* Chicago, Illinois State and American Bar Associations; American Health Lawyers Association. (Also Partner, Davis, Unrein, Hummer, McCallister, Biggs & Head, LLP, Topeka, Kansas). **PRACTICE AREAS:** Personal Injury; Pharmacy Law; Antitrust; Health Care; Multi-District and Class Action Litigation; Appellate Practice. **Email:** eunrein@davisunrein.com

THOMAS A. KELLIHER, born Santa Monica, California, June 6, 1964; admitted to bar, 1994, Wisconsin; 1995, Illinois, U.S. Court of Appeals, Seventh Circuit; U.S. District Court, Northern District of Illinois; U.S. District Court, Southern District of Indiana. *Education:* University of Virginia (B.A., 1989); John Marshall Law School (J.D., cum laude, 1994). Phi Delta Phi; Order of John Marshall. Staff Editor, John Marshall Law Review, 1992-1994. Law Clerk to Judge Robert D. Sundby, Wisconsin Court of Appeals, Fourth District, Madison, Wisconsin, 1994-1996. Associate Attorney, Cascino Vaughan Law Offices, 1996-1998. Assistant Corporation Counsel, City of Chicago Law Department, Torts Division, 1998-2000. *Member:* Chicago Bar Association; Association of Trial Lawyers of America; Illinois Trial Lawyers Association; American Health Lawyers Association. **PRACTICE AREAS:** Medical Malpractice; Product Liability; Personal Injury; Pharmaceutical; Antitrust; Multi-District and Class Action Litigation; Automobile Accidents; Truck Accidents. **Email:** tkelliher@gdmlawfirm.com

McCARTHY & ASSOCIATES

20 N. WACKER DRIVE, SUITE 1701
CHICAGO, ILLINOIS 60606
Telephone: 312-634-5200
Telecopier: 312-634-5220

Government and Legislative Relations, State and Local Taxation, General Corporate Law, Health Care and Aviation Law.

MEMBER OF FIRM

THOMAS J. McCARTHY, born Chicago, Illinois, August 21, 1947; admitted to bar, 1974, Illinois and U.S. District Court, Northern District of Illinois including Trial Bar. *Education:* University of Santa Clara; University of Notre Dame (A.B., 1969); John Marshall Law School (J.D., 1974). Past Member, Editorial Advisory Board, *Journal of Property Taxation.* Licensed Real Estate Broker, Illinois, 1973. Co-Author: "Property Tax Exemptions: Headed For Extinction?," Health Progress, December, 1988; "The Real Property Tax System in Chicago, Illinois: A Practical Overview," Financial Planning Committee for the City of Chicago, May, 1986. Member: Law Department, Cook County Assessor's Office, Chicago, Illinois, 1971-1973; Law Department, The City of Chicago Corporation Counsel's Office, Appeals and Review Division, SCR-711, 1973-1974; Trial Division, Cook County State's Attorney, Chicago, Illinois, 1974-1977. Commissioner, Attorney's Registration and Disciplinary Commission, Hearing Board of the Supreme Court of Illinois, 1986-1991. Former President, Worldwide Aviation Safety and Security Association. Director, Special Children's Charities, 1992—. Managing Partner, McCarthy & Associates, 1991—. President/CEO, TaxTech International, Inc., 1994—. Partner, Mayer, Brown, Rowe & Maw (formerly Mayer, Brown & Platt), Chicago, Illinois, 1985-1991. Associate and Partner, Gould & Ratner, Chicago, Illinois, 1977-1985. Alumni Member, Colorado Outward Bound School. *Member:* Chicago and Illinois State (Member, Real Estate Law Section) Bar Associations. **REPORTED CASES:** Lutheran General Health Care System v. Dept. of Revenue, 231 Ill.App. 3d 652, 595 NE 2d. 1214 (1992). **PRACTICE AREAS:** Tax Controversies; Tax Litigation; Government Relations. **Email:** tjmcc@mcalawyers.com

ASSOCIATE

RACHEL L. OESCH, admitted to bar, 2001, Illinois. *Education:* State University of New York at Buffalo (B.A., History and International Studies, 1993); Roosevelt University (Lawyers Assistant Program, 1995); Chicago-Kent College of Law, Illinois Institute of Technology (J.D., 2001). Associate Attorney, McCarthy & Associates, 2002—. Transaction Paralegal, Miner, Barnhill & Gallard, P.C., 1997-2001. Paralegal, Hymen & Blair, P.C., 1995-1997. Legal Assistant, Andrew J. Rukavina, 1995. **PRACTICE AREAS:** Tax Law; Real Estate. **Email:** roesch@mcalwyers.com

OF COUNSEL

JEFFREY W. FINKE, born Chicago, Illinois, April 2, 1950; admitted to bar, 1977, Illinois, U.S. Court of Appeals, Seventh Circuit and U.S. District Court, Northern District of Illinois; 1978, U.S. Court of Appeals for the District of Columbia Circuit; 1983, U.S. Court of Appeals, Federal Circuit and U.S. Court of Federal Claims; 1986, U.S. Supreme Court; 1990, U.S. District Court, Central District of Illinois. *Education:* University of Illinois (A.B., Economics, 1972); University of California at Berkeley (M.A., Economics, 1974); University of Chicago (J.D., 1977). Comment Editor, 1976-1977 and Staff Member, 1975-1976, University of Chicago Law School Law Review. Author: "State Financing: The State's Case," 79 Ill. Bar. J. 553, 1991. Co-Author: "Jurisdiction Over Nonresidents in Illinois — Recent Developments," 64 Chicago Bar Record 306, 1983. Assistant Attorney General, 1982-1991, Illinois. Arbitrator: National Association of Securities Dealers, 1993—. Of Counsel, McCarthy & Associates, 1999—. Principal, Jeffrey W. Finke Law Office, 1999—. *Member:* Chicago, Illinois State and American Bar Associations. **REPORTED CASES:** People ex. rel. Hartigan v. E& E Hauling, 153 Ill.2d. 473, 607 NE 2d. 165 (1992) (fraud in minority and women business enterprises); Darry H. v. Coler, 901 F.2d 893 (7th Cir. 1986), 93 ALR Fed 501 (1986) (defense of State officials in constitutional challenge to child protection program). **PRACTICE AREAS:** Real Estate Taxation; Commercial Litigation; Bankruptcy Litigation.

(This Listing Continued)

McCARTHY & ASSOCIATES, Chicago—Continued

EDWARD R. RABE, JR., born Chicago, Illinois, February 10, 1948; admitted to bar, 1974, Illinois and U.S. District Court, Northern District of Illinois. *Education:* North Park University (B.A., 1970); Illinois Institute of Technology, Chicago Kent College of Law (J.D., 1973). Delta Theta Phi. Co-Author: "Joan Documentation Handbook," Continental Bank N.A., 1981. Counsel, 1999-2003, and Associate, 1992-1999, Mayer, Brown, Rowe & Maw LLP, Chicago, Illinois. Member, Regional Counsel Division, Midwestern Regional Office, Federal National Mortgage Association, Chicago, Illinois, 1991-1992. Senior Attorney II, Law Department, 1978-1991, and Segal Advisor, General Banking Services-Operations Division, 1974-1978, Continental Bank N.A., Chicago, Illinois. *Member:* Chicago (Former Chair and Vice Chair, Commercial Finance and Transactions Committee) and American (Member, Business Law Section) Bar Associations. ***PRACTICE AREAS:*** Banking Law; Finance; Commercial Banking. ***Email:*** erabe@mcalawyers.com

REPRESENTATIVE CLIENTS: American Farm Bureau Federation; Alcoa, Inc.; Evanston Northwestern Healthcare; Unilever United States, Inc.; Joseph T. Ryerson & Son, Inc.; Sprint; Total Logistic Control; Roosevelt University.
REFERENCE: Bank One/Chase and The Northern Trust.

McCARTHY DUFFY

Established in 1886

180 NORTH LASALLE STREET
SUITE 1400
CHICAGO, ILLINOIS 60601
Telephone: 312-726-0355
Fax: 312-726-6383; 312-726-6609
URL: http://www.mccarthyduffylaw.com
URL: http://www.mccarthyduffy.com

Skokie, Illinois Office: 8022 Lincoln Avenue. Telephone: 847-673-0355. Fax: 847-673-2354.
Palos Park, Illinois Office: 8102 West 119th Street, Suite 800, 60464. Telephone: 708-923-7345. Fax: 708-923-0963.

Commercial Litigation. Banking, Real Estate, Probate, Trusts & Estates, Corporate, Employment, Appellate, Municipal and Bankruptcy Law.

MEMBERS OF FIRM

JOHN M. DUFFY, born Chicago, Illinois, August 1, 1930; admitted to bar, 1954, Illinois. *Education:* Loyola University (B.S., 1952); Loyola University Law School (J.D., 1954). *Member:* Chicago (Chairman, Circuit Court Operations Committee, 1974), Illinois State and American Bar Associations; Illinois Trial Lawyers Association; Legal Club of Chicago. (Also at Skokie Office). ***PRACTICE AREAS:*** Commercial Law; Personal Injury Law. ***Email:*** jduffy@mcdnslaw.com

FOREST J. MILES, born Evanston, Illinois, September 5, 1948; admitted to bar, 1977, Illinois. *Education:* University of Illinois and Fort Lewis College (B.A., 1971); John Marshall Law School (J.D., 1977; LL.M., Taxation, 1985). Member, National Moot Court Team. Village Attorney, University Park, 1985—. Chair Qualified Arbitrator, Circuit Court of Cook County Mandatory Arbitration Program. *Member:* Chicago, Illinois State and American Bar Associations. ***PRACTICE AREAS:*** Municipal Law; General Corporate Law; Taxation Law; Civil Litigation. ***Email:*** fmiles@mcdnslaw.com

THOMAS J. MONTGOMERY, born Chicago, Illinois, June 8, 1947; admitted to bar, 1973, Illinois. *Education:* University of Illinois (A.B., 1969); Loyola University (J.D., 1972). Member, 1970, and Managing Editor, 1971-1972, Loyola Law Journal. Law Clerk to Hon. John C. Hayes, Illinois Appellate Court, 1972-1974. *Member:* Chicago, Illinois State and American Bar Associations. ***PRACTICE AREAS:*** Estate Planning; Estate Administration; Banking Law; Real Estate. ***Email:*** tmontgomery@mcdnslaw.com

TERRENCE LEIGH SCHAUL, born Northbrook, Illinois, September 2, 1963; admitted to bar, 1988, Illinois; 1989, U.S. District Court, Northern District of Illinois and U.S. Tax Court. *Education:* University of Illinois (B.A., 1985); DePaul University (J.D., 1988). *Member:* Chicago, Illinois State and American Bar Associations; American Institute of Certified Public Accountants; Illinois CPA Society. ***PRACTICE AREAS:*** Taxation Law; Corporate Law; Banking Law; Real Estate Law. ***Email:*** tschaul@mcdnslaw.com

STEPHEN A. SNAKARD, born Chicago, Illinois, September 29, 1945; admitted to bar, 1970, Illinois. *Education:* University of Arizona (B.S., 1967); John Marshall Law School (J.D., 1970). Delta Theta Phi. *Member:* Chicago, Illinois State and American Bar Associations. (Also at Skokie Office). ***REPORTED CASES:*** Lipin v. Lee, 803 F.2d 322 (1986), aff'g 625 F. Supp. 1098 (1985); Hayna v. Arby's, Inc., 99 Ill. App. 3d 700 (1981); Corbett v. Devon Bank, 12 Ill. App. 3d 559 (1973). ***PRACTICE AREAS:*** Trials; Professional Malpractice; Personal Injury; Class Action; Construction; General Civil Litigation; Business Litigation; Appeals; Banking; Employment; Insurance; Trust; Real Estate; Commercial; Corporate Practice. ***Email:*** ssnakard@mcdnslaw.com

TIMOTHY E. WEILANDT, born Chicago, Illinois, December 30, 1961; admitted to bar, 1987, Illinois and U.S. District Court, Northern District of Illinois. *Education:* University of Wisconsin-Madison (B.B.A., 1984); DePaul University (J.D., 1987). *Member:* Chicago and American Bar Associations. ***PRACTICE AREAS:*** Commercial Law; Banking Law; Bankruptcy Law; Real Estate Law. ***Email:*** tweilandt@mcdnslaw.com

RICHARD J. WITRY, born Skokie, Illinois, April 8, 1950; admitted to bar, 1976, Illinois and U.S. District Court, Northern District of Illinois; 1983, U.S. Court of Appeals, 7th Circuit and U.S. Supreme Court. *Education:* College of Holy Cross (B.A., 1972); John Marshall Law School (J.D., 1976). Author: Illinois Revised Statutes, Chapter 26, Section 4-403(4). Commissioner, Skokie Park District, 1979-1985. Vice Consul, 1978-1990; Consul, 1990-1995, Luxembourg. President, Skokie Historical Society, 1988-1993. Director, Skokie Chamber of Commerce, 1991-1993. Member, Downtown Redevelopment Task Force, Skokie, Illinois, 1990-1996. Trustee, Skokie Public Library, October 1998-April 2005. *Member:* Illinois State Bar Association. (Also at Skokie Office). ***REPORTED CASES:*** Stein v. Galitz, et al. 478 F. Supp. 517; Segni v. Commercial Office of Spain, 650 F. Supp 1040, 650 F. Supp 1042, 650 F. Supp 1045, 816 F.2d 344, 835 F.2d 160; Knepper v. Automotion, 788 F. Supp 999; In re: Niteway Transportation Company, Inc., 96 B.R. 854; In re: Martin Grinding & Machine Works, Inc., 42 B.R. 888; Chapman v. Richey 78 Ill 2d 243. ***PRACTICE AREAS:*** Banking Law; Creditors Rights Law; ERISA; Foreign Sovereign Immunities Act Litigation; Probate; Estate Planning. ***Email:*** rwitry@mcdnslaw.com

(This Listing Continued)

STEVEN N. ZARIS, born Detroit, Michigan, January 27, 1957; admitted to bar, 1981, Illinois and U.S. District Court, Northern District of Illinois. *Education:* Columbia University (A.B., 1978); University of Michigan of Ann Arbor (J.D., 1981). *Member:* Chicago (Member, Real Property Committee) and American (Member, Sections on: Real Property, Probate and Trust Law) Bar Associations. ***PRACTICE AREAS:*** Real Estate; Banking Law. ***Email:*** szaris@mcdnslaw.com

ASSOCIATE

JULIE M. REALMUTO, born Chicago, Illinois, May 9, 1967; admitted to bar, 2000, Illinois. *Education:* DePaul University (B.S., 1997); Chicago-Kent College of Law (J.D., 2000). ***PRACTICE AREAS:*** Real Estate; Bankruptcy; Corporate Law. ***Email:*** jrealmuto@mcdnslaw.com

REPRESENTATIVE CLIENTS: Forest Park National Bank; John Burns Construction Co.; Marquette Bank; Village of University Park, Illinois; Maine-Niles Association of Special Recreation; Harris Bank and Trust; Associated Bank; Northern Trust Company; Bank One; American National Bank; First Suburban Bank; IBM.

McCRACKEN & FRANK LLP

Established in 2001

200 WEST ADAMS, SUITE 2150
CHICAGO, ILLINOIS 60606
Telephone: 312-263-4700
Fax: 312-263-3990
URL: http://www.pattm.com

Intellectual Property.

MEMBERS OF THE FIRM

WILLIAM E. McCRACKEN, born Elmhurst, Illinois, December 16, 1955; admitted to bar, 1980, Illinois; registered to practice before the U.S. Patent and Trademark Office. *Education:* University of Illinois (B.S.E.E., 1977); Loyola University (J.D., 1980). Eta Kappa Nu. *Member:* Chicago Bar Association; Intellectual Property Law Association of Chicago; American Intellectual Property Law Association; Federation Internationale des Conseils en Propriete Industrielle (FICPI). ***PRACTICE AREAS:*** Intellectual Property; Patents; Trademarks. ***Email:*** wmccracken@pattm.com

J. WILLIAM FRANK, III, born Darby, Pennsylvania, April 23, 1946; admitted to bar, 1973, Virginia; 1974, Wisconsin; 2002, Illinois; registered to practice before the U.S. Patent and Trademark Office. *Education:* Lehigh University (B.S.Ch.E., 1968); Georgetown University (J.D., 1973). Formerly with S.C. Johnson & Son, Inc. *Member:* American Bar Association (Member, Intellectual Property Law and Technology Law Sections); American Intellectual Property Law Association (Member, Board of Directors, 1994-1997; Chair, Industrial Designs, 1992-1993; Chair, Membership Committee, 1998-2000; Vice-Chair, Committee on Local Associations, 2002-2004; Fellows Committee, Vice-Chair 2004-2005, Chair 2005—); Association of Corporate Patent Counsel (Emeritus Member). Fellow, American Intellectual Property Law Association. ***PRACTICE AREAS:*** Intellectual Property; Patents; Trademarks; Trade Secrets; Copyrights. ***Email:*** jwfrank@pattm.com

ASSOCIATES

NICHOLAS P. SCHMIDBAUER, born Milwaukee, Wisconsin, November 27, 1977; admitted to bar, 2003, Illinois and U.S. District Court, Northern District of Illinois; registered to practice before U.S. Patent and Trademark Office. *Education:* University of Michigan at Ann Arbor (B.S.M.E., 2000); University of Illinois at Urbana/Champaign (J.D., cum laude, 2003). *Member:* Chicago and American Bar Associations; American Intellectual Property Law Association. ***PRACTICE AREAS:*** Intellectual Property; Patents; Trademarks; Copyrights. ***Email:*** nschmidbauer@pattm.com

THOMAS P. RILEY, born LaPorte, Indiana, March 27, 1973; admitted to bar, 2002, Indiana and U.S. District Court, Northern District of Indiana; 2003, U.S. Court of Appeals for the Federal Circuit; 2004, Illinois; registered to practice before U.S. Patent and Trademark Office. *Education:* Purdue University (B.S.C.E., 1998); Valparaiso University (J.D., 2002). Member, Valparaiso Law Review. Adjunct Professor of Law, Valparaiso University. Formerly with Botkin & Hall. ***PRACTICE AREAS:*** Intellectual Property; Patents; Trademarks; Copyrights; Trade Secrets. ***Email:*** triley@pattm.com

OF COUNSEL

THOMAS R. STIEBEL, JR., born St. Louis, Missouri, December 1, 1962; admitted to bar, 1999, Illinois; 2002, U.S. Court of Appeals for the Federal Circuit; registered to practice before U.S. Patent and Trademark Office. *Education:* Southern Illinois University (B.S. Botany, 1986); St. Louis University (M.S., Biology, 1989); Northwestern University (J.D., 1999). ***REPORTED CASES:*** Pfizer, Inc. v. Dr. Reddys' Labs. Ltd., 359 F3d. 1361 (Fed. Cir. 2004). ***PRACTICE AREAS:*** Intellectual Property; Patents; Biochemical Patents; Biotechnology Patents; Pharmaceutical Patents; Biotechnology Patent Prosecution; Pharmaceutical Patent Prosecution; Molecular Biology Patents; Immigration Rights; Human Rights. ***Email:*** tstiebel@pattm.com

McCULLOUGH, CAMPBELL & LANE

Established in 1987

205 NORTH MICHIGAN AVENUE, SUITE 4100
CHICAGO, ILLINOIS 60601
Telephone: 312-923-4000
Facsimile: 312-923-4329
Email: firm@mcandl.com

General Civil Trial and Appellate Practice in all State and Federal Courts. Aviation, Banking, Commercial, Corporation and Corporation Financing, Directors and Officers Liability, Employee Benefits, Employment Discrimination, Environmental, Insurance, Reinsurance and Insurance Defense, International Business, Medical Malpractice, Products Liability, Professional Liability, Real Estate, Securities and Taxation.

FIRM PROFILE: At McCullough, Campbell & Lane, we understand that the law is a means of achieving our clients' business objectives, not an end in itself. We strive to assist our clients in reaching their goals, by sharing with them the expertise and legal resources that we have accumulated in insurance law, litigation, and business counseling. We are dedicated to providing legal services of the highest quality, while remaining innovative, responsive, and cost-effective.

McCullough, Campbell & Lane, which now has over twenty-five lawyers, was established in 1987 in Chicago by founding partners who averaged more than ten years of experience. From the outset, the firm has had a national rather than local orientation, because much of its work is performed on behalf of foreign insurance organizations with legal questions arising under the laws of jurisdictions across the country. Today, the firm continues to be engaged in a diverse national and international practice focused on the following practice areas: Insurance Law, Litigation, Business Counseling.

Our attorneys possess specialized knowledge in a broad range of specific subjects that cut across these practice areas. These include professional liability, directors and officers liability, products liability, aviation, health care, and employment law. Within these subject areas, we can, for example, defend claims, counsel insurers, draft policies and contracts, set up corporations, or litigate coverage disputes. We believe this strengthens our capacity to assist our clients in achieving their business objectives.

PARTNERS

JOHN W. McCULLOUGH, born Miami, Oklahoma, August 10, 1940; admitted to bar, 1966, Illinois. *Education:* Northwestern University (B.A., 1962); University of Michigan (J.D., 1965). Member, Barristers. *Member:* Chicago, Illinois State, American and International Bar Associations; The Law Club of Chicago; Legal Club of Chicago; The Seventh Circuit Bar Association. ***PRACTICE AREAS:*** Commercial Litigation; Insurance; Reinsurance; Professional Liability; Accountants Liability.

JOHN G. CAMPBELL, born Chicago, Illinois, October 9, 1932; admitted to bar, 1961, Illinois. *Education:* Princeton University (A.B., cum laude, 1954); Harvard Law School (LL.B., 1961). *Member:* Illinois State Bar Association (Chairman, Federal Taxation Section, 1974-1975) and The Law Club of Chicago. ***PRACTICE AREAS:*** Banking; Corporate Finance; Real Estate; Taxation; Health Law. ***Email:*** jcampbel@mcandl.com

MICHAEL M. LANE, born Evanston, Illinois, August 11, 1941; admitted to bar, 1966, Illinois. *Education:* University of Notre Dame (A.B., cum laude, 1963); University of California (LL.B., 1966). *Member:* Society of Trial Lawyers. ***PRACTICE AREAS:*** Aviation Litigation; Commercial Litigation; Product Liability.

DENNIS L. FROSTIC, born Wyandotte, Michigan, February 8, 1943; admitted to bar, 1969, Michigan; 1972, Illinois. *Education:* University of Michigan (B.A., 1964; J.D., 1967). *Member:* State Bar of Michigan; American Bar Association. ***PRACTICE AREAS:*** Insurance; Litigation. ***Email:*** dfrostic@mcandl.com

JOHN A. HUBBUCH, born Jeffersonville, Indiana, February 28, 1949; admitted to bar, 1974, Illinois. *Education:* Vanderbilt University (B.A., cum laude, 1971); University of Chicago (J.D., 1974). Phi Beta Kappa. *Member:* American Bar Association. ***PRACTICE AREAS:*** Professional Liability; Insurance Law; Directors and Officers Liability. ***Email:*** jhubbuch@mcandl.com

F. DENNIS NELSON, born Highland Park, Michigan, July 9, 1952; admitted to bar, 1978, Illinois. *Education:* University of Michigan (A.B., with high distinction, 1974; J.D., cum laude, 1977). Law Clerk, Judge Donald Holbrook, Jr., Michigan Court of Appeals, 1977-1978. Member, Professional Liability Underwriting Society. *Member:* International Bar Association (Chairman, Professional Indemnity Subcommittee of Insurance Section, 1990-1994). ***PRACTICE AREAS:*** Professional Liability; Accountants Liability; Auditors Malpractice; Insurance Law. ***Email:*** fnelson@mcandl.com

PAUL S. TURNER, born New Castle, Indiana, October 11, 1953; admitted to bar, 1978, Ohio; 1982, Illinois. *Education:* Harvard University (A.B., 1975; J.D., 1978). *Member:* American Bar Association. ***PRACTICE AREAS:*** Insurance; Reinsurance; Medical Malpractice; Professional Liability. ***Email:*** pturner@mcandl.com

PATRICK M. GRABER, born Chicago, Illinois, March 1, 1950; admitted to bar, 1979, Illinois. *Education:* Purdue University (B.S.A.E., 1972); University of Notre Dame (J.D., 1979). *Member:* Illinois Association of Defense Trial Counsel; Defense Research Institute. (Member, Aerospace Committee); Trial Lawyers Club of Chicago. [Commander, U.S.N.R., Retired]. ***PRACTICE AREAS:*** Aviation; Products Liability. ***Email:*** pgraber@mcandl.com

ANN P. GOODMAN, born Winchester, Massachusetts, August 16, 1957; admitted to bar, 1984, Illinois; 1989, U.S. Court of Appeals, Seventh Circuit; 1995, U.S. Supreme Court. *Education:* Wellesley College (A.B., cum laude, 1979); Vanderbilt University (J.D., 1984). Arbitrator, Cook County Mandatory Arbitration Program, 1990—. *Member:* Chicago and American Bar Associations. ***PRACTICE AREAS:*** Civil Litigation; Aviation Defense; Products Liability. ***Email:*** agoodman@mcandl.com

(This Listing Continued)

ANNE E. LAVOIE, born Evergreen Park, Illinois, April 24, 1960; admitted to bar, 1985, Illinois. *Education:* University of Illinois (B.A., 1982, Bronze Tablet; J.D., cum laude, 1985). *Member:* Professional Liability Underwriting Society. ***PRACTICE AREAS:*** Accountants Liability; Insurance Law. ***Email:*** alavoie@mcandl.com

MARK D. SIEBERT, born New York, N.Y., October 5, 1960; admitted to bar, 1986, Illinois. *Education:* University of Illinois (A.B., 1983; J.D., magna cum laude, 1986). Order of the Coif. Harno Scholar. Associate Editor, University of Illinois Law Review, 1985-1986. *Member:* American Bar Association. ***PRACTICE AREAS:*** Professional Liability; Directors and Officers Liability; Insurance Law. ***Email:*** msiebert@mcandl.com

DEBRA A. EMRY, born Sioux City, Iowa, February 19, 1962; admitted to bar, 1987, Illinois. *Education:* University of Iowa (B.A., 1984); University of Illinois (J.D., 1987). *Member:* Chicago, Illinois State and American Bar Associations. ***Email:*** demry@mcandl.com

BART RINN, born Chicago, Illinois, December 23, 1963; admitted to bar, 1988, Illinois. *Education:* Northern Illinois University (B.S., summa cum laude, 1985); University of Illinois (J.D., cum laude, 1988). ***PRACTICE AREAS:*** Insurance Law; Litigation; Professional Liability. ***Email:*** mrinn@mcandl.com

MYRA J. BROWN, born Chicago, Illinois, September 15, 1950; admitted to bar, 1974, Illinois; 1977, U.S. Court of Appeals, Seventh Circuit; 1979, U.S. Supreme Court. *Education:* Drake University (B.A., 1971); DePaul University (J.D., 1974). National Institute of Trial Advocacy (Certificate, Teacher Training, Trial Advocacy Workshop). *Member:* Chicago, Illinois State and American Bar Associations; Illinois Association of Healthcare Attorneys; American Society for Healthcare Risk Management. ***PRACTICE AREAS:*** Health Care; Professional Liability; Insurance Law. ***Email:*** mbrown@mcandl.com

ASSOCIATES

STEPHEN D. KOSLOW, born Joliet, Illinois, January 8, 1969; admitted to bar, 1994, Illinois and U.S. District Court, Northern District of Illinois. *Education:* University of Illinois at Urbana-Champaign (B.S., with high honors, 1991); DePaul University (J.D., 1994). *Member:* Illinois State Bar Association. ***PRACTICE AREAS:*** Civil Litigation. ***Email:*** skoslow@mcandl.com

VERONICA NULMAN, born Moscow, Russia, May 3, 1973; admitted to bar, 1998, Massachusetts; 1999, New York; 2000, Illinois and U.S. District Court, Northern District of Illinois. *Education:* Northwestern University (B.A., 1995); Boston University School of Law (J.D., 1998). Note Editor, International Law Journal. *Member:* Chicago and Illinois State Bar Associations. ***LANGUAGES:*** Russian and French. ***PRACTICE AREAS:*** Civil Litigation. ***Email:*** vnulman@mcandl.com

BRIAN J. DUSEK, born Crookston, Minnesota, February 15, 1972; admitted to bar, 1998, Illinois. *Education:* University of Minnesota (B.A., 1994); DePaul University College of Law (J.D., 1998). Author: "Ghost in the Machinist," 10 DePaul Bus. L.J. 103 (1997). ***REPORTED CASES:*** Smith v. Union Avto. Indem. Co., 752 N.E.2d 1261 (2d Dist. 2001). ***Email:*** bdusek@mcandl.com

JULIE L. HENN, born Park Ridge, Illinois, February 22, 1970; admitted to bar, 2003, Illinois. *Education:* Hillsdale College (B.A., 1992); Boston University School of Law (J.D., 2003). Author: "Targeting Transnational Internet Content Regulation," 21 B.U. Int'l L.J. 157 (2003). *Member:* Chicago, Illinois State and American Bar Associations. ***LANGUAGES:*** French. ***PRACTICE AREAS:*** Professional Liability; General Litigation. ***Email:*** jhenn@mcandl.com

OF COUNSEL

MARVIN GREEN, born Wilkes-Barre, Pennsylvania, July 3, 1925; admitted to bar, 1950, Illinois. *Education:* University of Chicago (A.B., 1948; J.D., 1950). ***PRACTICE AREAS:*** Civil Practice; Federal Taxation; Estate Planning. ***Email:*** mgreen@mcandl.com

ANNE JENTRY-GREEN, born Chicago, Illinois, August 31, 1946; admitted to bar, 1976, Illinois and U.S. District Court, Northern District of Illinois; 1980, U.S. Tax Court; 1992, U.S. Court of Appeals, Seventh Circuit. *Education:* University of Illinois; Loyola University (J.D., 1976); DePaul University (LL.M., in Taxation, 1981). Member, Loyola University Law Journal, 1975-1976. *Member:* Chicago (Member: Federal Taxation Committee, 1978—; Federal Taxation Committee Executive Council, 1980-1982) and American (Member, Section of Taxation) Bar Associations; Chicago Council of Lawyers. ***PRACTICE AREAS:*** Corporate Law; Federal Taxation; Wills; Trust Law. ***Email:*** ajentry@mcandl.com

DAVID L. JOSLYN, born Glen Ridge, New Jersey, June 17, 1948; admitted to bar, 1975, Illinois and U.S. District Court, Northern District of Illinois; 1995, U.S. Court of Appeals, Seventh Circuit. *Education:* Northwestern University (B.A., 1970; J.D., cum laude, 1975). Member, National Moot Court. Assistant States Attorney, Cook County, 1976-1980. *Member:* Chicago and American (Member, Section on Tort and Insurance) Bar Associations. ***PRACTICE AREAS:*** Insurance Coverage; Architect and Engineer Malpractice Defense. ***Email:*** djoslyn@mcandl.com

CARL D. LIGGIO, SR., born New York, N.Y., September 5, 1943; admitted to bar, 1967, District of Columbia; 1967, New York; 1983, Wisconsin; 1997, Illinois. *Education:* Georgetown University (A.B., 1963); New York University (J.D., cum laude, 1967). Order of the Coif. Author, numerous articles on law firm management, securities lase, professional responsibility. Founding Member, 1982, Member, 1982-1995, Treasurer, 1982-1983, Director and Member of Executive Committee, 1982-1995 and Member, Policy Committee, 1985-1995, American Corporate Counsel Association. Chairman, Committee on Corporate Law Departments, Association of the Bar of the City of New York, 1993-1995. Trustee, 1987-1995 and Chairman, Audit Committee, 1989-1995, Fordham Preparatory School. Member, Disciplinary Committee, Appellate Division 1st Department, New York State Bar Association, 1985-1990. Member, Editorial Board, Accounting Regulation. General Counsel, Arthur Young/Ernst & Young, 1972-1994. *Member:* New York State, Illinois State and American Bar Associations; District of Columbia Bar; State Bar of Wisconsin; American Corporate Counsel Association. [U.S. Army, 1968-1969]. ***PRACTICE AREAS:*** Securities; Professional Liability; Corporate law; Litigation; Insurance Law. ***Email:*** cliggio@mcandl.com

McDONALD & McCABE, LLC

300 S. WACKER DRIVE, SUITE 1600
CHICAGO, ILLINOIS 60606
Telephone: 312-845-5190
Fax: 312-845-5825
Email: tmcdonald@mcdonaldmccabe.com
URL: http://www.mcdonaldmccabe.com

Complex Litigation, Technical Litigation, Fires, Explosions, Construction Failures; Construction Liability, Product Liability, Property Insurance Coverage and Litigation; Liability Insurance Coverage; Subrogation; Insurance Bad Faith, Civil RICO, Employment Law.

THOMAS A. McDONALD, born Chicago, Illinois, August 20, 1942; admitted to bar, 1969, Illinois and U.S. District Court, Northern District of Illinois including Trial Bar. *Education:* Georgetown University (A.B., 1965); Loyola University (J.D., 1968). *Member:* Chicago, Illinois State (Member, Insurance Law Section) and American (Member, Committee on Property Insurance Law, Tort and Insurance Practice and Litigation Sections) Bar Associations; Defense Research Institute. ***PRACTICE AREAS:*** Complex Civil Litigation; Fires; Explosions; Collapses; Floods; Construction and Design Law; Product Failure; Chemical and Electrical Plant Malfunctions; Industrial Accidents; Commercial Accidents; Subrogation; Self Insured Law; Boiler and Machinery Coverage and Litigation; Insurance Bad Faith; First and Third Party Coverage and Litigation; Third Party Insurance; Arbitration; Mediation; Commercial Arbitration. ***Email:*** tmcdonald@mcdonaldmccabe.com

JOHN B. McCABE, born Chicago, Illinois, January 17, 1945; admitted to bar, 1971, Illinois and U.S. District Court, Northern District of Illinois including Trial Bar. *Education:* Marquette University (B.C.E., 1967); John Marshall Law School (J.D., with honors, 1971). Associate Editor, The John Marshall Journal of Practice & Procedure, 1971. Licensed Engineer-in-Training, Wisconsin, 1967. Lecturer I.C.L.E., Tortious Damage to Business Property, 1979, Subrogation and Self-Insurance Recovery, 1988. Author: I.C.L.E.—Subrogation, 1990. *Member:* Chicago, Illinois State and American (Member, Insurance, Negligence and Compensation Law Section) Bar Associations; International Association of Defense Counsel; Defense Research Institute; Federation of Defense and Corporate Counsel; The National Association of Independent Insurance Adjusters Counsel. ***PRACTICE AREAS:*** Complex Litigation; Technical Litigation; Fire Insurance Litigation; Explosions; Flood; Insurance Defense; Construction Liability; Products Liability; Property Insurance Coverage; Insurance Bad Faith; Civil RICO; Subrogation. ***Email:*** jmccabe@mcdonaldmccabe.com

---

DAVID R. EDSEY, born Chicago, Illinois; admitted to bar, 1993, Illinois. *Education:* DePaul University (B.A., 1987); Loyola University (J.D., 1993). Member and Lead Articles Editor, Loyola Law Journal. Author: "Recent Developments in Trial Techniques," 38 Tort & Ins. L.J. 729 (2003); "That Delete Key May Bite You," Spoilation Claims Against Trucking Companies for Destructing Electronic Data," Handbook to ABA's Transportation Mega Conference III (March 1999); Case Note, Mu Min v. Virginia: The Supreme Court's Failure to Establish Adequate Procedure to Counter the Prejudicial Effects of Pretrial Publicity, 23 Loy.U.Chi.L.J. 57 (1992). *Member:* Illinois State and American Bar Associations (Member, Tort Insurance Practice Section, 2000-2003); Defense Research Institute. ***PRACTICE AREAS:*** Subrogation; Insurance Coverage; Construction Litigation; Professional Liability; Insurance Defense Litigation; Property Insurance Coverage. ***Email:*** dedsey@mcdonaldmccabe.com

JEREMY F. GOLDSTEIN, born Indianapolis, Indiana, April 15, 1971; admitted to bar, 1998, Illinois. *Education:* Ball State University (B.S., 1994); DePaul University (J.D., 1998). Certified Arbitrator, Cook County Circuit Court. *Member:* Illinois State (Member, Decalogue Society, 2003) and American Bar Associations. ***PRACTICE AREAS:*** Subrogation; Insurance Coverage. ***Email:*** jgoldstein@mcdonaldmccabe.com

MARK D. HOWARD, born Peoria, Illinois, June 9, 1956; admitted to bar, 1981, Illinois, U.S. District Court, Central and Northern Districts of Illinois and U.S. Court of Appeals, Seventh Circuit; 1985, U.S. Supreme Court; 1986, Trial Bar; 1989, U.S. District Court, Southern District of Illinois. *Education:* Northwestern University (B.A., 1978); University of Illinois (J.D., 1981). Featured Speaker Illinois Institute of Continuing Legal Education, 1999. *Member:* Chicago and Illinois State Bar Associations. (Certified as a Civil Trial Advocacy Specialist by the National Board of Trial Advocacy). ***PRACTICE AREAS:*** Property Insurance Coverage; Subrogation. ***Email:*** mhoward@mcdonaldmccabe.com

JAMES K. SCHULTZ, born Maywood, Illinois, September 23, 1971; admitted to bar, 1997, Illinois; U.S. District Court, Northern District of Illinois, U.S. District Court, Northern and Southern Districts of Indiana and U.S. Court of Appeals, Eleventh Circuit. *Education:* Marquette University (B.A., 1993); Depaul University (J.D., 1997). *Member:* Illinois State and American Bar Associations. ***PRACTICE AREAS:*** Property Subrogation; Insurance Coverage; Torts; Litigation. ***Email:*** jschultz@mcdonaldmccabe.com

THOMAS A. SMITH, born Blue Island, Illinois, May 5, 1963; admitted to bar, 1994, Illinois and U.S. District Court, Northern District of Illinois; 2001, California. *Education:* United States Naval Academy (B.S., 1985); Loyola University Chicago School of Law (J.D., cum laude, 1994). Editor-in-Chief, Loyola University Chicago Law Journal. *Member:* Illinois State Bar Association; California State Bar. [Lieutenant Commander, U.S. Naval Reserve (1985 —)]. ***PRACTICE AREAS:*** Insurance Coverage; Subrogation; Environmental. ***Email:*** tsmith@mcdonaldmccabe.com

McDONNELL BOEHNEN HULBERT & BERGHOFF LLP

300 SOUTH WACKER DRIVE
CHICAGO, ILLINOIS 60606-6709
Telephone: 312-913-0001
Fax: 312-913-0002
Email: info@mbhb.com
URL: http://www.mbhb.com

Intellectual Property Law, Federal Trial and Appellate Practice in Patent, Trademark, Trade Dress, Trade Secrets, International Trade, Unfair Competition, Copyright and Antitrust Causes before Federal and State Courts and Administrative Agencies; All phases of Prosecution before the United States and Foreign Patent and Trademark Offices.

FIRM PROFILE: McDonnell Boehnen Hulbert & Berghoff LLP is a progressive, mid-size intellectual property law firm located in downtown Chicago and Port Townsend, Washington. MBHB's practice focuses upon the intellectual property litigation, prosecution, and counseling needs of technology-driven companies. The Firm's clients range from Fortune 100 companies to entrepreneurial start-ups, and operate in areas from biotechnology, chemical, and pharmaceutical, to the electronic, computer, and telecommunications industries.

The Firm's attorneys are experienced in procurement, licensing, enforcement, and defense of patents, trademarks, copyrights, trade secrets and unfair competition in a number of technological disciplines and product categories. More than half of the Firm's professionals have a Ph.D. or other advanced technical degrees, and all are recognized in their fields as having outstanding technical and legal expertise.

JOHN J. McDONNELL, born Chicago, Illinois, March 21, 1939; admitted to bar, 1974, Illinois; registered to practice before U.S. Patent and Trademark Office. *Education:* Northern Illinois University (B.S., 1963); Iowa State University (Ph.D., 1968); Chicago-Kent College of Law (J.D., 1974).

DANIEL A. BOEHNEN, born Mitchell, South Dakota, August 5, 1950; admitted to bar, 1976, Illinois and U.S. District Court, Northern District of Illinois and Northern District of California; U.S. Court of Appeals, Federal, Seventh and Fifth Circuits; U.S. Supreme Court; registered to practice before U.S. Patent and Trademark Office. *Education:* University of Notre Dame (B.S. Ch.E., 1973); Cornell University (J.D., 1976).

BRADLEY J. HULBERT, born Minneapolis, Minnesota, November 16, 1952; admitted to bar, 1977, Minnesota; 1980, Illinois; 1983, U.S. Court of Appeals for the Federal Circuit and U.S. Supreme Court; 1987, Massachusetts; registered to practice before U.S. Patent and Trademark Office. *Education:* University of Minnesota (B.E.E., with distinction, 1974; M.B.A., 1978; J.D., cum laude, 1977).

PAUL H. BERGHOFF, born Chicago, Illinois, August 25, 1956; admitted to bar, 1981, Illinois and U.S. District Court, Northern District of Illinois; 1983, U.S. Court of Appeals for the Federal Circuit; 1986, U.S. Supreme Court; registered to practice before U.S. Patent and Trademark Office. *Education:* Lawrence University (B.A., in Chem., cum laude, 1978); University of Michigan (J.D., cum laude, 1981).

GRANTLAND G. DRUTCHAS, born Detroit, Michigan, January 22, 1961; admitted to bar, 1985, Illinois; U.S. District Court, Northern District of Illinois; U.S. Court of Appeals for the Federal Circuit; U.S. Supreme Court; registered to practice before U.S. Patent and Trademark Office. *Education:* Massachusetts Institute of Technology (B.S.M.E., 1982); University of Michigan (J.D., 1985).

JAMES C. GUMINA, born Washington, D.C., June 1, 1959; admitted to bar, 1987, Illinois and U.S. Court of Appeals for the Federal Circuit; U.S. District Court, Northern District of Illinois; U.S. District Court, Eastern District of Wisconsin; registered to practice before U.S. Patent and Trademark Office. *Education:* University of Notre Dame (B.S., 1981); John Marshall Law School (J.D., 1987).

DAVID M. FRISCHKORN, born Berkeley, California, August 22, 1957; admitted to bar, 1989, Illinois and U.S. District Court, Northern District of Illinois; U.S. Court of Appeals for the Federal Circuit; registered to practice before U.S. Patent and Trademark Office. *Education:* University of California at Berkeley (B.S. Ch.E., 1980); DePaul University (J.D., 1989).

LEIF R. SIGMOND, JR., born San Gabriel, California, February 20, 1965; admitted to bar, 1990, Illinois and U.S. District Court, Northern District of Illinois; 1992, U.S. Court of Appeals for the Federal Circuit; 1995, New Jersey and U.S. District Court, District of New Jersey; 1997, New York; 1998, U.S. District Court, Western District of Michigan and U.S. District Court, Eastern District of Wisconsin; 1999, U.S. Supreme Court; registered to practice before U.S. Patent and Trademark Office. *Education:* Lafayette College (B.S., Electrical Engineering, 1987); Widener University School of Law (J.D., magna cum laude, 1990).

A. BLAIR HUGHES, born Redwood City, California, October 7, 1958; admitted to bar, 1991, Illinois and U.S. District Court, Northern District of Illinois; 1992, U.S. Court of Appeals for the Federal Circuit; registered to practice before U.S. Patent and Trademark Office. *Education:* Rose-Hulman Institute of Technology (B.S., Ch.E., cum laude, 1980); DePaul University (J.D., with honors, 1991).

LAWRENCE H. AARONSON, born Shreveport, Louisiana, November 29, 1965; admitted to bar, 1991, Illinois; U.S. Court of Appeals for the Federal Circuit; U.S. District Court, Northern District of Illinois; registered to practice before U.S. Patent and Trademark Office. *Education:* University of Michigan (B.S.E.E., summa cum laude, 1987); University of Illinois (J.D., magna cum laude, 1991).

THOMAS A. FAIRHALL, born Seattle, Washington, December 31, 1959; admitted to bar, 1991, Illinois, Washington State, U.S. Court of Federal Claims, U.S. District Court, Northern District of Illinois; U.S. District Court, Western District of Michigan and U.S. Court of Appeals for the Federal Circuit; registered to practice before U.S. Patent and Trademark Office. *Education:* University of Colorado at Boulder (B.A., Physics and Mathematics, with distinction, 1988); John Marshall Law School (J.D., summa cum laude, 1991).

(This Listing Continued)

MATTHEW J. SAMPSON, born Evergreen Park, Illinois, January 7, 1963; admitted to bar, 1991, Illinois and U.S. District Court, Northern District of Illinois; registered to practice before U.S. Patent and Trademark Office. *Education:* University of Illinois (B.S.E.E., 1985); DePaul University, College of Law (J.D., with honors, 1991).

CURT J. WHITENACK, born Wausau, Wisconsin, September 14, 1961; admitted to bar, 1991, Illinois, Wisconsin, U.S. District Court, Western District of Wisconsin and U.S. District Court, Northern District of Illinois; registered to practice before U.S. Patent and Trademark Office. *Education:* University of Wisconsin (B.S., Bacteriology, 1984; J.D., cum laude, 1991); Michigan State University (M.S., 1988).

MICHAEL S. GREENFIELD, born Chicago Illinois, October 10, 1960; admitted to bar, 1992, Illinois; registered to practice before the U.S. Patent and Trademark Office. *Education:* University of Illinois (B.S., Chemistry, 1982, Phi Beta Kappa, Phi Kappa Phi); University of California, San Diego (M.S. Chemistry, 1984; Ph.D., Chemistry, 1987); University of California, Los Angeles (Post-Doctoral Fellow, Department of Chemistry, 1987-1989); Stanford University (J.D., 1992).

STEVEN J. SARUSSI, born Chicago, Illinois, June 24, 1960; admitted to bar, 1992, Illinois and U.S. District Court, Northern District of Illinois; registered to practice before U.S. Patent and Trademark Office. *Education:* Loyola University of Chicago (A.B., 1982; M.S., 1986); John Marshall Law School (J.D., magna cum laude, 1992).

CHRISTOPHER M. CAVAN, born Illinois, August 11, 1964; admitted to bar, 1992, Illinois; registered to practice before U.S. Patent and Trademark Office. *Education:* Northwestern University (B.S.M.E., 1986); Loyola University (J.D., cum laude, 1992).

KEVIN E. NOONAN, born Bronxville, New York, May 7, 1954; admitted to bar, 1993, Illinois, U.S. District Court, Northern District of Illinois and Massachusetts; registered to practice before U.S. Patent and Trademark Office. *Education:* State University of New York (B.S., 1978); Princeton University (Ph.D., Molecular Biology, 1987); John Marshall Law School (J.D., cum laude, 1993).

GEORGE I. LEE, born May 20, 1964; admitted to bar, 1994, Illinois and U.S. District Court, Northern District of Illinois; U.S. District Court, District of Arizona; registered to practice before U.S. Patent and Trademark Office. *Education:* University of Wisconsin (B.S.E.E., 1986); University of Illinois (J.D., magna cum laude, 1994).

JOSHUA R. RICH, born Washington, D.C., June 29, 1969; admitted to bar, 1994, Illinois; 1995, U.S. District Court, Northern and Central Districts of Illinois; 1996, U.S. Court of Appeals, Sixth Circuit; 1997, U.S. Court of Appeals, Seventh Circuit; 2001, U.S. Court of Appeals, Federal Circuit and U.S. District Court, Eastern District of Wisconsin; registered to practice before U.S. Patent and Trademark Office. *Education:* University of Maryland (B.S., Biochemistry, B.A., Government and Politics, 1991); University of Virginia (J.D., 1994).

JAMES M. McCARTHY, born Upper Saddle River, New Jersey, January 14, 1969; admitted to bar, 1994, Illinois and U.S. District Court, Northern District of Illinois; 1998, U.S. Court of Appeals for the Federal Circuit; 1999, U.S. District Court, Eastern District of Wisconsin; registered to practice before U.S. Patent and Trademark Office. *Education:* University of Notre Dame (B.S.E.E., 1991); University of Dayton (J.D., 1994).

ROBERT J. IRVINE, III, born Hinsdale, Illinois, November 7, 1962; admitted to bar, 1994, Illinois and U.S. District Court, Northern District of Illinois. *Education:* University of Illinois (B.S.E.E., 1989; M.S.E.E., 1992); Northwestern University (J.D., 1994).

THOMAS E. WETTERMANN, born Chicago, Illinois, March 29, 1964; admitted to bar, 1995, Illinois and U.S. District Court, Northern District of Illinois; 1996, U.S. Court of Appeals, Federal Circuit; registered to practice before U.S. Patent and Trademark Office. *Education:* Marquette University (B.S.E.E., 1987; B.A., German, 1987); University of North Carolina (M.B.A., 1992); DePaul University (J.D., 1995). ***LANGUAGES:*** German.

SEAN M. SULLIVAN, born Chicago, Illinois, May 11, 1970; admitted to bar, 1995, Illinois and U.S. District Court, Northern District of Illinois; registered to practice before U.S. Patent and Trademark Office. *Education:* University of Illinois (B.S.M.E., 1992); Loyola University (J.D., cum laude, 1995).

RICHARD A. MACHONKIN, born Rochester, New York, March 22, 1968; admitted to bar, 1996, Illinois and U.S. District Court, Northern District of Illinois; registered to practice before U.S. Patent and Trademark Office. *Education:* University of Michigan (B.S., 1989); Cornell University (M.S., 1992); Harvard University (J.D., cum laude, 1996).

EMILY MIAO, born New York, N.Y., December 3, 1960; admitted to bar, 1997, Illinois; registered to practice before U.S. Patent and Trademark Office. *Education:* New York University (Ph.D., 1991); Chicago-Kent College of Law, Illinois Institute of Technology (J.D., 1997).

PATRICK G. GATTARI, born Detroit, Michigan, August 15, 1962; admitted to bar, 1992, Illinois and U.S. District Court, Northern District of Illinois including Trial Bar; registered to practice before U.S. Patent and Trademark Office. *Education:* University of Michigan (B.S., 1985); Southern Methodist University (J.D., 1992).

DAVID S. HARPER, born Des Plaines, Illinois, June 1, 1961; admitted to bar, 1998, Illinois; registered to practice before U.S. Patent and Trademark Office. *Education:* Northern Illinois University (B.A., 1983); University of Illinois at Chicago (Ph.D., Molecular Biology, 1989); Chicago-Kent College of Law (J.D., 1998).

MARCUS J. THYMIAN, born St. Paul, Minnesota, January 31, 1972; admitted to bar, 1998, Illinois; U.S. District Court, Northern District of Illinois; registered to practice before U.S. Patent and Trademark Office. *Education:* University of Minnesota (B.S.E.E., 1995; J.D., cum laude, 1998).

STEPHEN H. DOCTER, born Park Ridge, Illinois, January 14, 1964; admitted to bar, 1999, Illinois; registered to practice before U.S. Patent and Trademark Office. *Education:* Loyola University of Chicago (M.S., Organic Chemistry, 1992; B.A., Chemistry, 1986); John Marshall School of Law (J.D., 1999). ***LANGUAGES:*** German.

LISA M. W. HILLMAN, born West Allis, Wisconsin; admitted to bar, 1999, Virginia and District of Columbia; 2001, Illinois; registered to practice before U.S. Patent and Trademark Office. *Education:* University of Florida (Ph.D., 1995; J.D., with honors, 1998).

(This Listing Continued)

ANITA J. TERPSTRA, born Lynn, Massachusetts, September 16, 1961; admitted to bar, 1998, Illinois; U.S. District Court, Northern District of Illinois. *Education:* Bates College (B.A., Biology, 1984); Boston University (Ph.D., Biochemistry, 1994); St. Louis University Law School (J.D., 1998).

S. RICHARD CARDEN, born Huntsville, Alabama, October 10, 1967; admitted to bar, 1999, Illinois and U.S. District Court, Northern District of Illinois; 2000, U.S. District Court, Eastern District of Wisconsin; U.S. Court of Appeals, Federal Circuit; registered to practice before U.S. Patent and Trademark Office. *Education:* Tulane University (B.S.E., cum laude, 1989); University of Pennsylvania (M.S.E., in Chemical Engineering, 1994); Washington University (J.D., 1999). ***LANGUAGES:*** French.

JEREMY EDWARD NOE, born Chicago, Illinois, March 11, 1963; admitted to bar, 2000, Illinois. *Education:* University of Illinois (B.S., Ch.E., 1984); Chicago-Kent College of Law (J.D., 2000).

PAUL S. TULLY, born Springfield, Illinois, April 4, 1967; admitted to bar, 2000, Illinois; U.S. District Court, Northern District of Illinois; U.S. Court of Appeals, Seventh and Federal Circuits; registered to practice before U.S. Patent and Trademark Office. *Education:* Eastern Illinois University (B.S., 1989); Northwestern University (M.S., 1990; Ph.D., 1992); John Marshall Law School (J.D., with honors, 2000).

ANTHOULA POMRENING, born Chicago, Illinois, September 1, 1967; admitted to bar, 1999, Illinois; registered to practice before U.S. Patent and Trademark Office. *Education:* Illinois Institute of Technology (B.S.M.E., 1989); John Marshall Law School (J.D., 1999).

ALISON JAMEEN BALDWIN, born Frankfurt, Germany, November 18, 1970; admitted to bar, 2000, Illinois and U.S. District Court, Northern District of Illinois. *Education:* Purdue University (B.S., 1994); North Carolina State University (M.Ag., 1996); Chicago-Kent College of Law (J.D., 2000).

NICOLE F. KEENAN, born Buffalo, New York, November 10, 1971; admitted to bar, 2000, Illinois. *Education:* University of New York at Buffalo (Pharmacy, B.S., 1995); DePaul University (J.D., 2000).

JEFFREY A. STECK, born Dayton, Ohio, December 16, 1972; admitted to bar, 2001, New York; 2002, Illinois; registered to practice before U.S. Patent and Trademark Office. *Education:* University of Chicago (B.A., Physics, 1994); University of California at Berkeley (J.D., 2000).

PAUL W. CHURILLA, born Detroit, Michigan, May 23, 1965; admitted to bar, 2000, Oregon; 2001, U.S. District Court, District of Oregon; 2001, U.S. Court of Appeals, Ninth Circuit; registered to practice before U.S. Patent and Trademark Office (Not admitted in Illinois). *Education:* Michigan State University (B.S.E.E., 1987); Northwestern School of Law of Lewis (J.D., 2000).

OF COUNSEL

DENIS A. BERNTSEN, born Chicago, Illinois, April 22, 1947; admitted to bar, 1972, Illinois; 1985, Massachusetts; registered to practice before U.S. Patent and Trademark Office. *Education:* University of Illinois (B.S.E.E., 1969; J.D., 1972).

ASSOCIATES

ERIC R. MORAN, born Winfield, Illinois, November 23, 1971; admitted to bar, 2001, Illinois; registered to practice before U.S. Patent and Trademark Office. *Education:* University of Notre Dame (B.S., 1994); Chicago-Kent College of Law (J.D., with high honors, 2001).

ANDREW W. WILLIAMS, born Columbus, Ohio, July 29, 1966; admitted to bar, 2001, Illinois; U.S. District Court, Northern District of Illinois; registered to practice before U.S. Patent and Trademark Office. *Education:* University of Iowa (B.S., 1988); Yale University (M.Phil., 1991; Ph.D., 1995); George Washington University (J.D., with highest honors, 2001).

DANIEL P. WILLIAMS, born Grand Rapids, Michigan, July 4, 1976; admitted to bar, 2001, Illinois. *Education:* University of Michigan (C.S.E., 1998); Harvard University (J.D., 2001).

AARON F. BARKOFF, born Madison, Wisconsin, July 4, 1971; admitted to bar, 2002, Illinois; registered to practice before U.S. Patent and Trademark Office. *Education:* Lawrence University (B.A., 1993); University of Wisconsin-Madison (Ph.D., 1999); University of Chicago Law School (J.D., 2002).

MARK L. CHAEL, born Hammond, Indiana, December 31, 1959; admitted to bar, 2002, Illinois; registered to practice before U.S. Patent and Trademark Office. *Education:* Purdue University (B.S., 1985); Northwestern University (Ph.D., 1994); John Marshall Law School (J.D., 2002).

DONALD L. ZUHN, born Evergreen Park, Illinois, January 10, 1962; admitted to bar, 2002, Illinois; registered to practice before U.S. Patent and Trademark Office. *Education:* Loyola University (B.S., 1984); University of Illinois at Chicago (Ph.D., 1996); John Marshall Law School (J.D., 2002).

BRADLEY W. CRAWFORD, born Berwyn, Illinois, December 15, 1966; admitted to bar, 2003, Illinois; registered to practice before U.S. Patent and Trademark Office. *Education:* University of Illinois at Chicago (B.S., 1991); University of Illinois at Urbana-Champaign (M.S., 1996); Chicago-Kent College of Law (J.D., 2002).

LISA SCHOEDEL, born Los Angeles, California; admitted to bar, 2003, Illinois; registered to practice before U.S. Patent and Trademark Office. *Education:* Washington University (B.S., 1987; M.S., 1991); DePaul College of Law (J.D., summa cum laude, 2003).

DENNIS D. CROUCH, born Columbia, South Carolina, April 30, 1975; admitted to bar, 2003, Illinois; registered to practice before U.S. Patent and Trademark Office. *Education:* Princeton University (B.S.E., honors, 1997); University of Chicago (J.D., honors, 2003).

(This Listing Continued)

McDONNELL BOEHNEN HULBERT & BERGHOFF LLP, Chicago—Continued

DAVID L. CIESIELSKI, born Gary, Indiana; admitted to bar, 2003, Illinois and U.S. District Court, Northern District of Illinois. *Education:* Purdue University, Calumet (B.S.E.E., 1991); GMI-Kettering University (M.S., Manufacturing Management, 1996); Indiana University (J.D., 2003).

VICTORIA FRIEDMAN, born Kiev, Ukraine; admitted to bar, 2003, Illinois. *Education:* DePaul University (CLS, 2000); John Marshall Law School (J.D., 2003). ***LANGUAGES:*** Russian and Ukrainian.

PAULA S. FRITSCH, born Milwaukee, Wisconsin; admitted to bar, 2003, Illinois. *Education:* Winona State University (B.S., 1994); University of Iowa (Ph.D., 2000; J.D., 2003).

JENNIFER M. KURCZ, born Lincoln, Nebraska; admitted to bar, 2003, Illinois; registered to practice before U.S. Patent and Trademark Office. *Education:* University of Nebraska at Lincoln (B.S., 2000; J.D., 2003).

RAEF SHALTOUT, born Alexandria, Egypt, January 18, 1969; admitted to bar, 2004, Illinois; registered to practice before U.S. Patent and Trademark Office. *Education:* Southwest Missouri State University (B.S., 1989); University of Missouri (Ph.D., 1996); Chicago-Kent College of Law, Illinois Institute of Technology (J.D., 2003).

McFADDEN & DILLON

A PROFESSIONAL CORPORATION

120 SOUTH LA SALLE, SUITE 1530

CHICAGO, ILLINOIS 60603

Telephone: 312-201-8300

Facsimile: 312-201-0535

Email: mcfaddendillonlaw@ameritech.net

General Civil Trial and Appellate Practice. Corporation, Securities, Estate Planning, Probate, Banking, Real Estate and Employment Law.

ROGER J. McFADDEN, born Evergreen Park, Illinois, September 14, 1945; admitted to bar, 1971, Illinois; 1973, U.S. District Court, Northern District of Illinois including Trial Bar; 1976, U.S. Court of Appeals, Seventh Circuit; 1986, U.S. Tax Court and U.S. Claims Court; 1990, U.S. Court of Appeals, Eighth Circuit. *Education:* University of Notre Dame (A.B., 1967); University of Illinois (J.D., 1971). Law Clerk to the Honorable William J. Lynch, U.S. District Court, 1971-1973. *Member:* Chicago and American (Member, Sections on: Litigation; Antitrust Law; Labor and Employment Law) Bar Associations; Bar Association of the Seventh Federal Circuit. ***REPORTED CASES:*** Shea v. Angulo, 19 F.3d 343 (7th Cir. 1994); Bruce Drugs, Inc. v. Hollister, Inc., 688 F.2d 853 (1st Cir. 1982); Tibbitts v. Van Den Bergh Foods Company, 859 F.Supp. 1168 (N.D. Ill. 1994); Rose Marine Transportation Corp. v. Kaiser Aluminum & Chemical Corporation, 778 F.Supp. 15 (N.D. Ill. 1991); Rose Marine Transportation v. Kaiser Aluminum & Chemical Corporation, 762 F.Supp. 757 (N.D.Ill. 1991); Rose Marine Transportation v. Kaiser Aluminum & Chemical Corporation, 758 F.Supp. 1218 (N.D. Ill. 1990); Craig v. First American Capital Research, Inc., et al., 740 F.Supp. 530 (N.D. Ill. 1990); George F. Harding Museum v. United States, 674 F.Supp. 1323 (N.D. Ill. 1987); Continental Illinois National Bank & Trust Co. v. Stanley, 606 F.Supp. 558 (N.D. Ill. 1985); Continental Illinois National Bank & Trust Co. v. Stanley, 585 F.Supp. 1385 (N.D. Ill. 1984); Continental Illinois National Bank & Trust Co. v. Stanley, 585 F.Supp. 610 (N.D. Ill. 1984); Oliff v. Exchange International Corporation, 449 F.Supp. 1277 (N.D. Ill. 1978); Radial Lip Machine, Inc. v. International Carbide Corp., 76 F.R.D. 224 (N.D. Ill. 1977); Lavin v. A.G. Becker, Inc., 60 F.R.D. 684 (N.D. Ill. 1973); Lurie v. Canadian Javelin, Ltd., 93 Ill.2d 231, 443 N.E.2d 592 (1982); Lurie v. Canadian Javelin, Ltd., 92 Ill.App.3d 15, 415 N.E.2d 1055 (1st Dist. 1980). ***PRACTICE AREAS:*** Employment Practices Law; Commercial Litigation.

THOMAS J. DILLON, born Evergreen Park, Illinois, May 16, 1954; admitted to bar, 1979, Illinois and U.S. District Court, Northern District of Illinois including Trial Bar, U.S. Tax Court and U.S. Claims Court; 1986, U.S. Court of Appeals, Seventh Circuit. *Education:* University of Chicago (B.A., 1976); Northwestern University (J.D., 1979). *Member:* Chicago, Illinois State and American (Member, Litigation Section) Bar Associations; Bar Association of the Seventh Federal Circuit. ***REPORTED CASES:*** Kusak v. Ameritech Information Systems, 80 F. 3d 199 (7th Cir. 1996); Fallimento C.Op.M.A. v. Fischer Crane Company, 995 F.2d 789 (7th Cir. 1993); Ashland Oil Co. v. Arnett, 875 F.2d 1271 (7th Cir. 1989); Furth v. Inc. Publishing Co., 823 F.2d 1178 (7th Cir. 1987); Searight v. Kaiser Aluminum & Chemical Corporation, 625 F.Supp. 17 (N.D. Ill. 1984); Jacobson v. Buffalo Rock Supply Co., 278 Ill. App. 3d 1084, 664 N.E.2d 328 (3rd Dist. 1996). ***PRACTICE AREAS:*** Civil Litigation; Employment Practices Law; Bankruptcy Law; Real Estate Law; Commercial Litigation; Banking Law; Estate Planning; General Practice.

WENDY KALETA SKROBIN, born Oak Lawn, Illinois, March 26, 1969; admitted to bar, 1994, Illinois and U.S. District Court, Northern District of Illinois. *Education:* Northwestern University (B.A., 1991); Loyola University (J.D., 1994). *Member:* Chicago and Illinois Bar Associations. ***REPORTED CASES:*** People v. LeCour, 273 Ill.App.3d 1003, 652 N.E.2d 1221 (1st Dist. 1995). ***PRACTICE AREAS:*** Real Estate Law; Probate; Estate Planning; Family Law; Corporate Law; Civil Practice; Trial Practice; Appellate Practice.

TIMOTHY J. SOMEN, born Maywood, Illinois, September 13, 1976; admitted to bar, 2003, Illinois and U.S. District Court, Northern District of Illinois. *Education:* St. Norbert College (B.B.A., 1998); John Marshall Law School (J.D., 2002). *Member:* Illinois State and American Bar Associations. ***PRACTICE AREAS:*** Civil Litigation; Commercial Litigation; Banking Law; Personal Injury; Real Estate; Estate Planning; General Practice.

McGUIREWOODS LLP

Established in 1834

77 WEST WACKER DRIVE

SUITE 4100

CHICAGO, ILLINOIS 60601-1815

Telephone: 312-849-8100

Fax: 312-849-3690

Email: info@mcguirewoods.com

URL: http://www.mcguirewoods.com

REVISER OF THE VIRGINIA LAW DIGEST FOR THIS DIRECTORY.

Atlanta, Georgia Office: The Proscenium, 1170 Peachtree Street, N.E., Suite 2100, 30309-7649. Telephone: 404-443-5500. Fax: 404-443-5599.

Baltimore, Maryland Office: 7 Saint Paul Street, Suite 1000, 21202-1671. Telephone: 410-659-4400. Fax: 410-659-4599.

Charlotte, North Carolina Office: Bank of America Corporate Center, Suite 2900, 100 North Tryon Street, 28202-4011. Telephone: 704-373-8999. Fax: 704-373-8935.

Charlottesville, Virginia Office: Court Square Building, 310 Fourth Street N.E., Suite 300, P.O. Box 1288, 22902-1288. Telephone: 434-977-2500. Fax: 434-980-2222.

Jacksonville, Florida Office: Bank of America Tower, 50 North Laura Street, Suite 3300, 32202-3661. Telephone: 904-798-3200. Fax: 904-798-3207.

Los Angeles, California Office: 11601 Wilshire Boulevard, 90025. Telephone: 310-575-1848.

McLean, (Tysons Corner) Virginia Office: 1750 Tysons Boulevard, Suite 1800, 22102-4215. Telephone: 703-712-5000. Fax: 703-712-5050.

New York, New York Offices: 1345 Avenue of the Americas, 10105-0106. Telephone: 212-548-2100. Fax: 212-548-2150.

Norfolk, Virginia Office: World Trade Center, 101 West Main Street, Suite 9000, 23510-1655. Telephone: 757-640-3700. Fax: 757-640-3701.

Pittsburgh, Pennsylvania Office: Dominion Tower, 23rd Floor, 625 Liberty Avenue, 15222-3142. Telephone: 412-667-6000. Fax: 412-667-6050.

Richmond, Virginia Office: One James Center, 901 East Cary Street, 23219-4030. Telephone: 804-775-1000. Fax: 804-775-1061.

Washington, D.C. Office: Washington Square, 1050 Connecticut Avenue, N.W., Suite 1200, 20036-5317. Telephone: 202-857-1700. Fax: 202-857-1737.

Almaty, Republic of Kazakhstan Office: McGuireWoods Kazakhstan LLP, 41B, Kazibek Bi Street, 5th Floor, 480100. Telephone: +7-3272-596-100. Fax: +7-3272-596-116.

Brussels, Belgium Office: Avenue Louise 250, bte 64, 1050. Telephone: +32-(0)2-629-42-11. Fax: +32 (0)2 629 42 22.

Accountants Liability, Administrative Law, Advertising Law, Affordable Housing, Alternative Dispute Resolution, Americans with Disabilities Act, Antitrust, Appellate Practice, Asbestos Litigation, Asset Based Finance, Automotive Products Liability, Bankruptcy, Banks and Banking, Business Acquisitions, Business Divestitures, Business Law, Business Litigation, Buying and Selling of Businesses, Capital Markets, Charitable Giving, Class Actions, Coal Mining, Cogeneration; College and University Law, Commercial Litigation, Commercial Real Estate, Communications and Media, Complex Commercial Litigation, Computer Contracts, Confidentiality Agreements, Construction Equipment Liability, Construction Litigation, Consumer Finance, Content Licensing, Contracts, Copyright Licensing, Corporate Control Contests, Corporate Finance, Corporate Governance, Corporate Investigations, Corporate Law, Corporate Reorganization, Covenants Not to Compete, Creditors Rights, Criminal Taxation, Digital Signatures, Domain Name Infringement, Domain Names, Drug and Medical Device Defense, Drug and Medical Device Litigation, E-Commerce, Education Law, Electric Utilities, Emerging Growth Companies, Employee Benefits, Employee Benefits Litigation, Employment Breach of Contract, Employment Contracts, Employment Discrimination, Energy, Energy Acquisitions, Energy Project Development, Energy Regulation, Entertainment Law, Environmental Administrative Law, Environmental Compliance, Environmental Land Use, Environmental Law, Environmental Litigation, Environmental Real Estate, ERISA, Executive Compensation, False Advertising, Family Business Law, Fiduciary Litigation, Finance, First Amendment Law, Franchises and Franchising, Gas Utilities, Government Investigations, Government Relations, Health Care, High Technology Contracts, Hospital Administration, Hospital Law, Hostile Takeovers, Immigration Law, Independent Power, Insurance Litigation, Intellectual Property, Intellectual Property Licensing, Intellectual Property Litigation, Intellectual Property Portfolio Management, Intellectual Property Procurement, Intellectual Property Rights, International Arbitration, International Mergers and Acquisitions, International Taxation, International Trade, Internet Licensing, Joint Venture Litigation, Joint Ventures, Labor and Employment, Labor Relations, Land Use, Latex Allergy Litigation, Lead Poisoning, Leasing, Legal Ethics and Professional Responsibility, Leveraged Buyouts, Litigation, Litigation Management, Lobbying, Local Taxation, Marketing Law, Media Law, Merger Reorganization, Mergers and Acquisitions Finance, Mergers, Acquisitions and Divestitures, Motorcycle Products Liability, Municipal Law, Music Law, Natural Gas, North American Energy Trade, Oil and Gas Law, Partnership Law, Partnership Litigation, Partnership Taxation, Patent Litigation, Patent Prosecution, Patents, Petroleum Trading, Products Liability, Products Liability Insurance Coverage, Project Finance, Promotion Law, Proprietary Rights, Proxy Contests, Public Finance, Public Utility Law, Railroad Law, Real Estate, Real Estate Acquisitions, Real Estate Development, Real Estate Investment Trusts, Real Estate Leasing, Regulatory Law, Resorts and Leisure, Securities, Securities Litigation, Securities Regulation, Securitization, Software Copyright, Software Licensing, Software Protection, Spin-Offs, Sponsorship Law, Sports Law, Sports Licensing, Sports Marketing Law, State Taxation, Structured Finance, Sweepstakes, Takeovers, Tax Audits, Tax Credits, Tax Exempt Organizations, Tax Litigation, Taxation, Technology Licensing, Telephone Utility Regulation, Toxic Tort Class Actions, Toxic Torts, Trade Regulation, Trade Secrets, Trademark Registration, Trademarks, Transportation, Trusts and Estates, Trusts and Estates Taxation, Union Labor Law, Utility Law, Utility Regulation, Vaccine Injury, Web Site Development, White Collar Crime, Wrongful Termination.

FIRM PROFILE: Whether assisting a Fortune 50 giant or a small start-up, our focus is on building relationships that drive results. Our clients' businesses and industries are as important to us today as they were when we began in 1834, proven by the fact that many of our client relationships have lasted for decades. With lawyers working from 15 strategically located offices worldwide, McGuireWoods uses client focused teams to serve public, private, government

(This Listing Continued)

and nonprofit clients from such industries as automotive, banking and financial services, chemicals, energy resources, food processing, general manufacturing, government, health care, insurance, real estate, retailing, sports and entertainment, technology and telecom, and transportation.

PARTNERS

RICHELLE L. ASCHENBRENNER, born Miami, Florida, 1969; admitted to bar, 1994, Illinois. *Education:* University of Notre Dame (B.B.A., 1991); Loyola University Chicago School of Law (J.D., 1994); DePaul University (LL.M., 1998). ***PRACTICE AREAS:*** Executive Compensation; ERISA; Employee Benefits. ***Email:*** raschenbrenner@mcguirewoods.com

SCOTT BECKER, born Chicago, Illinois, 1964; admitted to bar, 1989, Illinois; 2000, Wisconsin. *Education:* University of Illinois (B.S., 1986); Harvard University (J.D., 1989). Certified Public Accountant, Illinois. Author: Book, "Ambulatory Surgery Centers: Legal and Regulatory Issues,"; Book, "The Physician's Managed Care Success Manual"; Book, "Health Care Law: A Practical Guide". Co-Editor, Mathew Bender Health Law Monthly. Managing Editor of Outpatient Surgery Business and Legal News. Author of more than 50 articles related to regulatory and transitional issues. Adjunct Professor of Corporate Health Care Law, Chicago Kent Law School. ***PRACTICE AREAS:*** Health Care; Corporate Law; Securities. ***Email:*** sbecker@mcguirewoods.com

LONNI E. BERKLEY, born Chicago, Illinois, 1960; admitted to bar, 1983, Illinois. *Education:* University of Colorado (B.A., 1980); Northwestern University (J.D., 1983). ***PRACTICE AREAS:*** Partnerships; Joint Ventures; Sports Law; Emerging Growth Companies; Technology; Mergers and Acquisitions; Asset Securitization; Public Finance; Project Finance; Securities Compliance; Capital Markets; Real Estate; Construction Law; Leasing; Public Partnerships; Private Partnerships; Resorts and Leisure; Affordable Housing; Tax Credits; Business Acquisitions; Business Reorganization; Business Divestitures; Family Business. ***Email:*** lberkley@mcguirewoods.com

PATRICK E. BRADY, born Chicago, Illinois, 1954; admitted to bar, 1983, Illinois; 1984, U.S. District Court, Northern District of Illinois. *Education:* Northwestern University (B.A., 1976); John Marshall Law School (J.D., 1983). Order of John Marshall. Awarded the John N. Jewett Scholarship and The Arba N. Waterman Scholarship and The Graduate School Scholarship. Member, Taxation Committee, Illinois Chamber of Commerce, 1991—. ***PRACTICE AREAS:*** Real Estate Acquisitions; Real Estate Leasing; Real Estate Sales; Real Estate Taxation; Real Estate Financing. ***Email:*** pbrady@mcguirewoods.com

FREDERICK H. BRANDING, born Elgin, Illinois, 1944; admitted to bar, 1973, Illinois; U.S. District Court, Northern District of Illinois including Trial Bar. *Education:* Drake University (B.A., 1966; B.S., 1968); Illinois Institute of Technology, Chicago Kent College of Law (J.D., 1973). Registered Pharmacist, Illinois, 1968. Two Time Recipient, FDA Commissioner's Special Citation for Outstanding Contributions in the Field of Food and Drug Law Enforcement. Author: "Understanding and Working with the Food and Drug Administration," Chapter in Legal Handbook for Doing Business in the United States, Compiled by Consul General of Switzerland, Chicago, 2004; "Underdeveloped: FDA's Authority to Take Photographs During an FDA Establishment Inspection under Section 704," Food and Drug Law Journal, Washington, D.C., 2003; "Preparing for and Surviving FDA Investigations," Food and Drug Law Institute Update, 2002; "Evaluating and Responding to the Threat of Bioterrorism," Client Alert, 2002. Member, Bell, Boyd & Lloyd. Partner: Holleb & Coff; Johnson & Bell. Assistant U.S. Attorney, Chief, Civil Division. Chief, Psychotropic Substances Control Unit, United Nations International Narcotics Control Board, Vienna Austria. ***PRACTICE AREAS:*** Food, Drug and Cosmetic Law; Federal Litigation; Regulatory Investigations. ***Email:*** fbranding@mcguirewoods.com

MICHAEL A. CHABRAJA, born Indianapolis, Indiana, 1967; admitted to bar, 1992, Illinois, U.S. District Court, Northern District of Illinois and U.S. Court of Appeals, Seventh Circuit. *Education:* DePauw University (B.A., 1989); University of Illinois (J.D., 1992). ***PRACTICE AREAS:*** Commercial Litigation; Intellectual Property Litigation; Products Liability Defense. ***Email:*** mchabraja@mcguirewoods.com

LELAND H. CHAIT, born Atlanta, Georgia, 1959; admitted to bar, 1989, Louisiana; 1990, U.S. District Court, Eastern District of Louisiana; 1991, Illinois; 1992, U.S. Court of Appeals, 7th Circuit; 1994, U.S. District Court, Eastern District of Michigan; 2002, U.S. District Court, Northern District of Illinois and U.S. Supreme Court. *Education:* University of Chicago (B.A., 1981; J.D., 1988). ***PRACTICE AREAS:*** Antitrust and Trade Regulation; Class Action Defense; Complex and Multi-District Litigation; Consumer Finance; Partnerships; Joint Ventures; Securities Litigation. ***Email:*** lchait@mcguirewoods.com

JEFFREY C. CLARK, born 1965; admitted to bar, 1991, Illinois; U.S. District Court, Northern District of Illinois including Trial Bar. *Education:* University of Toledo (B.A., 1988); The Ohio State University College of Law (J.D., 1991). ***PRACTICE AREAS:*** Civil Litigation; Complex Litigation; Trial Practice; Hospital Risk Management; Hospital Liability. ***Email:*** jcclark@mcguirewoods.com

'CRAIG R. CULBERTSON, born Chicago, Illinois, 1955; admitted to bar, 1980, Illinois. *Education:* Davidson College (B.A., 1977); Loyola University (J.D., 1980). Executive Vice President and General Counsel, Castle Energy Corporation, 1993-1996. General Counsel, iTRACS Corporation, 2000—. ***PRACTICE AREAS:*** Mergers and Acquisitions; Banking Law; Corporate Finance; Emerging Growth Companies; Technology Law; Energy; Project Finance; Securities. ***Email:*** cculbertson@mcguirewoods.com

DARRYL R. DAVIDSON, born Chicago, Illinois, 1959; admitted to bar, 1983, Illinois. *Education:* University of Illinois at Chicago (B.A., 1980); University of Illinois College of Law (J.D., 1983). Phi Beta Kappa. Edmund J. James Scholar. ***PRACTICE AREAS:*** Municipal Bonds; Tax Increment Finance; Municipal Finance. ***Email:*** ddavidson@mcguirewoods.com

KEITH A. DORMAN, born Elmhurst, Illinois, 1957; admitted to bar, 1982, Illinois; U.S. District Court, Northern District of Illinois; 1988, U.S. District Court, Northern District of California; 1992, U.S. Court of Appeals, Seventh Circuit; 1994, U.S. District Court, Western District of Michigan; 1995, U.S. Court of Appeals, Eighth Circuit; 1996, U.S. Supreme Court; 1997, U.S. Court of Appeals, Eleventh Circuit. *Education:* Augustana College (B.A., 1979); University of Illinois (J.D., 1982). Phi Beta Kappa; Omicron Delta Kappa. Member, Mortar Board. ***PRACTICE AREAS:*** Labor and Employment; Age Discrimination in Employment; Employment Discrimination; Labor Law; Sexual Harassment; Wage and Hour Law; Trade Secrets; Non-Compete Agreements and Enforcement. ***Email:*** kdorman@mcguirewoods.com

SCOTT P. DOWNING, born Chicago, Illinois, 1966; admitted to bar, 1991, Illinois. *Education:* University of Illinois (B.A., 1988); University of Chicago (J.D., 1991). Phi Beta Kappa. Associate Editor, The Business Lawyer, 1993-1994. Co-Author: Protecting Your ASC: A Legal Handbook. ***PRACTICE AREAS:*** Health Care; Corporate. ***Email:*** sdowning@mcguirewoods.com

LINDA B. DUBNOW, born Rochester, Minnesota, 1963; admitted to bar, 1992, Arizona and U.S. District Court, District of Arizona; 1995, Illinois; 1996, U.S. District Court, Northern District of Illinois; 1999, U.S. Court of Appeals, Seventh Circuit; 2000, U.S. Court of Appeals, Ninth Circuit; 2003, U.S. Court of Appeals, Eleventh Circuit. *Education:* University of Pennsylvania (B.A., 1985); Boston University (J.D., 1992). ***PRACTICE AREAS:*** Appellate; Class Action Litigation; Complex Commercial Litigation; Consumer Financial Services. ***Email:*** ldubnow@mcguirewoods.com

PAUL D. DURBIN, born Springfield, Illinois, 1969; admitted to bar, 1994, Illinois and U.S. District Court, Central District of Illinois; 1995, U.S. Court of Appeals, Seventh Circuit; 2002, U.S. District Court, Northern District of Illinois. *Education:* Marquette University (B.A., 1991); University of Illinois (J.D., 1994). ***PRACTICE AREAS:*** Debt and Equity Finance; Commercial Transactions. ***Email:*** pdurbin@mcguirewoods.com

PAUL E. FISHER, born Boston, Massachusetts, 1947; admitted to bar, 1973, Illinois. *Education:* Rockford College (B.A., 1969); University of Michigan (J.D., 1973). Partner, Piper, Marbury, Rudnick & Wolfe, 1981-2001. Senior Attorney, The First National Bank of Chicago, 1975-1981. ***PRACTICE AREAS:*** Real Estate Finance; Real Estate Acquisitions; Leasing; Letters of Credit; Loan Workouts; Foreclosures; Mergers, Acquisitions and Divestitures; Banking; Project Finance; Affordable Housing; Tax Credits; Capital Markets; Real Estate; Environmental Law; Land Use; Public and Private Partnerships; Resorts and Hospitality; Real Estate Transactions; International Investment; International Taxation. ***Email:*** pfisher@mcguirewoods.com

KARA M. FRIEDMAN, born Kalamazoo, Michigan, 1967; admitted to bar, 1993, Illinois. *Education:* University of Michigan (B.A., 1989); Loyola University of Chicago (J.D., 1993). ***LANGUAGES:*** Spanish. ***PRACTICE AREAS:*** Health Care; Certificates of Need; Health Care Corporate Law; Health Care Licensing. ***Email:*** kfriedman@mcguirewoods.com

DONALD J. GIBSON, JR., born Kansas City, Missouri, 1958; admitted to bar, 1983, Illinois and U.S. District Court, Northern District of Illinois. *Education:* Loras College; Loyola University (B.A., 1980; J.D., 1983). General Counsel, Boulevard Bancorp, Inc., 1990-1994. ***PRACTICE AREAS:*** Banking; Commercial Lending; Real Estate; Commercial Leasing; Corporate. ***Email:*** dgibson@mcguirewoods.com

LARRY R. GOLDSTEIN, born Indianapolis, Indiana, 1948; admitted to bar, 1973, Illinois. *Education:* Indiana University (A.B., 1970); University of Michigan (J.D., 1973). Phi Beta Kappa. ***PRACTICE AREAS:*** Employee Benefits. ***Email:*** lrgoldstein@mcguirewoods.com

ARNOLD E. GRANT, born Chicago, Illinois, 1957; admitted to bar, 1984, Illinois. *Education:* Washington University (B.A., 1980); University of Chicago (J.D., 1984). ***PRACTICE AREAS:*** Corporate Law; Tax Planning; Litigation. ***Email:*** agrant@mcguirewoods.com

RICHARD T. GREENBERG, born Brooklyn, New York, 1952; admitted to bar, 1977, Illinois. *Education:* Northwestern University (B.A., 1974); New York University School of Law (J.D., 1977). ***PRACTICE AREAS:*** Business Litigation; Professional Liability; Corporate Governance; Insurance; Reinsurance. ***Email:*** rgreenberg@mcguirewoods.com

W. KIRK GRIMM, born Minneapolis, Minnesota, 1955; admitted to bar, 1980, Illinois. *Education:* Northwestern University (B.A., 1977); Stanford University (J.D., 1980). ***PRACTICE AREAS:*** Leasing; Lending; Mergers and Acquisitions; Emerging Growth Companies. ***Email:*** kgrimm@mcguirewoods.com

DAVID S. GUIN, born South Bend, Indiana, 1962; admitted to bar, 1989, Illinois. *Education:* University of Notre Dame (B.B.A., 1984); Notre Dame Law School (J.D., 1989). ***Email:*** dguin@mcguirewoods.com

JANICE K. HAMBLIN, born Crawfordsville, Indiana, 1961; admitted to bar, 1987, Illinois. *Education:* Iowa State University (B.B.A., 1983); University of Illinois (J.D., 1987). ***PRACTICE AREAS:*** General Corporate; Mergers and Acquisitions; International. ***Email:*** jhamblin@mcguirewoods.com

JAMES T. HARRINGTON, born Chicago, Illinois, 1942; admitted to bar, 1967, Illinois; 1968, Indiana; 1969, U.S. Supreme Court; 1983, U.S. Court of Appeals, Third, Fourth, Seventh and Eighth Circuits; U.S. District Court, Northern, Central and Southern Districts of Illinois including Trial Bar; U.S. District Court, Northern and Southern Districts of Indiana. *Education:* University of Notre Dame (B.A., 1964; J.D., 1967). Member, Board of Editors, Notre Dame Lawyer, 1966-1967. Law Clerk, The Honorable George N. Beamer, U.S. District Court, Northern District of Indiana, 1967-1969. Associate and Partner, Rooks, Pitts & Poust, 1969-1987. Partner: Ross & Hardies, 1987-2003; McGuireWoods LLP, 2003—. Vice President and Secretary, Mid-America Legal Foundation. Chairman, Board of Advisors, IIT Stuart School of Business, Masters in Environmental Management. Chairman, Board of Directors, Illinois Safety Council. Frequent author and speaker on envionrmental law. ***PRACTICE AREAS:*** Environmental Litigation; Air Pollution; Environmental Administrative Law; Hazardous Waste; Solid Waste; Water Pollution; Environmental Permitting. ***Email:*** jharrington@mcguirewoods.com

DAVID L. HARTSELL, born Detroit, Michigan, 1955; admitted to bar, 1983, Michigan; 1986, Illinois; 1997, Georgia. *Education:* University of Michigan (B.A., 1978; J.D., 1982). Research Attorney, Michigan Court of Appeals, 1983-1984. ***PRACTICE AREAS:*** Business Litigation; Class Action Defense; Professional Liability; Consumer Litigation. ***Email:*** dhartsell@mcguirewoods.com

GAIL CHANEY KALINICH, born Mattoon, Illinois, 1962; admitted to bar, 1987, Illinois. *Education:* University of Illinois (A.B., 1984; J.D., 1987). Co-Author: "Discrimination Based on Handicap," 1989 IICLE Employment Discrimination Handbook. Member,

(This Listing Continued)

McGUIREWOODS LLP, Chicago—Continued

American Psychology-Law Society. ***PRACTICE AREAS:*** Labor and Employment; Employment Litigation; Sexual Harassment; Internal Employment Investigations. ***Email:*** gkalinich@mcguirewoods.com

KIMBERLY J. KANNENSOHN, born Youngstown, Ohio, 1965; admitted to bar, 1990, Illinois; 1991, U.S. District Court, Northern District of Illinois. *Education:* University of Michigan (B.A., 1987); Harvard University (J.D., 1990). Phi Beta Kappa. ***PRACTICE AREAS:*** Health Care Regulation; Health Care Reimbursement; Health Care Fraud; Physician Contracts. ***Email:*** kkannensohn@mcguirewoods.com

MICHAEL E. KERNAN, born New York, 1958; admitted to bar, 1992, Illinois. *Education:* United States Air Force Academy (B.S., 1980); University of Illinois (M.B.A., 1992; J.D., 1992). ***PRACTICE AREAS:*** Mergers and Acquisitions; Corporate Governance; Securities. ***Email:*** mkernan@mcguirewoods.com

JACQUELYN F. KIDDER, born Darien, Connecticut, 1957; admitted to bar, 1981, Illinois and U.S. District Court, Northern District of Illinois; U.S. District Court, Central District of Illinois and U.S. Court of Appeals, Seventh Circuit. *Education:* University of Connecticut (B.A., 1978); John Marshall Law School (J.D., 1981). Executive Editor, John Marshall Law Review, 1981. Member, Gavel Society, 1981. Member, Order of John Marshall. Author: "Derivative Immunity Under Sec. 1983: Conspiracies Between Immune Judicial Officials and Private Persons," John Marshall Law Review, Vol. 14, Fall 1980. ***PRACTICE AREAS:*** Commercial Litigation. ***Email:*** jkidder@mcguirewoods.com

SALLY DOUBET KING, born Galesburg, Illinois, 1951; admitted to bar, 1989, Illinois. *Education:* Knox College (B.A., 1973); Illinois State University (M.A., 1974); DePaul University (J.D., 1989). ***PRACTICE AREAS:*** Employee Benefits Litigation; Executive Compensation; Employee Stock Ownership Plans; ERISA; COBRA; Employee Benefits; Retiree Medical Benefits; Health and Welfare Benefits; Fiduciary Law. ***Email:*** sking@mcguirewoods.com

HENRY DEVOS LAWRIE, JR., born Evanston, Illinois, 1942; admitted to bar, 1967, Illinois. *Education:* Bowdoin College (A.B., 1964); Northwestern University College of Law (J.D., 1967). Former Partner, Gardner, Carton & Douglas. ***PRACTICE AREAS:*** Employee Benefits; Executive Compensation. ***Email:*** hlawrie@mcguirewoods.com

RICHARD E. LIEBERMAN, born Akron, Ohio, 1946; admitted to bar, 1971, Ohio; 1975, Illinois. *Education:* Miami University (B.A., 1968); University of Cincinnati (J.D., 1971). Listed in: The International Who's Who of Business Lawyers, 2002—; Chambers USA's Leading Lawyers for Business, 2004, 2005; Best Lawyers in America, 2006. Author: "Personal Foul: Coach Joe Moore vs. Notre Dame," Academy Chicago Publishers (2001); "Litigation Strategies In Defending Wrongful Discharge Suits," Employee Relations Law Journal, 718, Spring, 1986. Co-Author: "Comparable Pay: A Management Perspective," Solving EEO Problems, 177, 1980. Attorney, National Labor Relations Board, 1971-1973. Trial Attorney, Equal Employment Opportunity Commission, 1973-1974. Trustee, Goodman Theatre of Chicago. Member, Board of Visitors, University of Cincinnati Law School. ***PRACTICE AREAS:*** Labor and Employment; Affirmative Action; Employment Litigation; Trade Secrets; Defamation; Complex Commercial Litigation. ***Email:*** rlieberman@mcguirewoods.com

LESLIE D. LOCKE, born Buffalo, New York, 1947; admitted to bar, 1975, Illinois; U.S. District Court, Northern District of Illinois including Trial Bar. *Education:* Washington & Lee University (B.A., 1968); Cornell University (J.D., 1975). Phi Kappa Phi. Co-Managing Editor, Cornell Law Review, 1974-1975. ***Email:*** llocke@mcguirewoods.com

WILLIAM MICHAEL LONG, born Decatur, Illinois; admitted to bar, 1986, Illinois; 1990, U.S. District Court, Northern District of Illinois and U.S. Tax Court. *Education:* Bradley University (B.S., 1981); John Marshall Law School (J.D., 1986); DePaul University (LL.M., Taxation, 1993). ***PRACTICE AREAS:*** Business and Corporate Law; Estate and Gift Taxation; Probate; Trust and Estate Administration. ***Email:*** wlong@mcguirewoods.com

AMY B. MANNING, born Des Moines, Iowa, 1967; admitted to bar, 1992, Illinois and U.S. District Court, Northern District of Illinois; 1993, U.S. Court of Appeals, Seventh Circuit; 1996, U.S. Court of Appeals, Sixth Circuit; 2000, U.S. Court of Appeals, Eighth Circuit. *Education:* Monmouth College (B.A., 1989); University of Chicago (J.D., 1992). Winner, University of Chicago Hinton Moot Court Competition, Justice Antonin Scalia presiding. Thomas P. McAulroy Award for Outstanding Appellate Advocacy With Highest Distinction. ***PRACTICE AREAS:*** Commercial Litigation; Antitrust; Class Action Defense; Health Care Litigation; Civil RICO; Commodities Fraud. ***Email:*** amanning@mcguirewoods.com

RICHARD J. MASON, P.C., born Syracuse, New York, 1951; admitted to bar, 1977, Illinois. *Education:* University of Illinois (B.A., 1973); University of Chicago (M.B.A., 1980); University of Notre Dame (J.D., 1977). Adjunct Professor of Business Law, Chicago-Kent College of Law, 1984—. Member, Board of Directors, Illinois Farm Legal Assistance Foundation, 1985-1988. ***PRACTICE AREAS:*** Commercial Transactions; Commercial Litigation; Bankruptcy Reorganization; Bankruptcy Litigation; International Insolvency. ***Email:*** rmason@mcguirewoods.com

MARK J. McGUIRE, born Middletown, Connecticut, 1953; admitted to bar, 1981, Michigan; 1983, Illinois; 1993, District of Columbia. *Education:* Southern Connecticut State College (B.A., 1974); St. Louis University (J.D., 1980). General Counsel, The Peoples Gas Light and Coke Co., North Shore Gas Co. Counsel, ANR/Michigan Consolidated Gas Company, 1980-1985. Assistant General Counsel, Peoples Energy, 1985-1993. Partner, Jenner & Block, 1993-2002. Member, Midwest Energy Association. ***PRACTICE AREAS:*** Administrative Law; Antitrust and Trade Regulation; Business Acquisitions; Cogeneration; Federal Energy Regulation; Oil and Gas Law; Public Utility Law; Energy; Corporate. ***Email:*** mmcguire@mcguirewoods.com

RICHARD L. MENSON, born Chicago, Illinois, 1943; admitted to bar, 1968, Illinois and U.S. Court of Military Appeals; 1973, U.S. Court of Federal Claims and U.S. District Court, Northern District of Illinois; 1975, U.S. Tax Court. *Education:* Ripon College (A.B., 1965); Northwestern University (J.D., 1968); George Washington University (LL.M., Taxation, 1973). Partner, Gardner, Carton & Douglas, 1977-1998. Member: Legal and Legislative Committee, ProfitSharing/401k Council of America; American Benefits Council. Fellow, American College of Employee Benefit Counsel. Member, Board of Directors and Legal and Legislative Committee, ProfitSharing/401k Council of America. Charter Fellow, American College of Employee Benefit Counsel. Member, International Pension and Employee Benefit Lawyers Association. [JAGC, U.S. Army, 1968-1973]. ***PRACTICE AREAS:*** Employee Benefits; Executive Compensation; Employee Stock Ownership Plans; Employee Benefits Litigation; ERISA; COBRA; Employee Contracts; ERISA Litigation. ***Email:*** rmenson@mcguirewoods.com

JOHN J. MICHELS, JR., born Ft. Monroe, Virginia, 1955; admitted to bar, 1985, Tennessee; 1992, Virginia; 1998, District of Columbia; 2003, Illinois. *Education:* U.S. Air Force Academy (B.S., 1977); Duke University (J.D., 1985). Editor, Air Force Law Review, 1989-1991. U.S. Air Force Trial Attorney, 1985-1991. Instructor, Federal Labor and Employment Law, United States Air Force JAG School, 1989-2003. Author: "The Long Reach of the NLRA," Legal Times, June 1996; "Declaring a Truce by Other Means," Legal Times, May 12, 1997; "The Anthrax Vaccine Controversy," Virginia Lawyer, December 2001. Co-Author with Rodney A. Satterwhite, "Employment Issues in Communications Technology," June 1998. Member: Board of Governors, Military Law Section, Virginia State Bar, 1996-2002; Labor and Employment Law Committee, American Bar Association, 1994—; Association of Graduates (USAFA), 1977—. [Officer, USAF, 1977-1991; Lt. Col., USAFR Retired]. ***LANGUAGES:*** Russian. ***PRACTICE AREAS:*** Labor and Employment; ERISA Litigation; Sports Law; Military Law. ***Email:*** jmichels@mcguirewoods.com

THOMAS R. MULROY, born Evanston, Illinois, 1946; admitted to bar, 1973, Illinois. *Education:* University of Santa Clara (B.A., 1968); Loyola University School of Law (J.D., 1972). Partner: Mulroy Scandaglia Marrinson Ryan, 2001-2003; Jenner & Block, 1976-2001. Assistant U.S. Attorney, Chicago, 1972-1976. Member: Attorney Registration and Disciplinary Commission, 1976-1989; Board of Directors, Illinois Institute for Continuing Legal Education, 1987-1991; Committee to Evaluate Federal Judges, 1989. Chairman, Judicial Evaluation Committee, Appellate Division. Chairman, McGuireWoods' Commercial Litigation Department, Chicago office. Fellow, American College of Trial Lawyers. ***PRACTICE AREAS:*** Commercial Litigation; Intellectual Property Law. ***Email:*** tmulroy@mcguirewoods.com

DONALD C. PASULKA, born Chicago, Illinois, 1961; admitted to bar, 1986, Illinois; 1989, California. *Education:* University of Chicago (A.B., 1983); Harvard University (J.D., 1986). ***Email:*** dpasulka@mcguirewoods.com

RUSSELL M. PELTON, born Chicago, Illinois, 1938; admitted to bar, 1963, Illinois; 1971, U.S. Court of Appeals, Seventh Circuit; 1979, U.S. Supreme Court; 1983, U.S. Court of Claims; 1997, U.S. Court of Appeals, Third Circuit. *Education:* DePauw University (B.A., 1960); University of Chicago (J.D., 1963). General Counsel: American Association of Neurological Surgeons, 1983—; Delta Dental Plan of Illinois, 1980-1995. Chairman, Wilmette, Illinois Zoning Board of Appeals, 1989-2000. [Captain, JAG, U.S. Air Force, 1963-1966]. ***PRACTICE AREAS:*** Health Care; Litigation. ***Email:*** rpelton@mcguirewoods.com

MICHAEL R. PHILLIPS, born Chicago, Illinois, 1969; admitted to bar, 1994, Illinois and U.S. District Court, Northern District of Illinois; 1998, U.S. Supreme Court; 2002, U.S. Court of Appeals, Third and Tenth Circuits; 2003, U.S. District Court, District of Colorado; 2004, U.S. Court of Appeals, Second Circuit and U.S. District Court, Southern District of Illinois; U.S. Court of Appeals, Sixth and Seventh Circuits; U.S. District Court, Central District of Illinois; U.S. District Court, Northern District of Indiana; U.S. District Court, Eastern District of Wisconsin. *Education:* University of California at Berkeley (A.B., 1991); University of Michigan (J.D., 1994). Associate Editor, 1992-1993; Contributing Editor, 1993-1994, Michigan Law Review. Recipient, American Bar Association, John R. Brown Award, 1994. Author: "The Constitutionality of Employer-Accessible Child Abuse Registries: Due Process Implications of Governmental Occupational Blacklisting," 92 Michigan Law Review, 139. ***PRACTICE AREAS:*** Labor and Employment; Commercial Litigation. ***Email:*** mphillips@mcguirewoods.com

JOHN F. POLLICK, born Detroit, Michigan, 1952; admitted to bar, 1980, Illinois and U.S. District Court, Northern District of Illinois. *Education:* Yale University (B.A., 1976); University of Michigan (J.D., 1980). Adjunct Professor of Bankruptcy Law, Chicago-Kent College of Law, (1992-1995; 1999—). ***PRACTICE AREAS:*** Secured Lending; Business Transactions; Bankruptcy. ***Email:*** jpollick@mcguirewoods.com

ROBERT J. PRISTAVE, P.C., born Fullerton, California, 1942; admitted to bar, 1967, Illinois. *Education:* University of Chicago (A.B., 1964); Northwestern University (J.D., 1967). ***PRACTICE AREAS:*** Health Care; Alternative Health Care Delivery Systems; Health Care Corporate Law; Health Care Fraud; Health Care Mergers and Acquisitions; Health Care Regulation. ***Email:*** rpristave@mcguirewoods.com

RICHARD J. RAPPAPORT, born Chicago, Illinois, 1943; admitted to bar, 1967, Illinois and U.S. District Court, Northern District of Illinois including Trial Bar; 1978, U.S. Court of Appeals, Seventh and Tenth Circuits; 1979, U.S. Supreme Court; 1986, U.S. Court of Appeals, Sixth Circuit; 1988, U.S. Court of Appeals, Fourth Circuit and U.S. Tax Court; 1993, Florida; 1997, U.S. Court of Appeals, Eleventh Circuit; 2000, U.S. Court of Appeals, Eighth Circuit. *Education:* Loyola University (B.S., 1966); Loyola University, School of Law (J.D., 1967). Associate Editor, Recent Decisions, Illinois Bar Journal, 1966-1967. Trial Attorney, Antitrust Division, U.S. Department of Justice, 1967-1969. Co-Chairman, ALI-ABA Course of Study, Potential Liability of Local Governments under Federal Antitrust and Civil Rights Laws, Atlanta, 1978; San Diego, 1980; Tampa, 1982. Co-Author: American Bar Association's Section of Antitrust Law Monograph on the Noerr-Pennington Doctrine, 1993. ***PRACTICE AREAS:*** Antitrust and Trade Regulation; Business Litigation; Contract Litigation; Complex and Multi-District Litigation; Alternative Dispute Resolution. ***Email:*** rrappaport@mcguirewoods.com

DAVID L. RIESER, born Chicago, Illinois, 1956; admitted to bar, 1980, Illinois; 1981, U.S. District Court, Central District of Illinois; 1985, U.S. District Court, Northern District of Illinois; 1986, Federal Trial Bar; 2003, U.S. District Court, Northern District of Indiana. *Education:* University of Chicago (A.B., 1977); Washington University (J.D., 1980). Appointed by Governor Edgar to the Illinois Site Remediation Advisory Committee, March, 1998—. Author: Illinois State Coordinator, "Brownfields Law & Practice," 2002—; "Proportionate Share Liability and its Impact on Real Estate Transaction," Illinois Real Estate Journal, Feb. 1, 1999; "Practical Approach to Brownfields: A Brief Overview of 'TACO' and the 'SRP'," Illinois Bar Journal, May 1998; "Crack New Markets, Seek Development

(This Listing Continued)

Opportunities," Crains's Small Business, Chicago Edition, Vol. 5, p.9, June 1997; "New Site Remediation Regulations Changes Rules for Environmental Professionals," Illinois Engineer, June/July 1997; "Brownfields Bill Promotes Sweeping Changes," 16 NIU L.Rev. 621, Summer 1996. *Member:* American Bar Association (Member, Environment and Natural Resources Section). ***PRACTICE AREAS:*** Hazardous Waste Regulation; Brownfields; Superfund; Underground Storage Tanks; Environmental Compliance; Environmental Corporate Law; Environmental Transactions; Clean Water Act; Clean Air Act. ***Email:*** drieser@mcguirewoods.com

JAMES B. RILEY, JR., born Evanston, Illinois, 1954; admitted to bar, 1979, Illinois and U.S. District Court, Northern District of Illinois; U.S. Court of Federal Claims. *Education:* University of Illinois (B.S., 1976); George Washington University (J.D., 1979). Co-Chariman, Health Care Department, McGuireWoods LLP. Certified Public Accountant, Illinois. Formerly with U.S. Department of Health and Human Services Centers for Medicare and Medicaid. ***PRACTICE AREAS:*** Corporate Law; Health Law. ***Email:*** jriley@mcguirewoods.com

JEFFREY E. ROGERS, born Chicago, Illinois, 1949; admitted to bar, 1976, Illinois and U.S. District Court, Northern District of Illinois including Trial Bar; 1979, U.S. Court of Appeals, Seventh Circuit; U.S. District Court, Central District of Illinois. *Education:* Loyola University (B.A., 1972); John Marshall Law School (J.D., 1976). Member, National Moot Court Team. Author: Manual for Staff Attorneys, U.S. Court of Appeals, 7th Circuit, Revised Edition, 1977. Co-Author: Chapter on Criminal Sentencing in Antitrust Counseling and Litigation Techniques (Matthew Bender, 1990); Revised Manual for Staff Attorneys, U.S. Court of Appeals for 7th Circuit (1977). Instructor, Appellate Advocacy, 1985 and Trial Advocacy, 1986, U.S. Department of Justice, Attorney General's Advocacy Institute. Staff Attorney, 7th Circuit, 1976. U.S. Attorney's Office, Northern District of Illinois, 1978-1987. Recipient, Awards: U.S. Department of Justice, Special Commendation Award, 1987; U.S. Department of Justice Special Achievement Award (1986). ***Email:*** jrogers@mcguirewoods.com

LAWRENCE R. SAMUELS, born Chicago, Illinois, 1946; admitted to bar, 1972, New York; 1976, Illinois. *Education:* University of Chicago (B.A., 1968); Harvard University (J.D., 1971). ***PRACTICE AREAS:*** Securities; Corporate Law; Mergers and Acquisitions; Litigation. ***Email:*** lsamuels@mcguirewoods.com

EDWARD W. SCHWARTZ, born Forest Hills, New York, 1963; admitted to bar, 1990, Illinois. *Education:* Northwestern University (B.S., 1984); University of Illinois (J.D., 1990). ***PRACTICE AREAS:*** Accountants Liability; Employment Discrimination; Insurance Coverage; Consumer Litigation; Fair Credit Reporting Act; Civil Litigation. ***Email:*** eschwartz@mcguirewoods.com

JOHN L. SENICA, born Chicago, Illinois, 1960; admitted to bar, 1985, Illinois; 1998, Indiana. *Education:* University of Notre Dame (B.A., 1982); Northwestern University (J.D., 1985). Recipient, Notre Dame Scholar Award. ***PRACTICE AREAS:*** Business Law; Corporate Law; Finance; Mergers, Acquisitions and Divestitures; Real Estate. ***Email:*** jsenica@mcguirewoods.com

WILLIAM D. SERRITELLA, born Chicago, Illinois, 1946; admitted to bar, 1971, Illinois; 1972, U.S. District Court, Northern and Central Districts of Illinois; 1974, U.S. Court of Appeals, Seventh Circuit; 1979, U.S. Supreme Court; 1995, U.S. District Court, Western and Eastern Districts of Wisconsin; 1997, U.S. District Court, Northern and Southern Districts of Indiana. *Education:* University of Illinois (B.A., 1968; J.D., 1971). *Member:* Society of Trial Lawyers; Trial Lawyers Club; National Association of Railroad Trial Counsel; Defense Research Institute. ***PRACTICE AREAS:*** Civil Litigation; Business Litigation; Products Liability; Toxic Torts; Federal Employers Liability Act (FELA). ***Email:*** wserritella@mcguirewoods.com

PATRICIA K. SMOOTS, born Oak Park, Illinois, 1954; admitted to bar, 1986, Illinois, U.S. District Court, Northern District of Illinois and U.S. Court of Appeals, Seventh Circuit. *Education:* University of Illinois (B.S., 1981); DePaul University (J.D., 1986). Author: "Members of the City Council vs. Taxpayers for Vincent: The Constitutionality of Prohibiting Temporary Sign Posting on Public Property to Advance Local Aesthetic Concerns," 34 De Paul Law Review 197, 1984. ***PRACTICE AREAS:*** Complex Civil Litigation; Creditors; Insolvency. ***Email:*** psmoots@mcguirewoods.com

JOEL H. SPITZ, born Wausau, Wisconsin, 1965; admitted to bar, 1990, Wisconsin and Illinois; U.S. Supreme Court; U.S. Court of Appeals, Sixth, Seventh and Ninth Circuits; U.S. District Court, Eastern and Western Districts of Wisconsin and Northern and Central Districts of Illinois, Northern District of Indiana, Western and Eastern Districts of Michigan, Northern District of Texas and District of Oregon. *Education:* University of Wisconsin (B.A., 1987); Marquette University (J.D., 1990). Adolph I. Mandelker Scholar. Executive Editor, Marquette Law Review. Member, National Sports Law Institute Journal. Author: Note, "Punitive Damages-Recovery of Compensatory Damages as a Prerequisite, Tucker v. Marcus," 142 Wis. 2d 425, 418 N.W. 2d 818 1988, 72 Marq. L. Rev., 609 (1987); Comment, "The Transent Rule of Personal Jurisdiction: A Well Intentioned Concept that has Overstayed Its Welcome," 73 Marq. L. Rev. 181 (1989). ***PRACTICE AREAS:*** Age Discrimination in Employment; Employment Litigation; Family and Medical Leave Act; Sexual Harassment; Title VII Discrimination; Wrongful Termination Defense; Americans with Disabilities Act; Restrictive Covenants. ***Email:*** jspitz@mcguirewoods.com

GARY L. STARKMAN, born Chicago, Illinois, 1946; admitted to bar, 1971, Illinois; 1972, U.S. Court of Appeals, Seventh Circuit and U.S. District Court, Northern District of Illinois; 1974, U.S. Supreme Court; 1984, U.S. Court of Appeals, Third, Fifth and District of Columbia Circuits. *Education:* University of Illinois (A.B., 1968); Northwestern University (J.D., 1971). Chairman, Article Editors, Journal of Criminal Law, Criminology and Police Science, 1970-1971. Co-Author: "Cases and Comments on Criminal Procedure," Foundation Press, 6th Edition, 2003. Assistant U. S. Attorney, Chief Appellate Division, Northern District of Illinois, 1971-1975. Counsel to the Governor of Illinois, 1977-1981. Director, Northwestern University School of Law Alumni Association, 1982-1985. Member, District Court Admissions Committee, Northern District of Illinois, 1983-1994. Chairman, Illinois Racing Board, 1990-1996; Director, International Association of Racing Commissioners, 1991-1994. ***PRACTICE AREAS:*** Civil Appeals; Federal Civil Practice; Commercial Litigation. ***Email:*** gstarkman@mcguirewoods.com

MARTA A. STEIN, born Akron, Ohio; admitted to bar, 1988, Illinois and U.S. District Court, Northern District of Illinois; U.S. District Court, Eastern District of Wisconsin; U.S. Court of Appeals, Seventh Circuit. *Education:* University of Michigan (B.A., 1985); Ohio State University (J.D., 1988). ***PRACTICE AREAS:*** Complex Commercial Litigation; Banking Litigation; Business Law; Life and Health Insurance. ***Email:*** mstein@mcguirewoods.com

ROBERT E. WANGARD, born Kennan, Wisconsin, 1941; admitted to bar, 1969, Illinois. *Education:* University of Wisconsin (B.A., 1966); University of Illinois (J.D., 1969). Staff Member, 1967-1968, and Articles Editor, 1968-1969, University of Illinois Law Review. Author: "Pre-Acquisition Agreements in Mergers and Acquisitions," International Financial Law Review Special Supplement: United States, A Legal Guide, June 1998; "Negotiated Mergers and Acquisitions," International Financial Law Review Special Supplement: A Legal Guide to Corporate Activity and Inward Investment, October 1995. Member, Board of Visitors, University of Illinois Law School, 1999—. ***PRACTICE AREAS:*** Mergers and Acquisitions; International Mergers and Acquisitions; International Business Law; Foreign Investment in the United States; Corporate Finance; Business Law; Strategic Alliances. ***Email:*** rwangard@mcguirewoods.com

JAY A. YALOWITZ, born Evanston, Illinois, 1967; admitted to bar, 1993, Illinois and U.S. District Court, Northern District of Illinois. *Education:* University of Michigan (B.A., 1989); Washington University (J.D., 1993). Primary Articles Editor, Washington University Law Quarterly, 1992-1993. ***PRACTICE AREAS:*** Health Care Corporate Law; Health Care Facility Licensing; Health Care Fraud; Health Care Mergers and Acquisitions; Integrated Health Care Delivery Systems. ***Email:*** jyalowitz@mcguirewoods.com

KEVIN J. YOUNG, born Peoria, Illinois, 1960; admitted to bar, 1986, Illinois; 1998, California; U.S. District Court, Northern District of Illinois and Eastern District of Wisconsin. *Education:* University of Illinois (B.A., 1982); John Marshall Law School (J.D., 1986). Justice, Moot Court Board. First Place, Chicago Bar Association Moot Court Competition. Publications: "After Deprizio—Will Waiver of Subrogation Survive?" IBA Law Watch, Illinois Bankers Association, 1992; "Internet Privacy: It's Not Just For B2C Anymore," eBiz Chronicle.com, September 6, 2001; "Spam: Should It Be Taken Off The E-mail Menu?" DM Enewsletter, a publication of the National School Supply and Equipment Association, 2002; "Open Source Software: Is It Really Free?" The John Marshall Law School, Center For Intellectual Property Law, News Source, Spring 2003. Speaker: "Perfecting Security Interests in Copyrights and Trade Secrets," Law Seminars International, Security Interests in Intellectual Property, June 9, 2003; "Collateral Documents, Credit Support and Third Party Documents, Commercial Lending Requirements and Loan Documnetation in Illinois," Lorman Education Series, November 2, 2003. ***PRACTICE AREAS:*** Corporate Law; Financial Services; Mergers and Acquisitions; International Mergers and Acquisitions. ***Email:*** kjyoung@mcguirewoods.com

PAUL C. ZIEBERT, born Milwaukee, Wisconsin, 1962; admitted to bar, 1990, Illinois and U.S. District Court, Northern District of Illinois. *Education:* Washington and Lee University (B.A., 1984); George Washington University (J.D., 1990). Member, Moot Court Board. ***PRACTICE AREAS:*** Fair Credit Reporting Act; Fair Debt Collection Practices Act; Litigation; Products Liability; Class Action Defense. ***Email:*** pziebert@mcguirewoods.com

ROBERT T. ZIELINSKI, born Chicago, Illinois, 1957; admitted to bar, 1982, Illinois; 1983, U.S. District Court, Northern District of Illinois including Trial Bar, 1990; U.S. Court of Appeals, Second, Fifth, Sixth, Seventh and Ninth Circuits. *Education:* Harvard College (B.A., 1979); New York University (J.D., 1982). Chair, Village of Winnetka Landmark Preservation Commission. ***PRACTICE AREAS:*** Employment Discrimination; Labor Management Relations; Americans with Disabilities Act; Family and Medical Leave Act; Wrongful Termination Defense; Collective Bargaining. ***Email:*** rzielinski@mcguirewoods.com

RETIRED PARTNERS

BRUCE J. McWHIRTER, born Chicago, Illinois, 1931; admitted to bar, 1955, Illinois and District of Columbia; 1990, U.S. Supreme Court. *Education:* Northwestern University (B.S., 1952); Harvard Law School (LL.B., 1955). Phi Beta Kappa.

DAVID F. STERLING, born Joliet, Illinois, 1936; admitted to bar, 1961, Illinois. *Education:* Northwestern University (B.S., 1958; J.D., 1961). Beta Gamma Sigma. Member, Board of Editors, Northwestern University Law Review, 1961. Illinois Certified Public Accountant, 1958. Fellow, American College of Trust and Estate Counsel: ***PRACTICE AREAS:*** Marital Agreements; Probate; Estate and Gift Taxation; Trusts and Estates Taxation; Trusts and Estates; Wills. ***Email:*** dsterling@mcguirewoods.com

OF COUNSEL

JOANN TANSEY ANGAROLA, born Toledo, Ohio, 1951; admitted to bar, 1977, Illinois. *Education:* University of Nebraska; University of Michigan (B.S., 1973); Loyola University (J.D., 1977). Assistant Cook County, Illinois State's Attorney, 1977-1985. ***PRACTICE AREAS:*** Civil Litigation; Land Use. ***Email:*** jangarola@mcguirewoods.com

DAVID N. McBRIDE, born Knox, Indiana, 1931; admitted to bar, 1955, Illinois; 1983, Wisconsin. *Education:* University of Notre Dame (A.B., 1954; J.D., 1955). Member, Board of Editors, Notre Dame Lawyer, 1954-1955. ***Email:*** dmcbride@mcguirewoods.com

JAMES C. WILLIAMS, born Kittery, Maine, 1955; admitted to bar, 1980, Connecticut; 1991, District of Columbia; 2002, Illinois. *Education:* Georgetown University (B.S., 1977); University of Connecticut (J.D., 1980); College of William & Mary (M.L.T., 1986). Partner, Deloitte & Touche, LLP. ***PRACTICE AREAS:*** Employee Benefits; Employee Stock Ownership Plans; ERISA; Executive Compensation; Employee Breach of Contract; COBRA; ERISA Litigation. ***Email:*** jwilliams@mcguirewoods.com

ASSOCIATES

TAMMY L. ADKINS, born Columbus, Ohio, 1970; admitted to bar, 1996, Illinois. *Education:* The Ohio State University (B.A., 1992; J.D., 1995). ***PRACTICE AREAS:*** Commercial Litigation; Consumer Litigation; Class Action Defense. ***Email:*** tadkins@mcguirewoods.com

(This Listing Continued)

McGUIREWOODS LLP, Chicago—Continued

DEBORAH BEERMAN, admitted to bar, 2003, Illinois. *Education:* University of Wisconsin-Madison (B.A., 1999); University of Illinois (J.D., 2003). ***Email:*** dbeerman@mcguirewoods.com

MELISSA M. BIEN, born Ashtabula, Ohio, 1974; admitted to bar, 2001, Illinois and U.S. District Court, Northern District of Illinois; 2003, U.S. Court of Appeals, Seventh Circuit. *Education:* Case Western Reserve University (B.A., 1997; J.D., 2001). ***PRACTICE AREAS:*** Labor and Employment. ***Email:*** mbien@mcguirewoods.com

PHILIP S. BREWSTER, born Lynn, Massachusetts; admitted to bar, 2003, Massachusetts (Not admitted in Illinois). *Education:* Syracuse University (B.A., 1999); Boston College (J.D., 2003). ***PRACTICE AREAS:*** Health Care. ***Email:*** pbrewster@mcguirewoods.com

DANIEL PHILIP BUBAR, born Allentown, Pennsylvania, 1979; admitted to bar, 2004, Illinois and U.S. District Court, Northern District of Illinois. *Education:* Taylor University (B.A., 2001); University of Notre Dame Law School (J.D., 2004). ***PRACTICE AREAS:*** Products Liability; Complex and Multi-District Litigation. ***Email:*** dbubar@mcguirewoods.com

ROBERT L. CARTER, born Alton, Illinois, 1953; admitted to bar, 1981, Illinois and Missouri; U.S. District Court, Southern District of Illinois; 1985, U.S. District Court, Eastern District of Missouri, U.S. Court of Appeals, Eighth Circuit; 1997, U.S. District Court, District of Colorado; 1992, U.S. Court of Appeals, Seventh Circuit; 1996, U.S. Court of Appeals, Federal Circuit. *Education:* Southern Illinois University (B.S., 1978); John Marshall Law School (J.D., 1981). Associate Editor, The John Marshall Law Review, 1980. Author: "Limitations on Recoverable Damages," The Construction Lawyer, Forum on the Construction Industry, Vol. 18, No. 2, 1998, Contributed Sections I, IV, VI and X; "Modifying Charitable Land Trusts," 74 Ill. Bar. J. 86, 1985; "Implied Causes of Action," 14 John Marshall L. Rev. 141, 1980. Assistant States Attorney, Ford County, January, 1988 to November, 1988; Special Public Defender, Madison County, Illinois, 1981-1985. ***PRACTICE AREAS:*** Franchise Litigation; Insurance Bad Faith Defense; Intellectual Property Litigation; Securities Litigation; Contract Litigation; Commercial Arbitration. ***Email:*** rcarter@mcguirewoods.com

CARLA M. CASAS, born Lima, Peru, 1975; admitted to bar, 2002, Florida; 2003, Illinois. *Education:* Andrews University (B.A., 1999); University of Florida (J.D., 2002). ***LANGUAGES:*** Spanish. ***PRACTICE AREAS:*** Health Care; Litigation. ***Email:*** ccasas@mcguirewoods.com

CHARLES A. CAVALLO, III, born Washington, D.C.; admitted to bar, 2005, Illinois. *Education:* University of Illinois, Urbana-Champaign (B.S., 1993); Northwestern University (M.B.A., 2003; J.D. 2003). ***PRACTICE AREAS:*** Corporate Governance; Corporate Finance; Securities; Mergers and Acquisitions; Joint Ventures; Private Equity; Banking. ***Email:*** ccavallo@mcguirewoods.com

BERNARD CHERKASOV, admitted to bar, 2004, Illinois. *Education:* University of Michigan (B.A., 1998; J.D., 2003); Harvard University (M.T.S., 2001). Director, Board of Directors, AIDS Legal Council of Chicago. International Law Clerk to Chief Justice Barak, Supreme Court of Israel, 2004. Mayor-Appointed Member, Executive Committee, City of Ann Arbor, Michigan, 2001-2003. ***LANGUAGES:*** Russian and French. ***PRACTICE AREAS:*** Commercial Litigation. ***Email:*** bcherkasov@mcguirewoods.com

LISA L. CLAY, born Pullman, Washington, 1969; admitted to bar, 2002, Illinois; U.S. District Court, Northern District of Illinois; U.S. Court of Appeals, Seventh Circuit. *Education:* Valparaiso University (B.A., 1992); University of Wisconsin (M.I.L.R., 1995); University of Iowa (J.D., 2001). ***PRACTICE AREAS:*** Class Action Litigation; Consumer Financial Services; Complex Commercial Litigation; Employment Litigation. ***Email:*** lclay@mcguirewoods.com

DAWN M. CUTLAN, born Oak Park, Illinois, June 1, 1974; admitted to bar, 2000, Illinois. *Education:* DePaul University (B.A., 1996); University of Illinois (J.D., 2000). ***PRACTICE AREAS:*** Labor and Employment; Employment Discrimination. ***Email:*** dcutlan@mcguirewoods.com

PAUL W. DOERSCHELN, admitted to bar, 1997, Illinois; U.S. District Court, Northern District of Illinois. *Education:* University of Illinois (B.A., 1994); Illinois Institute of Technology, Chicago-Kent College of Law (J.D., 1997). Member, Chicago-Kent Law Review, 1995-1997. ***PRACTICE AREAS:*** Products Liability; Commercial Law. ***Email:*** pdoerscheln@mcguirewoods.com

DONALD A. ENSING, born Chicago, Illinois, 1972; admitted to bar, 1998, Illinois. *Education:* University of Michigan (B.A., 1994); Chicago-Kent College of Law (J.D., 1998). Order of the Coif. Law Clerk, Hon. F. A. Little, U.S. District Court, Western District of Louisiana, 1998-1999. ***PRACTICE AREAS:*** Commercial Law; Corporate Law; Banks and Banking; Mergers, Acquisitions and Divestitures. ***Email:*** densing@mcguirewoods.com

STEVEN M. EVANS, born Columbus, Ohio; admitted to bar, 1989, Illinois; 1993, California; 1994, Florida; 1995, District of Columbia, Colorado and Hawaii; U.S. Court of Appeals for the Federal Circuit; U.S. District Court, Northern District of Illinois including Trial Bar; registered to practice before U.S. Patent and Trademark Office. *Education:* Purdue University (B.S.E.E., 1986); Indiana University School of Law (J.D., 1989). ***PRACTICE AREAS:*** Intellectual Property; Patents. ***Email:*** sevans@mcguirewoods.com

THOMAS B. FITZGIBBON, born Indianapolis, Indiana, 1979; admitted to bar, 2004, Illinois. *Education:* University of Pennsylvania (B.A., 2001); University of Chicago (J.D., 2004). ***PRACTICE AREAS:*** Commercial Litigation. ***Email:*** tfitzgibbon@mcguirewoods.com

JOHN CHARLES GARDNER, born Madison, Wisconsin, 1977; admitted to bar, 2004, Illinois and Wisconsin. *Education:* University of Wisconsin-Madison (B.S., 2000); Marquette University (J.D., 2004). Senior Note and Comment Editor, Marquette Law Review, 2003-2004. ***PRACTICE AREAS:*** Employment Discrimination; Government; Noncompete Litigation; Wrongful Termination. ***Email:*** jgardner@mcguirewoods.com

SAMANTHA C. GORDON, born Brawley, California, 1970; admitted to bar, 2000, Illinois and U.S. District Court, Northern District of Illinois; 2003, U.S. District Court, Northern District of Illinois including Trial Bar. *Education:* Stanford University (B.A., 1997); Northwestern University (J.D., 2000). Member, Northwestern National Trial Team, 1999-2000. [U.S. Army Reserve, 1993-1999]. ***PRACTICE AREAS:*** Commercial Litigation; White Collar Crime. ***Email:*** sgordon@mcguirewoods.com

BLAIR B. HANZLIK, born Chicago, Illinois, 1976; admitted to bar, 2003, Illinois and U.S. District Court, Northern District of Illinois. *Education:* Wesleyan University (B.A., 1998); University of Illinois College of Law (J.D., 2003). ***PRACTICE AREAS:*** Commercial Litigation. ***Email:*** bhanzlik@mcguirewoods.com

COLLEEN E. HELENHOUSE, born Chicago, Illinois, 1969; admitted to bar, 1998, Illinois and U.S. District Court, Northern District of Illinois; 2005, U.S. Court of Appeals, Seventh Circuit. *Education:* University of Illinois (B.A., 1990); DePaul University (M.A., 1994); IIT-Chicago Kent College of Law (J.D., 1998). Order of the Coif. Recipient, American Jurisprudence Award, Legal Writing I & II. Mediator, Center for Conflict Resolution. Certified Mediator. ***PRACTICE AREAS:*** Commercial Litigation; Intellectual Property Litigation; School Law. ***Email:*** chelenhouse@mcguirewoods.com

JAMES J. HENDRICKSON II, born Mankato, Minnesota, 1973; admitted to bar, 2004, Illinois. *Education:* St. John's University (B.A., 1995); University of Michigan (J.D., 2004). ***PRACTICE AREAS:*** Labor and Employment Litigation; Employment Discrimination. ***Email:*** jhendrickson@mcguirewoods.com

JAIME L. HOCHHAUSEN, born 1978; admitted to bar, 2004, Illinois. *Education:* University of Wisconsin-Platteville (B.A., 1999); The John Marshall Law School (J.D., 2003). ***PRACTICE AREAS:*** Complex Commercial Litigation; Intellectual Property; Securities Litigation. ***Email:*** jhochhausen@mcguirewoods.com

THOMAS H. HORENKAMP, admitted to bar, 2004, Illinois. *Education:* University of Notre Dame (B.A., 1996); University of Chicago (M.A., 1997); University of Miami (J.D., 2004). ***LANGUAGES:*** Portuguese. ***PRACTICE AREAS:*** Finance; Securities. ***Email:*** thorenkamp@mcguirewoods.com

CARA M. HOUCK, born Chicago, Illinois, 1965; admitted to bar, 1997, Illinois. *Education:* Northwestern University (B.S., 1990); Thomas M. Cooley Law School (J.D., 1996). ***PRACTICE AREAS:*** Civil Litigation; Business Litigation; Products Liability. ***Email:*** chouck@mcguirewoods.com

JOSEPH J. JANATKA, born Los Angeles, California, 1962; admitted to bar, 1987, Illinois and U.S. District Court, Northern District of Illinois. *Education:* Knox College (B.A., 1984); Washington University School of Law (J.D., 1987). Phi Beta Cappa; Order of the Coif. Schzold Distinguished Scholar in History. ***PRACTICE AREAS:*** Environmental Diseases; First Party Insurance; Products Liability; Asbestos Defense; Subrogation; Toxic Torts. ***Email:*** jjanatka@mcguirewoods.com

RACHEL GOLDSTEIN KEMPLER, born Highland Park, Illinois, 1974; admitted to bar, 1999, Illinois. *Education:* University of Illinois (B.A., 1996); University of Chicago (J.D., 1999). Phi Beta Kappa. ***PRACTICE AREAS:*** Health Care. ***Email:*** rkempler@mcguirewoods.com

ELISSA BOYSEN KOCH, born Hershey, Pennsylvania; admitted to bar, 2004, Illinois. *Education:* Northwestern University (B.S., 2000); University of Southampton, Southampton, England (M.Sc., 2002); Loyola University (J.D., 2004). ***PRACTICE AREAS:*** Health Care Regulation; Health Care Corporate Law. ***Email:*** ekoch@mcguirewoods.com

WILLIAM L. KUHN, born Frankfurt, Germany, 1975; admitted to bar, 1999, Illinois and U.S. District Court, Northern District of Illinois; 2001, U.S. Court of Appeals for the Seventh Circuit. *Education:* University of Arizona (B.A., 1996); Harvard University (J.D., 1999). ***PRACTICE AREAS:*** Appellate Practice; Class Action Litigation; Complex Commercial Litigation; Securities Litigation; Insurance Coverage Litigation; Drug and Medical Device Defense and Pharmaceuticals; Energy; Utilities. ***Email:*** wkuhn@mcguirewoods.com

JOHN A. LEJA, born Chicago, Illinois, 1969; admitted to bar, 1998, Illinois; U.S. Court of Appeals, Seventh Circuit; U.S. District Court, Northern District of Illinois. *Education:* Purdue University (B.S., 1991); Cornell University Law School (J.D., 1998). ***PRACTICE AREAS:*** Complex Commercial Litigation; Intellectual Property; Construction Litigation; Patents; Consumer Finance; Class Action Litigation; Appellate Practice. ***Email:*** jleja@mcguirewoods.com

GARY Y. LEUNG, JR., born Los Angeles, California, 1976; admitted to bar, 2002, Illinois. *Education:* Northwestern University (B.A., 1998; J.D., 2002). ***PRACTICE AREAS:*** Commercial Litigation. ***Email:*** gleung@mcguirewoods.com

LINCOLN J. LOUNSBURY, born Carbondale, Illinois, 1970; admitted to bar, 2001, Illinois. *Education:* Southern Illinois University (B.A., 1992; M.A., 1995); Northwestern University (J.D., 2001). ***PRACTICE AREAS:*** Employee Benefits; Executive Compensation. ***Email:*** llounsbury@mcguirewoods.com

RONALD EDWARD LUNDEEN, JR., born Charleston, Illinois, 1973; admitted to bar, 2004, Illinois. *Education:* University of Utah (B.S., 1997); University of Chicago Law School (J.D., 2004). ***PRACTICE AREAS:*** Health Care Regulatory; Health Care Financial Services; Corporate Services Health Care; Health Care. ***Email:*** rlundeen@mcguirewoods.com

RACHEL WILLIAMS MANTZ, born Madison, Wisconsin, 1972; admitted to bar, 1997, Wisconsin and Illinois. *Education:* Washington University (B.A., 1994); University of Wisconsin-Madison (J.D., 1997). ***PRACTICE AREAS:*** Mergers; Acquisitions; Securities; Corporate Finance. ***Email:*** rmantz@mcguirewoods.com

DAVID T. MEEHAN, born Elmhurst, Illinois, 1970; admitted to bar, 1998, Illinois and U.S. District Court, Northern District of Illinois. *Education:* Indiana University (B.A., 1994); DePaul University (J.D., 1997). *Member:* Chicago Bar Association (Chairman, Debtor-Creditor Rights Subcommittee). ***PRACTICE AREAS:*** Appellate Practice; Class Action Litigation; Complex Commercial Litigation; Consumer Financial Services; Consumer Law. ***Email:*** dmeehan@mcguirewoods.com

CARLIN R. METZGER, born Chicago, Illinois, 1976; admitted to bar, 2001, Illinois and U.S. District Court, Northern District of Illinois. *Education:* DePauw University (B.A., 1998); Illinois Institute of Technology, Chicago-Kent College of Law (J.D., 2001). ***LAN-***

(This Listing Continued)

GUAGES: French. **PRACTICE AREAS:** Complex Commercial Litigation; Intellectual Property; White Collar Crime; Government Investigations; Insurance. **Email:** cmetzger@mcguirewoods.com

ALISON VRATIL MIKULA, born Kansas City, Missouri; admitted to bar, 2004, Illinois. *Education:* Middlebury College (B.A., 1999); University of Michigan (M.H.S.A., 2004; J.D., 2004). ***PRACTICE AREAS:*** Health Care. ***Email:*** amikula@mcguirewoods.com

PETER A. MILIANTI, born Des Plaines, Illinois, 1972; admitted to bar, 1997, Illinois and U.S. District Court, Northern District of Illinois. *Education:* University of Iowa (B.A., 1994); Chicago-Kent College of Law, Illinois Institute of Technology (J.D., 1997). ***PRACTICE AREAS:*** Employment Discrimination; Labor Law. ***Email:*** pmilianti@mcguirewoods.com

PAMELA M. MILLER, born Newport News, Virginia, 1977; admitted to bar, 2002, Illinois. *Education:* University of Florida (B.S., B.A., 1999); University of Illinois (J.D., 2002). ***Email:*** pmiller@mcguirewoods.com

DAVID A. P. NEBOYSKEY, born Monroe, Michigan, 1969; admitted to bar, 2000, Illinois. *Education:* University of Michigan (B.A., 1993); Indiana University (J.D., 2000). ***PRACTICE AREAS:*** Real Estate; Mezzanine Financing. ***Email:*** dneboyskey@mcguirewoods.com

BRIAN P. O'MEARA, born Evanston, Illinois, 1975; admitted to bar, 2001, Illinois and U.S. District Court, Northern and Southern Districts of Illinois; 2002, Indiana and U.S. District Court, Northern and Southern Districts of Indiana; 2004, U.S. District Court, Central District of Illinois. *Education:* Boston College (B.A., 1997); Loyola University School of Law (J.D., 2001). ***PRACTICE AREAS:*** Commercial Litigation; Business Litigation; Unfair Competition; Class Action; Fair Credit Reporting Act. ***Email:*** bomeara@mcguirewoods.com

ANNE M. PETERSON, born Oak Lawn, Illinois; admitted to bar, 2002, Illinois. *Education:* University of Notre Dame (B.A., 1993); University of Michigan, Ann Arbor (M.A., 1999); University of Notre Dame Law School (J.D., 2002). ***PRACTICE AREAS:*** Labor and Employment. ***Email:*** apeterson@mcguirewoods.com

KATIE M. RAK, born East Chicago, Indiana, 1978; admitted to bar, 2004, Illinois. *Education:* University of Notre Dame (B.A., 2001); University of Notre Dame Law School (J.D., 2004). ***PRACTICE AREAS:*** Employee Benefits. ***Email:*** krak@mcguirewoods.com

NANCY MARY RILEY, born Evanston, Illinois, 1978; admitted to bar, 2004, Illinois and U.S. District Court, Northern District of Illinois; 2005, U.S. Court of Appeals, Seventh Circuit. *Education:* Northwestern University (B.A., 2000); University of Southern California (J.D., 2004). ***PRACTICE AREAS:*** Products Liability. ***Email:*** nriley@mcguirewoods.com

ANGELO M. RUSSO, born West Palm Beach, Florida, 1975; admitted to bar, 2000, Illinois and U.S. District Court, Northern District of Illinois; 2004, U.S. District Court, Eastern District of Wisconsin. *Education:* University of Illinois (B.S., 1997); DePaul University College of Law (J.D., 2000). ***PRACTICE AREAS:*** Complex Commercial Litigation; White Collar Crime; Antitrust and Trade Regulation; Contracts; Fiduciary Litigation; Government Investigations. ***Email:*** arusso@mcguirewoods.com

ANDREW S. RYERSON, born Park Ridge, Illinois, 1969; admitted to bar, 1995, Illinois. *Education:* Miami University (B.A., 1991); DePaul University (J.D., 1995). ***PRACTICE AREAS:*** Real Estate.

SCOTT A. SCHLAUTMAN, born St. Louis, Missouri; admitted to bar, 2003, Illinois. *Education:* Tulane University (B.S.M., 1995); University of Notre Dame (J.D., 2003). ***PRACTICE AREAS:*** Mergers and Acquisitions; Securities; SEC Enforcement; Corporate Governance; Corporate Finance; Business Law. ***Email:*** sschlautman@mcguirewoods.com

MICHAEL M. SCHMAHL, born Milwaukee, Wisconsin; admitted to bar, 2001, Illinois, Wisconsin and U.S. District Court, Northern District of Illinois. *Education:* Bowdoin College (A.B.,1997); University of Wisconsin (J.D., 2001). ***PRACTICE AREAS:*** Creditors Rights; Bankruptcy. ***Email:*** mschmahl@mcguirewoods.com

KAREN SEWELL, born San Jose, California, 1979; admitted to bar, 2004, Illinois. *Education:* Northwestern University (B.S., 2001); University of Illinois College of Law (J.D., 2004). ***PRACTICE AREAS:*** Commercial Litigation. ***Email:*** ksewell@mcguirewoods.com

JENNIFER A. STOJAK, born Chicago, Illinois, 1975; admitted to bar, 2001, Illinois. *Education:* Fairfield University (B.A., 1997); Georgetown University (J.D., 2001). ***PRACTICE AREAS:*** Employee Benefits; ERISA Litigation. ***Email:*** jstojak@mcguirewoods.com

MELISSA SZABAD, born Dayton, Ohio, 1973; admitted to bar, 2000, Illinois. *Education:* Kenyon College (B.A., 1996); DePaul University (J.D., 2000). General Editor, DePaul Law Review. ***PRACTICE AREAS:*** Health Care. ***Email:*** mszabad@mcguirewoods.com

ELIZABETH S. TENNEY, born East Lansing, Michigan, 1975; admitted to bar, 2001, Illinois; 2004, California. *Education:* Michigan State University (B.A., 1997; J.D., cum laude, 2000); Georgetown University (LL.M., Taxation, 2001). ***PRACTICE AREAS:*** Trusts and Estates; Private Wealth Services; Family Business; Partnerships; Joint Ventures; State Taxation; Local Taxation; Business Acquisitions; Business Reorganization; Business Divestitures. ***Email:*** etenney@mcguirewoods.com

JEFFREY C. TORRES, born Wailuku, Hawaii, 1967; admitted to bar, 1997, Illinois; 1998, District of Columbia; U.S District Court, Northern District of Illinois. *Education:* University of Notre Dame (B.B.A., 1989); Pacific Lutheran University (M.B.A., 1992); University of Michigan (J.D., 1996). Member: Lamba Legal Defense and Education Fund; Cooperating Attorney Network. ***PRACTICE AREAS:*** Complex Commercial Litigation. ***Email:*** jtorres@mcguirewoods.com

(This Listing Continued)

CAROLYN M. TRENDA, born Barrington, Illinois, 1977; admitted to bar, 2002, Illinois. *Education:* University of Notre Dame (B.A., 1999; J.D., 2002). ***PRACTICE AREAS:*** Employee Benefits; Executive Compensation. ***Email:*** ctrenda@mcguirewoods.com

CHRISTOPHER J. VERSTRATE, born Sheboygan, Wisconsin, 1974; admitted to bar, 1999, Illinois. *Education:* Trinity Christian College (B.A., 1996); Northwestern University (J.D., 1999). Coordinating Articles Editor, Journal of International Law and Business, 1998-1999. Co-author: "Open Source Software: Is It Really Free?" The John Marshall Law School Center for Intellectual Property Law News Source, Spring 2003; "Internet Privacy: It's Not Just for B2C Anymore," eBiz Chronicle, September 6, 2001. Speaker, "Security Interests in Intellectual Property," presented at Commercial Lending Requirements and Loan Documentation, Illinois, November 6, 2003. Adjunct Professor, Legal Environment of Business, Trinity Christian College, Spring 2004. ***PRACTICE AREAS:*** Corporate Law; Business Law; Intellectual Property. ***Email:*** cverstrate@mcguirewoods.com

BARTON C. WALKER, born Philadelphia, Pennsylvania, 1979; admitted to bar, 2004, Illinois. *Education:* University of North Carolina at Chapel Hill (B.A., 2001); University of Notre Dame (J.D., 2004). ***PRACTICE AREAS:*** Finance; Securities; Corporate Governance; Emerging Growth Companies; Technology Law; Regulatory Law; Mergers and Acquisitions; Joint Ventures; Private Equity; Telecommunications Law; Media Law; Health Care. ***Email:*** bwalker@mcguirewoods.com

AMBER McGRAW WALSH, born Sedalia, Missouri, 1976; admitted to bar, 2002, Missouri; 2003, Illinois. *Education:* University of Kansas (B.A., 1999); Washington University (J.D., 2002). ***PRACTICE AREAS:*** Health Care Law. ***Email:*** awalsh@mcguirewoods.com

JACOB A. WARDEN, born Pittsburgh, Pennsylvania; admitted to bar, 2004, Illinois. *Education:* University of Pennsylvania (B.A., 1999); Northwestern University School of Law (J.D., 2004). Executive Editor, 2003-2004 and Staff Member, 2002-2004, Northwestern Journal of International Law & Business. Author, "Open Skies at a Crossroads," Northwestern Journal of International Law & Business, Fall 2003. ***LANGUAGES:*** French. ***PRACTICE AREAS:*** Real Estate Transactions; Environmental Solutions. ***Email:*** jwarden@mcguirewoods.com

UNDRAY WILKS, born Chicago, Illinois, 1962; admitted to bar, 1987, Illinois. *Education:* Northwestern University (B.A., 1984); University of Michigan (J.D., 1987). Senior Contracts Manager, Motorola, Inc., 1996-2001. Associate, Kelley Drye & Warren, 1990-1995. ***PRACTICE AREAS:*** Automotive; Insurance Coverage Litigation; Drug and Medical Device Litigation; Pharmaceuticals; Products Liability; Toxic Torts; Real Estate Transactions. ***Email:*** uwilks@mcguirewoods.com

BRIANNA J. ZIELKE, born Presque Isle, Maine, 1975; admitted to bar, 2003, Illinois. *Education:* University of Notre Dame (B.A., 1997); Northwestern University School of Law (J.D., 2003). ***Email:*** bsmith@mcguirewoods.com

REVISER OF THE VIRGINIA LAW DIGEST FOR THIS DIRECTORY.

McKAY, NORA, TANZILLO, DADDINO & KOTT, LLP

10 SOUTH LASALLE STREET, SUITE 2700
CHICAGO, ILLINOIS 60603
Telephone: 312-650-7900
Fax: 312-650-7910

Insurance Defense, Medical Malpractice, Pharmacist Liability, Premises Liability, Insurance Fraud and Coverage Issues.

MEMBERS OF FIRM

TIMOTHY J. McKAY, born Chicago, Illinois, October 20, 1954; admitted to bar, 1979, Illinois; 1980, U.S. District Court, Northern District of Illinois including Trial Bar and U.S. Court of Appeals, Seventh Circuit. *Education:* University of Notre Dame (B.A., magna cum laude, 1976); Loyola University (J.D., 1979). Law Clerk to the Hon. William J. Bauer, U.S. Court of Appeals, Seventh Circuit, 1978-1979. Assistant State's Attorney, Appellate Division, 1979-1980, Felony Trial Division, 1981-1984, Cook County. *Member:* DuPage County, Illinois State and American Bar Associations; Trial Lawyers Club of Chicago; Defense Research Institute; Illinois Defense Counsel; Federal Trial Bar. ***PRACTICE AREAS:*** Hotel Innkeeper Litigation; Premise Liability Defense Litigation; Medical Malpractice Defense Litigation; Insurance Fraud and Coverage Litigation; Criminal Law. ***Email:*** tmckay@mckaynora.com

ROBERT L. NORA, born Chicago, Illinois, August 4, 1955; admitted to bar, 1980, Illinois and U.S. District Court, Northern District of Illinois including Federal Trial Bar. *Education:* Northwestern University (B.A., with honors, 1977); DePaul University (J.D., 1980). Listed in "Top Twenty Tort Defense Lawyers," Chicago Lawyer, January 2003. Author: "Dental Malpractice: Its Causes and Cures," Quintessence International, Vol. 17, No. 2/1986, reprinted Chicago Dental Society Review, July, 1986; "Medical Affidavit Requirement Held Unconstitutional," Risk Management Exchange Vol. 2, No. 2, Winter, 1989; "AIDS Confidentiality Act and Hospital Liability," Occurrence Vol. 11, No. 3, July-Sept., 1989. Speeches: Chicago Dental Society Midwinter Meeting, February, 1987; American Academy of General Dentistry, Annual Meeting, May, 1988; Chicago Dental Society Midwinter Meeting, February, 1989: "Market Share Liability: The Art of the Possible," September, 1989, videotaped for presentation by Chicago Bar Association and Continuing Legal Education Satellite Network; "Medical Malpractice from the Defense Perspective," Illinois Trial Lawyers Association, December 7, 1991. Moderator: "Current Trends in Medical Malpractice," Chicago Bar Association, June 1993; "The Preparation and Trial of Medical Negligence Cases: The Impact of HB20," Chicago Bar Association, June 14, 1995. *Member:* Chicago, Illinois State and American Bar Associations; Trial Lawyers Club of Chicago; Society of Trial Lawyers for the State of Illinois (Member, Board of Directors). ***PRACTICE AREAS:*** Medical Malpractice. ***Email:*** bnora@mckaynora.com

PAUL A. TANZILLO, born Chicago, Illinois, October 24, 1960; admitted to bar, 1986, Illinois and U.S. District Court, Northern District of Illinois. *Education:* Illinois

(This Listing Continued)

McKAY, NORA, TANZILLO, DADDINO & KOTT, LLP, Chicago—Continued

Benedictine College (B.A., 1982); IIT-Chicago Kent College of Law (J.D., 1986). Member, Justinian Society of Lawyers. *Member:* Chicago, Northwest Suburban, Illinois State and American Bar Associations; Illinois Association of Defense Trial Counsel; Defense Research Institute. ***PRACTICE AREAS:*** Civil Trial; Insurance Defense. ***Email:*** ptanzillo@mckaynora.com

CHRISTOPHER M. DADDINO, born Knob Noster, Missouri, October 4, 1966; admitted to bar, 1991, Illinois and U.S. District Court, Northern District of Illinois. *Education:* Miami University (B.A., 1988); Loyola University (J.D., 1991). ***PRACTICE AREAS:*** Medical Malpractice; Criminal Trial. ***Email:*** cdaddino@mckaynora.com

ANDREA H. KOTT, born Chicago, Illinois, March 24, 1964; admitted to bar, 1990, Illinois and U.S. District Court, Northern District of Illinois. *Education:* Washington University (B.A., cum laude, 1986); Case Western Reserve University (J.D., 1989). Philip C. Jessup International Moot Court Team. Author: "AIDS Confidentiality Act to Hospital Liability," Occurrence, Vol. 11, No. 3, July-September, 1989; "Federal Preemption of Medical Devices," IDC Quarterly, Vol. 2, No. 3, 1992. ***PRACTICE AREAS:*** Medical Malpractice; Pharmacist Liability. ***Email:*** akott@mckaynora.com

LYNNE M. REARDON DAMSMA, born Albany, New York, January 13, 1970; admitted to bar, 1995, Ohio; 1996, Illinois. *Education:* Ohio University (B.S., 1992); University of Akron (J.D., 1995). *Member:* Chicago and Illinois State Bar Associations. ***PRACTICE AREAS:*** Medical Malpractice; Insurance Defense. ***Email:*** lreardon@mckaynora.com

ASSOCIATES

VINCENT MICHAEL AURICCHIO, born Hempstead, New York, January 22, 1971; admitted to bar, 1997, Illinois. *Education:* Vanderbilt University (B.S., 1993); DePaul University College of Law (J.D., 1997). Faculty Member, National Business Institute: "Settlements in Illinois," February 2004; "Advanced Expert Witness Deposition Tactics in Illinois," November 2004. *Member:* Chicago Bar Association. ***PRACTICE AREAS:*** Medical Malpractice Litigation; Premises Liability Litigation; Commercial Litigation; Real Estate. ***Email:*** vauricchio@mckaynora.com

STUART L. BERMAN, born Baltimore, Maryland, December 30, 1971; admitted to bar, 1998, Illinois. *Education:* Bates College (B.A., 1994); Chicago-Kent College of Law, Illinois Institute of Technology (J.D., 1998). ***PRACTICE AREAS:*** Insurance Defense. ***Email:*** sberman@mckaynora.com

KEVIN M. BUGOS, born Chicago, Illinois, July 3, 1972; admitted to bar, 1997, Illinois; 2001, U.S. District Court, Northern District of Illinois, including Trial Bar. *Education:* University of Notre Dame (B.A., 1994); Chicago-Kent College of Law (J.D., 1997). *Member:* DuPage County and Illinois State Bar Associations. ***PRACTICE AREAS:*** Premises Liability; Personal Injury Defense; Criminal Law; Commercial Law. ***Email:*** kbugos@mckaynora.com

CAROLINE E. CARLSON, born Chicago, Illinois, November 26, 1972; admitted to bar, 1999, Illinois; 2003, U.S. District Court, Northern District of Illinois. *Education:* Colgate University (B.S.); DePaul University Law School (J.D., 1999). ***PRACTICE AREAS:*** Medical Malpractice. ***Email:*** ccarlson@mckaynora.com

RYAN T. JOHNSON, born Des Moines, Iowa, October 27, 1977; admitted to bar, 2003, Illinois and U.S. District Court, Northern District of Illinois. *Education:* University of Iowa (B.A., 2000); Drake University (J.D., 2003). *Member:* Illinois State Bar Association. ***Email:*** rjohnson@mckaynora.com

BRAD SCHULMAN, admitted to bar, 2005, Illinois and U.S. District Court, Northern District of Illinois. *Education:* Lehigh University (B.A., 2001); The John Marshall Law School (J.D., cum laude, 2005). *Member:* Chicago and Illinois State Bar Associations. ***PRACTICE AREAS:*** Medical Malpractice Litigation; Premises Liability. ***Email:*** bschulman@mckaynora.com

THE LAW FIRM OF MICHAEL R. McKENNA, P.C.

Established in 1976

500 WEST MADISON STREET, SUITE 3800
CHICAGO, ILLINOIS 60661
Telephone: 312-321-0123
Fax: 312-876-2020
URL: http://www.ChicagoPatent.com
Email: info@ChicagoPatent.com
URL: http://www.lawyers.com/mckennalawfirm

Patent, Trademark and Copyright Law, including prosecution, licensing and dispute resolution.

FIRM PROFILE: The firm represents a creative clientele of inventors and entrepreneurs, designers, manufacturers, authors, artists, and software developers.

MICHAEL R. McKENNA, born Chicago, Illinois, April 10, 1948; admitted to bar, 1976, Illinois; 1983, U.S. District Court, Northern District of Illinois including Trial Bar; 1985, U.S. Court of Appeals, 7th Circuit; 1987, U.S. Court of Appeals for the Fedreal Circuit and U.S. Supreme Court; 1994, Hawaii; registered to practice before the U.S. Patent and Trademark Office. *Education:* University of Illinois (B.S., Engineering, with honors, 1971); Illinois Institute of Technology, Chicago-Kent College of Law (J.D., 1976). *Member:* Chicago, Illinois State, Hawaii State and American Bar Associations; American Intellectual Property Law Association; Intellectual Property Law Association of Chicago; Society of Professionals in Dispute Resolution; Lawyers for the Creative Arts.

McKENNA STORER

Established in 1954

33 N. LA SALLE STREET
14TH FLOOR
CHICAGO, ILLINOIS 60602-2610
Telephone: 312-558-3900
Fax: 312-558-8348
Email: postmaster-@mckenna-law.com
URL: http://www.mckenna-law.com

Waukegan, Illinois Office: 33 North County Street, 6th Floor, 60085-4343. Telephone: 847-249-1620. Fax: 847-249-8457.

Woodstock, Illinois Office: 666 Russel Court, Suite 303, 60098-2672. Telephone: 815-334-9690. Fax: 815-334-9697.

Administrative Hearings, Appellate, Banking and Lending, Bankruptcy, Civil Rights, Commercial, Construction, Employment, Estate Planning, Fidelity, Insurance Coverage, Legal Malpractice, Mediation Services, Medical Malpractice, National Coordination, Personal Injury, Products Liability, Professional Liability, Surety, Tax and Toxic Tort.

FIRM PROFILE: McKenna Storer celebrated its 50th Anniversary in 2004. The Firm has a history and reputation for providing quality legal services to its clients. Our clients are individuals, corporations and insurance companies. We serve local, national and international clients from our offices in the Chicago, Illinois metropolitan area.

Client focused and service driven, the Firm is committed to cost-effective client services that are effective, personal and timely. Whether retained for litigation or consultation, McKenna Storer's philosophy is to consider traditional and creative solutions to our clients' legal needs.

WILLIAM J. McKENNA (1923-1975)
JOHN F. WHITE (1929-2002)

ATTORNEYS

RICHARD M. CLARK (Resident, Waukegan Office) (For complete biographical data, see Waukegan Office)

GREGORY L. COCHRAN, admitted to bar, 1980, Illinois. *Education:* University of Michigan (B.A., 1977; J.D., 1980). ***Email:*** gcochran@mckenna-law.com

SARA E. COOK (Resident, Woodstock Office) (For complete biographical data, see Woodstock Office)

JOHN A. CULVER, admitted to bar, 1988, Illinois. *Education:* St. Catharine's College, Cambridge University, England; Michigan State University (B.A., 1985); Mattias Concannon Programme of International Law, Notre Dame London Law Centre; University of Notre Dame (J.D., 1988). ***Email:*** jculver@mckenna-law.com

JAMES P. DeNARDO, admitted to bar, 1967, Illinois. *Education:* DePaul University (B.A., 1964; J.D., 1967). ***Email:*** jdenardo@mckenna-law.com

JOHN W. EGAN, admitted to bar, 1977, Illinois. *Education:* Xavier University (A.B., 1969); Fordham University (M.A., 1973); Northwestern University (J.D., 1977). ***Email:*** jegan@mckenna-law.com

DAWN E. EHRENBERG, admitted to bar, 1987, Illinois. *Education:* Joliet Junior College; Lewis University (B.A., 1984); University of Illinois (J.D., 1987). ***Email:*** dehrenberg@mckenna-law.com

TINA L. FINK, admitted to bar, 2002, Illinois. *Education:* Loras College (B.A.,1999); DePaul University (J.D., 2002). ***Email:*** tfink@mckenna-law.com

MARGARET MARIE FOSTER, admitted to bar, 1988, Illinois. *Education:* University of Arkansas (B.A., 1979; M.A., 1980; J.D., 1988). ***Email:*** mfoster@mckenna-law.com

TERRY A. FOX, admitted to bar, 1991, Illinois. *Education:* Iowa State University (B.A., 1985); University of Iowa (J.D., 1990). ***Email:*** tfox@mckenna-law.com

THOMAS W. HAYES, admitted to bar, 1986, Illinois. *Education:* U.S. Military Academy (B.S., 1978); DePaul University (J.D., 1986). ***Email:*** thayes@mckenna-law.com

PATRICIA C. KRAFT (Resident, Woodstock Office) (For complete biographical data, see Woodstock Office)

THOMAS F. LUCAS, admitted to bar, 1978, Illinois. *Education:* University of Illinois (B.A., 1975); Loyola University (J.D., 1978). ***Email:*** tlucas@mckenna-law.com

BRUCE B. MARR, admitted to bar, 1981, Indiana; 1983, Illinois. *Education:* University of Virginia (B.A., 1976; M.Ed., 1978); DePaul University (J.D., 1981). ***Email:*** bmarr@mckenna-law.com

TRACY McGONIGLE, admitted to bar, 1993, Illinois. *Education:* Loyola University, Chicago (B.A., 1990); DePaul University (J.D., 1993). ***Email:*** tmcgonigle@mckenna-law.com

TIMOTHY J. MURTAUGH, III, admitted to bar, 1962, Illinois. *Education:* University of Notre Dame (A.B., 1958); University of Michigan (LL.B., 1961). ***Email:*** tmurtaugh@mckenna-law.com

PAIGE MORAY NEEL, admitted to bar, 2001, Indiana; 2003, Illinois. *Education:* Indiana University, Bloomington (B.A., 1998; J.D., 2001). ***Email:*** pneel@mckenna-law.com

WILLIAM S. PIPER, admitted to bar, 1978, Illinois. *Education:* Loyola University (A.B., 1975; J.D., 1978). ***Email:*** wpiper@mckenna-law.com

ROBERT P. PISANI, admitted to bar, 1986, Illinois. *Education:* University of Wisconsin-Madison (B.A., 1983); DePaul University (J.D., 1986). ***Email:*** rpisani@mckenna-law.com

SAMUEL A. PURVES, admitted to bar, 1966, Illinois. *Education:* Stanford University (A.B., 1963); University of Michigan (J.D., with distinction, 1966). ***Email:*** spurves@mckenna-law.com

(This Listing Continued)

JULIE A. RAMSON, admitted to bar, 1982, Illinois. *Education:* University of Wisconsin (B.S.N., 1971); Loyola Law School (J.D., 1982). ***Email:*** jramson@mckenna-law.com

THOMAS A. REED, admitted to bar, 1975, Illinois. *Education:* University of Illinois (B.S., 1969); University of Texas at Austin (J.D., 1975). ***Email:*** treed@mckenna-law.com

RICHARD J. RETTBERG, admitted to bar, 1976, Illinois. *Education:* University of Illinois at Urbana-Champaign (B.A., 1973); IIT/Chicago-Kent College of Law (J.D., 1976). ***Email:*** rrettberg@mckenna-law.com

KRISTIN DVORSKY TAURAS, admitted to bar, 1993, Illinois. *Education:* University of Iowa (B.A., 1989); DePaul University (J.D., 1993). ***Email:*** ktauras@mckenna-law.com

JUSTIN L. TERRY, admitted to bar, 2000, Illinois. *Education:* Northwestern University (B.S., 1994); University of Notre Dame (J.D., 1999). ***Email:*** jterry@mckenna-law.com

McLACHLAN, RISSMAN & DOLL

Established in 1987

676 NORTH MICHIGAN AVENUE, SUITE 2800
CHICAGO, ILLINOIS 60611
Telephone: 312-266-2444
Telecopier: 312-266-3330

Acquisition and Financing Transactions; General Corporate; Railroads; Rail Equipment Finance; Commercial Transactions.

FIRM PROFILE: Prior to 1987 all members of McLachlan, Rissman & Doll were associated with Isham, Lincoln & Beale.

MEMBERS OF FIRM

DONALD J. McLACHLAN (1937-1992)

THOMAS W. RISSMAN, born Chicago, Illinois, May 19, 1957; admitted to bar, 1982, Illinois. *Education:* Cornell University (A.B., 1979); University of Chicago (J.D., 1982). Recipient, Distinguished Service Award. Director: Railroad Financial Corporation, 1989—; Shopper Trak RCT Corporation, 1995—; Arkansas & Missouri Railroad Company; Electro-Motive Diesel, Inc., 2004—. ***Email:*** trissman@mrdlaw.com

JOHN H. DOLL, born Marion, Michigan, July 24, 1944; admitted to bar, 1980, Illinois. *Education:* Calvin College (B.A., 1966); University of Chicago (M.A., 1968); IIT/Chicago-Kent College of Law (J.D., with high honors, 1980). Notes and Comments Editor, Chicago-Kent Law Review, 1979-1980. ***Email:*** jdoll@mrdlaw.com

LAURAL S. JIN, born Cleveland, Ohio, June 29, 1970; admitted to bar, 1997, Illinois. *Education:* University of Chicago (A.B., 1992; J.D., 1997). ***Email:*** ljin@mrdlaw.com

ASSOCIATE

ALISON C. MADAUSS, born Chicago, Illinois, June 13, 1978; admitted to bar, 2003, Illinois. *Education:* Vanderbilt University (B.A., 2000); University of Chicago (J.D., 2003). ***Email:*** amadauss@mrdlaw.com

COUNSEL

ANTHONY E. ROTHSCHILD, born Chicago, Illinois, May 16, 1957; admitted to bar, 1983, Illinois, U.S. District Court, Northern District of Illinois; 1984, U.S. Court of Appeals, Seventh Circuit. *Education:* Harvard College (A.B., 1979); Northwestern University (J.D., 1983). Member, Northwestern University Law Review, 1981-1983. Law Clerk to the Honorable Wilbur F. Pell, Jr., U.S. Court of Appeals, Seventh Circuit, 1983-1985. *Member:* Chicago Bar Association. ***PRACTICE AREAS:*** Corporate Law; Acquisitions and Dispositions; Venture Capital; Intellectual Property. ***Email:*** arothschild@mrdlaw.com

McNAMARA & AUSTIN, P.C.

25 EAST WASHINGTON - SUITE 1501
CHICAGO, ILLINOIS 60602
Telephone: 312-201-8850
Fax: 312-201-8853
Email: austin@mafirm.com
URL: http://www.mafirm.com

Civil Trial Practice, Criminal Defense, Driving While Intoxicated, Drug Crimes, Felonies, Homicide, Misdemeanors, Parole and Probation, Sexual Assault, Traffic Violations, Suspended License Offenses, Personal Injury, Automobile Accidents, Medical Malpractice and Real Estate Law.

EDWARD J. AUSTIN, born Chicago, Illinois, February 2, 1970; admitted to bar, 1996, Illinois. *Education:* Indiana University, Bloomington (B.A., 1992); Loyola University (J.D., 1996). Assistant States Attorney of Cook County, Illinois, 1996-2001. *Member:* Chicago Bar Association. ***PRACTICE AREAS:*** Criminal Defense; Personal Injury; Civil Litigation; Real Estate. ***Email:*** austin@mafirm.com

JOHN L. McNAMARA, born Evanston, Illinois, September 22, 1970; admitted to bar, 1995, Illinois. *Education:* University of Illinois, Urbana-Champaign (B.A., 1992); Chicago-Kent College of Law (J.D., 1995). Cook County States Attorney's Office, 1995-2001. ***PRACTICE AREAS:*** Criminal Defense; Personal Injury; Real Estate. ***Email:*** john@mafirm.com

KEVIN J. McNAMARA, born Evanston, Illinois, February 7, 1969; admitted to bar, 1995, Illinois. *Education:* Indiana University (B.A., 1991); John Marshall Law School (J.D., 1995). Formerly with Neville, Pappas & Mahoney, 1995-2001. *Member:* Illinois Trial Lawyers Association. ***PRACTICE AREAS:*** Personal Injury; Medical Malpractice; Real Estate. ***Email:*** kevin@mafirm.com

McPARLAND & PHILLIPS, LLC

221 N. LA SALLE STREET, SUITE 463
CHICAGO, ILLINOIS 60601
Telephone: 312-634-1100
Fax: 312-634-1101
Email: jmcpar8174@aol.com

Corporate, Commercial, Real Estate, Employment and Health Care Law.

JAMES E. McPARLAND, born Evansville, Indiana, October 2, 1946; admitted to bar, 1972, Illinois, U.S. District Court, Northern District of Illinois including Trial Bar; 1980, U.S. Supreme Court; 1973, U.S. Court of Appeals, 7th Circuit; 1986, U.S. District Court, Central District of Illinois. *Education:* St. Procopius College (B.A., 1968); John Marshall Law School (J.D., 1972). Member, Gavel Society. Associate Editor, John Marshall Journal of Practice and Procedure, 1971-1972. Member, Village of Downers Grove Zoning Commission, 1980-1986. *Member:* Illinois State and American Bar Associations; American Academy of Hospital Attorneys; Illinois Association of Healthcare Attorneys. ***PRACTICE AREAS:*** Corporate; Employment Management; Health Care. ***Email:*** jmcpar8174@aol.com

WILLIAM B. PHILLIPS, born Gorin, Missouri, May 31, 1946; admitted to bar, 1973, Illinois, U.S. District Court, Northern District of Illinois and U.S. Court of Appeals, Seventh Circuit. *Education:* Northwestern University (B.S., 1968); University of Illinois (J.D., 1973). *Member:* Chicago and Illinois State Bar Associations. ***PRACTICE AREAS:*** Real Estate; Corporate. ***Email:*** phillipswb@aol.com

GAYLE M. MEADORS, P.C.

20 SOUTH CLARK STREET, 25TH FLOOR
CHICAGO, ILLINOIS 60603
Telephone: 312-558-1255
Email: gmm@erisalaw-chicago.com
URL: http://www.erisalaw-chicago.com

Employee Benefits, ERISA.

FIRM PROFILE: Employee benefits and employment law representation for businesses.

GAYLE M. MEADORS, born Chicago, Illinois, 1946; admitted to bar, 1977, Illinois. *Education:* University of Illinois (A.B., with honors, 1969); University of Chicago (M.A., Lib. Sci., 1973); DePaul University (J.D., magna cum laude, 1977). Phi Beta Kappa. Author: "Compensation and Benefits Briefs," Journal of Medical Practice Management, Greenbranch Publishing. *Member:* Chicago and Illinois State Bar Associations. (Also Of Counsel to Ogletree, Deakins, Nash, Smoak & Stewart, P.C.). ***PRACTICE AREAS:*** Employee Benefits; ERISA; 401(k) Plans; Qualified Retirement Plans; Pension Taxation; Profit Sharing; Pension Plans; Pension and Profit Sharing Plans; Non-Qualified Benefits; Health Benefits; Flexible Benefit Plans; ERISA Compliance; Deferred Compensation; COBRA. ***Email:*** gmm@erisalaw-chicago.com

MECKLER BULGER & TILSON

123 NORTH WACKER DRIVE, SUITE 1800
CHICAGO, ILLINOIS 60606
Telephone: 312-474-7900
Facsimile: 312-474-7898
URL: http://www.mbtlaw.com

Practice concentrated in all areas of general commercial litigation, insurance, reinsurance, excess and professional liability coverage, labor and employment, product liability and white collar criminal litigation and counseling.

MEMBERS OF FIRM

JEFFREY A. BERMAN, born Chicago, Illinois, May 31, 1962; admitted to bar, 1987, Illinois and U.S. District Court, Northern District of Illinois including Trial Bar; 1990, U.S. Court of Appeals, Seventh Circuit and U.S. District Court, Central District of Illinois; 1995, U.S. District Court, District of Arizona. *Education:* University of Illinois (B.S., with honors, 1984; J.D., magna cum laude, 1987). Recipient: Harno Fellowship; American Jurisprudence Award, 1986. Associate Editor, University of Illinois Journal, 1986-1987. Certified Public Accountant, Illinois, 1984. Trustee, Buffalo Grove Board of Trustees, 1999—. *Member:* Illinois State and American Bar Associations. ***PRACTICE AREAS:*** Insurance Coverage; Business Litigation; Commercial Litigation. ***Email:*** jeffrey.berman@mbtlaw.com

ANNE L. BLUME, born Detroit, Michigan, January 31, 1963; admitted to bar, 1991, Illinois. *Education:* Michigan State University (B.A., 1985); John Marshall Law School (J.D., 1991). Chief Justice, The John Marshall Moot Court Executive Board, 1990-1991; ISBA Moot Court Competition Winning Team, 1st Place Brief, 3rd Place Oralist. ***REPORTED CASES:*** Dearborn Ins. Co. v. Int'l. Surplus Lines Ins. Co., 308 Ill. App. 3d 368 (1st Dist. 1999); Old Republic Ins.Co.v. Chuhak & Tecson, 84 F.3d 998 (7th Cir. 1996). ***PRACTICE AREAS:*** Construction Litigation; Commercial Litigation; Professional Liability; Insurance Coverage. ***Email:*** anne.blume@mbtlaw.com

BRIAN W. BULGER, born Chicago, Illinois, May 27, 1951; admitted to bar, 1977, Illinois, U.S. District Court, Northern District of Illinois and U.S. Court of Appeals, Seventh Circuit; 1980, U.S. Supreme Court. *Education:* Georgetown University (A.B., cum laude, 1972; J.D., 1977). Selected "Among Nation's Best Employment Litigators," National Law Journal, July 1992. Author: "Boys Markets Injunctions," 69 Ill. Bar J. 94, Oct. 1980; "Practice and Procedure Before the Office of Federal Contract Compliance Programs," Ill. Inst. for CLE. - Employment Law Handbook - Chapter, 1986. Co-Author: "Two Bites at the Apple: Termination of Grievance Proceedings When Employees File Discrimination Charges," Empl. Relations L.J. 1987; "Sign of the Times: Implementing Reductions in Force," Empl. Relations L.J. 1992. Adjunct Professor and Advisory Board Member, Univ. of Wisconsin Management Institute, 1980—. *Member:* American Bar Association (Member: Labor Law Section; Equal Employment Opportunity Committee, 1980—). ***SPECIAL***

(This Listing Continued)

MECKLER BULGER & TILSON, Chicago—Continued

AGENCIES: National Labor Relations Board; Office of Federal Contract Compliance Program; U.S. Department of Labor (Wage/Hour); Equal Employment Opportunity Commission. ***PRACTICE AREAS:*** Employment and Labor Law and Litigation representing Management. ***Email:*** brian.bulger@mbtlaw.com

JACK J. CARRIGLIO, born Chicago, Illinois, November 9, 1951; admitted to bar, 1978, Illinois and U.S. District Court, Northern District of Illinois including Trial Bar; 1980, U.S. Court of Appeals, Seventh Circuit; 1984, U.S. Supreme Court. *Education:* University of Illinois (B.A., 1974); Chicago-Kent College of Law, Illinois Institute of Technology (J.D., cum laude, 1978). Member of Staff, Chicago-Kent Law Review, 1977-1978. Special Assistant State's Attorney, Cook County, 1984-1985. *Member:* Chicago, Illinois State, Federal (Chicago Chapter Vice-President) and American Bar Associations; American College of Trial Lawyers. ***Email:*** jack.carriglio@mbtlaw.com

JANET R. DAVIS, born Caribou, Maine, March 28, 1955; admitted to bar, 1980, Illinois. *Education:* University of Michigan (B.S.A., with high distinction, 1977; J.D., 1980). Author: "Pleading and Motion Practice," in *Third Party Practice,* Illinois Institute for Continuing Legal Education, 1992. Co-Author: "Architects, Engineers and Surveyors," in *Professional Liability,* Illinois Institute for Continuing Legal Education, 1982. "CGL Coverage for Hazardous Substances Clean-Up," in March 1988, "For the Defense," Vol. 30, No. 3. Member, American Institute of Architects. *Member:* American Bar Association (Member: Standing Committee on Technology and Information Systems, 1997—; Tort and Insurance Practice Section; Insurance Coverage Litigation Committee, Chair, 1998-1999; Minorities and Women Involvement Committee, 1993-1997, Chair, 1995-1996); Defense Research Institute. ***PRACTICE AREAS:*** Insurance Coverage; Architect and Engineer Liability; Construction Law; Hotel Liability. ***Email:*** janet.davis@mbtlaw.com

JOHN E. DeLASCIO, admitted to bar, 1991, Illinois, U.S. District Court, Northern District of Illinois and U.S. Court of Appeals, Seventh Circuit; 1995, U.S. District Court, Central District of Illinois; 2002, U.S. District Court, Eastern District of Michigan. *Education:* DePaul University (B.A., 1988); John Marshall Law School (J.D., 1991). ***PRACTICE AREAS:*** Litigation; Insurance Coverage; Directors and Officers Insurance Coverage; Insurance Agents and Brokers Errors and Omissions; Employment Practices Liability Insurance; Commercial Liability; Fair Debt Collection Practices Act; Appellate Practice. ***Email:*** john.delascio@mbtlaw.com

KAREN M. DIXON, born Omaha, Nebraska, March 15, 1972; admitted to bar, 1997, Illinois and U.S. District Court, Northern District of Illinois; 1998, Nebraska. *Education:* University of Nebraska-Lincoln (B.A., 1993); Chicago-Kent College of Law, Illinois Institute of Technology (J.D., with high honors, 1997). Order of the Coif; Moot Court. *Member:* Chicago and Nebraska State Bar Associations; Defense Research Institute. ***PRACTICE AREAS:*** Insurance Coverage. ***Email:*** karen.dixon@mbtlaw.com

J. STUART GARBUTT, born Cleveland, Ohio, August 28, 1945; admitted to bar, 1971, Illinois, U.S. District Court, Northern District of Illinois and U.S. Court of Appeals, Seventh Circuit. *Education:* Purdue University (B.S.I.M., 1967); Northwestern University (J.D., 1970). General Counsel: Illinois Department of Human Rights, 1975-1984; Illinois Local Labor Relations Board, 1984-1989. Lecturer, Loyola University (Chicago) Institute of Human Resources and Industrial Relations. *Member:* Chicago and American Bar Associations. ***PRACTICE AREAS:*** Labor and Employment Law; Litigation. ***Email:*** stu.garbutt@mbtlaw.com

PAUL R. GARRY, born Kansas City, Missouri, May 21, 1952; admitted to bar, 1977, Illinois. *Education:* University of Wisconsin-Madison (B.A., 1974); Cornell University (J.D., 1977). Author: "Employment Discrimination Based on Disability," IICLE Employment Discrimination Handbook, 1989, updated 1992, 1996 and 1998. Lecturer on Employment Discrimination, University of Chicago Graduate School of Business. ***PRACTICE AREAS:*** Labor and Employment Law. ***Email:*** paul.garry@mbtlaw.com

BRENT J. GRABER, born Peoria, Illinois, September 3, 1956; admitted to bar, 1981, Illinois and U.S. District Court, Northern District of Illinois. *Education:* University of Iowa (B.B.A., with distinction, 1977); University of Michigan (J.D., 1981). ***PRACTICE AREAS:*** Insurance Coverage; Professional Liability. ***Email:*** brent.graber@mbtlaw.com

J. ROBERT HALL, born Toledo, Ohio, June 6, 1969; admitted to bar, 1997, Illinois and U.S. District Court, Northern District of Illinois. *Education:* University of Pennsylvania (B.A., 1991); Chicago-Kent College of Law, Illinois Institute of Technology (J.D., 1997). Recipient, Chicago-Kent Academic Merit Scholarship; Moot Court Honor Society Executive Board Scholarship. Vice President, Moot Court Honor Society. National Finalist and Midwest Regional Championship Team, National Best Petitioner's Brief, ABA National Appellate Advocacy Competition. Finalist, Charles Evans Hughes Moot Court Competition. Judicial Extern: Honorable Hubert L. Will, Senior U.S. District Judge, Northern District of Illinois (September - December 1995); Honorable David H. Coar, U.S. District Judge, Northern District of Illinois (May - August 1995). *Member:* Chicago, Illinois State and American Bar Associations. ***LANGUAGES:*** French. ***PRACTICE AREAS:*** Civil Litigation. ***Email:*** bob.hall@mbtlaw.com

REBECCA R. HALLER, born Chicago, Illinois, September 6, 1960; admitted to bar, 1989, Illinois. *Education:* University of Illinois (B.A., 1983); DePaul University (J.D., 1989). ***PRACTICE AREAS:*** Insurance Coverage. ***Email:*** rebecca.haller@mbtlaw.com

BRETT D. HEINRICH, born LaGrange, Illinois, April 17, 1959; admitted to bar, 1986, Illinois and U.S. District Court, Northern District of Illinois; 1987, Federal Trial Bar, Northern District of Illinois. *Education:* University of Illinois (B.S., 1982); DePaul University (J.D., 1985). Benton National Moot Court Competition. Author: "What Do You Do When the Deponent Takes the Fifth?", CBA Record, Vol. 3, No. 4, 1989; "Pre-Trial Motions Under Sections 2-615 and 2-619," CBA Record, Vol. 3 No. 10, 1989; "Diversity Jurisdiction and Professional Corporations," Young Lawyers Journal, CBA, Vol. 16, No. 4, 1987. Editor-in-Chief, Young Lawyers Journal, Chicago Bar Association Record, 1986-1990. Director, Young Lawyers Section, Chicago Bar Association, 1989-1990. Associate Attorney, Law Office of James T. J. Keating, 1990. Special Assistant, Revenue Prosecution, 1987-1990 and Assistant Attorney General, General White Collar Prosecutions, 1985-1987, Illinois Attorney General's Office. Environmental Counsel, 1991-1994, Senior Litigation Counsel, 1994-1996, Senior Area Counsel, 1996-1998, Waste Management, Inc. *Member:* Chicago (Member: Environmental Law Committee; Young Lawyers Section), Illinois State and American (Member, Sections on: Alternative Dispute Resolution; Energy) Bar Associations. ***PRACTICE AREAS:*** Litigation; Environmental; Corporate. ***Email:*** brett.heinrich@mbtlaw.com

CHRISTOPHER S. HENNESSY, born Chelsea, Massachusetts, December 16, 1967; admitted to bar, 1996, Illinois, U.S. District Court, Northern District of Illinois; 1997, U.S. District Court, Northern District of Indiana. *Education:* Northern Illinois University (B.S., 1991); John Marshall Law School (J.D., cum laude, 1996). ***PRACTICE AREAS:*** Insurance Coverage; Commercial Litigation; Municipal Liability; Municipal Defense. ***Email:*** chris.hennessy@mbtlaw.com

JAMES J. HICKEY, born Chicago, Illinois, March 1, 1962; admitted to bar, 1988, Illinois and U.S. District Court, Northern and Central Districts of Illinois; 2000, U.S. District Court, Northern and Southern Districts of Indiana. *Education:* University of Dubuque (B.A., 1984); Chicago-Kent College of Law, Illinois Institute of Technology (J.D., 1988). Member, Moot Court Society. Author: "Attacking the Testimony of Your Opponent's Accident Reconstructionist," For the Defense, Defense Research Institute, April, 1992; "Settling the Excess Insurance Claim: The Insurer's Perspective", 1999. ***PRACTICE AREAS:*** Insurance Coverage; Commercial Litigation; Insurance Defense; Products Liability; Environmental Law. ***Email:*** james.hickey@mbtlaw.com

RICHARD A. HODYL, JR., born Chicago, Illinois, 1964; admitted to bar, 1989, Illinois, U.S. District Court, Northern District of Illinois and U.S. Court of Appeals, Seventh Circuit; 1995, U.S. Supreme Court. *Education:* Western Illinois University (B.S., 1986); DePaul University (J.D., 1989). ***PRACTICE AREAS:*** Insurance Coverage; Commercial Litigation; Corporate Transactional; Regulatory. ***Email:*** richard.hoydl@mbtlaw.com

JAMES H. KALLIANIS, JR., born Chicago, Illinois, July 4, 1965; admitted to bar, 1990, California; 1992, Illinois, U.S. District Court, Northern, Central and Eastern Districts of California and U.S. Court of Appeals, Ninth Circuit. *Education:* University of Illinois (B.A., 1987); DePaul University (J.D., 1990). Associate Editor, DePaul Business Journal. Co-Author: "Discrimination, Sexual Harassment and Wrongful Termination: How to Minimize Your Risk and Exposure," Bank Director—White Paper (1994); "Professional Liability Insurance," Suing and Defending Professionals in Illinois, (IICLE, 1997); "Empowering Corporate Boards to Exercise Greater Control Over Shareholder Derivative Actions," Watson Wyatt's D&O Newsletter (Summer 1997). *Member:* American Bar Association; Professional Liability Underwriting Society; American Health Lawyers Association. ***PRACTICE AREAS:*** Insurance Coverage; Commercial Litigation. ***Email:*** james.h.kallianis@mbtlaw.com

CHRISTOPHER E. KENTRA, born Fort Wayne, Indiana, November 21, 1966; admitted to bar, 1992, Illinois and U.S. District Court, Northern District of Illinois; 1994, U.S. District Court, Central District of Illinois. *Education:* Miami University (B.S., Finance, 1989); Chicago-Kent College of Law, Illinois Institute of Technology (J.D., with honors, 1992). Member, Moot Court Society, 1991-1992. Co-Author: "Illinois Trade Secret Law," BNA/ABA Publication, 1995. *Member:* Chicago (Co-Chairman, Corporate Practice Committee, Young Lawyers Section, 1994-1995) and American Bar Associations. ***PRACTICE AREAS:*** Corporate Litigation; Insurance Litigation; Employment Law. ***Email:*** chris.kentra@mbtlaw.com

PHILIP R. KING, born Buffalo, New York, May 19, 1959; admitted to bar, 1984, Illinois, U.S. District Court, Northern and Central Districts of Illinois and U.S. Court of Appeals, Seventh and Ninth Circuits. *Education:* Grove City College (B.A., magna cum laude, 1981); Case Western Reserve University (J.D., 1984). Order of the Coif. Associate Editor, Case Western Reserve University Law Review, 1982-1983. Author, "Monetary Remedies Under The EAHCA," Tort and Insurance Law Journal, Spring, 1988. Co-Author: "Insurance Agents and Brokers in Professional Liability," Illinois Institute for Continuing Legal Education, 1991-1992. *Member:* Illinois State and American (Vice Chair, Tort and Insurance Practice Section; Associate Editor, Tort and Insurance Law Journal, 1986-1989) Bar Associations; Illinois Association of School Attorneys. ***PRACTICE AREAS:*** Professional Liability; Construction Law; Insurance Coverage; Employee Health Benefits Coverage. ***Email:*** phil.king@mbtlaw.com

MARI HENRY LEIGH, born Rensselaer, Indiana, March 28, 1958; admitted to bar, 1983, Ohio; 1984, U.S. District Court, Northern District of Ohio and U.S. Court of Appeals, Sixth Circuit; 1991, Illinois. *Education:* Purdue University (B.A., 1980); Case Western Reserve University (J.D., 1983). Order of the Coif. Recipient, American Jurisprudence Award. Author/Co-Author: "The Ethical Use of Outside Auditors and Billing Guidelines," Nov. 1998 ACE Annual Claims Exposition & Conference; "Litigating Fee Dispute Cases on Behalf of a Client or Third-Party Payer: Some Practical Tips," Apr. 1998 Mealey's Attorneys Fees Conference; "Legal Audits: Is the Defense Bar's Argument that the Insurer is an 'Outsider' to the Attorney-Client Relationship in Our Clients' Best Interests?" 1998 IADC Annual Meeting; "Your Bill: A Behind-the-Scenes Look at a Legal Audit," Nov. 1997, U.S. Business Litigation; "Survey of State Arbitration Provisions," Nov. 1997 Vol. 1, No. 4 Mealey's Attorney Fees; "Fee Dispute Tips for Insurers, Insureds and Counsel in *Cumis* Situations," Oct. 1997 Mealey's Attorney Fees; "The Insurability of Prevailing Party Legal Fees," Sept. 1997 Mealey's Attorney Fees; "The Ethics of Legal Fee Arrangements," Aug. 1997 Vol. 1, No. 1 Mealey's Attorney Fees; "Billing Judgement—What Is It? Do You Have It?" May 1997 Preview Issue, Mealey's Attorney Fees; "*Daubert* and Its Impact on the Admissibility of Expert Testimony in Motor Vehicle Product Liability Litigation: The Debate Over *Daubert's* Applicability to Cases Involving Technical or Specialized Knowledge," ABA's 1997 Emerging Issues in Motor Vehicle Product Liability Litigation Seminar; "Punitive Damages Update," IADC's 1997 Mid-Year Conference: "When the Parent is to Blame: A Commentary on Parental Responsibility in the '90's," Fall/Winter 1996 TIPS Committee News for ABA's Products, General Liability and Consumer Law Committee; "Defending Your Company's Destiny: Ten Tips for Reducing Risk and Improving Your Bottom Line in an Uncertain Legal Environment," Frank F. Haack & Associates' June 1996 Tort Reform Seminar; "Six Tips for Successfully Defending the Automotive Manufacturer in a Child Restraint Case," ABA's 1996 Emerging Trends in Automotive Product Liability Seminar; "Can *Daubert* Bar 'Witchcraft' From the Courtroom?" May 1995 Corporate Legal Times. Instructor, Trial Advocacy Short Course, 1988, 1990, Cleveland State John Marshall College of Law Simulation. Adjunct Instructor, Legal Research and Writing, Cleveland State John Marshall College of Law, 1984-1986. *Member:* Ohio State, Illinois State

(This Listing Continued)

and American Bar Associations; Defense Research Institute. ***PRACTICE AREAS:*** Commercial Litigation; Product Liability; Professional Liability. ***Email:*** mari.henry.leigh@mbtlaw.com

MICHAEL I. LEONARD, born Milwaukee, Wisconsin, December 7, 1965; admitted to bar, 1991, Illinois and U.S. District Court, Northern District of Illinois. *Education:* University of Iowa (B.A., 1988); Loyola University (J.D., 1991). Recipient, American Jurisprudence Award in Leadership and Service Award. Member, National Mock Trial Team. Author: "Combatting AIDS's Acoustic Shadow: Illinois Addresses the Problems of Criminal Transfer of HIV," Loyola University of Chicago Law Journal, Vol. 22, No. 2, Winter, 1991; "The Death Penalty: Personal Perspectives," Loyola University of Chicago Law Journal, Vol. 22, No. 1, Fall, 1990. *Member:* Chicago and American Bar Associations. ***LANGUAGES:*** French. ***PRACTICE AREAS:*** Labor and Employment Litigation. ***Email:*** michael.leonard@mbtlaw.com

MICHAEL S. LOEFFLER, born Chicago, Illinois, October 30, 1959; admitted to bar, 1985, Illinois and U.S. District Court, Northern District of Illinois; 1989, U.S. Court of Appeals, Seventh Circuit; 1990, U.S. Court of Appeals, Tenth Circuit; 1995, U.S. Supreme Court. *Education:* Loyola University; University of Illinois (B.S., Finance, with high honors, 1981); University of California, Los Angeles (J.D., 1985). Phi Kappa Phi. Member, Federal Communications Law Journal. *Member:* Chicago and American (Member: Litigation Section; Forum on Entertainment and Sports Industries) Bar Associations; Professional Liability Underwriting Society; Chicago Council on Foreign Relations. ***PRACTICE AREAS:*** Professional Liability; Directors and Officers Liability; Financial Institution Bonds; Commercial; General Liability Insurance Coverage; Professional Liability Defense; Employment Practice Liability; Employment Practice Defense. ***Email:*** mloeffler@mbtlaw.com

ERIC E. LYNCH, born Washington, D.C., July 30, 1967; admitted to bar, 1992, New Jersey and U.S. District Court, District of New Jersey; 1993, Illinois and U.S. District Court, Northern District of Illinois; 1995, New York. *Education:* Syracuse University (B.A., 1989); John Marshall Law School (J.D., 1992). Phi Alpha Theta. Judicial Externship, Hon. John W. Bissell, U.S. District Court, District of New Jersey, 1991. *Member:* Chicago Bar Association. ***PRACTICE AREAS:*** Commercial Litigation. ***Email:*** eric.lynch@mbtlaw.com

MICHAEL M. MARICK, born Chicago, Illinois, November 20, 1957; admitted to bar, 1982, Illinois; 1983, Florida; U.S. Supreme Court and U.S. Court of Appeals, Third and Sixth Circuits. *Education:* Denison University (B.A., 1979); Chicago-Kent College of Law, Illinois Institute of Technology (J.D., with honors, 1982). Member, IIT/Chicago-Kent Law Review, 1980-1982. Member, ABA National Trial Advocacy Team, 1982. Author: "Professional Liability Insurance," 'Suing and Defending Professionals', Chapter 1, Illinois Institute for Continuing Legal Education, 1997; "Making Sense of the Contra Proferentem Approach to Insurance Policy Construction," 5 CGL Reporter § 195 at p. 1 (Spring, 1993); "Untangling the Web of Confusion Surrounding Insurance Contract Construction," IDC Quarterly, Vol. 3, No. 2, at p. ii (2nd Quarter 1993); "Excess, Surplus Lines and Reinsurance: Recent Developments," 26 Tort and Ins. L.J. 231, 1991; "Professional Liability Insurance," Professional Liability Handbook, Illinois Institute for Continuing Legal Education, 1991; "Excess Insurance - An Overview of General Principles and Current Issues," 24 Tort and Ins. L.J. 715, 1989; "1987-1988 Illinois Law Survey: 'Insurance Law'," 20 Loy. U. Chi. L.J. 481, 1989; "Excess Insurance," Liability Insurance Handbook, Illinois Institute for Continuing Legal Education, 1989 (1992 Supp. and 1996); "Comprehensive General Liability, Professional and Excess Coverage," Attorneys Guide to Liability Insurance, Illinois Institute for Continuing Legal Education, 1985; "The Bad Faith Case" and "Primary and Excess Coverage Disputes," Practising Law Institute, Vol. 380, 1986. Adjunct Professor, Insurance Law, IIT/Chicago-Kent College of Law, 1987—. Vice-Chairman, ABA/TIPS Excess, Surplus Lines and Reinsurance Committee, 1990-1992. Membership Chairman, ABA Litigation Section Insurance Coverage Litigation Committee, 1992-1996. President, IIT/Chicago-Kent College of Law Alumni Association, 1994-1995, Board of Overseers, 1993-1995. Member, Panel of Arbitrators, American Arbitration Association. *Member:* Chicago, Illinois State (Chair, Insurance Law Section Council, 1995-1996) and American (Member, Sections on: Litigation; Tort and Insurance Practice) Bar Associations; The Florida Bar; International Association of Defense Counsel; Defense Research Institute. ***PRACTICE AREAS:*** Insurance Coverage; Reinsurance; Commercial Litigation. ***Email:*** michael.marick@mbtlaw.com

KENT MAYNARD, JR., born Bowling Green, Ohio, July 8, 1955; admitted to bar, 1990, Illinois and U.S. District Court, Northern District of Illinois; 1992, U.S. Court of Appeals, Seventh Circuit. *Education:* University of Chicago (A.B., with honors, 1978; M.B.A., 1981); John Marshall Law School (J.D., magna cum laude, 1990). *Member:* American Bar Association. ***LANGUAGES:*** Spanish. ***PRACTICE AREAS:*** Insurance Coverage; Litigation. ***Email:*** kent.maynard@mbtlaw.com

BRUCE R. MECKLER, born Silver Spring, Maryland, June 10, 1955; admitted to bar, 1981, Illinois and U.S. District Court, Northern District of Illinois; 1983, U.S. District Court, Northern District of Illinois, Trial Bar. *Education:* Bradley University (B.A., 1977); John Marshall Law School (J.D., with high distinction, 1981). Order of John Marshall. Justice, Moot Court Council. Irving Kaufman Securities Law Moot Court Competition. Faculty, Chicago Bar Association Trial Practice Course, 1985—. Faculty, Illinois Institute for Continued Legal Education, 1990—. Standing Member, Illinois Supreme Court Committee on Professional Responsibility, 1998—. Assistant States Attorney, States Attorneys Office of Cook County, 1981-1984. Co-Chairman, Illinois Legal Needs Study, 1988-1989. Board of Directors, John Marshall Law School Alumni Association. *Member:* Chicago (Chairman, Trial Practice Task Force, Young Lawyers Section, 1985-1986; Vice-Chairman, Tort Litigation Committee, 1987-1988; Chairman, Tort Litigation Committee, 1988-1991; Judicial Evaluation Committee, 1991-1994) and American (Member, Committee on the Prosecution and Defense of RICO, 1982-1985) Bar Associations; The Association of Trial Lawyers of America; Defense Research Institute. Faculty, National Institute for Trial Advocacy. ***PRACTICE AREAS:*** Commercial Litigation; Professional Liability; Litigation; Attorney Fee Disputes. ***Email:*** bruce.meckler@mbtlaw.com

ZIYAD I. NACCASHA, born Baghdad, Iraq, September 24, 1965; admitted to bar, 1990, Illinois. *Education:* California Polytechnic State University (B.S., Finance and Business Administration, 1987); University of Notre Dame (J.D., 1990). Author: "The Permissibility of Routine AIDS Testing in the Health Care Context," Notre Dame Journal of Law, Ethics & Public Policy, September 1990. Co-Author: "U.S. Legal Review," Reinsurance, November 1996 and 1997; *The Law of Reinsurance Claims,* 1997 Supplement, Andrews Publications. *Member:* Chicago and American Bar Associations; Arab-American Bar Association (Board Member); Arab-American Professional Association. ***LANGUAGES:*** Arabic. ***PRACTICE AREAS:*** Insurance; Reinsurance; Insurance Coverage; Insurance Litigation; Corporate Law; International Law; Contracts; Litigation. ***Email:*** ziyad.naccasha@mbtlaw.com

STEVEN D. PEARSON, born Elmhurst, Illinois, September 10, 1961; admitted to bar, 1985, Illinois, U.S. District Court, Northern District of Illinois, U.S. District Court, Western District of Michigan and U.S. Court of Appeals, Seventh Circuit; 1986, U.S. Court of Appeals, Second Circuit; 1988, U.S. Supreme Court; 1989, U.S. District Court, District of Arizona; 1991, U.S. Court of Appeals, Eleventh Circuit. *Education:* University of Minnesota (B.A., 1982); DePaul University (J.D., 1985). Omicron Delta Kappa. Author: "The Illinois Accountant Privilege - Whose Privilege is it and When may it be Invoked?" Young Lawyers Journal, Chicago Bar Association, Vol. 17, No. 3, 1988. Legal Writing Assistant Instructor, De Paul University College of Law, 1983-1984. Judicial Extern, Hon. Charles P. Kocoras, U.S. District Judge, Northern District of Illinois. Adjunct Professor, Insurance Law, IIT/Chicago-Kent College of Law, 1991—. *Member:* Chicago (Associate Editor, Young Lawyers Journal, 1988-1990), Illinois State and American Bar Associations; Defense Research Institute; Illinois Association of Defense Trial Counsel. ***PRACTICE AREAS:*** Insurance Coverage; Professional Liability; Commercial Litigation. ***Email:*** steve.pearson@mbtlaw.com

PAMELA G. PERRONE, born New York, New York, September 26, 1957; admitted to bar, 1981, Illinois. *Education:* State University of New York (B.A., 1977); George Washington University, National Law Center (J.D., 1981). *Member:* Illinois State Bar Association (Chair, Standing Committee on Legal Technology, 2001-2002; Assembly Members, 1997-2003). ***PRACTICE AREAS:*** Legal Fee Audit. ***Email:*** pamela.perrone@mbtlaw.com

ALAN M. POSNER, born Milwaukee, Wisconsin, June 8, 1953; admitted to bar, 1977, Illinois. *Education:* Harvard University (A.B., magna cum laude, 1974); University of Chicago (J.D., 1977). Author: "Factors To Consider in Bringing Federal Declaratory Judgment Actions in the United States," 7 Intl. Ins. Law Rev. 230 (1995); "Prematurity of Declaratory Judgment Actions," 25 The Brief 15 (1995). Visiting Professorial Lecturer in Law, Holland Law Center, University of Florida, 1980-1981. *Member:* Chicago, Illinois State and American Bar Associations. ***PRACTICE AREAS:*** Insurance Coverage; Litigation. ***Email:*** alan.posner@mbtlaw.com

DON R. SAMPEN, born Bloomington, Illinois, July 19, 1950; admitted to bar, 1975, Illinois and U.S. Court of Appeals, Seventh Circuit; 1977, U.S. Court of Appeals, Tenth Circuit; 1981, U.S. Supreme Court; 1982, U.S. Court of Appeals, Fifth Circuit; 1983, U.S. District Court, Northern District of Illinois including Trial Bar. *Education:* Northwestern University (B.A., 1972; J.D., magna cum laude, 1975). *Member:* Chicago, Illinois State and American Bar Associations. ***REPORTED CASES:*** Martin vs. Davies, 917 F.2d 336 (7th cir. 1990); Walsh vs. Mellas, 837 F2d 789 (7th cir. 1988); Dellcar vs. Hicks, 685 F.Supp. 679 (N.D. Ill. 1988); Brennan vs. Stanford, 600 N.E.2d 404 (1st Dist. Ill.App.. 1992); Import vs. Continental, 577 N.E.2d 1205 (1st Dist. Ill.App. 1991); Schuler vs. Beers, 510 N.E.2d 48 (1st Dist. Ill.App. 1987). ***PRACTICE AREAS:*** Insurance Defense; Commercial Litigation. ***Email:*** don.sampen@mbtlaw.com

JASON R. SCHULZE, born Red Oak, Iowa, August 12, 1970; admitted to bar, 1996, Illinois. *Education:* University of Iowa (B.A., 1992); DePaul University (J.D., 1996). Member, Law Review, De Paul University College of Law. Author: "United States v. Tucker: Can the Sixth Circuit Really Abolish the Outrageous Government Conduct Defense?" De Paul L.Rev. (Spring 1996). *Member:* Chicago and Illinois State Bar Associations. ***Email:*** jason.schulze@mbtlaw.com

SCOTT M. SEAMAN, born Chicago, Illinois, May 24, 1962; admitted to bar, 1987, Illinois, U.S. District Court, Northern and Central Districts of Illinois, U.S. Court of Appeals, Seventh and Tenth Circuits and U.S. Supreme Court. *Education:* Barat College (B.A., 1984); Loyola University (J.D., magna cum laude, 1987). Editor, Loyola University of Chicago Law Journal. Recipient: Chief Justice Roger B. Taney Award; Judge John C. Hayes Award; Thomas L. Owens Award; Judge John V. McCormack Award; Illinois Lawyers Auxiliary Scholarship; Loyola Leadership & Service Award. General Editor and Contributing Author: "Wrongful Death and Survival Actions in Illinois," Illinois Institute of CLE, 1993; "Using Surprise to Capture the Expert Witness," For The Defense, Vol. 35, No. 4, April 1993; "Achieving Case Objections Through Deposition Strategy," TIPS, Aug. 1990; "When the Other Side Sends You a Subpoena," The Brief, Vol. 19, No. 3, Spring 1990; "Think Proactively About Product Liability Management," Corporate Legal Times, Sept. 1994; "Can *Daubert* Bar 'Witchcraft' From The Courtroom: Or Does The Case Only Heighten The Level of Judicial Serving," Corporate Legal Times, May, 1995; "A Comprehensive Analysis of Allocation/Apportionment of Losses Involving Complex Insurance Coverage Claims," Focus on Excess Insurance (Lorman Education Services, Feb. 1999); "A Primer on Contemporary Umbrella & Excess Insurance Issues," 8th Annual Institute Contemporary Reinsurance & Excess Insurance Issues (Glasser Legal Works, 1998); "Substantive Coverage Issues in 'Long Tail' Claims: Trigger, Pollution Exclusion, and Duty to Defend," Environmental Coverage Litigation - From Soup to Nuts (ISBA Insurance Law Section, May 1997); "Environmental Coverage: Law and Litigation," Liability Insurance (IICLE 1996, 1998 Supp.); "Employing Discovery, Investigation and Surprise to Capture Plaintiff's Expert," Defense Practice Notebook (DRI 1996); "The Good, the Bad and the Ugly About Joint Defense," The Brief, ABA Tort & Insurance Practice Section, Vol. 28, No. 1, Fall 1998; "All Counsel for Insurers That Participated in a Joint Defense are Disqualified," For The Defense, Vol. 39, No. 8 (Aug. 1997); "Mounting the Joint Defense in Complex Insurance Coverage Litigation," For The Defense, Vol. 39, No. 7 (July 1997); "The Anatomy of a Joint Defense in Complex Insurance Coverage Litigation," For The Defense, Vol. 39, No. 6 (June 1997); "Excess Liability Insurance: Law and Litigation," Tort & Insurance Law Journal, Vol. 32, No. 3 (ABA, Spring 1997); "Excess Liability Insurance Issues in an Era of Increased Exposure and Visibility," 6th Annual Institute Contemporary Reinsurance and Excess Insurance Issues," (Glasser Legal Works, Chicago, Illinois, Sept. 1996). *Member:* Chicago, Illinois State and American (Member, Section on: Litigation; Tort and Insurance Practice; Committee on Product Liability) Bar Associations; Defense Research and Trial Lawyers Association; National Associations of Manufacturers. ***PRAC-***

(This Listing Continued)

MECKLER BULGER & TILSON, Chicago—Continued

TICE AREAS: Insurance Coverage; Reinsurance Law; Product Liability; Torts; Litigation; Business Litigation; Commercial Litigation. ***Email:*** scott.seaman@mbtlaw.com

MARK J. SEPLAK, born Berwyn, Illinois, November 30, 1959; admitted to bar, 1985, Illinois; 1996, California. *Education:* DePaul University (B.S., 1982); Northern Illinois University (J.D., 1985). ***PRACTICE AREAS:*** Insurance Coverage; Appellate. ***Email:*** mark.seplak@mbtlaw.com

JEROME C. STUDER, JR., born Minneapolis, Minnesota, July 27, 1964; admitted to bar, 1995, Illinois and U.S. District Court, Northern District of Illinois. *Education:* University of Chicago (B.A., cum laude, 1992); Chicago-Kent College of Law, Illinois Institute of Technology (J.D., cum laude, 1995). *Member:* American Bar Association. [With U.S. Army, 1983-1988]. ***REPORTED CASES:*** Maness v. Santa Fe Speedway, 298 Ill. App. 3d 1014, 700 N.E.2d 194 (Ill.App. 1998). ***PRACTICE AREAS:*** Legal Fee Disputes; Commercial Litigation; Insurance Coverage Litigation. ***Email:*** joe.studer@mbtlaw.com

JOSEPH E. TILSON, born Nashville, Tennessee, January 30, 1956; admitted to bar, 1981, Illinois. *Education:* University of Michigan (B.A., 1976; J.D., cum laude, 1979). Phi Beta Kappa. Co-Author: *Drug Testing In The Workplace,* BNA, 1989; "Employee Handbooks: Helpful Hints or Binding Contracts," Illinois Banker, May, 1987. *Member:* Chicago (Co-Chair, 1988-1989, Member, 1984 and Director, 1989, Labor and Employment Law Committee, Young Lawyers Section) and American (Chair: Age Discrimination Committee, 1994; Fair Labor Standards Act Committee, 1992-1993; Equal Pay Act Committee, 1990-1992) Bar Associations. ***PRACTICE AREAS:*** Labor and Employment Law. ***Email:*** joe.tilson@mbtlaw.com

JULIE L. TRESTER, born Waukegan, Illinois, October 9, 1964; admitted to bar, 1991, Illinois. *Education:* University of Illinois (B.A., cum laude, 1986; J.D., magna cum laude, 1989). Phi Beta Kappa. Phi Alpha Theta. Adjunct Professor, Chicago-Kent College of Law, Illinois Institute of Technology, 1996—. ***PRACTICE AREAS:*** Employment Law; Insurance Coverage; Appellate Practice. ***Email:*** julie.trester@mbtlaw.com

PETER J. VALETA, born Washington, Pennsylvania, November 13, 1953; admitted to bar, 1980, Illinois and U.S. District Court, Northern District of Illinois; 1981, Florida. *Education:* University of Pittsburgh (B.A., 1974); University of Miami (J.D., 1980). Member, University of Miami Law Review, 1978-1980. Author: "The Codification of Rule 10b-5 Private Actions in the Proposed Federal Securities Code," 33 University of Miami Law Review, September, 1979. ***PRACTICE AREAS:*** Insurance Defense. ***Email:*** peter.valeta@mbtlaw.com

MATTHEW R. WILDERMUTH, born Fort Wayne, Indiana, June 2, 1964; admitted to bar, 1989, Illinois and U.S. District Court, Northern District of Illinois; 1993, U.S. Court of Appeals, Seventh Circuit; 1997, U.S. District Court, Eastern District of Michigan. *Education:* Indiana University (B.A., with honors and distinction, 1986; J.D., magna cum laude, 1989). Phi Beta Kappa; Order of the Coif. Member, National Trial Team. Administrative Editor, Executive Board, Indiana Law Journal, 1987-1989. Author: "Blind Man's Bluff: An Analysis of the Discovery of Expert Witnesses Under Federal Rule of Civil Procedure 26(b)(4) and A Proposed Amendment," 64:4 Indiana Law Journal 925-963, 1989; "Strategic Considerations for Policyholders Pursuing Long-Tail Claims Against The Solvent London Market," Risk and Insurance Management Society Annual Convention, April, 1997. Co-Author: "Emerging Theories of Damages and the Role of Expert Witnesses: Seeing Through the Science," Defense Research Institute, Defense Practice Seminar, December, 1989. *Member:* Chicago (Secretary, Insurance Committee, Young Lawyers Section, 1991-1992; Trial Techniques Committee, 1992—), Seventh Circuit and American Bar Associations. ***Email:*** matthew.wildermuth@mbtlaw.com

BRIAN J. WILLIAMS, born Des Moines, Iowa, December 22, 1959; admitted to bar, 1986, Illinois and U.S. District Court, Northern District of Illinois; 1991, U.S. Court of Appeals, Seventh Circuit. *Education:* Western Illinois University (B.S., with high honors, 1982); Chicago-Kent College of Law, Illinois Institute of Technology (J.D., with highest honors, 1986). Recipient, American Jurisprudence Award; Corpus Juris Secundum Award. Author: "Seventh Circuit Review: Environmental Law," Chicago-Kent Law Review, Vol. 61, No. 2, 1985; "The Child's Action for Loss of Society and Companionship," Chicago-Kent Law Review, Vol. 62, No. 1, 1985; "Seventh Circuit Review: Environmental Law," Chicago-Kent Law Review, Vol. 62, No. 3, 1986. *Member:* Chicago, Illinois State and American Bar Associations. ***PRACTICE AREAS:*** Civil Litigation. ***Email:*** brian.williams@mbtlaw.com

TIMOTHY A. WOLFE, born Hammond, Indiana, May 22, 1963; admitted to bar, 1988, Illinois; 1989, U.S. District Court, Northern District of Illinois; 1991, Trial Bar; 1993, U.S. District Court, Central District of Illinois; 1996, U.S. Court of Appeals, Seventh Circuit; 1998, U.S. Court of Appeals, Eighth Circuit. *Education:* University of Illinois (B.A., cum laude, 1985; J.D., 1988). Phi Beta Kappa. Recipient, American Jurisprudence Award in Criminal Procedure. *Member:* Chicago Bar Association. ***PRACTICE AREAS:*** Employment Litigation; Commercial Litigation. ***Email:*** tim.wolfe@mbtlaw.com

ASSOCIATES

ROBERT J. AMBROSE, born Chicago, Illinois, May 18, 1969; admitted to bar, 1997, Illinois and U.S. District Court, Northern District of Illinois; 1998, U.S. Court of Appeals, Sixth Circuit. *Education:* Marquette University (B.A., 1991); John Marshall Law School (J.D., 1997). Moot Court Executive Board. Judicial Clerk for Chief Judge, U.S. Court of Appeals, Sixth Circuit, 1998-1999. *Member:* Chicago Bar Association. ***PRACTICE AREAS:*** Insurance Coverage; Commercial Litigation. ***Email:*** bob.ambrose@mbtlaw.com

JAMES G. ARGIONIS, born Chicago, Illinois, December 5, 1971; admitted to bar, 1995, Illinois. *Education:* Loyola University (B.A., summa cum laude, 1992; J.D., 1995). Member, 1993-1994 and Executive Editor, 1994-1995, Loyola University Chicago Law Journal. ***LANGUAGES:*** Greek. ***PRACTICE AREAS:*** Commercial Litigation; Construction Litigation; Products Liability. ***Email:*** jargionis@ngelaw.com

EILEEN E. BAKER, born Chicago, Illinois, October 14, 1973; admitted to bar, 1998, Illinois. *Education:* University of Illinois (B.S., 1995); Chicago-Kent College of Law, Illinois Institute of Technology (J.D., 1998). Order of the Coif. ***PRACTICE AREAS:*** Labor and Employment. ***Email:*** eileen.baker@mbtlaw.com

(This Listing Continued)

PHILLIP BETH, born Bethesda, Maryland, May 22, 1973; admitted to bar, 1998, Illinois and Indiana. *Education:* Valparaiso University (B.A., 1995; J.D., magna cum laude, 1998). ***PRACTICE AREAS:*** Insurance Coverage. ***Email:*** phillip.beth@mbtlaw.com

LAUREN W. BLATT, born June 7, 1975; admitted to bar, 2001, Illinois; 2002, U.S. Tax Court. *Education:* Emory University (B.A., 1997); Emory University School of Law (J.D., 2001). *Member:* Chicago and Illinois State Bar Associations. ***PRACTICE AREAS:*** Insurance Coverage. ***Email:*** lauren.blatt@mbtlaw.com

DAVID D. BROWN, born Hinsdale, Illinois, September 5, 1973; admitted to bar, 1998, Illinois and U.S. District Court, Northern District of Illinois. *Education:* Vanderbilt University (B.A., 1995); University of Illinois College of Law (J.D., magna cum laude, 1998). Order of the Coif. ***PRACTICE AREAS:*** Attorney Fee Disputes; Commercial Litigation. ***Email:*** david.brown@mbtlaw.com

ROBERT E. BROWNE, JR., born Evanston, Illinois, December 14, 1970; admitted to bar, 1997, Wisconsin; 1998, Illinois. *Education:* University of Notre Dame (B.A., 1993); Marquette University Law School (J.D., 1997). ***PRACTICE AREAS:*** Insurance Defense. ***Email:*** robert.browne@mbtlaw.com

YUKYONG CHOI, born Seoul, South Korea, May 13, 1973; admitted to bar, 2001, Illinois. *Education:* New York University (B.A., 1995); Loyola University of Chicago School of Law (J.D., 2001). ***PRACTICE AREAS:*** Labor and Employment. ***Email:*** yukong.choi@mbtlaw.com

MATTHEW C. COHN, born HIghland Park, Illinois, May 13, 1971; admitted to bar, 2001, Illinois and U.S. District Court, Northern District of Illinois. *Education:* Bucknell University (B.S., with honors, 1990); Indiana University (M.S., 1995); Chicago-Kent College of Law (J.D., with honors, 2000). ***PRACTICE AREAS:*** Environmental Law; Litigation. ***Email:*** matthew.cohn@mbtlaw.com

SETH E. DARMSTADTER, born Highland Park, Illinois, June, 16, 1979; admitted to bar, 2005, Illinois. *Education:* American University (B.A., 2000); Chicago-Kent College of Law (J.D., 2004). ***PRACTICE AREAS:*** Litigation. ***Email:*** seth.darmstadter@mbtlaw.com

BLAIR L. DAWSON, born Los Angeles, California, July 29, 1977; admitted to bar, 2002, Illinois. *Education:* Marquette University (B.A., 1999); Chicago-Kent College of Law, Illinois Institute of Technology (J.D., 2002). ***PRACTICE AREAS:*** Insurance Coverage. ***Email:*** blair.dawson@mbtlaw.com

VICTORIA DIZIK, born Odessa, Ukraine, February 25, 1979; admitted to bar, 2004, Illinois; 2005, U.S. District Court, Northern District of Illinois. *Education:* Brandeis University (B.A., magna cum laude, 2001); DePaul University College of Law (J.D., 2004). Phi Beta Kappa. Author: "Corporate Speech Under Fire-Has Nike Finally Done It?," DePaul University College of Law, Fall 2004. *Member:* Women's Bar Association of Illinois. ***LANGUAGES:*** Russian and Spanish. ***PRACTICE AREAS:*** Insurance Coverage.

MITCHELL J. EDLUND, born Morrison, Illinois, November 28, 1967; admitted to bar, 1995, Illinois, U.S. District Court, Northern and Central Districts of Illinois and U.S. Court of Appeals, Seventh Circuit. *Education:* Augustana College (B.A., 1990); Northern Illinois University (M.P.A., 1995); Valparaiso University (J.D., 1995). Member, Valparaiso University Law Review. Author, "In the Heat of the Chase: Determining Substantive Due Process Violations Within the Framework of Police Pursuits When An Innocent Bystander is Injured", 30 Val. U.L. Rev. 161 (1995). *Member:* Illinois State Bar Association. ***PRACTICE AREAS:*** Commercial Litigation; Complex Litigation; Construction Litigation; Insurance Coverage. ***Email:*** mitchell.edlund@mbtlaw.com

LYNN GEERDES-LUGO, born Grundy Center, Iowa, 1967; admitted to bar, 1997, Illinois; 1999, Iowa. *Education:* Drake University (B.S., 1990); University of Iowa (J.D., 1997). ***PRACTICE AREAS:*** Insurance Coverage. ***Email:*** lynn.geerdes@mbtlaw.com

JEREMY J. GLENN, born Atlanta, Georgia, March 1, 1972; admitted to bar, 1997, Illinois and U.S. District Court, Northern District of Illinois; 1999, U.S. Court of Appeals, Seventh Circuit. *Education:* Drake University (B.S.B.A., 1994); University of Iowa (J.D., with high distinction, 1997). Member, Journal of Corporation Law. Member, Executive Board, Moot Court. *Member:* Chicago and American Bar Associations. ***PRACTICE AREAS:*** Labor and Employment Law. ***Email:*** jeremy.glenn@mbtlaw.com

CARRIE L. GRAZIANI, born Pittsburgh, Pennsylvania, November 11, 1975; admitted to bar, 2001, Illinois and U.S. District Court, Northern District of Illinois. *Education:* Xavier University (B.A., 1998); DePaul University (J.D., 2001). *Member:* Illinois State Bar Association; Women's Bar Association. ***PRACTICE AREAS:*** Insurance Coverage. ***Email:*** carrie.graziani@mbtlaw.com

JEFFREY GREENSPAN, born September 30, 1977; admitted to bar, 2002, Illinois. *Education:* University of Illinois (B.A., 1999); Chicago-Kent College of Law, Illinois Institute of Technology (J.D., 2002). ***PRACTICE AREAS:*** Commercial Litigation; Legal Fee Dispute.

KENNETH J. HOGAN, born Chicago, Illinois, April 22, 1970; admitted to bar, 1995, Illinois and U.S. District Court, Northern District of Illinois; 2004, U.S. Court of Appeals, Seventh Circuit. *Education:* University of Illinois (B.A., 1992; J.D., 1995). ***PRACTICE AREAS:*** Insurance Defense. ***Email:*** kenneth.hogan@mbtlaw.com

ANDREW M. HUTCHISON, born Des Moines, Iowa, September 20, 1978; admitted to bar, 2004, Illinois. *Education:* Harvard University (B.A., cum laude, 2001); University of Iowa College of Law (J.D., with distinction, 2004). Author: "One Person, Five Votes: An argument for Applying the Equal Protection Clause to Iowa's Judicial Elections," 8 Journal of Gender, Race & Justice 211. ***PRACTICE AREAS:*** Insurance Coverage. ***Email:*** andrew.hutchison@mbtlaw.com

J. AARON JENSEN, born Price, Utah, November 30, 1969; admitted to bar, 1999, Illinois. *Education:* Utah State University (B.A., 1996); Loyola University Chicago School of Law (J.D., 1999). ***PRACTICE AREAS:*** Insurance Coverage; Litigation. ***Email:*** aaron.jensen@mbtlaw.com

GEORGE K. KATSOUDAS, born Argos, Greece, February 23, 1970; admitted to bar, 1995, Illinois and U.S. District Court, Northern District of Illinois. *Education:* Loyola University (B.A., 1992; J.D., 1995). Senior Member, Loyola Law Journal, 1994-1995. *Member:*

(This Listing Continued)

Chicago, Illinois State and American Bar Associations. ***LANGUAGES:*** Greek. ***PRACTICE AREAS:*** Commercial Litigation; Construction Law; Partnership Disputes. ***Email:*** george.katsoudas@mbtlaw.com

MELISSA A. KING, born Salinas, California, September 17, 1978; admitted to bar, 2004, Illinois. *Education:* Lake Forest College (B.A., 2000); Loyola University (J.D., 2004). *Member:* Illinois and American Bar Associations; Women's Bar Assocaition of Illinois. ***PRACTICE AREAS:*** Insurance Defense. ***Email:*** melissa.king@mbtlaw.com

CHARLOTTE KORMENDY, born Culver City, California, October 31, 1973; admitted to bar, 1998, Illinois and U.S. District Court, Northern District of Illinois; 2000, U.S. District Court, Northern District of Indiana. *Education:* University of Massachusetts (B.A., 1995); Chicago-Kent College of Law, Illinois Institute of Technology (J.D., 1998). ***PRACTICE AREAS:*** Insurance Coverage; Litigation.

JONATHAN D. LICHTERMAN, born St. Paul, Minnesota, May 26, 1969; admitted to bar, 1996, Illinois; 1997, Minnesota; 2002, U.S. District Court, Northern District of Illinois. *Education:* University of Michigan (B.A., 1991); Georgetown University (J.D., 1996). Assistant States Attorney: Peoria County, 1997-2000; Lake County, 2000-2001. ***PRACTICE AREAS:*** Commercial Litigation; Antitrust Litigation. ***Email:*** jonathan.lichterman@mbtlaw.com

CHAD W. MAIN, born Ft. Wayne, Indiana, May 25, 1970; admitted to bar, 1997, California; 2004, Ohio (Not admitted in Illinois). *Education:* University of Colorado (B.A., 1993); Valparaiso University (J.D., 1996). ***PRACTICE AREAS:*** Insurance Defense; Entertainment Litigation; Litigation.

SANDRA J. McMULLAN, born San Francisco, California, October 7, 1967; admitted to bar, 2002, Illinois. *Education:* University of California, Berkeley (B.A., 1990); University of California, San Diego (MA., 1993); University of Miami (J.D., 1996). ***PRACTICE AREAS:*** Commercial Litigation. ***Email:*** sandra.mcmullan@mbtlaw.com

ERIC E. NEWMAN, born Columbus, Ohio, January 3, 1970; admitted to bar, 1997, Illinois; 1998, U.S. District Court, Northern District of Illinois. *Education:* Miami University (B.A., 1992); University of Michigan (J.D., 1997). *Member:* Chicago, Illinois State and American Bar Associations. ***PRACTICE AREAS:*** Civil Litigation. ***Email:*** eric.newman@mbtlaw.com

OMAR S. ODLAND, born Chicago, Illinois, August 27, 1961; admitted to bar, 1996, Illinois; 1997, Florida. *Education:* Northern Illinois University (B.A., 1984); John Marshall Law School (J.D., 1996). ***PRACTICE AREAS:*** Insurance Defense. ***Email:*** omar.odland@mbtlaw.com

JACOB RUBINSTEIN, born Boulder, Colorado, May 14, 1968; admitted to bar, 1994, Illinois; 1996, U.S. District Court, Northern District of Illinois. *Education:* University of Illinois (B.A., 1991); Chicago-Kent College of Law (J.D., 1994). ***PRACTICE AREAS:*** Employment Discrimination; Commercial Litigation. ***Email:*** jacob.rubinstein@mbtlaw.com

MEAGHAN L. SCHNEIDER, born Miami, Florida, September 1, 1975; admitted to bar, 2001, Illinois. *Education:* University of Notre Dame, (B.A., 1997); Loyola University, Chicago (J.D., 2001). ***PRACTICE AREAS:*** Commercial Law; Products Liability Law. ***Email:*** meaghan.schneider@mbtlaw.com

E. LYNETTE STAFFORD, born Louisville, Kentucky, January 10, 1972; admitted to bar, 2000, Minnesota and Wisconsin; 2004, Illinois. *Education:* Fisk University (B.A. in English, magna cum laude, 1994); Lewis and Clark College (J.D., 1997). Phi Beta Kappa. Mock Trial Competition Finalist, 1997. *Member:* Minnesota State Bar Association; State Bar of Wisconsin; Minnesota Association of Black Lawyers; Minnesota Women Lawyers. ***PRACTICE AREAS:*** Insurance Coverage; Litigation. ***Email:*** lynette.stafford@mbtlaw.com

ELIZABETH J. M. STROBEL, born Ann Arbor, Michigan, May 9, 1972; admitted to bar, 2000, Illinois. *Education:* Tufts University (B.A., 1994); Loyola University Chicago School of Law (J.D., 2000). ***PRACTICE AREAS:*** Commercial Litigation; Labor and Employment. ***Email:*** ellie.strobel@mbtlaw.com

SARA G. UFFELMAN, born Indianapolis, Indiana, September 14, 1976; admitted to bar, 2004, Illinois. *Education:* North Central College (B.A., 1977); DePaul University College of Law (J.D., cum laude, 2004). ***PRACTICE AREAS:*** Insurance Coverage. ***Email:*** sara.uffelman@mbtlaw.com

TIMOTHY J. WALSH, born June 2, 1977; admitted to bar, 2002, Illinois; 2003, U.S. District Court, Northern District of Illinois; 2005, U.S. District Court, Northern District of Indiana. *Education:* University of Missouri-Columbia (B.S., 1999); Washington University (J.D., 2002).

KRISTEN A. WEISSE, admitted to bar, 2002, Illinois. *Education:* Loyola University at Chicago (B.A., 1999; J.D., 2002). *Member:* Chicago and American Bar Associations. ***PRACTICE AREAS:*** Labor and Employment. ***Email:*** kristen.weisse@mbtlaw.com

ANNELIESE WERMUTH, born South Bend, Indiana, July 9, 1969; admitted to bar, 1999, Illinois. *Education:* DePaul University (B.A., 1991); Northwestern University (M.A., 1992); Loyola University (J.D., 1999). *Member:* American Bar Association. ***PRACTICE AREAS:*** Labor and Employment. ***Email:*** anna.wermuth@mbtlaw.com

OF COUNSEL

LISA C. BREEN, born Madison, Wisconsin, April 16, 1967; admitted to bar, 1992, Illinois and U.S. District Court, Northern District of Illinois. *Education:* Northern Illinois University (B.A., 1989); Chicago-Kent College of Law, Illinois Institute of Technology (J.D., 1992). Order of the Coif. Member, Chicago-Kent College Law Review. *Member:* Chicago (Member, Insurance Coverage Section) and Illinois State Bar Associations. ***PRACTICE AREAS:*** Insurance Coverage. ***Email:*** lisa.breen@mbtlaw.com

JOHN K. DALY, born Los Alamos, New Mexico, November 11, 1963; admitted to bar, 1994, New Mexico; 1995, U.S. District Court, District of New Mexico; 1996, Illinois. *Education:* University of New Mexico (B.A., 1987); University of Arizona (M.A., 1989); Hastings College of the Law, University of California (J.D., 1994). Member, Hastings Communications and Entertainment Law Journal. *Member:* American Bar Association (Member, Litigation Section). ***PRACTICE AREAS:*** Insurance Coverage Litigation; Insurance Defense; Commercial Litigation. ***Email:*** john.daly@mbtlaw.com

THOMAS J. O'BRIEN, born Chicago, Illinois, October 16, 1932; admitted to bar, 1960, Illinois and U.S. District Court, Northern District of Illinois. *Education:* DePaul University (B.A., 1956; J.D., 1959). Author: "Tro Petitions," Illinois Bar Journal, Vol. 81, Nov. 1993. Circuit Judge, 1976-1994, Appellate Justice, 1994-1995. *Member:* Chicago Bar Association; Northwest Suburban Bar Association. ***PRACTICE AREAS:*** Arbitration; Mediation. ***Email:*** tom.obrien@mbtlaw.com

PETER PETRAKIS, born 1951; admitted to bar, 1976, Illinois. *Education:* Loyola University (B.A., with honors, 1973; J.D., cum laude, 1976). Student Article Editor, Loyola University Law Journal, 1975-1976. Author: "The Lot is Cast into the Lap; Federal Communications Commission Mistreatment of State Lottery Broadcasts," Loyola University of Chicago Law Journal, Vol. 6:2, 1976. Co-Author: "Healthcare Construction Projects," Construction Joint Ventures, Ch. 2, 1992. Law Clerk to Hon. Howard C. Ryan, Justice of Illinois Supreme Court, 1976-1977. ***LANGUAGES:*** Greek. ***Email:*** peter.petrakis@mbtlaw.com

GEORGENE M. WILSON, born Gary, Indiana, October 17, 1952; admitted to bar, 1981, Illinois, U.S. District Court, Northern District of Illinois including Trial Bar and U.S. Court of Appeals, Seventh Circuit; 1994, U. S. Supreme Court. *Education:* Indiana University (B.A., 1974; M.P.A., 1977); DePaul University (J.D., with honors, 1981). Adjunct Professor, DePaul University School of Law. *Member:* Chicago Bar Association. ***REPORTED CASES:*** Zavala v. Powermatic, 167 Ill. 2d 542 (1995); Kirk v. Michael Reese Hospital, 117 Ill. 2d 507 (1987); Statewide Insurance Co. v. Brendan Construction Co., 218 Ill. App.3d 1055 (1991). ***PRACTICE AREAS:*** Insurance Law; Professional Liability; Construction Litigation; Commercial Litigation. ***Email:*** georgene.wilson@mbtlaw.com

(This Listing Continued)

MEITES, MULDER, BURGER & MOLLICA

Established in 1980

208 S. LASALLE STREET, SUITE 1410
CHICAGO, ILLINOIS 60604-1003
Telephone: 312-263-0272
Fax: 312-263-2942
URL: http://www.mmbmlaw.com

Class Actions, Federal Practice, Employment Rights, Employment Law, Government Contracts, Toxic Torts, Employment Discrimination, Appellate Practice, ERISA, Consumer Law, Civil Rights, Environmental Litigation, Securities Litigation, Complex Litigation.

FIRM PROFILE: Meites, Mulder, Burger & Mollica represents plaintiffs in class actions and multi-plaintiff lawsuits in cases involving employment discrimination, ERISA, pension benefits, qui tam actions, and other complex litigation.

THOMAS R. MEITES, born Chicago, Illinois, September 27, 1943; admitted to bar, 1969, Illinois. *Education:* Harvard College (B.A., 1965); Harvard University Law School (J.D., magna cum laude, 1969). Editorial Board, Vols. 81 and 82, and Articles Editor, Vol. 82, Harvard Law Review, 1968-1969. Law Clerk to Judge J. Edward Lumbard, Chief Judge of the United States Court of Appeals for the Second Circuit, 1969-1970. Instructor, Northwestern School of Education and Social Policy, 1999—. Co-Author: with Daniel Kessler and Geoffrey Miller, "Explaining Deviations from the Fifty-Percent Rule: A Multimodal Approach of the Selection of Cases for Litigation," 25 Journal of Legal Studies 233 (1996). Formerly with: Businessmen for the Public Interest, 1970-1971; private practice in Chicago, 1971-1979; Partner, Meites, Frackman, Mulder & Burger (now Meites, Mulder, Burger & Mollica), 1980—. Appointed by President of the United States, to Board of Directors, Legal Services Corporation, 2003—. Member, Board of Governors, Chicago Counsel of Lawyers, 1977-1982. Chair, Appleseed Fund for Justice, 2000-2002. Director, Legal Assistance Foundation of Chicago, 1978-1979. Member, Hearing Board, Illinois Supreme Court Attorney Disciplinary Commission, 1975-1980. Member, Board of Directors, Citizens Schools' Committee, 1971-1972. Member, Chicago, Council of Lawyers, 1971—. Appointed Special Master, Mister v. I.C.G.R.R., 81-3006 (S.D.Ill.) 1989-1993. ***PRACTICE AREAS:*** Class Actions; Employment Discrimination; Federal Practice. ***Email:*** tmeites@mmbmlaw.com

MICHAEL M. MULDER, born Watertown, New York, December 17, 1949; admitted to bar, 1975, Illinois; 1979, U.S. Supreme Court; U.S. Court of Appeals, Fifth, Sixth, Seventh, Eighth, Ninth and Tenth Circuits and U.S. Court of Appeals for the District of Columbia. *Education:* Western Michigan University (B.A., with honors, Political Science, 1972); Valparaiso University School of Law (J.D., 1975). Adjunct Professor of Law, Appellate Practice Clinic, The John Marshall Law School, 1978-1980. Adjunct Professor of Law, Federal Court Clinical Program, Valparaiso University School of Law, 1980-1982. Assistant Defender, Illinois State Appellate Defender, 1975-1980. Legal Director, Project Justice and Equality, 1980-1982. Associate, Meites & Frackman, 1982-1986. Partner, Meites, Mulder, Burger & Mollica, 1986—. *Member:* National Legal Aid and Defender Association (Defender Amicus Brief Committee, 1978-1981); Chicago Council of Lawyers; National Employment Lawyers Association; American Bar Association (Member, Section on Labor and Employment). ***PRACTICE AREAS:*** Class Actions; Employment Discrimination; Federal Practice; ERISA. ***Email:*** mmmulder@mmbmlaw.com

PAUL W. MOLLICA, born Fairfax, Virginia, January 29, 1961; admitted to bar, 1986, Illinois; U.S. Court of Appeals, First, Fourth, Fifth, Seventh, Ninth and Tenth Circuits; U.S. Supreme Court. *Education:* University of Chicago (B.A., 1983); DePaul University (J.D., with honors, 1986). Managing Editor of Notes and Comments, De Paul Law Review, 1985-1986. Executive Editor, Lindemann & Grossman, "Employment Discrimination Law, 4th Ed.," 2006. Associate Editor, Lindemann and Kadue, "Attorneys' Fees," chapter, Age Discrimination in Employment Law, 2003. Associate Editor, Lindemann and Grossman," Employment Discrimination Law, 3d Ed., Third Supp.," 2002. Associate Editor, Schlei and Grossman, "Employment Discrimination Law, 3d Ed., Second Supp.," BNA, 2000; "Federal Summary Judgment at High Tide," 84 Marquette L. Rev. 139 (2000); "Employment Discrimination Law in the Seventh Circuit: 1992-1996," 1 Employee Rights and Employment Policy Journal 63 (1997). Associate, Sonnenschein, Carlin, Nath & Rosenthal (now

(This Listing Continued)

MEITES, MULDER, BURGER & MOLLICA, Chicago—Continued

Sonnenschein, Nath & Rosenthal), 1986-1990. Associate, Meites, Frackman, Mulder & Burger, 1990-1996. Partner, Meites, Frackman, Mulder & Burger (now Meites, Mulder, Burger & Mollica), 1997—. Member, U.S. District Court Merit Selection Panel, U.S. District Court, Northern District of Illinois, 1999-2000, 2000-2001. Member, Seventh Circuit Task Force, Draft Civil Jury Instructions, 2002. *Member:* Chicago Council of Lawyers (President, 1999-2001, Board of Governors, 1996-2001; Treasurer, 1998-1999; Chair, Federal Courts Committee, 1995-1999; Chair, Judicial Evaluation Committee, 2002; Board of Governors, Chicago Lawyers Committee for Civil Rights Under Law, 2001—); American Bar Association (Member, Labor and Employment Section); National Employment Lawyers Association (Seventh Circuit Representative, Amicus Advisory Committee, 2000—. ***PRACTICE AREAS:*** Class Actions; Employment Discrimination; Appellate Practice; Federal Practice. ***Email:*** pwmollica@mmbmlaw.com

JOAN H. BURGER, born Winston-Salem, North Carolina, October 27, 1945; admitted to bar, 1985, Illinois. *Education:* DePauw University (B.A., cum laude, 1967); Ohio State University (M.A., 1970); Loyola University of Chicago (J.D., 1985). Associate, Meites, Frackman & Mulder, 1985-1990. Partner, Meites, Mulder, Burger & Mollica, 1991—. *Member:* Illinois State Bar Association; Chicago Council of Lawyers; Chicago Bar Association. (Retired). ***PRACTICE AREAS:*** Class Actions; Employment Discrimination; Federal Practice; Toxic Torts.

SHONA B. GLINK, born Chicago, Illinois, October 28, 1966; admitted to bar, 1991, Illinois; 2000, Georgia; 2002, New York. *Education:* Tufts University (B.A., 1988); University of Illinois College of Law (J.D., summa cum laude, 1991). Order of the Coif. Recipient, Illinois Women's Bar Foundation Scholarship for Academic and Overall Achievement, 1991. Member, Editorial Board, 1990-1991 and Topics Editor, 1991, University of Illinois Law Review. Law Clerk to Judge George M. Marovich, District Judge, Northern District of Illinois, Eastern Division, 1991-1993. Author: Publications Note, "The Prosecution of Maternal Fetal Abuse: Is this the Answer?" 1991 U. Ill. L.Rev. 533. Assistant Corporation Counsel, Department of Law, Labor Division, City of Chicago, 1993-1998. Associate, 1998-2002 and Partner, 2003—, Meites, Mulder, Burger & Mollica. *Member:* New York State Bar Association; Illinois State Bar Association; American Bar Association; Chicago Council of Lawyers; National Employment Lawyers Association; Anti-Defamation League (Member, Civil Rights Executive Board, Chicago Chapter, 1997-2000). ***PRACTICE AREAS:*** Class Actions; Employment Discrimination; Federal Practice; Title VII Discrimination; Affirmative Action; Complex Litigation. ***Email:*** sbglink@mmbmlaw.com

ASSOCIATES

JOSIE RAIMOND, born Buffalo, New York, October 4, 1968; admitted to bar, 1995, Illinois; 1996, Massachusetts; U.S. Court of Appeals, Seventh Circuit. *Education:* Hamilton College (B.A., 1990); Vanderbilt University (J.D., 1995). Fellow, Public Interest Law Initiative, Northwestern University School of Law Legal Clinic, 1995. Author: Note, The Constitutionality of Student-Led Prayer at High School Graduation Ceremonies," Volume 48, Vanderbilt Law Review (1995). Associate, McDermott, Will & Emery, 1995-1997. Staff Attorney, Division of Enforcement, Securities and Exchange Commission, 1997-1999. Associate, Meites, Mulder, Burger & Mollica, 1999—. *Member:* Chicago Council of Lawyers; Illinois State Bar Association. ***PRACTICE AREAS:*** Class Actions; Employment Discrimination; Federal Practice; Commercial Litigation. ***Email:*** jraimond@mmbmlaw.com

JAMIE S. FRANKLIN, born Upland, California, November 2, 1969; admitted to bar, 1997, Illinois; U.S. Court of Appeals, Sixth and Seventh Circuits. *Education:* Duke University (B.A., 1992); University of Chicago Law School (J.D., 1997). Fellow, Consumer Law, Legal Assistance Foundation of Chicago, 1996-1997. Author: "Chapter 6: Fair Debt Collection Practices Act," Consumer Law Pleadings, Robert J. Hobbs & John Rao, eds., National Consumer Law Center, 1998. Associate, Edelman & Combs, 1997-1999. Associate, Meites, Mulder, Burger & Mollica, 1999—. *Member:* Chicago, Illinois State Bar Association; Chicago Council of Lawyers. ***PRACTICE AREAS:*** Class Actions; Employment Discrimination; Federal Practice; Environmental Litigation; Consumer Law. ***Email:*** jsfranklin@mmbmlaw.com

MERLO KANOFSKY BRINKMEIER & GREGG LTD.

208 SOUTH LA SALLE STREET, SUITE 950
CHICAGO, ILLINOIS 60604
Telephone: 312-553-5500
Facsimile: 312-553-1586
URL: http://www.merlolaw.com

Civil Trials and Appeals in State and Federal Courts. Aviation, Civil Rights, Excess Insurance, Insurance Coverage, Municipal Liability, Product Liability, Professional Liability, Reinsurance and General Civil Litigation.

FIRM PROFILE: Merlo Kanofsky Brinkmeier & Gregg Ltd. was established to provide the type of excellence in advocacy our clients expect from a large firm without the negatives normally associated with large firm retention.

We are committed to several interrelated objectives which we believe are important to our clients as they face business in 2004 and beyond. First, we are committed to fully involving our clients in thorough, thoughtful analysis, and strategic and tactical planning. We believe we serve our clients best when we first work to understand their business needs, servicing requirements, and overall dispute resolution philosophy, and then strive to communicate closely with them in advancing those needs. Second, we eschew the dogmatic or lock-step approaches some attorneys take to litigation in favor of specifically tailoring our approach to each piece of litigation to maximize our clients' representation. Finally, we are committed to flexibility: flexibility in fulfilling our clients' servicing needs; flexibility in litigation approach; flexibility in pricing; and flexibility in dispute resolution. In short, we strive to maximize our clients' representation while prudently expending their assets.

(This Listing Continued)

MICHAEL J. MERLO, born Chicago, Illinois, March 29, 1942; admitted to bar, 1967, Illinois; 1997, Florida; U.S. District Court, Central and Northern Districts of Illinois; U.S. District Court, District of South Dakota; U.S. District Court, Eastern District of Kentucky; U.S. District Court, Northern District of Texas. *Education:* John Carroll University (B.A., 1963); Northwestern University (J.D., 1966). General Counsel, Excess/Surplus Lines Claims Association, 1978—. Director, Illinois Insurance Exchange, 1981-1984. *Member:* Illinois State and American Bar Associations; International Association of Defense Counsel; Defense Research Institute; Private Pilot; Instrument Rating. ***PRACTICE AREAS:*** Commercial Law; Insurance Coverage; Environmental Law; Aviation Law; Professional Liability; Products Liability. ***Email:*** mjm@merlolaw.com

MARTIN A. KANOFSKY, born Chicago, Illinois, August 19, 1949; admitted to bar, 1981, Illinois and U.S. District Court, Northern District of Illinois including Trial Bar; 1982, U.S. Court of Appeals, Seventh Circuit. *Education:* Northeastern Illinois University (B.A., 1971); Northern Illinois University (J.D., 1981). Author, "Keeping Sensitive Information Confidential In Light of CPSC Reporting Requirements," Declarations, p. 30, Winter 1994-1995. Appointed Commercial Arbitrator, American Arbitration Association, 1985. *Member:* Chicago, Illinois State and American Bar Associations. ***SPECIAL AGENCIES:*** Federal Aviation Administration; Illinois Human Rights Commission; Maine Human Rights Commission. ***REPORTED CASES:*** Meyer v. Naperville Manor, 634 N.E.2d 411 (2d Dist. 1994); Balsamo/Olsen v. Bradley Place, 950 F.Supp. 896 (C.D. Ill. 1997); Voss v. Lincoln Mall Management Co., 519 NE 2d 1056 (1988); O'hearn v. Delta Airlines Inc., 838 F. Supp. 1264 (1993). ***PRACTICE AREAS:*** Civil Litigation; Insurance Law; Reinsurance. ***Email:*** mak@merlolaw.com

ALAN J. BRINKMEIER, born Lena, Illinois, November 11, 1954; admitted to bar, 1984, Illinois, U.S. District Court, Northern and Central District of Illinois, U.S. Court of Appeals, Seventh Circuit and U.S. Supreme Court. *Education:* Elmhurst College (B.A., with high honors, 1976); DePaul University (J.D., 1984). Phi Kappa Phi; Phi Alpha Delta. Co-Editor, "Digest of Insurance Laws," Illinois Digest Section, 55th Ed., p. 115s - Illinois, A.M. Best Co., 1984. Author: "The Question of X-Ray Ownership," *Chicago Bar Association Record,* Vol. 4, No. 5, p. 31, May 1990; "The Duty to Warn," *Illinois Parks and Recreation,* Vol. 21, No. 3, p. 9, May/June 1990; "Hague Convention: Service of Documents in Japan"; "Aon Aviation, Inc. Found Less Responsible than Alberto-Culver Has Owner/Operator Responsible in Palwaukee Crash Litigation," 'Resource Materials' Vol. 1 Ed. 5, May 6, 2003; "Damages: "A Few More Stitches for the Deep Pocket?" *The Brief of the DuPage County Bar Association,* Vol. 15 No. 2, p.11, February 2003; "Limited Public School Student Drug Testing Found Constitutional," 'Resource Material' Vo. 1 Ed. 2, July 2002, *Contributing Author:* "Family Awarded &10.45 Million in Crash Case" *Aviation Litigation Reporter, p. 5 May 27, 2003, Automotive Litigation Reporter,* p. 14439, December 1990; "Hague Convention: Commentary," *Aviation Litigation Reporter,* p. 12682, December 1990; "Conditions of the Land: Relationship of the Dangerous Condition Rule and the Open Danger Defense," *The Brief of the DuPage County Bar Association,* Vol. 2, No. 6, p. 9, February 1991; "Admissibility of NTSB Aircraft Accident Reports in Civil Litigation," *Aviation Litigation Reporter,* p. 15748, September 24, 1991; "Cross-Examination of Expert Witnesses From Discovery to Trial," *Illinois Trial Lawyers Association Course Handbook,* p. 87, May 2, 1992; "Give Up The Defense? - Not In Illinois," Declarations, p.8, Winter, 1993; "Government Immunity: A Summer of Planting Seeds," The Brief of the DuPage County Bar Association, Vol. 7, Issue 4, p. 21, December 1994; "Be 'FORE' warned. Golf Course Liability is Just a Stroke Away," PDRMA Risk Management Institute, p. 2, March 24, 1995; "Damages: Apportionment Among Joint Tortfeasors," The Brief of the DuPage County Bar Association, Vol. 10, Issue 3, 2.31, October 1997; "A Defense Perspective. "Insurance Law: Illinois' New Actual Notice and Deactivation of Tender Rules", *IDC Quarterly,* Vol. 11 No. 2, p. 16, Spring 2001. Contributing Author: ; "Forum Non Conveniens: Sponagle v. USAir/Piedmont Airlines Dismissal," *Aviation Litigation Reporter,* p. 11, 536, March 1990; "Cabin Door: Alumni v. Tracor Aviation, Inc. - Refurbisher Granted Summary Judgement in DC-10 Suit," *Aviation Litigation Reporter,* p. 12023, July 1990; "IL App. Ct. Affirms Plaintiff's Lack of Standing as 'Next of Kin,'" *Aviation Litigation Reporter,* p. 9, October 26, 1999; "Expert Cross-Examination and the Sole Proximate Cause Defense," The Brief of the DuPage County Bar Association, Vol.13. Issue 10, June 2001; "Redman v. United Airlines Class Certification Granted With Settlement Litigated Judgement" *Class Action Reports* Vol. 21, No. 6. pg. 767, November/December 2000; Resource Materials, www.merlowlaw.com: "Illinois Modifies Appeal Bond and Stay of Judgment Rules," Vol 2, Ed. 6, July 1, 2004; "Municipal Litigation," Vol. 3, Ed. 8, September 8, 2004; "Illinois Amends Disclosure Rules," Vol 3, Ed. 11, November 1, 2004. Arbitrator, Circuit Court of Cook County Mandatory Arbitration Program (IICLE). Past Member, Aviation Committee, Chicago Association of Commerce and Industry (CACI). Commissioner, City of Elmhurst, Board of Planning and Zoning, 1996—. *Member:* Chicago, DuPage County, Illinois State and American Bar Associations; Defense Research Institute; Appellate Lawyers Association. ***REPORTED CASES:*** In Re: Air Crash Disaster at Sioux City, Iowa on July 19, 1989, 631 N.E. 2d 1302 (1st Dist. 1994); Baby Ashley Doe v. Village of Highland Park, 1995 Lexis 1075 (N.D. Ill. January 30, 1995); Meyer v. Naperville Manor, 634 N.E. 2d. 411 (2d. Dist. 1994); Barrett vs. Forest Preserve District of Cook County, 593 N.E. 2d 990; Creekside Associates, Inc. vs. City of Wood Dale, 684 F. Supp. 201; Jane Doe Class Actions vs. City of Calumet City 128 F.R.P. 93 and Again at 754 F. Supp. 1211; Chrissafis v. Continental Airlines, 940 F.Supp. 1292 (1996); Houck v. TWA Flight 800, 947 F.Supp. 373 (N.D. Illinois 1996); Felder v. Town of Lowell, 934 F.Supp. 1032 (N.D. Indiana 1996); Chrissafis v. Continental Airlines, Inc., Case No. 95C 5080, United States District Court for the Northern District of Illinois, Eastern Division, 1998 U.S. Dist. Lexis 2384, February 20, 1998, Decided, February 23, 1998, Docketed; Dotson v. McDonald's Corp., No. 97C 1833, United States District Court for the Northern District of Illinois, Eastern Division, 1998 U.S. Dist. Lexis 4676, March 31, 1998, Decided, April 12, 1998, Docketed; Jo Lou Mio v. Alberto Culver Company, 715 N.E.2d 309 (2d Dist. 1999); Anderson v. Alberto-Culver USA Inc. _Ill. App. 3rd _, Docket Nos. 1-01-2181 (cons.) (Ill. App. March 6, 2003); Associated Aviation Underwriters, Inc. v. AON Aviation, Inc._Ill App.3d—, Docket No. 1-02-3815 (Ill. App. May 13, 2004). ***PRACTICE AREAS:*** Aviation Law; Products Liability; Insurance; Municipal Liability; Civil Practice. ***Email:*** ajb@merlolaw.com

MICHAEL R. GREGG, born Helena, Montana, July 13, 1959; admitted to bar, 1987, Illinois, U.S. District Court, Northern District of Illinois including Trial Bar, U.S. District Court, Southern District of Illinois, U.S. District Court Eastern District of Wisconsin and U.S. Court of Appeals, Fourth Circuit. *Education:* University of Illinois (B.S., 1981); John

(This Listing Continued)

Marshall Law School (J.D., with distinction, 1987). Member Editorial Staff, John Marshall Law Review, 1986-1987. *Member:* Chicago, Illinois State and American Bar Associations. ***PRACTICE AREAS:*** Complex Litigation; Insurance Coverage Litigation; Reinsurance; Appeals; Commercial Litigation. ***Email:*** mrg@merlolaw.com

LINDA J. SCHNEIDER, born Chicago, Illinois, April 7, 1960; admitted to bar, 1989, Illinois and U.S. District Court, Northern and Central Districts of Illinois. *Education:* Southern Illinois University (B.A., 1982); DePaul University (J.D., 1989). *Member:* Chicago, Illinois State and American Bar Associations. ***LANGUAGES:*** French. ***REPORTED CASES:*** O'Hern v. Delta Air Lines, Inc., 838 F.Supp. 1264 (N.D. Ill. 1993). ***PRACTICE AREAS:*** Aviation Litigation; Negligence; Products Liability; Professional Liability; Municipal Liability; General Civil Litigation. ***Email:*** ljs@merlolaw.com

DONALD G. MACHALINSKI, admitted to bar, 1989, Illinois and U.S. District Court, Northern and Central Districts of Illinois including Trial Bar. *Education:* Illinois State University (B.S., 1986); Loyola University (J.D., 1989). *Member:* American Bar Association. ***PRACTICE AREAS:*** Civil Litigation Defense; Aviation Liability; Premises Liability; Professional Liability; Nursing Home Litigation; Products Liability; Insurance Coverage Litigation; Trial Practice; Appellate Practice; Private Pilot. ***Email:*** dgm@merlolaw.com

JOHN D. DALTON, born Normal, Illinois, June 25, 1962; admitted to bar, 1987, Illinois; 1989, U.S. District Court, Northern District of Illinois. *Education:* Illinois Wesleyan University (B.A., 1984); John Marshall Law School (J.D., 1987). Certified Public Accountant, Illinois, 1989. Co-Author: "Excess Insurance: The Unique Duties Arising Out of an Excess Policy," *The Policy,* April 2001. Contributing Writer, "Environmental Liability and Insurance: A Guide to Obtaining Coverage, with Tax Analysis an Planning," Clark, Boardman, Callaghan, Oct. 1996. Co-Author, with Edwin J. Kula: "Flex Plans: A Benefit Option For Schools," The Journal of School Business Management, 1992; "Low-Cost Benefit Saves Taxes for Employees," Illinois School Board Journal, 1992. *Member:* Chicago (Member, Insurance and Securities Committee), Illinois State (Member, Insurance Section Counsel) and American (Member, Business Law Section) Bar Associations. ***PRACTICE AREAS:*** Insurance. ***Email:*** jdd@merlolaw.com

ROSS D. ROLOFF, born Bloomington, Minnesota, January 1, 1968; admitted to bar, 1993, Indiana, Illinois and U.S. District Court, Northern District of Illinois. *Education:* Wartburg College (B.A., 1990); Valparaiso University (J.D., 1993). Phi Delta Phi. Moot Court Society. Member, National Moot Court Team. *Member:* Chicago, Illinois State, Indiana State and American Bar Associations. ***PRACTICE AREAS:*** Insurance Coverage; Commercial Litigation. ***Email:*** rdr@merlolaw.com

MARK H. SHANBERG, born Chicago, Illinois, September 14, 1967; admitted to bar, 1992, Illinois; U.S. District Court, Northern District of Illinois. *Education:* Indiana University (B.A., 1989); John Marshall Law School (J.D., 1992). *Member:* Illinois State Bar Association; Illinois Trial Lawyers Association. ***REPORTED CASES:*** Cooksey v. Township of Schaumburg, slip op. 1-03-3302. ***PRACTICE AREAS:*** Medical Malpractice; General Liability; Products Liability; Premises Liability; Aviation Litigation. ***Email:*** mhs@merlolaw.com

---

MICHELLE B. BALFOUR, born Bemidji, Minnesota, February 14, 1974; admitted to bar, 2001, Illinois; 2002, U.S. District Court, Central District of Illinois. *Education:* North Dakota State University (B.A., 1997); DePaul University (J.D., 2000). Phi Alpha Delta. *Member:* Illinois State and American Bar Associations. [U. S. Army National Guard, 1995-2002.]. ***PRACTICE AREAS:*** Civil Practice; Insurance Coverage; Litigation. ***Email:*** mbb@merlolaw.com

ANTHONY N. BALICE, born Skokie, Illinois, March 24, 1973; admitted to bar, 2000, Illinois and U.S. District Court, Northern District of Illinois. *Education:* University of Illinois at Chicago (B.A., 1995); DePaul University School of Law (J.D., 2000). Dean's List. ***LANGUAGES:*** Italian. ***PRACTICE AREAS:*** Insurance Coverage; Civil Practice. ***Email:*** anb@merlolaw.com

AMELIA CHRISTENSEN, born LaPorte, Indiana, October 19, 1976; admitted to bar, 2004, Illinois and U.S. District Court, Northern District of Illinois. *Education:* University of Notre Dame (B.A., English, 1999); John Marshall Law School (J.D., 2004). Associate Justice, John Marshall Law School Moot Court. *Member:* Chicago and Illinois State Bar Associations; Illinois Association of Defense Trial Counsel. ***PRACTICE AREAS:*** Insurance Defense. ***Email:*** akc@merlolaw.com

MARY C. CLIFFORD, born Brooklyn, New York, April 1, 1974; admitted to bar, 2003, Illinois and U.S. District Court, Northern District of Illinois. *Education:* St. Francis College (B.A., magna cum laude, 1996); Washington University (J.D., 2003). ***PRACTICE AREAS:*** Insurance Coverage; Civil Litigation. ***Email:*** mcc@merlolaw.com

C. EDWARD CRAFT, born Southfield, Michigan, October 25, 1974; admitted to bar, 2000, Illinois. *Education:* University of Michigan (B.A., 1996); University of Illinois (J.D., 1999). ***PRACTICE AREAS:*** Insurance (100%). ***Email:*** cec@merlolaw.com

THOMAS D. DONOFRIO, born Oaklawn, Illinois, June 1, 1970; admitted to bar, 1995, Illinois and U.S. District Court, Northern District of Illinois. *Education:* University of Chicago (B.A., 1992); Washington University (J.D., 1995). ***Email:*** tdd@merlolaw.com

JASON R. DONOVAN, born Milwaukee, Wisconsin, March 3, 1977; admitted to bar, 2002, Wisconsin; 2003, Illinois; 2004, U.S. District Court, Northern District of Illinois. *Education:* Northwestern University (B.M., 1999); University of Wisconsin-Madison (J.D., 2001). ***LANGUAGES:*** French. ***PRACTICE AREAS:*** Insurance Law; Civil Litigation; Insurance Coverage. ***Email:*** jrd@merlolaw.com

MICHAEL G. PATRIZIO, born Steubenville, Ohio, March 17, 1952; admitted to bar, 1984, Illinois; 1999, U.S. Court of Appeals, 7th Circuit. *Education:* West Virginia University (B.A., 1974); DePaul University (J.D., 1984). Author: 79 Illinois Bar Journal 234. ***LANGUAGES:*** Italian. ***REPORTED CASES:*** Maka v. Illinois Farmers Inc. Co., 332 Ill.App.3d 447, 772 N.E.2d 895 (2002); Smith v. Industrial Commission, 308 Ill App. 3d 260, 719 N.E. 2d 329 (1999); Tribune Co. v. Allstate Ins. Co., 306 Ill.App.3d 779, 715 N.E.2d 263 (1999); Strickland v. Communications and Cable of Chicago, Inc., 304 Ill. App. 3d 679, 710 N.E.2d 55, 237 (1999); Netzel v. Industrial Commission, 286 Ill. App. 3d 550, 676 N.E. 2d 270 (1997); Berlak v. Villa Scalabrini Home For The Aged, Inc., 284 Ill. App. 3d 231, 671 N.E 2d 768 (1996); Farley Metals, Inc. v. Barber Colman Co., 269 Ill.App.3d 104, 645 N.E.2d 964 (1994); Miller v. Industrial Commission, 255 Ill.App.3d 947, 627 N.E.2d 676 (1993); Newbern v. Industrial Commission, 256 Ill.App.3d 1043, 628 N.E.2d 532 (1993); Little Company of Mary Hospital v. Industrial Commission, 256 Ill.App.3d 1036, 628 N.E.2d 537 (1993); Hartsfield v. Industrial Commission, 241 Ill.App.3d 1055, 610 N.E.2d 702 (1993); ARA Services, Inc. v. Industrial Commission, 226 Ill.App 3d 224, 590 N.E. 2d 78 (1992); Wolf v. Meister-Neiberg, Inc., 143 Ill. 2d 44, 570 N.E.2d 327 (1991); Balderos v. City Chevrolet, 214 F.3d 849, 7th Cir. Il. (2000); Staples v. Krack Corp., 186 F.2d 977, 7th Cir. Il. (1999); Flood v. Long Term Disability Plan for First Data Corp., 2003 WL 367063, N.D. Il. (2003) . ***PRACTICE AREAS:*** Insurance; Appellate Practice; Commercial Litigation. ***Email:*** mgp@merlolaw.com

(This Listing Continued)

CHRISTOPHER J. RAISTRICK, born Park Ridge, Illinois, October 31, 1971; admitted to bar, 1996, Illinois. *Education:* Illinois Wesleyan University (B.A., 1993); Loyola University (J.D., 1996). Member, Certified American Chemical Society. Chicago Legal Clinic. *Member:* Illinois State Bar Association. ***PRACTICE AREAS:*** Insurance Defense; Aviation Law; Insurance Coverage. ***Email:*** cjr@merlolaw.com

TODD M. ROWE, born Livonia, Michigan, December 2, 1974; admitted to bar, 2000, Wisconsin; 2003, Michigan (Not admitted in Illinois). *Education:* Eastern Michigan University (B.S., 1997); Marquette University (J.D., 2000). ***PRACTICE AREAS:*** Insurance; Complex Litigation; Products Liability. ***Email:*** tmr@merlolaw.com

THOMAS EDWARD SARIKAS, born Decatur, Illinois, April 16, 1958; admitted to bar, 1994, Illinois and U.S. District Court, Northern District of Illinois; 1995, U.S. District Court, Central District of Illinois. *Education:* University of Notre Dame (B.S.C.E., 1980); DePaul University School of Law (J.D., 1994). *Member:* American Bar Association. ***PRACTICE AREAS:*** Civil Litigation; Insurance Coverage; Commercial Litigation. ***Email:*** tes@merlolaw.com

REPRESENTATIVE CLIENTS: Acstar Insurance Co.; Adriatica Insurance Co.; AIG Aviation; American International Group; Delta Air Lines, Inc.; Farmers Insurance Group; First State Insurance Co.; Forest Preserve District of Cook County; General Reinsurance; Jefferson Insurance Co.; Jewel Foods, Inc.; Markel Rhulen; Mead Reinsurance; Pioneer Claim Mgmt., Inc.; Prudential Reinsurance Co.; Reliance National Insurance Co.; Scottsdale Insurance Co.; United States Aviation Underwriters, Inc.; Western World Insurance Co.;

ROBERT A. MERRICK, JR., LTD.

53 WEST JACKSON BOULEVARD
SUITE 1235
CHICAGO, ILLINOIS 60604
Telephone: 312-922-0772
Fax: 312-922-0851
Email: ramerrick@sbcglobal.net

Attorney Discipline Defense, Professional Responsibility, Legal Ethics.

ROBERT A. MERRICK, JR., born Camden, New Jersey, January 13, 1951; admitted to bar, 1977, Illinois and U.S. District Court, Northern District of Illinois; 1979, U.S. Court of Appeals, Seventh Circuit; 1982, U.S. Supreme Court. *Education:* Princeton University (A.B., 1973); Northwestern University (J.D., cum laude, 1977; Ph.D. in Clinical Psychology, 1981). Past Lecturer, Legal Ethics: Northwestern University School of Law; DePaul University College of Law; Loyola University School of Law. *Member:* Chicago, Illinois State and American Bar Associations. ***PRACTICE AREAS:*** Attorney Discipline; Legal Ethics and Professional Responsibility.

METGE, SPITZER & KREID

30 WEST MONROE STREET, SUITE 630
CHICAGO, ILLINOIS 60603
Telephone: 312-580-1710
Fax: 312-580-1711

Transportation, Freight Loss and Damage, Personal Injury, Property Damage, Contract and Regulatory Claims Disputes, Commercial Litigation, Construction Litigation, Commercial, Employment, ERISA, Health Care, Insurance, Banking, Environmental, Construction, Real Estate, Transactions and Corporate Law. Mediation, Arbitration and Litigation Practice.

MEMBERS OF FIRM

MARVIN F. METGE, born Hot Springs, Arkansas, September 10, 1929; admitted to bar, 1953, Illinois and U.S. District Court, Northern District of Illinois. *Education:* Vanderbilt University, Drake University and Northwestern University (B.S.L.); Northwestern University (J.D., 1953). Phi Delta Phi. *Member:* Chicago, Illinois State and American Bar Associations; Law Club of Chicago; The Society of Trial Lawyers. ***PRACTICE AREAS:*** Transportation; Environmental Law; Construction; Real Estate; Corporate Law; Estate Planning; Litigation; Mediation; Arbitration.

BRUCE C. SPITZER, born Chicago, Illinois, June 27, 1947; admitted to bar, 1972, Illinois and U.S. District Court, Northern District of Illinois. *Education:* University of Illinois (A.B., 1969; J.D., 1972). *Member:* Chicago and American Bar Associations; National Association of Railroad Trial Counsel; Conference of Freight Counsel (Chairman, 1986-1988); Transportation Lawyers Association. ***PRACTICE AREAS:*** Transportation; Freight Loss and Damage; Personal Injury; Property Damage; Contracts; Regulatory Law; Commercial Litigation; Litigation; Mediation; Arbitration. ***Email:*** bcspitzer@msklaw.com

CHRISTOPHER A. "KIT" KREID, born Alton, Illinois, October 19, 1961; admitted to bar, 1986, Illinois and U.S. District Court, Northern District of Illinois including Trial Bar; U.S. District Court, Central District of Illinois; U.S. Court of Appeals, Seventh Circuit. *Education:* University of Illinois (B.S., with honors, 1983); Washington University (J.D., 1986). *Member:* Chicago, Illinois State and American Bar Associations; National Association of Railroad Trial Counsel; Law Club of Chicago. (Managing Partner). ***PRACTICE AREAS:*** Contracts; Commercial Litigation; Transportation; Construction Litigation; Environmental Law; Employment Law; ERISA; Health Care; Personal Injury; Property Damage; Arbitration. ***Email:*** ckreid@msklaw.com

MICHAEL BEST & FRIEDRICH LLP

Established in 1990

401 NORTH MICHIGAN AVENUE

SUITE 1900

CHICAGO, ILLINOIS 60611

Telephone: 312-222-0800

Facsimile: 312-222-0818

Email: info@michaelbest.com

URL: http://www.michaelbest.com

Milwaukee, Wisconsin Office: 100 East Wisconsin Avenue, 53202-4108. Telephone: 414-271-6560. Telecopier: 414-277-0656.

Madison, Wisconsin Office: One South Pinckney Street, Firstar Plaza, P.O. Box 1806, 53701-1806. Telephone: 608-257-3501. Telecopier: 608-283-2275.

Manitowoc, Wisconsin Office: 1000 Maritime Drive, 54220. Telephone: 920-686-2800. Telecopier: 920-686-2810.

Waukesha, Wisconsin Office: Two Riverwood Place, Suite 200, N19 W24133 Riverwood Drive, 53188-1174. Telephone: 262-956-6560. Telecopier: 262-956-6565.

Center Valley, Pennsylvania Office: Stabler Corporate Center, 3773 Corporate Parkway, 18034. Telephone: 610-798-2170. Telecopier: 610-798-2180.

Litigation, Corporate and Commercial Law, Management Labor and Employment, Employee Benefits, Patents, Trademarks, Internet Law, Computer Technology, Intellectual Property, Financial Institutions, Securities and Mergers and Acquisitions, Real Property and Commercial, Industrial and Residential Land Development, Federal and State Taxation, Associations, Antitrust and Unfair Trade Practices, Public and Corporate Finance, Creditors' Rights, Bankruptcy and Insolvency, International Business, Estate and Trust Planning, Business Succession Planning, Health Care, Immigration, Environmental, Government Relations and Administrative, Retail Distribution, Communications, Sports and Entertainment, Trade and Professional, Alternative Dispute Resolution, Venture Capital, Insurance Defense, Law Firm Disputes, Divorce and Family Law, Construction Law.

LAW FIRM ALLIANCES/ASSOCIATIONS: **LEX MUNDI**

PARTNERS

REGINA W. CALABRO, born Bristol, Tennessee, August 9, 1965; admitted to bar, 1993, Illinois; 1994, North Carolina, U.S. District Court, Eastern and Middle Districts of North Carolina and U.S. District Court, Northern District of Illinois; 1997, U.S. Court of Appeals, Seventh Circuit and U.S. District Court, Northern District of Illinois including Trial Bar; 2000, Tennessee and U.S. District Court, Eastern District of Tennessee. *Education:* University of Tennessee at Knoxville (B.S., with honors, 1987); DePaul University (J.D., 1993). Order of the Barristers. Editor, Lead Articles, Journal of Art and Entertainment Law. Member, Moot Court Society. Past-Secretary/Treasurer, Bristol Bar Association (Virginia). *Member:* Chicago, Illinois State, Tennessee, and American Bar Associations; American Health Lawyers Association. ***PRACTICE AREAS:*** Labor and Employment. ***Email:*** rwcalabro@michaelbest.com

LISA C. CHILDS, admitted to bar, 1997, Illinois; U.S. District Court, Northern District of Illinois; U.S. Court of Appeals, Federal Circuit; registered to practice before U.S. Patent and Trademark Office. *Education:* Rice University (B.A., 1987); North Carolina State University (Ph.D., 1994); Loyola University (J.D., cum laude, 1997). Phi Lambda Upsilon; Alpha Sigma Nu. Member, Loyola University of Chicago Law Journal, 1995-1997. Author: "Protecting Your Seed Line Through Legal Channels," Seed World, 1997; "Plant Variety Protection Demonstrated," Seed World, 1997; "Rite-Hite Corp. v. Kelley Co: The Federal Circuit Awards Damages for a Patent Not In Suit," Loyola University of Chicago Law Journal, 1996. Co-Author, "Examination and Cross-Examination of Witnesses, The Inventor, Experts, Third Parties," Chapter 11, Patent Litigation, Practicing Law Institute, 1994. *Member:* American Bar Association; Intellectual Property Law Association of Chicago; Association of University Technology Managers. ***PRACTICE AREAS:*** Patents; Trademarks; Copyrights; Unfair Competition; Litigation. ***Email:*** lcchilds@michaelbest.com

RONALD S. COPE, admitted to bar, 1964, Illinois; U.S. District Court, Northern District of Illinois including Trial Bar; U.S. Court of Appeals, Fifth and Seventh Circuits; 1971, U.S. Supreme Court. *Education:* University of Chicago (B.A., 1961; J.D., 1963). *Member:* Chicago (Member, Local Government Committee), Illinois State and American (Member, Urban, State, and Local Government Section) Bar Associations; Illinois Municipal League (Member, Home Rule Attorneys Committee). ***PRACTICE AREAS:*** Land Use; Local Government; Finance. ***Email:*** rscope@michaelbest.com

G. A. FINCH, born Tacoma, Washington, May 4, 1955; admitted to bar, 1982, Illinois; 1984, District of Columbia; U.S. District Court, Northern District of Illinois including Trial Bar. *Education:* Amherst College (B.A., 1977); University of Michigan (J.D., 1980). Lambda Alpha International Land Economics Society. Salzburg Seminar Fellow in International Trade. Leadership Greater Chicago Fellow. Illinois Super Lawyer. Illinois Leading Lawyer. Recipient, The Chicago Jaycees Ten Outstanding Young Citizens Award. Judicial Law Clerk to Chief Judge James B. Parsons, U.S. District Court, Northern District of Illinois. Author: "Employment Contracts: More Than Just a Handshake," Consulting-Specifying Engineer, June 2005; "Attorney Billing Practices: What is a Consumer of Legal Services to Think," Illinois State Bar Association Real Property Newsletter, August 2003; "Employment Contracts, What You Should Know," Midwest Engineer, May/June 2003; "Talking Politics, Why Do We Need a Robust CTA? Entire Region's Health Depends on It," Crain's Chicago Business, December 16, 1996; "Lawyer's Forum: 'Block 37' Just One Piece of North Loop Project," Chicago Daily Law Bulletin 6, July 1, 1996; "Talking Development, Mickey on State: What Dealmakers Can Expect," Crain's Chicago Business, May 13, 1996; "Talking Politics, What Should Be Done With Block 37? Keep it Vacant," Crain's Chicago Business, February 5, 1996; "Effective Meetings," CBA Record, January 1990; "Illinois Public Bidding Statute: The Pitfalls," 78 Illinois Bar Journal 402, 1990; "Understanding the Other Sector in the Regulatory and Market Environments," The Journal of Real Estate Development, Spring 1988; "A Primer on Illinois Public Mechanics Liens," 75 Illinois Bar Journal 500, 1987; "Going to Leader School Makes Chicago Stronger, Your Turn," Crain's Chicago Business, November 2, 1987; "American Antidumping Law & Japanese Imports," Spring-Autumn Papers, Spring, 1981. Former Board Member: Illinois Human Rights Commission (Commissioner); Chicago Area Council Boy Scouts of America (Vice President); St. Joseph Seminary of Loyola (Chairman); University of Michigan Rackham Graduate School; Chicago Housing Authority Pension Fund; Commonwealth School (Boston); Journal of Real Estate Development; Journal of Real Estate Finance; Illinois Bar Journal (Secretary); CBA Record; Pegasus Players; Amherst Club of Chicago (Vice President); Chicago Sinfonietta; League of United Latin American Citizens Council 313 (Vice President). Past Member: Chicago Bar Association Real Property Committee Executive Council, 1987-1999; Cook County Recorder's Blue Ribbon Committee, 1989; Governor's Steering Committee on Housing, 1991; Cook County Board President's Transition Team, 1994; Illinois Agriculture Export Advisory Committee, 1994-1997; Governor Ryan's Transition Team, 1998; Governor Blagojevich's Transition Team, 2002; Lieutenant Governor Pat Quinn's Energy Working Group, 2003-2004; Illinois Delegation to 2004 National Republican Convention. Chicago Housing Authority General Counsel, 1999-2002. City of Chicago Deputy Planning Commissioner, 1986-1989. *Member:* Cook County Bar Association. ***PRACTICE AREAS:*** Corporate; Real Estate; Commercial; Construction; Government. ***Email:*** gafinch@michaelbest.com

JUDITH L. GRUBNER, born Detroit, Michigan, July 6, 1951; admitted to bar, 1976, District of Columbia; 1977, U.S. District Court, District of Columbia and U.S. Court of Appeals, District of Columbia Circuit; 1981, Illinois; 1982, U.S. District Court, Northern District of Illinois including Trial Bar and U.S. Court of Appeals, Seventh Circuit; 1993, U.S. Court of Appeals, Federal Circuit; 2001, U.S. District Court, Eastern District of Michigan. *Education:* Oberlin College (A.B., with honors in Economics, 1973); George Washington University (J.D., with honors, 1976). Editorial Board, The Intellectual Property Strategist, Law Journal Newsletter Publishing. Editor: "Flying Solo," 3d Ed., American Bar Association. Author: "Know the Law before Designing PR Games," O'Dwyer's PR Services Report, February 2004; "Suing Rebuilders for Trademark and Patent Infringement," Intellectual Property Strategist, May 2002; "Ensuring the Legality of a Company's Promotional Games," Start-Up and Emerging Companies Strategist, February 2002. *Member:* American Bar Association (Former Council Member and Co-Chair, Publishing Board of the Law Practice Management Section; Patent, Trademark and Copyright Section); Intellectual Property Law Association of Chicago (President, Educational Foundation). ***PRACTICE AREAS:*** Intellectual Property; Unfair Competition Law; Sweepstakes Law; Litigation; Licensing. ***Email:*** jlgrubner@michaelbest.com

KERRYANN M. HAASE, born Waukesha, Wisconsin, December 5, 1969; admitted to bar, 1996, Illinois; 1997, Wisconsin, U.S. District Court, Northern District of Illinois and U.S. Court of Appeals, Seventh Circuit. *Education:* University of Wisconsin, Madison (B.A., 1992); John Marshall Law School (J.D., 1996). Selected as one of Law Bulletin Publishing's "40 Illinois Attorneys Under Forty to Watch.". ***PRACTICE AREAS:*** Employment Relations Law; Labor Law. ***Email:*** kmhaase@michaelbest.com

LAUREL A. HASKELL, admitted to bar, 1997, Illinois, U.S. District Court, Northern District of Illinois and U.S. Court of Appeals, Seventh Circuit. *Education:* James Madison University (B.S., magna cum laude, 1992); University of Minnesota (J.D., magna cum laude, 1997). ***PRACTICE AREAS:*** Litigation. ***Email:*** lahaskell@michaelbest.com

PETER F. HERZOG, born Milwaukee, Wisconsin, April 20, 1959; admitted to bar, 1985, Illinois. *Education:* University of Wisconsin at Madison (B.S., 1982); Chicago-Kent College of Law (J.D., 1985). Co-Author: "Public/Private Construction Projects," Construction Superconference, San Francisco, CA, 1996; "Negotiating a Construction Contract Termination," ABA Forum on Construction Industry, Dallas, TX, 1996; "Minority/Majority Joint Ventures," Construction Superconference, San Francisco, CA, 1995; "Current Techniques of Joint Venturing," Construction Superconference, New York, NY, 1994. *Member:* Chicago (Member, Real Estate Committee; Past Chair, Construction Law Committee; Past Chair, Mechanics Lien Committee) and American (Member, Forum Committee, Construction, 1985—) Bar Associations. ***PRACTICE AREAS:*** Construction Law; Mechanics Liens; Litigation. ***Email:*** pfherzog@michaelbest.com

DANIEL A. KAUFMAN, born Chicago, Illinois, February 21, 1961; admitted to bar, 1987, Illinois, U.S. District Court, Northern District of Illinois and U.S. Court of Appeals, Seventh Circuit and U.S. Supreme Court. *Education:* Amherst College (B.A., with honors, 1983); University of Chicago (J.D., 1986). Phi Beta Kappa. Judicial Law Clerk for the Hon. Charles L. Levin, Supreme Court of Michigan. Selected to *Law Bulletin Publishing's* list of "40 Illinois Attorneys Under 40 Years Old to Watch," 2000. *Member:* Chicago and American (Member, Sections on: Employment Law; Litigation) Bar Associations; National Association of College and University Attorneys. ***PRACTICE AREAS:*** Labor and Employment Law; Litigation; Education Law. ***Email:*** dakaufman@michaelbest.com

CHARLES A. LAFF, born Chicago, Illinois, February 17, 1934; admitted to bar, 1959, Illinois, U.S. District Court, Northern District of Illinois, including Trial Bar; 1960, U.S. Court of Appeals, 7th, 9th and 11th Circuits; 1961, Florida; 1972, U.S. Supreme Court; 1982, U.S. Court of Appeals for the Federal Circuit; U.S. District Court, Eastern District of Michigan; 1997, U.S. District Court, Eastern District of Wisconsin; registered to practice before U.S. Patent and Trademark Office. *Education:* Purdue University (B.S., Ch.E., 1955); Harvard University (J.D., 1958). Co-Author: "Further Unraveling of Sears—Compco: Of Patches, Paladin and Laurel and Hardy," 7 Loyola University Law Journal 33, 1976 (reprinted in 66 Trademark Reporter 427, 1976); "Examination and Cross-Examination of Witnesses, The Inventor, Experts, Third Parties," with Lisa C. Childs, Ph.D., Practicing Law Institute Patent Litigation, Volume 1, 1994; "Handling Opinions of Counsel in Patent Trials," ALI-ABA Course of Study, Trial of a Patent Case, Chicago, Illinois, September 29-30, 1994; "Trade Dress: A Broad Cloak," The Plastics Distributor & Fabricator Magazine, Volume 18, Number 5, September/October 1997. Lecturer: "Science, Law and Technology," Illinois Math and Science Academy, 2000, 2001; "Beyond Trademarks," Annual INTA Meeting, 2001. Adjunct Professor, Intellectual Property Law, Loyola University of Chicago, School of Law, 1974-1998. *Member:* American (Member, Sections on: Patent, Trademark and Copyright Law; Litigation) and International Bar Associations; American Intellectual Property Law Association; Intellectual Property Law Association of Chicago (Vice President, 1991; President-Elect, 1992; President, 1993); International Trademark Association. ***PRACTICE AREAS:*** Patent, Trademark, Copyright and Unfair Competition Law; Litigation. ***Email:*** calaff@michaelbest.com

LAURA SHROYER LISS, admitted to bar, 1996, Illinois and U.S. District Court, Northern District of Illinois; 1999, Trial Bar. *Education:* University of Michigan (B.A., 1992); Chicago-Kent College of Law (J.D., 1995). Frequent speaker on employment law

(This Listing Continued)

and human resources issues. Selected as one of "40 Illinois Attorneys Under 40 Years Old To Watch," Law Bulletin Publishing, 2005. Volunteer and Junior Board Member, Working in the School (WITS - a tutoring and mentoring program in the Chicago Public Schools). ***PRACTICE AREAS:*** Labor and Employment Law. ***Email:*** lsliss@michaelbest.com

JOHN J. McHUGH, born Chicago, Illinois, April 2, 1934; admitted to bar, 1961, Illinois. *Education:* Loyola University, Chicago (B.S., 1956; J.D., cum laude, 1961). Alpha Sigma Nu; National Blue Key Society. Editor-in-Chief, Loyola University Law Review, 1960-1961. *Member:* Chicago, Illinois State and American Bar Associations; United States Supreme Court Bar Association; Lawyers Club of the City of Chicago.

BRIDGET M. O'KEEFE, born Chicago, Illinois, March 6, 1959; admitted to bar, 1987, Illinois. *Education:* St. Mary's College (B.A., 1981); Catholic University of America (M.A., 1984); Georgetown University (J.D., cum laude, 1987). Member: Chicago Real Estate Executive Women; Board of Advisors, Catholic Charities; The Economic Club of Chicago. Board Member, Parkways Foundation. Member, Leadership Greater Chicago, 1995-1996 Class. Former Board Member, Old St. Patrick's Church. *Member:* Chicago Bar Association. ***PRACTICE AREAS:*** Zoning, Planning and Land Use; Government; Regulatory Law; Historic Preservation. ***Email:*** bmokeefer@michaelbest.com

LARRY L. SARET, born Chicago, Illinois, August 27, 1950; admitted to bar, 1975, Illinois and U.S. District Court, Northern District of Illinois; 1976, U.S. Court of Appeals, 7th Circuit; 1982, U.S. Court of Appeals for the Federal Circuit; 1985, U.S. Supreme Court; registered to practice before U.S. Patent and Trademark Office. *Education:* Cornell University (B.A., Physics, 1972); Loyola University (J.D., 1975). Student Articles Editor, Loyola University Law Journal, 1974-1975. Adjunct Professor, Intellectual Property Law, Loyola University of Chicago School of Law, 1996-1997. *Member:* Intellectual Property Law Association of Chicago; AIPLA. ***PRACTICE AREAS:*** Patent Law; Trademark Law; Copyright Law; Unfair Competition Law; Litigation. ***Email:*** llsaret@michaelbest.com

JOSEPH F. SCHMIDT, born Chicago, Illinois, March 29, 1948; admitted to bar, 1973, Illinois and U.S. District Court, Northern District of Illinois, including Trial Bar, U.S. Supreme Court, U.S. Court of Appeals, 7th Circuit and U.S. Court of Appeals for the Federal Circuit. *Education:* Loyola University (B.A., 1970); Illinois Institute of Technology/Chicago-Kent College of Law (J.D., 1973). Co-Author: "Dilution Differences" - Analyzing TTAB and Supreme Court Standards, Intellectual Property Strategist, February 2004. Adjunct Professor, Program in Intellectual Property Law, Chicago-Kent College of Law, Illinois Institute of Technology. *Member:* Chicago, Illinois State and American Bar Associations; Intellectual Property Law Association of Chicago. ***PRACTICE AREAS:*** Trademark Law; Copyright Law; False Advertising; Unfair Competition Law; Litigation; Appellate Practice. ***Email:*** jfschmidt@michaelbest.com

MARTIN L. STERN, born Chicago, Illinois, May 26, 1952; admitted to bar, 1977, Illinois, U.S. District Court, Northern District of Illinois, including Trial Bar and U.S. Court of Appeals, 7th Circuit; 1982, U.S. Court of Appeals for the Federal Circuit; 1986, U.S. Supreme Court; registered to practice before U.S. Patent and Trademark Office. *Education:* Illinois Institute of Technology (B.S., with high honors, 1974); Northwestern University (J.D., cum laude, 1977). Tau Beta Pi; Chi Epsilon. ***PRACTICE AREAS:*** Patent Law; Trademark Law; Copyright Law; Unfair Competition Law; Litigation. ***Email:*** mlstern@michaelbest.com

MICHAEL A. STIEGEL, born Greenfield, Massachusetts, September 15, 1946; admitted to bar, 1971, Illinois; 1985, Wisconsin; 1987, Florida. *Education:* University of Arizona (B.A., 1968); Loyola University (J.D., cum laude, 1971). Comment Editor, Loyola University Law Review. Law Clerk, Judge Wm. Lynch, U.S. District Court, Northern District of Illinois, 1971-1972. Author: "Ex Parte Communications When a Corporate Litigant Is Involved," Business Laws, Inc., 1992; "Spoliation of Evidence in Civil Actions," ABA Monograph, 1993; Punitive Damages in Arbitration, an Approach to Review of Clearly Erroneous Awards," ABA Litigation Section, 1997; "30 (b)(6) Depositions-A Powerful Tool in a Litigation Arsenal," Tips From the Trenches, ABA Litigation Section, 2000. Author: "The Art of the Covenant," Workforce Magazine, July 2004. Adjunct Professor of Law, Northwestern University School of Law, 1994—. Appointed Northern District of Illinois Federal Court Merit Section Committee for Magistrate Vacancy, 1996-1998. Elected Economic Club of Chicago, 2001. *Member:* Chicago (Chair, Large Firm Committee 2003-2005), Illinois State and American (Member, ABA Sections of: Litigation, Business Law and Labor and Employment Law; Section Committees; Litigation Section; Member, Council, 1997-2000; Budget Officer, 2000-2002; Elected Revenue Officer, 2002-2004; Executive Committee, 2000— National CLE Programs Committee, 1995-1997; Trial Evidence; Co-Chair, 1991-1995; Labor and Employment Law, Section Committee on Equal Employment Opportunities; Lawyers Conference Standards for Admissibility of Technologically Sophisticated Evidence, ABA Judicial Administration Division-Lawyers Conference; Appointed to National Conference of Lawyers and CPAs) Bar Associations; The Florida Bar; State Bar of Wisconsin; Trial Attorneys of America; National Safety Council (ABA Litigation Section Advisor to the National Conference of Commissioners on Uniform State Laws, Drafting Committee on Model Law for Punitive Damages, 1994-1996). ***PRACTICE AREAS:*** Trial Practice; Alternative Dispute Resolution; Business Law; Tort Law; Employment Discrimination Law. ***Email:*** mastiegel@michaelbest.com

SARAH E. SWARTZMEYER, born Buffalo, New York, March 10, 1969; admitted to bar, 1995, New York and Illinois; 2004, Wisconsin. *Education:* State University of New York at Stony Brook (B.A., 1991); State University of New York at Buffalo (J.D., 1994); Loyola University (LL.M., in Healthcare, 1996). ***PRACTICE AREAS:*** Health Care Law. ***Email:*** seswartzmeyer@michaelbest.com

STEVEN J. TEPLINSKY, born Chicago, Illinois, June 13, 1953; admitted to bar, 1978, Illinois, U.S. Supreme Court and U.S. Court of Appeals, 7th and 8th Circuits; 1979, U.S. District Court, Central District of Illinois; 1980, U.S. District Court, Northern District of Illinois; 1982, U.S. District Court, Northern District of Illinois including Trial Bar. *Education:* Northern Illinois University (B.A., cum laude, 1974); Chicago-Kent College of Law, Illinois Institute of Technology (J.D., with honors, 1978). Frequent speaker on various employment issues. Instructor, Legal Writing, Chicago-Kent College of Law, 1977-1978; Adjunct Professor, The John Marshall Law School, 1984-1989. Assistant Attorney General, Illinois, 1978-1980. President, Northwest Suburban Jewish Community Center, 1990-1991; 1992-1994. *Member:* Illinois State (Member, Sections on: Labor and Employment) and American (Member, Sections on Labor Law and Litigation) Bar Associations; Appellate Lawyers Association of Illinois; Transportation Lawyers Association. ***PRACTICE AREAS:*** Labor and Employment; Appellate Practice. ***Email:*** sjteplinsky@michaelbest.com

OF COUNSEL

LOUIS ALTMAN, admitted to bar, 1959, New York; 1970, Connecticut, U.S. District Court, District of Connecticut, Southern and Eastern Districts of New York and U.S. Court of Appeals, 2nd Circuit; 1972, Illinois; 1975, U.S. Court of Appeals, 7th Circuit; 1980, U.S. Supreme Court; 1982, U.S. Court of Appeals for the Federal Circuit; registered to practice before U.S. Patent and Trademark Office. *Education:* Cornell University (A.B., 1955); Harvard University (LL.B., 1958). Associate Professor, 1976-1979 and Adjunct Professor, 1979-1996, John Marshall Law School. Adjunct Professor, Loyola University Law School, 1997. Recipient, Gerald Rose Memorial Award, 1988. Author: Callmann, Unfair Competition, Trademarks and Monopolies (4th Edition), 1981. *Member:* Chicago (Chairman, Patent, Trademark and Copyright Committee, 1982-1983) and American Bar Associations; Intellectual Patent Law Association of Chicago (Director, 1978-1979); New York Patent, Trademark and Copyright Law Association; Connecticut Patent Law Association; American Intellectual Property Law Association; United States Trademark Association; Institute of Electrical and Electronic Engineers. ***PRACTICE AREAS:*** Patent Law; Trademark Law; Copyright Law; Unfair Competition Law; Litigation. ***Email:*** laltman@michaelbest.com

JULIAN L. BERMAN, admitted to bar, 1948, Wisconsin; 1960, Illinois. *Education:* University of Wisconsin (Ph.B., 1943; LL.B., 1948; LL.M., 1949). Phi Alpha Delta. Law Clerk for Judge Eugene Black, U.S. Tax Court, 1949-51. Trial Attorney and Special Assistant to Regional Counsel, Office of Chief Counsel, Internal Revenue Service, 1951-61. *Member:* American Bar Association (Committee on Individual Income Tax Problems, 1981—); Chicago Council of Lawyers. ***PRACTICE AREAS:*** Federal Taxation; Estate Planning; Probate; Business. ***Email:*** jlberman@michaelbest.com

KENNETH H. DENBERG, born Chicago, Illinois, January 3, 1935; admitted to bar, 1959, Illinois; 1960, U.S. District Court, Northern District of Illinois; 1967, U.S. Court of Appeals, Seventh Circuit. *Education:* University of Illinois (B.A., 1956); DePaul University College of Law (J.D., 1959). Author: "Conventional Subrogation," Chicago Daily Law Bulletin, 1998. ***PRACTICE AREAS:*** Business; Corporate; Real Estate; Alcoholic Beverage Control. ***Email:*** khdenberg@michaelbest.com

S. RICHARD FINE, born Chicago, Illinois, March 19, 1925; admitted to bar, 1950, Illinois. *Education:* University of Chicago (Ph.B., 1946; J.D., 1950). *Member:* Chicago (Federal Tax Committee, 1964) and American (Section on Taxation) Bar Associations; Chicago Council of Lawyers. ***PRACTICE AREAS:*** Federal Taxation; Business. ***Email:*** srfine@michaelbest.com

JULIAN J. FRAZIN, born Chicago, Illinois, May 29, 1930; admitted to bar, 1956, Illinois; 1957, U.S. District Court, Northern District of Illinois; 1970, U.S. Supreme Court. *Education:* University of Illinois, Chicago; Roosevelt University (B.A., Political Science, 1952); Northwestern University School of Law (J.D., 1955). Columnist, Chicago Lawyer. Principal Writer and Producer, Chicago Bar Association, "Christmas Spirits," Political and Social Satire Revue, 1965—. Speaker: U.S. Information Agency, East China School of Politics And Law; International Conference on Crime And Justice, Shanghai, China; Chicago Bar Association, Matrimonial Law Committee; Chicago Bar Association, Justice for Youth Symposium. Former Judge, Circuit Court of Cook County, Illinois, 1990-1998: Civil Trial Section (Jury and Non-Jury) Municipal Department, 1990-1993; Child Protection Division of the Juvenile Court, 1993; Trial and Post Decree Motion Section of the Domestic Relations Division, 1994-1997; Traffic Division, 1997-1998. Adjunct Lecturer, University of Illinois, Chicago, 2000. Appointed, Illinois Supreme Court Planning and Oversight Committee for a Judicial Performance Evaluation Program, December, 1996. Member, University of Illinois, Chicago, Scholarship Association. Recipient, Chancellor's Award, University of Illinois, Chicago. Board of Directors, Illinois Parents' Care and Share; Participant, Renaissance Weekend; Founder, Herman Kogan Awards for Outstanding Reporting on Legal Issues. *Member:* Chicago Bar Association (Former Officer and Member of the Board of Managers); American Judges Association; Illinois Judges Association; The Law Club of Chicago; Decalogue Society of Lawyers. ***PRACTICE AREAS:*** Business Law; Civil Practice. ***Email:*** jjfrazin@michaelbest.com

RICHARD L. FREEMAN, born Chicago, Illinois October 29, 1932; admitted to bar, 1958, Illinois. *Education:* Harvard University (A.B., cum laude, 1954); Yale University (LL.B., 1957). *Member:* Chicago Bar Association (Committee on Probate Practice, 1974—; Chairman, Division V, 1985-86). Fellow, American College of Trust and Estate Counsel. ***PRACTICE AREAS:*** Probate; Estate Planning. ***Email:*** rlfreeman@michaelbest.com

STEVEN B. RANDALL, born Chicago, Illinois, September 14, 1936; admitted to bar, 1962, Illinois; 1964, U.S. District Court, Northern District of Illinois; 1977, U.S. Tax Court; 1991, U.S. Court of Appeals, Seventh Circuit. *Education:* Illinois Wesleyan University (B.S., 1958); University of Wisconsin-Madison (J.D., 1961). *Member:* Chicago (Corporate Law Committee) and American (Forum on the Entertainment and Sports Industries) Bar Associations. ***PRACTICE AREAS:*** Corporate; Securities; Business; Internet Law; Electronic Commerce; Media Law; Entertainment; Publishing. ***Email:*** sbrandall@michaelbest.com

WILLIAM L. SHARP, born Detroit, Michigan, December 2, 1939; admitted to bar, 1964, Illinois; 1966, U.S. District Court, Northern District of Illinois; 1974, U.S. Court of Appeals, Seventh Circuit. *Education:* Yale University (B.A., cum laude, 1961); University of Chicago (J.D., 1964). Lecturer, Joint Ventures for Financial Institutions, Work-out Techniques and Practices for Financial Institutions. ***PRACTICE AREAS:*** Real Estate; Business. ***Email:*** wlsharp@michaelbest.com

ASSOCIATES

GRETCHEN M. HOSTY, admitted to bar, 2003, Illinois, U.S. District Court, Northern District of Illinois and U.S. Court of Appeals, Seventh and Federal Circuits; registered to practice before U.S. Patent and Trademark Office. *Education:* University of Illinois (B.S., 2000); Illinois Institute of Technology, Chicago-Kent College of Law (J.D., 2003). Contributing Author: "Intellectual Property Law in Cyberspace," BNA Books, 2002 Supplement,

(This Listing Continued)

MICHAEL BEST & FRIEDRICH LLP, Chicago—Continued

2004 Supplement, 2005 Supplement; Co-Author: "Dilution Differences: Analyzing TTAB and Supreme Court Standards," Intellectual Property Strategist, February 2004. ***PRACTICE AREAS:*** Intellectual Property. ***Email:*** gmhosty@michaelbest.com

RAYMOND M. KRAUZE, admitted to bar, 2003, Illinois; U.S. District Court, Northern District of Illinois. *Education:* Boston University (B.A., Latin Honors, 1995); Georgetown University (J.D., 2003). ***PRACTICE AREAS:*** Litigation. ***Email:*** rmkrauze@michaelbest.com

CHRISTOPHER R. PARKER, admitted to bar, 1999, Illinois and U.S. District Court, Northern District of Illinois. *Education:* University of Wisconsin-Madison (B.A., 1992); University of Illinois (J.D., 1999). *Member:* Chicago, Illinois State and American Bar Associations. ***PRACTICE AREAS:*** Litigation. ***Email:*** crparker@michaelbest.com

BRIAN P. PAUL, admitted to bar, 2003, Illinois; U.S. District Court, Northern District of Illinois; U.S. District Court, Central District of Illinois. *Education:* Emory University (B.A., 2000); Vanderbilt University (J.D., 2003). ***PRACTICE AREAS:*** Labor and Employment Law. ***Email:*** bppaul@michaelbest.com

SUSAN D. REINECKE, admitted to bar, 1999, Illinois and U.S. District Court, Northern District of Illinois; registered to practice before U.S. Patent and Trademark Office. *Education:* Temple University (B.S., cum laude, 1988, M.S., Engineering, 1990); State University of New York at Buffalo (J.D., magna cum laude, 1999). ***PRACTICE AREAS:*** Intellectual Property. ***Email:*** sdreinecki@michaelbest.com

JAMIE A. ROBINSON, admitted to bar, 1999, Illinois and Wisconsin; U.S. District Court, Northern District of Illinois and U.S. Court of Appeals, Seventh Circuit. *Education:* University of Wisconsin-Madison (B.A., 1994; J.D., cum laude, 1999). ***PRACTICE AREAS:*** Litigation. ***Email:*** jarobinson@michaelbest.com

STEPHEN C. SMITH, born Hartford, Connecticut, May 3, 1950; admitted to bar, 2003, Illinois; U.S. District Court, Northern and Central Districts of Illinois; registered to practice before U.S. Patent and Trademark Office. *Education:* University of Illinois (B.S., Electrical Engineering, 1985; M.S., Electrical Engineering, 1986; J.D., 2003). Illinois Connection Ambassador, University of Illinois Alumni Association. Member: Institute of Electrical and Electronic Engineers (Laser and Electro-Optical Society, Electron Devices Society, Electronic Materials Division, Communications Society). [U. S. Air Force]. ***PRACTICE AREAS:*** Intellectual Property; Patent Prosecution. ***Email:*** scsmith@michaelbest.com

REPRESENTATIVE CLIENTS: Alliance Airlines; American National Bank and Trust Company of Chicago; Clear Channel Outdoor, Inc. (f/k/a Eller Media); Com-Pac International, Inc.; Blue Cross Blue Shield Association; Ecker Enterprises Inc.; Lincoln Property Company; Rush-Presbyterian-St. Luke's Medical Center; Storck, U.S.A.; Textron, Inc.; United Insurance Company of America; Unitrin, Inc.; University Healthcare Consortium; Wheaton Franciscan Services, Inc.

MICHAELS & MAY, P.C.

SEARS TOWER, SUITE 5620
233 SOUTH WACKER DRIVE
CHICAGO, ILLINOIS 60606
Telephone: 312-428-4720
Facsimile: 312-575-8679
URL: http://www.michaelsmay.com

Insurance Coverage, Commercial Litigation, Excess and Reinsurance, Environmental, Professional Liability Insurance Coverage, Directors and Officers Liability, Complex and General Civil Litigation, Insurance Bad Faith, Appellate Practice, International Dispute Resolution, Alternative Dispute Resolution, Class Action Defense, Intellectual Property Litigation, Product Liability.

MEMBERS

JAN M. MICHAELS, born New York, New York, March 6, 1963; admitted to bar, 1989, Illinois and U.S. District Court, Northern District of Illinois; 1998, U.S. District Court, Northern District of Illinois including Trial Bar. *Education:* State University of New York at Albany (B.A., magna cum laude, 1986); University of Notre Dame (J.D., magna cum laude, 1989). Recipient, American Jurisprudence Award, Business Organizations. Author: "Courts Stress Importance of Clear Clauses," National Law Journal, Sept. 22, 1997. Arbitrator, National Futures Association. *Member:* Chicago, Illinois State and American Bar Associations. ***REPORTED CASES:*** Harvard Indus., Inc. v. Aetna Cas. & Sur., 642 A.2d 438 (Super. Ct. N.J., 1993). ***PRACTICE AREAS:*** Commercial Litigation; Insurance Coverage; Trademarks; Class Action Defense; Alternative Dispute Resolution.

THEODORE J. MAY, born Cincinnati, Ohio, February 15, 1961; admitted to bar, 1987, Illinois and U.S. District Court, Northern District of Illinois. *Education:* University of Minnesota (B.A., 1983; J.D., cum laude, 1987). Associate Editor, University of Minnesota Law Review, 1986-1987. *Member:* Chicago and American Bar Associations. ***PRACTICE AREAS:*** Insurance Coverage; Excess and Reinsurance; Insurance Litigation; International Dispute Resolution; Directors and Officers Liability; Professional Errors and Omissions Liability; Commercial Litigation.

ALFRED L. BUCHANAN, born Lexington, Kentucky, September 1, 1959; admitted to bar, 1990, Illinois and U.S. District Court, Northern District of Illinois. *Education:* University of Kentucky (B.A., with distinction, 1987; J.D., with highest honors, 1990). Order of the Coif. Recipient: CJS Award for Significant Legal Scholarship; West Hornbook Award for Outstanding Scholastic Achievement; American Jurisprudence Awards in Civil Procedure I, Civil Procedure II, Administrative Law and Federal Courts. Member, Board of Editorial Advisors, Journal of Natural Resources and Environmental Law. Author: "Evolving RICO Issues for the Environmental/Natural Resources Practitioner," 6 Journal of Mineral Law & Policy, 1990-1991; "United States vs. Whizco: Are SMCRA Obligations Dischargeable Under the Bankruptcy Code?" 5 Journal of Mineral Law & Policy, 1989-1990. Fayette County Constable, First District, Lexington, Kentucky, 1986-1990. *Member:* Chicago Bar Association (Member, Committee on Insurance Law, 1993—). ***PRACTICE AREAS:*** Insurance Coverage; Complex Litigation.

(This Listing Continued)

STEVEN SCHULWOLF, born Chicago, Illinois, March 10, 1969; admitted to bar, 1994, Illinois. *Education:* University of Illinois (B.A., summa cum laude, 1991); University of Michigan (J.D., cum laude, 1994). Phi Beta Kappa. Teacher, University of Plodiv, 1998-2000. *Member:* Chicago Bar Association. ***LANGUAGES:*** Bulgarian. ***PRACTICE AREAS:*** Insurance Coverage; Litigation; Business Litigation.

ASSOCIATES

SCOTT M. SALERNO, born Chicago, Illinois, November 1, 1972; admitted to bar, 1998, Illinois; 1999, U.S. District Court, Northern District of Illinois. *Education:* Southern Illinois University (B.S., 1994); DePaul University (J.D., 1998). ***PRACTICE AREAS:*** Insurance Coverage; Insurance Defense; Commercial Litigation.

JOHN M. DUCZYNSKI, born Detroit, Michigan, November 12, 1948; admitted to bar, 1976, Illinois and U.S. District Court, Northern District of Illinois; 1996, U.S. Court of Appeals, 6th Circuit. *Education:* University of Michigan (A.B., 1973; J.D., cum laude, 1976). *Member:* Chicago and American Bar Associations. ***PRACTICE AREAS:*** Insurance Coverage; Professional Liability Insurance Coverage; Excess and Reinsurance; Insurance Litigation; Insurance Coverage Defense.

KATHRYN A'HEARN, born Indianapolis, Indiana; admitted to bar, 2003, Illinois. *Education:* Indiana University (B.S., 2000); Loyola University (J.D., 2003). ***PRACTICE AREAS:*** Insurance Defense; Commercial Litigation; Insurance Coverage.

STEPHEN A. SKARDON, born Dayton, Ohio, December 15, 1972; admitted to bar, 2003, Illinois. *Education:* The Ohio State University (B.A., 1995); University of Illinois (J.D., 2002). ***PRACTICE AREAS:*** Insurance Coverage; Excess and Reinsurance; Insurance Defense.

NEAL F. THOMPSON, born 1952; admitted to bar, 1981, Illinois. *Education:* University of Illinois (B.A.); Northwestern University (J.D.). ***PRACTICE AREAS:*** Commercial Litigation; Insurance Coverage; Insurance Defense.

JOHN A. LEE, born Chicago, Illinois, March 29, 1959; admitted to bar, 1998, Illinois. *Education:* University of Wisconsin (B.S., 1985; M.S., 1988); DePaul University College of Law (J.D., 1998). Author: "Special Report: Environmental Audit Immunity Laws: A State-By-State Comparison," 28 Env't Rep. (BNA) No. 7, at 331-56 (June 13, 1997), Reprinted in: 21 Chem. Reg. Rep. (BNA) No. 14, at 381-406 (July 4, 1997); (Law Research.com's Article of the Month for August, 1998); "The Underlying Legal Theory To Support a Well-Defined Human Right to a Healthy Environment as a Principle of Customary International Law," 25 Columbia Journal of Environmental Law, No. 2, at 283-346 (Spring 2000); "Environmental Audit Immunity Laws and Self-Disclosure Policies: A State-By-State Comparison," Env't Rep. (BNA), June 2004. ***PRACTICE AREAS:*** Insurance; Human Rights; Environmental Law.

MICHAEL McNAUGHTON, born Superior, Wisconsin, August 3, 1972; admitted to bar, 2000, Illinois; 2002, Minnesota. *Education:* University of Chicago (B.A., Political Science, 1994); Chicago-Kent College of Law, Illinois Institute of Technology (J.D., 2000). *Member:* Chicago Bar Association. ***PRACTICE AREAS:*** Insurance Coverage; Insurance Litigation; Commercial Litigation. ***Email:*** mmcnaughton@michaelsmay.com

WILLIAM D. ELLISON, born Moline, Illinois, December 29, 1951; admitted to bar, 1988, Illinois and U.S. District Court, District of Kansas; 1993, U.S. District Court, Northern District of Illinois and U.S. District Court, Western District of Missouri; 2003, Missouri. *Education:* Augustana College (B.A., 1974); Northern Illinois University (J.D., magna cum laude, 1988). ***PRACTICE AREAS:*** Insurance Coverage Litigation; Business Litigation. ***Email:*** wellison@michaelsmay.com

---

LAWRENCE T. MILLER

Established in 1978

230 WEST MONROE STREET, SUITE 250
CHICAGO, ILLINOIS 60606
Telephone: 312-236-2431
Fax: 312-641-6174
Email: ltmjd@aol.com

Civil Trial and Appellate Practice, Litigation, Business Law, Commercial Litigation, Creditors' Rights, Corporate Law, Real Estate Law, Elder Law, Trusts and Estates, Wills and Probate, Administrative Law, Medical Malpractice, Personal Injury, Premises Liability, Professional Liability, Libel, Slander, Insurance, Labor and Employment Law, Election, Campaign and Political.

LAWRENCE T. MILLER, born Oak Park, Illinois, November 9, 1942; admitted to bar, 1969, Illinois. *Education:* Saint Meinrad College; Marquette University (B.A., 1965); University of Illinois (J.D., 1968). *Member:* Chicago and Illinois State Bar Associations; Illinois Trial Lawyer's Association. ***PRACTICE AREAS:*** Civil Litigation; Civil Appeals; Administrative Law; Administrative Hearings and Appeals; Business Litigation; Commercial Litigation; Contracts; Contract Litigation; Corporate Litigation; Condominium Law; Wrongful Termination; Executive Compensation; Employment Litigation; Insurance; Insurance Coverage; Automobile Insurance; Casualty Insurance; General Liability; Libel; Slander; Defamation; Negligence; Personal Injury; Automobile Accidents and Injuries; Wrongful Death; Professional Liability; Federal Employers Liability Act; Americans with Disabilities Act; Discrimination; Probate; Estate Administration; Contested Trusts and Estates; Estate Litigation; Will Contests.

Language: English.

LAW OFFICES OF ROCHELLE C. MILLER

Established in 1992

155 NORTH MICHIGAN AVENUE, SUITE 500
CHICAGO, ILLINOIS 60601-7511
Telephone: 312-565-4800
Fax: 312-565-4810
Email: rochmiller@aol.com
URL: http://www.lawyers.com/rcmillerlaw

Estate Planning, Trusts and Estates, Wills and Probate, Estate and Gift Taxation, Fiduciary Income Tax, Generation-Skipping Tax, Charitable Giving.

ROCHELLE C. MILLER, born Flushing, New York, January 19, 1951; admitted to bar, 1986, Illinois. *Education:* University of Michigan (B.S., 1973); Illinois Institute of Technology, Chicago-Kent College of Law (J.D., with honors, 1986) Dean's List. Recipient, American Jurisprudence Award in Estate Planning. Listed as a Leading Attorney in Trusts and Estate Planning Law, The Guide to Leading Illinois Attorneys. *Member:* Chicago (Member, Sections on: Trust Law, Federal Tax - Estate, Gift and Generation Skipping Transfer Tax and Probate Practice), Illinois State and American (Member, Sections on: Real Property, Probate and Trust Law) Bar Associations; Chicago Estate Planning Council.

ALAN BENJAMIN MILLER

CHICAGO, ILLINOIS

(See Highland Park)

Business Litigation, Non-Consumer Collections, Probate Litigation, Insurance Fraud, Securities Fraud, Estate Planning and Administration, Real Estate, Small Business, Personal Injury.

MILLER FAUCHER AND CAFFERTY LLP

Established in 1992

30 NORTH LA SALLE STREET, SUITE 3200
CHICAGO, ILLINOIS 60602
Telephone: 312-782-4880
Telecopier: 312-782-4485
URL: http://www.millerfaucher.com

Philadelphia, Pennsylvania Office: One Logan Square, Suite 1700, 18th and Cherry Streets, 19103. Telephone: 215-864-2800. Telecopier: 215-864-2810.

Ann Arbor, Michigan Office: 101 North Main Street, 48104. Telephone: 734-769-2144. Telecopier: 734-769-1207.

Arbitration, Antitrust Class Actions, Deceptive Trade Practices, Appellate Practice, Federal Civil Practice, Commercial Fraud and Commercial Liability, Complex Commercial Litigation, Commodities Fraud, Complex and Multi-District Litigation, Consumer Fraud, Consumer Class Actions, ERISA Litigation, ERISA Class Actions, Civil Litigation, Federal Civil Litigation, Trial Practice.

FIRM PROFILE: Founded in 1992, Miller Faucher and Cafferty LLP combines the talents of attorneys with a wide range of experience in complex civil litigation. The firm has offices in Chicago, Illinois, Philadelphia, Pennsylvania and Ann Arbor, Michigan. Miller Faucher and Cafferty's primary expertise is in the area of federal and state securities, commodities, employee benefits and antitrust litigation. The skill and experience of attorneys now practicing with Miller Faucher has been recognized on repeated occasions by courts which have appointed these attorneys to major positions in complex multi-district or consolidated litigation. Attorneys from Miller Faucher and Cafferty LLP have taken a leading role in numerous important actions and have been responsible for a number of outstanding results and important decisions.

MEMBERS OF FIRM

MARVIN A. MILLER, born Brooklyn, New York, January 2, 1944; admitted to bar, 1970, Illinois; 1980, New York, U.S. District Court, Northern District of Illinois, U.S. Court of Appeals, Second, Third, Seventh and Eleventh Circuits and U.S. District Court, Eastern District of Michigan; 1989, U.S. District Court, Southern District of New York and U.S. District Court, Northern District of California; 1993, U.S. District Court, District of Arizona. *Education:* Hofstra University (B.B.A., 1967); IIT/Chicago-Kent College of Law (J.D., 1970). Phi Delta Phi (President, 1970). Member, Editorial Board, Chicago Kent Law Review. Author: "The Educational Paradox," 46 Chi-Kent L. Rev. 236 (1969). *Member:* Chicago and Illinois State Bar Associations. ***Email:*** mmiller@millerfaucher.com

PATRICK E. CAFFERTY, born Dearborn, Michigan, July 21, 1958; admitted to bar, 1983, Michigan; 1985, U.S. District Court, Eastern District of Michigan; 1986, Illinois, U.S. District Court, Western District of Michigan, U.S. District Court, Northern District of Illinois and U.S. Court of Appeals, Sixth Circuit; 1987, U.S. Court of Appeals, Seventh Circuit and U.S. Supreme Court; 1989, U.S. Court of Appeals, Third Circuit; 1992, U.S. Court of Appeals, Fourth Circuit; 1993, U.S. District Court, District of Arizona. *Education:* University of Michigan at Dearborn (B.A., with distinction, 1980); University of Exeter, England; Detroit College of Law at Michigan State University (J.D., cum laude, 1983). Recipient, American Jurisprudence Award, Commercial Transactions, 1982. Prehearing Attorney, Michigan Court of Appeals, 1983-1985. Clerk to Judge Glenn S. Allen, Jr., Michigan Court of Appeals, 1985. *Member:* Washtenaw County Bar Association; State Bar of Michigan. (Resident, Ann Arbor, Michigan Office). ***Email:*** pcafferty@millerfaucher.com

ELLEN MERIWETHER, born Darby, Pennsylvania, October 20, 1959; admitted to bar, 1985, Pennsylvania and U.S. District Court, Eastern District of Pennsylvania; 1989, U.S. Court of Appeals, Third Circuit. *Education:* La Salle University (B.A., maxima cum laude, 1981); George Washington University (J.D., magna cum laude, 1985). Order of the

(This Listing Continued)

Coif. Adjunct Professor, La Salle University Honors Program, Law and Society, 1988-1992. *Member:* Philadelphia (Member, Federal Courts Committee), Pennsylvania and American Bar Associations. (Resident, Philadelphia, Pennsylvania Office). ***Email:*** emeriwether@millerfaucher.com

BRYAN L. CLOBES, born Atlantic City, New Jersey, March 27, 1962; admitted to bar, 1990, New Jersey; 1993, Pennsylvania. *Education:* University of Maryland at College Park (B.A., 1984); Villanova University (J.D., 1988). Clerk: U.S. District Court, District of New Jersey, Judge Mitchell H. Cohen; U.S. Court of Appeals, Judge Arlin M. Adams, 1985-1986; Maryland Circuit Court Judge Joseph H.H. Kaplan, 1988-1989. Trial Attorney, Commodity Futures Trading Commission, 1989-1992. (Resident, Philadelphia, Pennsylvania Office). ***Email:*** bclobes@millerfaucher.com

JENNIFER WINTER SPRENGEL, born Chicago, Illinois, May 6, 1965; admitted to bar, 1990, Illinois. *Education:* Purdue University (B.A., 1987); DePaul University College of Law (J.D., 1990). Member, De Paul University Law Review, 1989-1990. *Member:* Chicago and American Bar Associations. ***Email:*** jsprengel@millerfaucher.com

WILLIAM R. KANE, born Philadelphia, Pennsylvania, March 6, 1961; admitted to bar, 1990, Pennsylvania and New Jersey; U.S. District Court, Eastern and Middle Districts of Pennsylvania; U.S. District Court, District of New Jersey; U.S. Court of Appeals, Third Circuit. *Education:* University of Pennsylvania (B.A., 1984); Temple University (J.D., cum laude, 1988). Recipient, American Jurisprudence Award for Secured Transactions, Temple University. Temple Law Review. (Resident, Philadelphia, Pennsylvania Office). ***Email:*** wkane@millerfaucher.com

MICHAEL J. WILLNER, born Bethlehem, Pennsylvania, April 26, 1962; admitted to bar, 1988, Pennsylvania and U.S. District Court, Eastern District of Pennsylvania; U.S. Court of Appeals, Third Circuit. *Education:* University of Pennsylvania (B.A., 1984); Temple University (J.D., cum laude, 1988). Judicial Clerk to Honorable John B. Hannum of United States District Court, Eastern District of Pennsylvania, 1988-1989. *Member:* Philadelphia Bar Association; Philadelphia Association of Defense Counsel. (Resident, Philadelphia, Pennsylvania Office). ***Email:*** mwillner@millerfaucher.com

ASSOCIATES

LORI A. FANNING, born Omaha, Nebraska, June 23, 1963; admitted to bar, 2000, Illinois and U.S. District Court, Northern District of Illinois. *Education:* University of Nebraska at Omaha (B.A., 1986); Central Michigan University (M.S.A., 1993); Chicago Kent College of Law (J.D., 2000). *Member:* Chicago, Illinois State and American Bar Associations. ***Email:*** lfanning@millerfaucher.com

MELODY FORRESTER, born Richmond, Virginia, May 1, 1963; admitted to bar, 1998, New York; 1999, U.S. District Court, Eastern District of New York; 2000, Pennsylvania and New Jersey. *Education:* University of Virginia (B.A., cum laude, 1985); Columbia University Law School (J.D., 1993). *Member:* New York State, American and National Bar Associations. (Resident, Philadelphia, Pennsylvania Office). ***Email:*** mforrester@millerfaucher.com

CHRISTOPHER B. SANCHEZ, born Albuquerque, New Mexico, January 15, 1974; admitted to bar, 2000, Illinois. *Education:* University of New Mexico (B.A, cum laude, 1996); DePaul University (J.D, 2000). *Member:* Chicago and Illinois State Bar Associations; Hispanic National Bar. ***Email:*** csanchez@millerfaucher.com

MICHAEL S. TARRINGER, born Philadelphia, Pennsylvania, October 9, 1965; admitted to bar, 1994, Pennsylvania; 1998, U.S. Court of Appeals, Third Circuit. *Education:* Philadelphia College of Textiles and Science (B.S., 1987); Villanova University (J.D., 1993). Delta Mu Delta; Business Honor Society; Sara Tyler Wister Award. (Resident, Philadelphia, Pennsylvania Office). ***Email:*** mtarringer@millerfaucher.com

ANTHONY F. FATA, born Pinesville, Ohio, July 29, 1973; admitted to bar, 1999, Illinois; U.S. District Court, Northern District of Illinois. *Education:* Miami University (B.A., 1995); Ohio State University (J.D., with honors, 1999). Order of the Coif. Managing Editor, Ohio State University Journal on Dispute Resolution, 1998-1999. Recipient: CALI Consumer Law Award; Excellence for the Future Award. Research Assistant to: Professor Robert C. Berry, Sports and Entertainment; Professor Arthur F. Greenbaum, Civil Procedure. Contributing Writer: IICLE Securities Law Handbook, Civil Liability fro Fraud: 1933 Act 17(a) and 1934 Act 10(b); Purchaser Remedies for Fraud, Misstatement, or Omission, Submitted January 2002 by Steven S. Scholes. Author: "Attaining Settlement Class Certification Under Amchem and Ortiz," Product Liability Law & Strategy, May 2001. Formerly with, McDermott, Will & Emory. *Member:* Chicago Bar Association.

NYRAN ROSE PEARSON, born 1974; admitted to bar, 1999, Oregon; 2002, Illinois and U.S. District Court, Northern and Southern Districts of Illinois. *Education:* Illinois Wesleyan University (B.A., 1995); University of Oregon (J.D., 1999). *Member:* Chicago and Oregon State Bar Associations. ***PRACTICE AREAS:*** Complex Commercial Litigation; Antitrust Class Actions; Consumer Litigation. ***Email:*** npearson@millerfaucher.com

OF COUNSEL

J. DENNIS FAUCHER, born Vancouver, Washington, October 29, 1936; admitted to bar, 1962, Idaho; 1973, Pennsylvania, U.S. Supreme Court, U.S. Court of Appeals, Second, Third and Ninth Circuits, U.S. District Court, Eastern District of Pennsylvania, U.S. District Court, District of Idaho and U.S. Tax Court. *Education:* University of Idaho (B.S., magna cum laude, 1960; LL.B., summa cum laude, 1962). Assistant Professor of Law, University of Idaho College of Law, 1962, 1963. Attorney for the Penn Central Trustees, 1971, 1972. *Member:* Philadelphia, Pennsylvania and American Bar Associations. (Resident, Philadelphia, Pennsylvania Office). ***Email:*** jdfaucher@millerfaucher.com

DOM J. RIZZI, born Chicago, Illinois, June 27, 1932; admitted to bar, 1961, Illinois. *Education:* DePaul University (B.S.C., 1957; J.D., 1961). ***Email:*** drizzi@millerfaucher.com

MATTHEW E. VAN TINE, born Tomahawk, Wisconsin, June 21, 1958; admitted to bar, 1983, Illinois and Massachusetts; 1984, U.S. District Court, District of Massachusetts; 1986, U.S. District Court, Northern District of Illinois. *Education:* Harvard University (A.B., cum laude, 1980); Boston University (J.D., magna cum laude, 1983). Edward F. Hennessey Scholar; Paul J. Liacos Scholar; G. Joseph Tauro Distinguished Scholar. Member,

(This Listing Continued)

MILLER FAUCHER AND CAFFERTY LLP, Chicago—Continued

1981-1982 and Executive Editor, 1982-1983, Boston University Law Review. Author: Note, "Application of the Federal Parole Guidelines to Certain Prisoners: An Ex Post Facto Violation," 62 Boston University Law Review 515, March, 1982. Law Clerk to the Honorable Raymond J. Pettine, U.S. District Judge, District of Rhode Island, 1983-1984. Assistant Corporation Counsel, City of Chicago, 1988-1992. *Member:* Chicago and American Bar Associations; American Inns of Court; Asian American Bar Association. ***LANGUAGES:*** Spanish. ***Email:*** mvantine@millerfaucher.com

MILLER SHAKMAN & HAMILTON LLP

Established in 1946

SUITE 3600
180 NORTH LA SALLE STREET
CHICAGO, ILLINOIS 60601
Telephone: 312-263-3700
FAX: 312-263-3270
URL: http://www.millershakman.com

Civil Trial and Appellate Practice in state and federal courts, as well as Arbitration and Mediation practice, in an array of commercial matters: Business Litigation; Corporate Litigation; Legal Malpractice and Legal Ethics; Representation of Lawyers and Law Firms; Bankruptcy Litigation and Creditors' Rights; Securities Litigation; Constitutional Litigation; Employment Litigation and Counseling; Environmental Litigation; Governmental and Regulatory Litigation; Intellectual Property and Media Litigation; Closely-Held Business and Partnership Disputes; Professional Malpractice and Directors and Officers Liability; Real Estate and Construction Litigation; Specialized Corporate Representations; Estate Planning; Counseling and Transactional Practice.

FIRM PROFILE: Since its founding nearly 60 years ago, Miller Shakman & Hamilton has become one of the most highly regarded small law firms in the country. The firm concentrates its practice on complex litigation matters. By assembling some of the brightest lawyers from the best law schools, and by maintaining a manageable size and structure, we are able to provide our clients personalized attention and top-level representation. Perhaps the most telling characteristic of the firm is the frequency with which it is chosen by the best-informed and most selective consumers of legal services-other lawyers. Top firms from Chicago and throughout the country regularly refer their clients to us when unable to handle cases themselves, and law firms of all sizes select us to represent them directly in legal malpractice and other matters. The "American Lawyer" once featured the firm as one of the nation's "Thirteen Great Small Law Firms.".

MEMBERS OF FIRM

MARC O. BEEM, born Chicago, Illinois, May 24, 1948; admitted to bar, 1975, Illinois. *Education:* Princeton University (A.B., high honors, 1970); University of Chicago (J.D., 1975). Order of the Coif. Law Clerk to Hon. Bernard M. Decker, U.S. District Court, Northern District of Illinois, 1975-1976. *Member:* American (Member, Section on Litigation) Bar Association; Chicago Council of Lawyers. ***PRACTICE AREAS:*** Professional Liability; Commercial Litigation; Constitutional Litigation; Corporate Litigation; Creditors Rights; Bankruptcy; Partnership Law. ***Email:*** mbeem@millershakman.com

STEPHEN J. BISGEIER, born Brooklyn, New York, July 27, 1943; admitted to bar, 1969, California; 1970, Illinois. *Education:* University of California at Berkeley (B.S., with honors, 1965); Boalt Hall School of Law, University of California (J.D., 1968). Order of the Coif. Note and Comment Editor, California Law Review, 1967-1968. *Member:* Chicago and American Bar Associations; Chicago Council of Lawyers. ***PRACTICE AREAS:*** Commercial Litigation; Legal Malpractice Defense; Corporate Litigation; Securities Litigation; Corporate Law. ***Email:*** sjbis@aol.com

DANIEL M. FEENEY, born Elmhurst, Ill., March 26, 1969; admitted to bar, 1994, Illinois; U.S. Court of Appeals, Seventh Circuit. *Education:* DePaul University (B.A., magna cum laude, 1991); University of Michigan (J.D., with honors, 1994). Member: Journal of Law Reform. Law Clerk to Hon. Barbara B. Crabb, U.S. District Court, Western District of Wisconsin; Special Assistant Illinois Attorney General, 1995. *Member:* Chicago and American Bar Associations; Chicago Council of Lawyers. ***PRACTICE AREAS:*** Commercial Litigation; Professional Liability; Bankruptcy Litigation; Trade Secrets; Business Arbitration; Partnership Law; Intellectual Property. ***Email:*** dfeeney@millershakman.com

EDWARD W. FELDMAN, born Chicago, Illinois, October 29, 1957; admitted to bar, 1984, Illinois. *Education:* University of Illinois (B.A., with high distinction in English, summa cum laude, 1979; B.S., in Physics, 1980); Harvard University (J.D., magna cum laude, 1984). Phi Beta Kappa. Adjunct Professor of Trial Advocacy, Northwestern University School of Law, 1988—. Faculty Member, National Institute for Trial Advocacy. Lecturer and Clinical Fellow, Northwestern University School of Law, 1986-1988. Law Clerk to Hon. Marvin E. Aspen, U.S. District Court, Northern District of Illinois, 1984-1986. Member, Advisory Committee on Rules and Practice, U.S. District Court, Northern District of Illinois. Member, Civil Justice Reform Act Advisory Group, Northern District of Illinois. *Member:* Chicago and American Bar Associations; Chicago Council of Lawyers. ***PRACTICE AREAS:*** Commercial Litigation; Legal Malpractice Defense; Legal Professional Liability; Professional Practices; Employment Litigation; Employment Discrimination; Corporate Litigation; Partnership Law; Civil Rights; Construction Litigation; Civil Appeals. ***Email:*** efeldman@millershakman.com

ARTHUR W. FRIEDMAN, born St. Louis, Missouri, March 19, 1943; admitted to bar, 1968, Illinois. *Education:* Brown University (A.B., 1965); London School of Economics (1964); University of Chicago (J.D., 1968). Cooperating Instructor, Pre-Law Education Program, Chicago-Kent College of Law and DePaul University School of Law, 1980. *Member:* Chicago and American Bar Associations; Chicago Council of Lawyers. ***PRACTICE AREAS:*** Commercial Litigation; Corporate Litigation; Professional Liability; Estate Planning. ***Email:*** afriedman@millershakman.com

(This Listing Continued)

R. DICKEY HAMILTON, born Chicago, Illinois, January 28, 1935; admitted to bar, 1960, District of Columbia; 1964, Illinois. *Education:* Oberlin College (B.A., 1957); University of Chicago (J.D., 1960). Managing Editor, University of Chicago Law Review, 1959. Author: "Taking and Defending Depositions," Litigation, Winter, 1985. Appointed by U.S. District Court for the Northern District of Illinois as chairperson of committee to develop guidelines for conduct of depositions, 1994. *Member:* Chicago and American Bar Associations. ***PRACTICE AREAS:*** Commercial Litigation; Construction Litigation; Libel and Slander; Securities Litigation; Zoning Law. ***Email:*** dhamilton@millershakman.com

DIANE F. KLOTNIA, born Chicago, Illinois, December 4, 1961; admitted to bar, 1988, Pennsylvania; 1989, Illinois. *Education:* University of Illinois (B.S., Highest honors, 1984); University of Chicago (J.D., 1987). Order of the Coif. Managing and Book Review Editor, University of Chicago Law Review. Law Clerk to Hon. Max Rosenn, U.S. Court of Appeals, Third Circuit. Member, Board of Directors of the University of Illinois College of Business Alumni Association, 2001—. Member, Board of Directors of the ACLU of Illinois, 1999— and Faculty of the Practising Law Institute. Member, Board of Directors, Chicago Council of Lawyers, 1999-2004. *Member:* Chicago, Illinois State and American Bar Associations. ***PRACTICE AREAS:*** Commercial Litigation; Legal Professional Liability; Construction Litigation; Corporate Litigation; Partnership Law; Mortgage Foreclosure; Civil Rights; Media Law. ***Email:*** dklotnia@millershakman.com

RONALD S. MILLER, born Chicago, Illinois, September 28, 1931; admitted to bar, 1955, Illinois; 1960, New York. *Education:* University of Illinois (B.S., 1953; LL.B., 1955). Member, Board of Editors, Illinois Law Forum, 1953-1954. Member, Chicago Lawyers Committee for Civil Rights Under Law (Chairman, 1977-1978). Member, Board of Directors, National Lawyers Committee for Civil Rights Under Law. Member, Illinois House Speaker's Amendatory Veto Task Force, 1984; Member and President, Board of Visitors, University of Illinois Law School, 1984-1989; Member, Board of Visitors, DePaul Law School, 1991-1997. Chairman, Human Behavior Institute. Member, Board of Advisors, Center for International Human Rights at Northwestern Law School. Co-Chair, Illinois ACLU Advisory Committee. Pro Bono Affairs, Senior Counsel, Center for Disability and Elder Law. *Member:* Chicago, Illinois State and American Bar Associations; Chicago Council of Lawyers. ***PRACTICE AREAS:*** Corporate Law; Real Estate Law; Insurance Law. ***Email:*** rmiller@millershakman.com

MICHAEL L. SHAKMAN, born Chicago, Illinois, August 31, 1942; admitted to bar, 1966, Illinois. *Education:* University of Wisconsin and University of Chicago (A.B., 1962; A.M., 1964); University of Chicago (J.D., cum laude, 1966). Order of the Coif. Managing Editor, University of Chicago Law Review, 1965-1966. Associate Editor, American Bar Association Litigation Journal, 1978-1983. Instructor, Litigation, IIT-Chicago Kent College of Law, 1977-1978. Lecturer, University of Chicago Law School, 1979-1980. Clerk to Hon. Walter V. Schaefer, Justice, Illinois Supreme Court, 1966-1967. Member, National Panel of Arbitrators, American Arbitration Association, 1973—. *Member:* Chicago, Illinois State and American Bar Associations; Chicago Council of Lawyers; American Law Institute. ***LANGUAGES:*** French. ***PRACTICE AREAS:*** Corporate Litigation; Partnership Litigation; Commercial Litigation; Legal Malpractice Defense; Legal Professional Liability; Professional Practices; Civil Rights Litigation; Construction Litigation; Arbitration; Zoning Litigation. ***Email:*** mlshak@aol.com

THOMAS M. STAUNTON, born Elmhurst, Illinois, November 12, 1963; admitted to bar, 1993, Illinois. *Education:* University of Illinois (B.A., 1986); New York University (J.D., 1993). Law Clerk to Hon. J.P. Stadtmueller, U.S. District Court, Eastern District of Wisconsin, 1993-1995. *Member:* Chicago, Illinois State and American Bar Associations; Chicago Council of Lawyers. ***PRACTICE AREAS:*** Commercial Litigation. ***Email:*** tstaunton@millershakman.com

STUART M. WIDMAN, born Cleveland, Ohio, July 1, 1948; admitted to bar, 1977, Illinois; 1987, U.S. Tax Court; 1988, Wisconsin; U.S. District Court, Northern District of Illinois including Trial Bar; U.S. Court of Appeals, Fourth and Seventh Circuits; U.S. Supreme Court. *Education:* University of Pennsylvania, Wharton School of Finance (B.S., 1970); Northwestern University (J.D., 1974). Selected as Leading American Attorney in ADR, Commercial Law by American Research Corporation, 1997-2001. Author of multiple articles and publications regarding ADR. Faculty Member: DePaul University College of Law, Commercial Arbitration, Spring 2002; American Arbitration Association training program of Commercial Arbitration Rules, Basic, 1998-2005 and Advanced, 2000-2005; National Institute of Trial Advocacy Program on Negotiation and Mediation, Northwestern University School of Law, June 1997. Member: Illinois Judicial Conference Alternative Dispute Resolution Coordinating Committee, 1990-2000; Chicago Mercantile Exchange Business Conduct Committee, 2001. *Member:* Chicago (Member: Arbitration and Alternative Dispute Resolution Committee, 1985—; Secretary, 1987-1988; Chairman, 1989-1990; Bankruptcy Law Committee; International Law Committee; Professional Responsibility Committee), Illinois State (Member: Alternative Dispute Resolution Committee; Member, Sections on: Commercial Law; Banking and Bankruptcy Law) and American (Member, Sections on: Business Law; Dispute Resolution; ADR Committee, Litigation Section; Natural Resources; Energy and Environmental Law; Center of Professional Responsibility); American Arbitration Association (Member, Chicago Regional Office; Member, Commercial Arbitration Advisory Committee); Society of Professionals in Dispute Resolution; The Association of Trial Lawyers of America. ***PRACTICE AREAS:*** Commercial Litigation; Arbitration; Mediation; Securities Litigation; Employment; Partnership; Commercial Code; Contracts; Trade Secrets. ***Email:*** swidman@millershakman.com

ASSOCIATES

JULIE H. FRIEDMAN, born Cincinnati, Ohio, May 28, 1944; admitted to bar, 1970, California and Illinois. *Education:* Smith College (B.A., 1966); Georgetown University (J.D., 1969). *Member:* Chicago Bar Association; State Bar of California; Chicago Council of Lawyers.

ROBERTA G. EVANS, born Chicago, Illinois, March 17, 1938; admitted to bar, 1961, Illinois; 2003, U.S. Supreme Court. *Education:* University of Illinois and University of Connecticut (B.A., with honors and distinction, 1958); University of Chicago (J.D., 1961). Phi Beta Kappa. Assistant Dean, Director, Graduate Student Affairs, University of Chicago

(This Listing Continued)

Law School, 1981-1996. *Member:* Chicago and Illinois State Bar Associations; Chicago Council of Lawyers; Decalogue Society of Lawyers. ***PRACTICE AREAS:*** Probate Law; Estate Planning Law. ***Email:*** revans@millershakman.com

JENNIFER E. SMILEY, born Pipestone, Minnesota, February 20, 1972; admitted to bar, 2001, Illinois. *Education:* Vassar College (B.A., 1994); Northwestern University School of Law (J.D., magna cum laude, 2001). Phi Beta Kappa; Order of the Coif. Senior Manuscript Editor, Northwestern University Law Review, 2000-2001. Law Clerk, Hon. Milton I. Shadur, U.S. District Court, Northern District of Illinois, 2001-2002. ***PRACTICE AREAS:*** Commercial Litigation. ***Email:*** jsmiley@millershakman.com

FREDRICK E. VARS, born Corvallis, Oregon, February 1, 1973; admitted to bar, 1999, Oregon; 2003, Illinois. *Education:* Princeton University (A.B., summa cum laude, 1995); Yale Law School (J.D., 1999). Phi Beta Kappa. Essays Editor, Yale Law Journal. Co-Author: "To Insure Prejudice: Racial Disparities in Taxicab Tipping," 114 Yale Law Journal, forthcoming 2005; "Determinants of Citations to Articles in Elite Law Reviews," 27 Journal of Legal Studies 427 (2000); "When Does Private Discrimination Justify Public Affirmative Action?," 98 Columbia Law Review 1577 (1998). Fellow, Yale Law School Center for the Study of Corporate Law, 2000-2001. Law Clerk: Hon. Bruce M. Selya, U.S. Court of Appeals, First Circuit, 1999-2000; Hon. Joan B. Gottschall, U.S. District Court, Northern District of Illinois, 2002. *Member:* Chicago, Illinois State and American Bar Associations; Oregon State Bar. ***PRACTICE AREAS:*** Commercial Litigation; Legal Ethics. ***Email:*** fvars@millershakman.com

ROGER J. PERLSTADT, born Lansing, Michigan, May 20, 1975; admitted to bar, 2002, Illinois. *Education:* Carleton College (B.A., 1997); University of Chicago (J.D., 2002). Member, University of Chicago Law Review. Law Clerk to Hon. Elaine E. Bucklo, U.S. District Court, Northern District of Illinois, 2002-2003. ***PRACTICE AREAS:*** Litigation. ***Email:*** rperlstadt@millershakman.com

ZACHARY J. FREEMAN, born Los Angeles, California, July 10, 1973; admitted to bar, 2003, Illinois; 2004, U.S. District Court, Northern District of Illinois. *Education:* Princeton University (A.B., 1995); Northwestern University School of Law (J.D., cum laude, 2003). Order of the Coif. *Member:* Chicago, Illinois State and American Bar Associations; Chicago Council of Lawyers. ***PRACTICE AREAS:*** Litigation. ***Email:*** zfreeman@millershakman.com

MILLER & SWEENEY

111 WEST WASHINGTON STREET, SUITE 1160
CHICAGO, ILLINOIS 60602
Telephone: 312-384-0500
Fax: 312-384-0600

Litigation, Commercial Litigation, Civil Practice, Appellate Practice.

MEMBERS OF FIRM

MATTHEW S. MILLER, born Baltimore, Maryland, March 24, 1971; admitted to bar, 1996, Illinois and U.S. District Court, Northern District of Illinois; 1999, U.S. District Court, Northern District of Illinois, including Trial Bar; 2002, U.S. Court of Appeals, Seventh Circuit. *Education:* University of Wisconsin (B.A., 1993); Loyola University (J.D., cum laude, 1996). Recipient, Kraft W. Eidman Award, American College of Trial Lawyers, 1996. National Champion, National Trial Competition, 1996. Editor-at-Large, Loyola University Law Journal. Philip H. Corboy Trial Advocacy Fellowship. Associate, Jenner & Block, 1996-2000. Volunteer Attorney, Chicago Volunteer Legal Services. *Member:* Chicago, Illinois State and American Bar Associations; Association of Trial Lawyers of America; Illinois Trial Lawyers Association; Barrister, American College of Barristers. ***PRACTICE AREAS:*** Litigation; Commercial Litigation; Civil Practice; Appellate Practice.

ROBERT D. SWEENEY, born St. Paul, Minnesota, January 16, 1971; admitted to bar, 1996, Illinois and U.S. District Court, Northern District of Illinois. *Education:* University of Notre Dame (B.A., 1993); Loyola University School of Law, Chicago (J.D., 1996). National Champion, National Trial Competition, 1996. Certified Instructor, National Institute of Trial Advocacy, 1997. *Member:* Chicago, Illinois and American Bar Associations. ***PRACTICE AREAS:*** Commercial Litigation.

MINER, BARNHILL & GALLAND, P.C.

Established in 1970
14 WEST ERIE STREET
CHICAGO, ILLINOIS 60610
Telephone: 312-751-1170
Facsimile: 312-751-0438
URL: http://www.lawmbg.com

Madison, Wisconsin Office: Suite 803, 44 East Mifflin Street. Telephone: 608-255-5200. Facsimile: 608-255-5380.

General Practice, Trial and Appellate Litigation, Commercial, Employment, Employee Benefits, Civil Rights and Securities Litigation, Banking Law, Single and Multi-Family Housing Finance and Development, Non-Profit Corporations.

CHARLES BARNHILL, JR., born Indianapolis, Indiana, May 22, 1943; admitted to bar, 1968, Illinois and U.S. District Court, Northern District of Illinois; 1969, U.S. Court of Appeals, Seventh Circuit; 1982, U.S. Supreme Court; 1987, Wisconsin. *Education:* University of Pennsylvania (B.S., Economics, 1965); University of Michigan (J.D., cum laude, 1968). Order of the Coif. Assistant Editor, Michigan Law Review, 1967-1968. Director, Legal Assistance Foundation, 1975. Special Master, Appointed by District Court, Northern District of Illinois in *Lumpkin, et al v. International Harvester, Re: Wisconsin Steel Co., et al. Member:* State Bar of Wisconsin; American Bar Association (Member, Litigation Section; Co-Chairman, Employment Litigation Committee, 1978-1980); Chicago Council of Lawyers (Member, Board of Directors, 1969-1971, 1974-1976). Fellow, American College of Trial Lawyers. (Resident, Madison, WI Office). ***PRACTICE AREAS:*** Employment Litigation; Consumer Litigation; Antitrust; Securities Litigation. ***Email:*** cbarnhill@lawmbg.com

JEFFREY I. CUMMINGS, born Fort Wayne, Indiana, September 24, 1962; admitted to bar, 1987, Illinois and U.S. District Court, Northern District of Illinois; 1991, U.S. Court of Appeals, Seventh Circuit; 1993, U.S. District Court, Central District of Illinois. *Education:* Michigan State University (B.A., high honors, 1984); Northwestern University (J.D., cum laude, 1987). Phi Beta Kappa; Order of the Coif. Member, Journal of Criminal Law and Criminology, 1985-1987. President, Chicago Lawyers' Committee for Civil Rights Under Law, 1999. Member, Board of Directors, Chicago Lawyers' Committee for Civil Rights Under Law, 1993—. Hearing Officer, City of Chicago, Commission on Human Relations, 1995—. ***PRACTICE AREAS:*** Employment Litigation; Civil Rights; Voting Rights; False Claims Act Litigation; Health Care Litigation; Commercial Litigation. ***Email:*** jcummings@lawmbg.com

WILLIAM P. DIXON, born Buffalo, New York; admitted to bar, 1970, Wisconsin; 1973, District of Columbia, U.S. District Court, Eastern and Western Districts of Wisconsin and U.S. Supreme Court. *Education:* State University of New York at Buffalo (B.S., Finance, 1965; J.D., cum laude, 1970). Member, Buffalo Law Review, 1968-1969. Chief Counsel, Office of the Governor, Wisconsin, 1972-1973. Counsel, U.S. House of Representatives Judiciary Committee, 1973-1974. General Counsel, U.S. House of Representatives Banking Committee, 1975-1977. U.S. Alternate Executive Director, The World Bank, 1977-1979. Commissioner of Banking, Wisconsin, 1983-1985. Chief of Staff, U.S. Senator Gary Hart, 1985-1987. Member: Wisconsin Supreme Court Board of Attorneys Professional Competence, 1976-1979; Governor's Blue Ribbon Commission on Ethics and Lobbying Legislation, 1989; Wisconsin Legislative Council Special Committee on Campaign Financing, 1992-1993. *Member:* State Bar of Wisconsin; The District of Columbia Bar. (Resident, Madison, WI Office). ***PRACTICE AREAS:*** Banking Law; Consumer Law; Antitrust; Commercial Litigation. ***Email:*** wdixon@lawmbg.com

GEORGE F. GALLAND, JR., born Washington, D.C., February 18, 1945; admitted to bar, 1973, Illinois and U.S. District Court, Northern District of Illinois; 1974, U.S. Court of Appeals, Seventh Circuit; 1982, U.S. Supreme Court. *Education:* Princeton University (A.B., 1967); University of Chicago (J.D., 1973). Order of the Coif. Acting General Attorney, Chicago Park District, 1986-1987. *Member:* Chicago Council of Lawyers (Chairman, Judicial Evaluation Subcommittee, 1977-1981; Member, Board of Governors, 1978-1983; President, 1983-1985). ***LANGUAGES:*** Spanish. ***PRACTICE AREAS:*** Employment Discrimination; Employment Law; Medical-Legal Law; Business Litigation. ***Email:*** ggalland@lawmbg.com

ROBERT S. LIBMAN, born Chicago, Illinois, April 28, 1963; admitted to bar, 1988, California; 1991, District of Columbia; 2004, Illinois. *Education:* Stanford University (B.A., 1985; J.D., 1988). Phi Beta Kappa; Omicron Delta Epsilon; Order of the Coif. Clerk to Honorable Joyce H. Green, U.S. District Court the District of Columbia, 1988-1990. Special Litigation Counsel, U.S. Department of Justice Civil Rights Division, Employment Litigation Section, 1991-2004. *Member:* American Bar Association; National Employment Lawyers Association. ***PRACTICE AREAS:*** Employment Discrimination; Civil Rights; Employment Law.

WILLIAM A. MICELI, born Evergreen Park, Illinois, September 30, 1958; admitted to bar, 1984, Illinois and U.S. District Court, Northern District of Illinois including Trial Bar. *Education:* Georgetown University; Loyola University of Chicago (B.A., cum laude, 1980; J.D., 1984). Alpha Sigma Nu. Recipient, Mellon Philosophy Prize. Member, Loyola University of Chicago Law Journal. Assistant Corporation Counsel, City of Chicago, 1984-1989. Member, Winfield Moody Health Center Advisory Board. ***PRACTICE AREAS:*** Affordable Housing; Real Estate; Partnership Law; Nonprofit Corporations. ***Email:*** wmiceli@lawmbg.com

JUDSON H. MINER, born Chicago, Illinois, April 13, 1941; admitted to bar, 1967, Illinois; 1968, U.S. District Court, Northern District of Illinois and U.S. Court of Appeals, Seventh Circuit; 1973, U.S. Supreme Court; 1977, U.S. Court of Appeals, Fifth Circuit; 1979, U.S. District Court, District of Columbia. *Education:* Northwestern University (B.A., 1963); London School of Economics, London, England; University of Chicago (J.D., 1967). Associate Editor, Chicago Law Review, 1966-1967. Chairman, Insurance Consumers Advisory Panel, Illinois Department of Insurance, 1969. Member: Illinois Supreme Court Advisory Committee on Judicial Vacancies, 1976; Executive Committee, Lawyers' Committee for Civil Rights Under Law, 1976-1985; NAACP Legal Defense Educational Fund, Inc.; United States Senate Judicial Nominations Commission for the State of Illinois, 1992-1996. Corporation Counsel, City of Chicago, 1985-1989. *Member:* American Bar Association; Chicago Council of Lawyers (President, 1969-1971; Member, Board of Governors, 1971-1975, 1978; Chairman, Judicial Evaluation Committee, 1971-1976). ***PRACTICE AREAS:*** Federal Litigation; Employment Discrimination; Civil Rights; False Claims Act Litigation. ***Email:*** jminer@lawmbg.com

SARAH E. SISKIND, born New York, N.Y., December 2, 1952; admitted to bar, 1978, New York; 1979, U.S. District Court, Eastern District of New York; 1982, U.S. District Court, Southern District of New York; 1984, U.S. Court of Appeals, Second Circuit; 1986, U.S. Court of Appeals, Fourth Circuit; 1987, Wisconsin and U.S. District Court, Western District of Wisconsin; 1988, U.S. District Court, Eastern District of Wisconsin; 1990, U.S. Court of Appeals, Seventh Circuit; 1992, U.S. Supreme Court; 1994, U.S. Court of Appeals, Third Circuit; 1995, U.S. Court of Appeals, Eighth Circuit. *Education:* Yale University (B.A., magna cum laude, 1974); Harvard University (J.D., 1977). *Member:* New York State and American Bar Associations; State Bar of Wisconsin; National Employment Law Association. (Resident, Madison, WI Office). ***PRACTICE AREAS:*** Class Actions; Consumer Law; Employee Benefits; Employment Law; Civil Rights. ***Email:*** ssiskind@lawmbg.com

PAUL L. STRAUSS, born Syracuse, New York, July 2, 1956; admitted to bar, 1981, Illinois; 1991, California. *Education:* Williams College (B.A., summa cum laude, 1978); Yale University (J.D., 1981). Phi Beta Kappa. Author: "Using Statistics In Employment Discrimination Cases," 1992 Civil Rights Litigation and Attorney' Fees Annual Handbook (National Lawyers Guild); "Handling A Plaintiff's Sexual Harassment Case," Litigation (ABA Section of Litigation, Vol. 26, No. 4 (Summer, 2000). Hearing Officer, Chicago Commission on Human Relations, 1991-1994. Leadership Greater Chicago, 1991-1992.

(This Listing Continued)

MINER, BARNHILL & GALLAND, P.C., Chicago—Continued

Member: Chicago Council of Lawyers (President, 1993-1994). ***PRACTICE AREAS:*** Federal and State Litigation; Employment Discrimination; Wage and Hour Law; Civil Rights; Medical Malpractice. ***Email:*** pstrauss@lawmbg.com

LAURA E. TILLY, born Wilmington, Delaware, February 26, 1959; admitted to bar, 1984, Illinois and U.S. District Court, Northern District of Illinois; 1985, U.S. Court of Appeals, Eleventh Circuit; 1986, U.S. Court of Appeals, Tenth Circuit. *Education:* Carleton College (B.A., magna cum laude, 1980); University of Michigan (J.D., cum laude, 1984). Phi Beta Kappa. Member, Advisory Committee, Community Economic Development Law Project. *Member:* American Bar Association (Member, Affordable Housing Forum); Chicago Council of Lawyers. ***PRACTICE AREAS:*** Real Estate; Nonprofit Corporations; Affordable Housing. ***Email:*** ltilly@lawmbg.com

---

LISA T. ALEXANDER, born New York, N.Y., October 26, 1972; admitted to bar, 2003, Illinois and U.S. District Court, Northern District of Illinois. *Education:* Wesleyan University (B.A., Government, with honors, 1994); Columbia University (J.D., 2002). Intern, U.S. Department of Justice, Civil Rights Division. Articles Editor, National Black Law Journal. *Member:* Chicago and American (Member, Affordable Housing Forum) Bar Associations. ***PRACTICE AREAS:*** Affordable Housing; Nonprofit and Charitable Organizations; Real Estate; Employment Discrimination; Civil Rights. ***Email:*** lalexander@lawmbg.com

ELIZABETH J. EBERLE, born Beaver Dam, Wisconsin, February 7, 1965; admitted to bar, 1998, California; 2000, Wisconsin; 2001, U.S. District Court, Western and Eastern Districts of Wisconsin; 2001, U.S. Court of Appeals, Seventh Circuit; 2002, U.S. District Court, Northern District of California (Not admitted in Illinois). *Education:* University of Wisconsin-Madison (B.S., 1987); Stanford Law School (J.D., 1998). *Member:* National Employment Law Association. (Resident, Madison, WI Office). ***PRACTICE AREAS:*** Consumer Law; Employment Discrimination; Class Actions. ***Email:*** beberle@lawmbg.com

NANCY L. MALDONADO, born Skokie, Illinois; admitted to bar, 2001, Illinois; 2004, U.S. District Court, Northern District of Illinois. *Education:* Harvard University (B.A., 1997); Columbia University Law School (J.D., 2001). Columbia Stone Scholar. *Member:* Chicago and American Bar Associations; Hispanic Lawyers' Association of Illinois. ***LANGUAGES:*** Spanish. ***PRACTICE AREAS:*** Federal and State Litigation; Employment Discrimination; Employment Law; Medical-Legal Law. ***Email:*** nmaldonado@lawmgb.com

REBECCA ONIE, born Brookline, Massachusetts, June 1, 1977; admitted to bar, 2003, Illinois, U.S. District Court, Northern District of Illinois; 2004, U.S Court of Appeals, Seventh Circuit. *Education:* Harvard University (B.A., magna cum laude, with highest honors, 1997); Harvard Law School (J.D., magna cum laude, 2003). Phi Beta Kappa. Editor, Harvard Law Review Symposium. Author, "When Hope Falls Short: Hope VI, Accountability, and the Privatization of Public Housing," Harvard Law Review, 1997, (2003). ***PRACTICE AREAS:*** Real Estate; Nonprofit Corporations; Affordable Housing; Employment Discrimination; Civil Rights. ***Email:*** ronie@lawmbg.com

OF COUNSEL

SHARON K. LEGENZA, born Germany, July 8, 1965; admitted to bar, 1991, Illinois. *Education:* University of Chicago (B.A., 1987); Northwestern University (J.D., 1991). Staff member, Northwestern Journal of International Law and Business, 1989-1991. ***LANGUAGES:*** French and Korean. ***PRACTICE AREAS:*** Litigation.

BRADLEY SCOTT WEISS, born Hammond, Indiana, May 28, 1954; admitted to bar, 1988, Illinois; 1991, District of Columbia; 1992, U.S. District Court, District of Columbia; 1992, U.S. District Court, District of Maryland; U.S. Court of Appeals, 7th Circuit; 1997, U.S. Court of Appeals, Federal Circuit. *Education:* Loyola University of Chicago (B.A., 1976); Chicago-Kent College of Law (J.D., 1987). Contributing Author: ABA Public Contract Section's First and Second Edition monograph on qui tam litigation; ABA report on qui tam litigation and voluntary disclosure. *Member:* American Bar Association (Member, Section on Public Contract Law; Former Vice Chair, Procurement Fraud Committee, Public Contract Section; Former Co-Chair, Procurement Fraud Subcommittee on Qui Tam Litigation and Voluntary Disclosure). ***PRACTICE AREAS:*** Whistleblower Litigation; False Claims Act; Retaliatory Discharge. ***Email:*** weiss@bsw-law.com

MIROBALLI, DURKIN & RUDIN

6 W. HUBBARD, SUITE 300
CHICAGO, ILLINOIS 60610
Telephone: 312-229-5555
Fax: 312-229-5556
URL: http://www.mdr-law.com

Personal Injury, Civil Torts.

MEMBERS OF FIRM

JOSEPH J. MIROBALLI, born Blue Island, Illinois, November 30, 1953; admitted to bar, 1979, Illinois. *Education:* Northern Illinois University (B.A., 1975); John Marshall Law School (J.D., 1979). Phi Delta Phi. Author: "Changing Anti-Coagulants and Frequent Monitoring," Medical Malpractice Prevention, June, 1992; "Medical Malpractice Trial Notebook," 1992-2000. *Member:* Chicago, Illinois State and American Bar Associations; The Association of Trial Lawyers of America; Illinois Trial Lawyers Association (Member, General Assembly); Justinian Society of Lawyers; Illinois State Bar Association (Member, Board of Governors). ***PRACTICE AREAS:*** Personal Injury; Civil Torts.

ALBERT E. DURKIN, JR., born Chicago, Illinois, June 5, 1952; admitted to bar, 1977, Illinois and U.S. District Court, Northern District of Illinois. *Education:* Lewis University (B.A., Public Administration, 1974); DePaul University (J.D., 1977). Phi Alpha Delta. Lecturer: "Demonstrative Evidence in Brain Injury Cases", Indiana Trial Lawyers Association and Indiana Brain Injury Association Annual Seminar, October 8, 2005; "Increased Risk of Future Injury," Illinois State Bar Association, May 2003; Traumatic Brain Injury Study Case,: Illinois Management Network, April 2003; "Trying an Arbitration Case - Plaintiff's Perspective," Illinois State Bar Association, May 30, 2002; "Catastrophic Brain Injury: A Legal Case Study and Implications for Case Managers," ATLA, March 15-16, 2002; "Voir Dire," Chicago Bar Association, October 2001; "Effective Use of Paralegals," Roosevelt University, 2001; "Construction Negligence," ITLA, September 18, 1999; "Special Interrogatories," ITLA, May 3, 1997. Judge: Student Trial Advocacy Competition, March 2000 and 2003; American Moot Trial Association Regional Competition, February 2002 and 2003. Elected to: Leading Lawyer's Network, 2004-2005. *Member:* Chicago (Member, Judiciary and Civil Practice Committees) and Illinois State (Member, Tort Section Council and Judicial Evaluation Committee) Bar Associations; Association of Trial Lawyers of America; Illinois Trial Lawyers Association (Member, Medical Negligence Committee). ***PRACTICE AREAS:*** Plaintiff's Personal Injury Law; Catastrophic Injury; Product Liability; Medical Malpractice; Aviation Law; Premises Liability; Transportation; Negligence.

SCOTT H. RUDIN, born Skokie, Illinois, November 28, 1964; admitted to bar, 1989, Illinois and U.S. District Court, Northern District of Illinois. *Education:* Illinois State University (B.S., 1986); IIT, Chicago-Kent College of Law (J.D., 1989). *Member:* Chicago, Illinois State and American Bar Associations; Illinois Trial Lawyers Association. ***PRACTICE AREAS:*** Personal Injury; Civil Torts.

JEROME MIRZA AND ASSOCIATES, LTD.

Established in 1973

THREE FIRST NATIONAL PLAZA
CHICAGO, ILLINOIS 60602
Telephone: 312-368-1903
Facsimile: 312-368-0528
URL: http://www.mirzalaw.com

Bloomington, Illinois Office: 705 East Washington Street. Telephone: 309-827-8011. Facsimile: 309-829-8638.

Trial and Appellate Practice. Products Liability, Malpractice and Railroad Law.

FIRM PROFILE: A small law office that handles only a select number of major personal injury cases throughout the state of Illinois and in adjoining states. The law firm has frequently secured verdicts for its clients which are among the largest awarded in the nation.

JEROME MIRZA, born Chicago, Illinois, November 3, 1937; admitted to bar, 1963, Illinois; 1972, U.S. Supreme Court; 1980, U.S. Court of Appeals, 7th Circuit. *Education:* Illinois Wesleyan University (B.S., 1960); University of Illinois (LL.B., 1963). Phi Alpha Delta. Author: "Preparation and Trial of a Railroad Crossing Case," *Illinois Bar Journal,* August 1970 and *The Practical Lawyer,* January 1971; The Practical Lawyer's Negligence Law Manual No. 2, November 1972; "Proving Damages to the Self-Employed Plaintiff," *Handbook on Damages* , Illinois Institute for Continuing Legal Education, 1974, 1981, 1987; "The Standard of Care," *Handbook on Medical Malpractice* , Illinois Institute for Continuing Legal Education, 1975; "Standard of Care and Duties," Handbook on Plaintiff's Medical Malpractice Litigation, Illinois Institute for Continuing Legal Education, 1981, 1984; "Malpractice Problems—Plaintiff's View," Representing Health Care Institutions Handbook, Illinois Institute for Continuing Legal Education, 1982; "Introduction—Some General Trial Techniques in Proving Damages," Handbook on Proof of Damages, Illinois Institute for Continuing Legal Education, 1987; "Railroad Crossing Litigation," American Jurisprudence Trials, 1976; "Illinois Tort Law and Practice," Lawyers Cooperative Publishing Company, 1974; "Illinois Tort Law and Practice, 2d Edition," Lawyers Cooperative Publishing Company, 1988; "Illinois Tort Law and Practice, 3d Edition," West Publishing, 2004; "Illinois Personal Injury," (10 Volumes), Lawyers Cooperative Publishing Company, 1989. "Winning Litigation The Mirza Way," The West Group, 1992. Co-Editor, 1972, and Editor, 1973-1976, *Tort Trends,* published by the Illinois State Bar Association. Editor, Trial Lawyers Journal, published by the Illinois Trial Lawyers Association, 1977-1981. Director and Principal Instructor: Illinois Trial Lawyers Association College of Advocacy, 1980-1987; Illinois Trial Lawyers Association—Association of Trial Lawyers of America College of Advocacy, 1988-1989, Jerome Mirza Professional Trial Lawyers College of Advocacy at the University of Illinois College of Law, 2000-2003. Member, Board of Directors, Illinois Institute for Continuing Legal Education, 1986-1988. *Member:* Illinois State (Member, 1970-1977, and Chairman, 1980-1981, Executive Council on Tort Law; Chairman, Committee on Specialization, 1975-1976; Third Vice President, 1985-1986; Second Vice President, 1986-1987; President Elect, 1987-1988; President, 1988-1989) and American (Member, House of Delegates, 1985-1989) Bar Associations; Illinois Trial Lawyers Association (Member: Board of Managers, 1967-1978; Chairman, Amicus Curiae, 1975-1978; Executive Committee, 1975-1977; Vice President, 1978-1980; President-Elect, 1980-1981; President, 1981-1982); The Association of Trial Lawyers of America (Member, Board of Governors, 1972-1975, 1981-1989); American Board of Trial Advocates (Advocate). Founder and Lifetime Member, Trial Lawyers for Public Justice; Inner Circle of Advocates (Member). Fellow: International Society of Barristers; International Academy of Trial Lawyers.

THOMAS M. HARRIS, JR., born Lincoln, Illinois, May 10, 1963; admitted to bar, 1988, Illinois. *Education:* University of Illinois (B.A., 1985); University of Colorado (J.D., 1988). Author: "Survey of Illinois Law: Tort Developments," Southern Illinois University Law Journal, Vol. 19, Summer 1995; "Zen and the Art of Motorcycle-Injury Litigation," Illinois Bar Journal, Vol. 88 No. 7, July 2000. Member, Editorial Board, Illinois Bar Journal. Assistant States' Attorney, Logan County, Illinois, 1989-1991. Faculty, Jerome Mirza Professional Trial Lawyers College of Advocacy at the University of Illinois College of Law, 2000-2003. Board of Directors, Illinois Bar Foundation. *Member:* Logan County, McLean County and Illinois State Bar Associations (Tort Law Section Council, Chair, 1995-1996; Civil Practice and Procedure Section Council: Chair, 1999-2000, Vice-Chair, 1998-1999, Secretary, 1997-1998; Allerton Conference, Chair, 2000; Committee on Leg-

(This Listing Continued)

islation, 1996-1998; Standing Committee on Legal Education; Standing Committee on Supreme Court Rules); Illinois Trial Lawyers Association (Co-Chair, 1995-1996, Seminar Planning). ***Email:*** tomharrisjr@hotmail.com

MITCHELL HOFFMAN & WOLF LLC

221 NORTH LASALLE, SUITE 1148
CHICAGO, ILLINOIS 60601
Telephone: 312-726-6722
Fax: 312-726-3220
URL: http://www.mitchellhoffmanwolf.com

Plaintiffs Personal Injury, Automobile Accidents, Wrongful Death, Medical Malpractice, Construction Accidents, Premises Liability.

J. WESLEY MITCHELL, born Lebanon, Indiana, 1960; admitted to bar, 1990, Illinois. *Education:* Indiana State University (B.S., 1983); Chicago-Kent College of Law, Illinois Institute of Technology (J.D., 1990). *Member:* Illinois State Bar Association; Illinois Trial Lawyers Association. ***PRACTICE AREAS:*** Plaintiffs Personal Injury; Automobile Accidents and Injuries; Wrongful Death; Medical Malpractice; Construction Accidents. ***Email:*** jwmatty@aol.com

KENNETH A. HOFFMAN, born Chicago, Illinois, April 14, 1966; admitted to bar, 1991, Illinois and U.S. District Court, Northern District of Illinois; 1998, Federal Trial Bar. *Education:* Indiana University (B.A., 1988); Washington University (J.D., 1991). Member, Wiley Rutledge Moot Court Board. Listed by, Chicago Daily Law Bulletin as one of Illinois "Top 40 Attorneys Under 40," 2003. Assistant Instructor, Legal Research and Writing, Washington University, St. Louis, 1990-1991. *Member:* Chicago (Chair, Tort Litigation Committee, 2002-2003), Illinois State and American Bar Associations; Illinois Trial Lawyers Association; The Association of Trial Lawyers of America. ***PRACTICE AREAS:*** Personal Injury; Medical Malpractice; Wrongful Death. ***Email:*** khofflaw@aol.com

PAUL P. WOLF, born New York, New York, April 27, 1959; admitted to bar, 1985, Illinois. *Education:* University of Indiana-Bloomington (B.A., 1981); John Marshall Law School (J.D., 1985). *Member:* Chicago and Illinois State Bar Associations; Illinois Trial Lawyers Association; Women's Bar Association; Anti-Defamation League. ***PRACTICE AREAS:*** Personal Injury; Medical Malpractice; Construction Accidents; Premises Liability; Automobile Accidents and Injuries.

AZITA M. MOJARAD

Established in 2000

THREE FIRST NATIONAL PLAZA
70 W. MADISON STREET, SUITE 3700
CHICAGO, ILLINOIS 60602
Telephone: 312-641-0771
Fax: 312-641-0480
Email: amojarad@aol.com
URL: http://www.azitalaw.com

Collections, Contracts, Family Law, Immigration and Naturalization and Real Estate.

AZITA M. MOJARAD, born Iran, 1965; admitted to bar, 2000, Illinois. *Education:* Cambridge University, Cambridge, England (English Proficiency Teaching Certificate, 1984); Tehran University (B.S., Business Administration, 1986); North Park University (M.B.A., 1995); Loyola University at Chicago (J.D., 2000). Credit and Collection Manager, MTH Industries, Chicago, Il, 1989-1999. Investigator, Chicago Board Options Exchange, 1999-2002. *Member:* Chicago, Illinois State and American Bar Associations; American Immigration Lawyers Association. ***LANGUAGES:*** English and Persian. ***PRACTICE AREAS:*** Collections; Contracts; Family Law; Immigration and Naturalization; Real Estate.

MONICO, PAVICH & SPEVACK

20 SOUTH CLARK STREET, SUITE 700
CHICAGO, ILLINOIS 60603-1894
Telephone: 312-782-8500
Fax: 312-759-2000

Federal Criminal and Civil Litigation. Products Liability and Medical Malpractice Law. Appellate Practice.

MEMBERS OF FIRM

MICHAEL D. MONICO, born Chicago, Illinois, December 16, 1947; admitted to bar, 1973, Illinois; 1982, U.S. Supreme Court; U.S. Court of Appeals, Second, Sixth and Seventh Circuits and U.S. District Court, Northern and Central Districts of Illinois. *Education:* Georgetown University (A.B., 1969); Northwestern University (J.D., 1973). Assistant United States Attorney, Northern District of Illinois, 1973-1977. Publications: Co-Author: "Federal Criminal Practice" A Seventh Circuit Handbook, 2005 Edition, Lexis Law Publishing, (February, 2005); "Federal Criminal Practice" A Seventh Circuit Handbook, 2004 Edition, Lexis Law Publishing, (February 2004); "Federal Criminal Practice" A Seventh Circuit Handbook, 2003 Edition, Lexis Law Publishing, (February, 2003); "Federal Criminal Practice," A Seventh Circuit Handbook, 2002 Edition, Lexis Publishing (February, 2002); "Seventh Circuit Criminal Law Handbook, 2001 Edition," Lexis Publishing, (February, 2001); "Seventh Circuit Criminal Law Handbook, 2000 Edition," Lexis Publishing, (February, 2000). Selected Articles and Lectures: "The Effective Closing Argument: How to Make Them Remember," Indiana Continuing Legal Education Forum (2005); "Staying on the Right Side of the OIG" 14th Annual International Heart and Vascular Conference, Las Vegas, Nevada (2005); "Recent Medicare Fraud Prosecutions: From Drug Companies To Doctors and Their Lawyers!" National CLE Conference, Aspen, Colorado (January, 2003); "The Defense of Medicare Fraud Prosecutions," NACDL Midwinter Meeting and Seminar, Cancun, Mexico, February 20, 2003; "The Defense of Insider Trading Prosecutions," National CLE Conference, Vail, Colorado (January, 2001); "The Art of Cross-Examination," Chicago Inn of Court, March 23, 1999; "Impeachment in White-Collar Crimes: Practical Ideas & Suggestions," The Champion, March, 1999; "Impeachment in White Collar Cases," NACDL Annual Meeting & Seminar, Denver, Colorado, August 6, 1998; "Federalization of State Crime," Seventh Circuit Bar Association Annual Meeting, Milwaukee, Wisconsin, May 23, 1994; "Do Numbers Lie?: The Financial Expert," NACDL, Fall Meeting, Chicago, Ill., Oct. 29, 1993; "Cross Examination of Expert Witnesses in Financial Crimes," IACJ Annual Meeting, Chicago, Ill., Oct. 9, 1993; "Mentors & Whistleblowers: Young Lawyers Ethical Concerns," American Inns of Court Annual Meeting, Chicago, Ill., June 11, 1993; "Civil Justice Reforms," ABA Symposium, San Francisco, Calif., Aug. 1992; "Closing Argument - Making Sense of It," Kane County Bar Association, Criminal Law Committee and IACJ, St. Charles, Ill., March 19, 1992; "The Federal Sentencing Guidelines for Organizations: Having the Government As Your Partner," ABA Annual Meeting, Chicago, Ill., Aug. 6, 1990; "Plea Bargaining Practice and Techniques in Federal Court," IICLE, Chicago, Ill., March 11, 1988; "Ethical Problems Not Made For Television," *Chicago Daily Law Bulletin,* April 14, 1987; "Reduction of Sentence Under the Comprehensive Crime Control Act of 1984," *Illinois State Bar Association, Newsletter,* December, 1986; "New Regime for Reporting of Currency Transactions," *The National Law Journal,* January 20, 1986; "Representing Corporations and Their Employees in Agency and Grand Jury Investigations," ABA Symposium, Chicago, Illinois, September 27, 1985; "Effects of the 1984 Comprehensive Crime Control Act on the Business Community," ABA, Washington, D.C., July 6, 1985; "Governmental Intervention with the Attorney-Client Relationship," Georgia Association of Criminal Defense Lawyers, Jekyll Island, Georgia, April 27, 1985; "Ethical Problems For Government Lawyers," ABA, Denver, Colorado, June 26, 1987; "Money Laundering: Present State of the Law," ISBA, Geneva, Illinois, March 20, 1987; "Undercover Investigations Involving the Judicial Process," ABA, Chicago, Illinois, August 5, 1984. Co-Author: "Congress Should Re-Think RICO," Chicago Lawyer, Sept. 1990. Instructor at the National Institute for Trial Advocacy, Midwest Regional Program, at Loyola University School of Law, 2001. Instructor in Trial Practice: Loyola University School of Law, 1977-1987, 1992; National Institute of Trial Advocacy, 1983-1984, 2001-2003; Selected for Inclusion in "Best Lawyer in America" From 1993—; American College of Trial Lawyers; "Elected to the American Board of Criminal Lawyers, 1989. Board of Governors (1996—; Vice-President, 2003—). *Member:* Chicago, Illinois State (Member, Board of Governors, 1987-1989; Chairman, Criminal Justice Section Council, 1986-1987), Seventh Circuit (Chairman, Criminal Law and Procedure, 1995-1996; Board of Governors, 2002—), Federal and American (Member: White Collar Crime Committee, 1985-1989) Bar Associations; Master of the Bench, Chicago Inn of Court (President, 1993); National Association of Criminal Defense Lawyers (Member, Board of Directors, 1989-1990); Illinois Attorneys for Criminal Justice (President, 1992); Chicago Council of Lawyers; Justinian Society of Lawyers (President, 1989). Fellow: Illinois Bar Foundation. [Captain, U.S. Army Reserve, J.A.G. Corps, 1974-1984]. ***PRACTICE AREAS:*** Criminal and Civil Trials; Appeals. ***Email:*** mdm@monico-law.com

ROBERT J. PAVICH, born Chicago, Illinois, December 25, 1947; admitted to bar, 1975, Illinois and U.S. District Court, Northern District of Illinois including Trial Bar; 1999, Indiana, U.S. District Court, Northern and Southern Districts of Indiana and U.S. Court of Appeals, Seventh Circuit. *Education:* Harvard University (B.A., 1969); DePaul University (LL.B., 1975). Lead Counsel, International Criminal Tribunal for the Former Yugoslavia, 2001. *Member:* Chicago, Illinois State, Indiana State and American Bar Associations; The Association of Trial Lawyers of America; Illinois Trial Lawyers Association (Member, Board of Managers, 1986); Indiana Trial Lawyers Association; Defense Bar Association. [With U.S. Army]. ***PRACTICE AREAS:*** Medical Malpractice; Products Liability; Personal Injury; Civil Litigation; Civil Trial Appeals; International Law; Plaintiffs Personal Injury. ***Email:*** rpavich@monicopavich.com

BARRY A. SPEVACK, born New York, N.Y., February 25, 1950; admitted to bar, 1978, Illinois and U.S. District Court, Northern District of Illinois including Trial Bar; 1979, U.S. Court of Appeals, Seventh Circuit; 1989, U.S. Court of Appeals, Sixth Circuit; 1992, U.S. Court of Appeals, Third Circuit. *Education:* American University (B.A., 1972); Loyola University (J.D., cum laude, 1978). Alpha Sigma Nu. Recipient: Chief Justice Edward D. White Scholarship Award, 1978; Loyola University Leadership and Service Award, 1978. Member, Loyola National Trial Practice Team. Editor-in-Chief, Loyola Law Journal, 1977-1978. Author: "Expanding State Constitutional Protections & the New Silver Platter," 8 Loyola Law Journal of Chicago, Vol. 8, 1978. Co-Author: "Federal Criminal Practice - A Seventh Circuit Handbook," Lexis Publishing, (2002 ed); "Seventh Circuit Criminal Handbook" (2001 ed.), Lexis Publishing; "Seventh Circuit Criminal Handbook (2000 ed.), Lexis Publishing; "New Regime for Reporting of Currency Transactions," National Law Journal, January 20, 1986; "Ethical Problems Not Made for Television," Chicago Daily Law Bulletin, April 14, 1987; "Government Intervention in the Attorney-Client Relationship," presented to Georgia Association of Criminal Defense Lawyers, Jekyll Island, Georgia, April 27, 1985; "Plea Bargaining Practice and Techniques in Federal Court," presented to Illinois Institute for Continuing Legal Education, Chicago, Illinois, March 11, 1988; "Summary of Recent Illinois Supreme Court Decisions," presented to Law Update Program, Illinois State Bar Association, Chicago, March 30, 1984; "Summary of Selected Provisions of the Anti-Drug Abuse Act of 1986," presented to Illinois State Bar Association, Chicago, February, 1987; "Money Laundering: Present State of the Law," presented to Illinois State Bar Association Law Update Program, Geneva, Illinois, March 20, 1987. Associate Editor of Illinois State Bar Association Criminal Justice Newsletter, 1986-1988, and Author of "From the Seventh Circuit: Instructions," Vol. 30, No. 3 (Sept. 1986); "From the Seventh Circuit: RICO," Vol. 30, No. 6 (Jan. 1987); "Recent Amendments to the Circuit Rules of Appellate Procedure," Vol. 30, No. 11 (June 1987); "The View of *McNally,* " Vol. 31, No. 6 (Feb. 1988); "Rule 404(b) on Appellate Review," Vol. 32, No. 1 (July, 1988). Panelist, Illinois State Bar Association, April 20, 1993, "Horizontal Restraints of Trade--Criminal and Civil Enforcement Action". Lecturer, Advanced Legal Writing for Paralegals, Institute for Paralegal Education, Chicago, June 19, 2001. Adjunct Professor, Loyola University School of Law, 1989—. Instructor: Legal Writing and Research, Loyola University of Chicago Law School, 1982-1986; Introduction to Legal Reasoning, Loyola University of Chicago Law School, 1982—; Legal Writing for Practicing Lawyers, Loyola University of Chicago (Continuing Education Program), 1983; Advanced Legal Writing and Drafting, Loyola University of Chicago Law School, 1983—; Legal Reasoning and Research for Health Care Professionals, 1987. *Member:* Chicago and American Bar Associations; Illi-

(This Listing Continued)

MONICO, PAVICH & SPEVACK, Chicago—Continued

nois Trial Lawyers Association; Association of Trial Lawyers of America; National Association of Criminal Defense Lawyers. ***PRACTICE AREAS:*** Criminal and Civil Trials; Appeals.

MARTHA A. MACALOON, born Detroit, Michigan, October 5, 1952; admitted to bar, 1984, Illinois. *Education:* Boston College (B.S., 1974); Yale University (M.S.N., 1978); DePaul University (J.D., with honors, 1984). *Member:* Chicago, Illinois State and American Bar Associations; Association of Trial Lawyers of America. ***PRACTICE AREAS:*** Medical Malpractice. ***Email:*** mmacaloon@monicopavich.com

MELANIE K. FAIRMAN, born Highland Park, Illinois, February 9, 1968; admitted to bar, 1994, Illinois and U.S. District Court, Northern District of Illinois. *Education:* George Washington University (B.A., cum laude, 1990); Loyola University of Chicago (J.D., cum laude, 1994). Beta Alpha Psi. Member: Loyola National Trial Practice Team; Loyola National Moot Court Team. Recipient: Loyola University Leadership and Service Award; American Jurisprudence Awards for Trial Practice/Advocacy, Appellate Advocacy, Moot Court and Legal Clinic. Part-time Faculty, Coach for Loyola Trial Practice Teams, 1994-2000. *Member:* Chicago, Illinois State and American Bar Associations; Illinois Trial lawyers Association; Decalogue Society of Lawyers; Women's Bar Association of Illinois; Chicago Council for Lawyers; Federal Trial Bar; Association of Trial Lawyers of America. ***PRACTICE AREAS:*** Plaintiffs Personal Injury; Medical Malpractice; Products Liability; Automobile Accidents and Injuries. ***Email:*** mfairman@monicopavich.com

JACQUELINE S. JACOBSON, born Chicago, Illinois, July 8, 1965; admitted to bar, 1990, Illinois, U.S. Court of Appeals, Seventh Circuit and U.S. District Court, Northern District of Illinois. *Education:* University of Wisconsin (B.A., with honors, 1987); London School of Economics; Loyola University of Chicago School of Law (J.D., cum laude, 1990). Student Articles Editor, Loyola University of Chicago Law Journal. Recipient: Loyola University Service and Leadership Award; American Jurisprudence Award for Constitutional Law; Manuel F. Cohen Award, Federal Securities Bar Association, 1996. Co-Author, "Juvenile Law, 1987-1988 Illinois Law Survey," Loyola University of Chicago Law Journal. Co-Author: "The Defense of Insider Trading Prosecutions," National CLE Conference, Vail, Colorado, (January 2001); "The Supreme Court Turns Insider Trading Inside Out," The Champion, (December, 1997). Law Clerk, United States Court of Appeals for the Seventh Circuit, 1990-1992. Senior Enforcement Attorney, United States Securities and Exchange Commission, Midwest Regional Office, 1992-1996; prosecuted case against PaineWebber, one of the largest securities fraud cases in SEC history. ***PRACTICE AREAS:*** White Collar Criminal Defense; Federal Criminal Law; Securities Regulation; Commodities Regulation; Professional Liability. ***Email:*** jjacobson@monicopavich.com

---

ANASTASIA PAVICH, born Chicago, Illinois, July 13, 1979; admitted to bar, 2004, Illinois, U.S. District Court, Northern District of Illinois; 2005, Indiana, U.S. District Court, Northern and Southern Districts of Indiana. *Education:* St. Norbert College (B.A., 2001); Loyola University (J.D., 2004). ***PRACTICE AREAS:*** Medical Malpractice; Personal Injury; Products Liability. ***Email:*** apavich@monicopavich.com

THEODORE EPPEL, born Detroit, Michigan, September 20, 1970; admitted to bar, 1997, Illinois. *Education:* University of Michigan (B.A., 1993); University of Indiana (J.D., cum laude, 1997). *Member:* Chicago Bar Association. ***PRACTICE AREAS:*** White Collar Crime (90%); Criminal Law (10%). ***Email:*** treppel@monicopavich.com

OF COUNSEL

STEVEN J. SEIDMAN, born Chicago, Illinois, April 10, 1956; admitted to bar, 1981, Illinois, U.S. District Court, Northern District of Illinois and U.S. Court of Appeals, 7th Circuit. *Education:* University of Illinois (B.S., 1978); DePaul University (J.D., 1981). *Member:* Illinois State Bar Association; The Association of Trial Lawyers of America; Workers Compensation Lawyers Association; Illinois Trial Lawyers Association. (Also Member, Seidman Law Offices). ***PRACTICE AREAS:*** Civil Litigation; Medical Malpractice; Litigation; Products Liability; Workers Compensation. ***Email:*** sseidman@seidmanlaw.net

JAMES D. MONTGOMERY & ASSOCIATES, LTD.

ONE NORTH LASALLE STREET SUITE 2450
CHICAGO, ILLINOIS 60602
Telephone: 312-977-0200
Fax: 312-977-0209
Email: missp@jdmlaw.com
URL: http://www.lawyers.com/jamesdmontgomery

Complex Litigation, including Personal Injury, Wrongful Death, Aviation, Medical Malpractice and Products Liability.

JAMES D. MONTGOMERY, born 1932; admitted to bar, 1956, Illinois. *Education:* University of Illinois (J.D., 1956). Corporation Counsel, City of Chicago, 1983-1986. Lecturer, National Association of Criminal Defense Attorneys. Instructor, Litigation, Illinois Institute for Continuing Legal Education and DePaul University College of Law. Fellow, International Academy of Trial Lawyers. ***PRACTICE AREAS:*** Personal Injury (20%, 50); Medical Malpractice (15%, 20); Municipal Law (35%, 100); Criminal Defense (5%, 2); Civil Rights (25%, 30). ***Email:*** james@jdmlaw.com

JAMES D. MONTGOMERY, JR., born Chicago, Illinois, October 21, 1957; admitted to bar, 1982, Illinois. *Education:* Stanford University (B.A., 1979); University of Illinois (J.D., 1982). ***PRACTICE AREAS:*** Plaintiffs Personal Injury; Wrongful Death; Police Misconduct. ***Email:*** James2@jdmlaw.com

THOMAS C. MARSZEWSKI, born Chicago, Illinois, September 23, 1966; admitted to bar, 1992, Illinois and U.S. District Court, Northern District of Illinois. *Education:* Northern Illinois University (B.A., 1988); Illinois Institute of Technology (J.D., 1992). ***PRACTICE AREAS:*** Personal Injury (40%); Wrongful Death (30%); Civil Rights (30%).

MELVIN BROOKS, born Chicago, Illinois, March 16, 1959; admitted to bar, 1985, Illinois and U.S. District Court, Northern District of Illinois. *Education:* Iowa State University (B.A., 1982); University of Iowa (J.D., 1985). ***PRACTICE AREAS:*** Personal Injury (80%); Products Liability (10%); Medical Malpractice (10%). ***Email:*** mbrooks@jdmlaw.com

ASSOCIATES

MARK PARTS, born Buffalo, New York, April 27, 1961; admitted to bar, 1990, Illinois. *Education:* Butler University (B.A., 1983); Northwestern University (M.A., 1984); University of Chicago (J.D., 1990). ***PRACTICE AREAS:*** Litigation.

JAMES M. SANFORD, born Columbus, Ohio, July 14, 1961; admitted to bar, 1987, Ohio and Illinois; 2004, Wisconsin. *Education:* Michigan State University (B.A., 1983); Capital University (J.D., 1986). ***PRACTICE AREAS:*** Medical Malpractice; Civil Litigation; Personal Injury. ***Email:*** Jims@jdmlaw.com

BEVERLY P. SPEARMAN, born St. Louis, Missouri, June 3, 1964; admitted to bar, 2001, Illinois. *Education:* St. Louis University (B.S.N., 1991); University of New Mexico School of Law (J.D., 2001). Registered Nurse, 1991. *Member:* Association of Trial Lawyers of America; Illinois Trial Lawyers Association (Member, Medical Malpractice Committee). ***PRACTICE AREAS:*** Medical Malpractice (75%); Wrongful Death (20%); Personal Injury (5%). ***Email:*** bspearman@jdmlaw.com

TRENT A. MCCAIN, born Gary, Indiana, February 26, 1974; admitted to bar, 2002, Illinois; 2003, Indiana, U.S. District Court, Northern and Southern Districts of Indiana and U.S. Court of Appeals, 6th Circuit. *Education:* Florida A & M University (B.S.B.A., cum laude, 1995); Valparaiso University (J.D., 2002). *Member:* American Bar Association; Association of Trial Lawyers of America. ***PRACTICE AREAS:*** Personal Injury (60%); Medical Malpractice (10%); Products Liability (10%); Wrongful Death (10%); Police Misconduct (10%). ***Email:*** tamccaine@jdmlaw.com

MOORE, STRICKLAND & WHITSON-OWEN

Established in 1985

ONE EAST WACKER DRIVE, SUITE 3510
CHICAGO, ILLINOIS 60601
Telephone: 312-464-1890
Fax: 312-464-1627
Email: attorneys@moore-strickland.com

Automobile Insurance Defense, Commercial Insurance Defense, General Liability Defense, Insurance Defense, Local Government Defense, Municipal Defense, Premises Liability Defense, Products Liability Defense, Property Insurance Defense, School District Liability, Self Insured Defense.

FIRM PROFILE: Moore, Strickland & Whitson-Owen is recognized as a quality defense firm. The firm has assembled partners with over 75 years of collective experience as defense trial lawyers and who have tried over 250 cases to verdict. The firm's small size and depth of experience make it somewhat unique in the field of defense work. The lawyers are able to work closely and efficiently with clients while providing a quality defense for high exposure claims. The firm defends claims in the areas of general liability, premises liability and products liability for insurance companies, retail, manufacturing and service corporations, medical device companies, academic institutions and municipal entities.

MEMBERS

GARY K. MOORE, born Oak Park, Illinois, July, 1946; admitted to bar, 1974, Illinois; 1975, U.S. District Court, Northern District of Illinois, including Trial Bar; 1992, U.S. Court of Appeals, Seventh Circuit. *Education:* University of Illinois (B.A., 1969; M.A., 1971); Loyola University (J.D., 1974). *Member:* Chicago and American (Litigation Section) Bar Associations; Defense Research Institute. ***REPORTED CASES:*** Vesey v. Chicago Housing Authority, 145 Ill. 2d 404 (1991); Trotter v. Chicago Housing Authority, 516 N.E. 2d 121 (1987); Loving v. Chicago Housing Authority, 560 N.E. 2d 1129 (1990); Hill v. Chicago Housing Authority, 233 Ill. App. 3d 923 (1992). ***PRACTICE AREAS:*** Litigation; Products Liability; Toxic Torts; Appellate Practice. ***Email:*** gmoore@moore-strickland.com

DARLENE STRICKLAND, born Elmhurst, Illinois, May 19, 1953; admitted to bar, 1992, Illinois. *Education:* Northern Illinois University (B.A., cum laude, 1977); Loyola University (J.D., 1992). *Member:* Illinois State and American (Member, Law Practice Management Section, 1988—) Bar Associations; Women's Bar Association of Illinois. ***REPORTED CASES:*** SCR Medical Transportation Services, Inc. v. Browne, 335 Ill. App. 3d 585 (2002). ***PRACTICE AREAS:*** Litigation; Products Liability; Toxic Torts; Appellate Practice; Construction Law. ***Email:*** dstrickland@moore-strickland.com

EUGENA A. WHITSON-OWEN, born Herrin, Illinois, January 6, 1970; admitted to bar, 1996, Illinois. *Education:* Eastern Illinois University (B.S., 1992); John Marshall Law School (J.D., 1996). Phi Alpha Delta. Associate Justice, Moot Court. *Member:* Illinois Association of Defense Trial Counsel; Women's Bar Association of Illinois. ***REPORTED CASES:*** Jakubowski, etc. v. Alden-Bennett Construction Co., 327 Ill. App. 3d 627 (2002). ***PRACTICE AREAS:*** Litigation; Products Liability; Toxic Torts; Appellate Practice; Construction Law; Insurance Coverage. ***Email:*** ewhitson-owen@moore-strickland.com

ASSOCIATES

THOMAS J. BRANIT (1958-1993)

ROBERT P. KILE [U.S. Army, 1983-1994, Captain; U.S. Army Reserve, 1995—, Lt. Col]. (1955-2005). ***REPORTED CASES:*** Connaghan v. Caplice, 325 Ill. App. 3d 245 (2001).

CHRISTINE M. QUINTOS, born Rochester, Michigan, March 23, 1976; admitted to bar, 2002, Illinois and U.S. District Court, Northern District of Illinois; 2003, Texas. *Edu-*

(This Listing Continued)

cation: University of Notre Dame (B.S., 1998); DePaul University (J.D., 2002). *Member:* Chicago Bar Association. ***PRACTICE AREAS:*** Litigation; Products Liability; Construction Law; Toxic Torts; Insurance Coverage. ***Email:*** cquintos@moore-strickland.com

RHETT STROM, born Elmhurst, Illinois, October 21, 1971; admitted to bar, 2004, Illinois. *Education:* Wittenberg University (B.A., 1994); DePaul University (J.D., 2004). ***PRACTICE AREAS:*** Litigation; Insurance Defense. ***Email:*** rstrom@moore-strickland.com

BRETT A. SKEAN, born Naperville, Illinois, March 27, 1973; admitted to bar, 2003, Illinois. *Education:* University of Iowa (B.A., 2000); Northern Illinois University (J.D., 2003). Northern Illinois University Law Review. ***PRACTICE AREAS:*** Litigation; Insurance Defense. ***Email:*** bskean@moore-strickland.com

All Attorneys are Members of Defense Research Institute.

EDMUND B. MORAN, JR.

Established in 1986

53 WEST JACKSON BOULEVARD, SUITE 857
CHICAGO, ILLINOIS 60604
Telephone: 312-408-1544
Fax: 312-408-1539
Email: moran_law@earthlink.net

General Civil Litigation. Trials and Appeals. Environmental, Commercial, Civil Rights and Torts, Criminal, Constitutional and Defamation.

EDMUND B. MORAN, JR., born Chicago, Illinois, January 6, 1947; admitted to bar, 1973, Illinois; 1976, U.S. Court of Appeals, Seventh Circuit; 1979, U.S. Supreme Court; 1973, U.S. District Court, Northern District of Illinois, including Trial Bar. *Education:* University of Notre Dame (B.B.A., 1969); Loyola University (J.D., 1973). Law Clerk to U.S. District Court Judge William J. Lynch, 1974-1976. Assistant Cook County Public Defender, 1973-1974. Assistant Illinois Attorney General (Environmental Control Division, 1984-1986) and Special Assistant Illinois Attorney General, 1986-1992. Member, Keck, Mahin & Cate, Chicago, Illinois, 1976-1983. Member, President, 1992-1993, Board of Governors, Loyola University School of Law Alumni Association, 1989-1994. President, 1990, City of Evanston Recreation Board, 1988-1991. Alderman, Evanston City Council, 1991—. [With U.S. Marine Corps, Reserve, 1970-1976]. ***SPECIAL AGENCIES:*** Delegate, Solid Waste Agency of Northern Cook County, 1993—. ***PRACTICE AREAS:*** Civil Litigation; Trials and Appeals; Environmental Law; Commercial Law; Civil Rights Law; Torts; Criminal Law; First Amendment.

JOHN T. MORAN & ASSOCIATES

Established in 1985

SUITE 900
309 WEST WASHINGTON
CHICAGO, ILLINOIS 60606
Telephone: 312-630-0200
Telefax: 312-630-0203
Email: j.moran@comcast.net
URL: http://www.lawyers.com/jmoran

Civil and Criminal Appeals, Labor and Employment, Discrimination Law, Wrongful Termination, State and Federal Criminal Law, Business Litigation.

JOHN THOMAS MORAN, JR., born Oak Park, Illinois; admitted to bar, 1969, Illinois; 1973, U.S. Supreme Court; 1976, Colorado and U.S. Court of Appeals, Sixth, Seventh and Ninth Circuits. *Education:* University of Notre Dame (A.B., cum laude, 1965); Georgetown University (J.D., 1968). Listed in Who's Who in American Law, 9th Ed., 1996-1997. Grantee: National Endowment for the Humanities, Law and Ethics, Harvard Law School, 1977; Ford Foundation, International Colloquium on the Common Law, London, 1976. *Member:* Illinois State Bar Association; Appellate Lawyers Association; National Legal Aid and Defenders Association; National Employment Lawyers Association; National Association of Criminal Defense Lawyers. ***LANGUAGES:*** French. ***REPORTED CASES:*** People v. R. Caballes, Illinois Supreme Court, on remand from the U.S. Supreme Court, 2005; United States v. Re, 401 F.3d 828 (7th Cir. 2005); People v. Durr, 2004 Ill. App. LEXIS 893 (2004)(state appeal, trial court affirmed); People v. A. Rodriguez, 312 Ill. App. 3d 920, 728 N.E.2d 635 (2000); United States v. Zizzo, 120 F.3d 1338 (7th Cir. 1997); Schweihs v. Burdick, 96 F.3d 917 (7th Cir. 1996); United States v. Sorensen, 58 F.3d 1154 (7th Cir. 1995); Doherty v. Caisley, 104 Ill. 2d 11 (1984); People ex rel. Davis v. Vazquez, 92 Ill. 2d 132; 441 N.E.2d 54 (1982); People ex rel. Mosley v. Carey, 74 Ill. 2d 527; 387 N.E.2d 325 (1979); Browder v. Ill. Dept of Corrections, 434 U.S. 257 (1978); Brown v. Illinois, 422 U.S. 590 (1975),. ***PRACTICE AREAS:*** Appellate Practice (30%, 200); Employment Law (25%, 50); Criminal Law (20%, 500); Litigation (20%, 150); Business Law (5%, 300). ***Email:*** jmoran@jtmoranlaw.com

MORGAN, LEWIS & BOCKIUS LLP

77 WEST WACKER DRIVE
CHICAGO, ILLINOIS 60601
Telephone: 312-324-1000
eFax: 877-432-9652;
Fax: 312-324-1001
Email: postmaster@morganlewis.com
URL: http://www.morganlewis.com

Philadelphia, Pennsylvania Office: 1701 Market Street, 19103-2921. Telephone: 215-963-5000. eFax: 877-432-9652; Fax: 215-963-5001.
Washington, DC Office: 1111 Pennsylvania Avenue, NW, 20004. Telephone: 202-739-3000. eFax: 877-432-9652; Fax: 202-739-3001.

(This Listing Continued)

New York, New York Office: 101 Park Avenue, 10178-0060. Telephone: 212-309-6000. eFax: 877-432-9652; Fax: 212-309-6001.
Los Angeles, California Office: 300 South Grand Avenue, Twenty-Second Floor, 90071-3132. Telephone: 213-612-2500. eFax: 877-432-9652; Fax: 213-612-2501.
San Francisco, California Office: One Market, Spear Street Tower, 94105. Telephone: 415-442-1000. eFax: 877-432-9652; Fax: 415-442-1001.
Miami, Florida Office: 5300 Wachovia Financial Center, 200 South Biscayne Boulevard, 33131-2339. Telephone: 305-415-3000. eFax: 877-432-9652; Fax: 305-415-3001.
Pittsburgh, Pennsylvania Office: One Oxford Centre, Thirty-Second Floor, 15219-6401. Telephone: 412-560-3300. eFax: 877-432-9652; Fax: 412-560-7001.
Princeton, New Jersey Office: 502 Carnegie Center, 08540-6241. Telephone: 609-919-6600. eFax: 877-432-9652; Fax: 609-919-6701.
Palo Alto, California Office: 2 Palo Alto Square, 3000 El Camino Real, Suite 700, 94306. Telephone: 650-843-4000. eFax: 877-432-9652; Fax: 650-843-4001.
Dallas, Texas Office: 1717 Main Street, Suite 3200, 75201-7347. Telephone: 214-466-4000. eFax: 877-432-9652; Fax: 214-466-4001.
Harrisburg, Pennsylvania Office: One Commerce Square, 417 Walnut Street, 17101-1904. Telephone: 717-237-4000. eFax: 877-432-9652; Fax: 717-237-4001.
Irvine, California Office: 5 Park Plaza, Suite 1750, 92614. Telephone: 949-399-7000. eFax: 877-432-9652; Fax: 949-399-7001.
Boston, Massachusetts Office: 225 Franklin Street, Suite 1705, 02110. Telephone: 617-451-9700. eFax: 877-432-9652; Fax: 617-451-9710.
London, England Office: Morgan, Lewis & Bockius, 2 Gresham Street, London EC2V 7PE. Telephone: 44-20-7710-5500. Fax: 44-20-7710-5600.
Paris, France Office: Morgan, Lewis & Bockius, 68, rue du Faubourg Saint-Honoré, 75008 Paris. Telephone: +33 (0) 1-53-30-43-00. Fax: +33 (0) 1-53-30-43-01.
Brussels, Belgium Office: Morgan, Lewis & Bockius, 7 Rue Guimard, B-1040. Telephone: 32-2-507-75-00. Fax: 32-2-507-75-55.
Frankfurt, Germany Office: Guiollettstraße 54, D-60325 Frankfurt am Main. Telephone: 49-69-714-007-0. Fax: 49-69-714-007-10.
Tokyo, Japan Office: Shin-Tokyo Building, 9th Floor, 3-1, Marunouchi 3-chome, Chiyoda-ku, Tokyo 100-0005. Telephone: 81-3-5219-2500. Fax: 81-3-5219-2501.

Acquisitions and Mergers, Antitrust, Banking, Bankruptcy, Civil Litigation, Construction, Corporate, Elections and Campaign Financing, Employee Benefits and Pensions, Environmental, Estate Planning, Government Regulation, Health and Biotechnology, Immigration, Intellectual Property, Insurance, Insurance Recovery, International Law, Investment Management and Financial Services, Labor and Employment, Legislative, Litigation, Municipal Finance, Natural Resources, Non-Profit Organizations, Partnerships, Patent Litigation, Patent Prosecution, Personal Injury, Personal Law and Probate, Product Liability, Public Utilities, Real Estate, Savings and Loan, Securities Offerings, Trademarks and Copyrights, Taxation and White Collar Defense. Unless otherwise indicated, lawyers listed are not certified by the Texas Board of Legal Specialization.

MEMBERS OF FIRM IN CHICAGO

DAVID ACKERMAN, born June 11, 1949; admitted to bar, 1974, Illinois. *Education:* Princeton University (A.B., 1971); Harvard Law School (J.D., 1974). Wilson Scholar. Author: "Questions and Answers Regarding the Duties of ESOP Fiduciaries," Journal of Employee Ownership Law and Finance, Winter, 2001; "Innovative Uses of ESOPs in Estate Planning for Business Owners," 33 Miami Estate Planning Institute, ch. 12, Matthew-Bender, 1999; "New Planning Opportunities for S Corporations: Tax-Favored ESOPs," Journal of Passthrough Entities, March-April 1999; "ESOPs and S Corporations," Journal of Employee Ownership Law and Finance, Winter, 1998; "Tax Considerations in Organizing Closely Held Corporations," Ch. 2 of *Closely Held Corporations* (Ill. Inst. for Cont. Legal Ed. 1995); "Tax-Favored Planning for Ownership Succession via ESOPs," Estate Planning, Nov./Dec. 1992; "Planning for Ownership Succession in the Closely Held Business," DePaul Business Law Journal, Spring 1991. *Member:* Chicago (Member, Federal Taxation Committee, 1984—), Illinois State and American Bar Associations. ***PRACTICE AREAS:*** Corporate Employee Benefits. ***Email:*** dackerman@morganlewis.com

SARI M. ALAMUDDIN, born December 6, 1968; admitted to bar, 1993, Illinois and Wisconsin; 1998, U.S. Supreme Court. *Education:* Princeton University (B.A., 1990); University of Wisconsin Law School (J.D., 1993). ***PRACTICE AREAS:*** Labor and Employment Law. ***Email:*** salamuddin@morganlewis.com

MIRIAM G. BAHCALL, born June 28, 1958; admitted to bar, 1985, Illinois. *Education:* University of Wisconsin (B.S., 1980); University of Chicago Law School (J.D., 1985). ***PRACTICE AREAS:*** Securities Litigation; Commercial Litigation; Regulatory Investigations. ***Email:*** mbahcall@morganlewis.com

THEODORE M. BECKER, born February 18, 1949; admitted to bar, 1975, Illinois, U.S. Court of Appeals, Seventh and Tenth Circuits; 1976, U.S. Court of Appeals, Ninth Circuit; 1978, U.S. Supreme Court; 1983, U.S. Court of Appeals for the Federal Circuit. *Education:* Washington University (A.B., 1970); Northwestern University (M.A., 1972; Ph.D., 1981); Northwestern University School of Law (J.D., 1974). Phi Beta Kappa; Order of the Coif. Fellow, Northwestern University Program in Law and the Social Sciences, 1970-1974. Russell Sage Fellow, Yale Law School, 1974-1975. *Member:* Chicago, Illinois State and American (Member, Sections on Litigation, Business Law, Real Property, Probate and Trust Law; Forum on Franchising) Bar Associations. ***PRACTICE AREAS:*** Litigation; Alternative Dispute Resolution; Employee Benefits; Labor and Employment; Franchises and Franchising; Business Law; Corporate Law; Commercial Law; Banks and Banking; Real Estate. ***Email:*** tbecker@morganlewis.com

BARRY A. HARTSTEIN, born May 25, 1951; admitted to bar, 1976, Illinois; 1982, California. *Education:* Cornell University, School of Industrial and Labor Relations (B.S., 1973); Northwestern University School of Law (J.D., 1976). Phi Kappa Phi. Author: "Telecommuting: The New Workplace of the '90's," Employee Relations Law Journal (Spring 1996); "Weeks v. Baker & McKenzie: A Potential 'Blueprint' for Sexual Harassment Litigation," Employee Relations Journal (Spring 1995); "The Broadening Scope of Harassment in the Workplace," Employee Relations Law Journal (Spring 1994); "Employer Audits of EEO Activities: Helpful or Hurtful," HR Focus, American Management Association (January 1993). Editorial Board, Employee Relations Law Journal, 1991—; Editorial Advisory Board, Employment Law Strategist, 1993—; Editorial Board, Employment Law

(This Listing Continued)

MORGAN, LEWIS & BOCKIUS LLP, Chicago—Continued

Counselor, Business Law, Inc., 1994—; Board of Editors, Employer's Guide to Equal Employment Opportunity Law, Business Laws, Inc., 1985—. ***PRACTICE AREAS:*** Employment Law; Labor Law; Employment Discrimination; Wrongful Termination; Labor and Employment. ***Email:*** bhartstein@morganlewis.com

BRIAN D. HECTOR, born May 3, 1961; admitted to bar, 1989, Illinois; 1999, U.S. Tax Court. *Education:* University of Illinois (B.A., 1983); Chicago-Kent College of Law, Illinois Institute of Technology (J.D., 1989). *Member:* Chicago (Member, Employee Benefits Committee), Illinois State (Member, Employee Benefits Section) and American (Member, Taxation Section) Bar Associations; The ESOP Association (Board Member, Illinois Chapter); National Center for Employee Ownership. ***PRACTICE AREAS:*** ERISA; Employee Benefits; ESOP; Executive Compensation; Taxation. ***Email:*** bhector@morganlewis.com

CHARLES C. JACKSON, born April 2, 1952; admitted to bar, 1977, Illinois; 1982, U.S. Supreme Court. *Education:* Bethel College (B.A., 1974); Northwestern University School of Law (J.D., 1977). ***PRACTICE AREAS:*** Labor and Employment Law. ***Email:*** charles.jackson@morganlewis.com

RICHARD B. LAPP, born September 20, 1958; admitted to bar, 1985, Illinois. *Education:* Michigan State University (B.A., 1981); University of Wisconsin Law School (J.D., 1985). Order of the Coif. Law Clerk, Hon. Daniel A. Manion, U.S. Court of Appeals for the Seventh Circuit. ***PRACTICE AREAS:*** Labor and Employment Law. ***Email:*** rlapp@morganlewis.com

STEVEN M. MALINA, born July 7, 1962; admitted to bar, 1987, Illinois. *Education:* University of Michigan (B.A., 1983); University of Illinois College of Law (J.D., 1987); University of Chicago (M.B.A., 1993). ***PRACTICE AREAS:*** Securities Litigation; Financial Services Regulation; Commercial Litigation. ***Email:*** smalina@morganlewis.com

THOMAS A. MARRINSON, born May 19, 1964; admitted to bar, 1993, Illinois. *Education:* Columbia University (A.B., 1986); University of California, Los Angeles School of Law (J.D., 1989). Chief Articles Editor, Federal Communications Law Journal, 1988-1989. Author: "Insurance Coverage Disputes," Law Journal Press, 1996; Co-Author: "Electronic Discovery: Get Used To It," Gavels & Gears, Fall 2003; Co-Author: "Beyond 'Sudden': The New Wave of Pollution Exclusion Litigation," Environmental Claims Journal, Spring 1995. *Member:* Chicago (Secretary, Insurance Law Committee) and American (Co-Chair, Technology for the Litigator, Past Co-Chair, Litigation Management and Economics Committee) Bar Associations; American Bar Foundation (Fellow). ***PRACTICE AREAS:*** Commercial Litigation; Insurance Coverage. ***Email:*** tmarrinson@morganlewis.com

PHILIP A. MISCIMARRA, born March 14, 1956; admitted to bar, 1982, Pennsylvania; 1986, Illinois; 1993, Wisconsin. *Education:* Duquesne University (B.A., 1978); The Wharton School, University of Pennsylvania (M.B.A., 1982); University of Pennsylvania Law School (J.D., 1982). Author: "The NLRB and Managerial Discretion: Plant Closings, Relocations, Subcontracting, and Automation," 1983. Co-Author: "Trading Spaces — What the Courts Say Now About Mandatory Arbitration," by Miscimarra and Bear (Amer. Empl. L. Council 2003); "The NLRB and Secondary Boycotts," by Miscimarra, Berkowitz, Wiener, and Ditelberg (3d ed. 2002); "Government Protection of Employees Involved in Mergers and Acquisitions," by Northrup and Miscimarra (1989 and 1989-1997 supplement); "Frozen in Time — The NLRB, Outsourcing and Management Rights," by Miscimarra and Schwartz, 18 J. Lab. Res. 561, (1997); "Multinational Union Organizations in the White-Collar, Service and Communications Industries," by Rowan, Pitterle, and Miscimarra (1983). Member: Editorial Advisory Board, Olin Institute for Employment Practice & Policy, George Mason University, 1997—; Editorial Advisory Board, University of Pennsylvania Journal of Labor & Employment Law, 1999—. Senior Fellow, The Wharton School, University of Pennsylvania, Center for Human Resources. ***PRACTICE AREAS:*** Labor and Employment Law. ***Email:*** pmiscimarra@morganlewis.com

GRADY B. MURDOCK JR., born June 10, 1948; admitted to bar, 1974, Illinois; 1986, U.S. Supreme Court. *Education:* Grinnell College (B.A., 1970); Northwestern University School of Law (J.D., 1973). ***PRACTICE AREAS:*** Labor and Employment Law. ***Email:*** gmurdock@morganlewis.com

ELIZABETH S. PERDUE, born May 7, 1954; admitted to bar, 1982, Illinois. *Education:* Pomona College (B.A., 1976); University of Chicago Law School (J.D., 1982). *Member:* Illinois State and American Bar Associations; United States Trademark Association. ***PRACTICE AREAS:*** Corporate Law; Mergers and Acquisitions; Commercial Lending. ***Email:*** eperdue@morganlewis.com

JOHN D. SHUGRUE, born August 30, 1962; admitted to bar, 1987, Illinois. *Education:* University of Denver (B.A., 1984); University of North Carolina School of Law (J.D., 1987). Member, University of North Carolina Law Review. Articles Editor, North Carolina Journal of International Law and Commercial Regulation. Author: "Insurance Coverage Disputes," Law Journal Press (co-author); "Illinois Environmental Insurance Coverage Law," 11 *Environmental Claims Journal* 113 (Winter 1999) (co-author); "Tips to Help Preserve Insurance Coverage," The Corporate Counsellor (May and June 1999) (co-author); "Parol Evidence Myths in Insurance Coverage Litigation," 1 *Journal Insurance Coverage* 1 (Summer 1998) (co-author); "Lloyd's Names Litigation in the United States: Is the Glass Half Empty of Half Full?" 4 *International Insurance Law Review* 91 (March 1996). *Member:* American Bar Association (Past Co-Chair, Insurance Coverage Litigation Committee, Litigation Section). ***PRACTICE AREAS:*** Insurance Coverage Advice and Litigation; Commercial Litigation. ***Email:*** jshugrue@morganlewis.com

NINA G. STILLMAN, born April 3, 1948; admitted to bar, 1973, Illinois. *Education:* Smith College (A.B., 1970); Northwestern University School of Law (J.D., 1973). Phi Beta Kappa; Moot Court; Order of the Coif. Author: "Occupational Health Issues Under Employment Discrimination Law," Occupational Medicine: Law and the Workplace, Hanley & Belfus, Inc., 1996; "The Occupational Safety and Health Act," Chap. 30, Employment Law Desk Book for Human Resources Professionals, West Group, 2001. Listed in the Best Lawyers in America, 1993—, Who's Who in America, 1994—, and Crain's Chicago Business' "100 Most Influential Women in Chicago," 1996. *Member:* Chicago Bar Association (Chairman, Labor and Employment Law Committee, 1986-1987). ***PRACTICE AREAS:*** Labor and Employment Law; Employment Litigation; Occupational Safety and Health; Wrongful Termination Defense. ***Email:*** nstillman@morganlewis.com

(This Listing Continued)

OF COUNSEL IN CHICAGO

ANDY R. ANDERSON, born September 9, 1959; admitted to bar, 1984, Illinois. *Education:* MacMurray College (B.S., 1981); University of Illinois College of Law (J.D., 1984). ***PRACTICE AREAS:*** Corporate Employee Benefits. ***Email:*** aanderson@morganlewis.com

MARY A. SMIGIELSKI, born March 2, 1968; admitted to bar, 1993, California; 1997, Illinois; 2004, U.S. Supreme Court. *Education:* University of San Diego (B.A., 1990); University of San Diego School of Law (J.D., 1993). ***PRACTICE AREAS:*** Labor and Employment Law. ***Email:*** msmigielski@morganlewis.com

ASSOCIATES IN CHICAGO

GREGORY P. ABRAMS, admitted to bar, 2003, Illinois. *Education:* University of Pennsylvania (B.A., 2000); University of Chicago Law School (J.D., 2003). ***Email:*** gabrams@morganlewis.com

JAMES E. BAYLES, JR., admitted to bar, 1991, Illinois. *Education:* University of Chicago (B.A., 1987; M.B.A., 1988); Boalt Hall School of Law, University of California at Berkeley (J.D., 1991). ***Email:*** jbayles@morganlewis.com

BETH A. BLACK, admitted to bar, 1999, Illinois. *Education:* Northern Illinois University (B.S., 1990); John Marshall Law School (J.D., 1999). ***Email:*** bblack@morganlewis.com

SHANNON CALLAHAN, admitted to bar, 2004, Illinois. *Education:* University of Michigan (B.A., 2000); Loyola University Chicago School of Law (J.D., 2004). ***Email:*** scallahan@morganlewis.com

DEBORAH S. DAVIDSON, admitted to bar, 1998, Illinois. *Education:* University of Tulsa (B.A., 1995); Washington University School of Law (J.D., 1998). ***Email:*** ddavidson@morganlewis.com

TODD E. DOMJAN, admitted to bar, 2000, Illinois. *Education:* University of Notre Dame (B.A., 1997); Pepperdine University School of Law (J.D., 2000). ***Email:*** tdomjan@morganlewis.com

KEVIN DREHER, admitted to bar, 2002, Illinois; 2003, Pennsylvania and New Jersey. *Education:* University of Michigan (B.A., 1993); University of Illinois College of Law (J.D., 2002). ***Email:*** kdreher@morganlewis.com

ROSS H. FRIEDMAN, admitted to bar, 2001, Illinois. *Education:* University of Illinois (B.S., 1997); University of Chicago Law School (J.D., 2001). ***Email:*** rfriedman@morganlewis.com

LAURA M. GEIGER, admitted to bar, 1999, Illinois. *Education:* University of Illinois (B.A., 1996); Chicago-Kent College of Law, Illinois Institute of Technology (J.D., 1999). ***Email:*** lgeiger@morganlewis.com

DANIEL A. HETZEL, admitted to bar, 2004, Illinois. *Education:* Northwestern University (B.A., 1997); University of Chicago Law School (J.D., 2003). ***Email:*** dhetzel@morganlewis.com

RENEE P. LEWIS, admitted to bar, 1997, Illinois. *Education:* DePaul University (B.S., 1992); DePaul University College of Law (J.D., 1997). ***Email:*** rlewis@morganlewis.com

TAMMARA M. LOVETT, admitted to bar, 1995, Illinois. *Education:* University of Wisconsin-Madison (B.A., 1992); Chicago-Kent College of Law, Illinois Institute of Technology (J.D., 1995). ***Email:*** tlovett@morganlewis.com

M. EMILY OSBORNE, admitted to bar, 2000, California; 2004, Illinois. *Education:* University of California, Santa Barbara (B.A., 1997); University of San Francisco School of Law (J.D., 2000). ***Email:*** eosborne@morganlewis.com

MICHAEL H. PEIPERT, admitted to bar, 1998, Illinois. *Education:* University of Illinois at Urbana-Champaign (B.S., 1987); Chicago-Kent College of Law, Illinois Institute of Technology (J.D., 1998). ***Email:*** mpeipert@morganlewis.com

CHRISTOPHER RIZZO, admitted to bar, 2003, Illinois. *Education:* Northwestern University (B.A., 1999); University of Illinois College of Law (J.D., 2003). ***Email:*** crizzo@morganlewis.com

CHARIS A. RUNNELS, admitted to bar, 1999, Illinois. *Education:* Marquette University (B.A., 1993); Chicago-Kent College of Law, Illinois Institute of Technology (J.D., 1999). ***Email:*** crunnels@morganlewis.com

DANIEL J. STRUCK, admitted to bar, 1994, New York; 1997, Illinois. *Education:* University of Dallas (B.A., 1988); New York University School of Law (J.D., 1993). ***Email:*** dstruck@morganlewis.com

HEATHER ANN WRIGHT, admitted to bar, 2001, Illinois. *Education:* Loyola University Chicago (B.A., 1997); Loyola University Chicago School of Law (J.D., 2000). ***Email:*** hwright@morganlewis.com

ETHAN G. ZELIZER, admitted to bar, 2003, Illinois. *Education:* Loyola University (B.A., 2000); Loyola University Chicago School of Law (J.D., 2003). ***Email:*** ezelizer@morganlewis.com

Members of the Firm, Counsel, Of Counsel and Associates in Philadelphia, Pennsylvania; Washington, DC; New York, New York; Los Angeles, California; San Francisco, California; Miami, Florida; Pittsburgh, Pennsylvania; Princeton, New Jersey; Palo Alto, California; Dallas, Texas; Harrisburg, Pennsylvania; Irvine, California; Boston, Massachusetts; London, England; Paris, France; Brussels, Belgium; Frankfurt am Main, Germany; and Tokyo, Japan are listed in the Biographical Section respectively.

THE LAW FIRM OF WENDY R. MORGAN

CHICAGO, ILLINOIS

(See Arlington Heights)

Family Law, Divorce, Child Custody, Interstate Custody, Adoptions, Child Support, Paternity, Premarital Agreements, Domestic Violence, Visitation Rights, Adoption Law, Domestic Violence, Visitation Rights.

JOHN F. MORREALE & ASSOCIATES, P.C.

CHICAGO, ILLINOIS

(See Glen Ellyn)

National and International Relocation Real Estate, Estate Planning, Trusts and Estates, Wills and Probate, Estate Planning, Financial Planning, Family, Divorce and Small Business, Bankruptcy, Civil and Criminal Law.

MORRIS & STELLA

SUITE 1200
200 WEST ADAMS STREET
CHICAGO, ILLINOIS 60606
Telephone: 312-782-2345
Telecopier: 312-750-0924
Email: morrisandstella@ameritech.net

Products Liability Litigation. General Civil and Commercial Litigation.

MEMBERS OF FIRM

WILLIAM J. MORRIS, born Chicago, Illinois, January 13, 1930;. admitted to bar, 1965, Illinois and U.S. District Court, Southern and Northern Districts of Illinois including Trial Bar; 1974, U.S. District Court, Eastern District of Kentucky and U.S. Court of Appeals, Seventh Circuit; 1975, U.S. Supreme Court; 1978, U.S. Court of Appeals, Fourth Circuit; 1980, U.S. District Court, Eastern District of Texas; 1981, U.S. District Court, Northern District of Texas; 1982, U.S. Court of Appeals for the Federal Circuit; 1994, New York; registered to practice before U.S. Patent and Trademark Office. *Education:* University of Illinois (B.S.M.E., 1952); John Marshall Law School (J.D., with honors, 1965). Member, Order of John Marshall. *Member:* Chicago, Illinois State, New York State and American Bar Associations; Association of the Bar of New York City; Illinois Association of Defense Trial Counsel; Defense Research Institute; Illinois Trial Lawyers Association. ***PRACTICE AREAS:*** Products Liability Litigation; General Civil and Commercial Litigation.

JOSEPH N. STELLA, born Buffalo, New York, May 25, 1947; admitted to bar, 1974, Illinois and U.S. District Court, Northern District of Illinois including Trial Bar; 1977, U.S. Court of Appeals, Seventh Circuit; 1985, U.S. District Court, Eastern District of Wisconsin. *Education:* St. Johns University (B.A., 1969); IIT/Chicago-Kent College of Law (J.D., with distinction, 1973). *Member:* Chicago, Illinois State and American Bar Associations; Defense Research Institute; Illinois Trial Lawyers Association. ***PRACTICE AREAS:*** Products Liability Litigation; General Civil and Commercial Litigation.

JEFFREY W. GUNN, born Arlington, Virginia, January 17, 1954; admitted to bar, 1984, Illinois; 1985, U.S. District Court, Northern District of Illinois. *Education:* Illinois Wesleyan University and Loyola University (B.A., summa cum laude, 1977); DePaul University (J.D., 1984). Phi Kappa Phi. *Member:* Chicago and American Bar Associations; Defense Research Institute. ***LANGUAGES:*** Spanish. ***PRACTICE AREAS:*** Products Liability Litigation; General Civil and Commercial Litigation.

ASSOCIATES

BRUCE J. MANOS, born Chicago, Illinois, June 21, 1953; admitted to bar, 1988, Illinois; 1989, U.S. District Court, Northern District of Illinois and U.S. Court of Appeals, Seventh and Federal Circuits; 1990, U.S. District Court, Western District of Wisconsin and Western District of Michigan. *Education:* United States Merchant Marine Academy (B.S. in Mech. Eng., with honors, 1974); John Marshall Law School (J.D., 1988). Phi Delta Phi. Adjunct Professor of Paralegal Studies, Robert Morris College, 1991. *Member:* Chicago (Member, Tort Litigation Committee, 1991) and Illinois State Bar Associations. [USNR, 1970-1980, Final Rank, Lt. (j.g.)]. ***PRACTICE AREAS:*** Products Liability Litigation; General Civil and Commercial Litigation.

WILLIAM F. McDERMOTT, born Rockville Center, New York, October 12, 1952; admitted to bar, 1978, Illinois and U.S. District Court, Northern District of Illinois; 1979, U.S. Court of Appeals, Seventh Circuit; registered to practice before U.S. Patent and Trademark Office. *Education:* Manhattan College (Bachelor of Engineering, 1975); Illinois Institute of Technology, Chicago-Kent College of Law (J.D., 1978). Author: "Intellectual Property," 59 IIT/Chicago-Kent Law Review 685 (1983). Intern Professional Engineer, New York, 1975. Private Pilot, Federal Aviation Administration, 1984. Adjunct Professor of Business Law, Lewis University, 1987-1988. *Member:* Society of Automotive Engineers. ***PRACTICE AREAS:*** Products Liability Litigation; General Civil and Commercial Litigation.

RONALD ERIC BENTSEN, born Chicago, Illinois, December 1, 1960; admitted to bar, 1992, Illinois and U.S. District Court, Northern District of Illinois. *Education:* University of Illinois (B.S.C.E., 1983; M.S.C.E., 1984); Loyola University (J.D., 1992). Tau Beta Pi; Chi Epsilon. *Member:* Chicago, Illinois State and American Bar Associations. ***PRACTICE AREAS:*** Products Liability Litigation; General Civil and Commercial Litigation.

KATHLEEN HOGAN MORRISON, P.C.

THREE FIRST NATIONAL PLAZA, SUITE 2100
70 WEST MADISON STREET
CHICAGO, ILLINOIS 60602
Telephone: 312-977-4477
Fax: 312-977-0872
Email: kmorrison@adoptionattorneys.org
URL: http://www.chicagoadoptionattorney.com

Adoption and Child Welfare.

KATHLEEN HOGAN MORRISON, born Davenport, Iowa, December 19, 1949; admitted to bar, 1976, Illinois and U.S. District Court, Northern District of Illinois; 1982, Trial Bar; 1987, U.S. Court of Appeals, Seventh Circuit. *Education:* St. Louis University (B.A., cum laude, 1972); John Marshall Law School (J.D., with distinction, 1976). Instructor: Legal Research and Writing, John Marshall Law School, 1982-1984; Secondary Education, Ohio, 1972-1973. Author: "Basic Concepts of Adoption," Ch. 1, Illinois Adoption Law, Illinois Institute for Continuing Legal Education, 2002; "Wrongful Adoption," Ch. 14, Adoption Law: Practice and Procedure in the 21st Century, New York State Bar Association, 2004. Board Member, Adoption Law, Leading Lawyers Network. Member, Adoption Law, Chicago Super Lawyers. Member, 1993— and Trustee, 2000-2004, American Academy of Adoption Attorneys. Board Member: Gift Adoption Fund, Illinois, 2001-2004; Chances By Choice; Illinois Adoption Registry Advisory Council; North American Council on Adoptable Children. *Member:* Chicago Bar Association (Member, 1990—; Chair, 1994-1995, 1999-2000; Adoption Law Committee). ***PRACTICE AREAS:*** Adoption Law; Litigation.

MOSKOVIC & ASSOCIATES

CHICAGO, ILLINOIS

(See Arlington Heights)

Civil Practice, Litigation, Commercial Law, Contracts, Personal Injury, Medical Malpractice, Divorce, Child Support, Child Custody, Visitation Rights, Family Law, Collections.

LAW OFFICES OF HAROLD MOSKOWITZ, L.L.C.

55 WEST MONROE STREET, SUITE 1100
CHICAGO, ILLINOIS 60603
Telephone: 312-977-0223
Fax: 312-422-8001
Email: hlmatty@aol.com

Civil Litigation in Federal and State Courts, Secured Lending, Real Estate, Banking, Bankruptcy, Breach of Contract, Business, Partnerships, Debtor and Creditor, Asset Protection, Estate Planning.

HAROLD L. MOSKOWITZ, born Cincinnati, Ohio, June 23, 1953; admitted to bar, 1977, Maryland; 1980, Illinois and District of Columbia. *Education:* Loyola College of Baltimore (B.A., magna cum laude, 1973); Ner Israel Rabbinical (B.S., 1973); University of Maryland (J.D., 1977); Georgetown University (LL.M., 1978). *Member:* American Bar Association; American Bankruptcy Institute. ***PRACTICE AREAS:*** Civil Litigation; Real Estate Law; Bankruptcy; Workouts; Corporate; Secured Lending. ***Email:*** harold.moskowitz@moskowitzlaw.com

MOSS AND BLOOMBERG, LTD.

CHICAGO, ILLINOIS

(See Tressler, Soderstrom, Maloney & Priess)

MOTHERWAY & NAPLETON

Established in 1982
100 WEST MONROE STREET
SUITE 200
CHICAGO, ILLINOIS 60603
Telephone: 312-726-2699
Fax: 312-726-6851
Email: mn@mnlawoffice.com
URL: http://www.mnlawoffice.com

General Civil Practice. Commercial, Negligence, Trial, Malpractice, Products Liability and Aviation Litigation.

MEMBERS OF FIRM

NICHOLAS J. MOTHERWAY, born Chicago, Illinois, January 21, 1940; admitted to bar, 1965, Illinois and U.S. District Court, Northern District of Illinois; U.S. District Court, Western District of Michigan; U.S. Court of Appeals, Seventh Circuit. *Education:* Loyola University (B.S.C., 1961); DePaul University (J.D., 1965). Phi Alpha Delta. Author: "Deposition and Discovery," Illinois Civil Practice, Illinois Continuing Legal Education, Vol. II, 1987; Supplemental, 1989; Revised, 1991, 1992-1995, 1997, 2000-2003; "Post-Traumatic Stress Disorder," Am. Jur. Proof of Facts 2d, Vol. 50, 1987. Contributing Author: "Products Liability Practice Guide," Matthew Bender, 1988; "Successful Discovery in Products Cases," The Trial Lawyer's Guide, Vol. 37, No. 4, 1994. Assistant State's Attorney, Cook County, Illinois, 1966-1973. Chief, Organized Crime and Special Prosecutions, 1971-1973. Chairman, DePaul University College of Law Advisory Council, 1998-1999. Member, Panel of Arbitrators, American Arbitration Association. *Member:* Chicago (Member, Select Committee to Study Illinois Insurance Crisis, 1987) and Illinois State (Elected Member, General Assembly, 1981-1986; Vice-Chairman, Tort Section Council, 1985, Chairman, 1986-1987; Editor, Tort Trends, 1985-1986) Bar Associations; Illinois Trial Lawyers Association (Chairman, Civil Practice Committee, 1982-1983; Chairman, Product Liability Committee, 1986; Co-Chairman, Constitutional Challenge Committee, 1992-1995; Board of Managers, 1990—); The Association of Trial Lawyers of America (State Delegate of Illinois, 1984-1988; Chairman, People's Law School Project, 1987; Regional Chairman, National Student Trial Advocacy Competition, 1988; Recipient, Wiedemann-Wysocki Citation for Excellence, 1992; Member, Board of Governors, 1990-1995); American Board of Trial Advocates (Vice-President, Illinois Chapter, 1993-1995; President 1995-1996); National Board of Directors (Member, Judicial Committee, 1995-1998; Civil Justice Committee, 1998—); Society of Trial Lawyers; Trial Lawyers for Public Justice. Fellow: Roscoe Pound Foundation; American College of Trial Lawyers (Member, Illinois State Committee, 1995-1998); Illinois Bar Foundation (Charter Member). ***PRACTICE AREAS:*** Personal Injury; Negligence; Malpractice; Products Liability; Aviation Litigation; Commercial. ***Email:*** nmotherway@mnlawoffice.com

(This Listing Continued)

MOTHERWAY & NAPLETON, Chicago—Continued

ROBERT J. NAPLETON, born Evergreen Park, Illinois, January 13, 1963; admitted to bar, 1988, Illinois and U.S. District Court, Northern District of Illinois including Trial Bar; 1989, U.S. District Court, Central District of Illinois; 1995, U.S. District Court, Western District of Wisconsin; 1999, U.S. Supreme Court; 2000, U.S. District Court, District of Colorado; 2004, U.S. Court of Federal Claims. *Education:* Loyola University (B.B.A., 1985; J.D., 1988). Author: Article, "An Analysis of the Proctor v. Davis Decision-Has it Reduced Recovery of Punitive Damages in Illinois to the Cost of Doing Business?" Illinois State Bar Association Tort Trends, December, 1994 . Lecturer: "Disability and Disfigurement," Illinois Trial Lawyers Association Seminar, February, 1994; "Wilful and Wanton Misconduct/Punitive Damages," Illinois Trial Lawyers Association, September, 1994; "Slip, Trip and Cases," Northwest Suburban Bar Association Seminar, February, 1995; "Proving Liability," Illinois Trial Lawyers Association Seminar, April, 1995; "Proving Disability and Pain and Suffering," Illinois State Bar Association Seminar, April, 1995; "Premises Liability," Illinois Trial Lawyers Association Seminar, September, 1995; "Hospital and HMO Liability," Illinois State Bar Association Seminar, November, 1995; "Managed Care Liability Issues, Point/Counterpoint," The Healthcare Risk Management Society of Metropolitan Chicago, March, 1996; "Effective Discovery Procedures in Illinois," National Business Institute Seminar, September, 1996; "Direct Examination of the Plaintiff on Injury/Damage Issues," Illinois Trial Lawyer Association Seminar, October, 1996; "HMO Liability," Illinois Trial Lawyers Association Seminar, September, 1998; "Depositions Options," Illinois State Bar Association Seminar, December, 1999; "HMO Liability, What Now Following Petrovich?" Illinois Trial Lawyers Seminar, December, 1999. "HMO Malpractice Liability," The Sedona Conference, March, 2000; "HMO Liability From Two Plaintiff's Perspective," Illinois State Bar Association, May, 2000; "HMO Liability," Illinois Trial Lawyers Association, December, 2000; "Establishing Medical Negligence," October, 2001; "Screening the Potential Case," January, 2002; "Liens," Illinois Trial Lawyers Association Seminar, October, 2002; "Managed Care Liability," Chicago-Kent College of Law Health Society Spring Symposium, April, 2003; "How to Decrease Your Chances of Being Sued and Still Practice Good Medicine from the Standpoint of a TTs Plaintiff's Attorney," American Society of Dermatopathology Annual Meeting, October, 2003. Member, States Attorney Office, Cook County, Markham, Illinois, 1987-1988. Member, Loyola University Law School Circle of Advocates, Deans Circle, 2001—. Member, Trial Lawyers Care, Inc. (Free Legal Help for 9-11 Victims). Bar Appointments: Illinois Supreme Court Committee on Professional Responsibility, 2003-2004; Illinois Supreme Court Committee on Jury Instructions in Civil Cases, 2005. *Member:* Chicago, Illinois State (Member: Board of Governors, 1994-2000; Tort Section Council, 1992-1995) and American Bar Associations; Southwest Bar Association; Illinois Trial Lawyers Association (Member: Board of Advocates, 1993-1997; Board of Managers, 1997—; Medical Negligence and Product Liability Committees, 1992—); The Association of Trial Lawyers of America; Trial Lawyers for Public Justice; American Board of Trial Advocates; Society of Trial Lawyers; Leading American Attorneys; Leading Illinois Lawyers Network; 40 Illinois Lawyers under 40 to Watch, 2000; Catholic Lawyers Guild of Chicago. Fellow: Roscoe Pound Foundation; American Bar Foundation; Illinois Bar Foundation (Life Fellow). ***PRACTICE AREAS:*** Catastrophic Personal Injury; Negligence; Medical Negligence; Products Liability; Aviation Litigation; Construction Accident Litigation; Wrongful Death. ***Email:*** bnapleton@mnlawoffice.com

ASSOCIATES

JOHN M. SALETTA, born Chicago, Illinois, July 20, 1961; admitted to bar, 1988, Illinois and U.S. District Court, Northern District of Illinois including Trial Bar; 1996, U.S. Court of Appeals, Seventh Circuit. *Education:* University of Notre Dame (B.A., 1983); Loyola University (J.D., 1988). Author: "Deposition and Discovery," Illinois Civil Practice, Illinois Continuing Legal Education, Vol. II, 1997. Lecturer: "Evidentiary Foundation," Northwest Suburban Bar Association, April, 1999; "Foundation and Rule 216," Ross and Hardies, July, 1999; "Overlooked But Powerful Discovery Devices," Illinois State Bar Association Seminar, December, 1999; "How to Maximize your Damages as Plaintiff," ITLA Education Fund, February, 2002; "Jury Instructions," ITLA Education Fund, September, 2002. *Member:* Illinois State Bar Association; Illinois Trial Lawyers Association; The Association of Trial Lawyers of America; Society of Trial Lawyers. ***PRACTICE AREAS:*** Catastrophic Injury; Negligence; Medical Negligence; Products Liability; Aviation Litigation; Construction Accident Litigation; Wrongful Death. ***Email:*** jsaletta@mnlawoffice.com

DANIEL T. MADIGAN, born Chicago, Illinois, June 5, 1968; admitted to bar, 1993, Illinois; 1995, U.S. District Court, Northern District of Illinois; 1996, U.S. District Court, Western District of Michigan. *Education:* University of Illinois (B.A., 1990; J.D., 1993). Assistant Corporation Counsel, City of Chicago, 1993-1996. *Member:* Illinois State Bar Association; Illinois Trial Lawyers Association; Association of Trial Lawyers of America. ***PRACTICE AREAS:*** Personal Injury; Malpractice; Products Liability; Negligence; Trucking Law. ***Email:*** dmadigan@mnlawoffice.com

KEVIN J. GOLDEN, born Denver, Colorado, January 29, 1966; admitted to bar, 1992, Illinois; 1993, U.S. District Court, Northern District of Illinois. *Education:* DePaul University (B.A., 1988; J.D., 1992). Lecturer, Voir Dire Illinois Trial Lawyers Association Seminar, December 2001. Assistant State Attorney, Cook County, 1992-2000. *Member:* Will County and Illinois State Bar Associations; Illinois Trial Lawyer Association; The Association of Trial Lawyers of America. ***PRACTICE AREAS:*** Personal Injury; Products Liability; Negligence; Medical Negligence; Civil Rights; Wrongful Death Law. ***Email:*** kgolden@mnlawoffice.com

NICHOLAS T. MOTHERWAY, born Chicago, Illinois, January 25, 1971; admitted to bar, 1998, Illinois and U.S. District Court, Northern District of Illinois. *Education:* Indiana University (B.A., 1993); DePaul University (J.D., 1997). *Member:* Illinois State Bar Association; Illinois Trial Lawyers Association; The Association of Trial Lawyers of America. ***PRACTICE AREAS:*** Personal Injury; Products Liability; Negligence; Medical Negligence; Wrongful Death Law. ***Email:*** ntm@mnlawoffice.com

MUCH SHELIST FREED DENENBERG AMENT & RUBENSTEIN, P.C.

191 NORTH WACKER DRIVE
SUITE 1800
CHICAGO, ILLINOIS 60606-1615
Telephone: 312-521-2000
Fax: 312-521-2100
URL: http://www.muchshelist.com

Irvine, California Office: 2030 Main Street, Suite 1200, 92614. Telephone: 949-851-7475. Fax: 949-250-1714.

Corporate, Secured Lending, Real Estate, Federal Taxation, Estate Planning and Probate Law, Business, Antitrust, Commodities and Securities Law, Litigation, Trade Regulations Law, Bankruptcy, Environmental Law.

FIRM PROFILE: Founded in 1970 and numbering two attorneys, Much Shelist Freed Denenberg Ament & Rubenstein, P.C., has grown steadily to the mid-sized firm we are today. Many of our attorneys concentrate their expertise in highly sophisticated practice areas. Our Clients include large national and multi-national corporations. And in both our business and nationwide litigation practices, we regularly-and successfully-oppose law firms many times our size.

Our firm represents a wide variety of business clients including institutional lenders, real estate developers, national retailers and apparel manufacturers, e-commerce start up companies, venture capitalists, individual entrepreneurs, attorneys and other professionals, and brokers and traders. To enable us to comprehensively serve our clients' needs, attorneys in our firm are admitted to practice in the District of Columbia and several states including Florida, Indiana, New York and Texas, as well as Illinois. We have the experience to explore innovative approaches based on firsthand experience. We use mediation, arbitration and other alternatives to resolve disputes when we believe they are in our clients' best interest.

DAVID ALAN ALMAN, born Illinois, December 19, 1971; admitted to bar, 1997, Illinois. *Education:* University of Illinois (B.A., 1994; J.D., magna cum laude, 1997). ***PRACTICE AREAS:*** Corporate; Finance. ***Email:*** dalman@muchshelist.com

JOSEPH D. AMENT, born Chicago, Illinois, October 14, 1936; admitted to bar, 1963, Illinois. *Education:* University of Illinois (B.S., 1958); Roosevelt University (M.B.A., 1959); John Marshall Law School (J.D., 1962). Nu Beta Epsilon; Beta Alpha Psi; Beta Gamma Sigma. Member, Order of John Marshall. Certified Public Accountant, Illinois, 1959. ***PRACTICE AREAS:*** Taxation Law; Business Acquisitions; Estate Planning; Commodities; Securities Class Action and Shareholder Derivative Matters; Reinsurance Matters. ***Email:*** jament@muchshelist.com

WILLIAM N. ANSPACH, JR., born Chicago, Illinois, May 22, 1949; admitted to bar, 1974, Illinois; 1975, District of Columbia. *Education:* University of Michigan (B.A., 1971); University of Illinois (J.D., 1974). ***PRACTICE AREAS:*** Employee Benefits; Corporate. ***Email:*** wanspach@muchshelist.com

MARVIN N. BENN, born Chicago, Illinois, September 24, 1944; admitted to bar, 1972, Illinois and District of Columbia; U.S. Court of Appeals for the Federal Circuit; registered to practice before the U.S. Patent and Trademark Office. *Education:* University of Illinois (B.S.E.E., 1966); University of Illinois Law School (J.D., 1971). Co-Author: "§117-The Right to Adapt into the Fourth Generation and the Source Code Generator's Dilemma," The John Marshall Journal of Computer & Information Law, Vol. XII, No. 4, Spring 1994; "Disablement of Software Risks and Potential Liabilities," Software Law Journal, Vol. VI, No. 1, February 1993. Adjunct Professor of Computer Law, John Marshall Law School, 1985—. *Member:* Chicago (Chairman, Computer Law Committee, 1992-1993), Illinois State (Chairman, Patent, Trademark & Copyright Council of Lawyers, 1986-1987; Chairman, Computer Law Committee, 1984-1988) Bar Associations; Patent Law Association of Chicago; American Intellectual Property Law Association. ***PRACTICE AREAS:*** Patents; Trademarks; Copyrights; Computer Law; Trade Secrets. ***Email:*** mbenn@muchshelist.com

STEVEN P. BLONDER, born Illinois, 1967; admitted to bar, 1993, Illinois. *Education:* University of Michigan (B.A., 1990); University of Chicago (J.D., 1993). ***PRACTICE AREAS:*** Litigation. ***Email:*** sblonder@muchshelist.com

STEVEN H. BLUMENTHAL, born Milwaukee, Wisconsin, July 10, 1953; admitted to bar, 1978, Illinois. *Education:* University of Wisconsin-Madison (B.A., 1975); Washington University (J.D., 1978). Notes and Comments Editor, Urban Law Annual, 1977-1978. ***PRACTICE AREAS:*** Real Estate; Corporate and Finance. ***Email:*** sblumenthal@muchshelist.com

LAWRENCE H. BRENMAN, born Gary, Indiana, September 3, 1957; admitted to bar, 1982, Colorado and U.S. District Court, District of Colorado; 1984, Illinois and U.S. Tax Court. *Education:* University of Colorado (B.S., 1979); University of Denver (J.D., 1982); New York University (LL.M., 1983). Order of St. Ives. Staff Member, University of Denver Law Review, 1981-1982. Graduate Editor, Tax Law Review, 1982-1983. Certified Public Accountant, Colorado, 1982. Adjunct Professor, IIT-Kent College of Law, 1995—. Co-Author, Limited Liability Companies—Law, Practice and Forms. Editor, Journal of Partnership Taxation. Co-Editor, Business Entities. ***PRACTICE AREAS:*** Business Law; Taxation. ***Email:*** lbrenman@muchshelist.com

DAVID T. BROWN, born Peoria, Illinois, July 17, 1960; admitted to bar, 1986, Illinois and U.S. Tax Court. *Education:* University of Illinois (B.S., with high honors, 1982); Loyola University of Chicago (J.D., 1986). Certified Public Accountant, Illinois, 1982. ***PRACTICE AREAS:*** Corporate; Real Estate; Taxation; Finance. ***Email:*** dbrown@muchshelist.com

PENNY BROWN, born Chicago, Illinois, July 31, 1948; admitted to bar, 1980, Illinois; 1983, U.S. District Court, Northern District of Illinois including Trial Bar. *Education:* Roosevelt University (B.A., 1969); IIT Chicago-Kent Law School (J.D., 1979). Charles Evans Hughes Moot Court Finalist. Member, Chicago-Kent Law Review. ***PRACTICE AREAS:*** Litigation. ***Email:*** pbrown@muchshelist.com

(This Listing Continued)

STEPHEN J. CASSIN, born Palestine, Illinois, July 14, 1953; admitted to bar, 1984, Missouri and U.S. District Court, Eastern and Western Districts of Missouri; 1985, Illinois, U.S. District Court, Southern and Northern Districts of Illinois and U.S. Court of Appeals, Seventh and Eighth Circuits; 1994, U.S. Court of Appeals for the Federal Circuit; registered to practice before U.S. Patent and Trademark Office. *Education:* United States Naval Academy (B.S., with high honors, 1975); University of Michigan (J.D., cum laude, 1984). Professor of Business Law, St. Louis University Business School, St. Louis, Missouri, 1988-1989. *Member:* Illinois State and American Bar Associations; The Missouri Bar; Intellectual Property Law Association of Chicago. [Lt., U.S. Navy, 1975-1980; "Operation Desert Storm" recall, CDR USNR, 1990-1991]. ***LANGUAGES:*** French. ***PRACTICE AREAS:*** Patent; Trademark; Copyright; Trade Secret; Admiralty Litigation. ***Email:*** scassin@muchshelist.com

LESLEE MOSS COHEN, born Skokie, Illinois, November 23, 1967; admitted to bar, 1993, New York; 1999, Illinois. *Education:* University of Michigan (B.A., with high distinction, 1989); New York University School of Law (J.D., 1992). ***PRACTICE AREAS:*** Securities; Mergers and Acquisitions; General Corporate. ***Email:*** lcohen@muchshelist.com

JAMES M. DASH, born Evanston, Illinois, June 20, 1959; admitted to bar, 1985, Texas; 1989, Illinois. *Education:* Loyola University of Chicago (B.A., 1982); University of Houston (J.D., 1985). *Member:* Chicago (Chair, Subcommittee on Construction and Mechanic's Liens, 1999-2000), Illinois State and American Bar Associations. ***PRACTICE AREAS:*** Commercial Litigation; Construction Law; Mechanics Liens. ***Email:*** jdash@muchshelist.com

SCOTT L. DAVID, born Chicago, Illinois, March 25, 1955; admitted to bar, 1979, Illinois and U.S. District Court, Northern District of Illinois. *Education:* Northern Illinois University (B.A., cum laude, 1976); Washington University (J.D., 1979). Associate Editor, Urban Law Annual, 1978-1979. ***PRACTICE AREAS:*** Tax Deferred Exchanges; Commercial Real Estate Law; Secured Transactions and Lending; Real Estate Tax Assessments. ***Email:*** sdavid@muchshelist.com

HOWARD M. DENENBERG, born Chicago, Illinois, June 19, 1934; admitted to bar, 1959, Illinois. *Education:* Northwestern University (B.S., 1956); University of Illinois (J.D., 1959). Phi Delta Phi. ***PRACTICE AREAS:*** Corporate Law; Tax Law; Estate Planning Law; Entertainment Law. ***Email:*** hdenenberg@muchshelist.com

RACHEL E. FELDSTEIN, born Detroit, Michigan, March 16, 1972; admitted to bar, 1997, Illinois. *Education:* University of Michigan (B.A., with distinction, 1994); Loyola University (J.D., cum laude, 1997). ***PRACTICE AREAS:*** Litigation. ***Email:*** rfeldstein@muchshelist.com

MICHAEL J. FREED, born Chicago, Illinois, February 13, 1938; admitted to bar, 1963, Illinois, District of Columbia, U.S. District Court, Northern District of Illinois and the District of Columbia and U.S. Court of Appeals for the District of Columbia; 1977, U.S. Court of Appeals, Seventh Circuit; 1983, U.S. Supreme Court. *Education:* University of Pennsylvania (B.S., 1959); University of Chicago (J.D., 1962). ***PRACTICE AREAS:*** Antitrust Litigation; Securities Litigation; Complex Litigation. ***Email:*** mfreed@muchshelist.com

IRVING M. GESLEWITZ, born New York, N.Y., May 17, 1950; admitted to bar, 1976, Illinois; U.S. District Court, Northern District of Illinois, Trial Bar; U.S. Supreme Court; U.S. Court of Appeals, Third, Fourth, Seventh and Eleventh Circuits. *Education:* Rutgers University (B.A., with highest honors, 1972); University of Chicago (J.D., 1976). Phi Beta Kappa. ***PRACTICE AREAS:*** Labor and Employment Law; Employment Related Litigation. ***Email:*** igeslewitz@muchshelist.com

CAROL V. GILDEN, born New York, New York, July 28, 1956; admitted to bar, 1983, Illinois and U.S. District Court, Northern District of Illinois. *Education:* University of Illinois (B.S., Business Administration, 1979); Chicago-Kent College of Law (J.D., with honors, 1983). Member, Chicago-Kent Law Review, 1982-1983. Staff Attorney, U.S. Securities and Exchange Commission, Division of Enforcement, Chicago Regional Office, 1983-1988. ***PRACTICE AREAS:*** Complex Litigation; Class Actions; Securities; Consumer Fraud; Antitrust Litigation; Arbitrations. ***Email:*** cgilden@muchshelist.com

NEAL T. GOLDSTEIN, born Chicago, Illinois, September 2, 1962; admitted to bar, 1989, Illinois. *Education:* University of Illinois (B.S., 1984); Loyola University (J.D., 1989). Certified Public Accountant, Illinois, 1984. ***PRACTICE AREAS:*** Corporate Law; Health Care. ***Email:*** ngoldstein@muchshelist.com

DAVID GOODMAN, born Blue Island, Illinois, December 23, 1963; admitted to bar, 1989, Illinois, U.S. District Court, Northern District of Illinois including Trial Bar and U.S. Court of Appeals, Seventh and Eighth Circuits. *Education:* Brandeis University (B.A., cum laude, 1986); Boston University (J.D., 1989). *Member:* Chicago (Vice-Chairman, Local Government Committee), Illinois State and American Bar Associations. ***PRACTICE AREAS:*** Intellectual Property; Labor and Employment; Litigation. ***Email:*** dgoodman@muchshelist.com

JULIE M. HANUSA, born Maquoketa, Iowa, May 15, 1964; admitted to bar, 1989, Illinois and U.S. District Court, Northern District of Illinois. *Education:* University of Iowa (B.A., with highest distinction, 1985); Northwestern University (J.D., 1989). Phi Beta Kappa. Associate Editor, Journal of Criminal Law and Criminology, 1988-1989. *Member:* Chicago and American Bar Associations. ***PRACTICE AREAS:*** Finance; Corporate; Mergers and Acquisitions; Health Care. ***Email:*** jhanusa@muchshelist.com

DON S. HERSHMAN, born Chicago, Illinois, August 26, 1957; admitted to bar, 1982, Illinois and U.S. District Court, Northern District of Illinois. *Education:* University of Illinois (B.S., in Accounting, with honors, 1979); Loyola University (J.D., 1982). Phi Kappa Phi; Beta Alpha Psi. Certified Public Accountant, Illinois, 1980. ***PRACTICE AREAS:*** Securities; Corporate; Finance; Mergers and Acquisitions. ***Email:*** dhershman@muchshelist.com

MICHAEL B. HYMAN, born Elgin, Illinois, July 26, 1952; admitted to bar, 1977, Illinois; U.S. District Court, Northern District of Illinois including Trial Bar; U.S. District Court, Central District of Illinois; U.S. Court of Appeals, Seventh and Tenth Circuits; U.S. Supreme Court. *Education:* Northwestern University (B.S.J., with honors, 1974; J.D., 1977). Kappa Tau Alpha. Assistant Attorney General, State of Illinois, Antitrust Division, 1977-1979. Editor-in-chief, Chicago Bar Association's CBA Record, 1988-1990; 1993—. ***PRACTICE AREAS:*** Consumer Rights; Class Action Litigation; Antitrust Law. ***Email:*** mbhyman@muchshelist.com

JEAN K. JANES, born Berlin, Wisconsin, February 7, 1954; admitted to bar, 1993, Minnesota; 1994, Ohio; 2000, Illinois. *Education:* Ripon College (B.A., summa cum laude, 1976); Eastman School of Music (M.A., Musicology, 1981); University of Minnesota (J.D., cum laude, 1993). Member, 1991-1992 and Note and Comment Editor, 1992-1993, Minnesota Law Review. *Member:* Chicago (Member: Class Action Litigation Committee; Alliance for Women) and American (Member, Sections on: Antitrust; Litigation, Center for Professional Responsibility) Bar Associations. ***PRACTICE AREAS:*** Complex Commercial Litigation; Commercial Litigation; Antitrust Class Actions; Securities Fraud Class Actions. ***Email:*** jjanes@muchshelist.com

STEVEN A. KANNER, born New York, N.Y., December 17, 1954; admitted to bar, 1979, Illinois. *Education:* Albright College (B.A., 1976); DePaul University (J.D., 1979). Phi Alpha Delta. *Member:* Chicago and Illinois State Bar Associations; Decalogue Society of Lawyers. ***PRACTICE AREAS:*** Class Action Litigation; Complex Litigation; Antitrust Law; Securities Regulation Law. ***Email:*** skanner@muchshelist.com

STEPHEN P. KIKOLER, born New York, N.Y., April 24, 1945; admitted to bar, 1969, Illinois. *Education:* University of Michigan (B.A., 1966; J.D., cum laude, 1969). [Capt., U.S. Army, JAGC, 1970-1973]. ***PRACTICE AREAS:*** Commercial Litigation; Construction Law; Mechanics Liens. ***Email:*** skikoler@muchshelist.com

ANDREW W. LAPIN, born Chicago, Illinois, February 2, 1953; admitted to bar, 1978, Illinois; U.S. District Court, Northern District of Illinois. *Education:* Indiana University (B.A., 1975); John Marshall Law School (J.D., 1978). *Member:* Chicago (Member: Real Property Committee; Real Property Finance Subcommittee; Commercial Finance Committee) and Illinois State Bar Associations. ***PRACTICE AREAS:*** Mergers, Acquisitions and Divestitures; Real Estate; Secured Transactions; Franchise Law; Corporate. ***Email:*** alapin@muchshelist.com

ANNE E. LARSON, admitted to bar, 1989, Illinois; 1998, Arizona. *Education:* University of Illinois (A.B., 1985); University of Michigan Law School (J.D., 1988). Phi Beta Kappa. Bronze Tablet. Edmund J. James Scholar. Law Clerk to Hon. George W. Lindberg, U.S. District Court, Northern District of Illinois. *Member:* Chicago, Illinois State and American Bar Associations. ***LANGUAGES:*** French. ***PRACTICE AREAS:*** Labor; Employment Law; Litigation. ***Email:*** alarson@muchshelist.com

MARK S. LITNER, born Boston, Massachusetts, June 23, 1959; admitted to bar, 1985, Illinois; 1986, U.S. District Court, Northern District of Illinois. *Education:* Tufts University (B.A., magna cum laude, 1981); Northwestern University (J.D., 1985); Kellogg Graduate School of Management (M.M., 1985). ***LANGUAGES:*** French. ***Email:*** mlitner@muchshelist.com

WILLIAM H. LONDON, born Chicago, Illinois, May 29, 1962; admitted to bar, 1987, Illinois, U.S. District Court, Northern District of Illinois, U.S. Court of Appeals, Seventh Circuit. *Education:* Syracuse University (B.A., magna cum laude, 1984); IIT Chicago-Kent College of Law (J.D., 1987). ***PRACTICE AREAS:*** Complex Litigation. ***Email:*** blondon@muchshelist.com

GREGORY B. MANN, born Chicago, Illinois, April 15, 1968; admitted to bar, 1993, Illinois. *Education:* University of Wisconsin, Madison (B.A., 1990); Chicago Kent College of Law (J.D., 1993; LL.M., Taxation, 1996). ***PRACTICE AREAS:*** Estate Planning. ***Email:*** gmann@muchshelist.com

BARAT S. McCLAIN, born Narberth, Pennsylvania, July 28, 1951; admitted to bar, 1990, Illinois and U.S. District Court, Northern District of Illinois; 1991, U.S. Court of Appeals, Seventh Circuit; 1993, U.S. District Court, Central District of Illinois; 1997, U.S. Court of Appeals, Eleventh Circuit. *Education:* San Francisco College for Women, Lone Mountain College; Mundelein College (B.A., 1987); IIT/Chicago-Kent College of Law (J.D., with honors, 1990). Staff Member, 1988-1989 and Executive Editor, 1989-1990, Chicago-Kent Law Review. *Member:* Chicago (Immediate Past Co-Chair, Alliance for Women), Illinois State and American Bar Associations. ***PRACTICE AREAS:*** Litigation; Antitrust; Complex Litigation. ***Email:*** bmcclain@muchshelist.com

DOUGLAS A. MILLEN, born New Haven, Connecticut, February 26, 1969; admitted to bar, 1994, Connecticut; 1995, New York and Illinois. *Education:* University of Michigan (B.G.S., 1991); University of Illinois (J.D., magna cum laude, 1994). ***PRACTICE AREAS:*** Complex Litigation; Antitrust; Securities; Consumer Rights. ***Email:*** dmillen@muchshelist.com

MELINDA J. MORALES, born Minneapolis, Minnesota, March 11, 1967; admitted to bar, 1994, Minnesota and U.S. District Court, District of Minnesota; 1998, Illinois and U.S. District Court, Northern District of Illinois. *Education:* Carleton College (B.A., 1989); University of Minnesota (J.D., 1994). Member, 1992-1993 and Director, 1993-1994, Phillip C. Jessup International Law Moot Court, University of Minnesota. ***PRACTICE AREAS:*** Complex Litigation; Consumer Law; Securities; Antitrust. ***Email:*** mmorales@muchshelist.com

JAMES E. MORGAN, born Indiana, 1968; admitted to bar, 1993, Ohio; 2001, Illinois. *Education:* Indiana University School of Law, Bloomington (B.S., 1989; J.D., 1992). ***Email:*** jmorgan@muchshelist.com

MICHAEL MOSKOVITZ, born Hammond, Indiana, October 6, 1970; admitted to bar, 1996, Illinois. *Education:* Indiana University (B.A., 1993); New York University School of Law (J.D., 1996). *Member:* Chicago and American Bar Associations. ***PRACTICE AREAS:*** Complex and Mulit-District Litigation; Antitrust Law; Securities Law. ***Email:*** mmoskovitz@muchshelist.com

MORRIE MUCH, born Chicago, Illinois, July 28, 1938; admitted to bar, 1962, Illinois. *Education:* University of Illinois (B.S., Finance, 1959); University of Chicago (J.D., 1962). Order of the Coif. Author and Lecturer: "Enforcing Security Agreements," I.C.L.E. Handbook Creditor's Rights in Illinois, 1974; Revised, 1995. ***PRACTICE AREAS:*** Real Estate Development and Lending; Secured Transactions; Business Law; Trade Associations. ***Email:*** mmuch@muchshelist.com

NORMAN B. NEWMAN, born Chicago, Illinois, February 18, 1951; admitted to bar, 1975, Illinois and U.S. District Court, Northern District of Illinois including Trial Bar. *Edu-*

(This Listing Continued)

MUCH SHELIST FREED DENENBERG AMENT & RUBENSTEIN, P.C., Chicago—Continued

cation: University of Illinois (B.A., 1972); John Marshall Law School (J.D., 1975). Appointed Member, Private Panel of Trustees, U.S. Bankruptcy Court, Northern District of Illinois, 1982, Chairman, Trustee Advisory Counsel, 1990. ***PRACTICE AREAS:*** Bankruptcy, Reorganization and Creditors' Rights. ***Email:*** nnewman@muchshelist.com

MICHAEL L. O'SHAUGHNESSY, born 1949; admitted to bar, 1987, Illinois; 1993, Wisconsin. *Education:* Christian Brothers University (B.A., 1973); University of Cincinnati (J.D., 1987). ***PRACTICE AREAS:*** Finance; Mergers, Acquisitions and Divestitures; Cross Border Finance. ***Email:*** moshaughnessy@muchshelist.com

JOEL S. POLISKY, born Chicago, Illinois, October 24, 1952; admitted to bar, 1979, Illinois and U.S. Tax Court. *Education:* University of Illinois (B.S., 1974); DePaul University (M.B.A., 1976); John Marshall Law School (J.D., 1979). Honors Recognition, Finance. ***PRACTICE AREAS:*** Real Estate Transactions; Acquisitions and Mergers; Estate Tax; Corporate. ***Email:*** jpolisky@muchshelist.com

MITCHELL S. ROTH, born Chicago, Illinois, May 28, 1967; admitted to bar, 1992, Illinois, U.S. District Court, Northern District of Illinois. *Education:* University of Illinois at Champaign (B.S., with high honors, 1989; J.D., with honors, 1992). ***PRACTICE AREAS:*** Mergers and Acquisitions; Corporate Law; Technology; Federal Taxation; Wealth Transfer; Succession Planning. ***Email:*** mroth@muchshelist.com

JEFFREY C. RUBENSTEIN, born Chicago, Illinois, January 27, 1942; admitted to bar, 1966, Illinois. *Education:* University of Michigan (A.B., 1963; J.D., 1966); Lawyers Institute, The John Marshall Law School (LL.M., 1983). ***PRACTICE AREAS:*** Corporation Law; Mergers and Acquisitions; Taxation; Real Estate. ***Email:*** jrubenstein@muchshelist.com

MICHAEL B. SADOFF, born Sioux City, Iowa, August 19, 1949; admitted to bar, 1975, Illinois. *Education:* University of Iowa (B.B.A., with honors, 1971); DePaul University (J.D., magna cum laude, 1975). Certified Public Accountant, Iowa, 1971. Author: Case Note, "Couch v. United States-Protection of Taxpayers' Records," 23 DePaul Law Review 810, 1973. Co-Author: Comment, "Abandonment of Residential Property in an Urban Context," 23 De Paul Law Review 1186, 1974; "The Apartment: Chicago Rewrites the Script," CBA Record, March, 1986. Executive Editor, De Paul Law Review, 1974-1975. Instructor, Legal Drafting, Illinois Institute of Technology/Chicago-Kent College of Law, 1983-1985. Member, DePaul University College of Law Dean's Council, 2000—. *Member:* Chicago, Illinois State and American Bar Associations. ***PRACTICE AREAS:*** Real Estate (Property) Law; Leases and Leasing; Secured Transactions Law; Business Law. ***Email:*** msadoff@muchshelist.com

JOANNE A. SARASIN, born Chicago, Illinois, October 27, 1960; admitted to bar, 1985, Illinois. *Education:* University of Illinois (B.A., 1982; J.D., summa cum laude, 1985). ***PRACTICE AREAS:*** Litigation. ***Email:*** jsarasin@muchshelist.com

SCOTT N. SCHREIBER, born Flint, Michigan, August 25, 1956; admitted to bar, 1985, Illinois and U.S. District Court, Northern District of Illinois, Eastern District of Wisconsin. *Education:* Michigan State University (B.A., 1978); IIT/Chicago-Kent College of Law (J.D., 1985). Member, Moot Court Society, 1983-1984. Member, Chicago-Kent Law Review, 1984-1985. (Certified in Business Bankruptcy Law by the American Board of Bankruptcy Certification). ***PRACTICE AREAS:*** Bankruptcy; Creditors Rights; Litigation. ***Email:*** sschreiber@muchshelist.com

STEVEN SCHWARTZ, born Chicago, Illinois, August 12, 1952; admitted to bar, 1977, Illinois. *Education:* University of Illinois (B.S., 1974); Northwestern University (J.D., highest honors, 1977). Bronze Tablet. ***PRACTICE AREAS:*** Mergers and Acquisitions; Corporate Finance; Federal Income Tax Law; Corporate Law. ***Email:*** sschwartz@muchshelist.com

THOMAS B. SHAPIRA, born Chicago, Illinois, January 18, 1967; admitted to bar, 1992, Illinois and U.S. District Court, Northern District of Illinois; 1994, U.S. Court of Appeals, Seventh Circuit. *Education:* Brown University (A.B., 1989); University of Pennsylvania (J.D., 1992). *Member:* Chicago and American Bar Associations; American Health Lawyers Association; Illinois Health Lawyers Association. ***PRACTICE AREAS:*** Health Care Transactional; Health Care Regulatory. ***Email:*** tshapira@muchshelist.com

EDWARD D. SHAPIRO, born Brooklyn, New York, June 4, 1962; admitted to bar, 1991, Massachusetts; 1992, U.S. District Court, District of Massachusetts; 1994, Illinois and U.S. District Court, Northern District of Illinois. *Education:* State University of New York at Binghamton (B.A., with honors, 1984); Boston University (J.D., 1991). *Member:* Chicago, Illinois State and American Bar Associations; International Alliance of Holistic Lawyers. ***PRACTICE AREAS:*** Civil Litigation; Mediation; Arbitration; Holistic Law; Collaborative Law. ***Email:*** eshapiro@muchshelist.com

MICHAEL R. SHELIST, born Chicago, Illinois, October 11, 1936; admitted to bar, 1961, Illinois and Florida. *Education:* Northwestern University (B.S., 1958; J.D., 1961). Tau Epsilon Rho (Chancellor, 1960-1961). Recipient, American Jurisprudence Prize in Evidence. ***PRACTICE AREAS:*** Corporate Law; Federal Income, Estate and Gift Taxation Law; Real Estate Development. ***Email:*** mshelist@muchshelist.com

NORMAN A. SHUBERT, born Peoria, Illinois, February 21, 1935; admitted to bar, 1960, Illinois. *Education:* University of Michigan (A.B., cum laude, 1957); Northwestern University (J.D., 1960). Associate Editor, Northwestern University Law Review, 1959-1960. ***PRACTICE AREAS:*** Banking Law; Corporate Law; Real Estate Law; Estate Planning. ***Email:*** nshubert@muchshelist.com

GREGG M. SIMON, born Chicago, Illinois, June 16, 1962; admitted to bar, 1987, Illinois. *Education:* University of Illinois (B.S., with honors, 1984); Loyola University (J.D., 1987). Member, 1985-1986 and Lead Articles Editor, 1986-1987, Loyola University of Chicago Law Journal. Certified Public Accountant, Illinois, 1984. Member, Professional Advisory Committee, Jewish Federation of Metropolitan Chicago. *Member:* Chicago and Illinois State Bar Associations; Chicago Estate Planning Counsel; Greater North Shore Estate and Financial Planning Counsel. ***PRACTICE AREAS:*** Estate Planning; Probate Administration; Trust Administration; Tax Planning; Business Planning. ***Email:*** gsimon@muchshelist.com

(This Listing Continued)

STEVEN A. STENDER, born Chicago, Illinois, September 21, 1955; admitted to bar, 1980, Illinois and U.S. District Court, Northern District of Illinois. *Education:* University of Illinois (B.A., 1977); Illinois Institute of Technology/Chicago-Kent College of Law (J.D., with honors, 1980). *Member:* Chicago Bar Association. ***PRACTICE AREAS:*** Real Estate Law; Zoning Law. ***Email:*** sstender@muchshelist.com

CHRISTOPHER J. STUART, born Elmhurst, Illinois, March 21, 1960; admitted to bar, 1985, Illinois and U.S. District Court, Northern District of Illinois. *Education:* University of Edinburgh; University of Illinois (B.A., with high honors, 1982; J.D., 1985). Delta Theta Phi. Member, National Moot Court Board of Editors, 1984-1985. Member, University of Illinois Law Review, 1983-1985. ***PRACTICE AREAS:*** Complex Commercial Litigation; Consumer Litigation; Securities Litigation. ***Email:*** cstuart@muchshelist.com

GLENN D. TAXMAN, born Skokie, Illinois, September 14, 1970; admitted to bar, 1996, Illinois; 2002, California. *Education:* University of California, Santa Barbara (B.A., 1992); John Marshall Law School (J.D., cum laude, 1996). Law Review. ***PRACTICE AREAS:*** Real Estate; Corporate; Commercial Lending. ***Email:*** gtaxman@muchshelist.com

ANTHONY C. VALIULIS, born Rockford, Illinois, May 12, 1947; admitted to bar, 1974, Illinois; U.S. Supreme Court; 1990, U.S. Tax Court; U.S. District Court, Northern District of Illinois, including Trial Bar; U.S. Court of Appeals, Seventh, Ninth, Tenth and Eleventh Circuits. *Education:* Marquette University (B.A., 1970); Loyola University (J.D., cum laude, 1974). Alpha Sigma Nu. Member, Loyola Law Journal, 1973-1974. *Member:* Chicago, Illinois State and American Bar Associations; Illinois Trial Lawyers Association; Association of Trial Lawyers of America. Fellow, American Bar Foundation. ***REPORTED CASES:*** Guillen v. Potomac, 203 Ill.2d 141 (2003); Brouwer v. Raffensperger, Hughes & Co., 199 F.3d 961 (7th Cir. 2000); Perry v. Economy Fire & Cas. Co., 724 N.E.2d 151 (1st Dist. 1999); Insurance Co. of Illinois v. Stringfield, 685 N.E.2d 980 (1st Dist. 1997). ***PRACTICE AREAS:*** Appellate Practice; Civil Practice; Complex and Multi-District Litigation; Commercial Law; Contracts; Fraud and Deceit; Insurance; Litigation; Unfair Competition. ***Email:*** tvaliulis@muchshelist.com

MICHAEL B. VINER, born Chicago, Illinois, July 1, 1963; admitted to bar, 1988, Illinois and U.S. District Court, Northern District of Illinois. *Education:* University of Illinois (B.S., with high honors, 1985; J.D., 1988). Beta Alpha Psi. Certified Public Accountant, Illinois, 1985. ***PRACTICE AREAS:*** Commercial Real Estate; Finance. ***Email:*** mviner@muchshelist.com

JOHN H. WARD, born Wilmington, North Carolina, September 23, 1942; admitted to bar, 1978, Illinois and U.S. District Court, Northern District of Illinois including Trial Bar; 1984, U.S. Court of Appeals, Seventh Circuit; 1988, U.S. Supreme Court; 1992, U.S. Tax Court; 1999, U.S. District Court, Eastern District of Wisconsin; U.S. Court of Appeals for the Federal Circuit. *Education:* United States Military Academy (B.S., with distinction, 1964); Armed Forces Language Institute (French, 1969); Institut Universitaire de Hautes Etudes Internationales, University of Geneva, Switzerland, Licence ès Sciences Politiques (études Internationales, 1971); DePaul University (J.D., with honors, 1978). Olmsted Scholar, 1969-1971. *Member:* Chicago, Illinois State and American Bar Association. [U.S. Army Officer, 1964-1977; Airborne, Ranger, Special Weapons qualifications; Combat in Vietnam 1967-1968; Combat Infantry Badge, bronze star, etc.]. ***LANGUAGES:*** French, Russian and German. ***PRACTICE AREAS:*** Civil Litigation; Class Action; Bankruptcy Litigation. ***Email:*** jward@muchshelist.com

ORAN F. WHITING, born Chicago, Illinois, 1961; admitted to bar, 1987, Illinois and U.S. District Court, Northern District of Illinois; 1992, U.S. Court of Appeals, Tenth Circuit; 1995, U.S. District Court, Central District of Illinois; U.S. Court of Appeals, Seventh Circuit. *Education:* University of Pennsylvania (B.S., Economics, 1983; B.A., International Business, 1983); Centro de Estudios Hispanicos, Madrid, Spain (1984); Georgetown University (J.D., 1986). *Member:* Cook County and American (Co-Chair, Electronic Publishing Committee, Litigation Section) Bar Associations; Chicago Bar Foundation (Board Member). ***LANGUAGES:*** Spanish. ***PRACTICE AREAS:*** Litigation; Regulatory Law; Government Land; Immigration Land. ***Email:*** owhiting@muchshelist.com

PHILIP WONG, born Evanston, Illinois, December 18, 1951; admitted to bar, 1977, Illinois. *Education:* Johns Hopkins University (B.A., 1973); John Marshall Law School (J.D., 1977). ***PRACTICE AREAS:*** Mortgage Law; Real Estate Law; Real Estate Development and Syndications Law. ***Email:*** pwong@muchshelist.com

---

LISA H. BEN-ISVY, born Skokie, Illinois, March 22, 1968; admitted to bar, 1993, Illinois. *Education:* University of Michigan (B.A., 1990); London School of Economics, London, England; Northwestern University (J.D., 1993). *Member:* Chicago Bar Association. ***PRACTICE AREAS:*** Commercial Litigation; Appellate Practice. ***Email:*** lben-isvy@muchshelist.com

MICHAEL D. BURSTEIN, born Yonkers, New York, November 4, 1972; admitted to bar, 1997, Illinois. *Education:* Stanford University (A.B., 1994); Northwestern University (J.D., cum laude, 1997). Associate Note and Comment Editor, Northwestern University Law Review, 1996-1997. ***PRACTICE AREAS:*** Real Estate. ***Email:*** mburstein@muchshelist.com

SOO CHOI, born Newburgh, New York; admitted to bar, 2002, Illinois. *Education:* Duke University (B.A, 1996); University of Chicago (M.A., 1997); Cornell University Law School (J.D., 2001). ***PRACTICE AREAS:*** Intellectual Property; Litigation. ***Email:*** schoi@muchshelist.com

JOSEPH L. COHEN, born January 22, 1977; admitted to bar, 2002, Ohio; 2003, Illinois and U.S. District Court, Southern District of Ohio. *Education:* Bradley University (B.S., Business Management and Administration, summa cum laude, 1999); Washington and Lee University School of Law (J.D., cum laude, 2002). ***Email:*** jcohen@muchshelist.com

JONNA DALEIDEN EIMER, born Evanston, Illinois, January 18, 1973; admitted to bar, 1997, Illinois. *Education:* Lake Forest College (B.A., summa cum laude, 1994); Northwestern University School of Law (J.D., 1997). Phi Beta Kappa. *Member:* Chicago Bar Association. ***PRACTICE AREAS:*** Corporate; Mergers and Acquisitions; Securities. ***Email:*** jeimer@muchshelist.com

(This Listing Continued)

WILLIAM SILAS HACKNEY, III, born San Francisco, California, 1972; admitted to bar, 1998, Illinois. *Education:* University of Illinois (B.A., 1994); St. John's University (J.D., 1997). ***PRACTICE AREAS:*** Bankruptcy; Reorganization; Creditors' Rights. ***Email:*** whackney@muchshelist.com

KIMBERLY A. KRUGMAN, born Chicago, Illinois, December 2, 1965; admitted to bar, 1995, California; 1998, Illinois. *Education:* Arizona State University (B.S., 1987); Southwestern University School of Law (J.D., 1995). Member: Southwestern University College of Law Review; Moot Court. ***PRACTICE AREAS:*** Commercial Litigation; Antitrust; Right of Publicity; Trademark Infringement; Copyright Infringement; False Advertising; Unfair Competition. ***Email:*** kkrugman@muchshelist.com

JASON L. LaBELLA, born Boston, Massachusetts, March 15, 1969; admitted to bar, 1997, Illinois. *Education:* Pennsylvania State University (B.A., 1992); Chicago-Kent College of Law (J.D., 1997). *Member:* Chicago and American Bar Associations. ***PRACTICE AREAS:*** Commercial Real Estate; Leasing; Lending. ***Email:*** jlabella@muchshelist.com

L. DANIEL LIUTIKAS, born Chicago, Illinois, December 24, 1971; admitted to bar, 2000, Illinois. *Education:* Chicago-Kent College of Law (J.D., 2000). Member, Chicago-Kent Law Review. Certified Mediator, Chicago Bar Association. ***LANGUAGES:*** Lithuanian. ***PRACTICE AREAS:*** Intellectual Property; Corporate Law; Entertainment Law. ***Email:*** dliutikas@muchshelist.com

DONAL M. O'BRIEN, born Dublin, Ireland, 1973; admitted to bar, 1998, Illinois. *Education:* University College Dublin, National University of Ireland (B.A., with honors, 1995); Loyola University (J.D., 1998). ***PRACTICE AREAS:*** Corporate Law; Mergers and Acquisitions; Telecommunications. ***Email:*** dobrien@muchshelist.com

TINA PARIES, born 1969; admitted to bar, 2001, Illinois. *Education:* Northern Illinois University (B.A., 1991); Chicago-Kent College of Law, Illinois Institute of Technology (J.D., 2001). ***PRACTICE AREAS:*** Litigation. ***Email:*** tparies@muchshelist.com

DAVID MATTHEW PILOTTO, born Hammond, Indiana, January 2, 1970; admitted to bar, 2000, Illinois. *Education:* Western Illinois University (B.B., 1992); Loyola University Chicago (J.D., cum laude, 2000). Certified Public Accountant, Illinois, 1994. ***PRACTICE AREAS:*** Corporate Law; Mergers and Acquisitions; Banking; Lender Law. ***Email:*** dpilotto@muchshelist.com

ADAM K. SACHAROFF, born Toronto, Canada, March 17, 1972; admitted to bar, 1998, Illinois; registered to practice before U.S. Patent and Trademark Office. *Education:* Purdue University (B.S.A.E., 1995); Franklin Pierce Law Center (J.D., 1998). *Member:* Chicago and American Bar Associations; American Intellectual Property Law Association. ***PRACTICE AREAS:*** Patents; Trademarks; Litigation; Trade Secrets. ***Email:*** asacharoff@muchshelist.com

LORNE T. SAEKS, born Skokie, Illinois, August 11, 1966; admitted to bar, 1991, Illinois. *Education:* University of Illinois (B.A., 1988); Indiana University (J.D., 1991). ***PRACTICE AREAS:*** Employment Law; Labor Law; Commercial Litigation. ***Email:*** lsaeks@muchshelist.com

MICHAEL B. SHAW, born Chicago, Illinois, 1973; admitted to bar, 1998, Illinois. *Education:* Northwestern University (B.A., cum laude, 1995, Phi Beta Kappa; J.D., cum laude, 1998); University of Chicago (M.B.A., 2002). *Member:* Chicago, Illinois State and American Bar Associations. ***PRACTICE AREAS:*** Corporate Law; Corporate Finance; Securities; Taxation; Business Planning. ***Email:*** mshaw@muchshelist.com

LISA MARIE SPELHAUG, born Rochester, Minnesota, 1969; admitted to bar, 1997, Minnesota; 1998, Illinois. *Education:* University of Minnesota (B.A., 1993); Hamline University (J.D., cum laude, 1997). Operations Editor, Hamline Law Review, 1996-1997. ***PRACTICE AREAS:*** Commercial Real Estate; Lender Law. ***Email:*** lspelhaug@muchshelist.com

ROBERT J. WOZNIAK, born December 19, 1966; admitted to bar, 2000, Michigan; 2001, District of Columbia (Not admitted in Illinois). *Education:* University of Michigan (B.A., 1988); Wayne State University (J.D., cum laude, 2000). Order of the Coif. Formerly with U.S. Department of Justice, Antitrust Division, 2000-2001. ***PRACTICE AREAS:*** Antitrust. ***Email:*** rwozniak@muchshelist.com

OF COUNSEL

JACK SHORE, born Toledo, Ohio, July 9, 1926; admitted to bar, 1952, District of Columbia; 1959, Wisconsin; 1961, Illinois and U.S. District Court, Northern District of Illinois; registered to practice before U.S. Patent and Trademark Office. *Education:* Illinois Institute of Technology (B.S., M.E., 1946); George Washington University (LL.B., 1951). Adjunct Professor, Licensing of Intellectual Property, John Marshall Law School, 1991—. *Member:* American Bar Association; Intellectual Property Law Association of Chicago; Licensing Executive Society. ***PRACTICE AREAS:*** Patent; Trademark; Copyright; Licensing Law. ***Email:*** jshore@muchshelist.com

REFERENCES: American National Bank; NBD Chicago Bank; Harris Trust and Savings Bank and Bank Hapoalim.

(For Other Personnel and Biographical Data, see Professional Biographies at other Chicago, Illinois Office, 10 South LaSalle Street, Suite 3300)

LAW OFFICES OF CHARLES LEE MUDD

Established in 2001

3344 NORTH ALBANY AVENUE
CHICAGO, ILLINOIS 60618
Telephone: 773-588-5410
Fax: 773-588-5440
URL: http://www.muddfirm.com
Email: cmudd@muddlawoffices.com
URL: http://www.muddlawoffices.com

Civil and Commercial Litigation, Internet Law, Intellectual Property, Technology Law, Privacy Law, Real Estate, Elder Law.

(This Listing Continued)

CHARLES LEE MUDD, born Louisville, Kentucky, June 16, 1968; admitted to bar, 1997, Indiana; 1999, Illinois; 2000, Connecticut. *Education:* Purdue University (B.A., 1990; M.A., 1994); Quinnipiac College (J.D., magna cum laude, 1997). Adjunct Faculty, John Marshall Law School. 2nd Vice-President, Board of Directors, Northcenter Chamber of Commerce, Chicago, Illinois. *Member:* Chicago, Illinois State (Member, Section Council, Intellectual Property Section), Indiana State, Connecticut and American Bar Associations; Computer Law Association. ***LANGUAGES:*** English. ***PRACTICE AREAS:*** Civil Litigation; Commercial Litigation; Internet Law; Intellectual Property; Technology Law; Privacy Law; Real Estate; Elder Law.

Language: English.

MULLEN & KELLIHER

A Partnership including Professional Corporations

THREE FIRST NATIONAL PLAZA
SUITE 2060
CHICAGO, ILLINOIS 60602
Telephone: 312-346-2998
Fax: 312-346-6024

Personal Injury, Wrongful Death, Product Liability, Malpractice and Railroad F.E.L.A. Cases, Civil and Trial Practice in all State and Federal Courts.

FIRM PROFILE: Mullen, Minella & Kelliher was established as a partnership in 1988 by John C. Mullen, Christopher Mullen and Mary R. Minella. Prior thereto the firm was in business under John C. Mullen since 1952. The firm specializes in plaintiff's personal injury and wrongful death, malpractice, product liability, and general negligence cases. It has a general civil trial practice, in all state and federal courts in negligence law and appeals.

MEMBERS OF FIRM

CHRISTOPHER MULLEN, (P.C.), born Pensacola, Florida, July 19, 1945; admitted to bar, 1980, Illinois. *Education:* Loyola University (B.S., 1967); Northern Illinois University (M.B.A., 1973); DePaul University (J.D., 1979). Cook County Assessor's Office, 1975-1981. *Member:* Illinois State Bar Association (Member, 1980-1986 and Chairman, 1985, State and Local Taxation Committee; Member, 1990— and Chairman, 1993-1994, ISBA Standing Committee on Judicial Appointments; Member, Board of Governors, 1994—); Illinois Trial Lawyers Association. [Capt., U.S. Marine Corps, 1969-1972]. ***SPECIAL AGENCIES:*** Board of Tax Review; Illinois Property Tax Appeal Board; Cook County Assessor. ***PRACTICE AREAS:*** Plaintiffs Personal Injury and Wrongful Death; Malpractice; Product Liability; Railroad; F.E.L.A.; Real Estate Tax Law. ***Email:*** cmullen@mullenfirm.com

SUZANNE DVORAK KELLIHER, born Chicago, Illinois, October 8, 1970; admitted to bar, 1996, Illinois. *Education:* University of Illinois (B.S, 1992); DePaul University (J.D., 1996). *Member:* Chicago and Illinois State Bar Associations; Illinois Trial Lawyers Association. ***LANGUAGES:*** Spanish. ***PRACTICE AREAS:*** Personal Injury; Wrongful Death; Products Liability; Workers Compensation. ***Email:*** skelliher@mullenfirm.com

OF COUNSEL

JOHN C. MULLEN, (LTD.), born Chicago, Illinois, December 24, 1922; admitted to bar, 1949, Illinois. *Education:* Loyola University (A.B., 1943); DePaul University (LL.B., 1948). Member, Illinois State Bar Association (President, 1979-1980: Member, Board of Governors, 1972-1978; Chairman, Committee to Advance Passage of Judicial Merit Selection through 1977-1978 Legislature; Secretary of Board and Secretary of Assembly, 1975-1976). Member, Board of Directors: Illinois Bar Foundation, 1976-1977; Illinois Institute for Continuing Legal Education, 1976-1979; Illinois Bar Automated Research Foundation, 1976-1979; Board of Directors, Mental Health Association of Greater Chicago, 1980. Recipient, Distinguished Alumni Award of DePaul University, 1979. Chairman, ISBA Judicial Merit Selection Committee, 1986. Chairman, ISBA Standing Committee on Federal Judicial and Related Appointments, 1987. Chairman, ISBA Committee on Judicial Appointments, 1988—. *Member:* Chicago (Member: Committee on Inquiry, 1962-1965: Tort Litigation Committee, Chairman, 1969-1970; Member, Judiciary Committee, 1973-1974), Seventh Judicial Circuit, Federal and American (Member, House of Delegates, 1978-1980) Bar Associations; Illinois Trial Lawyers Association (President, 1970); The Association of Trial Lawyers of America (Member, Board of Governors, 1975-1977); American Judicature Society; American Bar Foundation (Fellow); National Conference of Bar Presidents; Society of Trial Lawyers; International Academy of Trial Lawyers (Member, Board of Directors, 1985-1990); U.S.O. of Illinois, Inc. (Member, Board of Directors, 1986-1997; President, 1995, 1996); The Inner Circle of Advocates, 1973—. [1st. Lt., U.S. Marine Air Corps, 1943-1946]. ***PRACTICE AREAS:*** Personal injury and wrongful death, plaintiff; Malpractice; Product Liability; Railroad F.E.L.A. cases.

JON G. CARLSON (Also Member of Carlson & Carlson, P.C., Edwardsville, Illinois)

THE MULLER FIRM, LTD.

Established in 1990

THE MULLER BUILDING
110 WEST GRAND AVENUE
CHICAGO, ILLINOIS 60610-4269
Telephone: 312-467-6700
Facsimile: 312-467-0252
URL: http://www.mullaw.com
Email: kmuller@mullaw.com
URL: http://www.lawyers.com/mullerlaw

Practice concentrated in Trial/Settlement of High-Profile Domestic Relations Cases concerning Property Division, Child Custody, Child Support, Domestic Violence, Paternity, Alternative Living Arrangements, Adoption, Ante-and Post-Nuptial Agreements, Probate Matters including Guardianships, Wills and Trusts, Contract Preparation, Negotiation and Litigation, Crimi-

(This Listing Continued)

THE MULLER FIRM, LTD., Chicago—Continued

nal charge Trial and Settlement, analysis of Stock, Option, Commodity, Real Estate and Insurance Offerings and Holdings, Business Valuations, Hidden-Asset Discovery and Appellate Advocacy.

FIRM PROFILE: The Muller Firm, Ltd. offers clients exclusive legal experience in divorce and family law along with over fifteen consulting attorneys selected for their specific expertise in legal areas tangential to the assessment and distribution of marital assets, including tax, corporate, real estate, securities, bankruptcy, immigration, employment and pension rights, collection, wills and trusts, personal injury, criminal and intellectual property. Mr. Muller also practices Arts, Entertainment and Intellectual Property Law and Alternative Dispute Resolution.

As Mr. Muller regularly receives national recognition, his involvement carries authority recognized by his peers and the judiciary. He is listed in Illinois Law and Leading Attorneys, Super Lawyers, Who's Who in American Law, Who's Who in Practicing Attorneys, Who's Who in Emerging Leaders and Who's Who in America. Mr. Muller is a Family Law Commentator for FOX TV, past host of CBS radio's weekly show, UNCOMMON LAW on 105.0 FM WCKG-Chicago; Columnist for Chicago Social Magazine and frequent family law informational source for Time, Newsweek, USA Today, National Enquire, Chicago Tribune, Chicago Sun Times, Chicago Magazine, Milwaukee Journal, Milwaukee Sentinel, A Current Affair, the Oprah Winfrey Show and the Jerry Springer Show.

Although Mr. Muller focuses on high-profile family law matters, he recognizes that trouble has no socioeconomic boundaries. He is available to represent anyone with a legitimate problem which requires competent help. The initial retainer and hourly rate are individually tailored to the complexity of the matter and the particular client's ability to pay.

KURT A. MULLER, born Chicago, Illinois, June 21, 1955; admitted to bar, 1986, Illinois and U.S. District Court, Northern District of Illinois; 1987, Arizona; 1989, U.S. District Court, Eastern District of Wisconsin. *Education:* University of Wisconsin (B.S., Bio-Chemistry, 1977); John Marshall Law School (J.D., 1986). Member: The Marshall Opinion; Decalogue Society; Gifted Students Program; Student Senate; Debate Team. Author: "The Second Wives Club," *Divorce* 1997; "In Consideration Of Divorce," 1991, 1996 (2nd Edition) and 1999 (Third Edition); "Nobody's Angel," Chicago, November 1989; "Initiation Fees For The 'Second Wives Club'," *Divorce,* December, 1996, Vol. 1, No. 2; "Prenuptial Agreements," *National Enquirer,* September 5, 1989; "The Danger Zone of Divorce Work," *Chicago Tribune,* June 28, 1988; "Chicago Profile: Divorce Attorney," *Chicago Sun-Times,* January 1988; "Assessing Current Implications of Alternative Lifestyle Relationships," *American Journal of Family Law,* Winter, 1987; "Limiting Your Risk: An Investor's Guide To Options On Future Contracts," *Murlas,* 1982. Contributor: "The Jewish American Prince Handbook, *Turnbull & Willoughby,* 1986. *Presenter:* "Handling an Illinois Divorce Case From Start to Finish," National Business Institute, 2003. Family Law Commentator for Fox-Chicago News; Past Family Law Commentator for Dateline-NBC; Past Host of CAN TV 21 "Kurt Muller's CONSULTATION"; Past Host of WCKG-FM Radio's Kurt Muller's Uncommon Law, 1998-2003; Columnist for Chicago Social Magazine: "Ask Muller," 1999—. Member, Research Board of Advisors *The American Biographical Institute:* Fullerton Cenacle, Board of Directors, 1991—; Carl Sandburg Condominium Association II; Board of Directors, 1990. Cook County Domestic Relations Division Court Facilitator, 1998—. Illinois Superlawyers; Who's Who in America; Who's Who in Emerging Leaders; Who's Who in Practicing Attorneys; Who's Who in American Law; Illinois' Law & Leading Attorneys; Cook County Sheriff's Distinguished Service Award, 1983, 1979. Attorney: Law Offices of Richter-Muller, P.C., 1992-1995; Law Offices of Kurt A. Muller, P.C., 1990-1992; Harry M. Weiss & Associates, 1987; Gordon & Glickson, P.C. 1986-1987. Deputy Sheriff, Cook County Sheriff's Department, 1978-1987. Commodity Broker, 1980-1983. Associate Creative Director, 1977-1980. Member: Anti-Defamation League; Planned Parenthood. *Member:* Chicago (Member, Young Lawyers Section-Domestic Relations), Illinois State and American Bar Associations. Special Counsel: ACLU; The National Smoker's Alliance. ***LANGUAGES:*** Spanish, Russian, German and Yiddish. ***PRACTICE AREAS:*** Adoption Law; Child Abuse and Neglect; Child Custody; Child Custody Mediation; Child Sexual Abuse; Child Support; Grandparents Visitation Rights; Independent Adoptions; International Child Abduction; International Child Custody; Interstate Adoptions; Interstate Child Custody; Juvenile Criminal Law; Juvenile Law; Parental Kidnapping; Private Adoptions; Step Parent Adoptions; Termination of Parental Rights; Visitation Rights; Discrimination; Race Discrimination; Sex Discrimination; Age Discrimination; Womens Rights; Breach of Contract; Contract Fraud; Contract Litigation; Guardianship; Guardianship Administration; Alimony; Cohabitation Agreements; Divorce; Divorce Mediation; Divorce Taxation; Domestic Relations; Domestic Violence; Equitable Distribution; Family Mediation; Gay and Lesbian Family Law; International Family Law; Interstate Support; Marital Agreements; Marital Property Distribution; Marital Property Law; Marital Property Settlements; Matrimonial Law; Name Changes; Non-Traditional Family Law; Palimony; Paternity; Post Divorce; Postnuptial Agreements; Premarital Agreements; Qualified Domestic Relations Orders (QDROs); Separation Agreements; Spousal Support. ***Email:*** kmuller@mullaw.com

---

TODD A. WALTERS, born Livingston, New Jersey, September 19, 1969; admitted to bar, 1995, Illinois and U.S. District Court, Northern District of Illinois. *Education:* Ithaca College (B.A., 1991); Thomas M. Cooley Law School (J.D., 1995). Listed in: Who's Who in America Law Students; Illinois Superlawyers. *Member:* Chicago, Illinois State and American Bar Associations. ***PRACTICE AREAS:*** Matrimonial Law; Probate Litigation; Estate Planning; Adoption Law; Paternity Litigation; Child Support Litigation; Child Custody; Surrogacy Law. ***Email:*** twalters@mullaw.com

MICHAEL L. LODERMEIER, born St. Paul, Minnesota, July 26, 1974; admitted to bar, 1999, Illinois. *Education:* University of Wisconsin-Eau Claire (B.S., 1996); John Marshall Law School (J.D., 1999). *Member:* Chicago (Member, Family Law Committee), Illinois State and American Bar Associations. ***PRACTICE AREAS:*** Matrimonial Law; Domestic Relations; Child Support; Divorce; Child Custody; Family Law. ***Email:*** mlodermeier@mullaw.com

(This Listing Continued)

THE LAW OFFICES OF MUNDAY & NATHAN

33 NORTH DEARBORN STREET
SUITE 2220
CHICAGO, ILLINOIS 60602
Telephone: 312-346-5678
Fax: 312-346-8394

Plaintiff's Personal Injury Litigation, Negligence, Medical and Professional Negligence, Products Liability, Premises Liability, Construction Accidents, Railroad and Aviation Law and Police Pursuit Litigation.

FIRM PROFILE: John Munday and Thomas Nathan, former partners in the law firm Land & Munday, established Munday & Nathan in 1991. From the onset, Munday & Nathan has focused its practice on plaintiff personal injury litigation in both the state and federal courts and has successfully tried numerous cases to verdict. Additionally, Munday & Nathan engages in appellate practice and, in selected cases, personal injury litigation and trial practice throughout the country.

JOHN J. MUNDAY, born Mount Morris, Illinois, February 16, 1943; admitted to bar, 1968, Illinois and U.S. District Court, Northern District of Illinois. *Education:* Southern Illinois University (B.A., 1965); Chicago-Kent College of Law (J.D., 1968). Co-Author: "Opinion Evidence," Chapter of Illinois Civil Trial Evidence, 1986; "Production of Documents and Tangible Things," Chapter of Illinois Civil Discovery, 1996, 1999. Contributing Author of Goldstein Trial Technique, Callahan & Company, Second Edition, 1969. Contributing Author to Personal Injury Deskbook and Medical Trial Techniques Quarterly, 1982-1989. Guest Lecturer for Illinois State Bar Association, Illinois Institute for Continuing Legal Education, Illinois Trial Lawyers Association and Lawyers Post Graduate Clinic. Member, Panel of Arbitrators, American Arbitration Association. *Member:* Chicago, Illinois State and American Bar Associations; Illinois Trial Lawyers Association; The Association of Trial Lawyers of America; American Judicature Society. ***PRACTICE AREAS:*** Personal Injury; Medical Negligence; Professional Negligence; Aviation; Products Liability; Premises Liability; Construction Accidents; Police Pursuit Litigation. ***Email:*** jmunday@mundayandnathan.com

THOMAS J. NATHAN, born Chicago, Illinois, March 21, 1950; admitted to bar, 1978, Illinois and U.S. District Court, Northern District of Illinois. *Education:* Lawrence University (B.A., 1972); Northwestern University (M.A., 1975); John Marshall Law School (J.D., 1978). Gavel Society. Co-Author, "Production of Documents and Tangible Things," Chapter of Illinois Civil Discovery, 1996, 1999. Trustee, Francis Parker School, 1986-1989. Trustee, 1989-1997; President, 1993-1994, Board of Trustees, Wilmette District 39 Schools. Lecturer: 1989-1997, Lawyers Post Graduate Clinic, Chicago Bar Association, 1982-1987; Illinois Institute for Continuing Legal Education. *Member:* Chicago, Illinois State and American Bar Associations; Illinois Trial Lawyers Association; The Association of Trial Lawyers of America; The Society of Trial Lawyers. ***PRACTICE AREAS:*** Medical Negligence; Professional Negligence; Products Liability; Personal Injury; Civil Rights Litigation. ***Email:*** tnathan@mundayandnathan.com

EDWARD G. PROCTOR, JR., born Chicago, Illinois, February 2, 1962; admitted to bar, 1989, Illinois and U.S. District Court, Northern District of Illinois. *Education:* University of Illinois (B.S., 1985); Loyola University (J.D., 1989). Member: Legal Clinic for the Disabled, 1989—; Board of Governors, Loyola Chicago School of Law. *Member:* Chicago and Illinois State Bar Associations; The Association of Trial Lawyers of America; Illinois Trial Lawyers Association. ***PRACTICE AREAS:*** Personal Injury; Civil Rights; Commercial Litigation. ***Email:*** tproctor@mundayandnathan.com

---

JEFFREY A. SCHULKIN, born Skokie, Illinois, February 1, 1970; admitted to bar, 1995, Illinois and U.S. District Court, Northern District of Illinois. *Education:* University of Illinois (B.A., 1992); IIT-Chicago Kent College of Law (J.D., 1995). *Member:* Chicago and American Bar Associations; Illinois Trial Lawyers Association. ***PRACTICE AREAS:*** Personal Injury; Medical Malpractice; Products Liability; Professional Negligence. ***Email:*** jschu35@aol.com

ANDREW EISENBERG, born Highland Park, Illinois, June 17, 1971; admitted to bar, 1999, Illinois. *Education:* University of Illinois, Urbana-Champaign (B.A., 1994); John Marshall Law School (J.D., 1998). ***PRACTICE AREAS:*** Medical Malpractice; Personal Injury; Products Liability; Civil Rights. ***Email:*** aeisenberg@mundayandnathan.com

---

MURPHY & HOURIHANE, L.L.C.

77 WEST WACKER DRIVE, SUITE 4800
CHICAGO, ILLINOIS 60601
Telephone: 312-606-9300
Fax: 312-606-8765
Email: info@mhlitigation.com
URL: http://www.mhlitigation.com

Litigation Practice including Commercial Litigation, Government Relations, Contracts, Employment Agreements, Construction Disputes, Real Estate, White Collar Crime and Professional Malpractice.

FIRM PROFILE: Gene Murphy and John Hourihane excel at helping plaintiffs and defendants prosecute and defend their interests in litigation over contracts, employment agreements, construction problems, real estate deals, and white-collar investigations and lawsuits. They worked together at one of the world's largest law firms before starting their own practice, and have handled hundreds of jury and bench trials.

(This Listing Continued)

Our clients are global corporations and small businesses, public sector managers, medical and financial service professionals. We counsel them on transactions, regulatory problems, and civil and criminal litigation, whether it means defending them against allegations, or enforcing their rights as plaintiffs.

EUGENE E. MURPHY JR., admitted to bar, 1987, Illinois; 1989, U.S. District Court, Northern District of Illinois; 1997, U.S. Court of Appeals, Seventh Circuit. *Education:* Loras College (B.A., magna cum laude, 1984); Illinois Institute of Technology, Chicago-Kent College of Law (J.D., 1987). *Member:* Chicago and Illinois State Bar Associations. ***PRACTICE AREAS:*** Commercial Litigation; White Collar Crime; Government Relations; Municipal Law. ***Email:*** emurphy@mhlitigation.com

JOHN N. HOURIHANE, JR., admitted to bar, 1998, Illinois; U.S. District Court, Northern District of Illinois. *Education:* Loyola University, Chicago (B.B.A., 1991; M.B.A., 1996); Chicago-Kent College of Law, Illinois Institute of Technology (J.D., 1998). *Member:* Chicago (Secretary, USA Commercial Litigation Committee) and Illinois State Bar Associations. ***PRACTICE AREAS:*** Commercial Litigation; Real Estate; Real Estate Litigation. ***Email:*** h.hourihane@mhlitigation.com

LAW OFFICE OF BRENDA L. MURZYN

1255 NORTH STATE PARKWAY
CHICAGO, ILLINOIS 60610
Telephone: 312-330-3458
Fax: 312-266-5967
Email: brendamurzynlaw@ameritech.net
URL: http://www.lawyers.com/murzyn

Real Estate Closings, For Sale By Owner Investment Property, Foreclosure, Probate, Wills, Residential Real Estate, Commercial Real Estate, Real Estate Investment, Land Trusts, Land Sales, Real Estate Acquisitions, Real Estate Contracts.

BRENDA L. MURZYN, born Evansville, Indiana, October 10, 1954; admitted to bar, 1983, Illinois and U.S. District Court, Northern and Southern Districts of Indiana. *Education:* Indiana University (B.S., 1976); Northern Illinois University (J.D., 1982). Recipient, American Jurisprudence Award. *Member:* Kane County, DuPage County, Illinois State, Indiana State and American Bar Associations; Illinois Real Estate Lawyers Association.

LAW OFFICE OF DAVID MUSCHLER

135 SOUTH LASALLE STREET, SUITE 3950
CHICAGO, ILLINOIS 60603
Telephone: 312-759-0102
Fax: 312-629-0174
Email: cubmusch@aol.com
URL: http://www.lawyers.com/muschlerlaw

Construction, Real Estate, Litigation, Arbitration.

FIRM PROFILE: David Muschler practices in the general corporate and commercial areas with particular emphasis in construction and real estate matters. He has extensive experience in both transactional and litigation matters. For the past twenty years, he has specialized in arbitration, both as an advocate and as an arbitrator, and other alternative dispute resolution models. In addition, Muschler frequently serves as local counsel for firms needing representation in litigation and transactions in the Chicago area.

DAVID E. MUSCHLER, born Aurora, Illinois, October 29, 1946; admitted to bar, 1973, Illinois and U.S. District Court, Northern District of Illinois, including Trial Bar; 1988, U.S. Court of Appeals, Seventh Circuit. *Education:* DePauw University (B.A., 1968); Northwestern University (J.D., 1973). Member, Board of Arbitrators, National Association of Securities Dealers, 1985—. Member, Panel of Arbitrators, American Arbitration Association. *Member:* Chicago, Illinois State and American Bar Associations. [U.S. Army, 1969-1971]. ***PRACTICE AREAS:*** Arbitration (25%); Litigation (40%); Construction (30%); Real Estate (5%). ***Email:*** Cubmusch@aol.com

STEPHEN T. MYKING

300 SOUTH WACKER DRIVE
SUITE 3400
CHICAGO, ILLINOIS 60606-6785
Telephone: 312-786-6176
Fax: 312-986-9192
Email: smyking@cs.com

Immigration Law, Employment Relations Law (U.S. and International) confined to Management.

STEPHEN T. MYKING, born Benson, Minnesota, November 11, 1947; admitted to bar, 1972, Virginia; 1973, U.S. Court of Military Appeals; 1975, District of Columbia; 1976, U.S. Supreme Court; 1977, Illinois. *Education:* Washington College (B.A., 1969); University of Virginia (J.D., 1972). Omicron Delta Kappa; Phi Alpha Theta. *Member:* The District of Columbia Bar; Virginia State Bar; Inter-American (Member, Labor Committee) Bar Association. [Lieut., JAGC, USNR, 1972-1976]. ***LANGUAGES:*** Spanish.

JONATHAN NACHSIN, P.C.

105 WEST ADAMS STREET, SUITE 3000
CHICAGO, ILLINOIS 60603-6209
Telephone: 312-327-1777
Fax: 312-431-1456
Email: nachsin@att.net
URL: http://www.jonathannachsin.com

Class Actions, Consumer Litigation, Contract Litigation, Warranty Law.

JONATHAN NACHSIN, born Youngstown, Ohio, December 12, 1951; admitted to bar, 1985, Illinois and U.S. District Court, Northern District of Illinois; 1987, U.S. Court of Appeals, Seventh Circuit. *Education:* Case Western Reserve University (B.A., 1975); Illinois Institute of Technology, Chicago-Kent College of Law (J.D., with honors, 1985). Member, Moot Court Society. Member, National Constitutional Law Competition Team. *Member:* Chicago Bar Association. ***PRACTICE AREAS:*** Class Actions; Consumer Litigation; Contract Litigation; Warranty Law. ***Email:*** nachsin@worldnet.att.net

NADLER, PRITIKIN & MIRABELLI, L.L.C.

ONE PRUDENTIAL PLAZA
130 EAST RANDOLPH DRIVE, SUITE 1200
CHICAGO, ILLINOIS 60601
Telephone: 312-861-4600
Fax: 312-861-4666
Email: r.dorus@npmfamlaw.com
URL: http://www.npmfamlaw.com

Family Law and Domestic Relations Law including Dissolution of Marriage, Division and Valuation of Marital and Non-Marital Property, Maintenance and Support, Custody and Visitation, Domestic Violence, Establishment of Paternity, Prenuptial and Postnuptial Agreements and, When Necessary, Litigation of Cases and the Prosecution and Defense of Appeals. Mediation and Arbitration.

FIRM PROFILE: Resolving Difficult Situations with Integrity, Excellence and Experience.

Members of Nadler, Pritikin & Mirabelli, L.L.C. actively participate in the legal community. The firm includes the President-Elect of the International Academy of Matrimonial Lawyers, three past presidents of the Illinois Chapter of the American Academy of Matrimonial Lawyers, the past General Counsel of the American Academy of Matrimonial Lawyers, a Diplomat of the American College of Family Trial Lawyers, as well as one of the Members of the Board of Governors of the Illinois State Bar Association. The firm's attorneys lecture and publish individually and on behalf of the Chicago, Illinois and American Bar Associations as well as the Illinois Institute of Continuing Legal Education.

The firm represents clients throughout Cook, Lake, Will and DuPage Counties.

FLOYD N. NADLER, born Chicago, Illinois, 1934; admitted to bar, 1959, Illinois; 1973, Alabama; 1963, U.S. Supreme Court and U.S. Court of Military Appeals. *Education:* University of Illinois (A.B., 1956); John Marshall Law School (J.D., 1959). Recipient, Samuel S. Berger Award, 2004. Selected, Leading Lawyers Network. Fellow, American Academy of Matrimonial Lawyers (National Secretary, 1974-1978; National Legal Counsel, 1998-1999; Illinois Chapter President, 1991-1992). Member, International Academy of Matrimonial Lawyers (U.S.A. President, 2004—; President-Elect, 2002-2003; Former Secretary, U.S. Chapter, 2000-2001; National Delegate). Diplomat, American College of Family Trial Lawyers (Member, Executive Committee). *Member:* Chicago, American and Illinois State (Member, Family Law Section) Bar Associations. ***PRACTICE AREAS:*** Family Law; Domestic Relations; Matrimonial Law; Divorce; Child Support; Child Custody; Visitation Rights; Paternity; Premarital Agreements; Postnuptial Agreements. ***Email:*** f.nadler@npmfamlaw.com

JAMES B. PRITIKIN, born Chicago, 1939; admitted to bar, 1965, Illinois. *Education:* University of Illinois (B.S., 1961); DePaul University (J.D., 1965). Listed, Who's Who in American Law. Selected, Leading Lawyers Network and 100 Best Super Lawyers. Fellow, American Academy of Matrimonial Lawyers (Past President, Illinois Chapter, 1997-1998). Fellow, International Academy of Matrimonial Lawyers. Director, The American Academy of Matrimonial Lawyers Foundation. Certified Matrimonial Mediator and Arbitrator. Court-Appointed Children's Representative. Hearing Officer, Illinois Supreme Court, Attorney Registration and Disciplinary Commission. *Member:* Illinois State (Member, Family Law Section), American (Member, Family Law Section) and Chicago (Member, Family Law Section) Bar Associations. ***PRACTICE AREAS:*** Family; Domestic Relations; Matrimonial; Divorce; Child Support; Child Custody; Visitation Rights; Paternity; Premarital Agreements; Postnuptial Agreements. ***Email:*** j.pritikin@npmfamlaw.com

ENRICO J. MIRABELLI, born Chicago, Illinois, June 27, 1956; admitted to bar, 1981, Illinois and U.S. District Court, Northern District of Illinois. *Education:* St. Mary's College (B.A., magna cum laude, 1978); John Marshall Law School (J.D., 1981). Recipient: Chicago Volunteer Legal Services Corporation Distinguished Service Award, 1984, 1993; John Marshall Law School Distinguished Service Award, 1995; Award of Merit, National Center for Exploited and Missing Children, 2000; Certificate of Appreciation, Legal Assistance Foundation (ProBono, Baby Christopher Case), 1995. Member, Justinian Society (President, 1997, Member, Executive Committee). Co-Author: "Amendment to Code of Civil Procedure," Sec. 5/2-401(e). Leading Illinois Attorney, Family Law. Appointed, Illinois Supreme Court (1st District Member, Committee on Character and Fitness). Appointed Member by Mayor Richard M. Daley, Personnel Board of the City of Chicago, 1997—. Member, Board of Directors, 2004-2006, Illinois Bar Foundation. *Member:* Chicago, Illinois State (Member, Board of Governors, 1999-2005; Former Member, General Assembly and Family Law Section) and American Bar Associations; The Association of Trial Lawyers of America; Illinois Trial Lawyers Association. ***PRACTICE AREAS:*** Family; Domestic Relations; Matrimonial Law; Divorce; Child Support; Child Custody; Visitation Rights; Paternity; Premarital Agreements; Postnuptial Agreements. ***Email:*** e.mirabelli@npmfamlaw.com

(This Listing Continued)

NADLER, PRITIKIN & MIRABELLI, L.L.C., Chicago—Continued

ILENE E. SHAPIRO, born Chicago, Illinois, October 9, 1953; admitted to bar, 1978, Illinois and U.S. District Court, Northern District of Illinois. *Education:* Northwestern University (B.A., 1975); Loyola University (J.D., 1978). Recipient, Distinguished Service Award, Chicago Volunteer Legal Services Foundation, 1996. Certified Child's Representative, Circuit Court of Cook County. Author: "Discovery Procedure In Child Support Cases - Defendant's Case," Illinois Civil Discovery Practice, Illinois Institute of Continuing Legal Education, 1996. Lecturer: Illinois CPA Society, Divorce Tax Law Program, November 1994; Illinois Institute of Continuing Legal Education, Child Support Litigation, March 1988; Special Problems in Illinois Family Law-Privileges, September, 1988; Professional Education Systems, Inc., QDROS and Pensions, May, 1988; National Business Institute, Inc., Effective Family Law Practice in Illinois, June, 1993. Member, Circuit Court of Cook County, Illinois Domestic Relations Advisory Committee, 1996-1997. President, Board of Managers, Journeys of the Heart Adoption Services, Illinois, 1998-1999. American Academy of Matrimonial Lawyers (President-Elect, Illinois Chapter, 1998-2000; President, 2000-2002; Member, Board of Managers, 1990—). *Member:* Chicago, Illinois State and American Bar Associations;. ***Email:*** i.shapiro@npmfamlaw.com

JAMES A. NADLER, born Chicago, Illinois, November 12, 1963; admitted to bar, 1989, Alabama; 1991, Illinois. *Education:* University of Illinois (B.A., 1986); Cumberland School of Law of Samford University (J.D., 1989). Member, Board of Managers, 2000-2004 and Fellow, American Academy of Matrimonial Lawyers. Co-Creator, Juvenile Court Abuse and Neglect Training Simulation Program, Cook County Juvenile Court System. Named, One of Forty Attorneys Under Forty, Chicago Law Bulletin, 2003. Board Member, Family Law Section, Illinois Institute for Continuing Legal Education. *Member:* Chicago (Member, Family Law Committee, 1990; Chairman, Young Lawyers Section, 1993-1994; Director, Young Lawyers Section, 1994-1995), Illinois State and American Bar Associations. ***PRACTICE AREAS:*** Family; Domestic Relations; Matrimonial; Divorce; Child Support; Child Custody; Visitation Rights; Paternity; Premarital Agreements; Postnuptial Agreements. ***Email:*** j.nadler@npmfamlaw.com

FRANCIS A. GEMBALA, born Chicago, Illinois, February 1, 1947; admitted to bar, 1972, Illinois; 1979, U.S. Tax Court, U.S. Supreme Court. *Education:* Loyola University (A.B., 1970; J.D., 1972); DePaul University School of Law (LL.M., Taxation, 1983). Retired, Domestic Relations Associate Judge, Circuit Court of Cook County. Former Faculty Member, National Judicial College. Contributing Editor, Family Law Chapter on Obtaining Orders of Protection, Illinois Institute for Continuing Legal Education, 2003. Member, Editorial Board of the Family Violence and Sexual Assault Bulletin. Founding Member, Illinois State Domestic Violence Coordinating Council. *Member:* Chicago (Former Chair, Criminal Law Committee) and Illinois State Bar Associations (Former Member, Task Force for Technical Revisions to the Domestic Violence Act); Advocates Society (Past President); Justinian Society of Lawyers; Illinois Judges Association. ***PRACTICE AREAS:*** Family; Mediation; Arbitration; Domestic Relations; Matrimony; Divorce; Child Support; Child Custody; Visitation Rights; Paternity; Premarital Agreements; Postnuptial Agreements. ***Email:*** f.gembala@npmfamlaw.com

JACALYN BIRNBAUM, born Chicago, Illinois, March 25, 1951; admitted to bar, 1992, Illinois and U.S. District Court, Northern District of Illinois. *Education:* George Washington University (B.A., 1972); DePaul University (J.D., 1992). Co-Author with B. Richman: "The Innocent Spouse Exception and Wiksell: No Longer an All or Nothing Proposition," American Journal of Family Law, Vol. II, No. 2, Summer, 1997; "Life Insurance Trusts Can Protect Children," Chicago Daily Law Bulletin, January 27, 1997; "Doling Retirement Benefits After Divorce," Chicago Daily Law Bulletin, March 6, 1996. Co-Author: with Schatz, "New Statute Promotes Homemakers' Rights," Illinois Bar Journal, Vol. 80, No. 121, p. 610, December, 1992; "Dissipation in Illinois: Time for a More Flexible Approach," Illinois Family Law Report, Vol. XVI, NO. 1, January, 1993; with David H. Levy, "MMPI: Introduction and Overview," Fall CLE Conf. 1993 ABA Family Law Section, 11-93; "How Do You Spell Cash Relief? Q-D-R-O," Chicago Daily Law Bulletin, 5-19-94; with Michael S. Cohen, "Back to the Future: The Trend Toward (Maybe) Permanent Maintenance," Lake County Bar Association, Family Law Seminar, 4-29-94. Lecturer, "New Statute Promotes Homemakers' Rights," Northwest Suburban Bar Seminar, March, 1993. Fellow, American Academy of Matrimonial Lawyers (Illinois Chapter). *Member:* Chicago (Member, Matrimonial Law Committee, 1992—) and Illinois State (Member, Legal Admissions, Education and Competence Committee, 1992; Contributor, Family Law Section Newsletter) and American Bar Associations. ***PRACTICE AREAS:*** Family Law; Domestic Relations; Matrimonial Law; Divorce; Child Support; Child Custody; Visitation Rights; Paternity; Premarital Agreements; Postnuptial Agreements. ***Email:*** j.birnbaum@npmfamlaw.com

MATTHEW C. ARNOUX, born Evanston, Illinois, February 9, 1960; admitted to bar, 1984, Illinois. *Education:* Georgetown University (B.A., cum laude, Economics, 1981); University of Illinois (J.D., 1984). *Member:* Chicago and Illinois State Bar Associations. ***PRACTICE AREAS:*** Family Law; Domestic Relations; Matrimonial Law; Divorce; Child Support; Child Custody; Visitation Rights; Paternity; Premarital Agreements; Postnuptial Agreements. ***Email:*** m.arnoux@npmfamlaw.com

SAM F. CANNIZZARO, born Chicago, Illinois, March 13, 1959; admitted to bar, 1984, Illinois. *Education:* Loyola University (B.A., 1980; J.D., 1984). Associate Judge, Circuit Court of Cook County, 1998. Member, Edgebrook-Sauganas Chamber of Commerce (Past President, Chairman of the Board). Wish-Granter, Make-A-Wish Foundation of Northern Illinois. Member, Justinian Society of Lawyers. *Member:* Chicago (Member, Family Law Section), Illinois State (Assembly Member, Member, Family Law Section) and American (Member, Family Law Section) Bar Associations; Association of Trial Lawyers of America. ***PRACTICE AREAS:*** Family; Domestic Relations; Matrimonial; Divorce; Child Custody; Child Support; Visitation Rights; Paternity; Premarital Agreements; Postnuptial Agreements. ***Email:*** s.cannizzaro@npmfamlaw.com

STEVEN D. GERAGE, born Chicago, Illinois, November 30, 1964; admitted to bar, 1990, Illinois and U.S. District Court, Northern District of Illinois. *Education:* University of Illinois (B.S., 1987); Loyola University of Chicago School of Law (J.D., 1990). *Member:* Family Law Advocacy Institute; American, Illinois State and Chicago Bar Associations. ***PRACTICE AREAS:*** Family Law; Domestic Relations; Divorce Litigation; Domestic Violence; Matrimonial Law; Child Support; Child Custody; Visitation Rights; Paternity; Premarital Agreements; Postnuptial Agreements. ***Email:*** s.gerage@npmfamlaw.com

MICHAEL IAN BENDER, born Chicago, Illinois, October 18, 1965; admitted to bar, 1991, Illinois; 1993, U.S. District Court, Northern District of Illinois, including Trial Bar. *Education:* University of Illinois (B.A., 1988; LL.M., Information Technology Law, with honors, 2005); John Marshall Law School (J.D., cum laude, 1991). Past President, Decalogue Society of Lawyers. Facilitator, Cook County Domestic Relations Post Decree Court Rooms. Public Administrator for Cook County (Appointed by Governor Rod Blagojevich). Past President, Skokie Park District Board of Commissioners. *Member:* American, Illinois and Chicago (Former Co-Chair, Interfaith Law Committee) Bar Associations. ***PRACTICE AREAS:*** Family; Domestic Relations; Matrimonial; Divorce; Child Support; Child Custody; Visitation Rights; Paternity; Premarital Agreements; Postnuptial Agreements. ***Email:*** m.bender@npmfamlaw.com

AMY L. GERTLER, born November 10, 1957; admitted to bar, 1986, Illinois. *Education:* Tulane University (B.A., with honors, 1979); University of Illinois (M.S., Criminal Justice); John Marshall Law School (J.D., 1986). Certified: Basic Divorce Mediation Training, Mediation Training and Consultation Institute, Ann Arbor, Michigan; Representing Minor Children, Domestic Relations Division, Circuit Court of Cook County and Lake County. *Member:* Chicago, Lake County and Illinois State Bar Associations. ***PRACTICE AREAS:*** Collaborative Law; Mediation; Matrimonial Law; Family Law; Divorce.

SHALOM D. BERSSON, born New York, N.Y., July 12, 1976; admitted to bar, 2002, Illinois and U.S. District Court, Northern District of Illinois. *Education:* Yeshiva University (B.S., 1999); Chicago-Kent College of Law, Illinois Institute of Technology (J.D., 2002). *Member:* Chicago, Illinois State and American Bar Associations; Decalogue Society of Lawyers. ***PRACTICE AREAS:*** Family; Domestic Relations; Matrimonial Law; Divorce; Child Support; Child Custody; Visitation Rights; Premarital Agreements; Postnuptial Agreements; Divorce Litigation; Domestic Violence; Paternity. ***Email:*** s.bersson@npmfamlaw.com

CYNTHIA J. VOCAT, born February 25, 1970; admitted to bar, 2002, Illinois. *Education:* Illinois State University (B.S.Ed., 1992); DePaul University (J.D., summa cum laude, 2002). Order of the Coif. Associate Editor, DePaul Law Review, 2001-2002. National Moot Court Competition, 1999, 2000. *Member:* Chicago, Illinois State and American Bar Associations. ***PRACTICE AREAS:*** Family; Domestic Relations; Matrimonial; Divorce; Child Support; Child Custody; Visitation Rights; Paternity; Premarital Agreements; Postnuptial Agreements. ***Email:*** c.vocat@npmfamlaw.com

TANIA K. GRAY, born Ohio, June 16, 1978; admitted to bar, 2004, Illinois. *Education:* Miami University of Ohio (B.S., 2000); John Marshall Law School (J.D., 2003). Vice President, John Marshall Law School Student Bar Association, 2001-2002. *Member:* Illinois State, American and Chicago (Chair, YLS Family Law Section) Bar Associations; Women's Bar Association of Illinois. ***PRACTICE AREAS:*** Family; Domestic Relations; Matrimonial; Divorce; Child Support; Child Custody; Visitation Rights; Paternity; Premarital Agreements; Postnuptial Agreements. ***Email:*** t.gray@npmfamlaw.com

ERIN E. MASTERS, born San Juan, Puerto Rico, February 15, 1980; admitted to bar, 2004, Illinois. *Education:* University of California, San Diego (B.A., 2001); Loyola University, Chicago (J.D., 2004). Phi Alpha Delta. Recipient: Justian Society Scholarship, 2002; Daniel Ward Scholarship, 2001; Loyola University Pro Bono Award, 2004. *Member:* Chicago (Member, Family Law Section) and American (Member, Family Law Section) Bar Associations. ***PRACTICE AREAS:*** Family Law.

RACHEL C. HEYMAN, born 1963; admitted to bar, 1990, New York; 1997, Illinois. *Education:* University of Pennsylvania (B.A., cum laude, 1985); University of Chicago (J.D., 1989). ***PRACTICE AREAS:*** Matrimonial Law; Family Law; Divorce.

NASHARR & SHEA LLC

TWO PRUDENTIAL PLAZA
180 N. STETSON AVENUE, SUITE 4525
CHICAGO, ILLINOIS 60601
Telephone: 312-819-1900
Fax: 312-819-1910
Email: attorneys@nashea-law.com
URL: http://www.nasharr-law.com

Banking Law, Finance Law, Loans, Business Law, Corporate Law, Real Estate, Commercial Real Estate, Leasing, Commercial Landlord and Tenant Law, Civil Litigation, Eminent Domain, Employment Law, Wills, Trusts and Estates, Probate.

ANTHONY J. NASHARR, III, born Chicago, Illinois, August 9, 1958; admitted to bar, 1983, Illinois and U.S. District Court, Northern District of Illinois. *Education:* Miami University (B.S., Business, 1980); John Marshall Law School (J.D., 1983). *Member:* Chicago, Illinois State and American (Member, Business Advice and Financial Planning Committee) Bar Associations. ***PRACTICE AREAS:*** Banking Law; Corporate Law; Commercial Real Estate; Trusts and Estates; Estate Planning. ***Email:*** anasharr@nashea-law.com

BRIAN C. SHEA, born Chicago, Illinois; admitted to bar, 1986, Illinois and U.S. District Court, Northern District of Illinois. *Education:* Northwestern University (B.S., 1977); Loyola University of Chicago (M.B.A., 1979; J.D., 1986). Zeta Phi Eta. Evans Scholar. Adjunct Professor, John Marshall Law School. *Member:* Chicago (Member, Committees on: Real Property; Real Estate Taxation) and American (Member, Sections on: Business Law; Real Property) Bar Associations; Chicago Mortgage Attorneys Association (Past President); Leading Lawyers of Illinois. ***PRACTICE AREAS:*** Real Estate Law; Bank Lending; Business Law; Corporate Law; Finance Law; Leasing; Commercial Landlord and Tenant Law. ***Email:*** bshea@nashea-law.com

JOHN J. CURRY, JR., born Chicago, Illinois, June 13, 1953; admitted to bar, 1978, Illinois; 1981, U.S. Court of Appeals, Seventh Circuit; 1982, U.S. District Court, Northern District of Illinois including Trial Bar; 1986, District of Columbia. *Education:* Northwest-

(This Listing Continued)

ern University (B.A., 1975); Vanderbilt University (J.D., 1978). Assistant Attorney General, State of Illinois, 1981-1983. Trial Attorney, Civil Rights Division, United States Department of Justice, 1983-1986. Special Assistant Attorney General, State of Illinois, 1995-1998. *Member:* Chicago (Member, Civil Rights Committee, 1980), Lake County, Illinois State (Member, Civil Practice Section) and American (Member, Indo-Chinese Refugee Legal Assistance Program, 1979-1981) Bar Associations; The District of Columbia Bar. ***PRACTICE AREAS:*** Civil Litigation; Commercial Litigation; Government Law. ***Email:*** jcurry@nashea-law.com

---

BRYAN P. LYNCH, born Chicago, Illinois, January 27, 1971; admitted to bar, 1996, Illinois; 1998, U.S. District Court, Northern District of Illinois. *Education:* University of Illinois Urbana-Champaign (B.A., 1993); The John Marshall Law School (J.D., 1996). *Member:* Illinois State Bar Association (Elected Member of the Assembly); Cook County Justinian Society of Lawyers; Illinois Real Estate Lawyers Association. ***PRACTICE AREAS:*** Eminent Domain; Condemnation; Property Rights; Real Estate; Government Affairs; Commercial Law. ***Email:*** blynch@nashea-law.com

JONATHAN R. KOYN, born West Allis, Wisconsin, October 15, 1969; admitted to bar, 1998, Illinois; U.S. Court of Appeals; Seventh Circuit; U.S. District Court, Northern District of Illinois. *Education:* Northern Illinois University (B.A., 1992); DePaul University (J.D., 1998). *Member:* Chicago and Illinois State Bar Associations. ***PRACTICE AREAS:*** Real Estate; Corporate Law; Banking Law; Commercial Litigation; Sports Law. ***Email:*** jkoyn@nashea-law.com

---

NEAL, GERBER & EISENBERG LLP

Established in 1986
TWO NORTH LASALLE STREET
SUITE 2200
CHICAGO, ILLINOIS 60602
Telephone: 312-269-8000
FAX: 312-269-1747
URL: http://www.ngelaw.com

General Civil Practice. Corporate Law, Commodities, Securities, Governance, Bankruptcy, Real Estate, Labor and Employment, Employee Benefits, Estate Planning, Environmental Law, Federal, State and International Tax, Finance, Health Law, Information Technology, Intellectual Property, State and Local Property Law, Wealth Preservation, Insurance Coverage and Litigation including Antitrust, Commercial Litigation, White Collar Crime, Products Liability Defense, Exempt Organizations and Association Law.

FIRM PROFILE: Neal Gerber Eisenberg LLP is a Chicago firm providing legal services to a diverse group of clients in a wide array of domestic and global business transactions and litigation matters. Our clients include privately and publicly held companies, financial institutions, non-profit organizations and high net worth individuals. Our client base reflects virtually every business industry, including a number of Fortune 100 companies. Neal Gerber Eisenberg, a growing firm of over 175 attorneys, enjoys a reputation as one of the fastest growing law firms and is recognized throughout the Chicago area and nationally for its expertise in a number of key practice areas. Our mission is to deliver superior individualized client service in a thoroughly integrated manner that exceeds expectations.

PARTNERS OF FIRM

HARVEY M. ADELSTEIN, born Cleveland, Ohio, September 24, 1936; admitted to bar, 1961, Ohio; 1962, Illinois. *Education:* Kenyon College (A.B., cum laude, 1958); Case Western Reserve University (LL.B., 1961). Order of the Coif. Editor-in-Chief, Case Western Law Review, 1960-1961. Teaching Fellow, Northwestern University School of Law, 1961-1962. ***PRACTICE AREAS:*** Labor and Employment; Management Labor Law. ***Email:*** hadelstein@ngelaw.com

CLAUDIA HARRI ALLEN, born New York, New York, July 25, 1960; admitted to bar, 1987, New York; 1994, Illinois. *Education:* Yale University (B.A., magna cum laude, 1982); Columbia University (J.D., 1986). James Kent Scholar; Harlan Fiske Stone Scholar. ***PRACTICE AREAS:*** Corporate Law; Corporate Governance; Mergers, Acquisitions and Divestitures; Securities. ***Email:*** callen@ngelaw.com

DIANE M. ANDERSON, born Chicago, Illinois, July 25, 1959; admitted to bar, 1983, Illinois. *Education:* Loyola University of Chicago (B.B.A., summa cum laude, 1980); Columbia University (J.D., 1983). Beta Alpha Psi; Beta Gamma Sigma. AICPA Elijah Watt Sells Award. Editor, Columbia Law Review, 1982-1983. Certified Public Accountant, Illinois, 1980. ***PRACTICE AREAS:*** State and Local Taxation Law. ***Email:*** danderson@ngelaw.com

SCOTT J. BAKAL, born New York, New York, December 24, 1960; admitted to bar, 1985, Illinois. *Education:* Yale University (B.S., magna cum laude, 1982); Harvard University (J.D., magna cum laude, 1985). ***PRACTICE AREAS:*** Federal Taxation; Estate Planning Law; Corporate Law; Venture Capital. ***Email:*** sbakal@ngelaw.com

JEFFREY J. BAKKER, born Chicago Heights, Illinois, September 17, 1968; admitted to bar, 1997, Illinois and U.S. District Court, District of Illinois. *Education:* Monmouth College (B.A., magna cum laude, 1990); University of Illinois (J.D., magna cum laude, 1997). Co-Author: "HIPPA Privacy Compliance: It's Time To Take It Seriously," Benefits Law Journal, Spring 2004; "ERISA Issues In Insurance Company Demutualizations," Benefits Law Journal, Autumn, 2001. *Member:* American Bar Association (Member, Employee Benefits Committee, 1997—); National Association of Stock Plan Professionals (2001—). ***PRACTICE AREAS:*** Employee Benefits (50%); Executive Compensation (50%). ***Email:*** jbakker@ngelaw.com

PETER H. BARROW, born New York, New York, March 15, 1950; admitted to bar, 1976, Illinois; 1978, New York. *Education:* Washington University (B.A., summa cum laude, 1972); Syracuse University (J.D., cum laude, 1976). Phi Beta Kappa. Board Member, Syracuse University Law Review, 1975-1976. ***PRACTICE AREAS:*** Banks and Banking; Finance. ***Email:*** pbarrow@ngelaw.com

(This Listing Continued)

ROBERT A. BEDORE, born Chicago, Illinois, April 3, 1954; admitted to bar, 1980, Illinois. *Education:* DePaul University (B.S.C., with highest honors, 1975; J.D., 1980). Certified Public Accountant, Illinois, 1975. Adjunct Faculty, Federal Tax Procedure and Litigation: Loyola University School of Law, 1990—; Northwestern University, 1984-1993. ***PRACTICE AREAS:*** Tax Controversies; Taxation (Local, State, Federal and International) Law. ***Email:*** rbedore@ngelaw.com

WENDY L. BENDERSKY, born Dayton, Ohio, May 13, 1967; admitted to bar, 1993, California; 1999, Illinois. *Education:* Northwestern University (B.A., 1989); George Washington University (J.D., 1993). ***PRACTICE AREAS:*** Commercial Leasing; Leases and Leasing; Real Estate. ***Email:*** wbendersky@ngelaw.com

LAWRENCE M. BENJAMIN, born Miami, Florida, July 26, 1962; admitted to bar, 1987, Illinois. *Education:* Northwestern University (B.A., 1983); University of Chicago (J.D., 1987). ***PRACTICE AREAS:*** Real Estate; Banking Litigation; Commercial Litigation; Construction Law; Real Estate Litigation; Bankruptcy Law; Lenders Rights. ***Email:*** lbenjamin@ngelaw.com

H. NICHOLAS BERBERIAN, born Philadelphia, Pennsylvania, December 27, 1952; admitted to bar, 1978, Illinois. *Education:* Kenyon College (A.B., cum laude, 1974); University of Chicago (M.B.A., 1975; J.D., 1978). *Member:* American Bar Association (Co-Chair: Securities Litigation Committee, 2003—; Subcommittee on Broker-Dealer Litigation, 1993-2003). ***PRACTICE AREAS:*** Federal Securities Litigation; Regulatory Law; Commercial Litigation. ***Email:*** nberberian@ngelaw.com

PAULA KAPLAN BERGER, born April 18, 1952; admitted to bar, 1976, Illinois; 1980, Florida. *Education:* University of Missouri (B.J., 1973); DePaul University (J.D., magna cum laude, 1976). Mortar Board. *Member:* Chicago Bar Association; The Florida Bar. ***Email:*** pberger@ngelaw.com

STEPHEN L. BERGER, born Chicago, Illinois, March 14, 1945; admitted to bar, 1970, Illinois. *Education:* University of Illinois (B.A., 1967); Illinois Institute of Technology/Chicago-Kent College of Law (J.D., 1970). ***PRACTICE AREAS:*** Real Estate Law. ***Email:*** sberger@ngelaw.com

STEPHEN S. BERKELEY, born Washington, D.C., April 21, 1970; admitted to bar, 1995, Illinois; 1996, Arizona, U.S. District Court, District of Arizona and U.S. District Court, Northern District of Illinois. *Education:* Hamilton College (B.A., Political Science, 1992); Chicago-Kent College of Law, Illinois Institute of Technology (J.D., 1995). *Member:* Chicago (Member: Securities Law Committee; Financial and Investment Services Committee) and American (Member, Business Law Section) Bar Associations; State Bar of Arizona. ***PRACTICE AREAS:*** Securities; Securities Litigation and Arbitration; Investments. ***Email:*** sberkeley@ngelaw.com

HOWARD L. BERNSTEIN, born Chicago, Illinois, July 16, 1943; admitted to bar, 1968, Texas; 1971, U.S. Supreme Court; 1973, Illinois and U.S. Court of Appeals, Seventh Circuit; 1997, U.S. Court of Appeals, Fifth Circuit; 1999, U.S. Court of Appeals for the District of Columbia Circuit; 2004, U.S. Court of Appeals, Ninth Circuit. *Education:* University of Texas at Austin (B.B.A., 1965; J.D., 1968). Counsel to Chairman, National Labor Relations Board, 1970-1972. Fellow, College of Labor and Employment Lawyers. *Member:* American Bar Association (Member, Committee on Development of the Law Under the National Labor Relations Act, Labor Law Section). ***PRACTICE AREAS:*** Labor and Employment Law. ***Email:*** hbernstein@ngelaw.com

JERRY H. BIEDERMAN, born Chicago, Illinois, July 2, 1946; admitted to bar, 1971, Illinois. *Education:* Stanford University (B.A., 1968); University of Chicago (J.D., 1971). ***PRACTICE AREAS:*** Business Planning Law; Estate Planning; Corporate Law; Employee Benefits Law; Real Estate Acquisitions; Real Estate Development; Real Estate Leasing; Taxation (Federal and International) Law. ***Email:*** jbiederman@ngelaw.com

EUGENE A. BOYLE, born Fort Belvoir, Virginia, October 3, 1961; admitted to bar, 1986, Missouri; 1987, Illinois. *Education:* Lawrence University (B.A., 1983); Washington University (J.D., 1986). Executive Notes and Comments Editor, Washington University Journal of Urban and Contemporary Law, 1985-1986. ***PRACTICE AREAS:*** Labor; Employment Law. ***Email:*** eboyle@ngelaw.com

KAREN A. BROUCEK, born Joliet, Illinois, June 17, 1954; admitted to bar, 1979, Illinois. *Education:* Lewis University (B.A., 1976); DePaul University College of Law (J.D., 1979); John Marshall Law School (LL.M., Employee Benefits, 2000). ***PRACTICE AREAS:*** Employee Benefits. ***Email:*** kbroucek@ngelaw.com

SCOTT A. BROWDY, born Chicago, Illinois; admitted to bar, 1991, Florida; 1992, Illinois. *Education:* University of Virginia (B.A., 1988); Northwestern University (J.D., 1991). ***LANGUAGES:*** Italian. ***PRACTICE AREAS:*** Securities Litigation; Commercial Litigation. ***Email:*** sbrowdy@ngelaw.com

ALAN C. BROWN, born Rockford, Illinois, May 12, 1956; admitted to bar, 1981, Illinois. *Education:* Miami University (B.A., magna cum laude, 1978); University of Chicago (J.D., cum laude, 1981). Phi Beta Kappa; Order of the Coif. ***PRACTICE AREAS:*** Trusts and Estates; Estate and Gift Taxation; Life Insurance. ***Email:*** abrown@ngelaw.com

ROBERT E. BROWNE, born Lake Geneva, Wisconsin, April 2, 1945; admitted to bar, 1970, Wisconsin; 1971, Illinois; U.S. Supreme Court; U.S. District Court, Northern District of Illinois including Trial Bar, U.S. District Court, Southern District of Illinois, U.S. District Court, Western and Eastern Districts of Wisconsin, U.S. District Court, Eastern District of Michigan, U.S. District Court, Northern District of Texas, U.S. District Court, District of Colorado, U.S. Court of Appeals, Sixth, Seventh, Ninth, Eleventh and the Federal Circuits; registered to practice before U.S. Patent and Trademark Office. *Education:* University of Notre Dame (B.S.C.E., 1967); University of Wisconsin-Madison (J.D., 1970). *Member:* Chicago (Vice-Chairman, Section on Patent, Trademark and Copyright Law, 1980-1982) and American Bar Associations; State Bar of Wisconsin (Director, Non-Resident Lawyers Division, 1987-1995, 2001-2003); Intellectual Property Law Association of Chicago (Member, Board of Governors, 1992-1994). ***PRACTICE AREAS:*** Intellectual Property; Litigation. ***Email:*** rbrowne@ngelaw.com

CHRISTOPHER M. BURKY, born Utica, New York, December 26, 1970; admitted to bar, 1996, Illinois. *Education:* Loyola University of Chicago (B.A., magna cum laude, with

(This Listing Continued)

NEAL, GERBER & EISENBERG LLP, Chicago—Continued

distinction, 1993; J.D., 1996). ***PRACTICE AREAS:*** Securities Litigation; Commodities Litigation; Commercial Litigation; Securities Regulation; Commodities Regulation. ***Email:*** cburky@ngelaw.com

TIMOTHY W. BURNS, born December 20, 1963; admitted to bar, 1991, Missouri; 1997, Illinois. *Education:* Weber State University (B.A., 1991); University of Missouri at Columbia School of Law (J.D., 1991). Order of the Coif. Associate Managing Editor, Missouri Law Review, 1990-1991. Author: "D&O Insurance and 'Holding Claims'," The Insurance Coverage Law Bulletin, March 2005; "Conserving D&O Insurance Policies in Securities Fraud Litigation: A Common Interest of Policyholders and Institutional Shareholder Claimants," Coverage, July/August 2004; "Insurance Coverage for Blast Faxes," The Corporate Counselor, May 2004; "The D&O Insurance Audit: Are You Getting What You Paid For?" Coverage, Jan./Feb. 2004; "Advising Corporate Boards On Directors' And Officers' Insurance," LexisNexis Corporate Governance Report, September 2003; "E&O Coverage in the New Corporate Environment," Insurance Coverage Law Bulletin, May 2003; "D&O Policy Proceeds in Bankruptcy," Insurance Coverage Law Bulletin, September 2002; "SEC Certification Requirements Likely to Raise Important Issues Under Directors and Officers Liability Insurance Policies," Insurance Coverage Law Bulletin, August 2002; "Recent Developments in the Battle for D&O Coverage in the Wake of Bankruptcy," Insurance Coverage Law Bulletin, April 2002. Co-Author, "Directors and Officers Liability: Prevention, Insurance and Indemnification," American Lawyer Media Law Journal Press, 2000. Contributor and Update Editor, Insurance Coverage Disputes, American Lawyer Media Law Journal Seminars-Press, 1996. *Member:* American Bar Association (Chair, Insurance Coverage Litigation Committee, 2003—). ***PRACTICE AREAS:*** Insurance; Insurance Litigation; Corporate Law; Corporate Governance; Litigation.

PATRICIA S. CAIN, born Pittsburgh, Pennsylvania, January 30, 1953; admitted to bar, 1977, Illinois; 1984, New York. *Education:* Georgetown University (A.B., 1974); Northwestern University (J.D., 1977). Phi Beta Kappa; Pi Sigma Alpha; Order of the Coif. Member, 1975-1977 and Executive Editor, 1976-1977, Northwestern University Law Review. ***PRACTICE AREAS:*** ERISA; Employee Benefits Law; Executive Compensation. ***Email:*** pcain@ngelaw.com

SUSAN FEINGOLD CARLSON, born Chicago, Illinois, March 20, 1959; admitted to bar, 1984, Illinois. *Education:* Brown University (A.B., 1981); Vanderbilt University (J.D., 1984). Associate Editor, Vanderbilt Journal of Transnational Law, 1983-1984. ***PRACTICE AREAS:*** Trade and Professional Associations; Antitrust and Trade Regulation; Health Care. ***Email:*** scarlson@ngelaw.com

MICHAEL A. CARRILLO, born East Chicago, Indiana, October 22, 1969; admitted to bar, 1996, Illinois; registered to practice before U.S. Patent and Trademark Office. *Education:* Purdue University (B.S., 1993); University of Illinois (J.D., 1996). Phi Delta Phi. ***PRACTICE AREAS:*** Patents; Trademarks; Intellectual Property Licensing; Litigation; Copyrights. ***Email:*** mcarrillo@ngelaw.com

JILL ANN COLEMAN, born Pontiac, Michigan, August 31, 1955; admitted to bar, 1980, Illinois. *Education:* University of Michigan (B.A., with highest distinction, 1977; J.D., 1980). Order of the Coif. Senior Editor, Michigan Law Review, 1978-1980. ***PRACTICE AREAS:*** Finance. ***Email:*** jcoleman@ngelaw.com

ANDREA M. DESPOTES, born Chicago, Illinois, September 17, 1969; admitted to bar, 1995, Illinois. *Education:* Stanford University (A.B., with distinction, 1991); Harvard University (J.D., cum laude, 1995). Phi Beta Kappa. Author: "Assumptions of Liabilities in Corporate Nonrecognition Transactions: A Critique of the IRS's New Guidance," Journal of Taxation of Corporate Transactions, Vol. 1, No. 5, p. 9 (July-August 2003); "Assessing REIT Spin-Off Transactions," Journal of Taxation of Corporate Transactions, Vol. 1, No. 1, p. 17 (May-June 2002). ***PRACTICE AREAS:*** Taxation. ***Email:*** adespotes@ngelaw.com

JENNIFER DESSER, born Chicago, Illinois, July 21, 1970; admitted to bar, 1997, Illinois. *Education:* University of Michigan (B.A., with high distinction, 1992); Illinois Institute of Technology/Chicago-Kent College of Law (J.D., 1997). ***PRACTICE AREAS:*** Real Estate. ***Email:*** jdesser@ngelaw.com

VICTORIA L. DONATI, born Ashland, Ohio, August 3, 1967; admitted to bar, 1992, Ohio; 1994, Illinois. *Education:* Ashland College (B.A., summa cum laude, 1989); Case Western Reserve University (J.D., magna cum laude, 1992). Order of the Coif. Member, Editorial Board, Case Western Reserve Law Review. ***PRACTICE AREAS:*** Labor Law; Employment Law; Nonprofit and Charitable Organizations. ***Email:*** vdonati@ngelaw.com

MARSHALL E. EISENBERG, born Chicago, Illinois, July 16, 1945; admitted to bar, 1971, Illinois. *Education:* University of Illinois (B.S., 1967; M.A.S., 1968; J.D., with honors, 1971). Order of the Coif; Beta Alpha Psi. Notes and Comments Editor, University of Illinois Law Forum, 1970-1971. Certified Public Accountant, Illinois, 1967. ***PRACTICE AREAS:*** Corporate Law; Securities; Taxation; State Taxation; Federal Taxation; International Taxation; Estate Planning; Real Estate; Real Estate Investment Trusts. ***Email:*** meisenberg@ngelaw.com

DOUGLAS M. ELLIS, born Buffalo, New York, September 26, 1963; admitted to bar, 1988, Illinois. *Education:* State University of New York at Buffalo (B.A., summa cum laude, 1985); Harvard University (J.D., cum laude, 1988). ***PRACTICE AREAS:*** Real Estate; Real Property; Leasing. ***Email:*** dellis@ngelaw.com

ROSS D. EMMERMAN, born Chicago, Illinois, September 11, 1962; admitted to bar, 1987, Illinois. *Education:* University of Michigan (B.B.A., with honors, 1984); George Washington University (J.D., with honors, 1987). Beta Alpha Si. Certified Public Accountant, Illinois, 1984. ***PRACTICE AREAS:*** Corporate Law; Mergers, Acquisitions and Divestitures; Securities; Investments; Private Equity; Venture Capital; Emerging Growth Companies. ***Email:*** remmerman@ngelaw.com

LEE J. EULGEN, born West Allis, Wisconsin; admitted to bar, 1997, Illinois, Wisconsin and U.S. District Court, Northern District of Illinois and Western District of Wisconsin. *Education:* University of Notre Dame (B.B.A., 1994); University of Wisconsin (J.D., 1997). ***PRACTICE AREAS:*** Intellectual Property; Entertainment Law; Litigation. ***Email:*** leulgen@ngelaw.com

(This Listing Continued)

STEPHEN FEDO, born Duluth, Minnesota, November 11, 1950; admitted to bar, 1981, Illinois. *Education:* Macalester College (B.A., with distinction, 1971); State University of New York at Stony Brook (M.A., 1973); University of Chicago (J.D., 1981). ***PRACTICE AREAS:*** Litigation; Business Law; Trust Law; Civil Rights. ***Email:*** sfedo@ngelaw.com

AVRAM I. FELDMAN, born Pittsburgh, Pennsylvania, December 29, 1962; admitted to bar, 1988, Illinois. *Education:* University of Michigan (B.B.A., with high distinction, 1985; J.D., cum laude, 1988). Phi Beta Kappa. Certified Public Accountant, Illinois, 1989. ***PRACTICE AREAS:*** Corporate Law; Business Planning; Real Estate. ***Email:*** afeldman@ngelaw.com

BRUCE A. FOX, born Chicago, Illinois, January 10, 1957; admitted to bar, 1981, Illinois. *Education:* University of Illinois (B.S. and B.A., 1978); University of Michigan (J.D., cum laude, 1981). ***PRACTICE AREAS:*** Mergers and Acquisitions; Information Technology; Corporate Law. ***Email:*** bfox@ngelaw.com

TIMOTHY A. FRENCH, born New Britain, Connecticut, August 22, 1959; admitted to bar, 1985, Illinois. *Education:* Harvard University (A.B., cum laude, 1982); Northwestern University (J.D., 1985). Julius H. Miner Moot Court Board, 1984-1985. Author: "The Rise and Fall of the Doctrine of Equitable Subordination as Applied to Nonmanagement Creditors," 4 Journal of Bankruptcy Law and Practice 257 (1995). ***PRACTICE AREAS:*** Environmental Law; Debtor and Creditor; Bankruptcy Law; Creditors Rights Law; Commercial Litigation. ***Email:*** tfrench@ngelaw.com

ELLEN B. FRIEDLER, born Milwaukee, Wisconsin, October 11, 1958; admitted to bar, 1983, Illinois. *Education:* University of Wisconsin-Madison (B.A., 1980); Harvard University (J.D., 1983). ***PRACTICE AREAS:*** Commercial Real Estate; Leases and Leasing. ***Email:*** efriedler@ngelaw.com

JEFFREY M. GALKIN, born Chicago, Illinois, February 17, 1963; admitted to bar, 1989, Illinois. *Education:* University of Illinois (B.S., with high honors, 1985); Northwestern University (J.D., cum laude, 1989). Order of the Coif. Executive Editor, Journal of Criminal Law and Criminology, 1988-1989. Certified Public Accountant, Illinois, 1985. ***PRACTICE AREAS:*** Real Estate. ***Email:*** jgalkin@ngelaw.com

NORMAN J. GANTZ, born Chicago, Illinois, August 24, 1947; admitted to bar, 1972, Illinois. *Education:* University of Illinois (B.A., with honors, 1969); Northwestern University (J.D., cum laude, 1972). Pi Sigma Alpha. Senior Editor, Journal of Criminal Law, Criminology and Police Science, 1971-1972. Member, Securities Law Advisory Committee to the Secretary of State of Illinois, 1984-1990. Member, Revised Uniform Limited Partnership Act Committee to the Secretary of State of Illinois, 1985-1990. ***PRACTICE AREAS:*** Corporate Law; Securities; Mergers, Acquisitions and Divestitures. ***Email:*** ngantz@ngelaw.com

JAMES K. GARDNER, born Gary, Indiana, November 16, 1943; admitted to bar, 1968, Illinois and Indiana; 1972, District of Columbia. *Education:* Purdue University (B.A., 1965); Indiana University (J.D., cum laude, 1968). Order of the Coif; Omicron Delta Kappa. ***PRACTICE AREAS:*** Antitrust Law; Commercial Litigation; Mergers and Acquisitions Law. ***Email:*** jgardner@ngelaw.com

CHARLES E. GERBER (1941-1998)

ROBERT G. GERBER, born Chicago, Illinois, January 13, 1971; admitted to bar, 1998, Illinois. *Education:* Indiana University (B.A., 1994); John Marshall Law School (J.D., 1998). Phi Delta Phi. Order of John Marshall. Executive Editor, John Marshall Law Review, 1997-1998. Author: "Computers and the Year 2000: Are You Ready?" John Marshall Law Review, 1997. ***PRACTICE AREAS:*** Corporate Law; Mergers, Acquisitions and Divestitures; Business Law; Partnership Law. ***Email:*** rgerber@ngelaw.com

GERALD A. GOLDEN, born Chicago, Illinois, January 7, 1945; admitted to bar, 1972, Illinois. *Education:* Washington University (A.B., 1966); Northwestern University (M.B.A., 1968); DePaul University (J.D., 1972). Editor, DePaul Law Review, 1971-1972. Fellow, College of Labor and Employment Lawyers. ***PRACTICE AREAS:*** Labor and Employment; Contracts. ***Email:*** ggolden@ngelaw.com

DAVID V. GOODSIR, admitted to bar, 1991, Illinois. *Education:* University of Michigan (B.A., 1986); Loyola University (J.D., 1991). Member, Loyola University of Chicago Law Journal. Editor-in-Chief, Loyola Consumer Law Reporter. ***PRACTICE AREAS:*** Commercial Litigation; Insurance Coverage Litigation. ***Email:*** dgoodsir@ngelaw.com

JOHN W. GUARISCO, born Melrose Park, Illinois, May 27, 1970; admitted to bar, 1995, Illinois. *Education:* Stanford University (B.A., 1992); University of Illinois (J.D., 1995). Harno Scholar. Order of the Coif. Member and Managing Editor, University of Illinois Law Review. ***PRACTICE AREAS:*** Professional Liability; Insurance; Insurance Defense; Litigation; Civil Practice; Bankruptcy. ***Email:*** jguarisco@ngelaw.com

IRWIN I. GZESH, born Chicago, Illinois, October 12, 1954; admitted to bar, 1981, Illinois. *Education:* University of Illinois (B.S., with honors, 1976); Illinois Institute of Technology/Chicago-Kent College of Law (J.D., with high honors, 1981). Edmund J. James Scholar. Notes and Comments Editor, Chicago-Kent Law Review, 1980-1981. Instructor (Legal Drafting-Commercial Agreements and Negotiations) Illinois Institute of Technology/Chicago Kent College of Law, 1984-1987. ***PRACTICE AREAS:*** Business Law; Real Estate Law; Real Estate Development and Syndications Law. ***Email:*** igzesh@ngelaw.com

KENNETH L. HARRIS, born Chicago, Illinois, August 10, 1960; admitted to bar, 1985, Illinois. *Education:* Hamilton College (A.B., summa cum laude, 1982); University of Chicago (J.D., 1985); New York University (LL.M., 1988). Phi Beta Kappa. Co-Author: "Standards of Tax Practice," Tax Analysts, 6th edition, 2004; "Assessing The Long-Awaited LLC Classifications Guidelines," 73 Taxes 51, 1995. Adjunct Professor of Law: Northwestern University School of Law, 2004; IIT/Chicago-Kent, College of Law, 1991—. ***PRACTICE AREAS:*** Taxation; Corporate Law. ***Email:*** klharris@ngelaw.com

DAN J. HOFMEISTER, JR., born Park Ridge, Illinois, December 6, 1964; admitted to bar, 1990, Illinois. *Education:* University of Nebraska at Lincoln (B.J., 1987); Loyola University, Chicago (J.D., 1990). Member: National Moot Court Team and National Trial Team. Chief Articles Editor, Loyola Consumer Law Reporter. Recipient, Loyola University Leadership and Service Award. Adjunct Professor, Olivet Nazarene University. *Member:*

(This Listing Continued)

Chicago, Illinois State and American Bar Associations; American Health Lawyers Association. ***PRACTICE AREAS:*** Health Law; Managed Care; Insurance Coverage; Commercial Law; Litigation; Products Liability. ***Email:*** dhofmeister@ngelaw.com

MICHAEL J. HUGHES, born Lynn, Massachusetts, November 18, 1964; admitted to bar, 1989, Illinois. *Education:* University of Chicago (B.A., with honors, 1986); Washington University (J.D., 1989). Associate Editor, Washington University Law Quarterly, 1988-1989. ***PRACTICE AREAS:*** Environmental Law; Litigation. ***Email:*** mhughes@ngelaw.com

PHILIP M. KAYMAN, born Chicago, Illinois, December 6, 1941; admitted to bar, 1967, Illinois. *Education:* University of Michigan (B.B.A., with honors, 1963); Northwestern University (J.D., cum laude, 1967). Order of the Coif; Beta Alpha Psi. Associate Editor, Northwestern University Law Review, 1966-1967. Associate-in-Law, Boalt Hall, University of California, 1967-1968. ***PRACTICE AREAS:*** Real Estate (Property) Law; Corporate and Securities Law. ***Email:*** pkayman@ngelaw.com

MICHAEL G. KELBER, born Park Ridge, Illinois, November 6, 1967; admitted to bar, 1996, Illinois; registered to practice before the U.S. Patent and Trademark Office. *Education:* University of Illinois (B.S., 1989); Chicago-Kent College of Law, Illinois Institute of Technology (J.D., 1996). *Member:* Chicago, Illinois State and American Bar Associations; American Intellectual Property Law Association. ***PRACTICE AREAS:*** Intellectual Property; Intellectual Property Litigation; Trademarks; Patents; Copyrights; Intellectual Property Licensing. ***Email:*** mkelber@ngelaw.com

SYNDE B. KEYWELL, born Detroit, Michigan, September 26, 1950; admitted to bar, 1978, Michigan; 1983, Illinois and U.S. Court of Appeals, Sixth and Seventh Circuits. *Education:* University of Michigan (B.A., 1975; J.D., cum laude, 1978). Law Clerk to the Hon. Anna Diggs Tayler, U.S. District Court for the Eastern District of Michigan. *Member:* Member, Chicago Bar Association, Illinois State Bar Association, American Bar Association, American Bankruptcy Institute. ***PRACTICE AREAS:*** Bankruptcy; Reorganization; Creditors Rights; Litigation. ***Email:*** skeywell@ngelaw.com

PATRICK G. KING, born LaGrange Park, Illinois, May 19, 1967; admitted to bar, 1993, Illinois. *Education:* Illinois Benedictine College (B.A., 1989); John Marshall Law School (J.D., 1993). ***PRACTICE AREAS:*** Commodities; Securities Litigation. ***Email:*** pking@ngelaw.com

JOSHUA A. KLEIN, born New Haven, Connecticut, January 13, 1972; admitted to bar, 1997, Illinois. *Education:* Tufts University (B.A., 1994); University of Pennsylvania (J.D., 1997). ***PRACTICE AREAS:*** Corporate Law; Securities Law. ***Email:*** jklein@ngelaw.com

JEFFREY G. KRAFT, born New York, N.Y., June 17, 1949; admitted to bar, 1977, Massachusetts; 1983, Illinois. *Education:* City College of the City University of New York (B.A., cum laude, 1972); Case Western Reserve University (J.D., 1976); Harvard University (M.P.H., 1977). ***LANGUAGES:*** French and Spanish. ***PRACTICE AREAS:*** Corporate Law; Health Care; Hospital Law; Insurance; Mergers, Acquisitions and Divestitures; Regulatory Law. ***Email:*** jkraft@ngelaw.com

STEVEN A. LAMPERT, born Chicago, Illinois, November 11, 1944; admitted to bar, 1969, Illinois. *Education:* University of Illinois (B.S., 1966); Northwestern University (J.D., cum laude, 1969). Editorial Board, Northwestern University Law Review, 1968-1969. ***PRACTICE AREAS:*** Trusts and Estates; Probate; Taxation. ***Email:*** slampert@ngelaw.com

DOUGLAS J. LUBELCHEK, born Chicago, Illinois, August 15, 1963; admitted to bar, 1987, Illinois. *Education:* University of Illinois (B.S., with highest honors, 1984); University of Chicago (J.D., with honors, 1987). Certified Public Accountant, Illinois, 1984. ***PRACTICE AREAS:*** Real Estate Law; Finance. ***Email:*** dlubelchek@ngelaw.com

JED R. MANDEL, born Boston, Massachusetts, January 17, 1952; admitted to bar, 1977, Illinois. *Education:* University of Michigan (B.A., with honors, 1974); Northwestern University (J.D., 1977). Phi Eta Sigma. ***PRACTICE AREAS:*** Trade and Professional Associations; Antitrust and Trade Regulation; Health Care; Environmental Law. ***Email:*** jmandel@ngelaw.com

MIRANDA KISER MANDEL, born Indianapolis, Indiana, November 3, 1956; admitted to bar, 1981, Illinois. *Education:* Colorado College; Indiana University (B.A., 1977; J.D., summa cum laude, 1980). Order of the Coif. John H. Edwards Fellowship, 1979-1980. Law Clerk, Hon. Paul H. Roney, United States Court of Appeals, Eleventh Circuit, 1980-1981. ***PRACTICE AREAS:*** Business Law; Corporate Law; Mergers, Acquisitions and Divestitures. ***Email:*** mmandel@ngelaw.com

MARIA T. MANHART, born Inglewood, California, December 15, 1962; admitted to bar, 1988, Wisconsin; 1995, Illinois. *Education:* Creighton University (B.A., cum laude, 1985); Marquette University (J.D., 1988). Phi Delta Phi. Recipient, American Jurisprudence Award in Collective Bargaining. Member, Marquette University Law Review, 1987-1988. ***PRACTICE AREAS:*** Leases and Leasing; Real Estate. ***Email:*** mmanhart@ngelaw.com

MICHAEL P. MANLY, born Lincoln, Nebraska, March 21, 1971; admitted to bar, 1996, Illinois. *Education:* University of Nebraska (B.A., with distinction, 1993; J.D., with high distinction, 1996). ***PRACTICE AREAS:*** Securities Litigation. ***Email:*** mmanly@ngelaw.com

DAVID S. MARTIN, born Dekalb, Illinois, March 22, 1953; admitted to bar, 1982, Illinois. *Education:* Kalamazoo College (B.A., 1975); John Marshall Law School (J.D., 1982). Assistant Cook County State's Attorney, 1983-1985. ***PRACTICE AREAS:*** Real Estate Taxation; State and Local Property Taxation; Real Estate Law. ***Email:*** dmartin@ngelaw.com

THOMAS C. McDONOUGH, born St. Louis, Missouri, February 26, 1963; admitted to bar, 1988, Illinois and Wisconsin; 1989, U.S. District Court, Northern District of Illinois; 1990, U.S. District Court, Western District of Wisconsin; 1994, U.S. Court of Appeals, Federal Circuit; 2002, U.S. Supreme Court; registered to practice before U.S. Patent and Trademark Office. *Education:* University of Illinois (B.S., with honors, 1985); University of Wisconsin-Madison (J.D., with honors, 1988). Order of the Coif. *Member:* Chicago Bar Association; American Intellectual Property Law Association. ***PRACTICE AREAS:*** Patents; Intellectual Property. ***Email:*** tmcdonough@ngelaw.com

(This Listing Continued)

DIANA J.P. McKENZIE, born Detroit, Michigan, 1959; admitted to bar, 1986, Georgia; 1993, Illinois. *Education:* Kenyon College (B.A., magna cum laude, 1981); Emory University (M.B.A., 1985; J.D., 1985). Phi Beta Kappa. Author: "Preventative Law: Disentanglement Clauses in IT Outsourcing Agreement," published in the Computer Law Association Bulletin (September, 2005); "Controlling the Chaos: A New Approach to Streamlining Outsourcing Negotiations," published in Intellectual Property and Technology Law Journal (September, 2005); "Creating a Healthy Relationship with Your (Next) IT Vendor," published in Journal of Healthcare Information Management (Fall, 2003); "Legal Protections Related to Security Concerns," published in Journal of Healthcare Information Management (Summer, 2003); "Negotiating Web Host Development Agreements," published in The Computer & Internet Lawyer (February, 2003). Presentations and Speaker: "Transformational Outsourcing," presented at the Computer Law Association European Conference, Stockholm, Sweden (October, 2005); "Outsourcing: Doing It Right The First Time and Every Time," presented at the American Bar Association 2005 Annual Meeting, Chicago, Illinois (August, 2005); "A Practical Approach to Drafting Information Technology Contracts," presented via live teleconference for the Scottsdale Institute, Chicago, Illinois (June, 2005); "Exceeding Client Expectations: Winning Negotiating Strategies," presented at the Minority Corporate Counsel Association 2005 Annual Meeting, Chicago, Illinois (March, 2005). Member, Advisory Board, Intellectual Property Law Journal, 1995—. Member, Editorial Board: Performance Improvement Advisor, 1996—; Report on Healthcare Information Management, 1995—. Selected: as one of America's Leading Lawyers for Business in Technology and IT Outsourcing by Chambers USA in 2005; for inclusion in the 2006 edition of The Best Lawyers in America under Information Technology Law. *Member:* Computer Law Association (Member, Advisory Board, 2003—; President, 2002-2003; Officer, 2000-2003; Member, Board of Directors, 1997-2003); Healthcare Information & Management Systems Society (Senior Member, 2002—). ***PRACTICE AREAS:*** Information Technology; Computer Law; Outsourcing Law; High Technology; Health Care Technology; Internet Law; Privacy Law; Commercial Law; Security; Technology Law. ***Email:*** dmckenzie@ngelaw.com

THOMAS J. McNULTY, born Philadelphia, Pennsylvania, December 5, 1951; admitted to bar, 1976, Illinois and New Jersey. *Education:* University of Notre Dame (B.S., 1973); Rutgers University (J.D., magna cum laude, 1976). Associate Editor, Rutgers-Camden Law Review, 1975-1976. Assistant State's Attorney, Cook County, Illinois, Supervisor of Real Estate and Personal Property Tax Unit, 1981-1984. ***PRACTICE AREAS:*** Real Estate Law; Real Estate Taxation Law; Litigation. ***Email:*** tmcnulty@ngelaw.com

ANTONY J. McSHANE, born New York, New York, November 10, 1960; admitted to bar, 1985, Illinois and U.S. District Court, Northern District of Illinois. *Education:* University of Illinois (B.A., 1982); DePaul University (J.D., 1985). *Member:* International Trademark Association; American Intellectual Property Association of America. ***PRACTICE AREAS:*** Litigation; Intellectual Property Counseling and Litigation; Commercial Litigation; E-Business Law; Internet Law. ***Email:*** amcshane@ngelaw.com

EARL N. MELAMED, born Montreal, Canada, January, 18, 1957; admitted to bar, 1982, Illinois. *Education:* Northwestern University (B.S., with honors, 1979; J.D., 1982). ***PRACTICE AREAS:*** Business Law; Joint Ventures; Limited Liability Company Law; Partnership Law; Corporate Law; Taxation Law. ***Email:*** emelamed@ngelaw.com

CHAD W. MOELLER, born 1971; admitted to bar, 1997, Illinois and U.S. District Court, Northern District of Illinois; 2001, U.S. Court of Appeals, Seventh Circuit. *Education:* University of Wisconsin-Madison (B.A., 1994); DePaul University (J.D., 1997). Member, Moot Court Society, 1994-1997. ***PRACTICE AREAS:*** Labor and Employment. ***Email:*** cmoeller@ngelaw.com

MICHAEL L. MOLINARO, born Chicago, Illinois, December 13, 1957; admitted to bar, 1982, Illinois. *Education:* St. Joseph's College (B.S. cum laude, 1979); DePaul University (J.D., 1982). Editor, DePaul Law Review, 1981-1982. Law Clerk to Hon. F. Hertz, United States Bankruptcy Court, Northern District of Illinois, 1982-1983. Author: "Directors and Officers: Beware of the Vicinity of Insolvency," Corporate Officers & Directors Liability, April 5, 2004; "Defeating a Cramdown: Getting A Grip on the Indubitable Equivalent Standard," The Secured Lender, November/December 1994; "Single-Asset Real Estate Bankruptcies: Curbing An Abuse of the Bankruptcy Process," UCC Law Journal, Fall 1991; "Bankruptcy Wars!" The Secured Lender, May/June 1990; "The Threat of Cramdown: How Real Is It?" Real Estate Review, Fall 1989; "Tax Increment Financing: A New Source of Funds for Community Redevelopment in Illinois-City of Canton v. Crouch," 30 DePaul Law Review 459, 1981. Co-Author, "Documenting a Consensual Transfer of Distressed Real Estate," American Bar Association, Real Property, Probate & Trust Law Section, 1998. ***PRACTICE AREAS:*** Creditors' Rights; Bankruptcy Law; Financial Services Law. ***Email:*** mmolinaro@ngelaw.com

ARTHUR B. MUIR, born Denver, Colorado, January 9, 1946; admitted to bar, 1977, Illinois. *Education:* University of Pennsylvania (A.B., 1968; M.B.A., 1972); Northwestern University (J.D., 1976). Illinois Assistant Attorney General, Environmental Control Division, 1977-1979. *Member:* Chicago, Illinois State and American Bar Associations. ***PRACTICE AREAS:*** Commercial Finance; Real Estate Finance; Debt Finance; Leveraged Buyouts. ***Email:*** amuir@ngelaw.com

PHIL C. NEAL, born Chicago, Illinois, July 30, 1919; admitted to bar, 1943, Illinois; 1945, California. *Education:* Harvard University (A.B., 1940; LL.B., 1943). President, Harvard Law Review, 1943. Law Clerk to Mr. Justice Robert H. Jackson, 1943-1945. With U.S. Department of State, 1945. Professor of Law: Stanford University, 1948-1961; University of Chicago, 1962-1983. Dean, University of Chicago Law School, 1963-1975. Chairman, President's Task Force on Antitrust Laws, 1968. Executive Secretary, U.S. District Courts Coordinating Committee for Multiple Litigation, 1962-1965. Chairman, Pacific Regional Enforcement Commission, Wage Stabilization Board, 1950-1952. Fellow: American Bar Foundation (Director, 1964-1979). ***PRACTICE AREAS:*** Antitrust Law; Constitutional Law; Appellate Practice; Litigation. ***Email:*** pneal@ngelaw.com

MARLENE MATHES NELSON, born Germany, September 26, 1946; admitted to bar, 1995, Illinois. *Education:* DePaul University (B.A., 1991); Illinois Institute of Technology, Chicago-Kent College of Law (J.D., 1995). ***PRACTICE AREAS:*** Estate Planning; Estate Administration; Trust Administration; Estate and Gift Taxation. ***Email:*** mnelson@ngelaw.com

(This Listing Continued)

NEAL, GERBER & EISENBERG LLP, Chicago—Continued

PETER B. NEWTON, born Oak Park, Illinois, December 14, 1952; admitted to bar, 1983, Illinois. *Education:* Columbus College (B.S., 1979); Illinois Institute of Technology/ Chicago-Kent College of Law (J.D., with high honors, 1983). Member: Product Liability Advisory Council; Propane Gas Defense Association. ***PRACTICE AREAS:*** Products Liability Defense; Commercial Litigation; Securities Law. ***Email:*** pnewton@ngelaw.com

KIMBERLY A. PENDO, born Chicago, Illinois; admitted to bar, 1998, Illinois. *Education:* University of Illinois (B.A., summa cum laude, with distinction and honors, 1995); Northwestern University (J.D., 1998). Phi Beta Kappa; Bronze Tablet (University Honors); James Scholar. *Member:* Chicago Bar Association (Chair, Trade & Professional Associations Law Committee); Association Forum of Chicagoland (Member, Editorial Committee); American Society of Association Executives. ***LANGUAGES:*** Hebrew. ***PRACTICE AREAS:*** Trade and Professional Associations; Nonprofit and Charitable Organizations; Corporate Law; Entertainment and the Arts. ***Email:*** kpendo@ngelaw.com

MARK A. RABINOWITZ, born Chicago, Illinois, February 9, 1954; admitted to bar, 1978, Illinois and U.S. District Court, Northern District of Illinois; 1979, U.S. Court of Appeals, Seventh Circuit; 1987, U.S. District Court, Eastern District of Pennsylvania and U.S. Court of Appeals, Third Circuit; 2000, U.S. Court of Federal Claims; 2003, U.S. Court of Appeals, Second Circuit. *Education:* University of Illinois (B.A., summa cum laude, 1975); Harvard University (J.D., 1978). Phi Beta Kappa. Member, Bronze Tablet. ***REPORTED CASES:*** Commercial Union Insurance Co. v. David Lines, (2nd Cir. August 5, 2004); Silverstein v. Penguin Putnam, Inc. (2nd Cir. May 7, 2004); Weizeorick v. ABN AMRO Mortgage Group, Inc., 337 F.3d 827 (7th Cir. 2003); First Federal Savings Bank of Hegewisch v. United States, 52 Fed.Cl. 774 (2002); Northern Trust Company v. Bunge Corp., 899 F.2d 591 (7th Cir. 1990). ***PRACTICE AREAS:*** Commercial Litigation; Trial Practice; Insurance Litigation. ***Email:*** mrabinowitz@ngelaw.com

ROBERT RADASEVICH, born Chicago, Illinois, October 16, 1956; admitted to bar, 1981, Illinois. *Education:* Southern Illinois University (B.A., with honors, 1978); DePaul University (J.D., with honors, 1981). Note and Comment Editor, DePaul Law Review, 1980-1981. ***PRACTICE AREAS:*** Commercial Litigation; Bankruptcy Law. ***Email:*** rradasevich@ngelaw.com

TIMOTHY RAY, born Chicago, Illinois; admitted to bar, 1995, Illinois. *Education:* Xavier University of Louisiana (B.A.); University of Iowa (J.D.). Member, Iowa Moot Court Board. Member, Iowa Law Review. *Member:* Chicago, Cook County, Illinois State and American Bar Associations; National Bar Association. ***Email:*** tray@ngelaw.com

STEPHEN M. REICHES, born Baltimore, Maryland, November 16, 1961; admitted to bar, 1987, Illinois. *Education:* Northwestern University (B.A., 1983); The University of Chicago (J.D., 1987). Phi Beta Kappa. ***PRACTICE AREAS:*** Estate Planning Law; Probate Law; Trust Law; Charitable Trusts and Foundations Law. ***Email:*** sreiches@ngelaw.com

RAWN HOWARD REINHARD, born 1963; admitted to bar, 1989, Illinois. *Education:* Ohio State University; David Lipscomb College (B.A., magna cum laude, 1985); Duke University (J.D., with high honors, 1988). ***PRACTICE AREAS:*** Noncompetition and Nonsolicitation Agreements; Class Action Defense; Securities Arbitration; Securities Litigation; Products Liability; Complex Litigation. ***Email:*** rreinhard@ngelaw.com

MEG M. REYNOLDS, born Evanston, Illinois; admitted to bar, 1994, Illinois. *Education:* Northwestern University (B.A., 1980); University of Illinois (J.D., magna cum laude, 1994). Harno Scholar. Associate Editor, University of Illinois Law Review. ***PRACTICE AREAS:*** Employee Benefits; Health Care; ERISA; Pension Plans. ***Email:*** mreynolds@ngelaw.com

LAWRENCE I. RICHMAN, born Chicago, Illinois, August 8, 1954; admitted to bar, 1977, Illinois. *Education:* Columbia University (B.A., magna cum laude, 1974); University of Chicago (J.D., 1977). Phi Beta Kappa. ***PRACTICE AREAS:*** Business Law; Nonprofit and Charitable Organizations; Partnership Law; Probate; Taxation; Trusts and Estates; Wills. ***Email:*** lrichman@ngelaw.com

DAVID B. RITTER, born Queens, New York, August 21, 1958; admitted to bar, 1985, Illinois and U.S. District Court, Northern District of Illinois; 1986, U.S. Court of Appeals, Seventh Circuit; 1987, U.S. Court of Appeals, Sixth Circuit. *Education:* Cornell University (B.S., 1980); Case Western Reserve University (J.D., cum laude, 1985). Member, Case Western Reserve Law Review, 1983-1984. Author: "Insurance Coverage of Employee Claims," Employment Law Strategies, Vol. 1, No. 9, January 1994; "Employee Benefits and Collective Bargaining," Chapter 26, Employee Benefits Law IICLE; "Special Considerations in the Construction Industry," Chapter 15, Labor Law IICLE; "Making Family Leave Act Work," Crain's Small Business (May 1997); "Sexual Harassment Investigation Privileges: Tips and Traps," Sexual Harassment and Discrimination Newsletter, Vol. 1, No. 12 (May 1997); "Protections Afforded Accused Harassers and How Employers Can Avoid Suits From Them," Employment Law Strategist, Vol. 1, No. 6 (December 1996); "Do's and Don'ts of Interviewing in Compliance with the ADA," Employment Law Strategist, Vol. 3, No. 8 (December 1995); "When Could an Employer be Liable for Intoxicated Employees?" Employment Law Strategist, Vol. 2, No. 8 (December 1994); "Insurance Coverage of Employee Claims," Employment Law Strategist, Vol. 1, No. 9 (January 1994). Advisory Board, "You and the Law," National Institute of Business Management, 1998—; "Sexual Harassment and Discrimination," James Publishing Incorporated, 1996-1997; Board of Editors, "The Corporate Counselor," The New York Law Publishing Co., 1998—; Board of Editors, "Employment Law Strategist," The New York Law Publishing Co., 1995—. Contributing Editor: Employment Discrimination Law, American Bar Association Section of Labor and Employment Law, 1996; "AIDS and Public Policy Journal," University Publishing Group, 1988—; "The Developing Labor Law," American Bar Association Section of Labor and Employment Law, 1986-1989. *Member:* American Bar Association. ***PRACTICE AREAS:*** Employment Law. ***Email:*** dritter@ngelaw.com

KATHRYN A. ROE, born Macomb, Illinois; admitted to bar, 1991, Illinois and U.S. District Court, Northern District of Illinois. *Education:* University of Notre Dame (B.A., summa cum laude, 1988) Northwestern University (J.D., 1991). Phi Beta Kappa. *Member:* Chicago and American Bar Associations; American Health Lawyers Association. ***PRACTICE AREAS:*** Health Care. ***Email:*** kroe@ngelaw.com

(This Listing Continued)

JACK A. ROVNER, born Boston, Massachusetts, May 6, 1946; admitted to bar, 1976, Illinois and U.S. District Court, Northern District of Illinois including Trial Bar; 1979, U.S. Court of Appeals, Seventh and Ninth Circuits and U.S. Supreme Court. *Education:* Brandeis University (B.A., 1968); Boston University (J.D., 1976). Member, 1974-1976 and Articles Editor, 1975-1976, Boston University Law Review. Author: "The Privacy Crime: Justice Department Narrows the Targets of HIPAA Criminal Prosecutions," 8 CCH Health Care Compliance Letter No. 17, August 22, 2005; "Making Sense of HIPAA Privacy: Solutions for Complex Compliance Dilemmas," 37 Journal of Health Law 399, Summer 2004; "The Thin Line Between Malpractice and Benefit Determination," 12 Managed Care 31, No. 4, April 2003; "Don't Let Fear of HIPAA Keep You from Crucial Data," 12 Managed Care 56, No. 3, March, 2003; "Managing the Privacy Challenge: Compliance with the Amended HIPAA Privacy Rule," 15 The Health Lawyer 18, September 2002 (with K. Roe and R. Glover); "Commentary: Some Advice on Consent," 32 Modern Healthcare 21, No. 18, May 6, 2002; "Private Lives: Overview of the Final HIPAA Privacy Rules," 901 Legal Affairs Bulletin 10, February, 2001; "When Collaboration Becomes Collusion: State of New York ex rel. Spitzer v. Saint Francis Hospital," 12 The Health Lawyer 1, November 6, 2000; "Physician Unions: A Changing and Challenging Legal Landscape," 897 Legal Affairs Bulletin 7, September, 2000; "Federal Regulation Comes to Private Health Care Financing: The Group Health Insurance Provisions of the Health Insurance Portability and Accountability Act of 1996," 7 Annals of Health Law 183, 1998; "Managing Antitrust in Mergers and Acquisitions," Piper Jaffray Mergers & Acquisitions Quarterly 13, Fall, 1998; "Health Care Fraud and Abuse Control After HIPAA," 9 The Health Lawyer 1, No. 2, 1997; "Analysis of the Provisions of the Health Insurance Portability and Accountability Act of 1996," 9 The Health Lawyer 1, No. 3, 1996; "Physician-Hospital Organizations: Antitrust and PHO Contracting Activities," 8 The Health Lawyer 10, Early Winter, 1995; "Group Purchasing in Health Care Markets: An Ingredient in Health Care Reform," Antitrust and Evolving Health Care Markets 177, 1995; "Monopsony Power in Health Care Markets: Must the Big Buyer Beware Hard Bargaining?" 18 Loyola-Chicago Law Journal 857, 1987. Member, Secretary's Advisory Committee on Regulatory Reform, U.S. Department of Health and Human Services, 2002. Member, Editorial Board, The Health Lawyer, Health Law Section, American Bar Association, 1999-2002. Board Member, Bureau of National Affairs, Inc.'s (BNA) Health Law Reporter, 2005—. Selected for inclusion in the 2006 edition of The Best Lawyers in America under Health Care Law. [U.S. Coast Guard, 1968-1971]. ***PRACTICE AREAS:*** Antitrust; Antitrust and Trade Regulation; Business Law; Commercial Law; Contracts; Corporate Law; Health Care; Insurance; Litigation; Medicare and Medicaid; Mergers, Acquisitions and Divestitures; Privacy Law; Regulatory Law. ***Email:*** jrovner@ngelaw.com

RALPH T. RUSSELL, JR., born Waukegan, Illinois, July 1, 1948; admitted to bar, 1974, Illinois. *Education:* Ripon College (A.B., summa cum laude, 1970); University of Chicago (J.D., 1974). Phi Beta Kappa. Lecturer in Law, Trial Practice, University of Chicago Law School, 1981-1983. ***PRACTICE AREAS:*** Commercial Litigation; Antitrust Law; Banking Litigation; School Desegregation Law; Shareholder Derivative Actions. ***Email:*** rrussell@ngelaw.com

JOHN S. SANTA LUCIA, born Buffalo, New York, June 6, 1963; admitted to bar, 1988, California; 2000, Illinois. *Education:* Northwestern University (B.A., 1985; J.D., 1988). Member, Editorial Board, Northwestern Journal of International Law and Business, 1987-1988. ***PRACTICE AREAS:*** Real Estate; Partnership Law; Finance. ***Email:*** jsantalucia@ngelaw.com

JERRY M. SANTANGELO, born Nutley, New Jersey, August 20, 1959; admitted to bar, 1984, Illinois. *Education:* Miami University (B.S., 1981); DePaul University (J.D., 1984). Managing Editor, Lead Articles, Volume 33 Board, DePaul Law Review, 1983-1984. ***PRACTICE AREAS:*** Securities Regulation; Securities Litigation; Commodities Regulation; Commodities Litigation; Commercial Litigation; Trade Secrets Litigation; Employment Litigation. ***Email:*** jsantangelo@ngelaw.com

CHERYL KEHOE SCHAUL, born Chicago, Illinois, September 8, 1959; admitted to bar, 1985, Illinois. *Education:* Northern Illinois University (B.A., cum laude, 1981); Loyola University (J.D., 1985). Editor, Loyola Law Journal, 1984-1985. ***PRACTICE AREAS:*** Estate Planning and Probate Law. ***Email:*** cschaul@ngelaw.com

LEAH A. SCHLEICHER, born Flint, Michigan, December 24, 1971; admitted to bar, 1997, New Jersey; 1998, New York; 2002, Illinois. *Education:* Michigan State University (B.A., 1994); Fordham University (J.D., 1997). ***PRACTICE AREAS:*** Real Estate; Finance. ***Email:*** lschleicher@ngelaw.com

HARRY J. SECARAS, born Chicago, Illinois, May 19, 1963; admitted to bar, 1989, Illinois. *Education:* University of Illinois (B.A., 1985; M.B.A., 1989; J.D., 1989). Senior Editor and Chapter Author: "How to Take a Case Before the NLRB." *Member:* American Bar Association. ***LANGUAGES:*** Greek. ***PRACTICE AREAS:*** Labor and Employment Law (Management). ***Email:*** hsecaras@ngelaw.com

AUDREY E. SELIN, born Chicago, Illinois, 1952; admitted to bar, 1977, Illinois. *Education:* University of Illinois (B.S., cum laude, 1974); Loyola University (J.D., cum laude, 1977). Instructor, Loyola University School of Law, 1977-1979. *Member:* Chicago and American Bar Associations. ***PRACTICE AREAS:*** Real Estate; Corporate Law; Finance. ***Email:*** aselin@ngelaw.com

MICHAEL D. SHER, born Chicago, Illinois, July 27, 1950; admitted to bar, 1974, Illinois; U.S. District Court, Northern District of Illinois, U.S. District Court, Eastern District of Michigan, U.S. District Court, Eastern District of Wisconsin, U.S. Court of Appeals, Sixth, Seventh and Ninth Circuits, U.S. Tax Court and U.S. Supreme Court. *Education:* University of Michigan (B.A., with distinction, 1971); University of Wisconsin-Madison (J.D., cum laude, 1974). Lecturer in Law, Trial Practice, University of Chicago Law School, 1981-1983. Staff Attorney, Federal Defender Program, Northern District of Illinois, 1975-1977. ***PRACTICE AREAS:*** Litigation; White Collar Crime. ***Email:*** msher@ngelaw.com

LISA A. STEGINK, born Detroit, Michigan, 1962; admitted to bar, 1991, Illinois. *Education:* Calvin College (B.A., 1985); University of Chicago (J.D., 1991). ***PRACTICE AREAS:*** Associations; Not-For-Profit Organizations; Trademarks and Copyrights. ***Email:*** lstegink@ngelaw.com

(This Listing Continued)

DAVID S. STONE, born Detroit, Michigan, July 19, 1960; admitted to bar, 1985, Illinois. *Education:* University of Michigan (B.A., with distinction, 1982; J.D., cum laude, 1985). ***PRACTICE AREAS:*** Securities; Corporate Transactions; Venture Capital. ***Email:*** dstone@ngelaw.com

WILLIAM J. TARNOW, born Rantoul, Illinois, January 13, 1973; admitted to bar, 1997, Illinois. *Education:* University of Illinois (B.A., 1994; J.D., cum laude, 1997). Editor and Author, Elder Law Journal. ***PRACTICE AREAS:*** Labor and Employment; Litigation; Unfair Competition; Trade Secrets; Business Arbitration. ***Email:*** wtarnow@ngelaw.com

ELAINE M. TAUSSIG, born Chicago, Illinois, 1965; admitted to bar, 1995, Illinois and New York. *Education:* Barnard College (B.A., cum laude, 1987); Northwestern University (J.D., 1993). ***PRACTICE AREAS:*** Securities; Corporate Law. ***Email:*** etaussig@ngelaw.com

KEVIN D. TESSIER, born Fontana, California; admitted to bar, 1996, Illinois. *Education:* University of Redlands (B.A., 1992); Indiana University School of Law (J.D., 1996). Law Clerk, Hon. James D. Heiple, Illinois Supreme Court, 1998-2000. ***PRACTICE AREAS:*** Commercial Litigation; Health Law; Insurance Coverage. ***Email:*** ktessier@ngelaw.com

WINFIELD S. THOM, born Kenosha, Wisconsin, January 18, 1964; admitted to bar, 1997, Wisconsin; 2000, Illinois. *Education:* Stanford University (B.A.S., 1986); University of Wisconsin-Madison (J.D., cum laude, 1997). Order of the Coif. ***PRACTICE AREAS:*** Corporate Law; Mergers and Acquisitions; Securities; Venture Capital. ***Email:*** wthom@ngelaw.com

MARTIN H. TISH, born Chicago, Illinois, February 8, 1957; admitted to bar, 1981, Illinois. *Education:* Northwestern University (B.A., highest distinction, 1978; J.D., cum laude, 1981). Phi Beta Kappa; Order of the Coif. Lowden-Wigmore Award, First Prize. Alumni Scholar. Member of Staff, 1979-1980 and Note and Comment Editor, 1980-1981, Journal of Criminal Law and Criminology. ***PRACTICE AREAS:*** Estate Planning; Probate; Trusts and Estates; Wills; Asset Protection. ***Email:*** mtish@ngelaw.com

ELIZABETH MATICH TODOROVIC, born Chicago, Illinois, November 8, 1962; admitted to bar, 1987, Illinois. *Education:* Northwestern University (B.A., with honors, 1984); Boston University (J.D., 1987). ***PRACTICE AREAS:*** Real Estate Law. ***Email:*** etodorovic@ngelaw.com

JONATHAN D. WASSERMAN, born Chicago, Illinois, July 6, 1963; admitted to bar, 1988, Illinois. *Education:* University of California at Santa Cruz (B.A., with highest honors and comprehensive honors in Psychology, 1985); University of Chicago (J.D., 1988). Presidents Counsel Undergraduate Fellowship. Vice President and Group General Counsel, Allied Signal Safety Restraint Systems, Sterling Heights, Michigan, 1996. ***PRACTICE AREAS:*** Mergers and Acquisitions; Venture Capital; Business Law; Private Wealth Services. ***Email:*** jwasserman@ngelaw.com

ROBERT M. WEISS, born 1965; admitted to bar, 1990, Illinois; 1995, New York. *Education:* Dartmouth College (A.B., magna cum laude, 1987); Stanford University (J.D., 1990). Phi Beta Kappa. Named one of "40 Under 40" Outstanding Illinois Attorneys, Chicago Daily Law Bulletin, 2003. Contributing Editor, Computer Law Assocation Bulletin. Chairman, Computer Law Committee, Chicago Bar Association, 2002-2004. *Member:* Chicago Council on Foreign Relations. ***LANGUAGES:*** Spanish, French. ***PRACTICE AREAS:*** Computer Law; Information Technology; High Technology; Technology Contracts; Internet Law; Commercial Law; Health Information Technology; Outsourcing; Computers and Software; Corporate Law; Technology and Science. ***Email:*** rweiss@ngelaw.com

TERRY D. WEISSMAN, born Brooklyn, New York, April 6, 1957; admitted to bar, 1982, New York; 1993, Illinois. *Education:* Cornell University (B.A., 1978); Hofstra University (J.D., with distinction, 1981). Member, 1979-1980 and Student Project Editor, 1980-1981, Hofstra Law Review. ***PRACTICE AREAS:*** Securities Litigation; Commercial Litigation; Legal Malpractice Defense; Insurance Coverage. ***Email:*** tweissman@ngelaw.com

TINA L. WINER, born Chicago, Illinois, August 19, 1970; admitted to bar, 1994, Illinois. *Education:* University of Illinois (B.A., 1991; J.D., 1994). Law Clerk, Department of Justice, 1992. ***PRACTICE AREAS:*** Commercial Litigation; Securities Litigation; Employment Litigation. ***Email:*** twiner@ngelaw.com

THOMAS C. WOLFORD, born St. Louis, Missouri, October 31, 1960; admitted to bar, 1986, Illinois. *Education:* University of California, Berkeley (A.B., with honors, 1983); Boalt Hall School of Law, University of California(J.D., 1986). ***PRACTICE AREAS:*** Bankruptcy; Creditors Rights; Commercial Litigation; Secured Lending. ***Email:*** twolford@ngelaw.com

ELIZABETH D. WRIGHT, born Sioux Falls, South Dakota, July 29, 1971; admitted to bar, 1998, Illinois; 2001, Idaho. *Education:* University of South Dakota (B.A., 1993); University of Iowa (J.D., with high distinction, 1998). Editor-in-Chief, Iowa Law Review, 1997-1998. Law Clerk, Hon. William R. Price, Missouri Supreme Court, 1998-1999. ***PRACTICE AREAS:*** Commercial Law; Contracts; Construction Law. ***Email:*** ewright@ngelaw.com

AMY J. ZDRAVECKY, born Grand Rapids, Michigan, March 19, 1970; admitted to bar, 1995, Georgia; 1998, Illinois. *Education:* University of Michigan (B.A., with high distinction, 1992; J.D., 1994). ***PRACTICE AREAS:*** Labor and Employment Law. ***Email:*** azdravecky@ngelaw.com

LISA S. ZEBOVITZ, born Indianapolis, Indiana, December 30, 1955; admitted to bar, 1980, Illinois; 1981, Pennsylvania; 1982, New Jersey. *Education:* Lake Forest College (B.A., 1977); DePaul University (J.D., 1980). New Jersey Department of Environmental Protection, 1980-1981. U.S. Environmental Protection Agency, 1981-1986. Waste Management, Inc., 1987-1998. ***PRACTICE AREAS:*** Environmental Law; Mediation; Toxic Torts. ***Email:*** lzebovitz@ngelaw.com

ROBERT D. ZIMELIS, born New Rochelle, New York, March 25, 1950; admitted to bar, 1975, Illinois. *Education:* Northwestern University (B.A., with honors, 1972; J.D., cum laude, 1975). ***PRACTICE AREAS:*** Business Planning Law; Investments; Partnerships; Limited Liability Companies; Estate Planning; Taxation (Local, State, Federal and International) Law. ***Email:*** rzimelis@ngelaw.com

(This Listing Continued)

SENIOR COUNSEL

SARAH C. BENDER, born New York, N.Y., September 24, 1971; admitted to bar, 1999, Illinois. *Education:* Bradley University (B.A., cum laude, 1995) Phi Eta Sigma; University of Illinois College of Law (J.D., 1999); University of Illinois (M.S., 1999). Dean's List. Phi Alpha Delta (Treasurer, Bradley University Chapter). ***PRACTICE AREAS:*** Commercial Real Estate; Leases and Leasing; Real Estate. ***Email:*** sbender@ngelaw.com

THOMAS D. BIXBY, born Chicago, Illinois; admitted to bar, 2000, Wisconsin; 2005, Illinois. *Education:* Harvard University (A.B., with honors, 1978); University of Missouri (J.D., 1999). Order of the Coif. Member, University of Missouri Law Review. Author: "Employer Options Under Medicare Part D: Opportunities for Insurers and HMOs," American Health Care Lawyers Association, HMOs and Health Plans, June 2005; "Insurance Commissioners To the Left of Me, CMS to the Right, Here I Am, Stuck In the Middle With You," AHIP Coverage, September/October, 2004. ***PRACTICE AREAS:*** Health Law; Insurance; Medicare and Medicaid. ***Email:*** tbixby@ngelaw.com

ANGELA ELBERT, born Louisville, Kentucky, August 28, 1971; admitted to bar, 1996, Illinois. *Education:* Hanover College (B.A., cum laude, 1993); Indiana University School of Law - Bloomington (J.D., cum laude, 1996). Author, "Asbestos Stopgaps Useful as Congress Feuds," Business Insurance, August 30, 2004. Co-Author: "The Second Wave of Asbestos Litigation and Its Impact on Insurance," Coverage, Vol. 14, No. 6, November/December 2004; "Illinois Estoppel: Conduct that Causes an Insurer's Rights to be Forfeited," Coverage, Vol. 14, No. 3, May/June 2004; "The Plain Meaning of Wrongful Entry or Eviction or Other Invasion of the Right of Private Occupancy: Why Standard-Form Personal Injury Insurance Coverage Applies to Pollution Claims," Environmental Claims Journal, Vol. 12, No. 3, Autumn 1999. *Member:* American Bar Association. ***PRACTICE AREAS:*** Insurance Coverage; Litigation. ***Email:*** aelbert@ngelaw.com

CHRISTINE C. FRANKLIN, born Glens Falls, New York, 1949; admitted to bar, 1980, California; 1994, Illinois; 1995, District of Columbia and Colorado; U.S. District Court, Northern District of Illinois and Northern, Southern, and Central Districts of California; U.S. Court of Appeals, Ninth Circuit; U.S. Supreme Court. *Education:* Newton College of the Sacred Heart (B.A., cum laude, 1971); University of Virginia (M.A., 1974); University of California School of Law, Los Angeles (J.D., 1979). *Member:* State Bar of California; The District of Columbia Bar; American Bar Association (Member, 1993— and Council Member, 1996-1999, Administrative Law and Regulatory Practice Section). ***Email:*** cfranklin@ngelaw.com

JUDITH L. LANDESMAN, born Chicago, Illinois; admitted to bar, 1977, Illinois. *Education:* University of Illinois (B.A., with university honors, 1965); Illinois Institute of Technology/Chicago-Kent College of Law (J.D., with high honors, 1977). Phi Beta Kappa; Phi Kappa Phi; Bronze Tablet. Author: "Construction Trust Fund Provisions of the Mechanics Lien Act," 1998 ISBA Real Property Law Bulletin. *Member:* Illinois State Bar Association (Real Property Law Section). ***PRACTICE AREAS:*** Real Estate; Surety Law. ***Email:*** jlandesman@ngelaw.com

DAVID M. LAVIN, born Chicago, Illinois, January 13, 1959; admitted to bar, 1984, Illinois. *Education:* Illinois State University (B.S., 1981); DePaul University College of Law (J.D., 1984). Adjunct Professor, Advanced Trial Advocacy, Illinois Institute of Technology/Chicago-Kent College of Law. ***PRACTICE AREAS:*** Real Estate Taxation. ***Email:*** dlavin@ngelaw.com

BURTON H. LITWIN, born Chicago, Illinois, July 26, 1944; admitted to bar, 1970, Illinois. *Education:* Roosevelt University (B.S.B.A., with honors, 1966); Northwestern University (J.D., cum laude, 1970). Beta Gamma Sigma; Order of the Coif. Member, Board of Editors, Northwestern University Law Review, 1968-1970. Listed in Who's Who in American Law. Author: "The Protest and Administrative Appeals," Published as a chapter in Federal Civil Tax Practice, by the Illinois Institute for Continuing Legal Education. Certified Public Accountant, Illinois, 1966. *Member:* Chicago (Chairman, Administrative Practice Subcommittee, Federal Taxation Committee, 1982-1983) and American (Member, Administrative Practice Committee, Section of Taxation, 1980—) Bar Associations. ***PRACTICE AREAS:*** Taxation; Federal Taxation; International Taxation; Tax Controversies; Tax Litigation. ***Email:*** blitwin@ngelaw.com

TIMOTHY P. MAHONEY, born Chicago, Illinois, November 13, 1966; admitted to bar, 1993, Illinois. *Education:* Loyola University (B.A., 1989); Chicago-Kent College of Law, Illinois Institute of Technology (J.D., 1993); Case Western Reserve University (M.B.A., 2001). ***PRACTICE AREAS:*** General Litigation. ***Email:*** tmahoney@ngelaw.com

MILTON L. PETERSEN, born Adair, Iowa, August 10, 1958; admitted to bar, 2000, Illinois. *Education:* Iowa State University (B.S., with distinction, 1981); University of Minnesota (M.S., 1984); University of Michigan (J.D., cum laude, 2000). Author: "Preventative Law: Disentanglement Clauses in IT Outsourcing Agreement," Computer Law Association Bulletin, Vol. 20, No. 2 (2005); "Controlling the Chaos: A New Approach to Streamlining Outsourcing Negotiations," Intellectual Property and Technology Law Journal, Vol. 17, No. 11 (2005); "Legal Protections Related to Security Concerns," Journal of Healthcare Information Management (Summer, 2003); "Developing a Winning IT Negotiations Strategy," Journal of Healthcare Information Management (Winter, 2003); "Struggling to Comply with HIPAA Transactions and Code Set Standards by the Deadline? Consider Filing for an Extension," Inside HIPAA Compliance (Spring, 2002). Speaker: "Buyer Beware: Procuring Software and Services in an Unstable Industry," 98th Annual Conference of the GFOA (Government Finance Officers Association), Milwaukee, Wisconsin (June, 2004); "Compliance Countdown: Real World Strategies for Implementing the HIPAA Privacy Regulations in Illinois," Health Care Law Section, Illinois State Bar Association, Southern Illinois University School of Medicine Seminar, Chicago, Illinois (April, 2002). ***PRACTICE AREAS:*** Information Technology; Outsourcing Transactions; Healthcare Technology; Computer Law; Internet Law. ***Email:*** mpetersen@ngelaw.com

BETH J. ROSNER, born Chicago, Illinois, August 31, 1953; admitted to bar, 1978, Illinois. *Education:* Lake Forest College (B.A., 1975); Northwestern University (J.D., cum laude, 1978). Phi Beta Kappa; Order of the Coif. ***PRACTICE AREAS:*** Securities; Corporate. ***Email:*** brosner@ngelaw.com

FRANCIS J. WIRTZ, born 1954; admitted to bar, 1980, Illinois. *Education:* University of Illinois (B.S., with honors, 1975); University of Michigan (J.D., cum laude, 1979).

(This Listing Continued)

NEAL, GERBER & EISENBERG LLP, Chicago—Continued

Author: "An Update on the Consolidated Debt Discharge Regulations," Vol. 2, No. 4, Journal of Taxation of Corporate Transactions 5 (April-May, 2004); "The New Temporary Consolidated Debt Discharge Regulations," Vol. 2, No. 1, Journal of Taxation of Corporate Transactions 9 (October-November, 2003); "Treatment of Foreign Stapled Entity as Includable Corporation for Certain Foreign Tax Credit Purposes," Vol. 1, No. 6, Journal of Taxation of Corporate Transactions 9 (September-October), 2003; "Additional Rite Aid Developments," Vol. 1, No. 3 Journal of Taxation of Corporate Transactions 5 (January-February 2003); "Minority Interest Protections and the Voting Control Test," 2 Journal of Taxation of Corporate Transactions 17 (August-September 2002). *Member:* American Bar Association (Member: Federal Tax Law Section; Former Member: Task Force on Simplification of Subchapter K; Task Force on Aggregate v. Entity Treatment of Partnerships in International Tax Area; Former-Chair: Subcommittee on International Taxation of Partnerships, S Corporations and Trusts). ***PRACTICE AREAS:*** Taxation. ***Email:*** fwirtz@ngelaw.com

OF COUNSEL

SHERI E. WARSH, born Chicago, Illinois, June 27, 1964; admitted to bar, 1989, Illinois. *Education:* University of Michigan (B.B.A., 1986); University of Illinois (J.D., 1989). Member, Moot Court Team. ***PRACTICE AREAS:*** Trusts and Estates; Taxation; Estate Planning and Administration; Private Wealth Services. ***Email:*** swarsh@ngelaw.com

NEAL & LEROY, LLC

203 NORTH LASALLE, SUITE 2300
CHICAGO, ILLINOIS 60601
Telephone: 312-641-7144
Fax: 312-641-5137
Email: lneal@nealandleroy.com
URL: http://www.nealandleroy.com

Eminent Domain, Condemnation, Labor and Employment, Litigation, Public Finance and Project Finance, Real Estate and Real Estate Finance, Zoning, Development and Land Use, Business Reorganization and Bankruptcy and Construction Law.

FIRM PROFILE: Neal & Leroy, LLC is a minority owned firm with more than sixty years in the legal community.

The firm's commitment to each of its clients is to be a high-quality legal service provider, sensitive to issues of cost containment, accountability and the unique business concerns of each client.

EARL L. NEAL, admitted to bar, 1953, Illinois. *Education:* University of Illinois (B.A., 1949); University of Michigan (J.D., 1952). ***PRACTICE AREAS:*** Real Estate; Eminent Domain; Municipal; Litigation. ***Email:*** hsemprit@nealandleroy.com

LANGDON D. NEAL, admitted to bar, 1981, Illinois. *Education:* Cornell University (A.B., 1978); University of Illinois (J.D., 1981). ***PRACTICE AREAS:*** Zoning, Planning and Land Use; Eminent Domain; Litigation. ***Email:*** lneal@nealandleroy.com

MICHAEL D. LEROY, admitted to bar, 1968, Illinois. *Education:* University of Illinois (A.B., 1963); University of Michigan (J.D., 1966). ***PRACTICE AREAS:*** Eminent Domain; Real Estate; Municipal and Zoning; Litigation. ***Email:*** mleroy@nealandleroy.com

ANNE L. FREDD, admitted to bar, 1973, Illinois. *Education:* Bradley University (B.A., 1964); Loyola University (M.S.W., 1967); Northwestern University (J.D., 1973). ***PRACTICE AREAS:*** Eminent Domain; Real Estate; Municipal and Zoning; Municipal Finance; Litigation. ***Email:*** afredd@nealandleroy.com

RICHARD F. FRIEDMAN, admitted to bar, 1969, Illinois. *Education:* University of Illinois at Urbana (B.S., 1963); University of Chicago (J.D., 1968). ***PRACTICE AREAS:*** Eminent Domain; Real Estate; Municipal and Zoning; Municipal Finance; Litigation; Appellate Practice. ***Email:*** rfriedman@nealandleroy.com

ATTORNEYS

Lenny D. Asaro	***Jonathan D. Leach***
Paul E. Bennett, II	***Francine D. Lynch***
Nicole L. Castillo	***James G. McConnell***
Terrance L. Diamond	***Tobin M. Richter***
Thomas W. Goedert	***Lawrence K. Sezer***
Deborah F. Hamilton	***Jerome A. Siegan***
Ryan K. Harding	***Bradley A. Smith***
Renee F. Kessel	***Carol D. Stubblefield***

Jeanette Sublett

OF COUNSEL

Benjamin Ghess	***George N. Leighton***

NEAL & McDEVITT

CHICAGO, ILLINOIS
(See Evanston)

Intellectual Property Practice (including Trademarks, Copyrights, Unfair Competition, Licensing and Litigation).

JAY SCOTT NELSON

5757 NORTH LINCOLN AVENUE, SUITE 20
CHICAGO, ILLINOIS 60659-4720
Telephone: 773-907-9010
Fax: 773-907-9013

General Civil Practice in all State and Federal Courts, Business Transactions.

JAY SCOTT NELSON, born Chicago, Illinois, September 5, 1941; admitted to bar, 1975, Illinois; U.S. Court of Appeals, Seventh Circuit; U.S. District Court, Northern District of Illinois including Trial Bar. *Education:* Parsons College (B.A., 1964); University of Iowa (M.B.A., 1967); John Marshall Law School (J.D., 1975). *Member:* Chicago, Illinois State and American Bar Associations; Trial Lawyers Club of Chicago. ***REPORTED CASES:*** Malouskas v. Tishman, 81 Ill.App. 3d 759; Bednar v. Venture, 106 Ill.App. 3d 454; Woods v. North Pier, 131 Ill.App. 3d 21; Richardson V. v. Chapman, 175 Ill. 2d 98.

NETZEL & ASSOCIATES, P.C.

Established in 2003

211 E. ONTARIO STREET, SUITE 1800
CHICAGO, ILLINOIS 60611
Telephone: 312-283-5200
Fax: 312-283-5005
Email: tnetzel@whistlelaw.com
URL: http://www.whistlelaw.com

Whistle Blower, Qui Tam Litigation/Whistleblower Litigation, Health Care Fraud, Employment Retaliation, Class Action Litigation, Commercial Litigation.

FIRM PROFILE: Netzel & Associates, P.C. is a Chicago-based law firm specializing in the representation of whistleblowers under the False Claim Act and other anti-fraud statutes. The firm has particular expertise in prosecuting healthcare fraud cases including claims based on "upcoding" or falsely inflating charges in services rendered, the performance of medically unnecessary procedures, the provision of substandard patient care and the payment of illegal kickbacks and off label promotion activities of pharmaceutical manufactures.

Netzel & Associates, P.C. represents whistleblowers nation wide and works with a network of consulting experts and other law firms nation-wide. Our firm also represents consumers in class action litigation and commercial litigation matters on a case by case basis.

TRACY L. NETZEL, born Park Falls, Wisconsin, February 14, 1974; admitted to bar, 2000, Wisconsin, Illinois and U.S. District Court, Northern District of Illinois; 2004, U.S. District Court, Western District of Michigan; 2005, U.S. District Court, Central District of Illinois. *Education:* University of Wisconsin-Madison (B.A., with distinction, 1996; J.D., cum laude, 2000). *Member:* Chicago, Illinois State and American Bar Associations; State Bar of Wisconsin; Qui Tam Litigation Group; The Association of Trial Lawyers of America. ***PRACTICE AREAS:*** Qui Tam Litigation; Whistleblower Litigation; Health Care Fraud; Employment Litigation; Class Actions; Commercial Litigation. ***Email:*** tnetzel@whistlelaw.com

BERNARD R. NEVORAL AND ASSOCIATES LTD.

Established in 1974

ONE EAST WACKER DRIVE, SUITE 3610
CHICAGO, ILLINOIS 60601
Telephone: 312-263-7058
Fax: 312-263-4566
Email: brnltd@nevoral.com

General Civil Practice in all State and Federal Courts. Appellate Practice, Products Liability, Workers Compensation and Negligence Law. Federal Employers Liability Act.

FIRM PROFILE: Mr. Nevoral founded this firm over 30 years ago and his practice concentrates exclusively in plaintiff personal injury litigation. He routinely handles complex damages cases including claims for wrongful death and personal injury arising out of medical malpractice, product liability and railroad claims resulting in many million dollar verdicts and settlements. He is very knowledgeable in insurance litigation and has won many complex coverage cases.

BERNARD R. NEVORAL, born Brno, Czechoslovakia, December 25, 1943; admitted to bar, 1971, Illinois and U.S. District Court, Northern and Central Districts of Illinois; U.S. District Court, Northern District of Indiana; U.S. District Court, Western District of Wisconsin; 1974, U.S. Court of Appeals, 7th Circuit; 1980, U.S. Supreme Court; 1986, Wisconsin. *Education:* DePaul University (B.A., 1966; J.D., 1970). Phi Alpha Delta. *Member:* Chicago, Illinois State and American Bar Associations; State Bar of Wisconsin; Illinois Trial Lawyers Association; The Association of Trial Lawyers of America. ***PRACTICE AREAS:*** Personal Injury; Medical Malpractice; Products Liability; Civil Practice; Trial Practice. ***Email:*** brnltd@nevoral.com

---

DAVID F. SZCZECIN, born Chicago, Illinois, October 24, 1970; admitted to bar, 1998, Illinois. *Education:* University of Illinois (B.A., 1992); John Marshall Law School (J.D., 1998). ***PRACTICE AREAS:*** Civil Practice. ***Email:*** brnltd@nevoral.com

ANDREW A. GALICH, born Chicago, Illinois, May 17, 1931; admitted to bar, 1958, Illinois. *Education:* DePaul University (B.S.C., 1954; J.D., 1957). [U.S. Army, 1957-1959]. ***PRACTICE AREAS:*** Civil and Trial Practice; Workers Compensation.

ROBERT J. DRUMMOND, born Utica, New York, August 4, 1950; admitted to bar, 1979, Illinois and U.S. District Court, Northern District of Illinois. *Education:* Loyola Uni-

(This Listing Continued)

versity (B.A., 1972); DePaul University (J.D., with honors, 1979). Recipient, American Jurisprudence Awards in Torts and Evidence. Judicial Clerkship: Supreme Court Justice Thomas E. Kluczynski, 1979-1980; Nicholas J. Bua, Judge, Northern District of Illinois, 1981-1982. *Member:* Chicago, Illinois State and American (Member, Section of Litigation) Bar Associations; Illinois Trial Lawyers Association (Secretary, Amicus Curiae Committee, 1985—); The Association of Trial Lawyers of America; Illinois Appellate Lawyers Association. ***PRACTICE AREAS:*** Federal Employers Liability Act (FELA); Tort Litigation. ***Email:*** brnltd@nevoral.com

NILSON, STOOKAL, GLEASON & CAPUTO

205 WEST RANDOLPH STREET, SUITE 440
CHICAGO, ILLINOIS 60606
Telephone: 312-443-1331
Fax: 312-443-0746
Email: NSGCLaw@aol.com

Personal Injury, Workers Compensation, Medical Malpractice, Airplane Crash Litigation, Automobile Accidents and Injuries, Wrongful Death, Federal Employers Liability Act (FELA), Construction Accidents, Employment Law and Divorce Law.

FIRM PROFILE: The Firm founded in 1987 by Richard Nilson and Marc Stookal; Steven Gleason and William Caputo joined shortly thereafter. The Firm stated with a local practice and now represents clients across Illinois and Nationally. Members of the firm are published in their fields, hold elected office, participate in professional associations and are active in Pro Bono Associations.

RICHARD P. NILSON, born 1955; admitted to bar, 1981, Illinois. *Education:* Northern Illinois University (B.S., 1978); DePaul University (J.D., 1981). ***PRACTICE AREAS:*** Personal Injury Law; Workers Compensation Law; Product Liability Law. ***Email:*** rpnilson@aol.com

MARC B. STOOKAL, born Chicago, Illinois, February 14, 1956; admitted to bar, 1981, Illinois, U.S. District Court, Northern District of Illinois and U.S. Court of Appeals, Seventh Circuit. *Education:* University of Illinois (B.A., 1978); DePaul University (J.D., 1981). *Member:* Chicago and Illinois State Bar Associations; Illinois Trial Lawyers Association. ***PRACTICE AREAS:*** Workers Compensation Law; Personal Injury Law. ***Email:*** mbstookal@comcast.net

STEVEN M. GLEASON, born Newton, New Jersey, June 15, 1953; admitted to bar, 1980, Illinois and U.S. District Court, Northern District of Illinois. *Education:* University of Wisconsin (B.A., 1977); DePaul University (J.D., 1980). *Member:* Chicago Bar Association. ***PRACTICE AREAS:*** Personal Injury; Insurance; Alternative Dispute Resolution; Construction Law. ***Email:*** smgleas@aol.com

WILLIAM P. CAPUTO, born Chicago, Illinois, July 1, 1951; admitted to bar, 1982, Illinois and U.S. District Court, Northern District of Illinois; 1984, U.S. Court of Appeals, Seventh Circuit. *Education:* Northern Illinois University (B.S., 1972; M.S., 1974; C.A.S., 1975; Ed.D., 1977); DePaul University (J.D., with honors, 1982). *Member:* Chicago, Illinois State and American Bar Associations; American Trial Lawyers Association; Illinois Trial Lawyers Association; Justinian Society of Lawyers. ***PRACTICE AREAS:*** Construction Law; Medical Malpractice; Personal Injury. ***Email:*** wcaputo@aol.com

NIRO, SCAVONE, HALLER & NIRO

Established in 1976

181 WEST MADISON, SUITE 4600
CHICAGO, ILLINOIS 60602-4515
Telephone: 312-236-0733
Facsimile: 312-236-3137
URL: http://www.niroscavone.com

Intellectual Property and Technology-Related Law including Patent, Trademark, Trade Secret, Copyright, Licensing, Unfair Competition, Related Antitrust Matters.

FIRM PROFILE: NIRO, SCAVONE, HALLER & NIRO specializes in the trial of intellectual property cases, generally including patent, trademark, trade secret, unfair competition and busines torts. The firm's practice extends throughout the United States, with lawyers of the firm having extensive trial and appellate experience in nearly all of the federal judicial circuits and in various state trial and appellate courts. The firm also represents clients in a broad spectrum of related intellectual property matters including licensing and the procurement of domestic and international patents, trademark registrations and copyrights. Partners of the firm have written and lectured on trial advocacy at major law schools and the Practicing Law Institute, American, Federal and Illinois Bar Associations and elsewhere.

MEMBERS AND ASSOCIATES

RAYMOND P. NIRO, born Pittsburgh, Pennsylvania, December 6, 1942; admitted to bar, 1970, Illinois; 1987, Colorado, U.S. District Courts, Northern District of Illinois, Eastern District of Michigan, Western and Northern Districts of Texas, Northern District of New York, Northern District of California, Eastern and Western Districts of Wisconsin, District of Colorado; District of Minnesota, District of Connecticut and District of Arizona, U.S. Court of Appeals, Fourth, Fifth, Sixth, Seventh, Ninth, Tenth and Federal Circuits and U.S. Supreme Court; registered to practice before U.S. Patent and Trademark Office; State of Illinois Supreme Court; State of Colorado Supreme Court. *Education:* University of Pittsburgh (B.S. in Chem. Engr., magna cum laude, 1964); George Washington University (J.D., with honors, 1969). Member, George Washington Law Review, 1968-1969. Speaker on Trial Advocacy, Harvard University Law School, State Bar of Texas, American and Federal Bar Associations, the Practicing Law Institute and the Sedona Conference, 2002-2003. Named to National List of Top Ten Trial Lawyers, The National Law Journal, 1997 and Top Ten Trial Lawyers in Illinois, 1999. Listed in International Who's Who of Patent Lawyers. Chair, Intellectual Property Advisory Boards, George Washington and De Paul University Law Schools. *Member:* Federal Circuit, Chicago, Illinois State and American Bar Associations; Intellectual Property Law Association of Chicago; American Intellectual Property Law Association; The Association of Trial Lawyers of America. ***PRACTICE AREAS:*** Patent, Trade Secret, Antitrust, Trademark and Copyright Litigation.

THOMAS G. SCAVONE, born Flint, Michigan, September 4, 1946; admitted to bar, 1973, Illinois, U.S. District Courts, Northern District of Illinois, Eastern District of Michigan, Central and Northern Districts of California, Northern District of Texas, Northern District of Ohio, Southern District of New York, Western District of Pennsylvania, Eastern District of Wisconsin, U.S. Court of Appeals for the Federal and Seventh Circuits and U.S. Supreme Court; registered to practice before U.S. Patent and Trademark Office. *Education:* University of Detroit (B.S. in Chem. Engr., Master of Engr., magna cum laude, 1969); Georgetown University and Wayne State University (J.D., with honors, 1973). Tau Beta Pi; Omega Chi Epsilon. *Member:* Federal Circuit, Illinois State and American Bar Associations; American Intellectual Property Law Association; Intellectual Property Law Association of Chicago. ***PRACTICE AREAS:*** Patent; Trade Secrets; Trademark Litigation. ***Email:*** scavone@nshn.com

TIMOTHY J. HALLER, born Buffalo, New York, June 6, 1946; admitted to bar, 1975, New York; 1979, Illinois, U.S. District Courts, Northern District of Illinois, Eastern District of Michigan and Western and Southern Districts of New York, U.S. Court of Appeals for Federal, Second and Seventh Circuits and U.S. Supreme Court; registered to practice before U.S. Patent and Trademark Office. *Education:* Clarkson College (B.S.M.E., with distinction, 1968); Georgetown University (J.D., 1974). Editor, Georgetown Journal of Law and Policy in International Business, 1972-1974. *Member:* New York State, Illinois State and American Bar Associations; Intellectual Property Law Association of Chicago; American Intellectual Property Law Association; The Association of Trial Lawyers of America. [Lieut., U.S. Navy, 1969-1970]. ***PRACTICE AREAS:*** Patent, Trade Secret, Antitrust, Trademark and Copyright Litigation. ***Email:*** haller@nshn.com

WILLIAM L. NIRO, born Pittsburgh, Pennsylvania, December 13, 1945; admitted to bar, 1974, Illinois; 1975, District of Columbia; U.S District Court, Northern District of Illinois, District of Columbia; Northern District of Ohio; Northern District of Texas; Northern District o California; Western District of Kentucky; Central District of California; Northern District of Ohio; U.S. Court of Appeals Seventh and Federal Circuits and U.S. Supreme Court. *Education:* University of Pittsburgh (B.S. in Chem. Engr., 1967); DePaul University (J.D., 1974); George Washington University (LL.M. in Environmental Law, 1975). Harvard Law School, PIL, Negotiation and Mediation, 1993, 1996. Editor, DePaul L.Rev., 1974-1975. Assistant Professor of Law, Lewis University, College of Law, 1975-1978. Associate Professor of Law, Northern Illinois University College of Law, 1978-1981. Adjunct Professor of Law, DePaul University College of Law, 2001—. *Member:* Illinois State Bar Association (Member: Bar Publications Committee, 1980-1986; Member, Editorial Board and Editor, Illinois Bar Journal, 1991-1999; Member, ISBA Committee on Illinois Judicial Evaluation, 1999-2003; Committee on Legal Technology, 2002-2005); District of Columbia Bar; The Association of Trial Lawyers of America; American Intellectual Property Law Association; Justinian Society of Lawyers. ***PRACTICE AREAS:*** Patent; Trademark; Copyright; Trade Secret; Unfair Competition; Environmental Litigation; Arbitration and Mediation; Environmental. ***Email:*** wniro@nshn.com

JOSEPH N. HOSTENY, III, born Chicago, Illinois, April 13, 1945; admitted to bar, 1976, Illinois and U.S. District Court, Northern District of Illinois; 1977, U.S. Court of Appeals, Seventh Circuit; 1983, U.S. Court of Appeals for the Federal Circuit and U.S. Tax Court; registered to practice before U.S. Patent and Trademark Office. *Education:* Marquette University (B.S.M.E., 1967); DePaul University (J.D., summa cum laude, 1976). Tau Beta Pi; Pi Tau Sigma. Registered Professional Engineer, State of Illinois, 1976; Assistant U.S. Attorney, Northern District of Illinois, 1976-1983. Author: "Bank Crime: The 100 Yard Rule In The Boardroom," Litigation Magazine, Fall, 1984; "Fastener Loosening: The Effects - Part 2," Assembly Engineering, March, 1984; "Playing The Patenting Game," American Medical News, August, 1997; "Bullet-Proofing For Patent Litigation," Inventors' Digest, September/October, 1997; "Bullet-Proofing For License Litigation," Inventors' Digest, November/December, 1997; "Bullet-Proofing For Licensing," Inventors' Digest, January/February, 1998; "The Economic Espionage Act: A Very Mixed Blessing," Intellectual Property Today, February, 1998; "Thanks, But We'd Rather Do It Ourselves," Corporate Counsel Magazine, April, 1998; "Can a Trademark Be Used to Extend an Expired Patent?" Intellectual Property Today, August, 1998; "Corporate Espionage: Protecting Trade Secrets," The Journal of the American Corporate Counsel Association, January/February, 1999; "How Do You Pay When You Can't Afford to Pay?" Intellectual Property Today, January, 1999; "How to Minimize Discovery Wars in Contingent Fee Litigation," Intellectual Property Today, February, 1999; "How Important Is the Prosecution History?" Intellectual Property Today, March/April, 1999; Monthly Column, "Litigators Corner" in Intellectual Property Today, includes articles on topics relating to intellectual property litigation, such as "Markman", contingent fee intellectual property litigation and inventors depositions. Speaker: before numerous professional, legal and educational groups throughout the country. *Member:* American Intellectual Property Law Association; Intellectual Property Law Association of Chicago (Member, Federal Practice Committee, 1982; Chairman, Inventor Services Committee, 1986-1987); American Society of Mechanical Engineers. [Lieut., U.S.N., 1967-1971 (Submarine Service)]. ***REPORTED CASES:*** Beery v. Thomson Consumer Elecs., Inc., 218 F.R.D. 599 (S.D. Oh. 2003); TechSearch L.L.C. v. Intel Corp., 286 F.3d 1360 (Fed. Cir. 2002); Hunter Eng'g Co. v. ACCU Indus., 245 F. Supp. 2d 761 (E.D. Va. 2002); Emerson Elec. Co. v. Spartan Tool, 223 F.Supp. 2d 856 (N.D. Oh. 2002); Benedict v. GMC, 184 F.Supp. 2d 1197 (N.D. Fla. 2002); Benedict v. GMC, 184 F.Supp. 2d 1197 (N.D. Fla. 2001); Methode Electronics, Inc. v. Finisar Corp., 205 F.R.D. 552 (N.D. Cal. 2001); Methode Electronics, Inc. v. Hewlett-Packard Co., 55 U.S.P.Q.2d 1602, (N.D. Cal. 2000); Depuy Orthopedics, Inc. v. Androphy, 53 U.S.P.Q.2d 1941 (N.D. Ill. 2000); Anderson v. International Eng'g & Mfg., 160 F.3d 1345 (Fed. Cir. 1998); Atkinson v. General Research of Elecs., 24 F.Supp. 2d 894 (N.D. Ill. 1998); Wyttenbach v. Atoma Int'l, 997 F.Supp. 1037 (N.D. Ill. 1998); Clintec Nutrition Co. v. Baxa Corp., 988 F.Supp. 1109 (N.D. Ill. 1997); Amphenol Corp. v. Maxconn Inc., 43 U.S.P.Q.2d 1638 (N.D. Ill. 1997); Yosemite Inv. v. Floyd Bell, Inc., 943 F.Supp. 882 (S.D.Oh. 1996); In re Mahurkar Double Lumen Hemodialysis Catheter Patent Litigation, 71 F.3d 1573 (Fed. Cir. 1995); In re Mahurkar Double Lumen Hemodialysis Catheter Patent Litigation, No. MDL 853, 28 U.S.P.Q.2d 1801 (N.D.Ill. 1993); In re Mahurkar Double Lumen Hemodialysis Catheter Patent Litigation, 831 F.Supp. 1354 (N.D. Ill. 1993); Emhart Industries, Inc. v. Universal Instruments Corp., 25 U.S.P.Q.2d 1295, (N.D.N.Y. 1992); In re Mahurkar Double Lumen

(This Listing Continued)

NIRO, SCAVONE, HALLER & NIRO, Chicago—Continued

Hemodialysis Catheter Patent Litigation, No. MDL 853, 140 B.R. 969, 23 U.S.P.Q.2d 1903 (N.D.Ill. 1992); Vas-Cath, Inc. v. Mahurkar, 935 F.2d 1555 (Fed. Cir. 1991); Emhart Industries, Inc. v. D-Tech Corp., 21 U.S.P.Q.2d (BNA) 1953 (S.D.Ind. 1991); In re Mahurkar Double Lumen Hemodialysis Catheter Patent Litigation, No. MDL 853, 750 F. Supp. (N.D. Ill. 1990); Vas-Cath, Inc. v. Mahurkar, 745 F. Supp. 517 (N.D. Ill. 1990); Impra, Inc. v. Quinton Instruments Co., 17 U.S.P.Q.2d 1890 (D.Az. 1990); Joiher v. McEvers, 898 F.2d 569 (7th Circ. 1990); Westek Associates v. Tri-Lite Electronics, Inc. 722 F.Supp. 474 (N.D.Ill. 1989); National Business Systems, Inc. v. AM International, Inc., 109 F.R.D. 172 (N.D. Ill. 1986); United States v. Pizarro, 717 F.2d 336 (7th Cir. 1983); United States v. Theodorou, 576 F.Supp. 1007 (N.D. Ill., 1983); United States v. Johnston, 690 F.2d 638 (7th Cir. 1982) (en banc); United States v. Johnston, 664 F.2d 152 (7th Cir. 1981); United States v. Tucker, 581 F.2d 602 (7th Cir. 1978). ***PRACTICE AREAS:*** Trade Secrets; Patents; Trademarks; Copyright Litigation. ***Email:*** jhosteny@hosteny.com

ROBERT A. VITALE, JR., born Pittsburgh, Pennsylvania, March 31, 1960; admitted to bar, 1985, Pennsylvania; 1986, Illinois, U.S. District Courts, Northern District of Illinois, including Trial Bar, Eastern District of Wisconsin, Eastern District of Michigan, Northern District of Indiana and Northern District of California, U.S. Court of Appeals for the Federal, First and Seventh Circuits and United States Supreme Court; registered to practice before U.S. Patent and Trademark Office. *Education:* Bucknell University (B.S.C.E., 1982); Duquesne University (J.D., 1985). *Member:* Chicago, Pennsylvania, Illinois State, Federal and American Bar Associations; American Intellectual Property Law Association. ***PRACTICE AREAS:*** Intellectual Property Litigation.

JOHN C. JANKA, born Louisville, Kentucky, May 13, 1950; admitted to bar, 1987, Illinois and U.S. District Court, Northern District of Illinois; 1988, U.S. Court of Appeals, Seventh Circuit; 1989, U.S. Court of Appeals for the Federal Circuit; registered to practice before U.S. Patent and Trademark Office. *Education:* Illinois Institute of Technology (B.S., Chemical Engineering, 1970; M.S., Chemical Engineering, 1973); University of Chicago (J.D., with distinction, 1987). John M. Olin Fellow in Law and Economics. Comment Editor, University of Chicago Law Review, 1986-1987. Author: "Federal Disclosure Statutes and the Fifth Amendment; the New Status of Trade Secrets," 54 University of Chicago Law Review 334, Winter, 1987; "The Law and Economics of Reasonable Royalty Damages After Black & Decker's 'Snakelight ' Litigation," 7 Federal Circuit Bar Journal 373, Winter, 1997. *Member:* American Bar Association; American Chemical Society; American Institute of Chemical Engineers. ***PRACTICE AREAS:*** Trade Secret, Patent, Trademark and Copyright Litigation.

PAUL K. VICKREY, born Harvey, Illinois, October 28, 1955; admitted to bar, 1980, Illinois. *Education:* University of Illinois (B.A., 1977); Loyola University (J.D., 1980). Member, Loyola Law Journal, 1979-1980. Board of Editors, The Business Torts Reporter. Chairman, AIDS Legal Council of Chicago, 1990-1993. ***PRACTICE AREAS:*** Intellectual Property; Litigation.

DEAN D. NIRO, born Houston, Texas, February 22, 1965; admitted to bar, 1991, Illinois, U.S. District Court, Northern District of Illinois and U.S. Court of Appeals, Federal Circuit; registered to practice before U.S. Patent and Trademark Office. *Education:* University of Colorado (B.S., Civil Engineering, 1988); DePaul University (J.D., 1991). Author: "Protecting Characters Through Copyright Law: Paving A New Road Upon Which Literary, Graphic and Motion Picture Characters Can All Travel," DePaul Law Review, Vol. 41 No. 2 Winter, 1992. p. 359. *Member:* Chicago Bar Association; American Intellectual Property Law Association. ***PRACTICE AREAS:*** Intellectual Property Law.

RAYMOND P. NIRO, JR., born Pittsburgh, Pennsylvania, October 11, 1966; admitted to bar, 1991, Illinois, U.S. District Court, Northern District of Illinois, Eastern District of Michigan and U.S. Court of Appeals, Federal Circuit. *Education:* Indiana University (B.S., 1988); DePaul University (J.D., 1991). ***PRACTICE AREAS:*** Intellectual Property Law.

PATRICK F. SOLON, born Detroit, Michigan, October 27, 1964; admitted to bar, 1991, Illinois, U.S. District Court, Northern District of Illinois and U.S. Court of Appeals, Federal, Sixth, Seventh and Eighth Circuits. *Education:* University of Michigan (B.B.A., 1986; J.D., 1990). Phi Delta Phi. ***PRACTICE AREAS:*** Intellectual Property; Litigation.

ARTHUR A. GASEY, born Des Plaines, Illinois, October 16, 1967; admitted to bar, 1992, Illinois, U.S. District Court, Northern District of Illinois and U.S. Court of Appeals for the Federal Circuit; registered to practice before U.S. Patent and Trademark Office. *Education:* University of Notre Dame (B.S., Chemical Engineering, 1989); John Marshall Law School (J.D., magna cum laude, 1992). Staff Editor, John Marshall Law Review; National Champion, Giles S. Rich Patent Law Moot Court Competition. Co-author: "Trial of Inequitable Conduct, Laches and Prosecution History Estoppel Issues," Patent Litigation 1992, Vol. I, pp. 727-99 (PLI, 1992). ***PRACTICE AREAS:*** Litigation; Intellectual Property Law. ***Email:*** gasey@nshn.com

CHRISTOPHER J. LEE, born Seoul, Korea, December 10, 1964; admitted to bar, 1993, Illinois, U.S. Court of Appeals, Federal and Seventh Circuit, U.S. District Court, Northern District of Illinois including Trial Bar and U.S. District Court, District of Colorado; 2003, U.S. District Court, Eastern District of Wisconsin; registered to practice before U.S. Patent and Trademark Office. *Education:* University of Illinois (B.S., Chemical Engineering, 1990); Chicago-Kent College of Law (J.D., 1993). Co-author: "Update on Substantive Due Process in Land Use Cases in the Federal Courts," Land Use: ALI-ABA, Course Materials (Vol. 1)(1991); "Equitable Defense in Patent Cases: Equities Count," Patent Litigation 1994, PLI (Vol. 2)(1994); "A Perspective on Financing Intellectual Property Litigation," (1998). Operations Engineer, Coatings and Resins Division, PPG Industries, Pittsburgh, Pennsylvania, 1988-1990. *Member:* Federal Circuit, Chicago, Illinois State and American Bar Associations. ***LANGUAGES:*** Korean. ***PRACTICE AREAS:*** Intellectual Property Litigation. ***Email:*** clee@nshn.com

DAVID J. SHEIKH, born Peoria, Illinois, November 1, 1965; admitted to bar, 1992, Illinois; 1993, U.S. Court of Appeals, Seventh Circuit; 1994, U.S. Court of Appeals, Federal Circuit and U.S. District Court, Northern District of Illinois; 2003, U.S. District Court, Eastern District of Wisconsin. *Education:* University of Illinois (B.S., 1988); DePaul University (J.D., 1992). Editor-in-Chief, DePaul University Law Review, 1991-1992. Law Clerk, U.S. Court of Appeals, Seventh Circuit, 1992-1994. Author: "Survey of Illinois Law: Criminal Law and Procedure," 18 SIU L.J. 747 (1994); "Public School Finance Reform: Is Illinois 'Playing Hooky'?," 41 DePaul L. Rev. 195 (1992); "Trial of Inequitable Conduct, Laches and Prosecution History Estoppel Issues," I Patent Litigation 1992, 727 (practicing Law Institute ed.). *Member:* Federal Circuit, Chicago, Illinois State and American Bar Associations. ***PRACTICE AREAS:*** Patents; Trademark Litigation; Trade Secrets; Intellectual Property. ***Email:*** sheikh@nshn.com

VASILIOS (BILL) D. DOSSAS, born Polykastano, Kozani, Greece, September 18, 1952; admitted to bar, 1982, Illinois, U.S. District Court, Northern District of Illinois; 1995, U.S. Court of Appeals, Federal Circuit; 2001, U.S. District Court, Eastern District of Michigan; registered to practice before U.S. Patent and Trademark Office. *Education:* University of Illinois (B.S., with high honors, 1974; M.S., 1975); Loyola University (J.D., 1982). *Member:* Federal Circuit Bar Association; Intellectual Property Law Association of Chicago. ***LANGUAGES:*** Greek. ***PRACTICE AREAS:*** Intellectual Property; Litigation; Patent and Trademark Prosecution; Counseling. ***Email:*** dossas@nshn.com

ROBERT P. GREENSPOON, born January 16, 1970; admitted to bar, 1995, Illinois and U.S. District Court, Northern District of Illinois; 1996, U.S. District Court, District of Arizona; 1998, Minnesota, U.S. Court of Appeals for the Federal Circuit and U.S. District Court, Eastern Di strict of Michigan; registered to practice before U.S. Patent and Trademark Office. *Education:* University of Chicago (A.B., Physics, with honors, 1992); University of Michigan (J.D., 1995). Executive Production Editor, Michigan Journal of International Law. Author, Note, "U.S. Government Control over the Export of Scientific Data and Other Technical Information: Holes in the Sieve," 16 Michigan Journal of International Law, 583, 1995. Law Clerk to Judge Brian Barnett Duff, U.S. District Court, Northern District of Illinois, 1995-1996. ***PRACTICE AREAS:*** Patent Litigation; Patent Prosecution.

SALLY WIGGINS, born Harvard, Illinois, January 16, 1963; admitted to bar, 1994, Illinois and U.S. District Court, Northern District of Illinois; 1995, U.S. Court of Appeals, Seventh Circuit; 1996, U.S. District Court, Central District of Illinois; 1998, U.S. District Court, Western District of Wisconsin; 1999, U.S. Court of Appeals, Federal Circuit; 2000, U.S. District Court, District of Colorado; 2002, U.S. District Court, Eastern District of Michigan. *Education:* National College of Education (B.A., 1991); John Marshall Law School (J.D., 1994). Judicial Extern, Trial Advocacy, Moot Court. Judicial Law Clerk, U.S. District Court Judge Paul E. Plunkett, 1994-1995. Adjunct Professor. ***REPORTED CASES:*** Michlin v. Canon, Inc.; Illinois Toolworks v. MetroMark; Hunter Engineering v. ACCO Industry; Black & Decker v. Pro-tech Power. ***PRACTICE AREAS:*** Intellectual Property Litigation.

RICHARD BURNS MEGLEY, JR., born Boston, Massachusetts, November 22, 1967; admitted to bar, 1995, Illinois and U.S. District Court, Northern District of Illinois; 2000, U.S. Court of Appeals, Federal Circuit; registered to practice before U.S. Patent and Trademark Office. *Education:* University of Wisconsin-Madison (B.S.I.E., 1989); DePaul University (J.D., 1995). *Member:* American Bar Association; American Intellectual Property Lawyers Association; Federal Circuit Bar Association. ***PRACTICE AREAS:*** Patent Litigation; Intellectual Property Law. ***Email:*** megleyjr@nshn.com

MATTHEW G. McANDREWS, born Evergreen Park, Illinois, February 13, 1966; admitted to bar, 1995, Illinois, U.S. District Court, Central and Northern Districts of Illinois including Trial Bar, U.S. District Court, Western District of Wisconsin, U.S. District Court, District of Colorado and U.S. Courts of Appeals for the Federal, Ninth and Fourth Circuits. *Education:* University of Notre Dame (B.A., 1989); The John Marshall Law School (J.D., 1995). Phi Delta Phi. ***PRACTICE AREAS:*** Patent Litigation; Intellectual Property. ***Email:*** mmcandrews@nshn.com

PAUL C. GIBBONS, born Boston, Massachusetts, December 21, 1967; admitted to bar, 1997, Illinois, Massachusetts and U.S. District Court, Northern District of Illinois; 2000, U.S. Court of Appeals, Federal Circuit. *Education:* Worcester Polytechnic Institute (B.S.E.E., 1991); Suffolk University (J.D., cum laude, 1997). Executive Editor, Suffolk Transnational Law Review, 1996-1997. Author: "The Application Publication Dilemma," Vol. 20, No. 2, Suffolk Transnational Law Review, 449, 1997. *Member:* American Intellectual Property Lawyers Association; Institute of Electrical and Electronic Engineers. ***PRACTICE AREAS:*** Patent Litigation; Intellectual Property Law. ***Email:*** gibbons@nshn.com

WILLIAM W. FLACHSBART, born Omaha, Nebraska, November 28, 1967; admitted to bar, 1996, Illinois. *Education:* University of Chicago (B.S., Mathematics, 1991); University of Oregon (M.S., Mathematics, 1992); Loyola University of Chicago (J.D., 1996). ***PRACTICE AREAS:*** Intellectual Property; Intellectual Property Litigation; Technology Law. ***Email:*** flachsbart@nshn.com

BRADY J. FULTON, born Peoria, Illinois, June 3, 1970; admitted to bar, 1996, Illinois, Illinois Supreme Court and U.S. District Court, Northern District of Illinois; 1999, U.S. Court of Appeals, 7th Circuit; 2001, U.S. District Court, Southern District of Illinois; 2002, U.S. District Court, Central District of Illinois. *Education:* Loyola University (B.A., English Literature, 1992); Illinois Institute of Technology, Chicago-Kent College of Law (J.D., with honors, 1996). Recipient, Amjur Awards for highest grades in Legal Writing, Civil Procedure, and Personal Income Tax. Member, Moot Court Honor Society. Law Clerk: Honorable William J. Bauer, U.S. Court of Appeals, Seventh Circuit, 1999-2000; Honorable Ann Claire Williams, U.S. District Court, Northern District of Illinois, 1997-1999. *Member:* Chicago, Illinois State and American Bar Associations. ***PRACTICE AREAS:*** Commercial Litigation; Intellectual Property. ***Email:*** fulton@nshn.com

GREGORY P. CASIMER, born South Bend, Indiana, April 28, 1962; admitted to bar, 1999, Illinois. *Education:* Purdue University (B.S.C.E., 1985); DePaul University (J.D., 1998). Member, American Water Works Association, 1986. Professional Engineer, Illinois and Indiana, 1990. ***PRACTICE AREAS:*** Intellectual Property. ***Email:*** casimer@nshn.com

DINA PASCARELLI HAYES, born Princeton, New Jersey, March 21, 1973; admitted to bar, 1999, Illinois. *Education:* College of William and Mary (B.S., 1995); DePaul University (J.D., 1999). Editor, DePaul Journal of Art and Entertainment Law, 1998-1999. ***REPORTED CASES:*** Calabrese v. Square D; Smith Engineering v. Eisenmann. ***PRACTICE AREAS:*** Intellectual Property Litigation. ***Email:*** hayes@nshn.com

DOUGLAS M. HALL, born Pittsburgh, Pennsylvania, April 13, 1972; admitted to bar, 1999, Illinois. *Education:* Duke University (B.A., 1994); Duquesne University (J.D., 1999). Member, Duquesne Law Review, 1997-1999. ***PRACTICE AREAS:*** Intellectual Property Litigation. ***Email:*** dhall@nshn.com

(This Listing Continued)

FREDERICK C. LANEY, born Orangeburg, South Carolina, September 19, 1972; admitted to bar, 2001, Illinois. *Education:* Louisiana State University (B.S.M.E., 1995); Loyola University (J.D., 2001). Member, Loyola University Law Review. ***PRACTICE AREAS:*** Patents. ***Email:*** laney@nshn.com

DAVID J. MAHALEK, born Kearney, Nebraska, May 15, 1970; admitted to bar, 2003, Illinois. *Education:* University of Nebraska at Lincoln (B.A., 1993); DePaul University (J.D., 2003). Member, De Paul Law Review. ***PRACTICE AREAS:*** Intellectual Property Litigation. ***Email:*** mahalek@nshn.com

KARA L. SZPONDOWSKI, born Dearborn, Michigan, August 13, 1974; admitted to bar, 2004, Illinois; registered to practice before U.S. Patent and Trademark Office. *Education:* Purdue University (B.S.I.E., 1996); Chicago-Kent College of Law (J.D., 2004). ***PRACTICE AREAS:*** Intellectual Property Litigation; Patents; Trademarks; Copyrights. ***Email:*** szpondowski@nshn.com

ROBERT A. CONLEY, born Chicago, Illinois, October 11, 1976; admitted to bar, 2004, Illinois. *Education:* Marquette University (B.S., 1998; M.S., 2001); DePaul University (J.D., 2004). ***Email:*** rconley@nshn.com

REPRESENTATIVE CLIENTS: Black & Decker Corp.; Haden, Inc.; Miller Industries, Inc.; Schweitzer Corp.; B&J Manufacturing Co.;; C&F Packing Co., Inc.; Lucasey Manufacturing Co.; Nylok Corp.; Sears Manufacturing Co.; International Truck and Engine Corp.; Illinois Tools Works; Carrier Corp; Hurco Companies, Inc.; Schreiber Foods, Inc.; United Technologies Corporation; Pratt & Whitney; Anicom, Inc.; Al Tech Specialty Steel Corp.; The Kewanee Corp.; Monroe Truck Equipment; Niagra Blower; Quantum Group, Inc.; Thor Technologies Corp.; North American Capacitor Company; Dyadic Industries; Konstant Products; Old World Industries, Inc.; Splitfire, Inc.; Phonetel, Inc.; Thames Water Utilities, Ltd.; Aqua-Aerobic Systems, Inc.; Applica, Inc.; Regent Lighting, Inc.; Touchstone, Inc.; ATM Communications International, Inc.; TechSearch, LLC; Technology Licensing Corp.; Nevada SCSI Enterprises, Inc.; Rose Packing Co.; Lear Corporation; Soundview Technologies; Anatomic Research, Inc.; Snap-On Inc.; PhoneTel Communications; Technology Licensing Corporation; IP Innovation L.L.C.; Sunrise Medical Inc.; Kinectic Concepts Inc.; Simmons Bedding Company.

NISEN & ELLIOTT, LLC

Established in 1946

200 WEST ADAMS STREET, SUITE 2500
CHICAGO, ILLINOIS 60606
Telephone: 312-346-7800
Facsimile: 312-346-9316
URL: http://www.nisen.com

Corporate Law, Commercial Litigation in all Federal and State Courts, Insurance Coverage, Financial Services, Employee Benefits, Estate Planning and Administration, Health Care Law, Taxation, Transportation Law, Employment Law, Commodities Law, Real Estate, Mergers and Acquisitions, Exempt Organizations, Antitrust, International Litigation, Aviation Law, Bankruptcy Reorganizations and Family-Owned-Business Law.

FIRM PROFILE: Since its founding in 1946, Nisen & Elliott has strongly believed that the legal services delivered should enable businesses, and those who own and manage them, to achieve growth and financial success. To that end, all of our members have extensive experience with business transactions and with organizations engaged in various industries. The firm maintains relationships with allied professionals and professional organizations, including accounting firms, actuaries, valuation experts, financial and investment firms, laboratories, and scientific experts. In addition the firm maintains a network of recommended counsel in major cities throughout the United States and other countries to assist in serving the needs of our clients.

MEMBERS OF FIRM

PAUL F. GERBOSI, born Chicago, Illinois, December 12, 1944; admitted to bar, 1969, Illinois. *Education:* Northwestern University (B.S., 1966); Loyola University (J.D., cum laude, 1969). Alpha Sigma Nu. Member, John Evans Club of Northwestern University. Executive Editor, Board of Student Editors, Loyola University, 1968-1969. *Member:* American Bar Association. ***PRACTICE AREAS:*** Business Law; Corporate Law; Commercial Law; Taxation; Federal Taxation; Estate Planning; Probate. ***Email:*** PGERBOSI@NISEN.COM

EDWARD B. MUELLER, born Chicago, Illinois, May 8, 1947; admitted to bar, 1973, Wisconsin; 1977, Illinois. *Education:* Loyola University (B.S., 1970); Northwestern University School of Law (J.D., 1973). Blue Key, National Honor Fraternity. Special Projects Editor, Journal of Criminal Law and Criminology, 1972-1973. *Member:* Chicago (Member: Antitrust Committee) and American (Member, Sections on Anti-Trust, Insurance and Business Law) Bar Associations. ***PRACTICE AREAS:*** Commercial Transactions; Business Formation; Asbestos Litigation; Insurance Coverage. ***Email:*** EMUELLER@NISEN.COM

ANTHONY PACKARD, born Evanston, Illinois, July 1, 1942; admitted to bar, 1969, Illinois; 1972, U.S. District Court, Northern District of Illinois and U.S. Court of Appeals, Seventh Circuit; 1973, U.S. Supreme Court. *Education:* Amherst College (A.B., 1965); Northwestern University (J.D., 1968). *Member:* Chicago and Illinois State Bar Associations. ***PRACTICE AREAS:*** Corporate Law; Employment Law; Civil Litigation. ***Email:*** APACKARD@NISEN.COM

MARK F. ZAENGER, born Toledo, Ohio, January 11, 1954; admitted to bar, 1980, Illinois; 1981, U.S. District Court, Northern District of Illinois. *Education:* Illinois Benedictine College (B.A., 1976); Loyola University (J.D., 1980). *Member:* Chicago (Member, Employee Benefits Committee, 1983—), Illinois State (Member, Employee Benefits Section, 1982—) and American Bar Associations; Chicago Estate Planning Council. ***PRACTICE AREAS:*** Employee Benefits; ERISA; Executive Compensation Law; Estate Planning Law. ***Email:*** MZAENGER@NISEN.COM

MICHAEL J. DALEY, born Philadelphia, Pennsylvania, August 9, 1955; admitted to bar, 1980, Illinois and U.S. District Court, Northern District of Illinois including Trial Bar; 1985, U.S. Court of Appeals, Seventh Circuit and U.S. Supreme Court; 1994, U.S. District Court, Northern District of Indiana and U.S. Tax Court; 1998, U.S. Court of Appeals, Ninth Circuit. *Education:* University of Denver (B.A., with honors, 1977); Loyola University

(This Listing Continued)

(J.D., 1980). Regional Champion, 1980 National Mock Trial Competition. Recipient, 1995, Robert Bellarmine Award, Loyola University School of Law. Instructor: Trial Practice, Loyola University School of Law, 1983—; National Institute for Trial Advocacy, 1999—. Panel Arbitrator: National Futures Association, 1986—; Chicago Board of Trade, 1997—. Assistant States Attorney, Cook County, Illinois, 1981-1983. *Member:* Chicago Bar Association (Member, Committees on: Evaluation of Judicial Candidates, 1983-1989; Federal Civil Practice, 1983-1989); National Association of Railroad Trial Counsel; Bar Association of the Seventh Federal Circuit; Association of Transportation Practitioners. ***PRACTICE AREAS:*** Litigation. ***Email:*** MDALEY@NISEN.COM

JOHN FOSTER LESCH, born Chicago, Illinois, March 17, 1940; admitted to bar, 1966, Illinois; 1972, U.S. Tax Court; 1983, U.S. District Court, Northern District of Illinois and U.S. Court of Appeals, Seventh Circuit. *Education:* Northwestern University (B.S., 1962); Illinois Institute of Technology/Chicago-Kent College of Law (J.D., 1965). *Member:* Chicago (Member, Probate Practice Committee) and Illinois State (Member, Section on Federal Taxation) Bar Associations; Chicago Estate Planning Council. ***PRACTICE AREAS:*** Estate Planning; Estate Administration; Federal Taxation. ***Email:*** JLESCH@NISEN.COM

JOHN K. KNEAFSEY, born Chicago, Illinois, September 4, 1939; admitted to bar, 1965, Illinois; 1966, U.S. District Court, Northern District of Illinois and U.S. Court of Appeals, Seventh Circuit. *Education:* John Carroll University (B.S., 1962); Loyola University (J.D., 1965). Instructor, Probate and Federal Tax Law, Roosevelt University, 1973-1977. Alderman, City of Evanston, 1972-1976. Acting Chairman and Member, Illinois Liquor Control Commission, 1977-1996. Member, 1988— and Chairman, 1989—, Cook County Merit Board. *Member:* Chicago and Illinois State Bar Associations; Illinois Trial Lawyers Association; The Association of Trial Lawyers of America. [Capt., U.S. Army, 1965-1967]. ***PRACTICE AREAS:*** Commercial Litigation; Bankruptcy; Alcoholic Beverage Control. ***Email:*** JKNEAFSEY@NISEN.COM

MICHAEL H. MOIRANO, born Teaneck, New Jersey, July 25, 1952; admitted to bar, 1979, Illinois, U.S. District Courts, Northern District of Illinois, including Trial Bar, Northern District of Indiana, Eastern District of Wisconsin, U.S. Court of Appeals, Seventh Circuit and U.S. Supreme Court. *Education:* University of Illinois (B.A., 1976); Loyola University (J.D., 1979). Editor, Trial Briefs, Illinois State Bar Association Committee on Civil Practice and Procedure, 1987-1991. Author: "Mandatory Insurance Laws," INCL Brief, ABA Section on Insurance, Negligence and Compensation Law, Vol. 7, No. 4, August, 1978. *Member:* American Bar Association (Member, Committee on Aviation Law, Litigation Section). ***PRACTICE AREAS:*** Commercial Litigation; Aviation Law; International Litigation. ***Email:*** MMOIRANO@NISEN.COM

ROBERT O. MIDDLETON, born Evergreen Park, Illinois, October 13, 1953; admitted to bar, 1980, Washington; 1981, Illinois, U.S. Tax Court, U.S. District Court, Western District of Washington and U.S. Court of Appeals, Ninth Circuit. *Education:* Marquette University (B.A., 1975); Notre Dame Law School at London School of Economics; Gonzaga University School of Law (J.D., cum laude, 1979); University of Florida (LL.M., Taxation, 1981). Co-Author: "Income Taxation of Trusts," Trust Administration, Illinois Institute of Continuing Legal Education. Attorney for family-held enterprises. *Member:* Chicago and American Bar Associations; Washington State Bar Association; American Association of Individual Investors; Chicago Estate Planning Council; Family Firm Institute. ***PRACTICE AREAS:*** Federal Taxation Law; Family Business Law; Estate Planning Law. ***Email:*** RMIDDLETON@NISEN.COM

WILLIAM G. DALUGA, JR., born Chicago, Illinois, December 12, 1951; admitted to bar, 1981, Illinois; 1987, Florida; U.S. Tax Court; U.S. District Court, Northern District of Illinois. *Education:* University of Illinois, Champaign-Urbana (B.S., Accounting, 1973); DePaul University (M.S., in Taxation, 1976); Loyola University of Chicago (J.D., 1981). Certified Public Accountant, Illinois, 1974. *Member:* The Florida Bar; American Bar Association; American Institute of Certified Public Accountants. ***PRACTICE AREAS:*** Commercial Transactions; Closely Held Businesses; Federal Taxation; State Taxation; Estate Planning. ***Email:*** WDALUGA@NISEN.COM

KENNETH J. ROJC, born Oak Park, Illinois, July 27, 1955; admitted to bar, 1980, Illinois and U.S. District Court, Northern District of Illinois. *Education:* University of Illinois (B.A., with honors, 1977); Indiana University School of Law (J.D., 1980). Member, Law Review. Co-Author: "New Frontiers in Automotive Sale and Finance Products," The Business Lawyer, February 2005; "Business License Requirements for Lessors," Vehicle Leasing Today, Fourth Quarter, Volume 26, No. 4, Fall 2004; "Vicarious Liability of Motor Vehicle Lessors," The Business Lawyer, May 2004; "Sales and Financing of Off-Lease Vehicles: Key Legal Issues," The Business Lawyer, May 2003; "The Electronic Approach to Motor Vehicle Financing: An Emerging Road Map," The Business Lawyer, May 2002; "Motor Vehicle Financing Via the Internet," The Business Lawyer, May 2001; "Negative Equity in Trade-In Vehicles: Regulation Z and State Law Developments," The Business Lawyer, May 2000; "The New Approach to Trade-In Vehicle Disclosures Under Regulation Z," The Business Lawyer, May 1999; "State Law Response to the New Regulation M," The Business Lawyer, May 1998; "Impact of the New Regulation M on State Motor Vehicle Leasing Disclosure Laws," The Business Lawyer, May 1997. Author: "National Bank Lending Limits - A New Framework," The Business Lawyer, 1985; "New Legal Lending Limits For National Banks - An Overview," Illinois State Bar Association Commercial Banking and Bankruptcy Law Quarterly Report, 1984. *Member:* American Bar Association (Member, Section of Business Law); Consumer Bankers Association; Association of Consumer Vehicle Lessors. ***PRACTICE AREAS:*** Automotive Finance; Consumer Finance; Banking Law. ***Email:*** KROJC@NISEN.COM

THOMAS V. McCAULEY, born Oak Park, Illinois, May 25, 1950; admitted to bar, 1975, Illinois, U.S. District Court, Northern District of Illinois and U.S. Court of Appeals, Seventh Circuit. *Education:* Georgetown University (A.B., 1972); Loyola University (J.D., 1975). Instructor: Legal Writing, Loyola University, 1974-1978; Business Law, DePaul University, 1979. Trustee; Chairman, 1987-1991, Planning and Development, Village of River Forest. Member, Board of Governors, 1977-1983; President, 1982-1983, Loyola University School of Law. Trustee: Chairman, 1997-1999, Fenwick High School, 1991—. *Member:* Chicago (Member: Commodities Law Committee, 1978-1981; Corporation Law Committee, 1984-1987) and American (Member, Section on Business Law) Bar Associations. ***PRACTICE AREAS:*** Business Law; Corporate Law; Real Estate; Commercial Finance; Construction Law; Gaming Law. ***Email:*** TMcCAULEY@NISEN.COM

(This Listing Continued)

NISEN & ELLIOTT, LLC, Chicago—Continued

HELEN M. JENSEN, born Chicago, Illinois, August 24, 1947; admitted to bar, 1987, Illinois. *Education:* DePaul University (B.A., 1983; J.D., 1987). Member, Chicago Estate Planning Counsel. *Member:* Chicago (Sections on: Real Property), Illinois State (Real Estate) and American (Real Property, Trust and Probate Section) Bar Associations. ***PRACTICE AREAS:*** Real Estate; Estate Planning; Commercial Transactions. ***Email:*** HJENSEN@NISEN.COM

WILLIAM A. WALKER, born Chicago, Illinois, January 8, 1959; admitted to bar, 1987, Illinois. *Education:* University of Illinois (B.S., 1982; M.B.A., 1984); Loyola University (J.D., 1987). Panel Mediator, National Association of Securities Dealers, Center for Conflict Resolution, U.S Postal Services. *Member:* Chicago (Member, Sections on: Health Care; Commercial Finance & Transactions; Corporation & Business Law) and Illinois State (Member, Business Law Section) Bar Associations; Association for Conflict Resolution; American Health Lawyers Association. ***PRACTICE AREAS:*** Commercial Transactions; Closely Held Business; Health Care; Mediation. ***Email:*** WWALKER@NISEN.COM

DANIEL P. DAWSON, born Chicago, Illinois, July 8, 1963; admitted to bar, 1988, Illinois, U.S. District Court, Northern District of Illinois, including Trial Bar, U.S. Court of Appeals, Seventh Circuit. *Education:* University of Notre Dame (B.A., 1985); Loyola University (J.D., 1988). *Member:* Chicago (Former Member, Legislative Liaison, Young Lawyer Section, Bankruptcy Division), Illinois State and American Bar Associations. ***PRACTICE AREAS:*** Commercial Litigation; Bankruptcy Litigation; Litigation. ***Email:*** DDAWSON@NISEN.COM

WILLIAM J. RALEIGH, born Chicago, Illinois, December 25, 1953; admitted to bar, 1980, Illinois; 1982, U.S. District Court, Northern District of Illinois including Trial Bar and U.S. Court of Appeals, Seventh Circuit. *Education:* Loyola University (B.S., cum laude, 1976; M.A., 1978; J.D., 1980). Alpha Sigma Nu; Psi Chi. Recipient, Loyola University President's Medallion, 1975. Member, Editorial Board, Barrister Magazine, 1985-1988. Co-Author: "Overview of the RICO Act as Applied to Financial Institutions," Advising Financial Institution, IICLE, 1987. Author: "Attorney-Client Privileges," TRIAL, May, 1988; "Confronting the Fifth Amendment Privilege in Depositions," Barrister, Summer, 1985. Chairperson Arbitrator, Circuit Court of Cook County, 1990—. *Member:* Chicago, Illinois State and American Bar Associations. ***PRACTICE AREAS:*** Litigation; Bankruptcy; Financial Institution; Creditor Services; Employment; Banking; Securities Fraud; Corporate Law; Business; Civil Rights; Construction; Debtor and Creditor Rights; Real Estate. ***Email:*** WRALEIGH@NISEN.COM

MARY ROSE C. MANCZAK, born Chicago, Illinois, November 22, 1959; admitted to bar, 1986, Illinois and U.S. District Court, Northern District of Illinois. *Education:* DePaul University (B.A., with highest honor, 1982); Loyola University of Chicago (J.D., 1986). Delta Epsilon Sigma; Phi Alpha Theta. Recipient, American Jurisprudence Award for Excellent Achievement in the Study of Insurance Law. Co-Author: "A Commentary on the Final and Proposed COBRA Regulations," Benefit Plan Compliance, Volume 3, Issue No. 5, May, 1999 and Issue No. 6, June, 1999; Interview: "Risks and Concerns of Allocating COBRA Obligations By Contract," COBRA Guide Connections, Issue No. 80, Report No. 80, October 28, 1999. Speaker: "Nuts and Bolts of 401 (k) Plans in Illinois," Nov. 5, 2002. Member, Board of Advisors, Chicago Lawyers Chapter, the Federalist Society. ***PRACTICE AREAS:*** Employee Benefits; ERISA; Executive Compensation. ***Email:*** MMANCZAK@NISEN.COM

BRADLEY S. McCANN, born Rockford, Illinois, July 8, 1971; admitted to bar, 1998, Illinois and U.S. Tax Court. *Education:* Northern Illinois University (B.S., Accounting, 1993); DePaul University College of Law; Quinnipiac College School of Law (J.D., cum laude, 1998). Phi Delta Phi. Recipient: American Jurisprudence Award in Corporations; Distinguished Academic Achievement Award; Certified Public Accountant, 1994. Member, Estate Planning Counsel. *Member:* Chicago, Illinois State and American Bar Associations; American Institute of Certified Public Accountants. ***PRACTICE AREAS:*** Tax; Business Law; Corporate Law; Probate; Estate Planning; Real Estate. ***Email:*** BMCCANN@NISEN.COM

DONALD F. FROEHLKE, born Arlington Heights, Illinois, January 7, 1960; admitted to bar, 1994, Illinois; 1995, U.S. District Court, Northern District of Illinois. *Education:* University of Notre Dame (B.A., 1983); IIT Chicago-Kent College of Law (J.D., 1994). *Member:* Chicago (Member, Employee Benefits Committee) and American Bar Associations. ***PRACTICE AREAS:*** Employee Benefits; ERISA Law. ***Email:*** DFROEHLKE@NISEN.COM

PATRICK VINING, born West Orange, New Jersey; admitted to bar, 2000, Illinois. *Education:* College of the Holy Cross (A.B., 1992); Indiana University School of Law (J.D., cum laude, 2000). Fulbright Recipient, 1992-1993. Executive Problem Editor, Sherman Minton Moot Court, 1999-2000. Central Region Semi-finalist and Best Brief Honorable Mention, Jessup International Moot Court, 2000. Book Review Editor, Indiana Journal of Global Legal Studies, 1999-2000. Co-Author: "Business License Requirements for Lessons," Vehicle Leasing Today, Fourth Quarter Vol. 26, No. 4, Fall 2004; "Sale and Financing of Off-Lease Vehicles: Key Legal Issues," The Business Lawyer, May, 2003. *Member:* Chicago and Illinois State Bar Associations; Federalist Society. ***LANGUAGES:*** German. ***PRACTICE AREAS:*** Automotive Finance; Consumer Finance; Banking Law. ***Email:*** PVINING@NISEN.COM

D. ERIC MARTIN, born Chicago, Illinois, March 23, 1971; admitted to bar, 2001, Illinois; 2002, U.S. District Court, Northern District of Illinois, U.S. Court of Appeals, Seventh Circuit and U.S. Tax Court. *Education:* Loyola University (B.B.A., cum laude, Accounting, 1993; J.D., Certificate in Taxation, 2001). Alpha Sigma Nu Jesuit National Honor Society. Certified Public Accountant, 1994. Co-Author, "Tax Procedure and Administration Update, "ISBA Annual Federal Tax Conference, 2001, 2002; "Are Tax Returns Privileged Documents?" ISBA Federal Taxation Committee Newsletter, January, 2003. *Member:* Chicago, Illinois State and American Bar Associations. ***PRACTICE AREAS:*** Tax; Business Law; Corporate Law; Probate; Estate Planning. ***Email:*** EMARTIN@NISEN.COM

ELENA GALLO, born New York, N.Y., July 31, 1975; admitted to bar, 2001, Illinois, U.S. District Court, Northern District of Illinois and U.S. Court of Appeals, Seventh Circuit. *Education:* State University of New York at Stony Brook (B.S., 1996); Thomas M. Cooley Law School (J.D., Litigation Certification, with distinction, 2001); C.W. Post University (M.P.A., with honors, 2004). Editor, Thomas M. Cooley Law Journal, 1999-2001. *Member:* Chicago, Illinois State and American Bar Associations; The Association of Trial Lawyers of America. ***PRACTICE AREAS:*** Civil Litigation; Employment Litigation. ***Email:*** EGALLO@NISEN.COM

DAVID E. GEMPERLE, born Chicago, Illinois, November 29, 1977; admitted to bar, 2003, Illinois and U.S. District Court, Northern District of Illinois. *Education:* Boston University (B.A., 1999); University of Illinois College of Law (J.D., cum laude, 2003). ***PRACTICE AREAS:*** Automotive Finance; Consumer Finance; Banking Law; Employee Benefits; ERISA. ***Email:*** DGEMPERLE@NISEN.COM

JESSICA R. FALK, born Blue Island, Illinois, September 19, 1977; admitted to bar, 2003, Illinois; U.S. District Court, Northern District of Illinois, U.S. District Court, Northern District of Indiana and U.S. Court of Appeals, Seventh Circuit. *Education:* University of Illinois (B.A., 1999); University of Michigan (J.D., cum laude, 2003). Instructor, University of Michigan, 2002-2003. ***PRACTICE AREAS:*** Civil Litigation. ***Email:*** JFALK@NISEN.COM

CLAIRE E. GORMAN, born Evanston, Illinois, February 24, 1979; admitted to bar, 2004, Illinois and U.S. District Court, Northern District of Illinois. *Education:* Marquette University (B.A., 2001); DePaul University College of Law (J.D., magna cum laude, 2004). Order of the Coif. Member: DePaul Law Review and Moot Court Society. *Member:* Chicago, Illinois State and American Bar Associations. ***PRACTICE AREAS:*** Commercial Litigation. ***Email:*** CGORMAN@NISEN.COM

SARA B. ROBERTSON, born Flint, Michigan, November 29, 1976; admitted to bar, 2002, Illinois and U.S. District Court, Northern District of Illinois. *Education:* Albion College (B.A., summa cum laude, 1999) Phi Beta Kappa; Loyola University Chicago School of Law (J.D., 2002). Viola Player, Chicago Bar Association Symphony Orchestra. *Member:* Chicago, Illinois State and American Bar Associations. ***PRACTICE AREAS:*** Automotive Finance; Consumer Finance; Banking Law. ***Email:*** SROBERTSON@NISEN.COM

MATTHEW SOLLITTO, born Chicago, Illinois; admitted to bar, 2004, Illinois and U.S. District Court, Northern District of Illinois. *Education:* Georgetown University (B.A., 2000); University of Notre Dame (J.D., 2004). *Member:* Illinois State and American Bar Associations. ***PRACTICE AREAS:*** Litigation. ***Email:*** msollitto@yahoo.com

OF COUNSEL

DONALD C. SHINE, born Wilmette, Illinois, October 10, 1940; admitted to bar, 1970, Illinois, U.S. District Court, Northern District of Illinois including Trial Bar and U.S. Court of Appeals, Seventh Circuit; 1977, U.S. Supreme Court; 1982, U.S. Tax Court. *Education:* John Carroll University (B.S., 1962); Loyola University (J.D., 1969). Recipient: Francis J. Rooney-St. Thomas Moore Award, 1986; St. Thomas Moore Award, 1989. Author: "Commodities Law: Investor Protection of Abandonment?" Chicago-Kent Law Review 73, Vol. 55, 1979. Member, Board of Advisors, Loyola University, School of Law, 1978-1980. Member, Board of Governors, 1972-1978, President, 1979-1980 and Member, Dean Selection Committee, 1983, Loyola Law Alumni. Member, Panel Attorney Selection Committee, Federal Defender Program, 1978-2004. Assistant U.S. Attorney, Northern District of Illinois, 1970-1975. Member, State of Illinois Commodities Law Advisory Board, 1985-1990. ***PRACTICE AREAS:*** Commodities Law; Commercial Law; Criminal Law; Litigation; Federal Criminal Litigation. ***Email:*** DSHINE@NISEN.COM

NOLAN LAW GROUP

Established in 1981

20 NORTH CLARK STREET, 30TH FLOOR

CHICAGO, ILLINOIS 60602

Telephone: 312-630-4000
Toll Free: 888-630-9340
Facsimile: 312-630-4011
URL: http://www.nolanlawgroup.net
Email: contact@nolan-law.com
URL: http://www.lawyers.com/nolan-law

Plaintiff's Personal Injury, Aviation, Traumatic Brain Injury, Wrongful Death, Medical Malpractice, Product Liability, FELA, Construction Accidents, Transportation Law, Automobile Accidents, Civil Trial and Appellate Practice.

FIRM PROFILE: Donald Nolan and the firm's attorneys provide quality legal representation for victims of serious personal injury and wrongful death arising out of aviation disasters, medical malpractice, construction, railroad and product liability claims.

Nolan Law Group has litigated many high profile cases including representation of large family groups in aviation disasters such as American Airlines Flight 587, Singapore Air Flight SQ006, EgyptAir Flight 990, Swissair Flight 111, TWA Flight 800, USAir Flight 427 and others. The firm also represents survivors and families of victims of the September 11, 2001 terrorist attacks. In addition, Nolan Law Group handles cases for victims of the March 17, 2001, derailment of Amtrak's California Zephyr near Nodaway, Iowa; the March 15, 1999, crash of Amtrak's City of New Orleans train near Bourbonnais, Illinois; and Construction negligence lawsuits from the construction of the new U.S. Post Office in downtown Chicago.

Nolan Law Group is well established in its record of providing multi-million dollar verdicts and settlements in serous personal injury and wrongful death matters. Nolan Law Group enjoys Martindale-Hubbell's highest rating for legal ability and ethical standards, and Mr. Nolan has been voted a Leading American Attorney by his peers and appears in Who's Who in American Law.

DONALD J. NOLAN, born Chicago, Illinois, June 13, 1952; admitted to bar, 1977, Illinois and U.S. District Court, Northern District of Illinois; 1983, Trial Bar; 2003, New York. *Education:* Elmhurst College (B.A., with honors, 1974); DePaul University (J.D., 1977). Trial: "Hi Tech Proof in Brain Injury Cases," June 2005. Lecturer: "Putting It All

(This Listing Continued)

Together," North American Brain Injury Society (NABIS) Conference, October 9, 2004; "Airport Security," Emory Riddle Aviation Law Symposium, January 14, 2002; "Handling the Severe TBI Case: An Overview from an Attorney," ATLA, July 15, 2001; "Making the Complex Understandable: What to Use and When," ATLA, July 16, 2001; "Pre-Impact Terror," SMU Aviation Law Symposium, February 23, 2001; "Courtroom Presentation of Cranial Nerve and Brainstem Injury Cases," Utah Trial Lawyers Association, February 2, 2001; "Neuro and the Law: An Interdisciplinary Approach," The Rehabilitation Achievement Center, October 25, 2000; "Aviation Issues in the New Millennium," Moderator, American Bar Association, October 19-21, 2000; "Presentation of Cranial Nerve and Brain Stem Injury Cases," National Brain Injury Association, September 14-16, 2000; "Special Opening Statement Techniques in TBI Cases," Brain Injury Association of California, September 10-11, 2000; "Technology in the Courtroom," Chicago Bar Association Bootcamp, September 7, 2000; "Special Trial Tactics in a Case with a Mild Closed Head Injury," ATLA, July 29-August 2, 2000; "The Role of Professional Ethics in Treating Patients with Traumatic Brain Injury," Brain Injury Association of Illinois, July 29, 2000; "Pediatric Life Care Planning," Brain Injury Association of Illinois, October 16, 1999; "Special Opening Statement Techniques in the MTBI Case," Brain Injury Association of California, October 12, 1999; "Construction Negligence," Illinois Trial Lawyer Association, September 18, 1999; "Mild Traumatic Brain Injury," John Marshall Law School, September 9, 1999; "Technology in the Courtroom: Cutting Edge Tactics From Real Time Court Reporting to Computer Animation," Chicago Bar Association, August 25, 1999; "The Ultimate TBI Notebook," Traumatic Brain Injury Seminar, June 3-4, 1999; "Handling the Severe TBI Case: Settlement and Trial Perspectives," and "Direct Examination of Medical and Defense Experts in the Mild to Moderate TBI Case," Utah Trial Lawyers Association, January 28-29, 1999; "Opening Statements," Illinois Trial Lawyers Association, October 12, 1998; "Organizing the File and Preparing the Case for Settlement or Trial," Brain Injury Association, September 17-19, 1998; "What Health Care Providers Should Know About Legal Rights and Remedies," National Spinal Cord Injury Association, August 24-26, 1998; "Technology in the Courtroom: From Realtime Court Reporting to Computer Animation," Chicago Bar Association, August 13, 1998; "Handling High-Profile Cases," ATLA, July 11, 1998; "Dynamic Demonstrative Evidence," ATLA, April 17, 1998; "The Use of Demonstrative Evidence," Consumer Attorneys of California, November 15, 1997; "Lawsuits and Workers' Compensation Claims: What Brain Injury Patients and Health Care Providers Should Know About Legal Rights and Remedies," Brain Injury Association of Illinois, October 24, 1997; "Opening Statement," American Board of Trial Attorneys, October 9, 1997; "Organizing the File and Preparing the Case for Settlement and Trial," Brain Injury Association, Inc. Annual Conference for Attorneys, September 24-25, 1997; "Summation in the Mild Traumatic Brain Injury Case," and "The Use of Demonstrative Evidence in Construction Site Accidents," ATLA, July 19-23, 1997; Panel Discussion: "Issues of Professionalism and Expectation Between Lawyers and Judges," National Association of Women Lawyers, May 2, 1997; "Preparing the Case for Settlement and Trial," New Jersey Trial Lawyers Association, April 18, 1997; "Evaluation of Claims involving Brainstem Injuries," Brain Injury Association of North Carolina, January 24, 1997; "Voir Dire in the Mild Brain Injury Case," ATLA, January 20, 1997; "Unifying the Medical-Legal Approach to Traumatic Brain Injury," Brain Injury Association of Illinois, October 4, 1996; "Preparing the File for Settlement and Trial: The Post-Concussion Syndrome Case," Brain Injury Association Annual Conference for Attorneys, September 19, 1996; "Traumatic Brain Stem Injury," ATLA, July 29, 1996; "Case Selection and Development: Plaintiff's Perspective," Chicago Bar Association, April 17, 1996; "Handling Wrongful Death Cases," Mothers Against Drunk Driving (MADD) Video Presentation, March 1996; "Direct Examination of Vocational Economist Expert," Brain Injury Association of North Carolina, January 29, 1996; "Informed Court: What's It All About?" The National Head Injury Foundation 14th Annual National Symposium, December 3-5, 1995; "Opening Statement: Mock Trial Demonstration," ATLA, July 1995; "Structural Work Act Cases: Current Topics in Injury Victim Advocacy," Illinois Trial Lawyers Association, April 24, 1993; "Trial Demonstration and Techniques: An Automobile Case Study," Program Chair, Illinois Trial Lawyers Association, October 14, 1991; "Product Liability: How to Do It," Seminar Moderator, Chicago Bar Association, March 7, 1990; "The Wrongful Death Act: Obtaining the Successful Result," Program Moderator, Chicago Bar Association, February 14, 1990; "Tort Litigation: Important Answers to New Questions," Program Chair, Chicago Bar Association, February 1, 1990; "Tort Litigation: New Development and Trends," Chicago Bar Association, January 19, 1989; "Handling a Wrongful Death Case," Program Chair, Chicago Bar Association, November 3, 1988; "Product Liability Practice: How to Obtain the Successful Result," Program Chair, Chicago Bar Association, September 15, 1988; "Structural Work Act: Discovery," Illinois Trial Lawyers Association, June 4, 1988; "Insurance Law: Conflict of Interest Between Insured and Insurer," Illinois Trial Lawyers Association, October 18, 1986; "Sports Injury Law: Tort Litigation," Chicago Bar Association, February 18, 1986; "Damages Under Wrongful Death Act After Bullard v. Barnes," Chicago Bar Association, February 27, 1985. Member: The Roscoe Pound Association; Civil Justice Foundation (Treasurer and Honor Roll of Champions); Belli Society; Brain Injury Association of Illinois (Member, Board of Directors); National Spinal Cord Injury Association (Member, Board of Directors). Elected to: "Leading Lawyer's Network," Illinois, 2004-2005. *Member:* Chicago (Past Chair, Tort Litigation Committee; Past Member, Evaluation of Candidates Committee, 1990; Member, Public Affairs/Media Relations Committee, 1997; Chair, Long-Range Planning Committee, 1998), Illinois State (Appointed to Tort Section Council) and American (Member: Litigation Practice Group; Aviation and Space Law Committee) Bar Associations; Illinois Trial Lawyers Association (Past Secretary; Past Chair, Product Liability Committee; Member, Board of Managers; Past Member, Legislative Committee; Membership Committee; Civil Practice Committee and Public Relations Committee); Association of Trial Lawyers of America (Secretary/Treasurer, Aviation Section; Chair-Elect, Traumatic Brain Injury Litigation Group; Birth Trauma Litigation Group; Construction Site Accident Litigation Group; Membership Oversight Committee; National College of Advocacy; Chair, Railroad Law Section; Chairman, Aviation Section, 2004-2005); Trial Lawyers Club of Chicago; Lawyer-Pilot's Bar Association. ***PRACTICE AREAS:*** Plaintiff's Personal Injury Law; Aviation Law; Wrongful Death; Medical Malpractice; Product Liability; Premises Liability; FELA; Construction Accidents; Negligence. ***Email:*** djn@nolan-law.com

(This Listing Continued)

WILLIAM J. JOVAN, admitted to bar, 1961, Illinois; 1962, U.S. Court of Appeals, Seventh Circuit and U.S. District Court, Northern District of Illinois. *Education:* Northwestern University (B.S., 1958; J.D., 1961). Law Clerk to Judge Elmer J. Schnackenberg, U.S. Court of Appeals, 1961-1964. Appointed by Illinois Supreme Court to Illinois Supreme Court Rules Committee, 1982-1988. *Member:* Chicago Bar Association (Member: Judicial Evaluation Committee; Judiciary Committee; Past Chair, Circuit Court Committee, 1990-1991; Civil Practice Committee, 1998-1999); The Association of Trial Lawyers of America; Illinois Trial Lawyers Association; Appellate Lawyers Association. ***PRACTICE AREAS:*** Plaintiff's Personal Injury; Appeals; Product Liability; Premises Liability; Wrongful Death; Negligence. ***Email:*** wjj@nolan-law.com

FLOYD A. WISNER, admitted to bar, 1977, Illinois and U.S. District Court, Northern District of Illinois; 1988, Alabama and U.S. District Court, Northern District of Alabama; 1990, Louisiana and U.S. District Court, Eastern, Western and Middle Districts of Louisiana. *Education:* DePaul University (B.A., summa cum laude, 1974; J.D., magna cum laude, 1977). Executive Editor, De Paul Law Review, 1976-1977. Publications: "Insurers Liability for Insureds' Attorney Fees in Declaratory Judgment Actions," 1998 CGL Reporter. Lecturer: "The Victims Compensation Fund and the Liability of the Airlines," Southern Trial Lawyers Association, February 2002; "Airport Security," Embry-Riddle University Aviation Law Symposium, January 2002; "The Liability of an Aircraft Manufacturer," Florida and Louisiana Bar Association Blue Angels Seminar, November 2001. *Member:* New Orleans, Louisiana State and American Bar Associations; Alabama State Bar. ***PRACTICE AREAS:*** Aviation Law; Product Liability; Negligence; General Civil Litigation. ***Email:*** faw@nolan-law.com

JEROME L. SKINNER, born Dunkirk, New York, September 4, 1951; admitted to bar, 1979, Ohio and U.S. District Court, Southern District of Ohio; 1980, U.S. District Court, Eastern District of Kentucky; 1982, U.S. Court of Appeals, Sixth Circuit; 1986, U.S. Supreme Court; 1988, U.S. District Court, Eastern District of Michigan (Not admitted in Illinois). *Education:* State University of New York (B.A., 1974); Ohio Northern University (J.D., 1979). Phi Alpha Delta (Treasurer, 1977-1978; 1978-1979). American Jurisprudence Award, Administrative Law. Barrister, American Inns of Court. Plaintiff Steering Committee, Libyan Terror Litigation, Pan Am Flight 103, December 21, 1988. Plaintiffs' Executive Committee, Egypt Air Flight 990, October 31, 1999. *Member:* Cincinnati, Ohio State (Lawyer's Assistance Committee) and American Bar Associations; The Association of Trial Lawyers of America. ***REPORTED CASES:*** Trial Counsel for Plaintiffs, 'In Re: Bendectin Products Liability Litigation MDL 486'; Trial Counsel for Plaintiffs, 'In Re: Air Crash Disaster at Covington, Kentucky, June 2, 1983 MDL 569'; Trial Counsel for Plaintiffs, 'In Re: Air Crash Disaster at Gander, Newfoundland, December 12, 1985 MDL 683'; Trial Counsel for Plaintiffs and Member of Plaintiff's Reconstituted Steering Committee, 'In Re: Aircrash at Detroit Metropolitan Airport, Detroit Michigan, August 16, 1987 MDL 742'; Plaintiffs' Steering Committee in the Libyan Litigation, In Re: Air Crash Disaster at Lockerbie, Scotland, December 12, 1998, Pan Am Flight 103, MDL 799; In Re: Air Crash Disaster of United Airlines, Inc. on July 19, 1989 at Sioux City, Iowa, United Flight 232, MDL 817; Plaintiffs' Trial Team, In Re: Air Crash Disaster at La Guardia International Airport on March 22, 1992, MDL 936; In Re: Air Crash Disaster at Pittsburgh, Pennsylvania on September 8, 1994, U.S. Air Flight 427, MDL 1040; Plaintiffs' Steering Committee, In Re: Air Crash Disaster at Dubrovnik Airport, Croatia (Bosnia) on April 3, 1996, MDL 1180; In Re: Air Crash Disaster at New York, N.Y. on July 17, 1996, TWA Flight 800, PSC, MDL 1161; In Re: Air Crash Disaster at Peggy's Cove, Nova Scotia on September 28, 1998, Swiss Air Flight 111, MDL 1269; Greene v. B.F. Goodrich, et al. S-76A Sikorsky Helicopter Crash near Jackson, Kentucky on June 14, 1999; Member, PEC & PLC, In Re: Air Crash Disaster near Nantucket Isle, Massachusetts on October 31, 1999, Egypt Air Flight 990, MDL 1344; In Re: Air Crash Disaster at Charlotte International Airport, North Carolina on January 8, 2003, U.S. Airways Flight 5481, MDL 1558. ***PRACTICE AREAS:*** Complex and Multi-district Litigation; General Aviation Litigation; Commercial Air Crash Litigation.

JAMES H. LAWLOR, III, born Kankakee, Illinois, December 19, 1960; admitted to bar, 1987, Illinois. *Education:* Northeastern Illinois University (B.A., with high honors, 1983); John Marshall Law School (J.D., 1987). Author: "Loss of Society in Illinois: The Swing Toward Restricted Liability," Illinois Bar Journal, October, 1989; "The Right to Die in Illinois in the Wake of Cruzan, Longeway and Greenspan," Illinois Bar Journal, February, 1991. Lecturer: "Proving the Mild to Traumatic Brain Injury Case," ITLA, February 9, 2002. *Member:* Chicago and Illinois State Bar Associations; Illinois Trial Lawyers Association. ***PRACTICE AREAS:*** Plaintiff's Personal Injury; Product Liability; Premises Liability; FELA; Construction Accidents; Vehicular Collisions; Negligence. ***Email:*** jhl@nolan-law.com

ORLA M. BRADY, born Nashville, Tennessee, July 2, 1974; admitted to bar, 2001, Massachusetts; 2004, Illinois. *Education:* New England School of Law (J.D., cum laude, 2001); Trinity College, Dublin Ireland (LL.M., 2004). Honors Moot Court. Trinity College Law Review, Editorial Board. *Member:* Massachusetts and Illinois State Bar Associations. ***PRACTICE AREAS:*** Personal Injury; Aviation Law. ***Email:*** omb@nolan-law.com

OF COUNSEL

JOHN J. LOWREY, born Joliet, Illinois, October 28, 1939; admitted to bar, 1969, Colorado and U.S. District Court, District of Colorado; 1970, Illinois and U.S. District Court, Northern District of Illinois including Trial Bar; 1977, U.S. Supreme Court and U.S. Court of Appeals, Seventh Circuit; U.S. Court of Military Appeals. *Education:* Loyola University (B.S., 1961); University of Denver (J.D., 1969). Phi Alpha Delta. Author: "Limitations in Medical Malpractice Cases: A Plaintiffs View," Illinois Trial Lawyers Journal, Vol. 7, #1, Fall/Winter 1984; "Hospital Liability for Contract Emergency Room Physicians," Illinois Trial Lawyers Journal, Vol. 7, #2, Spring/Summer, 1985; "Making the Defense Expert Your Expert in Medical Malpractice Cases," Trial Diplomacy Journal, Vol. 9 #2, Summer, 1986; "A Medical Malpractice Trial Analyzed," American Journal of Trial Advocacy, Vol. 11:1, Summer, 1987; "Trial Techniques in Medical Malpractice, Opening Statement," Medical Trial Techniques Quarterly, Summer, 1985; Julien Opening Statements, §1.01.27 and §3.02, 1985; Stein Closing Argument, §§312.50, 315.50, 405.50, 1985; "Presenting the Medical Evidence: Testimony of Neuropsychologist in Retrolental Fibroplasia Malpractice Case: $17 Million Structured Settlement," A Case History Report, Trauma, No. 2, August,

(This Listing Continued)

NOLAN LAW GROUP, Chicago—Continued

1985; "Vicarious Liability and Corporate Negligence," Medical & Hospital Negligence, Chapters 13-14, 1988; "Statutory Considerations," IICLE Medical Malpractice Handbook, Chapter 13, 1989; "Examination of Neurosurgeon in Neurosurgery Anesthesiology Quadroplegia Malpractice Case," Medical Trial Techniques Quarterly, Vol. 36, 1989; "Averbach Handling Accident Cases—Medical, Hospital and Dental Malpractice," §83B Interrogatories Regarding Insurance Policies, 1990; "The Trial Brief: an Aid to Preparation and Persuasion," Trial Talk: CTLA, Vol. 39, Issue 34, 1990; "Plaintiffs Perspective in Products Liability, IICLE, 1990; "Opening Statements, Motions, Jury Instructions in Trial of Civil Lawsuit, CBA, 1990 and Economic and Financial Experts, ITLA, 1990. Lecturer: Midwest Deposition Program, NITA 1995; Effective use of Depositions at ISBA Trial 1991. Deposing Defense Experts, IICLE, 1989; Opening Statements, CBA, 1989; Pleadings after the Medical Malpractice Reform Act, ITLA, 1988; Packaging the Evidence, ITLA, 1987; Medical Malpractice Trials, Loyola University School of Law, 1986; Medical Negligence Practice under new statute, ITLA, 1986; Uninsured and underinsured motorist coverage, ITLA, 1986; Preparing the Expert for Deposition, ITLA, 1985; Medical Malpractice Reform Act, ITLA, 1985; Chancery Practice Seminar, CBA, 1985; Update on Professional Negligence, ITLA, 1984; Cross-examination of defendant's medical expert witness at trial, Young Lawyers Section, CBA, 1984; Deposing the medical expert, Young Lawyers Section, CBA, 1984; Comprehensive Evidence, ITLA, 1983; Current Practice in the First Municipal District, CBA, 1982; Direct and cross-examination of an economist in a personal injury action, IICLE, 1982; Medical expert witnesses, What attorneys should understand about doctors, IICLE, 1981; Illinois Civil Evidence Trial Skills Course, IICLE, 1979; Experts in Federal Discovery, CBA, 1979; Evidence and Procedure in Professional Malpractice Litigation, De Paul University School of Law, 1976; Recent developments in medical malpractice litigation, ISBA, 1976. Coordinator and Speaker of CBA-Bench/Bar Symposiums, 1989-1991. Deputy District Attorney, First Judicial District of Colorado, 1969-1970. Assistant Attorney General of the State of Illinois, 1970-1971. Special Assistant Attorney General of Illinois, 1970-1982. Special Assistant Corporation Counsel, City of Chicago, 1979-1986. *Member:* Chicago (Elected Member, Board of Managers, 1986-1988; Committee Chairman, Continuing Legal Education, 1991-1992; Illinois State (Elected Member of Assembly, Illinois State Bar Assembly, 1984-1990) and Federal (Board of Directors, Chicago Chapter) Bar Associations; Illinois Trial Lawyers Association (Elected Member, Board of Managers); Illinois Appellate Lawyers Association. [Col., U.S. Marine Corps Reserve, 1958-1983, Retired]. ***PRACTICE AREAS:*** Medical Malpractice; Legal Malpractice; Brain Injury; Business Litigation.

CHARLES RAYBURN BARNETT, III, born Elmhurst, Illinois, June 11, 1960; admitted to bar, 2001, Illinois; 2002, U.S. District Court, Northern District of Illinois. *Education:* University of Illinois (B.S., 1982); Northern Illinois University (J.D., 2000). Member, Aircraft Owners and Pilots Association; Aircraft Association; Allied Pilots Association. Pilot, Airline Transport, 1989. *Member:* Chicago, Illinois State and American Bar Associations; Lawyers Pilots Bar Association. [Captain, U.S. Air Force, 1982-1991]. ***PRACTICE AREAS:*** Aviation Law. **Email:** crb@nolan-law.com

NOONAN & LIEBERMAN, LTD.

105 WEST ADAMS STREET, SUITE 3000
CHICAGO, ILLINOIS 60603-6209
Telephone: 312-431-1455
Fax: 312-431-1456
Email: JNoonan@noonandlieberman.com

Real Estate Litigation, Lenders Rights and Lenders Litigation, Foreclosure, Commercial Litigation, and Civil Rights and Appellate Practice.

JAMES V. NOONAN, born Evergreen Park, Illinois, November 8, 1963; admitted to bar, 1989, Illinois and U.S. District Court, Northern District of Illinois; 1990, U.S. District Court, Northern District of Indiana. *Education:* Marquette University (B.A., 1985); De Paul University (J.D., 1988). Co-author, Illinois Mortgage Foreclosure Practice, IICLE (2003). *Member:* Chicago and Illinois State Bar Associations. ***PRACTICE AREAS:*** Real Estate Litigation; Lenders Rights; Lenders Liability; Foreclosure; Commercial Litigation; Civil; Appellate Practice; Class Action Litigation. ***Email:*** JNoonan@noonanandlieberman.com

MITCHELL A. LIEBERMAN, born 1961; admitted to bar, 1986, Illinois. *Education:* Indiana University (B.A., 1983); DePaul University (J.D., 1986). Co-author, Illinois Mortgage Foreclosure Practice, IICLE (2003). ***PRACTICE AREAS:*** Commercial Litigation; Bankruptcy; Lenders Rights; Real Estate Litigation; Foreclosures. ***Email:*** MLieberman@noonanandlieberman.com

---

PATRICK J. McCANN, II, born Arlington Heights, Illinois, April 9, 1975; admitted to bar, 2001, Illinois and U.S. District Court, Northern District of Illinois. *Education:* Arizona State University (B.S., 1997); The John Marshall Law School (J.D., 2000). ***PRACTICE AREAS:*** Commercial Litigation; Civil Litigation; Real Estate Litigation; Foreclosures. **Email:** PMccann@noonanandlieberman.com

CRAIG C. SMITH, born Vicenza, Italy, July 7, 1966; admitted to bar, 1996, Illinois and U.S. District Court, Northern District of Illinois. *Education:* University of Illinois (B.A., 1988); John Marshall Law School (J.D., 1996). ***PRACTICE AREAS:*** Lenders Rights; Lender Liability; Real Estate Litigation; Commercial Litigation; Foreclosures. ***Email:*** csmith@noonanandlieberman.com

JONATHAN D. NUSGART, born Winnipeg, Manitoba, June 24, 1966; admitted to bar, 1992, California and U.S. District Court, Southern District of California; 1993, Illinois and U.S. District Court, Northern District of Illinois; 2003, U.S. Court of Appeals, Seventh Circuit. *Education:* University of Florida (B.A., 1988); California Western School of Law (J.D., 1991). *Member:* Chicago, DuPage County and American Bar Associations; State Bar of California. ***PRACTICE AREAS:*** Commercial Litigation; Real Estate Law; Creditors Rights. ***Email:*** jnusgart@noonanandlieberman.com

(This Listing Continued)

RALPH T. WUTSCHER, born Weslaco, Texas, May 27, 1970; admitted to bar, 1998, Illinois. *Education:* University of California, Los Angeles (B.A., 1993); University of Illinois (J.D., 1998). *Member:* Chicago Bar Association (Chair and Legislative Liason, Consumer Credit Committee). ***REPORTED CASES:*** Jenkins v. Mercantile Mortgage Co., et al, WL 31163115 (N.D. Ill. 2002); Lahey v. JM Mortgage Services, U.S. Dist LEXIS 5221 (N.D. Ill 2000); Livingston v. Prime Auto Credit, Inc., U.S. Dist. LEXIS 18891 (N.D. Ill. 2000). ***PRACTICE AREAS:*** Consumer Finance; Class Actions; Regulatory Law. ***Email:*** RWutscher@noonanandlieberman.com

OF COUNSEL

MICHAEL J. WEIK, born Billings, Montana, April 10, 1953; admitted to bar, 1978, Illinois; 1981, U.S. District Court, Northern District of Illinois including Trial Bar; 1986, U.S. Court of Appeals, Seventh Circuit. *Education:* University of Illinois (B.S., 1975; J.D., 1978). Certified Mediator, DePaul. *Member:* Illinois State Bar Association. ***PRACTICE AREAS:*** Business Litigation; Commercial Litigation; Health Care Litigation; Trust Litigation; Probate Litigation. ***Email:*** MWeik@noonanandlieberman.com

REPRESENTATIVE CLIENTS: American Business Credit; Ameriquest Mortgage Company; Bank of New York; Bank One, N.A.; Bayview Financial; Business Loan Center; Chase Manhattan Mortgage Company; Citicapital Commercial Corporation; Citicorp Vendor Finance; Citifinancial Mortgage; CitiMortgage; Commercial Federal Bank; Concord Acceptance Corp.; Countrywide Financial Corp.; Countrywide Home Loan; EMC Mortgage Company; Fairbanks Capital Corporation; Fieldstone Mortgage Co.; First Financial Corp.; First National Bank of Arizona; First NLC Financial Services LLC; Fremont Investment and Loan; GMAC Residential Funding; Home Loan Corporation; Interbay Funding Corporation; Litton Loan Servicing LP; Manufacturers and Traders Trust; Midland Bank; Mortgage Lenders Network USA, Inc.; National City Mortgage Company; National City Home Loan Services, Inc.; Nationwide Mortgage Plan and Trust; New Century Mortgage; Ocwen Federal Bank, FSB; Option One; Provident Bank; Pullman Bank; Residential Title Services, Inc.; Security National Servicing Corporation; Superior Home Services, Inc.; Urban Equities; Virtual Bank (Lydian Private Bank FSB); Wells Fargo Co.; Wilshire Credit Corporation.

STEVEN K. NORGAARD, P.C.

CHICAGO, ILLINOIS

(See Glen Ellyn)

Real Estate, Estate Planning, Probate, Buying and Selling a Home, Commercial Real Estate, Trusts and Estates, Small Business Law, Wills, Probate.

NORTON, MANCINI, WEILER & DEANO

SUITE 835
111 WEST WASHINGTON STREET
CHICAGO, ILLINOIS 60602
Telephone: 312-807-4999
Fax: 312-807-4998
Email: firm@nortonmancini.com

Wheaton, Illinois Office: 109 North Hale Street. Telephone: 630-668-9440. Fax: 630-668-9489.

Trial Practice. Personal Injury, Malpractice, Products Liability, Corporate Litigation, Municipal Litigation, Insurance, Corporate, Probate and Environmental Law, Medical Malpractice.

JOHN E. NORTON, born Rockford, Illinois, August 14, 1949; admitted to bar, 1975, Illinois. *Education:* University of Notre Dame (A.B., 1971); DePaul University (J.D., 1975). *Member:* Chicago, DuPage County (Member, Board of Directors, 1987-1989), Illinois State and American Bar Associations; Illinois Association of Defense Trial Counsel. ***PRACTICE AREAS:*** Trial Practice; Corporate Litigation; Malpractice; Products Liability; Environmental Litigation; Medical Malpractice. ***Email:*** jnorton@nortonmancini.com

LORENZO A. MANCINI, born Mola Di Bari, Italy, July 15, 1946; admitted to bar, 1977, Illinois. *Education:* St. Mary's College (B.A., 1968); DePaul University (J.D., summa cum laude, 1977). *Member:* Chicago, Du Page County, Illinois State and American Bar Associations; Illinois Association of Defense Trial Counsel. ***PRACTICE AREAS:*** Trial Practice; Insurance Law; Malpractice; Products Liability; Environmental Litigation; Medical Malpractice; Automobile Liability. ***Email:*** lmancini@nortonmancini.com

THOMAS R. WEILER, born Chicago, Illinois, November 11, 1958; admitted to bar, 1983, Illinois. *Education:* University of Notre Dame (B.B.A., 1980); Loyola University of Chicago (J.D., 1983). *Member:* Chicago, Du Page County, Illinois State and American Bar Associations; Illinois Trial Lawyers Association; The Association of Trial Lawyers of America. ***PRACTICE AREAS:*** Trial Practice; Malpractice; Products Liability; Environmental Litigation. ***Email:*** tweiler@nortonmancini.com

JAMES L. DEANO, born Chicago, Illinois, October 28, 1956; admitted to bar, 1981, Illinois. *Education:* Western Illinois University (B.A., 1978); John Marshall Law School (J.D., with honors, 1981). Order of John Marshall. Member, John Marshall Law Review, 1980-1981. *Member:* Illinois State and American Bar Associations. ***PRACTICE AREAS:*** Trial Practice; Municipal Law; Products Liability; Employment Law. ***Email:*** jdeano@nortonmancini.com

THOMAS J. LONG, born Bangor, Maine, October 4, 1958; admitted to bar, 1983, Illinois. *Education:* University of Notre Dame (B.A., 1980); Loyola University (J.D., 1983). *Member:* Du Page County and Illinois State Bar Associations. ***PRACTICE AREAS:*** Trial Practice; Insurance; Legal Malpractice; Personal Injury. ***Email:*** tlong@nortonmancini.com

W. ANTHONY ANDREWS, born Folkston, Georgia, December 9, 1966; admitted to bar, 1993, Illinois; 1995, U.S. District Court, Northern District of Illinois. *Education:* Lewis University (B.A., 1990); DePaul University (J.D., 1993). *Member:* Dupage and Chicago Bar Associations. ***PRACTICE AREAS:*** Insurance Defense; Insurance Coverage; Municipal; Civil Rights Defense. ***Email:*** wandrews@nortonmancini.com

(This Listing Continued)

DANIEL M. LATREILLE, born Grosse Point, Michigan, September 11, 1964; admitted to bar, 1993, Michigan, Illinois and U.S. District Court, Eastern District of Michigan and Northern District of Illinois. *Education:* University of Michigan (B.A., 1986); University of Detroit (J.D., 1992). *Member:* State Bar of Michigan; Chicago, Illinois State and American Bar Associations. ***PRACTICE AREAS:*** Insurance Defense; Automobile Liability; Medical Malpractice. ***Email:*** dlatreille@nortonmancini.com

DAVID H. CAPIZZI, born Oak Park, Illinois, October 30, 1977; admitted to bar, 2003, Illinois. *Education:* Indiana University (B.S., Public Policy, 1999); John Marshall Law School (J.D., LL.M., Real Estate, 2003); Dominican University (M.B.A., 2003). ***PRACTICE AREAS:*** Insurance Defense; Automobile Liability; Casualty Insurance; Property Insurance; Litigation. ***Email:*** dcapizzi@nortonmancini.com

MARK W. CONRAD, born Toledo, Ohio, October 29, 1953; admitted to bar, 1979, Illinois and U.S. District Court, Northern District of Illinois including Trial Bar; 1983, Trial Bar. *Education:* Carthage College (B.A., magna cum laude, 1975); John Marshall Law School (J.D., with distinction, 1979). Phi Delta Phi. Member, Order of John Marshall. *Member:* Chicago, Lake County, Illinois State and American (Member, Sections on: Litigation; Torts and Insurance Practice) Bar Associations; Defense Research Institute. ***PRACTICE AREAS:*** Trial Practice; Insurance Defense; Professional Liability; Health Care; Probate; Premises Liability; Automobile Liability; Structural Work Act; Construction Law; Negligence. ***Email:*** mconrad@nortonmancini.com

REPRESENTATIVE CLIENTS: Allstate Insurance Company; American Family Insurance Group; Auto-Owners Insurance; Chicago Hospital Risk Pooling Program; County of DuPage; CNA Insurance Company; Custard Claims Management Service, Inc.; Gallagher Bassett Insurance Service; Gordon Food Ser vice Inc.; Great American Insurance Company; Illinois State Medical Insurance Services, Inc.; Intergovernmental Risk Management Agency; ISBA Mutual Insurance Company; McLarens Toplis North America, Inc.; Multi Systems Agency, Inc.; Ophthalmic Mutual Insurance Company; Oshkosh Truck Corporation; Parker Hannifin Corporation; Park District Risk Management Agency (PDRMA); St. Paul Travelers Insurance Company; Sentry Insurance Company; SRS Specialty Risk Services (Hartford); State Farm Insurance Company; Trammel Crow.

(For complete biographical data on all personnel, see Professional Biographies at Wheaton, Illinois)

NOTTAGE AND WARD

Established in 1988

TEN NORTH DEARBORN STREET, PENTHOUSE
CHICAGO, ILLINOIS 60602
Telephone: 312-332-2915
Fax: 312-332-3075

Family, Divorce, Child Custody, Premarital and Postnuptial Agreements, Visitation and Matrimonial Litigation, Appeals.

FIRM PROFILE: Nottage and Ward concentrates in divorce and family law; provides a commitment to negotiation and expertise in litigation; excels in the art of communication, the tactics of persuasion and the skills of pre-trial strategy; balances each clients unique, immediate, emotional needs with a realistic assessment of the client's future financial requirements and offers consultation and legal services for individuals in a range of living situations.

MEMBERS OF FIRM

ROSAIRE M. NOTTAGE, born Brooklyn, New York, October 7, 1948; admitted to bar, 1976, Illinois, U.S. District Court, Northern District of Illinois and Federal Trial Bar. *Education:* Michigan State University (B.A., cum laude, 1970); Loyola University (J.D., 1976). Associate, 1976-1983, and Partner, 1984-1987, Bell, Boyd & Lloyd. *Member:* Chicago, Illinois State and American Bar Associations; Women's Bar Association of Illinois. ***PRACTICE AREAS:*** Divorce; Family; Matrimonial Law. ***Email:*** rmn@nottawar.com

EUNICE WARD, born Chicago, Illinois, August 16, 1946; admitted to bar, 1980, Illinois; 1982, U.S. District Court, Northern District of Illinois and Federal Trial Bar. *Education:* The Ohio State University (B.S., with honors, 1968); Ohio State University (M.Ed., 1969); IIT-Chicago-Kent College of Law (J.D., 1979). Phi Alpha Delta. *Member:* Chicago and American Bar Associations; Women's Bar Association. ***PRACTICE AREAS:*** Divorce; Family; Matrimonial Law. ***Email:*** ew@nottawar.com

ASSOCIATES

JEFFREY J. KNIPMEYER, born Hannibal, Missouri, September 15, 1971; admitted to bar, 1996, Missouri; 1997, Illinois. *Education:* University of Missouri (B.A., 1993); DePaul University (J.D., 1996). Staff Writer, DePaul Environmental Law Digest. *Illinois State and American Bar Associations.* ***PRACTICE AREAS:*** Domestic Relations. ***Email:*** jk@nottawar.com

PATRICK B. MARKEY, born Milwaukee, Wisconsin, August 18, 1975; admitted to bar, 2002, Illinois. *Education:* University of Minnesota (B.A., International Relations, 1998); Chicago-Kent College of Law (J.D., 2002). *Member:* Chicago and Illinois State Bar Associations. ***LANGUAGES:*** Spanish. ***PRACTICE AREAS:*** Matrimonial Law; Litigation; Divorce; Family Law. ***Email:*** pbm@nottawar.com

ISA-LEE WOLF, admitted to bar, 1999, Illinois. *Education:* Indiana University (B.A., 1996); Case Western Reserve University (J.D., cum laude, 1999). ***PRACTICE AREAS:*** Matrimonial Litigation; Divorce; Family Law. ***Email:*** ilw@nottawar.com

ANNEMARIE TARARA, admitted to bar, 2003, Illinois. *Education:* DePaul University (B.S., 2000); Chicago-Kent College of Law (J.D., 2003). ***PRACTICE AREAS:*** Domestic Relations. ***Email:*** at@nottawar.com

NOVACK AND MACEY LLP

Established in 1984

100 NORTH RIVERSIDE PLAZA
CHICAGO, ILLINOIS 60606
Telephone: 312-419-6900
Fax: 312-419-6928
Email: nminfo@novackandmacey.com
URL: http://www.novackandmacey.com

General Trial and Appellate Practice in State and Federal Courts and in Arbitration, including Civil Appeals, Bankruptcy Litigation, Banks and Banking, Business Torts, Class Actions, Complex Commercial Litigation, Commercial Real Estate, Creditors' Rights, Energy, Environmental Litigation, Financial Institutions Litigation, Fraud and Deceit, including Art Fraud, Insurance Litigation, Lender Liability, Partnership Law, Professional Liability, Securities Litigation, Trademark Litigation, Trust Litigation, Unfair Competition.

FIRM PROFILE: Novack and Macey is defined by the level of intensity it brings to litigation -- a profound commitment to winning for clients. Novack and Macey's focused and thorough approach, together with its highly developed courtroom skills and a smart team of lawyers, is a powerful combination for its clients. This combination results in intelligent analyses, sound business strategies, and, if needed, a tough-as-nails approach to litigating. It also results in other lawyers hiring Novack and Macey to handle their own most important disputes.

Recently, Novack and Macey became a member of the Integrated Advisory Group, an international organization of small to medium-sized law, accounting and consulting firms. IAG provides its members with a network of qualified professional advisors all over the world from whom they can request assistance or to whom they can refer clients.

Reported Cases: Old Republic v. Ness Motley, No. 03 C 5238, 2005 U.S. Dist. LEXIS 160 (Jan. 4, 2005); Old Republic v. Ness Motley, No. 03 C 5238, 2004 U.S. Dist. LEXIS 5731 (April 5, 2004); Chicago Dist. Council of Carpenters Pension Fund v. Reinke Insulation Co., 347 F.3d 262 (7th Cir. 2003); United Phosphorus Ltd. v. Angus Chemical Co., 131 F. Supp. 2d 1003 (N.D. Ill. 2001); Owens v. McDermott, Will & Emery, 316 Ill. App. 3d 340, 736 N.E.2d 145 (1st Dist. 2000); Antler v. Classic Residence Management Limited Partnership, 315 Ill. App. 3d 259, 733 N.E.2d 393 (Ill. App. Ct. 1st Dist. 2000); Dumas v. Angus Chemical Co., 728 So.2d 441 (La. Ct. App. 2d Cir. 1999); Perlman v. Zell, 185 F.3d 850 (7th Cir. 1999); Golden v. McDermott, Will & Emery, 299 Ill. App. 3d 982, 702 N.E.2d 581 (1st Dist. 1998); Banks v. Hit or Miss, Inc., 996 F. Supp. 802 (N.D. Ill. 1998); City of Chicago v. Michigan Beach Housing Cooperative, 297 Ill. App. 3d 317, 696 N.E. 2d 804 (Ill. App. Ct. 1st Dist. 1998); Gaffney v. City of Chicago, 302 Ill. App. 3d 41, 706 N.E.2d 914 (Ill. App. Ct. 1st Dist. 1998); Angus Chemical Co. v. IMC Fertilizer, 939 S.W. 2d 138 (Tex. 1997); Brown v. United Missouri Bank, 78 F.3d 382 (8th Cir. 1996); Chase Manhattan Bank, N.A. v. American Nat'l Bank and Trust Co., 93 F.3d 1064 (2d Cir. 1996); MaGee v. Huppin-Fleck, 279 Ill. App. 3d 81, 664 N.E.2d 246 (Ill. App. Ct. 1st Dist. 1996); Petition of K.M. and D.M. to adopt Olivia M., 274 Ill. App. 3d 189, 653 N.E.2d 888 (Ill. App. Ct. 1st Dist. 1995); RTC v. Franz, 909 F. Supp. 1128 (N.D. Ill. 1995); Zielinski v. Henke, 275 Ill. App. 3d 128, 655 N.E.2d 1040 (Ill. App. Ct. 1st Dist. 1995); Lewis v. Long Grove Trading Co., 13 F.3d 1028 (7th Cir. 1994); Lawson v. Household Bank F.S.B., 20 F.3d 786 (7th Cir. 1994); Continental Bank N.A. v. Meyer, 10 F.3d 1293 (7th Cir. 1993); RTC v. Thompson, 989 F.2d 942 (7th Cir. 1993); Shields Enterprises, Inc. v. First Chicago Corp., 975 F.2d 1290 (7th Cir. 1992); Riney v. Wiess & Neuman Shoe Co., 217 Ill. App. 3d 435, 577 N.E.2d 505 (Ill. App. Ct. 4th Dist. 1991); Bastian v. Petren Resources Corp., 892 F.2d 680 (7th Cir. 1990); Gaff v. FDIC, 919 F.2d 384 (6th Cir. 1990); Ma v. Continental Bank N.A., 905 F.2d 1073 (7th Cir. 1990); Abrams v. Rappoport, 163 Ill. App. 3d 748, 516 N.E.2d 943 (Ill. App. Ct. 1st Dist. 1987); Singer v. Lexington Insurance Co., 658 F. Supp. 341 (N.D. Tex. 1986).

MEMBERS OF FIRM

P. ANDREW FLEMING, born Doncaster, England, March 20, 1958; admitted to bar, 1982, Illinois; U.S. District Court, Northern District of Illinois. *Education:* Leeds University, Leeds, England, (LL.B., with honors, 1979); Council of Legal Education, London, England (Barrister, 1980); Illinois Institute of Technology/Chicago-Kent College of Law (J.D., 1982). Awarded: Duke of Edinburgh Scholarship, 1980; Geoffrey Veale Scholarship, 1981. Member, Honourable Society of the Inner Temple, 1979. *Member:* Chicago and American Bar Associations. ***PRACTICE AREAS:*** Complex Commercial Litigation; Arbitration; Partnership Dissolution. ***Email:*** paf@novackandmacey.com

KAREN L. LEVINE, born New York, New York, March 10, 1952; admitted to bar, 1986, Illinois. *Education:* Grinnell College (B.A., with honors, 1974); University of Chicago (M.A., 1976); Northwestern University (J.D., cum laude, 1986). Order of the Coif. Staff Member, 1984-1985 and Articles and Symposium Editor, 1985-1986, Northwestern Law Review. Co-author with Professor Martin Redish: "Constitutional Federalism, Judicial Review and the Scope of the Commerce Power: The Role of Textual Analysis," New York University Law Review, April, 1987. Law Clerk to Justice Seymour Simon, Supreme Court of Illinois, 1986-1987. Member, Academy of Certified Social Workers, 1978-1985. *Member:* Chicago Council of Lawyers (Member, Board of Governors). ***PRACTICE AREAS:*** Civil Appeals; Complex Business Litigation; Directors and Officers Liability; Family Law; Trust Litigation. ***Email:*** kll@novackandmacey.com

ERIC N. MACEY, born Baltimore, Maryland, December 28, 1951; admitted to bar, 1978, Illinois; U.S. District Court, Northern District of Illinois; 1980, U.S. Court of Appeals, Seventh Circuit. *Education:* Princeton University (A.B., magna cum laude, 1973); Annenberg School of Communications, University of Pennsylvania (M.A., 1975); National Law Center, George Washington University (J.D., with high honors, 1978). Order of the Coif. Staff Member, The George Washington Law Review, 1976-1978. Instructor, National Institute of Trial Advocacy; Adjunct Professor, Northwestern University School of Law. Author: Note, "The Collateral Estoppel Effect of Administrative Agency Actions in Federal Civil Litigation," 46 The George Washington Law Review 65, 1977; "The Cost of Parting Ways," National Business Association Magazine, Vol. 2, No. 2. April 2001. Contributing Author to Law.com, including co-authoring article entitled "Appeals Court Warns a New

(This Listing Continued)

NOVACK AND MACEY LLP, Chicago—Continued

Retainer Agreement Pitfall." Co-Author: "Are Your Attorney-Client Retention Agreements Enforceable?," CBA Record, January 2001. Officer, Chicago-Lincoln Inn of Court. *Member:* American (Member: Litigation Section; Energy Litigation Committee), Chicago and Energy Bar Associations. ***PRACTICE AREAS:*** Arbitration; Business Torts; Complex Commercial Litigation; Energy Litigation; Financial Institution Litigation; Insurance Litigation; Partnership Law; Real Estate Litigation. ***Email:*** emacey@novackandmacey.com

MONTE L. MANN, born Skokie, Illinois, February 12, 1970; admitted to bar, 1995, Illinois and U.S. District Court, Northern District of Illinois; 1998, District of Columbia; 1999, U.S. Court of Federal Claims and U.S. Court of Appeals, Seventh Circuit. *Education:* University of Pennsylvania (B.A., magna cum laude, 1992); Northwestern University (J.D., 1995). Note and Comment Editor, Journal of Criminal Law and Criminology, Northwestern University Law School, 1994-1995. Author: "Choosing Counsel: How to Hire and Keep the Best Litigation Counsel," Small Business Opportunities Magazine, May, 2001; "So You Want to Take Your Business OnLine?" Chicago Software News, Nov. 1999. *Member:* Chicago Bar Association; Federal Trial Bar for the U.S. District Court for the Northern District of Illinois. ***PRACTICE AREAS:*** Litigation. ***Email:*** mmann@novackandmacey.com

MITCHELL L. MARINELLO, born Passaic, New Jersey, July 1, 1954; admitted to bar, 1981, New York and U.S. District Court, Southern and Eastern Districts of New York; 1984, U.S. Court of Appeals, Second Circuit; 1985, Illinois and U.S. District Court, Northern District of Illinois; 1986, U.S. Court of Appeals, Seventh Circuit; 2003, U.S. District Court, Western District of Michigan. *Education:* Wesleyan University (B.A., magna cum laude, with honors, 1976); New York University (J.D., 1980). Fellow, Thomas J. Watson Foundation, Wesleyan University, 1976-1977. Senior Writing Editor, New York University, Moot Court Board, 1980. Publications: "Playing Nice: Noncompete Terms In Physician Employment Agreements," 2005 MGMA Connexion; "Obtaining TROs and Preliminary Injunctions," 2004 Litigation Review; "Disputes About Common Area Maintenance Charges," 2001 Litigation Review; "Recent Supreme Court Rulings on the Americans with Disabilities Act," The Trial Lawyer's Guide, Vo. 43, No. 2, 1999; "Expanding Illinois' Service of Process on Individuals," CBA Record July/August 1991. Arbitrator: American Arbitration Association; Commercial Panel and NASD. *Member:* Chicago (Former Chair, Civil Litigation Committee, Div. III), American and Federal Bar Associations; Integrated Advisory Group International. ***PRACTICE AREAS:*** Commercial Litigation; Real Estate Litigation; Partnership Litigation. ***Email:*** mlm@novackandmacey.com

TIMOTHY J. MILLER, born Saginaw, Michigan, November 16, 1960; admitted to bar, 1985, Illinois; 1989, U.S. District Court, Northern District of Illinois. *Education:* Alma College (B.A., summa cum laude, 1982); Duke University (J.D., with high honors, 1985). Phi Beta Kappa; Order of the Coif. Managing Editor, Duke Law Journal, 1984-1985. Author: "The Attorneys' Duty to Reveal a Client's Intended Future Criminal Conduct," 1984 Duke Law Journal 582, and "7th Circuit gives Arbitrators Permission to Ignore the Law," Chicago Daily Law Bulletin, June 28, 2001. Co-Author: "An Unexpected Bite: An Explanation of the Fickle Fiduciary Rule," CBA Record, February/March 2000; "Are Your Attorney-Client Retention Agreements Enforceable?" CBA Record, January 2001. Contributing Author to Law.com, including co-authoring article entitled "Appeals Court Warns a New Retainer Agreement Pitfall." Former member of Editorial Board of Mealey's D&O Liability Litigation Reports. *Member:* American Bar Association. ***PRACTICE AREAS:*** Alternative Dispute Resolution; Civil Appeals; Complex Litigation; Partnership Dissolution; Directors and Officers Liability. ***Email:*** tjm@novackandmacey.com

STEPHEN NOVACK, born St. Louis, Missouri, July 22, 1946; admitted to bar, 1972, Illinois; U.S. District Court, Northern District of Illinois; 1976, U.S. District Court, Eastern District of Wisconsin; U.S. Court of Appeals, Seventh Circuit; U.S. Supreme Court; 1980, U.S. Court of Appeals, Fifth Circuit; 1982, U.S. District Court Trial Bar; U.S. Court of Appeals, First Circuit; 1986, U.S. Court of Appeals, Sixth Circuit; 1993, U.S. District Court, Central District of Illinois; U.S. Court of Appeals, Ninth Circuit; 1994, U.S. Court of International Trade; 1995, U.S. Court of Appeals, Eighth Circuit; 1996, U.S. Tax Court; U.S. Court of Appeals, Second Circuit; 1997, U.S. Court of Appeals, Federal Circuit. *Education:* University of Missouri at St. Louis (B.A., magna cum laude, 1968); Northwestern University Law School (J.D., magna cum laude, 1972). Order of the Coif. Recipient of Ford Foundation Fellowship in Criminal Law, 1970. Member, Northwestern University National Moot Court Team, 1972. Staff Member, 1970-1971 and Notes and Comments Editor, 1971-1972, Northwestern University Law Review. Author: "Javins v. First National Realty Corp.—The Implied Warranty of Habitability and Rent Withholding in Urban Leases," 66 Northwestern University Law Review 227, 1971; "Jack Spring, Inc. v. Little; Appeal Bonds, Implied Warranty of Habitability, Defenses to Actions for Eviction—New Principles of Landlord-Tenant Law," 66 Northwestern University Law Review 790, 1972. Lecturer, Illinois Institute of Continuing Legal Education, 1984. *Member:* Chicago Bar Association. ***PRACTICE AREAS:*** Complex Commercial Litigation; Civil Appeals; Real Estate Litigation; Banking Litigation; Insurance Litigation; Bankruptcy Litigation. ***Email:*** sn@novackandmacey.com

STEPHEN J. SIEGEL, born Chicago, Illinois, September 4, 1962; admitted to bar, 1992, Illinois and U.S. District Court, Northern and Central Districts of Illinois. *Education:* Middlebury College (B.A., cum laude, 1984); University of Michigan Law School (J.D., cum laude, 1990). Law Clerk, Honorable Morey L. Sear, U.S. District Court, Eastern District of Louisiana, 1990-1991. Author: "'Extrajudicial' Privilege Waiver Does Not Necessarily Result in Broad Subject Matter Waiver," ABA Committee on Corporate Counsel Newsletter, Fall 2004. Legislative Assistant, U.S. Rep. Harry M. Reid (D. Nev.), 1985-1986. *Member:* American Bar Association; Chicago Council of Lawyers. ***PRACTICE AREAS:*** Civil Litigation; Complex Commercial Litigation; Energy; Securities. ***Email:*** ssiegel@novackandmacey.com

DONALD A. TARKINGTON, born Evanston, Illinois, March 10, 1956; admitted to bar, 1983, Illinois. *Education:* Indiana University (B.S., 1978); Northwestern University (J.D., 1983). Member, Northwestern University National Moot Court Team, 1983. Recipient of William Jennings Bryan Award and Lowden Wigmore Prize for excellence in oral and written advocacy, 1982. Author: "Contractors Beware: Contract Liability Laws," Multifamily Executive Magazine, July, 2001; "Guarding Your Companies' Secrets in the Electronic Age," Accounting Today, Nov. 26, 2001. Member, Board of Education for the Evanston/Skokie Consolidated School District 65, 1995-1999; President of the Board of the District 65 Educational Foundation, 2001—. *Member:* American Bar Association. ***PRACTICE AREAS:*** Complex Business Litigation; Civil Appeals; Real Estate Litigation; Insurance Litigation; Bankruptcy Litigation. ***Email:*** dat@novackandmacey.com

MICHAEL A. WEINBERG, born Chicago, Illinois, June 10, 1952; admitted to bar, 1976, Illinois and U.S. District Court, Northern District of Illinois. *Education:* Vassar College (A.B., with honors and distinction, 1973); University of Michigan Law School (J.D., 1976). Associate Editor, 1974-1975 and Note Editor, 1975-1976, University of Michigan Law Review. *Member:* Chicago Bar Association. ***PRACTICE AREAS:*** Commercial Litigation; Lender Liability; Complex Business Litigation; Employment Litigation. ***Email:*** maw@novackandmacey.com

ASSOCIATES

KENNETH M. ABELL, born Chicago, Illinois, October 19, 1973; admitted to bar, 2001, Illinois. *Education:* University of Wisconsin-Madison (B.A., 1995); Northwestern University (J.D., 2001). Note and Comment Editor, Journal of Criminal Law and Criminology. Board Member, Chicago Area Project. *Member:* American Bar Association. ***PRACTICE AREAS:*** Commercial Litigation. ***Email:*** kabell@novackandmacey.com

ALLAN V. ABINOJA, born St. Louis, Missouri, March 2, 1976; admitted to bar, 2001, Illinois. *Education:* Yale University (B.A., 1998); University of Notre Dame (J.D., cum laude, 2001). *Member:* Chicago and American (Member, Litigation Section) Bar Associations. ***PRACTICE AREAS:*** Commercial Litigation. ***Email:*** aabinoja@novackandmacey.com

ANDREW D. CAMPBELL, born Lansing, Michigan, March 15, 1974; admitted to bar, 1999, Illinois. *Education:* University of Michigan (B.A., 1996); Loyola University, Chicago (J.D., magna cum laude, 1999). Author: "Kansas v. Hendricks: Absent a Clear Meaning of Punishment, States Are Permitted to Violate Double Jeopardy Clause," 30 Loyola University Chicago Law Journal No. 1. *Member:* Chicago Bar Association. ***PRACTICE AREAS:*** Commercial Litigation. ***Email:*** acampbell@novackandmacey.com

STEVEN J. CISZEWSKI, born Palos Park, Illinois, September 22, 1973; admitted to bar, 1998, Illinois. *Education:* University of Illinois (B.A., cum laude, 1995; J.D., magna cum laude, 1998). Member, Illinois' National Moot Court Team; Moot Court Board. Recipient, Rickert Award for Excellence in Oral Advocacy; American Jurisprudence Award for Excellence in Trial Advocacy. *Member:* Illinois and American (Member, Sections on: Tort and Insurance Practice) Bar Associations. ***PRACTICE AREAS:*** Litigation. ***Email:*** stevec@novackandmacey.com

KRISTEN WERRIES COLLIER, born Jacksonville, Illinois, July 6, 1971; admitted to bar, 2000, Illinois. *Education:* University of Illinois, Urbana-Champaign (B.A., 1993); Maxwell School of Citizenship and Public Affairs, Syracuse University (M.P.A., 1996); University of Illinois College of Law (J.D., 1999). Member, National Moot Court Team, 1998-1999. Moot Court Board. Recipient, Rickert Award for Excellence in Oral Advocacy, 1999. Member, University of Illinois Law Review, 1997-1999. ***PRACTICE AREAS:*** Litigation. ***Email:*** kwc@novackandmacey.com

RICHARD G. DOUGLASS, born Bloomington, Minnesota, July 12, 1974; admitted to bar, 2002, Georgia; 2004, Illinois. *Education:* University of Pittsburgh (B.A., magna cum laude, 1998); University of Georgia (J.D., magna cum laude, 2002). Order of the Coif. Articles Editor, Georgia Law Review. *Member:* State Bar of Georgia; Illinois State Bar Association. ***PRACTICE AREAS:*** Commercial Litigation. ***Email:*** rdouglass@novackandmacey.com

SHELBY L. DRURY, born Melrose Park, Illinois, May 5, 1973; admitted to bar, 1998, Illinois. *Education:* University of Illinois at Urbana-Champaign (B.S., 1995; Bronze Tablet); Northwestern University (J.D., cum laude, 1998). Co-Author: "An Unexpected Bite: An Explanation of the Fickle Fiduciary Rule," CBA Record, February/March, 2000. Member, Journal of International Law and Business, Northwestern University, 1996-1998. *Member:* Chicago Bar Association. ***PRACTICE AREAS:*** Litigation. ***Email:*** sdrury@novackandmacey.com

BRIAN M. DUNN, born Tampa, Florida, April 5, 1974; admitted to bar, 2003, Florida and New York; 2004, Illinois. *Education:* University of South Florida (B.A., summa cum laude, 1999); Georgetown University Law Center (J.D., 2002). Author: "The Mexicali Tire Pile: Smoke on the Horizon?" 14 Georgetown International Environmental Law Review 409-427, 2001. *Member:* The Florida Bar. ***PRACTICE AREAS:*** Commercial Litigation. ***Email:*** bdunn@novackandmacey.com

STEPHANIE J. HARRIS, born Spartanburg, South Carolina, August 17, 1976; admitted to bar, 2004, Illinois. *Education:* Converse College (B.A., 2001); University of Georgia (J.D., magna cum laude, 2004). Member, University of Georgia Law Review. *Member:* Illinois State and American Bar Associations. ***PRACTICE AREAS:*** Litigation. ***Email:*** sharris@novackandmacey.com

JULIE A. JOHNSTON-AHLEN, born New Hartford, New York, February 15, 1971; admitted to bar, 2002, Illinois; 2003, U.S. District Court, Northern District of Illinois. *Education:* Wells College (B.A., 1992); University of Minnesota, Minneapolis (M.B.A., 1994; J.D., magna cum laude, 2002). Phi Beta Kappa; Order of the Coif. ***LANGUAGES:*** Spanish. ***PRACTICE AREAS:*** Commercial Litigation; Bankruptcy. ***Email:*** jjohnston-ahlen@novackandmacey.com

ELIZABETH A. MAYER, born Macomb, Illinois, January 15, 1973; admitted to bar, 1997, Pennsylvania; 1998, Illinois; 1999, U.S. District Court, Northern District of Illinois. *Education:* Illinois Wesleyan University (B.A., summa cum laude, 1994); University of Michigan (J.D., cum laude, 1997). Law Clerk, Honorable Marvin Katz, U.S. District Court, Eastern District of Pennsylvania, 1997-1999. ***PRACTICE AREAS:*** Litigation. ***Email:*** emayer@novackandmacey.com

RICHARD L. MILLER II, born Danville, Illinois, June 4, 1970; admitted to bar, 1997, Illinois; 1998, Minnesota, U.S. District Court, Northern, Central Districts of Illinois including Trial Bar and U.S. Supreme Court. *Education:* University of Illinois (B.S., magna cum laude, 1992; J.D., cum laude, 1997). Author: "An Introduction to Opinion Testimony Disclosures in Illinois," Illinois Bar Journal, January, 2002. *Member:* Chicago and Illinois State Bar Associations. ***PRACTICE AREAS:*** Commercial Litigation; Criminal Law. ***Email:*** rmiller@novackandmacey.com

(This Listing Continued)

CHRISTOPHER S. MOORE, born Memphis, Tennessee, November 29, 1960; admitted to bar, 1998, Illinois. *Education:* University of Chicago (B.A., 1993); University of Illinois, Urbana-Champaign (J.D., summa cum laude, 1998). Member, Order of the Coif. Member, 1996-1997 and Editor-in-Chief, 1997-1998, University of Illinois Law Review. Visiting Assistant Professor of Law, University of Illinois College of Law, 2002-2004. *Member:* Illinois State Bar Association. ***PRACTICE AREAS:*** Commercial Litigation. ***Email:*** cmoore@novackandmacey.com

JOSEPH S. NACCA, admitted to bar, 2003, Illinois. *Education:* University of Virginia (B.A., with high honors, 2000); Columbia University Law School (J.D., 2003). Phi Beta Kappa; Echols Scholar; Hamilton Fellow; Harlan Fiske Stone Scholar. Staff, Columbia Business Law Review. Recipient, Lewis M. Hammond Award. Law Clerk, Honorable Lawrence E. Kahn, United States District Court, Northern District of New York, 2003-2004. ***PRACTICE AREAS:*** Litigation. ***Email:*** jnacca@novackandmacey.com

VINCENT M. ROCHE, born Yankton, South Dakota, September 7, 1977; admitted to bar, 2003, Illinois and U.S. District Court, Northern and Central Districts of Illinois. *Education:* Augustana College (B.A., 2000); University of Virginia (J.D., 2003). Order of the Coif; John M. Olin Law and Economics Fellow. Member, University of Virginia Law Review. Author: "Bashing the Corporate Shield: The Untenable Evisceration of Freedom of Contract in the Corporate Context," 28 J. Corp. L. 289, 2003; "Road Hunting Shot Down: Reflecting on the South Dakota Supreme Court's Opinion in State v. Rumpca," 7 Great Plains Nat. Resources J. 31, 2003. ***PRACTICE AREAS:*** Litigation. ***Email:*** vroche@novackandmacey.com

ALISON TALBERT SCHWARTZ, born Chicago, Illinois, November 12, 1974; admitted to bar, 1999, Illinois and U.S. District Court, Northern District of Illinois. *Education:* University of Illinois (B.A., 1996; J.D., magna cum laude, 1999). Member, Elder Law Journal, University of Illinois College of Law, 1997-1999, Legal Research and Writing Honors Distinction. Judicial Extern for Judge Ruben Castillo, U.S. District Court for the Northern District of Illinois, 1997. *Member:* Chicago Bar Association. ***PRACTICE AREAS:*** Litigation. ***Email:*** ast@novackandmacey.com

JOHN F. SHONKWILER, born Lansing, Michigan, March 26, 1970; admitted to bar, 1998, Illinois, U.S. District Court, Northern and Central Districts of Illinois, U.S. Court of Appeals, Seventh Circuit. *Education:* University of Michigan (B.A., 1992); University of Illinois (J.D., magna cum laude, 1998). Recipient, CALI Award in International Law, Fall 1996. Topic Editor, University of Illinois Law Review, 1997-1998. Author, "Causes of Action: Trademark Infringement," Illinois Institute for Continuing Legal Education, 2002, 2004; "Recent Decisions Section," Illinois Bar Journal, June 1998. *Member:* American Bar Association. ***PRACTICE AREAS:*** Commercial Litigation. ***Email:*** jfs@novackandmacey.com

LOUIS C. SZURA, born Rochester Hills, Michigan, February 2, 1976; admitted to bar, 2003, Ohio; 2004, Illinois. *Education:* University of Michigan at Ann Arbor (B.A., Political Science, 1998); Cornell University Law School (J.D., 2003). *Member:* Chicago and Illinois State Bar Associations. ***PRACTICE AREAS:*** Commercial Litigation. ***Email:*** lszura@novackandmacey.com

COURTNEY DOUGLASS TEDROWE, born Hinsdale, Illinois, June 23, 1970; admitted to bar, 2001, New York; 2002, Illinois. *Education:* Vassar College (B.A., 1992); Boston University (M.A., 1997); Cornell University (J.D., 2000). Recipient, Herbert Reif Prize. Editor, Cornell Law Review, 1999-2000. Judicial Extern, Hon. Stanley Sporkin, U.S. District Court, District of Columbia, 1999. Author, "Conceptual Severance and Takings in the Federal Circuit," 85 Cornell L. Rev. 586, 2000.*Member:* New York State and American Bar Associations. ***PRACTICE AREAS:*** Civil Litigation; Commercial Litigation. ***Email:*** cdt@novackandmacey.com

REPRESENTATIVE CLIENTS: Abbott Laboratories, Inc.; Activision, Inc.; American Honda Motor Co., Inc.; ANGUS Chemical Company; ATC/Vancom, Inc.; Checker Taxi Association, Inc.; Constellation Power Source Inc.; Exxon-Mobile Corporation; Equity Financial Group; Foot Locker Inc.; Home Depot U.S.A., Inc.; Hyatt Corporation; Hyatt Hotels Corporation; Jupiter Reality Corp.; Jupiter Brokerage Services, Inc.; Kohler Co.; The Lurie Company; The Marmon Group; McDonald's Corporation; Mirant Corporation; National Tax Credit Partners; OurHouse.com; Outboard Marine Corp.; Pritzker Family Members; Prudential Insurance Co. of America; Philip Rootberg; Shields Enterprises, Inc.; Time-Life Libraries, Inc.; Time Consumer Marketing, Inc.; TJX Companies; Tyson Foods, Inc.; Trans-Canada Pipelines; Sam Zell; Yahoo! Inc.

LAW OFFICES OF NEAL R. NOVAK LTD.

33 NORTH LASALLE STREET, SUITE 1900
CHICAGO, ILLINOIS 60602
Telephone: 312-425-2500
Fax: 312-425-2525
Email: novak@novakjuris.com
URL: http://www.lawyers.com/nealnovak

Insurance Coverage and Defense, Reinsurance and Fidelity/Crime Coverage Matters.

NEAL R. NOVAK, born Cincinnati, Ohio, March 13, 1951; admitted to bar, 1977, Ohio; 1978, U.S. District Court, Southern District of Ohio; 1980, Illinois and U.S. District Court, Northern District of Illinois including Trial Bar; 1992, Hawaii. *Education:* University of Cincinnati (B.A., 1973; J.D., 1977). *Member:* Hawaii State and American (Tort and Insurance Practice Section/Fidelity Surety Committee) Bar Associations. ***Email:*** novak@novakjuris.com

KAREN ANDERSEN MORAN, born Chicago, Illinois, November 20, 1966; admitted to bar, 1992, Minnesota; 1994, Illinois and U.S. District Court, District of Minnesota. *Education:* University of Illinois (B.S., with honors, 1988; J.D., cum laude, 1992). Law Clerk to The Honorable Robert Schumacher, Minnesota Court of Appeals, 1993-1995. *Member:* Chicago and American Bar Associations. ***Email:*** moran@novakjuris.com

REID J. ROZEN, born Chicago Heights, Illinois, December 7, 1960; admitted to bar, 1988, Illinois; 1989, U.S. District Court, Northern District of Illinois. *Education:* Illinois Wesleyan University (B.A., magna cum laude, 1983); Vanderbilt University; University of Michigan (J.D., 1988). ***LANGUAGES:*** German and French. ***Email:*** rozen@novakjuris.com

JULIA M. CORE, born Pittsburgh, Pennsylvania, April 15, 1956; admitted to bar, 1983, Louisiana; 1986, Illinois; U.S. District Court, Eastern, Western and Middle Districts of Louisiana and Northern District of Illinois. *Education:* Augustana College (B.A., 1978); Tulane University of Louisiana (J.D., cum laude, 1983).

LAURA E. PRYST, born Evanston, Illinois, December 14, 1974; admitted to bar, 2001, Illinois and U.S. District Court, Northern District of Illinois. *Education:* University of Iowa, Iowa City (B.A., 1997; J.D., 2000). ***Email:*** pryst@novakjuris.com

NOVOSELSKY LAW OFFICES

120 NORTH LA SALLE STREET, SUITE 1400
CHICAGO, ILLINOIS 60602-2401
Telephone: 312-346-8930
Fax: 312-346-9453
Email: mail@novoselsky.com
URL: http://www.novoselsky.com

General Civil Trial and Appellate Practice. Probate, Class Actions and Civil Rights Litigation.

MEMBER OF FIRM

DAVID A. NOVOSELSKY, born Chicago, Illinois, November 2, 1947; admitted to bar, 1973, Illinois, U.S. District Court, Northern District of Illinois and U.S. Court of Appeals, Seventh Circuit; 1978, U.S. Supreme Court. *Education:* Loyola University (A.B., 1969; J.D., 1973). Participant, National Moot Court Competition, 1972. Editor, Appellate Practice Handbook, Illinois Appellate Lawyers Association, 1977-1982. Author: "Basic Illinois Civil Practice," "Grounds for Reversal" and "Oral Argument," Illinois Civil Practice After Trial, 1980 and 1984 editions. Law Clerk to the Honorable Thaddeus V. Adesko, Justice, Illinois Appellate Court, 1973-1975. *Member:* Chicago, Illinois State and American Bar Associations; Illinois Trial Lawyers Association; Appellate Lawyers Association (President, 1984-1985). ***PRACTICE AREAS:*** Civil; Appellate; Class Actions; Civil Rights; Probate. ***Email:*** dnovoselsky@novoselsky.com

ASSOCIATES

LESLIE J. ROSEN, born March 31, 1953; admitted to bar, 1981, Massachusetts; 1982, Illinois and U.S. District Court, District of Massachusetts; 1985, U.S. District Court, Northern District of Illinois; 1993, U.S. Court of Appeals, Seventh Circuit; 1996, U.S. Court of Appeals, Eighth and Ninth Circuits. *Education:* University of Illinois, Urbana (B.A., 1974); Boston University (M.Ed., 1975); Northeastern University (J.D., 1981). Assistant Attorney General for the State of Illinois, Civil Appeals Division, 1982-1984. *Member:* Chicago Bar Association; Illinois Appellate Lawyers' Association. ***PRACTICE AREAS:*** Appellate Practice. ***Email:*** lrosen@novoselsky.com

JEFFREY M. BROWN, born Chicago, Illinois, February 1, 1959; admitted to bar, 1986, Illinois and U.S. District Court, Northern District of Illinois. *Education:* Hampshire College; Loyola University (J.D., 1986). ***PRACTICE AREAS:*** Catastrophic Injury; Commercial Litigation; Civil Rights. ***Email:*** jbrown@novoselsky.com

OF COUNSEL

LINDA A. BRYCELAND, born Brooklyn, New York, September 25, 1954; admitted to bar, 1986, Illinois and U.S. District Court, Northern District of Illinois. *Education:* University of Illinois (B.A., with distinction in History, 1977; M.A., 1979); DePaul University (J.D., 1986). Editor, DePaul Law Review, 1985-1986. *Member:* Chicago, Illinois State and American Bar Associations; Illinois Trial Lawyers Association. ***PRACTICE AREAS:*** Civil Trial; Appellate; Probate; Class Actions; Civil Rights Litigation. ***Email:*** lbryceland@novoselsky.com

JAMES J. AYRES, born Chicago, Illinois, November 1954; admitted to bar, 1984, Illinois; U.S. District Court, Northern District of Illinois and U.S. Court of Appeals, Seventh Circuit. *Education:* University of Illinois (B.A, 1980); DePaul University (J.D., 1984). Author: *Law Office Software:An Attorney's Guide to Selection*, John Wiley and Sons, Inc., New York, 1990-1995. Adjunct Professor of Law, DePaul College of Law, 1986-1996. *Member:* Illinois State Bar Association (Chairman, Bench and Bar Section Council, 1998-1999). (Also practicing individually). ***PRACTICE AREAS:*** Commercial Litigation. ***Email:*** jayres@novoselsky.com

WILLIAM P. OBERHARDT, LLC

2100 THREE FIRST NATIONAL PLAZA
70 WEST MADISON, SUITE 2100
CHICAGO, ILLINOIS 60602
Telephone: 312-251-1100
Fax: 312-251-1175
Email: wpoberhardt@aol.com
URL: http://www.wpoberhardt.com

Intellectual Property including Patents, Trademarks, Copyrights, Trade Secrets, and Unfair Competition, Litigation, Prosecution, Appeals, Licensing, Technology Transfer, Opinions, and Counseling.

WILLIAM P. OBERHARDT, born Chicago, Illinois, December 12, 1952; admitted to bar, 1978, Illinois, U.S. District Court, Northern District of Illinois including Trial Bar, U.S. Court of Appeals, Seventh and Federal Circuits and U.S. Court of Federal Claims; registered to practice before U.S. Patent and Trademark Office. *Education:* University of Notre Dame (B.S.M.E., with honors, 1975); DePaul University (J.D., 1978). Pi Tau Sigma. Assistant Attorney General, Consumer Fraud and Protection Division, 1978-1984. *Member:* Chicago, Federal Circuit and American Bar Associations; American Intellectual Property Law Association; Intellectual Property Law Association of Chicago.

(This Listing Continued)

DIANE DANZY ODELL
ATTORNEY AT LAW, P.C.

70 WEST MADISON STREET, SUITE 1400
CHICAGO, ILLINOIS 60602
Telephone: 773-624-9828
Fax: 773-624-0790
Email: odelldia@ameritech.net
URL: http://www.dianeodelllaw.com

Residential and Commercial Real Estate, Buying and Selling, Leasing, Real Estate Transactions, Housing Code Violations, Landlord/Tenant, Evictions, Disabled Estates, Guardianship.

DIANE DANZY ODELL, born 1952; admitted to bar, 1994, Illinois and U.S. District Court, Northern District of Illinois. *Education:* Governors State University (B.S., 1982; M.S., 1984); Chicago-Kent College of Law, Illinois Institute of Technology (J.D., 1993). *Member:* Chicago Bar Association.

OGLETREE, DEAKINS, NASH, SMOAK & STEWART, P.C.

TWENTY-FIFTH FLOOR
TWO FIRST NATIONAL PLAZA
20 SOUTH CLARK STREET
CHICAGO, ILLINOIS 60603-1891
Telephone: 312-558-1220
Telecopier: 312-807-3619
Email: clientservices@ogletreedeakins.com
URL: http://www.ogletreedeakins.com

Atlanta, Georgia Office: 600 Peachtree Street, N.E., Suite 2100. Telephone: 404-881-1300.
Austin, Texas Office: 301 Congress Avenue, Suite 1250. Telephone: 512-344-4700.
Birmingham, Alabama Office: One Federal Place, Suite 1000, 1819 Fifth Avenue North. Telephone: 205-328-1900.
Charleston, South Carolina Office: 134 Meeting Street, Suite 160, P.O. Box 1808. Telephone: 843-853-1300.
Charlotte, North Carolina Office: 400 West Trade Street. Telephone: 704-342-2588.
Columbia, South Carolina Office: 1320 Main Street, Suite 600. Telephone: 803-252-1300.
Dallas, Texas Office: 700 Preston Commons, 8117 Preston Road. Telephone: 214-987-3800.
Greensboro, North Carolina Office: 2725 Horse Pen Creek Road, Suite 101. Telephone: 336-375-9737.
Greenville, South Carolina Office: The Ogletree Building, 300 North Main Street, P.O. Box 2757. Telephone: 864-271-1300.
Houston, Texas Office: One Allen Center, 500 Dallas Street, Suite 3000. Telephone: 713-655-0855.
Kansas City, Missouri Office: 4717 Grand Avenue, Suite 300. Telephone: 816-471-1301.
Los Angeles, California Office: 633 West Fifth Street, Suite 5300. Telephone: 213-239-9800.
Indianapolis, Indiana Office: Suite 4600, 111 Monument Circle. Telephone: 317-916-1300.
Miami, Florida Office: 80 S.W. 8th Street, Suite 1830. Telephone: 305-374-0506.
Morristown, New Jersey Office: 10 Madison Avenue, Suite 402. Telephone: 973-656-1600.
Nashville, Tennessee Office: SunTrust Center, Suite 800, 424 Church Street. Telephone: 615-254-1900.
Phoenix, Arizona Office: 2415 East Camelback Road, Suite 800. Telephone: 602-778-3700.
Raleigh, North Carolina Office: 2301 Sugar Bush Road, Suite 600, P.O. Box 31608. Telephone: 919-787-9700.
San Antonio, Texas Office: 2600 Weston Centre, 112 East Pecan Street. Telephone: 210-354-1300.
St. Thomas, U.S. Virgin Islands Office: The Tunick Building, 1336 Beltjen Road, Suite 202. Telephone: 340-714-1235.
Tampa, Florida Office: 100 North Tampa Street, Suite 3600. Telephone: 813-289-1247.
Washington, D.C. Office: Fifth Floor, 2400 N Street, N.W. Telephone: 202-887-0855.

Labor Relations, Employment Litigation, Workers' Compensation. Civil Litigation in all State and Federal Courts and Administrative Agencies.

CHARLES E. MURPHY, born Stamford, Connecticut, June 23, 1942; admitted to bar, 1967, Illinois; 1973, Hawaii; 1977, California; U.S. Court of Appeals, 3rd, 7th, 9th and District of Columbia Circuits and U.S. Supreme Court. *Education:* Tulane University of Louisiana (B.S., 1964, Omicron Delta Kappa); University of Chicago (J.D., 1967). Trial Attorney, National Labor Relations Board, 1967-1971. Regional Labor Counsel, U.S. Postal Service, 1971-1973. Executive Committee and Past Chairman, AGC Labor and Employment Lawyers Council. *Member:* State Bar of California; Hawaii State and American Bar Associations. ***PRACTICE AREAS:*** Labor Law; Construction Labor Law; Collective Bargaining. ***Email:*** charles.murphy@ogletreedeakins.com

ARTHUR B. SMITH JR., born Abilene, Texas, September 11, 1944; admitted to bar, 1969, Illinois; 1976, New York; U.S. Supreme Court; U.S. Court of Appeals, 2nd, 5th, 6th, 7th, 11th and District of Columbia Circuits. *Education:* Cornell University (B.S., 1966); University of Chicago (J.D., 1969). Phi Eta Sigma; Phi Kappa Phi. Assistant Professor of Industrial and Labor Relations Law, Cornell University, 1975-1977. Co-Author: "Employment Discrimination Law, Cases and Materials," Lexis Law Publishing, 2000 and 2004 Supplement. Author: "Construction Labor Relations," Commerce Clearing House, 1984, 1993. Assistant Editor: "The Developing Labor Law," Section of Labor and Employment Law, American Bar Association, 4th Ed. 2000 and 2003 Supplement. Fellow: College of Labor Law and Employment Lawyers. Listed in The Best Lawyers in America and in Illinois Super Lawyers. *Member:* New York State and American (Co-Chairman, Committee on

(This Listing Continued)

Development of the Law Under the National Labor Relations Act, Section of Labor and Employment Law, 1976-1977) Bar Associations. College of Labor and Employment Lawyers. ***PRACTICE AREAS:*** Labor and Employment; Civil Rights; Legal Ethics; Professional Responsibility; Litigation. ***Email:*** arthur.smith@ogletreedeakins.com

ROBERT P. CASEY, born Northbridge, Massachusetts, May 28, 1951; admitted to bar, 1976, Illinois; U.S. Supreme Court; U.S. Court of Appeals, 7th, 10th, 11th and District of Columbia Circuits. *Education:* St. Anselm's College (B.A., summa cum laude, 1973); DePaul University (J.D., summa cum laude, 1976). Author: "Selected Age, Sex, and Disability Discrimination Issues in Employee Benefits," Chapter 27, Illinois Institute of Continuing Legal Education, Employee Benefits Law Handbook, 1994 and supp. 1997; "Labor Relations," Chapter 19, Construction Law (Matthew Bender). *Member:* American Bar Association. ***PRACTICE AREAS:*** Labor and Employment; Employee Benefits; ERISA Litigation. ***Email:*** robert.casey@ogletreedeakins.com

RICHARD L. SAMSON, born Chicago, Illinois, July 2, 1960; admitted to bar, 1985, Illinois, U.S. Court of Appeals, 7th Circuit. *Education:* University of Illinois (B.A., 1982); Illinois Institute of Technology-Chicago Kent College of Law (J.D., 1985). Co-Author: "Drug Testing of Public Employees: A Management Perspective," Journal of Law and Education, Vol. 17, No. 4, 703-716, Fall 1988. Contributing Editor, The Developing Labor Law, 1988-1992. Adjunct Professor of Law, Illinois Institute of Technology-Chicago Kent College of Law, 1994-1998. *Member:* Chicago and American Bar Associations. ***PRACTICE AREAS:*** Labor Law; Employment Law. ***Email:*** richard.samson@ogletreedeakins.com

CAROL A. POPLAWSKI, born Arlington Heights, Illinois, May 31, 1960; admitted to bar, 1986, Illinois; 1993, U.S. Court of Appeals, 7th Circuit. *Education:* University of Illinois (B.S., 1982); DePaul University (J.D., 1986). Member, DePaul Law Review, 1983-1984. *Member:* Illinois State and American (Member, Equal Employment Opportunity Committee, Labor and Employment Law Section, EEOC Liaison Committee) Bar Associations. ***PRACTICE AREAS:*** Employment Law; Labor Law; Civil Litigation. ***Email:*** carol.poplawski@ogletreedeakins.com

TRACEY L. TRUESDALE, born Fayetteville, North Carolina, August 17, 1967; admitted to bar, 1991, Illinois; 1996, U.S. Court of Appeals, Seventh Circuit; 1998, U.S. Court of Appeals, Fourth Circuit; 2005, U.S. Supreme Court. *Education:* Mundelein College (B.A., summa cum laude, 1988); IIT Chicago-Kent College of Law (J.D., with honors, 1991). Managing Editor, 1990-1991 and Member, 1989-1990, Law Review. Co-Author: "Pleadings, Discovery, and Settlement: Checklists and Forms," Employment Termination Practice Handbook, Chapter 17 (1994), Illinois Institute For Continuing Legal Education. *Member:* Chicago and American Bar Associations. ***PRACTICE AREAS:*** Labor Law; Employment Law. ***Email:*** tracey.truesdale@ogletreedeakins.com

RANDOLPH E. RUFF, born Denver, Colorado, October 16, 1958; admitted to bar, 1986, Illinois; U.S. District Court, Northern District of Illinois. *Education:* University of Colorado (B.A., 1981); Valparaiso University (J.D., 1986). Phi Alpha Delta. Articles Editor, Valparaiso University Law Review, 1985-1986. Co-Author: "Lender Liability," in Advising Illinois Financial Institutions, IICLE, 1993. Author: "Navigation Servitude: Post-Kaiser-Aetna Confusion," 20 Val. U.L. Rev. (1986). *Member:* Chicago (Chair, Construction and Mechanics Lien Subcommittee), Illinois State and American (Member, Forum on the Construction Industry) Bar Associations; Society of Illinois Construction Attorneys; Leading Lawyer's Network. ***PRACTICE AREAS:*** Construction Law and Litigation. ***Email:*** randolph.ruff@ogletreedeakins.com

THOMAS VASILJEVICH, born Chicago, Illinois, November 8, 1957; admitted to bar, 1982, Illinois; 1983, U.S. District Court, Northern District of Illinois; 1991, U.S. Tax Court. *Education:* University of Wisconsin, Madison (B.A., Economics, 1979); DePaul University College of Law (J.D., 1982); IIT - Chicago Kent College of Law (LL.M., Taxation, 1987). *Member:* Chicago (Member, Federal Tax and Employee Benefits Committees) and Illinois State (Vice Chair, Federal Taxation Section Council, 2005-2006; Former Chair, Employee Benefits Section Council, 1996-1997) and American (Member, Sections of Federal Tax, RPPTL and Labor and Employment) Bar Associations; International Foundation of Employee Benefit Plans; AGC Labor and Employment Law Council. ***PRACTICE AREAS:*** Employee Benefits; ERISA; Tax-Exempt Organizations; Healthcare Law; Multi-Employer Benefits; Executive Compensation. ***Email:*** thomas.vasiljevich@ogletreedeakins.com

MARGERY NEWMAN, born Brooklyn, New York; admitted to bar, 1983, Illinois and U.S. District Court, Northern District of Illinois; 1987, U.S. Court of Appeals, Seventh Circuit. *Education:* Brooklyn College (B.A., 1969); Roosevelt University (M.A., 1973); John Marshall Law School (J.D., with high distinction, 1983). Executive Director and Corporate Counsel, Federation of Women Contractors, 1988-2003. Member: American Subcontractors Association, 1986—; Association of Subcontractors and Affiliates, 1999— (Co-Chair, Government Relations Committee and Member, Professional Council); Lake County Contractors Association, 1999— (Government Relations and Education Committees); Chicago Real Estate Women, 2001—; Underground Contractors Association (Education Committee); Chairperson, National Public Relations, Women Construction Owners and Executives, U.S.A., Illinois Chapter, 1988-1992. Past Director, O'Hare Suburban Chapter, National Association of Women in Construction, 1990-1994. *Member:* Chicago (Member, 1986— and Chair, 1995-1997, Subcommittee on Mechanics' Liens), Illinois State (Section Council, Real Estate Law 2002—) and American (Member: Forum on the Construction Industry, 1990—; Committee on Construction Litigation, 2002—) Bar Associations. ***PRACTICE AREAS:*** Construction Law; Civil Litigation. ***Email:*** margery.newman@ogletreedeakins.com

MICHAEL H. CRAMER, admitted to bar, 1988, Illinois; U.S. District Court, Northern and Central Districts of Illinois; U.S. Court of Appeals, Seventh Circuit. *Education:* University of Michigan (B.A., with distinction, 1985; J.D., 1988). Named: Illinois Super Lawyer; 40 Illinois Attorneys Under 40 To Watch (Law Bulleting Publishing Company), 2003. President, 2004-2005 and Member, Board of Directors, CARPLS, Cook County's Legal Aid Hotline. President, 2003-2004, and Member, Board of Directors, Around The Coyote Arts Festival. Author: "Defending Wage and Hour Litigation" (Illinois Institute of Continuing Legal Education Annual Employment Law Update & Workshop, 2005). Co-author: "You Want What?! A Hands-on Guide to E-Discovery and Attorney-Client Communications" (Navigant Consulting Roundtable, 2005); "Anonymity, Immunity and Online Defamation: Managing Corporate Exposure to Reputation Injury" (The Sedona Confer-

(This Listing Continued)

ence Journal, Fall 2003). *Member:* American Bar Association (Member, Sections on: Litigation; Labor and Employment Law); Illinois Institute for Continuing Legal Education (Member, Labor and Employment Law Advisory Committee). ***REPORTED CASES:*** Spencer v. Illinois Community Action Association, 164 F.Supp.2d 1056 (C.D.Ill. 2001), aff'd., 51Fed. Appx. 973 (7th Cir. 2002); Nelson v. JC Penney Co., Inc., 75 F.3d 343 (8th Cir. 1996); Allen v. Quaker Oats Co., 1999 WL 787613 (N.D.Ill.,1999); Jones v. Sabis Educational Systems, Inc., 52 F.Supp.2d 868 (N.D.Ill. 1999); Cagle v. K-Five Construction Co., 954 F.Supp. 1267 (N.D.Ill. 1997). ***PRACTICE AREAS:*** Employment Litigation; Employment Law; Labor Law. ***Email:*** michael.cramer@ogletreedeakins.com

MICHAEL D. RAY, born Richmond, Virginia; admitted to bar, 2004, Pennsylvania and New Jersey; 2005, Illinois. *Education:* College of Wooster (B.A., cum laude, 2001); Indiana University-Bloomington (J.D., cum laude, 2004). Order of the Barristers. Articles Editor, Indiana Law Journal. Sherman Moot Court Champion. Author: "The Definition of 'Employee' in American Labor & Employment Law," (with K. Dau-Schmidt), in *Labour Law In Motion: Diversification of the Labour Force & Terms and Conditions of Employment* (Roger Blanpain, et al., Eds.), Hague: Kluwer Law International, 2005. ***PRACTICE AREAS:*** Labor and Employment. ***Email:*** michael.ray@ogletreedeakins.com

OF COUNSEL

GAYLE M. MEADORS, born Chicago, Illinois, September 13, 1946; admitted to bar, 1977, Illinois. *Education:* University of Illinois (A.B., in English, with honors, 1969); University of Chicago (M.A., in Lib. Sc., 1973); DePaul University (J.D., magna cum laude, 1977). Phi Beta Kappa. Author: Compensation and Benefits Briefs, Journal of Medical Practice Management. *Member:* Chicago and Illinois State Bar Associations. (Also Practicing Individually at Chicago, Illinois). ***LANGUAGES:*** French and German. ***PRACTICE AREAS:*** Employee Benefits; Employment Law. ***Email:*** gayle.meadors@ogletreedeakins.com

MATTHEW J. STRAUB, born St. Joseph, Michigan, October 17, 1974; admitted to bar, 2000, Illinois. *Education:* University of Notre Dame (B.A., cum laude, 1997); Case Western Reserve University School of Law (J.D., 2000). Contributing Author, Employment Law Section, Illinois Defense Counsel Quarterly. *Member:* Chicago and American Bar Associations. ***PRACTICE AREAS:*** Construction Litigation; Commercial Litigation. ***Email:*** matthew.straub@ogletreedeakins.com

JULIA A. DONNELLY, born Chicago, Illinois; admitted to bar, 1990, Illinois. *Education:* Marquette University (B.A., cum laude, 1984); Northern Illinois University (J.D., magna cum laude, 1990). Student Works Editor, Northern Illinois University Law Review. Co-author, Workers' Compensation in Illinois, Illinois State Chamber of Commerce, 1995. ***PRACTICE AREAS:*** Workers Compensation; ERISA. ***Email:*** julie.donnelly@ogletreedeakins.com

NANCY ANN CASE, born Chicago, Illinois; admitted to bar, 2002, Illinois. *Education:* University of North Florida (B.A., Literature and Communications, 1991); Chicago-Kent College of Law, Illinois Institute of Technology (J.D., 2000). *Member:* Chicago and Illinois State Bar Associations. ***REPORTED CASES:*** Santanna Natural Gas Corporation v. Wermers Floorcovering, 2003 WL 21783707 Ill. App. 2 Dist. ***PRACTICE AREAS:*** Subrogation; Litigation; Family Law. ***Email:*** nancy.case@ogletreedeakins.com

KAREN N. BRANDON, born Atlanta, Georgia, April 10, 1965; admitted to bar, 2000, Maryland; 2001, District of Columbia; 2002, Illinois. *Education:* Western Connecticut State University (B.S., magna cum laude, 1987); University of District of Columbia (M.B.A., summa cum laude, 1992); American University (J.D., 1999). Contributing Author, *Employee Benefits Law,* BNA 2003. *Member:* Chicago, Illinois State, Maryland State and American Bar Associations; District of Columbia Bar. ***PRACTICE AREAS:*** Employee Benefits. ***Email:*** karen.brandon@ogletreedeakins.com

MICHAEL R. CANNON, born Del Rio, Texas, November 20, 1969; admitted to bar, 2000, Illinois; U.S. District Court, Northern District of Illinois. *Education:* University of Texas (B.A., 1994); Loyola University (J.D., 2000). Corboy Fellowship. LEED Accredited Professional, 2000. *Member:* Chicago, Illinois State and American (Member, Forum on the Construction Industry) Bar Associations. ***PRACTICE AREAS:*** Construction Transactions; Construction Litigation. ***Email:*** michael.cannon@ogletreedeakins.com

REPRESENTATIVE CLIENTS: AGC Builders Association (Chicago); AGC Michigan; AGC Wisconsin; AGC Minnesota; AM General Corporation; Arch Technology Corp.; Boller Construction Co.; Capitol Construction Group, Inc.; Caremark, Inc.; Ceco Concrete Construction LLC; Central Illinois Builders AGC; CH2M Hill Constructors, Inc.; Chicago Bricklayers Employee Benefit Funds; Chicago Laborers Pension & Welfare Funds; Chicago Roofers Employee Benefit Funds; Commonwealth Edison Company; ConAgra; Crown Construction Enterprises, Inc.; Dynamic Health Care; Electrical Insurance Trustees Employee Benefit Funds; Elkay Manufacturing Company; Exelon Corp.; Fluor Maintenance Services, Inc.; Ford Motor; GE Consumer Finance; Genworth Financial, Inc.; Graycor, Inc. Greif Containers; Home Depot; Honeywell; Ispat Inland, a division of Mittal Steel Company; James McHugh Construction Co.; Lutheran Home & Services; Mariner; Material Service Corp.; MB Financial; McShane Construction Co.; Meyer Material Company; Mid-America Regional Bargaining Association; Nationwide Fixture Installers, Inc.; NISource; Northern Indiana Public Service Company; Ozinga Bros., Inc.; Pella Windows & Doors, Inc.; NTN Bearing Corp.; Pepper Construction Co.; SBC; SBC-Ameritech; Turner Construction Co.; Tyco Industries; Whiteco, Inc.; Wyndham International.

O'HAGAN, SMITH & AMUNDSEN

150 NORTH MICHIGAN AVENUE, SUITE 3300
CHICAGO, ILLINOIS 60601
Telephone: 312-894-3200
Fax: 312-894-3210
Email: choffice@osalaw.com
URL: http://www.osalaw.com

Rockford, Illinois Office: Stewart Square, 308 West State Street, Suite 320, 61101-1140. Telephone: 815-987-0441. Fax: 815-987-9891.

St. Charles, Illinois Office: 3815 E. Main Street, Suite A-1, 60174-2488. Telephone: 630-587-7910. Fax: 630-587-7960.

(This Listing Continued)

Waukegan, Illinois Office: 415 West Washington Street, Suite 204, 60079-0410. Telephone: 847-599-9503. Fax: 847-599-9525.

Woodstock, Illinois Office: 666 Russell Court, 60098. Telephone: 815-337-4900. Fax: 815-337-4910.

Milwaukee, Wisconsin Office: 4811 South 76th Street, Suite 305, 53220. Telephone: 414-282-7103. Fax: 414-282-1830.

Commercial; Commercial Transportation; Appellate; Complex Litigation; Construction; Corporate Transactions; Employment; Extra-Contractual/Insurance Litigation; Healthcare; Insurance Coverage; Personal Lines; Product Liability; Professional Liability; Property Litigation.

MEMBERS OF FIRM

GLEN E. AMUNDSEN, admitted to bar, 1980, Illinois. *Education:* Augustana College (B.A., cum laude, 1977); Chicago-Kent College of Law (J.D., with high honors, 1980). Phi Beta Kappa. *Member:* Lake County, Illinois State and American Bar Associations; Trial Lawyers Club of Chicago; Illinois Association of Defense Trial Counsel (Member, Board of Directors); Defense Research Institute. ***PRACTICE AREAS:*** Litigation; Premises Liability; Insurance Bad Faith; Insurance Coverage; Toxic Torts; Product Liability. ***Email:*** gamundsen@osalaw.com

JAMES P. BALOG, admitted to bar, 1983, Illinois and U.S. District Court, Northern District of Illinois. *Education:* University of Illinois (B.S., 1978); The John Marshall Law School (J.D., with distinction, 1983). *Member:* Chicago, Illinois State and American Bar Associations; Illinois Association of Defense Trial Counsel; Illinois Defense Counsel; The Trial Lawyer's Club of Chicago; Illinois Trial Lawyers Association. ***PRACTICE AREAS:*** Litigation; Premises Liability; Construction; Products Liability. ***Email:*** jbalog@osalaw.com

BENJAMIN A. BLUME, admitted to bar, 1989, Illinois; 1990, U.S. District Court, Northern District of Illinois; 1991, U.S. Court of Appeals, Seventh Circuit. *Education:* Knox College (B.A., 1985); Loyola University, Chicago (J.D., 1989). ***PRACTICE AREAS:*** Insurance Coverage; Toxic Torts; Environmental Law; Mass Torts; Construction; Products Liability; Commercial Transportation. ***Email:*** bblume@osalaw.com

LEW R.C. BRICKER, admitted to bar, 1991, Illinois and U.S. District Court, Northern District of Illinois. *Education:* University of Illinois (B.A., cum laude, with distinction in history, 1988; J.D., cum laude, 1991). *Member:* Chicago, Illinois State and American Bar Associations. ***PRACTICE AREAS:*** Litigation; Product Liability; Insurance; Transportation Litigation; Transportation Regulation. ***Email:*** lbricker@osalaw.com

PATRICK B. CAGE, admitted to bar, 1984, Illinois. *Education:* Illinois State University (B.S., 1981); Ohio Northern University (J.D., 1984). ***PRACTICE AREAS:*** Medical Malpractice. ***Email:*** pcage@osalaw.com

CRAIG A. CAPPAS, admitted to bar, 1993, Illinois. *Education:* University of Michigan (B.A., 1988); John Marshall Law School (J.D., 1993). Member, John Marshall Law Review. ***PRACTICE AREAS:*** Insurance Defense. ***Email:*** ccappas@osalaw.com

GERALD V. CLEARY, III, admitted to bar, 1989, Illinois. *Education:* University of Illinois (B.A., 1986); Loyola University School of Law (J.D., 1989). ***PRACTICE AREAS:*** Litigation; Automobile; Employment; Premises Liability; Products Liability; Aviation Liability. ***Email:*** gcleary@osalaw.com

CARMEL M. COSGRAVE, admitted to bar, 1980, Illinois. *Education:* Roosevelt University (B.A., with honors, 1977); Loyola University (J.D., with honors, 1980). Instructor, Loyola Law School, National Institute of Trial Advocacy. *Member:* Chicago, Illinois State and American Bar Associations; Trial Lawyers Club of Chicago; Illinois Defense Trial Counsel. ***PRACTICE AREAS:*** Litigation; Medical Malpractice; Employment. ***Email:*** ccosgrave@osalaw.com

DENNIS J. COTTER, admitted to bar, 1985, Illinois. *Education:* University of Notre Dame (B.B.A., 1981); DePaul University (J.D., 1985). *Member:* Chicago, Lake County, Winnebago County, Illinois State and American Bar Associations; The Association of Trial Lawyers of America. ***PRACTICE AREAS:*** Litigation; Professional Negligence; Commercial Defense; Insurance Defense. ***Email:*** dcotter@osalaw.com

RONALD L. DROZDZIK, admitted to bar, 1975, Illinois and U.S. District Court, Northern District of Illinois including Trial Bar; 1979, U.S. Court of Appeals, Seventh Circuit. *Education:* Knox College (B.A., 1968); IIT/Chicago-Kent College of Law (J.D., 1975). ***PRACTICE AREAS:*** Personal Injury Defense; Workers' Compensation Defense; Retaliatory Discharge Defense; Appellate Practice; Product Liability Defense. ***Email:*** rdrozdzik@osalaw.com

JEROME J. DUCHOWICZ, admitted to bar, 1976, Illinois and U.S. District Court, Northern District of Illinois. *Education:* Northern Illinois University (B.A., 1971); Loyola University of Chicago (J.D., 1976). *Member:* Chicago, Illinois State and American Bar Associations; Maritime Law Association; Illinois Defense Counsel. ***PRACTICE AREAS:*** Insurance Coverage; Trial Practice; Admiralty. ***Email:*** jduchowicz@osalaw.com

TIMOTHY J. FAGAN, admitted to bar, 1989, Illinois. *Education:* Marquette University (B.A., 1986); Loyola University (J.D., 1989). *Member:* Chicago and Illinois State Bar Associations; Illinois Association of Defense Trial Counsel; Defense Research Institute. ***PRACTICE AREAS:*** Litigation; Environmental; Appellate. ***Email:*** tfagan@osalaw.com

THOMAS F. FALKENBERG, admitted to bar, 1990, Illinois. *Education:* University of Notre Dame (B.B.A., 1987; J.D., 1990). **PRACTICE AREAS:** Professional Liability. ***Email:*** tfalkenberg@osalaw.com

JAMES W. FESSLER, admitted to bar, 1988, Illinois; 1990, U.S. District Court, Northern District of Illinois including Trial Bar; 1994, U.S. Court of Appeals, Seventh Circuit; 1995, U.S. District Court, Central District of Illinois. *Education:* University of Illinois/Urbana-Champaign (B.A., 1985); John Marshall Law School (J.D., with distinction, 1988). ***PRACTICE AREAS:*** Litigation; Appellate. ***Email:*** jfessler@osalaw.com

RITA M. FILIAGGI, admitted to bar, 1997, Illinois. *Education:* Washington University at St. Louis; Chicago-Kent College of Law, Illinois Institute of Technology (J.D., 1997). ***Email:*** rfiliaggi@osalaw.com

(This Listing Continued)

O'HAGAN, SMITH & AMUNDSEN, Chicago—Continued

ROSALYN M. GOLDEN, admitted to bar, 1984, Illinois and U.S. District Court, Eastern District of Illinois. *Education:* DePaul University (B.A., 1964); Illinois Institute of Technology/Chicago-Kent College of Law (J.D., with honors, 1984). *Member:* Chicago and Illinois State and American Bar Associations; Illinois Trial Lawyers Association; Illinois Defense Counsel; The Association of Trial Lawyers of America. ***PRACTICE AREAS:*** Personal and Commercial Lines Coverage Litigation. ***Email:*** rgolden@osalaw.com

ANITA SENESE JOHNSON, admitted to bar, 1976, Illinois; 1978, U.S. District Court, Northern District of Illinois including Trial Bar; U.S. Court of Appeals, Seventh Circuit. *Education:* Northwestern University (B.A., cum laude, 1973); DePaul University (J.D., summa cum laude, 1976). ***PRACTICE AREAS:*** Workers' Compensation Defense; Employment Law Defense; Tort Defense. ***Email:*** ajohnson@osalaw.com

ANTHONY G. KARAMUZIS, admitted to bar, 1991, Illinois. *Education:* Loyola University (B.A.,1988); DePaul University College of Law (J.D., 1991). ***Email:*** akaramuzis@osalaw.com

PATRICK KEATING, born Evergreen Park, Illinois, May 4, 1966; admitted to bar, 1992, Illinois, U.S. District Court, Northern District of Illinois, U.S. Court of Appeals, Second, Third, Seventh and Ninth Circuits and U.S. Supreme Court. *Education:* Princeton University (B.A., 1988); University of Notre Dame (J.D., 1992). Notre Dame Law School Scholar. Articles Editor, Notre Dame Journal of Legislation, 1991-1992. Member, St. Francis de Sales High School Governing Board. *Member:* American Bar Association (Member, Sections on: Aviation; Litigation; Tort and Insurance Practice); Traffic Club of Chicago; Regional Airline Association. ***REPORTED CASES:*** Fujitsu Ltd. v. Federal Express Corporation, F.3d, 2001 WL 40312 (2nd Cir. 2001); Hoogwegt U.S. Inc. v. Schenker International, Inc., 121 F. Supp. 2d 1228 (N.D. Ill. 2000)(on rehearing); Carle v. General American Life Insurance Co., 2001 W: 403012 (4th Cir. 1999); Insurance Co. of North America v. Federal Express Corporation, 189 F. 3d 914 (9th Cir. 1999); Byrton Dairy Products v. Harborside Refrigerated Services, 991 F. Supp. 977 (N.D. Ill 1997); Kinfe v. Port Authority of N.Y. & N.J., 232 A.D. 2d 373, 648 N.Y.S. 2d (2nd Dept. 1996). ***PRACTICE AREAS:*** Products Liability; Commercial Carrier Litigation; Cargo Claims; Appellate Practice. ***Email:*** pkeating@osalaw.com

THOMAS J. LYMAN, III, admitted to bar, 1987, Illinois and U.S. District Court, Northern District of Illinois including Trial Bar. *Education:* College of the Holy Cross (B.A., 1980); John Marshall Law School (J.D., 1987). *Member:* Chicago, Illinois State and American Bar Associations; The Association of Trial Lawyers of America. ***PRACTICE AREAS:*** Trial Litigation; Construction; Premises Liability; Product Liability; Automobile Liability; General Liability. ***Email:*** tlyman@osalaw.com

MICHAEL J. McGOWAN, admitted to bar, 1988, Illinois. *Education:* University of Notre Dame (B.A., cum laude, 1983); Loyola University (J.D., 1988). Recipient, American Jurisprudence Awards. Notre Dame Scholar. *Member:* Illinois State and American Bar Associations; Defense Research Institute; Illinois Defense Trial Counsel. ***PRACTICE AREAS:*** Product Liability; Structural Work Act; Premises Liability; Consumer Fraud; Construction Fraud; UCC; Premises. ***Email:*** mmcgowan@osalaw.com

THOMAS A. MEYER, admitted to bar, 1984, Illinois. *Education:* St. Norbert College (B.B.A., 1981); DePaul University (J.D., 1984). Recipient, American Jurisprudence Award for Excellence in Evidence. *Member:* Chicago and Illinois State Bar Associations; Illinois Association of Defense Counsel; Federal Trial Bar. ***PRACTICE AREAS:*** Litigation; Construction; Premises Liability. ***Email:*** tmeyer@osalaw.com

JAMES J. O'HAGAN, admitted to bar, 1963, Illinois. *Education:* DePaul University (B.S.C., 1958; J.D., 1962). Chairman, Suburban Committee, Committee on the Courts for the 21st Century. *Member:* Chicago, Illinois State and American Bar Associations; Illinois Defense Counsel; International Association of Defense Counsel; Defense Research Institute; Trial Lawyers Club of Chicago. ***PRACTICE AREAS:*** Litigation; Products Liability; Environmental; Insurance Coverage. ***Email:*** johagan@osalaw.com

KEVIN M. O'HAGAN, admitted to bar, 1992, Illinois and U.S. District Court, Northern District of Illinois; 1995, Virginia. *Education:* College of the Holy Cross (B.A., 1989); London University; DePaul College of Law (J.D., 1992). *Member:* Illinois State, Virginia and American (Chair Products Liability Yield Subcommittee; Vice Chair, YLD Litigation Committee) Bar Associations; Defense Research Institute; American Corporate Counsel Association. ***PRACTICE AREAS:*** Commercial Law; Transactional; Professional Liability; Securities; Consumer Fraud; Intellectual Property; Construction Contracts; Construction Litigation; Toxic Torts; Products Liability; Multi-District Litigation; Class Actions. ***Email:*** kohagan@osalaw.com

VICTOR J. PIEKARSKI, admitted to bar, 1974, Illinois; 1977, U.S. Court of Appeals, Seventh Circuit; 1978, U.S. Supreme Court. *Education:* Boston College (B.A., cum laude, 1971); University of Chicago (M.B.A., 1978); Northwestern University (J.D., cum laude, 1974). *Member:* American Bar Association; Illinois Association of Defense Trial Counsel; Defense Research Institute. ***PRACTICE AREAS:*** Litigation; Environmental; Coverage; Insurance; Re-Insurance. ***Email:*** vpiekarski@osalaw.com

JILL A. PIGNOTTI, admitted to bar, 1996, Illinois and U.S. District Court, Northern District of Illinois including Trial Bar. *Education:* University of Illinois (B.A., 1993); University of Notre Dame (J.D., 1996). ***Email:*** jpignotti@osalaw.com

MICHAEL RESIS, admitted to bar, 1981, Illinois, U.S. District Court, Northern District of Illinois and Eastern District of Wisconsin, U.S. Court of Appeals, Seventh Circuit and U.S. Supreme Court. *Education:* University of Illinois (B.A., 1978; J.D., 1981). Phi Beta Kappa. Rickert Scholarship Award. Law Clerk to Justice Glenn K. Seidenfeld, Illinois Appellate Court, 1981-1983. *Member:* Chicago, Illinois State and American Bar Associations; Illinois Defense Counsel; Trial Lawyers Club of Chicago; Appellate Lawyers Association. ***PRACTICE AREAS:*** Litigation; Appellate; Insurance Coverage. ***Email:*** mresis@osalaw.com

JULIE P. RUBIN, admitted to bar, 1992, Ohio; 1993, Illinois and U.S. District Court, Northern District of Illinois. *Education:* Colgate University (B.A., cum laude, 1989); Case Western Reserve University (J.D., cum laude, 1992). *Member:* Chicago and American Bar Associations. ***PRACTICE AREAS:*** Litigation; Environmental; Insurance Coverage. ***Email:*** jrubin@osalaw.com

(This Listing Continued)

ERIC L. SAMORE, admitted to bar, 1981, Wisconsin, Illinois and U.S. Court of Appeals, Seventh Circuit. *Education:* University of Wisconsin (B.S., 1978; J.D., 1981). Member, Order of the Coif. Law Clerk to Justice Allen Hartman, Illinois Appellate Court, 1981-1983. *Member:* Chicago and Illinois State Bar Associations; Trial Lawyers Club of Chicago. ***PRACTICE AREAS:*** Litigation; Premises Liability; Construction; Environmental. ***Email:*** esamore@osalaw.com

LARRY A. SCHECHTMAN, admitted to bar, 1983, Illinois and U.S. District Court, Northern District of Illinois. *Education:* Illinois State University (B.S., 1980); Illinois Institute of Technology/Chicago-Kent College of Law (J.D., with highest honors, 1983). *Member:* Chicago (Member, Young Lawyers Section), Illinois State and American Bar Associations; Illinois Association of Defense Trial Counsel; Trial Lawyers Club of Chicago (Director, 1990-1998); Defense Research Institute. ***PRACTICE AREAS:*** Litigation; Automobile; Construction; Premises Liability. ***Email:*** lschechtman@osalaw.com

JAMES S. SMITH, III, admitted to bar, 1990, Illinois. *Education:* Marquette University (B.A., 1986); John Marshall Law School (J.D., 1990). ***Email:*** jsmith@osalaw.com

LAWRENCE R. SMITH, admitted to bar, 1973, Illinois. *Education:* College of the Holy Cross (A.B., cum laude, 1970); University of Michigan (J.D., 1973). *Member:* Illinois State and American Bar Associations; Illinois Association of Defense Trial Counsel (President, 1988-1989); Defense Research Institute; American Law Firm Association (Board of Directors, 1994-1996). ***PRACTICE AREAS:*** Litigation; Automobile; Construction; Premises Liability; Products Liability. ***Email:*** lsmith@osalaw.com

MARCIE THORP, admitted to bar, 1994, Illinois. *Education:* University of Illinois (B.S.); Chicago-Kent College of Law (J.D.). ***PRACTICE AREAS:*** Appellate Practice; Complex Litigation. ***Email:*** mthorp@osalaw.com

RICHARD T. VALENTINO, admitted to bar, 1984, Illinois. *Education:* DePaul University (B.A., 1981); John Marshall Law School (J.D., 1984). ***PRACTICE AREAS:*** Insurance Coverage; Construction; Product Liability; Employment; Commercial. ***Email:*** rvalentino@osalaw.com

ALEEN R. TIFFANY, admitted to bar, 1993, Illinois and U.S. District Court, Northern District of Illinois. *Education:* University of Illinois (B.S., Mathematics, 1990); The John Marshall Law School (J.D., cum laude, 1993). *Member:* Chicago, McHenry County, Illinois State and American Bar Associations. ***PRACTICE AREAS:*** Litigation; Automobile Liability; Premises Liability. ***Email:*** atiffany@osalaw.com

ASSOCIATES

CHRISTINE V. ANTO, admitted to bar, 2001, Illinois. *Education:* Marquette University (B.A., 1997); DePaul University (J.D., 2001). ***Email:*** canto@osalaw.com

CYNTHIA L. BESECKER, admitted to bar, 1995, Illinois. *Education:* DePaul University (B.A., 1989; LL.M., 1999); Columbia University School of Social Work (M.S.S.W., 1990); John Marshall Law School (J.D. 1995). ***Email:*** cbesecker@osalaw.com

MOLLY A. CAPREZ, admitted to bar, 2003, Illinois. *Education:* Marquette University (B.A., 1998); University of Wisconsin (J.D., 2003). ***Email:*** macaprez@osalaw.com

JAMES CARONIS, admitted to bar, 1999, Illinois. *Education:* University of Illinois (B.A., 1996); Chicago-Kent College of Law (J.D., 1999). ***Email:*** jcaronis@osalaw.com

DANIEL P. DERECHIN, admitted to bar, 2001, Illinois. *Education:* Franklin & Marshall College (B.A., 1993); Georgetown University Law Center (J.D., 1998). ***Email:*** dpderechin@osalaw.com

ELIZABETH DILLON, admitted to bar, 1995, Illinois and U.S. District Court, Central District of Illinois; 2000, California. *Education:* Michigan State University (B.A., 1989); John Marshall Law School (J.D., 1995). ***Email:*** edillon@osalaw.com

JOSEPH M. EICHBERGER, admitted to bar, 1979, Illinois. *Education:* DePaul University (B.A., 1968); Lewis University (J.D., 1978). ***Email:*** jeichberger@osalaw.com

TIMOTHY LIAM EPSTEIN, admitted to bar, 2004, Illinois. *Education:* Boston College (B.A., 1999); University of Illinois (J.D., 2004). ***Email:*** tepstein@osalaw.com

KRISTINE S. ESTACIO, admitted to bar, 2000, Illinois and U.S. District Court, Northern District of Illinois. *Education:* University of Illinois (B.A., 1996); John Marshall Law School (J.D., 2000). ***Email:*** kestacio@osalaw.com

BRIAN T. FLOOD, admitted to bar, 2000, Illinois. *Education:* University of Wisconsin (B.S., 1997); Syracuse University (J.D., 2000). ***Email:*** bflood@osalaw.com

STEVEN FUOCO, admitted to bar, 1991, Illinois; 1997 U.S. District Court, Northern District of Illinois including Trial Bar. *Education:* Southwestern Oklahoma State University (1982-1984); University of Oklahoma (B.B.A., 1988); University of Tulsa (1988-1989); John Marshall Law School (J.D., 1991). ***Email:*** sfuoco@osalaw.com

FREDERIC C. GOODWILL, II, admitted to bar, 1992, Illinois. *Education:* University of Massachusetts (B.A., 1986); Vermont Law School (J.D., 1990). ***Email:*** fgoodwill@osalaw.com

WILLIAM P. HEFFERNAN, admitted to bar, 1992, Illinois. *Education:* University of Texas at Austin (B.B.S., 1989); St. Mary's University of San Antonio (J.D., 1992). ***Email:*** wheffernan@osalaw.com

KATIE A. IRVINE, admitted to bar, 1997, Illinois. *Education:* Miami University (B.A., 1994); John Marshall Law School (J.D., cum laude, 1997). ***Email:*** kirvine@osalaw.com

RYAN B. JACOBSON, admitted to bar, 1999, Illinois. *Education:* Indiana University at Bloomington (B.A., 1996); Illinois Institute of Technology, Chicago-Kent College of Law (J.D., 1999). ***Email:*** rjacobson@osalaw.com

LESLIE JOHNSON, admitted to bar, 1986, Illinois. *Education:* University of Illinois at Urbana-Champaign (B.A., 1981); Washington University (J.D., 1985); De Paul University (Masters of Law, Taxation, 1991). ***PRACTICE AREAS:*** Workers Compensation. ***Email:*** ljohnson@osalaw.com

CAROLYN KANG, admitted to bar, 2004, Indiana (Not admitted in Illinois). *Education:* Michigan State University (B.A. with honors, 1996); Indiana University School of Law (J.D., 2003). ***Email:*** ckang@osalaw.com

(This Listing Continued)

LISA G. KAUFMAN, admitted to bar, 2001, Illinois. *Education:* Indiana University (B.A., 1997); Brooklyn Law School (J.D., 2001). **Email:** lkaufman@osalaw.com

DAISY KHAMBATTA, admitted to bar, 2001, Texas; 2004, Illinois. *Education:* University of Texas at Austin (B.A, 1996); South Texas College of Law (J.D., 2000). **Email:** dkhambatta@osalaw.com

SOO JIN KIM, admitted to bar, 1998, Illinois. *Education:* Rutgers University (B.A., 1994); Valparaiso University School of Law (J.D., 1998). **Email:** skim@osalaw.com

HEATHER KINGERY, admitted to bar, 2001, Florida; 2004, Illinois. *Education:* Lipscomb University (B.A., 1997); University of Florida (J.D., 2000). **Email:** hkingery@osalaw.com

NICHOLAS G. KOURVETARIS, admitted to bar, 2000, Illinois. *Education:* Northwestern University (B.S., Speech, 1994; M.S., Integrated Marketing Communications, 1996); Chicago-Kent College of Law (J.D., 2000). **Email:** nkourvetaris@osalaw.com

JOHN D. LaBARBERA, admitted to bar, 2001, Illinois. *Education:* University of Illinois at Chicago (B.A., 1991); Chicago-Kent College of Law (J.D., 2001). **Email:** jlabarbera@osalaw.com

INHAK LEE, admitted to bar, 1999, Illinois. *Education:* University of Chicago (B.A., 1995); University of Iowa (J.D., 1999). *Member:* Chicago Bar Association. **Email:** ilee@osalaw.com

KATHERINE LENGIEWICZ, admitted to bar, 1999, Illinois. *Education:* Illinois State University (B.S., 1996); Northern Illinois University (J.D., 1999). **Email:** klengiewicz@salaw.com

RYAN A. MAHONEY, admitted to bar, 2001, Illinois. *Education:* University of Dayton (B.A., magna cum laude, 1998); University of Notre Dame (J.D., 2001). **Email:** rmahoney@osalaw.com

ANN McLELLAN, admitted to bar, 2002, Illinois. *Education:* University of Michigan (B.A., 1999); Northwestern University School of Law (J.D., 2002). **Email:** amclennan@osalaw.com

DANIEL B. MEYER, admitted to bar, 1996, Illinois; Pro Hac Vice: 2000, Pennsylvania. *Education:* Purdue University (B.A., 1992); DePaul University (J.D., 1996). **Email:** dmeyer@osalaw.com

LINDA F. NEWMAN, admitted to bar, 2002, Illinois. *Education:* University of Illinois (B.A.); Loyola University School of Law (M.A.); DePaul University College of Law (J.D., 2002). **Email:** lnewman@osalaw.com

DANIEL J. NOLAN, admitted to bar, 1997, Illinois. *Education:* St. Lawrence University (B.A., 1989); Chicago Kent College of Law (J.D., 1997). ***PRACTICE AREAS:*** Civil Litigation; Insurance Defense. **Email:** dnolan@osalaw.com

LISA M. PAGEL, admitted to bar, 2002, Illinois. *Education:* University of Kansas (B.G.S., 1998); John Marshall Law School (J.D., cum laude, 2002). **Email:** lpagel@osalaw.com

KENNETH PERRY, admitted to bar, 2004, Illinois. *Education:* Illinois Wesleyan University (B.A., 2001); University of Notre Dame (J.D., 2004). **Email:** tepstein@osalaw.com

TANYA PETERMANN, admitted to bar, 2004, Illinois. *Education:* University of Dayton (B.A., cum laude, 1998); John Marshall Law School (J.D. 2004). **Email:** tpetermann@osalaw.com

TROY S. RADUNSKY, admitted to bar, 1999, Illinois and U.S. District Court, Northern District of Illinois. *Education:* Arizona State University (B.A., 1994); John Marshall Law School (J.D., 1999). **Email:** tradunsky@osalaw.com

BRIAN A. ROSENBLATT, admitted to bar, 1997, Illinois and U.S. District Court, Northern District of Illinois. *Education:* Washington University (B.A., Economics, 1991); Chicago-Kent College of Law (J.D., 1997). **Email:** brosenblatt@osalaw.com

ANDREW C. SEIBER, admitted to bar, 1997, Illinois. *Education:* University of Illinois (B.A., 1993); John Marshall Law School (J.D., 1996). **Email:** aseiber@osalaw.com

ELANA K. SEIFERT, admitted to bar, 1998, Illinois. *Education:* Rutgers University (B.A., 1992); Loyola University of Chicago School of Law (J.D., 1997). **Email:** eseifert@osalaw.com

LUKE P. SHERIDAN, admitted to bar, 1992, Illinois. *Education:* University of Notre Dame (B.A., 1989); Loyola University (J.D., 1992). **Email:** lsheridan@osalaw.com

CARRIE A. VON HOFF, admitted to bar, 2003, Illinois. *Education:* Northwestern University; Vanderbilt University (J.D., 2003). **Email:** cvonhoff@osalaw.com

GINGER RAE WILEY, admitted to bar, 1997, Illinois. *Education:* Marshall University (B.A., 1997); Loyola University (J.D., 2001). **Email:** gwiley@osalaw.com

GARY ZHAO, admitted to bar, 2003, Illinois. *Education:* University of Michigan (B.A., 1999); Washington University (J.D., 2002). ***PRACTICE AREAS:*** Appellate Practice. **Email:** gzhao@osalaw.com

(For complete biographical data on other personnel, see Professional Biographies at other cities)

O'HALLORAN, KOSOFF, GEITNER & COOK, P.C.

CHICAGO, ILLINOIS

(See Northbrook)

Civil Trial and Appellate Practice in Federal and State Courts. Complex and Multi-District Litigation, Civil Rights and Government Tort Liability, Municipal Liability Defense, Construction, Insurance, Product Liability Defense, Securities, Estate Planning, Real Estate, Corporate, Commercial Transactions and Business Law.

O'KEEFE, LYONS & HYNES, LLC

Established in 1937

30 NORTH LA SALLE STREET, SUITE 4100
CHICAGO, ILLINOIS 60602
Telephone: 312-621-0400
Facsimile: 312-621-0297
Email: info@okeefe-law.com
URL: http://www.okeefe-law.com

Taxation (State and Local) Law, Ad Valorem Law, Finance Law, Finance: Mergers and Acquisitions, Health and Hospital Law, Litigation, International, Matrimonial Law, Estate Planning, Probate Law, Real Estate Law, Environmental Law.

CHRISTINE M. BIEBEL, born Evanston, Illinois, October 19, 1970; admitted to bar, 1995, Illinois and U.S. District Court, Northern District of Illinois. *Education:* Miami University (B.A., 1992); Georgetown University (J.D., 1995). ***PRACTICE AREAS:*** Finance; Mergers and Acquisitions; Health Law; Hospital Law. **Email:** christinebiebel@okeefe-law.com

JAMES E. CARROLL, born Evanston, Illinois, July 31, 1956; admitted to bar, 1982, Illinois and U.S. District Court, Northern District of Illinois; 1986, U.S. Court of Appeals, 7th Circuit; 1988, U.S. Supreme Court. *Education:* Loras College (B.A., maxima cum laude, 1978); Cambridge University (LL.M., in International Law, 1980); Northwestern University (J.D., 1982). ***PRACTICE AREAS:*** International Law; Finance; Mergers and Acquisitions. **Email:** jimcarroll@okeefe-law.com

DANIEL W. COYNE, born Chicago, Illinois, October 25, 1946; admitted to bar, 1971, Illinois, U.S. District Court, Northern District of Illinois and U.S. Court of Appeals, 7th Circuit; 1973, U.S. Court of Military Appeals; 1975, Massachusetts and U.S. District Court, District of Massachusetts; 1980, U.S. Supreme Court; 1986, U.S. Tax Court. *Education:* Marquette University (B.A., magna cum laude, 1968); Harvard University (J.D., cum laude, 1971). ***PRACTICE AREAS:*** Finance; Health Law; Hospital Law; Taxation. **Email:** dancoyne@okeefe-law.com

MARK R. DAVIS, born Hammond, Indiana, November 10, 1953; admitted to bar, 1979, Illinois and U.S. District Court, Northern District of Illinois including Trial Bar; 1981, U.S. Court of Appeals, Seventh Circuit; 1999, U.S. Supreme Court and U.S. Court of Appeals, Federal Circuit; 2000, U.S. Court of Federal Claims. *Education:* University of New Mexico (B.A., 1975); DePaul University (J.D., 1979). ***PRACTICE AREAS:*** State Taxation; Local Taxation; Litigation. **Email:** markdavis@okeefe-law.com

PATRICIA QUINN FORD, born Cleveland, Ohio, August 13, 1950; admitted to bar, 1978, Illinois and U.S. District Court, Northern District of Illinois. *Education:* University of Iowa (B.A., 1972); Loyola University (J.D., 1978). ***PRACTICE AREAS:*** State Taxation; Local Taxation. **Email:** patriciaford@okeefe-law.com

BRIAN P. FORDE, born Elmhurst, Illinois, July 29, 1971; admitted to bar, 1997, Illinois; 2000, U.S. District Court, Northern District of Illinois and U.S. Court of Appeals, Seventh Circuit. *Education:* Northern Illinois University (B.S., 1993); DePaul University (J.D., 1997). ***PRACTICE AREAS:*** State Taxation; Local Taxation. **Email:** brianforde@okeefe-law.com

ELIZABETH L. GRACIE, born Marathon, Ontario, Canada, September 22, 1957; admitted to bar, 1983, Wisconsin, Illinois and U.S. District Court, Northern District of Illinois. *Education:* University of Wisconsin (B.A., Honors, 1980; J.D., 1983). ***PRACTICE AREAS:*** State Taxation; Local Taxation. **Email:** elizabethgracie@okeefe-law.com

J. MICHAEL HEATON, born Seneca, Illinois, October 31, 1946; admitted to bar, 1971, Illinois and Iowa; 1972, U.S. Court of Military Appeals; 1975, U.S. District Court, Northern District of Illinois and U.S. Court of Appeals, 7th Circuit; 1980, U.S. Supreme Court. *Education:* University of Notre Dame (A.B., 1968; J.D., 1971). [Lieut., JAGC, USNR, 1971-1975]. ***PRACTICE AREAS:*** Ad Valorem Tax; State Taxation; Local Taxation. **Email:** mikeheaton@okeefe-law.com

KEVIN B. HYNES, born Evergreen Park, Illinois, March 14, 1966; admitted to bar, 1991, Illinois and U.S. District Court, Northern District of Illinois. *Education:* St. John's University (B.S., 1988); Loyola University (J.D., 1991); George Washington University (M.P.H., 1997). ***PRACTICE AREAS:*** Environmental Law; Ad Valorem Tax; State Taxation; Local Taxation; Litigation; Government Relations. **Email:** kevinhynes@okeefe-law.com

ROBERT E. HYNES, born Chicago, Illinois, April 5, 1944; admitted to bar, 1969, Illinois, U.S. District Court, Northern District of Illinois and U.S. Tax Court. *Education:* Loyola University (B.B.A., 1965; J.D., 1969). ***PRACTICE AREAS:*** State and Local Taxation; Property Taxation; Municipal Law; Governmental Relations. **Email:** roberthynes@okeefe-law.com

BARBARA JOHNSON, born Evergreen Park, Illinois, January 13, 1954; admitted to bar, 1980, Illinois, U.S. District Court, Northern District of Illinois and U.S. Court of Appeals, Seventh Circuit. *Education:* Quincy College (B.A., 1976); Loyola University of Chicago (J.D., 1980). ***LANGUAGES:*** Spanish. ***PRACTICE AREAS:*** Real Estate Law; Real Property Taxation; General Civil Practice. **Email:** barbarajohnson@okeefe-law.com

ALISON A. LEMMENS, born Green Bay, Wisconsin, November 19, 1974; admitted to bar, 2001, Illinois; 2001, U.S. District Court, Northern District of Illinois. *Education:* Marquette University (B.S., 1997); DePaul University (J.D., 2001). ***PRACTICE AREAS:*** State Taxation; Local Taxation. **Email:** alisonlemmens@okeefe-law.com

THOMAS G. LYONS, born Chicago, Illinois, May 24, 1931; admitted to bar, 1957, Illinois; 1958, U.S. District Court, Northern District of Illinois; 1968, U.S. Court of Appeals, 7th Circuit; 1972, U.S. Supreme Court. *Education:* Xavier University at Cincinnati and Loyola University at Chicago (B.S., 1954); Loyola University at Chicago (J.D., 1957).

MICHAEL L. McDERMOTT, born Chicago, Illinois, December 10, 1938; admitted to bar, 1963, Illinois. *Education:* Spring Hill College (B.S., 1960); Northwestern University (J.D., 1963). ***PRACTICE AREAS:*** Matrimonial Law; Estate Planning; Probate; Corporate Law; Real Estate. **Email:** mikemcdermott@okeefe-law.com

(This Listing Continued)

O'KEEFE, LYONS & HYNES, LLC, Chicago—Continued

KEVIN M. O'KEEFE, born Vincennes, Indiana, September 24, 1946; admitted to bar, 1973, Illinois; 1974, Florida. *Education:* University of Illinois (B.S., 1969); Chicago-Kent College of Law, Illinois Institute of Technology (J.D., cum laude, 1973). ***PRACTICE AREAS:*** Ad Valorem Tax; State Taxation; Federal Taxation. ***Email:*** kevinokeefe@okeefe-law.com

MARGUERITE QUINN, born Chicago, Illinois, June 13, 1959; admitted to bar, 1986, Illinois and U.S. District Court, Northern District of Illinois including Trial Bar; 1994, U.S. Supreme Court. *Education:* University of Iowa (B.A., 1981); Loyola University (J.D., 1985). ***PRACTICE AREAS:*** State Taxation; Local Taxation. ***Email:*** mquinn@okeefe-law.com

JASON T. SHILSON, born New York, N.Y., September 14, 1968; admitted to bar, 1993, Illinois and U.S. District Court, Northern District of Illinois; 1994, U.S. Court of Appeals, Seventh Circuit. *Education:* University of Michigan (B.A., 1990); DePaul University (J.D., 1993). ***PRACTICE AREAS:*** State Taxation; Local Taxation; Litigation. ***Email:*** jasonshilson@okeefe-law.com

JOHN F. WARD, JR., (P.C.), born Chicago, Illinois, September 5, 1941; admitted to bar, 1966, Illinois; 1970, U.S. District Court, Northern District of Illinois; 1976, U.S. Court of Appeals, 7th Circuit; 1980, U.S. Supreme Court; 1985, U.S. Court of Appeals, 6th Circuit. *Education:* University of Notre Dame (A.B., 1963); DePaul University (J.D., 1966). ***PRACTICE AREAS:*** Local Taxation; Telecommunications Law. ***Email:*** johnward@okeefe-law.com

REFERENCE: BankOne.

PAUL F. O'KEEFE, P.C.

Established in 2000

20 NORTH CLARK STREET, SUITE 2550

CHICAGO, ILLINOIS 60602

Telephone: 312-263-9200

Fax: 312-263-6245

Email: okeefelaw@msn.com

URL: http://www.okeefelawoffice.com

Waukegan, Illinois Office: 32 N. West Street. Second Floor. 60085. Telephone: 847-263-9262.

Arbitration, Business Law, Business Litigation, Complex Business Litigation, Federal Civil Practice, Commercial Law, Complex Commercial Litigation, Contracts, Breach of Contracts, Contract Litigation, Corporate Law, Corporate Litigation, Criminal law, Criminal Defense, Governmental Law, Labor and Employment, Employment Breach of Contract, Litigation, Civil Litigation, Complex Litigation, Defense Litigation, Federal Litigation, Trial Practice, Medical Malpractice, Personal Injury, Probate, Ancillary Probate, Probate Administration, Probate Litigation, Criminal Taxation, Trusts and Estates, Contested Trusts and Estates, Decedents Estates, Estate Litigation, Estate Settlements, White Collar Crimes, White Collar Criminal Defense, Wills, Contested Wills, Inheritance, Decedents Estates, Estate Administration, Estate Litigation, Estate Planning, Internet Crimes, Felonies.

FIRM PROFILE: We are dedicated to our clients.

PAUL F. O'KEEFE, born Evanston, Illinois, July 2, 1965; admitted to bar, 1990, Illinois; 2000, U.S. District Court, Northern District of Illinois and U.S. Court of Appeals, Seventh Circuit. *Education:* College of the Holy Cross (B.A., History, 1987); University of Illinois College of Law (J.D., 1990). Participant: National College of District Attorneys' two-week Trial Advocacy Course, 1999; Illinois Appellate Prosecutors' Trial Advocacy Seminar, 1995; National College of District Attorneys' Government Civil Practice Course, 1992. President, Paul F. O'Keefe, P.C., 2000-2004. Assistant State's Attorney, Civil Division and Criminal Division, Office of the Lake County State's Attorney, 1992-2000. Recognized by U.S. Department of Justice for an outstanding record in the prosecution of offenders brought to justice through the combined efforts of local law enforcement and the F.B.I. Associate, Siemon Larsen & Purdy, 1990-1991. *Member:* Chicago Bar Association (Civil Practice Committee Division II, Chairman, 2000-2001, 2002-2003, Vice-Chairman, 2001-2002; Civil Practice Executive Committee, 2000-2004; Civil Practice Committee; Probate Practice Committee; Criminal Law Committee); Lake County Bar Association (Member: Civil Trial and Appeal Committee, 2000-2005); Illinois State Bar Association (Member, Sections on: Civil Practice and Procedure; Trusts and Estates); The Lawyers Club of Chicago; American Inn's of Court - Jefferson Inn. ***REPORTED CASES:*** 246 Ill. App.3d 616; 616 N.E.2d 624. ***PRACTICE AREAS:*** Civil Litigation; White Collar Crime; Business Law; Probate. ***Email:*** okeefelaw@msn.com

LEGAL SUPPORT PERSONNEL

WANDA VICTORES

KIMBERLY PETRINA

STEVEN HAUBNER, Pi Gamma Mu. Chicago Marathon Finisher, 2001, 2002, 2004. (Law Clerk). ***PRACTICE AREAS:*** Legal Research. ***Email:*** shaubner@law.uiul.edu

Languages: Spanish.

JOHN J. O'LEARY

20 N. CLARK STREET, SUITE 1725

CHICAGO, ILLINOIS 60602

Telephone: 312-782-8807

Fax: 312-372-6067

Email: joleary@olearylawfirm.com

URL: http://www.olearylawfirm.com

Construction Law and Commercial and Residential Real Estate Law, Lending Law.

(This Listing Continued)

JOHN J. O'LEARY, admitted to bar, 1980, Illinois and U.S. District Court, Northern District of Illinois. *Education:* St. Mary's College (B.A., 1975); Northwestern University School of Law (J.D., 1980); John Marshall Law School (LL.M., Real Estate Law, 1999). Member, Editorial Board, Journal of Criminal Law and Criminology, 1979-1980. *Member:* Chicago, Illinois State and American Bar Associations. ***PRACTICE AREAS:*** Commercial Real Estate; Construction Law; Residential Real Estate; Lender Law.

OLSON & HIERL, LTD.

Established in 1986

20 NORTH WACKER DRIVE

36TH FLOOR

CHICAGO, ILLINOIS 60606-3181

Telephone: 312-580-1180

Telecopier: 312-580-1189

Email: firm@olsonhierl.com

URL: http://www.olsonandhierl.com

Intellectual Property and Technology-Related Law including Patents, Trademarks, Trade Secrets, Copyrights and Unfair Competition, Related Licensing and Litigation.

FIRM PROFILE: Olson & Hierl, Ltd. works closely with an active and established international network of law firms to offer its clients prompt and efficient service for intellectual property matters worldwide.

MICHAEL A. HIERL, born Chicago, Illinois, March 31, 1953; admitted to bar, 1980, Illinois and U.S. District Court, Northern District of Illinois including Trial Bar; 1981, U.S. Court of Appeals, Seventh Circuit; 1982, U.S. Court of Appeals, Federal Circuit; registered to practice before U.S. Patent and Trademark Office. *Education:* Southern Illinois University (B.S., 1975); Northwestern University (M.S., 1976); John Marshall Law School (J.D., 1980). Listed, Illinois Super Lawyers, Chicago Magazine, May 2005; Illinois Leading Lawyers Network, Law Bulletin Publishing Company, 2005. *Member:* Chicago, Federal Circuit and American Bar Associations; Intellectual Property Law Association of Chicago; American Intellectual Property Law Association; The Association of Trial Lawyers of America; American Chemical Society. ***Email:*** mhierl@olsonhierl.com

ARNE M. OLSON, born Elmhurst, Illinois, August 10, 1955; admitted to bar, 1980, Illinois and U.S. District Court, Northern District of Illinois including Trial Bar; 1981, U.S. District Court, Western District of Michigan and U.S. Court of Appeals, Seventh Circuit; 1982, U.S. Court of Appeals, Federal Circuit; registered to practice before U.S. Patent and Trademark Office. *Education:* University of Chicago (A.B. in Physics, 1977); DePaul University (J.D. with honors, 1980). Listed: Illinois Super Lawyers, Chicago Magazine, May 2005; Illinois Leading Lawyers Network, Law Bulletin Publishing Company, 2005. Author: "Design Your Patent Applications for Possible Fields-of-Use Licensing," Technology Transfer Manual, Vol. 3, Association of University Technology Managers, Inc., 1995. *Member:* Chicago and American Bar Associations; American Intellectual Property Law Association; International Trademark Association; American Association for the Advancement of Science. ***Email:*** aolson@olsonhierl.com

DOLORES T. KENNEY, born Chicago, Illinois; admitted to bar, 1984, Illinois and U.S. District Court, Northern District of Illinois; registered to practice before U.S. Patent and Trademark Office. *Education:* University of St. Francis (B.S., cum laude, 1956); Keller Graduate School of Management (C.B.A., 1977); Chicago-Kent College of Law, Illinois Institute of Technology (J.D., 1984). Phi Alpha Delta. Listed: Top Lawyers in Illinois, Leading Lawyers Law Bulletin Publishing Company, 2005. Author: "Intellectual Property Issues: Patents and Trade Secrets," Chapter 8 *Harry's Cosmeticology,* 8th Ed., Chemical Publishing Co., Inc., 2000; "Laboratory Notebooks: Valuable Indicators of Intellectual Property," Cosmetics and Toiletries, V120(5), pages 97-104 (2005). *Member:* Chicago, Illinois State and American Bar Associations; Women's Bar Association of Illinois; American Intellectual Property Law Association; American Chemical Society; Society of Cosmetic Chemists. ***LANGUAGES:*** Spanish. ***Email:*** dkenney@olsonhierl.com

TALIVALDIS CEPURITIS, born Plavinas, Latvia, April 15, 1935; admitted to bar, 1965, New York; 1967, Michigan; 1970, District of Columbia and U.S. Court of Appeals for the District of Columbia Circuit; 1971, U.S. Court of Appeals, Sixth Circuit; 1973, Illinois and U.S. Court of Appeals, Seventh Circuit; 1981, U.S. Supreme Court; 1982, U.S. Court of Appeals, Third Circuit and U.S. Court of Appeals, Federal Circuit; 1983, U.S. District Court, Northern District of Illinois including Trial Bar; registered to practice before U.S. Patent and Trademark Office. *Education:* University of Michigan (B.S.E., 1958; M.S.E., 1959); New York University (J.D., 1965). Listed: Top Lawyers in Illinois, Leading Lawyers Law Bulletin Publishing Company, 2005. *Member:* Chicago, Federal Circuit and American Bar Associations; Intellectual Property Law Association of Chicago; The Association of Trial Lawyers of America. ***LANGUAGES:*** German and Latvian. ***Email:*** tcepuritis@olsonhierl.com

KATHRYN E. GARIPAY, born Hanover, New Hampshire, July 22, 1959; admitted to bar, 1986, Illinois; 1989, U.S. District Court, Northern District of Illinois; 1998, U.S. Court of Appeals, Federal Circuit. *Education:* University of New Hampshire (B.A., cum laude, 1981); University of Puget Sound, School of Law (J.D., magna cum laude, 1986). *Member:* Chicago and Illinois State Bar Associations. ***Email:*** kgaripay@olsonhierl.com

JOSEPH M. KUO, born New Orleans, Louisiana, July 3, 1968; admitted to bar, 1993, Illinois and U.S. District Court, Northern District of Illinois including Trial Bar; 1998, U.S. Court of Appeals, Federal Circuit; registered to practice before the U.S. Patent and Trademark Office. *Education:* Northwestern University (B.S., Industrial Engineering, 1990); Tulane University of Louisiana (J.D., 1993). Author, "The Digital Copyright Act - A Balancing Act to Promote the Arts," 17 CBA Record 40, May 2003. *Member:* Chicago, Illinois State and American Bar Associations; American Intellectual Property Law Association. ***Email:*** jkuo@olsonhierl.com

DENNIS H. MA, born Hong Kong, China, October 18, 1976; admitted to bar, 2001, Illinois, U.S. District Court, Northern District of Illinois and U.S. Court of Appeals, Federal

(This Listing Continued)

Circuit; registered to practice before U.S. Patent and Trademark Office. *Education:* Northwestern University (B.A., Integrated Science and Biological Sciences, concentrating in Molecular/Cell Biology; B.S., Biomedical Engineering, specializing in Biotechnology, 1998); Cornell Law School (J.D. and LL.M. in International and Comparative Law, 2001). *Member:* Chicago and American Bar Associations; American Association for the Advancement of Science; American Intellectual Property Law Association. **Email:** dma@olsonhierl.com

BRUCE R. MANSFIELD, born Oak Park, Illinois, March 19, 1948; admitted to bar, 1975, Illinois; registered to practice before U.S. Patent and Trademark Office. *Education:* Illinois Institute of Technology (B.S.E.E., 1970); John Marshall Law School (J.D., with honors, 1975). Member, Order of John Marshall. *Member:* Illinois State Bar Association; Intellectual Property Law Association of Chicago. **Email:** bmansfield@olsonhierl.com

MARK R. BAGLEY, born St. Louis, Missouri, 1973; admitted to bar, 1999, Missouri; 2000, Illinois. *Education:* Harvard University (A.B., 1996); University of Chicago (J.D., 1999). Member, University of Chicago Law Review. **Email:** mbagley@olsonhierl.com

OF COUNSEL

SEYMOUR ROTHSTEIN, born Cleveland, Ohio, February 25, 1931; admitted to bar, 1958, District of Columbia; 1962, Illinois; U.S. District Court, Northern District of Illinois including Trial Bar; U.S. Court of Appeals, Federal Circuit; registered to practice before U.S. Patent and Trademark Office. *Education:* Case Institute of Technology (B.S., 1952); George Washington University (LL.B., 1958). Arbitrator, Circuit Court of Cook County. *Member:* Chicago, Seventh Federal Circuit and American Bar Associations; Intellectual Property Law Association of Chicago; International Trademark Association (Member, Panel of Neutrals); American Inn of Court (Counselor, 1994-1995). **Email:** srothstein@olsonhierl.com

PATENT AGENT

ROBERT J. ROSS, born Rockford, Illinois, August 18, 1959; admitted to bar, registered to practice before U.S. Patent and Trademark Office. *Education:* Northern Illinois University (B.S., summa cum laude, 1981); Ohio State University (Ph.D., 1986); John Marshall Law School (J.D., summa cum laude, 2005). John Marshall Distinguished Scholar. Inventor with 24 U.S. Patents, 1993-2001. *Member:* American Intellectual Property Law Association; American Chemical Society. (Patent Agent). **Email:** rross@olsonhierl.com

1-800-ASK-A-LAWYER & ASSOCIATES

aka David K. Kremin & Associates, A.P.C.

221 N. LA SALLE STREET, SUITE 1900
CHICAGO, ILLINOIS 60601
Telephone: 800-275-2529
Fax: 312-456-9900
Toll Free: 1-800-ASK A LAWYER (1-800-275-2529)
URL: http://www.askdavidkremin.com
URL: http://www.lawyers.com/davidkremin
Email: ASKALAWYER@aol.com
URL: http://www.1800askalawyer.com

Personal Injury, Litigation, Automobile Accidents, Work Accidents, Premises Liability, Product Liability, Fire and Casualty Cases, Medical Malpractice, Birth Defects, Dram Shop, Workers Compensation, Catastrophic Injuries, Spinal Cord, Airplane Crash and Slip and Fall, Wrongful Death.

DAVID K. KREMIN, born Chicago, Illinois, August 26, 1955; admitted to bar, 1983, Illinois and U.S. District Court, Northern District of Illinois. *Education:* University of Illinois (B.S., 1977); Illinois Institute of Technology, Chicago-Kent College of Law (J.D., highest honors, 1983). Law Clerk to Hon. Irving R. Norman, Circuit Court of Cook County, Illinois, 1982. Listed in: "Who's Who in American Law"; "Who's Who in Executives and Professionals"; " Million Dollar Plus List Published Chicago Lawyer Magazine Survey". Recent Recovery Clients' Awarded over $50 million. Awarded Leading Personal Injury Attorney Distinction 3 consecutive years. Admitted in the Million Dollar Advocates Forum. *Member:* Chicago and Illinois State Bar Associations; Decalogue Society of Lawyers; Illinois Trial Lawyers Association; The Association of Trial Lawyers of America; National Lawyers Association (Chairperson, Tort Division). (Also Member, David K. Kremin & Associates, P.C.). ***PRACTICE AREAS:*** Plaintiffs Personal Injury; Wrongful Death.

CLAUDIA ONEY & ASSOCIATES

Established in 1978

134 NORTH LA SALLE STREET, SUITE 300
CHICAGO, ILLINOIS 60602
Telephone: 312-782-1900
Fax: 312-782-1965
Email: claudiaoney@mac.com
URL: http://www.claudiaoney.com

Employment Law, Age, Race and Sex Discrimination, Family Law and Divorce.

FIRM PROFILE: Ms. Oney has practiced in the Cook County Domestic Relations Division for over 25 years. She has handled many difficult and contentious custody cases and complex property divisions. She also has extensive trial experience in the "roller coaster" area of maintenance awards. Following an initial consultation, Ms. Oney believes it is her job to advise a client whether or not their case has merit, based on a complicated array of circumstances. She ensures that each client understands the law as it relates to his or her particular circumstances, and she does not believe in making unrealistic promises. Since starting her own firm in 1978, most of her clients have been referrals from other clients. Ms. Oney utilizes a written retainer and her clients are thoroughly advised as to potential fees.

(This Listing Continued)

CLAUDIA ONEY & ASSOCIATES, P.C., born Lowell, Massachusetts, April 21, 1947; admitted to bar, 1978, Illinois and U.S. Court of Appeals, 7th Circuit; 1981, U.S. District Court, Northern District of Illinois including Trial Bar; 1983, U.S. Supreme Court. *Education:* University of Texas at Arlington (B.A., 1968); DePaul University (J.D., 1978). Named and Listed, One of the Best Attorneys in Illinois in Employment Law, Law and Leading Attorneys. Speaker, "The Top Ten Complaints of Angry Ex-Employees," Personnel Law Update, 1996. *Member:* Illinois State Bar Association; International Employment Lawyers Association; National Employment Lawyers Association (Member: Illinois Chapter; Computer Committee; Sexual Harassment Law Committee); Women's Bar Association; Leading American Attorneys. ***PRACTICE AREAS:*** Labor and Employment; Divorce; Child Custody. ***Email:*** claudiaoney@mac.com

O'ROURKE, HOGAN, FOWLER & DWYER

10 SOUTH LA SALLE STREET, SUITE 2900
CHICAGO, ILLINOIS 60603
Telephone: 312-739-3500
Fax: 312-739-3535

General Trial and Appellate Practice in all Courts, State and Federal Arbitrations and Dispute Resolution Board Proceedings. Our practice includes Construction Related (Public and Private) Contracts, Litigation, Claims, Bonds, Surety Law and Construction Liens. We also practice in the areas of Management Labor Relations Law, Employment Relations Law and Commercial Litigation.

MEMBERS OF FIRM

WILLIAM T. DWYER, JR., born Chicago, Illinois, July 12, 1947; admitted to bar, 1972, Illinois, U.S. District Court, Northern District of Illinois and U.S. Court of Appeals, Seventh Circuit. *Education:* University of Notre Dame (B.A., 1969); University of Illinois (J.D., 1972). *Member:* Chicago, Illinois State and American Bar Associations. ***PRACTICE AREAS:*** Commercial Litigation; Business Law; Banking Law. ***Email:*** wdwyer@ohfdlaw.com

W. CRAIG FOWLER, born Sandusky, Ohio, November 26, 1952; admitted to bar, 1978, Illinois; 1979, U.S. District Court, Northern District of Illinois. *Education:* University of Notre Dame (B.B.A., with high honors, 1975); Northwestern University (J.D., 1978). Beta Gamma Sigma. *Member:* Chicago, Illinois State, American (Member, Sections on: Corporation, Banking and Business Law; Real Property, Probate and Trust Law). ***PRACTICE AREAS:*** Corporation Law; Contracts Law; Real Estate Law. ***Email:*** wcfowler@ohfdlaw.com

MICHAEL A. GILMAN, born Chicago, Illinois, September 1, 1956; admitted to bar, 1982, Illinois; U.S. District Court, Northern District of Illinois including Trial Bar; 1991, U.S. District Court, Central District of Illinois. *Education:* University of Illinois (B.A., cum laude, 1978); Chicago-Kent College of Law (J.D., with high honors, 1982). Member, 1980-1981, Notes and Comment Editor, 1981-1982, Chicago-Kent Law Review. Co-Author: With William E. McNulty, "Reformation," Real Estate Litigation, Illinois Institute of Continuing Legal Education, Chapter 2, 1988. *Member:* Chicago, Illinois State and American Bar Associations. ***PRACTICE AREAS:*** Construction Law; Real Estate Law; Mechanics Lien Law; Contract Law; Appellate Practice Law. ***Email:*** mgilman@ohfdlaw.com

FREDERIC G. HOGAN, born Evergreen Park, Illinois, July 29, 1947; admitted to bar, 1973, Illinois; U.S. District Court, Northern District of Illinois including Trial Bar and U.S. Court of Appeals, Seventh Circuit. *Education:* University of Wisconsin, Madison (B.S.C.E., B.B.A., 1970); University of Notre Dame (J.D., 1973). *Member:* Chicago and American (Member, Real Estate Law Section) Bar Associations. ***PRACTICE AREAS:*** Contract Law; Real Estate; Real Estate Development Law; Title Insurance Law. ***Email:*** fhogan@ohfdlaw.com

JOHN C. O'ROURKE, JR., born Chicago, Illinois, November 13, 1947; admitted to bar, 1973, Illinois. *Education:* University of Notre Dame (B.A., 1969); DePaul University (J.D., 1973). Recipient, American Jurisprudence Award in Real Property. Law Clerk, Justice Edward Egan, Appellate Court of Illinois, 1973-1975. *Member:* Chicago, Illinois State and American (Member, Sections on: Litigation Law; Public Contract Law) Bar Associations. (Resident). ***PRACTICE AREAS:*** Construction Litigation; Public Contract Law. ***Email:*** jorourke@ohfdlaw.com

HOWARD I. GOLDBLATT, born Chicago, Illinois, October 13, 1962; admitted to bar, 1987, Illinois and U.S. District Court, Northern District of Illinois. *Education:* University of Pennsylvania (B.A., 1984); Northwestern University (J.D., 1987). *Member:* Chicago and American Bar Associations. ***PRACTICE AREAS:*** Commercial; Real Estate; Business; Corporate; Financial Institution. ***Email:*** hgoldblatt@ohfdlaw.com

OWENS, OWENS & RINN, LTD.

CHICAGO, ILLINOIS

(See Park Ridge)

Estate Planning, Probate, Taxation, Real Estate, Zoning, and Corporate Law. General Civil Trial and Appellate Practice in Federal and State Courts.

PACHTER, GREGORY & FINOCCHIARO, P.C.

CHICAGO, ILLINOIS

(See Deerfield)

Real Estate Finance, Real Estate Development and Commercial Litigation.

THE PAPE LAW FIRM

CHICAGO, ILLINOIS

(See Wheaton)

Real Estate Law, Construction Law.

PAPPAS, JACOBY & MARCUS

30 WEST MONROE STREET
SUITE 800
CHICAGO, ILLINOIS 60603
Telephone: 312-782-5363
Telecopier: 312-782-9590
URL: http://www.pjmlaw.net

Trial Practice in all State, Federal and Appellate Courts. Products Liability, Crashworthiness, Product Defects, Recreational Vehicle, Negligence, Personal Injury, Wrongful Death, Automobile Accidents, Pedestrian Injuries, Railroad Accidents, Medical Malpractice, Birth Trauma, Warranty Law, Insurance and Corporate Litigation.

FIRM PROFILE: Pappas, Jacoby & Marcus specializes in civil litigation, focusing primarily on personal injury matters. Our experience in representing clients runs the entire gamut, from serving as National or Regional counsel for Multi-National Corporations to representing individuals. All of the firm's attorneys have significant trial experience with excellent results. Our firm philosophy has been to remain small in order to assure flexibility, efficiency, personalized service and continuity of representation. Our size has allowed us to remain on the cutting edge of technological advances and to provide superior legal services within a very reasonable fee structure.

MEMBERS OF FIRM

JOHN J. PAPPAS, SR., born Detroit, Michigan, March 19, 1945; admitted to bar, 1970, Illinois. *Education:* University of Detroit and Michigan State University (B.A., 1967); University of Notre Dame (J.D., 1970). *Member:* Chicago, Illinois State and American Bar Associations; Defense Research and Trial Lawyers Association; The Association of Trial Lawyers of America; Trial Lawyers Club of Chicago; Illinois Trial Lawyers Association. ***PRACTICE AREAS:*** Products Liability; Personal Injury; Professional Negligence; Insurance Litigation. ***Email:*** jjp@pjmlaw.net

JOHN P. JACOBY, born Chicago, Illinois, December 29, 1957; admitted to bar, 1987, Missouri and U.S. District Court, Eastern District of Missouri; 1988, Illinois and U.S. District Court, Northern and Southern District of Illinois. *Education:* Southwest Missouri State University; Northwest Missouri State University (B.S., cum laude, 1982); Washington University School of Law (J.D., 1987). Recipient, American Jurisprudence Award. Author: "Saving the Golden Egg: Returning Sanity to the Discovery Process," The St. Louis Bar Journal, Summer 1992, Vol. XXXXIX No. 1; "How to Negotiate a Case in Civil Litigation," IICLE, Chicago, 2002-2005. *Member:* Chicago, Illinois State and American Bar Associations; The Missouri Bar; The Association of Trial Lawyers of America; Defense Research Institute. ***PRACTICE AREAS:*** Products Liability; Medical Malpractice; Personal Injury; Employment Litigation. ***Email:*** jpj@pjmlaw.net

DEBRA KRAMER MARCUS, born Chicago, Illinois; admitted to bar, 1981, Illinois; U.S. District Court, Northern District of Illinois; U.S. Court of Appeals, Seventh Circuit and U.S. Supreme Court. *Education:* University of Illinois (B.A., 1978); Chicago-Kent College of Law (J.D., 1981). Member, Chicago-Kent Law Review, 1980-1981. *Member:* Chicago, Illinois State and American Bar Associations; The Association of Trial Lawyers of America; Illinois Trial Lawyers Association. ***PRACTICE AREAS:*** Warranty Law; Products Liability; Professional Negligence; Class Actions; Personal Injury Litigation. ***Email:*** dkm@pjmlaw.net

ASSOCIATES

STEPHEN J. HEALY, born Chicago, Illinois, June 20, 1965; admitted to bar, 1992, Illinois and U.S. District Court, Northern District of Illinois. *Education:* Illinois State University (B.S., 1987); John Marshall Law School (J.D., 1992). *Member:* Chicago, Illinois State and American Bar Associations; Illinois Trial Lawyers Association. ***PRACTICE AREAS:*** Products Liability; Premises Liability; Personal Injury. ***Email:*** sjh@pjmlaw.net

JOHN J. PAPPAS, JR., born Evanston, Illinois, November 3, 1971; admitted to bar, 1997, Illinois. *Education:* Michigan State University (B.A., 1994); John Marshall Law School (J.D., 1997). *Member:* Chicago, Illinois State and American Bar Associations. ***PRACTICE AREAS:*** Personal Injury; Warranty Law; Automobile Accidents and Injuries. ***Email:*** jjr@pjmlaw.net

STEPHEN M. PASSEN, LTD.

ONE EAST WACKER, SUITE 2406
CHICAGO, ILLINOIS 60601
Telephone: 312-527-4500
Facsimile: 312-527-4435
URL: http://www.passenlaw.com
Email: spassen@passenlaw.com
URL: http://www.stephenmpassen.com

Practice Limited to Major Personal Injury Cases, Catastrophic Accidents and Injuries, Head Injuries, Spinal Cord Injuries, Paralysis, Surgical and Physician Malpractice, Automobile, Construction Accidents, Medical Malpractice, Work-Related Accidents, Products Liability Accidents.

STEPHEN M. PASSEN, born 1948, Chicago, Illinois; admitted to bar, 1973, Illinois and U.S. District Court, Northern District of Illinois; 1979, U.S. Court of Appeals, Seventh Circuit; 1980, U.S. Supreme Court. *Education:* University of California-Berkeley (B.A., 1970); University of Wisconsin Law School (J.D., 1973). Author: "Application of the Nursing Home Reform Act in Wrongful Death Actions: Further Legislation Required," published in Illinois Tort Reports, May 1989. Honored Member, Strathmore's Who Who, 2001 Edition. *Member:* Chicago, Illinois State (Former Member, Illinois Tort Council) and American Bar Associations; Illinois Trial Lawyers Association; Association of Trial Lawyers of America; American Arbitration Association (Former Member, Civil Practice Committee); Illinois Trial Lawyers Association. ***PRACTICE AREAS:*** Plaintiff's Personal Injury; Medical Malpractice; Product Liability. ***Email:*** spassen@passenlaw.com

JOHN J. DRISCOLL, born Elmhurst, Illinois, April 4, 1971; admitted to bar, 1997, Illinois. *Education:* University of Illinois (B.S., 1993); John Marshall School of Law (J.D., 1997). Member, Illinois State Bar Association Moot Court Team. Law Clerk to the Honorable William D. Maddux, Circuit Court, Cook County, Illinois, 1998-1999. *Member:* Chicago and Illinois State Bar Associations; Illinois Trial Lawyers Associations; The Association of Trial Lawyers of America. ***PRACTICE AREAS:*** Personal Injury; Medical Malpractice; Products Liability. ***Email:*** jdriscoll@passenlaw.com

(This Listing Continued)

PASULKA & WHITE, LLC

Established in 2004
THREE FIRST NATIONAL PLAZA
70 WEST MADISON STREET, SUITE 650
CHICAGO, ILLINOIS 60602
Telephone: 312-236-9150
Fax: 312-236-9157
Email: pasulkalaw@pasulkalaw.com
URL: http://www.pasulkalaw.com

Family Law including all phases of Matrimonial and Paternity Litigation, Custody, Visitation and Appeals.

FIRM PROFILE: Pasulka & White, LLC devotes its practice to family law. David P. Pasulka has extensive experience representing parents in custody and visitation disputes. He also is appointed regularly by the Courts to represent children in custody disputes. David P. Pasulka is a recognized expert on the issue of attorney's fees and has lectured and written extensively on the subject. William P White, III has extensive experience in divorce disputes involving complex financial litigation. William P. White III has represented litigants in some of the largest marital estates in the history of Illinois divorces.

MEMBERS OF FIRM

DAVID P. PASULKA, born Chicago, Illinois, August 29, 1959; admitted to bar, 1984, Illinois and U. S. District Court, Northern District of Illinois; 1985, California; 1993, U.S. Supreme Court. *Education:* University of Chicago (A.B., 1981); University of San Diego (J.D., 1984). Named among the 20 Top Divorce Attorneys by "North Shore Magazine," and among the 10 Top Divorce Lawyers by "The Chicago Sun Times." Recipient, The Chicago Volunteer Legal Services Distinguished Service Award. Author: 3 ICLE Chapters including Chapters on the Subjects of Attorney's Fees and Collection of Judgments; 2 Articles published in the "Illinois Bar Journal;" The "Amicus Curae" Brief on behalf of the American Academy of Matrimonial Lawyers and ISBA in the Illinois Supreme Court case of Nottage v. Jeka. Extensive Lecturer, Domestic Issues. *Member:* Chicago (Former Chair, Matrimonial Law Committee), North Suburban (Former President) and Illinois State (Former Member, Family Law Section Council) Bar Associations; American Academy of Matrimonial Lawyers, Illinois Chapter (Member: Board of Managers). ***PRACTICE AREAS:*** Family Law; Divorce; Child Custody; Attorney Fee Disputes; Paternity. ***Email:*** pasulkalaw@pasulkalaw.com

WILLIAM P. WHITE III, born Evanston, Illinois, December 9, 1947; admitted to bar, 1974, Illinois and U.S. District Court, Northern District of Illinois. *Education:* University of Notre Dame (B.B.A., 1969); DePaul University (J.D., 1974). *Member:* Illinois State Bar Association. ***PRACTICE AREAS:*** Matrimonial Law; Divorce; Paternity.

ASSOCIATES

WILLIAM K. BASS, born Lackawana, New York, December 15, 1955; admitted to bar, 1989, Illinois and U.S. District Court, Northern District of Illinois. *Education:* Kenyon College; New York University (B.F.A., 1982); University of Toledo (J.D., cum laude, 1989). Phi Kappa Phi; Order of the Coif. Provisional Member, University of Toledo Law Review, 1987-1988. Recipient, Burton A. Maddock Scholarship Award. Author: "Tison v. Arizona: A General Intent For Imposing Capital Punishment Upon An Accomplice Felony Murderer," 20 University of Toledo Law Review 255, Fall, 1988. ***PRACTICE AREAS:*** Family Law. ***Email:*** billbass@pasulkalaw.com

JANET L. MAZUREK, born Chicago, Illinois, October 23, 1965; admitted to bar, 1991, Illinois and U.S. District Court, Northern District of Illinois. *Education:* Southern Illinois University (B.S., 1987); John Marshall Law School (J.D., 1990). Member, Moot Court Executive Board. *Member:* Chicago (Member: Matrimonial Law Committee, 1991—; Fees & Ethics Subcommittee; Co-Chair, 1995-1996), Illinois State and American Bar Associations. ***PRACTICE AREAS:*** Family Law. ***Email:*** janetmazurek@pasulkalaw.com

MITCHELL B. GORDON, born July 29, 1975; admitted to bar, 2001, Illinois. *Education:* University of Iowa (B.A., 1997); Chicago-Kent College of Law of the Illinois Institute of Technology (J.D., 2001). ***PRACTICE AREAS:*** Family Law; Matrimonial Law; Litigation; Paternity.

PATENTS & TMS, P.C.

Established in 1998
1914 NORTH MILWAUKEE AVENUE
THIRD FLOOR
CHICAGO, ILLINOIS 60647
Telephone: 773-772-6009
Fax: 773-772-3210
URL: http://www.patents-tms.com
URL: http://www.lawyers.com/patentstmspc

Patent, Trademark and Copyright Law.

(This Listing Continued)

BRIAN M. MATTSON, born Zion, Illinois, January 23, 1964; admitted to bar, 1992, Illinois; registered to practice before U.S. Patent and Trademark Office. *Education:* Iowa State University (B.S.E.E., 1986); George Mason University (J.D., 1991). Partner, Hill, Steadman and Simpson, 1991-1998. Examiner, U.S. Patent and Trademark Office, 1986-1991. *Member:* Illinois State and American Bar Associations; American Intellectual Property Law Association; Intellectual Property Law Association of Chicago. ***PRACTICE AREAS:*** Patent Law; Trademark Law; Copyright Law. ***Email:*** bmattson@patents-tms.com

LAW OFFICES OF ROBERT B. PATTERSON, LTD.

Established in 1982

221 NORTH LA SALLE STREET, SUITE 1050
CHICAGO, ILLINOIS 60601
Telephone: 312-236-0995
FAX: 312-984-5791
Email: rbpltd@sbcglobal.net
URL: http://www.lawyers.com/pattersonfirm

Civil Trial Practice. Personal Injury, Medical Malpractice, Products Liability, Wrongful Death, Transportation, Railroad and Aviation Law. Appellate Practice.

FIRM PROFILE: This firm was established in 1982 when Mr. Patterson withdrew from 12 years of association with the plaintiff's practice of Louis G. Davidson & Associates, Ltd. We began and remain a small firm devoted to high quality, personally handled civil litigation on behalf of injured people. Our case load is deliberately restricted to allow personal attention of the attorneys to each file, adequate time for thorough preparation and the freedom to pursue novel claims of broad public interest such as the Laurie Dann case, first filed by this office, Red Cross distribution of HIV/Aids contaminated blood, and Air Carrier Defibrillation Cases.

ROBERT B. PATTERSON, born Brooklyn, New York, 1946; admitted to bar, 1971, Illinois and U.S. District Court, Northern District of Illinois; 1973, U.S. Court of Appeals, Seventh Circuit; 1978, U.S. Supreme Court; 1980, U.S. Court of Appeals, Eighth Circuit. *Education:* Pennsylvania State University (B.A., 1968); Northwestern University (J.D., cum laude, 1971). Phi Beta Kappa. Member, Board of Editors, Journal of Criminal Law, Criminology and Police Science, 1970-1971. Listed in Who's Who in American Law, 1983—. Author: "Criminal Contempt: A Proposal for Reform Providing the Least Possible Power Adequate to the End Proposed," 17 South Dakota Law Review 42, 1972; "Trends Toward Criminal Contempt Reform," 12 The Judges' Journal 37, 1973; "Products Liability: The Manufacturer's Continuing Duty to Improve His Product or Warn of Defects After Sale," 62 Illinois Bar Journal 92, October 1973. Co-Author: "Conflicts of Law: For the Plaintiff: Statute of Limitations Considerations in Choosing the Forum for Aircraft Disaster Litigation, Small Aircraft Accident Litigation," ch. 11, pp. 112-131, ABA Press, 1974; "Applicability of Admiralty Reparations Doctrine To Common Law Tort Theory," 6 University of Toledo Law Review 379, 1975; "Authentication of Tangible Evidence and the 'Best Evidence' Rule Under the Federal Rules of Evidence," The Federal Rules of Evidence, pp. 103-113, CBA, Committee for Continuing Legal Education, June 1975, January 1976, November 1976 and November 1978; "Analyzing The Medical Legal Aspects of a Claim," Medical Evidence, ch. 3, Illinois Institute for Continuing Legal Education, 1976, 1980; "Authentication of Tangible Evidence and the Best Evidence Rule," 57 Chicago Bar Rec. 247, 1976; "Techniques for Establishing Impaired Earning Capacity," Proof of Damages, ch. 4, Ill. Inst. for C.L.E., 1977, revised 1984, 1985 and 1990; "Parties to Product Liability Cases," Illinois Products Liability Practice, ch. 3, Ill. Inst. for C.L.E., 1977, revised, 1980, 1984 and 1990; "Recent Developments Relating to Civil Trial Practice," Illinois General Practice Review, ch. 2, Ill. Inst. for C.L.E., 1977; "Unique Sources of Discovery in Aircraft Accident Litigation," 13 INCL Forum 119 A.B.A., 1977; "Gathering Evidence and Analyzing the Medical-Legal Aspects of a Claim," Medical Evidence, ch. 2, Ill. Inst. for C.L.E., 1980, revised 1984 and 1985; "Anticipating and Avoiding Limitations Problems and Other Defenses, Plaintiff's Medical Malpractice Litigation," ch. 8, Ill. Inst. for C.L.E., 1981, revised 1984; "Professional Liability of Physicians," Professional Responsibility, ch. 10, Ill. Inst. for C.L.E., 1982, revised, 1985; Products Report: No "Social Justice" in the Proposed Federal Product Liability Statute, 5 Ill. T.L.J. 19, 1983; "Claims for Which Medical Evidence is Needed," Medical Evidence, ch. 3, Ill. Inst. for C.L.E. 1990; "Professional Liability of Physicians," Professional Liability, ch. 12, Ill. Inst. for C.L.E. 1991; "Physicians," Suing And Defending Professionals, ch. 12, Ill. Inst. for C.L.E, 1997, Supp. 2001. *Member:* Chicago (Member, 1973—, Secretary, 1975-1977, Vice-Chairman, 1977-1978, Chairman, 1978-1979, Medical Legal Relations Committee; Member, 1973-1987, Secretary, 1979-1980, Vice-Chairman, 1980-1981 and Chairman, 1981-1982, Federal Civil Practice Committee; Civil Procedure Committee, 1973-1987, Executive Committee, 1977-1986, Vice-Chairman, 1978-1979, Chairman, 1979-1980, 1984-1985 of Section II; Candidates Evaluation Committee, 1977-1981), Illinois State (Member: Standing Committee on ARDC, 1995-1996; J. Editorial Board, 1995-1996) and American Bar Associations; Illinois Trial Lawyers Association; The Association of Trial Lawyers of America; Appellate Lawyers Association. Fellow, Illinois State Bar Association. Life Fellow, Chicago Bar Association. Certified as a Civil Trial Advocate by the National Board of Trial Advocacy. ***REPORTED CASES:*** Bugno vs. Mt. Sinai Hospital & Medical Center, 201 Ill. App. 3d 245, 559 N.E.2d 1, 147 Ill. Dec. 1 (1st Dist. 1990); Davis vs. United States, 716 F.2d 418 (7th Cir. 1983); Roe v. O'Donohue, 38 F.3d 298 (7th Cir. 1994); Solich v. Portes Cancer Center, 158 Ill.2d 17 630 N.E.2d 820, 196 Ill. Dec. 655 (1994); Advincula v. United Blood Services 176 Ill. 2d 1, 678 N.E. 2d 1009, 223 Ill. Dec. 1 (1996).. ***PRACTICE AREAS:*** Personal Injury; Products Liability Law; Medical Malpractice; Railroad Law; Aviation Law. ***Email:*** rbpltd@sbcglobal.net

JOHN F. HEDRICH, born Princeton, Illinois, October 20, 1966; admitted to bar, 1992, Illinois and U.S. District Court, Northern District of Illinois; 1994, U.S. Court of Appeals, Seventh Circuit. *Education:* Iowa State University (B.A., 1989); Loyola University (J.D., 1992). Phi Kappa Phi; Pi Sigma Alpha. Co-Author, with Davidson Ream: "When Can a Bystander Recover," For the Defense, August 1990; "Deadman Switches and Defective Design," For the Defense, December 1990; "Physicians," Suing And Defending Professionals, Ch. 12, Ill. Inst. for C.L.E., 1997. *Member:* Illinois State Bar Association; Illinois Trial Lawyers Association. ***REPORTED CASES:*** Volpe v. IKO Industries, Ltd., 327 Ill. App. 3d 567, 763 N.E. 2d 870, 261 Ill. Dec. 621 (1st Dist. 2002); Damron vs. Micor Distributing, Inc. 276 Ill. App. 3d 901, 658 N.E.2d 1318, 213 Ill. Dec. 297 (1st Dist., 1995). ***PRACTICE AREAS:*** Personal Injury; Negligence; Products Liability; Medical Malpractice; Appellate. ***Email:*** jfhedrich@sbcglobal.net

PATTISHALL, McAULIFFE, NEWBURY, HILLIARD & GERALDSON LLP

Established in 1883

311 SOUTH WACKER DRIVE
SUITE 5000
CHICAGO, ILLINOIS 60606
Telephone: 312-554-8000
Facsimile: 312-554-8015
URL: http://www.pattishall.com

Alexandria, Virginia Office: 225 Reinekers Lane, Alexandria, VA 22314. Telephone: 703-684-7550. Fax: 703-684-7888.

Litigation and Counseling in the Areas of Domestic and International Trademark, Unfair Competition, Copyright, Internet, e-Commerce, Technology and Computer Law, Licensing, Advertising and Promotions, Right of Publicity, Counterfeiting and Trade Secrets.

MEMBERS OF FIRM

BRETT A. AUGUST, born Mattoon, Illinois, April 21, 1952; admitted to bar, 1977, Illinois. *Education:* University of Rouen, France; University of Illinois (B.A., magna cum laude, 1974); Yale University (J.D., 1977). Phi Beta Kappa; Phi Kappa Phi; Bronze Tablet. Associate Editor, Yale Studies in World Public Order, 1976-1977. President, Yale Association of International Law, 1976-1977. Adjunct Professor of Law, De Paul University School of Law, 1999-2005. Officer, 1981— and President, 2003-2005, French-American Chamber of Commerce. Chair, Chicago-Paris Sister Cities Committee. Chairman, Yale Law School Association of Chicago, 2000—. Secretary, Executive Committee, Yale Law School. U.S. Delegate, Committee for Trademark Law Harmonization, Association Internationale pour la Protection de la Propriete Intellectuelle. *Member:* Chicago, Federal and American (Chair, Subcommittee on Foreign Trademark Law, 1996-1998) Bar Associations; Intellectual Property Law Association of Chicago (Director, 2000-2003; Chair, Internet Committee, 1996-1998); American Intellectual Property Law Association. ***LANGUAGES:*** French. ***PRACTICE AREAS:*** Intellectual Property Litigation; Intellectual Property; Trademarks; Copyrights; Unfair Competition; Domain Name Dispute Resolution; Internet Law; International Law. ***Email:*** baugust@pattishall.com

DIANA LEE BIXLER, born Tulsa, Oklahoma, January 22, 1952; admitted to bar, 1981, District of Columbia; 1997, Illinois. *Education:* Southern Methodist University (B.A., with high honors, 1974); New York University Law School (J.D., 1980). Phi Beta Kappa. Formerly marketing counsel for BP/Amoco Corp., 1988-1999; FTC, Cleveland Regional Office, 1984-1988; U.S. Dept. of Energy, Office of Hearings and Appeals, 1980-1984. *Member:* American, Illinois State and Chicago Bar Associations; Intellectual Property Law Association of Chicago (IPLAC); International Association for the Protection of Intellectual Property (AIPPI). ***PRACTICE AREAS:*** Advertising and Promotion Law; Marketing Law; Trade Regulation; E-Commerce; Intellectual Property; Unfair Competition. ***Email:*** dbixler@pattishall.com

THAD CHALOEMTIARANA, admitted to bar, 1996, Illinois. *Education:* Pennsylvania State University (B.A., with highest distinction, 1993); Harvard University (J.D., cum laude, 1996). Phi Beta Kappa. *Member:* American Bar Association (Chair, Online Services Committee, Intellectual Property Law Section). ***PRACTICE AREAS:*** Intellectual Property Litigation; Intellectual Property; Trademarks; Copyrights; Unfair Competition; Domain Name Dispute Resolution; Trade Dress; Information Technology; E-Commerce; Internet Law; Trade and Professional Associations. ***Email:*** tc@pattishall.com

BRADLEY L. COHN, born Fort Lee, Virginia, January 7, 1968; admitted to bar, 1994, Illinois. *Education:* Duke University (B.A., with distinction, 1989); University of Michigan (J.D., cum laude, 1994). Law Clerk to the Honorable Anne C. Conway, U.S. District Court, Middle District of Florida, 1994-1995. Co-Author: "You Wrote It, But Who Owns It? A Copyright Overview," ACEP News, September 2004. Adjunct Professor, DePaul University College of Law. *Member:* Chicago (Director, 2004-2005 and Co-Chair, Intellectual Property Law Committee, 2002-2004, Young Lawyers Section), Illinois State and American Bar Associations. ***PRACTICE AREAS:*** Intellectual Property Litigation; Intellectual Property; Trademarks; Copyrights; Unfair Competition; Domain Name Dispute Resolution; Advertising Law. ***Email:*** bcohn@pattishall.com

RAYMOND I. GERALDSON, JR., born Racine, Wisconsin, October 19, 1940; admitted to bar, 1965, Illinois; 1966, District of Columbia. *Education:* DePauw University (B.A., 1962); Northwestern University (J.D., 1965). Phi Delta Phi. Adjunct Professor, Trademark Law and Practice, Trademark Litigation, John Marshall Law School, 1978—. Co-Author: "Review of the 1991 Trademark Decisions of the United States Court of Appeals for the Federal Circuit," The American University Law Review (Spring 1992); "Developments in Trademark and Unfair Competition Law," 24:1 The John Marshall Law Review, 1990. Member, Board of Directors, United States Trademark Association, 1985-1987. Editorial Board, Trademark Reporter, 1977-1981. Lawyers for the Creative Arts, Director, 1974— and President, 1976-1978. *Member:* Chicago, Illinois State (Member of Council, Section of Patent, Trademark and Copyright Law, 1978-1982; Chairman, 1980-1981), Seventh Circuit and American Bar Associations; Intellectual Property Law Association of Chicago (Member, Board of Directors, 1984-1986, 1992-1993; President, 1991-1992); American Intellectual Property Law Association; Legal Club of Chicago; Law Club of Chicago. ***PRACTICE AREAS:*** Intellectual Property Litigation; Intellectual Property; Trademarks; Copyrights; Unfair Competition; Domain Name Dispute Resolution; International Law. ***Email:*** rgeraldson@pattishall.com

(This Listing Continued)

PATTISHALL, McAULIFFE, NEWBURY, HILLIARD & GERALDSON LLP, Chicago—Continued

DAVID CRAIG HILLIARD, admitted to bar, 1962, Illinois and Supreme Court. *Education:* Tufts University (B.S.); University of Chicago Law School (J.D.). Recipient, Maurice Weigel Award as the Outstanding Young Lawyer in Illinois, Chicago Council of Lawyers Award for Leadership in Judicial Reform. Co-Author: "Trademarks and Unfair Competition," LexisNexis Publishing, (sixth edition, 2005); "Trademarks and Unfair Competition Deskbook," LexisNexis Publishing, (second edition, 2003; online edition, 2005). Adjunct Professor of Trademark, Unfair Competition and Federal Trade Commission Law, Northwestern University School of Law. Chairman, Northwestern University Symposium on Intellectual Property Law and the Corporate Client, 1987—; Lecturer on Advanced Trademark Law and on the Regulation of Information, on the Faculty of the University of Chicago School of Law. Member, Board of Directors, International Trademark Association, 1989-1991. CPR/INTA Alternative Dispute Resolution Distinguished Panel of Neutrals, 1994—. President, Chicago Bar Association, Founding Chairman, Young Lawyers Section. Editor-in-Chief, Chicago Bar Record. President, Lawyers Trust Fund of Illinois. Member: Illinois Commission on Rights of Women. Visiting Committees: University of Chicago Law School (Chairman), Northwestern University School of Law; De Paul University School of Law. Mediator and Arbitrator. *Member:* Chicago, Illinois State, Seventh Circuit and American (Chairman, Trademark Division; Member of Council) Bar Associations; Legal Club of Chicago (Past President); American Intellectual Property Law Association; Lawyers Club of Chicago; Wayfarers Club (Past President); American College of Trial Lawyers (Chairman, Courageous Advocacy Committee). [Judge Advocate General]. ***PRACTICE AREAS:*** Intellectual Property Litigation; Intellectual Property; Trademarks; Copyrights; Unfair Competition Law; Domain Name Dispute Resolution; International Law; Alternative Dispute Resolution. ***Email:*** dhilliard@pattishall.com

JONATHAN S. JENNINGS, born Cleveland, Ohio, July 11, 1964; admitted to bar, 1990, Illinois. *Education:* Emory University (B.A., 1986) Phi Beta Kappa; Trinity College, Dublin, Ireland; Rotary Scholar, 1986-1987; Northwestern University (J.D., 1990). Articles Editor, The Journal of Criminal Law and Criminology, 1989-1990. Adjunct Professor, The John Marshall Law School, 2003—. Member, Advisory Board for the DePaul University College of Law's Center for Intellectual Property Law & Information Technology. Author: "Domain Names and Trademarks on the Internet," ABA's IP Handbook (Fall 2005); "The Right of Publicity and the Internet," Advertising Compliance Service, Vol.24, page 5 (May 3, 2004); "The Right of Publicity and Cyberspace," IP Litigator (November/December 2003); "Significant Trademark/Domain Name Issues In Cyberspace," Understanding Basic Trademark Law, Practicing Law Institute Course Handbook (2002); "Recent Trends in Cybersquatting," E-Commerce Law, Vol.1, No. 3, page 1 (March 2001); "Trademark Infringement Primer," Understanding Basic Trademark Law, Practicing Law Institute Course Handbook (2000); "Copyright Pitfalls for Law Firms," CBA Record 42 (June/July 1996). Co-Author: "The Developing Right of Publicity," Performink Newspaper 2 (June 5, 1998); "A Short Guide to Identifying Intellectual Property Interests," Illinois Bar Journal (March 1996). *Member:* Chicago (Strategic Planning Committee), Illinois State, Federal and American (Chair, Trademark Division, Intellectual Property Law Section) Bar Associations; International Trademark Association (Member, Parallel Imports Committee); American Intellectual Property Law Association; Intellectual Property Owners Association (Member, Cybersquatting Committee); Intellectual Property Law Association of Chicago. ***PRACTICE AREAS:*** Intellectual Property Litigation; Intellectual Property; Trademarks; Copyrights; Unfair Competition; Domain Name Dispute Resolution; Trade Secrets; International Law; E-Commerce; Alternative Dispute Resolution. ***Email:*** jsj@pattishall.com

JANET A. MARVEL, born Lafayette, Indiana, January 27, 1961; admitted to bar, 1989, Illinois. *Education:* Indiana University (B.A., 1983); University of Michigan (J.D., cum laude, 1989). Phi Beta Kappa. *Member:* International Trademark Association. ***PRACTICE AREAS:*** Intellectual Property Litigation; Intellectual Property; Trademarks; Copyrights; Unfair Competition; Domain Name Dispute Resolution; Information Technology. ***Email:*** jmarvel@pattishall.com

JEREMIAH D. McAULIFFE, born Chicago, Illinois, October 1, 1921; admitted to bar, 1949, Illinois; 1971, District of Columbia. *Education:* Northwestern University (B.S., 1943; J.D., 1948). Phi Delta Phi. Member, U.S. Delegation to UNCTAD Conference on Role of Industrial Property System In Transfer of Technology, 1977. Founding Member, Treasurer and Member of Honour, Asociacion InterAmericana De La Propiedad Industrial, 1964-1976. *Member:* Chicago (Member, Board of Managers, 1970-1972), Illinois State, American, Inter-American, International and Seventh Circuit Bar Associations; Law Club of Chicago; Legal Club of Chicago; American Intellectual Property Law Association; International Trademark Association (Member, Board of Directors, 1973); International Patent and Trademark Association (Vice President, 1979; President, 1983-1989). [Commander, USNR, Retired]. ***LANGUAGES:*** Spanish. ***PRACTICE AREAS:*** Intellectual Property Litigation; Intellectual Property; Trademarks; Copyrights; Unfair Competition; Domain Name Dispute Resolution; International Law.

ROBERT M. NEWBURY, born Chicago, Illinois, November 27, 1931; admitted to bar, 1959, Illinois. *Education:* Carleton College (B.A., 1953); Yale University (LL.B., 1959). *Member:* Chicago, Illinois State, American (Chairman: Copyright Division, 1983-1984; Trademark Division, 1985-1986; Member of Council, 1986-1990) and Seventh Circuit Bar Associations; American Intellectual Property Law Association (Member, Board of Directors, 1984-1987; Fellow, 2003—); Copyright Society of the USA (Trustee, 1985-1988, 1995-1998); Legal Club of Chicago; American Bar Foundation. ***PRACTICE AREAS:*** Intellectual Property Litigation; Intellectual Property; Trademarks; Copyrights; Unfair Competition; Domain Name Dispute Resolution; Advertising Law. ***Email:*** rnewbury@pattishall.com

MARK V. B. PARTRIDGE, born Rochester, Minnesota, October 16, 1954; admitted to bar, 1981, Illinois. *Education:* University of Nebraska at Lincoln (B.A., with high distinction, 1978); Harvard University (J.D., 1981). Phi Beta Kappa. Vice President, Harvard Legal Aid Bureau, 1980-1981. Adjunct Professor, The John Marshall Law School, 1990—. Panelist, World Intellectual Property Organization Arbitration and Mediation Center, ICANN Domain Name Dispute Policy Panelist, 2000—. Mediator, Northern District of Illinois Lanham Act Mediation Panel, 1997—. International Trademark Association Panel of Neutrals, 2005. National Arbitration Forum Panel of Neutral Arbitrators and Mediators, 2004—. Arbitrator, Cook County Mandatory Arbitration Program, 1990-2003; Panel of Experts, World Intellectual Property Organization, Internet Domain Name Process, 1998-1999; National Chair, Brand Names Education Foundation, Saul Lefkowitz Moot Court Competition, 1998-1999; Advisory Board, *The IP Litigator,* 1997—; Editorial Board, Trademark Reporter, 1994-1997. Author: "Guiding Rights: Trademarks, Copyright and the Internet" (2003 iUniverse); "Trade Dress Protection and the Problem of Distinctiveness," The John Marshall Law School Review of Intellectual Property Law, Spring 2002; "Likelihood of Confusion: Understanding Trademark Law's Key Principle," IP Litigator, March/April 2000; "A Review of Recent Trademark Cases in the U.S.," 38.57 IDEA: The Journal of Law and Technology, 1997; "Trademark Parody and the First Amendment," 29.4 The John Marshall Law Review, 1996; "Managing Cases, Information and Yourself, Winning with Computers: Trial Practice in the 21st Century - Part 2" (ABA 1993). *Member:* Chicago, Illinois State and American Bar Associations; American Intellectual Property Law Association (Board of Directors, 1998-2001); International Trademark Association; Intellectual Property Law Association of Chicago; Legal Club (President, 1999); Lawyers Club of Chicago (President, 2000). ***PRACTICE AREAS:*** Intellectual Property Litigation; Intellectual Property; Trademarks; Copyrights; Unfair Competition; Domain Name Dispute Resolution; Computer Law; Internet Law; Advertising Law; International Law; Licensing Law. ***Email:*** mpartridge@pattishall.com

BEVERLY W. PATTISHALL (1916-2002)

ROBERT W. SACOFF, born Oak Park, Illinois, November 1, 1947; admitted to bar, 1973, Illinois; 1983, District of Columbia. *Education:* University of Notre Dame (A.B., 1969); Northwestern University (J.D., 1973). Editorial Board Member, Northwestern University Law Review, 1972-1973, Trademark Reporter, 1981-1984. Author: "Trademark Law in the Technology-Driven Global Marketplace," 4 Yale Symp. L & Tech. 8 (2001), http://lawtech.law.yale.edu/symposium/s01/comment_sacoff.htm; "Trademark and Unfair Competition Cases in the United States: 1994 in Review," 178 Revue Internationale de la Concurrence, No. 3, 41 (1995); "Multi-Million Dollar Judgment for Common Law Trade Mark Infringement Overturned: ZaZu Designs v. L'Oreal," 15 Euro. Int. Prop.Rev.104 (1993). Member, Public Advisory Committee on Trademark Affairs (1989-1995, 1997-2000). Advisor to U.S. Delegation to Geneva Diplomatic Conference on the Trademark Law Treaty (1994). *Member:* American Bar Association (Chair, Section of Intellectual Property Law, 2003-2004); Lawyers Club of Chicago (Board of Directors, 1999-2001); AIPPI US (US Group of Association Internationale pour la Protection de la Propriété Intellectuelle) (President, 2004-2006); American Intellectual Property Law Association (Board of Directors, 1990-1993); International Trademark Association (Board of Directors, 1987-1989). ***PRACTICE AREAS:*** Intellectual Property Litigation; Intellectual Property; Trademarks; Copyrights; Unfair Competition; Domain Name Dispute Resolution; International Law. ***Email:*** rsacoff@pattishall.com

SANJIV D. SARWATE, born Princeton, New Jersey, May 5, 1972; admitted to bar, 1997, Illinois. *Education:* University of Illinois (B.A., 1993); University of Chicago (M.A., 1995); University of Illinois College of Law (J.D., magna cum laude, 1997). ***PRACTICE AREAS:*** Intellectual Property Litigation; Intellectual Property; Trademarks; Copyrights; Unfair Competition; Domain Name Dispute Resolution; Computer Law; Technology Law; Communications and Media. ***Email:*** ssarwate@pattishall.com

BELINDA JAYNE SCRIMENTI, born Dayton, Ohio, January 30, 1956; admitted to bar, 1981, Ohio and U.S. District Court, Northern District of Ohio; 1984, U.S. District Court, Eastern District of Michigan; 1987, U.S. Court of Appeals, Sixth Circuit; 1988, U.S. Court of Appeals, Third Circuit; 1989, District of Columbia; 1995, U.S. Court of Appeals, Second Circuit; 2002, Virginia; 2003, U.S. District Court, Eastern District of Virginia (Not admitted in Illinois). *Education:* Ohio University (B.S. Journalism, summa cum laude, 1978); The Ohio State University (J.D., with honors, 1981). Note and Comment Editor, Ohio State Law Journal, 1980-1981. Author: "Defending Copyright Infringement Claims Involving the 'Total Look and Feel' of Literary or Artistic Works," XIV, No. 1 AIPLA Selected Legal Papers, 1995. Co-Author: "Counterfeiting and Piracy in the U.S.—A General Overview of the Law and Practice to Combat Counterfeiting and Piracy," 79 Piracy and Counterfeiting of Industrial Property and Copyright, 1983; "The Impact of the Temple Decision on Collegiate Licensing Programs," 10 The Licensing Journal 17, 1990; "Trademark Law Revision Act of 1988 and Its Impact of Trademark Prosecution and Enforcement in the United States," 3 The Corporate Analyst 176, 1991. Author: "A Journalist's View of The Progressive Case: A Look at the Press, Prior Restraint and the First Amendment from the Pentagon Papers Cases to the Future," 41 Ohio State L.J. 1165, 1980. International Trademark Association, Speaker, "Madrid 101, Filing and Prosecution Strategies" 2003; "'The Borders Beyond'—Using U.S. and Foreign Customs Agencies to Halt Exportation and Importation of Counterfeits Worldwide" 2005; International Anti-Counterfeiting Coalition (Meeting Co-Chair, 1998; Speaker, "Navigating Copyright and Trademark Basics," 2000; Speaker, "The Tools Plaintiffs Need to Improve Prospects for Monetary Relief," 1998). *Member:* Ohio State and American (Member: Sections on: Litigation; Intellectual Property Law; Forum on the Entertainment and Sports Industries) Bar Associations; District of Columbia Bar (Member, Sections on: Patent, Trademark and Copyright Law; Arts, Entertainment and Sports Law); Virginia State Bar (Member: Section on Intellectual Property); American Intellectual Property Law Association; International Trademark Association (Member, Committees on: Legislation, 1991; Public Relations, 1996; Publications, 1998; Information Services, 1997; Projects Editorial Board, 1998; Meetings, 2002-2003, Madrid Protocol 101, 2003; Meetings, 2004-2005, Anticounterfeiting Forum, 2005; Annual Meeting 2007 Project Team, Group Leader); Women's Bar Association of the District of Columbia. (Resident, Alexandria, Virginia Office). ***PRACTICE AREAS:*** Intellectual Property Litigation; Intellectual Property; Trademarks; Copyrights; Unfair Competition; Domain Name Dispute Resolution; Internet Law. ***Email:*** bscrimenti@pattishall.com

BENJAMIN S. WARREN III, born New York, N.Y., June 10, 1935; admitted to bar, 1963, Illinois; 1967, District of Columbia. *Education:* St. Paul's School; University of Virginia (B.A., 1960; J.D., 1963). Phi Alpha Delta. Member, Editorial Board, Trademark Reporter, 1985-1987. *Member:* The District of Columbia Bar; Bar Association of the District of Columbia; American Bar Association; American Intellectual Property Law Association; Lawyers Club of Chicago. [United States Marine Corps, 1956-1958]. (Resident Partner, Alexandria, Virginia Office). ***PRACTICE AREAS:*** Litigation; Trademark Law; Copyright Law; Unfair Competition Law; International Law. ***Email:*** bwarren@pattishall.com

(This Listing Continued)

JOSEPH N. WELCH II, born Ann Arbor, Michigan, July 30, 1954; admitted to bar, 1984, Illinois. *Education:* Harvard College (B.A., cum laude, 1976); Northwestern University (J.D., 1984). Adjunct Professor, Trademark and Unfair Competition Law, Northwestern University School of Law, 1989—. Co-Author: "Trademarks and Unfair Competition," LexisNexis Publishing, (sixth edition, 2005); "Trademarks and Unfair Competition Deskbook," LexisNexis Publishing, second edition, 2003. Mediator, Lanham Act Cases, Northern District of Illinois Voluntary Mediation Program. Member: Editorial Board of the Trademark Reporter; Projects Editorial Board of the International Trademark Association; American Intellectual Property Law Quarterly. *Member:* Chicago (Volunteer, Pro Bono Adoption Program), Illinois State and American (Co-Chair, Trademark Litigation Committee of Intellectual Property Law Section) Bar Associations; American Intellectual Property Law Association (Board of Directors); Seventh Circuit Bar Association; Lawyers For The Creative Arts; Intellectual Property Law Association of Chicago (Treasurer; Member, Board of Managers); Chicago Intellectual Property Alliance (Board of Directors). ***PRACTICE AREAS:*** Intellectual Property Litigation; Intellectual Property; Trademarks; Copyrights; Unfair Competition; Domain Name Dispute Resolution; International Law; Advertising Law. ***Email:*** jwelch@pattishall.com

ULI WIDMAIER, born Tübingen, Germany, April 27, 1962; admitted to bar, 1994, Illinois. *Education:* Brown University (B.A., magna cum laude, with honors, 1990; M.A., 1990); Yale University (J.D., 1994). Phi Beta Kappa. Author: "Use, Liability, and the Structure of Trademark Law," Hofstra Law Review, Winter 2005; "Jury und Medien—zu einem elementaren verfassungsrechtlichen Problem in den USA," Neue Juristische Wochenschrift, February 2004; "Jurisdiction and the Internet: The Ascendancy of In Rem Jurisdiction and the Decline of Zippo," ABA Intellectual Property Newsletter, Vol. 21, No. 3 (Spring 2003); "German Broadcast Regulation: A Model for a New First Amendment," Boston College International and Comparative Law Review, Winter 1998; "Covenants Not to Compete," in Antitrust and Unfair Competition, Illinois Institute of Continuing Legal Education, 1996, and 1999 Supplement. Co-Author: "Trademark Case Leaves Open Questions—Court Adopts Some of ABA's Analysis Despite Ruling for Victoria's Secret," ABA Journal eReport, Vol. 2, Issue 9 (March 7, 2003); "Trademark Dilution and the Plain Language Solution to Victoria's Secret," John Marshall Law School News Source, Vol. IV, No. 2 (Fall 2002). Lecturer in Law on Advanced Trademark Law, Intellectual Property Law, the Regulation of Information and the First Amendment in the Media, University of Chicago Law School. *Member:* Chicago, Federal and American (Section on Intellectual Property Law, Amicus Briefs Committee, 2003—) Bar Associations. ***LANGUAGES:*** German. ***PRACTICE AREAS:*** Intellectual Property Litigation; Intellectual Property; Trademarks; Copyrights; Unfair Competition; Domain Name Dispute Resolution; International Law. ***Email:*** uwidmaier@pattishall.com

OF COUNSEL

MELVYN A. SILVER, born Chicago, Illinois, April 3, 1940; admitted to bar, 1965, Illinois; 1969, U.S. Court of Appeals, Seventh Circuit; 1971, Indiana; 1986, Pennsylvania and U.S. Court of Appeals for the Federal Circuit and U.S. Supreme Court. *Education:* Northwestern University (B.A., 1962); Northwestern University (J.D., 1965). Adjunct Professor, Trademarks, Copyrights, Intellectual Property and Franchising, University of Notre Dame Law School, 1973-1976. Member, Board of Directors, 1987-1990 and Chairman, Education Committee, 1990-1991, International Trademark Association. *Member:* Chicago and American (Section on Intellectual Property Law; Antitrust Committee, 1973—) Bar Associations. ***PRACTICE AREAS:*** Intellectual Property Litigation; Intellectual Property; Trademarks; Copyrights; Unfair Competition; Domain Name Dispute Resolution. ***Email:*** msilver@pattishall.com

---

ANNIE L. ALBERTSON, born Taipei, Taiwan; August 3, 1978; admitted to bar, 2003 Illinois. *Education:* Stanford University (B.A., American Studies, 2000); Northwestern University School of Law (J.D., 2003). ***PRACTICE AREAS:*** Intellectual Property Litigation; Intellectual Property; Trademarks; Copyrights; Unfair Competition; Domain Name Dispute Resolution; Internet Law; Trade Secrets. ***Email:*** aalbertson@pattishall.com

PHILLIP BARENGOLTS, born Moscow, Russia, June 11, 1976; admitted to bar, 2001, Illinois. *Education:* Brown University (Sc.B., magna cum laude, 1998); Harvard University (J.D., 2001). ***PRACTICE AREAS:*** Intellectual Property Litigation; Intellectual Property; Trademarks; Copyrights; Unfair Competition; Domain Name Dispute Resolution; Information Technology; Internet Law; E-Commerce. ***Email:*** pbarengolts@pattishall.com

CHAD J. DOELLINGER, born Newton, Iowa; July 24, 1975; admitted to bar, 2001, Illinois. *Education:* University of Iowa (B.S., 1998; B.A., with honors, 1998); Yale Law School (J.D., 2001). Phi Beta Kappa. Editor-in-Chief, Yale Symposium on Law and Technology. Author: "Recent Developments in Trademark Law: The Ongoing Refinement of Rights," John Marshall Review of Intellectual Property Law (RIPL), Vol. 3, Issue 2 (Spring 2004); "Trademarks, Domain Names and Cyber-Infringement: A New Approach to an Old Problem," The IP Litigator, Vol. 10, No. 2 (March/April 2004); "Trademarks, Metatags, and Initial Interest Confusion: A Look to the Past to Reconceptualize the Future," 41 IDEA 173 (2001). ***PRACTICE AREAS:*** Intellectual Property Litigation; Intellectual Property; Trademarks; Copyrights; Unfair Competition; Domain Name Dispute Resolution; E-Commerce. ***Email:*** cdoellinger@pattishall.com

ANDREW N. DOWNER, born Iowa City, Iowa, December 5, 1974; admitted to bar, 2003, Illinois. *Education:* Northwestern University School of Law (J.D., 2003). ***PRACTICE AREAS:*** Intellectual Property Litigation; Intellectual Property; Trademarks; Copyrights; Unfair Competition; Domain Name Dispute Resolution. ***Email:*** adowner@pattishall.com

MATTHEW A. GRIFFIN, born Pittsburgh, Pennsylvania, August 25, 1969; admitted to bar, 2002, Illinois. *Education:* Miami University (B.A., magna cum laude, 1991); University of Michigan (M.A., in English Language and Literature, 1993); University of Chicago (J.D., cum laude, 2001). ***PRACTICE AREAS:*** Intellectual Property Litigation; Intellectual Property; Trademarks; Copyrights; Unfair Competition; Domain Name Dispute Resolution. ***Email:*** mgriffin@pattishall.com

(This Listing Continued)

KRISTEN S. KNECHT, born 1980; admitted to bar, 2004, Illinois. *Education:* University of Michigan (A.B. with distinction, Honors in English Literature, 2001); University of Michigan Law School (J.D., 2004). Executive Editor, Michigan Journal of Race and Law. ***PRACTICE AREAS:*** Intellectual Property Litigation; Intellectual Property; Trademarks; Copyrights; Unfair Competition; Domain Name Dispute Resolution.

SAPNA KUMAR, admitted to bar, 2003, Illinois. *Education:* University of Texas at Austin (B.S., Mathematics, 1999; B.A., Philosophy, with honors, 1999); University of Chicago Law School (J.D., 2003). ***PRACTICE AREAS:*** Intellectual Property Litigation; Intellectual Property; Trademarks; Copyrights; Unfair Competition; Domain Name Dispute Resolution; Computers and Software; Internet.

DANIELLE B. LEMACK, born Framingham, Massachusetts, May 1, 1972; admitted to bar, 1998, Illinois. *Education:* University of California at Berkeley (B.A., 1994); University of Michigan (J.D., 1998). Author and Panelist: "Keyword Advertising - Fair or Foul?" June 2004. ***PRACTICE AREAS:*** Intellectual Property Litigation; Intellectual Property; Trademarks; Copyrights; Unfair Competition; Domain Name Dispute Resolution; Advertising Law. ***Email:*** dlemack@pattishall.com

JARED D. SOLOVAY, admitted to bar, 1999, Illinois. *Education:* Columbia University (B.A.); University of California at Berkeley (J.D.). ***PRACTICE AREAS:*** Intellectual Property; Intellectual Property Litigation.

ANGELA K. STEELE, born Normal, Illinois, December 13, 1976; admitted to bar, 2002, Illinois. *Education:* University of North Carolina at Chapel Hill (B.S., with highest distinction, 1999); University of Chicago (J.D., 2002). Phi Beta Kappa. ***PRACTICE AREAS:*** Intellectual Property Litigation; Intellectual Property; Trademarks; Copyrights; Unfair Competition; Domain Name Dispute Resolution. ***Email:*** asteele@pattishall.com

TERESA D. TAMBOLAS, born Boonton, New Jersey, December 8, 1974; admitted to bar, 1999, Illinois and U.S. District Court, Northern District of Illinois; registered to practice before U.S. Patent and Trademark Office. *Education:* Columbia University (B.A., 1996); DePaul University (J.D., 1999). ***PRACTICE AREAS:*** Intellectual Property Litigation; Intellectual Property; Trademarks; Copyrights; Unfair Competition; Domain Name Dispute Resolution. ***Email:*** ttambolas@pattishall.com

PATTISHALL, MCAULIFFE HAS REPRESENTED: twenty of the Fortune 100; four of the top 9 U.S. Advertisers; two of the top 3 U.S. Megabrands; and twenty-one of the 23 Business Week Industry Groups.

PATTON & RYAN LLC

Established in 2004

ONE IBM PLAZA, SUITE 2900
CHICAGO, ILLINOIS 60611
Telephone: 312-261-5160
Fax: 312-261-5161
Email: jpatton@pattonryan.com
URL: http://www.pattonryan.com

Tort Litigation, Commercial Litigation, Product Liability Law, Environmental Law, Construction Law, Insurance Coverage, Civil Litigation, Insurance Defense, Professional Liability, Medical Malpractice.

FIRM PROFILE: A civil litigation defense firm specializing in defending insurers and self-insured in matters of catastrophic loss, professional liability, products and construction law, trucking and transportation, appellate litigation, environmental and toxic tort, and workers' compensation.

LANGUAGES: Spanish, French, German, Vietnamese and Urdu.

PARTNERS OF FIRM

JOHN W. PATTON, JR., born Evanston, Illinois, July 26, 1958; admitted to bar, 1983, Illinois and U.S. District Court, Northern District of Illinois; 1984, Federal Trial Bar; 1999, U.S. District Court, Western District of Michigan; 2001, U.S. District Court, Eastern District of Michigan, U.S. District Court, Northern and Southern Districts of Indiana and U.S. Court of Appeals, Seventh Circuit; 2002, U.S. District Court, Southern District of Illinois and U.S. District Court, Southern District of Texas. *Education:* Miami University (B.A., 1980); DePaul University (J.D., 1983). Author: "Tort Reform Issues and Trends," 1990; "Preparation and Trial of the Automobile Collision Case," 1992; "Preparing and Handling Toxic Tort Cases," 1993; "Handling Slip and Fall Cases," 1993; "Defending the Employer in Construction Cases," 1993, 1994; "Successful Preparation and Handling of Discovery Objections and Trial Motions," 1995; "Defense of the Catastrophic Loss Trucking Case," 1997; "Insurance Coverage Issues/Trucking Policies," 1997; "Placard/Logo Liability and Punitive Damage Liability of Motor Carriers," 1998; "Negligent Hiring and Negligent Entrustment as Causes of Action Against the Motor Carrier," 1998; "The Defense of the Employer Post-Kotecki, Braye, Briseno, and Lannom," 1999; "That Delete Key May Bite You: Spoliation Claims Against Trucking Companies for Destruction of Electronic Data," 1999; "Defending Employers In Third Party Liability Litigation," 2002; "Defending the Nuisance Value/Soft Tissue Claim," 2002; "Negligent Hiring and Negligent Entrustment," 2002; "Catastrophic Loss Cases," 2002. Speaker: Casualty Adjusters Association: Illinois Tort Reform Present and Future, 1996; Insurance and Transportation Industry Seminars on the investigation, defense and trial of catastrophic loss claims, cargo claims, insurance coverage, and compliance with Federal Motor Carrier Safety Regulations; The Investigation and Defense of Trucking Cases for the International Air Cargo Association of Chicago, 2002; Rusin Patton Maciorowski & Friedman's Successful Defense of Transportation and Tort Claims Seminar, 2002. Village Trustee, Village of Glenview. Alternate Director, Solid Waste Agency of Northern Cook County. Alternative Director, Board of Directors, Northwest Municipal Conference of Mayors. *Member:* Chicago (Mediator), Illinois State and American (Vice-Chair of Commercial Transportation Litigation Committee) Bar Associations; American Trucking Association; America Trial Association Litigation Center; Trucking Industry Defense Association; Professional Liability Association; Illinois Transportation Association; National Council of Self-Insurers; Chicago Casualty Adjuster Association. (Managing Partner). ***REPORTED CASES:*** Pehl v. Environmental Systems, Ill. App.

(This Listing Continued)

PATTON & RYAN LLC, Chicago—Continued

3d 218, 653 N.E. 2d 766 (1995). ***PRACTICE AREAS:*** Tort Litigation; Commercial Litigation; Product Liability Law; Environmental Law; Construction Law; Insurance Coverage. ***Email:*** jpatton@pattonryan.com

DAVID F. RYAN, born Evanston, Illinois, April 26, 1953; admitted to bar, 1985, Illinois and U.S. District Court, Northern District of Illinois; 1990, Federal Trial Bar; 1997, U.S. Court of Appeals, Seventh Circuit; 2002, U.S. District Court, Southern District of Texas; 2003, U.S. District Court, Northern District of Indiana. *Education:* University of Notre Dame (B.B.A., 1975); Quinnipiac College of Law (J.D., 1984). Associate Editor, Chicago Bar News. Arbitrator, Circuit Court of Lake County, 1989—. Author: "Imputed Negligence Doctrine in Automobile Cases," Illinois Bar Journal, October 1994. Speaker: "Civil Trial Support," The Illinois Paralegal Association Education Seminar, 2003; "The Law of Spoliation of Evidence," Rusin Patton Maciorowski & Friedman's Successful Defense of Transportation and Tort Claims Seminar, 2002; "Anatomy of a Personal Injury Lawsuit," Kiwanis Club Highland Park, 1995; "Jury Instruction," Landau, Omahana & Kopka Seminar, 1994; "Law Firm Marketing," Seminar, Chicago Bar Association News, Spring 1995. Member, Lake County Chamber of Commerce. *Member:* Chicago and Illinois State Bar Associations. ***REPORTED CASES:*** Indlecoffer v. Village of Wadsworth, 671 N.E.2d 1128 (2004); Wilson-McCray v. Strokes, 2003WL 22901569, N.D.Ill (2003); Bruce v. Diamond Transportation, Racine County, Wisconsin, 03 CV 0 (2004). A demand of $3 million, verdict of $560,000; Kimble v. Jorgenson Co., Cook County, Illinois, 00 L 010031 (2003). A demand of $10 million, verdict of $3 million; McCaffrey v. T & L Trucking, Cook County, Illinois, 97 L 1835 (2003). A demand of $3 million, verdict of $982,000; Quinn v. Kopf Trucking, Wayne County, Detroit, Michigan (1999) A demand of $2 million, verdict of $750,000. ***PRACTICE AREAS:*** Civil Litigation; Insurance Defense. ***Email:*** dryan@pattonryan.com

W. MARK SICKLES, born Aurora, Illinois; admitted to bar, 1991, Illinois and U.S. District Court, Northern District of Illinois; 2003, U.S. District Court, Northern District of Indiana; 2004, U.S. District Court, Southern District of Illinois. *Education:* Rush University (B.S., 1981); John Marshall Law School (J.D., 1991). Registered Nurse, 1981—. Trauma Nurse Specialist (TNA), 1985-1990. Advanced Cardiac Life Support Instructor (ACLS), 1986-1990. Presenter: EMTALA (Emergency Medical Treatment and Active Labor Act) Update for Emergency Department Medical and Nursing staff of Deaconess Hospital, Evansville, Indiana, 2002; EMTALA Update for Emergency Department Medical and Nursing Staff of Highland Park Hospital, Highland Park, Illinois, 1999; Effective Telephone Triage Assessment for Nurses in the Outpatient Setting, Wheaton Clinic, Wheaton, Illinois, 1998. Coach, American Youth Soccer Organization Coach, 1998—. *Member:* Chicago, Illinois State and American Bar Associations; National Association of Nurse Attorneys; Critical Care Nurses Association. ***REPORTED CASES:*** U.S. Bank, Administrator of the Estate of Roe Ann Lockhart, a minor v. YMCA of Metropolitan Chicago and Terrell Sanderson, 01 L 4891, a personal injury case. The demand was $35 Million; offers were for $1.7 million, $2.6 million, and $4.5 million and they were all rejected; $35.9 million was asked of the jury; the verdict was for the defense; Loukia Alafogianis v. George Bahramis and Michael O'Neil, 99 L 7031, a personal injury case. $300,000 was asked of the jury, the verdict was for the defense; Tamara Couch v. Madonna Arredondo, 99 L 3593, a personal injury case. Asked of jury $2.5 million, verdict $490,000; Ryszard Chrzanowski v. Sallie Ervin, 99 L 12832, a construction negligence case. $1.7 million was asked of the jury, the verdict was for the defense; Renee Wagner v. Gwillym Williams, 98 L 8884, a personal injury case. $9.9 million was asked of the jury, the verdict was for the defense. ***PRACTICE AREAS:*** Insurance Defense. ***Email:*** wmsickles@pattonryan.com

ASSOCIATES

DAVID S. ATLAS, born Chicago, Illinois; admitted to bar, 1979, Illinois and U.S. District Court, Northern District of Illinois. *Education:* University of Illinois (B.A., with honors, 1976); Chicago-Kent College of Law, Illinois Institute of Technology (J.D., with honors, 1979). Instructor in Law, 1979-1981. ***PRACTICE AREAS:*** Personal Injury; Medical Negligence. ***Email:*** datlas@pattonryan.com

FERNANDO M. BUSTAMANTE, born Lima, Peru, August 15, 1958; admitted to bar, 1983, Illinois and U.S. District Court, Northern District of Illinois. *Education:* Northern Illinois University (B.S., 1980); DePaul University (J.D., 1983). Hearing Officer, Chicago Park District, 1988-1997. *Member:* Chicago, Illinois State and American Bar Associations. ***LANGUAGES:*** Spanish. ***REPORTED CASES:*** In re Marriage of Callaway, 150 Ill.App.3d 712 (1986); Chavez v. Watts, 161 Ill.App.3d 664 (1987). ***PRACTICE AREAS:*** Insurance Defense; Civil Litigation; Transportation Law; Professional Liability; Appellate Practice. ***Email:*** fbustamante@pattonryan.com

ANDREW N. COLEMAN, born Chicago, Illinois, July 13, 1973; admitted to bar, 1998, Illinois. *Education:* Michigan State University (B.A., with honors, 1995); Vanderbilt University (J.D., 1998). Phi Beta Kappa. *Member:* Chicago, Illinois State and American Bar Associations. ***PRACTICE AREAS:*** Civil Litigation; Insurance Defense; Transportation; Professional Liability; Medical Malpractice; Premises Liability; Construction Defects. ***Email:*** acoleman@pattonryan.com

PAUL C. JAKUBIAK, born Lansing, Michigan, June 1, 1970; admitted to bar, 1997, Illinois; 1998, U.S. District Court, Northern District of Illinois. *Education:* University of Michigan at Ann Arbor (B.A., Political Science, 1994); Loyola University (J.D., 1997). ***LANGUAGES:*** French. ***REPORTED CASES:*** Van Meter v. City of Darien, 207 Ill. 2d 359 (2003). ***PRACTICE AREAS:*** Insurance Defense; Transportation Law; Construction Law; Products Liability. ***Email:*** pjakubiak@pattonryan.com

JAMES J. JOZEFOWICZ, born Chicago, Illinois, 1961; admitted to bar, 1989, Illinois; 1994, U.S. Court of Appeals, Seventh Circuit; 1998, U.S. District Court, Northern District of Illinois, including Trial Bar. *Education:* University of Chicago (B.A., Political Science, 1986; M.A., Social Science, 1993); Creighton University (1986); Northern Illinois University (J.D., 1988). Assistant State Attorney, Cook County States Attorney's Office, 1993-2001. Judicial Law Clerk, Chancery Division, Circuit Court of Cook County, 1989-1993. Special Project Director, Young Lawyers Section, Chicago Bar Association, 1995-1996. Chairman, Bench-Bar Relations Committee, Young Lawyers Section, Chicago Bar Association, 1994-1995. ***REPORTED CASES:*** Harriet Rizzo v. Michael Sheahan, et al., 266 F.3d 705 (7th Circuit 2001); Robert Simpson v. Tim Rowan, et al., 73 F.3d 134 (7th Circuit 1995); Marcy Jones and Votis Wilborn on their own behalf of other persons similarly situated v. Ross Takaki, Three Unknown Police Officers, Cook County, et al., 38 F.3d 321 (7th Circuit 1994). ***PRACTICE AREAS:*** Commercial Litigation; Municipal Liability; Federal Litigation; Labor and Employment Law; Insurance Defense Litigation; Professional Liability. ***Email:*** jjozefowicz@pattonryan.com

SARAH A. KENNEDY, born Saginaw, Michigan; admitted to bar, 1995, Illinois and U.S. District Court, Northern District of Illinois. *Education:* University of Michigan (B.A., 1990); DePaul University (J.D., 1995). *Member:* Chicago and Illinois State Bar Associations; Illinois Association of Defense Trial Counsel (Co-Chair, Young Lawyers Division, 2004—). ***PRACTICE AREAS:*** Civil Litigation; Transportation; Premises Liability; Fire Insurance; Medical Malpractice. ***Email:*** skennedy@pattonryan.com

FAWZIA MIRZA, born Ontario, Canada; admitted to bar, 2003, Illinois. *Education:* Indiana University at Bloomington (B.A., 1999); Chicago-Kent College of Law, Illinois Institute of Technology (J.D.). Recipient: Bar and Gavel Award for Outstanding Service to the Law School and Legal Community; CALI Award for highest achievement in Trial Advocacy's. Member, Chicago -Kent National Trial Advocacy Team, 2002-2003. *Member:* Muslim, Chicago and Indian State Bar Association; South Asian Law Students Association (President and Founder, 2002-2003). ***LANGUAGES:*** Urdu, French and English. ***PRACTICE AREAS:*** Civil Litigation. ***Email:*** fmirza@pattonryan.com

MARK R. PENNEY, born Lafayette, Indiana, 1974; admitted to bar, 2000, Indiana (Not admitted in Illinois). *Education:* Princeton University (B.A., magna cum laude, 1996);Harvard Law School (J.D., 2000); Northwestern University (M.A., 2002). *Member:* Indiana Bar Association. ***LANGUAGES:*** Latin, German. ***REPORTED CASES:*** Harris v. AC&S, Inc., 785 N.E. 2d 1087 (Ind., 2003); Jurich v. Garlock, Inc, 788 N.E. 2d 1093 (Ind., 2003); Harris v. AC&S, Inc., 766 N.E. 2d 383 (Ind. App., 2002); Jurich v. Garlock, 759 N.E. 2d 1066 (Ind. App., 2001). ***PRACTICE AREAS:*** Appellate Practice; Insurance Defense; Torts; Civil Litigation; Toxic Torts; Environmental Torts; Transportation. ***Email:*** mpenney@pattonryan.com

KATHRYN A. STARCK, born Ft. Worth, Texas; admitted to bar, 2002, Illinois and U.S. District Court, Northern District of Illinois. *Education:* DePaul University (English and Communications, 1995); Chicago-Kent College of Law, Illinois Institute of Technology (J.D., 2001). *Member:* Chicago and Illinois State Bar Associations; Women's Bar Association of Illinois; Hispanic Lawyers Association of Illinois. ***LANGUAGES:*** English and Spanish. ***PRACTICE AREAS:*** Civil Defense Litigation; Transportation Law; Professional Liability; Appellate Practice; Bankruptcy. ***Email:*** kstarck@pattonryan.com

PAUL S. STEINHOFER, born South Bend, Indiana, 1965; admitted to bar, 1993, Indiana; 1997, Illinois. *Education:* Indiana University, Bloomington (B.S., 1988; J.D., 1993). ***PRACTICE AREAS:*** Insurance Defense Litigation; Transportation Law; Civil Litigation; Professional Liability; Employment Law. ***Email:*** psteinhofer@pattonryan.com

BRIAN J. WEIG, born Aberdeen, South Dakota, August 8, 1964; admitted to bar, 1995, North Dakota; 2000, Illinois; 2003, U.S. District Court, Northern District of Illinois. *Education:* University of North Dakota (B.S., Psychology, 1987, Dean's List; J.D., 1995). *Member:* State Bar Association of North Dakota. ***PRACTICE AREAS:*** Civil Litigation; Insurance. ***Email:*** bweig@pattonryan.com

LEGAL SUPPORT PERSONNEL

TONET BALLARD
MICHAEL J. PATTON
NICOLE ZAMORA

Languages: Spanish, French, German, Vietnamese and Urdu.

PATZIK, FRANK & SAMOTNY LTD.

SUITE 900
150 SOUTH WACKER DRIVE
CHICAGO, ILLINOIS 60606
Telephone: 312-551-8300
Facsimile: 312-551-1101
Email: lawyers@pfs-law.com
URL: http://www.pfs-law.com

Corporate, Federal and State Securities, Federal Taxation, Estate Planning, Real Estate, Patent, Copyright and Trademark, Commercial and Business Law and Litigation.

FIRM PROFILE: Patzik, Frank & Samotny Ltd. represents a variety of clients in connection with a myriad of complex and demanding projects. Formed in 1991, Patzik, Frank & Samotny Ltd. represents public and private corporations, limited liability companies, partnerships, investment trusts, financial institutions, brokerage firms, investment banks, entrepreneurs and others. The firm's practice features a broad range of disciplines, including general corporate representation, securities law, federal and state taxation, business acquisition and disposition, public and private debt and equity financing (including private equity and venture capital), real estate acquisition and disposition, patent, trademark and copyright law (including prosecution, counseling and litigation), estate planning, commercial litigation and employment law and litigation. Patzik, Frank & Samotny Ltd. prides itself on being a "results oriented" law firm which focuses on attaining client objectives with an attention to detail and an understanding of the economic, political and interpersonal factors affecting a matter or transaction.

ALAN B. PATZIK, born Chicago, Illinois, 1959; admitted to bar, 1984, Illinois and U.S. District Court, Northern District of Illinois. *Education:* University of Illinois (B.S., in Accounting, with highest honors, 1981); Northwestern University (J.D., 1984). Beta Alpha Psi; Phi Eta Sigma; Phi Beta Gamma. Member: Bronze Tablet-University of Illinois; James Scholar. Certified Public Accountant, Illinois, 1981. Author: "The Model Control Share Statute of the North American Securities Administrators Association," 44 the Business Lawyer 577, 1989; "Strategic Land-Deal Planning," The National Law Journal, Summer, 1989; "Antitakeover Devices Used by REITs and RELPs," Real Estate Review, Fall, 1991.

(This Listing Continued)

Member: Chicago, Illinois State and American (Member, Sections of: Business Law; Taxation; Real Property) Bar Associations. ***PRACTICE AREAS:*** Corporate; Mergers and Acquisitions; Finance; Securities; Limited Liability Company Law; Partnership Law. ***Email:*** apatzik@pfs-law.com

STEVEN M. PREBISH, born Skokie, Illinois, 1965; admitted to bar, 1990, Illinois and U.S. District Court, Northern District of Illinois. *Education:* University of Illinois (B.A., 1987; J.D., cum laude, 1990). *Member:* Chicago, Illinois State and American Bar Associations. ***PRACTICE AREAS:*** Mergers and Acquisitions; General Corporate Law; Limited Liability Company Law; Securities Offerings; Securities Regulation; Private Equity; Investment Management; Broker-Dealer Regulation; Secured Lending; Real Estate Finance. ***Email:*** sprebish@pfs-law.com

MARC Z. SAMOTNY, born Chicago, Illinois, 1949; admitted to bar, 1975, Illinois; 1977, U.S. Tax Court. *Education:* Southern Illinois University (B.S., 1971); John Marshall Law School (J.D., with distinction, 1975). Certified Public Accountant, Illinois, 1974. Adjunct Professor of Law, The John Marshall Law School, 1984-1987. *Member:* Chicago, Illinois State and American (Member, Taxation Section) Bar Associations. ***PRACTICE AREAS:*** Business; Corporate; Strategic Alliances; Real Estate; Private Placement; Estate Planning; Federal Taxation; Partnership Law; Limited Liability Company Law. ***Email:*** msamotny@pfs-law.com

MAX SHAFTAL, born Havana, Cuba, 1956; admitted to bar, 1982, Illinois and U.S. District Court, Northern District of Illinois; 1984, U.S. Supreme Court and U.S. Court of Appeals, 7th Circuit; 1986, U.S. Court of Appeals for the Federal Circuit; 1986, U.S. Court of Appeals, 3rd Circuit; 1987, U.S. District Court, Eastern District of Michigan; registered to practice before the U.S. Patent and Trademark Office. *Education:* University of Illinois (B.S.C.E., 1978); DePaul University (J.D., 1982). Board Member, Northbrook School District No. 27, 2000-2004. Member, Intellectual Property Law Advisory Board, DePaul College of Law, 2000-2003. Guest Lecturer, Northern Illinois University College of Business, Entrepreneurship Class of 2004. *Member:* Chicago Bar Association (Member, Executive Board, 1985-1986 and Chairman, 1985-1986, Intellectual Property Law Committee, Young Lawyers Section, 1985-1986); Intellectual Property Law Association of Chicago (Secretary, 1997-1999; Board Member, 2000-2002). ***LANGUAGES:*** Spanish. ***PRACTICE AREAS:*** Patent, Trademark and Copyright; Unfair Competition; Trade Secrets. ***Email:*** mshaftal@pfs-law.com

JOEL G. SHAPIRO, born Chicago, Illinois, 1961; admitted to bar, 1985, Illinois. *Education:* Miami University (B.S., 1982); University of Illinois (J.D., magna cum laude, 1985). Certified Public Accountant, Illinois, 1984. *Member:* Chicago, Illinois State and American Bar Associations. ***PRACTICE AREAS:*** Tax; Partnerships; Limited Liability Company Law; General Corporate. ***Email:*** jshapiro@pfs-law.com

JAMES M. TEPER, born Milwaukee, Wisconsin, 1962; admitted to bar, 1987, Wisconsin, Illinois and U.S. District Court, Eastern District of Wisconsin and U.S. District Court, Northern District of Illinois. *Education:* University of Wisconsin-Madison (B.B.A., 1984; J.D., 1987). *Member:* State Bar of Wisconsin; American Bar Association. ***PRACTICE AREAS:*** Real Estate; Commercial Real Estate; Secured Lending; Banks and Banking. ***Email:*** jteper@pfs-law.com

THOMAS J. VERTICCHIO, born Litchfield, Illinois, 1960; admitted to bar, 1985, Illinois, U.S. Supreme Court, Illinois Supreme Court, U.S. Court of Appeals, Seventh Circuit and U.S. District Courts, Central and Northern Districts of Illinois including Trial Bar. *Education:* Illinois College (B.S., Economics, magna cum laude, 1982); Southern Illinois University (J.D., cum laude, 1985). ***PRACTICE AREAS:*** Commercial Litigation. ***Email:*** tverticchio@pfs-law.com

GARY IRWIN WALT, born Detroit, Michigan, 1957; admitted to bar, 1982, Illinois. *Education:* University of Michigan, Angell Scholar (B.A., with distinction, 1979); Cornell University (J.D., 1982). Member, Moot Court Board. *Member:* Chicago, Illinois State and American Bar Associations. ***PRACTICE AREAS:*** Corporate; Securities; Real Estate; Partnership; Mergers and Acquisitions; Arts and Entertainment Law; Commercial Workouts; Debtor and Creditor Reorganization. ***Email:*** gwalt@pfs-law.com

ALLAN L. YUSIM, born Chicago, Illinois, 1945; admitted to bar, 1970, Illinois. *Education:* University of Illinois (B.S., 1967; J.D., 1970). *Member:* Chicago and Illinois State Bar Associations. ***PRACTICE AREAS:*** Real Estate; Leases and Leasing; Construction Contracts; Estate Planning; Estate and Gift Taxation. ***Email:*** ayusim@pfs-law.com

CHADWICK I. BUTTELL, born Tucson, Arizona, 1968; admitted to bar, 1993, Illinois and U.S. District Court, Northern District of Illinois. *Education:* Northwestern University (B.A., Mathematics and Economics, 1990); Illinois Institute of Technology Stuart School of Business (M.B.A., 1993); Chicago-Kent College of Law (J.D., with honors, 1993; LL.M.in Taxation, 1998). Moot Court Society. *Member:* Chicago (Secretary, Federal Tax Committee) and American Bar Associations. ***PRACTICE AREAS:*** Business Law; Corporate Law; Securities Law; Mergers and Acquisitions; Taxation; Estate Planning. ***Email:*** cbuttell@pfs-law.com

SHERYL JAFFEE HALPERN, born Park Ridge, Illinois, 1969; admitted to bar, 1993, Illinois, U.S. District Court, Northern and Central Districts of Illinois, U.S. Court of Appeals, Seventh Circuit and U.S. Supreme Court. *Education:* University of Illinois (B.A., 1990); Chicago-Kent College of Law (J.D., 1993). Board Member, Moot Court Society. Teaching Assistant, Chicago-Kent College of Law Legal Writing Program, 1992-1993. Board Member, Midwest Center on Law and the Deaf, 2003—. *Member:* American Bar Association; Chicago-Lincoln Inn of Court; Society for Human Resource Management. ***PRACTICE AREAS:*** Employment Law; Employment Litigation; Commercial Litigation. ***Email:*** shalpern@pfs-law.com

---

PATRICK G. COOKE, born Evergreen Park, Illinois, 1967; admitted to bar, 1995, Illinois and U.S. District Court, Northern, Central and Southern Districts of Illinois. *Education:* University of Notre Dame (B.A., 1989; J.D., 1995). *Member:* Chicago and American Bar Associations. ***PRACTICE AREAS:*** Commercial Litigation; Insurance Coverage Litigation; Appellate Practice. ***Email:*** pcooke@pfs-law.com

SCOTT M. CURRAN, born La Grange, Illinois, 1976; admitted to bar, 2001, Illinois. *Education:* University of Illinois, Urbana-Champaign (B.A., with distinction, 1998); Chicago-Kent College of Law (J.D., with honors, 2001). Moot Court Honor Society. *Member:* Chicago and American Bar Associations. ***PRACTICE AREAS:*** Corporate Law; Business Law; Mergers and Acquisitions; Securities. ***Email:*** scurran@pfs-law.com

TAN H. LE, born Saigon, Vietnam, 1970; admitted to bar, 1996, Minnesota (inactive); 1999, Illinois. *Education:* Northwestern University (B.A., 1992); University of Wisconsin (J.D., 1996). ***PRACTICE AREAS:*** Mergers and Acquisitions; Private Equity; Securities; Corporate Law. ***Email:*** tle@pfs-law.com

DAVID J. SCHWARTZ, born Warsaw, Indiana, 1972; admitted to bar, 1998, Ohio; 2000, Illinois. *Education:* Liberty University (B.S., Government, magna cum laude, 1995); University of Dayton (J.D., cum laude, 1998). *Member:* Chicago and American Bar Associations. ***PRACTICE AREAS:*** State and Federal Securities Law; Corporate Law; Finance; Mergers and Acquisitions; Broker-Dealer Regulation; Investment Management. ***Email:*** dschwartz@pfs-law.com

SCOTT W. SMILIE, born LaGrange, Illinois, 1971; admitted to bar, 1997, Illinois and U.S. District Court, Northern District of Illinois; registered to practice before U.S. Patent and Trademark Office. *Education:* University of Illinois (B.S.G.E., 1993); Chicago-Kent College of Law, Illinois Institute of Technology (J.D., with honors, 1997). Member, Chicago-Kent Law Review. *Member:* Chicago Bar Association; Intellectual Property Law Association of Chicago. ***PRACTICE AREAS:*** Patents; Trademarks; Copyrights; Unfair Competition; Trade Secrets. ***Email:*** ssmilie@pfs-law.com

SEAN S. SWIDLER, born Skokie, Illinois, 1973; admitted to bar, 1999, Illinois and U.S. District Court, Northern and Central Districts of Illinois; registered to practice before U.S. Patent and Trademark Office. *Education:* University of Iowa (B.S.E., 1996); Chicago-Kent College of Law, Illinois Institute of Technology (J.D., 1999). Member: Moot Court Honor Society; Intellectual Property Moot Court Society. Treasurer, Intellectual Property Law Society, 1998-1999. Contributing Author: *Intellectual Property Law in Cyberspace,*BNA Publications, 1998. ***PRACTICE AREAS:*** Patents; Trademarks; Copyrights; Intellectual Property Litigation; Internet Law. ***Email:*** sswidler@pfs-law.com

JOSEPH C. VITEK, born Pontiac, Illinois, 1964; admitted to bar, 1989, Nebraska, U.S. District Court, District of Nebraska and U.S. Tax Court; 2001, Illinois. *Education:* University of Nebraska (B.A., 1986; J.D., 1989); University of Missouri (LL.M., in Taxation, 1992). *Member:* Chicago, Illinois State and Nebraska State Bar Associations; Chicago Estate Planning Council. ***PRACTICE AREAS:*** Estate Planning; Trust Law; Probate; Taxation; Corporate Law. ***Email:*** jvitek@pfs-law.com

OF COUNSEL

JEFFREY H. FRANK, born Sioux Falls, South Dakota, 1952; admitted to bar, 1980, Minnesota; 1981, Illinois; U.S. District Court, Northern District of Illinois; 1982, U.S. Tax Court; 1996, U.S. Court of Appeals, Seventh Circuit. *Education:* Macalester College (B.A., magna cum laude, 1974); University of Minnesota (J.D., cum laude, 1980); New York University (LL.M. in Taxation, 1981). Phi Beta Kappa. *Member:* Chicago (Member, Federal Tax Committee) and American (Member, Taxation Section) Bar Associations. ***PRACTICE AREAS:*** Federal and State Taxation; Partnership Law; Limited Liability Company Law; Corporate; Securities; Real Estate. ***Email:*** jhfrank@pfs-law.com

---

PAVALON, GIFFORD, LAATSCH & MARINO

TWO NORTH LA SALLE STREET, SUITE 1600
CHICAGO, ILLINOIS 60602
Telephone: 312-419-7400
Fax: 312-419-7408
Email: info@pglmlaw.com
URL: http://www.pglmlaw.com

Civil Trial and Appellate Practice in all Courts. Personal Injury, Wrongful Death, Railroad Injuries, (F.E.L.A.), Medical Malpractice, Products Liability, Aviation Law, Complex Commercial Litigation and Class Actions.

FIRM PROFILE: The law firm of Pavalon, Gifford, Laatsch & Marino concentrates in civil trial and appellate work in the areas of personal injury, medical malpractice, aviation, wrongful death and complex commercial matters in all state and federal courts. For many years, the members of the firm have obtained numerous multi-million dollar settlements and verdicts, some of which verdicts were the highest obtained regarding the specific issues tried. Messrs. Pavalon and Gifford are Fellows of the American College of Trial Lawyers and the International Society of Barristers. Mr. Pavalon has also been elected a Fellow of the International Academy of Trial Lawyers and to membership in the exclusive Inner Circle of Advocates. Mr. Pavalon and Mr. Gifford have been consistently listed in the "Best Lawyers in America." Mr. Gifford is also certified as a Civil Trial Advocate of the National Board of Trial Advocacy and by the American Board of Professional Liability Attorneys. The firm's members have also long been involved in leadership positions in the organized trial bar: Mr. Pavalon having served as President of the Association of Trial Lawyers of America, Trial Lawyers for Public Justice, The Roscoe Pound Foundation and the Illinois Trial Lawyers Association. Mr. Gifford also served as President of the Illinois Trial Lawyers Association .

The firm also has an expertise in Appellate matters. Mr. Laatsch, a counsel of record in over 20 appeals, is the partner who oversees the firm's appeals. Mr. Marino utilizes his experience from studying and traveling in Mexico and Spain as the firm attorney who represents its Spanish speaking clients.

The firm members collectively provide over 100 years of experience as trial lawyers working on behalf of plaintiffs in all the diversified areas of personal injury and wrongful death matters, as well as complex commercial cases and class actions. The vast majority of the firm's clientele is referred by other lawyers seeking the professionalism, experience and high degree of capabilities offered by the firm.

Pavalon, Gifford, Laatsch & Marino Selected Reported Cases:

(This Listing Continued)

PAVALON, GIFFORD, LAATSCH & MARINO, Chicago—Continued

Henry Burke v. 12 Rothschild's Liquor Mart, Inc. and City of Chicago, 209 Ill.App.3d 192, 568 N.E.2d 80 (1st Dist., 1991); 148 Ill.2d 429, 170 Ill.Dec. 633, 593 N.E.2d 522 (1992).

Gerrity v. Beatty, 71 Ill.2d 47, 373 N.E.2d 1323 (1978).

Brandt v. Sarah Bush Lincoln Health Center, 329 Ill.App.3d 348, 771 N.E.2d 470 (4th Dist., 2002); 204 Ill.2d 640, 792 N.E.2d 296 (2003).

Leone v. City of Chicago, 156 Ill.2d 33, 619 N.E.2d 119 (1993) (ITLA Amicus).

S.K. Hand Tool Corp. v. Dresser Industries, 284 Ill.App.3d 417, 672 N.E.2d 341 (1st Dist., 1996).

John Darrill Connelly v. General Motors Corp., 184 Ill.App.3d 378, 540 N.E.2d 370, 132 Ill. Dec. 630 (1st Dist. 1989).

Exchange National Bank of Chicago (Estate of Heagy) v. Air Illinois, Inc., 167 Ill.App.3d 1081, 522 N.E.2d 146 (1st Dist., 1988).

Northern Trust Company (Estate of Nardi) v. American Airlines, Inc., 142 Ill.App.3d 21, 491 N.E.2d 417 (1st Dist., 1985).

Harris Trust and Savings Bank (John Hopp, a Minor) v. Ali, et al, 100 Ill.App.3d 1, 425 N.E.2d 1359 (1st Dist., 1981).

In Re: Estate of Sue A. Bagus, 294 Ill.App.3d 887, 691 N.E.2d 401 (2nd Dist., 1998)

Young v. Gateway Transportation, 26 Ill.App.3d 864, 326 N.E.2d 222 (1st Dist., 1975).

Kenney v. Lakewood Engineering, 85 Ill.App.3d 790, 41 Ill.Dec. 53, 407 N.E.2d 551 (1st Dist., 1979).

Eva Ruff, Individually and as Special Administrator of the Estate of Sheldon Ruff, Deceased v. Northwestern Memorial Hospital, 159 Ill.App.3d 811, 513 N.E.2d 7, 111 Ill.Dec. 761 (1st Dist., 1987).

Lee v. Hyster Co., 156 Ill.App.3d 214, 509 N.E.2d 586 (1st Dist., 1987).

Jack Twitty v. American Gage & Machine Company, 105 Ill.App.3d 455, 434 N.E.2d 493, 61 Ill. Dec. 340 (1st. Dist., 1982).

Lounsbury v. Yorro, 124 Ill.App3d 745, 464 N.E.2d 866 (2nd Dist., 1984).

Colls v. City of Chicago, 212 Ill.App.3d 904, 156 Ill.Dec. 971, 571 N.E2d 951 (1st Dist., 1991).

Kelly v. Franco, 72 Ill.App.3d 642, 391 N.E.2d 54, 28 Ill.Dec. 855 (1st Dist., 1979).

Michael Salima v. Scherwood South, Inc., 38 F.3d 929 (7th Cir., 1994).

Will Holmes v. Elgin, Joliet & Eastern Railway Co., 18 F.3rd 1393 (7th Cir., 1994).

Shaffer v. Dalrymple, 507 S.W. 2d 65 (Mo. Ct. App., 1974).

Foster v. Henderson, 538 S.W.2d 910 (Mo. Ct. App., 1976).

MEMBERS OF FIRM

EUGENE I. PAVALON, born Chicago, Illinois, January 5, 1933; admitted to bar, 1956, Illinois. *Education:* Northwestern University (B.S.L., 1954; J.D., 1956). Recipient: Lifetime Achievement Award, Illinois Trial Lawyers Association, 1996; Champion of Justice Award, Trial Lawyers for Public Justice, 2000; Champion of Justice Award, Association of Trial Lawyers of America, 2003. Laureate, Academy of Illinois Lawyers, Illinois State Bar Association (ISBA), 2005. Author: "Human Rights and Health Care Law," American Journal of Nursing Co., 1980; "Your Medical Rights," Little Brown & Co., 1990. Member, Visiting Committee, Northwestern University School of Law, 1990-1996. Adjunct Professor (Trial Advocacy), Northwestern University School of Law. Member, Board of Overseers, Institute for Civil Justice, RAND, 1993-1999. *Member:* The Association of Trial Lawyers of America (President, 1987-1988); Illinois Trial Lawyers Association (President, 1980); Trial Lawyers for Public Justice (President, 1993-1994); Roscoe Pound Foundation (President, 1988-1990); American Board of Trial Advocates. Fellow: American College of Trial Lawyers; International Academy of Trial Lawyers; International Society of Barristers. The Inner Circle of Advocates. Listed, Best Lawyers in America. [Capt., U.S.A.F., 1956-1959]. ***PRACTICE AREAS:*** Personal Injury; Wrongful Death; Civil Trial Practice; Railroad Accidents and Injuries; Products Liability; Medical Malpractice; Aviation Litigation; Commercial Litigation; Class Actions. ***Email:*** pavalon@pglmlaw.com

GEOFFREY L. GIFFORD, born Kirksville, Missouri, November 26, 1946; admitted to bar, 1971, Missouri; 1972, Michigan; 1977, Illinois; 2001, U.S. Court of Appeals, 7th Circuit. *Education:* University of Missouri (B.A., 1968), University of Michigan (J.D., 1971). Phi Beta Kappa. University Scholar. Finalist for the 1998 Trial Lawyer of the Year Award given by the Trial Lawyers for Public Justice. Recipient: 1998 Public Justice Achievement Award as Chairman of the ITLA Constitutional Challenge Committee. Co-Author: "Illinois Practice Guide-Personal Injury," Second Edition, (Two Volumes), Lawyers Cooperative Publishing and Illinois State Bar Association, Copyright December, 1995. Certified by Loyola University Chicago School of Law and Institute for Health Law as a Qualified Medical Malpractice Case Mediator, 1995. Certified as a Civil Trial Advocate by the National Board of Trial Advocacy, 1989. Diplomate, American Board of Professional Liability Attorneys, 1992. Currently Listed in *The Best Lawyers in America,* 2003-2004 Edition. *Member:* Chicago, Illinois State and American Bar Associations; State Bar of Michigan; The Missouri Bar; Society of Trial Lawyers; Illinois Trial Lawyers Association (President, 1996-1997); The Association of Trial Lawyers of America (Member, Board of Governors, 1999-2004); American Board of Trial Advocates (Member, Illinois Chapter, 1998). *Fellow: American College of Trial Lawyers; International Society of Barristers.* ***PRACTICE AREAS:*** Civil Trial Practice; Medical Malpractice; Products Liability; Complex Commercial Litigation; Civil Litigation. ***Email:*** gifford@pglmlaw.com

GARY K. LAATSCH, born Chicago, Illinois, October 7, 1954; admitted to bar, 1979, Illinois. *Education:* Augustana College (B.A., cum laude, 1976); Loyola University (J.D., 1979). Contributing Author: "Medical Malpractice Trial Notebook," Illinois Trial Lawyers Association Education Fund, 1997-2004; "Illinois Products Liability Practice," Illinois Institute for Continuing Legal Education, 2003. *Member:* Chicago (Member, Judicial Evaluation Committee, 1993-1997), Illinois State and American Bar Associations; Illinois Trial Lawyers Association (Member, Amicus Curiae Committee, 1993—); The Association of Trial Lawyers of America; Appellate Lawyers Association. ***PRACTICE AREAS:*** Appellate Practice; Torts; Products Liability; Medical Malpractice. ***Email:*** laatsch@pglmlaw.com

FRANK C. MARINO, born Chicago, Illinois, August 27, 1948; admitted to bar, 1983, Illinois. *Education:* Lawrence University (B.A., 1970); Northwestern University (M.A., 1973); Illinois Institute of Technology/Chicago-Kent College of Law (J.D., with high honors, 1983). Lecturer: Transport Workers' Union Designated Counsel Meeting, "FELA" Case Law Update, February 1996. Member: Board of Trustees, Assisi Animal Foundation, Crystal Lake, Illinois; Executive Committee, Wheeling Township Democratic Party. *Member:* Chicago and Illinois State Bar Associations; Illinois Trial Lawyers Association; The Association of Trial Lawyers of America (ATLA). ***LANGUAGES:*** Spanish. ***PRACTICE AREAS:*** Medical Malpractice; Federal Employers Liability Act (FELA); Negligence; Appellate Practice. ***Email:*** marino@pglmlaw.com

ASSOCIATE

JOHN J. SIMONETTI, born Chicago, Illinois, June 6, 1968; admitted to bar, 1994, Illinois. *Education:* Boston College (B.A., History/Philosophy, cum laude, 1990); Loyola University Chicago (J.D., 1994). Co-Author: "Wrongful Death Actions and the Illinois Wrongful Death Act," "Damages in Wrongful Death Actions" and "Family Member Liabilities, Remedies, and Immunities," *IICLE Wrongful Death and Survival Actions in Illinois,* 2000. Legal Writing Instructor, Loyola University Chicago School of Law, 1998-1999. *Member:* Chicago Bar Association (Co-Chair, Young Lawyers Section Appellate Law Committee, 1997-1999); Illinois Trial Lawyers Association. ***PRACTICE AREAS:*** Medical Malpractice; Products Liability; Appellate Practice. ***Email:*** simonetti@pglmlaw.com

OF COUNSEL

MARTIN WHITTAKER, born Kansas City, Missouri, 1962; admitted to bar, 1991, Illinois; 1993, Missouri. *Education:* University of Notre Dame (B.A., 1984); National University of Ireland, University College Dublin (M.Phil., 1986); Illinois Institute of Technology, Chicago-Kent College of Law (J.D. with honors, 1991). *Member:* Chicago Bar Association; The Missouri Bar; West Suburban Bar Association. (Also Practicing Individually). ***Email:*** mwhittlaw@earthlink.net

Language: Spanish.

THE LAW OFFICES OF BRUCE D. PAYNTER

CHICAGO, ILLINOIS

(See Arlington Heights)

Criminal Law, Felonies, Misdemeanors, Drug Offenses, Driving While Intoxicated, Assaults, Weapons Charges, Drivers License Suspension, Traffic Violations, Sex Offenses, Personal Injury, Automobile Accidents, Motorcycle Accidents, Trucking Accidents, Wrongful Death, Real Estate Transactions, Buying and Selling Real Estate.

PECK, BLOOM, AUSTRIACO & MITCHELL, LLC

Established in 1998

105 WEST ADAMS, 31ST FLOOR
CHICAGO, ILLINOIS 60603
Telephone: 312-201-0900
Facsimile: 312-201-0803
URL: http://www.peckbloom.com

Northbrook, Illinois Office: 601 Skokie Boulevard, 60062. Telephone: 847-509-1099.

Probate, Estate Planning, Guardianship, Elder Law, Probate Litigation, Estate Administration, Asset Protection Planning, Real Estate, Real Estate Litigation, Corporate, Business Transactions, Public Aid Law, Medicaid Law.

FIRM PROFILE: The firm concentrates its practice in all aspects of probate, estate planning (wills and trusts), guardianship, and elder law with an emphasis on the litigation of contested wills. trusts and disabled persons' estates. Peck, Bloom, Austriaco & Mitchell, LLC is a boutique firm that prides itself in providing efficient, prompt and courteous service to clients through dedication, loyalty and close personal attention.

KERRY R. PECK, born 1952; admitted to bar, 1978, Illinois and U.S. District Court, Eastern District of Illinois; 1979, Florida. *Education:* Northern Illinois University (B.S., Ed.); Chicago-Kent College of Law, Illinois INstitute of Technology (J.D., with honors). Author: "A Hole In The Law", Article Series, Chicago Daily Law Bulletin, 1998; "Proceedings In The Probate Court for Disabled Adults," Chicago Bar Association Record; Blue Cross/Blue Shield; Chicago Tribune; Chicago Sun Times. Member, Board of Directors: The Center for Disability and Elder Law; Suburban Area Agency on Aging. *Member:* Chicago Bar Association (President, 1999-2000); North Suburban Bar Association; Illinois State Bar Association; Women's Bar Association of Illinois; National Academy of Elder Law Attorneys (President, Illinois Chapter). ***REPORTED CASES:*** Gebis v. Swietek, Supreme Court of Illinois, Docket No. 85909, (1999); Martzaklis v. 5559 Belmany Corp., 510 N.E. 2d 1148 (1987). ***PRACTICE AREAS:*** Trusts and Estates; Litigation; Probate; Estate Administration; Estate Planning. ***Email:*** rmallred@peckbloom.com

KENNETH M. BLOOM, born Evanston, Illinois, September 29, 1963; admitted to bar, 1988, Illinois. *Education:* University of Illinois (B.S., Acctg., 1985); Chicago-Kent College of Law, Illinois Institute of Technology (J.D., 1988). Moot Court. Recipient: Chicago Bar Association Milton H. Grat Award for Outstanding Project Leadership, 1997-

(This Listing Continued)

1998. Certified Public Accountant, Illinois, 1985—. Author: "Capital Gains Taxes on Pre-1997 Property," Chicago Bar Association Record, 1993; "Gallenstein v. U.S., Capital Gains Savings on Pre-1997 Property," American Bar Association Tax Newsletter. Director of Training, Hospice and Homebound Elderly Legal Assistance Program, 1995-1999. *Member:* Chicago (Member, Young Lawyers Section: Board of Directors, 1992-1999; Senior Project Coordinator, 1992-1999; Chairman, Estate Planning Committee, 1992-1999; Treasurer, 1997-1998), Illinois State and American (Member, Real Property, Probate and Trust Section, 1995-1999) Bar Associations; Chicago Estate Planning Council; Illinois Certified Public Accountants Society. ***PRACTICE AREAS:*** Estate Planning; Estate Administration; Probate; Real Estate; Corporate; Business Transactions. **Email:** kbloom@peckbloom.com

D. REBECCA MITCHELL, born Jamestown, New York, 1953; admitted to bar, 1980, Illinois and U.S. District Court, Northern District of Illinois. *Education:* Syracuse University (B.A., 1975); State University of New York at Buffalo (J.D., 1978). Phi Beta Kappa. Lecturer/Speaker: Guardianships; Elder Abuse; Medicaid; Estate Planning. Attorney: Illinois Guardianship and Advocacy Commission, 1980-1989; Legal Aid Bureau of Metropolitan Family Services, 1989-1993. *Member:* Chicago Bar Association (Chair, Elder Law Committee, 1996-1998); National Academy of Elder Law Attorneys (President Elect, 2000; Secretary, 1997-1998, Treasurer, 1996-1997 and Vice President, 1998-1999 Illinois Chapter). ***LANGUAGES:*** Spanish. ***PRACTICE AREAS:*** Elder Law; Probate; Estate Planning; Estate Administration. **Email:** dmitchell@peckbloom.com

---

RAY J. KOENIG III, born Pontiac, Michigan, October 5, 1973; admitted to bar, 1999, Illinois. *Education:* Michigan State University (B.A., 1995); DePaul University College of Law (J.D., 1999). Member, Moot Court Board. *Member:* Chicago, Illinois State and American (Member, Litigation Section, 1999-2000) Bar Associations. ***PRACTICE AREAS:*** Contested Wills; Contested Trusts and Estates; Guardianship; Corporate; Business; Litigation. **Email:** rkoenig@peckbloom.com

JEANINE M. CUNNINGHAM, admitted to bar, 1992, Illinois. *Education:* National College of Education (B.A., with honors, 1980); John Marshall Law School (J.D., 1991; LL.M., Taxation, 1999). *Member:* Chicago and Illinois State Bar Associations; North Suburban Bar Association (President-Elect); Women's Bar Association of Illinois. ***PRACTICE AREAS:*** Estate Planning; Estate Administration; Probate; Elder Law. **Email:** jcunningham@peckbloom.com

ALEXANDER DRAPATSKY, born Kiev, Ukraine, April 8, 1972; admitted to bar, 1997, Illinois. *Education:* University of Illinois at Urbana-Champaign (B.A., 1994); Chicago-Kent College of Law (J.D., 1997). Member, Chicago Kent Tax Society. *Member:* Chicago and American (Member, Committees on: Tax; Corporate Law) Bar Associations. ***PRACTICE AREAS:*** Corporate Law; Taxation; Estate Planning; Complex Business Litigation; Real Estate. **Email:** adrapatsky@peckbloom.com

MARISA T. CIPOLLA, born Chicago Heights, Illinois, April 30, 1976; admitted to bar, 2001, Illinois. *Education:* Northwestern University (B.A., 1998); Chicago-Kent College of Law, Illinois Institute of Technology (J.D., 2001). *Member:* Chicago, Illinois State and American Bar Associations. ***PRACTICE AREAS:*** Probate; Estate Administration; Guardianship; Contested Wills; Contested Trusts and Estates; Litigation. **Email:** mcipolla@peckbloom.com

OF COUNSEL

AURORA AUSTRIACO, born Philippines, January 19, 1965; admitted to bar, 1991, Illinois. *Education:* DePaul University (B.S., 1987; J.D., 1990). Recipient, American Jurisprudence Award, Torts. Author: Chapter, IICLE Real Estate Practice, 2003; "House Closing Repairs," American Bar Association Journal, July 1998. Member, Center for Conflict Resolution. Commissioner, Cook County Human Rights Commission, 1999—. *Member:* Chicago, Illinois State (Member, Real Estate Section Council) and American (Member, Real Estate Section) Bar Associations; Illinois Real Estate Lawyers. ***LANGUAGES:*** Tagalog. ***PRACTICE AREAS:*** Real Estate Litigation; Probate Litigation; Real Estate. **Email:** aaustriaco@peckbloom.com

---

PECK, SHAFFER & WILLIAMS LLP

11 SOUTH LASALLE STREET, SUITE 2100
CHICAGO, ILLINOIS 60603
Telephone: 312-372-6060; 877-372-6060
Fax: 312-372-6085
Email: lawinfo@peck-shaffer.com
URL: http://www.peck-shaffer.com

Atlanta, Georgia Office: Peck, Shaffer & Williams LLP, Atlanta Financial Center, Suite M20, 3353 Peachtree Road, N.E. Telephone: 404-995-3850. Fax: 404-995-3851.

Cincinnati, Ohio Office: Peck, Shaffer & Williams LLP, 201 E. 5th Street, Suite 900. Telephones: 513-621-3394; 800-927-2663. Telecopier: 513-621-3813.

Columbus, Ohio Office: Peck, Shaffer & Williams LLP, 175 South Third Street, Suite 600, 43215. Telephone: 614-224-5205; 888-900-5205. Telecopier: 614-224-0069.

Covington, Kentucky Office: Peck, Shaffer & Williams LLP, 118 West 5th Street, 41011. Telephones: 859-431-7000; 888-431-7511. Telecopier: 859-431-0673.

Denver, Colorado Office: Peck, Shaffer & Williams LLP, 555 17th Street, Suite 845 South, 80202. Telephone: 303-296-3996; 877-296-0333. Fax: 303-296-0344.

Louisville, Kentucky Office: Peck, Shaffer & Williams LLP, 239 S. Fifth Street, Suite 1603, 40202. Telephone: 502-561-0054. Telecopier: 502-561-0058.

Public Finance, Municipal Bonds, Municipal Bond Taxation, Municipal Securities. Tax Exempt Bonds, Housing and Urban Development, Health Care Finance, Tax Increment Finance, Municipal Leasing, Public Finance Taxation, Securities Finance, Blue Sky Law, Low Income Housing, Industrial Development Bonds, Municipal Bankruptcy, Public Construction Law.

FIRM PROFILE: Peck, Shaffer & Williams LLP (PS&W) is a law firm with the experience, knowledge and creativity to guide its clients (hundreds of municipalities, counties, school districts, townships, special districts and underwriters) in issuing bonds and other debt instruments. The capital improvements financed with the proceeds of this debt include traditional governmental projects, such as roads, sewers, water systems, all types of public buildings, public infrastructure facilities, such as stadiums, convention centers and single-, multifamily and public housing; facilities for 501(c)(3) organizations, such as hospitals, university and long term care facilities and "exempt facilities" for industrial and commercial users, such as factories, waste recovery plants and port facilities. PS&W's expertise also extends to lease transactions and public construction counsel matters and has helped finance thousands of low-income housing projects in virtually every state.

MEMBERS OF FIRM

BRUCE D. AGIN, born Cleveland, Ohio, September 13, 1961; admitted to bar, 1986, Illinois. *Education:* University of Michigan (B.A., Economics/Accounting, 1983) ; University of California School of Law, Los Angeles (J.D., 1986). ***PRACTICE AREAS:*** Municipal Bonds; Tax Exempt Bonds; Public Finance Taxation. **Email:** bagin@peck-shaffer.com

GEORGE D. BUZARD III, born Evanston, Illinois, January 31, 1953; admitted to bar, 1978, Illinois. *Education:* University of Illinois (B.S., 1975; J.D., 1978). ***PRACTICE AREAS:*** Municipal Bonds; Tax Exempt Bonds; Public Finance. **Email:** gbuzard@peck-shaffer.com

(For Additional Biographical Data on all Personnel, see Professional Biographies at http.www.peck-shaffer.com)

PEDERSEN & HOUPT

A PROFESSIONAL CORPORATION
Established in 1957
161 NORTH CLARK
SUITE 3100
CHICAGO, ILLINOIS 60601-3242
Telephone: 312-641-6888
Telecopier: 312-641-6895
URL: http://www.pedersenhoupt.com

Lake Forest, Illinois Office: One Westminister Place. Telephone: 708-295-4317.

Mergers and Acquisitions, Employee Benefits and Executive Compensation, Banking and Financing, Municipal Law and Land Use, Real Estate, Trusts and Estates, Taxation and Organizational Planning, Private Equity and Venture Capital, Public Securities, Litigation and Dispute Resolution, Family Law, Employment Law, Antitrust, Technology and Intellectual Property.

PEER PEDERSEN, admitted to bar, 1949, Illinois. *Education:* Carthage College, Newberry College; University of Illinois (B.S., 1947; J.D., 1948). ***PRACTICE AREAS:*** General Corporate; Real Estate; Estate Planning; Domestic Relations. **Email:** ppedersen@pedersenhoupt.com

JOHN H. MUEHLSTEIN, admitted to bar, 1980, Illinois. *Education:* University of South Florida (B.A., 1976); University of Dayton (J.D., 1980). ***PRACTICE AREAS:*** Commercial Transactions; Private Capital. **Email:** jmuehlstein@pedersenhoupt.com

PAUL S. ALTMAN, admitted to bar, 1969, Illinois. *Education:* University of Illinois (A.B., 1966; J.D., 1969). ***PRACTICE AREAS:*** Mergers and Acquisitions; Employment Law; Employee Benefits; Executive Compensation and Leveraged ESOPs. **Email:** paltman@pedersenhoupt.com

JOSEPH BENEDICT BROCATO, admitted to bar, 1992, Illinois and U.S. District Court, Northern District of Illinois. *Education:* Loyola University (B.A., summa cum laude, 1989); Northwestern University (J.D., cum laude, 1992). ***PRACTICE AREAS:*** Commercial Transactions; Real Estate; Franchise; Entertainment Law. **Email:** jbrocato@pedersenhoupt.com

LAWRENCE W. BYRNE, born Chicago, Illinois, March 1, 1962; admitted to bar, 1992, Illinois; U.S. District Court, Northern District of Illinois, including Trial Bar. *Education:* Creighton University (B.S., B.A., 1984); Loyola University (M.B.A., 1987); John Marshall Law School (J.D., 1992). *Member:* Chicago Bar Association; Illinois Trial Lawyers Association. ***PRACTICE AREAS:*** Family Law; Corporate Litigation; Consumer Fraud; Class Action Defense.

STACY P. CHRONOPOULOS, admitted to bar, 1997, Illinois. *Education:* Miami University (B.A., 1992); DePaul University (J.D., 1996). ***PRACTICE AREAS:*** Intellectual Property; Trademark; Copyright. **Email:** schronopoulos@pedersenhoupt.com

KIMBERLY J. CORNELL, admitted to bar, 1997, Illinois and Wisconsin. *Education:* University of Colorado at Boulder (B.A., 1994); University of Wisconsin-Madison (J.D., 1997). ***LANGUAGES:*** Spanish. ***PRACTICE AREAS:*** Commercial Litigation. **Email:** kstone@pedersenhoupt.com

STEPHEN A. FROST, admitted to bar, 1981, Iowa and Missouri; 1982, U.S. Court of Appeals, 8th Circuit; 1988, Illinois; 1996, U.S. Tax Court. *Education:* Iowa State University (B.S., 1978); University of Iowa (J.D., 1981). ***PRACTICE AREAS:*** Family Wealth Transfers; Estate Planning; Business Organization; Taxation; Probate. **Email:** sfrost@pedersenhoupt.com

JOHN J. HAYES, admitted to bar, 1983, Illinois; 1985, U.S. Tax Court. *Education:* Bradley University (B.S., 1980); DePaul University (J.D., 1983). Certified Public Accountant, Illinois, 1983. ***PRACTICE AREAS:*** Estate Planning; Taxation; Probate. **Email:** jhayes@pedersenhoupt.com

SUSAN M. HERMANN, admitted to bar, 1987, Illinois. *Education:* Barnard College (A.B., cum laude, 1984); Northwestern University (J.D., 1987). ***PRACTICE AREAS:*** Public Securities; Private Capital; Commercial Transactions; REITs. **Email:** shermann@pedersenhoupt.com

ARTHUR M. HOLTZMAN, admitted to bar, 1976, Illinois and U.S. District Court, Northern District of Illinois including Trial Bar; 1977, U.S. Court of Appeals, 7th Circuit;

(This Listing Continued)

PEDERSEN & HOUPT, A PROFESSIONAL CORPORATION, Chicago—Continued

1985, U.S. Tax Court; 1993, U.S. Court of Appeals, 3rd Circuit; 1994, U.S. Supreme Court; 1995, U.S. Court of Federal Claims. *Education:* Northwestern University (B.A., 1971; M.A.T., 1972); Washington University (M.B.A., 1976; J.D., 1976). ***PRACTICE AREAS:*** Commercial Law and Corporate Litigation; Commodity Futures Litigation; Municipal Law; Employment; Arbitration. ***Email:*** aholtzman@pedersenhoupt.com

MARC D. JANSER, admitted to bar, 1978, Illinois and U.S. District Court, Northern District of Illinois including Trial Bar; 1980, U.S. Court of Appeals, 7th Circuit. *Education:* Cornell College (B.A., 1974); University of Illinois (J.D., 1978). ***PRACTICE AREAS:*** Domestic Relations Law; Products Liability Law; Commercial and Corporate Litigation. ***Email:*** mjanser@pedersenhoupt.com

THOMAS J. KELLY, admitted to bar, 1962, Illinois. *Education:* University of Notre Dame (B.B.A., 1961; LL.D., 1962). ***PRACTICE AREAS:*** Secured Financings; Real Estate; Commercial Transactions. ***Email:*** tkelly@pedersenhoupt.com

HERBERT J. LINN, admitted to bar, 1969, Illinois; 2001, Texas. *Education:* University of Michigan (A.B., 1966); University of Illinois (J.D., 1969). ***PRACTICE AREAS:*** Real Estate; Corporate and Partnership Transactions; Finance. ***Email:*** hlinn@pedersenhoupt.com

DONALD J. MORAN, admitted to bar, 1977, Illinois and U.S. District Court, Northern and Central Districts of Illinois including Trial Bar; 1982, U.S. Court of Appeals, 7th Circuit; 1984, U.S. Tax Court; 1988, U.S. Supreme Court; 1997, Western District of Michigan; 1998, California; 2000, U.S. Court of Appeals, 6th and 11th Circuits. *Education:* Northwestern University (B.A., 1973); Syracuse University (M.R.P., 1977; J.D., 1977). ***PRACTICE AREAS:*** Civil Litigation; Appellate Practice; Environmental Law; Land Use; Zoning Law. ***Email:*** dmoran@pedersenhoupt.com

MARY C. MUEHLSTEIN, admitted to bar, 1985, Illinois. *Education:* University of Illinois (B.S., 1977); Illinois Institute of Technology, Chicago-Kent College of Law (J.D., 1985). ***PRACTICE AREAS:*** Banking; Finance; Real Estate; Secured Transactions. ***Email:*** mmuehlstein@pedersenhoupt.com

DAVID B. SOLOMON, admitted to bar, 1994, Illinois. *Education:* University of Michigan (B.B.A., 1991); DePaul University (J.D., 1994). ***PRACTICE AREAS:*** Banking Law; Finance; Employee Benefits; Executive Compensation; Corporate Law; Business Law. ***Email:*** dsolomon@pedersenhoupt.com

---

CHRISTINE DECKE ALT
LAUREN BLAIR
BRIAN P. COLLINS
RICHARD L. DiNARDO
ERIC J. KORDISH
ABAD LOPEZ
ERIK J. PEDERSEN
KELEE J. SCHWENN
MICHAEL P. SULLIVAN

OF COUNSEL

SHELDON DAVIDSON, admitted to bar, 1962, Illinois; 1965, U.S. District Court, Northern District of Illinois including Trial Bar; 1967, U.S. Court of Appeals, 7th Circuit; 1974, U.S. Court Tax; 1981, U.S. Court of Appeals, 8th Circuit; 2000, U.S. Court of Appeals, 11th Circuit. *Education:* DePaul University (B.S., in Com., 1960; J.D., 1962). ***PRACTICE AREAS:*** Complex Civil Litigation; Securities Litigation; Corporate Investigations; Criminal Defense.

RICHARD V. HOUPT, admitted to bar, 1952, Illinois. *Education:* University of Chicago (A.B., 1949); University of Illinois (LL.B., 1952). (Retired)

GARY S. MOSTOW, admitted to bar, 1980, Illinois. *Education:* Tulane University; University of Wisconsin-Madison (B.A., 1977); John Marshall Law School (J.D., 1980). ***PRACTICE AREAS:*** General Corporate. ***Email:*** gmostow@pedersenhoupt.com

GREGORY J. PERRY, admitted to bar, 1965, Illinois. *Education:* University of Wisconsin (B.S., 1961); Georgetown University (LL.B., 1965). (Also Of Counsel, Facio Abogados, San Jose, Costa Rica). ***PRACTICE AREAS:*** Taxation; Federal Taxation; State Taxation; Commercial Transactions. ***Email:*** gperry@pedersenhoupt.com

THOMAS F. SAX, admitted to bar, 1985, Illinois and U.S. District Court, Northern District of Illinois. *Education:* University of Michigan (A.B., 1981); University of Chicago (J.D., 1985). ***PRACTICE AREAS:*** Commercial Litigation; Construction Litigation; Securities Litigation. ***Email:*** tsax@pedersenhoupt.com

JAMES B. SLOAN, admitted to bar, 1962, Illinois; 1970, Wisconsin; U.S. District Court, Northern District of Illinois including Trial Bar. *Education:* Loyola University (A.B., 1957; J.D., 1962). (Resident, Lake Forest Office). ***PRACTICE AREAS:*** Antitrust Litigation; Commercial Litigation. ***Email:*** jsloan@pedersenhoupt.com

STANLEY C. SNEERINGER, born Philadelphia, Pennsylvania, October 23, 1972; admitted to bar, 1999, Illinois. *Education:* Harvard University (A.B., cum laude, 1994); Georgetown University (J.D., cum laude, 1998). Associate Editor, Georgetown Law Journal. ***PRACTICE AREAS:*** Commercial Litigation; Intellectual Property. ***Email:*** ssneeringer@pedersenhoupt.com

STEVEN M. STONE, admitted to bar, 1980, Illinois. *Education:* Southern Methodist University (B.A.S., 1976); DePaul University (J.D., 1980). (Also practicing individually). ***PRACTICE AREAS:*** Commercial Transactions; Corporate Law; Corporate Litigation; Commercial Litigation. ***Email:*** sstone@pedersenhoupt.com

PEDERSEN & WEINSTEIN LLP

Established in 2004
309 WEST WASHINGTON
SUITE 1200
CHICAGO, ILLINOIS 60606
Telephone: 312-855-1200
Fax: 312-855-1207
Email: info@pwllp.com
URL: http://www.pwllp.com

Employment Discrimination, Employment Litigation and Counseling, Mediation and Arbitration, Sexual Harassment, Employment Contracts, Executive Severance Contracts, Civil Rights.

MEMBERS OF FIRM

ERIKA E. PEDERSEN, born Atlanta, Georgia, May 8, 1970; admitted to bar, 1995, Illinois; 1996, U.S. District Court, Northern District of Illinois; 1998, U.S. Court of Appeals, Seventh Circuit. *Education:* Northern Illinois University (B.A., magna cum laude, 1992); DePaul University College of Law (J.D., with honors, 1995). Order of the Coif. Author: "You Only Get What You Can Pay For: Dziubak v. Mott and its Warning to the Indigent Defendant," 44 DePaul L. Rev. 499 (1995). *Member:* Chicago Bar Association. ***PRACTICE AREAS:*** Employment Discrimination; Employment Litigation and Counseling; Mediation and Arbitration; Sexual Harassment; Employment Contracts; Executive Severance Contracts; Civil Rights. ***Email:*** epedersen@pwllp.com

JILL S. WEINSTEIN, born Anderson, Indiana, June 24, 1972; admitted to bar, 1997, Indiana and U.S. District Court, Northern and Southern Districts of Indiana; 1999, California; 2000, Illinois; 2001, U.S. District Court, Northern District of Illinois; 2002, U.S. District Court, Central District of California. *Education:* Indiana State University (B.S., magna cum laude, 1994); Indiana University School of Law - Indianapolis (J.D., summa cum laude, 1997). *Member:* Chicago and Indiana State Bar Associations. ***PRACTICE AREAS:*** Employment Discrimination; Employment Litigation and Counseling; Mediation and Arbitration; Sexual Harassment; Employment Contracts; Executive Severance Contracts; Civil Rights. ***Email:*** jweinstein@pwllp.com

PEKIN LEVIN & ASSOCIATES

CHICAGO, ILLINOIS

(See Levin, Riback Lawgroup P.C.)

PERKINS COIE LLC

131 S. DEARBORN STREET, SUITE 1700
CHICAGO, ILLINOIS 60603-5559
Telephone: 312-324-8400
Facsimile: 312-324-9400
Email: perkins@perkinscoie.com
URL: http://www.perkinscoie.com

REVISER OF THE WASHINGTON LAW DIGEST FOR THIS DIRECTORY.

Other Offices: Anchorage, Alaska; Bellevue, Washington; Boise, Idaho; Denver, Colorado; Los Angeles, California; Menlo Park, California; Olympia, Washington; Phoenix, Arizona; Portland, Oregon; San Francisco, California; Seattle, Washington; Washington, D.C.

General Civil Trial and Appellate Practice in Federal and State Courts and before various Federal and State Administrative Tribunals. Administrative; Antitrust and Trade Regulation; Aviation and Aerospace; Banks and Banking; Bankruptcy; Biotechnology; Business Law; Commercial Law; Construction Law; Corporate Law; Employee Benefits; Energy; Environmental; Estate Planning; Federal Indian Law; Franchising; General Litigation; Government Contracts; Government Relations; Immigration; Intellectual Property; International Trade; International Law; Internet and Electronic Commerce; Labor and Employment; Land Use; Life Sciences; Mergers, Acquisitions and Divestitures; Municipal/Public Finance; Natural Resources; Nonprofit and Charitable Organizations; Probate; Patents; Products Liability; Project Finance; Political Law; Public Utility; Real Estate; School Law; Securities Law and Litigation; Taxation; Technology; Telecommunications; Toxic Torts; Trademarks and Copyrights; Venture Capital and Investment Funds; Water Rights; White-Collar Criminal Representation; Workers' Compensation.

FIRM PROFILE: Perkins Coie LLP is a leading, full-service international law firm. With more than 600 lawyers in 13 offices across the United States, the firm represents clients that range in size from Fortune 100 companies to start-ups, and has historically represented market leaders in traditional and cutting-edge technology industries.

PARTNERS

CRAIG BOGGS, born Havana, Illinois, November 15, 1963; admitted to bar, 1988, Illinois. *Education:* University of Illinois (B.S., 1985); University of Illinois College of Law (J.D., 1988). Speeches: "Workplace Investigations and Interview Techniques," Council on Education and Management's Illinois Personnel Law Update. *Member:* Illinois State and American Bar Associations. ***PRACTICE AREAS:*** Labor and Employment; Commercial Litigation. ***Email:*** cboggs@perkinscoie.com

BRUCE A. BONJOUR, born Kalamazoo, Michigan, November 24, 1949; admitted to bar, 1976, Michigan; 1985, Minnesota; 1986, California; 1993, Illinois. *Education:* Albion College (B.A., cum laude, 1971); State University of New York (M.A., 1972); George Washington University (J.D., with honors, 1976). Associate Legislative Representative for the County of San Diego, California, 1972-1976. Member, Committee on Public Borrowing, American Bar Association, 1982-1986. *Member:* Minnesota State and Illinois State Bar Associations; State Bar of California; State Bar of Michigan; National Association of Bond Lawyers. ***PRACTICE AREAS:*** Municipal Finance; Securitization. ***Email:*** bbonjour@perkinscoie.com

(This Listing Continued)

ERIC D. BRANDFONBRENER, born Chicago, Illinois, June 14, 1961; admitted to bar, 1987, Illinois. *Education:* Harvard College (A.B., cum laude, 1983); University of Michigan (J.D., 1986). Law Clerk to Hon. R. Allan Edgar, U.S. District Court, Eastern District of Tennessee, 1986-1987. ***PRACTICE AREAS:*** Commercial Litigation; Employment Litigation; Securities Litigation; Trusts and Estates. ***Email:*** ebrandfonbrener@perkinscoie.com

WILLIAM T. CAHILL, born Peoria, Illinois, June 23, 1947; admitted to bar, 1973, Illinois. *Education:* Loras College (B.A., maxima cum laude, 1969); University of Illinois (J.D., with honors, 1973). Order of the Coif. Member, Board of Editors, University of Illinois Law Review. *Member:* Chicago (Vice Chairman, 1985-1986, and Chairman, 1987-1988, Hearings Division, Chairman, Investigation Division, 1986-1987, General Chairman, 1988-1989, Judicial Evaluation Committee; Chairman, Appellate Committee, 1990-1991) and American Bar Associations; Illinois Trial Lawyers Association; The Association of Trial Lawyers of America. Fellow, International Academy of Trial Lawyers. ***PRACTICE AREAS:*** Litigation; Contract Law; Corporate Law; Insurance Law; Personal Injury; Intellectual Property. ***Email:*** wcahill@perkinscoie.com

ROBERT L. CAPIZZI, born 1959; admitted to bar, 1984, Illinois; 1994, Washington. *Education:* State University of New York at Buffalo (B.S., cum laude, 1981; J.D., 1984). ***PRACTICE AREAS:*** Tax-Exempt Finance; Taxation; Federal Income Tax; State Taxation. ***Email:*** rcapizzi@perkinscoie.com

JOHN M. CHRISTIAN, born Wichita, Kansas, September 15, 1948; admitted to bar, 1974, Illinois. *Education:* Princeton University (A.B., with honors, 1970); University of Michigan (J.D., with honors, 1973). Adjunct Professor, Product Liability, I.I.T. Chicago-Kent College of Law. *Member:* Chicago (Chairman: Tort Litigation Committee, 1986-1987; Special Task Force on Insurance, 1985-1986; Special Committee on Lawyers Professional Liability Insurance, 1987-1988) and American Bar Associations. ***PRACTICE AREAS:*** Commercial Law; Product Liability. ***Email:*** jchristian@perkinscoie.com

ALEXANDRA R. COLE, born Milwaukee, Wisconsin, September 12, 1955; admitted to bar, 1979, Illinois. *Education:* DePaul University (B.A., cum laude, 1976); University of Chicago (J.D., 1979). *Member:* American Bar Associations (Member, Committee on Design and Construction); Commercial Real Estate Women's Network - CREW (Board Member). ***PRACTICE AREAS:*** Domestic and International Real Estate; Construction Contracts; Hospitality Law; Commercial Transactions. ***Email:*** colea@altheimer.com

WILLIAM E. CORBIN, admitted to bar, 1980, Illinois. *Education:* Boston College (B.S., 1977); University of Michigan Law School (J.D., 1980). ***PRACTICE AREAS:*** Public Finance. ***Email:*** wcorbin@perkinscoie.com

KEN CRANE, born Highland Park, Illinois; admitted to bar, 1986, Illinois. *Education:* University of Illinois (B.S., 1980; J.D., cum laude, 1986). ***PRACTICE AREAS:*** Private Equity; International Corporate Law; International Transactions; Mergers and Acquisitions. ***Email:*** kcrane@perkinscoie.com

JAMES R. CRUGER, born Elmhurst, Illinois, July 6, 1961; admitted to bar, 1986, Illinois. *Education:* Loras College (B.A., cum laude, 1983); Northwestern University (J.D., cum laude, 1986). *Member:* Chicago and American Bar Associations. ***PRACTICE AREAS:*** Mergers and Acquisitions; Divestitures; Venture Capital. ***Email:*** jcruger@perkinscoie.com

SUSAN DALEY, born New Britain, Connecticut, May 27, 1959; admitted to bar, 1981, Illinois. *Education:* University of Connecticut (B.A., in Economics, summa cum laude, 1978); Harvard University (J.D., 1981). Member, BNA Pension & Benefits Reporter Advisory Board, 1995—. *Member:* Chicago (Chair, Employee Benefits Committee, 1990-1991 and Chair, Federal Taxation Committee, 1992-1993), Illinois State (Chair, Employee Benefits Section Council, 1995-1996) and American (Chair, Welfare Benefit Plans Committee, Section of Real Property, Probate and Trust Law, 1989-1995; Chair, EEOC Subcommittee, Section of Taxation, Employee Benefits Committee, 1999-2001; Chair, Securities Law Subcommittee, Section of Taxation, Employee Benefits Committee, 2001—) Bar Associations; American College of Employee Benefits Counsel; National Association of Stock Plan Professionals (Chicago Chapter President, 1995—). ***PRACTICE AREAS:*** Employee Benefits; Executive Compensation. ***Email:*** sdaley@perkinscoie.com

JAN FELDMAN, born St. Louis, Missouri, February 8, 1952; admitted to bar, 1981, Illinois. *Education:* Indiana University (B.A., with honors, 1975); University of Minnesota (M.A., 1978); Northwestern University (J.D., cum laude, 1981). ***PRACTICE AREAS:*** Litigation; Contract Law; Commercial Litigation; Patent Litigation; Intellectual Property Litigation; Environmental Liability; Toxic Torts. ***Email:*** jfeldman@perkinscoie.com

MATTHEW J. GEHRINGER, born Detroit, Michigan, August 22, 1958; admitted to bar, 1983, Illinois. *Education:* University of Michigan (B.B.A., magna cum laude, 1979; J.D., magna cum laude, 1983). Order of the Coif. Co-Author: "The Prima Facie Bad Faith Case," Illinois Institute for Continuing Legal Education, 1988. *Member:* Chicago, Illinois State and American Bar Associations. ***PRACTICE AREAS:*** Complex Litigation; Products Liability; Defense Litigation; Insurance Coverage; Professional Malpractice Law; Toxic Torts. ***Email:*** mgehringer@perkinscoie.com

PHILLIP GORDON, born Potgietersrus, South Africa, July 11, 1943; admitted to bar, 1969, Illinois; 1973, New York. *Education:* University of the Witwatersrand (B.A., 1964; B.A., with honors, 1965); Oxford University, England (B.A., 1967; M.S., 1973); University of Chicago (J.D., 1969). Editor, Midwest Transaction Guide, Matthew Bender, 1981. Teaching Associate, Northwestern University School of Law, 1967-1968. *Member:* Chicago, Illinois State and American Bar Associations; Urban Land Institute; International Council. ***PRACTICE AREAS:*** Hotel Acquisition; Financing; Hotel Management Contracts; Mergers and Acquisitions; Real Estate Financing. ***Email:*** gordon@perkinscoie.com

SCOTT B. GREENE, born Washington, D.C., August 24, 1953; admitted to bar, 1979, Illinois. *Education:* Indiana University (B.A., 1976); De Paul University (J.D., 1979). Recipient, American Jurisprudence Award in Commercial Transactions. Author, "Fiduciary Duties Owned a Corporation by its Directors and the Injunction Remedy," ISBA Corporation and Securities Law Newsletter, Vol. 34, No. 2, January, 1989. *Member:* Chicago (Computer Law Committee, 1987-1988), Illinois State and American (Litigation Committee, 1987-1993; Construction Industry Forum Committee, 1993; Labor and Employment Section, 1993) Bar Associations; The Association of Trial Lawyers of America. ***PRACTICE AREAS:*** Trial Practice; Construction Law; Employment Law; Commercial Law. ***Email:*** sgreene@perkinscoie.com

MARY KATHRYN KELLY, born Chicago, Illinois, April 14, 1954; admitted to bar, 1979, Illinois. *Education:* St. Mary's College (B.A., magna cum laude, 1976); Loyola University (J.D., 1979). *Member:* Chicago, Federal (Board of Directors, 1991—) and American Bar Associations; The Association of Trial Lawyers of America. ***PRACTICE AREAS:*** Litigation; Personal Injury; ERISA; Product Liability; Toxic Torts. ***Email:*** mkelly@perkinscoie.com

KENNETH T. LOPATKA, admitted to bar, 1971, Illinois; 1977, Massachusetts. *Education:* Illinois Benedictine College (B.A., 1968); Harvard Law School (J.D., 1971). ***PRACTICE AREAS:*** Labor and Employment Law. ***Email:*** klopatka@perkinscoie.com

C. VINCENT (VINCE) MALONEY, born Avon, Illinois, March 5, 1959; admitted to bar, 1987, Illinois; 1990, Missouri; 1992, Florida. *Education:* Marquette University (B.A., Political Science/Latin, 1981); University of Illinois (M.A.P.A., 1987; J.D., 1987). Articles Editor, University of Illinois Law Review. Speech, "Can't Win Without the Evidence: Winning Strategies Under Moorman," DuPage County Bar Association, October 1997. *Member:* Chicago, Illinois State and American Bar Associations. ***PRACTICE AREAS:*** Commercial Litigation; Product Liability; Hotel, Lodging and Travel. ***Email:*** cvmaloney@perkinscoie.com

DANIEL G.M. MARRE, born London, England, January 29, 1967; admitted to bar, 1992, Illinois. *Education:* University of Chicago (A.B., 1989); Northwestern University (J.D., 1992). Managing Editor, Northwestern University Law Review. Co-Author: "Comparative View of Laws Governing Condominium-Type Projects," The Construction Lawyer, Vol. 9, No. 3, July 1999. ***PRACTICE AREAS:*** Real Estate. ***Email:*** dmarre@perkinscoie.com

ROSEANN OLIVER, born Chicago, Illinois, October 7, 1947; admitted to bar, 1972, Illinois. *Education:* Northwestern University (B.A., 1969); Loyola University (J.D., 1972). Articles Editor, Loyola Law Journal. Co-Author: "Using Experts in Products Liability Cases," Idaho Law Review, Vol. 18, No. 3 (Summer 1982). Legal Writing Instructor, I.I.T. Chicago-Kent College of Law, 1973-1974; Loyola University, 1974-1975. *Member:* Chicago (Special Counsel, 1981-1982; Chairman, Standing Committee on Litigation, 1985-1988; Member, Amicus Curiae Committee, 1989—) and Illinois State Bar Associations. ***PRACTICE AREAS:*** Covenants Not to Compete; Litigation; Environmental Insurance Litigation; Products Liability. ***Email:*** roliver@perkinscoie.com

RICHARD E. PETERSON, born 1964; admitted to bar, 1989, Illinois. *Education:* De-Paul University (B.S., 1986); Columbia University (J.D., 1989). ***PRACTICE AREAS:*** Tax. ***Email:*** rpeterson@perkinscoie.com

ROBERT STEPHAN, admitted to bar, 1991, Illinois. *Education:* Northwestern University (B.A., 1988); Indiana University School of Law (J.D., 1991). ***PRACTICE AREAS:*** Public Finance; Structured Finance. ***Email:*** rstephan@perkinscoie.com

HUGH TOTTEN, admitted to bar, 1985, Illinois. *Education:* Purdue University (B.A., 1980); Northwestern University (J.D., 1985). ***PRACTICE AREAS:*** Litigation. ***Email:*** htotten@perkinscoie.com

EDWARD E. WICKS, born Woodstock, Illinois, November 11, 1950; admitted to bar, 1975, Illinois. *Education:* University of Illinois (A.B., magna cum laude, 1972); University of Chicago (J.D., 1975). Phi Beta Kappa; Phi Kappa Phi; Pi Sigma Alpha. Member of Staff, University of Chicago Law Review, 1973-1975. *Member:* Chicago (Member, Real Property Law Committee) and American Bar Associations. ***PRACTICE AREAS:*** Real Estate; Business. ***Email:*** wickse@perkinscoie.com

CHRISTOPHER B. WILSON, born Evanston, Illinois, July 29, 1962; admitted to bar, 1989, Illinois. *Education:* University of Michigan (B.A., 1984); Northwestern University (J.D., cum laude, 1989). Order of the Coif. Associate Note and Comment Editor, Northwestern Law Review. Law Clerk to Hon. William J. Bauer, Chief Judge, U.S. Court of Appeals, Seventh Circuit, 1989-1990. U.S. Senate Judiciary Committee, Legislative Aide to Senator Paul Simon, 99th Congress, 1985-1986. *Member:* American Bar Association. ***PRACTICE AREAS:*** Commercial Litigation; Products Liability; Antitrust; Securities Litigation; Employment Litigation; Trademark Licensing; Trademark Litigation. ***Email:*** cwilson@perkinscoie.com

DANIEL A. ZAZOVE, born Chicago, Illinois, October 30, 1947; admitted to bar, 1973, Illinois, U.S. District Court, Northern District of Illinois including Trial Bar and U.S. Court of Appeals, Seventh Circuit; 1998, U.S. Supreme Court. *Education:* University of Wisconsin (B.A., 1969); University of Illinois (J.D., 1973). Editor, Illinois Institute for Continuing Legal Education, *Bankruptcy Handbook. Member:* Chicago and American Bar Associations. ***PRACTICE AREAS:*** Bankruptcy Reorganization. ***Email:*** dzazove@perkinscoie.com

OF COUNSEL

DARRELL J. GRAHAM, born Mt. Clemens, Michigan, March 31, 1959; admitted to bar, 1985, Illinois. *Education:* University of Michigan (B.A., with highest distinction, 1981; J.D., 1985). Phi Beta Kappa. *Member:* American Bar Association. ***PRACTICE AREAS:*** Commercial Litigation; Antitrust; Insurance; Class Action; Employment Law. ***Email:*** DGraham@perkinscoie.com

KATHLEEN M. HOWARD, admitted to bar, 1991, Illinois; 1995, Hawaii. *Education:* Northeastern Illinois University (B.S., with highest honors, 1988); Loyola University (J.D., cum laude, 1991). Alpha Chi. Recipient: Judge Hayes Scholarship; American Jurisprudence Awards in: Contracts; Property; Criminal Procedure; Sales; Business Planning; Juvenile Law. Executive Editor, Publications, Loyola University of Chicago Law Journal, 1990-1991. Law Clerk to the Hon. E. John McConnell (Retired), Circuit Court of the Second Circuit, State of Hawaii, 1995-1998. Author, Comment, "Policing Discovery Under Illinois Supreme Court Rule 219(c): A Search for Judicial Consistency," 21 Loy.U.Chi.L.J. 973 (1990). *Member:* Chicago, Hawaii State and American Bar Associations. ***PRACTICE AREAS:*** Real Estate; Business Law; Health Care. ***Email:*** khoward@perkinscoie.com

(This Listing Continued)

PERKINS COIE LLC, Chicago—Continued

ASSOCIATES

AMINA ABRAHAMS, born Bloomfield Hills, Michigan, January 15, 1975; admitted to bar, 2002, Illinois. *Education:* Williams College (B.A., cum laude, 1997); University of Michigan (J.D., 2002). ***PRACTICE AREAS:*** Corporate Law. ***Email:*** aabrahams@perkinscoie.com

BEVIN M. BRENNAN, admitted to bar, 2000, Illinois. *Education:* Williams College (B.A., 1997); Harvard Law School (J.D., 2000). ***PRACTICE AREAS:*** Litigation. ***Email:*** bbrennan@perkinscoie.com

JONATHAN BUCK, admitted to bar, 2002, Washington (Not admitted in Illinois). *Education:* University of Puget Sound (B.A., cum laude, 1997); University of Michigan (J.D., magna cum laude, 2002). Associate Editor, Journal of Law Reform. ***PRACTICE AREAS:*** Commercial Litigation; Products Liability. ***Email:*** jbuck@perkinscoie.com

JASON BURLINGAME, admitted to bar, 1997, Illinois. *Education:* University of Chicago (B.A., 1993; J.D., 1997). ***PRACTICE AREAS:*** Commercial Litigation. ***Email:*** jburlingame@perkinscoie.com

JEANNE M. CULLEN, born Akron, Ohio, February 7, 1970; admitted to bar, 1997, Illinois. *Education:* Loyola University (B.B.A., cum laude, 1992; M.B.A., with honors, 1993); I.I.T. Chicago-Kent College of Law (J.D., 1997). ***PRACTICE AREAS:*** Commercial Litigation; Products Liability; White Collar Crime; Litigation. ***Email:*** jcullen@perkinscoie.com

SCOTT H. GINGOLD, admitted to bar, 1998, Illinois. *Education:* University of Michigan (B.A., 1995); Northwestern University (J.D., 1998). ***PRACTICE AREAS:*** Litigation; Intellectual Property; Antitrust. ***Email:*** sgingold@perkinscoie.com

JACLYN A. KIGHT, born Waterbury, Connecticut, July 19, 1977; admitted to bar, 2002, Illinois. *Education:* Loyola College, Maryland (B.A., cum laude, 1999); Loyola University, Chicago School of Law (J.D., 2002). Student Articles Editor, Loyola University, Chicago Law Journal. ***PRACTICE AREAS:*** Real Estate. ***Email:*** jkight@perkinscoie.com

SARAH R. KNIGHT, born Missoula, Montana, July 9, 1973; admitted to bar, 2001, Washington (Not admitted in Illinois). *Education:* Williams College (B.A., 1995); New York University School of Law (J.D., 2000). Editor-in-Chief, New York University Review of Law School Change, 1999-2000. ***PRACTICE AREAS:*** Land Use; Municipal Finance. ***Email:*** sknight@perkinscoie.com

J. BATES McINTYRE, admitted to bar, 2000, Illinois. *Education:* Grinnell College (B.A., 1995); University of Illinois (J.D., 2000). Order of the Coif. Associate Editor, University of Illinois Law Review. Law Clerk to Hon. Elaine E. Bucklo, U.S. District Court, Northern District of Illinois. ***LANGUAGES:*** German. ***PRACTICE AREAS:*** Commercial Litigation. ***Email:*** bmcintyre@perkinscoie.com

LAURENCE OLEKSA, born Minneapolis, Minnesota, April 29, 1975; admitted to bar, 2001, Illinois and Wisconsin. *Education:* University of Kansas (B.S., 1997); University of Wisconsin (J.D., cum laude, 2001). ***PRACTICE AREAS:*** Litigation; Labor and Employment. ***Email:*** loleksa@perkinscoie.com

CHAD D. STRIKER, born May 19, 1971; admitted to bar, 1997, Minnesota; 2002, Illinois. *Education:* University of Michigan (B.B.A., 1993; J.D., 1997). ***PRACTICE AREAS:*** Corporate Law; Mergers and Acquisitions. ***Email:*** cstriker@perkinscoie.com

THEODORE WERN, admitted to bar, 2000, Illinois. *Education:* Miami University (B.A., 1997); The Ohio State University College of Law (J.D., 2000). Order of the Coif. Articles Editor, Ohio State University Law Review. ***PRACTICE AREAS:*** Private Equity; Mergers and Acquisitions; Business Counseling. ***Email:*** twern@perkinscoie.com

RYAN WHITACRE, born Seoul, Korea, March 6, 1975; admitted to bar, 2000, Illinois. *Education:* Michigan State University (B.A., 1997); Cornell University Law School (J.D., 2000). ***PRACTICE AREAS:*** Litigation. ***Email:*** rwhitacre@perkinscoie.com

REVISER OF THE WASHINGTON LAW DIGEST FOR THIS DIRECTORY.

(For biographical data on other Perkins Coie personnel, see Professional Biographies for those offices)

LEONARD F. PERKINS & ASSOCIATES

CHICAGO, ILLINOIS

(See Arlington Heights)

General Business Law, State Taxation, Intellectual Property and Unclaimed Property, Corporations, Business Enterprises; Business Start-Ups, Promotion Law.

Y. JACQUELINE PERKINS

CHICAGO, ILLINOIS

(See Arlington Heights)

Family Law, Criminal, Murder, Homicide, Drug Crimes, Wrongful Felonies, Misdemeanors, Sex Assault, Police Misconduct, Divorce, Child Support, Domestic Violence.

PERRY & ASSOCIATES

CHICAGO, ILLINOIS

(See Spring Grove)

Land Use, Zoning, Municipal Law, Government, Employment Law, Civil Rights.

KEVIN R. PETERS

407 SOUTH DEARBORN STREET
SUITE 1675
CHICAGO, ILLINOIS 60605
Telephone: 312-697-0022; Cell: 312-543-6365
Fax: 312-697-0812
Email: kp6970022@aol.com
URL: http://www.kevinpeterslaw.com

Driving While Intoxicated, Drug Crimes, Felonies, Homicide, Misdemeanors, Sexual Assault, Traffic Violations, Police Misconduct, Civil Rights.

KEVIN R. PETERS, born Evergreen Park, Illinois, March 18, 1952; admitted to bar, 1983, Illinois; U.S. District Court, Northern and Central Districts of Illinois and Northern District of Indiana. *Education:* Millikin University (B.A., 1974); John Marshall Law School (J.D., 1983). Assistant State's Attorney, 1983-1984. Assistant Public Defender, 1984-1994. Private Practice, 1994—. *Member:* Chicago Bar Association; Chicago Council of Lawyers; National Association of Criminal Defense Lawyers. ***PRACTICE AREAS:*** Criminal Defense; Law Enforcement.

PETERS & LYONS, LTD.

Established in 1971
25 EAST WASHINGTON STREET, SUITE 1000
CHICAGO, ILLINOIS 60602
Telephone: 312-346-7300
Fax: 312-782-6690
URL: http://www.peterslyons.com
Email: Laborlaw@peterslyons.com
URL: http://www.lawyers.com/laborlaw

Management Labor Law, Employment Litigation, Opposition to Union Organization, Unfair Labor Practice Charges, Union Contract Negotiations, Employment Discrimination, Employment Contracts and Wage and Hour Law.

FIRM PROFILE: The firm concentrates its practice in assisting management in dealing with a wide variety of legal matters arising within the employment relationship, in both "union" and "non-union" settings.

We have chosen to practice as a small firm, to realize our goal of providing personal, practical and cost effective professional services of the highest quality to our clients.

Reported Cases: Acorn Corrugated Box Company v. Illinois Human Rights Commission, 181 Ill. App. 3d 122 (1989); Anooya v. Hilton Hotels Corporation, 733 F.2d 48 (7th Cir. 1984); Aurora Packing Company, Inc. v. NLRB, 904 F.2d 73 (D.C. Cir. 1990); Camacho v. Ritz-Carlton Water Tower, 786 F.2d 242 (7th Cir. 1982); Hong v. Childrens Memorial Hospital, 936 F.2d 967 (7th Cir. 1991); In re Hacienda Hotel and International Brotherhood of Teamsters, Local 995, 69 LA 939 (1977).

DONALD F. PETERS, born 1945; admitted to bar, 1971, Illinois and District of Columbia; U.S. District Court, Northern District of Illinois, including Trial Bar; U.S. Supreme Court. *Education:* University of Notre Dame (B.A., 1967); University of Illinois (J.D., 1970). Adjunct Professor of Law, DePaul University. Director, Little City Foundation. ***PRACTICE AREAS:*** Labor and Employment. ***Email:*** dpeters@peterslyons.com

CHRISTOPHER P. LYONS, born 1965; admitted to bar, 1990, Illinois and U.S. District Court, Northern District of Illinois; U.S. Court of Appeals, 6th and 7th Circuits. *Education:* University of Illinois (B.S., cum laude, 1987; J.D., 1990). Member, University of Illinois National Moot Court Team, 1989-1990. ***PRACTICE AREAS:*** Labor and Employment. ***Email:*** clyons@peterslyons.com

REPRESENTATIVE CLIENTS: Aargus Security Systems, Inc.; Airborne Express; Amalgamated Bank of Chicago; Aurora Packing Co.; Bodine Electric Co.; Boise Cascade Office Products; Burke Beverage Co., Inc.; Blackhawk Steel Corp.; Central Teaming, Inc.; Chicago Luggage Manufacturers Assn.; Chicago Steel Rule & Die Co.; The Chicago Yacht Club; Copper & Brass Servicenter Association, Inc.; Crane and Machinery, Inc.; DHL; Exhibit Installation Services, Inc.; The Freeman Cos.; Guardian Metal Sales, Inc.; Hostmark Hospitality Group; Metropolitan Bank & Trust Co.; Metroplex, Inc.; Oak Brook Bank; The Safer Foundation; Uno Restaurants, Inc.

PFAFF & GILL, LTD.

ONE EAST WACKER DRIVE, SUITE 3310
CHICAGO, ILLINOIS 60601
Telephone: 312-828-9666
Fax: 312-828-0880
Email: info@pfaffgill.com
URL: http://www.pfaffgill.com

Medical Malpractice including physician and surgical malpractice, birth defects, cerebral palsy, anesthesia negligence, failure to diagnose. Automotive Defects and Products Liability, Plaintiff Personal Injury including automobile accidents, catastrophic accidents, trucking accidents, head and spinal cord injuries, wrongful death.

FIRM PROFILE: We are proud to limit our work to representing people who have been harmed by wrongful conduct. As trial lawyers, we investigate potential cases, prepare evidence and take to trial all types of personal injury cases. We are best known for cases against doctors and hospitals as well as automobile manufacturers, but also represent people hurt by automobile and trucking negligence, premises liability, sexual assault, legal malpractice and all other torts. We refuse to represent corporations and insurance companies.

BRUCE R. PFAFF, born Glen Cove, New York, July 15, 1954; admitted to bar, 1979, California and U.S. District Court, Northern and Eastern Districts of California; 1984, Illinois; 1985, U.S. District Court, Northern District of Illinois; 1997, U.S. Supreme Court.

(This Listing Continued)

Education: Dartmouth College (A.B., 1976); Hastings College of the Law, University of California (J.D., 1979). President's Award, Illinois Trial Lawyers Association, 2000. Nominated for Trial Lawyer of the Year, Trial Lawyers for Public Justice, 1998. *Member:* Chicago Bar Association (Vice Chairman, 1986-1987 and Chairman, 1987-1988, Medical Relations Committee; Chairman, Tort Litigation Committee, 1992-1993); Illinois State Bar Association (Member, Legislation Committee, 2002—; Tort Law Section Council, 1999-2002. Medical Malpractice Committee, 1986-1988); American Board of Trial Advocates (National Board Member, 2001—; President, Illinois Chapter, 1999-2000); Trial Lawyers for Public Justice; Illinois Trial Lawyers Association (Chair, Medical Negligence Committee, 1989; Chair, Amicus Curiae Committee, 1994—; Legislation Committee); The Association of Trial Lawyers of America; Society of Trial Lawyers; Trial Lawyers for Public Justice. ***REPORTED CASES:*** DeYoung v. Alpha Construction Co, 186 Ill. App. 3d 758 (1989); Schaffner v. C&NW Transportation Co., 129 Ill. 2d 1 (1989); Carrillo v. Ford Motors Co. 325 Ill. App. 3d 455 (2001); Burger v. Lutheran General Hospital, 198 Ill. 2d 21 (2001). ***PRACTICE AREAS:*** Medical Malpractice; Legal Malpractice; Automotive Defects; Products Liability; Negligence; Wrongful Death. ***Email:*** bpfaff@pfaffgill.com

MICHAEL THOMAS GILL, born 1972; admitted to bar, 1997, Illinois and U.S. District Court, Northern District of Illinois. *Education:* Miami University (B.A., 1994); Loyola University (J.D., 1997). *Member:* Chicago Bar Association; Illinois State Bar Association; Illinois Trial Lawyers Association (Amicus Curiae Committee, 1997—; Medical Negligence Committee, 1997—); The Association of Trial Lawyers of America; Trial Lawyers for Public Justice; Leading Lawyers Network (Member, Sections on: Personal Injury; Professional Malpractice). ***REPORTED CASES:*** Bryant v. LaGrange Memorial Hosp., 345 Ill. App. 3d 565 (1st. Dist. 2003); Buckholtz v. MacNeal, 337 Ill. App. 3d 163 (lst Dist. 2003); Buckholtz v. MacNeal, 313 Ill. App. 3d 521 (1st Dist. 2000); Simmons v. Garces, 198 Ill. 2d 541 (2002); Simmons v. Garces, 319 Ill. App. 3d 308 (1st Dist. 2001); Carrillo v. Ford Motor Co., 325 Ill. App. 3d 955 (1st Dist. 2001); US v. Walker, 98 F.3d 944 (7th Cir. 1996). ***PRACTICE AREAS:*** Personal Injury; Medical Malpractice; Products Liability. ***Email:*** mgill@pfaffgill.com

---

MATTHEW DOUGLAS PORTS, born 1972; admitted to bar, 2000, Illinois and U.S. District Court, Northern District of Illinois. *Education:* University of Colorado at Boulder (B.A., 1994); DePaul University (J.D., 2000). *Member:* Chicago Bar Association (Co-Chair, Tort Litigation Committee, 2005—; Civil Practice Committee; Young Lawyers Society); Illinois State Bar Association (Civil Practice and Rules Committee); Illinois Trial Lawyers Association (Amicus Committee; Medical Negligence Committee; Young Lawyers Committee); Association of Trial Lawyers of America. ***PRACTICE AREAS:*** Personal Injury; Medical Malpractice; Products Liability. ***Email:*** mports@pfaffgill.com

MARK SZAFLARSKI, born Chicago, Illinois, March 11, 1957; admitted to bar, 1985, Illinois, U.S. District Court, Northern District of Illinois and U.S. Court of Appeals, Seventh Circuit. *Education:* University of Notre Dame (B.A., 1979); DePaul University (J.D., with honors, 1985). Editor, De Paul Law Review, Vol. 34, 1984-1985. *Member:* Chicago (Chair, Tort Litigation Committee, 2001-2002) and Illinois State Bar Associations; Illinois Trial Lawyers Association; The Association of Trial Lawyers of America. ***PRACTICE AREAS:*** Medical Malpractice; Products Liability; Personal Injury. ***Email:*** mszaflarski@pfaffgill.com

LAW OFFICES OF STEPHEN S. PHALEN LLC

77 W. WACKER, SUITE 4800
CHICAGO, ILLINOIS 60601
Telephone: 312-606-8718
Email: steve@phalenlaw.com
URL: http://www.stephenphalen.com

Personal Injury, Wrongful Death, Automobile Accidents, Boating Accidents, Motorcycle Accidents, Trucking Accidents, Bus Accidents, Train Accidents, Construction Accidents, Medical Malpractice, Head Trauma, Spinal Injuries.

MEMBER OF FIRM

STEPHEN S. PHALEN, born Boston, Massachusetts, September 5, 1960; admitted to bar, 1985, Illinois. *Education:* Miami University (B.A., 1982); University of Toledo (J.D., 1985). *Member:* Chicago and Illinois State Bar Associations; Illinois Trial Lawyers Association; The Association of Trial Lawyers of America. ***PRACTICE AREAS:*** Personal Injury; Medical Malpractice; Wrongful Death; Automobile Accidents; Construction Accidents; Head Trauma; Spinal Injury; Boating Accidents; Motorcycle Accidents; Truck Accidents; Bus Accidents; Train Accidents. ***Email:*** steve@phalenlaw.com

PIERCE, DALEY, BAFFES, O'SULLIVAN & MUSSAR

Established in 1913
LA SALLE PLAZA
180 N. LA SALLE STREET, SUITE 2320
CHICAGO, ILLINOIS 60601
Telephone: 312-236-7492
FAX: 312-236-2032

General Practice. Litigation. Medical Legal Law.

MEMBERS OF FIRM

ROBERT C. PIERCE (1935-1971)
DONAL D. O'SULLIVAN (1928-1995)
THOMAS G. BAFFES (1923-1998)

(This Listing Continued)

RICHARD J. DALEY, born Chicago, Illinois, April 1, 1935; admitted to bar, 1960, Illinois and U.S. District Court, Northern District of Illinois; 1965, U.S. Court of Appeals, 7th Circuit and U.S. Tax Court; 1976, U.S. Supreme Court. *Education:* Northwestern University (B.S., 1957); DePaul University (J.D., 1960). *Member:* Chicago and Illinois State Bar Associations; Illinois Trial Lawyers Association. ***PRACTICE AREAS:*** General Practice; Litigation; Medical-Legal Law.

MARTIN M. MUSSAR, born Chicago, Illinois, January 22, 1954; admitted to bar, 1979, Illinois. *Education:* Northwestern University (B.A., 1975); Loyola University (J.D., 1979). *Member:* Illinois State Bar Association.

PINDERSKI & PINDERSKI, LTD.

CHICAGO, ILLINOIS
(See Palatine)

WILLIAM G. PINTAS & ASSOCIATES, LTD.

368 WEST HURON STREET, SUITE 100
CHICAGO, ILLINOIS 60610
Telephone: 312-664-4411
Fax: 312-664-8833
URL: http://www.ineedanattorney.com
Email: pintas@msn.com
URL: http://www.mylawyerteam.com

Personal Injury, Workers Compensation, Accidents, Automobile Accidents and Injuries, Automobile Negligence, Bodily Injury, Brain Injury, Plaintiffs Personal Injury, Motorcycle Accidents, Head Injury, Electrical Injury, Slip and Fall, Spinal Injury, Medical Malpractice, Birth Trauma, Gynecology Malpractice, Medical Negligence, Physicians Professional Liability, Psychiatric Malpractice, Surgeons Liability.

WILLIAM G. PINTAS, born Chicago, Illinois, 1960; admitted to bar, 1985, Illinois. *Education:* University of Miami (B.A., Business Administration, 1982); Thomas M. Cooley Law School (J.D., 1984). *Member:* Illinois and American Bar Associations; The Association of Trial Lawyers of America; Illinois Trial Lawyers Association; National Spinal Cord Injury Association (Past Member, Board of Directors); Illinois Brain Injury Association (Past Member, Board of Directors). ***PRACTICE AREAS:*** Personal Injury; Workers Compensation; Automobile Accidents and Injuries; Automobile Negligence; Bodily Injury; Brain Injury; Plaintiffs Personal Injury; Motorcycle Accidents; Head Injury; Electrical Injury; Slip and Fall; Spinal Injury; Medical Malpractice; Birth Injuries; Gynecology Malpractice; Medical Negligence; Physicians Professional Liability; Psychiatric Malpractice; Surgeons Liability. ***Email:*** pintas@msn.com

ASSOCIATES

LAURA J. MULLINS, born New York; admitted to bar, 1995, Illinois. *Education:* Syracuse University (B.S., 1992); John Marshall Law School (J.D., 1995). ***PRACTICE AREAS:*** Personal Injury; Workers Compensation.

LINDA KECK, born Hinsdale, Illinois, 1974. *Education:* Loras College (B.S., Biology, Spanish, 1996); John Marshall Law School (J.D., 2000).

PINZUR, COHEN & KERR, LTD.

CHICAGO, ILLINOIS
(See Long Grove)

Administrative Matters, Adoption Law, Annexation, Appellate Practice, Arbitration, Asset Acquisitions and Sales, Banking and Loan Documentation, Banking Law, Business Law, Business Litigation, Business Planning and Formation, Business Successions, Buying and Selling of Businesses, Child Custody, Child Support, Civil Litigation in State and Federal Courts, Civil Rights, Class Actions, Closings, Collections, Commercial and Residential Development, Commercial Litigation, Commercial Real Estate, Community Association Law, Condemnation, Condominium Law, Contractual Disputes, Construction Law, Construction Arbitration, Construction Defects, Construction Litigation, Consumer Law, Contested Wills, Contracts, Cooperative Housing Law, Copyrights, Corporate Law, Corporations, Creditors Rights, Debtor and Creditor, Developer Disputes, Discrimination, Divorce, Domestic Violence, Elder Law, Employment Agreements, Employment Law, Entrepreneurial Ventures, Environmental Law, Equipment Leasing, Equitable and Injunctive Remedies, Estate Planning, Family Law, Family Business Law, Forcible Eviction Law, Foreclosures, Franchise Law, General Practice, Guardianship, Harassment, Homeowner's Association Law, Incorporation, Institutional Lending, Insurance Regulations, Workouts, Insurance, Land Development and Zoning, Landlord and Tenant Law, Leases and Leasing, Limited Liability Companies, Litigation, Matrimonial Law, Mechanics Liens, Mergers and Acquisitions, Mortgages, Municipal, Partnership Law, Personal Injury, Premarital Agreements, Probate Law, Real Estate, Real Estate Finance, Real Estate Litigation, Real Estate Tax Appeals, Real Estate Tax Assessment, Residential Real Estate, Sales Acquisitions, School Law, Secured Transactions, Small Business Law, Social Security, Spousal Support, Stock Acquisitions and Sales, Trademarks, Trusts and Estates, Uniform Commercial Code, Wills, Zoning, Planning and Land Use.

PIRCHER, NICHOLS & MEEKS

900 NORTH MICHIGAN AVENUE
CHICAGO, ILLINOIS 60611-1575
Telephone: 310-201-8900
FAX: 310-201-8922
URL: http://www.pircher.com

Los Angeles, California Office: 1925 Century Park East, Suite 1700. Telephone: 310-201-8900. FAX: 310-201-8922.

(This Listing Continued)

PIRCHER, NICHOLS & MEEKS, Chicago—Continued

Real Estate Law including Representation of Partnerships, Limited Liability Companies and Tax-Exempt Organizations in Acquisition, Development and Financing. Corporation, Federal and State Securities, Federal and State Taxation, Partnership, Environmental Law, Litigation, Bankruptcy and Limited Liability Company.

RESIDENT MEMBERS

MARC A. BENJAMIN, admitted to bar, 1989, Illinois. *Education:* University of Wisconsin (B.A., with honors, 1986); Harvard University (J.D., 1989). Phi Beta Kappa. *Member:* International Council of Shopping Centers. ***PRACTICE AREAS:*** Real Estate Law. ***Email:*** mbenjamin@pircher.com

EUGENE J. M. LEONE, admitted to bar, 1983, New York; 1995, Illinois. *Education:* Cornell University (B.A., 1979); George Washington University (J.D., 1982). Co-Author: "Friendly Foreclosures: A Borrower's Checklist," Real Estate Workouts and Asset Management, Vol. 5, No. 7, January, 1995. Author: "Financing a Regional Mall: Traditional Sources Versus Securitization," The Real Estate Finance Journal, Vol. II, No. 3, Winter 1996. *Member:* New York State and Illinois State Bar Associations. ***PRACTICE AREAS:*** Real Estate Law. ***Email:*** eleone@pircher.com

JONATHAN D. LEVY, admitted to bar, 1991, Illinois; U.S. District Court, Northern District of Illinois. *Education:* University of Michigan (B.A., with high distinction, 1986; J.D., 1991). ***PRACTICE AREAS:*** Real Estate Law. ***Email:*** jlevy@pircher.com

MICHAEL McKEEVER, admitted to bar, 1990, Illinois and U.S. District Court, Northern District of Illinois. *Education:* Stanford University (B.A., 1987); Northwestern University (J.D., 1990). ***PRACTICE AREAS:*** Real Estate. ***Email:*** mmckeever@pircher.com

MIRYAM ROSIE REES, admitted to bar, 1981, Illinois. *Education:* Northeastern Illinois University (B.A., with high honors, 1973); Loyola University (J.D., with honors, 1981). Recipient, Edward B. White Scholarship Award. Lead Article Editor, Loyola University Law Journal, 1980-1981. Teaching Assistant, Loyola University, September, 1980-1981. ***LANGUAGES:*** German. ***PRACTICE AREAS:*** Real Estate Law; Retail Leasing. ***Email:*** rrees@pircher.com

RESIDENT ASSOCIATES

ELCHANAN FINESTONE, admitted to bar, 2003, Illinois. *Education:* Touro College (B.A., summa cum laude, 1999); New York University Law School (J.D., 2003). *Member:* Illinois State Bar Association. ***PRACTICE AREAS:*** Real Estate Law; Commercial Real Estate Acquisitions; Commercial Real Estate Finance. ***Email:*** efinestone@pircher.com

JULIA L. HALPERN, admitted to bar, 2004, Illinois. *Education:* University of Illinois at Champaign-Urbana (B.A., 2000); Chicago-Kent College of Law (J.D., magna cum laude, 2004). Order of the Coif. Member, Moot Court Honor Society. *Member:* Illinois State Bar Association. ***PRACTICE AREAS:*** Real Estate. ***Email:*** jhalpern@pircher.com

JAY BYRON LEIBOVITZ, admitted to bar, 1996, Illinois. *Education:* University of Michigan (A.B., with high distinction, 1992; J.D., 1995). *Member:* Chicago and Illinois State Bar Associations; International Counsel of Shopping Centers. ***Email:*** jleibovitz@pircher.com

DIANNE M. LU, admitted to bar, 1999, Massachusetts; 2000, Illinois. *Education:* Yale University (B.A.); Northeastern University (J.D.). ***PRACTICE AREAS:*** Real Estate Law. ***Email:*** dlu@pircher.com

JENNIFER S. MANTER, admitted to bar, 2003, New York; 2005, Illinois. *Education:* Northwestern University (B.A., 1996); Washington University (M.A., 2000); Duke University School of Law (J.D., 2002). *Member:* Illinois State and New York State Bar Associations. ***Email:*** jmanter@pircher.com

PABLO L. PETROZZI, admitted to bar, 1999, Minnesota; 2001, Illinois. *Education:* University of Notre Dame (B.A., magna cum laude, 1995); University of Minnesota (J.D., cum laude, 1999). ***LANGUAGES:*** Spanish. ***PRACTICE AREAS:*** Real Estate Law. ***Email:*** ppetrozzi@pircher.com

AARON M. POTTER, admitted to bar, 2003, Illinois. *Education:* Biola University (B.M., magna cum laude, 1991); George Fox College (M.A., 1995); University of Notre Dame (J.D., magna cum laude, 2001). Judicial Clerk, U.S. Court of Appeals, Sixth Circuit, for Judges Alice M. Batchelder and John M. Rogers. ***PRACTICE AREAS:*** Real Estate. ***Email:*** apotter@pircher.com

JOHN M. VALENTINE, admitted to bar, 2001, Illinois and U.S. District Court, Northern District of Illinois. *Education:* University of Michigan (B.A., with distinction, 1997); Loyola University Chicago School of Law (J.D., magna cum laude, 2001). Recipient, CALI Awards for Property, Torts and Legal Writing, 1999 and Conflict of Laws, 2000. Lead Articles Editor, Loyola University Chicago Law Journal, 2000-2001. Adjunct Professor, Professional Skills, Loyola University Chicago School of Law, 2005. ***PRACTICE AREAS:*** Commercial Real Estate; Real Estate; Zoning, Planning and Land Use. ***Email:*** jvalentine@pircher.com

REPRESENTATIVE CLIENTS: AMB Property Corporation; American Fidelity Assurance Company; American General Investment Corporation; Apollo Real Estate Advisors; Arden Realty; Blackstone Real Estate Advisors; Eli Broad; The Broad Foundation; Builders Bank; CapitalSource Finance; Capital Guidance Corporation; Caruso Affiliated Holdings; Center Trust; Citibank (West), FSB; Columbia Group; Crescent Heights; The Common Fund; Continental American Properties; Countrywide Home Loans; Credit Suisse First Boston; Divco West Group; Essex Property Trust; Farallon Capital Management; Federal Home Loan Mortgage Corporation; First Boston Real Estate Fund; Fujita Corporation U.S.A.; GEM Investors; Highridge Partners; Hometown America; ING Barings; J.E. Robert Companies; JMB Realty Corporation; Lexington Commercial Holdings; Madison Marquette; Medallist Golf Developments; Morgan Stanley Dean Witter Mortgage Capital; Nomura Credit & Capital; Oaktree Capital Management; Pabst Brewing Company; Playa Capital Company; Regent Properties; The RREEF Funds; Salomon Smith Barney; The Shidler Group; Silvergate Bank; Starwood Capital Group; Stonebridge Associates; Storage Etc.; StorAmerica; Summit Commercial Properties; SunAmerica; Urban Retail Properties; Urban Shopping Centers; The Vons Companies; Walton Street Capital; Waterton Associates; Westcore Industrial Properties; Westfield Corporation; Whitehall Street Real Estate Limited Partnership; Zeller Realty Corporation.

(This Listing Continued)

(For complete biographical data on all personnel, see Professional Biographies at Los Angeles, California)

SCOTT D. POLLOCK & ASSOCIATES, P.C.

Established in 1990

105 WEST MADISON, SUITE 2200
CHICAGO, ILLINOIS 60602
Telephone: 312-444-1940
Fax: 312-444-1950
URL: http://www.lawfirm1.com
Email: info@lawfirm1.com
URL: http://www.lawyers.com/scottdpollock&assoc

Immigration and Nationality, Citizenship, Visas, Asylum, Deportation, Family and Litigation Practice.

FIRM PROFILE: Scott D. Pollock & Associates, P.C. provides legal representation in the area of Immigration and Nationality law to businesses and individuals, both in the United States and abroad. We are available for consultation and representation on a wide variety of matters, including family and employment-based immigration, immigrant and nonimmigrant visa processing, naturalization, employment authorization and employer sanctions, asylum, deportation/removal defense and advisals to criminal defense attorneys about the immigration consequences of criminal dispositions. By concentrating our practice in the area of Immigration and Nationality law, we can provide efficient and affordable services to an internationally diverse and growing client base.

SCOTT D. POLLOCK, born Washington, D.C., April 24, 1958; admitted to bar, 1986, New York and Illinois; U.S. Supreme Court; U.S. Court of Appeals, First, Sixth, Seventh, Eighth and Ninth Circuits; U.S. District Court, Northern District of Illinois; U.S. District Court, Western District of Michigan. *Education:* Antioch College (B.A., 1981); Brooklyn Law School (J.D., 1985, cum laude). *Member:* Chicago, New York State, Illinois State and American Bar Associations; American Immigration Lawyers Association. ***LANGUAGES:*** Spanish. ***REPORTED CASES:*** Bace v. Ashcroft, 352 F.3d 1133 (7th Cir. 2003); Bereza v. INS, 115 F.3d 458 (7th Cir. 1997); Boukhris v. Perryman, 2002 U.S. Dist LEXIS 1913 (N.D.IL); Bucur v. INS, 109 F.3d 399 (7th Cir. 1997); Cardona v. United State INS, 1995 U.S. Dist LEXIS 1853 (N.D. IL); Cervantes-Manzo v. INS, 2000 U.S. App. LEXIS 22406 (7th Cir. 2000); Kuhai v. INS, 199 F.3d 209 (7th Cir. 1999); Mazur v. INS, 1996 U.S. Dist. LEXIS 17936 (N.D. IL); Morales-Morales v. Ashcroft, 384 F.3d 418 (7th Cir. 2004); Palacios v. Perryman, 2000 U.S. App. LEXIS 18179 (7th Cir.); Pop v. INS, 279 F.3d 457 (7th Cir. 2002); Sileikis v. Perryman, 2001 U.S. Dist. LEXIS 12737 (N.D. IL); Singh v. Perryman, 1998 U.S. Dist. LEXIS 18481 (N.D. IL 1998); Stroe v. INS, 256 F.3d 498 (7th Cir. 2001); Wigglesworth v. INS, 319 F.3d 951 (7th Cir. 2003); Wlostowska v. INS, 2003 U.S. App LEXIS 2793 (9th Cir. 2003); Yang et al. v. INS, 109 F.3d 1185 (7th Cir. 1997). ***PRACTICE AREAS:*** Immigration Law; Litigation. ***Email:*** spollock@lawfirm1.com

---

MARTA DELGADO, born Chicago, Illinois; admitted to bar, 1996, Wisconsin; 1997, Illinois. *Education:* Northwestern University (B.A., 1993); University of Wisconsin-Madison Law School (J.D., 1996). *Member:* American Immigration Lawyers Association. ***LANGUAGES:*** Spanish. ***PRACTICE AREAS:*** Immigration Law. ***Email:*** mdelgado@lawfirm1.com

MARIA T. BALDINI-POTERMIN, born Chicago, Illinois; admitted to bar, 1997, Minnesota; 1999, Illinois; U.S. Supreme Court; U.S. Court of Appeals, Sixth and Seventh Circuits; U.S. District Court, Northern District of Illinois, District of Minnesota, Eastern District of Wisconsin, Western District of Michigan. *Education:* University of Dayton (B.A., magna cum laude, 1990); University of Minnesota Law School (J.D., cum laude, 1997). *Member:* Chicago and Illinois State Bar Associations; American Immigration Lawyers Association, National Immigration Project. ***LANGUAGES:*** Spanish. ***REPORTED CASES:*** Masok v. Achim, 2005 U.S. Dist. LEXIS 8108 (N.D.IL 2005); Yanez-Garcia & Masok v. Ashcroft, 388 F.3d 280 (7th Cir. 2004); Allabani v. Gonzales, 402 F.3d 668 (6th Cir. 2005). ***PRACTICE AREAS:*** Immigration Law; Deportation; Litigation. ***Email:*** mbaldini-potermin@lawfirm1.com

KATHRYN WEBER, born Milwaukee, Wisconsin; admitted to bar, 2004, Illinois. *Education:* Marquette University (B.A., magna cum laude, 1999); University of Minnesota Law School (J.D., cum laude, 2003). *Member:* American Immigration Lawyers Association. ***LANGUAGES:*** French. ***PRACTICE AREAS:*** Immigration Law. ***Email:*** kweber@lawfirm1.com

FATIMA G. MOHYUDDIN, born Alton, Illinois; admitted to bar, 2003, Missouri (Not admitted in Illinois). *Education:* St. Louis University (B.A., magna cum laude, 1998); American University (J.D., 2001). Recipient, Robert Bosch Foundation Fellowship in Germany, 2001-2002. *Member:* Missouri and American Bar Associations; American Immigration Lawyers Association. ***LANGUAGES:*** Urdu/Hindi and German. ***PRACTICE AREAS:*** Immigration Law. ***Email:*** fmohyuddin@lawfirm1.com

ANNE G. RELIAS, born Evanston, Illinois; admitted to bar, 2001, Illinois; 2002, U.S. District Court, Northern District of Illinois; 2003, U.S. Court of Appeals, Seventh Circuit; 2005, U.S. District Court, Eastern District of Wisconsin. *Education:* University of Michigan (B.A., History, with honors, 1998); DePaul University College of Law (J.D., 2001). *Member:* Chicago Bar Association; American Immigration Lawyers Association; National Immigration Project of the National Lawyers Guild. ***REPORTED CASES:*** O'Sullivan v. United States Citizenship & Immigration Services, 372 F.Supp. 2d 1097 (N.D. Ill. 2005); Ali v. Achim, 342 F. Supp. 2d 769 (N.D. Ill. 2004); Ali v. Achim, 2004 U.S. Dist. LEXIS 17352 (N.D. Ill. 2004); Ramirez-Vicario v. Achim, 2004 U.S. Dist. LEXIS 2798 (N.D. Ill. 2004); Kazarov v. Achim, 2003 U.S. Dist. LEXIS 22407 (N.D. Ill. 2003); Hmaidan v. Ash-

(This Listing Continued)

croft, 258 F. Supp. 2d 832 (N.D. Ill. 2003); Gill v. Ashcroft, 2002 U.S. Distr. LEXIS 9821 (N.D. Ill. 2002). ***PRACTICE AREAS:*** Immigration Law; Deportation. ***Email:*** arelias@lawfirm1.com

Languages: Spanish, French, Urdu/Hindi, German, Serbo-Croatian, Russian, Czech.

POLSKY & ASSOCIATES, LTD.

Established in 1986

205 NORTH MICHIGAN AVENUE
41ST FLOOR
CHICAGO, ILLINOIS 60601-5925
Telephone: 312-540-0200
Fax: 312-540-0207
Email: postmaster@polskylaw.com
URL: http://www.polskylaw.com

Tax Increment Finance, Commercial Real Estate Development, Commercial Real Estate Finance, Industrial Real Estate Law, Shopping Center Development, Municipal Finance, Redevelopment Law, Real Estate Development, Property Tax Abatement, Sales and Use Tax, Land Development, Land Entitlement.

FIRM PROFILE: Represents Fortune 500 companies and regional development companies, including industrial and commercial development companies, in all aspects of real estate development with an emphasis on tax increment financing (TIF), sales tax financing, governmental tax abatements, and other economic incentives. The firm has an extensive background in representing clients before state and municipal governmental bodies and in the negotiation and issuance of governmental obligations in conjunction with private development. It has counseled clients in the structuring and issuance of hundreds of millions of dollars of municipal TIF and sales tax bonds and notes on a national basis.

SAMUEL J. POLSKY, born 1950; admitted to bar, 1974, Illinois. *Education:* Roosevelt University (B.A., with honors, 1971); Northwestern University (J.D., cum laude, 1974). ***PRACTICE AREAS:*** Tax Increment Finance; Sales and Use Tax; Real Estate; Municipal Finance; Municipal Redevelopment; Property Tax Abatement; Zoning, Planning and Land Use. ***Email:*** spolsky@polskylaw.com

DEBORAH A. FAKTOR, born 1949; admitted to bar, 1989, Illinois. *Education:* University of Illinois (B.A., 1972); DePaul University (M.A., 1978); IIT/Chicago-Kent College of Law (J.D., cum laude, 1989). Member, Moot Court Society. *Member:* Chicago and Illinois State Bar Associations. ***PRACTICE AREAS:*** Commercial Transactions; Tax Increment Finance; Real Estate; Finance. ***Email:*** dfaktor@polskylaw.com

ASSOCIATE

LAUREN E. BRADY, born 1976; admitted to bar, 2003, Illinois and Wisconsin. *Education:* University of Chicago (B.A., cum laude, 1998); University of Wisconsin-Madison (M.B.A.; J.D., 2003). ***PRACTICE AREAS:*** Commercial Transactions; Tax Increment Finance; Real Estate; Finance. ***Email:*** lbrady@polskylaw.com

REPRESENTATIVE CLIENTS: Home Depot; Target Corporation; Kimco; IKEA; General Mills; Unilever; Archon Group; Ridge Property Trust.

POMERANTZ HAUDEK BLOCK GROSSMAN & GROSS LLP

Established in 1940

ONE NORTH LASALLE STREET, SUITE 2225
CHICAGO, ILLINOIS 60602-3908
Telephone: 312-377-1181
Fax: 312-377-1184
Email: pomerantz@pomlaw.com
URL: http://www.pomlaw.com

New York, New York Office: 100 Park Avenue, 10017. Telephone: 212-661-1100. Fax: 212-661-8665.
Washington, D.C. Office: 1025 Connecticut Avenue, N.W., Suite 1000. Telephone: 202-327-5420. Fax: 202-327-5422.

Corporate, Securities, Antitrust and Insurance Litigation.

(For complete biographical data on all personnel, see Professional Biographies at New York, New York)

POWER ROGERS & SMITH, P.C.

70 WEST MADISON STREET, 55TH FLOOR
CHICAGO, ILLINOIS 60602
Telephone: 312-236-9381
Fax: 312-236-0920
Email: law@prslaw.com
URL: http://www.prslaw.com

Plaintiffs Personal Injury and Wrongful Death, Litigation, Including Aviation, Medical and Professional Negligence, FELA, Products Liability, Premises Liability, Construction Accidents and Vehicular Accidents.

FIRM PROFILE: Power Rogers & Smith, P.C., represents individuals and families relating to tragedies that occurred due to the conduct of another in personal injury and wrongful death cases arising out of aviation and vehicular accidents, medical malpractice, FELA, product liability, premises liability, and construction accidents. The Firm was named in October, 2004, by "Chicago Lawyer" Magazine as Number One law firm with settlements over a million dollars, the only Illinois firm in the top two in "Chicago Lawyer" Magazine"'s annual survey for million-dollar settlements, for the fifth consecutive year. Power Rogers & Smith, P.C., and its trial lawyers have obtained for its clients more than 300 verdicts and settlements exceeding $1,000,000. In 1992, Mr. Power became Illinois Trial Lawyers Association President. In 1995, Mr. Power was named by "The National Law Journal" as one of the country's top ten trial lawyers. In 1998, "Chicago Lawyer" Magazine named Todd A. Smith as its Lawyer of The Year. In 1997, Mr. Smith was President of the Illinois State Bar Association. Mr. Power, Mr. Rogers and Mr. Smith are named in "The Best Lawyers in America." In 1999, Mr. Rogers became Illinois Trial Lawyers Association President, and was named by "The National Law Journal" as one of the country's top ten trial lawyers. He was President of the Cook County Bar Association in 1991. In 1999, Mr. Smith was elected Association of Trial Lawyers of America Parliamentarian. In 2002, Mr. Smith was elected Vice President of the Association of Trial Lawyers of America. In 1999, Mr. Power obtained a settlement of $100,000,000 for the wrongful death of six children and injuries to the parents, which settlement was the highest of its kind in Illinois history. This case led to the license-for-bribe scandal which involved the indictment of over 70 people and 57 convictions. Those indicted include the former governor of Illinois and his chief-of-staff. Also in 1999, Mr. Power was invited to become a member of The Inner Circle of Advocates and was selected by "The National Law Journal" as one of the top four plaintiff's personal injury trial lawyers in Illinois and one of the best trial lawyers in the country. In 2000, Mr. Power, along with Mr. Rogers, obtained an award in the amount $55,439,269.59, the largest personal injury award in Illinois history. In 2002, Mr. Power settled a case involving the death of a father and injuries to his wife and two children for the entire insurance coverage available in the amount $39,910,186.38. In 2004, a poll of Illinois attorneys published in "Chicago Magazine" named Mr. Power as the highest vote-getter of the top attorneys in Illinois. In 2004-2005, Mr. Smith served as President of the Association of Trial Lawyers of America. In 2005, he was also invited to membership in The Inner Circle of Advocates.

JOSEPH A. POWER, JR., born Chicago, Illinois, October 15, 1952; admitted to bar, 1977, Illinois and U.S. District Court, Northern District of Illinois; 1982, Federal Trial Bar; 1992, U.S. Supreme Court; 1994, U.S. Court of Appeals, Seventh Circuit. *Education:* University of Notre Dame (B.A., with high honors, 1974); Loyola University (J.D., 1977). Recipient: Medal of Merit Award, Illinois State Bar Association, 2003; Tribute for Leadership Award on behalf of social justice and progressive change, U.S. Action and U.S. Action Education Fund, 2003; Medal of Excellence Award, Loyola University School of Law, 2003; Citizen of the Year Award, The City Club of Chicago, 2003; "Protector of the Working Man" Award, Illinois State Crime Commission, 2001; "Board Member of the Year" Award, Little City Foundation, 2001; Special Commendation Award, Civil Justice Foundation, 2000. Named One of Top Trial Lawyers in the United States, The National Law Journal, 1999. Named, Chicago Lawyer Settlement Survey as No.1 Law Firm in Chicago, Chicago Magazine, 2003. Named, one of 30 Tough Lawyers, Chicago Magazine, 2002. Listed in Who's Who in American Law. Listed by Harvard Law Graduates Naifeh and Smith in their book "The Best Lawyers in America," 1987, 1989, 1990, 1991, 1992, 1993, 1995-1996, 1997-1998, 1999-2000, 2001-2002, and 2005-2006. Named, One of the Nation's Top Ten Litigators, National Law Journal, 1995. In a recent poll of Illinois attorneys published in "Chicago Magazine" rating the best attorneys in Illinois, Joe Power was the top vote-getter. Author of numerous articles relating to the trial of cases and related law subjects. Frequent presenter at seminars and meetings across the country. A representative listing of both articles and presentations may be found at the Power Rogers & Smith, P.C. web site (www-.prslaw.com). Chairman, Trial Bar Advocacy Program; Member, U.S. Senate Judiciary Committee, Chairman's Advisory Council, 1994; and Illinois Supreme Court Rules Committee, 1995-1997. *Member:* Chicago (Chairman, Federal Trial Advocacy Program, 1984), Illinois State and American Bar Associations; Illinois Trial Lawyers Association (President, 1992-1993; President Elect, 1991-1992; Second Vice President, 1990-1991; Third Vice President, 1989-1990; Board of Managers, 1984; Chairman, Committees on: Membership, 1985-1987; Legislative, 1987-1989; Member, Executive Committee, 1986-1988); Association of Trial Lawyers of America (Sustaining Member; Chairman, Insurance Practices Committee, 1986-1987); Trial Lawyers For Public Justice (President, 1998-1999; President Trial, 1997-1998; Vice-President, 1996-1997, Board of Directors, Lifetime Member, Benefactor and State Captain). The Inner Circle of Advocates. American College of Trial Lawyers, 1995—; International Academy of Trial Lawyers. ***REPORTED CASES:*** Tonarelli v. Gibbons, et al., 121 ILL App. 3d 1042, 460 N.E. 2d464 (1984); Harrington v. Rush Presbyterian-St. Luke's Medical Center, 210 Ill. App. 3d 183 580 N.E. 2d114 (1990); Carlson v. City Construction Co., 239 Ill.App.3d 211, 606 N.E.2d 400 (1992); Tierney v. Community Memorial General Hospital, 1994 WL 685073, 268 Ill.App.3d 1051 645 N.E.2d 284, Ill.App.3d (1st Dist. 1994), *Leave to Appeal Denied,* Ill.2d (April 5, 1995); Dahan v Uhs of Bethesda, Inc. et al 295 Ill.App. 3rd 770 692 N.E.2d 1303 (1998); Sprietsma v. Mercury Marine, a Division of Brunswick Corporation, 123 S.Ct. 518 (2002). ***PRACTICE AREAS:*** Plaintiff Personal Injury Litigation; Medical Malpractice; Product Liability; Aviation Litigation; Premises Liability; Wrongful Death Law; Vehicular Accident Law; Structural Work Act. ***Email:*** joepower@prslaw.com

LARRY R. ROGERS, born Chicago, Illinois, December 29, 1947; admitted to bar, 1983, Illinois; U.S. Supreme Court; U.S. District Court, Northern District of Illinois; U.S. District Court, Eastern District of Wisconsin; U.S. Court of Appeals, Sixth and Seventh Circuits. *Education:* St. Xavier College (B.A., Philosophy, 1974); DePaul University (J.D., 1983). Author of many articles on trial advocacy, and presenter at several seminars on trial practice. A representative listing of both articles and presentations may be found at the Power Rogers & Smith, P.C. web site (www.prslaw.com). Instructor, Federal Trial Advocacy Program, 1984. Member: Illinois Legal Needs Study Private Bar Committee; Teaching Team, Trial Advocacy Workshop: Harvard Law School, 1993; University of Chicago Law School, 1993. Trial Practice Workshop Teaching Team, University of Chicago Law School—Edwin F. Mandel Legal Aid Clinic: Topics, "Opening Statements," Direct and Cross-Examination of Lay and Expert Witnesses," "Closing Arguments," and "Mock Trial of Both Civil and Criminal Cases," 1995. Commissioner: Illinois Supreme Court Special Commission on the Administration of Justice, 1991—; U.S. Senate Judicial Nominations Commission for the Northern District of Illinois, 1993-1996. Member: Illinois Supreme Court Committee on Jury Instructions in Civil Cases; Board of Trustees, St. Xavier University, 1996—; Board of Directors, Legal Assistance Foundation of Chicago, 1996-2001. In 1999, named by "The National Law Journal" as one of the country's top ten trial lawyers. *Member:* Chicago, Cook County (President, 1991-1992; First Vice President, 1990; Second

(This Listing Continued)

POWER ROGERS & SMITH, P.C., Chicago—Continued

Vice President, 1989; Third Vice President, 2001-2002; Member: Board of Directors, 1985-1994; Nominating Committee, 1985; Education Committee, 1985; Judicial Evaluation Committee, 1986-1987); Illinois State and American Bar Associations; National Bar Association (Member, Board of Governors, 1990-1991); The Association of Trial Lawyers of America (Sustaining Member); Illinois Trial Lawyers Association (President, 2000; President Elect, 1999; Second Vice President, 1998; Third Vice President, 1997; Treasurer, 1989; Member: Board of Managers, 1987—; Legislative Committee, 1985; Co-Chair, 1996—; Membership Committee, 1985; Executive Committee, 1996—). ***PRACTICE AREAS:*** Plaintiff Personal Injury Litigation; Aviation Litigation; Medical Malpractice; Product Liability; Premises Liability; Wrongful Death Law; Automobile Accidents and Injuries; Vehicular Homicide; Structural Work Act. ***Email:*** larryrogers@prslaw.com

TODD A. SMITH, born Chicago, Illinois, August 27, 1949; admitted to bar, 1976, Illinois; 1980, U.S. District Court, Northern District of Illinois; U.S. Court of Appeals, Seventh Circuit; U.S. Supreme Court. *Education:* University of Kansas (B.S.B., 1971); Northwestern University Graduate School of Business (M.B.A., 1973); Loyola University School of Law (J.D., 1976). Member, Loyola Law Journal, 1975-1976. Appointment: State of Illinois Advisory Council on Spinal Cord-Head Injuries, 1995—. Author of numerous articles relating to the trial of cases and related law subjects. Frequent presenter at seminars and meetings across the country. A representative listing of both articles and presentations may be found at the Power Rogers & Smith P.C. web site (www.prslaw.com). Listed, Naifeh & Smith, The Best Lawyers in American, 1997-1998, 1999-2000, 2001-2002, 2003-2004, 2005-2006. Chicago Lawyer Magazine, "1998 Person of the Year." Member, Loyola Law Journal, Loyola University of Chicago School of Law. Recipient: 2005 Medal of Excellence, Loyola University of Chicago School of Law; Damien Award, Founders' Day, Loyola University of Chicago, 2002; Joe Tonahill Award, ATLA Annual Convention, 2002; American Legion Award of Excellence, C.D. Burton Post 808, 2002. Finalist, TLPJ Trial Lawyer of the Year, 1999. *Member:* Chicago Bar Association (Member: Tort Litigation Section; Judicial Evaluation Committee, 1985-1990; Past Chairman, Subcommittee on Legislation of Tort Litigation Section; Past Chairman, Subcommittee on Pending Legislation of Tort Litigation Section); Illinois State Bar Association (President, 1997- 1998; President Elect, 1996-1997; Second Vice President, 1995-1996, Third Vice President, 1994-1995; Treasurer, 1993-1994; Member, Editorial Board of Illinois Bar Journal, 1989; Associate Editor, 1990-1991; Elected Member, ISBA Assembly, 1990-1999; Elected Member, Board of Governors, 1991-1999; Board Liaison to: Illinois Bar Journal, 1991-1993; International and Immigration Law Section, 1991-1993; Health Care Section, 1991-1992; Bench and Bar Section, 1992-1993; Young Lawyers Section, 1993-1994; Civil Practice & Procedure 1993-1994; Member: Rules & By-Laws Committee, 1990-1991; Mutual Insurance Company Board Committee on Long Range Planning, 1992-1993; Life Fellow, Illinois Bar Foundation; Long Range Planning Committee, 1992-1993; Vice-Chair, Task Force on Minorities and the Justice System, 1993-1996; Elected Member, Scope & Correlation Committee, 1992-1993; Chair, Assembly Committee on Integrated Bar, 1993-1994; Chair, Standing Committee on Investments, 1993-1994; Member, Standing Committee on Budget & Audit, 1993-1994; Elected, Third Vice-President, 1994; Chairman, Standing Committee on ISBA Properties, 1994-1995; Board of Directors, ISBA Mutual Insurance Company, 1995—; Second Vice President, 1997-1998; First Vice President, 1998-1999; Chairman of the Board, 1999-2000); American Bar Association (Chairman of the Board, 1998-1999; Member, Sections on: Litigation; Space and Aviation; Tort and Insurance Practice; Member, Editorial Board of the "Brief," 1990-1992; Member, House of Delegates, 1995-1999); Fellow, American Bar Foundation; Illinois Trial Lawyers Association (Secretary, Amicus Curiae Committee, 1985-1987; Chairman, 1987-1989. Moderator, Trial Advocacy Seminar, December 1984; Member: Legislative Committee; Board of Managers, 1985—; Chairman: Legislative Committee, 1989-1995; Constitutional Challenge Committee, 1995-1997; Co-Chairman, Publications Committee, 1995-1997; Rules of Professional Conduct Committee, 1990-1992; Seminar Planning Chairman, 1992-1994; Executive Committee 1997-1998; Nominating Committee, 1998); Association of Trial Lawyers of America (Sustaining Member, Parliamentarian, 1999-2000; Treasurer, 2000-2001; Secretary, 2001-2002; Vice-President, 2002-2003; President-Elect, 2003-2004; President, 2004-2005; Member, Judicial Independence Committee, 1998-2000; Co-Chair, Legal Affairs Liaison Committee, 2000—; Chair, Public Affairs Committee, 2002-2003; Member: Amicus Curiae Committee, 1988-1993; Constitutional Litigation Committee, 1988-1995; Fellow, Trustee, Roscoe Pound Foundation; Fundraising Events Subcommittee, 1988-1989; Steering Subcommittee on Special Events; Board of Governors, 1989—; Member, Executive Committee, 1998—; ATLA Endowment Trustee, 1999—; Vice President, Board of Trustees, 2004-2005; Chair, Regional Judges Forum, Roscoe Pound Foundation, 2000—; Chair, Committee on Investments, 1999-2000; Co-Chair, Membership Oversight Committee, 1999-2000; Chair, Coordinating Committee of State Relations, 1999-2000; "M" Club, 1990—; ATLA PAC Committee, 1989-1991; Trial Lawyers for Public Justice, 1989—; Fellow, Civil Justice Foundation, 1989—; Chairman, Amicus Curiae Committee, 1990-1992; Member: Organizational Review Committee, 1991-1993; Aviation Advisory Committee, 1991-1993; Federal Rules Committee, 1991-1993; Vice-Chair; Legal Affairs Committee, 1992-1993 and 1996-1998; Vice-Chair, Aviation Law Section, 1992-1994; Chair Aviation Law Section, 1994-1995; Member: Mass Tort Sub-Committee, 1992-1993; Board of Trustees, National College of Advocacy, 1993-1996; Program Advisory Committee 1994 ATLA Annual Convention; Elected Member, Organization and Home Office Committee, 1994-1996); The Society of Trial Lawyers (Member, Board of Directors, 1992-1995); Trial Lawyers for Public Justice; Trial Lawyers Club of Chicago (Member, Board of Managers, 1987—); American Inn of Court-Markey Wigmore Chapter. Fellow, The Inner Circle of Advocates. Fellow, American College of Trial Lawyers. Fellow, International Academy of Trial Lawyers. Fellow, International Society of Barristers. ***REPORTED CASES:*** *Bullistron v. Northern Builders,* 127 Ill.App.3d 242 (1st Dist. 1984); *Cooper v. Chicago Transit Authority,* 153 Ill.App.3d 511 (1st Distr. 1987); *Chladek v. Albon,* 161 Ill.App.3d 884 (1st Dist. 1987); *Hinojosa v. City of Chicago Heights,* 166 Ill.App.3d 319 (1st Dist. 1988); *In re: Estate of Callahan,* 188 Ill.App.3d 323 (3d Dist. 1989), *aff'd.* 144 Ill.2d 32 (1991); (Amicus Counsel), *Lee v. Chicago Transit Authority,* 205 Ill.App.3d 163 (1st Dist. 1990) *Rev'd.* 152 Ill.2d 432 (1992); *Haight v. Aldridge Electric Co.,* 215 Ill.App.3d 353 (2d Dist. 1991); (Amicus Counsel), *Wolens v. American Airlines,* 147 Ill.2d 367 (1992); *Egan v. Chicago Transit Authority,* 240 Ill.App.3d 784 (1st Dist. 1993); Grutzius v. Franciscan Sisters Health Care, et 251 Ill.App. 3d 897; Depre v. Power Climber Incorporated, 23 Ill.App.3d, 116 (1st Dist. 1994); Barille v. Sears Roebuck and Company, 288 Ill.App.3d 171 (1st Dist. 1997); Cincinnati Ins. Co. (Ill St. Bar Assoc) v. Chapman (Mathis), 181 Ill.2d 65 (1998), and judgment reversed by; *Sprietsma v. Mercury Marine,* 123 S.Ct. 518 (2002); *Hallowell v. University of Chicago Hosp.,* 334 Ill.App.3d 206 (1st Dist. 2002); *Baseggio v. Sherman Hospital, Ill.App.3d (Docket No. 1-01-3593).* ***PRACTICE AREAS:*** Plaintiff's Personal Injury Litigation; Aviation Litigation; Medical Negligence; Professional Negligence; FELA; AIDS Litigation; Products Liability; Premises Liability; Construction Accidents; Structural Work Act; Wrongful Death Law; Automobile Accidents and Injuries. ***Email:*** tas@prslaw.com

---

THOMAS G. SIRACUSA, born Chicago, Illinois, May 23, 1961; admitted to bar, 1986, Illinois and U.S. District Court, Northern District of Illinois. *Education:* Loyola University (B.A., 1983); Illinois Institute of Technology/Chicago-Kent College of Law (J.D., with honors, 1986). Editor and Member of Staff, Chicago-Kent Law Review, 1984-1986. Author of numerous articles relating to the trial of cases and related law subjects. Frequent presenter at seminars and meetings across the country. A representative listing of both articles and presentations may be found at the Power Rogers & Smith, P.C. web site (www-.prslaw.com). *Member:* Chicago, Illinois State and American Bar Associations; The Association of Trial Lawyers of America (Board Member, Birth Trauma Litigation Group); Illinois Trial Lawyers Association (Board of Managers). ***PRACTICE AREAS:*** Plaintiff Personal Injury Litigation; Medical Malpractice; Product Liability; Premises Liability; Wrongful Death Law; Automobile Accidents and Injuries; Structural Work Act. ***Email:*** tsiracusa@prslaw.com

THOMAS M. POWER, born Chicago, Illinois, March 27, 1957; admitted to bar, 1985, Illinois and U.S. District Court, Northern District of Illinois. *Education:* St. Xavier College (B.A., 1980); John Marshall School of Law (J.D., 1985). Adjunct Professor, DePaul College of Law, January-May, 1996. *Member:* Chicago, Illinois State (Elected Member of the Assembly, 1994) and American Bar Associations; The Association of Trial Lawyers of America; Illinois Trial Lawyers Association (Member, Legislative Committee). ***REPORTED CASES:*** Gorlikowski v. Tolbert, et al., 52 F.3d 1439 (7th Cir. 1995); Gusich v. Metropolitan Pier & Exposition Authority, 326 Ill. App. 3d 1030 (1st Dist., 2001); Winters v. Kline, et al., 344 Ill. App. 3d 919 (1st Dist. 2003). ***PRACTICE AREAS:*** Plaintiff Personal Injury Litigation; Medical Malpractice; Product Liability; Premises Liability; Wrongful Death; Automobile Accidents; Structural Work Act. ***Email:*** tpower@prslaw.com

LARRY R. ROGERS, JR., born Chicago, Illinois, February 18, 1968; admitted to bar, 1994, Illinois and U.S. District Court, Northern District of Illinois. *Education:* University of California, Davis (B.S., 1990); IIT Chicago-Kent College of Law (J.D., 1993). Recipient, American Jurisprudence Award, Trial Advocacy II. *Member:* Cook County (President-Elect, 2004), Chicago, Illinois State, and American Bar Associations; National Bar Association (President, Young Lawyers Division, 2001-2002); Illinois Trial Lawyers Association (Member, Board of Advocates); The Association of Trial Lawyers of America (Member, Litigation Section). ***PRACTICE AREAS:*** Personal Injury; Litigation; Medical Malpractice; Products Liability; Premises Liability; Wrongful Death; Automobile Accidents and Injuries; Structural Work Act. ***Email:*** lrogersjr@prslaw.com

DEVON C. BRUCE, born Champaign, Illinois, December 8, 1969; admitted to bar, 1993, Illinois; 1994, U.S. District Court, Northern District of Illinois; U.S. District Court, Central District of Illinois; U.S. Court of Appeals, Seventh Circuit. *Education:* University College, Cork, Ireland; University of Illinois (B.A., 1990; J.D., 1993). Clerk to the Honorable Moses W. Harrison, II, Chief Justice, Illinois Supreme Court, 1993-1994. Recipient: 1998 Public Justice Achievement Award by the Trial Lawyers for Public Justice; Illinois Trial Lawyers Association Award for Volunteer work on behalf of the Amicus Curiae Committee, 1999. Author of numerous articles relating to the trial of cases and related law subjects. Frequent presenter at seminars and meetings across the country. A representative listing of both articles and presentations may be found at the Power Rogers & Smith, P.C. web site (www.prslaw.com). Judicial Advisory Council Pro Bono Volunteer, Appellate Defender Program, 1996—. Member, Board of Trustees, University of Illinois. Chairman, Legal Affairs Committee; Chairman, Budget and Audit Committee; Member, Sub-committee on President's Selection. Adjunct Professor of Law, University of Illinois, 2004, 2005. *Member:* Chicago and Illinois State (Former Chairman, Young Lawyers Division, 1993-2000) Bar Associations; Illinois Supreme Court Committee on Judicial Evaluation and Oversight; Chicago Inn of Court (Former Member); Illinois Trial Lawyers Association (Board of Advocates, 2001—); Trial Lawyers for Public Justice (Member, Lead Paint Committee). ***REPORTED CASES:*** Sprietsma v. Mercury Marine, 123 S.Ct. 518 (2002); Donaldson v. Central Illinois Public Service, 199 Ill.2d 63 (2002); Campuzano v. Il.State Bd. of Elections, No. 01C 50376; Bovara v. St. Francis Hospital, 298 Ill.App.3d 1025, 700 N.E.2d 143 (1st Dist. 1998); O'Banner v. McDonalds Corp, 173 Ill.2d 208, 670 N.E.2d 208 (1996); Lanphier v. Gilster Mary Lee Corp., 327 Ill.App. 3d. 801 (3rd Dist. 2002); Stein v. Chicago Park District, 323 Ill.App. 3d 574 (1st Dist. 2001); Gillen v. State Farm Insurance, 215 Ill.2d 381 (2005). ***PRACTICE AREAS:*** Personal Injury; Litigation; Medical Malpractice; Products Liability; Premises Liability; Wrongful Death; Automobile Accidents and Injuries; Construction Accidents; Clergy Sexual Misconduct. ***Email:*** dcbruce@prslaw.com

JOSEPH W. BALESTERI, born Maywood, Illinois, July 13, 1970; admitted to bar, 1995, Illinois and U.S. District Court, Northern District of Illinois. *Education:* Indiana University (B.S., 1992); DePaul University (J.D., 1995). Previous Employment: Hinshaw & Culbertson - Attorney - Practice concentration in Medical Malpractice Representation of Physicians, Nurses, HMO's and Hospitals (1995-2000). *Member:* Chicago, Illinois State and American Bar Associations; Illinois Trial Lawyers Association; The Association of Trial Lawyers of America. ***PRACTICE AREAS:*** Plaintiffs Personal Injury; Wrongful Death; Medical Malpractice; Products Liability; Premises Liability; Automobile Accidents and Injuries. ***Email:*** jbalesteri@prslaw.com

SEAN M. HOULIHAN, born Evergreen Park, Illinois, July 3, 1968; admitted to bar, 2002, Illinois and U.S. District Court, Northern District of Illinois. *Education:* University of Illinois-Chicago (B.A. with distinction, 1996) Golden Key Honor Society; DePaul University (J.D., 2001) Dean's List. *Member:* Chicago, Illinois State, Federal and American Bar Associations; Illinois Trial Lawyers Association; American Trial Lawyers Association.

(This Listing Continued)

PRACTICE AREAS: Plaintiffs Personal Injury; Products Liability; Medical Malpractice; Aviation Law; Automobile Accidents and Injuries; Commercial Fraud. **Email:** shoulihan@prslaw.com

BRIAN LaCIEN, born Chicago, Illinois, October 20, 1976; admitted to bar, 2002, Illinois. *Education:* University of Iowa (B.A., 1999); DePaul University (J.D., magna cum laude, 2002). Order of the Coif. ***PRACTICE AREAS:*** Personal Injury; Products Liability; Medical Malpractice; Construction Accidents; Automobile Negligence. **Email:** blacien@prslaw.com

RICHARD J. PRENDERGAST, LTD.

111 WEST WASHINGTON-SUITE 1100
CHICAGO, ILLINOIS 60602-2768
Telephone: 312-641-0881
Fax: 312-641-3562
Email: lawfirm@rjpltd.com
URL: http://www.rjpltd.com

General Trial and Appellate Practice. Personal Injury, Antitrust, Securities and Commercial Litigation.

RICHARD J. PRENDERGAST, born Chicago, Illinois, February 21, 1945; admitted to bar, 1969, Illinois; 1977, U.S. District Court, Northern District of Illinois including Trial Bar; 1978, U.S. Supreme Court and U.S. Court of Appeals, Seventh Circuit; 1979, U.S. Court of Appeals, Ninth Circuit and U.S. Tax Court; 1980, U.S. Court of Appeals for the District of Columbia Circuit; 1981, U.S. District Court, Eastern District of Wisconsin; 1999, U.S. Court of Appeals for the Federal Circuit. *Education:* Loyola University (B.B.A., 1968; J.D., 1969). *Member:* Chicago (President, 1994-1995), Illinois State and American Bar Associations; The Association of Trial Lawyers of America; Illinois Trial Lawyers Association; Appellate Lawyers Association of Illinois. Fellow: American College of Trial Lawyers; International Academy of Trial Lawyers; American Academy of Appellate Lawyers; Celtic Legal Society of Chicago (President, 1999); Illinois Board of Admissions to the Bar (President, 1997-1999). ***PRACTICE AREAS:*** Civil Litigation. **Email:** rprendergast@rjpltd.com

JAMES PRENDERGAST, born Evergreen Park, Illinois, March 22, 1953; admitted to bar, 1980, Illinois; 1981, U.S. District Court, Northern District of Illinois including Trial Bar and U.S. Court of Appeals, Seventh Circuit; 1997, U.S. Tax Court. *Education:* Quincy College (B.A., 1975); Northern Illinois University (J.D., 1980). Judge, Circuit Court of Cook County, Assigned to First Municipal Traffic, February 2000-December 2000. *Member:* Chicago, Illinois State and American Bar Associations; The Association of Trial Lawyers of America; Illinois Trial Lawyers Association. ***PRACTICE AREAS:*** Civil Litigation. **Email:** jprendergast@rjpltd.com

MICHAEL T. LAYDEN, born St. Louis, Missouri, June 8, 1970; admitted to bar, 1995, Illinois; 1997, U.S. District Court, Northern District of Illinois. *Education:* University of Wisconsin-Madison (B.A., 1992); Chicago-Kent College of Law, Illinois Institute of Technology (J.D., 1995). *Member:* Chicago Bar Association. **Email:** mlayden@rjpltd.com

DEIRDRE ANN CLOSE, born Chicago, Illinois, December 27, 1968; admitted to bar, 1995, Illinois; 1997, U.S. District Court, Northern District of Illinois; 1999, U.S. Court of Appeals for the Federal Circuit. *Education:* Loyola University (B.A., 1992); St. Thomas University (J.D., 1995). Phi Delta Phi. *Member:* Chicago Bar Association. **Email:** dclose@rjpltd.com

JENNIFER M. RYDER, born Milwaukee, Wisconsin; admitted to bar, 2004, Illinois and U.S. District Court, Northern District of Illinois. *Education:* University of Wisconsin-Madison (B.A., 2000); Loyola University Chicago (J.D., 2004). Golden Key; Philip H. Conboy Trial Team. *Member:* Chicago, Illinois State and American Bar Associations. ***PRACTICE AREAS:*** Civil Litigation. **Email:** jryder@rjpltd.com

PRETZEL & STOUFFER

CHARTERED
Established in 1946
ONE SOUTH WACKER DRIVE
SUITE 2500
CHICAGO, ILLINOIS 60606-4673
Telephone: 312-346-1973
FAX: 312-346-8242; 346-8060
URL: http://www.pretzel-stouffer.com

General Civil Litigation, Dispute Resolution, Trial and Appellate Practice. Insurance, Environmental, Corporate, Commercial, Probate, Tax, Real Estate, Employee Benefits, Construction and Admiralty Law.

FIRM PROFILE: Pretzel & Stouffer, Chartered is a Chicago-based law firm founded in 1946 to provide counsel in the areas of civil litigation, trials and appeals. Since our founding, we have expanded our civil litigation and trial practice with the changes in the law and the needs of our clients. We have also expanded our ability to serve the broad-based general business and personal legal needs of our corporate and individual clients.

Today the firm serves the litigation and general practice needs of hundreds of clients from most states and several foreign countries. We have expanded our practice to many areas beyond litigation and dispute resolution, slowly evolving into a full service firm capable of handling the diverse needs of individuals and businesses.

The firm includes within its list of litigation clients, companies engaged in manufacturing, service businesses, the pharmaceutical industry, the health care industry, the insurance industry, the financial industry, the construction industry and energy related concerns.

(This Listing Continued)

The clients served by our general practice attorneys represent diverse interests, including insurance, construction, general business, wholesale and retail sales, manufacturing, real estate development, health care providers and banks.

It is our goal to provide our clients creative legal representation of the highest quality in an efficient cost-effective manner that is sensitive to the changing needs of our clients.

CYNTHIA H. ALKHOUJA, born Chicago, Illinois, February 9, 1977; admitted to bar, 2002, Illinois. *Education:* Loyola University (B.A., 1999); Chicago-Kent College of Law (J.D., 2002).

SCOTT L. ANDERSON, born Morrison, Illinois, August 20, 1974; admitted to bar, 1999, Illinois; 2004, U.S. District Court, Northern District of Illinois. *Education:* Cornell College (B.A., 1996); Loyola University, Chicago School of Law (J.D., 1999). ***PRACTICE AREAS:*** Litigation; Medical Malpractice. **Email:** sanderson@pretzel-stouffer.com

DARRYL L. AWICK, born Lincoln, Illinois, July 10, 1959; admitted to bar, 1995, Illinois. *Education:* Illinois State University (B.S., 1981); Keller Graduate School of Management (M.B.A., 1984); John Marshall Law School (J.D., 1995). **Email:** dawick@pretzel-stouffer.com

RENA A. BALLARD, born Cleveland, Mississippi, August 18, 1960; admitted to bar, 1996, Illinois. *Education:* Delta State College (B.M., 1983); Florida State University (M.S., 1987); DePaul University (J.D., 1996). ***PRACTICE AREAS:*** Medical Malpractice Defense. **Email:** rballard@pretzel-stouffer.com

DAVID M. BENNETT, born Cleveland, Ohio, June 7, 1964; admitted to bar, 1989, Illinois and U.S. District Court, Northern District of Illinois. *Education:* Purdue University (B.A., 1986); IIT Chicago-Kent College of Law (J.D., 1989). Certified Arbitrator, Cook County Arbitration Program. *Member:* Chicago and Illinois State Bar Associations; Illinois Association of Defense Trial Counsel. ***PRACTICE AREAS:*** Tort Litigation. **Email:** dbennett@pretzel-stouffer.com

BRENDAN M. BURNS, born Oak Lawn, Illinois, November 3, 1977; admitted to bar, 2002, Illinois. *Education:* University of Wisconsin (B.B.A., 1999); Creighton University (J.D., 2002). Certified Mediator, Nebraska Mediation Center. *Member:* Illinois State Bar Association. ***PRACTICE AREAS:*** Civil Litigation; Commercial Litigation; Real Estate. **Email:** bburns@pretzel-stouffer.com

CHRISTOPHER C. CASSIDY, born Randolph, Vermont, September 25, 1969; admitted to bar, 1994, Vermont; 2000, Illinois. *Education:* Harvard University (B.A., 1991); Vermont Law School (J.D., 1994). ***PRACTICE AREAS:*** Insurance Coverage; Insurance Defense. **Email:** ccassidy@pretzel-stouffer.com

ROBERT MARC CHEMERS, born Chicago, Illinois, July 24, 1951; admitted to bar, 1976, Indiana, Illinois and U.S. District Court, Southern District of Indiana; 1977, U.S. Court of Appeals, Seventh Circuit and U.S. District Court, Northern District of Illinois including Trial Bar; 1981, U.S. District Court, Southern District of Illinois; 1985, U.S. Court of Appeals, Fifth Circuit; 1991, U.S. District Court, Central District of Illinois; 1992, U.S. Supreme Court. *Education:* University of Southern California (B.A., magna cum laude, 1973); Indiana University School of Law (J.D., cum laude, 1976). Phi Eta Sigma; Phi Alpha Delta. Member, Blackstonian. Member, Indiana Law Review, 1974-1976. ***PRACTICE AREAS:*** Insurance Coverage; Reinsurance Law; Declaratory Judgment; Professional Liability; Appellate Practice; Commercial Litigation. **Email:** rchemers@pretzel-stouffer.com

MICHAEL A. CLARKE, born 1961; admitted to bar, 1987, Illinois and U.S. District Court, Northern, Central and Southern Districts of Illinois. *Education:* University of Illinois (B.S., 1983); DePaul University (J.D., 1987). Order of the Barristers. Co-Author: *The Insurance Coverage Aspects of Environmental Claims,* Mid-American Press 1991; *Insurance Claims and the Construction Industry,* Mid-American Press 1992. *Member:* Illinois State Bar Association. ***PRACTICE AREAS:*** Insurance Coverage; Commercial Litigation. **Email:** mclarke@pretzel-stouffer.com

BRENDAN S. CROWLEY, born Duluth, Minnesota, April 18, 1978; admitted to bar, 2005, Illinois. *Education:* University of Illinois (B.S., 2000); DePaul University (J.D., 2005). ***PRACTICE AREAS:*** Civil Litigation; Commercial Litigation. **Email:** bcrowley@pretzel-stouffer.com

SUZANNE MARIE CROWLEY, born Chicago, Illinois, April 1, 1961; admitted to bar, 1987, Illinois and U.S. District Court, Northern District of Illinois. *Education:* Northern Illinois University (B.S., 1983); John Marshall Law School (J.D., 1986). ***PRACTICE AREAS:*** Civil Litigation; Products Liability; Insurance Coverage. **Email:** scrowley@pretzel-stouffer.com

MARY H. CUSACK, born Chicago, Illinois, March 6, 1978; admitted to bar, 2005, Illinois. *Education:* Marquette University (B.A., 2000); Loyola University (J.D., 2005). ***PRACTICE AREAS:*** Medical Malpractice Defense; Product Liability Defense; Tort Litigation; Insurance Coverage Law. **Email:** mcusack@pretzel-stouffer.com

MELISSA GIOVANINI DEPTULA, born Decatur, Illinois, April 10, 1972; admitted to bar, 1999, Illinois. *Education:* Northwestern University (B.A., 1994); John Marshall Law School (J.D., 1999).

MATTHEW J. EGAN, born Chicago, Illinois, December 4, 1957; admitted to bar, 1982, Illinois; U.S. District Court, Northern District of Illinois including Trial Bar; U.S. Court of Appeals, Seventh Circuit; U.S. Supreme Court. *Education:* University of Sterling, Scotland; University of Illinois (B.A., 1979); Loyola University (J.D., 1982). Assistant State's Attorney, Cook County, Illinois, 1982-1984. Trial Attorney, Hartford Insurance Group, 1984-1988. Special Assistant Attorney General, State of Illinois, 1992—. Member, Attorney Regulatory and Disciplinary Committee Hearing Board, 1991—. *Member:* Chicago and Illinois State Bar Associations. ***PRACTICE AREAS:*** Professional Liability Defense; Products Liability; Commercial Litigation; Insurance Litigation. **Email:** megan@pretzel-stouffer.com

WILLIAM W. ELINSKI, born Sayre, Pennsylvania, October 18, 1961; admitted to bar, 1998, Illinois. *Education:* University of New Hampshire (B.S., 1983); University of Pittsburgh (M.S., 1993); Lewis and Clark College (J.D., 1998). ***PRACTICE AREAS:*** Litigation. **Email:** welinski@pretzel-stouffer.com

(This Listing Continued)

PRETZEL & STOUFFER, CHARTERED, Chicago—Continued

MICHAEL A. FACCENDA, born South Bend, Indiana, October 21, 1970; admitted to bar, 1997, Illinois. *Education:* University of Notre Dame (B.A., 1993; J.D., 1996).

PATRICK F. HEALY, III, born Evergreen Park, Illinois, February 15, 1961; admitted to bar, 1986, Illinois and U.S. District Court, Northern District of Illinois. *Education:* Loras College (B.A., 1983); The John Marshall Law School (J.D., with distinction, 1986). ***PRACTICE AREAS:*** Construction Defense; Tort Defense; Product Liability Defense; Workers Compensation Defense; Broker's Error and Omissions Defense; Trucking Law; Automobile Liability Defense. ***Email:*** phealy@pretzel-stouffer.com

KIM M. HEFFERNAN, born Chicago, Illinois, March 23, 1967; admitted to bar, 1992, Illinois. *Education:* University of Colorado (B.S., 1989); St. Mary's University School of Law (J.D., 1992).

MARCIE L. HEFLER, born Baltimore, Maryland, September 9, 1968; admitted to bar, 1993, Illinois and U.S. District Court, Northern District of Illinois; 1999, U.S. Court of Appeals, Seventh Circuit; 2001, U.S. District Court, Northern District of Indiana. *Education:* University of Wisconsin-Madison (B.A., 1990); John Marshall Law School (J.D., 1993). ***PRACTICE AREAS:*** Medical Malpractice; Insurance Defense. ***Email:*** mhefler@pretzel-stouffer.com

BRIAN T. HENRY, born Chicago, Illinois, December 25, 1954; admitted to bar, 1980, Illinois and U.S. District Court, Northern District of Illinois. *Education:* Loyola University, Chicago (B.A., Honors Program Degree, magna cum laude, 1977); University of Illinois (J.D., 1980). Editor-in-Chief, Recent Decisions Section of Illinois Bar Journal, 1979-1980, Recipient: Paul S. Lietz Gold Key, 1977; Honors Program Gold Key, 1977; History Department Silver Key, 1977; Mellon Foundation Award, 1977; Rickert Award for Excellence in Legal Writing, 1980. Faculty Instructor: IADIC Trial Academy, 1990, 1992-2005; IADC Trial Academy, 2001. Fellow American College of Trial Lawyers. ***PRACTICE AREAS:*** Professional Liability; Products Liability. ***Email:*** bhenry@pretzel-stouffer.com

ANDREW J. HOLEN, born April 18, 1974; admitted to bar, 1999, Illinois. *Education:* Purdue University (B.S., 1996); University of Houston (J.D., cum laude, 1999). *Member:* Illinois State Bar Association. ***PRACTICE AREAS:*** Medical Malpractice Defense.

SCOTT LANGFORD HOWIE, born Seattle, Washington, November 13, 1966; admitted to bar, 1994, Illinois and U.S. District Court, Northern District of Illinois; 1996, U.S. Court of Appeals, Seventh Circuit. *Education:* Northwestern University (B.A., 1989); Chicago-Kent College of Law (J.D., 1994). *Member:* Appellate Lawyers Association. ***REPORTED CASES:*** Hoffman v. Orthopedic Sys., Inc., 327 Ill.App.3d 1004 (2002); Sinclair v. Berlin, 325 Ill.App.3d 458 (2001); Kass v. Resurrection Med. Ctr., 316 Ill.App.3d 1108 (2000); Benson v. SI Handing Systems, Inc., 188 F.3d 780 (7th Cir. 1999); Gavoni v. Dobbs Houses, Inc., 164 F.3d 1071 (7th Cir. 1999); Doe v. McKay, 183 Ill.2d 272(1998); Malkin v. Malkin, 301 Ill.App. 3d 303, 703 N.E.2d 460 (1st Dist. 1998); Pekin Ins. Co. v. L.J. Shaw & Co., 291 Ill.App.3d 888 (1997); Iser v. Copley Mem. Hosp., 288 Ill.App.3d 408 (1997); Towne Realty, Inc. v. Zurich Ins. Co., 548 N.W.2d 64 (Wisc. 1996); Oakley Transport, Inc. v. Zurich Ins. Co., 271 Ill.App.3d 716 (1995). ***PRACTICE AREAS:*** Appeals. ***Email:*** showie@pretzel-stouffer.com

CHRISTINE J. IVERSEN, born Lake Forest, Illinois, June 5, 1971; admitted to bar, 1998, Illinois and U.S. District Court, Northern District of Illinois. *Education:* Iowa State University (B.S., 1993); John Marshall Law School (J.D., cum laude, 1998). ***PRACTICE AREAS:*** Medical Malpractice; General Liability. ***Email:*** civersen@pretzel-stouffer.com

PRIYA K. JESANI, born New Delhi, India, December 31, 1974; admitted to bar, 1999, Illinois. *Education:* Miami University (B.S, 1996); University of Oklahoma (J.D., 1999). Order of the Barrister. ***Email:*** pjesani@pretzel-stouffer.com

BELLE L. KATUBIG, born Chicago, Illinois, February 11, 1966; admitted to bar, 1997, Illinois. *Education:* University of Illinois at Urbana-Champaign (B.S., 1988); John Marshall Law School (J.D., 1996). ***PRACTICE AREAS:*** Medical Malpractice Defense. ***Email:*** bkatubig@pretzel-stouffer.com

RICHARD P. KENYON, born Waukegan, Illinois, May 4, 1968; admitted to bar, 1995, Illinois and U.S. District Court, Northern District of Illinois. *Education:* University of Illinois (B.S., Kinesiology Bioscience, 1990); DePaul University (J.D., 1995). ***PRACTICE AREAS:*** Insurance Defense; Litigation. ***Email:*** rkenyon@pretzel-stouffer.com

JAMES A. LABARGE, born LaGrange, Illinois, June 7, 1962; admitted to bar, 1990, Illinois and U.S. District Court, Northern District of Illinois. *Education:* Michigan State University (B.A., 1984); DePaul University; Northern Illinois University (J.D., 1990). Member, National Mock Trial Team, 1990. President, 1991-1992, 1996-1997, Northeastern Illinois Propane Gas Association. Member, Illinois and National Propane Gas Associations. Vice-President, LaBarge Propane, Inc. *Member:* Illinois State Bar Association. ***PRACTICE AREAS:*** Products Liability; Gas Explosion; Fire Litigation; Structural Work Act Litigation. ***Email:*** jlabarge@pretzel-stouffer.com

THOMAS A. LANG, II, born Warrenville, Illinois, June 25, 1975; admitted to bar, 2000, Illinois. *Education:* University of Illinois at Urbana-Champaign (B.A., 1997); DePaul University (J.D., 2000). ***PRACTICE AREAS:*** Litigation. ***Email:*** tal@pretzel-stouffer.com

MATTHEW J. LIGDA, born Valparaiso, Indiana, January 31, 1968; admitted to bar, 1995, Illinois. *Education:* Emory University (B.B.A., 1990); DePaul University (J.D., 1995). ***PRACTICE AREAS:*** Insurance Defense. ***Email:*** mligda@pretzel-stouffer.com

DANIEL B. MILLS, born Country Club Hills, Illinois, May 25, 1963; admitted to bar, 1989, Illinois. *Education:* Eastern Illinois University (B.S., 1985); Northern Illinois University (J.D., cum laude, 1989). Managing Editor, Northern Illinois College of Law - Law Review, 1988-1989. Elected Life Member, Who's Who in America. *Member:* Chicago, DuPage County and Illinois State Bar Associations; Illinois Defense Counsel; American Trucking Association; Transportation Lawyers Association. ***PRACTICE AREAS:*** Tort Litigation. ***Email:*** dmills@pretzel-stouffer.com

LISA M. MOORE, born March 31, 1978; admitted to bar, 2003, Illinois and Wisconsin; 2005, U.S. District Court, Northern District of Illinois. *Education:* University of Illinois (B.S., 2000); University of Wisconsin (J.D., 2003). *Member:* Chicago and American Bar Associations. ***PRACTICE AREAS:*** Litigation. ***Email:*** lmoore@pretzel-stouffer.com

PATRICIA B. MUELLER, born Gary, Indiana, September 2, 1971; admitted to bar, 2004, Illinois. *Education:* Indiana University (B.S., 1994); John Marshall Law School (J.D., 2004).

BRENDAN J. NELLIGAN, born Chicago, Illinois, March 3, 1971; admitted to bar, 1996, Illinois. *Education:* University of Notre Dame (B.A., 1993); Georgetown University Law Center (J.D., 1996).

EDWARD H. NIELSEN, born Chicago, Illinois, January 22, 1946; admitted to bar, 1973, Illinois, U.S. District Court, Northern District of Illinois and U.S. Court of Appeals, Seventh Circuit. *Education:* Northern Illinois University (B.A., 1967); Valparaiso University (J.D., 1973). Phi Alpha Delta. Author: "Handling Insurance Claims in Illinois, publisher, Professional Educational Systems, Inc., 1985. Co-Author: Nielsen and Franco, "Purchased Testimony: The Problem of Professional Expert Witnesses," 57 Defense Counsel Journal, 525 (October, 1990). *Member:* DuPage County, Chicago, Illinois State and American Bar Associations; Illinois Defense Counsel; Defense Research Institute; Federation of Insurance and Corporate Counsel; Association of Ski Defense Attorneys; Trial Lawyers Club of Chicago; Society of Trial Lawyers. [With U.S. Army Military Intelligence, 1968-1971]. ***PRACTICE AREAS:*** Medical Malpractice; Products Liability. ***Email:*** enielsen@pretzel-stouffer.com

CAITLIN O'CONNOR, born St. Louis, Missouri, March 12, 1978; admitted to bar, 2003, Illinois. *Education:* Indiana University (B.A., 2000); Loyola University (J.D., 2003).

DONALD J. O'MEARA, JR., born Evanston, Illinois, May 1, 1966; admitted to bar, 1991, Illinois and U.S. District Court, Northern District of Illinois. *Education:* Fairfield University (B.A., 1988); The John Marshall Law School (J.D., 1991). *Member:* Chicago and American Bar Associations. ***PRACTICE AREAS:*** Medical Malpractice; Products Liability. ***Email:*** domeara@pretzel-stouffer.com

DAVID S. OSBORNE, born Somerset, Kentucky, July 9, 1968; admitted to bar, 1996, Illinois. *Education:* Washington University-St. Louis, Missouri (A.B., 1993); Northwestern University School of Law (J.D., 1996). ***PRACTICE AREAS:*** Insurance Coverage Litigation; Appellate Practice. ***Email:*** dosborne@pretzel-stouffer.com

HOWARD J. PIKEL, born Chicago, Illinois, July 6, 1953; admitted to bar, 1981, Illinois; 1999, Indiana. *Education:* University of Illinois (B.A., 1977); John Marshall Law School (J.D., 1981). ***PRACTICE AREAS:*** Medical Malpractice Defense; Insurance Defense; Products Liability.

NEIL K. QUINN, born Chicago, Illinois, April 8, 1929; admitted to bar, 1957, Illinois. *Education:* University of Illinois (B.A., 1951); DePaul University (J.D., 1957). By appointment of the Illinois Supreme Court, Member of the Review Board of the Attorney Registration and Disciplinary Commission, 1991—. Chairman of the Board, St. Francis Hospital of Evanston, Illinois, 1991-1994. *Member:* Chicago, Illinois State and American Bar Associations; Illinois Society of Trial Lawyers (President, 1979-1980); International Association of Defense Counsel (President, 1980-1981); Defense Research Institute (Member, Board of Directors, 1980-1982); Illinois Defense Counsel (Member, Board of Directors, 1974-1977). Fellow, American College of Trial Lawyers. [Ret. Capt., USMCR, 1951-1953]. ***PRACTICE AREAS:*** Medical Liability; Legal Professional Liability; Accountants Liability; Products Liability; Construction Liability; Commercial Litigation; ERISA. ***Email:*** nquinn@pretzel-stouffer.com

MARK S. RATNER, born Tucson, Arizona, March 18, 1968; admitted to bar, 1994, Michigan and U.S. District Court, Eastern District of Michigan; 1997, Illinois; 1999, Arizona and U.S. District Court, Northern District of Illinois. *Education:* Michigan State University (B.A., 1990); Detroit College of Law at Michigan State University (J.D., 1994). ***PRACTICE AREAS:*** Corporate Insurance Defense; Commercial Litigation. ***Email:*** mratner@pretzel-stouffer.com

CHARLES F. REDDEN, born Chicago, Illinois, March 11, 1958; admitted to bar, 1984, Illinois and U.S. District Court, Northern District of Illinois; 1986, Federal Court Trial Bar. *Education:* Boston University (B.A., 1980); Loyola University (J.D., 1984). Co-Author: "Qualifications to the Bar of Ex Parte Contacts," Vol. 79 Illinois Bar Journal 442, September, 1991. Author: "The Decline of Rule 220," Vol. 80 Illinois Bar Journal 440, September, 1992; "Limits on the Admission of Learned Treatises," Vol. 82, Illinois Bar Journal 186, April 1994. Assistant Corporation Counsel, City of Chicago, 1984-1986. ***PRACTICE AREAS:*** Professional Liability; Civil Appeals; Corporate Law; Employment Law. ***Email:*** credden@pretzel-stouffer.com

D. SCOTT RENDLEMAN, born Carbondale, Illinois, June 9, 1968; admitted to bar, 1993, Illinois and U.S. District Court, Southern District of Illinois; 1994, Missouri. *Education:* Illinois State University (B.S., cum laude, 1990); University of Illinois (J.D., 1993). ***PRACTICE AREAS:*** Medical Malpractice Defense; Product Liability Defense; Negligence Defense. ***Email:*** srendleman@pretzel-stouffer.com

BRIAN C. ROCCA, born Boston, Massachusetts, October 17, 1953; admitted to bar, 1982, Illinois and U.S. District Court, Northern District of Illinois including Trial Bar. *Education:* University of Northern Iowa (B.A., high honors, 1976); University of Iowa (J.D., with distinction, 1982). Lecturer: Illinois Bar Association on Trial Techniques, Injunctions and Healthcare; Medical Groups on Healthcare Law. *Member:* Chicago, Illinois State and American Bar Associations; Society of Trial Lawyers; Illinois Association of Defense Trial Counsel. ***PRACTICE AREAS:*** Medical Malpractice; Product Liability; Employment; Commercial Litigation. ***Email:*** brocca@pretzel-stouffers.com

EDWARD B. RUFF, III, born Oak Park, Illinois, October 15, 1954; admitted to bar, 1981, Illinois, U.S. Court of Appeals, Seventh Circuit; 1991, Wisconsin; U.S. District Court, Northern District of Illinois including Trial Bar; 2005, U.S. Supreme Court. *Education:* University of Wisconsin-Madison (B.S.M.E., 1977); DePaul University (J.D., 1981). Pi Tau Sigma, Honorary English Society. Authored many peer reviewed articles and lectured in many professional bar association and university settings. Some of the more recent articles include "Effective Use In House Engineering Experts," Presented Nov. 1995 Seventh Annual Product Liability Seminar, University of Wisconsin, Madison Department of Engineering. Author: "Failure to Read Warning Bars Claim of Inadequacy," Product Liability Update, IDC, Vol. 1, No. 1, Jan. 1996 Ruff, O'Meara; Illinois Tort Report §2013 and

(This Listing Continued)

(This Listing Continued)

2104; "Product Liability Update, IDC, Vol. 1, No. 1, Jan. 1996, Ruff, Schechter; "Legal Aspects of Construction Crane Safety," Paper Presented March, 2000; Restatement (third) of Torts: Products Liability; "Do we have a Post Sale Duty to Warn," FICC Semi-Annual Meeting; "The Restatement (Third) of Torts and its Effect on Products Liability Law," Vol. 49, No. 3, Page 265, FDCC Quarterly, Spring, 1999; "The Future of Our Courtrooms-Computer Generated Visual Evidence," FDCC Annual Meeting, July 1999; "Closing Argument Tactics Regarding Spoliated Evidence," FDCC Mid-Year Meeting, February 2000. *Member:* Chicago, Illinois State (Member: Products Liability and Toxic Tort Sections) and American Bar Associations; Seventh Circuit Bar Association (Member, Rules and Practice Committee); Defense Research Institute; Society of Trial Lawyers; FDCC (Vice President and Chair, Trial Tactics, Products Liability). ***PRACTICE AREAS:*** Civil Trial; Product Liability; Commercial Law; Insurance Coverage; Fire/Property Subrogation and Defense; Toxic Torts; Mass Torts; Construction; Intellectual Property. **Email:** eruff@pretzel-stouffer.com

MIGUEL A. RUIZ, born Mexico City, Mexico, October 31, 1963; admitted to bar, 1992, Wisconsin, Illinois and U.S. District Court, Northern District of Illinois. *Education:* University of Illinois (B.A., 1989); University of Wisconsin-Madison (J.D., 1992). ***PRACTICE AREAS:*** Medical Negligence Defense; General Casualty Defense. **Email:** mruiz@pretzel-stouffer.com

STEVEN W. RYAN, born Park Ridge, Illinois, March 12, 1968; admitted to bar, 1993, Illinois. *Education:* Loyola University (B.A., 1990; J.D., 1993). ***PRACTICE AREAS:*** Real Estate; Estate Planning; Probate. **Email:** sryan@pretzel-stouffer.com

LEWIS M. SCHNEIDER, born Chicago, Illinois; admitted to bar, 1973, Illinois; U.S. District Court, Northern District of Illinois. *Education:* Elmhurst College (B.A., Business Administration, 1968); The John Marshall Law School (J.D., with honors, 1973). Member: John Marshall Journal of Practice and Procedure; Order of John Marshall. *Member:* Chicago and American (Member, Sections on: Real Property, Probate and Trust Law; Corporate Law) Bar Associations; Chicago Estate Planning Council. ***PRACTICE AREAS:*** Business Transactions; Professional Practices; Estate Planning; Administration. **Email:** lschneider@pretzel-stouffer.com

ALAN J. SCHUMACHER, born Hammond, Indiana, April 21, 1959; admitted to bar, 1984, Illinois. *Education:* University of Notre Dame (B.B.A., magna cum laude, 1981); University of Illinois (J.D., 1984). *Member:* Chicago, Illinois State and American Bar Associations; Illinois Association of Defense Trial Counsel; The Association of Trial Lawyers of America; Defense Research Institute. ***PRACTICE AREAS:*** Professional Liability; Hospital Liability; Product Liability; Tort Litigation. **Email:** aschumacher@pretzel-stouffer.com

ROBERT E. SIDKEY, born Hammond, Indiana, March 19, 1974; admitted to bar, 1999, Illinois. *Education:* Valparaiso University (B.A., 1996); Chicago-Kent College of Law (J.D., 1999).

RICHARD J. SIEBERT, born Evergreen Park, Illinois, December 20, 1966; admitted to bar, 1991, Illinois and U.S. District Court, Northern District of Illinois. *Education:* DePaul University (B.S., magna cum laude, 1988); Northwestern University School of Law (J.D., 1991). ***PRACTICE AREAS:*** Insurance Law; Litigation; Appellate Practice. **Email:** rsiebert@pretzel-stouffer.com

JAMES J. SIPCHEN, JR., born Chicago, Illinois, January 8, 1968; admitted to bar, 1994, Illinois, U.S. District Court, Northern District of Illinois and U.S. Court of Appeals, Seventh Circuit. *Education:* Indiana University (B.A., Political Science, 1990); John Marshall Law School (J.D., 1994). ***PRACTICE AREAS:*** Corporate Litigation. **Email:** jsipchen@pretzel-stouffer.com

KATHRYN A. SMETANA, born Chicago, Illinois, November 25, 1973; admitted to bar, 2002, Illinois. *Education:* University of Illinois (B.S., 1995); Loyola University (J.D., 2002).

JOHN V. SMITH, II, born Washington, D.C., July 17, 1957; admitted to bar, 1982, Illinois; U.S. District Court, Northern District of Illinois including Trial Bar. *Education:* University of Notre Dame (A.B., 1979; J.D., 1982). Member, Notre Dame Law School National Mock Trial Team. Note Editor, Journal of Legislation, 1982. Author: "The Supreme Court Workload Problem: Current Congressional Reforms," Journal of Legislation, 1982. Co-Author: "Physician-Patient Privilege: Interviews Between Plaintiff's Physicians and Defense Attorneys," 66 Chicago Bar Journal 146, November, 1984; "Handling Insurance Claims in Illinois," Professional Education Systems, Inc., 1985; "Preparation of Defendant's Case," *Medical and Hospital Negligence,* Callaghan & Company, 1988; "Institutional Negligence," *Medical Malpractice,* Illinois Institute of Continuing Legal Education, 1989; "Hospital and Institutional Liability," Illinois Institute of Continuing Legal Education, 1996. *Member:* Chicago, Seventh Circuit, Illinois State and American Bar Associations; Defense Research Institute; The Society of Trial Lawyers. ***PRACTICE AREAS:*** Medical Malpractice; Hospital Liability; Professional Liability; Manufacturers' Liability; Commercial Litigation; Civil Litigation. **Email:** jsmith@pretzel-stouffer.com

JANE SOLMOR-MORDINI, born Carlisle, Pennsylvania, August 18, 1961; admitted to bar, 1990, Illinois. *Education:* University of Illinois (B.A., 1983); Art Institute (1984-1986); Illinois Institute of Technology (J.D., 1990).

BRIAN C. SUNDHEIM, born Chicago, Illinois, February 8, 1957; admitted to bar, 1986, Illinois. *Education:* Loyola University (B.A., 1980); John Marshall Law School (J.D., 1986). ***PRACTICE AREAS:*** Products Liability; Medical Malpractice; Professional Malpractice. **Email:** bsundheim@pretzel.stouffer.com

AMY J. THOMPSON, born Crown Point, Indiana, June 2, 1972; admitted to bar, 1997, Illinois. *Education:* Indiana University, Bloomington (B.S.Ph., 1994); Valparaiso University (J.D., 1997). ***PRACTICE AREAS:*** Insurance Defense; Health Law. **Email:** athompson@pretzel-stouffer.com

MICHAEL P. TURIELLO, born Newport, Rhode Island, July 17, 1970; admitted to bar, 1996, Illinois. *Education:* Bradley University (B.S., 1992); Villanova University (J.D., 1996). ***PRACTICE AREAS:*** Litigation; Medical Malpractice.

STEPHEN C. VELTMAN, born Chicago, Illinois, April 26, 1954; admitted to bar, 1979, Illinois and U.S. District Court, Northern District of Illinois; 1984, U.S. Court of Appeals, Seventh, Circuit; 1986, U.S. Court of Appeals, Second and Eleventh Circuits; 1988, U.S. Court of Appeals, Eighth Circuit. *Education:* Loyola University (B.A., 1976; J.D., 1979). Author: Chapter 5, Illinois Trial Practice and Procedure, *Third Party Practice,* Illinois Institute for Continuing Legal Education, 1987, 1989, 1992 and 2000. *Member:* Chicago (Chairman, Admiralty and Maritime Law Committee, 1987-1988) and Illinois State Bar Associations; Maritime Law Association of the United States; Propeller Club of the United States-Port of Chicago (President, 1991-1993). **Email:** sveltman@pretzel-stouffer.com

ANNE E. WALL, born December 25, 1976; admitted to bar, 2002, Illinois. *Education:* Miami University (B.A., 1999); DePaul University (J.D., 2002).

JOHN J. WALSH, III, born Oak Park, Illinois, February 23, 1946; admitted to bar, 1982, Illinois and U.S. District Court, Northern District of Illinois, 1983, Trial Bar; 1987, U.S. Court of Appeals, Seventh Circuit. *Education:* University of Notre Dame (B.A., magna cum laude, 1968); Loyola University (J.D., 1982). Phi Alpha Delta. Author: "Trial Techniques, Defense of a Medical Malpractice Case," ISBA, 1996; "Proving Fault in Auto Accident Cases," Chapters 1 and 6, Illinois Institute for Continuing Legal Education, 1988 ed., 1991 supp., 1994 ed. Assembly Delegate, ISBA, 1991-1997. *Member:* Chicago, Illinois State, Seventh Circuit and American Bar Associations; Society of Trial Lawyers. ***PRACTICE AREAS:*** Directors and Officers Liability; Hospital Liability; Nursing Liability; Products Liability; Civil Rights; Law Enforcement Liability; Employer Liability; Construction Liability; Contract Litigation; Commercial Litigation. **Email:** jwalsh@pretzel-stouffer.com

RICHARD M. WARIS, born St. Joseph, Missouri, December 30, 1954; admitted to bar, 1980, Illinois and U.S. District Court, Northern District of Illinois including Trial Bar. *Education:* University of Notre Dame (B.A., 1977); St. Louis University and University of Notre Dame (J.D., 1980). Member: The Order of the Barristers; National Mock Trial Team. Listed in: Who's Who in The Legal Profession; Marquis Who's Who in American Law; Who's Who in Practicing Attorneys. Managing Editor of the Journal of Legislation. Director of the Notre Dame Legislature Research Service. Master of the Bench, American Inn of Courts. *Member:* Chicago, Illinois State and American Bar Associations; LP Gas Joint Defense Counsel; Illinois Association of Defense Trial Counsel (Board of Directors, 1990-1991); International Association of Defense Counsel; General Counsel Professional Independent Insurance Agents of Illinois. ***PRACTICE AREAS:*** Medical Malpractice; Employer Liability; Civil Rights; Brokers and Agents Errors and Omissions; Trucking; Environmental Product Liability; Propane Litigation; Construction; Securities; Commercial; Civil Litigation. **Email:** rwaris@pretzel-stouffer.com

TIMOTHY A. WEAVER, born Elkhart, Indiana, November 30, 1948; admitted to bar, 1974, Illinois; 1975, U.S. District Court, Northern District of Illinois; 1982, Federal Trial Bar; 1999, Wisconsin and U.S. District Court, Eastern District of Wisconsin. *Education:* Brown University (A.B., cum laude, 1971); University of Illinois (J.D., 1974). Notes Editor, Recent Decisions Dept., Ill. Bar J., 1973-1974. Author: Casenote, Ill. Bar J., Vol. 62, 1973; "Preparation of Defendant's Case," *Medical and Hospital Negligence,* Callaghan, 1988, 1990; Chapt., "Informed Consent," *Medical Malpractice,* Illinois Institute for CLE, 1989; Chapt., "Hospital and Institutional Liability," *Medical Malpractice,* IICLE, 1996. General Editor, *Medical Malpractice,* IICLE, 1989 and 1996. *Member:* Illinois State and American Bar Associations; State Bar of Wisconsin; Illinois Association of Defense Trial Counsel; Civil Trial Counsel of Wisconsin. ***PRACTICE AREAS:*** Medical Malpractice; Civil Litigation. **Email:** tweaver@pretzel-stouffer.com

DANIEL G. WILLS, admitted to bar, 1990, Illinois and U.S. District Court, Northern District of Illinois. *Education:* DePaul University (B.S.Econ., 1984; J.D., 1990). ***PRACTICE AREAS:*** Insurance Coverage Litigation; Appellate Litigation. **Email:** dwills@pretzel-stouffer.com

ALAN S. ZELKOWITZ, born Brooklyn, New York, June 18, 1964; admitted to bar, 1989, Illinois and U.S. District Court, Northern District of Illinois; 1990, Missouri; 1991, U.S. District Court, Northern District of Illinois; 1997, U.S. Supreme Court. *Education:* University of Illinois (B.A., 1986); Washington University at St. Louis, Missouri (J.D., 1989). ***PRACTICE AREAS:*** Insurance Defense; Toxic Tort; Medical Malpractice. **Email:** azelkowitz@pretzel-stouffer.com

OF COUNSEL

PAULA MEYER BESLER, born Chicago, Illinois, August 2, 1964; admitted to bar, 1989, Illinois. *Education:* University of Illinois (B.S., 1986); Loyola University Chicago (J.D., 1989). Adjunct Professor, Loyola University Chicago School of Law. ***PRACTICE AREAS:*** Medical Malpractice. **Email:** pbesler@pretzel-stouffer.com

PAUL W. PRETZEL (1906-1987)

RALPH E. STOUFFER, JR., born Chicago, Illinois, 1917; admitted to bar, 1941, Illinois; 1956, U.S. District Court, Northern District of Illinois. *Education:* Northwestern University (B.S.L., 1939; J.D., 1941). Phi Delta Phi. *Member:* Chicago, Illinois State and American Bar Associations; Society of Trial Lawyers; Trial Lawyers Club of Chicago.

(This Listing Continued)

PRICE TUNNEY REITER

A PROFESSIONAL CORPORATION

123 N. WACKER DRIVE, SUITE 2220
CHICAGO, ILLINOIS 60606
Telephone: 312-230-9100
Fax: 312-230-9201
URL: http://www.ptrlaw.com

Trial and Appellate Practice in State and Federal Courts. Alternative Dispute Resolution, Litigation Prevention, Health Care Professionals Liability, Legal Malpractice, Accountant's Malpractice, Hospital Litigation, Products Liability, Premises Liability, Commercial Litigation, Fraud, Real Estate Broker and Insurance Agent Errors and Omissions, Nursing Home Litigation, Insurance Coverage Disputes, Breach of Lease, Toxic Tort Litigation, Contract Disputes, Environmental Litigation.

(This Listing Continued)

PRICE TUNNEY REITER, A PROFESSIONAL CORPORATION, Chicago—Continued

FIRM PROFILE: The firm was founded on the philosophy that lawyers are professionals first. We are straightforward, result oriented and dedicated to providing superior legal service. We focus primarily on litigation and alternative dispute resolution. The partners have over 90 years of litigation experience. Extensive trial experience in both state and federal courts.

PAUL L. PRICE, born Chicago, Illinois, April 21, 1945; admitted to bar, 1971, Illinois. *Education:* Loyola University (B.B.A., 1967); Chicago-Kent College of Law (J.D., with honors, 1971). Phi Alpha Delta. Recipient of 1992 National Law Journal List of Largest Defense Verdicts; John Guy Award, 2004. Member, IIT Kent College of Law Alumni Association (President, 1989-1990). *Member:* Illinois State and American Bar Associations; The Society of Trial Lawyers; Illinois Association of Defense Trial Counsel (IDC) (President, 1990-1991); Federation of Defense and Corporate Counsel (Member, Board of Directors, 1993-1997; President, 1999-2000); Defense Research Institute (Member, Board of Directors; Recipient, Fred Sievert 1991 Outstanding Defense Bar Leader Award); Association of Defense Trial Attorneys; Lawyers For Civil Justice (Member, Board of Directors). Fellow, American College of Trial Lawyers. [With U.S. Marine Corps, 1969-1975]. **PRACTICE AREAS:** Professional Liability; Commercial Litigation; Products Liability. **Email:** plprice@ptrlaw.com

ANTHONY J. TUNNEY, born Chicago, Illinois, November 6, 1947; admitted to bar, 1977, Illinois and U.S. District Court, Northern District of Illinois Trial Bar. *Education:* University of St. Thomas (B.A., 1969); The John Marshall Law School (J.D., 1977). Arbitrator, American Arbitration Association. *Member:* Chicago (Member, Judicial Candidate Evaluation Committee, 1980-1984), Illinois State and American Bar Associations; Illinois Association of Defense Trial Counsel (Member, Board of Directors, 1989-1993; President, 1997-1998; Co-Chairman, Trial Academy, 1992-1993; Chairman, Alternative Dispute Resolution Committee, 1991-1994; Chairman, Spring Seminar Committee, 1988); Defense Research Institute (Member, Board of Directors, 1999-2002; Association of Defense Trial Attorneys (Member, Executive Council, 1993-1999; President, 2000-2001). **PRACTICE AREAS:** Insurance Agents and Brokers Errors and Omissions; Nursing Liability; Professional Liability Defense; Product Liability; Civil Litigation; Commercial Litigation. **Email:** atunney@ptrlaw.com

CATHERINE COYNE REITER, born New York, N.Y., May 8, 1950; admitted to bar, 1981, Illinois. *Education:* University of Michigan (B.S.N., with honors, 1972); De Paul University (J.D., 1981). Sigma Theta Tau. Mortar Board. *Member:* Chicago Bar Association; American Bar Association; The American Association of Nurse Attorneys; Women's Bar Association of Illinois; Illinois Association of Defense Trial Counsel. Fellow, Illinois Association of Hospital Attorneys; Illinois Society of Trial Lawyers; Defense Research Institute. Fellow, American College of Trial Lawyers. **LANGUAGES:** Spanish. **PRACTICE AREAS:** Professional Liability; Commercial Litigation; Products Liability. **Email:** creiter@ptrlaw.com

STEVEN JOHN MARTIN, born Fairfax, Virginia, December 16, 1966; admitted to bar, 1992, Illinois and U.S. District Court, Northern District of Illinois. *Education:* Loyola University; University of Michigan (B.A., 1989); University of Illinois (J.D., cum laude, 1992). Reichert Scholar. Winner, Frederick H. Green Moot Court Competition. Member, National Moot Court Team. *Member:* Illinois Hospital Association; Illinois Association of Defense Trial Counsel (Chairman, Spring Seminar Committee, 2003; Co-Chairman, Public Relations Committee, 2000-2002); Chicago and Healthcare Risk Management Society. **PRACTICE AREAS:** Medical Malpractice; Environmental Litigation; Professional Liability; Commercial Litigation; Insurance Coverage. **Email:** sjmartin@ptrlaw.com

---

DINA L. TORRISI, born Chicago, Illinois, October 18, 1969; admitted to bar, 1994, Illinois and U.S. District Court, Northern District of Illinois; U.S. Supreme Court. *Education:* University of Illinois (B.A., 1991); The John Marshall Law School (J.D., 1994). Arbitrator, Cook County Mandatory Arbitration. *Member:* Chicago Bar Association. **PRACTICE AREAS:** Defense Litigation; Medical Malpractice; Commercial Litigation. **Email:** dtorrisi@ptrlaw.com

DANIEL J. DELEO, born Wilmington, Delaware, January 29, 1968; admitted to bar, 1999, Illinois and U.S. District Court, Northern District of Illinois. *Education:* Albertson College of Idaho (B.A., 1993); DePaul University College of Law (J.D., 1999). Law Clerk to Hon. Allen S. Goldberg, Circuit Court of Cook County. Arbitrator, Cook County Mandatory Arbitrator. *Member:* Chicago and Illinois State Bar Associations; National Association of Defense Trial Counsel. **PRACTICE AREAS:** Professional Liability; Commercial Litigation; Products Liability; Class Actions. **Email:** ddeleo@ptrlaw.com

ROBERT E. ELWORTH, born Omaha, Nebraska, June 10, 1967; admitted to bar, 1992, Nebraska; 1993, Illinois; 1997, California. *Education:* University of Nebraska at Lincoln (B.A., 1989); Creighton University (J.D., 1992). Illinois Defense Counsel, 2004. Instructor, Environmental Law, Business Law, Roosevelt University, 1997-1999. **LANGUAGES:** French. **REPORTED CASES:** Atkins v. Deere Co. 177 Ill. 2D 222 (1997); Roman v. Grafton Transit, 948 F. Supp. 736 (NO Ill. 1996); GPlo v. Work 901 F. Supp. 1370 (N.D. IU. 1995). **PRACTICE AREAS:** Professional Liability. **Email:** relworth@ptrlaw.com

CHRISTOPHER RICHARD REINKALL, born Chicago, Illinois, January 21, 1975; admitted to bar, 2002, Illinois. *Education:* Loyola University (B.A., 1999); Loyola University Chicago School of Law (J.D., 2002). **PRACTICE AREAS:** Medical Malpractice; Professional Malpractice; Insurance Fraud. **Email:** creinkall@ptrlaw.com

JEFFREY TABARES, *born Chicago, Illinois, June 3, 1970; admitted to bar, 2002,* Illinois. *Education:* Dallas Baptist University (M.A.. 1996); DePaul University (J.D., 2001). **LANGUAGES:** English, Spanish. **PRACTICE AREAS:** Medical Malpractice Defense; Transportation Defense; Real Estate. **Email:** jtabares@ptrlaw.com

LAW OFFICES OF VIRGINIA PRIHODA

7551 NORTH OAKLEY AVENUE
CHICAGO, ILLINOIS 60645
Telephone: 773-262-1712
Fax: 847-589-8072
URL: http://www.prihodalaw.com
Email: virginiaprihoda@hotmail.com
URL: http://www.virginiaprihoda.com

Taxation, Tax Consulting, Tax Audits, Collection Matters, Wills, Trusts, Living Trusts, Insurance Trusts, Guardianships, Powers of Attorney, Living Wills, Gifts to Minors, Probate, Tax Planning, Estate Planning, Tax and Estate Planning for Senior Citizens, Income Tax Return Preparation, Business Entity Planning, Business Succession Planning, Business Tax Planning, Representation before the Internal Revenue Service, IRS Liens, IRS Offers in Compromise.

VIRGINIA D. PRIHODA, born Chicago, Illinois, November 30, 1950; admitted to bar, 1992, Illinois. *Education:* Northwestern University (B.S., 1979); IIT Chicago-Kent College of Law (J.D., 1992). *Member:* Chicago and American Bar Associations. **SPECIAL AGENCIES:** Internal Revenue Service; Illinois Department of Revenue; Illinois Board of Appeals; Illinois Department of Employment Security. **PRACTICE AREAS:** Tax Law; Wills; Trusts; Probate; Guardianship; Estate Planning; Tax Defense; Real Estate; Bankruptcy. **Email:** virginiaprihoda@hotmail.com

---

PROPES & KAVENY, L.L.C.

833 WEST JACKSON, SUITE 200
CHICAGO, ILLINOIS 60607
Telephone: 312-334-3111
Fax: 312-829-3367
URL: http://www.pktrialaw.com
Email: propes@pktriallaw.com
URL: http://www.lawyers.com/propeskaveny

Medical Malpractice, including Failure to Diagnose, Birth Trauma, Obstetrics, Surgical, Oncological, Cardiac, Urological, Neurosurgical and Psychiatric Malpractice; Products Liability, Personal Injury.

LORNA E. PROPES, admitted to bar, 1975, Illinois, U.S. Court of Appeals, Seventh Circuit and U.S. District Court, Northern District of Illinois. *Education:* Indiana University (B.S., 1966); Columbia University (M.A., 1970); Loyola University (J.D., 1975). Assistant State's Attorney, Cook County State's Attorney's Office, 1975-1980. Contributor: "Master Advocates Handbook," National Institute for Trial Advocacy, 1986. Lecturer: International Society of Barristers, 1988 Annual Meeting. Faculty member: National Institute of Trial Advocacy, 1977—; Michigan Institute of Continuing Legal Education, Advocacy Institute, 1982-1984, 1986, 1990-1994, 1996; American Bar Association, Litigation Section Program in Trial Advocacy, Oxford, England, 1984; Pacific Law Institute, Trial Advocacy Training Institute for Honolulu Prosecutors, 1987. Demonstrator: Smithsonian Institute's and ATLA's Festival of American Folklife, Trial Lawyer's Exhibit, 1986; "Mastering the Art of Cross Examination," a videotape series produced by ABA and NITA, 1987; "The Art of Advocacy: Videotape Series: Selecting and Persuading the Jury," produced by NITA, 1988. I. Goodman Cohen Lecturer, Wayne State University School of Law, 1988. Recipient: Loyola University of Chicago School of Law St. Robert Bellarmine Award for distinguished service to the profession, 1988. *Member:* Chicago, Illinois State and American Bar Associations; Illinois Trial Lawyers Association (Member, Board of Managers); The Association of Trial Lawyers of America; Northwestern University Inns of Court; Illinois Racing Board. Fellow, International Academy of Trial Lawyers. **PRACTICE AREAS:** Personal Injury; Medical Malpractice; Products Liability.

ELIZABETH A. KAVENY, born Pittsburgh, Pennsylvania, September 24, 1965; admitted to bar, 1992, Illinois and U.S. District Court, Northern District of Illinois; 1993, U.S. Court of Appeals, Seventh Circuit. *Education:* Lehigh University (B.A., 1988); Case Western Reserve University (J.D., cum laude, 1992). Delta Theta Phi. Terese D. Norgar Scholar. Member, AULT National Trial Advocacy Team. Faculty: Instructor, Trial Tactics, Loyola University School of Law, 1996—. *Member:* Chicago Bar Association; Illinois Trial Lawyers Association; Women's Bar Association. **PRACTICE AREAS:** Personal Injury; Medical Malpractice.

DAVID R. NORDWALL, born Wichita, Kansas, July 1, 1968; admitted to bar, 1993, Illinois and U.S. District Court, Northern District of Illinois; 1995, U.S. Court of Appeals, 7th Circuit. *Education:* Auburn University (B.A., summa cum laude, 1990); Northwestern University (J.D., cum laude, 1993). *Member:* Chicago Bar Association; Illinois Trial Lawyers Association. **PRACTICE AREAS:** Appellate Litigation; Personal Injury; Medical Malpractice.

OF COUNSEL

PATRICIA C. BOBB, born Roswell, New Mexico, June 5, 1947; admitted to bar, 1972, Illinois. *Education:* New Mexico State University; College of Santa Fe (B.A., 1969); University of Notre Dame (J.D., 1972). Member, Board of Directors, National Institute of Trial Advocacy, 1987—. Adjunct Professor, Northwestern University Law School, Trial Advocacy I & II, 1981-1989. Faculty Member: American Trial Lawyers Association Advanced College of Advocacy, 1981-1989; American Bar Association Litigation Section, Advanced Trial Advocacy, Oxford, England, September, 1984. Appointed Member, Lawyers Advisory Subcommittee on Alternative Dispute Resolution, Illinois Judicial Advisory Council, 1985—. Listed in Best Lawyers in America, Personal Injury. *Member:* Chicago (Elected Member Board of Managers, 1992-1994; Elected Secretary, 1994-1995; President-Elect, 1996-1997; President, 1997-1998) and Illinois State (Member, Board of Governors, 1982-1984; Elected Member Assembly, 1984-1986; Member, Civil Practice and Procedure

(This Listing Continued)

Council, 1985—) Bar Associations; Illinois Trial Lawyers Association (Member, Board of Managers, 1982—; Member, Executive Committee); The Association of Trial Lawyers of America (Member, Board of Governors, 1989-1993). Fellow: American College of Trial Lawyers; International Academy of Trial Lawyers; International Society of Barristers. ***PRACTICE AREAS:*** Plaintiff's Personal Injury Law; Medical Malpractice Law.

PRUSIK SELBY DALEY & KEZELIS, P.C.

209 WEST JACKSON BOULEVARD, SUITE 900
CHICAGO, ILLINOIS 60606
Telephone: 312-427-4700
Fax: 312-427-8090
Email: advocates@psdlegal.com

Insurance Defense, Product Liability, Class Actions, Medical Negligence, Toxic Torts, Construction, Environmental, FELA, Asbestos, Contract Coverage, Consumer Products and Workers' Compensation, plus ADR and Arbitration, First Response Claim Investigation.

JOHN P. PRUSIK, born Evanston, Illinois, 1945; admitted to bar, 1975, Illinois and U.S. District Court, Northern District of Illinois including Trial Bar; 1978, U.S. District Court, Central District of Illinois; 1992, U.S. Court of Appeals, Seventh Circuit. *Education:* Mt. Carmel College (B.A., 1968); Loyola University (M.Ed., 1971; J.D., 1975). Public Defender, Effingham, Illinois, 1976. Assistant Attorney General, Criminal Division, State of Illinois, 1977-1979. Arbitrator, Illinois Mandatory Arbitration Program. *Member:* Chicago, Illinois State and American Bar Associations; Society of Trial Lawyers. ***PRACTICE AREAS:*** Civil Practice; Insurance Defense; Medical Malpractice; Products Liability; Personal Injury. ***Email:*** jprusik@psdlegal.com

TERENCE R. SELBY, born London, England; admitted to bar, 1986, Illinois and U.S. District Court, Northern District of Illinois. *Education:* Thurrock College (M.E., 1966); DePaul University (J.D., 1986). Professional Engineer, England, 1969. Graduate, Institution of Engineering Designers, 1966. Voting Member, Society of Engineers, 1970. Arbitrator, 1993. Instructor, Insurance School of Chicago. Speaker: N.F.P.A. *Member:* Chicago, Du Page, Illinois State and American Bar Associations. ***PRACTICE AREAS:*** Civil Practice; Insurance Defense; Products Liability; Toxic Torts; Construction Law; Environmental Law; FELA; Asbestos Litigation; Fire Investigation; Class Actions; Mass Torts; Complex Litigation; Alternative Dispute Resolution; Arbitration. ***Email:*** tselby@psdlegal.com

JOHN J. DALEY III, born Alexandria Bay, New York, 1956; admitted to bar, 1981, Illinois and U.S. District Court, Northern District of Illinois. *Education:* University of Notre Dame (B.A., 1978); DePaul University (J.D., 1981). Speaker, Insurance Law Seminar, Chicago Bar Association, 1997. Adjunct Professor of Law, Chicago-Kent College of Law, 1997-1999. Arbitrator, Illinois Mandatory Arbitration Program. Instructor, Insurance School of Chicago. *Member:* Chicago Bar Association (Member: Litigation Committee, 1987-1988; Insurance Committee, 1995-1997). ***PRACTICE AREAS:*** Civil Practice; Insurance Defense; Personal Injury; Medical Negligence; Products Liability. ***Email:*** jdaley@psdlegal.com

ALGIMANTAS KEZELIS, born Krakes, Lithuania; admitted to bar, 1955, Illinois, U.S. District Court, Northern District of Illinois including Trial Bar and U.S. Court of Appeals, Seventh Circuit. *Education:* University of Illinois; DePaul University; John Marshall Law School. Nu Beta Epsilon. Law Clerk, Judge Advocate's Office, United States Army, Ft. Benning, Georgia and Tokyo, Japan. Arbitrator, American Arbitration Association. Member, Committee on Jury Instructions in Civil Areas, Illinois Supreme Court, 1997—. *Member:* Chicago, Illinois State and American Bar Associations; Society of Trial Lawyers (Past President); Illinois Defense Counsel; Defense Research Institute. ***LANGUAGES:*** Lithuanian, German. ***PRACTICE AREAS:*** Products Liability; Construction Law; Insurance Law; Medical Malpractice; Appellate Practice; Civil Practice; Insurance Defense; Environmental Law; Toxic Torts; Trucking Law; Civil Rights; Commercial Litigation. ***Email:*** kezelis@psdlegal.com

---

LOUISE L. DALEY, born Washington, D.C., 1958; admitted to bar, 1985, Illinois and U.S. District Court, Northern District of Illinois. *Education:* Mount Mary College (B.A., 1980); DePaul University (J.D., 1981). ***PRACTICE AREAS:*** Civil Practice; Insurance Defense; Personal Injury; Medical Negligence; Products Liability. ***Email:*** lldaley@psdlegal.com

DANIEL J. CONNELL, born Park Ridge, Illinois, March 15, 1973; admitted to bar, 2000, Illinois. *Education:* University of Illinois, Urbana-Champaign (L.A.S., History, 1996); DePaul University (J.D., 2000). Formerly with Garretson & Santora, Ltd. ***PRACTICE AREAS:*** Construction Litigation; Commercial Litigation; Bankruptcy Law.

PUGH, JONES, JOHNSON & QUANDT, P.C.

Established in 1991
180 NORTH LA SALLE STREET, SUITE 3400
CHICAGO, ILLINOIS 60601
Telephone: 312-768-7800
Fax: 312-768-7801
URL: http://www.PJJQ.com

Complex Civil and White Collar Criminal Litigation, Employment Discrimination, Management and Labor Law, Drug and Medical Device Litigation, Pharmaceutical Litigation, Medical Malpractice, Trade Secrets, Contract and Commercial Litigation, Mediation and Arbitration, Products Liability, Patent Litigation, Antitrust, RICO, Securities, Banking Litigation, Business Fraud and Tort Litigation, Local Government Defense, Real Estate, Corporate Transactions and Public Finance.

FIRM PROFILE: Pugh, Jones, Johnson & Quandt provides quality litigation and corporate legal services to clients who value timely solutions delivered efficiently and cost-effectively. As a minority-owned and managed law firm of 21 attorneys, Pugh, Jones & Johnson provides its clients with both proven professional excellence as well as the added benefit of the firm's interpersonal diversity. Pugh, Jones & Johnson was established in 1991. Our named shareholders have more than 100 years of legal experience, and serve in various capacities in many professional and community organizations.

STEPHEN H. PUGH, JR., born Chicago, Illinois, October 17, 1942; admitted to bar, 1973, Illinois. *Education:* Loyola University. Clerk, Honorable James E. Parsons, U.S. District Court, Northern District of Illinois, 1973-1974. Special Trial Attorney, U.S. Department of Justice, 1974-1977. Associate, Chapman and Cutler, Chicago, Illinois, 1978-1983; Partner, Chapman and Cutler, 1983-1991. Board Member, Legal Assistance Foundation of Chicago, Illinois Institute for Continuing Legal Education. Panel Member, Hearing Board for the Attorney Registration and Disciplinary Commission of the Supreme Court of Illinois. Commissioner, Committee on Character and Fitness of the First Judicial District of the Illinois Supreme Court. Hearing Officer, Chicago Board of Education. ***PRACTICE AREAS:*** Litigation; Real Estate; Corporate Transactions; Public Finance. ***Email:*** spugh@pjjq.com

WALTER JONES JR., born Chicago, Illinois, October 7, 1946; admitted to bar, 1972, Illinois and U.S. District Court, Northern District of Illinois. *Education:* University of Illinois (B.A., 1969; J.D., 1972). Instructor, Trial Practice to Senior Harvard, Law School Seniors, January, 1982. Assistant U.S. Attorney, 1973-1986 and Chief of Criminal Division, 1980-1986. *Member:* Chicago, Illinois State, Federal (Member, Board of Directors, 1990-1004) and American (Elected Member of Criminal Justice Section's Council, 1982-1984; Member, Editorial Board, "Criminal Justice Magazine," 1986—; Chairman, Prosecution Function Committee, 1981-1984) Bar Associations; Seventh Circuit Bar Association (Illinois Chair, Committee on Criminal Law & Procedure, 1998—); American Board of Criminal Lawyers; American College of Trial Lawyers (Illinois Chair, 2001—). ***PRACTICE AREAS:*** White Collar Criminal Litigation; Complex Civil Litigation; Employment Discrimination. ***Email:*** wjones@pjjq.com

DENNIS P. W. JOHNSON, born Reading, Pennsylvania, December 31, 1954; admitted to bar, 1980, Illinois; U.S. District Court, Northern District of Illinois including Trial Bar; U.S. Court of Appeals, Seventh, First, Third, Fifth and Ninth Circuits; U.S. Supreme Court. *Education:* Albright College (A.B., magna cum laude, 1976); Georgetown University and University of Chicago (J.D., 1979). Associate, 1979-1986 and Equity Partner, 1987-1992, Bell Boyd & Lloyd, Chicago, Illinois. *Member:* Chicago, Illinois State and American Bar Associations. ***REPORTED CASES:*** Swanson v. Leggett & Platt, Inc., 154 F.3d 730 (7th Cir. 1998); Chiaramonte v. Fashion Group, Inc., 129 F.3d 391 (7th Cir. 1997), cert denied, 523 U.S. 1118 (1998); Howard v. Sweetheart Cup Company Inc., 2001 WL 1105092 (N.D.Ill. 2001); Shivakumar v. Abbott Laboratories, 2001 WL 775967 (N.D.Ill. 2001); Skaletsky and Jones v. City Colleges of Chicago, 75 F.Supp.2d 885 (N.D.Ill. 1999). ***PRACTICE AREAS:*** Complex Civil Litigation; Labor and Employment Litigation; Trade Secrets; Commercial Torts Litigation; Business Tort Litigation; Products Liability; Personal Injury. ***Email:*** djohnson@pjjq.com

ERIC F. QUANDT, born Beaver Dam, WI, June, 1951; admitted to bar, 1976, Wisconsin, Illinois and U.S. District Court, Northern District of Illinois. *Education:* Luther College; University of Wisconsin-Madison (B.S., 1973; J.D., 1976). ***PRACTICE AREAS:*** Drug and Medical Device Litigation; Medical Legal Law; Pharmaceutical. ***Email:*** equandt@pjjq.com

JORGE V. CAZARES, born Chicago, Illinois, October 2, 1963; admitted to bar, 1990, Illinois and U.S. District Court, Northern District of Illinois including Trial Bar; 1992, U.S. Court of Appeals, Seventh Circuit; 1993, U.S. Supreme Court and U.S. District Court, Central District of Illinois. *Education:* Yale University (B.S., 1985); Loyola University of Chicago (J.D., 1990). Arbitrator, Cook County Mandatory Arbitration Program (Chair-Qualified). *Member:* Illinois State and American Bar Associations; Hispanic National Bar Association; Hispanic Lawyers Association of Illinois. ***LANGUAGES:*** Spanish. ***PRACTICE AREAS:*** Complex Civil Litigation; Local Government Defense; Employment Litigation; Libel Defense; Personal Injury Defense; Eminent Domain. ***Email:*** jcazares@pjjq.com

SCOTT A. BREMER, born Chicago, Illinois, January 29, 1950; admitted to bar, 1975, Illinois. *Education:* St. Olaf College (B.A., 1972); Northwestern University (J.D., 1975); DePaul University (LL.M., Taxation, 1985). *Member:* Chicago and American Bar Associations; National Association of Bond Lawyers. ***PRACTICE AREAS:*** Public Finance. ***Email:*** sbremer@pjjq.com

LINZEY D. JONES, JR., admitted to bar, 1982, Illinois and U.S. District Court, Northern District of Illinois including Trial Bar; 1987, U.S. Court of Appeals, Third, Seventh and Eleventh Circuits; 1993, U.S. Supreme Court; 1999, U.S. District Court, Eastern District of Michigan; 2000, U.S. Court of Appeals, Sixth Circuit. *Education:* University of Illinois (B.A., 1979; J.D., magna cum laude, 1982). Order of the Coif. Member, Law Review. Mayor, Village of Olympian Fields, 1997—. Chicago Committee on Minorities in Large Law Firms, 1990-2000. *Member:* Chicago (Board of Managers, 1993-1995), Cook County (Board of Directors, 1993-1994) and American Bar Associations; South Suburban Mayors and Managers Association (President, 2002-2003). ***PRACTICE AREAS:*** Labor and Employment; Management Employment Law; Management Labor Law; Noncompetition and Non-Solicitation Agreements; Noncompete Litigation. ***Email:*** ljones@pjjq.com

MARY K. PERIOLAT, born Blue Island, IL, April, 1958; admitted to bar, 1983, Illinois and U.S. District Court, Northern District of Illinois. *Education:* Indiana University (B.A., 1980; J.D., cum laude, 1983). ***PRACTICE AREAS:*** Drug and Medical Device Litigation; Medical Malpractice; Pharmaceutical Litigation. ***Email:*** mperiolat@pjjq.com

CAROLE A. CORNS, born Westwood, New Jersey, April 8, 1963; admitted to bar, 1991, Illinois and U.S. District Court, Northern District of Illinois; 1992, U.S. Court of Appeals, 7th Circuit. *Education:* Indiana University (B.S., magna cum laude, 1985); University of Michigan (J.D., 1991). Beta Gamma Sigma. Contributing Editor, Michigan Journal of Law Reform. *Member:* Chicago Bar Association. ***LANGUAGES:*** French. ***Email:*** ccorns@pjjq.com

KIM BARKER LEE, born New York, N.Y., August 12, 1967; admitted to bar, 1993, Illinois. *Education:* Yale College (B.A., 1989); New York University (J.D., 1993). *Member:* Chicago and American Bar Associations; Black Women Lawyers' Association. ***PRACTICE AREAS:*** Public Finance; Government Law; Corporate. ***Email:*** kbarkerlee@pjjq.com

(This Listing Continued)

PUGH, JONES, JOHNSON & QUANDT, P.C., Chicago—Continued

DANIEL A. ROWIN, born Oakland, California, October, 1961; admitted to bar, 1989, Illinois; 1990, U.S. District Court, Northern District of Illinois. *Education:* University of California at Los Angeles (B.A., magna cum laude, 1986); Northwestern University (J.D., 1989). Phi Beta Kappa. ***PRACTICE AREAS:*** Litigation; Products Liability; Toxic Torts; Medical Negligence. ***Email:*** drowin@pjjq.com

LA VON M. JOHNS, born Chicago, Illinois, July 10, 1968; admitted to bar, 1996, Illinois; 1998, Nebraska. *Education:* Creighton University (B.A., cum laude, 1993); Northwestern University School of Law (J.D., 1996). *Member:* Chicago, Cook County and American (Member: Affordable Housing Subcommittee, 2002—; Women in Planning and Development, 1997— Bar Associations. ***PRACTICE AREAS:*** Commercial Real Estate Law; Real Estate Acquisitions; Leasing; Real Estate Finance. ***Email:*** ljohns@pjjq.com

MARK D. ANDREWS, born Evanston, Illinois, March 5, 1972; admitted to bar, 1997, Illinois and U.S. District Court, Northern District of Illinois; 1998, U.S. Court of Appeals, 7th Circuit. *Education:* Wheaton College (B.A., cum laude, 1994); University of Illinois College of Law (J.D., 1997). *Member:* Chicago and Illinois State Bar Associations. ***Email:*** mandrews@pjjq.com

EDUARDO M. COTILLAS. PRACTICE AREAS: Contracts; Computers and Software; Construction.

PAUL C. DO, born Saigon, Vietnam; admitted to bar, 2003, Illinois. *Education:* University of California of Berkeley (B.A. Political Science with distinction, 2000); University of California, Boalt Hall School of Law (J.D., cum laude, 2003). Member, Golden Key. *Member:* Chicago and Illinois State Bar Associations. ***LANGUAGES:*** Vietnamese and French. ***PRACTICE AREAS:*** Insurance Defense Litigation; Civil Litigation; Transportation Law; Employment Law; Commercial Litigation. ***Email:*** pdo@pattonryan.com

GIL R. CUBIA, admitted to bar, 1997, Illinois and U.S. District Court, Northern District of Illinois. *Education:* University of Michigan (B.B.A., 1989); Indiana University (J.D., 1996). ***PRACTICE AREAS:*** Real Estate; Commercial Transactions.

OF COUNSEL

THOMAS N. HARDING, born Rockford, Illinois, March 10, 1947; admitted to bar, 1973, Illinois. *Education:* University of Illinois (B.A., with distinction, 1969); University of Chicago (J.D., 1973). Phi Beta Kappa. Recipient, Carlson Prize, National Association of Bond Lawyers, 2001. Member, Board of Editors: *The Bond Lawyer,* 2001—; *National Association of Bond Lawyers Federal Securities Law of Municipal Bonds Deskbook.* Author, "The Effects of NSMIA on Blue Sky Requirements Applicable to Municipal Securities" and "Model Blue Sky Memoranda for Municipal Securities," published online at www.nabl.org under Resource Library/Securities Law Materials/Blue Sky, Sept. 2000. *Member:* National Association of Bond Lawyers (Chairman, Blue Sky Law Subcommittee, 2000—). [First Lt., U.S. Army Reserves, 1970-1976.]. ***PRACTICE AREAS:*** Municipal Finance. ***Email:*** tnharding@aol.com

PYES & CHERIN, LLP

Established in 1976

29 SOUTH LA SALLE STREET
SUITE 1100
CHICAGO, ILLINOIS 60603
Telephone: 312-236-5888
Fax: 312-236-1288
Email: pyescherin@usa.net

General, Civil Practice including Banking, Commercial, Collection, Personal Injury, Corporate, Family and Real Estate.

FIRM PROFILE: The law firm of Pyes & Cherin, LLP was founded in 1976 by Harvey Pyes and Steven Cherin. The firm represents clients throughout the Northern half of Illinois in all areas of legal services. The firm strongly believes in professional development and all partners and the associates attend continuing legal education and business seminars, professional association activities, client functions and civic affairs.

HARVEY PYES, born 1930; admitted to bar, 1954, Illinois and U.S. District Court, Northern District of Illinois. *Education:* Drake University (B.A.); DePaul University (J.D.). Author: "Confession of Judgement in Illinois," Illinois State Bar Journal, June, 1960. Chairman, Board of Trustees, Rush North Shore Medical Center, 1996-2001. Trustee, Rush-Presbyterian-St. Luke's Medical Center, 1996-2001. Trustee, Rush North Shore Medical Center, 1991—. Chairman of the Board: Bank of Highwood, 1974-1986; New Century Bank, 1975-1986. President, North Shore P.T.A. Association for the Retarded, 1972. Member, Bank Commissioner's Committee for a Dual Banking System, 1986-1987. Arbitrator, Cook County, Illinois Mandatory Arbitration Program. *Member:* Chicago, Illinois State (Chairman: Young Lawyers Section, 1962-1965; General Practice Section, 1970-1973; Commercial, Banking, and Bankruptcy Section, 1983-1985) and American Bar Associations. ***PRACTICE AREAS:*** Commercial Law; Real Estate Law; Corporate Law; Probate Law; Family Law. ***Email:*** PYESCHERIN@USA.NET

STEVEN CHERIN, born 1949; admitted to bar, 1975, Illinois and U.S. District Court, Northern District of Illinois; 1978, U.S. Tax Court. *Education:* Roosevelt University (B.S.B.A.); John Marshall Law School (J.D.). Delta Theta Phi. Licensed Real Estate Broker, Illinois, 1975. Instructor in Criminal Law and Real Estate, Triton College, River Grove, Illinois, 1976-1983. Instructor in Real Estate, City Colleges of Chicago, 1977-1994. Member, Chicago Volunteer Legal Services, 1976—. Volunteer Counsel, American Radio Relay League, 1980—. Volunteer Examiner, Amateur Radio Service, Federal Communications Commission, 2002—. Member, Panel of Arbitrators, American Arbitration Association. Arbitrator, Cook County, Illinois Mandatory Arbitration Program. *Member:* Chicago, Illinois State and American Bar Associations; Illinois Creditor's Bar Association. ***PRACTICE AREAS:*** Commercial Law; Real Estate Law; Corporate Law; Probate Law; Family Law; Personal Injury. ***Email:*** PYESCHERIN@USA.NET

CHARLES V. KWASNIEWSKI, born 1957; admitted to bar, 1996, Illinois; 1997, U.S. District Court, Northern District of Illinois. *Education:* Southern Illinois University (B.S., 1980); University of Illinois, Chicago (M.B.A., 1983); DePaul university (J.D., 1996). Recipient, American Jurisprudence Award for Evidence. *Member:* Chicago, Illinois State and American Bar Associations. ***PRACTICE AREAS:*** Commercial Law; Business Law; Family Law. ***Email:*** PYESCHERIN@USA.NET

MARIETTA L. KERR, born 1970; admitted to bar, 2002, New York and Illinois. *Education:* University of Western Ontario (B.A., 1993); McMaster University (B.A., 1995); John Marshall Law School (J.D., 2000). *Member:* Illinois State and New York State Bar Associations. ***LANGUAGES:*** French. ***PRACTICE AREAS:*** General Practice. ***Email:*** pyescherin@usa.net

REPRESENTATIVE CLIENTS: Alanson Manufacturing Co.; M. Block and Sons, Inc.; Belle-Aire Fragrances, Inc.

LAW OFFICES OF PETER Y. QIU

Established in 1999

736 W. 35TH STREET
CHICAGO, ILLINOIS 60616
Telephone: 773-843-9808
Fax: 773-843-9812
Email: pyqlawfirm@sbcglobal.net
URL: http://www.lawyers.com/pqiulaw

Business Litigation, Commercial Litigation, Collection of Judgments, Bankruptcy, Immigration, Civil Litigation, Personal Injury, Workers Compensation, Real Estate, Family Law, Wills and Probate, Trusts and Estates, Estate Planning, Criminal Defense, Copyrights.

PETER Y. QIU, born 1961; admitted to bar, 1998, Illinois. *Education:* Jilin University, China (B.A., English, 1982); University of Illinois at Chicago (M.A., American History, 1990); Chicago-Kent College of Law (J.D., 1998). *Member:* Chicago and American Bar Associations; The Association of Trial Lawyers of America. ***LANGUAGES:*** Chinese. ***PRACTICE AREAS:*** Business Litigation; Commercial Litigation; Copyrights; Civil Litigation; Immigration Law; Deportation; Family Law; Personal Injury; Workers Compensation; Real Estate; Evictions; Landlord and Tenant Law; Wills; Trust Law; Estate Planning; Criminal Defense.

Languages: Chinese and Spanish.

QUARLES & BRADY LLP

Established in 1892

CITICORP CENTER
500 WEST MADISON STREET, SUITE 3700
CHICAGO, ILLINOIS 60661-2511
Telephone: 312-715-5000
Fax: 312-715-5155
URL: http://www.quarles.com

REVISER OF THE WISCONSIN LAW DIGEST FOR THIS DIRECTORY.

Milwaukee, Wisconsin Office: Quarles & Brady LLP, 411 East Wisconsin Avenue, Suite 2040, 53202-4497. Telephone: 414-277-5000. Fax: 414-271-3552.
Madison, Wisconsin Office: One South Pinckney Street, Suite 600, P.O. Box 2113, 53701-2113. Telephone: 608-251-5000. Fax: 608-251-9166.
Naples, Florida Office: 1395 Panther Lane, 34109-7874. Telephone: 239-262-5959. Fax: 239-434-4999.
Boca Raton, Florida Office: One Lincoln Place, 1900 Glades Road, Suite 355, 33431. Telephone: 561-368-5400. Fax: 561-368-1996.
Phoenix, Arizona Office: Quarles & Brady Streich Lang, LLP, One Renaissance Square, Two North Central Avenue, 85004-2391. Telephone: 602-229-5200. Fax: 602-229-5690.
Tucson, Arizona Office: Quarles & Brady Streich Lang, LLP, One South Church Avenue, Suite 1700, 85701-1621. Telephone: 520-770-8700. Fax: 520-623-2418.

General Corporate Practice, including Administrative, Antitrust, Trade Regulation and Franchising, Creditors' Rights and Bankruptcy, Business Planning, Commercial, Community Associations and Country Clubs, Construction, Corporate Finance and Securities, E-Commerce, Employee Benefits, Energy and Telecommunications, Environmental, Estate Planning, Exempt Organizations, Family, Financial Institutions, Government Relations, Hospital and Health, Immigration, Insurance, Intellectual Property, International, Labor and Employment (Management), Litigation (Civil, Products Liability, Toxic Tort and Environmental Defense), Mergers and Acquisitions, Municipal, Privately Held Businesses, Public Finance, Real Estate and Land Use, School, Taxation and White Collar Crime.

FIRM PROFILE: Providers of the highest quality legal services since 1892. Quarles & Brady LLP offers a full array of legal services, helping businesses, governments and individuals find solutions to legal problems affecting entrepreneurial start-ups, international Fortune 500 companies and everything in between. With over 400 attorneys practicing from offices in Milwaukee and Madison, Wisconsin; Chicago, Illinois; Phoenix and Tucson, Arizona and Boca Raton and Naples, Florida; Quarles & Brady LLP represents a broad range of clients locally, nationally and internationally.

LAW FIRM ALLIANCES/ASSOCIATIONS: **STATE CAPITAL GLOBAL LAW FIRM GROUP**

UNITED STATES LAW FIRM GROUP

(This Listing Continued)

PARTNERS

PATRICK J. BITTERMAN, born Chicago, Illinois, August 30, 1965; admitted to bar, 1990, Illinois and U.S. District Court, Northern District of Illinois; 1995, U.S. Tax Court. *Education:* University of Illinois (B.A., 1987); Northwestern University (J.D., 1990). *Member:* Chicago, Illinois State and American Bar Associations. ***PRACTICE AREAS:*** Estate Planning; Taxation; Tax-Exempt Organizations. ***Email:*** pb2@quarles.com

THOMAS E. CHOMICZ, born Chicago, Illinois, April 9, 1941; admitted to bar, 1969, Illinois; 1970, U.S. Tax Court. *Education:* University of St. Thomas (B.A., 1963); University of Minnesota (J.D., cum laude, 1969). Certified Public Accountant, Minnesota, 1966. Author: "A Common Investment Fund For Foundations," Journal of Taxation for Exempt Organizations, Fall 1992; "How To Avoid Self-Dealing Issues When Providing Directors' and Officers' Liability Insurance," Journal of Taxation of Exempt Organizations, Summer 1996; Article, "How Foundations Decide Who Will Receive Grants," Grant Thornton, L.L.P., Accountants and Management Consultants (Fall 1997). *Member:* Chicago and American (Member, Tax Section, Tax-Exempt Organization Committee; Chairman, Private Foundation Subcommittee, 1985-1993; Co-Chairman: Joint Ventures Subcommittee, 1993-1999; Forms Ruling Subcommittee, 2000-2003) Bar Associations. ***PRACTICE AREAS:*** Tax-Exempt Organizations; Private Foundations; Tax; Estate Planning. ***Email:*** tc2@quarles.com

GARY R. CLARK, admitted to bar, 1997, Tennessee; 2000, Illinois. *Education:* Northwestern University (B.A., 1994); Washington University (J.D., 1997). *Member:* Chicago and American Bar Associations. ***Email:*** gclark@quarles.com

MELANIE ROVNER COHEN, born Chicago, Illinois, August 9, 1944; admitted to bar, 1977, Illinois; 1988, U.S. Court of Appeals, Seventh Circuit; 1998, U.S. Court of Appeals, Fifth Circuit and U.S. Supreme Court. *Education:* Brandeis University (A.B., with honors, 1965); DePaul University (J.D., magna cum laude, 1977). Frequent Lecturer and Author of numerous Published Articles. Instructor, John Marshall Law School, 1995—. Law Clerk to The Honorable Frederick J. Hertz, Bankruptcy Judge, U.S. District Court, Northern District of Illinois, 1976-1977. *Member:* Chicago (Chairman, Committee on Bankruptcy and Reorganization, 1983), Illinois State, Federal and American (Co-Chairman, Committee on Enforcement of Creditors' Rights) Bar Associations; Commercial Law League of America; Illinois Trial Lawyers Association; Turnaround Management Association (National and Chicago Director; International President, 1999-2000; Chairman, 2000-2002; Chicago President); Bankruptcy Arbitration and Mediation Services (Director). Fellow: American College of Bankruptcy; International Insolvency Institute; American Bankruptcy Institute; International Women's Insolvency & Restructuring Confederation. ***PRACTICE AREAS:*** Bankruptcy; Reorganization; Secured Lending; Debtor and Creditor. ***Email:*** mcohen@quarles.com

CHRISTOPHER COMBEST, born Jackson Heights, Queens, New York, October 1, 1960; admitted to bar, 1994, Illinois and U.S. District Court, Northern District of Illinois; 1998, U.S. Court of Appeals, Fifth Circuit. *Education:* Yale University (B.A., Summa cum laude, 1982; J.D., 1994); University of Washington (M.F.A., 1985). Phi Beta Kappa. Articles include: "Bankruptcy and Limited Liability Entities," The Practical Lawyer, April 1996 (Part I) and June 1996 (Part II) (with Melanie Rovner Cohen); "Real Estate in Bankruptcy," Chapter 16 in Volume II, Illinois Institute for Continuing Legal Education's handbook, Basic Real Estate Practice (IICLE 1995) (with Melanie Rovner Cohen and Michael M. Eidelman) and the 1998 Supplement thereto (sole author). Frequent teacher, law section of the one-day review course sponsored by the Turnaround Management Association for the certification exam sponsored by the Association of Certified Turnaround Professionals. *Member:* Chicago, Illinois State and American Bar Associations. ***REPORTED CASES:*** Mabey v. Southwestern Electric Power Company (In re Cajun Electric Power Cooperative, Inc.), 150 F.3d 503 (5th Cir. 1998). ***PRACTICE AREAS:*** Bankruptcy; Creditors Rights; Workouts; Insolvency. ***Email:*** ccombest@quarles.com

FAYE B. FEINSTEIN, born Brooklyn, New York, February 3, 1953; admitted to bar, 1984, Illinois and U.S. District Court, Northern District of Illinois; 1994, U.S. District Court, Eastern District of Wisconsin. *Education:* Brooklyn College (B.A., summa cum laude, phi beta kappa, 1973); Northwestern University Law School; New York University School of Law (J.D., 1984). Adjunct Faculty Member, John Marshall Law School. *Member:* Chicago (Former Chair, Committee on Bankruptcies and Reorganization; Former Vice Chair, Mediation Subcommittee) and American Bar Associations; International Women's Insolvency and Restructuring Confederation; Turnaround Management Association (Past President, Chicago Midwest Chapter; Past Chair: Professional Women's Networking Group; National Professional Women's Networking Group). ***PRACTICE AREAS:*** Institutional Lending; Workouts; Bankruptcy and Insolvency; Creditors Rights. ***Email:*** fbf@quarles.com

ROBERT F. FORRER, born Chicago, Illinois, October 3, 1945; admitted to bar, 1970, Illinois. *Education:* DePaul University (B.A., summa cum laude, 1967); Northwestern University (J.D., cum laude, 1970). Associate Editor, Northwestern University Law Review, 1969-1970. Member: Illinois Governor Edgar's Task Force on Higher Education; General Counsel, Illinois Retail Merchants Association. ***PRACTICE AREAS:*** Federal Securities Litigation; Complex Civil Litigation; General Commercial Litigation; Tax Litigation; Trust Construction Litigation. ***Email:*** rff@quarles.com

H. JAMES FOX, born New Orleans, Louisiana, November 27, 1943; admitted to bar, 1968, Illinois; 1969, U.S. District Court, Northern District of Illinois; 1973, U.S. Supreme Court; 1982, Florida. *Education:* Knox College (B.A., 1965); University of Illinois (J.D., 1968). ***PRACTICE AREAS:*** Business Law; Financial Services; Real Estate Law; Zoning; Land Use. ***Email:*** fox@quarles.com

ERIC J. FUGLSANG, born Arlington Heights, Illinois, April 15, 1971; admitted to bar, 1997, Illinois and U.S. District Court, Northern District of Illinois. *Education:* Elmhurst College (B.S., 1994); DePaul University (J.D., 1997). *Member:* Chicago, Illinois State and American Bar Associations. ***PRACTICE AREAS:*** Commercial Leasing, Sales and Acquisitions and Financing; Commercial Finance. ***Email:*** ejf@quarles.com

ROBERT L. GAMRATH III, born Salt Lake City, Utah, October 10, 1968; admitted to bar, 1994, Illinois, U.S. District Court, Northern District of Illinois and U.S. Court of Appeals, Seventh Circuit. *Education:* Indiana University (B.S., 1991); John Marshall Law School (J.D., 1994). Staff Editor, The John Marshall Journal of Computer and Information Law. Author: "Anatomy of Tax Increment Financing," Journal of Property Tax Management, Spring 1998; "Municipalities Keep Forgetting That Most Seniors Do Not Drive," Illinois Real Estate Journal, Sept. 13, 1999. Speaker: "Overview of Takings Law from Penn Coal to Del Monte Dunes," Holleb & Coff, 1999; "Update of Amendments to City of Chicago Landscape Ordinance, Parking Garage Ordinance and Streets and Sanitation Ordinance," Holleb & Coff, 1999; "Telecommunications 1997: Taking Your Governmental Client to Infinity and Beyond," Chicago Bar Association, 1997; "Should Your Governmental Client Get 'Tiffed'? How to Use Tax Increment Financing Without Creating Enemies," Chicago Bar Association, 1996. *Member:* Chicago, Illinois State (Member, Young Lawyers Division Council, 1997—) and American Bar Associations. ***REPORTED CASES:*** Amoco Oil Company v. Village of Schaumburg, 277 Ill.App. 3d 926, 661 N.E.2d 380, 214 Ill. Dec. 526 (1996). ***PRACTICE AREAS:*** Zoning and Land Use; Commercial Real Estate; Real Estate Finance. ***Email:*** rg2@quarles.com

JAMES J. GATZIOLIS, born Chicago, Illinois, April 1, 1948; admitted to bar, 1974, Illinois. *Education:* University of Illinois (B.S. in Accounting, 1970); IIT/Chicago-Kent College of Law (J.D., 1973). *Member:* Hellenic and American Bar Associations. ***PRACTICE AREAS:*** Corporate; Tax. ***Email:*** jjg@quarles.com

MARK J. HORNE, born Brainerd, Minnesota, August 23, 1946; admitted to bar, 1973, Illinois and U.S. District Court, Northern District of Illinois. *Education:* University of Southern Illinois (B.S., 1969); DePaul University (J.D., 1973). *Member:* Chicago and American Bar Associations. ***PRACTICE AREAS:*** Real Estate; Construction; Land Use; Real Estate Finance. ***Email:*** mjh@quarles.com

JOHN A. KLAGES, born Chicago, Illinois, May 4, 1962; admitted to bar, 1987, Illinois. *Education:* University of Illinois (B.S., 1984); Washington College of Law of American University (J.D., 1987). Member, Bronze Table. Co-Chairman, Chicago Volunteer Legal Services, 1991. *Member:* Illinois State Bar Association. ***PRACTICE AREAS:*** Employment; Labor. ***Email:*** jk2@quarles.com

GARY H. KLINE, born Sioux City, Iowa, October 1, 1939; admitted to bar, 1966, Iowa; 1967, Illinois. *Education:* University of Michigan (B.A., with high distinction, 1962); University of Edinburgh; Harvard University (J.D., 1965). Author: "Establishment of a Supporting Foundation to Raise Funds for a School District," The American School Board Journal, November, 1992. Co-Author: "Advocacy Activities of Charitable Organizations," Foundation Forum, Fall 1992; "When Is Expenditure Responsibility Necessary," Family Matters, Winter 1997. Selected as one of the top 5% of Illinois lawyers in survey of Illinois lawyers conducted by Law Bulletin Publishing Company, 2004. *Member:* American Bar Association. ***PRACTICE AREAS:*** Federal Income Taxation; Charitable Organizations; Foundations; Health Care; Trust and Estate Administration. ***Email:*** ghk@quarles.com

JANINE M. LANDOW-ESSER, born Omaha, Nebraska, September 23, 1951; admitted to bar, 1976, Virginia; 1977, District of Columbia; 1985, Illinois. *Education:* University of Wisconsin-Madison (B.A., 1973); George Washington University (J.D., with honors, 1976). Author: "Bridging the GAAP: Thoughts on Environmental Accounting," Brownfield News, November/December 2002; "Contracts to Keep Deals Alive," Brownfield News, January/February 2002; "While the Buyer Must Still Beware, Environmental Insurance May Provide What It Takes to Get Your Deal Closed," Corporate Real Estate Executive, October 2001; "Why You Shouldn't Play the 'Waiting Game,'" Opus Communications, January 2000; "OSHA's Proposed Ergonomics Standard, Letter to Editor, "Overfile Threat is Not Idle in Environmental Self-Audits," U.S. Business Litigation, July 1997; "Who Pays for Environmental Change?" American City & County, April 1992; "Insurance Coverage for Environmental Claims," Corporate Real Estate Executive, September 1992; "Audits and Accounting," Illinois CPA Society, Insight, August 1991. Contributor: "Getting the Green Light: Consultants Expedite Environmental Tasks," Plants, Site and Parks, January 2000; "Bond Sticking to Ergonomics Standard Opposition," Opus Communications, December 1999; "Environmental Law," Section of the Chicago Bar Association Young Lawyer Section's Guide to the Chicago Job Market, 1998, 1992; Making the Grade: Companies Ponder Environmental State of the States," Plants, Sites & Parks, Nov/Dec 1997; "Practice Points," Environmental Compliance & Litigation Strategy, November 1997; "Garbage Disposal: Fields of Dregs Save Dollars, Make Sense," Plants, Sites & Parks, March/April 1997; "Lender Liability to Illinois Institute for CLE/CBA's Commercial Finance and Transactions Committee Advanced Commercial Finance and Creditors' Rights in Illinois," 1993, 1996; "Waste From Manufacturing Plants," Waste Age, September 1993; "Environmental Liability Weighs Heavily On Minds of Property Owners," National Real Estate Investor, August 1993; "The Thin Green Line: Thinking Environmental," Midwest Real Estate News, August 1993; "Business Still Stinks," Merrill's Illinois Legal Times, July 1993; "Facing Environmental Liabilities in Business Transactions," The DuPont Company's Environmental Currents, December 1992; "Consultants Partnering With Real Estate To Write Environmental Success Stories," Site Selection, June 1992; "Environmental Audits and Expertise Have Become Industry Necessities," National Real Estate Investor, August 1991. Co-Author: "Environmental and Contracting Issues in Municipal Wastewater Treatment Outsourcing," America's Water and Wastewater Industries, January 2000; "It's Too Soon to Tell If PLI Can Reduce Disputes," The National Law Journal, January 25, 1999; "New Era for Responding to Environmental Risks in Real Estate Transactions," Officer and Industrial Properties, June 1998; "Closing the Deal in the Face of Environmental Contamination," Practical Real Estate Lawyer, July 1998; "Environmental Due Diligence: How To Obtain and Interpret Information, Part I; The Buyer's Perspective, Part II," Real Estate Environmental Liability News, March 1998; "Environmental Compliance Audits: A Tool To Manage Your Company's Regulatory Obligations," Real Estate Environmental Liability News, February 1998; "Federal Overfiling as a Trap for Unwary State Settlors," Illinois State Bar Association, Environmental Law Newsletter, September 1997; "Drafting the Best Possible Outsourcing Contract for the publication's Municipal Water/Wastewater Guide," American City & County, October 1997; "Guidelines: Contracting with an Environmental Consultant," AECRE Newsletter, Corporate Real Estate and the Law, Winter 1996; "Sauk County Landfill Superfund Settlement," American City & County, August 1993; "How to Insure Against Environmental Liability and Losses," The Mortgage and Real Estate Executives Report, August 1992; "Insurance Coverage For Environmental Claims," Journal of Property Management, May/June 1992. *Member:* Chicago (Chair, Environmental Law Committee 1991-1992) and American (Member: Commission on Women in the Profession; Environmental, Energy and Resources Section) Bar Associations; National Brownfield Association; Womens' Environmental Law Forum; Society of

(This Listing Continued)

QUARLES & BRADY LLP, Chicago—Continued

Women Environmental Professionals. ***LANGUAGES:*** French. ***PRACTICE AREAS:*** Environmental Law; Occupational Safety and Health Law; Insurance Coverage. ***Email:*** je3@quarles.com

SARAH M. LINSLEY, born Boston, Massachusetts, October 20, 1956; admitted to bar, 1984, Illinois; U.S. District Court, Northern District of Illinois; U.S. Court of Appeals, Seventh Circuit. *Education:* Harvard College (A.B., magna cum laude, 1979); Northwestern University School of Law (J.D., 1984). *Member:* Chicago and Illinois State Bar Associations. ***PRACTICE AREAS:*** Estate Planning; Employee Benefits; Not-for-Profit Organizations. ***Email:*** sl4@quarles.com

THOMAS J. MAGILL, born Springfield, Illinois, June 22, 1948; admitted to bar, 1977, Illinois and U.S. District Court, Northern District of Illinois; 1979, U.S. Court of Appeals, Seventh Circuit; 1993, U.S. District Court, Eastern District of Wisconsin; 1995, U.S. District Court, Western District of Michigan; 2001, U.S. District Court, Central District of Illinois; 2005, U.S. District Court, Northern District of Indiana. *Education:* University of Illinois (B.S., 1971); John Marshall Law School (J.D., with highest distinction, 1977). Certified Public Accountant, Illinois, 1970. Law Clerk to Senior U.S. District Judge Julius J. Hoffman, U.S. District Court, Northern District of Illinois, 1977-1979. *Member:* Chicago (Member, Bankruptcy Reorganization Section) and American (Member, Sections on: Litigation and Business Law) Bar Associations; American Bankruptcy Institute; American Association of Attorney-CPAs. ***PRACTICE AREAS:*** Commercial and Bankruptcy Litigation. ***Email:*** tjm@quarles.com

JOHN A. McDONALD, born February 22, 1940; admitted to bar, 1964, Illinois. *Education:* University of Michigan (A.B., 1961; J.D., 1963). *Member:* Chicago, Illinois State and American Bar Associations; Law Club of Chicago. ***PRACTICE AREAS:*** Labor and Employment; Discrimination Law; Litigation; Matrimonial Law. ***Email:*** j4m@quarles.com

KENDALL R. MEYER, born Hampton, Iowa, August 12, 1943; admitted to bar, 1968, Iowa and Minnesota; 1974, Illinois; U.S. District Court, Northern District of Illinois including Trial Bar; U.S. Court of Appeals, Seventh Circuit. *Education:* Cornell College (B.A., 1965); University of Iowa (J.D., summa cum laude, 1968). Member, Order of the Coif. Editor, University of Iowa Law Review, 1967-1968. Lecturer, Legal Writing, University of Minnesota, 1969-1970. Assistant Professor of Law, Washington University, 1970-1972. Associate Professor of Law, University of Iowa, 1972-1974. *Member:* American Bar Association. ***PRACTICE AREAS:*** Corporate Law; Securities Law; Litigation; Public Finance; International Law; International Arbitration. ***Email:*** krm@quarles.com

MICHAEL S. MOSTOW, born Chicago, Illinois, September 9, 1965; admitted to bar, 1991, Illinois and U.S. District, Northern District of Illinois. *Education:* University of Illinois (B.A., magna cum laude, 1987), Bronze Tablet; Northwestern University School of Law (J.D., 1991). Author/Co-Author: "Contracts to Keep Deals Alive," Brownfield News, January 2002; "Environmental Insurance May Provide What It Takes To Get Your Deal Closed," Corporate Real Estate Executive, October 2001; "Its Too Soon to Tell If PLI Can Reduce Disputes," The National Law Journal, January 1999; "Negotiating for Your Food Recall Insurance," Food Quality Magazine, May 1999; "Recall Insurance--Negotiate Specific Coverage Terms Before You Buy," Meat and Poultry, August 1999; "Closing the Deal in the Face of Environmental Contamination," Practical Real Estate Lawyer, July 1998. Speeches: "Solving Water Intrusion and Mold Problems," Lorman Education Services, July 2002 and July 2003; "Transaction Based Structured Settlements," Entech 2002, June 2002. Quoted in: "Pollution Risk Transfer Continuing to Evolve," Business Insurance, June 2002; "Determining Insurance Coverage Could Be A Tough Task for Businesses," Disaster Recovery Journal, Fall 2001; WGN Radio Spot Regarding Insurance Recovery for September 11 Losses, Fall 2001. *Member:* Chicago (Legislative Liaison, Environmental Law Committee), Illinois State (Member, Environmental Law Section) and American (Member, Tort and Insurance Practice Section) Bar Associations. ***PRACTICE AREAS:*** Environmental; Policyholders. ***Email:*** mmostow@quarles.com

THOMAS A. POLACHEK, born Chicago, Illinois, July 12, 1942; admitted to bar, 1968, Illinois; 1969, U.S. District Court, Northern District of Illinois; 1986, U.S. Tax Court. *Education:* Ripon College and Michigan State University (B.A., 1965); University of Illinois (J.D., 1968). Publications: Editorial Consultant for West Groups, Illinois Forms Legal and Business, Gifts and Trusts (1998 Ed.). Member, Advisory Editorial Board for Horner's Probate Practice and Estates (4th Ed., 1995); "Living (Revocable) Trusts for the Retiring Attorney," The Lawyer's Guide to Retirement (2d and 4th Eds., ABA Press, 1994 and 1998). "Suggested Appropriate Uses for Living (Revocable) Trusts," ISBA Estate Planning Probate & Trust Newsletter (September, 1991), reprinted in the Chicago Daily Law Bulletin (December 6, 1991). Speaker: "Yes Virginia, There is an Estate Tax—Myths and Mistakes and the Revocable Trust," Illinois State Bar Association's Law Ed. Series, 1999-2000; "Estate Planning and Gifts," Sponsored by the Ilinois State Bar Association and Lyric Opera of Chicago (Jan. 1997 & 1998); "Benefits For The Reluctant Donor (Legal and Otherwise) - An Overview of Charitable Giving and Some Traps To Avoid," Sponsored by the Illinois State Bar Association and Lyric Opera of Chicago (Feb. 1995); Panelist, Illinois Law, "Estate Planning," Chicago Access Cable (Nov. 1995); "Living (Revocable) Trusts for the Retiring Attorney," American Bar Association 1994 Annual Meeting, Senior Lawyers Division; "Appropriate Use of Living Trusts: When, How and Why?" Ill. State Bar Assoc. Law Ed. Series 1992/1993; "Living Trusts: When to Use, How to Fund and What Problems to Avoid," Illinois Institute for Continuing Legal Education's 35th Annual Estate Planning Short Course; "Administration of the Estate in Illinois," sponsored by the National Business Institute; "Intervivos Funding of the Unified Credit and GST Exemption, Irrevocable Insurance Trusts, Estate Freezes After 2036(c) and Investment Adviser Responsibilities and Liabilities," to the Greater Chicago Society of the Institute of Certified Financial Planners; "Estate Planning and Gifts (A Basic Outline)," American Back Society, Medical Legal Forum. Phi Delta Phi. Member, Board of Editors, University of Illinois Law Review. *Member:* Chicago and Illinois State (Member, 1988-1999, 2002— and Chair, 1997-1998, Trusts and Estates Section Council; Assembly Representative, 1998-2004) Bar Associations; The Chicago Estate Planning Council; The Lawyers Club of Chicago. American College of Trust and Estate Counsel; Illinois Bar Foundation. ***PRACTICE AREAS:*** Estate Planning; Trust and Estate Administration; Tax-Exempt Organizations. ***Email:*** tp2@quarles.com

(This Listing Continued)

JANICE E. RODGERS, born Evanston, Illinois, July 19, 1952; admitted to bar, 1976, Illinois and U.S. District Court, Northern District of Illinois; 1978, Florida (inactive). *Education:* University of Illinois (B.S., highest honors, 1973); Harvard University (J.D., cum laude, 1976). Lecturer on Law, Loyola University of Chicago School of Law, 1981-1983. Certified Public Accountant, Illinois, 1973. *Member:* Chicago (Member, Federal Taxation Committee; Past Chair, Exempt Organization Division) and American (Member, Section on Taxation, Tax Exempt Organization Committee) Bar Associations; The Florida Bar. ***PRACTICE AREAS:*** Tax-Exempt Organizations; Private Foundations; Personal Tax Planning. ***Email:*** jer@quarles.com

PETER A. SARASEK, born Milwaukee, Wisconsin, May 24, 1945; admitted to bar, 1974, Illinois and Wisconsin. *Education:* Catholic University of America (B.A., magna cum laude, 1967; M.A., cum laude, 1968); University of Wisconsin (J.D., cum laude, 1974). Order of the Coif. Editor, Wisconsin Law Review, 1972-1974. Author: "Who Foots The Bill for Capital Costs?" Commercial Investment Real Estate Journal, Summer, 1993; "When Your Building Is A Star," Journal of Property Management, Spring, 1994; Panel Member, and Chair of Practicing Law Institute Panels, including Negotiating Commercial Leases (Fall, 2000), Understanding the Sophisticated Real Estate Practice, Fall 2003. *Member:* Chicago, Illinois State (Member, Sections on: Real Property; Federal Taxation) and American (Member, Real Property, Probate and Trust; Corporation, Banking and Business Law) Bar Associations; State Bar of Wisconsin; Lender's Counsel Group (American Land Title Association); American College of Real Estate Lawyers; Commercial Real Estate Organization. (Managing Partner, Chicago Office). ***PRACTICE AREAS:*** Real Estate Finance; Commercial Leasing; Real Estate Acquisitions/Dispositions; Partnerships; Environmental. ***Email:*** psarasek@quarles.com

LEONARD S. SHIFFLETT, born Paris, Kentucky, January 1, 1949; admitted to bar, 1974, Illinois and U.S. District Court, Northern District of Illinois; 1977, U.S. Court of Appeals, 7th Circuit; 1983, U.S. Supreme Court; 1989, U.S. District Court, Eastern District of Wisconsin. *Education:* University of Illinois (A.B., high honors, 1971); University of Chicago (J.D., 1974). Phi Beta Kappa. *Member:* Illinois State and American Bar Associations; Illinois Association of Healthcare Attorneys. ***PRACTICE AREAS:*** Litigation; Health Care; Not-For-Profit; Corporate. ***Email:*** lss@quarles.com

JOHN P. VAIL, born Chicago, Illinois, August 21, 1955; admitted to bar, 1980, Illinois and U.S. District Court, Northern District of Illinois. *Education:* Loyola University (B.A., cum laude, 1977; J.D., 1980). Alpha Sigma Nu; Pi Sigma Alpha; Blue Key. Recipient: Lincoln Medallion Award, Lincoln Academy of Illinois, 1976-1977; Loyola University President's Medallion, 1976. *Member:* Chicago Bar Association. ***PRACTICE AREAS:*** Corporations; Mergers and Acquisitions; Exempt Organizations; Institutional Investment Law; Securities; Commercial Transactions. ***Email:*** jpv@quarles.com

D. SCOTT WATSON, born Danville, Illinois, March 23, 1963; admitted to bar, 1995, Illinois and U.S. District Court, Northern District of Illinois; 1996, U.S. Court of Appeals, Seventh Circuit; 1998, U.S. District Court, Eastern District of Wisconsin; 2000, U.S. District Court, Central District of Illinois; 2001, U.S. District Court, Northern District of Indiana. *Education:* Indiana State University (B.S., 1985; M.Ed., 1989); University of Illinois (J.D., 1995). ***PRACTICE AREAS:*** Labor and Employment Law. ***Email:*** dsw@quarles.com

ASSOCIATES

SOWMYA BHARATHI, born Chicago, Illinois, June 19, 1977; admitted to bar, 2004, Illinois and U.S. District Court, Northern District of Illinois. *Education:* University of Chicago (B.A., 1999); Chicago-Kent College of Law (J.D., with honors, 2004). *Member:* Chicago and Illinois State Bar Associations; Asian American Bar Association. ***PRACTICE AREAS:*** Labor and Employment; Litigation. ***Email:*** sbharath@quarles.com

JOEL A. BRODSKY, born Park Ridge, Illinois, January 12, 1970; admitted to bar, 1995, Illinois and U.S. District Court, Northern District of Illinois including Trial Bar, 2001. *Education:* Indiana University (B.A., with distinction, 1992); University of Illinois (J.D., 1995). Phi Beta Kappa. *Member:* Chicago Bar Association. ***Email:*** j8b@quarles.com

MERIDITH G. CANNON, born Royal Oak, Michigan; admitted to bar, 2000, Illinois and U.S. District Court, Northern District of Illinois. *Education:* University of Michigan (B.A., with distinction, 1997); Loyola University Chicago School of Law (J.D., magna cum laude, 2000). *Member:* Chicago, Illinois State and American (Member, Section on Business Law) Bar Associations. ***PRACTICE AREAS:*** Corporate Services. ***Email:*** mcannon@quarles.com

CHRISTOPHER T. DE MENT, born Kalamazoo, Michigan, April 21, 1972; admitted to bar, 1998, Michigan; 1999, Wisconsin; 2000, Illinois. *Education:* University of Michigan (B.A., with honors, 1994); University of Wisconsin-Madison (J.D., with honors, 1998). ***PRACTICE AREAS:*** Corporate Finance; Real Estate. ***Email:*** ctd@quarles.com

JENNIFER DORN, admitted to bar, 2002, Illinois. *Education:* University of Illinois (B.A., 1995; J.D., magna cum laude, 2002). ***PRACTICE AREAS:*** Real Estate. ***Email:*** jdorn@quarles.com

ELLEN MARIE GIRARD, born Fond du Lac, Wisconsin, February 15, 1972; admitted to bar, 2002, Illinois and U.S. District Court, Northern District of Illinois; 2003, U.S. District Court, Northern District of Indiana and U.S. District Court, Central District of Illinois; 2004, U.S. Court of Appeals, Seventh Circuit; 2005, U.S. Supreme Court. *Education:* Valparaiso University (B.A., 1994); Chicago-Kent College of Law, Illinois Institute of Technology (J.D., with high honors, 2002). *Member:* Chicago, Illinois State and American Bar Associations; Women's Bar Association of Illinois. ***PRACTICE AREAS:*** Labor and Employment. ***Email:*** egirard@quarles.com

CHARLES E. HARPER, JR., admitted to bar, 1999, Illinois. *Education:* Northwestern University (B.A., 1995); University of Illinois (J.D., 1999). ***PRACTICE AREAS:*** Litigation. ***Email:*** charper@quarles.com

JEREMY C. KLEINMAN, born Walnut Creek, California, May 15, 1974; admitted to bar, 1999, Illinois; 2001, U.S. District Court, Northern Dsitrict of Illinois. *Education:* University of California at Los Angeles (B.A., 1996); University of Michigan, Ann Arbor (J.D., 1999). *Member:* American Inns of Court (Marovitz Chapter). ***PRACTICE AREAS:*** Bankruptcy; Creditors Rights. ***Email:*** jkleinma@quarles.com

(This Listing Continued)

THOMAS A. McCARTHY, born 1974; admitted to bar, 2000, Illinois; 2001, Wisconsin; 2002, U.S. District Court, Northern District of Illinois. *Education:* University of Wisconsin-Madison (B.S., Economics, 1997; J.D., cum laude, 2000). Member: Moot Court Board; Wisconsin International Law Journal. *Member:* Chicago, Illinois State and American Bar Associations; State Bar of Wisconsin. ***PRACTICE AREAS:*** Commercial Real Estate Finance; Commercial Real Estate; Commercial Leasing. ***Email:*** thomas.mccarthy@quarles.com

DAVID T. MEEK, born Cincinnati, Ohio, May 2, 1969; admitted to bar, 1998, Illinois and U.S. District Court, Northern District of Illinois. *Education:* Wesleyan University (B.A., 1992); Chicago-Kent College of Law (J.D., 1998). Moot Court Honor Society. ***PRACTICE AREAS:*** Real Estate; Land Use; Zoning Law. ***Email:*** dmeek@quarles.com

BRENDAN O'CONNOR, born Evanston, Illinois, May 13, 1974; admitted to bar, 2002, Illinois. *Education:* Loyola University (B.A., cum laude, 1996; J.D., 2002). ***PRACTICE AREAS:*** Litigation. ***Email:*** boconnor@quarles.com

BENJAMIN L. SCHNEIDER, admitted to bar, 2003, Indiana; 2005, Illinois. *Education:* University of Wisconsin (B.S., 1999); University of Minnesota (J.D., 2003). *Member:* Chicago and Illinois State Bar Associations. ***PRACTICE AREAS:*** Bankruptcy. ***Email:*** bschneid@quarles.com

T. FRANK SHAW, born Stuttgart, Germany, July 6, 1979; (admission pending). *Education:* University of Wisconsin-Milwaukee (B.B.A., distinctive scholastic achievement, 2001); Loyola University-Chicago (J.D., cum laude, 2005). Dean's List, Loyola School of Law. CALI Award Winner in Legal Writing I and II, Criminal Procedure, and Advanced Legal Research; Pro Bono Recognition Award Winner. Student Clinician, Loyola Business Law Center Clinic; Student Research Assistant. *Member:* American Bar Association (Law Student Member); Chicago Bar Association (Law Student Member). ***PRACTICE AREAS:*** Real Estate. ***Email:*** fshaw@quarles.com

ANTHONY P. STEINIKE, born Chicago, Illinois, October 12, 1976; (admission pending). *Education:* DePaul University (B.A., with honors, 1999; J.D., 2003). Case Summaries Editor; DePaul -LLA Journal of Art and Entertainment Law 2002-2003. ***REPORTED CASES:*** Citation: 12 DPLJAEL 251 (2002); FNLW York Times Company v. Tasini DePavl; LLA Art and Entertainment Law Journal. ***PRACTICE AREAS:*** Litigation. ***Email:*** asteinik@quarles.com

MONICA MARIA TYNAN, born River Forest, Illinois; admitted to bar, 1992, Illinois and U.S. District Court, Northern District of Illinois; 1996, U.S. Court of Appeals, Seventh Circuit; 2003, U.S. Supreme Court. *Education:* University of Illinois (B.S., 1985); Chicago-Kent College of Law, Illinois Institute of Technology (J.D., 1992). *Member:* Chicago, Seventh Circuit and American Bar Associations. ***PRACTICE AREAS:*** Products Liability; Commercial Litigation. ***Email:*** mtynan@quarles.com

LEGAL SUPPORT

LEGAL ASSISTANTS

PAULA A. FEDOR

DAWN M. LAKOSKEY

LAURA A. MOORE

REVISER OF THE WISCONSIN LAW DIGEST FOR THIS DIRECTORY.

QUERREY & HARROW, LTD.

Established in 1939

175 WEST JACKSON BOULEVARD, SUITE 1600
CHICAGO, ILLINOIS 60604-2827
Telephone: 312-540-7000
Fax: 312-540-0578
URL: http://www.querrey.com

Crystal Lake, Illinois Office: 651 West Terra Cotta Avenue, Suite 221. Telephone: 815-479-1929. Fax: 815-479-1978.
Wheaton, Illinois Office: 310 South County Farm Road, Third Floor. Telephone: 630-653-2600. Fax: 630-653-0178.
Waukegan, Illinois Office: 415 West Washington Street, Suite 205. Telephone: 847-249-4440. Fax: 847-249-4932.
Joliet, Illinois Office: 2 Rialto Square, Suite 401, 116 North Chicago Street. Telephone: 815-726-1600. Fax: 815-726-1674.
Merrillville, Indiana Office: 8585 Broadway, Suite 510. Telephone: 219-738-1820. Fax: 219-738-1821.
New York, N.Y. Office: 120 Broadway, Suite 2800. Telephone: 212-233-0130. Fax: 212-233-0172.
London, England Office: 141-142 Fenchurch Street, Fifth Floor. Telephone: 207-929-6670. Fax: 207-929-6671.

General Civil and Trial Practice. Appellate, Banking, Commercial Litigation, Construction, Corporate, Dental, Employment, Environmental, Healthcare Liability, Insurance Coverage, Intellectual Property, Information Technology, Governmental Affairs/Government Procurement, Municipal Law, Personal Injury Defense, Product Liability, Professional Liability, Real Estate, Reinsurance, Tax, Transportation, Trusts, Estate Planning, Wills and Probate Law.

FIRM PROFILE: A TRADITION OF QUALITY. As one of Chicago's leading litigation firms, Querrey & Harrow maintains a proud tradition of responding quickly and efficiently to its clients' increasingly complex needs. Our multi-service law firm represents a wide range of individual, industrial, financial, governmental and commercial clients. We continue to offer a proven combination of professionalism and personal service. Our attorneys are experienced in handling litigation in both state and federal courts and alternative dispute resolutions. Our transactional lawyers include those with solid experience in banking, real estate, corporate law, health law, estate planning and governmental contracts. Querrey & Harrow combines the collective experience of these attorneys to deliver cost-efficient and timely resolutions of its clients' matters.

(This Listing Continued)

PAUL A. RETTBERG, admitted to bar, 1970, Illinois; 1977, U.S. Supreme Court. *Education:* DePaul University (B.A., 1966; J.D., 1970). Member, De Paul Law Review, 1969-1970. ***PRACTICE AREAS:*** Litigation; Construction; Product Liability; Municipal. ***Email:*** prettberg@querrey.com

RONALD M. JERRICK, admitted to bar, 1970, Illinois. *Education:* University of Notre Dame (A.B., 1966); DePaul University (J.D., 1970). (Also at Crystal Lake Office). ***PRACTICE AREAS:*** Litigation; Arbitration. ***Email:*** rjerrick@querrey.com

KEVIN J. CAPLIS, admitted to bar, 1973, Illinois. *Education:* University of Illinois, Chicago (B.A., 1970); DePaul University (J.D., 1973). ***PRACTICE AREAS:*** Litigation; Product Liability; Construction. ***Email:*** kcaplis@querrey.com

DENNIS A. MARKS, admitted to bar, 1974, Illinois. *Education:* Loyola University of Chicago (B.B.A., 1969); John Marshall Law School (J.D., 1974). (Managing Shareholder). ***PRACTICE AREAS:*** Litigation; Professional Liability; Admiralty and Maritime Law. ***Email:*** dmarks@querrey.com

ROBERT P. HUEBSCH, admitted to bar, 1975, Illinois. *Education:* University of Dayton (B.S., 1971); Chicago-Kent College of Law (J.D., 1975). ***PRACTICE AREAS:*** Litigation; Medical Malpractice. ***Email:*** rhuebsch@querrey.com

JAMES S. JENDRYK, admitted to bar, 1975, Illinois. *Education:* University of Notre Dame (B.B.A., 1972); John Marshall Law School (J.D., 1975). (Resident, Wheaton Office). ***PRACTICE AREAS:*** Litigation. ***Email:*** jjendryk@querrey.com

JAMES N. KOSMOND, admitted to bar, 1959, Illinois and U.S. Supreme Court; U.S. Court of Appeals, Seventh Circuit. *Education:* Bradley University (B.S., 1956); Northwestern University (J.D., 1959). ***PRACTICE AREAS:*** Litigation; Labor. ***Email:*** jkosmond@querrey.com

DANIEL F. GALLAGHER, admitted to bar, 1973, Illinois. *Education:* University of Illinois (B.A., with honors, 1970; J.D., 1973). ***PRACTICE AREAS:*** Litigation; Product Liability; Construction. ***Email:*** dgallagher@querrey.com

THOMAS P. BURKE, admitted to bar, 1984, Illinois. *Education:* St. Vincent College (B.A., high honors, 1976); Southern Illinois University (M.A., 1978); Loyola of Chicago (J.D., 1984). (Resident, Waukegan Office). ***PRACTICE AREAS:*** Litigation; Transportation; Construction; Employment. ***Email:*** tburke@querrey.com

ROGER LITTMAN, admitted to bar, 1979, Illinois; 2002, Wisconsin. *Education:* University of Illinois (B.A., 1976; J.D., 1979). ***PRACTICE AREAS:*** Litigation; Medical Malpractice; Commercial Fraud. ***Email:*** rlittman@querrey.com

CHARLES E. BLACKMAN, JR., admitted to bar, 1974, Illinois. *Education:* John Carroll University (A.B., 1971); Loyola University (J.D., 1974). ***PRACTICE AREAS:*** Litigation; Construction; Asbestos. ***Email:*** cblackman@querrey.com

THOMAS C. KAUFMANN, admitted to bar, 1984, Illinois. *Education:* University of Illinois (B.S., cum laude, 1979; J.D., 1983). ***PRACTICE AREAS:*** Estate Planning; Real Estate; Probate; Commercial. ***Email:*** tkaufmann@querrey.com

JAMES M. BREAM, admitted to bar, 1986, Illinois. *Education:* University of Wisconsin, Madison (B.A., with distinction, 1985); University of Minnesota (J.D., cum laude, 1986). ***PRACTICE AREAS:*** Litigation; Medical Malpractice; Health Care; Managed Care Defense. ***Email:*** jbream@querrey.com

JANET M. FARMANS, admitted to bar, 1982, Illinois. *Education:* Western Illinois University (B.A., 1974); Loyola University (M.A., 1979); Northern Illinois University (J.D., 1982). (Resident, Joliet Office). ***PRACTICE AREAS:*** Litigation; Product Liability; Construction; Eminent Domain. ***Email:*** jfarmans@querrey.com

ANTHONY J. MADORMO, admitted to bar, 1986, Illinois. *Education:* University of Illinois (B.A., with highest distinction, 1982); John Marshall Law School (J.D., with highest distinction, 1986). Member, John Marshall Law Review, 1984-1986. ***PRACTICE AREAS:*** Litigation; Construction; Insurance Coverage; Environmental. ***Email:*** amadormo@querrey.com

DAVID J. FLYNN, admitted to bar, 1990, Illinois. *Education:* Western Illinois University (B.A., magna cum laude, 1986); DePaul University (J.D., with honors, 1990). Order of the Coif. DePaul University Law Review, 1989-1990. ***PRACTICE AREAS:*** Litigation; Construction. ***Email:*** dflynn@querrey.com

CHARLES E. WHALEN, admitted to bar, 1964, Illinois; 1969, U.S. Supreme Court. *Education:* University of Illinois (B.A., with high honors, 1962; J.D., 1964). Phi Beta Kappa. Assistant Editor, University of Illinois *Law Forum,* 1962-1964. ***PRACTICE AREAS:*** Corporate Law; Commercial; Mergers and Acquisitions; Real Estate. ***Email:*** cwhalen@querrey.com

CHRISTOPHER R. JOHNSTON, admitted to bar, 1982, Illinois. *Education:* Elon College and Roanoke College (B.B.A., with honors, 1978); DePaul University (J.D., 1982). ***PRACTICE AREAS:*** Litigation; Municipal; Insurance; Fraud Investigations. ***Email:*** cjohnston@querrey.com

JOHN M. GREEN, admitted to bar, 1992, Illinois. *Education:* University of Notre Dame (B.S., 1982); Loyola University School of Dentistry (D.D.S., 1986); DePaul University College of Law (J.D., 1992). Licensed Dentist, Illinois, 1986. ***PRACTICE AREAS:*** Litigation; Dental Malpractice. ***Email:*** jgreen@querrey.com

DAVID E. NEUMEISTER, admitted to bar, 1991, Illinois and U.S. Court of Appeals, Seventh Circuit; 1998, U.S. Supreme Court; 2004, Solicitor in the Law Society of England and Wales. *Education:* University of Iowa (B.A., 1984); DePaul University (J.D., 1991). ***PRACTICE AREAS:*** Insurance Coverage; Appellate. ***Email:*** dneumeister@querrey.com

LARRY S. KOWALCZYK, admitted to bar, 1994, Illinois. *Education:* Loyola University (B.A., summa cum laude, 1992; J.D., cum laude, 1994). ***PRACTICE AREAS:*** Litigation; Product Liability; Construction; Elevator Liability. ***Email:*** lkowalczyk@querrey.com

MICHAEL B. STILLMAN, admitted to bar, 1994, Illinois. *Education:* Bradley University (B.A., 1991); DePaul University (J.D., 1994). (Resident, Joliet Office). ***PRACTICE AREAS:*** Litigation; Municipal Law. ***Email:*** mstillman@querrey.com

(This Listing Continued)

QUERREY & HARROW, LTD., Chicago—Continued

BRUCE H. SCHOUMACHER, admitted to bar, 1966, Nebraska (Inactive); 1971, Illinois. *Education:* Northwestern University (B.S., 1961); University of Chicago (M.B.A., 1963; J.D., 1966). ***PRACTICE AREAS:*** Litigation; Construction; Antitrust; Commercial; Professional Liability. ***Email:*** bschoumacher@querrey.com

THOMAS E. STAHR, admitted to bar, 1979, Illinois. *Education:* Eastern Illinois University (B.A., 1976); DePaul University (J.D., 1979). ***PRACTICE AREAS:*** Litigation; Product Liability. ***Email:*** tstahr@querrey.com

SCOTT B. KRIDER, admitted to bar, 1985, Illinois. *Education:* University of Wisconsin-Madison (B.S., Philosophy, 1978; B.S., Education, 1979); John Marshall Law School (J.D., 1985). Member, John Marshall Law Review, 1984-1985. ***PRACTICE AREAS:*** Litigation; Construction; Professional Liability; Real Estate Litigation. ***Email:*** skrider@querrey.com

JEROME M. SONNEFELDT, admitted to bar, 1987, Illinois. *Education:* Loyola University (B.A., 1984); DePaul University (J.D., 1987). ***PRACTICE AREAS:*** Litigation; Construction. ***Email:*** jsonnefeldt@querrey.com

GEORGE J. VOGRIN, JR., admitted to bar, 1987, Massachusetts; 1998, District of Columbia; 2000, New York. *Education:* University of Notre Dame (B.A., 1984); Boston University (J.D., 1987). (Resident, New York, N.Y. Office). ***PRACTICE AREAS:*** Insurance Coverage; Reinsurance; Litigation; Arbitration. ***Email:*** Gvogrin@QHNY.com

KEVIN T. SALTER, admitted to bar, 1978, New York. *Education:* Iona College (B.A., 1973); St. John's University (J.D., 1977). (Resident, New York, N.Y. Office). ***PRACTICE AREAS:*** International Insurance; Corporate Regulatory; Insurance and Reinsurance Law. ***Email:*** Ksalter@QHNY.com

STEVEN HELIS, admitted to bar, 1980, Illinois. *Education:* University of Illinois (B.A., 1977); DePaul University (J.D., 1980). ***PRACTICE AREAS:*** Litigation. ***Email:*** shelis@querrey.com

JONATHAN E. IRWIN, admitted to bar, 1989, Illinois. *Education:* Houghton College (B.A., 1985); Valparaiso University (J.D., 1989). ***PRACTICE AREAS:*** Litigation; Construction; Product Liability. ***Email:*** jirwin@querrey.com

KAREN M. VIVIAN, admitted to bar, 1989, Illinois. *Education:* Oakland University (B.S.N., 1983); Case Western Reserve University (J.D., cum laude, 1989). Registered Nurse, Illinois, 1983. ***PRACTICE AREAS:*** Medical Malpractice; Litigation. ***Email:*** kvivian@querrey.com

SYLVIA KARALEKAS, admitted to bar, 1993, Illinois. *Education:* Loyola University (B.B.A., 1990); John Marshall Law School (J.D., 1993). ***PRACTICE AREAS:*** Medical Malpractice; Dental Malpractice. ***Email:*** skaralekas@querrey.com

EDWARD J. KOZEL, JR., admitted to bar, 1992, Illinois. *Education:* Northern Illinois University (B.S., 1989); John Marshall Law School (J.D., 1992). ***PRACTICE AREAS:*** Litigation. ***Email:*** ekozel@querrey.com

JEFFREY W. CLYMER, admitted to bar, 1992, Indiana and Michigan. *Education:* Kalamazoo College (B.A., 1983); Valparaiso University (J.D., magna cum laude, 1992). (Resident, Merrillville, Indiana Office). ***PRACTICE AREAS:*** Litigation. ***Email:*** jclymer@querrey.com

LISSA L. HAMER, admitted to bar, 1987, Illinois. *Education:* Marquette University (B.S., 1981); Northern Illinois University (J.D., 1987). Medical Technologist, 1981. (Resident, Wheaton Office). ***PRACTICE AREAS:*** Litigation. ***Email:*** lhamer@querrey.com

R. JOHN ANDERSON, admitted to bar, 1983, Michigan; 1987, Illinois. *Education:* Wayne State University (B.A., cum laude, 1979; J.D., 1983). ***PRACTICE AREAS:*** Litigation. ***Email:*** randerson@querrey.com

THOMAS J. BRACKEN, admitted to bar, 1994, New Jersey; 1995, New York. *Education:* Boston College (B.A., 1990); Seton Hall University (J.D., 1994). (Resident, New York, N.Y. Office). ***PRACTICE AREAS:*** Insurance; Litigation; Reinsurance; Employment Law; Health Care. ***Email:*** Tbracken@QHNY.com

DAVID L. LAPORTE, admitted to bar, 1996, Illinois. *Education:* Michigan State University (B.A., with honors, 1989); DePaul University (J.D., with honors, 1996). Order of the Coif. ***PRACTICE AREAS:*** Litigation; Municipal; Construction; Transportation. ***Email:*** dlaporte@querrey.com

MIA M. LUCAS, admitted to bar, 1993, Florida; 1997, Illinois. *Education:* Florida State University (B.S., 1987); University of Denver; Nova University (J.D., 1992); Shepard Broad Law Center. (Resident, Crystal Lake Office). ***PRACTICE AREAS:*** Litigation. ***Email:*** mlucas@querrey.com

JENNIFER J. SACKETT POHLENZ, admitted to bar, 1994, Illinois; 1995, Indiana. *Education:* University of Colorado at Boulder (B.A., 1991); Valparaiso University (J.D., 1994). ***PRACTICE AREAS:*** Environmental; Litigation. ***Email:*** jpohlenz@querrey.com

TIMOTHY R. RABEL, admitted to bar, 1991, Illinois. *Education:* University of Illinois (B.A., 1988); John Marshall Law School (J.D., cum laude, 1991). ***PRACTICE AREAS:*** Litigation; Construction; Commercial; Corporate; Probate. ***Email:*** trabel@querrey.com

ELLEN E. GIBSON, admitted to bar, 1991, Illinois. *Education:* University of Michigan (B.A., 1986); University of Illinois (J.D., Honors, 1991). (Resident, Waukegan Office). ***PRACTICE AREAS:*** Litigation; Construction; Product Liability; Insurance Coverage. ***Email:*** egibson@querrey.com

ANNE M. BELANGER, admitted to bar, 1993, Illinois. *Education:* American University (B.A., 1990); Loyola University, Chicago (J.D., 1993). ***PRACTICE AREAS:*** Litigation. ***Email:*** abelanger@querrey.com

APRIL R. WALKUP, admitted to bar, 1996, Illinois. *Education:* Purdue University (B.A., 1993); John Marshall Law School (J.D., 1996). ***PRACTICE AREAS:*** Employment; Medical Malpractice. ***Email:*** awalkup@querrey.com

(This Listing Continued)

TERRENCE F. GUOLEE, admitted to bar, 1991, Illinois. *Education:* University of Wisconsin-Madison (B.A., 1987); DePaul University (J.D., 1991). ***PRACTICE AREAS:*** Litigation; Insurance Defense. ***Email:*** tguolee@querrey.com

CHRISTINE MCASEY, admitted to bar, 1995, Illinois. *Education:* Augustana College (B.A., Accounting, 1992); Valparaiso University (J.D., 1995). (Resident, Joliet Office). ***PRACTICE AREAS:*** Litigation. ***Email:*** cmcasey@querrey.com

GARY C. SACHS, admitted to bar, 1983, Connecticut; 1984, New York; 1999, Georgia. *Education:* Washington University (B.A., 1976); University of Colorado (J.D., 1983). (Resident, New York, N.Y., Office). ***PRACTICE AREAS:*** Civil Litigation; Insurance Coverage; Professional Liability; Reinsurance. ***Email:*** Gsachs@QHNY.com

DAVID R. PETERSON, admitted to bar, 1996, Illinois. *Education:* Iowa State University (B.S., 1986); Northern Illinois University (J.D., cum laude, 1996). ***PRACTICE AREAS:*** Litigation. ***Email:*** dpeterson@querrey.com

ROBERT ERIC TRAUL, admitted to bar, 1993, Illinois. *Education:* Florida State University (B.A., 1990); ITT Chicago-Kent College of Law (J.D., 1993). ***PRACTICE AREAS:*** Workers' Compensation; Litigation. ***Email:*** rtraul@querrey.com

GALEN A. BRADLEY, admitted to bar, 1995, Indiana; 1995, Illinois. *Education:* Eastern Illinois University (B.S., 1988); Valparaiso University School of Law (J.D., 1995). *Member:* Lake County, Porter County and Indiana State Bar Associations; Illinois Trial Lawyers Association. (Also at Merrilville, Indiana Office). ***PRACTICE AREAS:*** Insurance Defense; Workers Compensation.

DANIEL A. KIRK, admitted to bar, 1996, Illinois. *Education:* Eastern Illinois University (B.A., 1993); Chicago-Kent College of Law, Institute of Technology (J.D., 1996). ***PRACTICE AREAS:*** Litigation; Criminal. ***Email:*** dkirk@querrey.com

---

EMILY J. BARDELAS, admitted to bar, 2004, Illinois and Wisconsin. *Education:* Indiana University (B.A., 1998); University of Wisconsin (J.D., 2004). ***PRACTICE AREAS:*** Litigation. ***Email:*** ebardelas@querrey.com

BARRY C. BROTINE, admitted to bar, 2004, Illinois. *Education:* University of Illinois, Urbana-Champaign (B.A., with honors, 2001); Chicago-Kent College of Law (J.D., 2004). ***PRACTICE AREAS:*** Health Care; Professional Liability; Litigation. ***Email:*** bbrotine@querrey.com

MASON L. BUDELIER, admitted to bar, 2004, Illinois. *Education:* Iowa State University (B.A., 2001); Chicago-Kent College of Law (J.D., 2004). ***PRACTICE AREAS:*** Litigation. ***Email:*** mbudelier@querrey.com

ERNIE BURDEN, admitted to bar, 2000, Illinois. *Education:* Frostburg State College (B.S., 1994); John Marshall Law School (J.D., 2000). ***PRACTICE AREAS:*** Litigation; Medical Malpractice. ***Email:*** eburden@querrey.com

MEGAN A. BYRNES, admitted to bar, 2003, Illinois and Massachusetts; 2004, Connecticut. *Education:* Drake University (B.A., magna cum laude); Suffolk University Law School (J.D., summa cum laude). ***PRACTICE AREAS:*** Litigation. ***Email:*** mbyrnes@querrey.com

KEVIN M. CASEY, admitted to bar, 2004, Illinois. *Education:* DePaul University (B.A., 2001; J.D., 2004). ***PRACTICE AREAS:*** Litigation. ***Email:*** kcasey@querrey.com

THOMAS COMSTOCK, admitted to bar, 2002, Illinois. *Education:* Marquette University (B.S., 1998); John Marshall Law School (J.D., cum laude, 2002). ***PRACTICE AREAS:*** Litigation. ***Email:*** tcomstock@querrey.com

OMAR J. FAYEZ, admitted to bar, 1998, Illinois. *Education:* Wake Forest University (B.A., 1992); Appalachian State University (M.A., 1995); Loyola University School of Law (J.D., 1998). ***PRACTICE AREAS:*** Healthcare Liability; Litigation. ***Email:*** ofayez@querrey.com

PAUL L. FRIMAN, admitted to bar, 1988, Connecticut; 1990, New York; 1991, District of Columbia. *Education:* Indiana University (B.A., 1981); Baruch College of the City University of New York (M.B.A., 1988); New York Law School (J.D., 1988). (Resident, New York, N.Y. Office). ***PRACTICE AREAS:*** Commercial Litigation; Insurance Litigation. ***Email:*** pfriman@QHNY.com

MICHAEL J. FRIMET, admitted to bar, 1999, New York. *Education:* Syracuse University (B.S., 1995); Syracuse University (J.D., 1998). (Resident, New York, N.Y. Office). ***PRACTICE AREAS:*** Insurance; Litigation. ***Email:*** mfrimet@QHNY.com

CYNTHIA E. GARCIA, admitted to bar, 2002, Illinois. *Education:* DePaul University (B.A., 1998); Loyola University (J.D., 2001). ***LANGUAGES:*** Spanish. ***PRACTICE AREAS:*** Medical Malpractice; Litigation. ***Email:*** cgarcia@querrey.com

JENNIFER J. GROSS, admitted to bar, 2002, Illinois. *Education:* University of Michigan (B.A., 1999); DePaul University (J.D., 2002). ***PRACTICE AREAS:*** Litigation. ***Email:*** jgross@querrey.com

JOHN H. HALSTEAD, admitted to bar, 2002, Indiana. *Education:* Brigham Young University (B.A., cum laude, 1999); Indiana University School of Law - Bloomington (J.D., magna cum laude, 2002). (Resident, Merrillville, Indiana Office). ***PRACTICE AREAS:*** Litigation. ***Email:*** jhalstead@querrey.com

NICHOLAS JOHNSON, admitted to bar, 2005, Illinois. *Education:* University of Wisconsin (B.A., 2003); Thomas M. Cooley Law School (J.D., magna cum laude, 2005). (Resident, Waukegan Office). ***PRACTICE AREAS:*** Litigation. ***Email:*** njohnson@querrey.com

KONSTANTINOS KATSAROS, admitted to bar, 2004, New York and New Jersey. *Education:* Boston College (B.S., 2001); New England School of Law (J.D., 2004). (Resident, New York, N.Y. Office). ***PRACTICE AREAS:*** Insurance Coverage; Reinsurance. ***Email:*** kkatsaros@QHNY.com

BRANDON K. LEMLEY, admitted to bar, 2001, Illinois. *Education:* Indiana University School of Law (B.A., 1998); John Marshall Law School (J.D., 2001). ***PRACTICE AREAS:*** Litigation; Municipal Liability. ***Email:*** blemley@querrey.com

(This Listing Continued)

EILEEN E. MADDA, admitted to bar, 2003, Illinois. *Education:* Providence College (B.A., 1996); John Marshall Law School (J.D., 2002). ***PRACTICE AREAS:*** Litigation. ***Email:*** emadda@querrey.com

MEGHAN P. McCARTHY, admitted to bar, 2001, New York. *Education:* University of Notre Dame (B.A., 1997); St. John's University (J.D., 2000). (Resident, New York, N.Y., Office). ***PRACTICE AREAS:*** Insurance Coverage; Reinsurance; Appeals. ***Email:*** mmccarthy@QHNY.com

LAUREN McSWEENEY, admitted to bar, 1996, New York. *Education:* Baruch College of the City University of New York (B.A., 1989); Queens College of the City University of New York (J.D., 1996). (Resident, New York, N.Y., Office). ***PRACTICE AREAS:*** Litigation. ***Email:*** lmcsweeney@QHNY.com

JENNIFER L. MEDENWALD, admitted to bar, 2001, Illinois. *Education:* Indiana University (B.A., 1998); Indiana University School of Law (J.D., 2001). ***PRACTICE AREAS:*** Litigation; Employment Law; Appellate Practice. ***Email:*** jmedenwald@querrey.com

JEANNE M. MILLER, admitted to bar, 1998, Illinois. *Education:* Mundelein College (B.A., 1982; M.A., 1991); Loyola University (J.D., 1998). (Resident, Crystal Lake Office). ***PRACTICE AREAS:*** Litigation; Estate Planning; Insurance Coverage. ***Email:*** jmiller@querrey.com

CRYSTAL D. MONAHAN, admitted to bar, 2000, Michigan; 2003, New York. *Education:* Southeast Missouri State University (B.A., 1997); University of Michigan (J.D., 2000). (Resident, New York, NY Office). ***PRACTICE AREAS:*** Insurance; Litigation. ***Email:*** Cmonahan@GHNY.com

EVDOXIA C. NASSOPOULOS, admitted to bar, 2002, Illinois. *Education:* Loyola University (B.S., 1999; J.D. 2002). ***PRACTICE AREAS:*** Litigation. ***Email:*** ynassopoulos@querrey.com

ANGELIQUE PALMER, admitted to bar, 2004, Illinois. *Education:* University of Toronto (B.A.); Michigan State University College of Law (J.D.). ***PRACTICE AREAS:*** Litigation. ***Email:*** apalmer@querrey.com

NICKOLAS PAPPAS, admitted to bar, 1995, Illinois. *Education:* Loyola University Chicago (B.B.A., 1989); Loyola University Chicago College of Law (J.D., 1995). ***PRACTICE AREAS:*** Litigation; Criminal Law. ***Email:*** npappas@querrey.com

RYAN J. RODMAN, admitted to bar, 2004, Illinois. *Education:* University of Iowa (B.A. 2001); Chicago-Kent College of Law (J.D., 2004). ***PRACTICE AREAS:*** Litigation. ***Email:*** rrodman@querrey.com

JENNIFER M. SCARLETT, admitted to bar, 2003, Illinois. *Education:* Purdue University (B.A., 2000); The John Marshall Law School (J.D., 2003). ***PRACTICE AREAS:*** Litigation. ***Email:*** jscarlett@querrey.com

LAWRENCE A. STEINGOLD, admitted to bar, 2003, Illinois. *Education:* Indiana University (B.S., 1996); Chicago-Kent College of Law (J.D., 2002). (Resident, Waukegan Office). ***PRACTICE AREAS:*** Litigation. ***Email:*** lsteingold@querrey.com

JOAN R. STOHL, born Geneseo, Illinois, June 2, 1965; admitted to bar, 1991, Illinois. *Education:* North Central College (B.A., 1987); DePaul University (J.D., 1990). ***PRACTICE AREAS:*** Healthcare Liability. ***Email:*** jstohl@querrey.com

FUAD R. SULAYMAN, admitted to bar, 1999, Illinois. *Education:* Boston University (B.S.B.A., 1994); Chicago-Kent College of Law (J.D., 1999). ***PRACTICE AREAS:*** Litigation; Medical Malpractice. ***Email:*** fsulayman@querrey.com

MARIE J. TARASKA, admitted to bar, 1997, Illinois. *Education:* University of Illinois (B.A., with honors and highest distinction, 1994); DePaul University (J.D., 1997). ***PRACTICE AREAS:*** Litigation. ***Email:*** mtaraska@querrey.com

CYNTHIA D. TRAYNOR, admitted to bar, 1988, Illinois. *Education:* Ripon College (A.B., 1981); John Marshall Law School (J.D., 1988). ***PRACTICE AREAS:*** Litigation. ***Email:*** ctraynor@querrey.com

RICHARD J. TURIELLO, admitted to bar, 2001, Illinois. *Education:* Cazenovia College (B.P.S., 1997); Chicago-Kent College of Law (J.D., 2000). (Resident, Joliet Office). ***PRACTICE AREAS:*** Litigation. ***Email:*** rturiello@querrey.com

JOSEPH V. VITO, admitted to bar, 2004, Illinois. *Education:* University of Illinois (B.A., 2001); Chicago-Kent College of Law (J.D., 2004). ***PRACTICE AREAS:*** Litigation. ***Email:*** jvito@querrey.com

OF COUNSEL

THOMAS P. CARNEY, JR., admitted to bar, 1972, Illinois. *Education:* University of Notre Dame (B.A., 1967); Loyola University (J.D., 1972). Associate Editor, Loyola University Law Review, 1971-1972. ***PRACTICE AREAS:*** Litigation; Employment; Bankruptcy. ***Email:*** tcarney@querrey.com

DONALD C. GANCER, admitted to bar, 1957, Wisconsin; 1958, Illinois. *Education:* Marquette University (B.S., 1955; LL.B., 1957). Recent Decisions Editor, Marquette Law Review, 1956-1957. ***PRACTICE AREAS:*** Corporate; Commercial; Estate Planning; Real Estate.

NANCY M. HOFFMAN, admitted to bar, 1990, Illinois. *Education:* Kenyon College (B.A., 1985); Loyola University of Chicago (J.D., 1990). ***PRACTICE AREAS:*** Litigation. ***Email:*** nhoffman@querrey.com

ROBERT F. SHARP, admitted to bar, 1962, Illinois, U.S. Court of Appeals, Seventh Circuit, U.S. Supreme Court and U.S. Tax Court. *Education:* University of Illinois (B.S., 1958); DePaul University (J.D., 1962). ***PRACTICE AREAS:*** Litigation; Real Estate; Corporate. ***Email:*** rsharp@querrey.com

LAWRENCE S. SPEYER, admitted to bar, 1964, Illinois. *Education:* Roosevelt University (B.S.B.A., 1962); John Marshall Law School (J.D., 1964). ***PRACTICE AREAS:*** Litigation; Arbitration. ***Email:*** lspeyer@querrey.com

QUINLAN & CARROLL, LTD.

Established in 2001

30 NORTH LA SALLE STREET, SUITE 2900
CHICAGO, ILLINOIS 60602
Telephone: 312-263-0900
Telecopier: 312-263-5013
URL: http://www.qclaw.com

WILLIAM R. QUINLAN, born Chicago, Illinois; admitted to bar, 1964, Illinois, U.S. Court of Appeals, 7th Circuit, U.S. District Court, Northern District of Illinois, U.S. Court of Military Appeals, U.S. Court of Federal Claims and U.S. Supreme Court. *Education:* Loyola University (B.S.C., Accounting, 1961); Loyola University (J.D., cum laude, 1964); University of Virginia School of Law (LL.M., 1988). ***Email:*** wquinlan@qclaw.com

JAMES R. CARROLL, born Chicago, Illinois; admitted to bar, 1978, Illinois; 1979, U.S. District Court, Northern District of Illinois; 1982, U.S. Court of Appeals, 7th Circuit; 1987, U.S. Supreme Court; 1995, U.S. Court of Appeals, District of Columbia Circuit; 1997, U.S. District Court, Central District of Illinois. *Education:* North Park College (B.A., 1970); John Marshall Law School (J.D., 1978). ***Email:*** jcarroll@qclaw.com

THOMAS C. HYNES, born Chicago, Illinois, November 5, 1938; admitted to bar, 1962, Illinois. *Education:* Loyola University (B.S., 1959; J.D., cum laude, 1962). ***Email:*** thynes@qclaw.com

CHERYL I. NIRO, born Paso Robles, California, February 19, 1950; admitted to bar, 1981, Illinois. *Education:* University of Illinois (B.S., highest honors, 1972); Northern Illinois University (J.D., 1980). ***Email:*** cniro@qclaw.com

BRIAN J. ALESIA, born Minneapolis, Minnesota, October 22, 1970; admitted to bar, 1996, Illinois, U.S. District Court, Northern District of Illinois and U.S. Court of Appeals, Seventh Circuit. *Education:* University of Notre Dame (B.A., magna cum laude, 1993); Loyola University, Chicago (J.D., 1996). ***Email:*** balesia@qclaw.com

MICHAEL T. BEIRNE, born Morristown, New Jersey, February 4, 1966; admitted to bar, 1995, Illinois. *Education:* Boston College (B.A., 1991); Chicago-Kent College of Law (J.D., 1994). ***Email:*** mbeirne@qclaw.com

RICHARD C. BOLLOW, born Aurora, Illinois, February 25, 1945; admitted to bar, 1970, Illinois. *Education:* Brown University (A.B., 1967); University of Illinois (J.D., 1970). ***Email:*** rbollow@qclaw.com

NICHOLAS G. GRAPSAS, born Hammond, Indiana, December 6, 1961; admitted to bar, 1988, Illinois, U.S. District Court, Northern District of Illinois including Federal Trial Bar and U.S. Court of Appeals, 7th Circuit. *Education:* Loyola University of Chicago (B.A., 1984; J.D., 1988). ***Email:*** ngrapsas@qclaw.com

LISA M. HEGEDUS, born Hemet, California, September 8, 1970; admitted to bar, 1995, California; 1996, Illinois. *Education:* Loyola Marymount University (B.A., magna cum laude, 1992); Georgetown University (J.D., 1995). ***Email:*** lhegedus@qclaw.com

MATTHEW J. HYNES, born Evergreen Park, Illinois, March 31, 1971; admitted to bar, 1997, Illinois and U.S. District Court, Northern District of Illinois. *Education:* University of Notre Dame (B.A., 1993); Loyola University School of Law (J.D., 1996). ***Email:*** mhynes@qclaw.com

JAMES A. NIEWIARA, born Oak Park, Illinois; admitted to bar, 1993, Illinois and U.S. District Court, Northern District of Illinois, 1993. *Education:* University of Illinois (B.A., 1990); Harvard Law School (J.D., cum laude, 1993). ***Email:*** jniewiara@qclaw.com

MARTIN J. O'HARA, born Chicago, Illinois, November 14, 1968; admitted to bar, 1995, Illinois and U.S. District Court, Northern District of Illinois. *Education:* Illinois State University (B.A., 1990); John Marshall Law School (J.D., cum laude, 1995). ***Email:*** mohara@qclaw.com

WILLIAM J. QUINLAN, admitted to bar, 1995, Illinois. *Education:* University of Illinois (B.A., Political Science, 1992); Georgetown Law School (J.D., 1995). ***Email:*** wjquinlan@qclaw.com

JOHN H. SCHEID, JR., born Chicago, Illinois; admitted to bar, 1994, Illinois. *Education:* University of Illinois (B.A., 1990); John Marshall Law School (J.D., cum laude, 1994). ***Email:*** jscheid@qclaw.com

MICHAEL A. STEIGMANN, born Springfield, Illinois, June 24, 1969; admitted to bar, 1994, Illinois. *Education:* University of Illinois (B.A., magna cum laude, 1990); London School of Economics (M.Sc., 1991); Harvard School of Law (J.D., cum laude, 1994). ***Email:*** msteigma@qclaw.com

---

AMY E. BULLOCK, born Omaha, Nebraska, May 22, 1976; admitted to bar, 2003, Illinois and U.S. District Court, Northern District of Illinois. *Education:* Bradley University (B.S., 1998); University of Illinois (J.D., 2003). ***Email:*** abullock@qclaw.com

SHEILA A. LOOP, born St. Paul, Minnesota; admitted to bar, 2003, Illinois. *Education:* University of Minnesota (B.A., 1992); Loyola University (J.D., 2003). ***Email:*** sloop@qclaw.com

J. CHRISTOPHER MADDEN, born Evanston, Illinois, October 12, 1971; admitted to bar, 1997, Illinois. *Education:* Santa Clara University (B.A., 1993); Chicago-Kent College of Law (J.D., 1997). ***Email:*** cmadden@qclaw.com

JEANAH PARK, born Champaign, Illinois, April 12, 1976; admitted to bar, 2002, Illinois; U.S. District Court, Northern District of Illinois. *Education:* Northwestern University (B.A., 1998); University of Illinois (J.D., cum laude, 2002). ***Email:*** jpark@qclaw.com

JESSICA A. SOHL, born Waconia, Minnesota, August 2, 1977; admitted to bar, 2004, Illinois. *Education:* Gordon College (B.A., 1999); Loyola University School of Law, Chicago (J.D., 2004). ***Email:*** jsohl@qclaw.com

JOHN M. QUINN & ASSOCIATES, LTD.

CHICAGO, ILLINOIS

(See Bloomingdale)

Drivers License Suspension, Administrative Hearings, Driving While Intoxicated, Criminal Law, Traffic Violations, Criminal Defense, Misdemeanors.

RACHLIS DURHAM DUFF & ADLER

542 SOUTH DEARBORN STREET, SUITE 1310
CHICAGO, ILLINOIS 60605
Telephone: 312-733-3950
Fax: 312-733-3952
URL: http://www.rddlaw.net

Commercial Litigation, Corporate Litigation, Contract Litigation, Civil Appeals, Construction Litigation, Insurance Coverage, Securities, Employment, Consumer Fraud and Class Defense, Mass Torts, Accountants Liability.

PARTNERS

MICHAEL RACHLIS, born Chicago, Illinois, October 18, 1966; admitted to bar, 1990, Illinois and Wisconsin; 1996, U.S. District Court, Northern District of Illinois including Trial Bar; U.S. Court of Appeals, Seventh Circuit. *Education:* University of Illinois (B.A., 1987); University of Wisconsin (J.D., cum laude, 1990). Phi Beta Kappa. Member, Wisconsin International Law Journal, 1989-1990. *Member:* Chicago, Illinois State and American (Member, Litigation Section) Bar Associations; State Bar of Wisconsin. ***PRACTICE AREAS:*** Corporate Litigation; Contract Litigation; Civil Appeals. ***Email:*** mrachlis@rddlaw.net

EDWIN L. DURHAM, born Urbana, Illinois, September 6, 1957; admitted to bar, 1990, Illinois, U.S. District Court, Northern and Central Districts of Illinois and U.S. Court of Appeals, Seventh and Eighth Circuits. *Education:* University of Illinois (A.B., 1987; J.D., magna cum laude, 1990). Phi Beta Kappa. Harno Fellow. Recipient, Rickert's Award for Legal Writing and Academic Achievement. Editor-in-Chief, University of Illinois Law Review, 1989-1990. *Member:* Illinois State Bar Association. ***PRACTICE AREAS:*** Complex Commercial Litigation; Construction Litigation. ***Email:*** eldurham@rddlaw.net

KEVIN B. DUFF, born Chicago, Illinois, March 21, 1967; admitted to bar, 1992, Illinois, U.S. District Court, Northern District of Illinois, including Trial Bar, U.S. District Court, Northern District of Indiana, U.S. Court of Appeals, Sixth, Seventh and Eighth Circuits, U.S. Court of Appeals for the Federal Circuit and U.S. Supreme Court. *Education:* Georgetown University (A.B., 1989; J.D., 1992). Alpha Sigma Nu. Law Fellow. Managing Editor, Journal of Law and Policy in International Business, 1991-1992. Author/Presentor: "Class Acts: The Stage of Things to Come in Defending Class Actions," Price Waterhouse Coopers General Counsel Forum, Chicago, November 2003; "Putting Out and Preventing Fires: Prosecuting, Defending, and Anticipating Emergency Litigation" and "Preparation and Readiness for a TRO Motion," PriceWaterhouseCoopers General Counsel Forum, Chicago, June 2001; "Suing and Defending Fiduciaries," American Bar Association Real Estate and Probate Litigation Committee newsletter, Volume 2, Issue 1, (May 2002), at 8-18 (also presented at ABA Annual Meeting, August 2001). *Member:* Chicago, Seventh Circuit, Illinois State and American (Member, Litigation Section) Bar Associations. ***PRACTICE AREAS:*** Complex Litigation; Mass Torts; Accountants Liability. ***Email:*** kduff@rddlaw.net

MARION B. ADLER, born New York, N.Y., October 20, 1954; admitted to bar, 1982, Illinois and U.S. District Court, Northern District of Illinois including Trial Bar; U.S. District Court, Central District of Illinois; U.S. District Court, Northern District of Indiana; U.S. Court of Appeals, Fifth, Sixth, Seventh and Federal Circuits; U.S. Supreme Court. *Education:* Middlebury College (A.B., summa cum laude, 1976); Yale University (M.A., 1977); University of Chicago (J.D., with honors, 1982). Phi Beta Kappa. Order of the Coif. Member, University of Chicago Law Review, 1980-1981; Associate Editor, 1981-1982. Author: "Class Acts: The Stage of Things to Come in Defending Class Actions," Price Waterhouse Coopers General Counsel Forum, Chicago, November 2003; "Pursuing Insurance Coverage for Mold and 'Sick Building' Claims Under Tradition Liability Policies: Recent Developments in Applying the Pollution Exclusion," 12 Coverage No. 2 (March/April 2002) (also presented at ABA Section of Litigation Insurance Coverage Committee, 2002 midyear meeting); "Putting Out and Preventing Fires: Prosecuting, Defending, and Anticipating Emergency Litigation" (PriceWaterhouseCoopers General Counsel Forum, Chicago, June 2001); "Insurance Coverage 101 for Policyholders: The Basics of General Liability Policies," 11 Coverage No. 4, 22 (July/Aug. 2001) (also presented at ABA Section of Litigation Insurance Coverage Committee, 2001 midyear meeting); "Lessons Learned from the Bills (Clinton and Gates): When the CEO is Deposed" (PriceWaterhouseCoopers General Counsel Forum, Chicago, June 1999); "Legal Issues Involved in Long-Tail Insurance Disputes" (Mealey's Publications, Chicago, 1997); "An Overview of the Law of Privilege for Practitioners in Illinois" (Chi. Bar Ass'n 1997); "The Attorney-Client Privilege within the Corporation" (PriceWaterhouseCoopers General Counsel Forum, Chicago, December 1996); "Appellate Advocacy and Complex Insurance Coverage Disputes," in Trying Insurance Coverage Disputes (Law Journal Seminars-Press N.Y. June 1995). *Member:* Illinois State and American (Member, Litigation Section; Co-Chair, Practices and Procedures Subcommittee, Insurance Coverage Committee, 2000-2002) Bar Associations. ***PRACTICE AREAS:*** Commercial Litigation; Insurance Coverage. ***Email:*** madler@rddlaw.net

OF COUNSEL

ERIC S. NEWMAN, born Park Ridge, Illinois, June 30, 1966; admitted to bar, 1991, Illinois and U.S. District Court, Northern District of Illinois. *Education:* University of Michigan (B.B.A., with distinction, 1988); Northwestern University (J.D., 1991). ***PRACTICE AREAS:*** Corporate Law. ***Email:*** ericn1765@aol.com

KAY L. PICK, born Chicago, Illinois, June 24, 1944; admitted to bar, 1980, Illinois and U.S. District Court, Northern District of Illinois, including Trial Bar. *Education:* University of Rochester (B.A., with honors, 1966); DePaul University (J.D., 1980). Author: "Environmental Law," IICLE, Starting Points; "The Fundamentals of 11 Practice Areas," 1994, IICLE, 1997 Supplement.*Member:* Chicago, Illinois State and American (Member, Sections on: Litigation; Natural Resources; Energy and Environmental Law) Bar Associations. ***REPORTED CASES:*** Montgomery Ward v. The Home Insurance Co., 324 Ill. App.441, 753 N.E.2d 999 (1st Dist. 2001); Montgomery Ward v. Imperial Casualty & Indemnity Co., 81 Cal. App. 4th 356 (2000); People v. Dukes, 146 Ill. App. 3d 790, 497 N.E.2d 351 (1st Dist. 1986); United States v. Johns, 728 F.2d 953 (7th Cir. 1984). ***PRACTICE AREAS:*** Commercial Litigation (70%); Environmental Litigation (20%); Complex Litigation (10%). ***Email:*** kpick@rddlaw.net

---

RAKOCZY MOLINO MAZZOCHI SIWIK LLP

6 WEST HUBBARD STREET, SUITE 500
CHICAGO, ILLINOIS 60610
Telephone: 312-527-2157
Fax: 312-527-4205
URL: http://www.rmmslegal.com

Litigation, Intellectual Property, Antitrust and Complex Commercial. Patent and Regulatory Counseling, Licensing, Patent Prosecution.

PARTNERS

WILLIAM A. RAKOCZY, admitted to bar, 1995, Illinois; 2004, District of Columbia; U.S. Supreme Court; U.S. Court of Appeals, 3rd, 7th, District of Columbia and Federal Circuits; U.S. District Court for the District of Columbia; U.S. District Court, Northern District of Illinois; U.S. District Court, Western District of Wisconsin. *Education:* Wabash College (A.B., summa cum laude, 1992) Phi Beta Kappa; Vanderbilt University (J.D., 1995). Law Clerk to Hon. Wayne R. Andersen, U.S. District Court for the Northern District of Illinois, Eastern Division, 1995-1997. Associate, 1997-2001 and Partner, 2001-2004, Lord Bissell & Brook, LLP. *Member:* Chicago (Member, Judicial Evaluation Committee), Illinois State and American (Member, Sections on: Litigation; Intellectual Property) Bar Associations. ***REPORTED CASES:*** Warner-Lambert Co. v. Apotex Corp., 316 F.3d 1348; SmithKline Beecham Corp. v. Apotex Corp., 365 F.3d 1306; Knorr-Bremse Systeme Fuer Nutzfahrzeuge GmbH v. Dana Corp., 383 F. 3d 1337; Abbott Labs. v. TorPharm, Inc., 300 F.3d 1367; Adkins Energy, LLC v. Delta-T Corp., 347 Ill.App.3d 373; SmithKline Beecham Corp. v. Apotex Corp., 247 F.Supp.2d 1011; In re Gabapentin Patent Litig., 312 F.Supp.2d 653; Dietrich v. Trek Bicycle Corp., 297 F.Supp.2d 1122; SmithKline Beecham Corp. v. Apotex Corp., 193 F.R.D. 530; SmithKline Beecham Corp. v. Apotex Corp., 194 F.R.D. 624; In re Gabapentin Patent Litig., 214 F.R.D. 178; William Reber, LLC v. Samsung Elecs. Am., Inc., 220 F.R.D. 533. ***PRACTICE AREAS:*** Intellectual Property Litigation; Pharmaceutical Patents; Food and Drug Litigation; Antitrust; Complex Commercial Litigation.

PAUL J. MOLINO, admitted to bar, 1991, Illinois; U.S. Court of Appeals, 7th and Federal Circuits; U.S. District Court, Northern District of Illinois; U.S. District Court, Western District of Wisconsin; registered to practice before U.S. Patent and Trademark Office. *Education:* Drake University (B.S., 1987); DePaul University (J.D., 1991). Associate, 1994-2000 and Partner, 2000-2003, Lord Bissell & Brook, LLP. ***REPORTED CASES:*** SmithKline Beecham Corp. v. Apotex Corp., 365 F.3d 1306; Abbott Labs. v. Torpham, Inc., 309 F. Supp. 2d 1043; Glazo Group Ltd. v. Apotex, Inc., 272 F. Supp. 2d 772; In re Gabapentin Patent Litig., 214 F.R.D. 178; Asahi Glass Co. v. Pentech Pharms., Inc., 289 F. Supp. 2d 986; Abbott Labs. v. Torpham, Inc., 156 F. Supp. 2d 738. ***PRACTICE AREAS:*** Complex Commercial Litigation; Patent Litigation; Patents; Trade Secrets; Trademark Litigation.

DEANNE M. MAZZOCHI, admitted to bar, 1997, Illinois; U.S. Court of Appeals for the Federal Circuit; U.S. District Court, Northern District of Illinois; registered to practice before U.S. Patent and Trademark Office. *Education:* Boston University (B.A., Chemistry and Political Science, 1994); George Washington University (J.D., with honors, 1997). Named, "Defense Win of the Month," Trial Decision before Hon. Richard Posner, National Law Journal, April, 2003; Winner, GWU Giles S. Rich Moot Court Competition, 1996. Executive Managing Editor, American Intellectual Property Law Association Quarterly Journal, 1996-1997. *Member:* Chicago, Illinois State and American Bar Associations; American Intellectual Property Law Association. ***REPORTED CASES:*** SmithKline Beecham Corp. v. Apotex Corp., 365 F.3d 1306, 2004 U.S. App. LEXIS 8107; 70 U.S.P.Q. 2D (BNA) 1737; Abbott Labs. v. TorPham, Inc., 309 F. Supp. 2d 1043; In re Gabapentin Patent Litig., 214 F.R.D. 178; Tracy v. Jewel Food Stores, 62 U.S.P.Q. 2d (BNA) 1283, 2002 U.S. Dist. LEXIS 3806; 62 U.S.P.Q.2D (BNA) 1283. ***PRACTICE AREAS:*** Intellectual Property Litigation; Intellectual Property; Regulatory Law; Intellectual Property Licensing; Complex Commercial Litigation; Patent Litigation; Trademarks; Trade Secrets; Copyrights; Antitrust.

CHRISTINE J. SIWIK, admitted to bar, 1995, Illinois; U.S. Court of Appeals, 4th, District of Columbia and Federal Circuits; U.S. District Court, Northern District of Illinois. *Education:* Michigan State University (B.A., Social Science/Political Science, magna cum laude, 1992); Loyola University (J.D., magna cum laude, 1995). Recipient: Leadership & Service Award, Loyola University School of Law; Award for Outstanding Academic Achievement, Phi Alpha Delta; Outstanding Academic Senior Award, Michigan State University. Executive Editor, Loyola University Chicago Law Journal, 1994-1995. Former Partner, Winston & Strawn LLP. ***REPORTED CASES:*** aaiPharma Inc. v. Thompson, 296 F.3d 227; 3M v. Barr Labs., Inc., 289 F.3d 775; In re Tamoxifen Citrate Antitrust Litig., 222 F. Supp. 2d 326, 277 F.Supp. 2d 121; 3M v. Barr Labs., 139 F. Supp. 2d 1109; McCook Metals L.L.C. v. Alcoa, Inc., 192 F.R.D. 242; 277 F. Supp. 2d 121; TorPharm Inc. v. Shalala, 1997 U.S. Dist. LEXIS 21983. ***PRACTICE AREAS:*** Intellectual Property Litigation; Pharmaceutical Patents; Regulatory Law.

ASSOCIATES

AMY D. BRODY, admitted to bar, 2000, Illinois; 2002, District of Columbia; U.S. District Court, Northern District of Illinois. *Education:* University of Evansville (B.S., 1997); Indiana University (J.D., cum laude, 2000). Recipient, Scribe Award for Excellence in Legal Writing. Managing Editor, Global Legal Studies Law Journal, 1999-2000. Member: Law School Admissions Board; London (England) Law Consortium. Former Associate, Lord Bissell & Brook, LLP. *Member:* Chicago (Member, Litigation Section) and Illinois

(This Listing Continued)

State Bar Associations; District of Columbia Bar; Constitutional Rights Foundation. ***PRACTICE AREAS:*** Complex Commercial Litigation; Pharmaceutical Patents; Insurance Coverage; Reinsurance.

LARA MONROE-SAMPSON, admitted to bar, 2002, Illinois; U.S. District Court, Northern District of Illinois; U.S. Court of Appeals, Federal Circuit. *Education:* Northwestern University (B.S., Communications, 1993); George Washington University Law School (J.D., with honors, 2002). Member, Trial Court Board. Member, American Intellectual Property Law Association Quarterly Journal. Former Associate, Lord Bissell & Brook, LLP. *Member:* American Bar Association; American Intellectual Property Law Association; Defense Research Institute. ***PRACTICE AREAS:*** Patent Litigation; Regulatory Law.

TARA M. RAGHAVAN, admitted to bar, 2003, Illinois; registered to practice before U.S. Patent and Trademark Office. *Education:* University of Illinois (B.S., Chemistry and B.A., Economics, 2000; J.D., 2003). Notes Editor, Journal of Law, Technology & Policy, 2002-2003. Formerly with Dennison & Associates, Chicago. Member, Tyagaraja Utsavam, Indian Classical Music Organization. *Member:* American Intellectual Property Law Association; Illinois State Bar Association; Indian American Bar Association, Chicago. ***PRACTICE AREAS:*** Patent Litigation; Pharmaceutical Patents; Chemical Patents.

ALICE L. RIECHERS, admitted to bar, 2000, Wisconsin and Illinois; U.S. Court of Appeals, Federal Circuit; U.S. District Court, Northern District of Illinois. *Education:* University of Wisconsin-Eau Claire (B.A., Criminal Justice, summa cum laude, 1996); University of Wisconsin Law School (J.D., cum laude, 2000). Associate Editor, Wisconsin Law Review, 1999-2000. Former Associate, Winston & Strawn, LLP, Chicago. *Member:* Chicago, Illinois and American Bar Associations; State Bar of Wisconsin. ***PRACTICE AREAS:*** Complex Commercial Litigation; Pharmaceutical Patents.

RANDALL & KENIG LLP

NBC TOWER, SUITE 3160
455 NORTH CITYFRONT PLAZA DRIVE
CHICAGO, ILLINOIS 60611
Telephone: 312-822-0800
Fax: 312-822-0215

Commercial Real Estate, Commercial Law, Business Law, Banking Law, Construction Law, Zoning, Planning and Land Use, Real Estate.

BENJAMIN J. RANDALL, born Cleveland, Ohio, March 21, 1948; admitted to bar, 1972, Illinois. *Education:* The Ohio State University (B.A., 1969); Case Western Reserve University (J.D., 1972). Included: "Best Lawyers in America" and "The Leading Lawyers Network." Profiled and highly ranked by Chambers USA America's Leading Business Lawyers. Co-Author: "Landlord-Tenant Practice," Chapter 10 - Assignments and Subleases, Illinois Institute of Continuing Legal Education; "The Case for the Office Condominium," Real Estate Review, Vol. 13, No. 3. Lecturer, real estate law, Georgetown University Law Center Continuing Legal Education and Illinois Institute for Continuing Legal Education. *Member:* Chicago Bar Association (Member, Legal Opinions in Real Estate Transactions Sub-Committee); American College of Real Estate Lawyers; Commercial Real Estate Organization; Association of Industrial Real Estate Brokers. ***PRACTICE AREAS:*** Commercial Real Estate; Commercial Law; Business Law; Construction Law; Zoning, Planning and Land Use; Real Estate. ***Email:*** brandall@randall-law.com

SCOTT H. KENIG, born Chicago, Illinois, January 21, 1963; admitted to bar, 1988, Illinois; 1989, U.S. District Court, Northern District of Illinois. *Education:* Indiana University (B.A., 1985); Loyola University of Chicago School of Law (J.D., 1988). Editor, Loyola University's newspaper, "Blackacre". *Member:* Chicago, Illinois State and American Bar Associations. ***REPORTED CASES:*** Ortegel v. ITT Thorp Corporation, 210 Ill. App. 3d 669, 569 N.E. 2d 586 (2nd Dist. 1991); Michigan Avenue National Bank of Chicago v. Douglas A. Rogers, 1994 WL 390275 (N.D. Ill.); Boatmen's First National Bank of Kansas City v. David J. Wabick et al., 1996 WL 341451 (N.D. Ill.). ***PRACTICE AREAS:*** Commercial Real Estate; Commercial Law; Banking Law; Construction Law; Zoning, Planning and Land Use; Real Estate. ***Email:*** skenig@randall-law.com

---

WILLIAM H. RANSOM

415 NORTH LA SALLE STREET, SUITE 203
CHICAGO, ILLINOIS 60610
Telephone: 312-222-9120
Fax: 312-222-1656
Email: WRansom@aol.com
URL: http://www.williamhransom.com

Personal Injury, Automobile Accidents and Injuries, Wrongful Death, Collections, Workers' Compensation, Commercial Law, Business Law, Breach of Contract, Discrimination, Wrongful Termination, Family Law, Divorce, Adoption Law, General Practice, Appellate Practice, Criminal Practice, Driving While Intoxicated, Felonies, Traffic Violations, Homicide, Drug Crimes, Parole and Probation.

FIRM PROFILE: William H. Ransom is a solo practitioner in the Chicago area. He is an aggressive attorney with experience in many practice areas.

WILLIAM H. RANSOM, born St. Paul, Minnesota, June 12, 1960; admitted to bar, 1994, Illinois and U.S. District Court, Northern District of Illinois. *Education:* Loyola University (B.A., 1986); John Marshall Law School (J.D., 1994). Phi Delta Phi. Member, National Moot Court Team, 1993; Associate Justice, Moot Court Executive Board, 1993. Faculty, Truman College- City Colleges of Chicago. Arbitrator, Circuit Court of Cook County and the 19th Judicial Circuit. Exchequer of Stevens Inn, 1992. *Member:* Chicago and Illinois State Bar Associations.

RAPOPORT LAW OFFICES, P.C.

20 NORTH CLARK STREET, SUITE 3500
CHICAGO, ILLINOIS 60602
Telephone: 312-327-9880
1-800-545-6437
Fax: 312-327-9881
URL: http://www.rapoportlaw.com
Email: reception@rapoportlaw.com
URL: http://www.rapoportlaw.com

Plaintiffs' Personal Injury Litigation; Wrongful Death Litigation; Commercial Aviation Litigation; Medical Malpractice; General Aviation Litigation; Product Liability; Vehicular Accidents; Boating Accidents; Personal Watercraft Accidents; Construction Accidents; Premises Liability; Head and Spinal Injuries; Slip and Fall; Trucking Accidents; Drug and Medical Devices.

FIRM PROFILE: The attorneys at Rapoport Law Offices, P.C. represent individuals who have suffered serious personal injury and familes of those that suffered a wrongful death. Our practice concentrates on matters involving aviation accidents, medical malpractice, product liability, motor vehicle accidents, construction accidents, and premises liability. The skilled and experienced trial team at Rapoport Law Offices, P.C. has been providing providing personalized and exemplary legal counsel to clients involved in complex litigation matters since 1995.

The lawyers at Rapoport Law Offices, P.C. have extensive experience representing families of passengers and crew members killed in both commercial aviation and general aviation disasters. Mr. Rapoport has served a leadership role in the successful prosecution of many air crash cases including American Airlines flight 1420, United Airlines flight 232, EgyptAir flight 990, Swissair flight 111, American Eagle flight 3379 and USAir flight 1016.

DAVID E. RAPOPORT, born Chicago, Illinois, May 27, 1956; admitted to bar, 1981, Illinois; 1995, Wisconsin, U.S. Supreme Court, U.S. District Court, Eastern District of Wisconsin, U.S. District Court, Northern District of Illinois including Trial Bar, U.S. District Court, Central and Southern Districts of Illinois, U.S. Court of Appeals, Fourth, Seventh and Eleventh Circuits. *Education:* Northern Illinois University (B.S., Finance, 1978); Chicago-Kent College of Law (J.D., with highest honors, 1981); Lawyers Post Graduate Institute (One Year Post Graduate Training in Trial Advocacy, 1983); Graduate, Illinois Trial Lawyers College of Advocacy, 1984. Member Court Appointed Plaintiff's Steering Committees in litigation arising out of the crashes of EgyptAir Flight 990 near Nantucket Island on October 31, 1999, American Airlines Flight 1420 at Little Rock, Arkansas, on June 1, 1999, Swissair Flight 111 off the coast of Nova Scotia on September 2, 1998, American Eagle Flight 3379 near Raleigh, North Carolina on December 13, 1994 and USAir Flight 1016 at Charlotte, North Carolina on July 2, 1994. Co-Author, "Cockpit Image Recorders: A Picture is Worth a Thousand Words," Issues in Aviation Law and Policy, May 2005; "Punitive Damages After State Farm v. Campbell: The First Year," American Bar Association Aviation Litigation Section Meeting, N.Y, New York, 2004; "Attention All International Airlines and Flight Crews: Choosing Inaction Over Action No Longer Flies," Issues in Aviation Law and Policy, March 2004; "Will Boeing's Recent Move to Chicago Mean That More Commercial Airliner Crash Cases Will be Litigated There?" Issues in Aviation Law and Policy, April, 2003; "A 73-Year Odyssey: The Time Has Come for a New International Air Liability System," Issues in Aviation Law and Policy, October, 2002; "The Effect of Tort Litigation on the Airline Industry," DePaul Business Law Journal, Spring, 2002; "Trial and Evidentiary Considerations," Chapter in "Illinois Wrongful Death and Survival Actions," (IICLE), 1993, 1996, 2000, 2003; Trial techniques featured in: "The Lost Art: An Advocate's Guide to Effective Closing Argument," ch.2, p. 41 (1999); "Example of Direct Examination," published 7 Handling Accident Cases 154 (Cum. Supp. Jan., 1989); *Closing Arguments,* (West Cum. Supp. 1997). State Coordinator for National Board of Trial Advocacy; IIT Chicago Kent Law School Alumni Association Board of Directors; Guest Lecturer, Rights of Injured Workers, 1984-2005, Illinois Institute of Technology-Chicago Kent College of Law; Presenter, Association of Trial Lawyers of America and Illinois Institute for Continuing Legal Education; IIT Chicago Kent College of Law, Law Review 1980-1981; Legal Writing Instructor, 1981. *Member:* Chicago (Member: Aviation Litigation Section; Tort Litigation Committee), Illinois State and American Bar Associations; Illinois Trial Lawyers Association (Contributing Member); The Association of Trial Lawyers of America (Sustaining Member); Trial Lawyers for Public Justice; Lawyer-Pilot Bar Association; The Roscoe Pound Foundation. ***REPORTED CASES:*** Kemp v. Western Oilfields Supply Co., 2005 U.S. Dist. LEXIS 8670 (N.D. Ill., March 24, 2005); In re Air Crash Near Nantucket Island, Massachusetts on October 31, 1999, 307 F. Supp. 2d 465 (E.D.N.Y. 2004); Reliance Nat'l Ins. Co. v. Great Lakes Aviation, Ltd., 340 F. Supp. 2d 936 (C.D. Ill. 2004); Walter v. Bruhn, et al., 2002 U.S. App. Lexis 13168 (7th Cir. 2002); In Re Aircraft Accident at Little Rock, Arkansas on June 1, 1999, 231 F. Supp. 2d 852 (E.D. Ark. 2002); Rivas v. Doering, 2002 U.S. Dist. Lexis 9535 (W.D. Ky. 2002); Verbance v. Altman, 324 Ill. App. 3d 494, 754 N.E. 2d 856 (2d Dist. 2001); In Re Aircraft Accident at Little Rock, Arkansas on June 1, 1999, 118 F. Supp. 2d 916 (E.D. Ark. 2000); In Re Air Crash at Little Rock on June 1, 1999, 109 F. Supp. 2d 1022 (E.D. Ark. 2000); Miller v. Empress Casino Joliet Corp., 1999 U.S. Dist. Lexis 3531 (N.D. Ill. 1999); Reliance Nat'l Ins. Co. v. Great Lakes Aviation, Ltd., 12 F.Supp.2d 854 (C.D. Ill. 1998) (No. 97-3289); Josefson v. AMR Corp., No. 1:95CV00493, 1998 Lexis 12525 (M.D.N.C. April 23, 1998); In re Air Crash Near Morrisville, North Carolina on December 13, 1994, No. 1:95MD1084, 1997 Lexis 21827 (M.D.N.C. December 16, 1997); In re Air Crash at Charlotte, North Carolina on July 2, 1994, 982 F.Supp. 1092 (D.S.C. 1997) (MDL Docket No. 1041); In re Air Crash at Charlotte, North Carolina on July 2, 1994, 982 F.Supp. 1086 (D.S.C. 1997) (MDL Docket No. 1041); Ex parte Knight Ridder, Inc., 982 F.Supp. 1080 (D.S.C. 1997) (MDL Docket No. 3:95-1041-17); In re Air Crash at Charlotte, North Carolina on July 2, 1994, 982 F.Supp. 1060 (D.S.C. 1997) (MDL Docket No. 1041); In re Air Crash at Charlotte, North Carolina on July 2, 1994, 982 F.Supp. 1052 (D.S.C. 1997) (MDL Docket No. 1041); In Re Air Crash Near Morrisville, North Carolina on December 13, 1994, 1997 U.S. Dist. LEXIS 3809 (M.D.N.C. February 6, 1997); Lobocki v. Peabody Galion Corp., No. 95 C 5830, 1996 Lexis 6651 (N.D. Ill. May 14, 1996); Cheng v. United Air Lines, Inc., No. 93 C 149, 1995 Lexis 6943 (N.D. Ill. May 17, 1995); Cheng v. United Air Lines, Inc., No. 93 C 149, 1995 Lexis 1140 (N.D. Ill. January 25, 1995); Jackson v. Back of Yards Neighborhood Council, 240 Ill. App. 3d 128, 608

(This Listing Continued)

RAPOPORT LAW OFFICES, P.C., Chicago—Continued

N.E.2d 124, 181 Ill. Dec. 51 (1 Dist., Dec. 9, 1992) (No.1-90-1744); St. Louis v. Rockwell Graphic Systems, Inc., 153 Ill. 2d 1, 605 N.E.2d 555, 178 Ill. Dec. 761 (Oct. 22, 1992) (No.72779); In re Air Crash Disaster at Sioux City, Iowa, on July 19, 1989, 781 F.Supp. 1307 (N.D. Ill., Dec. 26, 1991) (No. MDL-817); Maki v. Keller Industries, Inc., 761 F. Supp. 66 (N.D. Ill., Mar 04, 1991) (No.91 C 1237); McKee v. Brady, 1990 WL 304242 (N.D. Ill., May 14, 1990) (No.88 C 20035); Houston vs. Quincy Post 5129, Veterans of Foreign Wars, 188 Ill. App. 3d 732, 544 N.E.2d 425, 135 Ill. Dec. 929 (4th Dist., Sept. 14, 1989) (No.4-89-0177); Courtney v. Allied Filter Engineering, Inc., 181 Ill. App. 3d 222, 536 N.E.2d 952, 129 Ill. Dec. 902 (1 Dist., Mar 27, 1989) (No.9 87-3622); Gonzalez v. Prestress Engineering Corp., 115 Ill. 2d 1, 503 N.E.2d 308, 104 Ill. Dec. 751, 55 USLW 2350, 124 L.R.R.M. (BNA) 2252, 105 Lab.Cas. P. 55,627, 1 IER Cases 1242 (Dec. 19, 1986) (No. 62644, 62645); Simpson v. Industrial Commission, 91 Ill. 2d 452, 440 N.E.2d 94 (1982). ***PRACTICE AREAS:*** Plaintiffs Personal Injury; Wrongful Death Litigation; Catastrophic Injury; Airplane Crash Litigation; Helicopter Crash Litigation; Medical Malpractice; Truck Accidents; Automobile Accidents and Injuries; Vehicle Accidents and Injuries; Construction Accidents; Product Liability; Premises Liability; Boating Accidents; Personal Injury Mediation; Personal Injury Arbitration; Personal Injury Appeals; Federal Civil Practice; Admiralty and Maritime Law; Jones Act; Railroad Accidents and Injuries; Federal Employers Liability Act (FELA). ***Email:*** drapoport@rapoportlaw.com

JON C. PAPIN, born St. Louis, Missouri, July 21, 1956; admitted to bar, 1984, Utah; 1989, Illinois. *Education:* Brigham Young University (B.S., 1980); University of Kentucky (J.D., 1983). *Member:* Chicago, Illinois State and American Bar Associations; Utah State Bar; Illinois Trial Lawyers Association. ***PRACTICE AREAS:*** Plaintiffs Personal Injury; Wrongful Death; Medical Malpractice; Catastrophic Injury; Birth Trauma; Obstetric Malpractice; Nursing Malpractice; Orthopedic Malpractice; Pediatric Malpractice; Physicians Professional Liability; Surgeons Liability; Products Liability; Automobile Accidents and Injuries; Automobile Negligence; Motor Vehicle Accidents and Injuries; Personal Injury Mediation; Personal Injury Arbitration. ***Email:*** jpapin@rapoportlaw.com

PAUL DAVID RICHTER, born Champaign, Illinois, November 21, 1969; admitted to bar, 1996, Illinois and U.S. District Court, Northern, Central and Southern Districts of Illinois. *Education:* University of Illinois (B.A., 1992); DePaul University (J.D., 1996). Co-Author, "Cockpit Image Recorders: A Picture is Worth a Thousand Words," Issues in Aviation Law and Policy, May 2005; "Punitive Damages After State Farm v. Campbell: The First Year," American Bar Association Aviation Litigation Section Meeting, N.Y, New York, 2004; "Attention All International Airlines and Flight Crews: Choosing Inaction Over Action No Longer Flies," Issues in Aviation Law and Policy, March 2004; "Will Boeing's Recent Move to Chicago Mean That More Commercial Airliner Crash Cases Will be Litigated There?" Issues in Aviation Law and Policy, April, 2003; "A 73-Year Odyssey: The Time Has Come for a New International Air Liability System," Issues in Aviation Law and Policy, October, 2002; Phi Alpha Delta. Extern, Federal Aviation Administration. *Member:* Chicago, Illinois State and American Bar Associations; Illinois Trial Lawyers Association; Lawyer-Pilot Bar Association; The Association of Trial Lawyers of America. ***REPORTED CASES:*** Reliance Nat'l Ins. Co. v. Great Lakes Aviation, Ltd., 340 F. Supp. 2d 936 (C.D. Ill. 2004); Rivas v. Doering, 2002 U.S. Dist. LEXIS 9535 (W.D.Ky. 2002); In Re Aircraft Accident at Little Rock, Arkansas on June 1, 1999, 231 F. Supp.2d 852 (E.D. Ark. 2002); In Re Aircraft Accident at Little Rock, Arkansas on June 1, 1999, 118 F. Supp. 2d 916 (E.D. Ark. 2000); In re Air Crash at Little Rock on June 1, 1999, 109 F. Supp.2d1022 (E.D. Ark. 2000); Miller v. Empress Casino Joliet Corp., 1999 U.S. Lexis 3531 (N.D. Ill. 1999); Reliance Nat'l Ins. Co. v. Great Lakes Aviation, Ltd., 12 F.Supp.2d 854 (C.D. Ill. 1998) (No. 97-3289); Josefson v. AMR Corp., No. 1:95CV00493, 1998 Lexis 12525 (M.D. N.C. April 23, 1998). ***PRACTICE AREAS:*** Plaintiffs Personal Injury; Wrongful Death Litigation; Catastrophic Injury; Airplane Crash Litigation; Helicopter Crash Litigation; Construction Accidents; Medical Malpractice; Product Liability; Truck Accidents; Premises Liability; Automobile Accidents and Injuries; Boating Accidents; Personal Injury Mediation; Personal Injury Arbitration; Personal Injury Appeals. ***Email:*** prichter@rapoportlaw.com

STEVEN M. SANDLER, born Chicago, Illinois, June 7, 1953; admitted to bar, 1978, Illinois and U.S. District Court, Northern District of Illinois; 1984, Federal Trial Bar. *Education:* University of Illinois (B.A, 1974); Chicago-Kent College of Law (J.D. with honors, 1978); National Institute of Trial Advocacy (Post Graduate Training, 1980). *Member:* Chicago (Chairperson, Aviation Law Committee), Illinois State and American Bar Associations; Illinois Trial Lawyers Association; American Trial Lawyers Association; Lawyer-Pilot Bar Association; National Transportation Safety Board Bar Association. ***REPORTED CASES:*** International Amphitheatre Company v. Vanguard Underwriters Insurance Company, 177 Ill. App. 3d 555; 532 N.E.2d 493; 1988 Ill. App. LEXIS 1771; 126 Ill. Dec. 808 (1988), The People of the State of Illinois v. Milton C. Jacobson, 119 Ill. App. 3d 103; 456 N.E.2d 218; 1983 Ill. App. LEXIS 2443; 74 Ill. Dec. 716 (1983). ***PRACTICE AREAS:*** Plaintiffs Personal Injury; Wrongful Death; Commercial Aviation Litigation; Aviation Litigation; Catastrophic Injury; Medical Malpractice; Products Liability; Automobile Accidents and Injuries; Motor Vehicle Accidents and Injuries; Commercial Vehicle Liability; Construction Accidents; Premises Liability; Personal Injury Mediation; Personal Injury Arbitration; Personal Injury Bench Trials; Personal Injury Appeals. ***Email:*** ssandler@rapoportlaw.com

JOSHUA L. WEISBERG, born Danbury, Connecticut, 1980; (admission pending). *Education:* University of Wisconsin (B.A., with distinction, 2002); University of Illinois (J.D., 2005). Phi Eta Sigma. Harno Scholar. High Honors: Legal Research and Writing; Introduction to Advocacy. Recipient, Rickert Award for Excellence in Oral Advocacy, 2005. Regional Champion, and National Finalist, National Moot Court Competition, 2004-2005. Best Overall and Best Brief, 2004 and Editor, 2005, Frederick Green Moot Court Competition. Teaching Assistant, Introduction to Advocacy, 2004. *Member:* American Bar Association; The Association of Trial Lawyers of America. ***PRACTICE AREAS:*** Plaintiffs Personal Injury; Wrongful Death.

OF COUNSEL

IRA J. FURMAN, born New York, N.Y., November 10, 1943; admitted to bar, 1987, New York; 1988, District of Columbia and U.S. District Court, Eastern and Southern Districts of New York; 1991, U.S. Supreme Court (Not admitted in Illinois). *Education:* Hunter College of the City University of New York (B.A., 1965); Catholic University of America (J.D., 1986). Recipient, Miller Cup, Moot Court Competition. Best-Written Legal Brief. Recipient, New Jersey Press Association Award, 1969. Deputy Director, Public Affairs, 1980-1988, National Transportation Safety Board (principal spokesman for the NTSB on scene for the investigation of major transportation accidents such as the Air Florida crash into the Potomac; the Delta Airlines windshear accident in Dallas; a fatal crash at Boston's Logan Airport; and the mid-air DC-9 collision over a Los Angeles suburb). Represented the NTSB in connection with its assistance to NASA during the investigation of the Challenger Space Shuttle disaster. Has testified as an expert on the shortcomings in Federal Aviation Administration management of aviation safety before the U.S. Senate Aviation Subcommittee. Licensed Private Investigator, New York, 1989. Reporter and Editor: *The Record,* Hackensack, New Jersey; *The Morning Call,* Paterson, New Jersey. Director of Communications, Consumer Union, Nonprofit Publisher of *Consumer Reports* Magazine. Public Information Officer and Deputy Director, Federal Trade Commission, Washington, D.C. Director of Communications, Consumers Union/Consumer Reports Magazine. Worked on scene as a reporter from Lockerbie, Scotland, scene of the tragic Pan Am explosion, from the Long Island site of the crash of the Avianca aircraft that ran out of fuel on its way to JFK International, at the Sioux City, Iowa DC-10 crash site and at a US Air collision in Los Angeles at New York's LaGuardia Airport. Special consultant for CBS News in connection with the mid-air fuel tank explosion of TWA Flight 800. Assisted in the SwissAir, Egyptair and American Airlines Little Rock lawsuits.*Member:* Nassau County (Member, Aviation Law Committee) and New York State Bar Associations; The District of Columbia Bar. ***PRACTICE AREAS:*** Aviation Litigation. ***Email:*** furman@furmanlaw.com

(This Listing Continued)

REARDON GOLINKIN & REED

Established in 1996

208 SOUTH LA SALLE STREET, SUITE 1290
CHICAGO, ILLINOIS 60604-1102
Telephone: 312-855-3700
Fax: 312-855-1089
Email: info@rgrlaw.com
URL: http://www.rgrlaw.com

Insurance Coverage, Litigation, Directors and Officers Liability, Professional Liability, Labor and Employment, Reinsurance, Alternative Dispute Resolution.

KAREN A. REARDON, born Philadelphia, Pennsylvania, February 20, 1959; admitted to bar, 1986, Illinois and U.S. District Court, Northern District of Illinois; 2000, U.S. District Court, Western District of Michigan; 2001, U.S. Court of Appeals, Third Circuit and U.S. District Court, Southern District of Indiana. *Education:* University of Pennsylvania (B.A., 1981); Franklin College, Lugano, Switzerland; University of Michigan (M.A., 1983); Vanderbilt University (J.D., 1986). Recipient: Chicago Bar Association Foundation "Lend-A-Hand" Award for founding "HighSight" inner-city mentoring program, 1995; Distinguished Public Interest Law Initiative (PILI) Alumni Award, 1994. Author: "Not All Settlements of Claims Are Covered 'Losses' Under D&O or E&O Policies," Mealey's Emerging Insurance Disputes, May 20, 2003; "Disqualifying an Opposing Party - Arbitrator Before the Arbitration," Mealey's Litigation Reports - Reinsurance, January 11, 2001; "A Critical Examination of Plaintiffs' Experts' Damage Analysis: An Important Defensive Tactic After Daubert and Kumho," Andrews Publications, December 1999 and January 2000; "When The Merits Don't Matter: Accounting For The Influence of Insurance on Settlement Dynamics In Securities Class Action Litigation," Andrews Corporate Directors and Officers Litigation Reporter, December 1998, August and September 1999; "A Hypothetical - Can A Professional Recover Under An Errors and Omissions Policy For Lost Business Resulting From An Employee's Negligence?", Mealey's Emerging Insurance Disputes, August 6, 1998; "If You Paid For Legal Services Recently, Chances Are You Paid Too Much: Hourly Billing and the 'Reasonable' Attorney Fee Standard," CPCU Journal, September 1995; reprinted in Insurance Law Review, 1996 Edition, Vol. 7. Speaker: "Under Fire: The D&O Criminal Defendant," at the PLUS International Conference, San Diego, 2004; "Ensuring Protection For D&O Coverage In Corporate Bankruptcies" at the Institute for International Research Seminar on D&O Liability in New York, September 2003; Is the Valuation of Damages in Securities Litigation Against Directors and Officers Junk Science? PLUS International Conference, New York, 1999; Valuing Damages In Securities Class Action Litigation, PLUS International Conference, Palm Springs, 1998; Assessing Damages in Employment Practices Claims Against Directors and Officers, PLUS, 1998. Lecturer: Law and Sociology, 1982-1983, University of Michigan; "Emerging Issues In Handling Professional Liability Claims" at the Professional Liability Underwriting Society's International Conference in Philadelphia, November 2003. *Member:* Professional Liability Underwriting Society (PLUS). ***PRACTICE AREAS:*** Insurance Coverage; Directors and Officers Liability; Professional Liability; Employment Discrimination; Reinsurance; Non-Profit and Charitable Organizations. ***Email:*** kreardon@rgrlaw.com

SCOTT G. GOLINKIN, born Chicago, Illinois, October 1, 1952; admitted to bar, 1984, Illinois and U.S. District Court, Northern District of Illinois; 1991, U.S. District Court, District of Arizona; 1993, U.S. District Court, Northern District of Illinois Trial Bar; 2001, U.S. District Court, Southern District of Indiana; 2002, U.S. Court of Appeals, Seventh Circuit; 2005, U.S. District Court, Eastern District of Wisconsin. *Education:* Northwestern University (B.M.E., 1974; M.M., 1975); DePaul University (J.D., cum laude, 1984). Editorial Board, DePaul Law Review. Recipient, Distinguished Public Interest Law Initiative (PILI) Alumni Award, 1997. Author: " A Hypothetical - Can A Professional Recover Under An Errors and Omissions Policy For Lost Business Resulting From An Employee's Negligence?", Mealey's Emerging Insurance Disputes, August 6, 1998; "If You Paid For Legal Services Recently, Chances Are You Paid Too Much: Hourly Billing and the 'Reasonable' Attorney Fee Standard," CPCU Journal, 1995; reprinted in Insurance Law Review, 1996 Edition, Vol. 7. Lecturer: The "Etc.": Exploring the New Contours and Dimensions of Miscellaneous Professional Liability Coverage, PLUS International Conference, New York, 1999; Damages In Employment Cases, PLUS Midwest Chapter Directors and Officers Insurance Seminar, May, 1998; Attorney Billing Practices, Central Illinois Chapter of Institute of Internal Auditors, April, 1996. Past President, Friends of Public Interest Law Initiative, 1993-1995. *Member:* Professional Liability Underwriting Society

(This Listing Continued)

(PLUS). **PRACTICE AREAS:** Insurance Coverage; Employment Discrimination; Professional Liability Insurance Coverage; Directors and Officers Liability; Alternative Dispute Resolution. **Email:** sgolinkin@rgrlaw.com

SCOTT O. REED, born Peoria, Illinois, September 24, 1957; admitted to bar, 1980, Illinois; 1988, U.S. District Court, Northern District of Illinois; 1989, U.S. Court of Appeals, Seventh Circuit; 1994, Northern District of Illinois Trial Bar; 2000, U.S. District Court, Western District of Michigan; 2001, U.S. District Court, Southern District of Indiana and U.S. Court of Appeals, Third Circuit; 2005, U.S. District Court, Eastern District of Wisconsin. *Education:* University of Illinois (B.A., 1976; J.D., 1980); University College of North Wales, Bangor Wales. Law Clerk, Hon. Thomas M. Welch, Illinois Appellate Court. Author: "Liability Insurance Coverage for Fair Debt Collection Practices Act Claims," Mealey's Emerging Insurance Disputes, December 14, 2004; "Not All Settlements of Claims Are Covered 'Losses' Under D&O or E&O Policies," Mealey's Emerging Insurance Disputes, May 20, 2003; "Disqualifying an Opposing Party - Arbitrator Before the Arbitration," Mealey's Litigation Reports - Reinsurance, January 11, 2001; "A Critical Examination of Plaintiffs' Experts' Damage Analysis: An Important Defensive Tactic After Daubert and Kumho," Andrews Publications, December 1999 and January 2000; "Disqualifying an Expert Witness," Trial, June 1997; "Insurance Company Insolvency the U.S. Perspective," 40 Insolvency Bulletin, October 1996; "The Impact of Derivative Securities Trading on Liability Insurers," International Insurance Law Review, May 1995; "Liability Insurance Coverage for the Tort of Conversion," Defense Counsel Journal, January 1995; "The Liability of Attorneys for Environmental Exposures," For the Defense, April 1994; "Actions Against Foreign Reinsurers in U.S. Courts," International Insurance Law Review, February 1994; "Developing Theories of Liability Against Reinsurers and Discovery Issues Affecting Reinsurers," Journal of Reinsurance, Summer 1994; "Discovery of Reserve and Reinsurance Information," 40 Federation of Insurance and Corporate Counsel Quarterly 372, Summer 1990 (Updated, Winter 1994); "Illinois Civil Voir Dire Outline," 78 Illinois Bar Journal 194, April 1990; "Discovery of Computerized Litigation Support Systems," 77 Illinois Bar Journal 306, February 1989 (First Place Article, Lincoln Legal Writing Contest); "Salvage and Subrogation," in Financial Institution Bonds (ABA, Tort and Insurance Practice Section), 1989; "Eavesdropping Regulation in Illinois," 21 John Marshall Law Review 251, Winter 1988; "Third Party Liability to the Surety," ABA Annual Meeting, Tort and Insurance Practice Section, August 9, 1988; "Market Share Liability," 75 Illinois Bar Journal 314, February 1987 (First Place Article, Lincoln Legal Writing Contest); "The Protected Class Under the Structural Work Act," 74 Illinois Bar Journal 186, December, 1985. *Member:* Professional Liability Underwriting Society (PLUS). **PRACTICE AREAS:** Insurance Coverage; Reinsurance; Directors and Officers Liability; Civil Appeals; Employment Discrimination. **Email:** sreed@rgrlaw.com

ASSOCIATES

KEITH W. MANDELL, born Chicago, Illinois, January 20, 1972; admitted to bar, 1999, Illinois; 2001, U.S. District Court, Northern District of Illinois and Southern District of Indiana. *Education:* Northwestern University (B.A., 1994); George Washington University (J.D., with honors, 1999). Author: "Liability Insurance Coverage for Fair Debt Collection Practices Act Claims," Mealey's Emerging Insurance Disputes, December 14, 2004. *Member:* American Bar Association. **PRACTICE AREAS:** Insurance Law; Corporate Law; Employment Law; Non-Profit Incorporation. **Email:** kmandell@rgrlaw.com

ERIC J. MARLER, born Des Moines, Iowa, June 29, 1976; admitted to bar, 2002, Illinois; 2003, U.S. District Court, Northern District of Illinois. *Education:* University of Iowa (B.S., 1998); University of Iowa College of Law (J.D., with distinction, 2001). Speaker: "Under Fire: The D&O Criminal Defendant," at the PLUS International Conference, San Diego, 2004. *Member:* Chicago and American Bar Associations. **PRACTICE AREAS:** Insurance Coverage; Directors and Officers Liability; Employment Law. **Email:** emarler@rgrlaw.com

NATALIA A. KOLASA, born Gdansk, Poland, April 6, 1979; admitted to bar, 2004, Illinois. *Education:* Truman State University (B.A., 2001); Cornell University Law School (J.D., 2004). *Member:* Chicago, Illinois State and American Bar Associations. **PRACTICE AREAS:** Insurance. **Email:** nkolasa@rgrlaw.com

OF COUNSEL

DANIEL V. MARSALLI, born Kankakee, Illinois, February 9, 1961; admitted to bar, 1987, Illinois; 2005, U.S. District Court, Eastern District of Wisconsin. *Education:* St. Louis University (B.A., 1983); University of Illinois (J.D., 1987). *Member:* Chicago Bar Association. **PRACTICE AREAS:** Insurance Coverage; Litigation; Appeals. **Email:** dmarsalli@rgrlaw.com

LAUREL BLACK RECTOR

53 W. JACKSON, SUITE 1118
CHICAGO, ILLINOIS 60604
Telephone: 312-322-7900
Fax: 312-922-8027
Email: laurelrector@lawyer.com
URL: http://www.laurelblackrector.com

Family Law, Divorce, Child Custody, Child Support, Visitation Rights, Domestic Violence, Spousal Support.

LAUREL BLACK RECTOR, born Chicago, Illinois, October 11, 1953; admitted to bar, 1978, Illinois; 1980, U.S. District Court, Northern District of Illinois; 1990, Missouri. *Education:* University of Rochester (B.A., with honors, 1975); Washington University School of Law (J.D., 1978). Assistant Editor: Developing Labor Law Institute Proceedings, 1977; Proceedings of Labor Law Section, American Bar Association, 1977. Recipient: Volunteer of the Year, Pro Bono Advocates, 1998; Distinguished Services Award, Chicago Volunteer Legal Services, 1998. Presenter, American Association of Public Welfare Attorneys National Training and Continuing Education Conference: Federal Court Sanctions Other Than Rule 11, Minneapolis, Minnesota, October 1988; The Basics of § 1983 - Review of the Fundamental Issues in Suits Brought Under § 1983, Charleston, South Carolina, November 1989. Staff Attorney, Illinois Department of Public Aid, 1978-1979. Illinois Assistant Attorney General, General Law Division, Chicago, Illinois, 1980-1985. Deputy Chief, Welfare Litigation Division, Illinois Attorney General's Office, 1985-1989. Staff Attorney, Legal Advocacy Services, Illinois Guardianship and Advocacy Commission, Fairview Heights, Illinois, 1990-1991. Assistant Prosecuting Attorney, St. Louis County, Missouri, 1991-1995. Assistant State's Attorney, Cook County, Illinois, 1995-1996. *Member:* The Missouri Bar; National Association of Women Business Owners; Women In Need Growing Stronger (Board Member). **PRACTICE AREAS:** Family Law; Divorce; Child Custody; Child Support; Visitation Rights; Domestic Violence; Spousal Support.

(This Listing Continued)

LAW OFFICES OF REED, CENTRACCHIO & ZAC, LLC

75 EAST WACKER DRIVE
4TH FLOOR
CHICAGO, ILLINOIS 60601
Telephone: 312-551-1552
Fax: 312-551-1559
Email: bvreed@bryanvreed.net
URL: http://www.rczlaw.com

Contract Litigation, Commercial Litigation, Creditor Rights, Debtor Rights, Divorce, Child Support, Child Custody, Visitation Rights, Personal Injury, International Advisement.

FIRM PROFILE: Law Offices of Reed, Centracchio & Zac, LLC was established in 1998. The Law Firm has its practice mainly in Chicago but also has an international clientele. The ability to speak foreign languages is an asset for our clients.

BRYAN V. REED, born Takoma Park, Maryland, August 25, 1967; admitted to bar, 1992, Illinois and U.S. District Court, Northern District of Illinois; 1997, U.S. Court of Appeals, Seventh Circuit. *Education:* University of Louisville (B.S., 1989); Northern Kentucky University, Salmon P. Chase College of Law (J.D., 1992). *Member:* Chicago, Illinois State and American Bar Associations. **LANGUAGES:** French. **PRACTICE AREAS:** Contract Litigation; Commercial Litigation; Collections; Family Law; International Advisement.

NICOLE CENTRACCHIO, born Chicago, Illinois; admitted to bar, 2000, Illinois; 2003, Massachusetts. *Education:* Lake Forest College (B.S., Philosophy, 1995); John Marshall Law School (J.D., 2000). *Member:* Chicago and Illinois State Bar Associations. **PRACTICE AREAS:** Family Law; Real Estate; Probate. **Email:** ncentracchio@rczlaw.com

ANTHONY ZAC, born Chicago, Illinois, 1970; admitted to bar, 1998, Illinois; 1999, Indiana; 2003, California. *Education:* Loyola University (B.A., 1992); DePaul University (J.D., 1998). Moot Court. *Member:* Illinois State and Indiana State Bar Associations; State Bar of California. **PRACTICE AREAS:** Real Estate; Commercial Litigation; Probate. **Email:** azac@rczlaw.com

Languages: French, Spanish, Arabic and Polish.

REIBMAN, HOFFMAN, BAUM, HIRSCH & O'TOOLE

Established in 1958

20 NORTH CLARK STREET, SUITE 1700
CHICAGO, ILLINOIS 60602
Telephone: 312-372-6367
Fax: 312-372-0531
Email: mailrhb@aol.com
URL: http://www.rhblawfirm.com

Construction Law, Construction Accidents and Defects, Legal Malpractice, Medical Malpractice, Personal Injury, Airplane Crash Litigation, Automobile Accidents, Truck Accidents, Dog Bites, Railroad Accidents, Sexual Abuse, Slip and Fall, Wrongful Death, Products Liability, Drug and Medical Device Litigation, Toxic Torts, Workers Compensation.

FIRM PROFILE: Established in 1958, our firm has always represented individuals who have been the victim of an accident. Throughout the years we have successfully handled matters for members of various unions, including the service and airline industries as well as the general public. We take pride in the fact that when you hire us, a member of our firm will handle the case from the claim through trial, if necessary. In addition, our firm has staff available to meet the language needs of our Spanish, Polish and Chinese clientele.

BURTON L. HOFFMAN, born 1932; admitted to bar, 1955 Illinois. *Education:* DePaul University (LL.B., J.D., 1954). Assistant States Attorney, Cook County, 1955-1959. Member, American Arbitration Association. *Member:* Chicago and Illinois Bar Associations; Illinois Trial Lawyers Association; Association of Trial Lawyers of America.

DAVID M. BAUM, born 1954; admitted to bar, 1979, Illinois and U.S. District Court, Northern District of Illinois. *Education:* Beloit College (B.A., 1975); Chicago-Kent College of Law (J.D., 1979). *Member:* Chicago and Illinois Bar Associations; Illinois Trial Lawyers Association; Association of Trial Lawyers of America.

NANCY L. HIRSCH, born 1957; admitted to bar, 1983, Illinois; 1988, U.S. District Court, Northern District of Illinois. *Education:* University of Iowa (B.A., 1979); John Marshall Law School (J.D., 1983). Moot Court Board. *Member:* Chicago and Illinois Bar Associations; Illinois Trial Lawyers Association; Association of Trial Lawyers of America.

PAUL G. O'TOOLE, born 1963; admitted to bar, 1990, Illinois. *Education:* Marquette University (B.A., 1986); John Marshall Hills Law School (J.D., 1990). Author, "Workplace Injury Report". Member, Clarendon Hills Zoning Board. *Member:* Illinois State Bar Association (General Assembly). **REPORTED CASES:** Dale Serani v. SPX, 2.7 million; T, Dvorak v. Djvelo, 2.25 million.

(This Listing Continued)

REIBMAN, HOFFMAN, BAUM, HIRSCH & O'TOOLE, Chicago—Continued

ASSOCIATE

MICHAEL S. HEDRICK, born 1969; admitted to bar, 2001, Illinois. *Education:* Appalachian State University (B.S., 1996); John Marshall Law School (J.D., 2001). *Member:* Chicago Bar Association.

LAW OFFICES OF SUSAN M. RENTSCHLER

203 NORTH LASALLE STREET, SUITE 2100
CHICAGO, ILLINOIS 60601
Telephone: 312-558-1457
Fax: 312-346-9603
Email: rentschlerlaw@aol.com

Estate Planning, Estate Administration, Wills and Probate, Trusts and Estates, Guardianship.

FIRM PROFILE: Susan M. Rentschler concentrates her practice in the areas of estate planning, probate and trust administration and related litigation.

Estate Planning: preparation of all types of estate planning tools, including revocable trusts, qualified domestic trusts, generation-skipping trusts, irrevocable insurance trusts, charitable remainder trusts, family foundations, trusts for minor children, supplemental needs trusts, family limited partnerships and LLCs.

Probate and Trust Administration: all aspects of probate and trust administration, independent and supervised probate proceedings, ancillary probate proceedings in other states, estate and income taxation; also experienced in guardianships for disabled adults and related issues for the elderly.

Estate and Trust Litigation: trial and appellate courts in contested estates and trusts, including will contests and construction actions, claims against estates, citations to discover and recover assets, trust reformations, actions for an accounting and breach of fiduciary duty.

SUSAN M. RENTSCHLER, born Hammond, Indiana, July 8, 1959; admitted to bar, 1990, Illinois, U.S. District Court, Northern District of Illinois and U.S. Court of Appeals, Seventh Circuit. *Education:* Purdue University (B.S., 1982); John Marshall Law School (J.D., magna cum laude, 1990). *Member:* Chicago and Illinois State Bar Associations; Chicago Estate Planning Counsel. ***PRACTICE AREAS:*** Trusts and Estates; Estate Planning; Estate Administration; Wills; Probate; Guardianship.

REOTT LAW OFFICES, LLC

35 EAST WACKER DRIVE, SUITE 650
CHICAGO, ILLINOIS 60601
Telephone: 312-332-7544
Fax: 312-782-4519
Email: rreott@reottlaw.com
URL: http://www.reottlaw.com

Environmental, Toxic Tort Defense, Environmental Bankruptcy, Environmental Insurance Coverage.

RAYMOND T. REOTT, born Pittsburgh, Pennsylvania, October 27, 1955; admitted to bar, 1980, Illinois; 1981, U.S. Court of Appeals, Seventh Circuit and U.S. District Court, Northern District of Illinois; 1984, U.S. Court of Appeals, Fourth and Sixth Circuits; 1986, U.S. Court of Appeals, Eleventh Circuit; 1988, U.S. Supreme Court; 1990, U.S. Court of Appeals, Tenth Circuit; 1994, U.S. Court of Appeals, Third Circuit; 1995, U.S. Court of Appeals, Eighth Circuit; 1997, U.S. Court of Appeals, Fifth Circuit. *Education:* Georgetown University (B.A., 1977); University of Chicago (J.D., cum laude, 1980). Order of the Coif. Member, University of Chicago Law Review, 1978-1980. Law Clerk, Hon. Richard D. Cudahy, United States Court of Appeals for the Seventh Circuit, 1980-1981. Selected by American Bar Association as one of 20 Young Attorneys Whose Work Stands Out, 1989. Co-Author: "Risk-Based Corrective Action: Lessons for Brownfields from the Illinois Rulemaking," EM Magazine, November 1998. ***Email:*** rreott@reottlaw.com

---

JORGE T. MIHALOPOULOS, born Chicago, Illinois, August 1, 1979; admitted to bar, 2004, Illinois and U.S. District Court, Northern District of Illinois. *Education:* DePaul University (B.S., with honors, 2001); Chicago-Kent College of Law, Illinois Institute of Technology (J.D., 2004). Dean's List, DePaul University. Recipient, Two-Time Winner of the CALI Award. Author: Illinois Bar Association's Newsletter on Environmental Law: Vol. 35 No. 1, Vol. 34, No. 3 and Vol. 34, No. 4. *Member:* Chicago and Illinois State Bar Associations. ***LANGUAGES:*** Greek. ***PRACTICE AREAS:*** Environmental Law. ***Email:*** jtm@reottlaw.com

LAW OFFICE OF GEORGE N. REVELIOTIS

30 N. MICHIGAN AVENUE, SUITE 1619
CHICAGO, ILLINOIS 60602
Telephone: 312-230-0160
Fax: 312-230-0161
Email: greveliotis@reveliotislaw.com
URL: http://www.reveliotislaw.com

Property Tax and Ad Valorem Tax.

(This Listing Continued)

GEORGE N. REVELIOTIS, born Brooklyn, New York, November 3, 1974; admitted to bar, 1999, Illinois. *Education:* University of Illinois (B.S., 1996); John Marshall Law School (J.D., 1999). Member, Greek American Restaurant Association. *Member:* Chicago and American Bar Associations. (Of Counsel, Peter G. Karahalios). ***LANGUAGES:*** Greek. ***PRACTICE AREAS:*** Property Tax; Ad Valorem Tax.

REVIS & WARD, LLC

123 WEST MADISON STREET
SUITE 950
CHICAGO, ILLINOIS 60602
Telephone: 312-701-0380
Fax: 312-701-1161
URL: http://www.revisandward.com

Family Law, Divorce, Child Custody, Child Support, Paternity, Premarital Agreements, Postnuptial Agreements.

COURTNEY A. REVIS, born Kettering, Ohio, August 20, 1968; admitted to bar, 1999, Ohio; 2002, Illinois. *Education:* Miami University (B.A., 1990); University of Cincinnati College of Law (J.D., 1999). Participant, The Saul Leftkowitz Moot Court Competition and Brooklyn Law School National Evidence Competition. *Member:* Chicago and Ohio State Bar Associations. ***PRACTICE AREAS:*** Family Law; Divorce; Child Custody; Child Support; Paternity; Premarital Agreements; Postnuptial Agreements. ***Email:*** revis@revisandward.com

JENNIFER R. WARD, born Lafayette, Louisiana, November 18, 1977; admitted to bar, 2002, Illinois. *Education:* University of Missouri-Columbia (B.A., 1999); John Marshall Law School (J.D., 2002). Council Member, The John Marshall Law School Moot Court. Participant, The August A. Rendigs, Jr. Moot Court Interscholastic Team Competition. Vice President and Class Representative, Student Bar Association. *Member:* Chicago and Women's Bar Associations. ***PRACTICE AREAS:*** Family Law; Divorce; Child Custody; Child Support; Paternity; Premarital Agreements; Postnuptial Agreements. ***Email:*** ward@revisandward.com

RICHARDS, RALPH & SCHWAB

CHARTERED

Established in 1976

39 SOUTH LASALLE STREET, SUITE 905
CHICAGO, ILLINOIS 60603
Telephone: 312-641-6696
Fax: 847-367-9621
Email: attorney@rrs-chtd.com
URL: http://www.lawyers.com/richardandschwab

Vernon Hills, Illinois Office: One Hawthorn Place, 175 East Hawthorn Parkway, Suite 345, 60061. Telephone: 847-367-9699. Fax: 847-367-9621. Email: attorney@rrs-chtd.com.

Corporate and Business. Banking and Finance. Bankruptcy and Creditors' Rights. Real Estate. Commercial Litigation.

REPRESENTATIVE CLIENTS: Amcore Bank, N.A.; A. E. Bancorp, Inc.; American Enterprise Bank; American Enterprise Leasing; Bank of Lincolnwood; Cambridge Bank; Des Plaines National Bank; First American Bank; Lakeland Community Bank; LaSalle Bank, N.A.; Libertyville Bank & Trust Company; Mt. Prospect National Bank; Mundelein Community Bank; National City Bank; Northside Community Bank; Lake County Partnership for Economic Development, Inc.; Midwest, Inc.; Riverside Foundation; Transamerica Small Business Capitol.

REFERENCES: American Enterprise Bank; LaSalle Bank, N.A.; Libertyville Bank & Trust Company.

(For complete biographical data on all personnel, see Professional Biographies at Vernon Hills, Illinois)

RICHARDSON, PATRICK, WESTBROOK & BRICKMAN, LLC

Established in 2002

218 N. JEFFERSON STREET, SUITE 400
CHICAGO, ILLINOIS 60661
Telephone: 312-466-1669
Fax:312-466-1513
URL: http://www.rpwb.com

Barnwell, South Carolina Office: 1730 Jackson Street, P.O. Box 1368, 29812. Telephone: 803-541-7850. Fax: 803-541-9625.

Mt. Pleasant, South Carolina Office: 1037 Chuck Dawley Boulevard, Building A, P.O. Box 1007, 29464. Telephone: 843-727-6500. Fax: 843-216-6509.

Charleston, South Carolina Office: 174 East Bay Street, P.O. Box 879, 29401. Telephone: 843-727-6541. Fax: 843-727-3103.

Antitrust and Trade Regulation, Business Torts, Class Actions, Commercial Litigation, Complex and Multi-District Litigation, Consumer Law, Drug and Medical Device Litigation, Environmental Law, Healthcare, Mass Torts, Medical Malpractice, Occupational Disease, Plaintiffs Personal Injury, Premises Liability, Products Liability, Securities, Railroad Accidents and Injuries, Tax Litigation, Toxic Torts, White Collar Criminal Defense.

(For complete biographical information on all personnel, see Professional biographies at Charleston, South Carolina Office)

RIEFF SCHRAMM & KANTER

100 NORTH LASALLE STREET, SUITE 2300
CHICAGO, ILLINOIS 60602-2402
Telephone: 312-372-2500
Fax: 312-372-2550
Email: mel@realproptax.com
URL: http://www.rieffschrammkanter.com

Real Estate Taxation, Property Tax Appeals, Property Tax Assessments, Tax Incentives, Tax Abatement, Exemption, Eminent Domain, Condemnation, Assessments.

FIRM PROFILE: The firm concentrates its practice in the areas of real estate taxation, eminent domain and governmental matters. We represent clients with all types of commercial, industrial and residential properties, concentrating in obtaining equitable assessments or, in eminent domain proceedings, fair compensation on their behalf. We also assist them in obtaining "assessment incentives" and "tax abatements" designed to encourage industrial, commercial, and multi-residential development. Our clients include developers, real estate investment trusts, banks, Fortune 500 companies and not-for-profit organizations, as well as individual property owners and small businesses. The firm represents clients with properties throughout Illinois as well as the Chicago metropolitan area. We also work with a network of real estate tax attorneys throughout the United States and Canada.

MEMBERS OF FIRM

MELVYN A. RIEFF, born Chicago, Illinois, January 31, 1944; admitted to bar, 1969, Illinois; 1977, U.S. District Court, Northern District of Illinois. *Education:* University of Illinois (B.A., 1965; J.D., 1968). Illinois State Scholar, 1961-1965. Adjunct Faculty, IIT/ Chicago-Kent College of Law, Spring 1978. Assistant and Acting City Attorney, Carbondale, 1969-1971. Assistant Attorney General, State of Illinois, Environmental Control Division, 1971-1973. Assistant State's Attorney, Cook County, 1973-1981. Supervisor, Environmental Law Section, 1973-1976. General Law and Special Litigation Section, 1976-1980; Real Estate Tax Section, 1980-1981. Chairman, Bench & Bar Advisory Committee on Tax Objections, Circuit Court of Cook County, 1993-1994. *Member:* Chicago (Chairman, Real Estate Taxation Committee, 1994-1995; Assessment and Appeals Sub-Committee Chairman, 1992-1993; Legislation Sub-Committee Chairman, 1991-1992), Illinois State and American Bar Associations. (Managing Partner). ***PRACTICE AREAS:*** Real Estate Taxation; Eminent Domain. ***Email:*** mel@realproptax.com

DONALD L. SCHRAMM, born Evanston, Illinois, December 9, 1949; admitted to bar, 1978, Illinois and U.S. District Court, Northern District of Illinois; 1982, U.S. District Court, Central District of Illinois. *Education:* Indiana University (B.A., 1972); John Marshall Law School (J.D., 1978). Phi Alpha Delta. General Counsel, Cook County Assessor's Office, 1978-1982. Author: "Assessment Incentive Classifications," Real Estate Journal, Vol. 1 No. 25 (December 7, 1998); "Taxation of Retirement Housing," Journal of Property Taxation, Vol. 1, No. 3, (1989). Lecturer, Seminar, Illinois Property Taxation; 1994. Special Assistant Attorney General, State of Illinois, 1985. *Member:* Chicago and Illinois State Bar Associations; Chamber of Commerce. ***PRACTICE AREAS:*** Real Estate Tax Assessment; Tax Incentives; Eminent Domain Law. ***Email:*** dschramm@realproptax.com

HERBERT KANTER, born Chicago, Illinois, June 5, 1939; admitted to bar, 1965, Illinois and U.S. District Court, District of Illinois; U.S. Supreme Court. *Education:* University of Illinois (B.S., 1962); John Marshall Law School (J.D., 1965). Assistant Supervisor, Capital Stock Tax Division, State of Illinois, Department of Revenue, 1962-1968. Author: "Pitfalls of Real Estate Taxation: Let the Buyer Beware," The REIT Report, 1997. Co-author: "Real Estate Taxes: Pitfalls for the Unwary Practitioner," Chicago Bar Record, June, 1991. Lectured: Chicago Bar Association Real Estate Taxation Programs. Moderator and Panelist: Real Estate Taxation Session, NARIET Law and Accounting Conference, 1997. *Member:* Chicago (Member, 1968— and Chairman, 1973-1974, State and Local Tax Committee) and Illinois State Bar Associations. ***PRACTICE AREAS:*** Real Estate Tax Assessment. ***Email:*** hkanter@realproptax.com

LAWRENCE B. BRODSKY, born Chicago, Illinois, August 1, 1934; admitted to bar, 1961, Illinois and U.S. District Court, Northern District of Illinois. *Education:* DePaul University (A.B., 1957; J.D., 1961). Phi Alpha Delta. Attorney Advisor, U.S. Army Materiel Command, 1961-1970. Assistant State's Attorney, Cook County, Real Estate Tax Unit, 1970-1987. Author: "Specific Objections to the County Collectors Application For Judgment of Real Estate Taxation," Illinois Institute for Continuing Legal Education, 1984, 1987, 1991 and 1997 and 2000. Instructor, Illinois Institute for Continuing Legal Education, 1984, 1986, 1987 and 1990. Lecturer, Illinois State Bar Association Law Education Series on Real Estate Taxation, 1992 and 1996. ***PRACTICE AREAS:*** Real Estate Taxation Law; Tax Exemptions. ***Email:*** lbrodsky@realproptax.com

GLENN S. GUTTMAN, born Chicago, Illinois; admitted to bar, 1993, Illinois and U.S. District Court, Northern District of Illinois. *Education:* University of Illinois (B.A., 1987); John Marshall Law School (J.D., 1990). Co-Author: "Tax Objection Complaints," and "Real Estate Tax Considerations," Illinois Institute for Continuing Legal Education, 2005. Member, International Association of Assessing Officers. *Member:* Chicago (Vice Chairman, Real Estate Taxation Committee, 2005-2006); Illinois State and American Bar Associations; Illinois Real Estate Lawyers Association. ***PRACTICE AREAS:*** Real Estate Tax Assessments; Real Estate Transactions; Tax Incentives; Eminent Domain; Condemnation Law. ***Email:*** gguttman@realproptax.com

MARGARET E. GRAHAM, born Oak Park, Illinois; admitted to bar, 1985, Illinois. *Education:* Dominican University (B.A., 1970); John Marshall Law School (J.D., 1984). Arbitration Panelist for the Circuit Court of Cook County. *Member:* Chicago, American and Women's Bar Associations. ***PRACTICE AREAS:*** Real Estate Tax Assessment; Tax Exemptions; Tax Incentives; Government Relations; Litigation; Arbitration. ***Email:*** mgraham@realproptax.com

MICHAEL T. REYNOLDS, born Chicago, Illinois, August 28, 1953; admitted to bar, 1981, Illinois; 1982, U.S. District Court, Northern District of Illinois; 1998, U.S. Supreme Court. *Education:* Loyola University (B.A., 1976; J.D., 1981). Deputy Member, Cook County Board of (Tax) Appeals, 1979-1982. Arbitrator, Cook County Mandatory Arbitration Program, 1994-2003. Lecturer: Real Estate Taxation Law, 1996, 1997, 1998, Continuing Legal Education Seminars, Chicago Bar Association. Executive Director, Lawyers' Assistance Program, Inc. *Member:* Chicago, Illinois State and American Bar Associations. ***PRACTICE AREAS:*** Real Estate Taxation; Real Estate Tax Exemptions. ***Email:*** mreynolds@realproptax.com

OF COUNSEL

STEPHANIE S. PARK, born Seoul, Korea; admitted to bar, 1996, Illinois and U.S. District Court, Northern District of Illinois. *Education:* University of Illinois (B.S., 1992); Illinois Institute of Technology, Chicago-Kent College of Law (J.D.). Phi Alpha Delta. Certified Public Accountant, Illinois, 1996. Licensed Real Estate Broker, Illinois, 1996. Hearing Officer, State of Illinois Property Tax Appeal Board. Treasurer, Asian American Health. Co-Author: "Real Estate Tax Considerations," Illinois Institute for Continuing Legal Education, 2005. *Member:* Chicago and Illinois State Bar Associations; Korean-American Bar Association. ***LANGUAGES:*** Korean. ***PRACTICE AREAS:*** Real Estate Tax Assessment; Real Estate Taxation; Commercial Real Estate; Industrial Real Estate Law; Residential Real Estate. ***Email:*** stephaniepark@realproptax.com

(This Listing Continued)

RIGGLE AND CRAVEN

SUITE 525
8430 WEST BRYN MAWR
CHICAGO, ILLINOIS 60631
Telephone: 312-368-8787
Telefax: 312-368-0939
Email: RandC@tradelaw.com
URL: http://www.tradelaw.com

Customs Law, International Trade, Export Regulation, Import and Export Law, Antidumping, International Law of the Sea. Federal, Administrative and Legislative Practice.

MEMBERS OF FIRM

DAVID A. RIGGLE, born Bloomington, Indiana, September 25, 1946; admitted to bar, 1978, Illinois, Michigan and U.S. District Court, Eastern District of Michigan; 1979, U.S. District Court, Northern District of Illinois and U.S. Court of Appeals, Seventh Circuit; 1979-1980, U.S. Customs Court; 1979-1982, U.S. Court of Customs and Patent Appeals; 1980, U.S. Court of International Trade; 1983, U.S. Court of Appeals for the Federal Circuit. *Education:* State University of New York at New Paltz (B.A., 1973); University of Michigan Rackman Graduate School, Center for Japanese Studies; University of Detroit (J.D., 1977). Japan American Society of Chicago (Vice-President, 1992-2002). *Member:* Chicago (Chair, 1992-1993, Customs and International Trade Law Committee), Illinois State and American Bar Associations; State Bar of Michigan. [With U.S. Army, 1967-1971]. ***PRACTICE AREAS:*** Customs Law; International Trade; Export Regulation; Import and Export Law; Antidumping. ***Email:*** riggle@tradelaw.com

DAVID J. CRAVEN, born Washington, D.C., September 25, 1958; admitted to bar, 1985, New York, U.S. Court of Appeals for the District of Columbia Circuit, U.S. Court of International Trade and U.S. Court of Appeals for the Federal Circuit; 1986, District of Columbia, Illinois, U.S. District Court, Northern District of Illinois and U.S. Court of Appeals, Seventh Circuit. *Education:* University of Iowa (B.A., 1981); The National Law Center, George Washington University (J.D., with honors, 1984). Phi Delta Phi. Member, George Washington University Journal of International Law and Economics, 1982-1983. Lecturer, Administrative and Judicial Relief From Export Sanctions, Chicago Bar Association, 1988. Author: "How a Customs Lawyer Can Assist in Import Transactions," U.S. Customs House Guide, 1994. Member: International Trade Club of Chicago (Contributor to Export Manual, 1991-1993); Law of the Sea Institute 1991-1993. *Member:* Chicago Bar Association (Member, Customs and International Trade Law Committee); The District of Columbia Bar. ***PRACTICE AREAS:*** Customs; International Trade and Export Control. ***Email:*** craven@tradelaw.com

OF COUNSEL

Jack D. Mlawski (Not admitted in IL; Also Member, Galvin & Mlawski, N.Y., N.Y.)

John J. Galvin (Not admitted in IL; Also Member, Galvin & Mlawski, N.Y., N.Y.)

John P. Craven (Not admitted in IL)

RIGHEIMER MARTIN & CINQUINO, P.C.

20 NORTH CLARK, SUITE 1900
CHICAGO, ILLINOIS 60602
Telephone: 312-726-5646
Telecopier: 312-609-2277

General Civil and Trial Practice. Eminent Domain, Banking, Probate, Health Care and Hospital Law, Corporate.

FRANK R. MARTIN, born Oak Park, Illinois, June 6, 1946; admitted to bar, 1972, Illinois; 1973, U.S. District Court, Northern District of Illinois. *Education:* Beloit College (B.A., 1968); Harvard University (J.D., 1972). Special Assistant Attorney General, 1974-1984. *Member:* Chicago, Illinois and American Bar Associations. ***PRACTICE AREAS:*** Banking Law; Corporate Law; Probate Law.

LEO N. CINQUINO, born Chicago, Illinois, November 14, 1947; admitted to bar, 1973, Illinois and U.S. District Court, Northern District of Illinois. *Education:* Northern Illinois University (B.S., 1969); Loyola University (J.D., 1973). Author: Chapter, "Discovery and Pre-trial Procedure: Illinois Eminent Domain Practice," IICLE, 1985, 1988. Guest Lecturer for: American Right of Way Association and American Institute of Real Estate Appraisers, 1979-1982; Illinois State Bar Association, 1988; Illinois Institute for Continuing Legal Education, 1988-1989, 1995 and 1998; Cumulative Supplement, Eminent Domain in Illinois, 1996 and 1998. Special Assistant Attorney General, 1973-1984. *Member:* Chicago (Chairman, Eminent Domain Subcommittee, 1977-1979) and Illinois State Bar Associations. ***PRACTICE AREAS:*** Eminent Domain Law.

(This Listing Continued)

RIGHEIMER MARTIN & CINQUINO, P.C., Chicago—Continued

DAVID A. MARTIN, born Oak Park, Illinois, October 21, 1951; admitted to bar, 1976, Illinois and U.S. District Court, Northern District of Illinois; 1977, Florida and U.S. Court of Appeals, Seventh Circuit; 1979, District of Columbia. *Education:* Princeton University (A.B., 1973); Indiana University (J.D., cum laude, 1976). Special Assistant Attorney General, 1978-1984. *Member:* Chicago and Illinois State Bar Associations; The Florida Bar; The District of Columbia Bar; American Society of Hospital Attorneys. ***PRACTICE AREAS:*** Health Care Law; Hospital Law; Probate Law; Banking Law.

SANDRA L. HEBENSTREIT, born Chicago, Illinois, November 29, 1950; admitted to bar, 1981, Illinois and U.S. District Court, Northern District of Illinois. *Education:* Indiana University (B.A., 1972); DePaul University (J.D., with honors, 1981). *Member:* Chicago and Illinois State Bar Associations. ***PRACTICE AREAS:*** Eminent Domain; Health Care Law; Hospital Law.

BRADLEY A. MUELLER, born Eau Claire, Wisconsin, July 31, 1960; admitted to bar, 1986, Illinois and U.S. District Court, Northern District of Illinois. *Education:* University of Wisconsin-Eau Claire (B.A., 1982); John Marshall Law School (J.D., 1986). *Member:* Chicago Bar Association. ***PRACTICE AREAS:*** Health Care Law; Hospital Law.

CELESTE P. CINQUINO, born Chicago, Illinois, May 19, 1945; admitted to bar, 1986, Illinois and U.S. District Courts, Northern District of Illinois and Eastern District of Wisconsin. *Education:* Northern Illinois University (B.A., 1967); IIT/Chicago-Kent College of Law (J.D., with high honors, 1986). *Member:* Chicago, Illinois State and American Bar Associations. ***PRACTICE AREAS:*** Eminent Domain Law; Real Property Law; Litigation.

FRANK S. RIGHEIMER (1882-1980)

ALVAH T. MARTIN (1908-1993)

FRANK S. RIGHEIMER, JR. (1909-1998)

REPRESENTATIVE CLIENTS: St. Paul Federal Bank for Savings; Illinois Masonic Medical Center; Scottish Rite Cathedral Association of Chicago; St. Paul Financial Development Co.; Mercy Hospital Medical Center; Corus Bank, N.A.

RINELLA AND RINELLA, LTD.

Established in 1940

ONE NORTH LA SALLE STREET
SUITE 3400
CHICAGO, ILLINOIS 60602-4094
Telephone: 312-236-5454
Fax: 312-236-6975
URL: http://www.rinellaandrinella.com
Email: donnaw@rinellaandrinella.com
URL: http://www.lawyers.com/rinellaandrinella

Practice Limited to Family Law and Divorce including the areas of Legal Separation, Negotiating and Drafting Premarital and Postnuptial Agreements, Judgment Enforcement, Child Custody and Child Support Actions, Domestic Violence, Spousal Support, Appeals, Adoption, Parentage Actions and Interstate Support Enforcement.

FIRM PROFILE: Rinella and Rinella, Ltd., is the oldest matrimonial law firm in Illinois. Founded by Samuel A. Rinella, a co-founder of the American Academy of Matrimonial Lawyers, and Kathryn Barasa Rinella, who served as President of the State of Illinois Women's Bar Association, the firm is nationally recognized as one of the premiere family law firms in the country.

The firm's clients range from captains of industry, television celebrities and sports stars, to small business owners, professionals, homemakers and working men and women.

SAMUEL A. RINELLA (1906-1982)

KATHRYN B. RINELLA (1906-1991)

BERNARD B. RINELLA, born Chicago, Illinois, April 15, 1936; admitted to bar, 1961, Illinois. *Education:* University of Michigan (B.A., 1958); DePaul University (J.D., 1961). Delta Theta Phi. Chapter Author: Legal Checklists, "Matrimonial Matters," 1983. Author: "Winning Cases Through Show and Tell," Family Advocate, Vol. 6, No. 1, 1983. Co-Author: "Illinois Child Custody Law: An Overview," Illinois Bar Journal, Vol. 76, No. 1, Sept. 1987; "Antenuptial Agreements and Malpractice: Is the Risk Worth the Reward?" American Journal of Family Law, Vol. 2, No. 2, Summer 1988; Illinois Domestic Relations Forms, Aspen Legal Publishers, 1989—; Hidden Assets, Family Advocate, Summer, 1989. Lecturer, Cambridge Institute, Family Law in Illinois, 1988-1989. Nominated: "The Best Lawyers In America, Woodward/White; Best Domestic Lawyers in America," National Law Journal; "Best Divorce Lawyers in America," Town and Country Magazine. Named to Leading Lawyers and Super Lawyers, 2004—. President, Justinian Society of Lawyers, 1977-1978. *Member:* Chicago (Member, 1963— and Chairman, 1980-1981, Matrimonial Law Committee), Illinois State (Member, 1965— and Chairman, 1971-1972, Council of Family Law Section) and American (Member, 1961—; Parliamentarian, 1988-1990; Associate Editor, Domestic Relations Section Law Notes, 1967-1974; Chairman, Divorce Law and Procedure Committee, 1987-1989; Member, Committee on Federal and International Law Taxation, Family Law Section, 1977; Committee, Task Force on the Needs of Children, Family Law Section, 1977) Bar Associations. Fellow: American Academy of Matrimonial Lawyers (Member, 1961—, Board of Governors, National Chapter, 1982-1984; Counsel to National Chapter, 1986; Member, 1990—; Member of Council, 1986—; President, Illinois Chapter, 1981-1983); American Academy of Matrimonial Lawyers Foundation (Member, 1990—; President, 2000-2002); International Academy of Matrimonial Lawyers (Member, 1990—; Council American Chapter, 1998); American College of Family Trial Lawyers (Member, 1994-2000). ***PRACTICE AREAS:*** Family Law; Premarital Agreements; Postnuptial Agreements; Adoption Law; Child Custody; Paternity. ***Email:*** donnaw@rinellaandrinella.com

(This Listing Continued)

JOSEPH G. PHELPS, admitted to bar, 1982, Illinois. *Education:* Loyola University (B.A., with honors, 1972; J.D., 1982). Chapter Author, Legal Checklists, "Matrimonial Matters—Tax Considerations," 1983. Guest Lecturer for the Chicago Volunteer Legal Services Foundation on: "The New Withholding Orders," June, 1984; "No Fault Divorce," September 25, 1984; "Mandatory Support Guidelines," December 18, 1984; "Maintenance and the 1984 Tax Reform Act," June, 1985; "Tax Reform Act of 1984 and Child Support," October, 1985; "Property Distribution and the New Tax Laws," January, 1986; "Qualified Domestic Relations Orders and the Valuations of Pensions," July 30, 1986; "Qualified Domestic Relations Orders," November 19, 1986 and "Court Procedures in Domestic Relations," January 28, 1987. Lecturer, "Family Law in Illinois," Cambridge Institute, July 14, 1988, April 26, 1989 and October 17, 1989 and April 18, 1989; "Child Custody and Visitation in Illinois," National Business Institute, Inc., April 19, 1995. Board Member, Chicago Volunteer Legal Services Foundation, 1989-1992. Commissioner, Chicago Park District, 1988-1994. Named to Super Lawyers, 2004—. *Member:* Chicago (Member, Matrimonial Law Committee, Subcommittee on Appellate Rules and Practices, 1983-1990; Subcommittee on Support Enforcement, 1984-1986; Subcommittee on the Courts, 1984-1991, Legislation Subcommittee, 1984-1991 and Current Law Reporting, 1986-1992), Illinois State (Member, Family Law Section; Associate Member, Family Law Section Council, 1988—) and American (Member, Family Law Section) Bar Associations; Catholic Lawyers Guild (Member, Board of Governors, 2003—). ***LANGUAGES:*** Italian and Latin. ***REPORTED CASES:*** People ex rel. Lionel I. Brazen v. Finley, 119 Ill.2d 485, 519 N.E.2d 898, 116 Ill.Dec.683 (1988); In Re The Marriage Of Savas, 139 Ill.App.3d 68, 486 N.E.2d 1318, 93 Ill.Dec 483 (1st Dist. 1985); In Re The Marriage Of Hilkovitch, 124 Ill.App.3d 401, 464 N.E.2d 795, 124 Ill.App.3d 401 (!st Dist. 1984); and In Re Marriage Of Ligas, 110 Ill.App.3d 1, 441 N.E.2d 1277, 65 Ill.Dec. 763 (1st Dist. 1982); In Re Marriage of Bielawski and Rycroft, N.D. 01-2193 (1st Dist. 2002). ***PRACTICE AREAS:*** Family Law; Premarital Agreements; Postnuptial Agreements; Adoption Law; Child Custody; Paternity; Probate; Real Estate. ***Email:*** josephp@rinellaandrinella.com

MARICAROL LACY, born Chicago, Illinois, May 21, 1960; admitted to bar, 1986, Illinois; U.S. District Court, Northern District of Illinois; U.S. Court of Appeals, 7th Circuit; U.S. Court of Claims. *Education:* Loyola University (B.S., magna cum laude, 1983); University of Notre Dame (J.D., 1986). Lecturer, Children and Family Law, Undergraduate and Graduate School of Social Work, Loyola University of Chicago, 1991—. Invited Lecturer, National Business Institute, University of Chicago; Dept. of Psychiatry: Legal Aspects of Confidentially Records, Reports and Testimony (2004). Lecturer: National Business Institute, Handling a Divorce Case from start to finish, 2002. Concern International 2002 Brigid Award Honoree. Chairperson, Concern Worldwide Brigid, 2004—. Certified Rape Victim Advocate. *Member:* Chicago and Illinois State Bar Associations; Women's Bar Association. ***PRACTICE AREAS:*** Family Law; Adoption Law; Child Custody; Paternity; Postnuptial Agreements; Premarital Agreements. ***Email:*** maricaroll@rinellaandrinella.com

KAREN J. BOWES, born Chicago, Illinois, March 10, 1956; admitted to bar, 1980, Illinois and Mississippi; U.S. District Court, Northern District of Illinois and U.S. District Court, Northern District of Mississippi. *Education:* University of Mississippi (B.A., 1977; J.D., 1980). Adjunct Professor, Loyola University of Chicago, Paralegal Institute, 1994—. Named to Super Lawyers, 2004—. *Member:* Chicago, Illinois State Bar Associations; The Mississippi Bar. ***PRACTICE AREAS:*** Family Law. ***Email:*** karenb@rinellaandrinella.com

MICHAEL J. CHIERO, born Oak Park, Illinois; admitted to bar, 1993, Illinois; 1994, California. *Education:* University of Michigan (B.A., English, 1989); John Marshall Law School (J.D., cum laude, 1993). Staff Member, John Marshall Law School, Law Review, 1991-1993. Recipient, Herzog Merit Scholarship, 1991. Lecturer, "Kids in a Divorcing Society," 1996—. *Member:* Illinois State Bar Association (Counsel Member, Family Law Section, 2003—). ***PRACTICE AREAS:*** Matrimonial Law; Child Custody; Paternity; Domestic Violence. ***Email:*** michaelc@rinellaandrinella.com

ASSOCIATE

NICOLE M. ONORATO, born Erie, Pennsylvania, May 20, 1975; admitted to bar, 2004, Illinois. *Education:* University of Wisconsin-Madison (B.A., 1997); DePaul University (J.D., 2004). *Member:* Chicago, Illinois State and American (Member, Family Law Section) Bar Associations; Women's Bar Association of Illinois. ***PRACTICE AREAS:*** Family Law (100%). ***Email:*** nicoleo@rinellaandrinella.com

RIORDAN, DONNELLY, LIPINSKI & McKEE, LTD.

Established in 1920

(Formerly McNeela & Griffin, Ltd.)

10 NORTH DEARBORN
4TH FLOOR
CHICAGO, ILLINOIS 60602
Telephone: 312-663-9400
Fax: 312-663-1028
Email: webbaddress@rdlmlaw.com
URL: http://www.rdlmlaw.com

Commercial and Tort Litigation, Construction, Mechanics Liens, Employment Practice, Surety and Fidelity Law, Insurance, Real Estate Law, Corporate Law; Estate Planning and Probate.

FIRM PROFILE: Riordan, Donnelly, Lipinski & McKeen continues a practice of law in civil litigation which began in 1920. For more than 80 years, the Firm has represented insurers, fidelity and surety bond issuers, manufacturers and contractors in trial and appellate courts. The Firm's construction, product liability and commercial litigation practices deliver high quality representation effectively and efficiently.

CORNELIUS F. RIORDAN, born Evergreen Park, Illinois, January 11, 1951; admitted to bar, 1976, Illinois. *Education:* University of Notre Dame (B.A., 1973); John Marshall Law School (J.D, 1976); DePaul University (M.S.A., 1982). Illinois Certified Public Ac-

(This Listing Continued)

countant, 1982. *Member:* Chicago and Illinois State Bar Associations. ***PRACTICE AREAS:*** Construction Law; Fidelity and Surety Law; Civil Litigation. ***Email:*** criordan@rdlmlaw.com

PATRICK G. DONNELLY, born Evergreen Park, Illinois, September 27, 1961; admitted to bar, 1986, Illinois. *Education:* Marquette University (A.B., 1983); DePaul University (J.D., 1986). ***PRACTICE AREAS:*** Construction Law; Civil Litigation. ***Email:*** pdonnelly@rdlmlaw.com

MARC S. LIPINSKI, born Parma, Ohio, September 30, 1954; admitted to bar, 1979, Illinois; 1980, U.S. District Court, Northern District of Illinois; 1982, U.S. Court of Appeals, Seventh Circuit. *Education:* University of Chicago (A.B., 1976); Stanford University (J.D., 1979). Phi Beta Kappa. *Member:* Chicago (Member: Real Property Committee; Mechanics' Lien Subcommittee), Illinois State and American (Member: Forum Committee on The Construction Industry; Tort and Insurance Practice Section) Bar Associations. ***PRACTICE AREAS:*** Fidelity and Surety; Construction Law; Insurance Law. ***Email:*** mlipinski@rdlmlaw.com

HAROLD E. McKEE, born South Bend, Indiana, October 3, 1960; admitted to bar, 1987, Illinois. *Education:* Saint Louis University (B.S.B.A., 1982); John Marshall Law School (J.D., 1987). Assistant States Attorney, Cook County, 1987-1991. *Member:* American Bar Association. ***PRACTICE AREAS:*** Construction Law; Fidelity and Surety Law; Commercial Litigation. ***Email:*** hmckee@rdlmlaw.com

MICHAEL A. PALERMO, JR., born River Forest, Illinois, December 27, 1965; admitted to bar, 1992, Illinois. *Education:* Bradley University (B.A., 1989); John Marshall Law School (J.D., 1992). *Member:* Chicago Bar Association. ***PRACTICE AREAS:*** Construction Law; Insurance; Labor and Employment; Civil Litigation. ***Email:*** mpalermo@rdlmlaw.com

JAMIE L. SCHWARTZ, born Chicago, Illinois, January 22, 1972; admitted to bar, 1997, Illinois. *Education:* Benedictine University (B.A., 1994); DePaul University (J.D., 1997). *Member:* American Bar Association; Defense Research Institute; National Association of Women in Construction. ***LANGUAGES:*** Spanish. ***PRACTICE AREAS:*** Fidelity and Surety; Construction Law. ***Email:*** jschwartz@rdlmlaw.com

GENEVIEVE M. LYNOTT, born Evanston, Illinois, September 28, 1974; admitted to bar, 2001, Illinois. *Education:* DePaul University (B.A., 1995; J.D., 2001). *Member:* Chicago, Illinois State and American Bar Associations; National Association of Women in Construction. ***PRACTICE AREAS:*** Surety Law; Construction Law; Real Estate; Insurance Defense. ***Email:*** glynott@rdlmlaw.com

BRIAN T. MILLER, born Rockford, Illinois, October 16, 1976; admitted to bar, 2002, Illinois. *Education:* Rutgers University (B.A., 1998); College of William & Mary (J.D., 2002). ***PRACTICE AREAS:*** Construction Law; Surety Law; General Corporate. ***Email:*** bmiller@rdlmlaw.com

OF COUNSEL

GARY L. GRIFFIN, born Pekin, Illinois, September 3, 1937; admitted to bar, 1961, Illinois. *Education:* DePaul University (J.D., 1961). Delta Theta Phi; Blue Key. Member, Board of Editors, De Paul Law Review, 1960-1961. *Member:* Chicago, Illinois State and American Bar Associations; International Association of Defense Counsel. ***PRACTICE AREAS:*** Fidelity, Surety and Casualty Defense Law; Construction Law. ***Email:*** ggriffin@rdlmlaw.com

REPRESENTATIVE CLIENTS: AC Pavement Striping Co., Inc.; Allstate Metal Fabricators; Allstate Steel Brectors, Inc.; American Home Assurance Co.; America Standard, Inc.; Arrow Road Construction Company; Banner Rebar; Belec Electrical, Inc; Boswell Building Contractors; Bond Safeguard Insurance Company; Central Blacktop, Inc.; Chicago Cooling, Corp.; Chicago Title Insurance Co.; CIGNA Co.; CNA Surety Corp./CNA; Connecticut Indemnity Company; Crawford & Company; Credit General Insurance Company, in Liquidation; Federated Mutual Insurance Company; Fidelity and Deposit Company of Maryland/Zurich North American; Fireman's Fund Insurance Company; Fisher Scientific Company; Frontier Insurance Company; Ganna Construction, Inc.; Gulf Insurance Company; Herlihy Mid-Continent Co.; Intercargo Insurance Co.; Irmscher, Inc.; James McHugh Construction Co.; JohnsonDiversey, Inc.; Liberty Mutual Insurance Company; Lurgi Lentjes North American; Mountbatten Surety Company/Zurich North American; National Construction Enterprises; NAS Surety; Michuda Construction Co.; RLI Insurance Company; S.C. Johnson & Son, Inc.; St. Paul Surety; The Dracket Products Company; Traveler's Bond; United States Fidelity & Guaranty Co.; Utica Mutual Insurance Co.; W.W. Granger; XL Specialty Insuranxe Company; XL Reinsurance America; XL Winterthur.

ROBINSON CURLEY & CLAYTON, P.C.

Established in 1987

300 SOUTH WACKER DRIVE
SUITE 1700
CHICAGO, ILLINOIS 60606
Telephone: 312-663-3100
Telecopier: 312-663-0303
URL: http://www.robinsoncurley.com

General Commercial Litigation, Litigation arising from Insurance Company and other Financial Institution Insolvencies, Reinsurance Recovery Disputes, RICO, Securities, Professional Liability, Intellectual Property, Class Actions, Civil Rights and Employment Litigation, Insurance Regulatory and Receivership Matters, Civil and Criminal Trial and Appellate Practice and Alternative Dispute Resolution in all State and Federal Courts and Tribunals.

C. PHILIP CURLEY, born Boston, Massachusetts, July 26, 1954; admitted to bar, 1979, Illinois and U.S. District Court, Northern District of Illinois; 1982, U.S. Court of Appeals, Seventh Circuit; 1992, U.S. Supreme Court. *Education:* Northwestern University (B.A., 1976); The National Law Center, George Washington University (J.D., with honors, 1979). Order of the Coif. Speaker: National Conference, Insurance Regulatory Examiners Society; Insolvency Workshop, National Association of Insurance Commissioners, 1999, 1996. Panelist: Regional Seminar, Society of Financial Examiners, 1996; Reinsurance Collections, Society of Insurance Receivers, 1995. Faculty, "Pleadings, Discovery and Jury Instructions in Statutory Causes of Action," Illinois Trial Lawyers Association Annual Convention, 1988. Litigation Seminar, National Association of Insurance Commissioners, Rehabilitator and Liquidators Task Force, 1985. "The Implications of Civil RICO," ABA Annual Convention, 1983. ***PRACTICE AREAS:*** Complex Commercial Litigation; Insurance and Reinsurance; Securities; Professional Liability Litigation; Civil RICO; Business Torts. ***Email:*** pcurley@robinsoncurley.com

FAY CLAYTON, born New Brunswick, New Jersey, November 19, 1946; admitted to bar, 1978, Illinois and U.S. District Court, Northern District of Illinois including Trial Bar; 1981, U.S. Court of Appeals, Seventh Circuit; 1982, U.S. Court of Appeals, Second Circuit; 1985, U.S. Court of Appeals, Sixth Circuit; 1986, U.S. Supreme Court. *Education:* New College (B.A., 1967); Chicago-Kent College of Law (J.D., with high honors, 1978). Member, Chicago-Kent Law Review, 1977. Author: "The Supreme Court's Decision in NOW v. Scheidler," 18 Private Antitrust Litigation News 37, 1994; "The Legality of the Chicago Nuclear Weapon Free Zone Ordinance," 17 Loyola Law Journal 553, 1986. Faculty, National Institute for Trial Advocacy, 1985. Adjunct Professor, Trial Advocacy, Northwestern University College of Law, 1989. Director, 2001—, Executive Committee Member, 2003—, and Regional Vice Chair, 2001—, Chicago Lawyers Committee for Civil Rights Under Law. Administrative Hearing Officer, Chicago Commission on Human Relations, 1991—. NASD Arbitrator. *Member:* American Bar Association; Chicago Council of Lawyers. ***PRACTICE AREAS:*** Complex Commercial Litigation; Civil RICO; Professional Liability Litigation; Business Torts; Employment and Civil Rights Litigation. ***Email:*** fclayton@robinsoncurley.com

ALAN F. CURLEY, born Akron, Ohio, September 22, 1958; admitted to bar, 1985, Illinois; 1987, U.S. District Court, Northern District of Illinois, including Trial Bar; 1988, U.S. Court of Appeals, Seventh Circuit; 1995, U.S. Court of Appeals, Fourth Circuit; 2003, U.S. Court of Appeals, Sixth Circuit; 2004, U.S. Court of Appeals, Fifth Circuit. *Education:* Tulane University of Louisiana (B.A., 1981); John Marshall Law School (J.D., with highest distinction, 1985). Editor, John Marshall Law Review, 1985. Author: "Rickey v. Chicago Transit Authority: Consistent Limitation on Recovery for Negligent Infliction of Emotional Distress in Illinois," 17 John Marshall Law Review 563, 1984. Law Clerk to the Honorable W. Eugene Davis, United States Court of Appeals, Fifth Circuit, 1985-1986. ***PRACTICE AREAS:*** Financial Institution Insolvency; Professional Liability Litigation; Director and Officer Liability Litigation; Complex Commercial Litigation; Business Torts; Employment Litigation; Complex Collections. ***Email:*** acurley@robinsoncurley.com

CYNTHIA H. HYNDMAN, born Gary, Indiana, October 12, 1956; admitted to bar, 1982, Wisconsin, Illinois and U.S. District Court, Northern District of Illinois; 1991, U.S. Court of Appeals, Seventh Circuit; 1992, Massachusetts and U.S. District Court, District of Massachusetts; 2000, U.S. Supreme Court. *Education:* Shimer College (A.B., with distinction, 1978); University of Wisconsin (J.D., cum laude, 1982). Member, 1996-2003 and Co-Chair, 1999-2001, Board of Directors, Lambda Legal Defense and Education Fund, Inc. ***PRACTICE AREAS:*** Professional Liability Litigation; Director and Officer Liability Litigation; Commercial Litigation; Civil RICO; Employment Litigation. ***Email:*** chyndman@robinsoncurley.com

SUSAN VALENTINE, born Lake Forest, Illinois, September 30, 1962; admitted to bar, 1987, Illinois and U.S. District Court, Northern District of Illinois, including Trial Bar; U.S. Supreme Court. *Education:* Albion College (B.A., magna cum laude, 1984); Chicago-Kent College of Law (J.D., with high honors, 1987). Order of the Coif. Visiting Assistant Professor of Law, Professional Responsibility and Legal Research and Writing, Chicago-Kent College of Law, 1997-2000. ***PRACTICE AREAS:*** Complex Commercial Litigation; Insurance Insolvency; Professional Liability; Civil RICO; Civil Rights. ***Email:*** svalentine@robinsoncurley.com

JOHN H. WICKERT, born Milwaukee, Wisconsin, August 1, 1960; admitted to bar, 1984, Illinois. *Education:* Marquette University (A.B., summa cum laude, 1981); Northwestern University (J.D., cum laude, 1984). Deputy General Counsel, Illinois Office of Special Deputy Receiver, Insurance, 1992-1994. *Member:* Chicago Bar Association (Chairman, Insurance Law Committee, 2001-2002). ***PRACTICE AREAS:*** Insurance Insolvency; Insurance Regulation and Coverage; Commercial Litigation. ***Email:*** jwickert@robinsoncurley.com

ALAN R. DOLINKO, born Chicago, Illinois, September 1, 1961; admitted to bar, 1986, Illinois and U.S. District Court, Northern District of Illinois; 1988, U.S. Court of Appeals, Third Circuit; 1991, U.S. Tax Court; 1994, U.S. Court of Appeals, Seventh Circuit. *Education:* University of Illinois (B.S., with highest honors, 1983); DePaul University (J.D., with honors, 1986). Kappa Tau Alpha. Communications Honor Society, 1983. Recipient, James Brady Award for Political Journalism, 1982. Member, De Paul College of Law Review, 1985-1986. *Member:* Chicago (Member, Civil Practice Committee, Dn III, 1988-1995, Chairman of Division Committee, 1992-1993 and Member Executive Section, 1992-1994), Illinois State and American Bar Associations. ***PRACTICE AREAS:*** General Commercial Litigation. ***Email:*** adolinko@robinsoncurley.com

ROBERT S. MICHAELS, born Detroit, Michigan, December 14, 1963; admitted to bar, 1991, Illinois; 1996, U.S. District Court, Northern District of Illinois; 1997, U.S. Court of Appeals, Seventh Circuit. *Education:* University of Michigan (B.A., 1986); Duke University (J.D., with high honors, 1989). Order of the Coif. Member, Duke Law Journal, 1989. Law Clerk, Honorable Robert H. Hall, U.S. District Court, Northern District of Georgia, 1989-1991. ***PRACTICE AREAS:*** Litigation. ***Email:*** rmichaels@robinsoncurley.com

ELIZABETH J. HUBERTZ, born Hillsborough, Florida, August 26, 1965; admitted to bar, 1993, Illinois, Alabama and U.S. District Court, Northern District of Illinois. *Education:* Wheaton College (B.A., cum laude, 1986); Northwestern University (M.A., 1988); University of Virginia (J.D., 1991). Law Clerk, Honorable Truman M. Hobbs, 1991-1992 and Honorable Ira DeMent, 1992-1993, U.S. District Court, Middle District of Alabama. ***PRACTICE AREAS:*** Complex Commercial Litigation; Employment Discrimination; Civil Rights; First Amendment Law. ***Email:*** ehubertz@robinsoncurley.com

CARL T. BERGETZ, born Melrose Park, Illinois, July 8, 1969; admitted to bar, 1996, Illinois; 2000, California. *Education:* Stanford University (B.A., 1991); University of Illi-

(This Listing Continued)

ROBINSON CURLEY & CLAYTON, P.C., Chicago—Continued

nois College of Law (J.D., magna cum laude, 1996). Summer Extern, Honorable Wayne R. Anderson, U.S. District Court, Northern District of Illinois, 1994. ***PRACTICE AREAS:*** Commercial Litigation. ***Email:*** cbergetz@robinsoncurley.com

ADAM N. HIRSCH, born Evanston, Illinois, October 4, 1976; admitted to bar, 2001, Illinois. *Education:* University of Texas at Austin (B.A., with highest honors, 1998); Harvard Law School (J.D., 2001). *Member:* Chicago and American Bar Associations. ***PRACTICE AREAS:*** Commercial Litigation. ***Email:*** ahirsch@robinsoncurley.com

ANGEL M. KRULL, born Bristol, Connecticut, January 16, 1976; admitted to bar, 2001, Illinois. *Education:* Bradley University (B.A., magna cum laude, 1998); Chicago-Kent College of Law (J.D., with highest honors, 2001). Staff Law Clerk, U.S. Court of Appeals, Seventh Circuit, 2001-2003. Judicial Extern, Hon. Blanche M. Manning, U.S. District Court, Northern District of Illinois, 1999. ***PRACTICE AREAS:*** Commercial Litigation. ***Email:*** akrull@robinsoncurley.com

ROBERT L. MARGOLIS, born New York, N.Y., March 6, 1963; admitted to bar, 1989, New York and U.S. District Court, Eastern and Southern Districts of New York; 1995, Illinois and U.S. District Court, Northern District of Illinois. *Education:* Duke University (B.A., 1985); University of Chicago (J.D., 1988). *Member:* Chicago and American Bar Associations. ***PRACTICE AREAS:*** Commercial Litigation; Civil RICO; Director and Officer Liability Litigation; Entertainment Litigation; Intellectual Property. ***Email:*** rmargolis@robinsoncurley.com

DARLENE M. OLIVER, born Cape Girardeau, Missouri, November 7, 1970; admitted to bar, 1994, Illinois and U.S. District Court, Northern and Southern Districts of Illinois, including Trial Bar. *Education:* Bradley University (B.S., magna cum laude, 1991); Georgetown University Law Center (J.D., 1994). Phi Kappa Phi. ***PRACTICE AREAS:*** Complex Commercial Litigation; Commodities Regulation; Securities Regulation; Environmental Law; Insurance. ***Email:*** doliver@robinsoncurley.com

OF COUNSEL

ELLEN G. ROBINSON, born San Antonio, Texas, April 23, 1944; admitted to bar, 1977, Illinois, U.S. Supreme Court, U.S. Court of Appeals, Seventh, Eighth, Ninth and Federal Circuits; U.S. District Court, Northern District of Illinois including Trial Bar. *Education:* University of Pennsylvania (B.A., 1966); DePaul University (J.D., summa cum laude, 1977). Adjunct Professor, Insurance Law, DePaul University, College of Law, 2000. Assistant State's Attorney, Cook County, Coordinator of Federal Litigation, 1977-1981. Author, "Directors of Insurance Companies, Do You Know To Whom Your Duties Run?" ABA Tips, 1999. Chapter Author, "Receiver's Handbook for Insurance Company Insolvencies." Director, Chicago Bar Foundation. ***PRACTICE AREAS:*** Insurance Insolvency; Insurance Regulation; Professional Liability Litigation; Director and Officer Liability Litigation; Complex Commercial Litigation; Civil RICO; Business Torts; Employment Litigation. ***Email:*** erobinson@robinsoncurley.com

LOIS J. LIPTON, born Chicago, Illinois, January 14, 1946; admitted to bar, 1974, Kentucky, U.S. District Court, Western District of Kentucky and U.S. Court of Appeals, Sixth Circuit; 1975, Illinois and U.S. District Court, Northern District of Illinois; 1976, U.S. Court of Appeals, Seventh Circuit; 1978, U.S. Supreme Court. *Education:* University of Michigan (B.A., 1966); Sheffield University, United Kingdom; DePaul University (J.D., summa cum laude, 1974). Staff, De Paul Law Review, 1972-1973. Delegate to White House Conference on Families, Appointed by Governor James Thompson, 1970. *Member:* Chicago, Kentucky and American Bar Associations; American Judicature Society; Chicago Council of Lawyers. ***PRACTICE AREAS:*** Complex Commercial Litigation; Class Actions. ***Email:*** llipton@robinsoncurley.com

REPRESENTATIVE CLIENTS: AT&T Corp.; National Association of Insurance Commissioners; National Organization for Women; Director of Insurance for the State of Illinios and Special Deputy Liquidator for the State of Illinois; Federal Deposit Insurance Corporation; Special Deputy Receiver, Insurance for the State of West Virginia; Louisiana Department of Insurance, Office of Receivership; Rhode Island Department of Business Regulation; Mississippi Insurance Department; Nevada Department of Business and Industry, Insurance Division; Swiss Reinsurance America Corp.; Wells Fargo Bank, N.A.

RODRIGUEZ O'DONNELL ROSS FUERST GONZALEZ WILLIAMS & ENGLAND, P.C.

8430 W. BRYN MAWR AVENUE, SUITE 525
CHICAGO, ILLINOIS 60631
Telephone: 312-372-7000
Fax: 312-372-1719
Email: rodriguez@rorfgw.com
URL: http://www.rorfgw.com

Washington, D.C. Office: 1211 Connecticut Avenue, N.W., Suite 800, 20036-3007. Telephone: 202-293-3300. Fax: 202-293-3307.
Miami, Florida Office: 1001 Brickell Bay Drive, Suite 2002, 33131. Telephone: 305-350-5690. Fax: 305-371-8989.
New York, New York Office: 45 Rockefeller Plaza, 10111. Telephone: 212-332-8136. Fax: 212-332-3401.
Los Angeles, California Office: 5777 W. Century Boulevard, Suite 1500, 90045-5659. Telephone: 310-410-4414. Fax: 310-410-1017.

International Transportation, Trade, Customs, Maritime, Commercial Transactions Law, Government Relations, Tax and Tax Litigation.

(For complete biographical data on all personnel, see Professional Biographies at Washington, D.C.)

ROOKS PITTS

CHICAGO, ILLINOIS

(See Dykema Gossett PLLC)

ROPER & QUIGG

CHICAGO, ILLINOIS

(See Jenner & Block LLP)

LAW OFFICES OF MARK J. ROSE

200 WEST ADAMS STREET, SUITE 2850
CHICAGO, ILLINOIS 60606-5206
Telephone: 312-704-1446
Fax: 312-704-8233
Email: MJRoseEsq@aol.com
URL: http://www.markjrose.com

Litigation Practice, including Bankruptcy, Creditor Rights, Mechanic's Lien Foreclosure, Mortgage Foreclosure and Commercial Law; Real Estate, Commercial Leasing, Buying and Selling of Businesses and Commercial Transactions.

MARK J. ROSE, born Chicago, Illinois, May 16, 1952; admitted to bar, 1977, Illinois and U.S. District Court, Northern District of Illinois; 1981, U.S. Court of Appeals, Seventh Circuit; 2002, U.S. District Court, Western District of Wisconsin. *Education:* University of Illinois (B.A., Political Science, magna cum laude, 1974); Northwestern University (J.D., 1977). Phi Beta Kappa; Phi Kappa Phi; Phi Eta Sigma; Pi Sigma Alpha. Member, Bronze Tablet. Edmund J. James Scholar. Participant, Julius Miner Moot Court Competition, 1976. *Member:* Chicago (Member, Bankruptcy and Reorganization Committee, 1982—), Illinois State and American Bar Associations; Decalogue Society of Lawyers.

REPRESENTATIVE CLIENTS: Adams Foam Rubber Co.; Allied Tube & Conduit; General Ceilings of Illinois, Inc.; Harris Bank/Bartlett; Hartney Fuel Oil Co.; Just Rite Acoustics, Inc.; Metropolitan Industries, Inc.; Midwest Acoustics, Inc.; Precision Midwest, Ltd.; Reinke Gypsum Supply Co., Inc.; Reinke Interior Supply Company, Inc.; RS Used Oil Services, Inc.; Safway Steel Products, Inc.; Slurry Systems, Inc.; Wheaton Associates, Inc.

LAW OFFICES OF CAREY S. ROSEMARIN, P.C.

CHICAGO, ILLINOIS

(See Northbrook)

Environmental Law.

MICHAEL C. ROSENBLAT, P.C.

CHICAGO, ILLINOIS

(See Glenview)

Criminal Law, Civil Practice, Qui Tam Litigation, False Claims Act, Whistleblower Litigation, White Collar Crimes, Drug Crimes, Parole and Probation, Juvenile Crimes, Driving While Intoxicated.

THE LAW OFFICE OF CURTIS BENNETT ROSS

19 SOUTH LA SALLE STREET, 13TH FLOOR
CHICAGO, ILLINOIS 60603
Telephone: 312-984-1514
Fax: 312-984-1504
Email: RossatLaw@aol.com
URL: http://www.divorce-chicago.com

Family Law, Divorce, Child Custody, Child Support, Paternity, Visitation.

CURTIS BENNETT ROSS, born Carbondale, Illinois, June 7, 1955; admitted to bar, 1980, Illinois. *Education:* University of Illinois (B.S., 1977; J.D., 1980). Teaching Assistant, Basic Financial Accounting and Federal Income Taxation, University of Illinois, 1979-1980. *Member:* Chicago Bar Association; Decalogue Society. ***PRACTICE AREAS:*** Family Law; Divorce; Child Custody; Child Support; Paternity; Visitation Rights.

ROSS, DIXON & BELL, LLP

55 WEST MONROE STREET
SUITE 3000
CHICAGO, ILLINOIS 60603-5758
Telephone: 312-759-1920
Fax: 312-759-1939
Email: info@rdblaw.com
URL: http://www.rdblaw.com

Washington, D.C. Office: 2001 K Street, N.W., 20006-1040. Telephone: 202-662-2000. Fax: 202-662-2190.
Irvine, California Office: 5 Park Plaza, Suite 1200, 92614-8592. Telephone: 949-622-2700. Fax: 949-622-2739.
San Diego, California Office: 550 West B Street, Suite 400, 92101-3538. Telephone: 619-235-4040. Fax: 619-231-8796.

Commercial Litigation and Appellate Practice, Insurance Coverage Litigation and Counseling, Directors and Officers Liability, Professional Liability, Environmental/Mass Tort Coverage, General Liability.

(This Listing Continued)

PARTNERS

EILEEN KING BOWER, born Naperville, Illinois, November 27, 1964; admitted to bar, 1988, Illinois; U.S. District Court, Northern District of Illinois. *Education:* Loyola University (B.A., cum laude, 1987; J.D., 1988). *Member:* Chicago, Illinois State and American Bar Associations. ***PRACTICE AREAS:*** Insurance Coverage Litigation and Counseling. ***Email:*** ebower@rdblaw.com

MICHAEL G. BRUTON, born Chicago, Illinois, May 6, 1960; admitted to bar, 1985, Illinois; U.S. District Court, Northern and Central Districts of Illinois; U.S. District Court, Northern District of Indiana; U.S. District Court, Eastern District of Michigan; U.S. District Court, Eastern District of Wisconsin; U.S. Court of Appeals, Seventh Circuit; U.S. Supreme Court. *Education:* University of Notre Dame (B.A., 1982; J.D., magna cum laude, 1985). Member, National Moot Court Team, 1984-1985. Judicial Law Clerk to the Honorable Kenneth F. Ripple, United States Court of Appeals for the Seventh Circuit, 1985-1986. Argued on Behalf of Petitioner Before U.S. Supreme Court in Milwaukee Brewery Workers v. Joseph Schlitz Brewing Co. No. 93-768. ***PRACTICE AREAS:*** Commercial Litigation; Insurance Coverage; Professional Liability. ***Email:*** mbruton@rdblaw.com

CLINTON E. CAMERON, born Indianapolis, Indiana, November 22, 1965; admitted to bar, 1991, Michigan; 1993, District of Columbia; 2001, Illinois; U.S. District Court for the District of Columbia; U.S. District Court, Western District of Michigan; U.S. District Court, Northern District of Illinois; U.S. Court of Appeals for the District of Columbia Circuit; U.S. Supreme Court. *Education:* University of Michigan (A.B., 1988; J.D., 1991); London Business School, University of London (M.S., 1999). Sloan Fellow. James B. Angell Scholar. Articles Editor, Michigan Journal of International Law, 1990-1991. *Member:* Chicago Bar Association. ***PRACTICE AREAS:*** Commercial Litigation; Environmental; Mass Tort Claims; Insurance Coverage Disputes; Professional Liability. ***Email:*** ccameron@rdblaw.com

HALLIE MILLER FAHEY, born McHenry, Illinois, July 2, 1965; admitted to bar, 1990, Illinois; U.S. District Court, Northern District of Illinois, including Trial Bar; U.S. Court of Appeals, Fifth and Seventh Circuits. *Education:* Butler University (B.S., cum laude, 1987); Boston College Law School (1987-1988); University of Illinois College of Law (J.D., cum laude, 1990). Delta Theta Phi. Harno Scholar. Recipient: American Jurisprudence Award, Legal Process. Member, University of Illinois Law Review. Editor, Illinois Bar Journal, 1989-1990. Author: Note, "DeBartolo Corp. v. Florida Gulf Building and Trades Council, 108 S. Ct. 1392, (1988)," 77 Ill. B.J. 613 (1989). Co-Author: "Tenders of Defense: Practical Solutions to Insurance Coverage Problems," IDC Journal (Spring 1994); "Interpleader," Chapter in Illinois Institute for Continuing Legal Education (2000). *Member:* Chicago, Illinois State and American Bar Associations; Defense Research Institute. ***REPORTED CASES:*** Chicago Hospital Risk Pooling Program v. Illinois State Medical Insurance Exchange, 325 Ill. App. 3d 970, 758 N.E.2d 353 (2001); Eastern Products Corp., et al. v. CNA Insurance Co., et al., No. 97-2376, Superior Court for the County of Essex, Massachusetts, reported in 14 Mealey's Litigation Report: Insurance 27 (May 16, 2000); Safeskin Insurance Management, Inc., et al. v. Pacific Indemnity Co., et al., No. 719448, Superior Court of San Diego County, California, reported in 14 Mealey's Litigation Report: Insurance 1 (November 2, 1999); Boyette v. Trans World Airlines, Inc. 954 S.W.2d 350 (Mo. App. 1997); Radic v. Chicago Transit Authority, 878 F. Supp. 1130 (N.D. Ill. 1995). ***PRACTICE AREAS:*** Construction Law; Employment; Insurance Coverage Litigation. ***Email:*** hfahey@rdblaw.com

REBECCA L. ROSS, born Lexington, Nebraska, March 16, 1951; admitted to bar, 1976, Nebraska; 1979, Minnesota; 1980, District of Columbia; 2001, Illinois; U.S. Court of Appeals for the District of Columbia; U.S. District Court for the District of Columbia; U.S. District Court, District of Maryland; U.S. Supreme Court. *Education:* Colby College (B.A., 1973); University of Nebraska (J.D., with distinction, 1976). Order of the Coif; The Order of Barristers. Member, National Moot Court Team, 1974-1975. Associate Editor, Nebraska Law Review, 1975-1976. Author: Note, "The Supreme Court Avoids Considering Sex-Based Classifications," 55 Nebraska Law Review 133, 1976. Co-Author: "Developments in West Virginia's Insurance Bad Faith Law—Where Do We Go From Here?" 98 West Virginia Law Review 267, 1995; "Handling a Complex General Liability Insurance Coverage Action," ABA Section of Litigation Insurance Coverage CLE Seminar, March 2004; "Spreading The Risk: Other Insurance Clauses," Insurance Coverage and Claims Institute Seminar, April 2005. Attorney: U.S. Department of Justice, Civil Division, 1976-1979; Briggs & Morgan, 1979-1980; U.S. Attorneys' Office, Civil Division, Washington, D.C., 1980-1987. *Member:* The District of Columbia Bar; Nebraska State and Minnesota State Bar Associations; Defense Research Institute. ***PRACTICE AREAS:*** Bad Faith Claims; Commercial Litigation; Complex Litigation; Environmental; Insurance Coverage; Mass Torts. ***Email:*** rross@rdblaw.com

MICHAEL P. TONE, born Washington, D.C., August 31, 1949; admitted to bar, 1974, Illinois; U.S. Court of Appeals, Fourth, Fifth, Seventh, Eighth, Ninth, Tenth and Eleventh Circuits; U.S. District Court, Northern and Southern Districts of Illinois; U.S. District Court, Western District of Michigan. *Education:* Denison University (B.A., 1971); University of South Carolina (J.D., 1974). *Member:* American Bar Association. ***PRACTICE AREAS:*** Bad Faith Claims; Directors and Officers Liability; Insurance; Litigation; Professional Liability. ***Email:*** mtone@rdblaw.com

DANIEL J. ZOLLNER, born Belleville, Illinois, May 6, 1956; admitted to bar, 1981, Illinois and U.S. District Court, Northern District of Illinois, including Trial Bar; 1986, U.S. Court of Appeals, Sixth, Seventh and Eighth Circuits. *Education:* University of Illinois (B.S., magna cum laude, with distinction in Finance, 1978; J.D., magna cum laude, 1981). Phi Beta Kappa; Mortar Board; Order of the Coif. Harno Scholar. ***PRACTICE AREAS:*** Insurance Coverage; Insurance Bad Faith; Insurance Professional Liability; Healthcare Coverage; ERISA; ERISA Litigation; Commercial Litigation. ***Email:*** dzollner@rdblaw.com

OF COUNSEL

SCOTT E. TURNER, born Phoenix, Arizona, October 9, 1968; admitted to bar, 1995, Illinois; U.S. Court of Appeals, Seventh Circuit; U.S. District Court, Northern District of Illinois. *Education:* University of Arizona (B.A., summa cum laude, 1990); University of Chicago (M.A., 1992); Northwestern University (J.D., 1995). Phi Beta Kappa. *Member:* Defense Research Institute. ***PRACTICE AREAS:*** Insurance Law; Professional Liability Defense; Professional Liability Coverage; Bad Faith. ***Email:*** sturner@rdblaw.com

ASSOCIATES

KIMBERLY E. BLAIR, born Pontiac, Illinois, July 30, 1975; admitted to bar, 2000, Illinois; U.S. District Court, Northern District of Illinois. *Education:* University of Illinois (B.A., magna cum laude, 1997); Vanderbilt University (J.D., 2000). Phi Beta Kappa. *Member:* Chicago and Illinois State Bar Associations. ***PRACTICE AREAS:*** Insurance Coverage; Litigation; Professional Liability. ***Email:*** kblair@rdblaw.com

JULIE L. BURGENER, born Joliet, Illinois, April 2, 1970; admitted to bar, 1999, Illinois; U.S. District Court, Northern District of Illinois. *Education:* Northern Illinois University (B.A., 1993); University of Illinois (J.D., magna cum laude, 1999). ***PRACTICE AREAS:*** Environmental Claims; Insurance Coverage Litigation and Counseling; Professional Liability. ***Email:*** jburgener@rdblaw.com

DAVID I. CURKOVIC, born May 3, 1977; admitted to bar, 2001, Illinois; U.S. District Court, Northern District of Illinois; U.S. Court of Appeals, Seventh Circuit. *Education:* University of Michigan (B.A., 1998; J.D., 2001). ***PRACTICE AREAS:*** Environmental Law; Insurance Law. ***Email:*** dcurkovic@rdblaw.com

DAVID F. CUTTER, admitted to bar, 1995, Maryland; 1997, District of Columbia; 2002, Illinois. *Education:* University of Michigan (B.G.S., 1989); Columbus School of Law of The Catholic University of America (J.D., magna cum laude, 1995). Law School Class Salutatorian. Executive Editor, Catholic University Law Review. Author: Note, 44 Catholic University Law Review 631, 1995. Law Clerk to the Hon. Aubrey E. Robinson, Jr., U.S. District Court for the District of Columbia, 1996-1997. ***PRACTICE AREAS:*** Insurance; Litigation. ***Email:*** dcutter@rdblaw.com

EÓIN M. DEMPSEY, born Evanston, Illinois, September 30, 1981; admitted to bar, 2005, Illinois. *Education:* University of Illinois (A.B., 2002; J.D., cum laude, 2005). ***PRACTICE AREAS:*** Insurance. ***Email:*** edempsey@rdblaw.com

PATRICK FRYE, born Charlotte, North Carolina, January 22, 1979; admitted to bar, 2004, Illinois. *Education:* University of North Carolina (B.A., with honors and highest distinction, 2001); Harvard Law School (J.D., 2004). Phi Beta Kappa. ***PRACTICE AREAS:*** Insurance Coverage Litigation and Counseling. ***Email:*** pfrye@rdblaw.com

TIMOTHY FURROW, born Flint, Michigan, October 23, 1976; admitted to bar, 2002, Illinois; U.S. District Court, Northern District of Illinois. *Education:* Indiana University (B.A., 1999); University of Iowa College of Law (J.D., with distinction, 2002). Author: "Canada Challenged as a Human Rights Leader: The Human Rights Committee's Decision in Waldman," 11 Transnational Law and Contemporary Problems, 225 (2001). *Member:* Chicago and American Bar Associations. ***PRACTICE AREAS:*** Litigation; Professional Liability; Insurance Coverage Litigation and Counseling; Mass Torts; Environmental Claims. ***Email:*** tfurrow@rdblaw.com

STEPHANIE HAAS, born Madison, Wisconsin, February 23, 1973; admitted to bar, 2002, Illinois; U.S. District Court, Northern District of Illinois. *Education:* University of Minnesota (B.A., 1996; J.D., 2002). *Member:* Chicago, Illinois State and American Bar Associations. ***PRACTICE AREAS:*** Bad Faith Claims; Environmental Claims; Insurance Coverage Litigation; Complex Litigation. ***Email:*** shaas@rdblaw.com

ADAM E. JONES, born Des Moines, Iowa, October 24, 1974; admitted to bar, 2002, Illinois and U.S. District Court, Northern District of Illinois. *Education:* University of Iowa (B.A., 1998); University of Iowa, College of Law (J.D., with distinction, 2002). *Member:* Chicago, Illinois State and American Bar Associations. ***PRACTICE AREAS:*** Insurance Coverage Litigation; Environmental; Antitrust; Civil Appeals; Complex and Multi-District Litigation. ***Email:*** ajones@rdblaw.com

PETER D. LINDAU, born New York, New York, September 18, 1963; admitted to bar, 1996, Illinois; U.S. District Court, District of Illinois; U.S. Court of Appeals, Seventh Circuit. *Education:* University of Vermont (B.A., 1985); Boston College (J.D., 1996). National Moot Court Team. ***PRACTICE AREAS:*** Environmental; Insurance Coverage; Media Law; Professional Liability. ***Email:*** plindau@rdblaw.com

ALEX MAHLER, born Scottsdale, Arizona, August 4, 1969; admitted to bar, 2000, Illinois. *Education:* Arizona State University (B.S., magna cum laude, 1992); Indiana University - Indianapolis (J.D., 2000). Chartered Property Casualty Underwriter. *Member:* Illinois State and American (Member, Tort and Insurance Practice Section) Bar Associations; American Institute for Chartered Property Casualty Underwriters (AICPCU). ***PRACTICE AREAS:*** Insurance Coverage; Professional Liability; General Liability; Environmental; Mass Tort Claims; Health Coverage; Lawyers Liability. ***Email:*** amahler@rdblaw.com

MELISSA McGUANE, born Wheeling, West Virginia, 1977; admitted to bar, 2002, Maryland; 2003, West Virginia; 2004, District of Columbia and Illinois. *Education:* Miami University (B.S., cum laude, 1999); American University, Washington College of Law (J.D., cum laude, 2002). Member, Moot Court Board. Member, American University Law Review. *Member:* West Virginia and Illinois State Bar Associations; The District of Columbia Bar. ***PRACTICE AREAS:*** Insurance; Litigation; Antitrust. ***Email:*** mmcguane@rdblaw.com

TYLER MERTES, born Arlington Heights, Illinois, April 22, 1979; admitted to bar, 2004, Illinois; U.S. District Court, Northern District of Illinois. *Education:* University of Illinois (B.A., 2001; J.D., 2004). ***PRACTICE AREAS:*** Insurance Coverage Litigation and Counseling. ***Email:*** tmertes@rdblaw.com

JESSIKA J. MOON, born Singapore, January 26, 1974; admitted to bar, 2000, New York; 2004, Illinois; U.S. District Court, Southern District of New York; U.S. District Court, Eastern District of New York; U.S. District Court, Northern District of Illinois. *Education:* Georgetown University (B.S., 1996); Boston University School of Law (J.D., 1999). Member, BUSL Labor Law Moot Court Team, 1998-1999; Law Clerk, United States Court of Appeals for the Second Ciruit, Staff Attorney's Office, March 2000-August 2001. *Member:* Association of the Bar of the City of New York; Illinois State, New York State and American Bar Associations. ***PRACTICE AREAS:*** Insurance Coverage. ***Email:*** jmoon@rdblaw.com

(This Listing Continued)

ROSS, DIXON & BELL, LLP, Chicago—Continued

EDWARD B. MULLEN, III, born Monmouth, Illinois, September 18, 1967; admitted to bar, 1998, California; 2004, District of Columbia; 2005, Illinois. *Education:* University of Pennsylvania (B.A.); George Washington University (J.D., 1997). Order of the Coif. ***PRACTICE AREAS:*** Commercial Litigation. ***Email:*** emullen@rdblaw.com

MILIND PAREKH, born Ottawa, Ontario, Canada, November 21, 1968; admitted to bar, 1995, New Jersey; 1997, Michigan and New York; 2003, Illinois; U.S. District Court, Eastern and Western Districts of Michigan; U.S. District Court, Northern District of Indiana; U.S. District Court, Eastern District of Wisconsin. *Education:* University of Michigan (A.B., with distinction, 1991); Fordham University (J.D., 1995). *Member:* American Bar Association. ***LANGUAGES:*** Gujarati. ***PRACTICE AREAS:*** Insurance Coverage Litigation and Counseling; Complex Litigation; Insurance Bad Faith. ***Email:*** mparekh@rdblaw.com

REGINA RIPLEY, born Berlin, Germany, December 20, 1971; admitted to bar, 2001, Illinois; U.S. District Court, Northern District of Illinois; U.S. Court of Appeals, Seventh Circuit. *Education:* University of Illinois at Urbana-Champaign (B.S., 1994; J.D., cum laude, 2001); Indiana University (M.A., 1998). *Member:* Chicago and American Bar Associations. ***LANGUAGES:*** Spanish. ***PRACTICE AREAS:*** Insurance Coverage. ***Email:*** rripley@rdblaw.com

CAROL THRELKELD, born Alton, Illinois, May 29, 1970; admitted to bar, 2002, Illinois; U.S. District Court, Northern District of Illinois. *Education:* Southern Illinois University (B.A., 1995); New Mexico State University (M.A., 1999); University of Illinois (J.D., 2002). *Member:* Chicago and Illinois State Bar Associations. ***PRACTICE AREAS:*** Insurance Coverage; Professional Liability. ***Email:*** cthrelkeld@rdblaw.com

CHRISTOPHER WHITE, born April 22, 1977; admitted to bar, 2004, Illinois; U.S. District Court, Northern District of Illinois and U.S. Court of Appeals, Seventh Circuit. *Education:* Princeton University (A.B., cum laude, 1999); Northwestern University (J.D., cum laude, 2003). Order of the Coif. Associate Editor, Northwestern University Law Review, 2002-2003. Staff Law Clerk, U.S. Court of Appeals for the Seventh Circuit, 2003-2005. Author, "No Good Deed Goes Unpunished: The Case for Reform of the Rescue Doctrine," 97 NW. U.L. Rev. 507, 2003. *Member:* American Bar Association. ***PRACTICE AREAS:*** Insurance Bad Faith; Insurance Coverage; Complex Litigation. ***Email:*** cwhite@rdblaw.com

(For complete biographical data on all personnel, see Professional Biographies at Washington, D.C.)

ROSS & HARDIES

CHICAGO, ILLINOIS

(See McGuireWoods LLP)

THE LAW OFFICE OF MARK L. ROTERT

11 SOUTH LASALLE STREET, SUITE 1200
CHICAGO, ILLINOIS 60603
Telephone: 312-236-8115
Fax: 312-236-8116
Email: mlr@markrotertlaw.com
URL: http://www.markrotertlaw.com

White Collar Criminal Defense, Commercial Litigation, Appellate Practice.

MARK L. ROTERT, born Sioux Falls, South Dakota, August 16, 1952; admitted to bar, 1977, Illinois and U.S. District Court, Northern District of Illinois; 1983, U.S. Supreme Court; 1995, U.S. District Court, District of Minnesota; 1998, U.S. District Court, Eastern District of Wisconsin; 1999, U.S. District Court, Central District of Illinois; 2003, U.S. District Court, Northern District of Indiana. *Education:* St. John's University (B.A., 1974); Loyola University (J.D., 1977). Assistant Attorney General, 1977-1987. Assistant U.S. Attorney, 1987-1994. Adjunct Professor: Appellate Advocacy, Loyola University School of Law, 1987-1989; Trial Advocacy, The John Marshall Law School, 1991-1993. Partner, Winston & Strawn, 1994-2004. *Member:* Illinois State Bar Association; Illinois Society of Trial Lawyers; National Association of Criminal Defense Attorneys. ***REPORTED CASES:*** Greer v. Miller, 483 U.S. 756 (1987); Allen v. Illinois, 478 U.S. 364 (1986). ***PRACTICE AREAS:*** White Collar Criminal Defense; Commercial Litigation; Appellate Practice.

ASSOCIATE

MATTHEW J. GULDE, admitted to bar, 2000, Illinois and U.S. District Court, Northern District of Illinois. *Education:* University of Notre Dame (B.S., cum laude, 1996); University of Texas (J.D., cum laude, 2000). Tau Beta Pi; Chi Epsilon. Kirkland & Ellis, 2000-2003; Law Clerk to the Honorable Amy J. St. Eve, District Court Judge for the Northern District of Illinois, 2003-2004. ***Email:*** mjgulde@markrotertlaw.com

THE ROTH LAW GROUP, LLC

Established in 2004

111 WEST WASHINGTON STREET, SUITE 1440
CHICAGO, ILLINOIS 60602
Telephone: 312-419-9599
Fax: 312-419-9559
Email: kwr@rothlawgroup.com
URL: http://www.rothlawgroup.com

Corporate Law: Business Litigation and Counseling, Prosecution and Defense of Contractual, Statutory and Common Law Claims, Equipment Leasing Contracts, Construction Contracts, Insurance Defense: Premises Liability, Coverage Analysis, Aviation: Prosecution and Defense of Mishap Claims, Real Estate: Buy-Sell Contracts, Closings, Condominium Conversions, Personal Injury: Accidents, Drug Injury.

(This Listing Continued)

FIRM PROFILE: The Roth Law Group, LLC represents and counsels small business and individual clients in commercial litigation and corporate transactions. The firm has an extensive Equipment Leasing practice representing defendants in contract disputes. We also offer Insurance Defense services specializing in Premises Liability and Aviation and are experienced in Real Estate and Personal Injury.

MEMBER OF FIRM

KARL W. ROTH, born Chicago, Illinois, November 12, 1965; admitted to bar, 2001, Illinois and U.S. District Court, Northern District of Illinois; U.S. Court of Appeals, District of Columbia Circuit. *Education:* Eastern Illinois University (B.S., 1987); Loyola University (J.D., 2001). *Member:* Chicago, Illinois State and American Bar Associations. [USMC, 1990-2003 Major KC-130 Pilot]. ***PRACTICE AREAS:*** Corporate Law; Business Law; Commercial Litigation; Insurance Defense; Aviation Law; Real Estate. ***Email:*** kwr@rothlawgroup.com

OF COUNSEL

BRAD JOHNSON, born Okmulgee, Oklahoma, May 2, 1971; admitted to bar, 2002, Illinois, U.S. District Court, Northern District of Illinois. *Education:* Northwestern University (B.A., 1993); Loyola University (J.D., 2002). *Member:* Chicago and Illinois State Bar Associations. ***PRACTICE AREAS:*** Real Estate; Corporate Law; Business Law; Commercial Litigation; Insurance Defense; Personal Injury. ***Email:*** rbj@rothlawgroup.com

JOEL S. ROTHMAN & ASSOCIATES, LTD.

55 WEST MONROE STREET, SUITE 3330
CHICAGO, ILLINOIS 60603
Telephone: 312-578-0900
Fax: 312-578-0905
Email: joel@rothmanlaw.com

Estate Planning, Estate and Trust Administration. Business Planning, Probate, Tax Planning, Corporate and Charitable Contribution Law.

JOEL S. ROTHMAN, born Chicago, Illinois, October 5, 1955; admitted to bar, 1980, Illinois. *Education:* Northwestern University (B.A., 1977; J.D., 1980). Assistant Instructor, Northwestern University School of Law, 1979-1980. Seminars: Credit Shelter Trusts, Decalogue Society of Lawyers, November 8, 2000; Drafting Wills and Trust Agreements, Decalogue Society of Lawyers, February 21, 1996, February 15, 1995, December 7, 1989; Gathering Client Information, Chicago Bar Association, April 23, 1997, April 12, 1996, April 30, 1991, May 2, 1990; Drafting in Consideration of Disclaimers, Chicago Bar Association, February 26, 1990; Basic Drafting Considerations, Chicago Bar Association, January 25, 1990. *Member:* Chicago (Member and Chairman, Trust Law Committee, 1997-1998, 2000-2002), Illinois State and American Bar Associations. (Also Of Counsel to Otis Law Offices, Mark T. Neil & Associates and Mitchell D. Pawlan, Ltd.). ***PRACTICE AREAS:*** Estate Planning; Probate; Estate and Trust Administration; Business Succession Planning; Charitable Trusts and Foundations; Closely Held Corporations. ***Email:*** joel@rothmanlaw.com

---

THOMAS D. STERLING, born Hinsdale, Illinois; admitted to bar, 1997, Illinois and U.S. District Court, Northern District of Illinois. *Education:* Northwestern University (B.A., 1993; J.D., 1996). *Member:* Chicago and Illinois State Bar Associations. (Also Of Counsel to Otis Law Offices, Mark T. Neil & Associates and Mitchell D. Pawlan, Ltd.). ***PRACTICE AREAS:*** Estate Planning; Probate; Trust Administration; Estate Administration. ***Email:*** tom@rothmanlaw.com

CHRISTOPHER R. FLECK, born Zionsville, Indiana, November 22, 1978; admitted to bar, 2004, Illinois. *Education:* DePauw University (B.A., 2001); Valparaiso University (J.D., 2004). *Member:* Chicago and Illinois State Bar Associations. (Also Of Counsel to Mark T. Neil & Associates and Mitchell D. Pawlan, Ltd.). ***PRACTICE AREAS:*** Estate Planning; Probate; Trust Administration; Estate Administration. ***Email:*** chris@rothmanlaw.com

OF COUNSEL

STUART A. COHN, born Chicago, Illinois, August 9, 1952; admitted to bar, 1980, Illinois. *Education:* University of Chicago (B.A., 1975; M.B.A., 1977; J.D., 1980). Certified Public Accountant, 1983. ***PRACTICE AREAS:*** Corporate Law; Securities.

MARK T. NEIL, born Peru, Illinois, November 23, 1949; admitted to bar, 1975, Illinois. *Education:* Shimer College (B.A., 1971); Oxford University, Oxford, England; Northwestern (J.D., 1974). *Member:* Chicago Bar Association. ***PRACTICE AREAS:*** Estate Planning; Estate Administration; Trust Administration; Probate.

ANITA S. RIDGE, born Hammond, Indiana, August 17, 1966; admitted to bar, 1991, Illinois and U.S. District, Northern District of Illinois. *Education:* Monmouth College (B.A., 1988); University of Chicago (J.D., 1991). *Member:* Chicago, Illinois State and American Bar Associations. ***PRACTICE AREAS:*** Estate Planning; Charitable Trusts and Foundations; Estate and Trust Administration.

ROBERT E. STIGGER, born Wilmington, Delaware, September 30, 1949; admitted to bar, 1976, Illinois. *Education:* Macalester College (B.A., 1971); University of Chicago (J.D., 1976). Peace Corps Volunteer, Afghanistan, 1971-1972. *Member:* Chicago and Illinois State Bar Associations. ***PRACTICE AREAS:*** Venture Capital Investments; Joint Ventures; Partnership Formation; Contracts; Business Transactions; Mergers and Acquisitions.

MICHEL WINKELSTEIN, born Zurich, Switzerland, October 10, 1951; admitted to bar, 1987, Illinois and U.S. District Court, Northern District of Illinois, including Trial Bar. *Education:* State University of New York at Buffalo (B.A., English, 1974); John Marshall Law School (J.D., 1987). *Member:* Chicago and Illinois State Bar Associations; National

(This Listing Continued)

Association of Consumer Bankruptcy Attorneys. ***PRACTICE AREAS:*** Real Estate; Consumer Bankruptcy; Bankruptcy; Probate.

ROTHSCHILD, BARRY & MYERS

A Partnership including Professional Corporations

Established in 1952

SUITE 3900

55 WEST MONROE STREET

CHICAGO, ILLINOIS 60603-5012

Telephone: 312-372-2345

FAX: 312-372-2350

Email: firm@rbmchicago.com

URL: http://www.rbmchicago.com

General Civil, Trial and Appellate Practice in Federal and State Courts. General, Corporate and Business Law, Real Estate, Estate Planning, Trusts and Probate, Antitrust, Aviation, Creditor, Bankruptcy, Class Actions, Constitutional Law, Construction Law, Employment Discrimination, Environmental, Franchising, Insurance, Intellectual Property, Pensions, Secured Transactions and Taxation.

FIRM PROFILE: The firm was founded in 1952 by Edward I. Rothschild, John Paul Stevens, and Norman J. Barry. Today, the firm continues its long tradition of representing clients with the quality and depth often associated with larger firms, but with the greater efficiency, responsiveness, and personal touch that the best small firms can provide. The firm's highly qualified group of attorneys work well together in serving their clients' needs. Representation of small to medium-sized businesses is a major part of the firm's business. The firm's clients also include large publicly held companies, trade associations, governmental bodies, and families and individuals.

MEMBERS OF FIRM

NORMAN J. BARRY (P.C.) (1921-1998)

EDWARD I. ROTHSCHILD (P.C.), born Chicago, Illinois, November 6, 1921; admitted to bar, 1949, Illinois. *Education:* Harvard University (A.B., magna cum laude, 1942); Harvard University Law School (LL.B., magna cum laude, 1948). Phi Beta Kappa. Member, Board of Editors, Harvard Law Review, 1947-1948. Chairman, Committee on Character and Fitness, Supreme Court of Illinois, 1959-1960. President, Harvard Law Society, 1961-1962. *Member:* Chicago (Member, 1949-1969, and Chairman, 1965-1967, Legislative Committee; Member: Board of Managers, 1960-1962; Committee on Candidates, 1962-1969) and American Bar Associations. ***PRACTICE AREAS:*** Estate Planning; Business Law; Real Estate; Trust Law; Probate.

WILLIAM G. MYERS (P.C.), born Chicago, Illinois, March 16, 1930; admitted to bar, 1953, Illinois. *Education:* Northwestern University (B.S., 1950; J.D., 1953). Phi Delta Phi. *Member:* Chicago, Illinois State and American Bar Associations. ***PRACTICE AREAS:*** Real Estate; Trusts and Estates; Business Law. **Email:** wgm@rbmchicago.com

MELVIN I. MISHKIN, born Brooklyn, New York, November 28, 1931; admitted to bar, 1957, Illinois. *Education:* Northwestern University (B.S.L., 1956; J.D., 1957). Tau Epsilon Rho; Order of the Coif. Member, Board of Editors, Northwestern University Law Review, 1956-1957. Attorney, Department of Justice, Antitrust Division, 1958-1959. *Member:* Chicago and American Bar Associations. ***PRACTICE AREAS:*** Automotive Franchises and Dealerships; Civil Litigation; Family Law.

JOHN J. COFFEY, III, born Evanston, Illinois, March 14, 1936; admitted to bar, 1961, Illinois. *Education:* St. Mary's College (B.A., cum laude, 1958); University of Notre Dame (J.D., 1961). Legislation Editor, Notre Dame Law Review, 1960-1961. *Member:* Chicago, Illinois State and American Bar Associations. ***PRACTICE AREAS:*** Business Law; Real Estate; Trusts and Estates. **Email:** coffey@rbmchicago.com

JOSEPH P. DELLA MARIA, JR., born Chicago, Illinois, October 11, 1940; admitted to bar, 1966, Illinois. *Education:* University of Notre Dame (A.B., 1962; J.D., 1966). Lead Articles Editor, Notre Dame Law Review, 1965-1966. Law Clerk to Judge Roger J. Kiley, U.S. Court of Appeals, Seventh Circuit, 1966-1967. *Member:* Chicago, Illinois State and American Bar Associations. [LCDR, JAGC, USNR, active duty, 1967-1971]. ***PRACTICE AREAS:*** Business Law; Business Litigation; Intellectual Property. **Email:** jpd@rbmchicago.com

MICHAEL J. WALL, born Chicago, Illinois, November 14, 1946; admitted to bar, 1975, Illinois. *Education:* University of Illinois (B.A., 1972); Chicago-Kent College of Law (J.D., with honors, 1975). Law Clerk to: Justice Edward J. Egan, Illinois Appellate Court, 1975; Justice John M. O'Connor, Jr., Illinois Appellate Court, 1976. *Member:* Chicago, Illinois State and American Bar Associations. ***PRACTICE AREAS:*** Construction Law; Litigation; Franchise Law and Litigation; Business Litigation; Environmental Litigation; Real Estate. **Email:** wall@rbmchicago.com

DANIEL CUMMINGS, born Joliet, Illinois, February 2, 1950; admitted to bar, 1975, Illinois. *Education:* Brown University (A.B., 1972); New York University (J.D., 1975). Assistant Defender, Office of State Appellate Defender, 1975-1978. *Member:* Chicago, Illinois State and American Bar Associations. ***PRACTICE AREAS:*** Commercial Litigation; Personal Injury Defense; Construction Litigation. **Email:** cummings@rbmchicago.com

KENNETH P. TAUBE, born St. Louis, Missouri, December 19, 1949; admitted to bar, 1979, Illinois. *Education:* Harvard College (B.A., 1976); University of Illinois (J.D., 1979). Managing Editor, University of Illinois Law Review, 1978-1979. Law Clerk to Justice Robert C. Underwood, Supreme Court of Illinois, 1979-1980. *Member:* Chicago, Illinois State and American Bar Associations. ***PRACTICE AREAS:*** Business Law; Intellectual Property; Civil Litigation; Construction Law. **Email:** taubek@rbmchicago.com

JONATHAN E. ROTHSCHILD, born Chicago, Illinois, September 4, 1954; admitted to bar, 1980, Illinois. *Education:* Kenyon College (B.A., cum laude, 1976); Northwestern University (J.D., 1980). *Member:* Chicago, Illinois State and American Bar Associations. ***PRACTICE AREAS:*** Real Estate; Business Law; Trusts and Estates. **Email:** rothj@rbmchicago.com

(This Listing Continued)

ALAN S. MADANS, born Brooklyn, New York, May 9, 1957; admitted to bar, 1982, New York; 1984, Illinois. *Education:* Northwestern University (B.A., with honors, 1978); Duke University (J.D., with distinction, 1981). Phi Beta Kappa; Order of the Coif. Editor-in-Chief, Duke Law Journal, 1980-1981. Law Clerk to: Judge James L. Oakes, U.S. Court of Appeals, Second Circuit, 1981-1982; Mr. Justice Harry A. Blackmun, 1982-1983. *Member:* Chicago and American Bar Associations. ***PRACTICE AREAS:*** Employment Law; Contracts; Business Litigation; Real Estate. **Email:** madans@rbmchicago.com

KEVIN J. MOORE, born Chicago, Illinois, November 13, 1958; admitted to bar, 1984, Illinois, U.S. District Court, Northern District of Illinois and U.S. Court of Appeals, Seventh Circuit. *Education:* Marquette University (B.A., 1980); DePaul University (J.D., 1984; M.B.A., 1985). Law Clerk to Justice Daniel P. Ward, Supreme Court of Illinois, 1984-1986. Assistant State's Attorney, 1986-1990. Member, Illinois Supreme Court Committee on Pattern Jury Instructions, Criminal, 1988-1995. *Member:* Chicago, Illinois State and American Bar Associations. ***PRACTICE AREAS:*** Business Litigation; Personal Injury; Insurance; Franchises and Franchising. **Email:** moore@rbmchicago.com

ROBIN K. POWERS, born Pittsburgh, Pennsylvania, June 27, 1967; admitted to bar, 1992, Illinois and U.S. District Court, Northern District of Illinois. *Education:* University of Pennsylvania (B.A., magna cum laude, 1989); Northwestern University (J.D., 1992). ***PRACTICE AREAS:*** Civil Litigation; Employment Law. **Email:** powers@rbmchicago.com

JOHN D. SILK, born Toledo, Ohio, April 3, 1970; admitted to bar, 1995, Ohio; 1997, Illinois. *Education:* University of Notre Dame (B.A., high honors, 1992); Boston College (J.D., 1995). ***PRACTICE AREAS:*** Civil Litigation; Business Law; Real Estate; Franchises and Franchising. **Email:** silk@rbmchicago.com

OF COUNSEL

SHEILA M. MURPHY, born Colorado Springs, Colorado, August 18, 1937; admitted to bar, 1970, Colorado, Illinois and U.S. District Court, District of Colorado; 1982, U.S. District Court, Northern District of Illinois, Trial Bar; 1985, U.S. Supreme Court. *Education:* Marquette University (B.A., 1959); DePaul University (J.D., 1970). Retired Illinois Circuit Court Presiding Judge, Sixth District. ***PRACTICE AREAS:*** Mediation; Arbitration; Litigation; Appellate Practice; Death Penalty. **Email:** murphy@rbmchicago.com

THE LAW OFFICES OF RUBIN & NORRIS, LLC

Established in 2002

205 WEST WACKER DRIVE, SUITE 705

CHICAGO, ILLINOIS 60606-1212

Telephone: 312-263-1360

Fax: 312-263-1368

URL: http://www.propertytaxattorneys.com

Email: johnknorrisattorney@msn.com

URL: http://www.lawyers.com/johnknorris

Wood Dale Office: 189 North Cedar Avenue, 60191-2084. Telephone: 630-787-1234. Fax: 630-787-1236.

Real Estate Taxation, Ad Valorem Property Taxation, Property Tax Assessments and Property Tax Appeals.

JOHN K. NORRIS, JR., born Tampa, Florida, March 28, 1954; admitted to bar, 1983, Illinois and U.S. District Court, Northern District of Illinois; 1984, Florida. *Education:* University of South Florida (B.A., in Political Science, 1980); IIT/Chicago-Kent College of Law (J.D., 1983). Phi Alpha Delta (Board of Directors). *Member:* Illinois State Bar Association (Ex-officio, State and Local Taxation Section Council, 2004-2005; Elected Assembly Member, 2001—); Illinois Property Tax Lawyers Association.

DONALD T. RUBIN, born 1950; admitted to bar, 1980, Illinois. *Education:* University of Illinois (B.A.); John Marshall Law School (J.D.). Member: Zoning Board of Appeals (Commissioner, 1990-2002), City of Highland Park, Illinois; Board of Directors, Youth Outreach Services, 1996-2004 (President, 2002—). *Member:* Chicago (Chairman, Real Estate Taxation Committee, 1986, 1993) and Illinois State (State and Local Taxation Section Council, 2000-2004; State Legislative Liaison from Section Council to Board of Governors, 2003-2004); Illinois Property Tax Lawyers Association (President, 2003-2004). ***PRACTICE AREAS:*** Real Property; Taxation; Zoning Law; Government; Local Government. **Email:** dtrtaxlaw@aol.com

DANIEL M. PIERCE, born Chicago, Illinois, March 31, 1928; admitted to bar, 1952, Illinois. *Education:* Harvard University (A.B., 1949; J.D., 1952). Member, 1965-1985 and Chairman, Revenue Committee, 1977-1985, Illinois House of Representatives, State Legislature. *Member:* Chicago (Chairman, Public Utilities Committee; State and Municipal Taxation Committee; Real Estate Taxation Committee), Illinois State and American Bar Associations. ***PRACTICE AREAS:*** State and Local Government Regulation; Legislative. **Email:** dpierce604@aol.com

OF COUNSEL

MARSHALL A. FLEISCHMAN, born Chicago, Illinois, February 21, 1937; admitted to bar, 1960, Illinois. *Education:* University of Illinois (B.S., 1958); DePaul University (J.D., 1960). Assistant Corporation Counsel, City of Chicago, Zoning, Extraordinary Remedies, Chancery, 1961-1963; Assistant States Attorney, Cook County, Criminal Felony Trial Division, 1963-1966. *Member:* Chicago (Member, Property Taxation Committee) and Illinois State Bar Associations. ***PRACTICE AREAS:*** Property Tax Appeals.

RUSIN MACIOROWSKI & FRIEDMAN, LTD.

Established in 1984

SUITE 1530
10 SOUTH RIVERSIDE PLAZA
CHICAGO, ILLINOIS 60606
Telephone: 312-454-5110
Fax: 312-454-6166
URL: http://www.rusinlaw.com

Champaign, Illinois Office: 2506 Galen Drive, Suite 104, 61821-7047. Telephone: 217-351-1700. Fax: 217-351-1732.

Carbondale, Illinois Office: 239 South Lewis Lane, Suite A, 62901-3443. Telephone: 618-351-8100. Fax: 618-351-8109.

Workers Compensation Law. Insurance Defense, Personal Injury, Products Liability, Auto and Trucking Liability, Structural Work Act, Commercial Litigation, Subrogation, Contract Insurance, Employment Discrimination. Wrongful Discharge.

FIRM PROFILE: Rusin Maciorowski & Friedman, Ltd. was founded in 1984 by Douglas F. Stevenson, Michael E. Rusin and Stephen J. Friedman (as Stevenson, Rusin & Friedman, Ltd.) with the goal of establishing a specialty firm focusing on representing employers and their insurance carriers in all of the varied legal aspects of the workplace injury, including Worker's Compensation, OSHA, personal injury, contribution liability and lien recovery, wrongful discharge and employment discrimination.

Through dedication to aggressive, result-oriented file handling and prompt, thorough client reporting, the firm grew from the original seven lawyers and continued to expand to serve its clients' needs throughout the state of Illinois and northern and northwestern Indiana. With the opening of our Champaign, Illinois office in 1999, and our Carbondale, Illinois office in 2003, the firm reinforced its commitment to efficient representation in our downstate venues.

With Douglas Stevenson's appointment to the Illinois Industrial Commission in 1998, the firm changed its name to reflect its current mission on providing a full service litigation practice to its client base of employers, industry and insurance carriers.

The firm's leadership role in Workers' Compensation and Employer Liability has carried over to its civil department. Initially developed to handle the claims evolving from the workplace accident, the firm has acquired a depth of experience in employment discrimination and wrongful discharge, product liability, and coverage issues. We have the unique ability to coordinate the handling of the Workers' Compensation claim and related civil actions including lien protection, third party practice including extensive remedy defenses and related insurance coverage issues, including the handling of Declaratory Judgement actions.

Our current civil department, managed by Gregory Vacala, has grown and provides seasoned trial attorneys handling cases throughout Illinois and surrounding states. These attorneys have a depth of experience in managing all phases of civil practice including transportation law (automobiles and trucking liability), commercial litigation, and insurance coverage.

The firm has earned a preeminent rating from Martindale-Hubbell.

MICHAEL E. RUSIN, born Chicago, Illinois, June 14, 1955; admitted to bar, 1978, Illinois. *Education:* Northwestern University (B.A., 1975; J.D., cum laude, 1978). Order of the Coif. Member, Editorial Board, Journal of Criminal Law and Criminology, 1976-1978. Legal Counsel Workers Compensation Claims Association. Member, Legislation Committee, International Association of Industrial Accident Boards and Commissions, 1983-1987. Member, Workers Compensation Committee, Illinois Manufacturers Association, 1984-1988. *Member:* Illinois State Bar Association; Workers Compensation Lawyers Association; Illinois Self-Insurers Association; National Council of Self-Insurers; Worker's Compensation Claim's Association. ***SPECIAL AGENCIES:*** Illinois Industrial Commission. ***REPORTED CASES:*** Carroll v. Industrial Commission, 563 N.E.2d 890 (1990); Waldschmidt v. Industrial Commission, 542 N.E.2d 726 (1989); Trans World Airlines v. Industrial Commission, 548 N.E.2d 367 (1989). ***PRACTICE AREAS:*** Workers' Compensation; Personal Injury Defense; Employment Liability Defense. ***Email:*** merusin@rusinlaw.com

STEPHEN J. FRIEDMAN, born Chicago, Illinois, March 30, 1950; admitted to bar, 1975, Illinois; 1980, U.S. Supreme Court; 1982, U.S. District Court, Northern District of Illinois including Trial Bar. *Education:* University of Illinois (A.B., with high honors, 1972; J.D., with honors, 1975). Order of the Coif. Author: "OSHA," IICLE, 1981, 1986. Lecturer, "Auto Liability," PLI, 1986; NBI "Labor & Employment Law." *Member:* Chicago, Illinois State and American Bar Associations; Illinois Defense Counsel; Workers Compensation Lawyers Association. ***SPECIAL AGENCIES:*** Illinois Industrial Commission. ***REPORTED CASES:*** Snoddy v. Teepak, 566 N.E.2d 682, 198 Ill. App.3d 966. ***PRACTICE AREAS:*** Workers Compensation; Intentional Tort; Wrongful Discharge; Employers Contribution Liability; Employment Discrimination; Americans with Disabilities Act. ***Email:*** sfriedman@rusinlaw.com

JOHN A. MACIOROWSKI, born Chicago, Illinois, June 15, 1955; admitted to bar, 1980, Illinois. *Education:* Illinois Benedictine College (B.A., summa cum laude, 1977); DePaul University (J.D., with honors, 1980). Member, Staff, De Paul Law Review, 1979. *Member:* American Bar Association. ***SPECIAL AGENCIES:*** Illinois Industrial Commission. ***REPORTED CASES:*** Pemble v. Industrial Commission of Illinois, 536 N.E.2d 1349; Hansel & Gretel Day Care Center v. Industrial Commission, 574 N.E.2d 1244. ***PRACTICE AREAS:*** Worker's Compensation. ***Email:*** jmaciorowski@rusinlaw.com

KENNETH N. MARSHALL, born Chicago, Illinois, October 2, 1948; admitted to bar, 1978, Illinois. *Education:* Illinois Benedictine College and Northern Illinois University (B.S.E., with high honors, 1970); University of Illinois (J.D., with high honors, 1978). *Member:* DuPage County and Illinois State Bar Associations. ***SPECIAL AGENCIES:*** Illinois Industrial Commission. ***REPORTED CASES:*** Illinois Bell Telephone Co. v. Industrial Commission, 131 Ill.2d 478, 137 IL. Dec. 658, 546 N.E.2d 603 (1989). ***PRACTICE AREAS:*** Workers Compensation. ***Email:*** kmarshall@rusinlaw.com

GREGORY G. VACALA, born Chicago, Illinois, August 19, 1958; admitted to bar, 1983, Illinois and U.S. District Court, Northern District of Illinois; 1985, Trial Bar; 1984, U.S. Tax Court; 1993, U.S. District Court, Southern District of Illinois; 1995, Missouri. *Education:* DePaul University (B.S., 1980; J.D., 1983). Recipient, U.S. Law Week Award. Licensed Certified Public Accountant, Illinois, 1983. *Member:* Illinois State, Missouri and American Bar Associations; The Association of Trial Lawyers of America. ***SPECIAL AGENCIES:*** Illinois Industrial Commission. ***REPORTED CASES:*** Armis Construction Co. v. Cosmopolitan Nat'l. Bank, 134 Ill. App.3d 1717, 479 N.E.2d 1111, 89 Il. Dec 105; Spencer v. Wandowski, 264 Ill App.3d 611, 636 N.E.2d 854 201 Ill. Dec. 422 (1994); Upchurch v. Ill. 261 Ill. App.3d 104 636 N.E.2d 434 199 Ill. Dec. 595 (1994); Hurt v. Ind. Comm., 191 Ill. App.3d 733, 548 N.E.2d 122, 138 Il. Dec 892; Colvin v. Hobart Bros., Ill. Supreme Court 156 Ill. 2d 166 620 N.E. 2d 375 189 Ill. Dec. 407 (1993). ***PRACTICE AREAS:*** Appellate Practice; Employment Related Torts; Occupational Disease; Commercial Litigation; American with Disabilities Act; Insurance Coverage; Indemnity; First Party Insurance; Torts; Personal Injury; Motor Vehicle Accidents and Injuries; Construction Insurance Defense; Class Actions. ***Email:*** gvacala@rusinlaw.com

DANIEL W. ARKIN, born Chicago, Illinois, February, 23, 1955; admitted to bar, 1987, Illinois and U.S. District Court, Northern District of Illinois. *Education:* College of Dupage (A.A., 1975); Northern Illinois University at DeKalb (B.S., 1977); Illinois Institute of Technology/Chicago-Kent College of Law (J.D., 1987). *Member:* Chicago and Illinois State Bar Associations. ***SPECIAL AGENCIES:*** Illinois Industrial Commission. ***REPORTED CASES:*** Hammel v. Ind. Comm., 253 Ill. App. 3d 900, 193 Ill. Dec. 201, 626 NE 2d 234 (1993). ***PRACTICE AREAS:*** Workers Compensation; Special Investigations; Fraud. ***Email:*** darkin@rusinlaw.com

RANDALL R. STARK, born Chicago, Illinois, October 4, 1961; admitted to bar, 1987, Illinois and U.S. District Court, Northern District of Illinois. *Education:* Marquette University (B.A., 1983); DePaul University (J.D., 1987). *Member:* Chicago, Illinois State and American Bar Associations. ***LANGUAGES:*** French. ***SPECIAL AGENCIES:*** Illinois Industrial Commission. ***PRACTICE AREAS:*** Workers Compensation; Personal Injury. ***Email:*** rstark@rusinlaw.com

MARK P. RUSIN, born Chicago, Illinois, June 22, 1963; admitted to bar, 1990, Illinois. *Education:* University of Illinois (B.A., 1987); Chicago-Kent College of Law (J.D., 1990). *Member:* Chicago and Illinois State Bar Associations. ***PRACTICE AREAS:*** Workers Compensation. ***Email:*** mprusin@rusinlaw.com

DANIEL R. EGAN, born Evanston, Illinois, June 8, 1963; admitted to bar, 1988, Illinois; 1989, U.S. District Court, Northern District of Illinois. *Education:* University of Notre Dame (B.A.G., 1985); Loyola University of Chicago (J.D., 1988). ***SPECIAL AGENCIES:*** Illinois Industrial Commission. ***REPORTED CASES:*** Zanger v. Industrial Commission, 306 Ill. App. 3d 887 715 N.E. 2d 764 240 Ill. Dec. 77 (4th Dist. Ind. Comm. Div. 1999). ***PRACTICE AREAS:*** Workers Compensation. ***Email:*** degan@rusinlaw.com

THEODORE J. POWERS, born Quincy, Illinois, November 30, 1955; admitted to bar, 1993, Illinois. *Education:* University of Illinois (B.A., 1984); IIT-Kent College of Law (J.D., 1993). *Member:* Chicago and Illinois State Bar Associations. ***LANGUAGES:*** Spanish. ***REPORTED CASES:*** Siddens v. Industrial Commission, 304 Ill. 3d 506 711 N.E. 2d 18 (1999); Funes v. B & B Equipment, Inc., 282 Ill. App. 3d 272, 688 N.E. 2d 54 (1996); Employers Mutual Companies v. Skilling, 163 Ill. 2d 284, 644 N.E. 2d 1163 (1994). ***PRACTICE AREAS:*** Personal Injury; Subrogation; Insurance Coverage; Employer's Liability; Workers Compensation. ***Email:*** tpowers@rusinlaw.com

GREGORY A. RODE, born Waukegan, Illinois, December 2, 1960; admitted to bar, 1988, Illinois. *Education:* North Central College (B.A., 1985); Northern Illinois University (J.D., cum laude, 1988). Delta Theta Phi. *Member:* Chicago, DuPage County, Cook County and Illinois State Bar Associations; Workers Compensation Lawyers Association. ***PRACTICE AREAS:*** Workers Compensation Defense. ***Email:*** grode@rusinlaw.com

R. MARK COSIMINI, born Chicago, Illinois, April 18, 1966; admitted to bar, 1992, Illinois; 1994, U.S. District Court, Central District of Illinois. *Education:* Northwestern University (B.A., 1988); Northern Illinois University (J.D., 1992). Delta Theta Phi. *Member:* Illinois State and American Bar Associations; Illinois Trial Lawyers Association. (Resident, Champaign Office). ***PRACTICE AREAS:*** Workers Compensation. ***Email:*** mcosimini@rusinlaw.com

JOSEPH N. CASCIATO, born Chicago, Illinois, December 2, 1949; admitted to bar, 1974, Illinois and U.S. District Court, Northern District of Illinois; 1981, U.S. Supreme Court. *Education:* Loyola University (B.A., 1971); DePaul University (J.D., 1974). Recipient, Bancroft Whitney Award in Commercial Law. Adjunct Professor, DePaul Law School, 1989—. Chairman, Illinois Supreme Court Discovery Commission. Member, Alternative Dispute Resolution Systems of American LLC. Circuit Judge, Cook County, Illinois, 1982-2004. *Member:* Chicago Bar Association; Justinian Society of Lawyers. ***REPORTED CASES:*** Abassi v. Paraskevollakos, Ill. Sup. Ct.; Sprietsma v. Mercury Marine, U.S. Sup. Ct.; Burger v. Lutheran General Hospital, Ill. Sup. Ct.; Varelis v. Northwestern Memorial Hospital, Ill. Sup. Ct. ***PRACTICE AREAS:*** Litigation; Mediation; Commercial Litigation. ***Email:*** jcasciato@rusinlaw.com

STUART PELLISH, born New York, New York, July 9, 1956; admitted to bar, 1985, Illinois. *Education:* University of Illinois (B.A., 1978); DePaul University (J.D., 1985). Commissioner, Illinois Industrial Commission, 1990-1991. ***PRACTICE AREAS:*** Workers Compensation. ***Email:*** spellish@rusinlaw.com

THOMAS E. MARGOLIS, born Perth Amboy, New Jersey, June 3, 1965; admitted to bar, 1993, Illinois. *Education:* National-Louis University (B.A., honors, 1989); Southern Illinois University (J.D., 1993). Former Assistant Attorney General, Illinois Attorney General's Office, 1995-2002. Keynote Speaker, Freshman Class Orientation, Southern Illinois School of Law, 1998, 1999, 2001. Author: "Health Care Workers and AIDS: HIV Transmission in the Health Care Environment," 13 Journal of Legal Medicine 357, Sept. 1992. Managing Attorney, Rusin Patton Maciorowski & Friedman's Carbondale Office. *Member:* Illinois State Bar Association. (Resident, Carbondale Office). ***Email:*** tmargolis@rusinlaw.com

---

FARRAH L. ANDERSON, born Savannah, Georgia, February 26, 1978; admitted to bar, 2002, Illinois. *Education:* Southern Illinois University (B.A., cum laude, 1999; J.D., 2001). Phi Kappa Phi; Phi Alpha Delta. (Resident, Carbondale Office). ***PRACTICE AREAS:*** Workers Compensation. ***Email:*** fanderson@rusinlaw.com

(This Listing Continued)

JOSEPH P. BASILE, born Chicago, Illinois, March 29, 1954; admitted to bar, 1979, Illinois; 1980, U.S. District Court, Northern District of Illinois. *Education:* St. Louis University (B.S.B.A., 1976); John Marshall Law School (J.D., with distinction, 1979). Author: "Workers' Compensation Flashpoints," Illinois Institute for Continuing Legal Education Monthly Articles, IICLE.COM; Chapter on Workers' Compensation for the Institute of Continuing Legal Education, 2005 Edition of Labor and Employment Issues In Transactions, Business Reductions and Workforce Reductions. *Member:* Chicago, Illinois State and American Bar Associations. ***LANGUAGES:*** French. ***PRACTICE AREAS:*** Workers Compensation; Civil Litigation. ***Email:*** jbasile@rusinlaw.com

AMBER M. CLARK, born Milwaukee, Wisconsin, September 22, 1967; admitted to bar, 1999, Illinois. *Education:* University of Colorado (B.A., Math, 1989); Oklahoma City University (M.B.A., 1993); DePaul University (J.D., 1999). *Member:* Illinois State and American Bar Associations. ***PRACTICE AREAS:*** Transportation; Torts; Insurance Defense. ***Email:*** aclark@rusinlaw.com

TIMOTHY D. DENNY, born Cape Giradeau, Missouri, September 12, 1976; admitted to bar, 2004, Illinois; 2005, U.S. District Court, Central and Southern Districts of Illinois. *Education:* Eureka College (B.S., 1999); Northern Illinois University (J.D., 2004). *Member:* Illinois State Bar Association. (Resident, Carbondale Office). ***PRACTICE AREAS:*** Workers Compensation. ***Email:*** tdenny@rusinlaw.com

STEVEN R. DYKI, born Grosse Pointe Farms, Michigan, January 8, 1974; admitted to bar, 1999, Illinois. *Education:* Central Michigan University (B.S., 1996); DePaul University (J.D., 1999). Sigma Iota Epsilon. Member, Board of Trustees Academic Honors Scholar, Central Michigan University, 1992. Dean's Scholar, DePaul University College of Law, 1996. National Honor Society in Business Administration and Management. President, DePaul Environmental Law Society, 1997-1999. Member, Chicago Junior Chamber of Commerce, 2003—. Author: Case Notes: ESA/Turtle Law: Earth Island Institute, et al. v. Christopher - DePaul Environmental Law Digest (Spring 1997); Case Notes: RCRA: Meghrig v. KFC Western, Inc., Environmental Law Digest (Fall 1996). ***PRACTICE AREAS:*** Workers Compensation.

BRENT W. HALBLEIB, born Manhattan, Kansas, February 20, 1969; admitted to bar, 1994, Missouri; 1995, Illinois. *Education:* University of Missouri (B.A., 1991); Washington University (J.D., 1994). *Member:* Bar Association of Metropolitan St. Louis; The Missouri Bar; Illinois State Bar Association. ***PRACTICE AREAS:*** Workers Compensation. ***Email:*** bhalbleib@rusinlaw.com

WILLIAM J. HARRINGTON, born Chicago, Illinois, April 6, 1965; admitted to bar, 1992, Illinois. *Education:* Indiana University (B.A., 1987); Thomas M. Cooley Law School (J.D., 1991). *Member:* Illinois Association of Defense Trial Counsel. ***PRACTICE AREAS:*** Insurance Defense. ***Email:*** wharrington@rusinlaw.com

LEAH L. MABERY, born Miami, Florida, December 14, 1974; admitted to bar, 2004, Illinois. *Education:* Clark Atlanta University (B.A., 1996); Valparaiso University School of Law (J.D., 2004). ***PRACTICE AREAS:*** Workers Compensation.

PHILIP MARCHION, born Columbus, Ohio, August 30, 1977; admitted to bar, 2004, Illinois. *Education:* Miami University (B.S., 2000); Loyola University School of Law, Chicago (J.D., 2004). *Member:* Chicago, Illinois State and American Bar Associations. ***PRACTICE AREAS:*** Workers Compensation Defense; Insurance Defense; Litigation. ***Email:*** pmarchion@rusinlaw.com

JOSEPH A. MARCINIAK, born Chicago, Illinois, February 13, 1963; admitted to bar, 1990, Illinois and U.S. District Court, Northern District of Illinois. *Education:* Illinois State University (B.S., Economics, 1985); IIT Chicago-Kent College of Law (J.D., with honors, 1990). Author: "Busque un banco para su negocia," LARAZA, 1992; "Anatomy of a Lawsuit," AE LawNews, 1992. Instructor, College of DuPage, 1993. Guest Lecturer, University of Illinois, 1992. Former Legal Counsel, Safeco Insurance. Former Senior Attorney, American States Insurance. Former Trial Attorney, American International Group. *Member:* Workers' Compensation Lawyers' Association; Chicago Bar Association. ***PRACTICE AREAS:*** Workers' Compensation. ***Email:*** jmarciniak@rusinlaw.com

NADINE NEUE, born Hamburg, Germany, January 29, 1976; admitted to bar, 2001, Illinois. *Education:* Hamilton College (B.A., 1998); DePaul University (J.D., 2001). ***LANGUAGES:*** German. ***PRACTICE AREAS:*** Workers Compensation (100%). ***Email:*** nneue@rusinlaw.com

IVAN NIEVES, born Chicago, Illinois, September 29, 1974; admitted to bar, 2000, Illinois. *Education:* Yale University (B.A., 1996); University of Illinois College of Law (J.D., 2000). ***LANGUAGES:*** Spanish. ***PRACTICE AREAS:*** Workers Compensation Defense. ***Email:*** inieves@rusinlaw.com

CRISTINA C. NOLAN, born Chicago, Illinois, February 25, 1972; admitted to bar, 1997, Illinois; 1998, Missouri. *Education:* DePaul University (B.A., 1994); St. Louis University (J.D., 1997). *Member:* The Missouri Bar; Illinois State Bar Association. ***LANGUAGES:*** French and Spanish. ***PRACTICE AREAS:*** Workers Compensation. ***Email:*** cnolan@rusinlaw.com

LUCAS M. ROTHAAR, born January 15, 1979; admitted to bar, 2004, Illinois. *Education:* Valparaiso University (B.A., 2001); Loyola University School of Law (J.D., 2004). ***PRACTICE AREAS:*** Workers Compensation. ***Email:*** lrothaar@rusinlaw.com

ROBERT P. SABETTO, born Cleveland, Ohio, September 15, 1970; admitted to bar, 2003, Illinois. *Education:* Kent State University (B.A., 1993); DePaul University College of Law (J.D., 2002). Author: "Sticks and Stones and Chips of Bone: Shock Humor and Emotional Distress," 10 DePaul-LCA Jael. ***PRACTICE AREAS:*** Workers Compensation. ***Email:*** rsabetto@rusinlaw.com

TERRY E. SCHROEDER, born Springfield, Illinois, October 13, 1956; admitted to bar, 2002, Illinois. *Education:* Eastern Illinois University (B.A., 1998); University of Illinois College of Law (J.D., 2002). Commercial Pilot's Certificate with Instrument and Multi-Engine ratings. Member, Aircraft Owners and Pilots Association.. *Member:* Illinois State and American Bar Associations. [U.S. Air Force, 1975-1979, 1981-1998. Master Sergeant.]. (Resident, Champaign Office). ***PRACTICE AREAS:*** Workers Compensation. ***Email:*** tschroeder@rusinlaw.com

(This Listing Continued)

DOUGLAS J. SULLIVAN, born Cedar Rapids, Iowa, July 10, 1964; admitted to bar, 1992, Illinois. *Education:* St. John's University (B.A., 1987); Regents College (1986); Drake University (J.D., 1991). ***PRACTICE AREAS:*** Civil Litigation; Employment Law; Labor Law. ***Email:*** dsullivan@rusinlaw.com

EDWARD R. TOMKOWIAK, born Thorp, Wisconsin, February 27, 1955; admitted to bar, 1980, Illinois. *Education:* St. Norbert College (B.A., 1976); University of Illinois (J.D., 1980). ***PRACTICE AREAS:*** Workers Compensation. ***Email:*** etomkowiak@rusinlaw.com

REPRESENTATIVE CLIENTS: *Insurance Companies:* American Country Insurance; American Family Insurance; American International Group; Argonaut Insurance Co.; Atlantic Mutual/ASIC; ACE/CIGNA; Empire Fire and Marine Insurance Co.; Employers Mutual Companies; Farmers Insurance Company; General Casualty; Harleysville Insurance; Indiana Lumbermens Insurance; Liberty Mutual Insurance; National Farmers Union; One Beacon; Protective Insurance/Sagamore Insurance; Republic Franklin Insurance; Safeco Insurance Co./American States; Sentry Insurance Company; Standard Mutual Insurance; State Farm Fire & Casualty Co.; St. Paul Travelers Insurance; Transguard Insurance; Utica Insurance; Virginia Surety; West Bend Insurance; Zurich Insurance Company. *Utilities, Business and Retail:* Al Transport; Allied Waste Industries; Armon/F.E. Moran; Central Leasing Management, Inc.; Claussen Pickle Company; Dominicks/Safeway Stores; Exelon/ Commonwealth Edison; Export Packaging; The Gap, Inc.; Kraft Foods, Inc.; J.S. Alberici; Lucent Technologies; MacMillan Bloedel; Qwest Communications; Sprint PCS; Swedish Covenant Hospital; U.S. Foodservice; Verizon/GTE; Wal-Mart Stores, Inc./Sam's Clubs; Weyerhaeuser. *Manufacturers:* ABC Rail/National Castings; Boise Cascade; Chrysler Corp.; Cooper Industries; Gardner Denver Machinery, Inc.; Georgia Pacific; Gunite Corp.; Intermatic, Inc.; Johns Manville; Johnson Controls; Keystone Consolidated Industries; Norcross Safety Products, LLC; Owens-Illinois, Inc.; Prairie Farms Dairy; Safway Steel/Safway Services; Sterling Steel; Vesuvius USA. *Motor Carriers and Insurers:* Aon Transportation Services; Conway Central Services; J.B. Hunt Transportation; Laidlaw Corporation; McLane Midwest. *Third Party Administrators and Agencies:* AIG Claims Service; Aon Risk Services; Brentwood Services Administrators; Broadspire; Cambridge Integrated Services; Cannon Cochran Management Services; Claimguard; Claims Management, Inc.; Constitution State Service Company; Crawford & Company; Cunningham Lindsey; Custard Risk Management; ESIS; Frank Gates Service Company; GAB Business Services; Gallagher Bassett Services; Gates McDonald; Hartford/SRS; Helmsman; Hinz Claims Management; Intergovernmental Risk Management Agency (IRMA); MAC Risk Management; Martin Boyer; National Employee Care Systems; PMA Management; RSKCo; Risk Enterprise Management; Sedgwick CMS; Underwriters Safety & Claims.

DAVID J. RYAN

111 WEST WASHINGTON STREET
SUITE 1900
CHICAGO, ILLINOIS 60602
Telephone: 312-782-7099
Facsimile: 312-807-4858

Civil Litigation, Health Care Law, Insurance Law, Arbitration, Mediation.

DAVID J. RYAN, born Oak Park, Illinois, May 27, 1953; admitted to bar, 1977, Illinois and U.S. District Court, Northern District of Illinois; 1978, U.S. Court of Appeals, Seventh Circuit; 1981, U.S. Supreme Court. *Education:* Northwestern University (B.A., 1974); Georgetown University (J.D., 1977); Loyola University (LL.M., 1995). Associate, Jacobs, Williams and Montgomery, Ltd., 1977-1985. Partner, Williams & Montgomery, Ltd., 1985-1993. Author, "The False Claims Act: An Old Weapon with New Firepower Is Aimed at Health Care Fraud," Annals of Health Law, Volume 4, pages 127-150, June 1995. Panelist: American Arbitration Association; American Health Lawyers Association, Alternative Dispute Resolution Service; Cook County Mandatory Arbitration Program. *Member:* Chicago (Member: Health Care and Hospital Law Committee), Illinois State (Member, Health Care, Civil Practice, Insurance and Tort Sections) and American Bar Associations; American Health Lawyers Association; Illinois Association of Healthcare Attorneys. (Also of Counsel, Huff & Gaines, Ltd.). ***PRACTICE AREAS:*** Civil Litigation; Health Care Law; Insurance; Arbitration; Mediation.

RYAN AND RYAN

33 NORTH DEARBORN STREET, SUITE 1530
CHICAGO, ILLINOIS 60602
Telephone: 312-236-1386
Fax: 312-236-2556
URL: http://www.ryanandryanchicago.com

Eminent Domain, Condemnation.

FIRM PROFILE: Over the past twenty years, our firm has concentrated our practice exclusively in the field of eminent domain. Ryan and Ryan is both the only firm in Illinois to limit its practice to this area of the law and to be listed as a member of the Owners Counsel of America. In addition, our firm has received the two highest jury verdicts in Illinois concerning eminent domain.

WILLIAM E. RYAN, born Chicago, Illinois, June 17, 1949; admitted to bar, 1975, Illinois. *Education:* Xavier University (B.A., 1971); DePaul Law School (J.D., 1975). *Member:* Illinois State and American Bar Associations; Owners' Counsel of America. ***PRACTICE AREAS:*** Eminent Domain; Condemnation. ***Email:*** william.ryan@ryanandryanchicago.com

TIMOTHY J. RYAN, born Chicago, Illinois, December 6, 1951; admitted to bar, 1978, Illinois. *Education:* Xavier University (A.B., 1974); John Marshall Law School (J.D., 1978). *Member:* Chicago, Illinois State and American Bar Associations. ***PRACTICE AREAS:*** Eminent Domain; Condemnation. ***Email:*** timothy.ryan@ryanandryanchicago.com

ASSOCIATES

TERRENCE D. McCABE, born Springfield, Illinois, June 3, 1959; admitted to bar, 1987, Illinois. *Education:* Illinois College (B.S., 1981); John Marshall Law School (J.D., 1987). *Member:* Chicago and American Bar Associations. ***PRACTICE AREAS:*** Eminent Domain; Condemnation. ***Email:*** terrence.mccabe@ryanandryanchicago.com

(This Listing Continued)

RYAN AND RYAN, Chicago—Continued

MICHAEL W. RYAN, born 1975; admitted to bar, 2002, Illinois. *Education:* Miami University (B.A., 1998); Northwestern University (J.D., 2002). ***Email:*** michael.ryan@ryanandryanchicago.com

LAUREN E. RYAN, born September 8, 1977; admitted to bar, 2002, Illinois. *Education:* Villanova University (B.S., 1999); DePaul University College of Law (J.D., 2002). ***Email:*** lauren.ryan@ryanandryanchicago.com

RYNDAK & SURI

Established in 1998

200 WEST MADISON STREET, SUITE 2100

CHICAGO, ILLINOIS 60606

Telephone: 312-214-7770

Fax: 312-214-7715

URL: http://www.ryndaksuri.com

Intellectual Property, Patents, Trademarks, Copyrights, Unfair Competition, Litigation, Computer Software.

FIRM PROFILE: Founded in 1998 by two partners from Jenner & Block, Ryndak & Suri specializes in intellectual property litigation, counseling and transaction work. The Firm provides a full range of services in the intellectual property area including patent, trademark and copyright prosecution, both domestically and internationally. The firm has a substantial client base including national and multinational corporations. Ryndak & Suri's clients are involved in chemical, computer, electronics, environmental, food products, heavy equipment, internet, pharmaceutical, medical products, software and telecommunication industries, among others.

JAMES D. RYNDAK, born Joplin, Missouri, April 11, 1952; admitted to bar, 1977, Illinois, U.S. Court of Appeals, Seventh Circuit and U.S. District Court, Northern District of Illinois including Trial Bar; 1979, Texas; 1980, U.S. Court of Appeals, Fifth Circuit, U.S. District Court, Northern District of Texas and U.S. Court of Appeals, Federal Circuit; registered to practice before U.S. Patent and Trademark Office. *Education:* Purdue University (B.S. Ch.E., 1973); Illinois Institute of Technology (J. D., with honors, 1977). Assistant Attorney General, Illinois, 1977-1978. Partner, Jenner & Block, Chicago, Illinois, 1986-1998. *Member:* State Bar of Texas; American Intellectual Property Law Association; Patent Law Association of Chicago. ***LANGUAGES:*** French. ***PRACTICE AREAS:*** Patents; Trademarks; Copyrights; Unfair Competition Law; Intellectual Property Litigation; Patent Litigation. ***Email:*** ryndak@ryndaksuri.com

MARK K. SURI, born Green Bay, Wisconsin, September 2, 1960; admitted to bar, 1988, Illinois; 1990, U.S. District Court, Northern District of Illinois, including Trial Bar; registered to practice before U.S. Patent and Trademark Office. *Education:* Luther College (B.A., magna cum laude, 1982); University of Iowa (M.S., 1985; J.D., summa cum laude, 1988). Order of the Coif. Partner, Jenner & Block, Chicago, Illinois, 1996-2000. Member, American Chemical Society. *Member:* Illinois State Bar Association; American Intellectual Property Law Association; Intellectual Property Law Association of Chicago. ***PRACTICE AREAS:*** Intellectual Property; Litigation; Licensing; Patents; Trademarks; Copyrights. ***Email:*** suri@ryndaksuri.com

ERIC H. WEIMERS, born Pensacola, Florida, August 2, 1958; admitted to bar, 1985, Louisiana; 1991, Illinois; U.S. Court of Appeals for the Federal Circuit; U.S. Court of Appeals, Fifth Circuit; U.S. District Court, Northern District of Illinois, including Trial Bar; U.S. District Court, Eastern, Middle and Western Districts of Louisiana; registered to practice before the U.S. Patent and Trademark Office. *Education:* Tulane University (B.S.E.E., 1980; B.S., 1980; J.D., cum laude, 1985). Eta Kappa Nu; Order of the Coif; Order of Barristers. Chief Justice, Tulane Moot Court Board, 1984-1985. Co-Author: "United States Patent Law and GATT," Chapter 4, International Intellectual Property Law 1997, Center for International Legal Studies, Wiley, 1998; "Changes in United States Patent Law as a Result of the General Agreement on Tariffs and Trade," International Legal Strategy, Vol. IV-7, July 1995. *Member:* Louisiana State Bar Association; The Federalist Society for Law and Public Policy Studies. ***PRACTICE AREAS:*** Intellectual Property; Technology Law. ***Email:*** weimers@ryndaksuri.com

SABO & ZAHN

401 N. MICHIGAN AVENUE, SUITE 2050

CHICAGO, ILLINOIS 60611

Telephone: 312-655-8620

Fax: 312-655-8622

Email: wsabo@sabozahn.com

URL: http://www.sabozahn.com

Construction Law, Construction Litigation, Construction Contracts, Construction Claims, Construction Defects, Construction Intellectual Property, Copyright Infringement, Architects and Engineers Liability, Mechanics Liens, Structural Work Act, Mediation, Arbitration.

FIRM PROFILE: Sabo and Zahn concentrates its practice in the resolution and prevention of disputes affecting the building and construction industry. The Firm represents contractors, subcontractors, suppliers, architects, engineers, owners, developers and others involved in the construction process. Mr. Sabo is the founding member of the Society of Illinois Construction Attorneys. In addition, the firm is one of a few in Chicago to be included in the Bar Register of Pre-Eminent Lawyers in the field of Construction Law.

WERNER A. SABO, born Wanfried, Germany, July 12, 1946; admitted to bar, 1981, Illinois and U.S. District Court, Northern District of Illinois. *Education:* Northwestern University (B.A., 1968); University of Illinois, Chicago-Kent College of Law (J.D., with high honors, 1981). Licensed Architect, Illinois. Author: "Legal Guide to AIA Documents," 4th Edition, published by Aspen Publishers, 1997. Author of a monthly law column for CSI Construction Specifier, AIA Focus and other publications. Contributing Author: "Architect's Guide to Design-Build Services," published by John Wiley, 2003. Vice-President and Director, Chicago Construction Specifications Institute, 1992-1994. *Member:* Chicago, Illinois State and American Bar Associations; Construction Specifications Institute. Fellow, American Institute of Architects. Fellow, Association of Licensed Architects. Founding Member, Society of Illinois Construction Attorneys. ***LANGUAGES:*** German. ***PRACTICE AREAS:*** Construction Law; Dispute Resolution; Arbitration; Mediation; Copyright Litigation. ***Email:*** wasbo@sabozahn.com

JAMES K. ZAHN, born Chicago, Illinois, January 2, 1943; admitted to bar, 1990, Illinois and U.S. District Court, Northern District of Illinois. *Education:* University of Illinois at Chicago (B.A. Architecture, 1967); Chicago-Kent College of Law (J.D., 1990). Licensed Architect, Illinois, 1971. Author: monthly law column for CSI Construction Specifier, AIA Focus and other publications. *Member:* Chicago Bar Association; Construction Specifications Institute; NCARB; Association of Licensed Architects (Founding Member); American Institute of Architects (Fellow); Association of Licensed Architects (Fellow). Certified Member, National Council of Architectural Accrediation Boards and the Society of Illinois Construction Attorneys. ***LANGUAGES:*** Polish. ***PRACTICE AREAS:*** Construction Law; Contract Negotiation; Contract Formation; Professional Licensing; Dispute Resolutions. ***Email:*** jzahn@sabozahn.com

SHAWN E. GOODMAN, born Elk Grove Village, Illinois, 1968; admitted to bar, 1993, Illinois and U.S. District Court, District of Illinois; 1999, U.S. Court of Appeals, Seventh Circuit. *Education:* University of Illinois, Urbana-Champaign (B.A., magna cum laude, highest distinction, 1989); Northwestern University School of Law (J.D., 1993). Associate: Blair & Cole, 1993-1996; Sabo & Zahn, 1996-2001; Cahill, Christian & Kunkle, 2001. Partner, Sabo & Zahn, 2002—. *Member:* Chicago and Illinois State Bar Associations; Association of Licensed Architects (Affiliate Member). ***LANGUAGES:*** Spanish. ***PRACTICE AREAS:*** Business Law; Construction Law; Criminal Law; Commercial Litigation; Personal Injury; Personal Injury Appeals; Copyright Infringement; Copyright Litigation; Copyright Prosecution; Copyrights. ***Email:*** sgoodman@sabozahn.com

SACHNOFF & WEAVER, LTD.

10 SOUTH WACKER DRIVE

CHICAGO, ILLINOIS 60606-7507

Telephone: 312-207-1000

Telecopier: 312-207-6400

URL: http://www.sachnoff.com

Antitrust Law, Appellate Practice, Arbitration, Bankruptcy/Creditors Rights, Business Planning Law, Class Actions, Commercial Litigation, Complex Litigation, Construction Litigation, Corporate Finance, Corporate Law, Electronic Commerce, Emerging Growth Companies, Employee Benefits, Environmental Law, ERISA, Executive Compensation, Family Business Law, Finance, Government Investigations, Health Care Regulation, Immigration, Information Technology, Insurance Coverage, International, Intellectual Property, Labor and Employment, Lending, Litigation, Mergers and Acquisitions, Patents, Probate Administration, Products Liability, Professional Liability, Real Estate, Securities Law, Tax, Technology, Transportation, Trusts and Estates, Venture Capital, White Collar Crime Defense, Workouts.

EVELYN C. ARKEBAUER, admitted to bar, 1986, Wisconsin; 1989, Illinois. *Education:* University of Wisconsin at Madison (B.A., 1983); University of Michigan Law School (J.D., 1986). ***LANGUAGES:*** French. ***PRACTICE AREAS:*** Corporate Law; Securities Law. ***Email:*** earkebauer@sachnoff.com

J. TODD ARKEBAUER, admitted to bar, 1988, Illinois. *Education:* University of Michigan (B.A., 1984); The Ohio State University (J.D., 1988). ***PRACTICE AREAS:*** Corporate; Securities; Information Technology; Computer. ***Email:*** tarkebauer@sachnoff.com

FRANK D. BALLANTINE, admitted to bar, 1985, Illinois and U.S. Court of Appeals, Sixth Circuit. *Education:* Manchester College, Oxford, England; Haverford College (B.A., 1978); Columbia University, New York, NY, Graduate School of Fine Arts-Film Division; University of Michigan (J.D., 1984). Law Clerk to Hon. Nathaniel R. Jones, U.S. Court of Appeals, Sixth Circuit, 1984-1985. ***PRACTICE AREAS:*** Information Technology; Venture Capital; Mergers and Acquisitions; Corporate; Securities Regulation. ***Email:*** fballantine@sachnoff.com

CAREY L. BARTELL, admitted to bar, 1998, Illinois. *Education:* Wesleyan University (B.A., 1995);University of Chicago Law School (J.D., 1998). ***PRACTICE AREAS:*** Labor and Employment; Litigation; Immigration. ***Email:*** cbartell@sachnoff.com

GREG L. BERENSTEIN, admitted to bar, 1985, Iowa; 1990, Illinois. *Education:* University of Iowa (B.A., 1982; J.D., 1985). ***PRACTICE AREAS:*** Information Technology; Biotechnology; Intellectual Property; Computer Law; Internet Law.

JEFFREY H. BERGMAN, admitted to bar, 1986, Wisconsin and Illinois. *Education:* University of Chicago (A.B., 1982); University of Wisconsin-Madison (J.D., 1986). ***PRACTICE AREAS:*** Civil Litigation; Arbitration. ***Email:*** jbergman@sachnoff.com

PETER T. BERK, admitted to bar, 1997, Illinois and U.S. District Court, Northern District of Illinois; 1998, U.S. Court of Appeals, Seventh Circuit. *Education:* University of Michigan (B.A., High Distinction, 1994); Northwestern University (J.D., cum laude, 1997). Phi Beta Kappa; Phi Alpha Delta, Justice, 1995-1996. Member, 1995-1997; Business Editor, 1996-1997, Journal of International Law & Business, Northwestern University School of Law. ***PRACTICE AREAS:*** Class Action Defense; Civil Litigation. ***Email:*** pberk@sachnoff.com

JACK L. BLOCK, admitted to bar, 1973, Illinois. *Education:* Washington University (A.B., 1967; MBA, 1968); Georgetown University (J.D., 1972). Law Clerk to the Hon. Hubert L. Will, Judge, U.S. District Court, Northern District of Illinois, 1973-1975. ***PRACTICE AREAS:*** Securities Regulation; Class Actions; Trial Practice. ***Email:*** jblock@sachnoff.com

STEPHEN T. BOBO, admitted to bar, 1981, District of Columbia; 1982, Illinois; U.S. District Court, Northern District of Illinois, U.S. District Court, Eastern District of Michigan including Trial Bar and U.S. Court of Appeals, Seventh Circuit. *Education:* Vanderbilt University (B.A., cum laude, 1977); George Washington University (J.D., 1980). Topics

(This Listing Continued)

Editor, Journal of International Law and Economics, 1979-1980. Former Senior Trial Attorney, U.S. Commodity Futures Trading Commission, Division of Enforcement, 1980-1985. ***PRACTICE AREAS:*** Financial Services. ***Email:*** sbobo@sachnoff.com

DAVID C. BOHAN, admitted to bar, 1978, Illinois and U.S. District Court, Northern District of Illinois; 1989, U.S. Court of Appeals, Seventh Circuit; 1994, U.S. Tax Court; 1996, U.S. Court of Appeals, Eighth Circuit. *Education:* Northwestern University (B.A., with distinction, 1975); Harvard Law School (J.D., cum laude, 1978). Law Clerk, Honorable John F. Grady, U.S. District Court, Northern District of Illinois, 1978-1979. ***PRACTICE AREAS:*** Complex Litigation; Securities Regulation. ***Email:*** dbohan@sachnoff.com

MARK A. BRAND, admitted to bar, 1979, Washington; 1981, Texas; 1988, Illinois. *Education:* Concordia College (B.A., cum laude, 1974); University of Notre Dame (J.D., 1979). ***PRACTICE AREAS:*** Products Liability; Toxic Torts; Complex Business Litigation; Complex Commercial Litigation; Intellectual Property. ***Email:*** mbrand@sachnoff.com

GARY S. CAPLAN, admitted to bar, 1988, Illinois. *Education:* University of Illinois (B.A., cum laude, 1985); Northwestern University (J.D., 1988). ***PRACTICE AREAS:*** Commercial Litigation; Class Action Defense. ***Email:*** gcaplan@sachnoff.com

H. BRIAN CENTENO, admitted to bar, 1995, Illinois and U.S. District Court, Northern District of Illinois. *Education:* University of Illinois-Champaign (B.S., 1990); Cornell University (J.D., 1995). ***PRACTICE AREAS:*** Commercial Litigation; Construction Litigation. ***Email:*** bcenteno@sachnoff.com

KIT CHASKIN, admitted to bar, 1990, Illinois. *Education:* Northwestern University (B.S., 1983; J.D., 1990). ***PRACTICE AREAS:*** Insurance; Insurance Coverage Litigation; Litigation. ***Email:*** chaskin@sachnoff.com

CHRISTOPHER R. CLARK, admitted to bar, 1996, Illinois. *Education:* Princeton University (A.B., cum laude, 1987); University of Chicago (J.D., with honors, 1996). ***PRACTICE AREAS:*** Commercial Litigation; Intellectual Property. ***Email:*** cclark@sachnoff.com

LOLETTA L. DARDEN, admitted to bar, 1991, Massachusetts; 1992, Rhode Island; 1999, Michigan; 2001, Illinois; registered to practice before U.S. Patent and Trademark Office. *Education:* Purdue University (B.S., 1982); Suffolk University (J.D., 1991). ***PRACTICE AREAS:*** Patents; Trademarks; Copyrights. ***Email:*** ldarden@sachnoff.com

CHARLES E. DOBRUSIN, admitted to bar, 1979, Illinois. *Education:* Brandeis University (B.A., 1974); Jewish Theological Seminary (M.A., 1976; Rabbi, 1980); New York University (J.D., 1979). ***PRACTICE AREAS:*** Estate Planning; Trusts and Estates. ***Email:*** cdobrusin@sachnoff.com

STEWART DOLIN, admitted to bar, 1977, Illinois and U.S. District Court, Northern District of Illinois. *Education:* University of Illinois (B.A., 1974); Loyola University (J.D., 1977). Edwin James Scholar. ***PRACTICE AREAS:*** Corporate Law; Corporate Finance; Mergers and Acquisitions. ***Email:*** sdolin@sachnoff.com

WILLIAM E. DORAN, admitted to bar, 1988, Illinois, Wisconsin and U.S. District Court, Western District of Wisconsin. *Education:* Ripon College (B.A., cum laude, 1985); University of Wisconsin (J.D., cum laude, 1988). ***PRACTICE AREAS:*** Corporate; Securities; Mergers and Acquisitions; Venture Capital. ***Email:*** wdoran@sachnoff.com

MARILYN P. DUNN, admitted to bar, 1990, Missouri; 1991, Kansas; 1996, Illinois. *Education:* Pitzer College (B.A., 1985); University of Kansas School of Law (J.D., 1990). Order of the Coif. ***PRACTICE AREAS:*** Real Estate. ***Email:*** mdunn@sachnoff.com

DAVID C. FUECHTMAN, admitted to bar, 1995, Illinois. *Education:* DePaul University (B.S., with honors, 1989); Loyola University of Chicago (J.D., 1995). Certified Public Accountant, Illinois, 1989. ***PRACTICE AREAS:*** Estate Planning; Trust Administration; Probate. ***Email:*** dfuechtman@sachnoff.com

ROSELYN L. FRIEDMAN, admitted to bar, 1977, Illinois and U.S. District Court, Northern District of Illinois. *Education:* University of Pittsburgh (B.S., 1964); Case Western Reserve University (M.A., 1967); Loyola University (J.D., cum laude, 1977). Elected Fellow, American College of Trust and Estate Counsel, 1999. *Member:* Chicago Bar Association (Chairman, Trust Law Committee, 1989-1990); Professional Advisory Committee of the Jewish Federation of Metropolitan Chicago (Chair, 1998—). ***PRACTICE AREAS:*** Estate Planning Law; Estate Administration Law; Estate and Gift Taxation Law; Family Business Law; Business Planning Law. ***Email:*** rfriedman@sachnoff.com

ARLENE N. GELMAN, admitted to bar, 1994, Illinois. *Education:* University of Illinois (B.A., 1989); Boston University (J.D., 1994). ***PRACTICE AREAS:*** Bankruptcy; Workouts; Equipment Leasing. ***Email:*** agelman@sachnoff.com

JEFFREY T. GILBERT, admitted to bar, 1980, Illinois, U.S. Court of Appeals, Seventh Circuit and U.S. District Court, Northern District of Illinois including Trial Bar. *Education:* Washington University (B.A., 1977); Northwestern University (J.D., 1980). Phi Beta Kappa. Law Clerk to Judge Marvin E. Aspen U.S. District Court, Northern District of Illinois, 1980-1982. ***PRACTICE AREAS:*** Litigation; Securities; Insurance Coverage Litigation. ***Email:*** jgilbert@sachnoff.com

NEIL GREENBAUM, admitted to bar, 1955, Illinois; 1958, U.S. District Court, Northern District of Illinois; 1964, U.S. Supreme Court; 1966, U.S. Court of Appeals, Seventh Circuit; 1977, U.S. Tax Court. *Education:* Northwestern University (B.S., 1953; J.D., 1955). President, Hebrew Immigrant Aid Society (HIAS), 1998—. Former President, Jewish Education Service of North America (JESNA), 1990-1993. [Veteran, U.S. Navy]. ***PRACTICE AREAS:*** Corporate; Partnership; Real Estate; Tax Exempt Organizations; Estate Planning. ***Email:*** ngreenbaum@sachnoff.com

JAMES J. GREENBERGER, admitted to bar, 1983, Illinois. *Education:* Haverford College (B.A., 1980); University of Michigan Law School (J.D., 1983). ***PRACTICE AREAS:*** Commercial Finance; Venture Capital; Mergers and Acquisitions. ***Email:*** jgreenberger@sachnoff.com

LEWIS B. GREENBLATT, admitted to bar, 1969, Illinois; 1975, U.S. District Court, Northern District of Illinois. *Education:* Miami University (B.A., 1966); University of Illinois (J.D., 1969). Author: "Firms' Failure to Address Post-Departure Fees, Responsibilities Can Yield Surprises," Law Firm Partnership and Benefits Report, 1995; "Issues Relating to Your Lateral Move," Chicago Daily Law Bulletin, 1996; "Dealing With Partner Defections When Economic Disincentives Are Unavailable," Law Firm Partnership and Benefits Report, 1998; "Dealing With Lawyer Mobility in a Changing Legal and Ethical Environment," Chicago Bar Association, 1998; "What to Watch Out For When Drafting Retirement Benefits Provisions," Law Firm Partnership and Benefits Report, 2000. Panelist and Author, "Law Firm Mergers," American Bar Association and CLESN Program, 1991. ***PRACTICE AREAS:*** Corporate Law; Mergers and Acquisitions; Private Equity; Partnership Law. ***Email:*** lgreenblatt@sachnoff.com

ROBIN HEISS, admitted to bar, 1969, Illinois. *Education:* University of Chicago (B.A., 1966); New York University (J.D., 1969). ***PRACTICE AREAS:*** Corporate. ***Email:*** rheiss@sachnoff.com

SETH M. HEMMING, admitted to bar, 1985, Illinois. *Education:* University of Illinois (B.S., with honors, 1982); Loyola University (J.D., cum laude, 1985). ***PRACTICE AREAS:*** Corporate; Mergers and Acquisitions; Securities. ***Email:*** shemming@sachnoff.com

MARK S. HERSH, admitted to bar, 1983, Illinois; 1985, District of Columbia. *Education:* University of Illinois (B.A., 1980); Stanford University (J.D., 1983). Assistant United States Attorney, Chicago, 1991-2000. ***PRACTICE AREAS:*** Civil Litigation; White Collar Crime Defense; Corporate Investigations; Government Investigations; Appellate Practice. ***Email:*** mhersh@sachnoff.com

JOHN L. HINES, JR., admitted to bar, 1981, Illinois and U.S. District Court, Northern District of Illinois; 1988, U.S. Court of Appeals, Seventh Circuit. *Education:* Princeton University (A.B., 1978); Northwestern University (J.D., 1981). Author: "Reciprocal Compensation," 4 Cyberspace Lawyer, No. 11, 2000. ***PRACTICE AREAS:*** Intellectual Property; Cyber Law; Electronic Commerce; Litigation. ***Email:*** jhines@sachnoff.com

AUSTIN L. HIRSCH, admitted to bar, 1973, Illinois. *Education:* University of Illinois (B.S. in Accounting, with high honors, 1970); Northwestern University (J.D., 1973). Certified Public Accountant, Illinois, 1972. Managing Partner, Sachnoff & Weaver, 1990—. Member of the Board of Managers, Chicago Bar Association, 1998—. Adjunct Professor of Law, Partnership Taxation, The John Marshall Law School, 1983-1992. Editorial Board, Northwestern Law Review, 1973. ***PRACTICE AREAS:*** Federal Tax; Partnership; Corporate Mergers; Corporate Planning; Family Business Law. ***Email:*** ahirsch@sachnoff.com

JAMES T. HULTQUIST, admitted to bar, 1990, Illinois and U.S. District Court, Northern District of Illinois; 1996, U.S. Court of Appeals, Seventh Circuit; 1997, U.S. District Court, Central District of Illinois and U.S. Court of Appeals, Fifth Circuit; 2000, Federal Trial Bar. *Education:* Illinois Wesleyan University (B.S., 1986); Loyola University (J.D., 1990). Recipient, Loyola University Leadership and Service Award. Student Editor, Business Lawyer Journal. Alternate, Chicago Bar Association Interschool Moot Court Team. Externship, U.S. Court of Appeals, Seventh Circuit, Chief Judge William Bauer, 1989-1990. *Member:* Licensing Executives Society; Computer Law Association. ***PRACTICE AREAS:*** Commercial Litigation; Products Liability; Toxic Torts; Intellectual Property. ***Email:*** jhultquist@sachnoff.com

ANNETTE BRANDS HURLEY, admitted to bar, 1995, Illinois and U.S. District Court, Northern District of Illinois; 1996, U.S. District Court, Central District of Illinois; 2002, Florida. *Education:* Loyola University at Chicago (B.A., cum laude, 1992); University of Notre Dame (J.D., 1995); Chicago-Kent College of Law (LL.M., in Taxation, 2000). ***PRACTICE AREAS:*** Estate Planning; Estate Administration. ***Email:*** abrands@sachnoff.com

JOSÉ A. ISASI, II, admitted to bar, 1992, Illinois and U.S. District Court, Northern District of Illinois Trial Bar; 1996, U.S. Court of Appeals, Seventh Circuit. *Education:* Duke University (A.B., 1989); Georgetown University Law Center (J.D., 1992). ***PRACTICE AREAS:*** Commercial Litigation; Construction Litigation; Products Liability; Insurance Coverage. ***Email:*** jisasi@sachnoff.com

CYNTHIA JARED, admitted to bar, 1980, Illinois. *Education:* Butler University (B.A., magna cum laude, 1970); DePaul University (M.A., 1973; J.D., with honors, 1980). ***PRACTICE AREAS:*** Commercial Real Estate; Real Estate Finance; Commercial Finance. ***Email:*** cjared@sachnoff.com

WADE S. LEATHERS, admitted to bar, 1986, Illinois; 1997, Washington. *Education:* University of Iowa (B.B.A., 1981; M.A., 1986; J.D., with distinction, 1986). ***PRACTICE AREAS:*** Taxation. ***Email:*** wleathers@sachnoff.com

MICHAEL P. LEE, admitted to bar, 1998, Illinois. *Education:* University of Washington (B.S., 1983); Stanford University (M.S., 1984; Ph.D., 1991); University of Chicago (J.D., Order of the Coif, high honors, 1998). Staff Member, University of Chicago Law Review. ***PRACTICE AREAS:*** Venture Capital; Finance; Intellectual Property; Information Technology; Mergers and Acquisitions; Securities. ***Email:*** mlee@sachnoff.com

RANDALL D. LEHNER, admitted to bar, 1996, Illinois; 1997, U.S. Court of Appeals, Seventh Circuit; 1998, U.S. District Court, Northern District of Illinois; 1999, U.S. Court of Appeals, Eleventh Circuit. *Education:* University of Michigan (B.A., with distinction and honors, 1993); Duke University School of Law (J.D., with high honors, 1996). Phi Beta Kappa. Order of the Coif. ***PRACTICE AREAS:*** Commercial Litigation. ***Email:*** rlehner@sachnoff.com

MICHAEL S. LEIB, admitted to bar, 1996, New Jersey and U.S. District Court, District of New Jersey; 1997, New York, Illinois and U.S. District Court, Northern District of Illinois; 2001, U.S District Court, Northern District of Indiana. *Education:* Duke University (B.A., 1991); Hebrew University, Jerusalem, Israel; Harvard University (J.D., 1996). Law Clerk to the Hon. Harry D. Leinenweber, U.S. District Court, Northern District of Illinois, 1997. Author, "E-Mail and the Wiretap Laws: Why Congress Should Add Electronic Communication to Title III's Statutory Exclusionary Rule and Expressly Reject a 'Good Faith' Exception," 34 Harv.J. on Legis. 393 (1997). ***PRACTICE AREAS:*** Commercial Litigation; Complex Litigation; White Collar Criminal Defense; Securities. ***Email:*** mleib@sachnoff.com

MICHAEL R. LIEBER, admitted to bar, 1996, Illinois and U.S. District Court, Northern District of Illinois. *Education:* Bates College (B.A., Rhetoric, 1992); Indiana University-Bloomington (J.D., 1996). ***PRACTICE AREAS:*** Civil Litigation. ***Email:*** mlieber@sachnoff.com

(This Listing Continued)

SACHNOFF & WEAVER, LTD., Chicago—Continued

DAVID E. LIEBERMAN, admitted to bar, 1992, Illinois. *Education:* Brown University (Sc.B., with honors, magna cum laude, 1984); University of Chicago (J.D., 1991). Member, University of Chicago Law Review, 1989-1991. Law Clerk to Hon. Albert J. Engel, U.S. Court of Appeals, Sixth Circuit, 1991-1992. S.K. Yee Scholar, Bradley Fellow, Criminal Justice. ***PRACTICE AREAS:*** Litigation. ***Email:*** dlieberman@sachnoff.com

JEFFREY L. LONDON, admitted to bar, 1984, Ohio; 1985, Illinois, U.S. District Court, Northern District of Illinois and U.S. Court of Appeals, Sixth Circuit; 1986, Minnesota and U.S. Court of Appeals, Seventh Circuit. *Education:* Haverford College (B.A., 1980); Duke University (M.B.A., 1984; J.D., with honors, 1984). ***PRACTICE AREAS:*** Employee Benefits; Executive Compensation. ***Email:*** jlondon@sachnoff.com

ROBERT D. LoPRETE, admitted to bar, 1989, Illinois. *Education:* DePauw University (B.A., cum laude, 1986); University of Michigan (J.D., cum laude, 1989). ***PRACTICE AREAS:*** Estate Planning; Wealth Planning. ***Email:*** rloprete@sachnoff.com

MICHAEL A. LoVALLO, admitted to bar, 1980, Illinois; U.S. District Court, Northern District of Illinois and U.S. Tax Court. *Education:* Georgetown University (A.B., cum laude, 1977); University of Sussex; Columbia University (J.D., 1980). Fellow, American College of Trust and Estate Counsel (ACTEC) (Chair, Trust Law Committee, 1993-1994). ***PRACTICE AREAS:*** Estate Planning; Probate; Trust Administration. ***Email:*** mlovallo@sachnoff.com

STEPHEN R. MILLER, admitted to bar, 1990, Illinois and U.S. District Court, Northern District of Illinois. *Education:* University of Illinois (B.S., Accounting, with highest honors, 1987); Harvard Law School (J.D., 1990). Recipient, Bronze Tablet, University of Illinois. Certified Public Accountant, Illinois, 1987. ***PRACTICE AREAS:*** Mergers and Acquistions; Corporate Law; Partnership Law. ***Email:*** nlong@sachnoff.com

STEVEN A. MILLER, admitted to bar, 1979, Illinois. *Education:* Washington University (B.A., 1975; J.D., 1979). Chief, Special Prosecutions Section, U.S. Attorney's Office, Northern District of Illinois, 1991-1995. ***PRACTICE AREAS:*** Civil Litigation; White Collar Defense. ***Email:*** smiller@sachnoff.com

MICHELLE L. MOORE, admitted to bar, 1997, Illinois. *Education:* University of California at Los Angeles (B.A., summa cum laude, 1994); University of Michigan (J.D., 1997). ***PRACTICE AREAS:*** Mergers and Acquisitions; General Corporate Law; Lending; Securities. ***Email:*** mmoore@sachnoff.com

JOHN W. MOYNIHAN, admitted to bar, 1993, Illinois and U.S. District Court, Northern District of Illinois. *Education:* St. Norbert College; University of Illinois at Champaign (B.S., with highest honors, 1988); University of Michigan (J.D., cum laude, 1992); Northwestern University. ***PRACTICE AREAS:*** Securities; Commercial Litigation; Class Action Litigation. ***Email:*** jmoynihan@sachnoff.com

ROBERT K. NEIMAN, admitted to bar, 1982, Illinois and U.S. District Court, Northern District of Illinois; 1983, U.S. Court of Appeals, Seventh Circuit. *Education:* University of Illinois (B.S.J., 1979); University of London; Washington University, St. Louis (J.D., 1982). ***PRACTICE AREAS:*** Commercial Litigation; Employment Defense; Health Care Regulation. ***Email:*** rneiman@sachnoff.com

DOUGLAS R. NEWKIRK, admitted to bar, 1982, Illinois. *Education:* Carleton College (B.A., magna cum laude, 1979); Yale University (J.D., 1982). Law Clerk to the Hon. John E. Simonett, Judge, Minnesota Supreme Court, 1982-1983. ***PRACTICE AREAS:*** Securities; Technology; Emerging Growth Companies. ***Email:*** dnewkirk@sachnoff.com

KEVIN M. NOONAN, admitted to bar, 1997, Illinois and U.S. District Court, Northern District of Illinois. *Education:* University of Cincinnati (B.B.A., 1992); Loyola University, Chicago (J.D., 1997). ***PRACTICE AREAS:*** Estate Planning; Probate Administration; Trust Administration. ***Email:*** knoonan@sachnoff.com

MATTHEW J. O'HARA, admitted to bar, 1996, Illinois and U.S. District Court, Northern and Central Districts of Illinois; 1998, U.S. District Court, Eastern District of Wisconsin and U.S. Court of Appeals, Seventh Circuit; 1999, U.S. District Court, Northern District of Illinois Trial Bar. *Education:* Northwestern University (B.A., with honors, 1983); Chicago-Kent College of Law, Illinois Institute of Technology (J.D., valedictorian, 1996). ***LANGUAGES:*** Spanish. ***PRACTICE AREAS:*** Commercial Litigation; Securities Litigation; Trade Secrets; ERISA Litigation; Criminal Defense. ***Email:*** mohara@sachnoff.com

ROBERT S. O'MEARA, admitted to bar, 1997, Michigan; 1998, Illinois. *Education:* Michigan State University (B.A., 1992); University of Illinois (J.D., 1996). ***PRACTICE AREAS:*** Commercial Litigation. ***Email:*** omeara@sachnoff.com

ARNOLD A. PAGNIUCCI, admitted to bar, 1974, Illinois. *Education:* DePaul University (B.A., 1970); Northwestern University (J.D., cum laude, 1974). ***PRACTICE AREAS:*** Business Litigation; Antitrust Law; Trial Practice. ***Email:*** apagniucci@sachnoff.com

BETH A. PETERSEN, admitted to bar, 1996, Illinois. *Education:* Northwestern University (B.A., 1990; J.D., 1996). ***PRACTICE AREAS:*** Corporate; Securities. ***Email:*** bpetersen@sachnoff.com

MATTHEW J. PETERSEN, admitted to bar, 1994, Illinois. *Education:* University of Illinois (B.A., 1991); Chicago-Kent College of Law (J.D., 1994). ***PRACTICE AREAS:*** Mergers and Acquisitions; Corporate Law; Securities; Venture Capital; Insurance Regulation. ***Email:*** mpetersen@sachnoff.com

HENRY PIETRKOWSKI, admitted to bar, 1995, Illinois. *Education:* Northwestern University (B.A., 1992); Chicago-Kent College of Law (J.D., 1995). ***PRACTICE AREAS:*** Litigation. ***Email:*** hpietrkowski@sachnoff.com

JONATHAN S. POLISH, admitted to bar, 1996, Illinois and U.S. District Court, Northern District of Illinois; 1998, U.S. Court of Appeals, Seventh Circuit. *Education:* University of Michigan (A.B., 1992); University of Michigan (J.D., cum laude, Order of the Coif, 1996). ***PRACTICE AREAS:*** Complex Commercial Litigation. ***Email:*** jpolish@sachnoff.com

NEIL B. POSNER, admitted to bar, 1996, Wisconsin, Illinois, U.S. District Court, Eastern District of Wisconsin and Northern District of Illinois, U.S. Tax Court. *Education:* New York University (B.A., 1971); Marquette University Law School (J.D., 1996). ***PRACTICE AREAS:*** Insurance Coverage; Commercial Litigation; Tax Controversies. ***Email:*** nposner@sachnoff.com

JONATHAN S. QUINN, admitted to bar, 1986, New York; 1988, U.S. District Court, Southern District of New York; 1989, Illinois and U.S. District Court, Northern District of Illinois including Trial Bar; 1993, U.S. District Court, Eastern District of Michigan and U.S. Court of Appeals, Seventh Circuit. *Education:* Haverford College (B.A., 1981); Northwestern University (J.D., 1985). ***PRACTICE AREAS:*** Commercial Litigation; Transportation; Securities Litigation; Class Action Defense. ***Email:*** jquinn@sachnoff.com

MICHAEL D. RICHMAN, admitted to bar, 1979, Illinois, U.S. District Court, Northern District of Illinois, U.S. Court of Appeals, Seventh Circuit, U.S. Court of Appeals, Eleventh Circuit; U.S. District Court, Eastern District of Wisconsin; U.S. District Court, Eastern District of Michigan; U.S. Supreme Court. *Education:* Indiana University (B.A., cum laude, 1976); Case Western Reserve University Law School (J.D., 1979). ***PRACTICE AREAS:*** Commercial Litigation; Appellate Practice. ***Email:*** mrichman@sachnoff.com

BRIAN D. ROCHE, admitted to bar, 1982, Illinois and U.S. District Court, Northern District of Illinois. *Education:* University of Chicago (A.B., with honors, 1978); Georgetown University (J.D., cum laude, 1982). ***PRACTICE AREAS:*** Securities Litigation; Intellectual Property; Commercial Litigation. ***Email:*** broche@sachnoff.com

LANCE R. RODGERS, admitted to bar, 1975, Illinois. *Education:* Harvard University (A.B., cum laude, 1971; J.D., cum laude, 1974). ***PRACTICE AREAS:*** Business; Federal and International Taxation. ***Email:*** lrodgers@sachnoff.com

JAMES A. ROLFES, admitted to bar, 1988, New York and U.S. District Court, Southern and Eastern Districts of New York; 1989, Illinois; 1991, U.S. District Court, Northern District of Illinois; 1996, U.S. District Court, Central District of Illinois. *Education:* University of Michigan (B.B.A., 1981); University of Illinois (J.D., magna cum laude, 1987). Certified Public Accountant, Michigan, 1981. ***PRACTICE AREAS:*** Complex Litigation; Professional Liability; Securities Litigation. ***Email:*** jrolfes@sachnoff.com

BARRY S. ROSEN, admitted to bar, 1977, Massachusetts; 1978, Illinois. *Education:* University of Illinois (B.S., summa cum laude, 1974); Harvard University (J.D., 1977). Assistant Attorney General, Antitrust Division, Commonwealth of Massachusetts, 1977-1979. ***PRACTICE AREAS:*** Complex Litigation; Attorney Liability; Accountant Liability; Directors and Officers Liability; Failed Bank Litigation. ***Email:*** brosen@sachnoff.com

CAROLYN HOPE ROSENBERG, admitted to bar, 1982, Illinois. *Education:* University of Michigan (B.A., with honors and highest distinction, 1979; J.D., 1982). Law Clerk to Hon. Frederick H. Weisberg, Superior Court of the District of Columbia, 1982-1983. Instructor: "Maximizing Coverage when Negotiating or Renewing Insurance," ACI 6th Annual D & O Liability Conference, May 2001. *Member:* American Bar Association (Co-Chair, Subcommittee on Directors' and Officers' Liability Insurance, 1990-1991; Co-Chair, Committee on Corporate Counsel's Subcommittee on Insurance Coverage, 1994—). ***PRACTICE AREAS:*** Insurance Coverage; Commercial Litigation; Director and Officer Liability. ***Email:*** crosenberg@sachnoff.com

HARRY B. ROSENBERG, admitted to bar, 1952, Illinois. *Education:* Oberlin College (B.A., cum laude, 1949); Harvard University (LL.B., 1952). ***PRACTICE AREAS:*** Estate Planning; Probate. ***Email:*** hrosenberg@sachnoff.com

ELLIS B. ROSENZWEIG, admitted to bar, 1965, Illinois. *Education:* John Marshall Law School (LL.B., 1965). ***PRACTICE AREAS:*** Real Estate.

ROBERT A. ROTH, admitted to bar, 1989, Illinois. *Education:* Lewis University (B.A., highest honors, 1985); John Marshall Law School (J.D., magna cum laude, 1989). ***PRACTICE AREAS:*** Products Liability; Commercial Litigation. ***Email:*** rroth@sachnoff.com

LOWELL E. SACHNOFF, admitted to bar, 1957, Illinois; U.S. District Court, Northern District of Illinois and U.S. Court of Appeals, Second, Third, Fifth and Seventh Circuits. *Education:* Harvard University (A.B., magna cum laude, 1952; LL.B., 1957). ***PRACTICE AREAS:*** Corporate; Securities; Litigation; Antitrust; Commercial Litigation. ***Email:*** lsachnoff@sachnoff.com

BINA SANGHAVI, admitted to bar, 1994, Illinois. *Education:* Illinois Institute of Technology (B.S., 1974; M.C.R.P., 1979); Loyola University (J.D., 1994). ***PRACTICE AREAS:*** Litigation. ***Email:*** bsanghavi@sachnoff.com

JOEL R. SCHAIDER, admitted to bar, 1982, Illinois and U.S. District Court, Northern District of Illinois. *Education:* University of Illinois (B.S., with honors, 1979); Illinois Institute of Technology/Chicago-Kent College of Law (J.D., 1982; LL.M., Taxation, 1993). Certified Public Accountant, Illinois, 1979. ***PRACTICE AREAS:*** Securities; Mergers and Acquisitions; Corporate. ***Email:*** jschaider@sachnoff.com

BRADLEY S. SCHMARAK, admitted to bar, 1987, Illinois. *Education:* University of Illinois (B.S., with high honors, 1984); Northwestern University (J.D., 1987). Certified Public Accountant, Illinois, 1984. ***PRACTICE AREAS:*** Secured Lending; Mergers and Acquisitions; Bankruptcy; Commercial Real Estate. ***Email:*** bschmarak@sachnoff.com

CHARLES P. SCHULMAN, admitted to bar, 1987, Illinois and U.S. District Court, Northern District of Illinois; 1988, U.S. Court of Appeals, Seventh Circuit. *Education:* Boston University (B.A., magna cum laude, 1984); American University (J.D., 1987). Law Clerk, Hon. Chief Judge John D. Schwartz, U.S. Bankruptcy Court, Northern District of Illinois, 1987-1988. ***PRACTICE AREAS:*** Bankruptcy/Creditors Rights; Commercial Litigation. ***Email:*** cschulman@sachnoff.com

JEFFREY A. SCHUMACHER, admitted to bar, 1980, Illinois. *Education:* Northwestern University (B.A., 1976; M.B.A., with distinction, 1983); Harvard University (J.D., cum laude, 1980). Phi Beta Kappa; Beta Gamma Sigma. F.C. Austin Fellow. ***PRACTICE AREAS:*** Corporate; Securities Regulation. ***Email:*** jschumacher@sachnoff.com

MARSHALL SEEDER, admitted to bar, 1980, Illinois. *Education:* University of Chicago (A.B., 1971); Illinois Institute of Technology/Chicago-Kent College of Law (J.D., cum laude, 1980). ***PRACTICE AREAS:*** Business Litigation; Transportation Litigation; Intellectual Property Litigation. ***Email:*** mseeder@sachnoff.com

(This Listing Continued)

CLIFFORD J. SHAPIRO, admitted to bar, 1982, Maryland; 1983, U.S. District Court, District of Maryland; 1984, Illinois and U.S. District Court, Northern District of Illinois including Trial Bar; 1985, U.S. Court of Appeals, Seventh Circuit. *Education:* Washington University (B.A., magna cum laude, 1978); George Washington University (J.D., with high honors, 1982). Order of the Coif. Member, George Washington Law Review, 1981-1982. Co-Chair: Construction Subcommittee, Insurance Litigation Committee; Insurance Subcommittee, Construction Litigation Committee, ABA. ***PRACTICE AREAS:*** Construction Litigation; Insurance Litigation; Complex Commercial Litigation. ***Email:*** cshapiro@sachnoff.com

DUANE F. SIGELKO, admitted to bar, 1986, Illinois and U.S. District Court, Northern District of Illinois. *Education:* University of Detroit (A.B., 1978); Northwestern University (J.D., cum laude, 1986). Order of the Coif. ***LANGUAGES:*** Spanish. ***PRACTICE AREAS:*** Litigation; Insurance; Immigration. ***Email:*** dsigelko@sachnoff.com

DANIEL J. SLATTERY, admitted to bar, 1985, Illinois. *Education:* Beloit College (B.A., cum laude, 1982); Washington University (J.D., 1985). ***PRACTICE AREAS:*** Real Estate Law; Land Use and Zoning Law. ***Email:*** dslattery@sachnoff.com

ABRAHAM J. STERN, admitted to bar, 1979, Illinois. *Education:* Roosevelt University (B.S.B.A., 1976); Chicago-Kent College of Law, Illinois Institute of Technology (J.D., with high honors, 1979); New York University (LL.M., in Taxation, 1980). ***PRACTICE AREAS:*** Long Term Care; Health Care; Business Planning; Real Estate Development and Syndication; Taxation. ***Email:*** astern@sachnoff.com

J. SAMUEL TENENBAUM, admitted to bar, 1973, Illinois; 1974, U.S. District Court, Northern District of Illinois including Trial Bar and U.S. Court of Appeals, Seventh Circuit; 1975, U.S. Court of Appeals, Tenth Circuit; 1976, U.S. Court of Appeals, Ninth Circuit; 1977, U.S. Supreme Court; 1979, U.S. District Court, Central District of Illinois; 1983, U.S. Court of Appeals for the Federal Circuit; 1994, U.S. Court of Appeals, Second Circuit. *Education:* The Ohio State University (B.A., 1970); Northwestern University (J.D., cum laude, 1973). Order of the Coif. Law Clerk, U.S. District Judge Richard W. McLaren, 1973-1975. Adjunct Professor of Clinical Trial Advocacy, Northwestern University School of Law, 1985—. ***PRACTICE AREAS:*** Litigation. ***Email:*** stenenbaum@sachnoff.com

GEORGE A. VINYARD, admitted to bar, 1977, Illinois. *Education:* Illinois Wesleyan University (B.A., magna cum laude, 1971); University of Michigan (J.D., cum laude, 1977). Phi Kappa Phi; Phi Alpha Delta. Vice President, General Counsel and Secretary, U.S. Robotics Corporation, 1994-1997. Vice President, Intellectual Property and Assoc. Gen. Counsel, 3Com Corporation, 1997-1999. ***PRACTICE AREAS:*** Intellectual Property; Information Technology; Internet Law; Corporate Law. ***Email:*** gvinyard@sachnoff.com

EDWARD V. WALSH, III, admitted to bar, 1983, Illinois and U.S. District Court, Northern District of Illinois. *Education:* Southern Illinois University (B.S., 1977); Northwestern University (J.D., 1983). ***PRACTICE AREAS:*** Environmental Law; Litigation. ***Email:*** ewalsh@sachnoff.com

ANGELA M. WASHELESKY, admitted to bar, 1992, Illinois. *Education:* DePaul University (B.A., 1988); DePaul College of Law (J.D., 1992); John Marshall Law School. ***PRACTICE AREAS:*** Intellectual Property; Internet Commerce; Advertising Law; Trade Practices Law. ***Email:*** awashelesky@sachnoff.com

WILLIAM N. WEAVER, JR., admitted to bar, 1964, Illinois. *Education:* Oberlin College (A.B., 1956); University of Chicago and John Marshall Law School (J.D., 1964). ***PRACTICE AREAS:*** Securities Offerings; Venture Capital; Private Placement Syndication. ***Email:*** wweaver@sachnoff.com

JEFFREY B. WHITT, admitted to bar, 1981, Illinois. *Education:* Illinois State University (B.S., 1978); Loyola University of Chicago (J.D., 1981). ***PRACTICE AREAS:*** Litigation; Products Liability. ***Email:*** jwhitt@sachnoff.com

SARAH R. WOLFF, admitted to bar, 1979, Illinois. *Education:* Northwestern University (B.S., with highest distinction, 1974; J.D., 1978). Member, Northwestern Journal of Criminal Law and Criminology. ***PRACTICE AREAS:*** Complex Commercial Litigation; Securities Litigation. ***Email:*** swolff@sachnoff.com

RICHARD K. WRAY, admitted to bar, 1974, Illinois; 1982, Florida. *Education:* Illinois Wesleyan University (B.A., magna cum laude, 1971); Vanderbilt University (J.D., 1974). ***PRACTICE AREAS:*** Litigation; Products Liability. ***Email:*** rwray@sachnoff.com

MARY LOU ZWICK, admitted to bar, 1995, Illinois. *Education:* University of Notre Dame (B.B.A., 1986); Loyola University (J.D., 1995). Certified Public Accountant, Illinois. ***PRACTICE AREAS:*** ERISA; Employee Benefits; Executive Compensation. ***Email:*** mzwick@sachnoff.com

ASSOCIATES

KATIE R. AUNE, admitted to bar, 2001, Illinois; 2002, Minnesota. *Education:* University of Iowa (B.A., 1998); University of Minnesota Law School (J.D., 2001). ***PRACTICE AREAS:*** Taxation. ***Email:*** kaune@sachnoff.com

MARY ANN BECKER, admitted to bar, 2002, Illinois. *Education:* Northwestern University (B.A., 1997); DePaul University (J.D., summa cum laude, 2002). Order of the Coif. ***PRACTICE AREAS:*** Commercial Litigation; Antitrust Law; Intellectual Property Litigation. ***Email:*** mbecker@sachnoff.com

BRADLEY JAMES BOLERJACK, admitted to bar, 2001, Illinois. *Education:* Lake Forest College (B.A., 1998); Loyola University (J.D., 2000). ***PRACTICE AREAS:*** Commercial Litigation. ***Email:*** bbolerjack@sachnoff.com

BENJAMIN L. BRIMEYER, admitted to bar, 2001, Illinois. *Education:* Northwestern University (B.S., cum laude, 1998); University of Minnesota (J.D., magna cum laude, 2001). ***PRACTICE AREAS:*** Corporate Finance; Mergers and Acquisitions. ***Email:*** bbrimeyer@sachnoff.com

ERICH S. BUCK, admitted to bar, 2001, Illinois. *Education:* Northwestern University (B.A., 1997); University of Iowa (J.D., 2001). ***PRACTICE AREAS:*** Litigation; Bankruptcy; Leasing. ***Email:*** ebuck@sachnoff.com

(This Listing Continued)

BRIGGITTE MARIE CARLSON, admitted to bar, 2001, Illinois and U.S. Court of Appeals, Seventh Circuit. *Education:* Vanderbilt University (B.A., 1998); Northwestern University (J.D., 2001). ***PRACTICE AREAS:*** Commercial Litigation. ***Email:*** bcarlson@sachnoff.com

HSING-HUA PAM CHEN, admitted to bar, 2001, Illinois. *Education:* University of Illinois (B.S., 1997; J.D., cum laude, 2001). ***PRACTICE AREAS:*** Corporate Law; Mergers and Acquisitions; Securities Law. ***Email:*** pchen@sachnoff.com

ADAM R. CHISS, admitted to bar, 2000, Illinois and U.S. District Court, Northern District of Illinois. *Education:* University of Wisconsin-Madison (B.A., 1994); University of Illinois at Urbana-Champaign (J.D., 2000). ***PRACTICE AREAS:*** Commercial Litigation; Employment Litigation. ***Email:*** achiss@sachnoff.com

JENNIFER YULE DePRIEST, admitted to bar, 2000, Illinois. *Education:* Indiana University (B.A., 1990); Loyola University at Chicago (J.D., 2000). ***PRACTICE AREAS:*** Commercial Litigation; Employment Law. ***Email:*** jdepriest@sachnoff.com

PATRICK J. ELDER, admitted to bar, 2001, Illinois. *Education:* Miami University (B.S., cum laude, 1997); University of Illinois (J.D., cum laude, 2001; M.B.A., 2001). ***PRACTICE AREAS:*** Commercial Real Estate; Corporate Law. ***Email:*** pelder@sachnoff.com

ROBIN J. ELOWE, admitted to bar, 2003, Illinois. *Education:* Northwestern University (B.A., 1997); Emory University School of Law (J.D., 2003). ***PRACTICE AREAS:*** Litigation. ***Email:*** relowe@sachnoff.com

TRACY GREGAR FERAK, admitted to bar, 2001, Illinois and U.S. District Court, Northern District of Illinois. *Education:* University of Illinois at Urbana-Champaign (B.A., 1998); Chicago-Kent College of Law, Illinois Institute of Technology (J.D., 2001). ***PRACTICE AREAS:*** Products Liability; Construction Litigation; Commercial Litigation. ***Email:*** tferak@sachnoff.com

ALEXANDRA GRIGORAS, admitted to bar, 2002, New York; 2003, Illinois. *Education:* University of Michigan (B.S., 1999; J.D., 2002). ***PRACTICE AREAS:*** Intellectual Property; Trademarks; Litigation; Media. ***Email:*** agrigoras@sachnoff.com

ALFRED E. HANNA, admitted to bar, 2004, Illinois. *Education:* Knox College (B.A., Chemistry, 1994); Loyola University (M.A., Community Counseling, 1998); The John Marshall Law School (J.D., 2004). ***PRACTICE AREAS:*** Intellectual Property; Internet Law; Technology Law. ***Email:*** ahanna@sachnoff.com

JOHN L. HAYES, admitted to bar, 2001, Illinois. *Education:* University of Illinois (B.A., 1994); University of Chicago Law School (J.D., 2001). ***PRACTICE AREAS:*** Litigation. ***Email:*** jhayes@sachnoff.com

KRISTEN E. HUDSON, admitted to bar, 2003, Illinois and U.S. District Court, Northern District of Illinois. *Education:* University of North Carolina at Chapel Hill (A.B., with honors, 1997); John Marshall Law School (J.D., magna cum laude, 2003). Member, The Order of John Marshall. ***Email:*** khudson@sachnoff.com

CAMILLE D. INOCELDA, admitted to bar, 2003, Illinois. *Education:* University of Wisconsin-Madison (B.A., 1998); University of Minnesota Law School (J.D., cum laude, 2003). ***PRACTICE AREAS:*** Corporate Finance; Mergers and Acquisitions; Securities Compliance. ***Email:*** cinocelda@sachnoff.com

MATTHEW M. JOHNSON, admitted to bar, 1995, Iowa; 2001, Illinois. *Education:* University of Notre Dame (B.A., 1990); Drake University (J.D., with honors, 1995); University of San Diego (LL.M., Tax, 2001). *Member:* Iowa State Bar Association. [With United States Navy Judge Advocate General's Corps, 1995-2001]. ***PRACTICE AREAS:*** Employment Law; Personnel Policies. ***Email:*** mjohnson@sachnoff.com

MEL M. JUSTAK, born Royal Oak, Michigan, May 4, 1974; admitted to bar, 2001, Indiana; 2002, Illinois. *Education:* University of Notre Dame (B.A., 1996); Indiana University School of Law-Indianapolis (J.D., magna cum laude, 2001); Georgetown University (LL.M., 2002). ***PRACTICE AREAS:*** Estate Planning; Wealth Planning. ***Email:*** mjustak@sachnoff.com

DANAIL KAZACHKI, admitted to bar, 2005, Illinois. *Education:* California Institute of Technology (B.S., 2002); Loyola University (J.D., cum laude, 2005). ***PRACTICE AREAS:*** Real Estate. ***Email:*** dkazachki@sachnoff.com

LISA KELLMEYER, admitted to bar, 2001, Illinois. *Education:* Duke University (B.A., 1995); University of Minnesota (M.A., 1997); University of Michigan at Ann Arbor (J.D., 2000). ***PRACTICE AREAS:*** Litigation. ***Email:*** lkellmeyer@sachnoff.com

SAFIA KHAN, admitted to bar, 1995, Illinois. *Education:* University of Chicago (B.A., with honors, 1992); University of Illinois (J.D., cum laude, 1995). *Member:* Chicago, Illinois State and American Bar Associations. ***LANGUAGES:*** Spanish, French and Urdu. ***PRACTICE AREAS:*** Real Estate; Business Law. ***Email:*** skhan@sachnoff.com

KENNETH G. KUBES, admitted to bar, 2002, Illinois. *Education:* Northwestern University (B.A., 1999); Indiana University School of Law - Bloomington (J.D., magna cum laude, 2002). Order of the Coif. ***PRACTICE AREAS:*** Financial Services Law. ***Email:*** kkubes@sachnoff.com

NICHOLAS A. LONG, admitted to bar, 1999, Wisconsin, Illinois, U.S. District Court, Western District of Wisconsin and U.S. District Court, Northern District of Illinois. *Education:* University of Wisconsin-Madison (B.A., with distinction, 1995; J.D., 1999). *Member:* State Bar of Wisconsin. ***PRACTICE AREAS:*** Corporate Law; Business Law; Mergers and Acquisitions; Trade Association Law. ***Email:*** nlong@sachnoff.com

ERICA E. LORD, admitted to bar, 2002, Illinois. *Education:* Michigan State University (B.A. in Political Theory and Constitutional Democracy, with high honors, 1996); George Washington University (J.D., with honors, 2002). ***PRACTICE AREAS:*** Estate Administration; Trust Administration. ***Email:*** elord@sachnoff.com

MYRA A. MARCAURELLE, admitted to bar, 2002, Illinois. *Education:* American University (B.A., 1997); Loyola University (J.D., 2001). ***PRACTICE AREAS:*** Commercial Litigation; Securities Litigation; Class Action Litigation. ***Email:*** mmarcaurelle@sachnoff.com

(This Listing Continued)

SACHNOFF & WEAVER, LTD., Chicago—Continued

VANESSA C. MARTI, admitted to bar, 2004, Illinois. *Education:* Emory University (B.A., magna cum laude, 1999); Georgetown University Law Center (J.D., cum laude, 2004). Phi Beta Kappa. ***PRACTICE AREAS:*** Commercial Litigation. ***Email:*** vmarti@sachnoff.com

ANDREW L. MATHEWS, admitted to bar, 2003, Illinois. *Education:* University of Michigan (B.A., 1999); Northwestern University School of Law (J.D., 2003). ***PRACTICE AREAS:*** Litigation. ***Email:*** amathews@sachnoff.com

KATHERINE A. MATHEWS, admitted to bar, 2003, Illinois. *Education:* Duquesne University (B.A., English; B.A., Communications Studies, summa cum laude, 1997); Northwestern University (J.D., 2003). ***PRACTICE AREAS:*** Corporate. ***Email:*** krowles@sachnoff.com

CHRISTOPHER A. McVETY, admitted to bar, 2001, Illinois. *Education:* University of Michigan at Ann Arbor (B.A., 1998; J.D., 2000). ***PRACTICE AREAS:*** Corporate Securities. ***Email:*** cmcvety@sachnoff.com

RAVEN MOORE, admitted to bar, 2003, Illinois. *Education:* University of Dayton (B.A., magna cum laude, 1998); Tulane Law School (J.D., cum laude, 2003). ***PRACTICE AREAS:*** Litigation. ***Email:*** moore@sachnoff.com

DANIEL MORRISON, admitted to bar, 1999, Illinois. *Education:* University of Michigan (J.D., 1999). ***PRACTICE AREAS:*** Litigation. ***Email:*** dmorrison@sachnoff.com

ANDREW MOSS, admitted to bar, 1999, Illinois and U.S. Court of Appeals, Seventh Circuit; 2002, U.S. District Court, Northern District of Illinois; 2003, California. *Education:* Tufts University (B.A., cum laude, 1989); The School of the Art Institute of Chicago (B.F.A., 1994); DePaul University (J.D., with honors, 1999). Order of the Coif. ***PRACTICE AREAS:*** Insurance Coverage. ***Email:*** amoss@sachnoff.com

CHARLOTTE S. POTUCEK, admitted to bar, 1997, Illinois. *Education:* Northwestern University (B.A., with honors, 1991); University of Illinois (J.D., magna cum laude, 1997). *Member:* Chicago, Illinois State and American Bar Associations. ***PRACTICE AREAS:*** Trusts and Estates; Decedents Estates; Estate Administration; Estate Planning; Family Trusts; Family Wealth Transfer; Living Trusts; Powers of Attorney; Retirement Planning; Trust Administration; Wealth Preservation. ***Email:*** cpotucek@sachnoff.com

VENUS McGHEE PRINCE, admitted to bar, 1998, Alabama; 2000, District of Columbia; 2001, Illinois. *Education:* Harvard University (B.A., 1995); Boalt Hall School of Law, University of California at Berkeley (J.D., 1998). ***PRACTICE AREAS:*** Insurance Coverage; Commercial Litigation. ***Email:*** vmcghee@sachnoff.com

KARLA RACHWALSKI, admitted to bar, 2004, Illinois. *Education:* Carleton College (B.A., 1998); Chicago-Kent College of Law, IIT (J.D., high honors, 2004). Order of the Coif. ***PRACTICE AREAS:*** Corporate Law; Mergers and Acquisitions; Securities Law Compliance. ***Email:*** krachwalski@sachnoff.com

LANA J. RAINES, admitted to bar, 2002, Illinois. *Education:* The University of Michigan School of Social Work (B.A., with distinction, 1997; M.S.W., 1999); The University of Michigan Law School (J.D., 2002). ***PRACTICE AREAS:*** Litigation; Insurance Coverage. ***Email:*** lkositzky@sachnoff.com

WILLIAM P. ROBISON, admitted to bar, 1998, Missouri; 2000, Pennsylvania; 2003, Illinois. *Education:* Duke University (A.B., in English, 1994); University of Pennsylvania Law School (J.D., 1998). ***PRACTICE AREAS:*** Class Actions; Product Liability; Commercial Litigation. ***Email:*** wrobison@sachnoff.com

ROBERT H. RUSH, admitted to bar, 2001, Illinois. *Education:* Bates College (B.A., 1988); University of Chicago (M.A., 1992); New York University (J.D., 2001). ***PRACTICE AREAS:*** Mergers and Acquisitions; Corporate Finance; Venture Capital. ***Email:*** rrush@sachnoff.com

DAVID Z. SMITH, admitted to bar, 1998, Illinois. *Education:* Brandeis University (B.A., magna cum laude, 1995); Harvard Law School (J.D., magna cum laude, 1998). ***PRACTICE AREAS:*** Litigation. ***Email:*** dsmith@sachnoff.com

MAX A. STEIN, admitted to bar, 2001, Illinois. *Education:* Carleton College (B.A., 1995); Chicago-Kent College of Law (J.D., 2001). ***PRACTICE AREAS:*** Commercial Litigation. ***Email:*** mstein@sachnoff.com

EMILY WOLF TORRE, admitted to bar, 2004, Illinois. *Education:* Georgetown University (A.B., summa cum laude, 1999); Harvard Law School (J.D., 2004). Phi Beta Kappa. ***PRACTICE AREAS:*** Litigation. ***Email:*** etorre@sachnoff.com

MICHELE L. WALTON, admitted to bar, 1999, Illinois. *Education:* Michigan State University (B.A., 1996); DePaul University (J.D., 1999). Order of the Coif. ***PRACTICE AREAS:*** Litigation. ***Email:*** mwalton@sachnoff.com

HILLARY A. WEIS, admitted to bar, 2002, Illinois. *Education:* University of Michigan (B.A., with honors, 1997) Phi Beta Kappa; Stanford University Law School (J.D., with distinction, 2002). ***PRACTICE AREAS:*** Commercial Litigation. ***Email:*** hweis@sachnoff.com

CASEY L. WESTOVER, admitted to bar, 2001, Illinois. *Education:* University of Illinois (B.S., 1998); Harvard Law School (J.D., magna cum laude, 2001). ***PRACTICE AREAS:*** Litigation; Class Action Litigation. ***Email:*** cwestover@sachnoff.com

MARYANNE C. WOO, admitted to bar, 1999, Illinois; 2001, U.S. District Court, Eastern District of Wisconsin; 2002, U.S. District Court, Northern District of Illinois. *Education:* Columbia College (B.A., magna cum laude, 1996); Columbia University (J.D., 1999). Harlan Fiske Stone Scholar. ***PRACTICE AREAS:*** Financial Law; Securities Litigation; Commercial Litigation. ***Email:*** mwoo@sachnoff.com

OF COUNSEL

JULES G. COGAN, admitted to bar, 1962, Illinois. *Education:* University of Illinois (B.A., 1958); Northwestern University (J.D., 1962). ***PRACTICE AREAS:*** Business; Corporate; Corporate Planning. ***Email:*** jcogan@sachnoff.com

FRANCES MEEHAN, admitted to bar, 1978, Illinois. *Education:* Northern Illinois University (B.A., 1971); Chicago-Kent College of Law (J.D., 1977). ***PRACTICE AREAS:*** Health Care; Administrative. ***Email:*** fmeehan@sachnoff.com

E. LEONARD RUBIN, admitted to bar, 1960, New York; 1962, Illinois; 1963, U.S. District Court, Northern District of Illinois; 1982, U.S. Court of Appeals, Seventh Circuit; 1999, U.S. Court of Appeals, Fifth Circuit. *Education:* University of Illinois; University of Miami (A.B., 1956; J.D., 1959). ***PRACTICE AREAS:*** Copyrights; Trademarks; Trade Secrets; Entertainment Law. ***Email:*** elrubin@sachnoff.com

ERNEST D. SIMON, admitted to bar, 1960, Illinois and U.S. Court of Appeals, Seventh Circuit; 1982, U.S. District Court, Northern District of Illinois including Trial Bar. *Education:* University of Illinois (B.A., 1956); Northwestern University (J.D., 1960). ***PRACTICE AREAS:*** Real Estate Law; Banking Law; Commercial Litigation. ***Email:*** esimon@sachnoff.com

SALVI, SCHOSTOK & PRITCHARD P.C.

Established in 2000

181 WEST MADISON, SUITE 3800
CHICAGO, ILLINOIS 60602
Telephone: 312-372-1227
Facsimile: 312-372-3720
Email: psalvi@salvilaw.com
URL: http://www.salvilaw.com

Waukegan, Illinois Office: 218 North Martin Luther King Jr. Avenue, 60085. Telephone: 847-249-1227. Telefax: 847-249-0138.

Concentration in representing Plaintiffs in personal injury, medical malpractice, wrongful death, transportation liability, aviation, product liability and commercial litigation.

FIRM PROFILE: Salvi, Schostok & Pritchard P.C. is proud of the reputation it has built over the years by representing victims of negligence. For over 22 years, the Firm has been dedicated to helping families recover both emotionally and economically by providing the highest professional and ethical legal representation. Since 1987, Salvi, Schostok & Prichard P.C. has successfully won 90 separate verdicts or settlements of $1 million or more totaling over $278 million. All the firm's attorneys are active participants in numerous professional legal associations. Patrick A. Salvi was recently inducted as a Fellow of the International Academy of Trial Lawyers (IATL) and is the Past President (1993-1994) of the Illinois Trial Lawyers Association (ITLA). Michael P. Schostok is also Past President of ITLA (2003-2004). David J. Prichard was recently elected to the Board of Directors for the Illinois Society of Trial Lawyers.

PATRICK A. SALVI, born Evanston, Illinois, February 10, 1953; admitted to bar, 1978, Illinois and U.S. District Court, Northern District of Illinois including Federal Trial Bar; 1979, Florida; 1985, Wisconsin and U.S. District Court, Eastern District of Wisconsin; U.S. Court of Appeals, Seventh Circuit. *Education:* St. Mary's College of Minnesota (B.A., cum laude, 1975; Doctor of Laws, honoris causa, 1999); University of Notre Dame (J.D., 1978). Ratings: "Leading American Attorneys of Illinois" by the Consumer Law Guidebook; "Top 5% of all Lawyers in Illinois" by the Leading Lawyers Network; "Best Lawyers in America" by Woodward/White, Inc. Cited in Countless Legal Publications and Gives Keynote Speeches Across the Country. Guest Lecturer at: University of Notre Dame; Harvard University; Northwestern University. *Member:* International Academy of Trial Lawyers; Illinois Trial Lawyers Association (Past President); Association of Trial Lawyers of America; Lake County, Cook County, Illinois State and American Bar Associations; State Bar of Wisconsin; The Florida Bar. ***REPORTED CASES:*** Skonieczny v.Gardner et al., 98 L 4578 (2001) Jury Verdict $13, 298, 052; Stelton v. Merchandise Mart et al., 91 L 14568 (1996) Settlement $12,560,000; Lay v. Good Samaritan, et al., 98 L 65 (2002) Jury Verdict $11,024,371; Wingo v. Rockford Memorial, et al., 92 L 345 (1996) Jury Verdict $10,232,523; Arredondo v. Westlake Hospital, et al., 00 L 13977 (2004) Settlement $8,300,000; Miroballi v. Estate of A. Locascio, et al., 88 L 11751 (1992) Jury Verdict $7,148,775; Donovan v. American Airport Limo, et al., 01 L 04242 (2003) Settlement $7,000,000; McDonald v. Freeport Memorial Hospital, et al., 99 L 17 (2002) Settlement $5,500,000; Cardenas v. Gibbons & Reed, et al., 96-16471 (1998) Settlement $5,000,000; Danao v. Lilien, et al., 98 L 151 (2000) Settlement $4,500,000. ***PRACTICE AREAS:*** Catastrophic Personal Injury; Wrongful Death; Medical Malpractice; Birth Injuries; Nursing Home Negligence; Transportation Liability; Aviation Litigation; Commercial Litigation. ***Email:*** psalvi@salvilaw.com

DAVID J. PRITCHARD, born Evanston, Illinois, August 15, 1952; admitted to bar, 1977, Illinois and U.S. District Court, Northern District of Illinois including Trial Bar; 1980, U.S. Court of Appeals, Seventh Circuit. *Education:* Loyola University (B.B.A., Economics, Alpha Sigma Nu, 1974; M.A., Theology, 1992); DePaul University (J.D., 1977). Ratings: "Top 5% of all Lawyers in Illinois" by the Leading Lawyers Network. Past President, Board of Directors, Legal Assistance Foundation, Chicago, 1985-1998. Member: Ethics Advisory Board, The Children's Memorial Hospital of Chicago, 1992-1999; Board of Directors, Gastro-Intestinal Research Foundation of the University of Chicago Hospitals, 1993-1995. Past Board President, Legal Assistance Foundation of Chicago. Currently Serves on Boards of United Cerebral Palsy of greater Chicago as well as Friends Without A Border, which founded Angkor Children's Hospital in Cambodia. *Member:* Illinois Trial Lawyers Association; Chicago Bar Association; Society of Trial Lawyers. (Resident). ***REPORTED CASES:*** Grant v. SSM Regional Health, et al., 00 L 6788 (2004) Settlement $10,000,000; Arredondo v. Westlake Hospital, et al., 00 L 13977 (2004) Settlement $8,300,000; McDonald v. Freeport Memorial Hospital, et al., 99 L 17 (2002) Settlement $5,500,000; Chandler v. Tajuddin, et al., 99 L 12889 (2001) Settlement $4,500,000; Pedroza v. Riverside OB GYN, et al., 99 L 14518 (2002) Settlement $4,300,000; Lawson v. Levie, et al., 01 L 13146 (2003) Settlement $3,500,000; Allen v. Bilyeu, et al., 96 L 180 (2000) Settlement $3,000,000; Washington v. Ladlad, et al., 99 L 12951 (2003) Settlement $2,925,000; Brantl v. Advocate Health, et al., 97 L 14691 (1999) Settlement $2,500,000; Parada v. Rush Presbyterian, et al., 00 L 12884 (2001) Settlement $1,450,000. ***PRACTICE AREAS:*** Catastrophic Injury; Wrongful Death; Medical Malpractice; Birth Injuries. ***Email:*** dpritchard@salvilaw.com

(This Listing Continued)

MARK N. SENAK, born Gary, Indiana, October 15, 1961; admitted to bar, 1987, Illinois and U.S. District Court, Northern District of Illinois, 1992, Trial Bar; 1992, U.S. District Court, Central District of Illinois and U.S. Court of Appeals, Seventh Circuit; 1994, U.S. District Court, Western District of Michigan; 1996, U.S. District Court, Southern District of Illinois; 1997, U.S. District Court, Southern District of Indiana. *Education:* Indiana University (B.A., English and Psychology, 1983); DePaul University College of Law (J.D., 1987). Member, Law Review, 1983-1987. Author: "Factual Investigation from the Insurer's Viewpoint," 1998 ed. of Property Insurance, Illinois Institute of Continuing Legal Education. Associate Instructor, Legal Writing, De Paul College of Law, 1984. *Member:* Chicago, Illinois State and American Bar Associations. ***PRACTICE AREAS:*** Commercial Litigation; Insurance Coverage; Property Subrogation; Employment Discrimination. ***Email:*** msenak@salvilaw.com

DONALD R. McGARRAH, born Norfolk, Virginia, July 5, 1953; admitted to bar, 1978, Missouri; 1979, Illinois and Trial Bar, U.S. District Court, Northern District of Illinois. *Education:* Spring Hill College (B.A., 1975); St. Louis University School of Law (J.D., 1978). Recipient, Everett Hulverson Award for Excellence in Trial Practice, St. Louis University School of Law, Spring 1978. Author: "When It's Not the Real Thing: The Sale of Counterfeit Sporting Goods Costs Trademark Owners and Retailers Millions of Dollars A Year, Here's How to Fight Back," NSGA Retail Focus (August, 1993); "Partnership Within the Law: Developing Legal Issues Among Manufacturers Agents and Retailers," Presentation to NSGA Management Conference (May 1993); "A Guide to the Cross-Examination of a Plaintiff's Economic Expert," Product Liability Advisory Council, April 1995; "Issues Regarding "Other Accident" Evidence," presentation at ABA Automobile Law Committee (August 1995). Panel Speaker: "Management of Catastrophic Damages," Trial Tactics Breakout Group, DRI Annual Product Liability Conference, Beverly Hills, CA, February 2002. Author and Speaker: "Management of Other Occurrence Evidence," DRI National Product Liability Meeting, New Orleans, LA, February 1998. Sustaining Member, Product Liability Advisory Council, 1990—. *Member:* Chicago, Illinois State and American (Member, Section of Litigation) Bar Associations; The Missouri Bar. ***PRACTICE AREAS:*** Medical Malpractice; Products Liability; Personal Injury; Wrongful Death; Aviation Law. ***Email:*** dmcgarrah@salvilaw.com

---

KATHLEEN A. MCGINTY, born Chicago, Illinois, 1963; admitted to bar, 1997, Illinois. *Education:* University of Illinois College of Nursing (B.S.N., with honors, 1987); Loyola University School of Law (J.D., 1997). *Member:* Illinois State Bar Association; Illinois Trial Lawyers Association; American Trial Lawyers Association. (Resident). ***PRACTICE AREAS:*** Health Care. ***Email:*** kmcginty@salvilaw.com

JOHN S. MUIR, born White Plains, New York, March 5, 1965; admitted to bar, 1993, Illinois, U.S. Court of Appeals, Seventh Circuit and U.S. Supreme Court. *Education:* Texas Christian University (B.S., 1988); John Marshall law School (J.D., with honors, 1993). Phi Delta Phi. Order of John Marshall. *Member:* Chicago Bar Association; Illinois Trial Lawyers Association. ***PRACTICE AREAS:*** Medical Malpractice; Wrongful Death; Personal Injury; Criminal Law. ***Email:*** jmuir@salvilaw.com

OF COUNSEL

JAMES H. CANEL, born Chicago, Illinois, February 26, 1944; admitted to bar, 1968, Illinois; 1969, U.S. District Court, Northern District of Illinois including Trial Bar; 1973, U.S. Court of Appeals, Seventh Circuit; 1974, U.S. Supreme Court. *Education:* Boston University; Washington University (B.A., 1964); DePaul University (J.D., 1968). Author, "The Standard of Care Instruction," Illinois Tort Report, Vol. 1, No. 3. Associate-in-Law, American College of Legal Medicine, 1980. Director, The Society of Trial Lawyers, 1991-1993. *Member:* Chicago (Member: Hearing Division, Judicial Candidate Evaluation Committee, 1976-1978; Investigative Division, 1982-1984; Medical Legal Relations Committee; Secretary, 1978-1979; Vice-Chairman, 1979-1980; Chairman, 1980-1981), Illinois State (Member: House of Delegates, 1978-1981; Sections on: Civil Practice; Tort Law; Civil Practice and Procedure) and American (Member, Sections on: Litigation; Tort and Insurance Practice; Vice-Chair, Committee on Medicine and Law, 1987-1988) Bar Associations; Illinois Trial Lawyers Association (Member, Board of Managers, 1985-1996); The Association of Trial Lawyers of America. (Also practicing individually, Chicago, Illinois). ***PRACTICE AREAS:*** Medical Malpractice; Personal Injury; Wrongful Death.

(For Complete Biographical Data on All Personnel, See Professional Biographies at Waukegan, Illinois)

SANCHEZ & DANIELS

Established in 1987

333 WEST WACKER DRIVE, SUITE 500

CHICAGO, ILLINOIS 60606

Telephone: 312-641-1555

Fax: 312-641-3004

Email: sd@sanchezdaniels.com

URL: http://www.sanchezdaniels.com

Wheaton, Illinois Office: 2100 Manchester Road, Suite 201. Telephone: 630-752-9880. Fax: 630-752-9881.

Defense Litigation, including Insurance Defense; Products Liability, including automobile, construction, pharmaceutical, medical devices, machines and mechanical devices; Transportation Liability, including automobiles, trucks, aircraft and watercraft; Construction Liability, including contractors, architects and owners; Warranty Liability, including the Magnuson-Moss Warranty Act and Lemon Law; Premises Liability, including landlord-tenant and hotel; Professional Liability, including attorneys, engineers, accountants, insurance agents and brokers, physicians and hospitals; Employer Liability, including wrongful termination; Commercial Liability, including breach of contract; Real Estate Liability; Environmental Liability, including pollution and toxic torts; Public Finance, including bond issues.

(This Listing Continued)

FIRM PROFILE: Founded in 1987, Sanchez & Daniels has grown from two to 37 attorneys. Saluted for its diversity and professionalism, Sanchez & Daniels maintains its position as the largest minority-owned and controlled law firm in the United States. Sanchez & Daniels is a full-service civil practice litigation law firm.

MEMBERS OF FIRM

MANUEL "MANNY" SANCHEZ, born Chicago, Illinois, December 1, 1947; admitted to bar, 1974, Illinois. *Education:* Northern Illinois University (B.A., 1970); University of Pennsylvania (J.D., 1974). Board Overseers, University of Pennsylvania Law School, January 1992-1998. Board of Trustees, Northern Illinois University. Board of Trustees, Benedictine University, 1993-1999. Board of Directors: Wheelabrator Technologies, Inc., 1992-1998; Metropolitan Bank and Trust Company, 1992—; Northwestern Memorial Foundation, 2002; United Community Bank, Chairman, 2000; Executives' Club of Chicago, 1993—; City of Chicago's Mayor's Fellows Program Board, 1994-2000; Board of Directors: Childrens Memorial Hospital 1996; Steppenwolf Theatre Company, 1994; The Alford Group, 1994. *Member:* Chicago, Illinois State and American Bar Associations; Chicago United (Co-Chair, 1996-1998); Trial Lawyers Club of Chicago, 1981-1989 President, 1989); Illinois Association of Defense Trial Counsel; Defense Research Institute; Society of Trial Lawyers; Hispanic National Bar Association (National Secretary, 1989-1992); Commercial Club of Chicago; Economic Club of Chicago. ***LANGUAGES:*** Spanish. ***PRACTICE AREAS:*** Insurance Defense; Employment Law; Products Liability; Medical Malpractice.

JOHN D. DANIELS, born Brooklyn, New York, February 11, 1939; admitted to bar, 1964, Illinois. *Education:* Princeton University (A.B., 1961); University of Chicago (J.D., 1964). Member, Panel of Arbitrators, American Arbitration Association. *Member:* Chicago, Illinois State and American (Chairman, Insurance Section Council, 1985) Bar Associations; Society of Trial Lawyers (Board of Directors, 1990-1992); Trial Lawyers Club of Chicago; International Association of Defense Counsel; Illinois Association of Defense Counsel; Defense Research Institute. ***PRACTICE AREAS:*** Commercial Law; Insurance; Employment Law; Tort Defense; Construction Law; Products Liability; Professional Liability.

TIMOTHY V. HOFFMAN, born Evanston, Illinois, December 3, 1958; admitted to bar, 1984, Illinois. *Education:* Indiana University (B.S., with high distinction, 1981); Loyola University of Chicago (J.D., 1984). Author: "Beware of the Super Lien - the Effect of Medicare on Personal Injury Settlements and Judgements." *Member:* Chicago and Illinois State Bar Associations; Illinois Association of Defense Counsel; Trial Lawyers Club of Chicago. ***REPORTED CASES:*** Stallman v. Youngquist, 531 N.E.2d 355 (1988); Rerack v. Lally, 609 N.E.2d 727 (1992); Bezan v. Chrysler, 636 N.E.2d 1079 (1994); Cruz v. Chrysler, 688 N.E. 653 (1997). ***PRACTICE AREAS:*** Tort Litigation; Commercial Litigation.

EDWARD M. ORDONEZ, born Miami, Florida, September 25, 1962; admitted to bar, 1988, Illinois; 1989, U.S. District Court, Northern District of Illinois. *Education:* University of Illinois (B.S., 1985); Indiana University School of Law (J.D., 1988). *Member:* Chicago (Section Council, Civil Practice and Procedure Committee, 1989-1991) and Illinois State Bar Associations. ***LANGUAGES:*** Spanish. ***PRACTICE AREAS:*** Litigation.

FRANKLIN U. VALDERRAMA, born Panama City, Panama, August 5, 1962; admitted to bar, 1988, Illinois and U.S. District Court, Northern District of Illinois. *Education:* University of Illinois (B.A., 1980); DePaul University (J.D., 1988). ***LANGUAGES:*** Spanish.

EDWARD N. ROBLES, born Chicago, Illinois, May 8, 1960; admitted to bar, 1988, Wisconsin, Illinois and U.S. District Court, Northern District of Illinois. *Education:* Wright Junior College (A.A., 1980); Loyola University (B.A., 1985); University of Wisconsin-Madison (J.D., 1988). *Member:* Chicago, Illinois State and American Bar Associations; State Bar of Wisconsin. ***LANGUAGES:*** Spanish.

HUGH C. O'DONNELL, born Detroit, Michigan, September 10, 1963; admitted to bar, 1989, Illinois and U.S. District Court, Northern District of Illinois, Indiana and U.S. District Court, Northern and Southern Districts of Indiana. *Education:* University of Chicago (A.B., with honors, 1985); University of Illinois (J.D., cum laude, 1989).

JOHN S. HUNTLEY, born Elgin, Illinois, June 7, 1949; admitted to bar, 1979, Illinois and U.S. District Court, Northern District of Illinois including Trial Bar. *Education:* University of Michigan (B.A., 1971); John Marshall Law School (J.D., with distinction, 1979). Delta Theta Phi. Member, The Order of John Marshall. Member, The John Marshall Journal of Practice and Procedure, 1977-1979. ***REPORTED CASES:*** Bohnen Intern. Inc. v. Liberty Mutual Ins. Co., 120 Ill. App. 3d 657 (2nd Dist., 1983); Frazer v. A.F. Munsterman, Inc., 123 Ill. 2d 245 (1985); Zavala v. Powermatic, Inc., 167 Ill.2d. 542 (1995). ***PRACTICE AREAS:*** Tort Litigation; Commercial Litigation; Insurance Law; Employment Law.

JOHN J. PIEGORE, born Chicago, Illinois, September 12, 1955; admitted to bar, 1981, Illinois and U.S. District Court, Northern District of Illinois including Trial Bar; 1986, U.S. Court of Appeals, Seventh Circuit. *Education:* Loyola University (B.S., with honors, 1977); Chicago Kent College of Law-Illinois Institute of Technology (J.D., with honors, 1981). *Member:* Illinois State Bar Association. ***REPORTED CASES:*** Hernon v. E.W. Corrgian Constr. Co., 149 Ill. 2d 190 (1992); Casualty Ins. Co. vs. E.W. Corrgian Constr. Co., 247 Ill. App. 3d 326 (1st Dist. 1993); Bass vs. Cincinnati, Inc. (Bass I), 180 Ill. App. 3d 1076 (1st Dist. 1989); Bass v. Cincinnati, Inc. (Bass II), 281 Ill. App. 3d 1019 (1st Dist. 1996); Chuhak vs. Kroll, 256 Ill. App. 3d 6 (1st Dist. 1994); Duncan v. Church, 278 Ill. App. 3d 588 (1st Dist. 1996); Knoblauch vs. DEF Transport, Inc., 86 F. 3d 684 (7th Cir. 1996); Davis v. Pak-Mor, 284 Ill. App. 3d 214 (1st Dist. 1996). ***PRACTICE AREAS:*** Insurance Coverage; Appellate Practice; Product Liability Law; Tort.

MARK S. VILIMEK, born Chicago, Illinois, August 24, 1956; admitted to bar, 1983, Illinois and U.S. District Court, Northern District of Illinois. *Education:* Lewis University (B.A., 1978); Illinois Institute of Technology/Chicago-Kent College of Law (J.D., with high honors, 1983). Phi Alpha Delta. Chair Qualified Arbitrator, Cook County Mandatory Arbitration. *Member:* DuPage County and Illinois State Bar Associations; Illinois Association of Defense Trial Counsel; Defense Research Institute. (Also at Wheaton, Illinois Office). ***REPORTED CASES:*** Cleggett vs. Zapianin, 187 Ill. App.3d 872 (1989); Glazewski vs. Allstate Insurance Company, 126 Ill. App.3d 471 (1984). ***PRACTICE AREAS:*** General Civil Trial; Appellate; Insurance Defense; Tort.

(This Listing Continued)

SANCHEZ & DANIELS, Chicago—Continued

GERALD M. DOMBROWSKI, admitted to bar, 1992, Illinois; U.S. District Court, Northern District of Illinois. *Education:* University of Illinois (B.A., 1986); Chicago-Kent College of Law (J.D., 1992). ***PRACTICE AREAS:*** Civil Litigation. ***Email:*** gdombrowski@sanchezdaniels.com

SUSAN K. CHAE, born Seoul, South Korea, March 17, 1967; admitted to bar, 1992, Illinois. *Education:* Loyola University (B.A., 1989); John Marshall School of Law (J.D., 1992). Formerly With: Kramer and Rosenberg, 1990-1993; Jones, Ware and Grenard, 1993-1996. Member, Medical Research Junior Board, 1993-1995. ***LANGUAGES:*** Korean.

PAIGE DONALDSON, born Burns Flat, Oklahoma, August 28, 1967; admitted to bar, 1993, Indiana; 1994, Illinois; 1993, U.S. District Court, Southern District of Indiana, U.S. District Court, Northern and Southern Districts of Indiana; 1994, U.S. District Court, Northern District of Illinois. *Education:* Indiana University (B.A., 1989; J.D., 1993). Phi Eta Sigma. Alpha Lambda Delta.

MARK E. WINTERS, born Chicago, Illinois, March 23, 1966; admitted to bar, 1991, Illinois. *Education:* Northwestern University (B.A., 1988); Loyola University (J.D., 1991). ***PRACTICE AREAS:*** Products Liability; Entertainment Law; Insurance Defense Law.

HUGO CHAVIANO, born Havana, Cuba, December 31, 1952; admitted to bar, 1979, Pennsylvania; 1980, Illinois and U.S. District Court, Northern District of Illinois; 1985, New York and U.S. Court of Appeals, Seventh Circuit. *Education:* Rutgers University (B.A., 1975); Northwestern University School of Law (J.D., 1978). Adjunct Professor of Law, Northwestern University School of Law. Arbitrator and Mediator, Hispanic Business Magazine 1997; 100 Most Influential Hispanics in the United States. *Member:* Chicago (Board of Managers, 1988-1990; Chair: Judicial Evaluation, Appellate Review Committee, 1992-1994; Chair, Insurance Law Committee, 1987-1988) and American (Member: House of Delegates, 1997-1999) Bar Associations; Hispanic National Bar Association (President, 1996-1997); Hispanic Alliance for Career Enhancement (President, 1988-1992). ***PRACTICE AREAS:*** Litigation; Insurance; Reinsurance.

NILGUN AYKENT ZAHOUR, born St. Louis, Missouri, September 12, 1963; admitted to bar, 1989, Wisconsin, Illinois, U.S. District Court, Eastern District of Wisconsin and U.S. District Court, Northern District of Illinois. *Education:* Northwestern University (B.A., 1985); Marquette University (J.D., 1989). Phi Delta Phi. Recipient: Departmental Awards in Law and Politics and Comparative Politics; American Jurisprudence Awards in Civil Procedure and Real Estate Development. *Member:* Chicago and American Bar Associations; State Bar of Wisconsin. ***LANGUAGES:*** Turkish. ***PRACTICE AREAS:*** Medical Malpractice.

LARRY C. JURGENS, admitted to bar, 1981, Illinois. *Education:* University of Illinois (B.S., 1971); Millikin University (B.A., 1972); University of Tulsa (J.D., 1981). *Member:* Decatur and Illinois State Bar Associations.

REPRESENTATIVE CLIENTS: Ace Hardware Corporation; Allstate Insurance Company; National Railroad Passengers Corporation (Amtrak); Borden, Inc.; Chevron Corporation; Chicago Housing Authority; Chicago Park District; CPC, International, Inc.; City of Chicago; Daimler Chrysler Corporation; Dayton Hudson; Dominick's Finer Foods, Inc.; Ford Motor Company; Frito-Lay, Inc.; General Mills, Inc.; General Motors Corporation; Hartford Insurance Company; Hughes Aircraft Company; Hyatt Corporation; Advocate Illinois Masonic Hospital; Iowa Interstate Railroad; Iowa Mutual Insurance Company; J.C. Penney Company; Kraft General Foods; Liberty Mutual Insurance Company; Lutheran General Hospital; Marriott Corporation; Marshall Field & Company; McDonald's Corporation; McHugh Construction; Motorola, Inc.; Norwegian American Hospital, Inc.; Option Care, Inc.; Phillip Morris, Inc.; Praxair, Inc.; Quaker Oats Company; Sara Lee Corporation; Simon Property Group; State Farm Insurance Company; Travelers Insurance; Turner Construction; United States of Mexico; USF&G; Waste Management, Inc.; Walsh Construction; Zurich American Insurance Company.

SANDLER, TRAVIS & ROSENBERG, P.A.

Established in 1977

225 WEST WASHINGTON STREET, SUITE 1550
CHICAGO, ILLINOIS 60606
Telephone: 312-641-0000
Telecopier: 312-641-0005
Email: info@strtrade.com
URL: http://www.strtrade.com

Miami, Florida Office: 5200 Blue Lagoon Drive, Suite 600, 33126-2022. Telephone: 305-267-9200. Telecopier: 305-267-5155.
Washington, D.C. Office: 1300 Pennsylvania Avenue, Suite 400, 20004. Telephone: 202-216-9307. Fax: 202-842-2247.
New York, New York Office: 551 Fifth Avenue, Suite 614, 10176. Telephone: 212-883-1300. Fax: 212-883-0068.
Baltimore, Maryland Office: 111 South Calvert Street, Suite 2700, 21202. Telephone: 410-385-5208. Fax: 410-837-2441.
San Francisco, California Office: Sandler, Travis & Rosenberg and Glad & Ferguson, P.C., 1 Sutter Street, 10th Floor, 94014. Telephone: 415-986-1088. Fax: 415-986-2271.
Los Angeles, California Office: Sandler, Travis & Rosenberg and Glad & Ferguson, P.C., 801 South Flower Street, Fifth Floor, 90017. Telephone: 213-327-0155. Telecopier: 213-327-0157.

Customs Law, International Trade and Transportation Law. International Corporate, Copyright and Trademark Law. Trial, Appellate, Federal and Administrative Practice. Immigration and Nationality Law. International Labor Law, NAFTA, Government Relations, Trade Negotiations, International Trade Policy, Intellectual Property, Import and Export Law, Foreign Trade Sanctions, Shipping Law, Surety.

GILBERT LEE SANDLER (Not admitted in Illinois; See Miami, Florida Listing)

THOMAS G. TRAVIS (Not admitted in Illinois; See Miami, Florida Listing)

LEONARD L. ROSENBERG *(Not admitted in Illinois; See Miami, Florida Listing)*

JEREMY R. PAGE, born Akron, Ohio, December 8, 1961; admitted to bar, 1986, Illinois and U.S. District Court, Northern District of Illinois; 1987, U.S. Court of International Trade and U.S. Court of Appeals for the Federal Circuit; 1993, Florida. *Education:* University of Illinois (B.A., 1983); University of Chicago (M.B.A., 1991); University of San Diego Institute on International and Comparative Law, Paris, France; IIT Chicago-Kent College of Law (J.D., cum laude, 1986). Licensed Customs Broker, 1997. ***LANGUAGES:*** French. ***PRACTICE AREAS:*** Customs and International Trade; Regulatory Law; Transportation. ***Email:*** jpage@strtrade.com

THOMAS E. JOHNSON, born Payson, Utah, January 11, 1948; admitted to bar, 1975, Illinois and U.S. District Court, Northern District of Illinois including Trial Bar; 1981, U.S. Court of International Trade; 1990, District of Columbia; 1998, U.S. Supreme Court. *Education:* Snow College (A.S., 1967); University of Utah (B.S., cum laude, 1969); Northwestern University (J.D., cum laude, 1975). Listed in: Who's Who in America Law; Who's Who in Emerging Leaders in America. Author: "Export/Import Procedures and Documentation," Amacom 4th ed., 2002; "Antitrust, Customs, Gray Market and Other Non-Tax Pricing Considerations," in Transfer Pricing: A Guide to the New Taxation Rules, John Wiley 1993. Member, Illinois District Export Council, 1985—. Past President, International Trade Club of Chicago. *Member:* Chicago and Illinois State Bar Associations; The District of Columbia Bar. ***LANGUAGES:*** Japanese. ***PRACTICE AREAS:*** Import and Export Law; Trade Regulation; Foreign Corrupt Practices Act; Antitrust Law; Unfair Trade Law. ***Email:*** tjohnson@strtrade.com

SHANNON E. FURA, born Alexandria, Virginia, June 18, 1971; admitted to bar, 2004, Illinois. *Education:* Appalachian State University, Boone, NC (B.A., 1993); George Mason University (M.A., 1995); Chicago-Kent College of Law, Illinois Institute of Technology (J.D., 2003). Licensed Customs Broker, Illinois, 1997. ***PRACTICE AREAS:*** Customs Law; International Trade; Regulatory Law; Transportation. ***Email:*** sfura@strtrade.com

ASSOCIATE

DONNA L. BADE, born St. Louis, Missouri, November 4, 1952; admitted to bar, 1998, Illinois; 1999, U.S. Court of International Trade; 2000, U.S. Court of Appeals for the Federal Circuit. *Education:* Hope College (B.A., 1974); John Marshall Law School (J.D., cum laude, 1998; LL.M., International Business and Trade, cum laude, 2000). Licensed Customs Broker, 1980. Adjunct Professor of Law, The John Marshall Law School. Past-President, Customs, Brokers and Freight Forwarders Association of Chicago. *Member:* Chicago, Illinois State and American Bar Associations; Customs and International Trade Bar Association. ***PRACTICE AREAS:*** Import and Export Law; Trade Regulation; Customs Law; Antiboycott Compliance; Regulatory Law. ***Email:*** dbade@strtrade.com

(For Complete Biographical Data on all Personnel, see Professional Biographies at Miami, Florida)

SARNOFF & BACCASH

ONE NORTH LA SALLE STREET
SUITE 1920
CHICAGO, ILLINOIS 60602-3907
Telephone: 312-782-8310
Fax: 312-782-8635
URL: http://www.sarnoffbaccash.com

Practice Limited to Real and Personal Property Taxation.

FIRM PROFILE: Sarnoff & Baccash represents clients in property tax matters only. As a property tax law firm, Sarnoff & Baccash represents properties in many states.

The partners in Sarnoff & Baccash were former government lawyers, with tax, trial and appellate experience. In addition to the attorneys, the firm employs property tax administrators who are trained in assessment and valuation procedures.

Sarnoff & Baccash represents Fortune 500 companies, insurance companies, banks and real estate developers, as well as industrial and corporate taxpayers. Properties represented include hotels, apartment complexes, nursing homes, shopping centers, office buildings and industrial properties such as warehouses and manufacturing facilities.

MEMBERS OF FIRM

MICHAEL F. BACCASH, admitted to bar, 1973, Illinois and U.S. District Court, Northern District of Illinois; 1977, U.S. Supreme Court; 1980, U.S. Court of Appeals, 7th Circuit; 1989, Colorado. *Education:* Princeton University (A.B., cum laude, 1970); University of Chicago (J.D., 1973). Author: "Can a State Constitutionally Levy Its Sales Tax on an Interstate Sale," New York University's Third Annual Institute on State and Local Taxation, 1985. Co-Author: Chapter entitled "Assessment of Taxable Property," "Attorney's Guide to Real Estate Taxation, Illinois Institute for CLE, 1987, 1991, 1993, 1997. Co-Author of Illinois Chapter on Sales-Use Taxation published by American Bar Association in "Handbook on Sales-Use Tax," 1986. Co-Editor, Legal Reporter of International Association of Assessing Officers, 1986-1989. Assistant State's Attorney, Cook County, Illinois, 1973-1981. *Member:* Chicago (Chairman, Sub-committee on Sales, Use and Miscellaneous Taxes, 1981-1982), Illinois State and American Bar Associations; Illinois Appellate Lawyers Association; Institute For Professionals in Taxation (Member); International Association of Assessing Officers (Member). ***PRACTICE AREAS:*** Real and Personal Property Taxation.

ROBERT M. SARNOFF, admitted to bar, 1968, Illinois and U.S. District Court, Northern District of Illinois; 1980, U.S. Supreme Court; 1988, Colorado. *Education:* University of Illinois (B.S., Finance, 1965); IIT Chicago-Kent College of Law (J.D., 1968). Author: Illinois Chapter of the American Bar Association Property Tax Deskbook; Chapter entitled "Assessment of Taxable Property," Attorneys' Guide to Real Estate Taxation, Illinois Institute for CLE, 1979, 1984; Co-Author, 1987, 1991, 1993, 1997. Co-Author of Illinois Chapter on Sales-Use Taxation published by American Bar Association in "Handbook on Sales-Use Tax," 1986. Co-Editor, Legal Reporter of International Association of Assessing Officers, 1986-1989. Editor, Tax Trends, Illinois State Bar Association, 1979-1980. Recipient, Institute of Property Taxation Literary Award, 1981. Assistant State's Attorney, Cook County, Illinois, 1970-1972. *Member:* Chicago (Chairman: Committee on State and Municipal Taxation, 1981-1982), Illinois State (Chairman, 1981-1982, State

(This Listing Continued)

Taxation Council; Member: Assembly, 1982-1985; Executive Committee of National Association of State and Local Bar Tax Sections, 1982-1986) and American (Member, State and Local Tax Committee, 1979—) Bar Associations; Institute For Professionals in Taxation (Member and designated Certified Member Institute-CMI); Real Estate Broker; C.I.A.O.A Certified Illinois Assessing Officer Associate; International Association of Assessing Officers (Member). ***PRACTICE AREAS:*** Real and Personal Property Taxation. ***Email:*** rsarnoff@sarnoffbaccash.com

ASSOCIATES

KENNETH R. SARNOFF, admitted to bar, 1998, Illinois. *Education:* Syracuse University (B.S., 1994); IIT Chicago-Kent College of Law (J.D., 1997). *Member:* Chicago, Illinois State and American Bar Associations; Institute For Professionals in Taxation (Member). ***PRACTICE AREAS:*** Real and Personal Property Taxation; Sports Law. ***Email:*** ksarnoff@sarnoffbaccash.com

STEVEN KANDELMAN, admitted to bar, 1998, Illinois. *Education:* Northwestern University (B.A., 1993); IIT Chicago-Kent College of Law (J.D., 1997). Phi Alpha Delta. *Member:* Chicago, Illinois State and American Bar Associations. ***PRACTICE AREAS:*** Real and Personal Property Taxation. ***Email:*** skandelman@sarnoffbaccash.com

CURTIS L. DURIK, born Oak Park, Illinois, March 18, 1973; admitted to bar, 1999, Illinois; 2000, Wisconsin. *Education:* University of Wisconsin-Madison (B.B.A., 1995); Illinois Institute of Technology, Chicago-Kent College of Law (J.D., 1998). ***Email:*** cdurik@sarnoffbaccash.com

ALLON D. SKIDELSKY, admitted to bar, 1998, Illinois. *Education:* University of Illinois (B.S., 1992); Illinois Institute of Technology, Chicago-Kent College of Law (J.D., 1997). ***PRACTICE AREAS:*** Real Estate Tax; Real Estate. ***Email:*** askidelsky@sarnoffbaccash.com

JAMES B. SARNOFF, admitted to bar, 2003, Illinois and U.S. District Court, Northern District of Illinois. *Education:* Syracuse University (B.S., 1999); Chicago-Kent College of Law, Illinois Institute of Technology (J.D., 2002). *Member:* Chicago (Member, Real Estate Taxation Committee, 2004—), Illinois and American Bar Associations. ***Email:*** jsarnoff@sarnoffbaccash.com

PROPERTY TAX ADMINISTRATOR

JEANINE MARIE HERZEG. *Education:* Mundelein College (B.A.); Loyola University (M.A.). Commercial, Industrial and Residential Property Tax Analyst. ***Email:*** jherzeg@sarnoffbaccash.com

SAUNDERS & DOYLE

20 SOUTH CLARK STREET
SUITE 1720
CHICAGO, ILLINOIS 60603
Telephone: 312-551-0051
Fax: 312-551-4467

Securities, Trade Regulation, Class Actions and Business Litigation.

TERRY ROSE SAUNDERS, born Philadelphia, Pennsylvania, July 13, 1942; admitted to bar, 1973, District of Columbia; 1976, Illinois; 1983, U.S. Supreme Court. *Education:* Goucher College and Barnard College (B.A., 1964); New York University (J.D., cum laude, 1973). Order of the Coif. Co-Author: "Securities Fraud: Litigating Under Rule 10b-5," Matthew Bender, 2001. *Member:* Chicago and American Bar Associations. ***PRACTICE AREAS:*** Securities; Antitrust; Class Actions; Complex Business Litigation.

THOMAS A. DOYLE, born Milwaukee, Wisconsin, November 25, 1965; admitted to bar, 1990, Illinois and U.S. District Court, Northern District of Illinois; 1991, U.S. Court of Appeals, Seventh Circuit; 1996, U.S. Supreme Court; 1998, Trial Bar; U.S. District Court, Northern District of Illinois. *Education:* Bradley University (B.S., cum laude, 1987); University of Illinois (J.D., 1990). *Member:* Chicago and American Bar Associations. ***PRACTICE AREAS:*** Securities; Antitrust; Class Actions; Complex Business Litigation.

LAW OFFICES OF MICHAEL T. SAWYIER

Established in 2002

150 NORTH MICHIGAN AVENUE, SUITE 2700
CHICAGO, ILLINOIS 60601
Telephone: 312-856-9741
Fax: 312-856-9743
Email: mtsawyier@mtsatlaw.com
URL: http://www.mtsatlaw.com

Highland, Indiana Office: 2646 Highway Avenue, Suite 201, 46322. Telephone: 219-923-8846. Fax: 219-838-0554.

Trusts and Estates, Asset Protection, Wills and Probate, Elder Law, Real Estate, Business Law.

FIRM PROFILE: While the firm has served and continues to serve a variety of high net-north clients, its focus is on providing high-quality estate and business planning services, including asset protection and related transactional and litigation services, including real estate, for the often - underserved middle economic class of clients. This focus has led to the firm's recent expansion by the addition of two associates and a northwestern Indiana office. More expansion is presently contemplated. Regardless of such expansion, the firm's total commitment is and will remain complete client service and satisfaction at an affordable cost.

MICHAEL T. SAWYIER, born Boston, Massachusetts, January 6, 1948; admitted to bar, 1972, Illinois; 1974, New York and District of Columbia; 1976, California; 1977, U.S. District Court, Northern District of Illinois; 1981, U.S. Court of Appeals, Seventh Circuit; 1983, Indiana; 1984, U.S. Supreme Court; 1989, Texas. *Education:* Harvard University (A.B., magna cum laude, 1969); University of Chicago (J.D., 1972); Yale University (LL.M., 1973). University of Chicago Law Review. ***REPORTED CASES:*** Treister v. American Academy of Orthopaedic Surgeons (U.S. Sup. Ct. 1984). ***PRACTICE AREAS:*** Commercial Real Estate; Trusts and Estates; Asset Protection; Business Law; Limited Liability Company Law; Tax Planning; Federal Income Tax; Estate and Gift Taxation.

ASSOCIATES

ROZINA GILANI, (admission pending). *Education:* DePaul University (B.S., 2002); The John Marshall Law School (J.D., 2005). ***LANGUAGES:*** Hindi, Urdu and Gujarati. ***PRACTICE AREAS:*** Real Estate; Trusts and Estates; Litigation. ***Email:*** rgilani@estateplanningattorneychicago.com

DANIELLE RICKARD, (admission pending). *Education:* Indiana University (B.A., 1994); Loyola University, Chicago (M.A., 2002; J.D., 2005). ***PRACTICE AREAS:*** Elder Law; Adoption Law; Litigation. ***Email:*** drickard@estateplanningattorneychicago.com

SPECIAL COUNSEL FOR: National Association of Financial and Estate Planners; United Landlords Association; American Konkani Association.

SCANDAGLIA & RYAN

55 EAST MONROE STREET, SUITE 3930
CHICAGO, ILLINOIS 60603
Telephone: 312-580-2020
Fax: 312-782-3806
Email: contact@scandagliaryan.com
URL: http://www.scandagliaryan.com

ADA Counseling/Litigation, Administrative Law, Admiralty Law, Antitrust, Commercial Litigation, Contracts, Copyright Law, Education Law, Employment Law, Environmental Law, Fiduciary Law, Government Contracts, Hospitality Law, Insurance Coverage, Intellectual Property Litigation, Not-for-Profit Corporate Law, Partnership Law, Product Liability, Real Estate Litigation, Securities Litigation, Technology Law, Trade Association Law, Trademark Law, UCC Sales, and White Collar Defense.

GREGORY J. SCANDAGLIA, born New York, N.Y., May 23, 1961; admitted to bar, 1987, Illinois. *Education:* State University of New York at Stony Brook (B.A., 1983); American University, Washington College of Law (J.D., 1986). Co-Author: "The Attorney and the Testifying Expert," 10 CBA Record No. 1, January 1996; "Express Preemption and Premarket Approval Under the Medical Device Amendments," 59 Food and Drug Law Journal No. 1, 245 (2004); "The Commercial Foreclosure Process in Illinois," 2 DePaul Business and Commercial Law Journal No. 2, 359 (Winter 2004). Lecturer, Working with Experts, John Marshall Law School, April 2000. Instructor, NITA Deposition Program, Jenner and Block, April 2000. Instructor, NITA Trial Advocacy, Midwest Region, 2003. *Member:* Chicago (Member, Judicial Evaluation Committee) and American Bar Associations. ***REPORTED CASES:*** Manning v. City of Chicago, 276 Ill.App.3d 260, 657 N.E. 2d 1123, 212 Ill. Dec. 778, 65 USLW 2352 (Ill. App. 1 Dist. Nov. 13, 1995) (No. 1-93-3647); Appeal Denied by Manning v. City of Chicago, 166 Ill.2d 542, 664 N.E. 2d 642, 216 Ill. Dec. 5 (Ill. Apr 03, 1996) (Table No. 80293); Certiorari Denied by Manning v. City of Chicago, 519 U.S. 862, 117 S. Ct. 168, 136 L.Ed.2d 110, 65 USLW 3253, 65 USLW 3261 (U.S. Ill. Oct 07, 1996) (No. 96-32). ***PRACTICE AREAS:*** Commercial Litigation; Real Estate Litigation; Patent Litigation; Product Liability; Antitrust; White Collar Crime; Employment Litigation; Contracts; Hospitality Litigation. ***Email:*** gscandaglia@scandagliaryan.com

WILLIAM J. RYAN, born New York, N.Y., April 14, 1963; admitted to bar, 1991, Illinois and U.S. District Court, Northern District of Illinois. *Education:* State University of New York at Albany (B.A., summa cum laude, 1988); Harvard University (J.D., cum laude, 1991). Article Editor, Harvard Journal of Law and Public Policy. Law Clerk, Hon. J. Daniel Mahoney, U.S. Circuit Judge, U.S. Court of Appeals, Second Circuit. Instructor, NITA Trial Advocacy, Midwest Region, 2003. [With U.S. Navy, 1980-1984]. ***REPORTED CASES:*** Lid Associates, et al. v. Dolan, 324 Ill.App.3d 1047, 756 N.E.2d 866 (1st Dist. 2001). ***PRACTICE AREAS:*** Commercial Litigation; Patent Litigation; Technology Law; Contracts; Antitrust. ***Email:*** wryan@scandagliaryan.com

ASSOCIATES

JAMES R. AHLER, born Ellsworth A.F.B., South Dakota, February 25, 1970; admitted to bar, 1997, Indiana and U.S. Court of Appeals, Seventh Circuit; 2000, Illinois. *Education:* Indiana University (B.A., 1992); St. Louis University (J.D., 1996). ***PRACTICE AREAS:*** Commercial Litigation; Trust Litigation; Construction Law. ***Email:*** jahler@scandagliaryan.com

AMY C. CRAWFORD, born Omaha, Nebraska, September 24, 1974; admitted to bar, 2000, Illinois. *Education:* University of Notre Dame (B.A., cum laude, 1996; M.A., 1997); University of Iowa (J.D., with distinction, 2000). Law Clerk, Hon. Harold F. See, Jr., Alabama Supreme Court, 2000-2001. *Member:* Chicago, Illinois State and American Bar Associations. ***PRACTICE AREAS:*** Complex Commercial Litigation. ***Email:*** acrawford@scandagliaryan.com

ERIC J. MUÑOZ, born Des Moines, Iowa, December 3, 1969; admitted to bar, 1999, Iowa; 2001, Illinois and U.S. District Court, Northern District of Illinois. *Education:* Stanford University (B.A., with honors, 1992); University of Iowa (J.D., with distinction, 1999). Law Clerk, Hon. Robert W. Pratt, U.S. District Court, Southern District of Iowa, 1999-2001. Symposium Editor, Journal of Transnational Law and Contemporary Problems, 1998-1999. Co-Author: "The Internal Corporate Investigation," 1 DePaul Bus. & Com. Law J. 49 (2002); "The Commercial Foreclosure Process in Illinois," 2 DePaul Business and Commercial Law Journal No. 2, 359 (Winter 2004). *Member:* Chicago and Illinois State Bar Associations; Hispanic Lawyers Association of Illinois. ***PRACTICE AREAS:*** Commercial Litigation; Intellectual Property Litigation; Employment Litigation; Professional Liability. ***Email:*** emunoz@scandagliaryan.com

ALAN W. NICGORSKI, born South Bend, Indiana, December 18, 1971; admitted to bar, 1997, Illinois; 1998, U.S. Court of Appeals, Seventh Circuit and U.S. District Court, Northern District of Illinois. *Education:* University of Notre Dame (B.A., with honors, 1994); Northwestern University (J.D., with honors, 1997). Order of the Coif. Law Clerk,

(This Listing Continued)

SCANDAGLIA & RYAN, Chicago—Continued

Hon. Kenneth F. Ripple, U.S. Court of Appeals, Seventh Circuit, 1997-1998. *Member:* Illinois State and American Bar Associations. ***REPORTED CASES:*** Lid Associates, et al. v. Dolan, No. 1-00-0162, 2001 WL 995001 (Ill.App.1 Dist Aug. 30, 2001). ***PRACTICE AREAS:*** Intellectual Property Litigation; Commercial Litigation; Antitrust; Employment Litigation. ***Email:*** anicgorski@scandagliaryan.com

MATTHEW B. STEFFENS, born Evanston, Illinois, March 17, 1971; admitted to bar, 2003, Illinois; 2004, U.S. District Court, Northern District of Illinois. *Education:* University of Notre Dame (B.A., B.S., 1993); University of Chicago (J.D., 2003). *Member:* Chicago and Illinois State Bar Associations. ***PRACTICE AREAS:*** Litigation. ***Email:*** msteffens@scandagliaryan.com

THERESE L. TULLY, born Chicago, Illinois, November 18, 1967; admitted to bar, 1996, Illinois, U.S. District Court, Northern District of Illinois and U.S. Court of Appeals, Seventh Circuit. *Education:* Oakland University (B.S., with honors, 1993); Loyola University (J.D., magna cum laude, 1996). Student Articles Editor, Loyola University Chicago Law Journal, 1995-1996. Law Clerk, Hon. Martin C. Ashman, U.S. District Court for the Northern District of Illinois, 1996-1998. Formerly with Jenner & Block, LLC, 1998-2001. Co-Author: "Express Preemption and Premarket Approval Under the Medical Device Amendments," 59 Food and Drug Law Journal No. 1, 245 (2004). *Member:* American Bar Association. ***PRACTICE AREAS:*** Commercial Litigation; Intellectual Property Litigation; Professional Liability. ***Email:*** ttully@scandagliaryan.com

COUNSEL

SCOTT E. ROGERS, born Kankakee, Illinois, July 31, 1956; admitted to bar, 1990, Florida; 1995, Missouri; 1996, Illinois. *Education:* University of Illinois-Champaign (B.A., 1984); University of Texas (M.A., 1987); Florida State University College of Law (J.D., with highest honors, 1990). Order of the Coif. Associate Editor, Florida State University Law Review, 1989-1990. *Member:* Illinois State and American Bar Associations; The Florida Bar; The Missouri Bar. ***PRACTICE AREAS:*** Intellectual Property; Trademarks; International Trademarks; Copyright Litigation; Unfair Competition Litigation; Prosecution; Counseling; Licensing; Trade Secrets; Right of Publicity; Employment Law; Labor and Employment; Commercial Litigation. ***Email:*** srogers@scandagliaryan.com

REPRESENTATIVE CLIENTS: Abbott Laboratories; A.L.F. Uno S.p.A.; Amtote International, Inc.; BB Five, Inc.; Cablevision Systems Corporation; Canali S.P.A.; Chicago Board of Education; Chicago Transit Authority; C.H. Robinson Worldwide, Inc.; CNH Global N.V.; Compass Environmental, Inc.; Estate of Robert Keck, Sr.; First Trust Corporation; Fortress Investments; Hotel Plaza Athenee; Illinois Tool Works Inc.; JMB Realty Corporation; Liberty Tax Service; Monsanto Company; Pactiv Corporation; Pass & Seymour, Inc.; Potter Roemer/ Fire Protection Equipment; Primestor Development, Inc.; Quantum Realty Services, Inc.; Recycled Paperboard Technical Association; San Ysidro Ranch; SBC Global Services, Inc./ Ameritech; Ty Inc.; Ty Warner Resorts & Hotel, LLC; Walton Street Capital, Inc.

SCANNICCHIO & ASSOCIATES, CHTD.

Established in 2000

SUITE 1210
33 NORTH LASALLE STREET
CHICAGO, ILLINOIS 60602
Telephone: 312-782-8274
Fax: 312-782-1595
Email: rscannicchio@aol.com

Family Law, Residential and Commercial Real Estate, Estate Planning, Appellate Practice, Probate.

REGINA A. SCANNICCHIO, born Chicago, Illinois, January 18, 1963; admitted to bar, 1989, Illinois, U.S. District Court, Northern District of Illinois; 1990, U.S. Court of Appeals, Seventh Circuit. *Education:* DePaul University (B.S., 1985); John Marshall Law School (J.D., 1988). Phi Alpha Delta. Justinian Society. Author: "Keys To Success in a Real Estate Transaction in Illinois," National Business Institute, 2001. *Member:* Chicago (Member, Matrimonial Committee), Illinois State (Member, General Assembly, Family Law Section) and American Bar Associations. ***REPORTED CASES:*** Bosch Die Casting Co., Inc. v. Lunt Manufacturing, 236 Ill. App. 3d 18, 603 N.E. 2d 546 (1992). ***PRACTICE AREAS:*** Family Law; Residential Real Estate; Commercial Real Estate; Estate Planning; Appellate Practice; Probate. ***Email:*** rscannicchio@aol.com

LEGAL SUPPORT PERSONNEL

KATHLEEN MINAHAN (Legal Assistant)

SCHAD, DIAMOND & SHEDDEN, P.C.

Established in 1980

332 SOUTH MICHIGAN AVENUE
SUITE 1000
CHICAGO, ILLINOIS 60604-4398
Telephone: 312-939-6280
Facsimile: 312-939-4661
URL: http://www.bsdlaw.com

Class Action Litigation (Securities, Insurance, Consumer Protection and Fair Debt Collection Practices), False Claims-Qui Tam Litigation, Whistleblower Litigation, Consumer Protection and Consumer Fraud Litigation, Business Transactions and Litigation, Environmental Law and Appellate Practice.

LAWRENCE W. SCHAD, born Milwaukee, Wisconsin, July 3, 1945; admitted to bar, 1970, Illinois and U.S. District Court, Northern District of Illinois including Trial Bar. *Education:* Denison University (B.A., with high honors, 1967); University of Michigan (J.D., 1970). Phi Beta Kappa; Phi Alpha Delta. Associate Editor, *Prospectus-Journal of Law Reform,* 1969-1970. *Member:* Chicago, American and International Bar Associations; Barrister American Inns of Court (Chicago Lincoln Inns Chapter); Taxpayers Against Fraud (TAF). ***PRACTICE AREAS:*** Class Actions; Consumer Fraud Litigation; Investment Fraud Litigation; Business Litigation; Commercial Litigation; False Claims Act; Qui Tam Litigation; Receiverships; Business Transactions; Real Estate Transactions; Commercial Transactions. ***Email:*** lwschad@bsdlaw.com

STEPHEN B. DIAMOND, born St. Clair, Michigan, July 10, 1943; admitted to bar, 1968, Illinois and U.S. District Court, Northern District of Illinois including Trial Bar. *Education:* Harvard University (A.B., 1965); University of Michigan (J.D., 1968). Phi Delta Phi. *Member:* Chicago, Illinois State and American Bar Associations. ***PRACTICE AREAS:*** Business Litigation; Investment Fraud; Consumer Class Actions; Whistleblower Litigation. ***Email:*** sdiamond@bsdlaw.com

JAMES SHEDDEN, born New York, N.Y.; admitted to bar, 1982, Illinois; 1987, U.S. District Court, Northern District of Illinois including Trial Bar. *Education:* University of Illinois at Chicago (A.B., 1973); University of Illinois (J.D., 1982). *Member:* Chicago (Member, Class Action Committee, 1989—), Illinois State and American Bar Associations; National Association of Consumer Advocates (Founding Member, 1994—); Illinois Trial Lawyers Association; The Association of Trial Lawyers of America. ***PRACTICE AREAS:*** Class Action Litigation; Consumer Protection Litigation; Consumer Fraud Litigation; Business Litigation; Commercial Transactions; Commercial Receivership; Real Estate; False Claims Act Litigation; Whistleblower Litigation; Qui Tam Litigation; Fair Debt Collection Practices Act; Fair Credit Reporting Act; Securities Fraud; Insurance Practices Litigation; Investment Fraud. ***Email:*** jshedden@bsdlaw.com

---

STEVEN J. TOMIELLO, born Chicago, Illinois; admitted to bar, 1993, Illinois and U.S. District Court, Northern District of Illinois. *Education:* DePaul University (B.A., 1990; J.D., 1993). *Member:* Chicago, Illinois State and American Bar Associations. ***PRACTICE AREAS:*** Class Action Litigation; Commercial Litigation; Securities Fraud; Consumer Protection Litigation; Deceptive Trade Practices; Unfair Trade; Complex Commercial Litigation; Consumer Fraud; Federal Civil Litigation; Qui Tam Litigation; Whistleblower Litigation. ***Email:*** stomiello@bsdlaw.com

MICHAEL S. HILICKI, born Granite City, Illinois, May 6, 1969; admitted to bar, 1994, Illinois; 1995, U.S. District Court, Northern District of Illinois. *Education:* University of Iowa (B.A., with distinction, 1991; J.D., with distinction, 1994). Phi Beta Kappa. *Member:* Chicago Bar Association. ***PRACTICE AREAS:*** Commercial Litigation; Consumer Litigation; Consumer Class Actions; Deceptive Trade Practices; Unfair Trade; Fair Lending; Federal Civil Practice; Complex Commercial Litigation; Consumer Credit; Consumer Fraud; Consumer Rights; Fair Credit Reporting Act; Fair Debt Collection Practices Act; Civil Litigation; Complex Litigation; Federal Civil Litigation. ***Email:*** mhilicki@bsdlaw.com

STANLEY W. PIERSON, born Mt. Carmel, Illinois; admitted to bar, 2002, Illinois; U.S. District Court, Northern District of Illinois. *Education:* University of California, Los Angeles (B.A., 1995); Loyola University (J.D., 2001). *Member:* Chicago, Illinois State and American Bar Associations. ***PRACTICE AREAS:*** Class Action Litigation; Qui Tam Litigation; Whistleblower Litigation; Commercial Litigation; Consumer Protection Litigation. ***Email:*** spierson@bsdlaw.com

TONY KIM, admitted to bar, 2003, Illinois and U.S. District Court, Northern District of Illinois. *Education:* Purdue University (B.A., 1999); The John Marshall Law School (J.D., 2002). *Member:* Chicago, Illinois State and American Bar Associations. ***PRACTICE AREAS:*** Class Action Litigation; Commercial Litigation; Consumer Protection Litigation; Investment Fraud Litigation; Securities Fraud Litigation; Qui Tam Litigation. ***Email:*** tkim@bsdlaw.com

KATHERINE A. HATHAWAY, admitted to bar, 2004, Illinois and U.S. District Court, Northern District of Illinois. *Education:* Washington University (B.A., 2000); Loyola University (J.D., cum laude, 2004). *Member:* Chicago and Illinois State Bar Associations. ***PRACTICE AREAS:*** Class Actions Litigation; Commercial Litigation; Consumer Protection Litigation; Qui Tam Litigation. ***Email:*** khathaway@bsd.com

SCHAIN, BURNEY, ROSS & CITRON, LTD.

Established in 1985

222 NORTH LA SALLE STREET, SUITE 1910
CHICAGO, ILLINOIS 60601-1102
Telephone: 312-332-0200
Fax: 312-332-4514

Real Estate practice including Contracts, Leases, Liens, Loans for Lenders, Borrower Financing, Lender Financing, Mezzanine and Conduit Financing, Residential, Industrial and Commercial Developments, Condominium Conversions and Tax Increment Financing.
Land Use Regulation practice including Annexations, Annexation Agreements, Zoning Relief including Planned Developments, Map Amendments, Subdivision Approvals, Variances, Licenses and Permits.
Environmental Law practice including Enforcement Defense, Permits and Transactions.
Commercial Litigation practice including Business, Bankruptcy and Creditor Litigation, Unfair Competition, Construction and Zoning Disputes and Property Rights Law.
Business and Corporate Law practice including Acquisitions, General Representation, LLC and Partnerships.
Municipal Law practice including Civil Rights, Condemnation, Contract, Annexation, Zoning, Negotiation and Enforcement of Intergovernmental Agreements and Special Financing Techniques including Special Service Areas and Tax Increment Financing districts.
Income and Estate Tax Law practice including Wealth Preservation, Estate Planning, Business Tax Planning and Contested Matters.

FIRM PROFILE: Schain, Burney, Ross & Citron, Ltd. concentrates its practice in all aspects of real estate matters including real estate transactions, land use and environmental law. Many of our attorneys specialize in more than one area of law, which allows us to provide our clients expertise in the areas of commercial litigation, business and corporate law, municipal law and real estate tax.

(This Listing Continued)

We currently represent the Village of Palatine (since 1991) and the Village of Vernon Hills (since 1995) and have represented as Special Counsel the Village of Hillside, the City of Naperville, the United City of Yorkville and the Village of LaGrange.

JOAN T. BERG, born Oak Park, Illinois, December 29, 1965; admitted to bar, 1992, Illinois and U.S. District Court, Northern District of Illinois. *Education:* Loyola University (B.S., 1988); IIT Chicago Kent College of Law (J.D., 1991). *Member:* Chicago, Illinois State and American Bar Associations. ***PRACTICE AREAS:*** Real Estate; Finance. ***Email:*** jberg@schainlaw.com

PATRICK T. BRANKIN, born Chicago, Illinois, April 7, 1970; admitted to bar, 1995, Illinois and U.S. District Court, Northern District of Illinois. *Education:* Eastern Illinois University (B.A., 1992); Loyola University (J.D., 1995). Co-Author: "Litigation of a Zoning Case," Chapter Nine, Illinois Land Use Law, 2004. Village Housing Court Prosecutor, Village of Palatine. *Member:* Chicago and Illinois State Bar Associations. ***PRACTICE AREAS:*** Land Use; Zoning Law; Municipal Law; Liquor Licensing; Business Law; Civil Litigation. ***Email:*** pbrankin@schainlaw.com

THOMAS R. BURNEY, born Chicago, Illinois, December 12, 1950; admitted to bar, 1977, Illinois and U.S. District Court, Northern District of Illinois. *Education:* University of Wisconsin-Madison (B.A., 1972); Loyola University (J.D., 1977). Guest Lecturer, "Trying a Zoning Case," Illinois Institute of Continuing Legal Education, Chicago and Springfield, Illinois, Spring 2004. Co-Author: "Litigation of a Zoning Case," Illinois Land Use Law (ICLE 2004). Village Attorney, Village of Palatine, 1990—. *Member:* Illinois State and American Bar Associations. (Managing Partner). ***REPORTED CASES:*** United States v. Palatine. ***PRACTICE AREAS:*** Land Use; Municipal Law; Environmental Law; Zoning Law; Property Rights Law; Annexation Agreements. ***Email:*** tburney@schainlaw.com

BERNARD I. CITRON, born Chicago, Illinois, June 30, 1957; admitted to bar, 1982, Illinois. *Education:* University of Illinois (B.S.A., 1978); John Marshall Law School (J.D., 1982). Adjunct Professor, Land Use Law, Master of Real Estate Program, The John Marshall Law School. Formerly with, City of Chicago Corporation Counsel's Office. Village Attorney, Vernon Hills. *Member:* Chicago and Illinois State Bar Associations. ***PRACTICE AREAS:*** Land Use; Municipal Law; Litigation. ***Email:*** bcitron@schainlaw.com

RICHARD G. GOLAB, born Detroit, Michigan, October 14, 1956; admitted to bar, 1990, Illinois. *Education:* Michigan State University (B.F.A., cum laude, 1979); DePaul University (J. D., 1990). *Member:* Illinois State Bar Association. ***PRACTICE AREAS:*** Real Estate; Business Law; Community Association Law. ***Email:*** rgolab@schainlaw.com

JAMES R. GRIFFIN, born Palo Alto, California, January 22, 1971; admitted to bar, 1997, Illinois; 1998, Indiana. *Education:* Purdue University (B.S.M.E., 1994); John Marshall Law School (J.D., cum laude, 1997). *Member:* Chicago and American Bar Associations. ***PRACTICE AREAS:*** Litigation; Municipal Law; Environmental Law. ***Email:*** jgriffin@schainlaw.com

TAMARA K. HIBBARD, born Holloman AFB, New Mexico, November 26, 1968; admitted to bar, 1993, Illinois; U.S. District Court, Northern District of Illinois. *Education:* Miami University (B.S., Business Administration, 1990); DePaul University (J.D., 1993). *Member:* American Bar Association. ***PRACTICE AREAS:*** Commercial Real Estate. ***Email:*** thibbard@schainlaw.com

ROBERT C. KENNY, born Evanston, Illinois, August 9, 1952; admitted to bar, 1979, Illinois and U.S. District Court, Northern District of Illinois including Trial Bar. *Education:* Georgetown University (A.B., 1974); John Marshall School of Law (J.D., 1978). Lecturer, First Amendment Right of Free Speech, Chicago Bar Association. Village Attorney, Village of Palatine. *Member:* Lake County, Illinois State and American Bar Associations; American Planning Association; Homebuilder Association of Lake County. ***PRACTICE AREAS:*** Land Use; Municipal Law. ***Email:*** rkenny@schainlaw.com

RICHARD J. LANG, born Chicago, Illinois, April 21, 1945; admitted to bar, 1970, Illinois; 2004, Wisconsin. *Education:* Loyola University (B.S., 1967); Northwestern University School of Law (J.D., cum laude, 1970). Former Lecturer, Loyola University School of Law. Assistant Professor, De Paul University College of Law. Former Chairman: Wilmette Fire and Police Commission; Wilmette Plan Commission. Member, Wilmette Zoning Board of Appeals. *Member:* Chicago and Illinois State Bar Associations; Chicago Estate Planning Council; American Health Lawyers Association. ***PRACTICE AREAS:*** Real Estate; Business Law; Health Care. ***Email:*** rlang@schainlaw.com

RICHARD H. LEVY, born Chicago, Illinois, September 15, 1943; admitted to bar, 1976, Illinois; 1994, Colorado. *Education:* Southern Illinois University (B.S., 1966); DePaul University (J.D., magna cum laude, 1976). Member, Home-Builders Association of Greater Chicago. Past Chairman, Association of Attorneys and Executives in Corporate Real Estate. Member, Advisory Board, Chicago School of Real Estate, Roosevelt University. Former Member, Real Estate Committee, Practicing Law Institute. *Member:* Colorado Bar Association. ***PRACTICE AREAS:*** Real Estate; Construction Law. ***Email:*** rlevy@schainlaw.com

JOHN D. MALARKEY, born New Haven, Connecticut, September 28, 1949; admitted to bar, 1983, Illinois. *Education:* Boston College (B.A., 1972); Northwestern University School of Law (J.D., 1983). ***PRACTICE AREAS:*** Real Estate Law; Transactional Law; Litigation; Leasing; Finance; Zoning. ***Email:*** jmalarkey@schainlaw.com

TIMOTHY J. McGONEGLE, born Fort Dodge, Iowa, August 22, 1952; admitted to bar, 1977, Illinois and U.S. District Court, Northern District of Illinois including Trial Bar; 1978, U.S. Court of Appeals, Seventh Circuit; 1981, U.S. Supreme Court; 1984, U.S. Tax Court; 1987, U.S. Court of Appeals for the Federal Circuit. *Education:* University of Iowa (B.A., with honors, 1974); Loyola University (J.D., 1977). Law Clerk to: Justice James A. Dooley, Illinois Supreme Court, 1977; Justice Robert Chapman Buckley, Illinois Appellate Court, 1978. *Member:* Chicago Bar Association. ***PRACTICE AREAS:*** Civil Litigation; Appellate Practice; Bankruptcy Litigation. ***Email:*** tmcgonegle@schainlaw.com

DAVID J. O'KEEFE, born Syracuse, N.Y., July 24, 1956; admitted to bar, 1981, Illinois. *Education:* University of Notre Dame (B.A., 1978); Loyola University (J.D., 1981). *Member:* Illinois State Bar Association. ***PRACTICE AREAS:*** Real Estate; Commercial Loans. ***Email:*** dokeefe@schainlaw.com

(This Listing Continued)

MICHAEL S. PINSKY, born Chicago, Illinois, July 25, 1945; admitted to bar, 1971, Illinois and U.S. District Court, Northern District of Illinois; 1973, U.S. Tax Court; 1974, U.S. Court of Federal Claims. *Education:* University of Illinois (B.S., 1967); DePaul University (J.D., 1971). Certified Public Accountant, Illinois, 1969. Conferee, Appeals Division, Internal Revenue Service. *Member:* Chicago (Member, Tax, Trusts and Probate Committees; Representative, Internal Revenue Service, District Director's Liaison Committee, 1984-1991; Chairman, Federal Tax Committee, 1985-1986; Procedure Subcommittee; Federal Tax Executive Committee), Illinois State (Tax Committee) and American (Member, Tax Committee) Bar Associations; Chicago Estate Planning Council. ***PRACTICE AREAS:*** Estate Planning; Tax Law; Business Law. ***Email:*** mpinsky@schainlaw.com

GARY L. PLOTNICK, born Lincolnwood, Illinois, January 18, 1962; admitted to bar, 1987, Illinois and U.S. District Court, Northern District of Illinois. *Education:* University of Illinois (B.A., 1984); DePaul University College of Law (J.D., 1987). *Member:* Chicago, Illinois State and American Bar Associations. ***PRACTICE AREAS:*** Real Estate; Estate Planning; Community Association Law. ***Email:*** gplotnick@schainlaw.com

MICHAEL E. ROSS, born Chicago, Illinois, August 14, 1951; admitted to bar, 1976, Illinois. *Education:* University of Illinois (B.A., with honors, 1973); Chicago-Kent University College of Law (J.D., 1976; LL.M., Taxation, 1988). Lecturer, Commercial Leasing, International Council of Shopping Centers Convention. *Member:* Chicago and Illinois State Bar Associations. ***PRACTICE AREAS:*** Real Estate; Commercial Leasing; Lender Law; Business Acquisitions. ***Email:*** mross@schainlaw.com

JEROME S. SCHAIN, born Chicago, Illinois, January 29, 1941; admitted to bar, 1966, Illinois. *Education:* University of Illinois, College of Pharmacy (B.S., Pharmacy, 1962); DePaul University (J.D., 1967). Supervisor, Zoning and Condemnation Departments, Cook County State's Attorney's Office. Legal Counsel in charge of preparation, 1976 Comprehensive Cook County Zoning Ordinance. ***PRACTICE AREAS:*** Land Use; Zoning Law; Real Estate Development. ***Email:*** jschain@schainlaw.com

GLENN C. SECHEN, born Chicago, Illinois, May 16, 1947; admitted to bar, 1974, Illinois and U.S. District Court, Northern District of Illinois including Trial Bar; 1976, U.S. Court of Appeals, Seventh Circuit; 1980, U.S. Supreme Court; 2001, U.S. District Court, Southern District of Illinois; 2002, U.S. District Court, Northern District of Indiana; registered to practice before U.S. Patent and Trademark Office. *Education:* Purdue University (B.S.E.E., 1969); John Marshall Law School (J.D., 1974; LL.M., 1987). Member, John Marshall Law Review, 1974-1975. Chief, Environmental Litigation Division, Cook County State's Attorney's Office. *Member:* Chicago and American Bar Associations. ***PRACTICE AREAS:*** Environmental Law; Land Use; Environmental Litigation. ***Email:*** gsechen@schainlaw.com

JEROME WIENER, born Johnstown, Pennsylvania, August 23, 1943; admitted to bar, 1968, Virginia; 1969, District of Columbia; 1983, Maryland; 1986, Illinois; U.S. District Court, Northern District of Illinois, U.S. Court of Appeals, Seventh Circuit and U.S. Supreme Court. *Education:* Lehigh University (B.S., 1965); Georgetown University Law Center (J.D., 1968). Assistant U.S. Attorney, District of Columbia, 1969-1973. Assistant General Counsel and Director, Office of Special Investigations, Department of Energy, 1978-1985. *Member:* Chicago and Virginia Bar Associations; Virginia State Bar; The District of Columbia Bar. ***PRACTICE AREAS:*** Civil Litigation. ***Email:*** jwiener@schainlaw.com

---

JENNIFER MORRISON BLOOM, born Rockford, Illinois, December 24, 1974; admitted to bar, 2004, Illinois. *Education:* University of Michigan, Ann Arbor (B.A., 1997); Chicago-Kent College of Law (J.D., 2002). Mediator, Center for Conflict Resolution. *Member:* Chicago Bar Association; Illinois State Bar; American Bar Association. ***PRACTICE AREAS:*** Real Estate. ***Email:*** jbloom@schainlaw.com

JESSICA MARIE BOUDREAU, born November 8, 1975; admitted to bar, 2003, California; 2004, Illinois; 2005, Wisconsin. *Education:* University of Wisconsin-Oshkosh (B.S., 1999); University of San Diego (J.D., 2003). Honored in recognition of work for San Diego City Attorney's Office and San Diego Councilman Scott Peters. Teaching Assistant to Prof. Dessent, Contract Law, University of San Diego, 2002-2003. Teaching Certification, 1999. *Member:* Chicago Bar Association (Member, Young Lawyer's Section); State Bar of California; State Bar of Wisconsin. ***PRACTICE AREAS:*** Land Use; Zoning Law; Commercial Real Estate; Residential Real Estate; Municipal Law; Real Estate; Corporate Law; Real Estate Litigation. ***Email:*** jboudreau@schainlaw.com

LINSEY N. COHEN, born February 12, 1973; admitted to bar, 1998, Illinois. *Education:* University of Illinois (B.A., 1995); Loyola University (J.D., 1998). *Member:* Chicago Bar Association. ***PRACTICE AREAS:*** Real Estate; Corporate Law. ***Email:*** lcohen@schainlaw.com

JAMES K. HENEGAN, born Chicago, Illinois, August 21, 1956; admitted to bar, 1981, Illinois. *Education:* University of Notre Dame (B.S., 1978); University of Illinois (J.D., 1981). Attorney, Pedersen & Houpt, Chicago, IL, 1981-1990. ***PRACTICE AREAS:*** Real Estate. ***Email:*** jhenegan@schainlaw.com

CHARLES D. MANGUM, born Houston, Texas, July 24, 1971; admitted to bar, 1998, Illinois. *Education:* University of Michigan (B.A., 1993); Case Western Reserve University (J.D., 1998). ***PRACTICE AREAS:*** Real Estate. ***Email:*** cmangum@schainlaw.com

COURTNEY E. MAYSTER, born Chicago, Illinois, May 30, 1976; admitted to bar, 2001, Illinois and U.S. District Court, Northern District of Illinois. *Education:* Georgetown University (B.A., Psychology, 1998); Loyola University (J.D., 2001). Formerly with Levenfeld Pearlstein. Real Estate Broker, Illinois, 2003. Member: Chicago Association of Realtors; National Association of Realtors; Illinois Association of Realtors. *Member:* Chicago (Member, Sections on: Real Estate Law; Condominium Law, 2001—), Illinois State and American Bar Associations. ***PRACTICE AREAS:*** Real Estate. ***Email:*** cmayster@schainlaw.com

KATRIINA S. McGUIRE, born Helsinki, Finland, September 17, 1968; admitted to bar, 1996, Illinois. *Education:* University of Washington (B.A., 1991); Loyola University (J.D., 1996). ***LANGUAGES:*** German and Finnish. ***PRACTICE AREAS:*** Zoning Law; Litigation. ***Email:*** kmcguire@schainlaw.com

(This Listing Continued)

SCHAIN, BURNEY, ROSS & CITRON, LTD., Chicago—Continued

CAROLINE A. NASH, born Chicago, Illinois, December 21, 1970; admitted to bar, 1996, Illinois. *Education:* University of Michigan (B.A., 1993); DePaul College of the Law (J.D., 1996). City of Chicago: Central Loop Project Manager, Special Project Coordinator, Department of Planning and Development; Assistant Corporation Counsel, Commercial and Policy Litigation Division. ***REPORTED CASES:*** Majeske v. City of Chicago. ***PRACTICE AREAS:*** Zoning Law; Land Use; Municipal Law. ***Email:*** cnash@schainlaw.com

DANIEL C. SHAPIRO, born Milwaukee, Wisconsin, December 23, 1961; admitted to bar, 1987, Illinois; 1988, U.S. District Court, Northern District of Illinois. *Education:* University of Michigan (B.A., 1984); American University (J.D., 1987). *Member:* Chicago, Illinois State and American Bar Associations. ***PRACTICE AREAS:*** Litigation; Zoning, Planning and Land Use; Municipal Law. ***Email:*** dshapiro@schainlaw.com

DONALD C. WENNLUND, born Joliet, Illinois, August 24, 1966; admitted to bar, 1991, Illinois. *Education:* University of Wisconsin, Whitewater (B.A., 1988); John Marshall Law School (J.D., 1991). Chief Counsel and Executive, Will County, 2000-2004. *Member:* Will County and Illinois State Bar Associations. ***PRACTICE AREAS:*** Zoning, Planning and Land Use; Litigation; Real Estate; Municipal Law. ***Email:*** cwennlund@schainlaw.com

MARIBETH HOPE WHITFIELD, born Winfield, Illinois, October 7, 1977; admitted to bar, 2004, Illinois. *Education:* University of Illinois (B.A., 2000); Chicago-Kent College of Law (J.D., 2004). ***Email:*** hwhitfield@schainlaw.com

KEVIN J. WOLFBERG, born Chicago, Illinois, April 1, 1972; admitted to bar, 1999, Illinois. *Education:* Indiana University at Bloomington (B.A., 1994); John Marshall Law School (J.D., LL.M., Taxation, 1999). ***PRACTICE AREAS:*** Zoning Law; Municipal Law; Taxation. ***Email:*** kwolfberg@schainlaw.com

SCHENK, ANNES, BROOKMAN & TEPPER, LTD.

Established in 1992

311 SOUTH WACKER DRIVE, SUITE 5125
CHICAGO, ILLINOIS 60606-6657
Telephone: 312-554-3100
Fax: 312-554-3115
URL: http://www.sabt.com
Email: sabt@sabt.com
URL: http://www.sabtlaw.net

Business and Commercial Litigation, Commercial Real Estate, including Representation of Management/Ownership, Estate Planning and Administration, Probate, Corporate Law, Corporate Planning, Financial Planning, Tax, Commercial Transactions, General Civil Trial/Litigation, Creditors Rights and Bankruptcy, Business Immigration, Insurance Law, including Insurance Coverage, Insurance Defense and Professional Liability and Employment Law.

FIRM PROFILE: Schenk, Annes, Brookman & Tepper, Ltd. was founded in 1992. Our attorneys have many years of experience and expertise in a wide range of legal and business areas. Our practice includes commercial real estate, including leasing, landlord/tenant relationships, real estate management issues, bankruptcy issues and real estate litigation, estate planning, probate, estate and gift tax, family law, corporate planning, financial planning, commercial litigation, tax and corporate transactional issues. Our attorneys have substantial support from our staff of paralegals and legal assistants. Firm clients include owners, managers and developers of major commercial real estate, individuals, entrepreneurs, small and large businesses, corporations and insurance companies. Our business philosophy is simple. The needs of our clients must come first along with the technical and legal expertise to provide the timely and cost effective service that our clients demand. We work to solve our clients' problems and meet their goals and needs quickly and efficiently.

GERALD L. SCHENK, born Chicago, Illinois, January 6, 1943; admitted to bar, 1968, Illinois; 1970, U.S. District Court, Northern District of Illinois; 1979, U.S. Tax Court; 1993, U.S. Court of Appeals, 7th Circuit. *Education:* University of Illinois (B.A., 1964; J.D., 1968). *Member:* Chicago (Member and Past Chairperson, Trust Law II Committee; Member and Past Chairperson, Probate Division I Committee) and Illinois State Bar Associations; Chicago Estate Planning Council. ***PRACTICE AREAS:*** Estate Planning; Probate; Probate Litigation; Estate and Gift Taxation; Business Planning and Transactions. ***Email:*** gschenk@sabt.com

ANDREW J. ANNES, born 1956; admitted to bar, 1982, Illinois and U.S. District Court, Northern District of Illinois including Trial Bar. *Education:* Loyola University (B.B.A., 1979); The John Marshall Law School (J.D., with distinction, 1982). Executive Editor, The John Marshall Law Review, 1981-1982. *Member:* Chicago and Illinois State Bar Associations. ***PRACTICE AREAS:*** Corporate Law; Litigation; Real Estate Law; Business Immigration; Family Law. ***Email:*** aannes@sabt.com

ROBERT K. BROOKMAN, born Detroit, Michigan, March 2, 1942; admitted to bar, 1970, Illinois and U.S. District Court, Northern District of Illinois; 1975, U.S. Tax Court; 1984, Wisconsin. *Education:* University of Michigan (A.B., 1964); University of Colorado at Boulder (J.D., 1969). Member, 1967-1969 and Associate Editor, 1968, University of Colorado Law Review. *Member:* Chicago (Vice Chairman, Probate Practice Committee, 1983; Chairman, Probate Practice Committee, 1995-1996), Illinois State and American Bar Associations; State Bar of Wisconsin. ***PRACTICE AREAS:*** Estate Planning; Probate; Taxation. ***Email:*** rbrookma@ix.netcom.com

ROBERT D. TEPPER, born 1949; admitted to bar, 1982, Illinois and U.S. District Court, Northern District of Illinois, including Trial Bar and U.S. Court of Appeals, 7th Circuit. *Education:* Southern Illinois University (B.A., 1975); The John Marshall Law School (J.D., with high distinction, 1982). Phi Alpha Delta (President, 1980-1981). The Order of John Marshall. Judicial Law Clerk to Chief Justice Howard C. Ryan, Illinois Superior Court, 1982-1983. Author: "Fire Safety In Transport Category Aircraft: Litigating A Post Crash Or In Flight Aircraft Fire," Journal of Air Law and Commerce, Vol. 49, No. 4. Member and Past President, Rotary Club of Lincolnshire, Illinois. *Member:* Chicago, Illinois State and American Bar Associations. ***PRACTICE AREAS:*** General Litigation; Commercial Litigation; Landlord and Tenant Law; Commercial Real Estate; Insurance Coverage; Family Law; Product Liability Defense; Employment Law; Bankruptcy; Creditors Rights. ***Email:*** rtepper@sabt.com

(This Listing Continued)

JOHN W. CAMPBELL, JR., born Albion, Michigan, August 26, 1974; admitted to bar, 2001, Illinois. *Education:* Michigan State University (B.S., Psychology, 1998); DePaul University College of Law (J.D., 2001). *Member:* Chicago and American Bar Associations. ***PRACTICE AREAS:*** Corporate Law; Litigation; Commercial Real Estate; Probate. ***Email:*** jcampbell@sabt.com

CHARLES G. BLAIR, born Chicago Heights, Illinois, January 22, 1969; admitted to bar, 2004, Illinois. *Education:* Northern Illinois University (B.S., 1992); The John Marshall Law School (J.D., cum laude, 2004). *Member:* Chicago Bar Association. ***PRACTICE AREAS:*** Estate Planning; Probate; Business Law; Commercial Litigation. ***Email:*** cblair@sabt.com

SCHIFF HARDIN LLP

A Limited Liability Partnership Including Professional Corporations

Founded in 1864

6600 SEARS TOWER
CHICAGO, ILLINOIS 60606-6473
Telephone: 312-258-5500
Facsimile: 312-258-5600
Email: attorneys@schiffhardin.com
URL: http://www.schiffhardin.com

Washington, D.C. Office: 1101 Connecticut Avenue, N.W. Telephone: 202-778-6400. Facsimile: 202-778-6460.
New York, New York Office: 623 Fifth Avenue, 28th Floor, 10022. Telephone: 212-753-5000. Facsimile: 212-753-5044.
Dublin, Ireland Office: 3 Burlington Road, Dublin 4 Ireland. Telephone: +011-353-1-202-6555. Facsimile: +011-353-1-668-1212.
Lake Forest, Illinois Office: One Westminster Place, 60045. Telephone: 847-295-9200. Facsimile: 847-295-7810.
Atlanta, Georgia Office: 1230 Peachtree Street, 18th Floor. Telephone: 404-806-3800. Facsimile: 404-806-3801.

General Practice.

LAW FIRM ALLIANCES/ASSOCIATIONS: ***TERRALEX, THE WORLDWIDE NETWORK OF INDEPENDENT LAW FIRMS***

UNITED STATES LAW FIRM GROUP

PARTNERS

THOMAS W. ABENDROTH, admitted to bar, 1984, Illinois. *Education:* Ripon College (B.A., summa cum laude, 1981); Northwestern University (J.D., magna cum laude, 1984). Phi Beta Kappa; Order of the Coif. Fellow, American College of Trust and Estate Counsel. ***PRACTICE AREAS:*** Trusts and Estates; Estate and Gift Taxation; Generation Skipping Tax; Business Succession Planning. ***Email:*** tabendroth@schiffhardin.com

JOHN F. ADAMS, admitted to bar, 1977, Illinois. *Education:* Princeton University (A.B., 1972); The Queen's College, Oxford University (B.A., 1974); University of Chicago (J.D., 1977). Law Clerk to Judge Hubert L. Will, (N.D., Ill.). ***PRACTICE AREAS:*** Corporate Law; Mergers, Acquisitions and Divestitures; Securities. ***Email:*** jadams@schiffhardin.com

BARRY S. ALBERTS, admitted to bar, 1971, Illinois and U.S. District Court, Northern District of Illinois. *Education:* Miami University (B.A., 1968); University of Chicago (J.D., 1971). Phi Beta Kappa. ***PRACTICE AREAS:*** Litigation; Legal Ethics and Professional Responsibility. ***Email:*** balberts@schiffhardin.com

KRISTY L. ALLEN, admitted to bar, 1996, Illinois. *Education:* Brown University (A.B., 1992); University of Michigan (J.D., 1996). Associate Editor, University of Michigan Journal of Law Reform. ***PRACTICE AREAS:*** Reinsurance; Civil Litigation. ***Email:*** kallen@schiffhardin.com

DAVID H. ANDERSON, admitted to bar, 1993, Minnesota and U.S. District Court, District of Minnesota; 1994, Illinois and U.S. District Court, Central District of Illinois; 1996, U.S. Court of Appeals, Seventh Circuit. *Education:* Northwestern University (B.S., 1986); University of Illinois (J.D., 1993). Chartered Property Casualty Underwriter (CPCU) Professional Designation, 1989. ***PRACTICE AREAS:*** Insurance Law; Commercial Litigation. ***Email:*** danderson@schiffhardin.com

DIRK W. ANDRINGA, admitted to bar, 1993, Illinois. *Education:* University of Illinois (B.A., magna cum laude, 1990); University of Illinois College of Law (J.D., magna cum laude, 1993). ***PRACTICE AREAS:*** Corporate; Mergers and Acquisitions. ***Email:*** dandringa@schiffhardin.com

DARREN C. BAKER, admitted to bar, 1998, Illinois. *Education:* Drury College (B.A., summa cum laude, with first honors, 1995); Northwestern University (J.D., cum laude, 1998). Articles Editor, Northwestern University Law Review. ***PRACTICE AREAS:*** Corporate and Securities; Intellectual Property. ***Email:*** dbaker@schiffhardin.com

JOHN A. BANNON, admitted to bar, 1991, Illinois and U.S. District Court, Northern District of Illinois. *Education:* University of Virginia (B.A., 1979); Marymount University (M.B.A., 1988); University of Chicago (J.D., with honors, 1991). ***PRACTICE AREAS:*** Litigation. ***Email:*** jbannon@schiffhardin.com

SVETLANA V. BEKMAN, admitted to bar, 1996, Illinois. *Education:* Brown University (B.A., 1988); Oxford University (M.Phil., 1990); Northwestern University (J.D., cum

(This Listing Continued)

laude, 1996). Phi Beta Kappa. Order of the Coif. Recipient, Keasbey Fellowship. ***LANGUAGES:*** Russian. ***PRACTICE AREAS:*** Estate Planning; Estate Administration. ***Email:*** sbekman@schiffhardin.com

LAURALYN G. BENGEL, admitted to bar, 1986, Illinois; 1990, U.S. District Court, Northern District of Illinois. *Education:* DePauw University (B.A., 1983); Washington University (J.D., 1986). ***PRACTICE AREAS:*** Employee Benefits. ***Email:*** lbengel@schiffhardin.com

ROBERT I. BERGER, admitted to bar, 1975, Illinois. *Education:* University of Illinois (B.A., 1971); Northwestern University (J.D., 1974). ***PRACTICE AREAS:*** Litigation. ***Email:*** rberger@schiffhardin.com

JILL B. BERKELEY, admitted to bar, 1975, Illinois, U.S. Court of Appeals, 7th Circuit and U.S. District Court, Northern District of Illinois and Indiana. *Education:* University of Michigan (B.A., magna cum laude, 1972); Northwestern University (J.D., 1975). Phi Beta Kappa. Recipient, Andrew C. Hecker Memorial Award, 2005. *Member:* American Bar Association. ***PRACTICE AREAS:*** Insurance Coverage; Insurance Litigation; Commercial Insurance; Self Insured Law; General Liability. ***Email:*** jberkeley@schiffhardin.com

SCOTT BIEBER, admitted to bar, 1979, Illinois and U.S. District Court, Northern District of Illinois; U.S. Tax Court. *Education:* University of Pennsylvania (B.A., Cum laude, 1976); University of Chicago (J.D., 1979). Fellow, American College of Trust and Estate Counsel. ***PRACTICE AREAS:*** Estate and Gift Taxation; Generation Skipping Tax; Family Partnerships; Charitable Trusts and Foundations; Family Business Law. ***Email:*** sbieber@schiffhardin.com

DAVID C. BLICKENSTAFF, admitted to bar, 1994, Illinois; 1995, U.S. District Court, Northern District of Illinois; 1996, U.S. Court of Appeals, Seventh Circuit; 1997, U.S. District Court, Central District of Illinois; 1998, U.S. Court of Appeals, Federal Circuit; 2004, U.S. Court of Appeals, Third Circuit. *Education:* Princeton University (A.B., with honors, 1990); Northwestern University (J.D., magna cum laude, 1994). Order of the Coif. Law Clerk to Hon. James B. Moran, U.S. District Court, Northern District of Illinois, 1994-1995. ***PRACTICE AREAS:*** Litigation; Trust Litigation; Estate Litigation; Class Action Defense; Appellate Practice. ***Email:*** dblickenstaff@schiffhardin.com

CHRIS L. BOLLINGER, admitted to bar, 1993, Illinois; 1995, U.S. District Court, Northern District of Illinois. *Education:* University of Michigan (B.S.E.E., magna cum laude, 1989; J.D., cum laude, 1992). ***PRACTICE AREAS:*** Intellectual Property; Computer Law; Internet Law; Information Technology Contracts; Electronic Commerce; Software Licensing. ***Email:*** cbollinger@schiffhardin.com

STEPHEN J. BONEBRAKE, admitted to bar, 1992, Illinois, U.S. District Court, Northern District of Illinois and U.S. District Court, Eastern District of Wisconsin; U.S. Court of Appeals, Seventh Circuit; U.S. District Court, Northern District of Indiana. *Education:* DePauw University (B.A., 1985); Loyola University (J.D., cum laude, 1992). ***PRACTICE AREAS:*** Environmental Law. ***Email:*** sbonebrake@schiffhardin.com

FELICE BRESSLER ROSE, admitted to bar, 1991, Illinois. *Education:* University of Michigan (B.A., 1988); University of Illinois (J.D., 1991). ***PRACTICE AREAS:*** Real Estate Development; Real Estate Acquisitions; Real Estate Sales; Real Estate Contracts; Real Estate Leasing. ***Email:*** fbressler@schiffhardin.com

MAX G. BRITTAIN, JR., admitted to bar, 1976, Illinois and U.S. District Court, Northern District of Illinois; 1978, U.S. Court of Appeals, Seventh Circuit; 1980, U.S. Supreme Court; 1984, U.S. Court of Appeals, Federal Circuit. *Education:* Bradley University (B.S., 1969); Loyola University (J.D., cum laude, 1976). Managing Editor, Loyola University of Chicago Law Journal, 1975-1976. Fellow, College of Labor and Employment Lawyers. ***PRACTICE AREAS:*** Management Labor Law; Employment Law; Employment Litigation. ***Email:*** mbrittain@schiffhardin.com

HARMON A. BROWN, admitted to bar, 1979, Illinois; 1995, Hawaii. *Education:* University of California at Los Angeles (A.B., summa cum laude, 1976; J.D., 1979); DePaul University (LL.M., 1984). Phi Eta Sigma; Omicron Delta Epsilon; Pi Gamma Mu; Phi Beta Kappa; Order of the Coif. Associate Managing Editor, University of California at Los Angeles Law Review. ***PRACTICE AREAS:*** Wills; Trusts and Estates; Closely Held Corporations; Family Limited Partnerships. ***Email:*** hbrown@schiffhardin.com

JAMES E. BROWN, admitted to bar, 1983, Illinois and U.S. District Court, Northern District of Illinois. *Education:* Ohio State University (B.A., summa cum laude, 1980); University of Chicago (J.D., with honors, 1983). Phi Delta Phi; Phi Beta Kappa. Associate Editor, University of Chicago Law Review. ***PRACTICE AREAS:*** Public Utility Law; Corporate Law. ***Email:*** jbrown@schiffhardin.com

LISA A. BROWN, admitted to bar, 1995, Illinois. *Education:* Wesleyan University (B.A., 1990); University of Chicago Law School (J.D., 1995). ***PRACTICE AREAS:*** Litigation. ***Email:*** lbrown@schiffhardin.com

ANTONY S. BURT, admitted to bar, 1983, Illinois; 1990, Colorado; 2004, New York. *Education:* Duke University (A.B., 1978); Northwestern University (J.D., 1982). Member, Northwestern University Law Review, 1981-1982. Adjunct Professor, Trial Advocacy, Northwestern University School of Law, 1994—. ***PRACTICE AREAS:*** Litigation; Reinsurance; Civil Investigations; Professional Liability; Directors and Officers Liability. ***Email:*** aburt@schiffhardin.com

KEVIN J. BYRNE, admitted to bar, 1981, Illinois and U.S. District Court, Northern District of Illinois. *Education:* Loyola University (B.A., magna cum laude, 1978); Northwestern University (J.D., cum laude, 1981). Recipient, Wolfe Award. Member, Northwestern University Law Review. ***PRACTICE AREAS:*** Litigation; Intellectual Property; Products Liability. ***Email:*** kbyrne@schiffhardin.com

JOSEPH A. CANCILA, JR., admitted to bar, 1986, Illinois; 1988, U.S. District Court, Northern District of Illinois including Trial Bar; 1992, U.S. Court of Appeals, Seventh Circuit. *Education:* University of Dayton (B.A., magna cum laude, 1974); Syracuse University (M.P.A., 1976); University of Chicago (J.D., cum laude, 1986). Member, University of Chicago Law Review. ***PRACTICE AREAS:*** Commercial Litigation; Class Actions; Antitrust; Fair Housing; Insurance; Employment Litigation. ***Email:*** jcancila@schiffhardin.com

JENNIFER M. CERVEN, admitted to bar, 1996, Illinois, U.S. Court of Appeals, Seventh and Eighth Circuits, U.S. District Courts, Northern and Central Districts of Illinois.

(This Listing Continued)

Education: Northwestern University Medill School of Journalism (B.S., 1985) University of Illinois College of Law (J.D., magna cum laude, 1996). ***PRACTICE AREAS:*** Labor and Employment; Civil Litigation. ***Email:*** jcerven@schiffhardin.com

EVERETT J. CYGAL, admitted to bar, 1993, Illinois. *Education:* University of Chicago (A.B., 1989); Northwestern University (J.D., cum laude, 1993). Order of the Coif. ***PRACTICE AREAS:*** Reinsurance Litigation; Commercial Litigation. ***Email:*** ecygal@schiffhardin.com

HEIDI DALENBERG, admitted to bar, 1989, Illinois, U.S. District Court, Northern District of Illinois, U.S. Supreme Court and U.S. Court of Appeals, Seventh, Eighth and Tenth Circuits. *Education:* University of Illinois (B.A., 1983); Loyola University (J.D., 1989). ***PRACTICE AREAS:*** Class Action Defense; Insurance Litigation; Antitrust; Commercial Litigation. ***Email:*** hdalenberg@schiffhardin.com

PAUL E. DENGEL, admitted to bar, 1979, Illinois. *Education:* Princeton University (A.B., 1976); University of Virginia (J.D., 1979). Order of the Coif. ***PRACTICE AREAS:*** Litigation; Securities; Commodities; Commercial Litigation. ***Email:*** pdengel@schiffhardin.com

SHARON A. DOHERTY, admitted to bar, 1996, Illinois; U.S. District Court, Northern District of Illinois. *Education:* University of Illinois (B.A., 1991); Chicago-Kent College of Law (J.D., 1996). Order of the Coif. ***PRACTICE AREAS:*** Litigation. ***Email:*** sdoherty@schiffhardin.com

PATRICIA DONDANVILLE, admitted to bar, 1981, Illinois; 2000, Indiana. *Education:* University of Notre Dame (B.A., 1978); University of Virginia (J.D., 1981). Phi Beta Kappa; Delta Theta Phi. ***PRACTICE AREAS:*** Finance; Energy; Utility Law; Corporate Law; Derivative Products. ***Email:*** pdondanville@schiffhardin.com

STEPHEN J. DRAGICH, admitted to bar, 1983, Illinois; 1984, U.S. District Court, Northern District of Illinois. *Education:* University of Illinois (B.S., with highest honors, 1980; J.D., magna cum laude, 1983). Business Manager, University of Illinois Law Review. ***PRACTICE AREAS:*** Mergers, Acquisitions and Divestitures; Business Law; Venture Capital. ***Email:*** sdragich@schiffhardin.com

MICHAEL W. DRUMKE, admitted to bar, 1991, Wisconsin; 1992, Illinois; 2001, Texas; U.S. Supreme Court, U.S. Court of Appeals, Seventh Circuit and U.S. District Court, Central and Northern Districts of Illinois including Trial Bar, Eastern and Western Districts of Wisconsin, Northern and Southern Districts of Indiana and Western District of Michigan. *Education:* Tufts University (B.A., cum laude, 1988); University of Wisconsin (J.D., 1991). Member and Senior Administrative Editor, Wisconsin Law Review. ***PRACTICE AREAS:*** Litigation; Products Liability; Mass Torts. ***Email:*** mdrumke@schiffhardin.com

MARCI A. EISENSTEIN, admitted to bar, 1979, Illinois. *Education:* Radcliffe College (B.A., 1976); New York University (J.D., 1979). Recipient, Moot Court Advocacy Award. ***PRACTICE AREAS:*** Litigation; Antitrust; Insurance; Class Action Litigation. ***Email:*** meisenstein@schiffhardin.com

JAMES F. X. FAHY, admitted to bar, 1988, Illinois. *Education:* DePaul University (B.A., 1983); Loyola University (J.D., 1986). (Resident at Dublin, Ireland Office). ***PRACTICE AREAS:*** Financial Institutions Law; International Business; College and University Law. ***Email:*** jfahy@schiffhardin.com

PETER V. FAZIO, JR., admitted to bar, 1964, Illinois; 1965, U.S. District Court, Northern District of Illinois; 1972, U.S. Court of Appeals, 7th Circuit; 1977, U.S. Supreme Court; 1981, District of Columbia and U.S. Court of Appeals, District of Columbia Circuit; 1993, Indiana. *Education:* College of the Holy Cross (A.B., 1961); University of Michigan (J.D., with distinction, 1964). Phi Delta Phi. Editor, Michigan Law Review. ***PRACTICE AREAS:*** Business Law; Public Utility Law. ***Email:*** pfazio@schiffhardin.com

ROBERT C. FELDMEIER, admitted to bar, 1990, Illinois. *Education:* University of Notre Dame (B.A., 1987); University of Illinois College of Law (J.D., 1990). ***PRACTICE AREAS:*** Litigation; Reinsurance Litigation. ***Email:*** rfeldmeier@schiffhardin.com

MATTHEW J. FISCHER, admitted to bar, 1994, Illinois. *Education:* University of Illinois (B.S., 1989); University of Michigan (J.D., 1994). ***PRACTICE AREAS:*** Products Liability Defense; Commercial Liability; Class Action Defense; Civil RICO. ***Email:*** mfischer@schiffhardin.com

J. MARK FISHER, admitted to bar, 1978, Illinois; 1990, U.S. Supreme Court; U.S. Court of Appeals, Second, Third and Seventh Circuits; U.S. Bankruptcy Court and U.S. District Court, Northern District of Illinois including Trial Bar, Northern District of Indiana, Eastern District of Wisconsin, Central District of Illinois and Western District of Michigan. *Education:* Yale University (B.A., magna cum laude, 1975); University of Virginia (J.D., 1978). Phi Beta Kappa; Order of the Coif. Winner of Traynor Award for Ablest Oral Argument in Lile Moot Court Competition. ***PRACTICE AREAS:*** Business Litigation; Commercial Credit; Lender Liability; Workouts; Commercial Bankruptcy. ***Email:*** mfisher@schiffhardin.com

STEVEN D. FRIEDLAND, admitted to bar, 1988, Illinois. *Education:* University of Illinois (B.A., cum laude, 1984; J.D., magna cum laude, 1988). Order of the Coif. ***PRACTICE AREAS:*** Real Estate; Zoning, Planning and Land Use; Local Government Law. ***Email:*** sfriedland@schiffhardin.com

MARK C. FRIEDLANDER, admitted to bar, 1982, Illinois, U.S. District Court, Northern District of Illinois and U.S. Court of Appeals, Seventh Circuit. *Education:* University of Michigan (B.A., magna cum laude, 1978); Harvard University (J.D., 1981). Phi Beta Kappa. James Barr Ames Moot Court Competition Finalist. *Member:* American College of Construction Lawyers. ***PRACTICE AREAS:*** Construction Law; Design-Build Projects; Alternative Dispute Resolution; Professional Liability; Civil Litigation. ***Email:*** mfriedlander@schiffhardin.com

JULIE J. FURER, admitted to bar, 1993, California; 1994, Illinois; 1996, U.S. District Court, Northern District of Illinois; U.S. Court of Appeals, Seventh Circuit. *Education:* University of Illinois (B.A., Secondary Education, 1989); DePaul University (J.D., 1993). ***LANGUAGES:*** Spanish. ***PRACTICE AREAS:*** Labor and Employment. ***Email:*** jfurer@schiffhardin.com

(This Listing Continued)

SCHIFF HARDIN LLP, Chicago—Continued

MATTHEW G. GALO, admitted to bar, 1998, Illinois; U.S. District Court, Northern District of Illinois. *Education:* University of Notre Dame (B.A., cum laude, 1989); Northwestern University (J.D., 1998). [Lieutenant, U.S. Navy, 1989-1993]. ***PRACTICE AREAS:*** Corporate; Securities. ***Email:*** mgalo@schiffhardin.com

JAMES P. GAUGHAN, admitted to bar, 1990, Illinois. *Education:* University of Chicago (B.A., 1987); Loyola University of Chicago (J.D., 1990). ***PRACTICE AREAS:*** Commercial Law; Class Actions Litigation. ***Email:*** jgaughan@schiffhardin.com

EUGENE J. GEEKIE, JR., admitted to bar, 1986, Missouri; 1987, Illinois; 1992, U.S. Supreme Court. *Education:* St. Louis University (B.S.B.A., summa cum laude, 1983; A.B., summa cum laude, 1983; J.D., cum laude, 1986). Alpha Sigma Nu; Phi Alpha Delta. Member, Order of the Woolsack. Articles Editor and Administrative Editor, St. Louis University Law Journal. ***PRACTICE AREAS:*** Bankruptcy; Creditors; Commercial Litigation; Real Estate Litigation; Equipment Finance and Leasing. ***Email:*** egeekie@schiffhardin.com

LAWRENCE M. GILL, admitted to bar, 1968, Illinois and U.S. District Court, Northern District of Illinois. *Education:* St. Louis University (A.B., cum laude, 1965); University of Michigan (J.D., cum laude, 1968). Alpha Sigma Nu. Certified Public Accountant, Illinois, 1973. Director, 1995-2000, President, 1998-1999, Illinois CPA Society. Director, 2001—, Member of Council, 1997—, American Institute of Certified Public Accountants. Co-Chair, National Conference of Lawyers and Certified Public Accountants, 2002—. ***PRACTICE AREAS:*** Corporate Law; International Law; Intellectual Property. ***Email:*** lgill@schiffhardin.com

WALTER C. GREENOUGH, admitted to bar, 1975, Illinois; U.S. Supreme Court; U.S. Court of Appeals, Second, Seventh, Ninth and Eleventh Circuits; U.S. District Court, Northern District of Illinois including Trial Bar, Central District of Illinois, District of Colorado, Western District of Wisconsin, Eastern District of Texas and District of Nebraska. *Education:* Amherst College (B.A., cum laude, 1972); University of Chicago (J.D., 1975). ***PRACTICE AREAS:*** Products Liability; Commercial Litigation; Securities Litigation. ***Email:*** wgreenough@schiffhardin.com

PAUL EDWIN GREENWALT, III, admitted to bar, 1992, Illinois. *Education:* Drake University (B.S.B.A., cum laude, Finance, 1989); University of Iowa (J.D., with high distinction, 1992). Phi Delta Phi. Recipient: American Jurisprudence Book Award in Constitutional Law. Member, University of Iowa Law Review. ***PRACTICE AREAS:*** General and Commercial Litigation; Energy and Public Utility Law; Criminal Law. ***Email:*** pgreenwalt@schiffhardin.com

DAVID A. GROSSBERG, admitted to bar, 1976, Illinois. *Education:* University of California at Berkeley (A.B., 1972); University of Chicago (J.D., 1975). Law Clerk the Hon. Judge Lewis R. Morgan, U.S. Court of Appeals, Fifth Circuit, 1975-1976. ***PRACTICE AREAS:*** Real Estate; Zoning, Planning and Land Use. ***Email:*** dgrossberg@schiffhardin.com

MICHAEL J. HANAHAN, admitted to bar, 1991, Illinois and U.S. District Court, Northern District of Illinois; 1998, U.S. District Court, Western District of Michigan and U.S. Supreme Court. *Education:* University of Notre Dame (B.A., Arch., 1987); Loyola University School of Law, Chicago (J.D., 1990). Recipient: Gertrude S. Sollitt Award for Best Architectural Thesis, American Institute of Architects; Loyola Academic Achievement Award in Mechanics Liens. ***PRACTICE AREAS:*** Construction Law; Products Liability; Intellectual Property; Litigation. ***Email:*** mhanahan@schiffhardin.com

WILLIAM M. HANNAY, admitted to bar, 1973, Missouri; 1974, District of Columbia; 1976, New York; 1980, Illinois. *Education:* Yale University (B.A., 1966); Georgetown University (J.D., 1973). Executive Editor, American Criminal Law Review. Law Clerk: Judge Myron H. Bright, U.S. Court of Appeals for the Eighth Circuit; Justice Tom C. Clark (Retired), U.S. Supreme Court. ***PRACTICE AREAS:*** Antitrust and Trade Regulation; Insurance Class Actions. ***Email:*** whannay@schiffhardin.com

STACIE R. HARTMAN, admitted to bar, 1996, Illinois, U.S. District Court, Northern District of Illinois, U.S. Court of Appeals, Seventh and Federal Circuits; 2004, New York. *Education:* St. Catherine's College, Oxford University, 1991-1992; Northwestern University (B.A., 1993; J.D., 1996). ***PRACTICE AREAS:*** Intellectual Property; Commodities Futures Trading Litigation. ***Email:*** shartman@schiffhardin.com

FREDERICK L. HARTMANN, JR., admitted to bar, 1969, Illinois. *Education:* Princeton University (A.B., cum laude, 1966); University of Chicago (J.D., 1969). ***PRACTICE AREAS:*** Corporate Law; Securities; Mergers, Acquisitions and Divestitures; Corporate Finance. ***Email:*** fhartmann@schiffhardin.com

SONDRA A. HEMERYCK, admitted to bar, 1991, Illinois; 1992, U.S. Court of Appeals, Seventh Circuit; 1995, U.S. District Court, Northern District of Illinois. *Education:* Yale University (B.A., summa cum laude, 1987); Harvard University (J.D., magna cum laude, 1991). Phi Beta Kappa. Member, Harvard University Law Review. ***PRACTICE AREAS:*** Intellectual Property Litigation; Libel and Slander; Defamation; Civil Litigation. ***Email:*** shemeryck@schiffhardin.com

THOMAS J. HENEHAN, admitted to bar, 1997, Illinois. *Education:* University of Illinois (B.S., summa cum laude, 1994); Harvard University (J.D., magna cum laude, 1997). Phi Beta Kappa. ***PRACTICE AREAS:*** Litigation; Product Liability. ***Email:*** thenehan@schiffhardin.com

DOUGLAS C. HOCHSTETLER, admitted to bar, 1977, Pennsylvania; 1986, Illinois; U.S. District Court, Northern District of Illinois, U.S. Court of Appeals, Seventh and Federal Circuits and U.S. Supreme Court; registered to practice before U.S. Patent and Trademark Office. *Education:* Princeton University (A.B., Chemistry, cum laude, 1974); Georgetown University (J.D., 1977). ***PRACTICE AREAS:*** Intellectual Property; Patent Infringement; Antitrust. ***Email:*** dhochstetler@schiffhardin.com

DAVID R. HODGMAN, admitted to bar, 1974, Illinois. *Education:* American College in Paris, Paris, France and Grinnell College (B.A., 1969); Yale University (J.D., 1974). Fellow, American College of Trust and Estate Counsel. ***PRACTICE AREAS:*** Contested Trusts and Estates; Estate Planning; Retirement Planning; Closely Held Business Estate Planning; Non-Profit and Charitable Organizations. ***Email:*** dhodgman@schiffhardin.com

PATRICIA BROWN HOLMES, admitted to bar, 1987, Illinois; U.S. District Court, Northern District of Illinois including Trial Bar, U.S. Court of Appeals, Seventh Circuit. *Education:* University of Illinois (B.S., 1983; J.D., 1986). ***PRACTICE AREAS:*** Litigation; White Collar Criminal Defense; Corporate Compliance. ***Email:*** pholmes@schiffhardin.com

ALLAN HORWICH, admitted to bar, 1969, Illinois, U.S. District Court, Northern District of Illinois; 1971, U.S. Court of Appeals, Seventh Circuit; 1976, U.S. Supreme Court; 1983, U.S. Court of Appeals, Tenth Circuit; 1989, U.S. District Court, Central District of Illinois; 1995, U.S. District Court, Eastern District of Wisconsin and U.S. District Court, Eastern District of Michigan. *Education:* Princeton University (A.B., cum laude, 1966); University of Chicago (J.D., 1969). Adjunct Professor, 1999-2000, Senior Lecturer, 2000—, Northwestern University School of Law. ***PRACTICE AREAS:*** Securities Class Actions; Securities Fraud; SEC Enforcement; Corporate Disclosure Counseling; Securities Law Compliance; Securities Litigation; Shareholder Derivative Actions; Utility Regulation. ***Email:*** ahorwich@schiffhardin.com

RICHARD J. HOSKINS, admitted to bar, 1971, New York; 1976, Illinois; 1982, U.S. Supreme Court. *Education:* University of Kansas (B.A., 1967); Northwestern University (J.D., 1970). Fellow, American College of Trial Lawyers. Senior Lecturer, Northwestern University Law School. ***PRACTICE AREAS:*** Litigation; Intellectual Property; Antitrust. ***Email:*** rhoskins@schiffhardin.com

DAVID A. HOWARD, admitted to bar, 1996, Illinois. *Education:* University of Iowa (B.A., 1990); DePaul University College of Law (J.D., 1996). Order of the Coif. ***LANGUAGES:*** Spanish. ***PRACTICE AREAS:*** Construction Litigation. ***Email:*** dhoward@schiffhardin.com

BARRY S. HYMAN, admitted to bar, 1984, Illinois. *Education:* Connecticut College (B.A., 1981); Case Western Reserve School of Law (J.D., 1984). ***PRACTICE AREAS:*** Energy; Business and Commercial Litigation; Bankruptcy Law; Alternative Dispute Resolution. ***Email:*** bhyman@schiffhardin.com

STEVE E. ISAACS, admitted to bar, 1995, Illinois; 1996, New York. *Education:* University of Illinois (B.A., cum laude, with honors, 1991); New York University (J.D., 1994). Edmund James Scholar. Journal of International Law and Politics. ***LANGUAGES:*** Spanish. ***PRACTICE AREAS:*** Corporate Law; Securities; Mergers, Acquisitions and Divestitures. ***Email:*** sisaacs@schiffhardin.com

LARRY JACOBSON, admitted to bar, 1981, Illinois; 1982, District of Columbia. *Education:* Washington University (B.A., magna cum laude, 1975); University of Chicago (M.B.A., 1977); Georgetown University (J.D., 1981). Certified Public Accountant, Illinois, 1978. ***PRACTICE AREAS:*** Federal, State and International Tax Planning and Litigation; Executive Compensation. ***Email:*** ljacobson@schiffhardin.com

JANET M. JOHNSON, admitted to bar, 1980, Iowa and Illinois. *Education:* University of Iowa (B.B.A., 1974; J.D., 1980). Phi Alpha Delta. Order of the Coif. Certified Public Accountant, Iowa, 1974. ***PRACTICE AREAS:*** Commercial Real Estate; Real Estate; Mortgages; Finance; Closely Held Corporations. ***Email:*** jjohnson@schiffhardin.com

TREVOR B. JOIKE, admitted to bar, 1970, Minnesota and U.S. District Court, District of Minnesota; 1988, Illinois; registered to practice before U.S. Patent and Trademark Office. *Education:* University of Illinois (B.S., Electrical Engineering, 1966); Washington College of Law of American University (J.D., 1970). ***PRACTICE AREAS:*** Intellectual Property; Intellectual Property Licensing. ***Email:*** tjoike@schiffhardin.com

THOMAS K. JUFFERNBRUCH, admitted to bar, 1995, Illinois. *Education:* University of Illinois (B.S., with honors, 1989); Indiana University (J.D., cum laude, 1995). Certified Public Accountant, Illinois. ***PRACTICE AREAS:*** Finance. ***Email:*** tjuffernbruch@schiffhardin.com

JAMES M. KANE, admitted to bar, 1979, Illinois and U.S. District Court, Northern District of Illinois. *Education:* DePaul University (B.A., summa cum laude, 1972); Syracuse University (M.P.A., 1973); DePaul University (J.D., 1979). ***PRACTICE AREAS:*** Real Estate; Zoning, Planning and Land Use; Eminent Domain; State Government; Local Government. ***Email:*** jkane@schiffhardin.com

NANCY L. KASKO, admitted to bar, 1978, Illinois. *Education:* University of Illinois (B.A., 1975); Northwestern University School of Law (J.D., cum laude, 1978). ***PRACTICE AREAS:*** Corporate; Securities; Finance. ***Email:*** nkasko@schiffhardin.com

PAULA M. KETCHAM, admitted to bar, 1994, Illinois. *Education:* Northwestern University (B.A., 1990); University of Chicago (J.D., 1994). ***PRACTICE AREAS:*** Labor and Employment; Class Action Litigation; Litigation. ***Email:*** pketcham@schiffhardin.com

ANDREW A. KLING, admitted to bar, 1984, Illinois. *Education:* University of Wisconsin (B.A., with distinction, 1978); University of Virginia (J.D., 1984). Editorial Board and Managing Board, Virginia Tax Review. Legislative Aide to U.S. Representative Bill Gradison. ***PRACTICE AREAS:*** Commercial Law; Corporate Finance; General Corporate; Mergers and Acquisitions. ***Email:*** akling@schiffhardin.com

BRIAN D. KLUEVER, admitted to bar, 1989, Illinois and U.S. District Court, Northern District of Illinois. *Education:* DePauw University (B.A., 1984); Northwestern University (J.D., 1989). ***PRACTICE AREAS:*** Commercial Real Estate; Property Law; Contracts. ***Email:*** bkluever@schiffhardin.com

WILLIAM I. KOHN, admitted to bar, 1976, Ohio; 1982, Indiana; 1992, District of Columbia; 1994, Illinois; U.S. District Court, Northern, Central and Southern Districts of Illinois, U.S. District Court, Northern and Southern Districts of Indiana, U.S. District Court, Northern District of Ohio, U.S. District Court, Northern District of Texas, U.S. Court of Appeals, Sixth, Seventh, Eighth, District of Columbia and Federal Circuits, U.S. Court of International Trade and U.S. Supreme Court. *Education:* University of Cincinnati (B.A., with honors, 1973); The Ohio State University (J.D., 1976). Omicron Delta Epsilon. Member, National Council, The Ohio State University College of Law. Member, Ohio State Law Journal. (Certified in Business Bankruptcy Law by the American Board of Certification). ***PRACTICE AREAS:*** Bankruptcy; Commercial Finance; Workouts. ***Email:*** wkohn@schiffhardin.com

(This Listing Continued)

APHRODITE KOKOLIS, admitted to bar, 1987, Illinois and U.S. District Court, Northern District of Illinois; 1989, U.S. Court of Appeals, Seventh Circuit; 2000, U.S. Supreme Court. *Education:* University of Illinois (B.A., 1984); Northwestern University (J.D., 1987). Bronze Tablet. Order of the Coif. Managing Editor, Northwestern University Law Review. ***LANGUAGES:*** Spanish. ***PRACTICE AREAS:*** Litigation; Class Action Defense; Appellate Practice. ***Email:*** akokolis@schiffhardin.com

ROBERT E. KOLEK, admitted to bar, 1968, Illinois; 1970, U.S. Court of Appeals, Seventh Circuit and U.S. Tax Court; 1978, U.S. Supreme Court; 1980, U.S. Court of Federal Claims and U.S. District Court, Northern District of Illinois; 2002, U.S. Court of International Trade. *Education:* Loyola University, Chicago (B.B.A., 1965; J.D., 1968). Alpha Sigma Nu; Blue Key. Law Clerk to Justice Thomas E. Kluczynski, Illinois Supreme Court. ***PRACTICE AREAS:*** Taxation; Tax Controversies; Tax Litigation; Cable TV; Business Taxation. ***Email:*** rkolek@schiffhardin.com

KEVIN L. KOLTON, admitted to bar, 1990, Illinois. *Education:* University of Illinois (B.S., Engineering, 1980); South Texas College of Law (J.D., magna cum laude, 1989). Order of the Lytae. Recipient, American Jurisprudence Award, Commercial Paper. Member, South Texas Law Review. ***PRACTICE AREAS:*** Construction Litigation; Energy; Insurance Litigation; Alternative Dispute Resolution. ***Email:*** kkolton@schiffhardin.com

MELISSA J. KRASNOW, admitted to bar, 1993, California, Illinois, U.S. District Court, Northern District of California and U.S. Court of Appeals, Ninth Circuit. *Education:* University of British Columbia (first class honors, 1987-1988); Wellesley College (A.B., Chinese Studies and Political Science, magna cum laude, 1989); Northwestern University School of Law (J.D., 1992). Phi Beta Kappa. ***PRACTICE AREAS:*** Corporate Law; Securities; Mergers, Acquisitions and Divestitures; International Law; Financial Institutions Law. ***Email:*** mkrasnow@schiffhardin.com

JOSEPH J. KRASOVEC, III, admitted to bar, 1989, Illinois and U.S. District Court, Northern District of Illinois; 1993, Colorado; 1994, U.S. District Court, Eastern District of Wisconsin; 1995, U.S. District Court, Central District of Illinois. *Education:* University of Denver (B.S., cum laude, 1986); Northwestern University (J.D., 1989). ***PRACTICE AREAS:*** Complex Litigation; Products Liability; Product Recall; Commercial Litigation. ***Email:*** jkrasovec@schiffhardin.com

RUTH E. KRUGLY, admitted to bar, 1983, Illinois and U.S. District Court, Northern District of Illinois. *Education:* Brandeis University (A.B., summa cum laude, with highest honors, 1980); University of Chicago (J.D., 1983). Phi Beta Kappa. ***PRACTICE AREAS:*** Municipal Law. ***Email:*** rkrugly@schiffhardin.com

JEFFREY KUTA, admitted to bar, 1972, Illinois. *Education:* University of Chicago (B.A., with honors, 1969; J.D., 1972). Managing Editor, University of Chicago Law Review, 1971-1972. Adjunct Professor, The John Marshall Law School, 1996—. ***PRACTICE AREAS:*** Real Estate; Real Estate Finance; Community Investment; Community Development; Urban Revitalization; Affordable Housing; Syndication; Tax Credits. ***Email:*** jkuta@schiffhardin.com

DENNIS G. LaGORY, admitted to bar, 1989, Illinois and U.S. District Court, Northern District of Illinois. *Education:* Wayne State University (B.A., 1973); Salmon P. Chase College of Law (J.D., summa cum laude, 1989). Author, "Federalism, Separation of Powers & Individual Liberties," 40 Vand. L. Rev. 1353 (1987). Editor, Law and Practice Regulation of Health Care Arrangements, American Bar Association, 1996. ***PRACTICE AREAS:*** Reinsurance Litigation; Reinsurance Arbitration; Insurance Regulation; Corporate Insurance; Insurance Coverage Litigation. ***Email:*** dlagory@schiffhardin.com

NEIL LLOYD, admitted to bar, 1994, Illinois. *Education:* Pomona College (B.A., 1988); Swarthmore College (1986); University of Chicago (J.D., with honors, 1994); University of Pennsylvania, Law School (1991-1992). Member, Editorial Board, University of Chicago Law Review. ***PRACTICE AREAS:*** Litigation; Appellate Practice; Products Liability; Labor and Employment. ***Email:*** nlloyd@schiffhardin.com

THOMAS P. LUNING, admitted to bar, 1968, District of Columbia and Illinois. *Education:* Xavier University (H.A.B., magna cum laude, 1964); Georgetown University (J.D., 1967). Managing Editor, The Georgetown Law Journal. Law Clerk to the Honorable Spottswood W. Robinson III, Circuit Judge and to the Court, United States Court of Appeals for the District of Columbia Circuit. ***PRACTICE AREAS:*** Litigation; Civil Litigation; Antitrust and Trade Regulation; Insurance; Professional Conduct. ***Email:*** tluning@schiffhardin.com

PAUL M. LURIE, admitted to bar, 1965, Illinois; 1971, U.S. Supreme Court. *Education:* University of Michigan (A.B., 1962; J.D., 1965). Member, Master Panel, American Arbitration Association. Member, Panel of Distinguished Neutrals, CPR Institute for Dispute Resolution. *Member:* Society of Illinois Construction Attorneys. Fellow: American College of Construction Lawyers; College of Commercial Arbitrators; International Academy of Mediators. ***PRACTICE AREAS:*** Construction and Design Law; Construction Arbitration; Construction Mediation; Construction Contracts; Construction Litigation. ***Email:*** plurie@schiffhardin.com

OWEN E. MacBRIDE, admitted to bar, 1975, Illinois. *Education:* The University of Michigan (B.A., 1971); The University of Michigan and Yale University (J.D., 1975). Phi Beta Kappa. Editorial Board, Yale Law Journal. Law Clerk to Hon. Robert P. Anderson, U.S. Circuit Judge, Second Circuit. ***PRACTICE AREAS:*** Electric Utilities; Gas Utilities; Energy Competition; Public Utility Regulation; Utility Contracts. ***Email:*** omacbride@schiffhardin.com

SEAN T. MALONEY, admitted to bar, 1987, Illinois. *Education:* University of Notre Dame (B.A., 1983); Indiana University (J.D., cum laude, 1986). ***PRACTICE AREAS:*** Real Estate Finance; Lease Finance. ***Email:*** smaloney@schiffhardin.com

PAUL C. MARENGO, admitted to bar, 1974, Illinois and U.S. District Court, Northern District of Illinois. *Education:* Princeton University (A.B., cum laude, 1971); University of Chicago (J.D., 1974). ***LANGUAGES:*** French. ***PRACTICE AREAS:*** Public Finance; Municipal Law; Health Care Finance; Tax Exempt Bonds; Corporate Finance. ***Email:*** pmarengo@schiffhardin.com

JOHN C. MARTIN, admitted to bar, 1994, Illinois and U.S. District Court, Northern District of Illinois; 1996, U.S. District Court, Central District of Illinois; 1998, U.S. Court of Appeals, Seventh Circuit. *Education:* Yale University (B.A., summa cum laude, 1991);

(This Listing Continued)

University of Chicago (J.D., with honors, 1994). Phi Beta Kappa; Order of the Coif. Law Clerk, The Hon. Suzanne B. Conlon, U.S. District Court, Northern District of Illinois. ***PRACTICE AREAS:*** Litigation; Class Action Defense; Commercial Law. ***Email:*** jmartin@schiffhardin.com

CATHERINE M. MASTERS, admitted to bar, 1983, Illinois; U.S. Supreme Court; U.S. Court of Appeals, Third, Fifth, Sixth, Seventh, Ninth and Eleventh Circuits; U.S. District Court, Northern District of Illinois. *Education:* University of Chicago (B.A., 1976); Yale University (M.A., 1977); University of Chicago (J.D., 1982). Phi Beta Kappa. Member, Editorial Board, University of Chicago Law Review. Law Clerk to Hon. Luther M. Swygert, U.S. Court of Appeals, Seventh Circuit. ***LANGUAGES:*** Greek and Latin. ***PRACTICE AREAS:*** General Litigation; Constitutional Law; Products Liability; Labor and Employment; Appellate Practice; Insurance Litigation. ***Email:*** cmasters@schiffhardin.com

DAVID S. McCARTHY, admitted to bar, 1988, New York; 1989, Illinois. *Education:* Yale University (B.A., magna cum laude, 1983); University of Chicago (J.D., 1987). ***PRACTICE AREAS:*** Corporate Law; Securities. ***Email:*** dmccarthy@schiffhardin.com

DAVID P. McHUGH, admitted to bar, 1997, Illinois, Florida and Vermont. *Education:* University of Vermont (B.A., 1994); Syracuse University College of Law (J.D., cum laude, 1997). ***PRACTICE AREAS:*** Corporate; Mergers and Acquisitions; Business Law; Commercial Contracts; Corporate Law. ***Email:*** dmchugh@schiffhardin.com

MICHAEL L. MEYER, admitted to bar, 1965, Illinois; 1978, District of Columbia. *Education:* Princeton University (A.B., 1962); Harvard University (LL.B., cum laude, 1965). ***PRACTICE AREAS:*** Broker-Dealer Regulation; Securities Regulation; Financial Services Regulation; Investment Company Law; Mutual Funds. ***Email:*** mmeyer@schiffhardin.com

WILLIAM E. MEYER, JR., admitted to bar, 1991, Illinois; 1992, U.S. District Court, Northern District of Illinois; U.S. Court of Appeals, Seventh and Fifth Circuits. *Education:* Harvard University (A.B., cum laude, 1988); Loyola University (J.D., magna cum laude, 1991). ***PRACTICE AREAS:*** Litigation. ***Email:*** wmeyer@schiffhardin.com

RICHARD T. MILLER, admitted to bar, 1998, Illinois. *Education:* Northwestern University (B.S., 1992); Loyola University Chicago (J.D., magna cum laude, 1998). ***PRACTICE AREAS:*** Corporate; Securities; Mergers and Acquisitions; Financings; Divestitures; Project Developments and Start-ups. ***Email:*** rmiller@schiffhardin.com

ROBERT J. MINKUS, admitted to bar, 1980, New York; 1984, Illinois. *Education:* Yale University (B.A., cum laude, 1976); University of Chicago (J.D., 1979). ***LANGUAGES:*** French. ***PRACTICE AREAS:*** Mergers, Acquisitions and Divestitures; Securities; Corporate Governance; Business Law. ***Email:*** rminkus@schiffhardin.com

JANE ELLEN MONTGOMERY, admitted to bar, 1990, Illinois. *Education:* University of Illinois (B.S., high honors, 1980); Northwestern University (J.D., 1990). ***PRACTICE AREAS:*** Environmental Law. ***Email:*** jmontgomery@schiffhardin.com

VIRGIL R. MONTGOMERY, JR., admitted to bar, 1992, Ohio; 2001, Illinois, U.S. District Court, Northern and Southern Districts of Ohio. *Education:* University of Colorado (B.A., 1989); Harvard Law School (J.D., 1992). ***PRACTICE AREAS:*** Construction; Construction Litigation. ***Email:*** vmontgomery@schiffhardin.com

PAULA J. MORENCY, admitted to bar, 1980, Illinois; 1980, U.S. District Court, Northern District of Illinois; 1982, Trial Bar; 1981, U.S. Court of Appeals, Seventh Circuit; 1990, U.S. Court of Appeals, Fifth Circuit; 1999, U.S. District Court, Central District of Illinois; 2000, U.S. District Court, Eastern District of Wisconsin; 2000, U.S. Supreme Court. *Education:* Princeton University (A.B., magna cum laude, 1977); University of Virginia (J.D., 1980). Winner, William Minor Lile Moot Court Competition. Member, Faculty, National Institute for Trial Advocacy, 1988—. Adjunct Professor of Trial Advocacy, Northwestern University School of Law, 1996—. ***PRACTICE AREAS:*** Commercial Litigation; Franchise and Distributor Disputes; Trade Secrets; Intellectual Property Litigation. ***Email:*** pmorency@schiffhardin.com

RALPH A. MORRIS, admitted to bar, 1970, Illinois; 1973, U.S. District Court, Northern District of Illinois; 1975, U.S. Court of Appeals, Sixth Circuit; 1976, U.S. District Court, Eastern District of Wisconsin; 1977, U.S. Court of Appeals, Seventh Circuit; 1982, U.S. Supreme Court; 1985, U.S. Court of Appeals, Eighth Circuit; 1990, U.S. Court of Appeals, Second Circuit. *Education:* Valparaiso University (B.A., 1967); University of Michigan (J.D., 1970). Order of the Coif. Adjunct Instructor, Loyola University Graduate School of Business. Fellow, College of Labor and Employment Lawyers. ***PRACTICE AREAS:*** Labor and Employment; Employer Rights; Management Labor Law; Title VII Discrimination; Wrongful Termination Defense; Mediation. ***Email:*** rmorris@schiffhardin.com

FRANCIS P. MORRISSEY, admitted to bar, 1993, Illinois and U.S. District Court, Northern District of Illinois; 1999, U.S. Court of Appeals, Seventh Circuit; 2002, U.S. District Court, Central District of Illinois; 2003, U.S. District Court, Southern District of Illinois; 2004, U.S. District Court, Northern District of Indiana. *Education:* College of the Holy Cross (B.A., 1990); Loyola University School of Law, Chicago (J.D., 1993). Member, Loyola Law Review. Named one of "40 Illinois Attorneys Under Forty To Watch," Chicago Daily Law Bulletin. ***PRACTICE AREAS:*** Products Liability; Personal Injury Litigation; Business Litigation; Corporate Fiduciary Defense; Class Action Defense. ***Email:*** fmorrissey@schiffhardin.com

GARY L. MOWDER (P.C.), admitted to bar, 1965, Illinois; 1966, U.S. District Court, Northern District of Illinois. *Education:* University of Illinois (B.S., 1963; LL.B., with honors, 1965). Order of the Coif; Phi Kappa Phi; Phi Delta Phi. Board of Editors, University of Illinois Law Review. ***PRACTICE AREAS:*** Corporate Law; Banking Regulation; Professional Sports Law. ***Email:*** gmowder@schiffhardin.com

STEVEN H. NOLL, admitted to bar, 1978, Ohio and Illinois; 1979, U.S. Court of Appeals, Seventh and Eighth Circuits; 1980, U.S. District Court, Northern District of Illinois, including Trial Bar; 1982, U.S. Supreme Court, U.S. Court of Appeals for the Federal Circuit and U.S. Court of Appeals, Sixth Circuit; 1984, U.S. Court of Appeals, Eleventh Circuit; 1985, U.S. Claims Court; registered to practice before U.S. Patent and Trademark Office. *Education:* Michigan State University (B.S., with honor, 1974); Ohio State University (J.D., 1977). ***PRACTICE AREAS:*** Industrial Property Law; Intellectual Property Law; Litigation; Patent Prosecution; Licensing Law. ***Email:*** snoll@schiffhardin.com

(This Listing Continued)

SCHIFF HARDIN LLP, Chicago—Continued

JOSEPH J. O'HARA, JR., admitted to bar, 1981, Illinois and U.S. District Court, Northern District of Illinois including Trial Bar; 1985, U.S. Court of Appeals, Seventh Circuit; 1990, U.S. District Court, Central District of Illinois; 1991, U.S. District Court, Western District of Wisconsin; 1992, New York. *Education:* Marquette University (B.S., 1975); Northwestern University (J.D., 1981). Member, Northwestern University Law Review. ***PRACTICE AREAS:*** Products Liability; Toxic Torts; Asbestos Defense Litigation. ***Email:*** johara@schiffhardin.com

ROGER PASCAL, admitted to bar, 1965, Illinois; 1969, U.S. Court of Appeals, Seventh Circuit; 1975, U.S. Supreme Court; 1985, Wisconsin; 1986, U.S. Court of Appeals, Second Circuit; 1987, U.S. Court of Appeals, Ninth Circuit; 1989, U.S. Court of Appeals, Sixth and Tenth Circuits. *Education:* University of Michigan (A.B., with distinction, 1962); Harvard University (J.D., cum laude, 1965). Phi Beta Kappa. Adjunct Professor of Law, Northwestern University School of Law. ***PRACTICE AREAS:*** Complex Litigation; Antitrust; Intellectual Property Litigation. ***Email:*** rpascal@schiffhardin.com

S. MICHAEL PECK, admitted to bar, 1973, Illinois. *Education:* University of Chicago (B.A., 1969); University of Michigan Law School (J.D., 1972). ***PRACTICE AREAS:*** Venture Capital; Private Equity; Leveraged Buyouts; Mergers and Acquisitions; Corporate; Securities. ***Email:*** speck@schiffhardin.com

RANDOLPH M. PERKINS, admitted to bar, 1982, Illinois. *Education:* Illinois State University (B.S., summa cum laude, 1977); University of Illinois (J.D., magna cum laude, 1982). Order of the Coif. Harno Fellow. Recipient, Rickert Award for Excellence in Legal Writing. Notes and Comments Editor, University of Illinois Law Review, 1981-1982. Judicial Law Clerk to Justice Robert C. Underwood, Illinois Supreme Court, 1982-1983. (Resident at Lake Forest, Illinois Office). ***PRACTICE AREAS:*** Corporate Law; Commercial Law; Commercial Leasing; Commercial Licensing; Real Estate; Business Dispute Resolution; Private Business Law. ***Email:*** rperkins@schiffhardin.com

CHARLES H.R. PETERS, admitted to bar, 1986, Illinois and U.S. District Court, Northern District of Illinois; 1992, U.S. Court of Appeals, Seventh Circuit; 2001, U.S. Supreme Court. *Education:* Miami University (B.S., magna cum laude, 1982); Northwestern University (J.D., cum laude, 1986). Beta Gamma Sigma. ***PRACTICE AREAS:*** Litigation; Communications and Media; Intellectual Property. ***Email:*** cpeters@schiffhardin.com

SCOTT E. PICKENS, admitted to bar, 1978, Illinois. *Education:* University of Illinois (B.S., 1972); University of Chicago (M.B.A., 1976); Loyola University (J.D., cum laude, 1978). Recipient, Chief Justice Edward D. White Scholarship Award. ***PRACTICE AREAS:*** Lending, Leasing; Mergers and Acquisitions; General Corporate. ***Email:*** spickens@schiffhardin.com

ROBERT R. PLUTH, JR., admitted to bar, 1980, Illinois and U.S. Tax Court. *Education:* University of Illinois; Lewis University (B.A., magna cum laude, 1976); Northwestern University (J.D., cum laude, 1980). Certified Public Accountant, Illinois, 1976. ***PRACTICE AREAS:*** Taxation. ***Email:*** rpluth@schiffhardin.com

CAROL R. PRYGROSKY, admitted to bar, 1987, Wisconsin; 1988, Illinois and U.S. District Court, Northern District of Illinois. *Education:* Indiana University (B.A., 1973); University of Wisconsin-Madison (J.D., 1987). Editor-in-Chief, Wisconsin Law Review. ***PRACTICE AREAS:*** Products Liability Defense; Civil Litigation; Complex Litigation; Intellectual Property Litigation; Environmental Litigation. ***Email:*** cprygrosky@schiffhardin.com

THOMAS B. QUINN, admitted to bar, 1978, California; 1979, Illinois; U.S. Supreme Court; U.S. Court of Appeals, Seventh, Eighth, Ninth and Federal Circuits; U.S. District Court, Northern, Central and Southern Districts of Illinois, Northern and Eastern Districts of California and Eastern District of Wisconsin. *Education:* Stanford University (B.A., with honors and distinction, 1974); Stanford Law School (J.D., 1978). ***PRACTICE AREAS:*** Complex Litigation; Federal Civil Litigation; ERISA Litigation; Intellectual Property Litigation. ***Email:*** tquinn@schiffhardin.com

PAUL A. RAHE, admitted to bar, 1996, Indiana; 2000, Illinois. *Education:* Indiana University (B.A., 1993); University of Virginia (J.D., 1996). ***PRACTICE AREAS:*** Corporate; Securities. ***Email:*** prahe@schiffhardin.com

ROBERT JOHN REGAN, admitted to bar, 1982, Illinois. *Education:* Colgate University (B.A., magna cum laude, Phi Beta Kappa, 1979); Cornell Law School (J.D., 1982). Member, Moot Court Board. ***PRACTICE AREAS:*** Corporate and Securities Law. ***Email:*** rregan@schiffhardin.com

ROBERT H. RILEY, admitted to bar, 1978, Illinois; 1985, Wisconsin. *Education:* Denison University (B.A., with highest honors, 1975); University of Chicago (J.D., 1978). Phi Beta Kappa. Hinton Moot Court Champion. ***PRACTICE AREAS:*** Civil Litigation; Product Liability; Complex Litigation; Toxic Torts; Mass Torts. ***Email:*** rriley@schiffhardin.com

KENNETH M. ROBERTS, admitted to bar, 1985, Missouri and U.S. District Court, Western District of Missouri; 1987, Illinois and U.S. District Court, Northern District of Illinois. *Education:* University of Iowa (B.G.S., with honors, 1982; J.D., with distinction, 1985). Omicron Delta Kappa. Associate Editor, Journal of Corporation Law. ***PRACTICE AREAS:*** Construction Law; Contracts Procurement; Government Contract Law; Insurance Law. ***Email:*** kroberts@schiffhardin.com

MELVIN A. ROBINSON, admitted to bar, 1984, Missouri and U.S. District Court, Western District of Missouri; 1985, Illinois; registered to practice before U.S. Patent and Trademark Office. *Education:* Southern Illinois University (B.S.E., in Electrical Engineering, 1980); St. Louis University (J.D., 1984). ***PRACTICE AREAS:*** Patent Law; Intellectual Property Law; International Patent Law. ***Email:*** mrobinson@schiffhardin.com

GABRIEL M. RODRIGUEZ, admitted to bar, 1984, Illinois; 1987, U.S. Court of Appeals, District of Columbia Circuit; 1989, U.S. District Court, Northern District of Illinois; 1991, U.S. Court of Appeals, Seventh Circuit; 1994, U.S. District Court, Western District of Michigan. *Education:* Northwestern University (B.A., 1979); Northern Illinois University (J.D., cum laude, 1984). Editor, Northern Illinois University Law Review. ***PRACTICE AREAS:*** Environmental Law; Litigation. ***Email:*** grodriguez@schiffhardin.com

(This Listing Continued)

PETER L. ROSSITER, admitted to bar, 1973, Illinois. *Education:* Princeton University (A.B., 1970); Yale University (J.D., 1973). Member, Board of Editors, Yale Law Journal, 1972-1973. Law Clerk to: U.S. District Judge Alvin B. Rubin, Eastern District of Louisiana, 1973-1975; Chief Justice Warren E. Burger, 1975-1976. ***PRACTICE AREAS:*** Corporate; Securities; Financial Institutions. ***Email:*** prossiter@schiffhardin.com

RONALD S. SAFER, admitted to bar, 1983, Illinois. *Education:* University of Pennsylvania (B.A., cum laude, 1979; B.S., cum laude, 1979); Georgetown University (J.D., magna cum laude, 1983). RICO Instructor, Federal Law Enforcement Training Center, 1994-1998. Assistant U.S. Attorney, 1989-1999. Chief, Criminal Division, 1998-1999. ***REPORTED CASES:*** U.S. v. Hoover, 95 CR 508 (N.D. Ill. 1997); U.S. v. Bailey (Helen Brach murder case), 892 F. Supp. 997 (N.D.L. 1995) aff'd, 97 F. 3d 982 (7th Cir. 1996). ***PRACTICE AREAS:*** White Collar Crime; Complex Litigation; Federal Criminal Law; Federal Practice; RICO. ***Email:*** rsafer@schiffhardin.com

JOHN N. SCHOLNICK, admitted to bar, 1979, Illinois; 1980, California. *Education:* Haverford College (B.A., 1976); Northwestern University School of Law (J.D., 1979). ***PRACTICE AREAS:*** Litigation. ***Email:*** jscholnick@schiffhardin.com

HENRY W. SLEDZ, JR., admitted to bar, 1974, Illinois and U.S. District Court, Northern District of Illinois; 1978, U.S. Court of Appeals, Seventh Circuit; 1993, U.S. District Court, Southern District of Illinois; 1997, U.S. District Court, Central District of Illinois; 1998, U.S. Court of Appeals, Eleventh Circuit; 2001, U.S. District Court, Northern District of Indiana. *Education:* University of Illinois (B.S., 1971); Loyola University (J.D., 1974). ***PRACTICE AREAS:*** Labor and Employment. ***Email:*** hsledz@schiffhardin.com

PATRICIA COSTELLO SLOVAK, admitted to bar, 1977, Illinois; 1981, New York and New Jersey. *Education:* St. Louis University (B.A., 1973); University of Chicago (J.D., 1977). Editor-in-Chief: "The Developing Labor Law," Third Edition, Cumulative Supplements, 1994-1996. Fellow, College of Labor and Employment Lawyers, 1997—. ***PRACTICE AREAS:*** Labor and Employment. ***Email:*** pslovak@schiffhardin.com

JEFFERY N. SMITH, admitted to bar, 1985, Illinois. *Education:* University of Michigan (B.B.A., 1982); Northwestern University School of Law (J.D., 1985). ***PRACTICE AREAS:*** Corporate; Securities; Private Equity; Venture Capital; Mergers and Acquisitions; Leveraged Buyouts. ***Email:*** jnsmith@schiffhardin.com

EDWARD SPACAPAN, JR., admitted to bar, 1979, Illinois. *Education:* Vanderbilt University (B.S., 1976); Northwestern University (J.D., 1979). Phi Beta Kappa. Member, Northwestern University Law Review, 1977-1979. ***PRACTICE AREAS:*** Employee Benefits; Executive Compensation; Qualified Retirement Plans; Health Benefits; ERISA Compliance. ***Email:*** espacapan@schiffhardin.com

DAVID M. SPECTOR, admitted to bar, 1971, Illinois and U.S. District Court, Northern District of Illinois; 2002, New York and U.S. District Court, Southern District of New York; U.S. District Court, Eastern District of New York; U.S. Court of Appeals, Seventh Circuit; U.S. District Court, Central District of Illinois; U.S. Court of Appeals, First, Second, Third and Fourth Circuits; U.S. Supreme Court. *Education:* Northwestern University (B.A., 1968); University of Michigan (J.D., magna cum laude, 1971). Order of the Coif. Notes and Comments Editor, Michigan Law Review, Vol. 69, 1970-1971. Editor: "Law and Practice of Life Insurance Company Insolvency," ABA, 1993. Law Clerk to Hon. Walter V. Schaefer, Justice of the Illinois Supreme Court, 1971-1972. *Member:* Chicago, Seventh Circuit and American (Chair, Committee on Public Regulation of Insurance, 1988-1989; Member, Sections on: Tort and Insurance Practice; Litigation; International Law) Bar Associations; Legal Club of Chicago; Federation of Regulatory Counsel; ARIAS (AIDA Reinsurance and Arbitration Society). ***PRACTICE AREAS:*** Insurance; Reinsurance Litigation. ***Email:*** dspector@schiffhardin.com

ROBIN M. SPENCER, admitted to bar, 1994, Minnesota; 1998, Illinois. *Education:* University of Utah (B.A., magna cum laude, 1990); University of Virginia (J.D., 1994). Phi Beta Kappa. ***PRACTICE AREAS:*** Franchise Law; Dealership Law; Commercial Litigation; Intellectual Property Litigation. ***Email:*** rspencer@schiffhardin.com

FREDERICK J. SPERLING, admitted to bar, 1980, Illinois, U.S. District Court, Northern District of Illinois including Trial Bar and U.S. Court of Appeals, Seventh Circuit; 1991, U.S. Supreme Court. *Education:* Amherst College (B.A., cum laude, 1975); University of Chicago (J.D., 1979). Associate Editor, University of Chicago Law Review. Law Clerk to Judge James Hunter, U.S. Court of Appeals for the Third Circuit. ***PRACTICE AREAS:*** Civil Litigation; Appellate Litigation; Business Litigation; Commercial Litigation; Libel, Slander and Defamation. ***Email:*** fsperling@schiffhardin.com

MARK A. STERNBERG, admitted to bar, 1988, Illinois. *Education:* University of Illinois (B.S., with high honors, 1985; J.D., magna cum laude, 1988). Order of the Coif. Harno Scholar. Certified Public Accountant, 1985.*Member:* American College of Investment Counsel. ***PRACTICE AREAS:*** Corporate Finance; Equipment Leasing. ***Email:*** msternberg@schiffhardin.com

DEBRA L. STETTER, admitted to bar, 1992, Illinois. *Education:* Bryn Mawr College (A.B., 1984); University of Chicago (M.B.A., 1987); Northwestern University (J.D., cum laude, 1992). Order of the Coif. Member, Northwestern, University Law Review. Fellow, American College of Trust and Estate Counsel. ***PRACTICE AREAS:*** Estate Planning; Estate Planning for Parents of Handicapped Children; Nonprofit and Charitable Organizations; Special Needs Trusts; Closely Held Business Estate Planning. ***Email:*** dstetter@schiffhardin.com

LINDA K. STEVENS, admitted to bar, 1987, Illinois and U.S. District Court, Northern District of Illinois including Trial Bar; 1993, U.S. Court of Appeals, Seventh Circuit. *Education:* Kalamazoo College (B.A., cum laude, 1984); University of Michigan (J.D., cum laude, 1987). *Member:* American Bar Association (Co-Chair, Intellectual Property/Trade Secrets Subcommittee, Litigation Section). ***PRACTICE AREAS:*** Litigation; Intellectual Property Litigation; Trade Secrets; Unfair Competition; Non-compete Litigation. ***Email:*** lstevens@schiffhardin.com

ROSS D. TAYLOR, admitted to bar, 1988, Illinois; 1992, Colorado (inactive). *Education:* Northern Illinois University (B.S., 1985); University of Virginia (J.D., 1988). Articles Editor, Virginia Tax Review. *Member:* American College of Investment Counsel. ***PRACTICE AREAS:*** Equipment Leasing; Corporate Finance. ***Email:*** rdtaylor@schiffhardin.com

(This Listing Continued)

PATRICIA J. THOMPSON, admitted to bar, 1988, Illinois; 1989, U.S. District Court, Northern District of Illinois; 1990, U.S. Court of Appeals, Seventh Circuit; 1991, U.S. District Court, Eastern District of Wisconsin; 1992, U.S. District Court, District of Colorado; 1994, U.S. District Court, Eastern District of Michigan and U.S. Court of Appeals for the Federal Circuit; U.S. District Court, District of Colorado, Western District of Oklahoma and Northern District of Texas. *Education:* University of California (B.S., 1984); Loyola University (J.D., magna cum laude, 1988). ***PRACTICE AREAS:*** Intellectual Property Litigation. ***Email:*** pthompson@schiffhardin.com

CLAY A. TILLACK, admitted to bar, 1982, Illinois and U.S. District Court, Northern District of Illinois. *Education:* Dartmouth College (A.B., 1979); University of Texas (J.D., with honors, 1982). ***PRACTICE AREAS:*** Intellectual Property; Litigation. ***Email:*** ctillack@schiffhardin.com

MICHAEL F. TOMASEK, admitted to bar, 1994, Illinois and U.S. District Court, Northern District of Illinois; 2001, U.S. Supreme Court. *Education:* Thornton Community College (A.A.S., 1986); Loyola University of Chicago (B.S., summa cum laude, 1989; J.D., magna cum laude, 1994). Recipient: Outstanding Criminal Justice Graduate Award; Chief Justice Edward D. White Scholarship Award; Loyola School of Law Merit Scholarship; West Publishing Company Award; American Jurisprudence Awards for Legal Writing and Research, Advanced Legal Bibliography, Constitutional Law II and Issues in Jurisprudence; Loyola Academic Achievement Award for Excellence in Environmental Law; Leadership and Service Award. Student Articles Editor, Loyola University Chicago Law Journal. Chair, Employee Benefits Committee, Chicago Bar Association, 2002. ***PRACTICE AREAS:*** Employee Benefits. ***Email:*** mtomasek@schiffhardin.com

SCOTT C. TOMASSI, admitted to bar, 1988, Illinois and U.S. District Court, Northern District of Illinois; 1992, U.S. Court of Appeals, Seventh Circuit; 1993, U.S. District Court, Central District of Illinois. *Education:* Loyola University of Chicago (B.B.A., 1985; J.D., 1988). Alpha Sigma Nu; Pi Sigma Alpha. Editor-in-Chief, Loyola University of Chicago Law Journal. ***PRACTICE AREAS:*** Litigation. ***Email:*** stomassi@schiffhardin.com

PATRICIA S. ULLMAN, admitted to bar, 2000, Illinois and Georgia. *Education:* College of William and Mary (B.A., 1973); Case Western Reserve University (M.B.A., 1979); Northwestern University (J.D., 1995). ***PRACTICE AREAS:*** Real Estate. ***Email:*** pullman@schiffhardin.com

BRETT A. VALIQUET, admitted to bar, 1975, Illinois and U.S. District Court, Northern District of Illinois including Trial Bar; 1980, U.S. Court of Appeals, Third Circuit; 1982, U.S. Court of Appeals for the Federal Circuit; 1989, U.S. Court of Appeals, Tenth Circuit; registered to practice before U.S. Patent and Trademark Office. *Education:* Illinois Institute of Technology (B.S.E.E., 1970); Kent College of Law (J.D., 1974). ***PRACTICE AREAS:*** Patent Law; Trademark Law; Copyright Law; Trade Secrets Law; Unfair Competition; Antitrust Law; International Trade Law; Licensing Law. ***Email:*** bvaliquet@schiffhardin.com

DARREN M. R. VAN PUYMBROUCK, admitted to bar, 1986, Illinois and U.S. District Court, Northern District of Illinois including Trial Bar; 1987, U.S. Court of Appeals, Seventh Circuit. *Education:* University of Washington (B.A., 1983); Loyola University (J.D., 1986). Editor, Loyola Law Journal. Law Clerk to the Honorable William J. Bauer, Chief Justice of the U.S. Court of Appeals, Seventh Circuit. ***PRACTICE AREAS:*** Mass Tort and Product Liability Litigation; General Commercial Litigation; Commodity and Securities Litigation; Insurance Coverage. ***Email:*** dvanpuymbrouck@schiffhardin.com

EVERETT S. WARD, admitted to bar, 1986, Illinois. *Education:* Princeton University (A.B., 1983); Harvard University (J.D., 1986). ***PRACTICE AREAS:*** Real Estate; Real Estate Finance. ***Email:*** eward@schiffhardin.com

THOMAS R. WECHTER, admitted to bar, 1966, Illinois. *Education:* University of Michigan (A.B., 1963); University of Chicago (J.D., 1966); New York University (LL.M. in Taxation, honors, 1968). Trial Attorney, Tax Division, Department of Justice, 1968-1974. ***PRACTICE AREAS:*** Federal Tax Controversies; Mergers, Acquisitions and Divestitures; Corporate Tax Planning; Partnership Law; Low Income Tax Credits. ***Email:*** twechter@schiffhardin.com

BRUCE P. WEISENTHAL, admitted to bar, 1983, Illinois. *Education:* University of Wisconsin-Madison (B.A., 1980; Omicron Delta Epsilon; Phi Kappa Phi); University of Pennsylvania (J.D., 1983). ***PRACTICE AREAS:*** Public Finance; Securities; Trust Administration; Workouts; Products Liability. ***Email:*** bweisenthal@schiffhardin.com

ADAM S. WEISS, admitted to bar, 1998, Illinois; U.S. District Court, Northern District of Illinois; registered to practice before U.S. Patent and Trademark Office. *Education:* University of Illinois (B.S., 1995); Chicago-Kent College of Law (J.D., with honors, 1998). Adjunct Professor, Advanced Legal Research and Drafting in Intellectual Property, IIT/Chicago-Kent College of Law. ***PRACTICE AREAS:*** Intellectual Property. ***Email:*** aweiss@schiffhardin.com

THOMAS P. WHITE, admitted to bar, 1984, Delaware; 1990, Illinois. *Education:* Earlham College (B.A., 1979); University of Chicago (J.D., 1984). Phi Beta Kappa. ***PRACTICE AREAS:*** Intellectual Property Law; Trademarks; Copyrights. ***Email:*** twhite@schiffhardin.com

ROBERT B. WILCOX, JR., admitted to bar, 1984, Illinois. *Education:* Harvard University (B.A., magna cum laude, 1970); University of California, Berkeley (J.D., 1984; M.B.A., 1984). ***PRACTICE AREAS:*** Market Regulation Law; Computer Law. ***Email:*** rwilcox@schiffhardin.com

ROGER R. WILEN, admitted to bar, 1988, Illinois. *Education:* University of Michigan (A.B., 1984; J.D., 1988). ***PRACTICE AREAS:*** Private Equity; Venture Capital; Corporate. ***Email:*** rwilen@schiffhardin.com

JAY WILLIAMS, admitted to bar, 1987, Illinois. *Education:* Northwestern University (B.A., 1980); State University of New York at Stony Brook (M.A., 1984; Ph.D., 1984); University of Illinois (J.D., 1987). Order of the Coif. Member, University of Illinois Law Review. ***PRACTICE AREAS:*** Intellectual Property Litigation; Class Action Defense; White Collar Criminal Defense; Contract Litigation; Criminal Appeals. ***Email:*** jwilliams@schiffhardin.com

HELEN T. WILSON, admitted to bar, 1988, Illinois and U.S. District Court, Northern District of Illinois. *Education:* Concordia University (B.A., 1979); DePaul University (J.D., 1988). Member, DePaul Law Review. Law Clerk to Hon. William G. Clark, Illinois Supreme Court. ***PRACTICE AREAS:*** Litigation; Complex Litigation with emphasis in defending Class Actions; Insurance; Products Liability; Antitrust Law. ***Email:*** hwilson@schiffhardin.com

BRENNA B. WOODLEY, admitted to bar, 1997, Illinois; U.S. District Court, Northern District of Illinois; U.S. District Court, Eastern District of Michigan. *Education:* University of Wisconsin (B.A., 1992, J.D., 1997). Phi Kappa Phi. Senior Managing Editor, Wisconsin Law Review. ***PRACTICE AREAS:*** ERISA litigation. ***Email:*** bwoodley@schiffhardin.com

MARK C. ZAANDER, admitted to bar, 1976, Illinois; 1995, Indiana. *Education:* University of Illinois (B.S., 1973); University of Chicago (J.D., 1976). Phi Beta Kappa. Member, Bronze Tablet. ***PRACTICE AREAS:*** Corporate Finance. ***Email:*** mzaander@schiffhardin.com

SHELDON A. ZABEL, admitted to bar, 1966, Illinois; 1976, U.S. Supreme Court. *Education:* Princeton University (A.B., 1963); Northwestern University (J.D., 1966). Order of the Coif. ***PRACTICE AREAS:*** Environmental Law; Natural Resources Law. ***Email:*** szabel@schiffhardin.com

KATHRYN D. ZALEWSKI, admitted to bar, 1997, Illinois and Michigan; U.S. District Court, Northern and Central Districts of Illinois; U.S. District Court, Eastern and Western Districts of Michigan; U.S. Court of Appeals, Sixth and Federal Circuits. *Education:* Purdue University (B.S., 1987); University of Michigan Law School (J.D., 1997). ***PRACTICE AREAS:*** Pharmaceutical Patent Litigation; Trademark; Unfair Competition; Copyright; Patent; Intellectual Property Litigation; Commercial Litigation. ***Email:*** kzalewski@schiffhardin.com

CHRISTOPHER J. ZINSKI, admitted to bar, 1987, Illinois; 1988, District of Columbia. *Education:* Marquette University (B.S., cum laude, 1984); Georgetown University Law Center (J.D., cum laude, 1987). Certified Public Accountant, Illinois, 1984. ***PRACTICE AREAS:*** Mergers and Acquisitions; Banks and Banking; Corporate Law; Executive Compensation; Business Law. ***Email:*** czinski@schiffhardin.com

SPECIAL PARTNERS

Lawrence Block (P.C.)
Stuart L. Goodman
Donald J. Kreger
Neal A. Mancoff
William A. Montgomery, (P.C.)
Guenther M. Philipp (P.C.)
James M. Van Vliet, Jr.
John J. Voortman
Ronald Wilder

RETIRED PARTNERS

Paul B. O'Flaherty
Mitchell S. Rieger
Burton R. Rissman (P.C.)
James B. Wilson (P.C.)

SENIOR COUNSEL

W. Donald McSweeney
Keith Shay

OF COUNSEL

HOWARD R. BARRON, admitted to bar, 1953, Illinois. *Education:* University of Chicago (Ph.B., 1948); Stanford University (B.A., 1950); Yale University (LL.B., 1953). Phi Alpha Delta; Pi Sigma Alpha. Associate Director, Yale Law School Moot Court of Appeals, 1952-1953. ***PRACTICE AREAS:*** Civil Litigation; Labor Law; Employment Law; Class Action Defense; Telecommunications Law; Proprietary Rights. ***Email:*** hbarron@schiffhardin.com

KATHLEEN C. BASSI, admitted to bar, 1985, Illinois. *Education:* Western Illinois University (B.A., with honors, 1969; M.A., 1981); Northern Illinois University (J.D., cum laude, 1985). Phi Alpha Theta. ***PRACTICE AREAS:*** Environmental. ***Email:*** kbassi@schiffhardin.com

SUSAN M. CARLSON, admitted to bar, 1975, Illinois. *Education:* Mundelein College (B.A., 1971); Northwestern University (J.D., cum laude, 1975). (Resident at Lake Forest, Illinois Office). ***PRACTICE AREAS:*** Taxation; Estate Planning; Private Business Law; Business Dispute Resolution. ***Email:*** scarlson@schiffhardin.com

JAMES A. CLARK, admitted to bar, 1977, Ohio; 1979, Illinois; 1986, Wisconsin. *Education:* Miami University (B.A., 1971; B.S., 1971); Cleveland State University (M.S., 1974); Case Western Reserve University (J.D., 1977). Order of the Coif. Executive Articles Editor, Case Western Reserve Law Review. Law Clerk, U.S. District Judge John M. Manos, Cleveland, Ohio. ***PRACTICE AREAS:*** Litigation. ***Email:*** jclark@schiffhardin.com

NICOLE FINITZO, admitted to bar, 1975, Illinois. *Education:* Northwestern University (B.S., Journalism, 1972; J.D., cum laude, 1975). Kappa Tau Alpha. (Resident at Lake Forest, Illinois Office). ***PRACTICE AREAS:*** Corporate Law; Nonprofit Organizations Law; Federal Taxation; Commercial Law; Business Dispute Resolution; Privately-Held Business Law; Employment Law. ***Email:*** nfinitzo@schiffhardin.com

BARBARA E. HERMANSEN, admitted to bar, 1982, Illinois; U.S. District Court, Northern District of Illinois including Trial Bar. *Education:* Cornell College, Mount Vernon (B.A., 1976); Northwestern University School of Law (J.D., 1982). ***Email:*** bhermansen@schiffhardin.com

LAEL F. JOHNSON, admitted to bar, 1963, Illinois; 1964; U.S. District Court, Northern District of Illinois; 1966, U.S. Court of Appeals, Seventh Circuit. *Education:* Wheaton College (A.B., 1960); Northwestern University (J.D., 1963). ***PRACTICE AREAS:*** Life Sciences; Biotechnology Licensing; Strategic Alliances; Technology Licensing; Business Start-Ups. ***Email:*** ljohnson@schiffhardin.com

KATHERINE J. LEVY, admitted to bar, 1980, Illinois. *Education:* DePaul University (B.S., Accountancy, with honors, 1969; M.S., Taxation, 1973; J.D., 1980). Beta Alpha Psi; Sigma Iota Epsilon. Recipient, American Jurisprudence Prize Award, 1979. Certified Public Accountant, Illinois, 1969. (Resident at Lake Forest, Illinois Office). ***PRACTICE AREAS:*** Taxation; Estate Planning; Estate Administration; Business Law. ***Email:*** klevy@schiffhardin.com

(This Listing Continued)

SCHIFF HARDIN LLP, Chicago—Continued

STEPHEN A. MARCUS, admitted to bar, 1968, Illinois; 1974, U.S. Supreme Court. *Education:* University of Illinois (B.S., Finance, 1965); Northwestern University (J.D., 1968). ***PRACTICE AREAS:*** Securities Regulation Law; Corporate Law; Business Law; Municipal Finance; Bond Finance. ***Email:*** smarcus@schiffhardin.com

KATHLEEN D. MATHEWSON, admitted to bar, 1985, Illinois and U.S. District Court, Northern District of Illinois. *Education:* DePaul University (B.S., with honors, 1981; M.S., Taxation, 1985); Loyola University School of Law (J.D., 1985). Certified Public Accountant. ***Email:*** kmathews@schiffhardin.com

KENDRA J. PANEK, admitted to bar, 1995, Illinois, U.S. District Court, Northern District of Illinois. *Education:* University of Illinois (B.A., 1992); Chicago-Kent College of Law (J.D., high honors, 1995). ***PRACTICE AREAS:*** Litigation. ***Email:*** kpanek@schiffhardin.com

CARL A. ROYAL, admitted to bar, 1974, Illinois. *Education:* Wabash College (B.A., magna cum laude, 1971); Yale University (J.D., 1974). Phi Beta Kappa. Member, Board of Editors, Futures and Derivatives Law Report. ***PRACTICE AREAS:*** Securities; Futures and Derivatives. ***Email:*** croyal@schiffhardin.com

JOHN D. SIMPSON, admitted to bar, 1961, Illinois and U.S. District Court, Northern District of Illinois including Trial Bar; 1969, U.S. Court of Appeals, Seventh Circuit; 1979, U.S. Court of Appeals, Sixth Circuit; 1981, U.S. District Court, Northern District of Texas; 1985, U.S. Claims Court and U.S. Court of Appeals for the Federal Circuit; 1988, Amtsgerichts München, Germany; registered to practice before U.S. Patent and Trademark Office. *Education:* Iowa State University (B.S., 1957); DePaul University (LL.B., 1961; J.D., 1969). ***PRACTICE AREAS:*** Patent Law; International Trade Regulation Law; Products Liability Law; High Technology Contracts; Patent Licensing; Patent Litigation; Licensing Law. ***Email:*** jsimpson@schiffhardin.com

RICHARD L. VERKLER, admitted to bar, 1962, Illinois. *Education:* University of Illinois (B.S., 1959); University of Wisconsin-Madison (J.D., 1962). Order of the Coif; Phi Alpha Delta. Member, Board of Editors, 1960-1962 and Articles Editor, 1961-1962, Wisconsin Law Review. (Resident at Lake Forest, Illinois Office). ***PRACTICE AREAS:*** Corporate Law; Federal Taxation; Private Business Law; Business Dispute Resolution; Commercial Law; Nonprofit Organizations Law. ***Email:*** rverkler@schiffhardin.com

COUNSEL

TODD D. FREER, admitted to bar, 1979, Illinois. *Education:* Cornell College (B.S.S., 1973); Loyola University Chicago School of Law (J.D., 1979). ***PRACTICE AREAS:*** Public Law; Public Finance; Corporate; Securities; Finance. ***Email:*** tfreer@schiffhardin.com

DANIEL J. DEEB, admitted to bar, 1996, Indiana and U.S. District Court, Southern and Northern Districts of Indiana; 2005, Illinois. *Education:* Aquinas College (B.S., magna cum laude, 1991); Indiana University School of Law - Bloomington (J.D., cum laude, 1996). ***PRACTICE AREAS:*** Environmental. ***Email:*** ddeeb@schiffhardin.com

MICHAEL J. HUFT, admitted to bar, 1995, Illinois and U.S. District Court, Northern District of Illinois. *Education:* University of Notre Dame (B.S. in Physics, cum laude, 1971); University of Michigan (Ph.D. in Biology, 1979); Northwestern University (J.D., 1995). Wigmore Scholar. Law Clerk to Hon. Judge Paul E. Plunkett, U.S. District Court, Northern District of Illinois. ***LANGUAGES:*** Swedish. ***PRACTICE AREAS:*** Estate Planning; Nonprofit and Charitable Organizations. ***Email:*** mhuft@schiffhardin.com

JOHN K. LINES, admitted to bar, 1984, Ohio; 2003, Colorado; 2005, Illinois. *Education:* Purdue University (B.S., with high honors, 1980); Indiana University (J.D., 1984). Member, Indiana Law Journal, 1983-1984. ***PRACTICE AREAS:*** Corporate; Securities; Real Estate. ***Email:*** jlines@schiffhardin.com

MARY ANNE MULLIN, admitted to bar, 1989, Colorado; 1990, Wisconsin; 1991, North Carolina; 2000, Illinois. *Education:* Lawrence University (B.A., 1984); University of Wisconsin-Madison (J.D., 1989). Articles Editor, Wisconsin Law Review, 1988-1989. ***PRACTICE AREAS:*** Environmental. ***Email:*** mmullin@schiffhardin.com

MICHAEL YETNIKOFF, admitted to bar, 1988, Illinois; 1989, U.S. District Court, Northern District of Illinois. *Education:* University of Chicago (B.A., with honors, 1985; J.D., with honors, 1988). ***PRACTICE AREAS:*** Bankruptcy; Workouts; Creditors. ***Email:*** myetnikoff@schiffhardin.com

ASSOCIATES

Ismail Alsheik (admission pending)
Andrew M. Alul
Mark A. Bergner
Elizabeth Anne Blackwood
Michael J. Boffa
Matthew Brett
Fiona A. Burke
Benjamin C. Butler
Tracy A. Campbell
John Capone
Edward M. Casmere
Jeffrey Colvin
Alexis Andrews Cooper
Erika Csicsila, L.
John C. deMoulpied
Nathan A. Engel (Resident at Lake Forest, Illinois Office)
Michelle J. Fisk
Patricia J. Fokuo
Aaron M. Forester
Laura B. Friedel
David C. Giles
M. Shawn Leist
Jonathan Mark Lively
Theresa M.H. Marx
Ramona Mateiu
Lisa J. Matyas
Heather R. McDonald
Kristen L. Mercado
Joshua R. More
Samantha C. Norris
Heidi Oertle
Carrie Lynn H. Okizaki (Not admitted in IL)
Binu George Palal
Avani A. Patel
Kavita Mukund Patel
Sailesh K. Patel
Holly A. Podulka
Linda Potapova
Lee Ann Rabe
Alex P. Rabinsky
Julie Claire Rising
Jessica Romero

(This Listing Continued)

ASSOCIATES (Continued)

Jason G. Harp
Lawrence H. Heftman
Kevin S. Hovis
Jennifer R. Izraelewicz
Ayad Paul Jacob
Matthew C. Jardine
Jonathan M. Judge
Jon K. Jurva
David G. Kairis
Charlene Q. Kalebic (Resident at Lake Forest, Illinois Office)
Kim A. Kamin
Brendan J. Kelly
Charlene M. Kelly
Ian T. Kelly
Kevin C. Knohl
Susan Kurzydlo Koci
Jo-Anne Kokoski
Matthew D. Lahey
Seth D. Lamden
Joshua Lee
Heidi Hennig Rowe
Amy M. Rubenstein
Andrew N. Sawula
Reid A. Schultz
David C. Scott
Marla R. Shade
Peter C. Spier
Sonia Macias Steele
Heidi Anne Steiner
Margaret Strothkamp
Jason M. Torf
Jon Carlo Vigano
Doug J. Wagenbach
Nora A. Kersten Walsh
Kelly M. Warner
Dorothy A. Weber (Not admitted in IL)
Alexander B. Young
Andrew P. Young
Jason L. Zgliniec
Jeanette Sanniola Zimmer
Gladys C. Zolna

STAFF ATTORNEYS

Andrew Finko
Theodora A. Karnegis
Margaret A. Nagela
Steven D. Welhouse

DIRECTOR OF MARKETING AND COMMUNICATIONS

DAVID A. MILBERG, admitted to bar, 1979, Illinois and U.S. District Court, Northern District of Illinois; 2001, Florida. *Education:* University of Michigan (A.B., 1970); John Marshall Law School (J.D., 1979). Member, John Marshall Law Journal. ***Email:*** dmilberg@schiffhardin.com

SCHIFF & HULBERT

Established in 1995

150 N. WACKER DRIVE, SUITE 1300
CHICAGO, ILLINOIS 60606
Telephone: 312-726-2800
Fax: 312-726-2100
Email: mschiff@schiffandhulbert.com
URL: http://www.schiffandhulbert.com

Labor and Employment Law, Workers Compensation.

FIRM PROFILE: Schiff & Hulbert is listed in the Bar Register of Preeminent Lawyers.

MEMBERS OF FIRM

MATTHEW B. SCHIFF, born Harvey, Illinois, May 18, 1957; admitted to bar, 1982, Illinois and U.S. District Court, Northern District of Illinois including Trial Bar; 1983, U.S. Court of Appeals, Seventh Circuit; 1999, U.S. Supreme Court. *Education:* Cornell University (B.A., 1979); Boston University (J.D., 1982). Author: "A Primer on Case Law Under the Americans with Disabilities Act," Tort Trial and Insurance Practice Law Journal, Vol. 39, No. 4 Summer 2004. Lead Author: Illinois Jurisprudence Encyclopedia, Volume 26 Workers Compensation, Matthew Bender, 2004; "Conducting Internal Investigations of Employee Theft and Other Misconduct," The Brief, Vol. 33, No. 3, Spring 2004; "Recent Developments in Employment Law," Tort and Insurance Law Journal, Vol. 37, No. 2, 2002. Lead Editor, Litigating The Sexual Harassment Case, American Bar Association, 2000. Lead Author: "Nine Steps to Conducting Harassment Investigations," The Brief, Vol. 29, No. 1, Fall 1999. Contributing Author: "Sexual Harassment in Employment Law," Barbara Lindemann et al. eds Supplement BNA, Chapters 14 and 27, 1997; "Survey of Illinois Law: Workers' Compensation" Southern Illinois University Law Journal, Vol. 19, 1995; "Illinois Jurisprudence," Labor and Employment, Vol. 22 Chapters 16, 17 and 18, 1995. Author: "A Primer on Case Law Under the Americans with Disabilities Act," Tort Trial and Insurance Law Journal, Vol. 39, No. 4, Summer 2004; "AIDS and The Health Care Worker," Gonzaga University Law Review, Vol. 29 No. 1 1994; "A Reasonable Accommodation Under The American with Disabilities Act," Gonzaga Law Review Vol. 28, No. 2 1993. Co-Author: "The Americans with Disabilities Act: A New Challenge for Employers," The Tort and Insurance Law Journal, Vol. XXVII, No. 1, Fall, 1991. Articles Editor, American Journal of Law & Medicine, 1981-1982. Seminar Faculty, University of Wisconsin Management Institute. Featured Speaker and Legal Issues Coordinator: past twelve LRP Annual National Workers' Compensation and Disability Conferences. *Member:* Chicago Bar Association; Illinois State Bar Association; American Bar Association (Past Management Chairman, Section on Labor and Employment Law, Committee on Workers Compensation, 1989-1991; Past Chair, Trial, Tort and Insurance Practice Section, Employer-Employee Relations Committee, Distance Learning Coordinator); Defense Research Institute; National Institute for Trial Advocacy; American Bar Foundation. ***REPORTED CASES:*** American Alliance Ins. Co. v. 1212 Restaurant Group, 342 111 App.3d 500 (1st Dist. 2003); McDermott v. City of Northwoods Police Department,103 S.W.3d 134 (Mo. App. E.D., 2002); National Manufacturing v. The Industrial Commission, 331 Ill.App. 3d 1045 (3rd. Dist. 2002); Illinois Institute of Technology Research Institute v. Industrial Commission, 314 Ill. App. 3d 149 (1st Dist. 2000); La Grange Memorial Hospital v. St. Paul Insurance Company, 317 Ill. App. 3d 863 (1st Dist. 2000); Palos Electric Company v. Industrial Commission, 314 Ill. App. 3d 920 (1st Dist. 2000); Efremidis v. Industrial Commission, 308 Ill. App 3d 915 (1st Dist. 1999); Kraft General Foods v. Industrial Commission, 287 Ill. App. 3d 526 (2d Dist.1997); Colvett v. L. Karp & Sons, 211 Ill. App. 3d 731 (1st Dist.1991); Wasielewski v.

(This Listing Continued)

HAVI Corp., 188 Ill App. 3d 340 (3d Dist.1989); Steel City National Bank of Chicago v. Aetna Insurance Company, 116 Ill. App. 3d 7 (1st Dist. 1983). ***PRACTICE AREAS:*** Collective Bargaining; Employment Contracts; Employment Discrimination; Employment Termination; Equal Employment Opportunity Law; Family and Medical Leave Act; Harassment; Retaliatory Discharge; Sexual Harassment; Title VII Discrimination; Wrongful Termination; Labor and Employment Law; Workers' Compensation Law. ***Email:*** mschiff@schiffandhulbert.com

JAMES W. HULBERT, born La Grange, Illinois, September 12, 1956; admitted to bar, 1982, Illinois and U.S. District Court, Northern District of Illinois. *Education:* University of North Carolina (B.A., magna cum laude, 1978); Boston College (J.D., cum laude, 1982). Phi Beta Kappa. Co-Author: Illinois Jurisprudence Encyclopedia Vo. 26 Workers Compensation, Matthew Bender, 2004; "Recent Developments in Employment Law," Tort and Insurance Law Journal, Vol. 37, No. 2, 2002; "Schools' Liability for Student-on-Student Sexual Harassment Under Title IX," Illinois Bar Journal, Vol. 88, February 2000. Speaker, LRP Annual National Worker's Compensation and Disabilities Conference, 2003. *Member:* Chicago, Illinois State and American Bar Associations; Defense Research Institute (Liaison for the State of Illinois, Workers Compensation Committee). ***REPORTED CASES:*** Robert Ross v. Industrial Commission No. 1-03-2999WC (1st. Dist. App. Ct.), August 4, 2004; American Alliance Ins. Co. v. 1212 Restaurant Group, 2003 342 Ill App. 3d 500 (2003); National Manufacturing v. The Industrial Commission, 331 Ill. App. 3d 1045 (3rd Dist., 2002); Hydraulics v. Industrial commission, 329 Ill. App. 3d 166 (2nd Dist., 2002); LaGrange Memorial Hospital v. St. Paul Insurance Co., 317 Ill. App. 3d 863 (1st Dist. 2000); Palos Electric Company v. Industrial Commission, 314 Ill App. 3d 920 (1st Dist. 2000); Efremidis v. Industrial Commission, 308 Ill.App.3d 915 (1st Dist. 1999); Kraft General Foods v. Industrial Commission, 287 Ill App 3d 526 (2d Dist. 1997); Holubek v. City of Chicago, 146 Ill App 3d 915 (1st Dist. 1986);. ***PRACTICE AREAS:*** Employment Law; Workers' Compensation Law; Commercial Litigation; Products Liability. ***Email:*** jhulbert@schiffandhulbert.com

SCHILLER, DUCANTO AND FLECK

Established in 1981

200 NORTH LA SALLE STREET, 30TH FLOOR
CHICAGO, ILLINOIS 60601
Telephone: 312-641-5560
Fax: 312-641-6361
Email: schillerducantoandfleck@sdflaw.com
URL: http://www.sdflaw.com

Lake Forest, Illinois Office: Suite 300, 207 East Westminster Avenue. Telephone: 847-615-8300. Fax: 847-615-8284.

Wheaton, Illinois Office: 311 South County Farm Road, Suite G. Telephone: 630-665-5800. Fax: 630-665-6082.

Family Law, Complex Domestic Relations Issues, Divorce/Dissolution of Marriage, Prenuptial Agreements/Premarital Agreements, Child Custody and Visitation, Spousal Support/Alimony/Maintenance, Matrimonial Law and Litigation, Appeals, Mediation-Family/ Divorce, Marital Settlement Agreements, Separation Agreements, Property Rights, Financial Discovery and Analysis Related to Divorce, and Tax Considerations Related to Divorce.

FIRM PROFILE: Schiller, DuCanto and Fleck is the largest law firm in the country to devote its practice exclusively to matrimonial law. The firm was founded in 1981 by Chicago attorneys Donald C. Schiller and Joseph N. DuCanto. Charles J. Fleck, former presiding judge of the Cook County Domestic Relations Division, joined in 1982. Firm members are nationally recognized experts in all aspects of matrimonial law, and many are current and past leaders of local, state and national bar associations. The biographies listed below contain specific references to articles authored, memberships and offices held by our attorneys within the last seven years. A more complete list can be found in the extended biographies listed on the firm's web page.

PARTNERS

JOSEPH N. DUCANTO, born Utica, New York, March 18, 1927; admitted to bar, 1955, Illinois; 1958, U.S. Tax Court; 1960, U.S. Supreme Court. *Education:* Antioch College (B.A., 1952); University of Chicago (J.D., 1955). Listed in Best Lawyers in America, by Neifeh and Smith, 1987-2002. Illinois Super Lawyers (Family Law) 2004—. Member of Leading Lawyers Network 2004—. Author of numerous journal articles respecting tax, financial and estate planning aspects of marital and matrimonial law. Author and Editor, Tax Financial and Estate Planning Developments in Connection With Divorce and Family Law (1970-1983). Visiting Lecturer in Family Law, Loyola University, 1968- 1992; Visiting Professor, 2002. Member, Scribes. Member, Board of Directors, Chicago Crime Commission, 1994—. Fellow: American Academy of Matrimonial Lawyers (National President, 1977-1979); American College of Trust and Estate Counsel (1970—). *Member:* Illinois State and American (Chairman, Family Law, Taxation Committee, 1982-1984) Bar Associations. American Academy of Matrimonial Lawyers (National President, 1977-1979); American College of Trust and Estate Counsel (1970—). [U.S. Marine Corps. WW II]. ***Email:*** jducanto@sdflaw.com

DONALD C. SCHILLER, born Chicago, Illinois, December 8, 1942; admitted to bar, 1966, Illinois and U.S. District Court, Northern District of Illinois; 1972, U.S. Supreme Court. *Education:* Lake Forest College; DePaul University (J.D., 1966). Recipient, Distinguished Alumni Award, De Paul University, 1988. Lecturer at Law, University of Chicago Law School (2001—). Listed in Best Lawyers in America, by Neifeh and Smith, 1987—; cited as one of the Nation's Top Lawyers by Town & Country Magazine, Worth Magazine, The National Law Journal, Crain's Chicago Business, Today's Chicago Woman & the Chicago Sun Times; Illinois Super Lawyers and Leading Lawyers; subject of book chapter in "The Divorce Lawyers", by Emily Couric. Chair, Domestic Relations Management Advisory Committee of the Circuit Court of Cook County (1993-2000). Faculty ABA Trial Advocacy Institute. Author of numerous articles and book chapters and frequent speaker at national CLE events. Diplomate, The American College of Family Trial Lawyers. President, ABA Retirement Funds (2005-2006). *Member:* Illinois State (President, 1987-1988; Board of Governors, 1977-1983; Chairman, Family Law Section, 1976-1977); American (Board of Governors, 1994-1997; House of Delegates, 1984-1988, 1997-2001, 2003—; Chairman, Family Law Section, 1985-1986); and Chicago (Member, 1971 and Matrimonial Law Committee Chairman, 1976-1977) Bar Associations; American Academy of Matrimonial Lawyers (National Chair of Continuing Legal Education, 1994-1995). ***Email:*** dschiller@sdflaw.com

CHARLES J. FLECK (Resident, Lake Forest Office)

DAVID H. HOPKINS, born Farragut, Idaho, March 19, 1944; admitted to bar, 1969, Illinois; 1971, U.S. Tax Court. *Education:* Duke University (A.B., 1966); Columbia University (J.D., 1969). Author of numerous papers in the divorce taxation area, including (i) Paper entitled, "Premarital Agreements Under Illinois Law," presented at the Twenty Eighth Annual Notre Dame Tax and Estate Planning Institute, 2002; (ii) Paper entitled, "Income Tax Land Mines in Divorce and Separation," presented at ABA Tax Section's mid-year meeting, 2000; and (iii) Chapter in IICLE Family Law Handbook (2003, plus Supplements), entitled "Tax Aspects of Dissolution of Marriage." Illinois Super Lawyers (Family Law) 2004—. Member of Leading Lawyers Network 2004—. Member, Board of Directors, Chicago Bar Foundation, 1998-2004. *Member:* Chicago Bar (Member, CBA Board of Managers, 1992-1994); Illinois State Bar (Chairman, Family Law Section Council, 1989-1990; Chairman, Joint ISBA/CBA Task Force on Illinois Domestic Violence Act, 1986-1992; and recipient of 1992 ISBA Board of Governors' Award); and American Bar (Chairman, ABA Domestic Relations Tax Simplification Task Force, 1980-1984, which drafted the reform proposals culminating in the 1984 and 1986 Amendments to the Internal Revenue Code in the divorce tax area; Chairman, 1982-1984 Section of Taxation Domestic Relations Tax Problems Committee). Fellow, American Academy of Matrimonial Lawyers. ***Email:*** dhopkins@sdflaw.com

ARNOLD B. STEIN, born Chicago, Illinois, October 2, 1948; admitted to bar, 1975, Illinois. *Education:* University of Illinois (B.S., 1970); Northwestern University (J.D., 1974). Phi Beta Kappa; Phi Alpha Theta. James Scholar. Listed: Best Lawyers in America, by Neifeh and Smith, 2003-2004 eds.; Illinois Super Lawyers (Family Law) 2004—. Member of Leading Lawyers Network, 2004—. *Member:* Northwest Suburban, Chicago, Illinois State and American (Member, Family Law Section, 1993; Co-Chair, Trial Practice Committee) Bar Associations; Illinois Trial Lawyers Association. ***Email:*** astein@sdflaw.com

BURTON S. HOCHBERG, born Chicago, Illinois, September 15, 1949; admitted to bar, 1974, Illinois; 1975, Florida and U.S. District Court, Northern District of Illinois. *Education:* University of Wisconsin (B.B.A., 1971); DePaul University (J.D., 1974). Listed: Best Lawyers in America, by Neifeh and Smith, 2003— eds.; Illinois Super Lawyers (Family Law) 2004—. Member of Leading Lawyers Network 2004—. Hearing Board Member, Illinois Disciplinary Commission, 1994-1997. *Member:* Illinois State Bar Association; American Academy of Matrimonial Lawyers (Chairman, Membership Committee, 1997-1998; Co-Chairman, Admissions Committee, 1998-2000). ***Email:*** bhochberg@sdflaw.com

CARLTON R. MARCYAN (Resident, Lake Forest Office)

TIMOTHY M. DAW (Resident, Wheaton Office)

BENJAMIN S. MACKOFF, born Chicago, Illinois, September 17, 1933; admitted to bar, 1958, Illinois; 1962, U.S. District Court, Northern District of Illinois; 1964, U.S. Supreme Court; 1982, Hopi Tribal Court; 1995, U.S. Court of the Armed Forces. *Education:* University of Chicago (B.A., 1953); Northwestern University (J.D., 1957); Editor, Northwestern University Law Review, 1956-1957. Judge, Circuit Court of Cook County 1973-1995; Presiding Judge, Domestic Relations Division, 1986-1995; Chair, Illinois Supreme Court Study Comm. on Mediation in Child Custody, Support and Visitation Disputes; Domestic Relations Chair, Illinois Judicial Conference Alternative Dispute Resolution Coordinating Comm. 1990-1993; Chair, Illinois State Bar Assn. Task Force on the Family, 1987-1990; Delegate, Illinois Conference of Chief Judges Child Support Enforcement Advisory Comm. 1988-1995; Adjunct Professor, John Marshall Law School (ADR), 1999-2003; President, Mediation Council of Illinois (2004-2005; Vice President, International Academy of Dispute Resolution, 2004-2005. Author: "Mediation and Family Law," Illinois Institute of Continuing Legal Education, 2001; "Domestic Violence, An International Problem," First World Congress on Family Law and the Rights of Children, Sydney, Australia, 1993. Recipient: Board of Governors Award, Illinois State Bar Association, 1988; Tom C. Clark Award, National Conference of Metropolitan Courts, 1991; Outstanding Contribution Award, Mediation Council of Illinois, 2002. Listed: Leading Lawyers of Illinois (Family Law, ADR), Chicago Lawyer, 2003-2005; Illinois Super Lawyers (Family Law) 2004—. Member of Leading Lawyers Network 2004—. *Member:* Illinois State Bar Association; Decalogue Society of Lawyers; Illinois Judges' Association. ***Email:*** bmackoff@sdflaw.com

JAMES B. O'BRIEN, born Chicago, Illinois, February 15, 1940; admitted to bar, 1964, Illinois and U.S. District Court, Northern District of Illinois; 1971, U.S. Supreme Court. *Education:* University of Illinois (B.A., 1962; J.D., 1964). Member: Leading Lawyers Network 2004—; American Academy Matrimonial Lawyers (inactive). *Member:* Illinois State Bar Association; Chicago Council of Lawyers. ***Email:*** jobrien@sdflaw.com

MICHAEL R. GALASSO (Resident, Wheaton Office)

SARANE CROWTHER SIEWERTH, born Chicago, Illinois, January 29, 1940; admitted to bar, 1981, Illinois and U.S. District Court, Northern District of Illinois; 1995, U.S. Court of Appeals, Seventh Circuit. *Education:* Northwestern University (B.S., 1961; M.A., 1962); Jesus College, Oxford, England; John Marshall Law School (J.D., with distinction, 1981). Member, Order of John Marshall. Listed: Leading Lawyer Network Top Lawyers, 2004; Illinois Super Lawyers (Family Law) 2004—. Member, Leading Lawyers Network 2004—. Author: Chapter, "Appeals in Custody and Visitation Cases," Child Custody Litigation, Illinois Institute of Continuing Legal Education, 1992, 1996, 2001. Adjunct Faculty, The John Marshall Law School, 1986—. Handles appeals in all types of Matrimonial law cases. *Member:* Chicago (Member: Matrimonial Law Committee, 1984-1994; Supreme Court Rules Subcommittee, 1986-1994; Current Law Subcommittee, 1986-1994), Illinois State and American Bar Associations. ***Email:*** ssiewerth@sdflaw.com

ANITA M. VENTRELLI, born Berwyn, Illinois, April 20, 1964; admitted to bar, 1990, Illinois. *Education:* University of Michigan (A.B., 1986); DePaul University (J.D., 1989). Recipient, Leading Lawyer Network Top Lawyers, 2004. Named as one of Forty

(This Listing Continued)

SCHILLER, DuCANTO AND FLECK, Chicago—Continued

Illinois Lawyers Under 40 to Watch in 2003 by Chicago Daily Law Bulletin; ISBA Outstanding Young Lawyer of the Year, 2001; Illinois Super Lawyers (Family Law) 2004—. Faculty Member of ABA Family Law Trial Advocacy Institute; Member, DePaul Law Review. Frequent Speaker and Author of articles and contributions to publications in the area of family law, ethics, trial practice, domestic violence and attorneys' fees; "Who's Who in American Law," Biography, 1994-1995. American Family Law Section (CLE Committee, 2001—; Long Range Planning Committee, Member, 2001—, Chair, 2003-2004, Vice Chair, 2002-2003; Governing Council, 1996-1998, 2001—; Marital Property Committee, Co-Chair 2001-2003, Vice Chair 2000-2001). *Member:* Chicago and Illinois State Bar Associations. ***Email:*** aventrelli@sdflaw.com

ANDREA K. MUCHIN, born Evanston, Illinois, February 13, 1962; admitted to bar, 1987, Illinois and U.S. District Court, Northern District of Illinois. *Education:* University of Michigan (B.A., 1984); Boston University (J.D., 1987). Recipient, Leading Lawyer Network Top Lawyers, 2004. Illinois Super Lawyers (Family Law) 2004—. Member of Leading Lawyers Network 2004—. Speaker: "Grandparents Rights" and "Joint Parenting," J.C.C. and Veterans of the Northwest Suburbs and Chicagoland area, 1994-1997. *Member:* Chicago (Family Law Committee), Illinois State (Member, Family Law Section) and American Bar Associations. ***Email:*** amuchin@sdflaw.com

DAVID A. KING (Resident, Wheaton Office)

KAREN PINKERT-LIEB, born Chicago, Illinois, March 5, 1966; admitted to bar, 1993, Illinois. *Education:* University of Texas at Austin (B.A., 1989); Chicago-Kent College of Law/IIT (J.D., with honors, 1993). Recipient, Leading Lawyer Network Top Lawyers, 2004. Illinois Super Lawyers (Family Law) 2004—. Selected as one of 40 attorneys under 40 by Chicago Lawyer Magazine, August 2000. Publications include chapter in Illinois Institute for Continuing Legal Education Family Law Edition and articles in Chicago Daily Law Bulletin and Divorce Magazine; Vice-Chair of Family Law Section, Illinois State Bar Association; former Chair of Continuing Legal Education Committee of Family Law Section. Frequent lecturer for Illinois State Bar Association and Illinois Institute of Continuing Legal Education on subjects such as Premarital Agreements, Litigating Domestic Relations Cases and Equalizing Access to Attorneys' Fees in Divorce. ***Email:*** kpinkert-lieb@sdflaw.com

DANIEL R. STEFANI, born Des Plaines, Illinois, November 30, 1966; admitted to bar, 1994, Illinois. *Education:* University of Illinois (B.A., 1988); John Marshall Law School (J.D., 1994). Author: "Discovering Employee Benefits," ABA Family Law Advocate, Winter 2001; "New Law Regarding Modification of Visitation Rights," Illinois State Bar Association Family Law Newsletter, January 2000. Speaker: "New Discovery Rules Including Supreme Court Rule 213," April 2003; "Use of Requests to Admit, Bills of Particular and Authentication of Corporate Records," CBA, Summer 2000; "Cohabitation Agreements," Illinois Institute of Continuing Legal Education, March/May 1999; "Accountants as Expert Witnesses in Valuation of Corporations," Institute Academy of Certified Public Accountants, 1997; Illinois Super Lawyers (Family Law) 2004—. Member of Leading Lawyers Network 2004—. *Member:* Chicago, Illinois State and American Bar Associations; American Inns of Court; Justinian Society of Italian American Lawyers. ***Email:*** dstefani@sdflaw.com

CELIA G. GAMRATH, born Park Ridge, Illinois, January 30, 1970; admitted to bar, 1994, Illinois and U.S. District Court, Northern District of Illinois. *Education:* Indiana University (B.S., 1991); John Marshall Law School (J.D., cum laude, 1994). Judicial Law Clerk, Appellate Court of Illinois. Adjunct Professor/Guest Lecturer, John Marshall Law School. Recipient: Leading Lawyers Network Top Lawyers; Chicago Magazine's Super Lawyers and Top Female Attorneys; JCCIA Impresa Award; ISBA Young Lawyer of the Year Award; Chicago Law Bulletin's 40 Under Forty Attorneys to Watch; CBA Alta May Hulett Award; ISBA Legal Writing Awards; Author and Lecturer (sampling includes): IICLE Family Law Flash Points; Illinois Bar Journal; ABA Lecture series; American Journal of Family Law; Annual Illinois Judicial Conference; Chicago Daily Law Bulletin; Appellate Law Review. Member: Illinois Supreme Court Character and Fitness Committee; Chicago Bar Foundation Board of Directors; ISBA Mutual Insurance Co.; Past President, John Marshall Law School Alumni Association. *Member:* Chicago Bar (Board of Directors); Illinois State Bar Association (Board of Governors); Appellate Lawyers Association (Past Director); Justinian Society Officer. Fellow, Illinois Bar Foundation. (Resident, Lake Forest Office). ***Email:*** cgamrath@sdflaw.com

ERIC L. SCHULMAN (Resident, Lake Forest Office)

MARIO R. VENTRELLI (Resident, Lake Forest Office)

MEIGHAN A. HARMON, born Hill, Utah, December 2, 1971; admitted to bar, 1996, Illinois. *Education:* University of Illinois (B.S., 1993); University of Notre Dame (J.D., 1996). Named as one of Forty Illinois Lawyers Under 40 to Watch in 2004 by Chicago Daily Law Bulletin; Illinois Super Lawyers (Family Law) 2005. *Member:* Chicago, Illinois State and American (Member, Sections on: Family Law; Litigation) Bar Associations; American Academy of Matrimonial Lawyers. ***REPORTED CASES:*** In re Marriage of Petersen, 744 N.E.2d 877, 319, Ill.App.3d 325, 253 Ill.Dec 144 (1st Dist. 2001). ***Email:*** mtemplin@sdflaw.com

ASSOCIATES

JASON N. SPOSEEP, born Marion, Indiana, November 9, 1977; admitted to bar, 2003, Illinois. *Education:* Indiana University (B.S., 2000); Chicago-Kent College of Law (J.D., 2003). *Member:* Chicago, Illinois State and American Bar Associations. ***Email:*** jsposeep@sdflaw.com

NEAL A. SIMON (Resident, Lake Forest Office)

JENNIFER L. DILLON KOTZ, born Barrington, Illinois, December 17, 1969; admitted to bar, 1998, Illinois. *Education:* Bucknell University (B.A., cum laude, 1992); Pepperdine University; Loyola University (J.D., 1998). Member, Pepperdine Law Review. *Member:* Chicago (Family Law Co-Chairman, Young Lawyers Section), Illinois State and American Bar Associations. ***Email:*** jkotz@sdflaw.com

DEBORAH A. CARDER (Resident, Wheaton Office)

(This Listing Continued)

CLAIRE R. McKENZIE, born Chicago, Illinois, October 24, 1960; admitted to bar, 1991, Illinois; 1992, U.S. District Court, Northern District of Illinois and U.S. Tax Court. *Education:* Northern Illinois University (B.A., cum laude, 1982); Loyola University (J.D., cum laude, 1991). Beta Alpha Psi. Certified Public Accountant, Illinois, 1982. Lecturer: "Tax Tips & Tricks", Illinois Society of Certified Public Accountants and Chicago Bar Association, 1998; "How to Keep Your Clients Out of the Line of Fire," National Association of Enrolled Agents, 1997; "Tax Law Changes & Updates," Chicago Bar Association, 1994 and 1996. *Member:* Chicago (Past Chair, Tax Committee), Illinois State and American Bar Associations; Illinois Society of Certified Public Accountants; American Institute of Certified Public Accountants. ***LANGUAGES:*** Italian. ***Email:*** cmckenzie@sdflaw.com

PATRICK THOMAS RYAN, born Chicago, Illinois, June 27, 1980; admitted to bar, 2005, Illinois. *Education:* University of Illinois (B.A., 2002); DePaul University College of Law (J.D., cum laude, 2005).

JESSICA BANK INTERLANDI, born Charleston, West Virginia, February 7, 1972; admitted to bar, 2001, Illinois. *Education:* Georgetown University (B.A., 1994); Chicago-Kent College of Law (J.D., 2001). Chicago-Kent Moot Court Honor Society. Recipient, Fay Clayton Award for Outstanding Oralist, November 15, 2000, Ninth Annual Ilana Diamond Rovner Appellate Advocacy Competition, Chicago Illinois. Author, "Requests to Admit Facts and For Genuineness of Documents", Illinois State Bar Association Family Law Newsletter, November 2001, Vol. 45. ***Email:*** jbank@sdflaw.com

JOSHUA M. JACKSON, born Burlington, Wisconsin, January 2, 1980; admitted to bar, 2005, Illinois. *Education:* University of Wisconsin (B.A. 2002); DePaul University College of Law (J.D., 2005).

STEWART J. AUSLANDER, born Park Ridge, Illinois, August 31, 1978; admitted to bar, 2003, Illinois. *Education:* University of illinois at Urbana-Champaign (B.S., 2000). *Member:* Chicago, Illinois State and American Bar Associations. ***Email:*** sauslander@sdflaw.com

ELIZABETH A. THEYSSEN, born September 12, 1975; admitted to bar, 2002, Illinois. *Education:* Indiana University (B.A., 1998); Loyola University (J.D., 2001). *Member:* Chicago, Illinois State and American Bar Associations. ***Email:*** etheyssen@sdflaw.com

MARY A. ZAMBRENO (Resident, Lake Forest Office)

MICHELLE A. LAWLESS, born Wichita Falls, Texas, December 9, 1973; admitted to bar, 1999, Illinois. *Education:* Indiana University (B.A., 1996); St. Louis University (J.D., 1999). *Member:* Chicago, Illinois State and American Bar Associations. ***Email:*** mlawless@sdflaw.com

ABIGAIL M. CHIESA (Resident, Wheaton Office)

JAY P. DAHLIN, born Paris, Illinois, January 12, 1976; admitted to bar, 2001, Illinois; 2002, U.S. District Court, Northern District of Illinois. *Education:* University of Illinois (B.A., magna cum laude, 1998); University of Illinois College of Law (J.D., 2001). Lincoln Scholar. James Scholar. Recipient: Rickert Award for Excellence in Oral Advocacy; CALI Award for Outstanding Performance in Estates and Trusts. First Place: University of Illinois Jessup International Moot Court Competition; University of Illinois ABA Negotiation Competition. *Member:* Illinois and American Bar Associations. ***Email:*** jdahlin@sdflaw.com

OF COUNSEL

HAROLD G. FIELD (Resident, Wheaton Office)

ANDREA M. SCHLEIFER & ASSOCIATES, P.C.

20 NORTH CLARK STREET, SUITE 2200
CHICAGO, ILLINOIS 60602
Telephone: 312-673-7373
Fax: 312-236-7660
Email: ams1esq@aol.com

Family Law, Divorce, Parentage, Child Custody, Visitation, Child Support, Contested Paternity, Contested Adoptions, Guardianship, Mediation, Alternative Dispute Resolution, Post Divorce Issues, Buying and Selling a Home, Buying and Selling a Business, Landlord Tenant Agreements and Residential Real Estate.

FIRM PROFILE: Awarded highest rating by peers as reflected in Martindale Hubbell, and named one of Illinois' Super Lawyers.

ANDREA M. SCHLEIFER, born Newark, New Jersey; admitted to bar, 1979, Illinois; U.S. Supreme Court. *Education:* Indiana University (B.A., 1970); Loyola University (J.D., 1979). *Member:* Illinois State Bar Association; Women's Bar Association of Illinois; Decalogue Society of Lawyers. ***PRACTICE AREAS:*** Divorce; Parentage; Child Custody; Visitation; Child Support; Adoption Law; Guardianship; Residential Real Estate. ***Email:*** ams1esq@aol.com

---

LINDA K. SCHNEIDER AND ASSOCIATES

CHICAGO, ILLINOIS

(See Palatine)

Adoption, Child Support, Custody and Visitation, Divorce, Family Law.

SCHOENBERG, FISHER, NEWMAN & ROSENBERG, LTD.

Established in 1946

222 SOUTH RIVERSIDE PLAZA
SUITE 2100
CHICAGO, ILLINOIS 60606-6101
Telephone: 312-648-2300
Fax: 312-648-1212
URL: http://www.sfnr.com

General Business Practice, including Corporate, Litigation, Trade Associations, Independent Manufacturers Representatives, Labor Law, Employee Benefits, Federal, State and Real Estate Taxation, Estate Planning, Probate, Real Estate, Environmental Law, Mergers and Acquisitions, Securities, Banking, Intellectual Property, Bankruptcy, Family Law, Unfair Trade Practices, Legal Ethics and Professional Responsibility.

KENNETH C. PRINCE (1912-2005)

SAMUEL SCHOENBERG (1913-1989)

DAVID L. FISHER (1929-1993)

MELVIN S. NEWMAN, born Chicago, Illinois, February 9, 1936; admitted to bar, 1960, Illinois, U.S. District Court, Northern and Eastern Districts of Illinois, U.S. Court of Appeals, Seventh, Eighth and Eleventh Circuits and U.S. Tax Court. *Education:* University of Illinois, Chicago Campus (B.S., 1957); University of Chicago (J.D., 1959). Certified Public Accountant, Illinois, 1958. *Member:* Chicago, Illinois State and American Bar Associations; The Bar Association of the Seventh Federal Circuit. **Email:** Mel.Newman@SFNR.com

GERALD M. NEWMAN, born Chicago, Illinois, June 29, 1939; admitted to bar, 1964, Illinois, U.S. District Court, Northern District of Illinois; registered to practice before U.S. Patent and Trademark Office. *Education:* University of Illinois (B.S.M.E., 1961); Northwestern University (J.D., 1964). *Member:* Chicago and Illinois State Bar Associations. **Email:** Gerry.Newman@SFNR.com

DANIEL E. BEEDERMAN, born Chicago, Illinois, December 29, 1952; admitted to bar, 1978, Illinois and U.S. District Court, Northern District of Illinois; U.S. Court of Appeals, Seventh Circuit. *Education:* University of Illinois at Chicago (B.A., with honors and distinction, 1975); Spertus College of Judaica (B.J.S., 1975); DePaul University (J.D., 1978). Phi Eta Sigma. *Member:* Chicago, Illinois State and American Bar Associations; Decalogue Society of Lawyers (Member, Board of Managers, 1979—; President, 1984-1985). **Email:** Daniel.Beederman@SFNR.com

ROBERT C. GOLDBERG, born Chicago, Illinois, April 27, 1948; admitted to bar, 1973, Illinois, U.S. District Court, Northern and Southern Districts of Illinois; U.S. Court of Appeals, Fifth, Seventh, Ninth and Eleventh Circuits. *Education:* University of Illinois (B.A., 1970); IIT-Chicago Kent College of Law (J.D., 1973). **Email:** Bob.Goldberg@SFNR.com

RICHARD R. PERLMAN, born Chicago, Illinois, January 29, 1952; admitted to bar, 1976, Illinois and U.S. District Court, Northern District of Illinois; 1983, Massachusetts. *Education:* Northwestern University (B.A., with highest distinction, 1973); Harvard University (J.D., 1976). Phi Beta Kappa; Phi Eta Sigma. *Member:* Chicago, Illinois State and American Bar Associations. ***PRACTICE AREAS:*** Business Law; Employee Benefits; Financing. **Email:** Rick.Perlman@SFNR.com

BRUCE E. BELL, born Chicago, Illinois, January 12, 1957; admitted to bar, 1982, Illinois and U.S. District Court, Northern District of Illinois; 1985, U.S. Tax Court. *Education:* University of Illinois (B.S. in Accounting, 1979); Loyola University (J.D., 1982). Recipient, American Jurisprudence Estate Plan Award. Certified Public Accountant, Illinois, 1979. *Member:* Chicago and Illinois State Bar Associations; Illinois CPA Society; American Institute of CPAs. ***PRACTICE AREAS:*** Corporate Law; Estate Planning Law; ERISA. **Email:** Bruce.Bell@SFNR.com

HERBERT B. ROSENBERG, born Chicago, Illinois, 1941; admitted to bar, 1967, Illinois. *Education:* DePaul University (B.Sc.; J.D.). Former Conferee, Internal Revenue Service. *Member:* Chicago and Illinois State Bar Associations. ***PRACTICE AREAS:*** Corporate; Property Tax; Estate Planning; Real Estate. **Email:** Herb.Rosenberg@SFNR.com

LEONARD J. GAMBINO, born Brooklyn, New York, August 26, 1956; admitted to bar, 1990, Illinois. *Education:* Case Western Reserve University (B.A., magna cum laude, 1979); John Marshall Law School (J.D., with high distinction, 1990). ***PRACTICE AREAS:*** Corporate; Tax; Mergers and Acquisitions. **Email:** Leonard.Gambino@SFNR.com

HENRY A. HAUSER, born St. Paul, Minnesota, February 21, 1945; admitted to bar, 1970, Illinois; 1975, U.S. Supreme Court; 1982, U.S. District Court, Northern District of Illinois. *Education:* College of St. Thomas (B.A., 1967); Loyola University (J.D., 1970). Chief Counsel, Assessor of Cook County, 1988-1995. Chief, Civil Division, Cook County State Attorney's Office, 1985-1986. ***REPORTED CASES:*** Rosewell v. LaSalle National Bank, 405 U.S. 503 (1981). ***PRACTICE AREAS:*** General Commercial Litigation; Real Estate Taxation. **Email:** Henry.Hauser@SFNR.com

ADAM J. GLAZER, born New York, N.Y., July 28, 1964; admitted to bar, 1988, Illinois and U.S. District Court, Northern District of Illinois including Trial Bar; 1990, U.S. Court of Appeals, Seventh Circuit. *Education:* Drew University (B.A., 1985); Northwestern University (J.D., 1988). Adjunct Professor, Trial Advocacy and Business Litigation, Northwestern University, 1998—. *Member:* Chicago and American Bar Associations. ***PRACTICE AREAS:*** Litigation; Business Law. **Email:** Adam.Glazer@SFNR.com

---

EILEEN B. COZZI, born Arlington Heights, Illinois, November 21, 1972; admitted to bar, 1997, Illinois. *Education:* Loyola University (BB.A., magna cum laude, 1994); DePaul University (J.D., 1997). Beta Alpha Psi. Alpha Sigma Nu. Golden Key. ***PRACTICE AREAS:*** Estate Planning; Tax Law. **Email:** Eileen.Cozzi@SFNR.com

DANIEL S. KLAPMAN, born Skokie, Illinois, March 1, 1972; admitted to bar, 1997, Illinois. *Education:* University of Illinois (B.S., 1994); Chicago-Kent College of Law (J.D., 1997). *Member:* Chicago, Illinois State and American Bar Associations. ***PRACTICE AREAS:*** Litigation. **Email:** Dan.Klapman@SFNR.com

DAVID S. MAKARSKI, born Chicago, Illinois, April 14, 1971; admitted to bar, 1996, Illinois; 1997, U.S. District Court, Northern District of Illinois; 1998, U.S. Court of Appeals, Seventh Circuit. *Education:* Northwestern University (B.A., 1993; J.D., 1996). ***PRACTICE AREAS:*** Litigation. **Email:** David.Makarski@SFNR.com

OF COUNSEL

PAUL W. GABLER, born Elgin, Illinois, August 8, 1931; admitted to bar, 1956, Illinois. *Education:* Harvard University (A.B., magna cum laude, 1953); University of Michigan (J.D., 1956). Phi Beta Kappa. Order of the Coif. *Member:* Illinois State and American Bar Associations. **Email:** Paul.Gabler@SFNR.com

(This Listing Continued)

SCHOPF & WEISS LLP

Established in 1987

312 WEST RANDOLPH STREET, SUITE 300
CHICAGO, ILLINOIS 60606-1721
Telephone: 312-701-9300
Fax: 312-701-9335
URL: http://www.sw.com

Business Litigation.

MEMBERS OF FIRM

PETER V. BAUGHER, born Chicago, Illinois, October 2, 1948; admitted to bar, 1974, Illinois; U.S. District Court, Central and Northern Districts of Illinois including trial bar and U.S. Court of Appeals, Seventh, Second and Eleventh Circuits; 1984, U.S. Court of International Trade; 1987, U.S. Supreme Court. *Education:* Princeton University (A.B., 1970); Yale University (J.D., 1973). Woodrow Wilson School Scholar. Law Clerk to Hon. Philip W. Tone, U.S. Court of Appeals for the Seventh Circuit, 1973-1974. President, Chicago International Dispute Resolution Association. Member, Advisory Committee, Northwestern Law School Center for International Rights. Co-Author: "A Trial Lawyer's Guide to Discovery in Federal and State Courts in Illinois" (1997, 2003); "Litigation Risk & Opportunity in the United States," (2003); "A Guide to Transnational Litigation," ABA International Litigation Quarterly, Vol. 13, No. 2, June 1997; "A New Way to Resolve International Disputes in Illinois," 88 Ill. Bar Journal 582, Oct. 2000. President, Chicago International Dispute Resolution Association. Arbitrator: National Association of Securities Dealers, National Futures Association. Past Chair, Chicago Bar Association Committee on International and Foreign Law and Chicago Bar Association Committee on Federal Civil Practice. *Member:* American Bar Association (Member, Sections on: Litigation; International Practice; Antitrust); American Law Institute; Chicago Lincoln Inn of Court (Past President).

IAN H. FISHER, born San Bernardino, California, June 27, 1969; admitted to bar, 1994, Illinois and U.S. District Court, Northern District of Illinois, including Trial Bar; 1998, U.S. District Court, Eastern District of Wisconsin; 2000, U.S. Supreme Court; 2005, U.S. Court of Appeals, Eighth Circuit. *Education:* The London School of Economics and Political Science (General Course, 1990); Grinnell College (B.A., honors, 1991); Northwestern University (J.D., cum laude, 1994). Phi Beta Kappa. Member, Mortar Board, Inc. *Member:* Chicago Bar Association (Chair, Federal Civil Practice Committee; Member, Commercial Litigation Committee); Illinois State Bar Association; American Bar Association (Co-Editor of ABA's Pretrial Practice & Discovery Newsletter; Co-Editor, ABA Business Torts Model Jury Instructions). ***PRACTICE AREAS:*** Commercial Litigation; Employment Litigation. **Email:** fisher@sw.com

TODD H. FLAMING, born Milwaukee, Wisconsin, August 31, 1966; admitted to bar, 1993, Illinois and U.S. District Court, Northern District of Illinois including Trial Bar; 2000, U.S. District Court, Eastern District of Michigan. *Education:* Loyola Marymount University (B.A., magna cum laude, 1988); University of Chicago (J.D., 1993). Member: University of Chicago Law Review, 1991-1993; University of Chicago Law School Roundtable, 1993. Board of Directors of Illinois Legal Aid Online, 2005. Adjunct Professor, Technology in the Practice of and Cyberspace Law, John Marshall Law School. Publications: Editor and Chapter Author: "Discovery in Federal and State Courts in Illinois" (2003); "A Lawyer's Guide to Using Computers," ISBA, 2000; "Survey of Illinois Law: Legal Technology," 24 S.Ill.U.L.J. 915 (2000); "Using Computers in Litigation, Business and Commercial Litigation," IICLE, 1999; "The Rules of Cyberspace: Informal Law in a New Jurisdiction," 85 Illinois Bar Journal 174, 1997; "The National Stolen Property Act and Computer Files: A New Form of Property, a New Form of Theft," U. Chi. L. Sch. Roundtable 255, 1993; "Laundering Illegally Seized Evidence Through the Federal Sentencing Guidelines," 59 U. Chi. L. Rev. 1209, 1992. Co-Author: "1998 Survey of Legal Technology," 23 S. Ill. U. L.J., 1183 (1999). Speaking Engagement and Television Appearances: First Business, NBC Nightly News; "Talk America," Radio program; "Tune In, Turn On, But Don't Drop Out," ISBA Annual Meeting, 1999; "The New Frontier: Schools, The Internet, and Liability," Illinois State Board of Education, 1999. Panelist, "Year 2000 Liability," You and The Law, CBA TV, 1999; "Anatomy of a Lawsuit," Independent Computer Consultants Association, 1998; "How to Evaluate Your Law Office for Y2K Problems," ISBA Mutual Insurance Company, 1998; "New Liability Risks: The Internet and Schools," ISBE, 1998; "Secrets of the Internet," Dupage Association of Women Lawyers, 1998; "Copyright Law," Illinois Law: Legal News You Can Use, ISBA TV, 1997; "What Lawyers Should Know About the Internet," ISBA Annual Meeting, 1997; "Tax Research and the Internet," Iowa State Bar Association, Spring Tax Institute, 1997; "Effective Discovery of Computer Stored Information," ILCLE, 1997; "The Internet for Judges," Illinois Judges Association Annual Meeting, 1996; "Electronic Lawyering," ISBA Annual Meeting, 1995. Chair, Committee on Legal Technology, Illinois State Bar Association, 1998-1999. *Member:* Illinois State (Chair, Committee on Legal Technology) and American (Co-Chair, Section of Litigation's Technology for the Litigator Committee; Web Site Editor, Business Torts Committee) Bar Associations.

(This Listing Continued)

SCHOPF & WEISS LLP, Chicago—Continued

VERÓNICA GÓMEZ, born Chicago, Illinois, July 25, 1969; admitted to bar, 1994, Illinois and U.S. District Court, Northern District of Illinois including Trial Bar; 1996, U.S. District Court, Eastern District of Wisconsin; U.S. Court of Appeals for the Seventh and Eleventh Circuits; 2001, U.S. District Court, Eastern District of Michigan and U.S. District Court, Southern District of Illinois; 2004, U.S. District Court, Northern District of Indiana. *Education:* Stanford University (A.B., with Departmental Honors, 1991); University of Chicago (J.D., 1994). *Member:* Chicago and American (Chair, Subcommittee on Membership & Diversity for the Technology for the Litigator Committee; Co-editor, "Expert Witnesses" Newsletter") Bar Association; Hispanic National Bar Association; Hispanic Lawyers Association of Illinois.

PATRICK J. HENEGHAN, born Chicago, Illinois, November 20, 1957; admitted to bar, 1983, Illinois; U.S. District Court, Northern District of Illinois and U.S. Court of Appeals, Third, Fifth, Seventh and Eleventh Circuits. *Education:* DePaul University; Southern Illinois University (B.S., 1980); Catholic University of America (J.D., 1983). Member, National Moot Court Team, 1981. Winner of the Sutherland Cup; Miller Cup; Bamberger Cup; Washington Regional ABA Moot Court Competitions. Member, 1981-1982 and Associate Editor, 1982-1983, Catholic University Law Review. Law Clerk to: Hon. Jerre S. Williams, U.S. Court of Appeals, Fifth Circuit 1984-1985; Hon. Robert L. Vining, U.S. District Court, Northern District of Georgia, 1983-1984. *Member:* American Bar Association (Member, Sections on: Litigation; Antitrust).

ARTHUR J. HOWE, born New Orleans, Louisiana, April 17, 1960; admitted to bar, 1985, Illinois; U.S. District Court, Central and Southern Districts of Illinois; U.S. District Court, Northern District of Illinois including Trial Bar; U.S. Court of Appeals, Fifth, Seventh, Ninth, Tenth and Eleventh Circuits; U.S. District Court, Northern District of Indiana; U.S. District Court, Western District of Michigan; U.S. District Court, District of Minnesota; U.S. District Court, Eastern District of Wisconsin. *Education:* London School of Economics, London, England; Wabash College (B.A., summa cum laude, 1982); Duke Law School (J.D., with honors, 1985). Phi Beta Kappa; Order of the Coif. Lilly Scholar. William Neal Reynolds Scholar. Member, Duke Law Journal, 1983-1985. Law Clerk to the Hon. Jesse E. Eschbach, U.S. Court of Appeals, Seventh Circuit, 1985-1986. *Member:* Chicago (Chair, Federal Civil Procedure Committee, 1994-1995), Illinois State and American Bar Associations; Chicago Council of Lawyers.

KENNETH E. KRAUS, born Chicago, Illinois, November 11, 1956; admitted to bar, 1986, Wisconsin, Illinois, U.S. District Court, Western District of Wisconsin, U.S. District Court, Eastern District of Michigan and U.S. District Court, Southern District of Illinois; U.S. District Court, Northern District of Illinois including Trial Bar; U.S. Court of Appeals, Seventh and Eleventh Circuits. *Education:* Ohio State University (B.A., 1981); University of Wisconsin (J.D., cum laude, 1986). Member, 1984-1985 and Editor-in-Chief, 1985-1986, Wisconsin Law Review. Adjunct Professor, Mass Media Law, De Paul College of Law, 1992—. Author: "Enforcement of Foreign Media Judgments in the Aftermath of Gutnick v. Dow Jones," 21 Communications Lawyer 1 (Spring 2003). *Member:* American Bar Association (Member, Forum on Communications Law).

PAULA E. LITT, born Cleveland, Ohio, December 17, 1952; admitted to bar, 1984, Illinois and U.S. District Court, Northern District of Illinois including trial bar; U.S. Court of Appeals, Fifth, Seventh, Eighth and Tenth Circuits. *Education:* Ohio State University (B.S., summa cum laude, 1973); University of Chicago (M.A., 1975); Harvard Law School (J.D., 1984). Author: "Securing Insurance Coverage for Your Corporate Client," *For the Defense* (2002).

JOSE A. LOPEZ, born Lockhart, Texas, February 8, 1970; admitted to bar, 1995, Illinois, U.S. District Court, Northern District of Illinois, including Trial Bar; U.S. Court of Appeals, Seventh and Eighth Circuits. *Education:* DePaul University (B.A., 1992); Northwestern University (J.D., 1995). Law Clerk, Honorable Morton Denlow, 1996-1997. Assistant State's Attorney, Cook County, 1997-1999. U.S Securities and Exchange Commission, Senior Attorney, Division of Enforcement, 1999-2000. *Member:* Chicago, Illinois State and American Bar Associations. ***PRACTICE AREAS:*** Commercial Litigation; Securities Litigation.

BRADLEY P. NELSON, born Green Bay, Wisconsin, September 17, 1960; admitted to bar, 1986, Wisconsin, Illinois and U.S. District Court, Western District of Wisconsin; 1987, U.S. District Court, Northern District of Illinois including trial bar; 1995, U.S. District Court, Eastern District of Michigan; U.S. District Court, Western District of Wisconsin; U.S. Court of Appeals, Seventh and Eighth Circuits. *Education:* University of Wisconsin-Oshkosh (B.S., summa cum laude, 1983); University of Wisconsin-Madison (J.D., cum laude, 1986). Order of the Coif. Articles Editor, Wisconsin Law Review, 1985-1986. *Member:* American Bar Association (Member: Professional Liability Committee; Business Torts Litigation Committee; Co-Editor ABA Business Torts Model Jury Instructions).

ROBERT J. PALMERSHEIM, born Milwaukee, Wisconsin, November 12, 1968; admitted to bar, 1996, Illinois, U.S. District Court, Central District of Illinois and U.S. District Court, Northern District of Illinois including Trial Bar; 1997, U.S. District Court, Eastern and Western Districts of Wisconsin; 1999, U.S. Court of Appeals, Seventh Circuit. *Education:* University of Wisconsin-Madison (B.A., 1990); DePaul University (J.D., with highest honors, 1996). Member: Order of the Coif; National Moot Court Team (Seventh Circuit Region Champion). Recipient, American Jurisprudence Awards: Evidence, Sales, Wills and Trusts, and Constitutional Law. Recipient, CALI Awards: Appellate Technique; Advanced Civil Litigation. *Member:* Chicago and American Bar Associations. ***PRACTICE AREAS:*** Commercial Litigation.

JASON M. ROSENTHAL, born Highland Park, Illinois, November 14, 1972; admitted to bar, 1997, Illinois, U.S. District Court, Northern and Central Districts of Illinois including Trial Bar; 1998, U.S. Court of Appeals, Seventh Circuit. *Education:* University of London, London, England (International Business, 1993); Indiana University (B.S. in Finance, 1994); Chicago-Kent College of Law, Illinois Institute of Technology (J.D., with highest honors, 1997). Order of the Coif. Notes and Comments Editor, Chicago-Kent Law Review, 1996-1997. Recipient: Ramsey-Burke Academic Scholarship, 1995-1997; American Jurisprudence Award, Trial Advocacy. Author of numerous published articles. *Member:* American Bar Association. ***PRACTICE AREAS:*** Business Litigation.

(This Listing Continued)

WILLIAM G. SCHOPF, born Michigan, September 7, 1948; admitted to bar, 1973, Illinois and U.S. District Court, Northern District of Illinois including trial bar; 1977, U.S. Supreme Court; 1989, Texas; 1995, U.S. District Court, Southern District of Texas; 1998, U.S. District Court, Eastern District of Texas; 2001, U.S. District Court, Southern District of Illinois; 2005, U.S. District Court, Western District of Michigan; U.S. Court of Appeals, Third, Fifth, Seventh, Eighth, Tenth and Eleventh Circuits. *Education:* Princeton University (A.B., 1970); Cornell University (J.D., 1973). Co-Author: "Litigation Risk and Opportunity in the United States," (2003); *Money In The Bank,* Dow Jones/BAI, 1988; "*Liquid Air v. Bridges:* A Plaintiff's Perspective on a Civil RICO Jury Trial," Rico Law Developments, 1986; "Discovery In Federal and State Courts In Illinois," Chicago Spectrum Press 1997.

STEVEN A. WEISS, born New York, N.Y., April 7, 1955; admitted to bar, 1980, Illinois and U.S. District Court, Northern District of Illinois including trial bar; 1988, U.S. Court of Appeals, Seventh Circuit; 1989, Texas; 1998, U.S. Supreme Court. *Education:* Cornell University (B.A., cum laude, 1977); University of Michigan (J.D., cum laude, 1980). Author: "Non-competes and Trade Secrets in a High Tech E-World," program materials for ABA presentation (Spring 2005); "Sanctions for Spoliation of Electronic Evidence," ABA Pretrial Practice Newsletter (Spring 2005); "Litigate or Arbitrate—Which Road to Choose," ABA Business Litigation Newsletter (Summer 2004); "Cost-Shifting for Electronic Evidence," ABA Technology for Litigator Newsletter (Spring 2004); "Joint Defense Agreements and Privileges," For the Defense Vol. 43 No. 12 (December 2001); "Alternative Dispute Resolution: A Lawyer's Perspective," Business Law Today, 1999; "Modification of Employment Restrictive Covenants," Illinois Bar Journal (1994). Co-Author: "A Trial Lawyer's Guide to Discovery in Federal and State Courts in Illinois," (2003, 1999, 1997). Speaker: "Non-Competes and Trade Secrets," ABA Litigation Annual Meeting (2005); "Electronic Discovery," CBA Federal Trial Bar (2005); "Misappropriation under the Trade Secrets Act," Law Seminar Institute (2004); "Electronic Document Preservation and Spoliation," Illinois CPA Society (2004); "Cost Shifting and Sanctions in E-Discovery," ABA Litigation Annual Meeting (2004); "Electronic Discovery," CBA Federal Trial Bar (2004); "Recent Developments in Trade Secrets Law," Law Seminar Institute 2003); "Intellectual Property Litigation," ABA Litigation Annual Meeting (1999,1998). *Member:* American Bar Association (Co-Chair, Section of Litigation Commercial and Business Litigation Committee; Past Co-chair, Technology Litigation Committee, Past Co-Chair, Internet Litigation Subcommittee of the Commercial and Business Litigation Committee).

ASSOCIATES

WILLIAM B. BERNDT, born Minneapolis, Minnesota, August 15, 1974; admitted to bar, 1999, Illinois and U.S. District Court, Northern District of Illinois including Trial Bar; 2000, U.S. Court of Appeals, Seventh Circuit; 2002, U.S. Court of Appeals, Third Circuit; 2003, U.S. District Court, Central District of Illinois. *Education:* Indiana University (B.A., magna cum laude, 1996); University of Michigan Law School (J.D., cum laude, 1999). ***PRACTICE AREAS:*** Litigation.

MARCUS D. FRUCHTER, born Chicago, Illinois, January 29, 1974; admitted to bar, 2004, Illinois and U.S. District Court, Northern District of Illinois. *Education:* Michigan State University (B.A., with honor, 1996); University of Chicago Law School (J.D., 2004). ***Email:*** fruchter@sw.com

ANNA EISNER SEDER, born Chicago, Illinois, May 31, 1974; admitted to bar, 2001, Illinois. *Education:* University of Illinois (B.A., 1996); Georgetown University (J.D., 2001).

AUTUMN L. SHARP, born San Rafael, California, October 5, 1976; admitted to bar, 2003, Ohio (Not admitted in Illinois). *Education:* Ohio University (B.S., summa cum laude, 1998); University of Virginia School of Law (J.D., 2003).

JENNIFER A. WATERS, born Oakville, Ontario, Canada, March 30, 1976; admitted to bar, 2002, Illinois. *Education:* Princeton University (A.B., 1998); Northwestern University School of Law (J.D., 2002). Dean's List. *Member:* Chicago, Illinois State and American (Member, Litigation Section) Bar Associations. ***PRACTICE AREAS:*** Business Litigation; Environmental Law.

COUNSEL

ELLEN S. MARTIN, born Pittsburgh, Pennsylvania, November 25, 1956; admitted to bar, 1989, Illinois. *Education:* University of Chicago (B.A., 1978); ITT Chicago Kent College of Law (J.D., with high honors, 1989). Order of the Coif. *Member:* Chicago, Illinois State and American Bar Associations; Women's Bar Association of Illinois. ***PRACTICE AREAS:*** Commercial Litigation.

RANA H. JANNEY, born Harvey, Illinois, February 19, 1974; admitted to bar, 2000, Illinois. *Education:* Northwestern University (B.A., 1996); Chicago-Kent College of Law, Illinois Institute of Technology (J.D., 2000). *Member:* American Bar Association. ***PRACTICE AREAS:*** Business Litigation.

KRISTEN N. PATE, born Jackson, Mississippi, May 15, 1976; admitted to bar, 2001, Louisiana; 2003, Illinois. *Education:* Louisiana State University (B.A., 1997; J.D., 2001). Former Member, Board of Directors, Childrens Bureau of Louisiana. *Member:* Louisiana State, Illinois State, Federal and American Bar Associations. ***PRACTICE AREAS:*** Commercial Litigation; Business Litigation; Securities Fraud; Class Actions; General Litigation.

SCHUELER, DALLAVO & CASIERI

233 SOUTH WACKER DRIVE, SUITE 6150
CHICAGO, ILLINOIS 60606
Telephone: 312-831-1099
Facsimile: 312-831-4144

Medical Malpractice, Products Liability, Directors and Officers Liability, Employment Law and Errors and Omissions.

FIRM PROFILE: Schueler, Dallavo & Casieri, is House Counsel for Chubb & Son, a division of Federal Insurance Company. In our practice we represent the interests of Chubb insureds in matters in litigation in Federal and State courts and agencies.

(This Listing Continued)

MATTHEW J. SCHUELER, born Oak Park, Illinois, September 13, 1960; admitted to bar, 1989, Illinois and U.S. District Court, Northern District of Illinois, 2002, U.S. District Court, Central District of Illinois. *Education:* Western Illinois University (B.S., with honors, 1982); Loyola University (J.D., 1989). Member, Trial Lawyers Club of Chicago. *Member:* Chicago, Illinois State and American Bar Associations; Defense Research Institute; Society of Trial Lawyers.

CHRISTOPHER J. DALLAVO, born Dearborn, Michigan, December 5, 1966; admitted to bar, 1992, Illinois and U.S. District Court, Northern District of Illinois; 1993, U.S. Court of Appeals, Seventh Circuit; 1999, U.S. District Court, Central District of Illinois. *Education:* University of Notre Dame (B.A., 1989); Loyola University (J.D., 1992). *Member:* Chicago and American Bar Associations.

VINCENT M. CASIERI, born Bronx, New York, June 11, 1966; admitted to bar, 1992, Illinois; 1994, U.S. District Court, Northern District of Illinois; 2000, Federal Trial Bar; 2001, Wisconsin; 2003, U.S. District Court, Central District of Illinois. *Education:* Johns Hopkins University (B.A., 1988); Loyola University School of Law (J.D., 1992). *Member:* Chicago and Illinois State Bar Associations; Illinois Association of Defense Counsel; Defense Research Institute.

KATHERINE ANN RODOSKY, born Evanston, IL March 15, 1967; admitted to bar, 1992, Pennsylvania; 1994, Illinois and U.S. District Court, Northern District of Illinois; U.S. Court of Appeals, Fifth and Seventh Circuits. *Education:* University of Colorado, Boulder, (BA, 1989); Penn State University Dickinson School of Law (JD, 1992); Georgetown University (LL.M., Constitutional and Civil Rights, with high honors, 1994). *Member:* Chicago Bar Association; Illinois Trial Lawyers Association.

MARK T. McANDREW, born Evergreen Park, Illinois, December 20, 1969; admitted to bar, 2001, Illinois and U.S. District Court, Northern District of Illinois. *Education:* University of Iowa (B.B.A., 1992); John Marshall law School (J.D., 2001).

SHIRLEY A. IRWIN, born St. Joseph, Missouri, July 28, 1966; admitted to bar, 1996, Tennessee; 1999, Illinois and U.S. District Court, Northern District of Illinois. *Education:* Rhodes College (B.A., 1988); University of Nottingham, Nottingham, England (LL.M. International Law, 1991); University of Memphis (J.D., 1995). Member, University of Memphis Law Review, 1993-1995. Best Oral Advocate, Philip C. Jessup International Law Moot Court Competition, 1994; United States Northwest Regional National Competition. Author: "Glass v. City of Chattanooga: The Abolishment of the Fellow - Servant Doctrine in Tennessee," University of Memphis Law Review, Vol. 25, Fall, 1994. ***REPORTED CASES:*** Seffernick v. Saint Thomas Hospital, 969 S.W.2d 391 (Tenn. 1998).

JENNIFER J. McFADDEN, born Chicago, Illinois, March 22, 1976; admitted to bar, 2001, Illinois and U.S. District Court, Northern District of Illinois. *Education:* Boston College (B.A., 1998); Loyola University (J.D., 2001). *Member:* Chicago and Illinois Bar Associations.

WILLIAM G. SCHUR

Established in 1981

111 WEST WASHINGTON STREET - SUITE 737
CHICAGO, ILLINOIS 60602
Telephone: 312-853-0156
FAX: 312-853-0158
Email: wgs1972@aol.com
URL: http://www.lawyers.com/schur

Commercial and Civil Litigation. Commercial Collection. Enforcement of Foreign Judgments. Real Estate.

FIRM PROFILE: The law firm of William G. Schur receives matters from lawyers and clients across the country and around the world. We respond quickly and thoroughly to the needs of out-of-town counsel and clients. We are the Chicago counsel of choice for many law firms whose clients have commercial collection and litigation problems.

WILLIAM G. SCHUR, born Cleveland, Ohio, April 26, 1950; admitted to bar, 1975, Illinois and U.S. District Court, Northern District of Illinois; 1978, U.S. Court of Appeals, Seventh Circuit. *Education:* Dartmouth College (A.B., magna cum laude, 1972); Cornell University (J.D., 1975). Phi Beta Kappa; Phi Delta Phi. Member, Board of Directors and Treasurer, 2400 North Lakeview Condominium Association, Chicago, Illinois, 1983-1986. Dartmouth College Alumni Council, 1999-2002. Pro Bono Counsel, Chicago Jaycees. *Member:* Chicago, Illinois State and American Bar Associations; Commercial Law League of America; Decalogue Society. ***REPORTED CASES:*** Kimco Corporation v. Murdoch, Coll and Lillibridge, Inc., 313 Ill. App. 3d 768, N.E.2d 1143, 246 Ill. Dec. 678; Armando Susmano, M.D. v. Associated Internists of Chicago, Ltd., 97 Ill. App. 3d 215, 422 N.E.2d 879, 52 Ill. Dec. 670; Rhea Coleman v. Paul Coleman, 66 Ill. App. 3d 694, 384 N.E.2d 116, 23 Ill. Dec. 480; Northlake Community Hospital v. Dr. Lawrence M. Cadkin, 55 Ill. App. 3d 344, 370 N.E.2d 1094, 13 Ill. Dec. 67. ***PRACTICE AREAS:*** Commercial Litigation; Civil Litigation; Commercial Collections; Enforcement of Foreign Judgments; Real Estate.

REPRESENTATIVE CLIENTS: The Northern Trust Co.; Bank of New York; Northwest Airlines; Clever Ideas, Inc.; Northwest Airlines Employees Credit Union; State of New York; Anspach Travel Bureau, Inc.; Studio 676, Inc. Group, Inc.; Storage Networks, Inc.; Bank One of Arizona; Abrams, Jossel and Knopfler, LLC; CBS, Inc.; The Amend Group; Ron Stonitsch Construction, Inc.; W.W. Grainger, Inc.; Empire Kosher Poultry, Inc.; Gulf States Paper Corporation; Crown Sportswear, Inc.; State Farm North Central Federal Credit Union; Veterinary Medicine Publishing Group; Houles, U.S.A., Inc.; Corporate Legal Times; Travelers Insurance Co.; Kimco Metal Systems, Inc.; Glenn Rieder, Inc.; Glidden Paint Company; American Express Company; Weigel Broadcasting Company; West Publishing Company; Midwest Mills, Inc.; Viacom International, Inc.; Aramark Uniform Services, Inc.; Southwest Airlines; United Airlines; Reynolds Aluimum Supply Company; Federal Express; Hilco Receivables, LLC.; Vulcan Material Company; Consolidated Freightway, Inc.; Aramark, Inc.; Robert Half International, Inc.; Nike USA, Inc.; Woman's Clinic; Clear Channel Communications; Kirk-Brummel, Inc.; Go Member, Inc.

SCHUYLER, ROCHE & ZWIRNER

A PROFESSIONAL CORPORATION

ONE PRUDENTIAL PLAZA, SUITE 3800
130 EAST RANDOLPH STREET
CHICAGO, ILLINOIS 60601
Telephone: 312-565-2400
Facsimile: 312-565-8300
URL: http://www.srzlaw.com

Evanston, Illinois Office: Suite 2050, 1603 Orrington Avenue. Telephone: 312-565-2400.

Business Enterprise: Closely Held Businesses, International Business Transactions, Structured Finance and Asset Securitization, Corporate and Personal Taxation, Employment and Benefits, Technology Startups and E-Commerce, Real Estate. Business Litigation: Securities and Commodities Litigation, Commercial and Employment Litigation, Labor Arbitration and Litigation, Professional Liability Litigation, Intellectual Property Litigation, Construction Contracts and Litigation. Estate Management: Estate Planning and Administration, Trusts, Probate and Trust Litigation, Estate and Transfer Taxation, Wealth and Health Planning.

FIRM PROFILE: Schuyler, Roche & Zwirner, a P.C., is one of the oldest law firms in Chicago. Our roots extend to the nineteenth century, but our midsize status endures by design, better enabling us to retain quality attorneys intent on partnering with clients and colleagues to achieve representation that is not only effective, but also cost-efficient.

Our concentration on closely held businesses and other startups has helped loyal clients to thrive and to enter the international marketplace; our services in asset securitization and structured finance are firmly established; and our expertise in taxation, employment, technology and real estate benefits both private individuals and companies. Equally important, our hard-won reputation for aggressive business defense litigation is a matter of public record, and our estate management team is unrivaled, we think, in planning for wealth and in bridging generations.

We also have an office in Evanston that serves Chicago's north suburban communities and concentrates on fostering and maintaining the close personal contact that clients value and have the right to expect.

SHAREHOLDERS

MICHAEL B. ROCHE, born Chicago, Illinois, December 15, 1941; admitted to bar, 1966, Illinois; 1967, U.S. District Court, Northern District of Illinois, Trial Bar, 1982 and U.S. Court of Appeals, Seventh Circuit; 1980, U.S. Supreme Court; 1984, U.S. District Court, Northern District of Indiana; 1994, U.S. District Court, Eastern District of Wisconsin. *Education:* University of Notre Dame (A.B., 1963; J.D., 1966). Staff Member, Notre Dame Lawyer, 1965-1966. Author: "The Plight of the Sexual Psychopath: A Legislative Blunder and Judicial Acquiescence," and "Ethical Problems Raised by The Neighborhood Law Office," Notre Dame Lawyer, 1966. Co-Author: "Securities Law: Seventh Circuit Review of Remedies, Definitions, Standing and Sanctions," Chicago-Kent Law Review, 1979. Arbitrator: National Association of Securities Dealers, 1988—; National Futures Association, 1988—; New York Stock Exchange, Inc., 1988—. *Member:* Chicago, Illinois State and American Bar Associations. ***REPORTED CASES:*** Elton Chaney and Amalgamated Transit Union, Local 1028, AFL-CIO v. Suburban Bus Division of the Regional Transportation Authority, d/b/a Pace Northwest Division, and Brett Burkhardt, Regional Manager, 52 F.3d 623 (7th Cir. 1995); Hard Rock Cafe Licensing Corporation, a New York Corporation v. Concession Services, Incorporated, 955 F.2d 1143 (7th Cir. 1992); Lawson Products, Inc., et al v. Avnet, Inc., 782 F.2d 1429 (7th Cir. 1986); Ellis v. City of Chicago, 272 F.Supp.2d 729 (N.D.Ill. 2003); Alfred N. Koplin v. Labe Federal Savings and Loan Association, 748 F.Supp. 1336 (N.D.Ill. 1990); Hyatt International Corporation v. Inversiones Los Jabillos, et al, 558 F.Supp. 932 (N.D. Ill. 1982); Winterland Concessions Company, d/b/a Winterland Productions, Raindrop Products, Inc., d/b/a Rolling Stones, et al v. Sileo, et al, 528 F.Supp. 1201 (N.D. Ill. 1981); Schaefer, et al v. First National Bank of Lincolnwood, et al, 509 F.2d 1287 (7th Cir. 1975); Forkin v. PaineWebber Incorporated, [1988-1989 Transfer Binder] Fed.Sec.L.Rep. (CCH) 97, 94, 128 and 129 (C.D. Ill. 1988); Geldermann, et al v. Stathis, et al, 177 Ill.App.3d 414, 532 N.E. 2d 366 (1st Dist. 1988). ***PRACTICE AREAS:*** Securities; Employment Law; Commercial Litigation; Business Law; Business Litigation. ***Email:*** mroche@srzlaw.com

RICHARD T. ZWIRNER, born Mt. Kisco, New York, July 8, 1943; admitted to bar, 1968, Illinois and U.S. District Court, Northern District of Illinois; 1973, U.S. Court of Appeals, Seventh Circuit; 1988, U.S. Court of Appeals for the Federal Circuit. *Education:* University of Michigan (B.A., 1965); Northwestern University (J.D., 1968). *Member:* Chicago, Illinois State and American (Member, Sections on: Antitrust Law; Corporation, Banking and Business Law; International Law and Practice; Patent, Trademark and Copyright Law) Bar Associations. ***LANGUAGES:*** French. ***PRACTICE AREAS:*** General Corporate; International Business Transactions. ***Email:*** zwirner@srzlaw.com

RALPH E. BROWN, born Chicago, Illinois, March 21, 1929; admitted to bar, 1956, Illinois; U.S. District Court, Northern District of Illinois including Trial Bar and Eastern District of Wisconsin; U.S. Court of Appeals, Sixth and Seventh Circuits; U.S. Supreme Court. *Education:* University of Illinois (B.S., 1949); University of Chicago (J.D., 1953). *Member:* Chicago and American Bar Associations; Chicago Council of Lawyers. ***PRACTICE AREAS:*** Corporate Litigation; Defense of Business Offenses; Business Enterprises. ***Email:*** rbrown@srzlaw.com

EDWARD J. COPELAND, admitted to bar, 1959, Illinois; 1981, New York. *Education:* Carleton College (B.A., 1955); University of London, London, England (Certificate, 1957); Northwestern University (J.D., 1958). Member, House of Representatives, Illinois General Assembly, 1967-1971. Chairman, Bank of the North Shore, Northbrook, Illinois, 1976-1981. Chairman, Board of Education, State of Illinois, 1981-1983. Member, State of Illinois Board of Education, 1974-1983. *Member:* Chicago, Illinois State and American Bar Associations. ***PRACTICE AREAS:*** Real Estate; Business Transactions; School Law. ***Email:*** ecopeland@srzlaw.com

(This Listing Continued)

SCHUYLER, ROCHE & ZWIRNER, A PROFESSIONAL CORPORATION, Chicago—Continued

HARRY C. BENFORD III, born Johnstown, Pennsylvania, April 26, 1937; admitted to bar, 1963, Illinois. *Education:* University of Pittsburgh (B.A., cum laude, 1958); Harvard University (LL.B., 1961). Pi Sigma Alpha. *Member:* Chicago (Member, Probate Practice and Elder Law Committees) and Illinois State Bar Associations; Chicago Estate Planning Council. [Lt. Col. (Ret.), U.S. Army Reserve, 1961-1984]. ***PRACTICE AREAS:*** Estate and Trust Administration; Trust and Estate Related Litigation; Estate Planning; Business Enterprises. ***Email:*** hbenford@srzlaw.com

JOSEPH J. STEVENS, born Chicago, Illinois, October 10, 1935; admitted to bar, 1964, Illinois. *Education:* St. Mary of the Lake Seminary (B.A., 1957); DePaul University (B.A., 1961; J.D., 1964). ***PRACTICE AREAS:*** Labor Law; Business Enterprises; Business Litigation. ***Email:*** jstevens@srzlaw.com

ROBERT A. MICHALAK, born Chicago, Illinois, October 28, 1945; admitted to bar, 1970, Illinois and U.S. District Court, Northeastern District of Illinois; 1973, U.S. Tax Court; 1978, U.S. Supreme Court. *Education:* University of Notre Dame (B.B.A., 1967); Loyola University (J.D., 1970). Certified Public Accountant, Illinois, 1972. *Member:* Chicago (Member, Committees on: Federal Taxation; Employee Benefits; Corporation Law), Illinois State (Member, Employee Benefits Section Council and Federal Taxation Section) and American (Member, Section of Taxation) Bar Associations; American Association of Attorney-Certified Public Accountants; Illinois Certified Public Accountant Society (Member, Federal Taxation Section). [Illinois National Guard, 1970-1976]. ***PRACTICE AREAS:*** Tax Law; Employee Benefits; General Corporate; Business Enterprises. ***Email:*** rmichalak@srzlaw.com

DAVID M. ALLEN, born Ithaca, New York, September 15, 1946; admitted to bar, 1972, Illinois and U.S. District Court, Northern District of Illinois; 1985, Trial Bar; 1980, U.S. Court of Appeals, Seventh Circuit; 1990, U.S. Supreme Court; 2000, U.S. Court of Appeals, Third Circuit. *Education:* Williams College (B.A., magna cum laude, 1968); University of Chicago (J.D., 1972). Phi Beta Kappa. Member, Panel of Arbitrators (Commercial Disputes), American Arbitration Association. *Member:* Chicago, Illinois State and American (Member, Sections on: Litigation; Health Care Law; Real Property, Probate and Trust Law) Bar Associations. ***PRACTICE AREAS:*** Commercial Litigation; Health Care Law; Estate and Trust Litigation; Business Enterprises. ***Email:*** dallen@srzlaw.com

ERNEST W. IRONS, born Chicago, Illinois, May 30, 1949; admitted to bar, 1976, Illinois and U.S. District Court, Northern District of Illinois including Trial Bar; 1991, U.S. District Court, Central District of Illinois and U.S. Court of Appeals, 7th Circuit; 1996, New York. *Education:* Wabash College (B.A., 1970); University of Michigan; Washington University (J.D., 1976). Associate Editor, Washington University Law Quarterly, 1975-1976. *Member:* American Bar Association; Lawyers Club of Chicago. ***PRACTICE AREAS:*** Securities Litigation; Employment Litigation; Business Law. ***Email:*** eirons@srzlaw.com

ALISON BARKLEY, born Chicago, Illinois, August 8, 1949; admitted to bar, 1977, Illinois. *Education:* Thornton Community College (A.A., 1969); University of Illinois (B.S., 1971); DePaul University (J.D., cum laude, 1976). *Member:* Illinois State and American Bar Associations. ***PRACTICE AREAS:*** General Corporate; Estates and Trusts; Estate Management; Estate Planning and Administration; Trusts; Wealth Planning; Health Planning; Business Enterprises. ***Email:*** abarkley@srzlaw.com

CHARLES H. COLE, born Chicago, Illinois, June 1, 1952; admitted to bar, 1977, Illinois and U.S. District Court, Northern District of Illinois including Trial Bar. *Education:* Illinois Institute of Technology (B.S., with honors, 1974); John Marshall Law School (J.D., with honors, 1977). Editor in Chief, John Marshall Journal of Practice and Procedure, 1976-1977. Author: "Developments in Property Damage Coverage Issues, an Examination of an Occurrence," IDC Quarterly, Third Quarter, 1992; "Fear of Future Harm: Stating A Claim for Damages," IDC Quarterly, Second Quarter, 1995. Columnist, Professional Liability, IDC Quarterly, 1996-1997. Adjunct Professor of Law, Products Liability and Trial Advocacy, Illinois Institute of Technology-Kent School of Law, 1980-1984. Instructor, IDC Trial Academy, 1992-1993. Lecturer: "Use of an Annuitant to Reduce Damages," IDC Annual Trial Tactics Seminar, 1989; "Civil Practice," Illinois Institute of Continuing Legal Education, 1978. President, Illinois Association of Defense Trial Counsel, 2001-2002. President-Elect, Illinois Association of Defense Trial Counsel, 2000-2001. Second Vice President, Illinois Association of Defense Trial Counsel, 1998-1999. Secretary-Treasurer, Illinois Association of Defense Trial Counsel, 1997-1998. Member, Board of Directors, Illinois Association of Defense Trial Counsel, 1993-1997; Chairman, Insurance Symposium, Illinois Association of Defense Trial Counsel, 1997. Chairman, Professional Liability Committee, Illinois Association of Defense Trial Counsel, 1994-1997. Chairman, Annual Trial Tactics Seminar, Illinois Association of Defense Trial Counsel, 1987. Member, Panel of Arbitrators, American Arbitration Association, 1987-1994. *Member:* Illinois State and American Bar Associations; International Association of Defense Counsel; Society of Trial Lawyers; Defense Research Institute (State Representative, 2001-2004; Annual Meeting Steering Committee, 2005—); Illinois Association of Defense Trial Counsel; Leading Illinois Attorneys; Trial Lawyers Club of Chicago. ***PRACTICE AREAS:*** Medical Malpractice; Insurance Coverage; Commercial Litigation; Products Liability; Professional Liability; Architectural Malpractice; Construction Litigation; Engineering Malpractice. ***Email:*** ccole@srzlaw.com

DANIEL V. KINSELLA, born Western Springs, IL, June 17, 1951; admitted to bar, 1977, Illinois and U.S. District Court, Northern District of Illinois including Trial Bar; U.S. District Court, Central District of Illinois; U.S. Court of Appeals, Seventh Circuit; U.S. Supreme Court. *Education:* Oakland University (B.A., 1973); University of Illinois (J.D., 1977). *Member:* American Bar Association (Member, Section on Labor and Employment Law). ***PRACTICE AREAS:*** Commercial Litigation; Business Law; Employment Litigation; Labor Arbitration; Labor Litigation; Business Litigation. ***Email:*** dkinsella@srzlaw.com

RICHARD E. MICHAELS, born Chicago, Illinois, June 10, 1952; admitted to bar, 1977, Illinois, U.S. District Court, Northern District of Illinois and U.S. Court of Appeals, Seventh Circuit. *Education:* DePaul University (B.S.C., summa cum laude, 1973); Northwestern University (J.D., 1977). Beta Gamma Sigma; Pi Gamma Mu; Beta Alpha Psi; Phi Eta Sigma; Delta Epsilon Sigma. Member, Northwestern University Law Review, 1976-1977. Author: "The Admissibility of Police Reports Under the Federal Rules of Evidence," 71 Northwestern University Law Review 691, 1976. Certified Public Accountant, Illinois, 1973. *Member:* Chicago, Illinois State, American (Member, Sections on: International Law and Practice; Antitrust Law; Corporation, Banking and Business Law) and International (Member, Committees on International Sales and Related Commercial Transactions and Antitrust Law and Monopolies) Bar Associations. Fellow, American Bar Foundation. ***LANGUAGES:*** Polish. ***PRACTICE AREAS:*** General Corporate; International Business Transactions; Business Enterprises. ***Email:*** rmichaels@srzlaw.com

L. ANDREW BREHM, born Dayton, Ohio, May 31, 1954; admitted to bar, 1979, Illinois and U.S. District Court, Northern District of Illinois, Trial Bar, 1985; 1982, U.S. Court of Appeals, Seventh Circuit; 1994, U.S. District Court, Eastern District of Wisconsin. *Education:* University of Notre Dame (A.B., with high honors, 1976); University of Michigan (J.D., cum laude, 1979). Arbitrator, National Association of Securities Dealers, 1987-1998. Member, Panel of Arbitrators, American Arbitration Association, 1987—. *Member:* Chicago and Illinois State Bar Associations. ***REPORTED CASES:*** PaineWebber v. Farnam, 870 F.2d 1286 (7th Cir. 1989); Hard Rock Cafe Licensing Corp. v. Concession Services, Inc., 955 F.2d 1143 (7th Cir. 1992); Weiss v. Ganz, 26 F.Supp.2d 655 (S.D.N.Y., 1998); Koplin v. Labe Federal Savings & Loan Ass'n, 748 F.Supp. 1336 (N.D. Ill. 1990); Capalbo v. PaineWebber Incorporated, 694 F.Supp. 1315 (N.D. Ill. 1988) and 672 F.Supp. 1048 (N.D. Ill. 1987); Wabash, Inc. v. Avnet, Inc., 516 F.Supp. 995 (N.D. Ill. 1981). ***PRACTICE AREAS:*** Securities; Commodities; Employment; RICO and other Commercial Litigation; Business Law. ***Email:*** lbrehm@srzlaw.com

DAVID M. GIANGROSSI, born Elmhurst, Illinois, March 23, 1952; admitted to bar, 1979, Illinois and U.S. District Court, Northern District of Illinois; 1992, U.S. Court of Appeals, Seventh Circuit; 1997, U.S. District Court, Eastern District of Wisconsin. *Education:* University of Wisconsin (B.A., 1974); John Marshall Law School (J.D., 1979). Chairman, Village of Cary Zoning Board of Appeals, 1992—. Chairman, Village of Cary Planning Commission, 1994—. *Member:* American Bar Association. ***PRACTICE AREAS:*** Probate Litigation; Commercial Litigation; Construction Law; Family Law; Business Enterprises. ***Email:*** dgiangrossi@srzlaw.com

JEFFREY E. SCHILLER, born Chicago, Illinois, September 13, 1954; admitted to bar, 1979, Illinois; U.S. District Court, Northern District of Illinois, Trial Bar, 1988; 1991, U.S. Tax Court; 1993, U.S. Court of Appeals, Seventh Circuit; 1994, U.S. Supreme Court; 1995, U.S. Court of Appeals, District of Columbia Circuit; 1997, U.S. District Court, Eastern District of Wisconsin; 2000, U.S. Court of Appeals, Third Circuit. *Education:* University of Michigan (B.A., 1976); Northwestern University (J.D., 1979). Recipient: William Jennings Bryan Award for Outstanding Achievement in Oral Advocacy; Lowden-Wigmore Prize for Achievement in Appellate Advocacy. *Member:* American Bar Association (Member, Sections on: Litigation; Intellectual Property; Civil Rights; Antitrust); International Trademark Association (Member, Membership Committee). ***REPORTED CASES:*** Edwards v. Cabrera, 58 F.3d 290 (7th Cir. 1995); Chaney v. Suburban Bus Division of Regional Transportation Authority, 52 F.3d 623 (7th Cir. 1995); Gordon v. Degelmann, 29 F.3d 295 (7th Cir. 1994); Willis v. Bell, 999 F.2d 284 (7th Cir. 1993); 784 F.Supp. 1360 (N.D. Ill. 1992); 731 F.Supp. 309 (N.D. Ill. 1990); 726 F.Supp. 1118 (N.D. Ill. 1989); 687 F.Supp. 380 (N.D. Ill. 1988); Prior Plumbing and Heating Co. v. Hagins, 258 Ill. App. 3d 683, 630 N.E.2d 1208 (1st Dist. 1994). ***PRACTICE AREAS:*** Intellectual Property Litigation; Commercial Litigation; Civil Rights Litigation.

THOMAS G. DRATHS, born Chicago, Illinois, July 8, 1952; admitted to bar, 1980, Illinois and U.S. District Court, Northern District of Illinois; U.S. District Court, Northern District of Illinois including Trial Bar; U.S. Claims Court; 1995, U.S. District Court, Eastern District of Michigan: 1998, U.S. District Court, Eastern District of Wisconsin. *Education:* Dartmouth College (A.B., 1975); DePaul University (J.D., 1980). ***PRACTICE AREAS:*** Labor and Employment; Civil Litigation; Construction; Real Estate; Business Enterprises. ***Email:*** tdraths@srzlaw.com

JOHN E. LOWE, born East St. Louis, Illinois, March 21, 1955; admitted to bar, 1980, Illinois. *Education:* University of Illinois at Urbana-Champaign (A.B., 1977); Harvard Law School (J.D., 1980). With Kevin R. Thieneman, the author of Chapter One, "Securities Overview," of the IICLE Securities Law Practice Handbook, and with William E. Turner the author of the 1997 supplement to that chapter. *Member:* Chicago and American (Member, Sections on: Securities; Negotiated Acquisitions and Business Law) Bar Associations. ***PRACTICE AREAS:*** Securities; Mergers, Acquisitions and Divestitures; Corporate Law; Business Law; Hedge Funds. ***Email:*** jlowe@srzlaw.com

MICHAEL F. BRAUN, born Joliet, Illinois, November 8, 1956; admitted to bar, 1981, Illinois and U.S. District Court, Northern District of Illinois; 1991, Trial Bar; U.S. Court of Appeals, Seventh Circuit; 1992, U.S. Court of Appeals, Eleventh Circuit; 1993, U.S. Supreme Court; 2001, U.S. District Court, Central District of Illinois. *Education:* University of Illinois (B.A., 1978; J.D., magna cum laude, 1981). Instructor, Northern Illinois University College of Law, 1985-1988. *Member:* Illinois State and American Bar Associations (Member, Sections on: Litigation; Labor and Employment Law; Business Law); Illinois Association of Defense Trial Counsel. ***REPORTED CASES:*** Gordon v. Degelmann, 29 F.3d 295 (7th Cir. 1994); Willis v. Bell, 999 F.2d 284 (7th Cir. 1993), 726 F.Supp. 1118 and 784 F.Supp. 1360 (N.D. Ill. 1992); Bordelon v. Chicago School Reform Board of Trustees, 8 F.Supp.2d 779 (1998); Midwest Decks, Inc. v. Butler & Baretz Acquisitions, Inc., 272 Ill.App.3d 370, 649 N.E.2d 511 (1st Dist. 1995); Dolezal v. Plastic and Reconstructive Surgery, S.C., 266 Ill.App.3d 1070, 640 N.E.2d 1359 (1st Dist. 1994). ***PRACTICE AREAS:*** General Civil Litigation; Employment Litigation and Counseling; Commercial Litigation; Restrictive Covenants; NASD Arbitration; Business Enterprises. ***Email:*** mbraun@srzlaw.com

ERIC M. FOGEL, born New York, March 15, 1955; admitted to bar, 1987, Illinois. *Education:* Pomona College (B.A., summa cum laude, 1977); The University of Michigan (M. A., 1980; M.B.A., 1986; J.D., 1986). Phi Beta Kappa. Adjunct Professor of Law, International Business, McGeorge University School of Law, Sacramento, California, 1996—. *Member:* American Bar Association. ***PRACTICE AREAS:*** Corporate Law; Securities; Business Law; Venture Capital; Business Enterprises. ***Email:*** efogel@srzlaw.com

DOUGLAS A. HANSON, born Park Ridge, Illinois, September 5, 1961; admitted to bar, 1987, Illinois. *Education:* University of Illinois (B.S., Accountancy with highest honors, 1983); Illinois Institute of Technology, Chicago-Kent College of Law (J.D., with high

(This Listing Continued)

honors, Valedictorian, 1987). Order of the Coif. Editor-in-Chief, Chicago-Kent Law Review, Volume 63, 1987. Certified Public Accountant, Illinois, 1983. Co-Author: "Taxation: Substance v. Form and Other Esoterica," 62 Chicago-Kent Law Review 657 (1986). *Member:* Chicago, Illinois State and American Bar Associations. ***PRACTICE AREAS:*** Commercial and Residential Real Estate; Real Estate Development; Construction Law; Condominium Law; General Corporate; Probate; Estate Planning; Estates and Trust; Business Enterprises. ***Email:*** dhanson@srzlaw.com

JAMES L. KOMIE, born Chicago, Illinois, June 23, 1962; admitted to bar, 1987, Illinois. *Education:* University of Michigan (B.A., with high distinction and high honors, 1984; J.D., cum laude, 1987). *Member:* Chicago, Illinois State and American Bar Associations. ***PRACTICE AREAS:*** Employment Law; Securities Litigation; Business Law. ***Email:*** jkomie@srzlaw.com

DAVID I. ADDIS, born Chicago, Illinois, April 16, 1963; admitted to bar, 1988, Illinois and U.S. District Court, Northern District of Illinois; 1992, U.S. Tax Court. *Education:* Indiana University (B.S., high distinction and departmental honors in Accounting, 1985); Boston University (J.D., cum laude, 1988). Certified Public Accountant, Illinois, 1985. Speaker: Limited Liability Companies and Limited Partnerships, National Business Institute, 1997. Illinois Secretary of State, Business Organizations Acts Advisory Committee, 2002-2005. *Member:* Chicago (Committees: Corporation and Business Law; Commercial Finance and Transactions; Securities Law; Patent, Trademark and Copyrights; Computer Law), Illinois State (Sections: Corporation and Securities Law; Intellectual Property) and American (Committees: Business Law; Intellectual Property) Bar Associations. ***PRACTICE AREAS:*** Domestic Business Transactions; Corporate Formation and Alteration; Limited Liability Company Law; Business Enterprises; Intellectual Property. ***Email:*** daddis@srzlaw.com

CAMILLE B. CONWAY, born Camp LeJeune, North Carolina, November 6, 1961; admitted to bar, 1989, Illinois. *Education:* North Park College (B.A., Economics, cum laude, 1984); Northwestern University (J.D., 1988). Adjunct Professor, Clinical Trial Advocacy, Northwestern University, 1996—. Instructor, Midwest NITA Program, 1999—. *Member:* American Bar Association (Member, White Collar Defense Section). ***PRACTICE AREAS:*** Commercial Litigation (92%); Employment Discrimination (4%); Municipal Defense (2%); Tort Defense; White Collar Criminal Defense (2%). ***Email:*** cconway@srzlaw.com

JUSTIN L. WEISBERG, born Chicago, Illinois, April 3, 1962; admitted to bar, 1992, Illinois and U.S. District Court, Northern District of Illinois; 2004, Trial Bar. *Education:* University of Illinois (B.S.E., 1987); IIT-Chicago Kent College of Law (J. D., 1992). Registered Professional Engineer: Illinois, 1991; Florida, 1992. Author: Securing United States Assets on Multinational Projects, International Project Finance Edited by Fiona Scott and Claus Peter Matins Transnational Publishers, 2000. Co-Author: "Knowing the Risks When Embarking on an International Venture," Proceedings of Construction Congress V, 1997; "Managing Risk: An Environmental Engineering Perspective," Proceedings of the National Conference of Environmental Engineers, 1998; *Professional Standards For The Geotechnical Engineer*, A Legal Perspective Geo-Engineering For Underground Facilities, Edited by Gabriel Fernandez and Robert A. Bauer, ASCE 1999; "Between A Rock and A Hard Place: Balancing the Interests of The Principal and Obligee," Construct!, Vol. 14, No. 1, published by the American Bar Association, Section of Litigation, Fall, 2004; "Keeping Your Complex Construction Case Under Control," Construct!, Vol. 14, No. 2, published by the American Bar Association, Section of Litigation, Winter, 2005. *Member:* Chicago and American Bar Associations; The American Society of Civil Engineers. ***PRACTICE AREAS:*** Construction Law; Complex Litigation; Insurance Coverage; Environmental Insurance Coverage; Commercial Litigation. ***Email:*** jweisberg@srzlaw.com

RONALD F. GEIMER, born Chicago, Illinois, July 18, 1968; admitted to bar, 1993, Illinois. *Education:* Northwestern University (B.A., 1990); University of Illinois (J.D., magna cum laude, 1993). Recipient: American Jurisprudence Award; Harno Scholar. Associate Editor, University of Illinois Law Review. *Member:* Chicago and Illinois State Bar Associations. ***PRACTICE AREAS:*** General Corporate; International Business Transactions; Business Enterprises. ***Email:*** rgeimer@srzlaw.com

LAUREN E. DEJONG, born Chicago, Illinois; admitted to bar, 1994, Illinois and U.S. District Court, Northern District of Illinois. *Education:* Hope College (B.A., magna cum laude, 1991); Northwestern University (J.D., 1994). *Member:* Chicago, Illinois State and American Bar Associations. ***PRACTICE AREAS:*** Probate; Estate Planning; Estate and Trust Administration. ***Email:*** ldejong@srzlaw.com

PARTNERS

CATHERINE C. GRYCZAN, born Knoxville, Tennessee, October 12, 1960; admitted to bar, 1985, Illinois and U.S. District Court, Northern District of Illinois. *Education:* University of Illinois (B.S., 1982); Tulane University School of Law (J.D., cum laude, 1985). *Member:* Chicago, Illinois State and American Bar Associations; Women's Bar Association of Illinois. ***LANGUAGES:*** French. ***PRACTICE AREAS:*** General Corporate; International Business Transactions; Business Enterprises. ***Email:*** cgryczan@srzlaw.com

DOUGLASS G. HEWITT, born Hinsdale, Illinois, September 10, 1955; admitted to bar, 1982, Illinois; U.S. District Court, Central District of Illinois; U.S. District Court, Northern District of Illinois including Trial Bar; U.S. Court of Appeals, Seventh Circuit. *Education:* University of Wisconsin (B.A., 1977); Loyola University (J.D., 1982). ***REPORTED CASES:*** Roth v. Lutheran General Hospital, 57 F.3d 1446 (7th Cir. 1995); SEC v. Danny O. Cherif, 933 F.2d 403 (7th Cir. 1991); Greg Daniel v. American Board of Emergency Medicine, et al., 988 F.Supp. 127 (W.D.N.Y. 1997); Koutsoubos v. Casanave, 816 F.Supp. 472 (N.D. IL 1993); Mosler v M/K Ventures International, Inc., 103 F.R.D. 385 (N.D. IL 1984); Susman v. Cypress Venture, 187 Ill.App.3d 312 (1st Dist. 1989); Van Dahm v. Novak, 174 Ill.App.3d 880 (2nd Dist. 1988); People v. Lewis, 103 Ill.2d 111 (1984); People v. McKinley, 115 Ill.App.3d 1095 (1st Dist. 1983). ***PRACTICE AREAS:*** Complex Commercial Litigation; Health Care Litigation; Employment Litigation. ***Email:*** dhewitt@srzlaw.com

RICHARD J. JUAREZ, born Chicago, Illinois, August 2, 1966; admitted to bar, 1992, Illinois. *Education:* University of Illinois (B.S., with honors, 1987); DePaul University (J.D., 1992). *Member:* Chicago and Illinois State Bar Associations; Illinois Association of

(This Listing Continued)

Defense Trial Counsel. ***PRACTICE AREAS:*** Medical Malpractice; Construction Law; Personal Injury; Premises Liability; Legal Malpractice; Business Litigation. ***Email:*** rjuarez@srzlaw.com

STEVEN P. PHERSON, born West Lafayette, Indiana, January 21, 1959; admitted to bar, 1994, Illinois, U.S. District Court, Northern District of Illinois and Trial Bar. *Education:* University of Vermont (B.A., 1981); John Marshall Law School (J.D., cum laude, 1994). ***PRACTICE AREAS:*** Securities Litigation; Commodities; Employment Litigation; Business Law. ***Email:*** spherson@srzlaw.com

ELISHA M. PRERO, born Detroit, Michigan, June 22, 1954; admitted to bar, 1981, Illinois. *Education:* Loyola University, Chicago (B.A., 1978); University of Michigan (J.D., 1981). ***PRACTICE AREAS:*** Corporate Law (40%); Real Estate (30%); Business Enterprises (30%). ***Email:*** eprero@srzlaw.com

ROBERT J. TRIZNA, born Joliet, Illinois, August 29, 1952; admitted to bar, 1979, Illinois; 1980, U.S. District Court, Northern District of Illinois including Trial Bar; 1985, U.S. Court of Appeals, Seventh Circuit; 1992, U.S. District Court, Eastern District of Wisconsin; 1997, U.S. Court of Appeals, Sixth Circuit and U.S. District Court, Eastern District of Michigan; 1999, U.S. Supreme Court. *Education:* University of Notre Dame (A.B., 1974); The John Marshall Law School (J.D., 1978). Member, John Marshall Law Review, 1977-1978. Adjunct Faculty, The John Marshall Law School, 1978-1979. Law Clerk to Hon. George N. Leighton, U.S. District Court, Northern District of Illinois, 1978-1980. *Member:* Chicago, Illinois State and American Bar Associations. ***REPORTED CASES:*** Bartsch v. Gordon N. Plumb, Inc., 138 Ill.App.3d 188, 485 N.E.2d 1105 (1st Dist. 1985); American Nat. Bank & Trust Co. v. Bentley, 159 Ill.App.3d 27, 512 N.E.2d 12 (1st Dist. 1987); Greer Properties, Inc. v. LaSalle Nat. Bank, 874 F.2d 457 (7th Cir. 1989); Marrocco v. General Motors Corp., 966 F.2d 220 (7th Cir. 1992); Duffy v. United States, 966 F.2d 307 (7th Cir. 1992); In re Baxco Corp., 148 B.R. 855 (Bkrtcy. N.D.Ill. 1992); In re Malcolm, 145 B.R. 259 (Bkrtcy. N.D.Ill. 1992); Creyts Complex, Inc. v. Marriott Corp., 98 F.3d 321 (7th Cir. 1996); Greenslade v. Chicago Sun-Times, 112 F.3d 853 (7th Cir. 1997); Board of Trustees v. Illinois Range, Inc., 71 F.Supp. 2d 864 (N.D.Ill. 1999); UAW v. BVR Liquidating, Inc., 190 F.3d 768 (6th Cir. 1999); International Armour & Limousine Company v. Moloney Coachbuilders, Inc., 272 F.3d 912 (7th Cir. 2001), cert. denied, 535 U.S. 1078 (2002); Trustees of AFTRA Health Fund v. Biondi, 303 F.3d 765 (7th Cir. 2002). ***PRACTICE AREAS:*** Civil Trial and Appellate Litigation; Corporate; Intellectual Property; Employment.

MARY K. WALTER, admitted to bar, 1990, Illinois. *Education:* University of Iowa (B.B.A., 1987); University of Notre Dame (J.D., 1990). ***PRACTICE AREAS:*** Securities; Asset-Backed Securitizations; Mergers and Acquistions.

ASSOCIATES

DOLORES AYALA, born Chicago, Illinois; admitted to bar, 1996, Illinois, U.S. District Court, Northern District of Illinois and U.S. Court of Appeals, Seventh Circuit. *Education:* Washington University (B.A., cum laude, 1982) Phi Beta Kappa; Universidad Complutense de Madrid, Spain; Universita Per Stranieri, Perugia, Italy; DePaul College of Law (J.D., 1996). Member, DePaul Law Review. *Member:* American Bar Association: Association of Defense Trial Counsel. ***LANGUAGES:*** Spanish, Italian, Hebrew. ***REPORTED CASES:*** T.H.E. Insurance Company v. City of Alton, 227 F.3d 802 (7th Cir. 2000); State ex rel. Harold D. Linthicum and Delmar Giles v. The Honorable Michael B. Calvin, Circuit Court of the City of St. Louis, Missouri, 57 S.W. 3d 855 (Mo. 2001); Smith v. Silver Cross Hospital, Habib Abbasi, M.D., 790 N.E.2d 77, 339 Ill.App.3d 67 (1st Dist. 2003); Ellis v. City of Chicago, 272 F.Supp.2d 729 (N.D. Ill. 2003); Bogacz v. Board of Education, Calumet Public School District 132, 2003 WL 22057026 (N.D. Ill. 2003). ***PRACTICE AREAS:*** Commercial Litigation; Employment Litigation; Education Law; Insurance Coverage. ***Email:*** dayala@srzlaw.com

JIN-HO CHUNG, born Seoul, Korea, August 25, 1971; admitted to bar, 1997, Minnesota; 1999, Illinois. *Education:* University of Michigan (B.A., 1994; J.D., 1996). *Member:* Chicago, Cook County, Illinois State and American Bar Associations. ***PRACTICE AREAS:*** Commercial Litigation; Arbitration. ***Email:*** jchung@srzlaw.com

ANDREW M. GEIER, admitted to bar, 2000, Illinois. *Education:* St. Norbert College (B.A., 1992); Loyola University (J.D., cum laude, 2000). *Member:* Chicago, Illinois State and American Bar Associations. ***PRACTICE AREAS:*** General Corporate; International Business Transactions; Business Enterprises. ***Email:*** ageier@srzlaw.com

MICHAEL D. LEE, born Brooklyn, New York, April 6, 1968; admitted to bar, 1994, Illinois and U.S. District Court, Northern District of Illinois; 1996, U.S. Court of Appeals, Seventh Circuit; 1997, U.S. District Court, Eastern District of Wisconsin. *Education:* University of Illinois (B.S., 1991); Chicago-Kent College of Law (J.D., 1994). *Member:* Chicago, Illinois State and American Bar Associations. ***PRACTICE AREAS:*** Commercial Litigation; General Litigation. ***Email:*** mlee@srzlaw.com

IAN S. LESCH, born Boston, Massachusetts, May 21, 1970; admitted to bar, 2000, Illinois. *Education:* DePaul University (B.A., 1994); Loyola University (M.B.A., 2000; J.D., 2000); Northwestern University (LL.M., 2003). ***PRACTICE AREAS:*** Federal Taxation; Estate Planning; ERISA; Corporate Law. ***Email:*** ilesch@srzlaw.com

JAMES D. MAHLO, born Moline, Illinois, October 12, 1976; admitted to bar, 2001, Illinois and U.S. District Court, Northern District of Illinois. *Education:* Augustana College (B.A., summa cum laude, 1998); Loyola University, Chicago (J.D., 2001; Certificate, Tax Law, 2001). ***LANGUAGES:*** German and Elementary Mandarin. ***PRACTICE AREAS:*** Corporate Formation; Corporate Organization; International Law; Taxation; Mergers and Acquisitions; Business Enterprises. ***Email:*** jmahlo@srzlaw.com

BRENDAN T. McMAHON, born Evanston, Illinois, December 21, 1971; admitted to bar, 2002, Illinois. *Education:* Miami University (B.A., 1994); Chicago-Kent College of Law (J.D., 2002). Co-Auther: "Between A Rock and A Hard Place: Balancing the Interests of The Principal and Obligee," Construct!, Vol. 14, No. 1, published by the American Bar Association, Section of Litigation, Fall, 2004. *Member:* Chicago and Illinois State Bar Associations. ***PRACTICE AREAS:*** Employment Litigation; Commercial Litigation; Labor Law; Real Estate Litigation; Business Enterprises. ***Email:*** bmcmahon@srzlaw.com

LAURIE MARTIN MONTPLAISIR, born Kouts, Indiana; admitted to bar, 1996, Illinois. *Education:* Purdue University (B.S., with distinction, 1988); Loyola University

(This Listing Continued)

SCHUYLER, ROCHE & ZWIRNER, A PROFESSIONAL CORPORATION, Chicago—Continued

(J.D., cum laude, 1996). *Member:* Chicago, Illinois State and American Bar Associations. ***PRACTICE AREAS:*** Corporate; Litigation; Transactions; Business Enterprises. ***Email:*** lhybl@srzlaw.com

RACHEL T. NGUYEN, born Saigon, Vietnam, July 14, 1973; admitted to bar, 1999, Illinois. *Education:* University of Michigan (B.A., 1995); Loyola University (J.D., 1999). *Member:* Chicago, Illinois State and American Bar Associations. ***PRACTICE AREAS:*** Commercial Litigation; Employment Litigation; Civil Litigation; Business Enterprises. ***Email:*** rnguyen@srzlaw.com

JENNIFER L. NORKUS, born Winthrop Harbor, Illinois, April 27, 1977; admitted to bar, 2004, Illinois. *Education:* University of North Carolina at Chapel Hill (B.A., 1999); University of Illinois (J.D., cum laude, 2004). ***PRACTICE AREAS:*** Business Enterprises. ***Email:*** jnorkus@srzlaw.com

MICHAEL T. ROCHE, born Evanston, Illinois, March 8, 1975; admitted to bar, 2002, Illinois. *Education:* Marquette University (B.S., 1997); Loyola University (J.D., 2002). Member, Loyola University Law Review. Co-Author: "Between A Rock and A Hard Place: Balancing the Interests of The Principal and Obligee," Construct!, Vol. 14, No. 1, published by the American Bar Association, Section of Litigation, Fall, 2004. *Member:* Chicago and Illinois State Bar Associations. ***PRACTICE AREAS:*** Commercial Litigation; Employment. ***Email:*** mtroche@srzlaw.com

GERALD T. ROHRER, JR., born Chicago, Illinois, February 7, 1968; admitted to bar, 1997, Illinois and U.S. District Court, Northern District of Illinois. *Education:* University of Dayton (B.A., 1991); John Marshall Law School (J.D., 1997). *Member:* Chicago, Illinois State (Member, Tort Law Council) and American Bar Associations. ***REPORTED CASES:*** Mercantile National Bank v. Metropolitan Water Reclamation District (Supreme Court Rule 23 Order issued April 27, 2001, 1st Dist. No. 1-00-2502); Robert Elsinga v. Kenny Kiewit Shea, a Joint Venture (Supreme Court Rule 23 Order issued December 30, 2002, 1st Dist. No. 1-01-3848); Michael Dahlen v. Metropolitan Water Reclamation District, et al. (Supreme Court Rule 23 Order issued April 21, 2003, 1st Dist. No. 1-01-3145); Paszkowski v. Metropolitan Water Reclamation District, et al., 789 N.E.2d 343 (1st Dist. 2003); Martens v. MCL Construction, et al. (1st Dist. No. 1-02-1557) 807 N.E.2d 480 (1st Dist. 2004); Paszkowski v. Metropolitan Water Reclamation District, et al. 820 N.E.2d 401 (Ill. 2004). ***PRACTICE AREAS:*** Defense Litigation; Construction Liability; Premises Liability; Automobile; Wrongful Death; Commercial Litigation; Insurance Coverage; Appellate Practice; Government Relations/Lobbying. ***Email:*** grohrer@srzlaw.com

JEFFREY R. ROSENBERG, born Chicago, Illinois, March 17, 1964; admitted to bar, 1997, Illinois. *Education:* Roosevelt University (B.A., 1992); Loyola University School of Law (J.D., cum laude, 1997). *Member:* Chicago and American Bar Associations; Illinois Association of Defense Trial Counsel. ***PRACTICE AREAS:*** Commercial Litigation; Securities Litigation; Employment Litigation. ***Email:*** jrosenberg@srzlaw.com

COUNSEL

WALTER L. ADAMS, born Middletown, New York, June 8, 1931; admitted to bar, 1958, Illinois. *Education:* Duke University (A.B., 1953); University of Michigan (J.D., 1958). Member, Editorial Board, University of Michigan Law Review, 1957-1958. *Member:* Chicago and American (Member, Labor and Employment Law Section) Bar Associations. ***PRACTICE AREAS:*** Labor Law; Employment Law; Business Litigation.

ROBERT M. HORWITCH, born Chicago, Illinois, February 12, 1931; admitted to bar, 1955, Illinois. *Education:* University of Michigan (B.B.A., 1952); Harvard University (J.D., 1955). Beta Gamma Sigma. *Member:* American Bar Association. [Sergeant, U.S. Army, 1955-1957]. ***PRACTICE AREAS:*** Real Estate; National and International Hotel Transactions; Business Law. ***Email:*** rhorwitch@srzlaw.com

THOMAS J. PARAVOLA, admitted to bar, 1981, Illinois. *Education:* Elmhurst College (B.A., 1978); University of Illinois (J.D., 1981). ***PRACTICE AREAS:*** Employee Benefits Law. ***Email:*** tparavola@srzlaw.com

RICHARD J. WALSH, born Oak Park, Illinois, June 1, 1926; admitted to bar, 1952, Illinois. *Education:* DePaul University; University of Michigan (LL.B., 1952). Delta Theta Phi. *Member:* Chicago and Illinois State Bar Associations. ***PRACTICE AREAS:*** General Corporate; Labor Law.

RICHARD S. WEINBERG, born Chicago, Illinois, August 9, 1936; admitted to bar, 1961, Illinois; 1993, North Carolina. *Education:* Harvard University (B.A., cum laude, 1958; J.D., cum laude, 1961). Trustee, Village of Wilmette, 1973-1975. Chairman, Wilmette Economic Development Commission, 1989-1992. ***PRACTICE AREAS:*** Acquisitions and Mergers; Secured Lending; Business Transactions; Estate Planning and Administration.

DAVID E. ZARSKI, born Chicago, Illinois, March 28, 1958; admitted to bar, 1983, Illinois. *Education:* Southern Illinois University (B.S., 1978); DePaul University College of Law (J.D., 1983). Visiting Lecturer, Center for International Sudies, Salzburg, Austria. Member: Governing Committee, National Conference on Consumer Finance Law; Financial Institutions Committee, Chicago Bar Association. Vice Chairman, 1998 and Chairman, 1999-2000, Consumer Law Committee, Chicago Bar Association. *Member:* American and International Bar Associations. Fellow, Center for International Legal Studies. ***PRACTICE AREAS:*** *Securitization; Structured Finance; Banking; Financial Institution Regulation;* Consumer Finance Law; Business Enterprises; Cross Border Finance; Debt and Equity Finance; Debt Finance; Commercial Finance; Asset Based Finance; Finance. ***Email:*** dzarski@srzlaw.com

SCHWARTZ COOPER CHARTERED

Established in 1921

180 NORTH LA SALLE STREET
SUITE 2700
CHICAGO, ILLINOIS 60601
Telephone: 312-346-1300
Telecopier: 312-782-8416
Email: postmaster@schwartzcooper.com
URL: http://www.schwartzcooper.com

Administrative and Regulatory, Banking, Corporate Finance, Corporate Law, Mergers and Acquisitions, Leveraged Buy-Outs, Private Equity and Venture Capital, Not-for-Profit Corporations, Bankruptcy, Creditors' Rights, Reorganizations, Workouts, Commodities, Employment Law, Estate Planning and Administration, Probate, Elder Law, Employee Benefits and Executive Compensation, Wealth Managment, Federal and State Tax, Commercial Litigation, White Collar Defense, Professional Liability, Appellate Law, Alternative Dispute Resolution, Asset Recovery, Franchise Law, Environmental Law, Real Estate, Condominiums, Leasing, Affordable Housing, Secured Transactions, Securities, Technology and Intellectual Property, Trademarks, Copyrights, Trade Secrets.

FIRM PROFILE: Schwartz Cooper Chartered is a premier business law firm providing services across a range of disciplines including commercial real estate, banking and finance, corporate and business law, private equity, litigation, bankruptcy, tax and estate planning, and technology and intellectual property. Our clients include commercial real estate developers and lenders, local and national banking institutions, investment funds, and small and mid-size public and private entities in industries ranging from manufacturing to technology to retail. We are committed to providing consistent quality and cost-effective personal service to each and every one of our clients.

DENNIS R. AINGER, born Harvard, Illinois, July 4, 1966; admitted to bar, 1991, Illinois and U.S. District Court, Northern District of Illinois; 1996, Wisconsin and U.S. District Court, Eastern District of Wisconsin; 1995, U.S. Court of Appeals, Seventh Circuit. *Education:* Northern Illinois University (B.A., summa cum laude, with honors, 1988); University of Illinois College of Law (J.D., magna cum laude, 1991). Order of the Coif. Harno Scholar. Member, University of Illinois Law Review, 1989-1990. *Member:* Chicago and Illinois State Bar Association; State Bar of Wisconsin. ***PRACTICE AREAS:*** Real Estate Development; Financing; Real Estate Acquisitions and Sales; Condominiums. ***Email:*** dainger@schwartzcooper.com

CHARLES M. BAUM, born Oak Park, Illinois, December 31, 1968; admitted to bar, 1995, Illinois and U.S. District Court, Northern District of Illinois; 2001, U.S. District Court, Southern District of Ilinois; 2002, U.S. Court of Appeals, 7th Circuit; 2004, U.S. Supreme Court. *Education:* DePaul University (B.S., 1991); John Marshall Law School (J.D., 1995). *Member:* Chicago, Illinois State and American Bar Associations. ***PRACTICE AREAS:*** Commercial Litigation; Civil Litigation; Criminal Litigation. ***Email:*** cbaum@schwartzcooper.com

RICHARD M. BENDIX, JR., born Chicago, Illinois, August 29, 1950; admitted to bar, 1975, Illinois. *Education:* University of Michigan (B.A., summa cum laude, 1972; J.D., cum laude, 1975). Phi Beta Kappa. Author: "Single Asset Real Estate Cases," in Bankruptcy Practice: The Nuts and Bolts of Life in a Chapter 11 Case, published by the Missouri Bar Association. *Member:* Chicago, Illinois State and American Bar Associations. Fellow, American College of Bankruptcy. ***PRACTICE AREAS:*** Bankruptcy; Debtor and Creditor. ***Email:*** rbendix@schwartzcooper.com

JAY S. BERLINSKY, born Joliet, Illinois, May 25, 1944; admitted to bar, 1969, Illinois. *Education:* Northwestern University (B.A., with honors, 1966); Stanford University (J.D., 1969). ***PRACTICE AREAS:*** Corporate Transactions; Acquisitions and Mergers; Real Estate Development Law; Commercial Contracts Law. ***Email:*** jberlinksy@schwartzcooper.com

MARK B. BUTTERMAN, born Chicago, Illinois, March 2, 1954; admitted to bar, 1980, Illinois and U.S. District Court, Northern District of Illinois. *Education:* Grinnell College (B.A., cum laude, 1976); Loyola University (J.D., 1980); Northwestern University (M.B.A., 1986). Director, Lawyers Committee for Better Housing, 1980-1983. *Member:* Chicago, Illinois State and American Bar Associations. ***PRACTICE AREAS:*** Real Estate Law; Commercial Transactions. ***Email:*** mbutterman@schwartzcooper.com

CARMEN D. CARUSO, born August 21, 1958; admitted to bar, 1983, Wisconsin; 1985, Illinois, U.S. District Court, Northern District of Illinois and U.S. Court of Appeals, Seventh Circuit; 1990, Trial Bar Northern District of Illinois; 1998, U.S. Supreme Court; 2002, U.S. District Court, District of Colorado. *Education:* Marquette University (B.A., cum laude, 1980); Loyola University of Chicago School of Law (J.D., 1983). Alpha Sigma Nu. Lecturer: "Encroachment-Let Me Count the Ways!" American Association of Franchisees and Dealers, 1999; "How to Use Class Actions, Association-Lawsuits and other Tools to Accomplish Systemwide Change," American Franchisee Association, 1999; "It's Not Over Until It's Over - Terminate, Transfer and Renewal," American Franchisee Association, 1998; "Collective Negotiation For Franchise Renewal," American Association of Franchisee and Dealers, 1998; "Rico Claims In Business Litigation," C.F.E. 1994. Author, "Fraud In Franchising," C.F.E. White Paper, 1998. Associate, 1985-1993, Partner, 1994-1997, Foran & Schultz. Publications: Program Chair, American Association of Franchisees & Dealers, Annual Meeting, Chicago, Illinois, 2002, and Moderator, "Dialogue with Regulators" and "Mediation in Franchising"; <"Expert Witness in Franchise Litigation" (paper & speech) and "Antitrust Concerns in Representing Franchisee Associations" (paper speech), American Franchisee Association, Philadelphia, May 2001; "Negotiate Now or Litigate Later: The problem of Ambiguity in Franchise Agreements," American Franchisee Association, Cour'd'elare (Idaho) May 2000; "Racial Discrimination in Franchising," Franchise Times, April 2000; "Encroachment-Let Me Count the Ways!" American Association of Franchisees and Dealers, 1999; "How to Use Class Actions, Association-Lawsuits and other Tools to Accomplish Systemwide Change," American Franchisee Association, 1999; "It's Not Over Until It's Over-Terminate, Transfer and Renewal," American Franchisee Association, 1998; "Collective Negotiation For Franchise Renewal," American Association of Franchisee and Dealers, 1998; "Rico Claims In Business Litigation," Certified Fraud Ex-

(This Listing Continued)

aminers, 1994; "Fraud Un Franchising," Certified Fraud, Examiners, Wjite Paper, 1998. *Member:* Chicago and American (Sections of Litigation and Forum on Franchising) Bar Associations. (Also of Counsel, Huff & Gaines, Ltd.). ***PRACTICE AREAS:*** Franchise Law; Franchise Litigation; Business Litigation; Trial Practice; Appellate Practice; Complex Commercial Litigation; Arbitration; Business Fraud; Commercial Fraud; Commercial Litigation; Commercial Torts; Commercial Real Estate Litigation; Construction Litigation; Corporate Litigation; Environmental Litigation; Dealer and Distributor Termination; Dealership Law; Franchise Termination; Intellectual Property Litigation; RICO.

JOHN L. CONLON, born Chicago, Illinois, November 26, 1940; admitted to bar, 1964, Illinois; 1979, California. *Education:* St. Joseph's College (B.A., magna cum laude, 1961); Georgetown University (J.D., 1964). Author: "Trial Hearsay: Objections and Exceptions," (2nd Ed., 2005). Contributor, ABA Section of Antitrust Law Sample Jury Instructions in Civil Antitrust Cases (1987, 1990 eds.). Handbook on Antitrust Grand Jury Investigations 2d Ed. (1988). Assistant States Attorney, Cook County, 1965-1967. Assistant U.S. Attorney, Northern District of Illinois, 1967-1968. *Member:* Chicago, Illinois State, Seventh Circuit and American (Antitrust Section, Chairman, Criminal Practice and Procedure Committee, 1989-1992) Bar Associations. American College of Trial Lawyers. ***PRACTICE AREAS:*** Commercial and Tax Litigation; Professional Malpractice; Antitrust. ***Email:*** jconlon@schwartzcooper.com

ANDREW H. CONNOR, born Chicago, Illinois, September 8, 1948; admitted to bar, 1979, Illinois and U.S. District Court, Northern District of Illinois. *Education:* University of Chicago (A.B., 1970; J.D., 1979); University of Arkansas at Fayetteville. Member, Arkansas Law Review, 1976. ***PRACTICE AREAS:*** Corporate Finance; Leveraged Buy-Outs; Mergers and Acquisitions; General Corporate Law. ***Email:*** aconnor@schwartzcooper.com

EDWARD A. COOPER (1897-1977)

DEREK L. COTTIER, born Toronto, Ontario, Canada, December 15, 1955; admitted to bar, 1984, Minnesota; 1987, Illinois. *Education:* St. Lawrence University (B.A., magna cum laude, 1976); Indiana University; University of Michigan (J.D., cum laude, 1984). Phi Beta Kappa; Order of the Coif. Law Clerk to Hon. Ilana D. Rovner, U.S. District Court, Northern District of Illinois, 1985-1987. *Member:* Chicago and American Bar Associations; Chicago Council of Lawyers. ***PRACTICE AREAS:*** Real Estate Finance (80%); Affordable Housing (10%); Real Estate (10%); Real Estate Development. ***Email:*** dcottier@schwartzcooper.com

C. ELIZABETH DARKE, born Sandusky, Ohio, December 30, 1969; admitted to bar, 1998, New York (Not admitted in Illinois). *Education:* Syracuse University (B.A., summa cum laude, 1992); State University of New York at Buffalo (J.D., cum laude, 1997). Phi Beta Kappa. ***LANGUAGES:*** Spanish. ***PRACTICE AREAS:*** Real Estate. ***Email:*** edarke@schwartzcooper.com

ROBERT G. DAVIDSON, born Indianapolis, Indiana, January 29, 1948; admitted to bar, 1974, Illinois; 1978, Florida. *Education:* Miami University and University of Wisconsin (B.A., with honors, 1971); Indiana University (J.D., cum laude, 1974). Member, Indiana Law Journal, 1972-1974. Associate Instructor, Indiana University Law School, 1973-1974. *Member:* Chicago and American Bar Associations. ***PRACTICE AREAS:*** Real Estate Development; Leasing; Finance; Construction; Workouts; General Corporate Law; Acquisitions. ***Email:*** rdavidson@schwartzcooper.com

JOAN M. EAGLE, born Chicago, Illinois, June 15, 1939; admitted to bar, 1983, Illinois and U.S. District Court, Northern District of Illinois; 1984, U.S. Court of Appeals, Seventh Circuit; 1992, U.S. District Court, Central District of Illinois; 2000, U.S. District Court, Northern District of Illinois including Trial Bar; U.S. District Court, Eastern District of Wisconsin. *Education:* University of Michigan (B.Mus., with distinction, 1961; M.Mus., with great distinction, 1962); Illinois Institute of Technology, Chicago-Kent College of Law (J.D., with high honors, 1983). ***PRACTICE AREAS:*** Labor and Employment; Employee Benefits; Education Law. ***Email:*** jeagle@schwartzcooper.com

RICHARD J. FIRFER, born Chicago, Illinois, January 30, 1943; admitted to bar, 1971, Illinois. *Education:* Northwestern University (B.A., 1964; J.D., cum laude, 1971). Order of the Coif. Law Clerk to Judge Thomas R. McMillen (dec'd), U.S. District Court, Northern District of Illinois, 1971-1972. ***PRACTICE AREAS:*** Corporate Transactions; Banking; Federal and State Taxes; Securities. ***Email:*** rfirfer@schwartzcooper.com

STEVEN H. GISTENSON, born Chicago, Illinois, September 18, 1960; admitted to bar, 1986, Illinois, U.S. District Court, Northern District of Illinois including Trial Bar, U.S. Supreme Court and U.S. Court of Appeals, Seventh Circuit; U.S. Court of the Armed Forces. *Education:* University of Illinois (B.A., 1983); John Marshall Law School (J.D., 1986). Associate Justice, Moot Court Executive Board, 1985. *Member:* Chicago, Illinois State and American Bar Associations; Illinois Trial Lawyers Association. ***PRACTICE AREAS:*** Litigation. ***Email:*** sgistenson@schwartzcooper.com

ROBERT DUNN GLICK, born Chicago, Illinois, January 31, 1936; admitted to bar, 1962, Illinois. *Education:* University of Pennsylvania (B.S., 1957); Michigan State University (M.B.A., 1961); University of Chicago (J.D., 1960). Attorney, Securities and Exchange Commission, 1962-1967. *Member:* Chicago, Illinois State and Federal Bar Associations. ***PRACTICE AREAS:*** Banking; Corporate. ***Email:*** rglick@schwartzcooper.com

RONALD B. GRAIS, born Chicago, Illinois, April 23, 1943; admitted to bar, 1968, Illinois and U.S. District Court, Northern District of Illinois. *Education:* Cornell University (B.A., 1965); University of Chicago (J.D., 1968). Member, Lambda Alpha International Honorary Land Economics Society, 1991—. Associate Editor, University of Chicago Law Review, 1966-1968. Commissioner: Illinois Guardianship and Advocacy Commission, 1993-2000; Winnetka Plan Commission, 1986-1993. Member: Economic Club of Chicago, 1991—; Chicago Metropolitan Planning Council, 1987-2000; Urban Development Committee, 1990-2000. *Member:* Chicago, Illinois State and American Bar Associations. (Administrative Managing Partner). ***PRACTICE AREAS:*** Real Estate Law (80%); Not for Profit Corporations (20%). ***Email:*** rgrais@schwartzcooper.com

MICHAEL B. GRAY, born Chicago, Illinois; admitted to bar, 1992, Illinois. *Education:* University of Chicago (B.A., Math, 1987); University of Illinois at Urbana-Champaign (M.S., Physics, 1988); Northwestern University School of Law (J.D., 1992). ***PRACTICE AREAS:*** Finance; Intellectual Property; Corporate Law; Mergers, Acquisitions and Divestitures; Internet Law; Securities; Joint Ventures; Strategic Alliances; Partnership Law; Technology Law; New Media Law. ***Email:*** mgray@schwartzcooper.com

ERNEST GREENBERGER (1923-2001)

STEPHEN S. HERSETH, born Boston, Massachusetts, November 15, 1947; admitted to bar, 1982, Illinois. *Education:* Yale University (B.A., 1969); Illinois Institute of Technology, Chicago-Kent College of Law (J.D., with high honors, 1982). Member, Oak Park Design Commission, Oak Park, Illinois, 1982-1984. Chairman, Oak Park Mall Commission, Oak Park, Illinois, 1985-1988. Governing Member, Chicago Symphony Orchestra, 1990—. *Member:* Chicago, Illinois State and American Bar Associations. ***PRACTICE AREAS:*** Real Estate Law; Construction Law; Environmental Law. ***Email:*** sherseth@schwartzcooper.com

WILLIAM M. HOLZMAN, born Milwaukee, Wisconsin, August 5, 1949; admitted to bar, 1975, Wisconsin; 1979, Illinois. *Education:* University of Wisconsin (B.A., with honors, 1971); University of San Diego (J.D., 1975). *Member:* Illinois State Bar Association. ***PRACTICE AREAS:*** Corporate Law; Mergers and Acquisitions; Securities Law. ***Email:*** wholzman@schwartzcooper.com

ANDREW W. KIM, born Bronx, New York, September 4, 1970; admitted to bar, 1997, New York; 2001, California; 2004, Illinois. *Education:* Yale University (B.A., 1992); Cornell Law School (J.D., 1996). Note Editor, Cornell International Law Journal. *Member:* New York State and American Bar Associations; State Bar of California. ***PRACTICE AREAS:*** Business Law; Corporate Law; Mergers and Acquisitions; Securities; Finance. ***Email:*** akim@schwartzcooper.com

IRA S. KOLB (1908-1988)

DANIEL J. KOPP, born Anderson, Indiana, September 18, 1962; admitted to bar, 1987, Illinois. *Education:* University of Notre Dame (B.A., 1984); Indiana University (J.D., magna cum laude, 1987). Order of the Coif. Managing Editor, Indiana Law Journal. ***PRACTICE AREAS:*** Commercial Real Estate. ***Email:*** dkopp@schwartzcooper.com

HYMAN J. KRAUSS (1922-1977)

MICHAEL S. KURTZON, born Chicago, Illinois, July 25, 1947; admitted to bar, 1973, Illinois. *Education:* Cornell University (A.B., 1969); University of Chicago (J.D., 1973). Author: "Representing Condominium Associations," Illinois Institute on Continuing Legal Education, 1999 Treatise on Illinois Condominium Law. President, 1981, Illinois Chapter, Community Associations Institute. *Member:* Chicago (Member, Executive Committee, Real Property Law Committee; Vice Chairman, 1978-1980 and Chairman, 1980-1982, Condominium Subcommittee of Real Property Committee), Illinois State and American Bar Associations; American College of Real Estate Lawyers. ***PRACTICE AREAS:*** Real Estate; Real Estate Finance; Real Estate Development; Real Estate Acquisitions; Condominium Law; Workouts. ***Email:*** mkurtzon@schwartzcooper.com

SCOTT M. LAPINS, born Fort Sill, Oklahoma, September 20, 1955; admitted to bar, 1980, Illinois. *Education:* University of Illinois (B.S., with highest honors, 1977); Northwestern University (J.D., cum laude, 1980). Beta Gamma Sigma; Phi Kappa Phi; Beta Alpha Psi. Listed in: Leading Lawyers Network; Superlawyers. Member, Editorial Board, Journal of Criminal Law and Criminology, 1979-1980. Certified Public Accountant, Illinois, 1977. Co-author: "Making Preservation an Economically Attractive Alternative," The Practical Guide to Illinois Preservation Law, published by Young Lawyers Division, Chicago Bar Association. *Member:* Chicago, Illinois State and American Bar Associations; Chicago Council of Lawyers; Illinois Institute of Certified Public Accountants. ***PRACTICE AREAS:*** Real Estate Finance (75%); Corporate Law (25%). ***Email:*** slapins@schwartzcooper.com

MICHAEL J. LEGAMARO, born Columbus, Ohio, February 2, 1961; admitted to bar, 1986, Illinois; 2001, Texas. *Education:* Washington University (A.B., summa cum laude, 1983); Northwestern University (J.D., 1986). Phi Beta Kappa; Omicron Delta Kappa. Executive Editor, Journal of Criminal Law and Criminology, 1985-1986. Co-Author, with Burton W. Kanter, "The Grantor Trust: Handmaiden to the IRS and Servant to the Taxpayer," 75 Taxes 706 (December 1997). [Captain, Judge Advocate General's Corps, United States Army: Trial Counsel, Mannheim, Germany, 1987-1988; Chief Legal Assistance, Supreme Headquarters, Allied Powers Europe, Mons, Belgium, 1988-1990]. ***Email:*** mlegamaro@schwartzcooper.com

SHARON ZABAN LETCHINGER, born Chicago, Illinois, October 18, 1968; admitted to bar, 1993, Illinois. *Education:* University of Illinois (A.B., 1990; J.D., magna cum laude, 1993). *Member:* Chicago and American Bar Associations. ***PRACTICE AREAS:*** Real Estate Finance; Real Estate Acquisitions and Dispositions. ***Email:*** sletchinger@schwartzcooper.com

ROBERT C. LINTON, born Evanston, Illinois, October 14, 1964; admitted to bar, 1989, Illinois. *Education:* University of Michigan (B.A., 1986); Georgetown University (J.D., cum laude, 1989). Member, The Tax Lawyer (Journal of ABA Tax Section), Georgetown University. *Member:* Chicago Bar Association. ***PRACTICE AREAS:*** Commercial Real Estate Transactions (100%). ***Email:*** rlinton@schwartzcooper.com

LAURA ANN LIPINSKI, born Chicago, Illinois, February 10, 1963; admitted to bar, 1987, Illinois and U.S. District Court, Northern District of Illinois. *Education:* Loyola University of Chicago (B.S., cum laude, 1984); University of Illinois (J.D., 1987). Alpha Sigma Nu. Licensed Real Estate Broker. Planning Commissioner, Western Springs, 2003—. *Member:* Chicago, Illinois State and American Bar Associations; National Association of Elder Lawyers. ***PRACTICE AREAS:*** Trusts and Estates (70%); Real Estate (20%); Elder Law (10%). ***Email:*** llipinski@schwartzcooper.com

NANCY R. LIVINGSTON, born Philadelphia, Pennsylvania, February 11, 1953; admitted to bar, 1983, Illinois; 2000, Colorado. *Education:* Wellesley College (B.A., 1975); DePaul University (J.D., with honors, 1983); New York University (LL.M. in Taxation, 1984). Assistant Professor, Clinical Practice, 1994-1999 and Adjunct Professor, IIT Chicago-Kent College of Law. ***PRACTICE AREAS:*** Estate Planning; Tax; Corporate. ***Email:*** nlivingston@schwartzcooper.com

JOSEPH Q. McCOY, born Inglewood, California, November 17, 1972; admitted to bar, 1998, Illinois. *Education:* University of Chicago (B.A., Public Policy Studies, 1994); University of Chicago, School of Social Sciences (M.A., Education, 1994); Northwestern

(This Listing Continued)

SCHWARTZ COOPER CHARTERED, Chicago—Continued

University School of Law (J.D., 1998). *Member:* Chicago and Illinois State Bar Associations; Urban Land Institute; National Association of Industrial and Office Properties. ***PRACTICE AREAS:*** Real Estate Lending (65%); Real Estate Acquisitions and Dispositions (25%); Real Estate Leasing (10%). ***Email:*** jmccoy@schwartzcooper.com

STANTON MILLER, born Chicago, Illinois, March 5, 1944; admitted to bar, 1969, Illinois; 1972, U.S. Court of Military Appeals. *Education:* Miami University (A.B., 1965); University of Illinois (J.D., 1968); John Marshall Law School (LL.M., Taxation, with honors, 1979). Phi Delta Phi. Instructor, Chicago-Kent College of Law, 1980-1982. Member: Board of Education District 108, Lake County, Illinois, 1985-1990; North Shore Special Education District, 1985-1990. *Member:* Chicago (Member: Probate Practice and Estate Planning Committee, 1978—; Patent, Trademark and Copyright, 1990—; Chairman, Division 2, 1986-1987), Illinois State and American Bar Associations; Chicago Intellectual Law Property Association (Chairman, Copyright Committee, 2001-2004); Copyright Society of the U.S.A. (Member, Board of Directors, 2001-2004). ***PRACTICE AREAS:*** Corporate Law; Copyrights. ***Email:*** sbmiller@schwartzcooper.com

ROBERT D. NACHMAN, born Chicago, Illinois, October 11, 1950; admitted to bar, 1983, Illinois and U.S. District Court, Northern District of Illinois; 1985, U.S. Court of Appeals, 7th Circuit. *Education:* University of Michigan (B.A., with high honors, 1972); University of Chicago (A.M., 1973); Harvard University (J.D., cum laude, 1983). Phi Beta Kappa. Co-Author, with Richard M. Bendix, "Bankruptcy Issues Related to Mortgage Foreclosure," Illinois Foreclosure and Related Bankruptcy and Title Issues, NBI, Inc., 2000. *Member:* Illinois State and American Bar Associations; Chicago Council of Lawyers; American Bankruptcy Institute. ***PRACTICE AREAS:*** Bankruptcy Law; Litigation. ***Email:*** rnachman@schwartzcooper.com

NEIL T. NEUMARK, born Geneva, Illinois, August 20, 1947; admitted to bar, 1973, Texas; 1977, Illinois. *Education:* Purdue University (B.S.I.E., 1970); Indiana University (J.D., magna cum laude, 1973). Phi Eta Sigma; Alpha Pi Mu; Tau Beta Pi. Member, Indiana Law Review, 1972-1973. *Member:* Illinois State Bar Association; State Bar of Texas. ***PRACTICE AREAS:*** Real Estate Development Law; Landlord and Tenant Transactions Law; Property Management Law; Leasing. ***Email:*** nneumark@schwartzcooper.com

JERROLD M. PEVEN, born Chicago, Illinois, September 13, 1955; admitted to bar, 1980, Illinois. *Education:* Washington University (B.A., 1977); Northwestern University (J.D., 1980). Member, Journal of Criminal Law and Criminology, 1978-1980. *Member:* Chicago and American Bar Associations. ***PRACTICE AREAS:*** Real Estate Development Law (75%); Finance and Workouts (25%). ***Email:*** jpeven@schwartzcooper.com

BRET A. RAPPAPORT, born Chicago, Illinois, April 24, 1961; admitted to bar, 1986, Illinois and U.S. District Court, Northern District of Illinois including Trial Bar, 1989; 1987, U.S. Court of Appeals, Seventh Circuit; 1989, U.S. Supreme Court. *Education:* Indiana University (B.S. in Finance, 1983); John Marshall Law School (J.D., 1986). Editor, John Marshall Law Review, 1985-1986. Field Editor, Wildflower Magazine. Author: "As Natural Landscaping Takes Root We Must Weed Out Bad Laws," 26 J. Marsh. L. Rev. 865, 1993; "LLC's and the Bankruptcy Code," Taxes, Vol. 74, No. 10, 1996. Intern, ACLU, Chicago, 1984-1986. Adjunct Professor, John Marshall Law School, 1989-1994. Assistant Illinois Attorney General, Civil Appeals Division, 1986-1988. Member, Lawyers Advisory Committee, Constitutional Rights Foundation, 1986-1996. Adjunct Professor DePaul Law School, 1999—. *Member:* Illinois State Bar Association. ***PRACTICE AREAS:*** Commercial Litigation; Employment Law; General Litigation; Civil Appeals. ***Email:*** brappaport@schwartzcooper.com

RICHARD T. REIBMAN, born Chicago, Illinois; admitted to bar, 1978, Illinois; 1979, Georgia. *Education:* New College (B.A., 1975); Illinois Institute of Technology, Chicago-Kent College of Law (J.D., highest honors, 1978). ***PRACTICE AREAS:*** Bankruptcy; Corporate Law; Creditors Rights; Futures; Securities Regulation; Securities Litigation. ***Email:*** rreibman@schwartzcooper.com

ERIC S. REIN, born Chicago, Illinois, June 16, 1956; admitted to bar, 1981, Illinois and U.S. District Court, Northern District of Illinois; 1982, Florida; 1983, U.S. Court of Appeals, Seventh Circuit; 2002, U.S. Court of Appeals, Fourth Circuit. *Education:* Washington University (B.A., 1978); University of Miami (J.D., 1981). *Member:* Chicago, Illinois State and American Bar Associations. ***PRACTICE AREAS:*** Commercial Litigation; Bankruptcy; Banking; Creditors Rights. ***Email:*** rrein@schwartzcooper.com

DINA B. ROSS, born 1963; admitted to bar, 1994, Illinois. *Education:* Brandeis University (B.A., 1985); University of Chicago Graduate School of Business (M.B.A., 1987); Loyola University of Chicago (J.D., cum laude, 1994). *Member:* Chicago and American Bar Associations. ***PRACTICE AREAS:*** Information Technology (60%); Intellectual Property (40%). ***Email:*** dross@schwartzcooper.com

MICHAEL D. ROTHSTEIN, born Bellville, Illinois, May 14, 1971; admitted to bar, 1997, Illinois. *Education:* University of Florida (B.S.B.A., high honors, 1993); University of Illinois (J.D., magna cum laude, 1997; M.B.A., 1997). *Member:* Chicago and Illinois State Bar Associations. ***PRACTICE AREAS:*** Real Estate; Corporate. ***Email:*** mrothstein@schwartzcooper.com

MARTIN W. SALZMAN, born Chicago, Illinois, June 9, 1945; admitted to bar, 1971, Illinois, U.S. District Court, Northern District of Illinois, U.S. Court of Appeals, Seventh Circuit and U.S. Supreme Court. *Education:* University of Illinois (B.A., 1968; B.S., 1968); Georgetown University (J.D., 1971). *Member:* Chicago and Illinois State Bar Associations. ***PRACTICE AREAS:*** Banking; Creditors Rights. ***Email:*** msalzman@schwartzcooper.com

RICHARD G. SCHULTZ, born Chicago, Illinois, July 23, 1938; admitted to bar, 1964, Illinois, U.S. District Court, Northern District of Illinois including Trial Bar and U.S. Court of Appeals, Seventh Circuit; 1970, U.S. Supreme Court; 1977, U.S. Court of Military Appeals. *Education:* University of Illinois; Northwestern University; DePaul University (J.D., 1963); New York University (LL.M. in Taxation, 1964). *Editor-in-Chief,* De Paul Law Review, 1962, 1963. Teaching Fellow, New York University, 1963-1964. Recipient: Taft Memorial Scholarship, 1963; United States Attorney General sustained Superior Performance Award, 1968; Federal Bar Association, 7th Judicial District Milton Gordon Award—Federal Employee of the Year, 1970. Lecturer on Trial Technique, 1985-1986 and Faculty

(This Listing Continued)

Member, 1985-1986, Illinois Institute for Continuing Legal Education. Assistant United States Attorney, Northern District of Illinois, 1964-1970; Chief of the Criminal Division, 1968-1970; Special Assistant Attorney, Metropolitan Water Reclamation District of Greater Chicago, 1970—. Special Assistant Attorney, Illinois Department of Children and Family Services, 1975-1977. Special Assistant Attorney, Chicago Board of Election Commissioners, 1973-1979 and Chicago Transit Authority, 1971-1982. *Member:* Chicago, Illinois State, Federal and American Bar Associations. Fellow, American College of Trial Lawyers. ***PRACTICE AREAS:*** Litigation. ***Email:*** rschultz@schwartzcooper.com

JOSEPH H. SCHWARTZ (1895-1971)

FRANKLIN S. SCHWERIN, born Gary, Indiana, July 17, 1939; admitted to bar, 1964, Illinois. *Education:* Indiana University (A.B., 1961); Harvard University (LL.B., 1964). Phi Beta Kappa. Author: "Judges Advice to Lawyers," CBA Record, April, 1996. Co-Author: "Preparing or Defending an Electoral Board Challenge," published in *Election Law,* Illinois Institute for Continuing Legal Education, Election Law, 1983. *Member:* Chicago and American Bar Associations; Chicago Council of Lawyers. ***PRACTICE AREAS:*** Litigation; Employment Law. ***Email:*** fschwerin@schwartzcooper.com

GARY P. SEGAL, born Chicago, Illinois, June 26, 1969; admitted to bar, 1995, Illinois. *Education:* University of Illinois (B.A., 1991; J.D., magna cum laude, 1995). *Member:* Chicago, Illinois State and American Bar Associations. ***PRACTICE AREAS:*** Commercial Finance; Corporate Law; Real Estate Finance; Real Estate. ***Email:*** gsegal@schwartzcooper.com

ROBERT A. SMOLLER, born Chicago, Illinois, June 9, 1946; admitted to bar, 1971, Illinois and U.S. District Court, Northern District of Illinois. *Education:* University of Illinois (B.S., cum laude, 1968); Northwestern University (J.D., cum laude, 1971). Certified Public Accountant, Illinois, 1969. *Member:* Chicago and American (Member, Business Law Section, 1982—) Bar Associations. ***PRACTICE AREAS:*** Securities Law; Corporate Law. ***Email:*** rsmoller@schwartzcooper.com

PATRICK T. STANTON, born Evergreen Park, Illinois, August 17, 1966; admitted to bar, 1993, Illinois and U.S. District Court, Northern District of Illinois. *Education:* University of Notre Dame (B.A., 1988); Loyola University, Chicago (J.D., cum laude, 1993). Senior Member, Loyola University Chicago Law Journal. Law Clerk to Judge George M. Marovich, U.S. District Court, Northern District of Illinois, 1995-1996. *Member:* American Bar Association. ***PRACTICE AREAS:*** General Litigation; Commercial Litigation. ***Email:*** pstanton@schwartzcooper.com

BRYAN R. SUP, born Berwyn, Illinois, September 16, 1970; admitted to bar, 1996, Illinois. *Education:* University of Michigan (B.A., 1992); DePaul University (J.D., 1996). Order of the Coif. Member, De Paul Law Review, 1994-1996. Author: "Mechanics Lien Law and Strategies in Illinois," National Business Institute Manual, 1996. *Member:* Chicago Bar Association. ***PRACTICE AREAS:*** Litigation; Bankruptcy. ***Email:*** bsup@schwartzcooper.com

STEVEN W. SWIBEL, born Chicago, Illinois, July 18, 1946; admitted to bar, 1971, Illinois and U.S. District Court, Northern District of Illinois; 1973, U.S. Tax Court; 1981, U.S. Court of Appeals, Seventh Circuit. *Education:* Massachusetts Institute of Technology (B.S., 1968); Harvard University (J.D., 1971). Adjunct Professor of Taxation, IIT/Chicago-Kent College of Law, 1989—. *Member:* Chicago (Chairman, Federal Taxation Committee, 1989-1990; Member, State and Local Tax Committee; Member, Executive Council, Federal Taxation Committee, 1984—; Chairman, Federal Taxation Committee Division on Partnerships and Real Estate, 1986-1987), Illinois State and American (Member, Partnership Committee, Section of Taxation) Bar Associations. ***PRACTICE AREAS:*** Federal Income Tax; General Corporate; State Tax; Estate Planning. ***Email:*** sswibel@schwartzcooper.com

EDWARD S. WEIL, born Highland Park, Illinois, October 3, 1960; admitted to bar, 1986, Illinois and U.S. District Court, Northern District of Illinois including Trial Bar and U.S. Court of Appeals, 7th Circuit. *Education:* Wesleyan University (B.A., 1982); Northwestern University (J.D., 1986). Member, Editorial Board, Northwestern University Law Review, 1985-1986. Co-Author: Chapter on Arbitration Proceedings and Discovery, Arbitration Handbook, Illinois Institute of Continuing Legal Education, 1989. *Member:* Chicago (Member, Real Property and Bankruptcy Committees) and Illinois State Bar Associations. ***PRACTICE AREAS:*** Litigation; Bankruptcy. ***Email:*** eweil@schwartzcooper.com

THOMAS M. WHITE, born New York, N.Y., September 4, 1949; admitted to bar, 1975, Illinois and U.S. District Court, Northern District of Illinois. *Education:* New College (B.A., 1971); Northwestern University (J.D., cum laude, 1975). *Member:* Chicago and American Bar Associations. ***PRACTICE AREAS:*** Employee Benefits; Executive Compensation. ***Email:*** twhite@schwartzcooper.com

---

HEATHER AESCHLEMAN, born Bloomington, Illinois, January 29, 1976; admitted to bar, 2001, Illinois. *Education:* University of Illinois at Urbana-Champaign (B.A., 1998; J.D., 2001). *Member:* Chicago, Illinois State and American Bar Associations. ***PRACTICE AREAS:*** Real Estate. ***Email:*** haeschleman@schwartzcooper.com

ROBERTO ANGUIZOLA, born Panama City, Republic of Panama, December 6, 1973; admitted to bar, 1999, Illinois and U.S. District Court, Northern District of Illinois; 2000, Minnesota and U.S. District Court, District of Minnesota; 2001, U.S. Court of Appeals, Fifth Circuit; 2002, Florida. *Education:* Northwestern University (B.A., 1995; J.D., 1999). ***LANGUAGES:*** Spanish. ***PRACTICE AREAS:*** Litigation. ***Email:*** ranguizola@schwartzcooper.com

DAVID E. BEKER, admitted to bar, 2003, Illinois. *Education:* Northwestern University (B.A., 1999); Loyola University (J.D., cum laude, 2002). Recipient: 2002 Hugh L. Dick Memorial Award for outstanding performance in the area of taxation; Chicago Bar Association Federal Taxation Committee Tax Student Award. ***LANGUAGES:*** Russian. ***PRACTICE AREAS:*** Bankruptcy; Corporate Law; Civil Litigation; Federal Taxation. ***Email:*** dbeker@schwartzcooper.com

MAGDA BOYLES, admitted to bar, 2003, Illinois. *Education:* Syracuse University (B.S.); Northwestern University (J.D.; B.A.). ***PRACTICE AREAS:*** Corporate; Finance. ***Email:*** mboyles@schwartzcooper.com

(This Listing Continued)

CHRISTOPHER CAHILL, born Los Angeles, California, 1961; admitted to bar, 1996, Ohio; 1999, Illinois and U.S. District Court, Northern District of Illinois. *Education:* University of Illinois (A.B., 1985) University of Michigan (J.D., 1996). *Member:* American and International Bar Associations; American Bankruptcy Institute. ***PRACTICE AREAS:*** Bankruptcy. ***Email:*** ccahill@schwartzcooper.com

B. WAYNE CREEL, born Dalton, Georgia, August 15, 1976; admitted to bar, 2003, Illinois. *Education:* Vanderbilt University (B.A., 1999); Loyola University (J.D., 2003). *Member:* Chicago and American Bar Associations. ***PRACTICE AREAS:*** Litigation (100%). ***Email:*** bcreel@schwartzcooper.com

PETER O. FARAH, born Cleveland, Ohio, September 14, 1975; admitted to bar, 2001, Massachusetts; 2005, Illinois. *Education:* Boston College (B.S., magna cum laude, 1997); Boston College Law School (J.D., magna cum laude, 2001). *Member:* Chicago, Illinois State and Massachusetts Bar Associations; Arab-American Bar Association of Illinois. ***LANGUAGES:*** Arabic. ***PRACTICE AREAS:*** Corporate Law (100%). ***Email:*** pfarah@schwartzcooper.com

JEREMY GOTTSCHALK, born Wauconda, Illinois, July 4, 1979; admitted to bar, 2004, Illinois. *Education:* Marquette University (B.A., magna cum laude, 2001); Loyola University Chicago School of Law (J.D., 2004). *Member:* Chicago and Illinois State Bar Associations; Lesbian and Gay Bar Association of Chicago. ***LANGUAGES:*** Spanish, American Sign Language. ***PRACTICE AREAS:*** Intellectual Property; Technology Transfers; Technology Licensing; Civil Litigation; Business Law; Corporate Law; Estate Planning; Nonprofit and Charitable Organizations. ***Email:*** jgottschalk@schwartzcooper.com

ROBERT GROHOLSKI, born Elk Grove, Illinois, July 27, 1975; admitted to bar, 2000, Illinois. *Education:* Northern Illinois University (B.S., 1997; J.D., 2000). *Member:* Chicago, Illinois State and American Bar Associations. ***PRACTICE AREAS:*** Litigation; Alternative Dispute Resolution. ***Email:*** rgroholski@schwartzcooper.com

DAVID HARPEST, born Aurora, Illinois, May 25, 1978; admitted to bar, 2004, Illinois. *Education:* DePaul University (B.M., with honors, 2000); University of Illinois (J.D., cum laude, 2004). *Member:* Chicago Bar Association. ***PRACTICE AREAS:*** Litigation; Banking Law; Franchises and Franchising. ***Email:*** dharpest@schwartzcooper.com

MICHAEL J. KARBER, born 1979; (admission pending). *Education:* University of Michigan (B.A., Psychology and Political Science, 2002); Northwestern University (J.D., 2005). ***Email:*** mkarber@schwartzcooper.com

HEATHER L. KRAMER, born Cedar Falls, Iowa, November 20, 1974; admitted to bar, 2000, Illinois and U.S. District Court, Northern, Southern and Central Districts of Illinois; 2004, U.S. Court of Appeals, Eighth Circuit. *Education:* University of Iowa (B.A., highest distinction, 1997); University of Texas (J.D., honors, 2000). Phi Beta Kappa. Law Clerk to the Hon. Steven M. Colloton, U.S. Court of Appeals, Eighth Circuit. *Member:* Illinois State and American Bar Associations. ***PRACTICE AREAS:*** Litigation. ***Email:*** hkramer@schwartzcooper.com

ALEEN LEE, born Chicago, Illinois, November 21, 1979; admitted to bar, 2004, Illinois. *Education:* Duke University (B.S., 2001); University of Michigan Law School (J.D., 2004). *Member:* Chicago and American Bar Associations; Korean American Bar Association. ***PRACTICE AREAS:*** Real Estate. ***Email:*** alee@schwartzcooper.com

DOROTHEA J. LIDD, born Chicago, Illinois, March 5, 1960; admitted to bar, 1987, Illinois. *Education:* University of Chicago (A.B., 1982); Loyola University (J.D., 1987). *Member:* Chicago, Illinois State and American Bar Associations. ***PRACTICE AREAS:*** Real Estate (100%). ***Email:*** dlidd@schwartzcooper.com

ROBERT M. MELLICAN, born Cambridge, Massachusetts, 1975; admitted to bar, 2005, Illinois and U.S. District Court, Northern District of Illinois. *Education:* University of Illinois (B.A., 1997); Monash University, Melbourne, Australia; Chicago-Kent College of Law, Illinois Institute of Technology (J.D., 2004). Notes & Comments Editor, Chicago-Kent Law Review, 2003. *Member:* Chicago, Illinois State and American Bar Associations. ***Email:*** mmellican@schwartzcooper.com

ARIKA J. OSACKY, born Chicago, Illinois; admitted to bar, 2001, Illinois; 2002, U.S. District Court, Northern District of Illinois. *Education:* Miami University (B.A., 1998); Chicago-Kent College of Law (J.D., 2001). *Member:* Chicago, Illinois State and American Bar Associations. ***PRACTICE AREAS:*** Litigation. ***Email:*** aosacky@schwartzcooper.com

IRENE M. REED, born Chicago, Illinois, January 8, 1974; admitted to bar, 1998, Illinois. *Education:* Harvard University (B.A., magna cum laude, 1995; J.D., 1998). ***PRACTICE AREAS:*** Real Estate. ***Email:*** ireed@schwartzcooper.com

AARON N. RICE, born Chicago, Illinois, July 19, 1977; admitted to bar, 2003, Illinois. *Education:* Emory University (B.A., 1999); University of Illinois (J.D., cum laude, 2003). ***PRACTICE AREAS:*** Corporate Law. ***Email:*** arice@schwartzcooper.com

SETH MANN ROSENBERG, born Park Ridge, Illinois; admitted to bar, 2003, Illinois. *Education:* University of Illinois (B.A., 2000); Chicago-Kent College of Law (J.D., high honors, 2003). Order of the Coif. Member, Chicago-Kent Law Review. ***PRACTICE AREAS:*** Commercial Litigation. ***Email:*** srosenberg@schwartzcooper.com

BETHANY SCHOLS, born Alma, Michigan, January 16, 1974; admitted to bar, 2001, Illinois and U.S. District Court, Northern District of Illinois; 2002, U.S. Court of Appeals, Seventh Circuit. *Education:* University of Illinois at Urbana-Champaign (B.S., 1996); Chicago-Kent College of Law (J.D., 2001). ***PRACTICE AREAS:*** Litigation. ***Email:*** bschols@schwartzcooper.com

JULIE B. SCHWARTZ, born Detroit, Michigan, 1980; (admission pending). *Education:* University of Michigan (A.B., Psychology, 2001); University of Illinois (J.D., cum laude, 2005). ***Email:*** jschwartz@schwartzcooper.com

DAVID SEIDMAN, born Flushing, New York, Septermber 9, 1972; admitted to bar, 1997, Illinois; 2001, District of Columbia. *Education:* University of Pennsylvania (B.A., 1994); Washington University (J.D., 1997). Law Clerk to the Hon. William D. Stiehl, U.S. District Court for the Southern District of Illinois, 1998-1999. Author: "Questioning the Retroactivity of CERCLA in Light of Landgraf v. USI Film Products," Wash. U. J. of Urb. and Contemp. L., 1997. *Member:* Chicago and Illinois State Bar Associations; The District of Columbia Bar. ***PRACTICE AREAS:*** Litigation; Appellate Practice; Transportation. ***Email:*** dseidman@schwartzcooper.com

MORGAN M. SMITH, born Ann Arbor, Michigan, April 16, 1980; (admission pending). *Education:* University of Michigan (B.S., 2003; J.D., 2005). ***Email:*** msmith@schwartzcooper.com

DIANA TSAI, born Hinsdale, Illinois, September 23, 1974; admitted to bar, 2000, Illinois. *Education:* University of Chicago (B.A., with honors, 1996); University of Illinois (J.D., cum laude, 2000). ***LANGUAGES:*** Chinese (Mandarin). ***PRACTICE AREAS:*** Lender Law; Banking Law; Corporate Law. ***Email:*** dtsai@schwartzcooper.com

SHANE T. YOUNG, born Clintonville, Wisconsin, June 6, 1973; admitted to bar, 2004, Illinois. *Education:* University of Chicago (A.B., with honors, 1995); University of Illinois (J.D., cum laude, 2004). *Member:* Chicago and American Bar Associations. ***PRACTICE AREAS:*** Real Estate (100%). ***Email:*** syoung@schwartzcooper.com

OF COUNSEL

ANNE KATHRYN BERG, born Danville, Illinois, March 14, 1968; admitted to bar, 1994, Illinois. *Education:* University of Illinois (B.S., 1991; J.D., 1994). Recipient, American Jurisprudence Award in Contracts/Sales. *Member:* Chicago, Illinois State and American Bar Associations. ***PRACTICE AREAS:*** Corporate Finance; Leveraged Buyouts; Banking; Corporate Law; Environmental Law. ***Email:*** aberg@schwartzcooper.com

HARRY G. COMERFORD, born Chicago, Illinois, March 19, 1921; admitted to bar, 1947, Illinois. *Education:* DePaul University (B.A., 1942; J.D., 1947). Judge, Circuit Court, State of Illinois, County of Cook, 1960-1994. Chief Judge, Circuit Court of Cook County, 1978-1994. *Member:* Chicago and American Bar Associations.

MALCOLM M. GAYNOR, born Chicago, Illinois, March 10, 1935; admitted to bar, 1958, Illinois. *Education:* University of Wisconsin; Northwestern University (B.S.L., 1955; J.D., 1958). Author, "Assignments for the Benefit of Creditors," published in *Creditors' Rights in Illinois,* Illinois Institute for Continuing Legal Education, 1969 and 1971. *Member:* Chicago (Chairman, Bankruptcy Committee, 1968) and Illinois State Bar Associations. Fellow, American College of Bankruptcy. ***PRACTICE AREAS:*** Bankruptcy; Reorganization; Commercial Litigation; Secured Transactions. ***Email:*** mgaynor@schwartzcooper.com

MARY LOUISE HADDAD, born Morristown, New Jersey, December 8, 1941; admitted to bar, 1976, Illinois. *Education:* Douglass College of Rutgers University (B.A., 1963); Northwestern University (J.D., cum laude, 1976). Phi Beta Kappa. Author: "Disclaimers: Still Many Unresolved Problems," Barrister, Fall 1980; "Disclaimer: Unresolved Problems After the Passage of New Federal and Illinois Statutes," Illinois Bar Journal, July 1979; "In Defense of the Marital/Residuary Trust," Illinois Bar Journal, March 1980; "The Joint Tenancy Account for Convenience: A Boon to Litigation," Illinois Bar Journal, June, 1984. Lecturer, IICLE Estate Planning Short Course, 1984, 1985, 1986, 1987. *Member:* Chicago, Illinois State and American Bar Associations. ***PRACTICE AREAS:*** Estate Planning; Probate. ***Email:*** mlhaddad@schwartzcooper.com

LLOYD S. KUPFERBERG, born Chicago, Illinois, May 11, 1931; admitted to bar, 1956, Illinois. *Education:* Northwestern University; University of Wisconsin (B.S., 1953); Harvard University (J.D., 1956). Phi Beta Kappa. *Member:* Chicago and Illinois State Bar Associations; Chicago Estate Planning Council. ***PRACTICE AREAS:*** Estate Planning; Corporate. ***Email:*** lkupferberg@schwartzcooper.com

SUSAN MEYER, born New London, Connecticut; admitted to bar, 1994, Illinois; 1995, Florida; U.S. District Court, Northern District of Illinois including Trial Bar. *Education:* State University of New York at Stony Brook (B.A., 1986); Chicago-Kent College of Law (J.D., 1994). *Member:* Chicago, Illinois State and American Bar Associations; The Copyright Society of the U.S.A. ***PRACTICE AREAS:*** Intellectual Property; Trademarks; Corporate Law; Franchises and Franchising. ***Email:*** smeyer@schwartzcooper.com

JOSEPH R. PODLEWSKI, JR., born Chicago, Illinois, January 8, 1953; admitted to bar, 1978, Illinois and U.S. District Court, Northern District of Illinois. *Education:* Northern Illinois University (B.A., 1975); Chicago-Kent College of Law, Illinois Institute of Technology (J.D., with honors, 1978). Phi Kappa Phi; Delta Theta Phi. Lead Articles Editor, Chicago-Kent Law Review, 1977-1978. Author: Comment, "Recovery For Mental Injury Resulting From Mental Stimulus Under Workmen's Compensation Laws," 53 Chicago-Kent L. Rev. 731 (1977). Lecturer, Environmental Institute, Moraine Valley Community College, 1991-2003. Legal Writing Instructor, IIT/Chicago-Kent College of Law, 1977-1978. *Member:* Chicago (Chairman, Environmental Law Committee, 1993-1994), Illinois State (Council Member, 2005-2006 and Member, Environmental Law Section) and American (Member, Environment, Energy and Resources Law Section) Bar Associations. ***PRACTICE AREAS:*** Environmental; Commercial Litigation. ***Email:*** jpodlewski@schwartzcooper.com

(This Listing Continued)

SCHWARTZ, COOPER, KOLB & GAYNOR

CHICAGO, ILLINOIS

(See Schwartz Cooper Chartered)

JOHN B. SCHWARTZ & ASSOCIATES

SUITE 408
THIRTY-NINE SOUTH LA SALLE STREET
CHICAGO, ILLINOIS 60603
Telephone: 312-332-1586
Fax: 312-332-7009
Email: JBSLAWOFF@aol.com

Civil Litigation Practice including Plaintiffs Personal Injury Litigation, Negligence, Medical and Professional Malpractice, Premises Liability, Wrongful Death Law, Vehicular Accident Law and Civil Appeals.

(This Listing Continued)

JOHN B. SCHWARTZ & ASSOCIATES, Chicago—Continued

JOHN B. SCHWARTZ, born Chicago, Illinois, December 30, 1939; admitted to bar, 1966, Illinois and U.S. District Court, Northern District of Illinois; 1971, U.S. Supreme Court; 1975, U.S. Court of Appeals, Seventh Circuit; 1978, U.S. Tax Court. *Education:* Northwestern University (B.A., 1962); DePaul University (J.D., 1966). Nu Beta Epsilon. Author: Supplement to Chapter 9, Medical Malpractice, Illinois Continuing Legal Education, 1984—. Lecturer, Illinois Civil Practice and Procedure Committee, 1997. *Member:* Chicago (Member, Committees of: Real Property Law, 1967-1969; Unauthorized Practice, 1971-1979; Negligence, 1972-1973; Tort Litigation, 1973-1974 and 1985-1996; Circuit Court, 1974-1977 and 1985-1996; Civil Practice, 1981-1983 and 1985-1996; Judicial Committee, 1985-1993; Subcommittee Judicial Ethics; Medical-Legal Committee), Illinois State (Auxiliary Member, Civil Practice Committee, 1984-1985; Member, Civil Practice & Procedure Law Council, 1995-1997) and American Bar Associations; Appellate Lawyers Association of Illinois; Illinois Trial Lawyers Association (Member: Rules Committee, 1992-1995; Medical Negligence Committee, 1996-2000; Civil Practice Committee, 1993-2000); The Association of Trial Lawyers of America (Member, Research Committee, 1971). Life Fellow, Chicago Bar Foundation. Fellow, Roscoe Pound Foundation. ***LANGUAGES:*** Italian, Spanish. ***PRACTICE AREAS:*** Personal Injury; Civil Litigation; Medical Malpractice; Civil Appeals. ***Email:*** JBSLAWOFF@aol.com

ASSOCIATE

DAVID J. SPIRA, born Milwaukee, Wisconsin, February 8, 1946; admitted to bar, 1993, Illinois. *Education:* University of Wisconsin (B.A., 1969; B.S., 1973); John Marshall Law School (J.D., magna cum laude, 1993). Member, John Marshall Law Review, 1992-1993. *Member:* Illinois and American Bar Associations; The Association of Trial Lawyers of America; Illinois Trial Lawyers Association. [Capt. U.S. Army, 1969-1973]. ***PRACTICE AREAS:*** Tort Litigation; Civil Appeals. ***Email:*** JBSLAWOFF@aol.com

MARTY J. SCHWARTZ, P.C.

Established in 1991

THREE FIRST NATIONAL PLAZA, SUITE 3700
CHICAGO, ILLINOIS 60602
Telephone: 312-558-4293
Fax: 312-558-7750
Email: sosueme@savaho.com
URL: http://www.savaho.com

Business Litigation, Commercial Litigation, Construction Litigation, Employment Litigation, Real Estate Litigation.

FIRM PROFILE: Marty J. Schwartz, P.C., established in 1991, represents entrepreneurs and corporations in business litigation. Success is measured by the end result, including the cost of litigation. As a sole practitioner, there is no delegation to inexperienced associates, no duplication of efforts and no interoffice conferences.

MARTY J. SCHWARTZ, born Chicago, Illinois, September 4, 1954; admitted to bar, 1979, Illinois; 1980, Florida. *Education:* Yale University (B.A., 1976); Washington College of Law of American University (J.D., magna cum laude, 1979). Collaborator with Robert Vaughn: "Financial Disclosure," Conflict-Of-Interest Regulation In The Federal Executive Branch, D.C. Health and Co., 1979. *Member:* Chicago and Illinois State Bar Associations; The Florida Bar; The Association of Trial Lawyers of America. ***REPORTED CASES:*** Door Sys. vs. Pro-Line Door Sys., 126 F.3d 1028 (7th Cir. 1997); Tadros vs. Kuzmak, 277 Ill.App.3d 301, 660 N.E.2d 162 (1st Dist., 1995); Hindin/Owen/Engelke, Inc. vs. Grm Indus., 869 F.Supp. 539 (N.D.Ill. 1994); IFC Credit Corp. vs. Nuovo Pasta Co., 815 F.Supp. 268 (N.D.Ill. 1993); Ross vs. Creighton Univ., 957 F2d 410 (7th Cir. 1992). ***PRACTICE AREAS:*** Business Litigation; Commercial Litigation; Construction Litigation; Employment Litigation; Real Estate Litigation. ***Email:*** sosueme@savaho.com

SCOPELITIS, GARVIN, LIGHT & HANSON, P.C.

Established in 1978

30 WEST MONROE STREET, SUITE 600
CHICAGO, ILLINOIS 60603-2427
Telephone: 312-422-1200
FAX: 312-422-1224
Email: chicago@scopelitis.com
URL: http://www.scopelitis.com

Indianapolis, Indiana Office: 10 West Market Street, Suite 1500, 46204-2968. Telephone: 312-637-1777. Fax: 317-687-2414.

Washington, D.C. Office: 1850 M Street, N.W., Suite 280, 20036-5804. Telephone: 202-783-9222. Fax: 202-783-9230.

Kansas City, Missouri Office: Two Pershing Square, 2300 Main Street, Suite 900, 64108. Telephone: 816-279-9835. Fax: 816-279-1973.

Pasadena, California Office: 790 East Colorado Boulevard, 9th Floor, 91101. Telephone: 626-795-4700. Fax: 626-795-4790.

General Civil Practice. Litigation in all State and Federal Courts, including Appellate Practice, Transportation, Motor Carrier, Corporate, Administrative, Antitrust and Trade Regulation, Business, Insurance Defense, Negligence, Labor and Employment, Environmental, Workers Compensation, Probate and Estate Planning and Public Utility Law.

FIRM PROFILE: Scopelitis, Garvin, Light & Hanson, P.C. is a full-service law firm that offers a wide range of legal services to clients in many industries, including manufacturing, pharmaceutical, e-commerce, retail products, construction, and environmental concerns. Of particular note is the firm's knowledge of the transportation industry and its long-standing history of service to motor carriers, shippers, brokers and insurance companies nationwide. From its offices in Indianapolis, Chicago, Washington, D.C., Kansas City and Pasadena, the firm offers clients knowledge and experience in many business-related disciplines and also seeks to meet its clients' more individual needs in such areas as personal injury litigation, estate planning and probate administration.

GERALD F. COOPER, JR., born Cleveland, Ohio, December 16, 1954; admitted to bar, 1980, Ohio; 1981, Florida; 1984, Illinois. *Education:* Miami University (A.B., 1977); DePaul University (J.D., 1980). White House Conference on Drug Free Transportation, 1987; Illinois Truck Safety Task Force, 1987-1988. Chairman, Model Policies Sub-group, American Trucking Association, Workers' Compensation Task Force. Member, Board of Directors, Illinois Transportation Association (Special Counsel to the Executive Director). Legal Technical Advisor to Republican Leader of the Illinois House of Representatives, 1995—. President Workers' Compensation Lawyers Association (1998-1999). *Member:* Chicago and Illinois State (Workers Compensation Council) Bar Associations; The Florida Bar. ***PRACTICE AREAS:*** Workers Compensation Defense; Labor. ***Email:*** jcooper@scopelitis.com

WILLIAM D. BREJCHA, born Chicago, Illinois, December 1, 1948; admitted to bar, 1973, Illinois and U.S. District Court, Northern District of Illinois; 1974, U.S. Court of Military Appeals; 1977, U.S. Court of Appeals, Seventh Circuit. *Education:* University of Notre Dame (B.A., cum laude, 1970); Loyola University (J.D., 1973). Recipient, F. A. Miller Journalism Award, University of Notre Dame. Editor, Loyola Law Journal, 1972-1973. Editor, Illinois State Bar Association, Public Utilities and Transportation Law Newsletter, 1992—. [Capt., U.S. Army, 1974-1977; Lt. Colonel, Illinois Army National Guard, 1977-1994 (Retired)]. ***PRACTICE AREAS:*** State and Federal Litigation; Transportation Law; Administrative Law; Military Law. ***Email:*** wdbrejcha@scopelitis.com

VICTOR P. SHANE, born Evanston, Illinois, November 1, 1957; admitted to bar, 1984, Illinois. *Education:* DePaul University (B.S., 1979); University of Santa Clara (J.D., 1984). Staff Attorney, Chicago Transit Authority, Tort Division, 1987-1991. Assistant State's Attorney, Cook County State's Attorney's Office, 1984-1987. *Member:* Chicago, Illinois State and American Bar Associations; Workers Compensation Lawyers Association; Chinese American Bar Association (President, 1992-1994). ***PRACTICE AREAS:*** Workers Compensation Defense; Labor and Employment; Civil Litigation Defense. ***Email:*** vshane@scopelitis.com

LEONARD R. KOFKIN, born Chicago, Illinois May 11, 1933; admitted to bar, 1958, Illinois. *Education:* Northwestern University (B.S./B.A., 1955; J.D., 1958; M.M., 1984). Phi Alpha Delta. *Member:* Illinois State Bar Association; Transportation Lawyer's Association (Distinguished Service Award 1987, Lifetime Acheivement Award 1998). ***PRACTICE AREAS:*** Transportation Law; Labor and Employment Law. ***Email:*** lrkofkin@mbf-law.com

DONALD J. VOGEL, born Fort Wayne, Indiana, July 10, 1959; admitted to bar, 1985, Indiana, Illinois; U.S. District Court, Northern and Central Districts of Illinois; U.S. District Court, Northern and Southern Districts of Indiana; U.S. Court of Appeals, Sixth, Seventh and Eighth Circuits. *Education:* Indiana University (B.S., 1981; J.D., 1985). *Member:* Chicago, Illinois State, Indiana State and American Bar Associations; Transportation Lawyers Association (First Vice President and Editor, The Transportation Lawyer, 2005-2006). ***PRACTICE AREAS:*** Labor and Employment Law; Transportation Law; Litigation.

ROBERT J. HENRY, born Chicago, Illinois, August 1, 1950; admitted to bar, 1975, Illinois and U.S. District Court, Northern District of Illinois. *Education:* Loyola University (B.A., cum laude, 1973; J.D., cum laude, 1975). Member, 1991-2005 and Chair, 2003-2004, American Moving and Storage Association Law Forum. *Member:* Chicago Bar Association. ***PRACTICE AREAS:*** Transportation; Surface Transportation; Contracts; Insurance; Commercial Law. ***Email:*** rhenry@scopelitis.com

OF COUNSEL

ROBERT C. RUBIN, born Chicago, Illinois, October 15, 1955; admitted to bar, 1983, Illinois. *Education:* Drake University (B.A., 1977); Tulane University of Louisiana (J.D., 1983). *Member:* Chicago (Member, Workers Compensation Section) and Illinois Bar Associations. ***PRACTICE AREAS:*** Workers Compensation.

MARIA ELENA PORTELA, born Havana, Cuba, May 26, 1958; admitted to bar, 1984, Illinois and U.S. District Court, Northern District of Illinois. *Education:* Northwestern University (B.A., 1980); Drake University (J.D., 1983). *Member:* Chicago, Illinois State and American Bar Associations. ***LANGUAGES:*** Spanish. ***PRACTICE AREAS:*** Workers' Compensation; Third-Party Liability.

DONALD W. DEVITT, born Chicago, Illinois; admitted to bar, 1984, Illinois. *Education:* Loyola University (B.A.; J.D.). ***PRACTICE AREAS:*** Highway Accident Defense; Transportation; Corporate; Business Transactions. ***Email:*** ddevitt@scopelitis.com

SARA L. PETTINGER, born Fullerton, California, March 9, 1965; admitted to bar, 1990, Illinois, U.S. District Court, Northern District of Illinois, and U.S. Court of Appeals, Seventh, Eighth and Eleventh Circuits. *Education:* University of Chicago (B.A., 1987); DePaul University (J.D., 1990). ***PRACTICE AREAS:*** Employment Litigation; Commercial Litigation.

JOHN S. MAGIERA, born Oak Park, Illinois, April 19, 1952; admitted to bar, 1979, Illinois; 2001, Wisconsin. *Education:* Northwestern University (B.A. 1974); Lewis University College of Law (J.D. 1978). *Member:* Illinois State Bar Association; Workers' Compensation Lawyers Association, Ltd. ***PRACTICE AREAS:*** Workers Compensation Defense; Civil Litigation Defense. ***Email:*** jmagiera@mnpclaw.com

JAMES D. ELLMAN, born Evanston, Illinois, March 30, 1965; admitted to bar, 1991, Illinois. *Education:* University of Iowa (B.B.A., 1987); Chicago-Kent College of Law, Illinois Institute of Technology (J.D., 1991). *Member:* Chicago, Illinois State and American Bar Associations. ***Email:*** jellman@scopelitis.com

ADAM C. SMEDSTAD, born Kettering, Ohio, September 21, 1967; admitted to bar, 1992, Illinois. *Education:* University of Chicago (B.A., 1989); George Washington University (J.D., 1992). ***PRACTICE AREAS:*** Commercial Litigation. ***Email:*** asmedstad@scopelitis.com

PHILLIP J. JOHNSON, born Chicago, Illinois, February 14, 1943; admitted to bar, 1969, Illinois. *Education:* Loyola University (B.S., 1965); Chicago-Kent College of Law,

(This Listing Continued)

Illinois Institute of Technology (J.D., 1968). Contributing Author, *Lane Medical Trial Technique*, quarterly; American Society of Law and Medicine. Past President, Illinois Workmen's Compensation Lawyer's Association. Member, Board of Governor's of the Illinois Workmen's Compensation Lawyer's Association. Past Member, Attorney's Advisory Board. Guest Speaker: Workmen's Compensation Law and Medical Malpractice, Loyola University School of Nursing; Workmen's Compensation Law, Chicago Bar Association; Workmen's Compensation Law, I.I.C.L.E. *Member:* Chicago Bar Association; Illinois Workers Compensation Lawyers Association. ***PRACTICE AREAS:*** Workers Compensation.

REPRESENTATIVE CLIENTS: Carey International, Inc.; Celadon Trucking Services, Inc.; Comcar Industries, Inc.; Dana Corporation; Dean Foods; Diakon Logistics, Inc.; Exel; FedEx; Graebel Van Lines; Great West Casualty Company; Hanjin Shipping Company; J.B. Hunt Transport, Inc.; Lancer Insurance; Landstar System, Inc.; Liquid Transport Corp.; Maersk, Inc.; Mansur Real Estate Services, Inc.; McLane Foodservices, Inc.; Northland Insurance; Overnite Transportation Company; Penske System, Inc.; Pepsi Americas, Inc.; Roadlink USA: Schneider National Inc.; SIRVA/Allied Van Line, Inc./North American Van Lines, Inc.; Steak 'n Shake; Swift Transportation, Co.; Tyson Foods, Inc.; USA Truck, Inc.; Unigroup, Inc./Mayflower Transit, LLC/United Van Lines, LLC; Watkins Associated Industries, Inc.; Yellow Roadway Corporation.

(For Complete Biographical Data on all personnel, See Professional Biographies, Indianapolis, Indiana)

SCOTT, HALSTED & BABETCH, P.C.

117 N. JEFFERSON STREET, SUITE 205
CHICAGO, ILLINOIS 60661
Telephone: 312-463-1045
Fax: 312-463-1046
Email: info@shblaw.net
URL: http://www.shblaw.net

Civil Litigation, Trials, Defense Litigation, Appeals, Personal Injury, Automobile, Premises Liability, Uninsured, Underinsured Motorists, Negligence, Strict Liability Law, Construction, Commercial and Insurance Law.

ROBERT K. SCOTT, born Evergreen Park, Illinois; admitted to bar, 1982, Illinois, U.S. District Court, Northern District of Illinois including Trial Bar and U.S. Court of Appeals, Seventh Circuit. *Education:* Southern Illinois University (B.A., 1979); DePaul University (J.D., 1982). *Member:* Illinois State Bar Association; Defense Research Institute. ***PRACTICE AREAS:*** Civil Litigation; Trials; Appeals. ***Email:*** bob@shblaw.net

KELLIE S. HALSTED, born Rockford, Illinois; admitted to bar, 1993, Illinois; 1994, Wisconsin; 1998, U.S. District Court, Northern District of Illinois including Trial Bar. *Education:* Marquette University (B.A., 1990); DePaul University (J.D., 1993). Phi Alpha Delta. *Member:* Chicago, Illinois State and American Bar Associations; State Bar of Wisconsin. ***PRACTICE AREAS:*** Civil Litigation; Trials; Appeals. ***Email:*** kellie@shblaw.net

DANIEL I. BABETCH, born Chicago, Illinois; admitted to bar, 1993, Illinois and U.S. District Court, Northern District of Illinois. *Education:* University of Kansas (B.A., 1990); John Marshall Law School (J.D., 1993). Member: John Marshall Law Review; John Marshall Moot Court Team. ***PRACTICE AREAS:*** Defense Litigation; Negligence; Strict Liability Law; Construction Law; Professional Liability Law; Corporate Law; Trials and Appeals. ***Email:*** dan@shblaw.net

MARK R. SANDRI, born Gaylord, Michigan; admitted to bar, 2005, Illinois and U.S. District Court, Northern District of Illinois. *Education:* University of Michigan (B.A., 2001); DePaul University (J.D., 2005). ***PRACTICE AREAS:*** Civil Litigation; Trial Practice; Appellate Practice. ***Email:*** mark@shblaw.net

LEGAL SUPPORT PERSONNEL

STACI L. VAZQUEZ

SCOTT & KRAUS, LLC

Established in 2003
150 SOUTH WACKER DRIVE, SUITE 2900
CHICAGO, ILLINOIS 60606
Telephone: 312-327-1050
Fax: 312-327-1051
URL: http://www.lawyers.com/skcounsel

Litigation, Corporate, Public Finance, Municipal Bonds, Commercial Litigation, Secured Lending, Real Estate and Health Care Law, General Business Practice.

DREW J. SCOTT, born Shelbyville, Illinois, August 27, 1960; admitted to bar, 1986, Illinois. *Education:* University of Illinois (B.S., B.A., magna cum laude, 1983; J.D., magna cum laude, 1986). Phi Beta Kappa. *Member:* Chicago, Illinois State and American Bar Associations. ***PRACTICE AREAS:*** Finance; Health Care Law; Corporate Law. ***Email:*** dscott@skcounsel.com

EUGENE S. KRAUS, born Chicago, Illinois, January 30, 1964; admitted to bar, 1989, Illinois, U.S. District Court, Northern District of Illinois and U.S. Court of Appeals, Seventh Circuit; 1995, U.S. District Court, Central District of Illinois. *Education:* University of Tulsa; Lake Forest College (B.A., 1986); DePaul University College of Law (J.D., 1989). *Member:* Chicago, Illinois State and American Bar Associations. ***PRACTICE AREAS:*** Commercial Litigation. ***Email:*** ekraus@skcounsel.com

THOMAS P. EGAN, born Chicago, Illinois, April 21, 1957; admitted to bar, 1987, Illinois. *Education:* DePaul University (B.S., cum laude, 1979; M.B.A., 1984; J.D., 1987). Bata Alpha Psi. Member, Law Review. Certified Public Accountant, 1980. *Member:* Chicago, Illinois State and American Bar Associations. ***PRACTICE AREAS:*** Finance; Corporate; Securities; Real Estate. ***Email:*** tegan@skcounsel.com

(This Listing Continued)

MILES V. COHEN, born September 25, 1973; admitted to bar, 1997, Illinois. *Education:* University of Illinois (B.S., 1994; J.D., cum laude, 1997). ***PRACTICE AREAS:*** Labor and Employment Law; Commercial Litigation; Real Estate Litigation. ***Email:*** mcohen@skcounsel.com

SONIA S. KINRA, admitted to bar, 2000, Illinois; 2001, U.S. District Court, Northern District of Illinois. *Education:* Emory University (B.A, 1996); South Texas College of Law (J.D., 1999). *Member:* American Bar Association. ***Email:*** skinra@skcounsel.com

JASON R. SLEEZER, born Ottowa, Illinois, March 3, 1979; admitted to bar, 2005, Illinois. *Education:* North Central College (B.A., 2001); DePaul University College of Law (J.D., 2004). ***PRACTICE AREAS:*** Litigation. ***Email:*** jsleezer@skcounsel.com

SVENERIK NILSEN, born Cambridge, Massachusetts, May 1, 1971; admitted to bar, 2000, Illinois. *Education:* Hamilton College (B.A., 1993); Vanderbilt University Law School (J.D., 1999). *Member:* Illinois State Bar Association. ***PRACTICE AREAS:*** Finance. ***Email:*** snilsen@skcounsel.com

JAMES M. McARDLE, admitted to bar, 1990, Illinois. *Education:* University of Illinois (A.B., 1983); University of Iowa (M.A., 1986); DePaul University (J.D., 1989). *Member:* Illinois State Bar Association; American Bankruptcy Institute. ***PRACTICE AREAS:*** Bankruptcy; Commercial Litigation. ***Email:*** jmcardle@skcounsel.com

LEGAL SUPPORT PERSONNEL

KIMBERLY FEARING, (Paralegal)
JEAN WATSON, (Paralegal)
KIRK WONIO, (Paralegal)
PAMELA COSTELLO, (Paralegal)
DION BRADLEY, (Law Clerk)

LAW OFFICES OF THOMAS J. SCULLY, III & ASSOCIATES

Established in 1975
53 WEST JACKSON, SUITE 523
CHICAGO, ILLINOIS 60604
Telephone: 800-628-1934
Fax: 219-836-5514
Email: tscully506@aol.com
URL: http://www.scullydisabilitylaw.com

Munster, Indiana Office: 506 Ridge Road, 46321. Telephone: 219-836-1380. Fax: 219-836-5514.

Chesterton, Indiana Office: 372 Indian Boundary Road, 46304. Telephone: 800-628-1934. Fax: 219-836-5514.

Practice limited to the area of Social Security Disability.

FIRM PROFILE: Practice primarily devoted to matters involving Social Security Disability.

THOMAS J. SCULLY, III, born Erie, Pennsylvania, February 14, 1945; admitted to bar, 1973, Pennsylvania; 1975, Indiana; 1977, Illinois. *Education:* Temple University (B.A., 1970); Rutgers University Law School (J.D., 1973). *Member:* Cook County (Vice Chair, Social Security Committee, 2005), Lake County, Chicago (Chair, Social Security Committee, 2005-2006), Illinois State, Indiana State and Federal Bar Associations; National Organization of Social Security Claimant Representatives (Sustaining Member). ***PRACTICE AREAS:*** Social Security; Social Security Disability.

VEDA PRAVEEN DASARI, admitted to bar, 2002, Indiana and Illinois. *Education:* St. Frances College, India (B.S., 1987); Purdue University (B.S., 1994); Valparaiso University School of Law (J.D., 2001) Dean's List. *Member:* Lake County, Indiana State and Illinois State Bar Associations. ***PRACTICE AREAS:*** Social Security Disability.

SEDGWICK, DETERT, MORAN & ARNOLD LLP

ONE NORTH WACKER DRIVE
SUITE 4200
CHICAGO, ILLINOIS 60606-2841
Telephone: 312-641-9050
Fax: 312-641-9530
Email: E-Mail@SDMA.com
URL: http://www.sdma.com

Dallas, Texas Office: 1717 Main Street, Suite 5400. Telephone: 469-227-8200. Fax: 469-227-8004.

Irvine, California Office: 3 Park Plaza, 17th Floor. Telephone: 949-852-8200. Fax: 949-852-8282.

London, England Office: Candlewick House, 120 Cannon Street, EC4N 6LR. Telephone: +011-44-20-7929-1829. Fax: +011-44-20-7929-1808. Telex: 927037.

Los Angeles, California Office: 801 South Figueroa Street, 18th Floor. Telephone: 213-426-6900. Fax: 213-426-6921.

Newark, New Jersey Office: Three Gateway Center, 12th Floor. Telephone: 973-242-0002. Fax: 973-242-8099.

New York, New York Office: 125 Broad Street, 39th Floor. Telephone: 212-422-0202. Fax: 212-422-0925.

Paris, France Office: 104 Avenue Kléber, 75116. Telephone/Fax: 011-33-1-4704-5502.

San Francisco, California Office: One Market Plaza, Steuart Tower, 8th Floor. Telephone: 415-781-7900. Cabel Address: "Sedma". Fax: 415-781-2635.

(This Listing Continued)

SEDGWICK, DETERT, MORAN & ARNOLD LLP, Chicago—Continued

Zurich, Switzerland Office: Spluegenstrasse 3, CH-8002. Telephone: +011-411-201-1730. Fax: +011-411-201-4404.

Advertising and Marketing, Agency and Distributorships, Agricultural Law, Alternative Dispute Resolution, Antitrust and Trade Regulation, Appellate Practice, Aviation and Aerospace, Bankruptcy, Banks and Banking, Business Law, Class Actions, Collections, Commercial Law, Commercial Real Estate, Communications and Media, Complex and Multi-District Litigation, Computers and Software, Construction Law, Consumer Law, Contracts, Copyrights, Corporate Law, Debtor and Creditor, Disabilities, Education Law, Employee Benefits, Entertainment and the Arts, Environmental Law, Equipment Finance and Leasing, Fidelity and Surety, Franchises and Franchising, Fraud and Deceit, Health Care, Hospital Law, Insurance, Insurance Defense, Intellectual Property, International Law, Labor and Employment, Leases and Leasing, Legal Ethics and Professional Responsibility, Libel, Slander and Defamation, Litigation, Media Law, Medical Practice, Natural Resources, Negligence, Patents, Personal Injury, Premises Liability, Privacy Law, Products Liability, Professional Liability, Real Estate, Regulatory Law, RICO, Securities, Technology and Science, Torts, Toxic Torts, Trade Secrets, Trademarks, Transportation, Unfair Competition, Zoning, Planning and Land Use.

PARTNERS

ANTHONY J. ANSCOMBE, born Philadelphia, Pennsylvania, February 7, 1961; admitted to bar, 1988, Illinois and California; 1989, U.S. District Court, Northern District of California and U.S. Court of Appeals, Ninth Circuit; 1994, U.S. District Court, Central District of California; 1997, U.S. District Court, Eastern District of California; 1999, U.S. District Court, Eastern District of Wisconsin and U.S. District Court, Northern District of Illinois, including Trial Bar, 2003; 2003, U.S. District Court, Southern and Central Districts of Illinois and U.S. Court of Appeals, Seventh Circuit. *Education:* Yale University (B.A., cum laude, 1983); University of Virginia (J.D., 1988). Notes Editor, Virginia Journal of Natural Resources Law, 1987-1988. Author, "Regulating Botanicals in Food", Food Technology (January 2003). *Member:* Chicago and Illinois State Bar Associations; Defense Research Institute. ***PRACTICE AREAS:*** Commercial Litigation; Class Actions; Complex Litigation; Food, Drug and Medical Device; Environmental and Toxic Tort. ***Email:*** anthony.anscombe@sdma.com

ERICA LEWIS BATTAGLIA, born Moscow, Idaho, December 20, 1970; admitted to bar, 1996, Illinois and U.S. District Court, Northern District of Illinois; 2002, U.S. Court of Appeals, Seventh Circuit. *Education:* Miami University (B.A., 1992); DePaul University (J.D., 1996). *Member:* American Health Lawyers Association; American Society for Healthcare Risk Management; Professional Liability Underwriting Society. ***PRACTICE AREAS:*** Health Care; Insurance. ***Email:*** erica.battaglia@sdma.com

THOMAS A. BRUSSTAR, born Detroit, Michigan, May 5, 1964; admitted to bar, 1989, Illinois. *Education:* Universität Freiburg, Freiburg, i.Br., Germany; University of Michigan (A.B., with high distinction, 1986; J.D., 1989). Editor-in-Chief, Michigan Journal of International Law, 1988-1989. *Member:* American Bar Association (Member, Tort and Insurance Practice and International Sections). ***LANGUAGES:*** German. ***PRACTICE AREAS:*** Insurance and Reinsurance Coverage; Commercial Litigation. ***Email:*** thomas.brusstar@sdma.com

RICHARD J. GEDDES, born Chicago, Illinois, July 25, 1948; admitted to bar, 1974, Illinois; U.S. District Court, Northern District of Illinois; U.S. Court of Appeals, Seventh Circuit. *Education:* LeMoyne College (B.A., 1969); Hastings College of Law, University of California (J.D., 1974). Listed in: Leading Lawyers in Illinois, ADR/International Law; Guide to the World's Leading Insurance and Reinsurance Lawyers. *Member:* Illinois State and American Bar Associations; Defense Research Institute; American Arbitration Association (Arbitrator, Commercial Panel); London Court of International Arbitration; ARIAS (US). ***PRACTICE AREAS:*** Insurance Coverage and Counseling; Arbitrations and Mediations; Complex Claims Management. ***Email:*** richard.geddes@sdma.com

KIRK C. JENKINS, born Elizabethtown, Kentucky, October 20, 1961; admitted to bar, 1986, District of Columbia; 1990, U.S. Supreme Court; 1994, California; 2004, Illinois. *Education:* Harvard University (B.A., magna cum laude, 1983); Harvard Law School (J.D., cum laude, 1986). *Member:* Bar Association of San Francisco; Illinois State and American (Member, Council of Appellate Lawyers) Bar Associations; California Academy of Appellate Lawyers; Appellate Lawyers Association. (Certified Specialist, Appellate Law, The State Bar of California Board of Legal Specialization). ***PRACTICE AREAS:*** Appellate Practice; Constitutional Law. ***Email:*** kirk.jenkins@sdma.com

ERIC C. SCHEINER, born Rockford, Illinois, December 25, 1969; admitted to bar, 1997, Illinois and Michigan. *Education:* University of Kentucky (B.A., 1992); John Marshall Law School (J.D., cum laude, 1996). Editor-in-Chief, The John Marshall Law Review, 1995-1996. Law Clerk, Michigan Court of Appeals, 1996-1997. Co-Author: with Jennifer Quinn Broda, "Recent Claim Trends in the Mutual Fund Industry," Directions and Outlooks - Professional Lines Perspectives, Benfield, Issue 1, July 2004, at 12-21; "Can an Act Be Both Negligent and Intentional?: Liability Insurance and the Adjudicated Dishonesty Exclusion," Mealey's: Emerging Insurance Disputes, Volume 9, Number 2, January 20, 2004. Author, "Taking the Public Out of Determining Public Policy: The Need for an Appropriate Scope of Bargaining Test in the Illinois Public Sector," 29 J. Marshall L. Rev. 531, 1996. *Member:* American Bar Association (Tort and Insurance Practice Section); Professional Liability Underwriting Society (PLUS). ***PRACTICE AREAS:*** Insurance and Reinsurance Coverage. ***Email:*** eric.scheiner@sdma.com

EVAN T. SMITH, born Akron, Ohio, December 19, 1961; admitted to bar, 1987, Illinois. *Education:* Harvard University (A.B., 1984); The Ohio State University (J.D., with honors, 1987). Co-Author: "Current Trends in Midwest Tort Reform," presented during the Marsh Healthcare Forum & Client Roundtable, September 23, 2005; "Wisconsin Supreme Court Finds Cap on Medical Malpractice Non-Economic Damages Unconstitutional," Sedgwick's Healthcare Law Newsletter, Summer 2005; "Are You Liable? A Guide for Consultants," Journal of AHIMA, November-December 2001 - 72/10. Author: "Is There an Insurance Response to Health Care Fraud and Abuse?," Journal of Health Care Compliance, Vol. 3, Number 4, July-August 2001; "Fraud and Abuse Settlements and Verdicts," Willis Health Trek Newsletter, December 1999; Presentations: Sedgwick's Third Annual Hot Topics Seminar for the Bermuda Insurance Market, panelist on "Reinsurance Audits: What to Expect and How to Make Them Pay Off," Bermuda, October 5, 2005; Marsh Healthcare Forum & Client Roundtable, panel moderator, "A Comparison of State Efforts in the Midwest-Tort Reform," Chicago, Illinois, September 23, 2005; Sedgwick's Second Annual Hot Topics Seminar for the Bermuda Insurance Market, "Health Care Tort Reform: The Erosion of MICRA and Other Tales," Bermuda, October 27, 2004; Sedgwick's 15th Annual Financial and Professional Services Insurance Seminar, "From Enron to WorldCom: The Perils of Participating in Accountants Professional Liability," London, England, October 8, 2002; Crittenden's Medical Insurance Conference, "Today's New Health Care Issues," and panelist, "Compliance Activities," May 11, 2000; Willis Health Care Seminar, "Recapping the Federal False Claims Act & DRG Upcoding," April 2000; Willis Re Spring Fling, "Insurability of False Claims Act Exposures," San Antonio, Texas, March 2000; Health Care Compliance Association, Third Annual Congress, "Insurability of False Claims Act Exposures," Washington, D.C., March 2000; Health Care Compliance Association, Annual Conference, "Insurability of False Claims Act Exposures," Chicago, Illinois, October 1999; Sedgwick's 12th Annual Financial and Professional Services Insurance Seminar, "Y2K Update," London, England, October 1999; Willis National Healthcare Conference, "Emerging Managed Care Exposures," Nashville, Tennessee, July 1999; Sedgwick's 7th Annual Financial and Professional Services Insurance Seminar, "Y2K Update," Morristown, New Jersey, June 1999; ABA Annual Conference, "Emerging D&O Exposures," New York, N.Y., February 1999; Illinois State Medical Society Annual Residency Program, "PATH Audits of Teaching Hospitals," Oak Brook, Illinois, February 1999; "Professional Liability Underwriting Society (PLUS) Annual Meeting, "Healthcare Fraud & Abuse: Detection, Prevention & Response," Palm Springs, California, November 1998. *Member:* Professional Liability Underwriting Society (PLUS); American Society of Healthcare Risk Management (ASHRM); Chicago Healthcare Risk Management Society (CHRMS); American Health Lawyers Association (AHLA); Health Care Compliance Association (HCCA); AIDA Reinsurance and Insurance Arbitration Society (ARIAS). ***PRACTICE AREAS:*** Insurance Coverage; Reinsurance Coverage; Healthcare; Professional Liability; Directors and Officers Liability. ***Email:*** evan.smith@sdma.com

FRED A. SMITH III, born Evergreen Park, Illinois, May 21, 1950; admitted to bar, 1982, Illinois; 1997, Indiana. *Education:* University of Illinois (B.S., 1972); Illinois Institute of Technology/Chicago-Kent College of Law (J.D., 1982). Law Clerk for Justice Thomas J. Moran, Illinois Supreme Court. Published articles on a variety of topics, including healthcare, insurance coverage and environmental issues. Frequent lecturer at private and professional seminar programs on various issues related to insurance and reinsurance contract disputes: "State Law Challenges in Managed Care," Chapter 4 of Managed Care Litigation (September 2005), published by the Bureau of National Affairs, Inc. (co-authored with members of Sedgwick's Healthcare Practice Group); Co-authored "An Overview of FEHBA and the Power of Its Preemption," The Health Lawyer (October 2005); Authored "Obtaining Dismissals for Healthcare Entities in Illinois: A Statutory Approach," Sedgwick's Healthcare Law Newsletter (Summer 2005); Presented "Why Are Silent PPOs Making So Much Noise?" Chubb Specialty's Managed Care Seminar (May 2005) with co-speaker Michael H. Bernstein (Partner, Sedgwick - New York); Presented "Medical Liability: The New Legal Landscape" at the Professional Liability Underwriting Society's fifth annual Medical Professional Liability Symposium held in Chicago, Illinois (March 2005); Authored "Creative D&O Settlements - Favorable for Insurers, Reinsurers, or Both?" appearing in Directions & Outlooks - Financial Lines Perspectives, a Benfield publication (Summer 2004); Presented "Creative D&O Settlements" at the annual Excess/Surplus Lines Claims Association Meeting held at General Reinsurance Corporation (May 2004); Presented "Emerging Issues - Attorney and Accountant Liability" at the Professional Liability Underwriting Society Midwest Chapter Seminar entitled State of the Reinsurance Marketplace and Emerging Issues, held in Chicago, Illinois (May 2002); Co-authored a chapter entitled "Extra-Contractual Damages" appearing in the Illinois Institute for Continuing Legal Education's Commercial and Professional Liability Insurance Practice Handbook (April 2002); Presented "Getting the Best Settlement Without Risking a Bad Faith Claim" at the Eighth National Conference of the American Conference Institute's Seminar entitled Advanced Forum on Litigating, Bad Faith and Punitive Damages, held in San Francisco, California (April 2002); Presented "Directors & Officers Liability from the Reinsurer's Perspective" at the Financial Institution Seminar held in London, England (October 2001); Presented "Walking the Settlement Minefield: Negotiating the Best Deal . . . Without Risking a Bad Faith Claim" at the American Conference Institute's Seminar entitled Advanced Forum on Bad Faith and Punitive Damages, held in San Francisco, California (March 2001); Co-authored with Zurich Re (North America) a booklet entitled BAD FAITH, a Fifty State Survey (October 1999); Authored an article entitled "Legislative Initiatives Affecting Managed Care Liability," published in Zurich-American Healthcare Managed Care Briefings (1998); Presented "Treaty and Ceding Company Policy Drafting Issues" at a Sedgwick reinsurance workshop for various reinsurance companies, entitled Multiple Year/Multiple Coverage Policies and Their Implications, held in Greenwich, Connecticut (November 1997); Spoke on various topics at a TIG Reinsurance Directors' & Officers' Liability Seminar, including: "EPL (Stand-Alone and by Endorsement/D&O v. Entity)"; "Entity/ Predetermined Allocation Issues"; "Non-Profit D&O" and "The Impact of the Securities Reform Act of 1995 on Insureds, Insurers and Reinsurers" (June 1997). *Member:* Chicago, Illinois State and American Bar Associations; Illinois Appellate Lawyers Association; Defense Research Institute, Inc.; Illinois Association of Defense Trial Counsel; Illinois Association of Healthcare Attorneys. ***PRACTICE AREAS:*** Healthcare, Business and Commercial Litigation; Class Action Litigation; Complex Insurance Litigation; Products Liability; Catastrophic Injury and Wrongful Death; Insurance Coverage and Reinsurance. ***Email:*** fred.smith@sdma.com

JAMES D. WANGELIN, born Evanston, Illinois, September 2, 1947; admitted to bar, 1974, Illinois. *Education:* University of Michigan (A.B., with distinction, 1969; J.D., 1974). Recipient, Chicago Bar Association's David C. Hilliard Award. Member, Governor's Advisory Board for Credit Unions, 1980-1981. Director, Chicago International Dispute Resolution Association. *Member:* Chicago (Member, Young Lawyers Section, 1979-1981), Illinois State and American Bar Associations; Defense Research Institute (Named Leading Lawyer, ADR and Insurance/Reinsurance); Chartered Institute of Arbitrators; ARIAS (Chairman, 1977-1982, and Director, 1979-1981, Lawyer Services Committee, Young Lawyers Section). ***PRACTICE AREAS:*** Insurance Coverage; Reinsurance; Alternative Dispute Resolution; Commercial Litigation; International Arbitration. ***Email:*** james.wangelin@sdma.com

(This Listing Continued)

SPECIAL COUNSEL

CAROL J. GERNER, born Chicago, Illinois; admitted to bar, 1981, Illinois. *Education:* Tufts University (B.A., cum laude, 1977); Washington University School of Law (J.D., 1981). Co-author: "The Rise in Breach of Fiduciary Duty Claims Against Managed Care Organizations Based Upon Healthcare Provider Financial Incentives," Willis - Health Trek, 2nd Quarter (1999). Associate Editor, *Health Care Liability Desk Book*, published by the West Group (1998). Co-author: "New Legislation Regarding Managed Care Liability," Willis - Health Trek, 1st Quarter (1997). Author: "A Physician's Guide to Avoiding Liability in Managed Care Settings," Chicago Medicine (March 1993); "AIDS in the Healthcare Workplace: Rights and Responsibilities," Loyola University Annals of Health Law, Vol. 1 (1992). Co-author: "Utilization Review: Erica's Preemptive Protection for Managed Care," Journal of the Institute for Behavioral Healthcare (September/October 1993). *Member:* Chicago, Illinois State and American Bar Associations; American Health Lawyers Association; Illinois Health Lawyers Association. ***PRACTICE AREAS:*** Insurance Coverage; Directors and Officers Liability; Professional Liability; Healthcare. ***Email:*** carol.gerner@sdma.com

RENEE S. LEVITT, admitted to bar, 1986, Illinois; U.S. District Court, Northern District of Illinois. *Education:* University of Illinois (B.A., 1983); IIT/Chicago-Kent College of Law (J.D., with honors, 1986). Omicron Delta Epsilon. Recipient, West Publishing Company Annual Hornbook Student Award. *Member:* Chicago, Illinois State and American Bar Associations. ***PRACTICE AREAS:*** Litigation; Insurance Coverage; Health Care; Toxic Torts; Construction Law; Professional Liability; Products Liability; Intellectual Property. ***Email:*** renee.levitt@sdma.com

MICHAEL B. SATZ, born Newark, New Jersey, July 15, 1953; admitted to bar, 1982, Illinois and U.S. District Court, Northern District of Illinois. *Education:* Northwestern University (B.A., 1975); John Marshall Law School (J.D., with distinction, 1982). *Member:* Professional Liability Underwriting Society (PLUS); Defense Research Institute. ***PRACTICE AREAS:*** Insurance and Reinsurance Coverage. ***Email:*** michael.satz@sdma.com

DAVID K. SUBRAMANIAN, admitted to bar, 1993, Illinois and U.S. District Court, Northern District of Illinois. *Education:* Augustana College (B.A., 1989); DePaul University (J.D., 1993). *Member:* American Bar Association; Defense Research Institute. ***REPORTED CASES:*** Weis v. State Farm Mutual Automobile Insurance Co., 333 Ill. App. 3d 402, 776 N.E.2d 309 (2nd Dist. 2002). ***PRACTICE AREAS:*** Insurance Coverage; Extra-contractual and Bad Faith Liability; Reinsurance. ***Email:*** david.subramanian@sdma.com

ASSOCIATES

SCOTT D. BRAUN, born Milwaukee, Wisconsin, October 20, 1971; admitted to bar, 1997, Illinois and U.S. District Court, Central and Southern Districts of Illinois; 1998, U.S. District Court, Northern District of Illinois. *Education:* University of Wisconsin-Madison (B.A., 1993); Washington University (J.D., 1996). ***PRACTICE AREAS:*** Insurance Coverage; Reinsurance; Professional Liability/E&O/D&O; Extracontractual/Bad Faith Liability; Commercial Litigation. ***Email:*** scott.braun@sdma.com

JENNIFER QUINN BRODA, born Chicago, Illinois, October 10, 1972; admitted to bar, 2000, Illinois and U.S. District Court, Northern District of Illinois. *Education:* Knox College (B.A., 1994); Loyola University - Chicago School of Law (J.D., 2000). Dean's List. Recipient, CALI awards in Legal Writing I, Legal Writing II and Employment Law. *Member:* Chicago Bar Association (Investigator, Judicial Evaluation Committee). ***PRACTICE AREAS:*** Directors and Officers Liability; Errors and Omissions Liability; Insurance Coverage Litigation; Bad Faith Litigation; Extracontractual Coverage Litigation. ***Email:*** jennifer.broda@sdma.com

MELANIE M. BROWN, born Columbus, Ohio, July 23, 1970; admitted to bar, 1997, Illinois and U.S. District Court, Northern District of Illinois; 1999, U.S. District Court, Eastern District of Wisconsin; 2003, U.S. District Court, Southern and Central Districts of Illinois; 2004, U.S. Court of Appeals, Seventh Circuit. *Education:* University of Virginia (B.A., with distinction, 1993); Washington & Lee University (J.D., 1997). Golden Key Honor Society; Phi Alpha Theta National Honor Society. *Member:* Chicago and Illinois State Bar Associations. ***PRACTICE AREAS:*** Mass Tort and Complex Litigation; Medical Malpractice; Commercial Litigation; Surety Litigation. ***Email:*** melanie.brown@sdma.com

JENNA L. BUDA, born South Bend, Indiana, April 17, 1975; admitted to bar, 2001, Illinois and U.S. District Court, Northern District of Illinois. *Education:* Indiana University (B.A., 1997); DePaul University (J.D., 2000). Phi Alpha Delta (Justice, 1999-2000). Note and Comment Co-Editor, DePaul University College of Law's Health Law Journal, 1999-2000. *Member:* Chicago, Illinois State and American Bar Associations; American Health Lawyers Association; American Society for Healthcare Risk Management. ***PRACTICE AREAS:*** Insurance Coverage; Health Care. ***Email:*** jenna.buda@sdma.com

NICHOLAS D. BUTOVICH, born Passaic, New Jersey, 1974; admitted to bar, 2002, Illinois. *Education:* Boston College (B.A., summa cum laude, 1996); Loyola University, Chicago School of Law (J.D., 2001). Phi Beta Kappa. Recipient: Patrick J. Durcan, S.J. Award for Excellence in History; CALI Award in Jurisprudence; CALI Award in Constitutional History. Editor-in-Chief, Forum of International Law. *Member:* Chicago and American Bar Associations. Phi Beta Kappa. ***LANGUAGES:*** Ukrainian, Croatian and Russian. ***PRACTICE AREAS:*** Insurance Coverage; Health Care. ***Email:*** nicholas.butovich@sdma.com

ELIZABETH J. COTTER, born Montague, Michigan, March 30, 1977; admitted to bar, 2003, Illinois. *Education:* Michigan State University (B.A., 1999); Hastings College of Law, University of California (J.D., 2003). *Member:* Chicago and Illinois State Bar Associations; Chicago Bar Foundation (Member, Young Professionals Board). ***PRACTICE AREAS:*** Complex Litigation and Class Action; International Arbitration and Insurance; Commercial Litigation. ***Email:*** elizabeth.cotter@sdma.com

GARY L. GASSMAN, born Chicago, Illinois, April 22, 1968; admitted to bar, 1993, Illinois. U.S. District Court, Northern District of Illinois including Trial Bar. *Education:* Indiana University - Bloomington (B.A., 1990); John Marshall Law School (J.D., 1993). Phi Delta Phi. Adjunct Professor, John Marshall Law School, 1996—. Author: "SYSOP, User and Programmer Liability: The Constitutionality of Computer Generated Child Pornography," 13 J. Marshall J. Comp. & Info 4810, 1995; "Internet Defamation: Jurisdiction in Cyberspace and the Public Figure Doctrine," 14 JMJCIL563, 1996. *Member:* Chicago and American (Member, Tort and Insurance Practice Section) Bar Associations; Professional Liability Underwriting Society (PLUS). ***PRACTICE AREAS:*** Directors and Officers Liability; Lawyers Professional Liability; Insurance and Reinsurance Coverage; Health Care. ***Email:*** gary.gassman@sdma.com

DAVID M. GOLDHABER, born Chicago, Illinois, February 12, 1971; admitted to bar, 1997, Illinois. *Education:* Purdue University (B.A., 1993); Loyola University Chicago School of Law (J.D., 1996). ***PRACTICE AREAS:*** Litigation; Health Care; Surety; Product Liability. ***Email:*** david.goldhaber@sdma.com

C. KINNIER LASTIMOSA, born Dallas, Texas, September 6, 1976; admitted to bar, 2002, Illinois and U.S. District Court, Northern, Central and Southern Districts of Illinois. *Education:* Northwestern University (B.A., 1998) Dean's list; Washington University (J.D., 2002) Dean's list. Phi Alpha Delta (Justice, 2001-2002). Executive Notes Editor, Washington University Law Quarterly, 2001-2002. Co-author, "Can an Act Be Both Negligent and Intentional?: Liability Insurance and the Adjudicated Dishonesty Exclusion," Mealey's: Emerging Insurance Disputes, Vol. 9, No. 2, (Jan. 20, 2004). Author: "One Man's Ceiling Is Another Man's Floor: The Effect of Post-Removal Damage Stipulations on the Amount in Controversy Requirement of a Diversity Case," Washington University Law Quarterly, Vol. 81, No. (2003); "Automatic for Removal?: The Use of Post-Petition Evidence to Establish the Amount of Controversy for Diversity Jurisdiction," Washington University Law Quarterly, Vol.80, No. 1 (2002). *Member:* Chicago and American Bar Associations. ***PRACTICE AREAS:*** Litigation; Insurance Law; Mass Tort and Complex Litigation. ***Email:*** kinnier.lastimosa@sdma.com

EILEEN NAVARRO, (admission pending). *Education:* Northern Illinois University (B.S., with honors, 2002); University of Illinois (J.D., 2005). Associate Editor, Elder Law Journal, University of Illinois College of Law, 2004-2005. ***LANGUAGES:*** Spanish. ***PRACTICE AREAS:*** Insurance; Health Care; Products Liability; Commercial Litigation. ***Email:*** eileen.navarro@sdma.com

JAMES M. PINKSTAFF, born Robinson, Illinois, April 23, 1977; admitted to bar, 2002, Illinois and U.S. District Court, Northern District of Illinois. *Education:* University of Illinois (A.B., with distinction, 1999; J.D., cum laude, 2002). Certified Public Accountant, 2003. *Member:* Chicago Bar Association; Chicago Council on Foreign Relations. ***LANGUAGES:*** Brazilian Portuguese. ***PRACTICE AREAS:*** Directors and Officers Liability; Corporate Governance; Healthcare; Insurance and Reinsurance Counseling. ***Email:*** james.pinkstaff@sdma.com

PETER J. PRESTON, born Pontiac, Michigan, May 19, 1970; admitted to bar, 1995, Tennessee; 1996, Michigan and U.S. District Court, Middle District of Tennessee; 1997, U.S. Court of Appeals, Ninth Circuit; 1998, Illinois and U.S. District Court, Northern District of Illinois; 1999, U.S. District Court, Western District of Michigan and U.S. District Court, Central District of Illinois. *Education:* University of Miami (B.B.A., 1992; J.D., cum laude, 1995). Phi Delta Phi. *Member:* American Bar Association (Litigation and Labor & Employment Sections); Illinois State Bar Association; State Bar of Michigan; Chicago Bar Association; Defense Research Institute. ***PRACTICE AREAS:*** Employment Litigation and Counseling; Professional Liability; Products Liability; Class Actions/Complex Litigation; Excess and Reinsurance; Excess Coverage; Insurance Arbitration. ***Email:*** peter.preston@sdma.com

SAMUEL B. RAINEY, born Philadelphia, Pennsylvania, August 20, 1976; admitted to bar, 2002, Illinois and U.S. District Court, Northern District of Illinois. *Education:* Miami University (Ohio) (B.A., 1999); University of Pittsburgh School of Law (J.D., 2002). Dean's List. Recipient: Health Law Certificate; CALI Awards in Advanced Legal Writing, Trademark Protection and International Law. *Member:* Chicago, Illinois State and American (Member, Health Law Division) Bar Associations. ***PRACTICE AREAS:*** Health Care; Insurance; Mass Tort and Complex Litigation. ***Email:*** samuel.rainey@sdma.com

IAN N. ROTHENBERG, born Skokie, Illinois, May 19, 1972; admitted to bar, 1997, Illinois; U.S. District Court, Northern District of Illinois. *Education:* University of Illinois at Champaign/Urbana (B.S., 1994); Loyola University, Chicago School of Law (J.D., 1997). Editor, Loyola University Law Review, 1996-1997. *Member:* Chicago and Illinois State Bar Associations. ***PRACTICE AREAS:*** Insurance Coverage; Insurance Litigation; Mass Tort and Complex Litigation. ***Email:*** ian.rothenberg@sdma.com

M. MILES SUKOVIC, born Chicago, Illinois, January 19, 1971; admitted to bar, 2000, Indiana; 2002, Illinois; U.S. District Court, Northern District of Illinois and U.S. District Court, Southern and Northern Districts of Indiana. *Education:* University of Illinois - Chicago (B.A., highest honors, 1995); Indiana University School of Law - Indianapolis (J.D., 1999). Phi Beta Kappa. Dean's List. Editor, International & Comparative Law Review. *Member:* Chicago, Indianapolis, Indiana State and American Bar Associations. ***LANGUAGES:*** French and Serbian. ***REPORTED CASES:*** Menefee v. Schurr, 751 N.E.2d 757 (Ind.Ct.App. 2001); Art Country Squire, L.L.C. v. Inland Mortg. Corp., 745 N.E.2d 885 (Ind.Ct.App. 2001). ***PRACTICE AREAS:*** Insurance Coverage and Litigation; Reinsurance; Commercial Litigation; Health Care; Insurance; Excess and Reinsurance; Excess Coverage; General Liability; Insurance Arbitration; Risk Management. ***Email:*** miles.sukovic@sdma.com

KRISTINE TEJANO, born Wichita, Kansas, February 7, 1971; admitted to bar, 2000, Illinois; 2001, U.S. District Court, Northern District of Illinois. *Education:* University of Pennsylvania (B.A., in Communications, 1993); DePaul University (J.D., 2000). *Member:* Chicago, Illinois State and American Bar Associations. ***PRACTICE AREAS:*** Directors and Officers Liability; Lawyers Professional Liability; Employment Practices Liability; Insurance Coverage; Reinsurance. ***Email:*** kristine.tejano@sdma.com

FRANK E. VALENTI, admitted to bar, 2002, Illinois and U.S. District Court, Northern District of Illinois. *Education:* Northern Illinois University (B.A., Business Management, 1998); University of Illinois College of Law (J.D., 2002). Dean's List. Member, University of Illinois Law Review. Member and Recipient, Best Brief Award, Frederick Green National Moot Court Team. Recipient, annual Rickert Award for Excellence in Oral Advocacy. ***PRACTICE AREAS:*** Insurance Coverage and Litigation; Class Actions/Complex Litigation; Commercial Litigation. ***Email:*** frank.valenti@sdma.com

REPRESENTATIVE CLIENTS: Abbott Laboratories Inc; Advocate Health Care Network; Aetna U.S. Healthcare, Inc.; American Airlines; American International Group; Bankers Insurance Service Corporation; Bayer Corporation; Bristol-Myers Squibb Company; Brown &

(This Listing Continued)

SEDGWICK, DETERT, MORAN & ARNOLD LLP, Chicago—Continued

Williamson Tobacco Corporation; Case Corporation; Caterpillar Inc.; Chevron Chemical Company; DaimlerChrysler Corporation; Chubb & Son Inc.; The Clorox Company; Collagen Corporation; Electric Insurance Company; Equiva Services LLC; Fidelity & Deposit Company of Maryland; Fisons Corporation; FOJP Service Corp.; Genentech, Inc.; General Motors; General Reinsurance Corporation; Hartford Insurance Company; Herman Miller, Inc.; Hewlett-Packard Company; Highlands Insurance Group; Hoffman-La Roche Inc.; Invacare Corporation; Isuzu Motors America, Inc.; Litton Industries Inc.; Lockheed Martin Corporation, Missiles & Space; Lorillard Tobacco Company; Metropolitan Life Insurance Co.; Monsanto Company; Morton International, Inc.; Optima Healthcare Ins. Services; Pacific Gas & Electric Company; The Permanente Medical Group Inc.; Pharmacia Corporation; Phillips Petroleum Company; Raytheon Aircraft Company; Schindler Elevator Corporation; Stanley Works Company; Stryker Corporation; Subaru of America, Inc.; Synthes USA; Tenet HealthSystem; The Tokio Marine and Fire Insurance Co., Ltd.; Toyota Motor Sales, U.S.A., Inc.; The Travelers Companies; Underwriters at Lloyd's; X.L. Insurance Company, Ltd.; Zurich-American Insurance Group.

(For complete biographical data on all personnel at Dallas, Texas; Irvine, California; Los Angeles, California; London, England; Newark, New Jersey; New York, New York; Paris, France; San Francisco, California; and Zurich, Switzerland, see Professional Biographies at those locations).

ALAN F. SEGAL

29 S. LA SALLE STREET, SUITE 334
CHICAGO, ILLINOIS 60603
Telephone: 312-444-1700
Fax: 312-444-1766
Email: asegal@megsinet.net
URL: http://www.asegal.com

Taxation, Individual Taxation, Business Taxation, Tax Audits, Employment Tax, Appellate Practice, Tax Law.

ALAN F. SEGAL, born Washington, D.C., May 12, 1945; admitted to bar, 1970, Illinois. *Education:* Georgetown University (B.S.B.A., Accounting, cum laude, 1967); University of Chicago (J.D., 1970). Alpha Sigma Nu. Member, District Director Advisory Committee, 1988—. Author: "Tax Aspects of Litigation," Vol. II, Illinois Civil Practice Handbook, Illinois Institute on Continuing Legal Education, 1991 and Law of Federal Income Taxation, Mertens, Vol. 5, Ch. 24A, 1991; "District Court and Claims Court Litigation," Federal Tax Practice and Procedure Practice Handbook, Illinois Institute on Continuing Legal Education, 1991. Formerly with Internal Revenue Service, Washington, D.C., 1966-1970. Associate and Partner, Levenfeld, Eisenberg et al, 1970-1988. Partner, Levin, Schreder & Segal, 1988-1990. *Member:* Chicago Bar Association (Member, Federal Taxation Committee, Division E, Practice and Procedure; Former Representative, District Director's Liaison Committee and Pre-Filing Advisory Group). ***PRACTICE AREAS:*** Taxation; Individual Taxation; Business Taxation; Tax Audits; Employment Tax; Appellate Practice; Trust Law.

SEGAL McCAMBRIDGE SINGER & MAHONEY, LTD.

Established in 1986
ONE IBM PLAZA, SUITE 200
330 NORTH WABASH
CHICAGO, ILLINOIS 60611
Telephone: 312-645-7800
Facsimile: 312-645-7711
URL: http://www.smsm.com

Brighton, Michigan Office: 7960 Grand River Ave., Suite 260, 48114. Telephone: 810-225-4227. Facsimile: 810-225-4201.
Austin, Texas Office: 100 Congress Avenue, Suite 700, 78701. Telephone: 512-476-7834. Facsimile: 512-476-7832.
Philadelphia, Pennsylvania Office: United Plaza 30 S. 17th Street, Suite #1700, 19103. Telephone: 215-972-8015. Facsimile: 215-972-8016.
Princeton, New Jersey Office: 103 Carnegie Center, Suite 103, 08540. Telephone: 609-452-1558. Facsimile: 609-452-1559.
Baltimore, Maryland Office: 217 Redwood Street, 21st Floor, 21202. Telephone: 410-779-3960. Fax: 410-779-3967.
New York, New York Office: 830 Third Avenue, Suite 400, 10022. Telephone: 212-651-7500. Fax: 212-651-7499.

Product Liability, Toxic Torts, General Insurance Defense, General Liability, Medical Malpractice, Professional Liability, Commercial Litigation, Coverage Issues, Municipal Liability, Law Enforcement Liability, Construction Litigation, Premises Liability, Employment Discrimination, Civil Rights, Automobile.

FIRM PROFILE: We specialize in litigation, concentrating primarily on the defense of product liability, environmental and toxic tort, medical and dental malpractice, municipal and public official liability, consumer warranty litigation and other tort litigation. The firm does not attempt to provide a complete spectrum of legal services, but instead focuses on limited practice areas, allowing us to stay abreast of the latest legal developments and industry trends within these select fields. By consistently providing aggressive and effective representation at reasonable rates, the firm has developed a reputation for excellence, and its roster of clients had grown impressively. In addition to regularly handling cases in various state and federal courts in Illinois, Indiana, Texas, Pennsylvania, New Jersey, New York, Maryland, Wisconsin, and Michigan, the firm serves as national trial and coordinating counsel for several clients. The firm maintains offices in Chicago; Austin; Philadelphia; Brighton; Michigan; Princeton; New Jersey; Baltimore; and New York.

(This Listing Continued)

PARTNERS

DONALD SEGAL, born Chicago, Illinois, July 23, 1938; admitted to bar, 1963, Illinois and U.S. District Court, Northern District of Illinois. *Education:* University of Illinois; University of Wisconsin (B.S., 1960); University of Chicago (J.D., 1963). Author: "Opening Statement," Chapter in Medical & Hospital Negligence, Callaghan and Company, 1988. Instructor, Medical Jurisprudence, Scholl College of Podiatric Medicine, 1979-1990. Member, Panel of Arbitrators, American Arbitration Association. *Member:* Chicago and Illinois State Bar Associations; Decalogue Society of Lawyers; Chicago Council of Lawyers; Japan-American Society of Chicago. ***PRACTICE AREAS:*** Products Liability Law; Medical Malpractice; Insurance Defense Litigation; General Liability; Toxic Tort. **Email:** dsegal@smsm.com

EDWARD J. McCAMBRIDGE, born Evergreen Park, Illinois, December 6, 1949; admitted to bar, 1975, Illinois, Michigan; U.S. District Court, Northern, Central and Southern Districts of Illinois and U.S. District Court, Eastern and Western Districts of Wisconsin. *Education:* University of St. Thomas (B.A., 1971); John Marshall Law School (J.D., 1975). Speaker, Asbestos Litigation, Illinois Association of Defense Counsel, 1984. Author: Section Trial Advocacy and Chairman in Illinois, 1991; Trial Advocacy In Illinois & Seminar Chairman, 1999. Chairman, Asbestos Defense Group of Cook County, 1981-1986. Member, Board of Directors, Chicago Asbestos Property Damage Defense Group, 1984—. Member, Panel of Arbitrators, American Arbitration Association. *Member:* Barien County (Member, Environmental and Toxic Tort Law Committees) and Illinois (Member, Sections on: Environmental and Business Torts) State Bar Associations; State Bar of Michigan; Illinois Defense Trial Counsel; Defense Research and Trial Lawyers Association; Chicago Trial Lawyers Club; National Business Institute (Toxic Mold Litigation, 2004). ***PRACTICE AREAS:*** Products Liability Law; Medical Malpractice; Toxic Tort; Insurance Defense Litigation; Environmental Litigation. **Email:** emccambridge@smsm.com

WILLIAM F. MAHONEY, born Chicago, Illinois, December 15, 1953; admitted to bar, 1978, Illinois; 1997, Michigan; 1998, Texas; U.S. District Court, Northern District of Illinois including Trial Bar; U.S. District Court, Southern District of Illinois; U.S. District Court, Central District of Illinois; U.S. District Court, Eastern District of Wisconsin; U.S. District Court, Northern District of Indiana. *Education:* Loyola University (B.A., Honors Degree, 1975); University of Illinois (J.D., 1978). Alpha Sigma Nu; Blue Key. Author: "Asbestos Trust: Time for a Decision," Harris Martin's COLUMNS-Asbestos, Vol. 5, No. 9, July 2005; Editor and Contributing Author, "Toxic Torts, Hazardous Substances and Environmental Law," Annual Survey, Tort and Insurance Law Journal, 1992-1996; Author and Speaker: "The Defense of Increased Risk and Fear of Cancer Claims," presented at American Bar Association National Institute on Toxic Torts, August, 1992; "Class Action and Mass Torts: History and Recent Developments," presented to Midwest Environmental Claims Association, September, 1997; Moderator: "Tort Reform in the New Millennium," American Bar Association Annual Meeting Presidential Showcase Program, 2001; Panelist: "Environmental Contamination, Litigation Strategies and Bankruptcy Considerations," American Bar Association Annual Meeting, 1996; Speaker: "The Case From Hell, Opening Statements for the Defendant in Toxic Tort Litigation," American Bar Association Annual Meeting, August, 1995; "Essentials of Daubert in Practice: The Role of Expert Scientific Proof at Trial," American Bar Association Annual Meeting, 1997; "Corporate Management of Toxic Tort Litigation," American Bar Association Annual Meeting, 1998; "Recent Appellate Developments in Asbestos Litigation," Mealey's National Asbestos Conference, 2000; "The Chrysotile Defense: Revisited," Defense Research Institute Asbestos Medicine Symposium, 2001; "Asbestos Litigation and Legislation," Defense Research Institute, Insurance Coverage and Claims Institute, 2003; "Medical Defenses in Asbestos Litigation," Mealey's National Asbestos Conference, 2003; "Ten Corporate Mistakes Leading to Punitive Damages," Defense Research Institute Damages Seminar, 2004; "Confronting Environmental, Asbestos, Mold and Other Organic Concerns," Defense Research Institute, Insurance Coverage and Claims Institute, 2004. *Member:* American Bar Association (Vice-Chairman, Toxic and Hazardous Substances Committee); Chicago Bar Association (Special Committee, Evaluation of Judicial Candidates); American Bar Foundation; Chicago Council of Lawyers; Defense Research Institute. ***REPORTED CASES:*** Kurrack v. ADT. ***PRACTICE AREAS:*** Toxic Torts; Environmental Litigation; Products Liability. **Email:** wmahoney@smsm.com

GREGORY E. ROGUS, born Chicago, Illinois, October 11, 1955; admitted to bar, 1980, Illinois and U.S. District Court, Northern District of Illinois including Trial Bar; 1981, U.S. Court of Appeals, Seventh Circuit; 1985, U.S. District Court, Central District of Illinois; 1994, U.S Supreme Court. *Education:* Loyola University (B.A., magna cum laude, 1977); University of Illinois (J.D., 1980). *Member:* Chicago Bar Association; Defense Research Institute. ***REPORTED CASES:*** Jaffee v. Redmond, 116 S. Ct. 1923 (1996). ***PRACTICE AREAS:*** Police and Public Official Liability Law; Premises Liability Law; Insurance Defense Litigation; Commercial Litigation; Appellate Advocacy; Employment Law; General Liability; Toxic Tort. **Email:** grogus@smsm.com

PHILLIP MARK CRANE, born Lafayette, Indiana, August 4, 1959; admitted to bar, 1984, Indiana; 1985, Illinois; 1987, U.S. District Court, Northern District of Indiana and Northern District of Illinois including Trial Bar; 1989, U.S. District Court, Central District of Illinois; 1992, U.S. District Court, Northern District of California. *Education:* Purdue University (B.A., 1981); Indiana University (J.D., cum laude, 1984). Author and Speaker: "Effective Cross-Examination Techniques," American Bar Association Annual Convention, 1995. Author: "Making Cross Examination Work," The Practical Litigator, Vol. 7, No. 4, July 1996; "The Data Bank: Is It Big Brother at Work?" ADA Legal Advisor, Vol. 1, No. 9, December, 1997; "Product Liability Defendants Discover Substantial Alteration Defense Has Been Substantially Altered," DRI Hand and Power Tools Newsletter, Spring 1998; "Keys to a Productive Relationship: National and Local Counsel in Mass Tort Litigation," For the Defense, Vol. 46, No. 5., May 2004. *Member:* Chicago Bar Association. ***PRACTICE AREAS:*** Products Liability; Medical and Dental Malpractice; Insurance Defense Litigation; Commercial Litigation; General Liability. **Email:** mcrane@smsm.com

ROBERT E. O'MALLEY, born Oak Park, Illinois, December 6, 1960; admitted to bar, 1986, Illinois and U.S. District Court, Northern District of Illinois including Trial Bar; 1992, U.S. District Court, Western District of Wisconsin and Central District of Illinois and U.S. District Court, Southern District of Illinois. *Education:* Marquette University (B.A., 1983); Chicago-Kent College of Law (J.D., 1986). Phi Sigma Alpha. Member, Panel of Ar-

(This Listing Continued)

bitrators, Cook County Mandatory Arbitration System. Author: "The Consumer Expectation Test - Has It Outlived Its Usefulness," For The Defense (DRI), September 2001. Speaker, "Claims: Offensive and Defensive Strategies," Scaffold Industry Association's (SIA) 33rd Annual Convention and Trade Show, Boston, MA, July 2005. *Member:* Chicago and Illinois State Bar Associations; Defense Research Institute (Industry-wide Litigation Committee); Product Liability Advisory Counsel (PLAC); International Association of Defense Counsel (IADC). ***REPORTED CASES:*** Navarro v. Fuji Heavy Industries, et al., 117 F.3d 1027, 925 F.Supp. 1323, 47 Fed. R. Evid. Serv. 446, (N.D.Ill. Apr 22, 1996); Costa v. Dresser Industries, et al., 205 Ill.Dec. 33, N.E.2d 898 (1994). ***PRACTICE AREAS:*** Products Liability; Toxic Tort; Construction Litigation; Medical Malpractice; Professional Liability; Commercial Litigation; General Liability. ***Email:*** romalley@smsm.com

PAUL E. WOJCICKI, born Chicago, Illinois, January 13, 1964; admitted to bar, 1989, Illinois; 1995, U.S. Supreme Court; 1990, U.S. District Court, Northern District of Illinois including Trial Bar and U.S. Court of Appeals, Seventh Circuit; 1991, U.S. District Court, Southern District of Indiana and U.S. District Court, Western District of Wisconsin; 1992, U.S. District Court, Eastern District of Wisconsin; 1995, U.S. District Court, Northern District of Indiana and U.S. District Court, Central District of Illinois; 1999, Michigan; 2001, U.S. District Court, Eastern District of Michigan. *Education:* Columbia University (A.B., 1986); DePaul College of Law (J.D., 1989). Author: "Is Illinois Supreme Court Rule 23(e)'s Denial of Precedential Effect to Appellate Court 'Orders' Constitutional," Chgo. Bar. Assn. Record, Jan. 2004, "A Note On Damges and Disclaimers in an Action for Breach of a Repair-or-Replacement Warranty," "Early Resolution Strategies in Warranty Litigation," "Attacking Breach of Implied Warranty Claims in Magnuson-Moss Actions," and "The Admissibility of Expert Evidence In the Seventh Circuit After Daubert," RV Defense; MV Defense.COM. Co-Author: "Ch. 5 Declaratory Relief," Illinois Civil Practice, Vol. II, 2003 and 1997 Practice Handbook, Illinois Institute of Continuing Education; "Ch. 3 Parties to Product Liability Cases," Illinois Product Liability Practice, 1996 Practice Handbook, Illinois Institute of Continuing Legal Education; "Defeating the Plaintiff's Automotive Products Case - Daubert Revisited," and "Do Vehicle Lessees Qualify As Consumers Under the Magnuson-Moss Act?". *Member:* Chicago, Illinois State and American (Member, Tort and Insurance Practice Sections) Bar Associations; Seventh Circuit Bar Association; Chicago Volunteer Legal Services Foundation; Appellate Lawyers Association; RV Defense.COM. ***PRACTICE AREAS:*** Appellate Advocacy; Products Liability; Commercial Law; Consumer Law; Toxic Tort. ***Email:*** pwojcicki@smsm.com

TIMOTHY L. KRIPPNER, born Hinsdale, Illinois, August 5, 1965; admitted to bar, 1990, Illinois and U.S. District Court, Northern District of Illinois; 1991, U.S. District Court, Southern and Central Districts of Illinois; 1991, U.S. District Court, Western District of Wisconsin; 2000, Texas. *Education:* University of Illinois (B.A., 1987); DePaul University (J.D., 1990). Alpha Lambda Delta. *Member:* Chicago and American Bar Associations. ***PRACTICE AREAS:*** Environmental Litigation; Products Liability; Toxic Tort; Medical Malpractice; General Liability. ***Email:*** tkrippner@smsm.com

STEVEN A. HART, born Flint, Michigan, October 18, 1967; admitted to bar, 1992, Illinois and U.S. District Court, Northern District of Illinois; 1995, U.S. District Court, Northern District of Illinois Trial Bar; 2004, New York and U.S. District Court, Eastern District of Wisconsin. *Education:* University of Wisconsin (B.A., 1989); John Marshall Law School (J.D., 1992). Author, "Using Expert Witnesses," IICLE, 1994. *Member:* Chicago, Illinois State, New York State and American Bar Associations; Illinois Trial Lawyers Association; The Association of Trial Lawyers of America. ***PRACTICE AREAS:*** Personal Injury; Products Liability; Environmental Torts; Transportation; Premises Liability; Medical Malpractice; Employment; Commercial; General Liability; Toxic Tort. ***Email:*** shart@smsm.com

KATHLEEN McDONOUGH, born February 19, 1969; admitted to bar, 1994, Florida; 1995, U.S. District Court, Southern District of Florida; 1996, Illinois; 1998, U.S. District Court, Northern District of Illinois including Trial Bar. *Education:* Saint Mary's College, Notre Dame, Indiana (B.A., cum laude, 1991); IIT Chicago-Kent College of Law (J.D., 1994). Member, Moot Court, University of Miami School of Law, visiting student, 1993-1994. Author, "Recent Developments in Toxic Tort Law," Tort & Insurance Law Journal, Vol. 32, No. 2, Winter 1997, "The Horwin SV40 Ruling and Its Impact on the Asbestos Litigation," HarrisMartin Columns, July 2003. *Member:* The Florida Bar; American Bar Association; Trucking Industry Defense Association. ***LANGUAGES:*** French. ***PRACTICE AREAS:*** Products Liability; Toxic Torts; Insurance Defense Litigation; Commercial Litigation; Corporate Law; Medical Malpractice Defense; General Liability. ***Email:*** kmcdonough@smsm.com

JOHN J. KOHNKE, born Chicago, Illinois, October 27, 1959; admitted to bar, 1984, Illinois; 1987, U.S. District Court, Northern District of Illinois. *Education:* Drake University (B.A., 1981; J.D., with honors, 1984). Member, Drake University Law Review, 1983-1984. Trustee, Glen Ellyn Village, 1999-2003. Author: "The Abolishment of Joint Liability and Its Effect on the Right of Contribution," Vol. 9, Issue 3 D.L.B.A., Brief 10/46 st 44; "The Contributory Negligence Doctrine and Maintenance of Municipal Property," Vol. 82, No 6 Ill. B. July 1994, 378. *Member:* Du Page County, Illinois and American Bar Associations. ***PRACTICE AREAS:*** Products Liability; Premises Liability; Lemon Law; Construction Law; Municipal Defense; Consumer Litigation; General Liability; Toxic Tort. ***Email:*** jkohnke@smsm.com

JASON L. KENNEDY, born Hammond, Indiana; admitted to bar, 1996, Indiana and Illinois; 2004, New York; U.S. District Court, Northern and Southern Districts of Indiana and U.S. Tax Court; 1997, U.S. District Court Northern and Central Districts of Illinois. *Education:* Indiana University (B.S., 1992; J.D., 1996). Order of Barristers. National Moot Court Competition, 1995. Finalist, Sherman Minton Moot Court Competition,1995. Member, Sherman Minton Moot Court Board 1995-1996. Author: "Recent Developments in Toxic Tort Law," Tort & Insurance Law Journal, Vol. 33, No. 2, Winter 1998. *Member:* Monroe County, Illinois State and Indiana State Bar Associations; Defense Research Institute; Defense Trial Counsel of Indiana. ***PRACTICE AREAS:*** Products Liability; Complex Mass Tort Litigation; Toxic Torts; Professional Liability; Commercial Litigation; General Liability. ***Email:*** jkennedy@smsm.com

SENIOR COUNSEL

JEFFREY SINGER, born Chicago, Illinois, August 26, 1950; admitted to bar, 1975, Illinois and U.S. District Court, Northern District of Illinois including Trial Bar; 1990, U.S. District Court, Northern District of California; 1992, U.S. Court of Appeals, Seventh Circuit; 1998, U.S. Supreme Court. *Education:* Drake University (B.A., 1972; J.D., 1975). Omicron Delta Kappa. Assistant State's Attorney, Cook County State's Attorneys Office, 1976-1980. Author: "Attacking Accident Reconstruction Testimony," presented at American Bar Association National Institute on Automotive Design Litigation, March 1991, Author and Lecturer, Illinois Institute of Continuing Legal Education, 1985—. Speaker: American Bar Association Annual Convention, 1986; Risk and Insurance Management Society Annual Convention, 1989; "Attacking Admissibility of Expert Witnesses," Automotive Liability Session, Defense Research Institute Product Liability Seminar, January, 1998; "Update on Latex Glove Allergy Litigation," Mass Torts Session, Defense Research Institute Product Liability Session, February 1999; "Update of Latex Glove Allergy Litigation," Defense Research Institute Product Liability Seminar, February, 1999; "Excluding and Defending the Expert under Daubert-A Demonstration," ABA 1999 Toxic Torts and Environmental Law Meeting, March, 1999; "Cross-examination/Trial Techniques," Defense Research Institute Products Liability Conference, January 2000. Defense Perspective on SSRI, Anti-Depressant Drugs, Mealey's Emerging Drug and Device Litigation Conference, December, 2002. Instructor, John Marshall Law School, 1978-1979. Instructor, Scholl College of Podiatric Medicine, 1981-1988. Sustaining Member, Product Liability Advisory Council, 1986—. Listed in Who's Who in American Law, 1992—. Co-Author: "Preemption of State Law Product Liability Claims by Medical Device Amendments of 1976," Product Safety and Liability Reporter, Vol. 23, No. 38, Sept. 29, 1995; Co-Author: "Attacking Accident Reconstruction Testimony," For the Defense, Vol. 34, No. 4, April, 1992. Author, "Parties to the Action," Illinois Product Liability Practice, 1996 & 1999 Practice Handbook, Illinois Institute of Continuing Legal Education; "Declaratory Relief," Illinois Civil Practice, Vol. II, 1997, 2002 and 2004 Practice Handbook, Illinois Institute of Continuing Legal Education. Author: "Recent Development in Products, General Liability and Consumer Law," 35 Tort & Insurance Law Journal, 553 (Winter 2000). *Member:* American (Member, Committees on: Products, General Liability and Consumer Law; Automobile Law; Pharmaceutical and Medical Device, Business Tort Law) Bar Association; Japan-America Society of Chicago; Association for the Advancement of Automotive Medicine; Defense Research Institute. ***PRACTICE AREAS:*** Products Liability Litigation; Commercial Litigation; Toxic Tort Litigation. ***Email:*** jsinger@smsm.com

ASSOCIATES

CHRISTY J. BENTON, born Grand Rapids, Michigan, June 11, 1970; admitted to bar, 1996, Michigan; 1997, Illinois and U.S. District Court, Northern District of Illinois. *Education:* Michigan State University (B.A., 1992); University of Detroit Mercy (J.D., 1995). Phi Delta Phi (Officer and Founding Member, 1993-1994). Member: Board of Directors, Moot Court, 1994-1995; Moot Court New York National Team, 1994-1995; Moot Court G. Mennen Williams Coach, 1994-1995. Member, American Inns of Court, 1994-1995. Co-Author: "The Consumer Expectation Test-Has It Outlived It's Usefullness?" DRI For the Defense, September 2001. Co-Author: "Keys to a Productive Relationship," DRI For the Defense, May 2004. *Member:* Chicago and Illinois State Bar Associations; State Bar of Michigan and DRI. ***PRACTICE AREAS:*** Product Liability Litigation; Toxic Tort Litigation; Medical Malpractice; Dental Malpractice; General Liability. ***Email:*** cbenton@smsm.com

NICHOLAS A. CAPUTO, born Illinois, November 16, 1976; admitted to bar, 2001, Illinois; 2003, Minnesota. *Education:* Villanova University (B.S., B.A., cum laude, 1998); Chicago-Kent College of Law (J.D., cum laude, 2001). Gamma Phi Honor Society. Chicago-Kent College of Law Bar and Gavel Society. Member, 2001 and Coach, 2002—, Chicago-Kent Trial Advocacy Team. *Member:* Chicago, Illinois State (Assemblyman) and American Bar Associations; Justinian Society of Lawyers. ***PRACTICE AREAS:*** Toxic Torts; Products Liability; General Liability. ***Email:*** ncaputo@smsm.com

AMINA S. CHOUDHRY, born Canton, Ohio, July 19, 1979; admitted to bar, 2004, Illinois. *Education:* University of Notre Dame (B.A. 2001); Case Western Reserve University (J.D. 2004). Phi Delta Phi (Historian, 2002-2004). ***PRACTICE AREAS:*** Toxic Tort; Civil Defense. ***Email:*** achoudhry@smsm.com

JOHN L. DILLENBECK, born Grand Rapids, Michigan, February 15, 1976; admitted to bar, 2001, Illinois and U.S. District Court, Northern District of Illinois. *Education:* Michigan State University (B.A., 1998); Chicago-Kent College of Law, Illinois Institute of Technology (J.D., 2001). ***Email:*** jdillenbeck@smsm.com

BRIAN H. ELDRIDGE, born Highland Park, Illinois, August 27, 1975; admitted to bar, 2002, California; 2003, Illinois. *Education:* University of Kansas (B.A., Psychology, 1997); University of California, Hastings College of the Law (J.D., 2003). Deputy District Attorney, Contra Costa County, California, 2003. *Member:* Illinois State and American Bar Associations; State Bar of California. ***PRACTICE AREAS:*** Transportation Liability; Commercial Litigation; Products Liability; General Liability. ***Email:*** beldridge@smsm.com

BERNARD GAWNE, III, born Hinsdale, Illinois, November 14, 1977; admitted to bar, 2004, Illinois. *Education:* University of Illinois (B.S., 2000); Chicago-Kent College of Law, Illinois Institute of Technology (J.D.,with High Honors, 2004). Order of the Coif. ***LANGUAGES:*** Spanish. ***PRACTICE AREAS:*** Litigation; Toxic Torts; Products Liability; Commercial Law; General Liability. ***Email:*** bgawne@smsm.com

CATHERINE E. BOYD GOLDHABER, born Michigan; admitted to bar, 1999, Illinois; 2002, U.S. District Court, Northern District of Illinois; 2004, Michigan. *Education:* Michigan State University (B.A., with honors, 1995); Loyola University Chicago School of Law (J.D., 1999). Contributing Author: *Jury Selection: Strategy and Science, Clark Boardman Callaghan, West Group, Second Edition, 1998. Co-Author:* "FOIA Disclosures: Restricting Their Discovery and Use by Opposing Counsel," The Toxic Tort Newsletter, Volume 4, Issue 1, (Spring 2005). Assistant State's Attorney, Cook County State's Attorney's Office, November 1999-February 2002. CIVITAS ChildLaw Fellow at Loyola. *Member:* Chicago Bar Association (Director, YLS; Current Board Member, Young Professionals Board); Illinois State Bar Association. ***REPORTED CASES:*** In re M.R., et al, 316 Ill.App.3d 399, 736 N.E.2d 167 (1st Dist., 2000); In re K.S. and J.S., 317 Ill.App.3d 830, 740 N.E.2d 425 (1st Dist., 2000). ***PRACTICE AREAS:*** Litigation; Toxic Torts; Products Liability; Child Welfare; Juvenile Law; General Liability. ***Email:*** cgoldhaber@smsm.com

KEITH J. HAYS, born Buffalo, New York, June 12, 1972; admitted to bar, 1998, Indiana (Not admitted in Illinois). *Education:* Wittenberg University (B.A., 1994); Indiana

(This Listing Continued)

SEGAL McCAMBRIDGE SINGER & MAHONEY, LTD., Chicago—Continued

University School of Law (J.D., 1998). *Member:* Indianapolis and Indiana State Bar Associations; Defense Trial Counsel of Indiana; Defense Research Institute. ***Email:*** khays@smsm.com

SCOTT W. HENRY, born Cleveland, Ohio, April 13, 1975; admitted to bar, 2000, Illinois and U.S. District Court, Northern and Central Districts of Illinois; 2001, Wisconsin and U.S. District Court, Eastern and Western Districts of Wisconsin. *Education:* Vanderbilt University (B.A., 1997); Case Western Reserve University (J.D., 2000). *Member:* State Bar of Wisconsin; Chicago Bar Association (Vice Chair; Member, Circuit Court Committee; Co-Editor, Young Lawyer's Journal). ***PRACTICE AREAS:*** Litigation; Products Liability; Toxic Torts; Commercial Litigation; General Liability. ***Email:*** shenry@smsm.com

MICAH R. INLOW, born Belleville, Illinois, November 29, 1974; admitted to bar, 2002, Illinois. *Education:* University of Illinois (B.S., 1996); Loyola University (J.D., 2002). Recipient, Cooney & Conway Scholarship. *Member:* Chicago and Illinois State Bar Associations. ***PRACTICE AREAS:*** Toxic Torts; Products Liability. ***Email:*** minlow@smsm.com

ADAM JAGADICH, born Hammond, Indiana, June 21, 1978; admitted to bar, 2003, Illinois. *Education:* Purdue University, West Lafayette (B.A., 2000); University of Wisconsin-Madison Law School (J.D., 2003). Phi Beta Kappa. ***PRACTICE AREAS:*** Litigation; General Liability; Toxic Tort. ***Email:*** ajagadich@smsm.com

KIMBERLY ALINA KAYIWA, born December 7, 1974; admitted to bar, 2000, New York; 2001, Illinois. *Education:* St. Bonaventure University (B.A., 1996); University of Buffalo School of Law (J.D., 1999). *Member:* Women's Bar Association. ***PRACTICE AREAS:*** Litigation; Toxic Torts; Medical Devices. ***Email:*** kkayiwa@smsm.com

SCOTT L. KELLOGG, born Monmouth, Illinois, August 18, 1975; admitted to bar, 2000, Illinois. *Education:* North Central College (B.A., Political Science, 1997); University of Notre Dame (J.D., 2000). ***PRACTICE AREAS:*** Toxic Tort Litigation; Products Liability; General Liability; Commercial. ***Email:*** skellog@smsm.com

TARA K. KENNEDY, born 1980; admitted to bar, 2005, Illinois. *Education:* Loyola University (B.A., 2002); Chicago-Kent College of Law, Illinois Institute of Technology (J.D., 2005).

CHAD J. LAYTON, born Hinsdale, Illinois, February 22, 1972; admitted to bar, 1997, Illinois. *Education:* University of Illinois (B.A., 1994); John Marshall Law School (J.D., cum laude, 1997). *Member:* Cook County and American Bar Associations. ***PRACTICE AREAS:*** General Practice; Commercial Litigation; Products Liability. ***Email:*** clayton@smsm.com

DAVID LEAVITT, born N.Y., N.Y., February 23, 1977; (admission pending). *Education:* New School for Social Research, Eugene Lang College, N.Y., N.Y. (B.A., 2000); Chicago Kent College of Law (J.D., 2005). ***Email:*** dleavitt@smsm.com

ROBERT JOHN McLAUGHLIN, born Evergreen Park, Illinois, January 15, 1975; admitted to bar, 2000, Illinois and U.S. District Court, Northern District of Illinois; 2005, U.S. District Court, Central District of Illinois. *Education:* Eastern Illinois University (B.S., Political Science, 1997); John Marshall Law School (J.D., 2000). Member, The John Marshall Law Review and Moot Court Trial Team. Co-Author: "Construction Crane Safety," presented to College of Engineering at the University of Wisconsin-Madison, 1991; "Discovery in Commercial Litigation," presented to Chicago Bar Association, 2000; "Homeria v. San Marcos," Best Brief, Georgetown Unversity International Law Moot Court Competition, 13 Georgetown International Law Review, 213 (2000). ***PRACTICE AREAS:*** Commercial Litigation; Products Liability. ***Email:*** rmclaughlin@smsm.com

GREGORY M. McMAHON, born Cleveland, Ohio, September 6, 1973; admitted to bar, 2002, Illinois. *Education:* University of Southern California (B.S., 1996); DePaul University College of Law (J.D., 2002). Symposium Editor, DePaul Business and Commercial Law Journal. ***PRACTICE AREAS:*** Toxic Tort Litigation. ***Email:*** gmcmahon@smsm.com

MARIA MENOTTI, born Melrose Park, Illinois, January 6, 1971; admitted to bar, 1995, Illinois and U.S. District Court, Northern District of Illinois; 1997, U.S. District Court, Central District of Illinois. *Education:* Purdue University at Lafayette (B.A., 1992); Chicago-Kent College of Law, Illinois Institute of Technology (J.D., 1995). Phi Alpha Delta. Justanian Society Scholarship, 1994. Bar & Gravel Society, 1995. *Member:* Chicago and Illinois State (Member, Young Lawyers Division) Bar Associations. ***REPORTED CASES:*** BNA-118 DEN A-5, 2002; Daily Environment Report News, June 19th 2002; US v Alpha Construction (ND IL # 02-C-3509). ***PRACTICE AREAS:*** Civil Litigation; Toxic Torts; Environmental. ***Email:*** mmenotti@smsm.com

KAREN RHEINGANS, born Milwaukee, Wisconsin, January 7, 1972; admitted to bar, 1999, Illinois; 2003, Wisconsin. *Education:* University of Wisconsin (B.A., 1994); John Marshall Law School (J.D., 1999). Member, Moot Court, Trial Team. ***PRACTICE AREAS:*** Toxic Torts. ***Email:*** krheingans@smsm.com

ALLISON SCOTT, born Berwyn, Illinois, June 30, 1979; admitted to bar, 2004, Indiana; 2005, Illinois. *Education:* University of Illinois, Champaign (B.S., Psychology, 2001); Indiana University, Bloomington (J.D., 2004). *Member:* Illinois State Bar Association; Indiana State Bar Association. ***PRACTICE AREAS:*** Toxic Torts; Asbestos; Products Liability; Civil Litigation. ***Email:*** ascott@smsm.com

KATHERINE L. SLEEKER, born Fairfax, Virginia, January 4, 1975; admitted to bar, 2002, Florida, Illinois and U.S. District Court, Northern District of Illinois. *Education:* College of William & Mary (B.A., 1997); University of Florida (J.D., 2002). *Member:* Chicago and Illinois State Bar Association; The Florida Bar. ***PRACTICE AREAS:*** Products Liability; Commercial Litigation; Toxic Tort; Consumer Litigation. ***Email:*** ksleeker@smsm.com

HOLLY R. STEVENS, born Battle Creek, Michigan, June 19, 1972; admitted to bar, 2000, Illinois; 2001 U.S. District Court, Northern District of Illinois; 2002 U.S. District Court, Northern District of Indiana; 2003, U.S. Court of Appeals, Seventh Circuit. *Education:* University of Michigan (B.A., 1994); John Marshall Law School (J.D., 1999). Member, American Bar Association, 2000-2003. *Member:* Chicago Bar Association. ***PRACTICE AREAS:*** Litigation; Consumer Litigation. ***Email:*** hstevens@smsm.com

BEN M. SWALLOW, admitted to bar, 2003, Illinois. *Education:* Indiana University (B.S., 1997); Chicago-Kent College of Law, Illinois Institute of Technology (J.D., 2002). ***PRACTICE AREAS:*** Product Liability; Toxic Tort Litigation; Hazardous Substances Litigation; General Liability. ***Email:*** bswallow@smsm.com

J. YASMIN TAYYAB, born New York, New York, December 16, 1973; admitted to bar, 1998 Massachusetts; 2003, Illinois. *Education:* Vanderbilt University (B.A., magna cum laude, 1995); Boston College at Chestnut Hill (J.D., 1998). Member, National Environmental & Administration Law Moot Court Team. *Member:* Massachusetts and Illinois State Bar Associations. ***PRACTICE AREAS:*** Products Liability; Toxic Torts. ***Email:*** ytayyab@smsm.com

CAMERON D. TURNER, born Scott Air Force Base, Illinois, August 20, 1972; admitted to bar, 1997, Illinois. *Education:* University of Notre Dame (B.A., cum laude, 1994); DePaul University (J.D., 1997). Recipient, CALI Award for Civil Rights Law, 1997. *Member:* Chicago and American Bar Associations. ***PRACTICE AREAS:*** Toxic Torts; Products Liability Defense; Commercial Litigation; Insurance Coverage; Insurance Defense. ***Email:*** cturner@smsm.com

SCOTT J. VOLD, born Chicago, Illinois; admitted to bar, 2003, Illinois and U.S. District Court, Northern District of Illinois; 2005, U.S. District Court, Central District of Illinois. *Education:* University of Illinois, Urbana-Champaign (B.A., 2000); Washington University School of Law, St. Louis (J.D., 2003). *Member:* Chicago Bar Association; Illinois State Bar Association; American Bar Association; The Association of Trial Lawyers of America. ***LANGUAGES:*** Spanish and English. ***PRACTICE AREAS:*** Toxic Torts Litigation; Products Liability; Civil Litigation; Class Actions; Commercial Torts; Business Torts; Consumer Class Actions; Consumer Fraud; Dental Malpractice; Plaintiffs Personal Injury. ***Email:*** svold@smsm.com

ALEXIS K. WEED, born Park Ridge, Illinois; admitted to bar, 2003, Illinois. *Education:* Michigan State University (B.A., Political Science, 1998); Loyola University School of Law (J.D., 2003). *Member:* Chicago Bar Association (Co-Chair, YLS Real Estate Committee); Illinois State Bar Association; American Bar Association. ***PRACTICE AREAS:*** Products Liability; Toxic Tort; Hazardous Substances Litigation; General Liability. ***Email:*** aweed@smsm.com

NANCY SUSAN WOODWORTH, born Terre Haute, Indiana, June 16, 1978; (admission pending). *Education:* Vanderbilt University (B.S., 2000); Indiana University (J.D., 2005). ***PRACTICE AREAS:*** Toxic Torts. ***Email:*** nwoodworth@smsm.com

REPRESENTATIVE CLIENTS: American LaFrance Corporation; Arrow International, Inc.; AW Chesterton Corporation; Barr Laboratories; Boston Scientific Corporation; Braun Corporation; Campbell Soup Company; Canal Insurance Company; Chubb Group of Insurance Companies; CNA Health Pro; COLTEC Industries; Congoleum Corporation; Countrywide Services Corporation; Cryolife, Inc.; C.R. Bard, Inc.; Cummins Engine Corp.; Delta International Machinery Corporation; Enpro Industries; Farnum Industries; Fleetwood Enterprises, Inc.; Flowserve Corporation; Foster Wheeler Energy Corp.; Freightliner Corporation; GAB Business Services, Inc.; Garlock Sealing Technologies; Greene Tweed Corp.; Hartford Insurance Company; Heritage Insurance Company; Horace Mann Insurance Company; Hyundai Motor America, Inc.; International Managers, Inc.; Isuzu Motors America, Inc.; JamSports and Entertainment, LLC; J.W. Harris Company; Kawasaki Motors Corporation, U.S.A.; Kimberly-Clark Corporation; Land Rover North America, Inc.; Liberty Mutual Insurance Company; Lincoln General Insurance Company; M+O Insulation Company; Makita Electric Corporation; Mallinckrodt, Inc.; Matsushita Electric Corporation of America; Mazda Motor Corporation; Mead/Westuaco Corporation; Medical Protective Company; MEDMARC Insurance Company; Miller Brewing Corporation; Minnesota Mining & Manufacturing; Mitsubishi Motor Sales of America; Mitsui Sumitomo Insurance Group; Monaco Coach Corporation; Navistar International Transportation Corporation; Nautilus Insurance Company; Nicor; Office Depot; PACCAR, Inc.; Panasonic; Plastics Engineering Inc.; Porsche Cars North America, Inc.; Porter/Cable Corporation; Quincy Compressor Inc.; Rockwell Automation Corporation; Rockwell International Corporation; Rogers Corporation; Safeskin Corporation; Scottsdale Insurance Company; Specialty Claims Management, LLC; St. Jude Medical, Inc.; St. Paul Travelers; Subaru of America, Inc.; Tokio Fire and Marine Insurance Company; Toyota Motor Corporation; Treesdale Inc.; United Technologies Corporation; Volvo North America Corporation; Warner-Chicott, Inc.; Wausau Insurance Company; Weil McLain Corp.; Winnebago Industries, Inc.; Zurn Industries.

(This Listing Continued)

SEIDMAN LAW OFFICES

20 S. CLARK STREET, SUITE 700
CHICAGO, ILLINOIS 60602
Telephone: 312-781-1977
Fax: 312-853-2187
URL: http://www.seidmanlawoffices.com

Insurance Defense; Corporate Litigation; Workers Compensation.

MEMBERS OF FIRM

STEVEN J. SEIDMAN, born Chicago, Illinois, April 10, 1956; admitted to bar, 1981, Illinois, U.S. District Court, Northern District of Illinois and U.S. Court of Appeals, 7th Circuit. *Education:* University of Illinois (B.S., 1978); DePaul University (J.D., 1981). *Member:* Illinois State Bar Association; The Association of Trial Lawyers of America; Workers Compensation Lawyers Association; Illinois Trial Lawyers Association. (Also Of Counsel, Monico Pavich & Spevack). ***PRACTICE AREAS:*** Civil Litigation; Medical Malpractice; Litigation; Products Liability; Workers Compensation. ***Email:*** sseidman@seidmanlaw.net

SEAN M. BAKER, born Baltimore, Maryland, 1966; admitted to bar, 1994, Illinois. *Education:* California State University, Long Beach (B.A., German, with honors, 1989); John Marshall Law School (J.D., 1994). ***LANGUAGES:*** French and German. ***PRACTICE AREAS:*** Insurance Defense; Corporate Litigation.

RYAN A. MARGULIS, born Chicago, Illinois, October 21, 1975; admitted to bar, 2001, Illinois. *Education:* Indiana University (B.S., Business, Sports Management, With Honors, 1998); Washington University School of Law, St. Louis (J.D., 2001). *Member:* Chicago and Illinois State Bar Associations; Worker's Compensation Law Association. ***PRACTICE AREAS:*** Workers Compensation; Personal Injury; Automobile Negligence; Medical Malpractice; Products Liability. ***Email:*** ramargulis@seidmanlaw.net

SEYFARTH SHAW LLP

Established in 1945

55 E. MONROE STREET, SUITE 4200
CHICAGO, ILLINOIS 60603-5803
Telephone: 312-346-8000
Fax: 312-269-8869
Email: seyfarthshaw@seyfarth.com

Washington, D.C. Office: 815 Connecticut Avenue, N.W. Telephone: 202-463-2400. Facsimile: 202-828-5393.

Los Angeles, California Office: 2029 Century Park East. Telephone: 310-277-7200. Facsimile: 310-201-5219.

New York, N.Y. Office: 1270 Avenue of the Americas, Suite 2500. Telephone: 212-218-5500. Facsimile: 212-218-5526.

San Francisco, California Office: 560 Mission Street, Suite 3100. Telephone: 415-397-2823. Facsimile: 415-397-8549.

Sacramento, California Office: 400 Capitol Mall, Suite 2350. Telephone: 916-448-0159. Facsimile: 916-558-4839.

Houston, Texas Office: 700 Louisiana Street, Suite 3700. Telephone: 713-225-2300. Facsimile: 713-225-2340.

Atlanta, Georgia Office: 1545 Peachtree Street, N.E., One Peachtree Pointe, Suite 700. Telephone: 404-885-1500. Facsimile: 404-892-7056.

Boston, Massachusetts Office: Two Seaport Lane, Suite 300. Telephone: 617-946-4800. Facsimile: 617-946-4801.

Brussels, Belgium Office: Avenue Louise 500, Box 8. Telephone: (32) (2) 647. 60. 25. Fax: (32) (2) 640. 70. 71.

Labor and Employment Law, Employee Benefits, Employment Discrimination, Employment-at-Will, Health Care, Occupational, Safety and Health, Worker's Compensation. Government Contracts. White-Collar Criminal. Litigation, Administrative Law, Business Contract Disputes, Construction, Corporations and Partnerships, General Tort, Insurance, Intellectual Property, Product Liability, Professional Liability, Securities and Commodities. Corporate, Acquisitions, Antitrust, Bankruptcy and Creditors' Rights, Commercial and Financial Transactions, Contracts, Divestitures, Joint Ventures, Mergers, Real Estate, Tax Law, Trust and Probate. Environmental, Safety and Toxic Torts.

PARTNERS

JOHN H. ANDERSON, born 1950; admitted to bar, 1976, Illinois; U.S. Supreme Court; U.S. Court of Appeals, Seventh and Federal Circuits; U.S. District Court, Northern District of Illinois; U.S. District Court, Northern District of Indiana; U.S. District Court, Eastern District of Wisconsin. *Education:* Williams College (B.A., cum laude, 1972) Phi Beta Kappa; John Marshall Law School (J.D., highest honors, 1976). *Member:* Chicago, Illinois State and American Bar Associations. ***PRACTICE AREAS:*** Litigation; Intellectual Property. ***Email:*** janderson@seyfarth.com

DAVID S. BAFFA, born 1969; admitted to bar, 1995, Illinois. *Education:* Princeton University (A.B., 1990); Chicago-Kent College of Law (J.D., with honors, 1995). ***PRACTICE AREAS:*** Labor and Employment. ***Email:*** dbaffa@seyfarth.com

JAMES BAIRD, born 1943; admitted to bar, 1968, Wisconsin; 1972, Illinois. *Education:* Michigan State University (B.A., 1965); University of Wisconsin (J.D., 1968); George Washington University (LL.M., with highest honors, 1970). *Member:* American Bar Association (Member, Board of Governors, 2004-2007); National Public Employer Labor Relations Association; Illinois Public Employer Labor Relations Association; Illinois State Chamber of Commerce; National Employment Law Institute (Member, Advisory Board); College of Labor and Employment Lawyers. ***PRACTICE AREAS:*** Labor and Employment Law. ***Email:*** jbaird@seyfarth.com

EDWARD W. BERGMANN, born 1941; admitted to bar, 1966, Illinois; U.S. Supreme Court; U.S. Court of Appeals, Seventh and Tenth Circuits. *Education:* Northwestern University (B.S., 1963); Cornell University (J.D., with distinction, 1966). Order of the Coif. *Member:* Chicago, Illinois State and American Bar Associations; American Academy of Hospital Attorneys; Illinois Hospital Association. ***PRACTICE AREAS:*** Labor and Employment; Fair Labor Standards Act. ***Email:*** ebergmann@seyfarth.com

DANIEL M. BLOUIN, born 1963; admitted to bar, 1988, Illinois; U.S. Court of Appeals, Seventh Circuit; U.S. District Court, Northern District of Illinois, including Trial Bar. *Education:* Purdue University (B.S., 1985); Loyola University (J.D., 1988). *Member:* Chicago and American Bar Associations; Defense Research Institute. ***PRACTICE AREAS:*** Litigation. ***Email:*** dblouin@seyfarth.com

MICHAEL E. BLOUNT, born 1949; admitted to bar, 1974, Texas; 1980, Illinois; 1981, District of Columbia. *Education:* University of Texas (B.A., 1971); University of Houston (J.D., 1974). Phi Alpha Delta; Order of the Barons. Attorney, Office of the General Counsel, Securities and Exchange Commission, 1977-1978. Legal Assistant to the Chairman of the Securities and Exchange Commission, 1978-1979. *Member:* Chicago and American (Member: Committee on Federal Regulation of Securities, 1981—; Section of International Law) Bar Associations; State Bar of Texas; District of Columbia Bar. ***PRACTICE AREAS:*** Business Law. ***Email:*** mblount@seyfarth.com

ERIC E. BOYD, born 1959; admitted to bar, 1986, Illinois; 2005, U.S. Court of Appeals, District of Columbia Circuit. *Education:* Northwestern University (B.S., with honors, 1981); Indiana University (J.D., cum laude, 1986). *Member:* Chicago and American Bar Associations. ***PRACTICE AREAS:*** Environmental Health and Safety; Administrative Law; Litigation. ***Email:*** eboyd@seyfarth.com

JEROME F. BUCH, born 1956; admitted to bar, 1982, Illinois; U.S. District Court, Northern, Central and Southern Districts of Illinois; U.S. District Court, District of New Jersey. *Education:* Loyola University of Chicago (B.B.A., 1979); DePaul University College of Law (J.D., 1982). *Member:* Chicago, DuPage County, Illinois State and American (Member, Forum on the Construction Industry) Bar Associations. ***PRACTICE AREAS:*** Litigation. ***Email:*** jbuch@seyfarth.com

J. KELLY BUFTON, born 1956; admitted to bar, 1980, Illinois. *Education:* Stanford University (B.A., 1977); University of Chicago (J.D., 1980). Phi Beta Kappa. *Member:* International Council of Shopping Centers; Pension Real Estate Association. ***PRACTICE AREAS:*** Real Estate; Real Estate Leasing; Land Use. ***Email:*** kbufton@seyfarth.com

SCOTT A. CARLSON, born 1965; admitted to bar, 1995, Illinois and U.S. District Court, Northern District of Illinois; 1998, U.S. Court of Appeals, Seventh Circuit; 1999, U.S. Supreme Court; 2002, U.S. District Court, Eastern District of Wisconsin. *Education:* University of Illinois (B.S., Computer Science and Mathematics, 1987); Southern Illinois University (J.D., summa cum laude, 1st in class, 1995). Adjunct Professor, The John Marshall School of Law, LLM Program in Information Technology and Privacy Law; Co-Chair, E-Discovery Task Force. *Member:* Kane County and Illinois State Bar Associations; International Association of Computer Investigative Specialists (IACIS) (Faculty Member); High Technology Crime Investigation Association (Midwest Chapter). [Lieutenant, U.S. Navy (1987-1991 Active Duty, 1991-1995 Reservist)]. ***PRACTICE AREAS:*** Litigation. ***Email:*** scarlson@seyfarth.com

PHILIP V. CARTER (Retired)

MARK CASCIARI, admitted to bar, 1979, Illinois; U.S. Supreme Court; U.S Courts of Appeals, First, Third, Fourth, Sixth, Seventh, Eighth, Ninth and District of Columbia Circuits; U.S. District Court, Northern (including Trial Bar) and Central Districts of Illinois, U.S. District Court, Northern District of Indiana, U.S. District Court, Eastern and Western Districts of Wisconsin, U.S. District Court, Western District of Tennessee, U.S. District Court, District of Colorado, U.S. District Court, District of Minnesota and U.S. District Court, District of Nebraska. *Education:* University of Southern California (B.A., magna cum laude, Phi Beta Kappa); Boston College (J.D., cum laude). *Member:* American Bar Association (Employee Benefits Committee, Labor and Employment Section; Litigation Section). ***PRACTICE AREAS:*** Litigation; ERISA/Employee Benefits Litigation; Employment Litigation; Class Action Defense. ***Email:*** mcasciari@seyfarth.com

BRENT I. CLARK, born 1961; admitted to bar, 1986, Illinois. *Education:* Kenyon College (B.A., with honors in History, with distinction in Economics, 1983); University of Virginia (J.D., 1986). Speeches: Environmental Avoits (June 1994); Managing Environmental Inspections (Exec. Enterprises July 1994); Redocine Environmental Liability, Community Right to Know (November 1994); Environmental and OSHA Compliance for Manufacturers (Tool Manufacturers Association, Jan., 1993); Effective OSHA Compliance, March 1994; The Legal Aspects of Managing Disasters (Feb., 1993); Developments in Superfund Litigation Strategies (Region V Environmental Law Conference, Executive Enterprises, Inc., May, 1991); OSHA Compliance and Managing OSHA Inspections and Litigation (National Forging Industry Association, April, 1991, February, 1992); Hazardous Waste Operations (Conference on OSHA Recordkeeping and Training Requirements, Executive Enterprises, May, 1992). Article: "Accidents, Injuries and Illnesses: Avoiding OSHA's Wrath," (Landscape Contractor, October 1992). ***PRACTICE AREAS:*** Environmental Health and Safety. ***Email:*** bclark@seyfarth.com

R. THEODORE CLARK, JR., born 1940; admitted to bar, 1965, Illinois. *Education:* Syracuse University (B.A., 1962); University of Michigan (J.D., 1965). Phi Beta Kappa. Fellow, College of Labor and Employment Lawyers. Co-author, "Determination of Appropriate Bargaining Units in the Public Sector," 51 Oregon Law Review 151, 1971; "The Practical Differences Between Public and Private Sector Collective Bargaining," 19 UCLA Law Review 867, 1972; "Labor Relations Law in Public Sector," Michie, 4th Ed. 1991. Author: "Public Employee Strikes: Some Proposed Solutions," 23 Labor Law Journal 111, 1972; "Public Sector Strikes: An Empirical Analysis," 2 Journal of Law and Education 217, 1973; "The Scope of the Duty to Bargain in Public Employment," Labor Relations Law in the Public Sector (ABA Section of Labor Relations Law, 1977); "Problems in Public Sector Collective Bargaining: A Management View," in Proceedings of New York University 32nd Annual National Conference on Labor 179, 1980; "A Guide to the Changing Court Rulings on Union Security in The Public Sector: A Management Perspective," 2 Journal of Law and Education, 71, 1985; "Privatization, Outsourcing, and Subcontracting in the U.S. Public Sector," Proceedings of the 41st Annual Meeting of the National Academy of Arbitrators, June 1998; "A Management View of Nonunion Employee Arbitration Procedures," in Labor Arbitration Under Fire, James Stern & Joyce Nojita, eds. 1997; "The Use of Economic Analysis in Postal Service Interest Arbitration, IRRA, 1997. *Member:* Chicago and American Bar Associations. ***PRACTICE AREAS:*** Labor and Employment. ***Email:*** tclark@seyfarth.com

PHILIP L. COMELLA, born 1955; admitted to bar, 1983, Illinois. *Education:* Beloit College (B.A., cum laude, 1978); George Washington University (J.D., with honors, 1983). Articles Editor, George Washington Journal of Int'l Law & Economics. Author: "Environmental Issues and Liability Considerations in Acquiring or Selling in the Privately Held Company (PLI 1998-2005); "EPA Cancels Invitations to its Own Program: The Agency's New Hazardous Waste Combustion Policy," 24 Envir. Law Rep. 10380 (July 1994); "Understanding a Sham: When is Recycling Treatment?" 20 B.C. Envir. Affairs L. Rev. 415 (1993); Regular Contributor, Brownfield News. *Member:* Illinois State and American Bar Associations. ***PRACTICE AREAS:*** Environmental, Safety and Toxic Tort; Construction Litigation; Landfill Gas. ***Email:*** pcomella@seyfarth.com

THEODORE E. CORNELL III, born 1949; admitted to bar, 1975, Illinois. *Education:* University of Notre Dame (A.B., cum laude, 1972); Northwestern University (J.D., with honors, 1975). Director: Daniel Murphy Scholarship Foundation; Continental Painting and Decorating, Inc. Member, Chicago Heart Walk Board, American Heart Association. *Member:* Chicago, Illinois State and American Bar Associations. ***PRACTICE AREAS:*** Business Law. ***Email:*** tcornell@seyfarth.com

JAMES L. CURTIS, born 1965; admitted to bar, 1990, Illinois; U.S. Supreme Court; U.S. Court of Appeals, Seventh and Eleventh Circuits; U.S. District Court, District of Colorado and Northern District of Illinois. *Education:* Albion College (B.A., 1987); Loyola University (J.D., 1990). *Member:* American Bar Association; American Trucking Association; Outdoor Advertising Association of America. ***PRACTICE AREAS:*** Environmental Health and Safety. ***Email:*** jcurtis@seyfarth.com

DOUGLAS A. DARCH, born 1951; admitted to bar, 1980, Illinois. *Education:* Georgia Institute of Technology (B.S., 1973); University of North Carolina (J.D., 1980). Author: "Implementing the Family and Medical Leave Acting a Union Workforce;" Update to The Developing Labor Law (BNA). Speaker, American Arbitration Assoc. Program, "Negotiating A Labor Agreement" on "Costing The Labor Agreement;" Loyola University-Chicago Conference "Labor Law and Collective Bargaining in the New Millennium." *Member:*

(This Listing Continued)

SEYFARTH SHAW LLP, Chicago—Continued

Chicago (Member and Former Chair, Labor and Employment Committee), Illinois State (Member and Former Chair, Individual Rights and Responsibilities Section Council; Former Member, Labor and Employment Section Council) and American Bar Associations. [U.S. Navy 1973-1977, Lt. Surface Warfare]. ***REPORTED CASES:*** Terracon, Inc., 339 NLRB #35 (2003), aff'd 361 F.3d 395 (7th Cir); Kinney v. Federal Security, 272 F.3d 924 (7th Cir. 2001); Dubuque Packing Co., 303 NLRB 386 (1991); Kyles v. Guardian Security, 222 F.3d 289 (7th Cir 2000) following remand 84 F.E.P. Cases (BNA) 928 (D.C. Ill. 2000); Safety Kleen, 279 NLRB 1117(1986). ***PRACTICE AREAS:*** Labor and Employment Law. ***Email:*** ddarch@seyfarth.com

GREGORY M. DAVIS, admitted to bar, 1997, Illinois and Wisconsin; U.S. District Court, Central, Northern and Southern Districts of Illinois and U.S. District Court, Eastern and Western Districts of Wisconsin; 2002, U.S. Court of Appeals, Seventh Circuit. *Education:* University of Michigan (B.A., with honors, 1989); Michigan State University, School of Labor & Industrial Relations (M.L.I.R., 1994); University of Wisconsin (J.D., cum laude, 1997). Co-Chair, Seyfarth Shaw LLP's Fair Credit Reporting Act Task Force; Society for Human Resource Management's Workforce Diversity Expert Panel; Co-Chair of the Advisory Board for Marriott Foundation's Bridges - From School to Work Program; Advisory Board for Michigan State University's School of Labor & Industrial Relations. *Member:* Illinois State Bar Association; State Bar of Wisconsin; American Bar Association. ***PRACTICE AREAS:*** Labor and Employment; Fair Credit Reporting Act; Privacy Law. ***Email:*** gmdavis@seyfarth.com

CHRISTOPHER J. DeGROFF, born 1970; admitted to bar, 1996, Indiana; 1998, Illinois; U.S. Court of Appeals, Seventh Circuit; U.S. District Court, Central and Northern Districts of Illinois; U.S. District Court, District of Colorado; U.S. District Court, Northern and Southern Districts of Indiana. *Education:* Indiana University (B.A., 1992; J.D., 1996). *Member:* Chicago and American Bar Associations. ***PRACTICE AREAS:*** Labor and Employment. ***Email:*** cdegroff@seyfarth.com

THOMAS G. DENT, born 1942; admitted to bar, 1970, Illinois. *Education:* University of Illinois; DePaul University (LL.B., 1970). ***PRACTICE AREAS:*** Litigation; White Collar Criminal Defense. ***Email:*** tdent@seyfarth.com

JOSHUA L. DITELBERG, born 1966; admitted to bar, 1991, Massachusetts; 1993, District of Columbia; 1997, Illinois; U.S. Court of Appeals, First, Sixth, Seventh, Eighth and District of Columbia Circuits; U.S. District Court, Northern and Southern Districts of Illinois; U.S. District Court, District of Massachusetts. *Education:* University of Pennsylvania (B.A., summa cum laude, 1987; M.A., 1987); University of Michigan (J.D., magna cum laude, 1991). Law Clerk to Judge Ralph B. Guy, Jr., U.S. Court of Appeals, Sixth Circuit, 1992-1993. Law Clerk to Justice Joseph R. Weisberger, Supreme Court of Rhode Island, 1991-1992. *Member:* American Bar Association (Member, Subcommittee on Practice and Procedure Under the National Labor Relations Act); Labor and Employment Relations Association (Executive Board, Chicago Chapter); Illinois Institute for Continuing Legal Education (Business Advisory and Planning Committee). ***PRACTICE AREAS:*** Labor and Employment; Labor/Employment Aspects of Transactions; Workforce Reductions. ***Email:*** jditelberg@seyfarth.com

KENNETH R. DOLIN, born 1955; admitted to bar, 1981, Illinois; 1985, U.S. District Court, Northern District of Illinois and U.S. Court of Appeals Seventh Circuit; U.S. District Court, Central District of Illinois. *Education:* University of Wisconsin at Madison (B.A., with honors, 1978); University of Illinois (J.D., cum laude, 1980); New York State School of Industrial and Labor Relations, Cornell University (M.I.L.R., 1981); New York University (LL.M., in Labor Law, 1987), Harno Scholar. Author, "The Supreme Court's Rejection of Excluding 'Ordinary Professional or Technical Judgment' as Independent Judgment When Directing Employee: Does Kentucky River Mean Lights Out For Mississippi Power?," 18 The Labor Lawyer 365 (Winter/Spring 2003); "Recent Developments and the Likely Effect of Changes at the National Labor Relations Board," (Lead Author) 54 Labor Law Journal 5 (Spring 2003); Lead Author: "Termination of Grievance Proceedings When Employees File Discrimination Charges," 13 Employee Relations Law Journal 249, Autumn, 1987; "Drafting Affirmative Action Plans and Practice Before the Office of the Federal Contract Compliance Programs," IICLE, Employment Discrimination, 2000; "Representation Case—Substantive Matters," IICLE, The Labor Law Handbook, 2002; "Recent Developments in The Area of Affirmative Action," Labor Law Journal, March, 1991; "Effects Bargaining—A Survey of the Rights and Obligations of Employers," 10 The Labor Lawyer 269, 1994. Associate Editor, Chapter 13 ("The Duty to Bargain"); Editor, The Developing Labor Law (4th Edition, 2002 Supplement, BNA); Associate Editor, The Developing Labor Law (4th Edition 2001, BNA). Adjunct Professor of Law, Northwestern University School of Law, 1990—. Trial Attorney, National Labor Relations Board, New York, 1982-1984. Columnist on current labor law issues for the National Law Journal, 2000—. *Member:* American Bar Association (Member, Committee on Development of the Law Under The National Labor Relations Act, Section of Labor and Employment Law, 1985—). ***PRACTICE AREAS:*** Labor and Employment Law. ***Email:*** kdolin@seyfarth.com

ARTHUR DON, born 1953; admitted to bar, 1978, Illinois. *Education:* Northwestern University (B.S., with distinction, 1975; J.D., cum laude, 1978). Member, Editorial Board, Northwestern University Law Review, 1977-1978. Member, Editorial Advisory Board, Journal of Mutual Fund Services, 1991-1997. Recipient, Wm. Jennings Bryan Moot Court Award, 1977. Author: "A Decade of Regulation: Protecting Investors While Permitting Investment," The Journal of Mutual Funds Services, 1996; "Fundamental Decisions: Setting A Mutual Fund's Investment Program," The Journal of Mutual Fund Services, 1995. Chairman, Chicago Bar Association Subcommittee on Investment Company Law, 1999-2001. ***PRACTICE AREAS:*** Securities; Corporate. ***Email:*** adon@seyfarth.com

GREGG M. DORMAN, admitted to bar, 1984, Illinois; U.S. District Court, Northern District of Illinois. *Education:* University of Illinois (B.A., 1981); Loyola University of Chicago School of Law (J.D., 1984). Member, University Club of Chicago. *Member:* Chicago, Illinois State and American Bar Associations; International Council of Shopping Centers. ***PRACTICE AREAS:*** Commercial Real Estate; Real Estate Development; Real Estate Acquisitions; Real Estate Leasing; Real Estate Finance. ***Email:*** gdorman@seyfarth.com

(This Listing Continued)

WILLIAM F. DUGAN, born 1970; admitted to bar, 1995, Illinois. *Education:* University of Illinois (B.A., 1992); University of Notre Dame School of Law (J.D., 1995). Member, Society for Human Resources Management. *Member:* Chicago and American Bar Associations; Human Resources Association of Greater Oak Brook (Board of Directors). ***PRACTICE AREAS:*** Labor and Employment. ***Email:*** wdugan@seyfarth.com

DIANE V. DYGERT, born 1962; admitted to bar, 1987, Illinois. *Education:* Cornell University (B.S., Industrial and Labor Relations, 1984); University of Michigan (J.D., 1987). ***PRACTICE AREAS:*** Employee Benefits. ***Email:*** ddygert@seyfarth.com

HILLARY A. EBACH, born 1963; admitted to bar, 1993, Illinois. *Education:* Northwestern University (B.A., 1985); University of Chicago (M.B.A., 1989); Northwestern University (J.D., magna cum laude, 1993). *Member:* American Bar Association, Chicago Bar Association. ***PRACTICE AREAS:*** Corporate Law; Finance. ***Email:*** hebach@seyfarth.com

WILLIAM J. FACTOR, born 1960; admitted to bar, 1991, Illinois. *Education:* University of Chicago (A.B., 1983); DePaul Law School (J.D., with high honors, 1990). Order of the Coif. *Member:* Chicago, Illinois State and American Bar Associations. ***REPORTED CASES:*** In re GGSI Liquidation, Inc., 313 B.R. 770, 43 Bankr.Ct.Dec. 151 (Bankr.N.D.Ill., Sep 01, 2004); In re Rasberry, 264 B.R. 495, 46 Collier Bankr.Cas.2d 939 (Bankr.N.D.Ill., Jul 10, 2001); In re Resource Technology Corp., 254 B.R. 215, Bankr. L. Rep. P 78,292 (Bankr.N.D.Ill., Oct 25, 2000); In re Montgomery Ward Holding Corp., 2000 WL 33712303 (Bankr.D.Del., Dec 11, 2000); Central States, Southeast and Southwest Areas Pension Fund v. Wintz Properties, Inc., 155 F.3d 868, 22 Employee Benefits Cas. 1880 (7th Cir.(Ill.), Sep 08, 1998); In re Chavin, 150 F.3d 726, Bankr. L. Rep. P 77,736 (7th Cir.(Ill.), Jul 22, 1998); In re Sardo Corp., 1996 WL 532315 (Bankr.N.D.Ill., Sep 19, 1996). ***PRACTICE AREAS:*** Bankruptcy; Bankruptcy Chapter 7; Bankruptcy Chapter 11; Bankruptcy Collections; Bankruptcy Fraud; Bankruptcy Litigation; Bankruptcy Mediation. ***Email:*** wfactor@seyfarth.com

WILLIAM J. FAIRBANKS, born 1952; admitted to bar, 1978, Illinois. *Education:* Brown University (A.B., 1974); University of Illinois (J.D., 1978). ***PRACTICE AREAS:*** Business Law. ***Email:*** wfairbanks@seyfarth.com

OWEN FAIRWEATHER (1913-1987)

JENNIFER KELLY FARDY, born 1970; admitted to bar, 1995, Illinois, U.S. District Court, Northern District of Illinois; 1996, Indiana, U.S. District Court, Northern and Southern Districts of Indiana; 1998, U.S. Court of Appeals, 7th Circuit; 2002, U.S. District Court, Eastern District of Wisconsin. *Education:* University of Iowa (B.A., 1992); Indiana University (J.D., 1995). *Member:* American Bar Association (Member, Litigation Section; Class Action and Derivative Suits Committee). ***PRACTICE AREAS:*** Litigation; Intellectual Property. ***Email:*** jfardy@seyfarth.com

BRENDA HOFMAN FEIS, born 1960; admitted to bar, 1985, Illinois; U.S. Court of Appeals, Seventh Circuit; U.S. District Court, Central and Northern Districts of Illinois, including Trial Bar. *Education:* Duke University (B.A., summa cum laude, 1982; J.D., 1985). *Member:* American Bar Association. ***PRACTICE AREAS:*** Labor and Employment. ***Email:*** bfeis@seyfarth.com

MICHEL J. FELDMAN, born 1943; admitted to bar, 1968, Illinois. *Education:* Northwestern University (B.S.B.A., 1965; J.D., cum laude, 1968). Order of the Coif. Member, Editorial Board, Northwestern Law Review, 1967-1968. Recipient, National Accounting Honorary and Honorable Mention for National Elijah Watt Sells Award, 1965. Certified Public Accountant, Illinois, 1965. Speaker: Art of Venturing Program - Northwestern University Kellogg School of Management. Participant in Stanford Law School's Program for Directors of NASDAQ Companies. Trustee, The Adler Planetarium 1986—. President, Avanti Communications, A Privately held telecommunications company, 1976-1981. President, Chicago Chapter of Association for Corporate Growth, 1996-1998. Founding Member, Director and Lecturer at the Entrepreneurship Institute, Chicago Chapter, Director, Watson Pharmaceuticals, Inc. (NYSE). ***PRACTICE AREAS:*** Mergers and Acquisitions (50%); Securities (10%); Corporate (40%); Tax Law. ***Email:*** mfeldman@seyfarth.com

IRA FIERSTEIN, born 1952; admitted to bar, 1977, Illinois. *Education:* University of Illinois (B.S., magna cum laude, 1974); Northwestern University (J.D., cum laude, 1977). Phi Beta Kappa. Board of Editors, Commercial Leasing Law and Strategy. Author: "The Pitfalls for Landlords to Avoid in Leases Involving New Construction, " Commercial Leasing Law & Strategy, 2005; "Proposed Revisions to the ADA's Physical Accessibility Guidelines Released," Retail Law Strategist, 2004: "It's Just a Phase - Issues and Answers for Landlords When Phasing A Project," Commercial Leasing Law & Strategy 2004: Authored Six chapters in the 2003 "Lease Negotiation Handbook" published by the International Association of Attorneys and Executives in Corporate Real Estate (AECRE) and the American Bar Association (ABA); "Five Deadly Sins: Lease Clauses A Landlord Should Refuse to Negotiate Under Any Circumstances," Commercial Law & Strategy 2003: "Mechanics' Lien Claims: How Can A Landlord Avoid 'Getting Stuck With the Bill'?" Commercial Leasing Law & Strategy 2002; "Criteria for Analyzing the Suitability of Buildings and Lease Forms for Carrier Hotels," Commercial Leasing Law and Strategy, 2001; "The Benefits and Pitfalls of Using Letters of Intent In Leasing Transactions," Commercial Leasing Law and Strategy, 2000; Note: "Commercial Leasing Law and Strategy," Crafting Lease Clauses, Volume II, 1999; "Lease Termination on Tenant Default," Commercial Leasing Law and Strategy, 1999; "Strategies for Lease Modification Following Tenant's Default," Commercial Leasing Law and Strategy, 1998, Shopping Center Legal Update, 1998; "Lease Negotiations: Landlord's Demand for Specialty Provisions in Anticipation of Major Tenant Defaults," Current Topics in Shopping Center Law, 1997. *Member:* International Council of Shopping Centers. ***PRACTICE AREAS:*** Real Estate; Land Development; Shopping Center; Telecommunications; Landlord-Tenant Law. ***Email:*** ifierstein@seyfarth.com

NOAH A. FINKEL, born 1968; admitted to bar, 1994, Illinois; U.S. Court of Appeals, Sixth, Seventh, and Tenth Circuits; U.S. District Court, District of Colorado; U.S. District Court, Central and Northern Districts of Illinois; U.S. District Court, Northern District of Indiana; U.S. District Court, Eastern District of Michigan; U.S. District Court, Eastern District of Wisconsin. *Education:* University of Michigan (B.A., with distinction, 1991; J.D., 1994). Law Clerk to the Hon. Nancy G. Edmunds, United States District Judge for U.S.

(This Listing Continued)

District Court for the Eastern District of Michigan, 1994-1995. *Member:* American Bar Association (Member, Labor Section, Committee on Federal Labor Standards Legislation). ***PRACTICE AREAS:*** Labor and Employment. ***Email:*** nfinkel@seyfarth.com

FREDRIC H. FISCHER, born 1942; admitted to bar, 1968, New York; 1973, Illinois; 1992, Wisconsin; U.S. Supreme Court; U.S. Court of Appeals, Second, Sixth and Seventh Circuits. *Education:* Cornell University (B.S., 1964); State University of New York at Buffalo (J.D., 1967); New York University (LL.M., Labor Law, 1968). Associate Editor, Buffalo Law Review, 1966-1967. Law Note Publications: 15 Buffalo L. Rev. 931 and 15 Buffalo L. Rev. 747 (1966). Co-Author: Fischer and Rapoport, "Protective Labor Legislation: Its Impact on Employee Terminations," and "Discharge for Contractual 'Just Cause'" Employee Termination Handbook—Legal and Psychological Guidelines for Employers (Executive Enterprises Publishing Co., Inc., 1981). Author: "Immigration Reform and Control Act of 1986 (IRCA)," Federal Employment Law and Regulations (Apland, 1999). Advice Branch, Office of General Counsel (Washington, D.C.), National Labor Relations Board, 1968-1970. Trial Attorney, National Labor Relations Board (Chicago, Illinois), 1970-1972. *Member:* New York State, Illinois State and American (Member: Management Spokesperson, NLRB Advisory Panel; Management Co-Chair, Practice and Procedure before the NLRB Committee, 1996-1998) Bar Associations; Immigration Lawyers Association. Fellow, College of Labor and Employment Lawyers. ***PRACTICE AREAS:*** Labor and Employment. ***Email:*** ffischer@seyfarth.com

ROBERT P. FLANAGAN, born 1965; admitted to bar, 1990, Illinois. *Education:* University of Illinois (B.A., 1987); IIT/Chicago-Kent College of Law (J.D., 1990). *Member:* Chicago (Member, Taxation Committee) and American (Member, Pension Committee) Bar Associations; IRS Great Lakes Area Tax Exempt and Government Entities (TE/GE) Council. ***PRACTICE AREAS:*** Employee Benefits; Executive Compensation. ***Email:*** rflanagan@seyfarth.com

ELIZABETH PFEILER FOLEY, born 1960; admitted to bar, 1985, Illinois. *Education:* Duke University (A.B., magna cum laude, 1981); University of Wisconsin Law School (J.D., 1985). *Member:* Chicago Bar Association; Chicago Commercial Real Estate Executive Women; Urban Land Institute. ***PRACTICE AREAS:*** Real Estate Secured Lending; Letters of Credit; Loan Restructuring; Loan Workouts. ***Email:*** efoley@seyfarth.com

JAMES R. FORTCAMP, admitted to bar, 1987, Illinois. *Education:* University of Illinois (B.S., Finance, honors, 1984; J.D., 1987). Recipient, American Jurisprudence Award; Judge James C. Connell Award. ***PRACTICE AREAS:*** Real Estate Tax. ***Email:*** jfortcamp@seyfarth.com

ELAINE S. FOX, born Chicago, Illinois; admitted to bar, 1975, Illinois; U.S. Court of Appeals, Seventh and Federal Circuits; U.S. District Court, Northern District of Illinois. *Education:* University of Illinois; Northwestern University (B.S); Illinois Institute of Technology Chicago-Kent College of Law (J.D., with honors, 1975). Gold Key; Pi Lamba Theta. Elected Member, College of Labor and Employment Lawyers, Inc. Author: "New Guidelines to Help You Weather the Storm of Independent Contractor Conundrum," Insight, Illinois Society of CPA's, December/January 1997. Management Co-Editor-in-Chief of the 2005 Supplement to the Seventh Edition of How to Take a Case to the NLRB; Management Co-Editor-in-Chief and Chapter Author, BNA's Seventh Edition of How to Take a Case Before the NLRB. Management Co-Editor of American Bar Association Labor and Employment Section's Quarterly Newsletter 2002 -2004. *Member:* Chicago Bar Association (Chair, Labor and Employment Law Committee, 1990-1991; Liaison Chair, Illinois Department and Commission of Human Rights Subcommittee, 1990-1992; Co-Chair, Alliance for Women, 1995-1996; Member, Board of Managers, 1996-1998); American Bar Association (Member, Labor Committee, Management Chair of NLRB Practice and Procedure Committee); Decalogue Society; Women's Bar Association; College of Labor and Employment Lawyers, Inc. Fellow American Bar Foundation. ***PRACTICE AREAS:*** Labor and Employment Relations Law. ***Email:*** efox@seyfarth.com

PAUL E. FREEHLING, born 1938; admitted to bar, 1962, Illinois. *Education:* Harvard University (A.B., cum laude, 1959; LL.B., 1962). Editor, ISBA Administrative Law Newsletter. Arbitrator, American Arbitration Association; Chicago Mercantile Exchange; National Futures Association. Mediator, CPR Institute for Dispute Resolution; Arbitrator, CPR Institute for Dispute Resolution. Distinguished Neutral, CPR Institute for Dispute Resolution. *Member:* Chicago, Illinois State and Federal Bar Associations; Chicago Council of Lawyers; Seventh Circuit Bar Association; Association for Conflict Resolution; American Law Institute; American Arbitration Association; American Judicature Association. American College of Trial Lawyers; American Bar Foundation; Illinois State Bar Foundation. ***PRACTICE AREAS:*** Litigation; Alternative Dispute Resolution. ***Email:*** pfreehling@seyfarth.com

JEFFREY D. FRIEDMAN, born 1966; admitted to bar, 1996, Illinois. *Education:* The Ohio State University (B.A., 1989); DePaul University (J.D., 1996). *Member:* American Bar Association (Member, Section on: Real Property, Probate and Trust), Illinois State Bar Association, Chicago Bar Association (Member, Section on: Real Property). ***PRACTICE AREAS:*** Commercial Real Estate; Real Estate; Leasing; Real Estate Finance; Business Law; Conveyancing; Easements; Homeowners Association Law; Land Acquisitions; Land Sales; Land Trusts; Planned Unit Development Law; Real Estate Acquisitions; Real Estate Contracts; Real Estate Development; Real Estate Exchanges; Real Estate Investment; Real Estate Joint Ventures; Real Estate Leasing; Real Estate Sales; Real Estate Partnerships; Real Estate Title; Real Property; Real Property Acquisitions; Real Property Development; Real Property Finance; Residential Real Estate; Residential Real Estate Acquisitions; Residential Real Estate Development; Residential Real Estate Finance; Residential Real Estate Sales; Right of Way Easements; Community Association Law; Condominium Association Law; Condominium Development; Conservation Easements; Condominium Law; Commercial Conveyancing; Commercial Real Estate Acquisitions; Commercial Real Estate Contracts; Commercial Real Estate Development; Commercial Real Estate Finance; Commercial Real Estate Sales; Industrial Real Estate Law; Retail Development; Shopping Center Acquisitions; Shopping Center Development; Shopping Center Law; Leases and Leasing; Commercial Landlord and Tenant Law; Commercial Leasing; Industrial Leasing; Office Leasing; Retail Leasing; Shopping Center Leasing; Property Law. ***Email:*** jfriedman@seyfarth.com

(This Listing Continued)

JOAN E. GALE, admitted to bar, 1979, Illinois. *Education:* Indiana University (A.B., 1973); DePaul University (J.D., with honors, 1979). *Member:* Chicago Bar Association. ***PRACTICE AREAS:*** Labor and Employment. ***Email:*** jgale@seyfarth.com

CHRISTOPHER A. GARCIA, born 1959; admitted to bar, 1994, Illinois and U.S. District Court, Northern District of Illinois; 2001, U.S. Court of Appeals, Seventh Circuit; 2002, U.S. Supreme Court; U.S. District Court, Northern District of Florida. *Education:* University of California at Santa Barbara (B.A., 1984); Cornell University Law School (J.D., 1993). Recipient, Cornell University: Certificate of Concentration in Trial Advocacy; Certificate of Recognition for Advocacy in Cornell Legal Aid Clinic, 1991-1993. *Member:* Chicago, Illinois State and American Bar Associations; Illinois Latino Bar Association; Hispanic National Bar Association. ***PRACTICE AREAS:*** Labor and Employment Law. ***Email:*** cgarcia@seyfarth.com

DURWARD J. (JAMES) GEHRING, born 1952; admitted to bar, 1977, Illinois. *Education:* University of Illinois (A.B., magna cum laude, 1974); University of Chicago (J.D., with honors, 1977). Law Clerk to Hon. Bernard M. Decker, U.S. District Court, Northern Division, Illinois, 1977-1978. ***PRACTICE AREAS:*** Employee Benefits. ***Email:*** dgehring@seyfarth.com

RAYMOND I. GERALDSON (Retired)

GEORGE H. GERSTMAN, born 1939; admitted to bar, 1964, Illinois. *Education:* University of Illinois (B.S. in E.E., 1960); George Washington University (J.D., cum laude, 1963). ***PRACTICE AREAS:*** Litigation; Intellectual Property. ***Email:*** ggerstman@seyfarth.com

JAY A. GITLES, born 1962; admitted to bar, 1987, Illinois; U.S. District Court, Northern District of Illinois. *Education:* University of Michigan (A.B., 1984); Northwestern University (J.D., 1987). Member, Board of Editors, Commercial Leasing Law & Strategy. Member, Northwestern University School of Law Fund Board. Co-Author, Article, "Eminent Domain: A Legal Look At The Ruling," Heartland Real Estate Business, August 2005. Author, Article, "Lease Termination Agreements: Get Out Quickly, But Carefully," Commercial Leasing Law & Strategy, April 2005. Author, Article, "Avoid Oversights In Lease Amendments," Commercial Leasing Law & Strategy, May 2004. Author, Book Chapter, "Preconditions To Exercise of Options," Lease Negotiation Handbook, published in 2003 by the International Association of Attorneys and Executives in Corporate Real Estate (AECRE) and the American Bar Association (ABA). Co-Author, Book Chapter, "Avoiding Battles of Attrition In CAM Negotiations," Crafting Lease Clauses - Meeting Shopping Center Landlord and Tenant Objectives, published in 2003 by the International Council of Shopping Centers ("ICSC"). Author, Article: "Know The Risks Before Signing Wireless Rooftop Leases," Real Estate Chicago, September 2001. Author, Article: "Streamlining The Negotiating Process By Using Either Flat CAM or Gross Leases," Commercial Leasing Law & Strategy, August 2000. Speaker: "Recent Trends in Telecommunications Site Leasing," Chicago Bar Association - Real Property Law Committee, April 26, 2000. Speaker: "Avoiding Battles of Attrition in CAM Negotiations," ICSC U.S. Shopping Center Law Conference, Scottsdale, Arizona, October 22, 1999. Instructor: "Leases; Landlord and Tenant Relationships," BOMA / Chicago Commercial Real Estate Law Course, Summer 1999. Speaker: "Lease Option Clauses," ICSC Chicago Retail Leasing Symposium, June 9, 1999. Speaker: "Wireless Telecommunication Site Leasing," ICSC U.S. Shopping Center Law Conference, Nashville, Tennessee, October 30, 1998. Author, Articles, "Wireless Telecom Sites Create Opportunity For Landlords (Two Parts)," The BOMA Chicago Report, September and October, 1998. Speaker: "Telecommunication Leases," ICSC U.S. Shopping Center Law Conference, Palm Desert, California, October 24, 1997. Speaker: "Current Trends In Commercial Lease Negotiations," Institute of Real Estate Management, Chicago Chapter, June 25, 1997. Speaker: "Common Area Maintenance Clauses," ICSC U.S. Shopping Center Law Conference, Orlando, Florida, October 26, 1996. Author, Article: "The Rezoning Amendment Process," Realty & Building, February 10, 1996. Author, Articles: "Commercial Real Estate Lease Analysis (Two Parts)," Realty & Building, July 10, 1993 and February 12, 1994. Note and Comment Editor, 1986-1987 and Staff Member, 1985-1986, Journal of Criminal Law and Criminology. Author, Note, "Fourth Amendment Reasonableness of Surgical Intrusions," Winston v. Lee, 105 S. Ct. 1611 (1985), 76 J. Crim. L. & Criminology 972 (1985). *Member:* Chicago Bar Association (Member, Real Property Law Committee); International Council Of Shopping Centers (ICSC); International Association of Attorneys and Executives in Corporate Real Estate (AECRE). ***PRACTICE AREAS:*** Commercial Real Estate; Leases; Real Estate; Zoning and Land Use; Business Law. ***Email:*** jgitles@seyfarth.com

WILLIAM I. GOLDBERG, born 1937; admitted to bar, 1962, Illinois. *Education:* Amherst College (B.A., cum laude, 1959); Harvard University (J.D., cum laude, 1962). Phi Beta Kappa. Counsel to the Governor of Illinois, 1973-1977. Member, 1967-1972; Vice President and Director, 1971 and 1972, Chicago Crime Commission. Advisory Commission with the Attorney General of the State of Illinois (Executive Committee), 1991-1994. ***PRACTICE AREAS:*** Civil Litigation. ***Email:*** wgoldberg@seyfarth.com

BETH T. GOLUB, admitted to bar, 1994, Georgia; 1997, Illinois; U.S. Court of Appeals, First and Seventh Circuits; U.S. District Court, Central, Northern and Southern Districts of Illinois; U.S. District Court, Eastern District of Michigan; U.S. District Court, District of Colorado. *Education:* Indiana University (B.S., with high honors, 1991); Emory University (J.D., 1994). ***LANGUAGES:*** Spanish. ***PRACTICE AREAS:*** Labor and Employment. ***Email:*** bgolub@seyfarth.com

DEBORAH C. GORDON, born 1969; admitted to bar, 1993, Illinois. *Education:* University of Illinois (B.A., 1990; J.D., 1993); University of Chicago (M.B.A., 2000). Author/Speaker: "Health Care Compliance," American Academy of Orthopaedic Surgeons, February 2005; "Overview of the Illinois Hospital Report Card Act," Metropolitan Chicago Healthcare Council webcast presentation, March 2004; "Hurray, I am an Entrepreneur...Now What?" The Exponent, June 2003; "I Can Do It Better: A Guide to Management Buyouts," The Exponent, April 2003; "Financing Long-Term Care Facilities," American Health Lawyers Association, February 2002; "Legal Considerations in Seeking Equity Financing," The Corporate Lawyer, August 2001; "Planting the Seeds for Start-up Money," E*Prairie Midwest Technology Business News, June 2001; "Beyond Your Investment: Management Compensation and Cooperation," Venture Forth, Spring 2001; "Merging or Selling a Medical Practice," Journal of Medical Practice Management, March/April 1999; "Selling or Merging Your Practice," Chicago Medicine, January 1999; "A Practical Guide

(This Listing Continued)

SEYFARTH SHAW LLP, Chicago—Continued

to Merging or Selling a Medical Practice," Health Finance Report, January 1999; "Insurance Restrictions on Provider Risk Assumption," Health Law Monthly, May 1997. *Member:* American Bar Association (Member, Health Law Section); American Health Lawyers Association; University of Chicago Women's Business Group; Turnaround Management Association; Women Health Executives Network; Chicago Health Executives Forum; Health Finance Management Association. ***PRACTICE AREAS:*** Health Care; Corporate; Finance. ***Email:*** dgordon@seyfarth.com

ADAM GREETIS, born 1972; admitted to bar, 1997, Illinois. *Education:* University of Illinois (B.A., 1994); Chicago-Kent College of Law, Illinois Institute of Technology (J.D., 1997). ***PRACTICE AREAS:*** Employee Benefits. ***Email:*** agreetis@seyfarth.com

GEOFFREY F. GROSSMAN, born 1935; admitted to bar, 1959, Illinois. *Education:* University of Michigan (B.B.A., 1956); Northwestern University (J.D., 1959). Order of the Coif. *Member:* Chicago, Illinois State and American Bar Associations. ***PRACTICE AREAS:*** Federal Tax; Estate Planning; Corporate; Partnerships; Limited Liability Company Law. ***Email:*** ggrossman@seyfarth.com

TIMOTHY F. HALEY, born 1951; admitted to bar, 1978, Illinois. *Education:* Washington & Lee University (B.A., 1973); University of Virginia (J.D., 1978). ***PRACTICE AREAS:*** Labor and Employment. ***Email:*** thaley@seyfarth.com

LINDA J. HAYNES, born 1965; admitted to bar, 1994, Illinois. *Education:* Purdue University (B.S., 1987); Loyola University (J.D., cum laude, 1994). *Member:* American Bar Association. ***PRACTICE AREAS:*** Employee Benefits (100%). ***Email:*** lhaynes@seyfarth.com

VALERIE J. HOFFMAN, born 1953; admitted to bar, 1978, Illinois; U.S. Court of Appeals, Third and Seventh Circuits. *Education:* University of Edinburgh, Edinburgh, Scotland and Union College (B.A., summa cum laude, 1975); Boston College (J.D., 1978). Founder and Chair, Seyfarth Shaw Affirmative Action Consulting Team. Member, Board of Managers, Worklab Consulting LLC. Trustee, Union College; Trustee, Graduate College of Union University. Director, Aids Foundation of Chicago. National Advisor and Chicago Region Director, National Conference for Community and Justice. Past President, Remains Theatre. Former Director, University Club of Chicago. *Member:* American Bar Association. ***PRACTICE AREAS:*** Labor and Employment. ***Email:*** vhoffman@seyfarth.com

EUGENE JACOBS, born 1947; admitted to bar, 1973, Illinois. *Education:* University of Wisconsin (B.A., 1969); New York University (J.D., 1973). ***PRACTICE AREAS:*** Employee Benefits; Executive Compensation; Executive Employment Agreements. ***Email:*** ejacobs@seyfarth.com

MARC R. JACOBS, born 1960; admitted to bar, 1985, Illinois; U.S. Court of Appeals, Fourth, Sixth and Seventh Circuits; U.S. District Court, Northern District of Illinois; U.S. District Court, Western District of Wisconsin. *Education:* Reed College; University of Wisconsin-Madison (B.A., 1982); Boston University (J.D., cum laude, 1985). Recipient, Bernard E. Farr Prize and Award, 1985. Edward Hennessey Distinguished Scholar; G. Joseph Tauro Scholar. Speaker, 1996 and 2005 National Academy of Arbitrators Annual Meeting. Member, Board of Directors: Jewish Vocational Service of Chicago, 2001—; Temple Sholom of Chicago, 2001—. *Member:* American Bar Association (Member, Employment Rights and Responsibilities Committee); Human Resources Management Association of Chicago. ***PRACTICE AREAS:*** Labor Relations Law; Employment Law. ***Email:*** mjacobs@seyfarth.com

JEFFREY JAHNS, born 1946; admitted to bar, 1971, Illinois. *Education:* Villanova University (A.B., 1968); University of Chicago (J.D., 1971). *Member:* Chicago and American Bar Associations. ***PRACTICE AREAS:*** Real Estate Law; Construction Law; Business Law. ***Email:*** jjahns@seyfarth.com

SHELDON LEIGH JETER, born 1969; admitted to bar, 1996, Illinois. *Education:* University of South Carolina (B.S./B.A., 1993); University of South Carolina School of Law (J.D., 1996). *Member:* American Bar Association (Member, Sections on Labor and Employment and Litigation). ***PRACTICE AREAS:*** Labor and Employment. ***Email:*** ljeter@seyfarth.com

MARK L. JOHNSON, born 1965; admitted to bar, 1990, Illinois; U.S. Court of Appeals, Fifth and Seventh Circuits; U.S. District Court, Northern District of Illinois; 2005, U.S. District Court, District of Colorado. *Education:* University of Illinois (B.A., 1987; J.D., 1990). Phi Sigma Alpha; Phi Alpha Delta. Member, University of Illinois Law Review, 1988-1990. Board of Directors, Rainbows. *Member:* Chicago, Federal and American Bar Associations; Builders Association of Greater Chicago (Member, Legal Advisory Council); The Lawyer's Club. ***PRACTICE AREAS:*** Commercial Litigation; Construction Law; Intellectual Property Law. ***Email:*** majohnson@seyfarth.com

ROBERT H. JOYCE (Retired)

GARY S. KAPLAN, born 1956; admitted to bar, 1984, New York, Illinois and U.S. District Court, Northern District of Illinois including Trial Bar; 1985, U.S. Court of Appeals, Sixth Circuit; 1987, U.S. Court of Appeals, Seventh Circuit; 1989, U.S. Court of Appeals, District of Columbia and Eighth Circuits; 1992, U.S. Supreme Court; 1994, U.S. District Court, Eastern District of Wisconsin; 2000, U.S. Court of Appeals, Fourth Circuit; 2005, U.S. Court of Appeals, Ninth Circuit. *Education:* Colgate University (B.A., cum laude, honors in Political Science, 1978); Northwestern University School of Law (J.D., cum laude, 1983). Senior Editor, The Railway Labor Act (BNA). Recipient, Neighborhood Action Group Pro Bono Recognition Award, 1992-1994. *Member:* American Bar Association (Member, Sections on: Labor and Employment Law and Litigation; Member, Committee on Railway and Airline Labor Law). ***REPORTED CASES:*** Lekas v. United Airlines, 282 F.3d 296 (4th Cir. 2002); Powell v. AT&T Communications, Inc., 938 F.2d 823 (7th Cir. 1991); Sladek v. Bell System Management Pension Plan, 880 F.2d 972 (7th Cir. 1989). ***PRACTICE AREAS:*** Labor and Employment. ***Email:*** gkaplan@seyfarth.com

JOEL H. KAPLAN, born 1946; admitted to bar, 1969, Illinois. *Education:* Cornell University (B.S., 1966); University of Chicago (J.D., 1969). ***PRACTICE AREAS:*** Labor and Employment. ***Email:*** jkaplan@seyfarth.com

(This Listing Continued)

EDWARD J. KARLIN, born 1952; admitted to bar, 1977, Illinois. *Education:* Indiana University (B.A., 1974); Northwestern University (J.D., cum laude, 1977). ***PRACTICE AREAS:*** Business Law. ***Email:*** ekarlin@seyfarth.com

JEFFREY C. KAUFFMAN, admitted to bar, 1983, Michigan; 1990, Illinois; U.S. Supreme Court. *Education:* Albion College (B.A., summa cum laude, 1977); University of Michigan (J.D., 1982). *Member:* Illinois State and American Bar Associations. ***PRACTICE AREAS:*** Labor and Employment. ***Email:*** jkauffman@seyfarth.com

TIMOTHY J. KEEFER, born 1964; admitted to bar, 1991, Illinois; registered to practice before U.S. Patent and Trademark Office. *Education:* University of Scranton (B.S., 1986); Franklin Pierce Law Center (J.D., 1990). *Member:* Chicago and American Bar Associations; Intellectual Property Law Association of Chicago; American Intellectual Property Law Association. ***PRACTICE AREAS:*** Litigation; Intellectual Property. ***Email:*** tkeefer@seyfarth.com

RAYMOND J. KELLY, JR., born 1940; admitted to bar, 1967, Illinois; U.S. Supreme Court; U.S. Court of Appeals, Sixth, Seventh, Eighth, Ninth, and Eleventh Circuits; U.S. District Court, Northern District, including Trial Bar and Central District of Illinois; U.S. District Court, Northern and Southern Districts of Indiana; U.S. District Court, Eastern and Western Districts of Michigan; U.S. District Court, Western District of Texas. *Education:* University of Notre Dame (B.A., 1962); DePaul University (J.D., 1967). *Member:* Illinois State, Federal and American Bar Associations; Defense Research Institute; National Health Lawyers Association. [United States Naval Officer, 1962-1964]. ***PRACTICE AREAS:*** Litigation; Labor and Employment. ***Email:*** rkelly@seyfarth.com

MARY KAY KLIMESH, born 1954; admitted to bar, 1986, Texas; 1992, Illinois. *Education:* Trinity University (B.A., 1977); University of Iowa College of Law (J.D., 1986). ***PRACTICE AREAS:*** Labor and Employment. ***Email:*** mklimesh@seyfarth.com

RONALD J. KRAMER, born 1966; admitted to bar, 1992, Illinois; U.S. Court of Appeals, Sixth, Seventh and Tenth Circuits; U.S. District Court, Northern District of Illinois, including Trial Bar; U.S. District Court, Eastern District of Michigan. *Education:* Michigan State University (B.A., 1988); Chicago-Kent College of Law (J.D., 1992). *Member:* Chicago, Illinois State and American (Member, Sections on: Labor and Employment Law; State and Local Government Law; Member, Council, and Vice-Chair, Government Operations Committee) Bar Associations. ***PRACTICE AREAS:*** Labor and Employment. ***Email:*** rkramer@seyfarth.com

ALVIN L. KRUSE, born 1943; admitted to bar, 1969, Illinois. *Education:* Northwestern University (B.A., 1965; J.D., 1968). Phi Beta Kappa; Order of the Coif. Member, Board of Editors, Northwestern University Law Review. Adjunct Professor, Northwestern University School of Law. *Member:* Chicago, Illinois State and American Bar Associations; National Association of Bond Lawyers. ***PRACTICE AREAS:*** Business Law. ***Email:*** akruse@seyfarth.com

ANDREW R. LAIDLAW, born 1946; admitted to bar, 1972, Illinois. *Education:* Northwestern University (B.A., 1969); University of North Carolina (J.D., 1972). Member, Barristers. Author: "Antitrust Problems," Labor Law for the General Practitioner, Illinois Institute for CLE, 1996; "Robinson-Patman Act," Antitrust for the General Practitioner, Illinois Institute CLE, 1977. *Member:* American Bar Association (Member, Antitrust Committee and Securities Law Committee, 1982—). ***PRACTICE AREAS:*** Litigation. ***Email:*** alaidlaw@seyfarth.com

ANDREW F. LAMPERT, admitted to bar, 1996, Pennsylvania (inactive); 1997, New Jersey (inactive); 1998, Illinois. *Education:* Tufts University (B.A., cum laude, 1993); George Washington University Law School (J.D., with high honors, Order of the Coif, 1996). ***PRACTICE AREAS:*** Real Estate. ***Email:*** alampert@seyfarth.com

DANIEL F. LANCILOTI, born 1967; admitted to bar, 1994, Illinois, U.S. District Court, Northern District of Illinois; 1997, U.S. District Court, Central District of Illinois; 2001, U.S. Court of Appeals, Seventh Circuit, U.S. Court of Appeals, Federal Circuit; 2002, U.S. District Court, Northern District of Illinois including Trial Bar. *Education:* Knox College (B.A., 1989); Valparaiso University (J.D., magna cum laude, 1994). *Member:* Illinois State Bar Association. ***PRACTICE AREAS:*** Litigation; Intellectual Property; Trade Secrets; Restrictive Covenants; Commercial Transactions. ***Email:*** dlanciloti@seyfarth.com

RICHARD S. LAUTER, born Chicago, Illinois; admitted to bar, 1982, Illinois, U.S. District Court, Northern District of Illinois and U.S. Court of Appeals, Seventh Circuit; 1986, Missouri. *Education:* University of Kansas (B.A. in Political Science and Communications, 1975); Northern Illinois University (J.D., 1982). Executive Editor, Northern Illinois University Law Review, 1981-1982. Speaker, Illinois Institute for Continuing Legal Education, Illinois Bankers Association and American Bankruptcy Institute. Law Clerk, Hon. Richard L. Merrick (ret.), U.S. Bankruptcy Court, Northern District of Illinois. *Member:* Chicago Bar Association; The Missouri Bar; American Bankruptcy Institute. ***PRACTICE AREAS:*** Bankruptcy; Workouts; Business Reorganization. ***Email:*** rlauter@seyfarth.com

BART A. LAZAR, born 1961; admitted to bar, 1987, Illinois; 1988, New York. *Education:* University of Chicago (B.A., 1982); Chicago-Kent College of Law (J.D., with honors, 1987); New York University (LL.M., Trade Regulation, 1988). Instuctor: Copyright, Trademark, Promotion and Privacy Issues, IIT/Chicago-Kent College of Law and Kellogg, Northwestern University, School of Management. Author: "Mickey and Vicky," IP Law and Business, May 2003; "Privacy Issues in the Workplace: A Post-Sept. 11 Perspective," Employee Relations Law Journal, Summer 2002; "Employee Privacy: Most Employers Need to Comply with HIPAA Health Care Privacy Regulations," E-Commerce Law & Strategy, May/June 2002; "Fundamental Issues in Copyright and Trademark Licensing," The Licensing Journal, August 2001; "New Laws Affect the Transfer of Information Across the Atlantic," The Corporate Lawyer; January 2001. Lecturer: "Battling Cybercrime," Chicago Crime Commission, November 2002; "Trademark and Copyright Licensing Issues," Practicing Law Institute, November 2002, 2001, 2000; "HIPAA Compliance-Managing Employee Health Data," Food Marketing Institute General Counsel Conference, June 2002; "Privacy Issues in the Workplace," ACCA-Boston, March 2002; "Privacy Issues in Promotions and Marketing," Promotion Marketing Association Annual Law Conference, December 2001; "Privacy Litigation Developments," Privacy By Design 2001, December 2001; "Privacy Strategies for Global Business," The Privacy Challenge: Chicago-Kent College of Law; April 2001; "What Marketers Need to Know About Privacy," Chicago Association of

(This Listing Continued)

Direct Marketing, February 2001. *Member:* International Trademark Association, Promotion Marketing Association, Lawyers for Creative Arts. ***REPORTED CASES:*** Bretford Mfg. v. Smith Sys. Mfg. Co., 116 F. Supp. 2d 951 (N.D. IL 2000); Pferdes v. International Sporthorse Registry, Inc., 1999 U.S. Dist. LEXIS 19448, 1999 WL 1206640 (N.D. Ill. 1999). ***PRACTICE AREAS:*** Intellectual Property; Privacy; Advertising and Marketing; Trademarks; Copyrights; Internet. ***Email:*** blazar@seyfarth.com

JILL LEKA, admitted to bar, 1985, Illinois; 1986, Missouri. *Education:* Southern Illinois University (B.S., 1980; J.D., 1985). *Member:* The Missouri Bar; Illinois State and American Bar Associations. ***PRACTICE AREAS:*** Labor and Employment. ***Email:*** jleka@seyfarth.com

H. DEBRA LEVIN, born 1950; admitted to bar, 1975, Illinois. *Education:* Cornell University (B.A., cum laude, 1972); Harvard University (J.D., cum laude, 1975). ***PRACTICE AREAS:*** Estate Planning; Probate; Employee Benefits; Non-Profit Organizations Law. ***Email:*** dlevin@seyfarth.com

MICHAEL R. LEVINSON, born 1954; admitted to bar, 1979, Illinois; U.S. Supreme Court; U.S. District Court, Central and Northern Districts of Illinois; U.S. District Court, Trial Bar, Northern District of Illinois; U.S. District Court, Eastern District of Wisconsin; U.S. District Court, Southern District of Indiana; U.S. Court of Appeals, Federal, Sixth and Seventh Circuits. *Education:* Claremont Men's College (B.A., summa cum laude, 1976); Harvard Law School (J.D., 1979); University of Chicago (M.B.A., 1997). *Member:* Chicago and American Bar Associations; National Institute of Trial Advocacy; National Association of Securities Dealers (Arbitrator). ***PRACTICE AREAS:*** Litigation; Intellectual Property. ***Email:*** mlevinson@seyfarth.com

MARK A. LIES, II, born 1946; admitted to bar, 1974, Illinois; U.S. Court of Appeals, Third, Fourth, Seventh and Eleventh Circuits; U.S. District Court, Northern District of Illinois; U.S. Court of Claims. *Education:* University of Notre Dame (B.A., 1968); DePaul University (J.D., 1974). *Member:* American National Standards Institute, Member Z244 Committee (1998-) ; Better Business Bureau of Chicago/Board of Directors (2005-) ; National Demolition Association, Adjunct Member (2001-); National Fire Prevention Association, Adjunct Member (1992-); Outdoor Advertising Association of America (2001-); Union League Club of Chicago, President (2001-02); Village of LaGrange, Police and Fire Commission (1998-); Workplace Violence Prevention Guidelines Committee, American National Standards Institute, ASIS (2005-). [Commissioned Officer U.S. Navy/Vietnam Veteran 1968-1974]. ***PRACTICE AREAS:*** Environmental Health and Safety; Litigation. ***Email:*** mlies@seyfarth.com

STEVEN R. LIFSON, born 1960; admitted to bar, 1987, Illinois. *Education:* Boston University (B.A., cum laude, 1982); University of Illinois (J.D., 1987); John Marshall Law School (LL.M., in Taxation, with honors, 1993). *Member:* Chicago, Illinois State and American Bar Associations; ESOP Association; National Center for Employee Ownership. ***PRACTICE AREAS:*** Employee Benefits; ERISA; Employee Stock Ownership Plans; Estate Planning; Probate. ***Email:*** slifson@seyfarth.com

RONALD L. LIPINSKI, born 1950; admitted to bar, 1976, Illinois and U.S. District Court, Northern District of Illinois; U.S. Court of Appeals, Seventh Circuit. *Education:* Kalamazoo College (B.A., 1972); John Marshall Law School (J.D., with high honors, 1976). *Member:* Illinois State, Federal and American Bar Associations; Defense Research Institute. ***PRACTICE AREAS:*** Litigation; Toxic Torts; Employment Litigation. ***Email:*** rlipinski@seyfarth.com

BRADFORD L. LIVINGSTON, born 1954; admitted to bar, 1979, Illinois; 1988, Wisconsin; U.S. Supreme Court; U.S. Court of Appeals, Third and Seventh Circuits; U.S. District Court, Central and Northern Districts of Illinois, including Trial Bar; U.S. District Court, Eastern District of Michigan; U.S. District Court, Eastern District of Wisconsin. *Education:* University of Michigan (B.A., with high distinction, 1976); University of Michigan (J.D., cum laude, 1979). *Member:* Chicago, Illinois State, American and International Bar Associations; State Bar of Wisconsin. ***PRACTICE AREAS:*** Labor and Employment. ***Email:*** blivingston@seyfarth.com

WALTER P. LOOMIS (Retired)

THOMAS D. LUPO, born 1959; admitted to bar, 1985, Illinois; U.S. Court of Appeals, Seventh Circuit; U.S. District Court, Central and Northern Districts of Illinois; U.S. District Court, Eastern District of Wisconsin; U.S. Army Court of Criminal Appeals. *Education:* University of Notre Dame (B.A., 1982; J.D., 1985). *Member:* American Bar Association. [Lieutenant Colonel, United States Army Reserve, Judge Advocate]. ***PRACTICE AREAS:*** Civil Litigation; Environmental Law. ***Email:*** tlupo@seyfarth.com

RICHARD M. LYON (Retired)

GERALD L. MAATMAN, JR., born 1956; admitted to bar, 1981, Illinois; U.S. District Court, Central, Northern, and Southern Districts of Illinois; U.S. Supreme Court; U.S. Court of Appeals, Seventh Circuit. *Education:* Washington and Lee University (B.A., 1978); Northwestern University (J.D., 1981). *Member:* Illinois State and American Bar Associations. ***PRACTICE AREAS:*** Labor and Employment; Litigation. ***Email:*** gmaatman@seyfarth.com

MARTIN P. MARTA, born 1942; admitted to bar, 1972, Illinois. *Education:* Roosevelt University (B.S., 1969); Duke University (J.D., 1972). Board of Directors: RAINBOWS; Greater O'Hare Association of Commerce and Industry; Volunteer Service Bureau. Member: Chicago Sister Cities Program (Milan Committee); Chicagoland Chamber of Commerce; Employment Ministry, St. Francis de Sales Catholic Church, Lake Zurich, Illinois (Committee Member); University Club of Chicago. *Member:* American Bar Association (Member, Labor and Employment Law Section, Committee on Labor Arbitration and Law of Collective Bargaining). ***PRACTICE AREAS:*** Labor; Public Employment Law; Arbitrations. ***Email:*** mmarta@seyfarth.com

RICHARD P. MCARDLE, born 1965; admitted to bar, 1993, Illinois. *Education:* Cleveland State University (B.B.A., cum laude, 1987); Case Western Reserve University (M.B.A., 1993; J.D., 1993). *Member:* American Bar Association. ***PRACTICE AREAS:*** Labor and Employment (100%). ***Email:*** rmcardle@seyfarth.com

CONDON A. MCGLOTHLEN, born 1961; admitted to bar, 1987, Illinois. *Education:* University of Kentucky (B.A., with honors and high distinction, 1984); University of Wisconsin-Madison (J.D., with honors, 1987). Order of the Coif. Author: "Layoffs and Litigation," House Counsel (May/June 2001); "New Rule May Jeopardize Settlement and Separation Agreements," ACCA Docket (July/August 2001); "Bragdon v. Abbott: The Supreme Court's First Take on the Americans With Disabilities Act," Employee Relations Law Journal (Spring 1999). ***PRACTICE AREAS:*** Labor and Employment. ***Email:*** cmcglothlen@seyfarth.com

ELLEN E. MCLAUGHLIN, born 1956; admitted to bar, 1981, Illinois; U.S. District Court, Central and Northern Districts of Illinois including Trial Bar; U.S. District Court, District of Colorado; U.S. District Court, Eastern District of Wisconsin; U.S. District Court, Northern District of Indiana; U.S. Court of Appeals, Fifth, Sixth and Seventh Circuits. *Education:* University of Notre Dame (B.A., cum laude, 1978; J.D., 1981). Chambers USA rated attorney. Member, Editorial Board: Americans with Disabilities Act Compliance Guide, Thompson Publishing; The Leave & Disability Coordination Handbook, Thompson Publishing. Guest lecturer for the American Bar Association, National Employment Law Institute, Society for Human Resource Management, Corporate Counsel Institute, American Arbitration Association, American Hospital Association, Illinois State Chamber of Commerce, Illinois State Bar Association, Hotel Human Resources Association of Chicago, Hotel Employers Labor Relations Association and Metropolitan Chicago Health Care Council. Co-author: "A Client's Guide to the ADA, FMLA and Workers' Compensation," The Journal of the American Corporate Counsel Association; "Training Becomes Important Step to Avoid Liability," The National Law Journal; "The Family and Medical Leave Act" chapter in Federal Employment Laws and Regulations and Employment Discrimination - How to Comply, both R.A. Apland publications. Author: "Physicians and the ADA: Examining Current Policies," Medical Staff Leader; "Status of Staff Physicians Uncertain under the ADA," Quality Management Update; "Physicians and the ADA," Hospitals Magazine. Co-authored comments to the EEOC's proposed regulations for the ADA and comments to the DOL's proposed regulations for the FMLA on behalf of national employer coalitions. Widely recognized as one of the nation's foremost ADA and FMLA experts. *Member:* Chicago and American (Member, Labor and Employment and Litigation Sections); National Employment Law Institute (Faculty and Advisory Board). ***PRACTICE AREAS:*** Labor and Employment; Age Discrimination in Employment; Employment Class Actions; Employment Disability Discrimination; Employment Law; Employment Litigation; Equal Employment Opportunity Law; Family and Medical Leave Act; Harassment; Labor Law; Management Employment Law; Personnel Policies; Personnel Training; Reductions in Force; Sexual Harassment; Title VII Discrimination; Labor Relations; Labor Arbitration. ***Email:*** emclaughlin@seyfarth.com

KRISTIN EDELL MICHAELS, born 1966; admitted to bar, 1991, Illinois. *Education:* Marquette University (B.A., magna cum laude, 1988); Northwestern University (J.D., 1991). ***PRACTICE AREAS:*** Labor and Employment. ***Email:*** kmichaels@seyfath.com

ROBERT J. MIGNIN, born 1948; admitted to bar, 1973, Illinois; U.S. District Court, Central and Northern Districts of Illinois; U.S. Court of Appeals, Seventh Circuit. *Education:* Knox College (B.A., cum laude, 1970); University of Illinois (J.D., 1973). *Member:* Chicago, Illinois State, American (Member, EEO and Labor Law Sections) and International (Officer of Committee) Bar Associations; Transportation Lawyers Association. ***PRACTICE AREAS:*** Labor and Employment. ***Email:*** rmignin@seyfarth.com

PETER C. MILLER, born 1965; admitted to bar, 1990, Illinois. *Education:* Marquette University (B.A., 1987); DePaul University (J.D., 1990). Chair, Employee Benefits Practice Group. *Member:* Chicago, Illinois State and American Bar Associations; The ESOP Association. ***PRACTICE AREAS:*** Employee Benefits; Executive Compensation. ***Email:*** pmiller@seyfarth.com

MICHAEL D. MISELMAN, born 1942; admitted to bar, 1967, Illinois. *Education:* University of Michigan (A.B., 1964); Harvard University (J.D., cum laude, 1967). Phi Beta Kappa. *Member:* Chicago, Illinois State and American Bar Associations. ***PRACTICE AREAS:*** Condominium Law; Real Estate. ***Email:*** mmiselman@seyfarth.com

IAN H. MORRISON, born 1970; admitted to bar, 1995, Missouri; 1996, Illinois; U.S. Supreme Court and U.S. Court of Appeals, Fifth, Sixth, Seventh, and Eighth Circuits; U.S. District Court, Northern and Central Districts of Illinois, U.S. District Court, Northern District of Indiana and U.S. District Court, Western District of Michigan. *Education:* University of Chicago (B.A., with honors, 1992); Washington University (J.D., 1995). Order of the Coif. Law Clerk to the Honorable Richard Mills, U.S. District Court, Central District of Illinois, 1995-1997. ***PRACTICE AREAS:*** Labor and Employment; ERISA Litigation; Class Action Defense. ***Email:*** imorrison@seyfarth.com

LAWRENCE J. MOSS, born 1955; admitted to bar, 1982, Illinois. *Education:* Columbia University (B.A., summa cum laude, 1977); Jewish Theological Seminary (M.A., 1979); University of Chicago (J.D., cum laude, 1982). Phi Beta Kappa; Order of the Coif. Member, University of Chicago Law Review, 1980-1981. ***PRACTICE AREAS:*** Real Estate Law; Government Pension Plans. ***Email:*** lmoss@seyfarth.com

DAVID L. NEWMAN, admitted to bar, 1992, Illinois; U.S. Court of Appeals, Federal Circuit; U.S. District Court, Northern District of Illinois; registered to practice before U.S. Patent and Trademark Office. *Education:* Ohio State University (B.S., 1986); DePaul University (J.D., 1992). *Member:* American Bar Association; American Intellectual Property Law Association; Intellectual Property Law Association of Chicago. ***PRACTICE AREAS:*** Litigation; Intellectual Property. ***Email:*** dnewman@seyfarth.com

ANDREA CAPLAN OKUN, admitted to bar, 1995, Illinois. *Education:* University of Michigan (B.A., with high distinction, 1992; J.D., 1994). *Member:* American Bar Association. ***PRACTICE AREAS:*** Complex Litigation; Products Liability; Securities Litigation and Arbitration; Trade Secrets; Class Action Defense; Insurance; Construction Law.

CAMILLE A. OLSON, born 1958; admitted to bar, 1983, California; 1985, Illinois. *Education:* University of Michigan (B.A., with high honors, 1980; J.D., 1983). ***PRACTICE AREAS:*** Labor and Employment. ***Email:*** colson@seyfarth.com

JERYL OLSON, born 1957; admitted to bar, 1985, Illinois. *Education:* Valparaiso University (B.S., 1979); Illinois Institute of Technology; DePaul University (J.D., 1985). *Member:* American Bar Association (Member, Department of Natural Resources Section); Air & Waste Management Association. ***PRACTICE AREAS:*** Environmental Law; Toxic Torts; Occupational Safety and Health. ***Email:*** jolson@seyfarth.com

JOHN J. O'MALLEY, born 1948; admitted to bar, 1974, Illinois. *Education:* College of the Holy Cross (B.A., 1971); DePaul University (J.D., cum laude, 1974). Member, De-

(This Listing Continued)

SEYFARTH SHAW LLP, Chicago—Continued

Paul University Law Review, 1972-1973. Author: "Summary Judgement," IDC Quarterly (First Quarter 1998); "Expert Witnesses: The Standard of Admissibility and the Standards Used in Testimony," IDC Quarterly (First Quarter 1995). *Member:* Chicago and American Bar Associations; Defense Research Institute; Illinois Association of Defense Trial Counsel (Co-Chairman, Practice and Procedure Committee, 1993—). ***PRACTICE AREAS:*** Litigation. ***Email:*** jomalley@seyfarth.com

RICHARD D. OSTROW (Retired)

CHRISTOPHER E. PAETSCH, born 1970; admitted to bar, 1995, Illinois; U.S. District Court, Northern District of Illinois; U.S. Court of Appeals, Seventh Circuit. *Education:* Duke University (B.A., magna cum laude, 1992); University of Michigan (J.D., cum laude, 1995). *Member:* Chicago, Illinois State and American Bar Associations. ***PRACTICE AREAS:*** Litigation; Intellectual Property. ***Email:*** cpaetsch@seyfarth.com

ROBERT J. PALEY, born 1933; admitted to bar, 1960, Illinois. *Education:* University of Michigan (B.B.A., 1955; J.D., with honors, 1960). Adjunct Professor, Taxation, DePaul Law School, 1984—. *Member:* Illinois State and American (Member, Tax Section) Bar Associations. ***PRACTICE AREAS:*** Business Law. ***Email:*** rpaley@seyfarth.com

GUS A. PALOIAN, born 1958; admitted to bar, 1984, Illinois. *Education:* Northwestern University (B.A., 1981); DePaul University (J.D., with honors, 1984). Law Clerk to Hon. Frederick J. Hertz, U.S. Bankruptcy Judge, Northern District of Illinois, 1984-1985. *Member:* Chicago (Member, Bankruptcy Committee), Illinois State and American (Member, Subcommittee on Partnership Bankruptcies and Use and Dispostion of Property) Bar Associations; American Bankruptcy Institute; Turn Around Management Association; National Association of Bankruptcy Trustees. ***PRACTICE AREAS:*** Litigation; Bankruptcy. ***Email:*** gpaloian@seyfarth.com

GERALD L. PAULING, II, born 1967; admitted to bar, 1992, Illinois; U.S. Court of Appeals, Seventh and District of Columbia Circuits; U.S. District Court, Northern District of Illinois. *Education:* University of Illinois (B.S., 1989); University of California School of Law (J.D., 1992). Winner, UCLA Moot Court Competition, 1990-1991. Member, UCLA National Team, National Moot Court Competition, 1991-1992. Business Managing Editor, National Black Law Journal, 1990-1991. Judicial Extern to Hon. Terry Hatter, U.S. District Court, Central District of California, 1991. Author: "The Implications of Crown Cork & Seal Co. for Employee Involvment Committees," The Labor Lawyer, Fall 2002. Speaker, "Conducting Employee Investigations," Illinois Institute for Continuing Legal Education conference, 2003. Board Member, Teen Living Programs of Chicago, 2001-2003. Board Member, Jackson Park Hospital Foundation, 2002-2003. *Member:* Chicago, Cook County, Illinois State and American Bar Associations. ***PRACTICE AREAS:*** Labor and Employment. ***Email:*** gpauling@seyfarth.com

THOMAS H. PECKHAM, born 1962; admitted to bar, 1987, Illinois. *Education:* Northwestern University (B.A., 1984; J.D., 1987). ***PRACTICE AREAS:*** Litigation; Intellectual Property. ***Email:*** tpeckham@seyfarth.com

ANDREW H. PERELLIS, born 1955; admitted to bar, 1981, Illinois; U.S. Supreme Court; U.S. Court of Appeals, Seventh and Ninth Circuits; U.S. District Court, Central and Northern Districts of Illinois (Trial Bar, 1986); U.S. District Court, Eastern District of Wisconsin. *Education:* University of Michigan (B.A., with distinction, 1977); George Washington University National Law Center (J.D., with high honors, 1981). *Member:* Chicago, Illinois State and American Bar Associations. ***PRACTICE AREAS:*** Environmental Health and Safety. ***Email:*** aperellis@seyfarth.com

THOMAS J. PISKORSKI, born 1955; admitted to bar, 1981, Illinois and U.S. District Court, Northern District of Illinois; 1982 U.S. Court of Appeals, Seventh Circuit; 1986, U.S. Court of Appeals, Tenth Circuit and U.S. District Court, Northern District of Illinois including Trial Bar; 1994, U.S. District Court, Northern District of California; 1995, U.S. District Court, Eastern District of Wisconsin; 1996, U.S. Court of Appeals, Fifth Circuit; 1997, U.S. Court of Appeals for the District of Columbia Circuit; 1988, U.S. District Court, Eastern District of Michigan and U.S. Court of Appeals, Sixth Circuit; 1998, U.S. Supreme Court; 1999, U.S. District Court, Central District of Illinois; 2000, U.S. Court of Appeals, Eighth Circuit; 2002, U.S. District Court, Western District of Michigan, U.S. Court of Appeals, First Circuit; 2004, U.S. District Court, Eastern District of Texas and U.S. Court of Appeals, Fourth Circuit. *Education:* Marquette University (B.S., magna cum laude, 1977); University of Notre Dame (M.B.A., high honors, 1981; J.D., 1981). Recipient, Chick Evans Scholarship, Marquette University. Associate Editor, University of Notre Dame Law Review. Law Clerk, Senior District Judge Robert A. Grant, U.S. District Court, Northern District of Indiana. Co-Author: "NLRB Breathes New Life Into Employee Participation Committees," Employee Relations Law Journal, p. 127, Winter 2001; "Levitz Furniture: NLRB Rewrites the Book on Employer Efforts to Oust Incumbent Unions," Employee Relations Law Journal, P. 31, Autumn 2001; "Navigating Through the Final and New COBRA Regulations," Employee Relations Law Journal, p. 77, Winter 1999; "Geissal v. Moore Medical Corp. - The Supreme Court Resolves Dual Coverage Issue," Benefits Law Journal, p. 97, Autumn 1998; "Employment Discrimiation Law in the Public Sector," Employment Discrimination (Ill. Inst. for CLE, 1996); "Managing the Risk and Liability of Wrongful Employment Practices through Insurance," Employee Relations Law Journal, p. 7, Autumn 1995; "Private Arbitration As The Exclusive Means Of Resolving Employment-Related Disputes," Employee Relations Law Journal, p. 205, Autumn 1993; "Federal Employment Laws and Regulations Chapter 3 - Discrimination in Employment," American Chamber of Commerce Publishers 1993; "Employment Discrimination, Chapter 1 - The Civil Rights Act of 1991 & Chapter 8 - Affirmative Action for Federal Contractors and Subcontractors," American Chamber of Commerce Publishers 1993; "More Lawsuits Forecast in Wake of Civil Rights Act of 1991," Chicago Lawyer, April 1992; "The Civil Rights Act of 1991: An Overview And Analysis," The Labor Lawyer 9, 1992; "Employment Discrimination Law in the Public Sector," Employment Discrimination, Ill. Inst. for CLE, 1989; "The Proper Role of Res Judicata and Collateral Estoppel in Title VII Suits," 79 Mich. L. Rev. 1485, 1981. Author: "*O'Connor v. Consolidated Coin Caterers Corp. - Supreme Court Establishes New Prima Facie Burden For ADEA Plaintiffs To Satisfy*," Employee Relations Law Journal, p. 95, Autumn 1996; "Minimizing Employee Benefits Litigation Through Effective Claims Adiministration Procedures," Employee Relations Law Journal, p. 421, Winter 1994/95; Illinois State Bar Association Labor and Employment Law Newsletter, February 1994;

(This Listing Continued)

"The Department of Human Rights' Power to Issue Complaints," Illinois Bar Journal, p. 78, February 1994; "Electromation: A Setback To Employee Participation Programs," The Labor Lawyer, 1993; "Reinstatement of The Sexual Harasser: The Conflict Between Federal Labor Law And Title VII," Employee Relations Law Journal, p. 617, Spring 1993; "The Growing Judicial Acceptance of Summary Judgments in Age Discrimination Cases," Employee Relations Law Journal, p. 245 Autumn 1992; "Fortino v. Quasar Co.: Are Japanese-Owned Companies Immune From Title VII?," Employee Relations Law Journal, p. 61, Summer 1992; "A Comprehensive Review of Seventh Circuit Labor and Employment Law Decisions," 1981-82 Term, 59 Chi. Kent L. Rev. 625, 1983. *Member:* Chicago Bar Association (Member, Labor and Employment Law Committee and Federal Civil Procedure Committee); Illinois State Bar Association (Member, Labor and Employment Law Section Council); American Bar Association (Member, Section of Labor and Employment Law, Litigation Committee on Employment and Labor Relations Law, Litigation Subcommittee of the Committee on Employee Rights and Responsibilities); Seventh Circuit Court of Appeals Bar Association. ***REPORTED CASES:*** Greviskes v. Universities Research Association, Inc. (Fermi National Accelerator Laboratory), Nos. 04-2784 & 04-3863 (7th Cir., August 8, 2005); Beasley v. Hub City Texas, L.P., 2003 WL 22254692 (State of Texas First District Court of Appeals, September 29, 2003); Dockery v. Dayton Hudson Corp., No. 97 C 6677, 2001 WL 693094 (7th Cir., June 18, 2001); Graduate Employees Organization v. Board of Trustees of the University of Illinois, 315 Ill.App.3d 278, 773 N.E.2d 759 (Ill. 1st Dist. App. Ct. 2000); Jay's Foods, L.L.C. v. Chemical & Allied Product Workers Union, 208 F.3d 610 (7th Cir. 2000), cert denied, 531 U.S. 927(2000); Graduate Employees Organization v. Board of Trustees of the University of Illinois, 309 Ill.App.3d 1071, 764 N.E.2d 597 (Ill. 1st Dist. App. Ct. 1999); Anaeme v. Diagnostek, Inc., 528 U.S. 814 (1999); Pokuta v. Trans World Airlines, Inc., 191 F.3d 834 (7th Cir. 1999); Doe v. Mutual of Omaha Insurance Co., 179 F.3d 557 (7th Cir. 1999); Vanderbilt University v. DiNardo, 174 F.3d 751 (6th Cir. 1999); Meier v. Coresource, Inc., No. 98-5364, 1999 WL 133255(6th Cir., February 23, 1999); Sheren v. Dayton-Hudson Corp., No. 98-3166, 1999 WL 89046 (7th Cir., February 18, 1999); Bradley v. Trans World Airlines, Inc., No. 1-97-2542 (Ill. App. 1st Dist, October 22, 1998); Couch v. Sprint Corporation, 524 U.S. 952 (1998); Burns International Security Services v. NLRB, 146 F.3d 873 (D.C. Cir. 1998); LCF, Inc. and Sprint Corp. v. NLRB, 129 F.3d 1276 (D.C. Cir. 1997); Bellows v. Amoco Oil Company, 118 F.3d 268 (5th Cir. 1997); University Professionals of Illinois, Local 4100, et al. v. Jim Edgar, et al., 114 F.3d 665 (7th Cir. 1997); Barefield v. Village of Winnetka, 81 F.3d 704 (7th Cir. 1996); Local 2, International Union of Security Officers v. Burns International Security Services, No. 94-15115, 1995 WL 411843 (9th Cir., July 12, 1995); Geise v. The Phoenix Co., 159 Ill. 2d 507, 639 N.E.2d 1273 (Ill. S. Ct., August 4, 1994); Hammond v. Trans World Airlines, Inc., 981 F.2d 1524 (7th Cir. 1992), rehearing en banc denied, 989 F.2d 944 (7th Cir. 1993), cert. denied, 114 S. Ct. 175 (1993); Board of Trustees of the University of Illinois v. Illinois Educational Labor Relations Board and Local 399, International Union of Operating Engineers, 235 Ill. App. 3d 709, 600 N.E.2d 1292 (4th Dist. 1992), appeal denied, 148 Ill. 2d 639, 610 N.E.2d 1260 (Ill. S. Ct. 1993); California School Employees Association v. ServiceMaster Company Limited Partnership, et al., 2 Cal. App. 4th 1396, 4 Cal. Rptr. 2d 35 (Cal. Ct. App. 1992), review denied, 1992 Cal. LEXIS 1796 (1992); Sexton v. Thermotron Industries, Inc., 502 N.W.2d 39 (Mich. Ct. App. 1992); Allied-Signal Inc. v. Acme Service Corp., 946 F.2d 1295 (7th Cir. 1991); Jane Doe v. Allied-Signal Inc., 925 F.2d 1007 (7th Cir. 1991); Washington v. St. Margaret Hospital, 904 F.2d 39 (7th Cir. 1990); AFSCME v. Board of Trustees of the University of Illinois, 197 Ill. App. 3d 521, 554 N.E.2d 476 (4th Dist. 1990); Haynes v. Alumax Recycling Group, Inc., 899 F.2d 16 (7th Cir. 1990); Williams v. Maremont Corp., 875 F.2d 1476 (10th Cir. 1989); Heussner v. National Gypsum Co., 887 F.2d 672 (6th Cir. 1989); Andre v. Bendix Corp., 841 F.2d 172 (7th Cir. 1988); Kelly v. Board of Trustees of the University of Illinois, 826 F.2d 1068 (7th Cir. 1987); Shasteen v. Wilson Sporting Goods Co., No. 87-5325 (6th Cir. 1987); Pesce v. J. Sterling Morton High School, 830 F.2d 789 (7th Cir. 1987); Wenthold v. AT&T Technologies, Inc., 142 Ill. App. 3d 612, 491 N.E.2d 1263 (1st Dist. 1986); Owens v. General Cable Company, No. 85-178 (Fla. Dist. Ct. App. 1985); Gaver v. GK Technologies, Inc., No. 84-1877 (Fla. Dist. Ct. App. 1985); Andre v. The Bendix Corp., 774 F.2d 786 (7th Cir. 1985); Fleischer v. Board of Community College District No. 519, 128 Ill. App. 3d 757, 471 N.E.2d 213 (2d Dist. 1984); Luckett, et al. v. Menasha Material Handling Corp., et al., No. 01 C 8967 (N.D. Ill. 2005); Parker v. City of Elgin, No. 03 C 0171 (N.D. Ill. 2005); Piggee v. Carl Sandburg College, et al., No. 03-1329 (C.D. Ill. 2005); Niu v. Revcor Molded Products Company, et al, Cause No. 153-202507-03 (Tarrant County, Texas 2005); Greviskes v. Universities Research Association, Inc. (Fermi National Accelerator Laboratory), 342 F.Supp.2d 763 (N.D. Ill. 2004), aff'd, Nos. 04-2784 & 04-3863 (7th Cir., August 8, 2005); Nielsen, et al. v. Devry, Inc., 302 F. Supp.2d 747 (W.D. Mich. 2003); Beasley v. Hub City Texas, L.P., Cause No. 2002-62901 (Harris County, Texas District Court March 6, 2003); Hub Group Tennessee, LLC v. Herzog, et al., No. CH-03-0166-2 (Chancery Court of Shelby County, Tennessee February 24, 2003); Lee v. McDonald's Corporation, No. 4:97CV1280 (E.D. Mo., December 11, 2002); Garren v. Molex Incorporated, No. 4:01CV00191 (E..D. Ark., November 13, 2002); Rodgers v. Metropolitan Water Reclamation District of Greater Chicago, et al., No. 01 C 2271 (N.D. Ill., December 14, 2001); Johnson v. City of Elgin, et al., No. 99 C 8288, 2002 WL 171971 (N.D. Ill., October 3, 2001); Bonne v. University of Illinois at Urbana-Champaign, No. UC-01-2 (State Universities Civil Service System September 19, 2001); Pettis v. McDonald's Corp., Charge No. 1991 CF 2143, ALS No. 10754 (ALJ Recommended Order and Decision, April 9, 2001); Graham v. City of Aurora, 156 F.Supp.2d 880 (N.D. Ill., March 28, 2001); Gates v. Molex Incorporated, No. 4:99CV892 SMR (E.D. Ark., March 2, 2001); Thompson v. Molex Fiber Optics, Case No. 99 C 5052 (N.D. Ill. 2000); Brown, et al. v. Nationscredit Commercial Corp., No. 3:99-CV-592, 2000 WL 887593 (D. Conn. 2000); Gorin v. Galileo International, Case No. 1:97-CV-348-JOF (N.D. Ga., July 21, 1999); Mason v. City of Elgin, Case No. 97 C 8088, 1999 WL 168818 (N.D. Ill., March 18, 1999); Switalski v. La Porte Transit Co., Inc., Cause No. 98-CV305RM (N.D. Ind., March 1, 1999); Switalski v. La Porte Transit Co., Inc., Cause No. 98-CV305RM, 160 LRRM 2763 (N.D. Ind., December 9, 1998); Pokuta v. Trans World Airlines, Inc., Case No. 97 C 5764, 1998 US Dist LEXIS 15726, 159 LRRM 2499 (N.D. Ill., September 25, 1998); Malesevic v. Tecom Fleet Services, Inc., et al., 72 F. Supp.2d 932 (N.D. Ind. 1998); Muska v. AT&T Corp., Case No. 96 C 5952, 1998 US Dist LEXIS 13215, 4 WH Cases 2d 1672 (N.D. Ill., August 24, 1998); Jay's Foods, L.L.C. v. Chemical & Allied Product Workers' Union, Local 20, a/w International Union of Allied Novelty and Production Workers, AFL-CIO, Case No. 97 C 6227, 1998 WL 265098, 162 LRRM 2675, 135 LC (CCH) 10,180 (N.D. Ill. May 11, 1998), aff'd, 208 F.3d 610 (7th Cir. 2000), cert. denied, 531 U.S. 427 (2000); Dotson & Nicholson v.

(This Listing Continued)

McDonald's Corporation, No. 97 C 1833, 1998 US Dist LEXIS 4676 (N.D. Ill., April 12, 1998); Lester v. Trans World Airlines, Inc., Case No. 95 C 2349, 1997 US Dist LEXIS 10857 (N.D. Ill., July 22, 1997); University Professionals of Illinois, Local 4100, et al. v. Jim Edgar, et al., 153 LRRM 2449 (N.D. Ill., September 27, 1996), aff'd, 114 F.3d 665 (7th Cir. 1997); Eugene v. McDonald's Corp., 1996 U.S. Dist. LEXIS 10193 (N.D. Ill., July 17, 1996); Thompson v. Borg-Warner Protective Services, Inc., No. C-94-4015 MHP (N.D. Cal., March 11, 1996); Huber v. Greyhound Lines, Inc., 926 F. Supp. 821 (E.D. Wis. 1996); Barefield, et al. v. Village of Winnetka, No. 93 C 1154 (N.D. Ill., August 28, 1995), aff'd, 81 F.3d 704 (7th Cir. 1996); Local 2, International Union of Security Officers v. Burns International Security Services, No. C 93-20151 JW (N.D. Cal., December 21, 1993), aff'd, No. 94-15115 (9th Cir., July 12, 1995); Susan Yule v. Burns International Security Services, Case No. 93-ERA-0012 (Secretary of Labor, May 24, 1995); Chaudhry v. Coca-Cola Bottling Co. of Chicago, 67 Fair Empl. Prac. Cases (BNA) 916, 1995 U.S. Dist. LEXIS 3039 (N.D. Ill., March 9, 1995); Signore v. Amoco Corp., No. 92 C 7220, 1994 U.S. Dist. LEXIS 10391 (N.D. Ill., July 29, 1994); Jacinto Mir. v. Coca-Cola Bottling Co. of Chicago, Case No. 1988 CF 1801, ALS No. 3183 (Illinois Human Rights Commission, April 5, 1994); Ballard v. Greyhound, Inc., No. 91 CA 15918 (D.D.C., December, 1993); Rodgers v. AlliedSignal Inc., et al., No. 3:93CV0421RM (N.D. Ind., September 27, 1993); Meyers v. Kawneer Co., Case No. IP 90-1980-C (S.D. Ind., October 6, 1992); Dockery v. Allied-Signal Inc., Case No. S92-30M (N.D. Ind., April 3, 1992); Ferran v. The ServiceMaster Company Limited Partnership, No. IP 90-2168-C (S.D. Ind., November 5, 1991); Hammond v. Trans World Airlines, Inc., 141 L.R.R.M. (BNA) 2063 (N.D. Ill. 1991), aff'd, 981 F.2d 1524 (7th Cir. 1992), rehearing en banc denied, 989 F.2d 944 (7th Cir. 1993), cert. denied, 114 S. Ct. 175 (1993); Carolyn Boles v. Sailor Mfging., Inc., Case No. S89-261 (N.D. Ind., March 28, 1990); Jane Doe v. Allied-Signal Inc., Case No. S88-449 (N.D. Ind., March 16, 1990), aff'd, 925 F.2d 1007 (7th Cir. 1991); Haynes v. Alumax Recycling Group, Inc., 719 F. Supp. 707 (N.D. Ill. 1989), aff'd without opinion, 899 F.2d 16 (7th Cir. 1990); Krizek v. Board of Education of Cicero-Stickney Township High School District No. 201, 713 F. Supp. 1131 (N.D. Ill. 1989); Kardynalski v. Trans World Airlines, Inc., 1988 WL 82576 (N.D. Ill. 1988); Chilbert v. Board of Trustees of the University of Illinois, 1986 WL 10052 (N.D. Ill. 1986) Pesce v. J. Sterling Morton High School District No. 201, 651 F. Supp. 152 (N.D. Ill. 1986), aff'd, 830 F.2d 789 (7th Cir. 1987); Kesterson v. Davenport, 647 F. Supp. 41 (N.D. Ill. 1986); Kelly v. Board of Trustees of the University of Illinois, 1986 WL 8356 (N.D. Ill. July 22, 1986); Hofmann v. AT&T Technologies, Inc., No. 84 C 7893 (N.D. Ill. March 21, 1986); Andre v. Bendix Corp., 42 Fair Empl. Prac. Cas. (BNA) 1895 (N.D. Ind. 1986), aff'd, 841 F.2d 172 (7th Cir. 1988); Grabb & Julow v. Bendix Corp., 666 F. Supp. 1223 (N.D. Ind. 1986); EEOC v. University of Notre Dame, 629 F. Supp. 837 (N.D. Ind. 1985); Gray v. Walgreen Co., 33 Fair Empl. Prac. Cas. (BNA) 835 (N.D. Ill. 1983); Crosby v. Bowater Inc., 382 F.3d 587 (6th Cir. 2004); BP Amoco Corp. v. NLRB, 217 F.3d 869 (D.C. Cir. 2000); Jenisio v. Trans World Airlines, Inc., 158 LRRM 3018, No. 98-858/RHK/FLN (D. Minn., July 23, 1998), aff'd, 187 F.3d 970 (8th Cir. 1999); Coker, et al. v. Trans World Airlines, Inc., et al., 957 F. Supp. 158 (N.D. Ill. 1997) & 959 F. Supp. 946 (N.D. Ill. 1997), aff'd, 165 F.3d 579 (7th Cir. 1999); Diehl, et al. v. Twin Disc, Inc., Case No. 94 C 50031, 1996 U.S. Dist. LEXIS 4117 (N.D. Ill., April 2, 1996); Redding v. AT&T Corporation, 124 F.3d 217 (10th Cir. 1997); Jones v. UOP, et al., No. 90 C 2243, 1993 U.S. Dist. LEXIS 911 & 4149 (N.D. Ill., March 30, 1993), aff'd, 16 F.3d 141 (7th Cir. 1994); Finnegan v. Trans World Airlines, Inc., 767 F. Supp. 867 (N.D. Ill. 1991), aff'd, 967 F.2d 1161 (7th Cir. 1992); UAW v. Keystone Consolidated Industries, Inc., 793 F.2d 810 (7th Cir. 1986); Vallone v. CNA Financial Corp., No. 98 C 7108, 2003 WL 1720020 (N.D. Ill. March 28, 2003), aff'd, 375 F.3d 623 (7th Cir. 2004), cert. denied, 125 S. Ct. 670 (2004); Vallone, et al. v. CNA Financial Corp., No. 98 C 7108, 2003 WL 1720020 (N.D. Ill., December 28, 2000); Vallone v. CNA Financial Corp., 76 F. Supp.2d 864 (N.D. Ill. 1999); Hutchins v. Caterpillar, Inc., et al., No. 98-1147, 2000 WL 33341459 (C.D. Ill. 2000); Johnson v. Republic Engineered Steels, Inc. & Metropolitan Life Insurance Company, Case No. 2:97-CV-170-TS (N.D. Ind., Sept. 20, 1999); Kolowski v. Metropolitan Life Insurance Co., 35 F. Supp.2d 1059 (N.D. Ill. 1998); Marciniak v. The Travelers Insurance Inc., 990 F. Supp. 1035 (N.D. Ill. 1998); Sullivan, as Plan Trustee v. Atlantic Plumbing, Case No. 95 C 4094 (N.D. Ill., December 5, 1995); Carr, et al. v. Burns International Security Services, Inc., et al., 848 F. Supp. 100 (S.D. Tex., March 31, 1994); Gaudiello v. AlliedSignal Inc., No. 90 C 20097, 1993 U.S. Dist. LEXIS 15812 (N.D. Ill., October 20, 1993); Dugan v. D & M Excavating, Inc., 12 Empl. Ben. Cases (BNA) 1748 (N.D. Ill. 1990). ***PRACTICE AREAS:*** Labor and Employment; Employee Benefits. ***Email:*** tpiskorski@seyfarth.com

J. STEPHEN POOR, born 1955; admitted to bar, 1980, Illinois; U.S. Supreme Court; U.S. Court of Appeals, Fourth, Sixth, Seventh, and Eighth Circuits; U.S. District Court, Central and Northern Districts of Illinois. *Education:* Indiana University (B.A., 1977); University of Virginia (J.D., 1980). *Member:* Chicago and American Bar Associations; Computer Law Association. ***PRACTICE AREAS:*** Labor and Employment. ***Email:*** spoor@seyfarth.com

JOHN W. POWERS, born 1949; admitted to bar, 1976, Illinois. *Education:* Harvard University (A.B., cum laude, 1971); Boston University (J.D., 1976). ***PRACTICE AREAS:*** Labor and Employment. ***Email:*** jpowers@seyfarth.com

ROGER L. PRICE, born 1944; admitted to bar, 1968, Illinois; U.S. Supreme Court; U.S. Court of Appeals, Fifth and Seventh Circuits; U.S. District Court, Northern District of Illinois, including Trial Bar. *Education:* University of Michigan (B.A., with high distinction, 1965); University of Chicago (J.D., 1968). Associate Editor, University of Chicago Law Review, 1967-1968. Law Clerk to Judge Abraham L. Marovitz, U.S. District Court for Northern District of Illinois, 1968-1971. Author: "Litigation Between Association Members for Breach of Condominium Provisions: Noise," 31 Am. Jur. Trials 193 (1984); Co-author: "The Illusory Promise of Best Efforts," 79 Ill. B.J. 356 (1991); "Understanding the Scheme to Defraud" Exception to Promissory Fraud in Illinois," 2 III B.J. 90 (2002); Author: "Is the Mechanics Lien Act Unconstitutional?" 93 Ill. B.J. 298 (2005). *Member:* Chicago and American (Member, Litigation Section and Construction Law Forum) Bar Associations; Association of Subcontractors and Affiliates; Builders Association of Greater Chicago. ***PRACTICE AREAS:*** Litigation; Construction Law; Intellectual Property. ***Email:*** rprice@seyfarth.com

MICHAEL J. QUINN, born 1952; admitted to bar, 1982, Wisconsin; 1984, Illinois. *Education:* Marquette University (B.A., 1974); University of Wisconsin at Milwaukee (M.U.P., 1977); University of Wisconsin at Madison (J.D., cum laude, 1982). Phi Kappa Phi. Note and Comment Editor, Wisconsin Law Review, 1981-1982. Adjunct Professor, Advanced Research (Environmental), ITT Chicago-Kent College of Law, 1994-2001. Adjunct Associate Professor, University of Wisconsin-Milwaukee (Lecturer, Land Use Law), 1989-1993. *Member:* American, Illinois State and Chicago Bar Associations; State Bar of Wisconsin; American Institute of Certified Planners. ***PRACTICE AREAS:*** Environmental Law; Real Estate; Land Use. ***Email:*** mquinn@seyfarth.com

(This Listing Continued)

ALLAN J. REICH, born 1948; admitted to bar, 1973, Illinois. *Education:* Cornell University (A.B., 1970); University of Michigan (J.D., cum laude, 1973). *Member:* Chicago and American Bar Associations. ***PRACTICE AREAS:*** Corporate; Securities; Finance Law. ***Email:*** areich@seyfarth.com

RICHARD L. REINISH, (P.C.), born 1941; admitted to bar, 1966, Illinois. *Education:* University of Michigan (B.B.A., 1963); Northwestern University (J.D., 1966). Lawyer's Institute - John Marshall Law School (postgraduate intellectual property courses). Trial Attorney, U.S. Department of Justice, Antitrust Division, 1966-1996. Adjunct Professor, Advanced Antitrust, Northwestern University School of Law, 2000—. Director: Jewish Federation of Metropolitan Chicago, 1984-1990; Jewish United Fund, 1984-1990; Jewish Family and Community Services, 1984-1990. *Member:* Chicago and American (Member, Antitrust Committee) Bar Associations. ***PRACTICE AREAS:*** Intellectual Property. ***Email:*** rreinish@seyfarth.com

JOHN E. ROGERS, admitted to bar, 1967, Illinois; 1987, Pennsylvania. *Education:* University of Notre Dame (B.A., 1964); Harvard University (J.D., 1967); University of Chicago (M.B.A., 1970). *Member:* International Fiscal Association (Member of Council); Attorneys in Corporate Real Estate (Founding Director). ***PRACTICE AREAS:*** Corporate; Real Estate. ***Email:*** jrogers@seyfarth.com

BURTON X. ROSENBERG, born 1941; admitted to bar, 1966, Illinois. *Education:* University of Pennsylvania (B.A., 1963); Northwestern University (J.D., 1966). ***PRACTICE AREAS:*** Business Law. ***Email:*** brosenberg@seyfarth.com

JEFFREY K. ROSS, born 1951; admitted to bar, 1976, Illinois; Federal Trial Bar; U.S. District Court, Northern District of Illinois; U.S. District Court, Eastern District of Wisconsin; U.S. Court of Appeals, Fourth, Sixth and Seventh Circuits. *Education:* Cornell University (B.S., 1973; J.D., 1976); Lehigh University. *Member:* Chicago and American (Member, Sections on: Labor and Employment Law; Litigation) Bar Associations. ***PRACTICE AREAS:*** Labor and Employment. ***Email:*** jross@seyfarth.com

DAVID J. ROWLAND, born 1962; admitted to bar, 1988, Illinois. *Education:* University of Michigan (A.B., 1985; J.D., 1988). ***PRACTICE AREAS:*** Labor and Employment. ***Email:*** drowland@seyfarth.com

JOEL D. RUBIN, born 1944; admitted to bar, 1968, Illinois; 2005, New York. *Education:* University of Pennsylvania (B.S., 1965); Northwestern University (J.D., cum laude, 1968). Law Clerk, U.S. Court of Appeals, Seventh Circuit, 1968-1970. *Member:* Chicago and American (Former Chairman: Committee on Pension Plan Investments in Real Estate, Real Property Division, Section on Real Property, Probate and Trust Law; Real Estate Syndications Committee) Bar Associations; Chairman, Governmental Affairs Committee, Pension Real Estate Association; The Economic Club of Chicago; American College of Real Estate Lawyers; Trustee of Jewish Publication Society. ***PRACTICE AREAS:*** Real Estate; Pension Investments; Corporate; Business Planning Law. ***Email:*** jrubin@seyfarth.com

CARL L. RUSSO, born 1946; admitted to bar, 1971, Illinois. *Education:* Marquette University (B.S., 1968); Northwestern University (J.D., 1971). ***Email:*** crusso@seyfarth.com

MICHAEL J. RYBICKI, born 1946; admitted to bar, 1970, Illinois. *Education:* St. Procopius College (B.A., 1967); University of Illinois (M.A., 1971; J.D., 1970). ***PRACTICE AREAS:*** Labor and Employment. ***Email:*** mrybicki@seyfarth.com

NATHANIEL SACK, born 1941; admitted to bar, 1965, Illinois. *Education:* University of Michigan (B.A., cum laude, 1962); Harvard University (J.D., 1965); DePaul University (LL.M., Taxation, 1982). Legal Counsel to Jewish Federation of Metropolitan Chicago, 1985—; Vice President, The Standard Club, 1988-1991. *Member:* Chicago (Member, Corporation Law, Federal Tax Law Committees) and American (Member, Federal and Tax Law and Exempt Organization Committees) Bar Associations. ***PRACTICE AREAS:*** Business Law; Exempt Organizations Law; Taxation; Personal Planning. ***Email:*** nsack@seyfarth.com

SUZANNE L. SAXMAN, born 1956; admitted to bar, 1981, Illinois. *Education:* University of Michigan (B.A., with honors, 1977); University of Illinois (J.D., with honors, 1981). Topics Editor and Member, University of Illinois Law Review, 1979-1981. Board Member, University of Illinois College of Law Board of Visitors, 1998-2001 and 2004-2006. Member, International Womens Insolvency and Restructuring Confederation. Managing Editor, Illinois Corporate Practice and Forms: The Seyfarth Shaw Manual (2001, 2002-2005 Supplements, DataTrace Publishing). Board Member, University of Illinois College of Law Alumni Association Board of Directors. Board Member, The Art Institute of Chicago Evening Associates Board of Directors. *Member:* Chicago (Member, Corporation Law Committee) and American (Member, Section on: Business Law, Small Business and Commercial Financial Services Committees; Vice Chair, Section of Business Law, Small Business Committee) Bar Associations. ***PRACTICE AREAS:*** Corporate; Mergers and Acquisitions; Commercial Transactions; Casinos and Gaming. ***Email:*** ssaxman@seyfarth.com

JEFFREY B. SCHAMIS, born 1947; admitted to bar, 1976, Illinois. *Education:* University of Rochester (A.B., with high honors, 1968); University of Chicago (Ph.D., 1972; J.D., 1976). Phi Beta Kappa. Recipient, Regents, Danforth and Ford Fellowships. *Member:* American Bar Association. ***PRACTICE AREAS:*** Real Estate; General Corporate; Finance and Restructuring Law. ***Email:*** jschamis@seyfarth.com

STEPHEN L. SCHAR, born 1945; admitted to bar, 1970, Illinois. *Education:* University of Chicago (B.A., 1967); DePaul University (J.D., 1970). Case Note Editor, De Paul Law Review, 1969-1970. Member of the Leading Lawyers Network-Wills, Trust and Estates, 2003—. *Member:* Chicago and Illinois State Bar Associations; Chicago Estate Planning Council. ***PRACTICE AREAS:*** Estate Planning; Probate; Taxation; General Corporate; Exempt Organizations. ***Email:*** sschar@seyfarth.com

(This Listing Continued)

SEYFARTH SHAW LLP, Chicago—Continued

JOHN S. SCHAUER, born 1940; admitted to bar, 1965, Illinois. *Education:* Michigan State University (B.A., 1962); Northwestern University (J.D., 1965). ***PRACTICE AREAS:*** Labor and Employment. ***Email:*** jschauer@seyfarth.com

RAY J. SCHOONHOVEN (Retired)

JAMES A. SCHRAIDT, born 1951; admitted to bar, 1978, Illinois; U.S. District Court, Southern District of Illinois. *Education:* University of Illinois (B.S., 1973); Southern Illinois University (J.D., 1978). *Member:* Chicago and American Bar Associations; National Association of Bond Lawyers. ***PRACTICE AREAS:*** Business Law. ***Email:*** jschraidt@seyfarth.com

RONALD SCHREIBER, born 1953; admitted to bar, 1977, Illinois; 1987, U.S. Tax Court. *Education:* Queens College of the City University of New York (B.A., magna cum laude, 1974); University of Chicago (J.D., 1977). Member: Leading Lawyers Network-Trusts, Wills and Estate Planning Law; and Tax Law: Individuals, 2003—. *Member:* Chicago (Member, Trust Law Committee, 1979—; Chairman, Division II, 1996-1997; Probate Practice Committee, 1978—), Illinois State (Member, Section on Estate Planning, Probate and Trust Law, 1979—) and American (Member, Section on Real Property, Probate and Trust Law, 1979—) Bar Associations. Chicago Estate Planning Council. ***PRACTICE AREAS:*** Probate; Estate Planning; Trust Law; Taxation; Exempt Organization. ***Email:*** rschreiber@seyfarth.com

WILLIAM P. SCHURGIN, born 1956; admitted to bar, 1980, Illinois. *Education:* University of Michigan (A.B., with high distinction, 1977); Boston University (J.D., cum laude, 1980). Editor: The Legal Aspects of AIDS, Thompson/West Publications 1991-2005. Author: "What Color is Your Collar," Corporate Counsel Magazine, 2004, "Understanding the New U.S. Department of Labor Overtime Regulations," "Physician and Resident Union Organizing" and "Trilogy of Supreme Court ADA Cases," CCH Compliance Letter, 2001-2004; "Drug and Alcohol Abuse in the Workplace," Federal Employment Laws and Regulations, 2001; "Disability Discrimination in the 1990's," Journal of Health and Hospital Law, 1991; "The Limits of Organized Employer/Employee Relations in Non-Union Facilities," Chicago Kent Law Review, 1981. Part Time Faculty: DePaul University College of Law, 1993—; Loyola University School of Law, 2000—. Member, Editorial Advisory Board, CCH Healthcare Compliance Guide, 2000—; Member: Editorial Advisory Board, Thompson Publishing Employer's Guide to the Fair Labor Standards Act, 2005—. Member: Leading Lawyers Network; Selected: Illinois Super Lawyers. *Member:* Chicago (Past Co-Chair, YLS Health Law Committee) and American Bar Associations; American Health Lawyers Association (Past Co-Chair, Labor and Employment Law Committee). Fellow, American College of Labor and Employment Lawyers. ***PRACTICE AREAS:*** Labor and Employment. ***Email:*** wschurgin@seyfarth.com

ROBERT J. SELL, born 1965; admitted to bar, 1990, Illinois. *Education:* University of Illinois (B.A., cum laude, with highest honors, 1987); Northwestern University (J.D., 1990). *Member:* Illinois State and American Bar Associations. ***PRACTICE AREAS:*** Business Law; Mergers, Acquisitions and Divestitures; Technology Contracts; Securities. ***Email:*** rsell@seyfarth.com

HENRY E. SEYFARTH (1908-1991)

JEREMY P. SHERMAN, born 1951; admitted to bar, 1976, Illinois. *Education:* American University (B.A., magna cum laude, 1973); George Washington University (J.D., with honors, 1976). National Chair of Seyfarth Shaw LLP's Labor and Employment Group. Fellow, College of Labor and Employment Lawyers. Member, Best Attorneys, Illinois Super Lawyer and Leading Lawyers networks. Featured in Who's Who Legal USA-Management Labour and Employment Lawyers and Marquis Who's Who in American Law (14th Edition). Author: "Bargaining Over the Terms and Conditions for Striker Replacements: Is the NLRB About to Change the Rules?" 47 Lab. L.J. 178 (1996); "Collective Bargaining Over Work Assignment Proposals, Differentiating Between Concepts of Jurisdiction and Unit Scope," 41 Lab. L.J. 3 (1990). George Washington Law Review, 1974-1976. ***PRACTICE AREAS:*** Labor and Employment. ***Email:*** jsherman@seyfarth.com

ROBERT J. SMITH, JR., born 1956; admitted to bar, 1981, Illinois and Indiana. *Education:* DePaul University (B.A., 1977; J.D., 1981). ***PRACTICE AREAS:*** Labor and Employment. ***Email:*** rsmith@seyfarth.com

HAROLD V. STOTLAND, born 1941; admitted to bar, 1966, Illinois. *Education:* Illinois Institute of Technology (B.S.E.E., 1963); DePaul University (J.D., 1966). *Member:* American Bar Association; American Intellectual Property Law Association; Intellectual Property Law Association of Chicago. ***PRACTICE AREAS:*** Litigation; Intellectual Property. ***Email:*** hstotland@seyfarth.com

JOSEPH S. TURNER, born 1961; admitted to bar, 1987, Illinois; 1993, Georgia. *Education:* University of North Carolina at Chapel Hill (B.A., 1983; J.D., 1987). ***Email:*** jturner@seyfarth.com

ALAN L. UNIKEL, born 1943; admitted to bar, 1968, Illinois. *Education:* Illinois Institute of Technology (B.S., Industrial Engineering, 1964); Georgetown University (J.D., 1968). ***PRACTICE AREAS:*** Litigation; Intellectual Property. ***Email:*** aunikel@seyfarth.com

MICHAEL A. WARNER, born 1941; admitted to bar, 1965, Illinois. *Education:* University of Wisconsin (B.S., 1962); University of Michigan (LL.B., 1964). Associate Editor, Michigan Law Review, 1963-1964. Co-Author: Employment Discrimination Law, BNA Corporate Practice Series (1999, 1993, 1984); How to Deal with Employment Issues under the Americans with Disabilities Act, Illinois Institute of Legal Education (1992); "The Civil Rights Act of 1991: Overview and Analysis," 8 Lab. Law. 9 (1992). Member of the College of Labor & Employment Lawyers, Inc. Voted one of the Best Litigators in Employment Law, 1992 Survey by National Law Journal. ***PRACTICE AREAS:*** Labor and Employment. ***Email:*** mwarner@seyfarth.com

ROBERT F. WEBER, born 1950; admitted to bar, 1976, New York; 1984, Illinois. *Education:* Georgetown University (A.B., cum laude, 1972); University of Chicago (J.D., 1975). ***PRACTICE AREAS:*** Business Law. ***Email:*** rweber@seyfarth.com

DAVID M. WEINER, born 1954; admitted to bar, 1980, Illinois. *Education:* University of Illinois (B.S., with honors, 1977); Loyola University (J.D., cum laude, 1980). Member, 1978-1980 and Lead Articles Editor, 1979-1980, Loyola University of Chicago Law Journal. Author: Note, "Residual Exception to the Hearsay Rule," 10 Loyola U. of Chicago L.J. 611, 1979. Co-Author: Nonqualified Deferred Compensation Arrangements, Callaghan and Company, 1987. *Member:* Chicago (Member, Employee Benefits Committee, 1982—) and American (Member, Sections of: Corporation, Banking and Business Law; Taxation) Bar Associations. ***PRACTICE AREAS:*** Employee Benefits. ***Email:*** dweiner@seyfarth.com

JOHN T. WEISE (Retired)

MICHAEL D. WEXLER, admitted to bar, 1991, Illinois; U.S. Court of Appeals, Seventh Circuit; U.S. District Court, Northern District of Illinois, Trial Bar; U.S. District Court, Central and Southern Districts of Illinois; U.S. District Court, Northern District of Indiana; U.S. District Court, Eastern District of Wisconsin. *Education:* University of Illinois (B.A., 1988); Illinois Institute of Technology, Chicago-Kent College of Law (J.D., with high honors, 1991). Order of the Coif. Kent Legal Scholar, Chicago-Kent Law Review, National Moot Court Competition Teams and Legal Writing Teaching Assistant. Felony Trial Attorney, Lake County States Attorney's Office, Illinois, 1992-1996. *Member:* Chicago, Illinois State and American Bar Associations. ***PRACTICE AREAS:*** Litigation; Intellectual Property; Trade Secrets; Unfair Competition; White Collar Crime; Complex Commercial Litigation. ***Email:*** mwexler@seyfarth.com

HANNAH B. WIDLUS, born 1955; admitted to bar, 1979, Texas; 1984, New York; 1988, Illinois; 1991, District of Columbia. *Education:* Miami University (B.S.B.A., 1976); George Washington University (J.D., with honors, 1979). *Member:* American Bar Association (Member, Section of Taxation Employee Benefits Committee); National Association of Public Pension Attorneys (NAPPA). ***PRACTICE AREAS:*** Employee Benefits; Executive Compensation Law. ***Email:*** hwidlus@seyfarth.com

PHILLIP SHAWN WOOD, born 1968; admitted to bar, 1992, Illinois; Federal Trial Bar; U.S. District Court, Northern District of Illinois; U.S. District Court, Eastern District of Wisconsin; U.S. Court of Appeals, Fourth, Fifth and Seventh Circuits. *Education:* University of Dayton (B.A., cum laude, 1989); Illinois Institute of Technology/Chicago-Kent College of Law (J.D., 1992). Order of the Coif. *Member:* Illinois State (Nominated to Civil Practice Council, 2005), Seventh Circuit, Federal and American (Member, Litigation Section) Bar Associations; Defense Research Institute; The Lawyers' Club of Chicago; National Society of Newspaper Columnists. ***PRACTICE AREAS:*** Commercial Litigation; Insurance Law; Professional Liability. ***Email:*** swood@seyfarth.com

PETER C. WOODFORD, born 1950; admitted to bar, 1978, Illinois; U.S. Supreme Court, U.S. Court of Appeals, Third, Fifth, and Seventh Circuits; U.S. District Court, Northern District of Illinois; U.S. District Court, Eastern District of Michigan; U.S. Tax Court. *Education:* Dartmouth College (A.B., 1971); George Washington University (J.D., with honors, 1978). *Member:* Chicago and American Bar Associations. [1st Lt, MPC, 1972-1975]. ***PRACTICE AREAS:*** Ethics and Professional Responsibility; Litigation. ***Email:*** pwoodford@seyfarth.com

JOSEPH E. WYSE (Retired)

SANDRA P. ZEMM, born 1947; admitted to bar, 1975, Florida and Illinois; U.S. Court of Appeals, District of Columbia, Sixth, Seventh and Tenth Circuits; U.S. District Court, District of Arizona; U.S. District Court, Northern District of Illinois. *Education:* University of Illinois (B.S., 1969); Florida State University (J.D., 1974). *Member:* Illinois State and American (Member, Labor and Employment Law Section; International Labor and Employment Law Committee) Bar Associations; The Florida Bar; College of Labor and Employment Lawyers; College of Labor and Employment Lawyers. ***PRACTICE AREAS:*** Labor and Employment (100%). ***Email:*** szemm@seyfarth.com

OF COUNSEL

GLENN I. BECKER, born 1961; admitted to bar, 1986, Illinois. *Education:* University of Michigan, Ann Arbor (B.A., highest distinction, 1983); University of Illinois (J.D., magna cum laude, 1986). ***PRACTICE AREAS:*** Real Estate. ***Email:*** gbecker@seyfarth.com

PAUL S. DRIZNER, born 1963; admitted to bar, 1988, Illinois. *Education:* University of Illinois (B.S., 1985); Loyola University of Chicago School of Law (J.D., 1988). ***PRACTICE AREAS:*** Business Law; Taxation. ***Email:*** pdrizner@seyfarth.com

ANN E. DUSTMAN, born 1967; admitted to bar, 1995, New York (Not admitted in Illinois). *Education:* Miami University (B.A., 1989); DePaul University College of Law (J.D., with honors, 1994). ***PRACTICE AREAS:*** Employee Benefits. ***Email:*** adustman@seyfarth.com

GARRETTSON ELLIS, born 1935; admitted to bar, 1963, Michigan; 1967, Illinois. *Education:* Princeton University (A.B., 1959); University of Michigan (LL.B., 1963). ***PRACTICE AREAS:*** Intellectual Property. ***Email:*** gellis@seyfarth.com

MERRILL A. FREED (Retired)

PATRICIA L. GILLMAN, born 1947; admitted to bar, 1973, District of Columbia; 1995, Illinois. *Education:* Smith College (B.A., cum laude, 1968); University of Pennsylvania (M.A., 1969); Georgetown University (J.D., 1972). *Member:* Illinois State Bar Association; District of Columbia Bar. ***PRACTICE AREAS:*** Corporate Law. ***Email:*** pgillman@seyfarth.com

CHERYL L. HAACK, born 1948; admitted to bar, 1994, Illinois. *Education:* University of Iowa (B.A., 1970); Northwestern University (M.Mu., 1974; M.Mgmt., 1978); The John Marshall Law School (J.D., 1994). *Member:* Chicago Bar Association. ***PRACTICE AREAS:*** Employee Benefits. ***Email:*** chaack@seyfarth.com

KAREN K. HARRIS, born 1969; admitted to bar, 1994, Illinois; 2004, Michigan. *Education:* Princeton University (B.A., with honors, 1991); Harvard University (J.D., 1994). Member, Editorial Board, Matthew Bender Health Law Quarterly, 2002-2003; Visiting Professor, Loyala Law School's Health Law Institute, 2002-2003. Editorial Advisory Board, "Private Payor Answer Book A-Z," Decision Health Publications, 2004. *Member:* Chicago (Member: Young Lawyers Section; Health and Hospital Law Committee), Illinois State and American (Member, Health Law Section) Bar Associations; America Health Lawyers Association. (Regional General Counsel). ***PRACTICE AREAS:*** Business; Hospital Law; Health Care; Medicare and Medicaid. ***Email:*** kharris@seyfarth.com

(This Listing Continued)

YVETTE HEINTZELMAN, admitted to bar, 1989, California; 1994, Illinois; U.S. Court of Appeals, Seventh, Eighth, Ninth and Eleventh Circuits; U.S. District Court, Northern and Southern Districts of California; U.S. District Court, Northern (Trial Bar), Southern and Central Districts of Illinois; U.S. District Court, Eastern District of Wisconsin. *Education:* Creighton University (B.A., 1986); Creighton University School of Law (J.D., cum laude, 1989). Member, Creighton Law Review, 1987-1989. Author: "Statutory Construction Controlling the Baby M Decision". *Member:* Illinois State Bar Association; American Bar Association; State Bar of California; Defense Research Institute. ***PRACTICE AREAS:*** Labor and Employment. **Email:** yheintzelman@seyfarth.com

SIDNEY J. HESS, JR., born 1910; admitted to bar, 1932, Illinois; U.S. Court of Appeals, Seventh Circuit; U.S. Supreme Court; U.S. Tax Court. *Education:* University of Chicago (Ph.B., 1930; J.D., 1932). Phi Beta Kappa. Member, University of Chicago Law Review. Listed in: Who's Who in America; Who's Who in the World; Who's Who in American Law. President and Board Member, Jewish Federation of Metropolitan Chicago; President and Board Member, Jewish United Fund of Metropolitan Chicago; President and Board Member, Schwab Rehabilitation Hospital; President and Board Member, Standard Club of Chicago; Board of Trustees Michael Reese Health Trust. *Member:* Chicago, Illinois State and American Bar Associations. and Charter Member, Illinois Bar Foundation. ***PRACTICE AREAS:*** Estate Planning Law; Corporate; Federal Taxation. **Email:** shess@seyfarth.com

R. THOMAS HOWELL, JR., born 1942; admitted to bar, 1968, Wisconsin and Illinois. *Education:* Williams College (B.A.); University of Wisconsin-Madison (J.D.). Vice President, General Corporate Counsel and Secretary, The Quaker Oats Company 1994-1996. Member, Advanced Management Program, Harvard Business School 1981. President, Chicago Bar Foundation 1991-1992. President, The Lawyers Club of Chicago 2004-2005. *Member:* Illinois State and American Bar Associations; State Bar of Wisconsin; The Economic Club of Chicago; The Lawyers Club of Chicago. ***PRACTICE AREAS:*** Business Law; Regulatory Law. **Email:** thowell@seyfarth.com

PATRICIA L. HUBBARD, born 1957; admitted to bar, 1992, Illinois; U.S. District Court, Northern District of Illinois including Trial Bar. *Education:* University of Illinois (B.S., 1980); Loyola University (J.D., cum laude, 1992). Contributor: The Family and Medical Leave Act, How to Comply, Seyfarth Shaw LLP, 2003. *Member:* Chicago Bar Association. ***PRACTICE AREAS:*** Labor and Employment Law. **Email:** phubbard@seyfarth.com

ANDI S. KENNEY, born 1962; admitted to bar, 1987, Illinois; U.S. District Court, Northern District of Illinois. *Education:* Duke University (A.B., magna cum laude, 1984); University of Michigan (J.D., cum laude, 1987). Associate Note Editor, Michigan Journal of Law Reform, 1986-1987. Author: "Reckless Endangerment of an Employee: A Proposal in the Wake of Film Recovery System to Make the Boss Responsible for His Crime," University of Michigan Journal of Law Reform 873, Vol. 20, No. 2., 1987; "Worker and Community Right-to-Know," Illinois Environmental Law Handbook, 1989. Associate, Sidley & Austin, 1987-1991. Secretary, CARPLS. *Member:* American Bar Association. ***PRACTICE AREAS:*** Environmental Health and Safety. **Email:** akenney@seyfarth.com

CYNTHIA C. MOONEY, born 1948; admitted to bar, 1988, Illinois. *Education:* Marygrove College (B.A., cum laude, 1970); DePaul University (M.S., 1973); Loyola University School of Law (J.D., cum laude, 1988). ***PRACTICE AREAS:*** Labor and Employment. **Email:** cmooney@seyfarth.com

DAVID J. PEZZA, SR., born 1960; admitted to bar, 1985, Illinois. *Education:* DePaul University (B.S., with highest honors, 1981); DePaul College of Law (J.D., 1985). ***PRACTICE AREAS:*** Real Estate. **Email:** dpezza@seyfarth.com

KEITH A. REED, born 1939; admitted to bar, 1963, Iowa and Illinois. *Education:* State University of Iowa (B.B.A., 1960; J.D., 1963). Author: "The National Labor Relations Act and Health Care Institutions; the Persistent Paradox," Employee Relations Law Journal, Vol. 4, No. 3, 1978-1979. Co-Author: *Arbitration in Health Care,* Aspen, 1981. Co-Editor: *Federal Employment Law and Regulations,* Apland; *Employment Discrimination: How to Comply,* Apland. *Member:* Chicago and American Bar Associations; Illinois Association of Hospital Attorneys. ***PRACTICE AREAS:*** Labor and Employment. **Email:** kreed@seyfarth.com

BRIAN P. ROCHE, admitted to bar, 1999, Illinois and U.S. District Court, Northern District of Illinois. *Education:* Marquette University (B.S., 1996); Chicago-Kent College of Law, Illinois Institute of Technology (J.D., 1999). *Member:* Chicago Bar Association. ***PRACTICE AREAS:*** Litigation. **Email:** broche@seyfarth.com

WALTER ROTH, born 1929; admitted to bar, 1952, Illinois. *Education:* University of Illinois; DePaul University; University of Chicago (J.D., 1952). Order of the Coif. Managing Editor, University of Chicago Law Review, 1951-1952. Law Clerk to Judge Luther M. Swygert, 1953-1954. President, American Jewish Congress Midwest Region, 1969-1973. President, Chicago Jewish Historical Society. Board Member, American Jewish Historical Society. *Member:* Chicago and American (Member, Tax Committee and Foreign Law Committee) Bar Associations. ***PRACTICE AREAS:*** Corporate; Estate Planning; Securities Law. **Email:** wroth@seyfarth.com

DAWN E. SELLSTROM, born 1966; admitted to bar, 1993, Illinois. *Education:* Northwestern University (B.A., 1988); Loyola University, Chicago (J.D., 1993). ***PRACTICE AREAS:*** Employee Benefits. **Email:** dsellstrom@seyfarth.com

JOY SELLSTROM, born 1958; admitted to bar, 1984, Illinois. *Education:* University of Florida (B.S., 1980); Nijenrode School of Business, Breukelen, The Netherlands (Diploma, 1980); Loyola University (J.D., 1984). *Member:* Chicago, Illinois State and American Bar Associations. ***PRACTICE AREAS:*** Employee Benefits. **Email:** jsellstrom@seyfarth.com

GERALD D. SKONING, born 1942; admitted to bar, 1967, Illinois. *Education:* Princeton University (A.B., cum laude, 1964); University of Michigan (J.D., 1967). ***PRACTICE AREAS:*** Labor and Employment. **Email:** gskoning@seyfarth.com

SHELDON R. STEIN, born 1928; admitted to bar, 1951, Illinois. *Education:* University of Chicago (B.A., 1948; J.D., 1951). Order of the Coif. Staff Attorney, Illinois Commerce Commission, 1951-1952; Chicago Land Clearance Commission, 1953-1955; Montgomery Ward & Company, Inc., 1955-1958. Trial Attorney, Securities and Exchange Commission, 1958-1961. Vice President, Secretary and General Counsel: Lincoln National Investment Management Company (named Security Supervisors, Inc. until 1973); The Selected Group of Funds (1961-1977); Lincoln National Direct Placement Fund (1973-1977). General Counsel, Ariel Capital Management. *Member:* Chicago Bar Association. ***PRACTICE AREAS:*** Investment Companies; Securities; Corporate Law. **Email:** sstein@seyfarth.com

(This Listing Continued)

JOSEPH L. STONE, born 1933; admitted to bar, 1959, Illinois; 1961, Florida. *Education:* University of Wisconsin (B.S., 1955); Northwestern University (J.D., 1959). Chairman, Board of Directors, Illinois Institute of Continuing Legal Education, 1984-1985. Panel Member, Resolute Systems, Inc. Member, Society of Professionals in Dispute Resolution. Arbitrator, Circuit Court of Cook County. Board of Directors, Chicago Bar Foundation, 1995-2000. President, Chicago Bar Association, 1986-1987. Chairman, State of Illinois ABA Membership Committee, 1989-1997. President, National Conference of Bar Presidents, 1986-1987. Member and Vice President, Chicago Board of Directors, American Ort Federation, 1991—. Vice President Board of Trustees, Zarem-Golde ORT Technical Institute, 1993—. Visiting Professor, Loyola University Chicago School of Law, Director, Business Law Center, 1999—. Member, Executive Council Senior Lawyers Division of the American Bar Association. Board Member, International Academy of Dispute Resolution Attorneys. Panel Member, ADR. *Member:* Decalogue Society of Lawyers; American Academy of ADR Attorneys; Women's Bar Association of Illinois; National Conference of Bar Presidents. [1st Lieutenant, U.S. Army Transportation Corps., 1955-1957]. ***PRACTICE AREAS:*** Real Estate; Real Estate Tax; Real Estate Tax Litigation; Corporate Law. **Email:** jstone@seyfarth.com

PAUL H. VISHNY, born 1931; admitted to bar, 1953, Illinois. *Education:* University of Illinois; DePaul University (J.D., cum laude, 1953). Member, Board of Editors, DePaul Law Review, 1952-1953. *Author:* "International Trade for the Nonspecialist," (ALI-ABA, Philadelphia, 1992) 2d ed., 1997; "Guide to International Commerce Law" (Shepard's/McGraw-Hill, Vol. 1, 1981; Vol. II, 1984). Planning Chairman, 1978-2004 and Faculty Member, 1978—, ALI-ABA Courses on International Trade. Member, Advisory Board, Centre for Telecommunications Development, Geneva Switzerland (1985-1991). Director: Jewish Welfare Fund of Metropolitan Chicago, 1967-1976; National Foundation for Jewish Culture, 1968-1989. *Member:* Chicago (Member, International and Foreign Law Committee, 1979-1985), Illinois State (Member, International and Immigration Law Section Council, 1986-1992) and American Bar Associations; American Society of International Law; Decalogue Society of Lawyers; International and Federal Communications Bar Associations. ***LANGUAGES:*** French, Hebrew. ***PRACTICE AREAS:*** International Law; Telecommunications; Trade Associations; Corporate Law. **Email:** pvishny@seyfarth.com

ASSOCIATES

STEPHAN W. ADDISON, born 1978; admitted to bar, 2004, Wisconsin and Illinois; U.S. District Court, Western District of Wisconsin. *Education:* Lewis University (B.S., with highest honors, 2000); University of Wisconsin at Madison (M.S. in Real Estate and Urban Land Economics, 2004; J.D., 2004). Licensed Real Estate Broker, Illinois. *Member:* Chicago and Illinois State Bar Associations; State Bar of Wisconsin; Urban Land Institute; Chicago Real Estate Council; Young Real Estate Professionals of Chicago; Wisconsin Real Estate Alumni Association. ***PRACTICE AREAS:*** Real Estate. **Email:** saddison@seyfarth.com

ALYSA M. BARANCIK, admitted to bar, 2000, Illinois. *Education:* Cornell University (B.S., 1995); Loyola University (J.D., 2000). ***PRACTICE AREAS:*** Labor and Employment. **Email:** abarancik@seyfarth.com

BRIAN WILLIAM BARRETT, born 1974; admitted to bar, 1999, Illinois and U.S. District Court, Central and Northern Districts of Illinois; 2000, U.S. Court of Appeals, Seventh Circuit; 2002, U.S. District Court, Northern District of Indiana. *Education:* Miami University (B.A., summa cum laude, 1996); University of Virginia (J.D., 1999). ***PRACTICE AREAS:*** Employee Benefits. **Email:** bbarrett@seyfarth.com

FRANK A. BEAR, born 1974; admitted to bar, 2003, Illinois; U.S. District Court, Northern District of Illinois and Eastern District of Michigan. *Education:* University of Illinois (B.S., 1997); DePaul University (J.D., cum laude, 2003). Member, Board of Directors, Lawyers' Committee for Better Housing. *Member:* Chicago (Young Lawyers Section), Illinois State and American Bar Associations. ***LANGUAGES:*** Spanish. ***PRACTICE AREAS:*** Labor and Employment. **Email:** fbear@seyfarth.com

JUSTIN K. BEYER, born 1979; admitted to bar, 2004, Illinois. *Education:* Beloit College (B.A., magna cum laude, 2001); University of Illinois (J.D., 2004). ***PRACTICE AREAS:*** Litigation. **Email:** jbeyer@seyfarth.com

TRACY M. BILLOWS, admitted to bar, 2001, Illinois. *Education:* De Paul University (B.A., 1995); Loyola University (M.S. Industrial Relations, 1997); Chicago-Kent College of Law, Illinois Institute of Technology (J.D., with honors, 2001; Certificate in Labor and Employment Law). Recipient, Edmund W. Burke Scholarship for Excellence in Forensic Oratory. *Member:* Chicago, Illinois State and American (Member, Practice and Procedure Under the NLRA Subcommittee) Bar Associations. ***PRACTICE AREAS:*** Labor and Employment. **Email:** tbillows@seyfarth.com

REBECCA PRATT BROMET, born 1973; admitted to bar, 2002, California; 2004, Illinois. *Education:* University of California, Berkeley (B.A., 1994); Vanderbilt University (J.D., 2001). ***PRACTICE AREAS:*** Labor and Employment. **Email:** rbromet@seyfarth.com

ANNE E. C. BRYNN, born 1970; admitted to bar, 2002, Illinois and U.S. District Court, Northern District of Illinois. *Education:* University of Vermont (B.A., cum laude, 1993); University of Illinois (J.D., cum laude, 2002). Co-Author: "Another Roadblock on the Way to Proving Trade Dress in Product Configuration: Traffix Devices, Inc. v. Marketing Displays, Inc.," Illinois State Bar Association Intellectual Property Newsletter, Volume 41, Issue 1 (December 2002); "Destructive Economic Policies in the Age of Terrorism: Government-Sanctioned Gambling as Encouraging Transboundary Economic Raiding and Destabilizing National and International Economies," Temple International & Comparative Law Journal, Volume 16, Number 2 (2002). ***PRACTICE AREAS:*** Estate Planning; Probate Administration. **Email:** abrynn@seyfarth.com

(This Listing Continued)

SEYFARTH SHAW LLP, Chicago—Continued

ALYSSA C. BURGHARDT, born 1974; admitted to bar, 2000, Illinois. *Education:* Wellesley College (B.A., 1997); Northwestern University School of Law (J.D., 2000). ***PRACTICE AREAS:*** Labor and Employment; Special Education. ***Email:*** aburghardt@seyfarth.com

SCOTT T. BUSER, born 1976; admitted to bar, 2001, Illinois and U.S. District Court, Northern District of Illinois. *Education:* University of Michigan, Ross School of Business (B.B.A., 1998); Emory University School of Law (J.D., 2001). *Member:* American Bar Association. ***PRACTICE AREAS:*** Real Estate. ***Email:*** sbuser@seyfarth.com

JESSICA E. CHMIEL, born 1976; admitted to bar, 2003, Illinois. *Education:* University of Wisconsin-Whitewater (B.A., 1999); DePaul University School of Law (J.D., 2003). ***PRACTICE AREAS:*** Labor and Employment. ***Email:*** jchmiel@seyfarth.com

JAMES R. CHO, born 1974; admitted to bar, 1999, Illinois; 2005, New York; U.S. Court of Appeals, District of Columbia and Seventh Circuits; U.S. District Court, Northern District of Indiana. *Education:* University of Michigan (B.A., high honors, 1996); University of Minnesota (J.D., cum laude, 1999). *Member:* American Bar Association, member; Korean American Bar Association, executive director (2002-2004); vice president (2004-2006); National Asian Pacific American Bar Association, Labor & Employment Section co-chair; Korean American Community Services, board member. ***PRACTICE AREAS:*** Labor and Employment. ***Email:*** jcho@seyfarth.com

SARAH NOREM CHOMIAK, admitted to bar, 2002, Illinois. *Education:* University of Illinois (B.S., 1996); Loyola University of Chicago (M.S.W., 1998); DePaul College of Law (J.D., 2002). ***PRACTICE AREAS:*** Labor and Employment Law. ***Email:*** schomiak@seyfarth.com

LOUIS S. CHRONOWSKI JR., born 1968; admitted to bar, 1999, Illinois. *Education:* Purdue University (B.S., 1990); DePaul University (M.B.A. 1995); Chicago-Kent College of Law, Illinois Institute of Technology (J.D., 1999). ***PRACTICE AREAS:*** Litigation; Intellectual Property; Real Estate. ***Email:*** lchronowski@seyfarth.com

COLIN M. CONNOR, (admission pending). *Education:* University of Michigan (B.A., 2002; J.D., 2005). *Member:* American Bar Association. ***PRACTICE AREAS:*** Labor and Employment. ***Email:*** cconnor@seyfarth.com

MICHAEL A. COX, born 1972; admitted to bar, 1999, Illinois. *Education:* Drake University (B.A., 1995); University of Illinois (J.D., 1999). ***PRACTICE AREAS:*** Labor and Employment. ***Email:*** mcox@seyfarth.com

RICHARD CUTSHALL, born 1979; admitted to bar, 2004, Illinois. *Education:* University of Minnesota (B.A., 2001); Loyola University Chicago (J.D., 2004). ***PRACTICE AREAS:*** Business Services; Corporate; Securities. ***Email:*** rcutshall@seyfarth.com

JOSHUA N. DALLEY, born 1977; admitted to bar, 2004, Illinois and Wisconsin. *Education:* Wake Forest University (B.A., cum laude, 1999); University of Wisconsin (J.D., cum laude, 2004). *Member:* Illinois State Bar Association; State Bar of Wisconsin. ***PRACTICE AREAS:*** Labor and Employment Law. ***Email:*** jdalley@seyfarth.com

PAMELA QUIGLEY DEVATA, born 1976; admitted to bar, 2001, Illinois; U.S. District Court, Northern District of Illinois; 2004, U.S. District Court, Eastern District of Michigan; 2005, U.S. District Court, Central District of Illinois; U.S. Court of Appeals, Sixth Circuit. *Education:* Washington University (B.A., 1998); Chicago-Kent College of Law (J.D., with high honors, 2001). Order of the Coif. *Member:* Chicago and American Bar Associations. ***PRACTICE AREAS:*** Labor and Employment. ***Email:*** pdevata@seyfarth.com

ROBERT W. DIEHL, born 1964; admitted to bar, 1997, Illinois and U.S. District Court, Northern District of Illinois; 2003, U.S. Court of Appeals, Federal Circuit. *Education:* Colorado State University (B.S. Chemistry, 1989); John Marshall Law School (J.D., 1997). ***PRACTICE AREAS:*** Intellectual Property. ***Email:*** rdiehl@seyfarth.com

ADA W. DOLPH, admitted to bar, 2004, Illinois and U.S. District Court, Northern District of Illinois; 2005, U.S. District Court, Central District of Illinois. *Education:* University of Wisconsin-Madison (B.A., 1999); Northwestern University (J.D., cum laude, 2004). Articles Editor, Northwestern University Law Review, 2003-2004. Published, Northwestern University Law Review, 2004. Member, Trial Advocacy Team, 2004. *Member:* Chicago (Member, Labor and Employment Practice Committee; Alliance for Women Service Committee; Alternative Dispute Resolution Practice Committee), Illinois State (Member, Labor and Employment Section) and American (Member, Labor and Employment Section) Bar Associations. ***PRACTICE AREAS:*** Labor and Employment. ***Email:*** adolph@seyfarth.com

W. ANDREW DOUGLASS, born 1973; admitted to bar, 2000, Missouri; 2001, Illinois; 2002, Ohio. *Education:* Miami University (B.S., magna cum laude, 1995); Saint Louis University (J.D., cum laude, 2000). Lead Articles Editor, Saint Louis University Public Law Review. Presentations: "Recent Changes in Employee Benefits Law," Thompson Hine LLP, May 2002. *Member:* American Bar Association. ***PRACTICE AREAS:*** Employee Benefits. ***Email:*** wadouglass@seyfarth.com

ANNE DUPREY, born 1972; admitted to bar, 1999, Illinois; U.S. Court of Appeals, Seventh Circuit; U.S. District Court, Central and Northern Districts of Illinois, including Trial Bar. *Education:* Kenyon College (B.A., cum laude, 1994); Washington & Lee University (J.D., cum laude, 1999). *Member:* Seventh Circuit Bar Association. ***PRACTICE AREAS:*** Labor and Employment Law. ***Email:*** aduprey@seyfarth.com

MOLLY EASTMAN, born 1978; admitted to bar, 2004, Illinois. *Education:* Boston University (B.A., Economics, B.M., Brass Performance, summa cum laude, 2001); Washington University (J.D., 2004). ***PRACTICE AREAS:*** Labor and Employment. ***Email:*** meastman@seyfarth.com

KATHLEEN M. EGGERS, born 1969; admitted to bar, 1996, Illinois and U.S. District Court, Northern District of Illinois. *Education:* Northeast Missouri State University (B.S., magna cum laude, 1993); University of Michigan Law School (J.D., cum laude, 1996). *Member:* Chicago Bar Association (Executive Board Member, Trust Law Committee). ***PRACTICE AREAS:*** Probate; Estate Administration; Trust Law; Estate Planning. ***Email:*** keggers@seyfarth.com

(This Listing Continued)

ROBIN FREEMAN, born 1979; (admission pending). *Education:* Washington University (B.A., 2001); Northwestern University School of Law (J.D., 2005). ***PRACTICE AREAS:*** Real Estate. ***Email:*** rfreeman@seyfarth.com

SARAH J. GOLDEN, born 1975; admitted to bar, 2002, Illinois. *Education:* Marquette University (B.A., 1998); Indiana University (J.D., 2002). ***PRACTICE AREAS:*** Employee Benefits. ***Email:*** sgolden@seyfarth.com

JOHN A. GRAHAM, admitted to bar, 1990, Illinois. *Education:* University of Wisconsin (B.A., with distinction, 1986); Loyola University of Chicago School of Law (J.D., 1990). *Member:* Illinois State (Member, Real Estate Law Section) and American (Member, Real Property, Probate and Trust Law Section) Bar Associations; International Council of Shopping Centers. ***PRACTICE AREAS:*** Commercial Real Estate. ***Email:*** jgraham@seyfarth.com

JASON GREIS, born 1976; admitted to bar, 2005, Illinois. *Education:* Emory University (B.A., 1998); DePaul University College of Law (J.D., cum laude, 2005). Human Resource/Staffing Certificates (CPC and CTS). *Member:* Chicago Bar Association. ***PRACTICE AREAS:*** Corporate Law. ***Email:*** jgreis@seyfarth.com

AMY L. GRIDER, born 1973; admitted to bar, 2004, Illinois. *Education:* University of California-Irvine (B.A., summa cum laude, 2000); University of Chicago Law School (J.D., 2003). *Member:* American Bar Association (Member, Employee Benefits Section); Chicago Bar Association; Illinois State Bar Association. ***PRACTICE AREAS:*** Employee Benefits. ***Email:*** agrider@seyfarth.com

JANESSA M. GRIFFIN, born 1970; admitted to bar, 2000, Illinois; 2003, England and Wales, Solicitor of the Supreme Court. *Education:* University of Notre Dame (B.A., 1992); Chicago-Kent College of Law (J.D., 2000); Northwestern University (LL.M., with honors, 2004). *Member:* American Bar Association (Member, Sections of Taxation and International Law Subcommittees: Partnerships and LLC; Foreign Activities of U.S. Taxpayers; U.S. Activities of Foreigners and Tax Treaties); International Fiscal Association (USA Branch); Law Society of England and Wales. ***PRACTICE AREAS:*** International Law; Tax Law. ***Email:*** jgriffin@seyfarth.com

BRIANNE GRUSZKA, born 1978; (admission pending). *Education:* University of Nevada - Las Vegas (B.A., summa cum laude, 2001); Loyola University Chicago School of Law (J.D., cum laude, 2005). ***PRACTICE AREAS:*** Labor and Employment.

BRUCE K. HARAGUCHI, born 1970; admitted to bar, 1998, Illinois. *Education:* Brigham Young University (B.A., cum laude, 1994); University of Virginia (J.D., 1997). *Member:* International Trademark Association; Intellectual Property Law Association of Chicago. ***PRACTICE AREAS:*** Intellectual Property; Trademarks; Trademark Prosecution; Trademark Litigation; Lanham Act. ***Email:*** bharaguchi@seyfarth.com

CHRISTOPHER S. HERMANSON, born 1969; admitted to bar, 2001, Illinois; registered to practice before U.S. Patent and Trademark Office. *Education:* University of Illinois (B.S., 1991); Chicago-Kent College of Law, Illinois Institute of Technology (J.D., 2000). Member, Big Brother and Big Sister Program of Du Page County. *Member:* Intellectual Property Law Association of Chicago. ***PRACTICE AREAS:*** Litigation; Intellectual Property.

DANA HILL, born 1974; admitted to bar, 1999, Illinois; U.S. District Court, Northern District of Illinois including Trial Bar; U.S. District Court, District of Colorado. *Education:* Drake University (B.A., summa cum laude, 1996); Northwestern University (J.D., 1999). *Member:* Chicago, Federal and American Bar Associations. ***PRACTICE AREAS:*** Litigation. ***Email:*** dhill@seyfarth.com

PATRICIA B. HILLIER, born 1979; admitted to bar, 2003, Wisconsin; 2005, Illinois. *Education:* Rutgers College (B.A., 2000); University of Chicago (J.D., 2003). ***PRACTICE AREAS:*** Employee Benefits.

CORY M. HIRSCH, born 1970; admitted to bar, 1999, Illinois; 2004, Pennsylvania. *Education:* Cornell University (B.S., 1992); Washington University (J.D., 1999; M.H.A., 1999). *Member:* American Bar Association. ***PRACTICE AREAS:*** Employee Benefits. ***Email:*** chirsch@seyfarth.com

J. SCOTT HUMPHREY, born 1971; admitted to bar, 1997, Illinois; 1998, U.S. District Court, Northern District of Illinois including Trial Bar. *Education:* Wittenberg University (B.A., 1993); John Marshall Law School (J.D., Dean's List, 1997); Northwestern University, Kellogg Graduate School of Management (M.B.A., 2002). *Member:* Chicago Bar Association (Member, Insurance, Business and Trial Techniques Committees); Defense Research Institute (Member, Construction Law, Product Liability and Toxic Tort Committees). Fellow, Chicago Bar Association College of Trial Lawyers. ***PRACTICE AREAS:*** Litigation; Trade Secret Misappropriation; Complex Litigation; Civil Litigation. ***Email:*** shumphrey@seyfarth.com

MOLLY M. JOYCE, born 1977; admitted to bar, 2002, Illinois. *Education:* DePaul University (B.A., with high honors, 1999); Chicago-Kent College of Law (J.D., with honors, 2002). ***PRACTICE AREAS:*** Litigation. ***Email:*** mjoyce@seyfarth.com

DAVID B. KAHNG, born 1967; admitted to bar, 1997, Oregon; 2001, Illinois; 2000, U.S. District Court, Northern and Middle Districts of Georgia, U.S. Court of Appeals, Fourth, Seventh and Eleventh Circuits, U.S. District Court, Northern, Central and Southern Districts of Illinois; 2002, U.S. District Court, Eastern District of Michigan and U.S. District Court, Eastern District of Wisconsin. *Education:* London School of Economics (General Course Certificate, 1989); University of Michigan (B.A., with distinction, 1989; J.D., 1996); Yonsei University (M.A., 1992). *Member:* Korean American Bar Association of Chicago (President); National Asian Pacific American Bar Association (Former Chair, Labor and Employment Section). ***LANGUAGES:*** Korean. ***PRACTICE AREAS:*** Labor and Employment. ***Email:*** dkahng@seyfarth.com

DINA M. KAPERNEKAS, born 1973; admitted to bar, 2000, Illinois; U.S. District Courts, Northern and Central Districts of Illinois. *Education:* University of Illinois (B.A., 1995); Chicago-Kent College of Law (J.D., 1999). Chicago-Kent Labor-Employment Law Certificate, 1999. *Member:* Chicago Bar Association; Womens' Bar Association; Illinois Public Employer Labor Relations Association. ***LANGUAGES:*** Greek. ***PRACTICE AREAS:*** Employment Law Counseling; Traditional Labor; USERRA and Military Leave; Wage and Hour. ***Email:*** dkapernekas@seyfarth.com

(This Listing Continued)

KRISTINA M. KERWIN, born 1968; admitted to bar, 1993, Texas; 2002, Illinois and California. *Education:* Texas A & M University (B.S., summa cum laude, 1990); University of Texas School of Law (J.D.,1993); University of Chicago Graduate School of Business (M.B.A., 2002). ***REPORTED CASES:*** Gonzalez v. The State Bar of Texas, 904 S.W.2d 823 (Tex. App. - San Antonio 1995); Old Republic Ins. Co. v. Ex-Im Svcs. Corp., et al., 920 S.W.2d 393 (Tex. App. - Houston 1996). ***PRACTICE AREAS:*** Labor and Employment; Commercial Litigation. ***Email:*** kkerwin@seyfarth.com

RACHEL KINDSTRAND, admitted to bar, 2003, Wisconsin and Illinois; U.S. District Court, Northern and Southern Districts of Illinois and Western District of Wisconsin. *Education:* Michigan State University (B.A., 2000); University of Wisconsin Law School (J.D., 2003). ***PRACTICE AREAS:*** Litigation. ***Email:*** rkindstrand@seyfarth.com

JENNIFER A. KRAFT, admitted to bar, 1996, Minnesota; 1998, Illinois. *Education:* University of Michigan (B.A., with distinction, 1993); University of Minnesota (J.D., magna cum laude, 1996). Order of the Coif. *Member:* Chicago Bar Association. ***PRACTICE AREAS:*** Employee Benefits. ***Email:*** jkraft@seyfarth.com

JOSEPH R. LANSER, born 1973; admitted to bar, 2000, Illinois; U.S. Court of Appeals, Seventh and Federal Circuits; U.S. District Court, Northern and Central Districts of Illinois; U.S. District Court, Northern District of Indiana; registered to practice before the U.S. Patent and Trademark Office. *Education:* Southern Illinois University (B.S., 1995); Chicago-Kent College of Law (J.D., 2000); John Marshall Law School (LL.M., with honors, 2001). *Member:* Intellectual Property Law Association of Chicago; High Technology Crime Investigation Association. ***PRACTICE AREAS:*** Intellectual Property Law; Litigation. ***Email:*** jlanser@seyfarth.com

RAFAEL E. LAZARO, admitted to bar, 2000, Puerto Rico and U.S. Court of Appeals, First Circuit; 2001, U.S. District Court, District of Puerto Rico; 2004, Illinois and U.S. District Court, Northern District of Illinois. *Education:* Cornell University (B.A., 1997; J.D., 2000). *Member:* Chicago, Illinois State and American (Member, Labor and Employment Section) Bar Associations. ***PRACTICE AREAS:*** Labor and Employment. ***Email:*** rlazaro@seyfarth.com

JEFFREY H. LIEBLING, born 1970; admitted to bar, 1998, Illinois and U.S. District Court, Northern District of Illinois. *Education:* Illinois State University (B.S., 1993); John Marshall Law School (J.D., magna cum laude, 1998). Phi Delta Phi. Member, Criminal Justice Association. Author, Comment, "Judicial Usurpation of the FTC's Authority: A Return to the Rule of Reason," John Marshall Law Review. *Member:* Illinois State and American Bar Associations. ***PRACTICE AREAS:*** Litigation. ***Email:*** jliebling@seyfarth.com

NOAH G. LIPSCHULTZ, admitted to bar, 2001, Illinois; U.S. District Court, Northern District of Illinois and Western District of Wisconsin; U.S. Court of Appeals, Seventh Circuit. *Education:* University of Wisconsin (B.A., with distinction, 1998); University of Chicago (J.D., 2001). *Member:* Chicago, Illinois State and American Bar Associations. ***PRACTICE AREAS:*** Labor and Employment Law. ***Email:*** nlipschultz@seyfarth.com

KATHRYN A. LLOYD, born Columbus, Ohio, April 10, 1974; admitted to bar, 2000, Illinois. *Education:* The Ohio State University (B.S., magna cum laude, 1996); Northwestern University School of Law (J.D., cum laude, 2000). *Member:* American Bar Association. ***LANGUAGES:*** French. ***PRACTICE AREAS:*** Corporate; Securities. ***Email:*** klloyd@seyfarth.com

SARA E. LORBER, born New York, N.Y., November 6, 1967; admitted to bar, 1995, Illinois; U.S. District Court, Northern District of Illinois; U.S. District Court, Northern District of Indiana; U.S. Court of Appeals, Seventh Circuit. *Education:* State University of New York at Binghamton (B.A., 1991); Case Western Reserve University (J.D., 1995). ***PRACTICE AREAS:*** Litigation; Bankruptcy; Workouts; Business Reorganization. ***Email:*** slorber@seyfarth.com

AMEENA Y. MAJID, admitted to bar, 1998, Illinois. *Education:* University of Iowa (B.A., 1994); Loyola University (J.D., 1998). ***PRACTICE AREAS:*** Employee Benefits; Tax Qualified Retirement Plans; Welfare Benefit Plans; Executive Compensation and Incentives. ***Email:*** amajid@seyfarth.com

EMILY M. MAKI-RUSK, born 1976; admitted to bar, 2002, Illinois. *Education:* Kalamazoo College (B.A., magna cum laude, 1999); Washington University School of Law (J.D., Order of the Coif, 2002). ***PRACTICE AREAS:*** Litigation. ***Email:*** emakirusk@seyfarth.com

ZACHARY S. MAY, born 1980; (admission pending). *Education:* Washington University in St. Louis (J.D., 2005); Indiana University, Bloomington (B.A., 2001). ***PRACTICE AREAS:*** Real Estate. ***Email:*** zmay@seyfarth.com

MICHELLE K. MELLINGER, born 1972; admitted to bar, 1997, Illinois; U.S. District Court, Central and Northern Districts of Illinois; U.S. Court of Appeals, Seventh Circuit. *Education:* University of Illinois (B.A., 1994); DePaul University (J.D., 1997). ***PRACTICE AREAS:*** Labor and Employment. ***Email:*** mmellinger@seyfarth.com

ALAYA B. MEYERS, born 1974; admitted to bar, 1998, California and U.S. District Court, Central District of California; 1999, U.S. District Court, Northern District of California; 2000, Illinois and U.S. District Court, Northern District of Illinois; 2001, U.S. Court of Appeals, Seventh Circuit; 2005, U.S. District Court, Central District of Illinois and U.S. District Court, District of Colorado. *Education:* University of California, Berkeley (B.A., summa cum laude, 1994) Phi Beta Kappa; Northwestern University School of Law (J.D., 1998). *Member:* Chicago (Seminar Chair, Labor and Employment Section), Los Angeles County and American Bar Associations; State Bar of California. ***PRACTICE AREAS:*** Labor and Employment. ***Email:*** ameyers@seyfarth.com

MEAGAN NOEL NEWMAN, born 1976; admitted to bar, 2003, Maryland; 2005, U.S. District Court, District of Maryland (Not admitted in Illinois). *Education:* University of Michigan (B.A. 1998); University of Maryland (J.D., with honors, 2003). ***PRACTICE AREAS:*** Environmental Law; Toxic Torts; OSHA. ***Email:*** mnewman@seyfarth.com

KAREN M. OSGOOD, admitted to bar, 2000, Illinois. *Education:* University of Colorado at Boulder (B.A., 1995); Loyola University (J.D., 2000). ***PRACTICE AREAS:*** Labor and Employment. ***Email:*** kosgood@seyfarth.com

(This Listing Continued)

ERNST H. OSTRAND, born 1973; (admission pending). *Education:* University of Iowa (B.A., 1996); National-Louis University (M.A.T., 1999); Chicago-Kent College of Law (J.D., high honors, 2005). *Member:* Chicago Bar Association. ***PRACTICE AREAS:*** Labor and Employment.

SCOTT PALER, born 1980; admitted to bar, 2005, Wisconsin (Not admitted in Illinois). *Education:* University of Wisconsin (B.A., with distinction, 2002; J.D., cum laude 2005). *Member:* American Bar Association; State Bar of Wisconsin. ***PRACTICE AREAS:*** Labor and Employment. ***Email:*** spaler@seyfarth.com

NICOLE K. PERACKE, admitted to bar, 2004, Illinois. *Education:* Northern Illinois University (B.S., 1993); DePaul University (M.B.A., HR Management, 1999); Loyola University - Chicago (J.D., cum laude, 2004). *Member:* Chicago, Illinois State and American (Member, Labor and Employment Section) Bar Associations. ***PRACTICE AREAS:*** Labor and Employment. ***Email:*** nperacke@seyfarth.com

JAMES J. POWERS, born 1970; admitted to bar, 1998, Illinois; U.S. District Court, Northern District of Illinois. *Education:* Northwestern University (B.A., 1992); Chicago-Kent College of Law (J.D., with high honors, 1998). Phi Beta Kappa. *Member:* Illinois State and American Bar Associations. ***PRACTICE AREAS:*** Labor and Employment. ***Email:*** jjpowers@seyfarth.com

STEPHANIE J. PULCANIO, admitted to bar, 2002, Illinois. *Education:* Denison University (B.A., 1996); Chicago-Kent School of Law (J.D., 2001). ***PRACTICE AREAS:*** Labor and Employment Law. ***Email:*** spulcanio@seyfarth.com

TRISHA M. RACHOY, born 1977; admitted to bar, 2004, Illinois. *Education:* DePaul University (B.S., high honors, 2001); Chicago-Kent College of Law (J.D., 2004). Order of the Coif. ***PRACTICE AREAS:*** Employee Benefits. ***Email:*** trachoy@seyfarth.com

CHARLES SANFORD RIECKE, admitted to bar, 1997, Louisiana, Minnesota (inactive) and North Dakota (inactive); 2001, Illinois; U.S. District Court, Northern and Central Districts of Illinois; U.S. District Court, Eastern District of Louisiana; U.S. Court of Appeals, Fifth and Seventh Circuits. *Education:* University of Oregon (B.A., 1993); Tulane University of Louisiana (J.D., 1996). Law Clerk: for the Honorable Carol A. Doyle, U.S. Bankruptcy Judge, Northern District of Illinois, Eastern Division (Chicago), 1999-2001; for the Honorable William A. Hill, U.S. Bankruptcy Appellate Panel Judge, Eighth Circuit, and U.S. Bankruptcy Judge, District of North Dakota, 1997-1999; for the Honorable Bruce M. Van Sickle, U.S. District Judge, District of North Dakota, 1996-1997. Annual Contributing Author, Norton Annual Survey of Bankruptcy Law. Author: "Postpetition Lenders: is Your Collateral at Risk?," 116 Banking Law Journal 53, January 1999 (Westlaw FIND Citation: 116 BLJ 53); "Equitable Mootness in Bankruptcy," 11 Norton Bankruptcy Law Adviser 7, 1998, (Westlaw FIND Citation: 11 NRTN-BLA 7); "Geiger Count: The Winter of Creditors' Discontent," 7 Consumer Bankruptcy News 3, June 4, 1998; "Sections 327 to 331- Attorney Fees," 2001-2002, Norton Annual Survey of Bankruptcy Law 467, William L. Norton, Jr., Editor, (Westlaw FIND Citation: 2002 NRTN-ASBL 467); "Sections 327 to 331-Attorney Fees," 2000-2001, Norton Annual Survey of Bankruptcy Law 387, William L. Norton, Jr., Editor; "Sections 327 to 331-Attorney Fees," 1999-2000, Norton Annual Survey of Bankruptcy Law 307, William L. Norton, Jr., Editor. *Member:* The Chicago Bar Association; The Abraham Lincoln Marovitz American Inn of Court; American Bankruptcy Institute. ***PRACTICE AREAS:*** Litigation. ***Email:*** criecke@seyfarth.com

STACEY L. ROBINSON, born 1964; admitted to bar, 1997, Georgia; 2001, Illinois. *Education:* Georgia Institute of Technology (B.C.E., 1986); Georgia State University (J.D., cum laude, 1997); John Marshall Law School (LL.M., Real Estate, with honors, 2004). Registered Professional Engineer: Georgia, 1992, South Carolina, 1993. *Member:* Illinois State Bar Association; State Bar of Georgia. ***PRACTICE AREAS:*** Real Estate (90%); Construction (5%); Environmental (5%). ***Email:*** srobinson@seyfarth.com

KRISTIN ROSELLA, born 1980; (admission pending). *Education:* University of Michigan (B.A., 2002); Chicago-Kent College of Law (J.D., 2005). ***PRACTICE AREAS:*** Litigation. ***Email:*** krosella@seyfarth.com

DOUGLAS S. RUPERT, born 1970; admitted to bar, 1997, Illinois; 1999, registered to practice before U.S. Patent and Trademark Office. *Education:* Michigan State University (B.S.E.E., 1994); Loyola University (J.D., 1997). *Member:* Chicago, Illinois State, and American Bar Associations; American Intellectual Property Law Association. ***PRACTICE AREAS:*** Litigation; Intellectual Property. ***Email:*** drupert@seyfarth.com

COLETTE M. SAVAGE, admitted to bar, 2001, Illinois; U.S. District Court, Northern District of Illinois. *Education:* University of Michigan (B.A., 1994); Indiana University School of Law - Bloomington (J.D., 2001). ***PRACTICE AREAS:*** Labor and Employment. ***Email:*** csavage@seyfarth.com

SCOTT A. SCHAEFERS, born 1977; admitted to bar, 2002, Illinois, U.S. District Court, Northern District of Illinois and U.S. Court of Appeals, Seventh Circuit. *Education:* University of Notre Dame (B.A., 1999); University of Illinois (J.D., 2002). *Member:* Chicago, Illinois State and American Bar Associations. ***PRACTICE AREAS:*** Litigation. ***Email:*** sschaefers@seyfarth.com

JAIME ERIN SCHNEIDER, born 1976; admitted to bar, 2001, Illinois. *Education:* University of Michigan at Ann Arbor (B.A., 1998); Chicago-Kent College of Law (J.D., high honors, 2001). Member, Chicago-Kent College Law Review. ***PRACTICE AREAS:*** Employee Benefits. ***Email:*** jschneider@seyfarth.com

SAM SCHWARTZ, born Minneapolis, Minnesota, July 4, 1979; (admission pending). *Education:* Tufts University (B.A., summa cum laude, 2001); Northwestern University School of Law (J.D., cum laude, 2005). ***PRACTICE AREAS:*** Labor and Employment. ***Email:*** sschwartz@seyfarth.com

SCOTT J. SMITH, admitted to bar, 1996, Illinois. *Education:* University of Michigan (B.S., 1990); IIT/Chicago-Kent College of Law (J.D., 1996). *Member:* American Bar Association (Construction Law Forum). ***PRACTICE AREAS:*** Commercial Litigation; Construction Law. ***Email:*** ssmith@seyfarth.com

AMANDA A. SONNEBORN, born 1978; admitted to bar, 2003, Illinois, U.S. District Court, Northern District of Illinois; 2004, U.S. District Court, Central and Southern Districts of Illinois and U.S. District Court, Western District of Wisconsin. *Education:* University of Illinois, Urbana-Champaign (B.A., high honors, 1999; Master's of Human Re-

(This Listing Continued)

SEYFARTH SHAW LLP, Chicago—Continued

sources and Industrial Relations, 2003; J.D., cum laude, 2003). *Member:* American Bar Association (Member, Labor and Employment Section). ***PRACTICE AREAS:*** Labor and Employment. ***Email:*** asonneborn@seyfarth.com

BRIAN M. STOLZENBACH, admitted to bar, 2000, Illinois; 2001, U.S. District Court, Northern District of Illinois; 2002, U.S. Court of Appeals, Seventh Circuit; 2003, U.S. District Court, Central District of Illinois; 2004, U.S. District Court, Northern District of Indiana; 2005, U.S. District Court, Eastern District of Michigan and U.S. Court of Appeals, Eighth and District of Columbia Circuits. *Education:* University of Missouri-Columbia (A.B., cum laude, 1997); University of Michigan (J.D., cum laude, 2000). *Member:* American Bar Association. ***PRACTICE AREAS:*** Labor and Employment. ***Email:*** bstolzenbach@seyfarth.com

DAVID L. STRECK, born 1970; admitted to bar, 1995, Illinois and U.S. District Court, Northern District of Illinois. *Education:* Northwestern University (B.A., 1992); Loyola University (J.D., 1995). *Member:* Illinois State and American Bar Associations. ***PRACTICE AREAS:*** Labor and Employment. ***Email:*** dstreck@seyfarth.com

DANIEL W. TARPEY, born 1972; admitted to bar, 1997, Illinois. *Education:* University of Illinois (B.A., 1994); University of Notre Dame (J.D., 1997). ***PRACTICE AREAS:*** Litigation. ***Email:*** dtarpey@seyfarth.com

MICHAEL D. THOMPSON, born 1975; admitted to bar, 2001, Illinois. *Education:* University of Iowa (B.B.A., 1997; J.D., with disninction, 2001). *Member:* Chicago and American Bar Associations. ***PRACTICE AREAS:*** Corporate Law; Securities. ***Email:*** mdthompson@seyfarth.com

JASON M. TORRES, admitted to bar, 2002, Illinois; U.S. District Court, Central and Northern Districts of Illinois; U.S. Court of Appeals, Seventh Circuit. *Education:* Indiana University (B.S., 1999; J.D., 2002). *Member:* Chicago Bar Association. ***PRACTICE AREAS:*** Labor and Employment. ***Email:*** jtorres@seyfarth.com

ANNETTE TYMAN, born 1969; admitted to bar, 2005, Illinois. *Education:* Indiana University (B.S., 1999); Loyola University of Chicago (M.B.A., 2004; J.D., cum laude, 2005). ***LANGUAGES:*** Spanish. ***PRACTICE AREAS:*** Labor and Employment. ***Email:*** atyman@seyfarth.com

JOHN M. VANDE WALLE, born 1960; admitted to bar, 1998, Illinois and U.S. District Court, Northern District of Illinois; 2000, U.S District Court, Central District of Illinois; 2002, U.S. Court of Appeals, Seventh Circuit; 2003, U.S. District Court, Eastern District of Michigan. *Education:* New College of Florida (B.A., 1984); Southern Methodist University (M.A./M.B.A., 1987); Chicago-Kent College of Law, Illinois Institute of Technology (J.D., with high honors, 1998). Order of the Coif. Author, "In the Eye of the Beholder: Issue of Distributive and Corrective Justice in the ADA's Employment Protection for Persons Regarded as Disabled," Chicago-Kent Law Review, 1998. *Member:* Chicago and American (Member, Section on Labor and Employment) Bar Associations. ***PRACTICE AREAS:*** Labor and Employment (100%). ***Email:*** jvandewalle@seyfarth.com

TYLER A. VanLONKHUYZEN, born 1974; admitted to bar, 2000, Illinois. *Education:* Hope College (B.A., 1997); DePaul University (J.D., 2000). ***PRACTICE AREAS:*** Corporate Law. ***Email:*** tvanlonkhuyzen@seyfarth.com

KIRSTEN K. WENDELA, born 1980; (admission pending). *Education:* University of Michigan (B.A., 2002); Chicago-Kent College of Law (J.D., honors, 2005). Managing Editor, Chicago-Kent Law Review, 2004-2005. Publication: "Context Is in the Eye of the Beholder: Establishment Clause Violations and the More-than-Reasonable Person," 80 Chi.-Kent L.Rev. 981 (2005). Legal Extern to Hon. Morton Denlow, U. S. District Court, N.D. Illinois, 2004. Finalist, Charles Evans Hughes Oral Argument Competition, 2003. *Member:* American Bar Association. ***PRACTICE AREAS:*** Litigation. ***Email:*** kwendela@seyfarth.com

MATTHEW A. WERBER, born 1974; (admission pending). *Education:* University of Michigan (B.S.E., 1997); Chicago-Kent College of Law (J.D., 2005). ***PRACTICE AREAS:*** Litigation; Intellectual Property. ***Email:*** mwerber@seyfarth.com

JUDITH L. WETHALL, admitted to bar, 1997, Illinois. *Education:* University of Wisconsin-Madison (B.A., 1985); Stetson University College of Law (J.D., cum laude, 1997). ***PRACTICE AREAS:*** Employee Benefits. ***Email:*** jwethall@seyfarth.com

ALISON B. WILLARD, born 1976; admitted to bar, 2001, Illinois. *Education:* Indiana University (B.A., 1998); University of Michigan Law School (J.D., 2001). ***PRACTICE AREAS:*** Labor and Employment Law. ***Email:*** abwillard@seyfarth.com

LINDSAY WOLTER, born 1978; admitted to bar, 2003, Illinois. *Education:* Yale University (B.A., 2000); Rosenstiel School of Marine and Atmospheric Science (M.A., 2003); University of Miami School of Law (J.D., 2003). *Member:* Chicago (Member, Environmental Law Committee) and American Bar Associations. ***PRACTICE AREAS:*** Environmental Safety and Toxic Torts. ***Email:*** lwolter@seyfarth.com

WINNIE WONG, born 1975; admitted to bar, 2004, Illinois; 2005, U.S. District Court, Northern District of Illinois. *Education:* Northwestern University (B.A., 1998); Loyola University Chicago School of Law (J.D., cum laude, 2004). Lead Articles Editor, Loyola Law Review, 2003-2004. *Member:* Chicago and American Bar Associations. ***PRACTICE AREAS:*** Labor and Employment. ***Email:*** wwong@seyfarth.com

JASON K. ZACHARY, born 1972; admitted to bar, 1999, Illinois. *Education:* Texas A & M University (B.B.A., 1995); Chicago-Kent College of Law (J.D., with honors, 1999); Georgetown University Law Center (LL.M., with distinction, 2002). *Member:* Chicago and American (Federal Regulation of Securities Committee) Bar Associations. ***PRACTICE AREAS:*** Corporate; Securities. ***Email:*** jzachary@seyfarth.com

PATRICK ZELLER, born 1970; admitted to bar, 1996, Illinois. *Education:* University of Illinois (B.A., 1992); John Marshall Law School (J.D., 1996). Adjunct Professor, LLM Program in Information Technology and Privacy Law, The John Marshall School of Law. Certified, EnCE (EnCase Examiner, Guidance Software); Certified, CFCE (Certified Forensic Computer Examiner); Certified, EECS (Electronic Evidence Collection Specialist). Member, The Sedona Conference. Member, FBI InfraGard Chapter. *Member:* Chicago and Illinois State Bar Associations; International Association of Computer Investigative Specialists (IACIS) (Instructor); High Technology Crime Investigation Association (Past President, Midwest Chapter). ***PRACTICE AREAS:*** Litigation; Intellectual Property. ***Email:*** pzeller@seyfarth.com

STAFF ATTORNEYS

MELANIE H. BERKOWITZ, born 1971; admitted to bar, 1996, Illinois and U.S. District Court, Northern District of Illinois; 1998, U.S. District Court, Central District of Illinois. *Education:* University of Pennsylvania (B.A., magna cum laude, 1993); New York University School of Law (J.D., 1996). *Member:* Chicago Bar Association (Alliance for Women). ***PRACTICE AREAS:*** Labor and Employment. ***Email:*** mberkowitz@seyfarth.com

JAMES L. FLATLEY, born 1947; admitted to bar, 1976, Illinois. *Education:* St. Norbert College (B.A., 1969); John Marshall Law School (J.D., 1976). ***PRACTICE AREAS:*** Real Estate. ***Email:*** jflatley@seyfarth.com

BRIAN J. HIPP, born 1974; admitted to bar, 1999, Illinois. *Education:* University of Wisconsin-Madison (B.A., 1996); University of Michigan (J.D., 1999). *Member:* American Bar Association. ***PRACTICE AREAS:*** Labor and Employment. ***Email:*** bhipp@seyfarth.com

MICHAEL E. ROMANI, born 1963; admitted to bar, 2002, Illinois and U.S. District Court, Northern District of Illinois; registered to practice before U.S. Patent and Trademark Office. *Education:* Northern Illinois University (B.S., Biological Sciences, 1987; M.S., Biological Sciences, 1990; M.S., Industrial Management, 1993); John Marshall Law School (J.D., 2002). *Member:* Illinois State and American Bar Associations. ***PRACTICE AREAS:*** Occupational Safety and Health; Environmental Law; Patent Prosecution; Trademark Prosecution. ***Email:*** mromani@seyfarth.com

(For complete biographical data on personnel at Washington, D.C., Los Angeles, California, New York, New York, San Francisco, California, Sacramento, California, Houston, Texas, Atlanta, Georgia, Boston, Massachusetts, and Brussels, Belgium, see Professional Biographies at those locations)

(This Listing Continued)

SHAHEEN, NOVOSELSKY, STAAT, FILIPOWSKI & ECCLESTON, P.C.

Established in 1961

20 NORTH WACKER DRIVE, SUITE 2900
CHICAGO, ILLINOIS 60606-3192
Telephone: 312-621-4400
Fax: 312-621-0268
Email: info@snsfe-law.com
URL: http://www.snsfe-law.com

Banking, Debtor and Creditor, Corporate Law, Commercial Law, Employee Benefits, Estate Planning, Estate Administration, Estate and Trust Litigation, Employment Relations Law, Litigation, Minority Business Law, Real Estate, Arbitration, Securities, Securities Industry Disputes, Taxation, Tax Exempt Organizations.

SHAREHOLDERS

RAYMOND SHAHEEN, born Deer Grove, Illinois, February 8, 1918; admitted to bar, 1949, Illinois. *Education:* DePaul University. Phi Alpha Delta. *Member:* Chicago, Illinois State and American Bar Associations. ***PRACTICE AREAS:*** Business Acquisitions Law; Corporate Law; General Business Law; Contracts Law. ***Email:*** RShaheen@snsfe-law.com

HENRY N. NOVOSELSKY, born Chicago, Illinois, January 19, 1942; admitted to bar, 1966, Illinois; 1967, U.S. District Court, Northern District of Illinois including Trial Bar and U.S. Court of Appeals, Seventh Circuit; 1971, U.S. Supreme Court. *Education:* Roosevelt University (B.A., Political Science, 1962); DePaul University (J.D., with honors, 1966). Hearing Examiner, State of Illinois, Illinois Commerce Commission, 1970-1973; Administrative Law Judge, State of Illinois, Illinois Department of Revenue, 1973-1976. *Member:* Illinois State and American Bar Associations; Appellate Lawyers Association of Illinois; Illinois Trial Lawyers Association. ***REPORTED CASES:*** Petersen v. Wallach, 764 N.E.2d 19 (Ill. 2002), affirming 733 N.E.2d 713; Woodfield Group v. DeLisle, 13 IER Cases, 693 NE.2d 464 (Ill. App. 1998); Trans-Aire International v. Northern Adhesive Co., 9 UCC Rep. Serv. 2d 878 F.2d 1259 (CCA 7th, 1989). ***PRACTICE AREAS:*** Commercial Litigation; Unfair Competition; Chancery and Extraordinary Remedies; Estate Litigation; Trust Litigation. ***Email:*** HNovoselsky@snsfe-law.com

LAWRENCE G. STAAT, born Chicago Heights, Illinois, July 2, 1949; admitted to bar, 1974, Illinois, U.S. Tax Court and U.S. Supreme Court. *Education:* University of Illinois (B.S., Finance, cum laude, 1971); DePaul University (M.S., Taxation, 1977); Tulane University and DePaul University (J.D., 1974). Trial Attorney, Office of Chief Counsel, Internal Revenue Service, Chicago District, 1977-1979. *Member:* Chicago (Member, Committee on Federal Taxation, 1976—) and American (Member, Section on Taxation, 1976) Bar Associations. ***PRACTICE AREAS:*** Federal and State Taxation Law; Real Estate; Business Transactions; Business Planning; Estate Planning. ***Email:*** LStaat@snsfe-law.com

STEVEN C. FILIPOWSKI, born Chicago, Illinois, February 19, 1950; admitted to bar, 1975, Illinois; 1979, U.S. District Court, Northern District of Illinois including Trial Bar; 1982, U.S. Court of Appeals, Seventh Circuit. *Education:* St. John's University (B.A., Humanities, 1972); Loyola University of Illinois (J.D., 1975). Member, Honors Program, St. John's University. Member: Union League Club; National Association of Wholesaler-Distributors. *Member:* Chicago (Member: Committees on: Corporate; Antitrust; Bankruptcy), Illinois State and American Bar Associations; The American Trial Lawyers Association; Defense Research Institute. ***REPORTED CASES:*** Harris Bank Hinsdale v. Caliendo, 601 NE2d 1330, 253 IllApp3d 1013 (1992); Lindsey v. Pate Foods Corporation, 1999 U.S. Dist. Lexis 7611. ***PRACTICE AREAS:*** Corporate Law; Product Distribution; Marketing Law; Commercial Litigation; Appellate Practice; Employment Law; Bankruptcy Litigation. ***Email:*** SFilipowski@snsfe-law.com

(This Listing Continued)

JAMES J. ECCLESTON, born Boston, Massachusetts, January 11, 1961; admitted to bar, 1987, Illinois, Massachusetts and U.S. District Court, Northern District of Illinois including Trial Bar; 1988, U.S. District Court, District of Massachusetts and U.S. Court of Appeals, Seventh Circuit; 1989, U.S. Tax Court. *Education:* University of Chicago (A.B., Politics, Economics, Rhetoric and Law, 1983); Boston College (M.A., 1984); Suffolk University (J.D., cum laude, 1987). Executive Member and Chief Editor, Suffolk University Law School Moot Court Board, 1987. Registered Investment Advisor, Illinois. Professional Licenses: NASD Series 7, Series 66 and Series 24, 1997—. Co-Editor and Contributing Author, "Securities Arbitration," Securities Law, Illinois Institute for Continuing Legal Education, 2003. Arbitrator and Mediator, National Association of Securities Dealers (NASD), Circuit Court of Cook County, Illinois, 1990—. *Member:* Chicago (Past Co-Chair, Securities Law Committee; Past Chair, Investment and Financial Services Committee; Past Co-Chair, Litigation and Enforcement Sub-Committee, Securities Law Committee) and American Bar Associations; Securities Industry Association (SIA); Public Investors Arbitration Bar Association (PIABA); Financial Planning Association (FPA) (Director, Chicago Chapter); Union League Club (Chair, Financial Services Committee). ***REPORTED CASES:*** Loren Griesberger, Multiple Color Systems, Inc., v. Orlando Scherling, John Kresz, 84 L-24909, Tried Feb. 19-25, 1991; In the Matter of the Arbitration Between Jay Kiessling and Sharon Kiessling, Claimants, v. E*Trade Securities, Inc., Respondent, 99-00839, 2000 NASD Arb. LEXIS 1296, Oct. 17, 2000; Taylor v. Salomon Smith Barney, 01-03676 2002 WL 321 68313 (NASD); Torrence v. Edward Jones & Co., 02-00061, 2003 WL 22288114 (NASD). ***PRACTICE AREAS:*** Securities Arbitration; Securities Litigation; Securities Regulation; Securities Fraud; Employment Law. ***Email:*** JEccleston@snsfe-law.com

PARTNERS

WILLIAM E. HOFMANN, born Chicago Heights, Illinois, March 12, 1949; admitted to bar, 1974, Illinois and U.S. District Court, Northern District of Illinois including Trial Bar; 1977, U.S. Tax Court; 1980, U.S. Supreme Court. *Education:* Carleton College (B.A., Government and International Relations, 1971); Washington University (J.D., 1974). *Member:* Chicago, Illinois State and American (Member, Sections on: Taxation; Real Property; Probate; Trust) Bar Associations; Chicago Estate Planning Council. ***PRACTICE AREAS:*** Federal Taxation; State Taxation; Business Planning; Estate Planning; Probate; Trust Law; Real Estate. ***Email:*** WHofmann@snsfe-law.com

SCOTT E. GALBREATH, born Chicago, Illinois, October 8, 1961; admitted to bar, 1986, Illinois and U.S. District Court, Northern District of Illinois; 1987, U.S. Tax Court; 1990, U.S. Claims Court. *Education:* Elmhurst College (B.A., Political Science and Urban Studies, with high honors, 1983); Illinois Institute of Technology/Chicago-Kent College of Law (J.D., 1986; LL.M. in Taxation with honors, 1991). Author: "Final Sponsorship Regulations Provide Some Guidance But Leave Hard Issues Unanswered," CCH Exempt Organizations Reports Tax-Exempt Advisor Newsletter Issue No.s 335, 336 (June, July, 2002); "Enron Debacle Will Be Catalyst for Reform of 401(k) Plan Laws," WLS-TVLaw.com, 2002. Contributing Author, *1996 Tax Legislation:* Law and Explanation, CCH Incorporated, 1996. *Articles:* "Trim Your Tax Bill" and "How to Choose a Tax Expert," February 2001; Practitioner Comment CCH State Tax Reporters, 1999; "Are Associate Member Dues Really Unrelated Business Income?" January 1995. Classes and Seminars: "The Basics of Forming a Tax-Exempt Charitable Organization," Chicago Bar Association Seminar (November, 2003); "The Effects of 9/11 On the Not-For-Profit Sector," Downers Grove Not For Profit Job Club, (September, 2003); "Payment of Taxes and Available Exemptions," "Taxes for Tax Exempt Organizations-the Unrelated Business Income Tax," and "IRS Consideration," National Business Institute's Illinois Nonprofits: Tax and Business Answers seminar (August 2003); "Aren't All NFPs The Same?" Woodridge Not For Profit Job Club (April, 2003); "Internet Issues Facing Charitable Organizations," CBA Continuing Legal Education Seminar speaker (September, 2002); "Unrelated Business Income" and "Balancing Private Inurement Against the Needs for Executive Compensation," National Business Institute's Exempt Organizations and Charitable Activities in Illinois seminar (September, 2002); "Retirement Plans for Exempt Organizations" and "Exempt Organizations and the Internet," Lorman Education Services Illinois Exempt Organizations seminar, August, 2002. "Panel Discussion on Tax Issues Regarding Internet Activities of Exempt Organizations," (March 2001); "Taxes for Tax Exempt Organizations," (February 2001); "Exempt Organizations and the Internet," (January 2001); "A Primer on Representing the Tax Exempt Charitable Organization," February 1997; "Taxes for Tax Exempt Organizations," December 1996; "Recent Legislation Affecting Exempt Organizations," September 1996. *Member:* Chicago, Illinois State and American Bar Associations. ***TRANSACTIONS:*** Successfully negotiated sale of popular Internet Domain name. ***PRACTICE AREAS:*** Tax Law; Employee Benefits; Real Estate; Nonprofit and Charitable Organizations; Business Law. ***Email:*** SGalbreath@snsfe-law.com

MICHAEL D. WEIS, born Chicago, Illinois, April 8, 1963; admitted to bar, 1988, Illinois; 1989, U.S. District Court, Northern District of Illinois. *Education:* University of Illinois (B.S., with high honors, 1985; J.D., cum laude, 1988). Certified Public Accountant, Illinois, 1985. *Member:* Chicago and American Bar Associations; Illinois Society of Certified Public Accountants; American Institute of Certified Public Accountants. ***PRACTICE AREAS:*** Real Estate; Corporate Law; Finance; Health Care; Tax Law. ***Email:*** mweis@snsfe-law.com

JACK L. HAAN, born Evergreen Park, Illinois, May 21, 1967; admitted to bar, 1992, Illinois; 1994, U.S. District Court, Central District of Illinois; 1995, U.S. District Court, Northern Districts of Illinois. *Education:* Hope College (B.A., Business Administration and Political Science, magna cum laude, 1989); American University, Washington College of Law (J.D., 1992). *Member:* Chicago and Illinois State Bar Associations. ***PRACTICE AREAS:*** Business Litigation; Arbitration; Chancery; Appeals; Estate Litigation; Trust Litigation. ***Email:*** JHaan@snsfe-law.com

SHARYN BETH ALPERT, born Chicago, Illinois, February 11, 1965; admitted to bar, 1993, Illinois and U.S. District Court, Northern District of Illinois. *Education:* Indiana University (B.S., Marketing, 1987); John Marshall Law School (J.D., 1993). ***PRACTICE AREAS:*** Business Litigation; Arbitration; Chancery Practice; Employment Law. ***Email:*** salpert@snsfe-law.com

(This Listing Continued)

JEFFREY M. GERSHON, born Plantation, Florida, December 21,1967; admitted to bar, 1996, Indiana and U.S. District Court, Southern and Northern Districts of Indiana; 2001, North Carolina; 2005, Illinois. *Education:* University of Arizona (B.A., 1991); Thomas M. Cooley Law School (J.D., 1996). With Indiana Securities Division, 1996-2000, Chief Deputy, 1998-2000. Associate, Wyrick Robbins Yates & Ponton LLP, Raleigh, North Carolina, 2000-2004. *Member:* Chicago Bar Association; National Society of Compliance Professionals. ***PRACTICE AREAS:*** Securities Regulation; Broker-Dealer Regulation; Investments Advisor Compliance; SEC Enforcement; Securities Arbitration; Securities Law. ***Email:*** jgershon@snsfe-law.com

RONALD M. AMATO, born Naperville, Illinois, October 9, 1969; admitted to bar, 1999, Illinois and U.S. District Court, Northern District of Illinois. *Education:* Northern Illinois University (B.A., 1993); Chicago-Kent College of Law (J.D., 1999). Winner, CALI Award, Advanced Research, Fall, 1997. Professional Licenses: NASD Series 7 and Series 63, 1993. *Member:* Chicago and American Bar Associations. ***PRACTICE AREAS:*** Securities Arbitration; Securities Regulation; Employment Law. ***Email:*** RAmato@snsfe-law.com

APRIL J. LINDAUER, born Phoenix, Arizona, April 27, 1974; admitted to bar, 2003, Illinois and U.S. District Court, Northern District of Illinois. *Education:* University of Chicago (A.B., Psychology, 1996); DePaul College of Law (J.D., 2003). Research Assistant, Professor N. Morrison Torrey, 2002-2003. *Member:* Chicago and American Bar Associations. ***PRACTICE AREAS:*** Securities Arbitration; Securities Litigation; Securities Regulation; Securities Fraud; Employment Law. ***Email:*** ALindauer@snsfe-law.com

SCOTT SISSEL, born 1979; admitted to bar, 2004, Illinois. *Education:* University of Iowa (B.B.A. in Accounting, 2001); University of Iowa (J.D., 2003); Northwestern University (LL.M. in Taxation, 2004). *Member:* American Bar Association; Illinois State Bar Association; Chicago Bar Association. ***PRACTICE AREAS:*** Taxation; Federal Income Tax; Tax Controversies; State Income Tax; Real Estate; Business Estate Planning; Business Succession Planning; Commercial Real Estate. ***Email:*** SSissel@snsfe-law.com

REPRESENTATIVE CLIENTS: The Northern Trust Company; JP Morgan Chase Bank; Roman, Inc.; The Huff Co.; LaSalle National Bank; Roman, Inc.; American Pacific Financial Corporation; Mid-States Wire Processing Co.; Bethlehem Industries, Inc.; Industrial Television Service, Inc.; Meyer Material Co.; Consolidated Steel & Supply Co.; Henry Technologies, Inc.; Liberty Lithographers, Inc., d/b/a Liberty Graphics, Inc.; Master Control Systems; Holum & Sons, Co. Inc.; Johnson Paving Company; Steve Foley Cadillac, Inc.; Waldmann Lighting Company; Bollinger, Lach & Associates; Luminair Film Productions, Inc.; Universal Electric Foundry, Inc.; Arrem Plastics, Inc.; County Line Properties, Inc.; Revere Electric Supply Company; Emercent, Inc.; Montessori Education Centers Associated, Inc.; Country Partners, Inc.; Country Gas Co.; Country Properties, LLC; Galloway Plastics, Inc.; U.S. Messenger & Logistics.
REFERENCE: Lincoln Financial Advisors.

SHANNON & ASSOCIATES, LTD.

8 SOUTH MICHIGAN, 26TH FLOOR
CHICAGO, ILLINOIS 60603
Telephone: 312-332-2804
Fax: 312-332-0600
Email: tshannon@shannonlawoffice.com
URL: http://www.shannonlawoffice.com

Business Law, Construction Law, Labor and Employment, Real Estate, Construction Defects, Mechanics Liens, Contracts, Franchises and Franchising, Employment Contracts, Personnel Policies, Mergers and Acquisitions.

FIRM PROFILE: Shannon & Associates was established by Thomas J. Shannon in 1976, when he left the firm of Epton, Mullin, Druth, Ltd. to start his own firm. Today his firm concentrates on Business matters involving corporate, real estate and employment law. Mr. Shannon has been recognized for his commitment to clients in Leadership and Management Directions, a publication of the American Bar Association.

THOMAS J. SHANNON, born Cleveland, Ohio, September 20, 1944; admitted to bar, 1973, Illinois, U.S. District Court, Northern District of Illinois including Trial Bar and U.S. Federal Court. *Education:* Loyola University (B.A., cum laude, 1968; J.D., 1973). Former Board Member: Illinois Credit Union Foundation; Five Hospital Home Bound Elderly Program. *Member:* Chicago Bar Association. ***PRACTICE AREAS:*** Business Law; Contracts; Franchises and Franchising; Mergers and Acquisitions; Labor and Employment; Wrongful Termination; Employee Benefit; Sexual Harassment; Real Estate; Condominium Law; Homeowners Association Law; Civil Rights; Media Law; Discrimination; Gay and Lesbian Rights; Communications and Media; Libel, Slander and Defamation; Privacy Law. ***Email:*** tshannon@shannonlawoffice.com

REPRESENTATIVE CLIENTS: Motorola Employees Credit Union; Speedsite On Line; Cereal Byproducts Company; Permaco Incorporated; Arlington Pediatric Therapy Management Services, Ltd.; PCS International; Pierce & Associates, P.C.

WAYNE S. SHAPIRO, P.C.

Established in 1978
111 WEST WASHINGTON STREET
SUITE 1028
CHICAGO, ILLINOIS 60602
Telephone: 312-704-8400
Fax: 312-704-0366
URL: http://www.honstlawyr.com
Email: honstlawyr@aol.com
URL: http://www.lawyers.com/wayneshapiro

Family, Divorce, Dissolution of Marriage, Paternity, Child Custody, Prenuptial Agreements, Postnuptial Agreements, Visitation, Real Estate, Landlord and Tenant, Commercial Real Estate, Residential Real Estate, Probate, Estate Planning, Guardianship, Wills and Litigation, Personal Injury, Medical Malpractice, Business, Bankruptcy, Felonies and Misdemeanors.

FIRM PROFILE: For over 25 years, Wayne S. Shapiro, P.C. has provided professional and personalized services to Chicago and has provided practical solutions where possible.

(This Listing Continued)

WAYNE S. SHAPIRO, P.C., Chicago—Continued

WAYNE S. SHAPIRO, born Chicago, Illinois, September 27, 1949; admitted to bar, 1978, Illinois and U.S. District Court, Northern District of Illinois. *Education:* University of Illinois (B.S., 1971); Loyola University (J.D., 1978). *Member:* Chicago, DuPage County and Illinois State Bar Associations. ***PRACTICE AREAS:*** Family Law; Real Estate; Probate.

SHAW GUSSIS FISHMAN GLANTZ WOLFSON & TOWBIN LLC

321 N. CLARK STREET
SUITE 800
CHICAGO, ILLINOIS 60610
Telephone: 312-541-0151
Fax: 312-980-3888
Email: info@shawgussis.com
URL: http://www.shawgussis.com

Bankruptcy and Insolvency Law, Creditors Rights, Real Estate and related services, Land Use and Zoning, Commercial Litigation, and Secured Lending.

MEMBERS OF FIRM

ROBERT M. FISHMAN, born Bloomington, Illinois, December 28, 1953; admitted to bar, 1979, Illinois and U.S. District Court, Northern District of Illinois; 1994, U.S. Court of Appeals, Seventh Circuit; 1998, U.S. District Court, Eastern District of Wisconsin; 2002, U.S. District Court, District of Minnesota; 2003, U.S. Court of Appeals, Eighth Circuit. *Education:* University of Illinois (B.A., 1976); George Washington University (J.D., 1979). Phi Eta Sigma; Pi Sigma Alpha; James Scholar. Member of the Advisory Board of BNA's Bankruptcy Law Reporter and The Bankruptcy Strategist. Listed in Euromoney's Guide to the World's Leading Insolvency Lawyers; Guide to Leading U.S. Insolvency Lawyers; The Best Lawyers in America and Leading Illinois Attorneys. Formerly with: Levit, Mason and Fishman, Ltd. and Ross & Hardies. *Member:* Chicago (Member, Bankruptcy and Reorganization Committee, 1980—), Illinois State (Member, Commercial Banking and Bankruptcy Law Council, 1998-2002) and American (Member, Section of Business Law, 1986—; Member: Business Bankruptcy Committee, 1986—; Subcommittees on Bankruptcy Administration and U.S. Trustee and Secured Creditors, 1986—) Bar Associations; American Bankruptcy Institute (Member: Board of Directors, 1989-2002; Executive Committee of Board, 1992-2000; Chairman, 1999-2000; Immediate Past President, 1998-1999; President, 1997-1998; President-Elect, 1996-1997; Vice President, Education, 1992-1996; Chairman, Programs and Seminars Committee, 1987-1992). Fellow, American College of Bankruptcy, 1998. ***PRACTICE AREAS:*** Bankruptcy; Bankruptcy Reorganization; Creditors Rights; Commercial Litigation; Business Law. ***Email:*** rfishman@shawgussis.com

SAMUEL GUSSIS, born Des Plaines, Illinois, July 18, 1973; admitted to bar, 1999, Illinois. *Education:* Dartmouth College (A.B., magna cum laude, 1995); University of Illinois (J.D., magna cum laude, 1999). Order of the Coif. Formerly with Sidley Austin Brown & Wood. ***PRACTICE AREAS:*** Real Estate. ***Email:*** sgussis@shawgussis.com

ROBERT W. GLANTZ, born Chicago, Illinois, May 4, 1964; admitted to bar, 1989, Illinois; 1990, U.S. District Court, Northern District of Illinois; 1998, U.S. District Court, Eastern District of Wisconsin. *Education:* University of Illinois (B.S., 1986; J.D., 1989). Certified Public Accountant, Illinois, 1986. Author: "Enforcing Judgments," Young Lawyers Handbook, 2001; "Creation of an Article of Security Interest," IICLE Secured Transactions 2001 Practice Handbook. Adjunct Professor of Law, Chicago-Kent College of Law (1995-1998). *Member:* Chicago Bar Association; American Bankruptcy Institute; Chicago Mortgage Attorneys Association. ***PRACTICE AREAS:*** Bankruptcy; Bankruptcy Reorganization; Creditors Rights; Real Estate Finance; Business Law; Commercial Litigation. ***Email:*** rglantz@shawgussis.com

RANDY S. GUSSIS, born Chicago, Illinois, August 4, 1948; admitted to bar, 1982, Illinois. *Education:* University of Illinois (B.A., 1969); Illinois Institute of Technology-Chicago Kent College of Law (J.D., summa cum laude, 1982). Moot Court; Kent Law Review. *Member:* Chicago and Illinois State Bar Associations. ***PRACTICE AREAS:*** Commercial Real Estate; Lender Representation; Finance Law; Leasing Law. ***Email:*** rgussis@shawgussis.com

PETER J. ROBERTS, born Providence, Rhode Island, July 19, 1966; admitted to bar, 1991, Massachusetts and U.S. District Court, District of Massachusetts; 1996, U.S. District Court, Northern District of Illinois; 1997, Illinois; 2000, U.S. District Court, District of Colorado; 2002, U.S. Court of Appeals, Seventh Circuit; 2004, U.S. District Court, Eastern District of Michigan, U.S. Tax Court and U.S. Supreme Court. *Education:* Boston College (A.B., cum laude, 1987); Duke University School of Law (J.D., 1990). Formerly with: D'Ancona & Pflaum LLC; Craig and Macauley P.C. *Member:* Chicago Bar Association; American Bankruptcy Institute. ***PRACTICE AREAS:*** Bankruptcy; Bankruptcy Reorganization; Creditors Rights; Commercial Litigation. ***Email:*** proberts@shawgussis.com

RICHARD A. SALDINGER, born Chicago, Illinois, May 30, 1966; admitted to bar, 1992, Illinois and U.S. District Court, Northern District of Illinois; 1998, U.S. Court of Appeals, Seventh Circuit; 2000, U.S. District Court, Central District of Illinois. *Education:* University of Illinois (B.S., magna cum laude, 1988; J.D., cum laude, 1992). *Member:* Chicago Bar Association. ***PRACTICE AREAS:*** Commercial Litigation; Bankruptcy Litigation.

BRIAN L. SHAW, born Chicago, Illinois, February 28, 1967; admitted to bar, 1993, Illinois and U.S. District Court, Northern District of Illinois; 1997, Federal Trial Bar; 1998, U.S. District Court, Eastern District of Wisconsin; 2001, U.S. District Court, Northern District of Indiana; 2003, U.S. Court of Appeals, Seventh and Eighth Circuits; 2004, U.S. Supreme Court. *Education:* Tufts University (B.A., cum laude, 1989); University of Illinois (J.D., magna cum laude, 1993). Co-Author: "Taxman Cometh: Are You Prepared?," Norton Bankruptcy Law Advisor, Issue No. 7, July 1995; "The Involuntary Bankruptcy Proceeding," Business Credit, October 1996; Chapter 4A, CLLA Bankruptcy Reform Act Manual, 5th ed., 1996; "Koopmans: The End Justifies The Means," Norton Bankruptcy Law Advisor, Issue No. 4, April 1997; "To File Or Not To File A Proof of Claim: Read On And Sleep Tight," Credit Today, August 1997; "New Value Is Alive, Well and Kicking at 203 North LaSalle Street Chicago," Norton Bankruptcy Law Advisor, Issue No. 2, February 1998; "Unexpired Leases and Retail Bankruptcy," The Bankruptcy Strategist, Vol. XV, No. 7, May 1998; "Business Bankruptcy Venue," Norton Bankruptcy Law Advisor, Issue No. 11, November 1998; "Proving Insolvency in Preference Actions", The Bankruptcy Strategist, Vol. XVI, No. 11, September 1999; "Dealing with the Overlap of a Bankruptcy Case and Employment Law," The Bankruptcy Strategist, Vol. XVII, No.4; 28 U.S.C. § 1930 (a)(b); "A Problem Worth Fixing," Norton Bankruptcy Law Advisor, Issue No.4, April, 2001; "A Tale of Two Chambers," Norton Bankruptcy Law Advisor, Issue No.7, July 2001; "Defending Officers and Directors in a Management Hostile Environment," The Bankruptcy Strategist, Vol. XX, Nos. 3 & 4; "Section 547 (c)(?) : Is the Critical Vendor order the New Preference Defense," The Bankruptcy Strategist vol. XXII, No.3. Former Member, University of Illinois College of Law Recent Alumni Advisory Board, 1997-2000. *Member:* Seventh Circuit, Chicago (Secretary, Bankruptcy Section), Illinois State and American Bar Associations; American Bankruptcy Institute (Co-Chair, Young and New member Committee, 2002—; Member, Board of Directors, 2005—; Program Chair, Chicago Consumer Conference, 2004). ***PRACTICE AREAS:*** Bankruptcy; Bankruptcy Reorganization; Creditors Rights; Commercial Litigation; Business Law. ***Email:*** bshaw100@shawgussis.com

DAVID L. SHAW, born Brooklyn, New York, February 7, 1943; admitted to bar, 1966, Illinois. *Education:* University of Michigan (A.B., with distinction, 1963; J.D., with distinction, 1966). Pi Sigma Alpha; Tau Epsilon Rho. Author, Handbook: "Illinois Land Use and Zoning," National Business Institute, 1991. *Member:* Chicago and Illinois State Bar Associations. ***PRACTICE AREAS:*** Real Estate Law; Zoning and Land Use; Financing Law. ***Email:*** dshaw1@shawgussis.com

GEORGE J. SPATHIS, born Chicago, Illinois, July 22, 1965; admitted to bar, 1990, Illinois and U.S. District Court, Northern District of Illinois, including Trial Bar; U.S. Court of Appeals, Seventh Circuit. *Education:* University of Illinois (B.A., 1987); Illinois Institute of Technology, Chicago-Kent College of Law (J.D., with high honors, 1990). Order of the Coif. Executive Articles Editor, Chicago Kent Law Review. Co-Author: "Antitrust, Association and the New Economy," Association Forum, January/February 2002. Formerly with Ross & Hardies. ***LANGUAGES:*** Greek. ***PRACTICE AREAS:*** Commercial Litigation; Bankruptcy Litigation; Trade Regulation; Antitrust; General Corporate Counseling. ***Email:*** gspathis@shawgussis.com

STEVEN B. TOWBIN, born Chicago, Illinois, October 7, 1949; admitted to bar, 1975, Illinois and U.S. District Court, Northern District of Illinois including Trial Bar; 1988, U.S. Court of Appeals, Seventh Circuit; 2003, U.S. Supreme Court. *Education:* University of Illinois (B.A., cum laude, 1971); DePaul University (J.D., cum laude, 1975). Named in Chambers' America's Leading Lawyers for Business in 2004 and 2005. *Contributing Author:* "Corporate Counsel's Guide to Bankruptcy Law," *Business Laws, Inc.* 1995-1997; "16th Annual Bankruptcy and Reorganization Institute," Manual, 1996; "Bankruptcy Litigation," The Newsletter of the Bankruptcy and Insolvency Committee of the Litigation Section of the American Bar Association. Panel Member, Chicago Bar Association Seminar (Basic Bankruptcy Practice), October, 1998. Presenter at: ABI 2004 Rocky Mountain Conference; 2004 ABI Annual Meeting on issue of Critical Vendor Payments under the Doctrine of Necessity; ABI Central States Seminar on Postpetition Transfers under § 549 of the Bankruptcy Code, 2005. Formerly with: D'Ancona & Pflaum LLC; Towbin & Zazove Ltd.; Gesas & Towbin. Fellow, American College of Bankruptcy. ***REPORTED CASES:*** Capital Factor v. Knmart Corp. (In re Kmart Corp.), 359 F.3d 866 (7th Cir. 2004); Bank of America v. Moglia (In re Outboard Marine Corporation), 330 F.3d 842 (7th Cir. 2003). ***PRACTICE AREAS:*** Bankruptcy; Commercial Litigation; Corporate Reorganization; Creditors Rights. ***Email:*** stowbin@shawgussis.com

JEFFREY L. WIDMAN, born Chicago, Illinois, November 12, 1967; admitted to bar, 1994, Illinois and U.S. District Court, Northern District of Illinois including Trial Bar; 2001, U.S. District Court, Eastern District of Wisconsin and U.S. Court of Appeals, Seventh Circuit. *Education:* University of Michigan (B.A., 1989); Loyola University (J.D., 1994). ***REPORTED CASES:*** Village of Lombard v. Intergovernmental Risk Management Agency, 288 Ill.App. 3D 1003 (2nd Dist. 1997); Sungard Data Systems v. Central Parking Corp., 214 F.Supp. 2d 878 (N.D. Ill. 2002); Truck Insurance Exchange v. Katka, 911 F.Supp. 313 (N.D.Ill. 1995); Baldi v. Lynch (In re McCook Metals L.L.C.), 319 B.R. 570 (N.D.Ill. 2002). ***PRACTICE AREAS:*** Commercial Litigation; Bankruptcy Litigation. ***Email:*** jlwidman@shawgussis.com

ASSOCIATES

JOHN M. SHELDON, born Chicago, Illinois, October, 28, 1969; admitted to bar, 1998, Illinois; 2001, U.S. District Court, Northern District of Illinois. *Education:* Syracuse University (B.S., 1991); Loyola University (J.D., 1998). Moot Court; Consumer Law Review; Phi Alpha Delta. Co-Author: "Are Payments Received During 90-Day Performance Period By A Creditor Holding A Floating Lien On Inventory Preferential?" Credit Today, March 2002. *Member:* Chicago and American Bar Associations. ***PRACTICE AREAS:*** Commercial Litigation; Bankruptcy; Bankruptcy Litigation; Creditors Rights. ***Email:*** jsheldon@shawgussis.com

ALLEN J. GUON, born New York, New York, August 10, 1970; admitted to bar, 1998, Illinois; U.S. District Court, Northern District of Illinois; 2003, U.S. Court of Appeals, Eighth Circuit. *Education:* Indiana University (B.S.P.A., with distinction, 1992); Indiana University School of Law - Bloomington (J.D., cum laude, 1997; M.S.E.S., 1997). *Member:* Chicago Bar Association; American Bankruptcy Institute. ***PRACTICE AREAS:*** Bankruptcy; Bankruptcy Reorganization; Creditors Rights; Commercial Litigation; Business Law. ***Email:*** aguon@shawgussis.com

JANICE A. ALWIN, born Park Ridge, Illinois, 1972; admitted to bar, 2002, Illinois, U.S. District Court, Northern District of Illinois and U.S. Court of Appeals, Seventh Circuit; U.S. Tax Court. *Education:* Northern Illinois University (B.S., 1999); DePaul University (J.D., cum laude, 2002). Certified Public Accountant, Illinois, 1999. Formerly with D'Ancona & Pflaum LLC. ***PRACTICE AREAS:*** Bankruptcy; Bankruptcy Reorganization; Creditors Rights; Commercial Litigation; Business Law. ***Email:*** jalwin@shawgussis.com

(This Listing Continued)

MARK L. RADTKE, born LaGrange, Illinois, March 19, 1975; admitted to bar, 2001, Illinois; 2002, U.S. District Court, Northern District of Illinois. *Education:* University of Iowa (B.B.A., 1997); Chicago-Kent College of Law (J.D., with high honors, 2001). Order of the Coif. Certified Public Accountant, Illinois, 1998. *Member:* Chicago Bar Association; American Bankruptcy Institute. ***PRACTICE AREAS:*** Bankruptcy; Bankruptcy Reorganization; Creditors Rights; Commercial Litigation. ***Email:*** mradtke@shawgussis.com

BRIAN M. GRAHAM, born Oak Park, Illinois, March 17, 1961; admitted to bar, 1997, Illinois, U.S. District Court, Northern District of Illinois and U.S. District Court, Eastern District of Michigan. *Education:* DePaul University (B.A., 1988); Chicago-Kent College of Law (J.D., 1997). Formerly with Katten Muchin Zavis Rosenman. ***PRACTICE AREAS:*** Bankruptcy; Bankruptcy Reorganization; Creditors Rights; Commercial Litigation. ***Email:*** bgraham@shawgussis.com

ANN STOCKMAN, born Burnsville, Minnesota; admitted to bar, 2000, Illinois and U.S. District Court, Northern District of Illinois. *Education:* Drake University (B.A., 1997); University of Minnesota (J.D., 2000). *Member:* Illinois State Bar Association; American Bankruptcy Institute. ***PRACTICE AREAS:*** Bankruptcy; Bankruptcy Reorganization; Creditors Rights; Finance. ***Email:*** astockman@shawgussis.com

PATRICK A. CLISHAM, born Naperville, Illinois; admitted to bar, 2002, Illinois; U.S. District Court, Northern District of Illinois; 2004, Arizona. *Education:* Northern Illinois University (B.A., 1992); DePaul University (J.D., cum laude, 2002). ***PRACTICE AREAS:*** Corporate Restructuring; Bankruptcy; Creditors Rights. ***Email:*** pclisham@shawgussis.com

SAMUEL A. LICHTENFELD, born St. Louis, Missouri, November 3, 1976; admitted to bar, 2002, Illinois. *Education:* Northwestern University (B.A., 1999); Boston University (J.D., 2002). ***PRACTICE AREAS:*** Real Estate. ***Email:*** slichtenfeld@shawgussis.com

MATTHEW A. SWANSON, born Urbana, Illinois, April 9, 1975; admitted to bar, 2000, Illinois; 2004, Colorado and U.S. District Court, District of Colorado;. *Education:* University of Michigan (B.A, with honors, 1997); University of Southern California (J.D., 2000). *Member:* American Bankruptcy Institute; American Bar Association. ***PRACTICE AREAS:*** Insolvency; Bankruptcy Reorganization; Creditors Rights; Commercial Litigation. ***Email:*** mswanson@shawgussis.com

KRISTINA M. SUMMERS, born Champaign, Illinois, December 19, 1975; admitted to bar, 2002, Illinois. *Education:* University of Illinois, Urbana-Champaign (B.A., 1998); Tulane University School of Law (J.D., cum laude, 2002). *Member:* Illinois State Bar Association. ***PRACTICE AREAS:*** Real Estate; Finance. ***Email:*** ksummers@shawgussis.com

THOMAS C. WENDT, born Chicago, Illinois, November 19, 1965; admitted to bar, 2002, Illinois. *Education:* Loyola University (B.A., 1998); Chicago-Kent College of Law (J.D., 2001). Recipient, CALI Award, Advanced Legal Writing for the International Business Attorney. *Member:* Chicago and American Bar Associations. ***PRACTICE AREAS:*** Commercial Real Estate. ***Email:*** twendt@shawgussis.com

STEVEN B. ISAACSON, born Chicago, Illinois, May 10, 1956; admitted to bar, 1981, Illinois. *Education:* University of Illinois at Champaign-Urbana (B.A., magna cum laude, 1978); Cornell University Law School (J.D., cum laude, 1981). Phi Beta Kappa. Member, Board of Editors, Cornell International Law Journal, 1980-1981. ***PRACTICE AREAS:*** Commercial Real Estate; Real Estate Finance; Banking Law. ***Email:*** sisaacson@shawgussis.com

GORDON E. GOUVEIA, born Hobart, Indiana, January 27, 1979; admitted to bar, 2004, Illinois. *Education:* Boston College (B.A., Political Science, 2001); Vanderbilt University (J.D., 2004). Phi Beta Kappa. Author: "Making a Mountain out of a Mogul: Jeremy Bloom v. NCAA and Unjustified Denial of Compensation under NCAA Amateurism Rules," 6 Vand. J. Ent. L. & Prac. 22 (2003). *Member:* Chicago Bar Association (Vice Chair, Young Lawyers Section Bankruptcy Committee, 2005-2006). ***PRACTICE AREAS:*** Corporate Reorganization; Creditors Rights; Bankruptcy Litigation; Commercial Litigation. ***Email:*** ggouveia@shawgussis.com

OF COUNSEL

RICHARD M. FOGEL, born Chicago, Illinois, June 4, 1955; admitted to bar, 1980, Illinois and U.S. District Court, Northern District of Illinois. *Education:* Northwestern University (B.S., 1977); University of Illinois (J.D., 1980). Member, Panel of Chapter 7 Bankruptcy Trustees, Northern District of Illinois, 1981—. *Member:* Chicago Bar Association; National Association of Bankruptcy Trustees; American Bankruptcy Institute. ***PRACTICE AREAS:*** Insolvency. ***Email:*** rfogel@shawgussis.com

JAY S. GELLER, born New York, N.Y., April 22, 1960; admitted to bar, 1985, Illinois and U.S. District Court, Northern District of Illinois; 1989, U.S. Court of Appeals, Sixth Circuit; 1992, U.S. Court of Appeals, Seventh Circuit; 1999, U.S. District Court, Northern District of Oklahoma; 2000, Maine; 2002, U.S. Court of Appeals, First Circuit and U.S. District Court, District of Maine. *Education:* Dartmouth College (A.B., magna cum laude, 1982), Phi Beta Kappa; Boston University (J.D., cum laude, 1985). Certified Business Bankruptcy Specialist. President, Pro Bono Advocates, 1994-1997. *Member:* Maine State and American Bar Associations; American Bankruptcy Institute. (Also practicing individually). ***PRACTICE AREAS:*** Bankruptcy; Bankruptcy Reorganization; Creditors Rights; Commercial Litigation. ***Email:*** jgeller@maine.rr.com

SHEEHAN & LOWER

CHICAGO, ILLINOIS

(See Cary)

Civil Trial Practice, Product Liability, Insurance Coverage, Defense of the Amusement Industry, Defense of Roller Skating Establishments, Aviation, Employment Discrimination and Employment Law.

SHEFSKY & FROELICH LTD.

Established in 1970

111 EAST WACKER DRIVE, SUITE 2800

CHICAGO, ILLINOIS 60601

Telephone: 312-527-4000
Fax: 312-527-4011
Email: sfltd@shefskylaw.com
URL: http://www.shefskylaw.com

Acquisitions, Divestitures and Mergers, Banking and Financial Institutions, Gaming, Food Industry, Construction, Corporate, Securities, Securitization and Financing, Venture Capital, Real Estate and Land Use, Employment, Employee Benefits and ESOPs, Franchise, Government, Health Care and Hospital, Insurance and Insurance Regulatory, State and Federal Litigation and Appellate Practice, Bankruptcy, Debtors'/Creditors' Rights, Partnerships, Estate Planning and Probate, Taxation, Technology.

FIRM PROFILE: Trained to approach lawsuits and transactions from a business perspective, the firm's attorneys handle cases and matters cost-effectively and with client goals in mind. We add value to growing companies by sharing their vision and providing creative ways to respond to ever-accelerating changes in business and finance.

RICHARD E. ADERMAN, born Chicago, Illinois, June 4, 1966; admitted to bar, 1992, Illinois and U.S. District Court, Northern District of Illinois; 1993, U.S. Tax Court. *Education:* Wesleyan University (B.A., 1989); University of Chicago (J.D., with high honors, 1992). ***PRACTICE AREAS:*** Tax; Corporate. ***Email:*** raderman@shefskylaw.com

JAMES D. ANDERSON, born 1972; admitted to bar, 1998, Illinois; U.S. District Court, Northern District of Illinois; U.S. Court of Appeals, Eighth Circuit. *Education:* Arizona State University (B.S., summa cum laude, 1994); University of Illinois (M.B.A., 1998); University of Illinois College of Law (J.D., 1998). Beta Gamma Sigma; Tau Kappa Epsilon; Order of the Coif. Harno Fellow. Member and Executive Administrative Editor, University of Illinois Law Review. *Member:* Chicago and American Bar Associations. ***PRACTICE AREAS:*** Venture Capital; Securities; Corporate Finance. ***Email:*** JAnderson@shefskylaw.com

KATHRYN KOVITZ ARNOLD, born Chicago, Illinois, September 24, 1965; admitted to bar, 1990, Illinois. *Education:* University of Illinois (B.S., high honors, 1987); Northwestern University (J.D., 1990). *Member:* Chicago, Illinois State and American Bar Associations. ***PRACTICE AREAS:*** Real Estate; Business Law. ***Email:*** karnold@shefskylaw.com

JAMES R. ASMUSSEN, born Evanston, Illinois, April 20, 1963; admitted to bar, 1989, Illinois. *Education:* Villanova University (B.S.A., magna cum laude, 1985); University of Illinois (J.D., with high honors, 1989). *Member:* Chicago Bar Association. ***PRACTICE AREAS:*** Corporate and Securities; Mergers and Acquisitions. ***Email:*** jasmussen@shefskylaw.com

MICHAEL J. CHOATE, born Milwaukee, Wisconsin, June 21, 1959; admitted to bar, 1989, Illinois. *Education:* Loyola University (B.B.A., in Economics, 1981); IIT Chicago-Kent College of Law (J.D., 1989). *Member:* Chicago and American Bar Association. ***PRACTICE AREAS:*** Securities; Corporate. ***Email:*** mchoate@shefskylaw.com

ERHARD R. CHORLÉ, born Linz, Austria, April 10, 1955; admitted to bar, 1984, Illinois. *Education:* DePaul University (B.S., 1978); John Marshall Law School (J.D., 1984). ***PRACTICE AREAS:*** Securities; Gaming. ***Email:*** echorle@shefskylaw.com

KIMBERLY M. COPP, born Milwaukee, Wisconsin, January 12, 1971; admitted to bar, 1997, Illinois. *Education:* Miami University (B.S., 1993); John Marshall Law School (J.D., magna cum laude, 1997). *Member:* Chicago and American Bar Associations. ***PRACTICE AREAS:*** Corporate; Securities. ***Email:*** kcopp@shefskylaw.com

MICHAEL A. CRAMAROSSO, born Chicago, Illinois, November 25, 1960; admitted to bar, 1985, Ohio; 1990, Illinois. *Education:* DePaul University (B.A., with highest honors, 1982); Duke University (J.D., with honors, 1985). *Member:* Chicago and American Bar Associations. ***PRACTICE AREAS:*** Business and Corporate; Mergers and Acquisitions; Commercial Finance; Financing and Secured Lending; Real Estate. ***Email:*** mcramarosso@shefskylaw.com

BRIAN L. CROWE, born Chicago, Illinois, January 28, 1939; admitted to bar, 1964, Illinois and U.S. District Court, Northern District of Illinois. *Education:* Loras College (B.A., 1960); Loyola University (J.D., 1964); University of Virginia (LL.M., 1982). Corporation Counsel, City of Chicago, 1997-1999; Judge, Cook County Circuit Court (appointed by Illinois Supreme Court, 1979); Presiding Judge of Real Estate Tax Court, 1986-1987. Law Jury Division 1980-1986. *Member:* Chicago, Illinois State and American Bar Associations; Illinois Judges Association; Illinois Trial Lawyers Association; Chicago Council of Lawyers; American Inns of Court; Chicago Inn of Court; Society of Professionals in Dispute Resolution; JAMS/Endispute; American Arbitration Association; National Association of Securities Dealers. ***PRACTICE AREAS:*** Chancery Practice; Commercial Litigation; Alternative Dispute Resolution. ***Email:*** bcrowe@shefskylaw.com

HOWARD A. DAVIS, born Chicago, Illinois, October 30, 1955; admitted to bar, 1980, Illinois; U.S. District Court, Northern District of Illinois including Trial Bar and U.S. Court of Appeals, Seventh Circuit. *Education:* University of Illinois (B.S., in Accounting, 1977); IIT Chicago-Kent College of Law (J.D., with highest honors, 1980). *Member:* Chicago, Illinois State and American Bar Associations; Illinois Restaurant Association. ***PRACTICE AREAS:*** Litigation; Corporate; Intellectual Property; Food Law. ***Email:*** hdavis@shefskylaw.com

CARY E. DONHAM, born East St. Louis, Illinois, November, 11, 1949; admitted to bar, 1988, Illinois and U.S. District Court, Northern District of Illinois. *Education:* Western Illinois University (B.A., 1974); IIT Chicago-Kent College of Law (J.D., 1988). *Member:* Illinois State and American Bar Associations. ***PRACTICE AREAS:*** Litigation; Employment. ***Email:*** cdonham@shefskylaw.com

LYNN A. ELLENBERGER, born Pittsburgh, Pennsylvania, April 22, 1965; admitted to bar, 1990, Pennsylvania; 1997, Illinois. *Education:* Washington & Jefferson College (B.A., magna cum laude, 1987); Vanderbilt University (J.D., 1990). Phi Beta Kappa. Re-

(This Listing Continued)

SHEFSKY & FROELICH LTD., Chicago—Continued

cipient, Junius I. Alison Prize for public interest service. Law Clerk to the Hon. Maurice B. Cohill, Jr., U.S. District Court, Western District of Pennsylvania, 1990-1992. ***PRACTICE AREAS:*** Litigation. ***Email:*** LEllenberger@shefskylaw.com

DAVID M. FRANEK, born Vernon, Connecticut, June 14, 1954; admitted to bar, 1980, New Hampshire; 1982, Connecticut; 1996, Massachusetts; 1998, Illinois. *Education:* University of Pennsylvania (B.A., magna cum laude, 1976); Duke University (J.D., 1980). *Member:* Connecticut and New Hampshire Bar Associations; International Council of Shopping Centers. ***PRACTICE AREAS:*** Real Estate Development; Leasing Law. ***Email:*** dfranek@shefskylaw.com

CEZAR M. FROELICH, born Deutsch Krone, Germany, January 1, 1946; admitted to bar, 1970, Illinois. *Education:* Loyola University (B.S., 1967; J.D., 1970). *Member:* Chicago, Illinois State and American Bar Associations. ***PRACTICE AREAS:*** Securities; Corporate. ***Email:*** cfroelich@shefskylaw.com

THEODORE G. GERTZ, born Chicago, Illinois, September 8, 1936; admitted to bar, 1962, Illinois. *Education:* University of Chicago (B.A., 1958); Northwestern University (J.D., 1962). *Member:* Chicago and Illinois State Bar Associations; Decalogue Society of Lawyers; Chicago Estate Planning Council. Fellow: Illinois Bar Foundation; Law Club of Chicago. ***PRACTICE AREAS:*** Estate Planning; Deferred Compensation; Trusts and Estates; General Corporate. ***Email:*** tgertz@shefskylaw.com

MITCHELL D. GOLDSMITH, born Chicago, Illinois, February 24, 1953; admitted to bar, 1978, Illinois. *Education:* University of Pennsylvania (B.A., summa cum laude, 1975); University of Chicago (J.D., 1978). *Member:* Illinois State Bar Association. ***PRACTICE AREAS:*** Securities; General Corporate. ***Email:*** mgoldsmith@shefskylaw.com

KAREN R. GOODMAN, born Chicago, Illinois, November 16, 1952; admitted to bar, 1977, Illinois and U.S. District Court, Northern District of Illinois including Trial Bar; U.S. Court of Appeals, Seventh Circuit. *Education:* University of Illinois (B.S., 1974); Loyola University of Chicago (J.D., 1977). ***PRACTICE AREAS:*** Bankruptcy; Commercial Law. ***Email:*** kgoodman@shefskylaw.com

JACK GUTHMAN, born Cologne, Germany, April 19, 1938; admitted to bar, 1963, Illinois. *Education:* Northwestern University (B.A., 1960); Yale University (LL.B., 1963). Member, 1970-1987 and Chairman, 1975-1987, Zoning Board of Appeals, City of Chicago. *Member:* Legal Club of Chicago; Economic Club of Chicago; Lambda Alpha International (Past President). Fellow, American Bar Foundation. ***PRACTICE AREAS:*** Zoning Law; Administrative Law; Government Regulatory Law; Legislative Law. ***Email:*** jguthman@shefskylaw.com

JACK J. HAGERTY, born Chicago, Illinois, May 3, 1958; admitted to bar, 1990, Illinois; U.S. District Court, Northern District of Illinois; U.S. District Court, Central District of Illinois; U.S. Court of Appeals, Seventh Circuit. *Education:* Elmhurst College; St. Mary's College (B.B.A., 1981); Chicago-Kent College of Law (J.D., with high honors, 1990). Certified Public Accountant, Illinois, 1983. *Member:* Chicago and Illinois State Bar Associations. ***PRACTICE AREAS:*** Civil and Criminal Litigation; Chancery; Commercial Litigation; Insurance Law; Securities Litigation; Class Action and Derivative. ***Email:*** jhagerty@shefskylaw.com

EDWARD J. HALPER, born Chicago, Illinois, November 4, 1946; admitted to bar, 1973, Illinois and U.S. District Court, Northern District of Illinois; 1978, U.S. Court of Appeals, Seventh Circuit. *Education:* St. Mary of the Lake Seminary (A.B., 1968); DePaul University (J.D., 1973). ***PRACTICE AREAS:*** Securities; Corporate Finance; Banks and Banking. ***Email:*** ehalper@shefskylaw.com

BRIAN F. HYNES, born Chicago, Illinois, November 29, 1970; admitted to bar, 1996, Illinois; U.S. District Court, Northern District of Illinois. *Education:* University of Illinois (B.A., Speech Communications, 1992); Loyola University (J.D., 1996). Listed in: Who's Who: American Law Students. Recipient: Illinois General Assembly Scholarship; Rose Marie Russo Scholarship. Research Editor, Consumer Law Reporter, 1995-1996. Lecturer: "Impact of Electric Deregulation on Municipalities," Illinois Government Finance Officers' Association Annual Meeting, June, 1999; "Electric Deregulation and Municipalities," Illinois Municipal League Annual Conference. Member, Board of Directors, International Visitors Center of Chicago. Commissioner, Southwest Home Equity Commission. Communications and Special Projects Coordinator, Office of the Speaker of the Illinois House of Representatives, 1992-1994. Statewide Coordinator, Friends of Michael J. Madigan, Democratic Party of Illinois, Chicago, Illinois, 1998—. ***REPORTED CASES:*** Schmude v. Michael Sheahan, 00 L 006557; Simmons et al. v. The Illinois State Police, et al., 99 CH 09799. ***PRACTICE AREAS:*** Government Relations; Land Use; Corporate Law. ***Email:*** BHynes@shefskylaw.com

RICHARD L. INGRAM, born Charleston, Illinois, August 6, 1956; admitted to bar, 1981, Illinois and U.S. District Court, Northern District of Illinois. *Education:* Eastern Illinois University (B.A., with honors, 1978); University of Tennessee at Knoxville (J.D., 1981). Managing Editor and Articles Editor, The Tennessee Law Review, 1980-1981. Author: "Municipal Corporations-Alienation of Property-Rejection of Governmental/Proprietary Test," 48 Tennessee Law Review 750. Member, Coles County Board, 1975-1978; Coles County Regional Planning Commission, 1975-1978. *Member:* American Bar Association. ***PRACTICE AREAS:*** Real Estate. ***Email:*** RIngram@shefskylaw.com

PAUL T. JENSON, born Arlington Heights, Illinois, June 18, 1971; admitted to bar, 1996, Illinois. *Education:* Marquette University (B.S., 1993); Loyola University of Chicago (J.D., 1996). Phi Alpha Delta. *Member:* Chicago, Illinois State and American Bar Associations. ***PRACTICE AREAS:*** Corporate; Securities; Estate Planning. ***Email:*** pjenson@shefskylaw.com

PAUL L. KELLEY, born Los Angeles, California, November 24, 1961; admitted to bar, 1986, Arizona 1987, Illinois. *Education:* Carthage College (B.A., summa cum laude, 1983); The John Marshall Law School (J.D., with high distinction, 1986). *Member:* Maricopa County and Illinois State Bar Associations; State Bar of Arizona. ***PRACTICE AREAS:*** Real Estate; Banking; Secured Transactions. ***Email:*** pkelley@skefskylaw.com

JOHN F. KENNEDY, born Chicago, Illinois, September 28, 1958; admitted to bar, 1987, Illinois and U.S. District Court, Northern District of Illinois. *Education:* Niles College of Loyola University (B.A., cum laude, 1980); DePaul University (J.D., with honors, 1987). Co-Author: "Guilty Pleas in Illinois," Loyola University Law Review, Judicial Conference Issue, Fall, 1987. *Member:* Chicago and Illinois State Bar Associations. ***PRACTICE AREAS:*** Municipal Law; Equitable Distribution; Shareholder Disputes; Restrictive Covenants; Trade Secrets; Zoning Law; Commercial Litigation; Constitutional Law; Appellate Practice. ***Email:*** jkennedy@shefskylaw.com

LAWRENCE M. KERN, born Harvey, Illinois, October 8, 1962; admitted to bar, 1988, Illinois. *Education:* University of Illinois (B.S., 1985; J.D., 1988). Certified Public Accountant, Illinois, 1985. *Member:* Chicago Bar Association. ***PRACTICE AREAS:*** Estate Planning; Probate and Trust Administration; Taxation. ***Email:*** lkern@shefskylaw.com

EDWARD J. KUS, born Chicago, Illinois, August 8, 1953; admitted to bar, 1978, Illinois; 1979, U.S. District Court, Northern District of Illinois; 1993, U.S. Supreme Court. *Education:* DePaul University (B.A., 1975); Northern Illinois University Law School (J.D., 1978). Executive Director, Mayor's Zoning Reform Commission, 2000-2004. City of Chicago Zoning Administator, 2001-2004. First Deputy Commissioner - City of Chicago Department of Planning and Development, 2003-2004. *Member:* Chicago and Illinois State Bar Associations; Advocats Society; Lambda Alpha International. ***PRACTICE AREAS:*** Zoning and Land Use Law; Government Regulatory Law; Municipal and Legislative Law. ***Email:*** EKus@shefskylaw.com

ANTHONY R. LICATA, born Du Quoin, Illinois, July 19, 1954; admitted to bar, 1979, Illinois. *Education:* MacMurray College (B.S., summa cum laude, 1976); Harvard University (J.D., cum laude, 1979). Director: Metropolitan Chicago Healthcare Council, Chicago, Illinois. Member, Highland Park Plan Commission, 1997—. Member, Board of Trustees, Kohl Children's Museum. ***PRACTICE AREAS:*** Real Estate Law; Land Use Regulation Law; Venture Capital Law. ***Email:*** alicata@shefskylaw.com

RALPH A. MANTYNBAND, born Chicago, Illinois, December 4, 1929; admitted to bar, 1953, Illinois. *Education:* University of Illinois (B.S., 1950); Harvard University; University of Chicago, Graduate School of Business; University of Chicago (J.D., 1952). *Member:* Chicago, Illinois State and American Bar Associations. ***PRACTICE AREAS:*** Litigation; International Law. ***Email:*** rmantynband@shefskylaw.com

JEFFRY A. MELNICK, born Chicago, Illinois, June 3, 1946; admitted to bar, 1972, Ohio; 1998, Illinois. *Education:* Carleton College (B.A., cum laude, 1968); University of Edinburgh, Scotland; Yale University (J.D., 1971). ***PRACTICE AREAS:*** Mergers and Acquisitions; Corporate Finance; Securities Law; International Transactions; Corporate. ***Email:*** jmelnick@shefskylaw.com

IRA S. NEIMAN, born Chicago, Illinois, January 25, 1960; admitted to bar, 1983, Illinois; U.S. District Court, Northern District of Illinois, U.S. Tax Court and U.S. Supreme Court. *Education:* Loyola University (B.B.A., 1980); DePaul University (J.D., 1983). Beta Alpha Psi. Certified Public Accountant, Illinois, 1981. *Member:* Chicago and American (Member, Real Property, Probate and Trust Law Section) Bar Associations; Chicago Estate Planning Council. ***PRACTICE AREAS:*** Probate; Taxation; Mergers, Acquisitions and Divestitures; Corporate Finance. ***Email:*** ineiman@shefskylaw.com

BRETT NOLAN, born Chicago, Illinois, August 15, 1973; admitted to bar, 1998, Illinois. *Education:* Middlebury College (B.A., 1995); Washington University (J.D., 1998). *Member:* Chicago and Illinois State Bar Associations. ***PRACTICE AREAS:*** Litigation. ***Email:*** bnolan@shefskylaw.com

DOUGLAS M. RAMSEY, born Tucson, Arizona, September 26, 1972; admitted to bar, 1998, Illinois. *Education:* Southern Methodist University (B.A., 1995); DePaul University College of Law (J.D., 1998). Phi Beta Kappa. Symposium Editor, DePaul Law Review. *Member:* Chicago, Illinois State and American Bar Associations. ***PRACTICE AREAS:*** Commercial Litigation; Municipal Law. ***Email:*** dramsey@shefskylaw.com

LAWRENCE C. RUBIN, born Chicago, Illinois, March 25, 1948; admitted to bar, 1972, Illinois. *Education:* University of Illinois (B.S., 1969); Northwestern University (J.D., 1972). Certified Public Accountant, Illinois, 1969. *Member:* Chicago and Illinois State Bar Associations. ***PRACTICE AREAS:*** Litigation. ***Email:*** lrubin@shefskylaw.com

MICHAEL J. SCHALLER, born Milwaukee, Wisconsin, January 16, 1950; admitted to bar, 1975, Illinois. *Education:* University of Illinois (B.S., with highest honors, 1971; J.D., 1975). Certified Public Accountant, Illinois, 1972. ***PRACTICE AREAS:*** Mergers and Acquisitions; Corporate Finance; Venture Capital; Gaming; Health Care. ***Email:*** mschaller@shefskylaw.com

JOHN C. SCIACCOTTA, born Chicago, Illinois, April 15, 1962; admitted to bar, 1987, Illinois and U.S. District Court, Northern District of Illinois including Trial Bar; 1991, U.S. Court of Appeals, 7th Circuit; 1993, U.S. Court of Federal Claims, U.S. Court of the Armed Forces and U.S. Supreme Court; 1995, U.S. Tax Court; 1998, U.S. District Court, District of Massachusetts, U.S. District Court, Western District of Ohio and U.S. District Court, Western District of Kentucky; U.S. District Court, Eastern District of Louisiana. *Education:* Creighton University (B.S.B.A., 1984); DePaul University (J.D., 1987). Listed in "40 Illinois Attorneys Under 40 Years Old to Watch," Chicago Daily Law Bulletin, 2000 Edition. Lecturer: Civil Practice Update, 1999 and General Practice Update, 1999, Illinois State Bar Association Seminars. Panel Participant, Illinois State Bar Association Cable T.V. Programs: "Anatomy of a Trial," 2003; "Looking for Mr. or Ms. Good Lawyer," 2003. *Member:* Chicago, Fenwick (Founding Director, 1997— Secretary), DuPage County, Illinois State (Member: Section on Civil Practice and Procedure Council), Federal and American Bar Associations; Justinian Society of Lawyers (President Elect, 2003-2004); Lawyers Club of Chicago; The Chicago Inn of Court; Catholic Lawyers Guild of Chicago. Fellow, Illinois Bar Foundation, 1998—. ***PRACTICE AREAS:*** Trial and Appellate Practice; Complex Commercial Litigation; Chancery Practice; Arbitration and Mediation. ***Email:*** jsci@shefskylaw.com

MICHAEL P. SHEEHAN, born February 22, 1971; admitted to bar, 1996, Illinois. *Education:* University of Illinois, Champaign (B.A., 1993); DePaul University (JD., 1996). Member, Law Review, De Paul University School of Law, 1995-1996. Author: "Retaliatory Discharge of In-House Counsel-Ethical Obligations v. Fiduciary Duties," 45 De Paul Law Review 859, 1996. ***PRACTICE AREAS:*** Litigation; Commercial Law. ***Email:*** msheehan@shefskylaw.com

(This Listing Continued)

JUDITH S. SHERWIN, born Chicago, Illinois, August 20, 1945; admitted to bar, 1978, Illinois, U.S. District Court, Northern District of Illinois and U.S. Court of Appeals, Seventh Circuit; 1979, U.S. Tax Court; 1982, U.S. Supreme Court; 1982, U.S. District Court, Northern District of Illinois, Trial Bar. *Education:* Roosevelt University (B.A., 1972; M.A., 1975); John Marshall Law School (J.D., 1978). Adjunct Professor: The John Marshall Law School, 1989-1992; Spertus College of Judaica, Master of Human Services Program, 1991-1993; Loyola University School of Law, 2001—. Instructor, Political Science, Oakton Community College, 1981-1983. Inquiry Board, 1991-1994 and Hearing Board, 1988-1991, Attorney Registration and Disciplinary Commission of The State of Illinois. *Member:* Decalogue Society of Lawyers. ***PRACTICE AREAS:*** Nursing Home Regulation; Real Estate; Corporate; Litigation; Attorney Discipline Defense. ***Email:*** jsherwin@shefskylaw.com

ALLAN T. SLAGEL, born Chicago, Illinois, March 16, 1960; admitted to bar, 1988, Illinois and U.S. District Court, Northern District of Illinois; U.S. District Court, Central District of Illinois; U.S. District Court, Eastern District of Michigan; U.S. District Court, District of Colorado; U.S. Court of Appeals, 7th Circuit. *Education:* Indiana University (B.S., 1985; J.D., magna cum laude, 1988). *Member:* Chicago, Illinois State and American Bar Associations; Association of Trial Lawyers of America. ***PRACTICE AREAS:*** Litigation. ***Email:*** aslagel@shefskylaw.com

PATRICIA S. SPRATT, born Aurora, Illinois, June 13, 1949; admitted to bar, 1991, Illinois; 1992, U.S. District Court, Northern District of Illinois and U.S. Court of Appeals, 7th Circuit; 1993, U.S. District Court, Northern District of Indiana; 1996, U.S. Supreme Court. *Education:* Loyola University Chicago School of Law (J.D., 1991). *Member:* Chicago, Illinois State and American Bar Associations. ***PRACTICE AREAS:*** Commercial Litigation. ***Email:*** pspratt@shefskylaw.com

JOEL J. SPRAYREGEN, born Jersey City, New Jersey, March 10, 1934; admitted to bar, 1958, Illinois. *Education:* Northwestern University (B.S., 1955); Yale University (LL.B., 1958). Member, Character and Fitness Commission of Illinois Supreme Court, 1985-1997. *Member:* Chicago (Chairman, Mental Health Committee, 1976), Illinois State and American (Chairman, Libel and Privacy Subcommittee, 1972) Bar Associations. ***PRACTICE AREAS:*** Litigation. ***Email:*** jsprayregen@shefskylaw.com

JEREMY STONEHILL, born Queens, New York, March 23, 1970; admitted to bar, 1997, Illinois. *Education:* University of Michigan (B.B.A., 1992); Loyola University (J.D., magna cum laude, 1997). Certified Public Accountant, Maryland, 1993. *Member:* Chicago and Illinois State Bar Associations. ***PRACTICE AREAS:*** Securities; Corporate; Tax. ***Email:*** jstonehill@shefskylaw.com

LAWRENCE J. SUFFREDIN, JR., born Evergreen Park, Illinois, October 5, 1947; admitted to bar, 1973, Illinois and U.S. District Court, Northern District of Illinois. *Education:* Loyola University (B.A., 1969); Georgetown University (J.D., 1972). Instructor, John Marshall Law School, 1975-1983. [U.S. Air Force, 1972-1973]. ***PRACTICE AREAS:*** Government Relations; Administrative Law. ***Email:*** lsuffredin@aol.com

STUART K. TAUSSIG, born Milwaukee, Wisconsin, December 19, 1937; admitted to bar, 1960, Illinois, Wisconsin and U.S. Tax Court; U.S. Court of Appeals, 7th Circuit and U.S. District Court, Northern District of Illinois. *Education:* University of Wisconsin (B.B.A., 1957; J.D., 1960). Member, Wisconsin Law Review, 1958-1959. Certified Public Accountant, Wisconsin, 1961. *Member:* Chicago and American Bar Associations; Chicago Council of Lawyers. ***PRACTICE AREAS:*** General Business; Closely Held Business; Mergers and Acquisitions; Tax; Estate and Succession Planning; Conflict Resolution. ***Email:*** staussig@shefskylaw.com

SUSAN W. WILES, born Berea, Ohio, October 25, 1964; admitted to bar, 1991, Illinois; U.S. District Court, Northern District of Illinois. *Education:* Baldwin-Wallace College (B.A., 1987); Northwestern University School of Law (J.D., 1991). Former In-house Counsel, Small Business Administration. Appointed by President George W. Bush to serve as Counselor to the Administrator of the U.S. Small Business Administration, 2001 to 2002. *Member:* Illinois State Bar Association. ***PRACTICE AREAS:*** Corporate Law; Securities Law. ***Email:*** SWiles@shefskylaw.com

JAMES D. WILSON, born Royal Oak, Michigan, November 7, 1950; admitted to bar, 1978, Illinois and U.S. District Court, Northern District of Illinois. *Education:* Oregon State University (B.S., 1973); IIT/Chicago-Kent College of Law (J.D., with high honors, 1978). *Member:* Chicago Bar Association; American Judicature Society. ***PRACTICE AREAS:*** Chancery; Business Litigation; Securities. ***Email:*** jwilson@shefskylaw.com

Ellen M. Avery
Susanna M. Brown
Christopher M. Gibbs
Elizabeth Harvey
Heather A. Jackson
Kristin A. Klaczek
Kevin M. Lippert
Megan L. McCoy
Ronald J. McDermott
Brian P. Monahan
Barton J. O'Brien
Thomas R. Pappas
Gabriel Reilly-Bates
Suzanne L. Sias
Nicolette L. Sonntag
Kim R. Walberg
Brent R. Walters

OF COUNSEL

PAUL D. FISCHER, born Chicago, Illinois, February 17, 1943; admitted to bar, 1968, Illinois; 1972, U.S. Court of Appeals, 7th Circuit and U.S. Supreme Court. *Education:* Loyola University (B.B.A., 1966; J.D., 1967). ***PRACTICE AREAS:*** Real Estate; Lender Finance. ***Email:*** pfischer@shefskylaw.com

CHANNING BLAIR HESSE, born Sherman, Texas, December 5, 1968; admitted to bar, 1994, Illinois and U.S. District Court, Northern District of Illinois. *Education:* Northern University (B.A., with honors, 1991); Chicago-Kent College of Law (J.D., with honors, 1994). *Member:* Chicago Bar Association. ***PRACTICE AREAS:*** Commercial Litigation. ***Email:*** cbhesse@shefskylaw.com

LLOYD E. SHEFSKY, born Lake Village, Arkansas, February 18, 1941; admitted to bar, 1965, Illinois; 1970, U.S. Tax Court; 1973, U.S. Supreme Court and Florida. *Education:* DePaul University (B.S.C., 1962); University of Chicago (J.D., 1965). Author: "*Entrepreneurs Are Made, Not Born,*" McGraw-Hill, 1994. Clinical Professor, Kellogg Graduate School of Management. *Member:* The Florida Bar. ***PRACTICE AREAS:*** Entrepreneurial Ventures; General Corporate; Tax. ***Email:*** lloyd@shefskyltd.com

SENIOR COUNSEL

ELIZABETH J. BODDY, admitted to bar, 1992, Illinois. *Education:* Augustana College (B.A., 1977); Northern Illinois University (J.D., 1992). Phi Alpha Delta. National Moot Court Team. Recipient: Outstanding Woman Student Award, Northern Illinois College of Law. Arbitration Panelist, DuPage Court Annexed Program. Former President, DuPage County American Inn of Court. *Member:* DuPage County (Former Director and Chair, Civil Practice Committee) and Illinois State Bar Associations. ***PRACTICE AREAS:*** Litigation. ***Email:*** eboddy@shefskylaw.com

JOSEPH P. GATTUSO, born Chicago, Illinois, June 27, 1959; admitted to bar, 1990, Illinois. *Education:* University of Illinois (B.A., 1984); DePaul University (J.D., 1990). Member: Woodstock Plan Commission, Woodstock, Illinois, 1994-1995; Advisory Committee on The Historical Woodstock Square, Woodstock, Illinois, 1994-1995. *Member:* Chicago and American Bar Associations. ***LANGUAGES:*** German. ***PRACTICE AREAS:*** Real Estate; Zoning, Planning and Land Use; Building and Public Safety Codes; Liquor Licensing; Licensing. ***Email:*** jgattuso@shefskylaw.com

KATHLEEN F. HOWLETT, born Chicago, Illinois, May 1, 1949; admitted to bar, 1985, Illinois; 1986, U.S. Court of Appeals, Seventh Circuit; 1991, U.S. Supreme Court; 1996, U.S. District Court, Northern District of Illinois. *Education:* Marquette University (B.S., 1970); Loyola University Institute for Health Law (LL.M., 1994); Loyola University of Chicago School of Law (J.D., 1985). ***PRACTICE AREAS:*** Health Care. ***Email:*** khowlett@shefskylaw.com

DAVID W. NYBERG, born 1955; admitted to bar, 1980, Illinois and Florida; U.S. Tax Court; U.S. District Court, Northern District of Illinois. *Education:* DePaul University (B.S.C., 1977; J.D., 1980). *Member:* Chicago and Illinois State Bar Associations; The Florida Bar. ***PRACTICE AREAS:*** Trusts and Estates; Probate. ***Email:*** dnyberg@shefskylaw.com

(This Listing Continued)

WILLIAM NEWELL SIEBERT

Established in 1969

307 NORTH MICHIGAN AVENUE, SUITE 924
CHICAGO, ILLINOIS 60601
Telephone: 312-329-0646
Fax: 312-553-4419
Email: wsiebert@siebert-immigrationlaw.com
URL: http://www.williamsiebert.com

Naturalization, Working Visas, Consular Practice, Family and Employment Based Permanent Residency Cases, PERM Labor Certification, Kennedy McCain.

FIRM PROFILE: Mr. Siebert has concentrated in immigration law since 1969, with an emphasis in representing health care professionals, hospitals, medical schools, physician recruiters and related health care providers. He also serves the needs of businesses seeking highly educated professionals of all disciplines. He is active as a speaker and author of immigration law topics as they relate to the needs of the health care industry.

Communication is primarily conducted telephonically. E-mail, fax and related electronic computerized communication is also a normal part of the practice.

WILLIAM NEWELL SIEBERT, born 1943; admitted to bar, 1969, Illinois; 1971, Florida. *Education:* Michigan State University (B.A., 1966); University of Detroit Mercy (J.D., 1969). *Member:* Chicago and American Bar Associations; Illinois State Bar Association; The Florida Bar; American Immigration Lawyers Association (Chicago and Miami Chapters). ***PRACTICE AREAS:*** Visas; Deportation; Consular Law; Family Immigration Law; Immigration Law; Employment Immigration; Permanent Visas.

ARNOLD G. SIEGEL

20 NORTH CLARK STREET, SUITE 2200
CHICAGO, ILLINOIS 60602
Telephone: 312-629-0222
FAX: 312-236-7660
Email: arnsiegel@aol.com
URL: http://www.lawyers.com/siegellaw

Real Estate Tax Assessment Law.

ARNOLD G. SIEGEL, born Chicago, Illinois, March 5, 1947; admitted to bar, 1976, Illinois. *Education:* Loyola University (B.A., 1969); DePaul University (J.D., 1976). Deputy Commissioner, Cook County Board of Appeals, 1979-1983. *Member:* Chicago (Member, Real Estate Taxation Committee, 1981—) and Illinois State Bar Associations; International Association of Assessing Officers.

ELAINE K. B. SIEGEL & ASSOCIATES, P.C.

39 SOUTH LA SALLE STREET, SUITE 617
CHICAGO, ILLINOIS 60603
Telephone: 312-236-8088
Facsimile: 312-236-3451
URL: http://www.siegeledlaw.com
Email: siegeledlaw@aol.com
URL: http://www.siegel-law.com

Skokie, Illinois Office: 5005 Touhy Avenue, 60076. Telephone: 847-329-7500. Facsimile: 847-675-1884.

(This Listing Continued)

ELAINE K. B. SIEGEL & ASSOCIATES, P.C., Chicago—Continued

Education, School Law, Discrimination.

ELAINE K. B. SIEGEL, born Detroit, Michigan, June 4, 1949; admitted to bar, 1982, Illinois. *Education:* University of Chicago; University of California at Los Angeles (A.B., summa cum laude, 1972); Harvard University (M.A., 1978); Indiana University (J.D., cum laude, 1982). Pi Gamma Mu; Phi Beta Kappa. Fulbright Fellow. *Member:* Illinois State Bar Association. ***LANGUAGES:*** Italian, Spanish, French and German. ***PRACTICE AREAS:*** Education Law; Employment Law; Civil Rights Law. ***Email:*** ekbsiegel@aol.com

---

KATHERINE J. EDER, born St. Cloud, Minnesota, July 19, 1977; admitted to bar, 2004, Illinois. *Education:* University of St. Thomas (B.A., cum laude, 2000); DePaul University College of Law (J.D., cum laude, 2004). Recipient: Certificate in International and Comparative Law. Publication, DePaul Journal of Health Care Law, 2003-2004. Judicial Extern, Honorable Judge Guzman, United States District Court, Northern District of Illinois, Fall, 2003. Sullivan Fellow, International Human Rights Law Institute, 2002-2003. *Member:* Chicago and American Bar Associations.

SIEGEL MOSES & SCHOENSTADT PC

Established in 1979

444 NORTH MICHIGAN AVENUE
SUITE 2600
CHICAGO, ILLINOIS 60611
Telephone: 312-658-2000
Fax: 312-658-2022
Email: sms@smslaw.com
URL: http://www.smslaw.com

Civil Trial and Appellate Practice in state and federal courts throughout the U.S. Alcoholic Beverages, Antitrust, Constitutional, Commercial, Administrative, Arbitration, Corporate, Licensing and Real Estate Law.

FIRM PROFILE: The Firm of Siegel Moses & Schoenstadt PC concentrates in the areas of litigation, regulatory, transactional and licensing all within the alcoholic beverage and hospitality industries. Also included therein are: advertising and marketing, administrative, antitrust, constitutional, franchise and e-commerce. The collective experience of our firm in these areas spans over 90 years.

Our clients are derived from all three "tiers" of the federal and state mandated alcoholic beverage industry. Within the supplier tier and on a national basis, include both domestic importers, as well as domestic and foreign, distilleries wineries and breweries. On the wholesale level, our clients include distributors of spirits, wine and beer located throughout the United States, and as well as those which operate statewide and locally throughout the metropolitan Chicagoland. At the retail level, they include regional, national and international, hotel and restaurant chains, as well as those local to the metropolitan Chicagoland area. In this regard, we secure the issuance and renewal of the requisite licenses to conduct business throughout the United States, as well as provide services with regard to acquisitions, zoning matters and obtaining leasehold interests for their locations.

As to the marketing and promotion of alcoholic beverages, we provide our supplier and national retail clients, as well as their respective advertising agencies, with an analysis or assistance in the development of specific programs on a 50-State basis. These programs may generally fall into the categories of consumer sweepstakes, contests of skill, instant cents-off coupons or supplier rebates, sponsorship of various events, consumer or retailer advertising specialties, point-of-sale materials or display activities.

From a litigation standpoint, we are thoroughly versed in the applicable laws of the various states which regulate the relationships between suppliers and wholesalers of alcoholic beverages. We have effectively handled cases at all levels of state and federal court systems throughout the United States. We have been directly (as lead counsel) or indirectly (as either a consultant or on behalf of amici curiae) involved in several of the key Supreme Court decisions which pertain to the interpretation of the Twenty-First Amendment and its interaction with the various other provisions of the United States Constitution. Internationally, we practice before the International Court of Commerce of The International Chamber of Commerce and the American Arbitration Association. During the 1970's, the firm legally structured the first wine auction event in the United States for Heublein, Inc. and Christie, Manson & Woods, International, and has taken the lead in developing the concept of direct marketing of wines. More recently, we have developed a compliant regulatory structure for marketing and selling alcoholic beverages through e-commerce. We have served as lead counsel in many industry cases initiated by state regulatory agencies (Florida, Georgia, Utah, Michigan and Alabama) against clients involved in direct marketing, e-commerce, etc. We maintain a thorough involvement with the regulatory schemes in each state and with their respective regulatory authority as well as the federal scheme and with the Bureau of Alcohol, Tobacco and Firearms.

Thus, the firm practices and has developed an expertise within the area of alcoholic beverages consisting of: litigation, administrative and antitrust law, constitutional law, licensing and marketing practices.

Supreme Court Cases: James B. Beam Distilling Co. v. Georgia, 501 U.S. 529, 111 S. Ct. 2439 (1991); South Dakota v. Dole, 483 U.S. 203, 107 S. Ct. 2793 (1987). Amicus; Rice v. Norman Williams Co., 458 U.S. 654, 102 S. Ct. 3294 (1982). Amicus.

Other Cases: Club Misty, Inc. v. Laski, 208 F.3d 615 (7th Cir. 2000); Valley Liquors, Inc. v. Renfield Importers, Ltd., 822 F.2d 656 (7th Cir. 1987); Valley Liquors, Inc. v. Renfield Importers, Ltd., 678 F.2d 742 (7th Cir. 1982); South Rothschild Liquor Mart v. Kozubowski, 752 F. Supp. 839 (N.D. Ill. 1990); Federated Distributors, Inc. v. Johnson, 530 N.E.2d 501, 125 Ill. 2d 1 (1988); North Sheffield, Inc. v. City of Chicago, 494 N.E.2d 711, 144 Ill. App.3d 913 (1986).

(This Listing Continued)

MORTON SIEGEL, born Chicago, Illinois, September 12, 1934; admitted to bar, 1960, Illinois; 1961, U.S. District Court, Northern District of Illinois; 1973, U.S. Court of Appeals, Fourth Circuit; 1980, U.S. Court of Appeals, Seventh Circuit; 1985, U.S. Court of Appeals, Eighth Circuit; U.S. Supreme Court. *Education:* University of Michigan (B.A., 1956); DePaul University (J.D., 1960). *Member:* Chicago, Illinois State and American (Member, Antitrust Law Section) Bar Associations. ***PRACTICE AREAS:*** Federal and State Litigation; Federal and State Alcoholic Beverage Regulation; Administrative Hearings and Civil Appeals; Constitutional Law; Internet Law. ***Email:*** ms@smslaw.com

MICHAEL A. MOSES, born Detroit, Michigan, March 11, 1950; admitted to bar, 1975, Illinois; 1976, U.S. District Court, Northern District of Illinois; 1980, U.S. Court of Appeals, Fourth Circuit; 1981, U.S. Court of Appeals, Seventh Circuit and U.S. Supreme Court; 1982, U.S. Court of Appeals, Fifth Circuit and U.S. District Court, Northern District of Illinois including Trial Bar; 1985, U.S. Court of Appeals, Eighth Circuit; 1996, U.S. Court of Appeals, Sixth Circuit. *Education:* University of Michigan (B.G.S., 1972); University of Detroit (J.D., 1975). *Member:* Chicago, Illinois State and American (Member, Sections on: Litigation; Administrative Law; Criminal Justice; Business and Franchise Law) Bar Associations; International Association of Gaming Attorneys. ***PRACTICE AREAS:*** Complex Commercial Arbitration; Commercial Litigation; Constitutional Law; Criminal Litigation; Administrative Law; Civil Appeals; Federal and State Alcoholic Beverage Regulation; Internet Law; Advertising and Marketing Law; Gaming Law. ***Email:*** mam@smslaw.com

RICHARD G. SCHOENSTADT, born Champaign, Illinois, February 16, 1953; admitted to bar, 1978, Illinois; 1979, U.S. District Court, Northern District of Illinois; U.S. Court of Appeals, Fourth and Seventh Circuits; U.S. Supreme Court. *Education:* University of Illinois (A.B. with highest honors, Finance, cum laude, Liberal Arts and Sciences, 1975); Loyola University, Chicago (J.D., 1978). Phi Beta Kappa; Phi Kappa Phi. James Scholar. Instructor: Legal Writing, Loyola University, School of Law, Chicago, 1977-1978. *Member:* Chicago (Member, Real Property Committee, 1978), Illinois State and American Bar Associations. ***PRACTICE AREAS:*** Federal and State; Complex Commercial Arbitration; Commercial Litigation; Administrative Law; Constitutional Law; Civil Appeals; Federal and State Alcoholic Beverage Regulation; Commercial Real Estate Transactions. ***Email:*** rgs@smslaw.com

---

JENNIFER G. GALLERY, born Chicago, Illinois, September 7, 1969; admitted to bar, 1994, Illinois and U.S. District Court, Northern District of Illinois. *Education:* University of Iowa (B.S., 1991); DePaul University (J.D., 1994). *Member:* Chicago, Illinois State and American Bar Associations. ***PRACTICE AREAS:*** Commercial Litigation; Administrative Law; Constitutional Law; Appellate Practice; Federal and State Alcoholic Beverage Regulation; Licensing; Commercial Real Estate Transactions. ***Email:*** jgg@smslaw.com

ZUBIN S. KAMMULA, born Radford, Virginia, March 4, 1970; admitted to bar, 1997, Illinois and California. *Education:* University of California at Los Angeles (B.S., 1992); California Western School of Law (J.D., 1996). *Member:* Chicago, Illinois State and American Bar Associations; State Bar of California. ***PRACTICE AREAS:*** Administrative Law; Litigation; Licensing; Federal and State Alcoholic Beverage Regulation; Advertising and Marketing Law. ***Email:*** zsk@smslaw.com

REPRESENTATIVE CLIENTS: Albertsons, Inc. d/b/a Jewel Foods & Osco Drugs; Atlantic Coastal Airlines; ARAMARK Corp.; Bennigan's Restaurants; Beverage Marketing, Inc.; BP Products North America, Inc.; BUCA, Inc.; Chicago Beverage Systems; Chipotle Mexican Grill,. Inc.; Coors Brewing Co.; Cost Plus, Inc.; Eskye.com; Freixenet U.S.A., Inc.; Four Seasons Hotel; The Gambrinus Co.; GMRI, Inc.; Harbor Distributing Co.; Hard Rock Cafe International; Houlihan's Restaurants; Hyatt Corporation; Ideal Promotions Inc.; InBev USA L.L.C.; Lettuce Entertain You Enterprises Inc.; Levy Organization; Lionstone International; Mach Robin, LLC; Max & Erma's Restaurants, Inc.; Midnight Oil Co, LLC; National Wine & Spirits, Inc.; Pete's Brewing Co.; Sam's Wine & Spirits, Inc.; Sidney Frank Import Co.; Sotheby's Inc.; Sovereign Brands; Spoetzel Brewery, Inc.; Starwood Hotels & Resorts Worldwide, Inc.; Travel Centers of America, Inc.; Union Liquors, Inc.

OFFICES OF CATHERINE SIMMONS-GILL, LLC

Established in 1997

221 NORTH LASALLE STREET
SUITE 850
CHICAGO, ILLINOIS 60601
Telephone: 312-609-6611
Fax: 312-609-6610
URL: http://www.simmonsgill.com
Email: csimmonsgil@netscape.net
URL: http://www.lawyers.com/simmons-gill

Intellectual Property, Trademark, Copyright, Internet, Trade Secret, Commercial Litigation, Corporate, Employment.

CATHERINE SIMMONS-GILL, born Rochester, New York, July 7, 1949; admitted to bar, 1975, Illinois, U.S. District Court, Northern District of Illinois and U.S. Court of International Trade. *Education:* Carleton College; University of Illinois (A.B., cum laude, 1971); Northwestern University (J.D., 1975). Adjunct Professor, John Marshall Law School Center for Intellectual Property, 1998—. Author: "Trademarks and Taxation," Committee on State and Local Taxation, 2001; "Litigating in Cyberspace", American Bar Association, 1996; "The Obverse Side of the Coin: The Right to Publicize vs. the Right of Privacy", Multimedia Law Institute, 1995; "Invasion of Privacy vs. Newsworthiness," The Multimedia Law Report, Vol. 1, No. 12, October 1995. *Member:* Chicago Bar Association; Intellectual Property Association of Chicago; International Trademark Association (President, 1995-1996). ***LANGUAGES:*** French and Spanish. ***PRACTICE AREAS:*** Intellectual Property; Trademarks; Copyrights; Internet Law; Commercial Litigation; Employment Law. ***Email:*** csimmonsgil@netscape.net

SIMON, LAPIDOS & SIMON, LLC

CHICAGO, ILLINOIS

(See Skokie)

Commercial Litigation, Residential and Commercial Real Estate, Business Transactions including Acquisitions and Mergers, Contracts, Taxation, Probate, Estate Planning including Guardianship and Elder Law, Landlord and Tenant Law, General Practice, Corporate Debtor and Creditor Reorganization and Bankruptcy, Pension and Profit Sharing Plans.

SKADDEN, ARPS, SLATE, MEAGHER & FLOM LLP

333 WEST WACKER DRIVE

CHICAGO, ILLINOIS 60606

Telephone: 312-407-0700
Fax: 312-407-0411
URL: http://www.skadden.com

Offices of Affiliates:
New York, New York: Four Times Square, 10036. Telephone: 212-735-3000. Fax: 212-735-2000.
Boston, Massachusetts: One Beacon Street, 02108. Telephone: 617-573-4800. Fax: 617-573-4822.
Washington, D.C.: 1440 New York Avenue, N.W., 20005. Telephone: 202-371-7000. Fax: 202-393-5760.
Wilmington, Delaware: One Rodney Square, 19801. Telephone: 302-651-3000. Fax: 302-651-3001.
Los Angeles, California: 300 South Grand Avenue, Suite 3400, 90071. Telephone: 213-687-5000. Fax: 213-687-5600.
San Francisco, California: Four Embarcadero Center, Suite 3800, 94111. Telephone: 415-984-6400. Fax: 415-984-2698.
Houston, Texas: 1600 Smith Street, Suite 4400, 77002. Telephone: 713-655-5100. Fax: 713-655-5200.
Palo Alto, California: 525 University Avenue, Suite 1100, 94301. Telephone: 650-470-4500. Fax: 650-470-4570.
Tokyo, Japan: Izumi Garden Tower, 21st Floor, 1-6-1 Roppongi, Minato-ku, 106-6021. Telephone: 011-813-3568-2600. Fax: 011-813-3568-2626.
London, England: Skadden, Arps, Slate, Meagher & Flom (UK) LLP, 40 Bank Street, Canary Wharf, E14 5DS. Telephone: 011-44-20-7519-7000. Fax: 011-44-20-7519-7070.
Hong Kong, China: 30/F Tower Two, Lippo Centre, 89 Queensway, Central. Telephone: 011-852-2820-0700. Fax: 011-852-2820-0727.
Sydney, New South Wales 2000, Australia: Skadden, Arps, Slate, Meagher & Flom (International), Level 13, 131 Macquarie Street. Telephone: 011-61-2-9253-6000. Fax: 011-61-2-9253-6044.
Toronto, Ontario, Canada: 222 Bay Street, Suite 1750, P.O. Box 258, M5K 1J5. Telephone: 416-777-4700. Fax: 416-777-4747.
Brussels, Belgium: 523 avenue Louise, Box 30, 1050. Telephone: 011-32-2-639-0300. Fax: 011-32-2-639-0339.
Frankfurt am Main, Germany: An der Welle 5, 60322. Telephone: 011-49-69-742200. Fax: 011-49-69-74220300.
Munich, Germany: Karl-Scharnagl-Ring 7, 80539. Telephone: +011-49-89-244-495-0. Fax: +011-49-89-244-495-300.
Paris, France: 68, rue du Faubourg Saint-Honoré, 75008. Telephone: 011-331-55-27-11-00. Fax: 011-331-55-27-11-99.
Beijing, China: East Wing Office, Level 4, China World Trade Center, No 1 Jian Guo Men Wai Avenue, 100004. Telephone: 011-86-10-6505-5511. Fax: 011-86-10-6505-5522.
Moscow, Russia: Degtyarniy Pereulok 4, Building 1, 125009. Telephone: 011-7-501-797-4600. Fax: 011-7-501-797-4601.
Singapore, Singapore: Skadden, Arps, Slate, Meagher & Flom (International), 9 Temasek Boulevard, Suite 29-01, Suntec Tower Two, 038989. Telephone: 011-65-6434-2900. Fax: 011-65-6434-2988.
Vienna, Austria: Schwarzenbergplatz 6, A-1030. Telephone: 011-43-1-710-77-300. Fax: 011-43-1-710-77-303.

General Practice.

PARTNERS

WAYNE W. WHALEN, born Hanover, IL, 1939; admitted to bar, 1967, Illinois. *Education:* United States Air Force Academy (B.S., 1961); Northwestern University (J.D., 1967).

CHARLES W. MULANEY, JR., born Chicago, IL, 1949; admitted to bar, 1975, Illinois. *Education:* Georgetown University (A.B., summa cum laude, 1971); Yale University (J.D., 1974). Phi Beta Kappa. Editor, Yale Law Journal, 1973-1974. Law Clerk, Hon. Edward Weinfeld, Southern District of New York (1974-1975).

TIMOTHY A. NELSEN, born Chicago, IL, 1947; admitted to bar, 1973, New York; 1986, Illinois. *Education:* Carleton College (B.A., 1969); University of Michigan (J.D., 1972).

MARIAN P. WEXLER, born Chicago, IL, 1951; admitted to bar, 1977, Illinois; 1981, New York. *Education:* University of Wisconsin-Madison; Lake Forest University (B.A., with highest honors, 1973); DePaul University (J.D., summa cum laude, 1977). Phi Beta Kappa.

WARREN G. LAVEY, born Chicago, IL, 1953; admitted to bar, 1979, Illinois. *Education:* Harvard University (B.A., summa cum laude, 1975; M.S., 1975; J.D., magna cum laude, 1979); Cambridge University, England (Dip. Econ., 1976). Phi Beta Kappa.

ANDREW S. KENOE, born Milwaukee, WI, 1956; admitted to bar, 1981, Illinois. *Education:* Northwestern University (B.A., with distinction, 1978); Columbia University (J.D., 1981); New York University (LL.M. in Taxation, 1982). Harlan Fiske Stone Scholar.

WILLIAM R. KUNKEL, born Oak Park, IL, 1956; admitted to bar, 1981, Illinois. *Education:* Creighton University (B.S., magna cum laude, 1978); Harvard University (J.D., cum laude, 1981). Editor-in-Chief, Harvard Environmental Law Review, 1980-1981.

JOHN D. RAYIS, born Baghdad, Iraq, 1954; admitted to bar, 1981, Michigan; 1985, Illinois; 1989, California. *Education:* Michigan State University (B.A., with honors, 1977; B.S., with honors, 1977); Wayne State University (J.D., cum laude, 1979); University of Michigan (LL.M., 1980).

DAVID E. SPRINGER, born Evanston, IL, 1952; admitted to bar, 1977, Illinois. *Education:* Yale College (A.B., summa cum laude, 1974); Yale Law School (J.D., 1977). Phi Beta Kappa.

JOHN WM. BUTLER, JR., born Detroit, MI, 1956; admitted to bar, 1980, Michigan; 1992, Illinois. *Education:* Princeton University (A.B., magna cum laude, 1977); University of Michigan (J.D., 1980).

EDWARD M. CRANE, born Chicago, IL, 1957; admitted to bar, 1982, Illinois. *Education:* DePaul University (B.S., 1979; J.D., 1982).

THOMAS A. HALE, born Appleton, WI, 1957; admitted to bar, 1982, Illinois. *Education:* Northwestern University (B.A., with distinction, 1979); Duke University (J.D., with distinction, 1982). Order of the Coif. Member, Editorial Board, Duke Law Journal, 1980-1982.

RANDALL J. RADEMAKER, born Peoria, IL, 1956; admitted to bar, 1982, Illinois. *Education:* Knox College (B.A., summa cum laude, 1979); University of Chicago (J.D., 1982). Phi Beta Kappa.

CHRISTINA M. TCHEN, born Columbus, OH, 1956; admitted to bar, 1984, Illinois. *Education:* Radcliffe College (A.B., cum laude, 1978); Northwestern University (J.D., cum laude, 1984).

GARY P. CULLEN, born Chicago, IL, 1960; admitted to bar, 1985, Illinois. *Education:* University of Illinois (B.A., 1982); Columbia University (J.D., 1985).

JOHN ANDRÉ LEDUC, born Oberlin, OH, 1954; admitted to bar, 1978, Ohio; 1984, Illinois. *Education:* Princeton University (A.B., summa cum laude, 1975); Harvard Law School (J.D., cum laude, 1978).

ANN H. POLLOCK, born Boston, MA, 1956; admitted to bar, 1982, New York; 1989, Illinois. *Education:* Yale University (B.A., magna cum laude, 1978); Harvard Law School (J.D., cum laude, 1981).

PETER C. KRUPP, born Grand Rapids, MI, 1961; admitted to bar, 1986, Illinois. *Education:* Albion College (B.A., 1983); University of Michigan (J.D., cum laude, 1986).

BRIAN W. DUWE, born Oshkosh, WI, 1960; admitted to bar, 1987, Illinois. *Education:* Dartmouth College (B.A., 1982); University of Chicago (J.D., 1987). Order of the Coif. Associate Editor, University of Chicago Law Review.

J. ERIC IVESTER, born Altus, OK, 1960; admitted to bar, 1985, Oklahoma; 1989, Texas; 1993, Illinois. *Education:* University of Oklahoma (B.A., 1982; J.D., with highest honors, 1985). Phi Delta Phi; Order of the Coif. Notes Editor, Oklahoma Law Review, 1984-1985.

CHARLES F. SMITH, born Pittsburgh, PA, 1962; admitted to bar, 1987, Illinois. *Education:* Knox College (B.A., cum laude, 1984); University of Chicago (J.D., cum laude, 1987). Order of the Coif. Comment Editor, University of Chicago Law Review.

SETH E. JACOBSON, born Fort Dix, NJ, 1963; admitted to bar, 1988, Illinois. *Education:* University of Michigan (B.A., 1985; J.D., 1988). Phi Beta Kappa.

MAXWELL M. MILLER, born Davenport, IA, 1958; admitted to bar, 1988, Illinois. *Education:* Drake University (B.A., magna cum laude, 1980; M.P.A., 1980); Yale University (J.D., 1988).

RODD M. SCHREIBER, born Flint, MI, 1961; admitted to bar, 1987, Illinois. *Education:* University of Michigan (B.A., 1984; J.D., 1987).

LOUIS S. FREEMAN, born Cincinnati, OH, 1940; admitted to bar, 1968, New York; 1975, Illinois. *Education:* University of Cincinnati (B.B.A., with high honors, 1963); Harvard University (J.D., 1966); New York University (LL.M., in Taxation, 1972).

MATTHEW R. KIPP, born Oak Park, IL, 1963; admitted to bar, 1989, Illinois. *Education:* Yale University (B.A., cum laude, 1985); Columbia University (J.D., 1989). Harlan Fiske Stone Scholar.

LYNN M. McGOVERN, born Chicago, IL, 1961; admitted to bar, 1986, Illinois. *Education:* University of Illinois (B.S., 1983); University of Michigan (J.D., 1986).

GEORGE N. PANAGAKIS, born Chicago, IL, 1965; admitted to bar, 1990, Illinois. *Education:* Northwestern University (B.A., 1987; J.D., 1990). Pi Sigma Alpha. Member, Northwestern University Law Review.

R. RYAN STOLL, born Boston, MA, 1964; admitted to bar, 1990, Illinois. *Education:* Stanford University (B.A., 1987; M.A., 1987); Harvard Law School (J.D., cum laude, 1990).

TIMOTHY R. POHL, born Cleveland, OH, 1966; admitted to bar, 1991, Illinois. *Education:* Amherst College (B.A., 1988); University of Chicago (J.D., 1991).

L. BYRON VANCE III, born Meridian, TX, 1968; admitted to bar, 1992, Texas; 2000, Illinois. *Education:* Baylor University (B.B.A., cum laude, 1990; J.D., cum laude, 1992).

JOHN K. LYONS, born Milwaukee, WI, 1964; admitted to bar, 1989, Illinois. *Education:* Georgetown University (B.S.F.S., 1986); Villanova Law School (J.D., cum laude, 1989).

FELICIA GERBER PERLMAN, born Chicago, IL, 1967; admitted to bar, 1992, Illinois. *Education:* University of Pennsylvania (B.A., B.S., 1989); Northwestern University (J.D., 1992).

FRANCES P.H. KAO, born Taipei, Taiwan, 1963; admitted to bar, 1992, California; 1999, Illinois. *Education:* Cornell College (B.S.S., 1985); Chicago-Kent College of Law, Illinois Institute of Technology (J.D., magna cum laude, 1992).

CHARLES B. TAYLOR, born Ottawa, IL, 1963; admitted to bar, 1992, Illinois. *Education:* University of Illinois (B.S., 1985); University of Chicago (J.D., 1992).

(This Listing Continued)

SKADDEN, ARPS, SLATE, MEAGHER & FLOM LLP, Chicago—Continued

SUSAN S. HASSAN, born Flint, MI, 1970; admitted to bar, 1996, Illinois. *Education:* University of Michigan (B.A., 1992; J.D., 1996). ***LANGUAGES:*** Arabic. ***PRACTICE AREAS:*** Corporate.

KIMBERLY A. DEBEERS, born Brooklyn, N.Y., 1966; admitted to bar, 1995, New York and Illinois. *Education:* University of Pennsylvania (B.A., 1989); Tulane Law School (J.D., 1993).

DAVID POLSTER, born Cleveland, OH, 1969; admitted to bar, 1994, Illinois. *Education:* Yeshiva University (B.A., 1991); Harvard University (J.D., 1994).

ALBERT L. HOGAN, III, born Columbus, OH, 1966; admitted to bar, 1997, Illinois. *Education:* The Ohio State University (B.S., 1989); The University of Chicago (J.D., 1997). Order of the Coif.

OF COUNSEL

ARTHUR S. ROLLIN, born Chicago, IL, 1932; admitted to bar, 1958, Illinois. *Education:* Michigan State University (B.A., 1954); Northwestern University (M.B.A., 1955; J.D., 1958). Certified Public Accountant, Illinois, 1956.

COUNSEL

ELIZABETH A. DEVINE, born Carbondale, IL, 1967; admitted to bar, 1995, New York; 2000, Illinois. *Education:* DePaul University (B.S., with highest honors, 1989); Columbia University (J.D., 1994).

STEVEN H. FORBES, born Sheboygan, WI, 1968; admitted to bar, 1997, Wisconsin; 1999, Illinois. *Education:* University of Wisconsin-Madison (B.B.A., with honors, 1990; J.D., magna cum laude, 1996; M.B.A., 1996). Order of the Coif. *Member:* State Bar of Wisconsin. ***PRACTICE AREAS:*** Corporate; Securities; Tax.

LEE P. GARNER, born Waycross, GA, 1968; admitted to bar, 1995, Connecticut; 1997, Illinois. *Education:* University of North Carolina at Chapel Hill (B.A., with distinction, 1990); Northwestern University (J.D., cum laude, 1995). Phi Beta Kappa.

ERIC J. GORMAN, born San Angelo, TX, 1969; admitted to bar, 1995, Illinois and U.S. District Court, Northern District of Illinois; 1996, U.S. Court of Appeals, Seventh Circuit; 1998, U.S. Court of Appeals, Tenth Circuit; 2001, U.S. Court of Appeals, Sixth Circuit; 2003, U.S. Supreme Court. *Education:* University of Chicago (A.B., with honors, 1992; A.M., with honors, 1992); University of Michigan (J.D., 1995).

SHILPI GUPTA, born Calcutta, India, 1969; admitted to bar, 1994, New Jersey; 1996, District of Columbia; 1997, Illinois. *Education:* Columbia University School of Engineering (B.S., 1991); Georgetown University (J.D., 1994). *Member:* New Jersey State and American Bar Associations. ***LANGUAGES:*** Hindi. ***PRACTICE AREAS:*** Corporate.

DAVID F. KOLIN, born Detroit, MI, 1955; admitted to bar, 1987, Illinois. *Education:* Michigan State University (B.A., 1984); University of Michigan (J.D., magna cum laude, 1987).

KAREN M. LEE, born New Haven, CT, 1969; admitted to bar, 1996, Illinois. *Education:* University of Washington (B.A., 1987); University of Chicago Law School (J.D., 1996). Phi Beta Kappa. ***LANGUAGES:*** Mandarin, Cantonese, Japanese. ***PRACTICE AREAS:*** Taxation.

MARK A. McDERMOTT, born Ft. Dodge, IA, 1966; admitted to bar, 1991, Iowa; 1992, Illinois. *Education:* Iowa State University (B.S., 1988); Northwestern University (J.D., cum laude, 1991). Phi Beta Kappa.

DONNA L. McDEVITT, born Philadelphia, PA, 1954; admitted to bar, 1988, Illinois. *Education:* University of Vermont (B.A., 1975); University of Illinois (M.A.S., 1978); University of Chicago (J.D., 1988).

STEVEN P. MIRIANI, born St. Louis, MO, 1963; admitted to bar, 1987, Illinois and U.S. District Court, Northern District of Illinois. *Education:* DePaul University; Tulane University (J.D., cum laude, 1986).

NANCY M. OLSON, admitted to bar, 1996, Illinois. *Education:* Northwestern University (B.A., 1993); Loyola University (J.D., 1996). ***PRACTICE AREAS:*** Real Estate. **Email:** nolson@skadden.com

MARK E. RAKOCZY, born Chicago, IL, 1952; admitted to bar, 1976, Illinois. *Education:* Kenyon College (B.A., 1973); John Marshall Law School (J.D., 1976).

DHANANJAI SHIVAKUMAR, born 1972; admitted to bar, 1998, New York (Not admitted in Illinois). *Education:* Harvard University (A.B., 1993); Yale Law School (J.D., 1996).

DEBORAH G. SOLMOR, admitted to bar, 1991, Illinois.

(For biographical data on other personnel, see firm's other Professional Biographies)

LAW OFFICES OF F. J. SKINNER-LEWIS

1 NORTH LA SALLE STREET, SUITE 1375
CHICAGO, ILLINOIS 60602
Telephone: 312-346-0336
Fax: 312-346-0192
Email: fjsl.law@attglobal.net
URL: http://www.lawyers.com/franceskinnerlewis

General Practice.

FRANCES J. SKINNER-LEWIS, born Chicago, Illinois; admitted to bar, 1980, Illinois, U.S. Court of Appeals, Seventh Circuit; U.S. District Court, Northern District of Illinois including Trial Bar. *Education:* University of Arizona (B.A., 1975); IIT-Chicago-Kent College of Law (J.D., with highest honors, 1980). Speaker: "Effective Discovery and Investigation Techniques," Illinois Association of Defense Trial Counsel; "Action Plans under Total Quality Management: Way to Eliminate the Glass Ceiling," Women in the Law Section, Young Lawyers Division, Chicago Bar Association; "Total Quality Management and Diversity in the Workplace," Professional Responsibility Section, American Bar Association; "Civility and the New Discovery Rules," Illinois State Bar Association/Illinois Judicial Association; "Third Party Actions: Strategies for Success," Tort Section, Illinois State Bar Association; "Effective Closing Arguments for the Defense," Trial Section, Illinois State Bar Association. *Member:* Chicago, Illinois State and American Bar Associations; Defense Research Institute; Trial Lawyers Club of Chicago; Federation of Women Contractors. ***PRACTICE AREAS:*** Civil Practice; Construction Law; Architectural Law; Construction Accidents; Construction and Design Law; Construction Arbitration; Construction Claims; Construction Contracts; Construction Defects; Complex and Multi-District Litigation; Civil Litigation; Complex Litigation; Defense Litigation; Federal Civil Litigation; Trial Practice; Medical Malpractice Defense; Insurance Defense; Labor and Employment.

SLOAN AND ASSOCIATES, INC.

111 WEST WASHINGTON STREET
SUITE 1020
CHICAGO, ILLINOIS 60602
Telephone: 312-332-3771
Fax: 312-332-1319
URL: http://www.lawyers.com/sloanandassoc

Family Law Practice including Child Custody, Divorce, Domestic Violence, Premarital Agreements, Paternity.

MEMBER OF FIRM

MAOL MURRAY SLOAN, born Chicago, Illinois, June 29, 1939; admitted to bar, 1969, Illinois. *Education:* Loyola University (LL.B., 1968). Publisher, "Illinois Trial Court Divorce Digest," 1986-1996. *Member:* Chicago and Illinois State Bar Associations; American Academy of Matrimonial Lawyers; American Bar Association. ***PRACTICE AREAS:*** Family Law; Child Custody; Divorce; Domestic Violence; Premarital Agreements; Paternity.

SMART & BOSTJANCICH

19 SOUTH LA SALLE STREET, SUITE 1300
CHICAGO, ILLINOIS 60603
Telephone: 312-857-2424
Facsimile: 312-201-0737

Litigation and Counseling. Domestic and International Trademark, Copyright, Unfair Competition and Computer Law, Licensing, Franchising, False Advertising, Right of Publicity, Counterfeiting and Trade Secrets.

JOHN BOSTJANCICH, born Cleveland, Ohio, January 29, 1947; admitted to bar, 1977, Illinois. *Education:* Carleton College (B.A., 1968); Ohio State University (M.S., 1970); Loyola University (J.D., cum laude, 1977). Member, Loyola University Law Journal, 1977. Adjunct Professor, John Marshall Law School. Member, Editorial Board, Trademark Reporter, 1988-1990, 1995-1998. *Member:* Chicago (Chair, Patents, Trademarks and Copyrights Committee, 1987-1988) Illinois State and American Bar Associations; American Intellectual Property Law Association; Intellectual Property Law Association of Chicago (Chair, Copyright Committee, 1991-1992). **Email:** JB@SmartBostjancich.com

PATRICIA S. SMART, born Waukegan, Illinois; admitted to bar, 1978, Illinois. *Education:* University of Illinois (B.A., 1975; J.D., magna cum laude, 1978). Order of the Coif. Adjunct Professor, John Marshall Law School. Co-founder, 1984; Secretary, 1984-1986; Advisory Board, 1986-1987, Legal Aid Clinic for the Disabled. Trustee, American Intellectual Property Law Education Foundation, 2002—. *Member:* Chicago (Chair, Patents, Trademarks and Copyrights Committee, 1989-1990), Illinois State (Intellectual Property Section Council, 1989-1996, Chair, 1994-1995), American (Member of Executive Committee, Section Of Intellectual Property Law, 2001-2003, Member of Council, Section of Intellectual Property Law, 1995-1998; Quarterly Contributor, Litigation Section, Intellectual Property Newsletter, 1993-2004) and Seventh Circuit Bar Associations; Copyright Society; Intellectual Property Law Association of Chicago (Member, Board of Managers, 1988-1990; 2002-2004; Secretary, 1998-2000). Fellow, American Bar Foundation. **Email:** PS@SmartBostjancich.com

LAW OFFICES OF GARY H. SMITH, P.C.

Established in 1990

180 NORTH LA SALLE STREET, SUITE 2001
CHICAGO, ILLINOIS 60601
Telephone: 312-236-7447
Fax: 312-236-7961
Email: gary@garyhsmith.com
URL: http://www.garyhsmith.com

Property Tax, Property Tax Appeals and Real Estate Law.

FIRM PROFILE: Gary H. Smith has been a practicing attorney for over twenty two years. His practice is comprised of handling property tax appeal matters for a variety of commercial and residential properties, including office and apartment buildings, business and industrial properties, homes and condominiums. Gary has successfully appealed the proposed assessments of thousands of commercial properties, as well as residences, resulting in millions of dollars in tax savings for his clients.

GARY H. SMITH, born Carrollton, Georgia, July 21, 1953; admitted to bar, 1980, Georgia and Illinois. *Education:* University of North Carolina (B.A., 1975); Washington

(This Listing Continued)

University (J.D., 1980). Member, Washington University Urban Law Review, 1978-1980. Member, Chicago Local School Council, 1991-1995. Secretary, Ravenswood Manor Improvement Association, 1991-1992. Registered Lobbyist, Property Tax, State of Illinois, 2004—. *Member:* Chicago (Chair, 2000-2001 and Vice Chair, 1999-2000, Real Estate Taxation Committee; Chair, 1997-1999 and Legislative Liaison, 1996, Assessment and Appeals Subcommittee; Member, Unauthorized Practice of Law Committee) and Illinois State Bar Associations; State Bar of Georgia; Illinois Property Tax Lawyers Association. **Email:** gary@garyhsmith.com

JENNIFER ALLEN-GOLDSTEIN, admitted to bar, 2003, Illinois. *Education:* Michigan State University (B.A., 1995); Illinois Institute of Technology, Chicago-Kent College of Law (J.D., 2003). *Member:* Chicago, Illinois State and American Bar Associations. ***PRACTICE AREAS:*** Property Tax Law; Real Estate; Tax Appeals. **Email:** jennifer@garyhsmith.com

SMITH, HEMMESCH, BURKE & BRANNIGAN

11 EAST ADAMS STREET, SUITE 1400
CHICAGO, ILLINOIS 60603
Telephone: 312-939-0100
Fax: 312-939-7765
URL: http://www.propertytaxlawfirm.com
Email: shb-law.com
URL: http://www.shbb-law.com

Real Property Taxation, General Civil Practice in State and Federal Courts, Real Estate and Personal Injury Law.

MEMBERS OF FIRM

WILLIAM L. SMITH, JR., born Melrose Park, Illinois, May 24, 1946; admitted to bar, 1971, Iowa and Illinois. *Education:* University of Iowa (B.A., 1968; J.D., with honors, 1971). Order of the Coif; Phi Delta Phi. Author: *Administrative Appeals and Procedures, Illinois Tax Service,* Matthew Bender, 1985. *Member:* Chicago (Member, Committees on: Civil Practice, 1973-1977; State and Municipal Taxation, 1977—) Bar Association; Illinois Institute of Property Taxation; International Association of Assessing Officers. ***SPECIAL AGENCIES:*** Cook County Board of Review, Illinois Property Tax Appeal Board. ***PRACTICE AREAS:*** Real Estate Taxation. **Email:** wls@shb-law.com

DONALD F. HEMMESCH, JR., born Chicago, Illinois, June 21, 1953; admitted to bar, 1978, Illinois. *Education:* Loras College (B.A., 1975); John Marshall University (J.D., 1978). Author: *Administrative Appeals and Procedures, Illinois Tax Service,* Matthew Bender, 1985. Special Assistant Attorney General, State of Illinois, 1980-1983. *Member:* Chicago and Illinois State Bar Associations; American Association of Homes for the Aging; Illinois Association of Homes for the Aging; Institute of Property Taxation. ***SPECIAL AGENCIES:*** Illinois Health Facilities Planning Board; Illinois Health Facilities Authority; Illinois Department of Public Health; Cook County Board of Review; Lake County Board of Review; Kane County Board of Review; Du Page County Board of Review; Illinois Property Tax Appeal Board. ***PRACTICE AREAS:*** Real Estate Taxation; Litigation; Retirement Housing; Health Care. **Email:** dfh@shb-law.com

KEVIN P. BURKE, born Cleveland, Ohio, May 20, 1959; admitted to bar, 1984, Illinois. *Education:* Cleveland State University (B.A., 1981); DePaul University College of Law (J.D., 1984). Cook County State's Attorney, 1984-1989. *Member:* Chicago and Illinois State Bar Associations; Institute of Property Taxation. ***SPECIAL AGENCIES:*** Cook County Board of Review; Lake County Board of Review; Du Page County Board of Review; Illinois Property Tax Appeal Board. ***REPORTED CASES:*** In re Application of County Treasurer, 175 Ill. App. 3d 564 (1988); Gaynor v. Walsh, 219 Ill. App. 3d 996 (1991); In re Application of County Treasurer, 186 Ill. App. 3d 597 (1989); Carswell v. Roswell, 150 Ill. App. 3d 168 (1986); In re Application of County Treasurer, 184 Ill. App. 3d 1048 (1989). ***PRACTICE AREAS:*** Real Estate Taxation. **Email:** kpb@shb-law.com

THOMAS E. BRANNIGAN, SR., born Chicago, Illinois, January 17, 1939; admitted to bar, 1963, Illinois; 1964, U.S. Court of Military Appeals; 1967, U.S. Supreme Court; 1979, Florida. *Education:* University of Notre Dame (A.B., 1961; LL.B., 1963). Assistant Attorney General, State of Illinois, 1967-1969. Assistant State's Attorney, Cook County, Illinois, 1969-1971. *Member:* Illinois State Bar Association; The Florida Bar. [With JAGC, U.S. Army, 1st Armored Division, 1964-1967]. ***REPORTED CASES:*** Boyle v. Landry, 401 U.S. 77(1971), Client Follow-Up Corp. v. Hynes, 390 N.E.2d 847 (1979); The Streeterville Corp. v. Dept. of Revenue, 714 N.E. 2d 497 (1999). ***PRACTICE AREAS:*** Property Taxation; Real Estate Taxation. **Email:** teb@shb-law.com

ASSOCIATE

CHRISTOPHER KACZYNSKI, born Park Ridge, Illinois, June 24, 1968; admitted to bar, 1993, Illinois and U.S. District Court, Northern District of Illinois. *Education:* University of Illinois, Urbana-Champaign (B.A., 1990); DePaul University College of Law (J.D., 1993). Pi Sigma Alpha (Membership, Chairperson, 1992). Articles Editor, Journal of Health and Hospital Law; Co-Author, "The Psychotherapist-Patient Privilege," 26 Journal of Health and Hospital Law 41. Author: "Computer-Stored Data Acquired From Real Estate Services: Should the Property Tax Appeal Board Allow It into the Record?" Vol. 46, No. 6 Tax Trends 4. Adjunct Professor, Paralegal Program, William Rainey Harper College, 1995—. Assistant States Attorney, Cook County States Attorney's Office, 1994-2000. *Member:* Chicago and Illinois State Bar Associations. ***REPORTED CASES:*** State Toll Highway Authority v. Amoco Oil Company and Mobil Oil Corp., 336 Ill.App. 3d 300, 783 N.E. 2d 658 (2nd Dist. 2003); People v Beard, 271 Ill. App. 3d 320, 648 N.E.2d 111 (1st District, 1995). ***PRACTICE AREAS:*** Real Estate Taxation; Litigation. **Email:** cbk@shb-law.com

REPRESENTATIVE CLIENTS: Allegiance Healthcare Corp.; Baxter Corp.; Bombardier Inc.; BP America, Inc.; Cardinal Healthcare; Central Steel & Wire Co.; Chicago Title Insurance Co.; Friendship Village of Schaumburg; Mid-America Savings & Loan; Mobil Oil Corp.; Northbrook Property & Casualty Co.; Peoples Gas Light & Coke Co.; Pepsi of America; SBC/Ameritech; Senior Lifestyle Corp.; Shell Oil Co.; 3M Company; Turtle Wax, Inc.; United States Steel Corp. REFERENCES: The Private Bank; Hinsbrook Bank; State Bank of the Lakes; Baxter Corp.; Weiss, Sugar, Dvorak & Dusek, Ltd.

(This Listing Continued)

SMITH O'CALLAGHAN & WHITE

33 NORTH LA SALLE STREET
SUITE 3800
CHICAGO, ILLINOIS 60602
Telephone: 312-419-1000
Facsimile: 312-419-1007
Email: socw@socw.com

Labor and Employment. Trial and Appellate Litigation: Federal and State Courts. Employment Litigation. Management Labor Law. Unfair Competition, Trade Secrets and Non-Compete Agreements. Administrative Agency: Federal, State and Local. Employment Mediation and Arbitration.

FIRM PROFILE: Smith O'Callaghan & White represents national and international corporations, including Fortune 500 and Global 500 companies, in legal matters arising in Chicago and the Midwest, mid-size corporations and professional entities such as other law firms. The firm's focus is in the areas of labor and employment law, and the full spectrum of employment-related litigation.

TERRY J. SMITH, born Wisconsin Rapids, Wisconsin, September 5, 1958; admitted to bar, 1984, Wisconsin, District of Columbia and U.S. Court of Appeals, Seventh Circuit; 1987, Illinois and U.S. District Court, Northern District of Illinois. *Education:* Lawrence University (B.A., magna cum laude, 1981); Cornell Law School (J.D., 1984). Phi Beta Kappa. Henry M. Wriston Scholar. *Member:* Chicago (Member: Labor and Employment Law and Federal Civil Practice Committees), Seventh Circuit and American (Member, Labor and Employment Law Section) Bar Associations. ***REPORTED CASES:*** Brill v. McDonald's Corporation, 28 F.3d 633 (7th Cir. 1994); Johnson v. Indopco, Inc., 79 F. 3d 1150, 1996 U.S. App. LEXIS 6313 (7th Cir. 1996); Wohl v. Spectrum Mfg., Inc., 94 F.3d 353 (7th Cir. 1996); Kelley v. Crosfield Catalysts, 135 F. 3d 1202 (7th Cir. 1998), 962 F. Supp. 1047 (N.D. Ill. 1997); Adamczyk, et al. v. Lever Brothers Co., 991 F. Supp. 931 (N.D.Ill. 1997), 33 F. Supp. 2d 679 (N.D.Ill. 1998) and 1999 U.S. Dist. LEXIS 3494 (N.D.Ill. 1999); Dikcis v. Indopco, Inc., 1997 U.S. Dist. LEXIS 5276 (N.D. Ill. 1997) and 1998 U.S. Dist. LEXIS 234 (N.D.Ill. 1998); Stevenson v. Unichema North America, 1995 U.S. Dist. LEXIS 10547 (N.D. Ill. 1995); Johnson and Wilkes v. Indopco, Inc., 887 F. Supp. 1092 (N.D. Ill. 1995), 846 F. Supp. 670 (N.D. Ill. 1994) and 834 F. Supp. 1039 (N.D. Ill. 1993); Messing v. InPhynet Medical Mgmt., et al., 872 F. Supp. 539 (N.D. Ill. 1995); Johnson v. Northern Indiana Public Service Co., 844 F. Supp. 466 (N.D. Ind. 1994); Rose, et al. v. Consolidated Elec. Distributors, Inc., 816 F. Supp. 489 (N.D. Ill. 1993); Layne v. Builders Plumbing Supply Co., Inc., 210 Ill. App. 3d 966, 569 N.E. 2d 1104 (2d Dist. 1991); Rolark v. University of Chicago Hospitals, 688 F. Supp. 401 (N.D. Ill. 1988) and 51 Fair Empl. Prac. Cas. (BNA) 1230 (N.D. Ill. 1989); Patton v. University of Chicago Hospitals, 706 F. Supp. 627 (N.D. Ill. 1989). ***PRACTICE AREAS:*** Labor and Employment; Employment Litigation; Management Labor Law; Litigation; Unfair Competition; Theft of Trade Secrets. **Email:** terry.smith@socw.com

MARY AILEEN O'CALLAGHAN, born Chicago, Illinois, July 24, 1945; admitted to bar, 1977, Illinois; 1988, U.S. District Court, Northern District of Illinois; 1990, U.S. District Court, Central District of Illinois; 1996 U.S. District Court, Northern District of Illinois Trial Bar. *Education:* Mundelein College (B.F.A., with honors, 1967); Loyola University School of Law (J.D., 1977). Associate Editor, Loyola University Law Journal, 1976-1977. Author: "Labor Law-Ominous Implication for Public Sector Collective Bargaining in Illinois," 8 Loy. Chi. L.J. 209 (1976); "Employment Discrimination Law," 2d edition, 1983-1985 cum. supplement, BNA Books, 1987-1990 (Contributing Editor). Speaker, Council on Education in Management, Executive Enterprises, American Bar Association, Section of Labor and Employment Law, Mid-Winter Meetings, American Management Association. Adjunct Professor, Loyola University of Chicago School of Law, 1980-1983; Adjunct Faculty, University of Wisconsin Management Institute, 1991-1998. Fellow, College of Labor and Employment Lawyers. *Member:* American Bar Association (Member: Section of Labor and Employment Law; Equal Employment Opportunity Law Committee; Employee Rights and Responsibilities Committee; International Labor Law Committee). ***REPORTED CASES:*** McEwen v. Delta Air Lines, Inc., 919 F.2d 58 (7th Cir. 1990); Taylor v. Canteen Corp., 789 F. Supp. 279 (C.D. Ill. 1992); Kohnke v. Delta Air Lines, Inc., 932 F. Supp. 1110 (N.D. Ill. 1996). ***PRACTICE AREAS:*** Management Labor Law; Labor and Employment; Employment Litigation; Affirmative Action Plans; Employee Handbooks; Employer Counseling; Employment Mediation; Executive Severance Contracts; Labor Relations; Collective Bargaining. **Email:** maoc@socw.com

LAURA A. WHITE, born Dayton, Ohio, November 24, 1969; admitted to bar, 1996, Illinois; U.S. District Court, Northern District of Illinois and U.S. Court of Appeals, Seventh Circuit. *Education:* University of Dayton (B.A., 1992); University of Dayton School of Law (J.D., 1996). Phi Alpha Delta. Office of the General Counsel, Loyola University of Chicago, 1996-1997. *Member:* Legal Assistance Foundation of Chicago, Volunteer Lawyers for the Homeless. *Member:* Chicago (Member, Labor and Employment Law Committee), Illinois State (Member, Labor & Employment Law and Civil Practice & Procedure Committees), Seventh Circuit and American (Member, Labor and Employment Law Section) Bar Associations. **PRACTICE AREAS:** Labor and Employment; Litigation; Employment Litigation; Employment Discrimination; Employment Class Actions; Management Employment Law; Wrongful Termination Defense. **Email:** laura.white@socw.com

OF COUNSEL

JOHN T. POWEN, born Chicago, Illinois, January 1, 1963; admitted to bar, 1988, Illinois. *Education:* University of Illinois (B.S., Finance, 1985); John Marshall Law School (J.D., 1988). Gavel Society; Phi Delta Phi. Partner, Kessler Smith & Powen, 1995-1999. President, 2002-2003, and Board of Directors, 1993-2004, Blind Service Association of

(This Listing Continued)

SMITH O'CALLAGHAN & WHITE, Chicago—Continued

Chicago. *Member:* Chicago and Illinois State Bar Associations. ***LANGUAGES:*** French. ***PRACTICE AREAS:*** Real Estate; Litigation; Real Estate Development. ***Email:*** john.powen@socw.com

DAVID ALAN SCHNEIDER, born Chicago, Illinois, July 16, 1969; admitted to bar, 1994, Illinois and U.S. District Court, Northern District of Illinois. *Education:* University of Wisconsin-Madison (B.S., 1991); Chicago-Kent College of Law (J.D., 1994). ***PRACTICE AREAS:*** Labor and Employment; Employment Litigation; Litigation; Employment Class Actions; Employment Discrimination. ***Email:*** david.schneider@socw.com

ASSOCIATES

ROBERT R. DUDA JR., born Hoffman Estates, Illinois, July 14, 1974; admitted to bar, 1999, Illinois and U.S. District Court, Northern District of Illinois. *Education:* University of Dayton (B.A., 1996); DePaul University (J.D., 1999). Phi Alpha Delta. *Member:* Chicago, Illinois State and American Bar Associations. ***PRACTICE AREAS:*** Labor and Employment; Litigation; Employment Litigation; Employment Discrimination; Theft of Trade Secrets; Unfair Competition. ***Email:*** robert.duda@socw.com

REBECCA A. FIGLER, born Park Ridge, Illinois, March 5, 1976; admitted to bar, 2001, Illinois and U.S. District Court, Northern District of Illinois. *Education:* Purdue University (B.S., with distinction, 1998); DePaul University (J.D., 2001). Phi Beta Kappa. Author: "Friends of Southeast's Future v. U.S. Forest Service," DePaul Environmental Law Digest, 1999. *Member:* Chicago, Illinois State and American Bar Associations. ***PRACTICE AREAS:*** Labor and Employment; Litigation. ***Email:*** rebecca.figler@socw.com

CHRISTINE E. NENTWIG, born York, Pennsylvania, February 26, 1971; admitted to bar, 2000, Pennsylvania; 2004, Illinois and U.S. District Court, Northern District of Illinois. *Education:* York College of Pennsylvania (B.A., cum laude, 1994); University of Maryland School of Law (J.D., 2000). *Member:* Chicago, Illinois State and American Bar Associations. ***PRACTICE AREAS:*** Labor and Employment; Litigation; Management Labor Law; Labor Relations; Employment Litigation. ***Email:*** christine.nentwig@socw.com

ELIZABETH M. LAUDERBACH, born Saginaw, Michigan, February 3, 1980; admitted to bar, 2005, Illinois and U.S. District Court, Northern District of Illinois. *Education:* University of Colorado (B.A., 2002); Loyola University Chicago School of Law (J.D., 2005). Law Clerk, Office of the Attorney General, State of Illinois, 2003. *Member:* Chicago, Illinois State and American Bar Associations. ***PRACTICE AREAS:*** Labor and Employment; Litigation; Employment Discrimination. ***Email:*** elizabeth.lauderbach@socw.com

SNOW & SNOW, LTD.

Established in 1975

33 N. LA SALLE STREET, SUITE 2000
CHICAGO, ILLINOIS 60602
Telephone: 312-263-4858
Facsimile: 312-263-4860
Email: martin.snow@snowandsnow.com
URL: http://www.snowandsnow.com

Estate Planning, Asset Protection, Wills and Probate, Trusts and Estates, Guardianships, Elder Law, Trust, Taxation, Small Closely Held Business Law, Business Succession Planning, Estate Planning, General Practice, Real Estate, Buying and Selling a Home, Buying and Selling a Business and IRS Audits.

ROBERT H. SNOW (1916-2003)

MARTIN B. SNOW, born Chicago, Illinois, 1948; admitted to bar, 1972, Illinois and U.S. District Court, Northern District of Illinois; 1979, U.S. Tax Court; 1988, U.S. Claims Court. *Education:* Drake University (B.S.B.A.); Loyola University (J.D.). ***PRACTICE AREAS:*** Probate; Estate Planning; Taxation; Real Estate; Corporate Law. ***Email:*** martin.snow@snowandsnow.com

SNYDER & McGOVERN, LLC

343 SOUTH DEARBORN STREET
SUITE 2015
CHICAGO, ILLINOIS 60604
Telephone: 312-447-0260
Fax: 312-447-0261
Email: shiplaw@juno.com
URL: http://www.snydermcgovern.com

Admiralty and Maritime Law, Civil Practice, Litigation, Commercial Litigation, Transportation, Torts.

MICHAEL A. SNYDER, born Evansville, Indiana, December 29, 1938; admitted to bar, 1968, Illinois and U.S. District Court, Northern District of Illinois; 1970, U.S. Court of Appeals, Seventh Circuit; 1972, U.S. Supreme Court; 1980, U.S. Court of Appeals, Fourth Circuit; 1981, U.S. Court of Appeals, Eighth Circuit. *Education:* United States Merchant Marine Academy (B.S., 1960); John Marshall Law School (J.D., 1968). Associate Editor, American Maritime Cases, 1977—. Author: "Maritime Collision Damage to Vessels and Fixed Structures," Tulane Law Review, Vol. 72 Pg. 881. Member, Permanent Advisory Board, Admiralty Law Institute Tulane University, 1985—. Adjunct Professor, Admiralty Law, The John Marshall School of Law, 1995—. *Member:* Chicago (Chairman, Maritime Law Committee, 1972-1973), Illinois State (Chairman, Admiralty and Maritime Law Section, 1970-1971, 1984) and American (Chairman, Admiralty Law Committee, Tort and Insurance Practice Section, 1992-1993) Bar Associations; Maritime Law Association of the United States; Society of Trial Lawyers. ***PRACTICE AREAS:*** Admiralty and Maritime Law; Civil Practice; Litigation. ***Email:*** shiplaw@juno.com

(This Listing Continued)

TIMOTHY S. McGOVERN, born Chicago, Illinois, June 25, 1975; admitted to bar, 2001, Illinois and U.S. District Court, Northern District of Illinois; 2002, U.S. District Court, Eastern District of Wisconsin and U.S. District Court, Northern District of Indiana; U.S. Court of Appeals, Seventh Circuit. *Education:* University of Illinois, Champaign-Urbana (B.A., English, 1997); John Marshall Law School (J.D., 2001). Master's License, Inland and Great Lakes, 1996. ***PRACTICE AREAS:*** Admiralty and Maritime Law; Commercial Litigation; Transportation; Torts; Litigation. ***Email:*** greatlakeslaw@aol.com

LAW OFFICES OF ALAN E. SOHN

Established in 1989

30 NORTH LA SALLE STREET, SUITE 2040
CHICAGO, ILLINOIS 60602
Telephone: 312-236-7005
Fax: 312-236-6906
Email: aeslaw@ameritech.net
URL: http://www.alansohnlaw.com

Closely Held Business Law, Estate Planning and Probate, Business Organizations, Real Estate, Litigation, Business Litigation, Representation of Child Day Care Centers.

FIRM PROFILE: Throughout his career for more than three decades, Alan has provided legal advice to a core clientele consisting of individuals and owners of privately-held companies. Alan can help you structure the business entity that best suits your particular needs for both the short and long term.

ALAN E. SOHN, born Chicago, Illinois, March 9, 1944; admitted to bar, 1968, Illinois; 1969, U.S. District Court, Northern District of Illinois including Trial Bar and U.S. Court of Appeals, Seventh Circuit; 1981, U.S. Supreme Court. *Education:* University of Illinois (B.A., 1965; J.D., 1968). Member, Chicago Estate Planning Council. *Member:* Chicago Bar Association.

SONNENSCHEIN NATH & ROSENTHAL LLP

SEARS TOWER, SUITE 8000
233 SOUTH WACKER DRIVE
CHICAGO, ILLINOIS 60606
Telephone: 312-876-8000
Cable Address: "Sonberk"
Telex: 25-3526
Telecopier: 312-876-7934
URL: http://www.sonnenschein.com

New York, N.Y. Office: 1221 Avenue of the Americas. Telephone: 212-768-6700. Facsimile: 212-768-6800.
Washington, D.C. Office: 1301 K Street, N.W., Suite 600 East Tower. Telephone: 202-408-6400. Facsimile: 202-408-6399.
San Francisco, California Office: 685 Market Street, 6th Floor. Telephone: 415-882-5000. Facsimile: 415-543-5472.
Los Angeles, California Office: 601 South Figueroa Street, Suite 1500. Telephone: 213-623-9300. Facsimile: 213-623-9924.
St. Louis, Missouri Office: One Metropolitan Square, Suite 3000. Telephone: 314-241-1800. Facsimile: 314-259-5959.
Kansas City, Missouri Office: Suite 1100, 4520 Main Street, 64111. Telephone: 816-460-2400. Facsimile: 816-531-7545.
West Palm Beach, Florida Office: Phillips Point, West Tower, 777 South Flagler Drive, Suite 1102. Telephone: 561-833-2410. Facsimile: 561-833-8387.
Short Hills, New Jersey Office: 101 JFK Parkway. Telephone: 973-912-7100. Fax: 973-912-7199.

Antitrust, Aviation Litigation, Banking, Bankruptcy, Commercial Financing, Corporate, Employee Benefits, Environmental, Estate Planning, Executive Compensation, First Amendment, Franchising, Government Contracts, Health Care, Insurance, Intellectual Property, International Trade, Labor and Employment, Land Use, Litigation, Media, Municipal Bonds, Outsourcing, Probate, Product Liability, Professional Liability, Real Estate, Securities, Taxation, Trade Regulation, Venture Capital, Workouts, Zoning.

FIRM PROFILE: Sonnenschein, Nath & Rosenthal LLP is a national law firm with 700 attorneys in nine U.S. offices and a global reach throughout Europe, Asia, the Middle East and Latin America. Sonnenschein serves many of the world's largest and best-known businesses, nonprofits and individuals. Founded in 1906, the firm is a leader in innovative legal services, serving its clients through integrated, inter-office cooperation and teamwork among practice groups to provide efficient, effective and timely legal services and business counseling.

Sonnenschein is a leader in the use of innovative service-enhancing technologies. Our leadership in the accomplished use of full, secure Extranet capabilities and our pioneering contributions to e-commerce are among reasons why our clients say the firm consistently and uniquely meets and exceeds their expectations. Clients also cite the firm's spirited and collegial partnering with them, and the remarkable degree of ownership each attorney brings to the important task of managing resources.

We value a diverse workforce and the inspired work our people do to improve the social and economic health of the communities in which we live and work. We are committed to helping nonprofit organizations achieve their service goals and individuals achieve justice under the law through pro bono work by our attorneys.

EDWARD SONNENSCHEIN (1881-1935)

HUGO SONNENSCHEIN (1883-1956)

(This Listing Continued)

PARTNERS

ROY M. ADAMS (Resident, New York, N.Y. Office)

NEAL AIZENSTEIN, born Chicago, Illinois, September 4, 1963; admitted to bar, 1987, Illinois. *Education:* University of Illinois (B.S. Accounting, 1984); Northwestern University (J.D., cum laude, 1987). Beta Alpha Psi; Beta Gamma Sigma. Member, Bronze Tablet. James Scholar. Note and Comment Editor, Journal of Criminal Law and Criminology, 1986-1987. Recipient, Lowden-Wigmore Prize. Certified Public Accountant, Illinois, 1984. Author: Note, "Searches By Public School Officials Valid On Reasonable Grounds," 76 Journal of Criminal and Criminology 898, Winter, 1985. *Member:* Chicago and American Bar Associations. ***PRACTICE AREAS:*** Corporate; Securities. ***Email:*** na@sonnenschein.com

DAVID ALBENDA (Not admitted in Illinois; Resident, New York, N.Y. Office)

MITCHELL EDWARD ALBERT (Not admitted in Illinois; Resident, Kansas City, Missouri Office)

CHRISTINE COMER ALFARO (Resident, St. Louis, Missouri Office)

JEAN ALLARD, born Trenton, Missouri, December 16, 1924; admitted to bar, 1953, Illinois; 1959, Ohio. *Education:* Culver-Stockton College (B.A., 1945); Washington University (M.A., 1947); University of Chicago (J.D., 1953). Awarded LL.D. by Culver-Stockton College, 1977 and Elmhurst College, 1979. Managing Editor, University of Chicago Law Review, 1952-1953. Member, Moot Court National Competition. *Member:* American Bar Association (Section of Business Law, Chair, 1989-1990, Member of Council, 1977-1981; Delegate to House of Delegates, 1991-1993; Editor, The Business Lawyer, 1987-1988; Member: Committee on Corporate Laws, 1975-1981; 1990-1996; Committee on Alternative Dispute Resolution, 1984-1986; Committee on Corporate Governance, 1997—); American Law Institute; American Judicature Society (Director, 1977-1981). Fellow, American Bar Foundation (1985—). ***PRACTICE AREAS:*** General Corporate Law. ***Email:*** ja@sonnenschein.com

MINA AMIR-MOKRI, born Chicago, Illinois, August 20, 1967; admitted to bar, 1994, Illinois. *Education:* University of Chicago (B.A., 1989); University of Illinois (J.D., 1993; M.S. Accy., 1996). ***LANGUAGES:*** French, Italian and Persian. ***PRACTICE AREAS:*** ERISA; Executive Compensation. ***Email:*** a4m@sonnenschein.com

ROBERT M. ANDALMAN, born Skokie, Illinois, April 26, 1966; admitted to bar, 1992, Illinois; 1993, Wisconsin. *Education:* University of Michigan (B.A., with honors and distinction, 1988); Boston University (J.D., cum laude, 1992). ***REPORTED CASES:*** In re: Witness Before the Special Grand Jury, 288 F.3d 289 (7th Cir. 2002); Chavez, et al v. Illinois State Police, 251 F.3d 612 (7th Cir. 2001); United States v. Pergler, 233 F.3d 1005 (7th Cir. 2001); In re: Impounded, 178 F.3d 150 (3rd Cir. 1999); Lyons, et al v. Ryan, et. al., 324 Ill. App. 3d 1094 (1st District 2001), eff'd 201 Ill 2d 529 (2002). ***PRACTICE AREAS:*** Litigation; White Collar Criminal Defense. ***Email:*** randalman@sonnenschein.com

THOMAS A. ANDREOLI, born March 13, 1963; admitted to bar, 1997, Illinois. *Education:* University of Texas (B.A., 1986); Northwestern University (M.S.J., 1987); Loyola University (J.D., 1997). Supervising Editor, Journal of The National Association of Administrative Law Judges, Spring 1997. Policy Director, Mayor's Office, City of Chicago, 1997-1998. Associate Editor, Crain's Chicago Business, 1991-1997. *Member:* Chicago and American Bar Associations. ***PRACTICE AREAS:*** Litigation. ***Email:*** tandreoli@sonnenschein.com

JOSEPH J. ANDREW (Not admitted in Illinois; Resident, Washington, D.C. Office)

REID L. ASHINOFF (Not admitted in Illinois; Resident, New York, N.Y. Office)

GAYLE M. ATHANACIO (Not admitted in Illinois; Resident, San Francisco, California Office)

KATHARINA E. BABICH (Not admitted in Illinois; Resident, Kansas City, Missouri Office)

JOHN R. F. BAER, born Melrose Park, Illinois, January 9, 1941; admitted to bar, 1966, Illinois. *Education:* University of Illinois (B.A., 1963; J.D., 1966). Phi Delta Phi. Member, 1964-1965 and Assistant Editor, 1965-1966, University of Illinois Law Forum. Chair, Illinois Attorney General's Franchise Advisory Board, 1996—. Secretary, 1993-1994 and Vice President, Franchising Committee, 1994-1997, Union Internationale des Avocats. Topics and Articles Editor, 1995-1996 and Associate Editor, 1996-1999, ABA Franchise Law Journal. Editor, CCH Sales Representative Law Guide, 1998—. Editor-in-Chief, The Franchise Lawyer, 1999—. Member, Legal/Legislative Committee, International Franchise Association. *Member:* Illinois State (Chairman, Professional Ethics Committee, 1982-1983), American (Member, Forum on Franchising), International and Interpacific Bar Associations. ***PRACTICE AREAS:*** Franchising; Distribution; International; General Corporate. ***Email:*** jbaer@sonnenschein.com

PAMELA BAKER, born Detroit, Michigan, April 6, 1951; admitted to bar, 1976, Illinois and Wisconsin. *Education:* Smith College (A.B., 1972); University of Wisconsin at Madison (J.D., 1976). Member, 1974-1975 and Managing Editor, 1975-1976, Wisconsin Law Review. Co-Author with Louis A. Freeman, "Pension Investments in Real Estate," 1 Journal of Taxation of Investments 155, 1984. Co-Author with Anita Gottlieb," Participating Loans-Unresolved Fiduciary and Tax Concerns," Journal Tax'n Investments 155, 1986. Author: "Pension Trusts as Limited Partners-Ruminations on UBI and Service Bolt and Nut," 1 Journal Tax'n Investments 348, 1984; "Enhanced Incentives for Leveraged ESOP's After the 1984 Tax Reform Act," 2 Journal Tax'n Investments 178, 1985; "Rules of Thumb for Choosing Between Ten-Year Averaging and Rollovers on a Retirement Plan Distribution," 2 Journal Tax'n Investments 330, 1985; "ERISA and Soft Dollars," 4 Journal Tax'n Investments 140, 1987; "Individual Retirement Arrangements and Simplified Employee Pension Plans," Illinois Institute for Continuing Legal Education Employee Benefits Law, 1987, 1991, 1994; "Executive Compensation in Mergers and Acquisitions (Part 1)," 39 The Practical Lawyer No. 4 75, 1993; "Executive Compensation in Mergers and Acquisitions (Part 2)," 39 The Practical Lawyer No. 5 45, 1993; "A Simple Approach To Pension Planning," 83 Illinois Bar Journal 37, 1995; "New New New Rule 16b-3," 4 Erisa and Benefits Law Journal 248, 1996; "Employee Benefit Plan Exemptions Under Section 16 of the Securities Exchange Act of 1934," 59 Employee Benefits and Executive Compensation Counselor, 9 (1998). Co-Author: "Executive Compensation: A 1987 Road Map for the Corporate Advisor," 43 The Business Lawyer 185, 1987. *Member:* Chicago (Member, Employee Benefits Committee, 1978—; Chairman, 1986-1987; Federal Taxation Committee, 1980—; Executive Council, 1982-1985), Illinois State (Member, 1988—, Chair, Employee Benefits Section Council, 1991-1992) and American (Vice Chair, Employee Benefits Committee, Taxation Section, 1995-1998, Chair-Elect, 1998-1999, Chair, 1999-2000; Chairman, Federal and State Securities Regulation Subcommittee of Employee Benefits Committee, 1985-1995; Member: Joint Committee on Employee Benefits, 1991—; Sections on: Real Property, Probate and Trust Law; Taxation; Business Law) Bar Associations. Charter Fellow, American College of Employee Benefits Counsel. ***PRACTICE AREAS:*** Employee Benefits; Executive Compensation. ***Email:*** pb@sonnenschein.com

MICHAEL A. BAMBERGER (Not admitted in Illinois; Resident, New York, N.Y. Office)

WILLIAM T. BARKER, born Pittsburgh, Pennsylvania, February 28, 1947; admitted to bar, 1975, California; 1976, Illinois. *Education:* Michigan State University (B.A., 1969; M.S., 1969); Boalt Hall School of Law, University of California (J.D., 1974). Associate Editor, California Law Review, 1973-1974. Editor, 2000— and Contributing Editor, 1990-1999 Bad Faith Law Report. Member: Board of Editors, Defense Counsel Journal, 1987—; Editorial Advisory Board, Insurance Litigation Reporter, 1987—; Editorial Advisory Board, Insurance Law Briefings, 1987-1988; Defense Research Institute Insurance Law Publications Board, 1992-1997; Editor Emeritus, Insurance Committee Newsletter of Defense Research Institute, 1995—(Regional Editor, 1990-1995; Editor, 1995-1996). Moderator, Insurance Law (General) and Illinois Insurance Law Discussion Groups on Counsel Connect, 1995-1997. Author: "'The Right and Duty to Defend': Conflicts of Interest and Insurer Control of the Defense, "In Litigating The Coverage Claim" (ABA Press, 1992); "Settling Without the Insurer's Consent" "In Litigating The Coverage Claim" (ABA Press, 1992); "Insurer Loss Of Defenses By Failure To State All Possible Grounds Of Claim Denial," in "Litigating The Coverage Claims II: Pretrial Procedures And Strategies," (ABA Press, 1993); "Reservation of Rights and Control of Settlement," in Donald J. Hirsch (ed.), Insurer's Duties: A Coverage Perspective (DRI 1995); "Combining Insurance and Self-Insurance: Issues in Handling Liability Claims," 61 Def. Coun. J. 352 (1994); "Insurance Defense Ethics and the Liability Insurance Bargain," 4 Conn. J. Ins. Law 75 (1997); "The Tripartite Relationship and the Protection of the Insured: Is There a Problem?" 21 Ins. Litig. Rptr. 533 (1999); "The Tripartite Relationship and Protection of the Insured: Beyond Professional Responsibility," 18 Ins. Litig. Rptr. 528 (1996); "Lobbying and the American Law Institute: The Example of Insurance Defense," 26 Hofstra L. Rev. 573 (1998); "Evidentiary Sufficiency In Insurance Bad Faith Suits," 6 Comm Ins. L.J. 82 (1999-2000); "Extrinsic Evidence and the Duty to Defend," 21 Ins. Litig. Rptr. 4 (1999); "Recoupment or Non Covered Settlements: Blue Ridge Ins. Co. v. Jacobson," 16 Bad Faith L. Rep. 29 (2000); "The Malicious Prosecution Analogy: A Reply to Quinn," 16 Bad Faith L. Rep. 72 (2000); "Lessons From A Claim Disaster: Capstick v. All State Ins. Co., 16 Bad Faith L. Rep. 75 (2000); "Archangel Insurance Co. v. Walter Raleigh: A Hypothetical Case on Recoupment of Defense Costs, 19 Ins. Litig. Rptr. 536 & 639 (1997); "Occurrence-Based Insurance: Scope of Coverage and Allocation of Losses," 18 Ins. Litig. Rptr. 652 (1996); "Insurability of Punitive Damages," 10 Bad Faith L. Rep. 207, 1994; "Bad Faith Cases & Bifurcation," 12 Bad Faith L. Rep. (1996); "Bad Faith: The Limits of the Advice of Counsel Defense," 12 Bad Faith L. Rep. 47 (1996); "Are Juries Competent to Find Judges Unreasonable," 16 Bad Faith L. Rep. 4 (2000); "Damages for Insurance Policy Breaches: A Reply to Ashley," 13 Bad Faith L. Rev. 109 (1997); "Defense Without Reserving Rights: When May Insurer Deny Coverage," 56 Def. Coun. J. 58 (1989); "Good Faith and Sale or Renewal of an Insurance Policy," 6 Bad Faith L. Rep. 167 & 192 (1990); "Defense Counsel and Policy Limits Settlement Offers: Another View," 6 Bad Faith L. Rep. 141 (1990); "King v. Meese: Does Compulsory Insurance Constitutionally Require Intensive Regulation of Ratemaking and Underwriting," 8 Ins. Litig. Rptr. 986 (1986); "Insurance Litigation, Diversity Jurisdiction, and the Direct Action Proviso," 35 Fed. Ins. Coun. Q. 225 (1985); "Control of The Defense and Control of Settlement: Need They Go Together?" 8 Bad Faith L. Rep., 59 (1992); "Coverage Disputes and Control of Settlement," 8 Bad Faith L. Rep., 77 (1992); "Claim Denials, Reconsideration, and Statutes of Limitation," 7 Bad Faith L. Rep. 108 (1991); "Fiduciary Duty, R.I.P." 6 Bad Faith L. Rep. 107 (1990); "Insurer Liability for Defense Counsel's Blunders," 9 Bad Faith L. Rep. 73, (1993); "Punitive Damages and Common Law Reform: Transportation Insurance Co. v. Moriel," 17 Ins. Litigation Reporter 3 (1995); "Post-Verdict Review of Punitive Damages: Honda Motor Co. v. Oberg," 16 Ins. Litigation Reporter 399 (1994); "Punitive Damages and the Constitution Revisited: Honda Motor Co. v. Oberg," 16 Ins. Litig. Rptr., 116 (1994); "Constitutional Constraints on Punitive Damages in the Wake of TXO," 15 Ins. Litig. Rptr. 373, (1993); "Whither Punitive Damages? TXO Production Corp. v. Alliance Resources Corp.," 15 Ins. Lit. Rptr. 210 (1993); "Notice When Representative Party Settles Uncertified Class Action," 57 Def. Coun. J. 476 (1990); "Managing the Discovery Process: Some Thoughts for In-House Counsel," 55 Def. Coun. Rev. 142 (1988) (reprinted in 32 Corporate Practice Commentator 603 (1991); "ALI Draft Questions Insurer's Right to Control The Defense," 60 Def. Coun. J. 611 (1993); "A Reservation of Rights Is Not Always Enough To Preserve Coverage Defenses," 16 Bad Faith L. Rep. 89 (2000); "The Texas Bad Faith Trilogy: Bombshell or Dud?" 13 Bad Faith L. Rep. 165 (1997); "Dissident Thoughts on The Duty of Defense," 9 Bad Faith L. Rep., (1994). Co-Author with Vobornik, "The Scope of the Emerging Duty of First-Party Insurers To Inform Their Insureds of Rights Under the Policy," 25 Tort & Ins. L.J. 749 (1990); with Wagner, "State Insurance Tax Differentials and Regulatory Objectives: A Constitutional Analysis, Part I, The Legal Standards," 8 J. Ins. Reg. 128 (1989); "Part II, Bases for Differentials & Retaliatory Considerations," 8 J. Ins. Reg. 258 (1990); with Glad & Levy, "Is an Insurer a Fiduciary to Its Insureds?" 25 Tort & Ins. L. J. 1 (1989); with Glad & Hassen, "Bad Faith Liability in the Absence of Coverage?" 7 Bad Faith L. Rep. 1 (1991); with Glad, "Bad Faith in the Absence of Coverage: The Insurer's Perspective," in Recurring Issues in Insurance Coverage Disputes (David R. Leitner, 2d. ABA 1996); "Use of Summary Judgment In Defense of Bad Faith Actions Involving First-Party Insurance," 30 Tort and Ins. L.J. 1 (1994); "Bad Faith Liability in the Absence of Coverage: A Reply," 7 Bad Faith L. Rep. 83 (1991); "Bad Faith Liability in the Absence of Coverage? Arizona Speaks Up," 7 Bad Faith L. Rep. 131 (1991); "Unfair Claims Practices Statutes and the Adjustment of Third Party Claims Against Insureds," 7 Bad Faith L. Rep. 237 (1991); "Summary Judgment In Bad Faith Litigation Arising From Suspicious Claims,: For The Defense, Vol. 35, No. 11, p. 20 (1994); "BMW of North America: Limitations on Punitive Damages Lotto," Underwriters Report (June 1996); with Glad & Barnes "Failure To Settle Third-Party

(This Listing Continued)

(This Listing Continued)

SONNENSCHEIN NATH & ROSENTHAL LLP, Chicago—Continued

Claims as Intentional Infliction of Emotional Distress," 8 Bad Faith L. Rep. 1 (1992); with Powell & Truesdale, "Too Many Claimants, Too Little Money: The Missed Opportunity of Trinity Universal Ins. Co. v. Bleeker," 14 Bad Faith L. Rep. 123 (1998); with Platto, "Mail Fraud Meets Insurance Law: United States v. Brennan," 20 Ins. Litg. Reptr. 905 (1998); with Estas, "Are Juries Competant to Find Judges Unreasonable," 16 Bad Faith L. Rep. 2 (2000); with Appelbaum, "Insurance Policy Changes at Renewal: What Must Be Explained?" 13 Ins. Litig. Rptr. 3 (1991); with Levy, New Perspective on Household Exclusions Where Liability Insurance Is Compulsory, 58 Def. Coun. J. 71 (1991); with Barnes, "The Standard for First-Party Bad Faith," 10 Bad Faith L. Rep. 69 (1994); with Barr "Recent Developments in New York Bad Faith Law," 10 Bad Faith L. Rep. 25 (1994); with Martin, "The Not-So-Peculiar Fate of Excess Insurers in the Laws of Bad Faith," 7 Bad Faith L. Rep. 162 (1991); with Kates, "Mootness in Judicial Proceedings: Toward a Coherent Theory, 62 Calif. L.J. 1385 (1974); with Silberman, "Courts Should Protect Pre-Existing Contract Rights From Redistributing Politics," Wash. Legal Found. Legal Op. Ltr., Vol. 7, No. 22 (Sept. 25, 1992). *Member:* Chicago (Insurance Law Committee and Constitutional Law Committee Chairman, 1984-1985 and Professional Responsibility Committee) and American (Member: Sections on Litigation, Committees on Insurance Coverage Litigation, Subcommittee Chair, 1990-1991, 1993-1996; Professional Responsibility and Appellate Practice; Tort and Insurance Practice, General Committee Board, 1995-1997, Chair, 1996-1997, Committees on Insurance Coverage Litigation, Vice Chair, 1993-1995, and Public Regulation of Insurance and Appellate Advocacy; Chair-Elect, 1994-1995, Chair, 1995-1996; Individual Rights and Responsibilities) Bar Associations; Chicago Council of Lawyers (Member, Board of Governors, 1989-1991; Secretary, 1987-1988; Co-Chair, Committee on Ethics and Professional Responsibility, 1990-1991; Chair, 1991-1995); International Association of Defense Counsel (Member, Committees on Casualty Insurance, Life, Health and Accident Insurance, Professional Responsibility; Amicus Curiae Chair, 1996-1997); Defense Research Institute (Member, Committees on Insurance Law, Business Litigation, Practice and Procedure); American Law Institute. Fellow, American Bar Foundation. ***PRACTICE AREAS:*** General Litigation; Insurance; Constitutional. ***Email:*** wtb@sonnenschein.com

MICHAEL A. BARNES (Not admitted in Illinois; Resident, San Francisco, California Office)

DANIEL D. BARNOWSKI (Not admitted in Illinois; Resident, Washington, D.C. Office)

MICHAEL H. BARR (Not admitted in Illinois; Resident, New York, N.Y. Office)

KARA S. BAYSINGER (Resident, San Francisco, California Office)

CAROL ANNE BEEN, born Peoria, Illinois, August 17, 1955; admitted to bar, 1983, Illinois and U.S. District Court, Northern District of Illinois; 1984, U.S. Court of Appeals, Seventh Circuit; 1996, U.S. District Court, Eastern District of Michigan. *Education:* University of Illinois (B.S., 1976; J.D., 1983); Northwestern University, 1982-1983. Bronze Tablet. Member, University of Illinois Law Review, 1982-1983. ***PRACTICE AREAS:*** Intellectual Property Litigation; Trademarks; Copyrights; Trade Secrets; Internet; Electronic Commerce; Computer Law; Advertising; Sweepstakes; Media; Entertainment. ***Email:*** cab@sonnenschein.com

RUDOLF H. BEESE, born Brantford, Ontario, Canada, December 18, 1956; admitted to bar, 1983, Kansas; 1991, Missouri. *Education:* Valparaiso University (B.S., Chemistry, 1979; J.D., 1982). ***PRACTICE AREAS:*** Construction; Real Estate; Economic Development Incentives. ***Email:*** rbeese@sonnenschein.com

CHERYL DYER BERG (Not admitted in Illinois; Resident, San Francisco, California Office)

JOSHUA G. BERMAN (Resident, Washington, D.C. Office)

AMY L. BESS (Resident, Washington, D.C. Office)

JANA COHEN BLACKMAN, born Miami Beach, Florida, August 30, 1962; admitted to bar, 1987, Illinois. *Education:* Northwestern University (B.A., with honors, 1984); University of Chicago Law School (J.D., 1987). *Member:* Chicago and American Bar Associations. ***PRACTICE AREAS:*** Affordable Housing; Real Estate; Corporate. ***Email:*** jcb@sonnenschein.com

ALLISON C. BLAKLEY, born Chicago, Illinois, April 26, 1956; admitted to bar, 1982, Illinois, U.S. District Court, Northern District of Illinois and U.S. Court of Appeals, Seventh Circuit; 1987, U.S. District Court, Eastern District of Michigan; 1988, U.S. Court of Appeals, Fifth and Ninth Circuits; 1989, U.S. Court of Appeals, Eleventh Circuit; 1990, U.S. District Court, Northern District of Illinois including Trial Bar; 1994, U.S. Court of Appeals, Third Circuit; U.S. District Court, District of Arizona. *Education:* University of California, Berkeley, College of Natural Resources (B.S., cum laude, 1978); University of Oregon School of Law (J.D., 1982). ***PRACTICE AREAS:*** Employment Litigation; Employment Counseling; Complex Civil Rights Litigation; Fair Housing; Arbitration. ***Email:*** ablakley@sonnenschein.com

G. HARLEY BLOSSER (Not admitted in Illinois; Resident, St. Louis, Missouri Office)

JOEL N. BOCK (Not admitted in Illinois; Resident, Short Hills, New Jersey Office)

VALARIE TATEM BOMAR, born Chicago, Illinois, March 2, 1969; admitted to bar, 1997, Illinois; 1998, Michigan. *Education:* Spelman College (B.S., cum laude, 1991); University of Michigan (J.D., 1997). *Member:* Wolverine, Illinois State and American Bar Associations; State Bar of Michigan. ***PRACTICE AREAS:*** Commercial Litigation. ***Email:*** vbomar@sonnenschein.com

DOUGLAS G. BONNER, born Washington, DC, September 28, 1958; admitted to bar, 1983, Florida; 1984, District of Columbia (Not admitted in Illinois). *Education:* Bucknell University (B.A., 1980); Catholic University of America (J.D., 1983). *(Resident, Washington, D.C. Office).* ***PRACTICE AREAS:*** Telecommunications; Litigation. ***Email:*** dbonner@sonnenschein.com

ALAN B. BORNSTEIN (Not admitted in Illinois; Resident, St. Louis, Missouri Office)

(This Listing Continued)

VICTOR H. BOYAJIAN (Not admitted in Illinois; Resident, New York, N.Y. and Short Hills, New Jersey Offices)

ROGER T. BRICE, born Chicago, Illinois, May 7, 1948; admitted to bar, 1973, Illinois and Iowa; 1974, U.S. Court of Appeals, 10th Circuit; 1975, U.S. Court of Appeals, 1st, 4th and 7th Circuits; 1976, U.S. District Court, Northern District of Illinois including Trial Bar; 1978, U.S. Supreme Court; 1995, U.S. District Court, Central District of Illinois. *Education:* DePaul University (A.B., summa cum laude, 1970); University of Chicago (J.D., 1973). Associate Editor, University of Chicago Law Review, 1972-1973. Author: "Grand Jury Proceedings: The Prosecutor, The Trial Judge and Undue Influence," 39 University of Chicago Law Review 761, 1972. Co-author: "NLRB v. Catholic Bishop of Chicago: Government Regulation v. First Amendment Religious Freedoms," 24 St. Louis University Law Journal 295, 1980. *Member:* American Bar Association (Member, Labor and Employment Law and Litigation Sections). [Lt., JAG, USNR, 1970-1978]. ***PRACTICE AREAS:*** Labor; Employment; Litigation. ***Email:*** rtb@sonnenschein.com

JEFFREY BRILL (Not admitted in Illinois; Resident, San Francisco, California Office)

LYNDA L. BROTHERS (Not admitted in Illinois; Resident, San Francisco, California Office)

RICHARD M. BROWN, born Chicago, Illinois, June 16, 1945; admitted to bar, 1970, Illinois. *Education:* Washington University (A.B., with honors, 1967); Northwestern University (J.D., 1970). Contributing Author: "Handling Business Interests and Estates," "Closely Held Corporation," "Illinois Estate Administration," "Life Insurance and Business Planning" and "Basic Estate Planning," Illinois Institute for Continuing Legal Education; "Recent Amendments to Federal Estate, Gift, and Generation Skipping Tax Provisions of the Internal Revenue Code," Illinois Bar General. Author and Lecturer, Estate Planning Short Course, University of Notre Dame. Member: Northwestern University Estate Planning Council; Professional Advisory Committee, Jewish United Fund; Gift Committee, Art Institute of Chicago. *Member:* Chicago, Illinois State and American Bar Associations. Fellow, American College of Trust and Estate Counsel. ***PRACTICE AREAS:*** Trusts and Estates; Tax Law; Corporate Law. ***Email:*** rbrown@sonnenschein.com

MARK S. BRYANT (Not admitted in Illinois; Resident, Kansas City, Missouri Office)

JEFFRY BUTLER (Not admitted in Illinois; Resident, San Francisco, California Office)

JOHN J. CALKINS (Not admitted in Illinois; Resident, Washington, D.C. Office)

DONALD M. CARLEY (Not admitted in Illinois; Resident, San Francisco, California Office)

LEO J. CARLIN (Deceased, 1988)

PHILLIP A. CASEY, born August 18, 1962; admitted to bar, 1988, Illinois. *Education:* Illinois State University (B.S., 1984); John Marshall Law School (J.D., 1988). ***PRACTICE AREAS:*** Energy; Telecommunications Law. ***Email:*** pcasey@sonnenschein.com

MARTIN R. CASTRO, born Chicago, Illinois, August 12, 1963; admitted to bar, 1988, Illinois. *Education:* DePaul University (B.A., Political Science, cum laude, 1985); University of Michigan Law School, Ann Arbor (J.D., 1988). ***PRACTICE AREAS:*** Corporate Diversity Counseling. ***Email:*** mcastro@sonnenschein.com

GINA M. CAVALIER (Resident, Washington, D.C. Office)

CARYN L. CHALMERS, born October 5, 1969; admitted to bar, 1994, Illinois. *Education:* University of Texas (B.S., 1991); Northwestern University (J.D., 1994). Coordinating Note and Comment Editor, Journal of International Law and Business. Author: Comment, 14.3 Northwestern Journal of International Law and Business 602, 1994. *Member:* Chicago and American Bar Associations. ***PRACTICE AREAS:*** Real Estate; Affordable Housing. ***Email:*** clf@sonnenschein.com

DEVEREUX CHATILLON (Resident, New York, N.Y. Office)

KEVIN P. CHAVOUS (Resident, Washington, D.C. Office)

WILLIAM W. CHOE (Not admitted in Illinois; Resident, San Francisco, California Office)

JOHN FRANKLIN CLARK (Resident, Washington, D.C. Office)

KIMANI CLARK (Resident, Washington, D.C. Office)

JOHN L. CLEARY (Not admitted in Illinois; Resident, Short Hills, New Jersey Office)

DENISE M. CLOLERY (Not admitted in Illinois; Resident, New York, N.Y. Office)

ROBERT W. COCKREN (Not admitted in Illinois; Resident, Short Hills, New Jersey Office)

DAVID E. CRAWFORD, JR. (Resident, St. Louis, Missouri Office)

SHIRLEY E. CURFMAN (Not admitted in Illinois; Resident, Los Angeles, California Office)

STEVEN R. DAVIDSON, born Chicago, Illinois, April 22, 1952; admitted to bar, 1977, Illinois. *Education:* University of Michigan (A.B., with high honors and high distinction, 1974); Harvard University (J.D., cum laude, 1977). Phi Eta Sigma. *Member:* Chicago and American Bar Associations. ***PRACTICE AREAS:*** Real Estate; Banking; Venture Capital. ***Email:*** srd@sonnenschein.com

LESLIE D. DAVIS, born Chicago, Illinois, February 21, 1971; admitted to bar, 1995, Illinois. *Education:* University of Iowa (B.A., 1992; M.A., 1995; J.D., 1995). Member, University of Iowa Law Review. ***PRACTICE AREAS:*** Litigation; Business Regulation. ***Email:*** ldavis@sonnenschein.com

BRUCE C. DAVISON (Not admitted in Illinois; Resident, Kansas City, Missouri Office)

ERIC R. DECATOR, born Philadelphia, Pennsylvania, October 9, 1957; admitted to bar, 1983, Colorado; 1987, Illinois; 1989, Pennsylvania; 1990, California; 1998, Missouri. *Education:* University of Michigan (B.A., 1978); Northwestern University, J.L. Kellogg School of Management (M.B.A., Hospital/Health Services Management, 1980); University of Colorado at Boulder (J.D., 1983). Order of the Coif. Visiting Instructor, University of Colorado School of Law, 1982. General Counsel and Chief Financial Officer, Delmed, Inc.,

(This Listing Continued)

1990-1991. First Assistant Attorney General, State of Colorado, 1991-1995. *Member:* National Association of College and University Attorneys. ***PRACTICE AREAS:*** Corporate; Health Care; Higher Education. ***Email:*** ewd@sonnenschein.com

DENNIS S. DIAZ (Not admitted in Illinois; Resident, Los Angeles, California Office)

J. ROSS DOCKSEY, born Milwaukee, Wisconsin, September 4, 1951; admitted to bar, 1981, Illinois. *Education:* U. S. Military Academy (B.S., 1973), Dean's List; University of Minnesota (J.D., cum laude, 1981). Member, Philip C. Jessup International Moot Court Team, 1980. Director, International Moot Court and National Moot Court Programs, University of Minnesota, 1980-1981. Director: Daubert Industries, Inc., 1996-2000; The Tim and Tom Gullikson Foundation, 1995-2000. Secretary, Daubert Industries, Inc. and subsidiaries, 1983-1997. Lecturer: Practising Law Institute, Georgetown Advanced Computer Law Institute, National Web Managers Conference; IT Mergers and Acquisitions Conference; Arthur Andersen Enterprise Awards Symposium. *Member:* American Bar Association. [Army, 1973-1978, Captain]. ***PRACTICE AREAS:*** Corporate; Information Technology; Outsourcing; Mergers and Acquisitions. ***Email:*** jrd@sonnenschein.com

MARK L. DOSIER, born Havana, Illinois, January 11, 1966; admitted to bar, 1991, Illinois and U.S. District Court, Northern District of Illinois. *Education:* University of Illinois at Champaign/Urbana (B.S., with highest honors, 1988); University of Chicago (J.D., 1991). Beta Gamma Sigma; Bronze Tablet. *Member:* Chicago and American Bar Associations. ***PRACTICE AREAS:*** Corporate; Securities. ***Email:*** mxd@sonnenschein.com

ARLENE G. DUBIN (Not admitted in Illinois; Resident, New York, N.Y. Office)

ROBIN M. EDWARDS (Not admitted in Illinois; Resident, San Francisco, California Office)

MICHAEL J. EMONT (Not admitted in Illinois; Resident, New York, N.Y. Office)

RALPH M. ENGEL (Not admitted in Illinois; Resident, New York, N.Y. Office)

TODD R. ESKELSEN (Not admitted in Illinois; Resident, Washington, D.C. Office)

PHYLLIS A. EWER, born Grant County, Indiana, February 27, 1939; admitted to bar, 1982, Illinois. *Education:* Indiana University (B.A., 1961; M.A., 1963); University of Washington (Ph.D., 1967); Northwestern University (J.D., cum laude, 1982). Articles Editor, Journal of Criminal Law and Criminology, 1980-1982. Author: "The Death Penalty," 71 JCLC 538, 1980; "Court Upholds Parental Notice Requirement before Allowing Abortions on Minors," 72 JCLC 1461, 1981; "Shedding Unwanted Retirement Plan Funds: A Problem In Need Of A Solution," 5 J. Tax'n Inv. 163, 1988. Adjunct Professor of Law, IIT/Chicago-Kent College of Law, 1990—. *Member:* Chicago (Member, Tax Committee and Employee Benefits Committee) and American (Member, Employee Benefits Committee of Tax Section) Bar Associations; Chicago Council of Lawyers. ***PRACTICE AREAS:*** Employee Benefits; Executive Compensation. ***Email:*** pae@sonnenschein.com

HOLLY S. FALKOWITZ WALLMAN (Not admitted in Illinois; Resident, New York, N.Y. Office)

CYNTHIA A. FAUR, born Medina, Ohio, June 11, 1967; admitted to bar, 1993, Illinois. *Education:* University of Michigan (B.A., 1989); University of Chicago (J.D., 1993). Phi Beta Kappa. James B. Angell Scholar. ***LANGUAGES:*** French. ***PRACTICE AREAS:*** Environmental. ***Email:*** cqf@sonnenschein.com

RICHARD L. FENTON, born Chicago, Illinois, April 6, 1954; admitted to bar, 1978, Illinois and U.S. District Court, Northern District of Illinois; 1980, U.S. Court of Appeals, Seventh Circuit; 1985, U.S. Court of Appeals, Second Circuit; 1990, U.S. Court of Appeals, Sixth Circuit; 1999, U.S. Tax Court. *Education:* University of Chicago (B.A., with honors, 1975; J.D., 1978). Author: "Rule 11: Stop, Think and Investigate," Litigation, Vol. 11, No. 2, Winter 1985. Recipient, William E. Goettler Political Institutions Award, University of Chicago, 1975. Student Officer, Mandel Legal Aid Clinic, 1977-1978. Member, 1992-1996, North Shore School District 112 Board of Education, Highland Park, Illinois (President, 1993-1994). *Member:* Chicago (Member, Judicial Evaluation Committee) and American (Member, Litigation Section) Bar Associations. ***PRACTICE AREAS:*** General Commercial Litigation; Real Estate Litigation. ***Email:*** rlf@sonnenschein.com

ELIZABETH A. FERRELL (Not admitted in Illinois; Resident, Washington, D.C. Office)

BRIAN W. FIELDS (Resident, Kansas City, Missouri Office)

SAMUEL FIFER, born Chicago, Illinois, May 5, 1950; admitted to bar, 1974, Illinois; 1977, U.S. Supreme Court. *Education:* Northwestern University (B.S., 1971); DePaul University (J.D., cum laude, 1974). Managing Editor, De Paul University Law Review, 1973-1974. Co-Author: "Y2K Claims Against the Computer Industry: Past as Prologue," Litigation, Winter 2000; "Defamation on the Internet: Nothing to Fear But New Ideas," presented to American Bar Association, 1997; "The Price of International Free Speech: Nations Deal with Defamation on the Internet," 8 DePaul Journal of Arts & Entertainment Law 1, 1997; "Internet's Global Marketplace of Ideas Faces Challenge from U.S. Defamation Law," IP Worldwide, March, 1996; "Taming a New Frontier: The Law Grapples with Online Defamation," presented to American Bar Association, 1995; "Courts Continue to Face Delicate Fair-Use Issues," National Law Journal, May 8, 1995; "Mpm-Compete Clauses Protect Trade Secrets," The National Law Journal, October 31, 1994; "The Acquisition and Disposition of Intellectual Property in Commercial Transactions: The U.S. Perspective," in The New Role of Intellectual Property in Commercial Transactions—Developing Trends in the Valuation, Exploitation and Protection of Intellectual Property, John Wiley & Sons, 1994. Contributor: State Trademark and Unfair Competition Law, International Trademark Association. Author: "On Trying to Protect Too Much," Remarks: Trademark News for Business," Vol. 4, No. 2, 1991; "Decision Backing Press Freedom Has Ominous Undertone," Chicago Tribune, August 17, 1990; Comment, "Musical Expression and First Amendment Considerations," 23 De Paul Law Review 143, 1974; Note, "United States v. Midwest Video, Cable Television and the Program Origination Rule," 22 De Paul Law Review 461, 1972. Adjunct Professor, Northwestern University School of Law, 1992—, (Entertainment Law). Member, Cyberlaw Committee, Libel Defense Resource Center, Defense Counsel Section. *Member:* Chicago, Illinois State (Chair, Copyright Committee, Intellectual Property Section Council, 1989-1990) and American (Member, Section of Patent, Trademark, and Copyright Law; Vice Chairman, Committee on Media Law and

(This Listing Continued)

Defamation Torts of the Section of Tort and Insurance Practice, 1990-1991) Bar Associations; International Trademark Association. ***PRACTICE AREAS:*** Defamation; Entertainment; Intellectual Property. ***Email:*** sxf@sonnenschein.com

SHELDON I. FINK, born Chicago, Illinois, May 12, 1930; admitted to bar, 1954, Illinois. *Education:* University of Wisconsin (B.B.A., 1952; LL.B., 1954). Order of the Coif. Editor, Wisconsin Law Review, 1953-1954. Trial Attorney, Tax Division, Department of Justice, 1956-1958. *Member:* Chicago and American Bar Associations. ***PRACTICE AREAS:*** Federal Income Tax. ***Email:*** sif@sonnenschein.com

JOHN F. FINSTON (Resident, San Francisco, California Office)

CHRISTINE BAY FISHER, born March 3, 1951; admitted to bar, 1981, Florida; 2000, Illinois. *Education:* University of the South (B.A., 1973); University of Florida (M.A., 1976; J.D., with honors, 1980). ***PRACTICE AREAS:*** Real Estate. ***Email:*** cfisher@sonnenschein.com

G. ROBERT FISHER (Not admitted in Illinois; Resident, Kansas City, Missouri Office)

MARK A. FLESSNER, born Kankakee, Illinois, 1954; admitted to bar, 1987, Illinois, U.S. District Court, Northern District of Illinois including Trial Bar and U.S. Court of Appeals, Seventh Circuit. *Education:* University of Illinois at Urbana-Champaign (B.A., with distinction in Political Science, 1976); University of Notre Dame (M. Div., 1980); DePaul University (J.D., 1986). Previous Employment: United States Attorney's Office, Chicago, Illinois, Criminal Division, 1990-2000 and Civil Division, 1987-1990, United States Attorney's Office, Chicago, Illinois. Recipient, Director's Award for Superior Performance from the United States Attorney General, 1996. *Member:* Chicago and American Bar Associations; Chicago Council of Lawyers (Member, Board of Governors). ***LANGUAGES:*** Spanish. ***REPORTED CASES:*** In re: Grand Jury Proceedings, 220 F.3d 568 (7th Cir. 2000); United States v. Ryan, 213 F.3d 34 (7th Cir. 2000); United States v. Cheska, 129 F.3d 1268 (7th Cir. 1997); United States v. Thompson, 76 F.3d 166 (7th Cir.1996); United States v. Saadeh, No. 93-2681, United States Court of Appeals for the Seventh Circuit, 1995 U.S. App. LEXIS 25289, September 7, 1995; United States v. Anderson, 61 F.3d 1290 (7th Cir. 1995); United States v. Saadeh, 61 F.3d 510 (7th Cir. 1995); United States v. Velez, 46 F.3d 688 (7th Cir. 1995); United States v. Burnom, 27 F.3d 283 (7th Cir. 1994); United States v. Daddino, 5 F.3d 262 (7th Cir. 1993); Allen v. Sullivan, 977 F.2d 385 (7th Cir. 1992); United States v. Schweihs, 971 F.2d 1302 (7th Cir. 1992); United States v. Zafiro, 945 F.2d 881 (7th Cir. 1991); United States v. Northlake, 942 F.2d 1164 (7th Cir. 1991); Thompson v. Sullivan, 933 F.2d 581 (7th Cir. 1991); United States v. Rodriguez, 929 F.2d 1224 (7th Cir. 1991); Savic v. United States, 918 F.2d 696 (7th Cir. 1990); Lewellen v. Morley, 909 F.2d 1073 (7th Cir. 1990); Carlson v. United States, 879 F.2d 261 (7th Cir. 1989); Lewellen v. Morley, 875 F.2d 118 (7th Cir. 1989); United States v. Fawell, No. 02 CR 310, United States District Court for the Northern District of Illinois, Eastern Division, 2002 U.S. Dist. LEXIS 10415, June 10, 2002, Decided, June 11, 2002; McCarroll v. United States, No. 99 CV 884/No. 95 CR 48-1, United States District Court for the Northern District of Illinois, Eastern Division, 2002; Profile Prods., LLC v. Soil Mgmt. Techs., Inc., 155 F. Supp. 2d 880 (ND IL 2001); Anderson v. United States, No. 97 C 2805, United States District Court for the Northern District of Illinois, Eastern Division, 1998; United States v. Cannon, No. 94 CR 277-2 (95 C 6769), United States District Court for the Northern District of Illinois, Eastern Division, 1997; United States v. Saadeh, Case No. 97 C 2798, United States District Court for the Northern District of Illinois, Eastern Division, 1997; United States v. MacCready, No. 96 C 525, United States District Court for the Northern District of Illinois, Eastern Division, 1997; United States v. MacCready, No. 96 C 525, United States District Court for the Northern District of Illinois, Eastern Division, 1996; United States v. Village of Oak Lawn, Civil Action No. 86-C-1745, United States District Court for the Northern District of Illinois, Eastern Division, 1996; United States v. McCarroll, No. 95 CR 48, United States District Court for the Northern District of Illinois, Eastern Division, 1996; United States v. Baiza, 94 CR 511, 96 C 1414, United States District Court for the Northern District of Illinois, Eastern Division, 1996; Carter v. Chater, No. 90 C 3489, United States District Court for the Northern District of Illinois, Eastern Division, 1996; Carter v. Chater, No. 90 C 3489, United States District Court for the Northern District of Illinois, Eastern Division, 1996; Carter v. Sullivan, 782 F. Supp. 1251 (ND IL 1991); Savic v. United States, 702 F. Supp. 695 (ND IL 1988); Savic v. United States, 689 F. Supp. 854 (ND IL 1988). ***PRACTICE AREAS:*** Complex Commercial Litigation; White Collar Criminal Defense. ***Email:*** mflessner@sonnenschein.com

MICHAEL R. FLYNN (Resident, New York, N.Y. Office)

MARTIN J. FOLEY (Not admitted in Illinois; Resident, Los Angeles, California Office)

JEFFREY C. FORT, born Burlington, Iowa, October 10, 1950; admitted to bar, 1975, Illinois; U.S. Supreme Court, U.S. Court of Appeals, Seventh and District of Columbia Circuits; U.S. District Court, Northern District of Illinois. *Education:* Monmouth College (B.A., 1972); Northwestern University (J.D., cum laude, 1975). Author: "Developing An Effective Environmental Compliance Program," (Clark Boardman Callaghan, 1993); "Decisions and Trends in Environmental Law," (Corporate Counsel Institute, October and December, 1992); "Due Diligence," Environmental Law for Transactional Attorneys (IICLE, 1991, republished ABA, 1992); "Overview of the Law Applicable to Insurance Coverage for Hazardous Waste Claims," in *Disputes Collateral to Superfund Proceedings,* (IICLE), 1988; "Responding to Section 104(e) Notice -- What To Do," in *The Effective Defense of a Hazardous Waste Case,* (IICLE), 1987; "Pollution Control Board," in *Chicago Lawyer's Court Handbook,* (CBA), 1981, rev. 1987-1991; "The Necessary Demise of Federal Common Law Nuisance," 12 Loy. U. Chi. L.J. 131, 1981; "Understanding Unconscionability: Defining the Principle," 9 Loyola U. Chi. Law Journal 765, 1978. Adjunct Professor for Environmental Law, Northwestern University School of Law, 1990-1993. Law Clerk for Justice John M. Karns, Jr., Fifth District, Illinois Appellate Court, 1975-1976. *Member:* Chicago (Chairman, Environmental Law Committee, 1986-1987) and American Bar Associations; Air & Waste Management Association (Chairman, Lake Michigan States Section, 1989-1990). ***PRACTICE AREAS:*** Environmental. ***Email:*** jcf@sonnenschein.com

GERALD E. FRADIN, born Urbana, Illinois, August 23, 1965; admitted to bar, 1990, Illinois and U.S. District Court, Northern District of Illinois; 1991, U.S. Court of Appeals, Seventh Circuit; 1996, U.S. Court of Appeals, Third Circuit. *Education:* University of Illinois at Champaign/Urbana (A.B., high distinction, 1987); University of Pennsylvania (J.D.,

(This Listing Continued)

SONNENSCHEIN NATH & ROSENTHAL LLP, Chicago—Continued

1990). Member, National Moot Court Team. *Member:* American Bar Association. ***PRACTICE AREAS:*** Commercial Litigation; Computer Litigation. ***Email:*** gef@sonnenschein.com

STEVEN H. FRANKEL (Resident, San Francisco, California Office)

BRUCE MERLIN FRIED (Not admitted in Illinois; Resident, Washington, D.C. Office)

MICHAEL M. FROY, born Evanston, Illinois, January 31, 1959; admitted to bar, 1983, Illinois. *Education:* University of Michigan (A.B., with honors and high distinction, 1979); University of Chicago, (J.D., 1983). Member, Planning Committee for the Ray Garrett, Jr. Corporate and Securities Law Institute. ***PRACTICE AREAS:*** Corporate; Securities. ***Email:*** mmf@sonnenschein.com

PAUL A. GAJER (Not admitted in Illinois; Resident, New York, N.Y. Office)

SARAH N. GALIOTO, born DuQuoin, Illinois, March 11, 1969; admitted to bar, 1996, Illinois. *Education:* University of Illinois, Urbana-Champaign, Illinois (B.A., 1991); Chicago-Kent College of Law, Illinois Institute of Technology (J.D., 1996). Recipient, American Jurisprudence Award, Advanced Research & Writing. *Member:* Energy Bar Association; Federal Telecommunications Bar Association. ***PRACTICE AREAS:*** Energy; Telecommunications; Environmental. ***Email:*** sgalioto@sonnenschein.com

PHILIP S. GALLAS (Resident, Kansas City, Missouri Office)

CATHERINE B. GARDNER (Not admitted in Illinois; Resident, Washington, D.C. Office)

BRIT L. GEIGER (Not admitted in Illinois; Resident, New York, N.Y. Office)

CHRISTIAN S. GENETSKI (Not admitted in Illinois; Resident, Washington, D.C. Office)

BRENT MATTHEW GIDDENS (Not admitted in Illinois; Resident, Los Angeles, California Office)

ALAN S. GILBERT, born Chicago, Illinois, April 1, 1949; admitted to bar, 1975, Illinois. *Education:* Princeton University (A.B., 1971); University of Chicago (J.D., 1975). Order of the Coif. Faculty, National Institute of Trial Advocacy, 1984—. Law Clerk to the Hon. William J. Bauer, U.S. Court of Appeals, Seventh Circuit, 1975-1977. *Member:* American Bar Association (Member: Section on Litigation, Committee on Commercial and Banking Litigation). ***PRACTICE AREAS:*** Trials; Complex Litigation; Class Actions. ***Email:*** agilbert@sonnenschein.com

JOHN T. GILBERTSON (Not admitted in Illinois; Resident, Los Angeles, California Office)

ROBERT D. GIRARD (Not admitted in Illinois; Resident, Los Angeles, California Office)

PAUL E. B. GLAD (Not admitted in Illinois; Resident, San Francisco, California Office)

MICHAEL M. GODSY (Resident, St. Louis, Missouri Office)

MARTIN R. GOLD (Not admitted in Illinois; Resident, New York, N.Y. Office)

ALVIN J. GOLDMAN (Not admitted in Illinois; Resident, New York, N.Y. Office)

JEFFREY S. GOLDMAN, born Chicago, Illinois, May 28, 1945; admitted to bar, 1970, Illinois; 1972, U.S. Court of Appeals, 4th Circuit; 1973, U.S. Court of Appeals, District of Columbia Circuit; 1974, U.S. Court of Appeals, 8th and 6th Circuits; 1974, U.S. Supreme Court; 1979, U.S. Court of Appeals, 2nd Circuit; 1982, U.S. Court of Appeals, 7th Circuit; 1993, U.S. Court of Appeals, 3rd Circuit; 1998, U.S. District Court, District of Arizona; U.S. District Court, Northern and Central Districts of Illinois, U.S. District Court, Northern District of New York and U.S. Court of Appeals, 9th and 11th Circuits. *Education:* Brown University (A.B., History, 1967); University of Chicago (J.D., 1970). Author: "Avoiding and Defending Wrongful Discharge Claims," The Brief, American Bar Association Tort and Insurance Practice Section, Spring, 1986; "Drug Testing in the Workplace," The Brief, American Bar Association Tort and Insurance Practice Section, Spring, 1988; "From Tiffs to RIFs: Counseling the Client on Terminating Employees," The Practical Lawyer, American Bar Association Committee on Continuing Professional Education, April 1991; "Fighting Over The Files," The Brief, American Bar Association Tort and Insurance Practice Section, Fall 1988. Speaker, "The Demise of White Collar Exemptions," TPA Alliance, May 2002. *Member:* American Bar Association (Past Member, Governing Council, Tort and Insurance Practice Section; Past Chairman, Employer-Employee Relations Committee; Member: Labor Section; Employment at Will Subcommittee, Litigation Section); National Association of College and University Attorneys; Chicago Association of Commerce and Industry (Member, Equal Employment Opportunity Subcommittee, 1981-1987). ***PRACTICE AREAS:*** Labor and Employment. ***Email:*** jgoldman@sonnenschein.com

JAMES A. GONIEA (Not admitted in Illinois; Resident, San Francisco, California Office)

GARY A. GOODMAN (Not admitted in Illinois; Resident, New York, N.Y. Office)

ROBERT N. GRANT, born Newburgh, New York, March 7, 1930; admitted to bar, 1956, Illinois; 1990, New York; 1995 United Kingdom. *Education:* Yale University (B.A., 1951); Harvard University (LL.B., 1956). Phi Beta Kappa. Member, 1975-1981 and President, 1980-1981, Board of Education, Winnetka, Illinois. President, Winnetka Public Schools Foundation, 1995-1998. Member, Legal Aid Committee, 1983—, Vice Chairman, 1986-1987, Chairman, 1988-1994 and Member, Board of Directors, 1984-1994, United Charities. President, Legal Aid Society of Illinois, 1988-1994. Trustee, The Nature Conservancy, 1978-1988. Member Designate, Board of Directors, Winnetka Community House, 2000. *Member:* Chicago and American (Member, Commercial Real Estate Lease Committee, 1980—) Bar Associations; Law Society of England and Wales. [U.S.A.F., Active duty, 1951-1953]. ***PRACTICE AREAS:*** Real Estate; Commercial Leasing; Commercial Real Estate Development; Corporate. ***Email:*** rng@sonnenschein.com

(This Listing Continued)

STEVEN J. GRAY, born Lincoln, Nebraska, April 24, 1957; admitted to bar, 1987, Ohio; 1988, Illinois; 1993, District of Columbia. *Education:* University of Notre Dame (B.A., 1979; M.B.A., with honors, 1982); Case Western Reserve University School of Law (J.D., 1987). ***PRACTICE AREAS:*** Corporate; Securities; Municipal Finance; Executive Compensation. ***Email:*** sgray@sonnenschein.com

RONALD GREENBERG (Not admitted in Illinois; Resident, New York, N.Y. Office)

ANDREW R. GREENE, born Canton, Ohio, June 19, 1967; admitted to bar, 1994, Illinois. *Education:* Miami University (B.A., 1989); Northwestern University (J.D., cum laude, 1994). ***PRACTICE AREAS:*** Litigation. ***Email:*** agreene@sonnenschein.com

KEVIN P. GROARKE (Not admitted in Illinois; Resident, New York, N.Y. Office)

JOHN I. GROSSBART, born Detroit, Michigan, February 19, 1954; admitted to bar, 1980, Illinois and U. S. Court of Appeals, Seventh Circuit. *Education:* University of Michigan (B.G.S., with distinction, 1976; J.D., cum laude, 1979). James Angell Scholar. *Member:* American Bar Association. ***PRACTICE AREAS:*** Commercial Litigation; Mass Tort; Insurance. ***Email:*** jig@sonnenschein.com

MICHAEL GUERRA, born Chicago, Illinois, September 1, 1963; admitted to bar, 1988, Illinois. *Education:* Loyola University (B.B.A., 1981); John Marshall Law School (J.D., 1988). Member: John Marshall Law Review, 1987-1988; Moot Court. *Member:* Chicago, Illinois State and American Bar Associations. ***PRACTICE AREAS:*** Telecommunications Law; Energy; Utility Regulation.

ROSEMARY L.L. GULLIKSON, born Chicago, Illinois, December 9, 1952; admitted to bar, 1994, Illinois. *Education:* Northern Illinois University (B.S., in Nursing, summa cum laude, 1974); Northwestern University (J.D., with honors, 1994). Registered Nurse, Illinois, 1974. ***PRACTICE AREAS:*** Corporate; Information Technology Contracts; Outsourcing; Venture Capital. ***Email:*** rlg@sonnenschein.com

KEVIN W. GUYNN, born Bremerhaven, Germany, December 9, 1952; admitted to bar, 1979, Wisconsin, Illinois and U.S. District Court, Northern District of Illinois, including Trial Bar; registered to practice before U.S. Patent and Trademark Office. *Education:* Purdue University (B.S.E., 1976); University of Wisconsin (J.D., 1979). Omicron Delta Kappa; Tau Beta Pi. Managing Editor, University of Wisconsin Law Review, 1978-1979. ***PRACTICE AREAS:*** Patent Law; Trademark Law; Copyrights; International Patent Law; Intellectual Property Law; Litigation; Licensing Law. ***Email:*** k2g@sonnenschein.com

FRANK H. HACKMANN (Resident, St. Louis, Missouri Office)

WAYNE R. HANNAH, JR., born Freeport, Illinois, August 18, 1931; admitted to bar, 1957, Illinois. *Education:* Illinois College (A.B., 1953); University of Bordeaux, France; New York University (J.D., 1957). Phi Beta Kappa. *Member:* Chicago (Member, Real Property Law Committee, 1970—), Illinois State (Member, Real Estate Committee, 1959—) and American Bar Associations. [With U.S. Marine Corps Reserve, 1957-1965]. ***LANGUAGES:*** French. ***PRACTICE AREAS:*** Corporate; Real Estate. ***Email:*** wrh@sonnenschein.com

MARK L. HANOVER, born Livingston, New Jersey, October 27, 1968; admitted to bar, 1993, Illinois. *Education:* University of Pennsylvania (B.A., cum laude, 1990); University of Minnesota (J.D., cum laude, 1993). Associate Editor, Minnesota Law Review. ***LANGUAGES:*** French. ***PRACTICE AREAS:*** Litigation. ***Email:*** myh@sonnenschein.com

MARK T. HANSEN (Not admitted in Illinois; Resident, Los Angeles, California Office)

KEVIN T. HAROFF (Resident, San Francisco, California Office)

LINDA CHAPLIK HARRIS, born Chicago, Illinois, May 21, 1949; admitted to bar, 1974, Illinois. *Education:* American University (1967-1969); University of Michigan (B.A., 1971); Catholic University of America (J.D., 1974). Phi Beta Kappa. Staff Law Clerk, 7th Circuit Court of Appeals, 1974-1976. *Member:* American Bar Association. ***PRACTICE AREAS:*** Corporate; Mergers and Acquisitions. ***Email:*** lch@sonnenschein.com

KENDRA KEKELIS HARTMAN, born Arlington Heights, Illinois, March 7, 1973; admitted to bar, 1998, Illinois. *Education:* Brandeis University (B.A., summa cum laude, 1995); Yale University (J.D., 1998). Phi Beta Kappa. ***PRACTICE AREAS:*** Litigation. ***Email:*** khartman@sonnenschein.com

HARUMI HATA (Not admitted in Illinois; Resident, Los Angeles, California Office)

SANDRA D. HAUSER (Not admitted in Illinois; Resident, New York, N.Y. Office)

JAMES A. HEETER (Not admitted in Illinois; Resident, Kansas City, Missouri Office)

ROGER K. HEIDENREICH (Resident, St. Louis, Missouri Office)

J. DEAN HELLER (Resident, Los Angeles, California Office)

FRANCES J. HENDERSON (Not admitted in Illinois; Resident, Washington, D.C. Office)

GARY A. HERNANDEZ (Not admitted in Illinois; Resident, San Francisco, California Office)

RAYMOND J. HESLIN (Not admitted in Illinois; Resident, New York, N.Y. Office)

ELLEN P. HESSION (Resident, New York, N.Y. Office)

WILLIAM REECE HIRSCH (Not admitted in Illinois; Resident, San Francisco, California Office)

HAROLD C. HIRSHMAN, born Durham, North Carolina, April 22, 1945; admitted to bar, 1969, Illinois. *Education:* Cornell University (B.S., 1966); University of Chicago (J.D., 1969). Member, University of Chicago Law Review, 1968-1969. Author: "Damages Recoverable in Commercial Cases and Their Proof," ICLE, 1978, 1981, 1985, 1988, 1990, 1993 and 1996; "Lender Liability and Settled Principles of Contract Law," Commercial Damages, 1989; "Breach by Customer of Services," Commercial Damages, Matthew Bender, 1987; "Evaluating the Case," Commercial Damages Reporter, March, 1986; "A Modest Proposal to Control Damage Evidence," Commercial Damages Reporter, 1991; "The Role of Good Faith in Lender Liability: A Reply to Professor Patterson," Commercial Damages Reporter, September, 1991. Member, Board of Editors, Commercial Damages

(This Listing Continued)

Reporter, 1986-1987. Adjunct Professor: IIT-Kent Law School, Securities Regulation, 1986; NITA Faculty, 1984—. ***PRACTICE AREAS:*** Litigation; Professional Liability; Banking; Securities. ***Email:*** hch@sonnenschein.com

KENNETH H. HOCH, born Buffalo, New York, January 7, 1947; admitted to bar, 1971, Illinois. *Education:* Canisius College (A.B., summa cum laude, 1968); University College of the University of London and University of Notre Dame (J.D., 1971). Midwest Region NITA Faculty, 1984—. *Member:* Chicago and American Bar Associations. ***PRACTICE AREAS:*** Commercial and Antitrust Litigation. ***Email:*** khh@sonnenschein.com

DONALD R. HOLLAND (Resident, St. Louis, Missouri Office)

DONALD P. HORWITZ, born Chicago, Illinois, 1936; admitted to bar, 1960, Illinois; 1961, District of Columbia; 1966, U.S. Supreme Court. *Education:* Northwestern University (B.S., with highest distinction, 1957); Yale Law School (J.D., with honors, 1960). Attorney General's Program for Honor Law Graduates, Tax Division, U.S. Department of Justice, 1961-1963. Co-Author: "Regulating The Franchise Relationship," 54 St. John's Law Review, 217; "Pricing Issues in Dealer and Franchise Relationships," 60 Antitrust Law Journal 491; "Franchising and Licensing in Canada," ABA-ALI; "Tax Aspects of Doing Business in Belgium," DePaul University Press. Member, Board of Directors, Chicago Medical School, 1999—. *Member:* Chicago, Illinois State and American Bar Associations; Chicago Bar Foundation (Trustee, 1991-1997); Chicago Cares (Board of Advisers, 1995—); Bernard Technologies, Inc. (Board of Directors, 1997—; Chairman of the Board, 1998—); Lakeland Health Ventures, Inc. (Board of Directors, 1994—); Northwestern Healthcare Network (Council of Governors, 1992-1999). ***PRACTICE AREAS:*** Corporate; Commercial; Franchising. ***Email:*** dph@sonnenschein.com

PAUL J. HOUSEY (Not admitted in Illinois; Resident, New York, New York Office)

JAMES L. HSU (Not admitted in Illinois; Resident, Los Angeles, California Office)

SUSAN M. HUGHES, born Chicago Heights, Illinois, September 2, 1968; admitted to bar, 1994, Illinois and U.S. District Court, Northern District of Illinois. *Education:* University of Illinois (B.A., 1990); DePaul University (J.D., 1994). Member, DePaul Law Review, 1992-1994. *Member:* Chicago and Illinois State Bar Associations. ***PRACTICE AREAS:*** Trusts and Estates. ***Email:*** smh@sonnenschein.com

MICHAEL D. HULTQUIST, born Chicago, Illinois, March 13, 1961; admitted to bar, 1986, Illinois and U.S. District Court, Northern District of Illinois including Trial Bar; 1988, U.S. Court of Appeals, Tenth Circuit; 1989, U.S. Court of Appeals, Third Circuit; 1991, U.S. Court of Appeals, Seventh Circuit; 1997, U.S. Court of Appeals, Eleventh Circuit. *Education:* Marquette University (B.S., summa cum laude, 1983); Loyola University (J.D., 1986). Assistant Editor, Women's Law Reporter, 1985-1986. *Member:* American Bar Association (Member, Tort and Insurance Practice Section; Chairman, Industry Involvement Subcommittee). ***PRACTICE AREAS:*** Litigation; Business Regulation. ***Email:*** hul@sonnenschein.com

DAVID C. JACOBSON, born Chicago, Illinois, October 9, 1951; admitted to bar, 1976, District of Columbia; 1977, New York; 1978, Illinois; 1990, California. *Education:* Johns Hopkins University (B.A., 1973); Georgetown University (J.D., 1976). Administrative Editor, Georgetown Law Journal, 1974-1976. Member, Board of Directors of the Legal Assistance Foundation of Chicago. *Member:* Chicago and American Bar Associations. ***PRACTICE AREAS:*** Internet; Electronic Commerce; Commercial Litigation. ***Email:*** dcj@sonnenschein.com

FRUMAN JACOBSON, born Chicago, Illinois, October 11, 1948; admitted to bar, 1973, Illinois. *Education:* University of Illinois (B.A., 1970); Northwestern University (J.D., cum laude, 1973). Phi Kappa Phi. James Scholar. Member, NITA Faculty; Board of Contributors, Bankruptcy Strategist; Faculty, Practising Law Institute. *Member:* American Bar Association (Member, Business Bankruptcy Committee). ***PRACTICE AREAS:*** Bankruptcy; Workouts. ***Email:*** fj@sonnenschein.com

MARIAN S. JACOBSON, born Cincinnati, Ohio, November 10, 1945; admitted to bar, 1972, Illinois. *Education:* Ohio Wesleyan University (B.A., with honors, 1967); University of Chicago (J.D., 1972). Member, The University of Chicago Law School Visiting Committee, 1992-1994. Member, Board of Governors, The Metropolitan Club of Chicago, 1998—. *Member:* American Bar Association; Chicago Council of Lawyers. ***PRACTICE AREAS:*** Corporate. ***Email:*** msj@sonnenschein.com

ROBERT J. JAKUBECK (Not admitted in Illinois; Resident, St. Louis, Missouri Office)

CHRISTOPHER G. JANNEY (Resident, Washington, D.C. Office)

THOMAS C. JENSEN (Resident, Washington, D.C. Office)

JOHN GRAYSON JOHNSON (Resident, San Francisco, California Office)

MARK P. JOHNSON (Not admitted in Illinois; Resident, Kansas City, Missouri Office)

ROBERT C. JOHNSON, born Chicago, Illinois, July 1, 1948; admitted to bar, 1973, Illinois, U.S. District Court, Northern District of Illinois and U.S. Court of Appeals, Second, Third, Seventh and Eleventh Circuits. *Education:* Cornell College (B.A., magna cum laude, 1970); New York University (J.D., 1973). Phi Beta Kappa. Articles Editor, Annual Survey of American Law, 1972-1973. *Member:* American Bar Association (Member, Tort and Insurance Practice Section). ***PRACTICE AREAS:*** Litigation; Insurance. ***Email:*** rcj@sonnenschein.com

ROBERT M. JOHNSON (Resident, Los Angeles, California Office)

ROBERT T. JOSEPH, born Detroit, Michigan, June 12, 1946; admitted to bar, 1971, Michigan; 1976, Illinois. *Education:* Xavier University (A.B., magna cum laude, 1968); University of Michigan (J.D., cum laude, 1971). Alpha Sigma Nu. Associate Editor, Michigan Law Review, 1970-1971. Assistant to the Director, Federal Trade Commission, 1972-1974. Author: "Vertical Maximum Price Fixing After State Oil Company v. Khan," Franchise Law Journal, Volume 17, No. 3, Winter 1998; "Resale Price Maintenance: Minimizing Risk When Communicating With Distributors About Prices," Antitrust, Fall, 1996; "Do Franchisors Owe A Duty of Competence?" 46 Business Lawyer 471. Co-Author: "Living With Kodak From The Seller's Standpoint," Antitrust, Fall/Winter, 1992; "Proof of The Meeting Competition Defense: Investigation and Verification of Reported Competing Offers," 62 Antitrust L.J. 127 (1993); "Functional Discounts and The Robinson-Patman Act After Texaco, Inc. v. Hasbrouck," Franchise Law Journal, Vol. 10, No. 2, Fall, 1990. *Member:* American Bar Association (Member, Section of Antitrust Law; Chair, Publications Committee, 1991-1994; Council Member, 1994-1997; Program Officer, 1997-1999; Committee Officer, 1999—; Member, Forum on Franchising; Governing Board Member, 1997—). ***PRACTICE AREAS:*** Antitrust; Trade Regulation; Franchising. ***Email:*** rtj@sonnenschein.com

KEVIN P. KAMRACZEWSKI, born Chicago, Illinois, May 19, 1956; admitted to bar, 1982, Illinois and U.S. District Court, Northern District of Illinois; 1987, California and U.S. District Court, Northern and Central Districts of California. *Education:* University of Chicago (A.B., with honors, 1978); University of Illinois (J.D., 1982). Phi Alpha Delta. *Member:* Los Angeles County and American Bar Associations; State Bar of California; Defense Research Institute. ***PRACTICE AREAS:*** Insurance Coverage; Reinsurance; Litigation. ***Email:*** kpk@sonnenschein.com

ARTHUR S. KATZ (Not admitted in Illinois; Resident, New York, N.Y. Office)

MICHELLE STARK KAUFMAN (Not admitted in Illinois; Resident, Kansas City, Missouri Office)

RONALD D. KENT (Not admitted in Illinois; Resident, Los Angeles, California Office)

MICHAEL L. KIKLIS (Not admitted in Illinois; Resident, Washington, D.C. Office)

CHRISTOPHER Q. KING, born Jerusalem, Israel, November 15, 1958; admitted to bar, 1983, Maryland; 1985, Illinois. *Education:* Northwestern University (B.A., 1980); Vanderbilt University (J.D., 1983). Phi Beta Kappa. Author: Case Comment, "Vanderbilt Journal of Transnational Law," Vol. 14, 1983; Article, "Claims For Failure to Liquidate (Margin Violations) and Wrongful Liquidation," in Securities Arbitration (PLI), 1996. Co-Author: Article, "Fine Tuning Advances Can Prove Dangerous," with Fruman Jacobson, 8 Bankruptcy Strategist No. 11, October, 1989; Article, "Funds Protections: An Overview of What Happens When Your Commodity Futures Broker Becomes Insolvent," with William F. Tueting, 7 Journal of the Futures Markets 93, Winter, 1987. Article, "A Checklist for the Compliance Officer or In-House Counsel Managing Customer-Broker Arbitration and Litigation" Securities Arbitration (PLI) 1997. Law Clerk for Hon. Robert C. Murphy, Chief Judge, Court of Appeals for Maryland, 1983-1984. *Member:* Chicago and American Bar Associations. ***PRACTICE AREAS:*** Securities; Commodity Futures; Litigation. ***Email:*** cqk@sonnenschein.com

ROBERT H. KING, JR., born Chicago, Illinois, May 19, 1953; admitted to bar, 1978, Illinois; 1989, California. *Education:* Dartmouth College (B.A., magna cum laude, 1975); University of Michigan (J.D., 1978). ***PRACTICE AREAS:*** Antitrust; Franchise Law; Distribution. ***Email:*** rking@sonnenschein.com

SANFORD KINGSLEY (Resident, San Francisco, California Office)

JAMES M. KIRKLAND (Not admitted in Illinois; Resident, Kansas City, Missouri Office)

MATT A. KIRMAYER (Not admitted in Illinois; Resident, San Francisco, California Office)

STEVEN B. KITE, born Chicago, Illinois, May 30, 1949; admitted to bar, 1974, Georgia; 1985, Illinois; 1986, Florida. *Education:* University of Illinois (B.A., with high honors, Liberal Arts and Sciences and distinction in Finance, 1971); Harvard Law School (J.D., 1974). *Member:* Chicago, Illinois State and American Bar Associations; The Florida Bar; State Bar of Georgia; National Association of Bond Lawyers. ***PRACTICE AREAS:*** Tax Exempt Finance. ***Email:*** skite@sonnenschein.com

LESLIE A. KLEIN, born New York, N.Y., August 2, 1955; admitted to bar, 1980, Illinois, U.S. District Court, Northern District of Illinois and U.S. Tax Court. *Education:* University of Illinois (B.S., with honors, 1977); Illinois Institute of Technology/ Chicago-Kent College of Law (J.D., with high honors, 1980). Adjunct Professor, Illinois Institute of Technology/Chicago-Kent College of Law. Certified Public Accountant, 1977. *Member:* Chicago, Illinois State and American Bar Associations. ***PRACTICE AREAS:*** Employee Benefits. ***Email:*** lk@sonnenschein.com

SHAUN M. KLEIN (Not admitted in Illinois; Resident, Kansas City, Missouri Office)

H. FRANCES KLEINER (Resident, New York, N.Y. Office)

JAMES A. KLENK, born Evergreen Park, Illinois, July 18, 1949; admitted to bar, 1974, Illinois; 1978, U.S. Supreme Court. *Education:* Beloit College (B.A., 1971); University of Wisconsin at Madison (J.D., 1974). Phi Beta Kappa; Order of the Coif. Articles Editor, Wisconsin Law Review, 1973-1974. Law Clerk to Chief Judge Thomas E. Fairchild, U.S. Court of Appeals, Seventh Circuit, 1974-1975. *Member:* Illinois State and American Bar Associations. ***PRACTICE AREAS:*** Litigation; Intellectual Property. ***Email:*** jak@sonnenschein.com

EDWARD KLIMERMAN (Not admitted in Illinois; Resident, New York, N.Y. Office)

ELAINE D. KOLISH (Resident, Washington, D.C. Office)

KENNETH G. KOLMIN, born New York, N.Y., October 22, 1951; admitted to bar, 1976, Illinois. *Education:* State University of New York at Albany (B.S., summa cum laude, 1973); Syracuse University (M.S., 1975; J.D., cum laude, 1975). Beta Gamma Sigma; Beta Alpha Psi; Phi Alpha Delta. Member, Justinian Society. Certified Public Accountant, Illinois, 1979. Author: "Temporary Regulations Resolve Some Problems for U.S. Persons Working Abroad," International Tax Journal, June 1979. *Member:* Chicago, Illinois State and American Bar Associations; American Institute of Certified Public Accountants; Illinois Society of Certified Public Accountants. ***PRACTICE AREAS:*** General Corporate; Taxation; Finance. ***Email:*** kgk@sonnenschein.com

JOHN C. KOSKI, born Charlotte, North Carolina, June 1, 1967; admitted to bar, 1992, Illinois and U.S. District Court, Northern District of Illinois; 1993, Florida; 1994, U.S. Court of Appeals, Seventh Circuit; 1995, U.S. Court of Appeals, Third Circuit; 1996, U.S. Supreme Court; 1997, U.S. District Court, Eastern District of Michigan and U.S. District Court, Northern District of Illinois including Trial Bar; 1999, U.S. Court of Appeals, Second Circuit; 2000, U.S. District Court, Eastern District of Wisconsin. *Education:* Vanderbilt University (B.A., 1989); University of Miami (J.D., cum laude, 1992). Order of the Coif. Senior Articles Editor, 1991-1992; Associate Articles Editor, Spring, 1991, University of Miami Law Review. Author: "Peril of the E-Mail Trail," National Law Journal, Jan.

(This Listing Continued)

SONNENSCHEIN NATH & ROSENTHAL LLP, Chicago—Continued

16, 1995, at CI (Co-Author); "Better Late Than Never? Timing, ADR and Litigation Costs," 9 Court Manager 16 (Spring 1994); "Mandatory Disclosure," 80 ABA Journal 85 (Feb. 1994); "From Hide-and-Seek to Show-and-Tell: Evidentiary Disclosure Rules," 17 American Journal of Trial Advocacy 497 (1993); "Idaho v. Wright: The Defenestration of Corroborating Evidence," 46 University of Miami Law Review 205 (1991). Intern to the Hon. Rosemary Barkett, Florida Supreme Court, 1991. Research Consultant, American Bar Association, Judicial Administration Division/Lawyers Conference Task Force on Reduction of Litigation Costs and Delay, 1993. *Member:* Illinois State and American Bar Associations; The Florida Bar. ***PRACTICE AREAS:*** Litigation. ***Email:*** jck@sonnenschein.com

THOMAS A. LABUDA, JR., born Chicago, Illinois, April 4, 1969; admitted to bar, 1994, Illinois. *Education:* Millikin University (B.A., magna cum laude, 1991); Loyola University Chicago (J.D., magna cum laude, 1994). Editor, Loyola University Chicago Law Journal. Co-author: "Ancillary Proceedings and Treatment of Foreign Debtors and Foreign Creditors Under the United States Bankruptcy Code," 23 Cal. Bankr. J. 275 (1997). ***PRACTICE AREAS:*** Bankruptcy; Litigation. ***Email:*** tal@sonnenschein.com

MARY KAY LACEY (Not admitted in Illinois; Resident, San Francisco, California Office)

DAVID S. LADWIG (Not admitted in Illinois; Resident, Kansas City, Missouri Office)

KEVIN C. LANE, born Evanston, Illinois, June 23, 1968; admitted to bar, 1996, Illinois. *Education:* University of Notre Dame (B.A., 1990); DePaul University (J.D., 1996). Certified Public Accountant. *Member:* Chicago Bar Association; American Institute of Certified Public Accountants. ***PRACTICE AREAS:*** Trust and Estates. ***Email:*** kcl@sonnenschein.com

ROBERT J. LANZA (Resident, New York, N.Y. Office)

JOHN J. LAWLOR, born Chicago, Illinois, September 16, 1951; admitted to bar, 1976, Illinois; 1989, Wisconsin. *Education:* Northwestern University (B.A., 1973; J.D., 1976). Phi Beta Kappa. Evans Scholar. Author: "Real Property Tax Delinquency and the Rehabilitation of Multi-Family Housing Stock in Chicago, Illinois: The Role of the Collection Provisions of the Illinois Revenue Act," 16 DePaul Law Review 1, 1976; "America's Low Income Housing Efforts: The Poor as Hostages of Fear and Misperception," Catholic University, Social Thought, Spring, 1977; "Tax Enforcement Programs and Neighborhood Revitalization: Mutually Compatible Goals?" American Society of Planning Officials, Land Use and Zoning Digest, Vol. 30, No. 5, 1978, pp. 6-9. Visiting Faculty, Lincoln Institute of Land Policy, 1977-1978. Faculty, Taxation as a Land Use Control, ALI-ABI, 1979. Lecturer, Public Policy and Inner-City Development, American Society of Planning Officials, 1978. Instructor, Land Development, Illinois Institute on Continuing Legal Education, 1986-1990. Faculty: The Real Estate Development Process, Prentice-Hall Law and Business, 1989-1990; Negotiating a Shopping Center Lease, Illinois Institute on Continuing Legal Education, 1990; Current Illinois Land Use Practices, Illinois Institute on Continuing Legal Education, 1990; Reciprocal Easement Agreement Site Planning Issues, International Council of Shopping Centers Law Conference, 1990. Urban Law Fellow, Northwestern University Center for Urban Affairs, 1974-1976. Special Assistant Attorney General, State of Illinois for condemnation matters, 1977-1982. Chairman, Greater State Street Council Real Estate Committee on the Chicago Central Area Plan for the 1990s, 1983. Member, Legal Club of Chicago, 1985-1992. Member, Chicago Bar Association, 1976-1992. *Member:* Illinois State and American Bar Associations; State Bar of Wisconsin; National Association of College and University Attorneys. ***PRACTICE AREAS:*** Zoning; Real Estate; Not-for-profit Corporations. ***Email:*** jxl@sonnenschein.com

MARK R. LEHRER (Not admitted in Illinois; Resident, New York, N.Y. Office)

J. BRADLEY LEITCH (Not admitted in Illinois; Resident, Kansas City, Missouri Office)

JEFFREY LENNARD, born New York, N.Y., August 21, 1948; admitted to bar, 1975, Illinois. *Education:* George Washington University (A.B., 1970); University of Chicago (1970-1972); University of Chicago (J.D., 1975). Recipient, Ford Foundation Fellowship, 1970-1972. *Member:* American Arbitration Association; National Mass Torts Panel. ***PRACTICE AREAS:*** Litigation. ***Email:*** jpl@sonnenschein.com

CHRISTINE LEPERA (Not admitted in Illinois; Resident, New York, N.Y. Office)

TRINA R. LERICHE (Not admitted in Illinois; Resident, Kansas City, Missouri Office)

ROBERT O. LESLEY (Resident, Kansas City, Missouri Office)

JACK B. LEVITT (Not admitted in Illinois; Resident, New York, N.Y. Office)

FRED L. LEVY (Not admitted in Illinois; Resident, Washington, D.C. Office)

STEVEN M. LEVY, born Chicago, Illinois, December 27, 1958; admitted to bar, 1982, Illinois. *Education:* Northwestern University (B.A., magna cum laude, 1979); Harvard University (J.D., cum laude, 1982). Phi Beta Kappa. *Member:* Chicago, Illinois State and American Bar Associations. ***PRACTICE AREAS:*** Litigation. ***Email:*** sml@sonnenschein.com

JULIUS LEWIS, born Omaha, Nebraska, November 29, 1931; admitted to bar, 1957, Illinois. *Education:* University of Chicago (B.A., 1950; M.A., 1954); Yale University (LL.B., 1957). Editor, Yale Law Journal, 1955-1957. *Member:* Chicago, Illinois State and American Bar Associations. ***PRACTICE AREAS:*** Corporate; Securities. ***Email:*** jl@sonnenschein.com

PAUL V. LICALSI (Not admitted in Illinois; Resident, New York, N.Y. Office)

YABO LIN (Resident, Kansas City, Missouri Office)

MARK J. LINDERMAN (Not admitted in Illinois; Resident, San Francisco, California Office)

SCOTT A. LINDQUIST, born Cleveland, Ohio, November 11, 1957; admitted to bar, 1982, Indiana; 1987, Illinois. *Education:* University of Michigan (B.A., with high honors in Economics and highest distinction, 1979; J.D., cum laude, with honors, 1982). Phi Beta Kappa. Recipient, Sims Prize, 1978. Author: "Creative Financing Techniques for Individual Properties," ABA 1993 Annual Meeting; "Loan Documents-The Next Generation," ABA Section of Real Property, Probate and Trust Law, 1993 Annual Conference; "Real Estate Lending Regulations: The New Ball Game," Probate & Property, May/June, 1993; "Loan Participations: What Happens When The Honeymoon Ends?" January/February, 1993. Co-Author: "Current Issues In Loan Participation and Co-Lending Agreements," ABA - Section of Real Property, Probate, and Trust Law 1992 Annual Conference; "Negotiating the Commercial Lease," Basic Real Estate Leasing, Indiana Continuing Legal Education Forum, 1987. Member, Indiana State Bar Association, 1982-1987. *Member:* American Bar Association. ***PRACTICE AREAS:*** Real Estate. ***Email:*** sal@sonnenschein.com

KAREN LITSINGER (Resident, Washington, D.C. Office)

LLOYD C. LOOMIS (Resident, Los Angeles, California Office)

MICHAEL B. LUBIC (Resident, Los Angeles and San Francisco CA, Offices)

DONALD G. LUBIN, born New York, N.Y., January 10, 1934; admitted to bar, 1957, Illinois. *Education:* University of Pennsylvania (B.S. in Econ., 1954); Harvard University (LL.B., 1957). Director and Member, Executive Committee, Finance Committee, Nominating and Corporate Governance Committee and Secretary, Audit Committee, McDonald's Corp. Director and Chairman, Audit Committee, Molex Incorporated. Director: Daubert Industries, Inc.; Chas Levy Company. Director, Chicago Foundation for Education. Member, Commercial Club, Executive Committee and Civic Committee. Trustee and Member, Executive Committee, Rush-Presbyterian-St. Luke's Medical Center. Chairman, Anchor Cross Society. Trustee, National Museum of American History. Life Trustee, The Chicago Symphony Orchestra. Director and Vice President, Ronald McDonald House Charities. Life Trustee and Former Chairman, Ravinia Festival Association and Life Trustee and Former Chairman, Highland Park Hospital. Former Director, National Board, Smithsonian Institution and Former Overseer of the University of Pennsylvania's College of Arts and Science. *Member:* Chicago Bar Association. ***PRACTICE AREAS:*** Corporate. ***Email:*** dgl@sonnenschein.com

HOLLEY T. LUTZ (Resident, Washington, D.C. Office)

Lisa A. MacVittie (Not admitted in Illinois; Resident, Washington, D.C. Office)

DAVID W. MAHER, born Chicago, Illinois, August 14, 1934; admitted to bar, 1960, New York; 1961, Illinois; 1996, Wisconsin; registered to practice before U.S. Patent and Trademark Office. *Education:* Harvard University (A.B., cum laude, 1955; LL.B., 1959). Author: "Purity Versus Plugola: A Study of the Federal Communications Commission's Sponsorship Identification Rules," DePaul Law Review, 1974; "The Shrink-Wrap License: Old Problems in a New Wrapper," Journal of the Copyright Society of the U.S.A., 1987; "Trademarks on the Internet: Who's in Charge?" The Data Law Report, Vol. 4, No. 1, July 1996; "Trademark Law on the Internet - Will it Scale?" John Marshall Journal of Computer & Information Law, 1997. Lecturer: DePaul University School of Law, 1973-1979; Loyola University of Chicago School of Law, 1980-1983. Chairman, Internet Policy Oversight Committee, 1997-2000. Vice President, Public Policy, Internet Society. Director, Better Business Bureau of Chicago and Northern Illinois. *Member:* Chicago and American (Member: Sections on: Science and Technology, Intellectual Property Law, Law Practice Management; Forum Committees on: Entertainment and Communications Law) Bar Associations; State Bar of Wisconsin; Federal Communications Bar Association; American Law Institute; Computer Law Association. [Lt., USAF, 1955-1956]. ***PRACTICE AREAS:*** Intellectual Property, Entertainment. ***Email:*** dmaher@sonnenschein.com

RICHARD L. MARCUS, born Chicago, Illinois, July 26, 1938; admitted to bar, 1962, Illinois. *Education:* Brown University; University of Chicago (A.B., 1960; J.D., 1962). Member, Editorial Board, University of Chicago Law Review, 1961-1962. Author: "Family and Medical Leave, Policies and Procedures," John Wiley & Sons, Inc., 1994. Member, Visiting Committee, The University of Chicago Law School, 1981-1984. Member, Visiting Committee, Division of Humanities, The University of Chicago, 1991—. *Member:* American Bar Association (Member: Section of Labor and Employment Law; Committee on Practice and Procedure before the National Labor Relations Board). ***PRACTICE AREAS:*** Labor and Employment. ***Email:*** rlm@sonnenschein.com

JEREMY MARGOLIS, born Chicago, Illinois, December 4, 1947; admitted to bar, 1973, Illinois. *Education:* University of Illinois (B.A., 1970); Northwestern University (J.D., cum laude, 1973).

I. EDWARD MARQUETTE (Not admitted in Illinois; Resident, Kansas City, Missouri Office)

DREW W. MARROCCO (Not admitted in Illinois; Resident, Washington, D.C. Office)

STEPHEN A. MARSHALL (Not admitted in Illinois; Resident, New York, N.Y. Office)

SONIA RENEE MARTIN (Not admitted in Illinois; Resident, San Francisco, California Office)

JOHN F. MARVIN (Not admitted in Illinois; Resident, Kansas City, Missouri Office)

MICHAEL R. MARYN (Not admitted in Illinois; Resident, Washington, D.C. Office)

SANDRA R. MCCANDLESS (Not admitted in Illinois; Resident, San Francisco, California Office)

FREDERICK D. MCCLURE (Resident, Washington, D.C. Office)

DOUGLAS MCCORMACK (Resident, Washington, D.C. Office)

THOMAS E. MCDONALD (Resident, San Francisco, California Office)

SEAN MCENEANEY (Not admitted in Illinois; Resident, San Francisco, California Office)

BRIAN R. MCGINLEY (Resident, Kansas City, Missouri Office)

MICHAEL T. MCNAMARA (Not admitted in Illinois; Resident, Washington, D.C. Office)

THOMAS K. MCQUEEN, admitted to bar, 1974, Illinois and U.S. District Court, Northern District of Illinois; 1975, U.S. Court of Appeals, Seventh Circuit; 1986, U.S. Court of Appeals, Fourth Circuit; 1996, U.S. Court of Appeals for the Federal Circuit; 1999, U.S. Court of Appeals, Fifth Circuit. *Education:* Colorado State University (B.A., 1971);

(This Listing Continued)

DePaul University (J.D., 1974). *PRACTICE AREAS:* White Collar Criminal Defense; Counseling; Health Care; Antitrust; Trade Regulation; Litigation. **Email:** tmcqueen@sonnenschein.com

MARK F. MEHLMAN, born Los Angeles, California, December 18, 1947; admitted to bar, 1973, Illinois. *Education:* University of Illinois (B.A., 1969); University of Michigan (LL.B., 1973). Administrative Editor, University of Michigan Journal of Law Reform, 1972-1973. *Member:* Illinois State and American (Council Member, Real Property and Probate Section) Bar Associations; American College of Real Estate Lawyers. *PRACTICE AREAS:* Real Estate; Financing. **Email:** mfm@sonnenschein.com

DONNA D. MELBY (Resident, Los Angeles, CA Office)

CYNTHIA L. MELLEMA (Not admitted in Illinois; Resident, San Francisco, California Office)

SHEPARD W. MELZER (Resident, New York, N.Y. Office)

SCOTT A. MEMMOTT (Not admitted in Illinois; Resident, Washington, D.C. Office)

ROBERT F. MESSERLY, born Lancaster, Ohio, March 10, 1962; admitted to bar, 1987, Illinois. *Education:* Xavier University (A.B., 1984); Northwestern University (J.D., 1987). *PRACTICE AREAS:* Real Estate. **Email:** rfm@sonnenschein.com

DAVID R. METZGER, born Akron, Ohio, November 28, 1959; admitted to bar, 1987, Illinois and U.S. District Court, Northern District of Illinois including Trial Bar; 1989, U.S. Court of Appeals for the Federal Circuit; 1992, U.S. Court of Federal Claims and U.S. District Court, District of Colorado; registered to practice before U.S. Patent and Trademark Office. *Education:* Purdue University (B.S.E.E., 1982); Case Western Reserve University (M.B.A., 1987; J.D., 1987). Chairman: Judicial Appointments and Patent Legislation Committee, 1992-1994; Newsletter Committee, 1994-1996; Member, 1998— and Chairman, 1996-1998, Litigation Committee, Board of Managers. *Member:* Chicago and American Bar Associations; Intellectual Property Law Association of Chicago. *LANGUAGES:* Spanish. *PRACTICE AREAS:* Patent Law; Trademark Law; Copyright Law; Litigation; International Patents; Unfair Competition Law; Electric Power; Electronics. **Email:** dvm@sonnenschein.com

TIMOTHY M. METZGER, born Evanston, Illinois, September 2, 1968; admitted to bar, 1993, Illinois. *Education:* University of Illinois (B.S., summa cum laude, accounting, 1990); Northwestern University (J.D., cum laude, 1993). Order of the Coif. Author: "Abandoning Accountants' Liability for Aiding and Abetting 10b-5 Securities Fraud," 87 Northwestern University Law Review, 1993. Certified Public Accountant, Illinois, 1990. *PRACTICE AREAS:* Corporate.

GARY MEYERHOFF (Not admitted in Illinois; Resident, New York, N.Y. Office)

MARTIN P. MICHAEL (Not admitted in Illinois; Resident, New York, N.Y. Office)

PAUL J. MILLER, born Boston, Massachusetts, March 27, 1929; admitted to bar, 1953, Massachusetts; 1957, Illinois. *Education:* Yale University (A.B., magna cum laude, 1950); Harvard University (LL.B., 1953). Phi Beta Kappa. *Member:* Chicago, Illinois State and American Bar Associations. [J.A.G.C., 1954-1957]. *PRACTICE AREAS:* Corporate; Securities. **Email:** pjm@sonnenschein.com

ROBERT B. MILLNER, born New York, N.Y., April 20, 1950; admitted to bar, 1975, Illinois. *Education:* Wesleyan University (B.A., magna cum laude, 1971); University of Chicago (J.D., 1975). Phi Beta Kappa. Law Clerk to Honorable George Edwards, United States Court of Appeals, Sixth Circuit, 1975-1976. *Member:* American Bar Association (Co-Chair, Bankruptcy and Insolvency Committee, Litigation Section, 1992-1995; Vice-Chair, Joint Ad Hoc Committee on Bankruptcy Court Structure and Insolvency Processes, 1993-1997). *PRACTICE AREAS:* Commercial Litigation; Bankruptcy. **Email:** rbm@sonnenschein.com

MARTIN J. MODERSON (Not admitted in Illinois; Resident, Kansas City, Missouri Office)

JAMES L. MOELLER (Not admitted in Illinois; Resident, Kansas City, Missouri Office)

PATRICK G. MORAN, born Boston, Massachusetts, December 9, 1950; admitted to bar, 1976, Illinois. *Education:* Harvard University (B.A., 1972); Georgetown University (J.D., 1976). Member, 1974-1975 and Notes Editor, 1975-1976, American Criminal Law Review. Author: "Mechanics' Liens," Basic Real Estate Practice, Illinois Institute for Continuing Legal Education. Co-author: "Office Leases," Commercial Landlord—Tenant Practice, Illinois Institute for Continuing Legal Education. *Member:* American Bar Association; American College of Real Estate Lawyers. *PRACTICE AREAS:* Real Estate Development; Financing. **Email:** pgm@sonnenschein.com

M. KEITH MOSKOWITZ, born Manhasset, New York, June 19, 1971; admitted to bar, 1998, Connecticut; 1999, New York; 2001, Illinois. *Education:* University of Michigan (B.A., with honors, 1993); University of Connecticut School of Law (J.D., 1998). *PRACTICE AREAS:* Litigation; Insurance; Class Actions. **Email:** mmoskowitz@sonnenschein.com

STACEY L. MURPHY (Resident, St. Louis, Missouri Office)

BERNARD NATH (1899-1996)

MARLENE D. NATIONS, born Chicago, Illinois, December 5, 1954; admitted to bar, 1982, Illinois. *Education:* University of Illinois (B.S., with high honors, 1975); Northwestern University (J.D., cum laude, 1982). *Member:* International Association of Attorneys and Executives in Corporate Real Estate. *PRACTICE AREAS:* Real Estate; Finance; Development. **Email:** mdn@sonnenschein.com

BARRY B. NEKRITZ, born Chicago, Illinois, December 16, 1938; admitted to bar, 1962, Illinois; 1969, Florida. *Education:* University of Illinois (B.A., 1959; LL.B., 1962). Trustee, Village of Northbrook, 1973-1981. Author: "Going Condo: How to Represent Tenants in Condominium Conversions," 8 Barrister 15, 1980; Matthew Bender Real Estate Transactions Introduction to Condominium Law, 1994; "Counseling the Shopping Center on Handling a Fire," AH-ABA Manual for Drafting Leases II, 1997; "Expectations for the Twenty-First Century: An Overview of the New Limited Partnership Act," Probate & Property, January/February 2002. *Member:* Chicago, Illinois State and American (Member, Supervisory Council) Bar Associations; The Florida Bar. *PRACTICE AREAS:* Real Estate. **Email:** bnekritz@sonnenschein.com

CAROLE NEVILLE (Not admitted in Illinois; Resident, New York, N.Y. Office)

DAVID B. NEWMAN (Not admitted in Illinois; Resident, New York, N.Y. Office)

DENNIS NATHAN NEWMAN, born New York, N.Y., August 16, 1946; admitted to bar, 1972, Illinois. *Education:* Brandeis University (B.A., 1969); University of Michigan (J.D., 1972). Adjunct Professor, Chicago-Kent Law School, Spring 2000. *Member:* American Bar Association. *PRACTICE AREAS:* Securities; Corporate. **Email:** dnn@sonnenschein.com

TERRANCE A. NORTON, born Oak Park, Illinois, January 3, 1945; admitted to bar, 1970, Illinois. *Education:* University of Notre Dame (B.A., Political Science, 1967); DePaul University (J.D., 1970). Managing Editor, De Paul Law Review. Honor Law Graduate, U.S. Department of Justice. *PRACTICE AREAS:* Pro Bono. **Email:** tnorton@sonnenschein.com

BERNARD J. NUSSBAUM, born Berlin, Germany, March 11, 1931; admitted to bar, 1956, New York; 1957, U.S. Court of Military Appeals; 1959, Illinois. *Education:* Knox College (A.B., 1952); University of Chicago (J.D., 1955). Phi Beta Kappa. Editor, University of Chicago Law Review, 1954-1955. Chairman, National Conference of Law Reviews, 1954-1955. Member, Board of Visitors, 1977-1983; President, Alumni Association, 1981-1983, University of Chicago Law School. Member, Committee on Civility of the Seventh Federal Judicial Circuit, 1990-1992. Member, National Panel of Arbitrators, American Arbitration Association. *Member:* Chicago (Member, 1962— and Chairman, 1968-1969, Committee on Federal Civil Procedure; Member, Committee on the Judiciary, 1970-1976), Illinois State (Member of Council, Antitrust Section, 1971-1973; Assembly Delegate, 1972-1980) and American Bar Associations. Fellow, American Bar Foundation. Charter Fellow, Illinois Bar Foundation. *PRACTICE AREAS:* Trials and Appeals. **Email:** bjn@sonnenschein.com

STEPHEN J. O'BRIEN (Not admitted in Illinois; Resident, St. Louis, Missouri Office)

PHILIP A. O'CONNELL, JR. (Resident, San Francisco, California Office)

ERIC A. OESTERLE, born Lafayette, Indiana, December 2, 1948; admitted to bar, 1973, Illinois. *Education:* University of Michigan (B.S., with honors, 1970; J.D., cum laude, 1973). Staff Editor, University of Michigan Journal of Law Reform, 1972-1973. *Member:* Chicago, Illinois State and American Bar Associations. *PRACTICE AREAS:* Litigation. **Email:** eao@sonnenschein.com

THOMAS G. OPFERMAN, born Oberlin, Ohio, February 11, 1956; admitted to bar, 1980, Illinois, U.S. District Court, Northern District of Illinois and U.S. Tax Court. *Education:* Ohio University (A.B., summa cum laude, 1977); Ohio State University (J.D., 1980). Phi Beta Kappa. Note and Comment Editor, Ohio State Law Journal, 1979-1980. Adjunct Professor for LLM Tax Program, IIT Chicago-Kent College of Law, 1991-1994. *Member:* Chicago and American Bar Associations. Fellow, American College of Trust and Estate Counsel. *PRACTICE AREAS:* Estate Planning; Family Offices; Charitable Planning; Tax Planning for Individuals. **Email:** tgo@sonnenschein.com

DAVID J. PAPIER (Not admitted in Illinois; Resident, Short Hills, New Jersey Office)

MICHAEL E. PAPPAS (Not admitted in Illinois; Resident, Los Angeles, California Office)

SANFORD M. PASTROFF, born Pittsburgh, Pennsylvania, August 8, 1963; admitted to bar, 1988, Illinois; 1989, U.S. District Court, Northern District of Illinois and U.S. Court of Appeals, Seventh Circuit. *Education:* University of Michigan (B.B.A., with high distinction, 1985); Northwestern University (J.D., cum laude, 1988). Author: "The Constitutional Rights of The Insane on Death Row," 77 J. Crim. L. & Criminology 884, 1986. *Member:* Seventh Circuit and American (Chair, Robinson-Patman Act Committee; Antitrust Section) Bar Associations. *PRACTICE AREAS:* Litigation; Antitrust. **Email:** sxp@sonnenschein.com

DEMIAN L. PAY (Not admitted in Illinois; Resident, San Francisco, California Office)

BARBARA LYNN PEDERSEN (Not admitted in Illinois; Resident, New York, N.Y. Office)

KENNETH J. PFAEHLER (Not admitted in Illinois; Resident, Washington, D.C. Office)

TIMOTHY PFISTER (Resident, New York, N.Y. Office)

ELLIOTT I. PORTNOY (Resident, Washington, D.C. Office)

CARYL A. POTTER, III (Resident, Washington, D.C. Office)

PAMELA K. PRICKETT (Not admitted in Illinois; Resident, Los Angeles, California Office)

CHRISTOPHER E. PRINCE (Resident, Los Angeles, CA Office)

DUANE C. QUAINI, born Napa, California, March 30, 1945; admitted to bar, 1970, Illinois. *Education:* Claremont Men's College (B.A., summa cum laude, 1967); Stanford University (J.D., 1970). Note Editor, Stanford Law Review, 1969-1970. *PRACTICE AREAS:* Litigation. **Email:** dcq@sonnenschein.com

EDWARD J. RADLO (Resident, San Francisco, California Office)

CHARLES A. REDD (Resident, St. Louis, Missouri Office)

EDWIN B. REESER, III (Not admitted in Illinois; Resident, Los Angeles, California Office)

EDWARD J. REICH (Not admitted in Illinois; Resident, New York, N.Y. Office)

PETER S. REICHERTZ (Resident, Washington, D.C. Office)

ALLEN G. REITER (Not admitted in Illinois; Resident, New York, N.Y. Office)

EDWARD H. RICE, born Chicago, Illinois, June 2, 1961; admitted to bar, 1988, Illinois; 1998, Missouri; U.S. District Court, Northern and Southern Districts of Illinois; U.S. District Court, Eastern District of Missouri; U.S. District Court, Eastern District of Michigan; U.S. Court of Federal Claims; U.S. Court of Appeals for the Federal Circuit. *Educa-*

(This Listing Continued)

SONNENSCHEIN NATH & ROSENTHAL LLP, Chicago—Continued

tion: University of Michigan (A.B., with honors, 1983; J.D., 1988). U.S. Department of Justice, Civil Division, Commercial Litigation Branch, Intellectual Property Section, Washington, D.C., 1991-1997. Law Clerk, Hon. Charles R. Norgle, Sr., U.S. District Court, Northern District of Illinois, 1990-1991. *Member:* American Bar Association. ***PRACTICE AREAS:*** Patent Litigation; Intellectual Property Litigation. ***Email:*** erice@sonnenschein.com

ROBERT E. RICHARDS, born Ann Arbor, Michigan, February 5, 1963; admitted to bar, 1988, Illinois; 1989, U.S. District Court, Northern District of Illinois and U.S. District Court, Eastern District of Wisconsin. *Education:* Johns Hopkins University (B.A., 1985); University of Michigan (J.D., cum laude, 1988). *Member:* Chicago and American Bar Associations. ***PRACTICE AREAS:*** Bankruptcy; Corporate. ***Email:*** rer@sonnenschein.com

STEVEN L. RIST (Not admitted in Illinois; Resident, Kansas City, Missouri Office)

GARY M. ROBERTS (Resident, Los Angeles, California Office)

JOHN E. ROONEY, born Oak Park, Illinois, July 13, 1963; admitted to bar, 1998, Illinois. *Education:* Loyola University (B.B.A., 1985); John Marshall Law School (J.D., 1988). Member, The John Marshall Law Review. *Member:* Chicago Bar Association (Chair, Public Utility Law Committee, 2000-2001). ***PRACTICE AREAS:*** Energy Regulation; Telecommunications; Administrative Law. ***Email:*** j7r@sonnenschein.com

MARTIN ROSEN (Not admitted in Illinois; Resident, New York, N.Y. Office)

ALLAN M. ROSENBLOOM (Not admitted in Illinois; Resident, New York, N.Y. Office)

KENNETH A. ROSENBLUM (Not admitted in Illinois; Resident, New York, N.Y. Office)

DOUGLAS E. ROSENTHAL (Not admitted in Illinois; Resident, Washington, D.C. Office)

MICHAEL D. ROSENTHAL, born New York, N.Y., December 21, 1964; admitted to bar, 1989, Illinois and U.S. Court of Appeals, Third Circuit; 1991, U.S. District Court, Northern District of Illinois; 1992, U.S. Court of Appeals, Seventh Circuit. *Education:* Washington University (A.B., magna cum laude, 1986); University of Michigan (J.D., magna cum laude, 1989). Phi Beta Kappa; Order of the Coif. Law Clerk to the Honorable Max Rosenn, U.S. Court of Appeals, Third Circuit, 1989-1990. ***PRACTICE AREAS:*** Venture Capital; Corporate; Securities. ***Email:*** mdr@sonnenschein.com

SAMUEL R. ROSENTHAL (1899-1994)

STEPHEN H. ROVAK (Resident, St. Louis, Missouri Office)

IRA I. ROXLAND (Not admitted in Illinois; Resident, New York, N.Y. Office)

HOWARD R. RUBIN (Resident, Washington, D.C. Office)

ARTHUR H. RUEGGER (Not admitted in Illinois; Resident, New York, N.Y. Office)

KIRK R. RUTHENBERG (Resident, Washington, D.C. Office)

W. MICHAEL RYAN, born Covington, Kentucky, February 10, 1965; admitted to bar, 1992, Illinois. *Education:* Yale University (B.A., 1987); University of Illinois (J.D., magna cum laude, 1992). *Member:* American Bar Association. ***PRACTICE AREAS:*** Corporate; Information Technology; Business Process Outsourcing. ***Email:*** wmr@sonnenschein.com

MARINA N. SAITO, born Chicago, Illinois; admitted to bar, 1995, Illinois; registered to practice before U.S. Patent and Trademark Office. *Education:* University of Illinois at Chicago (B.S., Math and Computer Science, 1986; B.S., Biology, 1986; M.S.E.E., 1991); Illinois Institute of Technology/Chicago Kent College of Law (J.D., 1995). *Member:* Chicago and American Bar Associations; American Intellectual Property Law Association; Intellectual Property Law Association of Chicago; Institute of Electrical and Electronics Engineers. ***PRACTICE AREAS:*** Patent Prosecution; Patent Litigation; Trademark Litigation; Trademark Prosecution; Intellectual Property Licensing. ***Email:*** mns@sonnenschein.com

MARC A. SALLE (Resident, Kansas City, Missouri Office)

IVOR E. SAMSON (Not admitted in Illinois; Resident, San Francisco, California Office)

CHARLES D. SATINOVER (1906-1998)

MITCHELL D. SCHEPPS (Not admitted in Illinois; Resident, West Palm Beach, Florida Office)

ERIC M. SCHILLER, born Detroit, Michigan, March 19, 1946; admitted to bar, 1971, Illinois. *Education:* Indiana University (A.B., with honors, 1968); Northwestern University (J.D., 1971). Editor, Northwestern University Law Review, 1970-1971. National Moot Court Team, 1971. Co-Author: "Loan Participation," Probate & Property, Jan./Feb. 1993. *Member:* Chicago and American Bar Associations; American College of Real Estate Lawyers. ***PRACTICE AREAS:*** Real Estate; Finance. ***Email:*** ems@sonnenschein.com

DONALD M. SCHINDEL, born Chicago, Illinois, January 5, 1932; admitted to bar, 1956, Illinois. *Education:* University of Illinois (B.S. Accy., 1953); University of Chicago (J.D., 1956). Author: "Estate Administration and Tax Planning for Survivors," Wiley Law Publications, 1987 and supplements. *Member:* Chicago (Member: Probate Practice Committee, 1966—, Chairman, 1981-1982; Federal Taxation Committee, 1976—), Illinois State and American Bar Associations; American College of Trust and Estate Counsel. ***PRACTICE AREAS:*** Trusts and Estates. ***Email:*** dms@sonnenschein.com

MICHAEL A. SCHLANGER (Not admitted in Illinois; Resident, Washington, D.C. Office)

KENNETH B. SCHNOLL (Resident, San Francisco, California Office)

IRA A. SCHREGER (Not admitted in Illinois; Resident, New York, N.Y. Office)

ROBERT L. SCHUCHARD (Not admitted in Illinois; Resident, Los Angeles, California Office)

(This Listing Continued)

ARNOLD P. SCHUSTER (Not admitted in Illinois; Resident, San Francisco, California Office)

JORDANA SCHWARTZ (Resident, New York, N.Y. Office)

LEWIS M. SCHWARTZ (Not admitted in Illinois; Resident, New York, N.Y. Office)

ROBERT F. SCOULAR (Not admitted in Illinois; Resident, Los Angeles, California Office)

GARY SENNER, born Chicago, Illinois, January 2, 1942; admitted to bar, 1968, Illinois. *Education:* University of Wisconsin (B.A., 1964; M.A., 1965); Northwestern University (J.D., 1968). Phi Beta Kappa; Phi Kappa Phi; Order of the Coif. Editor, Northwestern University Law Review, 1967-1968. Law Clerk to the Hon. John Paul Stevens, U.S. Circuit Judge, U.S. Court of Appeals, Seventh Circuit, 1970-1971. Attorney, Antitrust Division, Department of Justice, 1968-1970. *Member:* Chicago and American Bar Associations. ***PRACTICE AREAS:*** Antitrust Law; Litigation. ***Email:*** gs@sonnenschein.com

J. A. SHAFRAN (Not admitted in Illinois; Resident, Los Angeles, California Office)

HAROLD D. SHAPIRO, born Chicago, Illinois, April 15, 1927; admitted to bar, 1952, Illinois. *Education:* Northwestern University (B.S., 1949; J.D., 1952). Order of the Coif. Editor-in-Chief, Illinois Law Review and Northwestern University Law Review, 1951-1952. The Harriman Adjunct Professor, Northwestern University School of Law, 1959—. *Member:* Chicago, Illinois State and American Bar Associations; Legal Club of Chicago (Member, Executive Committee, 1982—; Vice President, 1983; President, 1984); Law Club of Chicago; Chicago Council of Lawyers. ***PRACTICE AREAS:*** Corporate; International. ***Email:*** hds@sonnenschein.com

ALBERT W. SHAY (Not admitted in Illinois; Resident, Washington, D.C. Office)

GERALD J. SHERMAN, born Chicago, Illinois, November 3, 1938; admitted to bar, 1963, Illinois. *Education:* University of Illinois (B.A., 1959) Phi Beta Kappa; University of Chicago (J.D., 1962). Order of the Coif. Editor, University of Chicago Law Review, 1961-1962. *Member:* Chicago and American Bar Associations; Chicago Council of Lawyers; American College of Real Estate Lawyers; International Association of Attorneys and Executives in Corporate Real Estate (AECRE). ***PRACTICE AREAS:*** Real Estate. ***Email:*** gjs@sonnenschein.com

JORDAN A. SIGALE, born Chicago, Illinois, February 2, 1967; admitted to bar, 1992, Illinois and U.S. District Court, Northern District of Illinois; 1995, Trial Bar; 1996, U.S. Court of Appeals, Federal Circuit; registered to practice before U.S. Patent and Trademark Office. *Education:* Hebrew University; University of Illinois (B.S., Computer Eng., 1989; J.D., magna cum laude, 1992). Phi Alpha Delta; Eta Kappa Nu. Best Oral Argument and Best Overall Score, University of Illinois Intellectual Property Moot Court Competition, 1991. Author of First Place paper from College of Law to ASCAPs Nathan Burkan Competition entitled, "Statutory (Copyright) Damages: What Process is Due?" 1992. *Member:* Chicago (Member, Antitrust, Intellectual Property and Trial Practice Sections); South Suburban and American Bar Associations. ***PRACTICE AREAS:*** Patent, Trademark and Copyright; Unfair Competition; Computer; Litigation. ***Email:*** 8js@sonnenschein.com

ALAN H. SILBERMAN, born Chicago, Illinois, October 22, 1940; admitted to bar, 1964, Illinois. *Education:* Northwestern University (B.A., with distinction, 1961); Yale University (LL.B., 1964). Member: Bureau of National Affairs Antitrust Advisory Board; Illinois Attorney General Franchise Advisory Board. *Member:* Chicago, Illinois State (Chairman, Antitrust Law Section, 1975-1976) and American (Chairman, Federal Trade Commission Committee, Antitrust Section, 1981-1983; Chairman, National Institute Programs, Antitrust Section, 1983-1985; Council Member, Antitrust Section, 1985-1988; Finance Officer, Antitrust Section, 1988-1990; Section Delegate, Antitrust Section, 1990-1992; Chair-Elect, 1992-1993; Chair, 1993-1994) Bar Associations; International Bar Association (Member, Antitrust and Franchising Committees). ***PRACTICE AREAS:*** Antitrust; Franchising; Litigation. ***Email:*** ahs@sonnenschein.com

ROGER C. SISKE, born Starkville, Mississippi, March 2, 1944; admitted to bar, 1969, Illinois. *Education:* Ohio State University (B.S., with honors in Corporate Finance, 1966); University of Michigan (J.D., magna cum laude, 1969). Phi Alpha Kappa; Order of the Coif. Associate Editor, University of Michigan Law Review, 1967-1969. *Member:* Chicago (Chairman, Employee Benefits Committee, 1979-1980), Illinois State (Former Chairman, Section Council on Employee Benefits, 1985-1986) and American (Chairman, Committee on Employee Benefits and Executive Compensation, 1982-1986; Business Law Section; Chairman, Joint Committee on Employee Benefits, 1983-1984; Chairman, Committee on Employee Benefits, 1990-1991, Tax Section) Bar Associations. [Captain, U.S. Army, 1970-1971]. ***PRACTICE AREAS:*** Employee Benefits; Pension; Profit Sharing; Executive Compensation; Employment Agreements; ESOPS. ***Email:*** rcs@sonnenschein.com

JANU SIVANESAN (Resident, New York, N.Y. Office)

SUSAN B. SLATER-JANSEN (Not admitted in Illinois; Resident, New York, N.Y. Office)

CHRISTOPHER SMITH (Not admitted in Illinois; Resident, Washington, D.C. Office)

JOHN L. SNYDER (Resident, Kansas City, Missouri Office)

STEPHEN L. SOLOMON (Not admitted in Illinois; Resident, New York, N.Y. Office)

MARGO C. SOULÉ (Not admitted in Illinois; Resident, Kansas City, Missouri Office)

ROCHELLE BUCHSBAUM SPANDORF (Not admitted in Illinois; Resident, Los Angeles, California Office)

NATALIE J. SPEARS, born Chicago, Illinois, December 10, 1970; admitted to bar, 1995, Illinois. *Education:* University of Iowa (B.B.A., 1992); Leiden School of Law, The Netherlands; University of Michigan (J.D., cum laude, 1995). Clerk to the Hon. Michael J. Melloy, Chief Judge, U.S. District Court, Northern District of Iowa, 1995-1996. ***PRACTICE AREAS:*** Litigation; Intellectual Property; Media. ***Email:*** nxs@sonnenschein.com

DARRY SRAGOW (Not admitted in Illinois; Resident, Los Angeles, California Office)

RONALD E. STAUFFER (Not admitted in Illinois; Resident, Washington, D.C. Office)

T. REED STEPHENS (Resident, Washington, D.C. Office)

(This Listing Continued)

THOMAS M. STEPHENS, born Brooklyn, New York, March 7, 1956; admitted to bar, 1982, Connecticut and U.S. District Court, District of Connecticut; 1987, Illinois. *Education:* University of Connecticut (B.A., 1979); Catholic University of America (J.D., 1982); New York University (LL.M. in Taxation, 1987). *Member:* Chicago and American Bar Associations. ***PRACTICE AREAS:*** Tax. ***Email:*** tms@sonnenschein.com

DAVID H. STERN (Not admitted in Illinois; Resident, Los Angeles, California Office)

JANE G. STEVENS (Not admitted in Illinois; Resident, New York, N.Y. Office)

DAVID P. STOEBERL (Resident, St. Louis, Missouri Office)

ERROL L. STONE, born Chicago, Illinois, December 14, 1939; admitted to bar, 1964, Illinois. *Education:* University of Pennsylvania (A.B., 1961); Harvard University (LL.B., magna cum laude, 1964). *Member:* Chicago, Illinois State and American Bar Associations. ***PRACTICE AREAS:*** Corporate Law; Securities; Real Estate. ***Email:*** els@sonnenschein.com

SARAH TOEVS SULLIVAN (Resident, Kansas City, Missouri Office)

KEVIN R. SWEENEY (Not admitted in Illinois; Resident, Kansas City, Missouri Office)

DANIEL R. SWETT, born Chicago, Illinois, September 17, 1936; admitted to bar, 1962, Illinois. *Education:* Harvard University (A.B., magna cum laude, 1958; LL.B., cum laude, 1961). *Member:* Chicago (Member: Committee on the Economics of the Legal Profession, 1966-1971; Professional Fees Committee, 1969-1971) and American (Member, Committee on Nonprofit Corporations, 1979—) Bar Associations; Chicago Council of Lawyers. ***PRACTICE AREAS:*** Corporate; Securities; Health Care. ***Email:*** drs@sonnenschein.com

LOUIS L.S. TAO (Not admitted in Illinois; Resident, Washington, D.C. Office)

MARC D. TEITELBAUM (Not admitted in Illinois; Resident, New York, N.Y. Office)

RHONDA C. THOMAS, born 1947; admitted to bar, 1973, Missouri; 2001, Illinois. *Education:* Drury College (A.B., cum laude, 1969); Yale University; University of Missouri (J.D., 1973). ***PRACTICE AREAS:*** Public Finance; Municipal; Real Estate. ***Email:*** rthomas@sonnenschein.com

ELIZABETH THOMPSON (Not admitted in Illinois; Resident, San Francisco, California Office)

D. McCARTY THORNTON (Not admitted in Illinois; Resident, Washington, D.C. Office)

DENISE M. TORMEY (Not admitted in Illinois; Resident, New York, N.Y. Office)

EILEEN BANNON TROST, born Teaneck, New Jersey, January 9, 1951; admitted to bar, 1976, Illinois; 1978, Minnesota. *Education:* Shimer College (B.A., with great distinction, 1972); University of Minnesota (J.D., cum laude, 1976). Author: "Supreme Court Rules Reliance on Counsel is Not Reasonable Cause to Abate Late Filing Penalty," Estate Planning, Warren, Gorham & Lamont, May, 1985; "Goodfellow Well Met: A Case Study on Disclaimers," Michigan Probate and Estate Planning Journal, State Bar of Michigan Probate and Estate Planning Section, June 1987; "Identifying Some Taxing Problems," Trusts and Estates, Communications Channels, Inc., July 1987; "'Hatching the Nest Egg' - Planning for Distributions from Qualified Plans and IRA's," The Compleat Lawyer (ABA Publication), October 1992. *Member:* Minnesota State Bar Association; International Academy of Estate and Trust Law; American College of Trust and Estate Counsel. ***PRACTICE AREAS:*** Trusts and Estates; Estate Taxation; Retirement Planning; Estate Planning. ***Email:*** ebt@sonnenschein.com

SCOTT TUROW, born Chicago, Illinois, April 12, 1949; admitted to bar, 1978, Illinois and U.S. District Court, Northern District of Illinois including Trial Bar; 1979, U.S. Court of Appeals, Seventh Circuit. *Education:* Amherst College (B.A., magna cum laude, 1970); Stanford University (M.A., 1974); Harvard University (J.D., cum laude, 1978). Phi Beta Kappa. Author: *ONE L:* An Inside Account of Life In The First Year at Harvard Law School, G. P. Putnam's Son, 1977; *Presumed Innocent,* Farrar, Straus & Giroux, 1987; *The Burden of Proof,* Farrar, Straus & Giroux, 1990; *Pleading Guilty,* Farrar Straus & Giroux, 1993; *The Laws of Our Fathers,* Farrar, Straus & Giroux, 1996; *Personal Injuries,* Farrar Straus & Giroux, 1999. Assistant United States Attorney, Northern District of Illinois, 1978-1986. *Member:* Chicago Bar Association; Chicago Council of Lawyers. ***PRACTICE AREAS:*** White Collar; Criminal Defense; General Litigation. ***Email:*** sft@sonnenschein.com

FRANK P. VANDERPLOEG, born Washington, D.C., June 8, 1944; admitted to bar, 1973, Illinois. *Education:* Northwestern University (B.A., 1965); University of Michigan (J.D., magna cum laude, 1973). Phi Alpha Delta; Order of the Coif. Administrative Editor, Michigan Law Review, 1972-1973. Chairman, Board of Directors, Project LEAP Educational and Research Fund, Inc., 1980-1982. Author: "How to Comply with Federal Election Campaign Requirements," Attorney's Guide to Illinois Election Law, IICLE, 1991 & Supp. 1998; "Managed Care Organizations Under ERISA: Protections and Pitfalls," 1993 Group Health Institute, Group Health Association of America; "Types of Plans - Nonqualified Deferred Compensation; Stock Options; and Related Plans," Employee Benefits Law, ICLE 1994; "Role-Playing Under ERISA: The Company as 'Employer' and 'Fiduciary,'" De Paul Business Law Journal, Spring/Summer 1997, Vol. 9, Number 2. Adjunct Professor, De Paul University College of Law, 1987—. *Member:* Chicago and American Bar Associations. [U.S. Navy, 1965-1970 LTJG]. ***PRACTICE AREAS:*** Employee Benefits; Executive Compensation. ***Email:*** fpv@sonnenschein.com

THOMAS K. VANDIVER (Resident, St. Louis, Missouri Office)

JACQUELINE M. VIDMAR, born Wurzburg, Germany, February 12, 1963; admitted to bar, 1988, Illinois; 1989, U.S. District Court, Northern District of Illinois. *Education:* University of Pennsylvania (B.A., 1985); Northwestern University (J.D., 1988). Contributing Author: Corrective Action Chapter, "Environmental Law in Illinois," (IICLE, 1993, 1996). Co-Author: "Illinois Pollution Control Board," Chapter of Chicago Lawyers Court Handbook (1996); Article, "What You Need to Know About Environmental Auditing," ALI-ABA The Practical Real Estate Lawyer, November 1998. *Member:* American Bar Association (Member, Section on Natural Resources Energy and Environmental Law). ***PRACTICE AREAS:*** Environmental. ***Email:*** jmv@sonnenschein.com

DONNA J. VOBORNIK, born Chicago, Illinois, February 21, 1962; admitted to bar, 1987, Illinois and Wisconsin. *Education:* Northwestern University (B.A., 1984); University of Wisconsin-Madison (J.D., 1987). *Member:* State Bar of Wisconsin; American Bar Associations. ***PRACTICE AREAS:*** Litigation; Insurance. ***Email:*** djv@sonnenschein.com

DAVID L. VOLK (Not admitted in Illinois; Resident, Los Angeles, California Office)

JOHN E. WALKER (Not admitted in Illinois; Resident, Los Angeles, California Office)

SUSAN M. WALKER (Not admitted in Illinois; Resident, Los Angeles, California Office)

THOMAS M. WALSH (Not admitted in Illinois; Resident, St. Louis, Missouri Office)

LORI ANNE WARD, born St. Louis, Missouri, September 22, 1966; admitted to bar, 1992, Arizona; 1993, U.S. District Court, District of Arizona; 1996, Illinois; 1999, U.S. Court of Appeals, Sixth Circuit, U.S. Tax Court and U.S. District Court, Northern District of Illinois. *Education:* University of Arizona (B.A. in Political Science and Philosophy, 1988; J.D., magna cum laude, 1991). *Member:* Maricopa County and American Bar Associations; State Bar of Arizona. ***PRACTICE AREAS:*** ERISA; Executive Compensation; Employee Benefits. ***Email:*** law@sonnenschein.com

PAIGE D. WATERS, born Kansas City, Missouri, January 17, 1964; admitted to bar, 1989, Illinois. *Education:* Miami University (B.A., 1986); Chicago-Kent College of Law, Illinois Institute of Technology (J.D., 1989). *Member:* Chicago Bar Association; National Association of Managed Care Regulators; International Association of Insurance Receivers; National Conference of Insurance Legislators-Industry Education Council; Interstate Insurance Receivership Commission, Receivership Law Advisory Committee. ***PRACTICE AREAS:*** Insurance. ***Email:*** pwaters@sonnenschein.com

ANDREW L. WEIL, born Highland Park, Illinois, December 19, 1960; admitted to bar, 1986, Illinois. *Education:* Northwestern University (B.A. in Economics, with honors, 1983; J.D., 1986). Phi Beta Kappa, Mortar Board. Member, 1984-1986 and Notes and Comments Editor, 1985-1986, Northwestern Journal of International Law and Business. *Member:* Chicago and American Bar Associations; American Society of Corporate Secretaries, and NAREIT. ***PRACTICE AREAS:*** Corporate; Securities; Mergers and Acquisitions; Public Offerings; Venture Capital; Electronic Commerce; Technology; Telecommunications Law; Real Estate; REITs. ***Email:*** alw@sonnenschein.com

MICHAEL J. WEINBERGER (Not admitted in Illinois; Resident, New York, N.Y. Office)

GADI WEINREICH (Resident, Washington, D.C. Office)

MARGO WEINSTEIN, born Chicago, Illinois, July 25, 1960; admitted to bar, 1988, Illinois. *Education:* Yale University (B.A., with honors, 1982); Northwestern University (J.D., cum laude, 1987). Order of the Coif. Member, Northwestern University Law Review. Law Clerk to Hon. Walter J. Cummings, U.S. Court of Appeals for the Seventh Circuit, 1987-1988. *Member:* Women's Bar Association of Illinois. ***PRACTICE AREAS:*** Litigation. ***Email:*** mxw@sonnenschein.com

JEROME P. WEISS (1934-1996)

BARRY LEIGH WEISSMAN (Resident, Los Angeles, California Office)

LINDA D. WHITE, born New York, N.Y., April 1, 1952; admitted to bar, 1976, Illinois. *Education:* University of Pennsylvania (A.B., 1973); Northwestern University (J.D., 1976). *Member:* Chicago, Illinois State and American (Member, Section on Real Property, Probate and Trust Law) Bar Associations. ***PRACTICE AREAS:*** Real Estate; Real Estate Finance; Telecommunications. ***Email:*** ldw@sonnenschein.com

G. MARC WHITEHEAD, born May 20, 1940; admitted to bar, 1964, Minnesota; 1997, Illinois. *Education:* Princeton University (B.A., 1961); Yale University (J.D., 1964). Author: "Jury Trial Innovations," National Center for State Courts. ***PRACTICE AREAS:*** Litigation. ***Email:*** whi@sonnenschein.com

JAMES G. WIEHL (Not admitted in Illinois; Resident, St. Louis, Missouri Office)

C. HUNTER WIGGINS, born St. Louis, Missouri, October 16, 1967; admitted to bar, 1995, Illinois; 1997, District of Columbia. *Education:* University of Iowa (B.A., English, 1990); University of Michigan (J.D., cum laude, 1993). ***PRACTICE AREAS:*** Litigation. ***Email:*** hwiggins@sonnenschein.com

JOHN LELAND WILLIAMS (Not admitted in Illinois; Resident, San Francisco, California Office)

MARY G. WILSON, born Minneapolis, Minnesota, May 31, 1967; admitted to bar, 1992, Illinois. *Education:* Yale University (B.A., cum laude, with distinction in American Studies, 1989); University of Chicago (J.D., with honors, 1992). ***PRACTICE AREAS:*** Health Care; Tax Exempt Organizations; Corporate Law. ***Email:*** mwilson@sonnenschein.com

ROBERT L. WINIKOFF (Not admitted in Illinois; Resident, New York, N.Y. Office)

BRADLEY A. WINTERS (Resident, St. Louis, Missouri Office)

JEROME T. WOLF (Not admitted in Illinois; Resident, Kansas City, Missouri Office)

BENJAMIN E. WOLFF III (Resident, New York, N.Y. Office)

PETER D. WOLFSON (Not admitted in Illinois; Resident, New York, N.Y. Office)

CLEMENT B. WOOD (Not admitted in Illinois; Resident, New York, N.Y. Office)

CURTIS E. WOODS (Resident, Kansas City, Missouri Office)

MELVIN M. WRIGHT, JR., admitted to bar, 1991, Illinois. *Education:* Rutgers University, Livingston College, New Brunswick (B.A., 1986); Seton Hall University School of Law, Newark (J.D., 1991). ***PRACTICE AREAS:*** Litigation. ***Email:*** mwright@sonnenschein.com

MICHAEL J. WYNNE, born California, October 31, 1959; admitted to bar, 1984, Illinois. *Education:* Southern Illinois University (B.S., Finance, 1981); John Marshall Law School (J.D., 1984). ***PRACTICE AREAS:*** Taxation. ***Email:*** mwynne@sonnenschein.com

LAURA ANN WYTSMA (Not admitted in Illinois; Resident, Los Angeles, California Office)

D. FARRINGTON YATES (Resident, New York, N.Y. Office)

(This Listing Continued)

(This Listing Continued)

SONNENSCHEIN NATH & ROSENTHAL LLP, Chicago—Continued

ALAN T. YOSHITAKE (Not admitted in Illinois; Resident, Los Angeles, California Office)

NICHOLAS C. YOST (Not admitted in Illinois; Resident, San Francisco, California Office)

PAULA M. YOST (Not admitted in Illinois; Resident, San Francisco, California Office)

HOWARD J. YOUNG (Resident, Washington, D.C.)

HENRY S. ZANGWILL (Not admitted in Illinois; Resident, Los Angeles, California Office)

MARJORIE J. ZESSAR, born Skokie, Illinois, March 18, 1967; admitted to bar, 1994, Illinois. *Education:* Stanford University (B.A., with university distinction, 1989); University of Chicago (J.D., 1994). ***PRACTICE AREAS:*** Real Estate. ***Email:*** mzessar@sonnenschein.com

JANICE H. ZIEGLER (Resident, Washington, D.C. Office)

ROBERT B. ZIMMERMAN (Not admitted in Illinois; Resident, New York, N.Y. Office)

KARL ZOBRIST (Resident, Kansas City, Missouri Office)

RICHARD M. ZUCKERMAN (Not admitted in Illinois; Resident, New York, N.Y. Office)

MARC ZWILLINGER (Resident, Washington, D.C. Office)

OF COUNSEL

YONG J. AN (Resident, Kansas City, Missouri Office)

JENNIFER A. BARRETT, born Manhassett, N.Y., December 15, 1964; admitted to bar, 1992, Illinois. *Education:* Barnard College, Columbia University (B.A., cum laude, with honors in English, 1987); University of Chicago Law School (J.D., 1992). *Member:* American Bar Association (Member: Litigation Section; Committee on Commercial and Business Litigation). ***PRACTICE AREAS:*** Complex Civil Litigation. ***Email:*** jbarrett@sonnenschein.com

THOMAS G. BARRETT (Not admitted in Illinois; Resident, New York, N.Y. Office)

BRIAN C. BEHRENS (Resident, St. Louis, Missouri Office)

CAMILLE E. BENNETT, admitted to bar, 1994, Illinois and U.S. District Court, Northern District of Illinois. *Education:* Wellesley College (B.A., 1978); Cornell University (M.A., Ph.d., 1985); University of Chicago (J.D., 1994). Phi Beta Kappa. Member, University of Chicago Law Review. ***PRACTICE AREAS:*** Litigation. ***Email:*** ceb@sonnenschein.com

BELINDA A. BOYER (Resident, St. Louis, Missouri Office)

AMADEO F. CANTU, JR. (Resident, Los Angeles, California Office)

CLARISSA CERDA, born Chicago, Illinois, October 17, 1964; admitted to bar, 1993, Illinois; 1994, U.S. District Court, Northern District of Illinois; 1996, District of Columbia. *Education:* Harvard University (A.B., 1986); University of Western Australia (M.Phil., 1988); University of Michigan (J.D., 1992); l'Université Libre de Bruxelles (Certificat, 1992). Ninth Best Oralist in World, Philip C. Jessup International Moot Court Competition. Former Assistant Counsel to the President of the United States at the White House. *Member:* American Bar Association (Commissioner, Opportunities for Minorities in the Profession); Hispanic National Bar Association (Regional President, Midwest). ***LANGUAGES:*** Spanish, French and Italian. ***PRACTICE AREAS:*** Mergers and Acquisitions; Securities; General Corporate. ***Email:*** cc@sonnenschein.com

DEBRA S. CLARK, born Galesburg, Illinois, June 16, 1955; admitted to bar, 1979, Illinois. *Education:* Southern Methodist University (B.B.A., 1976); University of Texas at Austin (J.D., 1979). ***PRACTICE AREAS:*** Banking; Finance; Corporate Law. ***Email:*** dclark@sonnenschein.com

JULIET A. COX (Resident, Kansas City, Missouri Office)

KAREN DAVIS (Resident, St. Louis, Missouri Office)

ZACK Z. DONG, born Shanghai, China, July 26, 1957; admitted to bar, 1998, Illinois. *Education:* East China Normal University, Shanghai, China; Purdue University (Ph.D., American Studies, 1993); Northwestern University (J.D., 1998). *Member:* Chicago, Illinois State and American Bar Associations. ***LANGUAGES:*** Chinese. ***PRACTICE AREAS:*** International Law. ***Email:*** zdong@sonnenschein.com

MARCO P. FERREIRA (Not admitted in Illinois; Resident, Los Angeles, California Office)

THERESA M. FITZGERALD (Not admitted in Illinois; Resident, San Francisco, California Office)

JULIE R. FORMWALT (Not admitted in Illinois; Resident, Kansas City, Missouri Office)

ALEXANDER H. FUKUI (Resident, Los Angeles, CA Office)

ANDREW I. GAVIL (Resident, Washington, D.C. Office)

STEPHEN L. GIBSON (Not admitted in Illinois; Resident, Washington, D.C. Office)

ALLISON T. GODFREY (Resident, Kansas City, Missouri Office)

DEBRA GOLDBERG (Not admitted in Illinois; Resident, New York, N.Y. Office)

HELISE HARRINGTON (Not admitted in Illinois; Resident, New York, N.Y. Office)

JACOB INWALD (Not admitted in Illinois; Resident, New York, N.Y. Office)

LARS E. JOHANSSON (Not admitted in Illinois; Resident, San Francisco, California Office)

DEE JOYCE-HAYES (Not admitted in Illinois; Resident, St. Louis, Missouri Office)

RALPH B. KELLEY (Not admitted in Illinois; Resident, New York, N.Y. Office)

(This Listing Continued)

ANDREW P. LEDERMAN (Not admitted in Illinois; Resident, New York, N.Y. Office)

CHUNLIN LEONHARD, born Hubei Province, China, March 8, 1964; admitted to bar, 1995, Massachusetts; 1997, Illinois; 1998, U.S. District Court, Northern District of Illinois. *Education:* Shanghai Foreign Language Institute (B.A., 1986); Boston University (J.D., magna cum laude, 1995). Paul J. Liacos Distinguished Scholar. *Member:* American and Chinese American Bar Associations. ***LANGUAGES:*** Mandarin Chinese. ***PRACTICE AREAS:*** Products Liability; Commercial Litigation; International Law. ***Email:*** cxl@sonnenschein.com

ARTHUR S. LEVINE (Not admitted in Illinois; Resident, Los Angeles, California Office)

MARCI ROSE LEVINE (Not admitted in Illinois; Resident, Washington, D.C. Office)

MATTHEW L. LIFFLANDER, born New York, N.Y., September 18, 1932; admitted to bar, 1958, New York. *Education:* New York University (B.A., 1954); Cornell University (J.D., 1957). Phi Delta Phi. Member, Board of Editors, New York Law Journal, 1986-1999. Assistant Counsel to the Governor of the State of New York, 1957-1958. Acting Village Justice, Hastings-on-Hudson, New York, 1969-1974. Minority Counsel, Select Committee on Election Law, New York State Legislature, 1973-1974. Special Counsel to the Speaker, New York State Assembly 1975-1978. Counsel and Director, New York State Assembly Medical Practice Task Force, 1977-1978. Counsel, New York State Commission on Health Education, 1979. Author: "Negotiating International Agreements," *International Franchising,* 1971; "Final Treatment, the File on Dr. X," *W.W. Norton,* 1979. *Member:* The Association of the Bar of the City of New York (Member, State Legislation Committee, 1960-1962); New York State, American and International Bar Association; New York State Magistrates Association. (Resident, New York, N.Y. Office). ***PRACTICE AREAS:*** Corporate Law; Government Relations; Litigation. ***Email:*** mlifflander@sonnenschein.com

HAROLD I. LORING (Not admitted in Illinois; Resident, Washington, D.C. Office)

JENNIFER A. MARLER (Resident, St. Louis, Missouri Office)

ERIC C. MARSHALL, born Oak Park, Illinois, June 21, 1958; admitted to bar, 1984, Illinois. *Education:* Yale University (B.A., 1980); University of Michigan (J.D., 1984). Phi Delta Phi. Former Employment: Kotten, Muchin & Zavis, 1984-1987; Amoco Corporation, 1987-1988; Amoco Chemical Co., 1988-1995; Amoco Chemical Europe, Geneva, Switzerland, 1995-1998; BP Amoco, Chicago, 1998. *Member:* Chicago and Illinois State Bar Associations. ***PRACTICE AREAS:*** Corporate Law. ***Email:*** emarshall@sonnenschein.com

WENDY BYERS MARVIN (Not admitted in Illinois; Resident, Kansas City, Missouri Office)

EDWARD J. McCAFFERY (Resident, Los Angeles, California Office)

JOHN GARY McDAVID (Resident, Washington, D.C. Office)

JANE A. MEYER (Not admitted in Illinois; Resident, New York, N.Y. Office)

ERIC T. MIKKELSON (Resident, Kansas City, Missouri Office)

GRACE E. MUELLER (Not admitted in Illinois; Resident, Los Angeles, California Office)

ROBERT P. MULVEY (Not admitted in Illinois; Resident, New York, N.Y. Office)

GREGORY R. NARON, born Kansas City, Missouri, February 1, 1966; admitted to bar, 1991, Illinois and U.S. District Court, Northern District of Illinois. *Education:* University of Kansas at Lawrence (B.A., with distinction, 1988); Columbia University (J.D., 1991). Phi Beta Kappa; Harlan Fiske Stone Scholar. Notes Editor, Columbia VLA Journal of Law and the Arts, 1990-1991. Author: "With Malice Toward All: The Political Cartoon and the Law of Libel," Colum-VLA J. Law & Arts, Vol. 15, No. 1 (Fall, 1990). Co-Author: "Depositions of Foreign Nationals: What Litigators Can Do," Inside Litigation," (April, 1994); "Summary Judgment and the First Amendment: A Decade After Anderson v. Liberty Lobby," Libel Defense Resource Center Bulletin, Issue No. 3 (1997); "www.jurisdiction.law: U.S. Courts' Responses to the Confounding Problem of Personal Jurisdiction in the Age of the Internet," In Brief Magazine World Legal Forum, www.worldlegalforum.co.uk/usachicago/articles (Nov. 1998); "Y2K Claims Against the Computer Industry: Past as Prologue," Litigation (Winter 2000); "Prior Restraint and Copyright Injunctions: Striking the Balance," Libel Defense Resource Center Bulletin, Issue No. 2 (2000). *Member:* American Bar Association. ***PRACTICE AREAS:*** Litigation; Intellectual Property. ***Email:*** gn@sonnenschein.com

ENRIQUE PEREZ, admitted to bar, 1995, Illinois; registered to practice before the U.S. Patent and Trademark Office. *Education:* Northwestern University (B.S.E.E., 1982); Illinois Institute of Technology (M.S., Electrical Engineering, 1989); Chicago-Kent College of Law, Illinois Institute of Technology (J.D., 1995). ***LANGUAGES:*** Spanish. ***PRACTICE AREAS:*** Intellectual Property; Technology Law. ***Email:*** eperez@sonnenschein.com

ABRAHAM D. PIONTNICA (Resident, New York, N.Y. Office)

DAVID C. REINTJES (Not admitted in Illinois; Resident, Kansas City, Missouri Office)

BURTON R. RUBIN, (P.C.) (Not admitted in Illinois; Resident, New York, N.Y. Office)

RICHARD L. SADOWSKY (Resident, New York, N.Y. Office)

JOSEPH H. SCHMITT (Not admitted in Illinois; Resident, New York, N.Y. Office)

MARTIN J. SCHWARTZ (Not admitted in Illinois; Resident, New York, N.Y. Office)

VICTOR H. SIM (Resident, Los Angeles, California Office)

DANIEL A. SPIRN (Resident, St. Louis, Missouri Office)

TODD M. STENNES, born Plum City, Wisconsin, September 24, 1966; admitted to bar, 1992, Illinois. *Education:* University of Illinois (B.S., Finance, 1989); University of Chicago (J.D., 1992). ***PRACTICE AREAS:*** Real Estate. ***Email:*** tstennes@sonnenschein.com

(This Listing Continued)

LETITIA REI TODD (Not admitted in Illinois; Resident, San Francisco, California Office)

ELIZABETH A. TOSARIS (Not admitted in Illinois; Resident, San Francisco, California Office)

WENDY S. WEINGART (Not admitted in Illinois; Resident, New York, N.Y. Office)

HOWARD H. WELLER (Not admitted in Illinois; Resident, New York, N.Y. Office)

DONNA M. WILSON (Resident, Kansas City, Missouri Office)

MORRIS K. WITHERS (Not admitted in Illinois; Resident, Kansas City, Missouri Office)

CHARLES M. YABLON (Not admitted in Illinois; Resident, New York, N.Y. Office)

DEBRA B. YALE, admitted to bar, 1988, Illinois. *Education:* Indiana University (B.S., 1985); Northwestern University (J.D., 1988). *Member:* Chicago Bar Association. ***PRACTICE AREAS:*** Real Estate. ***Email:*** dsy@sonnenschein.com

SPECIAL COUNSEL

DANIEL R. BROWN (Resident, San Francisco, California Office)

ASSOCIATES

JILL L. ABITBOL (Not admitted in Illinois; Resident, New York, N.Y. Office)

KIRILL Y. ABRAMOV (Resident, St. Louis, Missouri Office)

PHILIP F. ACKERMAN, born Port Washington, Wisconsin, November 14, 1968; admitted to bar, 1998, Illinois. *Education:* University of Wisconsin (B.B.A., 1991); Tulane Law School (J.D., magna cum laude, 1998). Order of the Coif; Beta Gamma Sigma. ***PRACTICE AREAS:*** Commercial Litigation; White Collar Criminal Litigation. ***Email:*** packerman@sonnenschein.com

JOSHUA AKBAR (Resident, New York, N.Y. Office)

DAVID S. ALVERSON (Not admitted in Illinois; Resident, Los Angeles, California Office)

ALEJANDRO AMEZCJA, born Chicago, Illinois, April 22, 1976; (admission pending). *Education:* DePauw University (B.A., 1998); Northwestern University (J.D., 2005). ***LANGUAGES:*** Spanish. ***Email:*** aamezcja@sonnenschein.com

LEANNA M. ANDERSON (Resident, Los Angeles, California Office)

MARY B. ANDERSON, born Evanston, Illinois, January 19, 1976; (admission pending). *Education:* University of Notre Dame (B.A., summa cum laude, 1998); DePaul University (J.D., 2004). Phi Beta Kappa. *Member:* American Bar Association. ***PRACTICE AREAS:*** Litigation. ***Email:*** manderson@sonnenschein.com

SHANNON SKINNER ANGLIN, admitted to bar, 2001, New York; 2002, Illinois; 2003, California. *Education:* Western Carolina University (B.A., 1992); Tulane University Law School (J.D., cum laude, 1998); Georgetown University Law Center (LL.M., Taxation, 1999). ***PRACTICE AREAS:*** Employee Benefits; Executive Compensation. ***Email:*** sanglin@sonnenschein.com

KATHRYN B. ASHTON, born St. Paul, Minnesota, May 3, 1972; admitted to bar, 1999, Illinois; 2001, Colorado. *Education:* Drake University (B.A., 1994); Chicago-Kent College of Law, Illinois Institute of Technology (J.D., 1999). Order of the Coif. ***PRACTICE AREAS:*** Tax Exempt Finance. ***Email:*** kashton@sonnenschein.com

ERIC M. BAIM (Resident, Washington, D.C. Office)

RACHEL G. BALABAN (Not admitted in Illinois; Resident, New York, N.Y. Office)

CAROLE BASS (Resident, New York, N.Y. Office)

DAVID R. BAUM (Not admitted in Illinois; Resident, New York, N.Y. Office)

LAURA BECKER (Resident, Los Angeles, California Office)

JASON BECKERMAN (Resident, Los Angeles, California Office)

IMANTA M. BERGMANIS (Not admitted in Illinois; Resident, Washington, D.C. Office)

WENYU HO BLANCHARD, born Taiwan, October 30, 1973; admitted to bar, 1999, Illinois and U.S. District Court, Northern District of Illinois. *Education:* Boston College (B.A., magna cum laude, 1995; J.D., 1999). Phi Beta Kappa; Phi Alpha Delta. *Member:* Chicago and American Bar Associations. ***LANGUAGES:*** Mandarin. ***PRACTICE AREAS:*** Intellectual Property. ***Email:*** wth@sonnenschein.com

KATHLEEN BOERGERS (Not admitted in Illinois; Resident, San Francisco, California Office)

HOWARD S. BONFIELD (Resident, New York, N.Y. Office)

RICHARD J. BRIGHTMAN (Not admitted in Illinois; Resident, Short Hills, New Jersey Office)

CHRISTOPHER A. BROWN, admitted to bar, 2001, Virginia; 2002, District of Columbia (Not admitted in Illinois). *Education:* University of Minnesota (B.A., 1995); George Washington University (J.D., 2000). ***PRACTICE AREAS:*** Food and Drug Law; Advertising Law; Trademark Law. ***Email:*** cbrown@sonnenschein.com

LEAH R. BRUNO, born Arlington Heights, Illinois, August 8, 1974; admitted to bar, 1999, Illinois. *Education:* Trinity College, Oxford University (A.S., 1995); Northwestern University (B.A., 1996); DePaul University (J.D., with highest honors, 1999). Order of the Coif. Member, Editorial Staff, De Paul Law Review. ***PRACTICE AREAS:*** Litigation. ***Email:*** l4b@sonnenschein.com

KATE BUCKLEY (admission pending), (Resident, New York, N.Y. Office)

KEVIN W. BUCKLEY (Not admitted in Illinois; Resident, St. Louis, MO Office)

JENNIFER A. BUNSHOFT (Not admitted in Illinois; Resident, San Francisco, California Office)

THOMAS J. BURTON, born Baton Rouge, Louisiana, September 16, 1962; admitted to bar, 2000, Illinois and U.S. District Court, Northern District of Illinois. *Education:* University of Missouri, Columbia (B.S.E.E. and B.S. Computer E., 1985); Washington University (M.B.A., 1992); St. Louis University Law School (J.D., cum laude, 2000). *Member:* St. Louis University Law Journal, 1998-1999. ***PRACTICE AREAS:*** Intellectual Property; Technology; Electronic Commerce; Patents; Litigation; Corporate. ***Email:*** t3b@sonnenschein.com

KWAME N. CAIN (Not admitted in Illinois; Resident, New York, N.Y. Office)

JULIE CALHOUN (Resident, St. Louis, Missouri Office)

MICHAEL CARNEY (admission pending), (Resident, New York, N.Y. Office)

LETISSA CARVER REID, born Milwaukee, Wisconsin, February 21, 1973; admitted to bar, 1998, Illinois; 2000, U.S. District Court, Northern District of Illinois. *Education:* University of Michigan (B.A., 1994); Indiana University School of Law (J.D., 1998). Member, Order of the Barristers. ***PRACTICE AREAS:*** Environmental. ***Email:*** lcarver@sonnenschein.com

PATRICIA N. CHOCK (Not admitted in Illinois; Resident, Los Angeles, California Office)

ZENAS J. CHOI (Resident, Washington, D.C. Office)

MICHAEL W. CHOU (Resident, Los Angeles, California Office)

KEVIN M. CHRISTENSEN (Not admitted in Illinois; Resident, San Francisco, California Office)

KEVIN J. CLANCY, born Indianapolis, Indiana, September 29, 1968; admitted to bar, 1993, Illinois, U.S. District Court, Central District of Illinois and U.S. Court of Appeals, Seventh Circuit; 1994, U.S. District Court, Northern District of Illinois. *Education:* University of Illinois (B.A., cum laude, 1990; J.D., magna cum laude, 1993). Phi Beta Kappa; Harno Scholar. Recipient, American Jurisprudence Award. ***PRACTICE AREAS:*** Commercial Litigation; Class Action Litigation. ***Email:*** kjc@sonnenschein.com

WILLIAM E. COPLEY, III (Not admitted in Illinois; Resident, Washington, D.C. Office)

MONA E. DAJANI, admitted to bar, 1996, Illinois. *Education:* University of Illinois (B.A., cum laude, 1988); University of St. Thomas, Cameron School of Business (M.B.A., with honors, 1992); Loyola University School of Law (J.D., 1996). Recipient, American Jurisprudence Awards in Computer Applications in the Law and Family Law, 1995. Case Note Writer, Loyola Consumer Law Reporter. Certified Public Accountant, Texas, 1993. *Member:* Chicago, Illinois State and American Bar Associations. ***PRACTICE AREAS:*** Real Estate; Corporate Transactions.

ANDREW DALIN (Not admitted in Illinois; Resident, New York, N.Y. Office)

KEITH A. DAVIDSON (Not admitted in Illinois; Resident, Los Angeles, California Office)

JEFFERY S. DAVIS, born January 29, 1977; admitted to bar, 2002, Illinois. *Education:* University of Illinois, Urbana-Champaign (B.S., 1999; J.D., 2002). ***PRACTICE AREAS:*** Corporate; Insurance Regulation.

DOMINIC J. DeMATTIES, born Newburgh, New York, July 30, 1971; (admission pending). *Education:* State University of New York College at Geneseo (B.A., 1994); Rochester Institute of Technology (M.S., 1997); Georgetown University (J.D., 2003). ***PRACTICE AREAS:*** Employee Benefits; Executive Compensation; ERISA. ***Email:*** ddematties@sonnenschein.com

DAVID ALOYSIUS DIEPENBROCK (Resident, San Francisco, California Office)

KATHERINE HALE DONNELLY, born Boston, Massachusetts, October 3, 1975; admitted to bar, 2001, Massachusetts (Not admitted in Illinois). *Education:* Boston University (B.A., 1997); Northeastern University School of Law (J.D., 2000). ***PRACTICE AREAS:*** Real Estate; Affordable Housing. ***Email:*** kdonnelly@sonnenschein.com

MICHAEL G. DONOHUE (Resident, Kansas City, Missouri Office)

STACI E. DRESHER (Resident, San Francisco, California Office)

DEBORAH DRULEY (Resident, St. Louis, Missouri Office)

STEPHANIE A. DUCHENE (Resident, San Francisco, California Office)

CHARLES A. DUFFIELD, born Canton, Illinois, November 2, 1970; admitted to bar, 2000, Illinois. *Education:* University of Illinois, Urbana-Champaign (B.S.,1993; J.D., 2000). *Member:* Chicago, Illinois State and American Bar Associations.

KATHERINE JEAN EDDY (Resident, San Francisco, California Office)

ANTHONY T. ELISEUSON, born Santa Monica, California, May 8, 1975; admitted to bar, 2002, Illinois. *Education:* Arizona State University (B.A., Political Science, 1999); University of Minnesota Law School (J.D., 2002). Pi Sigma Alpha. Associate Note & Comment Editor, Minnesota Journal of Global Trade. Extern, Honorable Franklin L. Noel, Magistrate Judge, District of Minnesota. *Member:* Chicago, Illinois State and American Bar Associations. ***PRACTICE AREAS:*** Litigation. ***Email:*** aeliseuson@sonnenschein.com

BENJAMIN S. ELLENBOGEN (Not admitted in Illinois; Resident, New York, N.Y. Office)

CYNTHIA J. EMRY (Resident, Los Angeles, California Office)

WENDY N. ENERSON, born Chicago, Illinois, December 30, 1969; admitted to bar, 2000, Illinois. *Education:* University of Illinois (B.A., 1993); Northwestern University (J.D., 2000). Member, Northwestern Law Review, 1998-2000. *Member:* American Bar Association. ***PRACTICE AREAS:*** Litigation. ***Email:*** wenerson@sonnenschein.com

LISA Z. FAIN, born Syracuse, New York, October 31, 1973; (admission pending). *Education:* Northwestern University (B.S., 1995; J.D., 2000). ***PRACTICE AREAS:*** Labor and Employment. ***Email:*** lisa_fain@sonnenschein.com

RAMY FAYED (Resident, Washington, D.C. Office)

DANIEL FEINBERG, born Chicago, Illinois, September 12, 1974; admitted to bar, 1999, Illinois and U.S. District Court, Northern District of Illinois. *Education:* Indiana University (B.A., Psychology and Criminal Justice, 1996); Loyola University (J.D., 1999). *Member:* Chicago and American Bar Associations. ***PRACTICE AREAS:*** Litigation. ***Email:*** dfeinberg@sonnenschein.com

(This Listing Continued)

SONNENSCHEIN NATH & ROSENTHAL LLP, Chicago—Continued

ROBERT L. FERNANDEZ, born Evanston, Illinois, October 31,1974; admitted to bar, 1999, Illinois. *Education:* DePaul University (B.A., with high honors, 1996); Northwestern University School of Law (J.D., 1999). Harold Washington Scholar. Member, Editorial board, Northwestern University Journal of International Law and Business. Extern Clerk, Hon. Ruben Castillo, U.S. District Court, Northern District of Illinois, Fall 1998. ***LANGUAGES:*** Spanish. ***PRACTICE AREAS:*** Real Estate Law; Secured Lending. ***Email:*** r2f@sonnenschein.com

A. WESLEY FERREBEE (Not admitted in Illinois; Resident, Washington, D.C. Office)

SCOTT T. FILMORE (Resident, St. Louis, MO Office)

ELIZABETH S. FINBERG (Resident, Washington, D.C. Office)

MARK A. FINK (Resident, New York, N.Y. Office)

JACQUELINE H. FINNEGAN (Resident, New York, N.Y. Office)

DEBRA L. FOGELMAN (Resident, Los Angeles, California Office)

STEPHEN E. FOX (Not admitted in Illinois; Resident, New York, N.Y. Office)

SAUNDRA N. FRIED, born Baton Rouge, Louisiana, March 8, 1969; admitted to bar, 1994, Ohio; 2003, Illinois. *Education:* University of Florida (B.A., 1991); Case Western Reserve University (J.D., 1994). Phi Beta Kappa. Chair, Government, School and Construction Law Committee, Ohio State Bar Association, 2002-2003. Vice Chair, Government Lawyers Committee, Ohio State Bar Association, 2001-2002. Board Member, Ohio Government Finance Officers Association, 2002-2003. Member, Chicago and Ohio Bar Associations; National Association of Bond Attorneys. Member, Women in Public Finance, 2005—. ***PRACTICE AREAS:*** Public Finance; Health Care; Corporate; Securities; Government Contracting. ***Email:*** sfried@sonnenschein.com

KATHERINE I. FUNK (Not admitted in Illinois; Resident, Washington, D.C. Office)

MICHAEL R. GALLIGAN (admission pending), (Resident, New York, N.Y. Office)

TODD A. GANGEL (Not admitted in Illinois; Resident, Kansas City, Missouri Office)

HECTOR GARCIA-SANTANA (admission pending), (Resident, Washington, D.C. Office)

R. MATT GARMS (Not admitted in Illinois; Resident, Kansas City, Missouri Office)

PATRICIA K. GARRINGER (Not admitted in Illinois; Resident, Kansas City, Missouri Office)

SUSAN J. GERMER (Not admitted in Illinois; Resident, San Francisco, California Office)

TERANCE A. GONSALVES, born Georgetown, Guyana, July 12, 1967; admitted to bar, 2000, Illinois. *Education:* University of Illinois, Urbana-Champaign (B.A., 1991); DePaul University College of Law (J.D., with honors, 2000). Member, Order of the Coif. ***PRACTICE AREAS:*** Litigation. ***Email:*** tgonsalves@sonnenschein.com

ANNE A. GONZALEZ (admission pending), (Resident, New York, N.Y. Office)

DINA GORODESS, born Tel Aviv, Israel; admitted to bar, 2000, Illinois. *Education:* Oberlin College (B.A., 1995); Northwestern University (J.D., 2000). ***PRACTICE AREAS:*** Litigation. ***Email:*** dgorodess@sonnenschein.com

AMANDA R. GRAINGER (Resident, Washington, D.C. Office)

THOMAS E. GREIFF (Resident, Los Angeles, CA Office)

WALTER C. HAZLITT, JR., born Port Jefferson, New York, June 18, 1969; admitted to bar, 1996, Virginia; 1997, District of Columbia; 2000, Illinois; U.S. District Court for the District of Columbia; U.S. District Court, Eastern District of Virginia; U.S. Court of Appeals, Fourth Circuit. *Education:* Dickinson College (B.A., Policy and Management Studies, 1991); George Washington University Law School (J.D., 1996). ***PRACTICE AREAS:*** Litigation; Energy. ***Email:*** whazlitt@sonnenschein.com

CHRIS S. HELLER (Resident, Kansas City, Missouri Office)

COURTNEY R. HENNING (admission pending), (Resident, Los Angeles, California Office)

ROBERT W. HOFFMAN (Not admitted in Illinois; Resident, San Francisco, California Office)

HILLARY HERA HUGHES (Not admitted in Illinois; Resident, New York, N.Y. Office)

ARETO A. IMOUKHUEDE, born Chicago, Illinois, November 7, 1977; admitted to bar, 2002, Illinois. *Education:* Northwestern University (B.A., 1999); Georgetown University (J.D., 2002). ***PRACTICE AREAS:*** Commercial Litigation. ***Email:*** aai@sonnenschein.com

LESA M. INGRAHAM, born Flint, Michigan, June 3, 1963; admitted to bar, 1993, Illinois. *Education:* Michigan State University (B.A., 1986); Chicago-Kent College of Law (J.D., magna cum laude, 1993). Order of the Coif. Executive Articles Editor, Chicago-Kent Law Review. Law Clerk to Honorable Hubert L. Will, U.S. District Court, Northern District of Illinois. *Member:* Chicago, Illinois State and American Bar Associations. ***PRACTICE AREAS:*** Corporate; Securities. ***Email:*** lmi@sonnenschein.com

JAMES E. JASAITIS (Not admitted in Illinois; Resident, Short Hills, New Jersey Office)

SANCHITHA JAYARAM (Not admitted in Illinois; Resident, Washington, D.C. Office)

JOMA R. JONES (Not admitted in Illinois; Resident, San Francisco, California Office)

KAREN M. JORDAN (Resident, St. Louis, Missouri Office)

JONATHAN KADEN, born Durham, North Carolina, August 7, 1974; admitted to bar, 1999, Illinois and U.S. District Court, Northern District of Illinois. *Education:* Duke University (A.B., magna cum laude, 1996); Northwestern University (J.D., cum laude, 1999). Author, 89 J. Crim. L. & Criminology 347 (1998). ***PRACTICE AREAS:*** Real Estate. ***Email:*** jkaden@sonnenschein.com

GAURAV KALRA (Resident, San Francisco, California Office)

CHRISTOPHER N. KANAGAWA (Resident, St. Louis, Missouri Office)

LEE KASTER (Not admitted in Illinois; Resident, San Francisco, California Office)

JUSTIN N. KATTAN (Resident, New York, N.Y. Office)

RAMJI B. KAUL, admitted to bar, 2005, Illinois. *Education:* University of Michigan (B.A., 2002; J.D., 2005). ***PRACTICE AREAS:*** Litigation. ***Email:*** rkaul@sonnenschein.com

NADIM KAZI, born Morristown, NJ, January 3, 1975; admitted to bar, 2001, Illinois. *Education:* St. Louis University (B.A., Accounting, 1998); Loyola University, Chicago School of Law (J.D., 2001). ***PRACTICE AREAS:*** Corporate and Securities; Bankruptcy. ***Email:*** nkazi@sonnenschein.com

DERRICK KEDZIORA, admitted to bar, 1997, Illinois and U.S. District Court, Northern District of Illinois. *Education:* Northwestern University (B.A., 1994; J.D., 1997). ***LANGUAGES:*** Polish. ***PRACTICE AREAS:*** Litigation.

LILLY KIM (Resident, Los Angeles, California Office)

LESLIE E. KLEIN (Not admitted in Illinois; Resident, Washington, D.C. Office)

JENNIFER B. KLEINER (Not admitted in Illinois; Resident, New York, N.Y. Office)

BEATA K. KRAKUS, born Taby, Sweden, December 2, 1973; admitted to bar, 2003, Illinois. *Education:* Stockholm University School of Law, Stockholm (LL.M., 1997); Loyola University (J.D., 2002). ***PRACTICE AREAS:*** Corporate. ***Email:*** bkrakus@hotmail.com

JANA KRUPOFF, born Syracuse, New York; admitted to bar, 2000, Illinois. *Education:* Indiana University (B.S., 1997); Chicago-Kent College of Law (J.D., 2000). ***PRACTICE AREAS:*** Corporate; Outsourcing. ***Email:*** jkrupoff@sonnenschein.com

AZNIV KSACHIKYAN (Not admitted in Illinois; Resident, Los Angeles, CA Office)

MERRILLYN ERSKINE KULIS (Resident, Los Angeles, California Office)

JOHN LABBE, admitted to bar, 2002, Illinois; U.S. District Court, Southern District of Ohio; registered to practice before U.S. Patent and Trademark Office. *Education:* Northwestern University (B.A., Biology, 1998; J.D., cum laude, 2002). Executive Editor, Northwestern University Law Review. *Member:* American Bar Association. ***PRACTICE AREAS:*** Intellectual Property; Technology. ***Email:*** jlabbe@sonnenschein.com

MELEANA E. LEAVERTON (Not admitted in Illinois; Resident, San Francisco, California Office)

SOOJUNG LEE, born October 19, 1973; admitted to bar, 2003, California (Not admitted in Illinois). *Education:* Yonsei University, Seoul, Korea (B.A., 1996); Loyola Law School, Los Angeles (J.D., 2003). (Resident, Los Angeles, California Office). ***PRACTICE AREAS:*** Corporate; Real Estate. ***Email:*** slee@sonnenschein.com

VERONICA M. LEI, born Pennsylvania, June 3, 1976; (admission pending). *Education:* Columbia University (B.A., 1998); Harvard Law School (J.D., 2004). Phi Beta Kappa. ***PRACTICE AREAS:*** Litigation. ***Email:*** vlei@sonnenschein.com

ELIZABETH A. LEIFEL, born Bloomington, Illinois, August 5, 1978; admitted to bar, 2003, Illinois. *Education:* University of Illinois (B.A., 2000); University of Michigan (J.D., 2003). ***Email:*** eleifel@sonnenschein.com

KEVIN D. LESH (Resident, San Francisco, California Office)

CLIONA A. LEVY (Not admitted in Illinois; Resident, New York, N.Y. Office)

RACHEL LEISER LEVY, born Washington, D.C., July 8, 1976; (admission pending). *Education:* Stern College for Women, Yeshiva University (B.A., 1998); University of Chicago (J.D., 2004). Law Review, 2004. Articles Editor, University of Chicago Legal Forum, 2002-2003. Author: "Judicial Interpretation of Employee Handbooks" University of Chicago Law Review, Spring 2005. ***LANGUAGES:*** German. ***PRACTICE AREAS:*** Litigation; Labor and Employment. ***Email:*** rlevy@sonnenschein.com

LISA M. LILLY, born Berwyn, Illinois, December 22, 1965; admitted to bar, 2000, Illinois. *Education:* Columbia College (B.A., 1988); DePaul University (J.D., 2000). Order of the Coif. *Member:* Women's Bar Association of Illinois. ***PRACTICE AREAS:*** Litigation. ***Email:*** lilly@ameritech.net

TALIA ANNA LISSNER, born Rehovot, Israel, January 23, 1972; admitted to bar, 2001, Illinois. *Education:* University of Illinois (B.S., 1994); Chicago-Kent College of Law, Illinois Institute of Technology (J.D., 2001). Chicago-Kent Honor Scholar. Member, Chicago-Kent Law Review, 1999-2000. ***LANGUAGES:*** Hebrew. ***PRACTICE AREAS:*** Real Estate. ***Email:*** tlissner@sonnenschein.com

KEITH LONDO, born Chicago, Illinois, March 20, 1973; (admission pending). *Education:* Western Michigan University (B.A., Accounting, 1995); Northwestern Law School (J.D., 2004). ***PRACTICE AREAS:*** Real Estate. ***Email:*** klondo@sonnenschein.com

EVA LOPEZ-PAREDES (admission pending), (Resident, New York, N.Y. Office)

STEVEN M. LUBEZNY, born Kiev, Ukraine, April 11, 1975; admitted to bar, 2001, Illinois. *Education:* University of Illinois, Champaign/Urbana (B.S.E.E., 1997); Chicago-Kent College of Law (J.D., 2001). Order of the Coif. ***PRACTICE AREAS:*** Patent; Trademark; Copyright; Unfair Competition. ***Email:*** slubezny@sonnenschein.com

MARK R. LUDWIKOWSKI (Resident, Washington, D.C. Office)

MONIKA J. MACHEN, admitted to bar, 2000, Illinois; 2001, Florida; 2002, U.S. District Court, Northern District of Illinois. *Education:* University of Pennsylvania (B.A., 1997); University of Michigan, Ann Arbor (J.D., 2000). ***PRACTICE AREAS:*** Bankruptcy; Creditors Rights. ***Email:*** mmachen@sonnenschein.com

KASHMIRA M. MAKWANA (Not admitted in Illinois; Resident, Washington, D.C. Office)

(This Listing Continued)

ERIC REED MANSELL, born Portland, Oregon, January 6, 1973; admitted to bar, 2001, Illinois. *Education:* University of Washington (B.A., 1995); Loyola University (J.D., 2001). Phi Delta Phi. *Member:* American Bar Association. ***PRACTICE AREAS:*** Corporate Law. ***Email:*** emansell@sonnenschein.com

MATTHEW MAROSTICA (admission pending), (Resident, San Francisco, California Office)

PATRICK C. MAXCY, born Presque Isle, Maine, July 22, 1970; admitted to bar, 1999, Maine and New Hampshire (Not admitted in Illinois). *Education:* University of Maine (B.A., 1993; J.D., 1999). ***PRACTICE AREAS:*** Bankruptcy. ***Email:*** pmaxcy@sonnenschein.com

KEVIN C. MAY (Resident, St. Louis, Missouri Office)

JOHNNY McCRAW, JR., admitted to bar, 2003, Illinois. *Education:* Middle Tennessee State University (B.A., 2000); University of Michigan Law School (J.D., 2003). Editor in Chief, University of Michigan Law Reform. ***PRACTICE AREAS:*** Litigation; Business Regulation. ***Email:*** jmmcraw@sonnenschein.com

JACQUE McCRAY, born Chicago, Illinois, February 17, 1979; admitted to bar, 2004, Illinois. *Education:* Harvard University (B.A., cum laude, 2001); Georgetown University (J.D., 2004). ***PRACTICE AREAS:*** Litigation; Intellectual Property. ***Email:*** jmccray@sonnenschein.com

ELIZABETH J. McCUBREY (Resident, Washington, D.C. Office)

SHANE M. McGEE (Not admitted in Illinois; Resident, Washington, D.C. Office)

STEVEN L. MEROUSE, born Detroit, Michigan, April 7, 1964; admitted to bar, 1997, Illinois. *Education:* Augustana College (B.A., magna cum laude, 1986); New York University (J.D., cum laude, 1997). Phi Beta Kappa; Omicron Delta Kappa. ***PRACTICE AREAS:*** Litigation; Antitrust. ***Email:*** s4m@sonnenschein.com

MARY L. MILLS, born Miami, Florida, March 9, 1961; admitted to bar, 1991, Illinois. *Education:* Washington University (B.A., 1984); Chicago-Kent College of Law (J.D., 1991). Order of the Coif. ***PRACTICE AREAS:*** Litigation. ***Email:*** mlm@sonnenschein.com

SARAH M. MINCHENER (Not admitted in Illinois; Resident, Washington, D.C. Office)

ANNE W. MITCHELL, born Chapel Hill, North Carolina, December 28, 1974; admitted to bar, 2002, Illinois and U.S. District Court, Northern District of Illinois; 2003, U.S. District Court, Central District of Illinois. *Education:* Agnes Scott College (B.A., 1997); Northwestern University (J.D., 2002). ***PRACTICE AREAS:*** Litigation. ***Email:*** amitchell@sonnenschein.com

MEREDITH A. MONACO, born Chicago Heights, Illinois, January 5, 1971; admitted to bar, 1997, Illinois; 1999, U.S. District Court, Northern District of Illinois and U.S. Court of Appeals, Seventh Circuit. *Education:* Miami University (B.A., magna cum laude, Phi Beta Kappa, 1993); Northwestern University (J.D., 1996). ***PRACTICE AREAS:*** Environmental Insurance Coverage; Litigation; Employment. ***Email:*** mm8@sonnenschein.com

KIM MORIMOTO (Not admitted in Illinois; Resident, San Francisco, California Office)

MIRELLA MOSHE SISKINDOVICH (admission pending), (Resident, New York, N.Y. Office)

JEFFREY MOVIT (admission pending), (Resident, New York, N.Y. Office)

M. QUINN MURPHY (Resident, St. Louis, Missouri Office)

MICKKI D. MURRAY (Resident, St. Louis, Missouri Office)

CATHERINE NASSER, born Melbourne, Australia, January 1, 1978; admitted to bar, 2004, Illinois. *Education:* University of Michigan (B.A., 2000); Northwestern University (J.D., cum laude, 2004). ***PRACTICE AREAS:*** Labor and Employment. ***Email:*** cnasser@sonnenschein.com

TARA A. NEALEY (Resident, St. Louis, Missouri Office)

JAMES C. NEELD (Resident, Kansas City, Missouri Office)

JESSICA M. NORRIS (Resident, Kansas City, Missouri Office)

MEGHAN E. NORTON, born February 12, 1979; (admission pending). *Education:* University of Pennsylvania (B.A., magna cum laude, 2001); Northwestern University (J.D., 2005). Phi Beta Kappa; Psi Chi; Phi Alpha Delta (Secretary, 1998-1999). ***PRACTICE AREAS:*** Litigation. ***Email:*** mnorton@sonnenschein.com

EMILY S. NOZICK (Resident, San Francisco, California Office)

STEPHANIE M. O'NEILL MACRO, born Minneapolis, Minnesota, January 5, 1970; admitted to bar, 1995, Illinois. *Education:* Boston University (B.A., 1992); Loyola University Law School (J.D., 1995). ***PRACTICE AREAS:*** Insurance Regulatory; Health Care; Corporate; E-Commerce; Privacy. ***Email:*** oneillmacro@sonnenschein.com

DANA ORR, admitted to bar, 2004, Illinois. *Education:* Université de Lyon; London School of Economics; Dartmouth College (B.A., African-American Studies, 2001); Georgetown University Law Center (J.D., 2004). ***PRACTICE AREAS:*** Litigation. ***Email:*** dorr@sonnenschein.com

ERIC I. ORSECK (Not admitted in Illinois; Resident, Short Hills, New Jersey Office)

ASHLEY H. OSBOURNE (Not admitted in Illinois; Resident, San Francisco, California Office)

MONICA PA (Resident, New York, N.Y. Office)

REID A. PAGE (Not admitted in Illinois; Resident, Washington, D.C. Office)

NADER PAKFAR (Resident, Los Angeles, California Office)

NICOLE S. PAKKALA, born Flint, Michigan, May 21, 1975; admitted to bar, 2000, Illinois, U.S. District Court, Northern District of Illinois and U.S. Court of Appeals, Seventh Circuit. *Education:* University of Michigan (B.A., 1997; J.D., 1999). ***REPORTED CASES:*** Hill v St. Paul Federal Bank, Nos. 1-00-2226; 00-3622; 00-3769(cons.) (Ill. App. Ct. 2002). ***PRACTICE AREAS:*** Litigation. ***Email:*** npakkala@sonnenschein.com

(This Listing Continued)

JAKE A. PALUMBO (Resident, St. Louis, Missouri Office)

DANIEL PANCOTTI (admission pending), (Resident, New York, N.Y. Office)

REGINALD L. PARKS, born Chicago, Illinois, 1971; admitted to bar, 2002, Illinois. *Education:* University of Illinois, Champaign-Urbana (B.A., 1995); DePaul University College of Law (J.D., 2002). *Member:* Chicago, Cook County, Illinois State and American Bar Associations. ***PRACTICE AREAS:*** Commercial Real Estate. ***Email:*** rparks@sonnenschein.com

LISA M. PEKKALA, born Superior, Wisconsin, August 2, 1971; admitted to bar, 1997, Wisconsin; 2001, Illinois. *Education:* University of Wisconsin-Eau Claire (B.A., Accountancy and Business Administration, cum laude, 1993); University of Wisconsin-Madison (J.D., 1997). *Member:* Chicago and Illinois Bar Associations; State Bar of Wisconsin. ***PRACTICE AREAS:*** Taxation. ***Email:*** lpekkala@sonnenschein.com

SHAHRZAD POORMOSLEH (Resident, Washington, D.C. Office)

AMY L. PUGLIANO (admission pending), (Resident, Washington, D.C. Office)

JUSTIN D. PULIKKAN (Resident, Kansas City, Missouri Office)

SARAH J. RATCLIFFE (Not admitted in Illinois; Resident, San Francisco, California Office)

CHRISTOPHER P. RAUCH, born Chicago, Illinois, October 30, 1969; admitted to bar, 2001, Illinois and U.S. District Court, Northern District of Illinois; registered to practice before U.S. Patent and Trademark Office. *Education:* Illinois Institute of Technology (B.S., 1991); John Marshall Law School (J.D., 1999; LL.M. in Intellectual Property Law, with honors, 1999). President, John Marshall Information Technology Law Society, 1998. Member, John Marshall Intellectual Property Law Society, 1998. *Member:* Chicago, Federal and American Bar Associations; Intellectual Property Law Association of Chicago. ***PRACTICE AREAS:*** Intellectual Property Law; Patents; Trademarks; Copyrights. ***Email:*** crauch@sonnenschein.com

JO CHRISTINE REED (Resident, New York, N.Y. Office)

KERRY E. REICHS (Not admitted in Illinois; Resident, Washington, D.C. Office)

JOSHUA REINERT (admission pending), (Resident, St. Louis, Missouri Office)

DEBORAH RENNER (Not admitted in Illinois; Resident, New York, N.Y. Office)

GEOFFREY J. REPO, born Montreal, Quebec, June 24, 1970; admitted to bar, 1999, Illinois. *Education:* University of California, Los Angeles (B.A., 1995); Boston University School of Law (J.D., 1999). ***PRACTICE AREAS:*** Commercial Litigation; Insurance Coverage; Reinsurance; Entertainment Law. ***Email:*** grepo@sonnenschein.com

MINDI RICHTER, born Indianapolis, Indiana, February 26, 1979; admitted to bar, 2004, Illinois. *Education:* Indiana University (B.S., Journalism, 2001); Loyola University (J.D., magna cum laude, 2004). ***PRACTICE AREAS:*** Intellectual Property; Media Law. ***Email:*** mrichter@sonnenschein.com

TRACI RITTENBERG (Resident, Washington, D.C. Office)

DAVID ROZENBLAT, born August 11, 1973; admitted to bar, 1998, Illinois and U.S. District Court, Northern District of Illinois; registered to practice before U.S. Patent and Trademark Office. *Education:* University of Illinois, Urbana-Champaign (B.S.M.E., 1994); Chicago-Kent College of Law, Illinois Institute of Technology (J.D., 1997). *Member:* Chicago, Illinois State and American Bar Associations; Intellectual Property Law Association of Chicago. ***LANGUAGES:*** Hebrew. ***PRACTICE AREAS:*** Patents; Trademarks; Copyrights. ***Email:*** drozenblat@sonnenschein.com

ANDREW L. RUBEN (Not admitted in Illinois; Resident, St. Louis, Missouri Office)

JASON L. RUBIN, born Philadelphia, Pennsylvania, February 8, 1973; admitted to bar, 1998, Illinois. *Education:* Cornell University (B.A., magna cum laude, 1995); University of Chicago (J.D., 1998). ***PRACTICE AREAS:*** Litigation. ***Email:*** j4r@sonnenschein.com

DANIEL SAKAGUCHI, admitted to bar, 2002, California; 2003, Missouri (Not admitted in Illinois). *Education:* University of California, Berkeley (B.A., German and Comparative Literature, 1995; M.A., German Studies, 1999; J.D., 2002). (Resident, St. Louis, Missouri Office). ***PRACTICE AREAS:*** Litigation. ***Email:*** dsakaguchi@sonnenschein.com

TIMOTHY J. SANTOLI (Not admitted in Illinois; Resident, New York, N.Y. Office)

TOBIAS SCHLUETER, born January 13, 1974; admitted to bar, 2002, Illinois, U.S. District Court, Northern District of Illinois and U.S. Court of Appeals, Seventh Circuit. *Education:* Franciscan University of Steubenville (B.A., Political Science, 1996); The John Marshall Law School (J.D., cum laude, 2002). Phi Delta Phi. Order of John Marshall. Member, The John Marshall Trial Advocacy Competition Team. Executive Student Publications Editor, John Marshall Law Review. ***PRACTICE AREAS:*** Litigation; Business Regulation; Labor and Employment. ***Email:*** tschlueter@sonnenschein.com

JAMES M. SCHOENECKER (Not admitted in Illinois; Resident, New York, N.Y. Office)

MARC L. SCHULTZ, born Chicago, Illinois, September 10, 1969; admitted to bar, 1997, Illinois. *Education:* Michigan State University (B.A., with honors, 1992); Chicago-Kent College of Law (J.D., with high honors, 1996); Order of the Coif; New York University (LL.M., Taxation, 1997). Extern, the Honorable Wayne R. Andersen, U.S. District Court, Northern District of Illinois. Recipient, American Jurisprudence Award in Bankruptcy, Academic Achievement Award in Legal Drafting. Class Representative, Student Bar Association, 1993-1994. Student Member, American Bar Association, 1993-1996. ***PRACTICE AREAS:*** Taxation. ***Email:*** mls@sonnenschein.com

ALISON POLLOCK SCHWARTZ, born Chicago, Illinois, January 10, 1972; admitted to bar, 1997, Illinois and U.S. District Court, Northern District of Illinois; registered to practice before U.S. Patent and Trademark Office. *Education:* University of Illinois (B.S.E.E., with highest honors, 1994); University of Chicago (J.D., with honors, 1997). Tau Beta Pi; Eta Kappa Nu; Order of the Coif. Member, Mortar Board. 1991-1992 *Member:* Chicago, Illinois State and American Bar Associations. ***PRACTICE AREAS:*** Intellectual Property. ***Email:*** 3as@sonnenschein.com

(This Listing Continued)

SONNENSCHEIN NATH & ROSENTHAL LLP, Chicago—Continued

RICHARD ADAM SENZER (Not admitted in Illinois; Resident, New York, N.Y. Office)

JOSEPH D. SERRANO (Not admitted in Illinois; Resident, Kansas City, Missouri Office)

AARON SHAFER (Not admitted in Illinois; Resident, New York, N.Y. Office)

CHARULATA (CHARU) JAIN SHAH, born Cleveland, Ohio, December 12, 1975; admitted to bar, 2002, New York; 2004, Illinois; registered to practice before U.S. Patent and Trademark Office. *Education:* Case Western Reserve University (B.S., magna cum laude, 1994; M.S. summa cum laude, Systems, Control, Industrial Engineering, 1998); University of Michigan, Ann Arbor (J.D., 2001). ***PRACTICE AREAS:*** Intellectual Property. ***Email:*** cshah@sonnenschein.com

ANDREA SHARETTA (Resident, New York, N.Y. Office)

JAMES A. SILVER (Not admitted in Illinois; Resident, Washington, D.C. Office)

DAVID R. SIMONTON (Not admitted in Illinois; Resident, San Francisco, California Office)

RON B. SITTON (Not admitted in Illinois).

HEATHER L. SKIDMORE (Resident, Los Angeles, California Office)

BARBARA LEE SMITH, born Highland Park, Illinois, October 18, 1967; admitted to bar, 1991, Illinois. *Education:* University of Chicago (A.B., with honors, 1988; J.D., with honors, 1991). Phi Beta Kappa. ***PRACTICE AREAS:*** Employee Benefits; Executive Compensation. ***Email:*** bqs@sonnenschein.com

DIANNE M. SMITH-MISEMER (Resident, Kansas City, Missouri Office)

SEKRET T. SNEED, born September 21, 1975; admitted to bar, 2001, California (Not admitted in Illinois). *Education:* Stanford University (B.A., 1997); Georgetown University Law Center (J.D., 2001). ***PRACTICE AREAS:*** Litigation. ***Email:*** ssneed@sonnenschein.com

PETER SOARES (Resident, San Francisco, California Office)

MILENA J. SPENCER, born Kiev, Ukraine, July 1, 1978; admitted to bar, 2004, Illinois. *Education:* Loyola University (B.S., magna cum laude, 2001); Boalt Hall School of Law, University of California (J.D., 2004). Presidential Scholar. Member, Golden Key. Winner, Best Oral Argument, Moot Court, UC Berkeley. Director, Appellate Advocacy Program, Moot Court Board, 2003-2004. Recipient: Bernstein Scholarship; Intellectual Property Certification, Berkeley Center for Law and Technology, 2004. Member, Berkeley Technology Law Journal, 2002-2003. Participant, Samuelson Law Technology & Public Policy Clinic, 2003-2004. ***LANGUAGES:*** Russian and Ukrainian. ***PRACTICE AREAS:*** Intellectual Property (80%); Litigation; Business Regulation (20%). ***Email:*** mspencer@sonnenschein.com

BRYAN P. STANLEY (Resident, Kansas City, Missouri Office)

KATHERINE E. STANTON, born Royal Oak, Michigan, August 21, 1980; (admission pending). *Education:* Central Michigan University (B.S., summa cum laude, 2002); University of Michigan (J.D., cum laude, 2005). Phi Alpha Delta. Member, National Society of Collegiate Scholars. Recipient: Michigan Competitive Scholarship; Board of Trustees Scholarship, 1998-2002, President's List and Dean's List, 1998-2002. Michigan Law School: Quarterfinalist, Campbell Moot Court Competition; Honors in Legal Practice. Member, Women Law Students Association. Associate Editor, Michigan Telecommunications and Technology Law Review, 2003-2004. ***PRACTICE AREAS:*** Litigation. ***Email:*** kstanton@sonnenschein.com

WILLIAM A. STETSON (Resident, West Palm Beach, Florida Office)

DANIELE B. STRAIN (Resident, New York, N.Y. Office)

REBECCA S. STRODER (Resident, Kansas City, Missouri Office)

KELLY S. SULLIVAN DEADY (Resident, Kansas City, Missouri Office)

DAPHNEE SURPRIS (Not admitted in Illinois; Resident, New York, N.Y. Office)

JADENE M.W. TAMURA (Resident, Los Angeles, CA Office)

TIMOTHY P. TERRY (Not admitted in Illinois; Resident, Los Angeles, California Office)

PIA N. THOMPSON, born Wiesbaden, Germany, September 13, 1969; admitted to bar, 1994, Illinois; 1995, U.S. District, Northern District of Illinois; 1999, U.S. Court of Appeals, Seventh Circuit. *Education:* Wellesley College (B.A., cum laude, 1991); University of Michigan (J.D., 1994). ***PRACTICE AREAS:*** Bankruptcy. ***Email:*** pthompson@sonnenschein.com

EMILIO TORRES-LUMSDEN (Resident, New York, N.Y. Office)

RHEANNA TOWNER, born Minneapolis, Minnesota, June 23, 1977; admitted to bar, 2004, Illinois. *Education:* Northwestern University (B.A., 1999; M.A., 1999; J.D., cum laude, 2004). ***PRACTICE AREAS:*** Corporate Litigation. ***Email:*** rtowner@sonnenschein.com

JOHNNY H. TRAN (admission pending), (Resident, Los Angeles, California Office)

MEI TSANG (Resident, Los Angeles, California Office)

PAUL R. TURVEY (admission pending), (Resident, Kansas City, Missouri Office)

MICHAEL RITCHIE Y. TY (Not admitted in Illinois; Resident, Los Angeles, California Office)

NOEL B. VALES (Not admitted in Illinois; Resident, New York, N.Y. Office)

CAREY P. WAGNER (Resident, New York, N.Y. Office)

ANAIS VIOLET WALLACH (admission pending), (Resident, Los Angeles, California Office)

ELIZABETH L. WARREN-MIKES, born Durham, North Carolina, February 10, 1969; admitted to bar, 1999, Illinois. *Education:* University of North Carolina at Chapel Hill (B.S.B.A., with distinction, 1991); Northwestern University (J.D., cum laude, 1999).

(This Listing Continued)

Law Clerk to John D. Butzner, Senior Circuit Judge, U.S. Court of Appeals, Fourth Circuit. ***PRACTICE AREAS:*** Intellectual Property; Real Estate. ***Email:*** ewm@sonnenschein.com

ANNE NICHOLSON WEBER, born Chicago, Illinois, July 9, 1957; admitted to bar, 1985, Massachusetts; 1990, Illinois. *Education:* Yale College (B.A., summa cum laude, 1979); Yale Law School (J.D., 1985). Bigelow Fellow, University of Chicago Law School, 1986-1987. Co-Author, with David C. Jacobson and Marshall S. Shapo, "International eCommerce: Business and Legal Issues," CCH Inc., 2001. ***PRACTICE AREAS:*** Litigation. ***Email:*** anw@sonnenschein.com

GRACE CATHERINE WEN (Not admitted in Illinois; Resident, Los Angeles, California Office)

JONATHAN R. WHITEHEAD (Resident, Kansas City, Missouri Office)

RODERIC M. WILLIAMS, born Frankfurt, Germany, February 10, 1976; admitted to bar, 2002, Illinois. *Education:* Northwestern University (B.S.E.D., 1998); University of Pittsburgh (J.D., 2002). ***PRACTICE AREAS:*** Business Litigation; Media and Entertainment Litigation; Commercial Litigation; Entertainment Law. ***Email:*** rwilliams@sonnenschein.com

FELIX T. WOO (admission pending), (Resident, Los Angeles, California Office)

LINDA YASSKY (Not admitted in Illinois; Resident, New York, N.Y. Office)

MICHELLE YIP (admission pending), (Resident, New York, N.Y. Office)

KATHY S. YOON (admission pending), (Resident, Los Angeles, California Office)

PAULA M. YOST (Not admitted in Illinois; Resident, San Francisco, California Office)

VIRGINIA K. YOUNG (Not admitted in Illinois; Resident, San Francisco, California Office)

JENNIFER S. YU (Not admitted in Illinois; Resident, Los Angeles, California Office)

SAUL L. ZACKSON (Resident, St. Louis, Missouri Office)

STEPHANIE L. ZEPPA (Not admitted in Illinois; Resident, San Francisco, California Office)

ELLEN PRINCE ZIVITZ, born Atlanta, Georgia, January 14, 1972; admitted to bar, 1997, Illinois. *Education:* Indiana University (B.A., Sociology and Psychology, with highest distinction, 1994), Phi Beta Kappa; Loyola University School of Law (J.D., magna cum laude, 1997). *Member:* Chicago and American Bar Associations. ***PRACTICE AREAS:*** Labor and Employment; Litigation. ***Email:*** epz@sonnenschein.com

MICHAEL ZOLANDZ (Not admitted in Illinois; Resident, Washington, D.C. Office)

(For Complete Biographical Data on all Personnel, See Los Angeles, San Francisco, California; New York, N.Y.; St. Louis, Kansas City, Missouri; Short Hills, New Jersey; Washington, D.C. and West Palm Beach, Florida Professional Biographies)

ROBERT A. SOUTHERN

CHICAGO, ILLINOIS

(See Grayslake)

Corporate, Securities and Finance.

DONALD F. SPAK

180 N. LASALLE STREET, SUITE 2510
CHICAGO, ILLINOIS 60601
Telephone: 312-214-1818
Fax: 312-609-0578
Email: don@spaklaw.com

Commercial Litigation, Real Estate Title Litigation, White Collar Crimes, Real Estate Tax Deed Litigation, Advertising and Copyright Law, Debtor and Creditor Law.

DONALD F. SPAK, admitted to bar, 1974, Illinois and U.S. District Court, Northern District of Illinois; 1983, U.S. Court of Appeals, Seventh Circuit. *Education:* Washington University (A.B., 1970); DePaul University (J.D., 1974). Member, De Paul Law Review, 1971-1973. Law Clerk to Justice T.A. McGloon, Illinois Appellate Court, 1974-1977. Adjunct Professor of Law, Chicago-Kent College of Law, 2001—. Formerly with, Arvey, Hodes, Costello & Burman, 1977-1990; Hamblet, Oremus & Little, 1991-2004. Illinois Human Relations Commission, Village of Skokie, 1983-2003. [Capt., JAGC, USAR, 1978-1982]

STEVEN SPECTOR LLC

Established in 1997

150 SOUTH WACKER DRIVE, SUITE 1200
CHICAGO, ILLINOIS 60606-4201
Telephone: 312-357-9408
Fax: 312-357-9404
Email: sspector@spectorllc.com
URL: http://www.spectorllc.com

Tax, Business Planning, Estate Planning, Tax Return Preparation, Probate, Wealth Management, Trust Administration, Corporate Formation, Limited Liability Companies.

STEVEN SPECTOR, born Davenport, Iowa, December 27, 1957; admitted to bar, 1981, Iowa; 1982, Illinois and U.S. District Court, Northern District of Illinois; 1997, U.S. Tax Court. *Education:* University of Illinois (B.S., Accounting, 1979); University of Iowa (J.D., 1981). Licensed, Certified Public Accountant. Arthur Andersen & Co., Tax Division, 1981-1990. Vice President of Taxes, Zunamon & Co., 1990-1997. *Member:* Chicago, Illinois State, Iowa State and American Bar Associations; American Institute of Certified Pub-

(This Listing Continued)

lic Accountants; Illinois Certified Public Accountants Society. ***PRACTICE AREAS:*** Tax Law; Real Estate Law; Probate Law; Corporate Law. ***Email:*** sspector@spectorllc.com

LEGAL SUPPORT PERSONNEL

MARY CICIORA, born Chicago, Illinois, February 16, 1959. Administrative Assistant to Chairman of Refco, Inc., 1985-1999. ***Email:*** mciciora@spectorllc.com

BETH LUBIN BLUM, born Des Moines, Iowa, May 4, 1961. *Education:* University of Arizona (B.S.B.A., cum laude, 1983). Beta Alpha Psi. Certified Public Accountant, Arizona, 1986. Formerly with Ernst & Young; PriceWaterhouseCoopers, 1994-2001; MGR Consulting Group, 1989-1994. ***PRACTICE AREAS:*** Tax and Accounting. ***Email:*** bblum@spectorllc.com

MARIOLA KARPIEL, born Poland, March 25, 1975. *Education:* Northeastern Illinois University (B.A., Accounting, 1997). Certified Public Accountant. Formerly with Arthur Andersen LLP. ***PRACTICE AREAS:*** Preparation of Tax Returns. ***Email:*** mstarmach@spectorllc.com

SPELLMIRE & SOMMER

77 WEST WACKER DRIVE, SUITE 4800
CHICAGO, ILLINOIS 60601
Telephone: 312-606-8721
Fax: 312-606-8731
Email: gws@spellmiresommer.com
URL: http://www.spellmireandsommer.com

Legal Malpractice, Accounting Malpractice, Insurance Coverage, Medical Hospital Malpractice, Professional Ethics and Attorney Discipline, Directors and Officers, Errors and Omissions, Insurance Law, General Litigation.

FIRM PROFILE: Spellmire & Sommer is uniquely qualified to advise and represent clients in legal ethics, professional liability, insurance and litigation matters. Spellmire & Sommer provides comprehensive representation to its clients. Spellmire & Sommer have successfully defended lawyers, law firms and other professionals that have been accused of negligence and have prosecuted lawyers, law firms and other professionals that have committed malpractice causing harm to their clients.

GEORGE W. SPELLMIRE, JR., admitted to bar, 1974, Illinois and U.S. District Court, Northern District of Illinois; 1984, U.S. Court of Appeals, Seventh Circuit; 1994, U.S. Supreme Court, Federal Trial Bar and U.S. Tax Court. *Education:* Ohio State University (B.A., 1970); DePaul University (J.D., 1974). Adjunct Professor, Northwestern University School of Law. *Co-author and Author:* "Accounting, Auditing and Financial Malpractice," (HBJ, 1998); "Accountant's Legal Liability" (HBJ, 1993); "Attorney Malpractice: Prevention & Defense," (Garland Publishing, 1990); "The Associates' Primer for the Prevention of Legal Defense," (Garland Publishing, 1990); "The Associates' Primer for the Prevention of Legal Malpractice," (Garland Publishing, 1987); " Illinois Handbook on Legal Malpractice," (Eterna Press, 1982); "Attorney Disciplinary Proceedings: Illinois Practice and Procedure," (Hinshaw & Culbertson, 1991); "Attorney Communications," (Chapter IADC Defense Management Manual, 1991). Listed in: *The Best Lawyers in America,* 8th Ed. and *Leading Illinois Attorneys. Presentations:* American Bar Association, Chicago Bar Association, Illinois State Bar Association, International Association of Defense Counsel, Illinois Institute for Continuing Legal Education, CNA (CLE) Lawyers Loss Control Seminars (Ariz., Ark., Cal., Colo., Ill., Ind., Kan., Mich., Minn., Mo., N.M., N.Y., Ohio, Tex., Wash., Wis.), Professional Liability Underwriter's Society, Workers Compensation Lawyers Association. *Member:* Chicago and Illinois State and American (Standing Committee on Professional Liability) Bar Associations; International Association of Defense Counsel (Advocacy Practice and Procedure Committee, Legal Malpractice Committee, Medical Malpractice Committee, Professional Errors and Omissions Substantive Law Committee); Defense Research Institute; Professional Liability Underwriting Society; Society of Trial Lawyers. Fellow, American College of Trial Lawyers. ***PRACTICE AREAS:*** Legal Ethics and Professional Responsibility; Accountant Professional Liability; Professional Ethics; Commercial Litigation; Securities Litigation. ***Email:*** gws@spellmiresommer.com

LISA MARRÉ SOMMER, admitted to bar, 1992, Pennsylvania; 1993, Illinois. *Education:* University of Illinois (B.A., cum laude, 1989); University of Notre Dame (J.D., cum laude, 1992). Golden Key National Honor Society. Author: "Risk Management Techniques in the Prevention of Malpractice," YLD News, December, 2001; Co-author: "Comparative Negligence In Accountants' Liability Actions". Speaker: "Ethical Fallout: What's Happening in the Service Industry," Executives Club of Chicago, March 2002; "Trends in the Professional Liability Arena," Northwest Suburban Chapter of Society of CPCU; Contributory Negligence 13th Annual ALI-ABA course of study regarding accountants liability. *Member:* Chicago, Illinois State and American Bar Associations; Illinois Defense Counsel (Former Associate Chair, Professional Liability Committee's Publications, Newsletter and Membership). ***PRACTICE AREAS:*** Legal Malpractice; Professional Liability; Complex Commercial Litigation; Professional Ethics. ***Email:*** lms@spellmiresommer.com

JOHN M. FOLEY, born Chicago Heights, Illinois, October 17, 1967; admitted to bar, 1992, Illinois, U.S. District Court, Northern District of Illinois and U.S. Court of Appeals, Seventh Circuit. *Education:* University of Illinois (B.S., with honors, 1989); DePaul University (J.D., 1992). *Author:* "Pushing the Envelope of FDCPA Liability: Recent Attempts to Apply the Telemarketing Sales Rule to Debt Collection," MAP Bulletin, June, 2001; "Lead Paint Litigation and 'Medical Monitoring' Class Actions," Toxic Exposure Litigation Newsletter, Vol. 1, Issue 2, November, 2000; "The Perils of Debt Collection by Attorneys: Ten Common Misconceptions about the FDCPA," ATLA Mutual Advisor, September, 1999; "Legal Malpractice Issues in Arizona Family Law," Family Law Section Seminar, Arizona State Bar Convention, June 1997. Employed by: Chukah & Tecson, PC, 1992-1996; Hinshaw & Culbertson LLP, 1996-2004. *Member:* Chicago and American Bar Associations; Illinois Association of Defense Trial Counsel. ***PRACTICE AREAS:*** Legal Malpractice; Medical Malpractice; Professional Liability; Commercial Litigation. ***Email:*** jmf@spellmiresommer.com

SPERLING & SLATER

A PROFESSIONAL CORPORATION
Established in 1976
55 WEST MONROE STREET
SUITE 3200
CHICAGO, ILLINOIS 60603
Telephone: 312-641-3200
Fax: 312-641-6492
URL: http://www.sperling-law.com

Commercial and Business Litigation, Antitrust, Intellectual Property, Appellate Practice.

FIRM PROFILE: Sperling & Slater limits its practice to complex commercial and business litigation. We have retained the vitality of a small firm while developing a "large firm" national practice. Our clients range from prominent publicly held corporations to mid-sized businesses to sole proprietors; included among them are several leading law firms. We represent both plaintiffs and defendants, at the trial as well as appellate level.

BRUCE S. SPERLING, born Pittsburgh, Pennsylvania, March 28, 1945; admitted to bar, 1970, New York; 1976, Illinois. *Education:* Northwestern University (B.S.M.E., 1967; J.D., 1970). ***REPORTED CASES:*** Johnson v. Levy Organization Development Company, Inc., 789 F.2d 601 (7th Cir. 1986); Olympia Equipment Leasing Company v. Western Union Telegraph Company, 797 F.2d 370 (7th Cir. 1986); Fishman v. Wirtz, 807 F.2d 520 (7th Cir. 1986); Heisley v. U.I.P. Engineered Products Corporation, 831 F.2d 54 (4th Cir. 1987); The Neiman-Marcus Group, Inc. v. David Dworkin, 919 F.2d 368 (5th Cir. 1990); Jeffery v. Sarasota White Sox, Inc., 64 F.3d 590 (11th Cir. 1995); Iowa Center Associates v. Watson, 456 F.Supp. 1108 (N.D. Ill. 1978); Coface v. Optique DuMonde, 521 F.Supp. 500 (S.D.N.Y. 1980); LaSalle National Bank v. County of Lake, 579 F.Supp. 8 (N.D. Ill. 1984); Clinton v. Janger, 583 F.Supp. 284 (N.D. Ill. 1984); Gallery House, Inc. v. Yi, 582 F.Supp. 1294 (N.D. Ill. 1984); Caliber Partners, Ltd. v. Affeld, 583 F.Supp. 1308 (N.D. Ill. 1984); Ovitz v. Jefferies & Company, Inc., 102 F.R.D. 242 (N.D. Ill. 1984); Fishman v. Wirtz, 594 F.Supp. 853 (N.D. Ill. 1984); FMC Corporation v. Manitowoc Company, Inc., 654 F.Supp. 915 (N.D. Ill. 1987); Ansbro v. Southeast Energy Group, Ltd., 658 F.Supp. 566 (N.D. Ill. 1987); E.T. Manufacturing Company, Inc. v. Xomed, 679 F.Supp. 1082 (M.D. Fla. 1987); Burger King Corporation v. American National Bank and Trust Company of Chicago, 119 F.R.D. 672 (N.D. Ill. 1988); ISC-Bunker Ramo Corporation v. Altech, Inc., 765 F.Supp. 1308, 1310, 1340 (N.D. Ill. 1990); In Re Nutri/System of Florida Associates, 178 B.R. 645 (E.D. Pa. 1995); Lake Shore Racquet Club, Inc. v. Fireman's Fund Insurance Companies, 91 Ill.App.3d 1118, 415 N.E.2d 625 (1980); Susman v. Cypress Venture, 114 Ill.App.3d 668, 449 N.E.2d 143 (1983); Statland v. Freeman, 112 Ill.2d 4, 493 N.E.2d 1075 (1986); Chariot Holdings, Ltd. v. Eastmet Corporation, 153 Ill.App.3d 50, 505 N.E.2d 1076 (1987); Capsonic Group v. Swick, 181 Ill.App.3d 988, 537 N.E.2d 1378 (1989); SPSS, Inc. v. Walsh, 267 Ill.App.3d 586, 641 N.E.2d 984 (1994); Wilkow v. Forbes, Inc., 241 F.3d 552 (7th Cir. 2001); Syndia Corp. v. Lemelson Medical, Education and Research Foundation, L.P. et al., 165 F.Supp. 2d 728 (N.D. Ill. 2001); Eisenberg v. Angelo, Gordon & Co., L.P., 82 F.Supp. 2d 180 (S.D.N.Y. 2000); Gregory v. Oiver, 226 F.Supp. 2d 943 (N.D. Ill. 2002); Symbol Technologies, Inc. v. Lemelson Medical, 277 F. 3d 1361 (Fed. Cir. 2002); Robertson-Ceco Corp. v. National Union Fire Ins. Co. of Pittsburgh, Pennsylvania, 292 F. Supp. 2d 1082 (N.D. Ill. 2003); HA 2003, Inc. v. Fed, Ins. Co. (In re HA 2003, Inc.), 310 B.R. 710 (Bankr. N.D. Ill. 2004); Wert v. Clear Channel Communs, Inc., 345 F.Supp.2d 909 (N.D. Ill. 2004); Jam Sports & Entm't, LLC v. Paradama Prods., 336 F.Supp.2d 824 (N.D. Ill. 2004); Chen v. Mayflower Transit, Inc.; 224 F.R.D. 415 (N.D. Ill. 2004); Symbol Techs, Inc. v. Lemelson, Med., Educ. & Research Found., Ltd. P'ship, 301 F.Supp.2d, 1147 (D. Nev. 2004). ***Email:*** bss@sperling-law.com

PAUL E. SLATER, born New York, N.Y., March 1, 1945; admitted to bar, 1970, Illinois. *Education:* Columbia University (B.A., 1967); Northwestern University (J.D., magna cum laude, 1970). Member, Order of the Coif. Member, Editorial Board, Northwestern University Law Review, 1970. Author: Comment, "The Supervising Architect: His Liability and Remedies When a Worker Is Injured," 64 Northwestern University Law Review 535, 1968; "Antitrust and Government Action: A Formula For Narrowing, Parker v. Brown," 69 Northwestern University Law Review 71, 1974. Associate Professor, Antitrust Law, 1972-1978 and Adjunct Professor, Antitrust Law, 1978—, Northwestern University School of Law. *Member:* Chicago (Member, Antitrust Committee, 1972—) and Illinois State (Member, Antitrust Section Council, 1978) Bar Associations. ***REPORTED CASES:*** Hewitt v. Joyce Beverages of Wisconsin, Inc., 721 F.2d 625 (7th Cir. 1983); Olympia Equipment Leasing Company v. Western Union Telegraph Company, 797 F.2d 370 (7th Cir. 1986); Fishman v. Wirtz, 807 F.2d 520 (7th Cir. 1986); Kowalski v. Chicago Tribune Company, 854 F.2d 168 (7th Cir. 1988); Chicago Ridge Theatre Limited Partnership v. M & R Amusement Corp., 855 F.2d 465 (7th Cir. 1988); Wilk v. American Medical Association, 895 F.2d 352 (7th Cir. 1990); T. Harris Young & Associates, Inc. v. Marquette Electronics, Inc., 931 F.2d 816 (11th Cir. 1991); Joyce Beverages of New York, Inc. v. Royal Crown Cola Co., 555 F.Supp. 271 (S.D.N.Y. 1983); Fishman v. Wirtz, 594 F.Supp. 852 (N.D. Ill. 1984); FMC Corporation v. Manitowoc Company, Inc., 654 F.Supp. 915 (N.D. Ill. 1987); Wilk v. American Medical Association, 671 F.Supp. 1465 (N.D. Ill. 1987); Return on Investment Systems v. Translogic Corporation, 702 F.Supp. 677 (N.D. Ill. 1988); O'Neill v. Davis, 721 F.Supp. 1013 (N.D. Ill. 1989); Chicago Ridge Theatre Limited Partnership v. M & R Amusement Corporation, 732 F.Supp. 1503 (N.D. Ill. 1990); Adams v. Towers, Perrin, Forster & Crosby, Inc., 793 F.Supp. 165 (N.D. Ill. 1992); In Re Brand Name Prescription Drugs, 867 F.Supp. 1338 (N.D. Ill. 1994); Farley, Inc. v. Chiappetta, 163 B.R. 999 (N.D. Ill. 1994); Fields Jeep-Eagle, Inc. v. Chrysler Corp., 163 Ill.2d 462 (1994); Mathews v. Sears Pension Plan, 144 F.3d 461 (7th Cir. 1998); C.R. Bard, Inc. v. M3 Systems, 157 F.3d 1340 (1998); DiMucci v. DiMucci, 91 F.3d 845 (7th Cir. 1996); Rybarczyk v. TRW, Inc., 235 F.3d 975 (6th Cir. 2000); C.R. Bard, Inc. v. M3 Systems, Inc., 120 F.Supp. 2d 1145 (N.D. Ill. 2000); Piggly Wiggly Clarksville, Inc. v. Interstate Brands Corp., 83 F. Supp. 2d 781 (N.D. Texas 2000); In re Brand Name Prescription Drugs Antitrust Litigation, 288 F. 3d 1028 (7th Cir. 2002); Drug Mart Pharmacy v. American Home Products, 296 F. Supp. 2d 423 (E.D. N.Y., 2003; In re Cardizem CD Antitrust Litigation, 332 F.3d 896 (6th Cir. 2003); Piggly Wiggly Clarksville, Inc. v. Interstate Brands Corp., 215 F. R. D. 523 (E.D. Tex. 2003). ***Email:*** pes@sperling-law.com

(This Listing Continued)

SPERLING & SLATER, A PROFESSIONAL CORPORATION, Chicago—Continued

EUGENE J. FRETT, born Chicago, Illinois, July 15, 1952; admitted to bar, 1978, Illinois. *Education:* Marquette University (B.A., summa cum laude, 1974); Northwestern University (J.D., cum laude, 1978). Phi Beta Kappa; Order of the Coif. Member, Editorial Board, Northwestern Law Review, 1977-1978. Teaching Fellow, Stanford University Law School, 1978-1979. *Member:* Chicago Bar Association; Chicago Council of Lawyers. ***REPORTED CASES:*** Kademian v. Ladish Co., 792 F.2d 614 (7th Cir. 1986); Adams v. Cavanagh Communities Corporation, 669 F.Supp. 870 (N.D. Ill. 1987); Burger King Corporation v. American National Bank and Trust Company of Chicago, 119 F.R.D. 672 (N.D. Ill. 1988); ISC-Bunker Ramo Corporation v. Altech, Inc., 765 F.Supp. 1308, 1310, 1340 (N.D. Ill. 1990); In Re Nutri/System of Florida Associates, 178 B.R. 645 (E.D. Pa. 1995); Exchange National Bank of Chicago v. Harris, 126 Ill.App.3d 382, 466 N.E.2d 1079 (1984); Mandalay Associates Limited Partnership v. Hoffman, 141 Ill.App.3d 891, 491 N.E.2d 39 (1986); Susman v. Cypress Venture, 187 Ill.App.3d 312, 543 N.E.2d 184 (1989); DiMucci v. DiMucci, 91 F.3d 845 (7th Cir. 1996); Scholes v. Stone, McGuire & Benjamin, 839 F.Supp. 1314 (N.D. Ill. 1993); Syndia Corp. v. Lemelson Medical, Education and Research Foundation, L.P., et al. 165 F.Supp. 2d 728 (N.D. Ill. 2001); Gregory v. Oliver, 226 F.Supp. 2d 943 (N.D. Ill. 2002); HPF, L.L.C. v. General Star Indem Co., 338 Ill. App. 3d 912, 788 N.E. 2d 753 (1st Dist. 2003). ***Email:*** gfrett@sperling-law.com

MITCHELL H. MACKNIN, born Cleveland Heights, Ohio, October 27, 1953; admitted to bar, 1978, Illinois. *Education:* Northwestern University (B.A., Economics, 1975); Northwestern University School of Law (J.D., cum laude, 1978). Order of the Coif. *Member:* Chicago, Illinois State and American (Member, Litigation Section) Bar Associations; Chicago Council of Lawyers. ***REPORTED CASES:*** Johnson v. Levy Organization Development Company, Inc., 789 F.2d 601 (7th Cir. 1986); Weigel Broadcasting Co. v. Smith, 289 Ill.App.3d 602, 682 N.E.2d 745 (1997); Doe v. Doe, 282 Ill.App.3d 1078, 668 N.E.2d 1160 (1996); Dearborn Wholesale Grocers, Inc. v. Whittler, 74 Ill.App.3d 813, 339 N.E.2d 1 (1979); Heisley v. U.I.P. Engineered Products Corporation, 831 F.2d 54 (4th Cir. 1987); The Neiman-Marcus Group, Inc. v. Dworkin, 919 F.2d 368 (5th Cir. 1990); Jeffery v. Sarasota White Sox, Inc., 64 F.3d 590 (11th Cir. 1995); Ovitz v. Jefferies & Company, Inc., 553 F.Supp. 300 (N.D. Ill. 1982); Besser Publishing Co. v. Pioneer Press, Inc., 571 F.Supp. 640 (N.D. Ill. 1983); LaSalle National Bank v. County of Lake, 579 F.Supp. 8 (N.D. Ill 1984); Caliber Partners, Ltd. v. Affeld, 583 F.Supp. 1308 (N.D. Ill. 1984); Ovitz v. Jefferies & Company, Inc., 102 F.R.D. 242 (N.D. Ill. 1984); ISC-Bunker Ramo Corporation v. Altech, Inc., 765 F.Supp. 1308, 1310, 1340 (N.D. Ill. 1990); Adams v. Towers, Perrin, Forster & Crosby, Inc., 793 F.Supp. 165 (N.D. Ill. 1992); Statland v. Freeman, 112 Ill.2d 4, 493 N.E.2d 1075 (1986); Chariot Holdings, Ltd. v. Eastmet Corporation, 153 Ill.App.3d 50, 505 N.E.2d 1076 (1987); SPSS, Inc. v. Walsh, 267 Ill.App.3d 586, 641 N.E.2d 984 (1994); Chicago Title & Trust Co. v. Ceco Corp., 92 Ill.App.3d 58, 415 N.E.2d 668 (1981); Eisenberg v. Angelo, Gordon & Co., L.P., 82 F.Supp. 2d 180 (S.D.N.Y. 2000); Robertson-Ceco Corp. v. National Union Fire Ins. Co. of Pittsburgh, Pennsylvania, 292 F. Supp. 2d 1082 (N.D. Ill. 2003); Symbol Techs, Inc. v. Lemelson, Med., Educ. & Research Found., Ltd. P'shing, 301 F.Supp.2d, 1147 (D. Nev. 2004). ***Email:*** mhmacknin@sperling-law.com

GREGG R. HAGUE, born Meadville, Pennsylvania, August 27, 1957; admitted to bar, 1984, Illinois and U.S. District Court, Northern District of Illinois. *Education:* Carleton College (B.A., cum laude, 1979); Washington University (J.D., 1984). Notes and Comments Editor, Washington University Law Quarterly, 1983-1984. *Member:* Chicago and American (Member, Sections on: Antitrust Law; Business Law; Litigation) Bar Associations. ***REPORTED CASES:*** Return on Investment Systems v. Translogic Corporation, 702 F.Supp. 677 (N.D. Ill. 1988); O'Neill v. Davis, 721 F.Supp. 1013 (N.D. Ill. 1989); Fields Jeep-Eagle, Inc. v. Chrysler Corp., 163 Ill.2d 462 (1994); Kohler Co. V. Kohler Int'l., Ltd., 196 F.Supp. 2d 690 (N.D., Ill. 2002); HPF, L.L.C. v. General Star Indem Co., 338 Ill App. 3d 912, 788 N.E. 2d 753 (1st. Dist. 2003). ***Email:*** grh@sperling-law.com

GREG SHINALL, born Valparaiso, Indiana, March 27, 1965; admitted to bar, 1990, Illinois and U.S. District Court, Northern District of Illinois. *Education:* University of Chicago (B.A., 1987); Valparaiso University (J.D., with highest honors, 1990). ***REPORTED CASES:*** In Re Carbon Dioxide Antitrust Litigation, 149 F.R.D. 229 (M.D. Fla. 1993) and 155 F.R.D. 209 (1993); In Re Brand Name Prescription Drugs, 867 F.Supp. 1388 (N.D. Ill. 1994); C.R. Bard, Inc. v. M3 Systems, 157 F.3d 1340 (1998) and 161 F.3d 1380 (1998); C.R. Bard, Inc. v. M3 Systems, Inc., 120 F.Supp. 2d 1145 (N.D. Ill. 2000); Ill. 2001); Board of Education v. Village of Robbins, 327 Ill.App.3d 599, 765 N.E.2d 449 (2001); Slamecka v. Empire Kosher Poultry, Inc., 290 F. Supp. 2d 934 (N.D. Ill. 2003); Wert v. Clear Channel Communs, Inc., 345 F.Supp.2d 909 (N.D. Ill. 2004); Jam Sports & Entm't, LLC v. Paradama Prods., 336 F.Supp.2d 824 (N.D. Ill. 2004); 2004 WL 2943649 (2004), 2005 WL 14917 (2005), and 2005 WL 589775 (2005). ***Email:*** shinall@sperling-law.com

STEVEN C. FLORSHEIM, born Milwaukee, Wisconsin, April 15, 1965; admitted to bar, 1991, Illinois. *Education:* Yale University (B.A., cum laude, 1987); University of Michigan (J.D., 1991). Order of the Coif. ***REPORTED CASES:*** In re Zenith Electronics Corp., 241 B.R. 92 (Bankr. D. Del. 1999); South Bay Chevrolet v. General Motors Acceptance Corporation, 85 Cal. Rptr. 2d 301, 72 Cal. App. 4th 861 (1999); In re Reliance Acceptance Corporation, 235 B.R. 548 (D. Del. 1999); Dreyfus v. Ameritech Mobile Communications, Inc., 298 Ill. App. 933, 700 N.E.2d 162 (1998); NL Industries, Inc. v. Commercial Union Ins. Co., 65 F.3d 314 (3rd Cir. 1995); Syndia Corp. v. Lemelson Medical, Education and Research Foundation, L.P. et al., 165 F.Supp. 2d 728 (N.D. Ill. 2001); Measurement Specialties, Inc., v. Taylor Precision Prods., L.P., 131 F.Supp. 2d 982 (N.D. Ill 2001); Lucini Italia Co. v. Grappolini, 231 F.Supp. 2d 764 (N.D., Ill. 2002); Coelho v. Park Ridge Oldsmobile, Inc., 247 F. Supp. 2d 1004 (N.D. Ill. 2003); Chen v. Mayflower Transit, Inc., 315 F.Supp.2d 886 (N.D. Ill. 2004); Chen v. Mayflower Transit, Inc., 224 FRD 415 (N.D. Ill. 2004); HA 2003, Inc. v. Fed, Ins. Co. (In re HA 2003, Inc.), 310 B.R. 710 (Bankr. N.D. Ill. 2004). ***PRACTICE AREAS:*** Commercial Litigation; Employment Law; Bankruptcy Litigation. ***Email:*** sflorsheim@sperling-law.com

CLAIRE P. MURPHY, born Spring Valley, Illinois, April 28, 1960; admitted to bar, *1989, Illinois. Education: University of Notre Dame (B.A., magna cum laude, 1982);* Loyola University of Chicago (J.D., 1989). Alpha Sigma Nu. Lead Articles Editor, Law Review. Co-Author: "Good Faith Settlement Under The Contribution Act: Do Trial Courts Have Too Much Discretion?" 20 Loyola U. Chi. Law Journal 961 (1989); "1986-1987 Illinois Law Survey: Torts," 19 Loyola U. Chi. Law Journal 751 (1988). ***REPORTED CASES:*** South Bay Chevrolet v. General Motors Acceptance Corporation, 85 Cal. Rptr. 2d 301, 72 Cal. App. 4th 861 (1999); Dawkins v. United Airlines, Inc., 1993 WL 339051 (N.D. Ill. Aug. 30, 1993); Dowlatshahi v. Motorola, 970 F.2d 289 (7th Cir. 1992); Lucini Italia Co. v. Grappolini, 231 F.Supp. 2d 764 (N.D., Ill. 2002); Gregory v. Oliver, 226 F.Supp. 2d 943 (N.D. Ill. 2002); Coelho v. Park Ridge Oldsmobile, Inc., 247 F. Supp. 2d 1004 (N.D. Ill. 2003); HA 2003, Inc. v. Fed, Ins. Co. (In re HA 2003, Inc.), 310 B.R. 710 (Bankr. N.D. Ill. 2004). ***PRACTICE AREAS:*** Commercial Litigation; Employment Law. ***Email:*** cmurphy@sperling-law.com

ROBERT D. CHEIFETZ, born Brooklyn, New York, October 13, 1966; admitted to bar, 1992, Illinois and U.S. District Court, Northern District of Illinois. *Education:* Brandeis University (B.A., magna cum laude, 1988); University of Chicago (J.D., 1992). *Member:* Chicago, Federal (Member, Intellectual Property Section) and American Bar Associations. ***REPORTED CASES:*** Newell Co. v. Lee, 950 F. Supp. 864 (N.D. Ill 1997); Eisenberg v. Angelo, Gordon & Co., L.P., 82 F.Supp. 2d 180 (S.D.N.Y. 2000); Lucini Italia Co. v. Grappolini, 231 F.Supp. 2d 764 (N.D., Ill. 2002); Wert v. Clear Channel Communs, Inc., 345 F.Supp.2d 909 (N.D. Ill. 2004); HA 2003, Inc. v. Fed, Ins. Co. (In re HA 2003, Inc.), 310 B.R. 710 (Bankr. N.D. Ill. 2004); Jam Sports & Entm't, LLC v. Paradama Prods., 336 F.Supp.2d 824 (N.D. Ill. 2004). ***Email:*** robc@sperling-law.com

THOMAS D. BROOKS, born Youngstown, Ohio, December 16, 1964; admitted to bar, 1995, Illinois. *Education:* Yale University (B.A., 1988); Northwestern University (J.D., cum laude, 1995). Senior Articles Editor, The Journal of Criminal Law and Criminology, 1994-1995. Author: Catching Jellyfish in The Internet: The Public-Figure Doctrine and Defamation on Computer Bulletin Boards, 21 Rutgers Computers and Technology Law Journal 461 (1995); First Amendment-Penalty Enhancement for Hate Crimes; Content Regulation, Questionable State Interests no non-Traditional Sentencing, 84 Journal Criminal Law & Criminology 703 (1994). *Member:* Chicago and Illinois State Bar Associations. ***REPORTED CASES:*** Archer-Daniels-Midland Co. v. Illinois Commerce Commission, 704 N.E. 2d 387 (Ill. 1998); In re: Union Electric Co., 81 FERC P. 61, 01111 (1997); In Re: Central Illinois Public Service Co., 180 PUR 4th 185 (Ill Comm'n., 1997); Abbott Labs v. TorPharm, Inc., 156 F.Supp. 2d 738 (N.D. Ill. 2001); Syndia Corp. v. Lemelson Medical, Education and Research Foundation, L.P. et al., 165 F.Supp. 2d 728 (N.D. Ill. 2001); Robertson-Ceco Corp. v. National Union Fire Ins. Co. of Pittsburgh, Pennsylvania, 292 F. Supp. 2d 1082 (N.D. Ill. 2003); Abbott Labs v. TorPharm, Inc., 309 F.Supp.2d 1043 (N.D. Ill. 2004); Jam Sports & Entm't, LLC v. Paradama Prods., 336 F.Supp.2d 824 (N.D. Ill. 2004). ***Email:*** tdbrooks@sperling-law.com

ADAM P. MERRILL, born Edison, New Jersey, October 18, 1968; admitted to bar, 1995, Illinois and U.S. District Court, Northern District of Illinois including Trial Bar; 1996, U.S. Court of Appeals, Seventh Circuit; 1999, U.S. Court of Appeals, Third Circuit. *Education:* Brigham Young University (B.S., Accounting, cum laude, 1992; J.D., 1995). Associate, 1995-2001 and Partner, 2001-2003, Kirkland & Ellis. ***REPORTED CASES:*** Williams v. Reliance Acceptance Corp. (In Re: Reliance Acceptance Corp.), 2000 WL 33712305 (Bankr. D.Del. 2000); Province v. Pep Boys -- Manny, Moe and Jack, 2000 WL 420626 (E.D. Pa. 2000); Reliance Acceptance Corp. v. Levin (In Re: Reliance Acceptance Corp.), 235 B.R. 548 (D. Del. 1999); Sanner v. board of Trade of City of Chicago, 181 F.R.D. 374 (N.D. Ill. 1998); U.S. v. Cunningham, 108 F.3d 120 (7th Cir. 1997). ***PRACTICE AREAS:*** Commercial Litigation; Corporate Investigations; Bankruptcy; Insurance Litigation; Professional Malpractice. ***Email:*** amerrill@sperling-law.com

---

CELIZA P. BRAGANÇA, born Menominee, Michigan, October 2, 1962; admitted to bar, 1992, Virginia (inactive); 1993, District of Columbia (inactive); 1995, Illinois and U.S. District Court, Northern District of Illinois; U.S. District Court, Eastern District of Wisconsin; 2002, Trial Bar, U.S. District Court, Northern District of Illinois. *Education:* University of Chicago (B.A., with honors, 1984; J.D., with honors, 1992); University of Chicago Graduate School of Business (M.B.A., 1992). Order of the Coif. Formerly with: Jenner & Block; Wiley, Rein & Fielding; Ungaretti & Harris. ***REPORTED CASES:*** Securities & Exchange Commission v. Terry Dowdell, et at., 175 F. Supp. 2d 850 W.D. Va. (Dec. 7, 2001); 2002 WL 236687 (Feb. 15, 2002); 2002 WL 424595 (Mar. 14, 2002; In the Matter of Laurie Canady, SEC Admin. Proceeding File No. 3-8531-D (Nov. 26, 2001); In the Matter of American Rice, Inc., et al., Exchange Act Release No. 47286, SEC Admin. Proceeding File No. 3-11024 (Jan. 30, 2003); American States Insurance Company v. Koloms, 177 Ill. 2d 473, 687 N.E.2d 72 (Ill. 1997) (filed amicus curiae brief); St. Paul Fire & Marine Insurance Company v. Warwick Dyeing Corporation, 26 F.3d 1195 (1st Cir. 1994) (filed amicus curiae brief). ***PRACTICE AREAS:*** Complex Commercial Litigation; Securities Litigation; Securities Regulation. ***Email:*** cbraganca@sperling-law.com

DANIEL A. SHMIKLER, born Gloversville, New York, July 7, 1969; admitted to bar, 1996, Illinois. *Education:* University of Chicago (B.A., 1991); Northwestern University (J.D., cum laude, 1996). Associate Note and Comment Editor, Northwestern University Law Review, 1995-1996. ***REPORTED CASES:*** Measurement Specialties, Inc., v. Taylor Precision Prods., L.P., 131 F.Supp. 2d 982 (N.D. Ill 2001); Kohler Co. V. Kohler Int'l., Ltd., 196 F.Supp. 2d 690 (N.D., Ill. 2002); Coelho v. Park Ridge Oldsmobile, Inc., 247 F. Supp. 2d 1004 (N.D. Ill. 2003). ***Email:*** dshmikler@sperling-law.com

MICHAEL G. DICKLER, born Chicago, Illinois, October 25, 1974; admitted to bar, 1999, Illinois. *Education:* University of Michigan (B.A., 1996; J.D., 1999). ***REPORTED CASES:*** Wert v. Clear Channel Communs., Inc., 345 F.Supp.2d (N.D. Ill. 2004); Abbott Labs v. TorPharm, Inc., 309 F.Supp.2d 1043 (N.D. Ill. 2004); Chen v. Mayflower Transit, Inc., 315 F.Supp.2d 886 (N.D. Ill. 2004); Symbol Techs, Inc. v. Lemelson. Med., Educ. & Research Found., Ltd. P'ship, 301 F.Supp.2d 1147 (D. Nev. 2004); WERTV Clear Communs., Inc., 345 F.Supp. 2d 909 (N.D.Ill. 2004); HA 2003, Inc. v. Fed, Ins. Co. (In re HA 2003, Inc.), 310 B.R. 710 (Bankr. J.D. Ill. 2004); JamSports & Entm't, LLC v. Paradama Prods., 336 F.Supp.2d 824 (N.D. Ill. 2004); Chen v. Mayflower Transit, Inc., 224 F.R.D. 415 (N.D. Ill 2004). ***PRACTICE AREAS:*** Complex Commercial Litigation; Class Action Litigation; Securities Litigation; Appellate Advocacy. ***Email:*** mdickler@sperling-law.com

MATTHEW WEISMAN, born Skokie, Illinois, December 10, 1972; admitted to bar, 2000, Illinois. *Education:* University of Pennsylvania (B.A., 1994); University of Chicago (J.D., 2000). ***REPORTED CASES:*** Wert v. Clear Channel Communs., Inc., 345 F.Supp.2d 909 (N.D. Ill. 2004). ***Email:*** mweisman@sperling-law.com

(This Listing Continued)

DINA G. ROLLMAN, admitted to bar, 2000, Illinois. *Education:* Oberlin College (B.A., 1995); Northwestern University (J.D., 2000). ***PRACTICE AREAS:*** Commercial Litigation. ***Email:*** drollman@sperling-law.com

MONAZZA ARAIN, born Chicago, Illinois, June 5, 1976; admitted to bar, 2001, Illinois. *Education:* Emory University School of Law (B.A., 1997); Northwestern University (J.D., 2001). *Member:* Chicago and Illinois State Bar Associations. ***PRACTICE AREAS:*** General Litigation. ***Email:*** marain@sperling-law.com

OF COUNSEL

HARVEY J. BARNETT, born Chicago, Illinois, May 22, 1943; admitted to bar, 1967, Illinois. *Education:* University of Illinois (B.A., 1964) Phi Beta Kappa; Northwestern University (J.D., with honors, 1967). Editor, Northwestern University Law Review, 1966-1967. ***Email:*** hbarnett@sperling-law.com

STEPHEN J. SPITZ, born Indianapolis, Indiana, December 2, 1944; admitted to bar, 1971, Ohio; 1975, Illinois. *Education:* Indiana University (B.A., 1967); Northwestern University (J.D., cum laude, 1971). Order of the Coif. Member, Board of Editors, Northwestern University Law Review, 1970-1971. Author: Comment, "Constitutional Reform of State Delegate Selection to National Political Party Conventions," 64 Northwestern University Law Review 915, 1970; "Investment Property, Fluctuating Value and the Cover Rule," 49 New York University Law Review 907, 1974; Co-Author: R. Childres and S. Spitz, "Status in the Law of Contract," 47 New York University Law Review 1, 1972. Clerk, U.S. Court of Appeals, Seventh Circuit, 1971. Assistant Professor, Corporation and Torts, The Ohio State University College of Law, 1971-1975. *Member:* Chicago, Illinois State and American Bar Associations. ***REPORTED CASES:*** LTD Commodities, Inc. v. Perederij, 699 F.2d 404 (7th Cir. 1983); Olympia Equipment Leasing Co. v. Western Union Telegraph Co., 797 F.2d 370 (7th Cir. 1986); Varhol v. National Railroad Passenger Corp., d/b/a Amtrak, 909 F.2d 1557 (7th Cir. 1990); National Tax Credit Partners, L.P. v. Havlik, 20 F.3d 705 (7th Cir. 1994); Kreindler v. Marx, 85 F.R.D. 612 (N.D. Ill. 1979); Great Western Cities, Inc. v. Binstein, 536 F.Supp. 808 (N.D. Ill. 1982); Clinton v. Janger, 583 F.Supp. 284 (N.D. Ill. 1984); Adams v. Cavanagh Communities Corporation, 669 F.Supp. 870 (N.D. Ill. 1987); Martin v. American Kennel Club, Inc., 697 F.Supp. 997 (N.D. Ill. 1988); Van Kampen Merritt, Inc. v. Avondale Properties Partnership, 702 F.Supp. 1412 (N.D. Ill. 1989); Herbstein v. Bruetman, 743 F.Supp. 184 (S.D.N.Y. 1990); Adams v. Cavanagh Communities Corp., 847 F.Supp. 1390 (N.D. Ill. 1994); Weiss Medical Complex, Ltd. v. Kim, 87 Ill.App.3d 111, 408 N.E.2d 959 (1980); People ex rel. Fahner v. Colorado City Lot Owners and Taxpayers Association, 108 Ill.App.3d 266, 438 N.E.2d 1273 (1982); Exchange National Bank of Chicago v. Harris, 141 Ill.App.3d 382, 466 N.E.2d 39 (1984); Newell Co. v. Lee, 950 F.Supp. 864 (N.D. Ill. 1997); Scholes v. Stone, McGuire & Benjamin, 839 F.Supp. 1314 (N.D. Ill. 1993). ***Email:*** sjspitz@worldnet.att.net

ANGIE A. CHEN, born Taiwan, June 9, 1969; admitted to bar, 1998, Georgia; 2000, Illinois. *Education:* University of Michigan (A.B., 1991; J.D., 1997); American University (M.F.A. in Creative Writing, 1994). ***REPORTED CASES:*** Gregory v. Oliver, 226 F.Supp. 2d 943 (N.D. Ill. 2002); Slamecka v. Empire Kosher Poultry, Inc., 290 F. Supp. 2d 934 (N.D. Ill, 2003). ***PRACTICE AREAS:*** Commercial Litigation; Employment Law. ***Email:*** achen@sperling-law.com

---

MARK L. SPIEGEL

25 EAST WASHINGTON, SUITE 1501
CHICAGO, ILLINOIS 60602
Telephone: 312-782-2860
Fax: 312-782-2870
Email: mark.spiegel@markspiegel.com
URL: http://www.markspiegel.com

Real Estate, including Residential, Commercial and Industrial, Condominium Development and Conversion, Leases and Leasing, Contract Negotiation and Disputes; Family Law, including Divorce, Child Custody, Child Support, Spousal Support/Alimony, Separation Agreements, Distribution/Separation of Property, Visitation Rights; Commercial Litigation, including Commercial Collections.

MARK L. SPIEGEL, born 1953; admitted to bar, 1978, Illinois. *Education:* Northeastern Illinois University (B.A., 1975); Chicago-Kent College of Law (J.D., 1978). *Member:* Illinois State Bar Association; Commercial Law League of America. ***PRACTICE AREAS:*** Real Estate; Family Law; Commercial Litigation.

SPRINGER, CASEY & DIENSTAG, P.C.

Established in 1945
100 WEST MONROE STREET
CHICAGO, ILLINOIS 60603
Telephone: 312-372-0800
Fax: 312-372-0842
Email: SCDCHGO@global.net

Barrington, Illinois Office: 509 West Old Northwest Highway 60010. Telephone: 847-382-9797.

General Practice. Civil Trial and Appellate Litigation in State and Federal Courts. Insurance Law, Regulatory Defense and Coverage Litigation. Administrative Agencies. Corporation, Estate Planning and Probate, Federal Taxation, Matrimonial, Municipal and Real Estate Law.

FIRM PROFILE: Commercial transactions and dissolution of marriage, insurance disputes and regulation, domestic relations, municipal law, real estate, estate planning.

WYATT JACOBS (1906-1994)

JOSEPH E. SPRINGER (1937-1983)

DONALD E. CASEY, born Chicago, Illinois, November 6, 1924; admitted to bar, 1957, Illinois and U.S. District Court, Northern and Central Districts of Illinois including Trial Bar, U.S. Court of Appeals, 5th and 7th Circuits. *Education:* Dartmouth College (A.B., Economics, 1948); Loyola University (J.D., 1957). Member, Board of Arbitrators, 1989— and Chair Qualified, National Association of Securities Dealers. Chairman, Insurance Law Section, Illinois State Bar Association, 1972-1973. *Member:* Chicago (Member: Securities Law Committee, 1963—; Civil Practice Committee; Insurance Law Committee, 1976—; Legislative Sub-Committee, 1995) and American Bar Associations. ***Email:*** scddchgo@aol.com

GARY E. DIENSTAG, born Chicago, Illinois, July 15, 1945; admitted to bar, 1969, Illinois and U.S. District Court, Northern District of Illinois including Trial Bar, U.S. Court of Appeals, 5th and 7th Circuits. *Education:* University of Wisconsin-Madison (B.S., with honors, 1966); Loyola University (J.D., cum laude, 1969). Alpha Sigma Nu; Pi Alpha Delta. Author: "The Short, Troubled Life of Elg v. Whittington: Amended Supreme Court Rule 304(a)," 77 Illinois Bar Journal 420, April, 1989; "The Spendthrift Trust: A Fortress Against Child Support and Maintenance?" 73 Illinois Bar Journal 648, August, 1985. Chairman, Village of Arlington Heights Zoning Board of Appeals, 1983-1992. Member, Panel of Arbitrators, American Arbitration Association. Member, Panel of Arbitration Cook County (Mandatory Arbitration Program). *Member:* Chicago, Illinois State and American Bar Associations; Illinois Appellate Lawyers Association. ***Email:*** scddchgo@aol.com

EDWARD M. SPRINGER, born Chicago, Illinois, January 20, 1942; admitted to bar, 1967, Illinois. *Education:* University of Illinois (A.B., 1963); DePaul University (J.D., 1967). Village Attorney: Village of Lake Barrington, Illinois, 1978-1987; Village of Barrington, 1991—. *Member:* Chicago and American Bar Associations. ***Email:*** scddchgo@aol.com

REPRESENTATIVE CLIENTS: American Claims Service, Inc.; AmeritasAcacia Companies; Federal Life Insurance Co. (Mutual); Great West Casualty Company; Guarantee Trust Life Insurance Company; Hanover Fire and Casualty Insurance Company; Illinois Casualty Company; Life and Health Insurance Company of America, Inc.; MONY Life Insurance Company; Mutual of Omaha Insurance Company; Old Republic Insurance Group; Systems Transport Company; Village of Barrington.

STACK & FILPI

CHARTERED
Established in 1976
SUITE 411, 140 SOUTH DEARBORN STREET
CHICAGO, ILLINOIS 60603-5298
Telephone: 312-782-0690
Facsimile: 312-782-0936
URL: http://www.stackfilpi.com

Federal and state commercial litigation with extensive experience in contract and intellectual property matters.

FIRM PROFILE: Founded in 1976, the firm concentrates in commercial litigation in federal and state trial and appellate courts, handling a variety of civil matters including commercial law, contracts, intellectual property and bankruptcy Located across the street from the federal courthouse, the firm provides convenient facilities, logistical support and substantial federal trial experience for out-of-state firms seeking local counsel to assist in litigation. Both partners are members of the federal trial bar and have appeared as counsel in more than 40 published decisions.

PAUL F. STACK, born Chicago, Illinois, July 21, 1946; admitted to bar, 1971, Illinois; 1972, U.S. District Court (Trial Bar); 1974, U.S. Tax Court; 1975, U.S. Claims Court and U.S. Supreme Court; 1977, U.S. Court of International Trade. *Education:* University of Arizona (B.S., 1968); Georgetown University (J.D., 1971). Editor, Georgetown University Law Journal, 1970-1971. Author: Note, "The Philadelphia Plan: Remedial Racial Classifications in Employment," 58 Georgetown University Law Journal 1158, 1971. Law Clerk, Honorable William J. Bauer, U.S. District Judge, 1971-1972. Assistant U.S. Attorney for Northern District of Illinois, 1972-1975. President, Village of Riverside, Illinois, 1997-2001. Member, Board of Education, Riverside-Brookfield Township High School District 208, Riverside, Illinois, 1989-1997. Member, Mayor Washington's Ad Hoc Advisory Committee on New Central Library, Chicago, Illinois, 1987-1989. Director, Suburban Library System, Burr Ridge, Illinois, 1979-1982. Trustee, Riverside Public Library Board, Riverside, Illinois, 1977-1983. *Member:* Chicago (Chairman, Customs Law Committee, 1979-1980) and American Bar Associations. ***PRACTICE AREAS:*** Commercial Litigation; Intellectual Property Rights; Intellectual Property Litigation; Trademark Infringement; Trademark Registration; Unfair Competition; Business Torts. ***Email:*** pstack@stackfilpi.com

ROBERT A. FILPI, born Chicago, Illinois, October 8, 1945; admitted to bar, 1970, Illinois; 1971, U.S. District Court (Trial Bar); 1975, U.S. Supreme Court; 1976, U.S. Tax Court; 1978, U.S. Claims Court; 1979, U.S. Court of International Trade. *Education:* Harvard University (B.A., magna cum laude, 1967); Northwestern University (J.D., 1970). Editor, Northwestern Journal of Criminal Law, Criminology and Police Science, 1969-1970. Assistant U.S. Attorney for Northern District of Illinois, 1971-1976 (Appellate Division, 1971-1972; Deputy Chief, Civil Division for U.S. Attorney's Office, 1975-1976). Trustee in Bankruptcy, 1976-1978; Member, Plan Commission, 1984-1994 (Chairman, Residential Subcommittee, 1986-1990), Village of Lincolnshire, Illinois. *Member:* Chicago and American Bar Associations. ***PRACTICE AREAS:*** Bankruptcy; Commercial Law; Contracts; Federal Civil Practice; Intellectual Property; Trusts and Estates. ***Email:*** rfilpi@stackfilpi.com

ASSOCIATE

CORI A. SZCZUCKI, born Cook County, Illinois, October 16, 1977; admitted to bar, 2002, Illinois and U.S. District Court, Northern District of Illinois; 2003, U.S. Court of International Trade. *Education:* University of Illinois at Urbana (B.A.S., 1999); University of DePaul (J.D., 2002). ***PRACTICE AREAS:*** Intellectual Property Rights; Intellectual Property Litigation; Trademark Infringement; Copyright Infringement; Trademark Registration; Copyright Registration. ***Email:*** cori@stackfilpi.com

(This Listing Continued)

STACK & FILPI, CHARTERED, Chicago—Continued

OF COUNSEL

JAMES A. McGURK, born Chicago, Illinois, March 22, 1948; admitted to bar, 1973, Illinois; 1974, U.S. Court of Appeals, Seventh Circuit; 1976, U.S. Supreme Court. *Education:* University of Illinois (B.A. with distinction in Political Science, 1970; J.D., 1973). Note and Comment Editor, University of Illinois Law Forum (now University of Illinois Law Review), 1972-1973. Author: "Criminal Procedure: The Seventh Circuit's Current Approach," 55 IIT/Chicago-Kent Law Review 95, 1979. Senior Law Clerk, Hon. Harlington Wood, Jr., U.S. District Judge, Springfield, Illinois, 1973-1974. Assistant U.S. Attorney, Northern District of Illinois, 1974-1979. Senior Trial Counsel, Commodity Futures Trading Commission, Division of Enforcement, Chicago, Illinois, 1981-1984. *Member:* Chicago (Chairman, Federal Civil Procedure Committee, 1995-1995), Seventh Circuit, Federal and American Bar Associations. ***PRACTICE AREAS:*** Securities; Commodities; Intellectual Property; Civil and Criminal Law. ***Email:*** jamcgurk@flash.net

STADHEIM & GREAR

WRIGLEY TOWER - 22ND FLOOR
400 NORTH MICHIGAN AVENUE
CHICAGO, ILLINOIS 60611-4102
Telephone: 312-755-4400
Fax: 312-755-4408

Patent Licensing and Litigation.

ROLF O. STADHEIM, born Kansas City, Missouri, May 3, 1940; admitted to bar, 1967, Illinois; 1970, U.S. Court of Appeals; 1974, U.S. Supreme Court; 1980, U.S. Court of Appeals, Fifth and Tenth Circuits; 1982, Trial Bar for Federal Circuit (N.D. Ill.) and U.S. Court of Appeals, Federal Circuit. *Education:* University of Wisconsin (B.S., 1962); University of Chicago (J.D., 1966). *Member:* The Federal Circuit Bar Association; Intellectual Property Law Association of Chicago; American Intellectual Property Law Association; Seventh Circuit Bar Association.

JOSEPH A. GREAR, born Chicago, Illinois, July 20, 1959; admitted to bar, 1984, Illinois, U.S. District Court, Northern District of Illinois including Trial Bar, and U.S. Court of Appeals for the Federal Circuit; 1987, U.S. Supreme Court. *Education:* Illinois State University (B.S., 1981); University of Illinois (J.D., 1984). Notes Editor, Recent Decisions, Illinois Bar Journal, 1983-1984. Author: "State Takeover Laws," Illinois Bar Journal, 1983. *Member:* Illinois State and American Bar Associations; Intellectual Property Law Association of Chicago.

GEORGE C. SUMMERFIELD, JR., born Berkeley, California, December 31, 1958; admitted to bar, 1987, Michigan, U.S. Supreme Court, U.S. Court of Claims, U.S. Court of Appeals, Seventh Circuit and U.S. Court of Appeals for the Federal Circuit (Not admitted in Illinois). *Education:* United States Naval Academy; Kings's College (B.A., magna cum laude, 1983); Wayne State University (J.D., 1987). Phi Delta Theta. Fulbright Scholar. Member: Jessup International Law Moot Court, Niagara International Law Moot Court Competitions and Zuber Moot Court Competition. *Member:* State Bar of Michigan; Federal Circuit and U.S. Court of Federal Claims Bar Associations; American Intellectual Property Law Association; Federation Internationale des Conseils en Propriete Industrielle. ***LANGUAGES:*** French, German, Romanian, Chinese. ***PRACTICE AREAS:*** Patents; Trademarks; Copyrights; General Business Law; Litigation. ***Email:*** gcsummerfield@stadlaw.com

KEITH A. VOGT, born Chicago, Illinois, January 30, 1961; admitted to bar, 1991, Illinois and U.S. District Court, Northern District of Illinois; registered to practice before U.S. Patent and Trademark Office. *Education:* University of Illinois (B.S., 1989): Illinois Institute of Technology, Chicago-Kent (J.D., 1991). [U.S.M.C., 1980-1983]. ***PRACTICE AREAS:*** Intellectual Property. ***Email:*** keithvogt@aol.com

STAES & SCALLAN, P.C.

111 W. WASHINGTON STREET
SUITE 1310
CHICAGO, ILLINOIS 60602
Telephone: 312-201-8969
Fax: 312-201-9233
Email: staesandscallan@earthlink.net

Business, Commercial and Federal White Collar Criminal Litigation. Appellate Practice in the Federal and State Courts of Appeals.

ANDREW T. STAES, born Blue Island, Illinois, May 23, 1958; admitted to bar, 1983, Illinois; 1984, U.S. District Court, Northern District of Illinois including Trial Bar; 1985, U.S. Court of Appeals, Seventh Circuit; 1991, U.S. Tax Court; 1992, U.S. Court Of Appeals, Ninth Circuit. *Education:* University of Illinois (B.S.B.A.); Illinois Institute of Technology/Chicago-Kent College of Law (J.D., with high honors, 1983). Member: Chicago-Kent Law Review, 1981-1982. Author: "Pleading Under The Federal Rules of Civil Procedure," in Federal Civil Practice, IICLE, 1987, 1989. ***REPORTED CASES:*** Altobello v. U.S. 125 S.Ct. 994 (2005); U.S. v. Handhart, 361 F.3d 382 (7th Cir. 2004); Zapata v. Hearthside Baking Co., 313 F. 3d 385 (7th Cir. 2003); United States v. Mietus, 237 F.3d 866 (7th Cir. 2001); United States v. Basinski, 226 F.3d 829 (7th Cir. 2000); United States v. Ienco, 182 F.3d 517 (7th Cir. 1999); United States v. Ienco, 126 F.3d 1016 (7th Cir. 1997); United States v. Ben-Hur (7th Cir. 1994); United States v. Cappas, 29 F.3d 1187 (7th Cir. 1994); Robinson v. Ada S. McKinley, 19 F.3rd 359 (7th Cir. 1994); Fred Smith Lumber v. Edidin, 845 F. 2d 750 (7th Cir. 1988); Walter v. Fiorenzo, 840 F.2d 427 (7th Cir. 1988). ***PRACTICE AREAS:*** Commercial Litigation; Complex Litigation; Civil Litigation; White Collar Crime. ***Email:*** andrewstaes@earthlink.net

STEPHEN SCALLAN, born Evanston, Illinois, October 20, 1969; admitted to bar, 1995, Illinois; 1996, Wisconsin and U.S. Court Eastern District of Wisconsin; 1997, U.S. District Court, Northern District Court of Illinois. *Education:* Northwestern University (B.A., 1992); University of Notre Dame (J.D., 1995). Author: "Proximate Cause Under Rico," Southern Illinois Law Journal, Vol. 20, Spring 1996. *Member:* Chicago Bar, Illinois State and American Bar Associations. ***REPORTED CASES:*** Zapata v. Hearthside Baking Co., 313 F.3d 385 (7th Cir., 2003); United States v. Basinski, 226 F. 3d 829 (7th Cir. 2000); United States v. Ionco, 182 F. 3d 517 (7th Cir. 1999); Director of Insurance for the State of Illinois v. O'Shaughnessy, 246 F. Supp. 935 (N.D. Ill. 2002); In the Matter of the Conservation of Alpine Insurance Company, 241 N.E. 2d 663 (1st Dist. 2000); Duggan v. Terzakis, 275 F. Supp. 2d 968, (N.D., Ill. 2003); Boss v. LaSalle Bank, 84 F.Supp.2d 947 (N.D. Ill. 1999); Lakeside Feeders, Ltd. v. Chicago Meat Processors, Inc., 35 F.Supp2d 638 (N.D. Ill. 1999); Goldsmith v. FADC, Ill. App. (2000). ***PRACTICE AREAS:*** Commercial Litigation; Complex Litigation; Civil Litigation; White Collar Crime. ***Email:*** stevescallan@earthlink.net

(This Listing Continued)

JOSEPH STALMACK & ASSOCIATES, P.C.

CHICAGO, ILLINOIS

(See Hammond, Indiana)

General Practice. Trials and Appeals. Insurance, Products Liability, Probate and Estate Planning, Transportation, Asbestos Litigation, Automobile, Common Carrier, Complex and Multi-District Litigation, Computer, Construction, Environmental and Industrial Disease, Environmental, Fire Insurance, Hazardous Materials, Legal Malpractice, Medical Malpractice, Mediation Services, Professional Malpractice, Subrogation, Toxic Substances and Toxic Torts Law, Personal Injury.

STAMOS & TRUCCO

Established in 1990
30 W. MONROE, SUITE 1600
CHICAGO, ILLINOIS 60603
Telephone: 312-630-7979
Telecopier: 312-630-1183

Commercial Litigation and Health Care Litigation.

FIRM PROFILE: Stamos & Trucco was founded in 1990. Its practice is concentrated in general commercial litigation, health care litigation, professional liability and discipline, toxic tort defense, corporate law, associations and commercial real estate.

JAMES J. STAMOS, born Chicago, Illinois, June 23, 1956; admitted to bar, 1980, Illinois and U.S. District Court, Northern District of Illinois; 1984, Trial Bar; 1985, U.S. Tax Court. *Education:* Valparaiso University (B.A., with distinction, 1977); University of Illinois (J.D., 1980). Phi Alpha Theta. Author: Chapter, "Claims of the Contractor, Architect or Engineer Against Their Respective Insurance Carriers," IICLE Construction Litigation Handbook, 2000; Chapter, "Rescission," IICLE Real Estate Litigation Handbook, 1999; Chapter, "Emergency Medicine," IICLE Medical Malpractice Handbook, 1998. ***REPORTED CASES:*** Haroco, Inc. v. American National Bank, 38 F.3d 1429 (7th Cir. 1994); Firstar Bank of Illinois v. Peirce, 306 Ill. App. 3d 525, 714 N.E.2d 116 (1st Dist. 1999). ***PRACTICE AREAS:*** Commercial Litigation; Health Care Litigation. ***Email:*** jstamos@stamostrucco.com

MICHAEL T. TRUCCO, born Chicago, Illinois, December 13, 1957; admitted to bar, 1982, Illinois and U.S. District Court, Northern District of Illinois; 1984, U.S. Court of Appeals, 7th Circuit; 1985, U.S. Tax Court and U.S. District Court, Northern District of Illinois, Trial Bar; 2002, U.S. District Court, Central District of Illinois. *Education:* Bradley University (B.S., 1979); DePaul University (J.D., 1982). Omicron Delta Kappa; Pi Sigma Alpha. Editor-in-Chief, De Paul Law Review, Volume 31, 1981-1982. Author: Note, "'Conditional' Res Ipsa Loquitur in Illinois Medical Malpractice Law: Proof of a Rare Occurrence as a Basis for Liability—Spidle v. Steward," 30 De Paul L. Rev. 413 (1981). Past President, DePaul University College of Law Alumni Board, 1993-1996. Faculty Member, National Institute for Trial Advocacy, 1995-1999. Clinical Instructor in Pretrial Litigation and Clinical Trial Advocacy, Northwestern University School of Law, 1994-1999, 2002. *Member:* Chicago, Illinois State and American Bar Associations; Defense Research Institute. ***REPORTED CASES:*** Lieberman & Kraff, M.D.S.C. v. Desnick, 224 Ill.App.3d 341, 614 N.E.2d 379 (1st Dist. 1993). ***PRACTICE AREAS:*** Commercial Litigation; Health Care Litigation; Toxic Tort Defense. ***Email:*** mtrucco@stamostrucco.com

GEORGE M. HOFFMAN, born Kansas City, Missouri, February 3, 1948; admitted to bar, 1981, Illinois. *Education:* California State University at Long Beach (B.A., 1970; M.A., 1977); DePaul University (J.D., 1981). Senior Note and Comment Editor, DePaul Law Review, 1980-1981. ***PRACTICE AREAS:*** Antitrust Law; Commercial Litigation. ***Email:*** ghoffman@stamostrucco.com

GUS J. ATHAS, born Chicago, Illinois, August 6, 1936; admitted to bar, 1965, Illinois and U.S. District Court, Northern District of Illinois; 1980, U.S. Court of Appeals, 7th Circuit. *Education:* University of Illinois (B.S., 1958); Loyola University (J.D., cum laude, 1965). *Member:* Chicago, Illinois State and American Bar Associations; American Corporate Counsel Association. ***PRACTICE AREAS:*** Mergers and Acquisitions; Corporate Law; Finance. ***Email:*** gathas@stamostrucco.com

RAYMOND GUPTA, born Hammond, Indiana, August 14, 1970; admitted to bar, 1995, Indiana; 2001, Illinois. *Education:* Indiana University (B.S., Biology, 1992); Vanderbilt University (J.D., 1995). ***PRACTICE AREAS:*** Health Care Litigation; Commercial Litigation. ***Email:*** rgupta@stamostrucco.com

ASSOCIATES

JOHN J. KAKACEK, born Waukegan, Illinois, December 3, 1958; admitted to bar, 1984, Illinois. *Education:* University of Illinois (B.S., Business Administration, with highest honors, 1981; J.D., 1984). ***PRACTICE AREAS:*** Commercial Litigation. ***Email:*** jkakacek@stamostrucco.com

(This Listing Continued)

JULIE N. HOWIE, born Evanston, Illinois, June 10, 1969; admitted to bar, 1994, Illinois and U.S. District Court, Northern District of Illinois. *Education:* Washington University (B.A., 1991); Chicago-Kent College of Law (J.D., 1994). Vice President, Moot Court Honor Society. *Member:* Chicago, Illinois State and American Bar Associations. ***LANGUAGES:*** German. ***PRACTICE AREAS:*** Appellate Practice; Torts; Commercial Litigation. ***Email:*** jhowie@stamostrucco.com

LAURA S. HUSEBY, born Kittery, Maine, October 20, 1971; admitted to bar, 1997, Pennsylvania and New Jersey; 2001, Illinois. *Education:* Villanova University (B.A.B.S., 1993); Villanova University School of Law (J.D., 1996). Author: Volume II, Issue 1, Villanova Sports & Entertainment Law Journal. ***LANGUAGES:*** French. ***PRACTICE AREAS:*** Health Care Litigation; Commercial Litigation. ***Email:*** lhuseby@stamostrucco.com

DANIEL R. SHAFFER, born Akron, Ohio, August 14, 1970; admitted to bar, 1995, Illinois and U.S. District Court, Northern District of Illinois. *Education:* Miami University (B.A., 1992); Chicago-Kent College of Law, Illinois Institute of Technology (J.D., with honors, 1995). *Member:* Illinois State Bar Association. ***PRACTICE AREAS:*** Health Care Litigation; Commercial Litigation.

JENNI L. YOUNG, born San Antonio, Texas, March 21, 1975; admitted to bar, 2000, Illinois. *Education:* Florida State University (B.S., 1997); DePaul University (J.D., 2000). Phi Alpha Delta. *Member:* American Bar Association. ***PRACTICE AREAS:*** Health Care Litigation; Asbestos Defense; Commercial Litigation. ***Email:*** jyoung@stamostrucco.com

JULIE BRUCE ZOGBAUM, born Columbus, Ohio, March 18, 1976; admitted to bar, 2001, Ohio; 2002, Illinois. *Education:* Miami University (B.A., 1998); Loyola University Chicago, School of Law (J.D., 2001; LL.M., Health Law, 2002). ***PRACTICE AREAS:*** Health Care Litigation; Commercial Litigation. ***Email:*** jzogbaum@stamostrucco.com

OF COUNSEL

JOHN J. STAMOS, born 1924; admitted to bar, 1949, Illinois. *Education:* DePaul University (LL.B.). States Attorney, Cook County, Illinois, 1966-1968; Justice, Illinois Appellate Court, 1968-1988; Justice, Illinois Supreme Court, 1988-1990.

KEITH L. MOORE, born Greencastle, Indiana, December 15, 1951; admitted to bar, 1977, Illinois; 1994, California. *Education:* Indiana University (B.A., 1974); Georgetown University (J.D., 1977). Staff Member, 1975-1976, Editor, 1976-1977, Georgetown Law Journal. *Member:* Illinois State Bar Association; State Bar of California. ***PRACTICE AREAS:*** Commercial Real Estate Law; Commercial Real Estate Transactions. ***Email:*** kmoore@stamostrucco.com

STATMAN, HARRIS, SIEGEL & EYRICH, LLC

333 WEST WACKER DRIVE, SUITE 1710
CHICAGO, ILLINOIS 60606
Telephone: 312-263-1070
Fax: 312-263-1201

Dayton, Ohio Office: Fifth Third Center, 110 North Main Street, Suite 1520, 45402. Telephone: 937-222-1090. Fax: 937-222-1046.
Cincinnati, Ohio Office: 2900 Chemed Center, 255 East Fifth Street, 45202-2912. Telephone: 513-621-2666. Telecopier: 513-621-4896.

General Civil Trial and Appellate Practice in Federal and State Courts. Commercial Litigation, Bankruptcy, Banking, Personal Injury and Family Law. Corporate Acquisitions, Dispositions, Spin-Offs, Corporate Formation, Financings, Real Estate, Banking and Commercial Law, Reorganizations, Restructurings, Bankruptcy, Civil Litigation, General Business, Intellectual Property, Taxation, Estate Planning.

MEMBERS OF FIRM

ALAN I. EHRENBERG, born Elizabeth, New Jersey, October 15, 1949; admitted to bar, 1975, Illinois and U.S. District Court, Northern District of Illinois. *Education:* University of Oklahoma (B.A., 1971); John Marshall Law School (J.D., 1975). Lecturer to Professional and Banking Groups on Bankruptcy Law and Creditors Rights. *Member:* Chicago and American Bar Associations. ***Email:*** aehrenberg@shsechicago.com

SCOTT C. FROST, born Poughkeepsie, New York, April 2, 1965; admitted to bar, 1991, New York, Illinois, District of Columbia and U.S. District Court, Northern District of Illinois; U.S. Court of Appeals, Seventh Circuit. *Education:* Emory University (B.A., 1987); Washington College of Law of American University (J.D., 1990). Articles Editor, American University Journal of International Law & Policy. Author: "Chapter 11 Friend or Foe to Health Care Providers?", First Illinois Speaks, November, 1994. Co-Author: "New Policy Grants Hospitals Greater Rights", First Illinois Speaks, May, 1994. Lecturer, Illinois Creditors Bar Association.*Member:* Chicago Bar Association (Member, Committee on Bankruptcy and Reorganization, 1992-1993; Commercial Law League, 1993). ***REPORTED CASES:*** Jeffrey Strange vs Monogram Credit Card Bank of Georgia, 129 F.3d 943 (7th Cir. 1997); William Duke v. Sears Roebuck and Co., 29 F.3d 43 (7th Cir. 1996); Rehabilitation Institute of Chicago v. Group Administrators, Ltd. 844 F.Supp. 1275 (N.D. Ill. 1994). ***PRACTICE AREAS:*** Commercial Litigation; Bankruptcy Litigation; Appellate Litigation; Banking Litigation; Secured Lending; Insolvency Litigation. ***Email:*** sfrost@shsechicago.com

ASSOCIATES

JOSHUA BERNSTEIN, born June 14, 1970; admitted to bar, 2002, Illinois; 2004, U.S. District Court, Northern District of Indiana; 2005, U.S. District Court, Northern, Southern and Central Districts of Illinois and Southern District of Indiana. *Education:* University of Wisconsin-Milwaukee (B.A., 1996); DePaul University (J.D., magna cum laude, 2002). *Member:* Illinois State Bar Association. ***PRACTICE AREAS:*** Appellate Litigation; Commercial Litigation; Banking Litigation. ***Email:*** jbernstein@shsechicago.com

DENISE D. KELIUOTIS, born Chicago, Illinois, February 17, 1968; admitted to bar, 2000, Illinois; U.S. District Court, Northern District of Illinois. *Education:* Loyola University (B.A., 1990); University of Michigan Law School (J.D., 2000). *Member:* Illinois State Bar Association. ***PRACTICE AREAS:*** Commercial Litigation; Class Action; Banking Litigation.

JULIE DAVIS EGAN, admitted to bar, 1995, Illinois; U.S. District Court, Northern District of Illinois. *Education:* Union College (B.A., 1991); University of Cincinnati College of Law (J.D., 1995). *Member:* Chicago Bar Association. ***PRACTICE AREAS:*** Commercial Litigation; Banking Litigation. ***Email:*** jdavis@bhlmlaw.com

REPRESENTATIVE CLIENTS: Bank One, N.A.; Schottenstein Stores Corporation; Value City Department Stores, Inc.; Crown Shoe Stores; American Eagle Outfitter Stores; Valley Fair Corporation; Gentry Clothiers, Inc.; Totes Incorporated; Tudor Properties, Inc.; Colerain Hills Shopping Center; St. Bernard Square Shopping Center; Skyway Luggage Company; Tampa Electric Company (TECO); Higher Education Assistance Foundation (HEAF); Roslyn Realty Company; Seneca Environmental Products, Inc.; Pipe Products, Inc.; Samex Trading Company, Inc.; Pella Window; AHF Industries; Peoples Bank Corporation (Indianapolis); HRC Limited Partnership (Hyatt Regency Cincinnati); The Fifth Third Bank; Rohr Corporation; H.R. Chally; Brennan Builders; K&L Investment Corp.
REFERENCES: The Fifth Third Bank; Bank One, N.A.

(This Listing Continued)

STEIN, RAY & HARRIS LLP

222 WEST ADAMS STREET, SUITE 1800
CHICAGO, ILLINOIS 60606
Telephone: 312-641-3700
Telecopier: 312-641-3701
URL: http://www.steinrayharris.com

Construction and Design Law, Mechanics Liens, Government Contracts, Insurance, Complex Litigation and Construction Related Insurance Bankruptcy.

MEMBERS OF FIRM

STEVEN G. M. STEIN, born State College, Pennsylvania, May 8, 1951; admitted to bar, 1976, Wisconsin; 1978, Illinois; 1980, U.S. Supreme Court. *Education:* University of Wisconsin (B.A., 1973); University of Chicago (J.D., 1976). Adjunct Professor, Illinois Institute of Technology/Chicago-Kent College of Law, 1979—. Lecturer, University of Illinois School of Architecture, 1991-1992. Editor-in-Chief, "Construction Law," Lexis Publishing, 1986; AIA Legal Citator, 1993; Construction Law Digest (Monthly). Co-Author: "Injured Workman: Loss Allocation Among Direct Participants in the Construction Process," St. Louis University Law Review, 1979; "Blueprint for the Liabilities of Design Professional After Moorman," 60 Chi. Kent L. Rev. 2, 1984; "Illinois Mechanics' Liens," PESI (1988); "Enforcing Provisions to Arbitrate in Construction Disputes," Wiley Law, 1991; "Legal Issues in Design Practice," McGraw Hill, 1992; "Design Professional Liability for Differing Site Conditions and the Risk-Sharing Philosophy," ABA Construction Lawyer, April 2000; "What's Mine is Mine: Copyright Protection for the Design Professional," chapter of Handling Construction Risks 2003, Allocate Now or Litigate Later, 2003; "Here Comes the Judge: The Duties and Responsibilities of Design Professional When Deciding Disputes," ASCE Journal of Professional Issues in Engineering Education and Practice, July 2003. Executive Director, Construction Law Institute, 1982-1993. Faculty Member, National Institute of Trial Advocacy (Midwest), 1981. Member, Board of Directors, Construction Specification Institute, Chicago Chapter, 1985-1986. Chairman, Legal Affairs Committee, 1987-1995 and Member of Board, 1991-1993, Builders Association of Greater Chicago. Division Chair and Member of Board, Chicago Building Congress, 1989-1993, President, 1993-1995. Trustee, 1995—, Chicago Architectural Foundation. Member: Board of Overseers, ITT School of Architecture, 2004—; Advisory Board, Chicago School of Real Estate, 2004—. *Member:* Chicago (Member, Forum Committee on Construction, 1978—; Litigation Section) and American Bar Associations; American College of Real Estate Lawyers; American College of Construction Lawyers (Fellow and Member, Board of Governors, 1988-1992, 1995-1998). ***PRACTICE AREAS:*** Construction and Design Law; Complex Litigation; Arbitration; Government Contracts; Insurance. ***Email:*** sgms@steinrayharris.com

STEPHEN E. RAY, born Exeter, New Hampshire, June 29, 1956; admitted to bar, 1981, Illinois and U.S. District Court, Northern and Central Districts of Illinois. *Education:* Colgate University (B.A., magna cum laude, 1978); Cornell University (J.D., 1981). Phi Beta Kappa. Co-Author: Revisions to Chapter Entitled "Documenting and Presenting Construction Claims," in Steven Stein's Four Volume Treatis Construction Law Published by Matthew Bender & Company, 2001; Chapter "Contractual Defenses," in Book Entitled "Architect and Engineer Liability: Claims Against Design Professionals," Aspen Publishers, Inc., 2005. Lecturer, Illinois Institute of Technology/Chicago Kent College of Law, 1988—. Member: Builders Association of Greater Chicago; Construction Financial Managers Association. Member, Board of Directors, Legal Counsel Forum, Mentor Program, American Consulting Engineers Council, Chicago Chapter. Member, Professional Services Division, Chicago Building Congress. *Member:* Chicago Bar Association. ***PRACTICE AREAS:*** Construction and Design Law; Complex Litigation; Arbitration; Government Contracts. ***Email:*** ser@steinrayharris.com

ROBERT J. HARRIS, born Chicago, Illinois, August 10, 1960; admitted to bar, 1985, Illinois and U.S. District Court, Northern District of Illinois; U.S. District Court, Central District of Illinois; U.S. Supreme Court. *Education:* Hamilton College (A.B., summa cum laude, 1982); Yale Law School (J.D., 1985). Phi Beta Kappa. Author: "Limitation of Liability Clauses: Allocating Risky Business," The Construction Lawyer, October, 1993. Co-Author: "State-By-State Guide to Design Licensing," Illinois Chapter, Aspen Law and Business, 1999. *Member:* American Bar Association (Member, Litigation Section). ***REPORTED CASES:*** Board of Managers v. IKO, et. al., 183 Ill.2d 66 (Ill. 1998); Vilas Development Corp. v. Ross, 179 Ill.2d 622 (Ill. 1998); Kleinschmidt v. Corporate 500 Centre Phase I, 678 N.E.2d 1065 (Ill.App.Ct. 1997); Union Switch & Signal, Inc. v. City of Chicago, 1993 WL 462832 (N.D.Ill. 1993); Balsamo Olsen v. Bradley Place, 966 F.Supp. 757 (C.D.Ill. 1996). ***PRACTICE AREAS:*** Complex Commercial Litigation; Intellectual Property Litigation; Real Estate Litigation; Construction Litigation. ***Email:*** rjh@steinrayharris.com

JEFFREY H. WINICK, born Iowa City, Iowa, August 4, 1963; admitted to bar, 1988, Illinois; 1989, U.S. District Court, Northern District of Illinois; 2002, Iowa. *Education:* University of Iowa (B.A., summa cum laude, 1985); University of Michigan (J.D., 1988).

(This Listing Continued)

STEIN, RAY & HARRIS LLP, Chicago—Continued

Phi Beta Kappa. Author: "CAD Law," Progressive Architecture, September, 1994. Lecturer: University of Illinois Graduate School of Architecture, 2002—. Adjunct Professor, Illinois Institute of Technology/Chicago Kent College of Law 2005—. Member, Chicago Committee on High Rise Buildings. *Member:* Chicago and American (Member, Construction Industry Forum) Bar Associations; Construction Specifications Institute; American Institute of Architects; Society of Illinois Construction Attorneys; Structural Engineers Association of Illinois; American Society of Testing and Measures. ***REPORTED CASES:*** Krusinski Construction Co. v. Northbrook Property and Casualty Co., 760 N.E.2d 530 (Ill.App. Ct. 2001); Angelo Mongiello's Children, LLC v. Pizza Hut, Inc., 70 F. Supp.2d 196 (E.D.N.Y. 1999); People of the State of Illinois v. Rolando Cruz, 643 N.E.2d 636 (Ill. 1994). ***PRACTICE AREAS:*** Complex Commercial Litigation; Real Estate Litigation; Construction Litigation; Contracts. ***Email:*** jhw@steinrayharris.com

JOEL J. RHINER, born Fort Dodge, Iowa, July 10, 1964; admitted to bar, 1990, Illinois, Iowa and U.S. District Court, Northern and Central Districts of Illinois. *Education:* University of Iowa (B.A., summa cum laude, 1987); University of California at Los Angeles (J.D., 1990). Phi Beta Kappa. Editor, UCLA Law Review, 1989-1990. Judicial Extern to the Honorable James B. Moran. Author: "Liability Exposures from Payment Certification," The Construction Specifier, October edition; "Enforcing Letters of Intent and Handshake Agreements," ABA Construction Lawyer, April 2000 edition; "Challenging the Finality of an Extended Change Order," Construction Change Order Claims, Aspen Publishers, 2005. Lecturer, Illinois Institute of Technology/Chicago Kent College of Law. *Member:* Chicago, Illinois State and American (Member, Construction Industry Forum) Bar Associations; Builders Association of Greater Chicago. ***PRACTICE AREAS:*** Complex Commercial Litigation; Construction and Design Law; Government Contracts. ***Email:*** jr@steinrayharris.com

CARL L. POPOVSKY, born St. Louis, Missouri, February 24, 1964; admitted to bar, 1991, Illinois and U.S. District Court, Northern District of Illinois; U.S. District Court, Central District of Illinois, U.S. District Court, Eastern District of Michigan, U.S. District Court, Northern District of Indiana and U.S. District Court, Eastern District of Wisconsin. *Education:* University of Illinois (B.S., Civil Engineering, 1986; J.D., magna cum laude, 1991). Chi Epsilon. Recent Decisions Notes Editor, Illinois Bar Journal, 1990-1991. Co-Author: "State-By-State Guide to Architect, Engineer and Contractor Licensing," Illinois Chapter, Aspen Publishers, 1999; "Design Professional Liability for Differing Site Conditions and the Risk-Sharing Philosophy," The Construction Lawyer, April 2000. Author: "Illinois Construction Law," Licensing Chapter, Aspen Publishers, 2003. Lecturer, Illinois Institute of Technology/Chicago Kent College of Law. *Member:* American Bar Association (Construction Industry Forum); American Society of Civil Engineers (Associate Member). ***PRACTICE AREAS:*** Construction and Design Law. ***Email:*** clp@steinrayharris.com

JEFFREY B. CHARKOW, born Meriden, Connecticut, March 6, 1966; admitted to bar, 1993, Illinois; 1995, U.S. District Court, Northern District of Illinois. *Education:* University of Wisconsin (B.A., 1988); Washington University (J.D., 1993). Order of the Coif. Member, Washington University Law Quarterly. Law Clerk to Honorable Carol E. Jackson, U.S. District Court, Eastern District of Missouri, 1993-1995. *Member:* American Bar Association. ***PRACTICE AREAS:*** Commercial Litigation; Construction and Design Law. ***Email:*** jbc@steinrayharris.com

JOHN N. WALKER, born Berwyn, Illinois, July 19, 1964; admitted to bar, 1992, Illinois and U.S. District Court, Northern District of Illinois; 1993, U.S. Court of Appeals, Seventh Circuit; 2002, U.S. District Court, Eastern District of Michigan. *Education:* University of Chicago (B.A., with special honors, 1986); Harvard University (J.D., cum laude, 1992). Phi Beta Kappa. *Member:* Chicago and Illinois State Bar Associations. ***LANGUAGES:*** Spanish and Portuguese. ***PRACTICE AREAS:*** Construction and Design Law; Civil Litigation; Complex Commercial Litigation; Information Technology; Intellectual Property. ***Email:*** jnw@steinrayharris.com

SCOTT R. FRADIN, born Chicago, Illinois, April 10, 1964; admitted to bar, 1996, Illinois. *Education:* University of Illinois (B.S.A.S., 1986; M. Arch., 1988); Chicago-Kent College of Law - IIT (J.D., with high honors, 1996). Order of the Coif. Member and Senior Associate, Chicago-Kent Law Review. Recipient, Ramsey-Burke Academic Scholarship. Registered Architect, Illinois, 1990. *Member:* Chicago and American (Construction Industry Forum) Bar Associations; American Institute of Architects. ***PRACTICE AREAS:*** Construction and Design Law; Construction Litigation; Contracts. ***Email:*** srf@steinrayharris.com

RYAN A. HISS, born Crystal Lake, Illinois, January 9, 1970; admitted to bar, 1995, North Carolina, U.S. District Court, Eastern District of North Carolina and U.S. Court of Appeals, Fourth Circuit; 2001, Illinois; U.S. District Court, Northern District of Illinois. *Education:* North Carolina State University (B.A., summa cum laude, 1992); University of North Carolina (J.D., with honors, 1995). Phi Kappa Phi. Staff Member, North Carolina Law Review, 1993-1994. Recipient, American Jurisprudence Award in Sales/UCC. Co-Author: "Here Comes the Judge - Duties and Responsibilities of Design Professionals When Deciding Disputes," ASCE Journal of Professional Issues in Engineering Education and Practice (July 2003). *Member:* Chicago, North Carolina and American (Member: Forum on the Construction Industry) Bar Associations; North Carolina State Bar. ***PRACTICE AREAS:*** Construction Litigation; Commercial Litigation; Construction and Design Law. ***Email:*** rxh@steinrayharris.com

ASSOCIATES

JOHN-PAUL LUJAN, born Evanston, Illinois, July 21, 1969; admitted to bar, 1997, Illinois. *Education:* University of Illinois (B.S., Architectural Studies, 1991; M.A., Architecture, 1993); DePaul University (J.D., 1997). *Member:* Chicago and American Bar Associations. ***PRACTICE AREAS:*** Litigation; Construction and Design Law. ***Email:*** jpl@steinrayharris.com

JEFFREY M. OSTERKAMP, born Tucson, Arizona, January 6, 1969; admitted to bar, 1998, Illinois. *Education:* Northwestern University (B.S.J., 1991; J.D., 1998). *Member:* Chicago and American Bar Associations. ***PRACTICE AREAS:*** Construction Law; Commercial Litigation. ***Email:*** jmo@steinrayharris.com

(This Listing Continued)

CARRIE L. BERGER, born Highland Park, Illinois, February 23, 1972; admitted to bar, 1997, Illinois and U.S. District Court, Northern District of Illinois. *Education:* Northwestern University (B.A., with departmental honors, 1994; J.D., 1997). Phi Eta Sigma. Judicial Extern to Honorable Ruben Castillo. Member, Julius H. Miner Moot Court Board. *Member:* Chicago, Illinois State and American Bar Associations. ***PRACTICE AREAS:*** Construction Law; Commercial Litigation. ***Email:*** clb@steinrayharris.com

CHARLES HENRY WAHTOLA, III, born Grand Forks, North Dakota, September 29, 1971; admitted to bar, 1998, Illinois. *Education:* University of Wisconsin (B.A., 1993); Loyola University (J.D, 1997). ***PRACTICE AREAS:*** Construction Law; Commercial Litigation; Complex Litigation. ***Email:*** chw@steinrayharris.com

MICHAEL J. KELLY, born Brooklyn, New York, January 16, 1965; admitted to bar, 1995, Massachusetts; 1997, U.S. District Court, District of Massachusetts; 2000, Illinois; 2001, U.S. District Court, Northern District of Illinois. *Education:* Williams College (B.A., cum laude, 1987); John Jay College of Criminal Justice (M.A., 1996); Harvard Law School (J.D., 1995). *Member:* Boston and American Bar Associations. ***PRACTICE AREAS:*** Litigation. ***Email:*** mjk@steinrayharris.com

PETER J. BEDARD, born Fitchburg, Massachusetts, September 10, 1969; admitted to bar, 1994, Illinois and Wisconsin; 1996, U.S. District Court, Northern District of Illinois. *Education:* Villanova University (B.A., 1991); University of Miami (J.D., cum laude, 1993). Member, University of Miami Entertainment and Sports Law Review. Author: "*A Moorman* - Doctrine Exception for Design Professionals and Construction Managers?" Illinois Bar Journal, August 2001; "Protecting Subcontractors' Rights Under Illinois Public Construction Bond Act," Illinois Bar Journal, October 2002. *Member:* Chicago (Vice-Chair, Construction Law and Mechanic's Lien Subcommittee, 2005-2006) and Illinois State Bar Associations. ***PRACTICE AREAS:*** Construction Litigation. ***Email:*** pjb@steinrayharris.com

KATE E. KIM, admitted to bar, 2003, Illinois; 2004, U.S. District Court, Northern District of Illinois. *Education:* University of California, Berkeley (B.A., 1997); University of Chicago Law School, Ruth Wyatt Rosenson Scholar (J.D., 2003). *Member:* Chicago and Illinois State Bar Associations; Asian American Bar Association. ***LANGUAGES:*** Korean. ***PRACTICE AREAS:*** Construction Litigation; Commercial Litigation. ***Email:*** kek@steinrayharris.com

LIZABETH A. MUNIZ, born Salt Lake City, Utah, May 1, 1976; admitted to bar, 2001, Illinois and U.S. District Court, Northern District of Illinois; 2003, U.S. District Court, Eastern District of Illinois and U.S. Court of Appeals, 7th Circuit. *Education:* University of Utah (B.S., Human Development, 1996); University of Michigan (M.S.W., 2001; J.D., 2001). Publication Manager, Michigan Journal of Gender & Law. Associate Editor, Journal of Law Reform. *Member:* Chicago and American Bar Associations. ***PRACTICE AREAS:*** Construction Litigation; Commercial Litigation. ***Email:*** lab@steinrayharris.com

SHORGE K. SATO, admitted to bar, 2002, Illinois. *Education:* Northwestern University (B.A., 1998); New York University (J.D., 2002). ***Email:*** sks@steinrayharris.com

EMILY K. MUCEUS, born Chicago, Illinois, August 7, 1975; admitted to bar, 2002, Illinois and U.S. District Court, Northern District of Illinois; 2004, U.S. Court of Appeals, Sixth Circuit. *Education:* Davidson College (B.S., 1997); Indiana University School of Law (J.D., cum laude, 2002). *Member:* Chicago and American Bar Associations. ***PRACTICE AREAS:*** Construction Litigation; Commercial Litigation. ***Email:*** ekm@steinrayharris.com

ALEXANDER KIPNIS, born 1980; (admission pending). *Education:* University of Chicago (J.D., 2005). ***Email:*** amk@steinrayharris.com

---

STEINBERG, POLACEK & GOODMAN

Established in 1931

309 WEST WASHINGTON STREET, SUITE 500
CHICAGO, ILLINOIS 60606
Telephone: 312-782-1386
FAX: 312-782-6739
URL: http://www.spglawyers.com
URL: http://www.lawyers.com/spg

Personal Injury, Automobile Accidents, Products Liability and Medical Malpractice Law.

MEMBERS OF FIRM

BRADLEY D. STEINBERG, born Chicago, Illinois, December 12, 1933; admitted to bar, 1958, Illinois. *Education:* Carleton College (B.A., 1955); Northwestern University (J.D., 1958); Harvard University (LL.M., 1959). Phi Beta Kappa. *Member:* Illinois State Bar Association. ***PRACTICE AREAS:*** Personal Injury Law; Product Liability Law; Medical Malpractice. ***Email:*** bsteinberg@spglawyers.com

BRUCE D. GOODMAN, born Chicago, Illinois, December 18, 1949; admitted to bar, 1974, Illinois. *Education:* University of Illinois (B.A., 1971); DePaul University (J.D., 1974). *Member:* Chicago, Illinois State and American Bar Associations. ***PRACTICE AREAS:*** Medical Malpractice; Personal Injury Law; Product Liability Law. ***Email:*** bgoodman@spglawyers.com

ASSOCIATE

RONALD KALISH, born Chicago, Illinois, June 8, 1967; admitted to bar, 1992, Illinois. *Education:* Miami University (B.S., 1989); John Marshall Law School (J.D., 1992). *Member:* Chicago, Illinois State and American Bar Associations; Illinois Trial Lawyers Association. ***PRACTICE AREAS:*** Personal Injury; Medical Malpractice; Products Liability; Real Estate; Commercial Litigation; Regulatory Law. ***Email:*** rkalish@spglawyers.com

STEJKOWSKI & ZAFFERE LLC

77 WEST WACKER DRIVE, SUITE 4800
CHICAGO, ILLINOIS 60601-1604
Telephone: 312-606-8611
Fax: 312-606-8608
URL: http://www.sandzlaw.com

Business Law, Commercial Real Estate, Mergers and Acquisitions.

MEMBERS OF FIRM

DAVID G. STEJKOWSKI, born Bolingbrook, Illinois, June 7, 1965; admitted to bar, 1993, California, U.S. District Court, Central District of California, U.S. Court of Appeals, Ninth Circuit; 1994, U.S. District Court, Southern District of California; 1996, Illinois. *Education:* Knox College (B.A., magna cum laude, 1987); University of Southern California (J.D., 1993). Phi Beta Kappa, Motar Board. Senior Articles Editor, Southern California Interdisciplinary Law Journal/Major Tax Planning. *Member:* The State Bar of California; The State Bar of Illinois. ***PRACTICE AREAS:*** Commercial Real Estate. ***Email:*** dstejkowski@sandzlaw.com

FRANK D. ZAFFERE, III, born Easton, Maryland, September 2, 1948; admitted to bar, 1974, New York; 1978, District of Columbia; 1980, Illinois. *Education:* University of Notre Dame (B.B.A., cum laude, 1970); Georgetown University (J.D., 1973). Beta Gamma Sigma. Editor, Law & Policy in International Business. *Member:* Chicago and American Bar Associations; Turnaround Management Association. ***PRACTICE AREAS:*** Business Law; Mergers and Acquisitions. ***Email:*** fzaffere@sandzlaw.com

R.M. STEPHENSON, LLC

CHICAGO, ILLINOIS

(See Oak Park)

Appellate Practice, Criminal Defense, Family Law, Wills, Trusts and Estates, Civil Litigation, Business Law, Real Estate Law.

DAVID M. STERNBERG

1 N. LASALLE AVENUE, SUITE 1525
CHICAGO, ILLINOIS 60602
Telephone: 312-372-6271
Fax: 312-333-6290
URL: http://www.davidsternberglaw.com

Automobile Accidents and Injuries, Slip and Fall, Wrongful Death, Personal Injury and Workers Compensation Law.

DAVID M. STERNBERG, born Chicago, Illinois, September 7, 1956; admitted to bar, 1983, District of Columbia and Illinois. *Education:* Brandeis University (B.A., 1978); Washington College of Law (J.D., 1982). *Member:* Illinois State Bar Association; The District of Columbia Bar. ***PRACTICE AREAS:*** Automobile Accidents and Injuries; Personal Injury Law; Slip and Fall; Workers Compensation; Wrongful Death.

STETLER & DUFFY, LTD.

11 S. LASALLE STREET, SUITE 1200
CHICAGO, ILLINOIS 60603
Telephone: 312-338-0200
Fax: 312-338-0070
URL: http://www.stetleranduffy.com

White Collar Criminal Defense; Commercial Litigation.

DAVID J. STETLER, born September 6, 1949; admitted to bar, 1974, Pennsylvania (inactive); 1975, District of Columbia (inactive); 1987, Illinois; U.S. Court of Appeals, Third, Seventh and Eighth Circuits; U.S. District Court, Northern and Central Districts of Illinois including Trial Bar; U.S. District Court, Northern District of Indiana. *Education:* Villanova University (B.A., 1971; J.D., 1974). Attorney, Office of Chief Counsel, Internal Revenue Service, 1974-1979. Special Attorney, United States Department of Justice, 1976-1978. Assistant United States Attorney, Northern District of Illinois, 1979-1988 (Deputy Chief, Special Prosecutions Division, 1983-1986; Chief, Criminal Receiving and Appellate Division, 1986-1988). Member, Wong Sun Society of San Francisco. *Member:* Illinois State and American Bar Assns.; National Assn. of Criminal Defense Lawyers; American College of Trial Lawyers. ***PRACTICE AREAS:*** White Collar Criminal Defense; Commercial Litigation.

JOSEPH J. DUFFY, born Chicago, Illinois, August 25, 1951; admitted to bar, 1979, Illinois; U.S. District Court, Northern District of Illinois including Trial Bar; U.S. Court of Appeals, Seventh Circuit; 1990, U.S. Tax Court. *Education:* DePaul University (B.S., cum laude, 1973); John Marshall Law School (J.D., 1979). Certified Public Accountant, Illinois, 1974. First Assistant U.S. Attorney, Northern District of Illinois, 1987-1989. Chief, Criminal Division, U.S. Attorney's Office, Northern District of Illinois, 1985-1986. *Member:* American Bar Association (Member, White Collar Crime Committee); American College of Trial Lawyers; National Association of Criminal Defense Lawyers. ***PRACTICE AREAS:*** Commercial Litigation; White Collar Criminal Defense.

JONATHAN M. CYRLUK, born Chicago, Illinois, July 1, 1967; admitted to bar, 1992, Illinois; U.S. District Court, Northern District of Illinois. *Education:* University of Illinois (B.A., 1989; J.D., magna cum laude, 1992). Topics Editor, University of Illinois Law Review, 1991-1992. Author, "U.S. v. Shork: Whatever You Do, Don't Trust Your Environmental Consultant," 4 Envir. Crimes and Enf. Newsletter, October 2002. *Member:* Chicago, Illinois State and American Bar Associations. ***PRACTICE AREAS:*** Commercial Litigation; White Collar Criminal Defense.

WILLIAM P. ZIEGELMUELLER, born Royal Oak, Michigan, April 28, 1969; admitted to bar, 1994, Illinois; U.S. District Court, Northern District of Illinois including Trial Bar; U.S. Court of Appeals, Seventh Circuit. *Education:* Wake Forest University (B.A., magna cum laude, 1991); Northwestern University (J.D., 1994). Phi Beta Kappa; Mortar Board. Author: Note, "Due Process on Drugs: The Implications of Forcibly Medicating Pretrial Detainees with Antipsychotic Drugs," 83 Northwestern Journal of Criminal Law, Criminology 836, 1993. *Member:* Chicago Bar Association; Wong Sun Society of San Francisco. ***PRACTICE AREAS:*** White Collar Criminal Defense; Commercial Litigation.

COREY B. RUBENSTEIN, born Syracuse, New York, July 9, 1970; admitted to bar, 1995, Illinois; U.S. District Court, Northern District of Illinois including Trial Bar; U.S. Court of Appeals, Seventh Circuit. *Education:* University of Michigan (A.B., 1992); Harvard University (J.D., cum laude, 1995). ***PRACTICE AREAS:*** White Collar Criminal Defense; Commercial Litigation.

JONI M. GREEN, born Cincinnati, Ohio, September 8, 1976; admitted to bar, 2001, Illinois. *Education:* Pennsylvania State University (B.S., with honors, 1998); Loyola University (J.D., cum laude, 2001). *Member:* Chicago and Illinois Bar Associations; American Bankruptcy Association. ***PRACTICE AREAS:*** White Collar Criminal Defense; Commercial Litigation.

TODD J. HAUGH, born Oregon, Illinois, December 14, 1976; admitted to bar, 2002, Illinois. *Education:* Brown University (B.A., with honors, 1999); University of Illinois College of Law (J.D., cum laude, 2002). ***PRACTICE AREAS:*** White Collar Criminal Defense; Civil Litigation.

(This Listing Continued)

STOLTMANN LAW OFFICES, P.C.

10 SOUTH LASALLE STREET, SUITE 3300
CHICAGO, ILLINOIS 60603-1002
Telephone: 312-332-4200
Fax: 312-332-4201
Email: stoltmann1234@hotmail.com

Securities Arbitration.

ANDREW J. STOLTMANN, born Milwaukee, Wisconsin, October 1, 1971; admitted to bar, 1999, Illinois; U.S. District Court, Northern District of Illinois. *Education:* University of Wisconsin (B.B.A., 1994); DePaul University (J.D., 1999). Author: "Investor Rights for the Year 2000 and Beyond,"; "Brokerage Firms Propose Hollow Solutions for Research Analyst Conflict of Interest." *Member:* Chicago (Member, Securities Law Committee) and American Bar Associations; Public Investor Arbitration Bar Association (Member, Federal Legislation and Arbitration Recruitment Committee); The Association of Trial Lawyers of America. ***PRACTICE AREAS:*** Securities Arbitration. ***Email:*** stoltmann1234@hotmail.com

STONE & ASSOCIATES L.L.C.

CHICAGO, ILLINOIS

(See Waukegan)

Practice limited to Criminal Law including White Collar Crime, Capital Offenses, Narcotics and Drugs, Death Penalty, Murder, Homicide and Federal Criminal Law.

STONE & MOORE

CHARTERED
Established in 1999

30 NORTH LA SALLE STREET, SUITE 4300
CHICAGO, ILLINOIS 60602
Telephone: 312-332-5656
Fax: 312-332-5858
URL: http://www.stonemoore.com

Products Liability, Mass Injury Litigation, Professional Malpractice Defense and Prosecution, Construction Litigation, Insurance Coverage Opinions and Litigation, Bad Faith, Reinsurance Arbitration, Personal Injury Defense, Appellate Practice, Workmans Compensation.

FIRM PROFILE: Stone & Moore, listed in the Bar Register of Preeminent Lawyers, is headquartered in Chicago (with two branch offices) serving a nation-wide clientele. The firm's mission is to provide aggressive, innovative and cost-effective service to its clients through the use of a skilled professional staff and cutting-edge technology. The firm has twenty-three attorneys whose personal histories are available by visiting the firm's website.

WILLIAM G. STONE, born Chicago, Illinois, October 10, 1949; admitted to bar, 1980, Illinois and U.S. District Court, Northern District of Illinois including Trial Bar; 1988, Indiana; 1999, Colorado. *Education:* University of South Florida (B.A., 1976); Phi Kappa Phi, University of Arkansas (J.D., 1980). Arkansas Law Review. Co-Author: "How to Prepare a Law Office Policy Manual," *Law Office Economics Section, Illinois State Bar Association,* Chairman's Column of Tort Law Section Newsletter, 1984-1985. Presenter: "Duty to Defend in Illinois"; "Bad Faith and How to Avoid It"; "Y2K Liability". *Member:* Chicago and Illinois State Bar Associations; Federal Defense Bar Association; Defense Research Institute; American Trial Lawyers Association. [U.S. Air Force, 1969-1973]. (Also at Merrillville, Indiana Office). ***PRACTICE AREAS:*** Civil Trial Practice; Insurance Coverage; Insurance Bad Faith; Environmental Litigation; Reinsurance; Reinsurance Arbitration; Legal Malpractice. ***Email:*** wstone@stonemoore.com

ROBERT CHARLES MOORE, born Chicago, Illinois, March 19, 1952; admitted to bar, 1977, Illinois, U.S. District Court, Northern District of Illinois, U.S. Court of Appeals, Seventh Circuit; 1983, U.S . Supreme Court; 1984, Trial Bar; 1987, Wisconsin; 1994, U.S. District Court, Central District of Illinois. *Education:* John Carroll University (B.S., B.A.,

(This Listing Continued)

STONE & MOORE, CHARTERED, Chicago—Continued

cum laude, 1974); Exeter University, Exeter, England (Program Award, 1975); Loyola University Law School (J.D., 1977). Recipient: John Carroll University Finance Scholar of Year Award; Business School Scholarship Award; First Year Representative to Student Bar Association, Loyola University Law School. Author: extensive publications in Risk Management, Contractual Transfer of Risk, Insurance and the Duty to Defend, Product Liability Tort Reform, Worker's Compensation. Featured Speaker: Joint Safety Conference of America; Safety Engineers of America; National Safety Council; Chicagoland Society of Casualty and Safety Engineers; Insurance Women of Suburban Chicago. Guest Lecturer: for numerous insurance carriers and third party administrators, including: American International Group; Great American Insurance Company; Alexis Risk Management; Crawford & Company; Tokio Fire & Marine Insurance Company; AON; Lloyd's of London Syndicate and Underwriters; Americas Insurance Company. Panel Counsel, Risk Management Task Force of Specialty Carriers & Riggers Association. Director, Society of Casualty and Safety Engineers. *Member:* DuPage County, Kane County, McHenry County, Chicago and Illinois State Bar Associations; Defense Research Institute. (Also at Wheaton, Illinois Office). ***PRACTICE AREAS:*** Products Liability; Construction Litigation; Insurance Coverage; Workers' Compensation; Professional Malpractice; Personal Injury Litigation; Appellate Practice. ***Email:*** rmoore@stonemoore.com

STONE, POGRUND & KOREY

A Partnership including Professional Corporations

Established in 1957

221 NORTH LA SALLE STREET, 32ND FLOOR
CHICAGO, ILLINOIS 60601
Telephone: 312-782-3636
Fax: 312-782-1482
Email: attorney@spklaw.com
URL: http://www.spklaw.com

General Practice. Corporate, Commercial, Banking, Real Estate, Litigation, Environmental, Construction, Employment Law, Commercial and Residential Real Estate, Business, Contract Law, Health Care Law, OSHA, Mechanic Liens, Government Liens, Employment Discrimination, Workers Compensation.

MEMBERS OF FIRM

BERTRAM A. STONE (1915-1994)

SHERWIN I. POGRUND, (P.C.), born Chicago, Illinois, September 4, 1934; admitted to bar, 1957, Illinois; 1961, U.S. District Court, Northern District of Illinois. *Education:* University of Illinois; Roosevelt University (B.A., 1955); Northwestern University (J.D., 1957); Oxford University. ***Email:*** sherwin@spklaw.com

MARTIN S. KOREY, born Chicago, Illinois, September 29, 1945; admitted to bar, 1970, Illinois, U.S. District Court, Northern District of Illinois including Trial Bar, U.S. Supreme Court, U.S. Court of Appeals, Seventh Circuit and U.S. Tax Court. *Education:* University of Illinois (B.S., 1967); DePaul University (J.D., 1970). ***Email:*** mkorey@spklaw.com

JAMES P. ZIEGLER, born Chicago, Illinois, August 31, 1952; admitted to bar, 1976, Illinois and U.S. District Court, Northern District of Illinois. *Education:* St. Michael's College and University of Toronto (B.A., with honors, 1973); DePaul University (J.D., summa cum laude, 1976). ***Email:*** jziegler@spklaw.com

DAVID B. POGRUND, born Chicago, Illinois, November 13, 1959; admitted to bar, 1983, Illinois; U.S. District Court Northern District of Illinois. *Education:* Tulane University (B.A., cum laude, 1981; J.D., 1983); Oxford University. Phi Eta Sigma. Tulane Scholar. ***Email:*** david@spklaw.com

CHRISTOPHER T. NOWOTARSKI, (P.C.), born Chicago, Illinois, July 6, 1958; admitted to bar, 1983, Illinois and U.S. District Court, Northern District of Illinois. *Education:* DePaul University (B.S.C., 1980; J.D., 1983). ***LANGUAGES:*** Polish. ***Email:*** cnowotarski@spklaw.com

LAWRENCE J. STARK, born New York, N.Y., December 18, 1960; admitted to bar, 1985, Illinois and U.S. District Court, Northern District of Illinois. *Education:* Brandeis University (B.A., 1982); IIT-Chicago-Kent College of Law (J.D., 1985). ***Email:*** lstark@spklaw.com

ASSOCIATE

CARTER ANDREW KOREY

LAW OFFICE OF HOWARD L. STOVALL

Established in 1996

2131 NORTH RACINE AVENUE
CHICAGO, ILLINOIS 60614
Telephone: 773-248-8896
Fax: 773-248-8897
Email: howard@stovall-law.com
URL: http://www.stovall-law.com

International Arbitration, International Commercial Law, International Business Law, International Distribution, particularly Commercial Law of the Arabic-Speaking countries of the Middle East.

FIRM PROFILE: For the past twenty-four years, Howard L. Stovall has assisted multinational companies on commercial law matters throughout the Arabic-speaking countries of the Middle East. Mr. Stovall has also served as an expert witness on Middle East commercial law, both before the U.S. federal (district and appellate) courts as well as in International Chamber of Commerce and American Arbitration Association arbitration proceedings. Formerly a partner in a large international law firm, Mr. Stovall established his own (solo) law office in Chicago, effective October 1996.

From his Chicago office, Mr. Stovall maintains a library of laws (in Arabic original and/or English translation) and precedents, as well as a close network of local correspondent counsel, for the following countries: Bahrain, Egypt, Iraq, Jordan, Kuwait, Lebanon, Libya, Oman, Palestine, Qatar, Saudi Arabia, Sudan, Syria, the United Arab Emirates (UAE), and Yemen.

Mr. Stovall advises on Middle East matters such as (i) companies and investment laws, and licensing; (ii) trade laws (including commercial agency, distributorship, customs duties, export/import); (iii) government contracts for goods and projects (including joint venture arrangements and the use of intermediaries); (iv) local laws and practices relevant to the Foreign Corrupt Practices Act (bribery laws, penal codes, civil service laws); (v) income tax and exchange control laws and regulations; (vi) labor laws, employment agreements and "second-ing" arrangements; and (vii) laws and regulations relevant to commercial disputes (both litigation and arbitration).

Mr. Stovall graduated from Albion College (Michigan), and then spent two years drilling water wells in North Yemen for the Ministry of Public Works (under a Peace Corps program). He studied Arabic language at the University of Michigan Rackham Graduate School, and obtained his law degree in 1981 from the University of Texas (Austin). Mr. Stovall spent two years in the Cairo office, and one year in the London office, of Baker & McKenzie law firm, and he travels regularly throughout the Middle East. He has also spoken and written extensively on various Middle East legal topics.

HOWARD L. STOVALL, born Grand Rapids, Michigan, September 29, 1952; admitted to bar, 1981, Illinois. *Education:* Albion College (B.A., 1974); University of Michigan; University of Texas (J.D., with honors, 1981). Formerly with Baker & McKenzie, Chicago, Cairo and London Offices, 1981-1996, Partner, 1989-1996. *Member:* Chicago, Illinois State, American (Chair, Middle Eastern Law Committee, 1999-2003) and International (Arab Regional Forum) Bar Associations. ***LANGUAGES:*** Arabic. ***PRACTICE AREAS:*** Middle East Trade (100%).

Languages: Arabic.

STRAUSS & MALK LLP

CHICAGO, ILLINOIS

(See Northbrook)

Estate Planning, Wealth Preservation, Probate, Business Succession Planning, Corporate Law, Business Acquisitions and Sales, Real Estate Acquisition and Development, Business and Real Estate Financing, ERISA, Executive Compensation, Professional Service Businesses, Tax Law, Litigation including Commercial, Business Transactions, Real Estate, Trusts and Estates and Torts.

STRIDE, CRADDOCK & STRIDE

111 WEST WASHINGTON STREET, SUITE 1837
CHICAGO, ILLINOIS 60602-2773
Telephone: 312-346-5800
Fax: 312-346-3870

General Civil and Trial Practice. Medical, Legal Malpractice and Negligence Law.

HERBERT F. STRIDE, born Chicago, Illinois, January 16, 1933; admitted to bar, 1957, Illinois. *Education:* Valparaiso University (B.A., 1954; J.D., 1957). Delta Theta Phi. Member, Panel of Arbitrators, American Arbitration Association. *Member:* Chicago, Illinois State and American Bar Associations; Illinois Trial Lawyers Association; The Association of Trial Lawyers of America. ***PRACTICE AREAS:*** Civil Trial; Medical Malpractice; Legal Malpractice; Negligence.

J. PATRICK CRADDOCK, born Chicago, Illinois, September 7, 1934; admitted to bar, 1968, Illinois; U.S. District Court, Northern and Central Districts of Illinois. *Education:* University of Notre Dame (B.S.C., 1956); Loyola University (M.S.I.R., 1965); John Marshall Law School (J.D., 1968). Phi Alpha Delta. Member, Panel of Arbitrators, American Arbitration Association. *Member:* Chicago and Illinois State Bar Associations. ***PRACTICE AREAS:*** Civil Trial; Medical Malpractice; Negligence.

HERBERT L. STRIDE, born Evanston, Illinois, November 2, 1960; admitted to bar, 1986, Illinois; U.S. District Court, Northern District of Illinois; U.S. Supreme Court. *Education:* Valparaiso University (B.A., 1982; J.D., 1985). *Member:* Chicago, Illinois State and American Bar Associations. ***PRACTICE AREAS:*** Civil Trial; Medical Malpractice; Legal Malpractice; Negligence.

NICHOLAS C. PANOS, born Princeton, Illinois, July 2, 1935; admitted to bar, 1967, Illinois. *Education:* Knox College (B.A., 1957); Northern Illinois University (M. S.Ed., 1962); John Marshall Law School (J.D., 1967). *Member:* Chicago and Illinois State Bar Associations. ***LANGUAGES:*** Greek. ***PRACTICE AREAS:*** Civil Trial; Medical Malpractice; Negligence; Probate; Real Estate.

DEBORAH A. STRIDE-SARAN, born Chicago, Illinois, December 10, 1959; admitted to bar, 1985, Illinois. *Education:* Valparaiso University (B.S., 1981); Loyola University (J.D., 1984). *Member:* Chicago and Illinois State Bar Associations; Illinois Trial Lawyers Association. ***PRACTICE AREAS:*** General Practice.

MICHAEL J. CRADDOCK, born Des Plaines, Illinois, July 14, 1967; admitted to bar, 1994, Illinois; U.S. District Court, Northern District of Illinois. *Education:* John Carroll

(This Listing Continued)

University (B.A., 1989); Thomas M. Cooley Law School (J.D., 1994). *Member:* Chicago and Illinois State Bar Associations. ***PRACTICE AREAS:*** Civil Trial; Medical Malpractice; Negligence.

JOSEPH P. GIAMANCO, born Mt. Vernon, Illinois, June 14, 1977; admitted to bar, 2002, Illinois. *Education:* University of Denver (B.A., 1999); DePaul University College of Law (J.D., 2002). Recipient, Outstanding Senior Award. *Member:* Chicago, Illinois State and American Bar Associations; Justinian Society (Law School Chapter President, 2001-2002). ***PRACTICE AREAS:*** Personal Injury; Insurance Defense; Negligence; Criminal Defense; Eminent Domain; General Practice.

SUGAR, FRIEDBERG & FELSENTHAL LLP

Established in 1981

30 NORTH LA SALLE STREET, SUITE 3000
CHICAGO, ILLINOIS 60602
Telephone: 312-704-9400
Facsimile: 312-372-7951
URL: http://www.sff-law.com

Business and Transactional Practice, including Corporate, Partnership and Securities Law, Mergers and Acquisitions, Securities and Futures Regulation, Real Estate, and Subsidized Housing, Federal Income Tax Planning and Litigation, Estate Planning and Administration, Commercial Litigation, Securities Litigation, Insolvency, Bankruptcy and Reorganization, Insurance Law, Franchise Law, Intellectual Property.

MEMBERS OF FIRM

RICHARD A. SUGAR, born Chicago, Illinois, May 22, 1947; admitted to bar, 1972, Illinois. *Education:* Indiana University (B.S., with honors, 1968) Beta Gamma Sigma; University of Chicago (J.D., 1972). ***Email:*** rsugar@sff-law.com

MICHAEL R. FRIEDBERG, born Chicago, Illinois, June 27, 1946; admitted to bar, 1971, Illinois. *Education:* Tulane University of Louisiana; Northwestern University (B.A., with honors, 1968); University of Chicago (J.D., 1971). ***Email:*** mfriedberg@sff-law.com

STEVEN A. FELSENTHAL, born Chicago, Illinois, May 21, 1949; admitted to bar, 1974, Illinois. *Education:* University of Illinois (A.B., with high honors, 1971); Harvard University (J.D., 1974) Phi Beta Kappa. ***Email:*** saf@sff-law.com

ANDREW B. DAVID, born Chicago, Illinois, August 14, 1954; admitted to bar, 1979, Illinois. *Education:* Colorado College (B.A., cum laude, 1976); Northwestern University (J.D., 1979). ***Email:*** adavid@sff-law.com

LESLIE J. WEISS, born Chicago, Illinois, August 14, 1957; admitted to bar, 1982, Illinois. *Education:* Smith College (A.B. cum laude, 1979); Northwestern University (J.D., 1982). ***Email:*** lweiss@sff-law.com

PAULA K. JACOBI, born La Porte, Indiana, May 31, 1950; admitted to bar, 1977, Illinois. *Education:* University of Michigan (B.Ed., 1972); University of Cincinnati and Northwestern University (J.D., 1977). Recipient, James B. Angell Scholar, University of Michigan. Member: University of Cincinnati Law Review. ***Email:*** pjacobi@sff-law.com

JONATHAN L. MILLS, born Chicago, Illinois, May 3, 1947; admitted to bar, 1977, Illinois. *Education:* University of Wisconsin-Madison (B.A., 1970); University of Chicago (J.D., 1977). ***Email:*** jmills@sff-law.com

HOWARD M. HELSINGER, born New York, N.Y., April 4, 1940; admitted to bar, 1978, Illinois. *Education:* Haverford College (B.A., 1962); Princeton University (Ph.D., 1970); University of Chicago (J.D., 1978). ***Email:*** hhelsinger@sff-law.com

MARTIN M. WEINSTEIN, born Baltimore, Maryland, July 24, 1943; admitted to bar, 1974, Maryland, 1975, District of Columbia; 1981, Illinois. *Education:* University of Maryland (B.S., 1967); Catholic University of America (J.D., 1974). Certified Public Accountant: Maryland, 1978; Illinois, 1983. ***Email:*** mweinstein@sff-law.com

ETAHN M. COHEN, born Columbus, Ohio, December 13, 1952; admitted to bar, 1984, Illinois. *Education:* Yale University (B.A., cum laude, 1975); Harvard University (Ph.D., 1981); University of Chicago (J.D., cum laude, 1984). ***Email:*** ecohen@sff-law.com

KATHRYN A. ERICKSON, born Milwaukee, Wisconsin, February 8, 1966; admitted to bar, 1991, Illinois. *Education:* Michigan State University (B.A., high honors, 1988); Northwestern University School of Law (J.D., 1991). ***Email:*** kerickson@sff-law.com

WILLIAM F. McGUINN, born Oak Park, Illinois, May 23, 1968; admitted to bar, 1993, Illinois. *Education:* Northern Illinois University (B.S., cum laude, 1990); University of Illinois (J.D., magna cum laude, 1993). Certified Public Accountant, Illinois, 1990. ***Email:*** wmcguinn@sff-law.com

ANDREW R. SCHWARTZ, born Chicago, Illinois, September 17, 1963; admitted to bar, 1988, Illinois. *Education:* University of Michigan (A.B., English, 1985); Loyola University (J.D., 1988). ***Email:*** aschwartz@sff-law.com

ADAM J. GRAIS, born Chicago, Illinois, January 30, 1968; admitted to bar, 1996, Illinois. *Education:* Columbia University (B.A., 1990); Chicago Law School (J.D., 1996). ***PRACTICE AREAS:*** Tax Law; Corporate Law. ***Email:*** agrais@sff-law.com

ASSOCIATES

ANDREW J. ABRAMS, born Evanston, Illinois, August 9, 1975; admitted to bar, 2000, Illinois. *Education:* University of Illinois-Urbana (B.A., cum laude, 1997); University of Chicago (J.D., 2000) Phi Beta Kappa. ***Email:*** aabrams@sff-law.com

BRETT N. CAGAN, born Columbus, Ohio, June 10, 1970; admitted to bar, 1997, Illinois. *Education:* Indiana University (B.S., 1992); Valparaiso University (J.D., magna cum laude, 1997). ***Email:*** bcagan@sff-law.com

PAMELA S. DiCARLANTONIO, born Washington, D.C., January 26, 1964; admitted to bar, 1996, Texas; 1997, Illinois. *Education:* University of Maryland (B.S., magna cum laude, 1986); University of Illinois (J.D., cum laude, 1996). ***Email:*** pdicarlantonio@sff-law.com

(This Listing Continued)

STEPHANIE P. LISTOKIN, born Montreal, Quebec, Canada, August 20, 1975; admitted to bar, 2002, New York and Massachusetts (Not admitted in Illinois). *Education:* Harvard University (A.B., cum laude, 1997); University of Pennsylvania Law School (J.D., 2001). ***PRACTICE AREAS:*** Estate Planning; Estate Administration; Trust Administration. ***Email:*** slistokin@sff-law.com

ELIZABETH A. SHEPARD, born Elk Grove, Illinois, June 16, 1971; admitted to bar, 1996, Illinois; 1998, Wisconsin. *Education:* University of Illinois (B.A., 1993); University of Notre Dame (J.D., cum laude, 1996). ***PRACTICE AREAS:*** Estate Planning; Estate Administration; Trust Administration. ***Email:*** eshepard@sff-law.com

MEGAN I. WITZEL, born St. Louis, Missouri, April 17, 1972; admitted to bar, 1997, Missouri; 1998, Illinois. *Education:* St. Mary's College (B.A., cum laude, 1994); Washington University (J.D., 1997). ***Email:*** mwitzel@sff-law.com

THE SULLIVAN FIRM, LTD.

CHICAGO, ILLINOIS

(See Rolling Meadows)

Litigation, Criminal Law, Family Law, Employment Law, Business Law, DWI and Real Estate.

LAW OFFICES OF SULLIVAN HINCKS & CONWAY

CHICAGO, ILLINOIS

(See Oak Brook)

Corporate and Business Law, Civil Litigation, Real Estate, Logistics, Transportation, Taxation, Administrative, Environmental, Employment and Related Litigation, Insurance Coverage, Insurance Regulatory Matters, Commercial Law, Equine Law.

SUSMAN & ASSOCIATES, P.C.

Established in 1986

203 NORTH WABASH AVENUE
14TH FLOOR
CHICAGO, ILLINOIS 60601
Telephone: 312-444-9600
Facsimile: 312-444-9612
Email: SusmanUSA@aol.com
URL: http://www.susmanlaw.com

Mexico Office: Lago Alberto 442-27, Col. Anahuac, 11320 Mexico, D.F.
Spain Office: Alejandro de Eguren Santisteban Abogado, Marqués del Puerto n° 9, 1° izda. Bilbao.
Belgian Office: Rue Faider 18, B 1060 Bruxelles, Belgium.
Peru Office: Calle 6, No. 193, Las Lilas, Santiago de Surco, Lima, Peru.

Customs, International Trade, International Transactions, Commercial and Foreign Trade Laws, Immigration Law, Visas, Work Permits, Employment Immigration, Related Administrative Law and Litigation, Commercial Transactions, Import and Export Law.

FIRM PROFILE: Susman & Associates is dedicated to providing clients with the highest quality of legal services possible, with a unique concentration in international matters, frequently involving more than one country or nation. Attorneys and staff are bilingual, and in many cases, multilingual. The firm also works through a wide network of high-caliber foreign attorneys practicing abroad who are well-known to the firm.

Ms. Susman concentrates her practice in customs and international trade law, international commercial transactions, foreign trade and immigration, with correspondent offices in Mexico, Spain and Belgium.

BARBARA A. SUSMAN, born Waukegan, Illinois, July 21, 1958; admitted to bar, 1983, Illinois and U.S. District Court, Northern District of Illinois; 1984, U.S. Court of International Trade and U.S. Court of Appeals for the Federal Circuit; 1987, U.S. Tax Court. *Education:* University of Illinois and University of Barcelona (A.B., with distinction, 1980); IIT Chicago-Kent College of Law (J.D., 1983). James Edmund Scholar; Abbott Laboratories Award (Spanish). Law Clerk, Honorable Jane A. Restani, U.S. Court of International Trade, 1983-1984. Intern, U.S. Customs Service, Office of the Regional Counsel (Chicago), 1982-1983. Special Merit Award, U.S. Customs Service, 1983. Adjunct Professor of Business Law, National College of Education, 1988-1990; Awarded "Best Teacher of the Year," 1989 and 1990; Leading Illinois Attorney, International Business and Imm Laio, 1996—. Author: "It's a Mod, Mod, Mod World: The Customs Modernization Act of 1993," American Bar Association, Canadian Law Newsletter, Vol. XX1 (Spring, 1994); "International Trade Requires Legal Eye," *Chicago Properties,* Vol. 5, No. 11, at 1 (Nov. 15, 1993); "New U.S. Immigration Opportunities for Scholars, Professors and Researchers," presented at 9th Annual conference, World Association of Case Method Research, University of Limerick, Ireland (June 21, 1992); "New Opportunities Under the U.S. Immigration Act of 1990," *Hong Kong Staff* (1992); "Take Another Look at Business Opportunities in the Caribbean Basin," *International Trade and Technology News ACTION,* (Northwestern University) Vol. 5, No. 1 at 24 (Winter, 1990); "Customs Enforcement of Trademarks of Configurations and Shape," *MIT Enterprise Forum,* Vol. 6, Iss. 4 (12/89); "Imports, Exports and U.S. Competitiveness in the European Market," Illinois Export Development Authority Newsletter, Fall, 1989; *Manufacturing Competitiveness Frontiers,* (IIT Research Institute), Vol. 14, No. 1 (January, 1990); "Export Licensing Controls," Vol. 13, No. 8, at 6 (August, 1989); "Progress of EC Common Market - '1992 Plan," Vol. 13, No. 1, at 17-19 (January, 1989); "Ongoing Trade Trends Between U.S. and Mexico," *The Globe* Vol. 26, No. 3 at 4-6 (November, 1988); "New Legal Developments in U.S.-Canada Trade," *The Globe,* Vol. 25, No. 6 at 1-3 (February, 1988); "The Immigration Reform and Control Act of 1986 ("IRCA"): Impact upon Employer/Employee Fourth Amendment Protections," Vol. 5, No. 1, *Hofstra Labor Law Journal,* (Fall, 1987); "Chandler v. Florida, 49 U.S.L.W. 4141 (1980);

(This Listing Continued)

SUSMAN & ASSOCIATES, P.C., Chicago—Continued

A Partial Answer to the Question of Cameras in the Courtroom," 28 *Decalogue Journal* 21 (Winter, 1982); Editor, *International Lawletter,* 1987—. *Lectures and Programs:* Speaker: "Valuation in Customs Import and Trade Cases," Nissan Conference, March 12, 1996; "American Association of Exporters and Importers," Regional Conference, November 7, 1995; "J-I Visa Waivers for Physicians and U.S. Immigration for Medical Workers," The Princeton Review, August 14, 1996; "Ethics: Don't Leave Home Without Them," American Immigration Lawyers Association-Indianapolis, July 27, 1994; Keynote Speaker, New International Challenges by the Year 2000, Purdue University, March, 1994, "Changes in International Business," Indiana World Trade Council, February 4, 1994; Panelist, "Immigration for Foreign Physicians, Nurses and Medical Professionals," American Immigration Lawyers Association National Conference and Stanley Kaplan Institute, Toronto, Canada, June 16, 1993; "Transatlantic Joint Ventures and Doing Business in the U.S.," "Illinois Heartland Global Summit," (Decatur), Illinois Power and Corporate Location (U.K.), May 6, 1993; "Legal Aspects of Export Sales and Distributor and Agency Agreements," at FMI/U.S. Food Export Show, May 8, 1993; Panelist, "EEC Harmonization," University of Dunedin, New Zealand, November, 1992; "Legalities of Exporting," College of Du Page (McDonald's) October 6, 1992; "Recent Developments in U.S.-Asia Pacific Trade," Chicago Association of Commerce and Industry, July 29, 1992; Moderator, "Customs and International Trade Law," Annual Conference, American Immigration Lawyers Association (New Orleans) June 11, 1992; Speaker, "Customs and International Trade: Recent Trends and Developments," Illinois State Bar, May 2, 1991; " Legal Requirements for International Business and Trade," J.L. Kellogg School of Management, Northwestern Univ., April 8 & 11, 1991 and Mundelein College, February 12, 1991; Radio Interview, "Leyes de Comercio a Nivel Internacional" (International Commercial Law), WOPA, August 2, 1990; Keynote Speaker, "Ethics and the Modern Woman," Mundelein College, March 3, 1991; Judge, Final Round, Midwest Regional Jessup International Moot Court Competition, February 16, 1991, February 21-22, 1989 and 1986 (Regionals); "Critical Developments in Immigration Law for Health Care," Metropolitan Chicago Healthcare Council, November 12, 1991, June 15 and July 9, 1990; Speaker, "U.S. Immigration & Nationality Laws," Chicago Bar Association (Labor Law), April 19, 1990; Speaker, "Selling Abroad: Legal Assistance Exporters Need," State of Illinois, March 20, 1990; Speaker, "Customs and Legal Aspects of Importing," American National Bank Seminar, February 27, 1990; Panelist, U. of I. Business Seminars, "Impacts of a United Europe," October 18, 1989 and "Legal Aspects of Customs and International Trade," Oct. 9, 1987; Speaker, EC 1992 "Customs Requirements, Procedures and Issues," Georgetown University Law Center/D.C.-Bar, "Expanding your Trade Practice: Keeping up with the Trends," June 8-9, 1989; Moderator, "Legal Aspects of Export - Expanding Strategic and Competitive Opportunities," 51st Annual Chicago World Trade Conference (ITC), May 23, 1989; Speaker, "U.S. Customs and Immigration Rules: Travelers and Foreign Personnel," Chicago Airline Managers Association, May 22, 1989; Faculty Papers and Presentations, National College of Education, March 22, 1990, May 11 and December 4, 1989; Speaker, "The New U.S. Trade Bill and Harmonized System of Tariff Classification," Korean Economic Council of Chicago, November 15, 1988; Speaker, "Customs Law and Practice/International Trade," Illinois State Bar "Law Ed" Series, May 4, 1990 and November 4, 1988; Speaker, "New Immigration Laws: Strategy and Planning," City Club of Chicago, October 3-4, 1988; Moderator and Chair, "Immigration Law Regional Issues Conference," American Immigration Lawyers Association, May 25, 1988; Co-moderator, "Intellectual Property Laws," CBA (YLS), May 3, 1988; Speaker, "International Legal Aspects of Exporting," U.S. Dept. of Commerce, Oct. 24, 1991 and May 1, 1985 and Chicago Chamber of Commerce, April 18, 1988; Lecturer, "Legal Aspects of International Trade and Transactions," Latin American Chamber of Commerce, February 19, 1988 and Oakton Community College, 1987-1988; Lecturer, "Legal Aspects of Foreign Investment in Illinois," "Recent customs and international trade cases," Chicago Bar Association, October 2, 1985; Lecturer, "Exports and Export Licensing," Chicago Chamber of Commerce, April 18, 1988 and Harper College, September 25, 1985; Panelist, "International Lawyer: Myth or Reality?" CBA, International and Foreign Trade Law Committee, September 6, 1985. Member: Chicago, Latin American, French and German Chambers of Commerce. *Member:* Illinois State (Chair, 1991-1992; Vice Chair, 1990; Secretary, 1989; International and Immigration Law Section Council), Chicago (Customs, International and Immigration Law Committees, 1984—; Vice Chair, Intellectual Property Law Committee, YLS, 1987-1988), Federal Circuit (Member, Hutchinson Writing Competition Committee, 1991) and American (Regional Coordinator, Canada Committee, 1993— and Member, U.S. Customs and International Law Committee); American Immigration Lawyers Association (Member, 1985—; Regional Chair, Business and Labor Law Committee, 1988-1989; Chair, INS District Director Liaison Committee, 1989-1990; Regional Chair, National Business and Congressional Network Committees, 1989-1992); Customs and International Trade (New York); Member, Union Internationale des Avocats; Asia-Pacific Lawyers Bar Associations; Chicago Council on Foreign Relations (Member, Committee on Foreign Affairs, 1986—); International Trade Club (Director, 1988-1990); Pan American Council (President, 1989-1990; Vice President and Secretary, 1986-1989); Customs Brokers and Foreign Freight Forwarders; International Trade (Greater Chicago) Associations; American Association of Exporters and Importers Associations; World Economic Development Forum. ***LANGUAGES:*** English, Spanish, Portuguese, French, Catalan. ***PRACTICE AREAS:*** Customs; International Trade; Commercial; Foreign Trade Laws; Immigration Law; Related Administrative Law; Litigation.

OF COUNSEL

DAVID G. DUGGAN, born Ottawa, Illinois, December 10, 1948; admitted to bar, 1981, Illinois. *Education:* Loyola University (A.B., 1970); John Marshall Law School (J.D., 1981). *Member:* Illinois State and American Bar Associations; The Association of Trial Lawyers of America.

MICHELE M. ROCAWICH, born Cleveland, Ohio, July 22, 1947; admitted to bar, 1994, Illinois and U.S. District Court, Northern District of Illinois; 1999, U.S. Court of Appeals, Sixth Circuit. *Education:* College of Mount St. Joseph on the Ohio (B.A., 1969); University of Chicago (M.A., 1972); Chicago-Kent College of Law (J.D., cum laude, 1994). Author, "Bleakhouse Then And Now," Illinois Bar Journal, 1996. ***PRACTICE AREAS:*** Environmental; Litigation; Antitrust; Securities; Employment. ***Email:*** rocawich@aol.com

ALEJANDRO DE EGUREN SANTISTEBAN, born Bilbao, Spain, April 21, 1956; admitted to bar, 1980, Spain (Not admitted in United States). *Education:* University of Deusto (J.D., 1980). Law Clerk, Military Court, 1980. Certified: Urban Planning, Instituto de Estudios Urbanisticos de Madrid, 1984; Commercial Society, Universidad de Navarra, 1990; Accountant and Economic Financial Analyst, Escuela Superior de Investigaciones y Técnicas Empresariales, 1992. Professor: Labor and Employment, Escuela de Formación Profesional - Academia San Luis de Bilbao, 1984; Civil, Commercial and Administrative Law, Centro de Estudios San Agustín (Bilbao). ***LANGUAGES:*** Spanish and French. ***PRACTICE AREAS:*** Commercial Law; Civil Law; Franchise Law; Administrative; Labor and Employment Law; National and International Franchise Law.

JOSÉ ANTONIO RODRÍGUEZ MARQUEZ, born Mexico City, Mexico, October 27, 1955; admitted to bar, 1978, Mexico (Federal and Local) (Not admitted in United States). *Education:* Amado Nervo University, Mexico (B.A., 1974); Universidad Nacional Autonoma de Mexico (J.D., magna cum laude, 1978); Pacific Western University (Ph.D. with Honors in International Business and Commerce).

BERNARD LAURENT, born Frameries, Belgium, September 21, 1962; admitted to bar, 1990, Belgium (Not admitted in United States) (Not admitted in Illinois). *Education:* Athenes Royal de Mons, Mons, Belgium; Faculte de Droit, Universite Catholique de Louvain, Louvain-La-Neuve, Belgium (Law, 1988). (Also practicing individually, Brussels, Belgium). ***PRACTICE AREAS:*** Contracts; Commercial Contracts; International Civil Practice.

JAMES GODWILL ISSA, born Accra, Ghana, July 14, 1964; admitted to bar, 1993, Ghana (Not admitted in the United States). *Education:* University of Ghana (B.A., honors, 1989); Ghana School of Law (J.D., 1995). ***LANGUAGES:*** French, Trui.

JULIE Y. LI, admitted to bar, 1995, Illinois. *Education:* Chinese University of Political Science and Law, Beijing, China (LL.B., 1984; LL.M., 1986); Washington University School of Law (J.D., 1994). Law Clerk, People's Appellate Court of Tangshan City, China, 1983. Assistant Law Professor, Central Institute for Nationalities, Beijing, China, 1986-1990. Associate, Susman & Associates. ***LANGUAGES:*** Chinese and Japanese.

JULIAN TORRES, born Yquitos, Peru, October 14, 1941; admitted to bar, 1966, Peru (Not admitted in United States) (Not admitted in Illinois). *Education:* University "Mayor De San Marcos" Lima, Peru (J.D., 1965); Diplomatic Career School for Graduates (1967). ***PRACTICE AREAS:*** Commercial Law; International Law.

Languages: English, Spanish, Portuguese, French, German, Polish.

Representative Clients and References upon request.

SUSMAN, WATKINS & WYLIE, LLP

Established in 1987

TWO FIRST NATIONAL PLAZA
20 SOUTH CLARK STREET, SUITE 600
CHICAGO, ILLINOIS 60603
Telephone: 312-346-3466
FAX: 312-346-2829
Email: chuckwatkins@ameritech.net

Securities, Corporate, Antitrust, Pension, Commodities, Antitrust and Class Action Litigation. General Civil and Trial Practice. Business and Corporation Law.

FIRM PROFILE: Susman, Watkins & Wylie, LLP represents individuals and businesses in securities, pension, consumer, antitrust, constitutional and related class action suits.

ARTHUR T. SUSMAN, born Chicago, Illinois, March 19, 1934; admitted to bar, 1958, Illinois; 1971, U.S. Supreme Court. *Education:* University of Illinois (B.S., with University honors, 1955); Northwestern University (J.D., 1958). Order of the Coif. Member, Board of Editors, Northwestern University Law Review, 1956-1958. ***PRACTICE AREAS:*** Securities; Corporate; Antitrust; Class Action; Business Law; Pension Litigation. ***Email:*** asusman@ameritech.net

CHARLES R. WATKINS, born Wichita, Kansas, November 2, 1953; admitted to bar, 1979, Illinois; 1981, Michigan. *Education:* Michigan State University (B.A., with high honors, 1975); University of Michigan (J.D., cum laude, 1978). Law Clerk to the Hon. John Feikens, Judge, U.S. District Court, Eastern District of Michigan, Detroit, Michigan, 1978-1979. ***PRACTICE AREAS:*** Securities; Corporate; Antitrust; Pension; Class Action; Business Law. ***Email:*** chuckwatkins@ameritech.net

JOHN R. WYLIE, born Chicago, Illinois, May 3, 1954; admitted to bar, 1984, California; 1985, Illinois. *Education:* Lawrence University (B.A., cum laude, 1977); University of California at Los Angeles School of Law (J.D., 1984). Law Clerk to the Honorable Joan Dempsey Klein, Chief Judge, California Court of Appeals, Second District, Los Angeles, California, 1983. *Member:* Chicago Bar Association; State Bar of California. ***PRACTICE AREAS:*** Class Actions; Securities; Antitrust; Pension; Constitutional Law; Tax Law. ***Email:*** johnwylie@ameritech.net

ASSOCIATES

MATTHEW T. HEFFNER, born Elkhart, Indiana, December 14, 1971; admitted to bar, 1997, Texas; 1999, Illinois. *Education:* Indiana University (B.A., with honors, 1994); University of Texas at Austin (J.D., 1997). *Member:* Chicago Bar Association; State Bar of Texas; Illinois Trial Lawyers Association. ***PRACTICE AREAS:*** Class Actions; Securities; Pension Litigation; Antitrust; Business Litigation. ***Email:*** mattheffner@ameritech.net

MATTHEW T. HURST, born Baltimore, Maryland, February 25, 1973; admitted to bar, 1999, Illinois. *Education:* Skidmore College (B.A., summa cum laude, 1995); Northwestern University (J.D., 1999). Extern to the Honorable Blanche Manning, Judge, U.S. District Court, Northern District of Illinois, 1997. *Member:* Chicago and American Bar Associations. ***PRACTICE AREAS:*** Class Action Litigation; Securities; Pension Plans; Antitrust; Business Litigation. ***Email:*** matthurst@ameritech.net

(This Listing Continued)

OF COUNSEL

WILLIAM T. GOTFRYD, born Chicago, Illinois, October 5, 1955; admitted to bar, 1980, Illinois and U.S. District Court, Northern District of Illinois. *Education:* Loyola University of Chicago (B.S., 1977; J.D., 1980). Member, Loyola Law Review. ***PRACTICE AREAS:*** Antitrust; Class Actions; Business Law. ***Email:*** wtglawproj@aol.com

LEGAL SUPPORT PERSONNEL

SANDRA PAVLAT
JULIE DIAZ
KATE KAMPHAUSEN
BARBARA DALLACOSTA
JORGE GALVAN

SWANSON, MARTIN & BELL

Established in 1992

330 NORTH WABASH
SUITE 3300
CHICAGO, ILLINOIS 60611
Telephone: 312-321-9100
Fax: 312-321-0990
URL: http://www.smbtrials.com

DuPage County, Illinois Office: 2525 Cabot Drive, Lisle, Illinois, 60532. Telephone: 630-799-6900. Fax: 630-799-6901.

Lake County, Illinois Office: 1860 West Winchester Road, Suite 201, Libertyville, Illinois, 60048. Telephone: 847-949-0025. Fax: 847-247-0555.

Waukegan, Illinois, Satellite Office: 415 Washington Street, Suite 1B, Waukegan, Illinois, 60085. Telephone: 847-949-0025. Fax: 847-247-0555.

Asbestos Litigation, Class Action Lawsuits, Commercial Litigation, Construction Litigation/ Disputes, Consumer and Warranty Law, Creditor's Rights, Drugs & Medical Devices, Employment Litigation, Environmental Law, Equipment Leasing, General Tort Liability, Healthcare, Insurance Coverage, Intellectual Property, Medical Negligence, Municipal Law, Product Liability, Professional Negligence, Real Estate Development/Zoning, Real Estate Litigation, Toxic and Mass Tort Litigation and White Collar Criminal Defense.

FIRM PROFILE: Swanson, Martin & Bell was founded in 1992 by a group of trial lawyers who left a large Chicago firm to better serve the needs of their clients. The firm is dedicated to resolving contested matters -- by trial, if necessary.

Jury trial experience is the hallmark of Swanson, Martin & Bell, a nationally-recognized litigation firm. Lawyers with the firm have tried hundreds of cases to verdict in a wide variety of commercial, equitable and casualty disputes in state and federal courts throughout the United States. As a result of the success the firm has enjoyed at trial, many Fortune 500 companies and prestigious institutions retain Swanson, Martin & Bell to handle their legal matters. The lawyers of the firm also serve as National Coordinating and Trial Counsel for numerous clients in complex product liability and mass tort litigation.

Because of the firm's size, efficiency and focus, Swanson, Martin & Bell is able to provide the highest quality of legal services at hourly rates lower than those offered by other, larger Chicago firms.

PARTNERS

BRIAN W. BELL, born Chicago, Illinois, March 13, 1952; admitted to bar, 1977, Illinois and Indiana. *Education:* Indiana University (B.A. 1974); Indiana University at Indianapolis (J.D., magna cum laude, 1977). Managing Editor, Indiana Law Review, 1976-1977. *Member:* Illinois State, Indiana State and American Bar Associations; Chicago Society of Trial Lawyers: Defense Research Institute; Product Liability Advisory Council. ***PRACTICE AREAS:*** Commercial Litigation; Products Liability; Professional Negligence. ***Email:*** bbell@smbtrials.com

STANLEY V. BOYCHUCK, born Chicago, Illinois, July 15, 1951; admitted to bar, 1979, Illinois, U.S. District Court, Northern District of Illinois, including Trial Bar, U.S. District Court, Eastern and Central Districts of Michigan and U.S. Court of Appeals, Sixth and Seventh Circuits. *Education:* Loyola University (B.A., 1973); John Marshall Law School (J.D., with distinction, 1979). Executive Editor, John Marshall Law Review, 1978-1979. Member: Blue Key National Honor Society; Order of John Marshall. Fellow: American College of Trial Lawyers. *Member:* Illinois State and American (Member, Section on Litigation) Bar Associations; American Board of Trial Advocates; American Trial Lawyers Association; Product Liability Advisory Council; Defense Research Institute (Member, Product Liability and Trial Practice Groups); Association for the Advancement of Automotive Medicine. [With USMC, 1973-1975; Capt., USMCR]. ***PRACTICE AREAS:*** Products Liability; Personal Injury; Negligence; Civil Litigation. ***Email:*** sboychuc@smbtrials.com

KEVIN V. BOYLE, born Evanston, Illinois, January 20, 1967; admitted to bar, 1992, Illinois and U.S. District Court, Northern District of Illinois. *Education:* University of Notre Dame (B.A., 1989); John Marshall Law School (J.D., 1992). Staff Editor, John Marshall Law Review, 1990-1992. *Member:* Illinois State Bar Association; Illinois Association of Defense Trial Counsel and Defense Research Institute. ***PRACTICE AREAS:*** Product Liability; Professional Liability; Commercial Litigation. ***Email:*** kboyle@smbtrials.com

MARGARET O. BYRNE, born Chicago, Illinois, October 11, 1962; admitted to bar, 1989, Illinois and U.S. District Court, Northern District of Illinois. *Education:* Roosevelt University (B.S.B.A., 1986); DePaul University College of Law (J.D., 1989). Editor, Journal of Health and Hospital Law, 1988-1989. ***PRACTICE AREAS:*** Asbestos Litigation; Toxic Tort Litigation; Products Liability; Premises Liability. ***Email:*** mbyrne@smbtrials.com

(This Listing Continued)

DAVID J. CAHILL, born Chicago, Illinois, August 5, 1955; admitted to bar, 1981, Illinois. *Education:* University of Illinois (B.A., magna cum laude, 1977); Illinois Institute of Technology/Chicago-Kent College of Law (J.D., with high honors, 1981). Phi Beta Kappa; Phi Kappa Phi. (Resident, Lisle Office). ***PRACTICE AREAS:*** Insurance Coverage; Personal Injury; Litigation; Products Liability; Medical Malpractice. ***Email:*** dcahill@smbtrials.com

STEVEN E. DANEKAS, born Rochelle, Illinois, November 7, 1955; admitted to bar, 1981, Illinois and U.S. District Court, Northern District of Illinois; 1982, U.S. Claims Court; 1984, U.S. Court of Appeals, Seventh Circuit; 1993, U.S. Court of Appeals, Fifth Circuit; 1996, U.S. Court of Appeals, Third and Eleventh Circuits; 2000, U.S. Court of Appeals, Eighth Circuit. *Education:* Northern Illinois University (B.S., magna cum laude, University Honors, 1977); University of Illinois (J.D., cum laude, 1981). Phi Kappa Phi. ***PRACTICE AREAS:*** Product Liability; Trial; Medical Malpractice Defense; Commercial Litigation; National Litigation. ***Email:*** sdanekas@smbtrials.com

P. STEPHEN FARDY, born Fullerton, California, July 10, 1969; admitted to bar, 1994, Indiana and U.S. District Court, Northern and Southern Districts of Indiana; 1996, Illinois and U.S. District Court, Northern District of Illinois. *Education:* Indiana University (B.A., with honors, 1991; J.D., 1994); John Marshall Law School-Center for Intellectual Property (LL.M., with honors, Intellectual Property, 2001). Member: Jessup International Moot Court Team, 1992-1994; Chicago Bar Association Moot Court Team, 1993-1994. Author, "Feet of Clay: How the Right of Publicity Exception Undermines Copyright Act Preemption," 12 Tex. Intell. Prop. L.J. 444 (2004). *Member:* Illinois State and Indiana State Bar Associations; Defense Research Institute; Intellectual Property Law Association of Chicago. ***PRACTICE AREAS:*** Commercial Litigation; Intellectual Property Transactions and Litigation; Products Liability. ***Email:*** sfardy@smbtrials.com

GEORGE F. FITZPATRICK, JR., born Elizabeth, New Jersey, March 30, 1954; admitted to bar, 1983, Illinois, U.S. District Court, Northern District of Illinois, including Trial Bar, U.S. District Court, Northern District of Indiana, U.S. Court of Appeals, 6th, 7th and 8th Circuits and the Supreme Court of the United States of America. *Education:* Purdue University (B.A., 1976); DePaul University (J.D., 1983). Executive Editor, De Paul Law Review, 1982-1983. Legislative Assistant and Federal Projects Coordinator, U.S. Congressman Adam Benjamin, Jr., lst District of Indiana, 1976-1980. *Member:* Chicago, Illinois State and American Bar Associations; Defense Research Institute; National Forum for Environmental and Toxic Tort Issues. ***PRACTICE AREAS:*** Products Liability; Environmental Law; Toxic Torts; Asbestos Litigation; Real Estate; Commercial Litigation; Construction Litigation; Lease Law; Transportation Law. ***Email:*** gfitzpat@smbtrials.com

ROBERT E. HALEY, born Chicago, Illinois, August 7, 1946; admitted to bar, 1972, Illinois, U.S. District Court, Northern and Central Districts of Illinois, U.S. District Court, Northern District of Indiana, U.S. Court of Appeals, Seventh Circuit and U.S. Supreme Court. *Education:* Loyola University (B.A., 1968); Northwestern University (J.D., cum laude, 1972). *Member:* Illinois State and American (Vice-Chair, ABA Committee on Automobile Law, 1995-1996) Bar Associations; Defense Research Institute. ***PRACTICE AREAS:*** Products Liability; Asbestos Defense; Personal Injury Defense; Aviation; Commercial Litigation. ***Email:*** rhaley@smbtrials.com

ELIZABETH SCHROER HARVEY, born Rockford, Illinois; admitted to bar, 1986, Illinois; 1990, U.S. District Court, Northern District of Illinois; 1995, U.S. District Court, Central and Southern Districts of Illinois; 2003. U.S. District Court, Northern District of Indiana. *Education:* University of Iowa (B.A., 1982); Southern Illinois University (J.D., 1986). Author: "Survey of Illinois Law: Environmental Law," S. Ill. U.L.J. 791, 1994; "Liability Issues in Private RCRA Suits Over Leaking Underground Storage Tank," 30 Chemical Waste Litigation Reporter 691, September, 1995. Attorney, Illinois Pollution Control Board, 1987-1994; Attorney Illinois Supreme Court, 1986-1987. *Member:* Chicago (Chairman, Practice & Procedure Subcommittee of Environmental Law Committee, 1989-1990) and Illinois State Bar Associations; Environmental Law Institute. ***PRACTICE AREAS:*** Environmental Law; Corporate Litigation; OSHA; Regulatory Law. ***Email:*** eharvey@smbtrials.com

LAWRENCE HELMS, born Martinsville, Virginia, October 7, 1951; admitted to bar, 1978, Illinois. *Education:* College of William & Mary (B.A., 1974); University of Virginia (J.D., 1978). Phi Beta Kappa; Order of the Coif. *Member:* Illinois State and American Bar Associations; Defense Research Institute; Illinois Association of Defense Trial Counsel. ***PRACTICE AREAS:*** Medical Malpractice Defense; Products Liability Defense; Health Care Law. ***Email:*** lhelms@smbtrials.com

MATTHEW D. JACOBSON, born Iowa City, Iowa, February 17, 1968; admitted to bar, 1993, Illinois and U.S. District Court, Northern District of Illinois. *Education:* University of Iowa (B.S., 1990; J.D., 1993). *Member:* DuPage County, Illinois State and American Bar Associations; Defense Research Institute. (Resident, Lisle Office). ***PRACTICE AREAS:*** Products Liability; Medical Malpractice; Commercial Litigation; Insurance Defense; Insurance Coverage. ***Email:*** mjacobso@smbtrials.com

DAVID E. KAWALA, born Evanston, Illinois, August 26, 1960; admitted to bar, 1985, Illinois, U.S. District Court, Northern and Central Districts of Illinois and U.S. Court of Appeals, Seventh Circuit. *Education:* Northwestern University (B.A., 1982); University of Illinois (J.D., 1985). Member, National Moot Court Team. Member, University of Illinois Law Review. *Member:* Chicago, Illinois State and American Bar Associations; Defense Research Institute (Member, Trucking Law Committee). ***PRACTICE AREAS:*** Product Liability; Transportation; Toxic Torts; Environmental Law; Insurance Defense; Legal Malpractice. ***Email:*** dkawala@smbtrials.com

JOSEPH P. KINCAID, born Midland, Michigan, December 11, 1961; admitted to bar, 1990, Illinois. *Education:* Illinois Wesleyan University (B.A., cum laude, 1984); Loyola University School of Law (J.D., 1989). Author: "Impact of Comparative Negligence Principles on Settlements in Multiple Defendant Cases," IICLE, February 19, 1990; "Obtaining Medical Evidence," IICLE, September, 1990; "The Personal Injury Paralegal in Illinois," IPE, 1998. Member, United Association of Equipment Leasing. *Member:* American Bar Association; Professional Liability Underwriting Society. ***PRACTICE AREAS:*** Commercial Litigation; Insurance Defense; Products Liability; Lease Law; Medical Malpractice. ***Email:*** jkincaid@smbtrials.com

PATRICIA S. KOCOUR, born Chicago, Illinois, August 30, 1966; admitted to bar, 1991, Illinois. *Education:* University of Illinois (B.S., 1988); University of Bath, England;

(This Listing Continued)

SWANSON, MARTIN & BELL, Chicago—Continued

Chicago-Kent College of Law (J.D., 1991). *Member:* Chicago, Illinois State and American Bar Associations; Defense Research Institute. ***PRACTICE AREAS:*** Medical Malpractice; Product Liability; Insurance Defense; Commercial Litigation. ***Email:*** pkocour@smbtrials.com

A. JAY KOEHLER, III, born Oak Lawn, Illinois, October 20, 1966; admitted to bar, 1991, Illinois; 1997, U.S. Court of Appeals, Seventh and Eighth Circuits. *Education:* Morehead State University (B.A., cum laude, 1988); John Marshall Law School (J.D., cum laude, 1991). Executive Editor, The John Marshall Law Review, 1990-1991. ***PRACTICE AREAS:*** Commercial Litigation; Products Liability; Construction Litigation; Insurance Defense. ***Email:*** jkoehler@smbtrials.com

STEVEN L. LARSON, born Elgin, Illinois, December 31, 1952; admitted to bar, 1977, Illinois and U.S. District Court, Northern District of Illinois. *Education:* University of Illinois (B.A., 1973); Washington University (J.D., 1977). Associate Notes and Comments Editor, Washington University Law Quarterly, 1976-1977; Author, Comment, "Prohibition of Religious Snakehandling," Washingtom University Law Quarterly, Volume 1976, Number 2. *Member:* Lake County and Illinois State Bar Associations; Illinois Association of Defense Trial Counsel; American Board of Trial Advocates; Illinois Society of Trial Lawyers. ***PRACTICE AREAS:*** Insurance Industry; Product Liability; Medical Malpractice; Trial Practice; Recreational Products; Commercial Litigation. ***Email:*** slarson@smbtrials.com

MICHAEL J. MAHER, born Chicago, Illinois, January 15, 1957; admitted to bar, 1985, Illinois; 1986, Florida; 1989, California. *Education:* Northern Illinois University (B.A., magna cum laude, 1982; J.D., 1985). Author: "Lessons in L.U.S.T.: The Complete Story of Liability for Leaking Underground Storage Tanks," Northern Illinois University College of Law, Law Review, Summer 1996 Issue; "Liability Issues in Private RCRA Suits Over Leaking Underground Storage Tanks," *Chemical Waste Litigation Reporter,* September, 1995; " Common Law Liability for Leaking Underground Storage Tanks," Northern Illinois University College of Law, Law Review, Fall 1993 Issue; "Lesson in L.U.S.T. - Cleaning Up Leaking Underground Storage Tanks," Illinois Bar Journal, March 1993; "Tax Ruling Could Discourage Environmental Remedies," Chicago Daily Law Bulletin, October 22, 1992; "Leaking Underground Storage Tanks - Cleanup Responsibilities and the Illinois Reimbursement Fund," Northern Lights, August, 1992; "Conflict-of-Law Rules In Environmental Coverage Disputes," *The Environmental Claims Journal,*Autumn, 1990; "A Guide Through Illinois' Environmental Regulatory Maze," *Illinois Bar Journal,* January, 1990; "The Responsible Property Transfer Act-Ready Or Not," *DuPage County Bar Journal,*December, 1989; "The Illinois Pollution Control Board-What Are Your Options When The IEPA Comes Knocking," *Illinois Municipal Review,*November, 1989. Professor, Kent/IIT College of Law, 1989-2000. *Member:* Chicago, Illinois State and American Bar Associations;. [USMC, Communications/Code Breaking, 1975-1978]. ***PRACTICE AREAS:*** Environmental Law; Corporate Litigation; OSHA; Labor Law; Regulatory Compliance. ***Email:*** mmaher@smbtrials.com

KEVIN T. MARTIN, born Springfield, Illinois, March 31, 1940; admitted to bar, 1967, Illinois. *Education:* Loyola University (B.S., 1963); Illinois Institute of Technology/Chicago-Kent College of Law (J.D., 1967). Phi Delta Phi. Recipient, Distinguished Service Award, Chicago Kent Board of Overseers, 1989. Member, Chicago-Kent Law Review, 1965-1967. President, Student Bar Association, 1966-1967. President, Chicago-Kent Alumni Association, 1985-1986. Member, Chicago-Kent Board of Overseers, 1986-1999. Author and Lecturer, *Medical Evidence,* IICLE, 1989. *Member:* Chicago (Member, Medical Legal Committee, 1980-1981) and Illinois State (Member, General Assembly, 1982-1987; Member: Council, Civil Practice and Procedures Section, 1982-1986, 1989-1994; Sections on: Torts; Civil Practice; Health Care; I.P.) Bar Associations; Institute For Public Affairs (Member, Board of Trustees, 1983-1986); American Board of Trial Advocates (National Board of Directors, 1993—); Trial Lawyers Club of Chicago (President, 1976-1977); Society of Trial Lawyers. Fellow, American College of Trial Lawyers. ***PRACTICE AREAS:*** Professional Liability; Products Liability; Medical Malpractice; Employment; Commercial Litigation; Toxic Torts; Consumer Fraud; Class Actions; Intellectual Property Litigation. ***Email:*** kmartin@smbtrials.com

ROBERT J. MEYER, born Chicago, Illinois, April 18, 1952; admitted to bar, 1987, Illinois and U.S. District Court, Northern District of Illinois; 1989, U.S. District Court, Central District of Illinois. *Education:* DePaul University (B.A., with honors, 1975; J.D., with honors, 1987). *Member:* Chicago, Illinois State and American Bar Associations; Illinois Trial Lawyers Association. ***PRACTICE AREAS:*** Medical Malpractice; Products Liability; Asbestos Litigation; Insurance Defense; Environmental Law; Real Estate; Intellectual Property. ***Email:*** rmeyer@smbtrials.com

TIMOTHY G. NICKELS, born Yokohama, Japan, October 7, 1957; admitted to bar, 1982, Illinois and U.S. District Court, Northern District of Illinois; 1986, U.S. Supreme Court. *Education:* University of Notre Dame (B.A., 1979; J.D., 1982). Member, National Moot Court Team. Recipient of A. Harold Weber Moot Court and William T. Kirby Awards, 1982. Co-author: with D.R. Carlson and R.J. Street, "A Model Antitrust Policy for College and Universities," Journal of Student Financial Aid, Vol. 22, No. 1 (Winter, 1992). Vice President - Development, Chicago Volunteer Legal Services Foundation. *Member:* Chicago (Member: Board of Managers; Nominating, Judicial Evaluation Committees), Illinois State and American (Member, Sections on: Litigation; Tort and Insurance Practice; Criminal Justice) Bar Associations; Notre Dame Law Association. ***PRACTICE AREAS:*** Medical Malpractice; Commercial Litigation; Product Liability; Toxic Torts; Trial; Criminal. ***Email:*** tnickels@smbtrials.com

JODY L. PABST, born Boston, Massachusetts, October 21, 1965; admitted to bar, 1993, Wisconsin and Illinois. *Education:* Vassar College (A.B., 1987); University of Wisconsin (J.D., 1993). Member and Note and Comment Editor, Wisconsin Law Review. *Member:* Defense Research Institute (Member: Medical Liability Committee; Medical Device Committee); American Association of Hospital Attorneys. ***PRACTICE AREAS:*** Civil Litigation; Professional Liability; Medical Negligence; Products Liability. ***Email:*** jpabst@smbtrials.com

DAVID F. PARDYS, born Chicago, Illinois, September 1, 1957; admitted to bar, 1982, Illinois and U.S. District Court, Northern District of Illinois; 1986, U.S. Court of Appeals,

(This Listing Continued)

Seventh Circuit and U.S. District Court, Eastern District of Wisconsin, U.S. District Court, Southern District of Indiana. *Education:* University of Illinois (B.A., 1979); IIT/Chicago Kent College of Law (J.D., with honors, 1982). *Member:* Lake County Bar Association. ***PRACTICE AREAS:*** Appellate; Health Care; Insurance Industry; Municipal; Product Liability; Trial. ***Email:*** dpardys@smbtrials.com

KAY L. SCHICHTEL, born Traverse City, Michigan, January 9, 1949; admitted to bar, 1974, Illinois. *Education:* Kalamazoo College (B.A., 1971); University of Chicago (J.D., 1974). Phi Beta Kappa. Member: Hinton Moot Court Managing Board; Osgoode Hall Moot Court Competition. Fellow, American College of Trial Lawyers. *Member:* Chicago, Illinois State and American Bar Associations; Defense Research Institute; Trial Lawyers Club of Chicago and Society of Trial Lawyers. ***PRACTICE AREAS:*** Products Liability Defense; Drugs and Medical Devices; Medical Malpractice. ***Email:*** kschicht@smbtrials.com

PETER G. SKIKO, born Poughkeepsie, New York, July 22, 1967; admitted to bar, 1992, Illinois. *Education:* University of Notre Dame (B.A., 1989; J.D., 1992). Eli Shaheen Fellowship. Journal of College and University Law, 1991. *Member:* Defense Research Institute. ***REPORTED CASES:*** 2003 U.S. Dist. Lexis, 14750. ***PRACTICE AREAS:*** Products Liability; Insurance Coverage; Insurance Defense; Construction Litigation. ***Email:*** pskiko@smbtrials.com

LINDA E. SPRING, born Bellefonte, Pennsylvania, September 17, 1945; admitted to bar, 1983, Illinois. *Education:* University of Minnesota (B.S., 1967; M.S., 1970); Loyola University (J.D., 1983). Law Clerk to Appellate Court Justice Hon. Glenn K. Seidenfeld, 1983-1984. *Member:* Lake County, Illinois State and American Bar Associations; Association of Women Attorneys of Lake County; Appellate Lawyers Association. ***PRACTICE AREAS:*** Medical Malpractice; Trial Practice; Appellate Practice; Governmental. ***Email:*** lspring@smbtrials.com

JOSEPH P. SWITZER, born Washington, D.C., July 29, 1955; admitted to bar, 1980, Illinois; U.S. District Court, Northern District of Illinois including Trial Bar. *Education:* University of Illinois (B.S., 1977; J.D., cum laude, 1980). Instructor, Business Administration 200, University of Illinois, College of Commerce, 1979-1980. *Member:* Chicago and Illinois State Bar Associations; Society of Trial Lawyers; American Board of Trial Advocates. ***PRACTICE AREAS:*** Product Liability; Medical Malpractice; Insurance Defense. ***Email:*** jswitzer@smbtrials.com

BRUCE S. TERLEP, born Elkhart, Indiana, October 29, 1958; admitted to bar, 1985, Illinois and U.S. District Court, Northern District of Illinois. *Education:* DePauw University (B.A., magna cum laude, 1981); University of Notre Dame (J.D., 1985). Phi Beta Kappa. *Member:* Du Page County and Illinois State Bar Associations. (Resident, Lisle Office). ***PRACTICE AREAS:*** Civil Litigation; Product Liability; Consumer Law; Civil Fraud; Automobile Warranty Law; Insurance Defense. ***Email:*** bterlep@smbtrials.com

JOHN A. TERSELIC, born LaSalle, Illinois, September 29, 1967; admitted to bar, 1992, Illinois. *Education:* Southern Illinois University (B.A., 1989); DePaul University (J.D., 1992). Law Clerk to Senior Judge Kenneth R. Harkins, U.S. Court of Federal Claims, 1992-1993. *Member:* Chicago, Lake County and Illinois State Bar Associations; U.S. Court of Federal Claims Bar Association. (Waukegan Office). ***PRACTICE AREAS:*** Insurance Defense; Medical Malpractice Defense. ***Email:*** jterseli@smbtrials.com

WILLIAM B. WEILER, born Aurora, Illinois, September 9, 1963; admitted to bar, 1989, Illinois, U.S. District Court, Northern District of Illinois and U.S. Court of Appeals, Seventh Circuit. *Education:* University of Notre Dame (B.A., 1985); John Marshall Law School (J.D., with high honors, 1989). Author, "Griffin v. Wisconsin: Do State's Needs Warrant Such Strict Measures?" 21 J. Marshall L. Rev. 921, 1988. *Member:* DuPage County, Kane County, Illinois State and American Bar Associations; Illinois Association of Defense Trial Counsel. ***PRACTICE AREAS:*** Medical Liability; Professional Liability; Insurance Coverage; Tort Defense; Commercial Litigation. ***Email:*** bweiler@smbtrials.com

DALE G. WILLS, born Ardmore, Oklahoma, July 7, 1955; admitted to bar, 1982, Missouri; 1983, Illinois. *Education:* Millikin University (B.S., summa cum laude, 1977); University of Illinois (J.D., magna cum laude, 1982). Phi Kappa Phi; Order of the Coif. University of Illinois Law Review, 1981-1982. Author: "Waiver of the Work Product Immunity," No. 3, University of Illinois Law Review, 1981. *Member:* Illinois State Bar Association; The Missouri Bar; Defense Research Institute; Products Liability Advisory Counsel. ***PRACTICE AREAS:*** Products Liability; General Civil Litigation. ***Email:*** dwills@smbtrials.com

ASSOCIATES

JAMES ADAMSON, born Chicago, Illinois, November 29, 1967; admitted to bar, 1994, Illinois and U.S. District Court, Northern District of Illinois; 1995, U.S. Court of Appeals, 7th Circuit. *Education:* University of Illinois (B.A., 1989); Chicago-Kent College of Law, Illinois Institute of Technology (J.D., with honors, 1994). Arbitrator, Circuit Court of Cook County. *Member:* Illinois State Bar Association; Illinois Association of Defense Trial Counsel; Defense Research Institute. ***PRACTICE AREAS:*** Medical Malpractice Defense; Environmental Litigation; Commercial Litigation. ***Email:*** jadamson@smbtrials.com

JOHN P. ARRANZ, born New York, N.Y., September 2, 1978; admitted to bar, 2003, Wisconsin, Illinois and U.S. District Court, Northern District of Illinois; 2004, Indiana and U.S. District Court, Northern District of Indiana. *Education:* University of Wisconsin - Madison (B.A., 2000; J.D., 2003). Phi Alpha Delta. Managing Editor, Wisconsin Law Review, 2001-2003. Managing Editor, Wisconsin International Law Journal, 2001-2002. *Member:* State Bar of Wisconsin; Illinois State Bar Association. ***LANGUAGES:*** Spanish. ***PRACTICE AREAS:*** Litigation; Medical Malpractice; Environmental Law; Products Liability. ***Email:*** jarranz@smbtrials.com

ROSS W. BARTOLOTTA, born Evergreen Park, Illinois, October 24, 1969; admitted to bar, 1994 Illinois, and U.S. District Court, Northern District of Illinois. *Education:* University of Illinois at Urbana-Champaign (B.A., 1991); Northern Illinois University (J.D., 1994). Dean's List. *Member:* Kane County and DuPage County Bar Associations; Justinian Society of Italian-American Lawyers. ***PRACTICE AREAS:*** Insurance Defense; Insurance Coverage; Medical Malpractice; Automobile Warranty Law; Civil Litigation; Construction Litigation; Mold Litigation. ***Email:*** rbartolo@smbtrials.com

(This Listing Continued)

NICOLE L. BJORK, born Green Bay, Wisconsin, August 25, 1978; admitted to bar, 2004, Illinois. *Education:* University of Wisconsin-Madison (B.A., 2000); Rutgers University (J.D., 2004). *Member:* American Bar Association. ***Email:*** nbjork@smbtrials.com

ELIZABETH A. BRUER, born Pontiac, Illinois, August 25, 1977; admitted to bar, 2002, Illinois. *Education:* University of Illinois at Urbana-Champaign (B.S., 1999); Loyola University (J.D., 2002). ***PRACTICE AREAS:*** Litigation. ***Email:*** ebruer@smbtrials.com

PATRICIA E. CHARLES, born Las Cruces, New Mexico, December 16, 1972; admitted to bar, 1999, Illinois; 2000, U.S. District Court, Northern District of Illinois; 2001, U.S. District Court, Central District of Illinois and U.S. Court of Appeals, Seventh Circuit; 2002, U.S. District Court, Southern District of Illinois. *Education:* University of Texas at Austin (B.S., Government, 1995); Vanderbilt University (J.D., 1999). *Member:* Chicago, Illinois State and American Bar Associations. ***PRACTICE AREAS:*** Medical Malpractice; Professional Negligence; Products Liability; Commercial Litigation. ***Email:*** pcharles@smbtrials.com

LEANNE W. CONN, born Urbana, Illinois, August 8, 1979; admitted to bar, 2004, Illinois. *Education:* Southern Illinois University (B.S., 2000); John Marshall Law School (J.D., cum laude, 2004). *Member:* Chicago and American Bar Associations. ***PRACTICE AREAS:*** Civil Litigation. ***Email:*** lconn@smbtrials.com

LINDSY A. ELKINS, born Kokomo, Indiana, August 6, 1977; admitted to bar, 2003, Illinois and U.S. District Court, Northern District of Illinois; 2004, Indiana and U.S. District Court, Northern and Southern Districts of Indiana. *Education:* Ball State University (B.S., 1999); University of Notre Dame (J.D., cum laude, 2003). Member, Golden Key. Author, Note, "Five Foot Two with Eyes of Blue: Physical Profiling and the Prospect of Genetics-Based Criminal Justice System," 17 Notre Dame J.L. Ethics and Pub. Poly. 269 (2003). *Member:* American Bar Association; Defense Research Institute. ***PRACTICE AREAS:*** Asbestos Litigation; Premises Liability; Medical Malpractice; Products Liability. ***Email:*** lelkins@smbtrials.com

SUZANNE M. FITCH, born Elgin, Illinois, August 9, 1975; admitted to bar, 2001, Illinois; U.S. District Court, Northern District of Illinois. *Education:* University of Illinois Urbana-Champaign (B.S., 1998); Northern Illinois University (J.D., magna cum laude, 2001). Member, Northern Illinois University Mock Trial Team. Lead Articles Editor, Northern Illinois University Law Review. *Member:* DuPage, Chicago and Illinois State Bar Associations. (Resident, Lisle Office). ***PRACTICE AREAS:*** Tort Liability; Automotive Warranty Law; Civil Litigation; Products Liability; Municipal Law. ***Email:*** sfitch@smbtrials.com

MISTI H. FLOYD, born Jackson, Tennessee, January 21, 1977; admitted to bar, 2002, Illinois, U.S. District Court, Northern District of Illinois. *Education:* Austin Peay State University (B.S., 1999); Chicago-Kent College of Law (J.D., with honors, 2002). Moot Court Honor Society. *Member:* Chicago, Illinois State and American Bar Associations. ***PRACTICE AREAS:*** Medical Malpractice; Tort Defense. ***Email:*** mfloyd@smbtrials.com

MEREDITH A. GAFFKE, born Wheeling, Illinois, January 17, 1979; admitted to bar, 2004, Illinois. *Education:* University of Missouri (B.S., 2001); Chicago-Kent College of Law, Illinois Institute of Technology (J.D., 2004). President, Moot Court Honor Society, 2003-2004. ***Email:*** mgaffke@smbtrials.com

DAVID S. GOLES, born Melrose Park, Illinois, May 7, 1972; admitted to bar, 1998, Illinois. *Education:* American University (B.A., 1994); Northern Illinois University (J.D., cum laude, 1998). Member, Law Review Editorial Board. Author: Smith v. Fair Employment and Housing Commission: Religious Freedom and Anti-Discrimination Laws Square Off in the Landlord/Tenant Setting, Northern Illinois University Law Review Vol. 18, Issue Number 1. *Member:* Lake County and Illinois State Bar Associations; Christian Legal Society. ***PRACTICE AREAS:*** Civil Litigation; Municipal; General Practice. ***Email:*** dgoles@smbtrials.com

JOHN A. GOLLWITZER, born Chicago, Illinois, August 14, 1971; admitted to bar, 2004, Illinois. *Education:* University of Illinois (B.A., 2001; J.D., 2004). ***PRACTICE AREAS:*** Civil Litigation. ***Email:*** jgollwitzer@smbtrials.com

RICHARD L. HAAS, born Kettering, Ohio, June 15, 1969; admitted to bar, 2002, Illinois; 2004, U.S. District Court, Northern District of Illinois. *Education:* Elmhurst College (B.S., 1992); DePaul University (J.D., magna cum laude, 2002). ***PRACTICE AREAS:*** Asbestos Litigation; Medical Malpractice; Tort Defense. ***Email:*** rhaas@smbtrials.com

JULIE R. HALPERIN, born Chicago, Illinois, September 29; admitted to bar, 2000, Illinois. *Education:* University of Illinois (B.A., 1996); Loyola University (J.D., 1999). ***PRACTICE AREAS:*** Medical Malpractice Defense. ***Email:*** jhalperi@smbtrials.com

CRAIG A. JACOBSON, born Fridley, Minnesota, July 19, 1976; admitted to bar, 2002, Illinois. *Education:* University of Michigan (B.A., 1999); Depaul University College of Law (J.D., 2002). *Member:* Chicago and American Bar Associations. ***PRACTICE AREAS:*** Products Liability; Medical Malpractice; Construction Litigation; Premises Liability; Commercial Litigation. ***Email:*** cjacobson@smbtrials.com

McRAY JUDGE, II, born Rocky Mount, North Carolina, June 2, 1969; admitted to bar, 1994, Illinois, U.S. District Court, Northern District of Illinois; 2001, North Carolina. *Education:* University of Iowa (B.S., 1991); University of Arkansas (J.D., 1994). Cook County States Attorney Office, 1995-2003. ***PRACTICE AREAS:*** Asbestos Defense; Medical Malpractice Defense; Casualty Insurance Defense; Products Liability Defense; Premises Liability Defense; Tort and Commercial Litigation. ***Email:*** mjudge@smbtrials.com

ANGELA ROSE KARRAS, born Oak Brook, Illinois, February 10, 1975; admitted to bar, 2000, Illinois; 2001, Indiana and U.S. District Court, Northern District of Illinois and U.S. District Court, Northern and Southern Districts of Indiana, U.S. District Court, Western District of Wisconsin. *Education:* Northwestern University, Medill School of Journalism (B.S.J., 1997); Indiana University School of Law, Bloomington (J.D., 2000). Member, Order of the Barristers. Notes Editor, Federal Communications Law Journal, 1999-2000. Author: "The Driver's Privacy Protection Act: A Fork in the Information Access Road," 52 Fed. Comm. L. J. 125 (1999). President, 1998-2000, Indiana University Student Law Association. *Member:* Chicago, Hellenic, Indiana State, Illinois State and American (Delegate, Law Student Division, ABA House of Delegates, 1999-2000) Bar Associations. ***PRACTICE AREAS:*** Products Liability; Professional Liability; Commercial Litigation. ***Email:*** akarras@smbtrials.com

RICHARD J. KEATING, JR., born Chicago, Illinois, April 15, 1969; admitted to bar, 1995, Illinois; U.S. District Court, Northern, Central and Southern Districts of Illinois. *Education:* Indiana University (B.S., 1991); Chicago-Kent College of Law (J.D., 1995). Formerly with Cook County States Attorney Office, 1995-2004. ***PRACTICE AREAS:*** Product Liability; Medical Malpractice; Torts; Commercial Litigation; Premises Liability. ***Email:*** rkeating@smbtrials.com

MICHAEL R. KLOTZ, born Cincinnati, Ohio, August 31, 1976; admitted to bar, 2004, Illinois. *Education:* Indiana University (B.A., 1999; J.D., 2004). Winner, Sherman Minton Moot Court Competition. Member, Indiana Law Journal, 2002-2004. ***Email:*** mklotz@smbtrials.com

MICHONE J. KUHLMAN, born Ames, Iowa, September 26, 1967; admitted to bar, 1996, Illinois; U.S. District Court, Northern District of Illinois and U.S. District Court, Southern District of Indiana. *Education:* Iowa State University (B.S., 1989); Georgia State University, College of Law (J.D., 1996). (Resident, Libertyville and Waukegan Offices). ***PRACTICE AREAS:*** Insurance Defense; Medical Malpractice Defense; Corporate Law. ***Email:*** mkuhlman@smbtrials.com

JOSHUA E. LIEBMAN, born Chicago, Illinois, November 22, 1976; admitted to bar, 2004, Illinois. *Education:* Tulane University (B.A., 1998); Loyola University (J.D., magna cum laude, 2004). ***Email:*** jliebman@smbtrials.com

DAVID M. MARCO, born London, England, September 19, 1970; admitted to bar, 2000, Illinois and U.S. District Court, Northern District of Illinois; 2004, U.S. Court of Appeals, 7th Circuit. *Education:* University of Bolton, England (B.S., 1994); Chicago-Kent College of Law (J.D., 2000). ***PRACTICE AREAS:*** Premises Liability; Products Liability; Commercial Litigation; Consumer Fraud. ***Email:*** dmarco@smbtrials.com

STEVEN P. MIKUZIS, born Chicago, Illinois, December 11, 1975; admitted to bar, 2003, Illinois, U.S. District Court, Northern District of Illinois. *Education:* University of Illinois (B.Arch., 1999); Chicago-Kent College of Law (J.D., with honors, 2002). Phi Delta Phi. *Member:* Hellenic, Chicago and Illinois State Bar Associations. ***PRACTICE AREAS:*** Tort Litigation; Commercial Litigation; Products Liability; Legal Malpractice. ***Email:*** smikuzis@smbtrials.com

AMY R. MILLER, born Joliet, Illinois, August 5, 1974; admitted to bar, 1999, Illinois and U.S. District Court, Northern District of Illinois. *Education:* Millikin University (B.A., cum laude, 1996); University of Illinois College of Law (J.D., magna cum laude, 1999). Recipient, Rickert Award for Oral Advocacy, 1999. *Member:* DuPage County and Illinois State Bar Associations. (Resident, Lisle Office). ***PRACTICE AREAS:*** Insurance Coverage; Medical Malpractice; Warranty Law; Products Liability; Commercial Litigation. ***Email:*** amiller@smbtrials.com

ANTHONY J. MONACO, born Chicago, Illinois, January 8, 1975; admitted to bar, 2003, Illinois; U.S. District Court, Northern, Central and Southern Districts of Illinois. *Education:* Marquette University (B.S., 1997); DePaul University (J.D., 2000). *Member:* Chicago, Illinois State and American Bar Associations; Justinian Society of Lawyers; Defense Research Institute. ***PRACTICE AREAS:*** Commercial Litigation; Products Liability; Professional Malpractice. ***Email:*** amonaco@smbtrials.com

ABOSEDE O. ODUNSI, born Chicago, Illinois, April 21, 1974; admitted to bar, 2001, Illinois and Wisconsin. *Education:* University of Illinois (B.A., 1996); Pennsylvania State University (M.A., 1998); University of Wisconsin-Madison (J.D., 2001). ***PRACTICE AREAS:*** Civil Litigation. ***Email:*** aodunsi@smbtrials.com

JOY I. PADNOS, born Chicago, Illinois, June 15, 1974; admitted to bar, 2000, Illinois, U.S. District Court, Northern District of Illinois. *Education:* Pitzer College (B.A., 1996); John Marshall Law School (J.D., cum laude, 2000). (Resident, Waukegan and Libertyville Offices). ***PRACTICE AREAS:*** Civil Litigation; Municipal Law; Insurance Defense; General Practice. ***Email:*** jpadnos@smbtrials.com

LOUIS J. PHILLIPS, born Melrose Park, Illinois, January 1, 1974; admitted to bar, 2003, Illinois; U.S. District Court, Northern and Central Districts of Illinois. *Education:* University of Illinois (B.A., 1997); John Marshall Law School (J.D., cum laude, 2003). Student Publication Editor, John Marshall Law Review, 2002-2003. ***PRACTICE AREAS:*** Medical Malpractice Defense; Products Liability; Premises Liability; Commercial; Litigation. ***Email:*** lphillip@smbtrials.com

PETER A. POGUE, born Evanston, Illinois, August 12, 1967; admitted to bar, 1994, California; 1996, U.S. District Court, Northern District of California; 1999, Illinois; 2003, Indiana. *Education:* Purdue University (B.S., 1989); Golden Gate University (M.B.A./J.D., 1993). Experience: With the firm since 2001; Attorney with a California litigation firm, 1992-2000. ***PRACTICE AREAS:*** Products Liability; Asbestos Litigation; Commercial Litigation; Insurance Defense. ***Email:*** ppogue@smbtrials.com

ARTHUR J. RELIFORD, JR., born Northampton, Massachusetts, August 7, 1974; admitted to bar, 1999, Illinois, U.S. District Court, Northern District of Illinois. *Education:* Hamilton College (B.A., 1996); DePaul University College of Law (J.D., 1999). *Member:* Cook County, Illinois State and American Bar Associations; Defense Research Institute. ***PRACTICE AREAS:*** Products Liability; Medical Malpractice; Legal Malpractice; Commercial Litigation; Tort Defense. ***Email:*** areliford@smbtrials.com

DAVID J. RISKI, born Crestwood, Illinois, November 24, 1975; admitted to bar, 2000, Illinois; 2001, U.S. District Court, Northern District of Illinois; U.S. District Court, Eastern District of Michigan. *Education:* Northern Illinois University (B.S., 1997); DePaul University (J.D., 2000). (Resident, Lisle Office). ***PRACTICE AREAS:*** Civil Litigation; Warranty Law; Products Liability; Insurance Defense.

G. CHRISTOPHER SLICK, born Tulsa, Oklahoma, September 10, 1971; admitted to bar, 1997, Illinois; 1998, U.S. District Court, Northern District of Illinois; 2001, U.S. District Court, Southern District of Illinois; 2004, U.S. District Court, Central District of Illinois. *Education:* Baylor University (B.A., 1993); University of Notre Dame (J.D., 1997). *Member:* Chicago Bar Association; Federalist Society. ***LANGUAGES:*** German. ***Email:*** cslick@smbtrials.com

(This Listing Continued)

SWANSON, MARTIN & BELL, Chicago—Continued

ALLISON Z. SULLIVAN, born Chicago, Illinois, July 29, 1976; admitted to bar, 2002, Illinois; U.S. District Court, Northern District of Illinois. *Education:* University of Michigan (B.A., 1998); Chicago-Kent College of Law (J.D., 2001). ***PRACTICE AREAS:*** Medical Malpractice; Insurance Defense. ***Email:*** asullivan@smbtrials.com

CHRISTIAN A. SULLIVAN, born Urbana, Illinois, November 30, 1974; admitted to bar, 2002, Illinois and U.S. District Court, Northern District of Illinois. *Education:* University of Illinois, Urbana-Champaign (B.A., 1999); Northern Illinois University College of Law (J.D., magna cum laude, 2002). Research Editor, Northern Illinois University Law Review. Extern, Philip G. Reinhard, United States District Court, Western District Illinois. Author: "Juvenile Delinquency in the Twenty-First Century: Is Blended Sentencing the Middle-Road Solution for Today's Violent Kids?", 21 N. Ill. U.L. Rev. 483, 2001. *Member:* DuPage County, Chicago and Illinois State Bar Associations. (Resident, Lisle Office). ***PRACTICE AREAS:*** Automobile Warranty Law; Insurance Defense; Products Liability; Appellate Litigation; Medical Malpractice Defense. ***Email:*** csulliva@smbtrials.com

KELLY SULLIVAN, born Hickory Hills, Illinois, June 24, 1975; admitted to bar, 2000, Illinois. *Education:* Loyola University (B.S., 1997); Chicago-Kent College of Law (J.D., 2000). Moot Court Honor Society. ***PRACTICE AREAS:*** Medical Malpractice Defense; Products Liability Defense; Tort Defense. ***Email:*** ksulliva@smbtrials.com

AIJU C. THEVATHERIL, born Bhopal, India, November 12, 1973; admitted to bar, 1999, Illinois and U.S. District Court, Northern District of Illinois. *Education:* University of Illinois (B.S., 1996); DePaul University College of Law (J.D., 1999). *Member:* Chicago, Illinois State and American Bar Associations. ***PRACTICE AREAS:*** Medical Malpractice Defense; Products Liability; Insurance Defense; Premises Liability; Health Care Law. ***Email:*** athevath@smbtrials.com

ALAIN VILLENEUVE, born Montreal, Canada, March 21, 1967; admitted to bar, 2003, Illinois. *Education:* University of Montreal - Polytechnique (B.E., 1991); University of Illinois (J.D., 2003). ***PRACTICE AREAS:*** Intellectual Property; International Law; Product Liability; Immigration Law. ***Email:*** avilleneuve@smbtrials.com

CATHERINE BASQUE WEILER, born Milwaukee, Wisconsin, November 19, 1974; admitted to bar, 2000, Illinois and U.S. District Court, Northern District of Illinois; 2003, U.S. District Court, Central District of Illinois and U.S. Court of Appeals, 7th Circuit. *Education:* University of Notre Dame (B.A., 1997); Loyola University, Chicago (J.D., 2000). *Member:* Chicago Bar Association; Appellate Lawyers Association. ***REPORTED CASES:*** Fillmore v. Page, 358 F.3d 496 (7th Cir. 2004); Vogue Tyre & Tubber Co. v. Office of the State Fire Marshal, 820 N.E.2d 15 (1st Dist. 2004); Village of Bolingbrook v. Bolingbrook Firefighters' Association, 347 Ill. App. 3d 434, (3rd Dist. 2004); Tinder v. Illinois Department of Public Aid, 346 Ill. App. 3d 510, N.E.2d 677 (3rd Dist. 2004); Gilbert v. Illinois Department of Human Rights, 343 Ill. App. 3d 904 (1st Dist. 2003); Dahman v. Illinois Department of Human Rights, 334 Ill. App. 3d 660 (4th Dist. 2002). ***PRACTICE AREAS:*** Civil Litigation. ***Email:*** cweiler@smbtrials.com

ANDREW M. WEISBERG, born Chicago, Illinois, December 16, 1970; admitted to bar, 1996, Illinois. *Education:* University of Illinois (B.A., 1993); University of Missouri, Columbia (J.D., 1996). ***PRACTICE AREAS:*** Civil Litigation. ***Email:*** aweisberg@smbtrials.com

OF COUNSEL

LENARD C. SWANSON, born Oak Park, Illinois, April 5, 1937; admitted to bar, 1967, Illinois. *Education:* University of Illinois (B.S., 1963; J.D., 1967). Order of the Coif. *Member:* Du Page County, Illinois State and American Bar Associations; Society of Trial Lawyers; Illinois Defense Counsel; Defense Research Institute. Fellow, American College of Trial Lawyers; Product Liability Advisory Council. ***PRACTICE AREAS:*** Products Liability; Professional Liability; Medical Malpractice; Insurance Defense; Commercial Litigation. ***Email:*** lswanson@smbtrials.com

EDWARD T. BUTT, JR., born Chicago, Illinois, October 27, 1947; admitted to bar, 1971, Illinois; 1975, Wisconsin; 1997, Michigan; U.S. District Court, Northern District of Illinois including Trial Bar; U.S. Court of Appeals, Sixth and Seventh Circuits; U.S. Claims Court; U.S. District Court, Eastern District of Wisconsin. *Education:* Lawrence University (B.A., 1968); University of Michigan (J.D., 1971). Recipient, American Jurisprudence Book Award in Land Finance Law. *Member:* Seventh Circuit and American (Member, Sections on: Litigation; Tort and Insurance Practice) Bar Associations; State Bar of Wisconsin (Member, Litigation and Non-Resident Lawyers Section); Defense Research Institute (Products Liability and Insurance Coverage Sections); State Bar of Michigan. ***PRACTICE AREAS:*** Product Liability; Insurance Coverage. ***Email:*** etbjrpc@aol.com

JOHN J. O'SULLIVAN, born Chicago, Illinois, July 20, 1964; admitted to bar, 1994, Illinois. *Education:* University of Illinois (B.A., 1990); Louisiana State University (J.D., 1993). ***PRACTICE AREAS:*** Toxic Tort; Environmental; Futures; Securities. ***Email:*** josullivan@smbtrials.com

JOHN C. CHURCH, born Evanston, Illinois, September 21, 1946; admitted to bar, 1978, Illinois. *Education:* Bradley University (B.S., 1975); Chicago-Kent College of Law (J.D., 1978). Phi Kappa Phi; Pi Sigma Alpha. [U.S. Army, 1969-1971.]. ***PRACTICE AREAS:*** Litigation; Corporate; Antitrust. ***Email:*** jchurch@smbtrials.com

THOMAS J. KOCH, born Des Moines, Iowa, March 29, 1955; admitted to bar, 1984, Illinois; U.S. District Court, Northern District of Illinois including Trial Bar. *Education:* Loras College (B.A., cum laude, 1977); Chicago-Kent College of Law (J.D., with high honors, 1984). Phi Alpha Delta. Notes and Comments Editor, IIT/Chicago-Kent Law Review, 1983-1984. Legal Writing Assistant, Chicago-Kent, 1983-1984. *Member:* Illinois State and American Bar Associations. ***PRACTICE AREAS:*** Medical Malpractice Defense; Products Liability; Entertainment Law. ***Email:*** tkoch@smbtrials.com

SYREGELAS LAW OFFICES

SUITE 1800, 180 N. LA SALLE STREET
CHICAGO, ILLINOIS 60601-2604
Telephone: 312-855-0400
Fax: 312-855-0535
Email: ns@syregelaslaw.com
URL: http://www.syregelaslawoffices.com

Medical Malpractice, Personal Injury, Premises Liability, Automobile Accidents, Commercial Litigation, White Collar Criminal Law.

MEMBER OF FIRM

NICHOLAS C. SYREGELAS, born 1944; admitted to bar, 1978, Illinois; 1987, U.S. District Court, Northern District of Illinois including Trial Bar. *Education:* Southern Illinois University (B.A., 1968); Northern Illinois University (J.D., 1975). *Member:* Illinois State Bar Association; Illinois Trial Lawyers Association; Hellenic Bar Association; Association of Trial Lawyers of America. ***PRACTICE AREAS:*** Medical Malpractice; Personal Injury. ***Email:*** ns@syregelaslaw.com

TABET DIVITO & ROTHSTEIN LLC

THE ROOKERY BUILDING
209 SOUTH LA SALLE STREET, SEVENTH FLOOR
CHICAGO, ILLINOIS 60604
Telephone: 312-762-9450
Fax: 312-795-9801
URL: http://www.tdrlawfirm.com
URL: http://www.lawyers.com/tabetdivito&rothsteinllc

General Civil Trial Practice, Commercial Litigation, Corporate Litigation, Appellate Practice, Arbitration and Mediation, Class Actions, Antitrust and Unfair Competition, Commercial Real Estate Litigation, Intellectual Property Litigation, Professional Liability, Product Liability, Insurance/Reinsurance Coverage, Trade Secret Misappropriation, Executive Compensation and Employment Litigation, Civil RICO, Construction Litigation, Constitutional Law, Governmental Litigation, Banking Litigation, Corporate Investigation, False Claims Act and Qui Tam Litigation, Securities Litigation, Sports Law.

CAESAR A. TABET, born Chicago, Illinois, July 23, 1960; admitted to bar, 1987, Illinois, U.S. District Court, Northern District of Illinois, and U.S. Court of Appeals, Seventh Circuit; Federal Trial Bar, Northern District of Illinois. *Education:* St. John's University (B.A., with honors, 1982); University of Minnesota (J.D., with honors, 1987). Staff Member, 1985-1986 and Note and Comment Editor, 1986-1987, Minnesota Law Review. Law Clerk to Hon. John A. Nordberg, U.S. District Court, Northern District of Illinois, 1987-1988. Adjunct Faculty, Loyola University of Chicago Law School, Advanced Trial Practice. *Member:* Chicago, Illinois State and American Bar Associations. ***PRACTICE AREAS:*** General Civil Trial Practice; Commercial Litigation; Corporate Litigation; Constitutional Law; Intellectual Property Litigation. ***Email:*** ctabet@tdrlawfirm.com

GINO L. DIVITO, born Chicago, Illinois, July 24, 1937; admitted to bar, 1963, Illinois, U.S. Court of Appeals, Seventh Circuit and U.S. District Court, Northern District of Illinois. *Education:* Loyola University (J.D., 1963). Recipient: Medal of Excellence, Loyola University of Chicago School of Law, 1995; Award of Excellence in the Field of Law, St. Ignatius College Prep, 1997; Award of Excellence, Justinian Society of Lawyers, 1997; Board of Governor's Award, Illinois State Bar Association, 2000; Lifetime Achievement Award, Illinois Judges Association, 2002; Virgil Tipton Publication Award, Illinois State Bar Association, 1999; Certificate of Appreciation, Appellate Lawyers Association, 1998; Award of Appreciation, Illinois Judges Association, 1994; Honorary Certificate for Teaching Trial Advocacy, Willamette University College of Law, 1992. Author: *Illinois Sentencing and Disposition Guide,* Illinois State Bar Association, 2001; *Adapting to the Illinois Compiled Statutes,* Illinois State Bar Association, 1993; *Crimes and Punishment and Criminal Procedure,* Illinois State Bar Association and Illinois Press Association, 1993, 2001; *HJR CA 20: ISBA's Resolution for Merit Selection of Judges by Appointment,* Illinois Bar Journal, 1987; *Discovery and Preparation for Trial,* Illinois Institute for Continuing Legal Education, 1983. Allerton House Conference: Participant and Speaker on the topic of News Media and the Courts, 1996; Participant, on the topics of: Multidisciplinary Practice, 2000; Expert Witnesses, 1994; Appellate Review, 1990. Adjunct Professor, Advanced Trial Advocacy, Loyola University School of Law, 1979—. Instructor, Willamette Law School, Salem, Oregon, Trial Advocacy and Advanced Trial Advocacy, 1982—. Instructor: New Judges Seminar, 1986-2000; National Judicial College, 1990-1994. Member: National Institute of Trial Advocacy (NITA). Justice, Illinois Appellate Court, 1989-1997. Judge, Circuit Court of Cook County, 1977-1989. Cook County Assistant State's Attorney, 1963-1977 (Chief, Criminal Division, supervisor of 330 attorneys, 1974-1977). Co-founder, Judicial Dispute Resolution, Inc., Formed November 1, 1997. President: Illinois Judges Association, 1993-1994; Markey-Wigmore Inn of Court, 1992-1993; Appellate Lawyers Association of Illinois, 2002-2003. Chairman, American Judicature Society, Illinois State Chapter, 1999-2002. Member: Illinois Planning and Oversight Committee for a Judicial Evaluation Program, 1998—; Illinois Supreme Court Committee on Rules of Evidence, 1975-1979; Board of Directors, Appellate Lawyers Association of Illinois, 1997-2004; Board of Directors, Chicago Bar Foundation, 1994-1995; Board of Directors, Chicago Chapter, Association for Conflict Resolution (formerly Society of Professionals in Dispute Resolution), 1998—; Board of Directors, Lawyers Assistance Program, Inc., 1996-1998; Board of Directors, The John Howard Association, 1987-1990, 1997-2001; Executive Committee, Justinian Society of Lawyers, 1984-1986, 1992-1995; Subcommittee on Criminal Rules for the Rules Committee of the Supreme Court of Illinois, 1989-1997; Judicial Administration Task Force of the Illinois Supreme Court Special Commission on the Administration of Justice, 1992-1993; Governor's Task Force Steering Committee on Judicial Merit Selection, 1987-1988; Special Commission on the Administration of Justice in Cook County, 1984-1986; Illinois Supreme Court Committee to Study Supreme Court Rule 23, 2003—; American Judicature Society, 1985—. Facilitating Judge, Supreme Court Committee on Judicial Performance Evaluation, 1989-1997. *Member:* Chicago (Member, Board of Man-

(This Listing Continued)

agers, 1993-1995), Illinois State (Member, Board of Governors, 1984-1990) and American Bar Associations; Appellate Lawyers Association; Illinois Judges Association. ***PRACTICE AREAS:*** Civil Litigation; Criminal Litigation; Appellate Practice; Complex Litigation; Commercial Litigation; Professional Liability; Alternative Dispute Resolution. ***Email:*** gdivito@tdrlawfirm.com

MICHAEL I ROTHSTEIN, born Louisville, Kentucky, March 26, 1960; admitted to bar, 1987, Illinois and U.S. District Court, Northern District of Illinois; 1993, U.S. Court of Appeals, Seventh Circuit; 1999, U.S. Supreme Court; Federal Trial Bar, Northern District of Illinois. *Education:* Indiana University (B.S., 1982); Boston University School of Law (J.D., 1987). Edward F. Hennessey Scholar. Assistant Special Outside Counsel, U.S. House Committee on Standards of Official Conduct in the Matter of Speaker James C. Wright, 1988-1989. Certified Public Accountant, Illinois, 1983. *Member:* Chicago, Illinois State and American Bar Associations; Illinois Appellate Lawyers Association (Director and Chairman, Appellate Rules Committee). ***PRACTICE AREAS:*** General Civil Trial Practice; Commercial Litigation; Governmental Litigation; Constitutional Law; Appellate Practice; Class Actions; Unfair Competition; Insurance/Reinsurance Coverage; Trade Secret Misappropriation; Construction Litigation; Banking Litigation. ***Email:*** mrothstein@tdrlawfirm.com

GARY L. PRIOR, born Niagara Falls, New York, June 26, 1943; admitted to bar, 1968, Illinois; U.S. District Court, Northern District of Illinois; Federal Trial Bar, Northern District of Illinois; U.S. Court of Appeals, Federal, Seventh and Third Circuits; U.S. District Court, Eastern and Western Districts of Wisconsin; U.S. Supreme Court. *Education:* Tulane University (B.S., 1965); University of Chicago (J.D., 1968). *Member:* Illinois State Bar Association; Illinois Appellate Lawyers Association. ***PRACTICE AREAS:*** General Civil Trial Practice; Commercial Litigation; Corporate Litigation; Governmental Litigation; Appellate Practice; Arbitration; Mediation; Professional Liability; International Law; Securities Litigation; False Claims Act; Qui Tam Litigation. ***Email:*** gprior@tdrlawfirm.com

J. JEFFREY PATTON, born Zanesville, Ohio, 1966; admitted to bar, 1994, Illinois and U.S. District Court, Northern District of Illinois; Federal Trial Bar, Northern District of Illinois. *Education:* Miami University (B.Phil., summa cum laude, 1988); University of Sheffield, Sheffield, England (M.Phil., with distinction, 1991); Harvard University (J.D., 1994). Visiting Lecturer, Peking University Law School, Beijing, China, 2001. *Member:* Chicago, Illinois State and American Bar Associations. ***PRACTICE AREAS:*** General Civil Trial Practice; Commercial Litigation; Professional Liability; Arbitration; Mediation. ***Email:*** jpatton@tdrlawfirm.com

DEBORAH E. DECKER, born Milwaukee, Wisconsin, October 14, 1972; admitted to bar, 1998, Illinois and U.S. District Court, Northern District of Illinois; 1999, Wisconsin and U.S. Court of Appeals, Seventh and Federal Circuits; 2000, U.S. District Court, Southern District of Illinois; U.S. Supreme Court. *Education:* North Central College (B.A., summa cum laude, 1994); University of Wisconsin Law School (J.D., cum laude, 1998). Order of the Coif. Moot Court Board, 1996-1998, Executive Board Vice President-Events, 1997-1998. Recipient, CALI awards for Evidence, Trial Advocacy, Advanced Legal Writing. Wisconsin Law Review, 1996-1998, Managing Editor, 1997-1998. Author, "Consent Decrees and the Prison Litigation Reform Act of 1995," 1997 Wis. L. Rev. 1275. *Member:* Chicago, Illinois State and American Bar Associations. ***PRACTICE AREAS:*** General Civil Trial Practice; Commercial Litigation; Corporate Litigation; Intellectual Property Litigation; Appellate Practice; Employment Litigation. ***Email:*** ddecker@tdrlawfirm.com

KARINA H. DEHAYES, born Detroit, Michigan, August 19, 1973; admitted to bar, 1998, Illinois and U.S. District Court, Northern District of Illinois; U.S. Court of Appeals, Seventh Circuit; Federal Trial Bar, Northern District of Illinois. *Education:* University of Michigan (B.A., with distinction, 1995); Loyola University of Chicago School of Law (J.D., 1998). *Member:* Chicago, Illinois State and American Bar Associations; Women's Bar Association (Board Member, 2003-2005). ***LANGUAGES:*** Polish. ***PRACTICE AREAS:*** Commercial Litigation; Business Litigation; Appellate Practice. ***Email:*** kdehayes@tdrlawfirm.com

---

STEPHEN J. KEELEY, born Fairbury, Illinois, 1970; admitted to bar, 1999, Illinois and U.S. District Court, Northern District of Illinois. *Education:* University of Illinois (B.A., summa cum laude, 1992); University of Virginia (J.D., 1999). Member, University of Virginia Law Review. Law Clerk to Hon. Harry D. Leinenweber, Northern District of Illinois. *Member:* Chicago and Illinois State Bar Associations. ***LANGUAGES:*** Spanish. ***PRACTICE AREAS:*** General Civil Trial Practice; Commercial Litigation; Intellectual Property Litigation; Securities Litigation; Arbitration; Mediation; Appellate Practice. ***Email:*** skeeley@tdrlawfirm.com

MARK H. HORWITCH, born Highland Park, Illinois; admitted to bar, 2000 Illinois; U.S. Court of Appeals, Seventh Circuit; U.S. District Court, Northern District of Illinois; U.S. District Court, Eastern District of Wisconsin. *Education:* University of Illinois at Urbana-Champaign (B.A., cum laude, 1997; J.D., magna cum laude, 2000). Phi Beta Kappa. ***PRACTICE AREAS:*** Litigation; Labor and Employment.

MICHAEL J. GRANT, born Chicago, Illinois, September 29, 1975; admitted to bar, 2001, Illinois and U.S. District Court, Northern District of Illinois. *Education:* University of Dayton (B.A., 1997); Chicago-Kent College of Law (J.D., with honors, 2001). Law Clerk to Stephen A. Schiller, Circuit Ct. of Cook County, Illinois, Chancery Division. *Member:* Chicago and Illinois State Bar Associations. ***REPORTED CASES:*** Illinois RSA No. 3, Inc. (U.S. Cellular) v. Dept of Cent. Mgmt. Servs., 2004 WL 433724 (Ill. App. Ct. 2004); Levenfeld v. Boyd, 2003 WL 22532801 (N.D. Ill. 2003); Caveney v. Bower, 797 N.E.2d 596 (Ill. 2003). ***PRACTICE AREAS:*** Commercial Litigation. ***Email:*** mgrant@tdrlawfirm.com

DANIEL I. KONIECZNY, born Erie, Pennsylvania, January 13, 1976; admitted to bar, 2001, Illinois; U.S. District Court, Northern District of Illinois and U.S. District Court, Northern District of Indiana; registered to practice before U.S. Patent and Trademark Office. *Education:* Princeton University (A.B., magna cum laude, 1998); Harvard Law School (J.D., 2001). *Member:* Chicago, Illinois and American Bar Associations. ***PRACTICE AREAS:*** General Civil Trial Practice; Commercial Litigation; Intellectual Property Litigation; Professional Liability; Products Liability; Appellate Practice. ***Email:*** dkonieczny@tdrlawfirm.com

(This Listing Continued)

HENRY H. HESS, born Columbus, Ohio, November 22, 1972; admitted to bar, 2002, Illinois and Wisconsin. *Education:* The Ohio State University (B.A., 1991); University of Wisconsin Law School (J.D., cum laude, 2002). *Member:* Chicago and American Bar Associations. ***PRACTICE AREAS:*** Litigation.

MARY BETH WYNN, born Michigan, 1973; admitted to bar, 2002, Illinois and U.S. District Court, Northern District of Illinois. *Education:* Haverford College (B.A., 1995); University of Chicago (J.D., 2002). *Member:* Chicago, Illinois and American Bar Association. ***PRACTICE AREAS:*** General Civil Trial Practice; Commercial Litigation; Employment Litigation. ***Email:*** mwynnsmith@tdrlawfirm.com

REEMA KAPUR, born India, 1978; admitted to bar, 2004, Illinois. *Education:* University of Chicago (B.A., 2001); Loyola University, Chicago (J.D., cum laude, 2004). ***Email:*** rkapur@tdrlawfirm.com

RACHEL N. CRUZ, born Miami, Florida, August 11, 1979; admitted to bar, 2004, Virginia; 2005, District of Columbia (Not admitted in Illinois). *Education:* Brown University (B.A., 2001); George Washington University (J.D., 2004). *Member:* Virginia State Bar. ***LANGUAGES:*** Spanish. ***PRACTICE AREAS:*** Real Property and Asset Management; Liability Insurance Coverage. ***Email:*** rcruz@tdrlawfirm.com

---

TAMARI & BLUMENTHAL, LLC

980 N. MICHIGAN AVENUE, 14TH FLOOR
CHICAGO, ILLINOIS 60611
Telephone: 312-922-8900

Commercial Litigation, Consumer Litigation, Corporate Law, Personal Injury Litigation, Business Litigation, Landlord Tenant Litigation.

MEMBERS OF FIRM

WALID JOSEPH TAMARI, born October 18, 1972; admitted to bar, 1999, Illinois. *Education:* Boston University (B.S.B.A., 1990); Loyola University of Chicago (M.B.A., 1996); John Marshall Law School (J.D., 1999);. Member, Law Journal (Journal of Computer and Information Law). Vice-President, Graduate Business Association, Graduate School of Business. *Member:* The Association of Trial Lawyers of America. ***PRACTICE AREAS:*** Commercial Litigation (40%); Consumer Litigation (40%); Corporate Law (20%). ***Email:*** wtamari@tamblum.com

GRANT BLUMENTHAL, born Cape Town, South Africa, 1971; admitted to bar, 1996, Illinois and U.S. District Court, Northern District of Illinois. *Education:* Miami University (B.S., 1993); John Marshall Law School (J.D., 1996). Staff Editor, John Marshall Law Review. Moot Court. ***PRACTICE AREAS:*** Commercial Litigation; Consumer Litigation; Personal Injury; Business Litigation; Landlord and Tenant Law.

PAUL M. NAPOLSKI, born Berwyn, Illinois, 1974; admitted to bar, 2000, Illinois. *Education:* Regis University (B.S., 1996); John Marshall Law School (J.D., 1999). ***PRACTICE AREAS:*** Commercial Real Estate; Residential Real Estate; Estate Planning; Probate. ***Email:*** pnapolski@tamblum.com

OF COUNSEL

CHRISTOPHER T. CONSIDINE, born Chicago, Illinois, February 21, 1969; admitted to bar, 1999, Illinois. *Education:* Marquette University (B.A., 1991); Loyola University (J.D., cum laude, 1998; M.B.A., 1998). *Member:* Chicago and American Bar Associations. ***PRACTICE AREAS:*** Business Law (20%); Corporate Law (20%); Intellectual Property (20%); Mergers and Acquisitions (20%); Securities Law (20%). ***Email:*** cconsidine@tamblum.com

---

TARADJI LAW OFFICES

Established in 2001

SUITE 1310, 205 WEST RANDOLPH
CHICAGO, ILLINOIS 60606
Telephone: 312-252-5252; 782-3400
Fax: 312-252-5253
Email: ntpc@taradji.com
Email: nbt@taradji.com
URL: http://www.taradji.com

Personal Injury, Workers Compensation, Premises Liability, Automobile Accidents, Negligence, Products Liability, Construction Accidents, Dog Bites, Slip and Fall, Wrongful Death, Medical Malpractice, Tort Law and Civil, Commercial and Business Litigation. Libel and Slander, Contracts and Small Business Law.

FIRM PROFILE: Chicago personal injury law firm.

NIMA B. TARADJI, admitted to bar, 1998, Illinois. *Education:* Texas Tech University (B.A., 1987); John Marshall Law School (J.D., 1998; LL.M., International Business and Trade, with honors, 1999). *Member:* Chicago, Illinois State and American Bar Associations; Illinois Trial Lawyers Association. ***LANGUAGES:*** French and Farsi. ***PRACTICE AREAS:*** Personal Injury. ***Email:*** nbt@taradji.com

Languages: French, Farsi and English.

TAXMAN & HURST

100 WEST MONROE STREET
SUITE 1605
CHICAGO, ILLINOIS 60603
Telephone: 312-263-3040
Fax: 312-263-7944
Email: info@taxmanlaw.com
URL: http://www.taxmanlaw.com

Tort Litigation Practice, Medical Malpractice, Negligence, Trials, Professional Malpractice and Products Liability Law.

PHILLIP TAXMAN, born February 21, 1936; admitted to bar, 1985, Illinois; U.S. District Court, Northern District of Illinois. *Education:* University of Illinois (B.S., Medicine, 1958; M.D., 1960); Loyola University (J.D.). *Member:* Illinois State and American Bar Associations; Illinois Trial Lawyers Association; Association of Trial Lawyers of America; Trial Lawyers Club of Chicago. Fellow: American College of Surgeons; International College of Surgeons; American College of Legal Medicine. Diplomat: American Board of Surgery.

BRIAN HURST, born June 15, 1970; admitted to bar, 1995, Illinois and U.S. District Court, Northern District of Illinois. *Education:* Eastern Illinois University (B.A., summa cum laude, 1992); Chicago-Kent College of Law, Illinois Institute of Technology (J.D., 1995). *Member:* Chicago, Illinois and American Bar Associations; Illinois Trial Lawyers Association; The Association of Trial Lawyers of America. **PRACTICE AREAS:** Tort Litigation; Medical Malpractice; Plaintiff's Personal Injury; Appellate Advocacy; Insurance Litigation.

OF COUNSEL

ERNEST W. BEUTEL, M.D., born Chicago, Illinois, February 14, 1946; admitted to bar, 1986, Illinois. *Education:* Loyola University (B.S., magna cum laude, 1967; M.D., 1971; J.D., 1985); University of Health Sciences, The Chicago Medical School (Hospital Risk Management Certificate). Alpha Omega Alpha; Phi Sigma Tau; Phi Beta Pi. Licensed Physician and Surgeon, Illinois, 1972. Clinical Assistant Professor of Surgery, Loyola University Stritch School of Medicine, 1985-2001. President, Medical Staff, Resurrection Medical Center, Chicago, 1998-1999. *Member:* Chicago, Illinois and American Bar Associations (Member, Torts and Science and Technology Law Sections); Association of Trial Lawyers of America; International Trial Lawyers Association; National Health Lawyers Association; American Medical Association; Chicago Surgical Society; Midwest Surgical Society. Fellow: American College of Surgeons; American College of Chest Physicians; American College of Legal Medicine. Associate Fellow, American College of Cardiology. [U.S. Naval Reserve Medical Corp., 1969-1980]. **PRACTICE AREAS:** Medical Malpractice; Tort Litigation; Negligence; Products Liability; Trial Practice.

FRANK A. TEDESSO

39 SOUTH LA SALLE, SUITE 808
CHICAGO, ILLINOIS 60603-1603
Telephone: 312-578-9770
Fax: 312-899-0048
Email: ftedesso@ameritech.net
URL: http://www.frankatedesso.com

Criminal Law, Traffic Violations, Domestic Violence, Driving While Intoxicated, Drug Crimes Sexual Assaults, Felonies, Misdemeanors, Armed Robbery, Robbery, Weapons Offense, Murder and Attempted Murder.

FIRM PROFILE: Frank A. Tedesso has specialized in the practice of Criminal Defense and Family Law within Chicago, IL over 10 years. He is a member of the American Bar Association and the Criminal Bar Association. Mr. Tedesso is a very aggressive attorney willing to get the job done. He has had numerous cases which support his diligent nature.

FRANK A. TEDESSO, born Oak Park, Illinois, June 20, 1968; admitted to bar, 1993, Illinois. *Education:* Northwestern University (B.A., 1990); DePaul University (J.D., 1993). *Member:* Chicago, Illinois State and American Bar Associations. **PRACTICE AREAS:** Criminal Law; Traffic Violations; Domestic Violence; Driving While Intoxicated; Drug Crimes; Sexual Assault; Felonies; Misdemeanors; Juvenile Law.

TEEPLE & LEONARD

175 W. JACKSON BOULEVARD, SUITE 240
CHICAGO, ILLINOIS 60604
Telephone: 312-986-3228
Fax: 312-986-3981

Commercial and Civil Litigation, Antitrust Law, Environmental Law, Intellectual Property Law.

RONALD W. TEEPLE, born July 10, 1942; admitted to bar, 1967, Illinois. *Education:* University of Chicago (B.A., 1964); University of Pennsylvania (LL.B., 1967). Author: "When, If Ever, Are Punitive Damages Recoverable in an Illinois Contract Action?" Illinois Bar Journal, Vol. 65, No. 3, November, 1976; "Keys to Controlling Outside Litigation Fees," CBA Record, Vol. 7, No. 6, September, 1993. *Member:* American Bar Association. **PRACTICE AREAS:** Commercial Litigation; Antitrust Law. **Email:** rwteeple@teeplelaw.com

JOHN L. LEONARD, born Berwyn, Illinois, June 20, 1946; admitted to bar, 1971, Illinois. *Education:* Loyola University (B.S., cum laude, 1968); Northwestern University (J.D., 1971). Weymouth Kirkland Scholar, 1969-1971. Russell Sage Fellow in Law and Social Sciences, 1969-1971. Recipient, Wigmore Key, 1971. *Member:* Chicago and American Bar Associations. **PRACTICE AREAS:** Litigation; Antitrust Law; Environmental Law; Intellectual Property Law; Real Estate Taxation; Contract Litigation; Personal Injury; Torts. **Email:** jlleonard@teeplelaw.com

MICHAEL H. ERDMAN, born Kansas City, Missouri, December 11, 1970; admitted to bar, 1996, Missouri; 1997, District of Columbia; 1998, Illinois. *Education:* Washington University (B.S.B.A., 1993); Boston University School of Law (J.D., cum laude, 1996). *Member:* Chicago and American Bar Associations. **PRACTICE AREAS:** Commercial Litigation; Civil Litigation; Antitrust; Intellectual Property; Copyright Infringement; Business Law; Freedom of Information (FOIA). **Email:** mherdman@teeplelaw.com

TELLER, LEVIT & SILVERTRUST, P.C.

11 EAST ADAMS, SUITE 800
CHICAGO, ILLINOIS 60603
Telephone: 312-922-3030
Toll-Free: 800-922-0342
Fax: 312-922-3048; 312-922-4105
URL: http://www.lawyers.com/tellerlevit&silvertrust
Email: TLS@TellerLevit.com
URL: http://www.TellerLevit.com

Creditors Rights, Collections, Civil Practice, Commercial Arbitration, Commercial Litigation, Preference Defense, Sale of Goods, Secured Transactions, Uniform Commercial Code, Breach of Contract, Commercial Contracts, Insurance Premium Collection, Mortgage Foreclosures, Construction Litigation, Mechanics Liens, Commercial Evictions, Post Judgment Collections, Appeals.

FIRM PROFILE: Teller, Levit & Silvertrust (TL & S). founded in 1920 by Carroll Teller, Louis Levit and Leon Silvertrust, has specialized in the practice of commercial law since its inception. With headquarters in the heart of Chicago, TL & S serves the commercial hub of northern Illinois. In cases over $75,000 where federal jurisdiction can be invoked, the range of TL & S extends to the outlying counties of DeKalb, Kane, Kendall, LaSalle, and McHenry. From this prime midwestern location, TL & S is well equipped to service clients throughout the entire nation.

ARTHUR RAPHAEL, born 1940; admitted to bar, 1965, Illinois and U.S. District Court, Northern District of Illinois; 1982, U.S. Supreme Court. *Education:* University of Illinois; DePaul University (J.D., 1965). Board Certified Creditors Rights Specialist of American Board of Certification and Bankruptcy Specialists. *Member:* Chicago and Illinois State Bar Associations; Commercial Law League of America. (Certified in Creditors' Rights Law by the American Board of Certification). **Email:** Araphael@TellerLevit.com

HAROLD STOTLAND, born 1940; admitted to bar, 1964, Illinois and U.S. District Court, Northern District of Illinois. *Education:* University of Chicago (B.A., 1961); John Marshall Law School (J.D., 1964). **PRACTICE AREAS:** Creditors Rights. **Email:** HStotland@TellerLevit.com

EDWARD S. MARGOLIS, born Chicago, Illinois, November 17, 1943; admitted to bar, 1968, Illinois; 1969, U.S. District Court, Northern District of Illinois; 1970, U.S. Court of Appeals, Seventh Circuit; 1987, U.S. Supreme Court. *Education:* University of Illinois (B.A., 1965; J.D., 1968). Phi Kappa Phi; Phi Eta Sigma. **PRACTICE AREAS:** Creditors Rights (40%); Commercial Litigation (45%); Civil Litigation (5%); Civil Appeals (10%). **Email:** EMargolis@TellerLevit.com

KEVIN E. POSEN, born Chicago, Illinois, June 20, 1961; admitted to bar, 1990, Illinois; 1991, U.S. District Court, Northern District of Illinois. *Education:* Loyola University of Chicago (B.A., 1983); The John Marshall Law School at Chicago (J.D., 1990). *Member:* DuPage County, Chicago (Member, Committees on: Civil Practice; Municipal Department; Circuit Court; Collection Law) and Illinois State Bar Associations; Commercial Law League of America (Member, Creditors Rights Section). **Email:** KPosen@TellerLevit.com

TENNEY & BENTLEY, LLC

Founded 1847

111 WEST WASHINGTON STREET
SUITE 1900
CHICAGO, ILLINOIS 60602
Telephone: 312-407-7800
Telefax: 312-807-4858
Email: TENBEN@interaccess.com

General Civil Practice, including Business and Personal Litigation, Corporate, Probate, Real Estate, Tax and Estate Planning.

HENRY F. TENNEY (1915-1971)

RICHARD BENTLEY (1922-1970)

MEMBERS OF FIRM

ARTHUR H. ANDERSON, JR., admitted to bar, 1970, Illinois and Massachusetts. *Education:* Tufts University (A.B., magna cum laude, 1967); University of Chicago (J.D., 1970). **PRACTICE AREAS:** Tax Law; Corporate Law. **Email:** aha@ahalaw.com

RICHARD J. COCHRAN, admitted to bar, 1967, Illinois. *Education:* Loyola University (B.S., 1964; J.D., 1967). Associate Editor, Loyola Law Review, 1966-1967. **PRACTICE AREAS:** Civil Litigation. **Email:** dickcochran@hotmail.com

(This Listing Continued)

EDWIN H. CONGER, admitted to bar, 1957, Illinois; 1963, Michigan; 1978, U.S. Supreme Court. *Education:* University of Michigan (A.B., 1954; M.B.A., 1955); Harvard University (LL.B., cum laude, 1957). ***PRACTICE AREAS:*** Business Counseling and Litigation. **Email:** conger@mindspring.com

JOHN S. ESKILSON, admitted to bar, 1964, Indiana; 1965, Illinois. *Education:* Carleton College and Brown University (A.B., 1957); University of Chicago (J.D., 1964). ***PRACTICE AREAS:*** Estate Planning Law; Probate Law. **Email:** sondervang@sblglobal.net

SOLOMON GUTSTEIN, admitted to bar, 1956, Illinois. *Education:* University of Chicago (A.B., with honors, 1953; J.D., 1956). Associate Editor, University of Chicago Law Review, 1955-1956. Co-Author: "Illinois Practice Guide- Real Estate," Lawyers Co-operative Publishing Co., 1995, and annual supplements to 2002. Consultant, Illinois Real Estate Service, Bancroft Whitney Company, 1988. Adjunct Professor, John Marshall Law School, 1994-1996. 40th Ward Alderman, Chicago, 1975-1979. ***LANGUAGES:*** Hebrew. ***PRACTICE AREAS:*** Real Estate; Health Care; Probate and Estate Planning. **Email:** tenben@interaccess.com

F. JAMES HELMS, admitted to bar, 1973, Illinois. *Education:* Purdue University (B.S., 1970); Indiana University (J.D., 1973). Order of the Coif. Associate Editor, Indiana Law Journal, 1972-1973. ***PRACTICE AREAS:*** Real Estate Law.

DAVID R. SHANNON, admitted to bar, 1990, Illinois. *Education:* Utah State University (B.S., cum laude, 1983); John Marshall Law School (J.D., cum laude, 1990; LL.M., Employee Benefits, with honors, 2003). ***PRACTICE AREAS:*** Commercial Litigation; Employee Benefits. **Email:** tenben@interaccess.com

TIMOTHY K. TRAVERS, admitted to bar, 1983, Illinois. *Education:* Loyola University (B.B.A., 1980); Chicago-Kent College of Law (J.D., with high honors, 1983). ***PRACTICE AREAS:*** Civil Litigation. **Email:** tenben@interaccess.com

OF COUNSEL

IRWIN J. ASKOW, admitted to bar, 1938, Illinois. *Education:* University of Chicago (A.B., 1936); University of Chicago Law School (J.D., 1938). ***PRACTICE AREAS:*** Corporate Law; Architectural and Construction Law. **Email:** ijaskow@aol.com

ALBERT L. FINSTON, admitted to bar, 1940, Illinois. *Education:* DePaul University (B.A., 1932; LL.B., 1940). ***PRACTICE AREAS:*** Corporate; Real Estate; Probate.

EDWARD J. KAHN, admitted to bar, 1955, Illinois; 1975, U.S. Supreme Court; U.S. District Court, Northern District of Illinois, including Trial Bar; U.S. Court of Appeals, Sixth and Seventh Circuits. *Education:* Northwestern University and University of Colorado (B.S., 1951); University of Michigan (J.D., 1954). Tau Epsilon Rho. First Place Winner, National Moot Court Competition. *Member:* Chicago (Member, Trust Law and Probate Practice Committees, 1985—); Illinois State (Member, Probate and Trust Law Committees, 1960—) and American (Member, Real Property, Probate and Trust Law Section, 1980—) Bar Associations; Chicago Estate Planning Council, 1984—. Fellow, American College of Trust and Estate Counsel, 1970—. ***PRACTICE AREAS:*** General Practice; Corporate Law; Tax Law; Probate Law; Estate Planning Law; Real Estate Law.

ASSOCIATES

ANN ADDIS PANTOGA, admitted to bar, 1997, Illinois. *Education:* St. Mary's College (B.M., 1979); Northwestern University (M.M., 1981); DePaul University, College of Law (J.D., 1997). ***PRACTICE AREAS:*** Civil Litigation. **Email:** tenben@interaccess.com

DAVID J. WOLF, admitted to bar, 1994, Illinois. *Education:* Northwestern University (B.S., 1986); DePaul University College of Law (J.D., 1994). ***PRACTICE AREAS:*** Corporate; Estate Planning; Taxation. **Email:** tenben@interaccess.com

THIEDMANN & EDLER

222 SOUTH RIVERSIDE PLAZA, SUITE 1410
CHICAGO, ILLINOIS 60606
Telephone: 312-831-4440
Fax: 312-831-4447
Email: thiedmann@thiedmannedler.com
URL: http://www.thiedmannedler.com

Corporate Law, Business Law, Mergers, Acquisitions and Divestitures, Finance, Securities, Business Immigration, Labor and Employment, Foreign Investment in the United States, Intellectual Property, International Commercial Arbitration.

MEMBERS OF FIRM

KLAUS U. THIEDMANN, born Frankfurt/Main, Germany, July 18, 1954; admitted to bar, 1983, Germany; 1985, Illinois. *Education:* University of Frankfurt, School of Law, Frankfurt, Germany; College of Europe, Bruges, Belgium; Cornell Law School; Northwestern University (J.D., 1985). *Member:* Chicago (Chair, International Law and Practice Committee, YLS Chicago Bar Association, 1991-1992) and Illinois State Bar Associations; National Association of Corporate Directors; Frankfurt Bar Association; German American Lawyers Association. ***LANGUAGES:*** German. ***PRACTICE AREAS:*** Corporate Law; Mergers and Acquisitions; Finance; Business Law; Foreign Investment. **Email:** thiedmann@thiedmannedler.com

ROBERT W. EDLER, born June 25, 1936; admitted to bar, 1962, Illinois and U.S. District Court, Northern District of Illinois. *Education:* Durham University, Durham, England; DePauw University (B.A. with highest distinction, 1958); University of Chicago (M.A., 1959); Stanford University (LL.B., 1962). Phi Beta Kappa. Author: "How to Write a Private Placement Memorandum-Disclosure Requirements of the Securities Law," IICLE Securities Law, 1997. Member, Panel of Arbitrators, National Association of Securities Dealers, 1985—. *Member:* Chicago, Illinois State and American Bar Associations. Fellow, Illinois Bar Foundation. ***SPECIAL AGENCIES:*** Securities and Exchange Commission. ***PRACTICE AREAS:*** Securities; Corporate Law; Mergers and Acquisitions; Finance; Arbitration. **Email:** edlerlaw@earthlink.net

(This Listing Continued)

SARAH A. A. AMES, born Heidelberg, Germany, December 16, 1968; admitted to bar, 1997, Illinois and U.S. District Court, Northern District of Illinois; 1998, Alabama. *Education:* University of Hamburg, School of Law, Hamburg, Germany; University of Alabama (M.A., 1994; J.D., 1997). *Member:* Chicago Bar Association; Alabama State Bar; American Immigration Lawyers Association. ***LANGUAGES:*** German. ***PRACTICE AREAS:*** Corporate Law; Immigration Law; Commercial Law. **Email:** ames@thiedmannedler.com

THOMAS W. SOSEMAN, born Cherokee, Iowa, April 21, 1966; admitted to bar, 1991, Iowa; 1993, Illinois. *Education:* Cornell College (B.S.S., magna cum laude, 1988); University of Iowa College of Law (J.D., with high distinction, 1991); University of Chicago, Graduate School of Business (M.B.A., 1995). *Member:* Iowa State and American Bar Associations. ***PRACTICE AREAS:*** Corporate Law; Finance; Business Law; Commercial Law; Arbitration; Mergers and Acquisitions; Secured Lending. **Email:** soseman@thiedmannedler.com

OF COUNSEL

ANNETTE E. GUSTAFSSON GUENTHER, born Eskilstuna, Sweden, April 6, 1962; admitted to bar, 1986, Sweden; 1992, Illinois. *Education:* University of Uppsala, School of Law, Uppsala, Sweden (LL.M., 1986); Illinois Institute of Technology, Chicago-Kent College of Law (J.D., 1992). *Member:* Chicago, Illinois State and American Bar Associations; Swedish American Bar Association; American Immigration Lawyers Association. ***LANGUAGES:*** Swedish. ***PRACTICE AREAS:*** General Corporate Law; Immigration Law; Swedish Business Law; Civil Law. **Email:** annette@lawgustafsson.com

ALAN B. SAMLAN, born Chicago, Illinois, January 19, 1948; admitted to bar, 1976, Illinois and U.S. District Court, Northern District of Illinois; 1982, U.S. Court of Appeals, Federal Circuit; registered to practice before U.S. Patent and Trademark Office. *Education:* University of Illinois (B.S.M.E., 1970); John Marshall Law School (J.D., 1976). Author: "Intellectual Property Rights," Legal Issues: International Investment in Illinois, 1984. *Member:* Chicago and Illinois State Bar Associations; American Intellectual Property Law Association; Intellectual Property Law Association of Chicago. (Also Member, Knechtel, Demeur & Samlan, Chicago, Illinois). ***PRACTICE AREAS:*** Patent; Trademark; Copyright; Real Estate Law; Commercial Law.

JAMIE S. FREVELETTI, born Oak Park, Illinois; admitted to bar, 1985, Illinois. *Education:* Northern Illinois University (B.A., 1981); Illinois Institute of Technology, Chicago-Kent College of Law (J.D., 1985); McGeorge School of Law, Salzburg, Austria (Diploma, International Studies, 1985). *Member:* Chicago and American Bar Associations. ***PRACTICE AREAS:*** Litigation; Food, Drug and Medical Device Litigation. **Email:** freveletti@thiedmannedler.com

DAVID J. HURLEY, born August 20, 1968; admitted to bar, 1999, Illinois and U.S. District Court, Northern District of Illinois; registered to practice before U.S. Patent and Trademark Office. *Education:* Virginia Polytechnic Institute and State University (B.S., Aerospace Engineering, 1991); John Marshall Law School (J.D., 1999). Article and Note Editor, John Marshall Law Review, 1997-1998. *Member:* Chicago and Illinois State Bar Associations; Intellectual Property Law Association of Chicago. (Also Member, Knechtel, Demeur & Samlan, Chicago, Illinois). ***PRACTICE AREAS:*** Patents; Trademarks; Copyrights; Internet Law; Real Estate Law; Commercial Law. **Email:** kd&slaw@xnet.com

LAW OFFICES OF SCOTT G. THOMAS

500 WEST MADISON STREET, SUITE 2790
CHICAGO, ILLINOIS 60661-2511
Telephone: 312-930-5500
Fax: 312-993-9896

Products Liability, Professional Liability, Securities Arbitration, Premises Liability, Automobile Accident Liability, Employment Law, General Liability, and Workers' Compensation.

STAFF COUNSEL
AMERICAN INTERNATIONAL COMPANIES

MANAGING ATTORNEY

SCOTT G. THOMAS, born Marshfield, Wisconsin, October 1, 1956; admitted to bar, 1982, Wisconsin and U.S. District Court, Eastern and Western Districts of Wisconsin; 1984, U.S. Court of Appeals, Seventh Circuit; 1987, U.S. Supreme Court; 1994, U.S. District Court, Northern District of Illinois including Trial Bar; 1999, Illinois. *Education:* University of Wisconsin-Eau Claire (B.A., summa cum laude, 1978); Marquette University (J.D., cum laude, 1982). Alpha Sigma Nu. Delta Theta Phi. Phi Kappa Phi. *Member:* Chicago, Milwaukee, Illinois State, Seventh Judicial Circuit and American Bar Associations; State Bar of Wisconsin; Civil Trial Counsel of Wisconsin; Wisconsin Academy of Trial Lawyers; Defense Research Institute; Illinois Association of Defense Trial Counsel. (Also Managing Attorney, Law Offices of Scott G. Thomas, New Berlin, Wisconsin)

SUPERVISING ATTORNEY

JAMES L. McKNIGHT, born Queens, New York, February 28, 1966; admitted to bar, 1991, Illinois, U.S. District Court, Northern District of Illinois and U.S. Court of Appeals, Seventh Circuit; 2002, U.S. District Court, Eastern and Western Districts of Wisconsin. *Education:* George Washington University (B.A., 1988); Boston University School of Law (J.D., 1991). *Member:* Chicago, Illinois State and American Bar Associations; Illinois Association of Defense Trial Counsel.

SENIOR TRIAL ATTORNEYS

JAMES P. HYNES, born Chicago Illinois, September 15, 1954; admitted to bar, 1981, Illinois and U.S. District Court, Northern District of Illinois. *Education:* Knox College (B.A., 1976); John Marshall Law School (J.D., 1981). Arbitrator, Cook and DuPage Counties. *Member:* Dupage County and Illinois State Bar Associations; State Bar of Wisconsin.

(This Listing Continued)

LAW OFFICES OF SCOTT G. THOMAS, Chicago—Continued

RICHARD M. JACOBSON, born Chicago, Illinois, September 9, 1954; admitted to bar, 1979, Illinois; 1988, Wisconsin. *Education:* University of Illinois (B.A., cum laude, 1976); DePaul University (J.D., 1979). *Member:* State Bar of Wisconsin.

PATRICIA J. KAMPSEN, born Dublin, Ireland, April 24, 1952; admitted to bar, 1985, Missouri; 1986, Illinois. *Education:* St. Mary's College (B.A., 1974); Washington University (M.S.W., 1976); St. Louis University (J.D., 1985). Phi Alpha Delta. *Member:* Bar Association of Metropolitan St. Louis; St. Louis County Bar Association; The Missouri Bar. ***PRACTICE AREAS:*** Workers Compensation.

MICHAEL F. LANIGAN, born Chicago, Illinois, October 12, 1946; admitted to bar, 1977, Illinois and U.S. District Court, Northern District of Illinois. *Education:* Loyola University (B.A., 1973; J.D., 1977). ***PRACTICE AREAS:*** Workers Compensation Defense.

ROBERT S. PHILLIPS, born Paris, Texas, November 22, 1948; admitted to bar, 1976, Illinois; U.S. District Court, Northern District of Illinois; 1986, U.S. Court of Appeals, 7th Circuit; 1987, U.S. Supreme Court; 1989, U.S. Army Court of Military Review and U.S. Court of Military Appeals; 1994, Wisconsin. *Education:* Indiana University (B.A., 1971); DePaul University (J.D., 1976). *Member:* McHenry County and Illinois State Bar Associations. [Lieut. Col., U.S. Army Reserve, 1971—]. ***PRACTICE AREAS:*** Professional Liability; Premises Liability; Motor Carrier Liability; Construction Accidents; Products Liability.

NANCY M. RUNDIN, born Chicago, Illinois, July 26, 1954; admitted to bar, 1980, Illinois; 1983, U.S. District Court, Northern District of Illinois including Trial Bar. *Education:* University of Illinois (B.A., 1976); John Marshall Law School (J.D., 1980). *Member:* Illinois State Bar Association.

TRIAL ATTORNEYS

MICHAEL F. MURPHY, born Oak Lawn, Illinois, August 27, 1967; admitted to bar, 1992, Illinois; 1995, U.S. District Court, Northern District of Illinois including Trial Bar. *Education:* Illinois State University (B.S.,1989); Loyola University School of Law (J.D., 1992).

ANDREW TOULOUPAKIS, born Chicago, Illinois; admitted to bar, 2000, Illinois. *Education:* University of Illinois at Chicago (B.A., 1995); John Marshall Law School (J.D., 2000). ***PRACTICE AREAS:*** Workers Compensation.

ASSOCIATE ATTORNEY

CLAUDIA HALLORAN, born Chicago, Illinois; admitted to bar, 1985, Illinois and U.S. District Court, Northern District of Illinois; 1996, U.S. Supreme Court. *Education:* University of Illinois (B.S., 1978); Chicago-Kent College of Law (J.D., high honors, 1985). *Member:* Chicago and Illinois State Bar Associations.

MICHAEL THOMPSON

401 NORTH MICHIGAN AVENUE, SUITE 1200
CHICAGO, ILLINOIS 60611
Telephone: 312-840-8556
Fax: 847-733-1807
Email: michaelthompsonlaw@earthlink.net
URL: http://www.michaelthompsonlaw.com

International Trade and Investment, Acquisition of Fine Art and Cultural Property, Transactions involving Literary and Artistic Property.

MICHAEL THOMPSON, born Des Moines, Iowa, August 2, 1951; admitted to bar, 1976, Iowa; 1979, New York; 1980, Missouri and U.S. Court of Appeals, 2d Circuit; 1981, U.S. Court of Appeals, District of Columbia Circuit; 1982, U.S. Court of Appeals, 7th Circuit; 1984, U.S. Supreme Court; 1988, U.S. Court of Appeals, Federal Circuit and U.S. Court of International Trade; 1994, Texas; 1999, Illinois. *Education:* University of Northern Iowa (B.A., magna cum laude, 1973); University of Iowa (J.D., cum laude, 1976; M.A., 1977). Co-Author: *Disbound and Dispersed:* The Leaf Book Considered, 2005; "Five Things Every Lawyer Should Know About Entertainment and Art Law," CBA Record, January 2004. Author: "Dealers in Cultural Property: UNIDROIT and UNESCO Code of Ethics," 13 The ABAA Newsletter 1, (Spring, 2002); "Economic Development in the Information Age: Investing in Telecommunications Infrastructure," Currents International Trade Law Journal (Fall 1995); "The Lawyer's Role When Business Expands Overseas," Texas Lawyer, Section Three (May 30, 1994); "The Relevance of Revenue/Variable Cost Ratios in Market Dominance Determinations," 23 Proceedings of the Transportation Research Forum 362 (1982). "Formerly, Adjunct Lecturer, Corporation Finance, Drake University. Executive Vice President and General Counsel, SBC International Development Corp. Commerce Counsel, Missouri Pacific Railroad Co. Special Assistant, New York Public Service Commission. *Member:* Chicago (Chair, Entertainment and Art Law Committee), Illinois State, New York State and American Bar Associations; State Bar of Texas (Chairman, Foreign Investment Committee, 1997); American Economic Association. ***PRACTICE AREAS:*** Art Law; Business Law; Communications Law; Contracts; International Law; International Trade; Investments; Mergers and Acquisitions.

FRANK P. TIGHE III

8700 WEST BRYN MAWR AVENUE, SUITE 800 SOUTH
CHICAGO, ILLINOIS 60631
Telephone: 630-574-5015
Fax: 630-574-1501

Trials and Appeals in Federal and State Courts.

FRANK P. TIGHE, III, admitted to bar, 1986, Illinois and U.S. District Court, Northern District of Illinois; 1987, U.S. Court of Appeals, Seventh Circuit; 1996, U.S. Supreme Court; 2000, U.S Court of Federal Claims. *Education:* University of Notre Dame (B.A.,

(This Listing Continued)

1982); Loyola University, Chicago (J.D., 1986). Member, Loyola University Chicago Law Journal, 1985-1986. Police Officer, City of Chicago, 1982-1985. *Member:* Chicago (Vice-Chairman, 1999-2000 and Chairman, 2000-2001, Professional Responsibility Committee), Illinois State and American Bar Associations; Illinois Trial Lawyers Association; Chicago Lincoln American Inn of Court. ***PRACTICE AREAS:*** Litigation.

TISHLER & WALD, LTD.

SUITE 3000
200 SOUTH WACKER DRIVE
CHICAGO, ILLINOIS 60606
Telephone: 312-876-3800
Telecopier: 312-876-3816
Email: tishlerandwald@tishlerandwald.com
URL: http://www.tishlerandwald.com

General Civil Practice. Bankruptcy and Reorganization, Corporate, Taxation, Estate Planning, Franchise, Probate, Real Estate, Banking, State and Federal Litigation.

KURT M. CARLSON, born Lake Forest, Illinois, November 18, 1965; admitted to bar, 1990, Michigan; 1996, Illinois. *Education:* Michigan State University (B.A., 1987); Thomas M. Cooley Law School (J.D., 1990). *Member:* Detroit, Illinois State and American Bar Associations; State Bar of Michigan (Member, Creditors Committee, 1995-1996). ***PRACTICE AREAS:*** Bankruptcy Reorganization; Commercial Litigation; Banking Law; Financial Institutions Law. ***Email:*** kcarlson@tishlerandwald.com

LAWRENCE R. DRUMM, born Cleveland, Ohio, December 8, 1969; admitted to bar, 1996, Illinois. *Education:* University of Notre Dame (B.A., with high honors, 1992); Chicago-Kent College of Law (J.D., 1996). Moot Court Honor Society. *Member:* Chicago, Illinois State and American Bar Associations. ***PRACTICE AREAS:*** Commercial Litigation. ***Email:*** ldrumm@tishlerandwald.com

DAVID A. KALLICK, born Chicago, Illinois, November 7, 1945; admitted to bar, 1971, Illinois; 1972, California. *Education:* Princeton University (A.B., 1967); Northwestern University (J.D., 1970). Judicial Law Clerk, Illinois Appellate Court, 1970-1971. *Member:* Chicago, Illinois State and American Bar Associations; State Bar of California. ***PRACTICE AREAS:*** Business Law; Business Transactions; Banking Law; Financial Institutions Law. ***Email:*** dkallick@tishlerandwald.com

ALEXANDER D. KERR, JR., born Pittsburgh, Pennsylvania, May 6, 1943; admitted to bar, 1968, Illinois; 1969, Pennsylvania. *Education:* Northwestern University (B.S., 1965; J.D., 1968). Assistant U.S. Attorney, Northern District of Illinois, 1974-1978.*Member:* Du Page County, Cook County, Chicago, Illinois State and American Bar Associations; Illinois Trial Lawyers Association; The Association of Trial Lawyers of America. [LCDR, JAGC, USNR, 1969-1973]. ***PRACTICE AREAS:*** Bankruptcy Reorganization; Business Law; Commercial Litigation. ***Email:*** akerr@tishlerandwald.com

STEVEN A. MIGALA, born Chicago, Illinois, November 15, 1971; admitted to bar, 1996, Illinois. *Education:* Bradley University (B.S., summa cum laude, 1993); University of Illinois (J.D., magna cum laude, 1996). Phi Kappa Phi; Beta Gamma Sigma; Omicron Delta Kappa. Member, Mortor Board. Administrative Editor, University of Illinois Law Review, 1995-1996. *Member:* Chicago, Kane County and Illinois State Bar Associations. ***PRACTICE AREAS:*** Business Transactions; Estate Planning; Estate Administration; Taxation. ***Email:*** smigala@tishlerandwald.com

JEFFREY B. ROSE, born Chicago, Illinois, January 31, 1952; admitted to bar, 1983, Illinois. *Education:* University of Illinois (B.A., 1973; M.A., 1974); DePaul University (J.D., 1983). *Member:* Chicago and Illinois State Bar Associations. ***PRACTICE AREAS:*** Bankruptcy Reorganization; Business Law; Business Transactions; Commercial Real Estate; Commercial Litigation. ***Email:*** jrose@tishlerandwald.com

NATALIA K. RZEPKA, born Rzeszow, Poland, February 7, 1977; admitted to bar, 2002, Illinois. *Education:* Loyola University (B.S., cum laude, 1999); Chicago-Kent College of Law, Illinois Institute of Technology (J.D., 2002). Member, Moot Court Honor Society. *Member:* Chicago, Illinois State and American Bar Associations. ***PRACTICE AREAS:*** Commercial Litigation; Bankruptcy Reorganization. ***Email:*** nrzepka@tishlerandwald.com

LOUIS B. TISHLER, JR., born Chicago, Illinois, August 31, 1933; admitted to bar, 1959, Illinois. *Education:* University of Michigan (A.B., 1955); Northwestern University (J.D., 1959). *Member:* Chicago and Illinois State Bar Associations. ***PRACTICE AREAS:*** Business Law; Business Transactions; Franchise Law; Estate Planning; Estate Administration; Commercial Real Estate. ***Email:*** ltishler@tishlerandwald.com

INEZ K. TREMAIN, born Syracuse, New York, July 30, 1940; admitted to bar, 1980, Illinois and U.S. District Court, Northern District of Illinois; 1983, District of Columbia. *Education:* Syracuse University (B.A., 1962); Loyola University (J.D., 1980). *Member:* Chicago, Illinois State and American Bar Associations; Bar Association of the District of Columbia. ***PRACTICE AREAS:*** Commercial Real Estate; Affordable Housing; Business Law; Business Transactions. ***Email:*** itremain@tishlerandwald.com

BRUCE L. WALD, born Chicago, Illinois, February 6, 1946; admitted to bar, 1972, Illinois. *Education:* University of Wisconsin (B.A., cum laude, 1968); Northwestern University (J.D., 1972). Phi Kappa Phi. Editor of ICCLE Bankruptcy Practice Handbook. *Member:* Chicago Bar Association (Member, Bankruptcy Committee, 1977—). ***PRACTICE AREAS:*** Bankruptcy Reorganization. ***Email:*** bwald@tishlerandwald.com

REFERENCE: Bank One, Chicago, Chicago, Illinois.

TOBIN PETKUS & MUÑOZ

Established in 1985

THREE FIRST NATIONAL PLAZA, SUITE 1950
CHICAGO, ILLINOIS 60602-4298
Telephone: 312-641-1321
Fax: 312-641-5220
Email: TomasPetkus@barristers.com
URL: http://www.barristers.com

Washington, DC Office: 1300 Pennsylvania Avenue, N.W., Suite 700, 20004-3024. Telephone: 202-204-2530. Fax: 202-347-2312.

Trial Practice, International Business Law, International Tax Law, Corporate Law, Commercial Law, Latin American Transactions, Civil Litigation.

FIRM PROFILE: Tobin Petkus & Muñoz is a nationally recognized litigation law firm that has achieved unprecedented results on behalf of its clients. The attorneys are recognized in the National Bar Registry of Preeminent Attorneys. In 1985 Craig D. Tobin left the Homicide Task Force of the Cook County Public Defender's Office for private practice. He was joined by the late Hon. Robert J. Collins. Judge Collins was a well-respected jurist the Chicago Tribune called 'the standard by which all other judges are to be measured.' Mr. Tobin has guided clients through cases which attracted intense media coverage. Mr. Tobin's peers have consistently voted him to the publication "Best Lawyers in America." Tomas Petkus, who joined the firm in 1995, pioneered the adaptation of computer technology to the practice of law. Mr. Petkus was instrumental in the development and use of computers and digital technology at trial. The firm is widely known for its trial expertise and the use of technology to enhance those skills. George Muñoz served in President Clinton's cabinet from 1993 to 1997 as Assistant Treasury Secretary and Chief Financial Officer of the U.S. Treasury Department. He was president and C.E.O. of the Overseas Private Investment Corporation, an independent Federal agency facilitating U.S. investments in developing countries from 1997-2001. Mr. Muñoz was formerly president of the Chicago Board of Education (1984-1987). Mr. Muñoz became of counsel to the firm in 2001 and a partner in 2003. Mr. Muñoz' unique expertise has allowed the firm to expand its national and international business consultation and litigation practice. All litigators have extensive trial experience on substantial cases. The firm concentrates its practice in the areas of complex civil litigation, white collar criminal representation, national and international business representation and transactions. The firm is dedicated to the delivery of the highest quality of litigation and legal services available.

HON. ROBERT J. COLLINS (1911-1997)

CRAIG DANIEL TOBIN, born Chicago, Illinois, 1954; admitted to bar, 1980, Illinois and U.S. Court of Appeals, Seventh Circuit. *Education:* University of Illinois (B.A., with honors); Chicago-Kent College of Law (J.D., with high honors, 1980). Trial Attorney: Felony Division, Cook County Public Defender's Office, 1980-1982. responsible for the handling of felonies from theft through murder; Homicide Task Force, Cook County Public Defender's Office, 1982-1985, responsible for the trial of capital cases and other homicides. Lecturer: "Effective Closing Arguments," Cook County Public Defender's Office, 1983; "Cross-Examination and Closing Arguments," Illinois Public Defenders Association, 1987; Illinois Continuing Legal Education, 1989. Instructor, National Institute for Trial Advocacy, Midwest Regional Programs, 1989, 1990, 1991. Lecturer and Demonstration on "The Art of Cross-Examination," Training Seminar, Cook County Public Defender. Listed, "The Best Lawyers in America." *Member:* American Bar Association; Chicago Bar Association; American Trial Lawyer's Association; Illinois State Bar Association. ***REPORTED CASES:*** Roberts v. Spears, et al., 02 L13204, successfully represented estate, widow and child of patient who died due to medical negligence and obtained a substantial settlement; Shumway v. Imanage, 01 L3350, successfully represented affected shareholder for claims arising from defendant's IPO and obtained substantial settlement; Busse v. UNUM Provident, et al., 98 L 11983, successfully represented a permanently disabled anesthesiologist in a substantial claim against his disability insurance carrier; People of the State of Illinois v. Steven Gianakis, No. 03 MC 5006013, successfully defended the prominent owner of Hickory Hills Country Club and numerous other restaurants against accusations that he had sexually assaulted and battered an employee. The complainant filed charges with the Hickory Hills Police Department as well as a complaint at the Equal Employment Opportunity Commission. The State sought to introduce evidence of similar acts which was blocked by motion. The case proceeded to Trial. Mr. Gianakis was acquitted on April 23, 2004; Berry, etal., v. Segal, etal., 02 CH 1595; successfully represented prominent businessman and owner of Near North National Group, Michael Segal, in a multi-million dollar racketeering and defamation claim filed against him; Nelson v. CoreComm, Ltd., et. al., No. 99 L 7051, successfully represented plaintiff in case involving failure of corporation to recognize shares in connection with a merger; McMahon v. DeJong, 99 L 646, obtained substantial settlement in a wrongful death medical malpractice claim for decedent's estate and family; Miller, et al. v. Endeavor Information Systems, et al., No. 00 L 7207, successfully represented plaintiffs' group in a large securities claim; Brown, et al., v. Ferrellgas, Inc. et al., No. 98VS1441870 (Georgia), successfully represented estate and children of heavy equipment operator killed in crash in a wrongful death suit; Williams v. University of Illinois, et al., No. 98 L 10732, obtained a substantial settlement in wrongful death medical malpractice claim for a 66 year old male with kidney and heart disease who died after elective surgery; People v. Mearday, No. 98 CR 12458, obtained acquittal of defendant in high profile case as with intense media coverage including interviews by ABC Network's "20/20"; Palka v. Cook County Hospital, et al., No. 97 L 14186, successfully represented plaintiff's estate and adult children in a medical malpractice wrongful death claim; Carpenter v. Nabong, No. 94 LA 83, obtained a record setting verdict in a medical malpractice action; People v. McManamon, obtained jury acquittal of a Cook County Sheriff's deputy charged with the murder of his wife; People v. Folaron, obtained jury acquittal of Viet Nam veteran accused of double homicide despite prosecution's use of nationally prominent expert previously undefeated in twenty jurisdictions; Abreu v. LaPreferida, et al., No. 88 CH 9342, successfully represented a shareholder in derivative suit, directors removed, trade secret ownership determined, damages and attorney's fees awarded to plaintiff; Torretto v. I.B. Diffusion, L.P., No. 92 C 2758, obtained a not guilty judgment for a company and its president against Title VII sexual harassment claim for eight million dollars alleging a hostile environment, sexual assaults and attempted rape; Munoz v. City of Chicago, No. 91 CH 1171, obtained a substantial judgment for a contractor in a major dispute with the city; Netzky v. Prudential, et al., No. 94-04918 (NASD Arbitration), A judgment for a sophisticated investor against brokerage firm for losses sustained for trades not performed. ***PRACTICE AREAS:*** Trial Practice. ***Email:*** ctobin@barristers.com

TOMAS PETKUS, born Chicago, Illinois, 1952; admitted to bar, 1980, Illinois and U.S. Court of Appeals, Seventh Circuit; Federal Trial Bar; U.S. District Court, Northern District of Illinois. *Education:* University of Illinois (B.A., with honors); Chicago-Kent College of Law (J.D.). Member, Moot Court Society. Private Practice, 1980—. Lecturer and Presenter, Computer Law and Technology, Chicago Bar Association and the Chicago Computer Society. Chairman, Law Office Technology Committee, Chicago Bar Association, Chicago Bar Association Long Range Planning Committee. Certified Arbitrator, Supreme Court of Illinois, 1990. Speaker, Chicago Bar Information Technology Show (C-BITS). *Member:* Illinois State Bar Association; Illinois Trial Lawyers Association; Chicago Bar Association; Baltic Bar Association. ***LANGUAGES:*** Lithuanian. ***REPORTED CASES:*** Roberts v. Spears, et al., 02 L13204, successfully represented estate, widow and child of patient who died due to medical negligence and obtained a substantial settlement; Shumway v. Imanage, 01 L3350, successfully represented affected shareholder for claims arising from defendant's IPO and obtained substantial settlement; Busse v. UNUM Provident, et al., 98 L 11983, successfully represented a permanently disabled anesthesiologist in a substantial claim against his disability insurance carrier; Berry, etal., v. Segal, etal., 02 CH 1595; successfully represented prominent businessman and owner of Near North National Group, Michael Segal, in a multi-million dollar racketeering and defamation claim filed against him; Nelson v. CoreComm, Ltd., et. al., No. 99 L 7051, successfully represented plaintiff in case involving failure of corporation to recognize shares in connection with a merger; McMahon v. DeJong, 99 L 646, obtained substantial settlement in a wrongful death medical malpractice claim for decedent's estate and family; Miller, et al. v. Endeavor Information Systems, et al., No. 00 L 7207, successfully represented plaintiffs' group in a large securities claim; Brown, et al. v. Ferrellgas, Inc. et al., No. 98VS1441870 (Georgia), successfully represented estate and children of heavy equipment operator killed in crash in a wrongful death action; Williams v. University of Illinois, et al., No. 98 L 10732, obtained a substantial settlement in wrongful death medical malpractice claim for a 66 year old male with kidney and heart disease who died due to elective surgery; Palka v. Cook County Hospital, et al., No. 97 L 14186, successfully represented plaintiff's estate and adult children in a medical malpractice wrongful death claim; Carpenter v. Nabong, No. 94 LA 83, obtained a record setting verdict in a medical malpractice action; Swihart v. Blades Machinery Co., et al., 3:95-CV-605RM (Northern District Indiana), successfully defended manufacturer of grinding equipment in multimillion dollar suit by worker sustaining traumatic amputation; Torretto v. I. B. Diffusion, L.P., No. 92 C 2758, obtained a not guilty judgment for a company and its president against Title VII sexual harassment claim seeking eight million dollars alleging a hostile environment, sexual assaults and attempted rape; A. Munoz General Contractors, Inc. v. City of Chicago. No. 91 CH 1171, obtained a substantial judgment for a contractor in a major dispute with the City; Netzky v. Prudential Securities, et al., No. 94-04918 (NASD Arbitration), judgment for a sophisticated investor against brokerage firm for losses sustained for trades not performed; Moreno v. Barber Coleman Co., et al., 85 L 28175, obtained substantial settlement in wrongful death suit on behalf of estate, wife and children of employee killed in a factory explosion; Mathers, et al. v. Holiday Inns, Inc. 80 L 01234, obtained a substantial settlement for a woman seriously injured while vacationing at a Holiday Inn. Concentration: Trial of Civil Matters. ***PRACTICE AREAS:*** Trial Practice; Civil Litigation. ***Email:*** TomasPetkus@barristers.com

GEORGE MUÑOZ, born 1951; admitted to bar, 1981, Illinois; 1994, District of Columbia. *Education:* University of Texas (B.B.A., with Honors, 1974); Harvard University (J.D., 1978). President, Chicago Board of Education, 1984-1987. Partner, Mayer, Brown & Platt, 1985-1989. George Muñoz and Associates, 1989-1993. Assistant Secretary and Chief Financial Officer of the U.S. Treasury Department, 1993-1997. President and Chief Executive Officer of the Overseas Private Investment Corporation, an independent federal agency facilitating U.S. investment in developing countries, 1997-2001. *Member:* Illinois State Bar Association; The District of Columbia Bar. ***LANGUAGES:*** Spanish. ***PRACTICE AREAS:*** International Business Law; International Tax Law; Corporate Law; Commercial Law; Latin American Transactions; Emerging Markets Transactions. ***Email:*** gmunoz@barristers.com

PAULA FULLER TOBIN, born St. Louis, Missouri; admitted to bar, 1987, Illinois. *Education:* University of Missouri-Columbia (B.S., 1977); Chicago-Kent College of Law (J.D., 1987). Former Partner, Hinshaw and Culbertson (1995-2000). Former elected representative to the General Assembly for the Illinois State Bar Association. *Member:* First Judicial District and Illinois State Bar Associations. ***PRACTICE AREAS:*** Trial Practice; Civil Litigation. ***Email:*** ptobin@barristers.com

FRANK A. MARINO, admitted to bar, 1975, Illinois; 1986, Wisconsin; 1987, Indiana; U.S. District Court, Northern District of Illinois; U.S. Court of Appeals, Seventh Circuit. *Education:* St. Mary's University (B.A., 1972); DePaul University (J.D., 1975). Recipient, United States Law Week Award. Former Member, Cook County Public Defender's Murder Task Force. Former Supervisor, Cook County Public Defenders Office. *Member:* Chicago, Illinois and Indiana State Bar Associations; State Bar of Wisconsin. ***REPORTED CASES:*** People v. Gonzalez, 87 CR 9034, obtained a jury acquittal in a capital case where client was charged with murder and armed robbery of a radio announcer in the Chicago area; People v. Booker, 87 CR 11032, obtained a dismissal of a murder indictment after two remands from the appellate court. ***PRACTICE AREAS:*** Trial Practice. ***Email:*** fmarino@barrister.com

Languages: Spanish and Lithuanian.

REPRESENTATIVE CLIENTS: I. B. Diffusion, L.P.; National Broadcasting Company; Garban-Intercapital PLC; Near North Insurance Agency, Inc.

(This Listing Continued)

TOOLE LAW OFFICES, LLC

1525 EAST 53RD STREET
CHICAGO, ILLINOIS 60615
Telephone: 773-684-5730
Fax: 773-684-5740
Email: info@toolelaw.com
URL: http://www.toolelaw.com

Corporate Law, Contracts, Commercial Transactions, Mergers and Acquisitions, Joint Ventures, Licensing, International Business Transactions, Foreign Investment, Trademarks, Copyrights, Entertainment Law, Employment Law, Civil Rights, Litigation.

FIRM PROFILE: Toole Law Offices, LLC, is an international law firm providing a full range of legal services to meet the diverse requirements of both individuals and businesses. Based in Chicago, Illinois, the firm advises local and international clients in general corporate matters, commercial transactions, entity formations, joint ventures, contracts, investment projects, licensing, employment law, and litigation. The firm is committed to providing its clients with the highest caliber legal service, by taking a genuine interest in the unique requirements of each client, demanding excellence of itself, and delivering a customized solution. Mr. Arnold E. Toole, the principal member of the firm, has experience in the legal markets of Singapore, Thailand, and Laos.

ARNOLD E. TOOLE, born 1965; admitted to bar, 1993, Illinois; 1996, U.S. Court of Appeals, Seventh Circuit; 2003, U.S. District Court, Northern District of Illinois. *Education:* Brandeis University (B.A., honors, 1987); University of Michigan (J.D., 1992). Author: "Doing Business in Myanmar." "Environmental Law in Thailand," copyright Baker & McKenzie, 1992; "Laos Legal Update," copyright DFDL, 1996, 1997. Presenter: The Economist Conferences: The First Roundtable with the Government of the Lao PDR, Topic: Human Resources in the Lao PDR, (1997). General Counsel, American Health Products Corporation, 1997—. *Member:* International Bar Association; Inter-Pacific Bar Association; American Bar Association; National Bar Association; Illinois State Bar Association; Cook County Bar Association; Chicago Bar Association. ***PRACTICE AREAS:*** Corporate Law; Contracts; Commercial Transactions; Mergers and Acquisitions; Joint Ventures; International Business Law; Foreign Investment; Trademarks; Copyrights; Entertainment Law; Employment Law; Civil Rights; Litigation. ***Email:*** aetoole@toolelaw.com

TORSHEN, SLOBIG, GENDEN, DRAGUTINOVICH & AXEL, LTD.

Established in 1963
105 WEST ADAMS STREET, SUITE 3200
CHICAGO, ILLINOIS 60603
Telephone: 312-372-9282
Fax: 312-372-7914
Email: law@torshen.com
URL: http://www.torshen.com

Trial and Appellate Practice in State and Federal Courts. Corporate and Insurance, Zoning and Land Use, Eminent Domain, Real Estate Litigation, Commercial Real Estate Litigation.

FIRM PROFILE: The firm concentrates its practice in high quality, high profile civil litigation and alternative dispute resolution. Members of the firm appear before state and federal trial and appellate courts, administrative agencies, and alternative dispute resolution tribunals in Illinois and other States in matters involving business torts, contracts, real estate, insurance, partnerships, securities and commodities, fraud, RICO, construction, corporations, banking, antitrust, professional malpractice and other business-related litigation including class actions. The firm and its individual members have been involved in over 300 reported decisions of the U.S. Supreme Court, various Circuit Courts of Appeals, U.S. District Courts and the Illinois Supreme and Appellate Courts. Representative of the firm's diverse clientele are businesses engaged in a wide variety of endeavors ranging from computer equipment leasing to scrap metal processing to soil testing, condominium and cooperative associations, insurance companies and agencies, long term care facilities, financial institutions, real estate developers, law firms, schools, political parties, governmental bodies, and religious organizations, as well as individuals involved in disputes arising from their official, professional or business pursuits. The firm also provides services in the areas of business and real estate transactions, probate, and corporate formation and is general, as well as litigation, counsel to a number of its clients. In all matters, close communication between lawyer and client is stressed.

JEROME H. TORSHEN (1929-2002)

ROBERT J. SLOBIG, born Chicago, Illinois, May 13, 1957; admitted to bar, 1982, Illinois. *Education:* Marquette University (A.B., magna cum laude, 1979); Northwestern University (J.D., cum laude, 1982). Phi Beta Kappa; Alpha Sigma Nu. Member, Northwestern Journal of International Law and Business, 1980-1982. Co-Author: "Subject Matter Jurisdiction of District Courts," *Federal Civil Practice,* IICLE, 1983; "Privileges," *Illinois Civil Trial Evidence,* IICLE, 1985. ***SPECIAL AGENCIES:*** U.S. Environmental Protection Agency, Illinois Environmental Protection Agency. ***PRACTICE AREAS:*** Commercial Litigation; Appellate Practice; Legal Professional Liability. ***Email:*** rslobig@torshen.com

JAMES K. GENDEN, born Chicago, Illinois, June 7, 1948; admitted to bar, 1975, Illinois. *Education:* Harvard University (B.A., magna cum laude, 1969); Harvard Law School (J.D., cum laude, 1975). Phi Beta Kappa. Author: "Separate Legal Representation for Children," 11 Harvard Civil Rights-Civil Liberties Law Review 565, 1976. Co-Author with Wayne W. Whalen: "White House Geographic Report Fails to Tackle the McFadden Issue," American Banker, February 19, 1981. Co-Author: "Motion Practice on Appeal," *Illinois Civil Appeals,* ILCLE (2002); "A Guide to the Illinois Franchise Disclosure Act," 20 Franchise L.J. 59 (2000). Law Clerk to Hon. Bernard M. Decker, Judge of United States District Court, Northern District of Illinois, 1975-1977. ***LANGUAGES:*** Spanish. ***PRACTICE AREAS:*** Commercial Litigation; Appellate Practice; Intellectual Property Litigation; Landlord and Tenant Law. ***Email:*** jgenden@torshen.com

ZORAN DRAGUTINOVICH, born Gevelsberg, Germany, June 22, 1946; admitted to bar, 1983, Illinois. *Education:* Roosevelt University (B.A., with honors, 1967); New York University (M.A., 1968); Illinois Institute of Technology/Chicago-Kent College of Law (J.D., with high honors, 1983). Executive Editor, Notes and Comments, Chicago-Kent Law Review, 1982-1983. Author: "Recovery of Court-Appointed Defense Costs: Framework for a Model Recoupment Statute," 57 Chicago-Kent Law Review, 457, 1981. Co-Author: "Liability Problems," Illinois Condominium Law IICLE (2003 Supp.). Law Clerk to the Hon. Allen Hartman, Justice of Illinois Appellate Court, 1983-1985. ***LANGUAGES:*** Serbo-Croatian. ***PRACTICE AREAS:*** Commercial Litigation; Condominium Law; Appellate Practice; Class Actions. ***Email:*** zdragutinovich@torshen.com

BRADLEY J. AXEL, born Milwaukee, Wisconsin, March 29, 1971; admitted to bar, 1996, Illinois. *Education:* University of Wisconsin (B.A., 1993); John Marshall Law School (J.D., 1996). Assistant State's Attorney, Peoria County, Illinois, 1997-1999. ***PRACTICE AREAS:*** Commercial Litigation; Complex Business Litigation; Legal Professional Liability; Appellate Practice. ***Email:*** baxel@torshen.com

(This Listing Continued)

LAW OFFICES OF KEVIN TOTTIS

ONE EAST WACKER DRIVE, SUITE 2420
CHICAGO, ILLINOIS 60601
Telephone: 312-923-9620
Fax: 312-923-9626
Email: ktottis@tottislaw.com

Commercial Litigation and Intellectual Property Litigation.

KEVIN TOTTIS, born Ferndale, Michigan, August 8, 1961; admitted to bar, 1986, Illinois. *Education:* University of Michigan (A.B., with distinction and honors, 1983; J.D., 1986). Author: "Unscrambling the Anti-Unscrambling Law: The Digital Millennium Copyright Act in Light of *Eldred v. Ashcroft,*" *IP Litigator,* January/February 2004. Organizer and Moderator: "E-Discovery Unplugged," AIPLA Spring 2005 Meeting; "Beyond the Preliminary Injunction: Trying the Trademark Infringement Case," AIPLA Annual Meeting, October 2003. Speaker Panelist: "The Year in Copyright Law," AIPLA Advanced Copyright/Trademark Seminar," June 2003; "Litigating Under the 'Anti-Trafficking' Sections of the DMCA," AIPLA Annual Meeting, October 2002. *Member:* American Bar Association; American Intellectual Property Law Association; Association Internationale pour la Protection de la Propriété Intellectuelle. ***LANGUAGES:*** German and French.

JAMIE M. TRAPP & ASSOCIATES

221 NORTH LA SALLE STREET, SUITE 2910
CHICAGO, ILLINOIS 60601
Telephone: 312-368-1444
Fax: 312-263-1108
URL: http://www.lawyers.com/jamietrapp
Email: trapplaw@yahoo.com
URL: http://www.trapplaw.com

Personal Injury, Catastrophic Accidents and Injuries, Head Trauma, Spinal Cord Injuries, Motorcycle Accidents, Tort Litigation, Medical Malpractice, Birth Defects, Physician and Obstetric Malpractice, Surgical Malpractice, Airplane Crash Litigation, Automobile Accidents, Dog Bites, Railroad Accidents, Sexual Abuse, Wrongful Death, Construction Negligence.

JAMIE M. TRAPP, born Chicago, Illinois, January 15, 1956; admitted to bar, 1981, Illinois and U.S. District Court, Northern District of Illinois including Trial Bar. *Education:* Western Illinois University (B.A., with highest honors, 1978); DePaul University (J.D., 1981). Phi Alpha Delta. Recipient, Presidents Award, Illinois Trial Lawyers Association, 2002. Editor, "Automobile Litigation in Illinois," 2002. *Member:* Chicago, Illinois State and American Bar Associations; Illinois Trial Lawyers Association (Seminar Planning Chairman, 2001). ***PRACTICE AREAS:*** Personal Injury; Products Liability; Medical Malpractice.

ASSOCIATES

DOUGLAS C. DORN, born Chilton, Wisconsin, February 5, 1967; admitted to bar, 1995, Illinois. *Education:* Illinois State University (B.S., 1992); DePaul University (J.D., 1995). *Member:* Illinois State Bar Association; Illinois Trial Lawyers Association. [Specialist 4, U.S. Army, 1985-1988]. ***PRACTICE AREAS:*** Personal Injury; Medical Malpractice; Automobile Accidents and Injuries; Construction Law; Workers Compensation.

JEREMY L. GELLER, born Connecticut, August 12, 1977; admitted to bar, 2002, Illinois. *Education:* University of Wisconsin-Madison (B.S., 1999); John Marshall Law School (J.D., 2002). *Member:* Chicago, Illinois State and American Bar Associations; Illinois Trial Lawyers Association; Association of Trial Lawyers of America. ***LANGUAGES:*** Spanish. ***PRACTICE AREAS:*** Personal Injury; Automobile Accidents and Injuries; Truck Accidents; Products Liability; Medical Malpractice; Wrongful Death.

TRESSLER, SODERSTROM, MALONEY & PRIESS

Established in 1986
233 SOUTH WACKER DRIVE
SEARS TOWER
22ND FLOOR
CHICAGO, ILLINOIS 60606
Telephone: 312-627-4000
FAX: 312-627-1717
Email: tsmp@tsmp.com
URL: http://www.tsmp.com

Wheaton, Illinois Office: 2100 Manchester Road, Suite 950, 60187. Telephone: 630-668-2800. FAX: 630-668-3003.

(This Listing Continued)

Bolingbrook, Illinois Office: 305 West Briarcliff Road, Suite 201, 60440-0858. Telephone: 630-759-0800. FAX: 630-759-8504.

Newark, New Jersey Office: 744 Broad Street, Suite 1510, 07102. Telephone: 973-848-2900. Fax: 973-623-0405.

Los Angeles, California Office: 1901 Avenue of the Stars, Suite 450, 90067. Telephone: 310-203-4800. Fax: 310-203-4850.

Costa Mesa, California Office: 3070 Bristol Street, Suite 450, 92626. Telephone: 714-429-2900. Fax: 714-429-2901.

General Civil Litigation and Trial Practice, Insurance, Reinsurance, Litigation, Insurance Bad Faith, Appellate Practice, Business Litigation, Business Transactions, Class Action Defense, Commercial Litigation, Complex Litigation, Directors and Officers Liability, Construction Law, Architects and Engineers, Fidelity and Surety, Real Estate Litigation and Transactions, Alternative Dispute Resolution, Product Liability, Intellectual Property, Internet Law, Electronic Commerce, Environmental Law, Asbestos Litigation, Health Care, ERISA, Labor and Employment, Technology Law, Securities Litigation, Health Care, Bankruptcy, Advertising Law, Personal Injury, Trusts and Estates, Contracts, Professional Liability, Regulatory, White Collar Crime, Corporate Law, Mergers and Acquisitions, Commodities, Condominium and Common Interest Community Law, Municipal Law.

FIRM PROFILE: Tressler, Soderstrom, Maloney & Priess is committed to preventive law and risk management for its clients and aggressive representation in litigation. Our experience in the trial and resolution of cases affords us the knowledge base to partner with clients effectively and efficiently to solve their business problems, optimize their profitability, and minimize their future risk and liability exposure. Expanding from its roots in insurance and reinsurance law, the firm works in a wide range of crucial practices to business and management. These include employment law, technology law, products liability, corporate and commercial and securities law, intellectual property, advertising injury and liability, bankruptcy, environmental and regulatory law, complex litigation, transportation and communications, fidelity and surety, advance trusts and estate planning. Our attorneys provide clients with consulting services and research analysis to avoid costly mistakes and respond quickly to business challenges and changing markets.

MEMBERS OF FIRM

JAY H. TRESSLER, born Chicago, Illinois, January 29, 1942; admitted to bar, 1967, Illinois. *Education:* DePauw University (A.B., 1964); University of Illinois (J.D., 1967). ***PRACTICE AREAS:*** Mediation; Complex Civil Litigation; Class Actions; Products Liability; Toxic Torts; Construction Law; Transportation; Commercial Disputes. ***Email:*** jtressler@tsmp.com

ROBERT S. SODERSTROM, born Chicago, Illinois, June 5, 1944; admitted to bar, 1969, Illinois. *Education:* Kenyon College (A.B., 1966); Loyola University (J.D., 1969). ***PRACTICE AREAS:*** Insurance; Reinsurance; Commercial Law; Environmental Law; Litigation; Class Actions; Appellate Practice. ***Email:*** rsoderstrom@tsmp.com

PATRICK E. MALONEY, born Chicago, Illinois, October 5, 1945; admitted to bar, 1970, Illinois. *Education:* University of Notre Dame (A.B., 1967; J.D., 1970). ***PRACTICE AREAS:*** Insurance; Environmental Law; Products Liability; Torts; Alternative Dispute Resolution; Toxic Torts; Litigation. ***Email:*** pmaloney@tsmp.com

HOWARD K. PRIESS II, born Chicago, Illinois, January 17, 1944; admitted to bar, 1971, Illinois. *Education:* Northwestern University (B.S., 1967); Chicago-Kent College of Law (J.D., 1971). ***PRACTICE AREAS:*** Products Liability; Construction Law; Commercial Litigation; Eminent Domain. ***Email:*** hpriess@tsmp.com

DANIEL R. FORMELLER, born Chicago, Illinois, August 15, 1949; admitted to bar, 1976, Illinois. *Education:* University of Illinois (B.A., 1970); DePaul University (J.D, 1976). ***PRACTICE AREAS:*** Directors and Officers Liability; Business Litigation; Professional Liability; Class Actions; Securities Litigation. ***Email:*** dformeller@tsmp.com

WILLIAM A. KINDORF, III, born St. Louis, Missouri, March 21, 1952; admitted to bar, 1977, Illinois. *Education:* University of Illinois (B.S., 1974); University of Michigan (J.D., 1976). (Also at Wheaton Office). ***PRACTICE AREAS:*** Business Law; Health Care; Estate Planning; Real Estate; Corporate Law. ***Email:*** bkindorf@tsmp.com

JUDITH FOURNIE HELMS, born Belleville, Illinois, October 12, 1952; admitted to bar, 1978, Illinois; 1984, Wisconsin. *Education:* DePaul University (B.A., 1973; J.D., 1978). ***PRACTICE AREAS:*** Insurance; Complex Litigation. ***Email:*** jhelms@tsmp.com

DAVID E. TRAINOR, born Pontiac, Illinois, May 25, 1949; admitted to bar, 1979, Illinois. *Education:* Illinois State University (B.S., 1973); The John Marshall Law School (J.D., 1979). ***PRACTICE AREAS:*** Insurance Coverage; Litigation; Directors and Officers Liability; Commercial Litigation. ***Email:*** dtrainor@tsmp.com

SHAUN McPARLAND BALDWIN, born Chicago, Illinois, October 19, 1954; admitted to bar, 1980, Illinois. *Education:* Northern Illinois University (B.S., 1976); John Marshall Law School (J.D., 1980). ***PRACTICE AREAS:*** Insurance Bad Faith; Insurance Coverage; Reinsurance; Litigation; Appellate Practice; Alternative Dispute Resolution; Class Action; Technology. ***Email:*** sbaldwin@tsmp.com

JACQUELINE A. CRISWELL, born Jersey City, New Jersey, January 23, 1956; admitted to bar, 1981, Illinois. *Education:* Wheaton College (B.M., 1978); DePaul University (J.D., 1981). ***PRACTICE AREAS:*** Litigation; Intellectual Property; Trademarks; Copyright Infringement; Patents; Internet Law; Advertising Law; Electronic Commerce; Professional Liability; Securities. ***Email:*** jcriswell@tsmp.com

STEPHEN T. GROSSMARK, born Chicago, Illinois, July 8, 1952; admitted to bar, 1977, Illinois. *Education:* University of Illinois (B.A., 1974); Washington University (J.D., 1977). ***PRACTICE AREAS:*** Environmental Law; Toxic Torts; Litigation; Products Liability; Commercial Litigation; Industry-wide Litigation. ***Email:*** sgrossmark@tsmp.com

MICHAEL W. MORRISON, born Kent, Ohio, April 8, 1953; admitted to bar, 1979, Illinois. *Education:* University of Illinois (B.A., 1976); Loyola University (J.D., 1979). ***PRACTICE AREAS:*** Insurance; Appellate Practice; Litigation. ***Email:*** mmorrison@tsmp.com

(This Listing Continued)

JOHN P. MANIATIS, born Evergreen Park, Illinois, September 8, 1956; admitted to bar, 1982, Illinois. *Education:* Illinois Institute of Technology (B.S., 1978); John Marshall Law School (J.D., 1982). ***PRACTICE AREAS:*** Personal Injury; Wrongful Death; Medical Malpractice; Commercial Litigation; Transportation. ***Email:*** jmaniatis@tsmp.com

JENNIFER JERIT JOHNSON, born Cortland, New York, April 23, 1960; admitted to bar, 1985, Illinois. *Education:* University of Illinois at Urbana-Champaign (B.A., 1982); Loyola University (J.D., 1985). ***PRACTICE AREAS:*** Torts; Litigation; Products Liability; Toxic Torts; Construction Litigation; Commercial Litigation. ***Email:*** jjohnson@tsmp.com

THOMAS K. HANEKAMP, born Chicago, Illinois, April 21, 1961; admitted to bar, 1986, Illinois. *Education:* Indiana University (B.A., 1983); DePaul University (J.D., 1986). ***PRACTICE AREAS:*** Insurance; Directors and Officers Liability; Reinsurance. ***Email:*** thanekamp@tsmp.com

MARY E. McPHERSON, born Fontana, California, March 1, 1961; admitted to bar, 1986, Colorado; 1989, Illinois; 1995, California. *Education:* Wellesley College (B.A., 1983); University of Notre Dame (J.D., 1986). (Resident Member, Los Angeles, California Office). ***PRACTICE AREAS:*** Insurance; Appellate Practice; Litigation; Insurance Bad Faith; Advertising Law; Intellectual Property. ***Email:*** mmcpherson@tsmp.com

JOHN H. HUSTON, born Dayton, Ohio, July 24, 1941; admitted to bar, 1976, Illinois. *Education:* Yale University (B.S., 1963; B.E., 1964); Loyola University (J.D., 1976). ***PRACTICE AREAS:*** Products Liability; Professional Liability; Architects and Engineers Liability; Commercial Litigation. ***Email:*** jhuston@tsmp.com

DION J. SARTORIO, born Ottawa, Illinois, September 5, 1956; admitted to bar, 1981, Illinois. *Education:* University of Illinois (B.S., 1978; J.D., 1981). ***PRACTICE AREAS:*** Insurance; Reinsurance; Professional Liability; Directors and Officers Liability; Litigation; Appellate Practice. ***Email:*** djsartorio@tsmp.com

JAMES R. MURRAY, born Oak Park, Illinois, March 22, 1960; admitted to bar, 1986, Illinois. *Education:* University of Illinois (B.S., 1983); John Marshall Law School (J.D., 1986). ***PRACTICE AREAS:*** Insurance Coverage; Insurance Bad Faith; Personal Injury; Environmental Insurance Coverage; Asbestos; Litigation. ***Email:*** jmurray@tsmp.com

MICHAEL J. DUFFY, born Evanston, Illinois, August 5, 1960; admitted to bar, 1987, Illinois. *Education:* Northern Illinois University (B.A., 1982); DePaul University (J.D., 1987). ***PRACTICE AREAS:*** Insurance; Commercial Law; Reinsurance; Contracts; Class Actions. ***Email:*** mduffy@tsmp.com

MAUREEN A. COLEMAN, born Chicago, Illinois, December 29, 1944; admitted to bar, 1988, Illinois. *Education:* College of St. Francis (B.S., 1982); Loyola University School of Law, Chicago (J.D., 1988). ***PRACTICE AREAS:*** Personal Injury; Medical Malpractice; Products Liability; Litigation. ***Email:*** mcoleman@tsmp.com

JAMES K. BORCIA, born Evanston, Illinois, March 30, 1964; admitted to bar, 1989, Illinois. *Education:* Northern Illinois University (B.S., 1986); Chicago-Kent College of Law (J.D., 1988). ***PRACTICE AREAS:*** Intellectual Property; Commercial Litigation; Contracts; Professional Liability; Directors and Officers Liability; Torts; Products Liability; Internet Law; Class Actions; Employment; Securities; Real Estate. ***Email:*** jborcia@tsmp.com

JAMES A. PINDERSKI, born Chicago, Illinois, August 12, 1964; admitted to bar, 1989, Illinois. *Education:* University of Illinois (B.A., 1986; J.D., 1989). ***PRACTICE AREAS:*** First and Third Party Insurance; Insurance Bad Faith; Insurance; Commercial Litigation; Products Liability; Appellate Practice. ***Email:*** jpinderski@tsmp.com

DURGA M. BHARAM, born Kakinada, Andhra Pradesh, India, April 12, 1966; admitted to bar, 1990, Illinois. *Education:* Andhra Pradesh University (B.Comm, 1986); Northwestern University (J.D., 1990). ***PRACTICE AREAS:*** Employment Law; Commercial Litigation. ***Email:*** dbharam@tsmp.com

DAVID L. KABAT, born Chicago, Illinois, July 6, 1946; admitted to bar, 1972, Illinois. *Education:* University of Notre Dame (B.A., 1968; J.D., 1972). ***PRACTICE AREAS:*** Commercial Real Estate; Construction Law; Financial Institutions Law; Business Law; Commercial Litigation; Franchise Law; Alternative Dispute Resolution. ***Email:*** dkabat@tsmp.com

DANIEL J. CUNNINGHAM, born Springfield, Pennsylvania, June 9, 1966; admitted to bar, 1991, Illinois. *Education:* University of Iowa (B.A., 1988); DePaul University (J.D., 1991). ***PRACTICE AREAS:*** Insurance Coverage; Insurance Bad Faith. ***Email:*** dcunningham@tsmp.com

CATHERINE CONNELLY-WARREN, born Detroit, Michigan, July 1, 1967; admitted to bar, 1991, Illinois. *Education:* University of Michigan (A.B., 1988); University of Notre Dame (J.D., 1991). ***PRACTICE AREAS:*** Insurance Coverage; Appellate Practice; Litigation. ***Email:*** cwarren@tsmp.com

ROBERT D. KOLAR, born Chicago, Illinois, August 21, 1938; admitted to bar, 1967, Illinois; 1994, Texas. *Education:* Roosevelt University (B.S., 1961); John Marshall Law School (J.D., 1967). ***PRACTICE AREAS:*** Products Liability; Complex Litigation; Intellectual Property; Technical Litigation; Professional Liability; Directors and Officers Liability. ***Email:*** rkolar@tsmp.com

ROBERT J. HEYNE, born Evergreen Park, Illinois, May 5, 1953; admitted to bar, 1979, Illinois. *Education:* Western Illinois University (B.B., 1976); The John Marshall Law School (J.D., 1979). ***PRACTICE AREAS:*** Commercial Litigation; Construction Litigation; Fidelity and Surety. ***Email:*** rheyne@tsmp.com

JAMES A. KNOX, JR., born Dallas, Texas, October 27, 1957; admitted to bar, 1984, Texas; 1985, Oklahoma; 1987, Illinois. *Education:* Southern Methodist University (B.A., 1980); University of Texas at Austin (J.D., 1984). ***PRACTICE AREAS:*** Fidelity and Surety; Construction Law; Professional Liability; Commercial Litigation; Directors and Officers Liability; Appellate Practice. ***Email:*** jknox@tsmp.com

KATHERINE E. TAMMARO, born New York, N.Y., January 28, 1967; admitted to bar, 1992, Illinois. *Education:* University of Notre Dame (B.A., 1989); Georgetown University (J.D., 1992). ***PRACTICE AREAS:*** Insurance; Litigation; Appellate Practice; Reinsurance; Internet Law. ***Email:*** ktammaro@tsmp.com

(This Listing Continued)

TRESSLER, SODERSTROM, MALONEY & PRIESS, Chicago—Continued

MARK T. BANOVETZ, born Evanston, Illinois, February 14, 1967; admitted to bar, 1992, Illinois. *Education:* Northern Illinois University (B.A., 1989); DePaul University (J.D., 1992). ***PRACTICE AREAS:*** Civil Litigation; Torts; Aviation Law; Construction Law; Commercial Litigation; Insurance Coverage; Professional Liability; Products Liability. ***Email:*** mbanovetz@tsmp.com

MICHAEL J. POLACHEK, born Chicago, Illinois, October 22, 1950; admitted to bar, 1976, Illinois. *Education:* University of Illinois at Urbana-Champaign (B.A., 1973); Chicago-Kent College of Law (J.D., 1976). (Resident Member, Wheaton Office). ***PRACTICE AREAS:*** Closely Held Business Law; Business Acquisitions; Business Divestitures; Commercial Real Estate; Zoning Law; Estate Planning. ***Email:*** mpolachek@tsmp.com

BRUCE M. ENGEL, born Chicago, Illinois, January 6, 1957; admitted to bar, 1984, Illinois. *Education:* University of Illinois (B.A., 1981; J.D., 1984). ***PRACTICE AREAS:*** Insurance Coverage; Reinsurance; Litigation. ***Email:*** bengel@tsmp.com

TODD S. SCHENK, born Joliet, Illinois, February 4, 1970; admitted to bar, 1995, Illinois. *Education:* Indiana University (B.A., 1992; J.D., 1995). ***PRACTICE AREAS:*** Insurance Coverage; Litigation; Commercial; Appellate Practice. ***Email:*** tschenk@tsmp.com

PAUL S. WHITE, born Salt Lake City, Utah, July 11, 1962; admitted to bar, 1990, California. *Education:* Brigham Young University (B.A., 1985); University of Utah (J.D., 1989). (Resident Member, Los Angeles, California Office). ***PRACTICE AREAS:*** Insurance Coverage; Insurance Bad Faith; Errors and Ommisions; General Liability; Intellectual Property Law; Media Law; Employment Law; Appellate Practice. ***Email:*** pwhite@tsmp.com

MARK R. VESPOLE, born Montclair, New Jersey, October 9, 1951; admitted to bar, 1977, New Jersey. *Education:* University of Notre Dame (B.S., 1973); Seton Hall University (J.D., 1977). (Resident Member, Newark, New Jersey Office). ***PRACTICE AREAS:*** Insurance Coverage; Products Liability; Professional Liability; Construction Law; Employment Law; Litigation; Toxic Tort; Mediation; Arbitration. ***Email:*** mvespole@tsmp.com

ANDREW S. BORIS, born Brookline, Massachusetts, May 19, 1967; admitted to bar, 1996, Illinois. *Education:* Boston College (B.A., 1989); DePaul University (J.D., 1996). ***PRACTICE AREAS:*** Insurance Coverage; Reinsurance; Litigation. ***Email:*** aboris@tsmp.com

RALPH J. KOOY, born Hinsdale, Illinois, October 9, 1967; admitted to bar, 1992, Illinois. *Education:* University of Illinois (B.A., 1989; J.D., 1992). ***PRACTICE AREAS:*** Fidelity and Surety; Commercial Litigation; Construction Law. ***Email:*** rkooy@tsmp.com

JOHN W. CARVER, born Elmhurst, Illinois, September 18, 1964; admitted to bar, 1990, Illinois. *Education:* Southern Illinois University (B.A., 1987); University of Iowa (J.D., 1990). ***PRACTICE AREAS:*** Construction Law; Employment Law; Professional Liability; Directors and Officers Liability; Litigation; Commercial. ***Email:*** jcarver@tsmp.com

DAVID SIMANTOB, born Tehran, Iran, October 7, 1966; admitted to bar, 1991, California. *Education:* Brown University (B.A., 1988); University of California at Los Angeles School of Law (J.D., 1991). (Resident Member, Los Angeles, California Office). ***PRACTICE AREAS:*** Insurance Coverage; Insurance Bad Faith; Litigation; Appellate Practice; Alternative Dispute Resolution. ***Email:*** dsimantob@tsmp.com

WEN-SHIN CHENG, born Kaohsiung, Taiwan, August 29,1971; admitted to bar, 1996, Illinois. *Education:* University of Illinois (B.A., 1992); College of William & Mary (J.D., 1996). ***PRACTICE AREAS:*** Insurance Coverage; Commercial Litigation; Insurance Bad Faith; Litigation. ***Email:*** wcheng@tsmp.com

CARRIE E. COPE, born Iowa, June 29, 1959; admitted to bar, 1991, Illinois. *Education:* Western Illinois University (B.A., 1981); University of Dayton (J.D., 1990). ***PRACTICE AREAS:*** Insurance Regulation; Directors and Officers Liability; Employment Practices Liability Insurance; Insurance Products; Professional Liability; Fiduciary Liability. ***Email:*** ccope@tsmp.com

LINDA TAI HOSHIDE, born New York, New York, June 10, 1970; admitted to bar, 1997, California. *Education:* University of California at Los Angeles (B.A., 1993); Loyola Marymount University (J.D., 1996). (Resident Associate, Los Angeles, California Office). ***PRACTICE AREAS:*** Commercial Litigation; Insurance Bad Faith; Environmental Insurance Coverage; Advertising and Personal Injury Coverage; Professional Liability; Errors and Ommisions. ***Email:*** lhoshide@tsmp.com

LINDA BONDI MORRISON, born Chicago, Illinois, January 18, 1965; admitted to bar, 1994, Illinois; 2000, California. *Education:* Loyola University (B.A., 1991; J.D., 1994). (Resident Member, Costa Mesa, California Office). ***PRACTICE AREAS:*** Litigation; Insurance; Insurance Bad Faith; Environmental Law; Toxic Torts; Construction Defects. ***Email:*** lmorrison@tsmp.com

JOANNA L. CROSBY, born Jersey City, New Jersey, November 6, 1962; admitted to bar, 1986, New Jersey. *Education:* St. Peter's College (B.A., 1983); Seton Hall University (J.D., 1986). (Resident Member, Newark, New Jersey Office). ***PRACTICE AREAS:*** Insurance Coverage; Personal Injury; Employment; Construction Law. ***Email:*** jcrosby@tsmp.com

THERESA E. MULLEN, born Staten Island, New York, January 23, 1967; admitted to bar, 1993, New Jersey; 1994, New York. *Education:* Lehigh University (B.A., cum laude, 1989); Albany Law School (J.D., 1993). (Certified by the Supreme Court of New Jersey as a Civil Trial Attorney) (Resident Member, Newark, New Jersey Office). ***PRACTICE AREAS:*** Insurance Coverage; Malpractice; Personal Injury; Premises Liability; Products Liability; Contractual and Indemnity Defense. ***Email:*** tmullen@tsmp.com

KATHERINE KLIMA LINER, born Prague, Czechoslovakia, July 23, 1964; admitted to bar, 1989, California. *Education:* University of Illinois (B.A., 1986; J.D., 1989). (Resident Member, Costa Mesa, California Office). ***PRACTICE AREAS:*** Insurance Coverage; Civil Litigation. ***Email:*** kliner@tsmp.com

(This Listing Continued)

DONALD W. McCORMICK, born Birmingham, Alabama, August 19, 1954; admitted to bar, 1981, Louisiana; 1982, Alabama; 1983, California. *Education:* Vanderbilt University (B.A., 1976); Tulane University School of Law (J.D., 1981). (Resident Member, Los Angeles, California Office). ***PRACTICE AREAS:*** Insurance Coverage; Insurance Bad Faith; Complex Litigation; Products Liability; Intellectual Property; Torts. ***Email:*** dmccormick@tsmp.com

ROBERT J. FETTWEIS, born Elizabeth, New Jersey, May 17, 1947; admitted to bar, 1972, New Jersey. *Education:* Seton Hall University (B.A., 1969); Cornell University (J.D., 1972). (Resident Member, Newark, New Jersey Office). ***PRACTICE AREAS:*** White Collar Crime; Commercial Litigation; Securities Arbitration; Directors and Officers Liability; Internal Investigations. ***Email:*** rfettweis@tsmp.com

IAN R. STEVENSON, born September 21, 1965; admitted to bar, 1991, Illinois and Wisconsin. *Education:* Lawrence University (B.A., 1987); University of Wisconsin-Madison Law School (J.D., 1991). ***PRACTICE AREAS:*** Insurance Coverage; Errors and Omissions Liability; Directors and Officers Liability; Insurance Law; Litigation. ***Email:*** istevenson@tsmp.com

STEVEN R. McMANNON, born 1957; admitted to bar, 1983, Idaho; 1986, Illinois. *Education:* Boise State University (B.B.A., 1979); University of Idaho (J.D., 1983). ***PRACTICE AREAS:*** Insurance; ERISA; Employment Benefits; Professional Liability; Commercial Civil Disputes. ***Email:*** smcmannon@tsmp.com

HARRY E. BARTOSIAK, born Hinsdale, Illinois, May 20, 1966; admitted to bar, 1992, Illinois. *Education:* Loyola University, Chicago (B.A., 1989; J.D., 1992). (Resident Member, Wheaton Office). ***PRACTICE AREAS:*** Corporate Law; Business Transactions; Health Care; Real Estate; HIPAA Compliance. ***Email:*** hbartosiak@tsmp.com

JANELLE K. CHRISTENSEN, born Denver, Colorado, March 25, 1966; admitted to bar, 1993, Colorado; 1994, Illinois. *Education:* University of Colorado at Boulder (B.F.A., 1988); University of Miami (J.D., 1993). ***PRACTICE AREAS:*** Civil Litigation; Insurance Defense; Insurance Bad Faith; Personal Injury. ***Email:*** jchristensen@tsmp.com

MICHAELA L. SOZIO, born Rochester, Minnesota, December 29, 1969; admitted to bar, 1995, California. *Education:* Villanova University (B.S., 1992); University of the Pacific, McGeorge School of Law (J.D., 1995). (Resident Member, Los Angeles, California Office). ***PRACTICE AREAS:*** Intellectual Property; Defamation; Employment; Business Litigation; Insurance Coverage; Commercial Law; Products Liability; Insurance Bad Faith. ***Email:*** msozio@tsmp.com

BARRY L. MOSS, born Chicago, Illinois, February 3, 1943; admitted to bar, 1968, Illinois. *Education:* Bradley University (B.S., 1964); Northwestern University Law School (J.D., 1967). (Resident Member, Bolingbrook Office). ***PRACTICE AREAS:*** Municipal Law; School Law; Local Government Law; Litigation; Corporate; Real Estate; Zoning. ***Email:*** bmoss@tsmp.com

STEVEN P. BLOOMBERG, born Chicago, Illinois, November 13, 1943; admitted to bar, 1969, Illinois. *Education:* University of Wisconsin (B.S., 1965); DePaul University (J.D., 1968). (Resident Member, Bolingbrook Office). ***PRACTICE AREAS:*** Condominium Law; Municipal Law; Local Government Law; Corporate Law; Litigation; Real Estate. ***Email:*** sbloomberg@tsmp.com

GEORGE A. MARCHETTI, born Chicago, Illinois, September 27, 1948; admitted to bar, 1978, Illinois. *Education:* University of Notre Dame (B.A., 1970); University of Chicago (M.A., 1972); Chicago-Kent College of Law (J.D., 1978). (Resident Member, Bolingbrook Office). ***PRACTICE AREAS:*** Municipal Law; School Law; Local Government Law; Litigation; Zoning. ***Email:*** gmarchetti@tsmp.com

DAVID J. FREEMAN, born Brooklyn, New York, December 14, 1958; admitted to bar, 1983, New Jersey and Pennsylvania; 1988, Illinois. *Education:* Georgetown University (A.B., 1979); Delaware Law School of Widener University (J.D., 1983). (Resident Member, Bolingbrook Office). ***PRACTICE AREAS:*** Litigation; Insurance Defense; Condominium; Municipal. ***Email:*** dfreeman@tsmp.com

JAMES BOAN, born Milwaukee, Wisconsin, May 27, 1951; admitted to bar, 1983, Illinois. *Education:* University of Illinois (B.S.L.A., 1973); Northern Illinois University (J.D., 1983). (Resident Member, Bolingbrook Office). ***PRACTICE AREAS:*** Municipal Law; Local Government Law; Zoning Law; Land Use; Litigation. ***Email:*** jboan@tsmp.com

OF COUNSEL

KATHERINE STREICHER ARNOLD, born Monroe, Michigan, January 11, 1961; admitted to bar, 1987, Illinois. *Education:* University of Michigan (A.B., 1993); Indiana University School of Law (J.D., 1987). ***PRACTICE AREAS:*** Insurance Coverage; Environmental Insurance Coverage.

SHERRIN ROSS INGRAM, born New Orleans, Louisiana, May 12, 1968; admitted to bar, 1993, Illinois. *Education:* Whittier College (B.A., 1989); University of Iowa (J.D., 1992). ***PRACTICE AREAS:*** Litigation; Environmental Insurance Coverage.

BERNARD E. DREW, JR., born Waukegan, Illinois, February 27, 1942; admitted to bar, 1968, Wisconsin; 1969, Illinois. *Education:* Miami University (B.S., 1965); Marquette University (J.D., 1968). Associate Judge, 1975-1984. Circuit Court Judge, 1984-1990. Chief Judge of the 19th Judicial Circuit (Lake and McHenry, IL Counties), 1988-1990. ***PRACTICE AREAS:*** Arbitration; Mediation. ***Email:*** bdrew@tsmp.com

C. DAVID SULLIVAN, born Fall River, Massachusetts, April 29, 1932; admitted to bar, 1969, Massachusetts; 1976, Illinois. *Education:* St. Bonaventure University (B.B.A., 1954); Suffolk University (J.D., 1966). Member, National Insurance Crime Bureau. *Member:* Massachusetts and Illinois State Bar Associations; Defense Research Institute; International Association of Defense Trial Counsel; Worker's Compensation Research Institute. ***PRACTICE AREAS:*** Fraud; Subrogation; First and Third Party Insurance; Insurance Litigation. ***Email:*** cdsullivan@tsmp.com

C. JACKSON DARNALL, born Waukegan, Illinois, January 14, 1934; admitted to bar, 1960, Illinois. *Education:* Northwestern University (B.A., 1957; J.D., 1960). (Resident Of Counsel, Wheaton Office). ***PRACTICE AREAS:*** Real Estate; Estate Planning; Closely Held Business Law; Credit Union Law. ***Email:*** cjdarnall@tsmp.com

(This Listing Continued)

ASSOCIATES

PETE V. ALBANIS, born Chicago, Illinois, January 31, 1977; admitted to bar, 2002, Illinois. *Education:* University of Chicago (B.A., 1999); DePaul University (J.D., 2002). ***Email:*** palbanis@tsmp.com

JEFFREY MARK ALPERIN, born Grosse Pointe, Michigan, February 25, 1968; admitted to bar, 1994, Michigan; 1995, Illinois; 2001, Wisconsin. *Education:* University of Michigan (B.A., 1990; J.D., 1993). ***Email:*** jalperin@tsmp.com

LARA A. ANDERSON, born Chicago, Illinois, August 19, 1967; admitted to bar, 1992, Illinois. *Education:* Northern Illinois University (B.S., 1989; J.D., 1992). (Resident Associate, Bolingbrook Office). ***Email:*** landerson@tsmp.com

JAMES P. ARRIGO, born Chicago, Illinois, February 6, 1960; admitted to bar, 1994, Illinois. *Education:* University of Illinois (B.S., 1982); DePaul University College of Law (J.D., 1994). (Resident Associate, Bolingbrook Office). ***Email:*** jarrigo@tsmp.com

JEFFREY D. BARCLAY, born Chicago, Illinois, April 14, 1964; admitted to bar, 1996, Illinois. *Education:* Loyola University (B.A., 1986); DePaul University (J.D., 1996). ***Email:*** jbarclay@tsmp.com

DANEEN FITZPATRICK BERRES, born Chicago, Illinois, May 5, 1975; admitted to bar, 2000, Illinois. *Education:* Marquette University (B.A., 1997); DePaul University (J.D., 2000). ***Email:*** dberres@tsmp.com

HEATHER M. BROWN-SMITH, born Los Angeles, California, February 14, 1966; admitted to bar, 1999, California. *Education:* University of California, Irvine (B.A., 1989); Western State University College of Law (J.D., magna cum laude, 1997). (Resident Associate, Costa Mesa, California Office). ***Email:*** hbrownsmith@tsmp.com

KRISTEN S. BURNS, born Salem, Massachusetts, March 20, 1973; admitted to bar, 1998, Illinois; 2001, Massachusetts. *Education:* Canisius College (B.A., 1995); DePaul University (J.D., 1998). ***Email:*** kburns@tsmp.com

MARCOS G. CANCIO, born San Juan, Puerto Rico, September 11, 1978; admitted to bar, 2003, Illinois. *Education:* Indiana University (B.A., 2000); Loyola University (J.D., 2003). ***Email:*** mcancio@tsmp.com

RINA CARMEL, born New York, New York, June 24, 1968; admitted to bar, 1998, Illinois; 2000, California. *Education:* Bryn Mawr College (A.B., 1990); University of Michigan (M.A., 1993; J.D., 1997). (Resident Associate, Los Angeles, California Office). ***Email:*** rcarmel@tsmp.com

JASON M. CRAFT, born Flat Rock, Michigan, November 30, 1975; admitted to bar, 2001, Illinois. *Education:* Michigan State University (B.A., 1998); DePaul University (J.D., 2001). ***Email:*** jcraft@tsmp.com

MATTHEW J. DEVEREUX, born Chicago, Illinois, February 20, 1970; admitted to bar, 1996, Illinois. *Education:* University of Notre Dame (B.A., 1992); DePaul University (J.D., 1996). ***Email:*** mdevereux@tsmp.com

THOMAS G. DRENNAN, born Blue Island, Illinois, October 17, 1976; admitted to bar, 2001, Illinois. *Education:* University of Illinois, Urbana-Champaign (B.A., 1998); Indiana University School of Law (J.D., 2001). ***Email:*** tdrennan@tsmp.com

JILL JENNINGS DRZEWIECKI, born Lawton, Oklahoma, February 13, 1971; admitted to bar, 1997, Illinois. *Education:* Oklahoma City University (B.S., 1993); Loyola University (J.D., 1997). ***Email:*** jdrzewiecki@tsmp.com

DONALD E. ELDER, born Frederick, Maryland, April 29, 1970; admitted to bar, 1998, Illinois. *Education:* University of Minnesota (B.A., 1993); Thomas M. Cooley Law School (J.D., 1998). ***Email:*** delder@tsmp.com

BONNY GARCHA, born New Delhi, India, August 15, 1974; admitted to bar, 1999, Illinois. *Education:* University of Illinois, Urbana-Champaign (B.A., 1996); Loyola University, Chicago (J.D., 1999). ***Email:*** bgarcha@tsmp.com

STEPHEN M. GREEN, born Westminster, California, September 25, 1970; admitted to bar, 1999, California. *Education:* Arizona State University (B.A., 1994); Whittier College School of Law (J.D., 1998). (Resident Associate, Los Angeles, California Office). ***Email:*** sgreen@tsmp.com

ADAM C. HACKETT, born Allentown, Pennsylvania, January 14, 1974; admitted to bar, 2002, California. *Education:* University of Notre Dame (B.B.A.; B.A., 1996); Georgetown University Law Center (J.D., 2002). (Resident Associate, Costa Mesa, California Office). ***Email:*** ahackett@tsmp.com

KATHERINE L. HAENNICKE, born Evergreen Park, Illinois, December 18, 1975; admitted to bar, 2000, Illinois. *Education:* Knox College (B.A., 1997); John Marshall Law School (J.D., 2000; LL.M., 2001). ***Email:*** khaennicke@tsmp.com

JAMES C. HAUSER, born Evanston, Illinois, August 19, 1950; admitted to bar, 1977, Illinois. *Education:* University of Illinois (B.A., 1972); Loyola University (J.D., 1977). ***Email:*** jhauser@tsmp.com

KAREN L. HEDEEN, born Dearborn, Michigan, February 16, 1967; admitted to bar, 1999, Illinois. *Education:* University of Illinois (B.S., 1992); Loyola University (J.D., 1999). ***Email:*** khedeen@tsmp.com

JOHN A. HUSMANN, born Louisville, Kentucky, November 13, 1969; admitted to bar, 2000, Illinois. *Education:* Creighton University (B.A., 1991); Loyola University (J.D., 2000). ***Email:*** jhusmann@tsmp.com

JAMIE C. KANDALEPAS, born Arlington Heights, Illinois, October 3, 1977; admitted to bar, 2002, Wisconsin; 2003, Illinois. *Education:* Northwestern University (B.A., 1999); Marquette University (J.D. 2002). ***Email:*** jkandalepas@tsmp.com

BASILEIOS KATRIS, born Waukegan, Illinois, November 20, 1971; admitted to bar, 1997, Illinois. *Education:* Loyola University-Chicago (B.A., 1994); Chicago-Kent College of Law (J.D., 1997). ***Email:*** bkatris@tsmp.com

MEGHAN M. KELLY, born Arlington Heights, Illinois, September 14, 1976; admitted to bar, 2004, Illinois. *Education:* Marquette University (B.S., 1998); University of Notre Dame (J.D., 2004). ***Email:*** mkelly@tsmp.com

(This Listing Continued)

DALE R. KURTH, born Fort Leonard Wood, Missouri, December 12, 1952; admitted to bar, 1984, Illinois. *Education:* University of Illinois (B.S., 1974; J.D., 1984). ***Email:*** dkurth@tsmp.com

MAUREEN LEPOCHAT, born Orange, New Jersey, November 20, 1957; admitted to bar, 1984, New Jersey. *Education:* C.W. Post Center of Long Island University (B.A., 1979); Seton Hall University (J.D., 1983). (Resident Associate, Newark, New Jersey Office). ***Email:*** mlepochat@tsmp.com

TIMOTHY R. LESSMAN, born Waukegan, Illinois, June 9, 1978; admitted to bar, 2005, Illinois. *Education:* University of Illinois at Urbana-Champaign (B.A., 1999); DePaul University College of Law (J.D., 2005). ***Email:*** tlessman@tsmp.com

CARI-ANN R. LEVINE, born New York, N.Y., September 12, 1977; admitted to bar, 2003, New York and New Jersey. *Education:* Rutgers University (B.A., 1999); St. John's University School of Law (J.D., 2002). (Resident Associate, Newark, New Jersey Office). ***Email:*** clevine@tsmp.com

TELLY J. LIAPIS, born Park Ridge, Illinois, October 16, 1972; admitted to bar, 1997, Illinois. *Education:* Loyola University (B.A., 1994); ITT/Chicago-Kent College of Law (J.D., 1997). ***Email:*** tliapis@tsmp.com

TORIA L. LUND, born Rockford, Illinois, August 25, 1980; admitted to bar, 2005, Illinois. *Education:* Marquette University (B.A., 2002); The John Marshall Law School (J.D., 2005). ***Email:*** tlund@tsmp.com

DEVIN C. MADDOX, born Chicago, Illinois, September 29, 1978; admitted to bar, 2004, Illinois. *Education:* University of Illinois (B.A., 2000); John Marshall Law School (J.D., 2004). ***Email:*** dmaddox@tsmp.com

ERIN L. MAJKA, born Abington, Pennsylvania, June 24, 1976; admitted to bar, 2002, Illinois. *Education:* DePauw University (B.A., 1999); DePaul University (J.D., 2002). ***Email:*** emajka@tsmp.com

KATHY KARABOYAS MALAMIS, born Chicago, Illinois, April 30, 1976; admitted to bar, 2001, Illinois. *Education:* Loyola University (B.A., 1998); DePaul University (J.D., 2001). ***Email:*** kkaraboyas@tsmp.com

KATHERINE E. MAST, born Jackson, Michigan, July 2, 1974; admitted to bar, 2002, California. *Education:* Pepperdine University (B.A., 1996); Loyola of Los Angeles Law School (J.D., 2002). (Resident Associate, Los Angeles, California Office). ***Email:*** kmast@tsmp.com

CHRISTIAN D. MOLLOY, born June 20, 1978; admitted to bar, 2005, California. *Education:* University of California at San Diego (B.A., 2000); Southwestern University School of Law (J.D., 2004). (Resident Associate, Los Angeles, California Office). ***Email:*** cmolloy@tsmp.com

MAURINE J. NEIBERG, born Cincinnati, Ohio, July 18, 1964; admitted to bar, 1996, Illinois. *Education:* Wellesley College (B.A., 1986); Brown University (M.S., 1988); University of Chicago (J.D., 1995). ***Email:*** mneiberg@tsmp.com

BURKE J. NIHILL, born Agana, Guam, July 9, 1978; admitted to bar, 2003, Illinois. *Education:* Illinois Wesleyan University (B.A., 2000); Chicago-Kent College of Law, Illinois Institute of Technology (J.D., 2003). ***Email:*** bnihill@tsmp.com

JOHN M. O'DRISCOLL, born Ponce, Puerto Rico, July 6, 1971; admitted to bar, 1996, Illinois. *Education:* University of Illinois, Urbana-Champaign (B.A., 1993); Indiana University (J.D., 1996). ***Email:*** jodriscoll@tsmp.com

DAVID J. OLMSTEAD, born Ann Arbor, Michigan, October 9, 1968; admitted to bar, 1995, Illinois. *Education:* University of Michigan (B.A., 1991); Catholic University of America (J.D., 1995). ***Email:*** dolmstead@tsmp.com

CRAIG GORDON PENROSE, born Winnipeg, Manitoba, Canada, July 15, 1962; admitted to bar, 1996, Washington; 1998, Illinois. *Education:* University of Toronto (B.M., 1985); Northwestern University (M.M., 1987); Seattle University School of Law (J.D., 1996). ***Email:*** cpenrose@tsmp.com

BARBORA PULMANOVA, born Prague, Czechoslovakia, November 3, 1977; admitted to bar, 2004, California (Not admitted in Illinois). *Education:* DePaul University (B.A., 1999; J.D., 2004). (Resident Associate, Costa Mesa, California Office). ***Email:*** bpulmanova@tsmp.com

ANDREW J. PURCELL, born Kankakee, Illinois, May 25, 1974; admitted to bar, 1999, Illinois. *Education:* Eastern Illinois University (B.A., 1995); The John Marshall Law School (J.D., 1999). ***Email:*** apurcell@tsmp.com

CARI JAY RAYMOND, born Chicago, Illinois, August 5, 1973; admitted to bar, 1999, Illinois. *Education:* Northern Illinois University (B.S., 1995); Widener University School of Law (J.D., 1998). ***Email:*** craymond@tsmp.com

JOE SADLER, born Mt. Zion, Illinois, August 16, 1976; admitted to bar, 2002, Illinois. *Education:* Indiana University, Bloomington (B.A., 1998); University of Illinois, Urbana-Champaign (J.D., 2002). ***Email:*** jsadler@tsmp.com

HUMA P. SHAH, born Clarinda, Iowa, April 6, 1971; admitted to bar, 1998, Illinois. *Education:* University of Kansas (B.S., 1993); Chicago-Kent College of Law (J.D., 1997). ***Email:*** hshah@tsmp.com

CONNIE J. SHENG, born October 21, 1974; admitted to bar, 2000, California. *Education:* Scripps College (B.A., 1996); Loyola Law School, Los Angeles (J.D., 2000). (Resident Associate, Los Angeles, California Office). ***Email:*** csheng@tsmp.com

SHEVONN K. SMITH, born Chicago, Illinois, September 10, 1978; admitted to bar, 2004, Illinois. *Education:* University of Illinois at Urbana-Champaign (B.A., 2000); IIT/Chicago-Kent College of Law (J.D., 2004). ***Email:*** ssmith@tsmp.com

EVAN B. SORENSEN, born Salt Lake City, Utah, October 6, 1967; admitted to bar, 1995, Utah; 1996, California. *Education:* University of Utah (B.S., 1992); Columbia University School of Law (J.D., 1995). (Resident Associate, Los Angeles, California Office). ***Email:*** esorensen@tsmp.com

HEATHER C. SULLIVAN, born Oak Lawn, Illinois, May 1, 1973; admitted to bar, 1998, Illinois. *Education:* University of Illinois (B.A., 1995); Loyola University (J.D., 1998). ***Email:*** hsullivan@tsmp.com

(This Listing Continued)

TRESSLER, SODERSTROM, MALONEY & PRIESS, Chicago—Continued

KATHLEEN ANN SWEITZER, born Chicago, Illinois, August 8, 1968; admitted to bar, 1994, Hawaii; 1995, Illinois. *Education:* University of Illinois at Urbana-Champaign (B.S., 1990); California Western School of Law (J.D., 1994). ***Email:*** ksweitzer@tsmp.com

DEAN J. TATOOLES, born Chicago, Illinois, March 23, 1973; admitted to bar, 1999, Illinois; 2000, District of Columbia. *Education:* Michigan State University (B.A., 1995); The John Marshall Law School (J.D., 1998). ***Email:*** dtatooles@tsmp.com

RYAN TAYLOR, born Macomb, Illinois, March 22, 1980; admitted to bar, 2005, Illinois. *Education:* University of Illinois at Urbana-Champaign (B.S., 2002); DePaul University College of Law (J.D., 2005). ***Email:*** rtaylor@tsmp.com

CHARMAGNE TOPACIO, born Chicago, Illinois, November 9, 1977; admitted to bar, 2002, Illinois. *Education:* Loyola University, Chicago (B.S., 1999); Chicago-Kent College of Law (J.D., 2002). ***Email:*** ctopacio@tsmp.com

BRIAN E. TURNAUER, born Scranton, Pennsylvania, November 22, 1970; admitted to bar, 2001, California. *Education:* Drexel University (B.S., 1994); Southwestern University School of Law (J.D., 1999). (Resident Associate, Los Angeles, California Office). ***Email:*** bturnauer@tsmp.com

DANA M. UGOLINI, born Highland Park, Illinois, July 21, 1970; admitted to bar, 2003, Illinois. *Education:* University of Illinois (B.A., 1992; M.S., 1997); Loyola University (J.D., 2003). ***Email:*** dugolini@tsmp.com

KELLY D. WALLER, born Chicago, Illinois, November 26, 1978; admitted to bar, 2003, Illinois. *Education:* University of Illinois (B.A., 1999; J.D., 2003). ***Email:*** kwaller@tsmp.com

DAVID O. YUEN, born Chicago, Illinois, April 2, 1968; admitted to bar, 1996, Illinois. *Education:* University of Illinois (B.S., 1989); Chicago-Kent College of Law (J.D., 1996). ***Email:*** dyuen@tsmp.com

Representatives Clients to be furnished upon request.

LAW OFFICES OF FERN N. TREVINO

Established in 1992

120 NORTH LASALLE STREET, SUITE 1050

CHICAGO, ILLINOIS 60602

Telephone: 312-630-4491

Fax: 312-630-9281

URL: http://www.chicagoemploymentlawyer.net

Email: ferntrevino@chicagoemploymentlawyer.net

URL: http://www.ferntrevinolaw.com

Employment Law, Employment Discrimination, Sexual Harassment, Retaliatory Discharge, Family and Medical Leave Act, Severance Agreements, Fair Labor Standards Act, Qui Tam, Whistleblower Law, Wrongful Termination and Civil Rights.

FERN N. TREVINO, born Memphis, Tennessee, June 29, 1945; admitted to bar, 1983, Illinois and U.S. District Court, Northern District of Illinois; 1990, Federal Trial Bar; 1992, U.S. District Court, Northern District of California; 1998, U.S. Court of Appeals, Seventh Circuit. *Education:* Loyola University of Chicago (B.A., 1968; M.S.W., 1978; J.D., 1983). Faculty Member, Illinois Institute for Continuing Legal Education, 1999. Employment History: Law Offices of Fern N. Trevino, 1992—; Banta Cox & Hennessey, 1990-1992; Employment Law Attorney, Regional Counsel's Office, Internal Revenue Service, 1987-1990 (received merit service awards, 1988 and 1989); Assistant Corporation Counsel, Employment Litigation Division, 1983-1987. *Member:* Chicago (Member: Labor and Employment Law Committee; Speaker's Bureau) and Illinois State Bar Associations; Women's Bar Association of Illinois (Member: Board of Directors, 1998-2000; Chair, Labor and Employment Law Committee, 1995, 1998-2000; Corresponding Secretary, 1999-2000); National Employment Lawyer's Association (Co-Chair, Programs Committee, 1997-1999); National Association of Women Business Owners (Member, Board of Directors, 1993-1995; Membership Retention Committee, Chair, 1993-1995; Member, Program Council, 1998-1999). ***LANGUAGES:*** Spanish.

ASSOCIATES

ALENNA K. BOLIN, born LaGrange, Illinois, November 6, 1958; admitted to bar, 1991, California; 1993, Illinois; 1994, U.S. District Court, Northern District of Illinois, including Trial Bar and U.S. Court of Appeals, Seventh Circuit; 2002, U.S. Court of Appeals, Eleventh Circuit. *Education:* Northern Illinois University (B.A., cum laude, 1981); University of California at Davis School of Law (J.D., 1990). Author: "An Ounce of Prevention: The Need for Source Reduction in Agriculture," Pace Environmental Law Review, Fall 1990. *Member:* American Bar Association; National Employment Lawyers Association (Member, Illinois Chapter). ***LANGUAGES:*** French. ***REPORTED CASES:*** Walters v. Metropolitan Educational Enterprises, Inc., 219 U.S. 202 (1997). ***PRACTICE AREAS:*** Employment Law; Employment Discrimination; Civil Litigation.

ANTOINETTE CHOATE, born Chicago, Illinois, February 14, 1979; admitted to bar, 2004, Illinois; 2005, U.S. District Court, Northern District of Illinois. *Education:* University of Chicago (A.B., 2001); Loyola University of Chicago School of Law(J.D., 2004). Author: "Alliances of Convenience: United States Ties with the Northern Alliance in Light of Human Rights Violations," The Forum of International Law, Volume IX, Number 1, 2001; "Global Justice: Fighting Terrorism with the International Criminal Court," The Forum of International Law, Volume IX, Number 2, 2002. *Member:* Chicago Bar Association; National Employment Lawyers Association (National and Illinois Chapters). ***PRACTICE AREAS:*** Employment Law; Employment Discrimination; Civil Litigation.

TREXLER, BUSHNELL, GIANGIORGI, BLACKSTONE & MARR, LTD.

Established in 1890

THE CLARK ADAMS BUILDING

105 WEST ADAMS STREET

SUITE 3600

CHICAGO, ILLINOIS 60603-6299

Telephone: 312-704-1890

Fax: 312-704-8023

Email: info@trexlaw.com

URL: http://www.trexlaw.com

Intellectual Property Law including Patent, Trademark, Trade Secrets, Copyright, Unfair Competition Law, all phases including Prosecution, Licensing and Litigation.

FIRM PROFILE: Trexler, Bushnell, Giangiorgi, Blackstone & Marr, Ltd. is one of the oldest intellectual property law firms in the country, with a history dating back to 1890. Our lawyers' comprehensive technical and legal expertise allows us to meet the most demanding intellectual property needs of our clients. We protect our client's domestic and international proprietary interests by procuring, enforcing, licensing and defending their patents, trademarks, copyrights and trade secrets. Existing clients range from Fortune 500 Corporations to the individual inventor. Our lawyers are committed to providing individualized, prompt and efficient legal services.

Dwight B. Cheever	1890
Cheever & Cox	1912
Cheever, Cox & Moore	1925
Cox & Moore	1932
Moore, Olson & Marzall	1936
Moore, Olson & Trexler	1942
Olson & Trexler	1953
Olson, Trexler, Wolters & Bushnell	1961
Olson, Trexler, Wolters, Bushnell & Fosse, Ltd.	1972
Trexler, Wolters, Bushnell & Fosse, Ltd.	1979
Trexler, Bushnell & Wolters, Ltd.	1981
Trexler, Bushnell, Giangiorgi & Blackstone, Ltd.	1987
Trexler, Bushnell, Giangiorgi, Blackstone & Marr, Ltd.	2000

RICHARD R. TREXLER (1906-1995)

RICHARD A. GIANGIORGI, born Highland Park, Illinois, 1939; admitted to bar, 1967, Illinois; 1968, U.S. District Court, Northern District of Illinois and U.S. Court of Appeals, 7th Circuit; 1978-1982, U.S. Court of Customs and Patent Appeals; 1982, U.S. Court of Appeals for the Federal Circuit. *Education:* Marquette University (B.S. Mechanical Engineering, 1962); Georgetown University (J.D., 1966). Pi Tau Sigma; Delta Theta Phi. Examiner, U.S. Patent Office, 1963-1966. *Member:* Chicago and Illinois State Bar Associations; Intellectual Property Law Association of Chicago. ***PRACTICE AREAS:*** Intellectual Property; Patent, Trademark and Copyright Law; Trade Secrets Law; Unfair Competition Law. ***Email:*** rgiangiorgi@trexlaw.com

RAIFORD A. BLACKSTONE, JR., born Detroit, Michigan, 1943; admitted to bar, 1970, Illinois, U.S. District Court, Northern District of Illinois, including Trial Bar and registered to practice before U.S. Patent and Trademark Office; 1975, U.S. Court of Appeals, 7th Circuit; 1976, U.S. Supreme Court; 1978-1982, U.S. Court of Customs and Patent Appeals; 1982, U.S. Court of Appeals for the Federal Circuit. *Education:* University of Cincinnati (B.S. Electrical Engineering, 1965); Loyola University (J.D., 1970). *Member:* Chicago (Chairman: Science, Technology and the Law Committee, 1975), Illinois State (Member, Patent and Trademark Section) and American Bar Associations; Intellectual Property Law Association of Chicago (Chairman: Computers and Electronics Committee, 1993). ***PRACTICE AREAS:*** Intellectual Property; Intellectual Property Licensing; Litigation; Trademarks; Copyrights; Trade Secrets Law; Unfair Competition. ***Email:*** rblackstone@trexlaw.com

DAVID J. MARR, born Chicago, Illinois, 1958; admitted to bar, 1987, Illinois and U.S. District Court, Northern District of Illinois including Trial Bar; U.S. Court of Appeals for the Federal Circuit; 1988, registered to practice before U.S. Patent and Trademark Office. *Education:* University of Illinois (B.S., General Engineering, 1980); Illinois Institute of Technology/Chicago-Kent College of Law (J.D., with honors, 1987). *Member:* Chicago, Illinois State and American Bar Associations; Intellectual Property Law Association of Chicago. ***PRACTICE AREAS:*** Intellectual Property; Patent, Trademark and Copyright Law; Trade Secrets Law; Unfair Competition Law; Licensing; Antitrust Law. ***Email:*** dmarr@trexlaw.com

LINDA L. PALOMAR, born Canton, Ohio, 1968; admitted to bar, 1994, Illinois and U.S. District Court, Northern District of Illinois; registered to practice before U.S. Patent and Trademark Office. *Education:* Purdue University (B.S., Aeronautical and Astronautical Engineering, 1990); Loyola University of Chicago (J.D., 1994). Examiner, U.S. Patent Office, 1990-1991. *Member:* Chicago Bar Association; American Intellectual Property Law Association. ***PRACTICE AREAS:*** Intellectual Property; Patent, Trademark and Copyright Law. ***Email:*** lpalomar@trexlaw.com

JAMES R. FOLEY, born Oak Lawn, Illinois, 1969; admitted to bar, 1995, Illinois; 1996, Iowa and U.S. District Court, Northern District of Illinois; registered to practice before U.S. Patent and Trademark Office. *Education:* University of Illinois (B.S., General Engineering, 1992); John Marshall Law School (J.D., cum laude, 1995). Associate Publications Editor, John Marshall Law Review, 1994-1995. *Member:* Chicago, Illinois State, and American Bar Associations. ***PRACTICE AREAS:*** Intellectual Property; Patent, Trademark and Copyright Law; Trade Secrets; Unfair Competition. ***Email:*** jfoley@trexlaw.com

JAMES A. O'MALLEY, born Elmhurst, Illinois, 1974; admitted to bar, 1999, Illinois and U.S. District Court, Northern District of Illinois; registered to practice before U.S. Patent and Trademark Office. *Education:* Marquette University (B.S.M.E., 1996); The John Marshall Law School (J.D., cum laude, 1999). Editor, The John Marshall Law Review, 1998-1999. *Member:* Chicago, Illinois State and American Bar Associations; Intellectual

(This Listing Continued)

Property Law Association of Chicago; American Intellectual Property Law Association. ***PRACTICE AREAS:*** Intellectual Property; Patent; Trademark; Copyright. ***Email:*** jomalley@trexlaw.com

TIMOTHY M. McCARTHY, born Chicago, Illinois, 1954; admitted to bar, 1981, Texas, U.S. District Court, Southern District of Texas; 1982, U.S. Court of Appeals, Fifth Circuit; 1984, Illinois, U.S. District Court, Northern District of Illinois and U.S. Court of Appeals, Seventh Circuit; 2001, U.S. Court of Appeals for the Federal Circuit; 2002, U.S. Supreme Court; registered to practice before the U.S. Patent and Trademark Office; Canada Intellectual Property Office. *Education:* University of Illinois (B.S. Chemical Engineering, 1976); University of Houston (J.D., 1981). Member, Faculty-Student Senate; Research Assistant, Illinois Lead Project, University of Illinois. Articles Editor, Houston Law Review, 1980-1981; Member, Interscholastic Mock Trial Team; Recipient, Fullbright & Jaworski Award and Butler, Binion, Rice, Cook & Knapp Award; Teaching Assistant, Legal Research, University of Houston. Adjunct Professor, Illinois Institute of Technology, Institute of Design. *Member:* American Bar Association; American Intellectual Property Law Association; American Institute of Chemical Engineers; Intellectual Property Law Association of Chicago. ***PRACTICE AREAS:*** Intellectual Property Prosecution, Litigation and Counseling.

PAIGE A. KITZINGER, born Green Bay, Wisconsin; admitted to bar, 1994, Illinois; 1995, Wisconsin and U.S. District Court, Northern District of Illinois; registered to practice before U.S. Patent and Trademark Office. *Education:* Marquette University (B.S., Electrical Engineering, 1991); DePaul University College of Law (J.D., 1994). *Member:* Chicago Bar Association; American Intellectual Property Law Association. ***PRACTICE AREAS:*** Intellectual Property; Patent, Trademark and Copyright Law. ***Email:*** pkitzinger@trexlaw.com

ROBERT J. DEPKE, born Chicago, Illinois, 1962; admitted to bar, 1992, Illinois; registered to practice before U.S. Patent and Trademark Office. *Education:* University of Illinois (B.S.E.E., 1986); Loyola University (J.D., 1992). ***Email:*** rdepke@trexlaw.com

LEWIS T. STEADMAN, SR., born Chicago, Illinois, 1926; admitted to bar, 1952, Illinois, District of Columbia and U.S. District Court, District of Columbia and U.S. District Court, Northern District of Illinois, including Trial Bar; 1962, U.S. Supreme Court and U.S. Court of Appeals, Sixth Circuit; 1966, U.S. Court of Appeals, Seventh Circuit; 1982, U.S. Court of Appeals for the Federal Circuit; registered to practice before U.S. Patent and Trademark Office. *Education:* Syracuse University (B.M.E., magna cum laude, 1946); George Washington University (J.D., with distinction, 1951). Order of the Coif; Tau Beta Pi; Omicron Delta Kappa; Sigma Xi; Pi Mu Epsilon; Phi Alpha Delta. Editor for Patents, George Washington University Law Review, 1950-1951. *Member:* American Bar Association; Intellectual Property Law Association of Chicago; American Intellectual Property Law Association; International Trade Commission Trial Lawyers Association; International Patent and Trademark Association (A.I.P.P.I.). ***PRACTICE AREAS:*** Intellectual Property Law; Patent; Trademark; Copyright; Litigation; Arbitration. ***Email:*** lsteadman@trexlaw.com

TRIBLER ORPETT & MEYER, P.C.

Established in 1984

30 NORTH LA SALLE STREET
SUITE 2200
CHICAGO, ILLINOIS 60602
Telephone: 312-201-6400
Fax: 312-201-6401
Email: admin@tribler.com
URL: http://www.tribler.com

General Civil Trial and Appellate Practice, including Professional Liability, Insurance Coverage, Reinsurance, Environmental, Municipal, School Board, Construction, Product Liability, Premises Liability, Petroleum Industry Practice, Labor and Employment, General Tort Defense, Unfair Competition, Corporate, Commercial and Business Law, Real Estate, and Administration.

LAW FIRM ALLIANCES/ASSOCIATIONS: **NETWORK OF LEADING LAW FIRMS**

DANIEL D. DREW, born Peoria, Illinois, June 20, 1960; admitted to bar, 1985, Illinois. *Education:* University of Illinois (B.S., Accounting, with high honors, 1982; J.D., 1985). *Member:* Illinois State and American Bar Associations. ***PRACTICE AREAS:*** Commercial Real Estate; Retail Development; Petroleum Marketing; Eminent Domain; Leasing; Secured Lending; Corporate; Mergers and Acquisitions; Outdoor Advertising; Business Planning; Business Law; Contracts; Nonprofit Corporations. ***Email:*** dddrew@tribler.com

HARLENE G. MATYAS, born Chicago, Illinois, October 21, 1949; admitted to bar, 1973, Illinois. *Education:* University of Illinois (B.S., 1969); New York Law School (J.D., 1973). Chair, Circuit Court Commission, 1998. Member, Judicial Evaluation Committee, 1995-2000. *Member:* Chicago Bar Association. ***PRACTICE AREAS:*** Construction Litigation; Products Liability Litigation; Mass Torts; Contract Litigation; Insurance Coverage. ***Email:*** hgmatyas@tribler.com

MICHAEL J. MEYER, born Houston, Texas, October 7, 1961; admitted to bar, 1986, Illinois. *Education:* University of Oregon; Illinois State University (B.S., 1983); Loyola University (J.D., 1986). Author: "Avoiding Coverage Litigation," in Illinois Insurance Broker, 1991. Co-Author: "Pick a Number - Any Number: The Illinois Law of Damages for Personal Injury and Death," International Bar Association, 1991; "Attorneys," in Suing and Defending Professionals in Illinois, Illinois Institute for Continuing Legal Education, 2001. Associate Editor, Illinois Tort Report, 1989. *Member:* Chicago, Illinois State and American Bar Associations; Illinois Association of Defense Trial Counsel; Defense Research Institute. ***PRACTICE AREAS:*** Professional Liability; Products Liability; Petroleum Law; Environmental Litigation; Construction Law; Municipal Liability. ***Email:*** mjmeyer@tribler.com

MITCHELL A. ORPETT, born Chicago, Illinois, July 9, 1954; admitted to bar, 1978, Illinois. *Education:* University of Illinois (B.A., cum laude with high distinction, 1974; M.A., 1975; J.D., 1978). Author: "Reinsurance in Law and Practice of Insurance Coverage Litigation," West Group, 2000; "Litigation Cost Control in the Tripartite Relationship: Is There a Professional in the House," In Attorneys Fees, Mealey Publication, 2000. Co-Author: "Insurance Agents and Brokers," in Suing and Defending Professionals in Illinois, Illinois Institute for Continuing Legal Education, 1996. *Member:* Illinois State (Insurance Law Section Council, 1985-1989) and American (Chair, Tort and Insurance Practice Section, 2000-2001) Bar Associations; Federation of Insurance and Corporate Counsel; International Bar Association; Illinois Association of Defense Trial Counsel; Decalogue Society of Lawyers (President, 1987-1988). ***PRACTICE AREAS:*** Insurance Coverage; Reinsurance; Professional and Product Liability; Municipal and School Liability; Employment Torts; General Civil Litigation. ***Email:*** maorpett@tribler.com

(This Listing Continued)

H. WESLEY SUNU, born Seoul, South Korea, November 3, 1960; admitted to bar, 1985, Illinois. *Education:* Ball State University; University of Wisconsin-Madison (B.A., with honors, 1982); Loyola University (J.D., 1985). Author: "Introduction to Professional Liability Coverages in Commercial and Professional Liability Insurance," Illinois Institute for Continuing Legal Education, 2002; "Motion Practice," Law and Practice of Insurance Coverage Litigation, West Publication, 2000; "Recent Trends in Excess Surplus Lines and Reinsurance," Tort & Insurance Law Journal, 1996 and 1998; "Reinsurance Issues" and "Coverage Issues for Insurers of Mobile Professional," Insurance Coverage Committee, Tort & Insurance Practice Section, American Bar Association, 1996 and 1998; "Discovery of Reinsurance Information in Coverage Litigation," Mealey's Reinsurance Reports, 1993. *Member:* Illinois State, American (Vice-Chair, Excess Surplus Lines and Reinsurance Committee, 1999-2000) and Asian-American Bar Associations. ***PRACTICE AREAS:*** Professional Liability; Insurance Coverage; Reinsurance; General Civil Litigation. ***Email:*** hwsunu@tribler.com

PANOS T. TOPALIS, born Chicago, Illinois, September 2, 1963; admitted to bar, 1989, Illinois. *Education:* Northern Illinois University (B.S., 1985); Illinois Institute of Technology, Chicago-Kent College of Law (J.D., 1989). Co-Author, "Attorneys in Suing and Defending Professionals in Illinois," Illinois Institute for Continuing Legal Education, 2001; "Venue and Forum Non Conveniens," in Illinois Civil Practice Vol. 1, Illinois Institute for Continuing Legal Education, 2000. *Member:* Chicago, Illinois State, Hellenic (President, 2000-2001) and American Bar Associations. ***LANGUAGES:*** Greek. ***PRACTICE AREAS:*** Professional Liability; Civil Litigation; Insurance Coverage. ***Email:*** pttopalis@tribler.com

WILLIS R. TRIBLER, born Galesburg, Illinois, March 6, 1934; admitted to bar, 1960, Illinois. *Education:* Bradley University (B.S., 1955); University of Illinois (J.D., 1960). Co-Author: "Venue and Forum Non Conveniens," in Illinois Civil Practice, Vol I, Illinois Institute for Continuing Legal Education, 2002; "Attorneys," in Suing and Defending Professionals in Illinois, Illinois Institute for Continuing Legal Education, 2001; "Methods and Sufficiency of Proof," in Illinois Civil Trial Evidence, Illinois Institute for Continuing Education, 2000; "Obligations of the Parties to the Insurance Contract," in Liability Insurance, Illinois Institute for Continuing Legal Education, 1998. Director, 1985-1991, Vice-Chairman, 1991-1992 and Chairman, 1992-1993, Illinois Institute For Continuing Legal Education. Director 1985-1990, Vice President, 1990-1992 and President, 1992-1994, Clients' Security Fund of the Bar of Illinois. *Member:* Chicago, Illinois State and American Bar Associations; American Judicature Society; Illinois Association of Defense Trial Counsel (President, 1984-1985); Academy of Illinois Lawyers, Laureate; Defense Research Institute; Society of Trial Lawyers; Appellate Lawyers Association; International Association of Defense Counsel; American Law Institute. ***PRACTICE AREAS:*** Insurance Coverage; Professional Liability; Insurance Agent and Broker Liability; General Civil Litigation. ***Email:*** wrtribler@tribler.com

DOUGLAS C. CRONE, born Freeport, Illinois, June 3, 1954; admitted to bar, 1979, Illinois. *Education:* Carthage College and University of Illinois (B.A., 1976); Northwestern University (J.D., 1979). Co-Author: "Methods and Sufficiency of Proof," Illinois Civil Trial Evidence, Illinois Institute for Continuing Legal Education, 2000; "Oil Refining and Marketing Annual Report," Natural Resources, Energy and Environmental Law, The Year in Review, 1996-1997. *Member:* Chicago (Chair, Insurance Law Committee, 1989-1990; Co-Chair, Young Lawyers Insurance Law Committee, 1985-1987), Illinois State (Co-Editor, Tort Law Section Newsletter, 1983-1984) and American (Chair, Petroleum Marketing Committee, 1997-1999; Vice-Chairman, Petroleum and Marketing Committee of the Section on Natural Resources, Energy, and Environmental Law, 1994-1997, 1999—) Bar Associations; Appellate Lawyers Association. ***PRACTICE AREAS:*** Professional Liability; Petroleum Law; Commercial Litigation; Insurance; Civil Litigation. ***Email:*** dccrone@tribler.com

---

DANIEL J. ARNETT, born Flint, Michigan, December 27, 1967; admitted to bar, 1994, Illinois and U.S. District Court, Northern District of Illinois; U.S. Court of Appeals, Seventh Circuit. *Education:* University of Michigan (B.A., 1990); DePaul University School of Law (J.D., 1994). *Member:* Defense Research Institute; Illinois Association of Defense Trial Counsel. ***PRACTICE AREAS:*** Products Liability; Transportation; Insurance Defense Litigation. ***Email:*** djarnett@tribler.com

PAUL R. GAMPERL, born Hinsdale, Illinois, March 1963; admitted to bar, 1997, Illinois and U.S. District Court, Northern District of Illinois. *Education:* University of Illinois, Chicago (B.A., 1986); DePaul University (J.D., 1996). *Member:* American Bar Association. ***PRACTICE AREAS:*** Insurance Defense; Commercial Litigation; Litigation. ***Email:*** gamperlp@jbltd.com

JENNIFER L. JACOBS, born Winfield Illinois, March 4, 1976; admitted to bar, 2001, Illinois. *Education:* Arizona State University (B.A., 1998); DePaul University College of Law (J.D., 2001). ***PRACTICE AREAS:*** Civil Litigation. ***Email:*** jljacobs@tribler.com

JENNIFER H. KAY, born New York, NY, May 27, 1966; admitted to bar, 1993, Texas; 1995, Illinois. *Education:* University of Texas (B.J., 1988); Southern Methodist University Law School (J.D., 1993). *Member:* Chicago and American Bar Associations; State Bar of Texas. ***PRACTICE AREAS:*** Employment Litigation; Employment Counseling; Tort Litigation. ***Email:*** jhkay@tribler.com

DAVID M. LEWIN, born Chicago, Illinois, December 22, 1965; admitted to bar, 1992, Illinois; U.S. District Court, Northern District of Illinois and U.S. District Court, Eastern District of Michigan. *Education:* Loyola University (B.A., honors, 1989); DePaul Univer-

(This Listing Continued)

TRIBLER ORPETT & MEYER, P.C., Chicago—Continued

sity (J.D., 1992). *Member:* Chicago and Illinois State Bar Associations; Illinois Association of Defense Trial Counsel. ***PRACTICE AREAS:*** Insurance Coverage; Insurance Defense. ***Email:*** dmlewin@tribler.com

ARLA G. ROSENTHAL, born Chicago, Illinois, May 18, 1963; admitted to bar, 1989, Illinois. *Education:* University of Wisconsin (B.B.A., 1985); Loyola University (J.D., 1988). *Member:* Chicago and Illinois State Bar Associations. ***PRACTICE AREAS:*** Litigation. ***Email:*** agrosenthal@tribler.com

LAWRENCE R. SCANLON, born South Bend, Indiana, May 3, 1969; admitted to bar, 1997, Illinois and U.S. District Court, Northern District of Illinois; 1999, U.S. District Court, Central District of Illinois. *Education:* University of Notre Dame (B.A., 1991); Loyola University, Chicago School of Law (J.D., 1997). ***PRACTICE AREAS:*** Litigation. ***Email:*** lrscanlon@tribler.com

KEVIN A. TITUS, born Peoria, Illinois, December 5, 1966; admitted to bar, 1993, Illinois; 1997, U.S. District Court, Northern District of Illinois. *Education:* Wharton School of the University of Pennsylvania (B.S., summa cum laude, 1989); University of Michigan (J.D., 1993). Phi Beta Kappa. Author: "Introduction to Professional Liability Coverages in Commercial and Professional Liability Insurance," Illinois Institute for Continuing Legal Education, 2002. ***PRACTICE AREAS:*** Civil Litigation; Reinsurance; Insurance Coverage; Petroleum Law; Eminent Domain. ***Email:*** katitus@tribler.com

STEPHEN S. WEISS, born Pierre, South Dakota, August 16, 1968; admitted to bar, 1994, Illinois and U.S. District Court, Northern District of Illinois. *Education:* University of Minnesota (B.S., 1990); DePaul University (J.D., 1994). Recipient, American Jurisprudence Award. *Member:* Chicago and Illinois State Bar Associations. ***PRACTICE AREAS:*** Litigation. ***Email:*** ssweiss@tribler.com

REPRESENTATIVE CLIENTS: American Alternative Insurance Corporation; Argonaut Insurance Company; Auto-Owners Insurance Company; AXA Global Risks Company; Celtic Life Insurance Company; Cincinnati Insurance Companies; CNA Insurance Company; Employers Reinsurance Corporation; Evanston Insurance Company; Fireman's Fund Insurance Co.; First Nonprofit Mutual Insurance Company; Gallagher Bassett Services, Inc.; Illinois Municipal League Risk Management Association; ISBA Mutual Insurance Co.; Markel Corp.; Martin Boyer Company; Media/Professional Insurance Agency, Inc.; R.D. Werner Company, Inc.; RHH Financial Services Group, Inc.; SAFECO Select Markets; St. Paul Companies; Sentry Insurance Company; Shand Morahan & Company, Inc.; Shell Oil Company; Statewide Insurance Group; United Rentals, Inc.; United States Liability Insurance Group; Unocal Corporation; Ward North America, Inc.; Wausau Insurance Companies; Westport Insurance Corporation; Winterthur Group; Yasuda Claims Service, Inc.; Zurich North America.

TROTT NELSON, P.C.

CHICAGO, ILLINOIS

(See Oak Brook)

Construction Law, Mechanics Lien, Construction Contracts, Construction Litigation.

TUCKER BOWER ROBIN & MERKER, LLC

Established in 2001

200 WEST MADISON
SUITE 1900
CHICAGO, ILLINOIS 60606
Telephone: 312-346-4700
Fax: 312-346-4711
Email: firm@tbrmlaw.com
URL: http://www.tbrmlaw.com

Insurance Coverage and Defense, Products Liability, Medical Malpractice, Labor and Employment, Civil Trial Practice, Construction Law, Liquor Liability, Toxic Torts, Medical Device Liability, Directors and Officers, Errors and Omissions.

FIRM PROFILE: Tucker Bower Robin & Merker, LLC is committed to providing the highest degree of legal representation and personal service to insurance carriers, their insureds and self-insured entities. Our relationship with clients is a key aspect of our organization. To that end, we focus on the client's goals, viewing issues from a business and a legal perspective. We offer timely legal analysis and recommendations so that the client can make informed decisions at every stage of the case. This includes a thorough evaluation of cases at the earliest possible time to provide our client with the necessary information to make an informed decision as to the likelihood of success in the litigation. As a case progresses, the client is timely informed of developments and their impact relative to defense strategy. We are ready, willing and able to try cases. All of our attorneys are litigators with substantial trial experience. We also have extensive experience in all forms of alternative dispute resolution. The firm provides affordable legal representation of the highest quality by combining integrity and professionalism with the cost-effectiveness of state-of-the-art computer technology. Our billing system can accommodate whatever format a client requires.

CREED T. TUCKER, born Urbana, Illinois, March 17, 1956; admitted to bar, 1985, Illinois; 1993, U.S. District Court, Northern District of Illinois including Trial Bar. *Education:* University of Illinois at Champaign-Urbana (A.B., with distinction, 1982); Northern Illinois University (J.D., 1985). Instructor, Advanced Research in Environmental Law, Chicago Kent College of Law, 1991-1993. Court Arbitration Chairman, Cook County Mandatory Arbitration Program. *Member:* Chicago (Member, Environmental Law and Energy, Insurance Law and Circuit Court Committees) Bar Association; Illinois Association of Defense Trial Counsel; Midwest Environmental Claims Association. ***REPORTED CASES:*** Forest Preserve District of DuPage County, et al, vs. Pacific Indemnity Co., et al, 665 N.E.2d 305; Laird vs. Baxter Health Care Corp., 650 N.E. 2d 215; KNS vs. Federal Insurance Company, 866 F.Supp. 1121 (N.D. IL). ***PRACTICE AREAS:*** Insurance Defense; Civil Trial Practice. ***Email:*** ctucker@tbrmlaw.com

ROBERT A. BOWER, born Chicago, Illinois, December 19, 1955; admitted to bar, 1985, Illinois and U.S. District Court, Northern District of Illinois; 1992, U.S. District Court, Central District of Illinois and U.S. Court of Appeals, Seventh Circuit. *Education:* Butler University (B.S. in Pharmacy, 1978); Loyola University (J.D., 1985). *Member:* Chicago Bar Association; Chicagoland Healthcare Risk Management Society. ***PRACTICE AREAS:*** Medical Malpractice; Product Liability Law; Employment Law; Health Care. ***Email:*** rbower@tbrmlaw.com

BARRY A. ROBIN, born Chicago, Illinois, April 23, 1957; admitted to bar, 1983, Illinois and U.S. District Court, Northern District of Illinois; 1984, U.S. Court of Appeals, Seventh Circuit; 1994, U.S. District Court, Central District of Illinois. *Education:* University of Illinois (B.S., 1979); John Marshall School of Law (J.D., 1983). Mentor, Moot Court Council. City Prosecutor, City of Wood Dale, Illinois, 1983-1984. *Member:* Chicago and DuPage County Bar Associations. ***REPORTED CASES:*** Buttita v. Stenberg, 246 Ill. App.3d 1012, 617 N.E.2d 122 (1st Dist. 1993), negligence case (auto). ***PRACTICE AREAS:*** Product Liability Law; Construction Law; Insurance Defense; Toxic Torts. ***Email:*** brobin@tbrmlaw.com

TIMOTHY G. MERKER, born Cleveland, Ohio, July 16, 1959; admitted to bar, 1984, Michigan and U.S. District Court, Eastern District of Michigan; 1990, Illinois and U.S. District Court, Northern District of Illinois. *Education:* University of Dayton (B.A., magna cum laude, 1981); University of Notre Dame (J.D., 1984). Pi Sigma Alpha; Alpha Sigma Tau. Author: "Working Toward Employee Ownership," Journal of Legislation, Vol. 11, No. 1, Winter 1984. *Member:* Chicago and American Bar Associations. ***REPORTED CASES:*** Allstate v. Sunbeam Corp., 53 F.3d 804 (1995). ***PRACTICE AREAS:*** Medical Malpractice; Health Care Law; Product Liability. ***Email:*** tmerker@tbrmlaw.com

REBECCA A. WEBER, born Santa Barbara, California, September 18, 1969; admitted to bar, 1996, Illinois and U.S. District Court, Northern District of Illinois. *Education:* Western Michigan University (B.S., 1992); DePaul University (J.D., 1996). *Member:* Illinois State and American Bar Associations. ***PRACTICE AREAS:*** Insurance Litigation; Employment Litigation; Construction Litigation; Medical Malpractice Defense; Products Liability; Insurance Defense. ***Email:*** rweber@tbrrlaw.com

CEASAR J. MELIDIS, born Patras, Greece, October 6, 1972; admitted to bar, 2001, Illinois. *Education:* Loyola University, Chicago (B.S., Biology, 1994); The John Marshall Law School (J.D., 2001). *Member:* Chicago and Illinois State Bar Associations; Hellenic Bar Association; Georgetown Chamber of Commerce. ***LANGUAGES:*** Greek, Spanish. ***PRACTICE AREAS:*** Insurance Defense Litigation; Contract Litigation; Workers Compensation Defense. ***Email:*** cmelidis@tbrmlaw.com

NANCY J. MESEROW, born Chicago, Illinois, December 27, 1949; admitted to bar, 1982, Oregon; 2000, Illinois. *Education:* Université de la Sorbonne, Paris, France; University of Colorado (B.A., 1972); Northwestern University (M.A., 1976); Northwestern School of Law of Lewis and Clark College (J.D., 1981). Author: "Claim Closure, Payment Methods and Recipients," 1990. *Member:* Oregon State Bar (Member: Committee on Racial /Ethnic Issues in the Judicial System, 1997; Loss Prevention Committee, 1998; Workers' Compensation Section, 1982—); Illinois State Bar Association. ***PRACTICE AREAS:*** Workers Compensation. ***Email:*** nmeserow@tbrmlaw.com

OF COUNSEL

RANDALL E. SERVER, born Chicago, Illinois, December 27, 1951; admitted to bar, 1976, Illinois; U.S. District Court, Northern and Central Districts of Illinois, including Trial Bar; 1977, U.S. Court of Appeals, Seventh Circuit. *Education:* Princeton University (A.B., cum laude, 1973); Northwestern University (J.D., 1976). Arbitration Panelist, Circuit Court, Cook County. *Member:* Chicago and Illinois State Bar Associations. ***PRACTICE AREAS:*** Business Litigation; Chancery; Insurance Defense; Class Action Defense. ***Email:*** rserver@tbrmlaw.com

MARY ELLEN ROSEN SWANSON, born Cincinnati, Ohio, October 30, 1939; admitted to bar, 1981, Illinois. *Education:* St. Louis University (B.S.R.N., 1962); Illinois Institute of Technology-Chicago Kent College of Law (J.D., 1981); Loyola University (LL.M., Health Care Law, 1990). *Member:* Chicago and Illinois State Bar Associations; American Association of Nurse Attorneys; Chicago Area Association Nurse Attorneys. ***PRACTICE AREAS:*** Medical Malpractice; Health Care Law; Nursing Liability; Professional Licensing. ***Email:*** mswanson@tbrmlaw.com

JESSICA B. TUCKER, born Detroit, Michigan, August 26, 1959; admitted to bar, 1985, Michigan and U.S. District Court, Eastern District of Michigan; 1986, Illinois and Colorado and U.S. District Court, Northern District of Illinois; 1993, U.S. Court of Appeals, Seventh Circuit. *Education:* University of Michigan, Ann Arbor (B.B.A., 1981); Thomas M. Cooley Law School (J.D., 1985). Village Trustee, Village of Winnetka, IL, 2004—. Arbitration Chair, Circuit Court, Cook County. *Member:* Appellate Lawyers Association of Illinois; Michigan Business School Club of Chicago. ***PRACTICE AREAS:*** Appellate Practice; Civil Litigation. ***Email:*** jtucker@tbrmlaw.com

LAW OFFICES OF
PHILLIP A. TURNER

Established in 1989

100 WEST MONROE STREET, SUITE 2204
CHICAGO, ILLINOIS 60603-1925
Telephone: 312-899-0009
Fax: 312-899-8087
Email: pturner98@sbcglobal.net

Civil Practice, Criminal Law, Trial Practice, Medical Malpractice, Administrative Law.

FIRM PROFILE: Mr. Turner is a respected trial attorney in Chicago, Illinois. He is a former Assistant United States Attorney. He is a specialist in federal criminal matters and provides representation before administrative boards and representation of federal employees in em-

(This Listing Continued)

ployment related matters. In addition, Mr. Turner provides representation in investigation conducted by governmental entities. Finally, Mr. Turner has an extensive knowledge of Latin America.

PHILLIP A. TURNER, born Milwaukee, Wisconsin, February 20, 1954; admitted to bar, 1978, Wisconsin; 1979, Illinois. *Education:* Marquette University (B.A., 1975); University of Wisconsin-Madison (J.D., 1978). Phi Beta Kappa. Assistant U.S. Attorney, Chicago, Illinois, 1980-1988. *Member:* Cook County, Illinois State and American Bar Associations; State Bar of Wisconsin; National Association of Criminal Defense Lawyers; The Association of Trial Lawyers of America; Illinois Trial Lawyers Association. ***LANGUAGES:*** Spanish. ***PRACTICE AREAS:*** Civil Practice; Criminal Law; Trial Practice; Medical Malpractice; Administrative Law.

Language: Spanish.

KATHARINE BARR TYLER

SUITE 725 - 53 WEST JACKSON BOULEVARD
CHICAGO, ILLINOIS 60604
Telephone: 312-663-1311
Fax: 312-663-1312
Email: KBTylerlaw@aol.com
URL: http://www.lawyers.com/katharinebarrtyler

Residential Real Estate, Commercial Real Estate, Estate Planning, Real Estate Tax Rate Objections.

KATHARINE BARR TYLER, born Moses Lake, Washington, February 11, 1956; admitted to bar, 1981, Illinois. *Education:* University of Illinois (B.A., 1978); John Marshall Law School (J.D., 1981). *Member:* Chicago, Cook County, Illinois State and American Bar Associations. ***PRACTICE AREAS:*** Residential Real Estate; Commercial Real Estate; Estate Planning; Real Estate Tax Rate Objections.

STEPHEN L. TYMA, P.C.

105 WEST MADISON STREET, SUITE 2200
CHICAGO, ILLINOIS 60602-4648
Telephone: 312-372-3920
Fax: 312-372-3780
URL: http://www.tymalaw.com
Email: STYMA@TYMALAW.COM
URL: http://www.lawyers.com/tymalaw

Federal and State Litigation, Trial and Appellate Practice, Business Law, Commercial Law, Construction Law, Contracts, Corporate Law, Environmental Law, Family Law, Divorce, Partnership Law, Probate, Professional Liability, Real Estate, RICO, General Practice.

STEPHEN L. TYMA, born Chicago, Illinois, March 12, 1950; admitted to bar, 1984, Illinois and U.S. District Court, Northern District of Illinois; 1988, U.S. Court of Appeals, Seventh Circuit; 1992, U.S. District Court, Eastern District of Michigan. *Education:* Michigan State University (B.A., cum laude, 1972; M.A., 1974; M.A., 1975); University of Michigan (C. Phil., 1978; J.D., 1984). *Member:* Chicago (Member and Chair, Constitutional Law Committee, 1997-1998, 2001-2002; Member, Nominating Committee, 1998), Illinois State and American Bar Associations. ***LANGUAGES:*** French and Spanish.

ULMER & BERNE LLP

Established in 1908
ONE N. FRANKLIN STREET, SUITE 1825
CHICAGO, ILLINOIS 60606-3401
Telephone: 312-324-8000
FAX: 312-324-8001
Email: infochicago@ulmer.com
URL: http://www.ulmer.com

Cleveland, Ohio Office: Skylight Office Tower, 1660 West 2nd Street, Suite 1100. Telephone: 216-583-7000. FAX: 216-583-7001.
Columbus, Ohio Office: 88 East Broad Street, Suite 1600. Telephone: 614-229-0000. FAX: 614-229-0001.
Cincinnati, Ohio Office: 600 Vine Street, Suite 2800. Telephone: 513-698-5000. FAX: 513-698-5001.

Antitrust; Banking and Commercial Lending; Broker/Dealer and Securities Litigation; Business Law; Business Litigation; Business Restructuring; Class Action Defense; Construction Law; Corporate Finance; Corporate Restructuring and Creditors' Rights; Corporate Succession Planning; Emerging Businesses; Employee Benefits; Employment and Labor; Environmental; Fair Housing; Financial Institution Compliance; General Counsel Services; Health Care; Income Tax; Insurance Coverage; Intellectual Property and Technology; Joint Ventures; Liability Defense; Mass Torts; Mergers, Acquisitions and Divestitures; Nonprofit; OSHA; Pharmaceutical; Product Liability; Public Law; Real Estate; Securities; Securities Regulatory Compliance; Subrogation; Tax; Technology Transactions; Toxic Tort Defense; Trade Secrets/Unfair Competition; Trusts and Estates; Venture Capital; Workers' Compensation; Trial and Appellate Practice in All Courts.

FIRM PROFILE: Ulmer & Berne LLP, established in 1908, is one of Ohio's largest law firms, as well as one of its fastest growing. The firm has doubled in size in the last five years and tripled in size in the last 10. In the last 18 months alone, the firm has added 47 new lawyers. A full-service firm with over 185 attorneys in Cleveland, Columbus, Cincinnati and Chicago, Ulmer & Berne represents publicly traded and privately held companies, financial institutions, pharmaceutical companies, family businesses, international joint ventures and affiliations, investor groups, start-ups and emerging businesses, public bodies and nonprofit organizations. For more information, visit www.ulmer.com.

(This Listing Continued)

LAW FIRM ALLIANCES/ASSOCIATIONS: ***LAWYERS ASSOCIATED WORLDWIDE (L.A.W.)***

BUSINESS COUNCIL, INC.

PARTNER

KENNETH F. BERG, born September 27, 1954; admitted to bar, 1979, Illinois. *Education:* Washington University (A.B., magna cum laude, 1976); Boston College (J.D., cum laude, 1979). Bigelow Fellow, University of Chicago, 1981-1982. ***LANGUAGES:*** Hebrew. ***PRACTICE AREAS:*** Business Litigation; Securities Litigation; Commodities Regulation; Trade Secrets. ***Email:*** kberg@ulmer.com

OF COUNSEL

PETER R. SONDERBY, born April 24, 1941; admitted to bar, 1967, Illinois. *Education:* University of Illinois (B.A., 1964); University of Illinois College of Law (J.D., 1967). ***PRACTICE AREAS:*** Securities Arbitration; Securities Litigation; General Commercial Litigation; Securities Regulatory Investigations; Commodities. ***Email:*** psonderby@ulmer.com

ASSOCIATE

SEAN M. DOWNEY, born August 9, 1976; admitted to bar, 2004, Illinois. *Education:* DePauw University (B.A., 1999); Indiana University School of Law - Bloomington (J.D., 2004). ***PRACTICE AREAS:*** Business Litigation; Financial Institutions Litigation. ***Email:*** sdowney@ulmer.com

UNGARETTI & HARRIS

3500 THREE FIRST NATIONAL PLAZA
CHICAGO, ILLINOIS 60602
Telephone: 312-977-4400
Fax: 312-977-4405
Email: info@uhlaw.com
URL: http://www.uhlaw.com

Washington, D.C. Office: 1500 K Street, N.W., Suite 250, 20005-1714. Telephone: 202-639-7500. Fax: 202-639-7505.

General Practice, including Business and Corporate, Financial Services and Securities, Litigation and Appeals, Real Estate, Health Care, Information Technology, Public Finance, Legislative and Regulatory Affairs, Labor and Employment, Employee Benefits, Taxation, Affordable Housing, Bankruptcy and Creditors' Rights, Estates and Trusts, Gaming Law, Intellectual Property and Patent Litigation, Class Actions and Securities Arbitration.

FIRM PROFILE: The Way Law Should Be Practiced.

Outstanding service. Experienced counsel. Innovative strategies. Focused advocacy. These are qualities that should characterize all law firms. Too often, they do not. At Ungaretti & Harris, they are a given. They define who we are.

We practice law the way it should be practiced. We listen to our clients. We learn their businesses. We fulfill their expectations.

Ungaretti & Harris represents clients nationally from our offices in Chicago and Washington, D.C. Whether we are representing a Fortune 500 corporation, regulated enterprise, emerging business or individual, we tailor our legal services to fit the client's unique needs.

The partners at Ungaretti & Harris are respected leaders in their fields. They are recognized for their knowledge, judgment, practicality and results. They work together across disciplines to assure that our clients are served efficiently and responsively.

At Ungaretti & Harris, we build and maintain exceptional client relationships. We do this by putting clients first. In fact, we are so committed to our clients that we were the nation's first law firm to guarantee our service in writing.

PARTNERS

R. SCOTT ALSTERDA, admitted to bar, 1980, Illinois. *Education:* Bowdoin College (B.A., 1976); John Marshall Law School (J.D., 1980). ***PRACTICE AREAS:*** Bankruptcy Reorganization; Commercial Bankruptcy; Out of Court Debt Restructuring; Workouts. ***Email:*** rsalsterda@uhlaw.com

NICHOLAS ANACLERIO, admitted to bar, 1984, Illinois. *Education:* University of Wisconsin (B.A., with honors, 1981); Loyola University School of Law, Chicago (J.D., 1984). ***PRACTICE AREAS:*** Litigation; Labor and Employment. ***Email:*** nanaclerio@uhlaw.com

VINCENT M. AQUILINO, admitted to bar, 1973, Illinois. *Education:* DePaul University (B.S.C., summa cum laude, 1969; M.B.A., 1971); Northwestern School of Law (J.D., 1973). ***PRACTICE AREAS:*** Taxation. ***Email:*** vmaquilino@uhlaw.com

STEPHEN H. ARMSTRONG, admitted to bar, 1980, Wisconsin; 1982, Illinois; U.S. District Court, Northern District of Illinois and U.S. District Court, Western District of Wisconsin. *Education:* Oberlin College (B.A., 1970); University of Wisconsin-Madison (M.A., 1972; J.D., 1980). *Member:* State Bar of Wisconsin. ***LANGUAGES:*** Italian. ***PRACTICE AREAS:*** Litigation. ***Email:*** sarmstrong@uhlaw.com

CHARLES R. BERNARDINI, admitted to bar, 1972, Illinois. *Education:* University of Illinois (B.S., 1968; J.D., 1972); John Marshall Law School (LL.M., State and Local Government Law, 1977). ***PRACTICE AREAS:*** Legislative Practice; Regulatory Law; Public Policy. ***Email:*** crbernardini@uhlaw.com

MICHAEL W. BLACK, admitted to bar, 1987, Missouri; 1988, Illinois. *Education:* University of Illinois (B.S., 1984; J.D., 1987). ***PRACTICE AREAS:*** Corporate Law; Finance. ***Email:*** mwblack@uhlaw.com

(This Listing Continued)

UNGARETTI & HARRIS, Chicago—Continued

DENNIS G. BOUXSEIN, admitted to bar, 1986, Georgia; 1993, Illinois. *Education:* St. Olaf College (B.A., cum laude, 1975); University of Illinois (J.D., magna cum laude, 1985). ***PRACTICE AREAS:*** Employee Benefits; Executive Compensation. ***Email:*** dgbouxsein@uhlaw.com

THOMAS F. BRETT, II, admitted to bar, 1978, Illinois and U.S. District Court, Northern District of Illinois; 1980, U.S. Tax Court. *Education:* University of Notre Dame (B.B.A., magna cum laude, 1975); Temple University (J.D., cum laude, 1978); DePaul University (LL.M. in Taxation, 1985). ***PRACTICE AREAS:*** Real Estate. ***Email:*** tfbrett@uhlaw.com

DAVID A. BRONNER, admitted to bar, 1973, Illinois; U.S. District Court, Northern District of Illinois. *Education:* New York University (B.A.); University of Chicago (J.D.). Phi Beta Kappa. ***PRACTICE AREAS:*** Corporate Law.

JOHN P. BUCKLEY, admitted to bar, 1985, Illinois; 1994, U.S. Supreme Court. *Education:* University of Michigan (B.A., with distinction and high honors, 1982; J.D., cum laude, 1985). ***PRACTICE AREAS:*** Products Liability Defense; Medical Malpractice; Torts; Appeals. ***Email:*** jpbuckley@uhlaw.com

STACEY CAVANAGH, admitted to bar, 1995, Illinois. *Education:* Boston College (B.A., 1992); IIT/Chicago-Kent College of Law (J.D., 1995). ***Email:*** sfcavanagh@uhlaw.com

KATHLEEN HOLPER CHAMPAGNE, admitted to bar, 1996, Illinois and Supreme Court of Illinois; 1997, U.S. District Court, Central District of Illinois. *Education:* University of Illinois (B.A., with departmental distinction, 1993); Chicago-Kent College of Law (J.D., with honors, 1996). ***Email:*** kholper@uhlaw.com

EDWARD CLANCY, admitted to bar, 1987, Illinois; U.S. District Court, Northern District of Illinois; U.S. Court of Appeals, Seventh Circuit. *Education:* University of Illinois (B.S., 1980); IIT Chicago-Kent College of Law (J.D., 1987). ***PRACTICE AREAS:*** Health Care.

KRIS E. CURRAN, admitted to bar, 1984, Illinois. *Education:* Bradley University (B.A., summa cum laude, 1981); Duke University (J.D., with honors, 1984). ***PRACTICE AREAS:*** Real Estate Workouts; Real Property Acquisitions; Real Property Development; Real Property Finance. ***Email:*** kecurran@uhlaw.com

LESLIE M. DARLING, admitted to bar, 1997, Illinois, U.S. District Court, Northern District of Illinois and Illinois Supreme Court. *Education:* Bradley University (B.S., summa cum laude, 1994); DePaul University (J.D., 1997). ***PRACTICE AREAS:*** Legislative; Regulatory. ***Email:*** lmdarling@uhlaw.com

CAROL M. DOUGLAS, admitted to bar, 1987, Illinois. *Education:* Loyola University of Chicago (B.A., cum laude, 1981; B.B.A., cum laude, 1981; J.D., 1987). ***PRACTICE AREAS:*** Litigation. ***Email:*** cmdouglas@uhlaw.com

JOHN J. DURSO, admitted to bar, 1977, Illinois and U.S. District Court, Northern District of Illinois; 1979, U.S. Supreme Court. *Education:* Northern Illinois University (B.A., magna cum laude, 1974); Loyola University (J.D., 1977). ***PRACTICE AREAS:*** Health Care.

JAMES T. EASTERLING, admitted to bar, 1974, Illinois. *Education:* Pepperdine University (B.A., summa cum laude, 1969); University of California at Los Angeles (M.A., summa cum laude, 1971); Harvard University (J.D., 1974). ***PRACTICE AREAS:*** Business Law; Corporate Law; Investments; Securities. ***Email:*** jteasterling@uhlaw.com

J. TIMOTHY EATON, admitted to bar, 1977, Illinois; U.S. Supreme Court, U.S. Court of Appeals, Seventh Circuit. *Education:* Miami University (B.A., 1973); Southern Illinois University (J.D., cum laude, 1977); Washington University (LL.M., 1979). Past President, Illinois State Bar Association; Past President, Appellate Lawyers Association. ***PRACTICE AREAS:*** Appellate Practice; Commercial Litigation; Products Liability. ***Email:*** jteaton@uhlaw.com

THEODORE T. EIDUKAS, admitted to bar, 1994, Illinois. *Education:* Augustana College (B.A., 1991); Northwestern University (J.D., 1994). ***PRACTICE AREAS:*** Litigation.

FRANCIS J. EMMONS, admitted to bar, 1977, Illinois; 1978, U.S. Tax Court; 1985, U.S. District Court, Northern District of Illinois; 1997, U.S. Court of Appeals, Seventh Circuit. *Education:* Marquette University (B.S., magna cum laude, 1974); Northwestern University (J.D., cum laude, 1977). ***PRACTICE AREAS:*** Taxation.

JOHN D. ENGLISH, admitted to bar, 1976, Illinois. *Education:* Drake University (B.A., with honors, 1971); Loyola University (J.D., 1976). ***PRACTICE AREAS:*** Estate Planning; Estate Administration; Estate Litigation; Trust Litigation. ***Email:*** jdenglish@uhlaw.com

THOMAS M. FAHEY, admitted to bar, 1980, Illinois. *Education:* University of Wisconsin (B.S., 1974); DePaul University (J.D., 1980). Listed in 1991-2004 Editions of "Best Lawyers in America," Illinois Health Care Attorneys Section. ***PRACTICE AREAS:*** Health Care Corporate Law; Health Care Finance; Public Finance. ***Email:*** tmfahey@uhlaw.com

SUSAN G. FEIBUS, admitted to bar, 1981, Pennsylvania and Illinois. *Education:* University of Pennsylvania (B.A., summa cum laude, 1977); Northwestern University (J.D., 1980). ***PRACTICE AREAS:*** Employment Litigation; Commercial Litigation; Healthcare Litigation. ***Email:*** sgfeibus@uhlaw.com

MICHAEL A. FICARO, admitted to bar, 1972, Illinois, U.S. Court of Appeals, Fifth, Sixth and Seventh Circuits and U.S. Supreme Court; U.S. District Court, Southern and Northern Districts of Illinois including Trial Bar. *Education:* DePaul University (B.A., 1969; J.D., 1972). ***PRACTICE AREAS:*** Litigation; Casino and Riverboat Gaming Law; White Collar Criminal Law. ***Email:*** maficaro@uhlaw.com

RAYMOND C. FRICKE, admitted to bar, 1990, Illinois. *Education:* Northwestern University (B.A., 1981); DePaul University (J.D., 1989). ***PRACTICE AREAS:*** Public Finance; Municipal Securities. ***Email:*** rcfricke@uhlaw.com

(This Listing Continued)

ROBERT H. GRIFFITH, admitted to bar, 1996, Illinois. *Education:* University of Iowa (B.B.A., 1993); Chicago-Kent College of Law (J.D., 1996). ***PRACTICE AREAS:*** Litigation. ***Email:*** rgriffith@uhlaw.com

THEODORE E. HARMAN, admitted to bar, 1989, Illinois. *Education:* Bradley University (B.S., summa cum laude, 1985); University of Illinois (J.D., magna cum laude, 1989). ***PRACTICE AREAS:*** Civil Appeals; Business Litigation; Commercial Arbitration; Commercial Litigation. ***Email:*** teharman@uhlaw.com

ALTON B. HARRIS, admitted to bar, 1967, Illinois. *Education:* Harvard University (B.A., 1962; LL.B., 1967). ***PRACTICE AREAS:*** Financial Services Regulation; Securities Fraud; Corporate Finance. ***Email:*** abharris@uhlaw.com

JOSEPH K. HASSON, admitted to bar, 1987, Illinois. *Education:* Duke University (B.A., magna cum laude, 1984); University of Illinois (J.D., 1987). ***PRACTICE AREAS:*** Business Law; Finance; Securities; Corporate Law. ***Email:*** jkhasson@uhlaw.com

ANNE M. HAULE, admitted to bar, 1981, Illinois. *Education:* Spring Hill College; Loyola University (B.A., 1970); John Marshall Law School (J.D., 1981). Past-President, Illinois Association of Health Care Attorneys. ***PRACTICE AREAS:*** Healthcare Law. ***Email:*** amhaule@uhlaw.com

F. THOMAS HECHT, admitted to bar, 1975, Illinois; 1981, U.S. District Court, Northern District of Illinois, U.S. Supreme Court and U.S. Court of Appeals, Seventh Circuit. *Education:* Stanford University (A.B., 1966); The John Hopkins School of Advanced International Studies (1968); University of Chicago (J.D., 1975). ***PRACTICE AREAS:*** Litigation. ***Email:*** fthecht@uhlaw.com

PAUL B. HOLMES, admitted to bar, 1981, Illinois; 1991, U.S. Tax Court. *Education:* Bradley University (B.S., magna cum laude, 1977); University of Illinois (J.D., 1981). Certified Public Accountant, Illinois, 1978. ***PRACTICE AREAS:*** Employee Benefits. ***Email:*** pbholmes@uhlaw.com

ROSS E. KIMBAROVSKY, admitted to bar, 1995, Illinois. *Education:* Northwestern University (B.A., 1992); University of Illinois (J.D., cum laude, 1995). ***LANGUAGES:*** Russian and Ukrainian. ***Email:*** rossk@uhlaw.com

SHANNON CAPONE KIRK, admitted to bar, 1998, Illinois. *Education:* St. John's University (B.A., magna cum laude, 1995); Suffolk University (J.D., cum laude, 1998). ***Email:*** scaponekirk@uhlaw.com

BRIAN E. KROB, admitted to bar, 1997, Illinois. *Education:* University of Kansas (B.A., with distinction, 1994); University of Illinois College of Law (J.D., magna cum laude, 1997). ***Email:*** bekrob@uhlaw.com

JAMES E. LENTZ, admitted to bar, 1975, Illinois. *Education:* Loras College (B.A., 1969); University of Iowa (J.D., 1975). ***PRACTICE AREAS:*** Real Estate Sales; Real Estate Acquisitions; Real Estate Workouts; Leasing; Real Estate Loan Securitization; Real Estate Loans. ***Email:*** jelentz@uhlaw.com

GARY I. LEVENSTEIN, admitted to bar, 1976, Illinois. *Education:* University of Illinois (B.A., with high honors, 1973); Northwestern University (J.D., 1976). Certified Public Accountant, Illinois, 1973. ***PRACTICE AREAS:*** Business Law; Investments; Securities. ***Email:*** gilevenstein@uhlaw.com

WILLIAM J. LEWIS, admitted to bar, 1995, Illinois. *Education:* Marquette University (B.S., 1991); Gonzaga University (J.D., 1995). ***PRACTICE AREAS:*** Real Estate. ***Email:*** wjlewis@uhlaw.com

BENJAMIN T. LO, admitted to bar, 1994, Illinois. *Education:* University of Michigan (B.A., 1991); Indiana University (J.D., 1994). ***PRACTICE AREAS:*** Litigation; Labor and Employment Law. ***Email:*** btlo@uhlaw.com

SAMERA S. LUDWIG, admitted to bar, 2000, New York; 2001, Illinois. *Education:* Wesleyan University (B.A., with high honors, 1994); Columbia University (J.D., 1997). ***PRACTICE AREAS:*** Finance; Litigation; Labor and Employment. ***Email:*** ssludwig@uhlaw.com

JAMES BRENT McCAULEY, admitted to bar, 1993, Indiana; 1994, Illinois. *Education:* Ball State University (B.S., 1987); Indiana University School of Law, Indianapolis (J.D., 1993). ***PRACTICE AREAS:*** Corporate Law; Securities; Financial Services Law. ***Email:*** jbmccauley@uhlaw.com

LORI R. McGUNN, admitted to bar, 1994, Kentucky; 2000, Illinois. *Education:* Indiana University, New Albany (B.S., 1989); Indiana University, Bloomington (J.D., cum laude, 1993; M.B.A., 1993). ***Email:*** lrmcgunn@uhlaw.com

CLAUDETTE P. MILLER, admitted to bar, 1988, Illinois and U.S. Court of Appeals, Seventh, Eighth and Tenth Circuits. *Education:* Oxford University, Oxford, England; Smith College (A.B., magna cum laude, 1985); University of Chicago (J.D., 1988). ***PRACTICE AREAS:*** Litigation. ***Email:*** cpmiller@uhlaw.com

JOHN G. NASSOS, admitted to bar, 1990, Illinois. *Education:* Indiana University (B.S., with high distinction,1987); Northwestern University (J.D., 1990). ***PRACTICE AREAS:*** Corporate Law.

WILLIAM H. NICHOLS, admitted to bar, 1979, Illinois; 1980, U.S. District Court, Northern District of Illinois. *Education:* Amherst College (B.S., with honors, 1976); Cornell University (J.D., 1979). ***PRACTICE AREAS:*** Employee Benefits.

FRANK E. PASQUESI, admitted to bar, 1990, Illinois. *Education:* Northwestern University (B.A., 1987); Boston University (J.D., 1990). ***LANGUAGES:*** Italian. ***PRACTICE AREAS:*** White Collar Crime; Commercial Litigation. ***Email:*** fepasquesi@uhlaw.com

FLOYD D. PERKINS, admitted to bar, 1977, Illinois. *Education:* University of Illinois (B.S., 1973); John Marshall Law School (J.D., 1977; LL.M., 1983). Certified Public Accountant, Illinois, 1975. ***PRACTICE AREAS:*** Litigation. ***Email:*** fdperkins@uhlaw.com

MICHAEL J. PHILIPPI, admitted to bar, 1984, Illinois and U.S. Supreme Court. *Education:* Illinois Wesleyan University (B.A., 1981); Valparaiso University (J.D., 1984). ***PRACTICE AREAS:*** Commercial Litigation; Environmental Litigation and Appeals; Products Liability; Complex Litigation. ***Email:*** mphilippi@uhlaw.com

(This Listing Continued)

ALEX PIROGOVSKY, admitted to bar, 1998, Illinois. *Education:* Northwestern University (B.A., 1994); Washington University School of Law (J.D., 1998). ***Email:*** apirogovsky@uhlaw.com

DEAN J. POLALES, admitted to bar, 1979, Illinois. *Education:* DePaul University; University of Chicago (B.A., 1975; J.D., 1979). ***PRACTICE AREAS:*** Litigation. ***Email:*** djpolales@uhlaw.com

CHRISTOPHER L. REXROAT, admitted to bar, 1993, Wisconsin; 2001, Illinois. *Education:* University of Wisconsin (B.A., 1988; J.D., cum laude, 1993). ***PRACTICE AREAS:*** Bankruptcy; Creditors Rights. ***Email:*** clrexroat@uhlaw.com

FRANK J. SAIBERT, admitted to bar, 1983, Illinois, U.S. Court of Appeals, Seventh Circuit and U.S. District Court, Northern District of Illinois. *Education:* University of Illinois (B.A., summa cum laude, 1980); University of Michigan (J.D., cum laude, 1983). ***PRACTICE AREAS:*** Labor and Employment Law. ***Email:*** fjsaibert@uhlaw.com

JULIE K. SEYMOUR, admitted to bar, 1990, Illinois. *Education:* Rockford College (B.A., 1985); University of Illinois (J.D., 1990; M.B.A., 1990). ***PRACTICE AREAS:*** Asset Based Finance; Secured Lending; Bond Finance; Health Care; Public Finance; Tax Exempt Finance. ***Email:*** jkseymour@uhlaw.com

KEVIN P. SHEA, admitted to bar, 1997, Illinois. *Education:* University Of Illinois (B.A., 1993; J.D., 1997). ***Email:*** kpshea@uhlaw.com

BARRY J. SHKOLNIK, born Chicago, Illinois, March 18, 1955; admitted to bar, 1980, Illinois. *Education:* University of Illinois (B.A., 1976); Stanford University (J.D., 1979). Phi Beta Kappa. ***PRACTICE AREAS:*** Corporate Securities; Finance. ***Email:*** bjshkolnik@uhlaw.com

JAMES B. SMITH, admitted to bar, 1974, Illinois. *Education:* Colgate University (B.A., 1968); Boston University (J.D., 1974). ***PRACTICE AREAS:*** Real Estate Contracts; Real Estate Finance; Real Estate Leasing; Real Estate Secured Lending. ***Email:*** jbsmith@uhlaw.com

TINA B. SOLIS, born Independence, Iowa, December 9, 1971; admitted to bar, 1997, Illinois and U.S. District Court, Northern District of Illinois; 1998, U.S. District Court, Central District of Illinois and U.S. District Court, Western District of Wisconsin. *Education:* University of Iowa (B.A., with high honors, 1994; J.D., with high honors, 1997). Phi Beta Kappa; Omicron Delta Kappa; Phi Delta Phi. Member, Mortar Board. *Member:* Chicago and Illinois State Bar Associations. ***PRACTICE AREAS:*** Litigation. ***Email:*** tbsolis@uhlaw.com

GREGG E. SZILAGYI, admitted to bar, 1988, Illinois and U.S. District Court, Northern District of Illinois. *Education:* University of Illinois (B.A., 1985; J.D., 1988). ***PRACTICE AREAS:*** Bankruptcy. ***Email:*** geszilagyi@uhlaw.com

THEODORE R. TETZLAFF, admitted to bar, 1969, Indiana and District of Columbia; 1974, Illinois. *Education:* Princeton University (B.A., 1966); Yale University (LL.B., 1969). ***PRACTICE AREAS:*** Litigation.

STEVEN J. THOMPSON, admitted to bar, 1987, Illinois and Wisconsin; U.S. Court of Appeals, Seventh Circuit. *Education:* University of Wisconsin-Madison (B.A., 1984; J.D., cum laude, 1987). ***PRACTICE AREAS:*** Litigation.

RICHARD A. UNGARETTI, admitted to bar, 1970, Illinois. *Education:* DePaul University (B.S.C., 1964; J.D., 1970). Fellow, American College of Real Estate Lawyers. ***PRACTICE AREAS:*** Real Estate Law; Real Property; Affordable Housing; Land Use; Real Estate Development. ***Email:*** raungaretti@uhlaw.com

SAM VINSON, admitted to bar, 1979, Illinois. *Education:* Dartmouth College (B.A., with honors, 1969); Georgetown University (J.D., 1977). ***PRACTICE AREAS:*** Legislative Practice; Health Care Law. ***Email:*** svinson@uhlaw.com

ROBERT S. WINNER, admitted to bar, 1997, Illinois. *Education:* Washington University, St. Louis (B.A., 1994); DePaul University College of Law (J.D., 1997). ***Email:*** rswinner@uhlaw.com

JENNIFER ZORDANI, admitted to bar, 1994, Illinois. *Education:* University of Chicago (B.A., 1985); IIT-Chicago Kent College of Law (J.D., 1994). ***PRACTICE AREAS:*** Corporate; Financial Services; Information Technology. ***Email:*** jlzordani@uhlaw.com

OF COUNSEL

KEVIN M. FOLEY, admitted to bar, 1972, Connecticut; 1973, District of Columbia; 1988, Illinois. *Education:* Georgetown University (B.A., 1969; J.D., 1972). (Also Principal, Quincy Law Group). ***PRACTICE AREAS:*** Commodities; Securities; Regulatory Law. ***Email:*** kmfoley@uhlaw.com

ERIC F. GREENBERG, admitted to bar, 1983, Illinois. *Education:* Northwestern University (B.A., 1980); Cornell Law School (J.D., 1983). ***PRACTICE AREAS:*** Food and Drug Law; Litigation. ***Email:*** efgreenberg@uhlaw.com

STEPHEN HOKE, admitted to bar, 1985, Illinois. *Education:* Indiana University (B.S., 1981); Georgetown University (J.D., 1985). Phi Beta Kappa. *Member:* Illinois State Bar Association. ***Email:*** shoke@uhlaw.com

DANIEL J. PIERCE, admitted to bar, 1972, Illinois. *Education:* DePaul University (B.S., 1969; J.D., 1972). ***PRACTICE AREAS:*** Real Estate Tax Appeals; Civil Litigation; Criminal Litigation. ***Email:*** dpjpierce@netzero.net

PATRICIA A. ROONEY, admitted to bar, 1985, Massachusetts; 1986, District of Columbia; 1987, Colorado; 1997, Illinois. *Education:* Georgetown University (B.S., cum laude, 1979); George Washington University (J.D., cum laude, 1984). ***PRACTICE AREAS:*** Corporate Law; Securities; Finance.

DEGEE D. WILHELM, admitted to bar, 2002, Illinois. *Education:* Baylor University (B.B.A., 1988); Chicago-Kent College of Law, Illinois Institute of Technology (J.D., with honors, 2002). ***Email:*** ddwilhelm@uhlaw.com

(This Listing Continued)

ASSOCIATES

BRIAN V. ALCALA, admitted to bar, 1997, Ohio, Indiana and Illinois. *Education:* University of Notre Dame (B.B.A., magna cum laude, 1994); Northwestern University (J.D., 1997). ***PRACTICE AREAS:*** Litigation.

ANNA L. BENJAMIN, admitted to bar, 2004, Illinois. *Education:* University of Notre Dame (J.D., 2004). ***PRACTICE AREAS:*** Litigation. ***Email:*** albenjamin@uhlaw.com

JOEL A. BLANCHET, admitted to bar, 1998, Illinois. *Education:* Canisius College (B.A., magna cum laude, 1995); University of Illinois College of Law (J.D., magna cum laude, Order of the Coif, 1998). ***Email:*** jablanchet@uhlaw.com

BRENDA N. BRODERICK, admitted to bar, 1997, Illinois. *Education:* St. Mary's College (B.A., 1990); Illinois Institute of Technology, Chicago-Kent College of Law (J.D., 1997). ***Email:*** bnbroderick@uhlaw.com

JAMES M. CARLSON, admitted to bar, 1999, Illinois. *Education:* Michigan State University (B.A., with high honors, 1996); University of Michigan (J.D., 1999). ***Email:*** jmcarlson@uhlaw.com

JOLYNN C. CAROLINE, admitted to bar, 2002, Illinois; U.S. District Court, Northern District of Illinois. *Education:* University of Illinois (B.S., with honors, 1999, J.D., 2002). *Member:* Chicago, Cook County and Illinois State Bar Associations. ***PRACTICE AREAS:*** Litigation; Labor and Employment. ***Email:*** jcaroline@uhlaw.com

KAMAU A. COAR, admitted to bar, 2003, Illinois and New York. *Education:* Johns Hopkins University (B.A., 1998); Duke University (J.D., 2001). ***Email:*** kacoar@uhlaw.com

BRECKEN JOY CUTLER, admitted to bar, 2003, Illinois. *Education:* Miami University (B.A., cum laude, 1997); University of Illinois (J.D., cum laude, 2002). ***Email:*** bjcutler@uhlaw.com

ELIZABETH A. DAVIS, admitted to bar, 2003, Illinois and U.S. District Court, Northern District of Illinois. *Education:* University of Iowa (B.A., 1997; J.D., with distinction, 2003). Executive Editor, University of Iowa Law Review, 2002-2003. *Member:* Chicago and American Bar Associations. ***LANGUAGES:*** Spanish. ***PRACTICE AREAS:*** Corporate Law.

HALLIE A. DIETHELM, admitted to bar, 1999, Illinois. *Education:* The Ohio State University (B.A., 1996; J.D., 1999). ***PRACTICE AREAS:*** Litigation. ***Email:*** hadiethelm@uhlaw.com

KEITH E. EDEUS, JR., admitted to bar, 1998, Illinois. *Education:* Truman State University (B.S., 1993); Northern Illinois University (J.D., magna cum laude, 1998). ***Email:*** keedeus@uhlaw.com

CATHERINE T. GONZALEZ, admitted to bar, 1989, Illinois. *Education:* Northeastern Illinois University (B.A., with high honors, 1982); Roosevelt University (Paralegal Certificate, 1982); Chicago-Kent College of Law, Illinois Institute of Technology (J.D., with high honors, 1989). ***Email:*** ctgonzalez@uhlaw.com

MICHAEL J. HAYES, JR., admitted to bar, 1996, Illinois and U.S. District Court, Northern District of Illinois. *Education:* University of Illinois (B.A., 1993); DePaul University (J.D., 1996). Assistant Editor, Journal of Health and Hospital Law, 1992-1993. Assistant Counsel to the Speaker of the Illinois House of Representatives, 1997. *Member:* Fenwick, Chicago and Illinois State Bar Associations. ***PRACTICE AREAS:*** Litigation.

TIMOTHY E. HORTON, admitted to bar, 2002, Illinois. *Education:* College of the Holy Cross (B.A., 1999); University of Notre Dame (J.D., 2002). ***Email:*** tehorton@uhlaw.com

DAVID LEVITT, admitted to bar, 2003, Illinois. *Education:* Loyola University (B.A., 2000); University of Chicago (J.D., 2003). ***Email:*** dlevitt@uhlaw.com

ANDREW B. LEVY, admitted to bar, 2000, Illinois, Massachusetts and New York. *Education:* State University of New York at Buffalo (B.A., cum laude, 1994); Cornell University (J.D., 1999). ***PRACTICE AREAS:*** Corporate Law.

MICHAEL P. McBRIDE, admitted to bar, 2004, Illinois. *Education:* University of Michigan (J.D., 2004). ***PRACTICE AREAS:*** Litigation. ***Email:*** mpmcbride@uhlaw.com

MELISSA GLASS MELSHER, admitted to bar, 1999, Illinois and New York. *Education:* American University (B.A., 1994); Benjamin N. Cardozo School of Law (Visiting Student, 1997-1998); Chicago-Kent College of Law (J.D., with honors, 1998). ***Email:*** mgmelsher@uhlaw.com

JACOB M. MIHM, admitted to bar, 2000, Illinois. *Education:* Loras College (B.A., cum laude, 1997); Southern Illinois University (J.D., 2000). ***Email:*** jmmihm@uhlaw.com

VALERIE BRESLIN MONTAGUE, admitted to bar, 2003, Illinois; U.S. District Court, Northern District of Illinois; U.S. Court of Appeals, Seventh Circuit. *Education:* Marquette University (B.A., cum laude, 2000); Georgetown University (J.D., 2003). ***PRACTICE AREAS:*** Health Care.

JENNIFER ORRICO, admitted to bar, 2000, Illinois. *Education:* Marquette University (B.A., magna cum laude, 1997); DePaul University (J.D., with honors, 2000). ***Email:*** jmjendusa@uhlaw.com

JENNIFER R. QUINN, admitted to bar, 1999, Illinois. *Education:* University of New Mexico (B.B.A., 1996); John Marshall Law School (J.D., 1999). ***Email:*** jrquinn@uhlaw.com

JOHN T. RUSKUSKY, admitted to bar, 1998, Illinois and U.S. District Court, Northern District of Illinois. *Education:* University of Notre Dame (B.A., cum laude, 1995); George Washington University (J.D., with highest honors, 1998). ***PRACTICE AREAS:*** Litigation.

JON P. SANDERS, admitted to bar, 2000, Illinois and New York. *Education:* Centre College (B.A., 1995); Vermont Law School (J.D., cum laude, 2000). ***PRACTICE AREAS:*** Environmental. ***Email:*** jpsanders@uhlaw.com

(This Listing Continued)

UNGARETTI & HARRIS, Chicago—Continued

SHANNON M. SCHAAB, born Wurzburg, West Germany, July 20, 1973; admitted to bar, 1998, Illinois. *Education:* University of Illinois (B.S., 1994); DePaul University (J.D., 1998). *Member:* Chicago and American Bar Associations. ***PRACTICE AREAS:*** Litigation. ***Email:*** smschaab@uhlaw.com

RACHEL C. STEINER, admitted to bar, 2004, Illinois. *Education:* University of Wisconsin (J.D., 2004). ***PRACTICE AREAS:*** Litigation. ***Email:*** rcsteiner@uhlaw.com

DANIEL P. STRZALKA, admitted to bar, 2003, Illinois. *Education:* University of Iowa (B.A., 2000); DePaul University (J.D., summa cum laude, 2003). ***Email:*** dpstrzalka@uhlaw.com

JESSICA K. THOMAS, admitted to bar, 1999, Illinois and U.S. District Court, Northern and Central Districts of Illinois. *Education:* University of Michigan (B.F.A., 1995); DePaul University College of Law (J.D., with honors, 1999). ***PRACTICE AREAS:*** Litigation. ***Email:*** jkthomas@uhlaw.com

JULIE E. TREUMANN, admitted to bar, 2001, Illinois. *Education:* St. Olaf College (B.A., magna cum laude, 1994); Loyola University (J.D., 2001). ***PRACTICE AREAS:*** Corporate Law.

ANGELA WILLIAMS-WALKER, admitted to bar, 2000, Wisconsin and Illinois. *Education:* Dartmouth College (B.A., 1993); University of Wisconsin-Madison (J.D., 2000). ***Email:*** awwalker@uhlaw.com

JEFFREY D. WOODS, admitted to bar, 2004, Illinois. *Education:* Valparaiso University (J.D., 2004). ***PRACTICE AREAS:*** Corporate Law. ***Email:*** jdwoods@uhlaw.com

LAW OFFICES OF
TOD M. URBAN, LTD.

Established in 1992

820 WEST JACKSON BOULEVARD
SUITE 310
CHICAGO, ILLINOIS 60607
Telephone: 312-474-1144
Fax: 312-993-1554
Email: Urbanlaw@ameritech.net
URL: http://www.lawyers.com/urbantod

Complex Criminal Law Practice including Capital Offenses, Murder, Drugs, Serious Felonies, Federal Criminal and Criminal Appeals.

TOD M. URBAN, born Evanston, Illinois, January 20, 1958; admitted to bar, 1984, Illinois; 1990, U.S. District Court, Northern District of Illinois; U.S. Court of Appeals, Seventh Circuit; U.S. District Court, District of Minnesota; U.S. District Court, Eastern District of New York. *Education:* Roosevelt University (B.S.B.A., 1981); Chicago-Kent College of Law (J.D., 1984). Certified Lead Counsel, Illinois Capital Litigation Trial Bar. Public Defender of Cook County, Felony Trial Division, 1985-1989. *Member:* Chicago Bar Association; National Institute for Trial Advocacy; National Association of Criminal Defense Lawyers; National Institute of Trial Advocacy (Faculty Member, 1990—). ***PRACTICE AREAS:*** Criminal Law; Appellate Practice.

VARGA BERGER LEDSKY HAYES & CASEY

A PROFESSIONAL CORPORATION

Established in 1996

SANTA FE BUILDING
224 SOUTH MICHIGAN AVENUE, SUITE 350
CHICAGO, ILLINOIS 60604-2507
Telephone: 312-341-9400
Fax: 312-341-2900

General Civil Practice in State and Federal Courts. Trials and Appeals in all Courts. General Commercial Litigation, Class Action Defense, Consumer Financial Services Litigation, Regulatory and Compliance, Environmental Safety and Health Law and Litigation, Real Estate, Insurance Coverage, Banking and Financial Institution Regulation, RICO, Civil Rights and Employment Litigation. Alternative Dispute Resolution.

FIRM PROFILE: Founded in April 1996 by four partners from two major Chicago law firms, Varga Berger Ledsky Hayes & Casey is committed to providing its clients with the highest quality representation in a cost-effective and service-oriented manner. Our founders, collectively, have substantial experience litigating a wide variety of complex business disputes in state and federal trial and appellate courts across the country, as well as before many regulatory authorities. Although we have broad experience in business litigation, we have special expertise in the areas of consumer financial services law and class action defense, as well as in environmental law. While seasoned trial lawyers, we also have considerable experience with various forms of alternative dispute resolution. In short, we know how to plead, discover, try and win lawsuits and how to otherwise achieve favorable results and fulfill clients' objectives--whether in litigation or in non-litigation compliance and regulatory contexts.

CRAIG A. VARGA, born Greensburg, Pennsylvania, March 22, 1954; admitted to bar, 1980, Illinois and U.S. District Court, Northern District of Illinois including Trial Bar; 1987, U.S. Court of Appeals, Seventh Circuit; 1998, U.S. Supreme Court. *Education:* Washington and Jefferson College (B.A., summa cum laude, 1976); Northwestern University (J.D., 1979). Phi Beta Kappa. Recipient, American Financial Services Association Distinguished Service Award, 2002. Note and Comment Editor, Journal of Criminal Law and Criminology, 1978-1979. General Counsel, Illinois Financial Services Association, 1995—. Member, Law Committee: American Financial Services Association. Member and Secretary, 2003—, Governing Committee, Conference on Consumer Finance Law. Member, Board of Advisors, *Consumer Financial Services Law Report;* State Editor, (Illinois) *Houselaw* and *Carlaw*. Member, Board of Trustees, Washington and Jefferson College, 2002-2007. Speaker: Conference on Consumer Finance Law, CLE Seminars, "Update on Litigation," 1992-2005; Practising Law Institute, "Consumer Financial Services Litigation," 1997-2000, 2004; American Conference Institute, "Class Actions," 2002-2004; "Consumer Finance Litigation and Class Actions," 2005. *Member:* American (Member, Business Law Section; Member, Committees on: Consumer Financial Services; Business and Corporate Litigation; Member, Litigation Section; Member, Committees on: Class Actions and Derivative Suits; Consumer Litigation; Commercial and Banking Litigation) and Illinois State Bar Associations. ***PRACTICE AREAS:*** Consumer Financial Services Litigation; Regulatory Compliance; Class Action Defense. ***Email:*** cvarga@vblhc.com

NORMAN B. BERGER, born Alexandria, Louisiana, September 7, 1956; admitted to bar, 1981, Illinois, U.S. District Court, Northern District of Illinois, U.S. Court of Appeals, Seventh Circuit; 1989, U.S. Supreme Court. *Education:* University of Wisconsin (B.A., 1978); DePaul University (J.D., 1981). Faculty Member, National Institute of Trial Advocacy, Midwest Region, 1989—. Assistant Attorney General, General Law Division, Special Litigation Section, Office of Attorney General of Illinois, 1983-1985. Chairman, Dean's Advisory Council, De Paul University College of Law. Chairman, Centennial Awards Program, Illinois State Historical Society, 2003. Member, Advisory Board, Illinois State Historical Society. *Member:* Chicago, Illinois State and American (Section of Litigation, Committee on Environmental Litigation; Section of Natural Resources, Energy and Environmental Law, Environmental Crimes Committee) Bar Associations. ***PRACTICE AREAS:*** Environmental Law; Environmental Litigation; Business Litigation; Real Estate Litigation; Class Actions; Products Liability. ***Email:*** nberger@vblhc.com

JONATHAN N. LEDSKY, born Washington, D.C., April 9, 1959; admitted to bar, 1986, Illinois and U.S. District Court, Northern District of Illinois; 1995, U.S. Court of Appeals, Seventh Circuit; 2001, U.S. District Court, Central District of Illinois. *Education:* University of Michigan; Franklin & Marshall College (B.A., 1982); Vanderbilt University (J.D., 1986). Phi Alpha Theta. State Editor (Illinois) "*Carlaw*". *Member:* Illinois State and American (Member, Business Law Section; Member, Committees on: Consumer Financial Services; Business and Corporate Litigation; Member, Litigation Section; Member, Committees on: Class Actions and Derivative Suits; Consumer Litigation; Commercial and Banking Litigation) Bar Associations. ***PRACTICE AREAS:*** Consumer Financial Services Litigation; Class Action Defense; Commercial Litigation. ***Email:*** jledsky@vblhc.com

MICHAEL D. HAYES, born Chicago, Illinois, July 16, 1959; admitted to bar, 1984, Illinois and U.S. District Court, Northern District of Illinois; 1988, U.S. Court of Appeals, Seventh Circuit; 1989, U.S. Supreme Court. *Education:* Bates College (B.A., 1981); DePaul University (J.D., 1984). Member, De Paul Law Review, 1983-1984. *Member:* Chicago (Member, Environmental Law Committee; Member, Class Litigation Committee), Illinois State and American (Member, Section on Natural Resources, Energy and Environmental Law) Bar Associations. ***PRACTICE AREAS:*** Environmental Law; Environmental Litigation; Class Actions; Commercial Litigation. ***Email:*** mhayes@vblhc.com

MICHAEL V. CASEY, born Washington, D.C., November 22, 1952; admitted to bar, 1981, Illinois, U.S. District Court, Northern District of Illinois and U.S. Court of Appeals, Seventh Circuit. *Education:* University of Wisconsin-Milwaukee (B.A., 1978); DePaul University (J.D., 1981). Trial Attorney, General Law Division, Office of the Attorney General of Illinois, 1983-1986. Chief, Legal Counsel Division, City of Chicago, Department of Law, 1989-1991. *Member:* Chicago, Illinois State and American Bar Associations. ***PRACTICE AREAS:*** Product Defect Litigation; Governmental Affairs; Commercial Litigation. ***Email:*** mcasey@vblhc.com

ANNE E. VINER, born Fort Wayne, Indiana, January 8, 1968; admitted to bar, 1993, Illinois. *Education:* Denison University (B.A., cum laude, 1990); Northwestern University (J.D., 1993). Phi Sigma Alpha; Phi Society; Phi Beta Kappa. Member, Editorial Board, Journal of Criminal Law & Criminology, 1992-1993. *Member:* Chicago (Member, Brownfields Subcommittee, Environmental Section, 1993—), Illinois State and American Bar Associations. ***PRACTICE AREAS:*** Environmental Law; Environmental Litigation; Class Actions; Commercial Litigation; Real Estate Litigation; Products Liability. ***Email:*** aviner@vblhc.com

JOSHUA D. DAVIDSON, born Salt Lake City, Utah, May 5, 1966; admitted to bar, 1993, Illinois; 1994, Utah; 1996, New York, U.S. District Court, Northern District of Illinois, Trial Bar and U.S. Court of Appeals, Seventh Circuit. *Education:* University of Utah (B.A., magna cum laude, 1990); Northwestern University (J.D., 1993). Phi Beta Kappa. Associate Note and Comment Editor, Northwestern University Journal of International Law and Business, 1992-1993. ***LANGUAGES:*** French. ***PRACTICE AREAS:*** Civil Litigation; Trials and Appeals; Commercial Litigation; Consumer Financial Services Litigation; Class Action Defense. ***Email:*** jdavidson@vblhc.com

---

HAROLD B. HILBORN, born Chicago, Illinois, November 1, 1970; admitted to bar, 1995, Illinois. *Education:* University of Michigan (B.A., summa cum laude, 1992); Northwestern University (J.D., 1995). Phi Beta Kappa; Order of the Coif. Associate Note and Comment Editor, Northwestern University Law Review, 1994-1995. ***PRACTICE AREAS:*** Commercial Litigation; Class Action Defense. ***Email:*** hhilborn@vblhc.com

JAIME S. ROGINSKI-KORD, born Kewanee, Illinois, May 5, 1976; admitted to bar, 2001, Illinois; 2003, U.S. District Court, Northern District of Illinois. *Education:* Western Illinois University (B.A., summa cum laude, 1997); Northwestern University School of Law (J.D., 2001). Phi Beta Kappa. *Member:* Chicago and Illinois State Bar Associations. ***PRACTICE AREAS:*** Commercial Litigation; Consumer Financial Services Litigation. ***Email:*** jroginskikord@vblhc.com

JULIE F. GROSCH, born Chicago, Illinois, March 1, 1977; admitted to bar, 2003, Illinois. *Education:* University of Illinois (B.A., 1999); Chicago-Kent College of Law (J.D., 2003). *Member:* Illinois State and American Bar Associations. ***PRACTICE AREAS:*** Commercial Litigation. ***Email:*** jgrosch@vblhc.com

(This Listing Continued)

OF COUNSEL

R. ELIZABETH TOPOLUK, born Key Biscayne, Florida, May 18, 1959; admitted to bar, 1985, Minnesota; 1999, Illinois. *Education:* College of St. Catherine (B.A., 1981); William Mitchell College of Law (J.D., 1985). Law Review. State Editor (Illinois) *Houselaw.* Member, Governing Committee, Conference on Consumer Finance Law. *Member:* Minnesota State and American (Chair, Consumer Litigation Subcommittee; Committees On: Consumer Financial Services) Bar Associations. ***PRACTICE AREAS:*** Financial Institution Regulation; Consumer Credit Compliance; Corporate Transactions. ***Email:*** btopoluk@vblhc.com

PETER E. MANIS, born Pittsburgh, Pennsylvania, August 16, 1957; admitted to bar, 1983, Illinois. *Education:* University of Michigan (B.A., with honors, 1980; J.D., 1983). *Member:* Chicago and Illinois State Bar Associations. ***PRACTICE AREAS:*** Real Estate Law.

LEGAL SUPPORT PERSONNEL

KENNETH J. JENSEN, born Chicago, Illinois, March 22, 1963. *Education:* University of Iowa (1981-1983); Kirkwood College (1983-1985); DePaul University (1989-1991). Member: Toastmasters International; Illinois Paralegal Association. (Legal Assistant). ***PRACTICE AREAS:*** Trial Preparation; Legal Research; Deposition Abstracts; Document Review; Correspondence Drafting; File Organization and Maintenance. ***Email:*** kjensen@vblhc.com

VEDDER, PRICE, KAUFMAN & KAMMHOLZ, P.C.

222 NORTH LA SALLE STREET
CHICAGO, ILLINOIS 60601-1003
Telephone: 312-609-7500
Fax: 312-609-5005
Email: See addresses for individual attorneys
URL: http://www.vedderprice.com

New York, New York Office: 805 Third Avenue. Telephone: 212-407-7700. Facsimile: 212-407-7799.

Roseland, New Jersey Office: Five Becker Farm Road. Telephone: 973-579-1100. Facsimile: 973-579-9607.

General Practice. Complex Litigation, Civil Litigation, Class Actions, Alternate Dispute Resolution, Corporate Law, Commercial Law, Equipment Finance and Leasing, Project Finance, Municipal Finance, Banking Law, International Trade, Labor and Employment, Employee Benefits, Occupational Safety and Health, Municipal Law, School Law, Securities, Investment Company Law, Professional Liability Defense, Insurance Coverage, Insurance Litigation, Tax Planning, Tax Litigation, Intellectual Property, Mergers and Acquisitions, Bankruptcy, Real Estate, Health Care, Trade and Professional Associations, Estate Planning, Trust Administration.

MEMBERS OF FIRM

THOMAS G. ABRAM, born Berwyn, Illinois, April 27, 1948; admitted to bar, 1973, Illinois and U.S. District Court, Northern District of Illinois including Trial Bar; 1982, U.S. Court of Appeals, 7th Circuit; 1986, U.S. District Court, Northern District of Indiana; 1989, U.S. District Court, Central District of Illinois. *Education:* Carleton College (B.A., cum laude, 1969); Stanford University (J.D., 1973; M.A. in Economics, 1977). ***PRACTICE AREAS:*** Class Actions; Affirmative Action; Labor and Employment Law. ***Email:*** tabram@vedderprice.com

BRUCE R. ALPER, born Chicago, Illinois, January 18, 1954; admitted to bar, 1978, Illinois and U.S. District Court, Northern District of Illinois including Trial Bar; 1979, U.S. Court of Appeals, 10th Circuit; 1984, U.S. Court of Appeals, 7th Circuit; 1986, Florida. *Education:* University of Illinois at Urbana (B.A., cum laude, 1975); Boston University (J.D., magna cum laude, 1978). Phi Beta Kappa. Member, University of Illinois Law Forum, 1976-1977. Co-Author: "Illinois Labor Law Survey," 19 Loyola University Law Journal 591 (1988); "Unions, Nurses and the Health Care Industry: Recent Administrative and Judicial Developments," Journal of Health and Hospital Law, Vol. 28, No. 2 (1995). ***PRACTICE AREAS:*** Labor and Employment; Labor Law; Employment Law; Employment Litigation; Employment Discrimination. ***Email:*** balper@vedderprice.com

DANA SIMAITIS ARMAGNO, born Chicago, Illinois, February 8, 1967; admitted to bar, 1992, Illinois and U.S. District Court, Northern District of Illinois. *Education:* University of Illinois (B.S., cum laude, 1989); DePaul University College of Law (J.D., 1992). Recipient, DePaul University College of Law Dean's Scholarship. Member, 1990-1992 and Notes and Comments Editor, 1991-1992, DePaul Law Review. ***PRACTICE AREAS:*** Business Law; Corporate Law; Commercial Finance; Debt and Equity Finance; Mergers, Acquisitions and Divestitures. ***Email:*** darmagno@vedderprice.com

JAMES A. ARPAIA, born Chicago, Illinois, December 4, 1953; admitted to bar, 1991, Illinois and U.S. District Court, Northern District of Illinois. *Education:* University of Illinois (B.S., 1975); IIT Chicago-Kent College of Law (J.D., 1991). ***PRACTICE AREAS:*** Investment Services; Mutual Funds; Broker-Dealer Regulation; Investment Management; Investments. ***Email:*** jarpaia@vedderprice.com

ANTHONY J. ASHLEY, born Abington, Pennsylvania, September 10, 1966; admitted to bar, 1992, Illinois and U.S. District Court, Northern District of Illinois, including Trial Bar; 1996, U.S. District Court, Central District of Illinois. *Education:* Miami University (B.S., 1988); DePaul University (J.D., 1992). President, Moot Court Executive Board, 1991; National Trial Team, 1990 and 1991. Anna Mansfield Fellowship, 1990. Recipient, Crowley Award for Trial Advocacy, 1992. Author: "Superfund Reauthorization or Reform: To Be or Not Be?" 3 Global Risk Manager, 1996. Extern, U.S. Attorney's Office, 1991. *Member:* Chicago and American Bar Associations. ***PRACTICE AREAS:*** Commercial Litigation; Trade Secrets Litigation; Intellectual Property Litigation; Technology Law; Environmental. ***Email:*** aashley@vedderprice.com

THOMAS A. BAKER, born Milwaukee, Wisconsin, March 10, 1948; admitted to bar, 1974, Illinois and U.S. District Court, Northern District of Illinois; 1980, District of Columbia and U.S. District Court, District of Columbia. *Education:* Marquette University (B.A., 1970); University of Chicago (J.D., 1974). Chartered Property and Casualty Underwriter (CPCU), Insurance Institute of America. ***PRACTICE AREAS:*** Insurance Contracts; Insurance Coverage; Insurance Litigation; Complex Litigation; Employment Litigation. ***Email:*** tbaker@vedderprice.com

ROBERT S. BEISER, born Chicago, Illinois, October 27, 1947; admitted to bar, 1976, Illinois; U.S. District Court, Northern and Southern Districts of Illinois; registered to practice before U.S. Patent and Trademark Office. *Education:* Michigan State University (B.A., cum laude, 1970; B.S., cum laude, 1970); Illinois Institute of Technology/Chicago-Kent College of Law (J.D., cum laude, 1976). Delta Theta Phi. Teacher, Intellectual Property Law, Roosevelt University, 1995. Speaker, Intellectual Property Association of Rotational Molders. *Member:* American Intellectual Property Law Association. ***PRACTICE AREAS:*** Patent, Trademark and Copyright Law. ***Email:*** rbeiser@vedderprice.com

DAVID E. BENNETT, born Chicago, Illinois, October 29, 1944; admitted to bar, 1969, Illinois, U.S. District Court, Northern District of Illinois including Trial Bar and U.S. Court of Appeals, 7th Circuit; 1980, U.S. Supreme Court. *Education:* DePaul University (B.A., 1966); Northwestern University (J.D., cum laude, 1969). Editor, Journal of Criminal Law, Criminology and Police Science, 1968-1969. *Member:* Illinois State Bar Association (Member, Antitrust Law Section Council, Chair, 1989-1990) Bar Association of the Seventh Federal Circuit (Meetings Program Chair, 1989; Member, Board of Governors, 1989-1990; Secretary, 1990-1994; First Vice President, 1995-1996; President, 1996-1997). ***PRACTICE AREAS:*** Commercial Litigation; Insurance Litigation; Antitrust; Securities Litigation; Appellate Practice. ***Email:*** dbennett@vedderprice.com

WILLIAM J. BETTMAN, born East Lansing, Michigan, October 21, 1963; admitted to bar, 1992, Illinois. *Education:* Northwestern University (B.A., 1986); Loyola University of Chicago (M.B.A., 1991; J.D., 1992). ***PRACTICE AREAS:*** Mergers and Acquisitions; Venture Capital; Executive Compensation; Corporate Law; Securities. ***Email:*** wbettman@vedderprice.com

GEORGE P. BLAKE, born Chicago, Illinois, January 22, 1934; admitted to bar, 1961, Illinois ; 1963, U.S. Court of Appeals, 7th Circuit and U.S. District Court, Northern District of Illinois including Trial Bar; 1971, U.S. Court of Appeals, 6th Circuit; 1974, U.S. Court of Appeals, 8th Circuit. *Education:* University of Notre Dame (B.Sc., 1956); University of Chicago (J.D., 1961). Phi Delta Phi (Magister, Douglas Inn, 1960-1961); Judicial Clerkship with the Indiana Supreme Court, 1961-1962. ***PRACTICE AREAS:*** Labor and Employment; Employment Discrimination; Employment Litigation; Management Labor Law; Wage and Hour Law. ***Email:*** gblake@vedderprice.com

JOHN T. BLATCHFORD, admitted to bar, 1991, New York (Not admitted in Illinois). *Education:* Tulane University (B.A.; J.D.). ***Email:*** jblatchford@vedderprice.com

STANLEY B. BLOCK, born Chicago, Illinois, January 9, 1933; admitted to bar, 1957, Illinois, U.S. District Court, Northern District of Illinois including Trial Bar and Central District of Illinois, U.S. Court of Appeals, 7th and 8th Circuits and U.S. Supreme Court. *Education:* Northwestern University (B.S., 1954); University of Chicago (J.D., 1957). Phi Alpha Delta; Beta Gamma Sigma. Editor, University of Chicago Law Review, 1956-1957. Member, Panel of Neutrals, 1995—, and Firm Representative, 1989—, to CPR Institute for Dispute Resolution. ***PRACTICE AREAS:*** Alternate Dispute Resolution; Mediation; Arbitration; Antitrust; Insurance Coverage; Insurance Bad Faith; Complex Commercial Litigation; Class Action Litigation; Commercial Transactions. ***Email:*** sblock@vedderprice.com

JONATHAN H. BOGAARD, born Humboldt, Iowa, March 25, 1957; admitted to bar, 1981, Illinois and Iowa. *Education:* University of Iowa (B.B.A., with distinction, 1978; M.A., 1981; J.D., with high distinction, 1981). Beta Gamma Sigma. Certified Public Accountant, Iowa, 1978. ***PRACTICE AREAS:*** Aircraft Finance and Leasing; Equipment Leasing; Equipment Finance; Corporate Tax Planning; Taxation. ***Email:*** jbogaard@vedderprice.com

MARK I. BOGART, born Cleveland, Ohio, July 10, 1957; admitted to bar, 1987, Illinois; 1994, Ohio. *Education:* Cleveland State University (B.A., 1979); Case Western Reserve University (J.D., 1983). Author: "Grantor Trust ESOP Financing: Proceed With Caution," *Journal of Pension Planning and Compliance* (Summer, 1991); "Determining Adequate Consideration in the Absence of Regulations: Have the Courts Clarified Matters or Added to the Confusion?" *Pension & Benefits Week* (June 3, 1996); "Seventh Circuit Affirms *Eyler* Tax Court Decision: ESOP Valuation Methods Could Be Impacted," *Pension & Benefits Week* (August 19, 1996); "Ninth Circuit Holds That Using an Independent Appraiser Number Does Not Ensure ERISA Compliance," *Pension & Benefits Week* (January 21, 1997); "Repeal of UBIT of S-ESOPs Creates Tax Planning Opportunities," *Pension & Benefits Week* (November 3, 1997); "Single-Employer Plan Termination," *Employee Benefits Law* , IICLE (1994, 1997). *Member:* American Bar Association. ***PRACTICE AREAS:*** ERISA; Executive Compensation; ESOPs. ***Email:*** mbogart@vedderprice.com

GABRIELLE M. BUCKLEY, born Oak Park, Illinois, July 29, 1956; admitted to bar, 1981, Illinois and U.S. District Court, Northern District of Illinois. *Education:* University of Illinois; Konan University, Kobe, Japan; Mundelein College (B.A., 1978); DePaul University (J.D., 1981). Phi Alpha Theta. Member, Research Staff, De Paul Law Review, 1980-1981. Author: "Fourth Circuit Finds Coercive Population Practices Insufficient to Grant Asylum," ABA International Law News, Section of International Law and Practice, Vol. 25 No. 1, Winter, 1996; "International Legal Developments in Review: 1997—Immigration and Nationality Law," The International Lawyer (Summer, 1998). Instructor, Business Law, Northwestern University, Chicago, 1984-1986. *Member:* Chicago (Co-Chair, International Law and Practice Committee, 1988-1990 and Special Projects Director, 1990-1991, Young Lawyers Division), American and International Bar Associations; Immigration Lawyers Association; Inter-Pacific Bar Association; Association Internationale des Jeunes Avocats. ***LANGUAGES:*** Japanese. ***PRACTICE AREAS:*** Business Immigration; Employment Immigration. ***Email:*** gbuckley@vedderprice.com

ANGELO J. BUFALINO, born Chicago, Illinois, December 15, 1954; admitted to bar, 1979, Illinois; registered to practice before U.S. Patent and Trademark Office. *Education:* University of Notre Dame (B.S.E.E., 1976); Loyola University (J.D., 1979). Member, National Patent Law Moot Court Competition. Winner, Midwest Regional Outstanding Brief. *Member:* Chicago and American Bar Associations; Intellectual Property Law Association

(This Listing Continued)

VEDDER, PRICE, KAUFMAN & KAMMHOLZ, P.C., Chicago—Continued

of Chicago; American Intellectual Property Law Association. ***PRACTICE AREAS:*** Patents; Trademarks; Copyrights; Trade Secrets; Unfair Competition. ***Email:*** abufalino@vedderprice.com

MITCHELL A. CARREL, born Buffalo, New York, February 12, 1968; admitted to bar, 1994, Illinois. *Education:* Miami University (B.S., 1990); Michigan State University DCL College of Law (J.D., cum laude, 1994). Co-Author: "Towers of Babble: The Continuing Struggle Over Wireless Siting Issues Under the Telecommunications Act of 1996," The Urban Lawyer, Fall 1999, Vol. 31, Number 4; Chapter 5, "Hot Topics in Land Use Law: From the Comprehensive Plan to Del Monte Dunes," Section of State and Local Government Law, American Bar Association, 2000; "Twin Towers: The Developing Split in Interpretations of Facility Siting Law Under the Telecommunications Act of 1996," The Urban Lawyer, Spring 2001; "Railroad Tracks by Walden Pond: The Ongoing Struggle Between Towers and Providers Under the Telecommunications Act of 1996," The Urban Lawyer, Summer 2001, Volume 33, Number 3; "Sprouting Towers: Resolving the Struggle Between Cellular Towers and Nature Under the Telecommunications Act of 1996," The Urban Lawyer, Fall 2002, Volume 34, Number 4. *Member:* Chicago and American Bar Associations. ***PRACTICE AREAS:*** Land Use; Real Estate; Zoning. ***Email:*** mcarrel@vedderprice.com

LAWRENCE J. CASAZZA, born Chicago, Illinois, December 13, 1946; admitted to bar, 1972, Illinois and U.S. District Court, Northern District of Illinois including Trial Bar; 1981, U.S. Court of Appeals, 7th Circuit. *Education:* Miami University (A.B., 1968); Loyola University (J.D., 1972). Note Editor, Loyola University Law Journal. Member, Editorial Review Board, The Illinois Labor Letter. Author: "Violence in the Workplace: How to Reduce an Employers Potential Liability," Illinois Public Employee Relations Report, Summer, 1997. Contributing Editor: *Discipline and Discharge in Arbitration*, BNA Books, 1998. Contributing Author: Labor Arbitration, *A Practical Guide for Advocates*, BNA Books, 1990; Elkouri & Elkouri, How Arbitration Works, 1985-1989 Supplement, BNA Books, 1991. Member, The National Registry of Who's Who. *Member:* American Bar Association (Co-Chairman, ADR in Labor and Employment Law Committee). Fellow: The College of Labor and Employment Lawyers; The American Bar Foundation. ***PRACTICE AREAS:*** Labor and Employment Law; Collective Bargaining; Labor Arbitration; Public Sector Employment Law. ***Email:*** lcasazza@vedderprice.com

THOMAS P. CIMINO, JR., born Chicago, Illinois, August 18, 1962; admitted to bar, 1987, Illinois and U.S. District Court, Northern District of Illinois; 1991, U.S. Court of Appeals, 7th Circuit; 1994, U.S. District Court, Central District of Illinois; 2001, U.S. District Court, Eastern District of Wisconsin; 2002, U.S. District Court, Southern District of Illinois. *Education:* Loyola University of Chicago (B.A., summa cum laude, 1984; J.D., magna cum laude, 1987). Alpha Sigma Nu; Alpha Delta Gamma. Senior Member, Loyola Law Journal. *Member:* Chicago and American Bar Associations; Justinian Society of Lawyers. ***PRACTICE AREAS:*** Commercial Litigation; Securities Litigation; Environmental Litigation; Professional Malpractice; Intellectual Property Litigation; Patent Litigation. ***Email:*** tcimino@vedderprice.com

MICHAEL G. CLEVELAND, born Chicago, Illinois, May 31, 1949; admitted to bar, 1974, Illinois and U.S. District Court, Northern District of Illinois including Trial Bar; 1977, U.S. District Court, Eastern District of Wisconsin and U.S. Court of Appeals, 7th Circuit; 1981, U.S. Court of Appeals, 9th Circuit; 1988, U.S. Court of Appeals, 11th Circuit; 1994, U.S. District Court, Central District of Illinois. *Education:* Loyola University (B.A., cum laude, 1971); University of Chicago (J.D. 1974). Member and Comment Editor, University of Chicago Law Review, 1972-1974. ***PRACTICE AREAS:*** Employment Law; Employment Litigation; Class Actions; Management Labor Law; Wrongful Termination Defense. ***Email:*** mcleveland@vedderprice.com

MARK A. DALLA VALLE, admitted to bar, 1989, California; 2001, Illinois; U.S. District Court, Northern, Central and Southern Districts of California and U.S. Court of Appeals, Ninth and Federal Circuits; registered to practice before the U.S. Patent and Trademark Office. *Education:* DeVry Institute of Technology (B.S.E.E., with honors, 1977); University of Southern California (M.S.E.E., 1983); Loyola Law School (J.D., 1989). *Member:* Institute of Electrical & Electronics Engineers. ***PRACTICE AREAS:*** Intellectual Property. ***Email:*** mdallavalle@vedderprice.com

JEFFREY C. DAVIS, born Woodstock, Illinois, December 15, 1961; admitted to bar, 1987, Illinois. *Education:* University of Arizona (B.S., 1984); Loyola University of Chicago (J.D., 1987). ***PRACTICE AREAS:*** Corporate Law; Mergers, Acquisitions and Divestitures; Computers and Software; Banks and Banking. ***Email:*** jdavis@vedderprice.com

THOMAS R. DEE, born Oak Park, Illinois, August 22, 1961; admitted to bar, 1993, Illinois and U.S. District Court, Northern District of Illinois, 1996, Trial Bar. *Education:* Dominican University (B.A., 1983; M.B.A., 1993); John Marshall Law School (J.D., cum laude, 1993). Associate Lead Articles Editor, John Marshall Law Review, 1992-1993. Author: "The Selling of Pollution: Unleashing Market Forces on the Acid Rain Problem," 25 J. Marshall L. Rev. 627 (1992). ***PRACTICE AREAS:*** Litigation; Intellectual Property; Trademark Infringement; Restrictive Covenant Litigation; Trade Secret Litigation. ***Email:*** tdee@vedderprice.com

THOMAS P. DESMOND, born South Charleston, West Virginia, May 6, 1956; admitted to bar, 1981, Illinois and U.S. District Court, Northern District of Illinois; 1994, U.S. Supreme Court. *Education:* University of Notre Dame (B.B.A., with honors, 1978); Northwestern University (J.D., 1981). Beta Gamma Sigma; Beta Alpha Psi (President, Beta Sigma Chapter, 1977-1978). Certified Public Accountant, Illinois, 1979. Author: "Deferred Compensation Arrangements," Chapter B:5, Bender's Federal Tax Service, 1995. Co-Author: *Fiduciary Responsibilities of Plan Sponsors,* 7th ed., Federal Publications Inc., 1997. ***PRACTICE AREAS:*** Executive Compensation; Securities; Employee Benefits; Corporate Finance. ***Email:*** tdesmond@vedderprice.com

DAVID L. DOYLE, born Cincinnati, Ohio, July 12, 1950; admitted to bar, 1975, Illinois and Georgia. *Education:* Miami University (B.S., 1972); Emory University (J.D., 1975); University of Chicago (M.B.A., 1980). *Member:* American Bar Association (Vice-Chairman, Oil Refining and Marketing Committee, 1986—). ***PRACTICE AREAS:*** Commercial Litigation; Antitrust; Franchise Litigation; Products Liability. ***Email:*** ddoyle@vedderprice.com

TERENCE M. DUNLEAVY, born Colorado Springs, Colorado, May 29, 1957; admitted to bar, 1982, Illinois; 1983, U.S. District Court, Northern District of Illinois, including Trial Bar; 1988, Wisconsin; U.S. Court of Appeals, Seventh Circuit. *Education:* Lewis University (B.A., 1979); Northern Illinois University (J.D., 1982). General Counsel, Illinois Racing Board, 1984-1988. Executive Director, Wisconsin Racing Board, 1988-1992. Member, Wisconsin Gaming Commission, 1992-1994. ***PRACTICE AREAS:*** Gaming Law; International Law; Corporate Law. ***Email:*** tdunleavy@vedderprice.com

DEBORAH BIELICKE EADES, born East St. Louis, Illinois, January 12, 1965; admitted to bar, 1990, Missouri; 1993, Colorado (Not admitted in Illinois). *Education:* University of Missouri (B.S.B.A., magna cum laude, 1986); Washington University School of Law (J.D., with honors, 1990). Staff Member, Washington University Law Review, 1991-1992. *Member:* American Bar Association. ***PRACTICE AREAS:*** Corporate Law; Securities. ***Email:*** deades@vedderprice.com

MICHAEL M. EIDELMAN, admitted to bar, 1988, Illinois. *Education:* University of Michigan (B.S., 1984); DePaul University (J.D., 1987). President, Decalogue Society of Lawyers, De Paul University, 1985-1986. *Member:* Chicago and Illinois State Bar Associations. ***PRACTICE AREAS:*** Bankruptcy and Creditors' Rights.

KARIN JAGEL FLYNN, born Groton, Connecticut, June 28, 1954; admitted to bar, 1982, Illinois. *Education:* Vassar College (A.B., 1976); The American University (J.D., 1982). *Member:* Chicago and American Bar Associations. ***PRACTICE AREAS:*** Investment Services. ***Email:*** kflynn@vedderprice.com

ANDREW M. GARDNER, born Evanston, Illinois, February 16, 1959; admitted to bar, 1986, Illinois; 1987, U.S. District Court, Northern District of Illinois; 1990, U.S. Court of Appeals, 7th Circuit; 1991, U.S. Supreme Court. *Education:* University of Chicago (B.A., 1981); DePaul University (J.D., 1986). Executive Editor, De Paul Law Review, 1985-1986. Co-Author: "Competition-Related Issues Under the Illinois Franchise Disclosure Act," Antitrust and Unfair Competition, IICLE, 1996; "Antitrust Exemptions and Immunities," Antitrust and Evolving Health Care Markets, DePaul University College of Law, 1995. ***PRACTICE AREAS:*** Antitrust; Commercial Litigation; Class Action Defense; Complex Litigation; Civil Appeals. ***Email:*** agardner@vedderprice.com

JAMES V. GARVEY, born Evergreen Park, Illinois, September 1, 1969; admitted to bar, 1994, Illinois and U.S. District Court, Northern District of Illinois; 1999, U.S. Court of Appeals, Ninth Circuit. *Education:* Santa Clara University (B.S., cum laude, 1991); University of Notre Dame (J.D., cum laude, 1994). Phi Beta Kappa; Phi Sigma Alpha. Member, Notre Dame Law Review, 1992-1994. Author: Note, "Health Care Rationing and the Americans with Disabilities Act: What Protection Should the Disabled Be Afforded?" Notre Dame Law Review, Vol. 68, No. 3, 1993. ***PRACTICE AREAS:*** Litigation; Commercial Litigation; Construction Law; Antitrust and Trade Regulation; Trade Secrets; Restrictive Covenants. ***Email:*** jgarvey@vedderprice.com

JOSHUA D. GENTNER, born South Bend, Indiana, August 8, 1972; admitted to bar, 1997, Illinois. *Education:* Indiana University (B.A., 1994); Northwestern University (J.D., cum laude, 1997). Order of the Coif. ***PRACTICE AREAS:*** Equipment Finance and Leasing; Equipment Finance. ***Email:*** jgentner@vedderprice.com

DEAN N. GERBER, born Chicago, Illinois, December 4, 1959; admitted to bar, 1985, Illinois. *Education:* University of Delaware (B.S., magna cum laude, 1982); University of Illinois (J.D., cum laude, 1985). Phi Kappa Phi; Omicron Sigma Delta. Certified Public Accountant, Illinois, 1984. ***PRACTICE AREAS:*** Equipment Finance; Equipment Leasing; Aircraft Finance and Leasing; Lease Finance; Leveraged Leasing. ***Email:*** dgerber@vedderprice.com

LYNNE A. GOCHANOUR, born Doylestown, Pennsylvania, March 24, 1961; admitted to bar, 1987, Arizona; 1989, Texas; 1993, Illinois. *Education:* Kalamazoo College (B.A., 1983); University of Michigan (J.D., 1986). Associate Editor, University of Michigan Journal of Law Reform. ***PRACTICE AREAS:*** Equipment Finance and Leasing. ***Email:*** lgochanour@vedderprice.com

STEVEN L. HAMANN, born Detroit, Michigan, October 10, 1952; admitted to bar, 1987, Illinois; U.S. District Court, Northern District of Illinois. *Education:* Michigan State University (B.A., with honors, 1974); University of Detroit (J.D., cum laude, 1987). Co-Author: "Better Late Than Never-After Acquired Evidence in Employment Discrimination Cases," Employee Relations Law Journal, Vol. 19, No. 2, Autumn, 1993. Member, American Inn of Court, 1987. *Member:* Chicago and American Bar Associations. ***PRACTICE AREAS:*** Labor Law; Employment Litigation. ***Email:*** shamann@vedderprice.com

DOUGLAS M. HAMBLETON, born Chicago, Illinois, November 25, 1955; admitted to bar, 1981, Illinois; 1982, U.S. District Court, Northern District of Illinois. *Education:* University of Virginia (B.A., 1977); Georgetown University (J.D., magna cum laude, 1981). Senior Case and Notes Editor, Law and Policy in International Business (1980-1981). *Member:* American Bar Association (Member, Young Lawyers Division Subcommittee on Financial Institutions Regulation, 1982-1992; Chairman, 1990; Member, Section of Business Law). ***PRACTICE AREAS:*** Banking Law; Corporate Law. ***Email:*** dhambleton@vedderprice.com

THOMAS G. HANCUCH, born Minneapolis, Minnesota, October 29, 1960; admitted to bar, 1988, Illinois; 1989, U.S. District Court, Northern District of Illinois and Eastern District of Wisconsin; 1991, U.S. Court of Appeals, 7th Circuit; 1992, U.S. Court of Appeals, 6th Circuit; 1993, U.S. District Court, Western District of Michigan; 1996, U.S. Court of Appeals, 8th Circuit; 2002, U.S. Court of Appeals, 5th Circuit. *Education:* University of Notre Dame (B.A., high honors, 1983); University of Wisconsin (J.D., magna cum laude, 1987). Order of the Coif. Associate Editor, Wisconsin Law Review, 1986-1987. Clerk to Minnesota Supreme Court, 1987-1988. ***PRACTICE AREAS:*** Labor and Employment; Employee Benefits; ERISA Litigation. ***Email:*** thancuch@vedderprice.com

RENEE M. HARDT, born Dearborn, Michigan, June 29, 1970; admitted to bar, 1997, Wisconsin; 2001, Illinois. *Education:* University of Michigan (A.B., with distinction, 1992); Boston University (J.D., 1997). Managing Editor, Boston University International Law Journal, 1996-1997. Author: "Kodak v. Fuji: A Test Case for the Extraterritorial Application of the Sherman Act," 15 Boston University International Law Journal 309 (1997).

(This Listing Continued)

Member: Chicago and American Bar Associations; State Bar of Wisconsin. ***PRACTICE AREAS:*** Investment Company Law; Investment Management; Corporate; Securities. ***Email:*** rhardt@vedderprice.com

J. KEVIN HENNESSY, born Chicago, Illinois, September 2, 1951; admitted to bar, 1976, Illinois and U.S. District Court, Northern District of Illinois. *Education:* University of Illinois (B.A., 1973); Loyola University of Chicago (J.D., 1976). Phi Beta Kappa; Phi Kappa Phi; Pi Sigma Alpha; Phi Alpha Delta. James Scholar. Co-Author: "Labor Law for the General Practitioner: Duty of Fair Representation," IICLE, 1980-2003. *Member:* Chicago, Illinois State (Member, Employment and Labor Law Section) and American (Member: Committee on Equal Employment Opportunity Law; Litigation Section, Committees on Alternative Dispute Resolution and Employment and Labor Relations Law) Bar Associations. ***PRACTICE AREAS:*** Labor Law; Employment Law. ***Email:*** khennessy@vedderprice.com

PAUL R. HOFFMAN, born Chicago, Illinois, January 3, 1962; admitted to bar, 1988, Illinois and U.S. District Court, Northern District of Illinois. *Education:* Marquette University (B.S., cum laude, 1984); DePaul University (J.D., with honors, 1988). Beta Gamma Sigma; Beta Alpha Psi. Certified Public Accountant, Illinois, 1985. Adjunct Professor, Accounting and the Law, DePaul University College of Law, 1994-1995. ***PRACTICE AREAS:*** Corporate Law; Corporate Finance; Mergers, Acquisitions and Divestitures; Bankruptcy; Workouts. ***Email:*** phoffman@vedderprice.com

JOHN M. HUGHES, born Chicago, Illinois, November 28, 1951; admitted to bar, 1986, Illinois; 1988, U.S. District Court, Northern District of Illinois; 1994, U.S. Tax Court. *Education:* University of Illinois (B.S., Accounting, 1980); Chicago-Kent College of Law (J.D., 1985). Member, Chicago-Kent Law Review. *Member:* Chicago, Illinois State and American Bar Associations. ***PRACTICE AREAS:*** Corporate Law; Energy; Tax Law. ***Email:*** jhughes@vedderprice.com

MICHAEL L. IGOE, JR., born Chicago, Illinois, April 24, 1930; admitted to bar, 1956, Illinois and U.S. District Court, Northern District of Illinois. *Education:* Georgetown University (B.S.S., 1952); University of Chicago (J.D., 1956). Member, City of Chicago Zoning Board of Appeals, 1959-1962. Secretary, Board of Cook County Commissioners, 1962-1990. Member, Committee on Courts, Cook County. ***PRACTICE AREAS:*** Corporate Law; Real Estate; Zoning. ***Email:*** migoe@vedderprice.com

JOHN J. JACOBSEN, JR., born Evergreen Park, Illinois, September 27, 1944; admitted to bar, 1975, Illinois and U.S. District Court, Northern District of Illinois including Trial Bar; 1983, U.S. Court of Appeals, 7th Circuit. *Education:* St. Mary of the Lake (B.A., 1966); University of Louvain (B. Theo., cum laude, 1968; B. Phil., cum laude, 1970; M.A., cum laude, 1970); University of Chicago (J.D., 1975). Co-Author: *Fiduciary Responsibilities of Plan Sponsors,* 7th ed., 1997; *ERISA Claims and Litigation,* 11th ed., 1996; *Effective Health Plan Design & Administration,* 1996. *Member:* Chicago (Member, Employee Benefits Committee) and American (Member, Federal Tax Section and Employee Benefit Committee) Bar Associations. ***PRACTICE AREAS:*** COBRA; Employee Health Benefits; ERISA Compliance; Public Pension Plans; Retirement Benefit Plans. ***Email:*** jjacobsen@vedderprice.com

JOHN JACOBY, born Chicago, Illinois, October 14, 1941; admitted to bar, 1965, Illinois; 1967, U.S. District Court, Northern District of Illinois including Trial Bar; 1970, U.S. Court of Appeals, 2nd Circuit; 1973, U.S. Court of Appeals, 7th Circuit; 1977, U.S. Court of Appeals, District of Columbia Circuit and U.S. Supreme Court; 1979, U.S. Court of Appeals, 10th Circuit and U.S. District Court, Eastern District of Wisconsin; 1987, U.S. District Court, Central District of Illinois. *Education:* University of Illinois (B.S., with honors, 1963; LL.B., 1965). Order of the Coif; Omicron Delta Kappa. Associate Editor, University of Illinois Law Forum, 1964-1965. Arbitrator, Mandatory Arbitration Program of the Circuit Court of Cook County, 1990—. *Member:* Chicago Bar Association; Lawyers Club of Chicago. ***PRACTICE AREAS:*** Collective Bargaining; Employment Civil Rights; Management Labor Law; Title VII Discrimination. ***Email:*** jjacoby@vedderprice.com

EDWARD C. JEPSON, JR., born Chicago, Illinois, October 25, 1955; admitted to bar, 1980, Illinois and U.S. District Court, Northern District of Illinois; 1982, U.S. Court of Appeals, 7th Circuit; 1984, U.S. Court of Appeals, 4th Circuit; 1985, U.S. Supreme Court; 1997, U.S. Court of Appeals, 3rd Circuit. *Education:* Knox College (B.A., magna cum laude, 1977); Harvard University (J.D., 1980). Phi Beta Kappa; National Merit Scholar. ***PRACTICE AREAS:*** Labor and Employment; Labor Law; Employment Law; Employment Litigation; Title VII Discrimination. ***Email:*** ejepson@vedderprice.com

NORMAN B. JULIUS, born Chicago, Illinois, February 1, 1956; admitted to bar, 1981, Illinois and U.S. District Court, Northern District of Illinois; 1988, U.S. Court of Appeals, 7th Circuit. *Education:* University of Illinois (B.S., magna cum laude, 1977); University of Chicago (J.D., 1980). Certified Public Accountant, Illinois, 1977. Beta Gamma Sigma; Beta Alpha Psi (President, Alpha Chapter, 1976-1977). *Member:* Chicago (Construction Law and Professional Fees Committee, Vice-Chair, 1992-1993, Chair, 1993-1994) and Illinois State Bar Associations; Decalogue Society of Lawyers. ***PRACTICE AREAS:*** Real Estate; Corporate Law; Real Estate Development; Real Estate Finance; Construction Law. ***Email:*** njulius@vedderprice.com

THEOPHIL C. KAMMHOLZ (1909-1992)

JAMES M. KANE, born Chicago, Illinois, December 15, 1952; admitted to bar, 1977, Illinois. *Education:* Loyola University (B.A., 1974); IIT/Chicago-Kent (J.D., 1977). Attorney, Comptroller of the Currency, 1977-1981. District Counsel, Comptroller of the Currency (Chicago), 1981-1993. *Member:* Chicago Bar Association (Chairman, Financial Institutions Committee, 1997-1998). ***PRACTICE AREAS:*** Banks and Banking; Bank Mergers and Acquisitions; Banking Regulation; Corporate Law. ***Email:*** jkane@vedderprice.com

GEOFFREY R. KASS, born Washington, D.C., March 24, 1964; admitted to bar, 1989, Illinois. *Education:* Williams College (B.A., cum laude, 1986); Northwestern University (J.D., 1989). Member, 1987, and Editorial Board, 1988, Northwestern Law Review. ***PRACTICE AREAS:*** Equipment Finance and Leasing; Equipment Finance; Equipment Leasing; Project Finance. ***Email:*** gkass@vedderprice.com

CHARLES R. KAUFMAN (1908-1990)

DIANE M. KEHL, born Chicago, Illinois, July 2, 1947; admitted to bar, 1985, Illinois and U.S. District Court, Northern District of Illinois including Trial Bar; U.S. Court of Appeals, Seventh Circuit. *Education:* University of Dayton (B.S., 1969); University of Illinois (M.Ed., 1979); IIT/Chicago-Kent College of Law (J.D., with high honors, 1985). ***PRACTICE AREAS:*** Commercial Litigation; Financial Institution Litigation; Consumer Class Actions; Restrictive Covenants. ***Email:*** dkehl@vedderprice.com

PETER J. KELLY, born Carroll, Iowa, April 21, 1947; admitted to bar, 1972, Illinois and U.S. District Court, Northern District of Illinois. *Education:* Loras College (B.S., 1969); Northwestern University (J.D., 1972). Member, John Henry Wigmore Key. *Member:* Chicago and Illinois State Bar Associations. ***PRACTICE AREAS:*** Environmental; Safety. ***Email:*** pkelly@vedderprice.com

LUDWIG E. KOLMAN, born Spittal, Austria, April 18, 1948; admitted to bar, 1975, Illinois and U.S. District Court, Northern District of Illinois, including Trial Bar; 1977, U.S. Court of Appeals, Seventh Circuit; 1980, U.S. Supreme Court; registered to practice before U.S. Patent and Trademark Office. *Education:* University of Illinois (B.S., with distinction, 1970); University of Rochester (M.S., 1972); Northwestern University (J.D., cum laude, 1975). Member, Editorial Board, Northwestern University Law Review, 1974-1975. Author: "In Patent Litigation, Can Teamwork Work?" The National Law Journal, January 1994. Assistant U.S. Attorney, Northern District of Illinois, 1978-1983. Pro Bono Attorney of the Year, 1992. ***PRACTICE AREAS:*** Commercial Litigation; Patent Infringement; Products Liability; White Collar Crime; Torts. ***Email:*** lkolman@vedderprice.com

KEVIN J. KUHN, born Evanston, Illinois, November 6, 1962; admitted to bar, 1992, Illinois and U.S. District Court, Northern District of Illinois; 1995, U.S. District Court, Southern District of Illinois; 1997, Territorial Court of the U.S. Virgin Islands. *Education:* Northern Illinois University (B.S., 1984); John Marshall Law School (J.D., cum laude, 1992). ***PRACTICE AREAS:*** Complex Litigation; Environmental Law; Environmental Insurance Coverage; Personal Injury Defense; Civil Appeals. ***Email:*** kkuhn@vedderprice.com

WILLIAM A. KUMMERER, born Clinton, Iowa, May 14, 1963; admitted to bar, 1988, Illinois; 1989, U.S. District Court, Northern District of Illinois; 1990, U.S. Court of Appeals, Seventh Circuit. *Education:* University of Iowa (B.A., with distinction, 1984); Georgetown University (J.D., 1988). Member, Georgetown Journal of Legal Ethics, 1986-87. ***PRACTICE AREAS:*** Corporate and Business Law; Mergers and Acquisitions; Trademark and Copyright Licensing; Audio and Video Publishing; Distribution and Manufacturing Contracts. ***Email:*** wkummerer@vedderprice.com

JEAN M. LANGIE, born July 21, 1960; admitted to bar, 1985, Illinois. *Education:* Iowa State University (B.S., with distinction, 1982); University of Iowa (J.D., with distinction, 1985). Order of the Coif. Recipient, University of Iowa Foundation Scholarship. Associate Editor, Journal of Corporation Law, 1984-1985. ***PRACTICE AREAS:*** Estate Planning; Probate; Taxation. ***Email:*** jlangie@vedderprice.com

KAREN P. LAYNG, born Chicago, Illinois, September 23, 1962; admitted to bar, 1987, Illinois and U.S. District Court, Northern District of Illinois; 1989, District of Columbia; 1991, U.S. District Court, Northern District of Illinois, Trial Bar and U.S. Court of Appeals, 7th Circuit; 1992, U.S. Court of Appeals, 9th Circuit; 2001, U.S. Court of Appeals, 6th Circuit. *Education:* University of Dijon, France; University of Illinois (B.A., 1984; J.D., 1987). Delta Theta Phi. Author: *IICLE Antitrust and Unfair Competition,* Chapter 15, "Competition-Related Issues Under the Illinois Franchise Disclosure Act," 1996 and 1998 Supplement; "How to Avoid Firestopping Liability," Insulation Outlook Magazine, June 2001, June 2000 and June 1997 Issues. President and former Secretary of the Seventh Circuit Bar Association. *Member:* Chicago and Illinois State Bar Associations; National Association of Women in Construction; Federation of Women Contractors. ***PRACTICE AREAS:*** Construction Law; Commercial Distributor Franchise and Litigation. ***Email:*** kplayng@vedderprice.com

RANDALL MARC LENDING, born St. Louis, Missouri, July 19, 1964; admitted to bar, 1988, Illinois and U.S. District Court, Northern District of Illinois including Trial Bar; 1989, Missouri and U.S. Court of Appeals, Seventh Circuit. *Education:* University of Michigan (B.A., magna cum laude, 1985); Vanderbilt Law School (J.D., 1988). Phi Delta Phi. Associate Articles Editor, Vanderbilt Law Review, 1987-1988. Author: "Protecting Hospitals from Judicial Narrowing of State Peer Review Statutes," Health Span, October, 1990. ***PRACTICE AREAS:*** Commercial Litigation; Securities Litigation; Employment Litigation. ***Email:*** rlending@vedderprice.com

DOUGLAS J. LIPKE, born Prairie du Chien, Wisconsin, May 7, 1953; admitted to bar, 1979, Illinois and U.S. District Court, Northern District of Illinois; 1982, U.S. Court of Appeals, Seventh Circuit; 1993, U.S. District Court, Eastern and Western Districts of Wisconsin. *Education:* Marquette University (B.S. cum laude, 1975); Loyola University of Chicago (J.D., 1979). Beta Alpha Psi. Member, Loyola University Law Journal, 1978-1979. *Member:* Chicago Bar Association; American Bankruptcy Institute. ***PRACTICE AREAS:*** Bankruptcy; Insolvency; Corporate Reorganization; Workouts; Bankruptcy Litigation. ***Email:*** dlipke@vedderprice.com

JOHN T. McENROE, born Oak Park, Illinois, February 9, 1952; admitted to bar, 1977, Illinois and U.S. District Court, Northern District of Illinois. *Education:* University of Illinois (B.S., magna cum laude, 1974); Yale University (J.D., 1977). ***PRACTICE AREAS:*** Corporate; Corporate Finance; Secured Finance; Leveraged Buyouts; Commercial Finance. ***Email:*** jmcenroe@vedderprice.com

DANIEL C. McKAY, II, born Chicago, Illinois, February 5, 1958; admitted to bar, 1984, Illinois; 1987, District of Columbia and U.S. Court of Appeals, District of Columbia Circuit; 1988, U.S. Supreme Court. *Education:* University of Notre Dame (B.A., with honors, 1980); Loyola University of Chicago School of Law (J.D., 1984); Loyola University of Chicago Graduate School (M.A., Political Science and Public Policy Analysis, magna cum laude, 1986). ***PRACTICE AREAS:*** Banking Law; Mergers and Acquisitions; Corporate. ***Email:*** dmckay@vedderprice.com

MAUREEN A. MILLER, born Milwaukee, Wisconsin, May 2, 1960; admitted to bar, 1986, Illinois, Wisconsin and U.S. District Court, Northern District of Illinois. *Education:* Marquette University (Honors B.A., cum laude, 1982; J.D., cum laude, 1986). Alpha Sigma Nu. *Member:* Chicago and American Bar Associations; State Bar of Wisconsin. ***PRACTICE AREAS:*** Securities; Corporate Law.

JAMES S. MONTANA, JR., born Chicago, Illinois, October 30, 1943; admitted to bar, 1969, New York and U.S. Court of Appeals, Second Circuit; 1970, U.S. District Court,

(This Listing Continued)

VEDDER, PRICE, KAUFMAN & KAMMHOLZ, P.C., Chicago— Continued

Southern District of New York; 1971, Illinois, U.S. Court of Appeals, Seventh Circuit and U.S. District Court, Northern District of Illinois; 1991, U.S. Supreme Court. *Education:* Georgetown University (A.B., 1965); Northwestern University (J.D., 1968). Assistant U.S. Attorney, 1971-1973 and Deputy Chief, Criminal Receiving & Appellate Division, U.S. Attorney's Office, Northern District of Illinois, 1973-1975; Chief Legal Counsel to the Governor of Illinois, 1993-1995; General Counsel, Bally Entertainment Corporation, 1995-1997. Adjunct Professor of Law (Trial Practice and Advanced Trial Practice), Loyola University School of Law, 1977-1993. Instructor: National Institute of Trial Advocacy, 1979-1982. 1985; Federal Practice, Illinois Institute of Continuing Education, 1984-1985. Special Assistant Attorney General of Illinois, 1980-1984. Judge, 1983— and Chief Justice, 1985-1993, Illinois Court of Claims, State of Illinois. Member: Board of Directors, Metropolitan Pier & Exposition Authority, Chicago (1996—); Board of Directors and Executive Committee, Chicagoland Chamber of Commerce (1995—); Board of Advisors, Institute of Metropolitan Affairs, Roosevelt University (1995—). Awards: Department of Justice Special Commendation for Outstanding Service in the Office of the U.S. Attorney, Northern District of Illinois (1974). *Member:* Association of the Bar of the City of New York; Chicago, Illinois State (Member, Assembly, 1980-1983; 1986-1993) and American (Sections on Litigation, Criminal Law and Gaming) Bar Associations; International Association of Gaming Attorneys. (Chairman, Litigation Department). ***PRACTICE AREAS:*** Civil Litigation; White Collar Criminal Litigation; Governmental Relations; Gaming. ***Email:*** jmontana@vedderprice.com

ROBERT J. MORAN, born Chicago, Illinois, December 21, 1945; admitted to bar, 1970, Illinois and U.S. District Court, Northern District of Illinois; 1973, U.S. Supreme Court; 1974, U.S. Court of Military Appeals. *Education:* University of Notre Dame (A.B., 1967); DePaul University College of Law (J.D., 1970). Delta Theta Phi Scholarship Key; Pi Gamma Mu. Member, De Paul University Law Review, 1969-1970. Judicial Clerkship, Illinois Appellate Court, 1970-1972. *Member:* Chicago Bar Association (Chairman, Investment Company Act Subcommittee, 1988-1990; Vice Chair, 1989-1990 and Chairman, 1990-1991, Securities Law Committee). ***PRACTICE AREAS:*** Corporate Law; Securities; Investment Management; Mutual Funds. ***Email:*** rmoran@vedderprice.com

PHILIP L. MOWERY, born Rockford, Illinois, July 20, 1963; admitted to bar, 1988, Illinois and U.S. District Court, Northern District of Illinois. *Education:* University of Chicago (A.B., 1985; J.D., 1988). ***PRACTICE AREAS:*** Employee Benefits; Employment Contracts; Executive Severance Contracts; Employment Litigation; Executive Compensation. ***Email:*** pmowery@vedderprice.com

LANE R. MOYER, born Madison, Wisconsin, June 4, 1963; admitted to bar, 1988, Wisconsin; 1989, Illinois. *Education:* Northern Illinois University (B.A., magna cum laude, 1985); Northwestern University (J.D., cum laude, 1988); University of Chicago (M.B.A., with honors, 1995). Beta Gamma Sigma; Phi Kappa Phi. Member, Mortar Board. Listed in Who's Who in American Colleges and Universities. Certified Public Accountant, Illinois, 1985. President, Young Executives Club. Alderman, City of Wood Dale. ***PRACTICE AREAS:*** Commercial Loans; Buying and Selling of Businesses; Closely Held Business Law; Entrepreneurial Business; Corporate Finance. ***Email:*** lmoyer@vedderprice.com

BRUCE C. NELSON, born Milwaukee, Wisconsin, July 14, 1961; admitted to bar, 1991, Illinois and U.S. District Court, Northern District of Illinois; 1996, U.S. Supreme Court; 1997, U.S. Court of Appeals, Seventh Circuit; 1998, U.S. District Court, Eastern District of Pennsylvania and U.S. Court of Appeals, Sixth Circuit. *Education:* Northwestern University (B.A., 1983); Boston University School of Law (J.D., 1991). Co-Author: "Quasi Discovery," *Civil Discovery Practice, Illinois,* Illinois Institute for Continuing Legal Education, 1996; "Making the Expert a Part of the Litigation Team," *Reengineering Healthcare Liability Litigation,* Michie 1997; "Educating the Defense Witness About the Litigation Process" *Reengineering Healthcare Liability Litigation,* Michie, 1997; 1997 Supplement to Vols. 3 and 4, *Medical & Hospital Negligence,* Michie, 1995; Liability Issues Facing Managed Care Organizations," *Legal Medicine,* 4th ed., Mosby, 1998; "Judicial, Attorney and Juror Misconduct," *Illinois Civil Trial Evidence,* Illinois Institute for Continuing Legal Education 1998; "ERISA Preemption in the Managed Care Context," *Tort & Insurance Law Journal,* Vol. 33, No. 2, American Bar Association, 1998; "Quasi-Discovery," *Civil Discovery Practice, Illinois,* Illinois Institute for Continuing Legal Education, 1999; "Telemedicine: Patient Convenience or Legal Minefield," *RX Law and Medicine Report,* Vol. 2, No. 3, LexisNexis, 2000; "Liability Exposure Facing Managed Care Organizations," *Legal Medicine,* 5th ed., Mosby, 2001. Contributing author of case reports for "In the Courts," American Medical News (American Medical Association 1999-2000). *Member:* Illinois State and American (Member, Sections on: Litigation and Tort and Insurance Practice) Bar Associations; American College of Legal Medicine. ***PRACTICE AREAS:*** Commercial Litigation; Healthcare Litigation; Trial and Appellate Practice. ***Email:*** bnelson@vedderprice.com

MICHAEL A. NEMEROFF, born Chicago, Illinois, October 5, 1963; admitted to bar, 1988, Illinois and U.S. District Court, Northern District of Illinois. *Education:* State University of New York at Binghamton (B.A., with honors, 1985); George Washington University (J.D., with honors, 1988). ***PRACTICE AREAS:*** Corporate Law; Mergers and Acquisitions; Commercial Finance; Emerging Growth Companies; Technology Law; Venture Capital; Private Equity. ***Email:*** mnemeroff@vedderprice.com

JOHN R. OBIALA, born Evergreen Park, Illinois, July 22, 1954; admitted to bar, 1979, Illinois and U.S. District Court, Northern District of Illinois; 1981, U.S. Court of Appeals, 7th Circuit. *Education:* University of Notre Dame (B.A., cum laude, 1976); Loyola University of Chicago (J.D., cum laude, 1979). ***PRACTICE AREAS:*** Corporate Law; Mergers and Acquisitions; Debt and Equity Finance; Joint Ventures; Venture Capital. ***Email:*** jobiala@vedderprice.com

TIMOTHY W. O'DONNELL, born Hillside, Illinois, June 17, 1961; admitted to bar, 1989, Illinois and U.S. District Court, Northern District of Illinois. *Education:* University of Iowa (B.B.A., 1983); DePaul University (J.D., 1989). Certified Public Accountant, Illinois. Co-Author: "Operating and Maintaining the S Corporation," (Ill. Inst. for CLE, 2000). ***PRACTICE AREAS:*** Tax Law; Equipment Finance and Leasing; Project Finance; Equipment Finance; Corporate Taxation; Partnership Taxation. ***Email:*** todonnell@vedderprice.com

CATHY G. O'KELLY, born Washington, D.C., May 30, 1953; admitted to bar, 1978, District of Columbia and Virginia; 1989, Illinois. *Education:* College of William & Mary (B.A., 1975); University of Virginia (J.D., 1978). Omicron Delta Kappa; Omicron Delta Epsilon. Staff Attorney, 1978-1981 and Special Counsel, 1981-1983, Division of Investment Management, Securities and Exchange Commission. ***PRACTICE AREAS:*** Investments; Securities; Investment Management; Mutual Funds. ***Email:*** cokelly@vedderprice.com

DANIEL O'ROURKE, born Evanston, Illinois, March 22, 1947; admitted to bar, 1972, Illinois. *Education:* College of the Holy Cross (A.B., 1969); Georgetown University Law Center (J.D., 1972). Omicron Delta Epsilon. Editor, Law and Policy in International Business, Georgetown University Law Center, 1971-1972. Co-Author: "A Never-Ending Story: BONY's Hostile Pursuit of Irving," Banking Expansion Reporter, June 1988; "Hostile Bank Takeovers: The Challenge of, and to, the Uninvited Bidder," Bowne & Co., April 1987; "Banks and Thrifts-Why Are You (still) Publicly Owned?" The Banking Law Journal, January 2001; Co Author: "Creating Capital and Providing Shareholder Liquidity for De Novo Banks - The Super De Novo Bank Solution," The Banking Law Journal, May 2001. *Member:* American Bar Association (Member: Banking Law Committee; Subcommittee on Bank and Bank Holding Company Acquisitions and Dispositions). ***PRACTICE AREAS:*** Banking Law; Corporate Finance; Securities; Executive Compensation. ***Email:*** dorourke@vedderprice.com

RICHARD W. PEARSE, born Detroit, Michigan, December 4, 1952; admitted to bar, 1984, Illinois. *Education:* Boston University (B.A., magna cum laude, with distinction in Psychology, 1976); University of Chicago (M.A., Organizational Psychology, 1980); Northwestern University (J.D., 1984). Author: "Uncovering Hidden Costs," Independant Energy, June 1997; "Efficient Allocation of Construction Risk in Engineering, Procurement, Construction, and Validation (EPCV) Contracts," Pharmaceutical Engineering, July/August 2000; "Compensation Arrangements in Design and Construction Agreements, and International Privatization," Stein, Steven Construction Law, *Matthew Bender,* 2002; "Vendor-Led Engineering - Procure - Construct (EPC) Projects," a Forthcoming Chapter in The Construction Business Handbook, *Aspen Law & Business,* 2003; "Selecting the Right Contracting Strategy," Inside Supply Management, October 2002; "Legal Issues of Outsourcing," Inside Supply Management, April 2003; "Optimizing Service Outsourcing Arrangements," Inside Supply Management, May 2003; "Legal Issues of Consortium or "Group" Purchasing," Inside Supply Management, October 2003. Previously with: Winston & Strawn; Friedman & Koven. *Member:* American; Inter-American and International Bar Associations. ***LANGUAGES:*** Spanish. ***TRANSACTIONS:*** Development, contracting and contract administration for infrastructure projects, power projects, chemical and pharmaceutical plants in U.S., Puerto Rico, Brazil, Argentina, Venezuela, Australia, Philippines, Canada, Mexico; Contracting for cogeneration projects in Italy, Mexico, Brazil, U.S.; Contracting for Pulp and Paper Projects in U.S., Spain, Colombia, Malaysia; development of hydroelectric power projects in Romania, Peru. Contracting for nuclear energy project in Taiwan; joint venture contracting for fertilizer complex in U.S., South Africa, India. ***PRACTICE AREAS:*** Commercial Law; Construction Law; Project Finance; Real Estate. ***Email:*** rpearse@vedderprice.com

JAMES S. PETRIE, born Newark, New Jersey, October 5, 1936; admitted to bar, 1961, Illinois; 1962, U.S. District Court, Northern District of Illinois including Trial Bar; 1968, U.S. Court of Appeals, 7th Circuit; 1978, New York; 1980, U.S. Court of Appeals, 6th Circuit; 1989, U.S. Court of Appeals, 8th Circuit. *Education:* University of Connecticut (A.B., 1958); University of Chicago (J.D., 1961). Phi Delta Phi. ***PRACTICE AREAS:*** Labor and Employment Law; Employment Litigation; Management Labor Law; Labor Arbitration. ***Email:*** jpetrie@vedderprice.com

THERESA M. PEYTON, born Ft. Belvoir, Virginia, September 8, 1963; admitted to bar, 1995, Illinois and U.S. District Court, Northern District of Illinois. *Education:* University of Virginia (B.A., 1985); IIT Chicago-Kent College of Law (J.D., with honors, 1995). ***PRACTICE AREAS:*** Equipment Finance and Leasing; Corporate; Aircraft Finance and Leasing. ***Email:*** tpeyton@vedderprice.com

IGOR POTYM, born Waukesha, Wisconsin, April 28, 1954; admitted to bar, 1980, Illinois and U.S. District Court, Eastern and Western Districts of Wisconsin. *Education:* University of Wisconsin at Milwaukee (B.A. in English, 1977); Marquette University (J.D., 1980); DePaul University College of Law (LL.M. in Taxation, 1985). Student Articles Editor, 1979-1980, and Member, 1978-1979, Marquette Law Review. Student Law Clerk to Hon. Robert C. Cannon, Judge, and Hon. John A. Decker, Chief Judge, Wisconsin Court of Appeals, District I, 1979-1980. ***PRACTICE AREAS:*** Estate Planning. ***Email:*** ipotym@vedderprice.com

ERIC S. PREZANT, born Poughkeepsie, New York, September 26, 1970; admitted to bar, 1997, Illinois and U.S. District Court, Northern District of Illinois. *Education:* Florida State University (B.S., 1992); Dominican University (M.B.A., 1995); John Marshall Law School (J.D., cum laude, 1997). Member, 1994-1997 and Staff Editor, 1996-1997, John Marshall Law Review. Co-Author: "Reclamation and Preference Defenses Primer," Commercial Law League of America, Young Lawyers Section, 1998; "Sections 303 and 305, Involuntary Cases and Abstention," Norton's Annual Survey of Bankruptcy Law, 1998-1999 Edition. ***PRACTICE AREAS:*** Bankruptcy; Insolvency; Corporate Reorganization; Bankruptcy Litigation; Creditors Rights. ***Email:*** eprezant@vedderprice.com

WILLIAM F. PRICE (1909-1973)

DONNA J. PUGH, born Baltimore, Maryland, April 14, 1958; admitted to bar, 1983, Illinois and U.S. District Court, Northern District of Illinois. *Education:* University of Florida (B.A., 1979); Loyola University of Chicago (J.D., 1983). Author: "Judicial Rulemaking: A Compendium," American Judicature Society, 1984. *Member:* Chicago (Past Chair, Local Government Committee) and American (Chair, Land Use Committee, State and Local Government Section) Bar Associations; Greater North Michigan Avenue Association (Chair, Planning and Zoning Committee). ***PRACTICE AREAS:*** Land Use Law; Zoning Law. ***Email:*** dpugh@vedderprice.com

CHRISTOPHER J. RECKAMP, born Barrington, Illinois, December 14, 1961; admitted to bar, 1991, Illinois and U.S. District Court, Northern District of Illinois; 1995, U.S.

(This Listing Continued)

Court of Appeals for the Federal Circuit. *Education:* Marquette University (B.S.E.E., 1985); DePaul University (J.D., M.B.A., 1991). *Member:* Chicago (Chairman, Patent, Trademark Copyright Committee, 1999-2000) and American Bar Associations; American Intellectual Property Law Association; Intellectual Property Law Association of Chicago. ***PRACTICE AREAS:*** Intellectual Property; Patents; Trademarks; Litigation. ***Email:*** creckamp@vedderprice.com

MICHAEL E. REED, born Fort Madison, Iowa, March 26, 1942; admitted to bar, 1968, Illinois and U.S. District Court, Northern District of Illinois. *Education:* Kenyon College (B.A., 1964); Northwestern University (J.D., cum laude, 1968). Phi Delta Phi. *Member:* Chicago, Illinois State and American Bar Associations; American Health Lawyers Association. ***PRACTICE AREAS:*** Trade and Professional Associations; Corporate Law; Antitrust; Taxation. ***Email:*** mreed@vedderprice.com

CHRISTINE M. RHODE, born Evanston, Illinois, May 15, 1948; admitted to bar, 1973, Illinois and U.S. District Court, Northern District of Illinois. *Education:* Northwestern University (B.A., 1970); University of Michigan (J.D., 1973). *Member:* Chicago Bar Association (Chairman, Division I of Probate Practice Committee, 1981-1982); Chicago Estate Planning Council. ***PRACTICE AREAS:*** Estate Planning; Family Wealth Transfer; Estate Administration; Federal Estate and Gift Taxation; Trust Law. ***Email:*** crhode@vedderprice.com

RICHARD C. ROBIN, born Brownwood, Texas, July 12, 1945; admitted to bar, 1970, Illinois and U.S. District Court, Northern District of Illinois; 1973, U.S. Court of Appeals, 7th Circuit; 1982, U.S. Court of Appeals, 6th Circuit; 1982, U.S. District Court, Northern District of Illinois including Trial Bar. *Education:* Tulane University of Louisiana (B.A., 1967); DePaul University (J.D., 1970). Trial Attorney, Office of the Illinois Attorney General, 1970-1974. ***PRACTICE AREAS:*** Real Estate Litigation; Restrictive Covenants; Employment Litigation; Toxic Tort Defense; Commercial Litigation. ***Email:*** rrobin@vedderprice.com

PAUL F. RUSSELL, born Kansas City, Missouri, February 3, 1948; admitted to bar, 1973, Illinois and U.S. District Court, Northern District of Illinois. *Education:* Northwestern University (B.A., 1970); University of Michigan (J.D., cum laude, 1973). ***PRACTICE AREAS:*** Employee Benefits; ERISA; Employee Stock Ownership Plans; Health Benefits; Pension and Profit Sharing Plans. ***Email:*** prussell@vedderprice.com

RICHARD H. SANDERS, born Chicago, Illinois, April 10, 1944; admitted to bar, 1969, Illinois; 1970, U.S. District Court, Northern District of Illinois; 1989, U.S. Court of Appeals, 7th Circuit and U.S. Supreme Court; 1990, Indiana, U.S. District Court, Northern and Southern Districts of Indiana and District of Columbia Court of Appeals. *Education:* Loyola University (B.S., 1967); Northwestern University (J.D., 1969). Nu Beta Epsilon. Adjunct Professor, Health Law, Northwestern University School of Law, 1994—. *Member:* Illinois State (Health Care Section Council, Member, 1984-1990, Vice-Chairman, 1987-1988, Chairman, 1988-1989) and American (Member, Health Law Section, 1994—) Bar Associations; American Health Lawyers Association. ***PRACTICE AREAS:*** Health Law; Health Care Regulation; Health Care Corporate Law; Medical Antitrust; Managed Care. ***Email:*** rsanders@vedderprice.com

CHAD A. SCHIEFELBEIN, born LaGrange, Illinois, February 2, 1970; admitted to bar, 1996, Illinois and U.S. District Court, Northern District of Illinois; 1998, U.S. Court of Appeals, 7th Circuit. *Education:* Valparaiso University (B.S., 1992; J.D., magna cum laude, 1996). National First Place, Giles Sutherland Rich Moot Court Competition, 1995. Chief Justice, Valparaiso Moot Court Society, 1995-1996. Note Editor, Valparaiso University Law Review, 1995-1996. Author: "Accepting an Exception to the 'Government Contracts Exception' of the District of Columbia's Long-Arm Statute," 30 Valparaiso Law Review 1032. ***PRACTICE AREAS:*** Commercial Litigation; Intellectual Property Litigation. ***Email:*** cschiefelbein@vedderprice.com

RICHARD H. SCHNADIG, born Chicago, Illinois, June 19, 1939; admitted to bar, 1965, Illinois; 1967, U.S. Court of Appeals, 7th, 8th and 11th Circuits; U.S. District Court, Northern, Central and Southern Districts of Illinois; 1984, U.S. Supreme Court. *Education:* Trinity College (B.A., cum laude, 1961); Harvard Law School (LL.B., 1964). Phi Beta Kappa. Special Counsel, Governor of Illinois, 1975-1976. Special Assistant to Director of Illinois Department of Personnel, 1973-1975. ***PRACTICE AREAS:*** Labor and Employment; Employment Litigation; Employment Law; Labor Law; Class Actions. ***Email:*** rschnadig@vedderprice.com

THOMAS E. SCHNUR, born Chicago, Illinois, April 23, 1961; admitted to bar, 1986, Illinois. *Education:* University of Illinois (B.S., with honors, 1983); DePaul University (J.D., 1986). Phi Eta Sigma; Alpha Kappa Psi. Member, De Paul Law Review, 1984-1986. *Member:* American Bar Association (Member, Business Law Section Committee on Commercial Financial Services). ***PRACTICE AREAS:*** Corporate Law; Commercial Law; Corporate Finance; Mergers and Acquisitions. ***Email:*** tschnur@vedderprice.com

DANIEL T. SHERLOCK, born Chicago, Illinois, January 19, 1956; admitted to bar, 1981, Illinois and U.S. District Court, Northern District of Illinois; 1989, U.S. Tax Court; 1990, U.S. Claims Court. *Education:* Loyola University of Chicago (B.A., cum laude, 1978); University of Notre Dame (J.D., cum laude, 1981); New York University (LL.M. in Taxation, 1987). Pi Sigma Alpha; Omicron Delta Epsilon; Alpha Sigma Nu; Phi Alpha Delta. Notes Editor, Notre Dame Law Review, 1980-1981. ***PRACTICE AREAS:*** Federal Income Tax; Corporate Tax Planning; Tax Deferred Exchanges. ***Email:*** dsherlock@vedderprice.com

ROBERT F. SIMON, born Chicago, Illinois, April 27, 1953; admitted to bar, 1982, Illinois, U.S. District Court, Northern District of Illinois; 1983, U.S. Tax Court; 1989, U.S. Court of Appeals, Tenth Circuit. *Education:* Miami University (B.A., cum laude, 1975); DePaul University (J.D., with honors, 1982). Author: "Final and Proposed COBRA Regulations," Employee Benefits Committee Quarterly, Illinois State Bar Association, Spring, 1999, presented at Benefits Committee, Chicago Bar Association, April 1999; "Qualified Employee Retirement Plan Benefit Distributions: A Survey of the Landscape," Benefits Committee, Chicago Bar Association, May 1994; "Buy-Sell Arrangements: Estate Planning for the Disposition of Business Interests," Estate Planning Committee, Chicago Bar Association, January 1991. Attorney, Office of District Counsel, Internal Revenue Service, 1982-1986. *Member:* Chicago (Chairman, Corporate Tax Division, 1993-1994 and Member, Executive Committee, 1992-1994, Taxation Committee) and American (Member, Sections on: Taxation; Real Property and Probate) Bar Associations. ***PRACTICE AREAS:*** Employee Benefits; Executive Compensation; Estate Planning; Taxation; Business Law. ***Email:*** rsimon@vedderprice.com

GUY E. SNYDER, born Oak Park, Illinois, March 11, 1954; admitted to bar, 1979, Illinois. *Education:* Marquette University (B.S., 1976); Loyola University of Chicago (J.D., 1979). Member, Loyola University Law Journal, 1979. Certified Public Accountant, Illinois, 1978. ***PRACTICE AREAS:*** Mergers and Acquisitions; Corporate Law; Business Law; Securities; Corporate Finance. ***Email:*** gsnyder@vedderprice.com

KENNETH F. SPARKS, born Anniston, Alabama, December, 31, 1963; admitted to bar, 1992, District of Columbia; 1997, Illinois, U.S. Court of Appeals for the District of Columbia, U.S. Court of Appeals, Fourth, Sixth, Seventh and Federal Circuits, U.S. District Court for the District of Columbia and U.S. District Court, Northern District of Illinois, including Trial Bar and U.S. District Court, Central District of Illinois. *Education:* Massachusetts Institute of Technology (B.S., 1986); University of Michigan (J.D., 1989). Order of the Coif. Judicial Law Clerk, Judge Cornelia Kennedy, U.S. Court of Appeals, Sixth Circuit, 1989-1990. *Member:* Illinois State Bar Association; The District of Columbia Bar. ***PRACTICE AREAS:*** Labor and Employment; Litigation. ***Email:*** ksparks@vedderprice.com

JAMES A. SPIZZO, born Chicago, Illinois, August 14, 1952; admitted to bar, 1979, Illinois, U.S. District Court, Central and Northern Districts of Illinois including Trial Bar and U.S. Court of Appeals, Seventh Circuit. *Education:* Illinois College (A.B., with honors, 1974); University of Iowa (J.D., 1978). Member, Board of Editors, Iowa Law Review, 1977-1978. Counsel to Illinois Senate Minority Leader, 1981-1983. Counsel to Illinois Manufacturers' Association. ***PRACTICE AREAS:*** Labor and Employment; Collective Bargaining; Employment Discrimination; Employment Litigation; Public Sector Collective Bargaining. ***Email:*** jspizzo@vedderprice.com

KELLY A. STARR, born Bridgeport, Connecticut, July 14, 1966; admitted to bar, 1995, Illinois and U.S. District Court, Northern District of Illinois. *Education:* Cornell University (B.S., 1988); University of Illinois College of Law (J.D., cum laude, 1995). ***PRACTICE AREAS:*** Employee Benefits; Executive Compensation. ***Email:*** kstarr@vedderprice.com

JOSEPH A. STRUBBE, born Evergreen Park, Illinois, May 1, 1959; admitted to bar, 1985, Illinois; 1990, U.S. District Court, Northern District of Illinois, including Trial Bar; 1991, U.S. Court of Appeals, 7th Circuit; 1992, U.S. Court of Appeals, 8th Circuit; 1993, U.S. District Court, Central District of Illinois. *Education:* Western Illinois University (B.A., highest honors, 1981); IIT/Chicago-Kent College of Law (J.D., highest honors, 1985). Editor, Notes and Comments, Chicago-Kent Law Review. 1984-1985. Judicial Clerk to Honorable Frank J. McGarr, Chief Judge, U.S. District Court, Northern District of Illinois, 1985-1987. ***PRACTICE AREAS:*** Environmental Litigation; Environmental Corporate Law; Complex Business Litigation; Complex Commercial Litigation. ***Email:*** jstrubbe@vedderprice.com

ROBERT J. STUCKER, born Chicago, Illinois, February 27, 1945; admitted to bar, 1970, Illinois and U.S. District Court, Northern District of Illinois; 1972, Maryland. *Education:* Georgetown University (A.B., cum laude, 1967); University of Chicago (J.D., 1970). Phi Beta Kappa; Phi Delta Phi. ***PRACTICE AREAS:*** Corporate Law; Executive Compensation; Financial Institutions; Securities; Business Law. ***Email:*** rstucker@vedderprice.com

DAVID A. STURMS, born Bay Shore, New York, June 6, 1960; admitted to bar, 1985, Illinois. *Education:* The Ohio State University (B.S., 1982); Loyola University (J.D., 1985). Author: "Enhancing the Effectiveness of Independent Directors: Is the System Broken, Creaking or Working?" Villanove Journal of Law and Investment Management, Fall, 1999. Member, Illinois Securities Advisory Committee. ***PRACTICE AREAS:*** Corporate Law; Investment Company Law; Investment Management; Mutual Funds; Securities. ***Email:*** dsturms@vedderprice.com

LAWRENCE L. SUMMERS, born Huntingburg, Indiana, June 6, 1948; admitted to bar, 1973, Illinois and U.S. District Court, Northern District of Illinois including Trial Bar; 1975, U.S. District Court, Northern District of Indiana; 1976, U.S. Court of Appeals, 7th Circuit; 1977, U.S. District Court, Eastern District of Wisconsin; 1981, U.S. Supreme Court. *Education:* Indiana University (A.B., 1970); Indiana University School of Law (J.D., magna cum laude, 1973). Order of the Coif. ***PRACTICE AREAS:*** Labor and Employment Law; Affirmative Action; Collective Bargaining; Employment Discrimination; Labor Arbitration. ***Email:*** lsummers@vedderprice.com

THEODORE J. TIERNEY, born Omaha, Nebraska, December 26, 1940; admitted to bar, 1964, Nebraska; 1967, U.S. Supreme Court; 1968, U.S. Court of Appeals, 8th Circuit; 1969, Illinois; 1978, U.S. Court of Appeals, 6th and 7th Circuits. *Education:* Creighton University (B.A., 1962; J.D., cum laude, 1964); Georgetown Law Center (LL.M., 1967). Alpha Sigma Nu; Phi Alpha Delta. Attorney, National Labor Relations Board, Kansas City, Missouri, 1967-1969. [Captain, USAF, Judge Advocate, 1964-1967]. ***PRACTICE AREAS:*** Labor and Employment Law; Labor Law; Union Elections; Union Contract Negotiations. ***Email:*** ttierney@vedderprice.com

ERNEST W. TORAIN, JR., born Baltimore, Maryland, January 19, 1965; admitted to bar, 1991, Illinois. *Education:* Dartmouth College (A.B., 1987); University of Michigan (J.D., 1991). Member: Dartmouth College Alumni Council; LaRabida Children's Hospital Business Council-Development Committee; Chiaravalle Montessori School-Development Committee; Union League Club; Chicago Urban League. *Member:* Chicago and American Bar Associations; Economic Club of Chicago. ***Email:*** etorain@vedderprice.com

MICHAEL J. TURGEON, born Richmond Heights, Missouri, January 1, 1968; admitted to bar, 1994, Missouri; 1995, Illinois; registered to practice before U.S. Patent and Trademark Office. *Education:* Marquette University (B.S.M.E., 1990); John Marshall Law School (J.D., 1994). Pi Tau Sigma; Phi Delta Phi. ***PRACTICE AREAS:*** Intellectual Property. ***Email:*** mturgeon@vedderprice.com

DALIUS F. VASYS, born Boston, Massachusetts, April 3, 1955; admitted to bar, 1980, Illinois and U.S. District Court, Northern District of Illinois. *Education:* Harvard College (B.A., magna cum laude, 1977); Northwestern University (J.D., 1980). ***PRACTICE AREAS:*** Mergers and Acquisitions; Corporate Finance; Commercial Law; Venture Capital; Private Equity. ***Email:*** dvasys@vedderprice.com

BEVERLY B. VEDDER (1887-1955)

(This Listing Continued)

VEDDER, PRICE, KAUFMAN & KAMMHOLZ, P.C., Chicago—Continued

WILLIAM F. WALSH, born Chicago, Illinois, December 20, 1947; admitted to bar, 1973, Illinois and U.S. District Court, Northern District of Illinois. *Education:* University of Michigan (B.A., with high distinction, high honors in history, 1969); Harvard Law School (J.D., cum laude, 1972). Phi Beta Kappa; National Merit Scholar. ***PRACTICE AREAS:*** Executive Compensation; Tax-Exempt Organizations; Nonprofit Corporations; Trade and Professional Association Law; Private Foundations. ***Email:*** wwalsh@vedderprice.com

CHARLES H. WIGGINS, JR., born Baltimore, Maryland, July 15, 1939; admitted to bar, 1965, Illinois; 1970, U.S. District Court, Northern District of Illinois; 1974, U.S. Tax Court; 1983, U.S. Court of Appeals, 7th Circuit. *Education:* University of Illinois (B.S.E.E., 1962; J.D., with honors, 1965). Phi Delta Phi; Order of the Coif. Member, Board of Student Editors, University of Illinois Law Forum, 1964-1965. [Capt., U.S. Judge Advocate Corps, 1966-1969]. ***PRACTICE AREAS:*** Closely Held Corporations; Federal Estate and Gift Taxation; Estate Planning; Estate Administration; Trust Administration. ***Email:*** cwiggins@vedderprice.com

THOMAS M. WILDE, born Chicago, Illinois, December 21, 1967; admitted to bar, 1993, Illinois and U.S. District Court, Northern District of Illinois; 1995, Massachusetts; 1998, U.S. Court of Appeals, 6th and 7th Circuits. *Education:* Northern Illinois University (B.A., cum laude, 1990); DePaul University (J.D., with honors, 1993). Order of the Coif. Member, De Paul University Law Review, 1991-1993. ***PRACTICE AREAS:*** Labor and Employment. ***Email:*** twilde@vedderprice.com

RICHARD L. WILLIAMS III, born Evanston, Illinois, October 30, 1940; admitted to bar, 1965, Illinois, U.S. District Court, Northern District of Illinois including Trial Bar and U.S. Court of Appeals, Seventh Circuit; 1966, U.S. Court of Military Appeals; 1968, District of Columbia and U.S. Supreme Court. *Education:* Princeton University (A.B., 1962); University of Virginia (LL.B., J.D., 1965). Phi Alpha Delta. Co-Head, Western Europe Special Interest Group of the International Committee of the Executive's Club of Chicago, 1991-1996. Former Senior Vice President-Administration, General Counsel and Director, Gould Inc. [Lt. JAG Corps. U.S. Navy, 1965-1968, Legal Officer]. ***PRACTICE AREAS:*** Buying and Selling of Businesses; Joint Ventures; Corporate Commercial Law; International Mergers and Acquisitions; Securities Offerings. ***Email:*** rwilliams@vedderprice.com

CHARLES B. WOLF, born Chicago, Illinois, April 16, 1950; admitted to bar, 1975, Illinois and U.S. District Court, Northern District of Illinois including Trial Bar; 1977, U.S. District Court, Eastern District of Wisconsin; 1978, U.S. Court of Appeals, 7th Circuit; 1984, U.S. Court of Appeals, 4th and 11th Circuits; 1985, U.S. Court of Appeals, 6th Circuit and U.S. Supreme Court; 1987, U.S. Court of Appeals, 5th Circuit; 1990, U.S. Court of Appeals, 9th Circuit; 1995, U.S. Court of Appeals, 10th Circuit. *Education:* Brown University (A.B., magna cum laude, 1972); University of Chicago (J.D., 1975). Author: "Preparing for IRS and DOL Audits," 1997 IFEBP Papers (1997). Co-Author: *ERISA Claims and Litigation,* 11th ed., 1996. Contributing Author: *Employee Benefit Law,* BNA Books (2d ed. 1999). *Member:* American Bar Association (Labor Section, Co-Chair, Subcommittee on Multi-Employer Benefit Plans). ***PRACTICE AREAS:*** Labor Law; Employment Law; Employee Benefits; Multi-Employer Pensions; Taft-Hartley Plans. ***Email:*** cwolf@vedderprice.com

GREGORY G. WROBEL, born Chicago, Illinois, December 19, 1954; admitted to bar, 1978, Illinois and U.S. District Court, Northern District of Illinois including Trial Bar; 1987, U.S. Court of Appeals, 7th Circuit; 1988, U.S. Supreme Court. *Education:* University of Chicago (B.A., with honors, 1975; J.D., 1978; M.B.A., 1979). Author: "Antitrust, Economic and Health Care Implications of Vertical Integration in Health Care," presented at "Antitrust and Health Care: Current Antitrust Issues for the Health Care Provider," FTC, Missouri Attorney General, St. Louis University Law School and ABA Antitrust Section, November 1997; "Antitrust Concerns in Managing the Managed Care Organization: Marshfield Clinic and Beyond," Thirteenth Annual Health Law Symposium, Illinois Association of Healthcare Attorneys, 1995. Member, Editorial Board and Contributing Author, "Annual Review of 1997 Antitrust Law Developments," ABA Section of Antitrust Law, 1998. *Member:* Chicago (Chair, Antitrust Law Committee, 1993-1994; Chair, Heath Law Committee, 2001-2002) and American (Contributing Editor and Editor, Antitrust Health Care Chronicle, 1993-2000; Vice Chair, Antitrust Section, Books and Treatises Committee, 1999—) Bar Associations. ***PRACTICE AREAS:*** Commercial Litigation; Antitrust and Trade Regulation; Health Law; Restrictive Covenants; Trade Secrets. ***Email:*** gwrobel@vedderprice.com

RICHARD A. ZACHAR, born Cedar Rapids, Iowa, April 17, 1942; admitted to bar, 1968, Illinois and U.S. District Court, Northern District of Illinois including Trial Bar; 1982, U.S. Court of Appeals, Federal Circuit; 1988, U.S. Court of Appeals, Seventh Circuit and U.S. Supreme Court; registered to practice before U.S. Patent and Trademark Office. *Education:* University of Notre Dame (A.B., 1964; B.S., 1965); Northwestern University School of Law (J.D., 1968). Pi Tau Sigma. ***PRACTICE AREAS:*** Intellectual Property; Patent Infringement; Trademark Infringement; Corporate. ***Email:*** rzachar@vedderprice.com

PEARL A. ZAGER, born West Bend, Wisconsin, October 15, 1955; admitted to bar, 1979, Wisconsin and U.S. District Court, Western District of Wisconsin; 1980, Illinois and U.S. District Court, Northern District of Illinois. *Education:* Florida Atlantic University (B.S., Finance, with honors, 1976); University of Wisconsin-Madison (J.D., 1979). ***PRACTICE AREAS:*** Business Organization; Commercial Real Estate Development; Commercial Real Estate Finance; Construction Contracts; Real Estate Leasing. ***Email:*** pzager@vedderprice.com

ASSOCIATES

PAIGE O. BARNETT, born Houston, Texas, March 12, 1972; (admission pending). *Education:* Vanderbilt University (B.A., cum laude, 1994); Northwestern University (J.D., 2001). ***PRACTICE AREAS:*** Labor and Employment.

(This Listing Continued)

CHRISTOPHER G. BARRETT, born New York, New York, October 9, 1970; (admission pending). *Education:* St. Lawrence University (B.A., 1992); Loyola University Chicago School of Law, Chicago, IL (J.D., 2004). ***PRACTICE AREAS:*** Corporate; Securities. ***Email:*** cbarrett@vedderprice.com

LESLIE ALLEN BAYLES, born Lansing, Michigan, November 16, 1963; admitted to bar, 2000, Illinois and U.S. District Court, Northern District of Illinois. *Education:* Central Michigan University (B.S., 1990; M.A., 1991); Loyola University, Chicago School of Law (J.D., magna cum laude, 2000). *Member:* Chicago, Illinois State and American Bar Associations. ***PRACTICE AREAS:*** Corporate Law; Bankruptcy. ***Email:*** lbayles@vedderprice.com

DAVID C. BLUM, born New York, N.Y., 1968; admitted to bar, 1997, Illinois. *Education:* University of Arizona (B.S.B.A., 1990); John Marshall Law School (LL.M., Taxation, with honors, 1997; J.D., cum laude, 1997). Business Managing Editor, The Journal of Computer and Information Law. Certified Public Accountant, Illinois, 1994. Author: "Final Tax Shelter List Maintenance Regulations: The IRS Narrows Its Scope," Journal of Taxation of Corporate Transactions, CCH, March-April 2003. *Member:* Chicago (Secretary, Federal Tax Committee; Former Chair, Partnership and Flow-Through Entry Subcommittee of the Federal Tax Committee) and American Bar Associations. ***PRACTICE AREAS:*** Taxation. ***Email:*** dblum@vedderprice.com

DAVID J. BORKON, born Dover, New Jersey, April 24, 1978; admitted to bar, 2003, New Jersey; 2004, New York (Not admitted in Illinois). *Education:* Northwestern University (B.A., 2000); Rutgers University School of Law - Newark (J.D., 2003). *Member:* New Jersey State and New York State Bar Associations. ***PRACTICE AREAS:*** Corporate Law; Mergers and Acquisitions; Finance. ***Email:*** dborkon@vedderprice.com

SARAH M. BROWN, born Cheboygan, Michigan, June 28, 1978; admitted to bar, 2004, Illinois. *Education:* Michigan State University (B.A., International Relations, 2000); University of Michigan Law School (J.D., 2004). ***PRACTICE AREAS:*** Labor and Employment. ***Email:*** sbrown@vedderprice.com

MARK A. CAMERO, born November 3, 1974; admitted to bar, 2002, Illinois. *Education:* Northern Illinois University (B.S., 1997); DePaul University (J.D., magna cum laude, 2002). Order of the Coif. ***LANGUAGES:*** Spanish. ***Email:*** mcamero@vedderprice.com

TIMOTHY J. CARROLL, born Oaklawn, Illinois, April 21, 1971; admitted to bar, 1999, Illinois. *Education:* College of St. Francis (B.A., 1993); DePaul University (J.D., 1999). Research and Writing Staff, De Paul Law Review, 1997-1999. President, Student Bar Association, 1998-1999. Listed in Who's Who in American College and University Students, 1993 and 1999. *Member:* Chicago, Illinois State and American Bar Associations; The Association of Trial Lawyers of America. ***PRACTICE AREAS:*** Intellectual Property Litigation; Products Liability; Tort; Commercial Litigation. ***Email:*** tcarroll@vedderprice.com

CHRISTOPHER T. COLLINS, born New York, N.Y., October 10, 1974; admitted to bar, 2002, Illinois. *Education:* University of Notre Dame (B.A., 1996); Chicago-Kent College of Law, Illinois Institute of Technology (J.D., with high honors, 2002). *Member:* Chicago Bar Association. ***PRACTICE AREAS:*** Employee Benefits. ***Email:*** ccollins@vedderprice.com

D. KATHRYN COLVIN, born Evanston, Illinois, November 27, 1971; admitted to bar, 1998, Illinois and U.S. District Court, Northern District of Illinois. *Education:* St. Mary's College, Notre Dame (B.B.A., 1993); Loyola University, Chicago School of Law (J.D., 1998). Recipient, Leadership and Services Award. Member, Wagner Labor Law Moot Court, 1998. *Member:* Chicago and American Bar Associations. ***PRACTICE AREAS:*** Labor and Employment. ***Email:*** kcolvin@vedderprice.com

LAURA CARROLL DEBOLT, born Chicago, Illinois, July 6, 1978; admitted to bar, 2003, Illinois. *Education:* Saint Mary's College (B.S., 2000); Northwestern University School of Law (J.D., 2003). ***PRACTICE AREAS:*** Commercial Real Estate (75%); Real Estate Finance (25%). ***Email:*** ldebolt@vedderprice.com

MICHAEL R. DEMNICKI, born October 24, 1968; admitted to bar, 1997, Illinois, District of Columbia and U.S. District Court, Northern District of Illinois. *Education:* Loyola University Chicago (B.S., Biology, 1990); Saint Louis University (J.D., 1996). ***PRACTICE AREAS:*** Equipment Finance. ***Email:*** mdemnicki@vedderprice.com

ROBERT W. DIXON, born Iowa City, Iowa, February 28, 1975; admitted to bar, 2001, Illinois. *Education:* University of Iowa (B.B.A., 1997); Drake University (J.D., with honors, 2001). Delta Theta Phi. Associate Editor, Drake Law Review, 2000-2001. Certified Public Accountant, Iowa, 1998. Author, "Gramm-Leach-Bliley Financial Modernization Act: Why Reform Was Necessary in the Financial Services Industry and the Act's Projected Effects on Community Banking," 49 Drake Law Review 671 (2001). ***PRACTICE AREAS:*** Corporate Law; Financial Institutions Law.

SCOT J. FOLEY, born Queens, New York, July 23, 1970; admitted to bar, 2004, New York (Not admitted in Illinois). *Education:* Hofstra University (B.A., 1994); Fordham University (J.D., 2002). ***PRACTICE AREAS:*** Mergers and Acquisitions; Private Equity; Corporate Securities. ***Email:*** sfoley@vedderprice.com

NICOLE A. FRANKEL, born Plantation, Florida, March 13, 1976; admitted to bar, 2003, Illinois and U.S. District Court, Northern District of Illinois; 2004, Wisconsin. *Education:* University of Wisconsin-Madison (B.A., 1997; J.D., 2003). Member: Moot Court, 2001-2003; Moot Court Executive Board, 2002-2003. Member, Wisconsin Women's Law Journal, 2001-2003. Law Clerk to the: Bankruptcy Court, Northern District of Illinois, 2003-2005; Title VII in the Seventh Circuit. *Member:* Illinois State and American Bar Associations. ***PRACTICE AREAS:*** Bankruptcy; Corporate Law. ***Email:*** nfrankel@vedderprice.com

DAVID W. FRENCH, born Evanston, Illinois, 1977; admitted to bar, 2002, Illinois and U.S. District Courts, Northern and Central Districts of Illinois. *Education:* DePaul University (B.S., Finance and Accounting, 1999); John Marshall Law School (J.D., 2002). Editor, The Journal of Computer and Information Law, 2001-2002. Certified Real Estate Broker, Illinois. Adjunct Professor, Real Estate Law, Illinois Central College, 2003-2005. Formerly

(This Listing Continued)

with Hinshaw & Culbertson LLP. *Member:* Chicago, Peoria County, Illinois State and American Bar Associations. ***PRACTICE AREAS:*** Corporate Finance; Real Estate Finance; Real Estate. ***Email:*** dfrench@vedderprice.com

ALLEN J. GABLE, born Port Huron, Michigan, August 10, 1970; admitted to bar, 1996, Michigan; 2001, Illinois. *Education:* University of Michigan (B.A., History, 1992); Michigan State University College of Law (J.D., 1996); New York University (LL.M., 1997). *Member:* State Bar of Michigan. ***PRACTICE AREAS:*** Finance; Secured Transactions; Health Care Finance; Mergers and Acquisitions. ***Email:*** agable@vedderprice.com

AARON R. GELB, born New York, New York, December 31, 1969; admitted to bar, 1995, Missouri and U.S. District Court, Eastern District of Missouri; 1996, Illinois; 1998, U.S. District Court, Western District of Texas and Southern District of Illinois; 1999, U.S. District Court, Northern District of Illinois. *Education:* University of Chicago (B.A., with honors, 1992); University of Texas (J.D., 1995). ***PRACTICE AREAS:*** Labor and Employment. ***Email:*** agelb@vedderprice.com

JENNIFER M. GOODMAN, born Indianapolis, Indiana, June 20, 1978; admitted to bar, 2005, Illinois. *Education:* Indiana University, Bloomington (B.A., Public Affairs, 2001); Northwestern Law School (J.D., 2005). ***PRACTICE AREAS:*** Investment Services. ***Email:*** jgoodman@vedderprice.com

NICHOLAS S. HARNED, born Detroit, Michigan, May 22, 1972; admitted to bar, 1998, Wisconsin and U.S. District Court, Western District of Wisconsin; 2000, Illinois and U.S. District Court, Northern District of Illinois. *Education:* University of Wisconsin-Madison (B.S., 1994; J.D., cum laude, 1998); Loyola University (LL.M., Health Law, 2001). Member, Wisconsin Law Review, 1997-1998. *Member:* Chicago and Illinois State Bar Associations; State Bar of Wisconsin; American Health Lawyers Association. ***PRACTICE AREAS:*** Health Care (50%); Finance (50%). ***Email:*** nharned@vedderprice.com

JEFFERY M. HEFTMAN, born Northbrook, Illinois, December 11, 1974; admitted to bar, 2002, Illinois. *Education:* University of Illinois, Urbana-Champaign (B.A., 1997); University of Illinois College of Law (J.D., 2002). ***PRACTICE AREAS:*** Litigation. ***Email:*** jheftman@vedderprice.com

BYRON D. HITTLE, born Indianapolis, Indiana, November 28, 1974; admitted to bar, 2002, Illinois. *Education:* DePauw University (B.A., 1997); Indiana University School of Law (J.D., cum laude, 2002). Order of the Coif. *Member:* Chicago Bar Association. ***PRACTICE AREAS:*** Investment Services; Investment Company Act of 1940; Corporate Law. ***Email:*** bhittle@vedderprice.com

P. MICHELLE JACOBSON, born Louisville, Kentucky, October 16, 1976; admitted to bar, 2001, Illinois. *Education:* Northwestern University (B.A., 1998); Boston University (J.D., 2001). *Member:* American Bar Association; American Immigration Lawyers Association. ***LANGUAGES:*** Spanish and French. ***PRACTICE AREAS:*** Business Immigration. ***Email:*** mjacobson@vedderprice.com

SUZANNE H. JOHNSON, born Columbia, Missouri, October 11, 1974; admitted to bar, 2000, Missouri; 2001, Illinois. *Education:* Florida State University (B.S., 1997); University of Missouri-Columbia (J.D., 2000). ***PRACTICE AREAS:*** Asset Based Finance; Finance and Transactions. ***Email:*** sjohnson@vedderprice.com

SARA J. KAGAY, born Clarinda, Iowa, December 12, 1974; admitted to bar, 2000, Missouri and U.S. District Court, Western District of Missouri; 2001, Kansas and U.S. District Court, District of Kansas; 2002, U.S. District Court, Southern District of Indiana; 2004, U.S. District Court, Eastern District of Missouri and Northern District of Indiana (Not admitted in Illinois). *Education:* Drake University (B.A., 1997); University of Iowa (J.D., 2000). Order of the Coif and Secretary of Phi Delta Phi. Formerly with Lathrop & Gage L.C. *Member:* American Bar Association. ***PRACTICE AREAS:*** Labor and Employment. ***Email:*** skagay@vedderprice.com

DAVID P. KAMINSKI, born Chicago, Illinois, May 21, 1971; admitted to bar, 1997, Illinois and U.S. District Court, Northern District of Illinois. *Education:* University of Illinois (B.A., with high distinction, 1993); DePaul University (J.D., 1997; M.B.A., 1997). DePaul Business Law Journal, 1994-1995. *Member:* Chicago and American Bar Associations. ***PRACTICE AREAS:*** Corporate; Finance; Mergers and Acquisitions. ***Email:*** dkaminski@vedderprice.com

JENNIFER DURHAM KING, born Chicago, Illinois, November 22, 1967; admitted to bar, 1998, Illinois. *Education:* Miami University of Ohio (B.A., 1989); Chicago-Kent College of Law (J.D., 1998). *Member:* Illinois State Bar Association. ***PRACTICE AREAS:*** Corporate; Securities. ***Email:*** jking@vedderprice.com

FREDERIC T. KNAPE, born Kansas City, Missouri, August 30, 1971; admitted to bar, 1998, Illinois. *Education:* University of Michigan (B.A., 1994); Chicago-Kent College of Law, Illinois Institute of Technology (J.D., 1998). Author: "Illinois Arbitration: Pre-Hearing Discovery and the Right to a Full and Fair Hearing," 13 CBA Record 32, September, 1999. *Member:* Chicago and American Bar Associations. ***REPORTED CASES:*** Pinilla v. Harza Eng'g Co., 755 N.E.2d 23 (Ill.App.Ct.), leave to appeal allowed, 763 N.E.2d 777 (Ill. 2001); Mitchell v. Banary, 759 N.E.2d 121 (Ill.App.Ct. 2001), affirmed in part reversed in part,---N.E.2d---, 2003 WL 253806 (Ill.Feb. 6, 2003). ***PRACTICE AREAS:*** Commercial Litigation; Appellate Practice. ***Email:*** fknape@vedderprice.com

JENNY FRIEDMAN KOERTH, born Milwaukee, Wisconsin, October 19, 1976; admitted to bar, 2002, Illinois and U.S. District Court, Northern District of Illinois; 2004, U.S. District Court, Southern District of Illinois. *Education:* University of Minnesota, Minneapolis (B.A., cum laude, 1998); Northwestern University School of Law (J.D., 2002). Phi Beta Kappa. Senior Editor, Northwestern Journal of International Law and Business. ***PRACTICE AREAS:*** Labor and Employment; Litigation. ***Email:*** jkoerth@vedderprice.com

JOSEPH H. KYE, born Chicago, Illinois, May 17, 1970; admitted to bar, 1997, Illinois. *Education:* Northwestern University (B.A., 1992); University of Chicago (J.D., 1997). *Member:* Chicago, Illinois State and American Bar Associations. ***PRACTICE AREAS:*** Securities; Mergers and Acquisitions; General Corporate.

JORDAN R. LABKON, born Skokie, Illinois, January 4, 1970; admitted to bar, 1995, Illinois; U.S. District Court, Northern District of Illinois; U.S. Court of Appeals, Seventh Circuit. *Education:* University of Pennsylvania (B.A., cum laude, 1992); Chicago-Kent College of Law (J.D., with honors, 1995). Phi Alpha Delta (Chapter President, 1993-1994).

(This Listing Continued)

Co-Founder, IIT/Chicago-Kent International Law Moot Court Honor Society. Champion and Best Brief, 1995 Niagara International Moot Court Competition. *Member:* Chicago, Illinois State and American Bar Associations; Decalogue Society of Lawyers. ***PRACTICE AREAS:*** Leveraged Leasing; Finance Transactions; Corporate Law. ***Email:*** jlabkon@vedderprice.com

JAMES P. LAMBE, born LaGrange, Illinois, March 23, 1974; admitted to bar, 2000, Illinois and U.S. District Court, Northern District of Illinois. *Education:* University of Notre Dame (B.B.A., cum laude, 1996); DePaul University-College of Law (J.D., 2000). Editor, DePaul Law Review. ***PRACTICE AREAS:*** Corporate; Equipment Finance. ***Email:*** jlambe@vedderprice.com

ADAM S. LEWIS, born Highland Park, Illinois, July 14, 1973; admitted to bar, 1998, Illinois. *Education:* University of Illinois (B.S., with honors, 1995); Loyola University, Chicago (J.D., cum laude, 1998). Certified Public Accountant, Illinois, 1995. ***PRACTICE AREAS:*** Corporate; Finance; Mergers and Acquisitions. ***Email:*** alewis@vedderprice.com

AMY ELIZABETH LEWIS, born Chicago Heights, Illinois, March 30, 1976; admitted to bar, 2003, Illinois. *Education:* University of Illinois (A.B., Economics, 1998; M.B.A., 2003; J.D., magna cum laude, 2003). Phi Beta Kappa; Beta Gamma Sigma. Recipient: George Huff Award for Excellence in Academics while Participating in Varsity Athletics, University of Illinois at Urbana-Champaign, 1996-1998; Arthur Andersen & Andersen Consulting Scholarship, University of Illinois at Urbana-Champaign; J. Nelson Young Scholarship, awarded for excellence in the study of tax law, University of Illinois College of Law. ***PRACTICE AREAS:*** Investment Company Law; Taxation. ***Email:*** amylewis@vedderprice.com

ALISON J. MAKI, admitted to bar, 2000, Illinois and U.S. District Court, Northern District of Illinois; 2001, U.S. Court of Appeals, 7th Circuit; 2002, U.S. District Court, Eastern District of Texas; 2003, U.S. District Court, Northern District of Indiana and U.S. District Court, Southern District of Illinois. *Education:* Northern Illinois University (B.Mus., 1990); University of Michigan Law School (J.D., cum laude, 2000). ***PRACTICE AREAS:*** Labor and Employment Law. ***Email:*** amaki@vedderprice.com

JOSEPH M. MANNON, born Wheaton, Illinois, June 11, 1976; admitted to bar, 2001, Illinois and U.S. District Court, Northern District of Illinois. *Education:* Michigan State University (B.A., with honors, 1998); Loyola University (J.D., 2001). Formerly with U.S. Securities & Exchange Commission. *Member:* Chicago Bar Association. ***PRACTICE AREAS:*** Financial Services Law; Securities Regulation; Securities Litigation. ***Email:*** jmannon@vedderprice.com

JOHN S. MARTEN, born Indianapolis, Indiana, August 1, 1977; admitted to bar, 2004, Illinois. *Education:* Loyola University (B.A., 2001; J.D., 2004). ***PRACTICE AREAS:*** Investment Company Law (100%). ***Email:*** jmarten@vedderprice.com

JON P. McCARTY, born Danville, Illinois, October 17, 1970; admitted to bar, 1998, Texas; 1999, Illinois and U.S. District Court, Western District of Texas; 2001, U.S. District Court, Northern District of Illinois. *Education:* Illinois State University (B.A., 1993; M.B.A., 1995); University of Illinois-College of Law (J.D., magna cum laude, 1998). Clerk, The Honorable David Briones, U.S. District Court, Western District of Texas. ***PRACTICE AREAS:*** Litigation. ***Email:*** jmccarty@vedderprice.com

COURTNEY ANNE McDONOUGH, born New York, N.Y., October 29, 1979; admitted to bar, 2004, Illinois. *Education:* University of Notre Dame (B.A., 2001; J.D., 2004). *Member:* Chicago Bar Association. ***PRACTICE AREAS:*** Labor and Employment (50%); Commercial Litigation (50%). ***Email:*** cmcdonough@vedderprice.com

MEGAN E. MEYERS, born Tulsa, Oklahoma, May 29, 1974; admitted to bar, 1999, Illinois. *Education:* University of Notre Dame (B.B.A., cum laude, 1996); Indiana University School of Law (J.D., cum laude, 1998). Delta Theta Phi. Sherman Minton Moot Court. Editorial Staff, Indiana Law Journal, 1997-1998. Author: "Where There's a Will, There's a Way: State Sales and Use Taxation of Electronic Commerce," Indiana Law Journal, Vol. 74, Issue 1, Winter 1998; "Tolling the Information Superhighway: State Sales and Use Taxation of Electronic Commerce," Harvard Journal of Law and Technology, Vol. 13, No. 3, Summer 2000. ***PRACTICE AREAS:*** Corporate Law; Mergers and Acquisitions; Executive Compensation. ***Email:*** mgroves@vedderprice.com

JAMES W. MORRISSEY, born Chicago, Illinois, April 19, 1971; admitted to bar, 2000, Illinois. *Education:* Boston College (B.A., cum laude, 1993); DePaul University College of Law (J.D., 2000); DePaul University, Kellstadt Graduate School of Business (M.B.A., 2000). Order of the Coif. Business Manager/General Editor, DePaul Law Review, 1998-1999. Author: "United States v. O'Hagan: A Results-Oriented Approach to Insider Trading Cases," DePaul Law Review, Fall, 1998. *Member:* Illinois State Bar Association. ***PRACTICE AREAS:*** Corporate Law; Mergers and Acquisitions; Financial Institutions Law. ***Email:*** jmorrissey@vedderprice.com

MICHAEL R. MULCAHY, born Chicago, Illinois, August 19, 1964; admitted to bar, 1993, Illinois and U.S. District Court, Northern District of Illinois; 1995, U.S. Court of Military Appeals. *Education:* Illinois State University (B.S., 1986); John Marshall Law School (J.D., 1993). *Member:* Chicago and American Bar Associations. [Major, Judge Advocate, U.S. Marine Corps, 1994-1998; U.S. Marine Corps Reserve, 1998—]. ***PRACTICE AREAS:*** Commercial Litigation; Intellectual Property Litigation. ***Email:*** mmulcahy@vedderprice.com

JOSEPH KEVIN MULHERIN, born Lakenheath AFB, England, January 22, 1974; admitted to bar, 2002, Illinois. *Education:* Marquette University (B.S., 1997); Pepperdine University (J.D., 2002). ***PRACTICE AREAS:*** Labor and Employment; Litigation. ***Email:*** jmulherin@vedderprice.com

CHRISTOPHER L. NYBO, admitted to bar, 2002, Illinois and U.S. District Court, Northern District of Illinois. *Education:* Dartmouth College (B.A., 1999); University of Chicago (J.D., 2002). Author: "Dialing M for Murder: Assessing the Interstate Commerce Requirement for Federal Murder-for-Hire," 2001 University of Chicago Legal F. 579, 2001. Member, DuPage County Zoning Board of Appeals, 2003—. *Member:* Chicago and Fenwick (Treasurer, 2002—) Bar Associations; Dartmouth Lawyers Association. ***PRACTICE AREAS:*** Labor and Employment (100%). ***Email:*** cnybo@vedderprice.com

(This Listing Continued)

VEDDER, PRICE, KAUFMAN & KAMMHOLZ, P.C., Chicago—Continued

MATTHEW T. O'CONNOR, born Rockford, Illinois, November 21, 1965; admitted to bar, 1994, Illinois. *Education:* Indiana University (B.S., 1988); Chicago-Kent College of Law (J.D, 1994). ***PRACTICE AREAS:*** Corporate Law; Corporate Finance; Mergers and Acquisitions. ***Email:*** moconnor@vedderprice.com

ANGELA C. PAVLATOS, born Evergreen Park, Illinois, March 22, 1975; admitted to bar, 2000, Illinois. *Education:* Millikin University (B.A., 1997); Loyola University School of Law (J.D., 2000). Moot Court. *Member:* Chicago and American Bar Associations. ***PRACTICE AREAS:*** Labor and Employment; Litigation. ***Email:*** apavlatos@vedderprice.com

JACOB C. POND, born Evansville, Illinois, October 12, 1974; admitted to bar, 2001, Illinois. *Education:* Washington University (B.S.B.A., 1997); Indiana University (J.D., 2001). Moot Court Octofinalist, 2000. Senior Articles Editor, Federal Communications Law Journal, 2000-2001. ***PRACTICE AREAS:*** Aircraft Finance and Leasing; Equipment Finance. ***Email:*** jpond@vedderprice.com

JENNIFER M.K. PROVENCHER, born Milwaukee, Wisconsin, May 9, 1977; admitted to bar, 2004, Illinois. *Education:* University of Minnesota, Twin Cities, MN (B.S., 1999); DePaul University, Chicago, IL (J.D., cum laude, 2004). ***PRACTICE AREAS:*** Corporate; Financial Institutions. ***Email:*** jprovencher@vedderprice.com

BRUCE A. RADKE, born Springfield, Illinois, July 16, 1968; admitted to bar, 1996, Illinois, U.S. District Court, Northern and Central Districts of Illinois and U.S. Court of Appeals, Seventh Circuit; 2001, U.S. District Court, Eastern District of Wisconsin. *Education:* University of Illinois (B.A., magna cum laude, 1990; J.D., cum laude, 1993). Phi Beta Kappa; Phi Kappa Phi. Author: "Meeting the Needs of Elderly Consumers: Proposed Reforms for the NAIC's Long-Term Care Insurance Model Act," 1 Elder Law Journal 227 (1993). ***PRACTICE AREAS:*** Commercial Litigation; Intellectual Property Litigation. ***Email:*** bradke@vedderprice.com

ERIC J. RIETZ, born Owatonna, Minnesota, January 14, 1967; admitted to bar, 1992, Illinois and U.S. District Court, Northern District of Illinois. *Education:* University of Wisconsin-Madison (B.A., honors, 1989); Northwestern University (J.D., 1992). Phi Kappa Phi. Licensed Real Estate Broker, Illinois. ***PRACTICE AREAS:*** Real Estate. ***Email:*** erietz@vedderprice.com

ALLYSON B. RUSSO, born Ann Arbor, Michigan, August 16, 1975; admitted to bar, 2001, Massachusetts; 2002, Illinois. *Education:* Boston College, Chestnut Hill (B.A., 1997); University of Michigan Law School, Ann Arbor (J.D., 2000). Formerly with: Wildman Harrold; Bingham McCutchen. ***PRACTICE AREAS:*** Bankruptcy; Corporate. ***Email:*** arusso@vedderprice.com

TIMOTHY M. SCHANK, born Evanston, Illinois, May 7, 1976; admitted to bar, 2001, Illinois; 2003, U.S. District Court, Northern District of Illinois. *Education:* University of Notre Dame (B.A., 1998; J.D., 2001). ***PRACTICE AREAS:*** Litigation. ***Email:*** tschank@vedderprice.com

DEREK M. SPYCHALSKI, born Salem, Massachusetts, July 2, 1971; admitted to bar, 2003, Illinois. *Education:* Johns Hopkins University (B.A., 1993); Loyola College (M.B.A., 1999); Chicago-Kent College of Law (J.D., 2003); Illinois Institute of Technology (M.S., 2003). Member and Executive Articles Editor, Chicago-Kent Law Review, 2000-2002. Certified Public Accountant, Illinois, 2002. ***PRACTICE AREAS:*** Corporate Law; Corporate Finance. ***Email:*** dspychalski@vedderprice.com

KATHRYN L. STEVENS, born Park Ridge, Illinois, January 31, 1975; admitted to bar, 1999, Illinois and U.S. District Court, Northern District of Illinois. *Education:* University of Wisconsin-Madison (B.A., 1996); DePaul University College of Law (J.D., 1999). Notes and Comments Editor, DePaul Journal of Healthcare Law. *Member:* Illinois State Bar Association. ***PRACTICE AREAS:*** Health Care; Trade and Professional Associations. ***Email:*** kstevens@vedderprice.com

PATRICK J. STOKLAS, born July 6, 1976; admitted to bar, 2004, Illinois. *Education:* Kenyon College (B.A., 1998); Loyola University (J.D., 2004). ***PRACTICE AREAS:*** Equipment Finance (100%). ***Email:*** pstoklas@vedderprice.com

CINDY S. STUYVESANT, born Grand Rapids, Michigan; admitted to bar, 2003, Illinois. *Education:* Michigan State University (B.A., Communications, 1988); Aquinas College (M.M., 1994); Chicago-Kent College of Law (J.D., with high honors, 2003). Member, Chicago-Kent Law Review. Member, Moot Court Honor Society. ***PRACTICE AREAS:*** Litigation. ***Email:*** cstuyvesant@vedderprice.com

MARYAM TABRIZI, born Esfehan, Iran, April 15, 1975; admitted to bar, 2003, Illinois. *Education:* University of California, Santa Barbara (B.S., 1997); University of Notre Dame (J.D., 2003). ***PRACTICE AREAS:*** Commercial Litigation; Product Liability. ***Email:*** mtabrizi@vedderprice.com

VENU V. TALANKI, born Ann Arbor, Michigan, November 10, 1976; admitted to bar, 2001, Michigan (Not admitted in Illinois). *Education:* University of Michigan (B.A., 1998); University of Illinois College of Law, Urbana-Champaign (J.D., 2001). ***PRACTICE AREAS:*** Mergers and Acquisitions; Finance. ***Email:*** vtalanki@vedderprice.com

KELLY A. TAUTGES, born St. Paul, Minnesota, May 26, 1975; (admission pending). *Education:* Marquette University (B.A., 1997); Loyola University (J.D., cum laude, 2001). ***PRACTICE AREAS:*** Litigation.

URSULA TAYLOR, born Niles, Michigan, February 17, 1980; admitted to bar, 2005, Illinois and U.S. District Court, Northern District of Illinois. *Education:* University of Michigan, Ann Arbor (B.A., 2002); Northwestern University School of Law (J.D., cum laude, 2005). Dean's List, Northwestern University School of Law, 2003-2005. ***PRACTICE AREAS:*** Civil Litigation. ***Email:*** utaylor@vedderprice.com

ANNE THERIEAU, born San Diego, California; admitted to bar, 2004, Illinois. *Education:* University of Notre Dame (B.A., 1996); Loyola University (J.D., cum laude, 2004). ***PRACTICE AREAS:*** Litigation (100%). ***Email:*** atherieau@vedderprice.com

JOHN B. THORNTON, born Manhasset, New York, May 28, 1959; admitted to bar, 2002, Illinois, and U.S. District Court, Northern District of Illinois. *Education:* University of Notre Dame (B.A., English, magna cum laude, 1981); University of Illinois (M.A., Applied Linguistics, 1983); Northwestern University (J.D., 2002). *Member:* Illinois State and American Bar Associations. ***PRACTICE AREAS:*** Litigation (100%). ***Email:*** jthornton@vedderprice.com

SARAH VANDERVEER, born Minneapolis, Minnesota, August 8, 1974; admitted to bar, 2003, Illinois. *Education:* DePauw University (B.A., 1997); George Washington University Law School (J.D., 2003). ***PRACTICE AREAS:*** Equipment Finance. ***Email:*** svanderveer@vedderprice.com

MICHAEL J. WATERS, born Midland, MI, June 14, 1978; (admission pending). *Education:* University of Michigan (B.S., Biology, 2000); Northwestern University School of Law (J.D., 2003). Recipient, Lewis Learned Coburn Scholarship. ***PRACTICE AREAS:*** Litigation. ***Email:*** mwaters@vedderprice.com

MARK L. WINGET, born New York, New York, December 21, 1968; admitted to bar, 1995, Illinois and U.S. District Court, Northern District of Illinois. *Education:* Johns Hopkins University (B.A., 1991); Harvard University (J.D., 1995). Phi Beta Kappa. ***PRACTICE AREAS:*** Corporate Law; Investment Company Law; Securities; Mutual Funds; Broker-Dealer Regulation. ***Email:*** mwinget@vedderprice.com

PETER T. WYNACHT, born Weymouth, Massachusetts; admitted to bar, 2001, Illinois. *Education:* University of Florida (B.A., 1996); Chicago-Kent College of Law, Illinois Institute of Technology (J.D., with honors, 2001); New York University (LL.M., Taxation, 2002). Honored by Chicago Bar Association for Outstanding Academic Achievement in Study of Tax Law. Member, Chicago-Kent Law Review. Member: Illinois State Bar Association, 2001-2002; American Bar Association, 2001-2002. ***PRACTICE AREAS:*** Taxation. ***Email:*** pwynacht@vedderprice.com

AMY L. YOUNG, born January 23, 1978; admitted to bar, 2004, Illinois. *Education:* North Central College (B.A., 1999); DePaul University College of Law (J.D., magna cum laude, 2004). ***PRACTICE AREAS:*** Health Law; Trade and Professional Associations; Corporate. ***Email:*** ayoung@vedderprice.com

JIN W. YUN, born Seoul, Korea, May 16, 1967; admitted to bar, 2001, Illinois. *Education:* Washington State University (B.B.A., 1989); University of Illinois, Urbana-Champaign (J.D., cum laude, 2001). Previously with Skadden Arps Slate Meagher & Flom LLP. ***LANGUAGES:*** Korean. ***PRACTICE AREAS:*** Equipment Finance. ***Email:*** jyun@vedderprice.com

MICHAEL DEREK ZOLNER, born Dennison, Ohio, September 16, 1973; admitted to bar, 1998, Missouri and U.S. District Court, Western District of Missouri; 1999, Illinois. *Education:* University of Oklahoma (B.A., with distinction, 1995; J.D., with honors, 1998). Order of the Coif.Member, Board of Advocates, Moot Court. Recipient: Paul K. Frost Memorial Scholarship; George B. Fraser Memorial Scholarship; Academic Achievement Awards in Contracts I and II, Civil Procedure I and II and Property II. Note Editor, University of Oklahoma Law Review, 1997-1998. Author: " Report a Crime, Lose Your Job: The Oklahoma Supreme Court Reigns in the Public Policy Exception to Employment-at-Will in Hayes v. Eateries, Inc.," 50 Okla. L. Rev. 585. ***PRACTICE AREAS:*** Commercial Litigation; Trade Secrets; Restrictive Covenants; Intellectual Property Litigation. ***Email:*** dzolner@vedderprice.com

OF COUNSEL

MARGARET A. ARNOLD, born Middletown, Connecticut, January 3, 1943; admitted to bar, 1977, Illinois; 1979, U.S. District Court, Northern District of Illinois. *Education:* Clarke College (B.A., cum laude, 1965); Loyola University of Chicago (J.D., 1977). ***PRACTICE AREAS:*** Insurance Coverage; Products Liability; Toxic Torts; Environmental Insurance Coverage; Litigation. ***Email:*** marnold@vedderprice.com

MICHAEL G. BEEMER, born Crawfordsville, Indiana, December 23, 1937; admitted to bar, 1963, Illinois, Indiana and U.S. District Court, Southern District of Indiana; 1964, U.S. District Court, Northern District of Illinois; 1965, Tax Court. *Education:* Williams College (B.A., magna cum laude, 1960); Harvard Law School (LL.B., cum laude, 1963). Phi Beta Kappa. President, Harvard Law Society of Illinois, 1982. ***PRACTICE AREAS:*** Mergers and Acquisitions; Taxation; Closely Held Business Law; Estate Planning; Nonprofit and Charitable Organizations. ***Email:*** mbeemer@vedderprice.com

BERNARD J. ECHLIN, born Chicago, Illinois, February 24, 1918; admitted to bar, 1953, Illinois and U.S. District Court, Northern District of Illinois. *Education:* DePaul University (B.S., 1948; J.D., 1952). Delta Theta Phi. Warvelle Senate: Tribune (1950-1951), Dean (1951-1952). Commissioner, Illinois Commission on Labor Law, 1969-1981. Trustee, Rush-Presbyterian-St. Luke's Medical Center, 1969—. Trustee, 1974-1989 and Chairman, 1985-1989, Anchor Organization for Health Maintenance. Member, Governing Board, Rush Home Health Service, 1983-1990. Director, 1983-1989 and Chairman, 1985-1986, Metropolitan Chicago Healthcare Council. Trustee, Ancilla Insurance Trust, 1985-1988. Director, Fox Valley Health Services Corporation, 1987-1992. Director, Copley Memorial Hospital, 1987-1992. Trustee, 1989-1992 and Chairman, 1989-1992, Rush-Presbyterian-St. Luke's Health Plans, Inc. Director and Vice Chairman, Rush Copley Health Care System, Inc., 1987—. *Member:* Chicago, Illinois State and American Bar Associations; American Academy of Hospital Attorneys; Illinois Association of Hospital Attorneys; Catholic Health Association of the United States. Honorary Fellow, American College of Health Care Executives. ***PRACTICE AREAS:*** Labor and Employment; Healthcare Law.

JAMES T. FITZGIBBON, born Sioux Falls, South Dakota, November 14, 1932; admitted to bar, 1960, Illinois; registered to practice before U.S. Patent and Trademark Office. *Education:* Loyola University (B.S., 1958; J.D., 1960). Contributor, 1958-1959; Associate Editor, "Recent Decisions," Section, 1959-1960, Illinois State Bar Journal. *Member:* Chicago and American Bar Associations; Intellectual Property Law Association of Chicago; American Intellectual Property Law Association; Law Club of Chicago. ***PRACTICE AREAS:*** Patents; Trademarks; Copyrights; Unfair Competition. ***Email:*** jfitzgibbon@vedderprice.com

PHILIP L. KENNEDY, born Berwyn, Illinois, January 8, 1932; admitted to bar, 1958, Illinois. *Education:* Northwestern University (B.S., 1954); University of Michigan (LL.B., 1957). *Member:* Chicago Bar Association. ***PRACTICE AREAS:*** Estate Administration; Estate Planning. ***Email:*** pkennedy@vedderprice.com

(This Listing Continued)

ALLAN E. LAPIDUS, born New York, New York, January 24, 1943; admitted to bar, 1967, Illinois; 1969, U.S. District Court, Northern District of Illinois; 1971, U.S. Court of Appeals, 7th Circuit; 1972, U.S. Supreme Court; 1975, U.S. District Court, Southern, Central and Northern Districts of Illinois including Trial Bar. *Education:* University of Wisconsin (B.S., 1964); University of Michigan (J.D., 1967). Trial Attorney, Federal Communications Commission, 1967-1969. Assistant United States Attorney, Northern District of Illinois, 1969-1973. Cooperating Attorney, American Civil Liberties Union, 1981—. Panel Attorney for Federal Defender Office, 1973—. ***PRACTICE AREAS:*** Complex Business Litigation; Employment Litigation; Federal Criminal Law; Occupational Safety and Health; Trial Practice. ***Email:*** alapidus@vedderprice.com

WILLIAM O. PETERSEN, born Chicago, Illinois, November 28, 1926; admitted to bar, 1952, Illinois; 1958, U.S. District Court, Northern District of Illinois. *Education:* Harvard College (A.B., cum laude, 1949); Harvard Law School (LL.B., 1952). ***PRACTICE AREAS:*** Corporate Law; Estate Planning.

COUNSEL

RONALD J. RAPP, born Chicago, Illinois, January 19, 1960; admitted to bar, 1985, Illinois and U.S. District Court, Northern District of Illinois. *Education:* Valparaiso University (B.A., summa cum laude, 1982); University of Minnesota Law School (J.D., cum laude, 1985). Appointed Colonel and Aide-de-Camp, Louisiana Governor's Staff, 1987. Associate: Foley & Lardner, Chicago, Il., 1988-1990; Skadden, Arps, Slate, Meagher & Flom, Chicago, Il., 1986-1988. Associate General Counsel, GE Capital Fleet Services, 2002-2003. Associate General Counsel and Assistant Secretary, Comdisco, Inc., 1990-2001. *Member:* National Business Aviation Association; Lawyer-Pilots Bar Association. ***PRACTICE AREAS:*** Aircraft Finance and Leasing; Corporate Aviation; Securitization; Equipment Finance and Leasing. ***Email:*** rrapp@vedderprice.com

THOMAS VEGA-BYRNES, LLC

Established in 2002

THE MONADNOCK BUILDING
53 WEST JACKSON BOULEVARD
SUITE 1057
CHICAGO, ILLINOIS 60604
Telephone: 312-360-1562
Mobile: 773-230-0228
Fax: 312-360-1607
Email: tvb@vegabyrnes.com
URL: http://www.vegabyrnes.com

International Construction Law, Electric Power, International Loans, International Investments, International Mergers and Acquisitions, International Joint Ventures, International Corporate Law, International Licensing.

FIRM PROFILE: Thomas Vega-Byrnes is a Chicago-based attorney with broad country and industry sector experience in international and US engineering and construction projects, in the areas of independent power generation, airports, pulp and paper and chemicals. He provides assistance to a wide range of clients throughout the United States and abroad, including Fortune 500 companies, major commercial and financial institutions, governments and governmental entities, as well as small and midsize companies.

Mr. Vega-Byrnes also advises commercial lenders on international secured lending, and represents clients in international mergers, acquisitions, joint ventures, licensing and the corporate law aspects of international reorganizations and restructurings for tax planning purposes.

THOMAS J. VEGA-BYRNES, born Chicago, Illinois, September 21, 1958; admitted to bar, 1990, Illinois; 2003, New York. *Education:* Loyola University (B.A., summa cum laude, 1980); University of Chicago (J.D., 1990). *Member:* Illinois State, New York State (Member, Business Law and International Law and Practice Sections) and American (Member, Construction Industry Forum; Sections on: Business Law, International Law and Practice) Bar Associations; CPR Institute for Dispute Resolution (Member and Panelist, Panels of Distinguished Neutrals). ***LANGUAGES:*** Spanish, Portuguese, French and Italian. ***PRACTICE AREAS:*** Construction Law; International Law; Energy; Finance; Investments; Mergers and Acquisitions; Joint Ventures. ***Email:*** tvb@vegabyrnes.com

Languages: Spanish, Portuguese, French and Italian.

REPRESENTATIVE CLIENTS: AES Panama, S.A.; Kawasaki Heavy Industries, Ltd.; RS Cogen, LLC; Shrimp Improvement Systems, LLC; Embotelladora La Cascada, S.A.; Yum! Brands, Inc.; ShoreCap International, Ltd.

LAW OFFICES OF LESLIE L. VEON

303 WEST MADISON STREET, SUITE 1150
CHICAGO, ILLINOIS 60606
Telephone: 312-578-1721
Facsimile: 312-578-1743
URL: http://www.lawyers.com/veonlaw

Practice limited to Matrimonial Law, Family Law, Domestic Relations Law, Trial and Appellate Practice.

FIRM PROFILE: The lawyers of the Law Offices of Leslie L. Veon practice matrimonial and family law, including divorce and dissolution of marriage; child support, custody and visitation; drafting of marital settlement agreements, premarital agreements and postnuptial agreements; paternity; and divorce appeals.

On both the trial and appellate levels, the Firm's attorneys handle cases involving substantial marital estates, valuation, tax, contested custody and issues of paternity.

Leslie L. Veon is a Fellow of the American Academy of Matrimonial Lawyers.

(This Listing Continued)

LESLIE L. VEON, born Kent, Ohio, July 14, 1953; admitted to bar, 1978, Illinois. *Education:* Miami University (A.B., cum laude, 1975); University of Cincinnati (J.D., 1978). Phi Beta Kappa. Author: "Doctrine of Forum Non Conveniens and Divorce Venue," Illinois Family Law Report, Vol. XIV, No. 8, August, 1991; "Verified Petitions For Exclusive Possession of the Marital Home," Illinois Family Law Report, Vol. XIV, No. 3, March, 1991. Co-Author: "Hidden Assets," A.B.A. Family Advocate, Summer 1989; "Illinois Child Custody Law: An Overview," Illinois Bar Journal, Vol. 76, No. 1, Sept. 1987; "Antenuptial Agreements and Malpractice: Is the Risk Worth the Reward?" American Journal of Family Law, Vol. 2, No. 2, Summer 1988; "Family Law in Illinois," The Cambridge Institute, 1988. Chapter Author: "How to Handle Goodwill Valuation Of Professional Practices," Handling Business Interest In Divorce Proceedings, Illinois Institute Of Continuing Legal Education, 1987; "Antenuptial Agreements: To Draft Or Not to Draft," Seminar On Matrimonial Law, American Academy of Matrimonial Lawyers, 1988; "Attorneys' Fees in Divorce Actions: Judicial Intervention and the Contingent Fee Bar," presentation to Illinois Chapter, American Academy of Matrimonial Lawyers, June, 1989; "Valuations Of Closely Held Corporations," Illinois Divorce Practice, Professional Education Systems, Inc., 1988. Seminar Lecturer: "Marital and Non-Marital Property: Issues of Transmutation, Reimbursement and Interspousal Gift," Chicago Bar Association, November 1995; "His, Hers and Ours: Divorce Planning and the Use of Premarital and Postnuptial Agreements," Chicago Estate Planning Council, April, 1995; "Professional Practice Goodwill," February 1988 and "Antenuptial Agreements," September 1988, Illinois Institute of Continuing Legal Education; "Goodwill Valuation," Professional Education Systems, Inc., May, 1988; "Illinois Family Law," The Cambridge Institute, July, 1988, April, 1989. *Member:* Chicago and Illinois State Bar Associations; Appellate Lawyers Association. Fellow, American Academy of Matrimonial Lawyers. ***REPORTED CASES:*** In Re Marriage of Singleteary, 293 Ill. App.3d 25, 687 N.E.2d 1080, 227 Ill. Dec. 598 (1st Dist. 1997); In Re Marriage of Schomburg, 269 Ill.App.3d 13, 645 N.E.2d 1005, 206 Ill. Dec. 753 (1st Dist. 1995); In Re Marriage of Leisner, 219 Ill.App.3d 752, 579 N.E.2d 1091, 162 Ill.Dec.277 (1st Dist. 1991); Licciardi v. Collins, 180 Ill.App.3d 1051, 536 N.E.2d 840, 129 Ill.Dec. 790, 57 USLW 2657 (1st Dist. 1989); In Re Marriage of Spomer, 123 Ill.App.3d 31, 462 N.E.2d 724, 78 Ill.Dec. 605 (5th Dist. 1984); St. Gemme v. Tomlin, 118 Ill.App.3d 766, 455 N.E.2d 294, 74 Ill.Dec. 264 (4th Dist. 1983). ***PRACTICE AREAS:*** Family Law; Domestic Relations; Matrimonial Law; Divorce.

ASSOCIATES

CHRISTINA M. DARDICK, born June 17, 1965; admitted to bar, 1995, Illinois. *Education:* Elmhurst College (B.S., 1987); DePaul University (M.B.A., 1990); Chicago-Kent College of Law (J.D., 1995). *Member:* Illinois State Bar Association. ***PRACTICE AREAS:*** Family Law; Domestic Relations; Matrimonial Law; Divorce.

DEBORAH L. DENCER, born Elgin, Illinois, March 24, 1978; admitted to bar, 2003, Illinois; 2004, Texas. *Education:* Augustana College (B.A., cum laude, 2000) Chicago-Kent College of Law, Illinois Institute of Technology (J.D., 2003). *Member:* Chicago, Illinois State and American Bar Associations. ***PRACTICE AREAS:*** Family Law; Domestic Relations; Matrimonial Law; Divorce.

KATE CURLER, born December 23, 1969; admitted to bar, 2002, Illinois. *Education:* Michigan State University (B.A., 1992); Santa Clara University (J.D., 2002). Member, Santa Clara University Honors Moot Court Competition, 2000. Participant, Oxford University Comparative Family Law Tutorial, 2000. *Member:* Chicago, Lake County and Illinois State Bar Associations; Association of Women Lawyers of Lake County (Board Member, 2004-2005); Jefferson Inns of Court. ***PRACTICE AREAS:*** Family Law; Domestic Relations; Matrimonial Law; Divorce.

THE LAW OFFICES OF MICHAEL J. VITALE

CHICAGO, ILLINOIS

(See Berwyn)

Family Law, Child Support, Domestic Relations, Divorce, Criminal Law, Felonies, Driving While Intoxicated.

VON MANDEL & VON MANDEL

79 WEST MONROE STREET, SUITE 1000
CHICAGO, ILLINOIS 60603
Telephone: 312-726-2145
Telecopier: 312-726-2261
Email: mvmtax@aol.com
URL: http://www.lawyers.com/mvmtax

Tax Controversies, Tax Litigation, Federal Taxation, Estate and Gift Taxation, State Tax Controversies, Employment Tax, Criminal Tax Audits.

FIRM PROFILE: Since 1976 the firm has concentrated in federal and state tax controversies and related litigation. Clients include corporations, partnerships, individuals and estates. The firm is available to act as co-counsel in tax matters. For reference see Franz v. United States, 94-1 USTC par. 50,113; 73 AFTR 2d par. 94-1485 (N.D. Ill. 1994).

MICHAEL J. VON MANDEL, born Yokohama, Japan, October 20, 1941; admitted to bar, 1969, District of Columbia and Connecticut; 1976, Illinois; 1977, Florida; U.S. District Court, Northern District of Illinois, Trial Bar. *Education:* Georgetown University (A.B., 1964); Catholic University of America (J.D., 1968); New York University (LL.M. in Taxation, 1970). Private law practice, Chicago, Illinois, 1976—. Author and Lecturer, Illinois Institute for Continuing Legal Education (Taxation), 1983—. Adjunct Professor, De Paul University, Graduate School of Law (Taxation), 1980-1983. Trial Attorney, Tax Division, U.S. Department of Justice, 1970-1976 (Chief, Chicago Civil Tax Docket, 1975-1976). Trial Attorney, Federal Trade Commission, 1968-1969. *Member:* Chicago (Committee on Federal Taxation), Federal (Board of Directors, 1980-1993; Chairman, Federal Tax Committee, 1980-1989), American (Sections on: Taxation; Litigation) and Seventh Circuit Bar

(This Listing Continued)

VON MANDEL & VON MANDEL, Chicago—Continued

Associations. **PRACTICE AREAS:** Tax Controversies; Tax Litigation; Federal Taxation; Estate and Gift Taxation; State Tax Controversies; Employment Tax; Criminal Tax Audits. **Email:** mvmtax@aol.com

MARY D. VON MANDEL, born Worcester, Massachusetts, September 27, 1952; admitted to bar, 1988, Illinois; 1989, Pennsylvania. *Education:* University of Pittsburgh (B.A., 1974); DePaul University (J.D., with honors, 1988; LL.M. in Taxation, 1994). Editor, DePaul Law Review, 1987-1988. Private law practice, Chicago, Illinois, 1988—. Associate, Chadwell & Kayser, Chicago, Illinois, 1988-1989. Author of articles on IRS Trust Fund Penalties and Employment Tax Classification issues. *Member:* Chicago, Illinois, Federal, American and Seventh Circuit Bar Associations. **PRACTICE AREAS:** Tax Controversies; Tax Litigation; Federal Taxation; Estate and Gift Taxation; State Tax Controversies; Employment Tax; Criminal Tax Audits. **Email:** mvmtax@aol.com

THE LAW OFFICES OF GEORGE J. VOURNAZOS

Established in 1998

2334 WEST LAWRENCE AVENUE, SUITE 100
CHICAGO, ILLINOIS 60625
Telephone: 708-636-5900; 773-784-5006
Fax: 773-784-5068
Email: LawFind@flash.net
URL: http://www.georgejvournazos.com

Personal Injury, Medical Malpractice, Legal Malpractice, Slip and Fall, Product Liability, Automobile Accidents, Workers Compensation, Assault and Battery, Consumer Bankruptcy, Business, Corporate, Contract Litigation, Chancery, Real Estate, Collections and Administrative Hearings.

GEORGE J. VOURNAZOS, born Chicago, Illinois, January 28, 1962; admitted to bar, 1987, Illinois; 1994, U.S. District Court, Northern District of Illinois including Trial Bar; 1997, U.S. Court of Appeals, Seventh Circuit; 1998, U.S. District Court, Central District of Illinois. *Education:* Loyola University (B.B.A., 1984; J.D., 1987). Law Clerk to Patrick J. Murphy, Cook County Public Guardian, 1986-1987. Listed in National Registry of Who's Who. *Member:* Association of Trial Lawyers of America. **PRACTICE AREAS:** Personal Injury; Medical Malpractice; Products Liability; Corporate Law; Contracts; Administrative Hearings; Real Estate; Personal Bankruptcy; Appellate Practice.

VURDELJA & HEAPHY

Established in 1991

120 NORTH LA SALLE STREET, SUITE 1150
CHICAGO, ILLINOIS 60602
Telephone: 312-345-2000
Fax: 312-345-2005

Civil Litigation including Insurance Coverage Litigation, Reinsurance Litigation and Arbitration, Bankruptcy Litigation, Breach of Contract, Construction Litigation, Commercial Torts, Employment Litigation, Collection, Personal Injury, Product Liability, Fraud, Probate Litigation.

JOHN M. HEAPHY, born Washington, D.C., November 20, 1955; admitted to bar, 1981, Illinois and U.S. District Court, Northern District of Illinois including Trial Bar (1987); 1983, U.S. Court of Appeals, Seventh Circuit. *Education:* University of Michigan (B.S.E., Chem. Eng., cum laude, 1978; J.D., magna cum laude, 1981). Order of the Coif; Tau Beta Pi. Mayer, Brown, Platt, Partner, 1988-1994 and Associate 1981-1987. *Member:* Illinois State Bar Association. **PRACTICE AREAS:** Commercial Litigation; Reinsurance Litigation and Arbitration; Bankruptcy Litigation; Products Liability; Employment Litigation. **Email:** jheaphy@vhlaw.net

GEORGE N. VURDELJA, JR., born Pittsburgh, Pennsylvania, December 4, 1956; admitted to bar, 1981, Illinois and U.S. District Court, Northern District of Illinois including Trial Bar (1984); 1986, U.S. Court of Appeals, Seventh Circuit. *Education:* James Madison College at Michigan State University (B.A., magna cum laude, 1978); University of Chicago (J.D., 1981). Phi Beta Kappa; Phi Kappa Phi. Previous Professional Experience: Mayer Brown & Platt, Partner, 1988-1991; Associate, 1981-1987. *Member:* Chicago, Illinois State, and American Bar Associations. **PRACTICE AREAS:** Commercial Litigation; Bankruptcy Litigation; Product Liability; Probate Litigation; Employment Litigation; Construction Litigation. **Email:** gvurdelja@vhlaw.net

GRISWOLD L. WARE, born Evanston, Illinois, June 24, 1963; admitted to bar, 1992, Illinois; 1993, U.S. District Court, Northern District of Illinois; 1994, U.S. Court of Appeals, Seventh Circuit. *Education:* Denison University (B.A., 1986); John Marshall Law School (J.D., 1992). *Member:* Chicago and American Bar Associations. **PRACTICE AREAS:** Commercial Litigation; Employment Litigation; Product Liability. **Email:** gware@vhlaw.net

LAW OFFICES OF MINH C. WAI

CHICAGO, ILLINOIS

(See Merrillville, Indiana)

General Practice, Personal Injury, Auto and Railroad Accidents, Construction Accidents, Property Damage, Slip and Fall, Unsafe Products, Wrongful Death, Bankruptcy, Insurance Defense and Coverage, Corporate Law, Contracts, Landlord-Tenant, Business Defense, Personal Injury Defense, Subrogation, Immigration Law.

WALKER WILCOX MATOUSEK LLP

Established in 2005

225 W. WASHINGTON STREET, SUITE 2400
CHICAGO, ILLINOIS 60606-3418
Telephone: 312-244-6700
Fax: 312-244-6800
URL: http://www.wwmlawyers.com

Insurance Law, Coverage, Counseling, Alternative Dispute Resolution, Litigation, Civil Trial Practice, Aviation Coverage and Defense, Casualty Insurance Coverage and Defense, Class Action Defense, Commercial Litigation, Construction Defense, Contract Litigation, Directors and Officers Liability Coverage, Employment Practices Liability Insurance Coverage and Defense, Environmental Insurance Coverage and Defense, Financial Institutions Liability Insurance Coverage and Defense, First and Third Party Insurance Coverage and Defense, Life, Accident and Health, and Disability Insurance Coverage and Defense, Media and Defamation Coverage and Defense, Medical Liability Insurance Coverage, Premises Liability Defense, Products Liability Defense, Professional Liability Insurance Coverage, Professional Liability Counseling and Defense, Property Insurance Coverage and Defense, Reinsurance Coverage and Arbitrations, Tort Defense, Accountants Liability, Insurance Agents and Brokers Liability, Attorneys, Data Processors, Tech and eBusiness, Directors and Officers Liability, Fiduciaries, Public Officials, School Boards, Real Estate Agents and Brokers, Registered Representatives, Third Party Administrators, Trustees.

FIRM PROFILE: Walker Wilcox Matousek LLP concentrates on sophisticated insurance matters and other complex commercial disputes, including counseling, alternative dispute resolution, litigation and trial. WWM attorneys are noted for their expertise in insurance and reinsurance coverage issues, all types of professional liability, defamation, and class action and tort defense. Along with in-depth expertise, WWM provides attentive and efficient service in a collegial environment.

WWM has been selected by many discerning clients, ranging from individuals to global enterprises, to represent their interests nationwide. Prior to establishing their own firm, the founders of WWM had spent their careers at one of the nation's largest and most prestigious insurance law firms.

PARTNERS OF FIRM

WILLIAM P. BILA, born Evergreen Park, Illinois, December 27, 1962; admitted to bar, 1988, Illinois, U.S. District Court, Northern and Central Districts of Illinois and U.S. Court of Appeals, Seventh Circuit. *Education:* University of Illinois-Urbana (B.A., 1985; J.D., cum laude, 1988). Pi Sigma Alpha (Honorary Member). Member, Law Review. Volunteer: Chicago Economic Development Law Project; Chicago Volunteer Legal Services. Member, Professional Liability Underwriting Society. *Member:* American Bar Association. **PRACTICE AREAS:** Directors and Officers Liability Insurance; Financial Institutions Errors and Omissions; Employment Practices Liability Insurance; Insurance Coverage Litigation. **Email:** wbila@wwmlawyers.com

JOSEPH J. BORDERS, born January 4, 1959; admitted to bar, 1993, Illinois. *Education:* Depaul University (B.S., 1988; J.D., with honors, 1993). Order of the Coif. Recipient: Michael Jaharis Scholarship, 1991; Thomas Heneghan Legal Scholarship, 1992. Member, Law Review. Extern Law Clerk: Honorable William T. Hart, District Judge, U.S. District Court, Northern District of Illinois; Honorable Kenneth F. Ripple, Circuit Judge, U.S. Court of Appeals, Seventh Circuit. **PRACTICE AREAS:** Insurance Coverage Defense; Professional Liability Insurance Coverage; Professional Liability Defense; Directors and Officers Insurance Coverage. **Email:** jborders@wwmlawyers.com

JOYCE F. CLOUGH, born Park Ridge, Illinois, July 2, 1964; admitted to bar, 1993, Illinois; 1994, U.S. District Court, Northern District of Indiana; 1997, U.S. District Court, Northern District of Illinois. *Education:* Northwestern University (B.S.I.E., 1986); DePaul University (J.D., with honors, 1993). Order of the Coif. Member, DePaul Law Review. Judicial Clerk to the Honorable William C. Lee, U.S. District Court, Northern District of Indiana, 1993-1994. Member, Professional Liability Underwriting Society. *Member:* Chicago and American Bar Associations. **PRACTICE AREAS:** Environmental Insurance Coverage; Toxic Tort Insurance Coverage; Professional Liability Insurance Coverage; Excess and Reinsurance; Insurance Litigation; Reinsurance; Employment Practices Liability Insurance; Insurance Coverage; General Liability. **Email:** jclough@wwmlawyers.com

ROBERT P. CONLON, born Elgin, Illinois, April 29, 1960; admitted to bar, 1985, Illinois and U.S. District Court, Northern District of Illinois including Trial Bar. *Education:* University of South Carolina (B.S., magna cum laude, 1982); DePaul University (J.D., with honors, 1985). Phi Beta Kappa. Author, "Illinois Product Liability Practice Handbook," IICLE, 2004. *Member:* Chicago, Illinois State and American Bar Associations; Defense Research Institute. **PRACTICE AREAS:** Aviation Litigation; Aviation Insurance; Class Action Defense; Complex and Multi-District Litigation; Construction Litigation; Professional Liability Insurance Coverage; Environmental Litigation; First Party Insurance; Insurance Bad Faith; Reinsurance Arbitration; Intellectual Property Litigation. **Email:** rconlon@wwmlawyers.com

EDWARD P. GIBBONS, born Manhasset, New York, July 18, 1963; admitted to bar, 1989, Illinois and U.S. District Court, Northern District of Illinois; 2002, U.S. District Court, Central District of Illinois; 2004, U.S. District Court, Southern District of Illinois; 2005, U.S. Court of Appeals, Seventh Circuit. *Education:* College of William & Mary (B.B.A., 1985); Notre Dame University (J.D., 1989). Author: "Successor Product Liability," MADDC Product Liability Seminar; "Product Liability for Sellers of Industrial Equipment," Chicago Industrial Truck Dealers Association; "Product Liability of Sellers of Industrial Equipment," Aerial Platform Trade Association. Member, St. Procopius Legal Pro Bono Legal Services. *Member:* Chicago, McHenry County, Illinois State and American Bar Associations; Defense Research Institute. **PRACTICE AREAS:** Product Liability Defense; Negligence Defense; Tort Defense; Libel and Slander; Defamation; Personal Injury Defense; Admiralty Law. **Email:** egibbons@wwmlawyers.com

JAMES J. HUBERTY, born February 26, 1969; admitted to bar, 1998, Illinois and U.S. District Court, Northern District of Illinois. *Education:* University of Iowa (B.S., Business Administration, 1991; M.B.A./J.D., 1998). Author: "Indemnification and Insurance for Di-

(This Listing Continued)

rectors and Officers," 54-2nd Corporate Practices Series (BNA). Investment Analyst, Old Republic International, Chicago; Chief Financial Officer, Liquidsite Corporation. Member, Professional Liability Underwriting Society. *Member:* American Bar Association. ***PRACTICE AREAS:*** Directors and Officers Liability; Insurance; Employment Practices Liability Insurance; Financial Institutions Law; Insurance Agents and Brokers Errors and Omissions; Insurance Coverage Litigation. ***Email:*** jhuberty@wwmlawyers.com

CELESTE M. KING, born Evergreen Park, Illinois, July 26, 1958; admitted to bar, 1983, Illinois and U.S. District Court, Northern District of Illinois; 1990, District of Columbia. *Education:* Purdue University (B.A., 1980); Loyola University (J.D., 1983). Phi Beta Kappa. Named Distinguished Student, Purdue University. Member, Loyola Law Review, 1982-1983. Author, Note, "Family Tort Immunity Doctrine in the Third Party Product Liability Claims," Loyola University School of Law, Law Review, 1983 Spring Symposium Issue. *Member:* American Bar Association. ***PRACTICE AREAS:*** Reinsurance; Arbitration; Professional Liability; Insurance Coverage. ***Email:*** cking@wwmlawyers.com

DAVID L. KOURY, born Oak Ridge, Tennessee, December 16, 1967; admitted to bar, 1993, Illinois and U.S. District Court, Northern District of Illinois; U.S. Court of Appeals, Seventh Circuit. *Education:* University of Iowa (B.B.A., 1990; J.D., 1993). Senior Note and Comment Editor, Iowa Law Review, 1992-1993. Co-Author, "Lloyd's and the London Market: Overview and Recent Developments," Understanding Lloyd's and the London Insurance Market: 1998 Update and Outlook, PLI, 1998. Member: Chicago Volunteer Legal Services; Professional Liability Underwriting Society. *Member:* American Bar Association. ***PRACTICE AREAS:*** Insurance Coverage; Business Litigation; Directors and Officers Liability; Complex Litigation. ***Email:*** dkoury@wwmlawyers.com

GARY L. LOCKWOOD, born Woodstock, Illinois, December 3, 1946; admitted to bar, 1976, Illinois and U.S. District Court, Northern District of Illinois; 2000, U.S. Court of Appeals, Seventh Circuit; 2002, U.S. Court of Appeals, Ninth Circuit. *Education:* Iowa Wesleyan College (B.A., magna cum laude, 1969); Albert Ludwig University, Germany; Northwestern University (J.D., 1976). Blue Key. Listed in: Who's Who in America; Who's Who in American Law; Who's Who in the Midwest. Author: "An Overview of Directors' and Officers' Liability Insurance for Illinois Corporations," Corporations & Securities, Illinois State Bar Association, Vol. 28, No. 3, January, 1983; "CERCLA Targets: The Expanding Scope of Superfund," Environmental Claims Journal, Vol. 3, No. 2, Winter 1990-1991; "A Battle Joined: The Looming Reinsurance War," Environmental Claims Journal, Vol. 5, No. 2, Winter 1992-1993; "Seeking Cover in the Age of Litigation," Business Law, Vol. 9, No. 1, September-October 1999; "Entity Coverage: A Nightmare For Directors and Officers?" Journal of the Professional Liability Underwriting Society, Vol. XIII, No. 5, May 2000; "Chapter 27: Business Risk and Insurance Coverage," in "Advising Small Businesses," West Group, April 2003. Co-Author: "Chapter 7 Professional Liability (IICLE, 1982, Supp. 1986)," 1985; Chapters 1-8, "Evaluating Business Insurance," CCH Solutions for Financial Planning (Electronic Library on CD-Rom, CCH Incorporated, November 1999; "Operator Liability for Directors and Officers Under CERCLA," Environmental Claims Journal, Vol. 9, No. 1, Austin, 1 996. Co-Author: "Chapter 9 Professional Liability," (IICLE 1991); "Allocation of Defense Costs and Settlements Under D & O Policies," Newsletter of the Professional Liability Underwriting Society, Vol. IV, No. 1, January, 1991; "The Duty to Defend the Corporate Insured under a DÆ Policy," PLUS Journal, Vol. XVIII, No. 11, November 1999. School Board Member, Consolidated School District 15, McHenry, Illinois, 1974-1985. Member, Professional Liability Underwriting Society. *Member:* American Bar Association. [U.S. Army, 1970-1972, Military Police-Sergeant]. ***LANGUAGES:*** German. ***PRACTICE AREAS:*** Directors and Officers Insurance Coverage; Corporate Insurance; Environmental Insurance Coverage; School Law; School Board Liability; Public Officials Liability; Professional Liability; Insurance Coverage; Employment Practices Liability Insurance Coverage; Reinsurance. ***Email:*** glockwood@wwmlawyers.com

PAUL F. MATOUSEK, born Cleveland, Ohio, October 8, 1962; admitted to bar, 1987, Illinois and U.S. District Court, Northern District of Illinois. *Education:* Baldwin-Wallace College (B.A., summa cum laude, 1984); University of Notre Dame (J.D., 1987). Author: "Indemnification and Insurance for Directors and Officers," The Bureau of National Affairs (BNA) Corporate Practice Series. Member, Professional Liability Underwriting Society. *Member:* American Bar Association. ***PRACTICE AREAS:*** Insurance Coverage; Directors and Officers Liability; Insurance Counseling and Litigation. ***Email:*** pmatousek@wwmlawyers.com

JILL A. O'DONOVAN, born Kansas City, Missouri, October 4, 1970; admitted to bar, 1995, Illinois and U.S. District Court, Northern District of Illinois. *Education:* George Mason University (B.S., with highest distinction, 1992); University of Iowa (J.D., with distinction, 1995). Member, Van Oosterhout Memorial Moot Court Competition. Note and Comment Editor, Journal of Corporation Law. Certified: Private Pilot, 1988; Glider Rating, 1986. Author: "Federal Preemption of Aircraft Design Certification Standards After Cleveland v. Piper Aircraft Corporation: Can General Aviation Manufacturers Recover?" 19 Journal of Corporation Law 665, 1994. *Member:* American Bar Association; International Aviation Women's Association. ***REPORTED CASES:*** 304 F.Supp.2d 758; 760 NE2d 319; 125 F3d 859. ***PRACTICE AREAS:*** Aviation Law; Insurance Coverage; Insurance Litigation; Professional Liability Insurance Coverage; Reinsurance. ***Email:*** jdonovan@wwmlawyers.com

KRISTINE M. SORENSON, born Green Bay, Wisconsin, March 17, 1963; admitted to bar, 1995, Illinois and U.S. District Court, Northern District of Illinois. *Education:* University of Wisconsin (B.A., 1985); DePaul University (J.D., 1995). National Moot Court Team. Contributor, "Coverage and Liability Issue in Sexual Misconduct Claims," American Re-Insurance Company (2002). Speaker, Seminar, "The Basics of Business Interruption Insurance" (2002). *Member:* Chicago Bar Association; Professional Liability Underwriting Society. ***PRACTICE AREAS:*** Insurance Coverage Litigation. ***Email:*** ksorenson@wwmlawyers.com

DAVID E. WALKER, born Omaha, Nebraska, November 5, 1964; admitted to bar, 1989, Illinois and U.S. District Court, Northern District of Illinois. *Education:* University of Colorado (B.A., with distinction, 1986); University of Illinois (J.D., magna cum laude, 1989). Phi Beta Kappa. Harno Fellow. Dean's List. Listed in, Illinois Super Lawyers. Member: St. Procopius Legal; University of Colorado Alumni Association; University of Illinois College of Law Alumni Association. *Member:* American Bar Association (Member: Litigation Section; Tort and Insurance Practice Section); Defense Research Institute; Professional Liability Underwriting Society. ***PRACTICE AREAS:*** Insurance Coverage Litigation; Professional Liability; First Party Property; Insurance Bad Faith. ***Email:*** dwalker@wwmlawyers.com

MARK D. WILCOX, born Chicago, Illinois, May 25, 1952; admitted to bar, 1976, Illinois and U.S. District Court, Northern District of Illinois including Trial Bar, 1982; 1987, U.S. Court of Appeals, 7th Circuit; 1989, U.S. Supreme Court. *Education:* University of Notre Dame (B.B.A., with high honors, 1973); Northwestern University (J.D., 1976); The American College, CLU, 1979 and ChFC, 1992. Beta Gamma Sigma. Member, Notre Dame National Monogram Club. Listed in: Illinois Super Lawyers; Who's Who in American Law; Who's Who in Finance and Industry. *Member:* Chicago (Member, Insurance Law Committee) and American (Member, Section on: Torts and Insurance Practice) Bar Associations; Trial Lawyers Club of Chicago; Defense Research Institute; Professional Liability Underwriting Society; American Society of CLU and ChFC; The National Association of Insurance and Financial Advisors; Society of Financial Service Professionals. ***PRACTICE AREAS:*** Insurance Counseling and Litigation; Professional Liability Counseling and Litigation; General Civil Litigation; Civil Trial Practice. ***Email:*** mwilcox@wwmlawyers.com

ASSOCIATES

ERIC D. BLANCHARD
MARNIE N. BOZIC
PETER G. DANIELS
JANNIS E. GOODNOW
JAMES W. KIENZLE, JR.
TIFFANY S. SALTZMAN-JONES
KARI A. TIMM
CHRISTOPHER A. WADLEY
DOUGLAS W. WALKER

WALLENSTEIN WAGNER & ROCKEY, LTD.

Established in 1935
SUITE 5300
311 SOUTH WACKER DRIVE
CHICAGO, ILLINOIS 60606-6630
Telephone: 312-554-3300
Facsimile: 312-554-3301
Email: iplaw@wwrfirm.com
URL: http://www.wwrfirm.com

Intellectual Property and Technology Related Law including Protection and Licensing of United States and International Patent, Trademark, Copyright Trade Secret and Unfair Competition Matters and Related Litigation in the Courts and United States International Trade Commission.

DANIEL N. CHRISTUS, born 1951; admitted to bar, 1980, Wisconsin and U.S. District Court, Eastern and Western Districts of Wisconsin; 1985, Illinois and U.S. District Court, Northern District of Illinois; U.S. Court of Appeals for the Federal Circuit; registered to practice before U.S. Patent and Trademark Office. *Education:* University of Wisconsin (B.S., Ch.E., 1973; J.D., 1980). ***PRACTICE AREAS:*** Intellectual Property Law. ***Email:*** dchristus@wwrfirm.com

THOMAS C. ELLIOTT, JR., born 1955; admitted to bar, 1981, Illinois, U.S. District Court, Northern District of Illinois and U.S. Court of Appeals, Seventh Circuit; U.S. Court of Appeals, Federal Circuit; U.S. District Court, Central District of Illinois. *Education:* DePauw University (B.A., 1977); Illinois Institute of Technology, Chicago-Kent College of Law (J.D., 1981). ***PRACTICE AREAS:*** Intellectual Property Litigation; Intellectual Property Counseling. ***Email:*** telliott@wwrfirm.com

JEFFREY R. GARGANO, born 1964; admitted to bar, 1992, Illinois, U.S. District Court, Northern District of Illinois including Trial Bar; U.S. Court of Appeals for the Federal Circuit; registered to practice before the U.S. Patent and Trademark Office. *Education:* Augustana College; University of Arizona (B.S., Ch.E., 1989); Illinois Institute of Technology, Chicago-Kent College of Law (J.D., 1992). ***PRACTICE AREAS:*** Intellectual Property Law. ***Email:*** jgargano@wwrfirm.com

MATTHEW J. GRYZLO, born 1969; admitted to bar, 1997, Illinois, U.S. District Court, Northern District of Illinois, Eastern District of Wisconsin and Middle District of Florida; U.S. Court of Appeals for the Seventh Circuit and Federal Circuit; registered to practice before the U.S. Patent and Trademark Office. *Education:* University of Illinois (B.S.M.E., 1991); John Marshall Law School (J.D., cum laude, 1997). ***PRACTICE AREAS:*** Intellectual Property Law. ***Email:*** mgryzlo@wwrfirm.com

BRENT A. HAWKINS, born 1971; admitted to bar, 1997, Illinois and Supreme Court of the State of Illinois; U.S. District Court, Northern and Central Districts of Illinois and Eastern District of Wisconsin; registered to practice before U.S. Patent and Trademark Office. *Education:* University of Michigan (B.S.E., 1994); University of Illinois (J.D., 1997). Adjunct Professor of Law, Advanced Patent Law, University of Illinois Law School. ***PRACTICE AREAS:*** Intellectual Property Law. ***Email:*** bhawkins@wwrfirm.com

RICHARD C. HIMELHOCH, born 1963; admitted to bar, 1990, Wisconsin, U.S. District Court, Western District of Wisconsin, Illinois and U.S. District Court, Northern District of Illinois; 1994, U.S. Court of Appeals, Federal Circuit; registered to practice before the U.S. Patent and Trademark Office. *Education:* University of Wisconsin (B.S., Applied Mathematics, Engineering & Physics, 1987; J.D., 1990). ***PRACTICE AREAS:*** Intellectual Property Law. ***Email:*** rhimelhoch@wwrfirm.com

PETER M. KLOBUCHAR, born 1962; admitted to bar, 1996, Illinois; U.S. District Court, Northern District of Illinois; registered to practice before U.S. Patent and Trademark Office. *Education:* Purdue University (B.S., Met.E., 1987); Chicago-Kent (J.D., 1996). ***PRACTICE AREAS:*** Intellectual Property Law. ***Email:*** pklobuchar@wwrfirm.com

(This Listing Continued)

WALLENSTEIN WAGNER & ROCKEY, LTD., Chicago—Continued

LINDA A. KUCZMA, born 1956; admitted to bar, 1981, Illinois and U.S. District Court, Northern District of Illinois; U.S. Court of Appeals for the Federal Circuit, Ninth Circuit and Seventh Circuit; U.S. Supreme Court; registered to practice before the U.S. Patent and Trademark Office. *Education:* St. Mary's College (B.A., Biology, magna cum laude, 1978); Loyola University (J.D., 1981). National Chair, Saul Lefkowitz Moot Court Competition, 1999-2000. Leading American Attorney in Illinois. ***PRACTICE AREAS:*** Intellectual Property Law. ***Email:*** lkuczma@wwrfirm.com

KATHLEEN A. LYONS, born 1954; admitted to bar, 1984, Illinois, U.S. District Court, Northern District of Illinois and U.S. Court of Appeals, Federal Circuit; registered to practice before U.S. Patent and Trademark Office. *Education:* Loyola University (B.S., Chemistry, 1977); DePaul University (J.D., with honors, 1984). ***PRACTICE AREAS:*** Intellectual Property Law. ***Email:*** klyons@wwrfirm.com

MONIQUE A. MORNEAULT, born 1962; admitted to bar, 1994, Illinois; U.S. District Court, Northern District of Illinois; registered to practice before U.S. Patent and Trademark Office. *Education:* University of Illinois (B.S., Microbiology, 1984); Illinois Institute of Technology, Chicago-Kent College of Law (J.D., 1993). ***PRACTICE AREAS:*** Intellectual Property Law. ***Email:*** mmorneault@wwrfirm.com

JAMES P. MURAFF, born 1967; admitted to bar, 1994, Illinois and U.S. District Court, Northern District of Illinois; U.S. Court of Appeals for the Federal Circuit; U.S. District Court, Central District of Illinois; registered to practice before the U.S. Patent and Trademark Office. *Education:* University of Illinois (B.S., Computer Engineering, 1990); John Marshall Law School (J.D., 1994). Adjunct Professor of Law, Patent Law, Intellectual Property Law, John Marshall Law School. ***PRACTICE AREAS:*** Intellectual Property Law. ***Email:*** jmuraff@wwrfirm.com

PAUL J. NYKAZA, born 1966; admitted to bar, 1993, Illinois, U.S. District Court, Northern District of Illinois and U.S. Court of Appeals, Seventh Circuit; registered to practice before the U.S. Patent and Trademark Office. *Education:* Illinois Institute of Technology (B.S.M.E., with honors, 1988); Loyola University (J.D., 1993). ***PRACTICE AREAS:*** Intellectual Property Law. ***Email:*** pnykaza@wwrfirm.com

BRADLEY F. RADEMAKER, born 1963; admitted to bar, 1991, Illinois and U.S. District Court, Northern District of Illinois; U.S. District Court for the Eastern District of Wisconsin; U.S. Court of Appeals for the Federal Circuit; registered to practice before U.S. Patent and Trademark Office. *Education:* Millikin University (B.S., Biology, 1985); Illinois Institute of Technology, Chicago-Kent College of Law (J.D., 1991). ***PRACTICE AREAS:*** Intellectual Property Law. ***Email:*** brademaker@wwrfirm.com

KEITH V. ROCKEY, born 1941; admitted to bar, 1967, District of Columbia; 1969, Illinois and U.S. District Court, Northern District of Illinois; U.S. Court of Appeals, Seventh Circuit; U.S. Supreme Court; U.S. Court of Appeals, Sixth and Federal Circuits and U.S. District Court, Eastern District of Michigan; U.S. District Court, Eastern District of Wisconsin; registered to practice before U.S. Patent and Trademark Office. *Education:* Purdue University (B.S., Ch.E., 1963); George Washington University (J.D., with honors, 1966). Fellow, American College of Trial Lawyers. ***PRACTICE AREAS:*** Intellectual Property Law. ***Email:*** krockey@wwrfirm.com

DAVID L. SCHWARTZ, born 1970; admitted to bar, 1995, Illinois; U.S. District Court, Northern District of Illinois and U.S. Court of Appeals, Seventh Circuit; registered to practice before U.S. Patent and Trademark Office. *Education:* University of Illinois (B.S., Ch.E., with high distinction, 1992); University of Michigan (J.D., cum laude, 1995). Adjunct Professor of Law, Advanced Patent Law, University of Illinois Law School. ***PRACTICE AREAS:*** Intellectual Property Law. ***Email:*** dschwartz@wwrfirm.com

ROGER H. STEIN, born 1958; admitted to bar, 1984, Illinois and U.S. District Court, Northern District of Illinois including Trial Bar; U.S. Court of Appeals for the Federal Circuit; U.S. Court of Appeals, Seventh Circuit; U.S. Supreme Court; registered to practice before U.S. and Canadian Patent and Trademark Offices. *Education:* University of Illinois (B.S.G.E., with honors, 1981; J.D., 1984). ***PRACTICE AREAS:*** Intellectual Property Law. ***Email:*** rstein@wwrfirm.com

SIDNEY WALLENSTEIN (1907-1999)

OF COUNSEL

ROBERT E. WAGNER, born 1930; admitted to bar, 1961, Iowa; 1964, Illinois; U.S. Supreme Court; U.S. District Court, Northern District of Illinois, Trial Bar; U.S. Court of Claims; registered to practice before U.S. Patent and Trademark Office and Canadian Patent Office. *Education:* Iowa State University (B.S., in Engineering, 1957); American University (J.D., 1961). Examiner, United States Patent Office, 1957-1961.

JOSEPH T. BERNSTEIN, born 1978; admitted to bar, 2003, Illinois. *Education:* University of Michigan (B.S., Computer Science, 2000; J.D., 2002). ***Email:*** jbernstein@wwrfirm.com

AMY M. CROUT ZIEGLER, born 1974; admitted to bar, 2002, Illinois. *Education:* DePaul University (B.S., Physics, 1997; J.D., 2002). ***Email:*** acrout@wwrfirm.com

AMOL A. PARIKH, born 1979; admitted to bar, 2005, Illinois. *Education:* Purdue University (B.S.E.E., 2001); DePaul University College of Law (J.D., 2005). Member, DePaul University Law Review. ***PRACTICE AREAS:*** Intellectual Property. ***Email:*** aparikh@wwfirm.com

AVANI C. PATEL, born 1977; admitted to bar, 2003, Illinois. *Education:* North Carolina State University (B.S., Biochemistry, 2000); DePaul University (J.D., 2003). ***Email:*** apatel@wwrfirm.com

NICHOLAS C. PRUHS, born 1973; admitted to bar, 2001, Illinois and Wisconsin. *Education:* University of Detroit Mercy (B.S., Ch.E., 1998); University of Wisconsin (J.D., 2001). ***Email:*** npruhs@wwrfirm.com

(This Listing Continued)

GREGORY G. SCHLENZ, born 1977; admitted to bar, 2002, Illinois. *Education:* University of Illinois (B.S., Materials Science and Engineering, 1999; J.D., 2002). ***Email:*** gschlenz@wwrfirm.com

PETER M. SIAVELIS, born 1971; admitted to bar, 2000, Illinois. *Education:* Michigan State University (B.S.M.E., 1994); Illinois Institute of Technology, Chicago-Kent College of Law (J.D., 1999). ***Email:*** psiavelis@wwrfirm.com

MAURICE E. TEIXEIRA, born 1971; admitted to bar, 1999, Illinois. *Education:* Purdue University (B.S.C.E., 1993); University of Illinois (J.D., 1999). Engineer-in-Training, 1994. ***Email:*** mteixeira@wwrfirm.com

HARVEY L. WALNER & ASSOCIATES, LTD.

123 N. WACKER DRIVE, SUITE 880
CHICAGO, ILLINOIS 60606
Telephone: 312-782-8550
Fax: 312-782-2646
Email: jon.walner@walnerlaw.com
URL: http://www.walnerlaw.com

Construction Accidents, Heath Insurance, Long Term Care, Nursing Home Litigation, Medical Malpractice, Personal Injury, Airplane Crash Litigation, Automobile Accidents, Dog Bites, Railroad Accidents, Sexual Abuse, Slip and Fall, Wrongful Death, Products Liability, Workers Compensation.

HARVEY L. WALNER, born 1936; admitted to bar, 1962, Illinois, U.S. Court of Appeals, Seventh Circuit, and U.S. District Court, Northern, Central and Southern Districts of Illinois. *Education:* Roosevelt University (B.A.); DePaul University College of Law (LL.B.). (Retired). ***Email:*** walner@walnerlaw.com

JONATHAN E. WALNER, admitted to bar, 1988, Illinois. *Education:* University of Michigan (B.B.A., 1984); Chicago-Kent College of Law, Illinois Institute of Technology (J.D., 1987). ***PRACTICE AREAS:*** Litigation. ***Email:*** jon.walner@walnerlaw.com

SHELBY H. KANARISH, admitted to bar, 1971, Illinois; U.S. Tax Court; U.S. Court of Appeals, Seventh Circuit; U.S. District Court, Northern District of Illinois. *Education:* University of Illinois (B.S., Accountancy, 1963); DePaul University College of Law (J.D., 1971). Instructor, New Arbitrators, American Arbitration Association. Attorney, Chicago Volunteer Legal Services Foundation. Judge, Law Schools Trial Competition, American Trial Lawyers Association. Consultant, Chicago Housing Authority Resident Organization. Arbitrator for Accident Claims, American Arbitration Association. *Member:* Chicago, Illinois State and American Bar Associations; Illinois Trial Lawyers Association; The Association of Trial Lawyers of America. (Also Member, Shelby H. Kanarish, P.C.). ***REPORTED CASES:*** Roy Gerald Hamrick v. Dennis Lewis, 515 F.Supp. 983 (U.S. Dis. N.D. of Ill. 1981). ***PRACTICE AREAS:*** Medical Malpractice; Police Brutality; Discrimination; Personal Injury. ***Email:*** shelby@walnerlaw.com

DEBRA I. CRYSTAL, admitted to bar, 1986, Illinois. *Education:* University of Illinois (B.A., History, 1983); John Marshall Law School (J.D., 1986). ***PRACTICE AREAS:*** Plaintiffs Personal Injury. ***Email:*** debrac@winstarmail.com

---

MARVIN S. LANSKY

CHRISTOPHER G. WALSH, JR.

Established in 2003
111 WEST WASHINGTON STREET, SUITE 1150
CHICAGO, ILLINOIS 60602
Telephone: 312-372-1155
Fax: 312-372-1974
Email: cgw@chriswalshlaw.com
URL: http://www.chriswalshlaw.com

Oak Park Office: 1111 South Boulevard, 60302. Telephone: 708-386-4571. Fax: 708-386-8413.

Property Tax Appeals and Civil Litigation.

CHRISTOPHER G. WALSH, JR., born Binghamton, New York, December 16, 1948; admitted to bar, 1976, Illinois; 1977, U.S. District Court, Northern District of Illinois and U.S. Court of Appeals, Seventh Circuit; 1983, U.S. Supreme Court. *Education:* Loyola University (A.B., Classics Honors, cum laude, 1970); University of Illinois-Springfield (M.A., 1972); New York University (J.D., cum laude, 1976, Order of the Coif). Law Clerk, Chief Justice Warren E. Burger, U.S. Supreme Court, 1978-1979; Law Clerk, Judge William J. Bauer, United States Court of Appeals, Seventh Circuit, 1976-1978. Managing Editor, New York University Law Review, 1975-1976. *Member:* Chicago and American Bar Associations. ***PRACTICE AREAS:*** Civil Litigation; Property Tax Appeals.

REPRESENTATIVE CLIENTS: Chicagoland Chamber of Commerce; Building Owners and Managers Association of Chicago; Chicago Development Council; INR Beatty Lumber Corp.; General Media Corp.; Teamsters Local 786 Lumber Employees Pension Fund.

LAW OFFICES OF LAURIE J. WASSERMAN

CHICAGO, ILLINOIS

(See Skokie)

Employment, Employment Discrimination, Employee and Employer Rights, Sexual Harassment, Americans With Disabilities Act, Family and Medical Leave Act, Whistle Blower Cases, Severance Agreements, Non-Compete Agreements, Retaliation.

WATSON-WESLEY COLEMAN, L.C.

CHICAGO, ILLINOIS

(See St. Louis)

Criminal Law, Driving While Intoxicated, Drug Crimes, Felonies, Homicide, Juvenile Law, Misdemeanors, Parole and Probation, Sexual Assault, Traffic Violations, Family Law, Personal Injury, Automobile Accidents, Dog Bites, Slip and fall, Wrongful Death, Real Estate, Trusts and Estates, Estate Planning, Wills and Probate, Business Law.

WEAVER LAW GROUP, LLC

549 WEST RANDOLPH STREET, SUITE 400
CHICAGO, ILLINOIS 60661
Telephone: 312-876-3686
Fax: 312-876-3680
Email: lramirez@weaverlawgroup.com
URL: http://www.weaverlawgroup.com

Regulatory and Administrative Practice to the Food, Drug, Cosmetic, Device and Dietary Supplement Industry. Trademark and Copyright Practice, Direct Sales, Telemarketing, Network Marketing, US Customs, Federal Trade Commission, Civil Litigation and Business Transactions.

MEMBERS OF THE FIRM

KAREN A. WEAVER, born Cleveland, Ohio, May 9, 1958; admitted to bar, 1994, Illinois and U.S. District Court, Northern District of Illinois; 1995, U.S. Court of Appeals, Tenth Circuit. *Education:* University of Toledo (B.S., Pharmacy, 1984); DePaul University (J.D., 1994). Author, "Cosmetic Label Regulations - Truth or Consequences", Global Cosmetic Industry. Registered Pharmacist, Illinois and Ohio, 1984. Secretary, Evening Law Student Society, 1993-1994. *Member:* Chicago (Member, Food, Drug and Consumer Product Regulatory Law Committee) and American Bar Associations; American Society of Pharmacy Law; National Nutritional Foods Association; American Herbal Products Association, Institute of Food Technologists. [Specialist 5, U.S. Army, 1976-1979]. ***PRACTICE AREAS:*** Food, Drug and Cosmetic Law; Federal Practice; Direct Marketing; Advertising Law; Promotion Law; Pesticide Regulation; Pharmacy Law; Trademarks; Civil Practice.

JAMES M. LANCHEROS, admitted to bar, 2001, Illinois. *Education:* Indiana University (B.A., Journalism, 1996); DePaul University College of Law (J.D., 2001). *Member:* Chicago, Illinois State, American and Hispanic Bar Associations. ***PRACTICE AREAS:*** Trademark Law; Copyright Licensing; Copyright Prosecution; Regulatory Compliance; Commercial Litigation; Direct Marketing; Advertising Law; Promotion Law.

Language: Spanish.

WEBSTER WILCOX CHRISTOPOULOS P.C.

320 WEST OHIO, SUITE 501
CHICAGO, ILLINOIS 60610
Telephone: 312-587-8800
Fax: 312-587-8808
Email: jwebster@wwclaw.com
URL: http://www.wwclaw.com

Beverage, Alcohol and Hospitality Industry Practice, including, Federal and State Alcoholic Beverage Regulation and Trade Practice, Administrative Hearings and Appeals, Excise and Sales Tax Litigation, Commercial Litigation, Commercial Transactions, Mergers and Acquisitions and Licensure.

JAMES L. WEBSTER, born Two Rivers, Wisconsin, April 20, 1953; admitted to bar, 1982, Illinois and U.S. District Court, Eastern District of Illinois; 1983, Wisconsin and U.S. Court of Appeals, Seventh Circuit; 1984, U.S. District Court, Eastern District of Wisconsin; 1987, U.S. Supreme Court; 1990, U.S. Tax Court. *Education:* University of Wisconsin (B.A., 1979); DePaul University (J.D., 1982). *Member:* Chicago, Illinois State, Wisconsin State and American (Member, Sections on: Litigation; Corporation, Banking and Business Law; Co-Chair, Alcoholic Beverages Practice Committee, 2000-2001) Bar Associations. ***PRACTICE AREAS:*** Alcoholic Beverages; Trade Practice; Excise Tax; Sales Tax Litigation. ***Email:*** jwebster@wwclaw.com

MARK WILCOX, born Chicago, Illinois, September 20, 1956; admitted to bar, 1982, Illinois. *Education:* University of Illinois (B.S., Accountancy, 1979); DePaul University (J.D., 1982); John Marshall University (LL.M., in Commercial Real Estate with honors, 1996). Phi Eta Sigma. Recipient, John Marshall Law School Excellence for the Future Award - Commercial Property Finance. Co-Author: "An Economic Analysis of Incest: Prohibition, Behavior and Punishment," St. Louis University Law Journal, Vol. 24 No. 4, 1982. *Member:* Chicago, Illinois and American Bar Associations. ***PRACTICE AREAS:*** Alcoholic Beverages; Commercial Transactions; Mergers and Acquisitions. ***Email:*** mwilcox@wwclaw.com

DIMITRIOS G. CHRISTOPOULOS, born Oak Park, Illinois, September 28, 1967; admitted to bar, 1992, Illinois and U.S. District Court, Northern District of Illinois; 1993, U.S. Court of Appeals, Seventh Circuit. *Education:* Loyola University (B.A., 1989); John Marshall Law School (J.D., cum laude, 1992). Member, John Marshall Law Review, 1991-1992. *Member:* Chicago, Illinois, American and Hellenic Bar Associations; Hellenic Professional Society. ***LANGUAGES:*** Greek. ***PRACTICE AREAS:*** Alcoholic Beverages; Commercial Litigation; Administrative Law Litigation. ***Email:*** dchristopoulos@wwclaw.com

HARLAN C. POWELL, born Las Cruces, New Mexico, September 17, 1969; admitted to bar, 1998, Illinois. *Education:* Northwestern University (B.A., 1992); McGeorge School of Law, University of the Pacific (J.D., 1997). ***PRACTICE AREAS:*** Alcoholic Beverages; Commercial Litigation; Administrative Law Litigation. ***Email:*** hpowell@wwclaw.com

REPRESENTATIVE CLIENTS: List Available Upon Request.

LAW OFFICES OF STEVEN C. WEISS

CHICAGO, ILLINOIS

(See Northbrook)

Logistics and Supply Chains, Third Party Supplier Contracting, Freight Forwarding, Freight Brokers, Admiralty and Maritime Law, Business Transactions, Corporate Law, Inland Marine Law, Marine Cargo, Air Cargo, Freight Loss and Damage, Insurance Coverage Disputes, Interstate Commerce, Motor Carrier Defense, Motor Carrier Liability, Shipping Regulation, Surface Transportation.

WELSH & KATZ, LTD.

120 SOUTH RIVERSIDE PLAZA
22ND FLOOR
CHICAGO, ILLINOIS 60606-3912
Telephone: 312-655-1500
Fax: 312-655-1501
URL: http://www.welshkatz.com

Arlington, Virginia Office: Crystal Plaza One, Suite 311, 2001 Jefferson Davis Highway, 22202-3603. Telephone: 703-415-4777.

Technology and Intellectual Property Law including Patent, Trademark, Copyright, Trade Secret, Unfair Competition and Related Antitrust Law, and Trials and Appeals.

FIRM PROFILE: Welsh & Katz, Ltd. is a full-service intellectual property law firm that focuses on technology and intellectual property law including patent, trademark, copyright, trade secret, unfair competition and related antitrust law, and trials and appeals. Its distinguished domestic and international clients have recognized the Firm for its counseling, strategic planning and litigation skills. The Firm's attorneys have educational backgrounds and experience in virtually all major areas of science and technology.

A. SIDNEY KATZ, born Melrose Park, Illinois, October 10, 1939; admitted to bar, 1966, Illinois; 1977, U.S. Supreme Court; 1991, District of Columbia; registered to practice before U.S. Patent and Trademark Office. *Education:* Illinois Institute of Technology (B.S.E.E., 1962); George Washington University (J.D., 1966). Tau Beta Pi; Eta Kappa Nu; Delta Theta Phi. Member, Advisory Board, The Licensing Journal, 1987—; Editorial Board, Mealey's Litigation Reports on Intellectual Property, 1992—; The IP Litigator. Co-Author: "Effective Litigation Against Knock-Offs," 3 Vols., 1983, "Chip, Mask & Program Protection," 1985, "Electronics & Computer Patent Practice," 1986, and "Electronics & Computer Patent & Copyright Practice," 2 Vols, 1987, 1990. Patent Examiner, U.S. Patent and Trademark Office, 1962-1965. *Member:* Chicago, Illinois State, and American Bar Associations; American Intellectual Property Law Association; Intellectual Property Law Association of Chicago; Licensing Executives Society; International Trademark Association; Institute of Electrical and Electronic Engineers; Union League Club of Chicago; American Friends of Hebrew University (Executive Committee, Midwest Region); The Standard Club of Chicago; Association of Patent Law Firms (President, 1999); George Washington University IP Advisory Board. (Managing Partner). ***PRACTICE AREAS:*** Intellectual Property. ***Email:*** askatz@welshkatz.com

RICHARD L. WOOD, born Detroit, Michigan, March 24, 1935; admitted to bar, 1964, Virginia and District of Columbia; 1966, Illinois; U.S. District Court, Northern District of Illinois including Trial Bar; U.S. Court of Appeals, Seventh, District of Columbia and Federal Circuits; registered to practice before U.S. Patent and Trademark Office. *Education:* University of Michigan (B.S.M.E., 1958; M.B.A., 1959); George Washington University (J.D., 1964). Delta Theta Phi. Law Clerk, Hon. Donald E. Lane, U.S. Court of Claims, 1964-1965. *Member:* Chicago and American Bar Associations; Virginia State Bar; Bar Association of the District of Columbia; Intellectual Property Law Association of Chicago (Treasurer, 1975-1977; Member, Board of Managers, 1992-1994); American Intellectual Property Law Association; The Lawyers Club of Chicago. ***PRACTICE AREAS:*** Intellectual Property. ***Email:*** rlwood@welshkatz.com

JEROLD B. SCHNAYER, born Chicago, Illinois, October 30, 1950; admitted to bar, 1977, Illinois; registered to practice before U.S. Patent and Trademark Office. *Education:* University of Illinois (B.S.E.E., 1972); Illinois Institute of Technology/Chicago-Kent College of Law (J.D., with honors, 1977). Lecturer, Patent Resources Group. *Member:* Chicago and Illinois State Bar Associations; Intellectual Property Law Association of Chicago. ***PRACTICE AREAS:*** Intellectual Property. ***Email:*** jbschnayer@welshkatz.com

JOSEPH R. MARCUS, born New York, N.Y., March 5, 1936; admitted to bar, 1965, Illinois and U.S. District Court, Northern District of Illinois; registered to practice before U.S. Patent and Trademark Office. *Education:* Carnegie-Mellon University (B.S. Ch.E., 1958); Illinois Institute of Technology/Chicago-Kent College of Law (J.D., 1965). *Member:* American Bar Association; American Intellectual Property Law Association. ***PRACTICE AREAS:*** Intellectual Property. ***Email:*** jrmarcus@welshkatz.com

GERALD S. SCHUR, born Chicago, Illinois, April 14, 1935; admitted to bar, 1963, Illinois and U.S. District Court, Northern and Central Districts of Illinois, including Trial Bar; U.S. Court of Appeals, Seventh and Federal Circuits; registered to practice before U.S. Patent and Trademark Office. *Education:* Purdue University (B.S. Ch.E., 1957); John Marshall Law School (J.D., 1963; M.P.L., 1968). *Member:* North Suburban, Illinois State and American Bar Associations; Intellectual Property Law Association of Chicago; Decalogue Society (President, 1999-2000). ***PRACTICE AREAS:*** Intellectual Property. ***Email:*** gsschur@welshkatz.com

GERALD T. SHEKLETON, born Phillipsburg, New Jersey, October 1, 1947; admitted to bar, 1973, Ohio; 1975, Illinois; registered to practice before U.S. Patent and Trademark Office. *Education:* Xavier University (B.S. in Chem., 1969); Cleveland State Univer-

(This Listing Continued)

WELSH & KATZ, LTD., Chicago—Continued

sity (J.D., 1973). *Member:* Chicago (Chairman: Intellectual Property Law Committee, 1980-1982; Copyright Committee, 1981-1982; Trademark Subcommittee, PTC Committee, 1982-1983), DuPage County and American Bar Associations; International Association for the Protection of Industrial Property; American Chemical Society; Intellectual Property Law Association of Chicago (Chairman, Copyright Committee, 1980, 1985). ***PRACTICE AREAS:*** Patents; International Patents; Trademarks; International Trademarks; Copyrights. **Email:** gtshekleton@welshkatz.com

JAMES A. SCHEER, born St. Joseph, Michigan, June 30, 1947; admitted to bar, 1978, Illinois and U.S. District Court, Northern District of Illinois and U.S. Court of Appeals for the Federal Circuit; registered to practice before U.S. Patent and Trademark Office. *Education:* University of Notre Dame (B.S., Eng. Sci., 1969; M.S.E.E., 1970); Northern Illinois University (J.D., 1978); John Marshall Law School (LL.M., Intellectual Property, 1991). Tau Beta Pi. Adjunct Professor of Intellectual Property, John Marshall Law School. *Member:* Intellectual Property Law Association of Chicago; Institute of Electrical and Electronic Engineers. ***PRACTICE AREAS:*** Intellectual Property. **Email:** jascheer@welshkatz.com

DANIEL R. CHERRY, born Minneapolis, Minnesota, December 31, 1948; admitted to bar, 1976, Ohio; 1987, Illinois and U.S. District Court, Northern District of Illinois including Trial Bar; U.S. Court of Appeals for the Federal Circuit; registered to practice before U.S. Patent and Trademark Office. *Education:* Massachusetts Institute of Technology (B.S., 1970); Harvard Law School (J.D., cum laude, 1976). Co-Author: *Patent Practice* (PRI 1997). *Member:* Chicago, Illinois State, Ohio State and American Bar Associations; American Intellectual Property Law Association; Federal Circuit Bar Association; Licensing Executives Society; Intellectual Property Law Association of Chicago. [U.S. Coast Guard, active duty, 1970-1973]. ***PRACTICE AREAS:*** Intellectual Property. **Email:** drcherry@welshkatz.com

ROBERT B. BREISBLATT, born Detroit, Michigan, September 22, 1948; admitted to bar, 1972, Florida; 1975, U.S. District Court, Southern District of Florida, U.S. Court of Appeals, Sixth Circuit and U.S. Supreme Court; 1976, Illinois; 1978, U.S. District Court, Northern District of Illinois including Trial Bar and U.S. Court of Appeals, Seventh Circuit; 1997, U.S. Court of Appeals for the Federal Circuit. *Education:* Florida State University (B.A., 1969); Duke University (J.D., 1972). Assistant U.S. Attorney, Northern District of Illinois, 1978-1987, Civil Division, 1978-1980, Criminal and Special Prosecutions Division, 1981-1987. Adjunct Professor of Law, IIT-Chicago Kent Law School for Trial Practice, 1991-1992. *Member:* Chicago, Illinois State, Federal and American Bar Associations; The Florida Bar. [U.S. Army, Active Duty, 1972-1974]. ***PRACTICE AREAS:*** Intellectual Property; Civil Trial Practice. **Email:** rbbreisblatt@welshkatz.com

JAMES P. WHITE, born Boston, Massachusetts, July 12, 1946; admitted to bar, 1973, Massachusetts; 1974, Illinois and U.S. District Court, Northern District of Illinois including Trial Bar; 1980, U.S. Court of Appeals, Seventh and District of Columbia Circuits and U.S. Supreme Court. *Education:* Michigan State University (B.S., 1969); Suffolk University Law School (J.D., 1973). Assistant U.S. Attorney, Northern District of Illinois, 1979-1987. Member, Human Relations Commission, Evanston, Illinois, 1976-1980. *Member:* Chicago, Federal and American Bar Associations; Intellectual Property Owners Association (Vice-Chair, Copyright Piracy and International Laws Committee). ***PRACTICE AREAS:*** Trademarks; Copyrights; Patent Litigation. **Email:** jpwhite@welshkatz.com

R. MARK HALLIGAN, born Cleveland, Ohio, September 11, 1953; admitted to bar, 1978, Ohio; 1979, U.S. District Court, Southern District of Ohio; 1984, U.S. District Court, Northern District of Ohio; 1988, U.S. Court of Appeals, Sixth Circuit; 1989, Illinois and U.S. District Court, Northern District of Illinois including Trial Bar; 1990, U.S. District Court, Northern District of California; 1991, U.S. Court of Appeals for the Federal and Seventh Circuits; 1992, U.S. District Court, Eastern District of Wisconsin; 2005, U.S. Supreme Court. *Education:* University of Cincinnati (B.A., summa cum laude, 1975); Northwestern University (J.D., 1978). Phi Beta Kappa. Articles Editor, Journal of Criminal Law and Criminology, 1977-1978. Author: "GTE Sylvania, The Case for Overruling Albrecht v. Herald Co.," 39 Ohio State Law Journal 196, 1978; "The Hidden Truth Behind Thermography," For The Defense, Defense Research Institute, Vol. 31, No. III 12-16, November 1989; "Cross Examination Of An Expert Witness," For The Defense, Defense Research Institute, Vol. 32, No. 9, 29-32, September 1990; "How to Identify and Protect Trade Secrets: The Illinois Trade Secrets Act," Ill. Inst. for CLE, 1992; "Protection of Trade Secrets: The Illinois Trade Secrets Act," DCBA Brief, DuPage County Bar Association Vol. 4, Issue 5 (May/June 1992); "PepsiCo, Inc. vs. Redmond: The Seventh Circuit"s Position on Threatened Misappropriation of Trade Secrets," DCBA Brief, Vol. 8, Issue 2 (December 1995); "Trade Secrets: Increasing Globalization, Corporate Demands Fuel Trend Toward Greater Protection," EuroWatch, Vol. 7, No. 20 (January, 1996); "The Economic Espionage Act of 1996," The National Law Journal, Vol. 19, No. 15 (December, 1996); "How Technology Escrow Accounts Can Protect Computer Software," The Intellectual Property Strategist, Vol. 3, No. 4 (January, 1997); "The Theft of Trade Secrets is Now a Federal Crime," Competitive Intelligence Review, Vol. 8(3) 7-12 (1997); "R. Mark Halligan, Esq. Trade Secrets Case Digest," James Publishing, Inc. (1999); "Safeguarding Secrets: Twelve Predictions for Trade Secret Law in The New Economy," Corporate Counsel Magazine, 44-46 (January, 2000); "Computers Spark Surge in Use of Trade Secrets," The National Law Journal, C12-13 (January 31, 2000); "Seven Safe Harbor Principles vs. Trade Secret Rights," The National Law Journal, Intellectual Property Section, C14-C15, C20 (December 18, 2000); "The Bite of Carnivore: Dark Days for Privacy," IP Worldwide, American Lawyers Media Publication pp. 48-53 (February, 2001); "Do Your Secrets Pass the Test?—Special Focus on Information Protection," Security Management (ISSN 145-9406) Volume 45, No. 3 American Society for Industrial Security (ASIS) pp. 53-58 (March 2001); "Trade Secrets and the Inevitable Disclosure Doctrine," National Legal Center for the Public Interest, www.nlcpi-.org., Vol. 5, No. 10 (October 2001); "Protecting Trade Secrets Online," Business, Law & The Internet (Chapter 14), Illinois Institute for Continuing Legal Education (IICLE) (2002 Edition); "Trade Secrets Case Digest," James Publishing, Inc. ISBN 1-58012-049-0 (1999); *"The Sorry State of Trade Secret Protection," (with Richard F. Weyand),* The Corporate Counsellor, Vol. 16, No. 3 (August 2001); "Want to Trade Secrets?" American Society for Industrial Security (ASIS), Security Management Magazine, Vol. 47, No. 1, pp. 67-75 (January 2003); "How to Identify and Protect Trade Secret Assets in the Information Age," BlueCross/BlueShield Association, Legal Affairs Bulletin, No. 932 (September 2003); "United States: The Identification and Protection of Trade Secrets," IP Value 2004: Building and Enforcing Intellectual Property Value, An International Guide for the Boardroom, ISBN 0-9535346-9-6 Globe White Page Ltd. (2004); "The Brave New World of Electronic Evidence Discovery," Illinois Bar Journal, Vol. 92, No. 6, p. 296 (June 2004); "Chapter 9: The Economic Valuation of Trade Secret Assets," (with Richard F. Weyand), Intellectual Property Valuation Primer, Fundamentals of Intellectual Property Valuation, American Bar Association, Intellectual Property Law (IPL) Section ISBN: 1-59031-430-1 Product Code: 5370143 (2005); "Duty to Identify, Protect Trade Secrets Has Arisen," The National Law Journal, Vol. 27, No. 52, p. S3 (August 29, 2005). Faculty: National Institute for Trial Advocacy, Midwest Regional, 1990—; The Centre; Operational Business Intelligence (Sarasota, Florida) www.the-centre.org/faculty.html. Adjunct Faculty, Center for Intellectual Property Law, John Marshall Law School, Advanced Trade Secrets Law and Trade Secrets Litigation. Part-Time Faculty, College of DuPage, Business and Professional Institute. Member, Board of Editorial Advisors: Intellectual Property LAWCAST, Vox Juris, Inc.; American Law and Policy Foundation (ALPF) www.legalpolicy.org. Round Table Scholar, Round Table Group www.roundtablegroup.com (Think Tank for professors and business thought leaders). WIPO Arbitration and Mediation Center-Domain Name Panel, www.arbiter.wipo.int/domains, 2002—. *Member:* Chicago, DuPage County, Ohio State, Illinois State (Member, Intellectual Property Law Section) and American (Member, Sections on: Antitrust Law; Business; Patent, Trademark and Copyright; Litigation; Chairman, ABA Intellectual Property Law Section, Committee 410, Trade Secrets and Interference with Contracts 1999-2001, Committee No. 403, Inequitable Conduct, 2001-2002, Committee No. 459, Special Committee on the Management of IP Assets, 2002-2003, Committee No. 408 Small Business, 2003-2005, Co-Chairman, Committee No. 410, Trade Secrets and Tortious Interference with Contracts, 2005-2006) Bar Associations; American Intellectual Property Law Association (Member, Trade Secret and Related Unfair Competition Committee); Intellectual Property Law Association of Chicago (Member, Board of Managers, 1992-1994; Secretary, 1994-1996; Vice-President, 1999-2000; President-Elect, 2000-2001; President, 2001-2002; Chairman, Trade Secret and Unfair Competition Committee, 1989-1992, 1996—); Licensing Executives Society, LES (Co-Chairman, Trade Secret Licensing Committee, 1997—); Leading Lawyer Network, The Top Lawyers in Intellectual Property Law, Law Bulletin Publishing Company, www.LeadingLawyers.com (2004); Illinois Super Lawyers List, Intellectual Property Litigation and Intellectual Property Law, www.superlawyers.com (2005); The Best Attorneys Network, www.bestattorneysnetwork.com. American Bar Foundation. ***PRACTICE AREAS:*** Intellectual Property. **Email:** rmhalligan@welshkatz.com

HARTWELL P. MORSE, III, born Brooklyn, New York, January 4, 1957; admitted to bar, 1982, Kentucky; 1983, U.S. District Court, Western District of Kentucky; 1984, U.S. District Court, Eastern District of Kentucky and U.S. Court of Appeals, Sixth Circuit; 1986, U.S. Court of Appeals for the Federal Circuit; 1988, Illinois; 1989, U.S. District Court, Northern District of Illinois. *Education:* Denison University (B.A., with honors, 1979); Dayton Law School (J.D., magna cum laude, 1982). Phi Alpha Delta. *Member:* Chicago, Kentucky and American Bar Associations; Federal Circuit Bar Association; American Intellectual Property Law Association. ***PRACTICE AREAS:*** Intellectual Property. **Email:** hpmorse@welshkatz.com

EDWARD P. GAMSON, born Chicago, Illinois, April 14, 1943; admitted to bar, 1978, Illinois; registered to practice before U.S. Patent and Trademark Office. *Education:* Trinity College (B.S., 1965); Northwestern University (Ph.D., 1970); John Marshall Law School (J.D., with distinction, 1978). *Member:* Association of University Technology Managers; Licensing Executives Society; American Chemical Society; Illinois State and American Bar Associations. ***PRACTICE AREAS:*** Intellectual Property. **Email:** epgamson@welshkatz.com

KARA EVE FOSTER CENAR, born Worcester, Massachusetts, April 4, 1963; admitted to bar, 1988, Illinois, U.S. District Court, Northern District of Illinois including Trial Bar and U.S. Court of Appeals, Seventh Circuit; 1993, U.S. Court of Appeals for the Federal Circuit, United States Supreme Court and U.S. Court of Federal Claims. *Education:* Loyola University (B.B.A., 1985; J.D., 1988). *Member:* Chicago and American Bar Associations. ***PRACTICE AREAS:*** Intellectual Property. **Email:** kecenar@welshkatz.com

KATHLEEN A. RHEINTGEN, born Dallas, Texas, April 5, 1963; admitted to bar, 1988, Illinois, U.S. District Court, Northern District of Illinois and U.S. Court of Appeals, Seventh Circuit; 1990, U.S. Court of Appeals for the Federal Circuit; registered to practice before U.S. Patent and Trademark Office. *Education:* University of Illinois (B.S., 1985); Loyola University (J.D., 1988). ***PRACTICE AREAS:*** Intellectual Property. **Email:** karheintgen@welshkatz.com

THOMAS W. TOLPIN, born Chicago, Illinois, July 15, 1945; admitted to bar, 1970, District of Columbia, Illinois; U.S. Court of Appeals for the Federal Circuit; U.S. Supreme Court; registered to practice before the U.S. Patent and Trademark Office. *Education:* University of Illinois (B.S., 1967); American University (J.D., 1970). Pi Tau Sigma, Tau Beta Pi, Phi Alpha Delta. *Member:* Chicago and American Bar Associations; American Intellectual Property Law Association; Intellectual Property Law Association of Chicago (Vice Chairman, U.S. Trademark Committee, 2000-2003; Chairman, Intellectual Property Licensing and Franchise Committee, 1999-2000; Member, Board of Managers, 1994-1995; Vice Chairman, Patent & Trademark Practice Committee; Chairman, Intellectual Property Tax Committee, 1990-1991, 1983-1984); Licensing Executives Society; International Trademark Association. [U.S. Navy, JAGC, Lieutenant, 1970-1974]. ***PRACTICE AREAS:*** Intellectual Property. **Email:** twtolpin@welshkatz.com

RICHARD W. McLAREN, JR., born Cincinnati, Ohio, May 15, 1945; admitted to bar, 1973, Ohio and U.S. District Court, Northern District of Ohio; 1978, U.S. Court of Appeals, Sixth Circuit; 1981, U.S. Supreme Court; 1997, Illinois and U.S. District Court, Northern District of Illinois including Trial Bar and U.S. Court of Appeals, Seventh Circuit; 1998, U.S. Court of Appeals for the Federal Circuit. *Education:* Yale University (B.A., 1967); Northwestern University (J.D., 1973). *Member:* Chicago, Illinois State (Member, Intellectual Property Law Section), Ohio State, Federal and American (Member, Sections on: Litigation; Intellectual Property Law; Business Law; Tort and Insurance Practice) Bar Associations; Federal Circuit Bar Association (Member, Intellectual Property Law Section); American Intellectual Property Law Association; Intellectual Property Law Associa-

(This Listing Continued)

tion of Chicago; American Judicature Society. [1st Lt., U.S. Army, 1967-1970]. ***PRACTICE AREAS:*** Intellectual Property; Civil Trial Practice. ***Email:*** rwmclaren@welshkatz.com

ELLIOTT C. BANKENDORF, born Chicago, Illinois, May 16, 1945; admitted to bar, 1969, Illinois; 1970, U.S. Tax Court and U.S. District Court, Northern District of Illinois. *Education:* DePaul University (B.S.C., 1966); University of Illinois (J.D., 1969); John Marshall Law School. Phi Alpha Delta. Certified Public Accountant, Illinois, 1968. Member, Private Practice Committee, Illinois Legal Needs Study. *Member:* Chicago (Chair, Corp. Law Depts. Committee, 1988-1989) and Illinois State Bar Associations; Intellectual Property Law Association of Chicago (Chair, U.S. Trademark Committee, 2005—; Member, International Trademark Committees); International Trademark Association (Member: International Trademark Committee, 1991; Finance Committee, 1992-2001; Meetings Committee, 2002-2003; Member Services Committee, 2004—; Board of Directors, 1994-1997). ***PRACTICE AREAS:*** Intellectual Property. ***Email:*** ecbankendorf@welshkatz.com

MITCHELL J. WEINSTEIN, born Bronx, New York, November 20, 1958; admitted to bar, 1993, Illinois and U.S. District Court, Northern District of Illinois; 1994, U.S. Court of Appeals, 7th Circuit; registered to practice before U.S. Patent and Trademark Office. *Education:* State University of New York (B.S.Ch.E., 1980); John Marshall Law School (J.D., cum laude, 1993). Giles Rich Moot Court National Championship, 1992. Professional Engineer, New York, Illinois, Michigan and Wisconsin. *Member:* American Bar Association; American Intellectual Property Law Association; Intellectual Property Law Association of Chicago. ***PRACTICE AREAS:*** Intellectual Property. ***Email:*** mjweinstein@welshkatz.com

ERIC D. COHEN, born New York, N.Y., June 10, 1955; admitted to bar, 1993, Illinois and U.S. District Court, Northern District of Illinois; 1998, U.S. Court of Appeals for the Federal Circuit; registered to practice before U.S. Patent and Trademark Office. *Education:* State University of New York at Buffalo (B.S.E.E., 1977); Pace University (M.S., computer science, with distinction, 1984); University of Dayton (J.D., 1993). Phi Alpha Delta. Co-Author: "U.S. Preliminary Injunction Granted Though French Counterpart Invalidated," Managing Intellectual Property - IP Strategy Yearbook, 1999. *Member:* Chicago and Illinois State Bar Associations; Intellectual Property Law Association of Chicago; American Intellectual Property Law Association; The Decalogue Society of Lawyers. ***PRACTICE AREAS:*** Intellectual Property. ***Email:*** edcohen@welshkatz.com

JOHN L. AMBROGI, born Evanston, Illinois, September 8, 1965; admitted to bar, 1990, Illinois, U.S. District Court, Northern District of Illinois including Trial Bar and U.S. Court of Appeals for the Federal Circuit. *Education:* Loyola University (B.S., cum laude, 1987; J.D., 1990). Alpha Sigma Nu. Co-Author: "Intellectual Property Rights and The Internet: The NSI Policy and Recent Case Law," Spring 1997. Author: "The Death Knell of Trademarks." *Member:* Chicago and American (Member, Tort and Insurance Practice Section) Bar Associations; Justinian Law Society; Intellectual Property Law Association of Chicago. ***LANGUAGES:*** Italian. ***PRACTICE AREAS:*** Intellectual Property. ***Email:*** jambrogi@welshkatz.com

JULIE A. KATZ, born Washington, D.C., April 15, 1965; admitted to bar, 1990, Illinois, U.S. District Court, Northern District of Illinois and U.S. Court of Appeals for the Federal and Seventh Circuits; 1991, U.S. Court of Appeals, Sixth Circuit; 1992, Tennessee, U.S. District Court, Eastern and Middle Districts of Tennessee. *Education:* Indiana University (B.A., 1987); University of Illinois (J.D., 1990). Recipient, Omicron Nu Scholarship. Author: "Civil Contempt/Copyright/Damages," July, 1989. Co-Author: "Protection of Trade Secrets: Parts I and II," Fall 1994, Spring 1995; "Intellectual Property Rights and The Internet: The NSI Policy and Recent Case Law," Spring 1997; "Battling the 'CompanyNameSucks.com' Cyberactivists," Intellectual Property & Technology Law Journal, Vol. 13, No. 3, March 2001. Speaking Engagements: Licensing Executive Society 2004 Spring Meeting, "Madrid Protocol: Successful Implementation in the U.S.?" (May 2004); ALI-ABA Intellectual Property Licensing Today Meeting, "Licensing—The Business Perspective: Why License/Accept a License for Use of IP," (August 2004). *Member:* Chicago, Illinois State and American Bar Associations; International Trademark Association; Brand Names Education Foundation (Past Chair, Saul Lefkowitz Moot Court Competition). ***PRACTICE AREAS:*** Intellectual Property. ***Email:*** jakatz@welshkatz.com

JON P. CHRISTENSEN, born Stoughton, Wisconsin, January 9, 1948; admitted to bar, 1989, Illinois and U.S. District Court, Northern District of Illinois; registered to practice before U.S. Patent and Trademark Office. *Education:* University of Wisconsin (B.S.E.E., 1972); Purdue University (B.S.M.E., 1983); John Marshall Law School (J.D., 1989; LL.M., 1995). Licensed Professional Engineer (Illinois), 1976-1989. *Member:* Chicago, Illinois State and American Bar Associations. ***PRACTICE AREAS:*** Intellectual Property. ***Email:*** jpchristensen@welshkatz.com

WALTER J. KAWULA, JR., born Lake Forest, Illinois, September 17, 1963; admitted to bar, 1994, Illinois and U.S. District Court, Northern District of Illinois; 2001, U.S. Court of Appeals for the Federal Circuit; registered to practice before U.S. Patent and Trademark Office. *Education:* University of Illinois (B.S.E.E., 1985); Chicago-Kent College of Law, Illinois Institute of Technology (J.D., with high honors, 1994). Order of the Coif. *Member:* Chicago and American Bar Associations. ***PRACTICE AREAS:*** Intellectual Property. ***Email:*** wjkawula@welshkatz.com

LEONARD FRIEDMAN, born Brooklyn, New York, December 5, 1948; admitted to bar, 1979, Illinois and U.S. District Court, Northern District of Illinois and Eastern District of Wisconsin; U.S. Claims Court; U.S. Court of the Armed Forces; U.S. Court of Appeals, Seventh and Federal Circuits; U.S. Supreme Court; registered as patent attorney with U.S. Patent and Trademark Office. *Education:* University of Rochester (B.S.E.E., with highest distinction, 1971); University of Chicago (J.D., 1979); George Washington University (LL.M., Intellectual Property, 1997). Phi Beta Kappa. Tau Beta Pi. Professional Engineer, Virginia. *Member:* Chicago, American and Federal Circuit Bar Associations; Decalogue Society; American Intellectual Property Law Association. [U.S. Navy, 1972-1992]. ***PRACTICE AREAS:*** Intellectual Property. ***Email:*** lfriedman@welshkatz.com

STEVEN E. FELDMAN, born Tacoma, Washington, July 19, 1970; admitted to bar, 1995, Illinois and U.S. District Court, Northern District of Illinois; 1997, U.S. Court of Appeals for the Federal Circuit; registered to practice before U.S. Patent and Trademark Office. *Education:* Northwestern University (B.S.M.Sc., 1992); George Washington University (J.D., 1995). Member, George Washington University Law Review. *Member:* Chicago, Illinois State and American Bar Associations; American Intellectual Property Law Association. ***PRACTICE AREAS:*** Intellectual Property. ***Email:*** sefeldman@welshkatz.com

JEFFREY W. SALMON, born Indianapolis, Indiana, October 24, 1966; admitted to bar, 1993, Illinois; 1994, Indiana; registered to practice before U.S. Patent and Trademark Office. *Education:* Northwestern University (B.S.E.E., 1989); Indiana University (J.D., 1992). *Member:* Chicago and Indiana State Bar Associations; Intellectual Property Law Association of Chicago. ***PRACTICE AREAS:*** Intellectual Property. ***Email:*** jwsalmon@welshkatz.com

THOMAS L. GEMMELL, born Royal Oak, Michigan, November 23, 1962; admitted to bar, 1995, Illinois; U.S. District Court, Northern District of Illinois, Eastern District of Michigan and Eastern District of Virginia. *Education:* University of Colorado (B.A., with honors, 1984); Stanford University (J.D., 1995). Phi Beta Kappa; Kappa Sigma. Managing Editor, Stanford Journal of Law, Business & Finance. Associate Editor, Stanford Journal of International Law. *Member:* Chicago, Illinois State and American (Member, Sections on Litigation; Air and Space Law) Bar Associations. [Lieutenant Colonel, USAFR, 1984—]. ***SPECIAL AGENCIES:*** Judge Advocate General, 1996-1997. ***PRACTICE AREAS:*** Intellectual Property. ***Email:*** tlgemmell@welshkatz.com

LOUISE T. WALSH, born Gary, Indiana, March 15, 1959; admitted to bar, 1995, Illinois and U.S. District Court, Northern District of Illinois; U.S. Court of Appeals, Seventh Circuit; U.S. Supreme Court; registered to practice before U.S. Patent and Trademark Office. *Education:* University of Notre Dame (B.S., 1981); Pace University (M.B.A., 1985); DePaul University (J.D., 1995). Order of the Coif. *Member:* Chicago Bar Association; Women's Bar Association of Illinois. ***PRACTICE AREAS:*** Intellectual Property. ***Email:*** ltwalsh@welshkatz.com

PAUL M. VARGO, born Jersey City, New Jersey, November 23, 1941; admitted to bar, 1977, Illinois and U.S. District Court, Northern District of Illinois; 1982, U.S. District Court, Northern District of Illinois including Trial Bar; registered to practice before U.S. Patent and Trademark Office. *Education:* Case Western Reserve University (B.S.E.E., 1963; M.S.E.E., 1965; Ph.D., 1969); Chicago-Kent College of Law, Illinois Institute of Technology (J.D., with high honors, 1977). Tau Beta Pi; Eta Kappa Nu; Sigma Xi. *Member:* Chicago, Illinois State and American Bar Associations. ***PRACTICE AREAS:*** Intellectual Property. ***Email:*** pmvargo@welshkatz.com

JOSEPH E. CWIK, born San Diego, California, January 3, 1969; admitted to bar, 1995, Illinois and U.S. District Court, Northern District of Illinois; 2002, U.S. Supreme Court and U.S. Court of Appeals, Eighth Circuit; 2003, U.S. Court of Appeals for the Federal Circuit; 2004, U.S. District Court, Northern District of Illinois including Trial Bar; registered to practice before U.S. Patent and Trademark Office. *Education:* University of Illinois (B.S.C.E., 1992); John Marshall Law School (J.D., cum laude, 1995). Chi Epsilon; Phi Delta Phi. Staff Editor, John Marshall Law Review. ***PRACTICE AREAS:*** Intellectual Property. ***Email:*** jecwik@welshkatz.com

J. ARON CARNAHAN, born Portland, Oregon, August 5, 1971; admitted to bar, 1997, Illinois and U.S. District Court, Northern District of Illinois; registered to practice before U.S. Patent and Trademark Office. *Education:* University of Illinois at Urbana (B.S.M.E., 1993; M.B.A., 1997; J.D., magna cum laude, 1997). Co-Author: "Battling the 'CompanyNameSucks.com' Cyberactivists," Intellectual Property & Technology Law Journal, Vol. 13, No. 3, March 2001. *Member:* Chicago, Illinois State and American Bar Associations. ***PRACTICE AREAS:*** Intellectual Property. ***Email:*** jacarnahan@welshkatz.com

ERIK B. FLOM, born Poughkeepsie, New York, April 18, 1963; admitted to bar, 1998, Illinois; registered to practice before U.S. Patent and Trademark Office. *Education:* Hope College (B.S., 1985); University of Chicago (Ph.D., 1993); Northwestern University (J.D., with honors, 1998). Note & Comment Editor, Northwestern Journal of International Law & Business. Member: American Chemical Society; American Association for the Advancement of Science. Author: "Patents," in Corporate Legal Compliance Handbook (Theodore L. Banks and Frederick Z. Banks eds., 2002). *Member:* Chicago and American Bar Associations. ***PRACTICE AREAS:*** Intellectual Property. ***Email:*** ebflom@welshkatz.com

---

RICHARD J. GURAK, born Chicago, Illinois, July 16, 1965; admitted to bar, 1997, Illinois; registered to practice before U.S. Patent and Trademark Office. *Education:* University of Illinois at Chicago (B.S., 1990); The John Marshall Law School (J.D., 1997). [U.S. Navy Reserves (Seabees), 1986-1993]. ***PRACTICE AREAS:*** Intellectual Property. ***Email:*** rjgurak@welshkatz.com

DANIEL M. GURFINKEL, born Havana, Cuba, May 12, 1961; admitted to bar, 1987, Illinois and U.S. District Court, Northern District of Illinois; 1990, U.S. Court of Appeals for the Federal Circuit; 2000, U.S. Supreme Court; registered to practice before U.S. Patent and Trademark Office. *Education:* University of Illinois (B.S.C.E., 1984); Indiana University (J.D., 1987). *Member:* Chicago and Illinois State Bar Associations; Intellectual Property Law Association of Chicago. ***PRACTICE AREAS:*** Intellectual Property. ***Email:*** dmgurfinkel@welshkatz.com

MICHELE S. KATZ, born Lake Forest, Illinois, September 14, 1975; admitted to bar, 2001, Illinois and Minnesota; 2002, District of Columbia. *Education:* Indiana University (B.A., 1997); Chicago-Kent College of Law (J.D., 2000). Mediator, Center for Conflict Resolution (Mediation). *Member:* Chicago, Illinois State and American Bar Associations; International Trademark Association; Decalogue Society of Lawyers; Women's Bar Association of Illinois; National Association of Women Business Owners. **LANGUAGES:** French, Hebrew and Spanish. ***PRACTICE AREAS:*** Intellectual Property. ***Email:*** mkatz@welshkatz.com

NATALIE A. REMIEN, born Evanston, Illinois, October 25, 1974; admitted to bar, 1999, Illinois. *Education:* University of Colorado at Boulder (B.S.B.A., cum laude, 1996); DePaul University (J.D., 1999). *Member:* Chicago and American Bar Associations. ***PRACTICE AREAS:*** Intellectual Property; Intellectual Property Litigation. ***Email:*** naremien@welshkatz.com

BRIAN J. SODIKOFF, born Chicago, Illinois, February 24, 1977; admitted to bar, 2003, Illinois and U.S. District Court, Northern District of Illinois; registered to practice

(This Listing Continued)

WELSH & KATZ, LTD., Chicago—Continued

before U.S. Patent and Trademark Office. *Education:* Vanderbilt University (B.S., Psychology, 1999); DePaul University School of Law (J.D., summa cum laude, 2003). Phi Kappa Phi. Order of the Coif. Member, De Paul University Law Review, 2001-2003. *Member:* American Bar Association. ***PRACTICE AREAS:*** Intellectual Property. ***Email:*** bsodikoff@welshkatz.com

BRETT M. TOLPIN, born Beaufort, South Carolina, August 5, 1971; admitted to bar, 1996, Washington; 1997, U.S. District Court, Western District of Washington; 2003, Illinois and U.S. Supreme Court. *Education:* University of Iowa (B.A., English, 1993); Gonzaga University (J.D., 1996). Recipient, Gonzaga Public Interest Law Project Scholarship, 1995. Formerly with: Federal Emergency Management Agency, 1997; Department of Energy, Office of Environmental Management, 1998. Trademark Attorney-Advisor, U.S. Patent and Trademark Office, 1998-2003. *Member:* Chicago (Young Lawyers Section, Vice-Chair, Intellectual Property Committee), Washington State and Illinois State Bar Associations; International Trademark Association; Intellectual Property Law Association of Chicago. ***PRACTICE AREAS:*** Intellectual Property. ***Email:*** bmtolpin@welshkatz.com

GEORGE S. PAVLIK, born Evanston, Illinois, November 23, 1974; admitted to bar, 2004, Illinois and U.S. District Court, Northern District of Illinois; registered to practice before U.S. Patent and Trademark Office. *Education:* University of Kansas (B.S., Human Biology, 1997); John Marshall Law School (J.D., Intellectual Property, 2004). Member, John Marshall Law Review. *Member:* Illinois State Bar Association; American Intellectual Property Law Association; Intellectual Property Law Association of Chicago. ***PRACTICE AREAS:*** Intellectual Property. ***Email:*** gpavlik@welshkatz.com

MICHAEL A. KROL, born Detroit, Michigan, October 25, 1965; admitted to bar, 2004, Illinois; registered to practice before U.S. Patent and Trademark Office. *Education:* University of Michigan (B.Sc., Microbiology, with highest distinctions, 1991; J.D., 2003); University of Wisconsin-Madison (Ph.D., Cellular and Molecular Biology, 2000). Phi Beta Kappa. Fellow, National Science Foundation. Recipient, Nadler Award for Achievement in Corporate Law. *Member:* American Bar Association; American Intellectual Property Law Association. ***PRACTICE AREAS:*** Intellectual Property. ***Email:*** makrol@welshkatz.com

SHERRY L. ROLLO, born Baytown, Texas, November 1, 1977; admitted to bar, 2004, Illinois. *Education:* University of Texas at Austin (B.S., Physics, 2001); John Marshall Law School (J.D., 2004). Recipient, Teagle Scholarship, University of Texas. Member, Review of Intellectual Property Law, John Marshall Law School. Author, "Hopping the HIPAA Hurdle: Proving Trademark Use in the Health Care Industry," Intellectual Property & Technology Law Journal. *Member:* Chicago and American Bar Associations. ***PRACTICE AREAS:*** Intellectual Property. ***Email:*** srollo@welshkatz.com

CHRISTOPHER K. MARLOW, born Ogdensburg, New York, October 31, 1974; admitted to bar, 2004, Illinois; registered to practice before U.S. Patent and Trademark Office. *Education:* University of Missouri (B.S.E.E., 1998); Northwestern University (J.D., 2004). ***PRACTICE AREAS:*** Intellectual Property. ***Email:*** ckmarlow@welshkatz.com

MAITREYA P. JANI, born Ahmedabad, India, May 29, 1974; admitted to bar, 1999, Illinois and U.S. District Court, Northern District of Illinois; 2003, California; registered to practice before U.S. Patent and Trademark Office. *Education:* University of Illinois (B.S.G.E., with honors, 1996); George Washington University (J.D., with honors, 1999). Tau Beta Pi. Member, George Washington Law School Trial Court Board, 1997-1999. Member, American Intellectual Property Law Association Quarterly Journal, 1997-1999. Author, "Intellectual Property and Unfair Competition," 2002 CA Litigation Review, May 2003. *Member:* State Bar of California. ***LANGUAGES:*** Spanish and Gujarati. ***PRACTICE AREAS:*** Intellectual Property. ***Email:*** mpjani@welshkatz.com

CRAIG M. KUCHII, born Wakayama, Japan, March 26, 1972; admitted to bar, 2004, Illinois. *Education:* Tulane University (B.S., 1994); Northwestern University (J.D., 2004). Phi Delta Phi. ***LANGUAGES:*** Japanese. ***PRACTICE AREAS:*** Intellectual Property. ***Email:*** ckuchii@welshkatz.com

STEPHEN P. BENSON, born Jackson, Michigan, July 28, 1970; admitted to bar, 2005, Illinois. *Education:* University of Michigan, Ann Arbor (B.S., Microbiology, 2001); Northwestern University (M.S., Neurobiology and Physiology, 2002); DePaul University (J.D., International and Comparative Law, 2005). Sigma Pi Sigma (Nominated to the University of Michigan Chapter). Recipient: Law Merit Scholarship; DePaul University College of Law; Summer Biomedical Research Grant, University of Michigan, 1999. Member, Honors Program in Biology and Physics, University of Michigan. Member, American Association for the Advancement of Science. ***PRACTICE AREAS:*** Intellectual Property. ***Email:*** sbenson@welshkatz.com

GREGORY J. SKONY, born Arlington Heights, Illinois, October 21, 1979; admitted to bar, 2005, Illinois. *Education:* University of Notre Dame (B.S., Electrical Engineering, cum laude, 2002); DePaul University (J.D., 2005). Member, DePaul Law Review, 2003-2005. ***PRACTICE AREAS:*** Intellectual Property. ***Email:*** gjskony@welshkatz.com

OF COUNSEL

LAURIE A. HAYNIE, born Salt Lake City, Utah, December 27, 1958; admitted to bar, 1985, Utah and U.S. District Court, District of Utah; 1987, Illinois and U.S. District Court, Northern District of Illinois; U.S. Court of Appeals for the Seventh and District of Columbia Circuits; 1995, U.S. Claims Court; 1996, U.S. Court of Appeals for the Federal Circuit; 2002, U.S. Supreme Court. *Education:* University of Utah (B.A., cum laude, 1981); Brigham Young University (J.D., 1984). Phi Kappa Phi. Author: "So The Copyright Office Has Refused To Register Your Claim To Copyright - What Does It Mean And What Can You Do About It?," Vol. 21 AIPLA Quarterly Journal, p.70 (1993). *Member:* Chicago Bar Association. ***PRACTICE AREAS:*** Intellectual Property. ***Email:*** lahaynie@welshkatz.com

JAMES J. MYRICK, born Wilmington, Delaware, September 12, 1943; admitted to bar, 1969, Illinois; 1982, U.S. Court of Appeals for the Federal Circuit; 1984, U.S. Supreme Court; registered to practice before U.S. Patent and Trademark Office. *Education:* University of Illinois (B.S., 1966); University of Michigan (J.D., 1969). Author: Article, "Patent Law for Programmed Computers and Programmed Life Forms," American Bar Association Journal, p. 920, 1982. Chief Patent Counsel, Kraft Foods, Inc., 1990-1996. *Member:* American Bar Association. ***PRACTICE AREAS:*** Intellectual Property. ***Email:*** jmyrick@welshkatz.com

THOMAS R. VIGIL, born Chicago, Illinois, March 20, 1938; admitted to bar, 1966, Illinois; 1967, U.S. District Court, Northern District of Illinois, including Trial Bar; 1982, U.S. Court of Appeals, Seventh and Ninth Circuits; registered to practice before U.S. Patent and Trademark Office. *Education:* Illinois Institute of Technology/Chicago-Kent College of Law (B.S.E.E., 1961); DePaul University College of Law (J.D., 1966). Phi Alpha Delta. *Member:* Chicago and American Bar Associations; Intellectual Property Law Association of Chicago; American Intellectual Property Law Association; International Trademark Association; International Patent & Trademark Association (American Branch of A.I.P.P.I.); Federation of International Counsel Property Industrial (FICPI-U.S. Section); Licensing Executives Society. ***PRACTICE AREAS:*** Intellectual Property. ***Email:*** trvigil@welshkatz.com

PHILIP D. SEGREST, JR., born Montgomery, Alabama, July 14, 1967; admitted to bar, 1992, Alabama and U.S. District Court, Middle District of Alabama; 1993, U.S. Court of Federal Claims; 1994, U.S. Court of Appeals for the Federal Circuit; 1996, Illinois and U.S. District Court, Northern District of Illinois; 2001, U.S. Supreme Court and U.S. Court of Appeals, 7th Circuit; registered to practice before U.S. Patent and Trademark Office. *Education:* University of Alabama (B.S., 1988, 1989; J.D., 1992). Member, University of Alabama Law Review, Editorial Board. Law Clerk to: Hon. Eric G. Bruggink, U.S. Court of Federal Claims, 1992-1993; Hon. John P. Wiese, U.S. Court of Federal Claims, 1993-1994; Hon. Marion T. Bennett, U.S. Court of Appeals for the Federal Circuit, 1994-1995. *Member:* Chicago, Illinois State, Federal Circuit and American Bar Associations; Alabama State Bar; Intellectual Property Law Association of Chicago. (Also Member of Segrest, Segrest & Weldon, Tuskegee, Alabama). ***PRACTICE AREAS:*** Intellectual Property. ***Email:*** pdsegrest@welshkatz.com

WALLACE L. OLIVER, born Chicago, Illinois, April 8, 1944; admitted to bar, 1974, Illinois; 1983, U.S. Court of Appeals for the Federal Circuit; registered to practice before the U.S. Patent and Trademark Office. *Education:* California Institute of Technology (B.S., Chemistry, 1966); Northwestern University (Ph.D., Physical Organic Chemistry, 1970); University of Liverpool, England (Post-Doctoral Fellow, 1971); Northwestern University School of Law (J.D., cum laude, 1974). *Member:* Illinois State, Federal Circuit and American Bar Associations; American Intellectual Property Law Association; Intellectual Property Law Association of Chicago; Licensing Executives Society. ***PRACTICE AREAS:*** Intellectual Property. ***Email:*** wloliver@welshkatz.com

LAURA A. LABEOTS, born Chicago, Illinois; admitted to bar, 2003, Illinois. *Education:* Indiana University (B.A., Chemistry, 1984); Northwestern University (M.S., Organic Chemistry, 1989; Ph.D., Organic Chemistry, 1992); The John Marshall Law School (J.D., 2003). *Member:* Chicago, Illinois State and American Bar Associations. ***LANGUAGES:*** Spanish and French. ***PRACTICE AREAS:*** Intellectual Property. ***Email:*** lalabeots@welshkatz.com

REPRESENTATIVE CLIENTS: Abbott Laboratories; Bally Total Fitness Corporation; Biovail Corporation; Fedders Corporation; General Electric Company; HEICO Corporation; Hillerich & Bradsby, Inc.; Northwestern University; Papst Licensing GmbH; Precious Moments, Inc.; Rockwell International Corporation; Samsonite Corporation; The Scripps Research Institute; Technomed Medical Systems, SA; Time Warner; Ty Inc.; Venture Industries; Xerox Corporation.

WELTMAN, WEINBERG & REIS CO., L.P.A.

10 S. LA SALLE STREET
SUITE 900
CHICAGO, ILLINOIS 60603
Telephone: 312-782-9676
Fax: 312-782-4201
Email: wwr@weltman.com
URL: http://www.weltman.com

Burlington, New Jersey Office: Telephone: 609-914-0437.
Deerfield, Illinois Office: Telephone: 847-940-9812.
Cincinnati, Ohio Office: Telephone: 513-723-2200.
Cleveland, Ohio Office: Telephone: 216-685-1000.
Columbus, Ohio Office: Telephone: 614-228-7272.
Philadelphia, Pennsylvania Office: Telephone: 215-599-1500.
Pittsburgh, Pennsylvania Office: Telephone: 412-434-7955.
Troy, Michigan Office: Telephone: 248-362-6100.

Creditors Rights, Collections, Creditor Bankruptcy, Foreclosure/Eviction, Title Insurance Law, Fair Debt Collections Practices Act, Probate/Deceased Collections, Subrogation, Credit Union Law, Banks and Banking, Creditor Defense, Complex Consumer and Commercial Litigation, Real Estate Title & Closing Services.

JEFFREY M. FEINGOLD, born Chicago, Illinois, 1950; admitted to bar, 1974, Illinois. *Education:* University of Illinois (B.A., 1971); DePaul University College of Law (J.D., 1974). *Member:* American, Illinois State and Chicago Bar Associations; Decalogue Society of Lawyers; American Association of Healthcare Administrative Management; Commercial Law League of America; Healthcare Financial Management Association; IN-SOL International; International Association of Commercial Collectors, Inc; National Association of Retail Collection Attorneys. ***PRACTICE AREAS:*** Commercial Litigation; Collection Services; Creditors Rights. ***Email:*** jfeingold@weltman.com

JOHN S. PUCIN, born Waukegan, Illinois, March 23, 1966; admitted to bar, 1992, Ohio and U.S. District Court, Southern District of Ohio; 2000, Illinois; 2003, Pennsylvania and U.S. District Court, Eastern District of Pennsylvania; 2004, U.S. District Court, Northern District of Illinois. *Education:* Xavier University (B.A., 1988); Capital University (J.D., 1992). Member, Franklin County Municipal Court Committee. *Member:* Illinois State and Chicago Bar Associations; Commercial Law League of America; Illinois Creditors Bar Association. ***PRACTICE AREAS:*** Creditors Rights. ***Email:*** jpucin@weltman.com

JAY K. LEVY, born 1949; admitted to bar, 1974, Illinois. *Education:* Northern Illinois University (B.S., 1971); Chicago-Kent College of Law, Illinois Institute of Technology

(This Listing Continued)

(J.D., 1974). *Member:* Illinois State and Chicago Bar Associations; American Association of Healthcare Administrative Management; Commerical Law League of America; Healthcare Financial Management Association; INSOL International; International Association of Commercial Collectors, Inc; National Association of Retail Collection Attorneys. ***PRACTICE AREAS:*** Creditors Rights; Collection Services; Legal Action Recovery. ***Email:*** jlevy@weltman.com

---

JOHN J. GRIEGER, JR., born Chicago Heights, Illinois, November 19, 1964; admitted to bar, 1990, Illinois and U.S. District Court, Northern District of Illinois; 2001, U.S. District Court, Central District of Illinois; 2004, U.S. District Court, Southern District of Illinois. *Education:* Northwestern University (B.A., 1986); University of San Diego School of Law (J.D., 1990). *Member:* Chicago Bar Association. ***LANGUAGES:*** Spanish, Lithuanian and French. ***PRACTICE AREAS:*** Bankruptcy. ***Email:*** jgrieger@weltman.com

DANIEL H. OLSWANG, born Skokie, Illinois, February 9, 1970; admitted to bar, 1996, Illinois and U.S. District Court, Northern District of Illinois; 2004, U.S. District Court, Southern District of Illinois. *Education:* University of Wisconsin-Madison (B.A., 1991); Chicago-Kent College of Law, Illinois Institute of Technology (J.D., 1996). *Member:* Chicago and Illinois State Bar Associations. ***PRACTICE AREAS:*** Foreclosures; Real Estate; Evictions; Creditors Rights. ***Email:*** dolswang@weltman.com

JOHN R. BOOKER, born Wichita Falls, Texas, June 30, 1963; admitted to bar, 1993, Illinois and U.S. District Court, Northern District of Illinois; 1997, U.S. Court of Appeals, Seventh Circuit; 1998, U.S. District Court, Northern District of Texas; 1999, U.S. District Court, District of Colorado. *Education:* University of Maryland (B.A., 1990); Southern Illinois University School of Law (J.D., 1993). [Sergeant, U.S.M.C., 1982-1990]. ***PRACTICE AREAS:*** Collections. ***Email:*** jbooker@weltman.com

(For complete biographical data on other personnel, see Professional Biographies at other locations)

WESSELS & PAUTSCH, P.C.

CHICAGO BAR ASSOCIATION BUILDING
321 SOUTH PLYMOUTH COURT, SUITE 900
CHICAGO, ILLINOIS 60604
Telephone: 312-461-0500
Fax: 312-461-0595
Email: wessels@stch.w-p.com
URL: http://www.w-p.com

St. Charles, Illinois Office: Dunham Center, 2035 Foxfield Drive. Telephone: 630-377-1554. Fax: 630-377-1653.
Milwaukee, Wisconsin Office: Two Plaza East, 330 East Kilbourn Avenue, Suite 1475. Telephone: 414-291-0600. Fax: 414-291-0200.
Davenport, Iowa Office: Northwest Bank Building, 101 W. Second Street, Suite 307. Telephone: 563-333-9102. Fax: 563-333-9105.
Minneapolis, Minnesota Office: MoneyGram Tower, 1550 Utica Avenue South, Suite 450. Telephone: 952-746-1700. Fax: 952-746-1704.
Indianapolis, Indiana Office: Market Tower, 10 West Market Street, Suite 1770. Telephone: 317-656-8800. Fax: 317-656-8855.

Representing Employers in Labor and Employment Law Matters. NLRA, RLA, all Federal and State Employment Discrimination Laws, Federal and State Disability Laws, Wrongful Discharge, Employment Contracts, Collective Bargaining Negotiations and Arbitrations, Employee Substance Abuse, Safety and Health, Unemployment Insurance, Benefits Law, Wage and Hour, and Employment-Based Immigration Matters. Litigation before all Federal and State Courts and Agencies, Trial and Appellate Practice.

FIRM PROFILE: Wessels & Pautsch, P.C.'s six offices in the Midwest serve a practice that is nationwide in scope. The Firm's maxim "we run through walls for our clients" reflects its aggressive advocacy of its clients' positions coupled with its broad knowledge of its clients' businesses. The Firm's aim is to provide cost-effective service together with personalized attention to matters assigned to it.

WALTER J. LISZKA, born Hammond, Indiana, July 28, 1945; admitted to bar, 1970, Illinois; U.S. District Court, Northern District of Illinois; U.S. Court of Appeals, Seventh Circuit; U.S. Supreme Court. *Education:* Northwestern University (B.A., 1967); Loyola University, Chicago (J.D., 1970). Alpha Sigma Nu. *Member:* Chicago, Illinois State and American Bar Associations. ***Email:*** waliszka@chgo.w-p.com

---

MICHAEL H. BERENDT, born Chicago, Illinois, September 2, 1976; admitted to bar, 2001, Illinois and U.S. District Court, Northern and Central Districts of Illinois. *Education:* State University of New York at Albany (B.A., 1998); John Marshall Law School (J.D., 2001). Phi Alpha Delta. Gibbons Criminal Procedures Moot Court. Candidacy and Production Editor, Journal of Computer and Information Law, 2000-2001. *Member:* Illinois, Chicago and American Bar Associations; Defense Research Institute. ***Email:*** miberendt@chgo.w-p.com

SEAN F. DARKE, born Detroit, Michigan, February 18, 1976; admitted to bar, 2005, Illinois. *Education:* State University of New York at Potsdam (B.A., 2001); Michigan State University College of Law (J.D., 2004). *Member:* Chicago, Illinois State and American Bar Associations.

(For complete biographical data on other personnel, see Professional Biographies at Chicago, Illinois; Milwaukee, Wisconsin; Davenport, Iowa; Minneapolis, Minnesota and Indianapolis, Indiana)

THE WEXLER FIRM LLP

Established in 2000
ONE NORTH LASALLE STREET, SUITE 2000
CHICAGO, ILLINOIS 60602
Telephone: 312-346-2222
Fax: 312-346-0022
Email: info@wexlerfirm.com
URL: http://www.wexlerfirm.com

Complex Multi-District Commercial Litigation, Class Actions, Consumer Litigation, Accountants' Liability, Defamation, Antitrust, Securities Fraud, Commodities, Fraud, RICO Litigation, Civil Rights, Legal Malpractice and Municipal Litigation.

FOUNDING PARTNER

KENNETH A. WEXLER, born Chicago, Illinois, March 15, 1955; admitted to bar, 1980, Illinois and Illinois Supreme Court; U.S. District Court, Northern District of Illinois; 1981, U.S. Court of Appeals, Seventh Circuit; 1989, U.S. Court of Appeals, Third Circuit; 1991, U.S. District Court, Northern District of New Mexico. *Education:* Washington University, St. Louis (B.A., summa cum laude, 1977); Georgetown University (J.D., 1980). Pi Sigma Alpha. Recipient, Arnold J. Lien Prize in Political Science. Member, American Constitution Society for Law and Policy. Member: People to People International; Chicago Coalition for the Homeless; The Hundred Club of Cook County. *Member:* Chicago, Illinois State and American Bar Associations; Chicago Council of Lawyers; The Association of Trial Lawyers of America; Roscoe Pound Institute; Illinois Trial Lawyers Association. ***PRACTICE AREAS:*** Complex and Multi-District Class Action Litigation; Complex Litigation; Commercial Litigation; Consumer Litigation; Civil Rights; Antitrust Litigation; Securities Litigation; Commodities Litigation; Defamation; Accountants' Liability; Legal Malpractice; Municipal Litigation; Discrimination. ***Email:*** kawexler@wexlerfirm.com

PARTNER

EDWARD A. WALLACE, born Sacramento, California, February 1, 1969; admitted to bar, 1995, Illinois and Illinois Supreme Court ; U.S. District Court, Northern District of Illinois; 1996, U.S. District Court, Southern District of Illinois; 2003, U.S. District Court, Western District of Michigan. *Education:* Eastern Illinois University (B.A., 1991); DePaul University (J.D., 1995). *Member:* Chicago, Illinois State and American Bar Associations. ***PRACTICE AREAS:*** Complex and Multi-District Class Action Litigation; Commercial Litigation; Consumer Litigation; Antitrust Litigation; Securities Litigation; Legal Malpractice. ***Email:*** eawallace@wexlerfirm.com

ASSOCIATES

JENNIFER FOUNTAIN CONNOLLY, born Austin, Texas, February 3, 1972; admitted to bar, 1998, Colorado and U.S. District Court, District of Colorado; 1999, U.S. Court of Appeals, Tenth Circuit; 2002, Illinois; 2003, U.S. District Court, Northern and Southern Districts of Illinois. *Education:* University of Chicago (A.B., with high honors, English, 1993); University of Denver (J.D., 1998). *Member:* Chicago, Illinois and American Bar Associations. ***PRACTICE AREAS:*** Antitrust and Trade Regulation; Consumer Protection; Commercial Litigation. ***Email:*** jfconnolly@wexlerfirm.com

ANTHONY J. SIEVERT, born Neenah, Wisconsin, January 9, 1976; admitted to bar, 2000, Wisconsin, Illinois and U.S. District Court, Northern District of Illinois. *Education:* University of Wisconsin-Madison (B.A., 1997; J.D., 2000). Phi Beta Kappa. ***PRACTICE AREAS:*** Antitrust; Consumer Law; Discrimination. ***Email:*** ajsievert@wexlerfirm.com

ANDRAE P. RENEAU, born Milwaukee, Wisconsin, June 15, 1978; admitted to bar, 2003, Illinois and Wisconsin. *Education:* Harvard University (B.A., cum laude, 2000); University of Wisconsin Law School (J.D., 2003). Member, Wisconsin Law Review, 2001-2003. ***PRACTICE AREAS:*** Civil Litigation. ***Email:*** apreneau@wexlerfirm.com

AMBER M. NESBITT, born Chicago, Illinois, August 14, 1978; admitted to bar, 2004, Illinois; 2005, U.S. District Court, Northern District of Illinois. *Education:* University of Michigan, Ann Arbor (B.A., 2000); Loyola University, Chicago School of Law (J.D., magna cum laude, 2004). Senior Member, Loyola University Chicago Law Journal, 2002-2004. *Member:* Chicago and Illinois State Bar Associations. ***PRACTICE AREAS:*** Complex and Multi-District Litigation; Consumer Protection; Civil Rights; Antitrust. ***Email:*** anesbitt@wexlerfirm.com

---

WHITING LAW GROUP, LTD.

ONE EAST WACKER DRIVE
SUITE 2300
CHICAGO, ILLINOIS 60601
Telephone: 312-372-1655
Toll Free: 877-936-7200
Fax: 312-279-1111
Email: twhiting@wlglaw.net
URL: http://www.wlglaw.net

Delavan, Wisconsin Office: 125 North Second Street, 53115. Telephone: 877-936-7200.

Personal Injury, wrongful death, automobile accidents, trucking accidents, slip and fall injuries, construction accidents, products liability and farming injuries; Medical Malpractice, including nursing home negligence, birth injuries, labor and delivery injuries, brain and spinal cord injuries, obstetric malpractice and hospital negligence.

TIMOTHY M. WHITING, born 1968; admitted to bar, 1994, Wisconsin; 1995, Illinois. *Education:* University of Wisconsin-Parkside (B.S., Business Administration, 1991); University of Wisconsin-Madison (J.D., 1994). Honored as one of the top forty lawyers under age forty in Illinois, 2002. ***Email:*** twhiting@wlglaw.net

MICHAEL J. GOLDBERG, born 1976; admitted to bar, 2002, Illinois. *Education:* University of Illinois (B.A., Speech Communications/Pre-Law, 1998); Chicago-Kent Col-

(This Listing Continued)

WHITING LAW GROUP, LTD., Chicago—Continued

lege of Law (J.D., 2002). Recipient, CALI Award Winner in Trial Advocacy, 2001. ***Email:*** mgoldberg@wlglaw.net

WIEDNER & McAULIFFE, LTD.

Established in 1972

ONE NORTH FRANKLIN
SUITE 1900
CHICAGO, ILLINOIS 60606
Telephone: 312-855-1105
Fax: 312-855-1792
URL: http://www.wmlaw.com

Workers' Compensation, Wrongful Discharge, ADA, Sexual Harassment and Human Rights Claims, Product Liability and Personal Injury Law. General Civil, Trial and Appellate Practice in both State and Federal Courts.

FIRM PROFILE: Wiedner & McAuliffe, Ltd. is a service oriented law firm specializing in various aspects of employment litigation and the defense of employers before the Illinois Industrial Commission and State and Federal Courts, and the Illinois Human Rights Commission, as well as general tort and commercial litigation.

FRANK J. WIEDNER, born Chicago, Illinois, July 3, 1923; admitted to bar, 1949, Illinois. *Education:* DePaul University (J.D., 1948); John Carroll University. Phi Alpha Delta. Contributor, Illinois Law Review, 1967. Faculty Member, Illinois Institute for Continuing Legal Education, 1970-1984. Columnist, Chicago Law Bulletin, Articles on Workers' Compensation, 1980. *Member:* Chicago (Member, Committee on the Industrial Commission, 1958-1963) and Illinois State (Council Chairman, Section on Workers' Compensation, 1976-1977; Editor, Newsletter on Workers' Compensation, 1963-1993; Member: Section of Workers' Compensation, 1971-1973; Committee on Unauthorized Practice of Law, Section of Workers' Compensation, 1973-1974) Bar Associations; Workers' Compensation Lawyers Association. ***PRACTICE AREAS:*** Workers' Compensation; Employment Litigation. ***Email:*** fjwiedner@wmlaw.com

JOHN P. McAULIFFE (Retired)

RUSSELL P. STANDLEE, born Chicago, Illinois, April 18, 1949; admitted to bar, 1975, Illinois; 1976, Florida. *Education:* Indiana University (B.S., 1971); Stetson University (J.D., 1975). Phi Delta Phi. *Member:* Chicago, Illinois State and American Bar Associations; Workers' Compensation Lawyers Association (Member, Board of Managers, 1976-1990; Officer, 1985-1987; President, 1988). ***PRACTICE AREAS:*** Workers' Compensation; Employment Litigation. ***Email:*** rpstandlee@wmlaw.com

PAUL W. WIEDNER, born Chicago, Illinois, January 11, 1951; admitted to bar, 1977, Illinois. *Education:* Colorado State University (B.S., 1973); DePaul University (J.D., 1977). Special Assistant State's Attorney, DuPage County. *Member:* DuPage County, Illinois State (Member, Workers' Compensation Committee) and American (Member, Tort and Insurance Practice) Bar Associations; Workers' Compensation Lawyers Association; Faculty Member for Illinois Institute of Continuing Legal Education. ***PRACTICE AREAS:*** Workers' Compensation; Employment Litigation. ***Email:*** pwwiedner@wmlaw.com

RICHARD J. LEAMY, JR., born Chicago, Illinois, May 9, 1952; admitted to bar, 1978, Michigan; 1979, Illinois and U.S. District Court, Northern District of Illinois including Trial Bar. *Education:* Western Michigan University (B.A., 1974); DePaul University (J.D., 1977). Clerk, Michigan Court of Appeals, 1977-1978. *Member:* Chicago, Illinois State and American (Member, Sections on: Litigation; Insurance, Negligence and Compensation Law) Bar Associations; Illinois Defense Counsel. ***PRACTICE AREAS:*** General Civil Trial Practice. ***Email:*** rjleamy@wmlaw.com

MARK C. WIEDNER, born Chicago, Illinois, August 9, 1955; admitted to bar, 1980, Illinois. *Education:* DePauw University (B.A., 1977); DePaul University (J.D., 1980). Phi Alpha Delta. *Member:* DuPage County, Chicago (Chairman, Young Lawyers Section for Workers' Compensation, 1987-1988) and Illinois State Bar Associations. ***PRACTICE AREAS:*** Workers' Compensation; Employment Litigation. ***Email:*** mcwiedner@wmlaw.com

TIMOTHY D. McMAHON, born Chicago, Illinois, September 26, 1952; admitted to bar, 1977, Illinois and U.S. District Court, Northern District of Illinois including Trial Bar. *Education:* John Carroll University (B.A., 1974); DePaul University (J.D., cum laude, 1977). Assistant State's Attorney, Cook County, Illinois, 1977-1983. *Member:* Chicago (Member, Circuit Court Committee, Tort Litigation Committee), DuPage County and Illinois State Bar Associations; Illinois Association of Defense Trial Counsel. ***PRACTICE AREAS:*** Employment Litigation; General Civil Trial Practice. ***Email:*** tdmcmahon@wmlaw.com

MARK D. WILKENING, born Chicago, Illinois, October 18, 1953; admitted to bar, 1980, Illinois and U.S. District Court, Northern District of Illinois. *Education:* Illinois State University (B.S., 1974); DePaul University (J.D., 1980). Instructor, Workers' Compensation, IICLE. Member, Illinois Self-Insured Association, 1987—. *Member:* Chicago (Member, Workers' Compensation Section) and Illinois State Bar Associations; Workers' Compensation Lawyers Association (Member, Board of Managers, 1995—; Officer, 1991-1993; President, 1994). ***PRACTICE AREAS:*** Workers' Compensation; Employment Litigation. ***Email:*** mdwilkening@wmlaw.com

MICHAEL F. DOERRIES, born Glen Ellyn, Illinois, February 15, 1959; admitted to bar, 1985, Illinois. *Education:* University of Iowa; University of Arizona; University of Illinois (B.S., 1981); Chicago-Kent College of Law (J.D., 1985). *Member:* Chicago and Illinois State Bar Associations; Workers' Compensation Law Association. ***PRACTICE AREAS:*** Workers' Compensation; Employment Litigation. ***Email:*** mfdoerries@wmlaw.com

JAMES W. STEVENSON JR., born Atlanta, Georgia, September 19, 1960; admitted to bar, 1987, Illinois, U.S. District Court, Western District of Illinois and U.S. Court of Appeals, Seventh Circuit. *Education:* DePauw University (B.A., 1982); John Marshall Law School (J.D., 1987). *Member:* Chicago, Illinois State and American Bar Associations; Workers' Compensation Lawyers Association. ***PRACTICE AREAS:*** Workers' Compensation; Employment Litigation. ***Email:*** jwstevenson@wmlaw.com

JANET D. PALLARDY, born Berwyn, Illinois, June 10, 1965; admitted to bar, 1990, Wisconsin and Illinois. *Education:* University of Illinois (B.S., with honors, 1987); University of Wisconsin-Madison (J.D., 1990). *Member:* Chicago, Illinois State and American Bar Associations; State Bar of Wisconsin; Workers' Compensation Lawyers Association. ***PRACTICE AREAS:*** Workers' Compensation Law. ***Email:*** jdpallardy@wmlaw.com

CATHERINE MAFEE LEVINE, born Rochester, New York, November 3, 1964; admitted to bar, 1991, Illinois. *Education:* Michigan State University (B.S., 1986); Roosevelt University (Paralegal Certificate, 1987); University of Detroit School of Law (J.D., 1991). Phi Alpha Delta (President, 1989-1990). Member, Moot Court. National Order of Barristers. American Inn of Court. Recipient, American Jurisprudence Award for Immigration Law. *Member:* Chicago, Illinois State and American Bar Associations; Illinois Worker's Compensation Lawyers Association. ***LANGUAGES:*** Farsi. ***PRACTICE AREAS:*** Workers' Compensation. ***Email:*** cmlevine@wmlaw.com

MARK P. MATRANGA, born Rockford, Illinois, December 28, 1947; admitted to bar, 1976, Illinois. *Education:* University of Illinois (B.A., cum laude, 1969); Chicago-Kent College of Law (J.D., cum laude, 1976). *Member:* Illinois State and American Bar Associations; Workers' Compensation Lawyers Association. ***PRACTICE AREAS:*** Workers' Compensation Law. ***Email:*** mpmatranga@wmlaw.com

ROBERT L. SMITH, born Rock County, Wisconsin, August 3, 1964; admitted to bar, 1989, Illinois and U.S. District Court, Northern District of Illinois. *Education:* Beloit College (B.A., 1986); Northern Illinois University (J.D., cum laude, 1989). *Member:* Chicago, Winnebago County, Illinois State and American Bar Associations; Workers' Compensation Lawyers Association; Illinois Association of Defense Trial Counsel. ***PRACTICE AREAS:*** Workers' Compensation (Management); Insurance Defense. ***Email:*** rlsmith@wmlaw.com

JAMES W. OZOG, born Chicago, Illinois, June 27, 1952; admitted to bar, 1977, Illinois, U.S. District Court, Northern District of Illinois including Trial Bar, U.S. District Court, Central District of Illinois and U.S. Court of Appeals, Seventh Circuit. *Education:* Northwestern University (B.S., 1974); Washington University (J.D., 1977). Evans Scholar, Northwestern University. Adjunct Faculty, Loyola University School of Law, Chicago, 1979-1981. Comments Editor, Urban Law Annual, 1976-1977. Product Liability Columnist, Illinois Defense Counsel Quarterly, 2001—. *Member:* Illinois State and American Bar Associations; Illinois Association of Defense Trial Lawyers; Propane Gas Defense Association (Member, Board of Directors, 2001—); Defense Research Institute. ***PRACTICE AREAS:*** Product Liability Defense; Insurance Defense; General Civil Litigation. ***Email:*** jwozog@wmlaw.com

DAVID J. O'CONNELL, born Wilmington, Delaware, October 12, 1962; admitted to bar, 1988, Illinois; 1990, U.S. District Court, Northern and Central Districts of Illinois, and U.S. Court of Appeals, Seventh Circuit. *Education:* Marquette University (B.S.M.E., 1985); St. Louis University (J.D., 1988). Co-Author: "Recognizing and Asserting the Spoliation Defense," Product Liability Update, Illinois Association of Defense Trial Counsel, Vol. 1, No. 2, July, 1996; "Federal Preemption Defenses in Product Liability Cases," IDC Quarterly, Vol. 6, No. 3, 1996; " Defending Product Liability Cases in Illinois after the Best Decision," IDC Quarterly, Vol. 8, No. 4, 1998. Judicial Internship, Illinois Circuit Court, Third Judicial Circuit. *Member:* Illinois State Bar Association. ***REPORTED CASES:*** Randell v. Wal-Mart Stores, Inc. 284 Ill. App.3d 970, 673 N.E.2d 452 (4 Dist. 1996); Shelbyville Mutual Insurance Co. v. Sunbeam Leisure Products Co., 262 Ill. App 3d 636, 634 N.E.2d 1319 (5Dist 1994); Robach v. V.I.P. Transportation, Inc. 930 F.3d 1207 (7 Cir. 1996); Allstate Insurance Company v. Sunbeam Corp., 53 F.3d 804 (7 Cir. 1995); Allstate Insurance Company v. Sunbeam Corp. 865 F.Supp. 1267 (N.D. Ill. 1994). ***PRACTICE AREAS:*** Professional Liability; Construction Law; Product Liability; Personal Injury Defense; Insurance Coverage; Appeals. ***Email:*** djoconnell@wmlaw.com

---

THOMAS W. WEBER, born Chicago, Illinois, March 21, 1956; admitted to bar, 1984, Illinois and U.S. District Court, Northern District of Illinois; 1994, U.S. Court of Appeals, Seventh Circuit. *Education:* Northern Illinois University (B.A., 1981); John Marshall Law School (J.D., 1984). *Member:* Chicago and Illinois State Bar Associations; Illinois Association of Defense Trial Counsel. ***PRACTICE AREAS:*** General Civil Trial Practice; Appellate Practice. ***Email:*** twweber@wmlaw.com

JAMES JASON COGGINS, born Asheboro, North Carolina, April 12, 1970; admitted to bar, 1997, Illinois; U.S. District Court, Northern District of Illinois. *Education:* University of Wisconsin-Madison (B.A., 1993); Chicago-Kent College of Law (J.D., with Honors, 1997). Recipient: CALI Award for Excellence for Justice and Legal System; Workers' Compensation; Advanced Research for Legal Scholars. *Member:* Chicago and American Bar Associations; National Employment Lawyers Association. ***Email:*** jjcoggins@wmlaw.com

BRIAN J. KOCH, born Evergreen Park, Illinois, December 21, 1970; admitted to bar, 1998, Illinois. *Education:* University of Illinois (B.S., 1993); DePaul University (J.D., 1997). Phi Alpha Delta. *Member:* Chicago and Illinois State Bar Associations; Workers' Compensation Lawyers Association. ***PRACTICE AREAS:*** Workers Compensation. ***Email:*** bjkoch@wmlaw.com

INGRID LULICH, born Baltimore, Maryland, December 14, 1967; admitted to bar, 1992, Illinois. *Education:* University of Maryland (B.A., 1989); DePaul University (J.D., 1992). ***PRACTICE AREAS:*** Workers Compensation. ***Email:*** imlulich@wmlaw.com

CHRISTINE M. JAGODZINSKI, born Evergreen Park, Illinois, June 20, 1976; admitted to bar, 2002, Illinois and U.S. District Court, Northern District of Illinois. *Education:* Loyola University (B.S., Criminal Justice, 1998; M.A., Criminal Justice Administration, 2000; J.D., 2002). Phi Alpha Delta. Chief Justice, Loyola University, 2001-2002. *Member:* Illinois State Bar Association; Workers' Compensation Lawyers Association. ***PRACTICE AREAS:*** Workers Compensation (100%). ***Email:*** cmjagodzinski@wmlaw.com

BRIAN H. DRISCOLL, born Chicago Heights, Illinois, October 25, 1961. *Education:* Marquette University (B.A., 1983); Illinois Institute of Technology - Chicago Kent College

(This Listing Continued)

of Law (J.D., 1987). Former Associate: Ed Malek and Associates; Jobin, Desveaux and Flynn. *Member:* Illinois State Bar Association; Workers' Compensation Lawyers Association. ***PRACTICE AREAS:*** Workers Compensation. **Email:** bhdriscoll@wmlaw.com

EMILY E. BORG, born Omaha, Nebraska, December 19, 1973. *Education:* Michigan State University (B.A., 1996); DePaul University (J.D., 2000). *Member:* Illinois State Bar Association; Workers' Compensation Lawyers Association. ***PRACTICE AREAS:*** Workers Compensation. **Email:** eeborg@wmlaw.com

JAMES M. ROZAK, born Chicago, Illinois, June 10, 1964; admitted to bar, 1991, Illinois and U.S. District Court, Northern District of Illinois. *Education:* Marquette University (B.S., 1987); John Marshall Law School (J.D., 1991). Member, Moot Court, Best Brief Chicago Bar Association, 1990. Recipient: Best Brief, Chicago Bar Association, 1990. Assistant States Attorney, DuPage County, 1991-1995. Member, Products Liability Section, Defense Research Institute, 2001—. Affiliate Member, Property Loss Research Bureau. ***PRACTICE AREAS:*** Products Liability Litigation (70%); Commercial Litigation (20%); Insurance Coverage (10%). **Email:** jmrozak@wmlaw.com

JAMES W. JANNISCH, born Chicago, Illinois, September 10, 1973; admitted to bar, 1999, Illinois and U.S. District Court, Northern District of Illinois. *Education:* North Central College (B.A., Economics, 1995); DePaul University (J.D., 1999). ***PRACTICE AREAS:*** Workers Compensation. **Email:** jwjannisch@wmlaw.com

KAREN E. COON, born Detroit, Michigan, June 20, 1972; admitted to bar, 1997, Michigan; 2002, Illinois. *Education:* Michigan State University (B.A., 1994); University of Michigan Law School (J.D., 1996). Former Associate, Law Offices of John J. Zacheira. *Member:* Chicago and Illinois State Bar Associations; State Bar of Michigan. ***PRACTICE AREAS:*** Workers Compensation; Insurance Defense. **Email:** kecoon@wmlaw.com

JASON R. SCHACHNER, born Arlington Heights, Illinois, May 10, 1977; admitted to bar, 2003, Illinois. *Education:* Michigan State University (B.S., Microbiology, 2000); Thomas M. Cooley Law School (J.D., 2003). *Member:* Chicago, Illinois State and American Bar Associations. ***PRACTICE AREAS:*** Products Liability; Civil Litigation. **Email:** jrschachner@wmlaw.com

ROBERT H. FREDIAN, born Evanston, Illinois, March 20, 1958; admitted to bar, 1993, Illinois; 1994, U.S. District Court, Northern District of Illinois. *Education:* Western Illinois University (B.S., 1980); Loyola University (J.D., 1993). *Member:* Illinois State Bar Association. ***PRACTICE AREAS:*** Civil Litigation; Insurance Defense; Employer Liability. **Email:** rhfredian@wmlaw.com

LINDA A. ROBERT, born Sri Lanka, July 8, 1977; admitted to bar, 2002, Illinois. *Education:* Loyola University (B.A., 1999; J.D., 2003). *Member:* Illinois State Bar Association; Workers Compensation Lawyers Association. ***PRACTICE AREAS:*** Workers Compensation. **Email:** larobert@wmlaw.com

DANIEL M. ANDERS, born Palos Heights, Illinois, November 1, 1975; admitted to bar, 2003, Illinois. *Education:* Loyola University (B.A., cum laude, 1998); Chicago-Kent College of Law, Illinois Institute of Technology (J.D., 2003). *Member:* Chicago, Illinois State and American Bar Associations. ***PRACTICE AREAS:*** Workers Compensation. **Email:** dmanders@wmlaw.com

TRICIA L. ANDERSON, born Urbana, Illinois, October 24, 1977; admitted to bar, 2003, Illinois. *Education:* Northwestern University (B.A., 2000); Washington University (J.D., 2003). ***PRACTICE AREAS:*** Workers Compensation. **Email:** tlanderson@wmlaw.com

BENJAMIN L. RIDDLE, born Portland, Oregon, March 3, 1977; admitted to bar, 2003, Illinois. *Education:* Indiana University (B.A., 2000); Indiana University School of Law (J.D., 2003). *Member:* Chicago and Illinois State Bar Associations. ***PRACTICE AREAS:*** Commercial Litigation; Products Liability. **Email:** blriddle@wmlaw.com

ERICA N. ROGINA, born Chicago, Illinois, July 20, 1958; admitted to bar, 1998, Illinois and U.S. District Court, Northern District of Illinois. *Education:* University of Wisconsin (B.A., Journalism, 1980); Loyola University of Chicago School of Law (J.D., 1988). *Member:* Chicago and Illinois State Bar Associations; Worker's Compensation Lawyers' Association. ***PRACTICE AREAS:*** Workers Compensation; Insurance Defense; Civil Litigation; Appellate Practice. **Email:** enrogina@wmlaw.com

LAW OFFICES OF MARK E. WIEMELT, P.C.

Established in 1993

10 SOUTH LA SALLE STREET, SUITE 3300
CHICAGO, ILLINOIS 60603
Telephone: 312-372-7664
Fax: 312-372-6568
URL: http://www.wiemeltlawoffices.com
Email: mark@wiemeltlaw.com
URL: http://www.wiemeltlaw.com

MARK E. WIEMELT, born Quincy, Illinois; admitted to bar, 1991, Illinois; 1992, U.S. District Court, Central and Southern Districts of Illinois and U.S. Court of Appeals, Seventh Circuit; 1993, U.S. District Court Northern District of Illinois; 2003, U.S. Court of Appeals, Federal Circuit; registered to practice before U.S. Patent and Trademark Office. *Education:* Bradley University (B.S.M.E., 1987); Southern Illinois University (J.D., 1991). Recipient, American Jurisprudence Award. Member, American Society of Mechanical Engineers, 1986—. *Member:* Chicago, Peoria County, DuPage County, Illinois State and American Bar Associations; American Intellectual Property Lawyers Association. ***PRACTICE AREAS:*** Intellectual Property; Internet Law; Litigation; Business Law; Commercial Law.

ROBERT L. KNECHTEL, born Elmhurst, Illinois, February 21, 1959; admitted to bar, 1989, Michigan; 1990, U.S. District Court, Eastern and Western Districts of Michigan; 1998, U.S. District Court, Central and Northern Districts of Illinois; registered to practice before U.S. Patent and Trademark Office (Not admitted in Illinois). *Education:* College of DuPage (A.A., 1979); Northern Illinois University (B.S., 1982); Universidad Technologica de Santiago (M.D., 1986); Thomas M. Cooley Law School (J.D., 1989). Pi Kappa Delta. Recipient: Debating Scholarship, Northern Illinois University; Scholastic Scholarship, Thomas M. Cooley Law School; American Jurisprudence Award. Member, Thomas M.

(This Listing Continued)

Cooley Law Review. Formerly with: Foster, Swift, Collins & Smith, P.C.; Knechtel, Demeur & Samlan. *Member:* State Bar of Michigan; American Bar Association; American Intellectual Property Law Association. ***PRACTICE AREAS:*** Intellectual Property; Litigation; Antitrust.

WILDMAN, HARROLD, ALLEN & DIXON LLP

Established in 1967

225 WEST WACKER DRIVE
SUITE 3000
CHICAGO, ILLINOIS 60606-1229
Telephone: 312-201-2000
Fax: 312-201-2555
Email: info@wildmanharrold.com
URL: http://www.wildmanharrold.com

Lisle, Illinois Office: 2300 Cabot Drive, Suite 455. Telephone: 630-955-0555. Fax: 630-955-0662.

General Practice. Accreditation, Alternative Dispute Resolution, Antitrust, Appellate, Asbestos, Automotive, Aviation, Banking, Bankruptcy, Business Organizations, Closely-Held Corporations, Commercial Litigation, Consumer, Corporate, Creditors' Rights, Criminal, Drug and Medical Device, E-Commerce, EMF, Employee Benefits, Environmental, Estate Planning, Family Law, Financial Services, Governmental Affairs, Health Care, Industrial Machinery, Insurance Industry, Intellectual Property, Labor and Employment, Land Use Regulation, Mergers and Acquisitions, Municipal Bonds, Patents, Probate, Probate Administration, Procurement and Contracting, Product Liability, Real Estate, Recreational Products, SBIC, Securities, Superfund, Tax, Toxic Torts, Trial, Venture Capital and Workouts.

FIRM PROFILE: Wildman, Harrold, Allen & Dixon LLP is a full-service law firm with over 220 attorneys. Its practice is local, regional and national, with clients ranging from Fortune 500 corporations to individual entrepreneurs. Over the firm's 38-year tenure, it has developed a broad national practice. Practice areas include mergers and acquisitions, real estate, intellectual property, corporate and securities, tax, finance, creditors' rights, employment, environmental, estate planning, probate and family law, governmental affairs and health care, patents, product liability, in addition to its national litigation practice. The firm maintains a suburban office in Lisle, Illinois.

Wildman, Harrold, Allen & Dixon LLP is firmly committed to providing superior client service and solving clients' problems in an efficient and cost-effective manner.

PARTNERS

ANTHONY L. ABBOUD, born Iowa City, Iowa, March 21, 1966; admitted to bar, 1994, Illinois and U.S. District Court, Northern District of Illinois; 2004, U.S. District Court, Central District of Illinois. *Education:* Carleton College (B.A., 1988); University of Iowa (J.D., with distinction, 1994). Member, National Moot Court Team. Board Member, Teachers' Retirement System and Former Deputy Director of Housing, State Treasurer's Office, State of Illinois. *Member:* Chicago and American Bar Associations. ***REPORTED CASES:*** Tasini v. New York Times, 206 F.3d 161 (2d Cir. 2000), aff'd, 533 U.S. 483 (2001). ***PRACTICE AREAS:*** Business Litigation; Complex Litigation; Government. **Email:** abboud@wildmanharrold.com

FRED M. ACKERSON, born 1956; admitted to bar, 1980, Illinois and U.S. District Court, Northern District of Illinois; 1982, U.S. Tax Court and U.S. Claims Court. *Education:* Hamilton College (B.A., 1977); University of Chicago (J.D., 1980). *Author:* "Multi-State Tax Planning in Illinois," Lorman, 2000; "Single Sales Factor Issues," (CBA, 1999); "Basic Principles of Federal Income Taxation of Real Estate Investment Trusts," Federal Tax Aspects of Real Estate Transactions (IICLE, 1987; Supplement 1990); "Application of the Personal Holding Company Tax to Affiliated Corporations Filing Consolidated Returns," Primer on Consolidated Returns (ABA Program, May 1989). Member, Illinois Department of Revenue Advisory Committee, 1990-1993. *Member:* Chicago (Member, Committee on State and Local Taxation) and American (Member, Section of Taxation, Committee on State and Local Taxation, 1991—; Committee on Affiliated and Related Corporations, 1987-1991; Author, Section of Taxation Comment on Dual Consolidated Loss Regulations, 1991; Chairman, Subcommittee on Affiliation and Control Issues, 1989-1990; Task Force on Section 382 and Consolidated Returns, 1988-1989; Committee on Partnership Taxation, 1985-1987) Bar Associations. ***REPORTED CASES:*** Hercules Incorporated v. Department of Revenue, _ Ill. App. 3d _, _ N.E.2d _ (1st Dist. 2001); Tyson Foods v. Department of Revenue, 312 Ill. App. 3d 64, 726 N.E.2d 12 (1st Dist. 2000); Communications & Cable of Chicago v. City of Chicago Department of Revenue, 275 Ill. App. 3d 680, 655 N.E.2d 1078 (1st Dist. 1995); Chicago Metropolitan Ski Council v. Commisioner, 104 T.C. 341 (1995); Drake v. United States, 642 F.Supp. 830 (N.D.Ill. 1986). ***PRACTICE AREAS:*** Federal Taxation; State Taxation; Corporate; Securities and Tax; Mergers and Acquisitions. **Email:** ackerson@wildmanharrold.com

STEPHEN A. ALLISON, born Nashville, Tennessee, August 19, 1957; admitted to bar, 1985, New York; 1988, Illinois. *Education:* Northwestern University (B.A., 1979; J.D., 1984); Kellogg Graduate School of Management (M.M., 1981). ***PRACTICE AREAS:*** Corporate Law; Corporate Finance; Project Finance. **Email:** allison@wildmanharrold.com

AIMEE B. ANDERSON, born Chicago, Illinois, August 9, 1950; admitted to bar, 1984, Illinois and U.S. District Court, Northern District of Illinois and U.S. Supreme Court; 1987, U.S. Court of Appeals, Seventh Circuit; 1988, U.S. District Court, Central District of Illinois; 1990, U.S. District Court, Northern District of Illinois including Trial Bar. *Education:* New College of the University of South Florida (B.A., 1972); Loyola University (J.D., 1984). Chairman, Legal Developments Subcommittee, Committee on Biased Enforcement and Racial Profiling, Illinois Law Enforcement Training and Standards Board, 2000-2001. *Member:* Federation of Defense and Corporate Counsel. ***PRACTICE AREAS:*** Product Liability Litigation; Local Government Liability Litigation; Civil Rights Litigation. **Email:** andersona@wildmanharrold.com

(This Listing Continued)

WILDMAN, HARROLD, ALLEN & DIXON LLP, Chicago—Continued

JOHN J. ARADO, born Chicago, Illinois, July 8, 1942; admitted to bar, 1967, Illinois. *Education:* University of Notre Dame (B.B.A., 1964); University of Michigan (J.D., 1967). Beta Gamma Sigma. Arbitrator, American Arbitration Association. *Member:* Chicago, Illinois State and American Bar Associations; International Trademark Association. ***PRACTICE AREAS:*** Commercial Litigation; Intellectual Property. ***Email:*** arado@wildmanharrold.com

BRENT R. AUSTIN, born November 21, 1964; admitted to bar, 1989, California; 1994, Illinois; U.S. District Court, Northern District of Illinois including Trial Bar, U.S. District Court, Southern District of Illinois, U.S. District Court, Northern District of California and U.S. Court of Appeals, Third, Fifth, Seventh and Ninth Circuits. *Education:* University of California at Los Angeles (B.A., History, summa cum laude, 1986); Boalt Hall School of Law, University of California (J.D., 1989). Phi Beta Kappa. Author: "Enough is Enough: Alleged Forum Manipulation and Class Certification Denial," BNA Class Action Litigation Report, September 10, 2004; "The Economic Loss Only Product Liability Class Action: Claim-Splitting as a Strategy for Obtaining Class Certification," ABA Class Actions and Derivative Suits Section, Spring 2004; "Mass Torts Disguised as Commercial Class Actions," Andrews Toxic Chemicals Litigation Reporter, September 4, 2003; Quote in "Class Denied in Tort Branded the Next Asbestos," Corporate Legal Times, June 2003; Quote in "The Poisoned Wood Mystery: Is it Unsafe? Is it 'the Next Asbestos'," National Law Journal, March 17, 2003. Co-Author: "Recent Pharmaceutical and Medical Devices: What St. Jude and Several State Court Cases Do and Don't Tell Us," Class Action Defense Section, Findlaw.com's Corporate Counsel Center, April 2004; "Using The Due Process Clause To Defend Claims For Class-Wide Punitive Damages," Findlaw.com, May 2003; "The Litigation Epidemic That Hasn't Come - Treated Wood and The Denial of Class Certification in Jacobs v. Osmose," Mealey's Litigation Report, March 2003; "ADR in Securities Class Actions," 3 Security News 7, 1994. Speaker, "Products Liability Class Actions: What You Need to Know," Class Action Litigation Summit, sponsored by Northstar Conferences LLC, June 2004. Moderator, "Class Action," CLE Symposium for In-House Counsel, sponsored by ACCA, Delaware Chapter and DuPont Legal, April 2004. Interview Subject, "The Present and Future State of Class Action Litigation," Forbes Channel (for American and Delta Airlines), January 2004. *Member:* Chicago, Illinois State and American (Member: Antitrust Committee; Litigation Committee; Class Action Committee; Corporate Counsel Committee; Mass Tort Committee) Bar Associations. ***REPORTED CASES:*** Ardoin v. Stine Lumber Co., 220 F.R.D. 459 (W.D. La. 2004) (Lead defense counsel in industry defeat of nationwide and statewide class certifications of breach of warranty, conspiracy and unjust enrichment claims); Jacobs v. Osmose, 213 F.R.D. 607 (S.D. Fla. 2003) (Lead defense counsel in defeating certification of nationwide false marketing, consumer fraud, nuisance and product liability class action involving industry-wide challenge to pressure treated wood); Sandwich Chef of Texas, Inc. v. Reliance National Indemnity Insurance Co., 319 F.3d 205 (5th Cir. 2003) (Principal counsel in successful appeal from nationwide RICO conspiracy class certification in action involving industry-wide challenge to workers' compensation rate-making practices); Ardoin v. Stine Lumber Co., 298 F. Supp. 2d. 422 (W.D. La. 2003) (Lead defense counsel in successful argument that exceptional equitable circumstances arising from plaintiffs' forum-shopping to defeat jurisdiction warranted removal of nationwide breach of warranty and product liability class action even after statutory deadline); In re Chromated Copper Arsenate (CCA) Treated Wood Prod. Liab. Litig., MDL Docket No. 1438 (MDL Feb. 15, 2002) (Lead defense counsel in defeating consolidation of putative nationwide class actions as multidistrict litigation) ; Miller v. Home Depot U.S.A., Inc., 199 F. Supp.2d 502 (W.D. La. 2001) (Defeat remand of nationwide toxic tort putative class action); AARP v. National Surety Corp., 98-820589-CZ, 2001 WL 1530348 (Mich. Cir. Ct. Oct. 23, 2001) (Defeated certification of nationwide conspiracy and breach of contract class action); Foodarama Supermarkets, Inc. v. American Insurance Co., 43 PA.D. & C.4th 467, 2000 WL 356697 (Pa. Comm. Pl. Jan. 10, 2000) (Defeated certification of nationwide conspiracy and breach of contract class action); Reap v. Continental Cas. Co., 199 F.R.D. 536 (D. N.J. 2001) (Defeated certification of nationwide employment discrimination class action); Sunbeam v. American Medical Association, No. 97 CV 6313 (N.D. Ill.) (Breach of trademark licensing agreement action); Hanson, et al. v. Hamot Medical Center, et al (Successful defense of claim of conspiracy to monopolize health care market.); In re Care Corporation Securities Litigation, (Successful defense of securities class action). ***PRACTICE AREAS:*** Class Actions; Consumer Fraud; Consumer Protection; Marketing Law; Marketplace Liability; Complex Commercial Litigation; Civil RICO; Antitrust; Products Liability. ***Email:*** austin@wildmanharrold.com

JOSEPH E. BENDER, born Chicago, Illinois, February 2, 1968; admitted to bar, 1993, Wisconsin; 1999, Illinois. *Education:* University of Illinois (B.A., 1990); Marquette University Law School (J.D., 1993); New York University School of Law (LL.M. in Taxation, 1995). Pi Sigma Alpha. Member, Marquette Law Review. Adjunct Professor, University of Illinois-Chicago. Seminar speaker on various tax related topics including Taxation of Electronic Commerce, Corporate Reorganizations and International Tax Planning, Guest Lecturer, Graduate Tax Program, University of Wisconsin-Milwaukee. ***PRACTICE AREAS:*** Domestic and International Taxation; State Taxation; Electronic Commerce. ***Email:*** bender@wildmanharrold.com

MICHAEL P. BENNETT, born Rantoul, Illinois, November 6, 1959; admitted to bar, 1989, Illinois. *Education:* University of Notre Dame (B.A., 1982); Loyola University (J.D., 1989). *Member:* Chicago, Illinois and American Bar Associations. ***LANGUAGES:*** Italian. ***PRACTICE AREAS:*** Software Licensing; High Technology; Internet Transactions; Information Technology; Intellectual Property; Marketing and Computer Law; Distribution; Strategies; Manufacturing; Outsourcing. ***Email:*** bennett@wildmanharrold.com

TODD A. BICKEL, born Sidney, Ohio, June 5, 1969; admitted to bar, 1994, Ohio; 1998, Illinois. *Education:* Ohio State University (B.A., summa cum laude, with honors, 1991); University of North Carolina (J.D., 1994). Phi Beta Kappa; Phi Kappa Phi. *Member:* Chicago and American Bar Associations. ***PRACTICE AREAS:*** Commercial Real Estate. ***Email:*** bickel@wildmanharrold.com

MICHAEL R. BLANKSHAIN, born Oak Park, Illinois, March 20, 1956; admitted to bar, 1981, Illinois; U.S. District Court, Northern District of Illinois; U.S. Court of Appeals, Seventh Circuit; U.S. Supreme Court. *Education:* Princeton University (A.B., cum laude, 1978); University of Illinois (J.D., summa cum laude, 1981). Order of the Coif. Member, University of Illinois Law Review, 1979-1981. *Member:* American Bar Association (Section of Antitrust Law). ***PRACTICE AREAS:*** Commercial Litigation; Antitrust Litigation. ***Email:*** blankshain@wildmanharrold.com

SCOTT R. BORSTEIN, born Cleveland, Ohio, June 22, 1963; admitted to bar, 1988, Illinois; 1992, California. *Education:* Miami University (B.A., cum laude, 1985); Georgetown University (J.D., 1988). *Member:* Chicago and Illinois State Bar Associations; State Bar of California. ***PRACTICE AREAS:*** Zoning; Real Estate; Entertainment; Business Law.

BRUCE L. BORUSZAK, born Chicago, Illinois, July 29, 1957; admitted to bar, 1982, Illinois; 2003, California. *Education:* University of Illinois (B.S. with highest honors, 1979); University of Michigan (J.D., cum laude, 1982). Beta Alpha Psi; Beta Gamma Sigma; Phi Kappa Phi; Omicron Delta Kappa; Order of the Coif. Member, 1980-1981 and Associate Editor, 1981-1982, University of Michigan Journal of Law Reform. Certified Public Accountant, Illinois, 1979. Commissioner, 1984-1987, Chairman. 1986-1987, North Shore Cable Commission. Member, 1997-1999 and Chairman, 1999, Deerfield Public School District 109 Caucus. Member, Board of Directors, University of Illinois Commerce Alumni Association, 1990—. President, University of Illinois Commerce Alumni Association, 2001-2003. Associate Member, International Council of Shopping Centers 1989—. *Member:* Illinois State Bar Association. ***PRACTICE AREAS:*** Real Estate. ***Email:*** boruszak@wildmanharrold.com

JOHN T. BROWN, born Oak Ridge, Tennessee, March 23, 1961; admitted to bar, 1986, Illinois. *Education:* University of Illinois (B.A., 1983); University of Virginia (J.D., 1986). Phi Beta Kappa. *Member:* Chicago, Illinois State, American and Seventh Circuit Bar Associations; Intellectual Property Law Association of Chicago. ***PRACTICE AREAS:*** Trademark; Copyright; Advertising; Unfair Competition; International Law; Litigation. ***Email:*** jbrown@wildmanharrold.com

CAL R. BURNTON, born Green Bay, Wisconsin, January 21, 1956; admitted to bar, 1981, Wisconsin; 1983, Illinois; U.S. District Court, Northern District of Illinois including Trial Bar; U.S. District Court, Eastern and Western Districts of Wisconsin. *Education:* University of Wisconsin (B.B.A., 1978); Marquette University (J.D., 1981). Alpha Sigma Nu. Marquette Law Review, 1980-1981. Intern, United States Attorney's Office, Milwaukee, Wisconsin (1980), Milwaukee County District Attorney's Office (1981). Staff Attorney, U.S. Court of Appeals, Seventh Circuit, 1981-1983. Conference, Simcom International, Using Safety Manuals to Avoid Litigation (July 1998). Regular Lecturer, Seminars on Product Liability, Warnings and Instructions, University of Wisconsin, Spring and Fall, 1990-2004; Lecturer, Conference on Product Liability and Accident Prevention, Japan Risk Management Association, Tokyo, Japan, August, 1991, 1992, October 1995 (Tokyo, Kyoto and Niigata); Lecturer, Conference on Risk Management and Product Liability, Nippon Fire and Marine Insurance Co. Ltd., Tokyo, Japan, October, 1993; Lecturer, Product Liability Prevention, AIRMIC Conference, University of Warwick, England, 1994. Lecturer, Loss Avoidance Through Product Warnings, Crum & Forster (1999). Contributing Author and Lecturer, Product Liability Prevention and Defense Association, 1989-2004. *Member:* Illinois State Bar Association; Defense Research Institute; International Association of Defense Counsel; Inter-Pacific Bar Association; The Association of Trial Lawyers of America. ***PRACTICE AREAS:*** Business Litigation; Products Liability Law; Environmental Law; Toxic Tort Litigation. ***Email:*** burnton@wildmanharrold.com

ADAM SCOTT CALISOFF, born Chicago, Illinois, June 20, 1969; admitted to bar, 1994, Illinois. *Education:* University of Southern California (B.S., 1991; J.D., 1994). Recipient: American Jurisprudence Award in Property. Managing Editor: Southern California Interdisciplinary Law Journal; Major Tax Planner, 1993-1994. Co-Chairman, Wildman Harrold Corporate, Securities and Tax Educational Program. ***PRACTICE AREAS:*** Mergers and Acquisitions; Corporate; Franchising. ***Email:*** calisoff@wildmanharrold.com

DOUGLAS R. CARLSON, born Joliet, Illinois, February 10, 1945; admitted to bar, 1969, Illinois. *Education:* Monmouth College (B.A., 1966); Northwestern University (J.D., 1969). Editorial Board Member, *Criminal Antitrust Litigation Manual,* published by American Bar Association, 1983. *Member:* Chicago, Illinois State and American Bar Associations; American Health Lawyers Association. ***PRACTICE AREAS:*** Health Care; Antitrust; Commercial Litigation; Accreditation. ***Email:*** carlson@wildmanharrold.com

JAMES A. CHRISTMAN, born Grand Haven, Michigan, October 15, 1948; admitted to bar, 1973, Illinois; U.S. District Court, Central and Northern Districts of Illinois including Trial Bar. *Education:* DePauw University (B.A.,1970); Washington University School of Law (J.D., 1973). Editor, Washington University Law Quarterly, 1972-1973. *Member:* Illinois State Bar Association; Chicago Council of Lawyers. ***PRACTICE AREAS:*** Health Care; Trial; Litigation. ***Email:*** christma@wildmanharrold.com

GEOFFREY C. COCKRELL, born Marion, Indiana, September 9, 1970; admitted to bar, 1997, Illinois. *Education:* Wheaton College (B.A., cum laude, 1993); Notre Dame Law School (J.D., magna cum laude, 1997). Author: "Batson Reform: A Lottery System of Affirmative Selection," Notre Dame Journal of Law, Ethics & Public Policy, Volume 11, Issue 1. ***PRACTICE AREAS:*** Venture Capital; Corporate/Securities; Mergers and Acquisitions; Small Business Investment Companies. ***Email:*** cockrell@wildmanharrold.com

WILLIAM J. COOK, admitted to bar, 1973, Nebraska; 1975, Illinois and U.S. Court of Appeals, Seventh Circuit; 1981, U.S. Supreme Court. *Education:* Creighton University (A.B., 1968; J.D., 1973). Vice President, Infragard (F.B.I. Computer Crime Unit Community Reach Out Program); Founding Member, Chicago Electronic Crimes Task Force. Member and Co-Author, National Science Foundation Critical Infrastructure Protection and the Law Committee Report. *Member:* Chicago, Illinois State and American Bar Associations; American Intellectual Property Law Association. [1st Lt. Infantry, U.S. Army 25th Infantry Division, 1968-1970]. ***PRACTICE AREAS:*** Intellectual Property; Information Technology; E-Commerce. ***Email:*** cook@wildmanharrold.com

JOHN W. COSTELLO, admitted to bar, 1972, Illinois. *Education:* John Carroll University (B.S., 1969); DePaul University Law School (J.D., 1972). ***PRACTICE AREAS:*** Financial Services; Creditor's Rights. ***Email:*** costello@wildmanharrold.com

PAUL R. DIAMOND, born Chicago, Illinois, July 19, 1955; admitted to bar, 1980, Illinois. *Education:* University of Illinois (B.S., with highest honors, 1977; J.D., 1980). *Member:* Chicago Bar Association; International Development Research Council. ***PRAC-***

(This Listing Continued)

TICE AREAS: Commercial Real Estate; Commercial Leasing; Industrial Real Estate Law; Real Estate Acquisitions and Sales; Shopping Center Law; Construction Law. ***Email:*** diamond@wildmanharrold.com

STEWART S. DIXON, born Evanston, Illinois, November 5, 1930; admitted to bar, 1957, Illinois and U.S. District Court, Northern District of Illinois; 1972, U.S. Supreme Court. *Education:* Yale University (B.A., 1952); University of Michigan (J.D., 1955). Independent Director for Lord, Abbett Managed Mutual Funds, 1976—. Member, Northwestern University Associates, 1965—. Trustee of Otho S.A. Sprague Institute Foundation, 1972—. Trustee, 1965—, Chairman of the Board, 1982-1987, Chicago Historical Society. *Member:* Chicago, Illinois State and American Bar Associations; American Law Institute. ***PRACTICE AREAS:*** Corporate Litigation; Antitrust; Tax; Estate Planning; Probate; Family Law. ***Email:*** dixon@wildmanharrold.com

MICHAEL DOCKTERMAN, born Rock Island, Illinois, December 14, 1954; admitted to bar, 1978, Illinois; U.S. District Court, Northern District of Illinois including Trial Bar; U.S. District Court, Central and Southern Districts of Illinois; U.S. District Court, Eastern and Western Districts of Michigan; U.S. District Court, Eastern District of Missouri; U.S. Court of Appeals, Seventh Circuit; U.S. Court of Appeals, Sixth Circuit; U.S. Court of Appeals, Fourth Circuit; U.S. Court of Appeals, Second Circuit; U.S. Court of Appeals for the Federal Circuit; U.S. Supreme Court. *Education:* Yale University (B.A., cum laude, 1975); Duke University (J.D., 1978). Recipient: International Academy of Trial Lawyers Award for Advocacy; B'nai B'rith Youth Organization Leadership Development Award. Instructor, National Institute for Trial Advocacy, Midwest Regional Program. Instructor, Kellogg School of Business Women's Director Development Program on Corporate Governance. Author: "How To Craft a Good Compliance Program Without Building a Bureaucracy," II CLE 1999; "The Convergence of Governance and Compliance," ABA Section of Business Law, 1999; "Designing and Implementing Effective Compliance Programs," ABA Section of Business Law 1998; "Compliance After Caremark," ABA Section of Business Law 1998; Review, Nafziger "International Sports Law," American J. Intl. L, 1989; "*Mechanik* "Two Years Later: Are Grand Jury Abuses Forever Safe From Review?" ABA Section of Antitrust Law Criminal Practice Newsletter, Summer, 1988. Co-Author: "Pleadings, Motions and Orders," IICLE Class Actions, 1979, 1986, 1990, 1993, 2001, 2004. Contributor, Criminal Antitrust Litigation Manual, ABA Section of Antitrust Law, 1983. Member, 1995— and President, 2000—, Board of Directors, Duke Law School Alumni Association; Member, 2002—, Board of Visitors, Duke Law School; Chair, Corporate Governance Subcommittee, ABA Section of Business Law Corporate Counsel Committee, 1997—; Member, 2002—, Fellow of the American Bar Foundation. *Member:* Chicago and American Bar Associations; Legal Club of Chicago; The Chicago Committee, Chicago Council on Foreign Relations. ***PRACTICE AREAS:*** Civil and Criminal Business Litigation; Corporate Governance. ***Email:*** dockterman@wildmanharrold.com

LEO P. DOMBROWSKI, born Evergreen Park, Illinois, November 27, 1956; admitted to bar, 1990, Illinois; U.S. District Court, Northern and Central Districts of Illinois, Eastern District of Wisconsin; U.S. Court of Appeals, Seventh Circuit, U.S. Court of Appeals for the Federal Circuit, U.S. Court of Appeals for Veterans Claims and U.S. Supreme Court. *Education:* University of Illinois (B.A., 1984); IIT Chicago-Kent College of Law (J.D., with high honors, 1990). Order of the Coif. Notes and Comments Editor, IIT Chicago-Kent Law Review. *Member:* Chicago, Illinois State and American Bar Associations. ***LANGUAGES:*** German. ***REPORTED CASES:*** Steel Co. v. Citizens for a Better Environment, 523 U.S. 83 (1998) on remand, 230 F. 3d 923 (7th Cir. 2000); A-C Reorganization Trust v. DuPont, 968 F.Supp. 423 (E.D. Wis. 1997). ***PRACTICE AREAS:*** Environmental; Toxic Torts; Commercial Litigation; Appellate. ***Email:*** dombrowski@wildmanharrold.com

JAMES P. DORR, born Storm Lake, Iowa, August 15, 1944; admitted to bar, 1969, Illinois. *Education:* Dartmouth College (B.A., 1966); University of Stockholm; Northwestern University (J.D., 1969). *Member:* American College of Trial Lawyers; Product Liability Advisory Council; International Association of Defense Counsel; Defense Research Institute. ***PRACTICE AREAS:*** Product Liability; National Litigation; Litigation Management; Trial; Commercial Litigation. ***Email:*** dorr@wildmanharrold.com

VILIA M. DRAZDYS, born Omaha, Nebraska, February 18, 1968; admitted to bar, 1992, Illinois and U.S. District Court, Northern District of Illinois; U.S. Court of Appeals, Seventh Circuit; U.S. Court of Appeals, Fourth Circuit. *Education:* Creighton University (B.S.B.A., summa cum laude, 1989); Harvard University (J.D., cum laude, 1992). *Member:* Chicago, Illinois State, and American Bar Associations. ***PRACTICE AREAS:*** Telecommunications Law; Commercial Litigation; Class Action Litigation. ***Email:*** drazdys@wildmanharrold.com

THOMAS P. DUFFY, admitted to bar, 1976, Illinois and U.S. District Court, Northern District of Illinois. *Education:* University of Pennsylvania (B.A., 1972); John Marshall Law School; DePaul University (J.D., cum laude, 1976). ***PRACTICE AREAS:*** Real Estate; Corporate Law; Litigation. ***Email:*** duffy@wildmanharrold.com

MARK L. DURBIN, born LaGrange, Illinois; admitted to bar, 1993, Illinois; U.S. District Court, Northern Districts of Illinois and Indiana; U.S. Court of Appeals, Seventh Circuit. *Education:* University of Illinois, Urbana (B.A., with distinction, 1988); DePaul University College of Law (J.D., 1993). *Member:* Chicago and American Bar Associations. ***PRACTICE AREAS:*** Commercial Litigation; Products Liability. ***Email:*** durbin@wildmanharrold.com

JAMES B. DURKIN, born Chicago, Illinois, January 28, 1961; admitted to bar, 1990, Illinois. *Education:* Illinois State University (B.S., 1984); The John Marshall Law School (J.D., 1989). Cook County State's Attorney. Illinois Attorney General. Member: Illinois House of Representatives, 1995-2002; Misericordia-Heart of Mercy Home Board of Advisors, 1996—. Republican Nominee for United States Senate, 2002. *Member:* Chicago Bar Association. (Lisle Office). ***PRACTICE AREAS:*** Government Affairs. ***Email:*** durkin@wildmanharrold.com

JOHN L. EISEL, born Akron, Ohio, January 18, 1949; admitted to bar, 1974, Illinois. *Education:* University of Illinois (B.S., 1971; J.D., magna cum laude, 1974). Order of the Coif. Member, Bronze Tablet, University of Illinois. Certified Public Accountant, Illinois, 1971. Articles Editor, University of Illinois Law Forum, 1973-1974. Law Clerk to Justice Walter V. Schaefer, 1974-1975. Illinois Secretary of State Business Corporation Acts Advisory Committee. *Member:* American Bar Association. ***PRACTICE AREAS:*** Mergers and Acquisitions; Securities; General Corporate. ***Email:*** eisel@wildmanharrold.com

DIANE G. ELDER, born Santa Monica, California, August 30, 1958; admitted to bar, 1983, California; 1984, Illinois. *Education:* University of California at Berkeley (A.B., 1980); University of Southern California (J.D., 1983). Phi Beta Kappa. Recipient: American Jurisprudence Award in Property; Nelson Justice Prize. *Member:* Chicago, Illinois State and American Bar Associations; The State Bar of California. ***LANGUAGES:*** Spanish. ***PRACTICE AREAS:*** General Practice; International Law; Intellectual Property; Trademark Law; Copyright Law; Unfair Competition Law; International Intellectual Property; Advertising Law. ***Email:*** elder@wildmanharrold.com

JERALD P. ESRICK, born Moline, Illinois, October 1, 1941; admitted to bar, 1966, Illinois and U.S. District Court, Northern District of Illinois including Trial Bar, U.S. Court of Appeals, Seventh and Ninth Circuits and U.S. Supreme Court. *Education:* Northwestern University (B.A., with honors, 1963); Harvard University (J.D., 1966). Chair, Diversity Committee of Firm, 1999—. Chairman, Management Committee of Firm, 1987-1990. Lecturer on Antitrust Law, Northwestern University, 1984-1992. Law Clerk to Hon. Abraham L. Marovitz, U.S. District Judge, Northern District of Illinois, 1966-1968. Member, Inquiry Board of the Supreme Court's Attorney Registration and Disciplinary Commission, 1973-1975. Secretary and Director, 1969-1985, The Fund for Justice. President, Board of Trustees, National Lekotek Center, 1989-1992. Board of Directors, Chicago Lawyers Committee for Civil Rights Under Law, 1974-1984; Friends Committee, Legal Assistance Foundation of Chicago, 1992—; Board of Visitors, Northwestern University College of Arts and Sciences, 1994—. National Panel of Commercial Arbitrators, American Arbitration Association. *Member:* Chicago (Member, 1970— and Chairman, 1980-1981, Antitrust Law Committee; Member: Securities Committee; Corporation Law Committee), Illinois State (Council Member, Antitrust Law Section, 1982-1985) and American (Member, Sections on: Business; Litigation; Antitrust) Bar Associations; Chicago Council of Lawyers (Founding Member; Secretary, 1969-1970; Member, Board of Governors, 1970-1972); Lawyer's Club of Chicago. Fellow, American College of Trial Lawyers. ***PRACTICE AREAS:*** Corporate and Securities; Antitrust; Commercial Litigation; Alternative Dispute Resolution. ***Email:*** esrick@wildmanharrold.com

LAWRENCE W. FALBE, born Chicago, Illinois; admitted to bar, 1994, Illinois and U.S. District Court, Northern District of Illinois; 1995, U.S. District Court, Eastern District of Wisconsin. *Education:* Augustana College (B.A., 1991); DePaul University College of Law (J.D., 1994). Phi Beta Kappa. *Member:* Chicago, Illinois State and American Bar Associations. ***PRACTICE AREAS:*** Environmental; Appellate; Commercial Litigation; Trial; Land Use. ***Email:*** falbe@wildmanharrold.com

BETH L. FANCSALI, admitted to bar, 1990, Texas and U.S. District Court, Northern District of Texas; 1994, U.S. Court of Appeals, Fifth Circuit; 1997, U.S. District Court, Southern and Western Districts of Texas; 2003, Illinois, U.S. District Court, Northern District of Illinois and U.S. Court of Appeals, Seventh Circuit. *Education:* Miami University of Ohio (B.S., magna cum laude, Business Administration, 1987); University of Texas (J.D., with honors, 1990). Order of the Coif. Associate Editor, Texas Law Review, 1989-1990. *Member:* Chicago and American (Member, Sections on: Antitrust; Criminal Justice; Litigation) Bar Associations; State Bar of Texas. ***PRACTICE AREAS:*** Complex Business Litigation; Antitrust Litigation; Class Action Litigation; Professional Liability; Ethics Issues; White Collar Criminal Defense; Corporate Investigations; Mass Tort Litigation. ***Email:*** fancsali@wildmanharrold.com

DAVID J. FISCHER, born Boston, Massachusetts, December 8, 1952; admitted to bar, 1977, Illinois. *Education:* Yale University (B.A., magna cum laude, 1974); Boston University (J.D., cum laude, 1977). Member, Boston University Law Review, 1976-1977. *Member:* Chicago and American Bar Associations. ***PRACTICE AREAS:*** Bankruptcy; Real Estate; Litigation. ***Email:*** fischer@wildmanharrold.com

DONALD FLAYTON, born New York, N.Y., October 3, 1947; admitted to bar, 1972, Illinois and U.S. District Court, Northern District of Illinois; 1981, U.S. Court of Appeals, Seventh Circuit; 1991, U.S. Court of Appeals, Federal Circuit; 1997, U.S. District Court, Southern District of Illinois; 2000, U.S. Court of Appeals, Eighth Circuit; 2002, U.S. Supreme Court. *Education:* University of Pittsburgh (B.A., 1969); Northwestern University (J.D., 1972). Author: "Consumer Protection Law in the United States," Center for International Studies (August 1994). *Member:* International Bar Association. ***PRACTICE AREAS:*** Commercial Litigation and Arbitration; Complex Business Litigation and Arbitration. ***Email:*** flayton@wildmanharrold.com

CRAIG STEVEN FOCHLER, born New York, N.Y., August 7, 1946; admitted to bar, 1971, Illinois. *Education:* Knox College (B.A., 1968); Northwestern University (J.D., 1971). *Member:* Chicago, Illinois State and American (Member: Litigation Section; Intellectual Property Law Section) Bar Associations; International Trademark Association; Intellectual Property Law Association; Promotion Marketing Association of America; Intellectual Property Law Association of Chicago; Law Club of Chicago. ***PRACTICE AREAS:*** Trademark; Copyright; Trade Secret; Unfair Competition; Franchise Law; Intellectual Property; Internet. ***Email:*** fochler@wildmanharrold.com

LISA M. FONTOURA, born September 8, 1971; admitted to bar, 1996, New Jersey and U.S. District Court, District of New Jersey; 2001, Illinois and U.S. District Court, Northern District of Illinois. *Education:* Franklin & Marshall College (B.A., 1993); Washington College of Law of American University (J.D., 1996). *Member:* Illinois State Bar Association. ***PRACTICE AREAS:*** Commercial Litigation; Employment Litigation.

KATHY PINKSTAFF FOX, born Indianapolis, Indiana, March 8, 1942; admitted to bar, 1979, Illinois and U.S. District Court, Northern District of Illinois; 1982, U.S. District Court, Northern District of Illinois including Trial Bar; 1989, U.S. Court of Appeals, Seventh Circuit; 1991, U.S. District Court, Central District of Illinois; 1993, U.S. Court of Appeals, Fifth Circuit; 1996, U.S. Supreme Court. *Education:* DePauw University (B.A., magna cum laude, 1964); Northwestern University (J.D., cum laude, 1979). Phi Beta Kappa. Notes and Comments Editor, Journal of Criminal Law & Criminology, Northwestern Law School, 1978-1979. *Member:* Inns of Court, Trial Lawyers Network. ***REPORTED CASES:*** Bogseth v. Emanuel, 166 Ill.2d 507, 655 N.E.2d 888 (1995); Neufville v. Diamond, 267 Ill.App.3d 1002, 638 N.E.2d 683 (1st Dist. 1994); Samansky v. Rush - Presbyterian - St. Luke's Medical Ctr., 208 IA3 377, 567 NE2 386 (1st Dist. 1990), rehearing denied, 1991; Rowan v. Novotny, 157 IA3 691, 510 NE2 1111 (1st Dist. 1987); Loizzo v. St.

(This Listing Continued)

WILDMAN, HARROLD, ALLEN & DIXON LLP, Chicago—Continued

Francis Hosp., 121 IA3 172, 459 NE2 314 (1st Dist. 1984); Inland Const. Co. v. Home Indem. Co., 113 IA3 558, 447 NE2 1023 (1st Dist. 1983); Plesnicar v. Kovac, 102 IA3 867, 430 NE2 648 (1st Dist. 1981); Fourfouris v. Standard Oil Realty Corp., 100 IA3 162, 426 NE2 915 (1st Dist. 1981), rehearing denied, 1981; Cirafici v. Goffen, 85 IA3 1102, 407 NE2 633 (1st Dist. 1980); Niehus v. Liberio 973 F.2d 526 (7th Cir. 1992); Harbor Insurance Co. v. Continental Bank Corp., 922 F.2d 357 (7th Cir. 1990), rehearing denied, 1991; Dileo v. Ernst & Young, 901 F.2d 624 (7th Cir. 1990), rehearing denied; In re Air Crash Disaster Near Chicago, on May 25, 1979, 644 F.2d 633 (7th Cir. 1981); In re Air Crash Disaster Near Chicago, 644 F.2d 594 (7th Cir. 1981); Motorola Credit Corp. v. Airstar Paging, Inc., 1997 U.S. Dist. LEXIS 6820; Holliday v. Timm, 2000 U.S. Dist LEXIS 13497; Momans v. St. John's Northwestern Military Academy, Inc., 2000 U.S. Dist. LEXIS 5129; Stonewall Insurance Co. v. Argonaut Insurance Co., 75 F.Supp.2d 893 (N.D. Ill. 1999); Motorola Credit Corp. v. Airstar Paging, 1997 U.S. Dist. Lexis 6820; Slijepcevich v. Caremark, Inc., 1996 U.S. Dist. LEXIS 110; National Union Fire Insurance Co. v. Continental Illinois Corp., 646 F.Supp. 746 (N.D. Ill. 1986); Reichert v. Urban Inv. & Dev. Co., 577 F.Supp. 971 (N.D. Ill. 1984); Pietruszynski v. McClier, 2002 Ill. App. Court, 1st Dist. ***PRACTICE AREAS:*** Commercial Litigation; Employment Litigation; Professional Malpractice. ***Email:*** fox@wildmanharrold.com

JOHN E. FREY, born East St. Louis, Illinois, February 17, 1951; admitted to bar, 1975, Illinois; 1977, New York. *Education:* Southern Illinois University (B.A., 1972); Georgetown University (J.D., 1975). Law Clerk, U.S. District Judge Richard B. Austin, 1975-1976. ***PRACTICE AREAS:*** Commercial Litigation; Environmental. ***Email:*** frey@wildmanharrold.com

HOWARD N. GILBERT, born Chicago, Illinois, August 19, 1928; admitted to bar, 1951, Illinois. *Education:* University of Chicago (Ph.B., 1947); Yale University (J.D., 1951). *Member:* Chicago and American Bar Associations; Chicago Council of Lawyers; National Health Lawyers Association. ***PRACTICE AREAS:*** Corporate Law; Business Law; Health Law; Real Estate; Trusts and Estates. ***Email:*** gilbert@wildmanharrold.com

GARY R. GILLEN, born Chicago, Illinois, May 25, 1965; admitted to bar, 1992, Illinois and U.S. District Court, Northern District of Illinois; 1993, U.S. Court of Appeals for the Federal Circuit; 1998, U.S. Court of Appeals, Seventh Circuit; registered to practice before U.S. Patent and Trademark Office. *Education:* Marquette University (Engineering); John Marshall Law School (J.D., 1992). Recipient, Evans Scholarship. *Member:* Illinois State Bar Association; American Intellectual Property Law Association; Intellectual Property Law Association of Chicago. ***PRACTICE AREAS:*** Patent; Trademark; Copyright; Intellectual Property Litigation. ***Email:*** gillen@wildmanharrold.com

KATHLEEN M. GILLIGAN, born Chicago, Illinois, November 4, 1961; admitted to bar, 1986, Maine; 1990, Illinois. *Education:* University of Notre Dame (B.A., with honors, 1983); Boston College Law School (J.D., cum laude, 1986). Staff Writer, 1984-1985 and Associate Editor, 1985-1986, Uniform Commercial Code, Reporter Digest at Boston College Law School. *Member:* Commercial Real Estate Executive Women. ***PRACTICE AREAS:*** Real Property; Real Estate; Leasing. ***Email:*** gilligan@wildmanharrold.com

KENNETH M. GORENBERG, born Philadelphia, Pennsylvania, March 18, 1965; admitted to bar, 1990, Illinois, U.S. District Court, Northern District of Illinois including Trial Bar, U.S. District Court, Central District of Illinois, U.S. District Court, Northern District of Indiana, U.S. District Court, Eastern and Western Districts of Wisconsin and U.S. Court of Appeals, Seventh and Tenth Circuits. *Education:* University of Pennsylvania (B.A., cum laude, 1987); University of Chicago (J.D., 1990). *Member:* American Bar Association; Defense Research Institute. ***REPORTED CASES:*** Copier v. Smith & Wesson Corp., 138 F.3d 833 (10th Cir. 1998). ***PRACTICE AREAS:*** Commercial Litigation; Insurance Coverage; Product Liability. ***Email:*** gorenberg@wildmanharrold.com

JEFFREY P. GRAY, born Chicago, Illinois, June 27, 1959; admitted to bar, 1984, Illinois and U.S. District Court, Northern District of Illinois; 1993, Colorado. *Education:* Indiana University (B.A., with distinction, 1981); Northwestern University (J.D., cum laude, 1984). Phi Beta Kappa; Order of the Coif. *Member:* Illinois State and American (Member, Business Law, Real Property & Probate and Financial Institutions and Commercial Finance Committees) Bar Associations. ***PRACTICE AREAS:*** Corporate, Securities, Tax; Banking and Creditors' Rights; Real Estate. ***Email:*** gray@wildmanharrold.com

JONATHAN A. HARRIS, born May 17, 1972; admitted to bar, 1998, Illinois, U.S. District Court, Northern District of Illinois and U.S. Court of Appeals, Federal Circuit; registered to practice before U.S. Patent and Trademark Office. *Education:* Duke University (B.S., 1994); University of Connecticut School of Law and School of Business (M.B.A., 1998; J.D., 1998). ***PRACTICE AREAS:*** Intellectual Property. ***Email:*** harrisj@wildmanharrold.com

H. RODERIC HEARD, born Bloomington, Indiana, October 10, 1946; admitted to bar, 1973, Illinois. *Education:* Northwestern University (B.S., 1968; M.S., 1969), Kappa Tau Alpha, journalism honorary fraternity; Marshall-Wythe School of Law, College of William and Mary (J.D., 1973). Member, Staff, William and Mary Law Review, 1972-1973. Faculty, National Institute of Trial Advocacy (NITA 1987—); Adjunct Professor of Law: DePaul University; Northwestern University. Member, Dispute Resolution Board, Kellogg School of Management, Northwestern University. Lecturer: "Tailoring Trial Advocacy for Mediation and Arbitration"; "Florida Election Contests," Network of Trial Law Firms, Palm Beach, Florida; "Federal Rules of Civil Procedure," National Business Institute; "Globalizing the Legal Process," International Bar Association, New Delhi, India. Distinguished Neutral, CPR Institute for Dispute Resolution. Lecturer "International Dispute Resolution," International Developing Law Institute, Rome, Italy. Co-Author "A Practical Guide To the Federal Rules of Civil Procedure," National Business Institute. Chairman, Network of Trial Law Firms, 2003. *Member:* Illinois State and American Bar Associations. ***PRACTICE AREAS:*** Commercial Litigation; Technology Litigation. ***Email:*** heard@wildmanharrold.com

HELAINE WACHS HEYDEMANN, born Long Beach, California; admitted to bar, 1973, California; 1975, Illinois; U.S. District Court, Central District of California; U.S. District Court, Northern District of Illinois. *Education:* University of California at Berkeley (A.B., 1968); Stanford University (J.D., 1971); Harvard University (LL.M., 1973).

(This Listing Continued)

Member: Chicago, Illinois State and American Bar Associations. ***PRACTICE AREAS:*** Litigation; Health Care; Employment Litigation. ***Email:*** heydemann@wildmanharrold.com

DAVID H. HIGHT, born Peoria, Illinois, August 5, 1955; admitted to bar, 1985, Illinois. *Education:* Millikin University (B.A., summa cum laude, 1976); Eastern Illinois University (M.A., 1980); DePaul University (J.D., with honors, 1985). Recipient, American Jurisprudence Award. Member, DePaul Law Review, 1982-1985. *Member:* Illinois State and American Bar Associations. (Lisle Office). ***PRACTICE AREAS:*** Corporate Law; Banking Law; Real Estate Law. ***Email:*** hight@wildmanharrold.com

RICHARD M. HOFFMAN, born Minneapolis, Minnesota, December 8, 1963; admitted to bar, 1990, Illinois and U.S. District Court, Northern District of Illinois, including Trial Bar. *Education:* University of Minnesota (B.S., 1987; J.D., magna cum laude, 1990). *Member:* Chicago and American Bar Associations. ***PRACTICE AREAS:*** Commercial Litigation; Real Estate Litigation. ***Email:*** hoffman@wildmanharrold.com

ANTHONY G. HOPP, born La Grange, Illinois, September 12, 1962; admitted to bar, 1988, Illinois and U.S. District Court, Central, Southern and Northern Districts of Illinois. *Education:* University of Illinois (B.A., summa cum laude, 1984; J.D., summa cum laude, 1988). University Honors, 1984; Order of the Coif. ***REPORTED CASES:*** Sirico v. Beckerle Lumber Supply, 624 N.Y.S. 2d (2nd Dept. 1996); Louisiana Pacific v. Koppers Company Inc., 38 Cal. Rptr. 2d 287 (1st District 1994). ***PRACTICE AREAS:*** Commercial Litigation; Toxic Tort Litigation; Environmental Litigation; Insurance Industry; Product Liability; Trial. ***Email:*** hopp@wildmanharrold.com

PETER M. HOWARD, born New York, N.Y., February 10, 1958; admitted to bar, 1985, New York; 1995, Illinois. *Education:* Antioch College (B.S., 1981); Yale University (J.D., 1984). ***PRACTICE AREAS:*** Corporate Law; Securities; Tax Law; Private Equity; Small Business Investment Companies (SBICs); Mergers and Acquisitions. ***Email:*** phoward@wildmanharrold.com

RICHARD C. JOHNSON, born Chicago, Illinois, February 28, 1957; admitted to bar, 1982, Illinois. *Education:* DePaul University (B.A., 1979); John Marshall Law School (J.D., 1982). *Member:* DuPage County Bar Association; DuPage County Estate Planning Council. (Lisle Office). ***PRACTICE AREAS:*** Estate Planning; Probate; Family Law; Real Estate Law. ***Email:*** johnson@wildmanharrold.com

MARTHA D. KANTER, born Boston, Massachusetts, September 11, 1964; admitted to bar, 1991, Illinois. *Education:* Boston College; College of the Holy Cross (B.A., 1986); Loyola University (J.D., 1991). ***PRACTICE AREAS:*** Commercial Litigation; Drug; Medical Device; Product Liability; Trial. ***Email:*** owensm@wildmanharrold.com

CHARLES C. KIM, born Seoul, South Korea, October 11, 1968; admitted to bar, 1995, Minnesota; 1999, Illinois. *Education:* Duke University (B.A., cum laude, 1991); Northwestern University (J.D., 1995). ***LANGUAGES:*** Korean. ***PRACTICE AREAS:*** Corporate; Securities; Mergers and Acquisitions. ***Email:*** kim@wildmanharrold.com

ANNE GIDDINGS KIMBALL, born Brooklyn, New York; admitted to bar, 1976, Illinois. *Education:* Smith College (B.A., magna cum laude, 1959); University of Vermont (M. A., 1960); University of Chicago (J.D., 1976). ***PRACTICE AREAS:*** Commercial Litigation; Consumer; Drug; Employment; Medical Device; Product Liability; Recreational Products. ***Email:*** kimball@wildmanharrold.com

STEVEN H. KLEIN, born Chicago, Illinois, May 20, 1965; admitted to bar, 1990, Illinois. *Education:* University of Michigan (B.A., with honors and distinction, 1987); Harvard University (J.D., 1990). Fellow, American Academy of Matrimonial Attorneys. *Member:* Chicago, Illinois State and American Bar Associations. ***PRACTICE AREAS:*** Family Law; Estate Planning; Probate. ***Email:*** klein@wildmanharrold.com

TIMOTHY K. KLINTWORTH, born Peoria, Illinois, December 7, 1970; admitted to bar, 1996, Missouri; 1997, Illinois; registered to practice before U.S. Patent and Trademark Office. *Education:* University of Illinois (B.S., Mechanical Engineering, 1993); University of Missouri-Columbia (J.D., 1996). Author: "The Enforceability of an Agreement to Submit to a Non-Arbitral Form of Dispute Resolution," Journal of Dispute Resolution, 1995. ***PRACTICE AREAS:*** Intellectual Property; Patent; Trademark. ***Email:*** klintworth@wildmanharrold.com

JOHN F. KUENSTLER, born Olney, Illinois, November 29, 1966; admitted to bar, 1993, Illinois; 1994, Missouri, U.S. District Court, Eastern District of Missouri, U.S. District Court, Northern, Central and Southern Districts of Illinois and U.S. Court of Appeals, Seventh Circuit. *Education:* University of Illinois (B.A., 1990); Washington University (J.D., 1993). Associate Editor, Journal of Urban and Contemporary Law. Law Clerk to the Hon. James L. Foreman, U.S. District Court, Southern District of Illinois, 1993-1994. *Member:* Bar Association of Metropolitan St. Louis; The Missouri Bar; Chicago, Illinois State and American Bar Associations. ***REPORTED CASES:*** Montgomery v. Pepsi-Cola General Bottlers, Inc., 2004 WL 2091483 (N.D.Ind. Sep 8, 2004); Raymond v. Ameritech Corp., 2004 WL 1381134 (N.D.Ill. May 7, 2004); Banks v. CBOCS West, Inc., 85 Empl. Prac. Dec. 41,663 (N.D.Ill. April 1, 2004); Torry v. Northrop Grumman Corp., 2003 WL 22595280 (N.D.Ill. Nov 7, 2003); Richardson v. Pepsi-Cola General Bottlers, Inc., 282 F.Supp.2d 855 (N.D.Ill. Sep 11, 2003); Rivera v. Cracker Barrel Old Country Store, Inc., 25 NDLR 238 (D.N.J. Mar 3, 2003); Davis v. Precoat Metals, 2002 WL 518141 (N.D.Ill., Mar 28, 2002); Davis v. Precoat Metals, 88 Fair Empl. Prac. Cas. (BNA) 495 (N.D.Ill., Feb 22, 2002); Rice-Bey v. Koppers Industries, Inc., 180 F.Supp.2d 988 (S.D.Ill., Jan 14, 2002); Florian v. Sequa Corp., 168 L.R.R.M. (BNA) 2389, 144 Lab.Cas. P 11, 134 (N.D.Ill., Aug 29, 2001); Reap v. Continental Casualty Co., 199 F.R.D. 536, (D.N.J., Mar. 21, 2001); Fox v. Koppers Industries, Inc., 79 Empl. Prac. Dec. 40, 361 (N.D. Ill., Jan. 3, 2001); Johnson v. LaSalle Partners, Inc., 82 Fair Empl. Prac. (as (BNA) 1746, 78 Empl. Prac. Dec. 40, 087 (N.D. Ill., May 23, 2000); Rotter v. Brinker Restaurant Corp., 1999 WL 1132989 (N.D.Ill. Dec. 10, 1999); Hearn v. Whirlpool Corp., 1998 WL 658260 (8th Cir., Sept. 16, 1998) (NO. 98-1464WA); Monks v. Bell & Howell Mail Processing Systems Co., 78 Fair Empl. Prac. Cas. (BNA) 29, 73 Empl. Prac. Dec. 45,467 (N.D.Ill. Aug 26, 1998); (NO. CIV. 97-C-4410); Randle El. v. Pizza Hut of America, Inc., 182 F.R.D. 542 (N.D.Ill., Aug 13, 1998); Ritter v. Whirlpool Corp., 1998 WL 469924, 135 Lab. Cas. 10,186 (W.D.Ark., Jun 10, 1998) (NO. CIV. 97-2167); Holt v. Whirlpool Corporation, 1998 WL 466643, 73 Empl. Prac. Dec. 45,357 (M.D.Tenn., Apr 30, 1998) (NO. 3:97-0502); Walther v. Everest & Jennings, Inc., 965 F.Supp. 1255, 70 Empl. Prac. Dec. 44,574 (E.D.Mo., Mar 21, 1997); (NO.

(This Listing Continued)

4:95CV2398-DJS); Rhoads v. Jones Financial Companies, 957 F.Supp. 1102, 73 Fair Empl. Prac. Cas. (BNA) 510, 70 Empl. Prac. Dec. 44,666 (E.D.Mo., Feb 11, 1997) (NO. 4:95CV836 FRB); Smith v. Clayco Accurate Const. Co., 1997 WL 106254, 69 Empl. Prac. Dec. 44,502, 9 NDLR 135 (E.D.Mo., Jan 23, 1997) (NO. 4:95-CV1819 CDP); Kramer v. K & S Associates, 942 F.Supp. 444, 70 Empl. Prac. Dec. 44,614, 7 A.D. Cases 59, 19 A.D.D. 487 (E.D.Mo., Sep 20, 1996) (NO. 4:94CV2239-DJS); Lewis v. Aerospace Community Credit Union, 934 F.Supp. 314, 74 Fair Empl. Prac. Cas. (BNA) 1339, 68 Empl. Prac. Dec. 44,069 (E.D.Mo., May 22, 1996) (NO. 4:95CV633 FRB); Kelleher v. Aerospace Community Credit Union, 927 F.Supp. 361, 70 Fair Empl. Prac. Cas. (BNA) 1279, 68 Empl. Prac. Dec. 44,039 (E.D.Mo., Mar 25, 1996) (NO. 4:95CV632 JCH); Rogic v. Mallinckrodt Medical, Inc., 917 F.Supp. 671, 67 Empl. Prac. Dec. 43,973 (E.D.Mo., Feb 8, 1996) (NO. 4:95CV597 FRB); Breeden v. Enterprise Leasing Co., 1995 WL 781700, 22 A.D.D. 541, 7 NDLR 352 (E.D.Mo., Dec 28, 1995) (NO. 4:95-CV-1821 CAS). ***PRACTICE AREAS:*** Employment Litigation; Labor Law; Commercial Litigation. ***Email:*** kuenstler@wildmanharrold.com

LEONARD S. KURFIRST, born Chicago, Illinois, October 10, 1959; admitted to bar, 1984, Illinois and U.S. District Court, Northern District of Illinois. *Education:* Stanford University (B.A., Economics, with honors, 1981); Indiana University (J.D., cum laude, 1984); DePaul University (L.L.M., Health Care Law, with honors, 2001). Phi Kappa Phi. Listed, *Who's Who in American Law.* Recipient, The CALI Award for Outstanding Achievement in Health Care Contracts, 1998; Medical Ethics, 1998 and Hospital Law, 1999. Wildman, Harrold, Allen & Dixon, 1986-1995; Elected to Partnership, 1992. Assistant Editor, "De Paul Journal of Health Care Law," 1998, 1999. Author: "The Duty to Disclose HMO Physician Incentives," The Health Lawyer, Vol. 13, No. 3 p. 18-27 (April 2001). *Member:* Chicago (Chair, Medical Legal Relations Committee, 1996, 2000), Illinois State and American Bar Associations; Illinois Association of Healthcare Attorneys. ***PRACTICE AREAS:*** Products Liability; Health Care; Commercial Litigation; Toxic Torts. ***Email:*** kurfirst@wildmanharrold.com

STEPHEN J. LANDES, born Chicago, Illinois, September 27, 1945; admitted to bar, 1970, Illinois; 1977, District of Columbia. *Education:* Northwestern University (B.A., with distinction, 1967; J.D., cum laude, 1970). Russell Sage Scholar, 1967-1970. Projects Editor, Northwestern University Law Review, 1969-1970. Assistant General Counsel, Bank of Israel (Jerusalem), 1974. *Member:* Chicago (Member, Antitrust Committee) and American (Member, Sections on: Antitrust; Litigation; Intellectual Property) Bar Associations; The District of Columbia Bar. ***PRACTICE AREAS:*** Antitrust Law; Litigation; Complex Litigation. ***Email:*** landes@wildmanharrold.com

DEAN J. LEFFELMAN, born Amboy, Illinois, June 23, 1953; admitted to bar, 1980, Illinois. *Education:* Northern Illinois University (B.S., 1976); John Marshall Law School (J.D., with distinction, 1979). Member: Order of John Marshall; John Marshall Law Review, 1978-1979. Author: "Avoiding Recognition of Income on Debt Cancellation," The Tax Advisor, February, 1980; "Planning Opportunities on Incorporation," Illinois Bar Journal, April, 1986; "Controlling A Corporation With Less Than Fifty-One Percent Ownership," Du Page Bar Journal, December, 1990. Past President, Fox Valley Estate Planning Council. Instructor of Business Law, Aurora University, 1981-1989. *Member:* Du Page County and Illinois State Bar Associations. (Lisle Office). ***PRACTICE AREAS:*** Corporate Law; Partnership Law; Real Estate Law; Estate Planning. ***Email:*** leffelman@wildmanharrold.com

JOHN S. LETCHINGER, born Chicago, Illinois, June 29, 1966; admitted to bar, 1991, Illinois and U.S. District Court, Northern and Central Districts of Illinois; U.S. Court of Appeals, Seventh and Federal Circuits. *Education:* Northwestern University (B.S., 1988); University of Illinois (J.D., 1991). ***PRACTICE AREAS:*** Intellectual Property Litigation; Commercial Litigation; General Litigation. ***Email:*** letchinger@wildmanharrold.com

BRIAN W. LEWIS, born Evergreen Park, Illinois, May 4, 1959; admitted to bar, 1985, Illinois; U.S. District Court, Northern District of Illinois including Trial Bar. *Education:* University of Illinois (B.A., cum laude, 1981); Loyola University (J.D., cum laude, 1985). Phi Beta Kappa; Phi Alpha Phi. *Member:* Chicago, Illinois State and American Bar Associations. ***PRACTICE AREAS:*** Complex Commercial Litigation; Product Liability Litigation; Contract Counseling; Consumer Products; Environmental Law; Recreational Products; Toxic Torts. ***Email:*** lewis@wildmanharrold.com

MICHAEL P. LUSK, admitted to bar, 1995, Kentucky; 1999, Illinois. *Education:* University of Louisville (B.S.B.A., 1986; J.D., cum laude, 1995). Phi Kappa Phi. Member, Brandeis Society. Managing Editor, Journal of Family Law, Vol. 33. Listed in "Who's Who Among Law Students". *Member:* Chicago, Kentucky, Illinois State and American Bar Associations. ***PRACTICE AREAS:*** Corporate; Tax. ***Email:*** lusk@wildmanharrold.com

THOMAS M. LYNCH, born Evergreen Park, Illinois, May 22, 1954; admitted to bar, 1984, Illinois and U.S. District Court, Northern District of Illinois including Trial Bar; 1987, U.S. Court of Appeals, Fourth Circuit; 1990, U.S. District Court, District of Arizona; 1996, U.S. Court of Appeals, Seventh Circuit; 1999, U.S. Supreme Court, and U.S. Court of Federal Claims; 2000, U.S. Court of Appeals, Eighth, Eleventh and Federal Circuits. *Education:* University of Dayton (B.A., summa cum laude, 1976); University of Chicago (M.A., 1978); Northwestern University (J.D., 1984). Recipient, A.H. Rose Award, 1976. Adjunct Professor, Northwestern University School of Law, 1996—; Instructor, National Institute for Trial Advocacy, 1995—. Participant, Advisory Committee, Illinois Secretary of State/Securities Department, 1997. *Member:* Chicago, Illinois State and American Bar Associations. ***PRACTICE AREAS:*** Commercial Litigation; Antitrust; Securities Litigation; Intellectual Property Litigation; Class Actions; Alternative Dispute Resolution; Business Law. ***Email:*** lynch@wildmanharrold.com

JOSEPH F. MADONIA, born Springfield, Illinois, November 17, 1959; admitted to bar, 1985, Illinois; 1989, U.S. District Court, Central District of Illinois; 1990, U.S. District Court, Northern District of Illinois including Trial Bar; 1996, U.S. District Court, Eastern District of Missouri. *Education:* University of Notre Dame (B.A., 1982); Southern Methodist University (J.D., 1985). Author: "SARA TITLE III: One State's Perspective," National Environmental Enforcement Journal, October 1989; "The OSHA/USEPA Final Rules: A Guide To Worker Protection Standards For Hazardous Waste And Emergency Response Operations," ELI's Environmental Law Reporter, April, 1990. Former Deputy Chief, Illinois Attorney General's Office, Environmental Division, 1989. Former Acting State's Attorney, Cumberland County, Illinois, 1988. *Member:* Illinois State (Environmental Law Section Council Appointee, 1994-1996) and American Bar Associations. ***PRACTICE AREAS:*** Environmental; Litigation. ***Email:*** madonia@wildmanharrold.com

THOMAS I. MATYAS, born Budapest, Hungary, August 25, 1947; admitted to bar, 1973, Illinois. *Education:* University of Illinois and Roosevelt University (B.A., 1970); New York Law School (J.D., 1973). Co-author: "Why Shareholders Have the Right to Accept Tender Offers," 61 Chicago Bar Record, No. 6, 1980. Member, Chicago Crime Commission, 1987—. Member, Volunteer Mediation Pilot Project, Law Division, Cook County Circuit Court. *Member:* Chicago (Member: Real Property Law Committee; Real Property Litigation Committee; Commercial Finance and Transactions Committee; Real Estate Legislation Committee) Illinois State (Member, Voluntary Fee Resolution Committee) and American (Member, Litigation Section; Co-Chair, Continuing Education Committee, Real Estate Management Committee) Bar Associations; Mortgage Bankers Association of America; Illinois Mortgage Bankers Association. ***PRACTICE AREAS:*** Commercial Litigation; Real Estate Litigation. ***Email:*** matyas@wildmanharrold.com

MICHAEL L. McCLUGGAGE, born Coshocton, Ohio, March 9, 1947; admitted to bar, 1972, Illinois and U.S. District Court, Northern District of Illinois; 1989, U.S. Court of Appeals, Seventh Circuit; 1993, U.S. Supreme Court. *Education:* Ohio Wesleyan University (B.A., 1969); University of Chicago (J.D., 1972). Phi Beta Kappa; Pi Sigma Alpha; Omicron Delta Kappa. Author: "How to Avoid Being Blindsided at Trial," Litigation (Fall, 1990). Speaker, "Antitrust Issues in Residual Insurance Markets," ABA Antitrust Section National Institute, February, 1994. *Member:* Chicago, Illinois State and American (Chairman, Insurance Industry Committee, Antitrust Section) Bar Associations; Chicago Council of Lawyers. ***PRACTICE AREAS:*** Antitrust; Commercial Litigation; Class Action Defense. ***Email:*** mccluggage@wildmanharrold.com

MARK P. MILLER, born Chicago, Illinois, August 30, 1960; admitted to bar, 1985, Illinois and U.S. District Court, Northern District of Illinois including Trial Bar; U.S. Court of Appeals, Seventh and Tenth Circuits; U.S. Supreme Court. *Education:* University of Illinois (A.B., cum laude, 1982; J.D., cum laude, 1985). Phi Beta Kappa. Associate Editor, University of Illinois Law Review, 1984-1985. *Member:* American Bar Association; Defense Research Institute. ***PRACTICE AREAS:*** Construction Equipment; Industrial Machinery; Insurance Industry; Appellate; Commercial Litigation; Intellectual Property Litigation; Product Liability; Real Estate Litigation; Trial. ***Email:*** millerm@wildmanharrold.com

BART T. MURPHY, born Chicago, Illinois, January 28, 1956; admitted to bar, 1981, Illinois and U. S. District Court, Northern District of Illinois including Trial Bar; 1982, U.S. Court of Appeals, 7th Circuit; 1987, U.S. Supreme Court; 1990, U.S. District Court, Central District of Illinois; 1998, U.S. District Court, Eastern District of Wisconsin and U.S. Court of International Trade; 1999, U.S. Tax Court. *Education:* St. Mary's College of Minnesota (B.A., 1978); Loyola University (J.D., 1981). Assistant State's Attorney, Cook County, 1982. Assistant Attorney General 1982-1991. Director, Catholic Lawyers Guild of Chicago. Director, Greater Illinois Chapter Cystic Fibrosis Foundation. *Member:* Chicago, DuPage County, Illinois State and American Bar Associations. (Lisle Office). ***REPORTED CASES:*** Chicago Dist. Council of Carpenters Pension Fund, et al. v. R.G. Construction Services, Inc., No 01 C 3976, 2002 U.S. Dist LEXIS 21001 (USDC ND IL 10/28/02); Construction Consulting v. Gersten Financial & Insurance, No. 02 C 3322, 2002 U.S. Dist LEXIS 11669 (USDC ND IL 6/27/02); Market Street Securities v. Racing Champions, No. 00 C 3267, 2000 U.S. Dist LEXIS 19103 (USDC ND IL 11/20/00). ***PRACTICE AREAS:*** Litigation. ***Email:*** murphy@wildmanharrold.com

ROBERT W. NEWMAN, admitted to bar, 1957, Illinois and U.S. District Court, Northern District of Illinois. *Education:* University of Illinois; DePaul University (LL.B., 1957). Lecturer, IICLE Demonstrating the Negotiation of a Loan Commitment, 1985. Chairman, Mayor's Navy Pier Task Force, Chicago, Illinois, 1985. Co-Chairman, Real Estate Group, Wildman, Harrold, Allen and Dixon, 1992—. *Member:* Chicago, Illinois State, and American Bar Associations. ***PRACTICE AREAS:*** Corporate; Tax; Real Estate. ***Email:*** newmanr@wildmanharrold.com

SARAH L. OLSON, born Boston, Massachusetts, December 27, 1953; admitted to bar, 1986, Illinois; U.S. District Court, Northern District of Illinois and Eastern District of Wisconsin; U.S. Court of Appeals, Second, Third, Fifth, Seventh and Eighth Circuits; U.S. Supreme Court. *Education:* Skidmore College; University of California at Berkeley (B.A., with high honors, 1975); Chicago-Kent College of Law (J.D., with honors, 1986). Author, "The 'Free Public Services Doctrine': Government Cost Recovery Claims," For the Defense (September 2001). Co-author with Helaine Heydemann, Richard Hickey, Mary Periolat, Patrick and Albert Salvi: "Specific Defenses," Chapter 7 in Illinois Institute for Continuing Legal Education Handbook titled Medical Malpractice, 1987, 1989; Washington Legal Foundation, "Uncertain Future for California EMF Litigation," Vol. 3, No. 4 (7/21/95); "Jurisdiction at Warp Speed: Alien Corporations and Cyberspace Torts," Defense Research Institute Seminar on Business Law, 1997; "'New' Theories of Liability for Manufacturers and Industries: Negligent Marketing, Public Nuisance and Fraud on the Marketplace," DRI Seminar on Industrywide Litigation, February, 1997; "Guilt by Association: Trade Association Liability," Defense Research Institute, 1997; S. Olson and A. Kimball, "The Limits On The Use of Tort Law To Encourage Consumer Safety," Loyola Consumer Law Review, 12(3):178, Spring 2000; A. Kimball and S. Olson, "Municipal Firearms Litigation: Ill-Conceived From Any Angle," Conn. Law Review 32(4):1277, Summer 2000; A. Kimball and S. Olson, "When All Else Fails, Blame Madison Avenue: Negligent Marketing Claims in Firearm Litigation," Tort & Insurance Law J. 36(4):981, Summer 2001. *Member:* Illinois State and American (Member, Litigation Section, Torts and Insurance Practice Section) Bar Associations; Defense Research Institute (Co-Chair, 1999-2001, Mass Torts Task Force; Chair, 1998-1999 and Vice-Chair, 1997-1998, Industrywide Litigation Committee; Member, Product Liability Committee, Drug and Device Committee; Co-Chair, Electromagnetic Field Litigation Subcommittee of Defense Research Institute 1994-1997). ***REPORTED CASES:*** First Commercial Trust Co. for Robin Leath v. Colt's Mfg. Co., Inc., 77 F3d 1081 (8th Cir. 1996); Yarbrough v. Sturm, Ruger & Co. Inc., 964 F.2d 376 (5th Cir. 1992); Lovett v. Sturm, Ruger & Co., Inc., 223 Mich.App. 374, 566 N.W. 2d 53 (1997), lv. denied, 586 N.W. 2d 918 (MI 1998); Morial v. Smith & Wesson Corp., 785 So.2d1 (La. 2001), cert. denied, 122 S.Ct. 346 (2001); Camden County Board of Chosen Freeholders, 123 F.Supp. 2d 245 (D.H.J. 2000), aff'd., 273 F.3d 536 (3d Cir. 2001). ***PRACTICE***

(This Listing Continued)

(This Listing Continued)

WILDMAN, HARROLD, ALLEN & DIXON LLP, Chicago—Continued

AREAS: Complex Product Liability; Drugs and Medical Devices; Recreational Products; Industry-Wide Litigation and Trade Association Liability; Appellate Practice. ***Email:*** olson@wildmanharrold.com

RICHARD C. PALMER, born Endicott, New York, March 26, 1957; admitted to bar, 1983, Illinois; U.S. District Court, Northern and Southern Districts of Illinois, Easter District of Wisconsin and U.S. Court of Appeals, Third and Seventh Circuits. *Education:* Aurora University (B.A., cum laude, 1980); DePaul University (J.D., cum laude, 1983). *Member:* Chicago, Illinois State, Federal and American Bar Associations; Trial Bar (N.D.Ill); Defense Research Institute; Illinois Association of Defense Trial Counsel; American Phytopathological Society; Airline Owners and Pilots Association Legal Panel. ***PRACTICE AREAS:*** Product Liability; Aviation; Agriculture; Trial; Toxic Torts; Drug; Medical Device. ***Email:*** palmer@wildmanharrold.com

DOUGLAS L. PROCHNOW, born Omaha, Nebraska, January 9, 1952; admitted to bar, 1977, Illinois. *Education:* University of Nebraska at Lincoln (B.A., with high distinction, 1974); Northwestern University (J.D., 1977). Phi Eta Sigma; Phi Beta Kappa. Member, Editorial Board, Journal of Criminal Law and Criminology, 1976-1977. Co-Author with Kevin T. Martin and Joseph P. Kincaid: Chapter, "Pretrial Preparation and Use of Medical Evidence," published by IICLE, 1984. Author of Supplements to Chapter in 1985, 1987 and 1990. Author with Denis M. Gravel: Chapter, "Obtaining Medical Evidence," published by IICLE, 1997. Author of Supplement to Chapter in 2000. Special Assistant Corporation Counsel to the City of Chicago, 1985-1986. *Member:* Chicago, Illinois State and American Bar Associations; Defense Research Institute; Association of Trial Lawyers of America (Associate Member); The Society of Trial Lawyers. ***REPORTED CASES:*** Smith v. American Arbitration Ass'n, Inc., 233 F. 3d 502 (7th Cir. (Ill.), Dec. 1, 2000) (NO. 00-1204); Alioto v. Marshall Field's & Co., 77 F.3d 934, Prod.Liab.Rep. (CCH) P 14, 514 (7th Cir. (Wis.), Feb. 21, 1996) (NO. 95-2139); Bombagetti v. Amine, 254 Ill.App.3d 817, 627 N.E.2d 230, 194 Ill.Dec. 114 (Ill.App. 1 Dist., Sept. 29, 1993) (NO. 1-91-1572); Grothen v. Marshall Field & Co., 253 Ill.App.3d 122, 625 N.E.2d 343, 192 Ill.Dec. 383 (Ill.App. 1 Dist., Sept. 9, 1993) (NO. 1-91-3797); Corgan v. Muehling, 143 Ill.2d 296, 574 N.E.2d 602, 158 Ill.Dec. 489, 59 USLW 2755 (Ill., May 30, 1991) (NO. 67123); Jackson v. Pellerano, 210 Ill.App.3d 464, 569 N.E.2d 167, 155 Ill.Dec. 167 (Ill.App. 1 Dist., Mar. 5, 1991) (NO. 1-89-0652); Meerbrey v. Marshall Field & Co., Inc., 139 Ill.2d 455, 564 N.E.2d 1222, 151 Ill.Dec. 560 (Ill., Nov. 30, 1990) (NO. 69652); Whiteco Metrocom Div. v. Village of Downers Grove, 197 Ill.App.3d 174, 553 N.E.2d 1145, 143 Ill.Dec. 159 (Ill.App. 2 Dist., Apr. 24, 1990) (NO. 2-89-0612); Smith v. American Arbitration Ass'n., Inc., 1999 U.S. Dist. LEXIS 19827 (N.D. Ill. 1999); Forum Ins. Co. v. First Horizon Ins. Co., 1989 U.S. Dist. LEXIS 6631 (N.D. Ill. 1989); Nelson v. Jain, 526 F. Supp. 1154 (N.E. Ill. 1981); Johnson v. Baldinger, 1990 U.S. Dist. LEXIS 4596 (N.D. Ill. 1990); Erkol v. Marshall Field & Co., 1989 U.S. Dist. LEXIS 2071 (N.D. Ill. 1989); Golden Rule Ins. Co. v. Elton, 328 Ill. App. 3d 444, 766 N.E.2d 269 (3rd Dist. 2002); Brokemond v. Marshall Field & Co., 612 N.E.2d 143 (3rd Dist. 1993); Meerbrey v. Marshall Field & Co., 189 Ill. App. 3d 1085, 545 N.E.2d 952 (1st Dist. 1989); Meerbrey v. Marshall Field & Co., 169 Ill. Appl 3d 1014, 524 N.E.2d 228 (1st Dist. 1988); Corgan v. Muehling, 167 Ill. App. 3d 1093, 522 N.E.2d 153 (1st Dist. 1988); Bryant v. Fox, 162 Ill. App. 3d 46, 515 N.E.2d 775 (1st Dist. 1987); Hammond v. Lane, 162 Ill. App. 3d 17, 515 N.E.2d 828 (1st Dist. 1987); Wysocki v. Upjohn Co., 157 Ill. App. 3d 868, 510 N.E.2d 994 (1st Dist. 1987); Hall v. Northwestern, 152 Ill. App. 3d 716, 504 N.E.2d 781 (1st Dist. 1987); Carlasare v. Wilhelmi, 134 Ill. App. 3d 1, 479 N.E.2d 1073 (1st Dist. 1985); Tatosian v. Graudins, 86 Ill. App. 3d 661, 408 N.E.2d 231 (1st Dist. 1980); Haas v. Westlake Hosp., 82 Ill. App. 3d 347, 402 N.E.2d 883 (1st Dist. 1980); Griffis v. Board of Ed. Dist. 122, 72 Ill. App. 3d 784, 391 N.E.2d 451 (1st Dist. 1979); Faust v. Michael Reese Hosp., 61 Ill. App. 3d 233, 377 N.E.2d 1030 (1st Dist. 1978); Rebecca Jackson v. Armando Pellerano, 210 Ill. App. 3d 464, 569 N.E.2d 167, 155 Ill. Dec. 167 (Mar. 05, 1991) (No. 1-89-0652); Linda Carlasare v. Gary G. Wilhelmi and Bhaskar Patel, 134 Ill App. 3d 479 N.E.2d 1073 (June 7, 1985); Michael Woods v. The Illinois State Toll Highway Authority (June 29, 2001) (No. 1-00-3377); Vincent Oliveri v. Balasubramaniam S. Iyer, M.D. (Jun. 27, 2000) (No. 1-99-2770); Michael Woods v. The Illinois State Toll Highway Authority (Mar. 9, 2000) (No. 1-98-4445); Robert Norwood v. The County of Berrian, David Chandler and William Doak (Nos. 97948 and 100344) (Oct. 3, 1989); Batus Health Care System, Inc. v. Ruy Burbano, Individually and d/b/a Amazonas Driving School (Oct. 13, 1987) (No. 87-2256); Eileen Ebel v. Edwin L. Falloon, M.D. (Nov. 4, 1982) (No. 81-2996). ***PRACTICE AREAS:*** Commercial Litigation; Insurance Industry; Product Liability; Toxic Tort; Trial. ***Email:*** prochnow@wildmanharrold.com

THOMAS J. RING, born Blue Island, Illinois, March 15, 1952; admitted to bar, 1978, Illinois; 1979, U.S. District Court, Northern District of Illinois including Trial Bar; U.S. Court of Appeals, Seventh Circuit; U.S. Court of Appeals for the Federal Circuit; registered to practice before U.S. Patent and Trademark Office. *Education:* University of Wisconsin (B.S.C.E.E., honors, (Bachelor of Science in Civil and Environmental Engineering) 1974); The John Marshall Law School (J.D., 1978). Phi Eta Sigma; Tau Beta Pi; Chi Epsilon. *Member:* Patent Law Association of Chicago; American Intellectual Property Law Association. ***PRACTICE AREAS:*** Patent; Intellectual Property. ***Email:*** ring@wildmanharrold.com

JOHN A. ROBERTS, born Rochester, New York, December 14, 1968; admitted to bar, 1994, Illinois, Kentucky and U.S. District Court, Northern District of Illinois; 2000, U.S. District Court, Central District of Illinois and U.S. Court of Federal Claims; U.S. District Court, Southern District of Illinois. *Education:* University of Michigan (B.A., 1990); University of Iowa (M.A., Hospital and Health Administration, 1993; J.D., 1993). Member, Iowa Law Review, 1992-1993. Appointed to University of Iowa Moot Court Board, 1992-1993. Co- Author: "Proposed Federal Statutes: Cardaveric Organ Donor Act and Living Donor Act," 18 Journal of Corporation Law 523 (1994); Speaking Engagement, June 2001, ISMIE "Sharing a Practice Sharing the Risk," Northbrook, IL.; Speaking Engagement, December 2001, Classic Insurance "Are You Sure Your Office is in Compliance?" (Dyer, Indiana). *Member:* Chicago (Member, Committees on: Health Care Law; Tort Law; Medical-Legal Relations Service), Illinois State (Member, Sections on: Health Care Law; Tort Law), Louisville and Kentucky Bar Associations; American Health Lawyers Association; Illinois Association of Healthcare Attorneys; Defense Research Institute. ***REPORTED CASES:*** Horbach v. Kaczmarek, 934 F. Supp. 981 (N.D. Ill., July 22, 1996) (NO. 95 C 5180). ***PRACTICE AREAS:*** Health Care Law; Health Care Regulatory; Fraud and Abuse; Health Insurance; Product Liability; Pharmaceutical and Medical Device Defense; General Litigation. ***Email:*** roberts@wildmanharrold.com

ALAN B. ROTH, born Brooklyn, New York, September 28, 1957; admitted to bar, 1984, Missouri, Illinois, U.S. District Court, Northern District of Illinois and U.S. Tax Court. *Education:* Duke University (B.A., 1978); Washington University (J.D., 1983); New York University (LL.M. in Taxation, 1984). Senior Editor, Washington University Law Quarterly, 1982-1983. Graduate Editor, Tax Law Review, 1984. Recipient, Kennesson Fellowship. Author: Comment, "Section 1985 (2) Clause One Does Not Require Allegations of Class or Race-Based Discriminatory Animus," Washington University Law Quarterly 849, 1983. Co-Author: "Federal Income Tax Considerations of Commercial Leasing," Illinois Institute for Continuing Legal Education, Commercial Landlord-Tenant Practice, 1996; Co-Author: "Ancillary Problems For Tax Preparers," Illinois Institute for Continuing Legal Education, Tax Preparer Liability, 1996. *Member:* Chicago, Illinois State and American Bar Associations. ***PRACTICE AREAS:*** Venture Capital; Small Business Investment Companies; Corporate, Securities, Tax; Financial Services; Creditors' Rights; Real Estate; Banking. ***Email:*** roth@wildmanharrold.com

MICHAEL M. ROTH, born Joliet, Illinois, January 15, 1954; admitted to bar, 1980, Illinois; 1981, U.S. District Court, Northern District of California. *Education:* University of Illinois at Champaign (B.S., 1976); The John Marshall Law School (J.D., 1980). Phi Delta Phi. Assistant State's Attorney, Cook County, 1980-1981. *Member:* Chicago, Illinois State and American Bar Associations; Illinois Trial Lawyers Association. (Lisle Office). ***PRACTICE AREAS:*** Local Government; Cable Communications; Telecommunications; Zoning and Land Development. ***Email:*** roth@wildmanharrold.com

FRED E. SCHULZ, born Chicago, Illinois, May 9, 1943; admitted to bar, 1970, Illinois. *Education:* Purdue University (B.S., with distinction, 1965); Northwestern University (J.D., 1968). *Member:* Chicago, Illinois State and American Bar Associations. ***PRACTICE AREAS:*** Commercial Litigation; Employment; Explosions; Fire; Product Liability. ***Email:*** schulz@wildmanharrold.com

CHRISTOPHER T. SHEEAN, born Detroit, Michigan; admitted to bar, 1992, Illinois and U.S. District Court, Northern District of Illinois including Trial Bar; 1994, U.S. District Court, Central District of Illinois; U.S. District Court, Southern District of Illinois, U.S. District Court, Eastern District of Michigan, U.S. District Court, Northern District of Oklahoma and U.S. Court of Appeals, Seventh Circuit. *Education:* University of Arizona (B.A., English, 1989; J.D., cum laude, 1992). Executive Note Editor, 1991-1992 and Writer, 1990-1991, Arizona Law Review. ***PRACTICE AREAS:*** Complex Litigation; Litigation; Products Liability; Toxic Torts. ***Email:*** sheean@wildmanharrold.com

ROBERT L. SHUFTAN, born Chicago, Illinois, May 3, 1954; admitted to bar, 1979, Illinois; 1983, U.S. District Court, Northern District of Illinois including Trial Bar; U.S. Supreme Court; U.S. Court of Appeals, Third, Fifth, Seventh, Ninth and Eleventh Circuits. *Education:* University of Illinois (B.A., summa cum laude, 1976); Harvard University (J.D., 1979). Managing Partner and Chairperson of the Executive Committee at Wildman, Harrold, Allen & Dixon. *Member:* American Bar Association (Member, Litigation and Natural Resources Energy and Environmental Law Sections). ***PRACTICE AREAS:*** Business Litigation; Environmental; Toxic Torts. ***Email:*** shuftan@wildmanharrold.com

LISA S. SIMMONS, born Milwaukee, Wisconsin, August 3, 1961; admitted to bar, 1986, Wisconsin, Illinois, U.S. District Court, Western District of Wisconsin and U.S. District Court, Northern and Central Districts of Illinois; U.S. Court of Appeals, Fourth, Seventh and Ninth Circuits. *Education:* University of Wisconsin-Madison (B.A., with distinction, 1983; J.D., cum laude, 1986). Phi Beta Kappa; Phi Kappa Phi. Managing Editor, Wisconsin Law Review, 1985-1986. *Member:* State Bar of Wisconsin; American Bar Association. ***LANGUAGES:*** French, Russian. ***PRACTICE AREAS:*** Appellate; Commercial Litigation; Criminal. ***Email:*** simmons@wildmanharrold.com

DAVID M. SIMON, born Urbana, Illinois, November 27, 1964; admitted to bar, 1989, Illinois, Wisconsin and U.S. District Court, Western District of Wisconsin; 1990, U.S. District Court, Northern District of Illinois; 1993, U.S. District Court, Central District of Illinois; 1994, U.S. District Court, Southern District of Illinois; 1995, U.S. District Court, Western District of Michigan; 1998, U.S. Court of Appeals, Fifth Circuit and U.S. District Court, District of Colorado. *Education:* Johns Hopkins University (B.A., 1986); University of Wisconsin-Madison (J.D. cum laude, 1989). Co-author: "The Ignored Effect: Taxes and the Calculation of Commercial Damages," Business Lawyer Update, September/October, 1991; "Avoid Windfall Commercial Damages: Consider Tax Benefits and Tax Law Changes," Inside Litigation, July, 1991; "The Effects of Regulations on State Liquor Prices," Empirica 23:303-316, 1996; "The Best Defense Against Lender Liability Claims," The Secured Lender, May-June, 1998; "Public Ownership versus Private Enterprise: State Liquor Distribution Systems Revisited," Volume 1 of "Economics Against the Grain" 1999. *Member:* Chicago, Illinois State and American Bar Associations; State Bar of Wisconsin. ***REPORTED CASES:*** *P.R.S International, Inc. v. Shred Pax Corp.,* 184 Ill.2d 224, 703 N.E.2d 71 (1998) (UCC and procedural issues); *Whirlpool Financial Corp. v. Sevaux,* 96 F.3d 216 (7th Cir. 1996) (lender liability issues); *Washington National Insurance Co. v. The Administrators,* 2F.3d 192 (7th Cir. 1993) (business defamation issues). ***PRACTICE AREAS:*** Commercial Litigation; Environmental Litigation. ***Email:*** simon@wildmanharrold.com

ERIC L. SINGER, born Pittsburgh, Pennsylvania, August 20, 1964; admitted to bar, 1988, Illinois. *Education:* University of Illinois (B.A., with distinction in Sociology, magna cum laude, 1985); University of Chicago (J.D., 1988). Phi Beta Kappa. *Member:* DuPage County and American (Member, Litigation Section; Forum on the Construction Industry) Bar Associations; American Institute of Architects Northeast Illinois; American Institute of Architects Chicago Professional Affiliate (Professional Affilliate Director American Institute of Architects Chicago, 1999-2001; American Institute of Architects (Allied Member). (Lisle Office). ***REPORTED CASES:*** Intergovernmental Risk Management v. O'Donnell Wicklund, Pigozzi and Peterson et al., 295 Ill. App. 3d 784, 692 N.E. 2d 739 (1st Dist. 1998); Onsite Engineering & Management, Inc. v. Illinois Tool Works, 744 N.E. 2d 928 (1st Dist. 2001). ***PRACTICE AREAS:*** Construction and Design Law; Complex Litigation; Mechanics Liens. ***Email:*** singer@wildmanharrold.com

ANDREW M. SLOBODIEN, admitted to bar, 1994, Illinois; 1995, New Jersey, U.S. Court of Appeals, Seventh and District of Columbia Circuits, U.S. District Court, Northern

(This Listing Continued)

District of Illinois including Trial Bar, U.S. District Court, Eastern District of Wisconsin, U.S. District Court, Northern District of Georgia and U.S. District Court, District of New Jersey. *Education:* Haverford College (B.A., 1986); University of Chicago - Divinity School (M.A., Religion, 1990); Chicago-Kent College of Law (J.D., with honors, 1994). ***PRACTICE AREAS:*** Labor and Employment Law. ***Email:*** slobodien@wildmanharrold.com

DEREK C. SMITH, born Toledo, Ohio, July 10, 1972; admitted to bar, 1998, Ohio; 1999, Illinois; 2000, U.S. District Court, Central District of Illinois; 2003, U.S. District Court, Southern District of Illinois; U.S. District Courts, Northern and Southern Districts of Ohio and U.S. District Court, Northern District of Illinois. *Education:* University of Toledo (B.B.A., 1994); University of Cincinnati (J.D., 1997). *Member:* Defense Research Institute. ***PRACTICE AREAS:*** Commercial Litigation; Product Liability; Toxic Tort Litigation. ***Email:*** smithd@wildmanharrold.com

JAMES M. SNYDER, born Lorain, Ohio, November 21, 1959; admitted to bar, 1987, Illinois. *Education:* Ohio State University (B.S., 1982; J.D., cum laude, 1986). Order of the Coif. *Member:* National Association of Bond Lawyers. (Lisle Office). ***PRACTICE AREAS:*** Municipal Finance; Taxation. ***Email:*** snyderj@wildmanharrold.com

CHARLES A. STERN, born Chicago, Illinois, July 27, 1930; admitted to bar, 1958, Illinois. *Education:* Northwestern University (B.S., with highest distinction, 1952); Harvard University (J.D., 1958). Phi Beta Kappa. *Member:* Chicago (Member, Securities Law Committee, 1959—), Illinois State and American Bar Associations. ***PRACTICE AREAS:*** Corporate and Business Law; Mergers and Acquisitions; Estate Planning. ***Email:*** stern@wildmanharrold.com

R. JOHN STREET, born Lancaster, Ohio, December 18, 1960; admitted to bar, 1986, Illinois. *Education:* Ohio University (B.S., cum laude, 1983); Case Western Reserve University (J.D., magna cum laude, 1986). Order of the Coif. ***PRACTICE AREAS:*** Antitrust; Commercial Litigation; Insurance. ***Email:*** street@wildmanharrold.com

PETER A. TOMARAS, born Oak Park, Illinois, July 8, 1952; admitted to bar, 1981, Illinois. *Education:* Elmhurst College (B.A., 1975); John Marshall Law School (J.D., 1981). Guest Lecturer, John Marshall Law School. *Member:* Chicago, Illinois State and American Bar Associations. ***PRACTICE AREAS:*** Products Liability; Toxic Tort; Health Care; Commercial Litigation. ***Email:*** tomaras@wildmanharrold.com

SHERRIE TRAVIS, born South Bend, Indiana; admitted to bar, 1976, Illinois and U.S. District Court, Northern District of Illinois. *Education:* University of Illinois (B.A., with honors, 1969; M.A., with high honors, 1970); IIT/Chicago-Kent College of Law (J.D., 1976). Delta Theta Phi. *Member:* Chicago (Member, Committee on Labor and Employment Law, 1976—) and American (Member, Labor Law Section, 1980—) Bar Associations. ***PRACTICE AREAS:*** Management Labor Law; Management Employment Law; Affirmative Action; Employment Discrimination; Personnel Policies; Employment Practices Liability Insurance. ***Email:*** travis@wildmanharrold.com

JAMES B. VOGTS, born Evanston, Illinois, April 29, 1958; admitted to bar, 1984, Illinois and U.S. District Court, Northern District of Illinois; U.S. District Court, Northern District of Indiana; U.S. Court of Appeals, Seventh Circuit. *Education:* Miami University (A.B., 1980); DePaul University (J.D., 1984). ***REPORTED CASES:*** Halliday v. Sturm, Ruger & Co., Inc., 770 A. 2d 1072 (Md. App. 2001); Bolduc v. Colt's Manufacturing Co., Inc., 968 F. Supp. 246 (D. Mass 1997); Cummins v. Lyle Industries, Inc., 93 F. 3d 362 (7th Cir. 1996); Cockrell v. Koppers Industries, Inc., 281 Ill. App. 3d 1009 (1996); Flynn v. Golden Grain Co., 269 Ill. App. 3d 871 (1995); Smith v. City of Evanston, 260 Ill. App. 3d 925 (1994); Awkwright Mut. Ins. v. Garrett & West, Inc., 782 F. Supp. 376 (N.D. Ill. 1992). ***PRACTICE AREAS:*** Litigation. ***Email:*** vogts@wildmanharrold.com

DAVID L. WEINSTEIN, born Chicago, Illinois, October 1, 1951; admitted to bar, 1979, Illinois and U.S. District Court, Northern District of Illinois including Trial Bar; 1980, U.S. Tax Court; 1981, U.S. Court of Appeals, Seventh Circuit; 1984, U.S. Court of Appeals, Eighth Circuit and U.S. Supreme Court; 1987, U.S. Court of Appeals, Sixth Circuit; 1989, U.S. Court of Appeals, Eleventh Circuit. *Education:* Southern Illinois University (B.A., 1973); Michigan State University (M.A., 1975); Northwestern University (J.D., 1979). Legal Writing Instructor, Northwestern University School of Law, 1978-1979. *Member:* Chicago, Illinois State and American (Member, Sections on: Labor and Employment; Litigation, 1984-2002) Bar Associations; American Arbitration Association. ***PRACTICE AREAS:*** Labor and Employment; Commercial Litigation. ***Email:*** weinstein@wildmanharrold.com

CRAIG M. WHITE, born Phoenixville, Pennsylvania, August 12, 1952; admitted to bar, 1977, Illinois; U.S. District Court, Central and Northern Districts of Illinois; U.S. District Court, Northern District of Indiana; U.S. Court of Appeals, Seventh and Eighth Circuits; U.S. Supreme Court. *Education:* Dartmouth College (B.A., magna cum laude, 1974); Indiana University (J.D., magna cum laude, 1977). Phi Beta Kappa; Order of the Coif. *Member:* American Bar Association (Member, Sections on: Litigation; Corporation, Banking and Business Law); The Legal Club of Chicago; Dartmouth Lawyers Association. ***PRACTICE AREAS:*** Commercial Litigation; Banking Litigation. ***Email:*** white@wildmanharrold.com

NEIL G. WOLF, born Chicago, Illinois, May 26, 1952; admitted to bar, 1991, Illinois and U.S. District Court, Northern and Central Districts of Illinois; 1998, U.S. District Court, Northern District of Indiana. *Education:* Indiana University (B.A., 1979); DePaul University College of Law (J.D., with honors, 1990). Order of the Coif. Article and Note Editor, DePaul Law Review. Author: "Boyle v. United Technologies Corp.: A Reasonably Precise Immunity-Specifying *The Defense Contractor's Shield,*" 39 DePaul L. Rev. 825 (1990); Chapter Editor, "The Fair Labor Standards Act," (BNA/ABA, 1999). *Member:* Illinois State (Member, Section on Labor and Employment) and American (Member, Section on Labor and Employment) Bar Associations. ***REPORTED CASES:*** Hirsch v. Corban Corp., 949 F.Supp. 296 (E.D. Pa. 1996); Gatewood v. Stone Container Corp., 170 F.R.D. 455 (S.D. Ia. 1996). ***PRACTICE AREAS:*** Labor and Employment. ***Email:*** wolf@wildmanharrold.com

ALLAN A. WULFSTAT, born Chicago, Illinois, January 29, 1939; admitted to bar, 1964, Illinois. *Education:* Northwestern University (B.S., 1961; J.D., 1964). ***PRACTICE AREAS:*** Employee Benefit Plans; Tax; Estate Planning; Corporate/Business Law; Wealth Preservation. ***Email:*** wulfstat@wildmanharrold.com

(This Listing Continued)

JONATHAN W. YOUNG, born Manhasset, New York, October 23, 1964; admitted to bar, 1990, Illinois and U.S. District Court, Northern District of Illinois; 1995, U.S. District Court, District of Nebraska; 1996, U.S. Court of Appeals, Eighth Circuit; 1999, U.S. Court of Appeals, Seventh Circuit. *Education:* Yale University (B.A., cum laude, 1986); Northwestern University (J.D., 1990). *Member:* American Bar Association. ***LANGUAGES:*** French. ***REPORTED CASES:*** In re MEI Diversified, Inc., 106 F.3d 829 (8th Cir. 1998). ***PRACTICE AREAS:*** Restructuring; Insolvency; Bankruptcy; Commercial Litigation. ***Email:*** young@wildmanharrold.com

JUSTINE YOUNG GOTTSHALL, born Washington, D.C., June 23, 1969; admitted to bar, 1994, Maryland; 1995, District of Columbia; 2003, Illinois. *Education:* University of Michigan (B.A., 1991); Stanford Law School (J.D., 1994). *Member:* Illinois State, Maryland State and American Bar Associations; The District of Columbia Bar. ***PRACTICE AREAS:*** Privacy; Marketing Law; Promotion Law; Information Technology; Intellectual Property; Business Continuity and Security; Business Security. ***Email:*** gottshall@wildmanharrold.com

ASSOCIATES

ANA L. ACENA, admitted to bar, 2001, New York (Not admitted in Illinois). *Education:* University of Chicago (B.A., with honors, 1993); Cornell Law School (J.D., 1998). *Member:* New York State and American Bar Associations. ***LANGUAGES:*** French. ***PRACTICE AREAS:*** Real Estate. ***Email:*** acena@wildmanharrold.com

NANCY F. AFRASIABI, (admission pending). *Education:* Northwestern University (B.A. in History and Communication Studies, 2002); University of Chicago (J.D., 2005). ***LANGUAGES:*** Farsi. ***PRACTICE AREAS:*** Litigation. ***Email:*** afrasiabi@wildmanharrold.com

REBECCA ALFERT, born Charlottesville, Virginia, May 17, 1969; admitted to bar, 1996, Georgia; 1997, Texas; 2003, Illinois. *Education:* University of Georgia (B.A., magna cum laude, 1991; J.D., cum laude, 1995). Phi Beta Kappa. Notes Editor, Georgia Law Review, 1994-1995. Law Clerk to the Hon. Jerry Buchmeyer, U.S. District Court, Northern District of Texas, 1995-1996. ***PRACTICE AREAS:*** Litigation. ***Email:*** alfert@wildmanharrold.com

ROBERT A. APONTE, (admission pending). *Education:* University of Michigan (B.A. in Economics, 2000); Northwestern University (J.D., 2005). ***PRACTICE AREAS:*** Litigation. ***Email:*** aponte@wildmanharrold.com

WILLIAM M. BARNES, JR., born Albany, Georgia, September 25, 1969; admitted to bar, 1999, Illinois. *Education:* Northwestern University (B.A., 1992; J.D., 1999). *Member:* Chicago and Illinois State Bar Associations. ***PRACTICE AREAS:*** Environmental Litigation; Litigation. ***Email:*** barnesw@wildmanharrold.com

P. AARON BASILIUS, (admission pending). *Education:* Brigham Young University (B.A. in History, 2001); University of Chicago (J.D., 2005). ***LANGUAGES:*** Spanish. ***PRACTICE AREAS:*** Litigation. ***Email:*** basilius@wildmanharrold.com

JENNIFER L. BAUGH, admitted to bar, 2004, Illinois. *Education:* Duke University (A.B., English, 1992); University of Iowa (J.D., with distinction, 2004). Member, 2002-2003 and Managing Editor, 2003-2004, Iowa Law Review. Author, "Punitive Damages and the Anti-Retaliation Penalties Provision of the Fair Labor Standards Act," Iowa Law Review, Vol. 89, Issue 5. ***PRACTICE AREAS:*** Labor and Employment; Litigation. ***Email:*** baugh@wildmanharrold.com

AMANDA A. BERNDT, (admission pending). *Education:* Lake Forest College (B.A. in Political Science and Philosophy, magna cum laude and with honors, 2001); Georgetown University (J.D., 2005). ***PRACTICE AREAS:*** Litigation. ***Email:*** berndt@wildmanharrold.com

JONATHAN A. BOHLEN, born May 20, 1969; admitted to bar, 1998, Illinois. *Education:* University of Chicago (B.A., 1995); Northwestern University School of Law (J.D., 1998). *Member:* Chicago and American (Member, Young Lawyers Division, Business Law Section, 1998—) Bar Associations. [U.S. Army, 1987-1991]. ***LANGUAGES:*** Czech. ***PRACTICE AREAS:*** Corporate; Securities; Tax. ***Email:*** bohlen@wildmanharrold.com

ALBERT M. BOWER, admitted to bar, 2001, Arizona; 2002, Illinois. *Education:* United States Air Force Academy (B.S., Legal Studies, 1994); University of Illinois, Urbana-Champaign (J.D., 2001). Order of the Coif. Recipient: CALI Awards for highest grades in Environmental Law, Evidence, Trademark and Unfair Competition, and Natural Resource Law; Ricket Award (Top 5% of the class). *Member:* Chicago and American Bar Associations. ***PRACTICE AREAS:*** Litigation. ***Email:*** bower@wildmanharrold.com

TODD M. BRANDEL, born 1976; (admission pending). *Education:* Miami University (B.S., Finance, 1999); Northwestern University (J.D., 2005). ***PRACTICE AREAS:*** Litigation. ***Email:*** brandel@wildmanharrold.com

MATTHEW J. CACCAMO, admitted to bar, 2004, Illinois. *Education:* University of Notre Dame (B.A., History & Government, summa cum laude, 2001); Harvard Law School (J.D., 2004). ***PRACTICE AREAS:*** Labor and Employment; Litigation; Government Affairs. ***Email:*** caccamo@wildmanharrold.com

BRIAN R. CARNIE, born Cherry Hill, New Jersey, October 17, 1968; admitted to bar, 1995, Illinois and U.S. District Court, Northern District of Illinois. *Education:* Northern Illinois University (B.S., magna cum laude, 1992); Case Western Reserve University (J.D., 1995). Legislative Aide for N. Duane Noland, State Representative, Illinois, 1990-1992. *Member:* Chicago (Member, Labor & Employment Law Committee) and Illinois State (Member, Civil Practice & Procedure Section) Bar Associations. ***REPORTED CASES:*** Adamczyk, et. al. v. Lever Brothers Co., 931 (N.D. III 1997), 33 F. Supp. 2d 679 (N.D. III 1998), and 1999 U.S. Dist. LEXIS 3494 (N.D. III. 1999); Kelley v. Crosfield Catalysts, 962 F. Supp. 1047 (N.D. III. 1997); Angara v. City of Chicago, 947 F. Supp. 1252 (N.D. III. 1996); Dikcis v. Indopco, Inc., 1997 U.S. Dist. LEXIS 5276 (N.D. III. 1997) and 1998 U.S. Dist. LEXIS 234 (N.D. III. 1998). ***PRACTICE AREAS:*** Labor and Employment Law. ***Email:*** bcarnie@wildmanharrold.com

MICHAEL J. CASTELLINO, born Durham, North Carolina, November 9, 1968; admitted to bar, 1994, Illinois and U.S. District Court, Northern District of Illinois. *Education:* University of Notre Dame (B.A., 1991); Notre Dame Law School (J.D., 1994). *Mem-*

(This Listing Continued)

WILDMAN, HARROLD, ALLEN & DIXON LLP, Chicago—Continued

ber: Chicago and Illinois State Bar Associations. ***PRACTICE AREAS:*** Government; Municipal Law; Land Use; Zoning Law; Litigation. ***Email:*** castellino@wildmanharrold.com

GINA M. CHANG, born Chicago, Illinois, July 27, 1974; admitted to bar, 1999, Illinois; U.S. District Court, Northern District of Illinois including Trial Bar, U.S. District Court, Central District of Illinois and U.S. Court of Appeals, Seventh Circuit. *Education:* Northwestern University (B.S., 1996); Loyola University (J.D., 1999). Author, "McInerney vs. Charter Golf: The Court Swings and Misses," 29 Loy. U. Chi. L.J. 907 (1998). *Member:* Korean American Bar Association; American Bar Association. ***PRACTICE AREAS:*** Labor and Employment; Litigation. ***Email:*** chang@wildmanharrold.com

DAVID J. CHROUST, born Berwyn, Illinois, December 22, 1955; admitted to bar, 1980, Illinois; 1981, U.S. District Court, Northern District of Illinois; 1982, U.S. Court of Appeals, Seventh Circuit. *Education:* Grinnell College (B.A., 1980); Columbia University (J.D., 1980). Phi Beta Kappa; Phi Delta Phi. *Member:* Illinois State Bar Association. (Lisle Office). ***PRACTICE AREAS:*** Appellate; Civil Litigation; Financial Services and Creditors' Rights. ***Email:*** chroust@wildmanharrold.com

CHAD E. CLARK, born Rock Island, Illinois, May 26, 1974; admitted to bar, 2001, Illinois. *Education:* University of Dubuque (B.S., 1997); University of Iowa (J.D., 2001). ***PRACTICE AREAS:*** Litigation. ***Email:*** clarkc@wildmanharrold.com

ALISON C. CONLON, admitted to bar, 2000, Illinois. *Education:* Yale University (B.A., English, cum laude, 1994); Georgetown University (M.A., English, 1997); Duke University (J.D., magna cum laude, 2000). Adjunct Professor, Legal Writing, The John Marshall Law School, 2001—. ***PRACTICE AREAS:*** Litigation. ***Email:*** conlon@wildmanharrold.com

DAVID A. COPLAND, born Connecticut, 1968; admitted to bar, 1996, Illinois; 1997, U.S. District Court, Northern District of Illinois. *Education:* Trinity College (B.A., 1990); Boston University School of Law (J.D., Intellectual Property, with honors, 1996). Paul J. Liacos Scholar. First-Place, ASCAP Nathan Burkan Memorial Writing Competition in Copyright Law, Boston University, 1995. *Member:* International Trademark Association. ***PRACTICE AREAS:*** Intellectual Property; Trademark; Unfair Competition; Internet; Advertising; Copyright. ***Email:*** copland@wildmanharrold.com

LOUIS DiSANTO, (admission pending), ; registered to practice before U.S. Patent and Trademark Office. *Education:* Michigan State University (B.S., Chemical Engineering, 1999); University of Illinois (J.D., 2005). ***PRACTICE AREAS:*** Patents. ***Email:*** disanto@wildmanharrold.com

MOHAMMED A. DIWAN, admitted to bar, 2004, Illinois. *Education:* University of Michigan (B.A., Political Science, African-American & African Studies, & French, with high distinction, 2001); Duke University (J.D., 2004). Phi Beta Kappa. Articles Editor, Duke Journal of Comparative & International Law, 2003-2004. ***LANGUAGES:*** French and Urdu. ***PRACTICE AREAS:*** Corporate Law; Securities; Tax Law. ***Email:*** diwan@wildmanharrold.com

CHRISTOPHER J. DOUGLASS, born Laurens, Iowa, June 30, 1977; admitted to bar, 2001, Illinois and U.S. District Court, Northern District of Illinois. *Education:* Northwestern University (B.A., cum laude, 1998); University of Iowa (J.D., with highest distinction, 2001). Order of the Coif. Senior Note and Comment Editor, Iowa Law Review. Author, "Objections, Renewals, and Preemptive Introduction," 86 Iowa Law Review 949, 2001. ***PRACTICE AREAS:*** Corporate Law; Securities; Mergers and Acquisitions; Private Equity; Health Care. ***Email:*** douglass@wildmanharrold.com

ERIN K. FERGUSON, (admission pending). *Education:* Washington & Lee University (B.A. in English, magna cum laude, 2001); Northwestern University (J.D., 2005). Phi Beta Kappa. National Merit Scholar. ***PRACTICE AREAS:*** Litigation. ***Email:*** erinferguson@wildmanharrold.com

NATHAN E. FERGUSON, born St. Louis, Missouri, November 6, 1969; admitted to bar, 2000, Illinois and U.S. District Court, Northern District of Illinois; 2001, U.S. Court of Appeals, Tenth Circuit; 2002, U.S. Court of Appeals, Ninth Circuit. *Education:* University of Chicago (B.A., 1992); Chicago-Kent College of Law, Illinois Institute of Technology (J.D., 2000). Editorial Board Member, The Journal of Intellectual Property, 1999-2000. *Member:* Chicago (Member, Entertainment Law Practice Committee) and Illinois State Bar Associations. ***PRACTICE AREAS:*** Intellectual Property; Litigation; E-Commerce; Real Estate. ***Email:*** ferguson@wildmanharrold.com

PAUL K. FREEBORN, admitted to bar, 2002, Illinois. *Education:* University of Wisconsin at Madison (B.A., Business, 1999); DePaul University (J.D., 2002). DePaul Law Review. *Member:* Chicago and American Bar Associations. ***PRACTICE AREAS:*** Litigation. ***Email:*** freeborn@wildmanharrold.com

JEFFREY L. GANSBERG, born Livingston, New Jersey, June 25, 1971; admitted to bar, 1997, Illinois; 1999, New Jersey; U.S. District Court, Northern District of Illinois. *Education:* University of Delaware (B.S., Accounting, 1993); Washington University (J.D., 1997). Recipient, Scholar in Law Award. Member, Board of Directors and Member, Finance Committee, Chicago Access Corporation. *Member:* Chicago and American Bar Associations; American Bankruptcy Institute. ***PRACTICE AREAS:*** Loan Restructuring; Insolvency. ***Email:*** gansberg@wildmanharrold.com

MATTHEW M. GARRETT, born Springfield, Illinois, January 1, 1975; admitted to bar, 2000, Illinois, U.S. District Court, Northern District of Illinois and U.S. Court of Federal Claims. *Education:* Quincy University (B.S., summa cum laude, 1997); University of Illinois, Champaign (J.D., magna cum laude, 2000). ***PRACTICE AREAS:*** Litigation. ***Email:*** garrett@wildmanharrold.com

CHRISTY S. GERST, born Evanston, Illinois, April 11, 1977; admitted to bar, 2001, Illinois and U.S. District Court, Northern District of Illinois. *Education:* Loyola University; Washington University (B.A., History and Political Science, with college honors, 1998); University of Illinois (J.D., magna cum laude, 2001). *Member:* Chicago and American Bar Associations. ***PRACTICE AREAS:*** Labor and Employment. ***Email:*** travisc@wildmanharrold.com

(This Listing Continued)

LESLIE GOGAN, (admission pending). *Education:* Ohio University, (B.S., Communications Systems Management, cum laude, 1994); Southeastern Paralegal Institute, Dallas, Texas (Paralegal Certificate, 1998); Chicago-Kent College of Law, Illinois Institute of Technology, (J.D., with high honors, 2003). Order of the Coif. Member, Chicago-Kent Law Review, 2002-2003. ***PRACTICE AREAS:*** Litigation. ***Email:*** gogan@wildmanharrold.com

JEREMY S. GOLDKIND, admitted to bar, 2004, Illinois. *Education:* University of Illinois (B.S., Advertising and Communications, with highest distinction, 2001); University of Iowa (J.D., with distinction, 2004). Co-President, Iowa Student Bar Association, 2004. Member, National Moot Court Team, University of Iowa, 2004. Member, Journal of Transnational Law and Contemporary Problems, 2003. ***PRACTICE AREAS:*** Litigation. ***Email:*** goldkind@wildmanharrold.com

JONATHAN S. GOODMAN, admitted to bar, 1998, Illinois and Wisconsin. *Education:* Emory University (B.A., summa cum laude, 1994); University of Wisconsin-Madison School of Law (J.D., cum laude, 1998). Member, Wisconsin Law Review. ***PRACTICE AREAS:*** Litigation. ***Email:*** goodmanj@wildmanharrold.com

ELIZABETH A. GUTIERREZ, (admission pending). *Education:* Northwestern University (B.A., English and Philosophy, 1999); University of Chicago (J.D, 2005). ***PRACTICE AREAS:*** Litigation. ***Email:*** gutierrez@wildmanharrold.com

VELISHA L. HADDOX, admitted to bar, 2002, Pennsylvania, New Jersey, U.S. District Court, Eastern District of Pennsylvania and U.S. District Court, District of New Jersey; 2003, Illinois. *Education:* University of Michigan (B.A., Political Science and Sociology, 1999) Temple University (J.D., 2002). ***LANGUAGES:*** Spanish. ***PRACTICE AREAS:*** Commercial Litigation; Products Liability; Toxic Torts. ***Email:*** vthomas@wildmanharrold.com

DAVID R. HALE, born Stillwater, Oklahoma, December 21, 1972; admitted to bar, 2000, New York and Maryland; U.S. District Court, District of Maryland (Not admitted in Illinois). *Education:* Rice University (B.A., Policy Studies, History and Anthropology, 1995); George Washington University Law School (J.D., 1999). Co-Author: "Snake-Oil Security Claims: The Systematic Misrepresentation of Product Security in the E-Commerce Arena," 9 Mich. Telecomm. Tech.L.Rev. 211 (2003). ***PRACTICE AREAS:*** Intellectual Property. ***Email:*** hale@wildmanharrold.com

JAMES J. HEGARTY, born March 22, 1971; admitted to bar, 1999, Wisconsin; 2004, Illinois. *Education:* Duke University (A.B., Public Policy Studies and Economics, cum laude, 1993); University of Chicago (J.D., 1999). Former Staff Attorney, Federal Trade Commission. *Member:* Illinois State and American Bar Associations; State Bar of Wisconsin. ***PRACTICE AREAS:*** Commercial Litigation; Antitrust. ***Email:*** hegarty@wildmanharrold.com

BETHANY L. HENGSBACH, born Michigan, 1972; admitted to bar, 1997, Illinois. *Education:* University of Illinois (B.A., 1994); DePaul University College of Law(J.D., 1997). ***PRACTICE AREAS:*** Litigation. ***Email:*** hengsbach@wildmanharrold.com

MEGHAN M. HUBBARD, admitted to bar, 2001, Illinois. *Education:* Western Michigan University (B.B., Business Administration, 1993); Chicago-Kent College of Law (J.D., cum laude, honors, 2001). ***PRACTICE AREAS:*** Litigation; Commercial Law; Landlord and Tenant Law; Construction Law; Insurance Coverage; Insurance Defense; Professional Malpractice; Trademark Litigation; Trial Practice. ***Email:*** hubbardl@wildmanharrold.com

MARK A. HUDDLE, born Dayton, Ohio, April 14, 1959; admitted to bar, 1992, Illinois. *Education:* Knox College (B.A., cum laude, 1981); School of the Art Institute of Chicago; University of Illinois (J.D., magna cum laude, 1992); University of Chicago (M.F.A., 1996). Assistant to the Governor of Illinois, 1983-1986. Member, Urban Gateways Board, Knox College Alumni Advisory Council. *Member:* Chicago, Illinois State and American Bar Associations. ***PRACTICE AREAS:*** Governmental; Municipal Bonds; Corporate Law; Child Care. ***Email:*** huddle@wildmanharrold.com

BRANDON G. HUMMEL, admitted to bar, 2004, Illinois. *Education:* Johns Hopkins University (B.A., History, cum laude, 2000); Northwestern University (J.D., 2004). Member, Moot Court. Participant: Civil Litigation Clinic; Bluhm Legal Clinic. Co-Author: "Recent Developments in Insurance Regulation," Tort & Ins. L.J., Winter 2005; Supplement to "Pleadings, Motions and Orders," in "Class Actions," Illinois Institute for Continuing Legal Education, 2004; "Recent Pharmaceutical and Medical Devices: What St. Jude and Several State Court Cases Do and Don't Tell Us," Class Action Defense Section, Findlaw.com's Corporate Counsel Center, April 2004; Case Study, "Employing Complex Financial and Operative Techniques to Keep a Troubled TIF Afloat: Sauk Village's Experience with Its Own TIF III," Local Government Law: The Newsletter of the ISBA's Section on Local Government Law, 2003. *Member:* Chicago and American Bar Associations. ***PRACTICE AREAS:*** Litigation; Government Affairs. ***Email:*** hummel@wildmanharrold.com

KATHERINE IVERS, (admission pending). *Education:* Yale University (B.A., Political Science, 1999); Loyola University; Chicago Law School (J.D., 2005). ***PRACTICE AREAS:*** Intellectual Property. ***Email:*** ivers@wildmanharrold.com

RICHARD J. JANCASZ, admitted to bar, 2002, Illinois. *Education:* University of Michigan (B.A., Sociology and History, 1999); DePaul University (J.D., cum laude, 2002). DePaul Law Review. *Member:* Chicago and American Bar Associations. ***PRACTICE AREAS:*** Litigation. ***Email:*** jancasz@wildmanharrold.com

JENNIFER A. JOHNSTON, born Cleveland, Ohio, October 7, 1973; admitted to bar, 2001, California; 2004, Illinois; U.S. District, Central District of California. *Education:* Case Western Reserve University (B.S.N., cum laude, 1997; J.D., 2000); Loyola University. Associate Editor, Health Matrix, Journal of Law and Medicine, Case Western Reserve University School of Law, 1998-1999. Registered Nurse: Ohio, 1997; California; Illinois. *Member:* Chicago Bar Association; State Bar of California; Southern California Association of Defense Counsel; American Association of Nurse-Attorneys; American Health Lawyers Association. ***PRACTICE AREAS:*** Litigation. ***Email:*** jjohnston@wildmanharrold.com

SUNITH V. KARTHA, born Trichur, Kerala, India, July 17, 1975; admitted to bar, 2002, Illinois. *Education:* Northwestern University (B.A., Political Science, 1997); Chicago-Kent College of Law (J.D., 2002). Order of the Coif. Editor-in-Chief, The Journal of

(This Listing Continued)

Intellectual Property. Staff Member, The Chicago-Kent Law Review. *Member:* Chicago, Illinois State and American Bar Associations. ***PRACTICE AREAS:*** Advertising, Promotion and Marketing; Privacy; Information Technology; Intellectual Property; Entertainment. ***Email:*** kartha@wildmanharrold.com

JEFFREY KOSC, born Belleville, New Jersey, July 7, 1971; admitted to bar, 1996, Illinois. *Education:* Colby College (B.A., 1993); DePaul University (J.D., 1996). *Member:* Illinois State and American Bar Associations. ***PRACTICE AREAS:*** Computers and Software; Intellectual Property; Advertising and Marketing. ***Email:*** kosc@wildmanharrold.com

MARK A. KROMKOWSKI, born South Bend, Indiana, April 25, 1970; admitted to bar, 1998, Illinois and U.S. Court of Appeals, Seventh Circuit. *Education:* University of Notre Dame (B.A., cum laude, 1992; J.D., 1998). Executive Editor, Notre Dame Law Review, 1997-1998. Author: "Collateral Order Doctrine as Applied to Discovery Request: The Third Circuit's Kelly v. Ford Motor Co. (In re: Ford Motor)," 73 Notre Dame L. Rev. 1119 (1998). Instructor, Legal Writing, University of Notre Dame, 1997-1998. Founder/President, The Irish Forum, 1997—. *Member:* Chicago Inn of Court. ***PRACTICE AREAS:*** Corporate; Securities; SBIC; Venture Capital; Gaming. ***Email:*** kromkowski@wildmanharrold.com

MICHELLE M. KUNDMUELLER, admitted to bar, 2004, Illinois. *Education:* Flagler College (B.A., Politics and Law, summa cum laude, 2000); University of Notre Dame (J.D., 2004). ***LANGUAGES:*** French. ***PRACTICE AREAS:*** Litigation. ***Email:*** kundmueller@wildmanharrold.com

MICHAEL R. LaPORTE, born Detroit, Michigan, April 19, 1969; admitted to bar, 1996, Illinois and U.S. District Court, Northern District of Illinois; 2002, U.S. District Court, Southern District of Illinois. *Education:* Williams College (B.A., 1991); Chicago-Kent College of Law, Illinois Institute of Technology (J.D., with high honors, 1996). Order of the Coif. Moot Court Honor Society, 1994-1996. Kent Legal Scholar, 1994-1996. Staff Member, Chicago-Kent Law Review, 1995-1996. ***PRACTICE AREAS:*** Intellectual Property Litigation; Litigation. ***Email:*** laporte@wildmanharrold.com

DENISE A. LAZAR, admitted to bar, 1998, Illinois and U.S. District Court, Northern District of Illinois including Trial Bar; 1999, U.S. Court of Appeals, Seventh Circuit; 2002, U.S. Supreme Court; 2003, U.S. District Court, Central District of Illinois; 2004, U.S. District Court, Southern District of Illinois. *Education:* Wheaton College (B.A., cum laude, Philosophy and Political Science, 1994); University of Sorbonne, Paris I (International Law Program, 1997); Cornell University (J.D., 1998). *Member:* Chicago, Illinois State, Seventh Circuit and American Bar Associations; Defense Research Institute. ***PRACTICE AREAS:*** Commercial Litigation; Professional Liability; Products Liability. ***Email:*** lazar@wildmanharrold.com

CAROL E. LIN, (admission pending). *Education:* University of Chicago (B.A. in English, with departmental honors, 2000; B.A. in Biology, 2000; J.D., 2005). ***PRACTICE AREAS:*** Litigation. ***Email:*** lin@wildmanharrold.com

LUCY LISIECKI, admitted to bar, 1998, Illinois and U.S. Court of Appeals, Seventh Circuit; 2000, U.S. District Court, Northern District of Illinois. *Education:* University of Chicago (B.A., 1995; J.D., 1998). Member, Chicago Council of Lawyers, 1999—. ***PRACTICE AREAS:*** Commercial Litigation. ***Email:*** lisiecki@wildmanharrold.com

REBECCA R. LONG, born Parma, Ohio, July 25, 1976; admitted to bar, 2001, Illinois. *Education:* University of Michigan (B.A., cum laude, with distinction, 1998); Loyola University, Chicago (J.D., 2001). Phi Alpha Delta (Vice-Justice, 1998-2000). James B. Angell Scholar, University of Michigan. Member: Mortar Board Senior Honor Society; Gamma Sigma Alpha Academic Honor Society. Member, National Mock Trial Team (Corboy Fellow), Loyola University. William W. Daniel National Competition Champion. ***PRACTICE AREAS:*** Litigation; Family Law. ***Email:*** longr@wildmanharrold.com

JOHN A. LUBURIC, born Hinsdale, Illinois, January 29, 1975; admitted to bar, 2000, Illinois and U.S. District Court, Northern District of Illinois. *Education:* DePaul University (B.S., Commerce, with high honors, 1997); Loyola University (J.D., cum laude, 2000). Dean's List. Member, Loyola University Chicago Law Journal, 1998-2000. ***PRACTICE AREAS:*** Litigation; Antitrust; Securities; Products Liability; Complex Litigation; Patent Litigation; Lender Law; Regulatory Law. ***Email:*** luburic@wildmanharrold.com

ASHANTI L. MADLOCK, admitted to bar, 2004, Illinois. *Education:* Northwestern University (B.S., Speech, 2001); George Washington University (J.D., 2004). Phi Alpha Delta International. *Member:* American Bar Association. ***PRACTICE AREAS:*** Labor and Employment; Litigation; Family Law. ***Email:*** madlock@wildmanharrold.com

SHANDELL S. MAGEE, born 1980; (admission pending). *Education:* University of Michigan (B.A. in English, 2002; J.D., 2005). ***PRACTICE AREAS:*** Corporate Law. ***Email:*** magee@wildmanharrold.com

JASON McCLAIN MAHONEY, admitted to bar, 2001, Illinois; 2002, Iowa. *Education:* Iowa State University (B.A., Rhetoric and Professional Communication, 1995); Loyola University of Chicago, Institute for Paralegal Studies (Certificate in Paralegal Studies, with honors, 1997); John Marshall Law School (J.D., 2001). *Member:* Chicago and Illinois State Bar Associations. ***PRACTICE AREAS:*** Real Estate. ***Email:*** jmahoney@wildmanharrold.com

R. MICHAEL McCANN, born Birmingham, Alabama, August 11, 1968; admitted to bar, 2001, Illinois and U.S. District Court, Northern District of Illinois. *Education:* Loyola University, New Orleans (B.B.A., 1990); Loyola University, Chicago (J.D., 2001). *Member:* Chicago, Illinois State and American Bar Associations. ***PRACTICE AREAS:*** Commercial Litigation. ***Email:*** mccann@wildmanharrold.com

JEFFREY K. McGINNESS, born Iowa City, Iowa, June 11, 1975; admitted to bar, 2001, Illinois. *Education:* University of Iowa (B.A., 1998; J.D., 2001). ***PRACTICE AREAS:*** Litigation; Environmental Law; Products Liability. ***Email:*** mcginness@wildmanharrold.com

ELIZABETH A. McKILLIP, admitted to bar, 2004, Illinois. *Education:* University of Illinois (B.A., Philosophy, 2001); Loyola University Chicago School of Law (J.D., magna cum laude, 2004). *Member:* DuPage County and Illinois State Bar Associations. (Lisle Office). ***PRACTICE AREAS:*** Estate Planning; Probate; Family Law. ***Email:*** mckillip@wildmanharrold.com

(This Listing Continued)

BRETT A. MIDDENDORF, born 1977; admitted to bar, 2005, Illinois. *Education:* Loyola University (B.B.A., Economics, cum laude, 2000); University of Iowa (J.D., 2005). ***PRACTICE AREAS:*** Litigation. ***Email:*** middendorf@wildmanharrold.com

LAURIE M. MILLER, born Chicago, Illinois, April 6, 1968; admitted to bar, 1995, Illinois. *Education:* University of Wisconsin (B.A., Political Science, 1990); Chicago-Kent College of Law (J.D., with honors, 1995). *Member:* American Corporate Counsel Association. (Lisle Office). ***PRACTICE AREAS:*** Corporate. ***Email:*** millerl@wildmanharrold.com

SHAWN MILLER, (admission pending), registered to practice before U.S. Patent and Trademark Office. *Education:* University of Notre Dame (B.S., Mechanical Engineering, 2000; B.A., Philosophy, cum laude, 2000; J.D., cum laude, 2004). ***PRACTICE AREAS:*** Patents. ***Email:*** shawnmiller@wildmanharrold.com

NICHOLAS R. MITCHELL, (admission pending). *Education:* Oakland University, (B.A., Political Science, cum laude, 2000); Chicago-Kent College of Law, Illinois Institute of Technology (J.D., 2003). Notes and Comments Editor, Chicago-Kent Law Review. Vice-President, Chicago-Kent Moot Court Honor Society. ***PRACTICE AREAS:*** Litigation. ***Email:*** nmitchell@wildmanharrold.com

DEBORAH L. MORGAN, admitted to bar, 2004, Illinois. *Education:* University of Illinois (B.A., Rhetoric, with distinction, 1998; B.A., Speech Communications, with distinction, 1998; J.D., 2004). ***PRACTICE AREAS:*** Litigation. ***Email:*** morgan@wildmanharrold.com

JULIE M. NICHOLS, born Buffalo, New York, December 4, 1968; admitted to bar, 1994, Illinois; 1999, U.S. District Court, Northern District of Illinois; 2000, U.S. District Court, District of Colorado; 2001, U.S. Supreme Court. *Education:* Duke University (A.B., 1991); Chicago-Kent College of Law (J.D., 1994); John Marshall Law School (LL.M., Intellectual Property Law, with honors, 1997). *Member:* Chicago and American Bar Associations; International Trademark Association; American Intellectual Property Law Association; Licensing Executives Society. ***PRACTICE AREAS:*** Intellectual Property. ***Email:*** nichols@wildmanharrold.com

MICHELLE NIJM, admitted to bar, 2004, Illinois. *Education:* Loyola University (B.A., Philosophy, magna cum laude, 2001); University of Chicago (J.D., 2004). ***LANGUAGES:*** French and Italian. ***PRACTICE AREAS:*** Intellectual Property. ***Email:*** nijm@wildmanharrold.com

NICOLE NOCERA, born Youngstown, Ohio, October 2, 1971; admitted to bar, 1998, Illinois; U.S. District Court, Northern District of Illinois; U.S. District Court, Northern and Southern Districts Indiana. *Education:* Ohio University (B.A., cum laude, 1994); Loyola University School of Law, Chicago (J.D., 1998). Member, Loyola University Chicago School of Law's National Trial Team and Chicago Bar Association Moot Court Team. *Member:* Chicago and Illinois State Bar Associations. ***PRACTICE AREAS:*** Commercial Litigation; Products Liability. ***Email:*** nocera@wildmanharrold.com

HEATHER E. NOLAN, admitted to bar, 2003, Illinois. *Education:* University of Wisconsin (B.S., Consumer Science and Personal Finance, with high honors, 2000); Loyola University Chicago School of Law (J.D., magna cum laude, 2003). Phi Upsilon Omicron. Editor-in-Chief, Loyola Consumer Law Review. Chicago Intellectual Property Colloquium Fellow. Saul Lefkowitz Trademark Moot Court Competition 2nd place Oral Advocate Team. Author: "Protecting Consumers from Cybersquatters: Is the ACPA Standing Up?" 14 Loyola Consumer Law Review 175 (March 2002). Co-Author, "Potential Liability for Marketing Your Business Electronically: The CAN-SPAM Act," Institute of Directors' Growing Business Handbook, 2004. Co-author, "Three Directions to Move in the Chicago Legal Market," Chicago Bar Association Record, at 42 (April 2002). *Member:* Chicago, Illinois State and American Bar Associations. ***PRACTICE AREAS:*** Intellectual Property; Intellectual Property Litigation; Information Technology. ***Email:*** hnolan@wildmanharrold.com

DAVID M. OPPENHEIM, admitted to bar, 2002, Illinois. *Education:* Yale University (B.A., Political Science with distinction and Economics, 1999); Harvard University (J.D., 2002). *Member:* Chicago and American Bar Associations. ***PRACTICE AREAS:*** Litigation. ***Email:*** oppenheim@wildmanharrold.com

MARCIA KLENK OWENS, born Cedar Rapids, Iowa, October 11, 1973; admitted to bar, 1998, Illinois. *Education:* University of Iowa (B.B.A., 1995; J.D., with high distinction, 1998). Order of the Coif. Student Writer and Note and Comment Editor, Iowa Law Review, 1996-1998. Member, International Council of Shopping Centers. *Member:* Chicago, Illinois State and American (Student Member, 1995-1998) Bar Associations. ***PRACTICE AREAS:*** Real Estate. ***Email:*** mowens@wildmanharrold.com

ALLYSON W. PAFLAS, admitted to bar, 2004, Illinois. *Education:* Wesley College (B.A., American Studies, with concentration in Political Science, cum laude, 2001); Duke University (J.D., 2004). Member, Moot Court Board. ***PRACTICE AREAS:*** Litigation. ***Email:*** paflasa@wildmanharrold.com

JOEL C. PASCHKE, admitted to bar, 1998, Minnesota; 2002, Illinois. *Education:* St. Cloud State University (B.A., English, summa cum laude, 1994); Hamlin University School of Law (J.D., cum laude, 1998). *Member:* Chicago (Member, Bankruptcy Committee, Young Lawyers Section), Illinois State and American (Member, Business Law Section) Bar Associations. ***PRACTICE AREAS:*** Restructuring; Insolvency. ***Email:*** paschke@wildmanharrold.com

RICHARD J. PEARL, admitted to bar, 2001, Illinois and U.S. District Court, Northern District of Illinois. *Education:* Northern Illinois University (B.S., Psychology/Philosophy, 1996); Loyola University of Chicago School of Law (J.D., cum laude, 2001; Certificate in Health Law). ***PRACTICE AREAS:*** Litigation; Insurance Coverage; Fiduciary Litigation; Breach of Contract; White Collar Crime; Products Liability; Complex Litigation; Commercial Litigation. ***Email:*** pearl@wildmanharrold.com

SANDRA S. PEDERSEN, admitted to bar, 2000, Illinois; 2001, U.S. District Court, Northern District of Illinois. *Education:* Miami University (B.S., cum laude, 1994); Villanova University School of Law (J.D., 2000). *Member:* Chicago and American (Member, Intellectual Property Law Section) Bar Associations; Intellectual Property Lawyers of Chicago. ***PRACTICE AREAS:*** Intellectual Property. ***Email:*** pedersen@wildmanharrold.com

(This Listing Continued)

WILDMAN, HARROLD, ALLEN & DIXON LLP, Chicago—Continued

WILLIAM R. POKORNY, admitted to bar, 2001, Illinois. *Education:* Augustana College (B.A., 1998); University of Chicago (J.D., 2001). ***PRACTICE AREAS:*** Labor and Employment. ***Email:*** pokorny@wildmanharrold.com

JAMES W. POLICHAK, admitted to bar, 2003, Illinois. *Education:* Union College (B.A., Psychology and English, magna cum laude, 1995); State University of New York (M.A., 1998; Ph.D., Experimental Psychology, 2000); University of Michigan Law School (J.D. 2003). *Member:* Chicago, Illinois State and American Bar Associations; American Intellectual Property Law Association; American Psychological Society; American Psychology-Law Society; European Association of Psychology and Law. ***LANGUAGES:*** French, Dutch. ***PRACTICE AREAS:*** Intellectual Property; Litigation. ***Email:*** polichak@wildmanharrold.com

MELISSA M. RIAHEI, born Tehran, Iran, December 12, 1973; admitted to bar, 1998, Illinois and U.S. District Court, Northern District of Illinois; 1999, U.S. District Court, Central District of Illinois; 2000, U.S. Court of Appeals, Seventh Circuit; 2001, U.S. Court of Appeals, Ninth Circuit; 2003, U.S. District Court, Southern District of Illinois and U.S. Court of Appeals, Federal Circuit. *Education:* George Mason University (B.A., 1995); University of Richmond (J.D., 1998). Member, University of Richmond Law Review. ***LANGUAGES:*** Farsi. ***PRACTICE AREAS:*** Appellate Practice; Complex Commercial Litigation; Corporate Litigation; Governmental Litigation. ***Email:*** riahei@wildmanharrold.com

DAVID M. ROTENBERG, admitted to bar, 2004, Illinois. *Education:* Vassar College (B.A., Political Science, 1999); University of Chicago (J.D., 2004). ***PRACTICE AREAS:*** Corporate Law; Securities; Tax Law. ***Email:*** rotenberg@wildmanharrold.com

JAMIE RUBIN, admitted to bar, 2000, Illinois. *Education:* University of Iowa (B.A., Economics, 1997); John Marshall Law School (J.D., 2000). Re-established and President, Entertainment and Media Law Society, 1997-1999. Guest Speaker, "You and The Law," Music Law and Television Production Issues, Chicago Bar Association. *Member:* Chicago (Vice Chairman, Computer Law Committee, 2002—), Illinois State and American Bar Associations; Promotion Marketing Association of America. ***PRACTICE AREAS:*** Advertising; Promotion Law; Marketing Law; Entertainment Law; Information Technology; Intellectual Property; Privacy Law. ***Email:*** rubinj@wildmanharrold.com

BEAU C. SEFTON, born Columbus, Ohio, August 7, 1974; admitted to bar, 1999, Illinois and U.S. District Court, Northern District of Illinois; 2000, U.S. District Court, Northern District of Indiana; 2001, U.S. District Court, Central and Southern Districts of Illinois. *Education:* Miami University (B.A., 1996); Harvard University (J.D., 1999). ***PRACTICE AREAS:*** Products Liability; Labor and Employment; Commercial Litigation. ***Email:*** sefton@wildmanharrold.com

MELISSA SUZANNE SKILKEN, born Dayton, Ohio, April 19, 1972; admitted to bar, 1998, Ohio and U.S. District Court, Southern District of Ohio; 1999, Illinois and U.S. District Court, Northern District of Illinois. *Education:* Kenyon College (B.A., cum laude, with high honors in history, 1994); University of Cincinnati College of Law (J.D., 1998). Executive Editor, University of Cincinnati Law Review. Author: "This Ban's For You: 44 Liquormart v. Rhode Island," 65 University of Cincinnati Law Review 1387, 1997. *Member:* Illinois State and American Bar Associations. ***PRACTICE AREAS:*** Commercial Litigation; Products Liability. ***Email:*** skilken@wildmanharrold.com

GREGORY M. SMITH, born Chicago, Illinois, October 31, 1968; admitted to bar, 1998, Illinois and U.S. Court of Appeals, Seventh Circuit; 1999, U.S. District Court, Northern District of Illinois including Trial Bar; registered to practice before U.S. Patent and Trademark Office. *Education:* University of Colorado at Boulder (B.S., Mechanical Engineering, 1992); John Marshall Law School (J.D., 1998). *Member:* Chicago, Illinois State and American Bar Associations; Justinian Society of Lawyers; American Intellectual Property Law Association; Chicago Intellectual Property Law Association. ***PRACTICE AREAS:*** Intellectual Property. ***Email:*** gsmith@wildmanharrold.com

JOSHUA L. SMITH, born Alexandria, Virginia, September 24, 1971; admitted to bar, 1996, Illinois and U.S. District Court, Northern District of Illinois; 1997, U.S. District Court, Central District of Illinois and U.S. Court of Appeals, Seventh Circuit. *Education:* University of Delaware (B.S., cum laude, 1993); Indiana University (J.D., cum laude, 1996). Kappa Delta Rho (National President, 2001—); Delta Theta Phi (Treasurer, 1995-1996). Member and Managing Editor, Indiana Law Journal. *Member:* American Bar Association; International Trademark Association; Chicago Software Association; International Association of Privacy Professionals. ***REPORTED CASES:*** Toney v. L'Oreal USA, Inc., --- F.3d ---, 2004 WL 2093265 (7th Cir Sept. 21, 2004); Toney v. L'Oreal USA, Inc., 64 U.S.P.Q.2d 1857 (N.D.Ill. 2002); Tasini v. New York Times, 206 F. 3d 161, (2nd Cir. 2000), aff'd, 533 U.S. 483 (2001); Chicago School Reform Board vs. Substance, Inc., 79 F. Supp. 2d 919 (N.D. Ill. 2000). ***PRACTICE AREAS:*** Privacy; Intellectual Property; E-Commerce. ***Email:*** smithj@wildmanharrold.com

MARTIN D. SNYDER, born Davenport, Iowa, December 29, 1970; admitted to bar, 1996, Illinois and U.S. District Court, Northern District of Illinois including Trial Bar; 2002, U.S. District Court, Central District of Illinois; 2003, U.S. District Court, Southern District of Illinois and U.S. District Court, Northern District of Indiana; 2004, U.S. Court of Appeals, Seventh Circuit. *Education:* University of Colorado (B.A., Political Science, 1993); Loyola University, Chicago School of Law (J.D., cum laude, 1996). Adjunct Professor, Trial Advocacy, Loyola University, Chicago School of Law, 2000—. *Member:* Chicago, Illinois State and American Bar Associations. ***PRACTICE AREAS:*** Commercial Litigation; Products Liability. ***Email:*** snyderm@wildmanharrold.com

AARON L. SOLOMON, admitted to bar, 2002, Illinois and U.S. District Court, Northern District of Illinois. *Education:* Wesleyan University College of Social Studies (B.A., with honors, 1997); University of Chicago (J.D., 2002). Comments and Developments Editor, *Chicago Journal of International Law,* 2001-2002. ***PRACTICE AREAS:*** Litigation; Health Care. ***Email:*** asolomon@wildmanharrold.com

JENEE M. STRAUB, born St. Charles, Illinois, May 17, 1973; admitted to bar, 1999, Illinois. *Education:* Bradley University (B.S., 1996); Northern Illinois University College of Law, (J.D., cum laude, 1999). (Lisle Office). ***Email:*** straub@wildmanharrold.com

(This Listing Continued)

PHILIP R. STRZALKA, born 1971; admitted to bar, 1998, Illinois; 2000, Virginia; 2001, District of Columbia. *Education:* University of Illinois (B.S., Finance, with honors, 1992); Chicago-Kent College of Law, Illinois Institute of Technology (J.D., with honors, 1998). *Member:* Virginia State Bar; The District of Columbia Bar. ***PRACTICE AREAS:*** Corporate Law; Securities; Tax Law. ***Email:*** strzalka@wildmanharrold.com

BRYAN PAUL SUGAR, born Skokie, Illinois, May 5, 1974; admitted to bar, 2001, Illinois; U.S. District Court, Northern District of Illinois. *Education:* University of Wisconsin (B.A., 1996); Chicago-Kent College of Law (J.D., 2001). *Member:* International Trademark Association; American Intellectual Property Law Association; American Society for the Technion. ***PRACTICE AREAS:*** Intellectual Property. ***Email:*** sugar@wildmanharrold.com

HELEN HYAE-JUNG SUH, born 1979; (admission pending). *Education:* Yale University (B.A., Economics, 2001); Northwestern University (J.D., 2005). ***LANGUAGES:*** Korean and Japanese. ***PRACTICE AREAS:*** Real Estate; Corporate Law. ***Email:*** suh@wildmanharrold.com

RYAN T. SULKIN, admitted to bar, 2004, Illinois. *Education:* Northwestern University (B.S.J., Journalism, summa cum laude, 2001; B.S., Psychology, 2001); Harvard Law School (J.D., 2004). Researcher and Presenter, "Legislating Through Proportionate and Congruent Review: A Guidebook for the Creation of Constitutional, Anti-Discrimination Legislation," 2004. ***PRACTICE AREAS:*** Intellectual Property; Intellectual Property Litigation; Information Technology; Privacy Law; Business Continuity; Business Security. ***Email:*** sulkin@wildmanharrold.com

DAVID P. VALLAS, born Buffalo, New York, July 7, 1973; admitted to bar, 2000, Illinois and U.S. District Court, Northern District of Illinois. *Education:* Williams College (B.A., Political Economy, 1995); Indiana University School of Law (J.D., 2000). Managing Editor, Federal Communications Law Journal, Indiana University School of Law. *Member:* Chicago and American Bar Associations. ***PRACTICE AREAS:*** Restructuring; Insolvency; Commercial Litigation. ***Email:*** vallas@wildmanharrold.com

CORRIE E. VALROSE, admitted to bar, 2000, Illinois. *Education:* Ball State University, College of Architecture and Planning (B.L.A., 1993); Chicago-Kent College of Law, Illinois Institute of Technology (J.D., 2000). Member, DePaul Environmental Law Journal. *Member:* Chicago and Illinois Bar Associations; American Institute of Architects (AIA); American Society of Landscape Architects (ASLA). (Lisle Office). ***PRACTICE AREAS:*** Litigation; Breach of Contract; Consumer Fraud; Truth in Lending; Mechanics Liens; Breach of Warranty; Design Professionals Liability; Contracts. ***Email:*** schafer@wildmanharrold.com

THERESA G. VAN VUREN, admitted to bar, 2003, Illinois. *Education:* University of Michigan (B.A., Political Science and Spanish, 1996); Chicago-Kent College of Law, Illinois Institute of Technology (J.D., high honors, 2003). Order of the Coif. Member, Chicago-Kent Law Review. Dean's List. Legal Intern, Legal Assistance Foundation of Metropolitan Chicago. Bilingual Advocate, Public Benefits Division. *Member:* Chicago, Illinois State and American Bar Associations. ***LANGUAGES:*** Spanish. ***PRACTICE AREAS:*** Labor and Employment. ***Email:*** vanvuren@wildmanharrold.com

ROBERT WAGNER, admitted to bar, 2001, Illinois; 2002, U.S. Court of Appeals, Sixth Circuit; 2003, U.S. District Court, Northern District of Illinois, U.S. District Court, Northern District of Ohio and U.S. Court of Appeals, Seventh Circuit. *Education:* Harvey Mudd College (B.S., Physics, 1992); University of Michigan (M.S., Applied Physics, 1995; Ph.D., 1998); Case Western Reserve University (J.D., magna cum laude, 2001). *Member:* Chicago, Illinois State and American Bar Associations; American Physical Society. ***PRACTICE AREAS:*** Litigation; Intellectual Property. ***Email:*** wagner@wildmanharrold.com

PEDRO J. WINDSOR, JR., admitted to bar, 2004, Illinois. *Education:* John Jay College of Criminal Justice of the City University of New York (B.A., Political Science, magna cum laude, 1999); University of Iowa (J.D., 2003). Elected Member, Iowa Student Bar Association. Member, Van Oosterhout Moot Court, University of Iowa Law School. ***PRACTICE AREAS:*** Litigation; Employment Law; Government Affairs. ***Email:*** windsor@wildmanharrold.com

WAYNE YAO, admitted to bar, 2004, Illinois. *Education:* Beijing Institute of Finance and Trade (B.A., Economic Law, 1992); Northwestern University (J.D., 2003; M.B.A., 2003). Member, BIFT Law Review. Member: Asian Pacific Law Students Association; Asian Management Association; Investment Banking Club; Consulting Club. *Member:* Chicago, Illinois State and American Bar Associations. ***LANGUAGES:*** Mandarin Chinese. ***PRACTICE AREAS:*** Corporate Law. ***Email:*** yao@wildmanharrold.com

JOHN W. YOUNG, admitted to bar, 2000, Illinois. *Education:* Duke University (B.A., 1994); University of Chicago (M.P.P., 1996); University of Virginia (J.D., 2000). *Member:* Chicago and Illinois State Bar Associations. ***PRACTICE AREAS:*** Litigation. ***Email:*** jyoung@wildmanharrold.com

EDWARD P. ZAENGLE, born Cooperstown, New York, June 25, 1963; admitted to bar, 1999, Illinois and U.S. District Court, Northern District of Illinois. *Education:* State University of New York at Oneonta (B.S., Geology and Water Resources, with honors, 1985); Southern Illinois University (M.S., Geology, 1992); University of Illinois (J.D., magna cum laude, 1999). Harno Scholar. Recipient: Academic Scholarship, University of Illinois; CALI Awards. Associate, Jenner & Block, Chicago, Illinois, 1999-2003. *Member:* Chicago and American Bar Associations. ***PRACTICE AREAS:*** Litigation; Products Liability; Toxic Torts; Commercial Litigation. ***Email:*** zaengle@wildmanharrold.com

OF COUNSEL

THOMAS D. ALLEN, born Detroit, Michigan, June 25, 1926; admitted to bar, 1952, Illinois. *Education:* Northwestern University (B.S., 1949); University of Michigan (J.D., 1952). Phi Delta Phi. *Member:* Chicago (Chair: Civil Practice Committee, 1975-1976; Legislative Committee, 1977-1979; Member, Board of Managers, 1989-1991), DuPage County, Illinois State, American and International Bar Associations; Lawyers Club of Chicago; Society of Trial Lawyers. Fellow, American College of Trial Lawyers (Illinois State Chair, 1984-1985; Chair, International Committee, 1997-1999). ***PRACTICE AREAS:*** Aviation; Product Liability; Trial; Appellate; Commercial Litigation. ***Email:*** allen@wildmanharrold.com

(This Listing Continued)

HOWARD ARVEY, admitted to bar, 1948, Illinois; 1981, New York. *Education:* Northwestern University (B.S., 1942); Harvard Law School and Northwestern University (J.D., 1948). Master in Chancery, Circuit Court, 1953-1965. *Member:* Chicago, Illinois State and American Bar Associations; Decalogue Society of Lawyers. ***PRACTICE AREAS:*** Corporate, Securities, Tax; Health Care. ***Email:*** arvey@wildmanharrold.com

MARSHALL L. BURMAN, born July 22, 1929; admitted to bar, 1954, Illinois. *Education:* Northwestern University (B.S., 1951); Yale University (LL.B., 1954). Phi Alpha Delta. Recipient, Judge Learned Hand Human Relations Award, 1983. Recipient, Order of Lincoln, 1990. Member, Financial Advisory Panel to Amtrak, 1970-1973. Regent, 1978—and Chancellor, 1979-1985, Lincoln Academy. Member, 1978-2001 and Chairman, 1984-1998, Illinois State Board of Investments. *Member:* Chicago and Illinois State Bar Associations. ***PRACTICE AREAS:*** Corporate; Securities. ***Email:*** burman@wildmanharrold.com

THOMAS R. FIELD, born Highland Park, Illinois, June 14, 1954; admitted to bar, 1980, Illinois and U.S. District Court, Northern District of Illinois. *Education:* University of Michigan (B.A., English, with distinction, 1976); Northwestern University (J.D., 1980). Member, Northwestern University Law Review, 1978-1980. *Member:* Chicago, Illinois State and American Bar Associations. ***PRACTICE AREAS:*** Real Estate. ***Email:*** field@wildmanharrold.com

LORI A. GOLDSTEIN, born Chicago, Illinois, October 8, 1959; admitted to bar, 1984, Illinois and U.S. District Court, Northern District of Illinois; 1990, U.S. Court of Appeals, Seventh Circuit. *Education:* University of Illinois (B.S., 1981; J.D., 1984). Index Editor, University of Illinois Law Review, 1983-1984. Author: "The Legal and Practical Reasons You Should Conduct Exit Interviews," Assisted Living, June 2000; "ADA Update: What Are The Courts Debating?" The Journal of Workers Compensation, Fall 1998; "Minimizing Your Employment Liability-Understanding the Interplay Among ADA, FMLA and Worker's Compensation," Food Industry News, Nov., 1996; "Complying with the FMLA May Not Be Enough-You May Need The ADA," Insight, The Magazine of the Illinois CPA Society, December/January 1995; Wildman Harrold Group Seminars, May 2001; Speaker: "Absences and Attendance: Navigating the Maze of the ADA, FMLA and Workers' Corporation," American Institute of Architects, June 2001; "FMLA and No-Fault Attendance, Association of Legal Administrators, January 2001; "Harassment Training," DuPage County Housing Authority, November 2000; "Reconciling ADA, FMLA, Workers Comp and COBRA," Annual EEO Conference, Loyola University, May 1999; "Sexual Harassment and General Employment Issues," Chicago Assn. of Industrial and Organizational Psychologists, Nov. 1996; "FMLA And ADA Update," Illinois Nursing Home Administrators Assn. August 1993. *Member:* Chicago (Member, Labor and Employment Law Section) and American (Member, Section on Labor and Employment Law) Bar Associations; Women's Bar Association of Illinois. ***PRACTICE AREAS:*** Employment Law. ***Email:*** goldstein@wildmanharrold.com

ROBERT M. GUNN, born Tientsin, China, September 6, 1927; admitted to bar, 1954, Iowa; 1955, Illinois. *Education:* Yale University (B.A., 1949); University of Iowa (J.D., 1954). *Member:* Chicago, Illinois State and American Bar Associations. ***PRACTICE AREAS:*** Corporate; Securities; Tax; Estate Planning; Probate; Family Law; Insurance Industry. ***Email:*** gunn@wildmanharrold.com

DUANE P. HAGERTY, born Dubuque, Iowa, June 5, 1966; admitted to bar, 1991, Minnesota; 1992, Iowa; 2005, Illinois. *Education:* University of Northern Iowa (B.A., with high honors, 1988); University of Minnesota (J.D., cum laude, 1991). Omicron Delta Epsilon. *Member:* Chicago, Polk County, Illinois State, Iowa State and American Bar Associations. ***PRACTICE AREAS:*** Real Estate. ***Email:*** hagerty@wildmanharrold.com

BERNARD HARROLD, born Wells County, Indiana, February 5, 1925; admitted to bar, 1951, Illinois. *Education:* Indiana University (A.B., 1949; LL.B., 1951). Fellow, Academy of Law Alumni Fellows, Indiana University School of Law. Phi Beta Kappa; Phi Eta Sigma; Order of the Coif. Note Editor, Indiana Law Journal, 1950-1951. Member, Winnetka Caucus Committee, 1967-1968. *Member:* Chicago (Member: Antitrust Committee, 1969—; Environmental Law Committee, 1971—; Chairman, Subcommittee on Private Remedies of Antitrust Committee, 1976-1977), Illinois State (Member, Antitrust Section; Chairman, Evidence Program, 1970) and American (Member, Sections on: Antitrust Law; Corporation, Banking and Business Law) Bar Associations; Lawyers Club of Chicago. Fellow, American College of Trial Lawyers. ***PRACTICE AREAS:*** Antitrust; Commercial Litigation; Criminal; Environmental; Insurance Industry; Intellectual Property. ***Email:*** harrold@wildmanharrold.com

MARSHALL M. HOLLEB, born Chicago, Illinois, December 25, 1916; admitted to bar, 1947, Illinois. *Education:* University of Wisconsin (B.A., 1937); Harvard Graduate School of Business Administration (M.B.A., 1939; I.A., 1941); Harvard Law School (J.D., 1942). U.S. State Department Consultant, Foreign Service Inspection Corps, Public Member, 1966. Member, National Committee, White House Conference on Aging, 1981. Member, Industry Sector Advisory Committee on Services for Trade Policy Matters, U.S. Department of Commerce, 1995-1998. Trustee, Acorn Fund, 1971-1995. General Counsel, Museum of Contemporary Art and Arts Club of Chicago. Member, National Panel of Arbitrators, American Arbitration Association. Chairman, Illinois State Council on Aging, 1973-1981. Member, Board of Directors, Harvard Law Society of Illinois, 1991. Overseer, Harvard Business School Club of Chicago, 1997—. ***PRACTICE AREAS:*** Corporate Law; Business Law; Real Estate Law; Estate Planning; Estate Administration; Wealth Preservation. ***Email:*** holleb@wildmanharrold.com

ELIZABETH KEILEY, born Chicago, Illinois, November 2, 1965; admitted to bar, 1990, Illinois and U.S. District Court, Northern District of Illinois; 2001, U.S. District Court, Northern District of Indiana; 2004, Indiana. *Education:* Boston College (B.A./B.S., magna cum laude, 1987); Loyola University (J.D., cum laude, 1990). *Member:* Illinois State Bar Association. ***PRACTICE AREAS:*** Appellate; Commercial Litigation; Products Liability. ***Email:*** keiley@wildmanharrold.com

KIPLUND R. KOLKMEIER, born Cedar Rapids, Iowa, July 18, 1962; admitted to bar, 1988, Illinois. *Education:* Stanford University (B.A., 1985); Loyola University of Chicago (J.D., 1988). Member, Historical Sites Commission, City of Springfield, 2003—; Legislative Counsel, Illinois Speaker of the House, Michael Madigan, 1989. Executive Director and General Counsel, Metro Counties Association, 1995-1998. Registered Lobbyist, Illinois. *Member:* Illinois State Bar Association. ***PRACTICE AREAS:*** Legislative Lobbying; Corporate Ethics; Government Ethics; Association Management; State and Federal Campaign Finance. ***Email:*** kolkmeier@wildmanharrold.com

CATHERINE MATHEWS GRAF, admitted to bar, 1995, Illinois, U.S District Court, Northern District of Illinois and Eastern District of Michigan. *Education:* Michigan State University (B.A., Journalism, Minor Political Science, 1991); DePaul University College of Law (J.D., 1995). Order of the Coif. President, Young Professionals Board for the Coordinated Advice and Referral Program for Legal Services (CARPLS), 1998-1999.*Member:* Chicago and American (Member, Corporate Counsel Committee) Bar Associations; American Corporate Counsel Association; Women's Bar Association of Illinois. ***PRACTICE AREAS:*** Commercial Litigation; Contracts; Intellectual Property; Internet Law. ***Email:*** mathewsgraf@wildmanharrold.com

JOHN E. McGOVERN, JR., born Chicago, Illinois, March 25, 1931; admitted to bar, 1959, Illinois. *Education:* Princeton University (B.S.E., cum laude, 1953); Harvard University (J.D., 1959). Alderman, City of Lake Forest, Illinois, 1978-1984; Trustee, Lake Forest College, 1972-1984; Trustee, Ravinia Festival Association, 1981-1985. Director, Lake Forest Hospital, 1972-1982. *Member:* Chicago (Chairman, Securities Law Committee, 1980-1981) and American (Member, Section on: Corporation, Banking and Business Law) Bar Associations. [U.S. Navy, 1953-1956]. ***PRACTICE AREAS:*** Securities; Corporate; Mergers and Acquisitions. ***Email:*** mcgovern@wildmanharrold.com

SHELDON P. MIGDAL, born Chicago, Illinois, July 3, 1936; admitted to bar, 1961, Illinois. *Education:* University of Illinois (B.S., 1958); Northwestern University (J.D., 1961). Special Trial Attorney, Tax Division, U.S. Department of Justice, 1961-1966. *Member:* Chicago, Illinois State and American Bar Associations; Chicago Council of Lawyers. ***PRACTICE AREAS:*** Tax; Corporate; Estate Planning; Real Estate. ***Email:*** migdal@wildmanharrold.com

SCOTT A. SEMENEK, born October 19, 1967; admitted to bar, 1992, Illinois and U.S. District Court, Northern District of Illinois. *Education:* University of Wisconsin-Madison (B.B.A., with distinction, 1989); Northwestern University (J.D., 1992). Beta Gamma Sigma; Phi Kappa Phi. Associate Articles Editor, Northwestern University Law Review. Author, "What Borrowers Can Reasonably Expect To Achieve Through Use of the Bankruptcy Tool," in *Playing the New Real Estate Game Successfully* (Prentice Hall 1993). Contributing Author, Wiley Bankruptcy Law Update, Aspen Law & Business, 1998; "The Prohibition of Fee Sharing: Words of Caution to Professionals,"American Bankruptcy Institute Journal, September, 1997; "Professional Liability in the United States, Professional Liability Lawyers," Lloyd's of London Press, Ltd., 1995; "Pro-ration of Rent Dead in Third and Sixth Circuits - Landlords Won the Battle, But Will They Lose the War," 19 Bankr. D.J. 123 (2002). Speaker, "Lender Liability: The Potential Threat Posed By Non-Traditional Plaintiffs," Chicago Bar Association Committee on Commercial Finance and Transactions, March 16, 2000. ***PRACTICE AREAS:*** Creditors Rights. ***Email:*** semenek@wilmanharrold.com

THOMAS H. SNYDER, born Chicago, Illinois, February 7, 1943; admitted to bar, 1968, Illinois. *Education:* Georgetown University (A.B., 1964); University of Michigan (J.D., 1967). Phi Delta Phi. *Member:* Illinois State and American Bar Associations; Chicago Council of Lawyers; Chicago Estate Planning Council. ***PRACTICE AREAS:*** Corporate; Tax; Estate Planning, Probate and Family Law; Real Estate. ***Email:*** snydert@wildmanharrold.com

CYNTHIA BUSHNELL STEVENS, born Chicago Heights, Illinois, July 22, 1956; admitted to bar, 1981, Illinois; U.S. Supreme Court; U.S. Court of Appeals for the Federal Circuit; U.S. District Court, Northern District of Illinois. *Education:* Indiana University (B.S., 1978); Illinois Institute of Technology/Chicago-Kent College of Law (J.D., 1981). *Member:* Chicago Bar Association; Womens Bar Association of Chicago; Intellectual Property Law Association of Chicago. ***PRACTICE AREAS:*** Trademark; Copyright; Unfair Competition. ***Email:*** stevens@wildmanharrold.com

LOUIS P. VITULLO, born Chicago, Illinois, October 15, 1944; admitted to bar, 1969, Illinois. *Education:* John Carroll University (B.A., 1966); Loyola University (J.D., 1969). Assistant and Counsel to the Governor of Illinois, 1974-1976. *Member:* Chicago and Illinois State Bar Associations. (Also at Lisle Office). ***PRACTICE AREAS:*** Commercial Litigation; Corporate, Securities, Tax; Governmental Practices; Real Estate. ***Email:*** vitullo@wildmanharrold.com

EDWIN A. WAHLEN, born Gary, Indiana, March 12, 1919; admitted to bar, 1948, Illinois. *Education:* University of Alabama; University of Chicago (A.B., 1942; J.D., cum laude, 1948). Phi Alpha Delta; Order of the Coif; Phi Beta Kappa. *Member:* Chicago, Illinois State and American Bar Associations. ***PRACTICE AREAS:*** Corporate, Securities, Tax; Real Estate Development.

MAX WILDMAN, born Terre Haute, Indiana, December 4, 1919; admitted to bar, 1948, Indiana and Illinois. *Education:* Butler University (B.S., 1941); University of Chicago (M.B.A., 1952); University of Michigan (J.D., 1947). Phi Delta Phi; Barristers Society. Special Assistant Attorney General, State of Illinois, 1957. *Member:* Chicago (Member, Antitrust Committee, 1967-1969), Illinois State and American Bar Associations; Trial Lawyers Club of Chicago; Law Club of Chicago; Legal Club of Chicago; National Association of Railroad Trial Counsel; Society of Trial Lawyers; International Association of Insurance Counsel. Fellow, American College of Trial Lawyers. ***Email:*** wildman@wildmanharrold.com

(For Biographical data on all firm personnel, see Professional Biographies at other office locations)

WILLIAMS & BAERSON, LLC

Established in 1995

ONE NORTH LASALLE STREET, SUITE 1350
CHICAGO, ILLINOIS 60602
Telephone: 312-629-9003
Fax: 312-629-9020

Trusts and Estates, Estate Planning and Administration, Taxation, International Taxation; Closely Held Businesses.

(This Listing Continued)

WILLIAMS & BAERSON, LLC, Chicago—Continued

H. RANDOLPH WILLIAMS, born Miami, Oklahoma, October 11, 1942; admitted to bar, 1967, Texas; 1970, Kansas; 1978, Illinois. *Education:* University of Kansas (A.B., 1964); Southern Methodist University (J.D., 1968); New York University (LL.M. in Taxation, 1971). Briefing Attorney, Texas Supreme Court, 1967-1968. Instructor: Trust Law, Washburn Law School, 1976; Estate Planning, Illinois Institute of Technology-Kent, 1980. Partner, Baker & McKenzie, 1985-1993. *Member:* Chicago (Member, State and Local Tax, Federal Tax and Trust Committee), American (Member, Sections on: Tax and Real Property; Probate and Trust) and International Bar Associations; Chicago Estate Planning Council; American College of Trust and Estate Counsel. ***LANGUAGES:*** French. ***PRACTICE AREAS:*** Estate Planning; Estate Administration; Trust Administration; Estate and Gift Taxation; Income Tax; International Tax; State Income Tax; Closely Held Business Law. ***Email:*** hrw@wb-legal.com

STEVEN L. BAERSON, born Chicago, Illinois, April 20, 1967; admitted to bar, 1992, Illinois and U.S. District Court, Northern District of Illinois; 1993, District of Columbia; 1994, U.S. Tax Court. *Education:* Indiana University (B.S., with high distinction, 1989); Cornell University (J.D., 1992). Certified Public Accountant, Illinois, 1989. Seminars: Effective Use of Technology, Chicago Bar Association, May 2, 1996; Estate Planning For The Protection of Assets, The Decalogue Society, January 17, 2001 and January 7, 1998 and Chicago Bar Association, November 8, 1999; Basic Estate Planning, Young Lawyers Section of the Chicago Bar Association, May 12, 1998; "Basic Estate Planning," Northwestern Medical Faculty Foundation, March 2000; "Choice of Entity," Chicago Bar Association, October 1, 2003. *Member:* Chicago (Director, Young Lawyer's Section, 1999-2001; Co-Chairman, Young Lawyers Section, Estate Planning Committee, 1997-1999) and American Bar Associations; Chicago Estate Planning Council. ***PRACTICE AREAS:*** Estate Planning and Probate; Trust and Estate Administration; Corporate Law; Federal Income Taxation; Business Succession Planning; Estate and Gift Taxation; Closely Held Business Law. ***Email:*** slb@wb-legal.com

OF COUNSEL

IRENE SHERIDAN BREWICK, born Chicago, Illinois, June 28, 1951; admitted to bar, 1983, Illinois. *Education:* College of Mt. St. Joseph (B.A., cum laude, 1973); Loyola University (J.D., cum laude, 1983). ***Email:*** isb@wb-legal.com

WILLIAMS MONTGOMERY & JOHN LTD.

Established in 1967

20 NORTH WACKER DRIVE
SUITE 2100
CHICAGO, ILLINOIS 60606
Telephone: 312-443-3200
Facsimile: 312-630-8500
Email: WMJINFO@WILLMONT.COM
URL: http://www.willmont.com

Miami, Florida Office: Clarke, Silverglate, Campbell, Williams & Montgomery, 799 Brickell Plaza, Suite 900. Telephone: 305-377-0700. Facsimile: 305-377-3001.

Commercial Litigation, Professional Liability (Accountants, Agents and Brokers, Architects and Engineers, Directors and Officers, and Lawyers), Antitrust, Securities Litigation, Class Actions, Mass Torts, Toxic Torts, Products Liability, Construction Liability, Employer Liability, Employment Discrimination, Environmental Insurance Coverage, Environmental Defense, Insurance Coverage, Automobile Liability Defense, General Liability, Insurance Bad Faith, Government Tort Liability, Police Liability, Railroad Accidents and Injuries, Trucking Liability, Maritime Negligence, Farm Equipment Liability, Premises Liability Defense, and Civil Appeals.

FIRM PROFILE: Since its formation in 1967, Williams Montgomery & John has developed a national reputation handling complex, high stakes commercial and tort litigation, including appeals. The firm has offices in Chicago, Illinois and Miami, Florida, and its attorneys have appeared in cases in all fifty states, the District of Columbia, Virgin Islands and Puerto Rico.

The Firm currently represents hundreds of corporations and partnerships as parties to lawsuits. It serves as national or regional coordinating or trial counsel to a number of these clients in the product liability and transportation-related areas.

In addition to its trial work, the Firm provides mediation and arbitration services, as well as expert witnesses in professional liability and insurance coverage matters.

The firm utilizes the latest and best in contemporary technology to enhance the traditional services it provides to its clients.

LLOYD E. WILLIAMS, JR., born Chicago, Illinois, 1934; admitted to bar, 1961, Illinois; 1970, U.S. Supreme Court; 2000, New Mexico. *Education:* Yale University (B.A., cum laude, 1956); University of Michigan (J.D., 1961). Fellow, International Academy of Trial Lawyers. ***PRACTICE AREAS:*** Commercial Litigation; Products Liability; Professional Liability; Construction Liability; Asbestos Litigation; Transportation Liability; Civil Rights Defense; Catastrophic Injury; Severe Burns; Insurance Bad Faith; Birth Trauma; Brain Injury; Spinal Injury; Wrongful Death. ***Email:*** lew@willmont.com

C. BARRY MONTGOMERY, born Latrobe, Pennsylvania, 1937; admitted to bar, 1962, Illinois; 1971, U.S. Supreme Court. *Education:* Muskingum College (B.A., cum laude, 1959); University of Michigan (J.D., 1962). Fellow, International Academy of Trial Lawyers. ***PRACTICE AREAS:*** Commercial Litigation; Products Liability; Professional Liability; Transportation Liability; Construction Liability; Catastrophic Injury; Severe Burns; Birth Trauma; Brain Injury; Spinal Injury; Wrongful Death; Directors and Officers Liability. ***Email:*** cbm@willmont.com

PETER C. JOHN, born Albany, New York, December 25, 1941; admitted to bar, 1966, Illinois; 1969, U.S. District Court, Northern District of Illinois. *Education:* Cornell University (A.B., 1963); Villanova University (J.D., 1966). Member, Illinois Supreme Court Committee on Jury Instructions, 1988-1998. *Member:* Chicago, Illinois State and American Bar Associations; International Academy of Trial Lawyers (President, 2001-2002); International Society of Barristers; Society of Trial Lawyers; American Board of Trial Advocates; American College of Trial Lawyers. [U.S.M.C., 1966-1967; U.S. Navy Commander-Reserves, 1967-1976]. ***PRACTICE AREAS:*** Commercial Litigation; Products Liability Defense; Attorney Malpractice Defense; Negligence. ***Email:*** pcj@willmont.com

THOMAS H. NEUCKRANZ, born Chicago, Illinois, November 29, 1947; admitted to bar, 1974, Illinois. *Education:* Princeton University (B.S.E., in Aeronautical Engineering, 1970); Northwestern University (J.D., 1974). Member: Product Liability Advisory Council; Federation of Defense and Corporate Counsel; Society of Trial Lawyers. ***PRACTICE AREAS:*** Products Liability; Civil Rights; Construction Liability; Employment Discrimination; Medical Malpractice; Commercial Litigation; Police Liability Defense; Marine Liability; Municipal Liability; Airplane Crash Litigation; Automotive Design Liability; Automotive Products Liability. ***Email:*** thn@willmont.com

EDWARD J. MURPHY, born Chicago, Illinois, March 18, 1947; admitted to bar, 1980, Illinois. *Education:* Illinois Institute of Technology (B.S., Mechanical and Aerospace Engineering, 1969); DePaul University (J.D., with honors, 1980). ***PRACTICE AREAS:*** Insurance Fraud Defense; Products Liability; Construction Liability; Transportation Liability; Fires and Explosions; Insurance Coverage. ***Email:*** ejm@willmont.com

DAVID E. STEVENSON, born Detroit, Michigan, May 20, 1952; admitted to bar, 1978, Michigan; 1979, Florida; 1981, Illinois. *Education:* Michigan State University (B.A., with high honors, 1973); Tulane University of Louisiana (J.D., 1978). ***PRACTICE AREAS:*** Commercial Litigation; Professional Liability; Reinsurance Coverage; Accountants Liability; Directors and Officers Liability; ERISA; Construction Liability. ***Email:*** des@willmont.com

JEFFREY H. LIPE, born Chicago, Illinois, May 13, 1958; admitted to bar, 1983, Illinois. *Education:* Tulane University of Louisiana (B.A., 1980); University of Illinois (J.D., 1983). ***PRACTICE AREAS:*** Products Liability; Construction Liability; Railroad Liability; Wrongful Death; False Arrest; False Imprisonment. ***Email:*** jhl@willmont.com

DEBORAH H. BORNSTEIN, born New York, N.Y., 1953; admitted to bar, 1978, District of Columbia; 1980, Illinois. *Education:* Bennington College (B.A., 1975); University of Chicago Law School (J.D., 1978). ***PRACTICE AREAS:*** Business Litigation; Antitrust; Energy Litigation; Appeals; Class Action Litigation. ***Email:*** dhb@willmont.com

STEVEN J. ROEDER, born Evergreen Park, Illinois, 1958; admitted to bar, 1984, Illinois. *Education:* University of Chicago (M.A., 1980); University of Illinois College of Law (J.D., 1984). *Member:* Chicago, Seventh Circuit, Illinois State and American Bar Associations; International Association of Defense Counsel. ***PRACTICE AREAS:*** Commercial Litigation; Securities Litigation; Professional Malpractice; Mass Torts Litigation; Class Action Litigation; Real Estate Litigation; Products Liability. ***Email:*** sjr@willmont.com

GREGORY J. BIRD, born Chicago, Illinois, March 10, 1960; admitted to bar, 1986, Illinois; 2000, Indiana. *Education:* Knox College (B.A., cum laude, 1982); University of Illinois (J.D., 1986). ***PRACTICE AREAS:*** Commercial Litigation; Construction Liability; Toxic Torts; Transportation Liability; Architects and Engineers Liability. ***Email:*** gjb@willmont.com

THOMAS J. PONTIKIS, born Chicago, Illinois, April 18, 1961; admitted to bar, 1986, Illinois. *Education:* DePaul University (B.A., with high honors, 1983; J.D., 1986). ***PRACTICE AREAS:*** Products Liability; Construction Liability; Welding Products Liability. ***Email:*** tjp@willmont.com

RAYMOND LYONS, JR., born Chicago, Illinois, March 16, 1951; admitted to bar, 1980, Illinois. *Education:* Loyola University (B.S., 1973); DePaul University (J.D., with honors, 1980). ***PRACTICE AREAS:*** Transportation Liability; Construction Liability; Products Liability; Premises Liability; Insurance Fraud Defense; Agricultural Tort Claims; Farm Equipment. ***Email:*** rl@willmont.com

BRIGID E. KENNEDY, born Fairfield, California, July 21, 1964; admitted to bar, 1989, Illinois. *Education:* Wellesley College (B.A., cum laude, 1986); University of San Diego - Institute on International and Comparative Law, Paris, France; Loyola University of Chicago (J.D., 1989). ***PRACTICE AREAS:*** Commercial Litigation; Legal Malpractice Defense; Insurance Coverage. ***Email:*** bek@willmont.com

BRADLEY C. NAHRSTADT, born Elmhurst, Illinois, October 21, 1967; admitted to bar, 1992, Illinois. *Education:* Monmouth College (B.A., summa cum laude, with distinction, 1989); University of Illinois (J.D., cum laude, 1992). ***PRACTICE AREAS:*** Automobile Liability Defense; Premises Liability Defense; Insurance Bad Faith Defense; Products Liability; Hotel Security. ***Email:*** bcn@willmont.com

ALYSSA M. CAMPBELL, born Brooklyn, New York, May 1, 1962; admitted to bar, 1987, Florida; 1997, Illinois. *Education:* University of South Florida (B.A., 1984); University of Florida (J.D., cum laude, 1987). ***PRACTICE AREAS:*** Civil Appeals; Trial Support; Insurance Coverage; Bad Faith. ***Email:*** amc@willmont.com

EDWARD R. MOOR, born Birmingham, Alabama, 1959; admitted to bar, 1990, Illinois and Indiana. *Education:* Indiana University (B.A., 1983; M.A., 1987; J.D., cum laude, 1990). Order of Barristers, 1990. Contributing Author: Indiana Trial Evidence Manual, A. Tanford and R. Quinlan, Michie, 2nd Edition, 1987 (Charlottesville, Virginia), 1987-1991. *Member:* Chicago and Illinois State Bar Associations; Illinois Trial Lawyers Association. ***REPORTED CASES:*** Cummings v. Gireesan, M.D. (1999). ***PRACTICE AREAS:*** Commercial Litigation; Products Liability; Construction Liability; Medical Malpractice; Catastrophic Injury; Wrongful Death. ***Email:*** erm@willmont.com

SUMMER E. HEIL, born Cedar Rapids, Iowa, December 1, 1969; admitted to bar, 1994, Illinois. *Education:* Indiana University (B.A., 1991); DePaul University (J.D., 1994). ***PRACTICE AREAS:*** Commercial Litigation; Employment Litigation; Health Care Fraud; Consumer Fraud Defense; ERISA Litigation. ***Email:*** seh@willmont.com

DAVID L. APPLEGATE, born Whitstable, Kent, England, 1953; admitted to bar, 1978, Illinois. *Education:* Yale University (B.A., cum laude, 1975); University of Chicago (J.D., 1978). ***PRACTICE AREAS:*** Trademark; Copyright; General Commercial; Business; Professional Liability; Employment; Insurance Law. ***Email:*** dla@willmont.com

(This Listing Continued)

THEODORE J. LOW, born Lake Forest, Illinois, October 26, 1952; admitted to bar, 1977, Illinois. *Education:* Wright State University (B.A., 1974); University of Michigan (J.D., magna cum laude, 1977). Order of the Coif. Associate Editor, University of Michigan Law Review, 1975-1977. ***PRACTICE AREAS:*** Commercial Litigation. ***Email:*** tjl@willmont.com

ERIC R. LIFVENDAHL, born Larchmont, New York, 1966; admitted to bar, 1992, Illinois; 1999, U.S. District Court, Northern District of Illinois. *Education:* Boston College (B.A., 1988); Loyola University (J.D., 1992). ***PRACTICE AREAS:*** Commercial Litigation; Bankruptcy Litigation; Civil Litigation. ***Email:*** erl@willmont.com

HANSON L. WILLIAMS, born Chicago, Illinois, 1968; admitted to bar, 1994, Illinois. *Education:* Colgate University (B.A., 1990); University of Denver College of Law (J.D., 1994). Member, University of Denver Law Review. ***PRACTICE AREAS:*** Commercial Litigation; Contracts; Products Liability; Torts; Medical Malpractice; Legal Malpractice. ***Email:*** hlw@willmont.com

THOMAS C. KOESSL, born Kenosha, Wisconsin, 1971; admitted to bar, 1996, Wisconsin; 1997, Illinois; 1999, U.S. Court of Appeals, Seventh Circuit. *Education:* University of Wisconsin-Parkside (B.A., with honors, 1993); Chicago-Kent College of Law, Illinois Institute of Technology (J.D., with highest honors, 1996). Order of Coif. Member, Chicago-Kent Law Review. *Member:* Illinois State Bar Association; State Bar of Wisconsin. ***PRACTICE AREAS:*** Commercial Litigation; Labor and Employment; Appeals. ***Email:*** tck@willmont.com

CHRISTINA D. KETCHAM, born Chicago, Illinois, December 28, 1971; admitted to bar, 1998, Illinois. *Education:* University of Illinois (B.S., 1994; J.D., magna cum laude, 1998). ***Email:*** cdk@willmont.com

CLAIRE L. LUNARDINI, born Chicago, Illinois, April 22, 1975; admitted to bar, 2000, Illinois. *Education:* DePaul University (B.A., 1997); DePaul University, College of Law (J.D., highest honors, 2000). Phi Kappa Phi; Sigma Tau Delta; Pi Sigma Alpha; Alpha Lambda Delta; Golden Key; Freshman Honor Society. Recipient, CALI Achievement Award for Legal Writing II and When Justice Fails. Article and Note Editor, De Paul Law Review, 1999-2000. *Member:* Chicago and American Bar Associations. ***LANGUAGES:*** French and Hebrew. ***PRACTICE AREAS:*** Insurance Defense; Personal Injury; Products Liability; Professional Malpractice; Torts. ***Email:*** cll@willmont.com

BRIAN Y. BOYD, born Geneva, Illinois, 1975; admitted to bar, 2002, Illinois. *Education:* Davidson College (B.A., 1997); Loyola University (J.D., 2002). ***PRACTICE AREAS:*** Commercial Litigation; Personal Injury; Products Liability. ***Email:*** byb@willmont.com

BETH B. WOODS, born Baltimore, Maryland, 1969; admitted to bar, 1998, Florida; 2002, Illinois. *Education:* University of Chicago (B.A., with honors, 1991); University of Miami (J.D., cum laude, 1998). ***LANGUAGES:*** French. ***PRACTICE AREAS:*** Insurance Defense; Commercial Litigation.

ALEX R. THIERSCH, born Evanston, Illinois, 1975; admitted to bar, 2001, Illinois and U.S. District Court, Northern District of Illinois. *Education:* University of Iowa (B.A., 1997); DePaul University (J.D., 2001). ***PRACTICE AREAS:*** Labor and Employment; Personal Injury; Tort Law.

BRIGITTE C. WEYLS, born Chicago, Illinois, 1976; admitted to bar, 2002, Illinois. *Education:* Denison University (B.A., 1999); De Paul University (J.D., 2002). ***LANGUAGES:*** French. ***PRACTICE AREAS:*** Construction Law; Products Liability; Insurance Law; Tort Law. ***Email:*** bcw@willmont.com

RODNEY C. BASHFORD, born Melbourne, Australia, 1967; admitted to bar, 1999, Illinois; 2001, Victorian Supreme Court, Australia. *Education:* Carthage College (B.A., magna cum laude, 1995); Loyola University, Chicago (J.D., 1999). ***PRACTICE AREAS:*** Litigation.

SEAN G. JOYCE, born Evergreen Park, Illinois, 1969; admitted to bar, 2003, Illinois and U.S. District Court, Northern District of Illinois. *Education:* DePaul University (B.S., 1991); Loyola University (J.D., 2003). ***PRACTICE AREAS:*** Litigation. ***Email:*** sgj@willmont.com

CHRISTINA M. ALDERFER, born Baltimore, Maryland; admitted to bar, 2002, Illinois. *Education:* Dickinson College (B.A., cum laude); Loyola University Chicago School of Law (J.D., cum laude, 2002). ***PRACTICE AREAS:*** Litigation. ***Email:*** cma@willmont.com

ANNDRA L. MASTERS, born Hinsdale, Illinois, 1977; admitted to bar, 2002, Illinois; 2004, U.S. District Court, Northern and Southern Districts of Illinois. *Education:* University of Illinois (B.A., with high distinction, 1999); DePaul University (J.D., 2002). ***PRACTICE AREAS:*** Litigation. ***Email:*** alm@willmont.com

MATTHEW B. ROSENTHAL, born Columbus, Ohio, 1975; admitted to bar, 2002, Missouri and U.S. District Court, Eastern District of Missouri; 2003, Illinois; 2004, U.S. District Court, Southern District of Illinois. *Education:* Miami University (B.A., cum laude, 1998); Duke University School of Law (J.D., 2002). ***PRACTICE AREAS:*** Commercial Litigation. ***Email:*** mr@willmont.com

MARGARET T. RODENBURG, born Harvey, Illinois; admitted to bar, 1997, Illinois; 2001, U.S. District Court, Northern District of Illinois; 2003, U.S. District Court, Northern District of Indiana. *Education:* University of Illinois, Champaign-Urbana (B.A., 1990); ITT - Chicago-Kent College of Law (J.D., 1997). ***PRACTICE AREAS:*** Commercial Litigation. ***Email:*** mtr@willmont.com

JAMES J. LUKAS, JR., born Flushing, New York, 1974; admitted to bar, 1999, Illinois and U.S. District Court, Northern District of Illinois; 2002, U.S. Court of Appeals, Federal Circuit. *Education:* Illinois Wesleyan University (B.A., 1996); DePaul University College of Law (J.D., 1999). *Member:* Chicago and American Bar Associations. ***PRACTICE AREAS:*** Patent, Trademark and Copyright; Patent Litigation; Intellectual Property; Unfair Competition. ***Email:*** jjl@willmont.com

PAUL J. RIPP, born 1967; admitted to bar, 2003, Illinois; registered to practice before U.S. Patent and Trademark Office. *Education:* University of Illinois at Urbana-Champaign (B.A., Economics, 1990; B.S., Mechanical Engineering, 1989; M.S., Mechanical Engineering, 1992); University of Chicago Law School (J.D., 2003). ***PRACTICE AREAS:*** Commercial Litigation; Patent Litigation. ***Email:*** pjr@willmont.com

RAMSEY L. MALLORY, born 1970; admitted to bar, 1999, Indiana and U.S. District Court, Northern and Southern Districts of Indiana; 2000, Illinois and U.S. District Court, Northern District of Illinois. *Education:* Eastern Illinois University (B.S., 1992); Valparaiso University (J.D., 1999). ***PRACTICE AREAS:*** Complex Litigation; Civil Litigation.

HOWARD L. HUNTINGTON, born Arlington Heights, Illinois, September 27, 1972; admitted to bar, 1998, Illinois; 1999, U.S. District Court, Northern District of Illinois; 2000, Indiana; 2002, U.S. District Court, Northern District of Indiana and U.S. Court of Appeals, Seventh Circuit; 2004, U.S District Court, Southern District of Illinois. *Education:* University of Illinois (B.A., 1995); Chicago-Kent College of Law, Illinois Institute of Technology (J.D., 1998). ***PRACTICE AREAS:*** Products Liability; Toxic Torts; Transportation Liability; Construction Litigation; Premises Liability; Commercial Litigation; Employment Litigation. ***Email:*** hlh@willmont.com

OF COUNSEL

ANTHONY P. KATAUSKAS, born Chicago, Illinois, November 26, 1938; admitted to bar, 1973, Illinois. *Education:* Loras College (B.A., 1960); John Marshall Law School (J.D., 1972). ***PRACTICE AREAS:*** Insurance Coverage; Toxic Torts; Reinsurance; International Arbitration; Environmental Law; Surety Defense; Excess and Reinsurance; Directors and Officers Liability. ***Email:*** apk@willmont.com

BARRY L. KROLL, born Chicago, Illinois, June 8, 1934; admitted to bar, 1958, Illinois; 1959, U.S. Court of Military Appeals; 1962, U.S. Supreme Court. *Education:* University of Michigan (A.B., 1955; J.D., with distinction, 1958). ***PRACTICE AREAS:*** Commercial Litigation; Civil Appeals; Insurance Coverage; Franchise Law. ***Email:*** blk@willmont.com

REPRESENTATIVE CLIENTS: *Corporate:* Alpha Therapeutics; Ameren-Cilco; American Engineering; Bank One; Bell Helicopter; Best Buy; Black & Decker; Blockbuster; CBS Broadcasting; Comdata Corp.; ConocoPhillips Co.; Cooper Tire & Rubber Co.; Dana Corporation; Diamond Computer Systems; Dunlop Tires; Fisher-Price; Ford Motor Company; Forsythe Solutions; Fortune Brands; General Electric; Glaxo SmithKline; Goodyear Tire & Rubber; Hendrickson International; IBM; Infinity Broadcasting; Inland Container Corp.; Jevic Transportation; Jordan Industries; JP Foodservice; Marten Transport; Metropolitan Water Reclamation District; PepsiAmerica; Premark International; Quest Diagnostics; Siemens Westinghouse Power Co.; Superior Ambulance; Terminix/Servicemaster; TruGreen/Chemlawn; U.S. Elevator; Viacom, Inc.; Walgreen Co.; Westinghouse Electric; Woodward Governor Company; Yellow Freight; Zenith Electronics. *Insurance:* Allianz; Allstate; Church Mutual; Cincinnati; Employers Reinsurance; Gallagher Bassett; Gainsco; Hanover; Infinity Group; Integrity Administrators; Jefferson; Lancer; NAS Insurance; Professional Underwriters: Progressive; RLI; Safeco; United National; Western National; Yasuda Fire & Marine; Zurich-American.

WILSON ELSER MOSKOWITZ EDELMAN & DICKER LLP

120 N. LA SALLE STREET
26TH FLOOR
CHICAGO, ILLINOIS 60602
Telephone: 312-704-0550
Facsimile: 312-704-1522
URL: http://www.wemed.com

Los Angeles, CA; San Diego, CA; San Francisco, CA; Washington, D.C.; McLean, VA; Newark, NJ; Philadelphia, PA; Baltimore, MD; Miami, FL; White Plains, NY; Dallas, TX; Houston, TX; Albany, NY; Garden City, NY; New York, NY; Boston, MA; Stamford, CT; Las Vegas, NV; London, England.

Affiliates: HPMBC/Clyde & Co.: Paris, France; Bach, Langheid Dallmayr: Cologne, Germany; Frankfurt/Main, Germany; Berlin, Germany; Munich, Germany.

Accounting Liability, Admiralty Law, Agents and Brokers Liability, Alternative Dispute Resolution, Appellate Practice, Architects and Engineers Liability, Asbestos Defense, Aviation Law, Commercial Law, Construction Law, D&O Liability, Employment Law, Environmental Law, General Liability, Health Care, Insurance Bad Faith, Insurance Coverage, Intellectual Property, Lawyers' Malpractice, Medical Malpractice, Municipal Law, Product Liability, Professional Liability, Toxic Torts, Trucking Law, Transportation Liability.

FIRM PROFILE: Our mission is to provide our clients with superior value and the very best in ideas, knowledge, counseling, auditing, exposure management, dispute prevention and resolution and to be responsive by setting benchmarks of excellence and exceeding them. Our success will be measured by having our clients choose us because of their belief in our ability to meet or exceed their expectations of price, service, quality, and expertise. Through our network of offices and affiliations, we are committed to being the leading and largest law firm in the world in our core practice areas. We also want to be profitable for our shareholders, increase our business, and provide the very best place to work by being caring to our colleagues and staff.

RESIDENT PARTNERS

ANJALI C. DAS, born Stillwater, Oklahoma; admitted to bar, 1993, Illinois. *Education:* University of Chicago (B.A., Political Science and South Asian Languages and Civilization, 1990); University of Notre Dame Law School (J.D., 1993); Northwestern University, Kellogg Graduate School of Management (M.B.A., 2001); University of Chicago, Graduate School of Business (Returning Scholar, 2005-2006). *Member:* Chicago (Co-Chairperson, Securities Law Committee, 2005-2006) and American (Member, Sections on: Tort and Insurance Practice; Business Law) Bar Associations. ***PRACTICE AREAS:*** Directors and Officers Liability; Employment Practices; Lawyers Professional Liability; Bankers Professional Liability. ***Email:*** dasa@wemed.com

(This Listing Continued)

(This Listing Continued)

WILSON ELSER MOSKOWITZ EDELMAN & DICKER LLP, Chicago—Continued

BENNETT R. HELLER, born Chicago, Illinois, November 2, 1959; admitted to bar, 1984, Illinois. *Education:* University of Illinois-Chicago (B.A., 1981); Loyola University (J.D., 1984). ***PRACTICE AREAS:*** Professional Liability; Insurance Coverage; Labor and Employment. ***Email:*** hellerb@wemed.com

DAVID M. HOLMES, born Utica, New York, October 30, 1962; admitted to bar, 1988, Illinois; U.S. District Court, Northern District of Illinois including Trial Bar; U.S. Court of Appeals, Seventh Circuit; U.S. District Court, Central District of Illinois; U.S. District Court, Western District of Wisconsin; U.S. District Court, Northern District of Indiana; U.S. District Court, Southern District of Indiana. *Education:* University of Illinois (B.S., 1985; J.D., 1988). Law Clerk to Justice Marvin Dunn, Illinois Appellate Court, 1988-1990. Author: "Fear of Contracting AIDS: When is it a Recognized Cause of Action?" The Trial Lawyer's Guide, Vol. 42, No. 4, 1999. Speaker: Expert Direct and Cross Examination, Federal Trial Bar Training Course, 2000; Employment Practices Liability Seminar, 1999, 2000; Persuasive Appellate Brief Writing, Illinois Attorney General's Office, Chicago, IL, 1988. *Member:* Illinois State and American Bar Associations; Defense Research Institute. ***REPORTED CASES:*** Johal v. Little Lady Foods, Inc. 2004 U.S. Dist. LEXIS 14777; Kahzinksy v. William Meyer & Sons, 2003 U.S. Dist. LEXIS 20715; Hausz v. Sunrise Chevrolet, 2003 U.S. Dist. LEXIS 21543; Cote v. MTP, Inc., 2003 U.S. Dist. LEXIS 4278; Randall v. Unitech Systems, Inc., 243 F.Supp.2d 822 (N.D. Ill. 2003); Davis v. Toshiba Machine Company, America, 186 Ill.2d 181 (1999); Yamada Corp. v. Yasuda Fire & Marine Ins. Co., 305 Ill.App.3d 362 (1999); Majca v. Estate of Dr. Lacher, 183 Ill. 2d 407 (1999); Cassidy v. Derek Bryant Insurance Brokers, Ltd., 244 Ill.App.3d 1054 (1993). ***PRACTICE AREAS:*** Products Liability; Employment; Professional Liability; Insurance. ***Email:*** holmesd@wemed.com

RAYMOND J. JAST, born Joliet, Illinois, July 14, 1947; admitted to bar, 1972, Illinois; 1973, District of Columbia. *Education:* MacMurray College (A.B., 1969); University of Michigan (J.D., 1972). *Member:* American Bar Association; Professional Liability Underwriting Society. ***PRACTICE AREAS:*** Professional Liability. ***Email:*** jastr@wemed.com

DANIEL J. McMAHON, born Rockville Centre, New York, November 5, 1963; admitted to bar, 1989, Illinois and U.S. District Court, Northern District of Illinois; 1991, U.S. Court of Appeals, Seventh Circuit; 1995, U.S. District Court, Southern and Central Districts of Illinois; 1997, U.S. District Court, Eastern and Western Districts of Wisconsin; 1999, U.S. Supreme Court; 2001, U.S. Court of Appeals, Sixth Circuit; 2004, U.S. District Court, Northern and Southern Districts of Indiana and U.S. District Court, Western District of Michigan; 2005, U.S. District Court, Eastern District of Michigan and U.S. Court of Appeals, Eighth Circuit. *Education:* University of Notre Dame (B.A., 1986; J.D., 1989). Listed in: Who's Who in American Law; Illinois Super Lawyers, Chicago Magazine, May 2005 and February 2006. Lecturer, "Anatomy of a Class Action," WEMED University-London, September 28, 2004. Speaker: "ERISA Update — What's New and What's Going on?" 37th Annual Midwest Claims Confernce, May 23, 2005; "Effective Use of Summary Judgment," Eastern Claims Conference, March 1, 2005; "Current Issues in Life, Health, Disability and ERISA Cases" Principal Life Insurance CE andCLE Lecture, November 30, 2004; "Litigation Cost Control: Early Evaluation Through the Trial Process," AIG CE and CLE Claims Seminar, August 3, 2004; "An Overview of ERISA from a Litigator's Perspective," Principal Outside Litigators Conference, October 17-18, 2002. Co-author: "Job Stress and Coronary Risk: Disability Claims Based on the Risk of Future Harm," Life, Health and Disability News (Summer 2004); "'Loss' Under Directors and Officers Liability Policy Does Not Include Section 11 Ill-Gotten Gain Settlement," Tort Trial & Insurance Practice Committee News (Summer 2003); "Life, Health, and Disability Claims Involving Intoxicated Motorists," Life, Health, and Disability News (Winter 2001); "Direct Liability Exposure to Insurers, Under the Americans With Disabilities Act," Health & Life Insurance Liability Reporter (Jan. 22 and Feb. 12, 1997). *Member:* Chicago, Illinois State and American (Member, Tort and Insurance Practice Section; Member: TIPS Insurance Coverage Litigation Committee; Lawyer's Professional Liability Committee); Defense Research and Trial Lawyers Association (Member: Life, Health, Disability & ERISA Committee; Professional Liability Committee; Fidelity & Surety Committee); Professional Liability Underwriting Society. ***REPORTED CASES:*** Conseco, Inc. v. National Union Fire Ins. Co. of Pittsburgh, PA, et al., 2002 WL 31961447 (Ind. Cir. December 31, 2002); Leipzig v. AIG Life Ins. Co., 362 F.3d 406 (7th Cir. 2004); O'Reilly v. Hartford Life & Acc. Ins. Co., 272 F.3d 955 (7th Cir. 2001), affirming, 1999 WL 15631 (N.D. Ill. March 3, 1999); Bock v. Computer Associates Intl., Inc. and Platinum Technology, Inc., No. 99 C 5967, 2000 WL 310288, 2000 WL 1053974, 257 F.3d 700 (7th Cir. 2001), 2001 WL 1195842 (N.D. Ill. Oct. 5, 2001), 2002 WL 511560 (N.D. Ill. Apr. 3, 2002); Much v. Pacific Mutual Life Ins. Co., 266 F.3d 637 (7th Cir. 2001), reversing, 1999 WL 146586 (N.D. Ill. Feb. 26, 1999); Sileo v. Principal Life Ins. Co., 2002 WL 355919 (2d Cir. March 6, 2002); Harper v. Yale Intl. Ins. Agency, Inc., 2004 U.S. Dist. LEXIS 8476 (N.D. Ill. May 12, 2004); Fisher v. PCI, 1999 U.S. Dist. LEXIS 14707 (N.D. Ill. Sept. 16, 1999); Silverstein v. J.C. Penney Financial Services, Inc., et al., 1999 WL 160232 (N.D. Ill. March 10, 1999); Bass v. Arrow Financial, 2002 U.S. Dist. LEXIS 12909 (N.D. Ill. July 15, 2002); Rush Presbyterian-St. Luke's Med. Center v. Prudential, 2004 U.S. Dist. LEXIS 5187 (N.D. Ill. March 30, 2004); Clark v. Anesi, Ozmon & Rodin, Ltd., 194 Ill.2d 566, 747 N.E.2d 352 (Ill. 2001); Golden Rule Insurance Company v. Schwartz, 203 Ill.2d 456, 786 N.E.2d 1010 (Ill. 2003); Southgate Bank v. Fidelity and Deposit Co. of Maryland, 794 P.2d 310 (Kan. App. 1990); Funeral Financial Systems, Inc. v. Pacific Mutual Life Ins. Co., 46 F.Supp.2d 801 (N.D. Ill. 1999); Newport v. Prudential Ins. Co. of America, 2004 U.S. Dist. LEXIS 14104 (E.D. Mich. July 21, 2004); Lyles v. Prudential Ins. Co. of America, 2004 U.S. Dist. LEXIS 11003 (E.D. Mich. June 14, 2004); Surgicore, Inc. v. Principal Life Ins. Co., 2002 U.S. Dist. LEXIS 9122 (N.D. Ill. May 21, 2002); Schluter v. Principal Life Ins. Co., 2001 U.S. Dist. LEXIS 5613 (N.D. Ill. May 1, 2001); Chambers v. Prudential, 2004 U.S. App. LEXIS 16264 (6th Cir. 2004); Welder-Kays v. Kleinert, et al., 2005 U.S. Dist. LEXIS 20247 (S.D. Ind. 2005); Tawse v. DHL Airways, 2005 U.S. Dist. LEXIS 13700 (N.D. Ill. 2005); Alberts v. Prudential, 2005 U.S. Dist. LEXIS 4250 (N.D. Iowa 2005); Riordan v. Golden Rule, 2005 U.S. Dist. LEXIS 10673 (S.D. Iowa 2005); Schwartz v. Prudential, 2005 U.S. Dist. LEXIS 3674 (N.D. Ill. 2005); White v. Prudential, 354 F.Supp.2d 1008 (S.D. Iowa 2005); Chimmy v. Prudential, 2004 U.S. Dist. LEXIS 23516 (N.D. Ill. 2004); Hedeen v. Aon Corp., 2004 Y.S. Dist. LEXIS 21706 (N.D. Ill. 2004); CNA Cas. v. E.C. Fackler, __ Ill.App. __, 2005 Ill.App. LEXIS 935 (Ill. App. 1st Dist. 2005). ***PRACTICE AREAS:*** Commercial Litigation; Insurance Defense; Professional Liability; Litigation; Employee Benefits; Appellate Practice; Civil Practice; Class Actions; Fidelity and Surety; Legal Ethics and Professional Responsibility; Life, Health, Disability Insurance and ERISA. ***Email:*** mcmahond@wemed.com

THOMAS MURRAY, born Evanston, Illinois, January 10, 1957; admitted to bar, 1984, Illinois; 1987, U.S. District Court, Northern District of Illinois; 1988, U.S. District Court, Eastern District of Wisconsin; 1992, Wisconsin. *Education:* University of Wisconsin (B.A., 1979); Loyola School of Law (J.D., 1984). ***PRACTICE AREAS:*** Products Liability. ***Email:*** murrayt@wemed.com

REBECCA ROTHMANN, born Chicago, Illinois, January 24, 1971; admitted to bar, 1996, Illinois and U.S. District Court, Northern District of Illinois including Trial Bar, 1998; 1998, U.S. District Court, Eastern and Western Districts of Wisconsin; 1999, U.S. Court of Appeals, Seventh Circuit; 2001, U.S. Supreme Court; 2002, U.S. District Court, Southern District of Illinois; 2005, U.S. District Court, Central District of Illinois. *Education:* University of Wisconsin-Madison (B.A. 1993); Chicago-Kent College of Law (J.D. 1996). *Member:* Chicago and American (Member, Tort and Insurance Practice Section) Bar Associations; Defense Research Institute (Member, Life, Health, Disability and ERISA Committee). ***PRACTICE AREAS:*** Professional Liability Defense (60%); Disability Insurance Defense (20%); Life Insurance Defense (20%). ***Email:*** rothmannr@wemed.com

CURT J. SCHLOM, born Chicago, Illinois, June 12, 1963; admitted to bar, 1990, Illinois and U.S. District Court, Northern District of Illinois including Trial Bar; U.S. District Court, Central and Southern Districts of Illinois, U.S. District Court, Eastern District of Wisconsin and U.S. District Court, Northern District of Indiana. *Education:* University of Wisconsin-Madison (B.A., 1985); DePaul University (J.D., 1990). Recipient, American Jurisprudence Award in Evidence. Legal Writing Teaching Assistant, DePaul University, 1989. *Member:* Chicago, Illinois State and American Bar Associations. ***PRACTICE AREAS:*** General Liability; Products Liability; Medical Malpractice; Construction Law. ***Email:*** schlomc@wemed.com

IAN A. STEWART, born St. Louis, Missouri, March 12, 1971; admitted to bar, 1996, Illinois; U.S. District Court, Northern and Central Districts of Illinois. *Education:* Washington University (B.A., 1993); St. Louis University School of Law (J.D., 1996). Order of Omega. Production Editor, Saint Louis Transatlantic Law Journal, 1995-1996. *Member:* Chicago Bar Association (Senior Investigator, Judicial Evaluation Committee, 2000-2005). ***PRACTICE AREAS:*** Litigation; Professional Liability; Construction Liability; Civil Practice; Products Liability; Medical Malpractice; Drug and Medical Device Litigation; OSHA. ***Email:*** stewarti@wemed.com

JAMES K. THURSTON, born New York, N.Y., July 1, 1962; admitted to bar, 1989, Wisconsin, Illinois and U.S. Court of Appeals, Fourth, Sixth and Ninth Circuits. *Education:* University of Pennsylvania (B.A., 1984); Yale Law School; Marquette University (J.D., magna cum laude, 1989). Author: "Directors and Officers' Liability," Illinois Institute of Continuing Legal Education (IICLE), 1991: "Chemical Warfare: Battling Steroids in Athletics," National Sports Law Institute, 1991. ***REPORTED CASES:*** National Sports Law Institute Article cited by: Richard McAdams, "Relative Preferences," 102 Yale Law Journal 1 (Oct. 1992). ***Email:*** thurstonj@wemed.com

RESIDENT ASSOCIATES

EDNA S. BAILEY, born Hannover, Germany, June 11, 1975; admitted to bar, 2002, Illinois and U.S. District Court, Central and Northern Districts of Illinois; U.S. District Court, Eastern and Western Districts of Wisconsin. *Education:* Georg-August Universitaet, Goettingen, Germany (law degree, 1999); University of Illinois, Urbana-Champaign (LL.M., 2000; J.D., 2002). ***Email:*** baileye@wemed.com

STEFAN R. DANDELLES, born Evanston, Illinois, April 26, 1973; admitted to bar, 1998, Illinois. *Education:* University of Wisconsin-Madison (B.A., 1994); University of Iowa (J.D., 1997). ***Email:*** dandelless@wemed.com

JAMES R. DOUGHERTY, born Hinsdale, Illinois, April 4, 1976; admitted to bar, 2002, Illinois; U.S. District Court, Northern District of Illinois. *Education:* Eastern Illinois University (B.A., 1999); John Marshall Law School, Chicago (J.D., 2002). ***Email:*** doughertyj@wemed.com

JACINTA EPTING, born Chicago, Illinois, June 17, 1975; admitted to bar, 2000, Illinois and U.S. District Court, Northern and Central Districts of Illinois. *Education:* Elmhurst College (B.A., 1997); University of Illinois (J.D., 2000). ***Email:*** eptingj@wemed.com

BENJAMIN FALLOON, born New Castle, Pennsylvania, July 18, 1975; admitted to bar, 2001, Illinois. *Education:* Haverford College (B.A., 1997); Northwestern University (J.D., 2000). ***Email:*** falloonb@wemed.com

JAMIE L. FILIPOVIC, born Dearborn, Michigan, July 21, 1977; admitted to bar, 2003, Illinois and U.S. District Court, Northern District of Illinois; U.S. District Court, Northern District of Texas. *Education:* University of Michigan, Ann Arbor (B.A., 1999); DePaul University College of Law (J.D., 2002). ***Email:*** filipovicj@wemed.com

ANTHONY M. GOLDNER, born Queens, New York, July 19, 1962; admitted to bar, 1994, Illinois and U.S. District Court, Northern District of Illinois. *Education:* University of Wisconsin-Madison (B.A., 1984); University of Chicago (M.A., 1986; Ph.D., 2002); Illinois Institute of Technology, Chicago-Kent College of Law (J.D., 1994). ***Email:*** goldnera@wemed.com

CINTHIA GRANADOS MOTLEY, admitted to bar, 2003, Illinois; U.S. District Court, Northern District of Illinois; U.S. District Court, Eastern and Western Districts of Wisconsin; U.S. Court of Appeals, Seventh Circuit. *Education:* Loyola University of Chicago (B.A., 1991); DePaul University College of Law (J.D., 2003). ***Email:*** motleyc@wemed.com

LISA HANDLER ACKERMAN, born Chicago, Illinois, June 26, 1974; admitted to bar, 1999, Illinois; U.S. District Court, Northern District of Illinois. *Education:* University of Illinois, Urbana-Champaign (B.A., with honors, 1996); Chicago-Kent College of Law (J.D., 1999). ***Email:*** ackermanl@wmed.com

(This Listing Continued)

PENELOPE S. HOPPER, born St. Louis, Missouri, September 19, 1968; admitted to bar, 1996, Missouri; 1997, Kansas; 2000, Illinois. *Education:* Washington University, St. Louis (B.A., 1990); Northwestern University, Medill School of Journalism (M.S.J., 1991); University of Missouri-Columbia, School of Law (J.D., 1996). **Email:** hopperp@wemed.com

JOHN C. HUNTER, born Iowa City, Iowa, October 5, 1974; admitted to bar, 2000, Illinois; U.S. District Court, Northern District of Illinois. *Education:* University of Iowa (B.A., 1997; J.D., 2000). **Email:** hunterj@wemed.com

NICHOLAS J. KAUFFMAN, born Syracuse, New York, November 12, 1969; admitted to bar, 1996, New York; 2003, Illinois; U.S. District Court, Southern and Eastern Districts of New York; U.S. District Court, Northern District of Illinois. *Education:* University of Denver (B.S.B.A., 1991); Albany Law School of Union University (J.D., 1995). **Email:** kauffmanN@wemed.com

KELLY A. KRAFT, born Howell, Michigan, January 29, 1974; admitted to bar, 1999, Illinois; 2000, Indiana. *Education:* Augustana College (B.A., 1996); Valparaiso University School of Law (J.D., 1999). **Email:** kraftk@wemed.com

JASON M. KUZNIAR, born Chicago, Illinois, August 15, 1973; admitted to bar, 1999, Illinois; U.S. Supreme Court; U.S. Court of Appeals, Seventh Circuit; U.S. District Court, Northern, Central, and Southern Districts of Illinois; U.S. District Court, Western District of Michigan; U.S. District Court, Eastern and Western Districts of Wisconsin. *Education:* Loyola University Chicago (B.A., 1996); Chicago-Kent College of Law (J.D., with honors, 1999). **Email:** kuzniarj@wemed.com

SHAWN P. LEE, born Fayetteville, Arkansas, August 12, 1975; admitted to bar, 2001, Missouri and Illinois. *Education:* Northwestern University (B.A., 1997); Washington University (J.D., 2000). **Email:** leesp@wemed.com

SMITA MOKSHAGUNDAM, born Montreal, Canada, August 20, 1975; admitted to bar, 2001, Illinois and U.S. District Court, Northern District of Illinois; U.S. Court of Appeals, Seventh Circuit. *Education:* University of Michigan, Ann Arbor (B.A., 1997); University of Illinois (J.D., 2001). **Email:** mokshagundams@wemed.com

CHRISTIAN NOVAY, born Brunswick, Maine, June 29, 1968; admitted to bar, 1998, New York; 2004, Illinois; U.S. District Court, Southern and Eastern Districts of New York; U.S. District Court, Southern and Northern Districts of Illinois. *Education:* Florida Southern College (B.S., 1991); Thomas Cooley Law School (J.D., 1997). **Email:** novayc@wemed.com

STEVEN D. SMIEJEK, born Chicago, Illinois, July 20, 1970; admitted to bar, 1997, Illinois and U.S. District Court, Northern District of Illinois. *Education:* Northern Illinois University (B.S., 1994); John Marshall Law School (J.D., 1997). **Email:** smiejeks@wemed.com

STACEY LYNN SMIRICKY, born Waukegan, Illinois, April 30, 1976; admitted to bar, 2002, Illinois; 2003, U.S. District Court, Northern District of Illinois and U.S. District Court, Eastern District of Wisconsin; 2004, U.S. District Court, Central District of Illinois and U.S. Court of Appeals, Seventh Circuit. *Education:* University of Iowa (B.A., 1999); Northern Illinois University College of Law (J.D., cum laude, 2002). **Email:** smiricks@wemed.com

DANIEL E. TRANEN, born St. Louis, Missouri, 1970; admitted to bar, 1997, Missouri and U.S District Court, Eastern District of Missouri; 1998, Illinois; 2000, Georgia, U.S. District Court, Northern and Middle Districts of Georgia; U.S. District Court, Southern, Northern and Central Districts of Illinois; U.S. District Court, Western District of Michigan; U.S. Court of Appeals, Eleventh Circuit. *Education:* University of Pennsylvania (B.A., 1992); University of Illinois (J.D., 1997). **Email:** tranend@wemed.com

BENJAMIN M. WHIPPLE, admitted to bar, 2004, Illinois, U.S. District Court, Northern District of Illinois and U.S. Court of Appeals, Seventh Circuit; U.S. District Court, Western District of Michigan; U.S. District Court, Southern District of Indiana. *Education:* University of Michigan (B.A., Philosophy, 2001); University of Notre Dame (J.D., cum laude, 2004). **Email:** whippleb@wemed.com

DANIEL A. WOLBERG, born Chicago, Illinois, July 7, 1971; admitted to bar, 2002, Illinois; U.S. District Court, Northern District of Illinois. *Education:* University of Wisconsin-Madison (B.A., 1993); Loyola University, Chicago (J.D., 2002). **Email:** wolbergd@wemed.com

RESIDENT OF COUNSEL

LOREN S. COHEN, born Chicago, Illinois, February 8, 1967; admitted to bar, 1992, Illinois. *Education:* University of Illinois (B.A., Accounting, 1989); DePaul University College of Law (J.D., 1992). *Member:* Chicago and Illinois State Bar Associations. ***PRACTICE AREAS:*** Architectural Law; Debtor and Creditor; General Liability Defense; Insurance Coverage and Bad Faith; Medical Malpractice Defense; Product Liability Defense; Trucking, Transportation and Cargo. **Email:** cohenl@wemed.com

CHARLES W. PLANEK, admitted to bar, 1981, Illinois. *Education:* DePaul University (B.A., Economics); DePaul University College of Law (J.D., 1981). *Member:* Illinois State Bar Association. ***PRACTICE AREAS:*** Insurance Defense (40%); Medical Malpractice (30%); Premises Liability Defense (20%); Trucking, Transportation and Cargo (10%). **Email:** planekc@wemed.com

WILSON & McILVAINE

CHICAGO, ILLINOIS

(See Quarles & Brady LLC)

THE LAW OFFICES OF RICHARD A. WILSON, P.C.

35 EAST WACKER DRIVE, SUITE 650
CHICAGO, ILLINOIS 60601
Telephone: 312-987-0191
Fax: 312-546-5140
URL: http://www.rwlex.com
Email: rwilson@rwlex.com
URL: http://www.richardwilsonlawoffice.com

Litigation and Appellate Practice concentrating in Domestic Relations Law, Same-Sex Law, including Marriage, Domestic Partnerships, Parentage, Custody and Visitation, Divorce, Custody and Visitation, and Related Matters, Pre- and Post-Decree, Pre- and Post-Nuptial Agreements, Cohabitation Agreements.

RICHARD ALLEN WILSON, born Aurora, Illinois, August 5, 1959; admitted to bar, 1992, Illinois and U.S. District Court, Northern District of Illinois. *Education:* Loyola University of Chicago (B.A., cum laude, 1982; J.D., 1992); School of the Art Institute of Chicago (Post-graduate, 1985-1987). *Member:* Chicago, Illinois State and American Bar Associations; Chicago Council of Lawyers; Appellate Lawyers Association. ***LANGUAGES:*** German. ***PRACTICE AREAS:*** Litigation; Appellate Practice; Domestic Relations; Gay and Lesbian Family Law; Gay and Lesbian Rights; Domestic Partnerships; Child Custody; Visitation Rights; Post Divorce Modification; Premarital Agreements; Cohabitation Agreements. **Email:** rwilson@rwlex.com

WINSTON & STRAWN LLP

Established in 1853
35 WEST WACKER DRIVE
CHICAGO, ILLINOIS 60601
Telephone: 312-558-5600
Facsimile: 312-558-5700
Email: postmaster@winston.com
URL: http://www.winston.com

Washington, D.C. Office: 1700 K Street, N.W., 20006-3817. Telephone: 202-282-5000. Telecopier: 202-282-5100.
New York, N.Y. Office: 200 Park Avenue, 10166-4193. Telephone: 212-294-6700. Telecopier: 212-294-4700.
Los Angeles, California Office: 333 South Grand Avenue, 38th Floor, 90071-1543. Telephone: 213-615-1700. Fax: 213-615-1750.
Geneva, Switzerland Office: 43 Rue du Rhone, CH 1204. Telephone: +41-22 317 75 75. Fax: +41-22 317 75 00.
Paris, France Office: 21 Avenue Victor Hugo. 75116. Telephone: 331-5364-8282. Fax: 331-5364-8220.
San Francisco, California Office: 101 California Street, 94111. Telephone: 415-591-1000. Fax: 415-591-1400.
London, England Office: Bucklersbury House, 3 Queen Victoria Street, EC4N 8NH. Telephone: 011-44-20-7429-0000. Fax: 011-44-20-7429-0100.

Alternative Dispute Resolution, Antitrust, Asset Securitization, Banking, Bankruptcy, Workouts and Financial Restructurings, Commercial Lending, Contracts, Corporate, Corporate Finance, E-Commerce, Employee Benefits and Executive Compensation, Energy, Environmental Law, Healthcare, Immigration, Intellectual Property, International, Labor and Employment Relations, Lease Finance, Litigation, Maritime, Mergers and Acquisitions, Product Liability, Project Finance, Public Finance, Real Estate, Securities, State and Federal Governmental Relations and Regulatory Affairs, Tax, Technology, Transportation, Trusts and Estates and White Collar Criminal Defense.

FIRM PROFILE: Winston & Strawn, founded in 1853, is one of the nation's oldest and largest law firms. With nearly 825 attorneys in offices in Chicago, New York, Washington, DC, Los Angeles, San Francisco, Geneva, Switzerland, Paris, France, and London, England, the firm provides a full range of legal services to clients throughout the United States and abroad, including Fortune 500 companies, major commercial and financial institutions, governments and governmental entities, as well as small and midsize companies, individuals and entrepreneurs from virtually every industry.

FREDERICK H. WINSTON (1853-1886)
FREDERICK S. WINSTON (1878-1909)
SILAS HARDY STRAWN (1891-1946)

PARTNERS

GEORGE B. CHRISTENSEN (1905-1997)
CALVIN P. SAWYIER (1921-2003)

THOMAS A. REYNOLDS, JR., born Chicago, Illinois, August 30, 1928; admitted to bar, 1951, Illinois. *Education:* Georgetown University (A.B., 1948); University of Michigan (J.D., 1951). Phi Delta Phi. *Member:* Chicago, Illinois State and American Bar Associations.

EDWARD L. FOOTE, born Ottawa, Illinois, November 6, 1928; admitted to bar, 1955, Illinois, U.S. Court of Appeals, Seventh Circuit and U.S. Supreme Court; U.S. Court of Appeals, Second, Eighth, Ninth, Tenth and Federal Circuits. *Education:* Harvard University (A.B., 1952; LL.B., 1955). Author: "Trial Techniques in Business and Commercial Cases," IICLE; "Cross Examination in Federal Courts," West Publishing. Faculty Member: American Intellectual Property Law Association; National Institute for Trial Advocacy; Advanced Institute for Trial Advocacy; Illinois Institute of Continuing Legal Education. Advisory Member, Loyola University Law School. Seminar Lecturer, Harvard Law School. *Member:* Illinois State and American Bar Associations; National Association of Criminal Defense Lawyers; American College of Trial Lawyers; International Academy of Trial Lawyers;

(This Listing Continued)

WINSTON & STRAWN LLP, Chicago—Continued

American Intellectual Property Association. Fellow: American College of Trial Lawyers; International College of Trial Lawyers. [U.S. Marine Corps]. ***PRACTICE AREAS:*** Jury Trial Litigation. ***Email:*** efoote@winston.com

BRUCE L. BOWER, born Chicago, Illinois, September 16, 1933; admitted to bar, 1960, Illinois. *Education:* University of Illinois (B.A., 1955); University of Michigan (J.D., with distinction, 1960). Member, University of Michigan Law Review, 1959-1960. *Member:* Chicago, Illinois State and American Bar Associations. (Retired)

M. FINLEY MAXSON, born Toledo, Ohio, August 9, 1934; admitted to bar, 1962, Illinois. *Education:* Duke University (A.B., 1956); Harvard University (LL.B., 1962). *Member:* Chicago, Illinois State and American Bar Associations. ***Email:*** mmaxson@winston.com

ROBERT G. LANE, born Chicago, Illinois, April 9, 1938; admitted to bar, 1963, Illinois. *Education:* Duke University (A.B., 1960); University of Michigan (J.D., with distinction, 1963). Phi Delta Phi; Order of the Coif. Member, University of Michigan Law Review, 1962-1963. *Member:* Illinois State and American Bar Associations. (Retired). ***PRACTICE AREAS:*** Employee Benefits Law; ERISA Transactions.

STEPHEN C. BRUNER, born Chicago, Illinois, November 11, 1941; admitted to bar, 1967, Illinois. *Education:* Yale University (B.A., summa cum laude, 1963); Harvard University (LL.B., cum laude, 1967). Phi Beta Kappa. Member, Panel of Arbitrators (Construction and Commercial), American Arbitration Association. *Member:* Chicago and American Bar Associations. (Retired). ***PRACTICE AREAS:*** Business Litigation; Business Arbitration; Construction Law; Government Contracts Law; Conflicts of Interest.

TERRY M. GRIMM, born Bloomington, Illinois, April 3, 1942; admitted to bar, 1967, Illinois. *Education:* Indiana University (B.A., 1964; J.D., cum laude, 1967); Durham University, England. Order of the Coif. Special Prosecutor, DuPage County, 1975-1976. *Member:* Illinois State Bar Association. ***PRACTICE AREAS:*** Litigation; Antitrust and Trade Regulation; Business Fraud; Business Litigation; Commercial Crimes; Complex Commercial Litigation; Commodities; Contracts. ***Email:*** tgrimm@winston.com

DUANE M. KELLEY, born Evanston, Illinois, June 20, 1947; admitted to bar, 1972, Illinois. *Education:* DePauw University (B.A., with high distinction, 1969); Northwestern University (J.D., cum laude, 1972). Phi Beta Kappa. Editor, Northwestern University Law Review, 1971-1972. *Member:* Seventh Circuit (Immediate Past President, Board of Governors) and American Bar Associations. Fellow, American College of Trial Lawyers. ***PRACTICE AREAS:*** Civil and Criminal Antitrust Litigation; Commercial Litigation. ***Email:*** dkelley@winston.com

ALBERT MILSTEIN, born Germany, December 29, 1946; admitted to bar, 1972, Illinois. *Education:* Yeshiva University (B.A., magna cum laude, 1969); University of Chicago (J.D., 1972). *Member:* Chicago and Illinois State Bar Associations. ***PRACTICE AREAS:*** Health Care Law; Real Estate Law. ***Email:*** amilstein@winston.com

KURT L. SCHULTZ, born Chicago, Illinois, February 13, 1946; admitted to bar, 1972, Illinois. *Education:* University of Pennsylvania (B.S., 1967); The Ohio State University (J.D., summa cum laude, 1972). *Member:* Chicago, Illinois State and American Bar Associations. [1st Lt., U.S. Army, 1967-1969]. ***PRACTICE AREAS:*** General Corporate Litigation; Business Arbitration; Federal Civil Practice; Commercial Law; Securities; Unfair Competition; Contested Trusts and Estates. ***Email:*** kschultz@winston.com

PAUL H. HENSEL, born Hinsdale, Illinois, April 11, 1948; admitted to bar, 1972, Illinois. *Education:* University of Illinois (B.S., with high honors in Finance, 1969); University of Michigan (J.D., cum laude, 1972). *Member:* Chicago and American Bar Associations. (Hiring Partner, Chief Administrative Partner). ***PRACTICE AREAS:*** Mergers and Acquisitions Law; Corporate Law; Real Estate Law. ***Email:*** phensel@winston.com

COLUMBUS R. GANGEMI, JR., born Philadelphia, Pennsylvania, August 6, 1947; admitted to bar, 1973, Illinois; 1979, U.S. Supreme Court. *Education:* Villanova University (A.B., cum laude, 1969; J.D., 1973); Temple University, doctoral fellow, 1970. Case and Comments Editor, Villanova Law Review, 1972-1973. Special Assistant Illinois Attorney General, 1989-1994. Author: Labor Dispute Planning Workbook, Labor Policy Association, 1999; "Insider Game Tactics: Understanding Work-to-Rule and Other Union In Plant Campaign Strategies," Labor Policy Association, 1997; "The Lockout as an Alternative to Union In Plant Campaign Tactics," NLRB Watch (LPA), Jan./Feb. 1999. Co-Author: (with William G. Miossi) "Retiree Health Plans: Look Back Before Going Ahead With Changes," Benefits Law Journal, Winter, 1990/91; (with Joseph J. Torres) "The Corporate Campaign at Caterpillar," Journal of Labor Research, Summer 1996; (with Derek G. Barella) "The Bargaining Order and Related Remedies Under the NLRA," IILCE Labor Law Handbook, 1999. *Member:* Chicago, Illinois State and American Bar Associations. Fellow, College of Labor and Employment Lawyers, 1998—. ***PRACTICE AREAS:*** Labor Law; Employment Relations Law; Litigation. ***Email:*** cgangemi@winston.com

CHRISTOPHER D. MURTAUGH, born Darby, Pennsylvania, October 25, 1945; admitted to bar, 1970, Illinois; 1973, Florida. *Education:* University of Illinois (A.B., 1967; J.D., 1970). Order of the Coif. *Member:* Chicago, Illinois State and American Bar Associations; The Florida Bar; American College of Real Estate Lawyers. [Lieutenant, U.S.N.R., 1971-1974]. ***PRACTICE AREAS:*** Real Estate; Commercial Real Estate. ***Email:*** cmurtaugh@winston.com

ROBERT F. DENVIR, born Chicago, Illinois, September 24, 1945; admitted to bar, 1971, Illinois. *Education:* University of Notre Dame (B.B.A., 1967); University of Illinois and DePaul University (J.D., 1971). Certified Public Accountant, Illinois, 1973. ***PRACTICE AREAS:*** Federal Income Tax; State Income Tax; Tax Audits; Tax Appeals; Tax Litigation. ***Email:*** rdenvir@winston.com

HURD BARUCH, born New York, N.Y., November 29, 1937; admitted to bar, 1960, Connecticut; 1964, U.S. Supreme Court; 1966, New York; 1971, District of Columbia; 1972, Pennsylvania; 1988, Illinois. *Education:* Hamilton College (B.A., 1957); Yale University (LL.B., 1960); Columbia University Graduate School of Business (M.B.A., 1961). Phi Beta Kappa; Order of the Coif; Beta Gamma Sigma. Member, Board of Editors, Yale Law Journal, 1959-1960. Author: "Wall Street: Security Risk," Acropolis Books Ltd., 1971 and Penguin Books, 1972; "The Audit Committee: A Guide for Directors," Harvard Business Review, June, 1980; "International Transactions Which Violate the Foreign Corrupt Practices Act or Other Criminal Statutes," Law and Practice of United States Regulation of International Trade (Oceana 1999). Special Counsel, Division of Trading and Markets, U.S. Securities and Exchange Commission, 1969-1972. *Member:* The District of Columbia Bar; Illinois State Bar Association. [Capt. USAFR, 1961-1964]. (Retired). ***PRACTICE AREAS:*** Securities Law; Litigation.

GREGORY S. MURRAY, born Philadelphia, Pennsylvania, April 19, 1949; admitted to bar, 1974, Illinois. *Education:* University of Notre Dame (A.B., 1971); University of Virginia (J.D., 1974). *Member:* Illinois State and American Bar Associations. ***PRACTICE AREAS:*** Corporate Law; Corporate Finance; Finance. ***Email:*** gmurray@winston.com

JAMES M. NEIS, born Chicago, Illinois, March 3, 1946; admitted to bar, 1973, Illinois; 1974, U.S. Tax Court. *Education:* DePaul University (B.A., 1969; J.D., 1973). Adjunct Faculty, De Paul University College of Law, 1979-1986. *Member:* Chicago, Illinois State and American Bar Associations. (Managing Partner). ***PRACTICE AREAS:*** General Corporate Law. ***Email:*** jneis@winston.com

MICHAEL V. HASTEN (1946-1997)

SUSAN E. CREMIN, born Chicago, Illinois, July 2, 1947; admitted to bar, 1977, Illinois. *Education:* Vassar College (A.B., cum laude, 1969); Northwestern University (J.D., 1976). Co-Author: "Registration and Reporting Under The Exchange Act," Understanding the Securities Laws 1996, Practicing Law Institute, 1996. *Member:* Chicago and American Bar Associations. ***PRACTICE AREAS:*** Corporate Law; Securities Law. ***Email:*** scremin@winston.com

ROBERT W. ERICSON, born Highland Park, Illinois, June 24, 1948; admitted to bar, 1976, Illinois; 1992, New York. *Education:* Johns Hopkins University (B.A., 1970; M.A., 1971); University of Virginia (J.D., 1976). *Member:* New York State Bar Association. (New York, N.Y. Office). ***PRACTICE AREAS:*** Mergers and Acquisitions; Mergers and Acquisitions Finance; Securities. ***Email:*** rericson@winston.com

NEIL E. HOLMEN, born Chicago, Illinois, March 23, 1950; admitted to bar, 1976, Illinois. *Education:* University of Illinois (B.S., 1971); DePaul University (J.D., magna cum laude, 1976). Phi Alpha Delta. *Member:* Chicago and American (Member, Antitrust and Litigation Sections) Bar Associations. ***PRACTICE AREAS:*** Commercial Litigation; Insurance Bad Faith; Chancery Practice. ***Email:*** nholmen@winston.com

GERALD C. PETERSON, born Chicago, Illinois, December 7, 1948; admitted to bar, 1977, Illinois and U.S. District Court, Northern District of Illinois including Trial Bar; 1978, U.S. Court of Appeals, Fifth Circuit; 1981, U.S. Court of Appeals, First Circuit; 1982, U.S. Court of Appeals, Seventh Circuit; 1985, U.S. Supreme Court; 1993, U.S. Court of Appeals, Third Circuit. *Education:* Loyola University (B.A., 1969); Loyola University (J.D., cum laude, 1977). Instructor, National Institute Trial Advocacy Program, 1989—. Member, ABA/National Conference of Minority Partners in Majority/Corporate Law Firms. *Member:* Cook County and American Bar Associations. [U.S. Army, 1970-1971, Rank E-4, Military Intelligence, Awarded Bronze Star]. ***PRACTICE AREAS:*** Employment Law; Labor Law. ***Email:*** gpeterson@winston.com

KIMBALL R. ANDERSON, born San Antonio, Texas, August 20, 1952; admitted to bar, 1977, Illinois and U.S. District Court, Northern District of Illinois including Trial Bar; 1979, U.S. Court of Appeals, 7th Circuit; 1982, U.S. Tax Court; 1987, U.S. Supreme Court. *Education:* University of Illinois (B.A., 1974; J.D., summa cum laude, 1977). Order of the Coif. Graduated First in the Class, University of Illinois College of Law. Recipient, ABA Pro Bono Publico Award, 2003. Editor, Illinois Law Review, 1976-1977. Certified Public Accountant, Illinois, 1974. Author: "The Legal Legacy of John Wayne Gacy: The Seventh Circuit's Irreputable Presumption that Juries Understand and Follow Jury Instructions," 78 Marquette Law Review 792, 1995; "Turf Wars—Can Non-Layers Represent Taxpayers in Real Property Tax Disputes?" Chicago Bar Record, June/July 1996; "Capitol Pro Bono Demand Is Up," National Law Journal, August 19, 1996; "Dealing With Jury Prejudice Against Big Corporations," Chicago Bar Record, March 1992; "The Scope of Attorneys' Responses To Auditors' Requests For Information—The ABA and AICPA Compromise," Univ. of Illinois Law Forum, 1976. Adjunct Professor of Law, Trial Advocacy, Northwestern University Law School. President, CBA Television Productions, Inc., 1988-1989. Member, Board of Directors: Public Interest Law Initiative, Chicago Bar Foundation, First Vice President; AIDS Legal Council of Chicago, 1988-1989. Treasurer, Chicago Bar Foundation. *Member:* Chicago (Member, Board of Managers, 1990-1992), Illinois State and American Bar Associations; Illinois CPA Society; American College College of Trial Lawyers (Fellow). ***REPORTED CASES:*** Shalala v. Illinois Council on Long Term Care, 2000 U.S Lexis 1734 (U.S. Supreme Court, 2/29/2000); U.S. ex rel. Harris v. Reed, 489 U.S. 255, 109 S. Ct. 1038 (1988); Heller International v. Lloyds, London, 974 F.2d 850 (7th Cir. 1992); Brockhouse v. United States, 749 F.2d 1248 (7th Cir. 1984); Portnoy v. Kawecki Berylco Industries, 607 F.2d 765 (7th Cir. 1979); Gunther v. Commissioner of IRS, 909 F.2d 291 (7th Cir. 1990); Freesen v. Commissioner of IRS, 798 F.2d 195 (7th Cir. 1986); McCoy v. Franklin Savings & Loan, 636 F.2d 172 (7th Cir. 1980); United States v. King, 613 F.2d (7th Cir. 1980); KOA v. New Mexico State Highway Dept. (N.M. Supreme Court); People v. White, 158 Ill. 2d 439 (1994); Swick v. Liautaud, 169 Ill. 2d 504 (1996); Commonwealth Edison Co. v. Ill. Dept. of Revenue, 197 Ill. App. 3d 968 (1st Dist. 1989); Carol Ann Dagon v. Caterpillar (Ill. App. Court, 3d Dist.); Pros and Callas v. Mid-America Computer Corp., 142 Ill. App. 3d (2d Dist. 1986); State of Illinois ex rel. Beauchamp v. Elrod, 137 Ill. App. 3d 208 (1st Dist. 1985); Harris Trust & Savings Bank v. Beach, 145 Ill. App. 3d 682 (1st Dist. 1986); Capsonic Group v. Swick, 181 Ill. App. 3d 988 (2nd Dist. 1989); Little City Foundation v. Capsonic Group, 231 Ill. App. 3d 122 (1st Dist. 1992); R.F. v. Abbott Laboratories, 709 A.2d 815 (N.J. Super A.D., 1998); R.F. Abbott Laboratories, 2000 N.J. Lexis 136 (N.J. Supreme Court, 2/29/2000); In re Detention of Bradley Lieberman, III. App. - (1st District 2001). ***PRACTICE AREAS:*** Commercial Litigation; Patent Infringement Litigation; Product Liability Defense; Professional Liability. ***Email:*** kanderso@winston.com

JEROME W. POPE, born Chicago, Illinois, July 30, 1951; admitted to bar, 1976, Illinois; 1977, U.S. District Court, Northern District of Illinois; 1978, U.S. Court of Appeals, 7th Circuit. *Education:* Purdue University; Bradley University (B.S., summa cum laude, 1973); DePaul University (J.D., with honors, 1976). *Member:* Illinois State and American Bar Associations. ***Email:*** jpope@winston.com

THOMAS A. REYNOLDS, III, born Evanston, Illinois, May 12, 1952; admitted to bar, 1977, Illinois; 1978, U.S. District Court, Northern District of Illinois; 1979, U.S. Court

(This Listing Continued)

of Appeals, 7th Circuit; 1983, U.S. District Court, Northern District of Illinois, Trial Bar. *Education:* Georgetown University (B.S.B.A., 1974); Emory University (J.D., 1977). **Email:** treynolds@winston.com

ROBERT F. WALL, born Chicago, Illinois, January 7, 1952; admitted to bar, 1977, Illinois and U.S. District Court, Northern District of Illinois. *Education:* University of Virginia; Northwestern University (B.A., with distinction, 1973); University of Santa Clara (J.D., summa cum laude, 1977). Comments Editor, University of Santa Clara Law Review, 1976-1977. Member, Editorial Board, M & A and Corporate Control Law Reporter, 1988—. Member, Executive Committee, Ray Garrett, Jr., Corporate and Securities Law Institute, 1994—. Listed in the Best Lawyers in America. *Member:* American Bar Association. ***PRACTICE AREAS:*** Takeovers; Mergers and Acquisitions; Mergers and Acquisitions Finance; Initial Public Offerings; Public Offerings. **Email:** rwall@winston.com

DAN K. WEBB, born Bushnell, Illinois, September 5, 1945; admitted to bar, 1970, Illinois; 1971, U.S. District Court, Northern District of Illinois and U.S. Court of Appeals, 7th Circuit; 1980, U.S. District Court, Southern District of Illinois. *Education:* Western Illinois University; Loyola University (J.D., cum laude, with honors, 1970). Phi Alpha Delta; Alpha Phi Sigma. Co-Author: with Scott F. Turow, "The Prosecutor's Function in Sentencing," Loyola University Law Journal, Vol. 13, No. 4, Summer, 1982; "Rico Forfeiture in Practice," University of Cincinnati Law Review, Vol. 52, No. 2, 1983; "Corporate Internal Investigations: Avoiding Criminal Liability, 1993. Member, National Institute of Trial Advocacy, 1979—. U.S. Attorney, Northern District of Illinois, 1981-1985; Director, State of Illinois Department of Law Enforcement, 1979-1980; Member and Vice-Chairman of the Chicago Metropolitan Fair and Exposition Authority, 1978-1981; Member, Attorney General's Advisory Committee, 1981-1984; Chairman, Illinois Hospital Association Governing Board Council, 1983—; Member and Treasurer of the Chicago Metropolitan Fair and Exposition Authority, 1985—; Chairman, Governor's Chicago Education Study Committee, 1985—. *Member:* Chicago, Illinois State, Federal and American Bar Associations; American College of Trial Lawyers; International Academy of Trial Attorneys. **Email:** dwebb@winston.com

WAYNE D. BOBERG, born Vincennes, Indiana, September 28, 1952; admitted to bar, 1978, Illinois. *Education:* Kansas State University; Indiana University (B.S., with distinction, 1975; J.D., magna cum laude, 1978). Beta Gamma Sigma. Recipient, American Jurisprudence Award in Corporations. *Member:* Chicago and American (Member, Business Law Section) Bar Associations. **Email:** wboberg@winston.com

MARK G. HENNING, born Evergreen Park, Illinois, September 8, 1953; admitted to bar, 1978, Illinois and U.S. District Court, Northern District of Illinois. *Education:* University of Illinois (B.A., magna cum laude, with distinction in Economics, 1975); Loyola University of Chicago (J.D., cum laude, 1978). Phi Beta Kappa. Editor, Loyola University of Chicago Law Journal, 1977-1978. Author: "Goffinet v. County of Christian: New Flexibility in Illinois Zoning Law," 8 Loyola University Law Journal, No. 3, 1977; "Lease Financing of Real Estate," Equipment Leasing-Leveraged Leasing, Practising Law Institute, 1999. Member, American College of Real Estate Lawyers. *Member:* American College of Real Estate Lawyers. **Email:** mhenning@winston.com

GREGORY J. MALOVANCE, born Munster, Indiana, June 29, 1954; admitted to bar, 1978, Illinois, U.S. District Court, Northern District of Illinois and U.S. Court of Appeals, Third and Seventh Circuit. *Education:* Emory University (B.A., Econ., magna cum laude, 1975); University of Chicago (J.D., 1978). Phi Beta Kappa. Author: "Impasse Resolution Procedures and Strikes Under the Illinois Educational Labor Relations Act," Life Under The Public Sector Labor Laws, Illinois Institute For Continuing Legal Education, June, 1985; "Teacher Evaluation Plans and The Duty To Bargain," Illinois Public Employee Relations Report, Institute of Labor and Industrial Relations, University of Illinois, Vol. 111, No. 3, Summer, 1986. *Member:* Illinois State and American (Member, Sections on: Litigation; Labor and Employment Relations) Bar Associations. ***PRACTICE AREAS:*** Labor and Employment. **Email:** gmalovance@winston.com

SCOTT J. SZALA, born Chicago, Illinois, May 30, 1953; admitted to bar, 1978, Illinois and U.S. District Court, Northern District of Illinois; 1979, U.S. Court of Appeals, Seventh Circuit. *Education:* American University; Knox College (B.A., 1975); Northwestern University (J.D., 1978). Phi Beta Kappa. Member, Moot Court Team, 1978. Accounting and Finance Intern, U.S. Air Force, Pentagon, Washington, D.C., Summer, 1974. Congressional Intern, Washington Semester Program, U.S. House of Representatives, 1973. Internship, Department of Justice, U.S. Attorney's Office, Chicago, 1977-1978. Law Clerk, Justice Dom J. Rizzi, Illinois Appellate Court, 1979-1980. *Member:* Chicago (Member, Young Lawyers Section; Co-Chairman: Law Explorers, 1982-1983; Moot Court, 1983-1984; Chairman, Bench/Bar Committee, 1984-1985; Member: Executive Council, 1982-1985; Senior Bar, Tort Litigation, 1978-1984), Illinois State and American (Member, Sections on: Litigation; Judicial Administration Division; Economics of Practice; Antitrust and Taxation; Young Lawyers Division; Trial Editor Barrister Magazine, 1982-1988; Speaker, ABA Convention, Sydney, Australia, 1980) Bar Associations; The Association of Trial Lawyers of America. [Capt., JAGC, USAR, 1985—]. **Email:** sszala@winston.com

CHARLES E. STAHL (1944-1998)

JAMES H. RUSSELL, born Oak Park, Illinois, August 22, 1943; admitted to bar, 1970, Illinois; 1982, Florida; 1985, Ohio. *Education:* Ohio Wesleyan University (B.A., 1965); The Ohio State University College of Law (J.D., 1969). Author: "Avoiding Corporate Successor Liability," Chemical Waste Litigation Reporter, 1988 with J. Blair Richardson, Jr.; "Basic Principles of Superfund Litigation," Vol. 5 Regulatory Toxicology and Pharmacology No. 1, 1985; "A Proposal to Repeal the Illinois Pollution Control Board's Construction Permit Regulations," Chicago Bar Record, November-December, 1980, with J. Huff (see also "Rebuttal to Construction Permit Water Regulations Article," by Illinois Environmental Protection Agency, Chicago Bar Record, May-June 1981); "Water Pollution," Chapter VI of Handbook on Environmental Law, Illinois Institute for Continuing Legal Education, 1978; "Common Law Environmental Liability under Federal Statutes," The Forum, American Bar Association, Vol. XI, No. 3, 1976; "Aircraft and Airport Noise: Current Legal Remedies and Future Alternatives," Insurance Counsel Journal, January 1975 (Yancey Memorial Award-Winning Article, 1976); "Inverse Condemnation of Airspace," Journal of Air Law and Commerce, Winter, 1973. *Member:* Chicago and American Bar Associations; The

(This Listing Continued)

Florida Bar. ***PRACTICE AREAS:*** Environmental Business Law; Environmental Cost Recovery; Environmental Lender Liability; Environmental Litigation. **Email:** jrussell@winston.com

THOMAS P. FITZGERALD, born Joliet, Illinois, June 14, 1954; admitted to bar, 1979, Illinois and U.S. District Court, Northern District of Illinois; 1984, U.S. Tax Court. *Education:* University of Notre Dame (B.B.A., 1976; J.D., cum laude, 1979). Managing Editor, 1977-1979 and Member, Board of Editors, 1978-1979, Notre Dame Law Review. Certified Public Accountant, Illinois, 1978. Author: "Federal Water Pollution Control Act of 1972 - Judicial Review of State Promulgated Pollution Regulations is not Available in Federal Court: Conflict Between State and Federal Pollution Regulations Cannot Be Judicially Resolved," 53 Notre Dame Law Review 595, 1978; "Qualifying Equity Interests in Reorganizations: A More Limited Species?" TAXES, The Tax Magazine, December, 1996; "Norwest Corp: Can You Bank on the Deductibility of Compensation Expense and Legal Costs Incurred Incident to an Acquisition?" TAXES, The Taxes Magazine, March 2000. ***PRACTICE AREAS:*** Federal Income Tax; Federal Tax Controversies. **Email:** tfitzger@winston.com

TIMOTHY J. RIVELLI, born Waukegan, Illinois, November 3, 1954; admitted to bar, 1979, Illinois, U.S. District Court, Northern District of Illinois, U.S. Court of Appeals, Seventh and Sixth Circuits and U.S. Supreme Court; 1993, U.S. Tax Court. *Education:* Northwestern University (B.A., 1976); Loyola University (J.D., valedictorian, cum laude, 1979). Assistant Editor, Loyola Law Journal, 1978-1979. Alumni Trustee, Northwestern University, Board of Trustees, 1986-1988. Adjunct Professor, Trial Practice, Northwestern University Law School, 1997. *Member:* American Bar Association (Member, Sections on: Litigation; Communications-Media Law; Copyright and Intellectual Property; Securities-Class Actions). ***PRACTICE AREAS:*** Commercial Litigation; Civil RICO; Defamation; False Advertising; Health Care Litigation; Intellectual Property Litigation; Professional Liability Defense; Copyright Litigation; Deceptive Trade Practices; Unfair Trade; Banking Litigation; Lender Liability; Media Law; First Amendment Law; Libel Defense; Privacy and Publicity; Entertainment Litigation; Shareholder Derivative Actions; Securities Fraud; Class Actions; Trademark Litigation; Securities. **Email:** trivelli@winston.com

STEPHEN C. SCHULTE, born Evanston, Illinois, June 26, 1952; admitted to bar, 1976, Illinois, U.S. Court of Appeals, Seventh Circuit and U.S. District Court, Northern and Southern Districts of Illinois including Trial Bar. *Education:* St. Louis University (A.B., magna cum laude, 1973, Phi Beta Kappa; J.D., 1976). Listed in: Who's Who of Lawyers in U.S.; International Who's Who of Product Liability Defense Lawyers. President and Commissioner, Glenview Park District. Founder of Greater Organization of the Less Fortunate (G.O.L.F.); Officer and President of OLPH Men's Club. *Member:* Illinois State Bar Association (Member, Committee on Certification and Specialization); Illinois Association of Defense Counsel. ***PRACTICE AREAS:*** Commercial Litigation; Contract Litigation; Intellectual Property Litigation; Tort Litigation; Civil Liability; Mass Torts; Tort Defense; Tort Liability; Asbestos Defense; Asbestos Litigation; Chemical Exposure; Toxic Tort Defense; Bank Fraud; Business Torts; Construction Accidents; Construction Contracts; Construction Litigation; Consumer Fraud; Bid Protests; Government Construction Contracts; Government Contract Arbitration; Insurance Litigation; Civil Litigation; Mortgage Banking Law; Negligence Defense; Industrial Accidents; Bodily Injury; Catastrophic Injury; Wrongful Death; Premises Liability Defense; Engineering Products Liability; Heavy Equipment Products Liability; Manufacturers Liability; Tobacco Litigation; FELA; FELA Occupational Hearing Loss; Railroad Crossing Accidents. **Email:** sschulte@winston.com

EDWARD F. GERWIN, JR., born Waldwick, New Jersey, February 14, 1955; admitted to bar, 1980, District of Columbia; 1981, U.S. District Court, District of Columbia, U.S. Court of Appeals, District of Columbia Circuit and U.S. Court of International Trade. *Education:* Villanova University (B.A., summa cum laude, 1977); Georgetown University (J.D., cum laude, 1980). Phi Kappa Phi. St. Thomas More Medal. Case and Notes Editor, Law and Policy in International Business, 1979-1980. Author: "The Special Prosecutor Provisions of the Ethics in Government Act of 1978," 36 Record of the Association of the Bar of the City of New York 420, 1981; "An Introduction to U.S. Export Control Laws," 32 The Practical Lawyer 25, 1986; "The Exxon-Florio Statute and Final Regulations," 7-8/1992 Der Schweizer Treuhänder 471; "International Trade Regulatory Considerations in Legal Auditing and Due Diligence," FindLaw.com, December, 2003. Teaching Fellowship in Legal Writing and Research, Georgetown University, 1978-1979. *Member:* The District of Columbia Bar. (Washington, D.C. Office). ***PRACTICE AREAS:*** International Trade; Administrative Law; Government. **Email:** egerwin@winston.com

F. ELLEN DUFF, born Portsmouth, Virginia, September 5, 1955; admitted to bar, 1980, California; 1981, U.S. District Court, Central District of California; 1982, Illinois; 1985, U.S. District Court, Northern District of Illinois. *Education:* University of Notre Dame (A.B., 1977); University of Chicago (J.D., 1980). *Member:* Chicago and American (Member, Section of Business Law) Bar Associations; The State Bar of California; Lawyers Club of Chicago. ***PRACTICE AREAS:*** Securities; Leveraged Leasing; Finance. **Email:** fduff@winston.com

TERRY JOHN MALIK, born Chicago, Illinois, May 1, 1951; admitted to bar, 1980, Illinois and U.S. District Court, Northern District of Illinois including Trial Bar; 1981, U.S. Court of Appeals, Seventh and Ninth Circuits; 1987, U.S. Supreme Court. *Education:* University of Notre Dame (B.A., with honors, 1973); Loyola University of Chicago (J.D., 1980). Lecturer, "Security Interests under Article 9 of UCC," Illinois Institute of Continuing Legal Education, 1988. ***PRACTICE AREAS:*** Bankruptcy; Finance; Business Law. **Email:** tmalik@winston.com

BRUCE A. TOTH, born Toledo, Ohio, February 14, 1953; admitted to bar, 1981, Illinois. *Education:* Georgia Institute of Technology (B.S., summa cum laude, 1976); Stanford University (M.B.A., 1980; J.D., 1980). Tau Beta Pi. Member, Stanford Law Review, 1979-1980. Author: "Section 1031 Extended to Nonsimultaneous Exchanges: Starker v. United States," Stanford Law Review, April, 1980. ***PRACTICE AREAS:*** Business Law; Corporate Law; Securities. **Email:** btoth@winston.com

ARNOLD G. GOUGH, JR., born Gary, Indiana, August 25, 1956; admitted to bar, 1981, Illinois. *Education:* Notre Dame (B.B.A., with high honors, 1978; J.D., 1981). Associate Editor, Notre Dame Lawyer, 1980-1981. Co-Author: with Michael G. Robinson, "Commercial Law Treatment of Synthetic Leases," Journal of Equipment Lease Financing, Vol. 13, No. 1 Spring 1995. Co-Editor, *Equipment Leasing-Leveraged Leasing,* PLI, 4th

(This Listing Continued)

WINSTON & STRAWN LLP, Chicago—Continued

Ed., 1999. *Member:* American Bar Association (Member: Section on Business Law; Aircraft Financing Subcommittee). ***PRACTICE AREAS:*** Leveraged Leasing; Lease Finance. ***Email:*** agough@winston.com

DENNIS J. KELLY, born Portland, Oregon, February 8, 1956; admitted to bar, 1981, Illinois; 1982, U.S. Tax Court. *Education:* University of Notre Dame (B.B.A., 1978); Loyola University (J.D., cum laude, 1981). *Member:* Chicago and American (Member: Tax Section; Tax-Exempt Financing Committee) Bar Associations; National Association of Bond Lawyers. ***PRACTICE AREAS:*** Taxation. ***Email:*** dkelly@winston.com

R. MARK McCAREINS, born Lake Forest, Illinois, July 27, 1956; admitted to bar, 1981, Illinois; 1982, U.S. District Court, Northern District of Illinois and U.S. Court of Appeals, 7th Circuit; 1984, California and U.S. Supreme Court; 1987, U.S. Court of Appeals for the Federal Circuit; 1988, U.S. Court of Appeals, 9th Circuit; 1989, U.S. Court of Appeals, 4th and 11th Circuits; 2000, U.S. Court of Appeals, 1st Circuit; 2002, U.S. Court of Appeals, Third Circuit; 2004, U.S. Court of Appeals, Tenth Circuit. *Education:* Northwestern University (B.A., with distinction, 1978); Washington University (J.D., 1981). Editor-in-Chief, 1980-1981 and Member, Advisory Board, 1982-2006, Washington University Law Quarterly. Member, Julius H. Minor Moot Court Judicial Panel, Northwestern University School of Law, 1984-2001. Editor: Health Care and Antitrust Manual, 1994-2002; Private Antitrust Litigation News, American Bar Association, 1992-1994. Senior Editor: Antitrust Discovery Handbook (ABA 2003); Task Force Report on Civil Litigation (ABA Antitrust Section, 2001). Author: "Transshipping Under the Antitrust Laws," 3 De Paul B.L.J. 285, 1991; "Arbitration Procedures: The Rules of the Road in Arbitrating Antitrust Disputes" (with Elizabeth McCallum), Antitrust Magazine at 15-23 (Fall 2004); "Issues Confronting the Terminated Dealer And Defensive Recommendations For The Manufacturer post-Spray-Rite," Distribution, National Law Journal Seminar Press at 417, 1987; "Business Information For Today's Practicing Lawyer," Utilization of Databases and Information Resources in Antitrust Litigation and Counseling at 405, PLI, 1984; "New Dimensions In The Robinson-Patman Act After Vanco Beverage," 1983 Duke Law Journal 1308; "Antitrust Legal Research: A Practitioner's Viewpoint," Vol. 6, No. 3-4 at 1-3 Legal Information Alert, 1987; Note, "Carve-Out: An Answer To The Contribution Question In Private Antitrust Litigation," 58 Washington University Law Quarterly 975, 1980; "Sanctions and Rule 11, Rule 11 and other Sanctions: New Issues in Federal Litigation," at 219, PLI, 1987; "State Law Alternatives to Federal Sherman Act Predatory Pricing Actions, Antitrust and Unfair Competition Law at 5," Vol. 29, No. 2, Illinois State Bar Association December, 1990; "State Tort Law: A Reasonable Alternative to a Federal Antitrust Predatory Pricing Claim," Competition, California State Bar Association, Vol. 1, No. 2, Fall, 1990; "The Antitrust Ramifications of Refusing to Deal with A Transshipper," National Law Journal, March 27, 1989; "Terminated Dealers Adopt New Tactics," National Law Journal, June 7, 1993. Co-Editor, ABA Antitrust Monograph, No. 18 on Non-Price Predation Under Section 2 of the Sherman Act, 1991; ABA Antitrust Section Practice Guide on Predatory Pricing Under Section 2(a) of the Robinson-Patman Act, 1995; "The Application of Antitrust to Non-Traditional Health Care Affiliations: Pounding a Square Peg Into a Round Hole," PAL News, Spring 1999, Evaluating Secular and Non Secular Hospital Affiliations Lessons from Poughkeepsie, Antitrust Health Care Chronicle (Fall 2000). Adjunct Professor, Antitrust Law, Kellogg Graduate School of Management, Northwestern University, 1988-2006. Instructor, National Institute and Trial Advocacy (NITA). President, Northwestern University Alumni Athletic (Football) Committee (Gridiron Network), 1994-1996. Board of Directors, Northwestern University Fast Break Club (Men's Basketball), 2005-2006. President, Northwestern University College of Arts and Sciences Alumni Board, 1990-1992. Member, Board of Regents (Chicago), Washington University, 1998-2006. Chair, Law Alumni Council (Chicago), Washington University, 1999-2001. Chair, Advisory Board, Washington University School of Law Center for Interdisciplinary Studies, 2003-2006. Listed in: Chambers Directory of America's Leading Business Lawyers (Antitrust, 2003-2006); Leading Lawyers Network (2005-2006); Best Lawyers in America (2005-2006); Illinois SuperLawyers (2005). Recipient: Alumnae Service Award, Northwestern University, 1994; Alumnae Award, Washington University School of Law, 2004. *Member:* Chicago (Member, Antitrust Section), Seventh Circuit and American (Member, Antitrust Section; Vice-Chair, Civil Practice and Procedure, 2004-2006; Member, Antitrust Civil Task Force, 2001; Chair, Private Antitrust Litigation, 1999-2001; Vice-Chair, Programs Committee, 2002-2003) Bar Associations; Federal Circuit Bar Association; State Bar of California (Member, Antitrust Section); American Inns of Court. American Bar Foundation. ***REPORTED CASES:*** Abbott Laboratories v. Baxter Healthcare, 334 F. 3d 1274 (Fed. Cir. 2003); Baxter Int'l v. Abbott Laboratories, 315 F. 3d 829 (7th Cir. 2003); In Re Linerboard Antitrust Litigation, 2004 U.S. Dist. Lexis 7202 (E. Penn.); Smurfit-Stone Container Corp. v. Southeast Paper, 368 F.3d 944 (7th Cir. 2004). ***PRACTICE AREAS:*** Antitrust (50%, 10); Intellectual Property (40%, 10); Commercial Law (10%, 10). ***Email:*** rmccareins@winston.com

STEPHEN P. DURCHSLAG, born Chicago, Illinois, May 20, 1940; admitted to bar, 1966, Illinois. *Education:* University of Wisconsin-Madison (B.S., 1962); Hebrew University, Jerusalem, Israel; Harvard University (LL.B., 1966). *Member:* Chicago and American Bar Associations. ***PRACTICE AREAS:*** Intellectual Property; Advertising and Marketing; Entertainment and the Arts. ***Email:*** sdurchl@winston.com

RICHARD B. TEIMAN, born Brooklyn, New York, May 19, 1938; admitted to bar, 1963, New York. *Education:* Princeton University (A.B., 1959); Harvard University (LL.B., 1962); Phi Beta Kappa. *Member:* The Association of the Bar of the City of New York (Member, Committee on Admiralty, 1975-1978, 1987; Chair, 1988-1991; 2003—); New York State and American Bar Associations; Maritime Law Association (Member, Committee on Marine Financing, 1980—). (New York, N.Y. Office). ***PRACTICE AREAS:*** Mergers and Acquisitions; Mergers and Acquisitions Finance; Debtor and Creditor Workouts. ***Email:*** rteiman@winston.com

ANTHONY J. D'AURIA, born Brooklyn, New York, March 3, 1937; admitted to bar, 1961, New York. *Education:* St. John's University (B.A., 1958; LL.B., 1960). Research Editor, St. John's Law Review, 1959-1960. Assistant U.S. Attorney, Southern District of New York, 1961-1964. Chairman, Committee on Character and Fitness, Supreme Court, Appellate Division, Second Judicial Department. Past-President, St. John's University Law School Alumni Association. Member, Board of Directors, Italy-American Chamber of Commerce. (New York, N.Y. Office). ***PRACTICE AREAS:*** Corporate Litigation. ***Email:*** adauria@winston.com

(This Listing Continued)

JONATHAN GOLDSTEIN, born New York, N.Y., November 20, 1943; admitted to bar, 1969, New York. *Education:* Yale University (B.A., magna cum laude, 1965); Harvard University (LL.B., 1968). Phi Beta Kappa. *Member:* New York State Bar Association. (New York, N.Y. Office). ***Email:*** jgoldst@winston.com

JOSEPH A. DiBENEDETTO, born New York, N.Y., July 5, 1946; admitted to bar, 1971, New York. *Education:* St. John's University (B.A., 1967; J.D., 1970). Managing Editor, St,. John's Law Review, 1968-1970. *Member:* New York State (Member, Committees on: Federal Courts, 1980; Civil Practice Law and Rules, 1980) and American Bar Associations. (New York, N.Y. Office). ***PRACTICE AREAS:*** Lender Liability; Class Action Defense; Commercial Arbitration; Commercial Litigation; Corporate Investigations; Corporate Litigation; Environmental Litigation; Solid Waste Management; Municipal Solid Waste; Accountants Liability; Securities Litigation; Estate Litigation; Real Estate Litigation. ***Email:*** jdibened@winston.com

JEFFREY H. ELKIN, born Brooklyn, New York, January 24, 1946; admitted to bar, 1971, New York; 1972, District of Columbia. *Education:* American University (B.A., 1967); Washington College of Law, American University (J.D., cum laude, 1971). Pi Gamma Mu; Pi Sigma Alpha; Phi Alpha Delta. Notes Editor, American University Law Review, 1970-1971. *Member:* The District of Columbia Bar; New York State and American Bar Associations; New York County Lawyers' Association. (New York, N.Y. Office). ***PRACTICE AREAS:*** Investments; Commercial Law; Securities; Public Finance; Mortgages. ***Email:*** jelkin@winston.com

SUSAN BERKWITT-MALEFAKIS, born Chicago, Illinois, November 13, 1955; admitted to bar, 1980, New York. *Education:* City College of the City University of New York (B.A., summa cum laude, 1976); University of Chicago (J.D., 1979). Phi Beta Kappa. Member, Committee on International Human Rights, The Association of the Bar of the City of New York, 1986-1989. (New York, N.Y. Office). ***PRACTICE AREAS:*** Corporate Law; Finance; Lenders Rights. ***Email:*** sberkwitt@winston.com

JOSEPH A. WALSH, JR., born Teaneck, New Jersey, July 19, 1949; admitted to bar, 1974, Illinois; 1988, Florida and U.S. District Court, Northern District of Illinois. *Education:* Indiana University (B.A., magna cum laude, 1971; J.D., magna cum laude, 1974). Associate Editor, Indiana Law Review, 1973-1974. *Member:* The Florida Bar; American Bar Association. ***Email:*** jwalsh@winston.com

MICHAEL G. ROBINSON, born Chicago, Illinois, July 28, 1957; admitted to bar, 1982, Illinois; 1984, U.S. Tax Court and U.S. District Court, Northern District of Illinois. *Education:* University of Illinois (B.S., with honors, 1979; J.D., magna cum laude, 1982). Recipient: Rickert Scholarship Award for Excellence in Legal Writing; Harno Scholar. Topics Editor, University of Illinois Law Review, 1981-1982. Certified Public Accountant, Illinois, 1979. Author: "Corporate Leasing Transactions," Research Institute of America, 1994. Co-Author: Article, "The Resurgence of Synthetic Leases," Vol. 12, No. 2, Journal of Equipment Lease Financing, Fall, 1994; Article, "The New Assault on Related Party Financing: How Far Will the Service Go?" Vol. 11, No. 3, The International Tax Journal, Summer, 1985. ***PRACTICE AREAS:*** Taxation; Equipment Finance and Leasing; Project Finance. ***Email:*** mrobinso@winston.com

MARK M. HEATWOLE, born Pittsburgh, Pennsylvania, January 28, 1948; admitted to bar, 1972, Illinois and U.S. District Court, Northern District of Illinois; 1974, U.S. Court of Appeals, Seventh Circuit; 1980, U.S. Supreme Court; 1987, U.S. Tax Court. *Education:* Washington & Lee University (B.A., 1969; J.D., cum laude, 1972). Phi Delta Phi. Member, Washington & Lee Law Review, 1971-1972. *Member:* American Bar Association (Member, Sections on: Business Law; Patent, Trademark and Copyright Law). ***PRACTICE AREAS:*** Corporate Finance; Securities; Mergers, Acquisitions and Divestitures; Computers and Software; Electronic Commerce. ***Email:*** mheatwole@winston.com

LEONARD W. BELTER, born Queens, New York, January 23, 1943; admitted to bar, 1968, New York and U.S. Court of Military Appeals; 1970, District of Columbia; 1973, U.S. Claims Court; 1974, U.S. Supreme Court. *Education:* St. Bonaventure University (B.A., 1964); Columbia University (LL.B., cum laude, 1967). Harlan Fisk Stone Scholar, Columbia University, 1966 and 1967. Assistant U.S. Attorney, 1970-1973. *Member:* The District of Columbia Bar. (Washington, D.C. Office). ***PRACTICE AREAS:*** Federal Energy Regulatory Law; Public Utility Law; Litigation. ***Email:*** lbelter@winston.com

THOMAS M. BUCHANAN, born Washington, D.C., December 28, 1953; admitted to bar, 1980, District of Columbia; 1981, U.S. Court of Appeals for the District of Columbia Circuit; 1982, Virginia, U.S. Court of Appeals, Fourth Circuit and U.S. District Court, Eastern District of Virginia; 1984, U.S. Supreme Court and Supreme Court of Virginia. *Education:* St. Louis University (B.A., magna cum laude, 1976); Georgetown Law Center (J.D., 1980). Author: "The Classified Information Procedures Act: A Shield Against Disclosure of Classified Information or Another Sword in Arsenal of the Prosecutor," ABA Complex Crimes Journal, 1989 and Corporate Criminal Liability Reporter, Vol. 3, No. 3, 1989. Assistant U.S. Attorney, Alexandria, Virginia, 1981-1984. *Member:* The District of Columbia Bar; Virginia State Bar; Maryland State Bar Association. (Washington, D.C. Office). ***PRACTICE AREAS:*** White Collar Crime; Complex Litigation; Civil Litigation; Banking Litigation. ***Email:*** tbuchana@winston.com

DONALD K. DANKNER, born Buffalo, New York, October 3, 1947; admitted to bar, 1973, District of Columbia. *Education:* University of Wisconsin (B.A., 1969); George Washington University (J.D., with honors, 1973). Member, Law Review, 1971-1973. Law Clerk to the Honorable Austin L. Fickling, Associate Judge, District of Columbia Court of Appeals, 1973-1974. *Member:* The District of Columbia Bar. (Washington, D.C. Office). ***PRACTICE AREAS:*** Energy Law; Litigation. ***Email:*** ddankner@winston.com

PETER N. HIEBERT, born Bakersfield, California, July 31, 1949; admitted to bar, 1981, District of Columbia. *Education:* Columbia University (B.A., 1972); Georgetown University (J.D., 1981). Member, 1979-1980 and Editor, 1980-1981, Georgetown Law Journal. *Member:* The District of Columbia Bar. (Washington, D.C. Office). ***PRACTICE AREAS:*** International Trade Law; Administrative Law; Legislative Practice. ***Email:*** phiebert@winston.com

(This Listing Continued)

ERIC L. HIRSCHHORN, born New York, N.Y., April 28, 1946; admitted to bar, 1968, New York; 1972, U.S. Supreme Court; 1973, District of Columbia. *Education:* University of Chicago (B.A., 1965); Columbia University (J.D., cum laude, 1968). Harlan Fiske Stone Scholar. Author, "The Export Control and Embargo Handbook, 2d Edition (Oceana 2004), and numerous other publications on export regulation and professional responsibility issues. Reginald Heber Smith Community Lawyer Fellow (MFY Legal Services, Inc.), 1968-1971. Counsel, Democratic Study Group, New York State Assembly, 1971. Legislative Assistant to Rep. Bella Abzug, U.S. House of Representatives, 1971-1973. Chief Counsel, Subcommittee on Government Information and Individual Rights, U.S. House of Representatives, 1975-1977. Deputy Associate Director for International Affairs and Trade, U.S. Office of Management and Budget (also Counsel, President's Reorganization Project), 1977-1980. Deputy Assistant Secretary for Export Administration, U.S. Department of Commerce, 1980-1981. Executive Secretary, Industry Coalition on Technology Transfer, 1986—. *Member:* The District of Columbia Bar (Member, 1997-1998, 1999-2001, Vice Chair, 2001-2003 and Chair, 2003-2005, Legal Ethics Committee; Member, 2004—, Rules of Professional Conduct Review Committee); The Association of the Bar of the City of New York; Thurgood Marshall American Inn of Court. (Washington, D.C. Office). ***REPORTED CASES:*** Boston & Maine Corp. v. STB, 364 F.3d 318 (D.C. Cir. 2004); Pejepscot Indus. Park, Inc. v. Maine Central R. Co., 281 F. Supp. 2d 311 and 297 F. Supp. 2d (D. Me. 2003); Rymes Heating Oils, Inc. v. Springfield Terminal Ry. Co., 358 F.3d 82 (1st Cir. 2004), aff'g 265 F. Supp. 2d 147 (D. Mass. 2003); Engelhard Corp. v. Springfield Terminal Ry. Co., 193 F. Supp. 2d 385 (D. Mass. 2002); Boston and Maine Corp. v. Town of Ayer, 191 F. Supp. 2d 257 (D. Mass. 2002); Olympic Chartering S.A. v. Ministry of Industry and Trade of Jordan, 134 F. Supp. 2d 528 (S.D.N.Y. 2001); In re Barr Labs., Inc., 930 F.2d 72 (D.C. Cir. 1991); Boston and Maine Corp. v. ICC, 911 F.2d 743 (D.C. Cir. 1990). ***PRACTICE AREAS:*** Export Regulation; Foreign Asset Control; Legal Ethics and Professional Responsibility; Federal Litigation; Railroad Law; Customs Law; Foreign Corrupt Practices Act; Foreign Sovereign Immunities Act. ***Email:*** ehirschhorn@winston.com

JOHN C. KIRTLAND, born Salina, Kansas, April 29, 1939; admitted to bar, 1971, District of Columbia; 1974, U.S. Supreme Court; 1977, U.S. Court of Appeals for the District of Columbia Circuit. *Education:* U.S. Naval Academy (B.S., 1961); George Washington University (J.D., 1971). Member, Order of the Coif. Counsel, U.S. Senate Committee on Commerce, Science and Transportation, 1971-1977. *Member:* The District of Columbia Bar; American Bar Association. [Lieutenant, U.S. Navy, 1961-1967; Naval Advisory Force, Vietnam, 1966-1967, Bronze Star (with Combat Distinguishing Device)]. (Washington, D.C. Office). ***PRACTICE AREAS:*** Legislative Practice; International Trade Law; Federal Regulatory Law. ***Email:*** jkirtland@winston.com

WILLIAM J. MADDEN, JR., born Washington, D.C., 1939; admitted to bar, 1965, District of Columbia; 1973, U.S. Supreme Court. *Education:* College of the Holy Cross (A.B., 1961); University of Michigan (J.D., 1964). Trial Attorney, Federal Power Commission, 1965-1968. *Member:* Federal Energy Bar Association (Member, Board of Directors, 1992-1994). (Washington, D.C. Office). ***PRACTICE AREAS:*** Energy Law; Environmental Law; Public Utility Law. ***Email:*** wmadden@winston.com

J. MICHAEL McGARRY, III, born Sacramento, California, July 30, 1943; admitted to bar, 1969, District of Columbia; 1972, Maryland. *Education:* University of Pennsylvania (B.S., 1965); University of Virginia (LL.B., 1969). Law Clerk to Judge Matthew F. McGuire, U.S. District Court, District of Columbia, 1969-1970. Assistant U.S. Attorney, 1970-1973. (Washington, D.C. Office). ***PRACTICE AREAS:*** Energy Law; Administrative Law; Natural Resources Law. ***Email:*** jmcgarry@winston.com

NICHOLAS S. REYNOLDS, born Grosse Pointe, Michigan, June 16, 1944; admitted to bar, 1971, Virginia; 1973, District of Columbia. *Education:* Wilkes College (B.S., 1968); College of William & Mary and George Washington University (J.D., with honors, 1971). Member, William & Mary Law Review, 1969-1970. *Member:* The District of Columbia Bar; Virginia and American (Vice Chairman, Atomic Energy Committee; Chairman, Programs & CLE Meetings Committee, Section on Public Utility, Communications and Transportation Law, 1980—) Bar Associations. (Washington, D.C. Office). ***PRACTICE AREAS:*** Energy Law; Public Utility Law; Nuclear Energy Law; Electric Power; Energy Acquisitions; Energy Regulation; Federal Energy Regulation; International Energy Law; Nuclear Energy. ***Email:*** nreynolds@winston.com

MARK J. WETTERHAHN, born New York, N.Y., June 13, 1944; admitted to bar, 1972, Maryland; 1973, District of Columbia; 1976, U.S. Supreme Court. *Education:* Queens College of the City University of New York (B.A., 1966); Columbia University (B.S., 1966; M.S., 1968); American University (J.D., 1972). Phi Beta Kappa. *Member:* The District of Columbia Bar; American Society of Mechanical Engineers; American Nuclear Society. (Washington, D.C. Office). ***PRACTICE AREAS:*** Nuclear Energy Law; Energy Law; Nuclear Waste. ***Email:*** mwetterh@winston.com

HOWARD M. PEARL, born Chicago, Illinois, June 18, 1954; admitted to bar, 1980, Illinois; 1982, U.S. District Court, Northern District of Illinois; 1987, U.S. Court of Appeals, Seventh Circuit. *Education:* Brown University (A.B., magna cum laude, 1976); Harvard University (J.D., cum laude, 1980). Phi Beta Kappa. Law Clerk to the Honorable Joseph L. Tauro, U.S. District Judge, District of Massachusetts, 1980-1982. Assistant U.S. Attorney, Northern District of Illinois, 1982-1987; Deputy Chief, Criminal Receiving and Appellate Division, U.S. Attorney's Office, 1987-1989. Associate Trial Counsel, Office of Independent Counsel (Iran/Contra), 1989-1990. General Counsel, National Basketball Referees Association, 1997-2004. ***PRACTICE AREAS:*** White Collar Criminal; Health Care; Commercial Litigation. ***Email:*** hpearl@winston.com

LAWRENCE R. DESIDERI, born Chicago, Illinois, June 6, 1958; admitted to bar, 1983, Illinois, U.S. District Court, Northern District of Illinois and U.S. Court of Appeals, Seventh Circuit. *Education:* Northern Illinois University (B.S., summa cum laude, with highest honors in Finance, 1980); University of Illinois (J.D., summa cum laude, 1983). Order of the Coif. Topics Editor, University of Illinois Law Review, 1982-1983. *Member:* Chicago and American Bar Associations. ***PRACTICE AREAS:*** Complex Commercial Litigation; White Collar Criminal Defense. ***Email:*** ldesider@winston.com

THOMAS J. QUIGLEY, born Brooklyn, New York, July 26, 1957; admitted to bar, 1984, New York and U.S. District Court, Southern and Eastern Districts of New York; 1986, U.S. Court of Appeals, Second Circuit; 1998, U.S. District Court, Western District of New York. *Education:* Fairfield University (B.A., 1979); St. John's University (J.D., 1983). Notes and Comments Editor, St. John's Law Review, 1982-1983. Member, Product Liability Advisory Council. *Member:* New York State and American Bar Associations; Federal Bar Council. (New York, N.Y. Office). ***PRACTICE AREAS:*** Products Liability Law; Commercial Law; Litigation. ***Email:*** tquigley@winston.com

DAVID A. REPKA, born Wilmington, Delaware, May 21, 1957; admitted to bar, 1981, District of Columbia. *Education:* Northwestern University (B.A., 1978); Georgetown University (J.D., cum laude, 1981). Phi Beta Kappa. Attorney, U.S. Nuclear Regulatory Commission, 1981-1984. (Washington, D.C. Office). ***PRACTICE AREAS:*** Nuclear Energy; Nuclear Waste; Administrative Agency Practice; Administrative Hearings and Appeals. ***Email:*** drepka@winston.com

NORMAN NEWMAN (1952-1998)

ANTHONY F. LoFRISCO, born Brooklyn, N.Y., 1933; admitted to bar, 1958, New York; 1960, U.S. Supreme Court. *Education:* Fordham University (B.S., 1955; LL.B., 1958). United Nations Delegate to the Diplomatic Conference on the Travel Contract Convention, 1970. (New York, N.Y. Office). ***Email:*** alofrisco@winston.com

JAMES R. THOMPSON, JR., born Chicago, Illinois, May 8, 1936; admitted to bar, 1959, Illinois and U.S. District Court, Northern District of Illinois; 1960, U.S. Court of Appeals, Seventh Circuit and U.S. Supreme Court. *Education:* University of Illinois; Washington University; Northwestern University (J.D., 1959). Editor-in-Chief, Journal of Criminal Law, Criminology and Police Science. Co-Author: with Inbau and Zagel, *Criminal Law and Its Administration,* Foundation Press, Fourth Edition, 1984; with Inbau, Haddad, Zagel and Starkman, *Cases and Comments on Criminal Procedure,* Foundation Press, Second Edition, 1980; with Inbau and Moenssens, *Cases and Comments on Criminal Law,* Foundation Press, Third Edition, 1983. Assistant and Associate Professor, Northwestern University Law School, 1964-1969. Assistant State's Attorney, 1959-1964. Assistant Attorney General, Illinois, 1969-1970. U.S. Attorney, Northern District of Illinois, 1971-1975. Governor of Illinois, 1977-1991. Chairman, President's Intelligence Oversight Board, 1989-1993. Member, Board of Directors: Chicago Board of Trade, 1991; FMC Corporation, 1991; FMC Technologies, Inc., 2001; Hollinger International, Inc., 1995; Maximus, Inc., 2001; Navigant Consulting Group, Inc., 1998; Chicago Climate Control; Abraham Lincoln Bicentennial Commission; Commission on Terrorist Attacks upon the United States; Lyric Opera, 1991; Music of Contemporary Art, 1991; Regent for Life, Lincoln Academy. *Member:* Chicago, Illinois State and American Bar Associations. ***PRACTICE AREAS:*** Government Regulatory; Corporate; Litigation. ***Email:*** jthompso@winston.com

THOMAS F. BLAKEMORE, born Oak Park, Illinois; admitted to bar, 1978, Illinois; 1989, Pennsylvania. *Education:* University of Illinois (B.S., with high honors, 1972; J.D., cum laude, 1978). Editor, University of Illinois Law Review, 1977-1978. *Member:* American Bar Association. ***PRACTICE AREAS:*** Commercial Lending. ***Email:*** tblakemo@winston.com

THOMAS J. FREDERICK, born Grand Rapids, Michigan, October 6, 1956; admitted to bar, 1984, Illinois and U.S. District Court, Northern District of Illinois; 1989, U.S. Court of Appeals, Seventh Circuit; 1993, U.S. Supreme Court. *Education:* Michigan State University (B.A., with high honors, 1978); University of Michigan (J.D., cum laude, 1984). Order of the Coif. Associate Editor, 1982-1983 and Article Editor, 1983-1984, Michigan Law Review. *Member:* Chicago and American Bar Associations. ***PRACTICE AREAS:*** Commercial Litigation; Product Liability Litigation; White Collar Criminal Litigation. ***Email:*** tfrederi@winston.com

GEORGE C. LOMBARDI, born Dallas, Texas, August 5, 1958; admitted to bar, 1984, Illinois and U.S. District Court, Northern District of Illinois; 1989, U.S. Court of Appeals for the Federal Circuit; 1993, U.S. Court of Appeals, Seventh Circuit. *Education:* Dartmouth College (A.B., cum laude, 1980); University of Michigan (J.D., magna cum laude, 1984). Order of the Coif. Associate Editor, 1982-1983 and Note Editor, 1983-1984, Michigan Law Review. ***PRACTICE AREAS:*** Complex Commercial Litigation; Intellectual Property Litigation; Securities Litigation; White Collar Criminal Defense. ***Email:*** glombard@winston.com

REX L. SESSIONS, born Lansing, Michigan, June 2, 1959; admitted to bar, 1984, Illinois and U.S. District Court, Northern District of Illinois; 1991, New York; 1992, U.S. District Court, Southern District of New York. *Education:* Northwestern University (B.A., 1981); University of Michigan (J.D., 1984). Kappa Alpha Pi; Alpha Lambda Delta. Mortar Board. ***PRACTICE AREAS:*** Labor and Employment Law. ***Email:*** rsession@winston.com

JOHN A. WAITS, II, born Greenville, Mississippi, June 6, 1947; admitted to bar, 1978, New York and U.S. District Court, Eastern and Southern Districts of New York; 1988, District of Columbia; 1989, U.S. Supreme Court. *Education:* University of Mississippi (B.A., summa cum laude, 1969); University of Virginia (M.A., with honors, 1972); New York University (J.D., 1977). Fulbright Scholar, University of Hamburg. Administrative Assistant to Congressman David R. Bowen, 1980-1982. Counsel to House Agriculture Subcommittee, 1979-1980. *Member:* The District of Columbia Bar. (Washington, D.C. Office). ***PRACTICE AREAS:*** Legislative Practice; Administrative/Regulatory Law; Agriculture; Economic Development; Trade; Political Law. ***Email:*** jwaits@winston.com

CHRISTINE L. ALBRIGHT, born June 21, 1951; admitted to bar, 1976, Illinois and U.S. District Court, Northern District of Illinois; 1985, Florida. *Education:* University of Michigan (B.A., with high distinction, 1973; J.D., magna cum laude, 1976). Order of the Coif. Recipient, American Jurisprudence Criminal Law Award. Associate Editor, 1974-1975 and Note Editor, 1975-1976, Michigan Law Review. Adjunct Professor, Northwestern University School of Law. *Member:* Chicago (Chairman, Trust Law Committee, 1994-1995), Illinois State (Member of Council, Trusts and Estates Section, 1995-1996) and American (Council Member, 1997—; Chairman, Committee on Estate Planning and Drafting: Marital Deduction, 1990-1995 and Committee on Tax Legislation and Regulations: Marital Deduction, 1995-1996 and Group Chair, Estate Planning for Families and Other Beneficiaries Committees, 1996-1997, Section of Real Property, Probate and Trust Law) Bar Associations; Chicago Estate Planning Council; Chicago Finance Exchange. Fellow, American College of Trust and Estate Counsel. ***PRACTICE AREAS:*** Estate Planning; Federal Estate and Gift Taxation; Generation Skipping Tax; Estate Administration; Trust Administration; Trusts and Estates; Wills; Probate; Trusts and Estates Taxation; Closely Held Business Estate Planning. ***Email:*** calbrigh@winston.com

(This Listing Continued)

WINSTON & STRAWN LLP, Chicago—Continued

MARC S. PALAY, born Chicago, Illinois, January 16, 1952; admitted to bar, 1977, Virginia; 1978, District of Columbia; 1979, U.S. District Court, District of Columbia; 1988, U.S. Court of Appeals, Ninth Circuit; 1990, U.S. Supreme Court and U.S. Court of Appeals, Federal Circuit. *Education:* Washington University (A.B., cum laude, 1973); George Washington University (J.D., with high honors, 1977). Order of the Coif. Member, The George Washington Law Review, 1976-1977. *Member:* The District of Columbia Bar. (Geneva, Switzerland Office). ***PRACTICE AREAS:*** Complex Litigation; International Commercial Arbitration; International Trade Law. ***Email:*** mpalay@winston.com

BENJAMIN P. FISHBURNE, III, born South Bend, Indiana, November 14, 1943; admitted to bar, 1971, District of Columbia. *Education:* University of Notre Dame (B.A., 1965); University of Virginia (LL.B., 1968). Order of the Coif. Professorial Lecturer, American University School of Law, 1973-1975. *Member:* The District of Columbia Bar. (Washington, D.C. Office). ***PRACTICE AREAS:*** International Commercial Transactions; Corporate Finance; High Technology; International Dispute Resolution. ***Email:*** bfishbur@winston.com

BARRY J. HART, born Philadelphia, Pennsylvania, February 26, 1948; admitted to bar, 1973, Pennsylvania; 1977, District of Columbia. *Education:* Dartmouth College (B.A., 1970); George Washington University (J.D., 1973); New York University (LL.M., 1976). (Washington, D.C. Office). ***PRACTICE AREAS:*** International Taxation; Tax Exempt Organizations; Nonprofit Corporations; International Corporate Law; International Corporate Transactions. ***Email:*** bjhart@winston.com

CHARLES L. KINNEY, born Parkersburg, West Virginia, May 31, 1952; admitted to bar, 1979, District of Columbia and U.S. District Court for the District of Columbia; 1986, U.S. Supreme Court. *Education:* Georgetown University (B.S.F.S., 1974; J.D., 1979). Chief Floor Counsel, U.S. Senate. (Washington, D.C. Office). ***PRACTICE AREAS:*** Federal Governmental Relations; Regulatory Affairs. ***Email:*** ckinney@winston.com

JAMES R. CURTISS, born Lincoln, Nebraska, December 20, 1953; admitted to bar, 1979, Nebraska and U.S. District Court, District of Nebraska; 1985, District of Columbia; 1992, U.S. Supreme Court. *Education:* University of Nebraska (B.A., 1976; J.D., 1979). Director: Baltimore Gas & Electric; Cameco Corporation. (Washington, D.C. Office). ***PRACTICE AREAS:*** Energy Law; Electric Power; Nuclear Energy Law. ***Email:*** jcurtiss@winston.com

NICOLAS C. ULMER, born August 5, 1952; admitted to bar, 1979, District of Columbia; 1980, California. *Education:* Brown University (A.B., honors, 1974); University of California at Hastings (J.D., 1979). Author: "Drafting the International Arbitration Clause," 20 International Lawyer 1335, 1986; "Winning the Opening Stages of an ICC Arbitration," Journal of International Arbitration 33, 1991. Co-Author: "Recognition and Enforcement of Foreign Civil Judgements in Switzerland," 27 International Lawyer 317, 1993; "Ethics and Effectiveness," The Commercial Way to Justice 167, Kluwer, 1997; "Claimants' Expectations from the United Nations Compensation Commission," 15 Journal of International Arbitration 7, 1998. *Member:* The District of Columbia Bar; State Bar of California; Association Suisse de l'Arbitrage. (Geneva, Switzerland Office). ***LANGUAGES:*** English, French, Spanish, German and Italian. ***PRACTICE AREAS:*** International Arbitration; International Commercial Law; World Trade Organization. ***Email:*** nulmer@winston.com

JULIE A. BAUER, born Elmhurst, Illinois, March 26, 1960; admitted to bar, 1985, Illinois; 1987, U.S. District Court, Northern District of Illinois; 1993, U.S. District Court, Central District of Illinois and U.S. Court of Appeals, Seventh Circuit; 2003, U.S. District Court, Southern District of Illinois. *Education:* University of Virginia (B.A., with distinction, 1982); University of Illinois (J.D., magna cum laude, 1985). Order of the Coif. Member, University of Illinois Law Review, 1983-1985. Law Clerk to the Hon. Charles P. Kocoras, U.S. District Court, Northern District of Illinois, 1985-1987. *Member:* Chicago, Seventh Circuit and American Bar Associations. Fellow, American Bar Foundation. ***PRACTICE AREAS:*** Litigation; Complex Commercial Litigation; Class Actions; Federal Civil Litigation; Libel, Slander and Defamation. ***Email:*** jbauer@winston.com

CHARLES B. BOEHRER, born Milwaukee, Wisconsin, December 5, 1959; admitted to bar, 1985, Illinois. *Education:* University of Wisconsin-Madison (B.B.A., 1982); University of Michigan (J.D., 1985). Member, Michigan Law Review, 1983-1985. ***PRACTICE AREAS:*** Corporate Law; Finance; Banks and Banking; Business Law. ***Email:*** cboehrer@winston.com

DEBORAH K. BOLING, born Okmulgee, Oklahoma, November 21, 1959; admitted to bar, 1984, Illinois and U.S. District Court, Northern District of Illinois. *Education:* University of Chicago (B.A., with general honors, 1980; J.D., 1984). *Member:* Chicago, Illinois State and American Bar Associations. ***PRACTICE AREAS:*** Employee Benefits; Executive Compensation Law. ***Email:*** dboling@winston.com

TERRENCE R. BRADY, born Evanston, Illinois, December 8, 1958; admitted to bar, 1985, Illinois and U.S. District Court, Northern District of Illinois. *Education:* Dartmouth College (A.B., 1982); University of Notre Dame (J.D., cum laude, 1985). Editor-in-Chief, Notre Dame Journal of Law, Ethics and Public Policy, 1984-1985. *Member:* Chicago, Illinois State and American Bar Associations. ***Email:*** tbrady@winston.com

STEVEN J. GAVIN, born Teaneck, New Jersey, February 17, 1960; admitted to bar, 1985, Illinois; 1986, U.S. District Court, Northern District of Illinois. *Education:* Yale University (B.A., 1982); Stanford University (J.D., 1985). Phi Beta Kappa. ***Email:*** sgavin@winston.com

JOHN L. MACCARTHY, born St. Louis, Missouri, December 26, 1959; admitted to bar, 1985, Illinois and U.S. District Court, Northern District of Illinois. *Education:* Williams College (B.A., magna cum laude, 1982); Stanford University (J.D., 1985). Phi Beta Kappa; Order of the Coif. ***PRACTICE AREAS:*** Securities; Mergers and Acquisitions. ***Email:*** *jmaccarthy@winston.com*

PETER C. McCABE, III, born Chicago, Illinois, June 29, 1960; admitted to bar, 1985, Illinois, U.S. District Court, Northern District of Illinois, U.S. Court of Appeals, 2nd, 7th, 9th and Federal Circuits and U.S. Supreme Court. *Education:* Harvard University (B.A., 1982); Indiana University (J.D., magna cum laude, 1985). Order of the Coif. Articles Editor, Indiana University Law Journal, 1984-1985. *Member:* Chicago and American Bar Associations. ***PRACTICE AREAS:*** Litigation; Intellectual Property Law. ***Email:*** pmccabe@winston.com

WILLIAM G. MIOSSI, born Evanston, Illinois, June 22, 1959; admitted to bar, 1985, Illinois; 1994, District of Columbia. *Education:* Georgetown University (B.S., 1981; M.A., 1983; J.D., 1985). Theta Phi Alpha. Law Clerk to Honorable June L.Green, U.S. District Judge, District of Columbia, 1985-1987. *Member:* The District of Columbia Bar. ***LANGUAGES:*** French. ***PRACTICE AREAS:*** Labor and Employment (100%). ***Email:*** wmiossi@winston.com

LOUIS J. WEBER III, born Davenport, Iowa, January 23, 1957; admitted to bar, 1985, Illinois and U.S. District Court, Northern District of Illinois. *Education:* University of Notre Dame (B.S.E.E., 1979; J.D., summa cum laude, 1985). Recipient, Farabaugh Prize for High Scholarship in Law. Staff Editor, Notre Dame Law Review, 1984-1985. ***PRACTICE AREAS:*** Federal Income Tax. ***Email:*** lweber@winston.com

JOHN C. LORENTZEN, born Fort Carson, Colorado, March 6, 1955; admitted to bar, 1980, Illinois, U.S. District Court, Northern District of Illinois and U.S. Tax Court. *Education:* Drake University (B.A., 1977; B.S.B.A., 1977); University of Chicago (J.D., 1980). Phi Beta Kappa; Beta Gamma Sigma. *Member:* American Bar Association (Member, Section on Taxation). ***PRACTICE AREAS:*** Corporate Tax Planning; Corporate Taxation; Federal Income Tax; Like Kind Exchanges; Tax Law; Corporate Law; Project Finance Law. ***Email:*** jlorentz@winston.com

JAMES M. REUM, born Oak Park, Illinois, November 1, 1946; admitted to bar, 1973, New York; 1979, Illinois. *Education:* Harvard University (B.A., cum laude, 1968); Harvard University (J.D., cum laude, 1972). Associate Counsel, Committee on the Judiciary, U.S. House of Representatives, 1974. Nominee, Commissioner, Securities and Exchange Commission, 1992. ***PRACTICE AREAS:*** Securities; Finance; Mergers, Acquisitions and Divestitures; Banks and Banking. ***Email:*** jreum@winston.com

WILLIAM D. BREWER, born Detroit, Michigan, October 30, 1961; admitted to bar, 1986, Illinois; 1995, New York. *Education:* Yale University (B.A., magna cum laude, 1983); Harvard University (J.D., 1986). *Member:* The Association of the Bar of the City of New York; Chicago, Illinois State, New York State and American Bar Associations. (New York, N.Y. Office). ***PRACTICE AREAS:*** Banking; Finance Law; Securities Law; Corporate Finance; Mergers and Acquisitions; Corporations; Secured Lending. ***Email:*** wbrewer@winston.com

CHRISTINA KARCHER CORSIGLIA, born Decatur, Illinois, December 26, 1962; admitted to bar, 1986, Illinois and U.S. Tax Court. *Education:* Grinnell College (B.A., 1982); Vanderbilt University (M.B.A., 1986; J.D., 1986). Senior Managing Editor, Vanderbilt Law Review, 1985-1986. *Member:* American Bar Association (Member, Section on Taxation). ***PRACTICE AREAS:*** International Corporate Taxation; Federal Tax Controversies; Leveraged Leasing. ***Email:*** ccorsigl@winston.com

W. GORDON DOBIE, born Detroit, Michigan, December 23, 1959; admitted to bar, 1986, Illinois. *Education:* Boston University (B.A., cum laude, 1982); Washington University (J.D., 1986). Order of the Coif. Managing Editor, Washington University Law Quarterly, 1985-1986. Frequent Author and Editor for several publications, including "Securities Litigation Practice Commentaries to United States Code," 15 U.S.C. §§ 77 and 78 (2002 and LEXIS electronic version); "Presumed Guilty, Assuming the Factual Truthfulness of Plaintiff's Complaint in the Class Certification Decision," United States Law Week (July 9, 2002); and "Strategic Use of Communications with Putative Class Members," Class Action Litigation Report (October 13, 2000). Serves on Advisory Board, BNA Class Action Litigation Report. Special Assistant Federal Defender, 1990-1993. ***PRACTICE AREAS:*** Securities; Class Actions; Commercial Litigation; Antitrust Litigation. ***Email:*** wdobie@winston.com

PATRICK O. DOYLE, born Fort Campbell, Kentucky, July 27, 1961; admitted to bar, 1986, Illinois. *Education:* University of Notre Dame (B.B.A., with highest honors, 1983); Northwestern University (J.D., cum laude, 1986). Order of the Coif. Coordinating Executive Editor, Northwestern University Journal of Criminal Law and Criminology, 1985-1986. *Member:* Chicago and Illinois State Bar Associations. ***PRACTICE AREAS:*** Mergers, Acquisitions and Divestitures; Private Equity. ***Email:*** pdoyle@winston.com

ANDREW J. McDONOUGH, born Fremont, Ohio, April 3, 1960; admitted to bar, 1986, Illinois. *Education:* The Ohio State University (B.A., 1983; J.D., 1986). Order of the Coif. Staff Member, 1984-1985 and Articles Editor, 1985-1986, Ohio State Law Journal. Author: "The 1984 Bankruptcy Amendments-Another Flawed Compromise," 46 Ohio State Law Journal, 1985. ***PRACTICE AREAS:*** Private Equity; Mergers and Acquisitions; Joint Ventures; Partnership Law; Limited Liability Company Law; Structured Finance. ***Email:*** amcdonou@winston.com

MICHAEL L. MULHERN, born Pittsburgh, Pennsylvania, December 1, 1961; admitted to bar, 1986, Illinois. *Education:* University of Notre Dame (B.A., cum laude, 1983; J.D., 1986). ***PRACTICE AREAS:*** Labor and Employment Law. ***Email:*** mmulhern@winston.com

LORI J. VAN AUKEN, born Catskill, N.Y., July 22, 1961; admitted to bar, 1987, New York and U.S. District Court, Northern, Southern and Eastern Districts of New York. *Education:* State University of New York at Albany (B.A., magna cum laude, 1983); Albany Law School (J.D., cum laude, 1986). Member, Justinian Society. *Member:* The Association of the Bar of the City of New York; The District of Columbia Bar; New York State and American Bar Associations. (New York, N.Y. Office). ***PRACTICE AREAS:*** Litigation. ***Email:*** lvanauke@winston.com

JOHN ALBERT WHITTAKER, IV, born Everett, Washington, December 5, 1950; admitted to bar, 1976, Washington; 1980, District of Columbia. *Education:* University of Washington (B.A., in Economics, with honors, 1973); University of Santa Clara (J.D., cum laude, 1976). *Member:* The District of Columbia Bar; Washington State Bar Association (inactive). (Washington, D.C. Office). ***PRACTICE AREAS:*** Federal Energy Regulation; Hydroelectricity Licensing; Hydroelectricity; Environmental Administrative Law; Administrative Agency Practice. ***Email:*** jwhittak@winston.com

GORDON ALAN COFFEE, born Dallas, Texas, September 9, 1958; admitted to bar, 1984, District of Columbia; 1986, Virginia. *Education:* University of Virginia (B.A., with

(This Listing Continued)

(This Listing Continued)

distinction, 1981); University of Texas (J.D., 1984). *Member:* The District of Columbia Bar; Virginia State Bar. (Washington, D.C. Office). ***PRACTICE AREAS:*** Commercial Litigation; Complex Litigation; Trial Practice. ***Email:*** gcoffee@winston.com

PATRICK F. MURRAY, born Detroit, Michigan, December 12, 1944; admitted to bar, 1972, Illinois; 1981, France, Conseil Juridique; 1992, France, Avocat. *Education:* University of Michigan (B.A., 1966; J.D., 1972). *Member:* Paris Bar Association. (Paris, France Office). ***LANGUAGES:*** French. ***PRACTICE AREAS:*** Corporate Law; Financial Markets; International Arbitration; International Law. ***Email:*** pmurray@winston.com

TIMOTHY M. BROAS, born Detroit, Michigan, March 21, 1954; admitted to bar, 1979, New Jersey; 1980, New York; 1981, U.S. District Court, Southern District of New York and U.S. Court of Appeals, First and Second Circuits; 1985, District of Columbia and U.S. District Court for the District of Columbia; 1986, U.S. Court of Appeals, Ninth Circuit; 1990, U.S. Court of Appeals, Sixth and Fourth Circuits. *Education:* Boston College (B.A., magna cum laude, 1976); College of William & Mary (J.D., 1979). Law Clerk to Justice Mark A. Sullivan, New Jersey Supreme Court, 1979-1980. Director, Council for Court Excellence, Washington, D.C. *Member:* The Association of the Bar of the City of New York; The District of Columbia Bar; American Bar Association. (Washington, D.C. Office). ***PRACTICE AREAS:*** Criminal Litigation; Civil Litigation. ***Email:*** tbroas@winston.com

LELAND E. HUTCHINSON, born South Haven, Michigan, July 3, 1948; admitted to bar, 1973, Michigan; 1974, Illinois. *Education:* Principia College (B.A., with highest honors, 1970); University of Chicago (J.D., 1973). ***PRACTICE AREAS:*** Securities; Mergers and Acquisitions; Venture Capital. ***Email:*** lhutchinson@winston.com

M. DAVID GALAINENA, born Cleveland, Ohio, November 9, 1957; admitted to bar, 1983, Illinois. *Education:* Tulane University (B.A., magna cum laude, 1980); University of Notre Dame (J.D., 1983). Phi Beta Kappa. ***PRACTICE AREAS:*** Securitization. ***Email:*** dgalainena@winston.com

WILLIAM A. CARMELL, born New York, N.Y.; admitted to bar, 1966, New York. *Education:* University of Michigan (B.A., 1961); Columbia Law School (LL.B., 1964). Listed in: The Best Lawyers in America, 2003-2004; 1995 Guide to the World's Leading Labour and Employment Lawyers, Euromoney Publications, PLC., 1995; Strathmore's Who's Who of Leading American Lawyers, 2003-2004. Lecturer: Recent Developments in American Employment Law as they Particularly Affect Japanese Companies Doing Business in the United States by Invitation of the Faculty of Law, University of Tokyo Law School, May 1994, published in Japan in the Japanese language, Spring 1996. Lecturer: Presentation in Tokyo, Japan to the Membership of the Keidanren (Japan Employers' Federation) on: "Reductions in Force/Legal and Pragmatic Considerations," Spring, 1998; "American Sexual Harassment Law," Fall 1996. Author: A Chapter for the International Human Resources Guide, which describes the International Implications of American Employment Law, published by Warren, Gorham & Lamont, 1997, republished in the April 2003 International Quarterly by Business Laws, Inc.; "Benefits of a Resolution—Centered ADR Program," Corporate Legal Times, December 1994; "Alternative Dispute Resolution," Journal Interworld's, March 15, 1994 and International Legal Strategy Publication (translated into the Japanese language); "The Affirmative Action Compliance Manual for Banks," published in February 1991 by The American Bankers Association; "Overview of Recent Federal Legislation and Court Decisions in the Employment Law Area," April 1992 and May 1993 presentation to the membership of the Keidanren on specific American employment law issues such as expatriate compensation and reduction in local staff; Affirmative Action Update," Proceedings of New York University—42nd Annual National Conference on Labor, December, 1989. *Member:* New York State (Member, International Employment Law Committee, 1989—) and American (Member, Labor Law Committee, 1981—and International Law and Practice Committee, 1990—) Bar Associations. [First Lt., Inf., U.S. Army Reserve National Guard, 1967-1970]. (New York, N.Y. Office). ***PRACTICE AREAS:*** Labor; Employment Law. ***Email:*** wcarmell@winston.com

MATTHIAS A. LYDON, born Chicago, Illinois, July 24, 1942; admitted to bar, 1969, Illinois and U.S. District Court, Northern District of Illinois; 1970, U.S. Court of Appeals, Seventh Circuit; 1975, U.S. Tax Court; 1977, U.S. Supreme Court. *Education:* DePaul University (B.A., 1965; J.D., 1969). Assistant U.S. Attorney, Northern District of Illinois, 1970-1975. *Member:* Chicago, Illinois State and American Bar Associations; National Association of Criminal Defense Lawyers. ***PRACTICE AREAS:*** Litigation. ***Email:*** malydon@winston.com

CHRISTOPHER C. McISAAC, born Rochester, New York, 1959; admitted to bar, 1985, Virginia; 1986, District of Columbia. *Education:* University of North Carolina (B.A., with highest honors, 1982), Morehead Scholar; University of Virginia (J.D., 1985). Phi Beta Kappa. Adjunct Professor of Law, Georgetown University Law Center. Member, Bretton Woods Committee. *Member:* The District of Columbia Bar; Virginia State Bar. (Washington, D.C. Office). ***PRACTICE AREAS:*** Project Finance; Corporate Finance; Banking. ***Email:*** cmcisaac@winston.com

ERIC W. BLOOM, born Philadelphia, Pennsylvania, April 19, 1962; admitted to bar, 1989, District of Columbia; 1992, U.S. Court of Appeals, Fourth and Sixth Circuits; 1993, U.S. District Court, District of Columbia; 1994, U.S. Court of Appeals, Federal Circuit; 1995, U.S. Court of Appeals, First and District of Columbia Circuits; 1996, U.S. Court of Federal Claims; 1997, U.S. District Court, District of Maryland; 2002, U.S. Court of Appeals, Second and Ninth Circuits. *Education:* George Washington University (B.A., magna cum laude, 1984; J.D., with honors, 1987). Author, "Petitioning the Government: Playing with Fire if You Don't Know the Ground Rules," Metropolitan Corporate Counsel (Dec. 2002/January 2003). Co-Author: "FDIC/RTC Suits Against Bank and Thrift Officers and Directors—Why Now, What's Left?," Fordham L. Review, May 1995. (Washington, D.C. Office). ***PRACTICE AREAS:*** Commercial Litigation; Criminal Litigation; Financial Institutions Litigation; Appellate Practice; Civil Appeals. ***Email:*** ebloom@winston.com

OSCAR A. DAVID, born 1962; admitted to bar, 1987, Illinois. *Education:* George Washington University (B.A.); University of Chicago (J.D.). Phi Beta Kappa. ***PRACTICE AREAS:*** Mergers and Acquisitions; Corporate Finance; Securities; Private Equity Transactions; Portfolio Investments; Private Equity; Venture Capital Fund Formation. ***Email:*** odavid@winston.com

ANTHONY DiSARRO, born Staten Island, N.Y., 1961; admitted to bar, 1987, New York. *Education:* State University of New York at Albany (B.A., magna cum laude, 1983); New York Law School (J.D., summa cum laude, 1986). *Member:* Federal Bar Council. (New York, N.Y. Office). ***PRACTICE AREAS:*** Commercial Litigation. ***Email:*** adisarro@winston.com

BRIAN S. HART, born Bloomington, Illinois, May 14, 1962; admitted to bar, 1987, California; 1989, Illinois. *Education:* University of Illinois, Champaign-Urbana (B.S. in Accountancy, with highest honors, 1984); University of California at Los Angeles (J.D., 1987). Certified Public Accountant, Illinois, 1984. ***PRACTICE AREAS:*** Corporate Finance; Mergers and Acquisitions; Venture Capital Investment; Joint Ventures. ***Email:*** bhart@winston.com

ELENI SKOULIKAS KOUIMELIS, born Greece, August 1, 1960; admitted to bar, 1985, Illinois. *Education:* University of Illinois (B.S., 1982); Loyola University (J.D., 1985). Phi Beta Kappa. Member, Loyola Law Review, 1984-1985. ***PRACTICE AREAS:*** Environmental Law. ***Email:*** ekouimel@winston.com

R. CABELL MORRIS, JR., born 1960; admitted to bar, 1987, Illinois. *Education:* Michigan State University (B.A.); DePaul University (J.D.). ***Email:*** rmorris@winston.com

JENNIFER T. NIJMAN, born August 27, 1962; admitted to bar, 1987, Illinois and U.S. District Court, Northern District of Illinois including Trial Bar; 1991, Wisconsin. *Education:* University of Illinois (B.A., 1984); University of Chicago (J.D., 1987). Member, University of Chicago Legal Forum, 1985-1987. *Member:* Chicago (President, 2002-2003), Illinois State and American (Member, Environmental Litigation Committee) Bar Associations. ***PRACTICE AREAS:*** Environmental Law; Environmental Litigation. ***Email:*** jnijman@winston.com

ANDREW W. RATTS, born St. Louis, Missouri, March 22, 1962; admitted to bar, 1987, Illinois. *Education:* University of Illinois (B.S., with highest honors, 1984); Harvard University (J.D., cum laude, 1987). Beta Gamma Sigma; Phi Kappa Phi. *Member:* American Bar Association. ***Email:*** aratts@winston.com

MICHAEL L. SIBARIUM, born Queens, New York, September 22, 1959; admitted to bar, 1985, Maryland and District of Columbia. *Education:* University of Connecticut (B.A., summa cum laude, 1981); George Washington University (J.D., with honors, 1984). Phi Beta Kappa. Member, The George Washington Journal of International Law and Economics, 1982-1984. *Member:* The District of Columbia Bar; American Bar Association. (Washington, D.C. Office). ***PRACTICE AREAS:*** Litigation; Antitrust; E-Commerce; Trade Regulation Law; Trade and Professional Associations. ***Email:*** msibariu@winston.com

THOMAS J. WIEGAND, born Lake Forest, Illinois, April 26, 1962; admitted to bar, 1987, Illinois. *Education:* Yale University (B.A., magna cum laude, 1983); Harvard University (J.D., 1986). ***PRACTICE AREAS:*** Commercial Litigation; White Collar Crime; Class Actions; Antitrust. ***Email:*** twiegand@winston.com

DANIEL C. BIRD, JR., born Pasadena, California, September 26, 1947; admitted to bar, 1977, Illinois. *Education:* United States Military Academy (B.S., 1969); University of Virginia (J.D., 1977). [Captain, U.S. Army Corps of Engineers, 1969-1974]. ***PRACTICE AREAS:*** Structured Finance; Asset Securitization; Investment Company Law; Securities. ***Email:*** dbird@winston.com

VINCENT SOL, born Brive, France, December 30, 1957; admitted to bar, 1989, France. *Education:* Institut D'Etudes Politiques (Dip., 1980); Paris Law University (J.D., 1984). Member, Environmental Law Committee, French Manufacturers Association (MEDEF). Vice President, Association Forum de l'environnement. Appointed in 1998 as a member of the French High Council for Regulated Facilities and in 2002 as Chairman of the Experts Group on Polluted Sites by the French Government. Associated Professor in environmental law on the postgraduate program at the University of Paris VII. (Paris, France Office). ***PRACTICE AREAS:*** Environmental Law. ***Email:*** vinsol@winston.com

THOMAS L. MILLS, born Elmira, New York, January 4, 1948; admitted to bar, 1975, District of Columbia. *Education:* United States Coast Guard Academy (B.S., 1970); George Washington University (J.D., with honors, 1975). Order of the Coif. Member, George Washington University Law Review, 1973-1975. [Lieut., U.S. Coast Guard, 1970-1975]. (Washington, D.C. Office). ***PRACTICE AREAS:*** Health Care; Maritime Law. ***Email:*** tmills@winston.com

CONSTANTINE G. PAPAVIZAS, born St. Paul, Minnesota, June 19, 1957; admitted to bar, 1984, Virginia; 1985, District of Columbia. *Education:* Georgetown University (B.A., 1978); Columbia University (M.I.A., 1981); George Washington University (J.D., with honors, 1984); University of Thessaloniki, Greece, International Public Law Institute. Pi Sigma Alpha. Author: "Coastwise Lease Finance Controversy Takes An Unexpected Turn," 1 Benedict's Maritime Bulletin, 2003; "1999-2000 U.S. Maritime Legislative Developments," 32 Journal of Maritime Law & Commerce, 2001; "New Developments in U.S.-Flag Vessel Financing and Citizenship Requirements," 24 Tulane Maritime Law Journal, 1999; "Penalty Enacted for Vessels Detained Under U.S. Port State Control Program," The International Journal of Shipping Law, March 1999; "Build and Charter Makes a Comeback," Marine Log, February 1998; "Foreign Crew Members Exempted from U.S. Tax," The International Journal of Shipping Law, December 1997; "Prevention of Biological Pollution — The U.S. National Invasive Species Act of 1996," The International Journal of Shipping Law, March 1997; "1995-1996 U.S. Maritime Legislative Developments," 28 Journal of Maritime Law and Commerce, January 1997; "The OECD Shipbuilding Agreement and its Effects on U.S. Law," 26 Journal of Maritime Law and Commerce, July 1995. Co-Author: "2001-2002 U.S. Maritime Legislative Developments," 34 Journal of Maritime Law and Commerce, July 2003; "1999-2000 U.S. Maritime Legislative Developments," 32 Journal of Maritime Law and Commerce, July 2001; "1997-98 U.S. Maritime Legislative Developments," 30 Journal of Maritime Law and Commerce, July 1999; "Compliance Tide Leaves Issues Open," The National Law Journal, July 6, 1998; "HMO Legislation Is Aimed at Protecting Patients," The National Law Journal, April 7, 1997; "Veering Off Course," Legal Times, March 20, 1995. Editor, Journal of Maritime Law & Commerce. (Washington, D.C. Office). ***LANGUAGES:*** Greek. ***PRACTICE AREAS:*** Health Care; Maritime Law; Securities. ***Email:*** cpapavizas@winston.com

JEFFREY G. BERMAN, born New York, N.Y., May 29, 1957; admitted to bar, 1982, District of Columbia; 1983, Florida. *Education:* Brown University (B.A., magna cum laude, 1979); Harvard University (J.D., 1982). Director, Harvard Legislative Research Bu-

(This Listing Continued)

WINSTON & STRAWN LLP, Chicago—Continued

reau, 1980-1981. *Member:* The District of Columbia Bar; The Florida Bar. (Washington, D.C. Office). ***PRACTICE AREAS:*** Energy Law; Communications Law; Government Relations; Corporate Law. ***Email:*** jberman@winston.com

JOHN FEHRENBACH, born Newark, New Jersey; admitted to bar, 1978, District of Columbia; 1979, U.S. District Court, District of Columbia and U.S. Court of Appeals, District of Columbia Circuit; 1994, U.S. Court of Appeals, Fifth Circuit; 1995, U.S. District Court, Northern District of Indiana; 2002, New York. *Education:* University of Delaware (B.A., 1974); Catholic University of America (J.D., 1978). Co-Author: ABA Annual Review of Business & Corporate Litigation, Environmental Chapter (2002, 2003, and 2004); "EPA Development of Revised Drinking Water Standards for Radionuclides," presented at Waste Management '99, Tuscon, AZ (March 1999); "The Waste Isolation Pilot Plant-A Paradigm for Meeting the Challenge of External Regulation," presented at Waste Management '98, Tuscon, AZ (March 1998); "Environmental Risks in Purchasing Properties from the RTC," in Journal of RTC Real Estate (May/June 1992). Contributor: "EPA's Final Rule on Lender Liability under Superfund," in Environmental Management Review (1992). Member, American Nuclear Society Public Policy Committee. Member, Environmental Law Institute. Vice-Chair, Environmental Policy Commission (1996-1998), Waste to Energy Task Force, Recycling Study Subcommittee (1996-1998), and Alternative Fuels Task Force (1997-1998), City of Alexandria, VA. *Member:* The District of Columbia Bar (Member, Section on Environment, Energy and Natural Resources); New York State Bar Association (Member: Environmental Law Section; Air Quality, Energy, and Transportation Committees). (Washington, D.C. Office). ***REPORTED CASES:*** U.S. v. G.E. and Town of Moreau, N.D.N.Y. (1988) (BNA, Toxic Law Reporter); Active Products Corp. v. A.H. Choitz & Co., 33 Chem. Waste Litig. Reporter 381 (N.D. IN., Ft. Wayne Div., Oct. 17, 1996). ***PRACTICE AREAS:*** Environmental Law; Transportation; Energy Law; Regulatory Law. ***Email:*** jfehrenbach@winston.com

WILLIAM N. HALL, born Stockholm, Sweden, January 5, 1953; admitted to bar, 1978, District of Columbia, U.S. Court of Appeals, Fifth, Ninth and District of Columbia Circuits, U.S. District Court, District of Columbia and U.S. District Court, Northern District of Indiana. *Education:* Bucknell University (B.A., cum laude, 1975); Georgetown University Law Center (J.D., 1978). Case and Note Editor, The Georgetown Law Journal, 1977-1978. Co-Author: "EPA's Final Rule on Lender Liability Under Superfund," Environmental Management Review, 3rd Quarter, 1992; "Environmental Risks in Purchasing Properties from the RTC," Journal of RTC Real Estate, May/June 1992. Author: "Environmental Audits—A Corporate Response to Bhopal," Environmental Forum, August, 1985. Co-Author: "Complying with EPA's Premanufacture Notification Requirements," Environmental Analyst, March and April, 1984; "Due Process at Sentencing: An Empirical and Legal Analysis of the Disclosure of Presentence Reports in Federal Courts," 93 Harvard Law Review 1613, June 1980. Member, Board of Directors: District of Columbia Sports and Entertainment Commission, 1995-1999; Federal City Council; National Capital Development Corp., 1994-1995. *Member:* Bar Association of The District of Columbia (Co-Chair, Environmental Law Committee, 1993-1995); The District of Columbia Bar (Member, Environmental Law Section); American Bar Association (Member, Section on Natural Resources, Energy and Environmental Law). (Washington, D.C. Office). ***PRACTICE AREAS:*** Environmental Law; Sports Law. ***Email:*** whall@winston.com

YOUNGHEE J. OTTLEY, born Pusan, Korea, March 3, 1951; admitted to bar, 1982, Illinois; 1987, New York. *Education:* Seoul National University (B.A., 1973); DePaul University (J.D., 1982); Columbia University (LL.M., 1986). Co-Author: with Bruce L. Ottley, "Liability for Defective Products in the Soviet Union: Socialist Law v. Soviet Realty," 8 Northwestern Journal of International Law and Business 627 (1987); with Bruce L. Ottley, "Product Liability Law in Japan: An Introduction to a Developing Area of Law," 14 Georgia Journal of International and Comparative Law 29 (1984); with Bruce L. Ottley and John B. Lewis, "New York Times v. Sullivan: A Retrospective Examination," 33 DePaul Law Review 741 (1984). ***LANGUAGES:*** Korean. ***PRACTICE AREAS:*** Mergers and Acquisitions; Corporate; Financing. ***Email:*** yottley@winston.com

ROBERT EVERETT BOSTROM, born Hartford, Connecticut, November 20, 1952; admitted to bar, 1981, New York and U.S. District Court, Eastern and Southern Districts of New York. *Education:* Franklin & Marshall College (B.A., with honors, 1974); The School of International Affairs, Columbia University (M.I.A., 1976); Boston College Law School (J.D., cum laude, 1980). Editor-in-Chief, Boston College International and Comparative Law Review, 1979-1980. Executive Vice President, Legal and Regulatory Affairs and General Counsel, National Westminster Bancorp, 1992-1996. Co-Editor, International Practitioner's Notebook, 1988-1993. Member, Board of Advisors, Mergers and Acquisitions, SNL Securities, 1994-1998. Author: "Nonbanking Activity Grandfather Rights of Foreign Banks Under Section 8 of the International Banking Act of 1978," 101 Banking Law Journal 468 (1984); "Asset Sales," Bankers Magazine 30-34, Nov.-Dec. (1987); "Guide for the Establishment of Asset Sale Programs," 4 Review of Financial Services Regulation 71 (1988); Non-Voting Equity Investments by Banks in Non-Bank Companies, 5 Review of Financial Services Regulation 43 (1989); "Mergers and Acquisitions: The Banking Industry," in R. Rupert (Ed.), The New Era of Investment Banking, (1993); "Foreigners Sidelined In Merger Game," American Banker, April 23, 1992; "Regulatory Clarification of the Applicability of the Risk-Based Capital Guidelines to Bank-Sponsored Asset-Backed Commercial Paper Programs and Credit Enhancement of Asset-Backed Securities," Duff & Phelps Structured Finance Quarterly, 1992; "Federal Banking Reform: Legislative Proposals," International Practitioner's Notebook (June, 1991). Lecturer: The SEC Institute: Bank Forum, "Risk-Based Capital Adequacy," 1987 and 1988; Lecturer and Co-Chairperson, Banking Law Institute, Leading Edge Developments in the Securitization of Financial Assets, 1988, 1989 and 1990. Moderator and Lecturer: Institute for International Research, Loan Asset Sales, 1988, 1989 and 1990. Chairperson and Lecturer: Banking Law Institute, Buying and Selling Loans, 1988, 1989 and 1990. Chairperson and Lecturer, InfoCast, Subordinated Debt and Equity Investments, 1989; Speaker, Investment Management Institute, *Cash Investment Strategies, 1989, 1990, 1991 and 1992. Chairperson and Lecturer,* Banking Law Institute, Foreign Banks in the United States, 1989; Speaker, Bankers Association for Foreign Trade: Living with the New U.S. Supervisory Regime: A BAFT Seminar for Senior U.S. Management of Foreign Banks, 1992, New York. Chairperson and Lecturer: Institute for International Research: Valuing, Investing, Trading and Selling Highly Leveraged Bank Debt, 1992, New York; Speaker, American Banker - Bond Buyer: Managing, Trading and Investing in LDC Debt, 1992, New York; Speaker: Bank & Financial Analysts Association, Twenty Second Annual Banking Symposium, 1992; Speaker, U.S. Banker Forum, 1993; Speaker, Practicing Law Institute, Bank Mergers and Acquisitions, 1994. Co-Chairman, Strategic Research Institute, Capital Markets Activities of International Banks, 1994 and 1995; Speaker, Bank Director, Bank Merger & Acquisition Forum, 1995 and 1996. Speaker, 6th Annual Foreign Bank Regulation Institute. Member, Executive Committee, American Branch, International Law Association, 1992-1994. (Managing Partner, New York Office) (New York, N.Y. Office). ***PRACTICE AREAS:*** Financial Institutions; Mergers and Acquisitions; Financial Institution Regulation; Corporate; Banking. ***Email:*** rbostrom@winston.com

(This Listing Continued)

WILLIAM A. ANDERSON, II, born Richmond, Virginia, January 9, 1947; admitted to bar, 1974, Virginia and U.S. Court of Appeals, Fourth, Tenth and District of Columbia Circuits; 2004, U.S. Supreme Court. *Education:* United States Air Force Academy; University of North Carolina (A.B., 1968); John F. Kennedy School of Government, Harvard University (M.P.P., 1973); Harvard University (J. D., cum laude, 1973). Phi Beta Kappa. *Member:* American Bar Association (Council, Section on Natural Resources, Energy and Environmental Law, 1981-1983; Liaison to Standing Committee on Environmental Law, 1983-1986; Chairman, Water Quality Committee, 1978-1980; Alternate, Coordinating Group on Regulatory Reform, 1981-1985; Liaison to Central and Eastern European Legal Initiative, 1990-1991; Co-Chair, Subcommittee on International Environmental Law, Environmental Controls Committee, Section of Business Law, 1990-2003; Member, Section on Administrative Law); Virginia State Bar (Environmental Law Section). (Washington, D.C. Office). ***PRACTICE AREAS:*** Environmental. ***Email:*** wanderso@winston.com

DANIEL R. MURDOCK, born New York, N.Y., August 15, 1937; admitted to bar, 1963, New York; 1964, U.S. District Court, Southern District of New York and U.S. Court of Appeals, Second Circuit; 1967, U.S. Supreme Court; 1969, U.S. District Court, Eastern District of New York; 1979, U.S. Court of Appeals, Fourth and Fifth Circuits; 1983, U.S. Court of Appeals, Eleventh Circuit; 1986, U.S. Court of Appeals, Ninth Circuit; U.S. Court of Appeals, First Circuit; 1999, U.S. Court of Appeals for the Federal Circuit. *Education:* Hamilton College (A.B., 1959); Harvard University (LL.B., 1962). Chief Assistant U.S. Attorney, Southern District of New York, 1976-1977. Assistant U.S. Attorney, 1963-1967. Trustee, Hamilton College, 1999-2003. *Member:* The Association of the Bar of the City of New York (Chair, Council on Judicial Administration, 2002-2005); New York State and American Bar Associations; Federal Bar Council. (New York, N.Y. Office). ***PRACTICE AREAS:*** Complex Litigation. ***Email:*** dmurdock@winston.com

JOAN B. TUCKER FIFE, born Knoxville, Tennessee, September 2, 1961; admitted to bar, 1986, Virginia; 1987, District of Columbia; 1989, California, U.S. Court of Appeals, Fourth and Eleventh Circuits, U.S. Court of Appeals for the District of Columbia Circuit, U.S. District Court, Eastern and Western Districts of Virginia, U.S. District Court, Central and Northern Districts of California and U.S. Supreme Court. *Education:* Northwestern University (B.A., 1983); Vanderbilt University (J.D., 1986). *Member:* State Bar of California; Virginia State Bar; The District of Columbia Bar. (San Francisco, California Office). ***PRACTICE AREAS:*** Employment Litigation; Employment Law; Title VII Discrimination; Sexual Harassment; Employment Disability Discrimination; Americans with Disabilities Act; Age Discrimination in Employment; Race Discrimination; Sex Discrimination; ERISA Class Actions; Whistleblower Litigation; Class Action Defense; Wage and Hour Litigation. ***Email:*** jfife@winston.com

WILLIAM A. KAPELL, born New York, N.Y., October 18, 1959; admitted to bar, 1986, New York and U.S. District Court, Southern and Eastern Districts of New York. *Education:* University of Pennsylvania (B.A., cum laude, 1981); Fordham University (J.D., 1985). *Member:* American Bar Association. (New York, N.Y. Office). ***Email:*** wkapell@winston.com

CATHERINE WOZNIAK JOYCE, born Chicago, Illinois, February 2, 1962; admitted to bar, 1988, Illinois. *Education:* Loyola University (B.B.A., summa cum laude, 1983); Loyola Law School (J.D., magna cum laude, 1988). Member, Loyola Law Review. Certified Public Accountant, Illinois, 1983. ***LANGUAGES:*** Italian. ***PRACTICE AREAS:*** Commercial Litigation; White Collar Criminal Defense. ***Email:*** cjoyce@winston.com

W. PAUL BISHOP, born February 14, 1948; admitted to bar, 1974, Georgia; 1977, District of Columbia; 1993, France. *Education:* University of Virginia (B.A., 1970); University of Georgia (J.D., 1974); George Washington University (M.S.A., 1977). Lecturer, Business Law, Boston University Graduate Business School, Brussels. *Member:* Paris Bar Association (Avocat); State Bar of Georgia; The District of Columbia Bar. [2nd Lt. Medical Service Corps, U.S. Army, 1971]. (Paris, France Office). ***LANGUAGES:*** French. ***PRACTICE AREAS:*** International Corporate Law; Business Law; Commercial Law; International Arbitration. ***Email:*** pbishop@winston.com

CAROL A. JOFFE, born Roslyn, New York, October 19, 1950; admitted to bar, 1979, Massachusetts; 1980, Maryland; 1981, District of Columbia. *Education:* Wheaton College (A.B., cum laude, with honors in Philosophy, 1972); Northeastern University (J.D., 1979). Mediator, Civil Division, Superior Court, District of Columbia. (Washington, D.C. Office). ***PRACTICE AREAS:*** Civil Litigation. ***Email:*** cjoffe@winston.com

CHARLES B. MOLSTER, III, born Richmond, Virginia, March 11, 1956; admitted to bar, 1984, Virginia; 1985, District of Columbia. *Education:* University of Virginia (B.A., 1979); University of Richmond (J.D., 1983). Law Clerk, Hon. James C. Cacheris, U.S. District Court, Eastern District of Virginia, Alexandria Division, 1983-1984. *Member:* The District of Columbia Bar; American Bar Association; Virginia State Bar; Virginia Trial Lawyers Association. (Washington, D.C. Office). ***REPORTED CASES:*** Hadeed v. Medic 24, 237 Va. 277, 377 S.E. 2d 589 (1989); Unlimited Screw Products v. MALM, et al., 781 F.Supp. 1121 (E.D. Va. 1991); Smith v. Allstate, 241 Va. 477, 403 S.E. 2d 696 (1991); Crowley v. NATA, 691 A.2d 1169 (D.C. App. 1997). ***PRACTICE AREAS:*** Complex Commercial Litigation; Business Litigation; Antitrust Litigation; Trade Secrets Litigation; False Advertising Litigation; Patent Litigation; Employment Defense. ***Email:*** cmolster@winston.com

STANFORD J. GOLDBLATT, born Chicago, Illinois, February 25, 1939; admitted to bar, 1963, Illinois. *Education:* Harvard University (B.A., magna cum laude, 1960; LL.B., magna cum laude, 1963). Author: "The Teaching Hospital under Medicare: A Prejudiced Position," Health Care Management Review, 4:3:67, Summer 1979; "The Medicare Sec-

(This Listing Continued)

tion 223 Schedule of Limits: A Continuing Struggle," Health Care Management Review 5:2:35, Spring 1980; "New Tax Law Hobbles Tax-Exempt Hospitals," Trustee, March 1982; "Avoiding Problems in Hospital-Physician Joint Ventures," Health Care Financial Management 38:2:88 February 1984. Law Clerk to Judge John M. Wisdom, U.S. Court of Appeals, Fifth Circuit, 1963-1964. ***PRACTICE AREAS:*** Corporate Law; Private Finance; Venture Capital; Business Transactions; Buying and Selling of Business; Entrepreneurial Business Law; Closely Held Corporations; Corporate Finance; Corporate Organization; Corporate Planning; Corporate Reorganization; Family Corporations; S Corporations; Investment Partnerships. ***Email:*** sgoldblatt@winston.com

MICHAEL S. MELBINGER, born Chicago, Illinois, September 5, 1958; admitted to bar, 1983, Illinois. *Education:* University of Notre Dame (B.A., 1980); University of Illinois (J.D., 1983). Author: "Executive Compensation," Commerce Clearing House, 2004; "Compliance Guide for Employee Benefit Trusts," American Bankers Association, Washington, D.C., 1997; "Protecting Yourself from the Tax on Excess Parachute Payments," Compensation & Benefits Management, Spring 2002; "Excess Pension Plan Assets Can Be Put to Various Uses," Practical Tax Strategies, October 2001; "Cross-Testing Final Regs. Validate New Comparability Plans," Tax Strategies, September 2001; "Why Not a Bill of Rights for Health Plan Sponsors?" Pension & Benefits Week, August 2001"; "Pack Tax Deductions into Employee Relocation Programs," Tax Strategies, July 2001; "Insurer Demutualizations Create Tax and ERISA Issues for Benefit Plans," Tax Strategies, March 2000; "Health Plan Compliance Gets Tougher Due to HIPAA," Benefit Plan Compliance, CCH Incorporated, June, 1997: "Stock-Based Executive Pay Plans Offer Choices," Taxation for Accountants, May, 1996; "What Your Plan Participants Know Could Hurt You," Profit Sharing, March, 1996; "Cases Highlight New Areas of Fiduciary Liability," Pension Management, October, 1995; "Gaining Assess to Excess Pension Assets," Pension Management, August, 1995; "Are You Acting As A Fiduciary," Pension Management, February, 1995; "Performance-Based Compensation Exception Increases in Importance," Journal of Taxation of Employee Benefits, November, 1994; "Avoiding Litigation Over Managed Health Care Decisions," Risk Management, October, 1994; "Stock Compensation Plans Get A Boost from RRA '93," Taxation for Accountants, November, 1993; "The Battle of the Rust Belt: Employers' Rights to Modify the Medical Benefits of Retirees," DePaul University Business Law Journal, February, 1993; "Supreme Court Protects Retirement Benefits from Creditors," Taxation for Lawyers, November, 1992; "The Maintenance, Funding and Modification of Retiree Medical Benefits," Employee Benefits Journal, September, 1992; "Rewarding Executives with Stock and Stock Value Arrangements," Taxation for Accountants, Taxation for Lawyers, May, 1992; "The High Stakes of Employee Benefit Plan Miscommunications," Journal of Compensation and Benefits, March, 1992; "Insurance Company Insolvency and Retirement Plans," Tax Management Compensation Planning Journal, October, 1991; "FASB Issues Statement on Employers' Account for Post-Retirement Medical Benefits," Tax Management Compensation Planning Journal, April 5, 1991; "Employee Benefits Plans and Corporate Transactions: Potential Liabilities," Employee Relations Law Journal, Spring, 1988. Adjunct Professor, Northwestern Universtiy School of Law. *Member:* American Bar Association; American College of Employee Benefit Counsel. ***PRACTICE AREAS:*** Executive Compensation; Employee Benefits; ERISA.

BRUCE R. BRAUN, born New Castle, Pennsylvania, May 3, 1963; admitted to bar, 1991, Illinois. *Education:* Haverford College (B.A., History, 1985); University of Virginia (J.D., 1989). Law Clerk, Chief Justice William H. Rehnquist, United States Supreme Court, October Term, 1990; Law Clerk, Judge Joel M. Flaum, United States Court of Appeals for the Seventh Circuit, 1989-1990; Editor in Chief, Virginia Law Review. Order of the Coif. Vinson & Elkins Scholarship (highest property law grade). CJS Award (Highest first year GPA). Selected for The American Lawyer's 45 Under 45: The Rising Stars of the Private Bar (2003). Selected, 40 Top Attorneys in Illinois to Watch Under the Age of 40, Chicago Lawyer (2000). Adjunct Professor of Law, Northwestern University School of Law, 2001—. Lecturer, Appellate Advocacy, Loyola University, 1992-1996. Recipient, Burton Award for Excellent in Legal Writing (2001). Author: "www.commercial_terrorism.com: A Proposed Federal Criminal Statute Addressing the Solicitation of Commercial Terrorism Through the Internet," 37 Harvard Journal of Legislation 159, Winter, 2000; "The Arbitration of Federal Domestic Antitrust Claims: How Safe is the American Safety Doctrine?" 16 Pepperdine L. Rev. S201, 1989; "Getting What You Paid For: The Judicial Cap on Attorney's Fees For Representing the Condemned Before the Supreme Court," 69 N.Y.U. L. Rev. 1014, 1994; "The Legal Legacy of John Wayne Gacy: The Irrebuttable Presumption That Jurors Understand Their Instructions," 78 Marquette L. Rev. 791, 1995; "Free at Last: Reflections on the Representation of a Death Row Inmate," Litigation, Winter, 1996; "Capital Pro Bono Demand is Up," The National Law Journal, August 19, 1996; "Litigating the Yankee Tax: Application of the Lodestar to Attorney's Fee Awards in Common Fund Litigation," 23 Florida State L. Rev. 897, 1996; "Trial Balloon: Life, Death, and Organ Donation Litigation," Summer 1998. ***REPORTED CASES:*** State of New York v. Microsoft (D.D.C. 2002)(Antitrust remedy trial); Hays v. General Electric, Co., 151 F. Supp.2d 1001 (N.D. Ill. 2001); Free v. Peters, 12 F.3d 700 (1993); F.J. Vollmer v. United States, 1 F.3d 1511 (7th Cir., 1993); Rostenkowski v. United States, 59 F.3d 1291 (D.C. Cir., 1995); Department of Revenue v. Kuhnlein, 646 So.2d 717 (Fla., 1994); St. Paul Marine v. Arntz, 54 Cal. Rptr. 2d 888 (1996); RTC v. Gallagher, 10 F.3d 46 (7th Cir., 1993); Harris v. Roderick, 126 F.3d 1189 (9th Cir., 1997); Heller v. Sharp, 974 F.2d 850 (7th Cir., 1992); Williams v. Continental Stock, 1 F.Supp. 836 (N.D. Ill. 1998); Owens Corning v. McClure, 188 IL.2d 102, 720 N.E.2d 242 (1999); Weiss v. Cooley, 230 F.3d 1027 (7th Cir. 2000); Spain v. Owens Corning, 710 N.E.2d 528 (Ill. 1999). ***PRACTICE AREAS:*** General Commercial Litigation; White Collar Criminal Defense; Appellate Practice. ***Email:*** bbraun@winston.com

RONALD H. JACOBSON, born Chicago, Illinois, July 23, 1963; admitted to bar, 1988, Illinois. *Education:* University of Illinois (B.A., with honors, 1985); Loyola University, Chicago (J.D., with honors, 1988); J.L. Kellogg Graduate School of Management, Northwestern University (M.B.A., with honors, 1990). Managing Editor, Loyola Law Journal, 1987-1988. Listed in Chamber's Global: The World's Leading Lawyers and Chamber's USA: America's Leading Lawyers for Business. Co-Author, "The Senior Debt Evolution: A Comparative Analysis of the Cash Flow CLO and the Synthetic Total Return Structure," Journal of Structured Finance, Summer 2005. Co-Presenter: Gold Sheets Corporate Finance Conferences, 2004 and 2005; Loan Syndication and Trading Association Conference, 2004. Member, Winston & Strawn Income Partner Compensation Committee, Associate Evaluation Committee, Billings and Collections Committee and Corporate Associate Training Program. Member, Executive Fund Raising Committee, Boy Scouts of America.

(This Listing Continued)

Member: American Bar Association (Business Law Section); Commercial Finance Association (Member, Founders Leadership Council); Loan Syndications and Trading Association; Association for Corporate Growth; Turnaround Management Association. ***PRACTICE AREAS:*** Banking Law; Corporate Law; Finance Law; Mergers, Acquisitions and Divestitures. ***Email:*** rjacobson@winston.com

ROBERT L. MICHELS, born Chicago, Illinois, January 24, 1963; admitted to bar, 1988, Illinois, U.S. District Court, Northern District of Illinois and U.S. Court of Appeals, Seventh Circuit. *Education:* University of Notre Dame (B.B.A., 1985); DePaul University (J.D., with honors, 1988). Judicial Clerk, Hon. Nicholas J. Bua, U.S. District Court, Northern District of Illinois, 1988-1990. Assistant U.S. Attorney, Chicago, Illinois, 1990-1995. ***PRACTICE AREAS:*** Commercial Litigation; White Collar Criminal Defense Law. ***Email:*** rmichels@winston.com

TIMOTHY P. O'CONNOR, born Chicago, Illinois, Jun 27, 1964; admitted to bar, 1989, Illinois and U.S. District Court, Northern District of Illinois; 1990, U.S. Court of Appeals, Seventh Circuit; 1993, U.S. District Court, Northern District of Illinois Trial Bar. *Education:* University of Illinois (B.A., cum laude with highest distinction in history, 1986); University of Michigan (J.D., cum laude, 1989). Phi Beta Kappa. ***PRACTICE AREAS:*** Commercial Litigation; Criminal Defense Law. ***Email:*** toconnor@winston.com

RONALD J. NYE, born May 11, 1964; admitted to bar, 1989, Illinois. *Education:* University of Notre Dame (B.B.A., with highest honors, 1986); University of Virginia (J.D., 1989). ***PRACTICE AREAS:*** Business Transactions; Leveraged Leasing; Lease Finance; Mergers and Acquisitions. ***Email:*** rnye@winston.com

PATRICK M. HARDIMAN, born Bridgeport, Connecticut, May 17, 1961; admitted to bar, 1987, Illinois. *Education:* University of Illinois (B.S., Finance, with high honors, 1983; M.B.A., 1987; J.D., cum laude, 1987). Co-Author, "The Senior Debt Evolution: A Comparative Analysis of the Cash Flow CLO and the Synthetic Total Return Structure," The Journal of Structured Finance, Summer 2005. Speaker: Gold Sheets Corporate Finance Conference, 2005; Loan Syndications and Trading Association Board Conference, 2004. *Member:* American Bar Association. ***PRACTICE AREAS:*** Corporate Law; Banks and Banking; Finance; Investments; Capital Markets; Derivative Products; International Capital Markets; Investment Management; Mezzanine Finance; Mutual Funds; Syndication; Structured Finance. ***Email:*** phardiman@winston.com

BRIAN T. BLACK, born St. Louis, Missouri, July 30, 1960; admitted to bar, 1989, Illinois. *Education:* University of Illinois (B.S.); Washington University (J.D.). ***PRACTICE AREAS:*** Public Offerings; Private Placement; Mergers and Acquisitions; Partnership Law. ***Email:*** bblack@winston.com

JAMES F. HURST, born Philadelphia, Pennsylvania, January 22, 1964; admitted to bar, 1989, Illinois; 1991, U.S. District Court, Northern District of Illinois, including Trial Bar; 1993, U.S. Court of Appeals, Seventh and Federal Circuits; 1999, U.S. Court of Appeals, District of Columbia Circuit; 2000, U.S. Supreme Court. *Education:* University of Delaware (B.S., magna cum laude); University of Pennsylvania (J.D., cum laude). Adjunct Professor, Appellate Advocacy, Northwestern University Law School; Selected in 2002 by the Chicago Law Bulletin as one of the 40 Illinois Attorneys Under 40 To Watch; Law Clerk, Hon. Marvin E. Aspen of the Northern District of Illinois; Moot Court Team Member; Associate Editor, Comparative Labor Law Journal; Author: "Understanding and Avoiding Corporate and Executive Criminal Liability," 49 The Business Lawyer 617, 1994; "Limiting Public Corruption Prosecutions Under The Hobbs Act: Will *United States v. Evans* be the Next *McNally?*," Chicago-Kent Law 29, 1992. ***REPORTED CASES:*** Eli Lilly and Co. v. Barr Laboratories, Inc., 251 F.3d 955 (Fed. Cir. 2001); Minnesota Mining And Mfg. Co. v. Barr Laboratories, Inc. --- F.3d ---, 2002 WL 826930 (Fed. Cir. 2002); Medeva Pharmaceuticals Mfg., Inc. v. Morton Grove Pharmaceuticals, Inc., 174 F. Supp.2d 802 (N.D.Ill. 2001). ***PRACTICE AREAS:*** Civil Litigation; Patent Litigation. ***Email:*** jhurst@winston.com

DAVID E. KOROPP, born Oak Park, Illinois, 1964; admitted to bar, 1989, Illinois; 1993, U.S. District Court, Northern District of Illinois, including Trial Bar; 1996, U.S. Court of Appeals, Seventh Circuit; 1997, U.S. Court of Appeals, Tenth Circuit. *Education:* University of Illinois, Urbana (B.A., 1986); University of Illinois (J.D., summa cum laude, 1989). Order of the Coif. Associate Editor, University of Illinois Law Review. ***PRACTICE AREAS:*** Commercial Litigation; Health Care Litigation; Media Law; Products Liability. ***Email:*** dkoropp@winston.com

KATHLEEN ANN SWIEN, admitted to bar, 1989, Illinois. *Education:* University of Michigan (A.B., 1979); University of Detroit (J.D., 1989); Loyola University at Chicago (Visiting Student, 1988-1989). Member, University of Detroit Law Review, 1987-1988. ***PRACTICE AREAS:*** Real Property; Real Estate Finance. ***Email:*** kswien@winston.com

ERIC J. MARCOTTE, born Pawtucket, Rhode Island, November 11, 1957; admitted to bar, 1988, Texas; 1993, U.S. Court of Appeals for the Federal Circuit; 1995, District of Columbia; 1997, U.S. District Court for the District of Columbia. *Education:* Park College (B.S., magna cum laude, 1982); University of Texas (J.D., with honors, 1987). *Member:* State Bar of Texas; The District of Columbia Bar; American Bar Association (Member, Public Contract Law Section, 1991—). [with U.S.A.F., 1979-1993; Air National Guard, 1993-2003; Lieutenant Colonel (ret.)]. (Washington, D.C. Office). ***PRACTICE AREAS:*** Government Contracts; Construction Law; Commercial Law. ***Email:*** emarcott@winston.com

VINCENT D. SALVATORE, JR., born Jakarta, Indonesia, June 29, 1954; admitted to bar, 1980, New York and U.S. District Court, Southern and Eastern Districts of New York; 1997, District of Columbia. *Education:* Dartmouth College (B.A., summa cum laude, 1976); Harvard University (J.D., 1979). Phi Beta Kappa. *Member:* Bar Association of the District of Columbia; American Bar Association; Washington Foreign Law Society. (Washington, D.C. Office). ***LANGUAGES:*** French and Italian. ***PRACTICE AREAS:*** International Project Finance; Structured Finance; Energy Finance; Renewable Energy. ***Email:*** vsalvatore@winston.com

BRADLEY E. LERMAN, born Chicago, Illinois, June 18, 1956; admitted to bar, 1981, District of Columbia; 1996, Illinois. *Education:* Yale University (B.A., summa cum laude, 1978); Harvard University (J.D., cum laude, 1981). Phi Beta Kappa. Adjunct Professor of

(This Listing Continued)

WINSTON & STRAWN LLP, Chicago—Continued

Law, Northwestern University School of Law, 1988-1994. ***PRACTICE AREAS:*** Complex Commercial Litigation; White Collar Defense; Products Liability. ***Email:*** blerman@winston.com

CHRISTOPH C. HEISENBERG, born Munich, Germany, June 30, 1965; admitted to bar, 1990, Massachusetts; 1991, New York; 1993, U.S. District Court, Southern District of New York; 1994, U.S. District Court, Eastern District of New York and U.S. Court of Appeals, Ninth Circuit; 1995, U.S. Court of Appeals, Second Circuit; 1996, U.S. District Court, District of Massachusetts. *Education:* University of New Hampshire (B.A., cum laude, 1987); Boston College (J.D., 1990). (New York, N.Y. Office). ***LANGUAGES:*** German. ***Email:*** cheisenberg@winston.com

DAVID B. LOVE, born Royal Oak, Michigan, October 23, 1956; admitted to bar, 1980, Illinois and U.S. District Court, Northern District of Illinois; 1985, U.S. Court of Appeals, Seventh Circuit; 1987, U.S. Court of Appeals, Tenth Circuit; 1989, U.S. Court of Appeals, Ninth Circuit; 2000, U.S. Court of Appeals, Eighth Circuit; 2003, U.S. Supreme Court. *Education:* Northwestern University (B.A., cum laude, 1977); University of Michigan (J.D., cum laude, 1980). ***PRACTICE AREAS:*** Litigation. ***Email:*** dlove@winston.com

MARY E. WALL, born Boston, Massachusetts; admitted to bar, 1986, District of Columbia, Virginia, U.S. Court of Appeals, Fourth and Fifth Circuits and U.S. Court of Appeals for the District of Columbia Circuit. *Education:* University of Massachusetts (B.S., cum laude, 1977); George Washington University (J.D., 1986). *Member:* The Virginia State Bar; American Bar Association; Women's Council on Energy and the Environment (Past President and Director). (Washington, D.C. Office). ***PRACTICE AREAS:*** Environmental Law; Environmental Compliance; Environmental Due Diligence; Environmental Insurance; Environmental Lender Liability; Environmental Permitting; Environmental Risk Management. ***Email:*** mwall@winston.com

JACK CROWE, born Chicago, Illinois, June 20, 1960; admitted to bar, 1989, Illinois; 1990, U.S. District Court, Northern District of Illinois, U.S. District Court, Northern District of Michigan and U.S. Court of Appeals, Seventh Circuit. *Education:* Boston College (B.A., cum laude, 1982); State University of New York at Buffalo; Loyola University (J.D., 1989). Symposium Editor, Loyola Law Journal, 1988-1989. Staff Attorney, Seventh Circuit Court of Appeals, 1989-1991. Law Clerk to the Honorable Ilana Rovner, U.S. District Court, Northern District of Illinois, 1991-1992 and Seventh Circuit Court of Appeals, 1992. Adjunct Faculty Member, Appellate Advocacy, Loyola University of Chicago, School of Law, 1990-1995. ***LANGUAGES:*** French. ***PRACTICE AREAS:*** Complex Litigation; Insurance Coverage; Securities Litigation; Mass Tort. ***Email:*** jcrowe@winston.com

SUSAN W. DREWKE, born Buffalo, New York, March 7, 1958; admitted to bar, 1990, Illinois. *Education:* Michigan State University; University of Illinois at Chicago (B.A., 1987); DePaul University College of Law (J.D., with honors, 1990). Order of the Coif. Staff Member, 1988-1989 and Article and Note Editor, 1989-1990, DePaul Law Review. *Member:* Chicago, Illinois State and American Bar Associations. ***PRACTICE AREAS:*** Trusts and Estate Litigation; Estate Planning and Administration. ***Email:*** sdrewke@winston.com

BRADLEY C. GRAVELINE, born Virginia, Minnesota, September 10, 1965; admitted to bar, 1990, Illinois, U.S. District Court, Northern District of Illinois and U.S. Court of Appeals, Seventh and Federal Circuits. *Education:* Depauw University (B.A., 1987); Northwestern University (J.D., 1990). Coordinating Note and Comment Editor, Journal of Criminal Law and Criminology, 1990. ***PRACTICE AREAS:*** Complex Commercial Litigation. ***Email:*** bgraveline@winston.com

ALEXIS MacDOWALL, born Brampton, Ontario, Canada, August 24, 1964; admitted to bar, 1989, Illinois, U.S. District Court, Northern District of Illinois, U.S. Court of Appeals, Seventh and Federal Circuits and U.S. Supreme Court. *Education:* University of Iowa (B.A. with honors, 1986; J.D., 1989). Phi Beta Kappa. Fellow, Leadership Greater Chicago, 2001-2002. Member, Mortar Board. Law Clerk to the Honorable George Marovich, U.S. District Court, Northern District of Illinois, 1998. Adjunct Faculty Member, Trial Advocacy, Northwestern University School of Law, 2000—. Board of Directors: AIDS Legal Counsel; YWCA. Board Member: The Children's Place; Chicago Counsel on Foreign Relations. *Member:* Chicago and American Bar Associations. ***LANGUAGES:*** French. ***PRACTICE AREAS:*** Products Liability; Patent Infringement; Complex Civil Litigation. ***Email:*** amacdowa@winston.com

DON JOSEPH MIZERK, born Chicago, Illinois, July 30, 1963; admitted to bar, 1988, Illinois; 2000, California; U.S. District Court, Northern District of Illinois, including Trial Bar, U.S. Court of Appeals, Sixth, Seventh and Federal Circuits and U.S. Supreme Court. *Education:* Illinois Wesleyan University (B.A., 1985); Vanderbilt University (J.D., 1988). Member, 1986-1988 and Senior Articles Editor, Vanderbilt Law Review. *Member:* Federal Circuit Bar Association. ***PRACTICE AREAS:*** Complex Commercial Litigation; Civil Litigation; Patent Litigation. ***Email:*** dmizerk@winston.com

KEVIN J. NARKO, born Chicago, Illinois, March 19, 1964; admitted to bar, 1989, Illinois, U.S. District Court, Northern District of Illinois and U.S. Court of Appeals, Third, Sixth, Seventh, Eighth and Eleventh Circuits. *Education:* University of Illinois (A.B., 1986); Northwestern University (J.D., 1989). Member, 1987-1989 and Articles Editor, 1988-1989, Northwestern Journal of International Law and Business. *Member:* Chicago, Seventh Circuit and American Bar Associations. ***PRACTICE AREAS:*** Complex Litigation; Civil Litigation. ***Email:*** knarko@winston.com

CHERYL TAMA OBLANDER, admitted to bar, 1988, Illinois; 1989, U.S. District Court, Northern and Central Districts of Illinois, U.S. District Court, Eastern District of Wisconsin and U.S. Court of Appeals, Seventh and Eleventh Circuits. *Education:* Southern Illinois University (B.A., 1980); Loyola University (J.D., 1988). *Member:* American Bar Association; National Association of Women Lawyers. ***PRACTICE AREAS:*** Labor and Employment; Bankruptcy. ***Email:*** ctama@winston.com

JOSEPH JAMES TORRES, *born Chicago, Illinois, April 22, 1963;* admitted to bar, 1990, Illinois, U.S. District Court, Northern and Central Districts of Illinois, U.S. Court of Appeals, Third, Sixth and Seventh Circuits and U.S. Supreme Court. *Education:* University of Chicago (B.A., 1985); University of Illinois (J.D., 1990). ***PRACTICE AREAS:*** Labor Law; Employment Law. ***Email:*** jtorres@winston.com

(This Listing Continued)

LOUISE REMBAR RADIN, born New York, N.Y.; admitted to bar, 1985, New York. *Education:* Harvard College (B.A., magna cum laude, 1976); Harvard Law School (J.D., 1984). Editor, Harvard Law Review. Law Clerk to Hon. Leonard I. Garth, U.S. Court of Appeals, Third Circuit, 1984-1985. Associate Counsel, Office of Independent Counsel (Iran/Contra), 1987-1991. Associate, Davis, Polk & Wardwell, 1986-1987; 1991-1995. *Member:* Association of the Bar of the City of New York (Member, Committee on Litigation, 1996-1999). (New York, N.Y. Office). ***LANGUAGES:*** French. ***PRACTICE AREAS:*** Complex Litigation; Civil Litigation; Securities Litigation; Corporate Investigations; White Collar Criminal Defense. ***Email:*** lradin@winston.com

LOREN A. WEIL, born Dayton, Ohio, April 21, 1961; admitted to bar, 1985, Ohio; 1988, Illinois. *Education:* Duke University (A.B., magna cum laude, 1982; J.D., 1985). ***PRACTICE AREAS:*** Debt Finance; Loan Restructuring. ***Email:*** lweil@winston.com

MATTHEW J. BOTICA, born Chicago, Illinois, January 11, 1951; admitted to bar, 1975, Illinois, U.S. District Court, Northern Districts of Illinois and Michigan and U.S. Court of Appeals, Seventh and Ninth Circuit. *Education:* Boston College (A.B., summa cum laude, 1972); Harvard University (J.D., 1975). Phi Beta Kappa. Member, American College of Bankruptcy, 1999. ***PRACTICE AREAS:*** Bankruptcy Reorganization; Secured Transactions; Bankruptcy Chapter 11; Out of Court Debt Restructuring. ***Email:*** mbotica@winston.com

MICHAEL L. BRODY, born Chicago, Illinois, July 29, 1952; admitted to bar, 1979, Illinois. *Education:* Wesleyan University (B.A., magna cum laude, 1974); University of Chicago (M.A., 1976; J.D., 1979). Phi Beta Kappa. *Member:* American Bar Association; American Intellectual Property Law Association. ***PRACTICE AREAS:*** Intellectual Property Litigation; Trial Practice; Federal Civil Litigation. ***Email:*** mbrody@winston.com

SUSAN F. KLEIN, born New York, N.Y., November 17, 1945; admitted to bar, 1971, New York. *Education:* Cornell University (B.S., 1967); Harvard Law School (J.D., cum laude, 1970). Assistant Professor, Taxation and International Law, Emory University, 1975-1978. Visiting Associate Professor, Taxation and International Law, Boston University School of Law, 1978-1979. *Member:* New York State (Vice Chairman, Tax Committee, International Section, 1988-1989) and American (Chairman, Canadian Law Committee, 1987-1990; Vice Chairman, Taxation Committee, 1990-1992, and Chairman, Taxation Committee, 1992-1994) Bar Associations; International Fiscal Association (Council, U.S. Branch, National Reporter, 1983 Congress; Executive Committee, U.S. Branch, 1997—); International Tax Association (President, 1983-1984). Fellow, American Bar Foundation. (New York, N.Y. Office). ***PRACTICE AREAS:*** Taxation; Private International Law. ***Email:*** sklein@winston.com

JOËL ALQUEZAR, born Dijon, France, May 16, 1952; admitted to bar, 1979, Paris. *Education:* Institut d'Études Politiques de Paris (Diploma, 1973); Faculté de Droit et des Sciences Economiques, University of Paris (D.E.A., Droit Fiscal, 1975; D.E.A., Sciences Économiques, 1977). Member, ICF. Former Professor, University of Paris. *Member:* Paris Bar Association (Member, Tax Committee, 1985-1990). (Paris, France Office). ***LANGUAGES:*** English, French and Spanish. ***PRACTICE AREAS:*** Complex Litigation; International Litigation; Business Arbitration; Business Litigation; Tax Litigation; International Arbitration. ***Email:*** jalqueza@winston.com

JAMES A. BEHA II, born New York, N.Y., July 3, 1949; admitted to bar, 1976, New York. *Education:* Princeton University (B.A., with high honors, 1971); Harvard University (M.A., 1974; J.D., magna cum laude, 1975; Ph.D, Sociology, 1986). Residency in Law and Social Science, Russell Sage Foundation, 1976. Special Consultant on Policy to New York City Criminal Justice Coordinating Council, 1978-1980. *Member:* The Association of the Bar of The City of New York (Chair, Committee on Legal Education and Admission to the Bar); New York State Bar Association (Member, Committee on Federal Procedure); New York County Lawyers Association (Member, Committee on Federal Courts). (New York, N.Y. Office). ***PRACTICE AREAS:*** Trial Practice; Commercial Litigation; Banking Litigation; Creditors Rights. ***Email:*** jbeha@winston.com

EDWARD G. H. CHIN, born Hong Kong, September 9, 1947; admitted to bar, 1978, New York; 1990, U.S. Supreme Court; registered to practice before U.S. Patent and Trademark Office (Not admitted in Illinois). *Education:* New York University (B.E., 1969; M.S., 1971); Fordham University (J.D., cum laude, 1977). Listed in the Guide to World's Leading Aviation Lawyers, Euromoney Legal Group, 1998, 2000, and 2002. Contributing Author: Negotiating Business Transactions, "Representing Buyers and Sellers in the Sale of Goods," Wiley Law Publications, 1989; Comment, "An Analysis and Review of School Financing Reform," 44 Fordham Law Review 773, 1976. *Member:* American Bar Association (Member, Section on Corporation, Banking and Business Law); New York County Lawyers Association. (New York, N.Y. Office). ***LANGUAGES:*** Mandarin and Cantonese. ***PRACTICE AREAS:*** Aircraft Finance and Leasing; Securities Offerings; Corporate Law. ***Email:*** echin@winston.com

STEVEN M. SCHWARTZ, born Queens, New York, September 9, 1962; admitted to bar, 1988, New York and U.S. District Court, Southern and Eastern Districts of New York; 1993, U.S. Court of Appeal, Second Circuit. *Education:* State University of New York at Binghamton (B.S., magna cum laude, 1984); Cornell University (J.D., magna cum laude, 1987). Order of the Coif. Editor, Cornell Law Review. *Member:* The Association of the Bar of the City of New York; New York State Bar Association; Federal Bar Council. (New York, N.Y. Office). ***PRACTICE AREAS:*** Commercial Litigation; Bankruptcy; Debtor and Creditor. ***Email:*** sschwart@winston.com

DAVID C. ROMM, born Washington, D.C., April 20, 1948; admitted to bar, 1977, Ohio; 1978, District of Columbia; 1990, Virginia. *Education:* University of Maryland (B.A., with high honors, 1973); The Ohio State University (J.D., 1977). Best Advocate, Moot Court Competition, 1977. Author: "Surety Bad Faith Claims-How to Avoid Them and How to Defend Them," Oct. 1993; "When Does the Owner Waive Its Right to Terminate the Principal for Default--How to Recognize a Waiver Against the Owner for the Non-Performing Principal, Or, How to Get Back Those Progress Payments," Northeast Surety & Fidelity Claims Conference, 1991; "Surety Recourse Against the Owner for the Non-Performance Principal, or, How to Get Back Those Progress Payments, Northeast Surety & Fidelity Claims Conference, 1991. Co-Author: "Construction Litigation Superconference," Andrews Publications, 1986-1989; "Owner Damages," American Construction Owners Association: Construction Owners Monograph Series, March 1986; "Recent Decisions Affecting Recovery of Home Office Overhead During Extended Performance Periods," Con-

(This Listing Continued)

struction Claims Monthly, August 1983. Speaker: National Association of Independent Sureties, West Palm Beach, 1999; Northeast Surety and Fidelity Claims Conference, 1991-1992; Construction Litigation, Super Conference 1986, Laguna Nigel, California and 1986 New York, New York; Seminar, University of Maryland "Successful Construction Claims Management," June and September 1982. *Member:* Ohio State and American (Member, Sections of: Surety and Fidelity; Public Contract Law; Litigation) Bar Associations; The District of Columbia Bar; Virginia State Bar. (Washington, D.C. Office). ***PRACTICE AREAS:*** Surety; Construction; Government Contracts; Civil Litigation. ***Email:*** dromm@winston.com

GARRY R. BOEHLERT, born Flushing, New York, January 30, 1956; admitted to bar, 1981, Virginia. *Education:* University of Virginia (B.A., with distinction, 1978); Marshall-Wythe School of Law, College of William and Mary (J.D., 1981). Law Clerk, Armed Services Board of Contract Appeals, 1980. Co-Author and Lecturer: "Public and Private Infrastructure Development," Federal Publications, 1996; Panelist, "The Future of Privatization," Federal Publications, 1996, Construction Contracts Year-in-Review. Author: "Building for the Government at a Profit: Public-Private Partnering," Virginia Business Law Journal, 1996. *Member:* Virginia State Bar. (Washington, D.C. Office). ***PRACTICE AREAS:*** Construction; Government Contracts; Litigation; Public-Private Development. ***Email:*** gboehler@winston.com

MANES M. MERRIT, born New York, N.Y., December 5, 1950; admitted to bar, 1977, North Carolina; 1978, New York and District of Columbia; 1979, U.S. Tax Court and U.S. Supreme Court. *Education:* University of Wisconsin (B.A., with distinction, 1972); New York University (M.B.A., 1975); Wake Forest University (J.D., 1977). *Member:* New York State and American Bar Associations; District of Columbia Bar; North Carolina State Bar. (New York, N.Y. Office). ***PRACTICE AREAS:*** Employee Benefits; Executive Compensation; Employee Stock Ownership Plans; Qualified Retirement Plans; Non-Qualified Retirement Plans; Health and Welfare Plans. ***Email:*** mmerrit@winston.com

STUART ALTSCHULER, born New York, N.Y., February 25, 1954; admitted to bar, 1979, New York; 1982, Illinois. *Education:* Princeton University (A.B., magna cum laude, 1975); Cornell University (J.D., cum laude, 1978); Oxford University. Managing Editor, Cornell Law Review, 1977-1978. ***PRACTICE AREAS:*** Complex Litigation. ***Email:*** saltschuler@winston.com

MARY PATRICIA BENZ, born Chicago, Illinois, April 18, 1951; admitted to bar, 1978, Illinois and U.S. District Court, Northern District of Illinois; 1996, U.S. District Court, Central District of Illinois. *Education:* Michigan State University; University of Illinois (B.A., 1973); Northwestern University (J.D., magna cum laude, 1978). Order of the Coif. Instructor, Legal Writing, Northwestern University School of Law, 1977-1978. Adjunct Professor of Law, Northwestern University School of Law, Trial Practice, 1989—. Instructor, National Institute of Trial Advocacy. *Member:* Chicago, Illinois State and Federal Bar Associations; Illinois Association of Defense Trial Counsel; Defense Research Institute; Women's Bar Association of Illinois; Appellate Lawyers Association. ***PRACTICE AREAS:*** Commercial Litigation; Products Liability Law; Insurance Law; ERISA Litigation; Civil Litigation; Civil Appeals. ***Email:*** mbenz@winston.com

TIMOTHY J. OXLEY, born Tokyo, Japan, July 9, 1953; admitted to bar, 1980, Illinois. *Education:* Wheaton College (B.A., 1975); John Marshall Law School (J.D., 1980). Managing Editor, John Marshall Law Review. ***LANGUAGES:*** Japanese. ***PRACTICE AREAS:*** Distribution Agreements; Commercial Credit; Commercial Loans; Loans; Business Formation; Business Organization; Buying and Selling of Business; International Business Law; International Joint Ventures; Joint Ventures; Limited Liability Company Law; Commercial Transactions; Sale of Goods; Secured Transactions; Uniform Commercial Code; Software Licensing; Commercial Contracts; International Commercial Contracts; International Contracts; Corporate Commercial Law; Corporate Contracts; Corporate Formation; Employment Contracts; Lease Finance; Technology Joint Ventures; Technology Licensing. ***Email:*** toxley@winston.com

E. KING POOR, born Flint, Michigan, February 8, 1954; admitted to bar, 1980, Illinois. *Education:* Dartmouth College (A.B., cum laude, with high distinction, 1976); Emory University (J.D., 1979). Instructor, National Institute of Trial Advocacy. Author: "Utility Rates Pending Judicial Review: A Riddle Wrapped in a Mystery in Illinois," 17 John Marshall L. Rev. 743 (1984). Assistant Illinois Attorney General, Illinois Commerce Commission Division, 1980-1984. ***PRACTICE AREAS:*** Civil Litigation; Appellate; Creditors Rights. ***Email:*** kpoor@winston.com

MARIE A. LONA, born St. Louis, Missouri, June 21, 1966; admitted to bar, 1991, Illinois. *Education:* Northwestern University (B.A., Psychology, with distinction, 1988); Stanford University (J.D., 1991). *Member:* Chicago, Illinois State and American (Member, Litigation Committee, Women's Advocate Subcommittee, Minority Trial Lawyer Subcommittee and First Amendment and Media Litigation Subcommittee, Forum on Communications Law) Bar Associations. ***PRACTICE AREAS:*** Litigation; Libel, Slander and Defamation; Securities; Professional Liability; White Collar Crime. ***Email:*** mlona@winston.com

SAMUEL MENDENHALL, born Chicago, Illinois, July 14, 1964; admitted to bar, 1991, Illinois. *Education:* University of Illinois (B.A., 1988; J.D., 1991). ***PRACTICE AREAS:*** Commercial Litigation; Products Liability; Insurance Coverage Disputes. ***Email:*** smendehn@winston.com

GRACE L. SHAFF, born Clinton, Iowa, July 21, 1966; admitted to bar, 1991, Illinois. *Education:* Northwestern University (B.A., 1988); University of Iowa (J.D., 1991). *Member:* Chicago and American Bar Associations. ***PRACTICE AREAS:*** Corporate Law. ***Email:*** gshaff@winston.com

COLLEEN T. SHAUGHNESSY, born Chicago, Illinois, June 21, 1966; admitted to bar, 1991, Illinois. *Education:* University of Illinois (B.S., 1988); DePaul University (J.D., 1991). ***Email:*** cshaughnessy@winston.com

JEFFREY M. WAGNER, born Chicago, Illinois, July 9, 1962; admitted to bar, 1988, Illinois and U.S. District Court, Northern District of Illinois; 1991, U.S. Court of Appeals, Seventh Circuit; 1995, U.S. Court of Appeals, Eleventh Circuit; 2001, U.S. Court of Appeals, Second Circuit; 2002, U.S. Court of Appeals, Fifth Circuit. *Education:* University of Redlands (B.A., magna cum laude, 1984); University of Chicago (M.A., 1986; J.D., 1988). Omicron Delta Kappa. Member, University of Chicago Legal Forum, 1987-1988. *Member:* Chicago and American Bar Associations. ***PRACTICE AREAS:*** Litigation; Business Law; Commercial Law; Complex and Multi-District Litigation; Products Liability; RICO; Securities; Toxic Torts. ***Email:*** jwagner@winston.com

JOSEPH J. ZAKNOEN, born Michigan City, Indiana, March 24, 1960; admitted to bar, 1991, Illinois, U.S. District Court, Northern District of Illinois and U.S. Court of Appeals, Sixth and Seventh Circuits. *Education:* Indiana University (B.A., magna cum laude, 1988; J.D., cum laude, 1991). *Member:* Illinois State Bar Association. ***PRACTICE AREAS:*** Litigation. ***Email:*** jzaknoen@winston.com

RAYMOND B. WUSLICH, born Hochwaldhausen, Germany, October 9, 1959; admitted to bar, 1988, Pennsylvania; 1989, District of Columbia. *Education:* University of Pittsburgh (B.A., 1981; M.P.I.A., 1986); American University, Washington College of Law (J.D., 1988). Senior Note and Comment Editor, The American University Law Review, 1987-1988. Law Clerk, Honorable Malcolm Muir, U.S. District Court, Middle District of Pennsylvania, 1988-1989. *Member:* The District of Columbia Bar; Pennsylvania and Energy Bar Associations. (Washington, D.C. Office). ***PRACTICE AREAS:*** Energy Law; Litigation. ***Email:*** rwuslich@winston.com

JOËLLE HERSCHTEL, born Neuilly, France, January 29, 1963; admitted to bar, 1988, Paris. *Education:* University of Paris X (Maîtrise en Droit, 1985; Diplome D'Etudes Approfondies de Droit des Affaires, 1987; German Licence, 1987); Institut d'Etudes Politiques de Paris (Diplome, 1986). (Paris, France Office). ***LANGUAGES:*** French, English and German. ***PRACTICE AREAS:*** Environmental Law; Business Law. ***Email:*** jherscht@winston.com

LEE T. PATERSON, born Washington, D.C., September 26, 1941; admitted to bar, 1967, California, U.S. District Court, Northern District of California and U.S. Court of Appeals, Ninth Circuit; 1979, U.S. Supreme Court; 1988, U.S. Court of Appeals, District of Columbia Circuit; 1989, U.S. District Court, Central District of California; 1992, U.S. Court of Appeals, Eighth Circuit; 2002 Hawaii and U.S. District Court, District of Hawaii. *Education:* St. Mary's College of California; Oregon State University (B.A., 1964; B.S., 1964); University of California at Los Angeles (J.D., 1967). Author: *California Unemployment Insurance Guide,* Parker Publications, 1990; *Cobra Compliance Manual,* J.W. Wiley, 1990; *Documenting Employee Discipline,* Parker Publications, 1988; *Employer's Compliance Review,* Parker Publications, 1992; *Employer's Wage Manual,* Parker Publications, 1992; *Employment Compliance Audit—California,* Parker Publications, 1989; *Federal Workplace Posters,* Parker Publications, 1989; *Mandatory Workplace Posters in California,* Parker Publications, 1988; *Negotiating Employee Resignations,* Parker Publications, 1990; *Public Employer's Compliance Review,* Parker Publications, 1990; *Public Employer's Wage Guide,* Parker Publications, 1990; *Sexual Harassment — What You Need to Know,* Crisp Publications, 1992; *Supervisors Guide to Documenting Employee Discipline,* Parker Publications, 1988; *Supervisors Guide to Employee Performance Reviews,* Parker Publications, 1990. General Counsel: Professionals in Human Resources Association, 1990; State Council Society of Human Resource Managers, 1990. *Member:* Hawaii State Bar Association; State Bar of California. (Los Angeles, California Office). ***PRACTICE AREAS:*** Labor and Employment. ***Email:*** lpaterso@winston.com

LAURA R. PETROFF, born Cleveland, Ohio, July 7, 1955; admitted to bar, 1980, Illinois, U.S. District Court, Northern District of Illinois; 1986, California, U.S. District Court, Central, Southern and Northern Districts of California and U.S. Court of Appeals, Ninth Circuit. *Education:* Denison University (B.A., 1977); Vanderbilt University (J.D., 1980). *Member:* Los Angeles County (Co-Chair, Education Committee, 1989-1991 and Member, Executive Committee, 1990-1992, Barristers) and American Bar Associations; State Bar of California. (Member, Executive Committee; Managing Partner, Los Angeles Office; Chair, Partner Compensation Committee). ***PRACTICE AREAS:*** Labor and Employment. ***Email:*** lpetroff@winston.com

SUSAN M. BENTON-POWERS, born St. Louis, Missouri, December 8, 1952; admitted to bar, 1982, Illinois, U.S. District Court, Northern District of Illinois and U.S. Court of Appeals, Seventh Circuit; 1984, U.S. Court of Appeals, Fourth Circuit. *Education:* University of Missouri-St. Louis (B.A., 1975; M.B.A., 1982); Boston University School of Law (J.D., 1982). *Member:* American Bar Association. ***PRACTICE AREAS:*** Labor and Employment. ***Email:*** sbenton@winston.com

DEBRA J. ALBIN-RILEY, born Culver City, California, February 26, 1959; admitted to bar, 1983, California, U.S. District Court, Central, Northern, Southern and Eastern Districts of California and U.S. Court of Appeals, Ninth Circuit. *Education:* University of California at Los Angeles (B.A., cum laude, 1980); University of Southern California Law Center (J.D., 1983). Lecturer, Business Litigation: Los Angeles County Bar Association, 1996—; California Continuing Education of the Bar, 1996—. Author: "Shade of Gray," Los Angeles Lawyers, September 1998; "San Francisco Superior Court Finds that Settlement Between California Attorney General and Computer Monitor Manufacturers Bars Private Action," California Manufacturers, Fall, 1996. *Member:* Los Angeles County (Chair, Programs Committee, 1999-2000 and Member, Litigation Section; Member, Intellectual Property Section) and American (Member: Litigation Section; Franchising Forum) Bar Associations; The State Bar of California. (Los Angeles, California Office). ***LANGUAGES:*** French. ***PRACTICE AREAS:*** Complex Business Litigation. ***Email:*** driley@winston.com

RICHARD F. WILLIAMSON, born Oakland, California, March 18, 1950; admitted to bar, 1975, Georgia (inactive); 1977, Virginia; 1996, District of Columbia. *Education:* University of Virginia (B.A., with high distinction, 1972; J.D., 1975). Phi Beta Kappa. *Member:* The District of Columbia Bar; Virginia and American Bar Associations; State Bar of Georgia; Virginia State Bar. (Washington, D.C. Office). ***PRACTICE AREAS:*** Commercial Real Estate; Corporate Finance. ***Email:*** rwilliamson@winston.com

SUSAN CANNON LONGSTREET, born Washington, D.C., July 18, 1944; admitted to bar, 1984, Virginia and U.S. Court of Appeals, Fourth Circuit; 1985, District of Columbia. *Education:* Duke University; George Washington University (B.A., 1967); Marshall Wythe School of Law, College of William & Mary (J.D., 1984). Phi Alpha Delta. Member, Board of Directors: Housing Opportunities for Women; Fractured Atlas Productions. *Member:* The District of Columbia Bar (Member, Real Estate Section); Bar Association of the District of Columbia; Virginia State Bar; American Bar Association (Member: Real Property, Probate and Trust Law Section; Forum on Affordable Housing and Community Development Law; Real Estate Committee); Women's Bar Association of the District of Co-

(This Listing Continued)

WINSTON & STRAWN LLP, Chicago—Continued

lumbia; National Association of Real Estate Investment Trusts. (Washington, D.C. Office). ***PRACTICE AREAS:*** Real Estate Finance; Commercial Real Estate; Real Estate Acquisitions; Real Estate Investment Trusts; Real Property; Affordable Housing. ***Email:*** slongstr@winston.com

NEAL R. MARDER, born Encino, California, July 8, 1960; admitted to bar, 1986, California; U.S. Court of Appeals, Ninth and Tenth Circuits ; U.S. District Court, Central, Southern and Northern Districts of California. *Education:* University of California at Los Angeles (B.S., cum laude, 1982); Loyola University School of Law, Los Angeles (J.D., cum laude, 1986). Member: Order of the Coif; St. Thomas More Law Honor Society. *Member:* Los Angeles County and American Bar Associations; State Bar of California (Member, Litigation Section); Inn of the Courts; Association of Business Trial Lawyers. (Los Angeles, California Office). ***PRACTICE AREAS:*** Complex Business Litigation; Intellectual Property; Class Actions; Antitrust and Unfair Competition; Toxic Tort; Products Liability. ***Email:*** nmarder@winston.com

KAY McNAB, born St. Louis, Missouri, December 9, 1962; admitted to bar, 1988, Illinois; 1989, U.S. District Court, Northern District of Illinois. *Education:* University of Illinois (B.A., 1985; J.D., magna cum laude, 1988). Order of the Coif. Notes and Comment Editor, University of Illinois Law Review. ***PRACTICE AREAS:*** Finance; Public Finance; Corporate Finance. ***Email:*** kmcnab@winston.com

MARIE C. OLDHAM, born Springfield, Illinois, January 20, 1961; admitted to bar, 1986, Illinois and U.S. District Court, Northern District of Illinois. *Education:* Southern Illinois University (B.S., summa cum laude, 1983); University of Illinois (J.D., magna cum laude, 1986). Certified Public Accountant, Illinois, 1983. ***PRACTICE AREAS:*** Banking; Bankruptcy. ***Email:*** moldham@winston.com

DAVID W. WIRT, born Santa Clara, California, August 9, 1965; admitted to bar, 1991, Illinois. *Education:* University of California at Berkeley (A.B., 1988); Northwestern University (J.D., 1991). ***PRACTICE AREAS:*** Corporate Reorganization; Bankruptcy; Commercial Litigation. ***Email:*** dwirt@winston.com

VIRGINIA R. RICHARD, born Mount Vernon, New York, August 6, 1943; admitted to bar, 1969, New York and U.S. District Court, Southern District of New York; 1973, Colorado; U.S. Supreme Court; U.S. Court of Appeals, Second, Third and Fifth Federal Circuits; 1980, U.S. District Court, Eastern District of New York. *Education:* Manhattanville College (A.B., 1965); New York University (J.D., 1969). Author: "Pros and Cons of Adherence to the Madrid Protocol," NYPTCLA Bulletin, 1993; Fordham University School of Law, Second Annual Conference, International IP Law and Policy, April, 1994; "Product Configuration Trademark Protection," Practicing Law Institute, 1995; "Injunctions in Software Copyright Cases," American Institute, 1995. Speaker: "The Duty to Search," All-Ohio Annual Institute on Intellectual Property, 1999; "Developments in Trademark Law," Practicing Law Institute, 1999; "A Guide to Internet Legislation," R.R. Donnelly Financial, 2000; "Developments in Entertainment Licensing," Product Marketing Association, 2000; "Legal Issues Relating to Digital Distribution of Content," International Quality and Productivity Center Conference, 2001; "Developments in U.S. Brand Management and Dilution Law," Building and Enforcing Intellectual Property Value, 2002; "The Dilution Chronicles," INTA 2002 Leadership Meeting. *Member:* Federal Circuit (Chairman, Trademark Appeals Committee, 1991-1993) and American (Member, Sections on: Patent, Trademark and Copyright Law; Antitrust Law) Bar Associations; International Trademark Association (Member, Editorial Board, Trademark Reporter, 1988-1989; Meetings Committee, 2000-2002); New York Intellectual Property Law Association (Member, Board of Directors, 1990-1993; Chair, Copyright Law Committee, 1994-1996). (New York, N.Y. Office). ***PRACTICE AREAS:*** Intellectual Property Portfolio Management; Intellectual Property Litigation; Intellectual Property Licensing; New Media Law. ***Email:*** vrichard@winston.com

VINCENT A. SAMA, born Brooklyn, New York, August 22, 1957; admitted to bar, 1983, New York and U.S. District Court, Southern District of New York; 1985, U.S. District Court, Eastern District of New York; 1989, U.S. Court of Appeals, Federal Circuit; 1991, U.S. Court of Appeals, Second Circuit; 2002, U.S. Court of Appeals, Third Circuit. *Education:* Columbia College (B.A., summa cum laude, 1979); Harvard Law School (J.D., cum laude, 1982). *Member:* The Association of the Bar of the City of New York; New York State Bar Association. (New York, N.Y. Office). ***PRACTICE AREAS:*** Commercial Litigation; International Litigation; International Arbitration; Entertainment Litigation; Securities Litigation; Insurance. ***Email:*** vsama@winston.com

WILLIAM C. SELIGMAN, born Brooklyn, New York, 1965; admitted to bar, 1989, New Jersey (inactive); 1990, New York (Not admitted in Illinois). *Education:* Columbia University (A.B., 1986; J.D., 1989). *Member:* American Bar Association (Vice-Chairperson, Committee on Commercial Real Estate Management, Section of Real Property, Probate and Trust Law, 1995-2000). (Los Angeles, California and New York, New York Offices). ***PRACTICE AREAS:*** Commercial Real Estate; Real Estate Finance; Mortgage-Backed Securitization. ***Email:*** wseligman@winston.com

COREY A. TESSLER, born Brooklyn, New York, 1961; admitted to bar, 1987, New York. *Education:* Tufts University (B.A., magna cum laude, 1983); Georgetown University Law Center (J.D., 1986). *Member:* The Association of the Bar of The City of New York. (New York, N.Y. Office). ***PRACTICE AREAS:*** Real Estate Law. ***Email:*** ctessler@winston.com

JAY GLADIS, born Washington, D.C., October 17, 1949; admitted to bar, 1975, New York. *Education:* Princeton University (A.B., 1971); University of Virginia (J.D., 1974). Notes Editor, Virginia Journal of International Law, 1973-1974. *Member:* New York State and American (Chairman, International Securities Transactions Committee, Section of International Law, 1991-1995) Bar Associations. (New York, N.Y. Office). ***PRACTICE AREAS:*** Business Transactions; Corporate Law; Mergers and Acquisitions; International Business Law; International Joint Ventures. ***Email:*** jgladis@winston.com

ALAN S. HOFFMAN, born Riverdale, New York, 1962; admitted to bar, 1988, New York; 1994, U.S. Supreme Court. *Education:* Purdue University (1980-1982); State University of New York at Albany (B.A., summa cum laude, 1984); Georgetown University (J.D., 1987). *Member:* New York State Bar Association. (New York, N.Y. Office). ***PRACTICE AREAS:*** Project Finance; Lease Finance; Secured Lending; Securitization; Corporate Finance; Financial Hedging Products. ***Email:*** ahoffman@winston.com

H. SIDNEY HOLMES III, born Flushing, N.Y. April 10, 1944; admitted to bar, 1980, New York. *Education:* Columbia University (B.A., 1976); Hofstra University (J.D., 1979). (New York, N.Y. Office). ***PRACTICE AREAS:*** Public Finance; Structured Finance; Bank Lending. ***Email:*** sholmes@winston.com

DAVID F. KROENLEIN, born Waverly, Iowa, 1943; admitted to bar, 1968, District of Columbia; 1972, New York. *Education:* Harvard College (B.A., with honors, 1964); Columbia University (LL.B., with honors, 1967). *Member:* Association of the Bar of the City of New York (Member: Corporation Law Committee, 1987-1988; Tri-Bar Opinion Committee, 1987-1988); American Bar Association. (New York, N.Y. Office). ***PRACTICE AREAS:*** Corporate Finance; Securities; Corporate Governance; Corporate Law; Mergers, Acquisitions and Divestitures; Partnership Organization. ***Email:*** dkroenlein@winston.com

ERIC M. NELSON, born New York, N.Y., June 6, 1947; admitted to bar, 1974, New York; 1975, U.S. District Court, Southern and Eastern Districts of New York and U.S. Court of Appeals, Second Circuit; 1995, U.S. Court of Appeals, Sixth Circuit; 1996, U.S. Court of Appeals, Third Circuit; 2001, U.S. Court of Appeals, Ninth Circuit. *Education:* Syracuse University (B.A., 1969); Brooklyn Law School (J.D., cum laude, 1973). Articles Editor, Brooklyn Law Review, 1972-1973. Law Clerk to Hon. Lee P. Gagliardi, Judge, U.S. District Court, Southern District of New York, 1973-1975. Member, Board of Trustees, Brooklyn Law School, 1975-1979. Associate Counsel, New York State Assembly Codes Committee, 1980. *Member:* Federal Bar Council. (New York, N.Y. Office). ***PRACTICE AREAS:*** Litigation; Commercial Litigation; Corporate Litigation; Securities Litigation; Employment Litigation; ERISA Litigation; Class Action Defense; Insurance Coverage Litigation; Probate Litigation; Civil Appeals. ***Email:*** emnelson@winston.com

JAMES S. NORMILE, born New York, N.Y., 1952; admitted to bar, 1977, New York and U.S. District Court, Southern and Eastern Districts of New York; 1992, U.S. Supreme Court. *Education:* Fordham University (B.A., 1973; J.D., 1976). (New York, N.Y. Office). ***PRACTICE AREAS:*** Project Finance; Public Finance; Municipal Finance (Bond) Law. ***Email:*** jnormile@winston.com

STEPHEN L. SHEINFELD, born Rochester, New York, October 1, 1958; admitted to bar, 1984, New York and U.S. District Court, Southern, Eastern and Western Districts of New York; 1986, District of Columbia; U.S. Court of Appeals, Second Circuit. *Education:* Cornell University (B.S., I.L.R., 1980); State University of New York at Buffalo (J.D., cum laude, 1983). Note and Comment Editor, Buffalo Law Review, 1982-1983. Founding Editor, Employment Law Strategist. *Member:* Association of the Bar of the City of New York; New York State (Member, Labor Law Section) and American (Member, Section on Labor and Employment Law) Bar Associations; The District of Columbia Bar; New York County Lawyers Association. (New York, N.Y. Office). ***PRACTICE AREAS:*** Labor and Employment Law. ***Email:*** ssheinfeld@winston.com

JOHN H. DENNE, born New York, N.Y., 1939; admitted to bar, 1965, New York. *Education:* Williams College (A.B., with honors, 1961); Columbia University (LL.B., 1965). Harlan Fiske Stone Scholar. Editor, Columbia Law Review, 1964-1965. *Member:* The Association of the Bar of the City of New York; American Bar Association. (New York, N.Y. Office). ***PRACTICE AREAS:*** Corporate Law; Mergers, Acquisitions and Divestitures; Corporate Finance; Securities. ***Email:*** jdenne@winston.com

WILLIAM F. DUDINE, III, born New York, N.Y., 1961; admitted to bar, 1987, New Jersey; 1988, New York; 1990, District of Columbia. *Education:* Dickinson College (B.A., 1983); St. John's University (J.D., 1987). *Member:* The Association of the Bar of the City of New York; New York State Bar Association. (New York, N.Y. Office). ***PRACTICE AREAS:*** Public Finance. ***Email:*** wdudine@winston.com

PATRICIA VAN B. MADSEN, born Lafayette, Indiana, 1958; admitted to bar, 1988, New York. *Education:* Harvard College (A.B., 1980); Columbia University (J.D., 1984). *Member:* Association of Real Estate Women (President, 2000-2001). (New York, N.Y. Office). ***PRACTICE AREAS:*** Commercial Real Estate; Commercial Real Estate Development; Commercial Real Estate Sales; Commercial Real Estate Finance. ***Email:*** pmadsen@winston.com

JOHN E. TARDERA, born Freeport, New York, May 16, 1957; admitted to bar, 1984, New York; U.S. District Court, Southern, Eastern, Northern and Western Districts of New York. *Education:* State University of New York at Stony Brook (B.A., 1979); Syracuse University (J.D., summa cum laude, 1983). Order of the Coif; Justinian Honorary Law Society. Managing Editor, Syracuse Law Review, 1982-1983. Author: "Education of Handicapped Students Under Education for All Handicapped Children Act and the Rehabilitation Act of 1973," 33 Syra. L. Rev. 657 (1982). *Member:* New York State Bar Association; New York County Lawyers Association. (New York, N.Y. Office). ***REPORTED CASES:*** Metro Indus.,Inc. v. Sammi Corp., 82 F.2d 839 (9th Cir.), cert. denied, 117 S.Ct. 181 (1996; Zucker v. Quasha, 891 F. Supp. 1010 (D.N.J. 1995. ***PRACTICE AREAS:*** Commercial Litigation; Trade Regulation Litigation. ***Email:*** jtardera@winston.com

ERIC P. TAYLOR, born Flushing, New York, 1963; admitted to bar, 1989, New York (Not admitted in Illinois). *Education:* Amherst College (B.A., 1985); New York University (J.D., 1988). (New York, N.Y. Office). ***PRACTICE AREAS:*** Public Finance; Municipal Finance. ***Email:*** etaylor@winston.com

LORAN T. THOMPSON, born New York, N.Y., December 23, 1947; admitted to bar, 1977, New York, U.S. Tax Court and U.S. Court of Claims. *Education:* Amherst College (B.A., magna cum laude, 1969); Harvard University (M.A., 1970; J.D., 1976). Phi Beta Kappa. *Member:* Association of the Bar of the City of New York; New York State (Member, Tax Section, Executive Committee 1991-1998; Co-Chair, Committee on Nonqualified Employee Benefits 1991-1995; Co-Chair, Committee on Qualified Plans, 1995-1998) and American (Member, Section on Taxation, Employee Benefits Committee) Bar Associations. (New York, N.Y. Office). ***LANGUAGES:*** French. ***PRACTICE AREAS:*** Executive Compensation; Employee Benefits; Federal Income Taxation. **Email:** lthompson@winston.com

ALEXANDER T. DELAND, born New York, N.Y., 1950; admitted to bar, 1976, Connecticut; 1983, New York. *Education:* Yale University (B.A., 1972); University of Con-

(This Listing Continued)

(This Listing Continued)

necticut (J.D., 1976); New York University (LL.M., 1978). *Member:* National Association of Bond Lawyers. (New York, N.Y. Office). ***PRACTICE AREAS:*** Municipal Finance (Bond) Law; Taxation Law. ***Email:*** adeland@winston.com

RICHARD F. LAWLER, born Providence, Rhode Island, March 24, 1945; admitted to bar, 1974, Connecticut, U.S. District Court, District of Connecticut and U.S. Court of Appeals, Second Circuit; 1979, U.S. District Court, Southern and Eastern Districts of New York; 1980, New York. *Education:* Yale University (B.A., 1967); Columbia University (J.D., 1973). Fulbright Scholar, 1968. Assistant U.S. Attorney, Southern District of New York, 1976-1980. [U.S. Navy, 1968-1970]. (New York, N.Y. Office). ***PRACTICE AREAS:*** Litigation; White Collar Criminal Defense; Products Liability Defense; Securities Litigation; Tort Defense. ***Email:*** rlawler@winston.com

C. MACNEIL MITCHELL, born New York, N.Y., September 22, 1942; admitted to bar, 1968, New York (1st Department); 1969, U.S. District Court, Southern and Eastern Districts of New York and U.S. Court of Appeals, Second Circuit; 1973, U.S. Supreme Court; 1982, U.S. Court of Appeals, Ninth Circuit. *Education:* Yale University (B.A., 1964); Boalt Hall School of Law, University of California (J.D., 1967). Associate, Breed, Abbott & Morgan, 1969-1975; Partner, Breed, Abbott & Morgan, 1975-1993; Partner, Whitman Breed Abbott & Morgan LLP, 1993-2000; Partner, Winston & Strawn LLP, 2000—. *Member:* The Association of the Bar of the City of New York; Federal Bar Council. [U.S. Army Reserves, 1967-1973]. (New York, N.Y. Office). ***LANGUAGES:*** French. ***REPORTED CASES:*** Carter-Wallace, Inc. v. Admiral Insurance Co., et al, 154 N.J. 312 (1998); Mobil Oil Indonesia, Inc. v. Asamera Oil (Indonesia) Ltd., 372 N.E.2d 21 (NY 1977); Valentino v. Carter-Wallace, Inc., 97 F.3d 1227 (9th Cir. 1996). ***PRACTICE AREAS:*** Litigation (30%); Bankruptcy Litigation (20%); Restructuring Transactions (15%); Insurance Coverage (15%); Products Liability Defense (10%); Environmental Defense (10%). ***Email:*** cmitchell@winston.com

BRIAN L. SULLIVAN, born New York, N.Y., July 19, 1948; admitted to bar, 1974, Connecticut; 1979, New York. *Education:* Wesleyan University (B.A., magna cum laude, 1970); Yale University (J.D., 1974). Phi Beta Kappa. Recipient, Carter Ledyard Prize. *Member:* American Bar Association. (New York, N.Y. Office). ***PRACTICE AREAS:*** Litigation; Antitrust and Trade Regulation; Franchise Litigation; Advertising and Marketing. ***Email:*** bsullivan@winston.com

NEIL UNDERBERG, born 1928; admitted to bar, 1952, New York; 1953, Republic of Korea; 1969, U.S. Supreme Court; 1980, U.S. District Court, Southern District of New York. *Education:* Syracuse University (B.A., 1949); Cornell Law School (LL.B., 1952; J.D., 1969); New York University Graduate School of Law (LL.M., 1957). Co-Author: "Business and Legal Problems of Shopping Centers," (2nd Edition) Practising Law Institute, 1968. Author: "Shopping Centers 1976," Practising Law Institute, 1976; "Shopping Centers Revisited 1979," Practising Law Institute, 1979; "Ground Leasing Makes Dollars and Cents for Developers," Real Estate Review, Volume 1, No. 2; "Environmental Laws and Overview," Shopping Center World, 1974; "Understanding the New Bankruptcy Act," National Mall Monitor, Volume 10, No. 2. Attorney Advisor, General Counsel of the Federal Housing Administration, 1954-1955. Member, Board of Directors: Alexander's, Inc., 1986—. Member, Panel of Arbitrators, American Arbitration Association. *Member:* The Association of the Bar of the City of New York; American Law Institute; American College of Real Estate Lawyers. [First Lieutenant, United States Air Force, 1952-1954-Staff Judge Advocate, 17th Bomb Wing (L), Pusan, Korea]. (New York, N.Y. Office). ***PRACTICE AREAS:*** Real Estate Law; Real Estate Finance Law. ***Email:*** nunderberg@winston.com

LINA M. VIVIANO, born New York, N.Y., December 10, 1959; admitted to bar, 1992, New York; 1995, U.S. District Court, Southern and Eastern Districts of New York. *Education:* Queens College of the City University of New York (B.A., summa cum laude, 1981); Harvard University (M.A., 1984); New York University (J.D., 1991). (New York, N.Y. Office). ***PRACTICE AREAS:*** Litigation; Arbitration. ***Email:*** lviviano@winston.com

WILLIAM A. HORIN, born Springfield, Illinois, August 21, 1954; admitted to bar, 1979, District of Columbia; 1980, U.S. District Court, District of Columbia and U.S. Court of Appeals, District of Columbia Circuit. *Education:* Northwestern University (B.S. Ch.E., 1976; M.S. Ch.E., 1977); Georgetown University (J.D., 1979). *Member:* The District of Columbia Bar (Member, Sections on Administrative Law; Energy Law); American Institute of Chemical Engineers; American Nuclear Society. (Washington, D.C. Office). ***PRACTICE AREAS:*** Energy Regulation; Nuclear Energy; Federal Administrative Law; Administrative Agency Practice. ***Email:*** whorin@winston.com

GERALD P. FARANO, born New York, N.Y., September 10, 1966; admitted to bar, 1992, Pennsylvania; 1993, District of Columbia. *Education:* Bucknell University (B.A., 1988); George Washington University (J.D., 1991); Georgetown University (LL.M., with distinction, 1992). (Washington, D.C. Office). ***PRACTICE AREAS:*** Corporate Law; Mergers and Acquisitions; Private Equity. ***Email:*** gfarano@winston.com

ANDREAS H. LESKOVSEK, born Silver Spring, Maryland, March 25, 1965; admitted to bar, 1990, Maryland; 1991, District of Columbia. *Education:* University of Maryland (B.A., summa cum laude, 1987); Georgetown University Law Center (J.D., magna cum laude, 1990). Phi Beta Kappa; Pi Sigma Alpha. Member, Law and Policy in International Business, 1988-1989. Author: "U.S.-Romanian Trade: Foreign Debt, Tariff and Future Prospects or Problems?" Law and Policy in International Business, Vol. 21, No. 1 (Fall, 1989). (Washington, D.C. Office). ***PRACTICE AREAS:*** Environmental Law. ***Email:*** jleskovsek@winston.com

JAY L. LEVINE, born Van Nuys, California, March 20, 1965; admitted to bar, 1991, New York and U.S. District Court, Southern and Eastern Districts of New York; 1998, District of Columbia and U.S. District Court, District of Columbia. *Education:* University of Maryland (B.A., 1987); Fordham University School of Law (J.D., cum laude, 1990). Staff Member, Fordham Law Review, 1988-1989; Dean's List, 1988-1990; Recipient, American Jurisprudence Awards in Civil Procedure, Constitutional Law, Contracts and Evidence; Recipient, Alumni Award for Excellence in Constitutional Law; Author, "Binding Absent Class Members To A Class Action Settlement Involving Money Damages," Private Antitrust Litigation News, August 1996; Drafter, Antitrust Law Developments (5th ed. 2002); Drafter, Annual Review of Antitrust Law Developments (2002 and 2003); Editor, Chapter on Monopolization, 2004 Annual Review of Antitrust Law Developments; Contributing Author, Model Jury Instructions in Civil Antitrust Cases (2005 Ed.). *Member:* American

(This Listing Continued)

Bar Association (Section on Antitrust Law). (Washington, D.C. Office). ***LANGUAGES:*** Hebrew. ***PRACTICE AREAS:*** Antitrust and Trade Regulation; Litigation. ***Email:*** jlevine@winston.com

MICHAEL P. O'BRIEN, born Chicago, Illinois, October 21, 1960; admitted to bar, 1985, Illinois; 1999, New York. *Education:* Loyola University (B.B.A., magna cum laude, 1982); Northwestern University (J.D., 1985). ***PRACTICE AREAS:*** Aircraft Finance and Leasing; Structured Finance; Derivative Products; Equipment Leasing. ***Email:*** mpobrien@winston.com

ANNE E. THAR, born Evanston, Illinois, September 7, 1957; admitted to bar, 1983, Illinois. *Education:* Mount Holyoke College (B.A., 1979); Northwestern University (J.D., 1983). Member, Northwestern Law Review. *Member:* Chicago, Illinois State and American Bar Associations. ***PRACTICE AREAS:*** Legal Ethics and Professional Responsibility. ***Email:*** athar@winston.com

GREGORY J. BYNAN, born Milwaukee, Wisconsin, October 6, 1966; admitted to bar, 1992, Wisconsin and Illinois. *Education:* Miami University; University of Wisconsin (J.D., 1992). ***PRACTICE AREAS:*** Securities Offerings; Mergers and Acquisitions; Private Equity; Venture Capital. ***Email:*** gbynan@winston.com

JOHN M. DICKMAN, born Chicago, Illinois, June 15, 1965; admitted to bar, 1992, Illinois. *Education:* University of Iowa (B.B.A., 1987); Loyola University (J.D., cum laude, 1992). ***Email:*** jdickman@winston.com

JOSEPH P. FRANKLIN, born Tampa, Florida, October 5, 1964; admitted to bar, 1992, Pennsylvania; 1997, Illinois. *Education:* Wabash College (B.A., summa cum laude, 1986); Vanderbilt University (M.S., 1988); University of Pennsylvania (J.D., 1992). Member: Phi Beta Kappa. Harold Sterling Vanderbilt University Fellow. ***PRACTICE AREAS:*** Commercial Litigation; Civil Litigation; Complex Litigation. ***Email:*** jfrankli@winston.com

JEFFREY A. LEON, born Chicago, Illinois, February 24, 1965; admitted to bar, 1991, Illinois. *Education:* University of Redlands (B.A., cum laude, 1987); Indiana University (J.D., summa cum laude, 1991). Order of the Coif. Managing Editor, Indiana Law Journal. ***PRACTICE AREAS:*** Antitrust; Commercial Litigation; Intellectual Property; Litigation. ***Email:*** jleon@winston.com

DAVID R. HAMBOURGER, born Chicago, Illinois, February 11, 1955; admitted to bar, 1980, Illinois. *Education:* University of Illinois (B.S., Finance, with honors, 1977); Loyola University (J.D., 1980); Northwestern University (M.B.A., 1986). *Member:* College of Law Practice Management; American Bar Association. (Technology Partner). ***PRACTICE AREAS:*** Technology. ***Email:*** dhambourger@winston.com

JAMES M. LYNCH, born Chicago, Illinois, September 22, 1951; admitted to bar, 1977, Illinois. *Education:* Xavier University (B.S.B.A., 1973); John Marshall Law School (J.D., 1976); Georgetown University (LL.M., 1980). Author: "McDonald's of Zion: Application of the Step Transaction Doctrine to the Continuity of Interest Test," The Tax Adviser, October, 1981; "The Assumption of Contingent Liabilities in Corporate Restructuring Transactions," Taxes Magazine, December, 1989; "Indianapolis Power & Light Company: Issues and Planning Opportunities Where the Government Seeks the Acceleration of Income," Taxes Magazine, December, 1990; "Taxing Major Corporate Distributions (Not Involving Changes In Control)," Taxes Magazine, December, 1993; "Back to the Code: A Reexamination of the Continuity Doctrines and Other Current Issues in Reorganizations," Taxes Magazine, December 1995; "Treatment of Options and Warrants in Taxable and Tax Free Acquisitions," University of Chicago Conference, published in Taxes Magazine, March, 1999. Certified Public Accountant, Illinois, 1977. Adjunct Professor, DePaul University College of Law, 1983-1990. *Member:* Chicago and American Bar Associations; American Institute of Certified Public Accountants. ***PRACTICE AREAS:*** Corporate Law; Tax Law. ***Email:*** jlynch@winston.com

ALLAN A. FANUCCI, born Scranton, Pennsylvania, January 25, 1953; admitted to bar, 1982, New Jersey and U.S. District Court, District of New Jersey; 1983, New York and U.S. District Court, Southern and Eastern Districts of New York; 1990, U.S. Court of Appeals for the Federal Circuit; 1996, District of Columbia; registered to practice before U.S. Patent and Trademark Office. *Education:* Wilkes College (B.S., Materials Engineering, 1974); Stevens Institute of Technology (M.S., Metallurgy, 1979); St. John's University (J.D., 1982). *Member:* Federal Circuit Bar Association; American Intellectual Property Law Association; New York Intellectual Property Law Association. (New York, N.Y. and Washington D.C. Offices). ***PRACTICE AREAS:*** Intellectual Property; Patents; Trade Secrets; Technology and Science. ***Email:*** afanucci@winston.com

DAVID M. TRAITEL, born Detroit, Michigan, January 7, 1968; admitted to bar, 1992, Michigan; 1996, New York. *Education:* University of Michigan (B.A., with high distinction, 1989; J.D., 1992). (New York, N.Y. Office). ***PRACTICE AREAS:*** Real Estate. ***Email:*** dtraitel@winston.com

PETER M. D'AMBROSIO, born Hartford, Connecticut, September 2, 1950; admitted to bar, 1976, Virginia and U.S. Court of Federal Claims. *Education:* Georgetown University (B.A., 1972; J.D., 1976). Editor, Law and Policy in International Business, International Law Review, 1975-1976. Co-Author: Chapter, "Claims Against the Government," in *Proving and Pricing Construction Claims,* 2d Edition (John Wiley & Sons, Inc.), 1996; "Dealing With International Contracting Risks," 86-5 Construction Briefings, Federal Publications, Inc., 1986; *The Electrical Contractor's Handbook of Claims Avoidance and Management,* Reston Publishing Company, 1984; "Project Scheduling and Construction Claims," Construction Consultants International Corp., 1978. Author: "Effective Procedures For Risk Management In International Construction," Engineering News-Record, 1984-1985; "Resolving International Construction Claims and Disputes," World Construction, 1983; "Construction Claims For The Owner," Practicing Law Institute, 1983-1984; The Project Schedule And The Claim," Engineering News-Record, 1978-1985. *Member:* Virginia State Bar; American Bar Association (Member: Litigation Section; Forum Committee on the Construction Industry); National and International Panels of Arbitrators; American Arbitration Association. (Washington, D.C. Office). ***REPORTED CASES:*** SAE/American Mid-Atlantic, Inc. GSBACA12294 et al., Lexis 390, October 23, 1998; G&M Electrical Contractors Co., GSBCA No. 4683, 79-1 BCA § 13,571 (1978); Daniel International Corp. v. Better Construction, Inc., 593 So. 2d 524 (1991); Premier Electrical Construction Co. v.

(This Listing Continued)

WINSTON & STRAWN LLP, Chicago—Continued

Morse Diesel, et al., 628 N.E. 2d 1090 (1993). ***PRACTICE AREAS:*** Construction Claims; Construction and Surety Law; Public Construction Law. ***Email:*** pdambros@winston.com

ALEXANDRE BRUE, born Paris, France, February 21, 1964; admitted to bar, 1993, France. *Education:* University of Paris II (Maîtrise en Droit des Affaires et Fiscalite, 1988). (Paris, France Office). ***LANGUAGES:*** French and English. ***PRACTICE AREAS:*** Corporate Law; Commercial Law; Labor Law; Consumer Law. ***Email:*** abrue@winston.com

JOHN W. CHRISTOPHER, born Honolulu, Hawaii, April 10, 1965; admitted to bar, 1992, Illinois; 1993, U.S. District Court, Northern District of Illinois; 2000, California; U.S. District Court, Central, Northern and Southern Districts of California. *Education:* University of Michigan (B.A., 1987; J.D., cum laude, 1992). ***PRACTICE AREAS:*** Litigation. ***Email:*** jchristopher@winston.com

TODD J. EHLMAN, born Chicago, Illinois, September 25, 1966; admitted to bar, 1989, Illinois; 1990, U.S. District Court, Northern District of Illinois; 1996, U.S. Court of Appeals, Seventh Circuit. *Education:* Northwestern University (B.A., 1986); University of Michigan (J.D., magna cum laude, 1989). Phi Beta Kappa; Order of the Coif. Michigan Law Review, 1987-1989. ***PRACTICE AREAS:*** Civil Litigation. ***Email:*** tehlman@winston.com

PAUL S. PILECKI, born Norristown, Pennsylvania, September 12, 1950; admitted to bar, 1978, Pennsylvania (inactive); 1985, District of Columbia. *Education:* St. Joseph's University (A.B., 1972); Temple University (J.D., 1978). Contributing Author, *Banking Law.* Bank Examiner, Federal Reserve Bank of Philadelphia, 1972-1978. Senior Counsel, Federal Reserve Board, 1978-1984. *Member:* Federal (Member, Executive Council, Banking Committee, 1995-1998, 2001—; Secretary-Treasurer, 2002-2004; Vice Chairman, 2004—) and American (Chairman, International Banking Subcommittee, Banking Law Committee, 1998-2002) Bar Associations. (Washington, D.C. Office). ***PRACTICE AREAS:*** Financial Institutions Regulation. ***Email:*** ppilecki@winston.com

STEPHEN J. SENDEROWITZ, born Allentown, Pennsylvania, April 13, 1949; admitted to bar, 1974, Illinois. *Education:* Northwestern University (B.A., 1971; J.D., 1974). Assistant United States Attorney, Northern District of Illinois, 1975-1983. Deputy Chief, 1979-1983 (Responsible for Securities, Commodities, Tax and Financial Crime cases). Trial Attorney, Equal Employment Opportunity Commission, 1974. Author: "Post-Enron 10b-5 Secondary Actor Liability: A New Standard for Attorneys," Illinois Bar Journal, Vol. 91, No.7, July, 2003 (co-author); "Finding Its Way; The Changing Face and Focus of the Office of the U.S. Attorney for the Northern District of Illinois," CBA Record, Vol. 12, No. 3, April, 1998; "Litigation Strategies in Criminal Commodity Fraud Cases," Illinois Bar Journal, Vol. 78, No. 12, December, 1990. "Defending Criminal Commodity Fraud Cases: An Overview," Prentice Hall Law and Business in "Commodities Trading: Trading Practices Under Scrutiny," pp. 86-134, 1989." Lecturer PLI, Commodity Futures Enforcement, 1989; Commodity Law Institute 1988; FBI Academy Commodity Fraud and White Collar Prosecution, 1980-1982. Chairman, U.S. Attorney General's Commodity Fraud Committee, 1982-1983. Deputy Special Prosecutor (Cook County), 1989. Named "Illinois Super-Lawyer" Securities Litigation, Chicago Magazine, 2005. *Member:* Chicago, Illinois State and American Bar Associations. ***PRACTICE AREAS:*** Securities and Commodities Litigation; Complex Civil Litigation; White Collar Criminal Defense; Corporate Internal Investigations. ***Email:*** ssendero@winston.com

TIMOTHY J. DABLE, born Chesterfield, England, May 11, 1968; admitted to bar, 1993, Illinois. *Education:* University of Michigan (B.S., 1990); Washington University (J.D., 1993). ***PRACTICE AREAS:*** Finance. ***Email:*** tdable@winston.com

DANE DROBNY, born Chicago, Illinois, July 21, 1967; admitted to bar, 1993, Illinois. *Education:* Colgate University (B.A., 1989); Washington University (J.D., 1993). ***Email:*** ddrobny@winston.com

JOHN R. GRIER, born Sioux City, Iowa, August 11, 1967; admitted to bar, 1993, Illinois. *Education:* University of Iowa (B.B.A., with honors, 1989; J.D., with high honors, 1993). *Member:* Chicago Bar Association. ***PRACTICE AREAS:*** Real Estate. ***Email:*** jgrier@winston.com

BRENDAN P. HEAD, born Chicago, Illinois, August 24, 1966; admitted to bar, 1993, Illinois; 1994, District of Columbia. *Education:* Georgetown University (B.A., 1988; J.D., 1993). ***PRACTICE AREAS:*** Mergers, Acquisitions and Divestitures; Securities. ***Email:*** bhead@winston.com

LAWRENCE I. KIERN, born New Orleans, Louisiana, December 29, 1952; admitted to bar, 1986, Michigan; 1994, District of Columbia. *Education:* United States Coast Guard Academy (B.S., 1974); Wesleyan University (M.A., 1979); University of Michigan (J.D., 1985); University of Connecticut (Ph.D., 1996). Phi Kappa Phi; Phi Alpha Theta. Author: "Liability, Compensation, and Financial Responsibility Under the Oil Pollution Act of 1990: A Review of the First Decade," Tulane Maritime Law Journal, Summer 2000. "Environmental Damages Under Federal Law," Tulane Law Review, Dec., 1997. Deputy Chief and Legislative Counsel, Coast Guard Congressional Affairs, 1994-1998. *Member:* State Bar of Michigan; Maritime Law Association. [U.S. Coast Guard, 1970-1998]. (Washington, D.C. Office). ***PRACTICE AREAS:*** Admiralty and Maritime Law; Environmental; Federal Legislative Practice; Oil Pollution; Regulatory; Litigation. ***Email:*** lkiern@winston.com

PETER J. KOCORAS, born Illinois, July 6, 1969; admitted to bar, 1993, Illinois. *Education:* Indiana University (B.S., 1990); DePaul University (J.D., 1993). ***REPORTED CASES:*** People v. Bohne, 312 Ill. App. 3d 705, 728 N.E.2d 509 (2000). ***PRACTICE AREAS:*** Complex Civil Litigation; Securities Litigation; Commercial Litigation; White Collar Crime; Corporate Investigations; Health Care Litigation. ***Email:*** pkocoras@winston.com

STEPHEN J. LEGATZKE, born Hinsdale, Illinois, May 24, 1967; admitted to bar, 1992, Illinois; 1993, U.S. Tax Court. *Education:* University of Notre Dame (B.A., 1989); University of Virginia (J.D., 1992). Phi Beta Kappa. Recipient, Cohen Tax Prize and Scholarship. Author: "The Equitable Recoupment Doctrine in United States v. Dalm," 10 Va. Tax Rev. 861 (1991). ***PRACTICE AREAS:*** Taxation. ***Email:*** slegatzke@winston.com

(This Listing Continued)

ROGER S. LUCAS, born Summit, New Jersey, October 17, 1966; admitted to bar, 1993, Illinois; 1999, Iowa. *Education:* University of Michigan (B.B.A., with high distinction, 1988; J.D., magna cum laude, 1992). ***PRACTICE AREAS:*** Taxation (100%). ***Email:*** rlucas@winston.com

BRIAN E. NEUFFER, born Fresno, California, June 12, 1963; admitted to bar, 1990, Illinois; U.S. District Court, Northern and Central Districts of Illinois; U.S. Court of Appeals, Seventh Circuit; U.S. Supreme Court. *Education:* Northwestern University (B.A., 1987); Brigham Young University (J.D., 1990). Lead Articles Editor, Brigham Young University Law Review, 1990. Law Clerk to Hon. Cathy R. Silak, Idaho Supreme Court, 1994-95. Co-Author: "Transshipping Under the Antitrust Laws," Vol. 3 DePaul Bus. L.J., Spring/Summer 1991. Author: "The Legality of Early Retirement Incentives Under the Age Discrimination in Employment Act," Vol. 3, Utah Bar J., Oct. 1990; Comment, "The Post-Expiration Duty to Arbitrate, Disregarding the Nolde Presumption After an Impasse in Negotiations," 1989 B.Y.U. L. Rev. 349. ***REPORTED CASES:*** Illinois Council on Long Term Care Inc. v. Shalala, 143 F.3d 1072 (7th Cir. 1998) (administrative procedure), rev'd in part 529 U.S. 1 (2000); United States v. Hunte, 196 F.3d 687 (7th Cir. 1999) (criminal); Alvarez v. Boyd, 225 F.3d 820 (7th Cir.) cert denied, 121 S.Ct. 1192 (2001) (habeas corpus); United States Fidelity & Guaranty Co. v. Old Orchard Plaza, 33 Ill. App. 3d 727, 776 N.E.2d 812 (1st Dist. 2002) (real estate); Fairfax Nursing Home, Inc. v. United States, 300 F.3d 835 (7th Cir. 2002) (administrative); Hoseman v. Weinschneider, 322 F.3d 468 (7th Cir. 2003) (bankruptcy - breach of contract); Weinschneider v. Hoseman, 395 F.3d 401 (7th Cir. 2005) (damages - attorney fees). ***PRACTICE AREAS:*** Litigation; Appellate Practice; Administrative Hearings. ***Email:*** bneuffer@winston.com

SUSAN A. PIPAL, born Evergreen Park, Illinois, December 19, 1967; admitted to bar, 1993, Illinois. *Education:* University of Notre Dame (B.A., 1990); Northwestern University (J.D., 1993). *Member:* Cook County Bar Association (Executive Committee Member, Alliance for Women). ***PRACTICE AREAS:*** Commercial Litigation; Products Liability Defense. ***Email:*** spipal@winston.com

J. DAVID REICH, born Winston-Salem, North Carolina, September 2, 1959; admitted to bar, 1988, New York; 1997, U.S. District Court, Southern and Eastern Districts of New York; 1998, U.S. Court of Appeals, Second Circuit. *Education:* Davidson College (B.A., magna cum laude, 1981); Columbia University (J.D., 1985). Charles Dana Scholar. Harlan Fiske Stone Scholar. Assistant U.S. Attorney, U.S. Attorney's Office, District of New Jersey, 1991-1997. (New York, N.Y. Office). ***PRACTICE AREAS:*** Civil Litigation; Corporate Investigations; White Collar Criminal Defense. ***Email:*** jreich@winston.com

MICHAEL P. ROCHE, born Chicago, Illinois, May 23, 1967; admitted to bar, 1993, Illinois. *Education:* University of Illinois (B.S., magna cum laude, 1989; J.D., magna cum laude, 1993). *Member:* Chicago and Illinois State Bar Associations. ***Email:*** mroche@winston.com

JULIE L. SOLOWAY, born Chicago, IL, August 20, 1967; admitted to bar, 1992, Illinois and U.S. District Court, Northern District of Illinois. *Education:* University of Michigan (A.B., with distinction, 1989); University of Illinois (J.D., magna cum laude, 1992). Member, Mortar Board, University of Michigan. ***Email:*** jsoloway@winston.com

MICHAEL E. EMRICH, admitted to bar, 1984, New York. *Education:* University of Albany (B.A., summa cum laude, 1980); Cornell Law School (J.D., 1983). Law Clerk for the Hon. Lawrence E. Howard, United States Bankruptcy Judge for the Western District of Michigan. *Member:* American Bankruptcy Institute; Association of Commercial Finance Attorneys; International Bar Association. (New York, N.Y. Office). ***PRACTICE AREAS:*** Creditors' Rights; Bankruptcy; International Bankruptcy; Claims Trading; Securitization. ***Email:*** memrich@winston.com

LANA C. MARINA, born Chicago, Illinois; admitted to bar, 1994, New York. *Education:* Northwestern University (Bachelor of Music, 1990); Cornell Law School (J.D., 1993). (New York, N.Y. Office). ***PRACTICE AREAS:*** Trademarks. ***Email:*** lmarina@winston.com

NIKOLAI KRYLOV, born Moscow, Russia, July 4, 1968; admitted to bar, 1983, Russia; 1995, New York. *Education:* Moscow University Law School (J.D., summa cum laude, 1983); Yale Law School (J.D., 1994). *Member:* New York State Bar Association (Member, Commonwealth of Independent States Committee). (New York, N.Y. Office). ***LANGUAGES:*** Russian. ***PRACTICE AREAS:*** Mergers and Acquisitions; Securities; International Law. ***Email:*** nkrylov@winston.com

ERIC M. ROBINSON, born Aberdeen, South Dakota, December 30, 1965; admitted to bar, 1993, California and U.S. District Court, Southern District of California; 1995, U.S. District Court, Central District of California; 1995, U.S. Court of Appeals, Ninth Circuit; 1999, U.S. Court of Appeals, Fourth and Sixth Circuits; 2003, New York and U.S. District Court, Southern and Eastern Districts of New York. *Education:* Carleton College (B.A., 1988); Temple University (J.D., 1993). *Member:* State Bar of California. (New York, N.Y. Office). ***PRACTICE AREAS:*** Commercial Litigation; Employment Law; Alternative Dispute Resolution; Entertainment Litigation; Sports Law. ***Email:*** erobinso@winston.com

HOWARD R. MAJEV, born New York, N.Y., December 10, 1952; admitted to bar, 1978, Maryland; 1995, District of Columbia. *Education:* The Johns Hopkins University (B.A., 1973); The University of Maryland School of Law (J.D., 1976). Omicron Delta Kappa. Articles Editor, Maryland Law Review, 1975-1976. Executive Assistant to the President of the Baltimore City Council, 1976-1979. *Member:* Maryland State and American Bar Associations; District of Columbia Bar. (Washington, D.C. Office). ***LANGUAGES:*** Polish. ***PRACTICE AREAS:*** Real Estate. ***Email:*** hmajev@winston.com

JEANNE M. DENNIS, born Rochester, New York, March 19, 1966; admitted to bar, 1993, District of Columbia. *Education:* Swarthmore College (B.A., 1988); University of California at Los Angeles (J.D., 1993). (Washington, D.C. Office). ***Email:*** jdennis@winston.com

ANNA SEGOBIA MASTERS, born Riverside, California, February 17, 1959; admitted to bar, 1984, California and U.S. District Court, Southern District of California; 1985, U.S. District Court, Central, Northern and Eastern Districts of California; 1990, U.S. Court of Appeals, 9th Circuit. *Education:* University of California at Riverside (B.A., 1981); University of California at Los Angeles (J.D., 1984). Recipient, Volunteer Attorney of the Year, Western Law Center for Disability Rights 2002. Speaker/Author, "Privacy in The New

(This Listing Continued)

Workplace," American Employment Law Council Ninth Annual Conference, 2001; Speaker/Author, "Sex, Race and Other Unlawful Harassment," National Employment Law Institute,Employment Conference, 2001; Speaker/Author, "Preparing A Sexual Harassment Case," National Employment Law Litigation Manual, 1999. Author: "Rights and Obligations Under The Americans With Disabilities Act," Defense Research Institute, 1997. Member, Board of Trustees, Mexican American Bar Association, 1995. Member, Board of Directors, Big Sisters of Los Angeles, 1995-2000. *Member:* Los Angeles County Bar Association (Labor and Employment Law Section); State Bar of California (Labor and Employment Section); Mexican American Bar Association of Los Angeles. (Los Angeles, California Office). ***PRACTICE AREAS:*** Labor and Employment Law. ***Email:*** amasters@winston.com

RONALD S. BETMAN, born Detroit, Michigan, February 26, 1961; admitted to bar, 1986, Illinois; 1987, Michigan; U.S. District Court, Northern District of Illinois, Trial Bar; U.S. Court of Appeals, Fifth, Seventh and District of Columbia Circuits. *Education:* University of Michigan (B.B.A., highest distinction, 1983; J.D., cum laude, 1986). Phi Beta Kappa. Contributing Editor, Michigan Law Review, 1984-1986. *Member:* Seventh Circuit Bar Association; American Bar Association; Defense Research Institute. ***PRACTICE AREAS:*** Securities; Consumer Class Actions; Business Litigation. ***Email:*** rbetman@winston.com

ROBERT Y. SPERLING, born Chicago, Illinois, July 14, 1947; admitted to bar, 1972, Illinois and U.S. District Court, Northern District of Illinois; 1975, U.S. Court of Appeals, Seventh Circuit; 1978, U.S. District Court, Eastern and Western Districts of Wisconsin; 1999, U.S. District Court, Southern and Central Districts of Illinois; 2001, U.S. Supreme Court. *Education:* University of Illinois (A.B., 1969); DePaul University (J.D., 1972). Member, DePaul Law Review. *Member:* Chicago, Illinois State and American (Member, Sections on: Civil Practice and Procedure; Litigation) Bar Associations. ***PRACTICE AREAS:*** Complex Litigation; Securities Litigation; Class Actions. ***Email:*** rsperling@winston.com

ANDREW P. BRIDGES, born Atlanta, Georgia, September 11, 1954; admitted to bar, 1984, Georgia; 1986, California; 1987, U.S. Supreme Court. *Education:* Stanford University (A.B., with distinction, 1976); Oxford University, Oxford, England (B.A., 1980; M.A., 1985); Harvard University (J.D., cum laude, 1983). Phi Beta Kappa. Law Clerk, Honorable Marvin H. Shoob, U.S. District Court, Northern District of Georgia, 1983-1985. Author: Article, "Cyber-Branding Holds Allure, Danger," Intellectual Property Supp. to S.F. Daily Journal, September 29, 1998; "Expert Advice," California State Bar Journal, October 1996; "Private RICO Litigation Based Upon 'Fraud in the Sale of Securities,'" 18 Georgia Law Review 43, 1983. Co-Author, Article, "Insurance Coverage for Trademark Litigation," Intellectual Property Strategist, October 1995. Lecturer: "Building Business Plans in an Uncertain Legal Environment: Aiming Plans at Moving Targets," eRisk Management Conference, International Quality and Productivity Center, San Francisco, November 2000; "Marketing and the Law," Third Annual Marketing and Sales Conference for Start-Up Internet and Software Companies, Software Development Forum, Mountain View, September 1998, June 1999, July 2000; "Brand Building: A Lasting Impression," Blueprint: The Business Strategy Summit for Internet Companies, co-sponsored by WSGR, San Francisco, June 2000; "Litigation Issues for the e-Commerce Company - From the Firing Line: Critical IP Issues for the Start-Up Company," State Bar of California Intellectual Property Section 2000 Spring Program, San Francisco, May 2000; "Music and the Internet," Association Literaire et Artistique Internationale, Canadian Chapter, Toronto, December 1999; "Music and the Internet," IBC UK Conferences, London, December 1999; "Strategic Issues in Trademark Law," Strategic Intellectual Property Planning Conference, CLE International, San Francisco, April 1998; "Jurisdictional Issues and the Internet," Practising Law Institute program on "Litigating Copyright, Trademark and Unfair Competition Cases for the Experienced Practitioner," San Francisco, December 1997; "Comparative Advertising under United States Law," Marques (Association of European Trademark Proprietors) Conference, Dublin, Ireland, September 1997; "Creative Strategies for Protection of Intellectual Property," American Bar Association Annual Convention, San Francisco, August 1997; "The European Community Trade Mark," American Bar Association Intellectual Property Law Conference, San Diego, June 1997; "International Considerations in Licensing," Practising Law Institute seminar on "Drafting Licensing Agreements," San Francisco, January 1997; "Discovery of Electronic Data in Litigation," International Trademark Association Mid-Year Meeting, Naples, Florida, November 1995; "Alternative Theories and Defenses," Practising Law Institute seminar on "Advanced Seminar on Trademark Law," San Francisco, April 1995. Co-Chair, Conference, "Digital Distribution of Music," American Conference Institute, February 2000. Moderator, "Copyright in an Internet World: Napster and Beyond," Fordham Conference on International Intellectual Property Law and Policy, New York, April 2001. Panelist, "Recording Industry Association of America v. Diamond Multimedia Systems," Loyola Law School Panel, Louisiana Music-New Orleans Pride Music Conference, New Orleans, April 1999. Instructor: University of Chicago Business School, 1999; Northwestern University Law School, 1999. Member, International Advisory Board, National Institute of Entertainment and Media Law, Southwestern University School of Law, Los Angeles. Domain Name Panelist, World Intellectual Property Organization Arbitration and Mediation Center, Geneva. *Member:* Bar Association of San Francisco (Co-Chair, Federal Courts Committee, 1989-1991); Atlanta, Federal and American (Sections on: Intellectual Property; Business Law; Litigation) Bar Associations; State Bar of Georgia; State Bar of California; International Trademark Association (Issues and Policy Committee; Chair, Emerging Issues Subcommitee); Copyright Society of the U.S.A.; Computer Law Association; European Communities Trademark Association; Marques (European Brand Owners Association); Hellenic Law Society of Northern California (Director, 1989-1994); World Trademark Law Report (Member, Board of Contributors); Berkeley Center for Law and Technology (Member, Executive Council). (San Francisco, California Office). ***LANGUAGES:*** Modern Greek, French and Italian. ***SPECIAL AGENCIES:*** Early Neutral Evaluator, U.S. District Court for the Northern District of California; Arbitrator (UDRP), World Intellectual Property Organization. ***REPORTED CASES:*** Recording Industry Association of America v. Diamond Multimedia Systems, 29 F. Supp. 2d 624 (C.D. Cal. 1998), aff'd, 180 F.3d 1072 (9th Cir. 1999); A&M Records, Inc. v. Napster, Inc., 239 F.3d 1004 (9th. Cir. 2001(for amicus curiae Digital Media Association); Quality Semiconductor, Inc. v. QLogic Corp., 31 U.S.P.Q.2d 1627 (N.D. Cal. 1994). ***Email:*** abridges@winston.com

(This Listing Continued)

JOHN D. FREDERICKS, born Castro Valley, California, February 28, 1964; admitted to bar, 1993, California. *Education:* University of California at Santa Cruz (B.A., 1987); University of San Francisco (J.D., cum laude, 1993). Author, "The Character of Section 357 (c): Why the Underlying Regulation is Capable of Producing Absurd Results," ABA Tax Lawyer, 167 Fall 1994. (San Francisco, California Office). ***PRACTICE AREAS:*** Finance; Bankruptcy; Commercial Law; Mortgages. ***Email:*** jfredericks@winston.com

AMANDA GROVES, born Fairbanks, Alaska, August 25, 1972; admitted to bar, 1996, California. *Education:* University of California at Los Angeles (B.A. in Communication Studies, cum laude, 1993); Santa Clara University (J.D., cum laude, 1996). (San Francisco, California Office). ***PRACTICE AREAS:*** Litigation. ***Email:*** agroves@winston.com

DEMETRA V. GEORGELOS, admitted to bar, 1992, California. *Education:* Yale University (B.A., cum laude, 1989); University of California School of Law, Los Angeles (J.D., 1992). Distinguished Advocate, UCLA Moot Honors Program; Selected to Roger J. Traynor Moot Court Competition Team. (Los Angeles, California Office). ***PRACTICE AREAS:*** Secured Finance; Commercial Loans; Workouts. ***Email:*** dgeorgelos@winston.com

DAVID A. HONIG, born Bangor, Maine, November 23, 1956; admitted to bar, 1992, California. *Education:* University of Oregon (B.A., magna cum laude, 1984); University of Chicago (J.D., 1991). Phi Beta Kappa. Law Clerk to the Hon. Charles L. Levin, Michigan Supreme Court, 1991-1992. Co-Author: "Chapter 9—Municipal Adjustment of Debts: An Overview," Central California Reorganization Conference, 1995. Chair, Barristers' Alternative Resolution Committee, 1995. *Member:* Bar Association of San Francisco (Delegate, State Bar Convention, 1999—); State Bar of California (Co-Chair, Business Law Section, Education Committee, 1999-2000; Member, Debtor-Creditor Relations and Bankruptcy Committee). (San Francisco, California Office). ***Email:*** dhonig@winston.com

ROBERT A. JULIAN, born Washington, D.C., April 5, 1954; admitted to bar, 1979, California. *Education:* University of San Francisco (B.A., 1976); Hastings College of Law, University of California (J.D., 1979). Alpha Sigma Nu. Author: "Tactical Considerations for Lenders Evaluating Counterclaims, Cross-Claims and Third Party Claims," in *Lenders on the Attack,* American Bar Association (1989), reprinted as "Defense Strategies for Lender Liability Cases," 1 Prac. Lit. 65 (1990); "Jurisdiction Under the Bankruptcy and Federal Judgeship Act of 1984," in *Fight or Flight: What to Do if Bankruptcy Strikes Your Lawsuit,* American Bar Association (1990); "Bankruptcy Litigation: More Than Voodoo," 21 Lit. 17 (Summer 1995). Co-Author with T. Keller, et al: "The Treatment of Insurance Policies and Proceeds in Bankruptcy," in *Resolving Insurer/Insured Business Insurance Disputes,* Exec. Ent. (1991). Lecturer: American Bar Association; Professional Education Systems; California Bankruptcy Forum; Association of Insolvency Accountants; Executive Enterprises. (San Francisco, California Office). ***REPORTED CASES:*** Bunker v. County of Orange, 183 Cal. App. 4th 542 (2002); Piombo Corp. v. Castlerock Properties (In re Castlerock Properties), 781 F.2d 159 (9th Cir. 1986); Gold Circle Stores v. Riviera Finance - East Bay, 540 F. Supp. 15 (N.D. Cal. 1982); Gauvin v. Wagner (In re Gauvin), 24 B.R. 578 (Bankr. 9th Cir. 1982). ***PRACTICE AREAS:*** Complex Business Trial Practice; Complex Business Litigation; Fiduciary Duty; Debtor and Creditor Remedies. ***Email:*** rjulian@winston.com

MICHAEL KIP MALY, born San Antonio, Texas, July 18, 1945; admitted to bar, 1975, California. *Education:* University of Texas (B.A., with honors, 1967); Hastings College of Law, University of California (J.D., 1975). Lecturer and Author: Practising Law Institute, American Law Institute/American Bar Association. Member, San Francisco Superior Court Arbitration Panel. [With U.S. Navy, 1967-1972 (LT)]. (San Francisco, California Office). ***PRACTICE AREAS:*** Commercial Trial Practice and Litigation. ***Email:*** mmaly@winston.com

PATRICK A. MURPHY, born Huntingdon, Pennsylvania, March 10, 1939; admitted to bar, 1966, California. *Education:* Williams College (B.A., 1961); Boalt Hall School of Law, University of California (J.D., 1965). Author: "Restraint and Reimbursement: The Secured Creditor in Arrangement and Reorganization Proceedings," 30 Bus. Law., 15, 1974; "Use of Collateral in Business Rehabilitations: A Suggested Redrafting of Section 7-203 of the Bankruptcy Reform Act," 63 Calif. L. Rev. 1483, 1975; "The United States Bankruptcy Reform Act of 1978," Int'l. Bus. Law, 182, 1979; *Creditors' Rights in Bankruptcy,* Second edition, Thomsen - West. Member, National Bankruptcy Conference, 1971. Lecturer and Author: American Law Institute/American Bar Association; Practising Law Institute; California Continuing Education of the Bar. Fellow, American College of Bankruptcy, 1990. Member, International Insolvency Institute. (San Francisco, California Office). ***PRACTICE AREAS:*** Business Workouts; Bankruptcy Reorganizations; Creditors Remedies; Secured Financing. ***Email:*** pmurphy@winston.com

JOHN C. NISHI, born Tokyo, Japan; admitted to bar, 1993, Illinois and U.S. District Court, Northern District of Illinois; 1995, California, U.S. District Court, Northern District of California and U.S. Court of Appeals, Ninth Circuit. *Education:* Yale University (B.A., cum laude, 1977); University of Southern California (M.M., 1980); University of Chicago (J.D., 1993). Recipient, Outstanding Graduate Award, University of Southern California. Associate Articles Editor, University of Chicago Legal Forum. Member, Editorial Board, Trademark Reporter. *Member:* American Bar Association; International Trademark Association (Member, Emerging Issues Committee, Fair Use and Other Boundaries Subcommittee; Subcommittee Chair, 2006). (San Francisco, California Office). ***PRACTICE AREAS:*** Trademarks; Unfair Competition; Advertising Law; Consumer Protection; Internet Law; Copyrights. ***Email:*** jnishi@winston.com

MARK A. OLSON, born Pittsburgh, Pennsylvania, March 31, 1954; admitted to bar, 1990, California. *Education:* St. Louis University (B.A., 1977); Northwestern University (M.A., 1978; Ph.D., 1983); University of California, Boalt Hall School of Law (J.D., 1990). Order of the Coif. Lecturer: Practicing Law Institute; Bar Association of San Francisco; Alameda County Bar Association. *Member:* Bar Association of San Francisco; Alameda County and Contra Costa County Bar Associations; State Bar of California; San Francisco Lawyers Club. (San Francisco, California Office). ***PRACTICE AREAS:*** Business Litigation; Complex and Multi-District Litigation; Unfair Competition; Commercial Litigation; Creditors Rights in Bankruptcy. ***Email:*** molson@winston.com

RANDY ROGERS, born Los Angeles, California, August 19, 1954; admitted to bar, 1980, California. *Education:* University of California at Santa Cruz (B.A., with honors, 1977); Hastings College of the Law, University of California (J.D., 1980). Senior Note and

(This Listing Continued)

WINSTON & STRAWN LLP, Chicago—Continued

Comment Editor, Hastings Law Journal, 1979-1980. Author: *Collier Farm Bankruptcy Guide,* Matthew Bender, 1989, 2nd ed., 1997; "Taking Security Interests in Personal Property," Cal. CEB 2001, 2nd ed., 2003; "Current Developments in Agricultural Bankruptcies and Insolvencies," 5 Drake J. of Ag. Law 137 (2000); Note, "Assignment of Rents Clauses Under California Law and in Bankruptcy: Strategy for the Secured Creditor," 31 Hastings Law Journal 1433, 1980. Adjunct Professor of Law, University of San Francisco, 1983. Contributor, *Collier on Bankruptcy* (rev. 15th ed.), *Collier Bankruptcy Manual, Collier Bankruptcy Practice Guide.* Lecturer and Author: Practising Law Institute; Central California Bankruptcy Association; American Agricultural Law Association; American Bar Association. Member, Board of Editors, *Collier on Bankruptcy,* 1996—. *Member:* Bar Association of San Francisco (Member, Commercial Law and Bankruptcy Section); State Bar of California (Member: Agribusiness Committee, 1996-1999; Uniform Commercial Code Committee, 1986-1988); American Bar Association (Member, Committee on Commercial Financial Services and Agricultural Financing and Real Estate Subcommittees, 1985—). Fellow, American College of Bankruptcy. (San Francisco, California Office). ***PRACTICE AREAS:*** Business Workouts; Bankruptcy Reorganizations; Creditors Remedies; Real Estate Finance; Secured Financing; Commercial Lending. ***Email:*** rrogers@winston.com

PAUL P. SAGAN, born Yonkers, New York; admitted to bar, 1991, California. *Education:* Brown University (B.A., 1984); John E. Anderson Graduate School of Management, University of California, Los Angeles (M.B.A., 1991); University of California, Los Angeles (J.D., 1991). Co-Author: "Charging the Secured Party's Collateral," in *Up The Downhill Slope,* Price Waterhouse Annual Reorganization & Bankruptcy Conference, 1992; "Valuation Issue in Bankruptcy," Association of Insolvency Accountants' 10th Annual Bankruptcy & Reorganization Conference, April 20-22, 1994. *Member:* State Bar of California. (Los Angeles, California Office). ***PRACTICE AREAS:*** Secured Finance; Commercial Loans; Workouts. ***Email:*** psagan@winston.com

ERIC E. SAGERMAN, born Brooklyn, New York, 1966; admitted to bar, 1991, California. *Education:* London School of Economics, London (G.C., List of Highly Commendable Exam Performances, 1986-1987); University of California at Santa Barbara (B.A., summa cum laude, 1988); University of California at Los Angeles (J.D., 1991). Cited in "Outstanding Young Lawyers," 15 *Turnarounds & Workouts* No. 4, April, 1999. Author: "The Ethics of Engagement: Getting In and Getting Out," *Bankruptcy Battleground West,* 1997. (Los Angeles, California Office). ***REPORTED CASES:*** In re Condor Systems, Inc., 290 B.R. 752 (Bankr. N.D. Cal. 2003). ***PRACTICE AREAS:*** Insolvency; Restructuring. ***Email:*** esagerman@winston.com

MARGARET SHENEMAN, born Richmond, California, January 25, 1949; admitted to bar, 1976, California. *Education:* University of California at Davis (A.B., 1970; M.A., 1972); Boalt Hall School of Law, University of California (J.D., 1976). Phi Beta Kappa; Order of the Coif. Articles Editor, California Law Review, 1975-1976. Author: *California Foreclosure,* Shepard's/McGraw Hill, 1991; "Equipment Leasing and the Bankruptcy Code," *Equipment Leasing - Leveraged Leasing,* Practising Law Institute, 1988; Note, "The Demise of the Due On Sale Clause," 64 Calif. L. R. 573, 1976. Co-Author: "The Secured Creditor's Complaint: Relief From the Automatic Stay in Bankruptcy Proceedings," 65 Calif. L. R. 1216, 1977; with C. Dumas, "Equipment Leasing and the Bankruptcy Code," in *Equipment Leasing - Leveraged Leasing* Practicing Law Institute, 1999. Lecturer, Stanford University, 1994-1997. Lecturer and Author: American Law Institute/American Bar Association; California Continuing Education of the Bar; National Conference of Bankruptcy Judges; Northwest Institute on Bankruptcy Law; Practising Law Institute; Bar Association of San Francisco; Association of Insolvency Accountants. Adjunct Professor of Law, University of San Francisco, 1978-1982. Member, Article 9 Study Committee for the Permanent Editorial Board for the Uniform Commercial Code, 1990-1993. *Member:* State Bar of California (Chair, Uniform Commercial Code Committee, 1981-1984; Executive Committee, 1985-1988; Co-Chair, Joint Committee on Anti-Deficiency Laws, 1986-1992); American Bar Association (Member, Personal Property Leasing Subcommittee of the Uniform Commercial Code Committee, 1984-present). Fellow, American Bankruptcy College, 1991. (San Francisco, California Office). ***PRACTICE AREAS:*** Venture Capital; Equipment Leasing; Restructuring; Insolvency; Bankruptcy Reorganization; Creditors Remedies; Real Estate Finance; Secured Financing; Commercial Lending. ***Email:*** msheneman@winston.com

ROLF S. WOOLNER, admitted to bar, 1983, New York; 1989, California. *Education:* University of Calgary, Calgary, Alberta (B.A., first class honors and gold medalist, 1979); Yale University (J.D., 1982). *Member:* Los Angeles County (Member, Trial Practice Inn of Court) and American (Member, Litigation Section, Bankruptcy and Insolvency Litigation Committee; Commercial and Banking Litigation Committee) Bar Associations; Association of Business Trial Lawyers. (Los Angeles, California Office). ***PRACTICE AREAS:*** Commercial Trial Practice and Litigation; Creditors Remedies. ***Email:*** rwoolner@winston.com

DEREK G. BARELLA, born Oak Park, Illinois, July 5, 1969; admitted to bar, 1994, Illinois. *Education:* Ball State University (B.S., cum laude, 1991); Indiana University (J.D., cum laude, 1994). Author: "Checking the Trigger - Happy Congress—The Extraterritorial Extension of Federal Employment Laws Requires Prudence," 69 Ind. L. J. 884, Summer 1994. ***PRACTICE AREAS:*** Labor and Employment Law. ***Email:*** dbarella@winston.com

MATTHEW F. BERGMANN, born Cincinnati, Ohio, March 26, 1969; admitted to bar, 1994, Illinois. *Education:* University of Michigan (B.B.A., with distinction, 1991; J.D., cum laude, 1994). ***PRACTICE AREAS:*** Mergers, Acquisitions and Divestitures; Securities. ***Email:*** mbergmann@winston.com

STEPHEN V. D'AMORE, born Chicago, Illinois, November 3, 1969; admitted to bar, 1994, Illinois; U.S. District Court, Northern District of Illinois; U.S. Court of Appeals, Seventh Circuit. *Education:* Loyola University, Chicago (B.A., summa cum laude, 1991); DePaul University College of Law (J.D., with honors, 1994). Order of the Coif. ***PRACTICE AREAS:*** Civil Litigation. ***Email:*** sdamore@winston.com

DAMON DiCASTRI, born Kenosha, Wisconsin, October 9, 1968; admitted to bar, 1994, Illinois. *Education:* University of Wisconsin (B.B.A., 1990); Northwestern University (J.D., 1994). ***PRACTICE AREAS:*** Corporate Finance. ***Email:*** ddicastri@winston.com

(This Listing Continued)

PATRICIA M. DINEEN, admitted to bar, 1990, New York; 1995, Florida. *Education:* Hunter College (B.A., 1986); New York University (J.D., 1989). Phi Beta Kappa. Member, New York University Law Review. *Member:* The Florida Bar. (New York, N.Y. Office). ***PRACTICE AREAS:*** Real Estate Finance; Real Estate Sales and Acquisitions; Leases and Leasing; Workouts; Joint Ventures. ***Email:*** pdineen@winston.com

DAVID J. DOYLE, born Lansing, Michigan, January 26, 1969; admitted to bar, 1994, Illinois. *Education:* Kalamazoo College (B.S., 1991); Northwestern University (J.D., 1994). ***Email:*** ddoyle@winston.com

M. CHRISTINE GRAFF, born McCook, Nebraska, January 2, 1969; admitted to bar, 1994, Illinois. *Education:* Creighton University (B.A., 1991); University of Chicago (J.D., 1994). *Member:* Chicago Bar Association (Co-Chair, YLS Real Estate Committee). ***PRACTICE AREAS:*** Commercial Real Estate; Real Estate. ***Email:*** mgraff@winston.com

BRIAN L. HEIDELBERGER, born Skokie, Illinois, April 10, 1969; admitted to bar, 1994, Illinois. *Education:* Indiana University (B.S., 1991); Chicago-Kent College of Law (J.D., 1994). Kent Legal Scholar. Member, Chicago-Kent Law Review. ***PRACTICE AREAS:*** Advertising Law; Marketing Law; Promotion Law; Sponsorship Law; Electronic Commerce; Copyrights; Trademarks. ***Email:*** bheidelberger@winston.com

LUKE ALLAN PALESE, born Milwaukee, Wisconsin, May 1966; admitted to bar, 1991, Wisconsin and U.S. District Court, Eastern and Western Districts of Wisconsin; 1999, Illinois. *Education:* Marquette University (B.S., cum laude, 1988; J.D., cum laude, 1991); New York University School of Law (LL.M., 1998). ***PRACTICE AREAS:*** Civil Litigation; Commercial Litigation. ***Email:*** lpalese@winston.com

RAYMOND PERKINS, born East St. Louis, Illinois, December 26, 1968; admitted to bar, 1994, Illinois. *Education:* University of Illinois (B.A., 1991; J.D., 1994). ***Email:*** rperkins@winston.com

TRACY A. O'FLAHERTY, born Evergreen Park, Illinois, February 6, 1969; admitted to bar, 1994, Massachusetts; 1995, U.S. District Court, District of Massachusetts; 1996, Illinois; U.S. Court of Appeals, First Circuit; 1998, U.S. District Court, Northern and Southern Districts of Illinois and U.S. Court of Appeals, Seventh Circuit. *Education:* Boston University (B.A., cum laude, 1991); Villanova University (J.D., 1994). Staff Member, 1992-1994 and Articles Editor, 1993-1994, Villanova Law Review. Author: 38 Villanova Law Review, 1579, 1993. Co-Author, "Playing Trade Secret Offense and Defense: Protecting Your Trade Secrets While Recruiting Your Industry's Best and Brightest." Board Member: Chicago Legal Clinic, Inc.; Intercultural Montessori Language Academy; Bradley Place Homeowners' Association. *Member:* Chicago Bar Association; Alliance for Women of the Chicago Bar Association. ***REPORTED CASES:*** Tice v. American Airlines, Inc.; Kalush v. Deluxe Corporation. ***PRACTICE AREAS:*** Labor and Employment Litigation. ***Email:*** toflaherty@winston.com

RONALD Y. ROTHSTEIN, born Winnipeg, Manitoba, Canada, August 3, 1969; admitted to bar, 1995, Illinois; 1996, District of Columbia. *Education:* University of Manitoba (B.A., with honors, 1991); Valparaiso University (J.D., cum laude, 1994); The George Washington University (LL.M., 1998). Editor-in-Chief, Canadian Law Newsletter, Section of International Law and Practice: Canadian Law Committee. *Member:* American Bar Association. ***PRACTICE AREAS:*** Litigation; Intellectual Property Law; Advertising Law. ***Email:*** rrothstein@winston.com

JOHN M. SCHLOERB, born Chicago, Illinois, May 2, 1962; admitted to bar, 1992, Illinois. *Education:* University of Michigan (B.A., with high honors, 1984); Columbia University (M.A., 1985); University of Pennsylvania (J.D., magna cum laude, 1992). Phi Beta Kappa. Staff Member, University of Pennsylvania Law Review, 1990-1992. ***PRACTICE AREAS:*** Corporate Law. ***Email:*** jschloerb@winston.com

JOSEPH A. SPIEGLER, born Long Island, New York, April 4, 1968; admitted to bar, 1994, Illinois. *Education:* New York University (B.A., 1990); University of Notre Dame (J.D., 1994). ***PRACTICE AREAS:*** Antitrust; Complex and Multi-District Litigation; RICO; White Collar Crime. ***Email:*** jspiegler@winston.com

JOHN J. TULLY, JR., born Chicago, Illinois, February 19, 1969; admitted to bar, 1994, Illinois and U.S. District Court, Northern District of Illinois; 2002, U.S. District Court, Eastern District of Michigan; 2005, U.S Court of Appeals, Ninth Circuit. *Education:* Yale University (B.A., magna cum laude, 1991); Northwestern University (J.D., cum laude, 1994). Associate Editor, Northwestern University Law Review, 1993-1994. ***PRACTICE AREAS:*** Litigation. ***Email:*** jtully@winston.com

RICARDO E. UGARTE, born Huanuco, Peru, September 1, 1968; admitted to bar, 1993, Illinois and U.S. District Court, Northern District of Illinois. *Education:* University of Chicago (B.A., with special honors, 1990); Northwestern University (J.D., 1993). Dean's List. Former Board Member, Pro Bono Advocates. *Member:* American and International Bar Associations. (Geneva, Switzerland Office). ***LANGUAGES:*** Spanish, French and Italian. ***TRANSACTIONS:*** Conducted Major International Arbitration Trials - IPOC v. LV Finance. ***PRACTICE AREAS:*** International Arbitration; International Litigation; Products Liability Litigation; Commercial Litigation. ***Email:*** rugarte@winston.com

MICHAEL D. WHITTY, born Lubbock, Texas, June 22, 1962; admitted to bar, 1989, Texas; 1993, Michigan; 1996, Illinois. *Education:* University of Texas at Austin (B.B.A., with honors, 1983; J.D., 1988). Certified Public Accountant, Texas, 1985-1993. Adjunct Professor, Northwestern University School of Law, 1998-2000. Certified Financial Planner, 2002—. *Member:* American Bar Association; International Bar Association; Family Firm Institute; Attorneys for Family Held Enterprises; Chicago Estate Planning Council. ***PRACTICE AREAS:*** Trusts and Estates; Family Wealth Transfer. ***Email:*** mwhitty@winston.com

FRANCISCO J. PAVIA, born San Juan, Puerto Rico, June 4, 1964; admitted to bar, 1991, Massachusetts and District of Columbia; 2000, Puerto Rico. *Education:* Princeton University (A.B., 1986); Harvard Law School (J.D., 1990). Fulbright Scholar, Bogota, Colombia, 1986-1987. (Washington, D.C. Office). ***LANGUAGES:*** Spanish. ***PRACTICE AREAS:*** Federal Government Relations; Corporate Law. ***Email:*** fpavia@winston.com

CHRISTINE A. EDWARDS, born Fort Monmouth, New Jersey, August 30, 1952; admitted to bar, 1983, Maryland; 1985, District of Columbia; 1990, Illinois. *Education:* University of Maryland at College Park (B.A., 1974); University of Maryland at Baltimore

(This Listing Continued)

(J.D., with honors, 1983). Author: "The CLO's Perspective on Managing Legal Risk," CLO Magazine, Spring 2002; "Seeing Around Corners - SOX Sections 302 and 906," CLE Magazine, Spring 2004; "New Accounting Rules: Miss the Issue, Fail the Exam," CLE Magazine, Winter 2004. Director, 2000—; Member, Audit Committee, Rush University Medical Center. Director, Board of Visitors, University of Maryland School of Law, 1997—. Board Member: Chicago Board Options Exchange, 1993-1999; SPS Transaction Services Inc., 1997. Member, Women in Housing and Finance, 1982—. Chairman: Financial Services Roundtable Public Policy and Legislative Committee, 2000-2003; Financial Services Roundtable Initiative for Class Action Reform, 2000-2003. Member: SIA Litigation Committee, 1995-1999; NYSE Legal Advisory Committee, 1992-1995; CLO Roundtable, 1995—2004; NASD Committee on Continuing Education, 1999. *Member:* The Association of the Bar of the City of New York; Illinois State, Maryland State and American (Member, Business Law Section on Securities) Bar Associations. ***TRANSACTIONS:*** Discover Financial Services (a subsidiary of Morgan Stanley) acquisition of Pulse Network, 2005. ***PRACTICE AREAS:*** Business Law; Corporate Governance; Securities Law; Banking Law; Securities Enforcement Actions; Legislative and Regulatory Policy; Financial Services. ***Email:*** cedwards@winston.com

RAUL R. HERRERA, born Republic of Panama, 1958; admitted to bar, 1984, District of Columbia. *Education:* George Washington University, Elliott School of International Affairs (B.A., 1981); George Washington University School of Law (J.D., 1984). Member, Executive Committee, International Council, Elliott School of International Affairs, The George Washington University. Chair, Advisory Committee, Latin American Studies Program, The George Washington University Elliott School of International Affairs. Former Member, Board of Directors: International Development Conference; Inter-American Bar Foundation; Federal Bar Association, District of Columbia Chapter; National Hispanic Student Network. *Member:* District of Columbia Bar (Former Chair, Investment and Finance Committee, International Law Section); American Bar Association (Advisory Committee, Latin American Legal Initiatives Council; Liaison to the Inter-American Bar Association); Inter-American Bar Association (Board of Directors; Chair, Corporate Counsel Committee); Southern Florida Regional Corporate Counsel Group; International Bar Association (Latin American Regional Counsel Committee). (Washington, D.C. Office). ***LANGUAGES:*** Spanish and Portugese. ***PRACTICE AREAS:*** International Project Finance; Capital Markets; Corporate Transactions; Commercial Arbitration. ***Email:*** rherrera@winston.com

JOHN L. CARR, JR., born Madison, Georgia, August 31, 1946; admitted to bar, 1978, District of Columbia and Georgia (inactive) (Not admitted in Illinois). *Education:* Auburn University (B.S., Aerospace Engineering, 1969); University of Georgia (J.D., 1978). Editor, University of Georgia Law Review, 1977-1978. Co-Author chapter examining the U.S. regulatory framework for foreign banks in "Regulation for Foreign Banks: United States and International," 2000. Co-Author: "The Indirect Foreign Tax Credit," BNA Tax Management Portfolio, 1997; "OCC Moving National Banks to the Forefront of Internet Banking," Electronic Banking Law and Commerce Report, 2000; "OCC Continues to Lead the Way on Internet Banking," Electronic Banking Law and Commerce Report, 2001; "Earnings Stripping Provisions: A Historical Perspective and Critque," Tax Management International Journal, 2003; "Capital Issues in the Attribution of Profits to Branches of International Banks," Tax Management International Journal, 2004. Member, International Fiscal Association. [Pilot, U.S. Air Force, 1969-1975]. ***PRACTICE AREAS:*** International Tax; Banking; Corporate. ***Email:*** jcarr@winston.com

NORMAN K. BECK, born Columbus, Ohio, May 27, 1970; admitted to bar, 1995, Illinois. *Education:* Occidental College (A.B., 1992); Washington University (J.D., 1995). ***PRACTICE AREAS:*** Complex and Multi-District Litigation; White Collar Criminal Defense; Securities. ***Email:*** nbeck@winston.com

JON MICHAEL BROWN, JR., born Bluffton, Indiana, April 27, 1970; admitted to bar, 1995, Illinois. *Education:* University of Notre Dame (B.A., magna cum laude, 1992); Northwestern University (J.D., 1995). ***Email:*** jbrown@winston.com

TARAS A. GRACEY, born Detroit, Michigan, August 2, 1969; admitted to bar, 1995, Illinois. *Education:* University of California, Berkeley (B.A., 1991); Duke University (J.D., 1995). ***PRACTICE AREAS:*** Civil Litigation; Complex Litigation; Patent Litigation. ***Email:*** tgracey@winston.com

DIANA JULIET HSU, born Detroit, Michigan, August 14, 1964; admitted to bar, 1993, Pennsylvania; 1994, Illinois; 1997 U.S. District Court, Northern District of Illinois. *Education:* University of Michigan (B.B.A., Marketing, 1986); DePaul University College of Law (J.D., with honors, 1993). Order of the Coif. Assistant Articles Editor, Journal of Hospital and Health Law. *Member:* American Bar Association; Chicago Bar Association. ***PRACTICE AREAS:*** Litigation; Products Liability. ***Email:*** dhsu@winston.com

BRIAN J. KOZLOWSKI, born LaGrange, Illinois, October 22, 1969; admitted to bar, 1995, Illinois. *Education:* University of Illinois (B.A., 1991); Loyola University (J.D., 1995). ***Email:*** bkozlowski@winston.com

MICHAEL J. LOTUS, born Boston, Massachusetts, April 22, 1963; admitted to bar, 1993, Illinois and U.S. District Court, Northern District of Illinois; 1995, U.S. Court of Appeals, Seventh Circuit. *Education:* University of Chicago (B.A., 1985); Indiana University (J.D., 1993). Law Clerk for Hon. Michael Kanne, U.S. Court of Appeals, Seventh Circuit, 1993-1994. ***PRACTICE AREAS:*** Litigation. ***Email:*** mlotus@winston.com

JOSEPH P. LUKAS, born Milwaukee, Wisconsin, October 9, 1970; admitted to bar, 1995, Wisconsin; 1997, Pennsylvania; 2000, Illinois. *Education:* Boston College (B.S., *summa cum laude,* 1992); University of Wisconsin (J.D., cum laude, 1995). Beta Gamma Sigma; Alpha Sigma Nu. ***PRACTICE AREAS:*** Mergers and Acquisitions; Securitization; Secured Lending. ***Email:*** jlukas@winston.com

TIMOTHY J. McCAFFREY, born Palatine, Illinois, August 11, 1970; admitted to bar, 1995, Illinois. *Education:* Indiana University (B.S., 1992; J.D., cum laude, 1995). ***PRACTICE AREAS:*** Commercial Litigation; Construction Law; White Collar Crime. ***Email:*** tmccaffrey@winston.com

DANIEL J. McGUIRE, born Rochester, New York, April 30, 1970; admitted to bar, 1996, New York; 1997, Illinois. *Education:* Villanova University (B.A., 1992); University of Chicago (J.D., 1995). ***Email:*** dmcguire@winston.com

(This Listing Continued)

RAYMOND W. MITCHELL, born Chicago, Illinois, November 11, 1969; admitted to bar, 1993, Illinois; U.S. Court of Appeals, Fifth, Sixth and Seventh Circuits. *Education:* Loyola University of Chicago (A.B., 1991); University of Chicago Law School and Loyola University of Chicago School of Law (J.D., 1993). Law Clerk, Judge James L. Ryan, U.S. Court of Appeals, Sixth Circuit, 1993-1994; Law Clerk, Hon. James D. Heiple, Illinois Supreme Court, 1996-1998. Research Editor, 1992-1993 and Staff Member, 1991-1992, Loyola Law Journal. Author: "A Small Departure from the Truth: When Private Religious Speech Runs Afoul of the Establishment Clause," 23 Loyola U. Chi L.J. 867, 1992. *Chicago, Illinois State and American (Member:* Appellate Rules & Statutes Subcommittee; Appellate Practice Committee) Bar Associations; Illinois Appellate Lawyers Association. ***PRACTICE AREAS:*** Appellate Practice; Commercial Litigation. ***Email:*** rmitchell@winston.com

JOHN E. MOONEY, born Evanston, Illinois, 1966; admitted to bar, 1995, Illinois. *Education:* Villanova University (B.A.); DePaul University (J.D.). *Member:* Seventh Circuit and American Bar Associations; Federal Circuit Bar Association. ***PRACTICE AREAS:*** Complex Litigation; Patent Litigation. ***Email:*** jmooney@winston.com

JOHN W. MOSS, born Kankakee, Illinois, September 24, 1964; admitted to bar, 1995, Illinois. *Education:* Northwestern University (B.A., 1986); DePaul University (J.D., with honors, 1995). Order of the Coif. Articles Editor, Journal of Health and Hospital Law. ***PRACTICE AREAS:*** Medical Litigation. ***Email:*** jmoss@winston.com

ADRIENNE BANKS PITTS, born Dayton, Ohio, June 19, 1968; admitted to bar, 1995, Illinois. *Education:* University of Pennsylvania (B.S., 1990); Boston University (J.D., with honors, 1995). Immediate Past Chair, Chicago Committee on Minorities in Large Law Firms. *Member:* Cook County (Committee Chair), Chicago, Illinois State and American Bar Associations. ***PRACTICE AREAS:*** Commercial Litigation; Complex and Multi-District Litigation; White Collar Crime. ***Email:*** apitts@winston.com

PETER W. POULOS, born Chicago, Illinois, July 29, 1968; admitted to bar, 1995, Illinois. *Education:* University of Illinois (B.S., 1990); Boalt Hall School of Law, University of California (J.D., 1995). ***Email:*** ppoulos@winston.com

TIMOTHY W. SMITH, born Des Moines, Iowa, January 25, 1970; admitted to bar, 1995, Illinois. *Education:* Purdue University (B.S., 1992); Columbia University (J.D., 1995). ***PRACTICE AREAS:*** Corporate Law. ***Email:*** tsmith@winston.com

ERIK W. SNAPP, born LaCrosse, Wisconsin, March 22, 1968; admitted to bar, 1995, Minnesota; 1996, Illinois and U.S. District Court, Northern District of Illinois; 1999, U.S. Court of Appeals, Seventh Circuit; 2004, U.S. District Court, Eastern District of Wisconsin and U.S. District Court, Southern District of Illinois. *Education:* St. John's University (B.S., cum laude, 1990); University of Minnesota (J.D., cum laude, 1995). ***PRACTICE AREAS:*** Complex Litigation; Appellate Practice; Health Care Fraud; Products Liability; White Collar Criminal Defense; Consumer Fraud Defense. ***Email:*** esnapp@winston.com

ERYK J. SPYTEK, born Melrose Park, Illinois, April 4, 1968; admitted to bar, 1994, Illinois. *Education:* Georgetown University, College of Arts & Science (B.A., 1992); Loyola University, Chicago (J.D., 1994); London School of Economics and Political Science, London, England (LL.M., with Merit, in International Business Law, 1995). *Member:* Chicago and American Bar Associations. ***LANGUAGES:*** Polish, Spanish and French. ***PRACTICE AREAS:*** Corporate. ***Email:*** espytek@winston.com

VICTORIA F. STACH, born Chicago, Illinois, November 5, 1966; admitted to bar, 1992, Illinois. *Education:* Northwestern University (B.A., 1988); Emory University School of Law (J.D., 1992). *Member:* American Bar Association. ***PRACTICE AREAS:*** Securitization; Corporate Finance. ***Email:*** vstach@winston.com

MARK A. DE BERNARDO, born Rochester, New York, December 27, 1953; admitted to bar, 1979, District of Columbia; 2001, U.S. Supreme Court. *Education:* Marquette University (B.A., cum laude, 1976); Georgetown University (J.D., 1979). (Washington, D.C. Office). ***PRACTICE AREAS:*** Labor and Employment; Drug and Alcohol Testing; Legislative.

H. ALLEN BLACK III, born Boston, Massachusetts, September 3, 1957; admitted to bar, 1991, Virginia, U.S. Court of Appeals, Fourth Circuit and U.S. Court of the Armed Forces; 1996, Maryland and U.S. District Court, District of Maryland; 2004, District of Columbia. *Education:* United States Coast Guard Academy (B.S., 1979); College of William & Mary (J.D., 1991). Order of the Coif. Member, William & Mary Law Review. Adjunct Professor, Maritime Law, University of Baltimore Law School, 1996—. Author: "The Illusion Qualified Immunity," William & Mary Law Review; Author: "Coast Guard Issues Maritime Security Regulations for Vessels," Benedict's Maritime Bulletin. *Member:* Virginia, Maryland State; District of Columbia Bar; Maritime Law Association; U.S. Naval Institute. [U.S. Coast Guard, 1975-1996, CDR]. (Washington, D.C. Office). ***LANGUAGES:*** Russian. ***PRACTICE AREAS:*** Maritime; Litigation; Admiralty Law; International Law; Health Care. ***Email:*** hblack@winston.com

M. CARTER DeLORME, born Washington, D.C., July 29, 1970; admitted to bar, 1995, Virginia; 1996, District of Columbia. *Education:* University of Pennsylvania (B.A., 1992); Georgetown University (J.D., 1995). *Member:* The District of Columbia Bar; Virginia State Bar; American Bar Association. (Washington, D.C. Office). ***PRACTICE AREAS:*** Labor and Employment. ***Email:*** mdelorme@winston.com

CATHERINE DiFIGLIA, born Queens, New York, July 19, 1966; admitted to bar, 1996, New York. *Education:* American University (B.S., 1988); Hofstra University (J.D., 1995). (New York, N.Y. Office). ***Email:*** cdifiglia@winston.com

MICHAEL T. DYSON, born Washington, D.C., October 13, 1966; admitted to bar, 1996, Maryland; 1997, District of Columbia and Virginia. *Education:* James Madison University (B.A., 1989); Georgetown University (J.D., 1995). Law Clerk to the Hon. James C. Cacheris, 1995-1996, Hon. Theresa Carroll Buchanan, 1996-1997, U.S. District Court, Eastern District of Virginia, Alexandria Division. Pro Bono Committee, Winston & Strawn LLP. *Member:* The District of Columbia Bar; Virginia State Bar; Maryland State Bar Association. (Washington, D.C. Office). ***PRACTICE AREAS:*** Litigation (100%). ***Email:*** mdyson@winston.com

MARION KRISTAL GOLDBERG, born New York, N.Y., September 30, 1947; admitted to bar, 1995, Maryland; 1997, District of Columbia. *Education:* University of Rochester (B.A., 1969); Columbia University (M.S., Social Work, 1973); University of Mary-

(This Listing Continued)

WINSTON & STRAWN LLP, Chicago—Continued

land (J.D., with honor, 1995). Order of the Coif. Associate Editor, Maryland Law Review. Judicial Law Clerk to the Hon. Lawrence F. Rodowsky, Court of Appeals of Maryland, 1995-1996. Author: "Stark (Proposed) Regulations Finally Issued," Maryland State Bar Association Bar Bulletin, April, 1998; "Maryland Rule 1-502: A Required Balancing Test Before Impeachment By Prior Criminal Conviction," 53 MD. L. REV. 844 (1994). *Member:* Maryland State (Member, Health Law Section) and American (Member, Health Law Section) Bar Associations; District of Columbia Bar (Member, Health Law Section; Member, Program & Education Committee); American Health Lawyers Association. (Washington, D.C. Office). ***LANGUAGES:*** Spanish. ***PRACTICE AREAS:*** Health Care; Health Care Fraud; Health Care Regulation; Health Care Mergers and Acquisitions; Health Care Corporate; Biotechnology. ***Email:*** mgoldberg@winston.com

CHARLES B. KLEIN, born New York, N.Y., May 27, 1970; admitted to bar, 1995, Virginia; 1996, District of Columbia. *Education:* University of Virginia (B.A., 1992); University of California, Hastings College of the Law (J.D., 1995). Associate Articles Editor, Hastings Law Journal, 1993-1995. Extern to Hon. Ronald M. George, Supreme Court of California, 1994. Author: "What Exactly is an Unlawful Gratuity After United States v. Sun-Diamond Growers of California," 68 Geo. Wash. L. Rev. 116 (1999). Co-Author: "Combating Cybertorts: An Examination of the Virginia Computer Crimes Act," Cybercrime Law Report, Nov. 4, 2002; VBA News Journal, Jan. 2003; Metropolitan Corporate Counsel, Mar. 2003. (Washington, D.C. Office). ***REPORTED CASES:*** United States v. Smith, 267 F.3d 1154 (D.C. Cir. 2001); Lopez v. United States, 201 F.3d 478 (D.C. Cir. 2000). ***PRACTICE AREAS:*** Complex Civil Litigation; White Collar Criminal Litigation; Appellate; Internal Investigations. ***Email:*** cklein@winston.com

JESSIE A. KOHLER, born Mt. Kisco, New York, September 11, 1970; admitted to bar, 1995, California. *Education:* University of California, Santa Barbara (B.A., magna cum laude, 1992); University of Southern California (J.D., 1995). Member, Southern California Interdisciplinary Law Journal. (Los Angeles, California Office). ***PRACTICE AREAS:*** Employment Law; Employment Breach of Contract; Employer Liability; Employment Arbitration; Employment at Will; Employment Litigation; Harassment; Fair Employment Practices; Employment Defense; Employment Class Actions; Fair Labor Standards; Wage and Hour Law; Wrongful Termination Defense; Reductions in Force; Personnel Policies; Whistleblower Litigation; Management Employment Law. ***Email:*** jkohler@winston.com

JAMES S. RICHTER, born Reading, Pennsylvania, 1967; admitted to bar, 1992, New Jersey and U.S. District Court, District of New Jersey; 1998, U.S. Court of Appeals, Third Circuit. *Education:* St. Joseph's University (B.S., Chemistry, 1989); University of Baltimore (J.D., 1992). *Member:* New Jersey State and American Bar Associations. (New York, N.Y. Office). ***PRACTICE AREAS:*** Commercial Litigation; Intellectual Property Litigation; Insurance Coverage; Complex and Multi-District Litigation; Environmental Litigation; Labor and Employment; Class Actions; Products Liability. ***Email:*** jrichter@winston.com

JEFFREY A. WOLFSON, born Washington, D.C., September, 1970; admitted to bar, 1995, Maryland; 1996, District of Columbia, U.S. District Court of the District of Columbia, and U.S. Court of Appeals for the Federal Circuit; registered to practice before U.S. Patent and Trademark Office. *Education:* Brown University (Sc.B., Chemical Engineering, 1992); The George Washington University National Law Center (J.D., with honors, 1995). Recipient: Chemical Engineering Award, American Institute of Chemists, 1992; West Publishing Award for Clinical Achievement in Consumer Law, 1994-1995. Member, 1993-1994 and Executive Managing Editor, 1994-1995, Geo. Wash. J. Int'l L. & Econ.; Publication Staff, 1994-1995, AIPLA Q.J.; Author: Note, "Patent Flooding in the Japanese Patent Offices," Geo. Wash. J. Int'l L. & Econ., 1994; Book Review, "Federal Broadband Law," Richmond J. Law & Tech., 1996; Area Chair, Brown Alumni Schools Coalition, 1997-2000; Regional Director and Executive Committee Member, Brown Alumni Schools Coalition, 2000-2003; Brown University Spotlight Award, 2003. Member, Brown Alumni Schools Coalition, 1992—. *Member:* The District of Columbia Bar (Member, Intellectual Property Section); American Intellectual Property Law Association; American Institute of Chemical Engineers. (Washington, D.C. Office). ***PRACTICE AREAS:*** Intellectual Property; Patents; Trade Secrets. ***Email:*** jwolfson@winston.com

STACY YAKABOSKI, born Riverhead, New York, December 9, 1969; admitted to bar, 1996, New York. *Education:* James Madison University (B.A., magna cum laude, 1992); St. John's University (J.D., cum laude, 1995). (New York, N.Y. Office). ***Email:*** syakaboski@winston.com

CHARLES S. BIRENBAUM, born May 14, 1957; admitted to bar, 1982, California. *Education:* Oberlin College (B.A., with honors in Government, 1979); Georgetown University Law Center (J.D., 1982). Dean's List. Special Study with John Fanning, Chairman, National Labor Relations Board. Adjunct Professor, Santa Clara University Law School, 1990. Member, Advisory Council and Arbitrator/Mediator, American Arbitration Association. Member, Board of Directors, Northern California Service League. Member, Northern California Advisory Board for Employment Law Panel. Past President, Lawyers Club of San Francisco, 1997. *Member:* Bar Association of San Francisco; American Bar Association. (San Francisco, California Office). ***PRACTICE AREAS:*** Labor and Employment. ***Email:*** cbirenbaum@winston.com

STEPHEN I. BERKMAN, born Chicago, Illinois, May 29, 1966; admitted to bar, 1992, California. *Education:* University of California, Berkeley (B.S., with honors, 1987); University of California at Los Angeles (J.D., 1992). Member, UCLA Law Review. *Member:* State Bar of California. (San Francisco, California Office). ***PRACTICE AREAS:*** Real Estate; Commercial Real Estate; Leases and Leasing; Mortgages; Property Law. ***Email:*** sberkman@winston.com

JEFFREY S. BOSLEY, admitted to bar, 1993, California and U.S. District Court, Northern and Eastern Districts of California; U.S. Court of Appeals, Ninth Circuit; U.S. Court of Appeals, District of Columbia Circuit. *Education:* Cornell University (B.S., Industrial and Labor Relations, 1988); Villanova University (J.D., 1993). (San Francisco, California Office). ***PRACTICE AREAS:*** Labor and Employment. ***Email:*** jbosley@winston.com

TYLER M. PAETKAU, born Hamilton, Ontario, Canada, 1965; admitted to bar, 1990, California and U.S. District Court, Northern District of California; U.S. Court of Appeals, Ninth Circuit. *Education:* University of Michigan (A.B., 1987); University of Michigan Law School (J.D., cum laude, 1989). *Member:* Bar Association of San Francisco; State Bar of California (Member and Secretary, Executive Committee, Labor and Employment Law Section, 2001—); American Bar Association (Member, Labor and Employment Law Section). (San Francisco, California Office). ***PRACTICE AREAS:*** Employment Law; Labor Law; Intellectual Property Litigation. ***Email:*** tpaetkau@winston.com

WILLIAM M. DOYLE, JR., born Chicago, Illinois, December 11, 1949; admitted to bar, 1976, Illinois. *Education:* John Carroll University (B.S. in Business Administration, 1972; B.A., 1972); Loyola University of Chicago (M.B.A., 1974); DePaul University (J.D., magna cum laude, 1976). *Member:* Chicago (Member: Probate Practice Committee, 1978-1980; Trust Law Committee, 1982—) and American (Member, Income Taxation of Trusts and Estates Committee) Bar Associations; Chicago Estate Planning Council. ***Email:*** bdoyle@winston.com

LINDA LEMEL HOSEMAN, born Dayton, Ohio; admitted to bar, 1989, South Carolina; 1991, Illinois and U.S. District Court, Eastern and Northern Districts of Illinois; U.S. District Court, District of South Carolina. *Education:* Vanderbilt University (B.A. in Communication, 1985); Tulane University (J.D., cum laude, 1989); New York University (LL.M. in Taxation, 1994). Adjunct Faculty Instructor, John Marshall Law School, 2000. *Member:* Illinois State Bar Association (Member, Employee Benefits Section Council, 1998, 1999 and 2000). ***PRACTICE AREAS:*** Employee Benefits. ***Email:*** lhoseman@winston.com

WILLIAM M. SULLIVAN, JR., born Norwalk, Connecticut, May 18, 1958; admitted to bar, 1985, Connecticut and U.S. District Court, District of Connecticut; 1986, New York and U.S. District Court, Southern and Eastern Districts of New York; 1992, U.S. Court of Appeals for the District of Columbia Circuit; 2000, District of Columbia; 2004, U.S. Court of Appeals, Fourth Circuit. *Education:* Tufts University (B.A., magna cum laude, 1980; M.A., 1981); Cornell University (J.D., 1985). Adjunct Associate Professor of Law, New York Law School, 1990-1991. Lecturer: Fordham Law School, 1990-1991; FBI Academy, Quantico, 1998-2001; Attorney General's Advocacy Institute, 1998. Assistant United States Attorney, District of Columbia, 1991-2001. Winner, numerous Department of Justice, and Metropolitan Police Department, Honors, Awards and Commendations. *Member:* The Association of the Bar of the City of New York; Bar Association of the District of Columbia; The District of Columbia Bar; American Bar Association; Edward Bennett Williams Inn of Court. (Washington, D.C. Office). ***PRACTICE AREAS:*** White Collar Criminal Defense; Complex Civil Litigation; Internal Investigations; Securities Regulation; Corporate Compliance; Export Control. ***Email:*** wsullivan@winston.com

DAVID E. MOLLÓN, born New York, N.Y., March 6, 1962; admitted to bar, 1989, New York and U.S. District Court, Southern and Eastern Districts of New York. *Education:* Columbia College (B.A., 1984); Fordham University (J.D., cum laude, 1987). Articles Editor, Fordham Law Review. Law Clerk, Hon. David N. Edelstein, U.S. District Court, Southern District of New York. *Member:* American Bar Association; Federal Bar Council. (New York, N.Y. Office). ***LANGUAGES:*** Spanish and French. ***PRACTICE AREAS:*** Complex Litigation; Products Liability; Securities Litigation; Litigation. ***Email:*** dmollon@winston.com

MARK S. WEISBERG, born New York, N.Y., June 21, 1963; admitted to bar, 1988, Illinois. *Education:* University of Pennsylvania (B.S., cum laude, 1985; J.D., 1988). *Member:* American Bar Association. ***PRACTICE AREAS:*** Employee Benefits and Executive Compensation. ***Email:*** mweisberg@winston.com

JAMES L. MALONE III, born Brighton, Massachusetts, August 5, 1947; admitted to bar, 1972, Virginia and U.S. Court of Federal Claims; 1978, U.S. Court of Appeals, Federal Circuit and U.S. Supreme Court; 1982, Illinois and U.S. Tax Court; 1983, U.S. District Court, Northern District of Illinois; 1984, U.S. Court of Appeals, Sixth Circuit; 1987, U.S. Court of Appeals, Seventh Circuit; 1990, U.S. Court of Appeals, Fourth Circuit; 1999, U.S. Court of Appeals, Ninth Circuit; 2003, New York. *Education:* Boston College (A.B., cum laude, 1969); University of Virginia (J.D., 1972); Georgetown University (M.L.T., 1978). Law Clerk to: Trial Judges, U.S. Court of Claims, 1972-1973; Judge Marion T. Bennett, U.S. Court of Claims, 1973-1974. Adjunct Professor, IIT Chicago-Kent College of Law, 1985-1990. Trial Attorney, 1974-1980 and Senior Trial Attorney, 1980-1982, United States Department of Justice, Tax Division, Court of Claims Section. *Member:* New York State, Illinois State, Virginia and American (Member, Taxation Section) Bar Associations; Virginia State Bar; U.S. Court of Federal Claims Bar Association (President, 1989-1990). (New York, N.Y. Office). ***PRACTICE AREAS:*** Federal Tax Controversies (70%, 200); Federal Taxation (15%); State Taxation (15%). ***Email:*** jlmalone@winston.com

ZOE J. ASHCROFT, born October 6, 1965; admitted to bar, 1989, England and Wales as a Solicitor. *Education:* University of Bristol (LL.B., Hons., 1986). *Member:* The Law Society. (London, England Office). ***Email:*** zashcroft@winston.com

PEGGY M. BALESTERI, born April 30, 1971; admitted to bar, 1996, Illinois. *Education:* Michigan State University (B.A., 1993); DePaul University (J.D., 1996). ***Email:*** pbalesteri@winston.com

KEVIN A. BANASIK, born Milwaukee, Wisconsin, December 18, 1970; admitted to bar, 2000, Illinois; U.S. Court of Appeals, Seventh Circuit and U.S. District Court, Northern and Southern Districts of Illinois, Northern District of Indiana and Eastern District of Wisconsin. *Education:* Marquette University (B.A., magna cum laude, 1993); Harvard University (J.D., 1996). Phi Beta Kappa. Harry S. Truman Scholar. ***PRACTICE AREAS:*** Civil Litigation; Consumer Fraud; SEC Enforcement; Product Defects. ***Email:*** kbanasik@winston.com

LORI A. BEAN, born Bethesda, Maryland, April 19, 1969; admitted to bar, 1994, Maryland; 1995, District of Columbia. *Education:* Vanderbilt University (B.A., cum laude, 1991); Cornell University (J.D., cum laude, 1994). Associate, 1992-1993, Editor, 1993-1994, Cornell Law Review. (London, England Office)

THOMAS J. BENZ, born October 29, 1948; admitted to bar, 1976, New York. *Education:* Georgetown University (B.S.F.S., 1970; M.S.F.S., 1973); Cornell Law School (J.D., 1975). Editor-in-Chief, Cornell International Law Journal, 1974-1975. Associate Member, The Law Society. (London, England Office). ***Email:*** tbenz@winston.com

CHRISTINE M. CAHILL, admitted to bar, 1996, Illinois; 2003, New York. *Education:* State University of New York at Binghamton (B.A., 1993); Indiana University (J.D., 1996). Editor, Indiana Law Journal, 1995-1996. (New York, N.Y. Office). ***PRACTICE AREAS:*** Corporate Finance; Commercial Loans.

(This Listing Continued)

JARED R. CLOUD, admitted to bar, 1995, Illinois. *Education:* University of Chicago (A.B., 1991; J.D., with honors, 1995). Member, Board of Directors, Chicago Volunteer Legal Services Foundation, 2004—. Member, Associate Board, Gilda's Club Chicago, 2004—. Arbitrator, Circuit Court of Cook County Mandatory Arbitration Program, 2005—. *Member:* Chicago, Illinois State and American Bar Associations. ***REPORTED CASES:*** Regnery v. Meyers, 345 Ill.App.3d 678 (Ill. App. Ct. 2003). ***PRACTICE AREAS:*** Trust Litigation; Estate Litigation; Contested Trusts and Estates; Fiduciary Litigation; Litigation. ***Email:*** jcloud@winston.com

LUKE A. CONNELLY, born New York, N.Y., August 15, 1969; admitted to bar, 1997, New York and U.S. District Court, Southern and Eastern District of New York. *Education:* Colorado College (B.A., 1991); Fordham University (J.D., 1996). (New York, N.Y. Office). ***PRACTICE AREAS:*** Litigation. ***Email:*** lconnell@winston.com

JEROME O. HERBET, born Neuilly-Sur-Seine, France, June 26, 1970; admitted to bar, 1998, France. *Education:* University of Paris, Paris X (LL.M., Business Law, 1993; Diploma, Anglo-American Studies, with honors, 1993; J.D., 1995); I.E.P., Paris Eco-Fi (Diploma, 1996). *Member:* Association Européene pour le Droit Bancaire et Financier (Member, France Chapter). (Paris, France Office). ***LANGUAGES:*** English, French and German. ***PRACTICE AREAS:*** Financial Law; Business Law; Mergers and Acquisitions. ***Email:*** jherbet@winston.com

LOUIS C. KATSORIS, born New York, N.Y.; admitted to bar, 1995, New York and New Jersey. *Education:* Fordham University (B.S., 1991; J.D., 1994). (New York, N.Y. Office). ***PRACTICE AREAS:*** Commercial Litigation; Civil Litigation.

DAVID NEIER, born New York, N.Y.; admitted to bar, 1986, New York; U.S. District Court, Southern and Eastern Districts of New York. *Education:* Hamilton College (B.A., summa cum laude, 1981); Harvard Law School (J.D., 1984). *Member:* American Bankruptcy Institute. (New York, N.Y. Office). ***PRACTICE AREAS:*** Bankruptcy. ***Email:*** neierd@gtlaw.com

ANTOINE MARTIN, born Brive, France, September 22, 1962; admitted to bar, 1987, Paris. *Education:* University of Paris (Maîtrise en Droit Privé, 1986; DEA English and American Business Law, 1987); ISA, Institut Supérieur des Affaires (Master, Business Administration, 1990). (Paris, France Office). ***LANGUAGES:*** French and English. ***PRACTICE AREAS:*** Mergers and Acquisitions; Business Start-Ups; International Business Law.

JOHN McMICKLE, born November 20, 1968; admitted to bar, 1995, Virginia. *Education:* University of Tennessee (B.A. in Political Science, magna cum laude, 1989); American University, Washington College of Law (J.D., 1994). (Washington, D.C. Office). ***PRACTICE AREAS:*** Public Law; Consumer Bankruptcy. ***Email:*** jmcmickle@winston.com

MATTHEW D. O'MEARA, born Chicago, Illinois, August 18, 1969; admitted to bar, 1996, Illinois. *Education:* Loyola University (B.A., 1991; J.D., cum laude, 1996). ***Email:*** momeara@winston.com

LAURETTE PETERSEN, born Sacramento, California, August 15, 1962; admitted to bar, 1996, Illinois. *Education:* Michigan State University (B.A., 1984); University of Chicago (J.D., 1996). ***Email:*** lpetersen@winston.com

KAREN CARAHER QUIRK, born Chicago, Illinois, April 4, 1968; admitted to bar, 1995, Illinois. *Education:* St. Mary's College (B.A., 1990); University of Notre Dame (J.D., magna cum laude, 1995). ***Email:*** kquirk@winston.com

BRIAN M. SCHAFER, born Chicago, Illinois, November 26, 1968; admitted to bar, 1996, Illinois. *Education:* Georgetown University (B.A., summa cum laude, 1991); Harvard University (J.D., cum laude, 1996). ***Email:*** bschafer@winston.com

SCOTT A. SCHIPMA, born Grand Rapids, Michigan, October 29, 1967; admitted to bar, 1993, Illinois; 1997, District of Columbia. *Education:* Trinity Christian College (B.A., with high honors, 1989); DePaul University (J.D., 1993). (Washington, D.C. Office)

AMANDA C. SOMMERFELD, born Ventura, California, November 30, 1970; admitted to bar, 1996, California. *Education:* University of California at Los Angeles (B.A., 1992); University of Southern California (J.D., 1996). Member, Hale Moot Court Honors Program. *Member:* Beverly Hills and Los Angeles County Bar Associations; State Bar of California; Women Lawyers of Los Angeles. (Los Angeles, California Office). ***PRACTICE AREAS:*** Employment Law (100%). ***Email:*** asommerf@winston.com

GAIL J. STANDISH, born Boston, Massachusetts, September 28, 1963; admitted to bar, 1993, California; registered to practice before U.S. Patent and Trademark Office. *Education:* Massachusetts Institute of Technology (S.B., 1985; S.M., 1990); University of California School of Law, Los Angeles (J.D., 1993). Order of the Coif. Articles Editor, U.C.L.A. Law Review, 1992-1993. Law Clerk to Honorable William J. Rea, U.S. District Court Judge, Central District of California, 1993-1994. Assistant U.S. Attorney, Central District of California, 1997-2001. [Officer, Flight Test Engineer, U.S. Air Force, Active Duty 1985-1988]. (Los Angeles, California Office). ***REPORTED CASES:*** In re Syncor Sec. Litig., 327 F. Supp. 2d 1149 (C.D. Cal. 2004). ***PRACTICE AREAS:*** Intellectual Property; Litigation; Securities Litigation. ***Email:*** gstandish@winston.com

STEPHEN R. SMEREK, born Dayton, Ohio, April 25, 1968; admitted to bar, 1994, Massachusetts; 1995, U.S. District Courts, District of Massachusetts; 2000, California, U.S. Courts of Appeals, First Circuit and U.S. District Court, Central District of California; 2004, U.S. Court of Appeals, Ninth Circuit and U.S. District Court, Southern District of California. *Education:* Indiana University (B.A., with distinction, 1990); Boston University (J.D., summa cum laude, 1993). Member and Topic and Book Review Editor, Boston University Law Review, 1992-1993. Law Clerk to Honorable Josesph L. Tauro, U.S. District Court, District of Massachsuetts, 1993-1994. Recipient: Dr. John Ordronaux Prize; Alumni Academic Achievement Award; West Publishing Awards (1991-1992, 1992-1993); American Jurisprudence Awards (Contracts, Constitutional Law, Family Law, Trusts & Estates). Daniel J. Dowd Distinguished Scholar; Edward F. Hennessey Distinguished Scholar; G. Joseph Tauro Distinguished Scholar. *Member:* State Bar of California (Member, Sections on: Litigation; Business Law; Intellectual Property); Massachusetts Bar Association. (Los Angeles, California Office). ***PRACTICE AREAS:*** Litigation; Class Actions; Securities; Intellectual Property; Business Law; Commercial Law; Consumer Law. ***Email:*** ssmerek@winston.com

(This Listing Continued)

BARRY S. VITOU, admitted to bar, 1994, England and Wales as a Solicitor. *Education:* University of Leicester (LL.B., Hons., 1990). (London, England Office). ***Email:*** bvitou@winston.com

PAUL J. COADY, born Yeadon, Pennsylvania, 1953; admitted to bar, 1978, California. *Education:* Dartmouth College (B.A., summa cum laude, 1975); Harvard University (J.D., cum laude, 1978). Phi Beta Kappa. *Member:* Los Angeles County (Member, Labor Law Section) and American (Member, Sections on: Labor Relations Law; Litigation; Individual Rights) Bar Associations; State Bar of California. (Los Angeles, California Office). ***PRACTICE AREAS:*** Labor Law; Employment Law.

GREGORY S. SHATAN, born New York, N.Y., August 11, 1958; admitted to bar, 1987, New York; 1989, U.S. District Court, Southern and Eastern Districts of New York. *Education:* Wesleyan University (B.A., 1981); Columbia University School of Law (J.D., 1986). Editor-in-Chief, Columbia-VLA Journal of Law & the Arts, 1985-1986. Harlan Fiske Stone Scholar, 1986. Recipient, Shubert Foundation Fellowship, 1985-1986. Speaker: "Avoiding Intellectual Property Liability," Practising Law Institute Conference on Protecting Your Intellectual Property Assets, 1999-2000; "Structuring and Negotiating the Transaction: Intellectual Property Issues in Mergers & Acquisitions," Intellectual Property Owners Association Annual Meeting, 2000; Moderator, "Speakers Workshop," INTA Annual Meeting, 2002; Speaker, "Trademark Issues in International Business Transactions," INTA Conference on International Trademark Issues, 2003. Co-Author, "Clorox Problems Can Harshly Effect M&A Deals," The National Law Journal, May 12, 1997; "Going, Going, Gone -- Legal Issues to Ponder in Running Online Auctions," Multimedia & Web Strategist, July 1, 1999; "Have You Checked Your Corporate Copyright Policy Lately?," The Metropolitan Corporate Counsel, February 1, 1999; "Year 2000 Readiness Disclosures -- New U.S. Legal Protections and Medical Device Marketing," 7 The Regulatory Affairs Journal (Devices) 56, February 1, 1999. Author: "ICANN Adopts New Policies for Domain Name Registrars," INTA Bulletin, November 1, 2004. *Member:* American Bar Association (Member, Sections on: Intellectual Property Law; Antitrust Law); New York State Bar Association (Member, Special Committee on Cyberspace Law); The Association of the Bar of the City of New York; International Trademark Assocation (Member, Internet Committee); Copyright Society of the United States; Media Law Resource Center. (New York, N.Y. Office). ***PRACTICE AREAS:*** Trademarks; Copyrights; Internet Law; Antitrust and Trade Regulation; Advertising and Marketing; Media Law; Computers and Software. ***Email:*** gshatan@winston.com

G. THOMAS STROMBERG, JR., born San Francisco, California, February 23, 1955; admitted to bar, 1982, Illinois; 1986, California. *Education:* Harvard University (B.A., with honors, 1979); University of Utah College of Law (J.D., 1982). *Member:* State Bar of California; Illinois State Bar Association. (Los Angeles, California Office). ***LANGUAGES:*** Japanese. ***PRACTICE AREAS:*** Private Equity; Mergers and Acquisitions; Corporate Finance. ***Email:*** tstromberg@winston.com

RANDA A. JAAFAR, born Freetown, Sierra Leone, March 12, 1961; admitted to bar, 1987, England; 1995, New York. *Education:* University of Essex, England (LL.B., 1983); College of Law (1987). (New York, N.Y. Office)

MICHAEL A. MOSER, born New York, N.Y., July 23, 1967; admitted to bar, 1994, New York and U.S. District Court, Southern District of New York. *Education:* Yale University (B.A., 1989); Vanderbilt University (J.D., 1994). (New York, N.Y. Office). ***PRACTICE AREAS:*** Real Estate.

ADAM J. SCHLATNER, born New York, N.Y., June 2, 1968; admitted to bar, 1995, New York. *Education:* State University of New York at Binghamton (B.A., with honors, 1990); University of Michigan (J.D., cum laude, 1993). (New York, N.Y. Office)

LINDA T. COBERLY, born Lansing, Michigan, March 24, 1967; admitted to bar, 1996, Illinois; U.S. Supreme Court; U.S. Court of Appeals, Sixth, Seventh, Eighth, and Federal Circuits; U.S. District Court, Northern District of Illinois; U.S. District Court, District of Colorado. *Education:* Princeton University (A.B., 1989); University of Michigan (J.D., magna cum laude, 1995). Order of the Coif. Editor-in-Chief, Michigan Law Review. Law Clerk to: the Hon. Douglas H. Ginsburg, U.S. Court of Appeals, District of Columbia Circuit, 1995-1996; the Hon. Stephen G. Breyer, U.S. Supreme Court, 1998-1999. Associate, 1996-1998, 1999-2003 and Partner, 2004, Mayer Brown Rowe & Maw LLP. *Member:* Appellate Lawyers Association; Defense Research Institute Appellate Advocacy Committee; National Association of Women Lawyers. ***PRACTICE AREAS:*** Appellate Practice. ***Email:*** lcoberly@winston.com

ROSS A. HONIG, born New York, N.Y., August 11, 1963; admitted to bar, 1989, New York. *Education:* State University of New York at Albany (B.A., cum laude, 1985); Boston University (J.D., 1988). G. Joseph Tauro Scholar. Recipient, American Jurisprudence Book Award in Civil Procedure. Editor, Probate Law Journal, 1987-1988. Author, "Baby's Desperate Cry," B.U. School of Law/Nat'l College Probate Judge's L. J., 1989. (New York, N.Y. Office). ***PRACTICE AREAS:*** Real Estate; Finance. ***Email:*** rhonig@winston.com

DAVID M. HICKEY, born Queens, New York, December 14, 1964; admitted to bar, 1989, California; 1990, U.S. Court of Military Appeals; 1993, U.S. District Court, Central District of California; 1994, U.S. District Court, Northern District of California; 1995, U.S. District Court, Southern District of California; 2004, New York; 2005, U.S. District Court, District of New Jersey, U.S. District Court, Northern District of Georgia. *Education:* Georgetown University (B.S., Finance and Economics, 1986); Stanford Law School (J.D., 1989). 15th Air Force Assistant Judge Advocate of the Year, 1993. Lecturer International Arbitration and Dispute Resolution (U.S., U.K., Japan, Republic of the Philippines, Republic of Indonesia, Singapore), 1995—. Keynote Speaker Telkom Indonesia, 2003. *Member:* State Bar of California; American Bar Association; London Court of International Arbitration; International Bar Association. [Captain, U.S. Air Force, 1990-1994]. (Los Angeles, California Office). ***PRACTICE AREAS:*** Class Actions; Consumer Class Actions; International Arbitration; Securities Litigation; Business Torts; Arbitration; Construction Arbitration; Trial Practice. ***Email:*** dhickey@winston.com

PAOLO DI ROSA, born Albuquerque, New Mexico, October 7, 1964; admitted to bar, 1991, Pennsylvania; 1992, District of Columbia. *Education:* Harvard University (B.A., magna cum laude, 1987; J.D., cum laude, 1991). Former Head, State Department Office, Legal Adviser for Western Hemisphere Affairs. Member, U.S. Senior Executive Service. Former Editor-in-Chief, Harvard Human Rights Journal. President, Chilean American Chamber of Commerce, Washington, D.C. *Member:* District of Columbia Bar; American Bar Associa-

(This Listing Continued)

WINSTON & STRAWN LLP, Chicago—Continued

tion (Member, International Law Section); Inter-American Bar Association; International Law Association; American Society of International Law. (Washington, D.C. Office). ***LANGUAGES:*** Spanish (native fluency), Portuguese and Italian (reading ability). ***PRACTICE AREAS:*** International Litigation; International Arbitration; Public International Law. ***Email:*** pdirosa@winston.com

SCOTT H. BLACKMAN, born Philadelphia, Pennsylvania, January 30, 1960; admitted to bar, 1989, New York and U.S. District Court, Southern and Eastern Districts of New York; 1992, U.S. Supreme Court; 1997, District of Columbia; U. S. Court of Appeals for the Federal Circuit; registered to practice before U.S. Patent and Trademark Office. *Education:* Philadelphia College of Pharmacy and Science (B.S., Chemistry, 1981; M.S., Medicinal Chemistry, 1984); Cornell University Law School (J.D., cum laude, 1988). Law Clerk to the Honorable S. Jay Plager, U.S. Court of Appeals for the Federal Circuit, 1990-1992. *Member:* New York State, Federal Circuit and American Bar Associations; The District of Columbia Bar; American Intellectual Property Law Association; American Chemical Society; Giles Sutherland Rich American Inn of Court. (Washington, D.C. Office). ***PRACTICE AREAS:*** Pharmaceutical Patents; Patent Litigation; Intellectual Property Rights; Intellectual Property Protection; False Advertising. ***Email:*** sblackman@winston.com

(MR.) THOMAS C. MAVRAKAKIS, born New York, N.Y., November 28, 1964; admitted to bar, 1994, Texas; 1995, California; registered to practice before U.S. Patent and Trademark Office. *Education:* Polytechnic Institute of New York (B.S., Electrical Engineering, 1989); St. John's University (J.D., cum laude, 1994). Eta Kappa Nu. *Member:* Bar Association of San Francisco; State Bar of California; State Bar of Texas; American Intellectual Property Lawyers Association; Silicon Valley Intellectual Property Law Association; San Francisco Intellectual Property Law Association. (San Francisco, California Office). ***PRACTICE AREAS:*** Litigation; Patents; Intellectual Property; Trade Secrets. ***Email:*** tmavrakakis@winston.com

EDMUND S. COHEN, born Newark, New Jersey, June 25, 1946; admitted to bar, 1972, New York and U.S. Court of Appeals, Second Circuit; 1973, U.S. Tax Court and U.S. Court of Federal Claims; 1975, U.S. District Court, Southern District of New York. *Education:* Dartmouth College (B.A., cum laude, 1968); Harvard Law School (J.D., cum laude, 1971); New York University (LL.M., Taxation, 1976). Adjunct Professor of Law, New York University Law School Graduate Tax Program, 1977—. *Member:* American Bar Association. (New York, N.Y. Office). ***PRACTICE AREAS:*** Taxation. ***Email:*** ecohen@winston.com

MILTON K. BUCKINGHAM, born 1967; admitted to bar, 1992, Illinois. *Education:* University of Arizona (B.A., cum laude, 1989); University of Illinois (J.D., 1992). ***Email:*** mbuckingham@winston.com

KURT STITCHER, born Plainfield, New Jersey, 1963; admitted to bar, 1990, Illinois; 2002, Pennsylvania. *Education:* Georgetown University (B.S. in Foreign Service, cum laude, 1985); Stanford University (J.D., with distinction, 1990). *Member:* American Bar Association (Member: Litigation Section; Criminal Justice Section). ***PRACTICE AREAS:*** Class Action Defense; Commercial Litigation; Litigation; Products Liability Defense; Toxic Torts; White Collar Criminal Defense; Corporate Investigations. ***Email:*** kstitcher@winston.com

BARBARA C. SESSIONS, admitted to bar, 1986, Illinois. *Education:* University of Michigan (B.A., 1983); DePaul University (J.D., 1986). *Member:* American Bar Association. ***Email:*** bsession@winston.com

OF COUNSEL

MARY HUTCHINGS REED, born Chicago, Illinois, March 7, 1951; admitted to bar, 1976, Illinois and U.S. District Court, Northern District of Illinois. *Education:* Brown University (B.A., with honors, 1973; M.A., 1973); Yale Law School (J.D., 1976). Phi Beta Kappa. Author: "The Legal Liability of Library Trustees," Journal of Library Administration, Vol. 3 (2), 1982; "Model Policy Concerning College and University Photocopying for Classroom, Research and Library Use," pamphlet published by American Library Association, 1982; "Sponsorship Agreements: Putting It in Writing," Special Events Report, September 30, 1985; "Remarks on MPAA Ratings," Newsletter on Intellectual Freedom, September, Vol. XXXIV, No. 5, p. 178, 1985; "Library and Classroom Use of Copyrighted Videotapes and Computer Software," American Libraries, February, 1986; "Discrimination and Related Litigation in Libraries," Journal of Library Administration, Vol. 7, No. 4, Winter, 1986; "How to Legally Protect a Public Event: Parts I and II," Special Events Report, May 18, 1987 and June 1, 1987; *The Copyright Primer for Librarians and Educators,* American Library Association and National Education Association, Chicago, 1987; "To Love a Parade," The Merchandising Reporter, Vol. 6, No. 8, September, 1987; "What is Right in Copyright?" American Libraries, February, 1989; *Business Torts* , Contributing Editor and Author of Chapters, "Privacy and Publicity" and "Trademarks," Matthew Bender, March, 1989; *The IEG Legal Guide to Sponsorship* , 498pp, International Events Group, Chicago, 1990; "The Legal Aspects of Promoting and Sponsoring Events," Special Events Group, March 26, 1990; "Monday Memo," Broadcasting, October 29, 1990; "Trademarks in the Sale of a Business: Concurrent Use and Licensing," The Trademark Reporter, Vol. 80, No. 5, p. 514, September-October, 1990; "Sponsorship Contracts: Drafting Challenges," The Licensing Journal, January 1995; "Sponsorship and the Arts: A Brief Overview of Legal Issues for Non-for-Profits," 13 Ent. 4 Spts. Lawyer 9, 1995; The Legal Guide to Cause Marketing, 256 pp., International Events Group, Chicago, 2001. Adjunct Professor: Northwestern University School of Law, 1988-1992; Columbia College, 1984-1987. *Member:* Chicago and American Bar Associations. ***PRACTICE AREAS:*** Trademark Law; Copyright Law; Advertising Law; Entertainment Law. ***Email:*** mreed@winston.com

J. ERICSON HEYKE, III, born Miami, Florida, May 17, 1943; admitted to bar, 1993, Illinois; 1995, District of Columbia. *Education:* Yale University (B.S., magna cum laude, 1964); Harvard Business School (M.B.A., 1966); University of Chicago (J.D., 1993). Phi Beta Kappa. Co-Author: with Robert L. Haig ed, "Valuation of a Business in an Acquisition Context," in Successful Partnering Between Inside and Outside Counsel, West Group and ACCA, 2000. *Member:* Illinois State and American Bar Associations; District of Columbia Bar. ***LANGUAGES:*** French, Spanish and Russian. ***PRACTICE AREAS:*** Mergers and Acquisitions; Corporate Finance; Structured Finance; International Project Finance; Securities; Private Equity. ***Email:*** rheyke@winston.com

JOHN M. HADLOCK, born Chicago, Illinois, 1937; admitted to bar, 1963, New York. *Education:* Colgate University (B.A., 1959); St. John's University (LL.B., 1962); New York University (LL.M., 1971). Associate Editor, St. John's Law Review, 1961-1962. Assistant Counsel, Majority Leader, New York State Senate, 1967. *Member:* Association of the Bar of the City of New York; American Bar Association. (New York, N.Y. Office). ***PRACTICE AREAS:*** Litigation; Antitrust Law; Publishing Law. ***Email:*** jhadlock@winston.com

JUDITH A. GELB, born New York, N.Y., April 5, 1935; admitted to bar, 1959, New York; 1960, U.S. Court of Appeals, 2nd Circuit, U.S. District Court, Southern and Eastern Districts of New York; 1962, U.S. Court of Military Appeals (Not admitted in Illinois). *Education:* Brooklyn College (B.A., 1955); Columbia University (J.D., 1958). Co-Author: "Avoiding U.S. Trust Wars," *Disputes Involving Trusts,* 1999 by Helbing & Lichtenhahn Verlag AG, Basle, Switzerland. *Member:* Association of the Bar of the City of New York; New York State (Member, Trusts and Estates Law Section, 1974—) and American (Member, Sections on Real Property; Probate; Trust Law) Bar Associations. (New York, N.Y. Office). ***PRACTICE AREAS:*** Estate Planning; Estate and Gift Taxation; Wills; Estate Administration; Trust Administration. ***Email:*** jgelb@winston.com

JOHN P. PROCTOR, born Kewaunee, Wisconsin, 1942; admitted to bar, 1968, District of Columbia; 1970, U.S. Court of Military Appeals; 1975, U.S. Court of Appeals for the District of Columbia Circuit; 1984, New York. *Education:* Princeton University (B.A., 1964); University of Pennsylvania (LL.B., 1967). Recipient, Bernard B. Payton Award, 1964. *Member:* Federal and American (Vice-Chairman, Air Quality Committee, Natural Resources Law Section, 1984—) Bar Associations. (Washington, D.C. Office). ***PRACTICE AREAS:*** Environmental Law; Energy Law. ***Email:*** jproctor@winston.com

HILL BLACKETT, III, born Chicago, Illinois, June 26, 1950; admitted to bar, 1977, Illinois; 1979, California. *Education:* Dartmouth College (B.A., with distinction, 1973); Hastings College of the Law, University of California (J.D., 1977). Phi Alpha Delta. Articles Editor, Hastings Law Journal, 1976-1977. Legal Extern to Hon. William W. Schwarzer, United States District Court, Northern District of California, 1977. Adjunct Professor of Law, University of San Francisco, 1982-1983. Author: "When an LBO Goes Sour: Assessing the Fraudulent Conveyance Risk in Leveraged Buy-Outs," 1 Banking L. Rev. 35, Winter 1989; "What Supreme Court Rulings on Adequate Protection and the Absolute Priority Rule Mean to Creditors," 1 Bankr. L. Rev. 47, Spring, 1989; "Supreme Court Rulings to Settle Major Issues for Secured Creditors," 1 Banking L. Rev. 49, Summer, 1988. Co-Author: "Federal Tax Liens," *Creditors' Rights in Illinois,* Illinois Institute of Continuing Legal Education, ed. 1980. Lecturer and Author, Executive Enterprises, California Continuing Education of the Bar, Professional Education Systems. *Member:* State Bar of California (Co-Chair: UCC Committee, 1997-1998; Intellectual Property Subcommittee, 1995-1996; Chair, Intellectual Property Subcommittee, 1994-1995); American Bar Association; National Business Institute. (San Francisco, California Office). ***PRACTICE AREAS:*** Secured Financing; Commercial Lending; Creditors Remedies. ***Email:*** hblackett@winston.com

S. SHANE SAGHEB, born Burbank, California, May 5, 1958; admitted to bar, 1983, California; U.S. District Court, Central, Northen, Eastern and Southern Districts of California; U.S. Court of Appeals, Ninth Circuit (Not admitted in Illinois). *Education:* University of California at Los Angeles (B.A., cum laude, 1980); Loyola Law School, Los Angeles (J.D., cum laude, 1983). Member, St. Thomas More Law Honor Society. *Member:* Los Angeles County and American Bar Associations; State Bar of California. ***Email:*** ssagheb@winston.com

GAELA K. GEHRING FLORES, born Peoria, Illinois; admitted to bar, 1996, Virginia; 1998, District of Columbia; U.S. District Court for the District of Columbia; U.S. District Court, District of Maryland; U.S. District Court, Eastern and Western Districts of Virginia; U.S. Bankruptcy Court, Eastern and Western Districts of Virginia; U.S. Court of Appeals for the District of Columbia and Fourth Circuits; U.S. Supreme Court. *Education:* University of Illinois at Urbana-Champaign (B.A., summa cum laude, with highest distinction, 1993); Georgetown University Law Center (J.D., cum laude, 1996). DC Street Law Project, 1994-1995. Recipient, American Jurisprudence Award for Legal Excellence in Clinical Work, 1995. Managing Articles Editor, The Georgetown Law Journal, 1995- 1996. Law Clerk to Hon. Paul L. Friedman, U.S. District Court for the District of Columbia, 1996-1998. Associate, Paul, Weiss, Rifkind, Wharton & Garrison, 1998-2002. Associate, White & Case LLP, 2002-2004. Member, D.C. Circuit Judicial Conference Standing Committee on Pro Bono Legal Services, 2004—. *Member:* District of Columbia Bar; Virginia State Bar; American Bar Association; American Society of International Law; Women's Bar Association; Hispanic Bar Association, District of Columbia. (Washington, D.C. Office). ***LANGUAGES:*** Spanish, French, Portuguese, Italian. ***REPORTED CASES:*** Eldred v. Reno, 239 F.3d 372 (D.C. Cir. 2001), aff'd 537 U.S. 186 (2003); Keefe Co. v. Americable Int'l, Inc., 219 F.3d 669 (D.C. Cir. 2000); In re Bray, 256 B.R. 708 (Bnkr. D. Md. 2000); Keefe Co. v. Americable Int'l, Inc., 169 F.3d 34 (1999); Ganesh, L.L.C. v. Computer Learning Centers, Inc., 183 F.R.D. 487 (E.D. Va. 1998). ***PRACTICE AREAS:*** International Arbitration; International Dispute Resolution; International Litigation; International Treaty Law; Federal Civil Litigation; Copyright Litigation; U.S. Supreme Court Litigation. ***Email:*** ggehringflores@winston.com

SENIOR COUNSEL

PETER WHITRIDGE WILLIAMS, born Charlottesville, Virginia, November 13, 1936; admitted to bar, 1967, Virginia and New York; 1968, District of Columbia; 1970, U.S. Supreme Court; 1973, France (as Conseil Juridique; not admitted to practice in French Courts). *Education:* University of Virginia (B.A., 1959; J.D., 1967). *Member:* International Bar Association. [LT. USNR US Naval Aviator, 1959-1967]. (New York, N.Y. Office). ***LANGUAGES:*** French. ***PRACTICE AREAS:*** International Banking Law; International Finance. ***Email:*** pwilliams@winston.com

SENIOR ATTORNEYS

BARRY L. SALKIN, born Bayonne, New Jersey, January 7, 1947; admitted to bar, 1977, New York; 1981, U.S. Tax Court; 2003, U.S. District Court, Southern District of New

(This Listing Continued)

York; 2004, U.S. Court of Appeals, Second Circuit. *Education:* Rutgers University (B.A., summa cum laude, 1968); Harvard University (M.A., 1969; Ph.D., 1974; J.D., cum laude, 1977). Phi Beta Kappa. (New York, N.Y. Office). ***PRACTICE AREAS:*** Employee Benefits. ***Email:*** bsalkin@winston.com

ALAN V. LINDQUIST, born Chicago, Illinois, March 2, 1954; admitted to bar, 1983, Illinois. *Education:* University of Illinois (B.S., 1976; J.D., magna cum laude, 1983). Phi Alpha Delta. Harno Fellow. Recipient, Elijah Watt Sells Award, CPA, 1979. Certified Public Accountant, Illinois, 1979. *Member:* Chicago Bar Association (Member, State and Local Taxation Committee, 1986—); Illinois CPA Society. ***PRACTICE AREAS:*** State Taxation Law; Local Taxation Law; State Income Tax Law; Sales and Use Tax Law; Transfer Tax Law. ***Email:*** alindqui@winston.com

DEBORAH S. K. JAGODA, born Orange, New Jersey, November 14, 1959; admitted to bar, 1985, New York and U.S. District Court, Southern and Eastern Districts of New York; 1995, District of Columbia. *Education:* Wharton School, University of Pennsylvania (B.S., summa cum laude, Economics, 1981); Harvard University (J.D., cum laude, 1984). Beta Gamma Sigma. Author: "Labor Law for Employment Lawyers: Watch Out for the NLRB in the Non-Union Context," Metropolitan Corporate Counsel, Sept., 1997; "Applying U.S. Discrimination Law to Overseas Business Operations," Employment Law Strategist, Jan., 1997. *Member:* American Bar Association (Member, Labor and Employment Law Section). (New York, N.Y. Office). ***PRACTICE AREAS:*** Employment Law; Employment Defense; Employment Discrimination; Employment Litigation; Employment Contracts; Collective Bargaining; Employee Leasing; Executive Severance Contracts; Fair Employment Practices; Fair Labor Standards; Labor Law; Labor Relations; Labor Arbitration; Personnel Policies; Personnel Training; Public Sector Collective Bargaining; Public Sector Employment Law; Public Sector Labor Relations; Wage and Hour Law; Confidentiality Agreements; Employee Discipline; Management Labor Law. ***Email:*** djagoda@winston.com

WILLIAM M. SUNKEL, born Bronx, New York, September 13, 1956; admitted to bar, 1988, Connecticut; 1989, New York; 1993, U.S. District Court, Southern and Eastern Districts of New York. *Education:* Fordham University; Hunter College of the City University of New York (B.A., summa cum laude, 1985); Pace University School of Law (J.D., cum laude, 1988). Ranking Scholar. Recipient, Merit Scholarship. Research & Writing Editor, Pace Law Review. Author: "City of Renton v. Playtime Theatres: Court-Approved Censorship Through Zoning," 7 Pace Law Review 251 (1986) (cited in Town of Islip v. Caviglia, 73 N.Y.2d 544 (1989)). (New York, N.Y. Office). ***REPORTED CASES:*** Rutlen v. Price-Waterhouse Coopers LLP, 726 N.Y.S. 2d 258 (1st Dept 2001); Continental Casualty Co. v. State of New York Mortgage Agency, No. 94 Civ. 8408 (KMW), 1998 WL 513054 (S.D.N.Y. Aug. 18, 1998); Baba v. Japan Travel Bureau International, Inc., 165 F.R.D. 398 (S.D.N.Y. 1993), aff'd, 111 F.3d (2d Cir. 1997); Geren v. Quantum Chemical Corp., 832 F.Supp. 798 (S.D.N.Y. 1993), aff'd 99 F.3d 401 (2d Cir., 1995); Breed, Abbott & Morgan v. Hulko, 74 N.Y.2d 686 (1989); Strougo v. Hoyt, 246 A.D.2d 320 (1st Dep't 1997); Quantum Chemical Corp. v. Reliance Group, Inc., 180 A.D.2d 548 (1st Dep't 1992). ***PRACTICE AREAS:*** Commercial Litigation; Labor and Employment Litigation. ***Email:*** wsunkel@winston.com

MARCIA R. GELMAN, born New York, N.Y., February 8, 1954; admitted to bar, 1985, District of Columbia; 1997, New York (Not admitted in Illinois). *Education:* Brandeis University (B.A., magna cum laude, with high honors, 1975); Boston University (J.D., 1980). Editor, Boston University Law Review, 1978-1980. ***Email:*** mgelman@winston.com

N. DWIGHT CARY, born Irvington, New Jersey, May 21, 1948; admitted to bar, 1975, California. *Education:* Pomona College (B.A., magna cum laude, 1970); Harvard University and Stanford University (J.D., 1975). Phi Beta Kappa. Consultant to 1981 Supplement and Author and Editor of 1982 and 1983 Supplements of *California Commercial Law: III,* published by California Continuing Education of the Bar. Author: *Legal Guide,* California Cattle Feeders Association, 1978. (San Francisco, California Office). ***PRACTICE AREAS:*** Secured Financing; Commercial Lending; Creditors Remedies; Real Estate Finance. ***Email:*** ncary@winston.com

ASSOCIATES

Maureen Aidasani; Lana Alamat; Laura J. Alexander; Tracy J. Allen; Brian N. Anderson; Stacey Austin; Courtney Engelbrecht Barr; Edward Berk (admission pending); ***Michael D. Bess; Matthew A. Bills; Monika M. Blacha; Kellie Blattner; Todd M. Bloomquist; Jason L. Booth; Katherine Borden; Lester G. Bovia, Jr.; David Bower*** (admission pending); ***Ryan Bowers*** (admission pending); ***Eric L. Broxterman*** (Not admitted in IL); ***Dean M. Burau; Alfonso Canela; Yoaldena Canela*** (admission pending); ***Romy Elisabeth Carr; Hortensia S. Carreira; Tracy S. Cassidy; Christine R. Chase; Pei Yuan Chung; Kevin M. Cloutier; Kendric M. Cobb; Danielle A. R. Coffman; Mindy D. Cohn; J. Erik Connolly; Larissa Cooper; Matthew D. Costigan; Kristen Cowan; Catherine L. Crisham; Christopher J. Cullen; Bryna Dahlin; David Dahlquist; Kareem A. Dale; Kyle DeJong; Joseph L. Devaney, III; Michael P. DiGiannantonio; Justin Endres; Elizabeth Epstein; Elizabeth Erickson; Christopher Blair Essig; Michael G. Falk; Jared R. Feehan; Brian D. Fergemann; Amy L. Flaherty; Stacy J. Flanigan; Michael A. Flomenhoft; Brian L. Franklin; Melissa Gadowski; Jennifer Gallinson; Rodger Lee Gardy, Jr.; Megan E. Gervase*** (Not admitted in IL); ***Gwenn E. Girard; Scott P. Glauberman; Anne Graber Blazek; Maria Guiao; Ankur Gupta; Adam K. Gusman; J. Eric Guth; L. Timothy Halleron; Katherine L. Harenza; James P. Healy, Jr.; James Franklin Herbison*** (admission pending); ***James M. Hilmert; Nathan E. Hoffman; Margaret Glunz Horton; M. Faiyaz Hussain; Eric L. Jacobson; Shelbee Jarol; Andrew M. Johnstone; Amit Kalra; Erin A. Kartheiser; Jai S. Khanna; Charles Kierpiec; Blaine C. Kimrey; Laura G. Klempay; Jennifer L. Kobayashi; Karen M. Kowalski; Jon J. Kramer; David Latchana; Arlene Lim; Derek P. Linde; Erik B. Lundgren; Lynn C. MacDonald; Katie Mackie; Robin Drey Maher; Julia Mano; Robyn Martin; Michael P. Mayer; Katherine A. McAvoy; Stephanie McCallum; Greg J. Miarecki; Ari D. Mintzer; Shannon Mudd Leutheuser; Michael T. Mullins; Cornelius M. Murphy; Elizabeth Anne Nemeth; Michael K. Nutter; Katherine O'Halleran; William O'Neil; Matthew R. Osenga*** (Not admitted in IL); ***Kevin J. O'Shea; Nicole J. Ottmer; Samuel S. Park; Christopher S. Perry; Theodore Zane Polley, III; Ivan M. Poullaos; Kenneth P. Purcell; Kimberly Reed; Michael Patrick Rohan; Robert T. Roos; Kevin M. Ryan; Rana H. Salti; Derek J. Sarafa; Nicholas J. Schuler, Jr.; Lisa K. Seilheimer; Vishal Raj Shani; Andrew D. Shapiro; Cardelle B. Spangler; Jennifer Spry; Chris Stathopoulos; Giel Stein; Shannon L. Stevens; Erin Glezen Stone; J. Andrew P. Stone; Matthew J. Sullivan; Michael J. Towne; Scott Walton; Brian Wanamaker; Andrew D. Wang; Brooke B. Ward; Andrew C. Warnecke; Matthew M. Wawrzyn; Anastasia G. Weis; Christopher A. Weller; Brian D. Werner; Nicole E. Wrigley; Ethan R. York.***

(This Listing Continued)

STAFF ATTORNEYS

Edward M. Coffman; Kelly Cordes; Jennifer L. Cuculich; Patrick Sean Ginty; Betsy L. Katten; Gregory A. McConnell; S. Charles Patel; Stephen N. Sher; Jonathon Treat; Paula Hudson Holderman.

LAW OFFICES OF WILLIAM H. WISE & ASSOCIATES

134 NORTH LASALLE STREET
SUITE 1515
CHICAGO, ILLINOIS 60602
Telephone: 312-346-4555
Fax: 847-272-4255
Email: william@wiseattorneys.net
URL: http://www.wiseattorneys.net

Schaumburg, Illinois Office: 1821 Walden Office Square, 4th Floor, 60173. Telephone: 847-397-1112. Fax: 847-272-4255.

Criminal Law, Driving While Intoxicated, Traffic Violations, Juvenile Law, Expungements, Parole and Probation, Drug Crimes, Felonies, Homicide, Misdemeanors, Secretary of State Drivers License Revocation, White Collar Crime, Personal Injury, Automobile Accidents, Constitutional Law and Workers Compensation.

WILLIAM H. WISE, born Chicago, Illinois, October 17, 1940; admitted to bar, 1965, Illinois; 1976, Colorado. *Education:* Roosevelt University (A.B., 1963); John Marshall Law School (J.D., 1965). Circuit Court Judge, State of Illinois, Criminal Division, 1995-1999. *Member:* Chicago, Northwest Suburban, North Suburban and Illinois State Bar Associations; American Academy of Trial Lawyers; National Association of Criminal Defense Lawyers; American Judicature Society; Decalogue Society of Lawyers. ***PRACTICE AREAS:*** Criminal Law; Driving While Intoxicated; Traffic Violations; Juvenile Law; Expungements; Parole and Probation; Drug Crimes; Felonies; Homicide; Misdemeanors; White Collar Crime; Personal Injury; Automobile Accidents; Constitutional Law; Workers Compensation.

ASSOCIATE

HOWARD J. WISE, born Des Plaines, Illinois, July 29, 1968; admitted to bar, 1997, Illinois. *Education:* University of Arizona (B.F.A., 1991); Thomas M. Cooley Law School (J.D., 1996). Assistant State Attorney, Cook County: Criminal Division, 2000-2001; Traffic Division, 1999-2000. Approved Bar Attorney, Chicago Bar Association. ***PRACTICE AREAS:*** Criminal Defense; Felonies; Misdemeanors; Traffic Violations; DUI; Drug Crimes; Juvenile Law; Expungements; Personal Injury; Workers Compensation. ***Email:*** howard@wiseattorneys.net

WITWER & WALDRON, LLC

CHICAGO, ILLINOIS

(See Evanston)

Wills, Trusts, Probate, Estate Planning, General Litigation, First Amendment and Religious Law, Municipal, Government, Corporate, Real Estate.

JOHN C. WOJTECZKO

77 WEST WASHINGTON STREET
CHICAGO, ILLINOIS 60602
Telephone: 312-782-4780
Fax: 312-372-9399
Email: jcwrefax@ameritech.net

Residential and Commercial Real Estate, Condominium, Real Estate Taxation, Income Tax, Business, Corporate, Estate Planning, Probate, Pension and Profit Sharing Law. Litigation.

JOHN C. WOJTECZKO, born Chicago, Illinois, July 11, 1946; admitted to bar, 1975, Illinois. *Education:* College of St. Thomas (B.A., 1968); Case Western Reserve University (J.D., 1975). Phi Delta Phi. *Member:* Chicago, Illinois State and American Bar Associations.

WOLF HALDENSTEIN ADLER FREEMAN & HERZ LLC

55 WEST MONROE STREET, SUITE 1111
CHICAGO, ILLINOIS 60603
Telephone: 312-984-0000
Fax: 312-984-0001
URL: http://www.whafh.com

New York, New York Office: 270 Madison Avenue, 10016. Telephone: 212-545-4600. Fax: 212-686-0114; 212-545-4653; 212-545-4677.
San Diego, California Office: Symphony Towers, Suite 2770, 750 B Street, 92101. Telephone: 619-239-4599. Fax: 619-234-4599.

(This Listing Continued)

WOLF HALDENSTEIN ADLER FREEMAN & HERZ LLC, Chicago—Continued

West Palm Beach, Florida Office: 625 North Flagler Drive, 9th Floor, 33401. Telephone: 561-833-1776.

Corporate and Securities, Estate and Trust, Real Estate, Licensing and Intellectual Property, Tax, Not-For-Profit, Employee Benefits, Labor, Commercial Collections, Elder Law and Litigation including Commercial, Securities and Class Actions.

MARY JANE EDELSTEIN FAIT, born New York, 1954; admitted to bar, 1980, New York and U.S. District Court, Southern and Eastern Districts of New York; 1982, Illinois and U.S. District Court, Northern District of Illinois; 1985, U.S. Court of Appeals, Seventh Circuit. *Education:* St. John's College and University of Illinois (B.A., Economics, 1976); Cornell Law School (J.D., 1979). *Member:* Chicago, Illinois State and American (Member, Antitrust Section) Bar Associations. ***PRACTICE AREAS:*** Antitrust; Securities Fraud; Consumer Fraud; Complex Litigation; Class Actions. ***Email:*** fait@whafh.com

ADAM J. LEVITT, born New York, 1969; admitted to bar, 1993, Illinois and U.S. District Court, Northern District of Illinois and U.S. Court of Appeals, Seventh Circuit; 1998, U.S. Supreme Court; 2000, U.S. District Court, District of Nebraska; 2001, U.S. District Court, Southern District of Illinois and U.S. District Court, Northern District of Indiana; U.S. District Courts, Northern and Eastern Districts of Texas; U.S. Court of Appeals, First and Seventh Circuits; U.S. Supreme Court. *Education:* Columbia University (A.B., magna cum laude, 1990); Northwestern University (J.D., 1993). *Member:* Chicago, Federal and American Bar Associations; American Law Institute; Lawyers for the Creative Arts. ***PRACTICE AREAS:*** Commercial Litigation; Securities Litigation; Consumer Litigation; Technology Law; Class Actions; Complex and Multi-District Litigation; Agricultural Law. ***Email:*** levitt@whafh.com

WOOD, PHILLIPS, KATZ, CLARK & MORTIMER

Established in 1876

CITICORP CENTER

SUITE 3800, 500 WEST MADISON STREET

CHICAGO, ILLINOIS 60661-2511

Telephone: 312-876-1800

Telecopier: 312-876-2020

Email: info@woodphillips.com

URL: http://www.woodphillips.com

Intellectual Property and Unfair Competition Law.

FIRM PROFILE: Founded in 1876 as Dyrenforth & Dyrenforth. Practice in all areas of patent, trademark, copyright and trade secret law and related aspects of contract, employment and unfair competition law.

MEMBERS OF FIRM

JEFFREY L. CLARK, born Garrett, Indiana, October 8, 1953; admitted to bar, 1979, Illinois; 1980, U.S. Court of Appeals, 7th Circuit; 1982, U.S. Court of Appeals for the Federal Circuit and U.S. District Court, Northern District of Illinois including Trial Bar; registered to practice before U.S. Patent and Trademark Office. *Education:* Purdue University (B.S., with Highest Distinction, 1975); Southern Illinois University (J.D., summa cum laude, 1979). Phi Kappa Phi; Chi Epsilon; Tau Beta Pi. Articles Editor, Southern Illinois University Law Review, 1978-1979. Author: "The Contract Clause Reemerges," Southern Illinois University Law Journal, Vol. 1978. *Member:* Illinois State and American Bar Associations; Intellectual Property Law Association of Chicago. ***PRACTICE AREAS:*** Patents; Trademarks; Copyrights. ***Email:*** jlclark@woodphillips.com

JEFFERY N. FAIRCHILD, born Nurnberg, Germany, February 2, 1962; admitted to bar, 1997, Illinois; 1998, U.S. District Court, Northern District of Illinois; registered to practice before the U.S. Patent and Trademark Office. *Education:* University of Illinois (B.S.M.E., with honors, 1984); John Marshall Law School (J.D., cum laude, 1997). *Member:* Chicago, Illinois State and American Bar Associations; Intellectual Property Law Association of Chicago; American Intellectual Property Law Association. ***PRACTICE AREAS:*** Patents; Trademarks; Copyrights. ***Email:*** jnfairchild@woodphillips.com

STEPHEN D. GEIMER, born Chicago, Illinois, July 14, 1952; admitted to bar, 1977, Illinois; 1982, U.S. Court of Appeals, Federal Circuit; registered to practice before U.S. Patent and Trademark Office. *Education:* University of Illinois (B.S.M.E., 1974); Loyola University (J.D., 1977). *Member:* Illinois State Bar Association; American Intellectual Property Law Association; Intellectual Property Law Association of Chicago. ***PRACTICE AREAS:*** Patents. ***Email:*** sdgeimer@woodphillips.com

ALLEN J. HOOVER, born Chicago, Illinois, December 17, 1940; admitted to bar, 1965, Illinois, U.S. District Court, Northern and Southern Districts of Illinois, U.S. Court of Appeals, Seventh Circuit and U.S. Court of Appeals for the Federal Circuit; registered to practice before U.S. Patent and Trademark Office. *Education:* Marquette University (B.M.E., 1962); DePaul University (J.D., 1965). Tau Beta Pi; Pi Tau Sigma; Phi Alpha Delta (Chapter Justice, 1964-1965); Blue Key. Member, Board of Editors, De Paul Law Review, 1964-1965. *Member:* Chicago, Illinois State and American Bar Associations; American Intellectual Property Law Association; Intellectual Property Law Association of Chicago (Member, Board of Managers, 1984-1985); Catholic Lawyers Guild of Chicago. ***PRACTICE AREAS:*** Patents; Trademarks; Copyrights. ***Email:*** ajhoover@woodphillips.com

MARTIN L. KATZ, born New York, N.Y., December 11, 1942; admitted to bar, 1968, District of Columbia; 1969, New Jersey; 1987, Illinois; registered to practice before U.S. Patent and Trademark Office. *Education:* University of Rhode Island (B.S., 1964); Georgetown University (J.D., 1968). *Member:* The District of Columbia Bar; Illinois State and American Bar Associations; American Intellectual Property Law Association; Intellectual Property Law Association of Chicago (Member, Board of Managers, 1987-1989). ***PRACTICE AREAS:*** Patents; Trademarks; Copyrights; Intellectual Property Licensing. ***Email:*** mlkatz@woodphillips.com

(This Listing Continued)

F. WILLIAM McLAUGHLIN, born Chicago, Illinois, April 9, 1956; admitted to bar, 1985, Illinois and U.S. District Court, Northern District of Illinois; 1989, U.S. Court of Appeals for the Federal Circuit; 1997, U.S. Court of Appeals, Seventh Circuit; registered to practice before U.S. Patent and Trademark Office. *Education:* University of Notre Dame (B.S.E.E., with honors, 1978); DePaul University (J.D., 1984). Tau Beta Pi; Eta Kappa Nu; Phi Alpha Delta. *Member:* Chicago, Illinois State and American Bar Associations; Intellectual Property Law Association of Chicago; American Intellectual Property Law Association. ***PRACTICE AREAS:*** Patents; Trademarks; Copyrights. ***Email:*** fwmclaughlin@woodphillips.com

DEAN A. MONCO, born Chicago, Illinois, August 6, 1950; admitted to bar, 1979, Illinois and U.S. District Court, Northern District of Illinois, including Trial Bar; U.S. Court of Appeals, Seventh Circuit; 1989, U.S. Court of Appeals for the Federal Circuit; registered to practice before U.S. Patent and Trademark Office. *Education:* Loyola University (B.S., 1973; M.B.A., 1977); DePaul University (J.D., 1979). Member, Board of Directors, Loyola University Graduate School of Business Alumni Association, 1979. *Member:* Chicago and Illinois State Bar Associations; Intellectual Property Law Association of Chicago; Justinian Society. ***PRACTICE AREAS:*** Patents; Trademarks; Copyrights. ***Email:*** damonco@woodphillips.com

JOHN S. MORTIMER, born Chicago, Illinois, October 20, 1954; admitted to bar, 1980, Illinois and Florida; registered to practice before U.S. Patent and Trademark Office. *Education:* University of Notre Dame (B.S.M.E., 1976); DePaul University (J.D., 1979). Tau Beta Pi; Pi Tau Sigma. *Member:* Chicago, Illinois State and American Bar Associations; American Intellectual Property Law Association; Intellectual Property Law Association of Chicago. ***PRACTICE AREAS:*** Patents; Trademarks; Copyrights. ***Email:*** jsmortimer@woodphillips.com

LISA VON BARGEN MUELLER, born Valparaiso, Indiana, February 17, 1967; admitted to bar, 1992, Illinois; registered to practice before U.S. Patent and Trademark Office. *Education:* Valparaiso University (B.S., magna cum laude, 1989; J.D., magna cum laude, 1992). *Member:* Illinois State and American Bar Associations. ***PRACTICE AREAS:*** Patents; Utility and Plant Patents; Trademarks; Intellectual Property; Plant Variety Protection; Licensing. ***Email:*** lvmueller@woodphillips.com

PAUL M. ODELL, born Oak Ridge, Tennessee, April 10, 1945; admitted to bar, 1973, Illinois; registered to practice before U.S. Patent and Trademark Office. *Education:* University of Wisconsin (B.S.N.E., 1968); DePaul University (J.D., 1973). Licensed Professional Engineer: Illinois, 1973; Indiana, 1975. *Member:* Chicago and Illinois State Bar Associations; Intellectual Property Law Association of Chicago; American Society of Mechanical Engineers. ***PRACTICE AREAS:*** Patents; Trademarks; Copyrights. ***Email:*** pmodell@woodphillips.com

JOEL E. SIEGEL, born New York, N.Y., March 23, 1943; admitted to bar, 1969, Illinois; registered to practice before U.S. Patent and Trademark Office. *Education:* Purdue University (B.S.I.E., 1964); Washington College of Law of American University (J.D., 1969). *Member:* Illinois State and American Bar Associations; American Intellectual Property Law Association. ***PRACTICE AREAS:*** Patents; Trademarks; Copyrights. ***Email:*** jesiegel@woodphillips.com

ASSOCIATE

MARK V. POLYAKOV, born Rostov-on-Don, Russia, June 15, 1978; admitted to bar, 2005, New York and Ohio (Not admitted in Illinois). *Education:* Case Western Reserve University (B.A., 1999; J.D., 2005). ***Email:*** mpolyakov@woodphillips.com

OF COUNSEL

RICHARD S. PHILLIPS, born Peoria, Illinois, April 11, 1926; admitted to bar, 1951, Illinois; registered to practice before U.S. Patent and Trademark Office. *Education:* Northwestern University and University of Illinois (B.S. in E.E., 1950); University of Illinois (LL.B., 1951). Phi Delta Phi; Eta Kappa Nu; Phi Mu Epsilon. *Member:* Chicago, Illinois State and American Bar Associations; Intellectual Property Law Association of Chicago; American Intellectual Property Law Association. ***PRACTICE AREAS:*** Patents; Trademarks; Copyrights. ***Email:*** rsphillips@woodphillips.com

WILLIAM A. VAN SANTEN (Retired)

LEGAL SUPPORT PERSONNEL

JOSEPH HERRON, born Chicago Heights, Illinois, July 17, 1978. *Education:* Case Western Reserve University (B.S., 2000). (Patent Agent). ***PRACTICE AREAS:*** Patent Prosecution; Legal Research. ***Email:*** jhherron@woodphillips.com

REPRESENTATIVE CLIENTS: Modine Manufacturing Company; Abbott Laboratories; General Kinematics Corporation; Hyatt International Corporation; Kone, Inc.; Siemens; International Business Machines; University of Chicago; University of Illinois; Southern Illinois University; Valent Biosciences Corporation; Encysive Pharmaceuticals Inc.; Tap Pharmaceuticals Products, Inc.; Wisconsin Alumni Research Foundation; Ball Horticultural Company; Johnson & Johnson; Seaquist Closures; SeaquistPerfect Dispensing.

CASEY WOODRUFF & ASSOCIATES

Established in 2000

155 N. MICHIGAN AVENUE, SUITE 500

CHICAGO, ILLINOIS 60601

Telephone: 630-585-2320

Fax: 630-585-2327

Email: cwoodruff@woodrufflawyers.com

URL: http://www.woodrufflawyers.com

Aurora, Illinois Office: Millennium Park Plaza, 75 Executive Drive, Suite 105, 60504. Telephone: 630-585-2320. Toll Free: 1-866-891-9211. Fax: 630-585-2327.

Workers Compensation, Personal Injury, Automobile Accidents, Social Security, Medical Malpractice, Products Liability.

(This Listing Continued)

FIRM PROFILE: Casey Woodruff & Associates is a statewide Plaintiff injury law firm. We protect the rights of workers injured on the job, motorists injured in accidents, victims of medical malpractice, and consumers hurt by faulty products. Winning cases is what we do at Casey Woodruff & Associates. Over the years we have recovered millions for our clients with our firm's practice of personal attention from the entire legal team at Casey Woodruff & Associates. Our initial consultation is free with no upfront out-of-pocket expenses to you. Our legal fee is based on what we recover for you. We handle every aspect of your case, from start to finish. Casey Woodruff & Associates is experience and professionalism.

CASEY (KENNETH) WOODRUFF, born 1962; admitted to bar, 1990, Illinois. *Education:* University of Illinois (B.A., 1986); Chicago-Kent College of Law, Illinois Institute of Technology (J.D., 1990). Phi Alpha Delta. Member, Moot Court Executive Board, 1989-1990. Winner, Novotny Moot Court Competition, 1989. Recipient, American Jurisprudence Award in Workers Compensation, 1989. Listed in "Leading American Attorneys," 1998. Author and Lecturer, "Workers Compensation: Getting Started," Illinois Institute of Continuing Legal Education, 1997. Guest Lecturer: Service Employees International Union (SEIU); Illinois Education Association; International Boilermakers Union. Associate, Katz, Friedman, Schur & Eagle, 1990-1997. Partner, 1997-2000 and Managing Partner, 2000—, Casey Woodruff & Associates. *Member:* Chicago, Illinois State and American Bar Associations; Illinois Trial Lawyers Association; American Trial Lawyers Association. ***LANGUAGES:*** Spanish. ***PRACTICE AREAS:*** Workers Compensation (75%); Social Security; Medical Malpractice; Products Liability; Automobile Accidents and Injuries (25%).

ASSOCIATES

JAY JOHNSON, born 1965; admitted to bar, 1998, Illinois. *Education:* University of Kentucky (B.A., 1988); John Marshall Law School (J.D., 1998). *Member:* Illinois Bar Association; Illinois Trial Lawyers Association. ***LANGUAGES:*** Spanish. ***PRACTICE AREAS:*** Workers Compensation (90%); Workers Compensation Appeals (5%); Social Security Disability (5%). ***Email:*** jjohnson@woodrufflawyers.com

MARIO C. PALERMO, born New York, New York, August 2, 1971; admitted to bar, 1996, Illinois. *Education:* Boston College (B.A., 1993); Chicago-Kent College of Law, Illinois Institute of Technology (J.D., 1996). *Member:* Chicago and DuPage County Bar Associations; Illinois Trial Lawyers Association; American Trial Lawyers of Association. ***REPORTED CASES:*** Evans v. Ford Motor Co., United States District Court for the Northern District of Illinois. ***PRACTICE AREAS:*** Automobile Accidents and Injuries (75%); Automobile Negligence (10%); Medical Malpractice (5%); Premises Liability (10%). ***Email:*** mpalermo@woodrufflawyers.com

Language: Spanish.

REPRESENTATIVE CLIENTS: Int'l Brotherhood of Teamster; United Auto Workers; Int'l Boilermakers Union; United Food & Commercial Workers; Service Employees Int'l Union (SEIU); Champaign County AFL-CIO; Illinois Education Association; Mexican Consulate; Garment & Leather Workers Union.

WORKER, SITKO & HOFFMAN, LLC

Established in 1993

150 N. WACKER DRIVE, SUITE 3100

CHICAGO, ILLINOIS 60606

Telephone: 312-345-1718

Fax: 312-345-1778

Email: dworker@wshlawfirm.com

URL: http://www.wshlawfirm.com

Phoenix, Arizona Office: 101 N. 1st. Avenue, Suite 2075, 85003. Telephone: 602-840-6101. Fax: 602-840-6102.

Insurance Defense, Civil Litigation, Coverage Litigation, Medical Malpractice, Appellate Practice. Civil and Commercial Litigation, Construction Litigation, Franchise Litigation, Distribution Law.

FIRM PROFILE: The law firm of Worker, Sitko & Hoffman, LLC. was formed on April 15, 2001 when the Chicago based firm of Worker & Power joined forces with Stephen D. Hoffman to expand its operations into the Phoenix, Arizona market. Worker & Power was founded in November, 1993 by Dan Worker. The firm attributes its consistent growth to a personalized approach, client satisfaction and diversity of practice areas. Worker, Sitko & Hoffman concentrates its practice on insurance defense, civil and commercial litigation, construction litigation, franchise litigation, and appellate practice. Our attorneys have complementary backgrounds which through their collective areas of expertise and extensive litigation experience, give us the ability to provide high quality representation.

Reported Cases: Reed v. Illinois Farmers Ins. Co., 188 Ill.2d 168, 720 N.E.2d (1999); Illinois Farmers Ins. Co. v. Cisco/Shane v. Illinois Farmers Ins. Co., 178 Ill.2d 386, 687 N.E.2d 807 (1997); Machulis v. Illinois Farmers Ins. Co., 281 Ill.App.3d 829, 667 N.E.2d 592 (1st Dist. 1996); Martin v. Illinois Farmers Ins. Co., 318 Ill.App.3d 751, 742 N.E.2d 848 (1st Dist. 2000); Zimmerman v. Illinois Farmers Ins. Co., 317 Ill.App.3d 360, 739 N.E.2d 990 (2d Dist. 2000); Illinois Farmers Ins. Co. v. Puccinelli, 276 Ill.App.3d 293, 657 N.E.2d 1062 (1st. Dist. 1995); Vanek v. Illinois Farmers Ins. Co., 268 Ill.App.3d 731, 644 N.E.2d 731, 644 N.E.2d 419 (2nd Dist. 1994); Bourbeau v. Illinois Farmers Ins. Co., Rule 23 Order, Appellate No. 94-0917; Hoyd v. Illinois Farmers Ins. Co., Rule 23 Order, Appellate No. 98-0017; Illinois Farmers Ins. Co. v. Downing, Rule 23 Order, Appellate No. 96-2564; Maka v. Illinois Farmers, 332 Ill. App.3d 447, 772 N.E.2d 895 (lst Dist. 2002); Lee v. John Deere Insurance Company, 208 Ill.2d 38, 802 N.E.2d 774 (2003); Discosola v. Bowman, 342 Ill.App.3d 530, 794 N.E.2d 875 (2003); Illinois Farmers Insurance Company v. Lynda Ricciardi, (Rule 23 order, 01CH 10113); Rebaque v. Forsythe Racing, Inc., 134 Ill.App.3d 778, 480 N.E.2d 1338 (1st Dist. 1985); Pyramid Controls, Inc. v. Siemens Indus. Automation, Inc., 172 F.3d 516 (7th Cir. 1999); Hartford Acc. and Indem. Co. v. Sullivan, 846 F.2d 377 (7th Cir. 1988); To-Am Equipment Co., Inc. v. Mitsubishi Caterpillar Forklift America, Inc., 152 F.3d 658 (7th Cir. 1998); Cleveland Wrecking Co. v. Central Nat. Bank in Chicago, 216 Ill.App.3d 279, 576 N.E.2d 1055, (1st Dist. 1991).

DANNY L. WORKER, born Oak Lawn, Illinois, March 15, 1963; admitted to bar, 1987, Illinois and U.S. District Court, Northern District of Illinois, including Trial Bar. *Education:* Loyola University (B.B.A., 1984; J.D., 1987). *Member:* Illinois State and American Bar Associations; Defense Research Institute. ***PRACTICE AREAS:*** Insurance Coverage; Insurance Bad Faith; Civil Litigation; Commercial Litigation; Construction Litigation; Franchise Litigation. ***Email:*** dworker@wshlawfirm.com

MARY F. SITKO, admitted to bar, 1991, Michigan and U.S. District Court, Eastern District of Michigan; 1995, Illinois. *Education:* Wayne State University; Detroit College of Law (J.D., 1991). ***PRACTICE AREAS:*** Insurance Defense; Coverage Litigation. ***Email:*** msitko@wshlawfirm.com

STEPHEN D. HOFFMAN, born Naperville, Illinois, July 25, 1966; admitted to bar, 1991, Arizona; 1992, U.S. District Court, District of Arizona; 1995, U.S. Court of Appeals, Ninth Circuit; 1996, New Mexico (Not admitted in Illinois). *Education:* Grand Canyon University (B.S., 1987); University of San Diego (J.D., 1991). Phi Delta Phi. Federalist Society. *Member:* Yavapai County, Maricopa County and American Bar Associations; State Bar of Arizona; State Bar of New Mexico. ***PRACTICE AREAS:*** Insurance Defense; Personal Injury. ***Email:*** shoffman@wshlawfirm.com

JAMES B. TOBIN, admitted to bar, 1987, Illinois; 2001, U.S. District Court, Northern District of Illinois. *Education:* Miami University (B.A., 1982); Loyola University (J.D., 1987). ***PRACTICE AREAS:*** Personal Injury Litigation. ***Email:*** jtobin@wshlawfirm.com

DAMON LAPORTE, born Chicago, Illinois, November 4, 1963; admitted to bar, 1995, Illinois. *Education:* Oberlin College (B.A., 1987); Chicago-Kent College of Law, Illinois Institute of Technology (J.D., 1995). ***PRACTICE AREAS:*** Litigation; General Practice.

ERIC ALVINE, born Moline, Illinois, November 30, 1975; admitted to bar, 2001, Illinois. *Education:* DePauw University (B.A., 1998); John Marshall Law School (J.D., 2001). ***Email:*** ealvine@wshlawfirm.com

BONNIE BERNADETTE BIJAK, born Chicago Heights, Illinois, August 10, 1958; admitted to bar, 1987, Illinois. *Education:* Eastern Illinois University (B.A., 1981); John Marshall Law School (J.D., 1987). ***PRACTICE AREAS:*** Civil Litigation.

JAMES J. CHANDLER, born Seoul, Korea, September 30, 1975; admitted to bar, 2000, Illinois. *Education:* Florida State University (B.S., 1997); Loyola University School of Law (J.D., 2000). ***PRACTICE AREAS:*** Insurance Defense Litigation. ***Email:*** jchandler@wshlawfirm.com

MARC ANTHONY CERVANTES, born Chicago, Illinois, September 25, 1975; admitted to bar, 2001, Illinois and U.S. District Court, Northern District of Illinois. *Education:* Indiana University (B.A., 1997); St. Louis University (J.D., 2000). Phi Alpha Delta. Formerly, Cook County States Attorney. ***PRACTICE AREAS:*** Insurance Defense; Tort Litigation; Insurance Coverage; Criminal Law. ***Email:*** mcervantes@wshlawfirm.com

MICHAEL SCHNITZER, born Chicago, Illinois, June 24, 1972; admitted to bar, 1997, Illinois. *Education:* The Ohio State University (B.A.S., 1994); The John Marshall Law School (J.D., 1997). ***PRACTICE AREAS:*** Insurance Defense; Contract Law; Toxic Tort Litigation; Plaintiff Class Action. ***Email:*** mschnitzer@wshlawfirm.com

OF COUNSEL

GARY W. LEYDIG, born Chicago, Illinois, July 26, 1955; admitted to bar, 1980, Illinois and U.S. District Courts, Northern District of Illinois including Trial Bar; U.S. Court of Appeals, Seventh and Eighth Circuits; U.S. Supreme Court. *Education:* University of Illinois (B.A., 1977); University of Edinburgh, Edinburgh, Scotland; Marshall-Wythe School of Law, College of William & Mary (J.D., 1980). Phi Delta Phi. Member: Moot Court Board, Order of Barristers. General Counsel, American Railway Corporation, 1990-1993. *Member:* Illinois State (Member, Sections on: Trial Practice and Procedure; Business Law) and American (Member, Sections on: Litigation; Business Law; Forum on Franchising) Bar Associations. ***PRACTICE AREAS:*** Commercial Litigation; Business Law; Commercial Law; Franchise Law; Distribution Law.

LEGAL SUPPORT PERSONNEL

NANCI E. KOLLER (Office Administrator)

JOSEPH WROBEL, LTD.

Established in 1980

105 WEST MADISON STREET, SUITE 700

CHICAGO, ILLINOIS 60602

Telephone: 312-781-0996

Fax: 312-606-0413

URL: http://www.chicagobankruptcy.com

URL: http://www.chicagobankruptcylaw.com

Email: j.wrobel.ltd@chicagobankruptcy.com

URL: http://www.chicagobankruptcylawfirm.com

Bankruptcy including Personal Bankruptcy, Business Bankruptcy, Chapter 7, Chapter 11, Chapter 13, Foreclosures and Garnishments and Business Dissolutions.

JOSEPH WROBEL, born 1948; admitted to bar, 1973, Illinois. *Education:* Northwestern University (B.A., 1969); DePaul University (J.D., 1973). ***LANGUAGES:*** German. ***Email:*** j.wrobel.ltd@chicagobankruptcy.com

(This Listing Continued)

LAW OFFICES OF PHILIP P. YANEZ

2400 N. WESTERN AVENUE, SUITE 201
CHICAGO, ILLINOIS 60647
Telephone: 773-772-0844
Fax: 773-772-0845
Email: pyanezlaw@hotmail.com
URL: http://www.pyanezlaw.com

Family Law, Criminal Law, Traffic, D.U.I., Residential Real Estate, Consumer Bankruptcy, Personal Injury, Slip and Fall, Auto Accidents, Dog Bites.

PHILIP P. YANEZ, born Chicago, Illinois, October 27, 1965; admitted to bar, 1990, Illinois. *Education:* University of Illinois (B.S., 1987); University of Michigan Law School (J.D., 1990). *Member:* Chicago Bar Association. ***LANGUAGES:*** Spanish. ***PRACTICE AREAS:*** Family Law; Criminal Law; Traffic Violations; Driving While Intoxicated; Residential Real Estate; Consumer Bankruptcy; Personal Injury; Slip and Fall; Automobile Accidents and Injuries; Dog Bites.

C. JOSEPH YAST

Established in 1992
WILLOW HILL EXECUTIVE CENTER
540 FRONTAGE ROAD
SUITE 2110 (NORTHFIELD)
CHICAGO, ILLINOIS 60093-1224
Telephone: 847-441-0357; 847-507-2167
Fax: 847-441-0359
Email: joeyastlaw@comcast.net

Business and Commercial Litigation, Including Contracts, Leases, RICO, Partnership, Corporations, Fiduciary Litigation, Fraud, Franchise Litigation, Injunctions and Litigations, Non-Compete Litigation and Civil Appeals.

C. JOSEPH YAST, born Chicago, Illinois, November 10, 1952; admitted to bar, 1977, Massachusetts; 1978, Illinois and U.S. District Court, Northern District of Illinois including Trial Bar; U.S. Court of Appeals, Fourth, Seventh, Eighth, Ninth and Tenth Circuits; U.S. District Court, Northern District of Indiana; U.S. District Court, District of Colorado. *Education:* Tufts University (B.A., cum laude, 1974); University of Chicago (J.D., cum laude, 1977). Order of the Coif. Law Clerk to the Hon. Herbert P. Wilkins, Supreme Judicial Court of Massachusetts, 1977-1978. Lord, Bissell & Brook, 1978-1992 (Partner, 1986-1992). *Member:* Chicago, Illinois State and American Bar Associations. ***REPORTED CASES:*** Gagan v. American Cablevision, 77 F.3d 951 (7th Cir. 1996); Stachon v. United Consumers Club, Inc., et.al., 229 F.3d 673 (7th Cir. 2000); Gagan v. Monroe, 269 F.3d 871 (7th Cir. 2001); Meehan v. United Consumers Club Franchising Corp., 312 F.3d 909 (8th Cir. 2002); Gagan v. Sharar, 376 F. 3d 987 (9th Cir. 2004).

YAVITZ & LEVEY, LLP

20 SOUTH CLARK STREET, SUITE 2200
CHICAGO, ILLINOIS 60603
Telephone: 312-924-4400
Fax: 312-924-4411
URL: http://www.yldivorce.com

Family Law, Divorce, Premarital Counseling and Agreements, Paternity, Adoption Law, Child Custody, Matrimonial Law, Domestic Relations, Appellate Practice.

MEMBERS OF FIRM

DAVID B. YAVITZ, born Chicago, Illinois, August 17, 1944; admitted to bar, 1969, Illinois. *Education:* Drake University (B.A., 1966); University of Illinois (J.D., 1969). Order of the Coif. Selected as one of Top 5% of Family Law Attorneys in Illinois by the Leading Lawyers Network, 2002-2006. Author: "Distinctions Between Marital and Nonmarital Property," (Chapter 19), "Marital Property Valuation," (Chapter 21), Illinois State Bar Association Family Law Handbook, 1994. Speaker, Illinois Institute Continuing Legal Education, 1985—. Represented Joint Illinois State Bar Association and Chicago Bar Association in Sponsorship and Passage of 1985 Spousal Health Insurance Rights Act in Illinois General Assembly. Law Office Computer Consultant, 1994—; Member, Apple Computer Consultants Network. *Member:* Chicago (Member, 1978—, Chairman, 1986-1987, Matrimonial Law Committee), Illinois State (Member, Assembly, 1988—; Family Law Section Council, 1979—, Chairman, 1984-1985, Secretary, 1982-1983, Editor-in-Chief, Newsletter, 1981-1984; Member, Special Committee on Gender Bias, 1991; Member, Standing Committee on Legal Technology, 1994—; Chairman, 1996—) and American (Member, American Family Law Section; Section Liaison to National Conference of Commissioners on Uniform State Laws, 1987—; Vice Chairman, Domestic Violence Committee, 1989—) Bar Associations. Fellow, American Academy of Matrimonial Lawyers (Member: Board of Directors, Illinois Chapter, 1986-1994). ***PRACTICE AREAS:*** Family Law; Divorce; Premarital Agreements; Paternity; Adoption Law; Child Custody; Matrimonial Law. ***Email:*** david@yldivorce.com

ROSS S. LEVEY, born Chicago, Illinois, September 18, 1968; admitted to bar, 1993, Illinois. *Education:* University of Illinois (B.S., with honors, 1990); DePaul University (J.D., 1993). Member, Journal of Arts and Entertainment Law. Newsletter Editor, Family Law Section, Illinois Bar Association, 2001-2006. Illinois Reporter, American Bar Association Family Law Quarterly, 2003-2004. *Member:* Chicago and Illinois State (Family Law Section Council, 2005—) Bar Associations. ***PRACTICE AREAS:*** Family Law; Divorce; Domestic Relations; Appellate Practice; Paternity; Child Custody. ***Email:*** ross@yldivorce.com

KEITH L. YOUNG

333 WEST WACKER DRIVE, SUITE 500
CHICAGO, ILLINOIS 60606
Telephone: 312-807-4777
Fax: 312-641-3004
Email: keithlyoung@prodigy.net
URL: http://www.lawyers.com/kyounglaw

Personal Injury, Automobile Accidents and Injuries, Slip and Fall, Wrongful Death, Insurance Bad Faith, Medical Malpractice, Products Liability, Negligence, Civil Rights, Automotive Products Liability and Drug and Medical Device Litigation.

KEITH L. YOUNG, born Chicago, Illinois, January 15, 1953; admitted to bar, 1977, Illinois, U.S. District Court, Northern District of Illinois and U.S. Court of Appeals, Seventh Circuit. *Education:* Iowa State University (B.S., 1974); Chicago-Kent College of Law (J.D., 1977). *Member:* Chicago (Member, Tort Litigation Committee), Illinois State and American Bar Associations; Illinois Trial Lawyers Association; The Association of Trial Lawyers of America.

YOUNG, ROSEN, FINKEL & SILBERT LIMITED

Established in 1956
33 NORTH LA SALLE STREET
SUITE 900
CHICAGO, ILLINOIS 60602
Telephone: 312-782-2555
Fax: 312-782-9360
Email: law@yrfs.com

Civil litigation practice in all Trial and Appellate Courts, Corporate, Real Estate and Other Business Transaction Matters. Incorporation, Estate Planning, Probate and Tax Planning, and Real Estate Property Tax Reduction.

HARRY A. YOUNG, JR., born Oak Park, Illinois, June 25, 1931; admitted to bar, 1958, Illinois and U.S. District Court, Northern District of Illinois; 1972, U.S. Court of Appeals, Seventh Circuit; 1973, U.S. Supreme Court; 1975, U.S. Claims Court and U.S. Tax Court; 1976, U.S. Court of Appeals, Fifth Circuit. *Education:* Grinnell College (B.A., 1953); Harvard University (LL.B., 1958). ***PRACTICE AREAS:*** Business Transactions; Business Litigation; Corporate Litigation. ***Email:*** hyoung@yrfs.com

ALAN ROSEN, born Chicago, Illinois, November 9, 1946; admitted to bar, 1974, Illinois and U.S. District Court, Northern District of Illinois; 1979, U.S. Supreme Court, U.S. Court of Appeals, Seventh Circuit, U.S. Tax Court and U.S. Claims Court; 1983, U.S. Court of Appeals for the Federal Circuit. *Education:* University of Illinois (B.S., Accounting, 1968); Loyola University (J.D., 1973). Internal Revenue Service, Revenue Agent, 1968-1974. Assistant States Attorney, Cook County, Illinois, 1974-1977. Chairperson, Illinois Supreme Court Committee on Character and Fitness, First District. Member: Public Integrity Transition Team, Illinois Attorney General Lisa Madigan, January 2003; ABA National Conference on Professional Responsibility, May 2003. ***PRACTICE AREAS:*** Business Litigation; Real Estate Taxation. ***Email:*** arosen@yrfs.com

NORMAN T. FINKEL, born Chicago, Illinois, July 5, 1957; admitted to bar, 1982, Illinois and U.S. District Court, Northern District of Illinois; 1983, U.S. Court of Appeals, Seventh Circuit; 1985, U.S. Supreme Court; 1991, U.S. Tax Court; 1997, U.S. Court of Federal Claims. *Education:* University of Illinois (B.S., Finance, with highest honors, 1979; J.D., 1982; M.B.A., with highest honors, 1983). Recipient: James Scholars; David Kinley Fellowship Award. ***LANGUAGES:*** Hebrew. ***PRACTICE AREAS:*** Business Litigation. ***Email:*** nfinkel@yrfs.com

WILLIAM R. KLEIN, born Chicago, Illinois, September 30, 1958; admitted to bar, 1983, Illinois; 1986, U.S. District Court, Northern District of Illinois; 1996, U.S. Supreme Court and U.S. Court of Appeals, Seventh Circuit, U.S. Tax Court; 1997, U.S. Court of Federal Claims. *Education:* University of Illinois (B.A., 1980; J.D., magna cum laude, 1983). Order of the Coif. Law Clerk to: Hon. Harold S. Trapp, Illinois Court of Appeals, Fourth District, 1983-1984; Hon. John T. McCullough, Illinois Court of Appeals, Fourth District, 1985-1986. ***PRACTICE AREAS:*** Business Litigation. ***Email:*** bklein@yrfs.com

RONALD G. SILBERT, born Chicago, Illinois, October 23, 1946; admitted to bar, 1972, Illinois and U.S. District Court, Northern District of Illinois; 1979, U.S. Supreme Court and U.S. Tax Court. *Education:* University of Illinois at Chicago (B.A., 1968); DePaul University (J.D., 1972). Editor-in-Chief, De Paul Law Review, Spring, 1972. ***PRACTICE AREAS:*** Estate Planning; Trust Law; Wills; Business Transactions; Incorporation. ***Email:*** rsilbert@yrfs.com

ASSOCIATE

G. TERENCE NADER, born Berwyn, Illinois, April 18, 1959; admitted to bar, 1987, Illinois. *Education:* Loyola University (A.B., 1981; B.S., 1981; J.D., 1987). Former Criminal Division Chief, McHenry County State Attorney's Office. Former Kane County State Attorney, Director of Child Advocacy Center. ***PRACTICE AREAS:*** Commercial Litigation; Business Litigation; Real Estate Taxation. ***Email:*** tnader@yrfs.com

OF COUNSEL

GEORGE E. SANG, born Chicago, Illinois, March 22, 1949; admitted to bar, 1973, Illinois. *Education:* Rutgers University (B.A., 1970); University of Chicago (J.D., 1973). Former Cook County Assistant States Attorney. Former Member: Bilandic, Neistein Richman, Hauslinger & Young. Member, Chicago Mercantile Exchange. ***PRACTICE AREAS:*** Commercial Litigation; Corporate Litigation; Commodities. ***Email:*** GSang@yrfs.com

ZAIDEMAN & ESRIG, P.C.

Established in 1985

10 SOUTH RIVERSIDE PLAZA, SUITE 1020
CHICAGO, ILLINOIS 60606-3827
Telephone: 312-207-0005
Fax: 312-207-1332
Email: ze@zelaw.com

Civil Trial and Appellate Practice in all courts. Commercial, Construction, Plaintiff Personal Injury, Medical Malpractice and Products Liability, Appeals.

FIRM PROFILE: The law firm of Zaideman & Esrig, P.C. was founded in 1985 to provide high quality trial and appellate work in a small firm setting. The firm has broad based trial experience in civil litigation including construction claims, medical malpractice, wrongful death, legal malpractice, product liability, other complex personal injury claims and other commercial litigation. The firm also represents doctors and lawyers in disciplinary and licensing proceedings and provides independent counseling in conflicts with insurance carriers. The firm is small enough to give each matter personal attention, but takes pride in its ability to handle the most sophisticated and complex litigation. The vast majority of the firm's clients are referred by other lawyers seeking the firm's experience and expertise in complex litigation.

ROBERT J. ZAIDEMAN, born Chicago, Illinois, June 16, 1953; admitted to bar, 1978, Illinois and U.S. District Court, Northern District of Illinois including Trial Bar; 1985, U.S. Court of Appeals, Seventh Circuit. *Education:* University of Illinois (B.A., 1975); Northwestern University (J.D., cum laude, 1978). Phi Eta Sigma. Faculty: Adjunct Professor of Pretrial Litigation, Northwestern University Law School, 1995—; National Institute for Trial Advocacy, Midwest Deposition Skills Program, 1994. *Member:* Chicago and Illinois State Bar Associations; Chicago Council of Lawyers; Illinois Trial Lawyers Association; The Association of Trial Lawyers of America. ***REPORTED CASES:*** Gomez v. Chody, 867 F.2d 395 7th Circuit, (1989); Turner Construction Co. v. Midwest Curtainwalls, Inc., 542 N.E.2d 249 (Ill.App.1989); People v. N.L. Industries, Inc., 673 N.E.2d 717 (Ill.App.1996); Schiff v. Friberg, 771 N.E.2d 517 (Ill. App. 2002); Sterdjevich v. RMK Management Corp., 796 N.E. 2d 1146 (2003). ***PRACTICE AREAS:*** Personal Injury Law; Professional Negligence; Commercial Litigation; Appellate Litigation. ***Email:*** rzaideman@zelaw.com

JERRY A. ESRIG, born Chicago, Illinois, February 17, 1953; admitted to bar, 1978, Illinois and U.S. District Court, Northern District of Illinois including Trial Bar; 1985, U.S. Court of Appeals, Seventh Circuit. *Education:* Northwestern University (B.A., 1974); University of Chicago (J.D., 1978). Phi Beta Kappa; Phi Eta Sigma. Faculty: Adjunct Professor of Pretrial Litigation, Northwestern University Law School, 1995—; National Institute for Trial Advocacy, Midwest Deposition Skills Program, 1994-1999; National Business Institute Premises Liability: Preparation and Trial of a Difficult Case in Illinois, 1994. Instructor, Illinois Institute for Continuing Legal Education, Construction Litigation, 1990; "Rights and Responsibilities of the Construction Lender vis a vis Contractors, Subcontractors, Material Suppliers and Third Parties," Construction Litigation, IICLE (1999). *Member:* Chicago and Illinois State Bar Associations; Chicago Council of Lawyers; Illinois Trial Lawyers Association; American Trial Lawyers Association. ***REPORTED CASES:*** Ampat/Midwest, Inc. v. Illinois Tool Works, Inc. 896 F2d 1035 (7th Cir. 1989); Turner Construction Co. v. Midwest Curtain Walls Inc., 543 NE2d 249 (Ill.App. 1989); Orrico v. Beverly Bank, 440 N.E.2d 253 (Ill.App. 1982). ***PRACTICE AREAS:*** Personal Injury Law; Construction Law; Commercial Litigation. ***Email:*** jesrig@zelaw.com

LEON ZELECHOWSKI, LTD.

Established in 1988

111 WEST WASHINGTON STREET, SUITE 1437
CHICAGO, ILLINOIS 60602
Telephone: 312-609-0022
Fax: 312-609-0626
Email: lzelech@comcast.net

Commercial Real Estate, Landlord and Tenant Law, Mortgages, Mechanics Liens, Breach of Contract, Creditors Rights, Collections, Buying and Selling of Businesses.

LEON ZELECHOWSKI, born Poland, June 6, 1948; admitted to bar, 1975, Illinois and U.S. District Court, Northern District of Illinois. *Education:* Southern Illinois University (B.S., 1971); Northwestern University (J.D., cum laude, 1975). Phi Beta Kappa. Lecturer, Business Law, Northwestern University, Summer, 1980. *Member:* Chicago and American (Member, Litigation Section) Bar Associations. ***LANGUAGES:*** Polish. ***REPORTED CASES:*** Wafra Leasing Corporation 1999-A-1 v. Prime Capital Corporation, et. al., 247 F.Supp.2d 987 (N.D. Ill 2002); Wafra Leasing Corporation 1999-A-1 v. Prime Capital Corporation, et. al., 204 F.Supp.2d 1120 (N.D. Ill 2002); Brown v. Farkas, 158 Ill. App. 3d 772 (1986); Cencula v. Keller, 180 Ill. App. 3d 645 (1989); Cencula v. Keller, 152 Ill. App. 3d 754 (1987). ***PRACTICE AREAS:*** Commercial Law; Commercial Litigation; Real Estate; Commercial Leasing; Creditors Rights; Buying and Selling of Businesses.

LLOYD L. ZICKERT

79 WEST MONROE STREET, SUITE 1100
CHICAGO, ILLINOIS 60603
Telephone: 312-236-1888
Fax: 312-236-1885
Email: zickert@compuserve.com

Patent, Trademark, Copyright and Unfair Competition Law.

LLOYD L. ZICKERT, born Beloit, Wisconsin, December 31, 1926; admitted to bar, 1953, Virginia; 1955, Illinois; 1960, U.S. Supreme Court; registered to practice before U.S. Patent and Trademark Office. *Education:* Purdue University (B.S.M.E., 1950); George Washington University (J.D., 1954). *Member:* Chicago, Illinois State, Federal Circuit and

(This Listing Continued)

American Bar Associations; Virginia State Bar; Chicago and American Intellectual Property Law Associations; The Lawyers Club of Chicago.

GEORGE M. ZUGANELIS ATTORNEY AT LAW, P.C.

3310 NORTH HARLEM AVENUE
CHICAGO, ILLINOIS 60634
Telephone: 773-237-3516
Fax: 773-237-3518
Email: gmzlawpc@aol.com

Criminal Defense, Real Estate, Personal Injury, Adoption, Workers Compensation.

FIRM PROFILE: The Past 26 years, I have developed a reputation for being a tenacious fighter for the legal rights of my clients. Our firm provides dedicated, individual legal attention in the following areas: Criminal Defense at both the State and Federal levels; Real Estate Transactions; Adoptions (in particular, international adoptions originating in Eastern Europe); Personal Injury Prosecution and Workers Compensation matters.

GEORGE M. ZUGANELIS, born Chicago, Illinois, April 11, 1948; admitted to bar, 1978, Illinois, U.S. District Court, Northern District of Illinois, U.S. Court of Appeals, Seventh Circuit and U.S. Supreme Court. *Education:* University of Michigan, Ann Arbor (B.S., 1970); Northern Illinois University College of Law, Glen Ellyn (J.D., 1978). *Member:* National Association of Criminal Defense Lawyers. ***PRACTICE AREAS:*** Criminal Defense; Real Estate; Adoption Law; Personal Injury; Workers Compensation. ***Email:*** gmzlawpc@aol.com

ZULKIE PARTNERS LLC

222 SOUTH RIVERSIDE PLAZA, SUITE 2300
CHICAGO, ILLINOIS 60606-6101
Telephone: 312-648-2244
Fax: 312-648-9848
URL: http://www.zulkiepartners.com
Email: pzulkie@zulkiepartners.com
URL: http://www.lawyers.com/zulkiepartners

Immigration and Naturalization Law.

PAUL L. ZULKIE, born 1952; admitted to bar, 1977, Illinois; U.S. District Court, Northern District of Illinois. *Education:* Northern Illinois University (B.A., summa cum laude, 1974); University of Illinois (J.D., 1977). Author: *Immigration Compliance in Employment and Business,* Callaghan and Co., 1987. *Member:* Illinois State Bar Association; American Immigration Lawyers Association (President, 2004-2005). ***PRACTICE AREAS:*** Immigration Law. ***Email:*** pzulkie@zulkiepartners.com

SUSAN M. MACLEAN, born 1963; admitted to bar, 1994, California; 1996, Illinois. *Education:* Oberlin College (B.A., government, 1986); London School of Economics and Political Science (Diploma, world politics, 1991); California Western School of Law (J.D., 1994). *Member:* Illinois State Bar Association; American Immigration Lawyers Association. ***PRACTICE AREAS:*** Immigration Law. ***Email:*** smaclean@zulkiepartners.com

ASSOCIATES

PAMELA MICK, born 1970; admitted to bar, 1996, Indiana; 1997, Illinois. *Education:* DePauw University (B.A., Asian Studies, 1992); Indiana University School of Law (J.D., 1996). *Member:* Illinois State Bar Association; American Immigration Lawyers Association. ***PRACTICE AREAS:*** Immigration Law. ***Email:*** pmick@zulkiepartners.com

TERRI BARTON BRAGGA, born Columbus, Ohio; admitted to bar, 1998, Ohio; 2001, District of Columbia (Not admitted in Illinois). *Education:* Vanderbilt University (B.A., Spanish and English, magna cum laude, 1995); The Ohio State University (J.D., 1998). *Member:* Ohio State Bar Association; American Immigration Lawyers Association. ***LANGUAGES:*** Spanish. ***PRACTICE AREAS:*** Immigration Law. ***Email:*** tbartonbragga@zulkiepartners.com

JENNIFER L. SIMUTIS, born 1972; admitted to bar, 2002, Illinois. *Education:* University of Illinois, Urbana-Champaign (B.A., Political Science and History, 1994); DePaul University College of Law (J.D., 2001). *Member:* Chicago and Illinois State Bar Associations; American Immigration Lawyers Association. ***PRACTICE AREAS:*** Immigration Law. ***Email:*** jsimutis@zulkiepartners.com

LAW OFFICE OF MITCHELL A. KLINE

CHICAGO HEIGHTS, ILLINOIS

(See Chicago)

Sexual Harassment, Discrimination, Age Discrimination, Sex Discrimination, Disability Discrimination, Race Discrimination, Religious Discrimination, Workers' Compensation.

LAW OFFICE OF JAMES J. SIWEK

CHICAGO RIDGE, ILLINOIS

(See Worth)

Bankruptcy - Chapters 7 and 13, Consumer Fraud, Criminal Law, Misdemeanors and Felonies, Driving While Intoxicated, Drug Crimes, Juvenile Law, Parole and Probation, Family Law, Adoptions, Child Custody, Child Support, Divorce, Domestic Violence, Visitation Rights, General Practice, Real Estate, Buying or Selling a Home, Construction, Landlord and Tenant, Trusts and Estates, Land Trusts, Living Trusts, Guardianships, Powers of Attorney, Wills and Probate.

MICHAEL T. MAHONEY, LTD.

Established in 1984

1011 NORTH SECOND STREET
CHILLICOTHE, ILLINOIS 61523
Telephone: 309-274-5451
Fax: 309-274-5405
Email: mahoney@mchsi.com
URL: http://www.mahoneyltd.com

Peoria Office: 414 Hamilton Boulevard, Suite 300. Telephone: 309-673-0375.

Civil Litigation, Wills and Probate, Trusts and Estates, Estate Planning, Family Law, Personal Injury, Juvenile Law, DUI, Divorce, Adoptions, Child Support and Custody, Visitation Rights, Automobile Accidents, Dog Bites, Slip and Fall, Wrongful Death, Real Estate, Buying and Selling, Construction Law, Workers Compensation, Title and Insurance, Domestic Relations, Corporations.

MICHAEL T. MAHONEY, admitted to bar, 1979, Illinois. *Education:* Loyola University (B.A., 1976; J.D., 1979). *Member:* Peoria County and Illinois State Bar Associations. ***REPORTED CASES:*** Proctor Hospital v. Taylor, 279 Ill. App.3d 624 (3rd Dist., 1996); Foreman v. Commonwealth Edison Co., 94 IIC 1324 (1994); In re Marriage of Good, 208 Ill. App.3d 775 (3rd Dist., 1999); In re Estate of Tulley, 171 Ill.App.3d 286 (3rd Dist., 1988); Greater Chillicothe Sanitary Dist. v. Prather, 157 Ill.App.3d 1086 (3rd Dist., 1987); City of Peoria v. Feuchter, 115 Ill.App.3d 177 (3rd Dist., 1983). ***Email:*** mmahoney@mchsi.com

REPRESENTATIVE CLIENTS: First National Bank of Chillicothe; Chillicothe Foundation, Inc.; Pearce Community Center; Chillicothe Park District; City of Lacon.

CHRISTENSEN & EHRET, LLP

CICERO, ILLINOIS

(See Chicago)

Admiralty and Maritime Law, Appellate Practice, Commercial Litigation, Construction Liability, Excess and Reinsurance, Insurance Coverage, Products Liability, Professional Malpractice, Transportation, Trial Practice.

GABRIELLE S. DAVIS, P.C.

CICERO, ILLINOIS

(See Oak Park)

Family Law.

KARLIN & FLEISHER, L.L.C.

CICERO, ILLINOIS

(See Chicago)

General Negligence, Trials and Appeals, Medical Malpractice and other Professional Liability, Products Liability, Railroad, Maritime and Aviation Negligence Law and Workers Compensation Law.

WALLENSTEIN WAGNER & ROCKEY, LTD.

CICERO, ILLINOIS

(See Chicago)

Intellectual Property and Technology Related Law including Protection and Licensing of United States and International Patent, Trademark, Copyright Trade Secret and Unfair Competition Matters and Related Litigation in the Courts and United States International Trade Commission.

HARVEY L. WALNER & ASSOCIATES, LTD.

CICERO, ILLINOIS

(See Chicago)

Construction Accidents, Heath Insurance, Long Term Care, Nursing Home Litigation, Medical Malpractice, Personal Injury, Airplane Crash Litigation, Automobile Accidents, Dog Bites, Railroad Accidents, Sexual Abuse, Slip and Fall, Wrongful Death, Products Liability, Workers Compensation.

MICHAEL T. BYRNE

115 WEST 55TH STREET, SUITE 400
CLARENDON HILLS, ILLINOIS 60514
Telephone: 630-654-8333
Fax: 630-654-0150
Email: michaeltbyrne@aol.com

Criminal Law, Driving While Intoxicated, Drug Crimes, Felonies, Homicide, Sexual Assault, Traffic Violations and Probation Violations.

MICHAEL T. BYRNE, born Evanston, Illinois, December 9, 1956; admitted to bar, 1982, Illinois and U.S. District Court, Northern District of Illinois. *Education:* University of Illinois, Urbana-Champaign (B.S., 1978); John Marshall Law School (J.D., 1981). Assistant Public Defender, 1981-1988 and Member Homicide Task Force, 1988, County Public Defender's Office. *Member:* Chicago and Du Page County Bar Associations.

IWAN CRAY HUBER HORSTMAN & VanAUSDAL LLC

115 WEST 55TH STREET, SUITE 400
CLARENDON HILLS, ILLINOIS 60514
Telephone: 630-789-8200
Email: attorneys@iwancray.com
URL: http://www.iwancray.com

Chicago, Illinois Office: 303 West Madison Street, Suite 2200, 60606-3315. Telephone: 312-332-8450. Fax: 312-332-8451.

Litigation Practice. Product Liability, Insurance Coverage, Complex Commercial, Professional Liability, Medical Malpractice, Transportation Liability, Premises Liability, Hospital Liability Defense, Environmental Litigation and Civil Appeals.

FIRM PROFILE: We recognize that purchasers of legal services today seek more resourceful, efficient and responsive lawyers than ever before. As a result, our litigation practice is designed to deliver the quality and value that our clients expect. The size, focus and technological commitment of our firm give us significant advantages over traditionally structured firms for achieving success in legal disputes. Although we are a litigation firm, we do not simply litigate; we work closely with our clients to provide individualized counseling, approaches and solutions to satisfy their unique legal and commercial needs.

DANIEL K. CRAY, born Quincy, Illinois, June 20, 1956; admitted to bar, 1981, Illinois. *Education:* Illinois State University (B.S., with high honors, 1978); University of Illinois (J.D., 1981). Co-Author: "Reimportation and It's Risks," For the Defense, June 2001. Author: "Motions to Remove," Defense Counsel Training Manual, International Association of Defense Counsel, 1995; "Federal Preemption Monograph," Illinois Association of Defense Trial Counsel Quarterly, Third Quarter, 1996; "Defending Product Liability Cases in Illinois After the *Best* Decision," Illinois Association of Defense Trial Counsel Quarterly, Fourth Quarter, 1998. Illinois Representative, National Jury Innovations Project. *Member:* DuPage County (Judicial Evaluation Committee), Illinois State and American Bar Associations; International Association of Defense Counsel (Chair, General Convention Committee 2005-2006; Vice-Chair, Products Liability Committee, 1998-1999; IADC Trial Academy Faculty, 2000); Defense Research Institute (Member, Sections on Medical Defense, Products Liability and Technology); Illinois Association of Defense Trial Counsel. ***PRACTICE AREAS:*** Commercial Litigation; Litigation; Legal Malpractice; Products Liability; Professional Liability; Medical Malpractice. **Email:** dkc@iwancray.com

(For Complete Biographical Data on all Personnel, see Professional Biographies at Chicago, Illinois)

LAMKIN & LAMKIN, P.C.

Established in 1948

200 SOUTH MONROE STREET
P.O. BOX 597
CLINTON, ILLINOIS 61727
Telephone: 217-935-3186
Fax: 217-935-8033

General Civil Practice. Trials. Real Estate, Taxation, DUI/DWI, Traffic Violations, Felonies, Criminal, Wills and Probate Law. Title Policies. Family Law, Debtor and Creditor, Estate Planning, Divorce, Adoptions, Child Support, Child Custody, Bankruptcy.

RAYMOND W. LAMKIN (1923-2001)

THOMAS M. LAMKIN, born Watson, Illinois, January 25, 1934; admitted to bar, 1960, Illinois. *Education:* University of Illinois (B.S., 1958; LL.B., 1960). State's Attorney, DeWitt County, Illinois, 1964-1968. *Member:* DeWitt County and Illinois State Bar Associations. ***PRACTICE AREAS:*** Estate Planning; Marital Law; Real Estate; Title Insurance.

PHILLIP R. LAMKIN, born DeWitt County, Illinois, November 22, 1952; admitted to bar, 1978, Illinois. *Education:* University of Illinois (B.A., magna cum laude, 1975; J.D., 1978). Phi Kappa Phi. Public Defender, DeWitt County, 1980-1988. *Member:* DeWitt County and Illinois State Bar Associations. ***PRACTICE AREAS:*** Litigation; Tax Law; Criminal Law; Creditor and Debtor Law.

REPRESENTATIVE CLIENTS: First National Bank & Trust of Clinton; Clinton Sanitary District; Village of Wapella; DeWitt County Public Building Co.; Bank of Chestnut.
APPROVED ATTORNEYS FOR: Attorneys Title Guaranty.
REFERENCE: First National Bank & Trust of Clinton, Clinton, Illinois.

MOSS, BRYAN & MOSS, P.C.

122 WARNER COURT
P.O. BOX 655
CLINTON, ILLINOIS 61727-0655
Telephone: 217-935-8341
Facsimile: 217-935-4416
Email: mbm@mbmpc.com

Personal Injury, Workers Compensation and General Litigation.

RAY MOSS, born 1932; admitted to bar, 1959, Illinois. *Education:* University of Illinois (B.S., 1956); John Marshall Law School (LL.B., 1958). State Attorney, 1960-1964. *Member:* De Witt County (President, 1968-1971), Illinois State and American Bar Associations; Illinois Trial Lawyers Association; The Association of Trial Lawyers of America.

GARRY W. BRYAN, born 1953; admitted to bar, 1980, Illinois. *Education:* Lewis University (B.A., 1977); John Marshall Law School (J.D., 1980). Staff Attorney, State Attorneys' Appellate Service Commission, 1980-1982. Law Clerk to Honorable A.G. Webber III, Fourth District Appellate Court, 1982-1984. *Member:* DeWitt County and Illinois State Bar Associations; Illinois Trial Lawyers Association.

(This Listing Continued)

DAVID M. MOSS, born 1954; admitted to bar, 1983, Illinois. *Education:* Western State College of Colorado (B.A., 1976); John Marshall Law School (J.D., 1983). *Member:* DeWitt County and Illinois State Bar Associations; Illinois Trial Lawyers Association.

BOGGS, BOGGS & BATES, LLC

120 EAST CHURCH STREET
COLLINSVILLE, ILLINOIS 62234
Telephone: 618-343-0031
Fax: 618-343-0177
Email: bbblawyers.com

Kansas City, Missouri Office: 1300 N.W. Jefferson Court, Kansas City, 64105. Telephone: 816-472-5599. Fax: 816-472-0870.
Belleville, Illinois Office: 23 South First Street, 62220-2029. Telephone: 618-746-9540. Fax: 618-746-9541.
St. Louis, Missouri Office: 7912 Bonhomme, Suite 400, 63105-1912. Telephone: 314-726-2310. Fax: 314-726-2360.

Insurance Defense, Workers Compensation Defense, Professional Liability, Employment Law, Environmental, Insurance Coverage, Products Liability, Negligence Defense, Corporate Law, Civil Trial Practice, Negligence Defense, Medical Malpractice, Commercial Litigation, Collections, Subrogation, Fraud, Arson, Trial and Appellate, Health Law, Construction, Fire and Marine, General Business Litigation, Creditor's Rights, Insurance, Bad Faith Defense, Self Insured Defense, Life Insurance Defense, Health Care Liability, Legal Malpractice.

(For Complete Biographical Data on all Personnel, See Professional Biographies at St. Louis, Missouri)

LAW OFFICES OF MICHAEL J. BRUNTON

100 E. CLAY STREET, SUITE 200
COLLINSVILLE, ILLINOIS 62234
Telephone: 618-343-0750
Fax: 618-343-0227
Email: mbrunton@ezl.com
URL: http://www.bruntonlawoffice.com

Personal Injury, Automobile Accidents, Wrongful Death, Slip and Fall, Workers Compensation, Repetitive Stress Injuries, Industrial Accidents, Construction Accidents, Products Liability, Insurance Dispute, Employment, Wrongful Discharge, Breach of Contract, Warranty Law and Class Actions.

MEMBER OF FIRM

MICHAEL J. BRUNTON, born Indianapolis, Illinois, June 14, 1961; admitted to bar, 1991, Illinois; 1992, Missouri and U.S. District Court, Southern and Central Districts of Illinois; U.S. Court of Appeals, Seventh Circuit; U.S. Supreme Court. *Education:* Indiana University (B.S., 1983); Indiana State University (M.B.A., with honors, 1986); Southern Illinois University (J.D., summa cum laude, 1991). Phi Alpha Delta; Beta Gamma Sigma; Phi Kappa Phi. Recipient, American Jurisprudence Awards. Staff Member, 1989-1990 and Notes and Comments Editor, 1990-1991, Southern Illinois University Law Journal. Moot Court Instructor, Southern Illinois University School of Law, Spring, 1991. *Member:* St. Clair County, Madison County and Illinois State Bar Associations; The Missouri Bar. ***PRACTICE AREAS:*** Personal Injury; Workers Compensation; Breach of Contract; Insurance; Wrongful Termination. ***Email:*** mbrunton@ezl.com

DUNHAM, BOMAN & LESKERA

300 WEST CLAY STREET
COLLINSVILLE, ILLINOIS 62234
Telephone: 618-344-7734
Telecopier: 618-344-3853
Email: dbl300@wberry.com

Belleville Office: 208 N. High. Telephone: 618-235-7222. Telecopier: 618-236-2800; 618-236-1899.

General Civil Trial and Appellate Practice. Negligence and Products Liability, Medical Malpractice, Probate, Insurance, Family, Real Estate, Environmental, School, Criminal and Bankruptcy Law.

JOHN W. LESKERA, born East Saint Louis, Illinois, June 19, 1931; admitted to bar, 1955, Illinois. *Education:* University of Illinois (A.B., 1953; J.D., 1955). Assistant Attorney General, 1968—. *Member:* Illinois State and American Bar Associations; Illinois Defense Counsel. Fellow, American College of Trial Lawyers. ***PRACTICE AREAS:*** Civil Litigation; Insurance Defense; Products Liability Defense; Negligence Defense; General Practice; School Law; Municipal Law; Litigation; Family Law; Matrimonial Law; Probate; Trust Law.

WILLIAM L. BERRY, born East Saint Louis, Illinois, July 7, 1948; admitted to bar, 1973, Illinois. *Education:* MacMurray College; Millikin University (B.A., 1970); Washington University (J.D., 1973). *Member:* Illinois State Bar Association. ***PRACTICE AREAS:*** Civil Litigation; Insurance Defense; Products Liability; Negligence; General Practice; Family Law; Probate; Trust Law. ***Email:*** wberry@wberry.com

ERIC C. YOUNG

JOHN L. BITZER, born Decatur, Illinois, October 21, 1952; admitted to bar, 1979, Illinois. *Education:* University of Illinois (B.S., 1974); John Marshall Law School (J.D., 1979). *Member:* Illinois State Bar Association. ***PRACTICE AREAS:*** Civil Litigation; Insurance Defense; Negligence Defense; Bankruptcy.

(This Listing Continued)

ASSOCIATES

JASON W. CORRAY, born Urbana, Illinois, May 29, 1973; admitted to bar, 2001, Illinois; 2002, Missouri. *Education:* University of Illinois, Urbana-Champaign (A.B., 1996); Southern Illinois University, Carbondale (J.D., 2000). ***PRACTICE AREAS:*** Corporate Law; Asbestos Litigation; Insurance Coverage Litigation; Subrogation; Plaintiffs Personal Injury. ***Email:*** jcorray@wberry.com

TAMARA R. CHANDLER, born Belleville, Illinois, November 10, 1974; admitted to bar, 2001, Illinois and U.S. District Court, Southern District of Illinois. *Education:* Deaconess College of Nursing (B.S.N., 1996); Southern Illinois University (J.D., 2001). Associate, Brown & James, P.C., 2001; Donovan, Rose, Nester & Joley, P.C., 2001-2003. Registered Professional Nurse, Illinois and Missouri, 1996—. *Member:* Illinois State and American Bar Associations. ***PRACTICE AREAS:*** Products Liability (40%); Automobile Liability (5%); Insurance Defense (50%); Insurance Coverage (5%).

HARVEY TAYLOR, JR., born East St. Louis, Illinois, February 4, 1977; admitted to bar, 2003, Illinois. *Education:* University of Illinois (B.A., 2000; J.D., 2003). *Member:* Illinois State and American Bar Associations. ***PRACTICE AREAS:*** Civil Litigation; Asbestos Litigation; Products Liability; Insurance Coverage. ***Email:*** htaylor@wberry.com

KEVIN J. NEWTON, born St. Louis, Missouri, January 23, 1975; admitted to bar, 2004, Illinois. *Education:* University of Illinois (B.A., 1997); St. Louis University (J.D., 2000).

ATTORNEYS FOR: Hartford Insurance Group; State Farm Insurance Cos.; The Travelers Indemnity Co.; Wausau Insurance Cos.; Nationwide Insurance Co.; RLI Ins. Group.

(For Personnel and Biographical data, see Professional Biographies at Belleville, Illinois)

JULIE HARPER

COLLINSVILLE, ILLINOIS
(See Alton)

Traffic, DWI, Bankruptcy, Estate Planning, Real Estate, Contracts, Wills, Probate, Trusts, General Practice, Criminal, Buying and Selling Homes, Guardianships, Automobile Accidents, Adoptions.

McMAHON, BERGER, HANNA, LINIHAN, CODY & McCARTHY

A PROFESSIONAL CORPORATION
Established in 1955
400 N. BLUFF ROAD
COLLINSVILLE, ILLINOIS 62234
Telephone: 618-345-5822
Fax: 618-345-6483
Email: lawfirm@mcmahonberger.com
URL: http://www.mcmahonberger.com

St. Louis, Missouri Office: 2730 N. Ballas Road, Suite 200, 63131-3039, PO Box 31901. Telephone: 314-567-7350. Fax: 314-567-5968.

Labor Relations, Civil Rights and Administrative Law, Employment Litigation in all Courts.

FIRM PROFILE: McMahon, Berger, Hanna, Linihan, Cody & McCarthy, A Professional Corporation was founded in 1955 as a law firm dedicated exclusively to the practice of labor relations law, representing management. The firm engages in every aspect of employment and labor relations law including: investigation and litigation of wrongful discharge and discrimination claims; representation and unfair labor practice charges and hearings before the NLRB, OSHA, MSHA, National Mediation Board and ERISA-MEPPA issues; federal and state appeals; collective bargaining; arbitration; and state employment issues, including unemployment compensation. The firm's practice is nationwide and embraces all agencies, as well as state and federal courts. The firm encourages its members to assume responsibility for leadership activities in its specialized area of practice, including the training of business and professional persons.

ALAN I. BERGER (1933-1999)

THOMAS M. HANNA, born Tulsa, Oklahoma, November 19, 1936; admitted to bar, 1960, Oklahoma; 1966, Missouri, U.S. District Court, Eastern District of Missouri, U.S. District Court, Southern District of Illinois and U.S. Court of Appeals, Sixth, Seventh and Eighth Circuits (Not admitted in Illinois). *Education:* University of Tulsa (B.S., 1958; LL.B., 1960). Phi Delta Phi. Author: "Labor Contract Reform," St. Louis Bar Journal, Spring, 1980. Trial Attorney, National Labor Relations Board, 16th Region, 1962-1966. *Member:* The Bar Association of Metropolitan St. Louis (Chairman, Labor Law Section, 1975-1976); The Missouri Bar. [USAF, 1961-1962; Lt., USNR-R, 1965-1971]. ***PRACTICE AREAS:*** Labor Law; Employment Law Litigation. ***Email:*** hanna@mcmahonberger.com

D. MICHAEL LINIHAN, born Oklahoma City, Oklahoma, August 30, 1941; admitted to bar, 1966, Kansas; 1969, Missouri (Not admitted in Illinois). *Education:* Westminster College (B.A., magna cum laude, 1963); University of Kansas (J.D., 1966). Phi Delta Phi. Contributing Editor, The Developing Labor Law. *Member:* The Bar Association of Metropolitan St. Louis; Kansas and American Bar Associations; The Missouri Bar. [Capt., U.S. Army, active duty, 1966-1968]. ***PRACTICE AREAS:*** Labor and Employment Law. ***Email:*** linihan@mcmahonberger.com

THOMAS O. McCARTHY, born Denver, Colorado, August 3, 1947; admitted to bar, 1973, Missouri (Not admitted in Illinois). *Education:* University of Missouri (B.S.E.E., cum laude, 1970; J.D., 1972). Tau Beta Pi; Eta Kappa Nu; Phi Delta Phi. Attorney, National Labor Relations Board, 14th Region, 1973-1974. *Member:* The Bar Association of Metropolitan St. Louis (Chairman, Labor Law Section, 1985-1986; Co-Chairman, Labor Arbi-

(This Listing Continued)

McMAHON, BERGER, HANNA, LINIHAN, CODY & McCARTHY, A PROFESSIONAL CORPORATION, Collinsville—Continued

trator Development Program, 1984-1985); The Missouri Bar; American Bar Association. ***PRACTICE AREAS:*** Labor and Employment Law; Litigation. ***Email:*** mccarthy@mcmahonberger.com

ROBERT W. STEWART, born Omaha, Nebraska, May 10, 1951; admitted to bar, 1975, Missouri; 1976, U.S. District Court, Eastern District of Missouri and U.S. Court of Appeals, Fourth, Seventh and Eighth Circuits (Not admitted in Illinois). *Education:* St. Louis University (B.S. in C., magna cum laude, 1973; J.D., cum laude, 1975). Beta Gamma Sigma; Alpha Sigma Nu. *Member:* The Bar Association of Metropolitan St. Louis; The Missouri Bar; American Bar Association. ***PRACTICE AREAS:*** Labor Law; Employment Law Litigation; ERISA. ***Email:*** stewart@mcmahonberger.com

JAMES N. FOSTER, JR., born St. Louis, Missouri, March 19, 1954; admitted to bar, 1979, Missouri, U.S. Supreme Court and U.S. Court of Appeals, Third, Fourth, Sixth, Seventh, Eighth and Ninth Circuits (Not admitted in Illinois). *Education:* St. Louis University (B.A., magna cum laude, 1976; J.D., cum laude, 1978). Alpha Sigma Nu; Phi Beta Kappa; Recipient, Danforth Foundation Metropolitan Leadership Fellowship, 1974-1976. Associate Editor, St. Louis University Law Journal, 1978. Intern, Missouri Court of Appeals, Eastern District, 1978. Instructor, Legal Research and Writing, St. Louis University School of Law, 1981-1982. Member, Federal Practice Committee, Eastern District of Missouri, 1990-1998. Trial Attorney, National Labor Relations Board, Fourteenth Region, 1979-1980. Board of Directors, St. Louis Youth Soccer Association, 2000-2003. Board of Directors, The University Club of St. Louis, 2003-2005. *Member:* The Bar Association of Metropolitan St. Louis (Chairman, Labor and Employment Law Section, 1990-1991); The Missouri Bar; American Bar Association. ***PRACTICE AREAS:*** Labor Law; Employment Law; Litigation. ***Email:*** foster@mcmahonberger.com

DANIEL R. BEGIAN, born Detroit, Michigan, March 30, 1953; admitted to bar, 1978, Illinois; 1979, Missouri and U.S. Court of Appeals, Seventh and Eighth Circuits. *Education:* University of Wisconsin (A.B., 1975); Southern Illinois University (J.D., 1978). Research Editor, Southern Illinois University Law Journal, 1977-1978. Trial Attorney, National Labor Relations Board, Region 14 (St. Louis) 1978-1981. *Member:* The Bar Association of Metropolitan St. Louis; The Missouri Bar; Illinois State and American Bar Associations. ***PRACTICE AREAS:*** Labor Law; Employment Law; Litigation. ***Email:*** begian@mcmahonberger.com

JOHN B. RENICK, born Harrisburg, Pennsylvania, December 31, 1945; admitted to bar, 1970, Missouri; 1972, U.S. District Court, Eastern and Western Districts of Missouri and U.S. Court of Appeals, Eighth Circuit (Not admitted in Illinois). *Education:* University of Missouri at Columbia (B.A., 1967; J.D., 1970). Attorney, 1971-1978 and Deputy Regional Solicitor, 1978-1985, U.S. Department of Labor, Office of Regional Solicitor, Kansas City, Missouri. Member, Board of Trustees, University of Missouri Law School Foundation, 1988-1991. *Member:* The Bar Association of Metropolitan St. Louis; The Missouri Bar. ***PRACTICE AREAS:*** Labor and Employment. ***Email:*** renick@mcmahonberger.com

PATRICIA M. McFALL, born New Castle, Pennsylvania, September 4, 1951; admitted to bar, 1981, Missouri and U.S. District Court, Western District of Missouri; 1985, U.S. District Court, Eastern District of Missouri; 1987, U.S. Supreme Court; 1988 U.S. Court of Appeals, Fourth, Sixth and Eighth Circuits (Not admitted in Illinois). *Education:* St. Louis University (A.B., 1973; J.D., 1980). Alpha Sigma Nu. Recipient, Caroline Knox Memorial Scholarship, 1969-1973. Participant, Leadership Training Institute, Stanford University Center for Research and Development in Teaching, 1975-1977. Lead Articles Editor, St. Louis University Law Journal, 1979-1980. Instructor, Legal Research and Writing, St. Louis University School of Law, 1979-1980. Intern: Hon. J. R. Reinhard, Missouri Court of Appeals, Eastern District, 1979; U.S. Equal Employment Opportunity Commission, 1979-1980. Director, Research Staff, Missouri Supreme Court, 1982-1985. Research Attorney, Missouri Supreme Court, 1980-1982. *Member:* The Bar Association of Metropolitan St. Louis; The Missouri Bar; American Bar Association. ***PRACTICE AREAS:*** Labor and Employment Law; Litigation. ***Email:*** mcfall@mcmahonberger.com

KEVIN J. LORENZ, born St. Louis, Missouri, February 28, 1955; admitted to bar, 1982, Missouri, U.S. District Court, Eastern District of Missouri and U.S. Court of Appeals, Eighth Circuit; 1983, Illinois. *Education:* St. Louis University (B.A., 1977; J.D., 1981). Phi Delta Phi. *The Member:* Bar Association of Metropolitan St. Louis; The Missouri Bar; Illinois State and American Bar Associations. ***PRACTICE AREAS:*** Labor Law; Employment Law; Litigation. ***Email:*** lorenz@mcmahonberger.com

THOMAS E. BERRY, born St. Louis, Missouri, June 20, 1962; admitted to bar, 1987, Ohio; 1988, U.S. District Court, Southern District of Ohio; 1989, Missouri; 1990, U.S. District Court, Eastern District of Missouri and U.S. Court of Appeals, Sixth, Seventh and Eighth Circuits (Not admitted in Illinois). *Education:* University of Illinois (A.B., 1984); The Ohio State University (J.D., with honors, 1987). Delta Theta Phi. *Member:* The Bar Association of Metropolitan St. Louis (Section Chair, Labor and Employment, 1998-1999); The Missouri Bar; Ohio State and American Bar Associations. ***PRACTICE AREAS:*** Employment Litigation. ***Email:*** berry@mcmahonberger.com

STANLEY G. SCHROEDER, born St. Louis, Missouri, June 28, 1952; admitted to bar, 1980, Missouri; 1982, U.S. Court of Federal Claims and U.S. District Court, Eastern District of Missouri (Not admitted in Illinois). *Education:* St. Louis University (B.S. in C., summa cum laude, 1974; J.D., cum laude, 1980). Beta Gamma Sigma. Order of the Woolsack. *Member:* The Bar Association of Metropolitan St. Louis (Member, Employee Benefits Committee); The Missouri Bar. ***PRACTICE AREAS:*** ERISA; Employee Benefits; Executive Compensation; Litigation; Collective Bargaining. ***Email:*** schroeder@mcmahonberger.com

GEOFFREY M. GILBERT, JR., born St. Louis, Missouri, July 29, 1966; admitted to bar, 1992, Missouri; 1993, U.S. District Court, Eastern District of Missouri (Not admitted in Illinois). *Education:* University of Colorado (B.A., 1988); St. Louis University (J.D., 1992). Recipient, Academic Achievement Award, English Legal History, Employment Law Certificate. *Member:* The Missouri Bar. ***PRACTICE AREAS:*** Labor and Employment Law. ***Email:*** gilbert@mcmahonberger.com

(This Listing Continued)

MICHELLE M. CAIN, born St. Charles, Illinois, November 7, 1958; admitted to bar, 1988, Illinois; 1994, Missouri, U.S. District Court, Eastern District of Missouri and U.S. Court of Appeals, Eighth Circuit; 1996, U.S. Supreme Court. *Education:* University of Illinois (B.A., 1981); John Marshall Law School (J.D., with highest distinction, 1988). Member: Order of John Marshall, 1988; Gavel Society, 1987-1988. Recipient: Dean's Academic Scholarship, 1985-1988; John N. Jewett Scholarship, 1988; Graduate School Scholarship, 1988; American Law Book Company Award, 1988. First Place: Best Brief, Region VIII, 1987 National Moot Court Competition (National Semifinalist); Best Memorials, West Central Region, 1987 Phillip C. Jessup International Law Moot Court Competition. Lead Articles Editor, The John Marshall Law Review, 1987-1988. Law Intern, Civil Rights Division, United States Department of Justice, 1987. Law Clerk to Hon. William O. Bertelsman, U.S. District Court, Eastern District of Kentucky, 1988-1989. Author: Note, "Abrogating the Political Offense Exception to Extradition," 20 John Marshall Law Review 653 (1987). *Member:* The Bar Association of Metropolitan St. Louis; The Missouri Bar; Illinois State and American Bar Associations. ***LANGUAGES:*** French. ***PRACTICE AREAS:*** Labor and Employment Law. ***Email:*** cain@mcmahonberger.com

STEPHEN B. MAULE, born Annapolis, Maryland, September 1, 1970; admitted to bar, 1995, Missouri; 1996, U.S. District Court, Eastern District of Missouri and U.S. Court of Appeals, Seventh and Eighth Circuits (Not admitted in Illinois). *Education:* University of California-Davis (B.A., 1992); University of Missouri-Columbia (J.D., 1995). Phi Alpha Delta. Member, The Journal of Dispute Resolution. *Member:* The Missouri Bar; American Bar Association. ***PRACTICE AREAS:*** Labor and Employment. ***Email:*** maule@mcmahonberger.com

ROBERT D. YOUNGER, born St. Louis, Missouri, February 2, 1965; admitted to bar, 1992, Missouri and U.S. District Court, Eastern District of Missouri (Not admitted in Illinois). *Education:* University of Missouri (B.S.B.A., 1989); St. Louis University (J.D., cum laude, 1992). *Member:* The Bar Association of Metropolitan St. Louis; The Missouri Bar; Missouri Organization of Defense Lawyers. ***PRACTICE AREAS:*** Employment Law; Labor Law. ***Email:*** younger@mcmahonberger.com

BURTON D. GARLAND, JR., born St. Louis, Missouri, September 14, 1970; admitted to bar, 1995, Missouri; 1996, Illinois; 1998, U.S. District Court, Southern District of Illinois and U.S. District Court, Eastern District of Missouri. *Education:* University of Arizona (B.S.B.A., 1992); St. Louis University (J.D.; M.B.A., 1995). Law Clerk to the Honorable William D. Stiehl, United States District Court, Southern District of Illinois, 1995-1998. Author: "The Role of American Antitrust Laws in Today's Competitive Global Marketplace," U. Miami Bus. L.J., Volume VI, Fall 1995/Spring 1996, Number 1&2. *Member:* The Missouri Bar (Member, Labor and Employment Law Section). ***PRACTICE AREAS:*** Employment Law; Labor Law. ***Email:*** garland@mcmahonberger.com

WILLIAM B. JONES, born South Bend, Indiana, October 17, 1968; admitted to bar, 1997, Missouri (Not admitted in Illinois). *Education:* University of Notre Dame (B.A., 1991; J.D., 1996). Phi Alpha Delta. Recipient, Moot Court Honor's Brief Award. Judicial Clerkship, Honorable James Pudlowski Missouri Court of Appeals, Eastern Districts. *Member:* The Bar Association of Metropolitan St. Louis; The Missouri Bar; American Bar Association. ***PRACTICE AREAS:*** Employment Law; Labor Law. ***Email:*** jones@mcmahonberger.com

MARY CARTER MARTIN, born St. Louis, Missouri, August 11, 1973; admitted to bar, 1998, Missouri and U.S. District Court, Eastern and Western Districts of Missouri; 1999, Illinois. *Education:* University of Missouri (B.S.B.A., 1995); University of Georgia (J.D., 1998). *Member:* The Missouri Bar. ***PRACTICE AREAS:*** Employment Law; Labor Law. ***Email:*** duncan@mcmahonberger.com

COREY L. FRANKLIN, born St. Louis, Missouri, January 29, 1977; admitted to bar, 2002, Missouri and U.S. District Court, Eastern and Western Districts of Missouri (Not admitted in Illinois). *Education:* Miami University (B.A., 1999); University of Missouri at Columbia (J.D., 2002). Associate Editor-In-Chief, Missouri Environmental Law and Policy Review. Formerly with Michael R. Painter & Associates, Chicago, Illinois. *Member:* Bar Association of St. Louis (Labor Law Section); The Missouri Bar. ***PRACTICE AREAS:*** Labor and Employment. ***Email:*** franklin@mcmahonberger.com

SUSAN C. FOX SCHULZE, born St. Louis, Missouri, November 15, 1975; admitted to bar, 2001, Missouri; 2002, Illinois. *Education:* St. Louis University (B.A., 1998); Washington University (J.D., 2001). Formerly with Brown & James. *Member:* American Bar Association. ***PRACTICE AREAS:*** Labor and Employment. ***Email:*** schulze@mcmahonberger.com

CHARLES H. MORGAN, born Orlando, Florida, December 19, 1970; admitted to bar, 2002, Missouri (Not admitted in Illinois). *Education:* Chaminade University of Honolulu (B.A., magna cum laude, 1999); University of Missouri at Kansas City (J.D., 2002). *Member:* Missouri Bar Association. [U.S. Army, 1992-1998]. ***PRACTICE AREAS:*** Employee Benefits; Employment Law. ***Email:*** morgan@mcmahonberger.com

CHRISTOPHER M. SANDERS, born St. Louis, Missouri, February 4, 1973; admitted to bar, 2003, Missouri and U.S. District Court, Eastern and Western Districts of Missouri (Not admitted in Illinois). *Education:* St. Louis University (B.S.B.A., magna cum laude, 1998; J.D., 2003). Phi Alpha Delta. Recipient, Employment Law Certificate. Judicial Law Clerk, U.S. District Court, Eastern District of Missouri. *Member:* The Missouri Bar. [With U.S. Air Force, 1992-1996]. ***PRACTICE AREAS:*** Labor and Employment. ***Email:*** sanders@mcmahonberger.com

LAURA B. STALEY, born St. Louis, Missouri, August 21, 1977; admitted to bar, 2002, Missouri (Not admitted in Illinois). *Education:* University of Missouri (B.A., 1999; J.D., 2002). Phi Alpha Delta. *Member:* Bar Association of Metropolitan St. Louis. ***PRACTICE AREAS:*** Employment Law; Labor Law. ***Email:*** staley@mcmahonberger.com

DANIEL G. FRITZ, born St. Louis, Missouri, July 16, 1977; admitted to bar, 2004, Missouri (Not admitted in Illinois). *Education:* Truman State University (B.A., 2000); St. Louis University School of Law (J.D., 2003). *Member:* Bar Association of Metropolitan St. Louis; The Missouri Bar; American Bar Association. ***PRACTICE AREAS:*** Labor and Employment. ***Email:*** fritz@mcmahonberger.com

STACIE A. OWENS, admitted to bar, 2003, Florida; 2005, Missouri (Not admitted in Illinois). *Education:* Drury College (B.A., English, 1997); University of Missouri-Kansas City (J.D., 2001). ***PRACTICE AREAS:*** Labor and Employment Law.

(This Listing Continued)

OF COUNSEL

WILLIAM W. CODY, born St. Louis, Missouri, March 22, 1935; admitted to bar, 1965, Missouri, U.S. District Court, Eastern District of Missouri, U.S. Court of Appeals, Seventh and Eighth Circuits and U.S. Supreme Court (Not admitted in Illinois). *Education:* Marquette University (B.S., 1957); St. Louis University (J.D., 1965). Trial Attorney, National Labor Relations Board, Regions 14 and 33, 1966-1970. *Member:* The Bar Association of Metropolitan St. Louis; The Missouri Bar; American Bar Association. [1st Lt., U.S. Army, 1957-1959]. ***PRACTICE AREAS:*** Labor Relations; Employment Law; Civil Litigation; National Labor Relations Act. **Email:** cody@mcmahonberger.com

RALPH E. KENNEDY, born Springfield, Missouri, November 20, 1919; admitted to bar, 1944, Missouri; 1976, District of Columbia (Not admitted in Illinois). *Education:* Southwest Missouri State University (A.B., 1942); Washington University (J.D., 1944). Delta Theta Phi; Order of the Coif. Regional Director, National Labor Relations Board, St. Louis, Missouri, 1955-1958. Regional Director, National Labor Relations Board, Los Angeles, California, 1958-1970. Member, National Labor Relations Board, 1970-1975. *Member:* The Bar Association of Metropolitan St. Louis; The Missouri Bar; District of Columbia Bar; Federal and American (Member, Labor Relations Law Section) Bar Associations.

REPRESENTATIVE CLIENTS: ATC/Vancom, Inc.; AT&T; Ameren UE; Bodine Aluminum, Inc. (A Subsidiary of Toyota Motor Corporate Services of North America, Inc.); Brinker International; Brown Group; Cooper Industries; Crane Co.; Dana Corporation; DT Industries; Electronic Data Systems; Emerson Electric Co.; Enterprise Rent-A-Car; Federal-Mogul Corporation; General American Life Insurance Co.; General Dynamics; General Tire, Inc.; Harbor Group Companies; Integram St. Louis Seating, a division of Intier Automotive; Jenny Craig Weight Loss Center; Kellwood Co.; Libby Owens Ford; Mallinckrodt Inc.; McDonald's Corp.; National Tooling and Machining Assn.; National Marine, Inc.; Nordyne, Inc.; ; Pettibone LLC.; Prairie Farms Dairy, Inc.; Ralston Purina; Ryan Walsh Stevedoring (Subsidiary of Ventura Corp.); Sabreliner; SAI Automotive USA, Inc.; Sara Lee Bakery Group; Sequa Corporation; Sigma/Aldrich Corp.; Siligan Plastics Corporation; Smurfit Stone Container Corp.; SNE Enterprises, Inc.; Solutia, Inc.; SuperValu, Inc. and its subsidiary Shop'n Save Warehouse Foods, Inc.; State Farm Insurance Companies; Travelers Insurance; Von Hoffmann Corporation, Inc.

BROWN & ASSOCIATES

COLUMBIA, ILLINOIS

(See Belleville)

Civil Litigation, Personal Injury, Medical Malpractice, Products Liability, Admiralty Law, Railroad Law and Commercial Law.

CROWDER & SCOGGINS, LTD.

Established in 1963

121 WEST LEGION AVENUE
P.O. BOX 167
COLUMBIA, ILLINOIS 62236
Telephone: 618-281-7111
Fax: 618-281-7115
Email: lawyers@crowderscoggins.com
URL: http://www.crowderscoggins.com

Trial and Appellate Practice in State and Federal Courts. Personal Injury, Workers Compensation, Commercial, Banking, Municipal, Corporate, Tax, Estate Planning and Family, Criminal and Real Estate Law.

FLOYD E. CROWDER, born Monroe County, Illinois, January 30, 1933; admitted to bar, 1957, Missouri and Illinois; 1959, U.S. Court of Military Appeals; 1960, U.S. District Court, Southern District of Illinois; 1968, U.S. Supreme Court; 1976, U.S. Court of Appeals, 7th Circuit. *Education:* University of Illinois; Washington University (B.A., 1955; J.D., 1957). States Attorney, Monroe County, Illinois, 1964-1968, 1976. Special Assistant Attorney General of Illinois, 1969-1983. *Member:* St. Clair County (President, 1981-1982), Monroe County (President, 1976-1977), Illinois State and American (Fellow) Bar Associations. [U.S. Air Force, Judge Advocate, 1957-1960, Captain]. ***PRACTICE AREAS:*** Business Law; Litigation; Banking Law; Corporate Law; Estate Planning Law; Estate Settlement Law; Municipal Law. **Email:** fcrowder@crowderscoggins.com

MARK C. SCOGGINS, born East St. Louis, Illinois, June 1, 1952; admitted to bar, 1977, Missouri; 1978, Illinois and U.S. District Court, Southern District of Illinois; 2001, U.S. District Court, Northern District of Illinois including Trial Bar. *Education:* Southern Illinois University (B.S., 1974); Tulsa University (J.D., 1977). *Member:* St. Clair County (Secretary, 1985-1987), Monroe County (President, 1982-1983), Illinois State and American Bar Associations; Illinois Trial Lawyers Association; The Association of Trial Lawyers of America. ***PRACTICE AREAS:*** Personal Injury Law; Workers Compensation Law; Criminal Law; Employment Law; Civil Rights Law; Labor Law. **Email:** mscoggins@crowderscoggins.com

MARK S. ROHR, born Belleville, Illinois, December 6, 1956; admitted to bar, 1981, Illinois; 1982, U.S. District Court, Central District of Illinois; 1983, U.S. District Court, Southern District of Illinois; 1989, U.S. Court of Appeals, Seventh Circuit. *Education:* Blackburn College (B.A., summa cum laude, 1978); St. Louis University (J.D., cum laude, 1981). Senior Staff Associate, St. Louis University Law Journal, 1979-1981. *Member:* Monroe County (President, 1986-1987), St. Clair County and Illinois State Bar Associations. ***PRACTICE AREAS:*** Creditors Rights; General Litigation; Family Law; Criminal Law; Municipal Law; Appellate Practice. **Email:** mrohr@crowderscoggins.com

TIMOTHY A. GUTKNECHT, born Detroit, Michigan, April 5, 1968; admitted to bar, 1993, Illinois; 1994, Missouri; 1996, U.S. District Court, Southern District of Illinois; 1997, U.S. Court of Appeals, 7th Circuit; 1998, U.S. Supreme Court. *Education:* Amherst College (B.A., 1990); Washington University (J.D., 1993). *Member:* Monroe County (President, 1998), St. Clair County, Illinois State and American Bar Associations. ***PRACTICE AREAS:*** Business Law; Litigation; Corporate Law; Estate Planning Law; Estate Settlement Law; Appellate Practice. **Email:** tgutknecht@crowderscoggins.com

(This Listing Continued)

ANDREA CROWDER KHOURY, born Belleville, Illinois, April 22, 1973; admitted to bar, 1998, Illinois; 1999, U.S. District Court, Southern District of Illinois. *Education:* St. Louis University (B.A., magna cum laude, 1995); Washington University (J.D., 1998). *Member:* Monroe County (Vice President, 2004-2005), St. Clair County and Illinois State Bar Associations. ***PRACTICE AREAS:*** Juvenile Law; Collections; Civil Litigation; Family Law. **Email:** akhoury@crowderscoggins.com

GREGORY J. HICKEL, born Town & Country, Missouri, January 29, 1973; admitted to bar, 1998, Illinois; 1999, Missouri; 2001, U.S. District Court, Northern District of Illinois. *Education:* Wheaton College (B.A., 1994); Washington University (J.D., 1998). *Member:* Monroe County (President, 2002-2004), St. Clair County and Illinois State Bar Associations; Bar Association of Metropolitan St. Louis; Christian Legal Society; Illinois Real Estate Lawyers Association; National Lawyers Association. ***PRACTICE AREAS:*** Estate Administration; Real Estate Law; Corporate Law; Estate Planning; Business Law. **Email:** ghickel@crowderscoggins.com

CLAY B. ST. CLAIR, born Bowling Green, Kentucky, August 14, 1975; admitted to bar, 2000, Illinois and U.S. District Court, Southern District of Illinois; 2001, Missouri and U.S. District Court, Northern District of Illinois; 2004, U.S. District Court, Eastern District of Missouri. *Education:* Truman State University (B.S., magna cum laude, 1997); Washington University (J.D., 2000). *Member:* Monroe County (Treasurer, 2004-2005), St. Clair County, Illinois State and American Bar Associations; The Association of Trial Lawyers of America; Illinois Trial Lawyers Association. ***PRACTICE AREAS:*** Personal Injury Law; Workers Compensation Law; Criminal Law; Employment Law; Civil Rights Law; Labor Law. **Email:** cstclair@crowderscoggins.com

COUNSEL FOR: Chicago Title Insurance Co.; First Bank; Luhr Bros., Inc.; Tower Rock Stone; Illinois Excavators, Inc.; Monroe County Title Co.; Columbia Quarry Co.; George Weber Chevrolet, Inc.; Columbia Rural Fire Protection District; Maeystown Rural Fire Protection District; Goley Insulation, Inc.; Rogers Redi-Mix, Inc.; Gateway FS, Inc.; Von Alst Holding Company.

DONALD R. BREWER

10 W. TERRA COTTA AVENUE
CRYSTAL LAKE, ILLINOIS 60014
Telephone: 815-356-6900
Fax: 815-459-1573
Email: luvtojogsz@aol.com,
URL: http://www.mchenryinjurylaw.com

Personal Injury including Catastrophic Injury, Wrongful Death, Automobile Accidents and Injuries, Head, Neck and Back Injury, Brain Injuries. Medical Malpractice including Failure to Diagnose or Misdiagnosis, Hospital Malpractice, Nursing Malpractice, Birth Trauma, Obstetric Malpractice, Nursing Home Abuse and Neglect, Elder Abuse, Malnutrition and Dehydration. Verbal and Sexual Abuse, Assault, Medication Errors and Burns, Products Liability, Defective Products and Patent Litigation.

FIRM PROFILE: Mr. Brewer began his career over thirty years ago in the field of patent litigation. Over time his focus began to shift as both fellow lawyers and individuals trusted him with their own and their families representation in injury matters.

Mr. Brewer is listed in the Bar Register of pre-eminet lawyers in the field of Personal Injury Law.

DONALD R. BREWER, born 1944; admitted to bar, 1974, Illinois; registered to practice before U.S. Patent and Trademark Office. *Education:* University of Iowa (B.S.E.E., 1967); University of Notre Dame (Overseas Studies, 1972); John Marshall Law School (J.D., 1973). Member, National Head Injury Foundation. Past-Member, Chicago Patent Law Association. *Member:* Chicago, Illinois State and American Bar Associations; Illinois Trial Lawyers Association; The Association of Trial Lawyers of America. ***PRACTICE AREAS:*** Personal Injury; Medical Malpractice; Patent Litigation; Products Liability.

STEVEN J. BRODY & ASSOCIATES, LTD

101 N. VIRGINIA STREET
SUITE 110
CRYSTAL LAKE, ILLINOIS 60014
Telephone: 815-479-8800
Fax: 815-479-8880
URL: http://www.sjbrodylaw.com
Email: steve@sjbrodylaw.com
URL: http://www.stevenjbrody.com

Family Law including Divorce, Separation Agreements, Child Custody, Child Support, Visitation Rights, Spousal Support, Restraining Orders, Paternity, Adoptions, Pre-nuptial / post-nuptial Agreements, Bankruptcy including Chapter 7 & 13, Consumer Bankruptcy, Small Business Bankruptcy, Foreclosures, Repossessions.

STEVEN J. BRODY, born August 27, 1961; admitted to bar, 1991, Illinois. *Education:* Arizona State University (B.S., Accounting, 1983); Loyola University School of Law (J.D., 1991). ***PRACTICE AREAS:*** Family Law; Divorce; Bankruptcy.

CAMPION, CURRAN, DUNLOP & LAMB, P.C.

Established in 1851

8600 US HIGHWAY 14, SUITE 201
CRYSTAL LAKE, ILLINOIS 60012
Telephone: 815-459-8440
Fax: 815-455-8134
Email: contact@ccdllaw.com
URL: http://www.ccdllaw.com

General Practice, Corporate Law, Trusts and Estate, Real Estate Law, Zoning, Planning and Land Use, Criminal Law, Appellate Practice, Insurance, Family Law, Labor and Employment, Administrative Law, Environmental Law, Personal Injury, Workers Compensation.

(This Listing Continued)

CAMPION, CURRAN, DUNLOP & LAMB, P.C., Crystal Lake—Continued

JAMES A. CAMPION, born Rockford, Illinois, February 2, 1947; admitted to bar, 1972, Illinois; 1979, U.S. District Court, Northern District of Illinois. *Education:* St. Norbert College (B.A., cum laude, 1969); Northwestern University (J.D., cum laude, 1972). *Member:* McHenry County and Illinois State Bar Associations; Illinois Appellate Lawyers Association. ***PRACTICE AREAS:*** Real Estate Litigation; Commercial Litigation; Civil Appeals; Business Arbitration. ***Email:*** jcampion@ccdllaw.com

DANIEL F. CURRAN, born Chicago, Illinois, September 30, 1949; admitted to bar, 1974, Illinois and U.S. District Court, Northern District of Illinois. *Education:* Loyola University (B.B.A., 1971); DePaul University (J.D., 1974). Member, De Paul Law Review, 1971-1974. *Member:* Chicago, McHenry County, Illinois State and American Bar Associations. ***PRACTICE AREAS:*** Real Estate; Zoning, Planning and Land Use Law; Trusts and Estates; Corporate Law; Environmental Law. ***Email:*** dcurran@ccdllaw.com

CHARLES A. DUNLOP, born Pontiac, Michigan, September 2, 1947; admitted to bar, 1981, Illinois and U.S. District Court, Northern District of Illinois. *Education:* University of Missouri-Columbia; Northern Michigan University (B.A., 1970); John Marshall Law School (J.D., 1981). Phi Delta Phi. Adjunct Faculty, John Marshall Law School, 1987—. Member: Woodstock Police Pension Board, 1987-1990; Woodstock Fire and Police Commission, 1988-1999. *Member:* Chicago, McHenry County, Illinois State and American Bar Associations; Illinois Trial Lawyers Association. ***PRACTICE AREAS:*** ARDC Defense; Estate Planning; General Corporate; Commercial Litigation. ***Email:*** cdunlop@ccdllaw.com

CYNTHIA D. LAMB, born Arlington Heights, Illinois, December 21, 1962; admitted to bar, 1988, Illinois; 1989, U.S. District Court, Northern District of Illinois and U.S. Court of Appeals, Seventh Circuit. *Education:* University of Illinois (B.A., 1985); DePaul University (J.D., 1988). Recipient, American Jurisprudence Award, 1986. *Member:* Chicago, McHenry County and Illinois State Bar Associations. ***PRACTICE AREAS:*** Criminal Defense; Civil Litigation; Family Law. ***Email:*** clamb@ccdllaw.com

---

LEE C. LOCKWOOD, born Elgin, Illinois, May 21, 1970; admitted to bar, 1999, Illinois. *Education:* Carthage College (B.A., 1992); DePaul University (J.D., 1999). *Member:* McHenry County Bar Association. ***PRACTICE AREAS:*** Business Law; Corporate Law; Real Estate. ***Email:*** lockwood@ccdllaw.com

THOMAS A. VACLAVEK, born Des Plaines, Illinois, April 9, 1974; admitted to bar, 2000, Illinois. *Education:* University of Arizona (B.S., 1998); Chicago-Kent College of Law (J.D., 2000). *Member:* Chicago, McHenry County and Illinois State Bar Associations. ***PRACTICE AREAS:*** Civil Litigation; Employment Law; Personal Injury; Zoning, Planning and Land Use; Bankruptcy Law. ***Email:*** tvaclavek@ccdllaw.com

LORI E. FULTON, born Rockford, Illinois, July 29, 1958; admitted to bar, 2002, Illinois. *Education:* DePaul University (B.A., highest honors, 1993); Loyola University (J.D., cum laude, 2002). Author: "Protective Custody of the Unborn: Involuntary Commitment of Pregnant Substance Abusing Mothers for the Protection of their Unborn Children," Children's Legal Rights Journal, Fall 2001. Instructor, Appellate Advocacy and Advanced Appellate Advocacy, Loyola University Chicago School of Law, 2002—. Court Approved Family Law Mediator. *Member:* Chicago, McHenry County, Illinois State and American Bar Associations; National Association of Council for Children; Illinois Appellate Lawyers Association. ***PRACTICE AREAS:*** Appellate Practice; Civil Litigation; Mediation. ***Email:*** 1fulton@ccdllaw.com

THOMAS D. ARADO, born Chicago, Illinois, September 30, 1968; admitted to bar, 2001, Illinois. *Education:* Valparaiso University (B.A., 1990); Northern Illinois University (J.D., magna cum laude, 2001). Delta Theta Phi Dean of Coke Senate Finalist, 1999-2000; NIU Moot Court Competition, 2000. Member, NIU Moot Court Society. Recipient, Outstanding Contribution To Scholarly Publications Award. Editor-in-Chief, Northern Illinois University Law Review, 2000-2001. Author: "Frozen Embryos and Divorce: Technological Marvel Meets the Human Condition," 21 N. Ill. U. L. Rev. 241 (2001). *Member:* Chicago, McHenry County, Illinois State and American Bar Associations. ***Email:*** tarado@ccdllaw.com

MEAGHAN ALEXANDER, born Elgin, Illinois, 1978; admitted to bar, 2004, Illinois; 2005, U.S. District Court, Northern District of Illinois. *Education:* Cornell College (B.A., 2000); Northern Illinois University (J.D., cum laude, 2004). Delta Theta Phi. Member, North Illinois University Moot Court Society, 2003-2004. Recipient: Carl W. Cicero Moot Court Award, 2003; Outstanding Contribution to Advocacy Programs Award, 2004. *Member:* Chicago, McHenry County, Illinois State and American Bar Associations. ***Email:*** malexander@ccdllaw.com

---

CARROLL & CARROLL

CRYSTAL LAKE, ILLINOIS

(See Woodstock)

Divorce, Custody, Paternity, Real Estate, Traffic, Criminal, Wills, Estate Planning, Probate.

THE LAW OFFICE OF H. CASE ELLIS

108 NORTH WALKUP AVENUE
CRYSTAL LAKE, ILLINOIS 60014
Telephone: 815-459-1001
Fax: 815-459-1249
Email: hcase@mc.net

Civil Practice, Arbitration/Mediation.

(This Listing Continued)

FIRM PROFILE: For twenty-five years Mr. Ellis' practice focused on civil litigation primarily involving business, premises, vehicle, product, professional liability and declaratory judgement actions to construe insurance coverage. His concentration is now in mediating civil cases both privately and as a court appointed mediator in Cook, McHenry, Lake and Winnebago Counties.

Mr. Ellis was one of the original mediators in the court annexed mediation program for the 19th Judicial Circuit and to date has mediated more than 900 court cases. In addition, he is certified in the 17th Circuit (state court) and on an original panel of mediators for the civil mediation program in the Federal District Court and the Cook County Circuit Court.

Mr. Ellis proposed and implemented a pilot program staffed by local bar association to mediate pro-se small claims disputes. He trained all volunteer mediators, drafted proposed rules and forms and is currently assisting the Small Claims Judge and Civil Practice Committee in developing a permanent program.

H. CASE ELLIS, born Middletown, Ohio, August 14, 1950; admitted to bar, 1976, Illinois and U.S. District Court, Northern District of Illinois; 1982, Federal Trial Bar. *Education:* Purdue University (B.S., 1972); Illinois Institute of Technology/Chicago-Kent College of Law (J.D., with honors, 1976). Law Clerk to Hon. Albert Hallett, Illinois Appellate Court, 1976-1977. Awarded: Center for Analysis of Alternative Dispute Resolution System 'Service to Community Award,' 2002; 'Distinguished Service Award,' McHenry County Bar Association, 2004. Appointed, Arbitrator, Manville Personal Injury Settlement Trust, 1989. Instructor, Conflict Resolution, North Central College, Naperville, Illinois (Graduate Studies, 2003—). Member, Panel of Arbitrators, American Arbitration Association. Board of Directors, International Academy of Dispute Resolution (2003—). Certified State Court Mediator: 19th Judicial Circuit (1997); 17th Judicial Circuit (2002); Cook County Circuit Court (2004). Certified Federal Civil Mediator, U.S. District Court, Northern District (2004). *Member:* McHenry County, Lake County, Winnebago County and Illinois State (Chairman, Tort Law Section, 1996-1997; Board of Governors, 2001—) Bar Associations. ***PRACTICE AREAS:*** Civil Practice; Mediation; Arbitration.

THE LAW FIRM OF FRANKS, GERKIN & McKENNA, P.C.

CRYSTAL LAKE, ILLINOIS

(See Marengo)

General, Civil & Criminal Trial Practice, Banking, Business Law, Commercial Real Estate, Corporate Law, Criminal Law, Debt Collections, Family Law, Personal Injury, Real Estate, Trusts & Estates, Immigration, Wills, Workers Compensation, Municipal Law, Traffic, Zoning, Planning and Land Use.

THE GARRY LAW FIRM, PC

Established in 2004

27 GRANT STREET
CRYSTAL LAKE, ILLINOIS 60014
Telephone: 815-356-8581
Fax: 815-356-8484
Email: rgarry@garrylaw.com
URL: http://www.garrylaw.com

Business/Corporate Law, Entity Planning Formation, Ownership Agreements, Business Transactions; Mergers/Acquisitions/Divestitures, U.S. and International Joint Ventures, Strategic Alliances and Partnerships, Commercial and Employment Contracts, Franchise Law, Conventional and SBA Financing, Private Placement Securities Law, Leasing, Commercial and Residential Real Estate Transactions, Land Use and Zoning, Estate Planning, Wills, Trusts, Probate, Business Succession Planning.

FIRM PROFILE: Strategic business-centric attorneys focused on all aspects of business, commercial and real estate transactions. Extensive experience working with all types of business entities across diverse industries. Prior to establishing her own practice, Ms. Garry was an associate with a large Chicago law firm working in complex business transactions and an intern with the US Securities and Exchange Commission. We are attorneys that understand the big picture and are dedicated to providing strategy, analysis and service to our business clients.

RITA W. GARRY, born Fairmont, Minnesota, June 22, 1957; admitted to bar, 1983, Illinois. *Education:* Lake Forest College (B.A., Political Science, with honors, 1979); Boston University School of Law (J.D., 1983). Phi Beta Kappa. Recipient: Solly A. Hartzo Award in Politics, 1979. Author: "The SEC and Small Business: An Overview of an Administrative Response to the Capital Needs of Small Business," New England Law Review, 1982-1983; "Cable Rate Regulation Update," ISBA, Local Government and Law, April, 1995; and "Ask the Expert," Contributor, The McHenry County Business Journal. Former Director: Lake Forest College Alumni Board of Governors; Metropolitan Family Services-Camp Algonquin Advisory Board; YMCA of McHenry County. Former Arbitrator: NASD. Certified Financial Planner, 1991. Lecturer and Advisor: Business Organization Law, McHenry County College, Small Business Development Center. *Member:* Illinois State (ISBA) and American (Member: Sections on: Federal Regulations of Securities; Business Law) Bar Associations (ABA). ***PRACTICE AREAS:*** Business Organization; Family Business Law; International Joint Ventures; Corporate Contracts; Small Business Corporations; Franchise Law; Partnership Organization; Real Estate; Estate Planning; Business Succession Planning. ***Email:*** rgarry@garrylaw.com

---

CAREY E. SCHULZE, born Elgin, Illinois, September 19, 1977; admitted to bar, 2002, Illinois. *Education:* Northern Illinois University (B.S., 1999); Chicago-Kent College of Law (J.D., 2002). *Member:* Illinois State (ISBA) and American Bar Associations (ABA); Illinois Real Estate Lawyers Association. ***PRACTICE AREAS:*** Corporate Law; Business

(This Listing Continued)

Transactions; Real Estate; Commercial Litigation; Employment Law. **Email:** cschulze@garrylaw.com

LAW OFFICES OF DAVID R. GERVAIS

4 EAST TERRA COTTA AVENUE
CRYSTAL LAKE, ILLINOIS 60014
Telephone: 815-459-2844
815-459-2848
Email: drglaw@sbcglobal.net

Business Law and Contracts, Business Formation, Commercial Law and Litigation, Real Estate Law and Litigation, Municipal Law, Land Use, Zoning, Divorce, Child Custody, Child Support, Visitation Rights, Spousal Support, Post Judgment Matters, Adoption, Guardianship, Misdemeanor and Felony Criminal Defense, Traffic Matters, Estate Planning, Probate and Probate Litigation, Bankruptcy.

DAVID R. GERVAIS, born Indianapolis, Indiana, March 12, 1953; admitted to bar, 1981, Illinois; 1982, U.S. District Court, Northern District of Illinois and U.S. Court of Appeals, Seventh Circuit. *Education:* Elgin Community College; Bucknell University (B.A., 1978); Illinois Institute of Technology/Chicago-Kent College of Law (J.D., 1981). Phi Alpha Delta. Past President: Cary Park District; McHenry County Historical Society; McHenry County Historic Preservation Commission. *Member:* Illinois State Bar Association. ***PRACTICE AREAS:*** General Practice; Litigation; Bankruptcy.

ASSOCIATES

MARY M.L. SPIEGEL, born South Bend, Indiana, May 15, 1966; admitted to bar, 1992, Michigan; 1995, Illinois. *Education:* St. Mary's College (B.A., 1988); Valparaiso University School of Law (J.D., 1991). Recipient, Vaughn Award for Trial Advocacy, 1991. Trustee, Fremont Public Library, 2000-2001. Author, "A Major Victory for Fire Protection Districts," The Call (publication of the Illinois Association of Fire Protection Districts) Spring 2005; "The Wauconda Case," The Gong (publication of the Illinois Fire Chiefs Association) Summer 2005. Speaker, Illinois Association of Fire Protection Districts, June 2005. Guest lecturer, Fire Service Management Courses, College of Lake County, 2002, 2003, 2004. *Member:* Illinois State Bar Association. ***REPORTED CASES:*** Wauconda Fire Protection District v. Stonewall Orchards L.L.P. and the County of Lake, 214 Ill2d 417, 293 IllDec. 246 (ILL Mar 24, 2005). ***PRACTICE AREAS:*** Municipal Law; Sexual Harassment; Family Law; Appellate Practice.

THOMAS J. LEAHY, born Chicago, Illinois; admitted to bar, 1972, Illinois. *Education:* Marquette University (B.S., 1969); Chicago-Kent College of Law (J.D., 1972). Trustee, McHenry County College, 1973-1976. *Member:* McHenry County (Member, Family Law Section; President 1982-1983) and Illinois State Bar Associations. ***REPORTED CASES:*** Guerra, In re Marriage of, 153 Ill. App.3d 550, (Ill. App. 2 Dist. 1987). ***PRACTICE AREAS:*** Family Law; Civil Litigation; Real Estate.

DAVID L. STRETCH, born Tampa, Florida, December 12, 1946; admitted to bar, 1978, New York; 1980, Hawaii; 1995, Illinois. *Education:* Yale University (B.A., 1970); Hastings College of the Law, University of California (J.D., 1976). *Member:* Illinois State Bar Association; Hawaii State and American Bar Associations. ***LANGUAGES:*** French. ***PRACTICE AREAS:*** Family Law; Bankruptcy. ***Email:*** stretchlaw@sbcglobal.net

OF COUNSEL

SCOTT A. NOLAN, admitted to bar, 1980, Illinois. *Education:* University of Illinois (B.A.); John Marshall Law School (J.D.).

GUMMERSON & RAUSCH

CRYSTAL LAKE, ILLINOIS

(See Woodstock)

Criminal Defense, Workers Compensation, Commercial Litigation, Family Law, Personal Injury, Medical Malpractice Defense, Zoning, Trusts and Estates, Corporate Law.

HINSHAW & CULBERTSON LLP

Hinshaw & Culbertson LLP is an Illinois registered limited liability partnership that has elected to be governed by the Illinois Uniform Partnership Act (1997)

Established in 1934

500 COVENTRY LANE
SUITE 205
CRYSTAL LAKE, ILLINOIS 60014-7504
Telephone: 815-459-5123
Facsimile: 815-459-5223.
Telex: 880248
Email: kfox@hinshawlaw.com
URL: http://www.hinshawlaw.com

Other Office Locations: Chicago, Illinois; Appleton, Wisconsin; Belleville, Illinois; Boston, Massachusetts; Champaign, Illinois; Edwardsville, Illinois; Fort Lauderdale, Florida; Jacksonville, Florida; Joliet, Illinois; Lisle, Illinois; Los Angeles, California; Miami, Florida; Milwaukee, Wisconsin; Minneapolis, Minnesota; New York, New York; Peoria, Illinois; Phoenix, Arizona; Portland, Oregon; Providence, Rhode Island; Rockford, Illinois; St. Louis, Missouri; San Francisco, California; Schererville, Indiana; Springfield, Illinois; Tampa, Florida; Waukegan, Illinois.

Appellate, Banking & Financing, Bankruptcy & Creditors' Rights, Class Action Litigation, Civil Rights Defense, Commercial Litigation, Corporate, Construction Law, Director & Officer Liability, Employee Benefits, Environmental, Fidelity & Surety, General Liability Litigation, Government, Health Care, Insurance Coverage, Insurance and Reinsurance, Labor & Employment, Legal Malpractice, Medical Malpractice, Mergers & Acquisitions, Municipal Liability, Personal Injury Defense, Public Law, Products Liability Litigation, Professional Liability, Regulatory, Real Estate, School Law, Securities, Taxation, Transportation, White Collar Crime and Workers' Compensation Defense.

FIRM PROFILE: Hinshaw & Culbertson LLP is a national AMLaw 200 firm with 425 lawyers in 27 offices coast-to-coast. The firm offers a full-service practice, with an emphasis in commercial and defense litigation, corporate, environmental, employment and construction law, as well as the representation of professionals in their liability and risk management matters.

Hinshaw provides services to a range of clients in financial services, construction, health care, not-for-profit, insurance, legal, manufacturing, real estate, transportation and other industries. Firm clients also include government agencies, municipalities and schools.

Hinshaw was founded in 1934. The firm is headquartered in Chicago, and maintains offices in 12 states: Arizona, California, Florida, Illinois, Indiana, Massachusetts, Minnesota, Missouri, New York, Oregon, Rhode Island and Wisconsin.

PARTNERS

JENNIFER L. JOHNSON, born Big Rapids, Michigan; admitted to bar, 1996, Indiana; 2002, Illinois. *Education:* Marian College (B.A., summa cum laude, 1993); Indiana University (J.D., 1996). Member: Defense Research Institute, 1996-2002; Defense Trial Counsel of Indiana, 1996-2002; Evansville Bar Association, 1996- 2002; Brooks Inns of Court, 1996-2001. *Member:* Illinois State Bar Association. ***PRACTICE AREAS:*** Insurance Defense; Insurance Coverage; Commercial Litigation; Medical Negligence. ***Email:*** jenjohnson@hinshawlaw.com

GREGORY T. SNYDER, born East Orange, New Jersey, September 27, 1959; admitted to bar, 1993, Illinois. *Education:* Southern Illinois University (B.S., 1982); DePaul University (J.D., 1993). *Member:* Winnebago County, Illinois State and American Bar Associations. ***PRACTICE AREAS:*** Medical Malpractice; Corporate Health Care Law; Risk Management; Civil Rights Defense Litigation; Personal Injury Litigation. ***Email:*** gsnyder@hinshawlaw.com

ASSOCIATES

MATTHEW F. LOGAN, born Arlington Heights, Illinois, February 12, 1973; admitted to bar, 1999, Illinois and U.S. District Court, Northern District of Illinois. *Education:* University of Illinois at Urbana-Champaign (B.A., English, 1995); The John Marshall Law School (J.D., 1999). ***PRACTICE AREAS:*** Commercial Litigation; Employment Litigation; Real Estate; Corporate Organizaton and Governance; Banking and Financing; Corporate Contracts; Real Estate Leasing. ***Email:*** mlogan@hinshawlaw.com

MICHELLE J. ROZOVICS, born 1971; admitted to bar, 1996, Illinois; 2004, U.S. District Court, Northern District of Illinois including Trial Bar. *Education:* University of Michigan (A.B., with Distinction, 1993; J.D., 1996). Author: "Preparing for Oral Depositions," Illinois Civil Discovery Practice, Ch. 5, Illinois Institute for Continuing Legal Education, 2003; Member, Civil Litigation Advisory Committee, Illinois Institute of Continuing Legal Education, 2003-2004; Co-Author: "Default and Default Judgment," Illinois Civil Practice, Vol. II, Ch. 7-S, Illinois Institute for Continuing Legal Education, 2000; Visiting Lecturer, Civic Education Project (Poland and Russia), Yale University/Central European University, 1996-1998; Intern, The Honorable Ann C. Williams, U.S. District Court, Northern District of Illinois, 1997; Intern, International Commission on Nuclear Policy, NGO, United Nations, 1994. *Member:* American Bar Association. ***LANGUAGES:*** Polish, Russian. ***PRACTICE AREAS:*** Medical Malpractice; Health Care Risk Management; International Law. ***Email:*** mrozovics@hinshawlaw.com

DAVID IAN WALTERS, born Chicago, Illinois, February 1, 1974; admitted to bar, 2002, Illinois; 2004, U.S. District Court, Northern District of Illinois. *Education:* Carthage College (B.A., 1997); DePaul University (J.D., 2002). Recipient: CALI Award for Academic Excellence in Antitrust; Marks Prize in Antitrust. *Member:* American Bar Association. ***PRACTICE AREAS:*** Medical Malpractice; Health Care; Risk Management; Commercial Litigation. ***Email:*** dwalters@hinshawlaw.com

OF COUNSEL

WILLIAM O. SHANK, born Hamilton, Ohio, January 11, 1924; admitted to bar, 1951, Ohio; 1955, Illinois and U.S. District Court, Northern District of Illinois; 1954, U.S. Supreme Court. *Education:* Miami University (A.B., 1947); Yale University (J.D., 1950). Listed in: Who's Who in America; Who's Who in American Law. Class Secretary, Yale University. Member: Civic Federation of Chicago; Chicago Crime Commission; Library of International Relations; Council of Community Services, Chicago; Senior Citizens Committee of the City of Crystal Lake. Member, Advisory Committee, eLawForum, Washington, D.C. *Member:* Legal Club of Chicago (Past President); Law Club of Chicago; Lawyer's Club of the City of Chicago; Chicago Bar Association (Chairman, Coproate Law Departments Committee); Yale Law School Association of Illinois (Former President). Life Fellow, American Bar Foundation. (Also at Chicago, Illinois Office). ***PRACTICE AREAS:*** Corporate Governance. ***Email:*** wshank@hinshawlaw.com

MADSEN, SUGDEN & GOTTEMOLLER

1 NORTH VIRGINIA STREET
CRYSTAL LAKE, ILLINOIS 60014
Telephone: 815-459-5152
Fax: 815-459-0290

Real Estate Law including Land Use, Zoning, Condemnation/Eminent Domain, Commercial Real Estate, Retail Development, Real Property Issues, Criminal Defense, Felonies, Misdemeanors, White Collar Criminal Defense, Fraud, Forgery, Assault and Battery, Manslaughter, Murder, Sex Crimes, Weapons Charges, Drugs and Narcotics, Parole and Probation Issues, Driving Under the Influence (DUI), Personal Injury, Automobile Accidents and Injuries, Workers Compensation, Head, Neck, Back and Shoulder Injuries, Repetitive Stress Injuries, Products Liability/Defective Products.

(This Listing Continued)

MADSEN, SUGDEN & GOTTEMOLLER, Crystal Lake—Continued

PARTNERS

HENRY H. SUGDEN, III, born Evanston, Illinois, May 10, 1949; admitted to bar, 1975, Illinois; 1976, U.S. District Court, Northern District of Illinois including Trial Bar; 1978, U.S. Court of Appeals, Seventh Circuit; 1980, U.S. Supreme Court; 2003, Capital Litigation Trial Bar. *Education:* Arizona State University (B.S., 1971); John Marshall Law School (J.D., 1975). *Member:* Chicago, McHenry County, Illinois State (Member, General Assembly) and American Bar Associations; National District Attorneys Association; Illinois Trial Lawyers Association; The Association of Trial Lawyers of America; American Judicature Society; Capital Litigation Bar of Illinois. ***PRACTICE AREAS:*** Personal Injury; Workers Compensation; Criminal Defense.

JOSEPH GOTTEMOLLER, born Streator, Illinois, October 29, 1957; admitted to bar, 1982, Illinois; U.S. District Court, Northern District of Illinois including Trial Bar. *Education:* University of Illinois (B.A., 1979); Washington College of Law (J.D., 1982). Trustee for McHenry County Conservation District, 2002—. Member, Board of Directors: Midwest Bank of McHenry County 2001-2003; McHenry County Gravel Task Force, 1990-1991; McHenry County Home Builders Association, 1993. *Member:* McHenry County (Member, 1984—; Secretary, Family Law Section, 1993—), Livingston County, Illinois State and American (Member, 1982—) Bar Associations. ***SPECIAL AGENCIES:*** Trustee for McHenry County Conservation District 2002 to Present. ***REPORTED CASES:*** HESSLER vs ROSENBERG 338 Ill.App.3d 1010, 788 N.E.2d 405, 273 Ill.Dec. 96, 50 UCC Rep.Serv.2d 330 Defined the term ASAP under the UCC. ***TRANSACTIONS:*** Example One Obtained annexation, zoning approval and final plat of Subdivision for Super-Walmart Center and 600 townhome units in Crystal Lake, Illinois September 2005. Example Two Otained annexation zoning and subdivision approval for Fairfield in site Crystal lake, Illinois September 2005. Exampl;e Three Obtained conditional use approval for Fraternite Notre Dame monastery in McHenry County June 2005. Example Four Annexed and zoned 130+ acre commercial development Huntley Illinois, July 2005. Example Five Annexed zoned and preliminary platted 212 single family and townhome site in the Village of Union Spring 2005. This was the first subdivision allowed in Union using a Schaefer system to treat and dispose of sanitary sewer. Example Six Annexed and approved 78 unit development in Ringwood, Illinois December 2004. ***PRACTICE AREAS:*** Zoning, Planning and Land Use (40%); Real Estate (25%); Civil Practice (25%); Commercial Real Estate Development (10%).

ASSOCIATE

KEITH D. SLOAN, born Bronx, New York, 1970; admitted to bar, 2005, Illinois. *Education:* Purdue University (B.A., History, 1992); Northern Illinois University (J.D., magna cum laude, 2001). Associate Editor, Law Review. Represented NIU college of Law Chicago Bar Association Moot Court Competition. Vice Justice of Phi Alpha Delta legal fraternity (Dooley Chapter). Commissioner for the Village of Lake In The Hills Parks and Recreation Board (1996-2000). *Member:* Illinois State Bar Association. McHenry County Bar Association. ***PRACTICE AREAS:*** Real Estate; Family Law; Corporate Law; Appellate Practice; Zoning Law.

MICHLING HOFMANN VINTON PLAZA & WICK, P.C.

CRYSTAL LAKE, ILLINOIS

(See Woodstock)

Personal Injury, Workers Compensation, Criminal Law, Family Law, Civil Litigation, Corporate Law, Residential Real Estate, Commercial Real Estate, Landlord and Tenant Law, Wills and Trusts, Land Use and Development, Zoning, Appellate Practice.

MILITELLO, ZANCK & COEN, P.C.

Established in 1974

40 BRINK STREET

CRYSTAL LAKE, ILLINOIS 60014

Telephone: 815-459-8800

FAX: 815-459-8429

URL: http://www.mzc.com

Trial Practice in all State and Federal Courts, Banking, Business Acquisitions, Corporation and Partnership, Employment Law, Environmental, Insurance Defense, Probate and Guardianship, Real Estate, Wills and Trusts and Zoning and Land Planning.

FIRM PROFILE: The firm was established by James G. Militello and Thomas C. Zanck in 1974 and has grown over the past 30 years to a full service law firm. The firm's objective is to provide the highest quality legal service to its clients in a timely, cost-effective and professional manner.

JAMES G. MILITELLO, born Chicago, Illinois, December 7, 1943; admitted to bar, 1968, Illinois; 1975, U.S. District Court, Northern District of Illinois and U.S. Supreme Court. *Education:* Marquette University (B.S., 1965); DePaul University (J.D., 1968). Commissioner of Planning Commission, McHenry County, 1972-1976. *Member:* McHenry County and Illinois State Bar Associations. ***PRACTICE AREAS:*** Business Acquisitions Law; Commercial Transactions; Environmental Law; Taxation Law; Zoning Law; Land Planning Law. ***Email:*** jgm@mzc.com

THOMAS C. ZANCK, born Chicago, Illinois, March 6, 1944; admitted to bar, 1968, Illinois; 1975, U.S. District Court, Northern District of Illinois including Trial Bar and U.S. Supreme Court; 2000, Wisconsin. *Education:* Loras College (B.A., cum laude, 1965); Georgetown University (J.D., 1968). *Member:* McHenry County (President, 1981-1982) and Illinois State Bar Associations; Illinois Trial Lawyers Association; Illinois Defense Counsel. ***PRACTICE AREAS:*** Banking Law; Commercial Litigation; Insurance Defense Law; Personal Injury Law; Trial Practice; Zoning Law. ***Email:*** tzanck@mzc.com

(This Listing Continued)

PATRICK D. COEN, born Oak Park, Illinois, March 17, 1951; admitted to bar, 1976, Illinois and U.S. District Court, Northern District of Illinois. *Education:* University of Notre Dame (B.A., cum laude, 1973); University of Illinois (J.D., 1976). *Member:* McHenry County (President, 1989-1990), Illinois State and American Bar Associations. ***PRACTICE AREAS:*** Business Law; Corporation and Partnership Law; Labor and Employment Law; Probate; Wills; Trusts and Estates. ***Email:*** patcoen@mzc.com

JAMES L. WRIGHT, born Oregon, Illinois, June 23, 1955; admitted to bar, 1980, Illinois and U.S. District Court, Central District of Illinois; 1982, U.S. District Court, Northern District of Illinois including Trial Bar. *Education:* University of Illinois (B.S., 1977; J.D., 1980). Author: "Environmental Regulation by Local Government after *Village of Carpentersville v. PCB*", Ill. Bar Journal (Oct. 1991, Vol. 79, No. 10). Member, Board of Directors, Crystal Lake Public Library, 1990-1999; President, 1993-1998. *Member:* McHenry County (President, 1996), Illinois State (Member, Environmental Law Section Council, 1991-1994) and American Bar Associations. ***PRACTICE AREAS:*** Civil Litigation; Environmental Law; Insurance Defense Law; Employment Law. ***Email:*** jlwright@mc.net

MARK S. SALADIN, born Woodstock, Illinois, October 1, 1958; admitted to bar, 1983, Illinois and U.S. District Court, Northern District of Illinois. *Education:* U.S. Air Force Academy; Illinois Benedictine College (B.A., summa cum laude, 1980); John Marshall Law School (J.D., 1983). *Member:* McHenry County and Illinois State Bar Associations. ***PRACTICE AREAS:*** Business Acquisitions Law; Corporation and Partnership Law; Real Estate Law; Zoning Law. ***Email:*** saladin@mzc.com

JAMES G. MILITELLO, III, born Des Plaines, Illinois, April 27, 1966; admitted to bar, 1991, Illinois and U.S. District Court, Northern District of Illinois. *Education:* Marquette University (B.S., 1988); John Marshall Law School (J.D., 1991). Former McHenry County Assistant States Attorney. *Member:* McHenry County, Illinois State and American Bar Associations. ***PRACTICE AREAS:*** Commercial Transactions; Corporation and Partnership; Environmental; Local Government Law; Real Estate; Trial Practice; Zoning and Land Planning. ***Email:*** jgm3@mzc.com

---

NANCY STINGLE PERKOSKI, born Detroit, Michigan, August 3, 1971; admitted to bar, 1996, Illinois and U.S. District Court, Northern District of Illinois. *Education:* University of Iowa (B.B.A., 1993); Valparaiso University School of Law (J.D., 1996). Delta Sigma Pi. *Member:* McHenry County and Illinois State Bar Associations. ***PRACTICE AREAS:*** Family Law; Estate Planning; Workers Compensation; Employment Law; Civil Litigation; Personal Injury. ***Email:*** nsp@mzc.com

DAVID G. PHOENIX, born Chicago, Illinois, May 16, 1964; admitted to bar, 1989, Illinois and U.S. District Court, Southern District of Illinois; 1990, Missouri; 1992, U.S. District Court, Eastern District of Missouri; 1998, U.S. District Court Northern District of Illinois. *Education:* University of Illinois (B.A., 1986); Northern Illinois University (J.D., 1989). Member, I.S.B.A. Moot Court Team, 1989. Member, Northern Illinois Law Review, 1988-1989. President, Moot Court Society, 1988-1989. Recipient, American Jurisprudence Book Award, in Criminal Procedure. *Member:* Illinois State Bar Association; The Missouri Bar. ***PRACTICE AREAS:*** Insurance Defense; Trial Practice; Personal Injury; Commercial Litigation; Landlord Tenant Law. ***Email:*** dgp@mzc.com

JILL J. STRUCK, born Park Ridge, Illinois, December 5, 1972; admitted to bar, 2000, Illinois. *Education:* Arizona State University (B.A., 1995); DePaul University (J.D., 1999). *Member:* McHenry County and Illinois State Bar Associations. ***PRACTICE AREAS:*** Estate Planning; Real Estate; Probate; Corporate Partnerships; Commercial Transactions. ***Email:*** jstruck@mzc.com

CATHERINE KEATING-HOWARD, born Oakland, California, December 25, 1944; admitted to bar, 1972, Illinois. *Education:* University of Illinois (B.A., 1969); DePaul University (J.D., 1972). Phi Alpha Delta. Cary School Board Member, 1985-1989. *Member:* Chicago and Illinois State Bar Associations. ***PRACTICE AREAS:*** Estate Planning; Probate; Real Estate; Business Law. ***Email:*** ckh@mzc.com

JEREMY W. SHAW, born Woodstock, Illinois, May 11, 1975; admitted to bar, 2002, Illinois. *Education:* Carthage College (B.A., 1997); Drake University School of Law (J.D., 2000). *Member:* McHenry County, Illinois State and American Bar Associations. ***PRACTICE AREAS:*** Zoning and Land Use; Civil Litigation; Municipal Law; Election Law. ***Email:*** jshaw@mzc.com

ADRIAN M. GOSCH, born Aberdeen, South Dakota, May 10, 1975; admitted to bar, 2000, Illinois. *Education:* Northern State University (B.S., 1997); University of South Dakota (J.D., 2000). *Member:* McHenry County, Illinois State, Federal and American Bar Associations. ***PRACTICE AREAS:*** Civil Litigation; Family Law; Personal Injury; Workers Compensation; Criminal Law. ***Email:*** agosch@mzc.com

A list of Representative Clients will be furnished upon request.
REFERENCES: American Community Bank & Trust; Home State Bank of Crystal Lake.

LAW OFFICES OF GARRY A. PAYTON

CRYSTAL LAKE, ILLINOIS

(See Waukegan)

Criminal Defense, Personal Injury, Medical Malpractice, Products Liability, Automobile Accidents, Wrongful Death, Construction Site Accidents, Driving While Intoxicated, Drug Crimes, Felonies, Homicide, Juvenile, Misdemeanors, Sexual Assault and Traffic Violations.

POLLOCK, MEYERS, EICKSTEADT & PULAK, LTD.

CRYSTAL LAKE, ILLINOIS

(See Marengo)

General Trial Practice, Appellate Practice, Estate Planning, Probate Law, Trust Law, Real Estate, Banking Law, Bankruptcy Law, Personal Injury, Workers Compensation, Administrative Law, Corporate Law, Contracts, Civil Litigation, Trusts and Estates, Real Estate Law.

QUERREY & HARROW, LTD.

Established in 1939

651 WEST TERRA COTTA AVENUE, SUITE 221

CRYSTAL LAKE, ILLINOIS 60014

Telephone: 815-479-1929

Fax: 815-479-1978

Email: rjerrick@querrey.com

URL: http://www.querrey.com

Chicago, Illinois Office: 175 West Jackson Boulevard, Suite 1600. Telephone: 312-540-7000. Fax: 312-540-0578.

Wheaton, Illinois Office: 310 South County Farm Road, Third Floor. Telephone: 630-653-2600. Fax: 630-653-0178.

Waukegan, Illinois Office: 415 West Washington Street, Suite 205. Telephone: 847-249-4440. Fax: 847-249-4932.

Joliet, Illinois Office: 2 Rialto Square, Suite 401, 116 North Chicago Street. Telephone: 815-726-1600. Fax: 815-726-1674.

Merrillville, Indiana Office: 8585 Broadway, Suite 510. Telephone: 219-738-1820. Fax: 219-738-1821.

New York, N.Y. Office: 120 Broadway, Suite 2800. Telephone: 212-233-0130. Fax: 212-233-0172.

London, England Office: 141-142 Fenchurch Street, Fifth Floor. Telephone: 207-929-6670. Fax: 207-929-6671.

General Practice and Trial Practice.

FIRM PROFILE: A TRADITION OF QUALITY. As one of Chicago's leading litigation firms, Querrey & Harrow, Ltd. maintains a proud tradition of responding quickly and efficiently to its clients' increasingly complex needs. Our multi-service law firm represents a wide range of individual, industrial, financial, governmental and commercial clients. We continue to offer a proven combination of professionalism and personal service. Our attorneys are experienced in handling litigation in both state and federal courts and alternative dispute resolutions. Our transactional lawyers include those with solid experience in banking, real estate, corporate law, health law, estate planning and governmental relations. Querrey & Harrow combines the collective experience of these attorneys to deliver cost-efficient and timely resolutions of its clients' matters.

RONALD M. JERRICK, admitted to bar, 1970, Illinois. *Education:* University of Notre Dame (A.B., 1966); DePaul University (J.D., 1970). (Also at Chicago Office). ***PRACTICE AREAS:*** Litigation; Arbitration.

MIA M. LUCAS, admitted to bar, 1993, Florida; 1997, Illinois. *Education:* Florida State University (B.S., 1987); University of Denver; Nova University (J.D., 1992); Shepard Broad Law Center. *Member:* Chicago Bar Association; The Florida Bar. (Resident). ***PRACTICE AREAS:*** Litigation. ***Email:*** mlucas@querrey.com

---

JEANNE M. MILLER, admitted to bar, 1998, Illinois. *Education:* Mundelein College (B.A., 1982; M.A., 1991); Loyola University (J.D., 1998). ***PRACTICE AREAS:*** Litigation; Estate Planning; Insurance Coverage. ***Email:*** jmiller@querrey.com

(For complete biographical data on all personnel, see Professional Biographies at Chicago, Illinois)

CURT P. REHBERG

64 EAST TERRA COTTA AVENUE

CRYSTAL LAKE, ILLINOIS 60014

Telephone: 815-444-1050

Fax: 815-444-1060

URL: http://www.rehberglawoffice.com

Real Estate, including Commercial and Residential, Contracts, Closings, Land Acquisition and Sales, Land Trusts, Development, Investment, Joint Ventures, Partnerships; Wills, Trusts and Estate Planning, including Family Trusts, Living Trusts, Powers of Attorney, Business Succession Planning, Retirement Planning, Wealth Preservation; Business Law, including Contracts, Business Formation, Sole Proprietorships, Partnerships, Business Incorporation, Joint Ventures, Business Fraud, Buy-Sell Agreements.

CURT P. REHBERG, born Woodstock, Illinois, January 31, 1964; admitted to bar, 1989, Illinois. *Education:* Eastern Illinois University (B.A., 1986); Northern Illinois University (J.D., 1989). *Member:* Chicago, Illinois State and American Bar Associations. ***PRACTICE AREAS:*** Real Estate Law; Taxation Law; Estate Planning Law.

ASSOCIATE

DOREEN T. PALUCH, born Chicago, Illinois, October 25, 1966; admitted to bar, 1991, Illinois. *Education:* University of Illinois (A.B., 1988; J.D., 1991). *Member:* McHenry County, Illinois State and American Bar Associations.

ZUKOWSKI, ROGERS, FLOOD & McARDLE

Established in 1957

50 VIRGINIA STREET

CRYSTAL LAKE, ILLINOIS 60014-4126

Telephone: 815-459-2050

Facsimile: 815-459-9057

Email: zrfm@stans.com

URL: http://www.zrfmlaw.com

General Practice, Banking and Finance, Bankruptcy, Commercial, Construction, Corporation, Environmental, Family, Government, Insurance, Labor and Employment, Litigation, Personal Injury and Torts, Probate, Trust and Estate, Real Property, Vehicle Warranty, Fraud Litigation.

PARTNERS

H. DAVID ROGERS, born Fort Worth, Texas, March 31, 1942; admitted to bar, 1969, Illinois. *Education:* Southern Methodist University (B.B.A., 1966; J.D., 1969). Delta Theta Phi. Member, Southwestern Law Journal. Municipal Attorney: Village of Algonquin, 1972—; Village of Algonquin Police Commission, 1981-1985. City Attorney, City of Harvard, 1978-1981. Village Attorney, McHenry Shores, 1977-1981. Co-Author: "A Case for Equal Treatment," Illinois Municipal Review, December, 1983; A List without Meaning: Eligibility Lists Pursuant to Public Act 888-440 Illinois Municipal Review, July 1994; "Legal Holidays and Special Meetings," Local Governments Law (April, 1996). Chairman, Southeastern McHenry County Unit of the American Cancer Society, 1986-1987, 1990-1991. Advisory Board Member, Crystal Lake Ambutal, 1985-1991. Vice-President, 1986-1990, President, 1990-1991, McHenry County Blood Commission. Board of Directors, The Greater Crystal Lake Area Chamber of Commerce and Industry, 1990-1992. *Member:* Chicago, McHenry County and Illinois State Bar Associations. ***PRACTICE AREAS:*** Alcoholic Beverages; Banks and Banking; Business Law; Commercial Real Estate; Contracts; Eminent Domain; Government; Leases and Leasing; Legal Ethics and Professional Responsibility; Municipal Law; Partnership Law; Real Estate; Utility Law; Zoning, Planning and Land Use. ***Email:*** drogers@zrfmlaw.com

RICHARD G. FLOOD, born Chicago, Illinois, April 11, 1949; admitted to bar, 1976, Illinois, U.S. District Court, Northern District of Illinois and U.S. Court of Appeals, Seventh Circuit; 1982, Federal Trial Bar. *Education:* University of Illinois (B.A., with honors, 1971); Illinois Institute of Technology, Chicago-Kent College of Law (J.D., with honors, 1976). Law Clerk, Appellate Court, State of Illinois, 1976-1978. Special Assistant Attorney General, 1983-1994. Author: "Photography in Illinois Litigation," Illinois Bar Journal (May, 1978), Vol. 1.66, No. 9; "Questions and Answers About Intergovernmental Agreements," Illinois Bar Journal (March, 1997); "A Case for Equal Treatment," Illinois Municipal Review (Dec., 1983); "Naperville Revisited?," Local Government Law (April, 1991); "What Constitutes an Indirect Interest Under the Corrupt Practices Act," Local Government Law (June, 1992); "Impact Fees: the Story Continues," Local Government Law (February, 1993); "The River Bend Decision And How It Affects Municipalities' Personnel Rules And Regulations," Illinois Municipal Review (June, 1993); "Municipal Regulation of Cable Television Under the 1992 Act," Illinois Municipal Review (November, December, 1993); "Consumer Protection and Customer Service Under the 1992 Cable Act," Illinois Municipal Review (January, 1994); "Franchising Issues Under the 1992 Cable Act," Illinois Municipal Review (February, 1994); "FCC Cable Television Regulation," Local Government Law (February, 1994); "The Appropriation and Levy Process," Local Government Law (November, 1994); Tax Trends (May 1995); Cable Rate Regulation Update, Local Government Law (April 1995); "Legal Holidays and Special Meetings," Local Government Law (April, 1996); "Notwithstanding Any Other Law to the Contrary..." Local Government Law (June, 1996); Community Development and Municipal Revenues, Local Government Law Section, Illinois State Bar Association Law Ed Series (October 26, 1992); School Impact Fee Update, Local Government Law, Vol. 33, No. 3 (October, 1996); "Meeting by Teleconference," Illinois Municipal Review (October, 1996); "Reducing Corruption in Government: The Amendment to the Public Officer Prohibited Activities Act," Local Government Law (November, 1997); "A List Without Meaning: Eligibility Lists Pursuant to Public Act 88-440," Illinois Municipal Review (July, 1994); "Negotiating the Maze of Land Division Regulation," National Business Institute, 1998; "Land Use: Current Issues in Subdivision Annexation and Zoning Law," National Business Institute, 1999; "Cable Television Franchising Issues," Illinois Municipal League (September 17, 1999); "Some Laws of 100 Years Ago Mirror Today's Laws," Illinois Municipal Review (September 2000); "Some Laws of 100 Years Ago Mirror Today's Laws," Local Government Law, (October, 2000); "Cable and Wireless Communications," Illinois Institute for Continuing Legal Education (October, 2000); Municipal Attorney: Village of Lake in the Hills, 1977-1997; Village of Johnsburg, 1983—; Village of Lakewood, 1984—; Village of Lake in the Hills Police Commission, 1981-1984; Village of Bull Valley, 1988—; Village of Hebron, 1988-1994; Village of West Dundee, 1994—; City of Woodstock, 1997—. Member, Board of Directors, Family Services and Community Mental Health Center for McHenry County, 1979-1986 (President, 1981-1986). *Member:* McHenry County (President, 1986-1987) and Illinois State (Member: Local Government Law Section Council, 1990-1996, Chairman, 1994-1995; Assembly, 1996—) and FCC Bar Associations; Illinois Municipal League (Member, Legislative Committee, 1993—). ***PRACTICE AREAS:*** Election, Campaign and Political Law; Eminent Domain; Family Law; Government; Municipal Law; Zoning, Planning and Land Use. ***Email:*** rflood@zrfmlaw.com

DAVID W. McARDLE, born Birmingham, Alabama, September 24, 1956; admitted to bar, 1981, Illinois; 1991, U.S. Court of Appeals, Seventh Circuit. *Education:* Indiana University (A.B., 1978); John Marshall Law School (J.D., 1981). Special Assistant Attorney General, 1985—. Author: "Stopping Illegal Sump Pump Hookups," Local Government Law (February, 1994); "The Supreme Court's Ratchet on Political Firings Tightens," Local Government Law (August, 1996). Municipal Attorney: City of Harvard, 1990—; City of McHenry, 1993—; City of Marengo, 2000—; Fox Waterway Agency, 2001—; Lake in the Hills Sanitary District, 1988—; Village of Lake in the Hills Police Commission, 1985—. Diplomat, Court Practice Institute, 1983. Board of Directors, Family Service and Commu-

(This Listing Continued)

ZUKOWSKI, ROGERS, FLOOD & McARDLE, Crystal Lake—Continued

nity Mental Health Center for McHenry County, 1985-1991; President, 1988-1991. Member: Illinois Road Builders Association. *Member:* McHenry County and Illinois State (Local Government Law Section Council, 1996—; Chairman, 1999—) Bar Associations. ***PRACTICE AREAS:*** Civil Rights; Class Actions; Construction Law; Election, Campaign and Political Law; Eminent Domain; Government; Insurance Defense; Litigation; Municipal Law; Negligence; Personal Injury; Utility Law; Zoning, Planning and Land Use. ***Email:*** dmcardle@zrfmlaw.com

JEANNINE A. THOMS, born Chicago, Illinois; admitted to bar, 1984, Illinois, U.S. District Court, Northern District of Illinois and U.S. Court of Appeals, Seventh Circuit; 1985, Federal Trial Bar. *Education:* Northern Illinois University (B.A., summa cum laude, 1981); Illinois Institute of Technology, Chicago Kent College of Law (J.D., with high honors, 1984). Phi Alpha Delta. Listed in Who's Who Among American Law Students. Law Clerk, Illinois Human Rights Commission, 1982. Arbitrator, 19th Judicial Circuit, State of Illinois. Certified Mediator, 19th Judicial Circuit, State of Illinois. Delegate, White House Conference on Families, 1980. Member, Illinois Courtwatching Project, Steering Committee, 1977-1979. Member, Womens' Advisory Council to the Governor of Illinois, 1979-1981. Member, League of Women Voters, Crystal Lake-Cary Area, President, 1977-1979. Member 1991-1998, Vice President 1993-1994 and President, 1995-1998, Board of Directors, McHenry County Mental Health Board. National Editorial Advisory Board, 1993-1994, Women's Investment Newsletter. Listed in: Who's Who in American Law, 1994-2000; Who's Who of American Women, 1997-2000. Municipal Attorney, Village of Richmond, 1993-1997. *Member:* Chicago, McHenry County, Illinois State (Member, Trust and Estates Council, 2000—) and American Bar Associations; The Association of Trial Lawyers of America. ***PRACTICE AREAS:*** Aged and Aging; Alternative Dispute Resolution; Children; Family Law; Guardianship and Conservatorship; Probate; Trusts and Estates; Wills. ***Email:*** jthoms@zrfmlaw.com

MELISSA J. COONEY, born Woodstock, Illinois, April 6, 1948; admitted to bar, 1991, Illinois and U.S. District Court, Northern District of Illinois. *Education:* Kent State University (B.G.S., 1985; M.A., 1987); University of Illinois College of Law (J.D., 1991). Adjunct Faculty, McHenry County College, 1997—. Executive Committee and Board Member, Woodstock Christian Care, Inc., 1997—. Secretary, 1995-1997 and President, 1997-1998, Woodstock Professional & Business Women. *Member:* McHenry County (Board of Governors, 1992-2001; President, 1999-2000) and Illinois State Bar Associations. ***PRACTICE AREAS:*** Aged and Aging; Children; Guardianship and Conservatorship; Probate; Trusts and Estates; Wills. ***Email:*** mcooney@zrfmlaw.com

MICHAEL J. SMORON, born Chicago, Illinois, October 15, 1966; admitted to bar, 1991, Illinois and U.S. District Court, Northern District of Illinois. *Education:* University of Notre Dame (B.A., 1988); Chicago-Kent College of Law, Illinois Institute of Technology (J.D., with high honors, 1991). Order of the Coif. Recipient: Kent Legal Scholar Award. Articles Editor, 1990-1991 and Staff Member, 1989-1991, Chicago Kent Law Review. Author: "Land Use: Current Issues in Subdivision Annexation and Zoning Law," National Business Institute, 1999. Co-Author: "Cable and Wireless Communications," Municipal Law and Practice in Illinois, Illinois Institute for Continuing Legal Education (2000); "Negotiating the Maze of Land Division Regulation," National Business Institute (1998). Municipal Attorney, Village of Johnsburg, 1995—. *Member:* Chicago, McHenry County, Illinois State and American Bar Associations; Illinois Institute for Local Government Law. ***PRACTICE AREAS:*** Election, Campaign and Political Law; Eminent Domain; Government; Municipal Law; Utility Law; Zoning, Planning and Land Use. ***Email:*** msmoron@zrfmlaw.com

REPRESENTATIVE CLIENTS: CNA Insurance Co.; Illinois Municipal League Risk Management Association — Martin Boyer Companies; Sherman Hospital; Harvard Memorial Hospital; Home State Bank/N.A.; Algonquin State Bank; Midwest Bank of McHenry County; Curran Group; Arrow Road Construction Company; Lowe Excavating Co., Inc.; Suntronic Technology Group; AstroCraft, Inc.; Power Conversion Products, Inc.
REFERENCE: Home State Bank/N.A.

ASHER, SMITH & ISAF

DANVILLE, ILLINOIS

(See Paris)

General Practice in all Courts. Trials and Probate Law. Corporation, Insurance and Commercial Banking Law and Workers Compensation Law, Personal Injury and Negligence Litigation. Divorce, Child Custody, Child Support.

DOBBINS, FRAKER, TENNANT, JOY & PERLSTEIN

A PROFESSIONAL CORPORATION

DANVILLE, ILLINOIS

(See Champaign)

General Practice, Trial and Appellate Practice in State and Federal Courts. Health Care, Privacy Law, Real Estate, Corporate, Estate Planning, Probate, Insurance Defense, Alternative Dispute Resolution, Family, Personal Injury, Medical Malpractice, Professional Liability, Products Liability, Commercial Litigation, Workers Compensation, Municipal and Drainage and Levee Law.

WILLIAM T. DONAHUE

1133 N. WALNUT
DANVILLE, ILLINOIS 61832
Telephone: 217-446-6403
217-446-6403
Email: bill@donahueweb.com
URL: http://www.donahueweb.com

General Practice. Juvenile, Adoption, Criminal Law, Personal Injury, Labor and Employment, Business Law and Civil Rights. Wills.

WILLIAM T. DONAHUE, born Evergreen Park, Illinois, December 18, 1957; admitted to bar, 1983, Illinois and U.S. District Court, Northern and Central Districts of Illinois. *Education:* University of Illinois (A.B., 1980); DePaul University (J.D., 1983). *Member:* Illinois State and American Bar Associations. ***PRACTICE AREAS:*** Juvenile Law; Adoption Law; Criminal Law; Personal Injury Law; Labor and Employment; Business Law; Civil Rights; Wills.

JOHN E. MARSZALEK

DANVILLE, ILLINOIS

(See Chicago)

Plaintiff Personal Injury including Automobile Accidents, Trucking Accidents, Motorcycle Accidents, Catastrophic Accidents, Wrongful Death, Medical Malpractice, Workers Compensation, Workplace Injuries.

PHEBUS & KOESTER

DANVILLE, ILLINOIS

(See Urbana)

Civil trial practice in all courts, including class actions, mass torts, personal injury, including products liability, medical malpractice, automobile accidents, slip and fall, and railroad.

JOHN T. PHIPPS LAW OFFICES, P.C.

DANVILLE, ILLINOIS

(See Champaign)

General Civil Trial Practice. Family, Personal Injury, Corporate, Banking, Paternity, Child Custody, Visitation, Divorce, Wills and Estate Planning, Domestic Relations, Probate, Elder Law, Traffic Defense, Business Fraud, White Collar Crimes, Mediation, Arbitration, Real Estate, Criminal Law, Domestic Violence, DUI.

SAIKLEY, GARRISON, COLOMBO & BARNEY, LLC

Established in 1938

208 WEST NORTH STREET
P.O. BOX 6
DANVILLE, ILLINOIS 61834-0006
Telephone: 217-442-0244
Fax: 217-442-0582
Email: sgclaw@sbcglobal.net

General Civil Practice. Tort, Bankruptcy, Commercial, Corporation, Taxation, Probate, Real Estate, Domestic Relations and Criminal Law.

FIRM PROFILE: Saikley, Garrison & Colombo, Ltd. was founded by Albert Saikley in 1938. The present lawyers have a combined experience of over 90 years in Danville, IL. Serving clients throughout Vermilion, Champaign, and surrounding counties, a General Practice with individuals focusing in specific areas of law.

ALBERT SAIKLEY (1912-1987)

WILLIAM L. GARRISON, born Herrin, Illinois, March 15, 1942; admitted to bar, 1967, Illinois; 1968, U.S. District Court, Central District of Illinois and U.S. Court of Appeals, Seventh Circuit. *Education:* University of Illinois (A.B., 1964; J.D., 1967). Phi Alpha Delta; Pi Sigma Alpha. *Member:* Vermilion County (President, 1987-1988) and Illinois State Bar Associations; National Consumer Finance Association. ***PRACTICE AREAS:*** Banking Law; Bankruptcy Law; Collections; Real Estate Law. ***Email:*** Williamlgarrison@sbcglobal.net

GILBERT H. SAIKLEY, born Danville, Illinois, January 8, 1948; admitted to bar, 1973, Illinois, U.S. District Court, Central District of Illinois and U.S. Tax Court. *Education:* University of Illinois (B.S., 1970; J.D., 1973). Phi Kappa Phi; Beta Alpha Psi; Beta Gamma Sigma. Member, Bronze Tablet. Member, Illinois Institute for Local Government Law. *Member:* Vermilion County (President, 1994-1995), Illinois State and American Bar Associations; Illinois Society of Certified Public Accountants; Sports Lawyers Association. ***PRACTICE AREAS:*** Commercial Law; Corporate Law; Taxation Law; Probate Law. ***Email:*** Gilbertsaikley@sbcglobal.net

KEVIN M. COLOMBO, born Chicago, Illinois, August 23, 1953; admitted to bar, 1982, Illinois, U.S. District Court, Central District of Illinois and U.S. Court of Appeals, Seventh Circuit. *Education:* University of Illinois (B.A., 1978); IIT/Chicago-Kent College of Law (J.D., with honors, 1982). *Member:* Vermilion County and Illinois State Bar Associations. ***PRACTICE AREAS:*** Personal Injury Law; Family Law; Criminal Law. ***Email:*** Kevincolombo@sbcglobal.net

(This Listing Continued)

EDWIN C. BARNEY, JR., born Danville, Illinois, April 6, 1974; admitted to bar, 1999, Illinois and U.S. District Court, Central District of Illinois. *Education:* Blackburn University (B.A., 1995); St. Louis University (J.D., 1998). Labor Law Certificate, 1998. *Member:* Vermilion County, Illinois State and American Bar Associations. ***PRACTICE AREAS:*** Employment Law; Labor Law; Traffic Violations; Family Law. ***Email:*** Edwincbarney@sbcglobal.net

REPRESENTATIVE CLIENTS: Community Bank; Danville Consolidated Credit Union; Danville Sanitary District; First Illinois Credit Union; First Midwest Bank; First National Bank of Danville; Old National Bank; First Financial Bank; New Horizon Credit Union; Iroquois Federal Savings & Loan Association; Landmark Credit Union; Lauhoff Credit Union; Personal Finance Co.; Midstate Collection Solutions; The First National Bank of Catlin; United Community Bank.
REFERENCES: Rent-A-Center; First Midwest Bank; Old National Bank; First National Bank of Danville.

MICHAEL OVERMANN, LTD.

7702 SOUTH CASS AVENUE, SUITE 135
DARIEN, ILLINOIS 60561
Telephone: 630-810-0316
Fax: 630-810-1984
Email: molawltd@aol.com
URL: http://www.lawyers.com/overmann

Estate Planning, Trust and Estate Administration; Probate, Guardianship, Estate Litigation.

MICHAEL OVERMANN, born St. Louis, Missouri, October 30, 1966; admitted to bar, 1995, Illinois. *Education:* Purdue University (B.S., with Distinction, 1989); St. Louis University (J.D., 1995). Attorney, The Northern Trust Company, Chicago, IL, 1995-1998. Counsel, Public Guardian of DuPage County, 2000-2002. *Member:* DuPage County (Member, Estate Planning and Probate Law Committee), Illinois State (Member, Trusts and Estate Section) and American (Member, Real Property, Probate and Trust Law Section) Bar Associations. ***PRACTICE AREAS:*** Estate Planning; Trust Administration; Estate Administration; Contested Trusts and Estates; Guardianship.

KATHERINE A. MARSHALL, born Boston, Massachusetts, 1965; admitted to bar, 1994, Illinois. *Education:* Columbia University (B.A., 1988); Loyola University, Chicago School of Social Work, (M.S.W., 1994); Loyola University, Chicago School of Law (J.D., 1994). Trust Officer, Fifth Third Bank, Rolling Meadows, 2001-2003. Attorney, Peck, Bloom, Miller & Mitchell, LLC, Chicago, 1995-2001. *Member:* Chicago and Illinois State Bar Associations; DuPage Association of Woman Lawyers. ***LANGUAGES:*** Hebrew. ***PRACTICE AREAS:*** Trust Administration; Estate Administration; Guardianship.

BEAVERS, GRAHAM & FINES

DECATUR, ILLINOIS

(See Taylorville)

HARRINGTON & TOCK

DECATUR, ILLINOIS

(See Champaign)

General Practice. Business, Partnership Law, Small Business Law, Family Business Law, Business Formation, Commercial Litigation, Probate, Tax, Corporation, Real Estate, Eminent Domain and Drainage Law, Shopping Center Law, Commercial Leasing, Commercial Landlord and Tenant Law, Tax Planning, IRS Controversies, Trials, Appeals and Commercial Arbitration.

HOLLEY & ROSEN

DECATUR, ILLINOIS

(See Springfield)

JEFFRY A. JUSTICE

SUITE 515 MILLIKIN COURT
132 SOUTH WATER STREET
DECATUR, ILLINOIS 62523
Telephone: 217-422-9800
Fax: 217-428-9742
Email: jeff@jeffryjustice.com

Commercial Litigation, Uniform Commercial Code & Banking, Bankruptcy including Chapter 11 Cases, Commercial & Construction Litigation.

JEFFRY A. JUSTICE, born Columbus, Ohio, June 3, 1951; admitted to bar, 1978, Illinois, U.S. District Court, Central and Northern Districts of Illinois, U.S. Court of Appeals, Seventh Circuit and U.S. Supreme Court. *Education:* University of Illinois (B.S., 1973); John Marshall Law School (J.D., 1978). Research Editor, John Marshall Law Review, 1977-1978. ***PRACTICE AREAS:*** Commercial Litigation; Construction Litigation; Collection Litigation; Bankruptcy; Business Formation; Uniform Commercial Code Law; Mortgage Foreclosure.

KEHART, PECKERT & BOOTH

A Partnership including a Professional Corporation
Established in 1879
132 SOUTH WATER STREET, SUITE 200
P.O. BOX 860
DECATUR, ILLINOIS 62525-0860
Telephone: 217-428-4689
Telecopier: 217-422-7950
Email: mjk@kehart.com
URL: http://www.kehart.com

Litigation, Business Litigation, Commercial Litigation, Corporate Litigation, Class Actions, Banking Law, Banking Institutions, Business Transactions, Domestic Relations, Estate Planning, General Civil and Trial Practice, Lenders Rights, Labor and Employment, Real Estate Transactions, Medical Malpractice Defense, Insurance Defense, Municipal Law, Probate Law, Workers Compensation.

EDWARD BOOTH, born Ft. Pierre, South Dakota, July 28, 1926; admitted to bar, 1954, Illinois, U.S. District Court, Central District of Illinois, U.S. Court of Appeals, Seventh Circuit and U.S. Supreme Court. *Education:* Indiana University (A.B., 1950); Harvard University (LL.B., 1953). Assistant State's Attorney, Macon County, 1957-1960. *Member:* Decatur, Illinois State and American Bar Associations. ***PRACTICE AREAS:*** Probate; Wills; Trusts; Estates; Municipal Law.

MICHAEL J. KEHART, born Pleasant Hill, Illinois, December 24, 1942; admitted to bar, 1967, Illinois and U.S. District Court, Central District of Illinois; 1981, U.S. Court of Appeals, Seventh Circuit. *Education:* Illinois College (A.B., 1964); University of Michigan (J.D., 1967). Phi Beta Kappa. *Member:* Decatur and Illinois State Bar Associations. ***PRACTICE AREAS:*** Medical Malpractice Defense; Insurance Defense; Litigation; Commercial Litigation. ***Email:*** mjk@kehart.com

JAMES E. PECKERT, born Decatur, Illinois, September 22, 1962; admitted to bar, 1986, Illinois; 1987, U.S. District Court, Central District of Illinois; 1990, U.S. Court of Appeals, Seventh Circuit; 1994, U.S. District Court, Southern District of Illinois. *Education:* Millikin University (B.S., 1983); Southern Illinois University (J.D., 1986). *Member:* Decatur, Illinois State and American Bar Associations. ***PRACTICE AREAS:*** Litigation; Commercial Litigation; Labor and Employment; Insurance Defense. ***Email:*** jep@kehart.com

HEIDI R. BALSLEY, born Spring Valley, Illinois, October 6, 1971; admitted to bar, 1996, Illinois; 1997, U.S. District Court, Central District of Illinois. *Education:* Millikin University (B.A., cum laude, 1993); Southern Illinois University (J.D., 1996). Editor, Southern Illinois University Law Journal, 1995-1996. Recipient, American Jurisprudence Award in Trusts & Estates. *Member:* Decatur and Illinois State Bar Associations. ***PRACTICE AREAS:*** General Civil and Trial Practice; Labor and Employment; Workers Compensation; Insurance Defense; Probate Law. ***Email:*** hrb@kehart.com

WILLIAM D. TRIMBLE, born Bexar County, Texas, January 20, 1969; admitted to bar, 1998, Illinois and U.S. District Court, Central District of Illinois. *Education:* Grinnell College (B.A., 1991); University of Illinois (J.D., magna cum laude, 1998). *Member:* Decatur and Illinois State Bar Associations; Illinois Trial Lawyers Association. ***PRACTICE AREAS:*** Litigation; Medical Malpractice Defense; Personal Injury; Commercial Litigation. ***Email:*** wdt@kehart.com

JASON B. SMALL, born Galesburg, Illinois, March 5, 1973; admitted to bar, 1999, Illinois. *Education:* DePauw University (B.A., 1995); Yale Law School (J.D., 1998). Phi Sigma Alpha; Phi Beta Kappa; Gold Key. Recipient, State Finalist Rhodes Scholar. Member: DePauw Alumni Board of Directors; DePauw Board of Visitors. ***PRACTICE AREAS:*** Litigation; Corporate Law. ***Email:*** jsmall@kehart.com

(MS) CYNTHIA M. CUSTER, born Boise, Idaho, 1958; admitted to bar, 2005, Illinois. *Education:* St. Francis Medical Center College of Nursing (B.S.N., 1994); University of Illinois at Chicago (M.S., 1996); Chicago-Kent College of Law, Illinois Institute of Technology (J.D., 2004). Registered Professional Nurse, Illinois, 1984. Certified Nurse Midwife, 1996. Member: American College of Nurse Midwives, 1996; American College of Legal Medicine, 2003. *Member:* Illinois State Bar Association; American Bar Association. ***PRACTICE AREAS:*** Corporate Law; Medical Malpractice; Litigation. ***Email:*** cc@kehart.com

OF COUNSEL

ROBERT W. OHLSEN, born Downers Grove, Illinois, June 18, 1931; admitted to bar, 1957, Illinois. *Education:* Bradley University (B.S., 1953); University of Illinois (J.D., 1957). Phi Delta Phi; Order of the Coif. Member, Board of Student Editors, University of Illinois Law Forum, 1956-1957. *Member:* Decatur, Illinois State and American Bar Associations. ***PRACTICE AREAS:*** Wills; Trusts and Estates; Real Estate; General Practice. ***Email:*** wcoc122@aol.com

REPRESENTATIVE CLIENTS: *Corporations:* Archer-Daniels-Midland Co.; A.E. Staley Manufacturing Co.; Bodine Electric of Decatur; Cub Foods; Kelly Construction, Inc.; Lincoln Diagnostics; Mueller Co.; PPG Industries, Inc.; Decatur Memorial Hospital; Wabash Memorial Hospital Association; *Insurance Companies:* American International Adjustment Co.; Countrywide Services Co.; GAB Business Services, Inc.; MMI Companies; Frontier Insurance; St. Paul Insurance; Medical Protective; Metropolitan Life. *Financial Institutions:* Hickory Point Bank and Trust; Central Illinois Bank, MC.; Union Planters Bank, N.A. *Municipalities:* City of Decatur, Illinois; Decatur Park District; Decatur Public Library; Decatur Public Building Commission.
REFERENCES: Union Planters Bank, N.A.; Hickory Point Bank and Trust.

METNICK, CHERRY, FRAZIER & SABIN, L.L.P.

DECATUR, ILLINOIS

(See Springfield)

General Trial and Appellate Practice. Criminal Defense, Workers Compensation, Personal Injury, Family Law, Labor and Employment Law, Estate Planning, Business Law.

MOSS, BRYAN & MOSS, P.C.

DECATUR, ILLINOIS

(See Clinton)

Personal Injury, Workers Compensation and General Litigation.

ROBERTS LAW OFFICE, LTD.

SUITE 300, MILLIKIN COURT
132 SOUTH WATER STREET
DECATUR, ILLINOIS 62523-1399
Telephone: 217-428-4385
Fax: 217-428-4387
Email: attybobob@aol.com
URL: http://www.lawyers.com/robertrobertslaw

Estate Planning, Wills, Probate, Trusts, Real Estate, Agricultural Law, Business Law.

ROBERT H. ROBERTS, born Decatur, Illinois, December 29, 1928; admitted to bar, 1955, Missouri, Illinois and U.S. Tax Court. *Education:* Millikin University (B.S., 1950); University of Michigan and University of Missouri (J.D., 1955). Phi Alpha Delta. Member, Board of Trustees, Lincoln College, Lincoln, Illinois, 1980—, Chairman 1985-1987. Member, Community Board of Directors, Union Planters Bank N.A. *Member:* Decatur, Illinois State and American Bar Associations; The Missouri Bar. ***PRACTICE AREAS:*** Estate Planning; Wills; Trusts; Probate; Real Estate; Agricultural Law.

SAMUELS, MILLER, SCHROEDER, JACKSON & SLY, LLP

Established in 1888

225 NORTH WATER STREET, SUITE 301
P.O. BOX 1400
DECATUR, ILLINOIS 62525
Telephone: 217-429-4325
Telecopier: 217-425-6313
Email: law@smsjslaw.com
URL: http://www.smsjslaw.com

Arthur, Illinois Office: 131 B South Vine Street, 61911. Telephone: 217-543-3403.

General Civil Trial and Appellate Practice, Personal Injury, Auto Accidents, Medical Malpractice, Workers Compensation, Corporate, Commercial, Employment, Banking, Finance, Mergers and Acquisitions, Health Care, Real Estate and Environmental, Trusts, Estates, Wills and Estates Planning.

MEMBERS OF FIRM

JERALD E. JACKSON, born St. Marys, Illinois, April 25, 1922; admitted to bar, 1949, Illinois. *Education:* Western Illinois University (B.S., 1946); University of Chicago (J.D., cum laude, 1949). Pi Kappa Delta; Order of the Coif. Member, Illinois Supreme Court Committees on: Pattern Jury Instructions, 1973-1994; Character and Fitness, 1974-1995. *Member:* Decatur, Illinois State and American Bar Associations. Fellow: American College of Trial Lawyers; Illinois Bar Foundation; American Bar Foundation; Laureate of the Academy of Illinois Lawyers. ***PRACTICE AREAS:*** Medical Malpractice Litigation; General Civil Litigation. ***Email:*** jejackson@smsjslaw.com

GUY E. WILLIAMS, born Chicago, Illinois, June 18, 1940; admitted to bar, 1965, Illinois. *Education:* University of Illinois (B.S., 1962; J.D., 1965). Phi Delta Phi. *Member:* Decatur and Illinois State Bar Associations. ***PRACTICE AREAS:*** Probate; Wills; Estate Planning; Real Estate. ***Email:*** gewilliams@smsjslaw.com

JOHN S. COBB, born Urbana, Illinois, March 25, 1946; admitted to bar, 1971, Illinois. *Education:* University of Illinois (B.S., 1968; J.D., 1971). Member, Illinois Secretary of State's Corporation Acts Advisory Committee, 1986-2003, and Chairman, 1993-1995. *Member:* Decatur, Illinois State and American Bar Associations. ***PRACTICE AREAS:*** General Corporate Law; Banking Law; Health Care Law; Mergers/Acquisitions. ***Email:*** jscobb@smsjslaw.com

MARK E. JACKSON, born Decatur, Illinois, March 30, 1949; admitted to bar, 1974, Illinois. *Education:* Lawrence University (B.A., 1971); University of Illinois (J.D., 1974). *Member:* Decatur, Illinois State and American Bar Associations. ***PRACTICE AREAS:*** Workers Compensation Law; Personal Injury Litigation; Medical Malpractice Litigation. ***Email:*** mejackson@smsjslaw.com

KEITH W. CASTEEL, born Decatur, Illinois, August 13, 1950; admitted to bar, 1975, Illinois. *Education:* Purdue University (B.S.I.E., with honors, 1972); University of Illinois (J.D., 1975). Tau Beta Pi; Iron Key. Recipient, Illinois State Bar Association Lincoln Award. Member, Illinois Secretary of State's Corporation Acts Advisory Committee, 2003. *Member:* Decatur, Illinois State and American Bar Associations. (Also at Arthur Office). ***PRACTICE AREAS:*** Banking Law; Commercial Law; Real Estate Law; Environmental Law; Probate; Estate Planning. ***Email:*** casteel@smsjslaw.com

DARRELL A. WOOLUMS, born Decatur, Illinois, September 24, 1947; admitted to bar, 1976, Illinois. *Education:* Ventura Junior College; Illinois State University (B.S., 1971); John Marshall Law School (J.D., 1976). *Member:* Decatur, Illinois State Bar Associations. ***PRACTICE AREAS:*** Tax Free Exchanges; Probate; Trust Law; Banking Law; Commercial Law. ***Email:*** woolums@smsjslaw.com

JOHN E. SANNER, born Decatur, Illinois, May 31, 1959; admitted to bar, 1984, Illinois. *Education:* Southern Illinois University (B.A., 1981; A.A., 1981; J.D., summa cum laude, 1984). *Member:* Decatur, Illinois State and American Bar Associations. ***PRACTICE AREAS:*** Corporate Law; Commercial Law; Mergers/Acquisitions; Health Care. ***Email:*** jesanner@smsjslaw.com

(This Listing Continued)

EDWARD Q. COSTA, born Springfield, Illinois, October 31, 1958; admitted to bar, 1984, Illinois. *Education:* St. Louis University (B.A., 1980); Creighton University (J.D., 1983). *Member:* Decatur, Illinois State Bar Associations. ***PRACTICE AREAS:*** General Civil Litigation; Personal Injury; Commercial Litigation; Creditors Rights; Bankruptcy; Foreclosures. ***Email:*** costa@smsjslaw.com

JAMES T. JACKSON, born Decatur, Illinois, December 31, 1961; admitted to bar, 1988, Illinois. *Education:* Wheaton College (B.A., with high honors, 1984); University of Colorado (J.D., 1988). *Member:* Decatur and Illinois State Bar Associations; National Association of College and University Attorneys. ***PRACTICE AREAS:*** Education Law; Medical Malpractice Litigation; Commercial Litigation; Employment Law. ***Email:*** jtjackson@smsjslaw.com

RHONDA L. HEINZ, born Springfield, Illinois, December 21, 1964; admitted to bar, 1991, Illinois. *Education:* University of Illinois (B.S., 1987; J.D., 1990). *Member:* Decatur, Macon County, Illinois State and American Bar Associations. ***PRACTICE AREAS:*** Employment Law; Personal Injury; Commercial Litigation; General Civil Litigation; Appellate Practice. ***Email:*** heinz@smsjslaw.com

BRIDGET C. HOGAN, born St. Louis, Missouri, February 21, 1961; admitted to bar, 1997, Illinois; 1998, Missouri. *Education:* Rockhurst College (B.S./B.A., 1983); St. Louis University (J.D., cum laude, 1997). *Member:* Decatur, Illinois State Bar Associations; The Missouri Bar. ***PRACTICE AREAS:*** Corporate Law; General Practice; Civil Litigation; Employment Law; Real Estate Law; Appellate Practice. ***Email:*** hogan@smsjslaw.com

ASSOCIATES

BRIAN T. HAIR, born Jamestown, New York, February 24, 1970; admitted to bar, 2001, Illinois; 2002, U.S. District Court, Central District of Illinois. *Education:* Hiram College (B.A. with honors, 1992); University of Illinois College of Law (J.D., 2001). Phi Beta Kappa. Recipient, Rickert Award. ***PRACTICE AREAS:*** Mergers and Acquisitions; Business Law; Commercial Law; Civil Litigation; Real Estate; Collections. ***Email:*** hair@smsjslaw.com

SCOTT E. GARWOOD, born Springfield, Illinois, November 14, 1976; admitted to bar, 2002, Illinois. *Education:* University of Illinois, Urbana-Champaign (B.S., Agriculture, 1999; J.D., 2002). *Member:* Decatur and Illinois State Bar Associations. ***PRACTICE AREAS:*** Probate; Wills; Trusts and Estates; Estate Planning; Business Law; Corporate Law; Mergers and Acquisitions; Agricultural Law; Real Estate; Municipal Law. ***Email:*** sgarwood@smsjslaw.com

PHOEBE S. BOWERS, born Mattoon, Illinois, May 30, 1978; admitted to bar, 2003, Illinois. *Education:* Millikin University (B.S., cum laude, 2000); Southern Illinois University School of Law (J.D., cum laude, 2003). *Member:* Decatur and Illinois State Bar Associations. ***PRACTICE AREAS:*** Estate Planning; Probate; Family Law; Environmental Law. ***Email:*** psbowers@smsjslaw.com

OF COUNSEL

NICHOLAS J. NEIERS, admitted to bar, 1960, Illinois. *Education:* University of Notre Dame (A.B., magna cum laude, 1959; J.D., 1960). Case Editor, Notre Dame Lawyer, 1959-1960. *Member:* Decatur, Illinois State Bar Associations;. American College of Trial Lawyers. [Retired USAR, Colonel]. ***PRACTICE AREAS:*** General Civil Litigation; Real Estate Law.

REPRESENTATIVE CLIENTS: Illinois Power Company; Millikin University; Lincoln College; Richland Community College; Decatur Memorial Hospital; Huston - Patterson Corporation; State Bank of Arthur; Village of Forsyth; Grinnell Insurance Co.; Cincinnati Insurance Company; Gallagher-Bassett; Bachrach Clothing, Inc.; Medical Protective Co.; K's Merchandise Mart, Inc.; DeMirco Industries, L.L.C., and its divisions Airfloat Systems and Climate Control; Sloan Implement Company.

SHAY & PERBIX

260 EAST WOOD STREET
DECATUR, ILLINOIS 62523
Telephone: 217-425-5900
Fax: 217-425-5901
Email: shayperb@insightbb.com
URL: http://www.shayandperbix.com

Plaintiffs Personal Injury, Workers Compensation, Medical Malpractice, Products Liability.

TIMOTHY M. SHAY, born Peoria, Illinois, February 16, 1961; admitted to bar, 1986, Illinois and U.S. District Court, Central District of Illinois; 1987, Missouri. *Education:* University of Illinois (B.S., 1983); University of Missouri at Columbia (J.D., 1986). Phi Delta Phi. Recipient, Golden Key National Honor Society Outstanding Teaching Assistant Award. Teaching Assistant, Business Law, University of Missouri, 1984-1986. President, University of Missouri Student Bar Association, 1985-1986. *Member:* Macon County, Sangamon County and Illinois State Bar Associations; The Missouri Bar; Illinois Trial Lawyers Association. ***PRACTICE AREAS:*** Personal Injury; Workers Compensation; Family Law; Medical Malpractice; Products Liability. ***Email:*** shayperb@insightbb.com

STEVEN W. PERBIX, born Havana, Illinois, May 14, 1962; admitted to bar, 1986, Illinois; 1989, U.S. District Court, Central District of Illinois. *Education:* Arizona State University (B.A., 1983); University of San Diego (J.D., 1986). Golden Key. Recipient, The Bishop Buddy Trial Advocacy Award, University of San Diego. Assistant State's Attorney, Jackson County, 1986-1988. *Member:* Macon County and Illinois State Bar Associations. ***PRACTICE AREAS:*** Family Law; Workers Compensation; Criminal Law; Medical Malpractice; Personal Injury. ***Email:*** shayperb@insightbb.com

ASSOCIATE

DENNIS R. ATTEBERRY, born Decatur, Illinois, February 15, 1972; admitted to bar, 2001, Illinois. *Education:* Blackburn College (B.A., Political Science, 1994); Southern Illinois University, Carbondale (J.D., 2001); University of Illinois, Springfield (M.A., Political Science, 2001). Phi Alpha Delta. Member, 1993— and Former Secretary, Project 29-Grassroots Lobbyist Group, Taylorville, Illinois. Former Associate, Londrigan, Potter&

(This Listing Continued)

Randle, 2001-1005. *Member:* Illinois Trial Lawyers Association; The Association of Trial Lawyers of America; Christian Legal Society. ***PRACTICE AREAS:*** Personal Injury (40%); Workers Compensation (30%); Probate (10%); Traffic Violations (10%); Civil Litigation (10%). ***Email:*** shayperb@aol.com

CHRISTOPHER M. TIETZ

132 S. WATER STREET, SUITE 444
DECATUR, ILLINOIS 62523
Telephone: 217-425-4910
Email: cmt@tietzlaw.com
URL: http://www.lawyers.com/tietz

Civil Litigation. Business Transactions, Real Estate, Corporate, Commercial, International, Employment, Construction, Technology, Insurance Defense, Products Liability, Professional Liability, Estate Planning, Trust and Probate Law.

FIRM PROFILE: Tietz Law Office is an aggressive business transactions and litigation firm, combining real estate, corporate, commercial, and litigation elements for best effect. The firm emphasizes personal service to a wide range of individual, industrial, financial, commercial and insurance clients throughout central Illinois. My extensive trial experience enhances the ability both to obtain favorable verdicts and to settle disputes efficiently and economically.

CHRISTOPHER M. TIETZ, born Tampa, Florida, September 18, 1952; admitted to bar, 1976, Illinois and U.S. District Court, Central District of Illinois; 1979, U.S. Court of Appeals, Seventh Circuit. *Education:* University of Illinois (B.S., 1973; J.D., 1976). *Member:* Decatur, Chicago (Commercial Transactions Committee, 1994—) and Illinois State (Commercial and Banking Law Council, 1987—, Chair, 1991-1992; Real Estate Law Council, 1993—, Chair, 1999-2000; Trusts and Estates Council, 2000—) Bar Associations; Illinois Defense Trial Counsel; Central Illinois Estate Planning Council (President, 1989-1990). ***LANGUAGES:*** German.

REPRESENTATIVE CLIENTS: *Corporate/Financial:* Benefit Planners, LLC; Craftmasters, Inc.; Doughboy Recreational Co.; Franz Kessler GmbH; Material Handling Systems, Inc.; National Startch and Chemical Co.; RTW Machine Tools, Inc.; Skeff Distributing Co.; The Northern Trust Co.; *Insurance:* Canal Insurance Co.; Cincinnati Insurance Co.; Farmers Insurance Group; Gulf Insurance Group; Illinois Mine Subsidence Insurance Fund; MetLife; St. Paul Fire & Marine Insurance Co.; Standard Mutual Insurance Co.

JOSEPH W. VIGNERI, LTD.

A PROFESSIONAL CORPORATION
Established in 1988
136 W. WASHINGTON STREET
DECATUR, ILLINOIS 62522
Telephone: 217-422-9992
Fax: 217-422-8669
Email: jvigneri@earthlink.net

Criminal Defense.

JOSEPH W. VIGNERI, born Decatur, Illinois, July 28, 1956; admitted to bar, 1983, Illinois; 1984, U.S. District Court, Central District of Illinois; 1991, U.S. Supreme Court. *Education:* Millikin University (B.A., 1980); St. Louis University (J.D., cum laude, 1983). Member, Order of the Woolsack. *Member:* Christian, Decatur (Chairman, Continuing Legal Education Committee, 1990-1991, 1994-1995; Technology Committee, 1996-1997), Illinois State (Secretary, Council on Individual Rights, 1985-1986) and American Bar Associations. ***Email:*** jvigneri@earthlink.net

LEGAL SUPPORT PERSONNEL

JENNIFER E. SHELTON (Legal Assistant)

WINTERS, FEATHERSTUN, GAUMER, POSTLEWAIT, STOCKS & FLYNN

225 N. WATER STREET, SUITE 200
P.O. BOX 1760
DECATUR, ILLINOIS 62525-1760
Telephone: 217-429-4453; 429-5213
Telecopier: 217-425-8892
URL: http://www.lawyers.com/wfgpsf

General Practice. Trials. Insurance Defense, Legal and Medical Malpractice, Workers Compensation, Probate, Real Estate, Corporations, Labor Strikes.

MEMBERS OF FIRM

ROBERT P. VAIL (1877-1964)

WALKER H. MILLS (1893-1962)

THOS. H. ARMSTRONG (1897-1981)

ROSWELL C. PRINCE (1919-1994)

GLEN A. FEATHERSTUN, born Mt. Vernon, Illinois, August 1, 1941; admitted to bar, 1966, Illinois and Missouri. *Education:* Washington University (B.S.B.A., 1963; J.D., 1966); University of Michigan (LL.M., 1967). Phi Delta Phi; Beta Gamma Sigma; Order of the Coif. Editor-in-Chief, Washington University Law Quarterly, 1965-1966. *Member:* Decatur, Illinois State and American Bar Associations; The Missouri Bar; Illinois Association of Defense Trial Counsel. ***PRACTICE AREAS:*** Trial Practice; Insurance Law; Workers Compensation Law; Probate; Construction. ***Email:*** gfeatherstun@family-net.net

DANIEL L. GAUMER, born Peoria, Illinois, August 1, 1950; admitted to bar, 1976, Illinois. *Education:* Bradley University (B.S., 1972); Southern Illinois University (J.D., summa cum laude, 1976). Phi Alpha Delta. Articles Editor, Southern Illinois Law Review, 1975-1976. Hearing Officer Claims Committee, State Universities Retirement System. *Member:* Decatur and Illinois State Bar Associations. ***PRACTICE AREAS:*** Workers Compensation Law; Insurance Law; Trial Practice; Probate; Real Estate. ***Email:*** dgaumer@family-net.net

R. SAMUEL POSTLEWAIT, born Urbana, Illinois, September 4, 1956; admitted to bar, 1985, Illinois. *Education:* Eastern Illinois University (B.S., 1978); Oklahoma City University (J.D., 1984). Phi Delta Phi. Recipient, American Jurisprudence Awards in Civil Procedure and Constitutional Law. *Member:* Decatur and Illinois State Bar Associations; Illinois Association of Defense Trial Counsel. ***PRACTICE AREAS:*** Trials; Insurance; Probate; Real Estate; Business Transactions; Health Care. ***Email:*** spostlewait@family-net.net

JERROLD H. STOCKS, born Decatur, Illinois, March 13, 1964; admitted to bar, 1989, Illinois and U.S. Court of Appeals, Seventh Circuit. *Education:* University of Illinois (B.A., 1986); Drake University (J.D., 1989). *Member:* Decatur Bar Association. ***PRACTICE AREAS:*** Civil Trial Practice; Insurance Defense; Estates; Construction; Agricultural Law. ***Email:*** jstocks@family-net.net

EDWARD F. FLYNN, born South Bend, Indiana, March 18, 1957; admitted to bar, 1986, Illinois and U.S. District Court, Central District of Illinois. *Education:* Illinois College (B.S., 1979); John Marshall Law School (J.D., 1986). Bureau of National Affairs Senior Scholar. ***PRACTICE AREAS:*** Commercial Transactions; Municipal Law; Real Estate Law; Workers Compensation; Civil Litigation. ***Email:*** eflynn@family-net.net

ASSOCIATES

ERICK F. HUBBARD, born Decatur, Illinois, October 25, 1968; admitted to bar, 2003, Illinois; 2004, U.S. District Court, District of Illinois. *Education:* Millikin University (B.A., 2000); Southern Illinois University School of Law (J.D., 2003). Phi Delta Phi. Member, American Inn of Court. *Member:* Illinois State Bar Association. ***PRACTICE AREAS:*** Civil Practice. ***Email:*** ehubbard@family-net.net

JOSEPH R. WETZEL, born Berrien Springs, Michigan, May 31, 1980; admitted to bar, 2004, Illinois. *Education:* Richland Community College (A.A., 1999); Millikin University (B.A., 2001); Southern Illinois University, Carbondale (J.D., 2004). ***PRACTICE AREAS:*** Civil Litigation. ***Email:*** jwetzel@family-net.net

OF COUNSEL

ROBERT D. WINTERS, born Robinson, Illinois, December 6, 1926; admitted to bar, 1950, Illinois. *Education:* Purdue University (B.S.; B.N.S. & T.); University of Michigan (J.D., 1950). *Member:* Decatur and American Bar Associations. Fellow, American College of Trial Lawyers. ***PRACTICE AREAS:*** Probate; Real Estate.

REPRESENTATIVE CLIENTS: Allstate Insurance Co.; American Family Insurance Group; CSX Transportation, Inc.; The Cincinnati Insurance Co.; Employers Mutual Cos.; Bridgestone/Firestone, Inc.; Gallagher Bassett Services, Inc.; Hawkeye-Security Insurance Co.; Millers Mutual Insurance Assn. of Illinois; National Farmers Union Property & Casualty Co.; Nationwide Mutual Insurance Co.; Old Republic Insurance Co.; Pekin Insurance Co.; Ryder Truck Rental, Inc.; American National Property & Casualty Co.; Archer-Daniels-Midland Co.; Brotherhood Mutual Insurance Co.; Country Mutual Insurance Co.; Crawford & Co.; The Farmers Auto Insurance Assoc.; Houston General Insurance Co.; Northland Insurance Cos.; Park District Risk Management Agency; Union Insurance Group; Western States Insurance Co.; Unitrin Property & Casualty Insurance Company; Iowa Mutual Ins. Co.; St. Paul; Monroe Guaranty Ins. Co.; Secura Insurance; Metropolitan Property & Casualty Insurance Company; United Heartland Insurance; Sanitary District of Decatur; Village of Mt. Zion; The GSI Group, Inc.; Heartland Express; Decatur Foundry, Inc.; Cambridge Integrated Services group, Inc.; Cannon, Cochran Management Services, Inc.; Cunningham, Lindsey; TIG Specialty; CSC Claims Company; Crown Cork & Seal; Traveler's Insurance Company; Liberty Mutual Insurance; Zurich North America; Ecompass Insurance; Acuity Mutual Insurance; ESIS; PPG Industries, Inc.; Regions Bank; Providence Property and Casualty Insurance Co.
REFERENCES: Main Street Bank & Trust; National City Bank.

BEERMANN & DeBRUYNE

DEERFIELD, ILLINOIS
(See Libertyville)

Family Law, Divorce, Adoption, Separation Agreements, Child Custody, Child Support, Domestic Violence, Visitation Rights, Family Mediation Adoption Law, Juvenile Law, Real Estate.

LYON & CARON LLP

790 ESTATE DRIVE, SUITE 180
DEERFIELD, ILLINOIS 60015
Telephone: 847-945-8810
Fax: 847-945-8812
URL: http://www.lc-law.com

Business Law, Corporate Law, Partnership Law, Limited Liability Companies, Private Placements, Taxation, Real Estate and Estate Planning.

MEMBERS OF FIRM

MICHAEL M. CARON, born December 14, 1955; admitted to bar, 1980, Illinois and U.S. District Court, Northern District of Illinois. *Education:* University of Illinois (B.S., magna cum laude, 1977; J.D., magna cum laude, 1980). Certified Public Accountant, Illinois, 1977. Author: "Tax Considerations in Condominium Development," Condominium Law, Illinois Institute of Continuing Legal Education, 2002; "Like-Kind Exchanges - New IRS Regulations Aid in Implementing a Vital Tax Planning Strategy," Illinois Realtor, 1991. Speaker, Like-Kind Exchanges, Lorman Education Services, 1999-2002, 2004, 2005. ***PRACTICE AREAS:*** Real Estate; Partnership Law; Taxation; Low Income Tax Credits; Private Placements; Estate Planning. ***Email:*** mcaron@lc-law.com

JEFFREY S. LYON, born Chicago, Illinois, August 30, 1949; admitted to bar, 1975, Illinois and U.S. District Court, Northern District of Illinois. *Education:* Drake University (B.A., 1971); DePaul University (J.D., 1975). Village Prosecutor, Morton Grove, Illinois, 1979-2001. ***PRACTICE AREAS:*** Commercial Real Estate; Leasing; Low Income Tax Credits. ***Email:*** jlyon@lc-law.com

(This Listing Continued)

LYON & CARON LLP, Deerfield—Continued

WILLIAM BRADLEY FOX, born Washington, D.C., January 26, 1966; admitted to bar, 1992, Illinois. *Education:* University of Michigan (B.A., 1988); Duke University (J.D., 1991); New York University (LL.M., Taxation, 1995). Phi Beta Kappa. ***PRACTICE AREAS:*** Taxation; Charitable Giving; Charitable Organizations Law; Estate Planning; Corporate Law. ***Email:*** wfox@lc-law.com

ASSOCIATE

MARY T. MANTHY, admitted to bar, 1995, Illinois. *Education:* Loyola University (B.A., 1989); Chicago-Kent College of Law (J.D., 1995). ***PRACTICE AREAS:*** Commercial Real Estate. ***Email:*** mmanthy@lc-law.com

REPRESENTATIVE CLIENTS: Aries Capital; Citadel Realty, Inc.; First Hospitality Group; La Salle Systems Leasing, Inc.; McDonald's Corp.; National Property Services, Inc.; Pathway Senior Living, LLC; Valenti Builders, Inc.; World Duty Free America, Inc.
REFERENCE: Citibank, FSB.

PACHTER, GREGORY & FINOCCHIARO, P.C.

790 ESTATE DRIVE, SUITE 150
DEERFIELD, ILLINOIS 60015
Telephone: 847-317-7350
Fax: 847-317-7355

Real Estate Finance, Real Estate Development and Commercial Litigation.

FIRM PROFILE: Pachter, Gregory & Finocchiaro, P.C., is a law firm concentrating in Real Estate transactions and Litigation. The firm represents national and regional development companies, financial institutions, and industrial and commercial owners and users of real estate in transactions across the United States. The scope of the firm's representation includes: annexations, acquisitions, dispositions, leasing, financings, commercial and real estate litigation, governmental economic incentives and zoning. The firm also represents clients in a variety of commercial matters, including corporate and partnership organization and operation matters.

LARRY H. PACHTER, born Grand Rapids, Michigan, March 29, 1957; admitted to bar, 1982, Illinois and U.S. District Court, Northern District of Illinois. *Education:* University of Michigan (B.B.A., with high distinction, 1979); Hebrew University; University of Michigan (J.D., cum laude, 1982). Certified Public Accountant, Michigan, 1979. ***PRACTICE AREAS:*** Mortgage Financing; Real Estate Development and Leasing. ***Email:*** larryp@realestatelaw.com

PATRICIA BALDWIN GREGORY, born Bronx, New York, November 2, 1960; admitted to bar, 1987, Connecticut; 1988, New York; 1989, Illinois. *Education:* Manhattan College (B.S., magna cum laude, 1982); Northwestern University (J.D., 1987). Certified Public Accountant, Illinois, 1984. *Member:* Chicago and American Bar Associations. ***PRACTICE AREAS:*** Real Estate Development and Leasing; Economic Development; Mobile Home Law. ***Email:*** patg@realestatelaw.com

PETER D. FINOCCHIARO, born Omaha, Nebraska, January 9, 1962; admitted to bar, 1987, Illinois. *Education:* University of Notre Dame (B.B.A., cum laude, 1984); Loyola University (J.D., 1987). Alpha Sigma Nu. Member: National Moot Court Team; Chicago Bar Association Moot Court Team. Recipient, American Jurisprudence Award For: Evidence; Corporate Tax; Leadership and Service Award. ***PRACTICE AREAS:*** Real Estate; Commercial Litigation; Corporate. ***Email:*** petef@realestatelaw.com

BARBARA C. RAFFALDINI, born Hagerstown, Maryland, January 22, 1962; admitted to bar, 1987, Maryland; 1988, District of Columbia; 1990, Illinois. *Education:* Georgetown University (B.S.F.S., cum laude, 1984; J.D., 1987). Pi Sigma Alpha. *Member:* The District of Columbia Bar; Maryland and Illinois State Bar Associations. ***PRACTICE AREAS:*** Mortgage Financing; Real Estate Development; Leasing; Mobile Home Law. ***Email:*** barbarar@realestatelaw.com

ANTHONY PERRELLI

510 LAKE ROAD, SUITE 105
DEERFIELD, ILLINOIS 60015
Telephone: 847-317-1451
847-236-9901
Email: perrelli@ameritech.net

Business Corporate, Small Business, Contracts, Business Planning, Real Estate, Commercial Litigation and Taxation.

ANTHONY PERRELLI, born Melrose Park, Illinois; admitted to bar, 2005, Illinois. *Education:* Dominican University (B.S., 2001); John Marshall Law School (J.D., 2004); Dominican University (M.B.A., 2005). *Member:* Chicago and DuPage County Bar Associations. ***PRACTICE AREAS:*** Business Law; Corporate Law; Real Estate; Taxation; Estate and Gift Taxation; Trusts and Estates; Estate Planning; Living Trusts; Financial Planning; Wealth Preservation; Contracts.

LAW OFFICES OF STEVEN I. RAPAPORT

DEERFIELD, ILLINOIS

(See Northbrook)

Workers Compensation, Personal Injury, Automobile Accidents, Construction Accidents, Criminal Law, Traffic Violations, DWI, Insurance, Legal Malpractice, Estate Planning.

BOYLE, CORDES, WITHEFT & BROWN, LLC

Established in 1934
301 EAST LINCOLN HIGHWAY
DEKALB, ILLINOIS 60115-3307
Telephone: 815-756-6328
Fax: 815-756-8842
URL: http://www.boylelawdekalb.com
URL: http://www.bcwblaw.com

General Civil Trial Practice in State and Federal Courts. Probate, Corporate, Trust and Estate Planning, Real Estate, Zoning and Planning, Secured Lending.

FIRM PROFILE: Boyle, Cordes, Witheft & Brown was founded by John G. Boyle in 1934 and is listed in the Bar Register of Preeminent Lawyers serving clients in De Kalb, Ogle and Kane Counties, engaging in a focus in Estate Planning, Probate and Real Estate.

MEMBERS OF FIRM

JOHN G. BOYLE (1907-1996)

GARY W. CORDES, born Eldora, Iowa, August 14, 1933; admitted to bar, 1962, Iowa and Illinois. *Education:* State University of Iowa (B.S.C., 1959; J.D., 1962). *Member:* Illinois State and American Bar Associations. ***PRACTICE AREAS:*** Probate Law; Real Estate Law; Zoning and Planning Law. ***Email:*** gcordes@boylelawdekalb.com

CHARLES G. BROWN, born DeKalb, Illinois, November 21, 1951; admitted to bar, 1976, Illinois; 1980, U.S. District Court, Northern District of Illinois. *Education:* University of Illinois (B.S., 1973); Loyola University (J.D., 1976). Associate Editor, Law Review, 1976. Law Clerk to Hon. Thomas J. Moran, Justice of the Illinois Supreme Court, 1976-1978. Co-Author: "Declaratory Relief" and "Motions, Requests and Notices Immediately Prior to and on the Eve of Trial," Illinois Civil Practice, Volume II (II Inst. for CLE, 1991). President, DeKalb County Estate Planning Council, 1999-2000. *Member:* DeKalb County (President, 1995-1996), Kane County (Member, Probate and Estate Committee), Illinois State (Member: Committee on Character and Fitness of the Illinois Supreme Court, 1990-1997 and Vice Chairman, 1996-1997; Trusts and Estates Section Council, 1994-1999; Editor, Trust and Estates Newsletter, 1997-1999; Assembly Representative, 1990-1994) and American Bar Associations; Illinois Township Attorneys Association; American Agricultural Law Association. ***PRACTICE AREAS:*** Trust and Estate Litigation; Estate Planning and Probate; Real Estate Law; Eminent Domain. ***Email:*** cbrown@boylelawdekalb.com

DAVID J. WITHEFT, born New London, Connecticut, August 29, 1945; admitted to bar, 1971, Illinois; 1986, North Carolina; 2000, Illinois. *Education:* Northern Illinois University (B.A., with honors, 1967); University of Illinois (J.D., 1970). Phi Alpha Delta. Listed in The Best Lawyers in America, Narfeh and Smith, 1995—. Lecturer or Co-Course Planner, North Carolina Bar Foundation Seminars, 1993, 1994 and 1996. *Member:* Illinois State Bar Association; North Carolina Bar Association (Member: Real Property Section Council, 1994-1997; Real Property Curriculum Committee, 1992-2000); North Carolina State Bar (Member, Real Property Specialization Committee; Committee Chairman, 1995-2000). American College of Real Estate Lawyers. (Board Certified Specialist in Real Property Law-Business, Commercial and Industrial Transactions, North Carolina State Board of Legal Specialization). ***PRACTICE AREAS:*** Real Estate Law; Secured Transactions; Secured Lending. ***Email:*** dwitheft@boylelawdekalb.com

REPRESENTATIVE CLIENTS: Castle Bank, N.A.; National Bank and Trust Company of Sycamore; De Kalb Park District; LNB National Bank; Sycamore Township; De Kalb Community Fire Protection District; Eagle Homes, Inc.; Dekalb County Building and Development Association; The Mecom Corporation; Rivermist Development Corporation; The Northern Trust Company.
REFERENCES: Castle Bank, N.A.; National Bank and Trust Company of Sycamore.

CLIFFE, FOSTER, CORNEILLE, BUICK & BUICK, LLC

151 WEST LINCOLN HIGHWAY
DEKALB, ILLINOIS 60115
Telephone: 815-758-6616
URL: http://www.cfcbb.com

Sycamore, Illinois Office: 331 West State Street. Telephone: 815-895-7411.
Shabbona, Illinois Office: 110 West Comanche. Telephone: 815-824-2258.
Waterman, Illinois Office: 200 West Lincoln. Telephone: 815-264-3340.
Hinckley, Illinois Office: 165 Lincoln. Telephone: 815-286-3501.

General Civil and Criminal Practice. Probate, Real Estate, Family Law, Municipal Law, Business and Estate Planning, Commercial Law, Personal Injury, Insurance and Corporation Law. Practice in all State and Federal Courts, including Federal Trial Practice.

MEMBERS OF FIRM

KEITH L. FOSTER, born Aurora, Illinois, April 2, 1950; admitted to bar, 1979, Illinois and U.S. District Court, Northern District of Illinois. *Education:* Northern Illinois University (B.A., 1974); Illinois Institute of Technology (J.D., with high honors, 1979). ***Email:*** k-foster@cfcbb.com

KEVIN E. BUICK, born Merced, California, March 25, 1964; admitted to bar, 1990, Illinois and U.S. District Court, Northern District of Illinois. *Education:* University of Colorado (B.A., 1987); Northern Illinois University (J.D., 1990). (Resident, Sycamore Office). ***SPECIAL AGENCIES:*** Alternate Zoning Hearing Officer, DeKalb County. ***Email:*** k-buick@cfcbb.com

MARCY L. BUICK, born Lincoln, Illinois, April 24, 1964; admitted to bar, 1990, Illinois and U.S. District Court, Northern District of Illinois. *Education:* University of Illinois (B.S., 1986); Northern Illinois University (J.D., 1990). (Resident, Sycamore Office). ***Email:*** m-buick@cfcbb.com

(This Listing Continued)

ASSOCIATE

HEATHER M. FRITSCH, born DeKalb, Illinois, March 19, 1975; admitted to bar, 2000, Illinois; 2001, U.S. District Court, Northern District of Illinois. *Education:* University of Illinois, Urbana-Champaign (B.A., English, with distinction, 1997); Chicago-Kent College of Law (J.D., 2000). **Email:** h-fritsch@cfcbb.com

CHARLES E. CRONAUER

DEKALB, ILLINOIS

(See Sycamore)

General Civil Trial and Appellate Practice in State and Federal Courts. Real Estate, Zoning Planning, Land Use, Business, Corporation, Commercial, Probate, Estate Planning, Trust, Personal Injury, Products Liability, Workers Compensation, Insurance, and National and International Franchising and Agricultural Law, Elder Law, Business Law, Environmental Law.

POLLOCK, MEYERS, EICKSTEADT & PULAK, LTD.

DEKALB, ILLINOIS

(See Marengo)

General Trial Practice, Appellate Practice, Estate Planning, Probate Law, Trust Law, Real Estate, Banking Law, Bankruptcy Law, Personal Injury, Workers Compensation, Administrative Law, Corporate Law, Contracts, Civil Litigation, Trusts and Estates, Real Estate Law.

THOMPSON, LAMONT, FLAHERTY & MASUR

A PROFESSIONAL CORPORATION

DEKALB, ILLINOIS

(See Aurora)

Practice limited to Personal Injury Litigation, including General Negligence, Automobile Accidents, Medical Malpractice, Product Liability, Wrongful Death and Workers Compensation, Transportation, Negligence, Slip and Fall, Dog Bites, Sexual Abuse. Serving all clients in DuPage, Kane, Kendall, DeKalb, Will and Cook Counties.

THE LAW OFFICES OF MARC L. BROWN

DES PLAINES, ILLINOIS

(See Park Ridge)

Elder Law, Real Estate, Trusts and Estates, Wills, Probate, Living Trusts, Guardianship, Nursing Home Abuse and Neglect, Health Care.

CIRIGNANI HELLER HARMAN & LYNCH LLP

DES PLAINES, ILLINOIS

(See Chicago)

Medical Malpractice, Wrongful Death, Cerebral Palsy, ERBS Palsy, Brain Damage, Anesthesia Injury, Improper Medication, Operating Room Death, Misdiagnosis, Birth Injuries, Retardation, Surgical Error, Medical Product Failure, Nursing Errors, Hospital Negligence, Head and Spinal Injuries, Automobile Accidents, Truck Accidents, Construction Accidents, Product Liability, Labor and Employment Litigation, Commercial Litigation, Insurance Coverage, Torts. Litigation.

CUTLER & ASSOCIATES, LTD.

DES PLAINES, ILLINOIS

(See Skokie)

Bankruptcy, Consumer Bankruptcy, Bankruptcy Chapter 7, Foreclosures, Small Business, Buying and Selling of Businesses, Family Business, Limited Liability, Partnership, Corporate, Contract, Breach of Contract, General Practice, Debtor and Creditor, Collections, Creditors, Rights and Civil Litigation.

THE LAW OFFICES OF ANTHONY B. FERRARO

DES PLAINES, ILLINOIS

(See Rosemont)

Wills, Trusts, Estates, Estate Planning, Estate Taxation, Probate and Trust Administration, Medicaid, Guardianship, Elder Law, and Trust and Estate-Related Commercial Transactions including Business Acquisitions and Real Estate, Commercial Arbitration.

LAW OFFICES OF DAVID H. LOCKS

DES PLAINES, ILLINOIS

(See Chicago)

Contested Wills, Trusts and Estates, Real Estate Transactions and Litigation, Mechanics Liens, Encroachments, Business and Commercial Transactions and Litigation and Insurance Coverage.

PTASINSKI & SMITH, P.C.

DES PLAINES, ILLINOIS

(See Niles)

Probate, Estate Planning and Administration, Trusts and Estates, Wills, Elder Law, Real Estate, Business Law, Divorce.

SEIDMAN LAW OFFICES

DES PLAINES, ILLINOIS

(See Chicago)

Insurance Defense; Corporate Litigation; Workers Compensation.

JAY A. SLUTZKY

DES PLAINES, ILLINOIS

(See Niles)

Wills, Living Trusts, Estate Planning, Residential Real Estate, Commercial Real Estate, Divorce, Personal Injury, Bankruptcy Law, Elder Law, DUI, DWI, Business Law, Commercial Law, Commercial Litigation, Business Organization, Business Transactions, Business Counseling, Business Advice, Real Estate Law, Real Estate Litigation, Commercial Transactions, Contracts, Construction Law, Litigation, Motor Vehicle Accidents, Personal Injury Defense, Plaintiffs Personal Injury, Probate, Estate Administration, Trusts, By-Pass Trusts, Credit Shelter Trusts, Special Needs Trusts, Testamentary Trusts, Ancillar Administration, Durable Powers of Attorney, Medical Powers of Attorney, Living Wills, Pour-Over Wills, Marital Deduction Trusts, Beneficiary Designations, Irrevocable Life Insurance Trusts, Split Dollar Purchase Agreements, Crummey Trusts, Workers Compensation, Civil Litigation, Criminal Defense, Pre-Marital Agreements, Planning for Disabled Spouses, Planning for Disabled Children, Estate Tax Return Preparation, Second Marriage Issues, Contested Wills and Trusts, Partnerships, Corporations, Limited Liability Companies.

TUTTLE, VEDRAL & COLLINS PC

Established in 1970

733 LEE STREET, SUITE 210
DES PLAINES, ILLINOIS 60016
Telephone: 847-824-0124
Fax: 847-824-7905
URL: http://www.tvclaw.com

Residential and Commercial Real Estate, Foreclosures, Banking Law, Trust and Estate Planning, Probate, Family Law, Divorce, Equitable Distribution, Corporate Law.

MILTON H. TUTTLE (Retired)

BARRY G. COLLINS, admitted to bar, 1967, Illinois. *Education:* Lawrence University (B.A., 1964); Northwestern University (J.D., 1967). *Member:* Chicago and Illinois State Bar Associations. ***PRACTICE AREAS:*** Real Estate; Probate; Estate Planning; Business Law; Limited Liability Company Law; Corporate Law.

WILLIAM D. VEDRAL, admitted to bar, 1968, Illinois. *Education:* University of Illinois at Champaign (B.A., 1965; J.D., 1968). *Member:* Chicago and Illinois State and Northwestern Suburban Bar Associations. ***PRACTICE AREAS:*** Real Estate; Buying and Selling a Home; Probate; Trust Law; Civil Litigation.

THOMAS YOUNG LAW FIRM

DES PLAINES, ILLINOIS

(See Palatine)

DIXON & GIESEN

Established in 1869

121 EAST FIRST STREET
P.O. BOX 389
DIXON, ILLINOIS 61021
Telephone: 815-284-2288
Fax: 815-284-1338
Email: lag@hsdixonlaw.com
URL: http://www.hsdixonlaw.com

General Civil, Criminal Trial and Appellate Practice in all State and Federal Courts. Banking, Corporation, Insurance, Workers Compensation and Family Law. Personal Injury. Probate and Estate Planning, Municipal and Environmental Law.

FIRM PROFILE: Dixon & Giesen descend directly from the Law Office of Eustace, Barge & Dixon, which firm dates to 1861. The law firm has operated from the same location at 121 East First Street in Dixon since 1861 although the first building there has been replaced with the present structure. Since this firm's inception, there has always been at least one member of the Dixon family as a firm partner at all times.

HENRY S. DIXON, born Dixon, Illinois, May 19, 1934; admitted to bar, 1963, Illinois. *Education:* University of Notre Dame (B.A., 1956); John Marshall Law School (J.D., 1963). Nu Beta Epsilon. U.S. Army Command & General Staff College, Ft. Leavenworth, KS; U.S. Army War College, Carlisle, Pennsylvania. Assistant Attorney General, 1963-1964. Lee County States Attorney, 1965-1968. *Member:* Lee County (Secretary-Treasurer, 1969-1973; President, 1974-1975; Vice-President, 1973-1974), Ogle County, Whiteside County, Winnebago County, Illinois State and American Bar Associations; Illinois Trial Lawyers Association (Member, Board of Managers, 1985-1989). ***REPORTED CASES:***

(This Listing Continued)

DIXON & GIESEN, Dixon—Continued

Home Federal Savings & Loan v. Burke, (1990) 3-88-0103; Kinkin v. Marchesi, (1992) 3-92-0009; Nauman v. McCaffrey, (1994) 2-94-21; Birdsley Trucking v. Industrial Commission (Philhower), (1990) 3-89-218 WC.; McCaffrey v. Nauman, (1993) 2-92-480; Hahnamann Albrecht Stebbins, 3-95-0785; Diana Johnson v. County of Lee, 2-96-0942; Priscilla Reuter v. Edward Reuter, 2-96-0281; People v. Alan Walker, 3-97-0206; Brills v. Amboy Fire Protection, 3-97-0391; IRM: Molln 3-98-0340; LaShelle v. LaShelle, 2-98-1360. ***PRACTICE AREAS:*** General Civil Law; Criminal Trial and Appellate Practice in all State and Federal Courts; Banking Law; Corporation Law; Insurance Law; Workers Compensation Law; Family Law; Personal Injury Law; Probate Law; Estate Planning Law; Municipal Law. ***Email:*** sc@hsdixonlaw.com

LINDA A. GIESEN, born Minneapolis, Minnesota, November 28, 1951; admitted to bar, 1991, Illinois. *Education:* Southern Illinois University (B.A., 1973); Indiana State University (M.S., 1974); University of Iowa (J.D., 1991). Phi Kappa Phi. Assistant Professor of Criminal Justice, Sauk Valley Community College, 1986-1992. Dixon Park Board Commissioner, 1987-1989. President, Dixon United Way Board, 1997-1998. Member, Dixon Rotary. Member, Dixon Family YMCA Board. Lee County State's Attorney, 2000-2004. *Member:* Lee Ogle County, Illinois State and American Bar Associations; American Association of University Women (President, 1994-1997). ***PRACTICE AREAS:*** Family Law; Personal Injury; Workers Compensation; Estate Planning; Probate; Corporate Law. ***Email:*** lag@hsdixonlaw.com

HENRY SHERWOOD DIXON, JR., born Dixon, Illinois, July 15, 1967; admitted to bar, 1997, Illinois. *Education:* University of Illinois (B.S., 1990); John Marshall Law School (J.D., 1997). *Member:* Lee County and Illinois State Bar Associations. ***PRACTICE AREAS:*** Civil Practice; Corporate Law; Family Law; Personal Injury; Probate; Estate Planning; Appellate Practice. ***Email:*** hsdii@hsdixonlaw.com

EHRMANN GEHLBACH BADGER & LEE

COMMERCE TOWERS
SUITE 100
215 E. FIRST STREET
DIXON, ILLINOIS 61021
Telephone: 815-288-4949
Fax: 815-288-3068
URL: http://www.egbbl.com

Criminal and Civil Litigation. Personal Injury, Corporate, Family, Insurance Defense, Real Estate, Estate Planning, Banking, Probate Law, Bankruptcy/Creditor's Rights Law and Worker's Compensation.

MEMBERS OF FIRM

ROLFE F. EHRMANN, born 1949; admitted to bar, 1975, Illinois; 1980, U.S. Supreme Court. *Education:* Northeastern Illinois University (B.A., with honors, 1971); DePaul University (J.D., 1975). Law Clerk to Justice Eberspacher, Illinois Appellate Court, 1976-1978. ***REPORTED CASES:*** Peo v. Ortiz (1992), 151 Ill.2d 1; In re Marriage of Perino (1992), 224 Ill.App.3d 605. ***PRACTICE AREAS:*** Family Law; Criminal Law. ***Email:*** ehrmann@egbbl.com

GARY R. GEHLBACH, born Lincoln, Illinois, March 8, 1949; admitted to bar, 1978, Illinois. *Education:* Knox College (B.A., 1971); Chicago-Kent College of Law (J.D., with high honors, 1978). *Member:* Lee County, Illinois State (Member of Council, Real Estate Section, 1985—; Chair, 1994-1995; Editor, "Real Property" Newsletter) and American Bar Associations. ***PRACTICE AREAS:*** Real Estate Law; Probate Law; Estate Planning Law; Business Law. ***Email:*** gehlbach@egbbl.com

DAVID W. BADGER, born Dixon, Illinois, August 13, 1954; admitted to bar, 1979, Illinois and U.S. District Court, Northern District of Illinois. *Education:* Millikin University (B.A., summa cum laude, 1976); University of Illinois (J.D., 1979). Phi Kappa Phi; Phi Alpha Delta. Harno Fellow. *Member:* Lee County, Illinois State and American Bar Associations. ***PRACTICE AREAS:*** Estate Planning; Real Estate; Probate; Trusts; Taxation. ***Email:*** badger@egbbl.com

DOUGLAS E. LEE, born 1962; admitted to bar, 1987, Virginia; 1991, Illinois. *Education:* University of Illinois (B.A., 1984); Northwestern University (J.D., 1987). Order of the Coif. Author: "Sealed Documents, Closed Hearings, and the Public's Right to Know," Illinois Bar Journal, September 1993. *Member:* Virginia State Bar. (Managing Partner). ***REPORTED CASES:*** USF&G v. Open Sesame Child Care Center, 819 F. Supp. 756 (N.D. Ill. 1993). ***PRACTICE AREAS:*** Commercial and Civil Litigation; Employment Law. ***Email:*** lee@egbbl.com

WARREN H. BADGER (1911-2005)

ASSOCIATES

MEGAN G. HEEG, born Oak Park, Illinois, May 18, 1956; admitted to bar, 1990, Illinois. *Education:* Rockford College (B.S., 1979); Northern Illinois University (J.D., magna cum laude, 1990). Lead Articles Editor, Northern Illinois University Law Review, 1989-1990. *Member:* Lee County, Illinois State and American Bar Associations. ***PRACTICE AREAS:*** Civil Litigation; Family Law. ***Email:*** heeg@egbbl.com

DANA M. CONSIDINE, born Mendota, Illinois, January 23, 1979; admitted to bar, 2003, Illinois. *Education:* Western Illinois University (B.B., 2000); Drake University (J.D., 2003). Delta Theta Phi; Drake Law Women. *Member:* Lee County, Illinois State and American Bar Associations. ***PRACTICE AREAS:*** Collections; Workers Compensation; Real Estate; Family Law. ***Email:*** considine@egbbl.com

REPRESENTATIVE CLIENTS: AMCORE Bank N.A., Dixon; Bradford Mutual Insurance Co.

MARY L. COLLINS

6912 S. MAIN STREET, SUITE 200
DOWNERS GROVE, ILLINOIS 60516
Telephone: 630-969-3903
Fax: 630-969-3931
URL: http://www.marycollinsdisabilitylaw.com
URL: http://www.collinsdisabilitylaw.com

Social Security Disability, Real Estate, Wills, Medicare, Medicaid, Elder Law.

MARY L. COLLINS, born Milwaukee, Wisconsin, April 24, 1955; admitted to bar, 1980, Wisconsin; 1987, Illinois. *Education:* University of Wisconsin-Madison (B.A., 1977); Marquette University (J.D., 1980). *Member:* National Organization of Social Security Representatives. ***PRACTICE AREAS:*** Social Security Disability; Real Estate; Wills; Medicare and Medicaid; Elder Law.

NANCY FALLON-HOULE, P.C.

5449 BENDING OAKS PLACE
DOWNERS GROVE, ILLINOIS 60515-4456
Telephone: 630-963-0439
URL: http://www.nfhlaw.com
Email: nfallon@nfhlaw.com
URL: http://www.lawyers.com/nfallon

Entrepreneur, Entrepreneurship, Starting a Business, Incorporation, Corporation, Corporations, Limited Liability Company, Limited Liability Companies, LLC, Entity, Partnership, Partnerships, Business Enterprises, Start-Up, Start Up, Early Stage, Early-Stage, Small Business, Business, Emerging Growth, Emerging Company, Corporate, Corporate Law, Corporate Lawyer.
Venture Capital, Raising Capital, Investor, Investing, Angel Investor, Seed Capital, Regulation D, Form D, Rule 506, Rule 504, SCOR, U-7, Form U-7, Business Plan, Business Planning, Disclosure, Due Diligence, Securities Disclosure, Private Placement, Private Offering, Private Offering Memo, Private Offering Memorandum, Private Placement Memo, Private Placement Memorandum, PPM, Subscription Agreement, Investor Agreement, Equity, Equity Financing, Financing, Stock, Shares, Stock Option, Option, Options, Warrants, Stock Offering, Securities Law, Securities Offering, Securities Exemption, Exemption, Exempt Offering, SEC, Securities and Exchange Commission, Securities Registration, Securities Regulation, Registration, Compliance, Reg D, Blue Sky, Blue Sky Law, State Securities, State Securities Law, State Registration, Federal Securities, Regulation A, Regulation SB, IPO, NASDAQ, Securities Lawyer, Securities and Investments.
Investment Adviser, Investment Advisor, Financial planner, Financial Planning, IARD, ADV, Form ADV, WebCRD, CRD, NASD, Finder, Money Finder, Private Placement Broker, NFA, Managed Funds, Hedge Fund, Trading Fund, Securities Fund, Futures Fund, Commodities Fund, Commodity Trading Advisor, CTA, Commodity Pool, CPO, Futures, Fund, Funds, CFTC, Disclosure Document, Compliance Audits, Regulatory Audits.
Business Law, Business Lawyer, Contract, Contracts, Agreement, Stockholder, Shareholder; Shareholder Agreement, Stockholder Agreement, LLC Agreement, Operating Agreement, Executive Agreement, Stock Option Agreement, Nondisclosure Agreement, Confidentiality Agreement, Closely-held, Closely held, Closely Held Businesses, Officers, Directors, Resolutions, Minute Book, Stock Ledger, Corporate Maintenance, Qualification, State Qualification, Business License, Annual Report.
Venture, Joint Venture, Joint Ventures, Strategic Alliance, Strategic Alliances, Film Financing.

FIRM PROFILE: We are a boutique Corporate Law, Securities Law, Futures Law, and Business Law firm, practicing in the niche legal areas described on our firm's website: www.nfhlaw.com. We focus in eight narrow areas of law, in depth in those areas.

We are located in west-suburban Chicago, and are connected to, and represent clients in, the entrepreneurial and trading communities in downtown Chicago, suburban Chicago, and on both U.S. coasts. Our firm was formed in 1998. The founding attorney has been practicing securities and corporate law for 16 years, including 12 years at a large national law firm, Katten Muchin & Zavis.

We created the long buzz-word list above to ensure that your Internet search would readily find us. We included words that you might use in your search: Not only words covering subject matters in which we practice, but also words describing the types of documents we prepare, transactions we handle, securities & corporate filings we make, and government agencies with which we file.

If your search term hit this page, chances are we do the type of legal work you seek. If not, we will refer you to someone who does. Now that you've found us, please visit our firm's website: www.nfhlaw.com, for the specifics of our practice areas. Our firm site provides links to full biographies, related sites, and complimentary summaries of corporate law and securities law information that we've prepared for prospective clients. Info: nfallon@nfhlaw.com.

NANCY FALLON-HOULE, born Indiana, 1956; admitted to bar, 1986, Illinois. *Education:* Roosevelt University (B.S., Accounting, with high honors, 1982); Chicago-Kent College of Law, Illinois Institute of Technology (J.D., 1986). Beta Gamma Sigma. *Member:* Chicago, DuPage, Illinois State (Member, Section Council on Corporate, Securities and Business Law) and American (Member: Small Business Committee; Federal Regulation of Securities Committee) Bar Associations. ***Email:*** nfallon@nfhlaw.com

RICHARD L. HIRSH & ASSOCIATES, P.C.

DOWNERS GROVE, ILLINOIS

(See Hinsdale)

Bankruptcy, Personal Bankruptcy, Debtor and Creditor, Foreclosures and Buy-Sell Agreements.

McJOYNT & KRISTUFEK, P.C.

1131 WARREN AVENUE
DOWNERS GROVE, ILLINOIS 60515
Telephone: 630-971-0100
Fax: 630-960-0263
URL: http://www.mcjoyntlaw.com
URL: http://www.mcjoyntkristufek.com

General Civil Practice, Litigation, Criminal, Matrimonial, DUI, Real Estate, Probate, Estate Planning, Corporate and Transactional and Small Business Law.

FIRM PROFILE: The Law Offices is equipped to handle your matter. Attorneys in the firm are former state's attorneys with vast experience in criminal, juvenile and traffic matters. Whether it be obtaining adequate compensation from a personal injury case or advance planning to provide smooth transfer of assets upon the death of family member involving estates, the attorneys of the firm are prepared. Protecting your real estate interests, family law concerns and commercial law issues is additionally handled with our utmost diligence.

TIMOTHY J. McJOYNT, born Aurora, Illinois, August 4, 1951; admitted to bar, 1977, Illinois and U.S. District Court, Northern District of Illinois including Trial Bar. *Education:* Western Illinois University (B.S., 1973); John Marshall Law School (J.D., 1977). Chairman, Downers Grove Township Youth Commission, 1985. Chairman, Director and General Counsel, Downers Grove Chamber of Commerce, 1988-2001. Attorney, Downers Grove Downtown Management Company, 1999—. Member, District 99 Foundation and District 58 Foundation. President, Grove Foundation, 1997—. *Member:* Chicago, DuPage County (Chairman: Real Estate Law and Practice Committee, 1985-1986, 2000-2001; Director, 1988-1991) and Illinois State (Delegate to the Assembly, 1984-1990 and 1992-1998) Bar Associations; DuPage County Criminal Defense Attorneys Association; Attorneys' Title Guaranty Fund, Inc. Fellow: Illinois Bar Foundation (Life Member). (Managing Partner). ***PRACTICE AREAS:*** Buying and Selling of Businesses; Family Business Law; Limited Liability Company Law; Partnership Law; Professional Practices; Small Business Law; Breach of Contract; Adoptions; Child Custody; Child Support; Divorce; Domestic Violence; Premarital Agreements; Spousal Support; Commercial Real Estate; Condominium Law; Landlord and Tenant Law; Mortgages; Asset Protection; Charitable Giving; Estate Litigation; Estate Planning; Guardianship and Conservatorship; Contested Wills; Zoning, Planning and Land Use. ***Email:*** legal@mcjoyntlaw.com

LYNNE KRISTUFEK, born Erie, Pennsylvania, September 18, 1950; admitted to bar, 1989, Illinois. *Education:* Southern Illinois University (B.S., 1986); John Marshall Law School (J.D., 1989). *Member:* DuPage County and Illinois State Bar Associations; DuPage Criminal Defense Bar Association. ***PRACTICE AREAS:*** Driving While Intoxicated; Drug Crimes; Felonies; Juvenile Law; Misdemeanors; Sexual Assault; Traffic Violations; Adoptions; Child Custody; Child Support; Divorce; Domestic Violence; Premarital Agreements; Spousal Support; Landlord and Tenant Law; Mortgages; Residential Real Estate. ***Email:*** 1.kristufek@mcjoyntlaw.com

---

MARY COX COFFEY, born Oak Brook, Illinois; admitted to bar, 1990, Illinois. *Education:* Woodlands Academy of the Sacred Heart, Lake Forest; St. Mary's College (B.B.A. and B.A. in Spanish); University of Valencia, Spain; John Marshall Law School (J.D., 1990). Member, Law Review, John Marshall Law School. Intern, DuPage County State's Attorney's Office, Civil Division. *Member:* DuPage County Bar Association. ***PRACTICE AREAS:*** Real Estate.

MOMKUS McCLUSKEY MOLTZEN MONROE MARSH & SPYRATOS, LLC

Established in 1990
3051 OAK GROVE ROAD, SUITE 220
DOWNERS GROVE, ILLINOIS 60515
Telephone: 630-434-0400
Fax: 630-434-0444
URL: http://www.momlaw.com

Chicago, Illinois Office: 33 North LaSalle Street, 34th Floor, 60606. Telephone: 312-279-1940. Fax: 312-279-1941.

General Civil Practice, Corporate Practice with particular expertise in Corporate and Transactional Law, Civil Litigation, Commercial Litigation, Product Liability Defense, Insurance Defense and Coverage, Personal Injury and Property Damage, Appeals, Mediation, Arbitration, Commercial and Residential Real Estate, Tax-Based Transactions, Employment Law, Environmental Law, Construction, Collections, Financing, Estate Planning, Catastrophic Injuries, Intellectual Property and Covenants Not to Compete, Premises Liability, Injunctive Remedies, and Real Property Owner Disputes.

FIRM PROFILE: MOMKUS McCLUSKEY MOLTZEN MONROE MARSH & SPYRATOS, LLC is a law firm dedicated to serving the business law and litigation needs of corporate and insurance clients, large and small. Established in 1990, we have offices in both DuPage County and downtown Chicago, Illinois. Our firm's mission is to provide clients with high quality legal service at reasonable fees through efficient operation. We believe in a close relationship with our clients with frequent communication aimed at developing a "team approach" between lawyer and client. In addition to getting results for our clients in litigation, we strive to prevent legal problems and disputes through advance planning and counseling.

Our local trial practice covers all Courts, State and Federal, in the greater Chicago area. This includes DuPage, Cook, Kane, Will, Lake and Winnebago Counties. We also cover matters pending in other courthouses in Northern and Central Illinois.

Our transactional practice covers a wide range of sophisticated matters for a variety of national and international companies and includes mergers and acquisitions, business succession planning, financing and other matters affecing business.

(This Listing Continued)

The firm is fully computerized for billing, legal research, case management and document retrieval. Our state-of-the-art resources enable the delivery of legal services to our clients promptly at a reasonable cost.

For more information visit our website at http://www.momlaw.com.

MEMBERS OF FIRM

EDWARD J. MOMKUS, born Chicago, Illinois, November 11, 1953; admitted to bar, 1977, Illinois; 1978, Ohio. *Education:* Elmhurst College (B.A., summa cum laude, 1974); Northwestern University (J.D., 1977). ***PRACTICE AREAS:*** Business Transactions; Business Acquisitions; Business Reorganizations; Corporate Law; Real Estate; Contracts; Estate Planning; Product Liability Defense. ***Email:*** emomkus@momlaw.com

JAMES F. McCLUSKEY, born Oak Park, Illinois, February 10, 1954; admitted to bar, 1979, Illinois and U.S. District Court, Central District of Illinois; U.S. Court of Appeals, Seventh Circuit and U.S. District Court, Northern District of Illinois including Trial Bar. *Education:* Triton College (A.A., 1974); Elmhurst College (B.S., 1976); Northern Illinois University (J.D., 1979); John Marshall Law School (LL.M., 1988). ***PRACTICE AREAS:*** Insurance Defense Trial Litigation; Commercial Litigation; General Civil Litigation; Professional Liability. ***Email:*** jfmccluskey@momlaw.com

MARK W. MONROE, born New Brunswick, New Jersey, August 17, 1955; admitted to bar, 1986, Illinois, U.S. District Court, Northern and Central Districts of Illinois including Trial Bar and U.S. Court of Appeals, Seventh Circuit. *Education:* University of Dayton; Trenton State College (B.S., 1977); Northern Illinois University (J.D., summa cum laude, 1986). ***PRACTICE AREAS:*** Insurance Coverage; Commercial Litigation; Insurance Litigation; Defense Litigation; Appeals; General Civil Litigation; Professional Liability. ***Email:*** mmonroe@momlaw.com

JAMES P. MARSH, born Elk Grove Village, Illinois, May 29, 1961; admitted to bar, 1988, Illinois and U.S. District Court, Northern District of Illinois. *Education:* Eastern Illinois University (B.A., 1983); John Marshall Law School (J.D., 1988). ***PRACTICE AREAS:*** Insurance Defense Litigation; Professional Liability Defense; Products Liability; Appeals; Insurance Coverage. ***Email:*** jmarsh@momlaw.com

JOHN D. PURDY, JR., born Chicago, Illinois, February 13, 1941; admitted to bar, 1966, Illinois and U.S. District Court, Northern District of Illinois. *Education:* Yale University (B.A., 1963); University of Chicago (J.D., 1966). ***PRACTICE AREAS:*** Real Estate; Corporate Law; Business Law. ***Email:*** jdpurdy@momlaw.com

E. ANGELO SPYRATOS, born Athens, Greece, January 26, 1966; admitted to bar, 1991, Illinois and U.S. District Court, Northern and Central Districts of Illinois. *Education:* Elmhurst College (B.A., 1988); Valparaiso University (J.D., 1991). ***PRACTICE AREAS:*** Insurance Defense; Civil Litigation; Personal Injury. ***Email:*** aspyratos@momlaw.com

KIMBERLY A. DAVIS, born Chicago, Illinois, November 12, 1965; admitted to bar, 1997, Illinois. *Education:* Morton College (A.A., 1985); Southern Illinois University (B.S., 1987); Chicago-Kent College of Law (J.D., with honors, 1997). ***PRACTICE AREAS:*** Insurance Defense Litigation; Plaintiffs Bodily Injury Litigation; Subrogation. ***Email:*** kdavis@momlaw.com

STEVEN B. EKKER, born Sharon, Pennsylvania, September 5, 1966; admitted to bar, 1993, Illinois and U.S. District Court, Northern District of Illinois. *Education:* University of Michigan (B.A., 1989); Northern Illinois University (J.D., cum laude, 1993). ***PRACTICE AREAS:*** Insurance Defense Litigation; Personal Injury; Commercial Litigation; Real Estate. ***Email:*** sekker@momlaw.com

OF COUNSEL

MARY CAFFREY MORRISSY, born Chicago, Illinois, April 1, 1951; admitted to bar, 1977, Illinois. *Education:* Webster College (B.A., cum laude, 1973); St. Louis University (M.A., History, 1974); Washington University (J.D., 1977). ***PRACTICE AREAS:*** Real Estate Law; Contract Law. ***Email:*** mmorrissy@momlaw.com

CRAIG S. STEVENS, born Tryon, North Carolina, April 21, 1947; admitted to bar, 1974, Indiana; 1992, Illinois. *Education:* Indiana University (B.S., 1969; J.D., 1974). ***PRACTICE AREAS:*** Mergers, Acquisitions and Divestitures; Contracts; Business Transactions; Corporate Organization; Intellectual Property. ***Email:*** cstevens@momlaw.com

HEATHER L. GENCK, born 1971; admitted to bar, 1997, Illinois and U.S. District Court, Northern and Central Districts of Illinois. *Education:* Purdue University (B.A., Secondary Education and French, 1993); John Marshall Law School (J.D., 1997; LL.M. Taxation, 2000). ***PRACTICE AREAS:*** Civil Litigation; Commercial Litigation; Mechanics Liens; Collections; Premises Liability. ***Email:*** hgenck@momlaw.com

ASSOCIATES

LORI N. CARROZZA, born El Paso, Texas, February 18, 1977; admitted to bar, 2002, Illinois. *Education:* University of Illinois in Champaign (B.A., Political Science, 1999); St. Louis University School of Law (J.D., 2002). ***PRACTICE AREAS:*** Insurance Defense; Premises Liability; Business Law; Corporate Law. ***Email:*** lcarrozza@momlaw.com

NEIL T. GOLTERMANN, born Maracaibo, Venezuela, August 15, 1955; admitted to bar, 1980, Illinois and U.S. District Court, Northern District of Illinois; 1981, U.S. Court of Appeals, Seventh Circuit; 1988, U.S. Supreme Court; 1994, U.S. District Court, Northern District of Texas; 1996, U.S. District Court, Central District of Illinois. *Education:* DePauw University (B.A., 1977); DePaul University (J.D., 1980). ***PRACTICE AREAS:*** Business Transactions; Corporate Law; Real Estate; Estate Planning. ***Email:*** ngoltermann@momlaw.com

JAMES S. HARKNESS, born Des Moines, Iowa, January 7, 1971; admitted to bar, 1996, Illinois; 1997, U.S. District Court, Northern District of Illinois; 1999, U.S. Court of Appeals, Seventh Circuit and U.S. District Court, District of Colorado. *Education:* Valparaiso University (B.A., Political Science and Philosophy, 1993); Valparaiso University School of Law (J.D., 1996). ***PRACTICE AREAS:*** Employment Law; Commercial Litigation; Civil Litigation; Class Actions; Professional Liability. ***Email:*** jharkness@momlaw.com

(This Listing Continued)

MOMKUS McCLUSKEY MOLTZEN MONROE MARSH & SPYRATOS, LLC, Downers Grove—Continued

CHRISTOPHER MICHAEL LUNARDINI, born Chicago, Illinois, March 4, 1975; admitted to bar, 2000, Illinois. *Education:* DePaul University (B.A., Political Science, 1977); DePaul University College of Law (J.D., 2000). ***PRACTICE AREAS:*** Civil Litigation; Insurance Defense; Contract Litigation; Premises Liability; Mold Litigation; Personal Injury. ***Email:*** clunardini@momlaw.com

KAREN T. McDONNELL HILLIGOSS, born Oak Lawn, Illinois, September 7, 1971; admitted to bar, 1996, Illinois and U.S. District Court, Northern District of Illinois including Trial Bar. *Education:* University of Illinois (B.S., 1993); John Marshall Law School (J.D., cum laude, 1996). ***PRACTICE AREAS:*** Products Liability; Personal Injury; Truck Accidents; Construction Accidents; Catastrophic Injury; Wrongful Death; Employment Law; Business Law; Corporate Law. ***Email:*** khilligoss@momlaw.com

EDWARD R. PSENICKA, born Berwyn, Illinois, September 26, 1970; admitted to bar, 1998, Illinois. *Education:* Northern Illinois University (B.A., English, 1992); University of Illinois College of Law, Champaign (J.D., 1998). ***PRACTICE AREAS:*** Insurance Coverage; Insurance Defense. ***Email:*** epsenicka@momlaw.com

JAMES K. THEISEN, born Leyden Township, Illinois, December 7, 1970; admitted to bar, 2003, Illinois; 2004, Missouri. *Education:* Western Illinois University (B.S., Law Enforcement Administration, 1994); Southern Illinois University School of Law (J.D., 2002). ***PRACTICE AREAS:*** Insurance Defense; Subrogation; Plaintiffs Personal Injury. ***Email:*** jtheisen@momlaw.com

REPRESENTATIVE CLIENTS: Allied Signal, Inc.; American Family Mutual Insurance Co.; American Standard Insurance Co.; American States Insurance; Apropos Technologies, Inc.; Birdview Internet Properties, Inc.; Bituminous Insurance; Camcraft Corporation; Catholic Mutual Insurance Company; CNA Insurance Company; Crawford & Co.; Design Professional Insurance Corp.; Diversified Products Corp.; DuPage Airport Authority; Dynamic Staffing Network, Inc.; Electric Conduit Construction Company; Engineering Systems, Inc.; Famer's Insurance Companies; Federal Signal Corp.; Gallagher Bassett; Glenborough Realty Trust; Grinnell Mutual Reinsurance Group; Illinois State Medical Insurance Services, Inc.; Institutional Equipment Company; Insurance Company of Illinois; Jing Mei Industrial (USA) Inc.; KI Industries, Inc.; Krups North American Inc.; Liberty Mutual Insurance Co.; Lindy Manufacturing, Inc.; McCann Concrete Specialties, Inc.; Meadowbrook Insurance Group; Millennium Information Services, Inc.; Mionix Corporation; Monitor Liability Managers; National Union Fire Insurance; Oakley Steel Products Company; Pekin Insurance Company; Private Bank and Trust Company; Republic Western Insurance Co.; Schulstad USA, Inc.; Sedona Land Company; State Farm Insurance Company; Sunbeam Corporation; Sykora & Company, LLC; U-Haul International, Inc.; USAA; US Bank, N.A.; Vanguard Archives, Inc.; Wal-Mart Stores, Inc.; Zenith Electronics Corp.

WILLIAM C. NORTH

Established in 1985

947 MAPLE AVENUE
DOWNERS GROVE, ILLINOIS 60515-4930
Telephone: 630-960-1242
Fax: 630-960-3760
Email: williamnorth@wcnorth.com
URL: http://www.lawyers.com/williamnorth

Personal Injury, Automobile Accidents, Medical Malpractice, Business Litigation, Employment Law, Human Rights, Discrimination, Divorce.

WILLIAM C. NORTH, admitted to bar, 1971, Illinois; 1977, U.S. District Court, Northern District of Illinois including Trial Bar. *Education:* Ripon College (A.B., 1968); University of Illinois (J.D., 1971). Listed in Who's Who in American Law, 1995—. Assistant Attorney General, 1972. Public Defender, Cook County, Illinois, 1973-1976. Associate and Partner, Hultman, North & Wuttke, 1977-1984. Insurance Defense Attorney, Terrel & Flynn, 1984-1985. *Member:* DuPage County Bar Association (Member: Civil Law Committee, 1995-1998; Legal Aid Committee, 1998—); The Association of Trial Lawyers of America. ***PRACTICE AREAS:*** Personal Injury Law; Medical Malpractice; Civil Litigation; Family Law; Divorce; Business Litigation.

JOHN R. WIMMER

928 WARREN AVENUE
DOWNERS GROVE, ILLINOIS 60515
Telephone: 630-810-0005
Fax: 630-960-5852
Email: JWimmerLaw@aol.com
URL: http://www.johnwimmer.com

Trials and Appeals in all State and Federal Courts, Civil Rights, Discrimination, Criminal, Felonies and Misdemeanors, Juvenile, Personal Injury and Commercial Disputes.

JOHN R. WIMMER, born Gary, Indiana, December 28, 1954; admitted to bar, 1979, Illinois; 1981, U.S. District Court, Northern District of Illinois; 1987, U.S. Court of Appeals, Seventh Circuit; 1999, U.S. Supreme Court and U.S. District Court, District of Arizona. *Education:* Cornell University (B.A., with distinction, 1976); University of Illinois (J.D., 1979). Law Clerk for: Hon. Paul Schnake, Justice of the Illinois Appellate Court, 1984-1986; Hon. Richard Stengel, Justice of the Illinois Appellate Court, 1979-1980. Assistant Defender, Officer of the State Appellate Defender, 1980-1984. *Member:* Chicago and Illinois State Bar Associations. ***LANGUAGES:*** German. ***REPORTED CASES:*** Village of Willowbrook v. Olech, — U.S. —, 120 S.Ct. 1073, 145 L.Ed.2d 1060 (2000).

HART AND HART

DU QUOIN, ILLINOIS

(See Benton)

General Trial and Appellate Practice in State and Federal Courts. Probate, Trust, Real Estate Deeds and Title Insurance, Bankruptcy (Creditors), Traffic, Banking, Business, Commercial and Corporation Law and Creditor Collections, Employment Law.

DEAN L. SUTTON, PC

1608 EIGHTH STREET
EAST MOLINE, ILLINOIS 61244
Telephone: 309-755-5239
Fax: 309-755-0966
Email: deansutton@dlsuttonpc.com
URL: http://www.dlsuttonpc.com

General Practice, Bankruptcy, Zoning and Land Use, Business Law, Starting a Business, Corporate and Small Business, Buying and Selling a Business, Business Planning, Contracts, Buying and Selling a Home, Eminent Domain, Guardianships, Social Security Disability, Commercial and Residential Real Estate, Wills and Probate, Trusts and Estates, Estate Planning, Municipal Law.

DEAN L. SUTTON, born Moline, Illinois, October 29, 1948; admitted to bar, 1975, Indiana and U.S. District Court, Northern District of Indiana; 1976, U.S. Court of Appeals, Seventh Circuit; 1979, Illinois and U.S. District Court, Central District of Illinois. *Education:* Black Hawk College; Augustana College (A.B., 1970); Valparaiso University (J.D., 1975). City Attorney, Silvis, Illinois. Special Assistant Attorney General, State of Illinois. *Member:* Rock County (Legal Aid-Pro Bono Committee, 1986—), Rock Island County and Illinois State Bar Associations; National Organization of Social Security Claimant's Representatives. ***Email:*** deansutton@dlsuttonpc.com

REPRESENTATIVE CLIENTS: City of Silvis; Attorney Title Guarantee Corp.; Moline Township; South Moline Township; Hampton Township.

BURROUGHS, HEPLER, BROOM, MacDONALD, HEBRANK & TRUE, LLP

EAST ST. LOUIS, ILLINOIS

(See Edwardsville)

General Civil Trial and Appellate Practice. Personal Injury, Negligence, Products Liability, Structural Work Act, Admiralty, Professional Malpractice, Insurance, Employment Law, Environmental, Asbestos and Toxic Tort, School, Municipal, Corporate, Tax, Real Estate and Probate Law.

BENJAMIN F. EDWARDS

Established in 1990

THE 1ST ILLINOIS BANK BUILDING
327 MISSOURI AVENUE, SUITE 402
EAST ST. LOUIS, ILLINOIS 62201
Telephone: 618-274-3063
Fax: 618-875-5241
Email: bedwa10613@yahoo.com
URL: http://www.bedwardslaw.com
Mailing Address: Post Office Box 306, East St Louis, IL 62202

The Edwards' Law Office provides legal services in the following areas of practice: Bankruptcy, Real Estate, Probate, Guardianship, Wills, Powers of Attorney, Family Law, Divorce, Traffic Violations, Automobile Accidents and Injuries and General Practice.

BENJAMIN F. EDWARDS, admitted to bar, 1975, U.S. Court of Appeals, Seventh Circuit; 1976, Illinois; 1977, U.S. District Court, Southern District of Illinois; U.S. District Court, Eastern District of Missouri; 1986, Missouri. *Education:* St. Louis University (B.A., 1970); Washington University (J.D., 1974). *Member:* Illinois State Bar Association; The Missouri Bar; Metro East Bar Association. ***PRACTICE AREAS:*** Bankruptcy; Real Estate; Probate; Estate Planning; Family Law; Traffic Violations; Automobile Accidents and Injuries.

GLASS & KOREIN, LLC

412 MISSOURI AVENUE
EAST ST. LOUIS, ILLINOIS 62201
Telephone: 618-274-0434
Fax: 618-274-8369

Workers Compensation, Personal Injury.

MEMBERS OF THE FIRM

MARK GLASS, born St. Louis, Missouri, November 12, 1947; admitted to bar, 1974, Illinois; 1983, Missouri. *Education:* University of Illinois (B.S., 1969); St. Louis University (J.D., 1974). Workers' Compensation Seminar Lecturer: National Business Institute; Lorman Education Services; Illinois Trial Lawyers Association. Member, Workplace Injury Litigation Group. Member, Panel of Arbitrators, American Arbitration Association. *Member:* Illinois State Bar Association (Member, Workers Compensation Section); Illinois Trial Lawyers Association (Member, Workers Compensation Committee, 1987—); Workplace Injury Litigation Group (Board of Directors, 1998-2001); American Civil Liberties Union. (Also Member, Carr Korein, LLC). ***PRACTICE AREAS:*** Workers Compensation Law; Personal Injury Law. ***Email:*** mglass@legal-matters.com

MICHAEL H. KOREIN, born St. Louis, Missouri, January 28, 1964; admitted to bar, 1991, New York; 1992, U.S. District Court, Southern and Eastern Districts of New York; 1995, U.S. District Court, Southern District of Illinois; 1995, U.S. District Court, Central District of Illinois; 1995, Illinois; 1996, Missouri. *Education:* University of Arizona (B.S./B.P.A., 1986); Washington University (J.D., 1990). Author: "Maritime Causes of Action for Personal Injury Available to Seaman," The Illinois Institute Continuing Legal Education, 2002; "Employment Issues in Workers' Compensation," Lorman Education Services, 2002; "Ethical Issues - Getting By in a Less Thank Perfect World," Lorman Education Services, 2002. Visiting Student, New York University School of Law, 1989-1990. Featured as

(This Listing Continued)

key speaker on Illinois worker rights before various labor and trade unions. *Member:* Madison County, St. Clair County, Illinois State (Member, Workers Compensation Committee) and American Bar Associations; Illinois Trial Lawyers Association; The Association of Trial Lawyers of America; Workplace Injury Litigation Group, Inc. (Also Member, Carr Korein, LLC). ***PRACTICE AREAS:*** Plaintiff's Personal Injury Litigation; Workers Compensation; Maritime Law; Negligence. ***Email:*** mkorein@legal-matters.com

GOLDSTEIN AND PRICE, L.C.

EAST ST. LOUIS, ILLINOIS

(See St. Louis, Missouri)

Admiralty and Maritime Law, Business Litigation including Products Liability, Insurance Coverage, Toxic Torts and Environmental Law, Subrogation, Contracts, Administrative Law, Unfair Competition and Professional Liability, Corporate.

HOAGLAND, FITZGERALD, SMITH & PRANAITIS

EAST ST. LOUIS, ILLINOIS

(See Alton)

General Practice and Trials in all Federal and State Courts. Insurance, Litigation, Negligence, Product Liability, Malpractice, Employment Discrimination, Corporate, Banking, Probate, Trusts, Estates, Labor Relations, Tax Law, Workers Compensation, Commercial Transactions, Real Estate, Governmental, Bankruptcies and Foreclosures.

KUNIN LAW OFFICE, LLC

412 MISSOURI AVENUE
EAST ST. LOUIS, ILLINOIS 62201
Telephone: 618-274-0434
Fax: 618-274-8369

Bankruptcy, Commercial and Debtors & Creditor Rights Law.

JOEL A. KUNIN, born St. Louis, Missouri, March 3, 1938; admitted to bar, 1962, Missouri; 1964, District of Columbia; 1965, Illinois. *Education:* Washington University (B.S.M.E., 1959; J.D., 1962). Lecturer on Bankruptcy Programs, CLE, 1990—. Member, Federal Trade Commission, 1962-1965. Assistant U.S. Attorney, 1965-1968. *Member:* St. Clair County, Illinois State, Federal and American Bar Associations; The Bar Association of Metropolitan St. Louis (Chairman, Bankruptcy Committee, 1984); Commercial Law League of America (Chairman, Midwest Region, 1986); The Association of Trial Lawyers of America; American Bankruptcy Institute. ***PRACTICE AREAS:*** Bankruptcy Law; Commercial Law; Debtor and Creditor Rights Law.

MICHELLE A. KUNIN, born Belleville, Illinois, September 30, 1967; admitted to bar, 1993, Missouri; 1994, Illinois and Kansas. *Education:* Boston University (B.A., 1990); University of Missouri, Columbia (J.D., 1993). Phi Delta Phi. Order of the Barristers. Law Clerk to the Honorable Harold Lowenstein, Missouri Court of Appeals, 1993-1994. *Member:* Bar Association of Metropolitan St. Louis; The Missouri Bar; Illinois State Bar Association. ***PRACTICE AREAS:*** Employment Law; Debtor and Creditor Rights; Commercial Law; Social Security Disability; Litigation.

MARK M. SILVERMINTZ, born St. Louis, Missouri, December 3, 1952; admitted to bar, 1978, Missouri; 1979, U.S. District Court, Eastern District of Missouri; 1982, Illinois and U.S. District Court, Southern District of Illinois; 1987, U.S. Court of Appeals, Seventh Circuit. *Education:* University of Pennsylvania; Washington University (A.B., 1975); George Washington University (J.D., 1978). *Member:* St. Clair County and Illinois State Bar Associations; The Missouri Bar; Bar Association of Metropolitan St. Louis. ***PRACTICE AREAS:*** General Practice; Commercial Law; Debtor and Creditor Rights; Litigation.

ASSOCIATE

STEVEN M. WALLACE, born East St. Louis, Illinois, May 5, 1959; admitted to bar, 1988, Illinois and U.S. District Court, Southern District of Illinois; 1989, Missouri; 1990, U.S. District Court, Eastern District of Missouri and U.S. Court of Appeals, Seventh Circuit; 1995, U.S. District Court, Central District of Illinois. *Education:* St. Louis University (A.B., 1981; J.D., magna cum laude, 1988); Southern Illinois University (M.B.A., 1987). ***PRACTICE AREAS:*** Bankruptcy (70%); Creditors Rights (5%); Debtors Rights (5%); Commercial Transactions (10%); Commercial Litigation (10%). ***Email:*** swallace@legal-matters.com

LUCCO, BROWN, THRELKELD & DAWSON, LLP

EAST ST. LOUIS, ILLINOIS

(See Edwardsville)

General Civil and Criminal Litigation in State and Federal Courts. Federal Criminal Defense including White Collar Criminal Defense, Corporate Internal Investigations, and Health Care Fraud Defense; State Criminal Defense including all Felonies, DUI, Traffic and Juvenile Law. Civil Litigation including Intellectual Property Litigation (Patents); Construction, Contracts, Corporations, Wrongful Death, Personal Injury, Workman's Compensation and UCC litigation.

THE REX CARR LAW FIRM, LLC

412 MISSOURI AVENUE
EAST ST. LOUIS, ILLINOIS 62201
Telephone: 618-274-0434
800-333-5297
Fax: 618-274-8369
URL: http://www.rexcarr.com
URL: http://www.lawyers.com/rexcarr

St. Louis, Missouri Office: 1 Metropolitan Square, 211 North Broadway, Suite 2970, 63102. Telephone: 1-800-333-5297.
Belleville, Illinois Office: 7012 West Main Street, 62223. Telephone: 618-397-9191.

Railroad, Medical Malpractice, Product Liability, Toxic Torts, Nursing Home Negligence, General Negligence, Trial Practice, Workers Compensation, Class Actions, Complex Litigation, Automobile Litigation.

FIRM PROFILE: The firm serves both Missouri and Illinois in a specialized Tort Practice maintaining three staffed offices in East St. Louis, Illinois, Belleville, Illinois and St. Louis, Missouri. Its partners are instructors at both National Seminars and those conducted on State levels in Missouri and Illinois.

The firm is included in the Martindale-Hubbell Bar Register of Preeminent Lawyers.

MEMBERS OF FIRM

REX CARR, born Carbondale, Illinois, December 29, 1926; admitted to bar, 1950, Illinois; 1984, Missouri. *Education.* Washington University and University of Illinois (A.B., 1948); University of Illinois (J.D., 1949). Phi Alpha Delta. Author: "Need for Revision of Discovery Procedure in Illinois," University of Illinois Law Forum, Summer 1949; "Attachment," Illinois Bar Journal, July 1954; "Measuring Damages in the Family Context," University of Illinois Law Forum, Winter 1962. Lecturer: Jury Selection in Negligence Cases, University of Illinois College of Law, February 1962; Trial Advocacy University of Illinois College of Law, 1969, 1971; "Closing Argument," Illinois Trial Lawyers College of Advocacy, July, 1988; "Final Argument Comparative Fault Cases," Illinois Trial Lawyers Seminar, October, 1988; "Use of Expert Witnesses," St. Louis University Law School, May, 1988; "The Judge's Participation in the Trial-How Far May the Judge Go?" Illinois Judges' Association, December, 1984; "How to Obtain Punitive Damages in Tort Litigation," Illinois Trial Lawyers Seminar, June, 1981; "Techniques in Personal Injury Litigation," Practicing Law Institute, April, 1981; "How to Prove Pain and Suffering," Illinois State Bar Association, April, 1990; "Use of Expert Testimony," Illinois Trial Lawyers Seminar, February, 1990; "Handling Defense Experts," Illinois Trial Lawyers Seminar, December, 1990; "Trial Workshop," American Board of Trial Advocates, June, 1991; "Direct Examination," American Board of Trial Advocates, May 1992; "Cross Examination of Defense Experts," American Board of Trial Advocates, June 1993; "Premises Liability," March 1989, Missouri Association of Trial Attorneys; "Argument," Illinois Trial Lawyers Journal, Fall/Winter Issue 1988; "The Law of Libel," Illinois Trial Lawyers Seminar, June, 1982; "Libel Law," Illinois Judges' Association, December, 1985; "Libel Law Reformation Conference," March, 1989, The Annenberg Program, Northwestern University, Chicago, Illinois; "Conduct of the Lawyer and Witnesses," Illinois State Bar Association, November, 1988; Participant, Illinois Trial Lawyers Association Seminars: "The Federal Employers Liability Act," October 1970; "The Unusual Case," June 1974; "Discovery-Medical Negligence," November 1974; "The Art of Summation," November 1978 and May 1979; "The Million Dollar Verdict," Maryland Trial Lawyers Seminar, February 1979; "Libel and Malpractice," Kansas Trial Lawyers Seminar, June 1983; "Trial Advocacy Skills," Georgetown University Law Center, November, 1990. Chairman, Human Relations Commission, City of East St. Louis, 1964-1972. Member, Board of Law Visitors, University of Illinois College of Law, 1983-1986. *Member:* St. Clair County (President, 1982-1983), Illinois State (Member: Education Committee, 1956-1957; Unauthorized Practice Committee, 1957-1959; Executive Committee, Junior Bar Section, 1959; Chairman, Illinois Supreme Court Committee, Rules of Evidence, 1975-1978) and American Bar Associations; Illinois Trial Lawyers Association (Member: Board of Governors, 1959—; Legislative Committee, 1959-1965); Missouri Trial Lawyers Association; The Association of Trial Lawyers of America (Member: Legislative Committee, 1965-1971; Charitable Immunity Committee, 1970-1973); Inner Circle of Advocates (Member, Board of Directors, 1984—; President, 1987-1990); American Board of Trial Advocates; American Board of Professional Liability Attorneys. ***PRACTICE AREAS:*** Medical Malpractice; Legal Malpractice; General Negligence Law; Products Liability; Complex Civil Litigation; Railroad Law.

STACI M. YANDLE, born Centreville, Illinois, July 27, 1961; admitted to bar, 1987, Illinois; 1988, U.S. District Court, Southern District of Illinois; 1991, U.S. Court of Appeals, Seventh Circuit; 2003, Missouri. *Education:* University of Illinois (B.S., 1983); Vanderbilt University (J.D., 1987). *Member:* Metro-East, Chicago, East St. Louis, St. Clair County, Illinois State and American Bar Associations; Illinois Trial Lawyers Association; The Association of Trial Lawyers of America. ***PRACTICE AREAS:*** Products Liability Law; Personal Injury Law; General Negligence Law; Medical Malpractice; Nursing Home Litigation; Wrongful Death.

ROSS T. ANDERSON, born St. Louis, Missouri, December 10, 1952; admitted to bar, 1978, Illinois; 1984, Missouri; U.S District Courts, Southern District of Illinois; U.S. District Court, Eastern District of Missouri; U.S. Court of Appeals, Seventh and Eighth Circuits and U.S Supreme Court. *Education:* University of Illinois (A.B., 1975; J.D., 1978). Phi Delta Phi. Author/Presenter: Lecturer Legal Seminar, Bar Association of Metropolitan St. Louis and National Business Institute. Author: "Use of Medical Records for Illinois Attorneys," October 2003 and "Dealing With Destruction-Spoliation of Evidence in Missouri," February 2005. *Member:* The Bar Association of Metropolitan St. Louis; St. Clair County, Madison County (Secretary, 1980-1981), Illinois State and American Bar Associations; The Missouri Bar; Illinois Trial Lawyers Association; Missouri Association of Trial Lawyers; The Association of Trial Lawyers of America. ***PRACTICE AREAS:*** Class Action Litigation; Medical Malpractice; Products Liability; Personal Injury; Catastrophic Injury; Nursing Home Abuse and Neglect.

PAUL G. SCHOEN, born St. Louis, Missouri, June 30, 1945; admitted to bar, 1970, Illinois and U.S. District Court, Southern District of Illinois; 1980, U.S. Supreme Court;

(This Listing Continued)

THE REX CARR LAW FIRM, LLC, East St. Louis—Continued

1982, U.S. Court of Appeals, Seventh Circuit; 2002, Missouri and U.S. District Court, Eastern District of Missouri. *Education:* Southern Illinois University (B.S., with honors, 1967); University of Illinois (J.D., 1970). Co-Author: "Pleadings, Illinois Civil Practice Before Trial," Chapter 9 Illinois Institute for Continuing Legal Education, 1978. Member, Board of Directors, 1970-1978 and President, 1975-1976, Southern Illinois University Alumni Association. Member, Board of Directors, Landmark Bank of Carbondale, 1979-1991. Commissioner, 1971-1980 and Chairman, 1972-1973; 1975-1976; 1979-1980, Southern Illinois Airport Board of Commissioners. Member: American Association of Airport Executives, Great Lakes Region, 1975-1995; Illinois Council of School Attorneys, 1991-1992; National Council of School Attorneys, 1991-1992. Formerly with: Feirich, Schoen, Mager, Green; Mitchell & Schoen; Donald R. Mitchell Law Firm; Medlin, Zimmer & South. *Member:* St. Clair County (Law Day Chairman, 1973), Illinois State (Member, School Law and Insurance Sections, Council Member: 1977-1982; 1991-1993) and American Bar Associations; The Missouri Bar; Illinois Trial Lawyers Association; The Association of Trial Lawyers of America. ***PRACTICE AREAS:*** Medical Malpractice; Nursing Home Abuse and Neglect; Personal Injury; Wrongful Death. ***Email:*** pschoen@rexcarr.com

TROY E. WALTON, born Chatham, Illinois; admitted to bar, 2000, Missouri and U.S. District Court, Eastern and Western Districts of Missouri; 2001, Illinois and U.S. District Court, Southern District Of Illinois; 2002, U.S. District Court, Central District of Illinois. *Education:* University of Illinois (B.A., 1997); St. Louis University School of Law (J.D., cum laude, 2000). Senior Editor, St. Louis-Warsaw Transatlantic Law Journal, 1999-2000. Team Representative, St. Louis University School of Law, Trial Advocacy, 2000. Formerly with, Reinert and Rourke, P.C. *Member:* Bar Association of Metropolitan St. Louis; Madison County, St. Clair County, Illinois State and American Bar Associations; The Missouri Bar; The Association of Trial Lawyers of America; Missouri Association of Trial Attorneys; Lawyers Association of St. Louis; Illinois Trial Lawyers Association; The Bar Association of Central and Southern Federal Districts of Illinois. ***PRACTICE AREAS:*** Catastrophic Injury; Medical Malpractice; Products Liability; Nursing Home Negligence; Class Action Litigation.

ALAN G. PIRTLE, born Merced, California, February 13, 1965; admitted to bar, 1991, Illinois; 1993, Missouri and U.S. District Court, Southern District of Illinois; 2004, U.S. District Court, Eastern District of Missouri. *Education:* Eastern Illinois University (B.A., 1987); St. Louis University (J.D., 1991). Lecturer, legal seminars, Illinois Trial Lawyers Association and National Business Institute. Chairman, Democratic party, Monroe County, Illinois, 2004—. *Member:* St. Clair County (Co-Chair, Legal-Medical Committee, 2004), Monroe County (President, 1995-1996), Madison County (Illinois), Illinois State and American Bar Associations; The Missouri Bar; Illinois Trial Lawyers Association (Member, Legislative and Medical Negligence Committees); Missouri Association of Trial Attorneys; The Association of Trial Lawyers of America. ***PRACTICE AREAS:*** Personal Injury Law; Nursing Home Litigation; General Civil Litigation; Medical Malpractice; Products Liability; Catastrophic Injury. ***Email:*** apirtle@rexcarr.com

MICHAEL B. MARKER, born Memphis, Tennessee, June 19, 1957; admitted to bar, 1990, Missouri; 1991, Illinois; U.S. District Court, District of Missouri and U.S. District Court, District of Illinois. *Education:* Middlebury College; Memphis State University (B.A., 1986); Washington University School of Law (J.D., 1989). Law Clerk to Hon. Harold L. Satz, Missouri Court of Appeals, 1989-1990. *Member:* Bar Association of Metropolitan St. Louis; St. Clair County and American Bar Associations. ***LANGUAGES:*** French, Spanish, German. ***REPORTED CASES:*** Goede v. Aerojet General Corp., 143 S.W.3d 14 (Mo.App.E.D., May 11, 2004); State v. Payne, 910 S.W.2d 318 (Mo.App.E.D., Sep 26, 1995); Shah v. Nangle, 859 S.W.2d 276 (Mo.App.E.D., Aug 24, 1993); Gulmen v. Gulmen, 851 S.W.2d 37 (Mo.App.E.D., March 30 1993); Heisler v. Jetco Service, 849 S.W.2d 91 (Mo.App.E.D., Jan 26, 1993); McMurray v. Director of Revenue, State of Mo., 800 S.W.2d 820 (Mo.App.E.D., Dec. 31,1990); Morris v. Margulis, 307 Ill.App.3d 1024, 718 N.E.2d 709 (Ill.App. 5 Dist., Sep 30, 1999); Swearingen v. Industrial Com'n, 298 Ill.App.3d 666, 699 N.E.2d 237 (Ill.App. 5 Dist., Aug 24, 1998); Cummis v. Country Mut. Ins. Co., 178 Ill.2d 474, 687 N.E.2d 1021 (Ill., Oct 02, 1997); Ragan v. Columbia Mut. Ins. Co., 219 Ill.App.3d 1088, 684 N.E.2d 1108 (Ill.App. 5 Dist., Sep 16, 1997); Estate of Hicks, 174 Ill.2d 433, 675 N.E.2d 89 (Ill., Dec 19, 1996); Granberry by Granberry v. Carbondale Clinic, S.C., 285 Ill.App.3d 54, 672 N.E.2d 1296 (Ill.App. 5 Dist., Nov 13, 1996); Richter v. Standard Mut. Ins. Co., 279 Ill.App.3d 501, 664 N.E.2d 1140 (Ill.App. 5 Dist., May 2, 1996); Wilson v. Missouri Pacific R. Co., 169 Ill.2d 170, 661 N.E.2d 282 (Ill., Jan 18 1996); Peile v. Skelgas, Inc., 163 Ill.2d 323, 645 N.E.2d 184 (Ill., Dec. 22, 1994); Pruett v. Norfolk and Western Ry. Co., 261 Ill.App. 3d 29, 632 N.E.2d 652 (Ill.App. 5 Dist., Apr 7, 1994); Worthy v. Norfolk and Western Ry. Co., 249 Ill.App.3d 1096, 619 N.E.2d 1371 (Ill.App. 5 Dist., Sep 13, 1993); Boatmen's Nat. Bank of Belleville v. Martin, 155 Ill.2d 305, 614 N.E.2d 1194 (Ill., May 20, 1993); Martinez v. Industrial Com'n, 242 Ill.App.3d 981, 611 N.E.2d 545 (Ill.App. 4 Dist., Mar 18, 1993); Roth v. St. Elizabeth's Hosp., 241 Ill.App.3d 407, 607 N.E.2d 1356 (Ill.App. 5 Dist., Feb. 10, 1993); Taylor v. Martin County Canvassing Bd., 773 So. 2d 517 (Fla., Dec 12, 2000). ***PRACTICE AREAS:*** Class Actions. ***Email:*** mmarker@rexcarr.com

DONNA M. ANDERSON, born St. Louis, Missouri, July 17, 1965; admitted to bar, 1997, Missouri; 2001, U.S. District Court, Eastern District of Missouri; 2004, U.S. District Court, Southern District of Illinois; 2005, Illinois. *Education:* Maryville University (B.S.N., 1993); St. Louis University (J.D., 1997; Certification in Health Law, 1997). Registered nurse, 1994. *Member:* The Missouri Bar (Member, Committee on Minority Issues; Committee on Health and Hospital Law); Mound City and Illinois State Bar Associations; Association of Trial Lawyers of America. ***PRACTICE AREAS:*** Nursing Home Abuse and Neglect; Medical Malpractice; Nursing Home Litigation. ***Email:*** danderson@rexcarr.com

OF COUNSEL

LAWRENCE ALAN WALDMAN, born St. Louis, Missouri, October 12, 1937; admitted to bar, 1962, Missouri; 1973, Illinois. *Education:* Washington University (B.S.B.A., 1959; J.D., 1962). Phi Delta Phi; Order of the Coif. Member, Washington University Law Quarterly, 1961-1962. *Member:* Missouri Bar; The Bar Association of Metropolitan St. Louis; St. Clair County and American Bar Associations. (Resident). ***PRACTICE AREAS:*** Probate Law; Estate Planning Law; Corporate Law; Real Estate Law.

ARMSTRONG LAW OFFICES

SOUTH MAIN AND SCHWARZ STREET
P.O. BOX 565
EDWARDSVILLE, ILLINOIS 62025
Telephone: 618-656-6770
Facsimile: 618-656-6808
URL: http://www.tadarmstrong.com
Email: tad@armstronglaw.net
URL: http://www.armstronglaw.com

Personal Injury, Medical Malpractice, Products Liability, General Civil Trial Practice, Wrongful Death, Dog Bites, Slip and Fall, Automobile Accidents.

BENTON TAD ARMSTRONG, born Andrews, Texas, March 30, 1951; admitted to bar, 1976, Illinois. *Education:* University of Illinois (B.S., 1973); University of Texas; University of Illinois (J.D., 1976). Phi Eta Sigma; Beta Alpha Psi; Beta Gamma Sigma. Author: "Punitive Damages and Breach of Contract: Mr. Corbin, Say It Isn't So," Illinois Bar Journal, February, 1997. Member, Million Dollar Advocates Forum. *Member:* Madison County, Illinois State and American Bar Associations; Illinois Trial Lawyers Association; The Association of Trial Lawyers of America; American Board of Trial Advocates.

ARMSTRONG TEASDALE LLP

A Partnership including Professional Corporations
Established in 1901
241 NORTH MAIN STREET
EDWARDSVILLE, ILLINOIS 62025
Telephone: 618-650-7087
Facsimile: 618-655-4004
Email: armstrongteasdale@armstrongteasdale.com
URL: http://www.armstrongteasdale.com

St. Louis, Missouri Office: One Metropolitan Square, Suite 2600, 63102. Telephone: 314-621-5070. Facsimile: 314-621-5065.
Kansas City, Missouri Office: 2345 Grand Boulevard, Suite 2000, 64108. Telephone: 816-221-3420. Facsimile: 816-221-0786.
Jefferson City, Missouri Office: 3405 West Truman Blvd., Suite 210, 65109-5713. Telephone: 573-636-8394. Facsimile: 573-636-8457.
Washington, D.C. Office: 1747 Pennsylvania Avenue, N.W., Suite 300, 20006. Telephone: 202-454-2800. Facsimile: 202-454-2805.
Springfield, Illinois Office: 3201 Pleasant Run, Suite A, P.O. Box 13317, 62791-3317. Telephone: 217-726-8200. Facsimile: 217-726-8300.
Belleville, Illinois Office: 23 South First Street, 62220. Telephone: 618-397-4411.
Overland Park, Kansas Office: 7400 West 132nd Street, Suite 200, 66213.
Henderson, Nevada Office: 701 North Green Valley Parkway, Suite 200, 89074. Telephone: 702-678-5070. Facsimile: 702-990-3003.
Sydney, Australia Office: C/Clayton Utz, Level 31, No. 1 O'Connell Street, Sidney, NSW 2000, Australia. Telephone: 61-29-262-6700. Facsimile: 61-29-262-3263.
New York, New York Office: 230 Park Avenue, Suite 2300, 10169. Telephone: 212-867-9500. Facsimile: 212-599-1759.
Shanghai, China Office: 1376 Nan Jing Xi Lu, Shanghai Center - Suite 718, Shanghai 200040, P.R. China. Telephone: 011-8621-6279-8808. Facsimilie: 011-8621-6279-8866.

General Civil Practice. Administrative Law, Agricultural Law, Alternative Dispute Resolution, Antitrust and Trade Regulation Law, Appellate Practice, Banking and Financial Services, Biotechnology/Life Sciences, Business Law, Civil Rights, Class Actions, Communications Law, Computer, Constitutional Law, Construction Law, Corporate Compliance and Governance, Corporate Law, Corporate Finance, Education Law, Eminent Domain, Employee Benefits, Employment and Labor, Energy, Entertainment & Sports, Environmental Law, Financial Restructuring, Reorganization and Bankruptcy, Distribution and Franchise, Government Contracts, Governmental Relations, Health Care, Immigration and Naturalization, Insurance Coverage/Reinsurance and Extracontractual Liability, International Law, International Trade, Internet Law, Investments, Litigation, Medical Malpractice, Mergers & Acquisitions, Natural Resources, Occupational Safety & Health Administration, Patent, Trademark and Intellectual Property, Pension and Executive Compensation, Personal Injury, Products Liability, Professional Liability, Public Law and Finance, Real Estate, Securities, Taxation, Technology and Science, Toxic Torts, Transportation, Trusts and Estates, White Collar Crime, Workers Compensation and Zoning, Planning & Land Use and Development.

FIRM PROFILE: Armstrong Teasdale LLP conducts a comprehensive nationwide civil law practice from offices in St. Louis, Kansas City and Jefferson City, Missouri; Overland Park, Kansas; Edwardsville, Belleville and Springfield, Illinois; Las Vegas, Nevada; Washington, D.C.; New York, New York; Shanghai, P.R.C.; and Sydney, Australia. The firm is the Missouri member of Lex Mundi, an international association of independent law firms, as well as State Law Resources, Inc. and United States Law Firm Group, both national networks of independent law firms.

MEMBERS OF FIRM

KAREN A. BAUDENDISTEL (Resident, St. Louis, Missouri Office)

MARK A. BOATMAN, born Minneapolis, Minnesota, June 4, 1958; admitted to bar, 1994, Missouri; 1995, Illinois. *Education:* University of Missouri-St. Louis (B.G.S., summa cum laude, 1991); Saint Louis University (J.D., cum laude, 1994). Alpha Sigma Nu. Faculty Fellow, Dean John B. Attanasio. Student Marshall, University of Missouri-St. Louis, Class of 1991. Managing Editor, Saint Louis University Law Journal. Author, "Lee v. Weisman: In Search of a Defensible Test for Establishment of Religion," 37 Saint Louis University Law Journal 773, 1993. *Member:* Bar Association of Metropolitan St. Louis; Illinois State and American Bar Associations; The Missouri Bar; National Association of Bond Lawyers. (Also at St. Louis, Missouri Office). ***PRACTICE AREAS:*** Public Law and Finance; Municipal Law. ***Email:*** mboatman@armstrongteasdale.com

(This Listing Continued)

DAVID W. BRASWELL (Resident, St. Louis, Missouri Office)

ANN E. BUCKLEY (Resident, St. Louis, Missouri and Belleville, Illinois Offices)

MICHAEL A. CHIVELL (Resident, St. Louis, Missouri and Belleville, Illinois Offices)

CLARK H. COLE, born St. Louis, Missouri, January 10, 1955; admitted to bar, 1980, Missouri; 1981, Illinois. *Education:* Louisiana State University (B.A., 1977); University of Missouri (J.D., 1980). Order of the Coif; The Order of Barristers. Missouri Law Review, Note and Comment Editor, 1979-1980. Recipient: Ike Skelton Trial Practice Award, 1980. *Member:* Bar Association of Metropolitan St. Louis (Chair, Bench and Bar Committee, 1996-1999); Illinois State and American (Chair, Health and Disability Insurance Law Committee, 1998-1999) Bar Associations; The Missouri Bar (Chair, Insurance Law Committee, 1990-1992; Chair, Medical-Legal Relations Committee, 1997-1998); Federation of Defense and Corporate Counsel (Chair, Life, Health and Disability Section, 1995-1998; Chair, Trial Tactics, Practice and Procedures Section, 2004—); International Association of Defense Counsel; Missouri Organization of Defense Lawyers (President, 2002-2003; Defense Research Institute (Missouri Representative, 2003—); International Association for Insurance Law. (Also at St. Louis, Missouri and Belleville, Illinois Offices). ***PRACTICE AREAS:*** Life Insurance; Health Insurance; Professional Liability; Disability Insurance; Personal Injury; Products Liability; Insurance Litigation; Commercial Litigation; Business Litigation. ***Email:*** ccole@armstrongteasdale.com

O. KIRBY COLSON, III (Resident, St. Louis, Missouri Office)

WILLIAM M. CORRIGAN, JR. (Resident, St. Louis, Missouri Office)

GLENN E. DAVIS, born St. Louis, Missouri, November 1, 1956; admitted to bar, 1982, Missouri; 1983, Illinois. *Education:* DePauw University (B.A., 1979); Washington University (J.D., 1982). Delta Theta Phi. Notes and Comments Editor, Washington University Law Quarterly, 1981-1982. Member, Antitrust Committee of the Bar Association of Metropolitan St. Louis. *Member:* Illinois State and American (Antitrust Section) Bar Associations; The Missouri Bar; Missouri Organization of Defense Lawyers. (Also at St. Louis, Missouri and Belleville, Illinois Offices) (Assistant Chair, Litigation Department; Business Litigation Section; Chair, Antitrust Trade Regulation and Distribution Law Practice Group). ***PRACTICE AREAS:*** Antitrust; Securities; Commercial Litigation; Professional Liability; Business Litigation; Corporate Compliance; White Collar Crime. ***Email:*** gdavis@armstrongteasdale.com

RICHARD W. ENGEL, JR. (Resident, St. Louis, Missouri and Belleville, Illinois Offices)

RAYMOND R. FOURNIE, born Belleville, Illinois, January 3, 1951; admitted to bar, 1979, Missouri; 1980, Illinois, U.S. District Court, Eastern District of Missouri and Southern and Central Districts of Illinois and U.S. Court of Appeals, Seventh Circuit. *Education:* University of Illinois (B.S., 1973); Saint Louis University (J.D., 1979). Alpha Sigma Nu. Member, Governing Committee on the Forum Committee for Sports and Entertainment Industries Law, American Bar Association, 1984-1990. General Counsel for the St. Louis Municipal Theatre Association (The Muny Opera). *Member:* The Bar Association of Metropolitan St. Louis; St. Clair County, Illinois State and Federal Bar Associations; The Missouri Bar; The Lawyers Association of St. Louis (President, 1990-1991); Defense Research Institute; Association of Defense Trial Counsel; Illinois Association of Defense Counsel; The Bar Association of the Central and Southern Federal Districts of Illinois. (Also at St. Louis, Missouri and Belleville, Illinois Offices). ***PRACTICE AREAS:*** Toxic Tort; Asbestos Defense; Medical Malpractice Defense Law; Products Liability Litigation. ***Email:*** rfournie@armstrongteasdale.com

TIMOTHY J. GEARIN (Resident, St. Louis, Missouri Office)

DAVID L. GOING (Resident, St. Louis, Missouri and Belleville, Illinois Offices)

ROBERT C. GRAHAM, III (Resident, St. Louis, Missouri Office)

FRANK N. GUNDLACH, (P.C.), born St. Louis, Missouri, April 26, 1938; admitted to bar, 1963, Missouri (Not admitted in Illinois). *Education:* Colgate University (A.B., 1960); Washington University (J.D., 1963). Selected to *Best Lawyers in America, Business and Personal Injury Litigation*, 1997—. Trial Attorney, Tax Division, Department of Justice, 1964-1966. *Member:* International Association of Insurance Counsel; National Defense Research Institute. American College of Trial Lawyers (Regent, 1998-2002). (Also at St. Louis, Missouri Office). ***PRACTICE AREAS:*** Business Litigation; Products Liability. ***Email:*** fgundlach@armstrongteasdale.com

ROBERT A. KAISER (Resident, St. Louis, Missouri Office)

PATRICK J. KENNY (Resident, St. Louis, Missouri Office)

ANITA M. KIDD, born Chicago, Illinois, May 10, 1960; admitted to bar, 1989, California; 1995, Missouri and Illinois. *Education:* Loyola University, Chicago (B.S.R.N., cum laude, 1983); Loyola Law School, Los Angeles (J.D., 1988). Alpha Sigma Nu. Registered Nurse: Illinois, 1983; California, 1985. *Member:* Illinois State Bar Association; The Missouri Bar; State Bar of California. (Also at St. Louis, Missouri Office). ***PRACTICE AREAS:*** Medical Malpractice; Product Liability; Litigation. ***Email:*** akidd@armstrongteasdale.com

DAVID G. LOSEMAN (Resident, St. Louis, Missouri and Belleville, Illinois Offices)

PHILIP G. LOUIS, JR. (Resident, St. Louis, Missouri Office)

ANDREW B. MAYFIELD (Resident, St. Louis, Missouri Office)

TIMOTHY R. McFADDEN (Resident, St. Louis, Missouri Office)

CONNIE McFARLAND-BUTLER (Resident, St. Louis, Missouri Office)

JEFFERY T. McPHERSON (Resident, St. Louis, Missouri Office)

JAMES E. MELLO (Resident, St. Louis, Missouri Office)

DANIEL C. NELSON (Resident, St. Louis, Missouri Office)

JOHN J. O'BRIEN (Resident, St. Louis, Missouri Office)

JULIE EMMERICH O'KEEFE (Resident, St. Louis, Missouri Office)

DANIEL K. O'TOOLE (Resident, St. Louis, Missouri Office)

DAVID G. OTT, (P.C.) (Resident, St. Louis, Missouri Office)

(This Listing Continued)

PATRICK W. RASCHE (Resident, St. Louis, Missouri Office)

JOHN TALBOT SANT, JR., (P.C.) (Resident, St. Louis, Missouri and Belleville, Illinois Offices)

ROBERT G. SCHWENDINGER (Chairman of the Health Care Practice Group) (Resident, St. Louis, Missouri Office)

AMIT B. SHAH (Resident, St. Louis, Missouri Office)

DEAN D. SMALL (Resident, St. Louis, Missouri Office)

MARK D. SOPHIR, (P.C.) (Resident, St. Louis, Missouri and Belleville, Illinois Offices)

JAMES L. STOCKBERGER, born Fort Wayne, Indiana, January 17, 1958; admitted to bar, 1988, Missouri; 1989, Illinois and Kansas. *Education:* Saint Louis University (B.A., cum laude, 1981; J.D., cum laude, 1988). Order of the Woolsack. *Member:* The Missouri Bar; Illinois State Bar Association; Bar Association of the Central and Southern Federal Districts of Illinois; International Association of Defense Counsel (IADC); National Institute of Trial Advocacy (NITA); Lawyers Association of St. Louis; National Association of Railroad Trial Counsel (NARTC). (Also at St. Louis, Missouri Office). ***PRACTICE AREAS:*** Products Liability Law; Transportation Law; Insurance Litigation; Medical Malpractice Defense. ***Email:*** jstockberger@armstrongteasdale.com

MARK L. STONEMAN (Resident, St. Louis, Missouri Office)

JOHN L. SULLIVAN (Resident, St. Louis, Missouri Office)

WILBUR L. TOMLINSON, (P.C.) (Resident, St. Louis, Missouri Office)

THERESE ROLUFS TRELZ (Resident, St. Louis, Missouri and Belleville, Illinois Offices)

TIMOTHY J. TRYNIECKI, born St. Louis, Missouri, December 30, 1956; admitted to bar, 1981, Missouri; 2005, Illinois. *Education:* University of Missouri (A.B., cum laude, 1978); Saint Louis University (J.D., cum laude, 1981). Co-Author, *Land Use Regulation,* American Bar Association, 1999. Research Fellow to Prof. John Griesbach, St. Louis University Law School, 1980. *Member:* American College of Real Estate Lawyers. (Also at St. Louis, Missouri Office). ***PRACTICE AREAS:*** Real Estate Law; Land Use. ***Email:*** ttryniecki@armstrongteasdale.com

JAMES J. VIRTEL, born Joliet, Illinois, May 15, 1944; admitted to bar, 1969, Missouri and Illinois; U.S. District Court, Eastern District of Missouri and Southern District of Illinois. *Education:* Loras College (B.A., cum laude, 1966); Saint Louis University (J.D., cum laude, 1969). Phi Delta Phi. Selected to *Best Lawyers in America, Personal Injury Litigation* 1997-1998 Edition. Editor, Saint Louis University Law Journal, 1968-1969. *Member:* Illinois State Bar Association; The Missouri Bar; International Association of Defense Counsel; The Defense Research Institute. Fellow, American College of Trial Lawyers. Regent, Loras College. (Also at St. Louis, Missouri and Belleville, Illinois Offices). ***PRACTICE AREAS:*** Business Litigation; Utility Litigation; Product Liability Litigation. ***Email:*** jvirtel@armstrongteasdale.com

GEORGE M. VON STAMWITZ (Resident, St. Louis, Missouri and Belleville, Illinois Offices)

THOMAS B. WEAVER (Resident, St. Louis, Missouri and Belleville, Illinois Offices)

MICHAEL E. WHITTLE (Resident, St. Louis, Missouri Office)

LISA M. WOOD, born Milwaukee, Wisconsin, February 8, 1961; admitted to bar, 1989, Missouri; 1990, Illinois, U.S. District Court, Eastern District of Missouri and Southern District of Illinois; U.S. Court of Appeals, Seventh, Eighth and Federal Circuits. *Education:* Saint Louis University (B.A., 1984; J.D., cum laude, 1989). Order of the Woolsack. Managing Editor, Saint Louis University Law Journal, 1988-1989. *Member:* Bar Association of Metropolitan St. Louis; Illinois State and American Bar Associations; The Missouri Bar; Defense Research Institute; Women Lawyers Association of Greater St. Louis. (Also at St. Louis, Missouri Office). ***PRACTICE AREAS:*** Commercial Litigation. ***Email:*** lwood@armstrongteasdale.com

JASON ZELLERS (Resident, St. Louis, Missouri Office)

ASSOCIATES

MARY L. BORDNER (Resident, St. Louis, Missouri Office)

KRISTIN D. BYRD (Resident, St. Louis, Missouri Office)

DORI B. DETHEROW (Resident, St. Louis, Missouri Office)

DANIEL M. FITZGERALD (Resident, St. Louis, Missouri Office)

JOVITA M. FOSTER (Resident, St. Louis, Missouri Office)

TYLER J. FRANK (Resident, St. Louis, Missouri Office)

VIRGINIA H. HOWELL (Resident, St. Louis, Missouri Office)

GREGORY A. IKEN (Resident, St. Louis, Missouri Office)

MICHAEL S. JEFFERIES (Resident, St. Louis, Missouri Office)

DAVID B. JENNINGS (Resident, St. Louis, Missouri Office)

JEFFREY H. KASS (Resident, St. Louis, Missouri Office)

MICHAEL B. KASS (Resident, St. Louis, Missouri Office)

MICHAEL H. KAUFFMAN (Resident, St. Louis, Missouri Office)

HEIDI P. KLOSTERMAN (Resident, St. Louis, Missouri Office)

SCOTT K. G. KOZAK (Resident, St. Louis, Missouri Office)

BRUCE D. LeMOINE (Resident, St. Louis, Missouri Office)

JACQUELINE P. ULIN LEVEY (Resident, St. Louis, Missouri Office)

MARY M. MACHON (Resident, St. Louis, Missouri Office)

LAURA L. McLAUGHLIN (Resident, St. Louis, Missouri Office)

CRAIG G. MOORE (Resident, St. Louis, Missouri Office)

HARRY M. (MARK) MURRAY, IV (Resident, St. Louis, Missouri Office)

(This Listing Continued)

ARMSTRONG TEASDALE LLP, Edwardsville—Continued

BRYAN D. NICHOLSON (Resident, St. Louis, Missouri Office)

TODD R. NISSENHOLTZ (Resident, St. Louis, Missouri Office)

SUSAN K. OLSEN (Resident, St. Louis, Missouri Office)

JILL M. PALMQUIST (Resident, St. Louis, Missouri Office)

CYNTHIA A. PETRACEK (Resident, St. Louis, Missouri Office)

STEVEN E. POZARIC (Resident, St. Louis, Missouri Office)

MATTHEW J. REH (Resident, St. Louis, Missouri Office)

RUSSELL C. RIGGAN (Resident, St. Louis, Missouri Office)

ANNA T. SELBY (Resident, St. Louis, Missouri Office)

JARROD H. SHARP (Resident, St. Louis, Missouri Office)

MATTHEW S. SHOREY (Resident, St. Louis, Missouri Office)

JOHN H. STOCKMAN, born Troy, New York, August 20, 1964; admitted to bar, 1990, New York; 1999, Illinois. *Education:* Rochester Institute of Technology (B.S., high honors, 1986); Albany Law School of Union College (J.D., 1989). *Member:* Illinois State Bar Association. (Also at Springfield, Illinois Office). ***PRACTICE AREAS:*** Public Law; Finance. ***Email:*** jstockman@armstrongteasdale.com

JOY L. VOKAC (Resident, St. Louis, Missouri Office)

ROGER A. WALKER (Resident, St. Louis, Missouri Office)

DEANNA M. WENDLER MODDE (Resident, St. Louis, Missouri Office)

LEEANN R. ZIGLER (Resident, St. Louis, Missouri Office)

OF COUNSEL

SUSAN BRADLEY BUSE (Resident, St. Louis, Missouri and Belleville, Illinois Offices)

THEODORE H. HELLMUTH, (P.C.) (Resident, St. Louis, Missouri Office)

THOMAS W. KELTY, born Springfield, Illinois, January 8, 1945; admitted to bar, 1971, Illinois; 1982, U.S. Supreme Court; 1985, Missouri and U.S. Tax Court. *Education:* Creighton University (B.A., 1967); University of Missouri at Kansas City (J.D., 1971). Phi Alpha Delta; Sigma Alpha Epsilon. Contributing Editor: "Illinois Jurisprudence - Municipal Law," Lawyers Cooperation Publishing, 1995. Author: "Special District Government in Illinois," Illinois Institute for Continuing Legal Education. *Member:* Sangamon County, Illinois State and American Bar Associations; The Missouri Bar; Illinois Trial Lawyers Association; National Association of Bond Lawyers; National Institute of Municipal Law Officers. (Also at Springfield, Illinois Office). ***PRACTICE AREAS:*** Municipal Law; Municipal Bonds; Municipal Finance; Corporate Finance; Corporate Law; Insurance; Workers Compensation; Estate Planning; Trusts and Estates; Wills; Probate; Commercial Real Estate; Commercial Litigation; Antitrust; Securities; Class Actions. ***Email:*** tkelly@armstrongteasdale.com

ROBERT G. RALEIGH (Resident, St. Louis, Missouri Office)

MELANIE B. TAMSKY (Resident, St. Louis, Missouri Office)

SENIOR COUNSEL

DONALD U. BEIMDIEK (Resident, St. Louis, Missouri and Belleville, Illinois Offices)

(For Biographical data on other Personnel, see Professional Biographies at St. Louis, Kansas City and Jefferson City, Missouri; Washington, D.C.; Belleville and Springfield, Illinois; Henderson, Nevada; and Shanghai, China Offices)

BLACKWELL SANDERS PEPER MARTIN LLP

EDWARDSVILLE, ILLINOIS

(See St. Louis, Missouri)

BURROUGHS, HEPLER, BROOM, MACDONALD, HEBRANK & TRUE, LLP

Established in 1896

TWO MARK TWAIN PLAZA, SUITE 300
103 WEST VANDALIA STREET
P.O. BOX 510
EDWARDSVILLE, ILLINOIS 62025-0510
Telephone: 618-656-0184
Telecopier: 618-656-1364
Email: firm@ilmolaw.com
URL: http://www.ilmolaw.com

St. Louis, Missouri Office: 1010 Market Street, Suite 500, 63101. Telephone: 314-355-6160.

General Civil Trial and Appellate Practice. Personal Injury, Negligence, Products Liability, Structural Work Act, Admiralty, Professional Malpractice, Insurance. Employment Law, Environmental, Asbestos and Toxic Tort, School, Municipal, Corporate, Tax, Real Estate and Probate Law.

FIRM PROFILE: The law firm of Burroughs, Hepler, Broom, MacDonald, Hebrank & True, LLP has a history spanning nearly One Hundred Years. Today, a primarily Trial Practice Firm with an emphasis on Defensive Civil Litigation, the firm serves a practice area extending throughout Central and Southern Illinois as well as St. Louis County in Eastern Missouri.

(This Listing Continued)

MEMBERS OF FIRM

G. GORDON BURROUGHS (1909-2000)

LARRY E. HEPLER, born Meadville, Pennsylvania, August 10, 1943; admitted to bar, 1968, Missouri and Illinois; 1971, U.S. District Court, Southern and Central Districts of Illinois; U.S. District Court, Eastern District of Missouri; U.S. Court of Appeals, Seventh Circuit. *Education:* Bucknell University (A.B., 1965); Washington & Lee University (J.D., magna cum laude, 1968). Order of the Coif; Omicron Delta Kappa; Phi Alpha Delta. Articles Editor, Washington & Lee Law Review, 1967-1968. Board of Directors, Illinois Institute of Continuing Legal Education, 1992-1994. *Member:* Bar Association of Metropolitan St. Louis; Madison County, Illinois State and American Bar Associations; The Missouri Bar; Federation of Insurance and Corporate Counsel; Defense Research Institute; Illinois Association of Defense Trial Counsel; American Board of Trial Advocates. [Capt., U.S. Army, 1968-1970]. ***PRACTICE AREAS:*** Negligence; Products Liability; Insurance; School; Personal Injury; Construction; Toxic Tort. ***Email:*** larry.hepler@ilmolaw.com

GORDON R. BROOM, born Effingham, Illinois, February 15, 1944; admitted to bar, 1969, Illinois; 1971, U.S. District Court, Southern and Central Districts of Illinois; U.S. Court of Appeals, Seventh Circuit; U.S. Supreme Court. *Education:* University of Illinois (A.B., 1966; J.D., 1969). Omicron Delta Kappa. Assistant Dean, University of Illinois College of Law, 1969-1971. *Member:* Madison County, Illinois State and American Bar Associations; Association of Defense Trial Attorneys (Member, Executive Council, 1998—); Illinois Association of Defense Trial Counsel (Board of Directors, 1986-1996; President, 1995-1996); Defense Research Institute; American Board of Trial Advocates (Chapter President, 2000-2001). Fellow: American Bar Foundation; American College of Trial Lawyers. ***PRACTICE AREAS:*** Negligence; Product Liability; Professional Malpractice; Insurance; Personal Injury. ***Email:*** gordon.broom@ilmolaw.com

THEODORE J. MACDONALD, JR., born Rochester, New York, May 11, 1951; admitted to bar, 1978, New York and Missouri; 1979, Illinois; 1982, U.S. District Court, Southern and Central Districts of Illinois; U.S. District Court, Eastern District of Missouri; U.S. Court of Appeals, Seventh and Eighth Circuits. *Education:* University of Pennsylvania (B.A., 1973); St. Louis University (J.D., 1977). Adjunct Professor, Washington University School of Law, 1989—. Assistant U.S. Attorney, Southern District of Illinois, 1978-1982. *Member:* Bar Association of Metropolitan St. Louis; New York State, Illinois State and American Bar Associations; The Missouri Bar; The Lawyers Association of St. Louis, Missouri; International Association of Defense Trial Counsel; Illinois Association of Defense Trial Counsel. ***PRACTICE AREAS:*** Personal Injury; Negligence; Products Liability; Insurance; Employment; Criminal; Toxic Tort. ***Email:*** ted.macdonald@ilmolaw.com

JEFFREY S. HEBRANK, born Highland, Illinois, February 6, 1957; admitted to bar, 1982, Illinois and U.S. District Court, Southern District of Illinois; 1983, Missouri and U.S. District Court, Eastern District of Missouri. *Education:* University of Dayton (B.A., 1979); Washburn University; St. Louis University (J.D., 1982). *Member:* Illinois State and American Bar Associations; The Missouri Bar; Illinois Association of Defense Trial Counsel (Member, Board of Directors, 1995—); Defense Research Institute. ***PRACTICE AREAS:*** Personal Injury; Negligence; Asbestos; Toxic Tort. ***Email:*** jeff.hebrank@ilmolaw.com

GARY E. TRUE, born Belleville, Illinois, September 19, 1954; admitted to bar, 1991, Missouri, U.S. District Court, Eastern District of Missouri and U.S. Court of Appeals, Eight Circuit; 1992, Illinois. *Education:* Southern Illinois University at Edwardsville (B.S., 1975; M.B.A., 1981); St. Louis University (J.D., summa cum laude, 1991). Delta Chi. Author: "Survey of Illinois Law: Corporate Law," Southern Illinois University Law Journal, Volume 17, Summer, 1993; "Metro Broadcasting v. FCC: A Dilution of the Right of Nonminorities to Equal Protection under the Fifth Amendment or a Temporary Aberration in Affirmative Action Jurisprudence?" St. Louis University Law Journal Volume 35, No. 3, 1990-1991. *Member:* The Missouri Bar; Illinois State and American Bar Associations; Bar Association of Metropolitan St. Louis; Missouri Society of Certified Public Accountants; American Institute of Certified Public Accountants; Estate Planning Council of St. Louis. ***PRACTICE AREAS:*** Estate Planning; Corporate Law. ***Email:*** gary.true@ilmolaw.com

STEPHEN R. KAUFMANN, born Jacksonville, Illinois, December 9, 1952; admitted to bar, 1978, Arizona; 1980, Illinois; 1988, U.S. Supreme Court; 2004, Missouri. *Education:* Knox College (B.A., Economics and Business Administration, 1975); Northwestern University (J.D., 1978). Phi Beta Kappa. Note and Comment Editor, Journal of Criminal Law and Criminology, 1978. Author: "Liability Insurance Coverage in Illinois for Environmental Damages," 12 Illinois Trial Lawyers Journal 25, Fall-Winter, 1989. Member, U.S. District Court, Central District of Illinois Advisory Committee on Local Rules of Procedure. Member, Illinois Supreme Court Rules Committee, 1992—. Barrister, Lincoln-Douglas Inn of Courts. *Member:* Sangamon County and Illinois State Bar Associations; State Bar of Arizona. ***REPORTED CASES:*** Simplex, Inc. v. Diversified Energy Systems, Inc., 847 F. 2d 1290 (7th Cir. 1988); Anderson Electric, Inc. v. Ledbetter Erection Corporation, 115 IL 2d 146 (1986); Heyen v. Sanborn Mfg. Co., 223 Il App. 3d 307 (4th Dist. 1992); Donaldson v. Central Illinois Public Service Company, 767 N.E. 2d 314 (Ill. 2002). ***PRACTICE AREAS:*** Toxic Torts; Products Liability Law; Medical Negligence; Class Actions; General Liability. ***Email:*** srk@ilmolaw.com

GERARD T. NOCE, born St. Louis, Missouri, December 18, 1951; admitted to bar, 1979, Missouri and U.S. District Court, Western and Eastern Districts of Missouri; 1980, Illinois; 1991, U.S. Court of Appeals, Eighth Circuit; 2000, U.S. Supreme Court. *Education:* University of Missouri (B.J., 1974; J.D., 1979). Phi Delta Phi. Recipient: American Jurisprudence Awards in Agency and Partnership and in Property: Evans Scholar, University of Missouri-Columbia, 1970-1974. Missouri Judicial Commission, Twenty Second Circuit, 2004—. Member, American Board of Trial Advocates, 2001—. *Member:* The Bar Association of Metropolitan St. Louis; The Missouri Bar; Lawyers Association of St. Louis; Missouri Organization of Defense Lawyers (Board Member, 1991—; Treasurer, 1996-1997; Secretary, 1997-1998; Vice President, 1998-1999; President, 1999-2000); International Association of Defense Counsel; Defense Research Institute (Missouri State Representative, 1998—). ***PRACTICE AREAS:*** Personal Injury; Toxic Torts; Professional Liability; Products Liability; Education Law. ***Email:*** gtn@ilmolaw.com

MICHAEL REDA, born Easton, Pennsylvania, November 8, 1956; admitted to bar, 1983, Illinois, Missouri and U.S. District Court, Southern District of Illinois. *Education:* University of Notre Dame (B.A., 1978); St. Louis University (J.D., 1982). *Member:* The Bar

(This Listing Continued)

Association of Metropolitan St. Louis; Madison County, Illinois State and American Bar Associations; The Missouri Bar; Illinois Association of Defense Trial Counsel. (Resident). ***PRACTICE AREAS:*** Civil Insurance Litigation. ***Email:*** mreda@ilmolaw.com

PAUL W. JOHNSON, born Milwaukee, Wisconsin, May 5, 1960; admitted to bar, 1985, Missouri and U.S. District Court, Eastern District of Missouri; 1986, Illinois. *Education:* University of Missouri at Columbia (B.A., 1982; J.D., 1985). Phi Delta Theta. *Member:* Bar Association of Metropolitan St. Louis; Illinois State Bar Association; The Missouri Bar; Illinois Association of Defense Trial Counsel. ***PRACTICE AREAS:*** Negligence; Products Liability; Insurance Defense; Insurance Coverage Disputes. ***Email:*** paul.johnson@ilmolaw.com

JOHN D. WENDLER, born Poplar Bluff, Missouri, January 22, 1952; admitted to bar, 1977, Illinois; 1983, Missouri. *Education:* University of Missouri and Southern Illinois University (B.A., 1974); St. Louis University (J.D., 1977). Recipient: Lloyd Harris Government Award, Southern Illinois University, 1974; Outstanding Teacher Award, Construction Department, Southern Illinois University, 1988. Adjunct Lecturer, Southern Illinois University School of Engineering, 1984—. *Member:* Madison County, St. Clair County and Illinois State Bar Associations; Bar Association of Metropolitan St. Louis; The Missouri Bar; American Corporate Counsel Association; Illinois Association of Defense Trial Counsel. ***Email:*** john.wendler@ilmolaw.com

LISA K. FRANKE, born Staunton, Illinois, September 11, 1957; admitted to bar, 1982, Illinois; 1983, Missouri and U.S. District Court, Southern District of Illinois. *Education:* Southern Illinois University at Carbondale (B.S., 1979; J.D., 1982). Phillip C. Jessup International Moot Court Team 1980-1981. Assistant State's Attorney, St. Clair County, Illinois, 1982-1988. *Member:* St. Clair County and Illinois State Bar Associations; The Missouri Bar. ***PRACTICE AREAS:*** Negligence; Medical Malpractice. ***Email:*** lisa.franke@ilmolaw.com

BRENDA G. BAUM, born Keokuk, Iowa; admitted to bar, 1988, Missouri; 1989, Illinois and U.S. District Court, Eastern District of Missouri. *Education:* Grinnell College (B.A., in English, 1985); Washington University (J.D., 1988). *Member:* Bar Association of Metropolitan St. Louis; The Missouri Bar; Illinois State and American Bar Associations. ***PRACTICE AREAS:*** Litigation. ***Email:*** brenda.baum@ilmolaw.com

DANIEL W. FARROLL, born Centreville, Illinois, January 7, 1966; admitted to bar, 1992, Illinois; 1993, Missouri, U.S. District Court, Southern District of Illinois and U.S. District Court, Eastern District of Missouri. *Education:* University of St. Thomas (B.A., 1988); Southern Illinois University at Carbondale (J.D., 1992). Member: Order of the Barristers; Philip C. Jessup Moot Court, 1991-1992. *Member:* Illinois State and American Bar Associations; The Missouri Bar; Illinois Association of Defense Trial Counsel. ***PRACTICE AREAS:*** Construction; Injury; Negligence; Products Liability; Insurance. ***Email:*** dan.farroll@ilmolaw.com

THOMAS SCOTT STEWART, born Columbus, Georgia, April 1, 1963; admitted to bar, 1995, Illinois; 1996, Missouri and U.S. District Court, Southern District of Illinois; U.S. District Court, Central District of Illinois and Eastern District of Missouri; U.S. Court of Appeals, Seventh Circuit. *Education:* St. Lawrence University (Govt., cum laude, 1985); St. Louis University (J.D., magna cum laude, 1995). Author: 13 St. Louis U. Publ. L. Rev. 887. *Member:* Illinois State and American Bar Associations. [Capt., U.S. Army, 1985-1989]. ***PRACTICE AREAS:*** Employment Law; Negligence; Civil Litigation. ***Email:*** scott.stewart@ilmolaw.com

TROY A. BOZARTH, born Bloomington, Illinois, October 29, 1969; admitted to bar, 1996, Illinois and U.S. District Court, Southern District of Illinois. *Education:* Illinois Wesleyan University (B.A., 1992); Drake University (J.D./M.B.A., 1996). *Member:* Illinois Association of Defense Trial Counsel. ***PRACTICE AREAS:*** Civil Litigation. ***Email:*** troy.bozarth@ilmolaw.com

WAYNE D. SKIGEN, born Stamford, Connecticut, April 16, 1956; admitted to bar, 1981, California; 2001, Illinois. *Education:* Tufts University; Colorado College (B.A., cum laude, 1978); Georgetown University (J.D., cum laude, 1981). Member, 1979-1980 and Editor, 1980-1981, Georgetown Law Journal. Member, Georgetown Criminal Justice Clinic, 1980-1981. Instructor, Legal Research, Writing and Oral Advocacy, Georgetown University Law Center, 1979-1980. *Member:* Bar Association of San Francisco; Los Angeles County Bar Association; State Bar of California. ***SPECIAL AGENCIES:*** Medical Board of California. ***PRACTICE AREAS:*** Commercial Litigation. ***Email:*** wayne.skigen@ilmolaw.com

ANNE B. SCHMIDT, born St. Louis, Missouri, March 2, 1954; admitted to bar, 1984, Missouri; 1995, Illinois. *Education:* University of Missouri (B.S., 1976); Washington University (J.D., 1984). Commissioner, Missouri Housing Development Commission, 2000—. *Member:* The Missouri Bar; Illinois State Bar Association. ***PRACTICE AREAS:*** Asbestos Defense (100%). ***Email:*** anne.schmidt@ilmolaw.com

ASSOCIATES

Paul B. Hunker, Jr. (Not admitted in IL); ***William L. Hanks; Joseph F. Grabowski; Kenneth E. Dick; George A. Kiser; Carl P. McNulty, II; Musette H. Vogel; Gregg A. Kinney; David Laurent; Gary A. Meadows; Stephen C. Morgan*** (Not admitted in IL); ***Robert H. Sands; Sean P. Sheehan; Michael J. Chessler; Anna R. Grabowski; W. Jason Rankin; Katherine M. Smith; Kristen Lynn Dieterich; Jennifer J. Scheibal; J. Phillip Steinman; Cassandra J. Hansell; Laura A. Hoffstetter*** (Not admitted in IL); ***Rebecca A. Nickelson; Matthew W. Potter; Bharat Varadachari*** (Not admitted in IL); ***Gretchen Wallace*** (Not admitted in IL); ***Beth A. Bauer; Brandy R. Beger; Thomas Patrick Briddick; Amanda M. Mueller; Nicholas V. Voswinkel*** (Not admitted in IL); ***Regina Lynn Lewis Wells; Jarrod P. Beasley; Candice D. Bennett; Dallas W. Cupp; James R. Grabowski; Eric P. Hall; Brian J. Huelsmann; Marc Jacob; Thomas H. Marrs; Noel L. Smith, Jr.; Allison Sonneveld; Erin Lyn Weber; E. Timothy Assouad*** (Not admitted in IL); ***Steven R. Belcher; Kurt Christian Benecke*** (Not admitted in IL); ***Daniel H. Cuneo*** (admission pending); ***Douglas J. McCarty; Edna L. McLain; Kevin N. Mellick; Rachel D. Silger; Patrick W. Stufflebeam; Jill R. Sundberg; Michael L. Young; Dede K. Zupanci; John H. Bornhofen; Matthew B. Champlin; Peter A. Corsale; Carolyn M. Husmann; Kelly M. Plummer; Benjamin W. Powell; Eric D. Rosser; Dougglas A. Stultz; J. Michael Ward; Michael R. Wesley; Olga Camp; Amy L. Gervich*** (Not admitted in IL); ***Michael P. Murphy; Kathleen M. Nester; Michael C. Schroer*** (Not admitted in IL); ***Carol L. Sparks; Michael T. Harvath*** (Not admitted in IL).

REPRESENTATIVE CLIENTS: Ameritech; Bituminous Insurance Company; BJC Health Systems; Cincinnati Insurance Company; CNA; Illinois State Bar Association Mutual Insurance Company; Kemper Insurance Company; Laclede Gas Company; Prairie Farms Dairy, Inc.; St. Paul Fire and Marine Insurance Company; The Tobacco Institute; W.R. Grace.

CALLIS, PAPA, HALE, SZEWCZYK, RONGEY & DANZINGER, P.C.

EDWARDSVILLE, ILLINOIS

(See Granite City)

General Civil, Trial and Appellate Practice. Federal Employers Liability Law, Negligence, Labor and Personal Injury, Workers Compensation, Probate, Estate Planning, Municipal and School, Criminal Law, Family Law.

CARLSON & CARLSON, P.C.

90 EDWARDSVILLE PROFESSIONAL PARK
P.O. BOX 527
EDWARDSVILLE, ILLINOIS 62025
Telephone: 618-656-0066
Fax: 618-656-0009
URL: http://www.carlsoninjurylaw.com
Email: ecarlson@mcleodusa.net
URL: http://www.lawyers.com/carlson&carlson

Personal Injury. Trial Practice. Federal Employers Liability. Toxic Torts. Products Liability, Premises Liability, Medical Malpractice, Car and Truck Accident Litigation, Civil Litigation, and Aviation Law.

FIRM PROFILE: Carlson & Carlson, P.C. is comprised of Jon G. Carlson and Eric J. Carlson. Together the firm has handled diverse cases involving railroad and truck accident litigation, products liability, industrial accidents, premises liability and medical malpractice. Numerous large verdicts have been attained. The firm represents clients nationwide. Jon Carlson challenged the Tort Reform Act in Illinois which was overturned by the Supreme Court in its entirety in the case of Vern Best vs. Taylor Machine Works, Inc., et al, 179 Ill.2d 367, 689 N.E.2d 1057 (Ill. 1997). In 2004 Jon G. Carlson was the recipient of the Leonard M. Ring Lifetime Achievement Award presented by the Illinois Trial Lawyers Association.

JON G. CARLSON, born Wakefield, Michigan, June 25, 1943; admitted to bar, 1967, Illinois; 1968 U.S. District Court, Eastern District of Illinois; 1977, U.S. District Court, Southern District of Illinois; 1983, U.S. Court of Appeals, Eighth Circuit; 1990, Missouri; 1993, U.S. Court of Appeals, Seventh Circuit; 1993, U.S. Supreme Court; 1994, U.S. District Court, Central District of Illinois; 1997 U.S. District Court, Eastern District of Missouri. *Education:* University of Illinois (A.B., 1965; J.D., 1967). Recipient, Leonard M. Ring Lifetime Achievement Award, Illinois Trial Lawyers Association, 2004. Finalist, Trial Lawyer of the Year, Trial Lawyers for Public Justice, 1998. Author: "Products Liability Crisis: Fact or Fantasy?" Litigation, 1978 and Chapter 7, "Protecting Litigation Rights," 1978, 1985, 1988, 2003 Illinois Civil Practice Before Trial; "Consulting Editor, Nichols Illinois Civil Practice," 1A General Considerations Summons and Appearances, 2001; ITLA Seminar speaker at the following: "How to Do it Seminar" Chicago, 1973; "Revolutionary Seminar" Fairview Heights, 1976; "The Bread & Butter Seminar for Practicing Attorneys" St. Louis & Chicago, 1979; "College of Advocacy Seminar" Bloomington 1980, 1981, 1982, 1986, 1987; "Basic Trial Advocacy Seminar, Cross Examination" Chicago 1980; "How to get the Six Figure Verdict in the Soft Tissue Injury Case" Chicago & St. Louis 1981; "Damages in Wrongful Death & Trial and Pre-Trial Techniques Seminar" St. Louis, 1983; "Case Evaluation and Negotiations, Products Liability" Lincolnshire, 1983; "Highway Safety" Chicago, 1985; "Forum Non Conveniens" 1986; "Trial Preparation" Chicago, 1988; "Trial Notebook Series, Privilege" St. Louis, 1991; "Presidential Face-Off Seminar" Chicago, 1993; "Hot Tips - Proven & Winning Ways in Personal Injury Cases" Bloomington, 1993; "Discovery", Chicago, 1995; "A Winning Game Plan" Springfield, 1996; "Negotiating & Settling Personal Injury Cases" Chicago, 1998; "Past Presidents Seminar", Chicago, 2000; "Workshop 2000 — Practical Tips for the Busy Plaintiff's Attorney" St. Louis, 2000; "How to Handle Accident Cases Efficiently, Economically and Expertly" St. Louis, 2001; "Past President's Seminar" Chicago 2002; "Point/Counterpoint" St. Louis, 2003; "Past Presidents Seminar" Chicago, 2004; "Wrongful Death", St. Louis, 2005. *Member:* Tri-City, Madison County, Illinois State (Member: Tort Section Council, 1972-1980; Admiralty Section, 1984-1985) and American Bar Associations; Illinois Trial Lawyers Association (Member, Board of Managers, 1971-1984; Secretary, 1972-1973; Treasurer, 1973-1974; Third Vice President, 1984-1985; Second Vice President, 1985-1986; President-Elect, 1986-1987; President, 1987-1988); The Association of Trial Lawyers of America; Missouri Trial Lawyers Association. Life Fellow: Illinois Bar Foundation; American Bar Foundation. (Also Of Counsel to Mullen & Minella). ***REPORTED CASES:*** Vern Best vs. Taylor Machine Works, Inc., et al; Isbell v. Union Pacific Railroad Co., 318 Ill. App.3d 1011 (Ill. App. 5th Dist. 2001); Ficken v. Alton & Southern Ry. Co. 291 Ill. App.3d 365 (Ill. App. 5th Dist. 2001); Miller v. Alton & Southern Ry. Co., 233 Ill. App.3d 896 (Ill. App. 5th Dist. 1992). ***PRACTICE AREAS:*** Personal Injury Law; Federal Employers Liability Law; Products Liability Law; Aviation Law; Medical Malpractice; Truck Accidents; Toxic Torts. ***Email:*** jcarlson@mcleodusa.net

ERIC JON CARLSON, born Belleville, Illinois, March 16, 1970; admitted to bar, 1995, Illinois; 1996, Missouri. *Education:* University of Illinois (B.A., cum laude, 1992); Southern Illinois University (J.D., magna cum laude, 1995). Phi Kappa Phi. Order of Barristers. Finalist, Trial Lawyer of the Year, Trial Lawyers for Public Justice, 1998. Articles Editor, Southern Illinois University Law Journal. Member: Southern Illinois Inn of Court, 1994-1995; National Products Liability Moot Court Team, 1993-1995. Author: Casenote, "Premises Liability: The Exception That Swallowed the Rule, Lee v. CTA," 19 S.Ill.L.J. 217. Speaker, "Offensive Use of Supreme Court Rule 237 (b)," Illinois Trial Lawyers Association, 2002; "Testimonial Evidence and Direct Examination" Illinois Trial Lawyers As-

(This Listing Continued)

CARLSON & CARLSON, P.C., Edwardsville—Continued

sociation, 2004. Consulting Editor, Nichols Illinois Civil Practice, Vol. 1A, General Considerations Summons and Appearances, 2001; Nichols Illinois Civil Practice," Vol. 5, Enforcement of Judgments - Costs, 2004. *Member:* Madison County, Illinois State and American Bar Associations; Illinois Trial Lawyers Association (Member: Board of Advocates, 2000-2001; Board of Managers, 2002—); The Association of Trial Lawyers of America. ***REPORTED CASES:*** Best v. Taylor Machine Works, Inc., 179 Ill.2d 367, 689 N.E.2d 1057 (Ill. 1997); Isbell v. Union Pacific Railroad Co., 318 Ill. App.3d 1011 (Ill. App.5th Dist. 2001). ***PRACTICE AREAS:*** Personal Injury; Federal Employees Liability; Products Liability; Medical Malpractice; Truck Accidents; Premises Liability; Civil Litigation; Toxic Torts. ***Email:*** ecarlson@mcleodusa.net

OF COUNSEL TO

MULLEN & MINNELLA, Chicago, Illinois.

CATES, KUROWSKI, BAILEY & SHULTZ, LLC

EDWARDSVILLE, ILLINOIS

(See Belleville)

Civil Litigation Practice. Toxic Tort, Asbestos, Insurance, Bad Faith Claims, Insurance Defense, Employment Law, Family Law.

COFFEY LAW FIRM

PROFESSIONAL CORPORATION

125 NORTH BUCHANAN STREET
P.O. BOX 247
EDWARDSVILLE, ILLINOIS 62025-0247
Telephone: 618-656-2244
Fax: 618-656-1307
Email: info@midwestlawfirm.com
URL: http://www.midwestlawfirm.com

Business Law, Corporate Law, Contracts, Mergers, Acquisitions and Divestitures, Trusts and Estates, Wills and Probate, Real Estate.

GARY R. COFFEY, born Sullivan County, Indiana, February 13, 1932; admitted to bar, 1955, Illinois. *Education:* University of Illinois (B.S. in Commerce and Law, 1953; J.D., 1955). [Major, USMCR, Retired]. ***PRACTICE AREAS:*** Trusts and Estates; Wills; Probate; Real Estate. ***Email:*** garycoffey@midwestlawfirm.com

GREGORY W. COFFEY, born Alton, Illinois, November 1, 1959; admitted to bar, 1985, Illinois. *Education:* University of Illinois (B.S., Accountancy, 1982); Northern Illinois University (J.D., cum laude, 1985). Member, Estate Planning Council of St. Louis. *Member:* American Bar Association; American Institute of Certified Public Accountants; Illinois C.P.A. Society. ***PRACTICE AREAS:*** Business Law; Corporate Law; Trusts and Estates; Real Estate; Wills; Probate. ***Email:*** gregcoffey@midwestlawfirm.com

JOHN W. McCRACKEN, born Downers Grove, Illinois, 1967; admitted to bar, 1997, Illinois; 1998, Missouri. *Education:* Millikin University (B.S., 1990); Southern Illinois University - Edwardsville (M.P.A., 1992); St. Louis University (J.D., 1997). *Member:* Madison County and Illinois State Bar Associations; The Missouri Bar. ***PRACTICE AREAS:*** Business Law; Corporate Law; Contracts; Mergers, Acquisitions and Divestitures; Real Estate; Mortgage Foreclosure; Real Estate Litigation; Probate Litigation; Civil Litigation. ***Email:*** johnmccracken@midwestlawfirm.com

---

SANDRA J. TATOIAN, born St. Louis, Missouri, October 24, 1975; admitted to bar, 2002, Illinois; 2003, Missouri. *Education:* Truman State University (B.S., 1998); Southern Illinois University, Carbondale (J.D., 2002). *Member:* Madison County and Illinois State Bar Associations. ***PRACTICE AREAS:*** Real Estate; Real Estate Litigation; Civil Litigation; Corporate Law; Business Law; Probate; Guardianship; Collections. ***Email:*** sandratatoian@midwestlawfirm.com

DANIELLE ANGELIQUE LA CHANCE-YATES, born San Bernardino, California, January 15, 1972; admitted to bar, 1999, Illinois; 2004, U.S. District Court, Southern District of Illinois. *Education:* William Woods College (B.A., 1993); Southern Illinois University (J.D., M.B.A., 1999). *Member:* Madison County and Illinois State Bar Associations. ***PRACTICE AREAS:*** Probate; Estate Planning; Municipal Law; State Government Law; Business Law; Corporate Law. ***Email:*** daniellelachance@midwestlawfirm.com

DIXON & JOHNSTON, P.C.

EDWARDSVILLE, ILLINOIS

(See Belleville)

Family Law, Social Security Disability, Personal Injury, Bankruptcy, Mortgage Foreclosure.

JULIE HARPER

EDWARDSVILLE, ILLINOIS

(See Alton)

Traffic, DWI, Bankruptcy, Estate Planning, Real Estate, Contracts, Wills, Probate, Trusts, General Practice, Criminal, Buying and Selling Homes, Guardianships, Automobile Accidents, Adoptions.

HEYL, ROYSTER, VOELKER & ALLEN

PROFESSIONAL CORPORATION

SUITE 100, MARK TWAIN PLAZA II
103 WEST VANDALIA STREET
P.O. BOX 467
EDWARDSVILLE, ILLINOIS 62025
Telephone: 618-656-4646
Telecopier: 618-656-7940
Email: firm@hrva.com
URL: http://www.hrva.com

Peoria, Illinois Office: Suite 600, Chase Building, 124 S.W. Adams, 61602. Telephone: 309-676-0400. Telecopier: 309-676-3374.
Springfield, Illinois Office: Suite 575, National City Center, P.O. Box 1687, 62705. Telephone: 217-522-8822. Telecopier: 217-523-3902.
Urbana, Illinois Office: Suite 300, 102 East Main Street, P.O. Box 129, 61803-0129. Telephone: 217-344-0060. Telecopier: 217-344-9295.
Rockford, Illinois Office: Second Floor, National City Bank Building, 120 West State Street, P.O. Box 1288, 61105-1288. Telephone: 815-963-4454. Telecopier: 815-963-0399.

General Civil Trial and Appellate Practice in all Courts, Insurance Defense, Workers' Compensation Defense, Professional Liability Defense, Truck Accidents, Construction Law, Railroad Accidents and Injuries, Insurance Coverage, Self Insured Defense, Products Liability Defense, Civil Rights, Asbestos Defense, Class Action Defense, Corporate Law, Health Care, Banking, Government, Employment, Environmental, Probate, Elder Law, Agribusiness, Immigration, Religious Institutions, Nonprofit and Charitable Organizations, College and University Law, and Real Estate.

PARTNERS

ROBERT H. SHULTZ, JR., born December 8, 1952; admitted to bar, 1978, Illinois. *Education:* University of Illinois (A.B., 1975; J.D., 1978). *Member:* DRI; Illinois Association of Defense Trial Counsel; American Board of Trial Advocates; Federation of Defense and Corporate Counsel. ***PRACTICE AREAS:*** Class Action Defense; Mass Torts Defense; Professional Liability Defense; Products Liability Defense; Insurance Defense. ***Email:*** rshultz@hrva.com

KENT L. PLOTNER, born July 13, 1958; admitted to bar, 1985, Illinois; 1998, Missouri. *Education:* Illinois State University (B.S., 1980); St. Louis University (J.D., 1985). *Member:* DRI; Illinois Association of Defense Trial Counsel. ***PRACTICE AREAS:*** Asbestos Defense; Toxic Tort Defense; First and Third Party Insurance Defense. ***Email:*** kplotner@hrva.com

RICHARD K. HUNSAKER, born June 2, 1960; admitted to bar, 1986, Illinois; 1992, Wisconsin. *Education:* University of Illinois (B.A., with high distinction, 1982; M.A., 1983); Washington University at St. Louis (J.D., 1986). *Member:* Illinois Association of Defense Trial Counsel; DRI. ***PRACTICE AREAS:*** Medical Malpractice Defense; Class Action Defense; Professional Liability Defense; Construction Accidents. ***Email:*** rhunsaker@hrva.com

JAMES A. TELTHORST, born July 2, 1962; admitted to bar, 1992, Illinois; 1993, Missouri. *Education:* University of Missouri, Rolla (B.S., 1985); St. Louis University (J.D., 1992). ***PRACTICE AREAS:*** Workers Compensation Defense.

JOSEPH P. WHYTE, born October 4, 1962; admitted to bar, 1990, Missouri; 1991, Illinois. *Education:* University of Missouri (B.S., 1984); St. Louis University (J.D., 1990). ***PRACTICE AREAS:*** Product Liability Defense; Class Action Defense; Professional Liability. ***Email:*** jwhyte@hrva.com

MICHAEL T. KOKAL, born May 28, 1965; admitted to bar, 1992, Illinois; 1993, Missouri. *Education:* University of Notre Dame (B.S.E.E., 1987); Washington University (M.L.A., 1989); University of Missouri (J.D., 1992). Law Clerk, Hon. Richard Mills, U.S. District Judge, Central District of Illinois, 1992-1994. [Capt., U.S.Air Force Reserve, 1987-1992]. ***PRACTICE AREAS:*** Medical Malpractice Defense; Products Liability Defense; Construction Law. ***Email:*** mkokal@hrva.com

OF COUNSEL

EDWARD E. JOHNSTON, born January 6, 1960; admitted to bar, 1986, Illinois; 1992, Missouri. *Education:* University of Illinois (B.A., 1982); Washington University (J.D., 1985). ***PRACTICE AREAS:*** Toxic Tort Defense; Asbestos Litigation Defense; Workers Compensation Defense. ***Email:*** eejohnston@hrva.com

TIMOTHY A. GRAHAM, born February 5, 1955; admitted to bar, 1984, Missouri; 2002, Illinois. *Education:* Illinois State University (B.S., 1981); Washington University (J.D., 1984). ***PRACTICE AREAS:*** Toxic Tort Defense; Asbestos Litigation Defense. ***Email:*** tgraham@hrva.com

WILLIAM J. DYE, JR., born 1947; admitted to bar, 1972, Illinois; 1974, Missouri. *Education:* Washington University (B.A., 1969; J.D., 1972). ***PRACTICE AREAS:*** Toxic Tort Defense; Asbestos Litigation Defense. ***Email:*** wdye@hrva.com

PHILIP M. EISELE, born November 3, 1953; admitted to bar, 1979, Missouri; 2005, Illinois. *Education:* University of Missouri (B.A., 1976; J.D., 1979). ***PRACTICE AREAS:*** Toxic Tort Defense; Civil Litigation Defense. ***Email:*** peisele@hrva.com

DOUGLAS R. HEISE, born April 8, 1958; admitted to bar, 1983, Illinois. *Education:* Eastern Illinois University (B.S., 1980); John Marshall School of Law (J.D., 1983). ***PRACTICE AREAS:*** Civil Litigation Defense; Municipal Law; Employment Law. ***Email:*** dheise@hrva.com

MICHAEL D. CLARK, born September 17, 1950; admitted to bar, 1984, Illinois; 1993, Missouri. *Education:* Southern Illinois University (B.A., 1979); Northern Illinois University (J.D., 1984). ***PRACTICE AREAS:*** Civil Litigation Defense; FELA Defense; Railroad Law. ***Email:*** mclark@hrva.com

(This Listing Continued)

MICHAEL D. SCHAG, born December 10, 1967; admitted to bar, 1994, Illinois; 1995, U.S. Court of Appeals for the Armed Forces; 2001, Colorado and U.S. Court of Federal Claims. *Education:* University of Illinois (B.S., 1989); Oklahoma City University (J.D., cum laude, 1994). *Member:* National Contract Management Association. [Major, Judge Advocate, U.S. Air Force Reserve]. ***PRACTICE AREAS:*** Toxic Tort Defense; Civil Litigation Defense; Commercial Law; Government Contracts; Military Law. ***Email:*** mschag@hrva.com

JAMES J. BENTIVOGLIO, born September 13, 1955; admitted to bar, 1995, Illinois; 1996, Missouri. *Education:* San Francisco State University (B.S., summa cum laude, 1977); Southern Illinois University-Carbondale (J.D., magna cum laude, 1995). *Member:* DRI; International Association of Defense Lawyers; Missouri Organization of Defense Counsel. ***Email:*** jbentivoglio@hrva.com

JANE M. BOARDMAN, born February 5, 1965; admitted to bar, 1993, Missouri; 1994, Illinois. *Education:* Central Missouri State University (B.S., 1987, M.S., 1988); Saint Louis University (J.D., 1993). ***Email:*** jboardman@hrva.com

ASSOCIATES

Christine M. McClimans
Michael F. Daniels
Aaron J. Bryant
Deborah A. Hawkins
Gray M. Magee, III
Laura L. Althardt
Mary Jo Kuca
John C. Craig
Jeffrey T. Bash
Patrick D. Cloud (admission pending)
Patrick E. Foppe
W. Wylie Blair
Christine A. Heinsz
Matthew J. Morris

Our lawyers are members of the American, state and local bar associations and, in many cases, are members of the local American Inn of Court chapters; where applicable, leadership positions in these organizations are listed.

(For Other Biographical Information, see Professional Biographies at Peoria, Rockford, Springfield and Urbana)

HINSHAW & CULBERTSON LLP

Hinshaw & Culbertson LLP is an Illinois registered limited liability partnership that has elected to be governed by the Illinois Uniform Partnership Act (1997)

Established in 1934

156 NORTH MAIN STREET
SUITE 206
EDWARDSVILLE, ILLINOIS 62025
Telephone: 618-655-0342
Facsimile: 618-655-0467
Email: kfox@hinshawlaw.com
URL: http://www.hinshawlaw.com

Other Office Locations: Chicago, Illinois; Appleton, Wisconsin; Belleville, Illinois; Boston, Massachusetts; Champaign, Illinois; Crystal Lake, Illinois; Fort Lauderdale, Florida; Jacksonville, Florida; Joliet, Illinois; Lisle, Illinois; Miami, Florida; Milwaukee, Wisconsin; Minneapolis, Minnesota; New York, New York; Peoria, Illinois; Phoenix, Arizona; Portland, Oregon; Providence, Rhode Island; Rockford, Illinois; St. Louis, Missouri; San Francisco, California; Schererville, Indiana; Springfield, Illinois; Tampa, Florida; Waukegan, Illinois.

Appellate, Banking & Financing, Bankruptcy & Creditors' Rights, Class Action Litigation, Civil Rights Defense, Commercial Litigation, Corporate, Construction Law, Director & Officer Liability, Employee Benefits, Environmental, Fidelity & Surety, General Liability Litigation, Government, Health Care, Insurance Coverage, Insurance and Reinsurance, Labor & Employment, Legal Malpractice, Medical Malpractice, Mergers & Acquisitions, Municipal Liability, Personal Injury Defense, Public Law, Products Liability Litigation, Professional Liability, Regulatory, Real Estate, School Law, Securities, Taxation, Transportation, White Collar Crime and Workers' Compensation Defense.

FIRM PROFILE: Hinshaw & Culbertson LLP is a national AMLaw 200 firm with 425 lawyers in 27 offices coast-to-coast. The firm offers a full-service practice, with an emphasis in commercial and defense litigation, corporate, environmental, employment and construction law, as well as the representation of professionals in their liability and risk management matters.

Hinshaw provides services to a range of clients in financial services, construction, health care, not-for-profit, insurance, legal, manufacturing, real estate, transportation and other industries. Firm clients also include government agencies, municipalities and schools.

Hinshaw was founded in 1934. The firm is headquartered in Chicago, and maintains offices in 12 states: Arizona, California, Florida, Illinois, Indiana, Massachusetts, Minnesota, Missouri, New York, Oregon, Rhode Island and Wisconsin.

PARTNERS

MARK D. BAUMAN, born St. Louis, Missouri, February 23, 1959; admitted to bar, 1984, Illinois and U.S. District Court, Southern District of Illinois; 1985, Missouri, U.S. District Court, Central District of Illinois and U.S. Court of Appeals, Seventh Circuit. *Education:* St. Louis University (B.A., 1981); Southern Illinois University (J.D., 1984). *Member:* St. Clair County (Member, Membership Committee, 1985-1986) and Illinois State Bar Associations; The Missouri Bar; Defense Research Institute; Association of Defense Trial Attorneys (Member, Executive Council, 1995-1998). (Also at Belleville, Illinois Office). ***PRACTICE AREAS:*** Product Liability Litigation; Personal Injury Defense Litigation; Legal Negligence Defense; Medical Negligence Defense; Construction Injury Litigation; Commercial Litigation; Class Action Defense; Insurance; Professional Liability Defense. ***Email:*** mbauman@hinshawlaw.com

JAMES F. CLAYBORNE, JR., born St. Louis, Missouri, December 29, 1963; admitted to bar, 1988, Illinois; 1991, U.S. District Court, Southern District of Illinois; 1994, Missouri and U.S. District Court, Eastern District of Missouri. *Education:* Tennessee State University (B.S., Political Science, 1985); University of Miami (J.D., 1988). State Senator, 1995—. Member, St. Louis Sports Commission. Delegate, American Bar Association House of Delegates. NFL Agent. *Member:* Metro-East and Illinois State (Member, Board of Governors, 1995—) Bar Associations. (Also at Belleville, Illinois Office). ***PRACTICE AREAS:*** Products Liability Litigation; Class Action Litigation; Commercial Litigation; Personal Injury Litigation; Municipal Law. ***Email:*** jclayborne@hinshawlaw.com

JOHN L. GILBERT, born Alton, Illinois, November 18, 1950; admitted to bar, 1975, Illinois and U.S. District Court, Southern District of Illinois; 1979, U.S. Supreme Court; 1983, U.S. Court of Appeals, Seventh Circuit; 1987, U.S. District Court, Central District of Illinois; 1990, Missouri. *Education:* University of Illinois (B.A., Phi Beta Kappa, high honors with distinction, 1972); Washington University (J.D., 1975). Phi Eta Sigma; Phi Beta Kappa; Phi Delta Phi. Illinois Civil Service Commissioner, 1978-1991. Adjunct Assistant Professor of Management, Southern Illinois University at Edwardsville. Former Chairman, Mercantile Bank, Edwardsville. Assistant State's Attorney, Madison County, Illinois. Member, National Association of College and University Attorneys. Member, Hearing Panel, Illinois Attorney Registration and Disciplinary Commission, Former Member, SIUE School of Business Advisory Committee. Board Member, St. Louis Metropolitan Major Case Squad. Former President and Secretary, Edwardsville, Illinois Rotary Club. *Member:* Madison County and Illinois State Bar Associations. (Also at Belleville, Illinois Office). ***PRACTICE AREAS:*** Labor Law; Civil Rights Defense; Class Actions; College and University Law. ***Email:*** jgilbert@hinshawlaw.com

JEFFREY R. GLASS, born Xenia, Ohio, July 7, 1953; admitted to bar, 1978, Illinois; 1980, U.S. District Court, Southern District of Illinois; 1987, Missouri; U.S. District Court, Eastern District of Missouri; U.S. District Court, Central District of Illinois. *Education:* St. Louis University (B.A., magna cum laude, 1974; J.D., 1978). Phi Delta Phi. Assistant State's Attorney, St. Clair County, Illinois, 1978-1982. *Member:* Madison County, St. Clair County and Illinois State Bar Associations; Defense Research Institute; Association of Defense Trial Attorneys; Missouri Organization of Defense Lawyers. (Partner-in-Charge of Hinshaw Offices in Belleville, Illinois and Edwardsville, Illinois. Chairman on Hinshaw's Diversity Committee). ***LANGUAGES:*** French. ***PRACTICE AREAS:*** Professional Liability Litigation; Medical Malpractice; Class Actions; Products Liability Litigation; Personal Injury Litigation. ***Email:*** jglass@hinshawlaw.com

DENNIS J. GRABER, born Manhattan, Kansas, September 23, 1959; admitted to bar, 1984, Illinois; 1986, U.S. District Court, Southern District of Illinois and U.S. Court of Appeals, Seventh Circuit; 1992, Missouri; 1994, U.S. District Court, Central District of Illinois. *Education:* Illinois College (B.A., 1981); Southern Illinois University School of Law (J.D., 1984). Phi Alpha Theta; Phi Alpha Delta. *Member:* Bar Association of Metropolitan St. Louis; St. Clair County and Illinois State Bar Associations; Workers' Compensation Claims Association. (Also at Belleville, Illinois Office). ***PRACTICE AREAS:*** Commercial Litigation; Complex and Multi-District Litigation; Insurance Defense; Labor and Employment. ***Email:*** dgraber@hinshawlaw.com

CHARLES A. PIERCE, born Dunlap, Illinois, March 21, 1966; admitted to bar, 1991, Illinois; 1992, Missouri; 1993, U.S. District Court, Southern District of Illinois; 2001, U.S. District Court, Central District of Illinois; 2002, U.S. Court of Appeals, Seventh Circuit. *Education:* University of Iowa (B.S., 1988); Southern Illinois University School of Law (J.D., magna cum laude, 1991). Order of the Barristers. Law Clerk, Illinois Appellate Court, Third District, 1991-1992. Editor, 1991 and Member, 1990-1991, Survey of Illinois Law, Southern Illinois University Law Review. *Member:* St. Clair County and Illinois State Bar Associations; The Missouri Bar; Defense Research Institute; Illinois Association of Defense Trial Counsel. (Also at Belleville, Illinois Office). ***REPORTED CASES:*** Sneed v. Howell, 306 Ill.App.3d 1149, 716 N.E.2d 336, 240 Ill.Dec. 203, (5th Dist. 1999); Burris v. Shaw, 124 Fed.Appx. 431 (7th Cir. 2004); Johnny Vegas, Inc. v. City of Alton, Ill., 2005 WL 578966, (S.D.Ill. 2005). ***PRACTICE AREAS:*** Civil Rights Defense Litigation; Civil Rights Section 1983; Municipal Liability; Products Liability Litigation; Personal Injury Litigation; General Liability Litigation; Insurance Coverage Litigation; Professional Liability Litigation. ***Email:*** cpierce@hinshawlaw.com

JOHN E. SABO, born St. Louis, Missouri, January 6, 1957; admitted to bar, 1987, Illinois and U.S. District Court, Southern District of Illinois; 1988, Missouri; 1990, U.S. Court of Appeals, Seventh Circuit. *Education:* McKendree College (B.B.A., 1983); Southern Illinois University (J.D., 1987). Appointed: Administrative Law Judge, Illinois Department of Public Health, 1999-2001; Special Assistant Attorney General by the Illinois Attorney General to represent the Office of the Governor in civil action, 2002; Special Assistant States Attorney for Madison County, Illinois to represent the County in a civil action, 2002. Court Appointed Arbitrator, Circuit Court, St. Clair County, Illinois, 1999—. Voted one of the leading lawyers in Illinois by Illinois attorneys, 2003. *Member:* St. Clair County and Illinois State Bar Associations; The Missouri Bar. (Also at Belleville, Illinois Office). ***PRACTICE AREAS:*** Banks and Banking; Class Actions; Commercial Law; Complex and Multi District Litigation; Contracts; Insurance; Litigation; Personal Injury; Products Liability. ***Email:*** jsabo@hinshawlaw.com

DAWN A. SALLERSON, born Terre Haute, Indiana, April 18, 1961; admitted to bar, 1986, Illinois; 1987, Missouri and U.S. District Court, Southern District of Illinois. *Education:* St. Mary-of-the-Woods College (B.A., 1983); St. Louis University School of Law (J.D., cum laude, 1986). Kappa Gamma Pi. U.S. District Court Rules Committee, U.S. District Court Magistrate Selection Panel, 1994. Speaker: "Your Deposition, Preparation and Examination: Defense of Company Procedures," 1995; "Limitations of Actions in Medical Malpractice Claims"; "Illinois Uninsured and Underinsured Motorist Provisions"; "Illinois Tort Reform, The Practical Effects," 1996; "Illinois Code of Civil Procedure, New Provisions, and the Impact Upon Claim Handling"; "Major Provisions and Immunities in the Illinois Tort Immunity Act," 1997; "Jury Instructions, Their Use and Effect, Under the Tort Reform Act"; "Significant Recent Decisions Impacting the Tort Immunity Act"; "Impact of Unconstitutionality of the Tort Reform Act"; "The Future of Tort Reform," 1998; "Municipal Immunities"; "Petrillo Violations," 2000; "Discovery and Investigation in Tort Actions," 2002; "Settlement/Release Protection"; "Pleadings: A Practitioner's View"; "Pleading Issues in Tort Defense," 2004; "Spoliation of Evidence," 2005; "Responsive Pleadings". *Member:* Illinois State Bar Association; American Bar Association; St. Clair County Bar Association. (Also at Belleville, Illinois Office). ***PRACTICE AREAS:*** Medical Negligence Defense; Class Actions Defense; Product Liability Litigation; Personal Injury De-

(This Listing Continued)

HINSHAW & CULBERTSON LLP, Edwardsville—Continued

fense Litigation; Legal Negligence Defense; Municipal Law; Insurance Defense. **Email:** dsallerson@hinshawlaw.com

HOAGLAND, FITZGERALD, SMITH & PRANAITIS

EDWARDSVILLE, ILLINOIS

(See Alton)

General Practice and Trials in all Federal and State Courts. Insurance, Litigation, Negligence, Product Liability, Malpractice, Employment Discrimination, Corporate, Banking, Probate, Trusts, Estates, Labor Relations, Tax Law, Workers Compensation, Commercial Transactions, Real Estate, Governmental, Bankruptcies and Foreclosures.

HUMES LAW OFFICE

515 ST. LOUIS STREET
P.O. BOX 201
EDWARDSVILLE, ILLINOIS 62025
Telephone: 618-656-0616
Fax: 618-656-3166
URL: http://www.jackhumeslaw.com

Municipal, Public Finance, Construction, Corporate, Real Estate, Wills and Probate, Trusts and Estates, Commercial and Residential Real Estate, Buying and Selling a Home, Buying and Selling a Business.

JACK H. HUMES, JR., born St. Louis, Missouri, August 7, 1952; admitted to bar, 1985, Illinois; 1987, Missouri; 1986, U.S. District Court, Southern District of Illinois. *Education:* Southern Illinois University at Edwardsville (B.A., 1974; M.S., 1975); St. Louis University (J.D., 1985). Phi Delta Phi. *Member:* Bar Association of Metropolitan St. Louis; The Missouri Bar; American Bar Association; Illinois State Bar Association; American Planning Association; American Institute of Certified Planners. ***PRACTICE AREAS:*** Municipal; Public Finance; Construction; Corporate; Real Estate; Probate. ***Email:*** jack@humeslawoffice.com

JOHNSON & ANDERSON

201 HILLSBORO AVENUE
EDWARDSVILLE, ILLINOIS 62025
Telephone: 618-659-1400
Fax: 618-659-1700
URL: http://www.johnsonandersonlaw.com
URL: http://www.j-a-law.com

Appellate Practice, Bankruptcy, Probate, Estate Planning, Estate Administration, Trusts and Estates, Asset Protection, Guardianship, General Civil, Family Law, Adoptions, Child Custody, Child Support, Domestic Violence, Divorce, Personal Injury, Wrongful Death, Medical Malpractice, Auto Accidents, Sexual Abuse, DWI, Drug Crimes, Juvenile Crimes, White Collar Crime, Traffic Violations, Elder Law, Parole Violation/Probation, Real Estate, Buying and Selling a Home.

BILLIE L. JOHNSON, born Lincoln, Nebraska, October 19, 1947; admitted to bar, 1986, Nebraska and U.S. District Court, District of Nebraska; 1995, Missouri; 1996, Illinois; 1997, U.S. District Court, Southern District of Illinois. *Education:* Wartburg College (B.A., 1969); Creighton University (M.A., 1975; J.D., 1986). Member, Creighton University Law Review, 1985-1986. Author: "Nebraska's 'Mysterious'New Tax Valuation System: L.B. 271, The Agricultural Land Valuation Law," Creighton Law Review, Vol. 19, No. 3, 1985-1986. *Member:* Madison County, Illinois State and American Bar Associations; The Missouri Bar; Nebraska State Bar Association. ***PRACTICE AREAS:*** Appellate Practice; Bankruptcy; Probate; Estate Planning; Estate Administration; General Civil. ***Email:*** bjohnson@j-a-law.com

KAREN A. ANDERSON, born Omaha, Nebraska, June 16, 1960; admitted to bar, 1989, Nebraska; 2002, Texas; 2003, Illinois. *Education:* University of Nebraska at Lincoln (B.A., 1983); Creighton University (J.D., 1986). *Member:* Madison County, Nebraska State and Illinois State Bar Associations; State Bar of Texas. ***PRACTICE AREAS:*** Family Law; Toxic Torts; Asbestos; Personal Injury. ***Email:*** kanderson@j-a-law.com

KNAPP, OHL & GREEN

6100 CENTER GROVE ROAD
P.O. BOX 446
EDWARDSVILLE, ILLINOIS 62025
Telephone: 618-656-5088
Fax: 618-656-5466
Email: wjk@knappohlgreen.com

Negligence, Products Liability, Insurance Coverage, Personal Injury, Workers Compensation, School Law, Municipal Law, Admiralty, Consumer Law, Medical Malpractice, Toxic Torts.

MEMBERS OF FIRM

WILLIAM J. KNAPP, born Xenia, Illinois, June 20, 1960; admitted to bar, 1985, Illinois and U.S. District Court, Southern District of Illinois; 1986, Missouri; 1995, U.S. Court of Appeals, Seventh Circuit; 1997, U.S. Supreme Court. *Education:* Graceland College (B.A., cum laude, 1982); Southern Illinois University at Carbondale (J.D., 1985). Member, Order of Barristers. Recipient, Hiram H. Lesar and Rosalee Lesar Scholarship. Member, 1983-1985 and Captain, 1984-1985, Jessup International Moot Court Team.

(This Listing Continued)

Member: Madison County and Illinois State Bar Associations; The Missouri Bar; Illinois Association of Defense Trial Counsel. ***PRACTICE AREAS:*** Negligence; Products Liability; Insurance; Personal Injury. ***Email:*** wjk@knappohlgreen.com

DONALD J. OHL, born Highland, Illinois, March 16, 1963; admitted to bar, 1993, Illinois and Missouri; U.S. District Court, Southern and Central Districts of Illinois; U.S. District Court, Eastern District of Missouri; U.S. Court of Appeals, Seventh Circuit. *Education:* Illinois State University (B.S., magna cum laude, 1985); St. Louis University (J.D., 1993). Recipient, American Jurisprudence Award, Civil Procedure. *Member:* Madison County (Secretary, 2004-2005; Treasurer, 2005-2006) and Illinois State Bar Associations. ***PRACTICE AREAS:*** Negligence; Insurance; Personal Injury; Product Liability. ***Email:*** djo@knappohlgreen.com

L. DAVID GREEN, born Benton, Illinois, August 23, 1960; admitted to bar, 1986, Nevada and U.S. District Court, District of Nevada; 1988, Illinois; 1989, Missouri; U.S. District Court, Southern District of Illinois and U.S. Court of Appeals, Seventh Circuit; 1998, U.S. District Court, Eastern District of Missouri. *Education:* Southern Illinois University at Carbondale (B.S., 1982; J.D., 1986). *Member:* Bar Association of Metropolitan St. Louis; Madison County and Illinois State Bar Associations; State Bar of Nevada; The Missouri Bar. ***PRACTICE AREAS:*** Negligence; Employer Liability; Workers Compensation. ***Email:*** ldg@knappohlgreen.com

ASSOCIATES

ELIZABETH A. BRADLEY, born Alexander, Illinois, July 27, 1971; admitted to bar, 1997, Illinois and U.S. District, Southern District of Illinois; 1999, Missouri. *Education:* Eastern Illinois University (B.A., cum laude, 1993); Southern Illinois University (J.D., cum laude, 1997). Member: International Moot Court Team; Southern Illinois University Law Journal. *Member:* Madison County and Illinois State Bar Associations; Illinois Association of Defense Trial Counsel. ***PRACTICE AREAS:*** Insurance Coverage; Insurance Defense. ***Email:*** eab@knappohlgreen.com

MICHAEL S. PRATER, born Alton, Illinois, February 21, 1971; admitted to bar, 2001, Illinois; 2002, U.S. District Court, Southern District of Illinois; 2003, Missouri; 2004, U.S. District Court, Eastern District of Missouri. *Education:* University of Missouri at St. Louis (B.A., 1994); Southern Illinois University (J.D., 2001). *Member:* Madison, St. Clair County and Illinois State Bar Associations. ***PRACTICE AREAS:*** Workers Compensation; Civil Litigation. ***Email:*** msp@knappohlgreen.com

CARLA C. STORM, born Mattoon, Illinois, May 17, 1978; admitted to bar, 2003, Missouri; 2004, Illinois. *Education:* University of Illinois (B.S., 2000); St. Louis University (J.D., 2003). *Member:* Bar Association of Metropolitan St. Louis; Illinois State Bar Association; The Missouri Bar. ***PRACTICE AREAS:*** Negligence; Personal Injury; Insurance Defense; Products Liability. ***Email:*** ccs@knappohlgreen.com

JOHN JOSEPH LEE, born Kansas City, Missouri, September 8, 1971; admitted to bar, 1997, Missouri and U.S. District Court, Eastern District of Missouri; 1998, Illinois and U.S. District Court, Southern District of Illinois. *Education:* Truman State University (B.A., 1994); Washington University School of Law (J.D., 1997). *Member:* Illinois State Bar Association; The Missouri Bar. ***LANGUAGES:*** French. ***PRACTICE AREAS:*** Workers Compensation; Appellate Practice; Civil Litigation. ***Email:*** jjl@knappohlgreen.com

REPRESENTATIVE CLIENTS: American Service Insurance Co.; Aon Risk Services; Apex Oil Company; Aramark Uniform and Career Apparel, Inc.; Bituminous Insurance Companies; Carlisle Syntec Inc.; Cassens Transport Co.; Chubb Group of Insurance Companies; Cincinnati Insurance Company; Crawford & Company; Edwardsville Community Unit School District; El Torito Restaurants; Employers Mutual Companies; Federation of American Consumers and Travelers; Fireman's Fund Insurance Company; Gallagher Bassett Services, Inc.; Grinnell Mutual Reinsurance Company; Henderson Trucking Company; Holland Construction, Inc.; Illinois Founders Insurance Company; Johnson Controls, Inc.; Lewis Bakeries; Matrix Service Co.; Millers American Group; North American Risk Services, Inc.; Northstar Dairy; Ohio Casualty Group; P. I. & I. Motor Express; Prairie Farms Dairy, Inc.; Safeco Insurance Co.; Sentry Insurance; Sovereign General Insurance Co.; St. Paul Travelers Insurance Co.; Tower Automotive; Transport Service Company of Hinsdale.

THE LAKIN LAW FIRM, P.C.

EDWARDSVILLE, ILLINOIS

(See Wood River)

General Trial Practice. Admiralty, Federal Employers Liability Act (FELA), Personal Injury and Workers Compensation.

PAUL H. LAUBER

3B CLUB CENTRE COURT
EDWARDSVILLE, ILLINOIS 62025-3519
Telephone: 618-692-9080
Fax: 618-692-9105
Email: plauber@cbnstl.com
URL: http://www.lauberlaw.com

Business and Real Estate Transactions, Wills, Trusts, Estate Planning and Probate, Commercial and Business Litigation, Estate Planning.

PAUL H. LAUBER, born St. Louis, Missouri, February 4, 1953; admitted to bar, 1978, Illinois; 1979, Missouri and U.S. District Court, Southern District of Illinois; 1987, U.S. Court of Appeals, Seventh Circuit. *Education:* Valparaiso University (B.A., 1975; J.D., 1978). Real Estate Broker, Illinois, 1990. Instructor, Real Estate Continuing Education, Illinois, 1991. *Member:* Bar Association of Metropolitan St. Louis; Madison County and Illinois State Bar Associations; The Missouri Bar. ***REPORTED CASES:*** Groetken v. Illinois Department of Revenue (7th Cir. 1988).

REPRESENTATIVE CLIENTS: Best Western Camelot Inn; R.P. Lumber Co; Ford Motor Credit Co.; Amsted Industries Inc.; Coldwell Banker Brown Realtors; First American Title Insurance Company; X2 Collision, Inc.; Prime Development, Inc.; Carrington Homes, Inc.; Home Nursery, Inc.; Shell Community Federal Credit Union.

LUCCO, BROWN, THRELKELD & DAWSON, LLP

P.O. BOX 539
EDWARDSVILLE, ILLINOIS 62025
Telephone: 618-656-2321
Fax: 618-656-2363
URL: http://www.lbtdlaw.com

General Civil and Criminal Litigation in State and Federal Courts. Federal Criminal Defense including White Collar Criminal Defense, Corporate Internal Investigations, and Health Care Fraud Defense; State Criminal Defense including all Felonies, DUI, Traffic and Juvenile Law. Civil Litigation including Intellectual Property Litigation (Patents); Construction, Contracts, Corporations, Wrongful Death, Personal Injury, Workman's Compensation and UCC litigation.

FIRM PROFILE: The firm's origins go back to the early 1900's when Judge Dick H. Mudge first opened his law practice in Edwardsville. Today, Lucco, Brown, Threlkeld & Dawson LLP situated half a block from the Madison County Court House, maintains a civil and criminal practice in State and Federal Court. The firm represents individuals, small businesses, and corporations in Madison, St. Clair, Bond, Clinton and Macoupin Counties and throughout the Federal District of Southern Illinois. The firm is well known and is listed in the Martindale-Hubbell Bar Register of Preeminent Lawyers.

DICK H. MUDGE (1879-1952)

DICK H. MUDGE, JR. (1919-1978)

J. WILLIAM LUCCO, born Alton, Illinois, November 5, 1947; admitted to bar, 1972, Illinois; 1974, Texas. *Education:* University of Illinois (A.B., 1969; J.D., 1972). Assistant Public Defender, Madison County, Illinois, 1976-1980. Member: Board of Directors, Land of Lincoln Legal Aid, 1979-2000; Madison County Civic Center Authority Board, 1986-1990. Municipal Counsel, Village of Livingston, 1985—. Chairman, U.S. Senate Judicial Nominations Commission for Southern District of Illinois, 1997-1999. Member, Inquiry Board, Attorney Regulatory and Disciplinary Commission, 1987—. Member, Supreme Court of Illinois Committee on Judicial Performance Evaluation, 1992—. CJA Panel Committee for Southern District of Illinois. Listed, Top 5% of Lawyers, Leading Lawyers Network. *Member:* Madison County (President, 2005-2006), Illinois State and American Bar Associations; State Bar of Texas; Illinois Trial Lawyers Association (Member, Illinois Capital Litigation Trial Bar Screening Committee); The Association of Trial Lawyers of America; National Association of Criminal Defense Lawyers. ***PRACTICE AREAS:*** White Collar Criminal Defense; General Criminal Defense; Personal Injury; General Civil. ***Email:*** jlucco@lbtdlaw.com

JOSEPH R. BROWN, JR., born Kansas City, Missouri, June 6, 1949; admitted to bar, 1974, Illinois; 1991, Missouri. *Education:* Tulane University of Louisiana (B.A., 1971); University of Illinois (J.D., 1974). Phi Eta Sigma; Phi Delta Phi. Assistant States Attorney, Madison County, Illinois, 1974-1978. Member, Criminal Justice Defense Panel, U.S. District Court, Southern District of Illinois, 1981—. Listed, Top 5% of Lawyers, Leading Lawyers Network. *Member:* Madison County (President, 1987-1988), Seventh Circuit, Illinois State and American Bar Associations; Illinois Trial Lawyers Association; The Association of Trial Lawyers of America. ***PRACTICE AREAS:*** Personal Injury; Worker's Compensation; Criminal; General Civil. ***Email:*** jbrown@lbtdlaw.com

CHRISTOPHER P. THRELKELD, born Centralia, Illinois, September 8, 1968; admitted to bar, 2000, Illinois, Missouri and U.S. District Court, Southern District of Illinois. *Education:* The Citadel (B.A., 1990); Southern Illinois University of Edwardsville (M.B.A., 1993); St. Louis University (J.D., 2000; Certificate in International and Comparative Law, Center for International and Comparative Law). *Member:* Madison County, Illinois State and American (Member, Business Law Section) Bar Associations; The Missouri Bar. ***PRACTICE AREAS:*** Business Litigation; Civil Litigation; Appellate Practice; International Law; White Collar Criminal Defense; Business Associations Law; Intellectual Property Litigation. ***Email:*** cthrelkeld@lbtdlaw.com

CURTIS M. DAWSON, born Springfield, Illinois, March 1, 1967; admitted to bar, 1995, Illinois. *Education:* Eastern Illinois University (B.A., 1989); Southern Illinois University at Carbondale (J.D., magna cum laude, 1995). Law Clerk, Hon. Robert W. Cook, Illinois Appellate Court, Fourth District, 1995-1997. Assistant State's Attorney, Peoria County, 1997-2000. *Member:* Madison County and Illinois State Bar Associations. ***PRACTICE AREAS:*** Criminal Defense; Personal Injury; Driving While Intoxicated; Appellate Practice. ***Email:*** cdawson@lbtdlaw.com

ASSOCIATES

JESSICA J. KOESTER, born Granite City, Illinois, June 14, 1977; admitted to bar, 2002, Illinois. *Education:* University of Illinois, Urbana-Champaign (B.A., 1999); University of Notre Dame (J.D., 2002). ***PRACTICE AREAS:*** Criminal Law; Traffic Violations; Juvenile Law; Civil Practice; Appellate Practice. ***Email:*** jkoester@lbtdlaw.com

DEBRA KELLY ZAHALSKY, admitted to bar, 2001, Illinois; 2002, Missouri. *Education:* Southern Illinois University, Edwardsville (B.S., magna cum laude, 1998); Washington University (J.D., 2001). *Member:* Bar Association of Metropolitan St. Louis; Madison County, Illinois State and American Bar Associations. ***PRACTICE AREAS:*** Civil Practice; Intellectual Property; Class Actions; Litigation. ***Email:*** dzahalsky@lbtdlaw.com

OF COUNSEL

JAMES E. GORMAN, born Summit, Illinois, November 9, 1930; admitted to bar, 1956, Illinois. *Education:* St. Ambrose College (B.A., 1952); University of Illinois (J.D., 1955). Phi Delta Phi. Member, Hearing Panel, Illinois Attorneys Regulatory and Disciplinary Commission, 1978-1998. *Member:* Illinois State and American Bar Associations; Defense Research Institute; Illinois Defense Counsel. Fellow, American College of Trial Lawyers. [U.S. Army Security Agency, 1955-1957]. ***PRACTICE AREAS:*** Negligence; Construction Law; Product Liability; Insurance; Automobile; Malpractice; Personal Injury. ***Email:*** jgorman@lbtdlaw.com

(This Listing Continued)

REPRESENTATIVE CLIENTS: McCann Concrete Products, Inc.; Pfizer Inc.; Quigley Company, Inc.; GEICO General Insurance Company; Highland Supply Corporation.
REFERENCES: Firstar Bank; Bank of Edwardsville.

McMAHON, BERGER, HANNA, LINIHAN, CODY & McCARTHY

A PROFESSIONAL CORPORATION

EDWARDSVILLE, ILLINOIS
(See Collinsville)

Labor Relations, Civil Rights and Administrative Law, Employment Litigation in all Courts.

THOMAS J. NOONAN, P.C.

EDWARDSVILLE, ILLINOIS
(See St. Louis, Missouri)

Asbestos Litigation, Bankruptcy Litigation, Civil Litigation, Commercial Bankruptcy, Creditor Bankruptcy, Foreclosures, General Liability Defense, Insurance, Insurance Defense, Insurance Litigation, Litigation, Personal Injury, Personal Injury Defense, Products Liability, Mold Litigation, Motor Carrier Defense, Real Estate Bankruptcy, Real Estate Foreclosure, Tort Defense, Workers Compensation Defense.

POLSINELLI SHALTON WELTE SUELTHAUS PC

MARK TWAIN PLAZA
SUITE 225
101 WEST VANDALIA STREET
EDWARDSVILLE, ILLINOIS 62025
Telephone: 618-655-9500
Fax: 618-655-9640
Email: pswslaw@pswslaw.com
URL: http://www.pswslaw.com

Kansas City, Missouri Office: 700 West 47th Street, Suite 1000. Telephone: 816-753-1000. Fax: 816-753-1536.
St. Louis, Missouri Office: 100 South Fourth Street, Suite 1100. Telephone: 314-889-8000. Fax: 314-231-1776.
Other St. Louis, Missouri Office: 7733 Forsyth Boulevard, Suite 1200. Telephone: 314-889-8000. Fax: 314-727-7166.
Overland Park, Kansas Office: 6201 College Boulevard, Suite 500. Telephone: 913-451-8788. Fax: 913-451-6205.
Topeka, Kansas Office: 555 Kansas Avenue, Suite 301. Telephone: 785-233-1446. Fax: 785-233-1939.
New York Office: 292 Madison Avenue, 17th Floor, 10017. Telephone: 212-684-0199. Fax: 212-684-0197.
Washington, D.C. Office: 555 Twelfth Street N.W., Suite 710, 20004. Telephone: 202-783-3300. Fax: 202-783-3535.

Class Action Defense, Commercial Litigation, Employment Litigation, ERISA Litigation, Insurance, Mass Torts, Product Liability Defense, Toxic Torts, Toxic Torts Defense.

Nicole Cress Behnen (Also at Kansas City and St. Louis, Missouri Offices)
Stephen R. Clark (Also at Kansas City and St. Louis, Missouri Offices)
Andrew J. Cross (Resident)
Dennis J. Dobbels (Also at Kansas City and St Louis, Missouri Offices)
Joseph T. Porter, Jr. (Also at Kansas City and St Louis, Missouri Offices)
Eric M. Trelz (Also at Kansas City and St. Louis, Missouri Offices)

REPRESENTATIVE CLIENTS: LITIGATION: Alliance Medical Corp.; American Medical Systems, Inc.; Amoco Pipeline Co.; ARDI Exchange; Bayer Corp.; Exxon Company, U.S.A.; Howmedica Inc.; Bristol-Myers Squibb Co.; Honeywell International Inc. PRODUCTS LIABILITY DEFENSE: Bristol-Myers Squibb Co.; General Electric Company; Mazda Motor of America, Inc.; Nissan Motor Co., Ltd.; Toyota Motor Sales, Inc.; Honda Motor Corp.

REED, ARMSTRONG, GORMAN, MUDGE & MORRISSEY

PROFESSIONAL CORPORATION
Established in 1927
115 NORTH BUCHANAN STREET
P.O. BOX 368
EDWARDSVILLE, ILLINOIS 62025
Telephone: 618-656-0257
Facsimile: 618-692-4416
Email: info@reedarmstrong.com
URL: http://www.reedarmstrong.com

General Civil Trial and Appellate practice in all State and Federal Courts, including Missouri, Personal Injury, Negligence, Premises Liability, Products Liability, Insurance, Automobile, Construction, Commercial Litigation, Workers Compensation, Employment, Discrimination, Dram Shop/Liquor Liability, Marine/Water Recreational Boating, Wrongful Discharge, Extra Contractual Liability/Bad Faith, Property Damage, Fraud/Arson/Fire, Non-Vehicle General Liability, Eminent Domain, Civil Rights, Class Action, Environmental, Toxic Tort, School, Corporate, Probate, Estate Planning, Real Estate Law.

(This Listing Continued)

REED, ARMSTRONG, GORMAN, MUDGE & MORRISSEY, PROFESSIONAL CORPORATION, Edwardsville—Continued

FIRM PROFILE: The law firm of REED, ARMSTRONG, GORMAN, MUDGE & MORRISSEY is primarily a civil trial practice firm with an emphasis on the defense of all types of personal and property damage litigation as well as employment, environmental, toxic tort, construction injury and class action litigation. The firm also practices business law and other related areas. The firm is listed in the Bar Register of Preeminent Lawyers.

HARRY C. ARMSTRONG, born Peoria, Illinois, January 19, 1932; admitted to bar, 1955, Illinois. *Education:* University of Illinois (B.S. in Comm. & Law, 1953; J.D., 1955). Phi Alpha Delta. *Member:* Illinois State and American Bar Associations; American Board of Trial Advocates; Defense Research Institute; Illinois Trial Lawyers Association; The Association of Trial Lawyers of America. Fellow, American College of Trial Lawyers. [J.A.G.D., U.S.A.F., 1955-1957]. ***PRACTICE AREAS:*** Negligence; Automobile; Insurance; Personal Injury. ***Email:*** harmstrong@reedarmstrong.com

STEPHEN C. MUDGE, born Alton, Illinois, September 23, 1952; admitted to bar, 1977, Illinois. *Education:* St. Ambrose College (B.A., with honors, 1974); St. Louis University (J.D., 1977). Assistant States Attorney, Madison County, 1977-1980. *Member:* Illinois State and American Bar Associations; The Missouri Bar; Illinois Association of Defense Trial Counsel; The Association of Trial Lawyers of America. ***PRACTICE AREAS:*** Negligence; Construction Law; Insurance; Automobile; Premises; Product Liability; Dram Shop Liability; Personal Injury; Class Actions. ***Email:*** smudge@reedarmstrong.com

MARTIN K. MORRISSEY, born Rock Island, Illinois, September 25, 1959; admitted to bar, 1985, Illinois. *Education:* University of Illinois (B.A., magna cum laude, 1982); Southern Illinois University (J.D., 1985). *Member:* American Bar Association; Illinois Association of Defense Trial Counsel; American Board of Trial Advocates. ***PRACTICE AREAS:*** Personal Injury; Negligence; Automobile; Premises; Construction; Malpractice; Defamation; Insurance Law; Products Liability; Commercial Litigation; Business Litigation. ***Email:*** mmorrissey@reedarmstrong.com

MICHAEL J. BEDESKY, born Joliet, Illinois, March 26, 1966; admitted to bar, 1991, Illinois. *Education:* Loyola University (B.A., 1988); University of Illinois (J.D., 1991). Alpha Sigma Nu; Phi Alpha Delta. *Member:* Illinois State Bar Association. ***PRACTICE AREAS:*** Negligence; Insurance; Automobile; Dram Shop Liability; Defamation; Class Actions; Products Liability; Workers Compensation; Civil Appeals. ***Email:*** mbedesky@reedarmstrong.com

BRYAN L. SKELTON, born Aurora, Illinois, November 3, 1960; admitted to bar, 1993, Illinois; 1994, U.S. District Court, Southern District of Illinois. *Education:* Mid-America Nazarene College (B.A., 1983); University of Missouri, Kansas City (M.A., 1990); St. Louis University (J.D., cum laude, 1993). *Member:* Illinois State Bar Association. ***PRACTICE AREAS:*** Negligence; Personal Injury; Insurance; Toxic Tort; Products Liability; Premises; Automobile; Class Actions; Commercial Litigation. ***Email:*** bskelton@reedarmstrong.com

WILLIAM B. STARNES, II, born Kansas City, Missouri, January 31, 1962; admitted to bar, 1989, Illinois and U.S. District Court, Southern and Central Districts of Illinois; 1995, Missouri; U.S. Court of Appeals, 7th Circuit. *Education:* University of Kansas (B.S., Bus. Adm., 1984); University of Missouri-Kansas City (J.D., 1988). *Member:* St. Clair County and Illinois State Bar Associations. ***PRACTICE AREAS:*** Civil Litigation; Insurance Defense; Appellate Practice. ***Email:*** wstarnes@reedarmstrong.com

---

MICHAEL HOBIN, born Peoria, Illinois, August 17, 1970; admitted to bar, 2000, Illinois. *Education:* Bradley University (B.S., Political Science, 1992); Illinois State University, Normal (M.S., History, 1994); Southern Illinois University, Carbondale (J.D., 2000). Phi Delta Phi. *Member:* Illinois State Bar Association. ***Email:*** mhobin@reedarmstrong.com

DOMINIQUE N. SEYMOURE, born Rota, Spain, March 25, 1976; admitted to bar, 2001, Illinois. *Education:* Southern Illinois University (B.A., 1998; J.D., 2001). Phi Delta Phi. Order of Barristers, 2001. ***PRACTICE AREAS:*** Civil Litigation. ***Email:*** dseymoure@reedarmstrong.com

JOHN F.X. McCORD, born Rantoul, Illinois, March 22, 1963; admitted to bar, 1999, Illinois, U.S. District Court, Central District of Illinois and U.S. Court of Appeals, Seventh Circuit. *Education:* United States Naval Academy (B.S., 1985); University of Illinois (J.D., cum laude, 1999). *Champaign County and Illinois State Bar Associations. [Lt., U.S. Navy, 1985-1996].* ***PRACTICE AREAS:*** General Civil Litigation; Employment; Estate Planning; Business; Corporate. ***Email:*** jmccord@reedarmstrong.com

STEPHEN MICHAEL SZEWCZYK, born East St. Louis, Illinois, March 8, 1949; admitted to bar, 1982, Illinois. *Education:* St. Louis University (A.B., 1972; M.B.A., 1976; J.D., 1981); Washington University (LL.M., 1984). Licensed Real Estate Broker, Illinois, 1979. Instructor, Business Law, Belleville Area College, Belleville, Illinois, 1980-1982. *Member:* St. Clair County, Illinois State and American Bar Associations. ***LANGUAGES:*** Spanish. ***Email:*** sszewczyk@reedarmstrong.com

TORI L. COX, born Alton, Illinois, June 9, 1978; admitted to bar, 2003, Illinois and U.S. District Court, Southern District of Illinois. *Education:* Illinois College (B.A., English Literature, 2000); Southern Illinois University School of Law (J.D., 2003). Phi Alpha Delta. *Member:* Madison County and Illinois State Bar Associations. ***PRACTICE AREAS:*** Civil Litigation; Insurance Defense. ***Email:*** tcox@reedarmstrong.com

MARK B. MORAN, born St. Louis, Missouri, March 2, 1958; admitted to bar, 1987, Missouri; 1989, Illinois and U.S. District Court, Southern District of Illinois. *Education:* University of Missouri (B.S., 1983); St. Louis University School of Law (J.D., 1986). ***PRACTICE AREAS:*** Personal Injury; Workers Compensation; Criminal Law. ***Email:*** mmoran@reedarmstrong.com

CHRISTOPHER M. GARCIA, admitted to bar, 2004, Illinois. *Education:* The Ohio State University (B.S., 2001); Tulane University (J.D., 2004). Law Clerk, Honarable Clifford J. Proud, Southern District of Illinois, 2003.

(This Listing Continued)

ROY D. ANDERSON, born Chicago, Illinois, May 22, 1955; admitted to bar, 1994, Illinois and Missouri; 1997, U.S. District Court, Eastern District of Missouri; 1999, U.S. Court of Appeals, Eighth Circuit; 2005, U.S. District Court, Southern District of Illinois. *Education:* Wheaton College (B.A., 1977); Eden Theological Seminary (M.D., 1981); St. Louis University (J.D., 1994). Law Clerk: Paul E. Riley, U.S. District Court, Southern District of Illinois, 1994-1996; G. Patrick Murphy, 2002. Ordained Elder with Methodist Church 1981. *Member:* Madison County, Illinois; Missouri and American Bar Associations. ***LANGUAGES:*** German. ***PRACTICE AREAS:*** Personal Injury; Workers Compensation; Estates. ***Email:*** randerson@reedarmstrong.com

REPRESENTATIVE CLIENTS: State Farm Insurance Cos.; Country Companies; Standard Mutual Casualty Co.; General Casualty Co. of Wisconsin; Employers Casualty Insurance Co.; Western States Mutual Insurance Co.; Allstate Insurance Co.; Lloyds of London; Ohio Casualty Co.; Hawkeye Security Insurance Co.; Shelter Insurance Companies; Millers Mutual Insurance Co.; Pekin Insurance Cos.; New Hampshire Insurance Group; American International Adjusting Co.; Illinois Agricultural Association; Indiana Insurance Co.; Standard Oil Co.; CNA; General American Insurance Co.; Employers Reinsurance Corp.; Marinco; Millers National-Illinois Group; Thomas T. North, Inc.; Toplis & Harding, Inc.; Martin Boyer Co.; Reliance Insurance Co.; Indiana National Insurance Co.; National Farmers Insurance Co.; Millers National Insurance Co.; Southern Illinois University at Edwardsville; Dresser Industries, Inc.; Crawford & Companies; Unitrin Insurance Group; Indresco, Inc.; Home Nursery, Inc.; Industrial Electric Co.; World Color Press; Prudential Life Insurance Co. of America; TIG Ins. Companies (Trans-America); Great West Casualty Co.; K & K Insurance Companies; Inter-City Products Corp. (USA); Calvert Ins., Co.; B.A.S.F. Corp.; Tri-Star Business Communities; Capital Indemnity Insurance Co.; Beall Manufacturing; Columbia Ins. Co.; Otis Elevator Co.; Tyssen Dover Elevator Co.; Claims America; Allied Ins. Co.; Tarkett, Inc.; Fluor International.

REEG & NOWOGROCKI, L.L.C.

EDWARDSVILLE, ILLINOIS

(See St. Louis, Missouri)

Asbestos Defense, Silicosis Litigation, Toxic Tort Class Actions, Toxic Tort Defense, Products Liability Defense, Drug and Medical Device Defense, Food Borne Disease, Food Products Liability, Welding Products Liability, Torts, Insurance, Insurance Coverage, Environmental Law, Environmental Crimes and Litigation, Personal Injury, Alternative Dispute Resolution, Civil Litigation, Class Action Defense, Complex Litigation, Defense Litigation, Federal Civil Litigation, Trial Practice, Commercial Law, Fraud and Deceit, Employment Law, Appellate Practice, Trusts and Estates, Wills and Probate Law.

JENNIFER A. SHAW, P.C.

Established in 2003

201 HILLSBORO AVENUE
EDWARDSVILLE, ILLINOIS 62025
Telephone: 618-655-0555
Fax: 618-659-1700
Email: j_a_shaw@yahoo.com
URL: http://www.jashawlaw.com

Family Law, Divorce, Child Custody, Child Support, Domestic Violence, Visitation Rights, Adoption Law, General Practice.

JENNIFER A. SHAW, born Belleville, Illinois, June 10, 1971; admitted to bar, 1996, Illinois. *Education:* University of Mississippi (B.S., Biology, 1993; J.D., 1996). Beta Beta Beta. Recipient, Illinois State Young Careerist, Business and Professional Women, 2002. Member, 1998-2004, Vice President, 1999-2003 and President, 2003-2004, Board of Directors, Phoenix Crisis Center, Inc.*Member:* Madison County and Illinois State (Member, Standing Committees on: ARDC 2000; Minority and Women Participation, 2003—; Delivery of Legal Services, 2005—; Secretary, Sexual Orientation and Gender Identity, 2004—; Council Member, Human Rights Section, 2005—; Member, Special Committee on Online Legal Research) Bar Associations. ***PRACTICE AREAS:*** Family Law; Divorce; Child Custody; Child Support; Domestic Violence; Adoption Law; Same Sex Law; Domestic Partnerships; Parental Rights; Custody Law; Visitation Rights; Premarital Agreements; Postnuptial Agreements; Cohabitation Agreements. ***Email:*** jennifer-shaw@sbcglobal.net

---

STEIGER LAW OFFICES

101 WEST VANDALIA, SUITE 150
EDWARDSVILLE, ILLINOIS 62025
Telephone: 618-656-2122
Fax: 618-656-2112
Email: steigerlaw@sbcglobal.net
URL: http://www.steigerlawfirm.com

Domestic Relations, Child Custody, Divorce, Civil trial Practice, Business Litigation, Corporate Law.

FIRM PROFILE: Mr. Steiger for the past eleven years has maintained his law offices in Madison County, Illinois, while maintaining an "Of Counsel" relationship with the firm Meness, Whitney, Burnet & Trog in Clayton, Missouri. Mr. Steiger maintains an active license for the practice of law in both Illinois and Missouri. Mr. Steiger has concentrated his practice for the past twelve years in all aspects of domestic relations litigation. Steiger Law Offices ws recognized for high professional legal standards and ethics in the 2005 Bar Register Preeminent Lawyers 89th edition. Mr. Steiger's practice includes contested litigation in dissolution of marriage, paternity, modificatioin of dissolution judgments, and post-judgment enforcement actions in all areas of domestic relations litigation.

FREDERICK M. STEIGER, born San Francisco, California, April 8, 1951; admitted to bar, 1979, Missouri; 1980, Illinois. *Education:* Southern Illinois University (B.A., 1974); Washington University (J.D., 1979). *Member:* The Madison County Bar Association; The St. Clair County Bar Association; The Missouri Bar; and The Bar Association of Metropolitan St. Louis. (Also Of Counsel, Menees, Whitney & Burnet, St. Louis, Missouri).

(This Listing Continued)

PRACTICE AREAS: Family Law; Divorce; Civil Practice, including business litigation, general business and corporate litigation. ***Email:*** steigerlaw@sbcglobal.net

THOMSON LAW OFFICE

A Professional Corporation

Established in 1995

1 SUNSET HILL PROFESSIONAL CENTRE
SUITE D
P.O. BOX 538
EDWARDSVILLE, ILLINOIS 62025
Telephone: 618-692-0028
Telecopier: 618-692-0269
Email: firminfo@thomsonlaw.com
URL: http://www.lawyers.com/thomsonlaw

Insurance Defense Trial Law, Civil Trial, Personal Injury, Insurance Coverage.

STEPHEN W. THOMSON, born Sullivan, Indiana, August 16, 1946; admitted to bar, 1975, Illinois. *Education:* United States Air Force Academy (B.S., in Engineering Management, 1968); Indiana University (J.D., 1975). Adjunct Associate Professor, Trial Advocacy, St. Louis University, 1994. *Member:* Madison County (President, 1990-1991), Illinois State and American Bar Associations; Illinois Defense Counsel; Defense Research Institute. [Capt., U.S. Air Force, 1968-1972]. ***REPORTED CASES:*** State farm Fire & Cas. Co. v. Martin, 186 Ill.2d 367, 710 N.E.2d 1228, 238 Ill.Dec. 126 (Ill. Apr. 15, 1999); Logan v. Old Enterprise Farms, Ltd., 139 Ill.2d 229, 564 N.E.2d 778, 151 Ill.Dec. 323 (Ill. Nov. 21, 1990); Lamkin v. Towner, 138 Ill.2d 510, 563 N.E.2d 449, 150 Ill.Dec. 562, Prod.Liab.Rep. (CCH) P 12,593 (Ill. Oct. 04, 1990); Koch v. Spalding. 174 Ill.App.3d 692, 529 N.E.2d 19, 124 Ill.Dec. 302 (Ill.App. 5 Dist. Sep. 26, 1988); Cullen v. Olin Corp., 195 F.3dd 317, 81 Fair Empl. Prac.Cas. (BNA) 190, 77 Empl. Prac. Dec. P 46, 315 (7th Cir.(Ill.) Oct. 25, 1999); Waggoner v. Olin Corp., 169 F.3d 481, 9 A.D. Cases 88, 14 NDLR P 203 (7th Cir-.(Ill.) Feb. 26, 1999); Webb v. City of Chester, Ill., 813 F.2d 824, 43 fair Empl.Prac.Cas. (BNA) 507, 42 Empl. Prac. Dec. P 36,869, 7 Fed.R.Serv.3d 549, 22 Fed. R. Evid, Serv. 948 (7th Cir.(Ill.) Mar. 06, 1987); Garris v. Schwartz, 551 F.2d 156 (7th Cir.(Ill.) Mar. 14, 1977); Allen v. Godar, 476 F.Supp. 172 (S.D.Ill. Aug.21, 1979). ***PRACTICE AREAS:*** Personal Insurance Defense; Insurance Coverage Defense; Construction Accidents; Personal Injury Defense; Insurance Coverage.

ERIC D. BERG, born Champaign, Illinois, December 21, 1976; admitted to bar, 2004, Illinois. *Education:* University of Illinois (B.S., 1998; J.D., 2004). Member, University of Illinois Law Review. ***PRACTICE AREAS:*** Personal Injury Defense; Insurance Coverage Defense. ***Email:*** eberg@thomsonlaw.com

OF COUNSEL

JONATHAN W. FOREMAN, born May 7, 1970; admitted to bar, 1997, Illinois; 1998, Missouri. *Education:* Cornell University (B.S., 1991); University of Texas at Austin School of Business Administration (M.B.A., 1994); University of Illinois (J.D., cum laude, 1997). *Member:* Illinois State Bar. ***PRACTICE AREAS:*** Insurance Contracts; Personal Injury; Workers Compensation; Criminal Law; Real Estate. ***Email:*** jwforeman@mchsi.com

REPRESENTATIVE CLIENTS: American International Group; Country Companies; Olin Corp.; Pekin Insurance Co.; State Farm Insurance Co.; Underwriters at Lloyds, London; Zurich American Insurance Group; National Farmers Union Insurance Company; General American Life Insurance Company; American Family Insurance; Travelers Insurance; General Casualty Company; CUNA Mutual Group; United Coastal Insurance Company; Gallagher Bassett Services, Inc.; Madison Mutual Insurance Company; Standard Mutual Insurance Company; West Group, Thompson Corporation; State Farm Mutual Automobile Insurance Company.

WILLIAMS VENKER & SANDERS LLC

Established in 2001

111 E. VANDALIA STREET
SUITE 3
EDWARDSVILLE, ILLINOIS 62025
Telephone: 618-659-9100
Fax: 618-659-9125
Email: wvs@wvslaw.com
URL: http://www.wvslaw.com

Belleville, Illinois Office: 23 South First Street, 62220. Phone: 314-345-5000. Fax: 314-345-5055.

St. Louis, Missouri Office: 10 South Broadway, Suite 1600, 63102. Phone: 314-345-5000. Fax: 314-345-5055.

Aviation, Business Litigation, Employment Discrimination Litigation, Environmental Litigation, FELA, Health Care Litigation, Insurance Defense, Labor and Employment, Maritime, Medical Malpractice Defense, Occupational Disease Litigation, Premises Liability Defense, Product Liability Defense, Railroad Litigation, Toxic Torts, Transportation Litigation.

REPRESENTATIVE CLIENTS: AIG Insurance; AIMCO, Anheuser-Busch Companies, Inc.; AON Corporation; Arkansas & Missouri Railroad Company; Baker-Hughes, Inc.; Bayer Corporation; BJC HealthCare; Bridgestone/Firestone, Inc.; Caterpiller Inc.; CNA Excess and Select; Dell Computer Corporation; Electric Insurance Company; Encompass Insurance; Freeman Energy Corporation; GE Power Systems; General Electric Company; The Goodyear Tire and Rubber Company; Group Health Plan, Inc.; Harrah's Entertainment, Inc.; Kraft Foods North America, Inc.; Lear Operations Corporation; Manufacturers Railway; Marathon Oil Company; Maxon Corporation; Mine Safety Appliances; Missouri Baptist Medical Center; National Railroad Passenger Corporation (Amtrak); Owens-Corning Fiberglass Corporation; Physicians Group, LC (PGLC); The Procter & Gamble Manufacturing Company; The Purdue Frederick Company; Rockwell International Corporation; St. Anthony's Medical Center; St. John's Mercy Medical Center; Saint Louis University; Shell Oil Company.; Sisters of Mercy Health System; South Kansas & Oklahoma Railroad; Swift & Company; The Travelers Insurance Company; Unilever United States, Inc.;Valero Market & Supply Company; Wabash National Corporation; Waste Management, Inc.

(For complete biographical data on all personnel, see Professional Biographies at St. Louis, Missouri)

CRAIG & CRAIG

EFFINGHAM, ILLINOIS

(See Mattoon)

General Practice in State and Federal Courts. Coal, Oil, Gas, Mining, Oil and Gas Transportation, Insurance, Drainage and Levee Law, Environmental, Corporation, Labor Relations, Workers Compensation and Real Estate Law. Estate Planning, Probate and Bankruptcy Law. Trials and Appeals.

HELLER, HOLMES & ASSOCIATES, P.C.

EFFINGHAM, ILLINOIS

(See Mattoon)

General Civil and Trial Practice in all State, Federal and Appellate Courts. Personal Injury, Medical Negligence, Criminal Defense, Insurance, Litigation, Probate, Workers Compensation, Corporation, Commercial, Family Law, Oil and Gas.

McMAHON, BERGER, HANNA, LINIHAN, CODY & McCARTHY

A PROFESSIONAL CORPORATION

EFFINGHAM, ILLINOIS

(See Collinsville)

Labor Relations, Civil Rights and Administrative Law, Employment Litigation in all Courts.

RYAN, BENNETT & RADLOFF

EFFINGHAM, ILLINOIS

(See Mattoon)

General, Civil and Criminal Practice. Trials in all Courts. Insurance Defense, Workers Compensation, Negligence, Corporation, Probate, Estate Planning, Bankruptcy, Taxation and Oil and Gas Law. Domestic Relations, Divorce, Child Custody and Adoption Law.

LAW OFFICE OF TERRY SHARP, P.C.

EFFINGHAM, ILLINOIS

(See Mount Vernon)

Bankruptcy, Creditor's Rights, Commercial, Banking, Real Estate, Corporate, Probate and Estate Planning Law. No small collections.

SIEMER, AUSTIN, RESCH, FUHR & TOTTEN

Established in 1896

307 NORTH THIRD STREET
P.O. BOX 607
EFFINGHAM, ILLINOIS 62401-0607
Telephone: 217-342-9291
Fax: 217-342-9295
Email: attorneys@psarf.com
URL: http://www.lawyers.com/psarf

Casey, Illinois Office: 14 North Central, Room 204. Telephone: 217-932-2158. Fax: 217-932-2159. Email: psarf@joink.com

General Civil Practice. Real Estate, Corporate, Estate Planning, Probate, Insurance Defense, Banking, Family Law, Children, Commercial, Collections, Criminal Defense, Personal Injury Law, Social Security Law, Oil and Gas Law. Trial and Appellate Practice in all Courts.

FIRM PROFILE: Established in 1896, the firm has grown in size and developed and expanded its resources to serve its clients throughout South Central Illinois, the Midwest United States, and worldwide.

MEMBERS OF FIRM

HARRY S. PARKER (1871-1963)

GEORGE H. BAUER (1895-1963)

HOWARD S. PARKER (1903-1978)

JAMES S. PARKER (1933-1981)

Q. ANTHONY SIEMER, born Teutopolis, Illinois, February 29, 1944; admitted to bar, 1969, Illinois; 1976, U.S. District Court, Central and Southern Districts of Illinois; 1981, U.S. Court of Appeals, Seventh Circuit. *Education:* University of Illinois (B.A., Economics, 1966); University of Notre Dame (J.D., 1969). Member, Leading Lawyers Network. *Member:* Effingham County, Illinois State (Assembly Member, 1981-1988; Member, Sections on: Banking; Taxation; Business Advice Financial Planning; Business and Financial Planning Section Council, 2004—) and American Bar Associations. (Also at Casey Office). ***PRACTICE AREAS:*** Business Law; Estate Planning; Commercial Real Estate; Eminent Domain. ***Email:*** qsiemer@psarf.com

(This Listing Continued)

SIEMER, AUSTIN, RESCH, FUHR & TOTTEN, Effingham—Continued

WILLIAM W. AUSTIN, born Effingham, Illinois, June 18, 1945; admitted to bar, 1970, Illinois; 1979, U.S. District Court, Central District of Illinois; 1983, U.S. Court of Military Appeals; 1986, U.S. District Court, Central and Southern Districts of Illinois; 1991, U.S. Court of Appeals, Seventh Circuit; 2005, U.S. Supreme Court. *Education:* University of Illinois (B.S., 1967; J.D., 1970). Assistant Attorney General, Illinois, 1971. Special Assistant Attorney General, Illinois, 1971-1983. Director, Attorneys' Title Guaranty Fund, 1986—. Director, ATG Trust Co., 1998—. *Member:* Effingham County, Illinois State (Member: Real Estate Law Section Council, 2001—; Mineral Law Subcommittee, 1981-1983; Law Office Economics, Section Council, 1985-1989; Standing Committee on Military Affairs, 2001—; Assembly Member, 1993-2001) and American (Member, Sections on: Real Property, Probate and Trust Law; Business Law; Litigation) Bar Associations; Illinois Real Estate Lawyers Association. Fellow, Illinois Bar Foundation. [Brigadier General, AUS, 1970-2001]. (Also at Casey Office). ***PRACTICE AREAS:*** Real Estate; Business Law; Related Civil Litigation. ***Email:*** waustin@psarf.com

MARILYN B. RESCH, born Madison, Indiana, December 5, 1948; admitted to bar, 1973, Illinois. *Education:* College of Wooster (B.A., 1970); Indiana University (J.D., 1973). Phi Beta Kappa. Field Attorney, National Labor Relations Board, 1973-1974. Assistant Attorney General, Illinois, 1974-1975. *Member:* Clark County, Effingham County, Illinois State (Member, Family Law Section) and American Bar Associations. (Also at Casey Office). ***PRACTICE AREAS:*** Divorce; Family Law; Children. ***Email:*** mresch@psarf.com

RONALD E. FUHR, born Dixon, Illinois, June 1, 1954; admitted to bar, 1984, Illinois; 1986, U.S. District Court, Central and Southern District of Illinois. *Education:* Central Michigan University (B.S., 1977); Southern Illinois University (J.D., cum laude, 1984). Editor, Southern Illinois Law Journal, 1983. *Member:* Effingham County, Illinois State (Member, Section on, Commercial, Banking and Bankruptcy Law) and American Bar Associations; Southern Illinois Bankruptcy Institute. (Also at Casey Office). ***PRACTICE AREAS:*** Commercial Law; Bankruptcy Law; Insurance Defense; Litigation. ***Email:*** rfuhr@psarf.com

WILLIAM B. TOTTEN, born Urbana, Illinois, September 20, 1960; admitted to bar, 1991, Illinois. *Education:* College of Wooster (B.A., 1983); Indiana University (M.S., 1985; J.D., 1991). *Member:* Effingham County (President, 2002-2003), Illinois State (Member, Sections on: Civil Practice & Procedure; Elder Law; Family Law) and American (Member, Tort and Insurance Practice Section) Bar Associations; Association of Trial Lawyers of America; Illinois Trial Lawyers Association; National Organization of Social Security Claimants' Representatives. (Also at Casey Office). ***PRACTICE AREAS:*** Civil Litigation; Social Security; Family Law; Criminal Law. ***Email:*** wtotten@psarf.com

MARTIN W. SIEMER, born Teutopolis, Illinois, August 11, 1967; admitted to bar, 1994, Illinois; 1998, U.S. District Court, Southern District of Illinois; 1999, U.S. Court of Appeals, Seventh Circuit. *Education:* University of Illinois (B.S., 1991); St. Louis University (J.D., summa cum laude, 1994). Alpha Sigma Nu; Order of the Woolsack. Staff, 1993 and Articles Editor, 1994, St. Louis University Law Journal. Author: "Tortious Interference with Contract: A Tort on the Brink of Extinction," 85 Ill. Bar Journal 322 July, 1997. *Member:* Effingham County, Illinois State and American Bar Associations; Appellate Lawyers Association; National Academy of Elder Law Attorneys. (Also at Casey Office). ***PRACTICE AREAS:*** Elder Law; Appellate Practice; Estate Administration; Estate Planning. ***Email:*** msiemer@psarf.com

TAYLOR LAW OFFICES, P.C.

122 EAST WASHINGTON
P.O. BOX 668
EFFINGHAM, ILLINOIS 62401-0668
Telephone: 217-342-3925
Fax: 217-342-2341
Email: attorneys@taylorlaw.net
URL: http://www.taylorlaw.net

Altamont, Illinois Office: 200 North Main Street, P.O. Box 350. Telephone: 618-483-6119. Fax: 618-483-5665.

Trial Practice in State and Federal Courts. Insurance, Personal Injury, Trusts, Probate, Estate Planning, Commercial, Municipal, Corporate, Bankruptcy, Real Estate, Oil and Gas, Criminal Law, Family Law, Collections, Utility, Energy and Power Generation Law, Land Use Law, Water Cooperatives.

DALE F. WOLFF, born Fayette County, Illinois, March 16, 1948; admitted to bar, 1975, Illinois; 1977, U. S. District Court, Southern District of Illinois. *Education:* University of Illinois (B.S., 1970); Valparaiso University (J.D., 1975). Assistant State's Attorney, Effingham County, 1977-1978. Past President, Illinois Land Title Association. *Member:* Effingham County and Illinois State Bar Associations. ***LANGUAGES:*** Spanish. ***PRACTICE AREAS:*** Living Trusts; Wills; Estate Planning; Probate; Real Estate. ***Email:*** wolff@taylorlaw.net

BRUCE A. BURKEY, born Princeton, Illinois, August 19, 1945; admitted to bar, 1976, Illinois; 1980, U. S. District Court, Southern District of Illinois. *Education:* U. S. Air Force Academy (B.S., 1968); Southern Illinois University; University of Illinois (J.D., 1976). *Member:* Effingham County, Illinois State and American Bar Associations. ***PRACTICE AREAS:*** Estate Planning; Probate; Bankruptcy; Real Estate; Business Planning. ***Email:*** burkey@taylorlaw.net

LOU J. VIVERITO, born Chicago, Illinois, January 1, 1953; admitted to bar, 1982, Illinois. *Education:* Eastern Illinois University (B.S., 1974); John Marshall Law School (J.D., with highest distinction, 1982). Order of John Marshall. Member, The John Marshall Law Review, 1981-1982. Author: Comment, "The Shared Appreciation Mortgage: A Clog on the Equity of Redemption?" 15 John Marshall Law Review 131 (1982). Assistant States Attorney, Marion County, Illinois, 1982-1983. *Member:* Illinois State Bar Association; Illinois Trial Lawyers Association; Illinois Association of Criminal Defense Lawyers; Association of Trial Lawyers of America; National Association of Criminal Defense Lawyers. ***PRACTICE AREAS:*** Criminal Law; Civil Litigation. ***Email:*** viverto@taylorlaw.net

MATTHEW R. HORTENSTINE, born Vandalia, Illinois, December 15, 1967; admitted to bar, 1993, Illinois and U.S. District Court, Central and Southern Districts of Illinois. *Education:* Eastern Illinois University (B.A., 1989); Washington University (J.D., 1993). *Member:* Effingham, Illinois State and American Bar Associations. ***PRACTICE AREAS:*** Municipal; Corporate Law; Real Estate; Litigation. ***Email:*** hortenstine@taylorlaw.net

DAVID A. McDEVITT, born Effingham, Illinois, November 18, 1966; admitted to bar, 1992, Illinois. *Education:* Eastern Illinois University (B.S., 1989); St. Louis University (J.D., 1992). *Member:* Effingham and Illinois State Bar Associations; Illinois Trial Lawyers Association. ***PRACTICE AREAS:*** Family Law (70%, 56); Civil Practice (15%, 12); Workers Compensation (15%, 12). ***Email:*** mcdevitt@taylorlaw.net

CHRISTOPHER A. KOESTER, born Effingham, Illinois, July 29, 1965; admitted to bar, 1990, Missouri; 1991, Illinois. *Education:* Eastern Illinois University (B.A., 1987); Southern Illinois University (J.D., 1990). *Member:* Effingham, Illinois State and American Bar Associations; Illinois Association of Defense Counsel; Association of Trial Lawyers of America. ***PRACTICE AREAS:*** Personal Injury; Insurance Litigation; Commercial Litigation. ***Email:*** koester@taylorlaw.net

---

TRACY A. BERBERICH, born Evansville, Indiana, November 14, 1978. *Education:* University of Southern Indiana (B.S., magna cum laude, 2000); Southern Illinois University (J.D., magna cum laude, 2003). Phi Alpha Delta. *Member:* Effingham, Illinois State and American Bar Associations. ***PRACTICE AREAS:*** Collections; Municipal Law; General Civil Litigation. ***Email:*** berberich@taylorlaw.net

ARIANO, HARDY, NYULI, JOHNSON, RICHMOND & GOETTEL, P.C.

Established in 1981
474 SUMMIT STREET
ELGIN, ILLINOIS 60120
Telephone: 847-695-2400
Telecopy: 847-695-8397
Email: aah@attorneys-illinois.com
URL: http://www.attorneys-illinois.com

Huntley, Illinois Office: 13300 Route 47, P.O. Box 487, 60142. Telephone: 847-669-5020.
Geneva Office: 22 S. 4th Street, Suite B, 60134.

General Civil and Criminal Practice in all Courts. Banking, Probate, Real Estate, Corporation, Federal Taxation, Transactional, Employment, Family, Personal Injury, Collections, Creditor Bankruptcy, Foreclosures, Landlord and Tenant Law, Workers Compensation Law, Mediation, Zoning, Planning and Land Use.

RALPH C. HARDY, born LaGrange, Georgia, June 25, 1943; admitted to bar, 1968, Illinois and Missouri. *Education:* Beloit College (B.A., 1965); Washington University (J.D., 1968). Note Editor, Washington University Law Quarterly, 1967-1968. Law Clerk to Judge Henry S. Wise, U.S. District Court, Eastern District of Illinois, 1968-1970. *Member:* Elgin, Kane County, McHenry County, Illinois State and American Bar Associations. ***TRANSACTIONS:*** Merger of State Bank of Huntley and Suburban Bancorp., Inc. for State Bank of Huntley, 1993 and Sale of State Bank of Paw Paw to NBE Bancshares, Inc. 1996. ***PRACTICE AREAS:*** Real Estate Law; Trusts and Estates; Wills; Elder Law; Probate Law; Corporate Law; Taxation Law; Zoning, Planning and Land Use; Banking Law. ***Email:*** rch@attorneys-illinois.com

LISA M. NYULI, born 1964; admitted to bar, 1989, Illinois and U.S. District Court, Northern District of Illinois. *Education:* University of Illinois (B.S., 1986); Northern Illinois University (J.D., 1989). Family Law Mediator, Kane County. *Member:* Kane County (Past President), Elgin (Past President) and Illinois State Bar Associations (Assembly Member, Judicial Advisory Polls Committee, CLE Committee). ***REPORTED CASES:*** Hoffmann v. Lyon Metal Products, Inc., et al 217 Ill. App. 3d 490 (2d Dist. 1991); People v. Picou, 260 Ill. App. 3d 35, 692 (2d Dist, 1994); First National Bank of Geneva v. Lively, 211 Ill. App. 3d 1 (2d Dist, 1991). ***PRACTICE AREAS:*** Family Law and Mediation; Creditor Bankruptcy; Commercial Law (Collections); Landlord/Tenant Law; Foreclosures. ***Email:*** lmn@attorneys-illinois.com

RANDY K. JOHNSON, born Chicago, Illinois, December 28, 1952; admitted to bar, 1978, Illinois, U.S. District Court, Northern District of Illinois and U.S. Court of Appeals, Seventh Circuit. *Education:* Carthage College (B.A., cum laude, 1975); John Marshall Law School (J.D. with distinction, 1978). *Member:* Kane County Bar Association (Chair, Appellate Practice Committee, 1998-2002). ***REPORTED CASES:*** In re Reliford, 65 Ill.App.3d 177 (1st Dist., 1978); People v. Rodgers, 92 Ill.2d 283 (1982); People v. Columbo, 118 Ill.App.3d 882 (1st Dist., 1983); People v. Hoffer, 106 Ill.2d 186 (1985); Heiden v. Ottinger, 245 Ill.App.3d 612 (2d Dist., 1993); Marriage of Weisbruch, 304 Ill. App.3d 99, 73 A.L.R. 5th 805 (2d Dist., 1999); Marriage of Henke, 313 Ill.App.3d 159 (2d Dist., 2000). ***PRACTICE AREAS:*** Family Law; Appellate Practice; Real Estate; Litigation. ***Email:*** rkj@attorneys-illinois.com

SCOTT G. RICHMOND, born Boston, Massachusetts, April 17, 1968; admitted to bar, 1995, Illinois and U.S. District Court, Northern District of Illinois. *Education:* Michigan State University (B.A., Accounting, 1990); Chicago-Kent College of Law (J.D., high honors, 1995). Order of the Coif. Moot Court (Vice-President, 1994-1995). *Member:* Chicago, Kane County (Co-Chair, New Lawyers Division), Illinois State and American Bar Associations; Illinois Trial Lawyers Association. ***PRACTICE AREAS:*** General Civil Litigation; Corporate Law; Business Law; Contracts; Personal Injury; Zoning, Planning and Land Use; Worker's Compensation. ***Email:*** sgr@attorneys-illinois.com

KARRSTEN GOETTEL, born Libertyville, Illinois, April 25, 1971; admitted to bar, 1997, Illinois. *Education:* University of Wisconsin-Madison (B.S., 1993); Loyola Univer-

(This Listing Continued)

sity (J.D., 1997). *Member:* Chicago, Kane County and Illinois State Bar Associations. ***PRACTICE AREAS:*** Real Estate; Commercial Real Estate; Business Law; Corporate Law; Wills; Trusts and Estates; Zoning, Planning and Land Use. ***Email:*** kg1@attorneys-illinois.com

---

JANE CRADDOCK RYAN, born Bloomington, Illinois, December 24, 1960; admitted to bar, 1988, Illinois. *Education:* Illinois State University (B.A., 1982); Northern Illinois University (J.D., 1987). Arbitrator, Civil Matters. Mediator, Complex Civil. *Member:* Kane County Bar Association. ***PRACTICE AREAS:*** Civil Litigation; Probate Litigation; Guardianship; Personal Injury; Collections. ***Email:*** jcr@attorneys-illinois.com

TODD E. WALLACE, born Des Moines, Iowa, July 7, 1975; admitted to bar, 2003, Illinois and U.S. District Court, Northern District of Illinois. *Education:* University of Illinois (B.S., 1998); Chicago-Kent College of Law (J.D., 2002). Real Estate Broker, Illinois, 2003. Member, Board of Trustees, University of Illinois, 1996-1997. *Member:* Kane County, Illinois State and American Bar Associations. ***PRACTICE AREAS:*** Real Estate; Estate Planning; Probate; Corporate Law; Litigation. ***Email:*** tew@attorneys-illinois.com

CELESTE M. WALKER, born Mendota, Illinois, February 25, 1959; admitted to bar, 2000, Illinois. *Education:* Drake University (B.A., 1986); Northern Illinois University College of Law (J.D., 2000). ***PRACTICE AREAS:*** Local Government Law; Real Estate; Litigation; General Practice. ***Email:*** cmw@attorneys-illinois.com

OF COUNSEL

FRANK V. ARIANO, born Chicago, Illinois, August 21, 1945; admitted to bar, 1970, Illinois; 1988, Colorado. *Education:* University of Wisconsin (B.S., 1967); Illinois Institute of Technology; Chicago-Kent College of Law (J.D., with distinction, 1970). Associate Editor, Chicago-Kent Law Review, 1969-1970. Fellow, American Academy of Matrimonial Lawyers. Certified Family Law and Major Civil Case Mediator, Family Law Section Counsel, Illinois State Bar Association. Certified Arbitrator, Kane and McHenry Counties. *Member:* Kane County (Past President), Elgin (Past President), Chicago, McHenry County, Illinois State (Assembly Member and Continuing Education Committee) and American Bar Associations; Commercial Law League of America; American Judicature Society; Illinois Trial Lawyers Association; The Association of Trial Lawyers of America; Academy of Family Mediators; Mediation Council of Illinois. ***PRACTICE AREAS:*** Family Law; Divorce Mediation; Civil Mediation; Commercial Law; Civil Practice. ***Email:*** fva@attorneys-illinois.com

Languages: Spanish.

GENERAL COUNSEL: Z Hardware Co.; Sybaquay Girl Scout Council, Inc.
REPRESENTATIVE CLIENTS: Bank One, Illinois, N.A.; Amcore Bank; Merchants Bank; Laboratory Corporation of America; Joseph Corporation.

BRADY & JENSEN

Established in 1951

2425 ROYAL BOULEVARD
ELGIN, ILLINOIS 60123
Telephone: 847-695-2000
Fax: 847-695-3243
URL: http://www.bradylaw.com

General Practice in all Courts. Trial and Appellate Practice. Corporation Law, Federal Taxation, Real Estate and Probate Law, Estate Planning, Personal Injury.

FIRM PROFILE: The roots of the firm go back to 1868. At present four partners and one associate concentrate in the trial area and six partners and one associate in the areas of business law, real estate, tax planning, estate planning and probate.

MEMBERS OF FIRM

WAYNE M. JENSEN, born Elgin, Illinois, November 23, 1940; admitted to bar, 1964, Illinois; U.S. District Court, Northern District of Illinois. *Education:* Valparaiso University (B.A., 1962; LL.B., 1964). Phi Alpha Delta. Special Assistant Attorney General, Illinois, 1971-1978. Appointed by Supreme Court of Illinois to Illinois Pattern Jury Instruction Committee, 1993—. *Member:* Elgin, Kane County, Illinois State and American Bar Associations; American Judicature Society; The Association of Trial Lawyers of America; Illinois Trial Lawyers Association. ***PRACTICE AREAS:*** Personal Injury and Related Cases; Products Liability; Medical Negligence; Worker's Compensation. ***Email:*** jensen@bradylaw.com

RICHARD L. HEIMBERG, born Valparaiso, Indiana, June 25, 1941; admitted to bar, 1966, Illinois. *Education:* Eastern Illinois University and Valparaiso University (B.A., 1965); Valparaiso University (LL.B., 1965). Phi Alpha Delta. *Member:* Elgin, Kane County and Illinois State Bar Associations. ***PRACTICE AREAS:*** Real Estate; Estate Planning. ***Email:*** rheimberg@bradylaw.com

ROGER K. FRANDSEN, born Springfield, Illinois, February 12, 1948; admitted to bar, 1974, Illinois; 1980, Florida. *Education:* DePauw University (B.A, 1970); University of Illinois (J.D., 1973). Notes and Comments Editor, University of Illinois Law Forum, 1972-1973. Author: "The Enforcement Powers of the Secretary of Labor under Section 402 of the LMRDA," University of Illinois Law Forum, Vol. 4, 1971. *Member:* Elgin, Kane County (General Counsel, 1994), Illinois State and American Bar Associations; The Florida Bar. ***PRACTICE AREAS:*** Real Estate; Corporate Law; Business Law. ***Email:*** frandsen@bradylaw.com

RONALD E. RASMUSSEN, born Chicago, Illinois, August 10, 1947; admitted to bar, 1974, Illinois. *Education:* Western Illinois University and Northeastern Illinois University (B.A., 1968); Illinois Institute of Technology and Chicago-Kent College of Law (J.D., 1974). Member, Chicago-Kent Law Review, 1973-1974. *Member:* Elgin, Kane County, Illinois State and American Bar Associations. [With U.S. Army, 1969-1970]. ***PRACTICE AREAS:*** Estate Planning; Probate; Trust Administration. ***Email:*** rasmussen@bradylaw.com

(This Listing Continued)

ALFRED Y. KIRKLAND, JR., born Elgin, Illinois, September 21, 1944; admitted to bar, 1974, Illinois and Indiana. *Education:* Williams College (B.A., 1966); Valparaiso University (J.D., 1974). Editor-in-Chief, Valparaiso University Law Review, 1973-1974. Author: Note, "The Bank Credit Card and the Consumer: Programming Justice into the Cashless Society," 7 Vol. Valparaiso University Law Review 503, 1973. Clerk to Luther M. Swygert, United States Court of Appeals, Seventh Circuit, 1974-1975. *Member:* Elgin, Kane County, Illinois State, Indiana State and American Bar Associations; The Association of Trial Lawyers of America; Illinois Trial Lawyers Association. ***PRACTICE AREAS:*** Civil; Commercial Trial Matters. ***Email:*** kirkland@bradylaw.com

GLEN T. DOBOSZ, born Chicago, Illinois, December 14, 1954; admitted to bar, 1979, Illinois; 1981, U.S. Tax Court; 1982, U.S. District Court, Northern District of Illinois including Trial Bar. *Education:* Valparaiso University (B.S., 1976; J.D., with high distinction, 1979). Associate Editor, Valparaiso University Law Review, (1978-1979). Certified Public Accountant, Illinois, 1976. Life Member, National Registry of Who's Who 2000. Instructor: Accounting and Taxation, Valparaiso University, 1977-1979; Paralegal Program, Taxation, Elgin Community College, 1991—. Named Leading American Attorney, Tax Law, American Research Corp., August 1998. *Member:* Elgin, Chicago (Member, Committee on Federal Taxation, 1980-1982), Kane County, Illinois State and American Bar Associations. ***PRACTICE AREAS:*** Taxation; Estate Planning; Corporations. ***Email:*** taxman@bradylaw.com

MICHAEL C. DEUTSCH, born Elgin, Illinois, October 19, 1954; admitted to bar, 1982, Illinois. *Education:* Bradley University (B.S., 1976); John Marshall Law School (J.D., 1982; LL.M., 1991). Certified Public Accountant, Illinois, 1978. *Member:* Elgin, Kane County and Illinois State Bar Associations. ***PRACTICE AREAS:*** Business Law; Corporate Law; Estate Planning; Probate. ***Email:*** deutsch@bradylaw.com

KEITH A. SPONG, born Somerville, New Jersey, April 25, 1963; admitted to bar, 1988, Illinois. *Education:* Iowa State University (B.S., 1985); University of Iowa (J.D., with distinction, 1988). Phi Alpha Theta. *Member:* Elgin, Kane County and Illinois State Bar Associations. ***PRACTICE AREAS:*** Real Estate; Business Transactions; Corporate Law. ***Email:*** spong@bradylaw.com

MARIOS NICHOLAS KARAYANNIS, born Athens, Greece, March 11, 1961; admitted to bar, 1986, Illinois and U.S. District Court, Northern District of Illinois including Trial Bar; 1996, U.S. Supreme Court; 1997, U.S. Tax Court. *Education:* University of Illinois (B.S., 1983); John Marshall Law School (J.D., with distinction, 1986). Order of John Marshall Honorary Society. Law Review, 1986. *Member:* Kane County and Illinois State Bar Associations; American Trial Lawyers Association; Illinois Trial Lawyers Association. ***LANGUAGES:*** Greek. ***PRACTICE AREAS:*** Personal Injury; Medical Malpractice; Toxic Torts; Family Law. ***Email:*** karayannis@bradylaw.com

FRED J. BEER, born Chicago, Illinois, September 22, 1965; admitted to bar, 1990, Illinois and U.S. District Court, Northern District of Illinois; 1992, U.S. Tax Court. *Education:* Valparaiso University (B.S., 1987); John Marshall Law School (J.D., cum laude, 1990). Member, John Marshall Law Review. Certified Public Accountant, Illinois, 1987. *Member:* Elgin, Kane County and Illinois State Bar Associations; American Trial Lawyers Association. ***PRACTICE AREAS:*** Employment Law; Workers Compensation; Personal Injury; Commercial Litigation; Civil Litigation; Taxation; Corporate Law. ***Email:*** beer@bradylaw.com

ASSOCIATES

BRIAN L. HEIMBERG, born Elgin, Illinois, May 9, 1970; admitted to bar, 1995, Illinois. *Education:* University of Illinois (B.A., 1992); Chicago Kent College of Law (J.D., 1995). *Member:* Kane County and Illinois State Bar Associations. ***PRACTICE AREAS:*** Real Estate; Corporate; Probate. ***Email:*** bheimberg@bradylaw.com

PATRICK J. CRIMMINS, born Chicago, Illinois, February 23, 1961; admitted to bar, 1987, Illinois. *Education:* Northern Illinois University (B.A., 1983); John Marshall Law School (J.D., 1986). *Member:* Illinois State Bar Association; Illinois Trial Lawyer Association. ***PRACTICE AREAS:*** Wrongful Death; Premises Liability; Personal Injury; Products Liability; Medical Malpractice; Toxic Torts; Workers Compensation; Litigation; Appellate Practice; Criminal Defense; Automobile Accidents; Truck Accidents; Construction Accidents; Nursing Home Litigation. ***Email:*** crimmins@bradylaw.com

REPRESENTATIVE CLIENTS: A.J. Funk & Co.; Artistic Carton Company; Association of Mid-Continent Universities; Batavia Container, Inc.; Center Homes; Chicago Title Insurance Co.; Church of the Brethren General Board; Colonial Ice Cream, Inc.; Concord Development Group; Elgin Corrugated Box Co.; Elgin Industries, Inc.; Elgin Paper Co.; First Community Financial Corp.; Haeger Industries; Hoffer Plastics Corp.; IHC Construction Companies, LLC; Illinois Hydraulic Construction Co.; Kenyon Brothers Co.; Lamp Construction Co.; Pulte Home Corporation; Residential Development Group, Inc.; Richmar Construction Co.; Valley Creek of Elgin, Inc.; W.R. Meadows, Inc.; Weldstar Company; Windsor Development Corp.; Wispark Corporation; Winspark Lifecare, LLC; Wyndham Deepoint Homes.

BRITTAIN & KETCHAM, P.C.

85 MARKET STREET
ELGIN, ILLINOIS 60123
Telephone: 847-742-6100
FAX: 847-742-6152
Email: jrif@msn.com

General Civil Practice in all Courts. Probate, Estate Planning, Health Care Law, Collections, Chancery, Corporate, Banking and Insurance Law, Real Property, Municipal Law. Trials, Trusts. Domestic Relations. Elder Law, Family Law.

LEWIS W. TERLIZZI (Retired)

WILLIAM R. KETCHAM (Retired)

RANDLE E. JOHNSON (Retired)

JOHN J. BRITTAIN (Retired)

LEO M. FLANAGAN, JR., born Chicago, Illinois, October 4, 1942; admitted to bar, 1969, Illinois; 1982, U.S. District Court, Northern District of Illinois including Trial Bar. *Education:* Lewis University (B.A., 1965); DePaul University (J.D., 1969). *Member:* Kane

(This Listing Continued)

BRITTAIN & KETCHAM, P.C., Elgin—Continued

County (Member: Committee on Legal Economics, 1980; Real Estate Practice Committee) and Illinois State Bar Associations. ***PRACTICE AREAS:*** Real Estate; Probate; Estate Planning; Corporate; Family Law; Partnership. ***Email:*** lflanagan@brittainketcham.com

JEFF RIFKEN, born Chicago, Illinois, January 4, 1946; admitted to bar, 1973, Illinois. *Education:* University of Illinois (B.A., 1968; J.D., 1973). *Member:* Kane County (Member, 1980— and Chairman, 1985, Matrimonial Law Committee), Illinois State (Member, Section on Health Law) and American Bar Associations. ***PRACTICE AREAS:*** Health Care; Family Law; Real Estate; Civil Litigation; Mediation; Collections; Probate. ***Email:*** jrif@msn.com

DANIEL ERVIN COMPTON, born Oak Park, Illinois, October 22, 1960; admitted to bar, 1987, Illinois. *Education:* Southern Illinois University; Valparaiso University (B.S., 1987); John Marshall Law School (J.D., with high distinction, 1982). *Member:* Illinois State Bar Association; Illinois Trial Lawyers Association. ***PRACTICE AREAS:*** Workers Compensation; Personal Injury; Commercial Litigation; Insurance Defense. ***Email:*** dancom@msn.com

---

PATRICK FLANAGAN, born Fort Lee, Virginia, February 12, 1955; admitted to bar, 1999, Illinois. *Education:* University of Illinois (B.A., 1977); Governor's State University (M.A., 1994); Chicago-Kent College of Law, Illinois Institute of Technology (J.D., 1998). Professor of Military Science Taught Military Law, Law of War Ethics, Standards of Conduct, Leadership and Decision Making. Adjunct Professor of Political Science Teaching Constitutional Law. [Military Lieutenant Colonel (Retired U.S. Army)]. ***PRACTICE AREAS:*** Real Estate; Personal Injury; Foreclosures; Insurance Defense.

REPRESENTATIVE CLIENTS: Economy Fire & Casualty Co.; The Cincinnati Insurance Co.; Rockford Mutual Insurance Co.; Elgin Financial Center, S.B.; Provena; Saint Joseph Hospital of Elgin; Manor Enterprises, Inc.; Preferred Risk Insurance; American States Insurance; Max McGraw Wildlife Foundation; Dundee Township Park District.
REFERENCES: Elgin Financial Center, S.B.; Bank One, Elgin; Old Kent Bank, Elgin; Home Federal Savings and Loan Association of Elgin; Union National Bank and Trust Co.; The Elgin State Bank; First American Bank of Dundee; American National Bank, Elgin; Amcore Trust Company, Elgin.

STEPHEN A. BRUNDAGE

ELGIN, ILLINOIS

(See Wheaton)

Criminal Law, Driving While Intoxicated, Drug Crimes, Felonies, Homicide, Juvenile Law, Misdemeanors, Parole and Probation, Sexual Assault, Traffic Violations, Assault and Battery, Burglary, Criminal Defense, Drivers License Suspension, Forgery, Manslaughter, Search and Seizure, Sex Crimes, Theft, Juvenile Law, Family Law, Divorce, Child Custody, Child Support, Domestic Violence, Premarital Agreements, Spousal Support, Martial Agreements, Marital Property Distribution, Martial Property Law, Marital Property Settlements, Matrimonial Law, Paternity, Post Divorce Modification, Real Estate, Real Estate Sales, Residential Real Estate, Residential Real Estate Sales, Personal Injury, Automobile Accidents and Injuries, Dog Bites, Sexual Abuse, Slip and Fall and Wrongful Death Law.

CAMIC, JOHNSON, WILSON & McCULLOCH, P.C.

ELGIN, ILLINOIS

(See Sycamore)

Criminal Trial Practice, including Assault, Batter, Burglary, Driver's License Suspension, Driving While Intoxicated (DUI), Forfeiture, Fraud, Death Penalty, Felonies, Forgery, Manslaughter, Misdemeanors, Murder, Parole and Probation, Post-Conviction Remedies, Search and Seizure, Sex Crimes, Theft, Traffic Violations, and Weapons Charges. Expungements and Secretary of State hearings. Family Practice, including Child Custody and Visitation, Divorce, Child Support and Adoption. Real Estate.

LAW OFFICES OF RICHARD HANUS

ELGIN, ILLINOIS

(See Chicago)

Immigration and Naturalization, Business Immigration, Citizenship, Consular Law, Deportation, Employment Authorizations, Employment Immigration, Employment Visas, Family Immigration Law, Immigration Law, Investor Vistas, Labor Certifications, Permanent Visas, Political Asylum, Refugee Law, Religious Visas, Visas.

JUERGENSMEYER AND ASSOCIATES

Established in 1963

1275 DAVIS ROAD, SUITE 131
ELGIN, ILLINOIS 60123-1304
Telephone: 847-695-9800
Toll Free: 1-888-695-9822
FAX: 847-695-9818
Email: juerlaw@sbcglobal.net
URL: http://www.juergensmeyerlawfirm.com

Chicago, Illinois Office: 39 South La Salle Street, Suite 915. Telephone: 312-332-1114.

General, Civil Trial and Appellate Practice. Personal Injury, Governmental, Real Estate, Family, Workers Compensation Law, Municipal, Divorce, Chancery, Commercial, Insurance, Banking, Corporation, Trust and Probate Law.

FIRM PROFILE: Spanish translation available.

(This Listing Continued)

JOHN E. JUERGENSMEYER, born Stewardson, Illinois, May 14, 1934; admitted to bar, 1963, Illinois; 1964, U.S. District Court, Northern District of Illinois and U.S. Court of Appeals, Seventh Circuit; 1968, U.S. Supreme Court; 1970, U.S. Tax Court; 1975, U.S. Court of Claims. *Education:* University of Illinois (B.A., with high honors, 1955; J.D., 1963); Princeton University (M.S., 1957; Ph.D., 1960). Phi Beta Kappa; Phi Alpha Delta. Professor of Constitutional Law and Political Science, Judson College, 1963—. Assistant Public Defender, Kane County, 1964-1967. Assistant States Attorney, Kane County, 1977-1978. Special Assistant Attorney General, State of Illinois, 1979-1986. Commissioner, U.S. National Commission for Libraries and Information Sciences, 1981-1988. Arbitrator, American Arbitration Association, 1979—. Arbitrator: Cook County Mandatory Arbitration Program; Kane County Mandatory Arbitration Program. *Member:* Chicago, (Chairman, Local Government Committee, 1974-1975), Kane County (Chairman, Municipal Law Committee, 1994-1995), Northwest Suburban, Illinois State (Chairman, Local Government Section, 1975-1976), Federal and American Bar Associations. [With USAFR, 1955-1958; USAF Active Duty, 1958-1960]. ***PRACTICE AREAS:*** Personal Injury; Local Government; Corporate Law; Business Law; Probate; Civil Litigation; Elder Law. ***Email:*** juerlaw@sbcglobal.net

ASSOCIATES

RICHARD P. BINGHAM, born Chicago, Illinois, October 7, 1966; admitted to bar, 1992, Illinois; 1994, U.S. District Court, Northern District of Illinois. *Education:* University of Illinois (B.A., 1988); University of Virginia (J.D., 1992). Phi Beta Kappa; Phi Kappa Phi. *Member:* Chicago, Kane County and Illinois State Bar Associations; Illinois Trial Lawyers Association; The Trial Lawyers Association of America. ***REPORTED CASES:*** In re Adoption of S. S. and R.S., 166 Ill. 2d 250, 657 N.E. 2d 935 (1995). ***PRACTICE AREAS:*** Personal Injury; Civil Litigation; Workers Compensation. ***Email:*** juerlaw@sbcglobal.net

DANELLE WOZNIAK OILSCHLAGER, born Elgin, Illinois, April 17, 1979; admitted to bar, 2005, Illinois. *Education:* University of Iowa (B.A., 2001); John Marshall Law School (J.D., 2005). Formerly with Kane County State's Attorney's Office. *Member:* Chicago, Kane County and Lake County Bar Associations. ***PRACTICE AREAS:*** Family Law; Criminal Defense; Bankruptcy; Real Estate. ***Email:*** juerlaw@sbcglobal.net

LEGAL SUPPORT PERSONNEL

PARALEGALS

SUSAN K. LORANG
NORINE D. OLSON
KELLY A. ZABRAN
LETICIA MARTINEZ, (Legal Assistant/Translator). ***LANGUAGES:*** Spanish.

Language: Spanish.

REPRESENTATIVE CLIENTS: Elgin Broadcasting Co.; Big Broadcasting Co.; Las Vegas Radio Co.; Schaumburg Township District Public Library; Illinois Library Assn.; St. Charles Public Library District.
REFERENCE: First Community Bank, Elgin.

LAW OFFICES OF GARRY A. PAYTON

ELGIN, ILLINOIS

(See Waukegan)

Criminal Defense, Personal Injury, Medical Malpractice, Products Liability, Automobile Accidents, Wrongful Death, Construction Site Accidents, Driving While Intoxicated, Drug Crimes, Felonies, Homicide, Juvenile, Misdemeanors, Sexual Assault and Traffic Violations.

LAW OFFICES OF HENRY REPAY

ELGIN, ILLINOIS

(See Belvidere)

General Practice, Real Estate, Commercial Real Estate, Residential Real Estate, Mortgages, Personal Bankruptcy, Consumer Bankruptcy, Debtor Bankruptcy, Chapter 7, Chapter 13, Nonprofit and Charitable Organizations, Guardianship, Adoptions.

SCHEFLOW & RYDELL

SUITE 200, 63 DOUGLAS AVENUE
ELGIN, ILLINOIS 60120
Telephone: 847-695-2800
Telecopier: 847-695-4547
Email: scheflowrydell1@aol.com

General Practice, Litigation, Corporate Law, Banks and Banking, Business Law, Commercial Law, Partnership Law, Nonprofit and Charitable Organizations, Wills, Trusts and Estates, Probate, Estate Planning, Real Estate, Commercial Real Estate, Mortgage Foreclosure, Zoning, Planning and Land Use, Leases and Leasing, Municipal Law, Trademarks, Taxation, Bankruptcy, Collections, Family Law, Adoptions.

MEMBERS OF FIRM

RICHARD S. SCHEFLOW, born Elgin, Illinois, November, 16, 1924; admitted to bar, 1953, Illinois. *Education:* Beloit College (B.A., 1950); University of Illinois (LL.B., 1953). *Member:* Kane County, Illinois State and American Bar Associations.

THOMAS C. RYDELL, born Elgin, Illinois, October 29, 1936; admitted to bar, 1966, Illinois. *Education:* Bradley University (B.S., 1960); Chicago-Kent College of Law (J.D., with honors, 1966). *Member:* Kane County, Elgin and Illinois State Bar Associations.

DOUGLAS J. SCHEFLOW, born Elgin, Illinois, June 10, 1957; admitted to bar, 1983, Illinois; registered to practice before U.S. Patent and Trademark Office. *Education:* University of Michigan (B.S., in Engineering, cum laude, 1979); University of Illinois (J.D., 1983). *Member:* Kane County and Illinois State Bar Associations.

(This Listing Continued)

REPRESENTATIVE CLIENTS: Sherman Hospital; State Financial Bank; Welch Bros. Concrete, Inc.; Shales McNutt Construction; West Elgin Apartments; Parr Electric Inc.; Fox River Water Reclamation District.

LAW OFFICES OF RICHARD E. TRAVIS

Established in 1997

2425 ROYAL BOULEVARD
ELGIN, ILLINOIS 60123
Telephone: 847-289-3390
Fax: 847-695-3243
Email: richard@travislaw.net
URL: http://www.richardtravislaw.com

General Practice in all Courts. Personal Injury, Wrongful Death, Commercial Litigation, Medical Malpractice, Products Liability and Worker's Compensation Law. Civil Litigation Practice, Automobile Accidents, Dog Bites, Slip and Fall.

RICHARD E. TRAVIS, born Detroit, Michigan, August 8, 1945; admitted to bar, 1972, Illinois. *Education:* University of Wisconsin-Whitewater (B.S., 1968); Illinois Institute of Technology; Chicago-Kent College of Law (J.D., 1972); The John Marshall Law School (LL.M., Taxation, 1983). Member, Chicago-Kent Law Review, 1971-1972. Author: "Wrongful Refusal to Settle by a Liability Insurer: The Standard for Illinois," 48 Chicago Kent Law Review 115, 1971; Note, "Torts—Strict Liability—A Hospital vs. Strict Liable for Transfusions of Hepatitis Infected Blood," 48 Chicago-Kent Law Review 292, 1971. Former Board Member, Oak Crest Residence Home. Board Member, Bethesda Community Development Center. Member: First Congregational Church of Elgin; Elgin Country Club. *Member:* Kane County and Illinois State Bar Associations; Illinois Trial Lawyers Association; The Association of Trial Lawyers of America. ***PRACTICE AREAS:*** Automobile Accidents and Injuries; Medical Malpractice; Wrongful Death; Personal Injury; Workers Compensation; Commercial Litigation; Dog Bites; Slip and Fall; Civil Litigation.

LEGAL SUPPORT PERSONNEL

ANNE HENNESSEY. *Education:* Judson College (B.A., Business Administration). 16 years' experience in all areas of law. (Legal Secretary)

JELLIFFE, FERRELL, MORRIS & DOERGE

ELIZABETHTOWN, ILLINOIS

(See Harrisburg)

Insurance Law, Negligence and Personal Injury, Litigation, Workers' Compensation Law, and Employment Law. Commercial Collection and DUI's. General Civil Practice in State and Federal Courts. Trials and Appeals.

CUTLER & ASSOCIATES, LTD.

ELK GROVE VILLAGE, ILLINOIS

(See Skokie)

Bankruptcy, Consumer Bankruptcy, Bankruptcy Chapter 7, Foreclosures, Small Business, Buying and Selling of Businesses, Family Business, Limited Liability, Partnership, Corporate, Contract, Breach of Contract, General Practice, Debtor and Creditor, Collections, Creditors, Rights and Civil Litigation.

KLEST LAW FIRM

ELK GROVE VILLAGE, ILLINOIS

(See Schaumburg)

Personal Injury, Medical Malpractice, Products Liability, Legal Malpractice, Construction Accidents, Airplane Crash Litigation, Insurance Bad Faith, Automobile Accidents, Motorcycle Accidents, Birth Trauma, Sexual Abuse, Child Abuse and Neglect, Slip and Fall, Wrongful Death, Dog Bites, Railroad Accidents and Injuries, Automobile Products, Liability and Drug and Medical Device Litigation, Trial Practice.

DANIEL K. ROBIN, LTD

ELK GROVE VILLAGE, ILLINOIS

(See Arlington Heights)

Bankruptcy, Chapter 7, Chapter 13, Divorce, Family Law, Child Support, Separation, Prenuptial Agreements, Equitable Distribution, Driving While Intoxicated, Traffic Violations, Criminal Law, Wills and Trusts, Estate Planning, Asset Protection.

MICHAEL W. FLEMING ATTORNEY AT LAW

360 W. BUTTERFIELD, SUITE 200
ELMHURST, ILLINOIS 60126
Telephone: 630-833-8400
Fax: 630-941-2852
Email: mfleminglaw@sbcglobal.net
URL: http://www.fleminglaw-firm.com

Criminal Defense Litigation, Felonies, Misdemeanors, DUI and Juvenile Law.

MICHAEL W. FLEMING, born Oakpark, Illinois, September 28, 1959; admitted to bar, 1984, Illinois, U.S. District Court, Northern District of Illinois; 1998, U.S. District Court, Central District of Illinois. *Education:* University of Illinois (B.S., 1981; CPA, 1983); John Marshall Law School (J.D., 1983). Certified Public Accountant, 1983. Dupage County States Attorney Office, Misdemeanor, Juvenile, Felony, Reckless Homicides, Drug and Death Penalty Prosecutions, 1984-1990. *Member:* Dupage County (Former Chairman, Criminal Law Committee) and Illinois State Bar Associations. ***PRACTICE AREAS:*** Criminal Defense; Felonies; Misdemeanors; Driving While Intoxicated; Juvenile Law.

KUBIESA, SPIROFF, GOSSELAR & ACKER, P.C.

533 W. NORTH AVENUE
SUITE 204
ELMHURST, ILLINOIS 60126
Telephone: 630-516-1800
Fax: 630-516-1808
URL: http://www.ksgalaw.net
Email: thefirm@ksgalaw.com
URL: http://www.ksgaklaw.com

Municipal Law, Business Law, General Civil and Trial Practice in all Courts, Public Finance, Land Use Law, Administrative Law, Employment Law, Corporate Law, Civil Litigation, Appeals, Real Estate, General Practice, Criminal Law, Eminent Domain.

FIRM PROFILE: Since 1976, the lawyers of this firm have developed reputations for responding quickly and effectively to an increasingly complex set of legal needs associated with an ever-changing municipal, business and legal environment. We are a west suburban Chicago firm with a long history of solid partnerships with area individuals, businesses, local governments and park districts. Our resources, experience and talent make for a commanding presence in the broader legal community. We deliver sophisticated and timely legal representation, along with a genuine thoughtfulness for our clients who are our partners in community, family and business success.

KENNETH T. KUBIESA, born Chicago, Illinois, November 30, 1950; admitted to bar, 1975, Illinois and U.S. District Court, Northern District of Illinois including Trial Bar. *Education:* University of Wisconsin-Madison (B.A., with honors, 1972); University of Illinois Loyola University of Chicago (J.D. 1975). City Attorney, Elmhurst and Oakbrook Terrace, Illinois. Village Attorney, Village of Oak Brook. Director: Ray Graham Association for People with Disabilities; Elmhurst Economic Development Commission. *Member:* DuPage County and Illinois State (Member, Public Utilities Section) Bar Associations; International Municipal Lawyers Association; Illinois Municipal League Home Rule Attorneys Committee; National Association of Bond Lawyers. ***PRACTICE AREAS:*** Municipal Law; Public Finance; Business Law; Civil Litigation. **Email:** kubiesa@ksgalaw.com

HARLAN J. SPIROFF, born Elmhurst, Illinois, May 19, 1952; admitted to bar, 1982, Illinois. *Education:* Roosevelt University (B.A., 1974; M.P.A., 1975); Northern Illinois University (J.D., 1982). Village Attorney, Wayne, Illinois. *Member:* Chicago, DuPage County and Illinois State Bar Associations. ***PRACTICE AREAS:*** Municipal Law; Land Use Law; Administrative Law; Employment Law; Real Estate Law. **Email:** spiroff@ksgalaw.com

BARBARA J. GOSSELAR, born Holland, Michigan, October 14, 1946; admitted to bar, 1979, Illinois and U.S. District Court, Northern District of Illinois; 1991, U.S. Court of Appeals, Seventh Circuit and U.S. Supreme Court. *Education:* Wheaton College (B.A., 1968); Northeastern University (M.A., in Guidance and counseling, 1973); Loyola University School of Law (J.D., 1979). Attorney for Westmont Roselle, Streamwood and Oak Brook, Illinois Park Districts. Village Attorney, Downers Grove, Illinois, 1981-1990. *Member:* Du Page County, Illinois State and American Bar Associations; Du Page Women Lawyers Association. ***PRACTICE AREAS:*** Municipal Law; Land Use Law; Appeals; Employment Law. **Email:** gosselar@ksgalaw.com

ANDREW Y. ACKER, born Sharon, Pennsylvania, February 22, 1961; admitted to bar, 1991, Michigan; 1992, Pennsylvania; 1993, Illinois, U.S. District Court, Northern District of Illinois including Trial Bar, and U.S. Court of Appeals, Seventh Circuit. *Education:* Denison University (B.A., 1983); Thomas M. Cooley Law School (J.D., cum laude, 1991). Associate, Thomas M. Cooley Law Review, 1989-1991. Research Attorney, Michigan Court of Appeals, 1991-1992. Law Clerk to Justice Tom M. Lytton, Illinois Appellate Court, 1993-1994. *Member:* Illinois State and American Bar Associations. ***PRACTICE AREAS:*** Civil Litigation; Appeals. **Email:** acker@ksgalaw.com

---

JOAN E. MULLINS, born Oak Park, Illinois; admitted to bar, 1991, Illinois. *Education:* St. Marys College (B.A., 1988); DePaul University, College of Law (J.D., 1991). *Member:* DuPage County and Illinois State Bar Associations. ***PRACTICE AREAS:*** Municipal Prosecution; Litigation. **Email:** mullins@ksgalaw.com

MARGARET M. O'CONNELL, born Chicago, Illinois, October 4, 1964; admitted to bar, 1991, Illinois and U.S. District Court, Northern District of Illinois; 1996, U.S. District Court, Southern District of Illinois. *Education:* Bradley University (B.S., 1986); John Marshall Law School (J.D., 1991). Instructor, Lawyering Skills II, John Marshall Law School, 2001. *Member:* Dupage County and Illinois State Bar Associations; Illinois Capital Litigation Trial Bar. ***REPORTED CASES:*** U.S. ex. rel. Bell v. Pierson, 157 F Supp 896 (7th Cir. 2000); In Re The Detention of Samuelson, 189 Ill. 2d 548 (2000). ***PRACTICE AREAS:*** Municipal Law; Family Law; Criminal Defense. **Email:** oconnell@ksgalaw.com

JOHN R. KELLY, born Cleveland, Ohio, June 24, 1978; admitted to bar, 2003, Illinois. *Education:* University of Illinois (B.S., 2000; J.D., 2003). **Email:** kelly@ksgalaw.com

MIA S. MCPHERSON, born 1973; admitted to bar, 1998, Illinois. *Education:* Purdue University (B.A., 1995); DePaul University (J.D., 1998). *Member:* DuPage County Bar Association. ***PRACTICE AREAS:*** Criminal Prosecution; Criminal Defense. **Email:** mcpherson@ksgalaw.com

JONATHAN P. STRINGER, born 1975; admitted to bar, 2001, Illinois and U.S. District Court, Northern District of Illinois. *Education:* Bowling Green State University (B.A., 1998); The John Marshall Law School (J.D., 2001). *Member:* DuPage County and Illinois State Bar Associations. ***PRACTICE AREAS:*** Civil Litigation; Transportation.

(This Listing Continued)

KUBIESA, SPIROFF, GOSSELAR & ACKER, P.C., Elmhurst—Continued

OF COUNSEL

DONALD S. NATHAN, born Chicago, Illinois, August 18, 1945; admitted to bar, 1975, Illinois and U.S. District Court, Northern District of Illinois; 1976, U.S. Court of Appeals, Seventh Circuit; 1988, U.S. Supreme Court; 2001, U.S. Court of Appeals, Ninth Circuit. *Education:* University of Illinois (B.A., cum laude, 1971); Loyola University (J.D., 1975). Formerly with: Nathan & Taradji; Donald S. Nathan, P.C.; Nathan, Florio & Maramba, P.C.; Grubman & Nathan, P.C.; Arnold Grubman & Associates; Sodak, Grubman, Pritikin, Rosenthal & Feldman. ***PRACTICE AREAS:*** Plaintiffs Personal Injury; Personal Injury Defense; Workers Compensation; Litigation. ***Email:*** nathan@ksgalaw.com

MICHAEL V. FAVIA

ELMWOOD PARK, ILLINOIS

(See Chicago)

Civil Litigation, Personal Injuries, Automobile Accidents, Medical Malpractice, Products Liability, Work Injuries, Health Law, Medicare and Medicaid Fraud, Medical and Health Related Regulatory Issues, Professional Licensure Matters.

SPINA, McGUIRE & OKAL

A PROFESSIONAL CORPORATION

Established in 1965

7610 W. NORTH AVENUE

ELMWOOD PARK, ILLINOIS 60707-4195

Telephone: 708-453-2800

FAX: 708-452-5088

Email: spinalaw@aol.com

URL: http://www.lawyers.com/spinamcguire&okal

Civil (State and Federal) Litigation, Commercial and Corporate Law, Family Law, Real Estate (Commercial and Residential), Real Estate Development, Family Law, Trusts, Estate and Probate, Union Labor Law, Appellate Practice, Personal Injury (including Product Liability).

ANTHONY F. SPINA, born Chicago, Illinois, August 15, 1937; admitted to bar, 1962, Illinois and U.S. District Court, Northern District of Illinois. *Education:* Loyola University (B.S., 1959); DePaul University (J.D., 1962). Delta Theta Phi. *Member:* Chicago, Illinois State and American Bar Associations; State Association of Township Attorneys (President, 1982-1985); National Association of Township Attorneys (Secretary, 1985-1988; Vice President, 1988-1993; President, 1993-1995); Justinian Society; Judicature Society. ***PRACTICE AREAS:*** Corporate Law; Commercial Law; Trusts and Estates; Township Law.

JAMES T. McGUIRE, born Evergreen Park, Illinois, September 9, 1949; admitted to bar, 1976, Illinois and U.S. District Court, Northern District of Illinois. *Education:* University of Illinois (B.A., 1971); John Marshall Law School (J.D., 1976). Phi Alpha Theta. Member, Order of John Marshall. *Member:* Illinois State and American Bar Associations. ***PRACTICE AREAS:*** Contracts; Real Estate; Probate; Transactional Law; Community Association Law; Real Estate Development.

TIMOTHY H. OKAL, born Chicago, Illinois, June 14, 1950; admitted to bar, 1976, Illinois and U.S. District Court, Northern District of Illinois including Trial Bar. *Education:* Loyola University (B.A., 1973); John Marshall Law School (J.D., 1976). *Member:* Chicago, Illinois State and American Bar Associations; The Association of Trial Lawyers of America; Illinois Trial Lawyers Association. ***REPORTED CASES:*** Arnold v. Village of Chicago Ridge, 181 Ill.App.3d 778; Canzoneri v. Village of Franklin Park, 161 Ill.App.3d 33; In re Estate of Roeseler, 287 Ill.App.3d 1003; VanMeter v. Darien Park District 297 Ill. 2d 273 (2003). ***PRACTICE AREAS:*** Civil Practice; Federal Litigation; Personal Injury; Labor Law; Criminal Defense; Products Liability; Appellate Practice; Commercial Litigation; Administrative Law.

JOHN D. SPINA, born Oak Park, Illinois, January 8, 1963; admitted to bar, 1988, Illinois and U.S. District Court, Northern District of Illinois including Trial Bar; 1989, Florida. *Education:* Loyola University of Chicago (B.A., 1985); Loyola School of Law (J.D., 1988). *Member:* Chicago, Illinois State and American Bar Associations; The Florida Bar; Illinois Trial Lawyers Association; Illinois Township Attorneys Association (President, 1999-2001; Director, 1996—); Justinian Society; American Judicature Society. ***REPORTED CASES:*** Cannizzo v. Berwyn Township 708 Community Mental Health Board, 251 Ill.Dec. 889, 741 N.E.2d 1067 (Ill.App 1 Dist. 2000); Granata vs. Allied American Insurance Ill.App. CT. 1st. Div. #1-00-0398 (8/19/02). ***PRACTICE AREAS:*** Litigation; Civil Practice; Township Law; Family Law; Bankruptcy.

FELICIA M. DiGIOVANNI, born Maywood, Illinois, September 18, 1973; admitted to bar, 1998, Illinois. *Education:* Dominican University (B.A., 1995); John Marshall Law School (J.D., 1998). Phi Delta Phi. *Member:* Chicago and West Suburban Bar Associations; Illinois State Bar Association (Assembly Member); Justinian Society. ***PRACTICE AREAS:*** Real Estate; Civil Practice; Family Law.

LYNCH AND BLOOM, P.C.

EUREKA, ILLINOIS

(See Peoria)

Matrimonial and Family Law, Divorce, Adoptions, Child Support, Child Custody, General Civil Litigation, Personal Injury Law.

WESTERVELT, JOHNSON, NICOLL & KELLER, LLC

EUREKA, ILLINOIS

(See Peoria)

General Civil Trial and Appellate Practice in State and Federal Courts, Insurance Defense, Health and Health Care, Labor Relations, Employment Discrimination and Affirmative Action, Products Liability Litigation, ERISA and Benefits Plans, Corporate, Agricultural, Bankruptcy, Creditors' Rights, Banking, Real Estate, State and Federal Taxation, Estate Planning, Trusts and Probate, Workers Compensation, Environmental, Commercial.

ALEXANDER LAW OFFICE

1603 ORRINGTON AVENUE

EVANSTON, ILLINOIS 60201

Telephone: 847-475-5010

Fax: 847-328-1928

Email: argalexander@earthlink.net

Real Estate, Zoning, Arbitration and Mediation.

MEMBER OF FIRM

ELLEN J. ALEXANDER, born Detroit, Michigan; admitted to bar, 1975, Illinois. *Education:* University of Michigan (B.A.); University of Illinois (M.A.); DePaul University (J.D., 1975). *Member:* American Bar Association; National Academy of Arbitrators. ***LANGUAGES:*** French. ***Email:*** argalexander@earthlink.net

ASHER, GITTLER, GREENFIELD & D'ALBA, LTD.

EVANSTON, ILLINOIS

(See Chicago)

Labor Relations, Employment and Employee Benefit Law, General Trial Practice in all Courts.

ATKINSON & ATKINSON

1603 ORRINGTON AVENUE, SUITE 2080

EVANSTON, ILLINOIS 60201

Telephone: 847-864-0070

Facsimile: 847-864-0588

Email: AandA@ameritech.net

URL: http://www.lawyers.com/atkinson&atkinson

Association Law, Business Law including Corporate, Real Estate, Estate Planning, Estate and Trust Administration, Labor and Employee Benefits, Professional Associations, Professional Licensure and Certification, Administrative, Tax and Litigation related to these areas of practice.

FIRM PROFILE: Atkinson & Atkinson was founded in Evanston in 1989 by John F. and Dale J. Atkinson. The firm concentrates on many areas including corporate, commercial and estate planning. It is most respected for its unique experience in professional licensure and certification; members of the firm regularly speak around the county regarding this area of law.

MEMBERS OF FIRM

JOHN F. ATKINSON, born Evanston, Illinois, February 19, 1932; admitted to bar, 1958, Illinois; 1961, U.S. District Court, Northern District of Illinois; 1969, U.S. Supreme Court; 1981, U.S. Court of Appeals, 7th Circuit; 1996, Wisconsin. *Education:* University of Rochester (B.A., 1954); Ohio State University (J.D., 1957). *Member:* Chicago, Illinois State and American Bar Associations. ***PRACTICE AREAS:*** Professional Licensure and Certification; Association Law; Corporate Law; Commercial and Business Law; Real Estate Law; Employment Law; Estate Planning; Probate; Trust Administration. ***Email:*** aanda@ameritech.net

DALE J. ATKINSON, born Evanston, Illinois, January 22, 1958; admitted to bar, 1987, Illinois and U.S. District Court, Northern District of Illinois; 1992, U.S. Court of Appeals, 7th Circuit. *Education:* Denison University; Ball State University (B.S., 1981); Northwestern School of Law, Portland, Oregon (J.D., 1987). Co-Author: "Professional Responsibility of a Pharmacist vs. Legal Liability," American Society on Pharmacy Law," 1988; "Pharmacist Liability - A Dilemma," Pharmacist's Life, Vol. 2, No. 4, April/May 1988. Author, "Legal Perspectives of Examination Security," The Bar Examiner Vol. 65 No. 4, 1996; Clear Exam Review Vol. VII No. 1, 1996. *Member:* Chicago, Illinois State and American Bar Associations; Sports Lawyers Association. ***PRACTICE AREAS:*** Professional Licensure and Certification; Association Law; Corporate Law; Commercial and Business Law; Real Estate; Employment; Estate Planning; Probate; Trust Administration. ***Email:*** aanda@ameritech.net.

JULIA C. WORKS, born Summit, New Jersey, December 29, 1967; admitted to bar, 1996, Texas; 1998, Illinois. *Education:* University of Pennsylvania (B.A., 1989); University of Connecticut (J.D., with honors, 1996). *Member:* Chicago, Illinois State and American Bar Associations. ***PRACTICE AREAS:*** Professional Licensing and Certification; Association Law; Corporate Law; Employment; Estate Planning; Probate; Trust Administration. ***Email:*** aanda@ameritech.net

A list of Representative Clients will be furnished upon request.

LAW OFFICE OF MARC N. BLUMENTHAL

EVANSTON, ILLINOIS

(See Chicago)

Franchise Law, Start-Up Franchisors and Franchisees, Leasing, Licensing, Trademarks, Trademark Information, Copyrights, Breach of Contract, Corporate Law, Business Formations, Business Transactions, Litigation, Arbitration.

CARDINAL LAW GROUP, LTD.

1603 ORRINGTON AVENUE
EVANSTON, ILLINOIS 60201
Telephone: 847-905-7111
Fax: 847-905-7113
URL: http://www.cardinallawgroup.com/lawyers/cook/
Email: info@cardinallawgroup.com
URL: http://www.cardinallawgroup.com

Chicago, Illinois Office: 720 South Dearborn Street, Suite 503, 60605. Telephone: 847-905-7111. Fax: 847-905-7113. URL: http://www.cardinallawgroup.com

Technology and Intellectual Property Law Including U.S. and International Patents, Patent Preparation, Patent Prosecution, Patent Litigation, Intellectual Property Licensing, Intellectual Property Litigation, Trademark, Copyright, Trade Dress, Trade Secret, Unfair Competition, Antitrust, Cyberlaw, Biotech, Mechanical, Electrical, Computer and Software Patents.

FIRM PROFILE: Cardinal Law Group specializes in intellectual property law including patent, trademark, copyright, trade secret and related areas.

With more than 20 lawyers and specialized professionals of varying backgrounds and experience, Cardinal Law Group is prepared to prosecute patent applications in all fields, including mechanical, electrical, software, biotech, and Internet related matters.

Our client base ranges from Fortune 500 companies to individual inventors.

FRANK C. NICHOLAS, born Chicago, Illinois, June 12, 1961; admitted to bar, 1989, Illinois and Wisconsin; registered to practice before U.S. Patent and Trademark Office. *Education:* Marquette University (B.S.M.E., 1983); University of Wisconsin-Madison (J.D., 1989). Extern Clerkship, U.S. Court of Appeals, Seventh Circuit. *Member:* Chicago and American Bar Associations; State Bar of Wisconsin; American Intellectual Property Law Association.

REPRESENTATIVE CLIENTS: General Motors; Motorola; SBC; Philips Electronics; IBM; Medtronic; Agilent Technologies; Gritwire; Clear Lam Packaging.

JOHN W. COOLEY

2106 ORRINGTON AVENUE
EVANSTON, ILLINOIS 60201-2914
Telephone: 847-328-7285
Fax: 847-864-1586

Arbitrator-Mediator.

JOHN W. COOLEY, born St. Louis, Missouri, October 28, 1943; admitted to bar, 1973, Missouri, Illinois, U.S. District Court, Northern District of Illinois and U.S. Court of Appeals, Seventh Circuit; 1982, U.S. Supreme Court. *Education:* U.S. Military Academy (B.S., 1965); Notre Dame Law School (J.D., 1973). Editor, Notre Dame Law Review, 1972-1973. Author: Callaghan's Appellate Advocacy Manual, 1989; Mediation Advocacy (NITA, 2002); Arbitration Advocacy (NITA, 2003); The Arbitrator's Handbook (NITA, 1998); The Mediator's Handbook (NITA, 2000). Lecturer, Appellate Advocacy, Alternatives to Litigation, Loyola School of Law, Chicago, 1979—. Assistant U.S. Attorney, Chicago, 1974-1977. Senior Staff Attorney, U.S. Court of Appeals, Seventh Circuit, 1977-1979. U.S. Magistrate, 1979-1981; Partner, Stone, McGuire & Benjamin, 1981-1984.

DAVID A. CULPEPPER

EVANSTON, ILLINOIS

(See Chicago)

Bankruptcy, Personal Injury, Wrongful Death, Automobile Accidents, Truck Accidents, Negligence, Probate, Chapter 7, Foreclosures, Domestic Relations, Family Law, Divorce, Adoptions.

CUTLER & ASSOCIATES, LTD.

EVANSTON, ILLINOIS

(See Skokie)

Bankruptcy, Consumer Bankruptcy, Bankruptcy Chapter 7, Foreclosures, Small Business, Buying and Selling of Businesses, Family Business, Limited Liability, Partnership, Corporate, Contract, Breach of Contract, General Practice, Debtor and Creditor, Collections, Creditors, Rights and Civil Litigation.

EVAN LAW GROUP, LLC

EVANSTON, ILLINOIS

(See Chicago)

Intellectual Property.

EVANSTON MAIN LAW OFFICE

ONE ROTARY CENTER
1560 SHERMAN AVENUE, SUITE 301
EVANSTON, ILLINOIS 60201
Telephone: 847-475-4474
Fax: 847-475-0286
Email: EvanstonMainLaw@sbcglobal.net
URL: http://www.evanstonmainlaw.com

Bankruptcy, Consumer Bankruptcy, Family, Divorce, Child Custody, Child Support, Premarital Agreements, Spousal Support, Corporate, Business, Contract, Wills, Trusts, Estate Planning, Probate, Criminal, Driving While Intoxicated, Traffic Violations, Misdemeanors, Felonies and Civil Litigation Practice.

(This Listing Continued)

ROGER H. SIMON, born Camp LeJeune, North Carolina, July 20, 1944; admitted to bar, 1970, Illinois; U.S. District Court, Northern District of Illinois. *Education:* Loyola University (B.A., 1966; J.D., 1970). *Member:* Illinois State and American Bar Associations. ***PRACTICE AREAS:*** Divorce; Family; Real Estate; Bankruptcy; Criminal; Business; Wills; Trusts and Estates; Probate. ***Email:*** EvanstonMainLaw@sbcglobal.net

STUART A. FELDMAN

EVANSTON, ILLINOIS

(See Wilmette)

Wills and Probate, Estate Planning, Trusts and Estates, Guardianships, Tax Planning, Taxation, IRS Audits, Business Planning, Small Business, General Business and Real Estate.

FREDDI L. GREENBERG

Established in 1983
1603 ORRINGTON AVENUE
SUITE 1050
EVANSTON, ILLINOIS 60201
Telephone: 847-864-4010
Fax: 847-864-4037
Email: flgreenberg@flglaw.com

Energy Law, Non-Utility Electric Generation and Power Marketing, Landfill Gas and Natural Gas, Public Utility Law, Municipal Electric Utilities, Business Law.

FREDDI L. GREENBERG, born Chicago, Illinois, April 9, 1946; admitted to bar, 1975, Illinois, U.S. District Court, Northern District of Illinois and U.S. Court of Appeals, Seventh Circuit. *Education:* University of Michigan (B.A., 1967); University of Chicago (M.A.T., 1971); Loyola University (J.D., 1975). Member, Loyola University of Chicago Law Review, 1974-1975. Reports Editor, Energy Law Journal, 1987—. Author: Chapter, "Cogeneration," *Natural Gas Yearbook,* Executive Enterprises, 1988-1992; "The Alcon Decision: Disincentive to Cogeneration," Energy Law Journal, Volume 7, 1986. *Member:* Chicago (Member, Public Utility Law Committee, 1989—), Illinois State (Member, Section Council, Public Utility and Transportation Law, 1991—; Chair, 1996-1997) and American (Member, 1983—, Chair, 1996-1997 and 2003-2004, Section on Natural Resources, Energy and Environmental Law) Bar Associations; Energy Bar Association (Member, Board of Directors, 2003—; Chairperson, Committee on Non-Utility Generation, 1984-1985); Midwest Cogeneration Association (Director, 1988—; Vice President, 1992-1993; President, 1994; Director, 1988-2003); Solid Waste Association of North America. ***PRACTICE AREAS:*** Energy Law; Municipal Utility Law; Utilities Law; Natural Resources; Oil & Gas Law; Business Law.

MARC H. HEISLER

2820 LINCOLN STREET
EVANSTON, ILLINOIS 60201-2045
Telephone: 847-328-2238
Fax: 847-328-7795
Mobile: 847-971-4492
Email: counselmhh@aol.com
URL: http://www.heislernet.com

Real Estate, Residential Real Estate, Buying and Selling a Home, Commercial Real Estate, Condominium Law and Mortgages. Business, Small Business, Partnership, Family Business and Buying and Selling a Business. Probate and Wills. Adoption Law. Civil Litigation, Chancery Practice, Collections, Personal Injury and Automobile Accidents.

FIRM PROFILE: Providing Legal Representation and Counseling to the Chicago Metro area since 1975.

MARC H. HEISLER, born Chicago, Illinois, February 2, 1944; admitted to bar, 1975, Illinois and U.S. District Court, Northern District of Illinois; 1983, U.S. District Court, Northern District of Illinois, Trial Bar. *Education:* Northwestern University (B.A., 1970); Loyola University (J.D., 1975). *Member:* Illinois State Bar Association. ***PRACTICE AREAS:*** Real Estate; Condominium Law; Business Law; Probate; Wills; Civil Litigation; Collections; Contracts; Chancery Practice; Personal Injury.

HURLEY, McKENNA & MERTZ

EVANSTON, ILLINOIS

(See Chicago)

Personal Injury, Plaintiff, Medical Negligence, Nursing Home Abuse.

KEIL M. LARSON

EVANSTON, ILLINOIS

(See Chicago)

Real Estate Litigation, Condominium Disputes, Real Estate Transactions, Probate Litigation, Partition Suits, Foreclosures, Lien Litigation, Specific Performance, Contract Litigation, Appraisal Litigation, Builder Litigation, Construction Defects, Landlord Tenant Law, Fraud Litigation, Immigration.

LESAVICH HIGH-TECH LAW GROUP, PC

EVANSTON, ILLINOIS

(See Chicago)

Software Patents, High-Tech Patents, Patent, Trademark Copyright Law, Licensing, Litigation, Internet Law, E-Commerce Law, Business Method Patents.

LAW OFFICE OF EMILY LOVE, P.C.

Established in 1997

621 MADISON STREET

EVANSTON, ILLINOIS 60202-2202

Telephone: 847-492-1612

Facsimile: 847-492-1618

Email: emily@emilylove.com

URL: http://www.emilylovelaw.com

Immigration and Naturalization.

EMILY LOVE, born Chicago, Illinois, 1963; admitted to bar, 1993, Illinois and U.S. District Court, Northern District of Illinois. *Education:* Haverford College (B.A., in Latin American Studies, 1985); Loyola University (J.D., 1993). Author: "Equality in Political Asylum Law: For a Legislative Recognition of Gender-Based Persecution," Harvard Women's Law Journal, Vol. 17, Spring, 1994. *Member:* Chicago Bar Association; American Immigration Lawyer's Association. ***LANGUAGES:*** Spanish. ***PRACTICE AREAS:*** Immigration and Naturalization. ***Email:*** emily@emilylove.com

Language: Spanish.

MACIOROWSKI, SACKMANN & ULRICH

EVANSTON, ILLINOIS

(See Chicago)

Worker's Compensation Defense Law, including Hospital, Corporations and Business Defense and Labor and Employment Law.

MANDELL MENKES LLC

EVANSTON, ILLINOIS

(See Chicago)

General Civil Practice, Class Action Defense, Consumer Finance and Banking, Corporate, Commercial Litigation, Employment, Media, Entertainment and Intellectual Property Law including Copyright and Trademark Law, Computer and Technology Law, Health Care, Captive Insurance and Purchasing and Risk Retention Groups and Insurance Coverage, Directors and Officers Liability, Professional Liability, Casualty, Life, Health and Disability.

MATEK LAW OFFICES, P.C.

EVANSTON, ILLINOIS

(See Chicago)

Subrogation, Collections, Commercial Litigation, Bankruptcy, Commercial Law.

MORRIS & STELLA

EVANSTON, ILLINOIS

(See Chicago)

Products Liability Litigation. General Civil and Commercial Litigation.

SCHOENBERG, FISHER, NEWMAN & ROSENBERG, LTD.

EVANSTON, ILLINOIS

(See Chicago)

General Business Practice, including Corporate, Litigation, Trade Associations, Independent Manufacturers Representatives, Labor Law, Employee Benefits, Federal, State and Real Estate Taxation, Estate Planning, Probate, Real Estate, Environmental Law, Mergers and Acquisitions, Securities, Banking, Intellectual Property, Bankruptcy, Family Law, Unfair Trade Practices, Legal Ethics and Professional Responsibility.

SCHUYLER, ROCHE & ZWIRNER

A PROFESSIONAL CORPORATION

SUITE 2050

1603 ORRINGTON AVENUE

EVANSTON, ILLINOIS 60201

Telephone: 312-565-2400

URL: http://www.srzlaw.com

Chicago, Illinois Office: One Prudential Plaza, Suite 3800, 130 East Randolph Street. Telephone: 312-565-2400. Facsimile: 312-565-8300.

General Practice: Estate Management: Estate Planning and Administration, Trusts, Probate and Trust Litigation, Estate and Transfer Taxation, Wealth and Health Planning; General Corporate; Tax; Commercial and Residential Real Estate.

SHAREHOLDER

ALISON BARKLEY, born Chicago, Illinois, August 8, 1949; admitted to bar, 1977, Illinois. *Education:* Thornton Community College (A.A., 1969); University of Illinois (B.S., 1971); DePaul University (J.D., cum laude, 1976). *Member:* Illinois State and American Bar Associations. ***PRACTICE AREAS:*** General Corporate; Estates and Trusts; Estate Management; Estate Planning and Administration; Trusts; Wealth Planning; Health Planning; Business Enterprises. ***Email:*** abarkley@srzlaw.com

SCOTT, HALSTED & BABETCH, P.C.

EVANSTON, ILLINOIS

(See Chicago)

Civil Litigation, Trials, Defense Litigation, Appeals, Personal Injury, Automobile, Premises Liability, Uninsured, Underinsured Motorists, Negligence, Strict Liability Law, Construction, Commercial and Insurance Law.

SHAW GUSSIS FISHMAN GLANTZ WOLFSON & TOWBIN LLC

EVANSTON, ILLINOIS

(See Chicago)

Bankruptcy and Insolvency Law, Creditors Rights, Real Estate and related services, Land Use and Zoning, Commercial Litigation, and Secured Lending.

LAW OFFICES OF JEFF SMITH

1603 ORRINGTON, SUITE 800

EVANSTON, ILLINOIS 60201

Telephone: 847-372-9324

Fax: 847-332-1171

Email: jsmith@jefflaw.com

Computer Law, Internet Law, Business Law, E-Commerce, Contract Litigation, Intellectual Property, Estate Planning, Domestic Relations, Municipal Law, Employment Law and Real Estate.

JEFF SMITH, born Chicago, Illinois; admitted to bar, 1983, Illinois; 1989, U.S. District Court, Northern District of Illinois and U.S. Court of Appeals, Seventh Circuit. *Education:* Northwestern University (B.A., 1977); Harvard University (J.D., 1982). Member: Editorial Board, Harvard Civil Rights - Civil Liberties Law Review, 1981-1982. Author: "No Substitution: Legal Clinics and Public Interest Law," 11 Loy. Q. Pub. Issues and L. 23, Fall, 1986; "Committee Campaigns: A Loophole in Illinois Disclosure Law," 2 Chi. Coun. Law. Coun. News 1, March, 1986. Faculty in Clinical Law, 1985-1987 and Lecturer, Election Law, 1989, Loyola University School of Law. Democratic State Central Committeeman, 1986-1990. Assistant Corporation Counsel, City of Chicago, 1987-1988. Former-Associate: Jenner and Block, LLC, 1982-1984; Gottlieb and Schwartz, 1988-1990. Director, Medicare Project, Loyola University of Chicago School of Law. *Member:* Illinois State and American Bar Associations. ***REPORTED CASES:*** Lake Michigan Federation v. U.S. Army Corps of Engineers; Baksinski v. Carey; South Austin Community Council v. I.C.C.; Coleman v. Vincent Lane, et al. ***PRACTICE AREAS:*** Computer Law; Internet Law; Business Law; E-Commerce; Contract Litigation; Intellectual Property; Estate Planning; Domestic Relations; Municipal Law; Employment Law; Real Estate.

LAW OFFICES OF GARY H. SMITH, P.C.

EVANSTON, ILLINOIS

(See Chicago)

Property Tax, Property Tax Appeals and Real Estate Law.

DAVID M. STERNBERG

EVANSTON, ILLINOIS

(See Chicago)

Automobile Accidents and Injuries, Slip and Fall, Wrongful Death, Personal Injury and Workers Compensation Law.

MICHAEL THOMPSON

EVANSTON, ILLINOIS

(See Chicago)

International Trade and Investment, Acquisition of Fine Art and Cultural Property, Transactions involving Literary and Artistic Property.

TISHLER & WALD, LTD.

EVANSTON, ILLINOIS

(See Chicago)

General Civil Practice. Bankruptcy and Reorganization, Corporate, Taxation, Estate Planning, Franchise, Probate, Real Estate, Banking, State and Federal Litigation.

WALLENSTEIN WAGNER & ROCKEY, LTD.

EVANSTON, ILLINOIS

(See Chicago)

Intellectual Property and Technology Related Law including Protection and Licensing of United States and International Patent, Trademark, Copyright Trade Secret and Unfair Competition Matters and Related Litigation in the Courts and United States International Trade Commission.

WEIL & ASSOCIATES

EVANSTON, ILLINOIS

(See Northbrook)

Family Law, Divorce, Collaborative Law, Adoptions, Child Custody, Child Support, Divorce, Domestic Violence, Premarital Agreements, Spousal Support.

WITWER & WALDRON, LLC

1603 ORRINGTON AVENUE, SUITE 2080
EVANSTON, ILLINOIS 60201
Telephone: 847-332-2020
Fax: 847-332-2002
URL: http://www.lawyers.com/witwer&waldron

Wills, Trusts, Probate, Estate Planning, General Litigation, First Amendment and Religious Law, Municipal, Government, Corporate, Real Estate.

FIRM PROFILE: Witwer & Waldron, LLC is a descendant of the original Gallagher-Witwer law firm founded in 1895. The firm has relocated from Chicago to Evanston, Illinois, combining its suburban practice with its pre-existing downtown practice.

SAMUEL W. WITWER, JR., born Chicago, Illinois, August 5, 1941; admitted to bar, 1967, Illinois and U.S. Supreme Court; 1973, U.S. District Court, Eastern District of Michigan; 1985, U.S. District Court, Northern District of Illinois including Trial Bar and U.S. Court of Appeals, Sixth and Seventh Circuits. *Education:* Dickinson College (A.B., with honors, 1963); University of Michigan (J.D., 1966). Phi Delta Phi. General Counsel: United Methodist Bishop, Chicago Area, 1976—; Glenview Park District, 1982—. Court Appointee, Trial Bar Admissions Committee of U.S. District Court, Northern District of Illinois, 1982-1997. Special Assistant Attorney General, State of Illinois, 1985-1991. Listed in Who's Who in America, 1995—. *Member:* Chicago (Member, Constitutional Law Committee, 1977-1980), Illinois State and American Bar Associations; Lawyers Club of Chicago; Methodist Bar Association (President, 1972). ***PRACTICE AREAS:*** Litigation; First Amendment Law; Church Law; Probate; Trust Law; Municipal Law; Government. ***Email:*** witwer@wpglawyers.com

BRIAN M. WALDRON, born Chicago, Illinois, November 14, 1944; admitted to bar, 1973, Illinois and U.S. District Court, Northern District of Illinois; 1973, U.S. Tax Court. *Education:* Loyola University (B.S., 1968; J.D., 1972). *Member:* Chicago Bar Association. ***PRACTICE AREAS:*** Wills; Estate Planning; Probate; Trusts; Real Estate; Corporate Law. ***Email:*** bwaldron@wpglawyers.com

FORST LAW OFFICES

EVERGREEN PARK, ILLINOIS

(See Oak Lawn)

Divorce, Debtor Bankruptcy.

JULIE HARPER

FAIRVIEW HEIGHTS, ILLINOIS

(See Alton)

Traffic, DWI, Bankruptcy, Estate Planning, Real Estate, Contracts, Wills, Probate, Trusts, General Practice, Criminal, Buying and Selling Homes, Guardianships, Automobile Accidents, Adoptions.

THE PEITHMANN LAW OFFICE

Established in 1948
111 SOUTH MAIN STREET
P.O. BOX 228
FARMER CITY, ILLINOIS 61842-1453
Telephone: 309-928-3390
Fax: 309-928-2731
Email: peithmannlawoffice@excite.com

Wealth Management, Asset Protection, Basic, Intermediate and Advanced Estate Planning, Trust and Estate Administration, Contested Estates, Elder Law, Closely Held Businesses, Farm and Commercial Real Estate, Gift, Estate and Income Taxation of all types.

FIRM PROFILE: The Peithmann Law Office was founded in 1948 by Ortheldo A. Peithmann and his non-attorney wife, Winona C. Peithmann, as a general practice law firm with a tilt towards municipal law, farm estate planning and tax matters. William A. Peithmann joined the firm full time in 1985, following a stint as international corporate counsel in California. Since 1985 the firm has developed a purposeful concentration in providing elite wealth management and related services to select high net worth clients throughout Illinois and Colorado. The Firm is dedicated to providing only the highest quality legal services, equivalent or superior to that provided by larger firms in more urban venues, and proudly stands behind its work. As a result The Peithmann Law Office is regularly cited by its peers as among the very best in Illinois. Referrals and requests for co-counsel are gladly accepted where appropriate.

ORTHELDO A. PEITHMANN, born 1917; admitted to bar, 1948, Illinois; 1966, U.S. Supreme Court. *Education:* University of Illinois (B.S., Agriculture, 1939; M.S., Agriculture, 1942; J.D., 1947). Phi Kappa Phi. Self-employed Attorney, Farmer City, 1948—. Life Member, American Legion and Veterans of Foreign Wars. *Member:* DeWitt County (Past President), Illinois State and American Bar Associations. [Captain, U.S. Army, 1942-1946, Okinawa Campaign and Korean Peninsula]. ***PRACTICE AREAS:*** Probate; Trusts and Estate Planning; Real Estate; Tax; Estate Administration; Civil Practice; Agricultural Law; Drainage Law.

(This Listing Continued)

WILLIAM A. PEITHMANN, born 1954; admitted to bar, 1978, Colorado; 1979, Illinois; 1980, California; 1995, U.S. Supreme Court. *Education:* DePauw University; Loretto Heights College (B.A., International Relations, 1975); University of Illinois Law School; University of Denver (J.D., 1978). Recipient, ISBA Board of Governors Award, 1998. Listed in: Best Lawyers in America (1999—, Trust and Estate Matters; 2003—, Tax Matters); Who's Who in American Law, 2002—; Who's Who in America, 2003—. Author: "Dispute Resolution Under Foreign Petroleum Concessions: A Review With Focus on Arbitration," 8 Century City Bar Association Journal 25, 1983; "An Introduction to the Rules of Disclaimers," ISBA Law Ed Series, Estate Planning, Probate & Trust Update, at 121, February 1991; "An Introduction to the Principles, Use and Consequences of Powers of Appointment," ISBA Law Ed Series, Estate Planning, Probate & Trust Update, at 87, February 1992; reprinted as "A Look At The Principles and Uses of Powers of Appointment," Trusts & Estates, August 1993, at 38; Chapter 15, "Disclaimers," Illinois Estate Administration (two vol.), Illinois Institute for Continuing Legal Education, 1993, rev'd 1995 and 1999; "An Introduction to the Principles, Planning, Drafting and Benefits of the GST Exempt Trust," ISBA LawEd Series, Trusts and Estates Section, at 87, March 1994, rev'd and repr. for American Bar Association, Section of Real Property, Probate and Trust Law annual program, "Generation Skipping for the General Practitioner," August 1995, rev'd and repr. for Colorado Bar Association 98th Annual Convention, Probate and Trust Law Section annual program, September 1996. Attorney, Getty Oil Co., International Exploration and Production Division, Los Angeles, California, 1980-1983. International Legal Counsel, Computer Land Corporation, Hayward, California, 1983-1985. Fellow, American College of Trust and Estate Counsel, 1994—. *Member:* Will County, DeWitt County (President, 1986-1992), The Colorado (Member, Trust and Estate Section), Illinois State (Member, 1988-2001 and 2002— and Chair, 1994-1995, Trusts and Estates Section Council; Member, Special Committee on Living Trusts, 1992-1994; Special Task Force and Standing Committee on Public Protection from Unauthorized Practice of Law, Member, 1995-2003 and Chair, 1995-1997; Board of Governors, 1995-2001; Committee on Scope and Correlation; Board Liaison to Real Estate Law, Agricultural Law, Trusts and Estates, Mineral Law and Federal Tax Law Section Councils) and American (Member, Section on: Real Property, Probate and Trust Law; Vice Chair, B-1 Generation Skipping Transfer Committee, 1994-1998) Bar Associations; State Bar of California. Life Fellow and Silver Fellow, Illinois Bar Foundation (Member, Board of Directors, 1997-1998 and 2001-2003). (Also Counsel to the firm of Mahoney, Silverman & Cross, Ltd., Joliet). ***PRACTICE AREAS:*** Asset Protection; Wealth Preservation; Contested Trusts and Estates; Probate; Trusts and Estate Planning; Real Estate; Tax; Estate Administration; Civil Practice. ***Email:*** bpeithmann@excite.com

LEGAL SUPPORT PERSONNEL

WINONA C. PEITHMANN. *Education:* MacMurray College (B.A., 1940); University of Illinois (M.A., English, 1947; M.Ed., 1948). Illinois Certified Public Accountant certificate, 1977. Internal Revenue Service Enrolled Agent, 1976—.

AMY L. JONES, (since 1996)

JAMES & ASSOCIATES

412 S. 2ND AVENUE
P.O. BOX 398
FORRESTON, ILLINOIS 61030-9536
Telephone: 815-938-3241
Email: jameslaw1@aol.com
URL: http://www.jamesandassociateslaw.com

Family Law, Civil Litigation, Professional Liability, Divorce, Debtor and Creditor, Tax Lien, Real Estate.

MEMBER OF FIRM

THOMAS H. JAMES, born December 31, 1960; admitted to bar, 1986, North Dakota; 1987, Minnesota; 1989, Illinois. *Education:* University of North Dakota (B.B.A., 1983; J.D., 1986).

LAW OFFICE OF PAUL R. IDLAS

FOX LAKE, ILLINOIS

(See Grayslake)

Bankruptcy, Real Estate, Chapter 7 Bankruptcy, Real Estate Closings.

DOBBS AND HUTCHISON

FRANKFORT, ILLINOIS

(See Chicago)

Personal Injury, Automobile Accidents, Trucking Accidents, Motorcycle Accidents, Head Trauma, Spinal Cord Injuries, Premises Liability, Wrongful Death, Social Security, Social Security Disability Benefits, Children's Benefits.

THERESA M. MALYSA

FRANKFORT, ILLINOIS

(See Orland Park)

Family Law, Divorce, Tax Considerations, Retirement Benefits, Child Custody, Parenting Time, Visitation, Child Support, Domestic Violence, Paternity, Matrimonial Litigation, Premarital Agreements.

McKEOWN, FITZGERALD, ZOLLNER, BUCK, HUTCHISON & RUTTLE

28 KANSAS STREET
FRANKFORT, ILLINOIS 60423
Telephone: 815-469-2176
Fax: 815-469-0295
URL: http://www.mckeownlawfirm.com

Joliet Office: 2455 Glenwood Avenue. Telephone: 815-729-4800. Fax: 815-729-4711.

General Civil, Trial and Appellate Practice. Corporation, Municipal, Probate, Estate Planning, Real Estate, Taxation, Employment, Healthcare, School and Personal Injury Law.

(For Complete Biographical data on all personnel, See Professional Biographies at Joliet, Illinois)

WILLIAM J. PETERS

237 SOUTH LAGRANGE ROAD
FRANKFORT, ILLINOIS 60423
Telephone: 815-469-1399
Fax: 815-469-0822
Email: wjplaw@aol.com
URL: http://www.lawyers.com/wjplaw

Trusts and Estates, Estate Planning, Asset Protection, Estate Litigation, Estate and Gift Taxation, Charitable Giving, Wills, Real Estate, Residential Real Estate, Commercial Real Estate, Condominium, Landlord and Tenant, Business, Small Business, Business Formations, Limited Liability, Buying and Selling of Businesses, Zoning and Land Use, Elder and Elder Care Law.

WILLIAM J. PETERS, born Waukegan, Illinois, May 8, 1949; admitted to bar, 1978, Illinois; 1986, U.S. District Court, Northern District of Illinois including Trial Bar; 1988, U.S. Tax Court; 2001, U.S. Supreme Court. *Education:* University of Illinois, Chicago (B.A.; with honors and distinction, 1974); University of Illinois, Urbana-Champaign (J.D., 1978). *Member:* Will County (Member, Real Estate Committee) and Illinois State Bar Associations. [U.S. Marine Corps, 1967-1971]. ***PRACTICE AREAS:*** Trust and Estates; Real Estate.

LAW OFFICE OF ROSEMARIE HEIDENREICH PARKER

Established in 1994

P.O. BOX 125
FREEBURG, ILLINOIS 62243
Telephone: 618-539-9956
Fax: 618-539-9954
Email: parkerrobtrosie@juno.com
URL: http://www.parkerlawoffice.net

Mailing Address: P.O. Box 125, Freeburg, IL 62243

Real Estate, Wills, Trusts, Probate Estates, Bankruptcy, Small Business Law, Water Law, General Practice.

FIRM PROFILE: Handling all your family's legal needs including Real Estate, Bankruptcy, Estate Planning including Trust and Wills, Probate Estates, and Small Business Transactions.

ROSEMARIE HEIDENREICH PARKER, born Belleville, Illinois; admitted to bar, 1994, Nevada; 2000, Colorado; 2003, Illinois. *Education:* University of Missouri (B.A., 1972); St. Louis University (J.D., 1994). *Member:* Illinois State and Colorado Bar Associations. ***PRACTICE AREAS:*** Real Estate; Wills; Probate; Trusts and Estates; Business Law; Bankruptcy; General Practice; Water Law. ***Email:*** parkerrobtrosie@juno.com

LAW OFFICES OF RALPH E. ELLIOTT

A PROFESSIONAL CORPORATION

1005 WEST LORAS DRIVE
P.O. BOX 1149
FREEPORT, ILLINOIS 61032
Telephone: 815-233-1022
Telecopier: 815-233-1988
Email: ree.elliottlawfirm@insightbb.com
URL: http://www.lawyers.com/elliottlaw

General Civil and Criminal Trial and Appellate Practice in State and Federal Courts. Commercial, Business, Personal Injury, Wills, Trusts, Estate Planning, Estate Administration, Real Estate, Financial Institutions, Collections, Agriculture, Bankruptcy and Family Law.

RALPH E. ELLIOTT, born Siler City, North Carolina, August 12, 1956; admitted to bar, 1981, Illinois; 1982, U.S. District Court, Northern District of Illinois including Trial Bar; 1985, U.S. Court of Appeals, Seventh Circuit. *Education:* University of Illinois (B.S., magna cum laude, 1978; J.D., 1981). Phi Beta Kappa. Member, Freeport Chamber of Commerce Board, 1991-1992, 2000—. *Member:* Stephenson County (President, 1997-1998), Winnebago County (Member, Bankruptcy Section), Illinois State and American Bar Associations; Illinois Trial Lawyers Association; The Association of Trial Lawyers of America.

MARK R. CELICHOWSKI, born Fond du Lac, Wisconsin, September 27, 1975; admitted to bar, 2003, Illinois and Wisconsin; 2004, U.S. District Court, Northern District of Illinois and U.S. Court of Appeals, Seventh Circuit. *Education:* University of Wisconsin (B.B.A., 1998; J.D., 2003). Member, Freeport Area Chamber of Commerce Ambassadors, 2003—. *Member:* Stephenson County (Treasurer, 2004—), Winnebago County and Illinois State Bar Associations; State Bar of Wisconsin.

(This Listing Continued)

REPRESENTATIVE CLIENTS: Fifth Third Bank; FS Credit Corporation; Growmark, Inc.; Borell Farms, Ltd.; Quality Electric; Rite-Way Furniture & Appliance Mart, Inc.; Laufenberg Feed & Agri-Service, Inc.; Stephenson Service Company; Conserv FS, Inc.; Christopher Fye & Associates Architects; United Agri-Products, Inc.; Floor Covering Plus, Inc.; Jewel Digital Design, Inc.; Security First Title Co.; Elgin State Bank; J.H. Barkau & Sons, Inc.; Gastel & Associates, P.C.; F.I.R.S.T. NCB, Inc.; Goldridge Group; Landmark National Corporation; Sherwood Valley Foods, Inc.; Berner Foods, Inc.; Heller Farms, LLC; The Flash, Inc.; Roughing It In Style, Inc.; Willowglen Academy-Illinois, Inc.; CB Engineering Pacific, Inc.; Dar-She Farms, Inc.; Preferred Concrete & Excavating, Inc.; Daniel G. Kamin, Freeport, LLC-Freeport Lincoln Mall; Mary's Fast License Service; Covenant Insurance Group, Inc.; Rock River Lubrication, L.L.C.; SBT Services, Inc.

JOHN GILBERT

FREEPORT, ILLINOIS

(See Rockford)

Criminal Law, DUI/DWI, Drug Crimes, Parole and Probation, Juvenile Law, Traffic Violations, Bankruptcy, Real Estate, Criminal Leasing, Residential, Family Law, Child Custody, Child Support, Divorce, Visitation Rights, Domestic Violence, Adoption, Wills and Probate, Trusts and Estates, Estate Planning, Business Law, Business Planning, Contracts, Business Litigation, Business Enterprises.

MAHONEY & HAUSER, LTD.

204 WEST STEPHENSON STREET
P.O. BOX 158
FREEPORT, ILLINOIS 61032
Telephone: 815-235-1515
Fax: 815-235-9657
Email: t.s.mahoney@prodigy.com

Civil Litigation, Personal Injury, Workers Compensation, Probate, Wills, Automobile Accidents, Wrongful Death, DUI, Juvenile Crimes, Divorce, Child Custody, Family and Real Estate Law, Criminal, Corporate.

FIRM PROFILE: Mahoney & Hauser, Ltd. has been serving clients for over forty years throughout Stephenson, Jo Daviess, Winnebago, Carroll, Ogle and surrounding counties. The firm is a general practice with individual lawyers focusing on specific areas of law.

RICHARD J. HAUSER, JR., born Freeport, Illinois, March 9, 1959; admitted to bar, 1984, Iowa and Nebraska; 1986, Illinois; 1992, U.S. District Court, Northern District of Illinois including Trial Bar. *Education:* Highland Community College (A.A.S., 1979); Creighton University (B.A., cum laude, 1981; J.D., cum laude, 1984). Assistant County Attorney, Pottawattamie County Attorney's Office, Council Bluffs, Iowa, 1985-1986. *Member:* Stephenson County, Iowa State, Nebraska State, Illinois State and American Bar Associations; The Association of Trial Lawyers of America. ***PRACTICE AREAS:*** Personal Injury; Family Law; Workers Compensation; Real Estate. ***Email:*** hauser5@aeroinc.net

TIMOTHY S. MAHONEY, born Davenport, Iowa, March 9, 1967; admitted to bar, 1992, Illinois; 1995, U.S. District Court, Northern District of Illinois. *Education:* St. Ambrose College University (B.A., 1989); Northern Illinois University (J.D., 1992). Recipient, Freeport Journal Standard Best of the Region Reader's Choice Awards: voted one of top 3 attorneys in region, 1999, 2000, 2002. President, Student Bar Association. Member of NIU College of Law Moot Court Hall of Fame. *Member:* Stephenson County, Illinois State and American Bar Associations; The Association of Trial Lawyers of America. ***PRACTICE AREAS:*** Criminal Law; Family Law; Personal Injury; Real Estate. ***Email:*** tsmahoney@prodigy.net

JAMES M. HAUSER, born Freeport, Illinois, August 3, 1963; admitted to bar, 1988, Illinois, Wisconsin and U.S. District Court, District of Wisconsin; 1989, Colorado and U.S. District Court, District of Colorado; 1990, U.S. Court of Appeals, Seventh Circuit; 1997, U.S. District Court, Northern District of Illinois. *Education:* University of Iowa (B.A., 1985); Marquette University (J.D., 1988). Delta Theta Phi. Law Clerk, Hon. P. Michael Mahoney, Magistrate Judge, U.S. District Court, Northern District of Illinois, 1986-1988; Hon. Donald E. Abram, Magistrate, U.S. District Court, District of Colorado, 1988-1990. *Member:* Stephenson County, Illinois State and American Bar Associations; State Bar of Wisconsin; Civil Trial Counsel of Wisconsin; The Association of Trial Lawyers of America. ***PRACTICE AREAS:*** Personal Injury; Family Law; Criminal Law; Juvenile Law.

OF COUNSEL

FRANCIS X. MAHONEY, born Peabody, Massachusetts, March 21, 1922; admitted to bar, 1948, Wisconsin, Illinois and U.S. District Court, Northern District of Illinois, including Trial Bar. *Education:* St. John's Preparatory School (1939); Boston College (A.B., 1943); Northwestern University (J.D., 1948). Sanborn, Lamoreux & Pray, Ashland, Wisconsin, 1948-1951; DeBardeleben & Mahoney, Park Falls, Wisconsin, 1951-1954; General Casualty Company of Illinois, Freeport, Illinois, 1955-1960; Nettles & Mahoney, Freeport, Illinois, 1960-1971; Part-time Public Defender, 1964; Member, Illinois House of Representatives, 1965-1967; Nettles, Mahoney & Mahoney, Freeport, Illinois, 1971-1978; Circuit Judge of the 15th Judicial Circuit, Stephenson County, Freeport, Illinois, 1978-1991; Mahoney & Hauser, Ltd., 1991—. Member, Retired Judge's Committee of IGA. *Member:* Stephenson County, Illinois State and American Bar Associations; The Association of Trial Lawyers of America; Alternate Dispute Resolution Committee of Illinois Judge's Association (Mediator and Arbitrator). [U.S. Navy, 1943-1946]. ***PRACTICE AREAS:*** Alternative Dispute Resolution; Probate; Personal Injury; Trusts and Estates; Will.

REPRESENTATIVE CLIENTS: Economy Excavating, Freeport, Illinois; Bee-Line Service, Freeport, Illinois; Hasken Construction, Freeport, Illinois; Township of Freeport; Kneller Plumbing; Morse Electric; United Rubber Workers Union Local 745.

THE LAW OFFICES OF NACK, RICHARDSON & NACK, P.C.

Established in 1896

106 NORTH MAIN STREET
P.O. BOX 336
GALENA, ILLINOIS 61036
Telephone: 815-777-1218; 777-1219
Fax: 815-777-2609
Email: offices@nack.com
URL: http://www.nack.com

Elizabeth, Illinois Office: Elizabeth State Bank Building. Telephone: 815-858-3712. Fax: 815-858-2571.

General Civil and Criminal Trial and Appellate Practice, Personal Injury, Corporate, Banking, Real Estate, Estate Planning and Probate, Family, Municipal, Creditor's Rights, Insurance Defense, DUI and Commercial Collections, Divorce, Custody, Adoption.

JOS. M. NACK (1865-1939)

LOUIS A. NACK (1901-1981)

JAMES W. RICHARDSON (1925-1988)

LOUIS A. NACK, JR., born Dubuque, Iowa, February 27, 1935; admitted to bar, 1966, Illinois. *Education:* College of the Holy Cross (B.S., 1956); University of Illinois (J.D., 1966). Phi Delta Phi. *Member:* Jo Daviess County and Illinois State Bar Associations. ***Email:*** lanack@nack.com

JAMES J. NACK, born Dubuque, Iowa, August 2, 1940; admitted to bar, 1964, Illinois. *Education:* University of Notre Dame (B.A., 1961); University of Michigan (J.D., with distinction, 1964). Order of the Coif; Phi Delta Phi. Galena City Attorney, 1975-1989. *Member:* Jo Daviess County and Illinois State Bar Associations. ***Email:*** jimnack@nack.com

JOSEPH E. NACK, born Indianapolis, Indiana, May 14, 1963; admitted to bar, 1989, Illinois. *Education:* Spring Hill College (B.S., 1985); Creighton University (J.D., 1988). Member, Moot Court Board. Assistant State's Attorney, Peoria County State's Attorney's Office, 1989-1992. *Member:* Jo Daviess County and Illinois State Bar Associations. ***Email:*** joenack@nack.com

THOMAS J. NACK, born Urbana, Illinois, August 5, 1965; admitted to bar, 1996, Nebraska and U.S. District Court, District of Nebraska; 1997, Colorado; 2000, Illinois. *Education:* University of Illinois (B.A., 1987); Creighton University (J.D., cum laude, 1996). *Member:* Omaha, Nebraska State and Colorado Bar Associations. ***PRACTICE AREAS:*** General Litigation; Commercial Law; Commercial Litigation; Personal Injury Litigation.

REPRESENTATIVE CLIENTS: Elizabeth State Bank; Mercantile Bank Midwest; Union Bank Northwest; ; City of East Dubuque; Village of Scales Mound; Village of Elizabeth; Village of Hanover; CNA Insurance; Sears; Hanover Fire District.

BARASH & EVERETT, LLC

256 S. SOANGETAHA ROAD
SUITE 108
GALESBURG, ILLINOIS 61401
Telephone: 309-341-6010
Fax: 309-341-1945
URL: http://www.barashlaw.com

Galva, Illinois Office: Yocum Bank Building, 110 N. Exchange Street, P.O. Box 165, 61434. Telephone: 309-932-2001. Fax: 309-932-3151.

Kewanee, Illinois Office: 211 W. 2nd Street, 61443. Telephone: 309-852-5555. Fax: 309-853-8135.

Agricultural Law, Bankruptcy, Commercial Law, Probate, Real Estate, Workers Compensation, Computers and Internet, Corporate and Business, Estate Planning and Administration, Family Law and Child Custody, Personal Injury and Title Insurance Law.

MEMBERS OF FIRM

BARRY M. BARASH, born Galesburg, Illinois, May 6, 1938; admitted to bar, 1963, Illinois; 1970, U.S. Supreme Court; 1976, U.S. Court of Appeals, Seventh Circuit; 1996, U.S. Tax Court. *Education:* Cornell University (B.A., 1960); University of Chicago (J.D., 1962). Assistant Attorney General, State of Illinois, 1963-1964. *Member:* Knox County, Illinois State and American Bar Associations; American Bankruptcy Institute. Fellow: American College of Bankruptcy. ***PRACTICE AREAS:*** Agricultural Law; Bankruptcy; Commercial Law. ***Email:*** barashb@barashlaw.com

REYNOLDS M. EVERETT, born Davenport, Iowa, January 29, 1946; admitted to bar, 1973, Illinois. *Education:* University of Illinois (B.S., 1968); University of Tulsa; Loyola University (J.D., 1972). Phi Delta Phi. *Member:* Henry County, Illinois State (Member: Real Estate Law Section Council, 1976-1982; General Assembly, 1976-1982; Probate, Trust and Estate Planning Law Section Council) and American (Vice-Chairman, Probate and Estate Planning Law Committee, General Practice Section, 1986—) Bar Associations. Fellow: American College of Trust and Estate Counsel. ***PRACTICE AREAS:*** Agricultural Law; Probate; Real Estate; Business Law. ***Email:*** everettr@barashlaw.com

ASSOCIATES

KEITH A. LUYMES, born Ames, Iowa, March 25, 1949; admitted to bar, 1974, Illinois. *Education:* Iowa State University (B.S., 1971); University of Illinois (J.D., 1974). Assistant States Attorney, 1977-1980. *Member:* Henry County and Illinois State Bar Associations. ***PRACTICE AREAS:*** General Practice; Commercial Law; Collections; Family Law; Litigation. ***Email:*** luymesk@barashlaw.com

CLINTON A. BLOCK, born Kewanee, Illinois, March 29, 1959; admitted to bar, 2001, Illinois; 2002, U.S. District Court, Central and Northern Districts of Illinois. *Education:* University of Illinois, Urbana-Champaign (B.S., 1982); Northern Illinois University,

(This Listing Continued)

DeKalb (J.D., 2001). Delta Theta Phi. Member, Federalist Society, 2000-2001. *Member:* Henry County and Illinois State Bar Associations. ***PRACTICE AREAS:*** Probate; Bankruptcy; Real Estate; Family Law; Wills; Trusts and Estates. ***Email:*** blockc@barashlaw.com

GRANT R. GULOVSEN, born New York, N.Y., September 30, 1968; admitted to bar, 1998, Illinois; 2003, U.S. District Court, Central, Northern and Southern Districts of Illinois and U.S. Court of Appeals, Seventh Circuit. *Education:* Trinity University (B.A., 1991); University of Illinois, Urbana-Champaign (J.D., 1998). ***PRACTICE AREAS:*** Aviation Tax; Consumer Bankruptcy; Commercial Law; Information Technology; Contracts; Internet Law; Litigation; Personal Injury; Sales and Use Tax; Workers Compensation. ***Email:*** gulovseng@barashlaw.com

THOMAS A. HILL, born Davis, California, January 16, 1978; admitted to bar, 2003, Illinois. *Education:* St. Olaf College (B.A., 2000); University of Minnesota (J.D., 2003). *Member:* Illinois State and American Bar Associations; West Central Illinois Association of Realtors. ***PRACTICE AREAS:*** Bankruptcy; Bankruptcy Reorganization; Commercial Litigation; Real Estate; Title Insurance; Employment Defense; Bankruptcy Litigation; Fraudulent Conveyance. ***Email:*** hillt@barashlaw.com

MAYA P. PAREKH, born Montreal, Quebec, December 19, 1978; admitted to bar, 2004, Illinois. *Education:* Loyola University (B.A., 2001); University of Minnesota (J.D., 2004). *Member:* Illinois State and American Bar Associations. ***PRACTICE AREAS:*** Business Associations Law; Commercial Litigation; Civil Litigation; Family Law; Estate Litigation. ***Email:*** parekhm@barashlaw.com

MUSTAIN LINDSTROM & HENSON

1865 NORTH HENDERSON STREET, SUITE 11B
GALESBURG, ILLINOIS 61401
Telephone: 309-344-5252
Facsimile: 309-344-3939

General Civil Practice in State and Federal Courts, Trials and Appeals, Personal Injury, Workers Compensation, Real Estate, Insurance, Corporation, Commercial Law, Bankruptcy and Probate Law.

MEMBERS OF FIRM

DOUGLAS D. MUSTAIN, born Shreveport, Louisiana, November 2, 1945; admitted to bar, 1974, Iowa, Illinois and U.S. District Court, Central District of Illinois; 1980, U.S. Court of Appeals, 7th Circuit; 1986, U.S. Supreme Court. *Education:* Knox College, Murray State University and University of Illinois (B.S., 1971); University of Iowa (J.D., with distinction, 1974). Phi Alpha Delta; Phi Delta Phi. Recipient, Outstanding Senior Award, University of Illinois, College of Commerce, 1971. Trustee, Cottage Care Corporation, 1984-1991. President, Galesburg Public Schools Foundation, 1987-1995. *Member:* Knox County (President, 1980-1982), Illinois State and American Bar Associations. [With U.S. Army, 1966-1969]. ***PRACTICE AREAS:*** Personal Injury Law; Civil Litigation; Commercial Law; Probate; Workers' Compensation.

ROBERT LINDSTROM, born Galesburg, Illinois, February 15, 1948; admitted to bar, 1975, Illinois and Iowa; 1976, Florida; 1979, U.S. District Court, Central District of Illinois; 1986, U.S. Court of Appeals, 7th Circuit; 2000, U.S. District Court, Northern District of Illinois. *Education:* University of Iowa and Coe College (B.A., 1971); Drake University (J.D., 1975). Special Assistant Attorney General, 1981-1982. Member, Illinois Savings and Loan Board, 1984-1990. Trustee, Cottage Health Care Systems, 1988-1991. Trustee, Cottage Health Care Foundation, 1991-2004. Member, Galesburg Community Unit District 205 Board of Education, 1997— (President, 2003-2004). *Member:* Knox County, Illinois State and Iowa State Bar Associations; The Florida Bar. ***PRACTICE AREAS:*** Commercial Litigation; Bankruptcy; Banking Law; Real Estate Law; Corporation Law.

RONALD HENSON (1942-2004)

REPRESENTATIVE CLIENTS: AgriBank; FCB; Wells Fargo Bank, N.A.; First Bank; Community National Bank in Monmouth; Rabo AgServices, Inc.; Pottery Workers Credit Union; Altona, Henderson and Victoria-Copley Fire Protection Districts; Cameron Grain Corp.; G & M Distributors, Inc.; Kleine Equipment, Inc.; Miller-Dredge Insurance Agency; Louis Lakis Ford, Inc.; Steve Lakis Dodge, Inc.; People's Do-It Center; Alexis Fire Equipment Co.; RFMS, Inc.

REFERENCES: Wells Fargo Bank, N.A.; Farmers and Mechanics Bank; First Bank; McGladrey and Pullen, LLP.

PRUSAK, WINNE & GORMAN, LTD.

GALESBURG, ILLINOIS

(See Peoria)

General Practice. Trial, Insurance, Workers Compensation, Personal Injury, Probate, Corporate, Construction Litigation, Fire Loss, Professional Liability, Real Estate Law, Automobile Liability Defense, Insurance Coverage, Uninsured and Underinsured Motorists Arbitration, Products Liability Defense, Professional Liability Defense.

JOHN R. REHN

311 E. MAIN STREET, SUITE 412
GALESBURG, ILLINOIS 61401-4867
Telephone: 309-342-4200
Fax: 309-341-2462
URL: http://www.johnrehn.com

Criminal Law, Personal Injury and Insurance Litigation.

JOHN R. REHN, born Geneseo, Illinois, June 20, 1967; admitted to bar, 1995, Illinois, U.S. District Court, Central District of Illinois and U.S. Court of Appeals, Seventh Circuit. *Education:* University of Illinois (B.S., magna cum laude, 1989); University of Notre Dame (J.D., cum laude, 1995). *Member:* Knox County and Illinois State Bar Associations; Illinois

(This Listing Continued)

JOHN R. REHN, Galesburg—Continued

Association of Defense Trial Counsel. ***PRACTICE AREAS:*** Criminal Law; Personal Injury; Insurance Litigation.

STANSELL, WHITMAN & BABER

GALESBURG, ILLINOIS

(See Monmouth)

Personal Injury, Banking, Bankruptcy, Collections, Criminal, Divorce, Probate and Wills, Real Estate, Workers Compensation Law. Civil Litigation.

STOERZBACH MORRISON P.C.

Established in 1929

139 SOUTH CHERRY STREET

P.O. BOX 1328

GALESBURG, ILLINOIS 61402-1328

Telephone: 309-341-6000

Telecopier: 309-343-7500

URL: http://www.galesburglaw.com

General Trial and Appellate Practice in State and Federal Courts. Corporation, Estate Planning, Estate Administration, Real Estate, Bankruptcy, Family Law, Personal Injury, Workers Compensation, Insurance Law.

FIRM PROFILE: The firm was founded in 1929. Serving clients regionally inclusive of west central Illinois, eastern Iowa in federal courts and the Quad Cities, it is a full-service firm with individuals concentrating in different areas of law as well as all lawyers being litigators.

ROBERT C. STOERZBACH, born Galesburg, Illinois, December 21, 1923; admitted to bar, 1949, Illinois. *Education:* Knox College and University of Illinois (B.S., 1947); University of Illinois (J.D., 1949). Phi Delta Phi; Order of the Coif. *Member:* Knox County (President, 1958), Illinois State and American Bar Associations. ***PRACTICE AREAS:*** Wills; Trusts; Estate Planning; Estate Administration; Real Estate; Corporate Law. ***Email:*** stoerzr@galesburglaw.com

DWAYNE I. MORRISON, born Canton, Illinois, October 22, 1947; admitted to bar, 1973, Illinois and U.S. Court of Appeals, Seventh Circuit; 1980, U.S. Tax Court. *Education:* University of Illinois (B.S., 1970; J.D., 1973). Order of the Coif. Assistant Editor, University of Illinois Law, 1972-1973. *Member:* Knox County and Illinois State Bar Associations. ***PRACTICE AREAS:*** Domestic Relations; Probate; Estate Planning. ***Email:*** morrison@galesburglaw.com

DANIEL B. STOERZBACH, born Galesburg, Illinois, April 7, 1958; admitted to bar, 1983, Illinois. *Education:* Illinois Wesleyan University (B.S., 1980); University of Illinois (J.D., 1983). Certified Public Accountant, Illinois, 1980. Agent: Attorneys' Title Guaranty Fund, Inc.; Chicago Title; TICOR; ATG Trust Company. *Member:* Knox County and Illinois State Bar Associations; Community Association Institute. ***PRACTICE AREAS:*** Real Estate; Title Insurance; Estate Planning and Administration; Corporate Law; Adoption; Social Security Disability; Workers' Compensation; Personal Injury. ***Email:*** stoerzd@galesburglaw.com

JOHN W. ROBERTSON, born Moline, Illinois, August 30, 1946; admitted to bar, 1975, Illinois; 1982, U.S. Court of Appeals, Seventh Circuit. *Education:* Ripon College (A.B., 1968); University of Illinois (J.D., 1975). Phi Beta Kappa; Phi Alpha Theta. Member, Illinois Supreme Court Committee on Jury Instructions in Civil Cases, 1979-1996. Member, Advisory Committee on Local rules of Procedure, Central District of Illinois, 1994—. *Member:* Knox County, Illinois State (Member, Insurance Law Section Council, 1979-1983; Standing Committee on Public Relations, 1982-1983) and American Bar Associations; Illinois Association of Defense Trial Counsel; Appellate Lawyers Association of Illinois; Community Associations Institute; The Bar Association of the Central and Southern Districts of Illinois. [Capt., Armor, U.S. Army, 1968-1972]. ***PRACTICE AREAS:*** Civil Trial Practice; Appellate; Insurance Defense and Coverage; ERISA. ***Email:*** jwr@galesburglaw.com

PAMELA S. WILCOX, born Galesburg, Illinois, October 4, 1954; admitted to bar, 1989, Illinois, U.S. District Court, Central and Southern Districts of Illinois and U.S. Court of Appeals, Seventh Circuit. *Education:* Illinois State University (B.A., 1975); Southern Methodist University (J.D., 1989). *Member:* Knox County, Illinois State and American Bar Associations; American Bankruptcy Institute; The Bar Association of the Central and Southern Federal Districts of Illinois; National Association of Consumer Bankruptcy Attorneys. (Certified in Consumer Bankruptcy Law by the American Board of Certification). ***PRACTICE AREAS:*** Bankruptcy Chapter 7; Bankruptcy Chapter 13; Debtor and Creditor. ***Email:*** wilcoxp@galesburglaw.com

DANIEL S. ALCORN, born Oakland, California, April 2, 1966; admitted to bar, 1991, Iowa; 1992, Illinois; 1995, U.S. District Court, Central District of Illinois; 1998, U.S. Court of Appeals, Seventh Circuit; 2004, U.S. District Court, Northern District of Illinois including Trial Bar. *Education:* Knox College (B.A., 1988); Drake University (J.D., 1991). Member, Blackstone Inn of Court. Articles Editor, Drake Law Review, 1990-1991. Managing Editor, Drake Legal Research Service. Law Clerk to Honorable Allen L. Donielson, Iowa Court of Appeals, 1991-1992. Author: Casenote, 40 Drake Law Review, 415 (1991); "No-Fault Attendance Policies: How Employers Can Avoid FMLA Violations," 88 Illinois Bar Journal 597 (Oct. 2000). *Member:* Knox County and Illinois State (Section Council, Labor and Employment Section) Bar Associations; Illinois Association of Defense Trial Counsel; Community Association Institute; The Bar Association of the Central and Southern Federal Districts of Illinois. ***PRACTICE AREAS:*** Employment Law; ERISA; Commercial Litigation; Civil Trial Practice; Appellate Practice. ***Email:*** alcornd@galesburglaw.com

JEREMY S. KARLIN, born Stamford, Connecticut, October 12, 1969; admitted to bar, 1994, Wisconsin and U.S. District Court, Eastern and Western Districts of Wisconsin; 1995, Illinois; 1997, U.S. District Court, Central District of Illinois; 2000, U.S. Court of Appeals, Seventh Circuit. *Education:* Syracuse University (B.A., 1991); Loyola University of Chicago (J.D., 1994). Member, Moot Court Team, 1993. Recent Cases Editor, Consumer Law Reporter, 1992-1993. *Member:* Knox County and Illinois State Bar Associations; The Bar Association of the Central and Southern Federal Districts of Illinois; State Bar of Wisconsin; Illinois Association of Defense Trial Counsel; Illinois State Bar Association General Assembly; Criminal Justice Section Counsel; Trial Counsel; Illinois Capital Litigation Trial Bar. ***PRACTICE AREAS:*** Civil Litigation; Workers Compensation; Family Law; Criminal Defense. ***Email:*** karlinj@galesburglaw.com

H. WAYNE STATHAM, born Cincinnati, Ohio, January 15, 1960; admitted to bar, 1986, Illinois. *Education:* Illinois State University (B.S., summa cum laude, 1982); University of Illinois (J.D., 1986). Delta Theta Phi. Member, Mortar Board. Knox County Assistant State's Attorney, 1986-1988. *Member:* Knox County and Illinois State Bar Associations. ***PRACTICE AREAS:*** Domestic Relations; Civil Trial Practice; Criminal Trial Practice; Adoption Law; Real Estate; Collections. ***Email:*** stathamw@galesburglaw.com

REPRESENTATIVE CLIENTS: City of Knoxville, IL; City of Oneida, IL; Dexter Farm Equipment; Spoon River FS, Inc.; Farmers & Mechanics Bank; First Bank; Galesburg Clinic Association; General Casualty Ins. Co.; Grinnell Mutual Ins. Co.; Knox College; Knox County, IL; Knoxville Fire Protection Dist.; Medical & Surgical Specialists; Oak Run Property Owners Assn.; Rockford Mutual Ins. Co.; Sandburg Village Apartments; State Farm Insurance Cos.

BROWN AND RAY

Established in 1884

115 NORTH STATE STREET

P.O. BOX 238

GENESEO, ILLINOIS 61254-1345

Telephone: 309-944-5115

Fax: 309-944-5261

Email: bandr@netexpress.net

General Civil Practice. Real Estate, Estate Planning and Probate, Drainage and Levee, Family and Taxation Law, Domestic Relations, Divorce, Wills and Trusts.

FIRM PROFILE: Brown and Ray was founded by Harry E. Brown in 1884. Mabel W. Brown and Roger Ray have been the partners since 1980, serving clients in Henry, Rock Island, Whiteside, Bureau, Knox and Mercer Counties. Brown and Ray engages in a General Practice.

MEMBERS OF FIRM

HARRY E. BROWN (1872-1944)

MABEL W. BROWN, born Geneseo, Illinois, December 7, 1916; admitted to bar, 1941, Illinois. *Education:* Oberlin College (B.A., 1938); University of Chicago (J.D., 1941). Chairman, Geneseo Planning Commission, 1962-1968. *Member:* Henry County (President, 1973-1976), Illinois State and American Bar Associations; American Judicature Society. ***Email:*** mbrown@netexpress.net

ROGER RAY, born Elmhurst, Illinois, December 27, 1948; admitted to bar, 1974, Illinois. *Education:* Hamilton College (B.A., 1971); John Marshall Law School (J.D., with honors, 1974). *Member:* Henry County and Illinois State Bar Associations. ***PRACTICE AREAS:*** Estate Planning; Probate; Domestic Relations; Wills; Trusts; Family Law; Real Estate; Tax Law. ***Email:*** rray@netexpress.net

REFERENCES: Central Trust & Savings Bank, Geneseo, Illinois; Farmers National Bank of Prophetstown, Geneseo Banking Center.

ARIANO, HARDY, NYULI, JOHNSON, RICHMOND & GOETTEL, P.C.

Established in 1981

22 S. 4TH STREET, SUITE B,

GENEVA, ILLINOIS 60134

Telephone: 847-695-2400

Email: aah@attorneys-illinois.com

URL: http://www.attorneys-illinois.com

Huntley, Illinois Office: 13300 Route 47, P.O. Box 487, 60142. Telephone: 847-669-5020.
Elgin, Illinois: 474 Summit Street. Telephone: 847-695-2400. Telecopy: 847-695-8397.

General Civil and Criminal Practice in all Courts. Banking, Probate, Real Estate, Corporation, Federal Taxation, Transactional, Employment, Family, Personal Injury, Collections, Creditor Bankruptcy, Foreclosures, Landlord and Tenant Law, Workers Compensation Law and Mediation.

LISA M. NYULI, born 1964; admitted to bar, 1989, Illinois and U.S. District Court, Northern District of Illinois. *Education:* University of Illinois (B.S., 1986); Northern Illinois University (J.D., 1989). Family Law Mediator, Kane County. *Member:* Kane County and Illinois State Bar Associations. (Also at Elgin Office). ***REPORTED CASES:*** Hoffmann v. Lyon Metal Products, Inc., et al 217 Ill. App. 3d 490 (2d Dist. 1991); People v. Picou, 260 Ill. App. 3d 35, 692 (2d Dist, 1994); First National Bank of Geneva v. Lively, 211 Ill. App. 3d 1 (2d Dist, 1991). ***PRACTICE AREAS:*** Family Law and Mediation; Creditor Bankruptcy; Commercial Law (Collections); Landlord/Tenant Law; Foreclosures. ***Email:*** lmn@attorneys-illinois.com

KARRSTEN GOETTEL, born Libertyville, Illinois, April 25, 1971; admitted to bar, 1997, Illinois. *Education:* University of Wisconsin-Madison (B.S., 1993); Loyola University (J.D., 1997). *Member:* Chicago, Kane County and Illinois State Bar Associations. (Also at Elgin Office). ***PRACTICE AREAS:*** Real Estate; Commercial Real Estate; Business Law; Corporate Law; Wills; Trusts and Estates; Zoning, Planning and Land Use. ***Email:*** kg1@attorneys-illinois.com

GENERAL COUNSEL: Z Hardware Co.; Sybaquay Girl Scout Council, Inc.

(This Listing Continued)

REPRESENTATIVE CLIENTS: Bank One, Illinois, N.A.; Amcore Bank; Merchants Bank; Laboratory Corporation of America; Joseph Corporation.

(For Complete Biographical Data on all Personnel, see Professional Biographies at Elgin, Illinois)

BROOKS, ADAMS AND TARULIS

GENEVA, ILLINOIS

(See Naperville)

General Practice including Trial and Appellate Litigation. General Business, Business/Commercial Litigation, Employment, Corporation, Municipal, School, Park, Condemnation, Real Estate, Environmental, Land Developments, Zoning, Probate, Wills, Trusts, Special Needs Trusts, Adoptions, Estate Planning, Banking, Commercial, Personal Injury, Condominium Law and Civil Rights Law, Consumer Protection, Consumer Fraud, Consumer Litigation, Family Law, Divorce, Matrimonial Law, Criminal/Traffic Defense, Juvenile Representation and School Law Matters.

LAW OFFICE OF BRUCE A. BROWN

GENEVA, ILLINOIS

(See Aurora)

Corporate Law, Banks and Banking, Business Law, Construction Law, Commercial Real Estate, Real Estate, Mortgages, Contracts, Contested Estates, Litigation.

STEPHEN A. BRUNDAGE

GENEVA, ILLINOIS

(See Wheaton)

Criminal Law, Driving While Intoxicated, Drug Crimes, Felonies, Homicide, Juvenile Law, Misdemeanors, Parole and Probation, Sexual Assault, Traffic Violations, Assault and Battery, Burglary, Criminal Defense, Drivers License Suspension, Forgery, Manslaughter, Search and Seizure, Sex Crimes, Theft, Juvenile Law, Family Law, Divorce, Child Custody, Child Support, Domestic Violence, Premarital Agreements, Spousal Support, Martial Agreements, Marital Property Distribution, Martial Property Law, Marital Property Settlements, Matrimonial Law, Paternity, Post Divorce Modification, Real Estate, Real Estate Sales, Residential Real Estate, Residential Real Estate Sales, Personal Injury, Automobile Accidents and Injuries, Dog Bites, Sexual Abuse, Slip and Fall and Wrongful Death Law.

DONAHUE, SOWA AND BROWN

216 CAMPBELL STREET
GENEVA, ILLINOIS 60134
Telephone: 630-232-1780
Fax: 630-232-9671
Email: gsowa@dsbb-law.com
URL: http://www.lawyers.com/dsbblaw

Lisle Office: 3030 Warrenville Road, Suite 215, 60532. Telephone: 630-505-5200. Fax: 630-505-4250.

Criminal Defense, DUI, Traffic, Drivers License Reinstatement, Appellate Law, Juvenile Law.

(See Lisle)

DRENDEL & DRENDEL

A PROFESSIONAL CORPORATION

GENEVA, ILLINOIS

(See Batavia)

Family Law, Real Estate Development, Zoning, Sales and Acquisitions, Corporate, Business, Planning Sales and Acquisitions, Estate and Trust Planning and Administration, Commercial and other Civil Litigation, Banking and Collection Law, Trials and Appeals in all State Courts and Mediation Services, Municipal Law and Local Government Law.

MICHAEL W. FLEMING ATTORNEY AT LAW

GENEVA, ILLINOIS

(See Elmhurst)

Criminal Defense Litigation, Felonies, Misdemeanors, DUI and Juvenile Law.

JONES LEMON GRAHAM & CLANCY LLP

Established in 1995

223 EAST STATE STREET
GENEVA, ILLINOIS 60134
Telephone: 630-208-0805
Fax: 630-208-4651
URL: http://www.joneslemon.com

Corporate Law, Litigation, Trusts and Estates, Environmental Law, Probate, Employment Law, Professional Liability, Insurance, Excess and Reinsurance, HealthCare, Medical Malpractice, Nursing Home Liability, Products Liability.

W. CLYDE JONES, III, born Evanston, Illinois, October 14, 1937; admitted to bar, 1967, Illinois; 1970, U.S. Court of Appeals, Seventh Circuit. *Education:* Yale University (B.A., 1959); Northwestern University (J.D., 1967). *Member:* Kane County, Illinois State and American Bar Associations; Fox Valley Estate Planning Council. ***PRACTICE AREAS:*** Estate Planning; Trust Administration; Corporate; Probate; Real Estate. ***Email:*** ClydeJ@joneslemon.com

(This Listing Continued)

STEVEN J. LEMON, born Elgin, Illinois, May 12, 1961; admitted to bar, 1990, Illinois and U.S. District Court, Northern District of Illinois. *Education:* Bethel College (B.A., in Chemistry, 1983); Harvard University (M.P.P., 1990); University of Illinois (J.D., 1990). Author: "The Risk Advisors Survival Guide to Mold Exclusions," 15 Environmental Claims Journal 1, 2003; "The First Applications of the Nollan Nexus Test: Observations and Comments," 13 Harvard Environmental Law Review 585, 1989. *Member:* Kane County (Member: Sections on: Environmental Law, Committee Chair, 1993-1998; Business Law), Illinois State and American (Member, Sections on: Natural Resources; Environmental; Energy Law; Probate and Property) Bar Associations; Environmental Risk Resources Association. ***PRACTICE AREAS:*** Environmental Compliance; Superfund; Property Remediation; Trusts and Estates; Closely Held Corporations. ***Email:*** StevenL@joneslemon.com

CHRISTOPHER J. GRAHAM, born Chicago, Illinois, September 14, 1958; admitted to bar, 1983, Illinois and U.S. District Court, Northern District of Illinois including Trial Bar; 1990, U.S. Court of Appeals, Ninth Circuit; 1991, U. S. District Court, Central District of Illinois and U.S. District Court, Eastern District of Wisconsin; 1992, U.S. Court of Appeals, Seventh Circuit. *Education:* Loyola University (B.B.A., magna cum laude, 1980); University of Michigan (J.D., 1983). Beta Alpha Psi; Alpha Sigma Nu; Beta Gamma Sigma. Associate Editor, University of Michigan Journal of Law Reform. Certified Public Accountant, Illinois, 1980. *Member:* Kane County, Illinois State and American Bar Associations; Illinois CPA Society; Professional Liability Underwriting Society. ***REPORTED CASES:*** Anglo-American Ins. Co. and Underwriters at Lloyd's v. Molin, 670 A.2d 194 (1995); Anglo-American Ins. Co. and Underwriters at Lloyd's v. Molin, 673 A.2d 986 (1996); Anglo-American Ins. Co., Zurich Re (UK) Ltd., and Underwriters at Lloyd's v. Molin, 691 A.2d 929 (1997); In re Carnation Co. Securities Litigation, 904 F.2d 40 (9th Cir. 1990); V. Chatman v. Skadden, Arps, Slate, Meagher & Flom, 1994 WL 478591 (N.D.Ill., Sept. 1, 1994); FDIC v. Greenwood, 701 F.Supp. 691 (C.D.Ill. 1988); FDIC v. Greenwood, 719 F.Supp. 749 (C.D.Ill. 1989); FDIC v. Greenwood, 739 F.Supp. 450 (C.D.Ill. 1989); Underwriters at Lloyd's v. Neumann and Arnstein and Lehr, 225 Ill.Dec. 168, 682 N.E.2d 1245 (2nd Dist. 1997); Basic v. Fitzroy Eng., 949 F.Supp. 1333 (N.D.Ill. 1996), aff'd, 132 F.3d 36 (7th Cir. (Ill.). In re: Arbitration between Fitzroy Eng. v. Flame Eng., Inc., No. 94 C. 2029, 1994 WL 700173 (N.D.Ill.,); Technic Eng. v. Basic Envirotech, 1998 WL 173240 (N.D.Ill., 1998); Technic Eng. v. Basic Envirotech, 53 F. Supp. 2d 1007 (N.D.Ill. 1999); Walsh v. Employers Ins. of Wausau (1985 U.S. Dist. LEXIS (Nov. 7, 1985); Thompson v. Allied Bank of Texas, (U.S.D.C. M.D.La.), 1991 U.S. Dist. LEXIS 20247 (Oct. 21, 1991). ***PRACTICE AREAS:*** Civil Litigation; Professional Liability; Employment Law; Corporate Law; Insurance Coverage. ***Email:*** ChrisG@joneslemon.com

PETER F. CLANCY, born Newburyport, Massachusetts, March 19, 1958; admitted to bar, 1984, Illinois. *Education:* Harvard University (A.B., 1980); Loyola University (J.D., 1984). *Member:* Kane County and Illinois State Bar Associations; Defense Research Institute; Professional Liability Underwriting Society; American Society for Healthcare Risk Management; Illinois Association of Healthcare Attorneys. ***PRACTICE AREAS:*** Captive Insurance; Excess and Reinsurance; Insurance Coverage; Health Care; Medical Malpractice; Professional Liability; Products Liability; Nursing Home Liability; Managed Care Liability. ***Email:*** PeteC@joneslemon.com

ROBERT PAUL NORMAN, born Morrison, Illinois, January 24, 1953; admitted to bar, 1989, Illinois and U.S. District Court, Northern District of Illinois and District of Oklahoma; U.S. District Court, Eastern District of Michigan. *Education:* Western Illinois University (B.A., 1975); John Marshall Law School (J.D., cum laude, 1989). Seminars, Speaking and Articles: Speaks and writes extensively on the California Statute, SB 1386, and other state statutes that require notification to persons whose personal information or identity is compromised through the hacking of a database; "Virtual Insurance: Is Your Old Policy from invisibleINC.com" PLI Seminar (Paper and Presentation), April 2002, New York, NY - ABC's of Insurance; "Virtual Insurance: Is Your Old Policy from INVISIBLEinc.com," ABA Annual Meeting, August 2002; Washington, D.C. (Paper and Presentation for E-Commerce Insurance Committee of the ABA); "E-Commerce Insurance and Coverage for Identity Theft," October 2005, Boston, Massachusetts (Paper and Presentation for Center for International Legal Studies). Author: "Using E-Commerce Insurance to Minimize Liability," Internet Law & Practice, by West. *Member:* Kane County, Illinois State and American Bar Associations. ***PRACTICE AREAS:*** Insurance Coverage Defense; E-Commerce; Insurance and Transactions; Computer Software; Technology Law; Professional Liability; Sports Law; Entertainment Law. ***Email:*** bobn@joneslemon.com

SPECIAL COUNSEL

MATTHEW J. NIELSEN, born Chicago, Illinois, August 12, 1967; admitted to bar, 1994, Illinois; 1995, Missouri, U.S. District Court, Southern District of Illinois and Eastern District of Missouri; 2001, U.S. District Court, Northern District of Illinois; 2002, U.S. Court of Appeals, Seventh Circuit. *Education:* Northern Illinois University (B.S., 1989); Southern Illinois University (J.D., magna cum laude, 1994). Phi Kappa Phi. Business Editor, Southern Illinois University Law Journal, 1993-1994. Recipient, Moot Court Best Advocate Award, 1993. Co-Author: W. Eugene Basanta, "The Latest Developments in Health Care Law," 9-12 Health Care Lawyer/ISBA (1992, 1993, 1994). *Member:* Kane County, Illinois State and Federal Bar Associations; Defense Research Institute (Insurance Law Section); Illinois Association of Healthcare Attorneys; Professional Liability Underwriting Society. ***PRACTICE AREAS:*** Medical Malpractice; Commercial Litigation; Insurance. ***Email:*** mattn@joneslemon.com

ASSOCIATE

JOSEPH P. KELLY, born Geneva, Illinois, February 3, 1979; admitted to bar, 2004, Illinois; 2005, U.S. District Court, Northern District of Illinois. *Education:* University of Illinois (B.S., Political Science, History, 2001); Chicago-Kent College of Law (J.D., 2004). *Member:* Kane County, Illinois State and American Bar Associations. ***PRACTICE AREAS:*** Insurance Coverage; Litigation; Professional Liability; Employment Law; Corporate Law. ***Email:*** jkelly@joneslemon.com

MULHERIN, REHFELDT & VARCHETTO, P.C.

GENEVA, ILLINOIS

(See Wheaton)

Commercial and Business Transactions, Health Care, Estate Planning, Litigation, Business, Tax, Employment, Insurance Defense, Medical Malpractice Defense and Employment Litigation.

O'HAGAN, SMITH & AMUNDSEN

GENEVA, ILLINOIS

(See St. Charles)

Commercial; Commercial Transportation; Appellate; Complex Litigation; Construction; Corporate Transactions; Employment; Extra-Contractual/Insurance Litigation; Healthcare; Insurance Coverage; Personal Lines; Product Liability; Professional Liability; Property Litigation.

LAW OFFICE OF BRENT E. OHLMANN, P.C.

GENEVA, ILLINOIS

(See Naperville)

Trademarks, Copyrights, Business Transactions, S-Corporation and LLC Issues, Entertainment Contracts, Software Licensing, Confidentiality Agreements, Strategic Alliances, Business Succession Planning, Internet Law.

RINELLA AND RINELLA, LTD.

GENEVA, ILLINOIS

(See Chicago)

Practice Limited to Family Law and Divorce including the areas of Legal Separation, Negotiating and Drafting Premarital and Postnuptial Agreements, Judgment Enforcement, Child Custody and Child Support Actions, Domestic Violence, Spousal Support, Appeals, Adoption, Parentage Actions and Interstate Support Enforcement.

SWANSON, MARTIN & BELL

GENEVA, ILLINOIS

(See Chicago)

Asbestos Litigation, Class Action Lawsuits, Commercial Litigation, Construction Litigation/ Disputes, Consumer and Warranty Law, Creditor's Rights, Drugs & Medical Devices, Employment Litigation, Environmental Law, Equipment Leasing, General Tort Liability, Healthcare, Insurance Coverage, Intellectual Property, Medical Negligence, Municipal Law, Product Liability, Professional Negligence, Real Estate Development/Zoning, Real Estate Litigation, Toxic and Mass Tort Litigation and White Collar Criminal Defense.

VAN DER SNICK LAW FIRM, LTD.

1795 WEST STATE STREET, SUITE B
GENEVA, ILLINOIS 60134
Telephone: 630-845-8200
Fax: 630-845-1060
URL: http://www.vandersnicklaw.com
Email: bvandersnick@vandersnicklaw.com
URL: http://www.lawyers.com/vandersnicklaw

Family Law, DUI and Traffic Law. Trials and Appeals. Criminal and Civil Trials. Divorce, Child Custody, Child Support.

FIRM PROFILE: J. Brick Van Der Snick concentrates his practice in the defense of DUI, Traffic and Family Law. He is a former prosecutor for the Kane County State's Attorneys Office and is recognized statewide as an expert in DUI/Traffic Defense. He has represented numerous clients in trials and appeals in Kane, Kendall, and DeKalb County.

J. BRICK VAN DER SNICK, admitted to bar, 1980, Illinois; 1981, U.S. District Court, Northern District of Illinois and U.S. Court of Appeals, Seventh Circuit. *Education:* Carthage College (A.B., 1976); John Marshall Law School, Chicago (J.D., 1980). Adjunct Instructor: "Paralegal Studies" and "Legal Environment of Business," Elgin Community College, 1983-1998; Instructor, Illinois State's Attorneys' Appellate Prosecutor's Trial School, 1983—. Guest Lecturer, Illinois State Bar Association Continuing Legal Education. Guest Speaker and Panel Participant, Chicago Cable Network on DUI, 1996. Lecturer, "D.U.I. and Criminal Law," Kane County Bar Association, 1992. Assistant State's Attorney, Kane County, 1980-1984. Certified in Standard Field Testing, National Highway Traffic Safety Administration. *Member:* Kane County (Member, Committees on: Family Law, 1995—; Criminal Law, 1991-1999; Co-Chair, Criminal Law Committee, 1998-1999), DuPage County, DeKalb County, Illinois State (Member, 1992-2000, Chair, 1998-1999, Vice Chair, 1997-1998 and Secretary, 1996-1997, Traffic and Court Section); National College of DUI Defense. ***REPORTED CASES:*** People v. O'Brien, 227 Ill. App. 3d 302, (2nd Dist. 1992); People v. Askland, 166 Ill. App. 3d 78 (2d Dist., 1988); People v. Lisa Fortney, 297 Ill. App. 3d 79, 697 N.E. 2d 1, 231 Ill. Dec. 720 (2nd Dist., 1998). ***PRACTICE AREAS:*** DUI; Traffic; Criminal Defense; Family Law; Real Estate. ***Email:*** bvandersnick@vandersnicklaw.com

POLLOCK, MEYERS, EICKSTEADT & PULAK, LTD.

GENOA, ILLINOIS

(See Marengo)

General Trial Practice, Appellate Practice, Estate Planning, Probate Law, Trust Law, Real Estate, Banking Law, Bankruptcy Law, Personal Injury, Workers Compensation, Administrative Law, Corporate Law, Contracts, Civil Litigation, Trusts and Estates, Real Estate Law.

LAW OFFICE OF GREGORY J. MARTUCCI, P.C.

GLENDALE HEIGHTS, ILLINOIS

(See Roselle)

Bankruptcy, Criminal Law, Driving While Intoxicated, Juvenile Criminal Law, Traffic Violations, Domestic Violence, Personal Injury, Automobile Accidents and Injuries, Slip and Fall, Workers Compensation.

TERRENCE J. BENSHOOF

Established in 1971
170 SPRING AVENUE
GLEN ELLYN, ILLINOIS 60137
Telephone: 630-605-6684
Fax: 630-469-1835
Email: tbenshoof@earthlink.net
URL: http://www.terrencebenshoof.com

Taxation, Federal Taxation, State Taxation, Tax Audits, Property Tax Appeals, Tax Planning, Tax Litigation, Estate Planning.

FIRM PROFILE: Over 20 years of practice in all areas of state, local and federal taxation. Representation of clients in audit, appeals, and courts at all levels. Strategic tax planning for small businesses and their owners.

TERRENCE J. BENSHOOF, born Chicago, Illinois, April 6, 1946; admitted to bar, 1971, Illinois and U.S. District Court, Northern District of Illinois including Trial Bar; 1972, U.S. Court of Appeals for the Armed Forces; 1976, U.S. Supreme Court; 1983, U.S. Court of Appeals, 8th and 9th Circuits; 1991, U.S. Tax Court; 1992, U.S. District Court, Western District of Michigan and U.S. Court of Appeals, 7th Circuit; 1994, U.S. District Court, Northern District of California and U.S. Court of Appeals, 6th Circuit; 1995, U.S. Court of Federal Claims; 2001, U.S. Court of Appeals for the Federal Circuit. *Education:* University of Illinois (B.A., with honors, 1968); DePaul University (J.D., 1971; LL.M., Tax, 1980). *Member:* DuPage County Bar Association. [LTC, USAR, retired]. ***PRACTICE AREAS:*** Taxation; Ad Valorem Tax; Property Tax Appeals; Sales and Use Tax.

BRUCAR & YETTER, P.C.

Established in 1999
500 ROOSEVELT ROAD, SUITE 330
GLEN ELLYN, ILLINOIS 60137
Telephone: 630-858-8840
Fax: 630-858-5299
Email: brucaryetter@hotmail.com
URL: http://www.brucarandyetter.com

Rolling Meadows, Illinois Office: 1600 Golf Road, Corporate Center, Suite 1200, 60008. Telephone: 847-490-9140.

Criminal Law, Federal Criminal Law, State Criminal Law, Appellate Practice, Drug Crimes, Drunk Driving, Extradition, Felonies, Homicide, Juvenile Criminal Law, Misdemeanors, Parole and Probation, Post Conviction Remedies, Search and Seizure, Traffic Violations.

FIRM PROFILE: Full service criminal defense practice featuring concentrations in federal, state, juvenile, traffic and appellate practice. Also working in the area of driver's license reinstatement practice. Individuals or corporations charged with criminal or traffic offenses in trial or appellate court.

WAYNE ELI BRUCAR, born 1953; admitted to bar, 1983, Illinois. *Education:* Loyola University; Chicago-Kent College of Law. (Also at Rolling Meadows). ***PRACTICE AREAS:*** Criminal Law; Federal Criminal Law; Appellate Practice; Drug Crimes; Driving While Intoxicated; Felonies; Homicide; Juvenile Criminal Law; Misdemeanors; Parole and Probation; Traffic Violations; State Government Law. ***Email:*** brucarandyetter@hotmail.com

JOHN P. YETTER, born 1971; admitted to bar, 1996, Illinois. *Education:* Northern Illinois University (B.S., 1993); University of Dayton (J.D., 1996). (Also at Rolling Meadows). ***PRACTICE AREAS:*** Criminal Law; Federal Criminal Law; Appellate Practice; Drug Crimes; Driving While Intoxicated; Felonies; Homicide; Juvenile Criminal Law; Misdemeanors; Parole and Probation; Traffic Violations; State Government Law. ***Email:*** brucarandyetter@hotmail.com

Language: Spanish.

THE COFFEY LAW OFFICE, P.C.

577 PENNSYLVANIA AVENUE, SUITE 204
GLEN ELLYN, ILLINOIS 60137
Telephone: 630-534-6300
Fax: 630-534-6400
Email: tcofflaw@sbcglobal.net
URL: http://www.lawyers.com/timcoffeylaw

Employment Law, Real Estate Law, Contract Litigation.

TIMOTHY J. COFFEY, born Chicago, Illinois, July 26, 1968; admitted to bar, 1994, Illinois. *Education:* Northern Illinois University (B.S., 1987); John Marshall Law School (J.D., 1994). ***PRACTICE AREAS:*** Employment Law; Contract Litigation; Real Estate Law.

MICHAEL P. MAZZA, LLC

686 CRESCENT BOULEVARD
GLEN ELLYN, ILLINOIS 60137
Telephone: 630-858-5071
Fax: 630-282-7123
URL: http://www.mazzalawfirm.com

FIRM PROFILE: The firm concentrates its practice in intellectual property law, and has significant experience in the litigation and trial of such matters, as well as the procurement of patents, trademarks and copyrights.

MICHAEL P. MAZZA, born Chicago, Illinois, May 19, 1964; admitted to bar, 1989, Illinois, U.S. District Court, Northern District of Illinois including Trial Bar and Supreme Court; 1990, U.S. Court of Appeals, Federal Circuit; registered to practice before U.S. Patent and Trademark Office. *Education:* University of Notre Dame (B.S., Civil Eng., 1986); University of Illinois; Loyola University (J.D., 1989); John Marshall Law School (Master of Laws, in I.P., 1995). Chi Epsilon. *Member:* Chicago and Illinois State Bar Associations; American Society of Civil Engineers; Trial Bar Association. ***PRACTICE AREAS:*** Intellectual Property Law. ***Email:*** mazza@mazzallc.com

---

JOHN M. MICHALIK, born Chicago, Illinois; admitted to bar, 2003, Illinois. *Education:* Georgetown University (B.S., Chem., cum laude, 2000); University of Notre Dame (J.D., 2003). *Member:* Illinois State Bar Association. ***PRACTICE AREAS:*** Intellectual Property Law. ***Email:*** john@mazzallc.com

OF COUNSEL

LAWRENCE E. THOMPSON, born Evergreen Park, Illinois; admitted to bar, 1997, Arizona; registered to practice before U.S. Patent and Trademark Office (Not admitted in Illinois). *Education:* University of Illinois (B.S.E.E., 1986); Arizona State University (J.D., 1996). *Member:* Chicago and Illinois State Bar Associations. ***PRACTICE AREAS:*** Intellectual Property Law. ***Email:*** ILIPCounselor@comcast.net

JOHN F. MORREALE & ASSOCIATES, P.C.

GOLF PLACE
449 TAFT AVENUE
GLEN ELLYN, ILLINOIS 60137-6209
Telephone: 630-790-6300
Fax: 630-790-1081
Email: Law@mmtpc.com
URL: http://www.morrealelaw.com

National and International Relocation Real Estate, Estate Planning, Trusts and Estates, Wills and Probate, Estate Planning, Financial Planning, Family, Divorce and Small Business, Bankruptcy, Civil and Criminal Law.

FIRM PROFILE: While the State of Illinois Supreme Court does not allow for specialization, this law firm has an extraordinary concentration of its practice in relocation real estate including document preparation and title placement on a national and international basis. The firm represents several relocation companies on a permanent basis and does ad hoc relocation work for many others.

In addition, several members of the firm conduct a general practice involving family law, wills and probate, civil practice, trusts and estates, relocation, real estate, financial planning, corporation, small business, civil and criminal law, title insurance defense.

Several members of the firm have taught at local colleges and conducted seminars for clients and other interested parties.

JOHN F. MORREALE, born Chicago, Illinois, January 3, 1939; admitted to bar, 1966, Illinois and U.S. District Court, Southern and Northern District of Illinois; 1990, Texas. *Education:* Loyola University (B.S., 1961); Northwestern University (J.D., 1965). Charter Member, Justinian Society, 1982. Attorney, Lazzara & Narusis, 1965-1967; Fred B. Hanson Associated, 1967-1971. Instructor, Contracts & Conveyancing and Real Estate Licensing, College of DuPage, 1980-1989. *Member:* DuPage County, Illinois State and American Bar Associations. ***PRACTICE AREAS:*** Real Estate; Wills; Probate; Corporate Law. ***Email:*** johnf@morrealelaw.com

STEVEN M. MACK, born Palo Alto, California, December 31, 1947; admitted to bar, 1978, Illinois and U.S. District Court, Northern District of Illinois; 1992, Wisconsin. *Education:* University of Illinois (B.A., 1970); Northern Illinois University College of Law

(This Listing Continued)

(J.D., 1978). *Member:* DuPage County, Illinois State and American Bar Associations. ***PRACTICE AREAS:*** Probate; Corporate Law; Trusts and Estates; Wills; Lifetime Planning; Estate Planning. ***Email:*** stevem@morrealelaw.com

JOAN M. BRADY, born Chicago, Illinois, December 27, 1958; admitted to bar, 1983, Illinois. *Education:* Illinois Benedictine College (B.A., 1980); The John Marshall Law School (J.D., 1983). ***PRACTICE AREAS:*** Real Estate; Wills; Trusts and Estates. ***Email:*** joanb@morrealelaw.com

KARI A. MALONE, born DeKalb, Illinois, September 9, 1977; admitted to bar, 2002, Illinois. *Education:* Northern Illinois University (B.S., 1999; J.D., 2002). *Member:* DuPage County and Illinois State Bar Associations. ***PRACTICE AREAS:*** Real Estate. ***Email:*** karim@morrealelaw.com

PATRICK F. CLEARY, born Chicago, Illinois, 1950; admitted to bar, 1976, Illinois and U.S. District Court, Northern District of Illinois. *Education:* Western Illinois University (B.A., with honors, 1973); Chicago-Kent College of Law (J.D., with honors, 1976). Licensed Illinois Insurance Producer. *Member:* DuPage County and Illinois State (Member, General Practice Solo and Small Firm Section) Bar Associations. ***PRACTICE AREAS:*** Real Estate; Professional Liability; Professional Liability Insurance Coverage; Employment. ***Email:*** patc@morrealelaw.com

JULIE E. CWIK, born Westchester, Illinois, September 30, 1972; admitted to bar, 2004, Illinois. *Education:* Indiana University (B.A., 1999); John Marshall Law School (J.D., 2004). *Member:* DuPage County, Illinois State and American Bar Associations. ***PRACTICE AREAS:*** Real Estate. ***Email:*** juliec@morrealelaw.com

KATHLEEN J. KWAK, born Chicago, Illinois, June 5, 1977; admitted to bar, 2005, Illinois. *Education:* Indiana University-Bloomington (B.A., 1999); Valparaiso University School of Law (J.D., 2004). *Member:* Chicago, DuPage County, Illinois State and American Bar Associations; Illinois Real Estate Lawyers Association. ***PRACTICE AREAS:*** Real Estate. ***Email:*** kathyk@morrealelaw.com

REPRESENTATIVE CLIENTS: A list of representative clients is available upon request.

STEVEN K. NORGAARD, P.C.

493 DUANE STREET, SUITE 400
GLEN ELLYN, ILLINOIS 60137
Telephone: 630-545-1005
Fax: 630-545-1051
Email: sn@norgaardlaw.com
URL: http://www.norgaardlaw.com

Real Estate, Estate Planning, Probate, Buying and Selling a Home, Commercial Real Estate, Trusts and Estates, Small Business Law, Wills, Probate.

STEVEN K. NORGAARD, born Chicago, Illinois, December 10, 1964; admitted to bar, 1990, Illinois. *Education:* University of Illinois (B.S., with highest honors, 1987); University of Chicago (J.D., 1990). Certified Public Accountant, Illinois, 1990. *Member:* Chicago and American Bar Associations. ***PRACTICE AREAS:*** Real Estate; Estate Planning; Probate; Buy-Sell Agreements; Commercial Real Estate; Trusts and Estates; Small Business Law; Wills.

DEBRA A. THOMAS, P.C.

800 ROOSEVELT ROAD, BUILDING B
SUITE 110
GLEN ELLYN, ILLINOIS 60137
Telephone: 630-790-0800
Fax: 630-790-3480
Email: debra@thomaslaws.com
URL: http://www.debrathomaslaws.com

Medical Malpractice, Products Liability, Personal Injury and Commercial Litigation.

DEBRA A. THOMAS, born Chicago, Illinois, February 1, 1950; admitted to bar, 1984, Illinois and U.S. District Court, Northern District of Illinois. *Education:* University of Illinois (B.A., 1981; J.D., 1984). Member, Board of Editors, National Moot Court Competition, 1984. Co-Author: "Representing the Hemophiliac with AIDS: An Overview," Courts, Health, Science & the Law: Vol. II, No. 1, Summer 1991; "Groundwater Pollution Cases With Many Victims," TRIAL, Vol. 27, No. 9, September 1991. Previous professional experience, Leonard M. Ring & Associates, P.C., 1984-1994. *Member:* Illinois State and American (Vice-Chair, Committee on Toxic and Hazardous Substances, Section of Tort and Insurance Practice, 1990-1993) Bar Associations; The Association of Trial Lawyers of America; Sustaining Member, Illinois Trial Lawyers Association. ***REPORTED CASES:*** Savage v. Martin, 628 N.E.2d 606 (1st Dist. 1993); Atwood v. Warner Elec. Brake & Clutch Co., 605 N.E.2d 1032 (2nd Dist. 1992); Hugley v. Alcarez, 494 N.E.2d 706 (1st Dist. 1986); Wadleigh v. Rhone-Poulene Rorer, Inc., 157 F.R.D. 410 (N.D. Ill. 1994); Poole v. Alpha Therapeutic Corp., 696 F.Supp. 351 (N.D. Ill. 1988); Ransom v. A.B. Dick Co., 682 NE2d 314 (1st Dist. 1997); Matter of Rhone-Poulenc Rorer, Inc., 51 F.3d 1293 (7th Cir. 1995); Harbor Ins. Co. v. Continental Bank Corp., 922 F.2d 357 (7th Cir. 1990); Erickson v. Baxter Healthcare, Inc. 151 F.Supp. 2d 952 (N.D.Ill. 2001); 131 F.Supp. 2d 995 (N.D. Ill. 2001); 94 F.Supp. 2d 904 (N.D.Ill. 2000); poole v. Alpha Therapeutic Corp., 698 F.Supp. 1387 (N.D. Ill. 1988). ***PRACTICE AREAS:*** Medical Malpractice; Products Liability; Personal Injury; Commercial Litigation.

THE LAW OFFICES OF MARC L. BROWN

GLENVIEW, ILLINOIS

(See Park Ridge)

Elder Law, Real Estate, Trusts and Estates, Wills, Probate, Living Trusts, Guardianship, Nursing Home Abuse and Neglect, Health Care.

THOMAS P. CERNEK, & ASSOCIATES

1701 EAST LAKE AVENUE, SUITE 460
GLENVIEW, ILLINOIS 60025
Telephone: 847-998-1400
Facsimile: 847-998-8690
Email: tpcernek@quixnet.net

Trial and Appellate Practice in State and Federal Courts, Personal Injury, Negligence, Medical Malpractice, Criminal, Real Estate, Corporation and Probate Law.

THOMAS P. CERNEK, born Mohawk, Michigan, April 13, 1927; admitted to bar, 1953, Illinois and Illinois Supreme Court; 1954, U.S. District Court, Northern District of Illinois; 1961, U.S. Supreme Court and U.S. Court of Appeals, Seventh Circuit. *Education:* University of Illinois; John Marshall Law School (J.D., 1952). Author: "Freedom of the Press" and "Speedy and Public Trial," published in Your Bill of Rights, Illinois State Bar Association, 1967. Member, John Howard Association (Prison Reform), Board of Directors, 1977-1982; Executive Committee, 1978-1982; Vice President, 1979-1982. Arbitrator, Commercial Panel, American Arbitration Association. *Member:* Chicago (Member, 1956-1965; Chairman, 1960, Defense of Prisoners Committee and Member, 1957-1961; Division Chairman, 1958-1961 Member, Unauthorized Practice of Law Committee; Committee on Inquiry, 1960-1964; Insurance Law Committee, 1971-1974; Committee on Narcotics and Drug Abuse, 1972; Evaluation of the Candidates Committee, Judiciary 1976-1980, 1990—, Executive Committee 1990—. Member, Real Property Law Section; Vice Chair, Investigation Committee, 1991—; Appellate Review Committee, 1995—; Judicial Evaluation Committee, 1995—), Illinois State (Member, Junior Bar Section, 1956-1958; Member, 1960-1970 and Chairman, 1967-1968-1969, American Citizenship Committee; Member, Criminal Law Committee, 1960) and American (Member, Section on Individual Rights and Responsibilities) Bar Associations; American Judicature Society; Illinois Trial Lawyers Association. **REPORTED CASES:** Whiterspoon v. Illinois, 391 U.S. 510, 88 U.S. 1770.

JEFFREY T. CERNEK, born Chicago, Illinois, June 25, 1958; admitted to bar, 1984, Illinois; 1985, U.S. District Court, Northern District of Illinois. *Education:* Knox College (B.A., 1980); Chicago-Kent College of Law (J.D., 1984). *Member:* Chicago (Member, 1985-1992 and Chairman, 1989-1990, Bench/Bar Relations; Member: Tort Litigation, 1985-1990; Defense of Prisoners Committee, 1987-1990; Director, 1990-1991, Young Lawyers Section, Secretary, 1991-1992 and Vice Chairman, 1992-1993) and Illinois State Bar Associations; Illinois Trial Lawyers Association. **PRACTICE AREAS:** Real Estate.

CAROL DI GIACOMO & KATHRYN SOMERS, L.L.C.

GLENVIEW, ILLINOIS

(See Northfield)

Family Law, Divorce, Collaborative Law, Child Custody, Child Support, Spousal Support, Visitation, Adoption, Mediation and Complex Family Law relating to Valuation and Tax Considerations, Estate Planning, Real Estate, Contract and Bankruptcy Law.

STUART A. FELDMAN

GLENVIEW, ILLINOIS

(See Wilmette)

Wills and Probate, Estate Planning, Trusts and Estates, Guardianships, Tax Planning, Taxation, IRS Audits, Business Planning, Small Business, General Business and Real Estate.

THE FIRM OF PER K. HANSON ASSOCIATED

Established in 1985
2222 CHESTNUT AVENUE, SUITE 201
GLENVIEW, ILLINOIS 60026
Telephone: 847-486-9960
Fax: 847-486-9970
Email: firm@pkhpc.com
URL: http://www.pkhpc.com

Estate Planning, Trusts, Asset Protection, Charitable Giving, Guardianship and Conservatorship, Wills and Probate, Corporate, Real Estate, Business Law, and Collections.

PER K. HANSON, born Evanston, Illinois, August 13, 1940; admitted to bar, 1965, Illinois. *Education:* University of Michigan (B.A., 1962); Northwestern University (J.D., 1965). Co-Author: "Law Office Efficiency and Economics," Illinois Institute of Continuing Legal Education, March, 1977. Author: Chapter, "Attorneys Fees," Illinois Institute of Continuing Legal Education, 1983. *Member:* Chicago (Chairman, Economics of the Legal Profession Committee, 1980-1981), North Suburban Lake County, Illinois State (Member, Law Office Economics Section Council, 1993—) and American Bar Associations; Chicago Estate Planning Council; Greater North Shore Estate Planning Council. **PRACTICE AREAS:** Estate Planning; Corporate Law; Real Estate; Probate. **Email:** perh@pkhpc.com

ASSOCIATES

MARY A. LONG, born Glenview, Illinois, July 24, 1935; admitted to bar, 1985, Illinois. *Education:* Northeastern Illinois University (B.A., 1980); John Marshall Law School (J.D., 1985). *Member:* Chicago, (Member: Probate Committee; Matrimonial Law Committee) Northwest Suburban (Member, Probate, Trust, Elder Law Committee), North Suburban and Illinois State Bar Associations; Greater North Shore Estate Planning Council. **PRACTICE AREAS:** Real Estate; Probate; Estate Planning. **Email:** maryl@pkhpc.com

(This Listing Continued)

TIMOTHY J. EDMIER, admitted to bar, 2001, Illinois. *Education:* University of Illinois (B.S., 1996); Kent Law School (J.D., 2001). **PRACTICE AREAS:** Estate Planning; Collections; Real Estate. **Email:** timothy@pkhpc.com

MARC H. HEISLER

GLENVIEW, ILLINOIS

(See Evanston)

Real Estate, Residential Real Estate, Buying and Selling a Home, Commercial Real Estate, Condominium Law and Mortgages. Business, Small Business, Partnership, Family Business and Buying and Selling a Business. Probate and Wills. Adoption Law. Civil Litigation, Chancery Practice, Collections, Personal Injury and Automobile Accidents.

BARRY LOCKE & ASSOCIATES, LTD.

GLENVIEW, ILLINOIS

(See Chicago)

Family Law, Divorce, Child Custody, Child Support, Paternity, Parentage, Visitation Rights.

MICHAEL C. ROSENBLAT, P.C.

2400 RAVINE WAY, SUITE 200
GLENVIEW, ILLINOIS 60025
Telephone: 847-657-0006
Fax: 847-657-7776
Email: MikeRLaw@msn.com
URL: http://www.rosenblatlaw.com

Criminal Law, Civil Practice, Qui Tam Litigation, False Claims Act, Whistleblower Litigation, White Collar Crimes, Drug Crimes, Parole and Probation, Juvenile Crimes, Driving While Intoxicated.

MICHAEL C. ROSENBLAT, born Chicago, Illinois, July 18, 1960; admitted to bar, 1985, Illinois and U.S. District Court, Northern District of Illinois including Trial Bar; 2004, Capital Litigation Trial Bar. *Education:* University of Illinois (B.A., Political Science, 1982); John Marshall Law School (J.D., 1985). Member, John Marshall Law Review. Co-Author: "Prosecuting a Claim Under the Illinois Whistleblower Reward and Protection Act," Employment Termination, IICLE, 2002, updated 2005; "The Attorney General's Medicaid Fraud Unit, Prosecuting Health Care Fraud" the Small Hospital Compliance Seminar, 1998, Illinois Hospital and Health Systems Association, Health Care Compliance Plans: Spanning the Continuum, 1998; "Filing a False Claims Case in the Northern District of Illinois," Chicago Bar Association, Committee on Federal Civil Procedure, 2000; "False Claims and Class Actions," Chicago Bar Association, Committee of Class Actions, 2001. Judge Advocate General, 1990-1993. Assistant Illinois Attorney General, 1993-2001 (including Deputy Bureau Chief, Criminal Prosecution, Deputy Bureau Chief, Special Litigation and Deputy Bureau Chief, Medicaid Fraud Unit). *Member:* American Bar Association (Member, Criminal Litigation Committee); National Association of Criminal Defense Lawyers; Illinois State Bar Association (Member, Criminal Justice Section). [United States Army, 1987-1993, Reserves 1993-2002. Infantry Officer 1988-1990. JAG, 1990-2002.]. **PRACTICE AREAS:** Criminal Law; Civil Practice; Drug Crimes; Driving While Intoxicated; Parole and Probation; Juvenile Criminal Law; White Collar Crime; Qui Tam Litigation; False Claims Act; Whistleblower Litigation; Military Courts Martial; Military Justice; Military Criminal Law; Military Administrative Law; Employment; Wrongful Termination. **Email:** mikerlaw@msn.com

LAW OFFICES OF DAVID M. SHULTS

GLENVIEW, ILLINOIS

(See Northbrook)

Commercial Law, Civil Litigation, Real Estate, and Family Law.

JELLIFFE, FERRELL, MORRIS & DOERGE

GOLCONDA, ILLINOIS

(See Harrisburg)

Insurance Law, Negligence and Personal Injury, Litigation, Workers' Compensation Law, and Employment Law. Commercial Collection and DUI's. General Civil Practice in State and Federal Courts. Trials and Appeals.

LAW OFFICES OF MICHAEL J. BRUNTON

GRANITE CITY, ILLINOIS

(See Collinsville)

Personal Injury, Automobile Accidents, Wrongful Death, Slip and Fall, Workers Compensation, Repetitive Stress Injuries, Industrial Accidents, Construction Accidents, Products Liability, Insurance Dispute, Employment, Wrongful Discharge, Breach of Contract, Warranty Law and Class Actions.

CALLIS, PAPA, HALE, SZEWCZYK, RONGEY & DANZINGER, P.C.

1326 NIEDRINGHAUS AVENUE
P.O. BOX 1326
GRANITE CITY, ILLINOIS 62040
Telephone: 618-452-1323; 1-800-851-3105
Fax: 618-452-8024

General Civil, Trial and Appellate Practice. Federal Employers Liability Law, Negligence, Labor and Personal Injury, Workers Compensation, Probate, Estate Planning, Municipal and School, Criminal Law, Family Law.

LANCE CALLIS, born Norfolk, Virginia, August 12, 1935; admitted to bar, 1959, Missouri and Illinois; 1968, U.S. Supreme Court. *Education:* St. Louis University (B.S., 1956; J.D., 1959). Phi Delta Phi. Counsel, Democratic Party, Madison County, Illinois. *Member:* East St. Louis, Tri-City (President, 1964-1965), Madison County (President, 1976-1977), Illinois State and American Bar Associations; The Missouri Bar; Illinois Trial Lawyers Association (Member, Board of Managers, 1982—); The Association of Trial Lawyers of America. Fellow: Illinois State Bar Foundation. ***PRACTICE AREAS:*** F.E.L.A. Law; Personal Injury Law. ***Email:*** lance@callislaw.com

JOHN T. PAPA, born Granite City, Illinois, October 3, 1951; admitted to bar, 1976, Illinois; 1977, U.S. District Court, Southern District of Illinois; 1982, U.S. Court of Appeals, Sixth Circuit; 1985, U.S. District Court, Northern District of Illinois and Eastern District of Kentucky; 1986, Missouri, U.S. District Court, Central District of Illinois and Western District of Kentucky; 1990, U.S. Court of Appeals, Seventh Circuit; 1994, U.S. District Court, Eastern District of Missouri; 1998, U.S. Court of Appeals, 8th Circuit. *Education:* University of Notre Dame (B.A., magna cum laude, 1973); University of Illinois (J.D., 1976). Designated Legal Counsel, United Transportation Union. Academy of Rail Labor Attorneys. City Attorney, Madison, Illinois. Vice-Chairperson, Committee on Character and Fitness, Fifth District Illinois, 2003. Attorney, Tri City Regional Port District, 2004. *Member:* Bar Association of Metropolitan St. Louis; Tri-City (President, 1984-1985), Madison County, Illinois State and American Bar Associations; The Missouri Bar; Illinois Trial Lawyers Association; Association of Trial Lawyers of America; National School Boards Association; Council of School Attorneys; Illinois Council of School Attorneys. (Resident). ***PRACTICE AREAS:*** F.E.L.A. Law; Personal Injury; Municipal and School Law. ***Email:*** jtp@callislaw.com

RAND S. HALE, born Wood River, Illinois, April 5, 1951; admitted to bar, 1976, Illinois; 1981, U.S. District Court, Southern District of Illinois; 1982, U.S. Court of Appeals, Seventh Circuit; 1985, Missouri. *Education:* University of Missouri (B.A., 1973); University of Tulsa (J.D., 1976). Real Estate Broker, Illinois, 1981. Assistant State's Attorney, Madison County, Illinois, 1976-1980. Special Defender, Madison County, Illinois. *Member:* Madison County (Secretary, 1985-1986) and Illinois State Bar Associations; Bar Association of Metropolitan St. Louis; The Missouri Bar. ***PRACTICE AREAS:*** Workers Compensation; Personal Injury; Criminal Law; Family Law. ***Email:*** rand@callislaw.com

EDWARD J. SZEWCZYK, born East St. Louis, Illinois, March 8, 1952; admitted to bar, 1976, Illinois; 1978, U.S. District Court, Southern District of Illinois; 1982, U.S. Court of Appeals, 7th Circuit; 1988, U.S. District Court, Central District of Illinois and U.S. Supreme Court. *Education:* University of Notre Dame (B.S., 1973); University of Illinois (J.D., 1976). Attorney, Metro East Park and Recreation District, 2005. *Member:* East St. Louis (Secretary-Treasurer, 1978-1979), Tri-City, Madison County, St. Clair County (Secretary-Treasurer, 1978-1979), Illinois State and American Bar Associations; Illinois Trial Lawyers Association; The Association of Trial Lawyers of America. ***PRACTICE AREAS:*** F.E.L.A. Law; Personal Injury; Medical Malpractice; Employment Discrimination. ***Email:*** ejs@calislaw.com

ROBERT W. RONGEY, II, born Madison County, Illinois, January 20, 1960; admitted to bar, 1987, Illinois; 1988, U.S. District Court, Southern District of Illinois; 1995, U.S. Court of Appeals, 7th Circuit; U.S. Supreme Court. *Education:* University of Missouri; Southern Illinois University (B.A., 1982; J.D., 1986). Phi Alpha Delta (President, 1985-1986). Assistant Attorney, Metro East Sanitary District. Attorney, Venice Township and Road and Bridge District. *Member:* Madison County, St. Clair County, Tri City and Illinois State Bar Associations; Illinois Trial Lawyers Association. ***PRACTICE AREAS:*** Personal Injury. ***Email:*** rwr@callislaw.com

KENNETH P. DANZINGER, born Cincinnati, Ohio, March 17, 1972; admitted to bar, 1997, Illinois; 1998, Missouri. *Education:* Kenyon College (B.A., 1994); St. Louis University (J.D., cum laude, 1997). Assistant City Attorney, Madison, Illinois. *Member:* Tri-City, Madison County, Illinois State and American Bar Association; The Missouri Bar; Illinois Trial Lawyers Association. ***PRACTICE AREAS:*** Personal Injury; F.E.L.A.; Municipal Law. ***Email:*** kpd@callislaw.com

ASSOCIATE

TODD A. NEILSON, born Centralia, Illinois, August 9, 1977; admitted to bar, 2002, Illinois; 2003, Missouri and U.S. District Court, Southern District of Illinois. *Education:* Southern Illinois University (B.A., magna cum laude, 1999); St. Louis University (J.D., cum laude, 2002). *Member:* Illinois State Bar Association; Illinois Trial Lawyers Association, The Missouri Bar; Association of Trial Lawyers of America. ***PRACTICE AREAS:*** Personal Injury. ***Email:*** todd@callislaw.com

OF COUNSEL

GEORGE FILCOFF, JR., born Granite City, Illinois, March 11, 1934; admitted to bar, 1957, Missouri and Illinois; 1958, U.S. District Court, Southern and Eastern Districts of Illinois; 1968, U.S. Supreme Court. *Education:* Washington University (A.B., 1955; J.D., 1957). Phi Delta Phi; Phi Delta Theta. Hearing Officer, Illinois Department of Revenue, 1968-1978. City Attorney, Madison, Illinois. City Attorney, Granite City, Illinois, 1963-1978. Associate and Circuit Judge for the Third Judicial Circuit, Madison County, Illinois, 1978-1995. *Member:* Tri-City (President, 1961-1962); Madison County (President, 1975-

(This Listing Continued)

976); Illinois State Bar Associations; The Missouri Bar; Association of Trial Lawyers of America. Fellow, American Academy of Matrimonial Lawyers. [Captain, U.S. Army]. ***Email:*** gfilcoff@callislaw.com

PHILIP J. RARICK, born Troy, Illinois, November 10, 1940; admitted to bar, 1966, Illinois and U.S. District Courts, Southern and Eastern District of Illinois. *Education:* Southern Illinois University (B.A., 1962); St. Louis University (J.D., 1966). Assistant State's Attorney, Madison County, Illinois, 1967-1975. Township Attorney, Collinsville, Illinois, 1967-1975. Township Attorney, Jarvis, Illinois, 1967-1975. City Attorney, Collinsvill, Illinois, 1966-1975. Associate and Circuit Judge, Third Judicial Circuit, Madison County, Illinois, 1975-1988. Appellate Judge, Fifth District, 1988-2002. Industrial Commission Division of the Appellate Court, 1992-2002. Justice of Illinois Supreme Court, 2002-2004. *Member:* Illinois State Bar Association; Illinois Trial Lawyers Association. ***PRACTICE AREAS:*** Workers Compensation; Personal Injury; Criminal Law.

REPRESENTATIVE CLIENTS: Paper, Allied-Industries, Chemical & Energy Workers Locals 7-663, 7-214 and 1347; Lovejoy School District; Madison School District; City of Madison, Il.
COUNSEL FOR: United Transportation Union; Democratic Party of Madison County, Illinois.
REFERENCES: Bank of Alton, Alton, Illinois; Union Planters Bank of Madison County, Granite City, Illinois; Bank of Edwardville, Edwardville, Il.

LUEDERS, ROBERTSON & KONZEN LLC

Established in 1923
1939 DELMAR AVENUE
GRANITE CITY, ILLINOIS 62040
Telephone: 618-876-8500
Telecopier: 618-876-4534
Email: lrk@lrklaw.com
URL: http://www.irkllc.com

General, Trial and Appellate Practice. Utility and Energy Law, Corporation and Banking and Trust Law, Estate, Probate, Real Estate and Administrative Law, Environmental Law, Municipal, Third Party Defense, Bankruptcy and Workers Compensation.

FIRM PROFILE: From its beginning more than 80 years ago as a respected law firm in Granite City, Illinois, Lueders, Robertson & Konzen LLC has grown to serve a full range of clients, ranging from Fortune 500 corporations and major regional industrial companies to small businesses and individuals. The firm has developed an excellent reputation as a small firm capable of handling large matters. The firm's clientele ranges from multi-national corporations to first-time legal consumers seeking simple wills.

MEMBERS OF FIRM

WESLEY LUEDERS (1896-1957)

RANDALL ROBERTSON, born Granite City, Illinois, July 11, 1920; admitted to bar, 1947, Illinois. *Education:* Westminster College; St. Louis University (B.S., 1943); Washington University; St. Louis University (J.D., 1947). Attorney: Granite City Park District, 1949-1995; Tri-City Regional Port District, 1961-1995. Assistant Attorney General, State of Illinois, 1953-1960. Member, Human Relations Commission of the City of Granite City, 1967-1968. Appointed by the Governor of the State of Illinois, Member, Illinois Board of Ethics, 1977-1978. *Member:* Tri-City, Madison County, Illinois State and American Bar Associations. ***PRACTICE AREAS:*** Energy; Public Utilities. ***Email:*** rrobertson@lrklaw.com

LEO H. KONZEN, born Alton, Illinois, December 22, 1929; admitted to bar, 1953, Illinois and Missouri. *Education:* St. Louis University (B.S., 1951; J.D., 1953). Phi Delta Phi. Special Assistant Illinois Attorney General, 1969-1983. City Attorney, Granite City, 1993-1997. Member, Board of Governors, St. Elizabeth's Medical Center, Granite City, Illinois, 1972-2001. Member, Board of Directors of East-West Gateway Coordinating Counsel, 1977-1979. Member, Board of Trustees, Southwestern Illinois College, 1987-1988. *Member:* Tri-City (President, 1962-1964), Madison County (Secretary, 1958-1959; Chairman, Grievance Committee, 1971-1973), Illinois State (Member: Attorney Registration and Discipline Commission Inquiry Board, 1983-1990; Hearing Panel, 1990—) and American (Vice Chair, Corporation, Banking and Business Law Committee, 1987-1988) Bar Associations. ***PRACTICE AREAS:*** General Practice; Probate; Real Estate. ***Email:*** lkonzen@lrklaw.com

R. ERIC ROBERTSON, born Granite City, Illinois, May 1, 1946; admitted to bar, 1973, Illinois. *Education:* DePauw University (B.A., 1968); St. Louis University (J.D., 1973). Delta Theta Phi. Assistant City Attorney, City of Granite City, 1973-1975. Special Assistant Illinois Attorney General, 1975-1983. Attorney: Tri-City Regional Port District, 1994—; Granite City Park District, 1994—. Member: Board of Directors, Coro Foundation, St. Louis, Missouri, 1986-1987; Lay Advisory Board and Ethics Committee, St. Elizabeth Medical Center, Granite City, Illinois, 1986-2001; Board of Directors: Tri-City Area United Way, 1991-1998; Alcoholic Rehabilitation Community House, 1985—. *Member:* Tri-City, Madison County, Illinois State and American Bar Associations. ***PRACTICE AREAS:*** Energy; Public Utilities; General Practice. ***Email:*** erobertson@lrklaw.com

BRIAN E. KONZEN, born St. Louis, Missouri, November 15, 1959; admitted to bar, 1984, Illinois. *Education:* St. Patrick's College, Maynooth, Ireland; University of Notre Dame (B.A., 1981); St. Louis University (J.D., 1984). Recipient, Kneip Award for Appellate Advocacy, 1983. Author, "Does the Eighth Circuit Abuse the Writ of Habeas Corpus," St. Louis University Public Law Forum, Vol. 4, No. 1, 1984. Member, Governing Board, Granite City Public Library, 1986-1987. Assistant City Attorney, 1987—. *Member:* Tri-City, Madison County, Illinois State and American Bar Associations. ***PRACTICE AREAS:*** Environmental; Employment Law; Municipal Law; General Practice; Commercial Litigation. ***Email:*** bkonzen@lrklaw.com

ASSOCIATES

LAUREN K. SMITH, born Bradenton, Florida, May 17, 1978; admitted to bar, 2003, Illinois. *Education:* Southern Illinois University (B.S.W., 1999); Southern Illinois Univer-

(This Listing Continued)

LUEDERS, ROBERTSON & KONZEN LLC, Granite City—Continued

sity School of Law (J.D., 2002). *Member:* Tri-City, Madison County, Illinois State and American Bar Associations. ***PRACTICE AREAS:*** General Practice. **Email:** lsmith@lrklaw.com

RYAN E. ROBERTSON, born Granite City, Illinois, August 3, 1976; admitted to bar, 2004, Illinois. *Education:* St. Louis University (B.A., 1998; J.D., 2004). *Member:* Tri-City, Madison County, Illinois State and American Bar Associations. ***PRACTICE AREAS:*** General Practice.

REPRESENTATIVE CLIENTS: Granite City Works; U.S. Steel Corporation; Allied Waste Industries, Inc.; Illinois Industrial Energy Consumers (IIEC) including Olin Corp.; Archer-Daniels-Midland Company; General Motors Corporation; Ford Motor Company; Corn Products International Inc.; Abbott Laboratories, Inc.; Caterpillar Inc.; A.E. Staley Manufacturing Co.; PPG Industries, Inc.; Continental General Tire Company; Cargill, Inc.; Solutia, Inc.; Deere & Company; Air Products & Chemicals; Mototola, Inc.; R.R. Donnelley & Sons; University of Illinois; Bunge North America, Inc.

ROTH & EVANS

2421 CORPORATE CENTRE DRIVE
SUITE 200
GRANITE CITY, ILLINOIS 62040
Telephone: 618-931-5000
Fax: 618-931-6474
Email: rothlaw@rothlaw.com
URL: http://www.rothlaw.com

General Civil Trial and Appellate practice in all State and Federal Courts, including Missouri.. Personal Injury, Negligence, Premises Liability, Products Liability, Insurance, Automobile, Construction, Commercial Litigation, Workers Compensation, Employment, Discrimination, Civil Rights, Class Action, Environmental, Toxic Tort, Municipal, Corporate, Probate, Real Estate Law.

FIRM PROFILE: Roth and Evans is an established firm which maintains a prominent litigation practice, with an emphasis in the area of personal injury defense. The firm has extensive trial experience in Illinois and Missouri, handling product liability, premises liability, medical malpractice, personal injury and municipal/government matters. Our attorneys combine academic performance with outstanding law practice accomplishments. The firm prides itself on being small enough to give each matter personal attention, while maintaining the ability to handle the most sophisticated and complex litigation.

RONALD A. ROTH, born Danville, Illinois, January 5, 1953; admitted to bar, 1978, Illinois and U.S. District Court, Southern District of Illinois; 1987, U.S. Court of Appeals, Seventh Circuit; 2000, Missouri. *Education:* DePauw University (B.A., 1975); Washington University (J.D., 1978). Delta Theta Phi. Recipient, American Jurisprudence Award, Civil Procedure, 1976. Member, Illinois State Bar Council on Insurance Law. *Member:* Tri-City, Madison County, Illinois State and American Bar Associations; Illinois Association of Defense Trial Counsel; Defense Research Institute. ***PRACTICE AREAS:*** Medical Malpractice; Commercial Litigation; Products Liability; Negligence. **Email:** raroth@rothlaw.com

ERIC W. EVANS, born Minneapolis, Minnesota, January 30, 1968; admitted to bar, 1993, Missouri; 1994, Illinois, Minnesota and U.S. District Court, Southern District of Illinois and U.S. District Court, Eastern District of Missouri. *Education:* Washington University (B.S. and A.B., 1990); St. Louis University (J.D., cum laude, 1993). Articles Editor, St. Louis University Law Journal, 1993. Staff Attorney, United State's Court of Appeals for the Eighth Circuit, 1993-1994. City Attorney, Pontoon Beach, Illinois, 1999—. Attorney, Long Lake Fire District, 2000—. *Member:* St. Louis, Tri Cities, Madison County, Illinois, Missouri and Minnesota Bar Associations; Illinois Association of Defense Counsel; Defense Research Institute. ***PRACTICE AREAS:*** Commercial Litigation; Products Liability; Premises Liability; Negligence; Municipal Law; Real Estate. **Email:** ewevans@rothlaw.com

ASSOCIATES

PHILIP J. LADING, born Effingham, Illinois, March 8, 1974; admitted to bar, 1999, Missouri, U.S. District Court, Eastern District of Missouri and U.S. Court of Appeals, Eighth Circuit; 2000, Illinois; 2001, U.S. District Court, Southern District of Illinois. *Education:* Illinois Wesleyan University (B.A., 1996); St. Louis University (J.D., cum laude, 1999). City Attorney, Staunton, Illinois, 2004—. *Member:* Madison County Bar Association. ***PRACTICE AREAS:*** Negligence; Products Liability; Premises Liability; Municipal Law. **Email:** pjlading@rothlaw.com

DAWN KAMADULSKI O'LEARY, born Granite City, Illinois, April 14, 1969; admitted to bar, 1999, Illinois; 2000, Missouri. *Education:* Monmouth College (B.A., 1991); Minnesota State University (M.F.A., 1996); Washington University (J.D., 1999);. Sigma Gamma Epsilon. National Merit Finalist. Law Clerk, Justice Gordon Maag, Illinois Appellate Court, Fifth District, 1999-2000. *Member:* Madison County and Tri Cities Bar Associations. ***PRACTICE AREAS:*** Personal Injury; Products Liability; Negligence. **Email:** dkoleary@rothlaw.com

PETER S. BLASI, born Chicago, Illinois, July 24, 1974; admitted to bar, 2000, Illinois and U.S. District Court, Northern District of Illinois; 2001, Missouri. *Education:* St. Louis University (B.A., 1996); John Marshall Law School (J.D., 1999). *Member:* Illinois State Bar Association; The Missouri Bar. ***PRACTICE AREAS:*** Personal Injury; Maritime Law; Property Damage; Workers Compensation. **Email:** psblasi@rothlaw.com

GEORGE H. ALBERS, born St. Louis, Missouri, 1966; admitted to bar, 2001, Illinois; 2000, Missouri. *Education:* St. Louis University (B.A., History, 1997; J.D., magna cum laude, 2000). Order of the Woolsack. Recipient, Dean's Scholarship. Co-Author: "State Rehabilitation Tax Creditors: A Rebirth of History Across the United States," The Journal of Multi-State Taxation and Incentives," November/December 2000; "The Rebirth of Historic Restoration in Missouri," Missouri Business Law Quarterly, August 2000. ***PRACTICE AREAS:*** Litigation; Negligence; Insurance; Real Estate.

(This Listing Continued)

REPRESENTATIVE CLIENTS: Allstate Insurance Company; Allstate Indemnity Company; Automobile Club Inter-Insurance Exchange; ACE USA; Mid-Continent; GMAC/Integon; Bankers & Shippers; Scottsdale Insurance Co.; Village of Pontoon Beach; Lumberman's Underwriting; Safety-Kleen Corporation.

WILLIAM W. SCHOOLEY

2038 EDISON AVENUE
P.O. BOX 1289
GRANITE CITY, ILLINOIS 62040
Telephone: 618-877-2142; 452-7122
800-942-7122
Fax: 618-452-9612
Email: barnone@granitecity.com

Plaintiff, Trial and Appellate Practice. Workers Compensation Law.

FIRM PROFILE: The firm was established in the early 1950's. Focusing primarily in the areas of personal injury and workers compensation. The attorneys handle matters throughout central and southern Illinois. 75% of the firms clients are union members.

WILLIAM W. SCHOOLEY, born Granite City, Illinois, April 2, 1929; admitted to bar, 1961, Illinois. *Education:* United States Military Academy (B.S., 1951); St. Louis University (J.D., 1961). Phi Delta Phi. *Member:* Tri-City, Madison County (President, 1971-1972), Illinois State and American Bar Associations; The Association of Trial Lawyers of America; Illinois Trial Lawyers Association. ***PRACTICE AREAS:*** Trial and Appellate Practice; Workers Compensation Law; Personal Injury.

THOMAS E. SCHOOLEY, born Granite City, Illinois, July 20, 1957; admitted to bar, 1983, Illinois and Alabama; 1997, Missouri. *Education:* University of Illinois (B.A., 1980); St. Louis University (J.D., 1983). *Member:* Tri-City, Madison County, Illinois State and American Bar Associations; Alabama State Bar. ***PRACTICE AREAS:*** Trial and Appellate Practice; Workers Compensation Law; Personal Injury.

REPRESENTATIVE CLIENT: Iron Workers Local 392, East St. Louis, Illinois.
ATTORNEYS FOR: Granite City Township; Pontoon Beach Water District; Community Unit School District 9; International Boilermakers Local 363.

RICHARD A. ANDERSON

11 N. SLUSSER STREET
GRAYSLAKE, ILLINOIS 60030
Telephone: 847-223-7011
Fax: 847-223-7012
URL: http://www.richardandersonattorney.com

Criminal Law, Driving While Intoxicated, Misdemeanors, Felonies, Real Estate, Buying and Selling of Businesses, Juvenile Criminal Law.

RICHARD A. ANDERSON, born Chicago, Illinois, December 8, 1952; admitted to bar, 1994, Wisconsin and Illinois. *Education:* Northeastern Illinois University (B.A., 1991); Marquette University (J.D., 1994). *Member:* State Bar of Wisconsin. Chicago, Lake County and Illinois State Bar Associations. ***PRACTICE AREAS:*** Criminal Law; Driving While Intoxicated; Traffic Violations; Misdemeanors; Felonies; Real Estate; Buying and Selling of Businesses; Juvenile Criminal Law.

LAW OFFICE OF PAUL R. IDLAS

1099 NORTH CORPORATE CIRCLE
GRAYSLAKE, ILLINOIS 60030
Telephone: 847-223-5555
Fax: 847-223-5583
URL: http://www.paulidlas.com
Email: pidlas@aol.com
URL: http://www.idlas.com

Bankruptcy, Real Estate, Chapter 7 Bankruptcy, Real Estate Closings.

PAUL R. IDLAS, born Morristown, New Jersey, January 4, 1956; admitted to bar, 1982, Illinois. *Education:* University of Illinois, Urbana-Champaign (B.S., 1978; J.D., 1982). *Member:* Illinois State Bar Association. ***PRACTICE AREAS:*** Bankruptcy; Real Estate; Bankruptcy Chapter 7; Bankruptcy Chapter 13; Debtor Bankruptcy; Personal Bankruptcy; Repossessions.

ROBERT A. SOUTHERN

28 BOBOLINK DRIVE
GRAYSLAKE, ILLINOIS 60030
Telephone: 919-969-8292
Fax: 919-969-8293
Email: rsouthern@nc.rr.com

Corporate, Securities and Finance.

ROBERT A. SOUTHERN, born Independence, Missouri, July 17, 1930; admitted to bar, 1955, Illinois. *Education:* Northwestern University (B.S., 1952; LL.B., 1954). Order of the Coif. Editor-in-Chief, Northwestern University Law Review, 1953-1954. Retired Managing Partner, Mayer, Brown, Rowe & Maw (Formerly, Mayer, Brown & Platt), 1978-1991. *Member:* Chicago Bar Association. ***PRACTICE AREAS:*** Corporate; Securities; Finance.

BEERMANN & DeBRUYNE

GURNEE, ILLINOIS

(See Libertyville)

Family Law, Divorce, Adoption, Separation Agreements, Child Custody, Child Support, Domestic Violence, Visitation Rights, Family Mediation Adoption Law, Juvenile Law, Real Estate.

ERIN E. CARTWRIGHT

GURNEE, ILLINOIS

(See Waukegan)

General Practice.

MICHAEL T. CAVANAUGH

4193 GROVE AVENUE
GURNEE, ILLINOIS 60031
Telephone: 847-263-8820
Fax: 847-336-2629
Email: mcavanaugh@cavanaughlawfirm.com
URL: http://www.cavanaughlawfirm.com

Criminal Law.

FIRM PROFILE: The Law Firm of Michael T. Cavanaugh has always taken pride in service to the client. All clients receive the individual attention and personal oversight of Mr. Cavanaugh. You can rely on the same experienced attorney appearing with you on each and every court date. Mr. Cavanaugh strongly feels that every case is important and should not be serviced by a revolving door of attorneys, or junior associate. Every phone call is returned by the end of the business day and you will always be kept informed about the progress of your case. Mr. Cavanaugh's goal is to treat everyone the way he would like to be treated.

MICHAEL T. CAVANAUGH, born Waukegan, Illinois, October 18, 1954; admitted to bar, 2000, Illinois. *Education:* Oregon State University (B.S., 1980); Northern Illinois University (J.D., cum laude, 2000). Mr. Cavanaugh is a lifelong resident of Lake County, IL. After twenty years in the business sector, Mr. Cavanugh graduated Cum Laude from Law School and joined the Lake County State's Attorneys Office as a Prosecutor. Mr. Cavanaugh thereafter entered private practice as a defense attorney: a practice concentrated in Felony, Misdemeanor, DUI, Traffic Law, and Driver's License Reinstatements. Mr. Cavanaugh currently serves as a Teen Court judge and is chairman of the Teen Court Advisory Board. *Member:* Lake County Bar Association, LCBA Legal Aid Committee, Volunteer Lawyer's Program. ***PRACTICE AREAS:*** Drugs and Narcotics; Drug Crimes; Drug Forfeiture; Drug Trafficking; Controlled Substances Law; Civil Drug Forfeiture; Alcoholic Beverages; Alcoholic Beverage Control; Criminal Law; Assault and Battery; Burglary; Civil Forfeiture; Criminal Fraud; Criminal Forfeiture; Criminal Defense; Criminal Conspiracy; Criminal Investigation; Drivers License Suspension; Driving While Intoxicated; Electronic Surveillance; Extortion; Extradition; Felonies; Forgery; Habeas Corpus; Homicide; Manslaughter; Misdemeanors; Murder; Parole and Probation; Post-Conviction Remedies; Malicious Prosecution; Sex Crimes; Sexual Assault; Theft; Traffic Violations; Search and Seizure; Weapons Charges; Criminal Appeals; Driver; Capital Offenses.

Languages: Spanish and Italian interpreters are available.

THE LAW OFFICES OF DAVID R. DEL RE

A PROFESSIONAL CORPORATION

GURNEE, ILLINOIS

(See Waukegan)

Criminal Defense, Family Law.

FERRIS, THOMPSON & ZWEIG, LTD.

Established in 1989

103 SOUTH GREENLEAF AVENUE, SUITE G
GURNEE, ILLINOIS 60031
Telephone: 847-263-7770
Fax: 847-263-7771
Email: mzweig@injurylawyershotline.com
URL: http://www.ftzlaw.net

Personal Injury, Airplane Crashes, Medical Malpractice, Construction Site Accidents, Nursing Home Abuse and Neglect, Property Damage, Railroad Accidents and Injuries, Slip and Fall, Unsafe Products, Wrongful Death, Automobile Accidents, Workers Compensation, Criminal Defense, Drug Crimes, Drunk Driving, Felonies, Homicides, Juvenile Crimes, Misdemeanors, Parole and Probation, Traffic Violations.

FIRM PROFILE: Personal Injury, Medical Malpractice, Auto Accidents, Slip and Fall, Products Liability, Workers' Compensation, Probate, Real Estate, Criminal Defense, Traffic Defense, DUI Defense.

SAUL FERRIS, born Chicago, Illinois, September 20, 1959; admitted to bar, 1985, Illinois. *Education:* Illinois State University (B.S., 1981); Thomas M. Cooley Law School (1982); Northern Illinois University (J.D., 1985). *Member:* American Bar Association. ***PRACTICE AREAS:*** Personal Injury Law; Criminal Law. ***Email:*** sferris@injurylawyershotline.com

GARY R. THOMPSON, born Chicago, Illinois, May 13, 1961; admitted to bar, 1987, Illinois. *Education:* University of Iowa (B.A., 1984); Northern Illinois College of Law

(This Listing Continued)

(J.D., 1987). Phi Alpha Delta. *Member:* Lane County, Chicago, Illinois State and American Bar Associations. ***LANGUAGES:*** Spanish. ***PRACTICE AREAS:*** Personal Injury; Criminal Defense; Bankruptcy. ***Email:*** gthompson@injurylawyershotline.com

MICHAEL L. ZWEIG, born Chicago, Illinois, October 10, 1958; admitted to bar, 1985, Illinois and U.S. District Court, Northern District of Illinois. *Education:* Arizona State University (B.S., 1980); The American University (M.A., 1985); California Western School of Law (J.D., 1985). *Member:* Chicago, Illinois State, American and International Bar Associations. ***LANGUAGES:*** Russian. ***PRACTICE AREAS:*** Probate (90%); Real Estate (10%). ***Email:*** mzweig@injurylawyershotline.com

JOHN STERGIOU, born Chicago, Illinois, August 18, 1972; admitted to bar, 2001, Illinois. *Education:* DePaul University (B.S., 1990); Thomas M. Cooley Law School (J.D., 2000). ***LANGUAGES:*** Spanish, Greek. ***PRACTICE AREAS:*** Criminal; Traffic; Real Estate; Personal Injury.

Languages: Spanish and Russian.

MATTHEW KAPLAN & ASSOCIATES

GURNEE, ILLINOIS

(See Libertyville)

Family Law, Divorce, Adoptions, Child Custody, Child Support, Domestic Violence, Spousal Support.

MAY & BUEGE

GURNEE, ILLINOIS

(See Waukegan)

Personal Injury, Workers Compensation and Insurance Law. Litigation.

JOSEPH P. McCAFFERY
ATTORNEY AT LAW

GURNEE, ILLINOIS

(See Aurora)

Criminal Litigation, White Collar, Felonies, Misdemeanors, Civil Defense, Legal Malpractice Defense, Insurance Defense, Medical Malpractice, Personal Injury, Divorce, Wills and Trusts, Real Estate Transactions, Banking, Securities, Corporate and Commercial Litigation.

LAW OFFICES OF
ELLIOT HEIDELBERGER

Established in 1985

7225 LONGMEADOW LANE
HANOVER PARK, ILLINOIS 60133
Telephone: 630-289-4000
Fax: 630-289-3444
URL: http://www.heidelbergerlaw.com
Email: elliot@heidelbergerlaw.com
URL: http://www.lawyers.com/eheidelberger

Chicago, Illinois Office: 20 North Clark Street, Suite 1725, 60602-4101. Telephone: 312-443-8003.

Family Law, Divorce, Child Custody, Child Support, Premarital Agreements, Spousal Support, Parentage, Real Estate Closings.

FIRM PROFILE: After 18 years as the managing partner of Heidelberger and Leibsker, Attorneys at Law, Elliot Heidelberger established a solo practice concentrating his work in the areas of Matrimonial and Family Law including Divorce, Child Custody, Child and Spousal Support, Property Division, Child Visitation, Pre Nuptial Agreements, Enforcement of Divorce Judgments, Adoption, Property Division in Dissolution of Marriage Cases, Divorce Mediation and Parenting Cases.

ELLIOT HEIDELBERGER, born Chicago, Illinois, October 2, 1942; admitted to bar, 1966, Illinois. *Education:* University of Illinois (B.A., 1964; J.D., 1966). Associate, The Law Office of Herbert F. Stride, 1967-1969. Managing Partner, The Law Offices of Heidelberger and Leibsker, 1969-1985. *Member:* Illinois State and American Bar Associations; Decalogue Society of Lawyers. Fellow, American Academy of Matrimonial Lawyers. ***PRACTICE AREAS:*** Family Law; Divorce; Child Custody; Child Support; Visitation Rights; Spousal Support; Premarital Agreements; Adoption Law; Marital Property Distribution; Divorce Mediation.

KLEST LAW FIRM

HANOVER PARK, ILLINOIS

(See Schaumburg)

Personal Injury, Medical Malpractice, Products Liability, Legal Malpractice, Construction Accidents, Airplane Crash Litigation, Insurance Bad Faith, Automobile Accidents, Motorcycle Accidents, Birth Trauma, Sexual Abuse, Child Abuse and Neglect, Slip and Fall, Wrongful Death, Dog Bites, Railroad Accidents and Injuries, Automobile Products, Liability and Drug and Medical Device Litigation, Trial Practice.

LAW OFFICE OF GREGORY J. MARTUCCI, P.C.

HANOVER PARK, ILLINOIS

(See Roselle)

Bankruptcy, Criminal Law, Driving While Intoxicated, Juvenile Criminal Law, Traffic Violations, Domestic Violence, Personal Injury, Automobile Accidents and Injuries, Slip and Fall, Workers Compensation.

HOWERTON, DORRIS & STONE

HARRISBURG, ILLINOIS

(See Marion)

Plaintiff's Personal Injury, Workers Compensation Law, Insurance Bad Faith, Breach of Contract, Criminal Defense, Medical Malpractice, General Civil and Trial Practice.

JELLIFFE, FERRELL, MORRIS & DOERGE

108 EAST WALNUT STREET
P.O. BOX 406
HARRISBURG, ILLINOIS 62946
Telephone: 618-253-7153; 253-7647
Telecopier: 618-252-1843
Email: jfmdf@neondsl.com

Insurance Law, Negligence and Personal Injury, Litigation, Workers' Compensation Law, and Employment Law. Commercial Collection and DUI's. General Civil Practice in State and Federal Courts. Trials and Appeals.

FIRM PROFILE: The Practice of Jelliffe, Ferrell, Morris & Doerge in Harrisburg, Illinois, through its former partners, has been in existence since 1920. The firm serves, and is engaged in, litigation in the southern one-third of the State of Illinois. The firm is actively involved in litigation regarding all areas related to personal injury, insurance and employment.

RETIRED

CHARLES R. JELLIFFE, born Springfield, Illinois, December 6, 1925; admitted to bar, 1953, Illinois. *Education:* University of Illinois (B.S., 1949; J.D., 1951). Fellow, American College of Trial Lawyers. (Retired)

MEMBERS OF FIRM

DONALD V. FERRELL, born Eldorado, Illinois, September 5, 1944; admitted to bar, 1969, Illinois and U.S. District Court, Southern District of Illinois; U.S. Court of Appeals, Seventh and Eighth Circuits; U.S. District Court, Western District of Indiana. *Education:* Southern Illinois University and University of Illinois (B.S., 1966); University of Alabama (J.D., 1969). Phi Alpha Delta. *Member:* Illinois State and American Bar Associations. Fellow, American College of Trial Lawyers. ***LANGUAGES:*** German. ***PRACTICE AREAS:*** Personal Injury; Civil Jury Trial; Insurance Contract Construction; Employment Law; Civil Rights Litigation. ***Email:*** dvf@neondsl.com

WALDEN E. MORRIS, born Harrisburg, Illinois, February 4, 1949; admitted to bar, 1976, Illinois and U.S Supreme Court; U.S. District Court, Southern District of Illinois. *Education:* Southern Illinois University (B.A., 1971); University of Tulsa (J.D., 1975). States Attorney, Saline County, Illinois, 1976-1980. *Member:* Saline County and Illinois State Bar Associations. ***PRACTICE AREAS:*** Personal Injury; Civil Trial; Workers Compensation; Insurance Contract Construction; Probate. ***Email:*** wem@neondsl.com

MICHAL DOERGE, born Harrisburg, Illinois, December 31, 1958; admitted to bar, 1984, Illinois; U.S. District Court, Southern District of Illinois, U.S. Supreme Court and U.S. Court of Appeals, Seventh Circuit. *Education:* Murray State University (B.S., 1981); Southern Illinois University (J.D., 1984). Lobbyist and State Agency Liaison, Illinois Education Association, 1985-1986. *Member:* Saline County and Illinois State Bar Association. ***PRACTICE AREAS:*** Insurance Law; Personal Injury; Workers' Compensation; Civil Litigation; Real Estate Development and Construction. ***Email:*** md@neondsl.com

ASSOCIATE

KELLY R. PHELPS, born Eldorado, Illinois, April 24, 1970; admitted to bar, 1995, Illinois; 1996, U.S. District Court, Southern District of Illinois; 1998, U.S. Court of Appeals, Seventh Circuit. *Education:* University of Illinois (B.A., 1992); Southern Illinois University (J.D., 1995). Phi Delta Phi. Legal Intern, Saline County State's Attorney's Office, 1994. *Member:* The Association of Trial Lawyers of America; Southern Illinois Workers' Compensation Bar Association (President). ***PRACTICE AREAS:*** Personal Injury; Civil Practice; Workers Compensation; Insurance.

REPRESENTATIVE CLIENTS: Auto-Owners Insurance; Country Companies; Bituminous Insurance; Kemper Insurance Co.; Midwestern Insurance Alliance; National Liability & Fire Insurance; Ohio Casualty Group; Sentry Insurance; Shelter Ins. Co.; Standard Mutual Ins. Co.; State Auto Insurance; State Farm Companies; Unitrin Insurance; Universal Underwriters; USAA Insurance; Westfield Insurance; The Hartford/Omni Automobile.

MITCHELL & MITCHELL

HARRISBURG, ILLINOIS

(See Marion)

General Trial and Appellate Practice. Insurance, Personal Injury, Medical Malpractice, Products Liability, Commercial Law, Litigation and Divorce.

ELMAN & EHARDT, LTD.

100 SOUTH AYER STREET-UNIT E
HARVARD, ILLINOIS 60033-2900
Telephone: 815-943-4051
Fax: 815-943-4086
Email: elman@owc.net

General Practice. Trials, Negligence Law, Worker's Compensation, Real Estate and Probate. Mediation.

WILLIAM ELMAN, born Evanston, Illinois, January 6, 1932; admitted to bar, 1959, Illinois; 1960, U.S. District Court, Northern District of Illinois; 1964, U.S. District Court, Southern District of Illinois; 1965, U.S. District Court, Western District of Wisconsin; 1971, U.S. Supreme Court and U.S. Court of Appeals, Southern District; 1976, U.S. District Court, Eastern District of Wisconsin; 1982, U.S. District Court, Northern District of Illinois Trial Bar. *Education:* Grinnell College (B.A., 1953); Harvard University (J.D., 1956). Author: "Case of the Defaulted Defendant," Illinois State Bar Journal, June, 1964; "Suvada At Two," Chicago Bar Record, May, 1967. City Attorney, City of Harvard, 1985-1989. Special Assistant States Attorney, McHenry County, 1992—. Arbitrator and Court Certified Mediator, 19th Judicial Circuit. Member, Panel of Arbitrators, American Arbitration Association. *Member:* Chicago (Member, Civil Practice Committee, 1971-1973), McHenry County (Member, Board of Governors, 1973-1978; 1985-1986) and Illinois State Bar Associations, Workers Compensation Lawyers Association; Illinois Trial Lawyers Association. [With U.S. Army, 1956-1958]

POLLOCK, MEYERS, EICKSTEADT & PULAK, LTD.

HARVARD, ILLINOIS

(See Marengo)

General Trial Practice, Appellate Practice, Estate Planning, Probate Law, Trust Law, Real Estate, Banking Law, Bankruptcy Law, Personal Injury, Workers Compensation, Administrative Law, Corporate Law, Contracts, Civil Litigation, Trusts and Estates, Real Estate Law.

MICHAEL V. FAVIA

HARWOOD HEIGHTS, ILLINOIS

(See Chicago)

Civil Litigation, Personal Injuries, Automobile Accidents, Medical Malpractice, Products Liability, Work Injuries, Health Law, Medicare and Medicaid Fraud, Medical and Health Related Regulatory Issues, Professional Licensure Matters.

LAW OFFICES OF LEYNAUD & LEYNAUD

A PROFESSIONAL CORPORATION

HENNEPIN, ILLINOIS

(See Peru)

General Civil and Trial Practice, Personal Injury, Mediation, Worker's Compensation, Real Estate, Criminal, Landlord/Tenant and Family Law. Business/Banking Litigation, DUI and Traffic. Insurance, General Practice, Medical Malpractice, Zoning and Land Use. Bad Faith, Drug Crimes, Juvenile Crimes, White Collar, Adoptions, Child Custody, Divorce, Child Support, Visitation Rights, Domestic Violence. Auto Accidents, Dog Bites, Slip and Fall, Wrongful Death, Buying and Selling, Wills and Probate.

HART AND HART

HERRIN, ILLINOIS

(See Benton)

General Trial and Appellate Practice in State and Federal Courts. Probate, Trust, Real Estate Deeds and Title Insurance, Bankruptcy (Creditors), Traffic, Banking, Business, Commercial and Corporation Law and Creditor Collections, Employment Law.

THOMAS A. HILL

Established in 1987
100 EXECUTIVE DRIVE
P.O. BOX 141
HIGHLAND, ILLINOIS 62249
Telephone: 618-654-9787; 654-6551
Fax: 618-654-4827
Email: hill-law@highlandil.com

Real Estate, Trusts and Estates, Business Law, Civil Practice, Corporate Law, Personal Injury.

THOMAS A. HILL, born Granite City, Illinois, February 24, 1948; admitted to bar, 1975, Illinois; 1990, Missouri. *Education:* Regis College and University of Illinois (B.S., 1970); John Marshall Law School (J.D., cum laude, 1975). *Member:* Tri-City (President, 1981-1982), Madison County (President, 1988-1989), Illinois State (Member, Corporation and Securities, Real Estate and Probate Sections) and American (Vice-Chairman, Bankruptcy Committee, General Practice Section, 1990-1991) Bar Associations; Missouri Bar;

(This Listing Continued)

Illinois Trial Lawyers Association; The Association of Trial Lawyers of America. ***PRACTICE AREAS:*** Estate Planning; Wills and Probate; Automobile Accidents; Buying and Selling of Homes.

A list of Representative Clients and References will be provided upon request.

BAIZER & KOLAR, P.C.

513 CENTRAL AVENUE, FIFTH FLOOR
HIGHLAND PARK, ILLINOIS 60035
Telephone: 847-433-6677
Fax: 847-433-6735
Email: bk@baizlaw.com
URL: http://www.baizlaw.com

Plaintiff's Personal Injury, Medical Malpractice and Aviation Negligence Trials.

ROBERT S. BAIZER, born Chicago, Illinois, December 3, 1946; admitted to bar, 1972, Illinois and U.S. District Court, Northern District of Illinois. *Education:* University of Illinois (B.A., 1969); Northwestern University (J.D., 1972). Member, Northwestern University Law Review, 1971-1972. Assistant State's Attorney, Lake County, Illinois, 1975-1978. *Member:* Lake County, Illinois State and American Bar Associations; Illinois Trial Lawyers Association (Member, Board of Managers); The Association of Trial Lawyers of America; Trial Lawyers for Public Justice (Member, Board of Directors). ***PRACTICE AREAS:*** Personal Injury; Medical Malpractice; Aviation Liability. ***Email:*** bob@baizlaw.com

JOSEPH E. KOLAR, born Waukegan, Illinois, August 21, 1960; admitted to bar, 1985, Illinois and U.S. District Court, Northern and Southern Districts of Illinois. *Education:* Illinois State University (B.S., 1982); Northern Illinois University (J.D., cum laude, 1985). Author, "Adoption of a Flexible Standard for Analyzing Informant's Tips in Illinois vs. Gates," 4 Northern Illinois University Law Review 179-202, 1983. Lake County Assistant States Attorney, Civil Division, 1985-1989. *Member:* Lake County and Illinois State Bar Associations; Illinois Trial Lawyers Association; The Association of Trial Lawyers of America. ***REPORTED CASES:*** County of Lake v. Zenko, 174 Ill. App. 3d 54, 528 NE. 2d 869 (1988); Salvation Army v. Department of Revenue, 170 Ill. App. 3d 336, 524 N.E. 2d 628 (1988); Poeta v. Sheridan Point Shopping Plaza Partnership, 195 Ill. App. 3d 852, 552 N.E. 2d 1248 (1990); Commonwealth Edison Company v. County of Lake, 183 Ill. App. 3d 1060, 540 N.E. 2d 6 (1989); Lake County Board of Review v. Property Tax Appeal Board, 172 Ill. App. 3d 851, 527 N.E. 2d 84 (1988); Kankakee County Board of Review v. Property Tax Appeal Board, 131 Ill. 2d 1, 544 N.E. 2d 762 (1989); Pace Realty Group Inc. v. Property Tax Appeal Board, 306 Ill. App. 3d 718, 713 N.E. 2nd 1249 (1999). ***PRACTICE AREAS:*** Personal Injury; Medical Malpractice; Aviation Liability. ***Email:*** joe@baizlaw.com

---

BETH GREENBERG PRAGER, born Fort Leonard Wood, Missouri, September 21, 1960; admitted to bar, 1986, Illinois and U.S. District Court, Northern District of Illinois. *Education:* University of Michigan (B.S.E., cum laude, 1982); University of Illinois (J.D., magna cum laude, 1986). Member, 1984-1986 and Notes and Comments Editor, 1985-1986, University of Illinois Law Review. Author, Note, "Are Applicants For Section 8 Housing "Entitled" To The Benefits," 3 University of Illinois Law Review 757, 1985. Legal Writing Instructor, De Paul College of Law, 1990. *Member:* Illinois State Bar Association. ***PRACTICE AREAS:*** Personal Injury; Medical Malpractice; Aviation Liability. ***Email:*** beth@baizlaw.com

BRIAN J. LEWIS, born Chicago, Illinois, November 13, 1971; admitted to bar, 1997, Illinois and U.S. District Court, Northern District of Illinois. *Education:* University of Michigan (B.A., 1994); University of Illinois (J.D., 1997). Member, Moot Court Invitational Team and Moot Court Board, 1996-1997. *Member:* Chicago, Lake County and Illinois State Bar Associations; Illinois Trial Lawyers Association (Member, Board of Advocates); The Association of Trial Lawyers of America. ***LANGUAGES:*** Spanish. ***PRACTICE AREAS:*** Personal Injury; Medical Malpractice; Aviation Liability. ***Email:*** brian@baizlaw.com

EMALFARB, SWAN & BAIN

440 CENTRAL AVENUE
HIGHLAND PARK, ILLINOIS 60035
Telephone: 847-432-6900
Fax: 847-432-8950

Construction Law, Mechanics Liens, Construction Defects, Bankruptcy, Creditor Rights, Real Estate Law, Zoning Law, Contracts.

MEMBERS OF FIRM

HAL A. EMALFARB, born Chicago, Illinois, July 2, 1952; admitted to bar, 1977, Illinois and U.S. District Court, Northern District of Illinois, U.S. Court of Appeals, 7th Circuit and U.S. Supreme Court. *Education:* University of Iowa (B.A., 1974); Loyola University (J.D., 1977). Author: Mechanic's Lien summaries for National Association of Credit Management Manual of Commercial Law; several chapters in Matthew Bender's Construction Litigation Treating Illinois Construction Law, McGraw-Hill, 1989. Highland Park City Councilman. Founder and General Counsel Network 50, Inc. Seminars: "Designing a National Receivable Recovery Management System for the State Subcontractor and Supplier," 1990-1991. *Member:* Chicago, Illinois State, American and International Bar Associations; Illinois Land Surveyor Association. ***PRACTICE AREAS:*** Construction Law. ***Email:*** hal@esb-law.com

PETER G. SWAN, born Park Forest, Illinois, January 20, 1959; admitted to bar, 1984, Illinois. *Education:* University of Illinois (B.A., 1981); Loyola University (J.D., 1983). Author: various authorships, Construction Law, Matthew Bender Publications; "Evidence in America," Michic Publications. *Member:* Chicago and American Bar Associations. ***PRACTICE AREAS:*** Construction Law; Mechanics Liens; Real Estate. ***Email:*** peter@esb-law.com

(This Listing Continued)

HOWARD M. BAIN, born July 24, 1948; admitted to bar, 1978, Illinois and U.S. District Court, Northern District of Illinois, including Trial Bar; 1978, U.S. Court of Appeals, Seventh Circuit; 1983, U.S. Tax Court. *Education:* University of Illinois (B.S., with honors, 1971); Northern Illinois University (J.D., 1978). Law School and Bar Exam tutor, 1978-1980, 1982, 1985-1987. Author: "The Lien Guide," 1988; Buildings Magazine Article, "Network 50 News." General Counsel to "Network 50 News." Seminars: "Designing a Nationwide Receivable Recovery Management System for the Multi-State Subcontractor and Supplier," 1990-1991. Chair, annual construction attorney's seminar for a panel of National Construction attorneys. *Member:* Chicago, Illinois State and American Bar Associations. ***PRACTICE AREAS:*** Construction Law; Mechanics Liens; Real Estate. ***Email:*** howard@esb-law.com

ASSOCIATES

WILLIAM J. BRODERICK, born July 19, 1970; admitted to bar, 2003, Illinois and U.S. Tax Court. *Education:* Marquette University (B.A., 1992); Chicago-Kent College of Law (J.D., 2003). ***PRACTICE AREAS:*** Construction Law. ***Email:*** william@esb-law.com

MICHAEL L. CUMMINGS, born Inglewood, California, July 31, 1959; admitted to bar, 1995, Illinois and U.S. District Court, Northern District of Illinois; 1997, Wisconsin, U.S. District Court, Central and Southern Districts of Illinois, U.S. District Court, Eastern and Western Districts of Wisconsin and U.S. District Court, Northern and Southern Districts of Indiana. *Education:* Northern Illinois University (B.A., 1984); Chicago-Kent College of Law, Illinois Institute of Technology (J.D., 1995). *Member:* Illinois State Bar Association. ***PRACTICE AREAS:*** Construction Law; Mechanics Liens. ***Email:*** michael@esb-law.com

FRED SHESTOPAL, born 1977; admitted to bar, 2002, Illinois. *Education:* DePaul University (B.A., 1999); John Marshall Law School (J.D., 2003; LL.M., 2003). ***PRACTICE AREAS:*** Construction Law. ***Email:*** fred@esb-law.com

TARA A. MORAN, born LaGrange, Illinois, August 11, 1967; admitted to bar, 1994, Illinois; U.S. District Court, Northern District of Illinois; 1999, U.S. District Court, Central District of Illinois and U.S. Court of Appeals, Seventh Circuit. *Education:* University of Notre Dame (B.A., Philosophy, 1989); John Marshall Law School (J.D., 1994). *Member:* Chicago and Illinois State Bar Associations. ***PRACTICE AREAS:*** Commercial Litigation; Construction Litigation. ***Email:*** tara@esb-law.com

GRANT AND GRANT

PROFESSIONAL CORPORATION
HIGHLAND PARK, ILLINOIS
(See Chicago)

Complex Family Law including Divorce, Dissolution of Marriage, Marital Property Distribution including Retirement Benefits, Spousal Support, Alimony, Maintenance, Child Custody, Visitation, Child Support, Domestic Violence, Paternity, all phases of Matrimonial Litigation, Post Divorce Modification, Premarital Agreements, Separation Agreements, Marital Settlement Agreements, Postmarital Agreements and Appeals.

HARRIS KESSLER & GOLDSTEIN LLC

HIGHLAND PARK, ILLINOIS
(See Chicago)

General Business Practice including Litigation, Secured Lending, Real Estate, Health Care and Estate Planning.

MARC H. HEISLER

HIGHLAND PARK, ILLINOIS
(See Evanston)

Real Estate, Residential Real Estate, Buying and Selling a Home, Commercial Real Estate, Condominium Law and Mortgages. Business, Small Business, Partnership, Family Business and Buying and Selling a Business. Probate and Wills. Adoption Law. Civil Litigation, Chancery Practice, Collections, Personal Injury and Automobile Accidents.

KENNETH A. HENRY

HIGHLAND PARK, ILLINOIS
(See Chicago)

Labor and Employment Law, OSHA, Wage and Hour Matters, Sexual Harassment, Employment Discrimination, Wrongful Termination, Union Management Relations, Real Estate, Commercial Real Estate, Residential Real Estate, Buying and Selling a House or Business, Bankruptcy, Chapter 7, Chapter 11, Corporate and Commercial Law, Litigation, Alternative Dispute Resolution, Mediation.

KLEIN DUB & HOLLEB, LTD.

660 LA SALLE PLACE, SUITE 100
HIGHLAND PARK, ILLINOIS 60035
Telephone: 847-681-9100
Fax: 847-681-1600
Email: info@labor-law.com
URL: http://www.labor-law.com

Chicago, Illinois Office: 222 North La Salle Street, Suite 1900, 60601. Telephone: 312-464-9400.

(This Listing Continued)

KLEIN DUB & HOLLEB, LTD., Highland Park—Continued

Private and Public Sector Labor Law, Employment Law, Employment Discrimination and Affirmative Action. Litigation in State and Federal Courts and before Administrative Agencies in all listed practice areas.

FIRM PROFILE: Klein Dub & Holleb, Ltd. offers full-service, prevention-focused labor and employment law counseling for management clients located throughout the United States. Our experience enables us to emphasize early case evaluation and the delivery of cost-effective representation. When defending employers before administrative agencies or in court, we are pro-active and forceful, consistent with the client's business philosophy. We approach all matters with thorough preparation, diligent follow-through, creativity and unparalleled personal service.

(For Biographical Data on all Personnel, see Professional Biographies at Chicago, Illinois)

LEWINTHAL, SKLAMBERG & ASSOCIATES

HIGHLAND PARK, ILLINOIS

(See Northbrook)

Family Law, Divorce, Child Custody, Child Support, Spousal Support, Domestic Relations, Alimony, Matrimonial, Palimony, Paternity, Premarital Agreements and Separation Agreements, Divorce Tax Considerations.

LAWRENCE A. MANSON

1445 ST. JOHNS AVENUE
HIGHLAND PARK, ILLINOIS 60035-3428
Telephone: 847-681-8734
Fax: 847-681-8735

Health Care Law, Litigation, Corporate Law.

LAWRENCE A. MANSON, born Port Arthur, Texas, November 12, 1948; admitted to bar, 1974, Illinois and U.S. District Court, Northern District of Illinois; 1978, U.S. Court of Appeals, Seventh Circuit. *Education:* Vanderbilt University (B.A., cum laude, 1971); Columbia University (J.D., 1974). Associate Editor, Columbia Journal of Transnational Law, 1973-1974. General Counsel, Office of Federal Law and Regulation, American Hospital Association, 1978-1980. Editor, The Health Lawyer of the American Bar Association's Health Law Forum, 1984-1990. *Member:* American Bar Association (Immediate Past Chair - Health Law Section, 1995-1997; Member, House of Delegates, 1997-1999; Chairman, Governing Committee, Health Law Forum, 1991-1995); Illinois Association of Hospital Attorneys (Director, 1982-1989; President, 1983-1984). ***PRACTICE AREAS:*** Health Care Law; Litigation; Corporate Law.

ALAN BENJAMIN MILLER

1954 FIRST STREET
SUITE 245
HIGHLAND PARK, ILLINOIS 60035
Telephone: 847-721-5050
Fax: 847-831-9902
Email: alanlaw@TheRamp.net
URL: http://www.lawyers.com/alanmiller

Business Litigation, Non-Consumer Collections, Probate Litigation, Insurance Fraud, Securities Fraud, Estate Planning and Administration, Real Estate, Small Business, Personal Injury.

ALAN BENJAMIN MILLER, born Chicago, Illinois, February 25, 1944; admitted to bar, 1968, Illinois and U.S. District Court, Northern District of Illinois including Trial Bar; 1973, U.S. Court of Military Appeals. *Education:* University of Illinois (A.B., 1965); Northwestern University School of Law (J.D., 1968); University of Chicago, Graduate School of Business (M.B.A., 1976). Instructor in Business Law, Evening Division, Northwestern University, 1979. *Member:* Chicago and American Bar Associations. [Capt., JAGC, USAR, 1968-1975]. ***PRACTICE AREAS:*** Business Litigation; Commercial Collections; Probate Litigation; Insurance Fraud; Securities Fraud; Estate Planning and Administration; Real Estate; Small Business; Personal Injury.

SCHIFFMAN & JACOBS, P.C.

660 LASALLE PLACE, SUITE 100
HIGHLAND PARK, ILLINOIS 60035
Telephone: 847-433-4300
Fax: 847-433-4328
Email: msjlaw4334300@aol.com
URL: http://www.sjlawoffices.com

Commercial Litigation, Family Law, Divorce, Real Estate, Franchise Law, Condominium Law, Corporate Transactions, Construction Defects, Child Rights, Criminal Defense, Driving While Intoxicated, Secretary of State License Reinstatements, Appellate Work.

REENA J. SCHIFFMAN, born Chicago, Illinois; admitted to bar, 1985, Illinois and U.S. District Court, Northern District of Illinois. *Education:* University of Southern California (B.A., 1981); John Marshall Law School, Chicago (J.D., 1984). *Member:* Chicago and Lake County Bar Associations. ***PRACTICE AREAS:*** Family Law; Traffic Violations; Criminal Law; Adoption Law; State Government Law; Divorce. ***Email:*** rjslaw4334300@aol.com

MICHAEL S. JACOBS, born Chicago, Illinois, August 12, 1967; admitted to bar, 1992, Illinois and U.S. District Court, Northern District of Illinois. *Education:* University of Wisconsin-Madison (B.A., 1989); John Marshall Law School, Chicago (J.D., 1992). *Member:* Chicago and Illinois State Bar Associations. ***PRACTICE AREAS:*** Real Estate Law; Condominium Law; Corporate Transactions; Franchise Law. ***Email:*** msjlaw4334300@aol.com

OF COUNSEL

C. COREY S. BERMAN, born Oakland, California, March 11, 1965; admitted to bar, 1990, Illinois; U.S. District Court, Northern District of Illinois and U.S. Court of Appeals, Seventh Circuit. *Education:* Northwestern University (B.M.E., 1986); Indiana University at Bloomington (J.D., 1990). Order of the Barristers. *Member:* Chicago Bar Association (Member, Trial Techniques and Entertainment Committee). ***PRACTICE AREAS:*** Commercial Litigation; Construction Defects; Civil Litigation. ***Email:*** cwcsb1@sbcglobal.net

LAW OFFICES OF DAVID M. SHULTS

HIGHLAND PARK, ILLINOIS

(See Northbrook)

Commercial Law, Civil Litigation, Real Estate, and Family Law.

WEIL & ASSOCIATES

HIGHLAND PARK, ILLINOIS

(See Northbrook)

Family Law, Divorce, Collaborative Law, Adoptions, Child Custody, Child Support, Divorce, Domestic Violence, Premarital Agreements, Spousal Support.

THE CHAWLA GROUP, LTD.

15 SPINNING WHEEL ROAD
SUITE 126
HINSDALE, ILLINOIS 60521
Telephone: 630-325-5557
Fax: 630-325-6666
URL: http://www.chawlagroup.com

Entertainment Law, Corporate Law, Civil Practice, Domestic Relations, Personal Injury, Medical Malpractice.

MEMBERS OF FIRM

TARRAN PAUL S. CHAWLA, born Bangkok, Thailand, April 3, 1966; admitted to bar, 1991, Illinois. *Education:* University of Illinois (B.A., 1988); Washington University (J.D., 1991). *Member:* American, Asian American, Chicago and Illinois State Bar Associations. ***PRACTICE AREAS:*** Entertainment Law; Corporate Law; Civil Practice; Domestic Relations; Personal Injury; Medical Malpractice.

CRAIG CARNELL CUNNINGHAM, born St. Louis, Missouri, October 29, 1965; admitted to bar, 1994, Illinois. *Education:* University of Southern California (B.A., cum laude, 1990); University of Chicago (J.D., 1993). *Member:* Chicago and American Bar Associations. ***PRACTICE AREAS:*** Litigation.

ANDREW B. SPIEGEL, born 1949; admitted to bar, 1974, Illinois. *Education:* University of Illinois (B.A.); Loyola University (J.D., 1974). ***PRACTICE AREAS:*** Taxation Law; Federal Practice; Litigation.

RICHARD L. HIRSH & ASSOCIATES, P.C.

15 SPINNING WHEEL ROAD
SUITE 128
HINSDALE, ILLINOIS 60521
Telephone: 630-655-2600
Fax: 630-655-2636
URL: http://www.bankruptcy-dupage.com
URL: http://www.hirshlawfirm.net

Bankruptcy, Personal Bankruptcy, Debtor and Creditor, Foreclosures and Buy-Sell Agreements.

RICHARD L. HIRSH, born 1951; admitted to bar, 1976, Illinois; 1980, U.S. District Court, District Court of Illinois; 1984, U.S. District Court, District Trial Bar. *Education:* State University of New York at Stony Brook (B.A.); Illinois Institute of Technology, Chicago-Kent College of Law (J.D., with Honors). ***PRACTICE AREAS:*** Bankruptcy; Personal Bankruptcy; Debtor and Creditor; Foreclosures; Buy-Sell Agreements. ***Email:*** richala@sbcglobal.net

ARNSTEIN & LEHR LLP

2800 WEST HIGGINS ROAD, SUITE 425
HOFFMAN ESTATES, ILLINOIS 60195-5224
Telephone: 847-843-2900
Fax: 847-843-3355
Email: mail@arnstein.com
URL: http://www.arnstein.com

Chicago, Illinois Office: Suite 1200, 120 South Riverside Plaza, 60606-3910. Telephone: 312-876-7100. Fax: 312-876-0288. Internet: mail@arnstein.com.

Boca Raton, Florida Office: 2424 North Federal Highway, Suite 462, 33431. Telephone: 561-322-6900. Fax: 561-322-6940.

Miami, Florida Office: Miami Center, 201 South Biscayne Boulevard, Fourth Floor, 33131. Telephone: 305-374-3330. Fax: 305-374-4744.

Tampa, Florida Office: 300 South Hyde Park Avenue, Suite 180, 33606. Telephone: 813-259-9964. Fax: 813-259-9724.

(This Listing Continued)

West Palm Beach, Florida Office: 515 North Flagler Drive, Suite 600, 33401-4323. Telephone: 561-833-9800. Fax: 561-655-5551.
Milwaukee, Wisconsin Office: 7161 North Port Washington Road, 53217. Telephone: 414-351-2440. Fax: 414-352-6901.

General Practice.

MEMBERS OF FIRM

J. WILLIAM BRAITHWAITE, admitted to bar, 1956, Illinois, Connecticut and U.S. District Court, Northern District of Illinois; 1960, U.S. Court of Appeals, 7th Circuit. *Education:* University of Santo Tomas, Manila and University of Connecticut (B.A., 1950); Columbia University (J.D., 1955). ***PRACTICE AREAS:*** Municipal and Land Use Law; Estate Planning; General Civil Practice; Real Estate (Property) Law. ***Email:*** jwbraithwaite@arnstein.com

LAWRENCE E. GRELLE, admitted to bar, 1968, Illinois. *Education:* Arizona State University and Northwestern University (B.S., 1965); University of Illinois (J.D., 1968). (Also at Chicago Office). ***PRACTICE AREAS:*** Business Law; Real Estate (Property); Estate Planning. ***Email:*** legrelle@arnstein.com

NANCY S. HARBOTTLE, admitted to bar, 1987, Illinois and Massachusetts. *Education:* DePauw University; Northern Illinois University, DeKalb (B.A., magna cum Laude, 1984); Chicago-Kent College of Law; Illinois Institute of Technology (J.D., 1987). ***PRACTICE AREAS:*** Local Government and Land Use; Real Estate; Estate Planning. ***Email:*** nsharbottle@arnstein.com

(For Complete Biographical data on all Personnel, see Chicago, Illinois Professional Biographies).

DZIEZAK LAW FIRM, P.C.

2300 NORTH BARRINGTON ROAD, SUITE 400
HOFFMAN ESTATES, ILLINOIS 60195
Telephone: 847-490-5370
Fax: 847-490-5378
Email: jdziezak@dziezak-law.com

Intellectual Property Law, including Patent, Trademark, Trade Secret, and Copyright Law, Licensing, and Unfair Competition.

JUDIE D. DZIEZAK, admitted to bar, 1994, Illinois and U.S. District Court, Northern District of Illinois; registered to practice before U.S. Patent and Trademark Office and the Canadian Patent Office. *Education:* Marian College (B.S., Chemistry & Biology, 1977); Purdue University (M.S., Food Science, 1980); Loyola University (J.D., 1994). Iota Sigma Pi; Kappa Gamma Pi; Phi Tau Sigma. Recipient: Williams Fellowship for Legal Writing; Loyola's Leadership and Service Award; American Jurisprudence Awards for Moot Court, Legal Writing and Advanced Legal Bibliography: National Institutes of Health Fellowship (Pharmacology). Recipient, Writing Awards, American Society of Business Press Editors (National and Chicago Chapters). Formerly, Chemist, Morton Chemical Co., 1981; Scientist, The Quaker Oats Company, 1981-1985. Technical Editor/Writer with an international scientific publication, 1985-1991. Author, Undergraduate Honors Thesis: "Electrophoretic analysis of alcohol dehydrogenase isozymes in C56Blk and DBA Mouse Strains." Graduate Thesis: "Stabilization of chromatographically isolated and purified anthocyanins (plant pigments) by complexation with flavonols." Author: articles, *Intellectual Property Litigation, Food Technology, Prepared Foods,* "Encyclopedia of Food Science, Food Technology and Nutrition," Academic Press Ltd., 1994 and 2003 editions and *Research Communications in Chemical Pathology and Pharmacology.* Certified Arbitrator, 18th Judicial Circuit, DuPage County, 1997-1998. *Member:* Chicago, Illinois State and American (Member: Intellectual Property Law Section, Chemical Practice and Biotechnology Committees) Bar Associations; American Intellectual Property Law Association (Member, Chemical Practice Committee); American Chemical Society; Institute of Food Technologists (Professional Member); American Association of University Women (Member, 1980-1985; Board of Directors and Chair, Legislative Committee, 1984-1985). ***PRACTICE AREAS:*** Intellectual Property; Patents; Trademarks; Trade Secrets; Copyrights; Licensing; Unfair Competition. ***Email:*** jdziezak@dziezak-law.com

LAW OFFICES OF CARYL JACOBS GABE & ASSOCIATES, INC.

HOFFMAN ESTATES, ILLINOIS

(See South Barrington)

Family, Divorce, Paternity, Mediation, Child Custody, Child Support, Matrimonial Law, Domestic Relations, Orders of Protection, Prenuptial Agreements, Adoptions, and Injunctions.

KLEST LAW FIRM

HOFFMAN ESTATES, ILLINOIS

(See Schaumburg)

Personal Injury, Medical Malpractice, Products Liability, Legal Malpractice, Construction Accidents, Airplane Crash Litigation, Insurance Bad Faith, Automobile Accidents, Motorcycle Accidents, Birth Trauma, Sexual Abuse, Child Abuse and Neglect, Slip and Fall, Wrongful Death, Dog Bites, Railroad Accidents and Injuries, Automobile Products, Liability and Drug and Medical Device Litigation, Trial Practice.

ROBINSON, PLUYMERT, PIERCEY, MACDONALD & AMATO, LTD

Established in 1989

2300 BARRINGTON ROAD, SUITE 220
HOFFMAN ESTATES, ILLINOIS 60195-2034
Telephone: 847-310-0025
Fax: 847-310-0054
Email: info@rppmalaw.com
URL: http://www.rppmalaw.com

Des Plaines Office: 733 Lee Street, Suite 100, 60016-6405. Telephone: 847-298-5030. Fax: 847-298-0169.

Business Law, Corporate Law, Banking Law, Estate Planning, Charitable Planning, Probate and Trust Administration, Family Law, Commercial Real Estate, Residential Real Estate, Condominium Law, Church Law, Non Profit Law, Litigation, Mediation and Arbitration.

MEMBERS OF FIRM

RUSSEL G. ROBINSON, born Minneapolis, Minnesota, October 17, 1957; admitted to bar, 1982, North Dakota; 1989, Illinois. *Education:* St. Paul Bible College (B.A., 1979); University of North Dakota (J.D., 1982). *Member:* Illinois State Bar Association. ***PRACTICE AREAS:*** Estate Planning; Business Law; Corporate Law. ***Email:*** rrobinson@rppmalaw.com

JAMES H. PLUYMERT, born Chicago, Illinois, April 19, 1956; admitted to bar, 1981, Illinois and U.S. District Court, Northern District of Illinois. *Education:* Calvin College (B.A., Political Science, 1978); DePaul University (J.D., 1981). *Member:* Lake County Bar Association. ***PRACTICE AREAS:*** Civil Litigation; Church Law; Nonprofit and Charitable Organizations; Mediation; Arbitration. ***Email:*** jpluymert@rppmalaw.com

RODNEY H. PIERCEY, born January 21, 1946; admitted to bar, 1973, Illinois. *Education:* Indiana University (B.A., Philosophy, 1969); Indiana University School of Law (J.D., 1973). ***PRACTICE AREAS:*** Estate Planning; Charitable Planning. ***Email:*** rpiercey@rppmalaw.com

GREGORY A. MACDONALD, born Evanston, Illinois, October 29, 1958; admitted to bar, 1984, Illinois. *Education:* University of Illinois (B.S., 1980); John Marshall Law School (J.D., 1984). *Member:* Chicago Bar Association. ***PRACTICE AREAS:*** Estate Planning; Probate; Trust Administration; Corporate Law; Real Estate. ***Email:*** gmacdonald@rppmalaw.com

BRENT L. AMATO, born Kansas City, Missouri, December 30, 1949; admitted to bar, 1975, Illinois. *Education:* University of Michigan (B.A., 1971); John Marshall Law School (J.D., 1975). ***PRACTICE AREAS:*** Business Law; Corporate Law; Commercial Law; Construction Law; Corporate Governance. ***Email:*** bamato@rppmalaw.com

RICHMOND A. PAYNE, born Jackson, Mississippi, May 15, 1962; admitted to bar, 1987, Missouri and U.S. District Court, Eastern District of Missouri; 1988, Illinois; 2000, U.S. District Court, Northern and Southern Districts of Illinois. *Education:* Westminster College (B.A., Political Science, 1984); St. Louis University (J.D., 1987). Articles Editor, St. Louis University Law Journal, 1986-1987. *Member:* Illinois State Bar Association; The Missouri Bar. ***PRACTICE AREAS:*** Banking Law; Financial Institutions Law; Corporate and Business Planning; Mergers, Acquisitions and Divestitures; Creditors Rights; Commercial Law; Media Law; Business Law; Business Organization; Secured Lending. ***Email:*** rpayne@rppmalaw.com

RONALD J. SENECHALLE, born December 27, 1958; admitted to bar, 1986, Illinois. *Education:* University of Illinois (B.A., 1981); Loyola University (J.D., 1986). ***PRACTICE AREAS:*** Residential Real Estate; Commercial Real Estate; Zoning Law; Land Use; Real Estate Development; Condominium Law. ***Email:*** rsenechalle@rppmalaw.com

ARIANO, HARDY, NYULI, JOHNSON, RICHMOND & GOETTEL, P.C.

Established in 1981

13300 ROUTE 47
P.O. BOX 487
HUNTLEY, ILLINOIS 60142
Telephone: 847-669-5020
Email: aah@attorneys-illinois.com
URL: http://www.attorneys-illinois.com

Geneva Office: 13 S. 7th Street, 60134. Telephone: 630-208-0674.
Elgin, Illinois: 474 Summit Street. Telephone: 847-695-2400. Telecopy: 847-695-8397.

General Civil and Criminal Practice in all Courts. Banking, Probate, Real Estate, Corporation, Federal Taxation, Transactional, Employment, Family, Personal Injury, Collections, Creditor Bankruptcy, Foreclosures, Landlord and Tenant Law, Workers Compensation Law and Mediation.

RALPH C. HARDY, born LaGrange, Georgia, June 25, 1943; admitted to bar, 1968, Illinois and Missouri. *Education:* Beloit College (B.A., 1965); Washington University (J.D., 1968). Note Editor, Washington University Law Quarterly, 1967-1968. Law Clerk to Judge Henry S. Wise, U.S. District Court, Eastern Division of Illinois, 1968-1970. *Member:* Elgin, Kane County, McHenry County, Illinois State and American Bar Associations; The Missouri Bar. ***TRANSACTIONS:*** Merger of State Bank of Huntley and Suburban Bancorp, Inc. for State Bank of Huntley, 1993 and Sale of State Bank of Pawpaw to NBE Bancshares, Inc. 1996. ***PRACTICE AREAS:*** Real Estate Law; Trusts and Estates; Wills; Elder Law; Probate Law; Corporate Law. ***Email:*** rch@attorneys-illinois.com

SCOTT G. RICHMOND, born Boston, Massachusetts, April 17, 1968; admitted to bar, 1995, Illinois and U.S. District Court, Northern District of Illinois. *Education:* Michigan State University (B.A., Accounting, 1990); Chicago-Kent College of Law (J.D., high

(This Listing Continued)

ARIANO, HARDY, NYULI, JOHNSON, RICHMOND & GOETTEL, P.C., Huntley—Continued

honors, 1995). Order of the Coif. Moot Court (Vice-President,1994-1995). *Member:* Chicago, Kane County (Co-Chair, New Lawyers Division), Illinois State and American Bar Associations; Illinois Trial Lawyers Association. ***PRACTICE AREAS:*** General Civil Litigation; Corporate Law; Business Law; Contracts; Personal Injury; Zoning, Planning and Land Use; Worker's Compensation. ***Email:*** sgr@attorneys-illinois.com

(For Complete Biographical Data on all Personnel, see Professional Biographies at Elgin, Illinois)

LAW OFFICE OF MICHAEL J. FLECK, P.C.

10771 ROUTE 47
P.O. BOX 992
HUNTLEY, ILLINOIS 60142
Telephone: 847-669-2558
Fax: 847-669-2564
Email: michaelfleck@earthlink.net
URL: http://www.flecklawoffice.com

Real Estate, Estate Planning, Estate Administration, Wills, Probate Law, Trusts and Estates, Corporate Law, Business Law, General Practice.

MICHAEL J. FLECK, born Hinsdale, Illinois, February 4, 1965; admitted to bar, 1995, Illinois and U.S. District Court, Northern District of Illinois. *Education:* University of Illinois (B.S., 1987); Chicago-Kent College of Law, Illinois Institute of Technology (J.D., 1995). Order of the Coif. *Member:* McHenry County (Vice President, 2004—), Seventh Circuit and Illinois State Bar Associations.

MILITELLO, ZANCK & COEN, P.C.

HUNTLEY, ILLINOIS

(See Crystal Lake)

Trial Practice in all State and Federal Courts, Banking, Business Acquisitions, Corporation and Partnership, Employment Law, Environmental, Insurance Defense, Probate and Guardianship, Real Estate, Wills and Trusts and Zoning and Land Planning.

ANGELINA & PALMER, P.C.

A Professional Corporation
Established in 1990
1626 W. COLONIAL PARKWAY
INVERNESS, ILLINOIS 60067-4724
Telephone: 847-359-0010
Fax: 847-359-0011
Email: info@apclaw.com
URL: http://www.apclaw.com

Family Law, including Divorce, Child Support, Child Custody, Alimony/Maintenance, Division of Property and Debt, Parentage, Grandparents' Rights, Visitation, Post Decree/Post Divorce Disputes, Separation, Uncontested Divorce, Divorce Settlements. Commercial Real Estate and Residential Real Estate Transactions, including Contract Drafting and Negotiation, Real Estate Closings, Real Estate and Construction Litigation, Zoning, Commercial and Residential Landlord/Tenant, Evictions, Commercial Lease Negotiation and Drafting. Business Law, including Formation of Corporations, Limited Liability Companies (LLC), and Limited Liability Partnerships (LLP). Advice for Business Legal Problems and Business Litigation. Employment Law, Executive Employment Agreements, Buy-Sell Agreements, Operating Agreements, Partnership Agreements, Asset Sales, Sales of Business.Estate Planning, including Wills, Trusts, Power of Attorney, Health Care Power of Attorney, Living Will, Special Needs Trust, Tax Avoidance Trust, Irrevocable Trust, Codicil, Probate.Criminal Law, including Criminal Defense, Felony, including Unlawful Use of Weapons, Battery, Theft, Burglary, Assault, DUI, Driving Under the Influence, Drug Possession, Drug Manufacture, Misdemeanor, Traffic, Ordinance Violation. Personal Injury for Serious Injuries and Wrongful Death.

FIRM PROFILE: Angelina & Palmer, P.C. (http://www.aplawyers.com) is a full-service firm geared to the needs of individuals and businesses in the northwest suburban Chicago area. Our firm has old-fashioned private service coupled with the high technology processes of the 21st Century. We aim for client satisfaction in everything we do. Since our firm has the ability to handle a wide variety of legal matters, we want to forge long-term relationships with our clients. We encourage our clients to call any time with their questions and concerns. We never charge for an initial consultation--the first call and meeting are always free of charge. We aren't bogged down with a lot of staff and high overhead. Attorneys will work on your matter--and a lawyer will call you back to discuss your question. Our goal is to return all calls and emails by the next business day. Our service separates us from our competition. There may be better lawyers--but no better service than ours.

DIRECTORS

MICHAEL J. ANGELINA, born Arlington Heights, Illinois, January 19, 1965; admitted to bar, 1990, Illinois. *Education:* University of Notre Dame (B.B.A., 1987); Illinois Institute of Technology, Kent College of Law (J.D., 1990). *Member:* Chicago Bar Association; Illinois Real Estate Lawyers Association. ***PRACTICE AREAS:*** Real Estate (60%); Estate Planning (30%); Corporate Law (10%). ***Email:*** mja@apclaw.com

RAIFORD D. PALMER, born Fort Benning, Georgia, August 16, 1969; admitted to bar, 1994, Illinois and U.S. District Court, Northern District of Illinois; 2003, U.S. District Court, Northern District of Illinois Trial Bar. *Education:* University of Illinois, Urbana-Champaign (B.A., 1991); Loyola University, Chicago (J.D., 1994). Former Coach, Lewis University Mock Trial Team. Created fast food business during college ("Sea Dog"). Student Ambassador, Soviet Union, 1987. Former Associate Attorney, Momkus Ozog & McCluskey LLC., 1994-1998. Certified Arbitrator, DuPage County Mandatory Arbitration Program. *Member:* Illinois State Bar Association, Northwest Suburban Bar Association. ***PRACTICE AREAS:*** Civil Litigation (20%); Family Law (40%); Business Law (40%). ***Email:*** rdp@apclaw.com

ATTORNEYS

KYLE F. FRACCARO, born Akron, Ohio, January 26, 1973; admitted to bar, 2004, Illinois. *Education:* Beloit College (B.A., 1995); Chicago-Kent College of Law, Illinois Institute of Technology (J.D., 2003). ***PRACTICE AREAS:*** Criminal Defense (50%); Divorce (30%); Litigation (20%). ***Email:*** kff@apclaw.com

JASON M. CHMIELEWSKI, born Hobart, Indiana, November 2, 1974; admitted to bar, 2002, Illinois. *Education:* Clemson University (B.A., 1998); De Paul University (J.D., 2002). *Member:* Chicago Bar Association. ***PRACTICE AREAS:*** Real Estate (65%); Probate (15%); Corporate Law (20%). ***Email:*** jmc@apclaw.com

ASHLEY HARRIS COLES, born Lawton, OK; admitted to bar, 2004, Illinois; 2004, U.S. District Court, Northern District of Illinois. *Education:* Oklahoma State University (B.A., 2001); University of Oklahoma (J.D., 2004). *Member:* Illinois State Bar Association, Chicago Bar Association. ***PRACTICE AREAS:*** Family Law (50%); Business Law (20%); Estate Planning (30%). ***Email:*** ahc@apclaw.com

LESLIE ANNE SLOMKA, born Palos Heights, Illinois, October 13, 1978; admitted to bar, 2004, Illinois and U.S. District Court, Northern District of Illinois. *Education:* University of St. Thomas (B.A., 2000); DePaul College of Law (J.D., 2003). *Member:* Chicago Bar Association; Illinois State Bar Association. ***PRACTICE AREAS:*** Real Estate (100%). ***Email:*** las@aplawyers.com

REPRESENTATIVE CLIENTS: Stucchi USA, Inc.; Espresso Best, Inc.; Car Boutique, Inc.; Responsive Network Systems, Inc.

EDDIE CARPENTER

305 WEST STATE STREET
P.O. BOX 871
JACKSONVILLE, ILLINOIS 62651
Telephone: 217-245-7015
FAX: 217-243-7725

Real Estate, Probate Law. Collections, Trusts, General Civil Practice.

EDDIE CARPENTER, born Jacksonville, Illinois, April 15, 1948; admitted to bar, 1980, Illinois. *Education:* Illinois College (B.A.,1970); University of Iowa (M.A., 1973); University of Illinois (J.D., 1980). City Attorney, 1982-1993. *Member:* Morgan County, Illinois State and American Bar Associations. ***PRACTICE AREAS:*** Real Estate Law; Probate Law; Collections; Trusts; General Civil Practice.

REPRESENTATIVE CLIENTS: Franklin Bank; Village of Franklin; Jacksonville Airport Authority; Jacksonville Savings Bank.; Passavant Area Hospital.

RAMMELKAMP BRADNEY, P.C.

Established in 1895
232 WEST STATE STREET
P.O. BOX 550
JACKSONVILLE, ILLINOIS 62651
Telephone: 217-245-6177
Fax: 217-243-7322
Email: info@rblawyers.net
URL: http://www.rammelkamplaw.com

Springfield, Illinois Office: 520 East Allen Street. 62703. Telephone: 217-522-6000. Fax: 217-522-6018.

Winchester, Illinois Office: 46 South Hill Street, 66666. Telephone: 217-742-5215. Fax: 217-742-3537.

General Practice. Insurance, Municipal, Probate, Estate Planning, Trusts, Tax, Real Estate and Corporation Law.

LARRY D. KUSTER, born Kewanee, Illinois, July 27, 1947; admitted to bar, 1973, Illinois. *Education:* Augustana College (B.A., 1969); University of Iowa (J.D., with honors, 1973). Master (Barrister), Lincoln-Douglas Inn of Court. *Member:* Federation of Defense and Corporate Counsel. (Also Practicing at Springfield Office). ***PRACTICE AREAS:*** Insurance; Education Law; Construction Law. ***Email:*** lkuster@rblawyers.net

FORREST G. KEATON, admitted to bar, 1977, Illinois and Iowa. *Education:* Bradley University (B.A., summa cum laude, 1974); University of Illinois (J.D., cum laude, 1977). Member, Illinois Supreme Court Character and Fitness Committee, 2001—. *Member:* Illinois Association of Defense Trial Counsel. [Judge Advocate, U.S. Air Force, 1977-1982; Col. USAFR, 1982—]. ***PRACTICE AREAS:*** Insurance; Utility Law; Commercial Law; Corporate Law. ***Email:*** fkeaton@rblawyers.net

BARBARA FRITSCHE, admitted to bar, 1977, Illinois. *Education:* Valparaiso University; Ohio State University; Cleveland State University (B.A., 1972); Marshall College of Law; DePaul University (J.D., 1977). Fullbright Scholar, 2002. Assistant Attorney General, 1977-1982. Chief Civil Rights Division, 1980-1981. Deputy Chief, General Law, 1981-1982. Illinois Supreme Court Committee on Character and Fitness, 1991-2000. ***PRACTICE AREAS:*** Insurance; Labor and Employment; Civil Rights; Education Law. ***Email:*** bfritsche@rblawyers.net

NANCY LINDSAY, admitted to bar, 1983, Illinois. *Education:* Illinois College (B.A., summa cum laude, 1979); Sangamon State University (M.A., 1980); St. Louis University

(This Listing Continued)

(J.D., 1983). Phi Beta Kappa. Instructor, Business Law, Illinois College, 1987—. Member, Workers' Compensation Section Council, 1999—. ***PRACTICE AREAS:*** Workers Compensation; Labor and Employment; Trial Practice. ***Email:*** nlindsay@rblawyers.net

MARIA M. GONZALEZ, admitted to bar, 1987, Illinois; 1991, U.S. District Court, Central District of Illinois. *Education:* Millikin University (B.A., summa cum laude, 1984); University of Illinois (J.D., 1987). Phi Alpha Delta. James Millikin Scholar. Member, Illinois Supreme Court Screening Committee for Capital Litigation Trial Bar, 2001—. ***PRACTICE AREAS:*** Family Law; Children; Employee Benefits; General Practice; Litigation. ***Email:*** mgonzalez@rblawyers.net

RICHARD R. FREEMAN, admitted to bar, 1988, Illinois. *Education:* Bradley University (B.S., magna cum laude, 1985); Washington University (J.D., 1988). ***PRACTICE AREAS:*** Municipal Law; Real Estate Law; Trusts and Estates; Corporate Law; Estate Planning. ***Email:*** rfreeman@rblawyers.net

H. ALLEN YOW, admitted to bar, 1989, Illinois; 1990, Missouri. *Education:* Wabash College (A.B., 1986); University of Aberdeen, Scotland; Southern Illinois University School of Law (J.D., 1989). Recipient, Lawyers Publishing Company Award for the Study of Family Law. Student Articles Editor, Southern Illinois University Law Journal. (Also Practicing at the Winchester Office). ***PRACTICE AREAS:*** Family Law; Municipal Law; Litigation; Education Law; Insurance. ***Email:*** ayow@rblawyers.net

GARY L. CLINE, admitted to bar, 1981, Illinois. *Education:* University of Illinois (B.A., 1977; J.D., 1981). *Member:* Illinois State Bar Association; Illinois Trial Lawyers Association; Lincoln-Douglas Inn of Court. ***PRACTICE AREAS:*** Workers Compensation; Litigation; Trial Practice. ***Email:*** gcline@rblawyers.net

BRADLEY W. WILSON, admitted to bar, 1998, Illinois. *Education:* University of Illinois (B.S., Agriculture, 1989); Chicago-Kent College of Law (J.D., 1998). Order of the Coif. Member, Christian Legal Society. ***PRACTICE AREAS:*** Corporate Law; Real Estate; Trusts and Estates; Taxation. ***Email:*** bwilson@rblawyers.net

AMY L. JACKSON, admitted to bar, 1993, Missouri; 1994, Illinois. *Education:* Illinois Wesleyan University (B.A., History, 1990); St. Louis University School of Law (J.D., 1993). ***PRACTICE AREAS:*** Insurance Defense; Environmental Law; Landlord and Tenant Law; Collections. ***Email:*** ajackson@rblawyers.net

ANTHONY J. DELGIORNO, admitted to bar, 2002, Illinois; 2003, U.S. Tax Court. *Education:* Illinois College (B.A., magna cum laude, Political Science, History, International Studies, 1999); American University Washington College of Law (J.D., 2002). Law and Government Society President. Member, NAACP, 2003—. ***PRACTICE AREAS:*** Taxation; Tax Litigation; Tax Planning; Estate Planning; Probate; Municipal Law; Government Law; Litigation; Business Law. ***Email:*** tdelgiorno@rblawyers.net

OF COUNSEL

ROBERT E. BRADNEY, admitted to bar, 1950, Illinois. *Education:* Illinois College (B.A., 1947); Harvard Law School (LL.B., 1950). *Member:* Academy of Lawyers (Inaugural Class). ***Email:*** rbradney@rblawyers.net

RICHARD E. MANN, admitted to bar, 1948, Illinois. *Education:* University of Illinois (A.B., 1946; J.D., 1947). States Attorney, Scott County, Illinois, 1948-1960. Circuit Judge, Seventh Circuit, Illinois, 1980-1988. (Resident, Winchester Office). ***Email:*** rmann@rblawyers.net

REPRESENTATIVE CLIENTS: American International Adjustment Co.; American States/Safeco; Atlanta Casualty Company; Auto Owners Insurance; Bank of Bluffs; Barry Community Unit School District; CIGNA; City of Waverly; Coon Run Drainage and Levee District; Country Mutual Insurance Co.; EMI Manufacturing; Federated Insurance; Franklin Community Unit School District No. 1; Fulton County Community Unit School District (Cuba); Fulton Area Vocational System; General Casualty of Wisconsin; Griggsville School District No. 4; Grinnell Mutual Insurance; Illinois Road Contractors; Illinois State Police Merit Board; Illinois State Historical Society; ILL-MO Welding Products; Infinity Insurance; Jacksonville School District 117; Meredosia Community Bank; Meredosia-Chambersburg Community School District; Milwaukee Insurance; Morgan Scott Regional Superintendent of Schools; National American Insurance Co.; National Union Insurance; Pekin Insurance Co.; Pleasant Hill Community Unit School District; Premier Bank of Jacksonville; Scott-Morgan Community Unit School District No. 2; Selective Insurance Co.; Shelby Electric Cooperative, Inc.; Shelby Insurance; Soyland Power Cooperative, Inc.; State Farm Fire and Casualty Co.; State Auto of Ohio; State Farm Mutual Auto Insurance Co.; St. Paul Fire and Casualty Company; Town of Naples; Travelers Insurance Co.; Two Rivers Vocational Education System; Union Automobile Insurance Co.; Village of Bluffs; Village of Chapin; Village of Meredosia; Village of Murrayville; Village of Woodson; Village of South Jacksonville; Virginia Community Unit School District; Waverly Community School District; Willow Creek Drainage and Levee District.

JULIE HARPER

JERSEYVILLE, ILLINOIS

(See Alton)

Traffic, DWI, Bankruptcy, Estate Planning, Real Estate, Contracts, Wills, Probate, Trusts, General Practice, Criminal, Buying and Selling Homes, Guardianships, Automobile Accidents, Adoptions.

RICHARD L. BERDELLE, JR., P.C.

JOLIET, ILLINOIS

(See Chicago)

Medical Malpracticing including: Surgical and Physician Malpractice, Obstetric Malpractice, Hospital Malpractice, Birth Defects and Birth Trauma. Plaintiff Personal Injury including: Automobile Accidents, Trucking Accidents, Motorcycle Accidents, Head Injuries, Catastrophic Accidents and Wrongful Death.

BRENNER, FORD, MONROE & SCOTT, LTD.

JOLIET, ILLINOIS

(See Chicago)

Insurance Defense, Personal Injury, Medical Malpractice, Construction Law, Product Liability, Uninsured/Underinsured Motorist Arbitrations and Litigation of Contested Coverage Issues.

CHUCK BRETZ & ASSOCIATES, P.C.

58 NORTH CHICAGO STREET, 2ND FLOOR
JOLIET, ILLINOIS 60432
Telephone: 815-740-1545
Fax: 815-740-1546
Email: cbretz@bretzlawoffice.com
URL: http://www.bretzlawoffice.com

Trial Practice, Criminal Defense, Family Law, and Complex Personal Injury Law. DUI/DWI, White Collar Crime, Felonies, Murder, Homicide, Misdemeanors, Traffic, Suspended License, Drug Crimes, Juvenile Law, Divorce, Contested and Uncontested Divorce, Child Custody, Child Support, Visitation, Post Decree, Orders of Protection, Domestic Violence, Automobile Accidents, Wrongful Death and Medical Malpractice.

FIRM PROFILE: Spanish Language Support Available.

CHARLES L. BRETZ, born McPherson, Kansas, November 7, 1957; admitted to bar, 1982, Illinois. *Education:* Trinity College (B.A., summa cum laude, 1979); University of Illinois (J.D., 1982). Phi Delta Phi. Assistant State's Attorney, 1982-1986 and First Assistant, 1992-1994, Will County. *Member:* Will County, Illinois State and American Bar Associations; Illinois Trial Lawyers Association. ***Email:*** cbretz@bretzlawoffice.com

COSMO J. TEDONE, born Manchester, Connecticut, December 13, 1966; admitted to bar, 1999, Illinois, Connecticut and U.S. District Court, Northern District of Illinois including Trial Bar. *Education:* Rochester Institute of Technology (B.S., 1990); Thomas Cooley Law School (J.D., cum laude, 1999). Member, Law Review, Thomas Cooley Law School. Assistant Public Defender, Will County, 2001-2004. *Member:* Will County Bar Association. ***PRACTICE AREAS:*** Criminal; Personal Injury. ***Email:*** ctedone@bretzlawoffice.com

ERIN W. O'SULLIVAN, born Olympia Fields, Illinois, November 27, 1978; admitted to bar, 2004, Illinois. *Education:* Lewis University (B.A., with highest honors, 2000); DePaul University (J.D., 2004). Delta Epsilon Sigma National Catholic Honors Society; Phi Alpha Theta National History Honors Society. Member: Lewis University Scholars Academy. ***PRACTICE AREAS:*** Family Law; Divorce; Child Support; Child Custody; Post Divorce Modification; Personal Injury. ***Email:*** eosullivan@bretzlawoffice.com

BRUMUND, JACOBS, HAMMEL & DAVIDSON, LLC

Established in 1960
EXECUTIVE CENTRE, SUITE 200
58 EAST CLINTON STREET
JOLIET, ILLINOIS 60432-4193
Telephone: 815-723-0628
FAX: 815-723-1371
Email: garykdavidson@aol.com
URL: http://www.lawyers.com/brumund&jacobs

The firm has a general practice with individual lawyers specializing in specific areas of the law, including Commercial and Residential Real Estate, Land Use and Zoning, Condominium and Homeowners Association Law, Contract Law, Personal Injury, Commercial Litigation, Corporate Law, Criminal Law, Aggravated Traffic, including DUI, Collection Law, Probate and Estate Planning, Family, Divorce, Adoptions and Juvenile Law, Landlord and Tenant Law.

FIRM PROFILE: The Law Firm of Brumund, Jacobs, Hammel and Davidson, LLC traces its roots to one of Will County's oldest law firms. Its attorneys collectively, have nearly one hundred years of experience in the practice of law. Our Law Firm prides itself in the success we achieve in meeting client goals through conflict resolution strategies which seek to maximize our clients return on their investment in us. The firm services clients throughout Will, Dupage, Kendall, Grundy, Kankakee and surrounding counties.

MEMBERS OF FIRM

PAUL F. BRUMUND (1916-2000)

MYLES L. JACOBS, born New York, New York, 1932; admitted to bar, 1960, New York, Illinois and U.S. District Court, Northern District of Illinois. *Education:* Dartmouth College (A.B., 1954); New York University School of Law (J.D., 1959). Panel Member, Will County Pro-Bono program. Co-Author, Will-Grundy Association of Realtors approved Real Estate Contract and its subsequent revision. Editor, Illinois Institute of Continuing Legal Education reference manual "Residential Real Estate." Lecturer, Section Council's annual Real Estate Update Seminars for the past ten years. Program coordinator, Real Estate Update Seminars. Frequent contributor, Real Estate Section Council's Newsletter. Member: Task Force on Unauthorized Practice of Law; Voluntary Fee Arbitration Committee and Judicial Evaluation Committee, Illinois State Bar Association. *Member:* Will County (President; Member and Past Chair, Real Estate Law Committee, 1985-2004), Illinois State (Member, Real Estate Section Council, 1993—; Chairman, 2001-2002; Co-Chairman, Continuing Legal Education Committee; Member, Assembly) Bar Associations. ***PRACTICE AREAS:*** Residential Real Estate; Commercial Real Estate; Land Development; Condominium Law; Zoning Law; Leases and Tax Appeals; Corporate Law; Estate Planning. ***Email:*** jacobs1404@aol.com

(This Listing Continued)

BRUMUND, JACOBS, HAMMEL & DAVIDSON, LLC, Joliet—Continued

JAMES R. BRUMUND, born Joliet, Illinois, 1948; admitted to bar, 1979, Illinois and U.S. District Court, Northern District of Illinois. *Education:* Augustana College (B.A., 1970); Northern Illinois University of Law (J.D., 1979). Former Special Assistant Attorney General, Department of Transportation of Illinois, 1979-1980. Former Attorney, Joliet Junior College. Former Attorney, Villages of Rockdale and Manhattan. Former Prosecutor for City Joliet. Founding Member and Past President, Joliet Park Foundation, Inc. *Member:* Will County (Member, Pro Bono Program), Illinois State and American Bar Associations; Illinois Trial Lawyers Association. ***PRACTICE AREAS:*** Personal Injury; Family Law; Eminent Domain; Aggravated Traffic Defense; Insurance Defense; Landlord and Tenant Law. ***Email:*** jrbatlaw@aol.com

TED P. HAMMEL, born Joliet, Illinois, 1963; admitted to bar, 1989, Illinois and U.S. District Court, Northern District of Illinois. *Education:* Marquette University (B.S., 1985); John Marshall Law School (J.D., 1989). Formerly with Hammel Law Offices, P.C., 1989-2004. *Member:* Will County and Illinois State Bar Associations. ***PRACTICE AREAS:*** Construction Law; Title and Foreclosure law; Zoning Law; Residential Real Estate; Commercial Real Estate; Criminal Law; Aggravated Traffic Defense; DUI; Landlord and Tenant Law. ***Email:*** tedhammel@comcast.net

GARY K. DAVIDSON, born Aurora, Illinois, 1973; admitted to bar, 1999, Illinois, Wisconsin and U.S. District Court, Northern District of Illinois. *Education:* Illinois College (BA, 1995); Northern Illinois University College of Law (JD, 1998); Universitiet Libre De Bruxelles, Brussels, Belgium, Law and Institutions of European Union (1997); Ritsumeikan University, Kyoto, Japan, Japanese Language Studies (1994). Fellow, Office of the Governor of the State of Illinois, 1993. Legislative Liaison, Illinois, State Representative Tom Ryder, 1994-1995. Board of Directors, West Central Illinois Council on Foreign Affairs, 1993-1995. Law Clerk to The Chief Judge of the Sixteenth Judicial Circuit, Illinois, 1996-1999. Member, Federalist Society, Lawyers Division. Deputy Court Administrator, Sixteenth Judicial Circuit, DeKalb, Kane and Kendall Counties, Illinois, 1999-2000. Member, Mahoney, Silverman and Cross, Ltd, 2000-2004. *Member:* Will County, Kane County, Illinois State (Member, Bar Activities and Services Committee) and American (Member, House of Delegates) Bar Associations; State Bar of Wisconsin. ***PRACTICE AREAS:*** Commercial Real Estate; Residential Real Estate; Land Development Law; Land Use and Zoning Law; Collections Law; Landlord and Tenant Law; Government Law; Corporate Law. ***Email:*** garykdavidson@aol.com

REPRESENTATIVE CLIENTS: Allstate Insurance Co.; Chicago Title Insurance Co.; Continental Casualty Co.; L.J. Crowther Roofing; Darryl Dupre, Inc.; Dempsey Chrysler Plymouth, Jeep Eagle; Firemen's Fund American Insurance Co.; First American Title Company; First Financial Security; GAB Business Services; General Casualty Company of America; Gould Excavating & Trucking, Inc.; Government Employees Insurance Co.; Indemnity Insurance Co. of N.A.; Fred Kehl & Associates; Krause Enterprises Limited; Motorist Insurance Companies; ProTown Properties; Remax Realty of Joliet; Royal-Liverpool Group; Standard Mutual Insurance Co.; Ticor Title Insurance Co.; Timberview Development Corp.; Will-Grundy Association of Realtors; Crestlake Holdings, LLC; DTD Investments, LLC; The Tomich Group.
REFERENCE: First Midwest Bank/Illinois.

LAW OFFICES OF SUSAN G. CASTAGNOLI, P.C.

JOLIET, ILLINOIS

(See Naperville)

Bankruptcy, Commercial Bankruptcy, Consumer Bankruptcy, Foreclosures, Debt Management, Family, Divorce, Divorce Planning, Premarital Agreements, Custody, Adoptions, Child Support, Real Estate, Financial Planning, Wills and Probate, Estate Planning, Trusts and Estates, Equine Law.

CETINA & JACQUES, P.C.

JOLIET, ILLINOIS

(See Oakbrook Terrace)

Personal Injury, Personal Injury Appeals, Personal Injury Arbitration, Personal Injury Defense, Personal Injury Mediation, Plaintiffs Personal Injury, Medical Malpractice, Nursing Home Abuse and Neglect, Driving While Intoxicated, Drug Crimes, Traffic Violations.

CHICAGO INTERNET ATTORNEYS

JOLIET, ILLINOIS

(See Chicago)

Personal Injury, Spinal Cord Injury, Automobile Accidents, Wrongful Death, Products Liability, Medical Malpractice, Corporate, Business, Real Estate, Criminal and Civil Litigation.

MARY L. COLLINS

JOLIET, ILLINOIS

(See Downers Grove)

Social Security Disability, Real Estate, Wills, Medicare, Medicaid, Elder Law.

JOHN J. CORBETT & ASSOCIATES

JOLIET, ILLINOIS

(See Chicago)

Personal Injury, Medical Malpractice, Products Liability, Negligence, Construction Accidents, Wrongful Death and Automobile Accidents, Nursing Home Litigation, Airplane Crash Litigation, Maritime Personal Injury, Railroad Accidents, Police Misconduct, Sexual Harassment.

CORBOY & DEMETRIO, P.C.

JOLIET, ILLINOIS

(See Chicago)

Plaintiff's Personal Injury and Wrongful Death Litigation, with an emphasis on Commercial and General Aviation, Professional and Hospital Negligence, FELA, Product Liability, Premises, Construction, Vehicular, Railroad and Commercial Litigation.

DAVIS, DYSTRUP, HOSTER & JAROT, P.C.

Established in 1977

181 NORTH HAMMES AVENUE
JOLIET, ILLINOIS 60435
Telephone: 815-744-6550
Fax: 815-744-4518
Email: ddho@davis-dystrup-law.com
URL: http://www.davis-dystrop-law.com

Administrative Law, Banking Law, Business Law. Civil Litigation before all courts, departments and administrative agencies. Commercial Law, Construction Law, Corporations, Criminal Defense, Employee Benefits and Executive Compensation, Employment Law, Environmental Law; Estates, Trusts and Financial Planning, Mergers and Acquisitions, Partnership Law, Real Estate Law, Rezoning and Land Use, Taxation Law.

FIRM PROFILE: Davis, Dystrup, Hoster, Osterberger and Jarot, P.C., was founded by L. Park Davis and Andrew C. Dystrup in 1977. Serving clients throughout Will and surrounding counties. The firm has a general practice with a focus on business, estate planning and real estate.

L. PARK DAVIS, born Springfield, Illinois, May 14, 1939; admitted to bar, 1965, Illinois; 1966, U.S. District Court, Northern District of Illinois; 1971, U.S. Supreme Court. *Education:* Illinois College (B.A., 1961); University of Illinois (J.D., 1964). *Member:* Chicago, Will County, Illinois State and American Bar Associations. (Retired). ***PRACTICE AREAS:*** Business Law. ***Email:*** lpd@davis-dystrup-law.com

ANDREW C. DYSTRUP, born Joliet, Illinois, June 27, 1945; admitted to bar, 1970, Illinois. *Education:* University of Illinois (B.S., 1967; J.D., 1970). Member, Attorney's Title Guaranty Fund, Inc., 1976—. Board of Directors and Chairman, Attorney's Title Guaranty Fund, Inc. *Member:* Will County, Illinois State and American Bar Associations. ***PRACTICE AREAS:*** Real Estate Law; Zoning Law. ***Email:*** acd@davis-dystrup-law.com

SCOTT HOSTER, born Joliet, Illinois, October 17, 1960; admitted to bar, 1985, Illinois; U.S. District Court, Northern District of Illinois including Trial Bar; U.S. Court of Appeals, Seventh Circuit. *Education:* Bob Jones University (B.A., 1982); DePaul University (J.D., 1985). Assistant States Attorney, Will County, 1985-1987. *Member:* Chicago, Will County and Illinois State Bar Associations; Appellate Lawyers Association. ***REPORTED CASES:*** Suburban Federal v. Weber 697 N.E. 2d 302; People v. CJR 647 N.E. 2d 1035; Petition of Gacki 634 N.E. 2d 1281; Orloff v. Petak 587 N.E. 2d 37; Knowles v. Westbrook Builders 544 N.E. 2d 121; Perivdiotis v. Pierson 521 N.E. 2d 254; Gretencord v. Cryder, 784 N.E.2d 384, In re CDT Landfill, U.S. Environmental Board of Appeals, 11 E.A.D.—. ***PRACTICE AREAS:*** Civil Litigation; Criminal Litigation. ***Email:*** smh@davis-dystrup-law.com

EDWARD J. JAROT, JR., born Joliet, Illinois, September 6, 1971; admitted to bar, 1996, Illinois. *Education:* Indiana State University (B.A., 1993); Loyola University, Chicago (J.D., 1996); John Marshall Law School (LL.M. with honors, 2001). *Member:* Chicago, Will County, Illinois State and American Bar Associations. ***PRACTICE AREAS:*** Estate Planning; Estate Administration; Taxation; Employee Benefits. ***Email:*** ejj@davis-dystrup-law.com

REPRESENTATIVE CLIENTS: UIC, Inc.; A & D Erectors; Tordai Brother Farms; RBK, LLC.; Knowles Printing Corp.; Chuck Dzak Motors, Inc.; Enterprise Land Title, LTD.; National City Bank; Johansen & Anderson, Inc.; Wille Brothers Co.; McLuckie Oil Co., Inc.; Ruettiger, Tonelli & Associates, Inc.; Jason Mechanical; WCFL-FM; Attorney's Title Guaranty Fund, Inc.; Corsetti Structural Steel; Rho Chemical Co.; Elliott Electric, Inc.; Commercial Electronics; Foxford Development, LLC.; Lyons Lumber; Gassensmith & Associates; Bailey's Carpets; Mechanical & Industrial Steel; Sharp Homes; PARADOX Properties; Ford Motor Credit Company; Doede Nursery; GALARZA Motorsport; DQM, Inc.; Founder's Bank; Oakhurst Builders; Camelot Homes; Pan-Tech, Inc., MPG Industries.
REFERENCES: First Midwest Bank of Joliet; Harris Bank of Joliet.

DOUGLAS G. DEBOER

54 NORTH OTTAWA STREET, SUITE 260
JOLIET, ILLINOIS 60432
Telephone: 815-724-1807
Fax: 815-727-5458
Email: dtdeboer@comcast.net
URL: http://www.deboerlaw.com

Criminal Defense, Driving While Intoxicated, Homicide, Drug Crimes, Felonies, Juvenile Law, Misdemeanors, Sexual Assault, Traffic Violations, Personal Injury, Auto Accidents, Wrongful Death.

DOUGLAS G. DEBOER, born Cicero, Illinois, May 20, 1962; admitted to bar, 1987, Illinois. *Education:* North Central College (B.A., 1984); IIT Chicago-Kent College of Law (J.D., 1987). First Assistant State's Attorney, 1994-2000 and Assistant State's Attorney, Will County State's Attorney's Office, Joliet, Illinois. *Member:* Will County and Illinois State Bar Associations. ***REPORTED CASES:*** People v. Lynn. 585 N.E. 2d 1204, 223 Ill. App. 3d 688, 166 Ill. Dec. 182 (3rd Dist., 1992); People v. Elston, 584 N.E. 2d 531, 223 Ill. App. 3d 186 165 Ill. Dec. 352 (3rd Dist., 1991); People v. Robinson, 579 N.E. 2d 579, 219 Ill. App. 3d 235, 161 Ill. Dec. 908 (3rd Dist., 1991); People v. Robinson, 589 N.E. 2d 1093, 226 Ill. App. 3d 649, 168 Ill. Dec. 693 (3rd Dist., 1992); People v. Mitchell, 572 N.E. 2d 1229,

(This Listing Continued)

213 Ill. App. 3d 1078, 157 Ill. Dec. 765 (3rd Dist., 1991). **PRACTICE AREAS:** Criminal Defense.

DYKEMA GOSSETT PLLC

Established in 1926

111 NORTH OTTAWA STREET

JOLIET, ILLINOIS 60432

Telephone: 815-727-4511

Facsimile: 815-727-1586

URL: http://www.dykema.com

Ann Arbor, Michigan Office: 2723 South State Street, Suite 400, 48104. Telephone: 734-214-7660. Fax: 734-214-7696.

Aurora, Illinois Office: 2 Hankes Road. Telephone: 630-844-2200. Facsimile: 630-844-2277.

Bloomfield Hills, Michigan Office: 39577 Woodward Avenue, Suite 300, 48304-2820. Telephone: 248-203-0700. Fax: 248-203-0763.

Chicago, Illinois Office: 10 South Wacker Drive, Suite 2300. Telephone: 312-876-1700. Fax: 312-876-1155.

Detroit, Michigan Office: 400 Renaissance Center, 48243-1668. Telephone: 313-568-6800. Fax: 313-568-6545.

Grand Rapids, Michigan Office: Suite 700, 300 Ottawa Avenue, N.W., 49503-2306. Telephone: 616-776-7500. Fax: 616-776-7573.

Lansing, Michigan Office: 124 W. Allegan Street, Suite 800, 48933-1742. Telephone: 517-374-9100. Fax: 517-374-9191.

Lisle, Illinois Office: 4200 Commerce Court, Suite 300. Telephone: 630-245-0400. Facsimile: 630-245-0140.

Los Angeles, California Office: 333 South Grand Avenue, Suite 2100, 90071. Telephone: 213-457-1800. Fax: 213-457-1850.

Washington, D.C. Office: Franklin Square, Suite 300 West, 1300 I Street, N.W., 20005-3353. Telephone: 202-906-8600. Fax: 202-906-8669.

Antitrust and Trade Regulation, Automotive, Banking and Financial Services, Bankruptcy, Biotechnology and Life Sciences, Casino Gaming, Class Action Defense, Computer and Software Law, Construction, Consumer Financial Services, Corporate Finance, E-Commerce, Emerging Business and Technology, Employee Benefits, Entertainment and Sports, Environmental Law, Family Law, Franchise Law and Regulation, Government Contracts, Government Policy and Practice, HealthCare, Indian Law, Insurance, Intellectual Property, International Law, Labor and Employment, Litigation and Dispute Resolution, Mergers and Acquisitions, Products Liability Defense, Public Finance, Real Estate, Retail Law, Securities, Taxation and Estates, Trade Associations.

FIRM PROFILE: Dykema Gossett PLLC represents the interests of domestic and foreign-based companies and institutions on a broad array of matters. Our diversified practice and Midwest work ethic have long made Dykema the choice of Fortune 100 companies, privately-held businesses, entrepreneurial enterprises and emerging businesses. With offices in Michigan, California, Illinois and Washington, D.C., Dykema has expanded beyond its original Michigan roots to become one of the largest firms in the United States. Our recent merger with Rooks Pitts in Illinois, effective April 1, 2004, is a significant milestone in our continued growth in the Midwest. We are proud to be recognized by area businesses as a corporate leader, and our broad-based litigation practice is routinely chosen by clients and peers alike as one of the best in the nation. Dykema is equally well known for our experienced government relations specialists, whose experience at the national, state and local levels is unrivalled. From manufacturers and automotive suppliers to financial institutions, from patent and trademark disputes to complex class action defense, from startups to large multinational corporations, our clients repeatedly look to Dykema to help them navigate through an ever-increasing stream of complex litigation and changing business environments.

MEMBERS OF FIRM

ROBERT R. GORBOLD, born St. Charles, Illinois, May 30, 1952; admitted to bar, 1979, Illinois. *Education:* Wheaton College (B.A., 1974); John Marshall Law School (J.D., with distinction, 1979). *Member:* Will County Bar Association. **PRACTICE AREAS:** Commercial Litigation; Complex Litigation; Medical Malpractice Defense; Insurance Coverage; Products Liability. ***Email:*** rgorbold@dykema.com

JAMES D. GRUMLEY, born Chicago, Illinois, May 30, 1950; admitted to bar, 1976, Illinois and U.S. District Court, Northern District of Illinois, including Trial Bar. *Education:* University of Notre Dame (B.B.A., 1972); Loyola University (J.D., 1976). **PRACTICE AREAS:** Insurance Defense Litigation; Products Liability. ***Email:*** jgrumley@dykema.com

RICHARD J. KAVANAGH, born Brooklyn, New York, June 9, 1944; admitted to bar, 1974, Illinois; 1979, U.S. Tax Court; 2000, U.S. Supreme Court. *Education:* Georgetown University (B.S.F.S., 1965); University of Chicago (M.B.A., 1970); DePaul University (M.S., Taxation, with distinction, 1978); Loyola University (J.D., cum laude, 1974). Beta Alpha Psi. Chairman, Plan Commission, Village of New Lenox, 2003—. Member, 1974-1983 and 1985-1997 and President, 1981-1983 and 1987-1997, Board of Education, Valley View Community School District 365-U. Alternate Delegate, Republican National Convention, 1988 and 2000. [First Lieutenant, U.S. Army, 1968-1970]. **PRACTICE AREAS:** Zoning, Planning and Land Use; Real Estate; Probate; Trusts and Estates; Municipal Law. ***Email:*** rkavanagh@dykema.com

BRYAN W. KOPMAN, born Harvey, Illinois, April 14, 1970; admitted to bar, 1995, Illinois. *Education:* Northwestern University (B.A., 1992); University of Notre Dame (J.D., 1995). *Member:* Will County Bar Association. **PRACTICE AREAS:** Insurance Defense; Medical Negligence; Commercial Litigation; Construction Litigation. ***Email:*** bkopman@dykema.com

OF COUNSEL

WILLIAM T. KAPLAN, born Chicago, Illinois, June 7, 1940; admitted to bar, 1966, Illinois and Missouri. *Education:* Grinnell College (B.A., 1962); New York University (M.B.A., 1963); Washington University (J.D., 1966). Staff Member and Editor, Business Advice and Financial Planning Newsletter, Illinois State Bar Association. *Member:* Illinois State Bar Association (Council Member, Corporation, Securities & Business Law Section). **PRACTICE AREAS:** Corporate Law (34%); Commercial Real Estate (34%); Estate Planning (32%). ***Email:*** wkaplan@dykema.com

GEORGE J. VOSICKY, born Chicago, Illinois, June 23, 1955; admitted to bar, 1979, Illinois and U.S. District Court, Northern District of Illinois. *Education:* University of Notre Dame (B.A., cum laude, 1976); DePaul University (J.D., 1979). **PRACTICE AREAS:** Litigation; Business; Commercial; Construction; Real Estate; Chancery and Equity; Commercial Real Estate; Leases and Leasing; Mortgages. ***Email:*** gvosicky@dykema.com

ASSOCIATES

MATTHEW W. CAMPBELL, born Elyria, Ohio, October 13, 1965; admitted to bar, 1993, Illinois. *Education:* Illinois State University (B.S., 1988); Thomas M. Cooley Law School (J.D., 1992). **PRACTICE AREAS:** Municipal Law; Probate; Real Estate. ***Email:*** mcampbell@dykema.com

PAMELA DAVIS GORCOWSKI, born New Orleans, Louisiana, February 6, 1956; admitted to bar, 1981, Illinois; U.S. Supreme Court; U.S. Court of Appeals, Seventh Circuit. *Education:* MacMurray College (B.A., summa cum laude, 1978); University of Illinois (J.D., 1981). *Member:* Will County Bar Association; Appellate Lawyers Association. **PRACTICE AREAS:** Appellate Practice (70%, 75). ***Email:*** pgorcowski@dykema.com

PAUL J. RICHARDS, born August 11, 1970; admitted to bar, 1995, Illinois. *Education:* Loyola University (B.A., 1992); Valparaiso University School of Law (J.D., 1995). **PRACTICE AREAS:** Corporate Law; Insurance Coverage; Real Estate; Commercial Litigation. ***Email:*** prichards@dykema.com

FABRIZIO, HANSON, PEYLA & KAWINSKI, P.C.

Established in 1966

TWO RIALTO SQUARE

116 N. CHICAGO STREET, SUITE 301

JOLIET, ILLINOIS 60432

Telephone: 815-727-5445

Fax: 815-727-1224

Email: mhanson-fhandp@attglobal.net

General Civil and Trial Practice. Insurance Defense, Personal Injury, Automobile Accidents, Products Liability, Wrongful Death, Construction Accidents, Workers Compensation, Corporate, Business, Probate, Real Estate, Health Care and Construction Litigation.

FIRM PROFILE: Fabrizio, Hanson, Peyla & Kawinski, P.C. was founded by George O'Brien in 1966. Serving clients for 40 years throughout Will, Kankakee, Grundy, DuPage and Kane Counties, the firm has a general practice with an emphasis on Civil Litigation.

GEORGE M. O'BRIEN (1917-1986)

JAMES R. FABRIZIO, born Chicago, Illinois, November 21, 1949; admitted to bar, 1976, Illinois and U.S. District Court, Northern District of Illinois. *Education:* University of Illinois (B.A., 1971); Chicago-Kent College of Law (J.D., with high honors, 1976). Notes and Comments Editor, Chicago-Kent Law Review, 1976. Instructor, Legal Writing, Chicago-Kent College of Law, 1975-1976. Law Clerk To Hon. Howard C. Ryan, Illinois Supreme Court, 1976-1977. *Member:* Will County, Illinois State and American Bar Associations; Illinois Defense Counsel; Defense Research and Trial Lawyers Association. **PRACTICE AREAS:** Insurance Defense; Personal Injury Litigation; Insurance Coverage Litigation. ***Email:*** jfabrizio-fhandp@attglobal.net

MARK E. HANSON, born Joliet, Illinois, April 16, 1952; admitted to bar, 1977, Illinois and U.S. District Court, Northern District of Illinois. *Education:* University of Notre Dame (B.A., cum laude, 1974); Loyola University (J.D., 1977). *Member:* Will County and Illinois State Bar Associations. **PRACTICE AREAS:** Real Estate; Health Care Law; Civil Litigation. ***Email:*** mhanson-fhandp@attglobal.net

GREGORY L. PEYLA, born Joliet, Illinois, June 18, 1953; admitted to bar, 1980, Illinois and U.S. District Court, Northern District of Illinois. *Education:* University of London and Tulane University (B.A., 1975); Tulane University (J.D., 1978). *Member:* Will County, Illinois State and American Bar Associations; American Judicature Society. **PRACTICE AREAS:** Workmen's Compensation; Probate; Civil Law. ***Email:*** gpeyla-fhandp@attglobal.net

MR. MARK KAWINSKI, born Oaklawn, Illinois, June 15, 1964; admitted to bar, 1991, Illinois. *Education:* University of Oklahoma (B.A., 1986); Illinois Institute of Technology, Chicago Kent College of Law (J.D., 1991). *Member:* Chicago, DuPage County, Kane County and Illinois State Bar Associations; Illinois Trial Lawyers Association. **PRACTICE AREAS:** Insurance Defense; Real Estate; Civil Litigation. ***Email:*** mkawinski-fhandp@attglobal.net

MR. JEREMIAH K. O'CONNOR, born Evergreen Park, Illinois, May 27, 1969; admitted to bar, 1994, Illinois and U.S. District Court, Northern District of Illinois. *Education:* Illinois State University (B.A., 1991); Northern Illinois University (J.D., 1994). **PRACTICE AREAS:** Insurance Defense; Civil Litigation.

OF COUNSEL

LAWRENCE E. MORRISSEY, born Joliet, Illinois, July 19, 1936; admitted to bar, 1964, Illinois. *Education:* University of Illinois (B.S., 1958); John Marshall Law School (LL.B., 1964). (Also practicing individually at 135 South La Salle Street, Chicago). **PRACTICE AREAS:** Trusts and Probate; Real Estate; Sports Law; Criminal Defense; Civil Litigation.

(This Listing Continued)

FABRIZIO, HANSON, PEYLA & KAWINSKI, P.C., Joliet—Continued

REPRESENTATIVE CLIENTS: *Insurance Clients:* Cincinnati Insurance Co.; The General Casualty Company of Wisconsin; Gallagher-Bassett Ins.; Wausau Insurance Co.; State Farm Insurance; Continental National American Group; Westfield Insurance Co.; Kemper Insurance; Jewel Cos.; Liberty Mutual Insurance Co.; U.S.F. & G. Insurance; Lumbermans Mutual Insurance Co.; Capitol Indemnity; TIG Insurance; Albertsons. *General Clients:* An Association of Franciscan Sisters of the Sacred Heart; Saint Joseph Medical Center; SaCor Systems; Illinois Securities Co.; Wilhelmi Beverage Co.; Brakur Custom Cabinetry Co.; Provena Saint Joseph Medical Center; Provena United Samaritans Medical Center; Provena Saint Joseph Hospital (Elgin); Provena Health Corporation; Senior Services Center of Will Country.
REFERENCE: The First National Bank of Joliet.

MICHAEL W. FLEMING
ATTORNEY AT LAW

JOLIET, ILLINOIS

(See Elmhurst)

Criminal Defense Litigation, Felonies, Misdemeanors, DUI and Juvenile Law.

MICHAEL N. GORCOWSKI, P.C.

Established in 1993

8 WEST CASS STREET
JOLIET, ILLINOIS 60432
Telephone: 815-740-5900
Fax: 815-740-5903
Email: mngorcow@sbcglobal.net
URL: http://www.gorcowskilaw.com

Landlord and Tennant Law, Family, Divorce, Child Custody, Child Support, Adoption, Traffic Violations, Driving While Intoxicated, Misdemeanors, Wills, Estate Planning, Commercial Real Estate, Residential Real Estate, Real Estate Closings, Personal Injury, Automobile Accidents, Workers Compensation.

FIRM PROFILE: This is a general practice firm. Our mission is to provide outstanding counsel, assuring that our clients and their legal matters are treated promptly, personally and professionally.

MICHAEL N. GORCOWSKI, born Harvey, Illinois, July 6, 1956; admitted to bar, 1981, Illinois; 1986, U.S. District Court, Northern District of Illinois. *Education:* University of Illinois (B.A., 1977; J.D., 1981). Edmund J. James Scholar. *Member:* Will County (Chairman, Law Day Committee, 1991-1993) and Illinois State Bar Associations. ***LANGUAGES:*** Spanish.

Language: Spanish.

REPRESENTATIVE CLIENT: The Colonies Apartments, Steger, Illinois; Foundation Housing, LLC; Three Brothers Enterprises, Inc.

LAW OFFICES OF
GRAY & IDRIS, P.C.

54 N. OTTAWA STREET, SUITE B80
JOLIET, ILLINOIS 60640
Telephone: 815-723-4543
Fax: 815-723-4922
URL: http://www.grayidrislaw.com

General Practice.

SARA J. GRAY, born 1974; admitted to bar, 2000, Illinois. *Education:* Northern Illinois University (B.A., 1997; J.D., 2000).

KAYODE R. IDRIS, born 1963; admitted to bar, 2000, Illinois. *Education:* University of Illinois (B.A., 1988); Northern Illinois University (J.D., 2000).

MICHAEL W. HANSEN, P.C.

Established in 2001

320 WATERSTONE WAY, SUITE 200
JOLIET, ILLINOIS 60431
Telephone: 815-744-9500
Fax: 815-744-4515
Email: mikehansen@core.com

Corporate, Real Estate, Estate Planning, Zoning, Planning and Land Use, Gaming Law, Closely Held Business Law, Limited Liability, Buying and Selling Businesses, Business Formation, Joint Ventures.

MICHAEL W. HANSEN, born Burlington, Iowa, 1951; admitted to bar, 1976, Illinois and Iowa. *Education:* University of Notre Dame (B.B.A., with honors, 1973); Drake University (J.D., 1975). Delta Theta Phi. Partner, Herschbach, Tracy, Johnson, Bertani and Wilson, 1976-1994. General Counsel, Chief Legal Officer, Vice-President and Secretary for Empress Entertainment, Inc., Empress Casino Joliet Corporation and Empress Casino Hammond Corporation, 1994-1999. Chief Executive Officer, Joliet Professional Baseball Club, LLC, 2001—. Founding Organizer and Director, First Community Bank of Joliet, 2004—. *Member:* Chicago, Will County, Illinois State (Chairman, Corporation and Securities Law Section Council 1989-1990; Member, Secretary of State's Corporate Acts Advisory Committee, 1990-1994, 2001-2005) and Iowa State Bar Associations. ***PRACTICE AREAS:*** Corporate Law; Real Estate; Estate Planning; Zoning, Planning and Land Use; Gaming Law; Closely Held Business Law; Limited Liability Company Law; Buying and Selling of Businesses; Business Formation; Joint Ventures. ***Email:*** mikehansen@core.com

COLLEEN M. WENGLER, born 1965; admitted to bar, 2001, Illinois. *Education:* University of Illinois (B.S., 1997); DePaul University (J.D., 2000). *Member:* Will County and Illinois State Bar Associations. ***PRACTICE AREAS:*** Business Litigation; Estate Planning; Real Estate.

(This Listing Continued)

HINSHAW & CULBERTSON LLP

Hinshaw & Culbertson LLP is an Illinois registered limited liability partnership that has elected to be governed by the Illinois Uniform Partnership Act (1997)

Established in 1934

57 NORTH OTTAWA STREET
SUITE 314
JOLIET, ILLINOIS 60432
Telephone: 815-726-5910
Facsimile: 815-726-0353
Telex: 880248
Email: kfox@hinshawlaw.com
URL: http://www.hinshawlaw.com

Other Office Locations: Chicago, Illinois; Appleton, Wisconsin; Belleville, Illinois; Boston, Massachusetts; Champaign, Illinois; Crystal Lake, Illinois; Edwardsville, Illinois; Fort Lauderdale, Florida; Jacksonville, Florida; Lisle, Illinois; Los Angeles, California; Miami, Florida; Milwaukee, Wisconsin; Minneapolis, Minnesota; New York, New York; Peoria, Illinois; Phoenix, Arizona; Portland, Oregon; Providence, Rhode Island; Rockford, Illinois; St. Louis, Missouri; San Francisco, California; Schererville, Indiana; Springfield, Illinois; Tampa, Florida; Waukegan, Illinois.

Appellate, Banking & Financing, Bankruptcy & Creditors' Rights, Class Action Litigation, Civil Rights Defense, Commercial Litigation, Corporate, Construction Law, Director & Officer Liability, Employee Benefits, Environmental, Fidelity & Surety, General Liability Litigation, Government, Health Care, Insurance Coverage, Insurance and Reinsurance, Labor & Employment, Legal Malpractice, Medical Malpractice, Mergers & Acquisitions, Municipal Liability, Personal Injury Defense, Public Law, Products Liability Litigation, Professional Liability, Regulatory, Real Estate, School Law, Securities, Taxation, Transportation, White Collar Crime and Workers' Compensation Defense.

FIRM PROFILE: Hinshaw & Culbertson LLP is a national AMLaw 200 firm with 425 lawyers in 27 offices coast-to-coast. The firm offers a full-service practice, with an emphasis in commercial and defense litigation, corporate, environmental, employment and construction law, as well as the representation of professionals in their liability and risk management matters.

Hinshaw provides services to a range of clients in financial services, construction, health care, not-for-profit, insurance, legal, manufacturing, real estate, transportation and other industries. Firm clients also include government agencies, municipalities and schools.

Hinshaw was founded in 1934. The firm is headquartered in Chicago, and maintains offices in 12 states: Arizona, California, Florida, Illinois, Indiana, Massachusetts, Minnesota, Missouri, New York, Oregon, Rhode Island and Wisconsin.

PARTNERS

WILLIAM R. CASSIAN, born Evergreen Park, Illinois, October 26, 1969; admitted to bar, 1994, Illinois. *Education:* Illinois State University (B.S., 1991); John Marshall Law School (J.D., 1994). *Member:* Will County Bar Association; Defense Research Institute; Illinois Association of Defense Trial Counsel. ***PRACTICE AREAS:*** Medical Malpractice; General Liability Litigation; Personal Injury Defense; Products Liability Litigation; School Law. ***Email:*** wcassian@hinshawlaw.com

JOHN R. FELTON, born Hartford, Wisconsin, September 1, 1963; admitted to bar, 1990, Illinois; 1991, U.S. District Court, Northern District of Illinois; 1994, U.S. Court of Appeals, Seventh Circuit; 2004, U.S. District Court, Central District of Illinois. *Education:* Carthage College (B.S., 1986); Chicago-Kent College of Law, Illinois Institute of Technology (J.D., 1990). *Member:* Kane County, Will County and Illinois State Bar Associations. [U.S. Army Reserves, 1983-1989]. ***PRACTICE AREAS:*** Insurance Defense; Medical Malpractice. ***Email:*** jfelton@hinshawlaw.com

MICHAEL GAHAN, born Joliet, IL, January 10, 1953; admitted to bar, 1978, Illinois; 1979, U.S. District Court, Northern District of Illinois. *Education:* Lewis University (B.A., 1975); University of Notre Dame (J.D., 1978). *Member:* Will County and Illinois State Bar Associations. ***PRACTICE AREAS:*** Medical Malpractice; Professional Liability Litigation; General Liability Litigation. ***Email:*** mgahan@hinshawlaw.com

SCOTT E. NEMANICH, born Joliet, Illinois, July 29, 1952; admitted to bar, 1978, Illinois. *Education:* Lewis University (B.A., 1974); Northwestern University (J.D., 1977). Phi Alpha Theta. Vice President, Lewis University Alumni Association, 1983-1984; Will County Juvenile Officers Association, 1980; Illinois State Board on Child Abuse and Neglect, 1980-1982. Honorary Chairman, Trinity School Bike-A-Thon, 1983. *Member:* Illinois State Bar Association; Will County Bar Association. ***PRACTICE AREAS:*** School Law; Real Estate Taxation; State and Federal Lobbying; Corporate; Wills; Living Wills. ***Email:*** snemanic@hinshawlaw.com

PETER G. PANNO, born Pontiac, Illinois, October 5, 1954; admitted to bar, 1979, Illinois. *Education:* University of Illinois (B.S., 1976); Loyola University (J.D., 1979). Beta Gamma Sigma; Phi Kappa Phi. *Member:* Will County and Illinois State Bar Associations. ***PRACTICE AREAS:*** Insurance Defense Litigation. ***Email:*** ppanno@hinshawlaw.com

DANIEL P. SLAYDEN, born Alton, Illinois, November 16, 1961; admitted to bar, 1987, Illinois and U.S. District Court, Northern District of Illinois; 1988, U.S. Court of Appeals, Seventh Circuit; 1993, U.S. District Court, Central District of Illinois. *Education:*

(This Listing Continued)

Elmhurst College (B.A., 1984); Southern Illinois University (J.D., 1987). Recipient, American Jurisprudence Second Book Award for Civil Pro. and Advanced Civil Pro. *Member:* Will County and Illinois State Bar Associations. ***PRACTICE AREAS:*** Medical Malpractice; Personal Injury Litigation. ***Email:*** dslayden@hinshawlaw.com

DANIEL J. SOFTCHECK, born Joliet, Illinois, January 23, 1954; admitted to bar, 1984, Illinois including Federal Trial Bar; U.S. District Court, Northern District of Illinois; 1990, U.S. District Court, Central District of Illinois. *Education:* University of Hawaii (B.A., with distinction, 1979); Loyola University (J.D., 1984). Attorney General, State of Illinois, 1987-1991. ***LANGUAGES:*** Russian. ***PRACTICE AREAS:*** Personal Injury; Employment Law. ***Email:*** dsoftshe@hinshawlaw.com

ASSOCIATES

CHARLES A. EGNER, born Chicago, Illinois, May 2, 1968; admitted to bar, 1995, Illinois and U.S. District Court, Northern District of Illinois. *Education:* Bradley University (B.S., summa cum laude, 1991); John Marshall Law School (J.D., cum laude, 1995). Member, John Marshall Law Review. Recipient: West Publishing's Award for Outstanding Achievement in Civil Procedure. *Member:* Illinois State Bar Association. ***PRACTICE AREAS:*** Medical Malpractice; Professional Liability Litigation. ***Email:*** cegner@hinshawlaw.com

MICHAEL J. VINES, born Evergreen Park, Illinois, 1970; admitted to bar, 2003, Illinois. *Education:* Northern Illinois University (B.A., 1998); John Marshall Law School (J.D., 2002). *Member:* Chicago, Will County and Illinois State Bar Associations. ***PRACTICE AREAS:*** Medical Malpractice; Tort Litigation. ***Email:*** mvines@hinshawlaw.com

TAMMY S. WARDEN, born Hinsdale, Illinois, May 31, 1973; admitted to bar, 1998, Illinois and U.S. District Court, Northern District of Illinois; 1999, U.S. District Court, Southern District of Illinois. *Education:* College of St. Francis (B.A., summa cum laude, Political Science, 1995); Loyola University (J.D., 1998). *Member:* Illinois State Bar Association. ***PRACTICE AREAS:*** Medical Malpractice; General Liability Litigation; Products Liability Litigation; Personal Injury Litigation. ***Email:*** twarden@hinshawlaw.com

HUGHES SOCOL PIERS RESNICK & DYM, LTD.

JOLIET, ILLINOIS

(See Chicago)

General Civil and Litigation Practice in all Courts. Insurance and Reinsurance. Personal Injury, Immigration, Civil Rights, Class Actions, Labor and Employment, Commercial, Professional Liability, Litigation.

JUNE, PRODEHL & RENZI, L.L.C.

1861 BLACK ROAD
JOLIET, ILLINOIS 60435
Telephone: 815-725-8000
Fax: 815-725-6126
URL: http://www.jprllc.com
Email: main@jprlaw.net
URL: http://www.lawyers.com/jprllc

General Civil and Trial Practice. Elder Law, Family, Divorce, Child Custody, Real Estate, Tax, Estate Planning, Personal Injury, Automobile Accidents, Criminal.

MEMBERS OF FIRM

DAVID A. JUNE, born Joliet, Illinois, May 27, 1956; admitted to bar, 1981, Illinois. *Education:* Drake University (B.A., cum laude, 1978); University of Iowa (J.D., with high distinction, 1981). *Member:* Will County, Illinois State and American Bar Associations; Association of Trial Lawyers of America. ***PRACTICE AREAS:*** Family Law; Personal Injury Law; Real Estate; Custody; Support; Civil Litigation; Adoption Law; Divorce; Visitation Rights; Spousal Support; Premarital Agreements; Domestic Violence; Automobile Accidents and Injuries. ***Email:*** dajune@jprlaw.net

FORD C. JUNE, III, admitted to bar, 1972, Iowa; 1977, Illinois. *Education:* Monmouth College (A.B., 1969); University of Iowa (J.D., 1972). Faculty Member, Illinois Institute of Continuing Legal Education, Elder Law, 1994—. Member, 1994-1998 and Vice President, 1996-1998, National Academy of Elder Law Attorneys, Illinois Chapter Board of Directors. Member, 1993, 1995—, and Vice President, 2001—, Joliet Township High School, District 204 Board of Education. Member, Board of Directors, Will County Legal Assistance, 1991—. Member, Board of Directors, Prairie State Legal Services, 1991-1996. Co-Editor, "How to Select a Nursing Home and Alternatives to Nursing Home Care ... A Guide," Illinois Department of Aging, 1985. Co-Author, "Manual of Public Interest Lobbying in Illinois, 1978. *Member:* Will County (Member, Probate Committee) and Illinois State (Chair, Elder Law Section Council, 2000—) Bar Associations; National Academy of Elder Law Attorneys. ***PRACTICE AREAS:*** Elder Law; Government; Probate; Real Estate; Long Term Care; Medicare and Medicaid; Guardianship; Estate Planning; Wills; Residential Real Estate; Landlord and Tenant Law. ***Email:*** fcjune@jprlaw.net

STEVEN J. PRODEHL, born September 16, 1953; admitted to bar, 1980, Illinois. *Education:* Lewis University (B.A., 1976); Northern Illinois University (J.D., 1979). ***PRACTICE AREAS:*** Criminal Law; Real Estate Law; Municipal Law; Driving While Intoxicated; Traffic Violations; Misdemeanors; Felonies. ***Email:*** sjprodehl@jprlaw.net

JOHN C. RENZI, born Chicago Heights, Illinois, August 20, 1954; admitted to bar, 1979, Illinois. *Education:* University of Illinois (B.A., with high honors in History, 1976); George Washington University (J.D., 1979). Plainfield Dist. 202 School Bd., 1999—. *Member:* Will County, Illinois State and American Bar Associations. ***PRACTICE AREAS:*** Family Law; Bankruptcy; Real Estate; Personal Injury; Divorce; Child Support; Residential Real Estate; Landlord and Tenant Law. ***Email:*** jcrenzi@jprlaw.net

(This Listing Continued)

MARILYN L. WYSOCKI, born Elgin, Illinois, April 4, 1963; admitted to bar, 1988, Illinois. *Education:* University of Illinois (B.S., 1985); Northern Illinois University (J.D., 1988). *Member:* Will County Bar Association. ***PRACTICE AREAS:*** Probate; Real Estate; Family Law; General Practice. ***Email:*** mlwysocki@jprlaw.net

JENNIFER M. LYNCH, born Rockford, Illinois, May 3, 1973; admitted to bar, 2001, Illinois and U.S. District Court, Northern District of Illinois. *Education:* University of Illinois (B.S.W., with honors, 1995); Chicago-Kent College of Law (J.D., 2001). *Member:* Will County, Illinois State and American Bar Associations; Will County Women's Bar Association; National Academy of Elder Law Attorneys. ***PRACTICE AREAS:*** Elder Law; Probate Administration; Real Estate; General Practice; Adoption Law; Long Term Care; Medicare and Medicaid; Guardianship; Estate Planning; Wills; Probate; Residential Real Estate; Landlord and Tenant Law. ***Email:*** jmlynch@jprlaw.net

KIESLER & BERMAN

57 NORTH OTTAWA STREET
SUITE 210
JOLIET, ILLINOIS 60432
Telephone: 815-723-2755
FAX: 815-723-2763
Email: info@thekillerbees.com
URL: http://www.kieslerberman.com

Chicago Office: 70 West Madison, Suite 4200. Telephone: 312-332-2840. Fax: 312-332-4547.

General Civil Trial and Appellate Practice. Insurance, Construction Litigation, Corporation, Real Estate and Probate Law. Asbestos Litigation, Civil Rights Law, Estate Planning, Insurance Coverage, Insurance Defense Law, Medical Malpractice Law, Police Misconduct, RICO, Surety and Fidelity Bond Law, Tort Law, Toxic Substances Law and Toxic Torts, Lanham Act Litigation, Condemnation Litigation, Arbitration.

FIRM PROFILE: Kiesler & Berman was founded April 16, 1963 by Robert L. Kielser and Marvin D. Berman, former classmates and graduates of the University of Illinois College of Law. The practice was started primarily as an insurance defense and subrogation firm with a sub-emphasis on corporate and real estate. The firm now services the entire Cook County area, as well as the collar counties of Lake, McHenry, Boone, Winnebago, Kane, DeKalb, LaSalle, DuPage, Will, Kendall, Grundy and Kankakee through its office located in Chicago, Illinois. The firm specializes in all phases of insurance defense and coverage work and continues its practice in corporate, real estate and probate.

PARTNER

DAVID A. BECK, born Chicago, Illinois, April 16, 1954; admitted to bar, 1979, Illinois and U.S. District Court, Northern District of Illinois. *Education:* University of Illinois (B.A., 1976); John Marshall Law School (J.D., 1979). ***PRACTICE AREAS:*** Tort Defense. ***Email:*** dab@thekillerbees.com

ASSOCIATE

EDWIN J. OLSON, admitted to bar, 1994, Illinois; U.S. District Court, Northern District of Illinois. *Education:* Michigan State University (B.A., 1989); Chicago-Kent College of Law, Illinois Institute of Technology (J.D., 1994). *Member:* Will County Bar Association. ***PRACTICE AREAS:*** Civil Litigation; Insurance Defense. ***Email:*** ejo@thekillerbees.com

KROCKEY, CERNUGEL, COWGILL, CLARK & PYLES

Established in 1972
3100 THEODORE STREET, SUITE 101
JOLIET, ILLINOIS 60435
Telephone: 815-729-3600
Fax: 815-729-4280
URL: http://www.kcccp.com

Corporate and Tax, Probate, Estate Planning, Real Estate, Banking, Municipal, Family, Divorce, Child Support, Child Custody, Domestic Violence, Visitation Rights, Adoption, Workers Compensation, Personal Injury Law, Auto Accidents, Dog Bites, Sexual Abuse, Slip and Fall, Wrongful Death, Buying and Selling a Home, Construction, Eminent Domain, Environmental Law, Landlord and Tenant, Zoning and Land Use.

MEMBERS OF THE FIRM

ROBERT S. KROCKEY, born Chicago, Illinois, December 6, 1940; admitted to bar, 1966, Illinois; 1975, U.S. District Court, Northern District of Illinois; 1977, U.S. Tax Court; 1978, U.S. Supreme Court. *Education:* University of Illinois (B.S.C., 1962); DePaul University (J.D., 1966). Certified Public Accountant, Illinois, 1965. ***PRACTICE AREAS:*** Corporate Law; Probate; Trust Law; Real Estate; Banking Law.

JOSEPH M. CERNUGEL, born Joliet, Illinois, March 23, 1950; admitted to bar, 1975, Illinois, U.S. Court of Appeals, Seventh Circuit and U.S. District Court, Northern District of Illinois. *Education:* Northwestern University (B.A., 1972); University of Illinois (J.D., with honors, 1975). ***PRACTICE AREAS:*** Real Estate; Family Law; Civil Litigation; Social Security Disability.

THOMAS E. COWGILL, born Cody, Wyoming, August 25, 1946; admitted to bar, 1975, Illinois; 1978, U.S. District Court, Northern District of Illinois. *Education:* Concordia College (B.M., summa cum laude, 1968); John Marshall Law School (J.D., with honors,

(This Listing Continued)

KROCKEY, CERNUGEL, COWGILL, CLARK & PYLES, Joliet—Continued

1975). *Member:* Illinois Trial Lawyers Association; American Trial Lawyers Association. [With U.S. Army, 1968-1971]. ***PRACTICE AREAS:*** Municipal Law; Civil Litigation; Workers Compensation; Personal Injury.

TIMOTHY A. CLARK, born Clinton, Iowa, December 4, 1962; admitted to bar, 1989, Illinois and U.S. District Court, Northern District of Illinois. *Education:* Augustana College (B.A., 1985); Northern Illinois University (J.D., 1989). ***PRACTICE AREAS:*** Municipal Law; Civil Litigation; Bankruptcy; Real Estate; Family Law.

GARY SCOTT PYLES, born Joliet, Illinois, December 10, 1965; admitted to bar, 1991, Illinois and U.S. District Court, Northern District of Illinois; 2001, U.S. Supreme Court. *Education:* Illinois State University (B.S., 1988); Northern Illinois University (J.D., 1991). *Member:* Illinois Trial Lawyers Association; The Association of Trial Lawyers of America. ***PRACTICE AREAS:*** Personal Injury; Traffic Violations.

GEORGE D. LENARD

CRYSTAL SQUARE BUILDING
81 NORTH CHICAGO STREET, SUITE 206
JOLIET, ILLINOIS 60432
Telephone: 815-723-9016
Fax: 815-723-7119
Email: LenardLaw@aol.com
URL: http://www.lawyers.com/lenardlaw

Criminal Defense, Felonies, Homicide, Sexual Assault, Drug Crimes, Misdemeanors, Driving While Intoxicated, Traffic Violations and Juvenile Law.

FIRM PROFILE: Experienced, aggressive legal representation; licensed in California, Arizona, Florida, Illinois and Michigan.

GEORGE D. LENARD, born Joliet, Illinois, August 26, 1957; admitted to bar, 1984, Illinois and U.S. District Court, Northern District of Illinois;; 1990, U.S. Supreme Court; 1998, Michigan and U.S. Court of Appeals, Sixth Circuit; 1999, Arizona; 2001, California; 2003, Florida. *Education:* Illinois State University (B.S., 1979); Thomas M. Cooley Law School (J.D., 1984). Phi Alpha Delta. Felony Prosecutor, Will County States Attorneys Office, 1984-1988. Member, Capital Litigation Trial Bar, Certified Lead Counsel, 2002—. *Member:* State Bar of Arizona; State Bar of Michigan; State Bar of California; The Florida Bar; National Association of Criminal Defense Lawyers; Illinois Association of Criminal Defense Lawyers. ***REPORTED CASES:*** People v. Mario Godina, Jr., 584 N.E.2d 523; People v. Thomas Pomykala 784 N.E. 2d 784 (Trial Counsel).

MAHONEY, SILVERMAN & CROSS, LTD.

822 INFANTRY DRIVE, SUITE 100
JOLIET, ILLINOIS 60435
Telephone: 815-730-9500
Fax: 815-730-9598
URL: http://www.mscltdlaw.com

Administrative Law; Appellate Practice; Banking Law; Business Law, including Business Formation, Maintenance and Planning, Financing, Acquisitions, Licensing and Business Transactions; Civil Litigation in State and Federal Courts, including Commercial, Construction, Personal Injury, Eminent Domain, Alternative Dispute Resolution, Zoning and Land Use; Construction Law; Land Use Law, including Zoning, Planning and Land Development; Local Governmental Law, including cities, villages, townships, fire protection, library and park districts, and governmental financing including tax increment financing districts; Real Estate Law; Tax Law; Traffic Law; Estate Planning; Trust Administration; Estate Administration; Contested Trusts and Estates; Elder Law; Gift, Estate and Income Tax Law.

FIRM PROFILE: The Law Firm of Mahoney, Silverman & Cross, Ltd. is comprised of eleven attorneys who, collectively, have more than ninety years of experience in the practice of law. Our Law Firm strives to provide excellent legal representation with the objective of exceeding client's expectations.

Some of our Firm's representative clients include: Marathon-Ashland Petroleum Company, ExxonMobil Corporation, Crosfield Chemicals, Inc., Waste Management, Inc., Ron Tirapelli Ford, Inc., Bill Jacobs Joliet, LLC, Gallagher & Henry, Ozinga Bros., Inc., T.H. Davidson & Co., Inc., 84 Lumber Company, Phoenix Developers Company, LLC, Mirant Co., Ryan Companies, Standard Bank and Trust Company, Good Will Industries of Southeast Wisconsin, Caterpillar, Inc., Chicago Title Insurance Company, Bridgeview Bank and Trust Company, James D. Fiala Paving Company, Inc., HomeStar Bank, Founders Bank, PPL Global, LLC, Illinois American Water Company, and Midwestern Generation EME, LLC. Some of our Firm's governmental clients include: Housing Authority of Joliet, Kankakee County Housing Authority, Village of Channahon, Village of Elwood, Village of Frankfort, Village of Oswego, Village of Shorewood, Village of Somonauk, City of Aurora, City of Wilmington, Frankfort Fire Protection District, Fox Township, Troy Fire Protection District, Troy Township, Plainfield Township, Sandwich Park District, Lemont Public Library District and Wheatland Township.

GEORGE F. MAHONEY, III, born Joliet, Illinois, 1949; admitted to bar, 1974, Illinois and U.S. District Court, Northern District of Illinois including Trial Bar; 2002, U.S. Supreme Court. *Education:* Lewis College (B.A., with high honors, 1971); DePaul University (J.D., 1974). Co-Author, with David J. Silverman, "Tax Increment Financing District Subchapter of Chapter of Governmental Finance of Development Illinois Land Use Law," Illinois Institute of Continuing Legal Education, 2005. *Member:* Illinois Judicial Ethics Committee, 1997—; Board of Directors of Will County Center for Economic Development, 1996-1998; Board of Trustees of Silver Cross Hospital 1983— (First Vice-Chair 1998—); Board of Directors of Northwestern HealthCare, 1996-2000; Board of Directors, Illinois Institute of Continuing Legal Education, 1999— (Executive Committee, 2004—); The Supreme Court of Illinois Committee on Judicial Performance Evaluation, 1999—. Board of Illinois Bar Foundation. Listed in: Martindale-Hubbell; Outstanding Lawyers of America; The Leading Lawyers Network of Illinois - The Top Lawyers; Chicago Magazine Illinois Super Lawyers. Member, Illinois Supreme Court Rules Committee, 1995-2003. Special Assistant Illinois Attorney General, 1984—. *Member:* Will County (President, 1984), and Illinois State (Member of Assembly, 1986-1992; Member, Standing Committee on Judicial Evaluations 1992—; Chair, Standing Committee, Judicial Evaluations 1995, 1997 and 2005—; Standing Committee on Legislation 1997—; Chair, Conference of the Future of the Legal Profession, 2004) Bar Associations. ***PRACTICE AREAS:*** Civil Litigation; Governmental Law; Zoning and Land Development Law; Municipal Law; Appellate Practice. ***Email:*** gmahoney@mscltdlaw.com

DAVID J. SILVERMAN, born Joliet, Illinois, 1952; admitted to bar, 1988, Illinois; 1989, U.S. District Court, Northern District of Illinois including Trial Bar; 2002, U.S. Supreme Court. *Education:* Lewis University (B.A., 1983); The John Marshall Law School (J.D., with high distinction, 1988). Co-Author, with George F. Mahoney, "Tax Increment Financing District Subchapter of Chapter of Governmental Finance of Development Illinois Land Use Law," Illinois Institute of Continuing Legal Education, 2005. Member, Illinois Supreme Court Committee on Character and Fitness, 1999-2001. *Member:* Will County and Illinois State (Member, Local Government Law Section Council, 1997—) Bar Associations. ***PRACTICE AREAS:*** Governmental Law; Zoning and Land Development Law; General Litigation. ***Email:*** dsilverman@mscltdlaw.com

THOMAS H. CROSS, III, born Nashville, Tennessee, 1958; admitted to bar, 1983, Illinois and U.S. District Court, Northern District of Illinois including Trial Bar. *Education:* Illinois Wesleyan University (B.A., 1980); Cumberland School of Law of Samford University (J.D., 1983). Member, Illinois General Assembly, 84th Legislative District, 1992—. Minority Leader of the Illinois House of Representatives, 2003—. Deputy Minority Leader of the Illinois House of Representatives, 2001-2002. Assistant Minority Leader, Illinois House of Representatives, 1999-2001. Member: Conflicts Committee, 1999—. Judicial Reappointment Committee, 1999—; Joint Committee on Administrative Rules, 1999—; Member, 1992-1998 and Chair, 1994-1997, House Judiciary Civil Law Committee. Minority Spokesperson, 1997-1998. Member, Constitutional Officers Committee, 1994-1998. Assistant State's Attorney, Kendall County, Illinois, 1983-1992. ***PRACTICE AREAS:*** Commercial Litigation; Personal Injury Litigation; Real Estate Law; Corporate Law. ***Email:*** tcross@mscltdlaw.com

ERIC P. HANSON, born Joliet, Illinois, 1969; admitted to bar, 1997, Illinois. *Education:* University of Illinois (B.A., 1991); John Marshall Law School (J.D., cum laude, 1995). Executive Editor, The John Marshall Law Review, 1994-1995. Judicial Law Clerk to Honorable Rita B. Garman, Illinois Appellate Court, 1995-1997. Member, Order of John Marshall. Assistant State's Attorney, Will County, Illinois, 1997-1998. Member, Appellate Lawyers Association. Member, Housing and Development Law Institute. Member: Board of Directors, Greater Joliet Area YMCA 2002—; Board of Directors, CASA Kendall County 2003-2004. *Member:* Will County, Illinois State (Member: Special Committee on Appellate Practice, 2001-2002; Special Committee on the Future of the Courts, 2001-2002; Standing Committee on Insurance Programs and Services, 2003—; Young Lawyers Division Council, 2000-2005) and American Bar Associations. ***PRACTICE AREAS:*** Governmental Law; Land Use Law; Municipal Law; Appellate Practice. ***Email:*** ehanson@mscltdlaw.com

JAMES A. MURPHY, born Chicago, Illinois, 1960; admitted to bar, 1987, Illinois and U.S. District Court, Northern District of Illinois including Trial Bar; 1993, U.S. Court of Appeals, Seventh Circuit. *Education:* Knox College (B.A., 1982); Illinois Institute of Technology (J.D., with honors, 1987). Judicial Law Clerk to Honorable Lawrence D. Inglis, Illinois Appellate Court, Second District, 1987-1989. Author, "Recent Public Contracting Cases, Trends and Strategies," ICLE Municipal Litigation Update, May 2003; "Pleadings, The Road Map for Trial," ISBA Law Ed, Successfully Navigating Civil Litigation, January 2004; "Motions for Summary Judgment Pursuant to 735 ILCS 5/2-1005 and Illinois Supreme Court Rule 191," ISBA Law Ed Civil Litigation Update and Overview of Civil Practice and Procedure, April 2005; "Enforcing Covenants Not to Compete." *Member:* Will County and Illinois State (Member, Civil Procedure Section Council, 2001—) Bar Associations. ***PRACTICE AREAS:*** Commercial Litigation; Personal Injury Litigation; Appellate Practice. ***Email:*** jmurphy@mscltdlaw.com

SEAN D. BRADY, born Chicago, Heights, Illinois, 1970; admitted to bar, 1997, Illinois. *Education:* Eastern Illinois University (B.A., 1992); University of Illinois (J.D., magna cum laude, 1997). Author: "A Preliminary Breath Screening Test (PBT) is Admissible by State in a Motion to Quash Arrest and Suppress Evidence"; "Is the Breathalyzer Mouthpiece a foreign substitute requiring a new 20 minute observation period?"; "A Citizens Tip is Not Enough to Justify a Stop of a Motor Vehicle without Sufficient Detail or Corroboration". Assistant State's Attorney, Will County, Illinois, 1997-2001. *Member:* Will County and Illinois State (Member, Traffic and Courts Section Council) Bar Associations. ***PRACTICE AREAS:*** Civil and Selected Criminal Litigation; General Practice; Appellate Practice. ***Email:*** sbrady@mscltdlaw.com

WALTER J. YURKANIN, born Joliet, Illinois, 1965; admitted to bar, 1994, Illinois and U.S. District Court, Northern District of Illinois. *Education:* St. Xavier University (B.A., 1987); Loyola University of Chicago (M.B.A., 1990); John Marshall Law School (J.D., 1994). Certified Public Accountant, State of Illinois (1988). DOMAIN INFRINGEMENT.COM: Trademark Cyberpiracy Prevention; Can Digital Signatures be Forged?; A Summary of Business and Taxation Issues Affecting Farming Operations; Limited Liability Companies: Liability Limitations and Dispute Resolution. *Member:* Member: Will County, Chicago and Illinois State (Member, Corporation Law Section Council, 2002—) Bar Associations. ***PRACTICE AREAS:*** Corporate Law; Securities Law; Finance Law; Labor and Employment Law; Real Estate Law; Individual Taxation; Corporate Taxation. ***Email:*** wyurkanin@mscltdlaw.com

KEVIN D. YUSMAN, born St Louis, Missouri, 1998; admitted to bar, 1998, Texas; 2000, California; 2004, Illinois and U.S. District Court, Northern District of Illinois including Trial Bar; U.S. Court of Appeals for the Armed Forces; U.S. Court of Appeals, Fifth, Eighth and Ninth Circuits. *Education:* University of Kansas (B.A., 1995); Southern Methodist University (J.D., cum laude, 1998). *Member:* Chicago, DuPage County and Illinois State Bar Associations. [U.S. Navy: Active Duty, 1999-2004; Reserve, 2005—]. ***PRACTICE AREAS:*** Commercial Litigation; Personal Injury Litigation.

(This Listing Continued)

ANGELA E. HART, born Baltimore, Maryland, 1975; admitted to bar, 2004, Illinois. *Education:* Eckerd College (B.A., 1997); University of Iowa (J.D., 2003). Member: Council for Working Women; Joliet Area Young Professionals; Joliet Region Chamber of Commerce Industry. *Member:* Will County and Illinois State Bar Associations; Will County Women's Bar Association. ***PRACTICE AREAS:*** Real Estate; Estate Planning; Commercial Transactions; General Corporate Law.

JUSTIN M. FREDIN, born Joliet, Illinois, 1977; admitted to bar, 2004, Illinois. *Education:* Brigham Young University (B.S., cum laude, 2001); University of Iowa (J.D., with distinction, 2004). *Member:* Will County and Illinois State Bar Associations. ***PRACTICE AREAS:*** Governmental Law; Zoning Law; Development Law. ***Email:*** jfredin@mscltdlaw.com

COUNSEL

WILLIAM A. PEITHMANN, born 1954; admitted to bar, 1978, Colorado; 1979, Illinois; 1980, California; 1995, U.S. Supreme Court. *Education:* DePaul University; Loretto Heights College (B.A., 1975); University of Illinois; University of Denver (J.D., 1978). Recipient, 1998 Board of Governors Award. Listed in The Best Lawyers in America, 1999—. *Member:* Member: Illinois State Bar Association (Board of Governors 1995-2001; Assembly 1994-2001; Various committees and section councils, including Trusts & Estates Section Council, 1988—; Chair, 1994-1995; Special Committee on Living Trusts, 1993 -1994; Chair, Task Force on Protection of Public from Unauthorized Practice of Law, 1995 -1997); Colorado Bar Association (Trust & Estate Section); American Bar Association (Member: Sections on: Real Property; Probate & Trust Law; Vice-Chair, B-1 Generation Skipping Transfers Committee, 1994-1998); American College of Trust and Estate Counsels (1994 —). (Also Member, Peithmann Law Office, Farmer City). ***PRACTICE AREAS:*** Estate Planning; Trust and Estate Administration; Wealth Management; Tax.

McKEOWN, FITZGERALD, ZOLLNER, BUCK, HUTCHISON & RUTTLE

Established in 1900

2455 GLENWOOD AVENUE

JOLIET, ILLINOIS 60435

Telephone: 815-729-4800

Fax: 815-729-4711

URL: http://www.mckeownlawfirm.com

Frankfort Office: 28 Kansas Street. Telephone: 815-469-2176. FAX: 815-469-0295.

General Civil, Trial and Appellate Practice. Corporate, Business, Municipal, Probate, Estate Planning, Real Estate, Taxation, Employment, Healthcare, School and Personal Injury.

FIRM PROFILE: Founded in 1900 by John Savage, McKeown, Fitzgerald, Zollner, Buck, Hutchison & Ruttle has provided high quality legal services to clients in Will and surrounding counties for over 100 years. The Firm engages in a general practice, with each attorney specializing in individual areas of law.

MEMBERS OF FIRM

CHARLES J. McKEOWN (1908-1985)

PAUL O. McKEOWN (1913-1982)

RICHARD T. BUCK (1936-1992)

DOUGLAS P. HUTCHISON (1939-1998)

STEWART C. HUTCHISON (1912-2002)

JOSEPH C. FITZGERALD (Retired)

DAVID L. RUTTLE, born Pembroke, Ontario, Canada, February 6, 1945; admitted to bar, 1971, Illinois. *Education:* DePauw University (B.A., 1967); University of Texas (J.D., 1970). Phi Delta Phi. *Member:* Will County and Illinois State Bar Associations. ***PRACTICE AREAS:*** Corporate Law; Municipal Law; School Law; Commercial Law. ***Email:*** dave@mckeownlawfirm.com

DOUGLAS J. McKEOWN, born Joliet, Illinois, July 4, 1949; admitted to bar, 1974, Illinois. *Education:* Western Illinois University (B.B.A., 1971); Chicago-Kent College of Law, Illinois Institute of Technology (J.D., 1974); DePaul University (M.S., Taxation, 1976). *Member:* Will County and Illinois State Bar Associations. ***PRACTICE AREAS:*** Probate; Estate Planning. ***Email:*** doug@mckeownlawfirm.com

JAMES B. HARVEY, born Joliet, Illinois, May 10, 1955; admitted to bar, 1980, Illinois. *Education:* Lewis University (B.A., with high honors, 1976); John Marshall Law School (J.D., with distinction, 1980). Delta Epsilon Sigma. Member, Order of John Marshall. Member, Illinois Supreme Court Committee on Professionalism. Trained Intervener, Lawyers Assistance Program. Trustee, Lewis University. Board Member, Cornerstone Services, Inc. *Member:* Will County and Illinois State Bar Associations; IL Township Attorneys Association; IL Institute for Local Government Law. ***TRANSACTIONS:*** Village of Plainfield Tax Increment Financing District. ***PRACTICE AREAS:*** Municipal Law; School Law; Public Law; Nonprofit Corporations. ***Email:*** jim@mckeownlawfirm.com

KENNETH A. GREY, born Waukegan, Illinois, November 16, 1951; admitted to bar, 1983, Illinois and U.S. District Court, Northern District of Illinois. *Education:* Western Illinois University (B.A., with honors, 1977); John Marshall Law School (J.D., 1983). Phi Alpha Delta. Member, Will County States Attorneys Office, 1983-1985. *Member:* Will County, Illinois State and American Bar Associations; Christian Legal Society (President, 1981-1983). [U.S. Army, 1970-1974]. ***PRACTICE AREAS:*** Municipal Law; Real Estate; Estate Planning. ***Email:*** ken@mckeownlawfirm.com

CHRISTOPHER N. WISE, born Princeton, Illinois, February 24, 1961; admitted to bar, 1986, Illinois; 1987, U.S. District Court, Western District of Tennessee. *Education:* Augustana College (B.A., cum laude, 1983); Valparaiso University (J.D., 1986). Phi Alpha Delta. *Member:* Will County and Illinois State Bar Associations. [JAGC, US Navy, 1986-1990; Final Rank, Lieutenant]. ***PRACTICE AREAS:*** Probate; Estate Planning; Real Estate. ***Email:*** chris@mckeownlawfirm.com

NICHOLAS E. SAKELLARIOU, born Columbus, Ohio, April 10, 1946; admitted to bar, 1974, Illinois; U.S. District Court, Northern District of Illinois and Trial Bar; 1977, U.S. Court of Appeals, Seventh Circuit; 1980, U.S. Court of Appeals, Eighth Circuit; 1981, U.S. Supreme Court. *Education:* University of Illinois (B.S.E.E., 1968); DePaul University (J.D., 1974). Corporation Counsel, City of Joliet, 1978-1986. *Member:* Will County, Illinois State and American Bar Associations. ***REPORTED CASES:*** Jackson v. City of Joliet, 715 F.2nd 1200 (7th Cir.). U.S. Court of Appeals, 7th Circuit; People ex rel. Rudman v. Rini, 64 Ill.2d 321, Illinois Supreme Court; City of Joliet v. Bosworth, 64 Ill.2d 516, Illinois Supreme Court; In re Appointment of Special State's Attorneys, 42 Ill. App.3d 176, Ill. Appellate Court, 3rd Dist.; Bowers v. DuPage County Regional Board of School Trustees, 183 Ill. App.3d 367, Ill. Appellate Court, 2nd Dist.; Quist v. Board of Trustees of Community College District No. 525, 258 Ill. App.3d 814, Ill. Appellate Court, 3rd Dist.; Bank of Elk Grove v. City of Joliet, 167 Ill. App.3d 457, Ill. Appellate Court, 3rd Dist.; Webber v. Michela, 633 F.2nd 518 (8th Cir.), U.S. Court of Appeals, 8th Circuit. ***PRACTICE AREAS:*** Municipal Law; Labor and Employment; Education Law; Government; Civil Rights. ***Email:*** nick@mckeownlawfirm.com

ARTHUR J. WILHELMI, born Joliet, Illinois, May 14, 1968; admitted to bar, 1993, Illinois and U.S. District Court, Northern District of Illinois. *Education:* Loyola University (B.A., cum laude, 1990); Joliet Junior College; Chicago-Kent College of Law, Illinois Institute of Technology (J.D., 1993). Member, National Jesuit Honor Society. Illinois State Senator, 43rd District. *Member:* Will County Bar Association. ***PRACTICE AREAS:*** Contracts; Residential Real Estate; Commercial Real Estate; Corporate Law. ***Email:*** arthur@mckeownlawfirm.com

CHRISTOPHER S. WARD, born Joliet, Illinois, November 4, 1970; admitted to bar, 1997, Illinois and U.S. District Court, Northern District of Illinois. *Education:* St. John's University (B.A., 1992); John Marshall Law School (J.D., 1996). Member, Moot Court Council. *Member:* Chicago and American Bar Associations. ***PRACTICE AREAS:*** School Law; Corporate. ***Email:*** ward@mckeownlawfirm.com

OF COUNSEL

GEORGE E. SANGMEISTER, born Joliet, Illinois, February 16, 1931; admitted to bar, 1960, Illinois. *Education:* Elmhurst College (B.A., 1957); John Marshall Law School (J.D., 1960). Magistrate, Circuit Court, 1961-1964 and States Attorney, 1964-1968, Will County. State Representative, 1973-1976 and State Senator, 1977-1986, 42nd District. United States Congressman, 4th District, 1988—. *Member:* Will County, Illinois State and American Bar Associations; Illinois Trial Lawyers Association.

MAX E. ZOLLNER, born Evanston, Illinois, December 3, 1938; admitted to bar, 1963, Illinois. *Education:* Knox College (A.B., 1960); University of Illinois (J.D., 1963). *Member:* Will County and Illinois State Bar Associations. (Retired). ***PRACTICE AREAS:*** Probate; Estate Planning; Real Estate. ***Email:*** mezollner@comcast.net

ASSOCIATES

KIM M. KAPSOS, born Milwaukee, Wisconsin, March 30, 1971; admitted to bar, 2002, Illinois and U.S. District Court, Northern District of Illinois. *Education:* University of Wisconsin-Milwaukee (B.S., 1994); Loyola University Chicago School of Law (J.D, 2002). Instructor, Legal Studies, Northwestern Business College, 2002-2005. *Member:* Will County and Illinois State Bar Associations. ***PRACTICE AREAS:*** Criminal Prosecution; Criminal Defense; Litigation. ***Email:*** kimk@mckeownlawfirm.com

JEAN A. KENOL, born Brooklyn, New York, August 2, 1976; admitted to bar, 2001, Illinois. *Education:* University of Notre Dame (B.A., 1998); University of Illinois (J.D., 2001). *Member:* Will County Bar Association. ***PRACTICE AREAS:*** Criminal Prosecution; Commercial Collections; Civil Litigation; Medical Malpractice Defense. ***Email:*** jean@mckeownlawfirm.com

RACHAEL GOULD, born Buffalo, New York, May 15, 1976; admitted to bar, 2002, Illinois. *Education:* Cornell University (B.S., 1998); George Washington University Law School (J.D., 2001). Golden Key National Honor Society. Member, Public Contracts Law Journal. *Member:* Chicago, Illinois State and American Bar Associations. ***PRACTICE AREAS:*** Residential Real Estate; Commercial Real Estate; Criminal Prosecution; Civil Litigation; Municipal Law. ***Email:*** rachael@mckeownlawfirm.com

TIFFANY R. GORMAN, born Kankakee, Illinois, July 10, 1978; admitted to bar, 2003, Illinois. *Education:* University of Illinois, Urbana-Champaign (B.A., 2000); Loyola University (J.D., 2003). *Member:* Illinois State and American Bar Associations. ***PRACTICE AREAS:*** Real Estate; Litigation; Municipal Law. ***Email:*** Tiffany@mckeownlawfirm.com

ATTORNEYS FOR: Amstek Metal; Charles G. Stevens Co.; Lockport Steel Fabricators; Silver Cross Hospital; Villages of: Plainfield and Mokena; Industrial Colors Co.; Walco Tool & Engineering; Healy, Snyder, Bender & Associates, Inc.; Plainfield Molding, Inc.; Southwest Agency for Risk Management; Joliet Junior College; Cornerstone Services Inc.; Plainfield Stamping-Illinois, Inc.; Plainfield Stamping-Texas, Inc.; Joliet Country Club; Kipling Development, Inc.; Will County Center for Community Concerns; Joliet YMCA; Executive Flight Mgt.; Joliet Public Grade School # 86; Lewis University; Merchants and Manufacturers Bank; DTE Energy Services, Inc.; Platinum Aviation LLC.

LAW OFFICE OF PATRICK A. MESZAROS

1256 WEST JEFFERSON STREET

JOLIET, ILLINOIS 60435

Telephone: 815-722-4001

Fax: 815-722-4007

URL: http://www.meszaroslaw.com

Personal Injury, Automobile Accidents and Injuries, Slip and Fall and Real Estate Law.

(This Listing Continued)

LAW OFFICE OF PATRICK A. MESZAROS, Joliet—Continued

PATRICK A. MESZAROS, born Joliet, Illinois, August 9, 1967; admitted to bar, 1997, Illinois and U.S. District Court, Northern District of Illinois. *Education:* Joliet Junior College; College of St. Francis (B.A., 1989); DePaul University (J.D., 1997). *Member:* Will County and Illinois State Bar Associations. ***PRACTICE AREAS:*** Personal Injury; Real Estate; Bankruptcy.

MITCHELL, BOLDEN & MELTON, P.C.

54 NORTH OTTAWA STREET, SUITE 245
JOLIET, ILLINOIS 60432
Telephone: 815-723-2895
Fax: 815-723-5136
Email: attorneymitchell@aol.com
URL: http://www.mgblawoffices.com

Criminal Law, Civil Law, Traffic Violations, Real Estate, Employment Law, Family Law.

ERIC A. MITCHELL, born Hampton, Virginia, July 15, 1971; admitted to bar, 1998, Illinois. *Education:* Purdue University (B.A., 1993); Indiana University (J.D., 1996). *Member:* Illinois State Bar Association. [U.S. Army Reserve, 1989-1997]. ***PRACTICE AREAS:*** Civil Law; Criminal Law; Traffic Violations. **Email:** AttorneyMitchell@aol.com

RAYMOND A. BOLDEN, born Chicago, December 17, 1933; admitted to bar, 1962, Illinois; 1964, U.S. District Court, Northern District of Illinois. *Education:* University of Illinois, Urbana-Champaign (B.S., Business; LL.B., 1981). Associate Judge, 12th Judicial District, 1986-2001. [U.S. Air Force, 1953-1957]. ***PRACTICE AREAS:*** Criminal Law; Real Estate; Family Law; Civil Law.

AMY MELTON, born Madison, Wisconsin, May 21, 1969; admitted to bar, 1998, Illinois; 2004, U.S. District Court, Northern District of Illinois. *Education:* University of Wisconsin-Madison (B.A., 1992); Northern Illinois University, DeKalb (J.D., 1998). Member, Northern Illinois Law Review. Author: "Blind Leading the 'Colorblind'-Affirmative Action and a Dream Still Deferred." *Member:* Will County Women's Bar Association (Secretary, 2003-2005). ***PRACTICE AREAS:*** Criminal Law; Traffic Violations; Real Estate; Employment Law.

MOSS AND BLOOMBERG, LTD.

JOLIET, ILLINOIS

(See Tressler, Soderstrom, Maloney & Priess)

NADLER, PRITIKIN & MIRABELLI, L.L.C.

JOLIET, ILLINOIS

(See Chicago)

Family Law and Domestic Relations Law including Dissolution of Marriage, Division and Valuation of Marital and Non-Marital Property, Maintenance and Support, Custody and Visitation, Domestic Violence, Establishment of Paternity, Prenuptial and Postnuptial Agreements and, When Necessary, Litigation of Cases and the Prosecution and Defense of Appeals. Mediation and Arbitration.

LAIRD M. OZMON, LTD.

54 NORTH OTTAWA STREET, SUITE B-5
JOLIET, ILLINOIS 60432
Telephone: 815-727-7700
FAX: 815-727-7800
Email: injury@ozmonlaw.com
URL: http://www.ozmonlaw.com

Civil Trial Law, State and Federal Courts with emphasis on Serious Personal Injury, Products Liability, Wrongful Death and Medical Negligence.

FIRM PROFILE: Laird M. Ozmon has served clients throughout, but not limited to, the state of Illinois. The firm was established in 1983 and focuses its practice in the areas of personal injury litigation.

LAIRD M. OZMON, born Chicago, Illinois, July 7, 1954; admitted to bar, 1979, Illinois; 1980, Florida, U.S. District Court, Northern District of Illinois and U.S. Court of Appeals, Seventh Circuit; 1983, U.S. Supreme Court. *Education:* Lewis University (B.A., with high honors, 1977); Loyola University (J.D., 1979). Co-Author: Chapter, "Trial Tactics in Medical Malpractice"; Illinois Institute for Continuing Legal Education, 1989 and 1992. *Member:* Illinois State (Assemblyman, 1998—) and American Bar Associations; The Florida Bar; American Board of Trial Advocates; The Society of Trial Lawyers; Illinois Trial Lawyers Association (President, 1997-1998); The Association of Trial Lawyers of America (Committee Chair, 1988-1989). ***REPORTED CASES:*** Jerry L. Ross v. Black and Decker, Inc., 977 F2d 1178 (7th Cir., 1992). ***PRACTICE AREAS:*** Civil Litigation; Appellate; Product Liability; Medical Malpractice; Personal Injury Law. **Email:** injury@ozmonlaw.com

PARALEGAL

VIVIAN KING

REFERENCE: First Midwest Bank/Joliet.

CYNTHIA L. PETERSEN

JOLIET, ILLINOIS

(See Blue Island)

Divorce, Qualified Domestic Relations Order (QDRO), Paternity, Premarital Agreements, Child Support.

LAW OFFICES OF STEPHEN S. PHALEN LLC

JOLIET, ILLINOIS

(See Chicago)

Personal Injury, Wrongful Death, Automobile Accidents, Boating Accidents, Motorcycle Accidents, Trucking Accidents, Bus Accidents, Train Accidents, Construction Accidents, Medical Malpractice, Head Trauma, Spinal Injuries.

POOL, LEIGH & FABRICIUS

JOLIET, ILLINOIS

(See Ottawa)

General Civil Trial and Appellate Practice in all Courts, Insurance, Real Estate and Family Law.

QUERREY & HARROW, LTD.

Established in 1939
2 RIALTO SQUARE
SUITE 401
116 NORTH CHICAGO STREET
JOLIET, ILLINOIS 60432
Telephone: 815-726-1600
Fax: 815-726-1674
Email: jfarmans@querrey.com
URL: http://www.querrey.com

Chicago, Illinois Office: 175 West Jackson Boulevard, Suite 1600. Telephone: 312-540-7000. Fax: 312-540-0578.
Crystal Lake, Illinois Office: 651 West Terra Cotta Avenue, Suite 221. Telephone: 815-479-1929. Fax: 815-479-1978.
Waukegan, Illinois Office: 415 West Washington Street, Suite 205. Telephone: 847-249-4440. Fax: 847-249-4932.
Wheaton, Illinois Office: 310 South County Farm Road, Third Floor. Telephone: 630-653-2600. Fax: 630-653-0178.
Merrillville, Indiana Office: 8585 Broadway, Suite 510. Telephone: 219-738-1820. Fax: 219-738-1821.
New York, N.Y. Office: 120 Broadway, Suite 2800. Telephone: 212-233-0130. Fax: 212-233-0172.
London, England Office: 141-142 Fenchurch Street, Fifth Floor. Telephone: 207-929-6670. Fax: 207-929-6671.

General Practice and Trial Practice.

JANET M. FARMANS, admitted to bar, 1982, Illinois. *Education:* Western Illinois University (B.A., 1974); Loyola University (M.A., 1979); Northern Illinois University (J.D., 1982). (Resident). ***PRACTICE AREAS:*** Litigation; Product Liability; Construction; Eminent Domain.

MICHAEL B. STILLMAN, admitted to bar, 1994, Illinois. *Education:* Bradley University (B.A., 1991); DePaul University (J.D., 1994). (Resident). ***PRACTICE AREAS:*** Litigation; Municipal Law. **Email:** mstillman@querrey.com

CHRISTINE McASEY, admitted to bar, 1995, Illinois. *Education:* Augustana College (B.A., Accounting, 1992); Valparaiso University (J.D., 1995). (Resident). ***PRACTICE AREAS:*** Litigation. **Email:** cmcasey@querrey.com

RICHARD J. TURIELLO, admitted to bar, 2001, Illinois. *Education:* Cazenovia College (B.P.S., 1997); Chicago Kent College of Law (J.D., 2000). (Resident). ***PRACTICE AREAS:*** Litigation. **Email:** rturiello@querrey.com

(For complete biographical data on all personnel, see Professional Biographies at Chicago, Illinois)

RATHBUN, CSERVENYAK & KOZOL, LLC

3260 EXECUTIVE DRIVE
JOLIET, ILLINOIS 60431
Telephone: 815-730-1977
Fax: 815-730-1934
Email: webmail@rcklawfirm.com
URL: http://www.rcklawfirm.com

Plainfield, Illinois Office: 618 West Main Street, 60544. Telephone: 815-577-9763. Fax: 815-577-9769.
Mokena Office: 9450 Enterprise Drive, 60448. Telephone: 708-479-9949. Fax: 708-479-0503.

Civil Practice. Insurance Defense, Commercial Litigation, Personal Injury, Labor and Employment, Construction Law, Workers' Compensation, Criminal Law, Education Law, FELA, Real Estate, Family Law, Estate Planning, Bankruptcy, Medical Malpractice, Zoning, Planning and Land Use, Wills, Immigration.

(This Listing Continued)

FIRM PROFILE: We specialize in the trial of civil lawsuits. Our staff is aggressive and responsive to the needs of our clients. When clients enter our office they have a conflict, when they leave they have a resolution. We accomplish our mission because we have a plan, a purpose, and dedication.

MEMBERS OF FIRM

TIMOTHY J. RATHBUN, born Evanston, Illinois, January 27, 1950; admitted to bar, 1974, Illinois; 1983, U.S. District Court, Northern District of Illinois, including Trial Bar. *Education:* Tulane University (B.A., 1972; J.D., 1974). *Member:* Will County, Illinois State and American Bar Associations; The Association of Trial Lawyers of America; Illinois Trial Lawyers Association. [JAGC, U.S. Navy, 1974-1977]. ***PRACTICE AREAS:*** Commercial Litigation; Construction Litigation; Personal Injury Law; Workers' Compensation Defense. ***Email:*** trathbun@rcklawfirm.com

FRANK S. CSERVENYAK, JR., born Chicago, Illinois, October 16, 1963; admitted to bar, 1988, Illinois and U.S. Court of Appeals, Seventh Circuit. *Education:* Illinois Wesleyan University (B.A., 1985); Drake University (J.D., 1988). Phi Alpha Delta (Vice-President, 1988). *Member:* Illinois State and American Bar Associations; Illinois Trial Lawyers Association; Association of Trial Lawyers of America. ***PRACTICE AREAS:*** Personal Injury Law; Criminal Law; Construction Litigation; Commercial Litigation. ***Email:*** frank@rcklawfirm.com

WILLIAM V. KOZOL, born Joliet, Illinois, May 16, 1953; admitted to bar, 1978, Illinois and U.S. District Court, Northern District of Illinois. *Education:* University of Illinois (B.S., 1975); Loyola University of Chicago (J.D., 1978). Phi Beta Kappa; Phi Kappa Phi; Pi Sigma Alpha. *Member:* Will County and Illinois State Bar Associations. ***PRACTICE AREAS:*** Insurance Defense Litigation; Personal Injury; Medical Malpractice; FELA. ***Email:*** wkozol@rcklawfirm.com

CARL R. BUCK, born Plainfield, Illinois, December 19, 1968; admitted to bar, 1997, Illinois. *Education:* Citadel Military College (B.A., Political Science, 1991); John Marshall Law Schools Center (J.D., 1997). President, Plainfield Chamber of Commerce. Trustee, Dist 202 Foundation of Excellence. *Member:* Will County, Illinois State and American Bar Associations. ***PRACTICE AREAS:*** Commercial Law; Contracts; Zoning; Corporate Law; Real Estate Litigation. ***Email:*** cbuck@rcklawfirm.com

KATHERINE L. MALONEY, born Joliet, Illinois, June 18,1967; admitted to bar, 1994, Illinois; U.S. District Court, Northern District of Illinois. *Education:* Northern Illinois University (B.A., International Relations/Economics, 1990); George Washington University (J. D., 1994). Recipient: Will County Outstanding Pro Bono Volunteer Award, 1998. *Member:* Will County, Illinois State and American Bar Associations; Illinois Trial Lawyers Association; American Association of University Women. ***PRACTICE AREAS:*** Family Law; Estate Planning; Real Estate; Bankruptcy; Probate. ***Email:*** kmaloney@rcklawfirm.com

ASSOCIATES

ERIC SWANSON, born Elgin, Illinois, October 23, 1968; admitted to bar, 1993, Illinois; 2001, U.S. District Court, Northern District of Illinois including Trial Bar. *Education:* Valparaiso University (B.A., 1990; J.D., 1993). *Member:* Will County and Illinois State Bar Associations. ***PRACTICE AREAS:*** Civil Litigation; Insurance Defense; Criminal Law. ***Email:*** eswanson@rcklawfirm.com

KEVIN MALCOLM ROSNER, born Vancouver, B.C., Canada, July 7, 1970; admitted to bar, 2002, Illinois and U.S. Court of Appeals, 7th Circuit. *Education:* University of British Columbia (B.A., 1993); Illinois Institute of Technology, Chicago-Kent College of Law (J.D., 2000). *Member:* Will County and Illinois State Bar Associations; Illinois Trial Lawyers Association. ***PRACTICE AREAS:*** Criminal Defense; Personal Injury. ***Email:*** krosner@rcklawfirm.com

ELIZABETH Z. LeBARON, born Cleveland, Ohio, August 21, 1955; admitted to bar, 1980, Illinois. *Education:* Miami University (B.A., magna cum laude, 1977); Indiana University (J.D., summa cum laude, 1980). Phi Beta Kappa. Member, Order of the Coif. Formerly with Sonnenschein Carlin Nath & Rosenthal. *Member:* Chicago, Illinois State and American Bar Associations. ***PRACTICE AREAS:*** Workers' Compensation; Civil Litigation. ***Email:*** elebaron@rcklawfirm.com

LISA GRAY CHASTAIN, born Tonawanda, New York, March 22, 1972; admitted to bar, 1999, Illinois; 2001, Texas. *Education:* Texas A & M University (B.B.A., 1993); California Western School of Law (J.D., 1997). *Member:* Illinois State and Will County Bar Associations; Womens Bar of Illinois; State Bar of Texas. ***PRACTICE AREAS:*** Civil Litigation; Commercial Litigation. ***Email:*** lchastain@rcklawfirm.com

LAWRENCE M. KASCHAK, born Streator, Illinois, July 29, 1966; admitted to bar, 1991, Illinois. *Education:* Northern Illinois University (B.S., 1988); John Marshall Law School (J.D., 1991). Formerly with Myers, Berry, O'Conor and Kuzma Herbolsheimer Law Offices. *Member:* LaSalle County and Illinois State Bar Associations. ***REPORTED CASES:*** People v. Dilworth, 169 Ill.2d 195, 661 N.E.2d 310 (1996); People v. Ross, 168 Ill.2d 347, 659 N.E.2d 1319 (1995). ***PRACTICE AREAS:*** Litigation (100%).

DONALD P. JONKER, born Chicago, Illinois, June 30, 1957; admitted to bar, 1984, Illinois; 1992, U.S. District Court, Northern District of Illinois; 2004, U.S. Court of Appeals, Seventh Circuit. *Education:* University of Illinois (B.A., 1980); Thomas M. Cooley Law School (J.D., 1984). *Member:* Will County and Illinois State Bar Associations. ***PRACTICE AREAS:*** Civil Litigation; Commercial Litigation; Attorney Discipline. ***Email:*** djonker@rcklawfirm.com

REPRESENTATIVE CLIENTS: American Electric, Inc.; American Redi-Mix; Attorneys' Title Guaranty Company; Auto Owners Insurance Company; Village of Braidwood Fire and Police Board; Brakur Custom Cabinetry, Inc.; Capital Indemnity; Menards; Caterpillar Inc.; Chicago Title Insurance Company; Cleary Building Corporation; Dockside Marina, Inc.; Gallagher Bassett Services, Inc.; George Rydman & Associates; Grinnell Mutual Insurance Company; Intercounty Title Company of Illinois; Iowa Mutual Insurance Company; Joilet Orthopedic and Sports Medicine Center, Ltd.; Joliet Township High School; Lindblad Construction Company of Joliet, Inc.; Lockport Steel Fabricators, Inc.; Material Distribution, Inc. (MDI); National Land Title Insurance Company; Numark Credit Union; Plainfield Construction Company; R.A. Ubert Construction, Inc.; Raytheon Engineers & Constructors, Inc.; Rod Baker Ford Sales, Inc.; Ron Stonitsch Construction, Inc.; Service Industrial Supply; State Farm Insurance Company; Stewart Title Guaranty Company; Ticor Title Company; West Bend Mutual Insurance.

(This Listing Continued)

RINELLA AND RINELLA, LTD.

JOLIET, ILLINOIS

(See Chicago)

Practice Limited to Family Law and Divorce including the areas of Legal Separation, Negotiating and Drafting Premarital and Postnuptial Agreements, Judgment Enforcement, Child Custody and Child Support Actions, Domestic Violence, Spousal Support, Appeals, Adoption, Parentage Actions and Interstate Support Enforcement.

RYAN AND RYAN

JOLIET, ILLINOIS

(See Chicago)

Eminent Domain, Condemnation.

LAW OFFICES OF MICHAEL T. SAWYIER

JOLIET, ILLINOIS

(See Chicago)

Trusts and Estates, Asset Protection, Wills and Probate, Elder Law, Real Estate, Business Law.

GREGORY R. SKUBISZ

JOLIET, ILLINOIS

(See Calumet City)

Criminal, Personal Injury, General Civil Litigation, Family, Real Estate, Estate Planning and Probate, Driving Under Influence, Traffic and Felonies.

SPESIA, AYERS & ARDAUGH

Established in 1899

TWO RIALTO SQUARE
116 NORTH CHICAGO STREET, SUITE 200
JOLIET, ILLINOIS 60432
Telephone: 815-726-4311
Fax: 815-726-6828
URL: http://www.spesia-ayers.com

General Trial and Appellate Practice in State and Federal Courts. Insurance, Medical Malpractice, Corporate, Personal Injury, Real Estate Taxation, Probate, Municipal Law.

FIRM PROFILE: Founded in 1899, originally as Barr & Barr, the law firm of Spesia, Ayers & Ardaugh has built a reputation for quality and aggressive legal representation in the Will, Cook, DuPage, Kane, Kendall, Grundy, LaSalle, DeKalb and Kankakee areas. Spesia, Ayers & Ardaugh offers representation in commercial, civil, personal, and municipal matters and is a full service law firm.

Senior partner, Douglas F. Spesia heads the commercial division of the firm, working with partners, John Ardaugh, Christian Spesia, Martin J. Shanahan, Jr. and Gabriel G. Orenic. Together, these attorneys concentrate in the fields of municipal law, condemnation, zoning, taxation and related litigation, as well as estate planning, real estate, and commercial matters. They have represented some of the largest companies in the State of Illinois while also serving the needs of individual clients.

Senior partner, E. Kent Ayers heads the civil trial division of the firm, working with attorneys John Spesia, Dinah Lennon Archambeault, Thomas M. Ewert, Jeffrey S. Taylor and Mark A. Lichtenwalter. These attorneys have represented individuals, corporations, insurance companies, utilities, school districts, school boards and municipalities in almost every area of civil law, including personal injury, property loss, condemnation, municipal, products liability, and medical malpractice. They are a team of seasoned trial attorneys having litigated matters involving major personal injuries, commercial disputes and catastrophic accidents.

The attorneys of Spesia, Ayers & Ardaugh remain available to offer outstanding representation in a fair and efficient manner.

MEMBERS OF FIRM

DOUGLAS F. SPESIA, born Joliet, Illinois, October 11, 1940; admitted to bar, 1965, Illinois. *Education:* University of Illinois (B.S., 1962); University of Notre Dame (LL.B., 1965). Staff Member, 1962-1964 and Member, Board of Editors, 1964-1965, Notre Dame Lawyer. Secretary, Will County Zoning Board of Appeals, 1967-1977. *Member:* Will County (President, 1978-1979) Illinois State and American Bar Associations. ***PRACTICE AREAS:*** Elder Law; Corporate Law; Condemnation; Partnership Law; Local Government Law; Easements; Real Estate Taxation; Probate; Trusts and Estates; Wills; Taxation; Municipal Law; Zoning, Planning and Land Use. ***Email:*** dspesia@spesia-ayers.com

E. KENT AYERS, born Canton, Illinois, March 7, 1942; admitted to bar, 1969, Illinois. *Education:* Wabash College (A.B., 1964); University of North Dakota (J.D., 1968). Phi Delta Phi. Will County Assistant State's Attorney, 1974-1975. Member of Panel, American Arbitration Association. *Member:* Will County, Illinois State (Member, House of Delegates, 1974-1978 and 1988-1990) and American Bar Associations; Illinois Trial Lawyers Association (Member, Board of Advocates); The Association of Trial Lawyers of America. Fellow, American College of Trial Lawyers. ***PRACTICE AREAS:*** Trial Practice; Medical Malpractice; Bodily Injury; Brain Injury; Catastrophic Injury; Wrongful Death; Products Liability. ***Email:*** kayers@spesia-ayers.com

(This Listing Continued)

SPESIA, AYERS & ARDAUGH, Joliet—Continued

JOHN R. "JACK" ARDAUGH, born Joliet, Illinois, January 4, 1959; admitted to bar, 1986, Illinois. *Education:* Illinois State University (B.S., 1980); John Marshall Law School (J.D., with distinction, 1986). Who's Who Among American Law Students. Illinois Lawyers Auxiliary Scholar. Robert G. Bone Scholar Nominee. Author: "Mandatory Disclosure: The Key to Real Estate Brokers' Conflicting Obligations," The John Marshall Law Review, 19:1 (Fall, 1985). Staff Editor, The John Marshall Law Review. Member: Moot Court Executive Council; J. Braxton Craven, Jr. Memorial Moot Court Competition. *Member:* Will County, Illinois State and American Bar Associations. ***PRACTICE AREAS:*** Elder Law; Business Dissolutions; Business Organization; Business Sale; Small Business Law; Commercial Real Estate; Commercial Contracts; Corporate Law; Small Business Corporations; Condemnation; Land Annexation; Local Government Law; Township Law; Guardianship; Leasing; Municipal Law; Partnership Law; Probate Administration; Property Rights; Boundary Disputes; Easements; Real Estate Development; Sports Contracts; Trusts and Estates; Wills; Zoning, Planning and Land Use. ***Email:*** jardaugh@spesia-ayers.com

JOHN M. SPESIA, born Joliet, Illinois, February 24, 1967; admitted to bar, 1993, Illinois; 1994, U.S. District Court, Northern District of Illinois. *Education:* The University of Iowa (B.A., Economics, 1989); The University of Denver (J.D., 1993). Order of St. Ives. Law Clerk to the Honorable Harry D. Leinenweber, United States District Judge for the Northern District of Illinois, 1994. *Member:* Will County and Illinois State Bar Associations; Illinois Trial Lawyers Association. ***PRACTICE AREAS:*** Trial Practice; Appellate Practice; Business Litigation; Commercial Litigation; Construction Litigation; Contract Litigation; Corporate Litigation; Condemnation; Local Government Law; Public Officials Liability; Automobile Liability; General Liability; Personal Injury; Premises Liability; Products Liability; Real Estate Litigation; Tort Liability. ***Email:*** jspesia@spesia-ayers.com

CHRISTIAN G. SPESIA, born Joliet, Illinois, September 1, 1968; admitted to bar, 1994, Illinois and U.S. District Court, Northern and Central Districts of Illinois. *Education:* The Colorado College (B.A., 1990); University of Denver (J.D., 1994). Order of St. Ives. *Member:* Will County and Illinois State Bar Associations. ***PRACTICE AREAS:*** Trial Practice; Appellate Practice; Business Litigation; Civil Rights; Local Government Law; Public Officials Liability; Condemnation; Employment Discrimination; Property Rights; Boundary Disputes; Easements; Real Estate Development; Tax Litigation; Zoning, Planning and Land Use. ***Email:*** cspesia@spesia-ayers.com

JEFFREY S. TAYLOR, born Chicago, Illinois, May 2, 1967; admitted to bar, 1995, Illinois and U.S. District Court, Northern District of Illinois. *Education:* Colorado State University (B.A., 1991); John Marshall Law School (J.D., cum laude, 1995). Moot Court Council. Order of John Marshall. Author: "Defending Product Liability Cases in Illinois After the Best Decision," IDC Quarterly, Fourth Quarterly, 1998. *Member:* Will County Bar Association; Illinois Trial Lawyers Association; The Association of Trial Lawyers of America. ***PRACTICE AREAS:*** Trial Practice; Business Litigation; Commercial Litigation; Personal Injury; Products Liability; Construction Law; Catastrophic Injury; Wrongful Death; Insurance Litigation; Real Estate Litigation. ***Email:*** jtaylor@spesia-ayers.com

ASSOCIATES

MARTIN J. SHANAHAN, JR., born Joliet, Illinois, July 19, 1972; admitted to bar, 1998, Illinois and U.S. District Court, Northern and Central Districts of Illinois. *Education:* College of St. Francis (B.A., cum laude, 1994); John Marshall Law School (J.D., 1998). Adjunct Professor, The College of St. Francis, 1999—. *Member:* Will County and Illinois State Bar Associations. ***PRACTICE AREAS:*** Trial Practice; Insurance Litigation; Local Government Law; Personal Injury; Elder Law. ***Email:*** mshanahan@spesia-ayers.com

MARK A. LICHTENWALTER, born Joliet, Illinois, January 29, 1970; admitted to bar, 2003, Illinois. *Education:* University of Illinois (B.S., 1992); John Marshall Law School (J.D., 2003). Order of John Marshall. Member, John Marshall Law School Law Review. Adjunct Professor, Trial Advocacy, University of St. Francis, 2004—. *Member:* Chicago, Will County, Illinois State and American Bar Associations; Illinois Trial Lawyers Association; Association of Trial Lawyers of America. ***PRACTICE AREAS:*** Trial Practice; Tort Liability; Local Government Law; Litigation. ***Email:*** mlichtenwalter@spesia-ayers.com

GABRIEL G. ORENIC, born Joliet, Illinois, February 25, 1967; admitted to bar, 2003, Illinois. *Education:* Barry University (B.A., 1989); John Marshall Law School (J.D., 2003). *Member:* Will County, Illinois State and American Bar Associations. ***PRACTICE AREAS:*** Tort Liability; Local Government Law; Eminent Domain; Probate Administration; Estate Planning. ***Email:*** gorenic@spesia-ayers.com

OF COUNSEL

DINAH LENNON ARCHAMBEAULT, born Washington, D.C., January 12, 1952; admitted to bar, 1988, Illinois; 1989, U.S. District Court, Northern District of Illinois; 1990, U.S. Court of Federal Claims; 1991, U.S. Court of Appeals, Seventh Circuit; 1992, U.S. Supreme Court; 2003, U.S. District Court, Central District of Illinois. *Education:* Lewis University (B.A., 1974); John Marshall Law School (J.D., with distinction, 1988). Member: Phi Delta Phi; The Gavel Society. Adjunct Professor, The John Marshall Law School, 1999. *Member:* Will County and Illinois State Bar Associations; Illinois Appellate Lawyers Association. ***PRACTICE AREAS:*** Medical Malpractice; Negligence; Personal Injury; Trial Practice; Appellate Practice; School Law. ***Email:*** dla@spesia-ayers.com

THOMAS M. EWERT, born Chicago, Illinois, 1946; admitted to bar, 1971, Illinois. *Education:* Northern Illinois University (B.S. 1968); University of Illinois (J.D., 1971). First Assistant State's Attorney, Kankakee County, 1971-1976. Associate Judge (Presiding Judge of Civil Division), Twelfth Judicial Circuit, 1976-2001. Member: Joint Committee on Judicial Ethics. Chairman, Illinois Supreme Court Capital Litigation Screening Committee. Mediator, ADR Systems of America, L.L.C. *Member:* Will County and Illinois State Bar Associations; Illinois Judges Association. ***PRACTICE AREAS:*** Trial Practice; Personal Injury; Medical Malpractice; Products Liability; Condemnation; Arbitration; Mediation. ***Email:*** tewert@spesia-ayers.com

(This Listing Continued)

ATTORNEYS FOR: A.N.R. Pipeline Co.; Advance Building Systems; Alliance Pipeline, L.P.; Aux Sable Liquid Products, LP; Blue Ribbon Products Co.; Caterpillar Tractor Co.; Catholic Diocese of Joliet; Commonwealth Edison Co./Exelon; Crossfield Chemicals, Inc.; ENPRO, Inc.; Fantastic Electric Inc.; First Group America; Goeken Group Corp.; Guardian Pipeline; IBM Corp.; Indiana Consolidated Insurance Cos.; Infinite INet, Inc.; J.U.L.I.E. Inc.; Joliet Catholic Academy; Kinder Morgan Inc.; Lakehead Pipeline Co.; Liberty Mutual Insurance Co.; Manhattan Township; Metropolitan Life Insurance Co.; Mickey Oil Cos.; MidCon Corp.; Natural Gas Pipeline Co. of America; Next, Inc.; Nicor Gas Company; Our Lady of Angeles Retirement Home; PDK Development; Peoples Energy Corp.; S&K Excavating & Trucking, Inc.; SBC Ameritech; Seagull Products Corp.; TE Products Pipeline Co., L.L.C.; Telecab, Inc.; Telecom Relay Services; Texas Eastern Pipeline Co.; The Inland Group, Inc.; United HealthCare Insurance Co.; Utilities, Inc.; Village of Manhattan; Village of Minooka; Village of New Lenox; Village of Rockdale; Walcrest, Ltd.; Williams Communications; Williams Pipe Line Co.

JAMES P. STEVENSON

54 NORTH OTTAWA STREET, SUITE 260
JOLIET, ILLINOIS 60432
Telephone: 815-727-7879
Fax: 815-727-5458

General Civil Trial and Appellate Practice, State and Federal Courts with emphasis on Personal Injury, Automobile Accidents, Slip and Fall, Wrongful Death, Municipal Law, Zoning, Insurance Disputes, Construction Disputes.

FIRM PROFILE: Available for services in Will, Grundy, La Salle, Kankakee and Kendall Counties.

JAMES P. STEVENSON, born East Chicago, Indiana, December 9, 1953; admitted to bar, 1984, Illinois and U.S. District Court, Northern District of Illinois; 1988, U.S. District Court, Northern District of Illinois Trial Bar; 1991, U.S. Court of Appeals, Seventh Circuit; 1993, U.S. Supreme Court; 1998, U.S. District Court, Central District of Illinois. *Education:* St. Joseph Calumet College; Governors State University; IIT/Chicago-Kent College of Law (J.D., 1984). Adjunct Professor, Graduate Studies, "Legal Aspects of Healthcare Administrations," University of St. Francis, Joliet. Co-Author: Chapter, "Trial Tactics in Medical Malpractice", Illinois Institute for Continuing Legal Education, 1989 and 1992. Assistant State's Attorney, Cook County, Illinois, 1984-1988. *Member:* Will County, Illinois State and American Bar Associations. ***REPORTED CASES:*** Jerry L. Ross v. Black and Decker, Inc., 977 F2d 1178 (7th Cir., 1992).

STUHR & DRELL

Established in 1984

54 N. OTTAWA STREET, SUITE 200
JOLIET, ILLINOIS 60432
Telephone: 815-722-2252
Fax: 815-722-3809
Email: stuhr_drell@earthlink.net
URL: http://www.struhrdrell.com

Family Law, Aviation and Aerospace Law, Criminal Law, Juvenile Law, Real Estate, Bankruptcy, Business Law, Juvenile, Guardianship and Adoptions.

MEMBERS OF FIRM

GEORGE M. STUHR, born Weehawken, New Jersey, June 21, 1937; admitted to bar, 1984, Illinois. *Education:* Seton Hall University (B.A., 1960); John Marshall Law School (J.D., 1984). *Member:* Will County, Illinois State and American Bar Associations; Lawyer Pilot Bar Association. ***PRACTICE AREAS:*** Real Estate (20%); Bankruptcy (20%); Business Law (30%); Federal Aviation Licenses (5%); General Practice (25%). ***Email:*** stuhr_drell@earthlink.net

LEA ARMSTRONG DRELL, born Chicago, Illinois, October 16, 1934; admitted to bar, 1985, Illinois. *Education:* National College of Education (B.A., 1970; M.Ed., 1977); John Marshall Law School (J.D., 1985). *Member:* Will County, Cork County, Illinois State and American Bar Associations. ***PRACTICE AREAS:*** Family Law; Juvenile Law; Real Estate; Guardianship; Adoption Law. ***Email:*** stuhr_drell@earthlink.net

TRACY, JOHNSON & WILSON

FIRST COMMUNITY BANK BUILDING
2801 BLACK ROAD, 2ND FLOOR
JOLIET, ILLINOIS 60435
Telephone: 815-723-8500
Fax: 815-727-4846
Email: jolietlaw@tracylawfirm.com

General Civil and Appellate Practice in all Courts, Corporation, Business, Pension and Profit Sharing, Banking, Commercial, Bankruptcy, Probate, Estate and Tax Planning, Real Estate, Real Estate Taxation, Personal Injury, Workers' Compensation, Employment, Eminent Domain, Municipal, Land Development, Zoning and Governmental Law.

RICHARD H. TEAS, born Streator, Illinois, 1930; admitted to bar, 1960, Illinois. *Education:* University of Illinois (A.B., 1957; LL.B., 1960). Phi Delta Phi. *Member:* Will County and Illinois State (Member, Trust & Estates Section Council, 1984-1990, 1994-2004, Secretary, 2000-2001, Chair, 2002-2003, Committee on Legislation, 1996—, Task Force on Unauthorized Practice of Law, 2000-2004) Bar Associations. Fellow, American College of Trust and Estate Counsel. ***PRACTICE AREAS:*** Trusts and Estates; Probate; Estate Planning; Tax Planning; Real Estate. ***Email:*** rteas@tracylawfirm.com

RAYMOND E. MEADER, born Joliet, Illinois, 1947; admitted to bar, 1979, Illinois. *Education:* Beloit College (B.A., 1969); Purdue University (M.S., 1975); Lewis University (J.D., with honors, 1978). Sigma Pi Sigma. Special Assistant Illinois Attorney General, 1980-1984, 1995—. *Member:* Will County, Illinois State (Member, Municipal Law Section

(This Listing Continued)

Council, 1995-1996) and American Bar Associations. ***PRACTICE AREAS:*** General Practice; Eminent Domain; Commercial Litigation; Zoning, Planning and Land Use; Municipal Law; Real Estate Taxation. ***Email:*** rmeader@tracylawfirm.com

A. MICHAEL WOJTAK, born Joliet, Illinois, 1955; admitted to bar, 1980, Illinois and U.S. District Court, Northern District of Illinois. *Education:* Lewis University (B.A., with honors, 1977); Loyola University-Chicago (J.D., 1980). Certified Public Accountant, Illinois, 1987. *Member:* Will County (President, 1991-1992) and Illinois State Bar Associations; Estate Planning Council of Greater Joliet (President, 1990-1991). ***PRACTICE AREAS:*** Real Estate; Estate Planning; Probate; Trusts; Commercial and Banking Law. ***Email:*** mwojtak@tracylawfirm.com

KENNETH A. CARLSON, born Joliet, Illinois, 1960; admitted to bar, 1986, Illinois and U.S. District Court, Northern District of Illinois including Trial Bar. *Education:* University of Illinois (B.A., 1981); Mississippi College School of Law (J.D., 1986). *Member:* Will County (Director, 1999—) and Illinois State Bar Associations. ***PRACTICE AREAS:*** Commercial; Employment; Municipal Law; Construction; Corporate Law; Real Estate; Zoning; Zoning Litigation; Real Estate Development. ***Email:*** kcarlson@tracylawfirm.com

JOHN S. GALLO, born Joliet, Illinois, 1958; admitted to bar, 1985, Illinois and U.S. District Court, Northern District of Illinois. *Education:* Lewis University (B.A., with high honors, 1981); Loyola University-Chicago (J.D., 1985). Certified Public Accountant, Illinois, 1982. *Member:* Will County and Illinois State (Member, Corporation, Securities and Business Law Section Council, 1995-1999) Bar Associations. ***PRACTICE AREAS:*** Business; Corporate; Pension and Profit Sharing; Federal Income Taxation; Estate Taxation; Gift Taxation; Real Estate. ***Email:*** jgallo@tracylawfirm.com

ASSOCIATES

RICHARD E. VOGEL, born Hinsdale, Illinois, 1970; admitted to bar, 1995, Illinois. *Education:* University of Illinois (B.S., with highest honors, 1992; J.D., summa cum laude, 1995). Beta Gamma Sigma; Alpha Lambda Delta; Golden Key. Order of the Coif. Recipient, Rickert Award. Member, University of Illinois Law Review, 1993-1995. Research and Editorial Assistant to Professor Ralph Reisner, Northwestern University School of Law, 1993—. Author: "Institutional Liability for ATM Attacks," University of Illinois Law Review, 1995. *Member:* Will County and Illinois State Bar Associations. ***LANGUAGES:*** Spanish. ***PRACTICE AREAS:*** Municipal; Zoning Law; Land Use; Real Estate. ***Email:*** rvogel@tracylawfirm.com

CORY D. LUND, born Joliet, Illinois, November 21, 1957; admitted to bar, 1982, Illinois and U.S. District Court, Northern and Central Districts of Illinois. *Education:* Northern Illinois University (B.A., 1979); Southern Illinois University (J.D., 1982). Review Editor, Southern Illinois University Law Journal. Author, "The Standard of Appellate Review for Criminal Sentences in Illinois," Southern Illinois University Law Journal, 1982. Mediator, Will County Large Case Mediation Program. Arbitrator, Will County Mandatory Arbitration Program. Plan Commission, Village of New Lenox, 1991-2003. *Member:* Will County and Illinois State Bar Associations. ***PRACTICE AREAS:*** Litigation; Personal Injury; Business Law; Municipal Law. ***Email:*** clund@tracylawfirm.com

MELANIE D. MANNING, born Joliet, Illinois, May 29, 1975; admitted to bar, 2001, Illinois and U.S. District Court, Northern District of Illinois. *Education:* University of Illinois (B.A., 1998); John Marshall Law School (J.D., 2001). *Member:* Will County and Illinois State Bar Associations. ***PRACTICE AREAS:*** Commercial Law; Business Law; Real Estate; Litigation. ***Email:*** mmanning@tracylawfirm.com

JOEL P. MURPHY, born Chicago Heights, Illinois, November 29, 1978; admitted to bar, 2004, Illinois and U.S. District Court, Northern District of Illinois. *Education:* Southern Illinois University, Carbondale (B.A., 2001; J.D., 2004). *Member:* Will County, Illinois State and American Bar Associations. ***PRACTICE AREAS:*** General Practice. ***Email:*** jmurphy@tracylawfirm.com

REPRESENTATIVE CLIENTS: Citgo; The Copley Press, Inc.; Citizens Utilities Co.; Harris Bank Joliet, N.A.; Packard Transport, Inc.; Joliet Franciscan Sisters; Bill Jacobs, Joliet, L.L.C.; BP Amoco Corporation; Route 66 Raceway, L.L.C.; Raceway Associates, L.L.C., d/b/a Chicagoland Speedway; J. Merle Jones & Sons, Inc.; Alexander Lumber Co., Inc.; Northern Illinois Steel Supply Co.; Crowther Roofing and Sheet Metal Inc.; Empress River Casino Corporation; Vulcan Materials Company; Prairie Material Sales, Inc.; T.J. Lambrecht Construction, Inc.; Tope Corporation; Boughton Trucking and Materials Inc.; Valley Concrete Co.; North Central Materials/PrairieGroup; Village of Romeoville; Village of Homer Glen; Joliet Regional Port District; Frankfort Township; Channahon Township; Wolf Point Condominium Association; Rogina & Associates, Ltd; Land Rover Hoffman Estates, L.L.C.; Bill Jacobs Naperville, L.L.C.; Chicago Bridge and Iron Company; The Barr Group; First Community Bank of Joliet; Bank of Shorewood; Green Garden Township; MGM Construction, Inc.; Kipling Development.

LAW OFFICES OF PHILLIP A. TURNER

JOLIET, ILLINOIS

(See Chicago)

Civil Practice, Criminal Law, Trial Practice, Medical Malpractice, Administrative Law.

LAWRENCE E. VARSEK

1403 ESSINGTON ROAD, SUITE 400
JOLIET, ILLINOIS 60431
Telephone: 815-744-3323
Fax: 815-744-3325
Email: Kesrav@aol.com
URL: http://www.lawyers.com/lawrenceevarsek

Estate Planning, Probate, Wills, Trusts and Estates, Guardianships, Corporate Law, Business Law, Family Business Law, Contested Trusts and Estates, Business Succession Planning.

LAWRENCE E. VARSEK, born Waukegan, Illinois, May 24, 1942; admitted to bar, 1967, Illinois; 1971, U.S. District Court, Northern District of Illinois and U.S. Supreme Court; 1986, U.S. Tax Court. *Education:* Wisconsin State University (B.A., 1964); University of Illinois (J.D., 1967). Secretary, Will County Zoning Board of Appeals, 1977-1978. Member: Will County Building Commission, 1989-1998; Police and Fire Commission, Village of Shorewood, Illinois, 1990-1999. *Member:* Will County and Illinois State Bar Associations; Will County Estate Planning Council. ***PRACTICE AREAS:*** Estate Planning; Probate; Wills; Trusts and Estates; Guardianship; Elder Law; Corporate Law; Business Law; Contested Estates and Trusts; Business Succession Planning.

(This Listing Continued)

JOSEPH WROBEL, LTD.

JOLIET, ILLINOIS

(See Chicago)

Bankruptcy including Personal Bankruptcy, Business Bankruptcy, Chapter 7, Chapter 11, Chapter 13, Foreclosures and Garnishments and Business Dissolutions.

FEIRICH/MAGER/GREEN/RYAN

JONESBORO, ILLINOIS

(See Carbondale)

General Trial and Appellate Litigation, Business, Probate, Trust, Real Estate, Insurance Law, Worker's Compensation, Banking and Corporation Law, Intellectual Property and Healthcare Law.

LAW OFFICES OF CHADWICK & LAKERDAS

JUSTICE, ILLINOIS

(See Chicago)

Criminal Law, Driving While Intoxicated, Drug Crimes, Felonies, Homicide, Juvenile Law, Misdemeanors, Parole and Probation, Sexual Assault, Traffic Violations, Personal Injury, Airplane Crash Litigation, Automobile Accidents, Dog Bites, Railroad Accidents, Sexual Abuse, Slip and Fall, Wrongful Death.

ACKMAN, MAREK, MEYER & BOYD, LTD.

Established in 1959

SUITE 400, ONE DEARBORN SQUARE
KANKAKEE, ILLINOIS 60901
Telephone: 815-933-6681
Fax: 815-933-6623
Email: ammb@amb-ltd.com

General Civil and Trial Practice. Probate, Real Estate, Insurance, Medical Malpractice, Workers Compensation and Corporation Law.

FIRM PROFILE: Ackman, Marek, Meyer & Boyd, Ltd., was founded in 1959 by Richard L. Ackman, the senior member of the firm. The firm's current professional corporation was reorganized at the end of 1996. Since its inception, the firm has focused on civil trial work with a strong emphasis in insurance defense. At the present time, attorneys of the firm provide individual concentrations in civil litigation, medical malpractice law, banking law, insurance law, probate and estate planning law and workers compensation law. A fully staffed office in Kankakee has been maintained since 1964. All partners and associates participate in continuing legal education seminars, serve as officers and committee members of professional organizations, of local and state bar associations and are actively engaged in community affairs.

J. DENNIS MAREK, born Chicago, Illinois, February 19, 1943; admitted to bar, 1967, Illinois. *Education:* DePauw University (B.A., 1964); Durham University, Durham, England; Northwestern University (J.D., 1967). Phi Delta Phi. Lecturer, Trial Practice, Illinois Institute of Continuing Legal Education, 1987. Instructor, Illinois Defense Counsel Trial Academy, 1993—. Public Defender, Iroquois County, 1971-1982. Civil Practice & Procedure Committee, 2003—. *Member:* Kankakee County (President, 1994), Iroquois County and Illinois State (Member: Public Relations Committee, 1975-1981; Judicial Evaluation Committee, 2001—; Civil Practice and Procedure Committee, 2003—) Bar Associations; Illinois Defense Counsel (Member: Membership Committee, 1984-1986; Board of Directors, 1992-2001); American Board of Trial Advocates; Association of Defense Trial Attorneys; Defense Research Institute. Fellow, American College of Trial Lawyers. ***PRACTICE AREAS:*** Medical Malpractice; General Civil Defense Law; Real Estate Law; Probate; Corporate Law. ***Email:*** dmarek@amb-ltd.com

JOHN J. BOYD, born Kankakee, Illinois, September 14, 1962; admitted to bar, 1989, Illinois. *Education:* Eastern Illinois University (B.A., 1984); John Marshall Law School (J.D., 1989). Counsel, Joliet Chamber of Commerce, 1989-1994. Assistant Public Defender, Felonies, Will County, 1989-1994. Attorney: Village of St. Anne; Godley Park District; Godley Public Water District; St. Anne Fire Protection District. *Member:* Kankakee County, Will County and Illinois State Bar Associations; Illinois Trial Lawyers Association; Illinois Defense Counsel; Association of Defense Trial Attorneys; Defense Research Institute. ***PRACTICE AREAS:*** General Civil Trial Law; Real Estate Law; Criminal Defense Law; Municipal Law. ***Email:*** jjboyd@amb-ltd.com

DANA M. MEYER, born Chicago Heights, Illinois, August 24, 1972; admitted to bar, 1997, Illinois. *Education:* Kankakee Community College (A.A., 1992); Valparaiso University (B.A., 1994; J.D., 1997). Instructor, Kankakee Community College, Civil Litigation, 2003—. *Member:* Kankakee County, Illinois State and American Bar Associations; Illinois Association of Defense Trial Counsel; Defense Research Institute. ***PRACTICE AREAS:*** General Civil Trial Law; Family Law; Zoning Law. ***Email:*** dmeyer@amb-ltd.com

(This Listing Continued)

ACKMAN, MAREK, MEYER & BOYD, LTD., Kankakee—Continued

MICHAEL T. JENEARY, born Kankakee, Illinois, November 21, 1970; admitted to bar, 1995, Illinois; 2003, U.S. District Court, Central District of Illinois. *Education:* Illinois Wesleyan University (B.A., 1992); DePaul University School of Law (J.D., 1995). Pi Sigma Alpha. Assistant States Attorney, Kankakee County, 1995-2000. Assistant Attorney General, State of Illinois, 2000-2002. Instructor, Juvenile Justice, Criminal Law and Procedure, Olivet Nazarene University. *Member:* Kankakee County Bar Association. **PRACTICE AREAS:** Civil Trial Law; Real Estate; Criminal Defense; Family Law. **Email:** mjeneary@amb-ltd.com

OF COUNSEL

RICHARD L. ACKMAN, born Belvidere, Illinois, September 23, 1927; admitted to bar, 1950, Illinois; 1960, U.S. Supreme Court. *Education:* St. Thomas College, University of Kansas (B.S., 1949); University of Illinois (J.D., 1951). Phi Alpha Delta. Public Defender, Kankakee County, 1955-1969. Special Assistant Attorney General, State of Illinois, Workmen's Compensation, 1969-1981. *Member:* Kankakee County (President, 1975-1976) and Illinois State Bar Associations. Fellow, American College of Trial Lawyers. **PRACTICE AREAS:** Corporate Law; Real Estate Law; Workers Compensation Law; Probate and Estate Planning. **Email:** rackman@amb-ltd.com

ROBERT W. BOYD, born Wetaug, Illinois, November 27, 1933; admitted to bar, 1966, Illinois; 1968, U.S. District Court, Eastern District of Illinois. *Education:* Murray State University; John Marshall Law School (J.D., 1966). Lecturer, Trial Practice, Illinois Institute of Continuing Legal Education, 1987. Associate Judge, Twelfth Judicial Circuit of Illinois, 1968-1973. *Member:* Iroquois County, (President, 1974-1975), Kankakee County (President, 1992-1994) and Illinois State Bar Associations; Illinois Defense Counsel; Defense Research Institute; Appellate Lawyers Association. **TRANSACTIONS:** Represented Consumers Illinois Water Company in Sale of Sewage System to Village of Bourbonnais, Illinois. **PRACTICE AREAS:** Banking Law; Civil Appellate Practice.

REPRESENTATIVE CLIENTS: American States Insurance Co.; Auto Owners Insurance Co.; Consumers Illinois Water Company; Country Mutual Insurance Co.; Economy Fire & Casualty Co.; EMCASCO; Employers Mutual Co.; Farmers Insurance Group; Gulf Insurance Group; Grinnell Mutual Insurance; Home Insurance Co.; Illinois Guaranty Fund; Illinois State Medical Insurance Services; Indiana Insurance Group; Insurance Company of North America; Madison Mutual Insurance Co.; Medical Protective Co.; Ohio Farmers Group; Perin Insurance; Physician's Mutual Insurance Co.; Ranger Insurance; Rockford Mutual Insurance Co.; Statesman Insurance Group; Underwriters Insurance Co.; Union Insurance Group; Western Casualty & Surety Co.; Western States Insurance Company; Zurich Insurance Co.

BARMANN, BOHLEN & WOODRUFF, P.C.

SUITE 602, 200 EAST COURT STREET
P.O. BOX 1787
KANKAKEE, ILLINOIS 60901
Telephone: 815-939-1133
Fax: 815-939-0994
Email: law@bbwlaw.net

General Practice. Trial, Probate, Estate Planning, Taxation, Real Estate, Corporate and Commercial Law, Health Law, Municipal, Appellate Practice in all Courts.

FIRM PROFILE: The firm was founded in 1978, being a merger of Blanke & Blanke and Norden & Barmann. Barmann, Bohlen & Woodruff, P.C., now consists of three partners who each concentrate practice in the areas listed below. The firm's practice covers the entire State of Illinois. Civil Litigation, Health Care Law, Estate Planning and Probate, Banking Law, Corporate Law and Municipal Law are the firm's principal areas of expertise.

GLEN R. BARMANN, born Chicago, Illinois, November 30, 1943; admitted to bar, 1969, Illinois; 1974, U.S. District Court, Central District of Illinois; 1979, U.S. Supreme Court. *Education:* Northern Illinois University (B.S., 1965); University of Illinois (J.D., 1968). Standing Trustee, U.S. Department of Justice, Central District of Illinois, 1974—. *Member:* Kankakee County (President, 2001-2003), Illinois State (Member, Probate and Trust Council) and American (Member, Probate and Trust Council) Bar Associations; National Association of Bankruptcy Trustees. **PRACTICE AREAS:** Estate Planning; Probate Law; Corporate Law; Bankruptcy Law; Real Estate. **Email:** barmann@bbwlaw.net

CHRISTOPHER W. BOHLEN, born Decatur, Illinois, July 24, 1949; admitted to bar, 1973, Ohio; 1977, Illinois, U.S. District Court, Central District of Illinois, U.S. District Court, Northern District of Illinois including Trial Bar, U.S. Court of Appeals, Seventh Circuit and U.S. Supreme Court. *Education:* University of Illinois (B.A., cum laude, 1970); Northwestern University (J.D., 1973). Member, Public Defenders Office, Cleveland, Ohio, 1973-1977. Assistant Public Defender, Kankakee County, 1977-1980. City of Kankakee Assistant City Attorney, 1993-1997 and City of Kankakee Corporation Counsel, 1997—, Kankakee, Illinois. *Member:* Kankakee County, Illinois State, Ohio State and American Bar Associations; Illinois Trial Lawyers Association. **PRACTICE AREAS:** Commercial Litigation; Personal Injury Litigation; Municipal Law. **Email:** bohlen@bbwlaw.net

DEBORAH A. WOODRUFF, born Peoria, Illinois, July 19, 1957; admitted to bar, 1985, Illinois. *Education:* University of Illinois; Southern Illinois University (B.S., 1981; J.D., 1985). Phi Alpha Delta (Treasurer, 1983-1984 and Justice, 1984-1985). Public Guardian and Public Administrator, Kankakee County, 1990-1992; 2001—. *Member:* Kankakee and Illinois State Bar Associations; Illinois Trial Lawyers Association; Society of Women In Law; Illinois Guardianship Association. **PRACTICE AREAS:** General Practice; Probate Law; Elder Law; Personal Injury. **Email:** woodruff@bbwlaw.net

REPRESENTATIVE CLIENTS: Centrue Bank; First American Bank; Triangle Construction Company, Inc.; Cognis Corp.; Illinois Municipal League Risk Management Association; Sun Chemical Corp.; Clifton Chemical Company; Servants of the Holy Heart of Mary; Wisco Envelope Co.; West Laboratories, Inc.; Armour Employees Credit Union; ABC Disposal Inc.; Armour Pharmaceutical Corp.; Electron Beam Technologies, Inc.; LaBeau Bros., Inc.; Meier Oil Service; City of Kankakee; First National Bank of Grant Park; Capstone Bank; Provena Health; Provena Hospitals; Provena Senior Services; U.S. Filter/Stranco; Central Community Healthcentre; Ravens Trucking, Inc.; Bourbonnais Township Park District; Kankakee County Visitor's Bureau.

(This Listing Continued)

BRENNER, FORD, MONROE & SCOTT, LTD.

KANKAKEE, ILLINOIS

(See Chicago)

Insurance Defense, Personal Injury, Medical Malpractice, Construction Law, Product Liability, Uninsured/Underinsured Motorist Arbitrations and Litigation of Contested Coverage Issues.

DECK & BARON

Established in 1976
200 EAST COURT STREET
SUITE 408
P.O. BOX 693
KANKAKEE, ILLINOIS 60901-5133
Telephone: 815-939-7373
Fax: 815-939-3737
URL: http://www.pdrblaw.com

General Civil Practice. Banking, Real Estate, Wills, Probate, Estate and Gift Taxation, Trust, Living Wills, Elder Law, Nursing Home Abuse, Estate Planning, Administration, Corporate and Commercial Law. Commercial Personal Injury Litigation.

FIRM PROFILE: The firm serves a wide variety of individual and corporate clients throughout Kankakee, Iroquois and surrounding counties. Each of the firm partners has various areas of expertise which when combined allow the firm to offer a full range of legal services.

GREGORY A. DECK, born Fort Wayne, Indiana, May 29, 1950; admitted to bar, 1975, Illinois. *Education:* Valparaiso University (B.A., 1972; J.D., 1975). Articles Editor, Valparaiso University Law Review, 1974-1975. *Member:* Kankakee County, Illinois State and American Bar Associations. **PRACTICE AREAS:** Real Estate Law; Estate Planning Law; Estate Administration Law; Commercial Law; Wills; Probate; Elder Law.

DENNIS J. BARON, born Kankakee, Illinois, November 14, 1951; admitted to bar, 1977, Illinois. *Education:* University of Illinois (B.A., 1973); University of Michigan (J.D., 1977). Phi Beta Kappa. Assistant Public Defender, Kankakee County, 1981-1984. Alderman, City of Kankakee, 1987—. *Member:* Kankakee County and Illinois State Bar Associations. **PRACTICE AREAS:** Commercial Litigation; Personal Injury Litigation; Family Law; Divorce; Custody; Visitation Rights; Support; Adoption Law.

REPRESENTATIVE CLIENTS: CommonWealth Credit Union; Armour Kankakee Credit Union; Kankakee County Federal Employees Credit Union; Riverside Hospital Employees Credit Union; Riverside Medical Center; Olivet Nazarene University; Standard Title Guaranty Co.; First American Bank; Kankakee Federal Savings Bank.

FABRIZIO, HANSON, PEYLA & KAWINSKI, P.C.

KANKAKEE, ILLINOIS

(See Joliet)

General Civil and Trial Practice. Insurance Defense, Personal Injury, Automobile Accidents, Products Liability, Wrongful Death, Construction Accidents, Workers Compensation, Corporate, Business, Probate, Real Estate, Health Care and Construction Litigation.

HOOKS LAW OFFICES, P.C.

KANKAKEE, ILLINOIS

(See Chicago)

Federal and State Criminal Defense Trial and Appellate Practice (all Felony Crimes including: White Collar, Fraud, Sexual, Weapons, Homicide, Bribery, Conspiracy and Drug Offenses; all Misdemeanor Crimes, including D.U.I., D.W.I. and D.W.B., involving: professionals, doctors, lawyers, business owners/executives, clergy and law enforcement officials). Commercial Litigation, Contract Litigation, Corporate Internal Investigations, Major Incident Management, Civil Fraud, Class Action, Defamation, Election Law and Sexual Harassment Defense. Premises Liability Defense, serious Personal Injury, Wrongful Death, selective Police Misconduct Litigation (Plaintiff and Defense), selective Professional Liability and Governmental Liability. Representation before Military Criminal Courts Martial and Administrative Boards, Disciplinary Labor Arbitrations, Professional Disciplinary License Boards, Academic/Disciplinary hearing/appeals panels (undergraduate, graduate and professional schools); Liquor Licensing Boards and Zoning and Permit Boards.

DAVID M. JAFFE

200 EAST COURT STREET, SUITE 212
KANKAKEE, ILLINOIS 60901
Telephone: 815-936-9186
Fax: 815-936-9765
URL: http://www.davidmjaffelaw.com
Email: jaffelaw@keynet.net
URL: http://www.davidjaffelaw.com

Probate, Real Estate, Estate Planning, Trusts and Estates, Elder Law, Corporate and Commercial Law, Banking Law, Business Law, Land Use.

DAVID M. JAFFE, born Kankakee, Illinois, September 18, 1941; admitted to bar, 1966, Illinois. *Education:* Indiana University (B.A., 1963; J.D., 1966). Phi Delta Phi. Faculty Research Associate, Indiana University Law School, 1966-1968. Assistant Attorney General, 1970-1983. *Member:* Kankakee County and Illinois State Bar Associations.

(This Listing Continued)

PRACTICE AREAS: Real Estate; Estate Planning; Elder Law; Estate & Trust Administration; Banking; Commercial; Probate; Corporate Law; Land Use.

TINA M. OLTON
KANKAKEE, ILLINOIS

(See Momence)

Real Estate, Social Security Disability, Family Law, Divorce, Child Custody, Bankruptcy, Wills, Probate.

LAW OFFICES OF LINDSAY A. PARKHURST
Established in 2001

1 DEARBORN SQUARE, SUITE 320
KANKAKEE, ILLINOIS 60901-3957
Telephone: 815-933-0114
Fax: 815-933-7658
Email: parkhurstlaw@yahoo.com
URL: http://www.parkhurstlaw.com

Family Law, Personal Injury, Bankruptcy, Traffic, Employment Law, Health Law, Social Security Disability, Real Estate, Small Business, Criminal.

FIRM PROFILE: A results driven general practice firm that regularly counsels and represents clients in personal injury, family law, traffic, bankruptcy, real estate, employment, criminal law, business law and health law matters.

LINDSAY A. PARKHURST, born LaGrange, Illinois; admitted to bar, 1989, Illinois and U.S. District Court, Northern and Central Districts of Illinois. *Education:* University of Illinois (B.A., with distinction in Honors English, 1985); Chicago-Kent College of Law, Illinois Institute of Technology (J.D., 1989); DePaul University College of Law, Health Law Institute (LL.M., Health Law, 1991). *Member:* Kankakee and Illinois State Bar Associations; Illinois Trial Lawyers Association; Society of Women in Law. ***LANGUAGES:*** English. ***PRACTICE AREAS:*** Family Law; Personal Injury; Bankruptcy; Traffic; Employment Law; Health Law; Social Security Disability; Real Estate; Small Business; Criminal.

Language: English.

ALAN F. SMIETANSKI
KANKAKEE, ILLINOIS

(See Bradley)

General Civil and Trial Practice. Corporate, Real Estate, Probate, Collections, Personal Injury, Municipal and Domestic Relations Law, Estate Planning, Wills, Probate, Trusts and Estates, Adoption Law, Child Custody, Child Support, Wrongful Death Automobile Accidents, Medical Malpractice.

DALE STROUGH ATTORNEY AT LAW
KANKAKEE, ILLINOIS

(See Watseka)

Bankruptcy, Family, Divorce, Adoption, Visitation Rights, Criminal, DWI, Drug Crimes, Juvenile Crimes, Traffic Violations, White Collar Crimes, Domestic Violence, Personal Injury, Medical Malpractice, Wrongful Death, Trusts and Estates, Estate Planning and Wills and Probate Law. General Practice.

SWANSON, MARTIN & BELL
KANKAKEE, ILLINOIS

(See Chicago)

Asbestos Litigation, Class Action Lawsuits, Commercial Litigation, Construction Litigation/Disputes, Consumer and Warranty Law, Creditor's Rights, Drugs & Medical Devices, Employment Litigation, Environmental Law, Equipment Leasing, General Tort Liability, Healthcare, Insurance Coverage, Intellectual Property, Medical Negligence, Municipal Law, Product Liability, Professional Negligence, Real Estate Development/Zoning, Real Estate Litigation, Toxic and Mass Tort Litigation and White Collar Criminal Defense.

KRUGER, HENRY & HUNTER
KARNAK, ILLINOIS

(See Metropolis)

Civil and Criminal Trial and Appellate Practice. Negligence, Product Liability, Wrongful Death, Workman's Compensation, Criminal, Family, Real Estate, Corporate, Probate, Bankruptcy, Divorce, Driving While Intoxicated.

MICHAEL T. MAHONEY, LTD.
LACON, ILLINOIS

(See Chillicothe)

Civil Litigation, Wills and Probate, Trusts and Estates, Estate Planning, Family Law, Personal Injury, Juvenile Law, DUI, Divorce, Adoptions, Child Support and Custody, Visitation Rights, Automobile Accidents, Dog Bites, Slip and Fall, Wrongful Death, Real Estate, Buying and Selling, Construction Law, Workers Compensation, Title and Insurance, Domestic Relations, Corporations.

(This Listing Continued)

WESTERVELT, JOHNSON, NICOLL & KELLER, LLC
LACON, ILLINOIS

(See Peoria)

General Civil Trial and Appellate Practice in State and Federal Courts, Insurance Defense, Health and Health Care, Labor Relations, Employment Discrimination and Affirmative Action, Products Liability Litigation, ERISA and Benefits Plans, Corporate, Agricultural, Bankruptcy, Creditors' Rights, Banking, Real Estate, State and Federal Taxation, Estate Planning, Trusts and Probate, Workers Compensation, Environmental, Commercial.

BOLLMAN, LESSER & McGLYNN, LLP
Established in 1996

582 NORTH OAKWOOD ROAD
SUITE 100
LAKE FOREST, ILLINOIS 60045
Telephone: 847-295-8800
Fax: 847-295-8886
URL: http://www.bollman-lesser.com

Probate, Probate Litigation, Estate Planning, Trusts and Estates, Wills, Federal Estate and Gift Taxation, Guardianship, Commercial Law, Labor and Employment, Real Estate.

MEMBERS OF FIRM

FREDRIC BRYAN LESSER, born Chicago, Illinois, May 1, 1955; admitted to bar, 1980, Illinois and U.S. District Court, Northern District of Illinois; 1984, U.S. Court of Appeals, Seventh Circuit; 1986, U.S. Court of Appeals, Ninth Circuit and U.S. Supreme Court; 1996, Wisconsin. *Education:* University of Illinois (B.A., 1976); London School of Economics; University of Michigan (J.D., 1980). Vice-President, LCBA. Elected, Village Board of Trustees for Lake Bluff, Illinois, April, 2003. Speaker to the Illinois Certified Public Accountants Association and the Illinois Safe Deposit Association. Past-President: Lake County Estate Planning Council; Lake Forest/Lake Bluff Chamber of Commerce; Deerfield Optimist Club. *Member:* Lake County (Second Vice-President) and Illinois State Bar Association. ***PRACTICE AREAS:*** Probate Litigation; Trusts and Estates; Contested Trusts and Estates; Estate Planning; Family Trusts; Fiduciary Law; Fiduciary Litigation; Powers of Attorney; Special Needs Trusts; Trust Administration; Trust Law; Trust Litigation; Living Trusts; Trust Planning; Trust and Estate Collections; Estate Planning for Unmarried Couples; Estate Planning for the Elderly; Estate Planning for the Disabled; Estate Planning for Parents of Handicapped Children; Estate Litigation; Estate Administration; Decedents Estates; Business Law; Business Enterprises; Business Estate Planning; Business Formation; Business Litigation; Business Organization; Business Start-Ups; Business Succession Planning; Business Transactions; Business Transfers; Buy-Sell Agreements; Buying and Selling of Businesses; Closely Held Business Estate Planning; Closely Held Business Law; Family Business Successions; Family Business Law; Limited Liability Company Law; Small Business Law; Sole Proprietorships; Chancery and Equity; Ancillary Probate; Probate Administration; Probate Taxation; Wills; Contested Wills; Inheritance; Living Wills. **Email:** Lesser@Bollman-Lesser.com

EDMUND R. McGLYNN, JR., born Chicago, Illinois, November 7, 1948; admitted to bar, 1977, Illinois and U.S. District Court, Northern District of Illinois; 1908, U.S. Tax Court; 1981, U.S. Court of Appeals, Seventh Circuit. *Education:* Illinois Institute of Technology (B.S., Business and Economics, 1970); John Marshall Law School (J.D., distinction, 1977). **Email:** mcglynn@bollman-lesser.com

ASSOCIATES

DAVID M. LUTREY, born Evanston, Illinois, November 28, 1968; admitted to bar, 1996, Illinois. *Education:* University of Illinois, Chicago (B.S., Marketing, 1993); Kelstadt Graduate School of Business, DePaul University (M.B.A., Emphasis Finance, 1996); DePaul College of Law (J.D., 1996). Arbitrator, 19th Judicial Circuit, Lake County, Illinois. *Member:* Illinois and Lake County (Member, Wills, Trusts and Probate Committee) Bar Associations; Lake County Estate Planning Council (Past President). ***REPORTED CASES:*** In Re Estate of Weiland, 788 N.E.2d 811, 273 Ill. Dec. 220 (2nd Dist. 2003). ***PRACTICE AREAS:*** Probate; Probate Litigation; Contested Trusts and Estates; Estate Planning; Estate Administration; Business Law; Business Transactions; Real Estate. **Email:** Lutrey@Bollman-Lesser.com

MARK T. CHAVIN, born Park Ridge, Illinois, March 23, 1970; admitted to bar, 2000, Illinois. *Education:* Northwestern University (B.A., 1991); DePaul University College of Law (J.D., 2000). *Member:* Illinois State Bar Association; Lake County Bar Association. ***PRACTICE AREAS:*** Trusts and Estates; Estate Planning; Probate; Trust Administration; Taxation; Real Estate; Commercial Real Estate; Business Law; Business Transactions. **Email:** chavin@bollman-lesser.com

JENNIFER J. HOWE, born New York, N.Y., October 12, 1965; admitted to bar, 1992, Michigan; 1998, Illinois. *Education:* University of Notre Dame (B.A., 1987); University of Detroit (J.D., cum laude, 1992). **Email:** howe@bollman-lesser.com

ELIZABETH L. HOLLAND, born Wright-Patterson Air Force Base, January 16, 1963; admitted to bar, 2002, Illinois and U.S. District Court, Northern District of Illinois. *Education:* Wittenberg University (B.A., 1985); William Mitchell College of Law (J.D., 2001). *Member:* Illinois State Bar Association; American Bar Association; Lake County Bar Association. ***PRACTICE AREAS:*** Business Law; Commercial Law; Estates, Wills and Trusts; Real Estate. **Email:** holland@bollman-lesser.com

(This Listing Continued)

BOLLMAN, LESSER & McGLYNN, LLP, Lake Forest—Continued

OF COUNSEL

ALBERT L. HALL, born Chicago, Illinois, June 17, 1926; admitted to bar, 1955, Illinois. *Education:* University of Illinois (B.S., 1949; M.S., 1950); Northwestern University (J.D., 1955). Phi Alpha Delta.

ROBERT M. BOLLMAN, born Harvey, Illinois, March 20, 1932; admitted to bar, 1956, Illinois; 1976, U.S. Supreme Court. *Education:* Albion College (A.B., 1953); Northwestern University (J.D., 1956). Arbitrator and Mediator, 19th Judicial Circuit, Lake County, Illinois. ***Email:*** Bollman@Bollman-Lesser.com

RICHARD B. KUSESKI, born Waukegan, Illinois, February 5, 1937; admitted to bar, 1963, Illinois. *Education:* Illinois Wesleyan University (B.S., 1959); John Marshall Law School (J.D., 1963). Public Defender, Lake County, 1964-1969. Arbitrator, 19th Judicial Circuit, Lake County, Illinois.

GEORGE M. COVINGTON

500 NORTH WESTERN AVENUE
SUITE 204
LAKE FOREST, ILLINOIS 60045
Telephone: 847-735-8764
Fax: 847-735-8770
Email: gcovington@sbcglobal.net

Real Estate, Land Use and Zoning Law, Conservation Law.

GEORGE M. COVINGTON, born Lake Forest, Illinois, October 4, 1942; admitted to bar, 1967, Illinois. *Education:* Yale University (A.B., 1964); University of Chicago (J.D., 1967). Lambda Alpha (honorary Land Economics Society). Author: Chapter on Surveys in Basic Real Estate Practice, Published by Illinois Institute for Continuing Legal Education; Conservation Easements: A Win/Win for Preservationists and Real Estate Owners, Illinois Bar Journal, December, 1996. Lecturer, Boundary Law in Illinois, National Business Institute, 1992; Advanced Real Estate Law in Illinois, National Business Institute, 1993. *Member:* Chicago, Lake County, Illinois State and American Bar Associations. ***PRACTICE AREAS:*** Real Estate Law; Conservation Easements; Land Use and Zoning; Environmental Land Use; Historic Preservation.

REPRESENTATIVE CLIENTS: Baytree National Bank; Dearpath Farm LLC; Horizon Farms, Inc.; Lake Forest College; Lake Forest Graduate School of Management;Lake Forest Open Lands Association; Landmarks Preservation Council of Illinois; Presbyterian Homes; Randall Metals Corp.; Fox Valley Land Foundation; Barrington Hills Conservation Trust; Lake Forest Academy.

LAW OFFICE OF ROLAND A. ECKERT

222 EAST WISCONSIN AVENUE, SUITE 210
LAKE FOREST, ILLINOIS 60045-1721
Telephone: 847-615-1474
Fax: 847-615-1476
Email: r.eckert@eckertlawfirm.com
URL: http://www.eckertlawfirm.com

General Business Practice, Corporate, Contracts, Zoning, Planning and Land Use, Environmental, Hazardous Materials and Substances, Hazardous Materials Management, Hazardous Materials Transportation, Construction Defects, Mechanics Liens, Buying and Selling of Businesses, Family Business, Limited Liability Company, Partnership, Small Business, Real Estate, Commercial Real Estate, Condominium and Mortgages.

ROLAND A. ECKERT, born Chicago, Illinois, November 12, 1946; admitted to bar, 1976, Illinois; 1978, District of Columbia. *Education:* University of Illinois (B.S., with honors in Economics, 1973); Case Western Reserve University (J.D., 1976). Counsel to the Administrator, Federal Aviation Administration, 1977-1980. Director, Office of International Aviation, Federal Aviation Administration, 1980-1981. General Counsel, Illinois Department of Transportation, 1981-1984. Counsel, Illinois Export Development Authority, 1985-1986. Special Assistant Attorney General, 1985—. *Member:* Lake County (Chairman, Environmental Law Committee), Illinois State and American (Member, Forum Committee on Construction Law) Bar Associations. ***PRACTICE AREAS:*** General Practice.

FULLIN LEGAL SERVICES LLC

LAKE FOREST, ILLINOIS

(See Libertyville)

Patents, Trademarks, Licensing, Copyrights, Trade Secrets.

LEWINTHAL, SKLAMBERG & ASSOCIATES

LAKE FOREST, ILLINOIS

(See Northbrook)

Family Law, Divorce, Child Custody, Child Support, Spousal Support, Domestic Relations, Alimony, Matrimonial, Palimony, Paternity, Premarital Agreements and Separation Agreements, Divorce Tax Considerations.

LAW OFFICES OF STUART A. REID

222 EAST WISCONSIN AVENUE, SUITE 305
LAKE FOREST, ILLINOIS 60045
Telephone: 847-295-0566
Fax: 847-295-0577
Email: reidlaw@comcast.net
URL: http://www.reidlawoffice.com

Matrimonial Law, Family Law, Domestic Relations, Divorce/Dissolution of Marriage, Child Custody, Child Support, Visitation Rights, Spousal Support/Alimony/Maintenance, Juvenile Law.

STUART A. REID, born Arlington Heights, Illinois, August 19, 1970; admitted to bar, 1997, Illinois. *Education:* University of Iowa (B.A., 1992; J.D., 1997).

SCHIFF HARDIN LLP

A Limited Liability Partnership Including Professional Corporations

Founded in 1864

ONE WESTMINSTER PLACE
LAKE FOREST, ILLINOIS 60045
Telephone: 847-295-9200
Facsimile: 847-295-7810

General Practice.

LAW FIRM ALLIANCES/ASSOCIATIONS: ***TERRALEX, THE WORLDWIDE NETWORK OF INDEPENDENT LAW FIRMS***

UNITED STATES LAW FIRM GROUP

PARTNER

RANDOLPH M. PERKINS, admitted to bar, 1982, Illinois. *Education:* Illinois State University (B.S., summa cum laude, 1977); University of Illinois (J.D., magna cum laude, 1982). Order of the Coif. Harno Fellow. Recipient, Rickert Award for Excellence in Legal Writing. Notes and Comments Editor, University of Illinois Law Review, 1981-1982. Judicial Law Clerk to Justice Robert C. Underwood, Illinois Supreme Court, 1982-1983. ***PRACTICE AREAS:*** Corporate Law; Commercial Law; Commercial Leasing; Commercial Licensing; Real Estate; Business Dispute Resolution; Private Business Law. ***Email:*** rperkins@schiffhardin.com

OF COUNSEL

SUSAN M. CARLSON, admitted to bar, 1975, Illinois. *Education:* Mundelein College (B.A., 1971); Northwestern University (J.D., cum laude, 1975). ***PRACTICE AREAS:*** Taxation; Estate Planning; Private Business Law; Business Dispute Resolution. ***Email:*** scarlson@schiffhardin.com

NICOLE FINITZO, admitted to bar, 1975, Illinois. *Education:* Northwestern University (B.S., Journalism, 1972; J.D., cum laude, 1975). Kappa Tau Alpha. ***PRACTICE AREAS:*** Corporate Law; Nonprofit Organizations Law; Federal Taxation; Commercial Law; Business Dispute Resolution; Privately-Held Business Law; Employment Law. ***Email:*** nfinitzo@schiffhardin.com

KATHERINE J. LEVY, admitted to bar, 1980, Illinois. *Education:* DePaul University (B.S., Accountancy, with honors, 1969; M.S., Taxation, 1973; J.D., 1980). Beta Alpha Psi; Sigma Iota Epsilon. Recipient, American Jurisprudence Prize Award, 1979. Certified Public Accountant, Illinois, 1969. ***PRACTICE AREAS:*** Taxation; Estate Planning; Estate Administration; Business Law. ***Email:*** klevy@schiffhardin.com

RICHARD L. VERKLER, admitted to bar, 1962, Illinois. *Education:* University of Illinois (B.S., 1959); University of Wisconsin-Madison (J.D., 1962). Order of the Coif; Phi Alpha Delta. Member, Board of Editors, 1960-1962 and Articles Editor, 1961-1962, Wisconsin Law Review. ***PRACTICE AREAS:*** Corporate Law; Federal Taxation; Private Business Law; Business Dispute Resolution; Commercial Law; Nonprofit Organizations Law. ***Email:*** rverkler@schiffhardin.com

ASSOCIATES

Nathan A. Engel ***Charlene Q. Kalebic***

SCHILLER, DuCANTO AND FLECK

Established in 1981

SUITE 300, 207 EAST WESTMINSTER AVENUE
LAKE FOREST, ILLINOIS 60045-1857
Telephone: 847-615-8300
Fax: 847-615-8284
Email: schillerducantoandfleck@sdflaw.com
URL: http://www.sdflaw.com

Chicago, Illinois Office: 200 North La Salle Street, 30th Floor. Telephone: 312-641-5560. Fax: 312-641-6361.

Wheaton, Illinois Office: 311 South County Farm Road, Suite G. Telephone: 630-665-5800. Fax: 630-665-6082.

Family Law, Complex Domestic Relations Issues, Divorce/Dissolution of Marriage, Prenuptial Agreements/Premarital Agreements, Child Custody and Visitation, Spousal Support/Alimony/Maintenance, Matrimonial Law and Litigation, Appeals, Mediation-Family/ Divorce, Marital Settlement Agreements, Separation Agreements, Property Rights, Financial Discovery and Analysis Related to Divorce, and Tax Considerations Related to Divorce.

(This Listing Continued)

FIRM PROFILE: Schiller, DuCanto and Fleck is the largest law firm in the country to devote its practice exclusively to matrimonial law. The firm was founded in 1981 by Chicago attorneys Donald C. Schiller and Joseph N. DuCanto. Charles J. Fleck, former presiding judge of the Cook County Domestic Relations Division, joined in 1982. Firm members are nationally recognized experts in all aspects of matrimonial law, and many are current and past leaders of local, state and national bar associations. The biographies listed below contain specific references to articles authored, memberships and offices held by our attorneys within the last seven years. A more complete list can be found in the extended biographies listed on the firm's web page.

PARTNERS

CHARLES J. FLECK, born Evanston, Illinois, May 1, 1940; admitted to bar, 1967, Illinois and U.S. District Court, Northern District of Illinois. *Education:* Northwestern University (B.A., 1963); Valparaiso University (J.D., 1967). Listed: Best Lawyers of America, by Neifeh and Smith, 1987-2001 eds.; Illinois Super Lawyers (Family Law) 2004—. Member of Leading Lawyers Network 2004—. Author: "FinPlan's Divorce Planner," American Bar Association Family Advocate, Winter, 1992-2002 issues; Chapter 18, Illinois Family Law, "Marital Settlement Agreements," IICLE, 1992. Lecturer and Seminar Panelist: American Academy of Matrimonial Lawyers, Illinois Chapter, September, 1991 "Contributions Pursuant to Sec. 503(c)(1) & (2) and 503 (d)(1) of the IMDMA". Judge: Circuit Court of Cook County, Trial Section, Domestic Relations Division, 1978-1979. Chief Presiding Judge, Domestic Relations Division, Circuit Court of Cook County, 1979-1982. Seminar Panelist, Illinois Institute, Legal Education, "Marital Settlement Agreements"; Lake County Bar Association Annual Seminar, Napa, California, 1998. *Member:* Illinois State (Member: Bench and Bar Section-Council, 1983-1987, Chairman, 1987; Family Law Section, 1982-1989) and American (Member, Family Law Section, 1982—) Bar Associations; Illinois Judges Association (Member, Board of Directors, 1978—). **Email:** cfleck@sdflaw.com

CARLTON R. MARCYAN, born Chicago, Illinois, January 27, 1955; admitted to bar, 1981, Illinois. *Education:* Kalamazoo College; DePaul University (B.S.C., 1976); John Marshall Law School (J.D., 1980). Beta Alpha Psi. Delta Theta Phi. Recipient: Chicago Volunteer Legal Services Foundation Distinguished Service Award 2000; The John Marshall Law School Alumni Association Distinguished Service Award 2003. Listed, Illinois Super Lawyers (Family Law) 2004—. Member of Leading Lawyers Network 2004—. Certified Public Accountant, Illinois, 1978. Certified Financial Planner, 1991. Certified Divorce Planner, 2000. Contributing Author: Tax Matters, American Journal of Family Law, Aspen Law & Business, 1999—. Lecturer: Trial Techniques and Divorce Taxation, American Bar Association, 1993-1994. Instructor: Northeastern Illinois University, 1981-1986; Taxation and Trial Practice, Illinois Institute for Continuing Legal Education, 1988—; Valuation and Financial Planning, Illinois Society of Certified Public Accountants, 1990. Diplomate, American Board of Forensic Accounting, 1998. President, The Advocates Society, 1988; President, ISBA Family Law Section Board Member, 2002—; ICPAS Special Interest Group Executive Committee 2002—; The John Marshall Law School Alumni Association Board Member, 2003. *Member:* Illinois State and American Bar Associations; American Academy of Matrimonial Lawyers (Governor and Officer, 1996-1998); American Institute of Certified Public Accountants; Illinois Society of Certified Public Accountants; American Association of Attorney - Certified Public Accountants. [With U.S. Marine Corps, 1973-1975]. **Email:** cmarcyan@sdflaw.com

ERIC L. SCHULMAN, born Chicago, Illinois, March 12, 1971; admitted to bar, 1997, Illinois; 1998, U.S. District Court, Northern District of Illinois. *Education:* University of Iowa (B.A., 1994); John Marshall Law School (J.D., cum laude, 1997). Author: "Sleeping with the Enemy: Combating the Sexual Spread of HIV-AIDS," The John Marshall Law Review, Summer 1996. *Member:* Chicago (Family Law Co-Chairman, Young Lawyers Section; Judicial Evaluation Committee), Illinois State (Family Law Section) and American Bar Associations. **Email:** eschulman@sdflaw.com

MARIO R. VENTRELLI, born Chicago, Illinois, May 28, 1968; admitted to bar, 1995, Illinois. *Education:* DePaul University (B.A., 1991; J.D., 1995). Pi Sigma Alpha. Justinian Society of Lawyers. Golden Key National Honor Society. Recipient, John G. Phillips Scholarship. Author: "Practice Tips: Hearsay," Kane County Bar Journal, February 1997; "A Leveling-of-the-Playing Field Primer," Kane County Bar Journal, June 1997. Speaker: K.I.D.S., Kids in a Divorcing Society Program: David Peskind Annual Family Law Seminar; Family Law Update, Illinois State Bar Association Annual Meeting, 1999, 2000. *Member:* Illinois State (Member, Family Law Section) and American (Member, Family Law Section) Bar Associations. **Email:** mventrelli@sdflaw.com

RESIDENT ASSOCIATES

NEAL A. SIMON, born Harvey, Illinois, January 31, 1978; admitted to bar, 2003, Illinois. *Education:* University of Illinois (B.S., 2000); DePaul University (J.D., 2003). **Email:** nsimon@sdflaw.com

MARY A. ZAMBRENO, born October 3, 1978; admitted to bar, 2004, Illinois. *Education:* Northwestern University (B.A., 2001); DePaul University (J.D., 2004). **Email:** mzambreno@sdflaw.com

SEMMELMAN & SEMMELMAN, LTD.

191 EAST DEERPATH, SUITE 301
LAKE FOREST, ILLINOIS 60045
Telephone: 847-234-4438
Fax: 847-234-4674
URL: http://www.semmelmanlaw.com

Estate Planning, Wills, Trusts, Probate, Real Estate and Business Matters.

ANDREW A. SEMMELMAN, born Libertyville, Illinois, June 20, 1931; admitted to bar, 1959, Illinois. *Education:* Lake Forest College (B.A., 1953); University of Illinois (LL.B., 1959). Phi Alpha Delta. Assistant State's Attorney, Lake County, 1959-1963. Magistrate of Circuit Court, Lake County, 1963-1966. *Member:* Lake County and Illinois State Bar Associations. ***PRACTICE AREAS:*** Zoning Law; Subdivision Law; Probate Law; Estate Planning Law; Real Estate. **Email:** andrew@semmelmanlaw.com

(This Listing Continued)

DAVID A. SEMMELMAN, born Lake Forest, Illinois, September 1, 1957; admitted to bar, 1983, Illinois. *Education:* University of Wisconsin-Madison (B.S., 1979); John Marshall School of Law (J.D., 1983). Assistant States Attorney, Lake County, 1983-1985. Certified Public Accountant, Illinois, 1990. Certified Mediator, Center for Conflict Resolution. *Member:* Lake County and Illinois State Bar Associations. ***PRACTICE AREAS:*** Real Estate Law; Estate Planning Law; Business Enterprises; Business Law. **Email:** david@semmelmanlaw.com

KIMBERLY SMORON WISNESKI, born Chicago, Illinois, October 19, 1972; admitted to bar, 1997, Illinois. *Education:* University of Iowa (B.A., Philosophy, with honors, 1994); Illinois Institute of Chicago-Kent College of Law (J.D., 1997). Author: "Conflicting Rules in Child Custody Mediation: Impartiality/Neutrality and the Best Interests of the Child," Family & Conciliation Courts Review (April, 1998); Certified Mediator Trainer, Center for Conflict Resolution, 1995—. *Member:* Lake County and Illinois State Bar Associations; Society of Professionals in Dispute Resolution; Academy of Family Mediators; Mediation Council of Illinois; Advocates Society. ***PRACTICE AREAS:*** Real Estate Law; Estate Planning; Business Law; Mediation. **Email:** kim@semmelmanlaw.com

REFERENCES: Northern Trust Bank/Lake Forest; Lake Forest Bank & Trust.

DAVID DEROSE

LAKE VILLA, ILLINOIS

(See Lindenhurst)

Personal Injury, Real Estate, Estate Planning, Wills, Corporate Law, Evictions, Foreclosures.

ARMSTRONG & SURIN

LA SALLE, ILLINOIS

(See Ottawa)

Personal Injury, Workers Compensation, Corporation, Probate, Real Estate, Negligence, Family Law, Bankruptcy, Criminal, Traffic, Wills and Trusts.

HERBOLSHEIMER, LANNON, HENSON, DUNCAN AND REAGAN, P.C.

Established in 1916
STATE BANK BUILDING
SUITE 400, 654 FIRST STREET
P.O. BOX 539
LA SALLE, ILLINOIS 61301
Telephone: 815-223-0111
Fax: 815-223-5829

Ottawa, Illinois Office: First Federal Savings Bank Building, 633 La Salle Street, Suite 409. Telephone: 815-434-1400. Fax: 815-434-2423.

Corporate Law, Business Law, Criminal Law, DWI/DUI, Juvenile Law, Employment Law, Administrative Law, Employment Termination, Sexual Harassment, Estate Planning, Probate, Tax Planning, Wills and Trusts, Family Law, Divorce, Adoption, Prenuptial Agreements, Health Care, Civil Litigation, Insurance Defense, Products Liability, Insurance, Subrogation, Real Estate, Boundary Disputes, Easements.

FIRM PROFILE: Herbolsheimer, Lannon, Henson, Duncan and Reagan was founded by J.E. Malone in 1916 serving clients throughout Illinois. The firm is a General Practice firm with a focus on Insurance Defense, and Civil Litigation.

GEORGE L. HERBOLSHEIMER (1911-1992)

R. JAMES LANNON, JR., born Springfield, Illinois, May 5, 1934; admitted to bar, 1960, Illinois. *Education:* University of Illinois (B.S., 1956; J.D., 1960). Phi Delta Phi; Order of the Coif. *Member:* LaSalle-Peru-Oglesby-Spring Valley (President, 1965-1981), Tri-City, La Salle County (President, 1964-1966), Illinois State and American Bar Associations. ***PRACTICE AREAS:*** Civil Trial; Insurance Defense; Administrative Law; Workers Compensation; Appellate Practice; Professional Liability; Divorce; Real Estate. **Email:** jlannon@hlhdr.com

T. DONALD HENSON, born Murray, Kentucky, July 24, 1942; admitted to bar, 1967, Illinois. *Education:* Murray State University and University of Illinois (B.S., 1964); University of Illinois (J.D., 1967). Phi Delta Phi. *Member:* La Salle County (President, 1980-1981), Illinois State (Member, Board of Governors, 1975-1978) and American Bar Associations. Fellow, American College of Trial Lawyers; Defense Research Institute; Illinois Trial Lawyers Association; Illinois Defense Counsel; Association of Insurance Attorneys. Charter Fellow, Illinois Bar Foundation. ***PRACTICE AREAS:*** Civil Litigation; Health Care; Product Liability; Insurance Defense; Will Contests. **Email:** dhenson@hlhdr.com

JOHN S. DUNCAN, III, born La Salle, Illinois, September 6, 1948; admitted to bar, 1973, Illinois. *Education:* John Carroll University (B.S.B.A., 1970); Loyola University (J.D., 1973). *Member:* La Salle County and Illinois State Bar Associations. ***PRACTICE AREAS:*** Corporate Law; Real Estate; Taxation; Probate; Estate Planning; Financial Planning. **Email:** jduncan@hlhdr.com

MICHAEL T. REAGAN, born Charleston, West Virginia, July 22, 1947; admitted to bar, 1972, Illinois. *Education:* Purdue University (B.S.M.E., 1969); Georgetown University (J.D., 1972). Pi Tau Sigma; Omicron Delta Kappa. Member, Illinois Supreme Court Committee on Pattern Jury Instructions, 1985-1995; Reporter, 1996—. *Member:* Chicago, La Salle County, Illinois State (Chair, Tort Law Section Council, 1989) and American Bar As-

(This Listing Continued)

HERBOLSHEIMER, LANNON, HENSON, DUNCAN AND REAGAN, P.C., La Salle—Continued

sociations; Appellate Lawyers Association (President, 1995-1996); Illinois Association of Hospital Attorneys; Illinois Defense Counsel; Defense Research Institute; Association of Insurance Attorneys. Fellow, Illinois Bar Foundation. (Resident, Ottawa Office). ***PRACTICE AREAS:*** Health Care; Civil Trial; Insurance Defense; Appellate; Administrative Law. ***Email:*** mreagan@hlhdr.com

DOUGLAS A. GIFT, born Freeport, Illinois, February 17, 1950; admitted to bar, 1975, Illinois. *Education:* Illinois State University (B.S., with honors, 1972); University of Illinois (J.D., with honors, 1975). Phi Delta Phi; Order of The Coif. *Member:* La Salle County, Illinois State and American Bar Associations; Illinois Association of Healthcare Attorneys (Member, Board of Directors, 1985-1989). ***PRACTICE AREAS:*** Hospital Law; Health Care; Civil Trial; Insurance Defense; Employment Law; Administrative Law; Adoption Law. ***Email:*** dgift@hlhdr.com

GARY R. EITEN, born Spring Valley, Illinois, January 24, 1954; admitted to bar, 1980, Illinois. *Education:* University of Illinois (B.S., 1976); Chicago-Kent College of Law (J.D., 1980). *Member:* La Salle County and Illinois State Bar Associations; Illinois Defense Counsel; Illinois State Bar Association Assembly. ***PRACTICE AREAS:*** Civil Trial; Insurance Defense; Real Estate; Administrative Law; Employment Law. ***Email:*** geiten@hlhdr.com

KAREN C. EITEN, born Oak Park, Illinois, September 12, 1958; admitted to bar, 1983, Illinois; 1984, Nebraska. *Education:* Western Illinois University (B.A., 1980); DePaul University College of Law (J.D., 1983). *Member:* LaSalle County, Illinois State, Nebraska State and American Bar Associations. ***PRACTICE AREAS:*** Family Law; Dissolution of Marriage; Divorce; Post Decree Modifications; Civil Litigation; Insurance Defense. ***Email:*** keiten@hlhdr.com

MICHAEL C. JANSZ, born Freeport, Illinois, January 1, 1963; admitted to bar, 1988, Illinois. *Education:* Loras College (B.A., 1985); Northern Illinois University (J.D., 1988). Phi Alpha Delta. *Member:* La Salle County (President, 1996—), Illinois State and American Bar Associations; Illinois Association of Defense Trial Counsel. (Resident, Ottawa Office). ***PRACTICE AREAS:*** Civil Trial; Insurance Defense; Employment Law; DUI; DWI; Litigation; Criminal Misdemeanor. ***Email:*** mjansz@hlhdr.com

---

JILL W. KLEIN, born Rockford, Illinois, November 25, 1967; admitted to bar, 1992, Illinois and U.S. District Court, Northern District of Illinois. *Education:* Illinois State University (B.S., cum laude, 1989); Northern Illinois University (J.D., cum laude, 1992). Delta Theta Phi. Member, National Mock Trial Team. Editor, Notes and Comments, Northern Illinois Law Review, 1991-1992. Author: "Michigan Department of State Police v. Sitz: Suspicionless Seizures and The Fourth Amendment," Vol. 11, Northern Illinois University Law Review, 349. *Member:* LaSalle County (Vice President, 1994-1996; Secretary, 1997—), Illinois State and American Bar Associations. ***PRACTICE AREAS:*** Real Estate; Financial Planning; Corporate Law; Taxation; Probate; Estate Planning; Insurance Defense; Employment Law. ***Email:*** jklein@hlhdr.com

TODD L. MARTIN, born Mendota, Illinois, November 30, 1965; admitted to bar, 1994, Illinois; 1995, U.S. District Court, Northern District of Illinois. *Education:* Southern Illinois University at Carbondale (B.A., 1990); Thomas M. Cooley Law School (J.D., 1994). *Member:* LaSalle County and Illinois State Bar Associations. ***PRACTICE AREAS:*** Insurance Defense; Criminal Law. ***Email:*** tmartin@hlhdr.com

WILLIAM P. HINTZ, born Chicago, Illinois, November 9, 1958; admitted to bar, 1983, Illinois. *Education:* DePaul University (B.A., 1980; J.D., 1983). *Member:* LaSalle County Bar Association. ***LANGUAGES:*** Spanish. ***PRACTICE AREAS:*** Personal Injury; Real Estate; Civil Rights; Municipal Law. ***Email:*** bhintz@hlhdr.com

STEPHEN M. OSBORNE, born July 13, 1961; admitted to bar, 1986, Illinois. *Education:* University of Illinois (A.B., 1983); Southern Illinois University (J.D., 1986). ***PRACTICE AREAS:*** Insurance Defense. ***Email:*** sosborne@hlhdr.com

REPRESENTATIVE CLIENTS: Aetna Life and Casualty Insurance Company; American States Insurance Co.; Badge-A-Minit, Inc.; Bituminous Casualty Insurance Cos.; Cincinnati Insurance Company; ComEd; Commercial Union Insurance Company; Community Hospital of Ottawa; Crum & Forster Insurance Company; Eureka Savings Bank; Farmers Insurance Group; General Casualty; Great Central Insurance Company; Hawkeye-Security Insurance Company; Home Insurance Company; Illinois Founder Insurance Company; Illinois Cement Company; Illinois Valley Community Hospital; Illinois Valley Contractor's Association; Indiana Insurance Company; LaSalle State Bank; Liberty Mutual Insurance Company; Lumbermen's Mutual (Kemper Group); Milwaukee Mutual Insurance Company; Ohio Casualty Group; Ottawa Community Hospital; Pekin Insurance Company; Rokford Mutual; Sauer-Sundstrand; St. Paul Insurance Company; Standard Mutual Insurance Company; State Farm Insurance Company; Transamerica Insurance Group; Travelers Insurance Company; U.S.F.& G.; Insurance Company; Western States Insurance Company; Zurich Insurance Company.

LAW OFFICES OF LEYNAUD & LEYNAUD

A PROFESSIONAL CORPORATION

LA SALLE, ILLINOIS

(See Peru)

General Civil and Trial Practice, Personal Injury, Mediation, Worker's Compensation, Real Estate, Criminal, Landlord/Tenant and Family Law. Business/Banking Litigation, DUI and Traffic. Insurance, General Practice, Medical Malpractice, Zoning and Land Use. Bad Faith, Drug Crimes, Juvenile Crimes, White Collar, Adoptions, Child Custody, Divorce, Child Support, Visitation Rights, Domestic Violence. Auto Accidents, Dog Bites, Slip and Fall, Wrongful Death, Buying and Selling, Wills and Probate.

THE BRAINARD LAW OFFICES

LAWRENCEVILLE, ILLINOIS

(See Charleston)

General Practice. Insurance Defense, Personal Injury, Products Liability, Probate, Trusts, Real Estate, Taxation, Municipal, Family and Health Law. Trials in all State and Federal Courts.

EMISON DOOLITTLE KOLB & ROELLGEN

LAWRENCEVILLE, ILLINOIS

(See Vincennes, Indiana)

General Practice. Trials, Estate Planning and Administration, Family Law, Bankruptcy, Corporation, Commercial and Insurance Law.

GOSNELL, BORDEN, ENLOE & SLOSS, LTD.

815 12TH STREET
P.O. BOX 737
LAWRENCEVILLE, ILLINOIS 62439-2496
Telephone: 618-943-2338
Fax: 618-943-2080
Email: gbes@midwest.net
URL: http://www.lawyers.com/gbes

General Practice. Insurance Defense. Trials. Probate Law. Oil and Gas Law. Personal Injury, Family Law.

JOHN F. BORDEN, born Vincennes, Indiana, October 2, 1945; admitted to bar, 1970, Illinois. *Education:* Greenville College (B.A., cum laude, 1967); University of Illinois (J.D., 1970). Phi Alpha Theta. Assistant Attorney General, Inheritance Tax Division, 1971-1982. Executive Secretary, Lawrence County Housing Authority, 1971-1973. *Member:* Lawrence County, Illinois State and American Bar Associations. ***PRACTICE AREAS:*** Probate; Oil and Gas Law; General Practice.

DOUGLAS A. ENLOE, born Vincennes, Indiana, July 14, 1948; admitted to bar, 1973, Illinois. *Education:* Eastern Illinois University (B.S., 1970); University of Illinois (J.D., 1973). City Attorney, 1974-1997; 2001— *Member:* Lawrence County, Illinois State and American Bar Associations; International Association of Insurance Counsel. Fellow: American College of Trial Lawyers; Illinois Association of Defense Trial Lawyers. ***PRACTICE AREAS:*** Insurance Defense; Personal Injury.

LARRY N. SLOSS, JR., born Mt. Carmel, Illinois, January 26, 1962; admitted to bar, 1987, Illinois. *Education:* Southern Illinois University (B.A., 1984; J.D., 1987). *Member:* Lawrence County, Illinois State and American Bar Associations; Illinois Association of Defense Trial Lawyers. ***PRACTICE AREAS:*** Insurance Defense; Oil and Gas Law; Family Law.

DARIN K. RICE, born Eldorado, Illinois, May 6, 1974; admitted to bar, 2000, Illinois. *Education:* Judson College (B.A., with high distinction, 1996); Southern Illinois University (J.D., 1999). ***PRACTICE AREAS:*** Insurance Defense; General Practice. ***Email:*** drice@midwest.net

OF COUNSEL

MAURICE E. GOSNELL, born Lawrenceville, Illinois, February 7, 1911; admitted to bar, 1934, Illinois. *Education:* University of Illinois (B.S., 1932; J.D., 1934). Member, Ohio River Valley Sanitation Commission, 1955-1966. Assistant Attorney General, 1969-1985. U.S. Magistrate, 1971-1975. Member, Board of Trustees, Vincennes University, 1952-1975. City Attorney, Lawrenceville, 1935-1941, 1953-1961, 1973-1974. Member, Illinois Supreme Court Committee to Recommend Rules for Implementation of Mandatory Court-Annexed Arbitration, 1985—. *Member:* Lawrence County, Illinois State (Member, Board of Governors, 1959-1965) and American Bar Associations; Society of Trial Lawyers; International Association of Insurance Counsel; Lawyer-Pilots Bar Association (President, 1974-1978). Fellow: Illinois Bar Foundation; American College of Trial Lawyers; American Bar Foundation.

LOCAL COUNSEL FOR: First Bank of Lawrence County; Old National Bank; First Federal Bank of Vincennes, Indiana; American Federal Credit Union; Rockford Mutual Insurance Co.; Hartford Accident & Indemnity Co.; Aetna Casualty & Surety Co.; State Farm Insurance Cos.; Country Mutual Insurance Cos.; Farm Credit System; Met/Life Insurance Co.; Bituminous Casualty Co.; Millers Mutual Insurance Assn.; Continental Insurance Co.; Crum & Forster Group; Indiana Industrial Insurance Co.; General Casualty Co.; Standard Mutual Insurance Co.; Safeco Insurance Co.; Illinois Municipal League; Risk Management Association; Toirma.

HART BELL LLC

LAWRENCEVILLE, ILLINOIS

(See Vincennes, Indiana)

General Practice. Litigation, Insurance, Banking, Corporate, Employment, Probate and Estate Planning, State and Federal Tax Law, Real Estate, Construction, Commercial, Business, Elder, Creditors Rights, Personal Injury, Family Law and Criminal Defense.

THE CHAWLA GROUP, LTD.

LEMONT, ILLINOIS

(See Hinsdale)

Entertainment Law, Corporate Law, Civil Practice, Domestic Relations, Personal Injury, Medical Malpractice.

MASARU K. TAKIGUCHI

LEMONT, ILLINOIS

(See Oak Brook)

Real Estate, Probate and Estate Planning, Civil Litigation, Commercial Transactions.

WESTERVELT, JOHNSON, NICOLL & KELLER, LLC

LEWISTOWN, ILLINOIS

(See Peoria)

General Civil Trial and Appellate Practice in State and Federal Courts, Insurance Defense, Health and Health Care, Labor Relations, Employment Discrimination and Affirmative Action, Products Liability Litigation, ERISA and Benefits Plans, Corporate, Agricultural, Bankruptcy, Creditors' Rights, Banking, Real Estate, State and Federal Taxation, Estate Planning, Trusts and Probate, Workers Compensation, Environmental, Commercial.

ASHMAN LAW OFFICES, LLC

LIBERTYVILLE, ILLINOIS

(See Chicago)

Business, Corporate and Commercial Litigation, Securities Litigation, Class Actions, Internet Law, Insurance Litigation, Employment Litigation, Civil Rights, Intellectual Property Litigation, Corporate Counseling, and Foreign Corrupt Practices Act Litigation and Counseling.

BEERMANN & DeBRUYNE

728 FLORSHEIM DRIVE
LIBERTYVILLE, ILLINOIS 60048
Telephone: 847-680-7070
Fax: 847-816-6122
URL: http://www.beermanndebruyne.com

Family Law, Divorce, Adoption, Separation Agreements, Child Custody, Child Support, Domestic Violence, Visitation Rights, Family Mediation Adoption Law, Juvenile Law, Real Estate.

JON L. BEERMANN, born Chicago, Illinois, December 1, 1939; admitted to bar, 1964, Illinois. *Education:* University of Wisconsin-Madison (B.B.A., 1961); University of Chicago (J.D., 1964). *Lake County (Member, Family Law Committee, 1980—), Chicago, Illinois State and American Bar Associations.* ***PRACTICE AREAS:*** Family Law; Real Estate. ***Email:*** jbeermann@aol.com

KATHY J. DEBRUYNE, admitted to bar, 1993, Illinois. *Education:* National College of Education, Evanston (B.A., 1987); Loyola University (J.D., 1992). *Member:* Lake County (Member, Family Law Section) and Illinois State Bar Associations; Association of Women Attorney Lake County. ***PRACTICE AREAS:*** Family Law; Divorce; Separation Agreements; Child Custody; Family Mediation; Adoption Law; Juvenile Law; Real Estate. ***Email:*** kathy@beermanfamilylaw.com

MARC J. BEERMANN, born Chicago, Illinois, December 30, 1971; admitted to bar, 2002, Illinois. *Education:* University of Wisconsin-Madison (B.S., 1994); DePaul University, College of Law (J.D., 2002). *Member:* Lake County, Chicago, Illinois State and American Bar Associations; Association of Women Attorneys of Lake County. ***PRACTICE AREAS:*** Divorce; Real Estate; Family Law. ***Email:*** marc@beermannfamilylaw.com

CASSIDAY, SCHADE & GLOOR, LLP

Established in 1979

1870 WEST WINCHESTER ROAD
SUITE 148
LIBERTYVILLE, ILLINOIS 60048-5353
Telephone: 847-932-6922
Fax: 847-932-6947
URL: http://www.cassiday.com

Chicago, Illinois Office: 20 North Wacker Drive, Suite 1040, 60606-2903. Telephone: 312-641-3100. Fax: 312-444-1669.
Naperville, Illinois Office: 1230 East Diehl Road, Suite 202, 60563-9362. Telephone: 630-328-2970. Fax: 630-328-2979.
Rockford, Illinois Office: 120 West State Street, Suite 401, 61101-1159. Telephone: 815-962-8301. Fax: 815-962-8401.

General Practice. Civil Trial Practice, Civil Appellate Practice, Insurance Coverage, Environmental, Medical and Professional Malpractice, Products Liability, Structural Work Act, Railroad, Employment, Corporate and Health Care Law, Commercial Litigation, Construction, Workers Compensation, Intellectual Property, Municipalities, Transportation, Patent Law.

FIRM PROFILE: Serving Boone, Lake, Kane, McHenry and Winnebago Counties, State of Wisconsin and associated Federal District Courts and National Trial Practice.

The firm also has an established Quality Control Department.

MEMBERS OF FIRM

MARC F. BENJOYA, born Chicago, Illinois, July 3, 1958; admitted to bar, 1983, Illinois including Federal Trial Bar, U.S. District Court, Northern District of Illinois and Wisconsin; 1999, U.S. District Court, Southern District of Indiana. *Education:* Northern Illinois University (B.A., cum laude, 1980); IIT/Chicago-Kent College of Law (J.D., 1983). *Member:* Lake County, Illinois State and Wisconsin State Bar Associations; Illinois Association of Hospital Attorneys; Illinois Association of Defense Trial Counsel. (Also at Rockford). ***PRACTICE AREAS:*** Professional Negligence; Professional Liability Defense; Insurance Defense. ***Email:*** mfb@cs-g.com

JOHN R. DAVIS, born Sterling, Kansas, December 19, 1951; admitted to bar, 1983, Illinois; U.S. District Court, Northern District of Illinois; U.S. District Court, Eastern District of Wisconsin; U.S. Court of Appeals, Seventh Circuit. *Education:* University of Illinois (B.S., 1974); John Marshall Law School (J.D., 1983). *Member:* Illinois State Bar Association; Defense Research Institute; Christian Legal Society. ***PRACTICE AREAS:*** Personal Injury Defense; Professional Liability Defense; Insurance Defense. ***Email:*** jrd@cs-g.com

JOHN J. REID, born Park Ridge, Illinois, January 17, 1971; admitted to bar, 1996, Illinois. *Education:* Northwestern University (B.A., 1993); IIT/Chicago-Kent College of Law (J.D., 1996). *Member:* Lake County and Illinois State Bar Associations; Defense Research Institute; Illinois Association of Defense Trial Counsel. ***PRACTICE AREAS:*** Medical Malpractice Defense; Products Liability Defense. ***Email:*** jjr@cs-g.com

ASSOCIATES

JAMES A. BERGLUND, born Chicago, Illinois, March 5, 1961; admitted to bar, 1986, Illinois. *Education:* Drake University (B.A., 1983); Chicago-Kent College of Law, Illinois Institute of Technology (J.D., 1986). *Member:* Chicago Bar Association. ***PRACTICE AREAS:*** Defense Litigation. ***Email:*** jb@cs-g.com

ANDREW T. FLEISHMAN, born Boston, Massachusetts, September 15, 1968; admitted to bar, 2001, Illinois. *Education:* New York University (B.A., 1991); Illinois Institute of Technology, Chicago-Kent College of Law (J.D., 1995). (Also at Chicago Office). ***Email:*** atf@cs-g.com

JAMIE H. GOLDSTEIN, born Skokie, Illinois, January 28, 1979; admitted to bar, 2004, Illinois. *Education:* University of Wisconsin-Madison (B.S., 2001); Illinois Institute of Technology, Chicago-Kent College of Law (J.D., 2004). Order of the Coif. (Also at Chicago Office). ***Email:*** jhg@cs-g.com

ROBIN B. LEVIN, born Skokie, Illinois, June 7, 1968; admitted to bar, 1999, Illinois. *Education:* University of Illinois (B.S., 1990); John Marshall Law School (J.D., 1999). ***Email:*** rbl@cs-g.com

DANIEL E. WIESCH, born Chicago, Illinois, March 4, 1975; admitted to bar, 2001, Illinois. *Education:* Northwestern University (B.A., 1997); University of Illinois (J.D., cum laude, 2001). ***Email:*** dew@cs-g.com

OF COUNSEL

TAMI J. REDING-BRUBAKER, born Chicago, Illinois, November 20, 1958; admitted to bar, 1983, Illinois. *Education:* North Central College (B.A., cum laude, 1980); IIT/Chicago-Kent College of Law (J.D., 1983). *Member:* Lake County and Illinois State Bar Associations. ***PRACTICE AREAS:*** Medical Malpractice Defense. ***Email:*** tjr@cs-g.com

References Available Upon Request.

(For complete biographical data on all personnel, see Professional Biographies at Chicago, Illinois)

DeSANTO, MORGAN & MITTELMAN

AN ASSOCIATION OF PROFESSIONAL CORPORATIONS

An Association of Professional Corporations

712 FLORSHEIM DRIVE
LIBERTYVILLE, ILLINOIS 60048-5270
Telephone: 847-816-8100
Facsimile: 847-816-8126
Email: desanto@iconnect.net
URL: http://www.lawyers.com/desantolaw

Plaintiff's Personal Injury, Automobile Accidents and Injuries, Slip and Fall, Wrongful Death, Insurance Bad Faith, Products Liability, Commercial Litigation, Employment Litigation, Discrimination, Harassment, Wrongful Termination.

JAMES J. DeSANTO, P.C., born Chicago, Illinois, October 12, 1943; admitted to bar, 1969, Illinois and U.S. District Court, Northern District of Illinois; 1972, U.S. Court of Appeals, Seventh Circuit; 1975, U.S. Supreme Court. *Education:* University of Illinois (B.A., 1965); DePaul University College of Law (J.D., 1969). Listed in: Who's Who in American Law, 1987—; Who's Who in America, 2000—; Guidebook of Law and Leading Attorneys, 1995. Co-Editor, Tort Trends, Illinois Bar Association, 1987-1990. Chairman, Tort Section Council, Illinois State Bar Association, 1991-1992. Panel of Arbitrators, American Arbitration Association, 1978—. Certified Arbitrator and Mediator, 19th Judicial Circuit, 1997. Trustee, Village of Libertyville, 1992-1994. Elected Director, 1988-1999, Secretary/Treasurer, 1999—, Third Vice President, 2000— and Board of Directors Chairman, 2003—, Illinois State Bar Association Mutual Insurance Company. *Member:* Chicago, Lake County (President, 1993-1994) and Illinois State (Chairman, Finance and Budget Committee, 1988-1989; Chairman, Tort Law Section Council, 1991-1992; Member, Ad Hoc Committee on Professional Quality in the Practice of Law, 1994-1996) Bar Associations; Illinois Trial Lawyers Association; The Association of Trial Lawyers of America. Fellow: Illinois Bar Foundation; Jefferson Inns of Court (1992—). ***PRACTICE AREAS:*** Personal Injury; Wrongful Death; Professional Liability; Commercial Litigation; Construction Law; Employment Law. ***Email:*** desanto@iconnect.net

VERNON E. MORGAN, P.C., born Adrian, Michigan, March 9, 1947; admitted to bar, 1977, Iowa; 1979, Illinois. *Education:* University of Illinois (B.A., 1972); Drake University (J.D., 1976). ***LANGUAGES:*** Russian. ***PRACTICE AREAS:*** Business; Corporate; Transactions; Contracts; Real Estate. ***Email:*** morganv@lightfirst.com

RICHARD S. MITTELMAN, P.C., born Chicago, Illinois, December 11, 1951; admitted to bar, 1983, Illinois and U.S. District Court, Northern District of Illinois. *Education:* University of Illinois (B.A., 1974); DePaul University; IIT/Chicago-Kent College of Law (J.D., with honors, 1983). Certified Arbitrator, 19th Judicial Circuit; Hearing Officer, School District Student Expulsion Cases. *Member:* Lake County (Member, Family and Em-

(This Listing Continued)

DESANTO, MORGAN & MITTELMAN, AN ASSOCIATION OF PROFESSIONAL CORPORATIONS, Libertyville—Continued

ployment Law Committee) Bar Association. ***PRACTICE AREAS:*** Divorce (25%); Personal Injury (30%); Commercial Litigation (15%); Education Law (5%); Labor and Employment (10%). ***Email:*** mittelmanr@lightfirst.com

DUDLEY & LAKE LLC

100 EAST COOK AVENUE, 2ND FLOOR
LIBERTYVILLE, ILLINOIS 60048
Telephone: 847-362-5385
Fax: 847-362-5386
URL: http://www.dudleylake.com

Personal Injury, Wrongful Death, Medical Malpractice, Products Liability, Workers' Compensation, Construction Litigation.

J. MATTHEW DUDLEY, born Springfield, Missouri, August 26, 1967; admitted to bar, 1993, Illinois and U.S. District Court, Northern District of Illinois; 1997, U.S. District Court, Southern District of Wisconsin. *Education:* University of Southern Mississippi (B.S., 1989); University of Tulsa College of Law (J.D., 1993). Moderator: Practical Considerations In Handling Personal Injury Cases, Illinois Trial Lawyers Association, Urbana, Illinois, February, 2001; "What Not to Miss" Springfield, IL v. Illinois, Trial Lawyers Association. Lecturer: "How to Deal with Prior and Subsequent Treaters," Medical Malpractice Seminar, Illinois Trial Lawyers Association, Chicago, Illinois, December 7, 2002; "How to Depose a Treating Physician, Deposing Doctors: How to Avoid the Land Mines", Illinois Institute for Continuing Legal Education, Springfield, Illinois, November 15, 2001; "Agency, Civil Practice Update and Review Seminar", Illinois Trial Lawyers Association, Chicago, Illinois, September 15, 2001; "Practical Considerations in Handling Personal Injury Cases, Illinois Trial Lawyers Association, Urbana, Illinois, February 3, 2001; "Damages," Civil Practice Updates & Review Seminar, Illinois Trial Lawyers Association, Chicago, Illinois, September, 2000; "Bad Faith and Punitive Damages," Winning Personal Injury Settlement Strategies, Illinois Institute for Continuing Legal Education, Bloomington, Illinois, October, 1999; "Bad Faith and Punitive Damages," Winning Personal Injury Settlement Strategies, Illinois Institute for Continuing Legal Education, Chicago, Illinois, October, 1999; "Local Governmental Tort Immunity," Civil Practice Updates & Review Seminar, Illinois Trial Lawyers Association, September, 1999; "Premises Liability," Tort Law Section Seminar, Illinois State Bar Association, February, 1998; "Uninsured/Underinsured Motorist Claims," Civil Practice Updated Review Seminar, Illinois Trial Lawyers Association, Chicago, Illinois, September, 1998; "Understanding Tort Law," Kellogg Graduate School for Management, Northwestern University, August, 1997; "Supreme Court Rule 213," Civil Practice Seminar, Lake County Bar Association, February, 1996; "Premises Liability," Civil Practice Updates and Review Seminar, Illinois Trial Lawyers Association, Chicago, Illinois, September, 1996. Author: "Attacking Defense Attempts to Avoid Apparent Agency: The Evolution Continues," Trial Journal, Illinois Trial Lawyers Association, Summer, 2000. Co-Author: Medical Malpractice Notebook, Illinois Trial Lawyers Association, Settlement, "Empty Chair Defense," 1994; Medical Malpractice Notebook, Illinois Trial Lawyers Association, "Locality Rule,"1994; Medical Malpractice Notebook, Illinois Trial Lawyers Association, Settlement "Empty Chair Defenses," 1993; Medical Malpractice Notebook, Illinois Trial Lawyers Association, "Locality Rule," 1993.*Member:* Lake County, Illinois State (Member, Continuing Legal Education Committee, 1993-1994; Young Lawyers, Division Counsel, 1997-1998) and American Bar Associations; Illinois Trial Lawyers Association (Member, Board of Advocates, 1997-1999; Board of Managers, 2000—); Million-Dollar Advocates Forum. ***PRACTICE AREAS:*** Personal Injury; Wrongful Death; Medical Negligence; Trucking Litigation. ***Email:*** mdudley@dudleylake.com

THOMAS M. LAKE, born Chicago, Illinois, August 11, 1964; admitted to bar, 1989, Illinois and U.S. District Court, Northern District of Illinois; 2003, Trial Bar. *Education:* Millikin University (B.A., 1986); John Marshall Law School (J.D., 1989). Lecturer, Tort Principals, Chicago Bar Association. *Member:* Chicago (Member, Young Lawyers Committee), Lake County (Member, Trial and Appellate Law and Workers Compensation Law Committees) and Illinois State Bar Associations; Illinois Trial Lawyers Association (Member, Amicus Committee); Workers' Compensation Lawyers Association; Association of Trial Lawyers of America. ***PRACTICE AREAS:*** Personal Injury; Wrongful Death; Medical Negligence; Workers' Compensation. ***Email:*** tlake@dudleylake.com

ASSOCIATES

JACQUELYN DOLORES MELIUS, born Waukegan, Illinois, August 17, 1974; admitted to bar, 2000, Illinois and U.S. District, Northern District of Illinois. *Education:* Northwestern University (B.A., 1996); John Marshall Law School (J.D., 2000). *Member:* Lake County, Illinois State (Member: Young Lawyers Division), and American Bar Associations; Illinois Trial Lawyers Association. ***PRACTICE AREAS:*** Personal Injury; Wrongful Death; Medical Negligence. ***Email:*** jmelius@dudleylake.com

GREGORY G. BALOS, born Chicago, Illinois, February 27, 1966; admitted to bar, 1991, Illinois and U.S. District Court, Northern District of Illinois. *Education:* Purdue University (B.A., 1988); Chicago-Kent College of Law, Illinois Institute of Technology (J.D., 1991). Prosecutor, Village of Alsip, 2000-2002. *Member:* Hellenic Bar Association (Board of Directors, 2001-2005). ***LANGUAGES:*** Greek. ***REPORTED CASES:*** Moran v. Gust K. Newburg/Dugan & Meyers 268 ILL. App. 3d 999, 645 NE 2d 489 (1st Dist 1994). ***PRACTICE AREAS:*** Personal Injury; Wrongful Death; Medical Negligence. ***Email:*** gbalos@dudleylake.com

PETER M. SCHLAX, born Evanston, Illinois, April 3, 1959; admitted to bar, 1986, Illinois. *Education: University of California at Berkeley (B.A., 1982); University of Illinois at Champaign* (J.D., 1986). Assistant States Attorney, Lake County, 1986-1988. Lecturer, " Worker's Compensation Issues," Lake County Civil Practice Committee Seminar, 2005. Board of Directors, Prairie State Legal Services, 2004—. Certified Mediator, Arbitrator, 19th Judicial Circuit Committee, Civil Practice. *Member:* Lake County (Chairman, Legal Aid Committee, 2003—) and Illinois State Bar Associations; Worker's Compensation Lawyers Association; Million Dollar Advocate Forum. ***PRACTICE AREAS:*** Workers Compensation; Personal Injury; Civil Litigation. ***Email:*** pschlax@dudleylake.com

OF COUNSEL

THOMAS M. SCHIPPERS, born 1960; admitted to bar, 1993, Illinois, U.S. District Court, Northern District of Illinois and Federal Trial Bar, Northern District of Illinois. *Education:* Northern Michigan University (B.S., 1984); Loyola University School of Law (J.D., cum laude, 1993). Illinois Attorney General's Office, 1999-2002. Investigative Counsel, Judiciary Committee, U.S. House of Representatives. Lecturer, Northeast Multi-Region Training. Adjunct Faculty: Loyola University School of Law, Advanced Trial Practice; Columbia College of Missouri, Business Law. Instructor: National Institute for Trial Advocacy; Illinois Appellate Prosecutor Trial Practice. Investigative Counsel, United States House of Representatives Judiciary Committee. ***PRACTICE AREAS:*** Personal Injury; Wrongful Death; Medical Negligence; Commercial Litigation; Civil Litigation; Appellate Practice. ***Email:*** tschippers@dudleylake.com

JOHN M. BURKE, born Evergreen Park, Illinois, October 9, 1941; admitted to bar, 1965, Illinois and U.S. District Court, Northern District of Illinois; 1966, U.S. Court of Appeals, Seventh Circuit; 1987, U.S. District Court, Northern District of Indiana. *Education:* Loyola University (B.B.A., 1964; J.D., cum laude, 1965). Member, Loyola Law Review, 1964-1965. Author: "Torts of Minors," Illinois Bar Journal, May, 1964. Lecturer: 1979-Chicago Bar Association-Toxic Torts; 1980-Illinois State Bar Association-Update Seminar; 1981-Illinois State Bar Association-Update Seminar; 1982-Illinois State Bar Association-Insurance and Tort Law Seminar; 1983-Illinois State Bar Association-Update Seminar; 1984-Illinois Institute for Continuing Legal Education-Trial Demonstration-Psychic Trauma; 1985-Illinois Trial Lawyers Seminar-Examination of Expert Witnesses; 1987-Chicago Bar Association-Tort Reform; 1997-Illinois Bar Association-Settlement Seminar. Attorney, Village of Wheeling, 1975-1977. Member, National Panel of Arbitrators, American Arbitration Association. *Member:* Chicago, Illinois State (Member, Tort Section Council, 1978-1988; Chairman, 1984) and American (Member, Litigation Section, Products Liability Committee) Bar Associations; The Association of Trial Lawyers of America; Appellate Lawyers Association of Illinois; Illinois Trial Lawyers Association (Member, Board of Managers, 1988—). ***REPORTED CASES:*** Predny v. Village of Park Forest, 164 Ill. App. 3d 688; Lipke v. Celotex, 153 Ill. App. 3d 498; Wyness v. Armstrong, 131 Ill. 2d 403. ***PRACTICE AREAS:*** Personal Injury Law; Product Liability Law; Medical Malpractice Law; Appellate Practice Law.

FULLIN LEGAL SERVICES LLC

711 NORTH MILWAUKEE AVENUE
LIBERTYVILLE, ILLINOIS 60048
Telephone: 847-573-9880
Fax: 847-573-9882
Email: tjfullin@fullinlegal.com

Patents, Trademarks, Licensing, Copyrights, Trade Secrets.

TIMOTHY J. FULLIN, born Columbus, Ohio, September 19, 1966; admitted to bar, 2001, Illinois and U.S. District Court, Northern District of Illinois; registered to practice before U.S. Patent and Trademark Office. *Education:* Ohio Dominican College (B.S., 1988); John Marshall Law School (J.D., 2001; LL.M., 2002). *Member:* Illinois State and American Bar Associations; Intellectual Property Law Association of Chicago. ***PRACTICE AREAS:*** Patents; Trademarks; Copyrights; Trade Secrets.

PATRICK J. HART

Established in 1994

728 FLORSHEIM DRIVE
LIBERTYVILLE, ILLINOIS 60048-2015
Telephone: 847-680-7240
Fax: 847-816-6122
URL: http://www.patrickhartlaw.com

General Practice, Bankruptcy, Family Law, Estate Planning, Taxes, Real Estate.

FIRM PROFILE: Patrick J. Hart is a CPA as well as an attorney. He is a former attorney for the internal revenue service. He is admitted to the Illinois Supreme Court, Federal District Court, and U.S. Tax Court.

PATRICK J. HART, born Omaha, Nebraska, June 18, 1949; admitted to bar, 1972, Illinois. *Education:* DePaul University (B.A., 1971; J.D., 1972).

MATTHEW KAPLAN & ASSOCIATES

Established in 1981

611 S. MILWAUKEE AVENUE, SUITE 5
LIBERTYVILLE, ILLINOIS 60048
Telephone: 847-918-7077
Fax: 847-918-0974
Email: matt@mkaplanlaw.com
URL: http://www.matthewkaplanlawfirm.com

Family Law, Divorce, Adoptions, Child Custody, Child Support, Domestic Violence, Spousal Support.

MATTHEW KAPLAN, born Chicago, Illinois, 1948; admitted to bar, 1979, Illinois and U.S. District Court, Northern District of Illinois. *Education:* Lake Forest College (B.A., 1970); Chicago-Kent College of Law (J.D., 1979). *Member:* Lake County and Illinois State Bar Associations. ***PRACTICE AREAS:*** Family Law; Divorce; Adoption Law; Child Custody; Child Support; Domestic Violence; Spousal Support.

(This Listing Continued)

SARA L. ROBERTS, born Detroit, Michigan, August 25, 1973; admitted to bar, 2001, Illinois and U.S. District Court, Northern District of Illinois. *Education:* Illinois State University (B.S., Education, 1995); Chicago-Kent College of Law (J.D., 2001). *Member:* Lake County and Illinois State Bar Associations; Association of Women Attorneys of Lake County (Board Member, 2002; 2004). ***PRACTICE AREAS:*** Family Law; Divorce; Child Support; Child Custody; Paternity; Adoption Law. ***Email:*** sarasilverton@aol.com

BOGDAN MARTINOVICH

611 S. MILWAUKEE AVENUE
LIBERTYVILLE, ILLINOIS 60048
Telephone: 847-970-3845
Fax: 847-680-9756
Email: martinovichlaw@earthlink.net
URL: http://www.bogdanmartinovich.com

Personal Injury, Automobile Accidents, Dog Bites, Nursing Home Abuse, Slip and Fall, Products Liability, Wrongful Death, Medical Malpractice, Head and Spinal Injuries, Commercial Litigation.

BOGDAN MARTINOVICH, born Landshut, Germany, April 12, 1950; admitted to bar, 1974, Illinois; 1975, U.S. District Court, Northern District of Illinois; 1977, U.S. Tax Court. *Education:* Northeastern Illinois University (B.A., 1971); DePaul University (J.D., 1974). *Member:* Lake County, Illinois State and American Bar Associations; Illinois Trial Lawyers Association; American Trial Lawyers Association. ***LANGUAGES:*** German and Serbo-Croatian. ***PRACTICE AREAS:*** Personal Injury (70%, 50); Commercial Litigation (30%, 20).

LAW OFFICES OF STEVEN P. McCOLLUM, P.C.

LIBERTYVILLE, ILLINOIS
(See Waukegan)

Criminal Law, Felonies, White Collar Crime, Juvenile Law, Termination of Parental Rights, Misdemeanors, Driving While Intoxicated, Drug Crimes, Homicide, Parole and Probation, Sexual Assault, Traffic Violations, Domestic Violence, Assault and Battery, Grand Jury Practice, Capital Offences, Construction Accidents, Personal Injury, Products Liability, Wrongful Death, Automobile Accidents and Injuries, Sexual Abuse. General Practice.

NEWLAND, NEWLAND & NEWLAND

1512 ARTAIVS PARKWAY
LIBERTYVILLE, ILLINOIS 60048
Telephone: 847-549-0000
Fax: 847-549-1908
Email: newlandglaw@aol.com
URL: http://www.newlandlawfirm.com

General Practice, Personal Injury, Slip & Fall, Auto Accidents.

GARY A. NEWLAND, born Chicago, Illinois, February 6, 1968; admitted to bar, 1993, Illinois. *Education:* Loyola University (B.S., 1990; J.D., 1993). ***PRACTICE AREAS:*** Criminal Law; Personal Injury; Real Estate.

CHARLES T. NEWLAND, born Chicago, Illinois, May 12, 1962; admitted to bar, 1988, Illinois; 1989, U.S. District Court, Northern District of Illinois. *Education:* University of Illinois (B.S., 1984); John Marshall Law School (J.D., with highest distinction, 1988). Phi Delta Phi. Member, Order of John Marshall. Member, Creighton International Moot Court Board. Recipient, West Publishing Award for Outstanding Scholastic Achievement. *Member:* Illinois State and American Bar Associations.

STEPHEN S. NEWLAND, born February 24, 1966; admitted to bar, 1991, Illinois. *Education:* University of Illinois (B.A.); DePaul University (J.D.).

ANTHONY PERRELLI

LIBERTYVILLE, ILLINOIS
(See Deerfield)

Business Corporate, Small Business, Contracts, Business Planning, Real Estate, Commercial Litigation and Taxation.

RICHARDS, RALPH & SCHWAB

CHARTERED

LIBERTYVILLE, ILLINOIS
(See Veronon Hills)

Corporate and Business. Banking and Finance. Bankruptcy and Creditors' Rights. Real Estate. Commercial Litigation.

CAREY J. SCHIEVER, LTD.

Established in 1981
1512 ARTAIUS PARKWAY, SUITE 300
LIBERTYVILLE, ILLINOIS 60048
Telephone: 847-680-1123
FAX: 847-680-1124
Email: cjschiever@ameritech.net
URL: http://www.lawyers.com/schieverlaw

General Business Practice. Corporate, Estate Planning, Business Planning, Real Estate, Construction, Probate and Financial Institutions and Foreclosure.

CAREY J. SCHIEVER, born Chicago Heights, Illinois, January 2, 1948; admitted to bar, 1973, Illinois and U.S. District Court, Northern District of Illinois. *Education:* DePauw University (B.A., 1970); Washington University (J.D., 1973). *Member:* Chicago, Lake County and Illinois State Bar Associations; Chicago Estate Planning Council; Lake County Estate Planning Council (President, 1983).

REPRESENTATIVE CLIENTS: Interlacken Construction Co.; Waukegan Safe & Lock, Ltd.; Hallen Products, Ltd.; Herky's Trucking, Inc.; Liberty Coach, Inc.; Maneval Construction; Wercheck Development Co.; Gewalt Hamilton Associates Engineering; The Synchronicity Group, Inc.; Laser Tech. LLC; Estate Installations, Inc.; Integration Ware, Inc.; Capitol Graphics and Promotions, Inc.; Liberty Medical Services, Inc.; JC Contracting, Inc.; Brauhaus Properties, LLC.; Libertyville Brewing Co.; Hitch Inn Post Motel, Inc.; Nedza Food Shop, Inc.; King Trucking, Inc.; Pat's Grayslake Pizza Shop, Ltd.; Ace Hardware of Lake Co., Inc.

GARY L. SCHLESINGER

Established in 1986
SUITE 300
1512 ARTAIUS PARKWAY
P.O. BOX 6229
LIBERTYVILLE, ILLINOIS 60048
Telephone: 847-680-4970
Fax: 847-680-5459
Email: glschles@lawoffice.com
URL: http://www.lawyers.com/schlesingerlaw

Trials and Appeals of Divorce, Custody, Support, Paternity, Adoption, Family Law and Domestic Relations.

GARY L. SCHLESINGER, born Chicago, Illinois, December 10, 1945; admitted to bar, 1971, Illinois. *Education:* Loyola University of Chicago (B.S., 1967); Northwestern University (J.D., 1970). Instructor in Family Law: Illinois State Bar Association, 1987-1991; Illinois Institute for Continuing Legal Education, 1988. Lake County Annual Family Law Speaker, 1974—. Certified Arbitrator and Mediator, Child's Representative, Circuit Court of the 19th Judicial Circuit, Lake County, Illinois, 1989. Member, Illinois State Bar Association Assembly, 1992-2001, 2004-2007. Faculty Member: Adult Education Program, Mundelein High School; Family Institute for Family Law Associates, 2001, 2002, 2004, 2005. *Member:* Lake County (Chairman, Family Law Committee, 1978-1982 and 1999-2000), Illinois State (Member, Family Law Section Council, 1987-1991 and 2005-2006) and American Bar Associations. Fellow, American Academy of Matrimonial Lawyers (Vice President, Illinois Chapter, 1990-1991, 2004-2006; Board Member, 1991-1995 and 2001-2004). [U.S. Army Reserve, 1969-1975]. ***PRACTICE AREAS:*** Trials and Appeals of Divorce Law; Custody Law; Support Law; Paternity; Adoption Law; Family Law; Domestic Relations.

ASSOCIATE

KEVIN ROSS JOHNSON, born Grand Forks, North Dakota, February 14, 1959; admitted to bar, 1987, Minnesota and North Dakota; 1999, Illinois. *Education:* North Dakota State University (B.A., 1984); University of North Dakota School of Law (J.D., 1987). Student Director, Legal Aid Association Clinic and Senior Law Student Teaching Assistant, Legal Writing, University of North Dakota School of Law, 1986-1987. Formerly with Chicago Legal Clinic, Inc. *Member:* Illinois State Bar Association. ***PRACTICE AREAS:*** Family Law; Domestic Relations.

MARLON T. SUSKIN

731 N. MILWAUKEE AVENUE
LIBERTYVILLE, ILLINOIS 60048
Telephone: 847-680-1902
Email: msk@yahoo.com
URL: http://www.marlonsuskinlawoffice.com

Real Estate, Collection, Family Law.

MARLON T. SUSKIN, born 1971; admitted to bar, 1996, Illinois. ***PRACTICE AREAS:*** Real Estate; Collections; Family Law.

SWANSON, MARTIN & BELL

Established in 1992
1860 WEST WINCHESTER ROAD
SUITE 201
LIBERTYVILLE, ILLINOIS 60048
Telephone: 847-949-0025
Fax: 847-247-0555
URL: http://www.smbtrials.com

Chicago, Illinois Office: 330 North Wabash, Suite 3300, 60611. Telephone: 312-321-9100. Fax: 312-321-0990.

(This Listing Continued)

SWANSON, MARTIN & BELL, Libertyville—Continued

Waukegan, Illinois, Satellite Office: 415 Washington Street, Suite 1B, Waukegan, Illinois, 60085. Telephone: 847-949-0025. Fax: 847-247-0555.
DuPage County, Illinois Office: 2525 Cabot Drive, Lisle, Illinois, 60532. Telephone: 630-799-6900. Fax: 630-799-6901.

Class Action Lawsuits, Commercial Litigation, Construction Litigation/Disputes, Consumer and Warranty Law, Creditor's Rights, Drugs & Medical Devices, Employment Litigation, Environmental Law, Equipment Leasing, General Tort Liability, Healthcare, Insurance Coverage, Intellectual Property, Medical Negligence, Municipal Law, Product Liability, Professional Negligence, Real Estate Development/Zoning, Real Estate Litigation, Toxic and Mass Tort Litigation, and White Collar Criminal Defense.

PARTNERS

STEVEN L. LARSON, born Elgin, Illinois, December 31, 1952; admitted to bar, 1977, Illinois and U.S. District Court, Northern District of Illinois. *Education:* University of Illinois (B.A., 1973); Washington University (J.D., 1977). Associate Notes and Comments Editor, Washington University Law Quarterly, 1976-1977; Author, Comment, "Prohibition of Religious Snakehandling," Washington University Law Quarterly, Volume 1976, Number 2. *Member:* Lake County and Illinois State Bar Associations; Illinois Association of Defense Trial Counsel; American Board of Trial Advocates; Illinois Society of Trial Lawyers. ***PRACTICE AREAS:*** Insurance Industry; Product Liability; Medical Malpractice; Trial Practice; Recreational Products; Commercial Litigation. ***Email:*** slarson@smbtrials.com

DAVID F. PARDYS, born Chicago, Illinois, September 1, 1957; admitted to bar, 1982, Illinois and U.S. District Court, Northern District of Illinois; 1986, U.S. Court of Appeals, Seventh Circuit and U.S. District Court, Eastern District of Wisconsin, U.S. District Court, Southern District of Indiana. *Education:* University of Illinois (B.A., 1979); IIT/Chicago Kent College of Law (J.D., with honors, 1982). *Member:* Lake County Bar Association. ***PRACTICE AREAS:*** Appellate; Health Care; Insurance Industry; Municipal; Product Liability; Trial. ***Email:*** dpardys@smbtrials.com

LINDA E. SPRING, born Bellefonte, Pennsylvania, September 17, 1945; admitted to bar, 1983, Illinois. *Education:* University of Minnesota (B.S., 1967; M.S., 1970); Loyola University (J.D., 1983). Law Clerk to Appellate Court Justice Hon. Glenn K. Seidenfeld, 1983-1984. *Member:* Lake County, Illinois State and American Bar Associations; Association of Women Attorneys of Lake County, Appellate Lawyers Association. ***PRACTICE AREAS:*** Medical Malpractice; Trial Practice; Appellate Practice; Governmental. ***Email:*** lspring@smbtrials.com

JOHN A. TERSELIC, born LaSalle, Illinois, September 29, 1967; admitted to bar, 1992, Illinois. *Education:* Southern Illinois University (B.A., 1989); DePaul University (J.D., 1992). Law Clerk to Senior Judge Kenneth R. Harkins, U.S. Court of Federal Claims, 1992-1993. *Member:* Chicago, Lake County and Illinois State Bar Associations; U.S. Court of Federal Claims Bar Association. ***PRACTICE AREAS:*** Insurance Defense; Medical Malpractice Defense. ***Email:*** jterseli@smbtrials.com

ASSOCIATES

DAVID S. GOLES, born Melrose Park, Illinois, May 7, 1972; admitted to bar, 1998, Illinois. *Education:* American University (B.A., 1994); Northern Illinois University (J.D., cum laude, 1998). Member, Law Review Editorial Board. Author: Smith v. Fair Employment and Housing Commission: Religious Freedom and Anti-Discrimination Laws Square Off in the Landlord/Tenant Setting, Northern Illinois University Law Review Vol. 18, Issue Number 1. *Member:* Lake County and Illinois State Bar Associations; Christian Legal Society. ***PRACTICE AREAS:*** Civil Litigation; Municipal; General Practice. ***Email:*** dgoles@smbtrials.com

MICHONE J. KUHLMAN, born Ames, Iowa, September 26, 1967; admitted to bar, 1996, Illinois; U.S. District Court, Northern District of Illinois and U.S. District Court, Southern District of Indiana. *Education:* Iowa State University (B.S., 1989); Georgia State University, College of Law (J.D., 1996). ***PRACTICE AREAS:*** Insurance Defense; Medical Malpractice Defense; Corporate Law. ***Email:*** mkuhlman@smbtrials.com

JOY I. PADNOS, born Chicago, Illinois, June 15, 1974; admitted to bar, 2000, Illinois, U.S. District Court, Northern District of Illinois. *Education:* Pitzer College (B.A., 1996); John Marshall Law School (J.D., cum laude, 2000). ***PRACTICE AREAS:*** Civil Litigation; Municipal Law; Insurance Defense; General Practice. ***Email:*** jpadnos@smbtrials.com

---

ROBBIN D. VANDERWOUDE

1580 SOUTH MILWAUKEE AVENUE, SUITE 403
LIBERTYVILLE, ILLINOIS 60048
Telephone: 847-680-8508
Fax: 847-680-8878
URL: http://www.lawyers.com/rvanderwoude

Family Law, Divorce, Child Support, Child Custody, Visitation Rights, Legal Separation, Alimony, Post Divorce Modification.
Know Your Rights! Caring Female Attorney Concentrating in all Areas of Family Law.

ROBBIN D. VANDERWOUDE, born Chicago, Illinois, May 14, 1954; admitted to bar, 1981, Illinois. *Education:* Northeastern Illinois University (B.A., 1976); John Marshall Law School (J.D., 1981). Former Divorce Commentator, "News Segment," Radio Program, 100.3 Radio Station, Chicago, Illinois, 1993-1995. *Member:* Chicago (Member, Lawyer Referral Panel, 1982-1987), Lake County (Member: Family Law Section; Pro-Bono, Volunteer Lawyers Program) and Illinois State Bar Associations; Association of Women Attorneys of Lake County. ***PRACTICE AREAS:*** Family Law; Divorce; Child Support; Post Divorce Modification; Domestic Relations; Alimony; Marital Agreements; Child Custody; Visitation.

THE LAW OFFICE OF THOMAS W. FUNK

Established in 1989
427 PULASKI STREET
LINCOLN, ILLINOIS 62656
Telephone: 217-735-1000
Fax: 217-735-5752
URL: http://www.tfunklaw.com
Email: tfunk@verizon.net
URL: http://www.funklaw.com

Family Law, Adoption Law, Criminal Law, Real Estate, Probate, Bankruptcy, Social Security Disability, Wills, Trusts, Estates.

THOMAS W. FUNK, born Lincoln, Illinois, February 14, 1959; admitted to bar, 1984, Illinois; 1988, U.S. District Court, Central District of Illinois. *Education:* Eastern Illinois University (B.S., 1981); Indiana University (J.D., 1984). *Member:* Logan County and Illinois State Bar Associations; Christian Legal Society. ***PRACTICE AREAS:*** Family Law; Criminal Law; Real Estate.

REPRESENTATIVE CLIENTS: City of Pulaski; Modern Brake & Aligment; Logan County Board of Realtors; Lincoln Lakes Condominium Association; Illinois Christian Childrens Ministry.

WOODS & BATES

Established in 1971
306 CLINTON STREET
LINCOLN, ILLINOIS 62656
Telephone: 217-735-1234
Fax: 217-735-1236
Email: bilbates@ccaonline.com

General Practice. Probate, Trusts and Estates, Wills, Real Estate and Collections.

WILLIAM B. BATES, born Lincoln, Illinois, September 27, 1954; admitted to bar, 1979, Illinois. *Education:* Westminster College (B.A. in Acct. and Econ., 1976); Drake University (J.D., with honors, 1978). Order of the Coif. Recipient, American Jurisprudence Award. *Member:* Logan County, Illinois State and American Bar Associations. (Also of Counsel to Sorling, Northrup, Hanna, Cullen and Cochran, Ltd., Springfield, Illinois). ***PRACTICE AREAS:*** General Practice; Probate; Trusts and Estates; Wills; Real Estate; Collections. ***Email:*** bilbates@ccaonline.com

REPRESENTATIVE CLIENTS: Illico Incorporated; The Abraham Lincoln Memorial Hospital; Lincoln Firemen's Pension Fund; Mt. Pulaski Products; Lincoln Christian College and Seminary; Lincoln Police Pension Fund; Construction Equipment Federal Credit Union; City of Lincoln.
REFERENCE: State Bank of Lincoln.

TRESSLER, SODERSTROM, MALONEY & PRIESS

LINCOLNSHIRE, ILLINOIS

(See Chicago)

General Civil Litigation and Trial Practice, Insurance, Reinsurance, Litigation, Insurance Bad Faith, Appellate Practice, Business Litigation, Business Transactions, Class Action Defense, Commercial Litigation, Complex Litigation, Directors and Officers Liability, Construction Law, Architects and Engineers, Fidelity and Surety, Real Estate Litigation and Transactions, Alternative Dispute Resolution, Product Liability, Intellectual Property, Internet Law, Electronic Commerce, Environmental Law, Asbestos Litigation, Health Care, ERISA, Labor and Employment, Technology Law, Securities Litigation, Health Care, Bankruptcy, Advertising Law, Personal Injury, Trusts and Estates, Contracts, Professional Liability, Regulatory, White Collar Crime, Corporate Law, Mergers and Acquisitions, Commodities, Condominium and Common Interest Community Law, Municipal Law.

CUTLER & ASSOCIATES, LTD.

LINCOLNWOOD, ILLINOIS

(See Skokie)

Bankruptcy, Consumer Bankruptcy, Bankruptcy Chapter 7, Foreclosures, Small Business, Buying and Selling of Businesses, Family Business, Limited Liability, Partnership, Corporate, Contract, Breach of Contract, General Practice, Debtor and Creditor, Collections, Creditors, Rights and Civil Litigation.

SHERYL RAE GHEZZI

Established in 1986
4433 WEST TOUHY, SUITE 301
LINCOLNWOOD, ILLINOIS 60712
Telephone: 847-675-7570
Fax: 847-673-0948
Email: ghezziatlaw@aol.com
URL: http://www.ghezzilaw.com

Civil Litigation, Family Law, Child Custody, Divorce, Premarital Agreements, D.U.I., Drug Crimes, Juvenile Crimes, Misdemeanors, Traffic, DUI Defense, Immigration, Wills and Probate, Divorce, Child Support, Visitation Interference, Visitation Abuse, Personal Injury Defense, Property Damage Defense, Estate Planning, Real Estate Litigation.

FIRM PROFILE: Twenty years of experience representing clients and their families.

(This Listing Continued)

SHERYL R. GHEZZI, born Chicago, Illinois, November 12, 1955; admitted to bar, 1984, Illinois. *Education:* Lake Forest College (B.A., 1977); John Marshall Law School (J.D., 1984). Justinian Society. Charter Member, A.F.C.C., Illinois Chapter. Child's Representative, Domestic Relations Division, Circuit Court of Cook County, 1992—. Board Member, Lincolnwood School Foundation, 2003—. Commissioner, Lincolnwood Human Relations Commission, 2005—. *Member:* Chicago, Illinois State (Member: Military Affairs Committee, 2002—) and American Bar Associations; Justinian Society; Women's Bar Association; American Trial Lawyers Association (Faculty, National Business Institute). ***LANGUAGES:*** Italian. ***PRACTICE AREAS:*** Civil Litigation; Family Law; Divorce; Child Custody; Child Support; Visitation Rights; Premarital Agreements; Traffic Violations; Criminal Law; Driving While Intoxicated; Wills; Trust Law; Estate Planning; Probate Litigation; Immigration Law. ***Email:*** ghezziatlaw@aol.com

Languages: Romanian, English, Aramic and Italian.

REPRESENTATIVE CLIENTS: Lincolnwood School Foundation; Evangers Dog Food Co., Inc.; Three Twins, Inc.; We'll Clean, Inc.; Dossier; Fifth Avenue, Inc.; The Cleaning Crew of Chicago, Inc.

DAVID DeROSE

2592 GRAND AVENUE, SUITE 201
LINDENHURST, ILLINOIS 60046
Telephone: 847-265-6700
Fax: 847-265-6701

Personal Injury, Real Estate, Estate Planning, Wills, Corporate Law, Evictions, Foreclosures.

DAVID A. DeROSE, born Oak Park, Illinois, April 1, 1956; admitted to bar, 1981, Illinois and U.S. District Court, Northern District of Illinois. *Education:* University of Illinois (B.A., 1978); John Marshall Law School (J.D., 1981). *Member:* Lake County and Illinois State Bar Associations. ***PRACTICE AREAS:*** Personal Injury; Real Estate; Estate Planning; Wills; Corporate Law; Evictions; Foreclosures.

ANDREWS KOEHLER & PASSARELLI, P.C.

4343 COMMERCE COURT, SUITE 615
LISLE, ILLINOIS 60532
Telephone: 630-505-9939
Fax: 630-505-9969
URL: http://www.akplaw.com

Representing Employers in Labor and Employment Law; Employment Discrimination and Employment-Related Litigation.

GREGORY H. ANDREWS, born Berwyn, Illinois, August 15, 1958; admitted to bar, 1992, Illinois, U.S. District Court, Northern District of Illinois and U.S. District Court, Central District of Illinois. *Education:* Luther College (B.A., 1980); University of Illinois (M.S., 1987); Chicago-Kent College of Law (J.D., 1992). Chief Justice, Moot Court, 1991-1992. Teaching Assistant, Legal Writing, Chicago-Kent College of Law, 1991-1992. *Member:* Chicago, Kane County (Chair, Labor and Employment Law Committee, 1996-2002), DuPage County, Illinois State and American Bar Associations. ***Email:*** gandrews@akplaw.com

RENÉE KOEHLER, born Blue Island, Illinois, January 6, 1966; admitted to bar, 1991, Illinois and U.S. District Court, Northern District of Illinois, Western and Eastern Districts of Wisconsin and Northern District of Indiana; 1998, U.S. Court of Appeals, Seventh Circuit. *Education:* Northern Illinois University (B.A., 1988); The John Marshall Law School (J.D., cum laude, 1991). Associate Candidacy Editor, John Marshall Law Review, 1990-1991. Author: "The State of Unions in America: Chipping Away at the Union Block", The John Marshall Law Review, Volume 23, Number 4. *Member:* Chicago, Kane County and Illinois State Bar Associations. ***Email:*** rkoehler@akplaw.com

RONALD J. PASSARELLI, born Berwyn, Illinois, June 8, 1963; admitted to bar, 1990, Illinois, U.S. District Court, Northern District of Illinois and U.S. Court of Appeals, Seventh Circuit. *Education:* Northern Illinois University (B.A., 1985); DePaul University, College of Law (J.D., 1990). Former Labor Relations Counsel, Chief Judge's Office, Circuit Court of Cook County. Guest Speaker, Northern Illinois University, College of Law. *Member:* Chicago, DuPage and American Bar Associations. ***Email:*** rpassarelli@akplaw.com

ISHAM R. JONES, III, born Chicago, Illinois, August 12, 1969; admitted to bar, 1997, Missouri and Illinois; 1999, U.S. District Court, Northern District of Illinois. *Education:* Illinois State University (B.S., 1991); University of Missouri, Columbia (J.D., 1996). Editor-in-Chief, Journal of Dispute Resolution, 1995-1996. *Member:* Chicago (Chair, Trade and Professional Associations Law Committee, 2003-2004) and Illinois State Bar Associations; The Missouri Bar. ***LANGUAGES:*** Portuguese.

KERRY L. DAVIDSON, born Carmel, California, April 3, 1972; admitted to bar, 2002, Illinois; 2004, U.S. District Court, Northern District of Illinois. *Education:* Valparaiso University (B.A., 1994; J.D., 2001). Teaching Assistant, Legal Writing, Valparaiso University College of Law, 1998-1999. *Member:* Illinois State Bar Association; Chicago Bar Association. ***Email:*** kdavidson@akplaw.com

CHITKOWSKI LAW OFFICES

801 WARRENVILLE ROAD, SUITE 620
LISLE, ILLINOIS 60532
Telephone: 630-824-4808
Facsimile: 630-824-4809
URL: http://www.chitkowskilaw.com

Business, Construction, Transportation, Corporate, Labor and Employment and Real Estate, Litigation and Transactions.

(This Listing Continued)

JOHN J. CHITKOWSKI, born Chicago, Illinois, December 2, 1963; admitted to bar, 1991, Illinois and U.S. District Court, Northern District of Illinois; 1993, U.S. Court of Appeals, 7th Circuit including Trial Bar; 2004, Michigan. *Education:* Valparaiso University (B.A., 1986); John Marshall Law School (J.D., 1991). *Member:* Chicago, DuPage County and American (Member, Construction and Industry Forum) Bar Associations; American Subcontractors Association; Construction Industry Affairs Council. ***PRACTICE AREAS:*** Business Law; Construction Law; Transportation Law; Corporate Law; Real Estate. ***Email:*** jjc@chitkowskilaw.com

COREY B. STERN, born Chicago, Illinois, August 16, 1972; admitted to bar, 2000, Illinois. *Education:* Northern Illinois University (B.S., Sociology, 1994); DePaul University (J.D., 2000). Dean's List. Member, DePaul Business Law Journal. *Member:* Illinois State Bar Association; Illinois Home Builders Association. ***PRACTICE AREAS:*** Construction Law; Corporate Law; Business Law; Real Estate. ***Email:*** cbs@chitkowskilaw.com

JASON M. LOEBACH, born LaSalle, Illinois, September 4, 1976; admitted to bar, 2001, Illinois. *Education:* North Central College (B.A., 1998); Northern Illinois University College of Law (J.D., 2001). Phi Delta Phi. *Member:* Chicago, Illinois State and American Bar Associations. ***PRACTICE AREAS:*** Corporate Law; Construction Law; Civil Litigation. ***Email:*** jml@chitkowskilaw.com

JOSEPH D. PERROTTA, born Elmhurst, Illinois, May 15 ,1972; admitted to bar, 1999, Illinois and U.S. District Court, Northern District of Illinois. *Education:* DePaul University (B.S., 1994); Loyola University (J.D., 1997). *Member:* DuPage County Bar Association. ***PRACTICE AREAS:*** Business Transactions; Real Estate; Estate Planning; Construction Law. ***Email:*** jdp@chitkowskilaw.com

OF COUNSEL

STEVEN C. BOREN, born Chicago, Illinois, October 26, 1949; admitted to bar, 2002, Illinois and U.S. District Court, Northern District of Illinois. *Education:* University of Illinois at Chicago (B.S., with honors, 1985); Chicago-Kent College of Law, Illinois Institute of Technology (J.D., with honors, 2002). Deans List. *Member:* Chicago, Illinois State and American Bar Associations. ***PRACTICE AREAS:*** Construction Law; Corporate Law; Real Estate; Civil Litigation. ***Email:*** scboren@earthlink.net

DONAHUE, SOWA AND BROWN

Established in 1985

SUITE 215, LISLE EXECUTIVE CENTER
3030 WARRENVILLE ROAD
LISLE, ILLINOIS 60532
Telephone: 630-505-5200
Fax: 630-505-4250
Email: gsowa@dsbb-law.com
URL: http://www.lawyers.com/dsbblaw

Geneva Office: 216 Campbell Street, 60134. Telephone: 630-232-1780. Fax: 630-232-9671.

Criminal Defense, DUI, Traffic, Drivers License Reinstatement, Appellate Law, Juvenile Law.

FIRM PROFILE: The firm carries the highest available rating by Martindale-Hubbell.

JOHN F. DONAHUE, born Chicago, Illinois, November 23, 1944; admitted to bar, 1971, Illinois. *Education:* Loyola University (B.S., 1967; J.D., 1971). Blue Key Honor Society. Lawyer of the Year, DuPage County Bar Association, 2000. Chosen as one of Illinois Super Lawyers by Chicago Magazine, 2005. See www.superlawyers.com. Author: "Emergency Blood Tests: New Road Around Fourth Amendment," DuPage Bar Brief, 1992; "Sufficiency of Criminal Complaints: A Separate Standard for Traffic Offenses?," Illinois State Bar Section Newsletter, 1988. Professor of Criminal Justice, Triton College, 1971-1974. Special Prosecutor, Dupage County, 1982-1984. Lead Attorney, People v. Marilyn Lemak. Lead Counsel, Certified by Illinois Supreme Court in capital cases as Lead Counsel. Member, Illinois Supreme Court Capital Litigation Screening Committee. *Member:* DuPage County (President, 1992-1993; Chairman, Judiciary Committee, 1992-1993; Chairman, Criminal Law Committee), Kane County, Chicago (Chairman, Criminal Justice Section, 1992-1993) and Illinois State (Chairman, Criminal Justice Section, 1992-1993) Bar Associations; DuPage County Criminal Defense Lawyers Association (Charter President, 1975-1976 and 1978-1979); Capital Litigation Bar of Illinois; National Association of Criminal Defense Lawyers. American College of Trial Lawyers. ***PRACTICE AREAS:*** Criminal Defense Law; Appeals. ***Email:*** jdonahue@dsbb-law.com

GLENN M. SOWA, born Chicago, Illinois, September 16, 1948; admitted to bar, 1983, Illinois and U.S. Court of Appeals, 7th Circuit. *Education:* Northern Illinois University (B.S., 1971; M.S., 1974; J.D., 1983). DuPage County State's Attorney's Office, 1983-1985. Illinois State Police, 1971-1983. *Member:* DuPage County, Kane County and Illinois State Bar Associations; Capital Litigation Bar of Illinois (Lead Counsel). ***PRACTICE AREAS:*** Criminal Defense Law; Traffic Law. ***Email:*** gsowa@dsbb-law.com

DANIEL E. BROWN, born Chicago, Illinois, November 8, 1964; admitted to bar, 1996, Illinois. *Education:* North Central College (B.A., 1987); Northern Illinois Law School (J.D., 1996). DuPage County State's Attorney Office, 1996-1997. DuPage County Sheriff's Office, 1989-1996. Secretary, State Drivers' License Reinstatement Hearings. *Member:* DuPage County and Illinois State Bar Associations; DuPage Criminal Defense Association. ***PRACTICE AREAS:*** Traffic Violations; Driving While Intoxicated; Criminal Law. ***Email:*** dbrown@dsbb-law.com

ASSOCIATE

PATRICIA MAGANA, born Sterling, Illinois, February 26, 1971; admitted to bar, 2001, Illinois. *Education:* Western Illinois University (B.A., 1993); Northern Illinois University (J.D., 1996). *Member:* DuPage County, Kane County, Illinois State Bar Associa-

(This Listing Continued)

DONAHUE, SOWA AND BROWN, Lisle—Continued

tions; Hispanic Lawyers Association of Illinois; DuPage Association of Women Lawyers (Member, Board of Directors, Third Vice-President, 2005-2006). ***LANGUAGES:*** Spanish. ***PRACTICE AREAS:*** Criminal Defense; Traffic Violations; Juvenile Law; Appellate Practice. ***Email:*** pmagana@dsbb-law.com

DYKEMA GOSSETT PLLC

Established in 1926

4200 COMMERCE COURT
SUITE 300
LISLE, ILLINOIS 60532
Telephone: 630-245-0400
Facsimile: 630-245-0140
URL: http://www.dykema.com

Ann Arbor, Michigan Office: 2723 South State Street, Suite 400, 48104. Telephone: 734-214-7660. Fax: 734-214-7696.

Aurora, Illinois Office: 2 Hankes Road. Telephone: 630-844-2200. Facsimile: 630-844-2277.

Bloomfield Hills, Michigan Office: 39577 Woodward Avenue, Suite 300, 48304-2820. Telephone: 248-203-0700. Fax: 248-203-0763.

Chicago, Illinois Office: 10 South Wacker Drive, Suite 2300. Telephone: 312-876-1700. Fax: 312-876-1155.

Detroit, Michigan Office: 400 Renaissance Center, 48243-1668. Telephone: 313-568-6800. Fax: 313-568-6545.

Grand Rapids, Michigan Office: Suite 700, 300 Ottawa Avenue, N.W., 49503-2306. Telephone: 616-776-7500. Fax: 616-776-7573.

Joliet, Illinois Office: 111 North Ottawa Street. Telephone: 815-727-4511. Facsimile: 815-727-1586.

Lansing, Michigan Office: 124 W. Allegan Street, Suite 800, 48933-1742. Telephone: 517-374-9100. Fax: 517-374-9191.

Los Angeles, California Office: 333 South Grand Avenue, Suite 2100, 90071. Telephone: 213-457-1800. Fax: 213-457-1850.

Washington, D.C. Office: Franklin Square, Suite 300 West, 1300 I Street, N.W., 20005-3353. Telephone: 202-906-8600. Fax: 202-906-8669.

Antitrust and Trade Regulation, Automotive, Banking and Financial Services, Bankruptcy, Biotechnology and Life Sciences, Casino Gaming, Class Action Defense, Computer and Software Law, Construction, Consumer Financial Services, Corporate Finance, E-Commerce, Emerging Business and Technology, Employee Benefits, Entertainment and Sports, Environmental Law, Family Law, Franchise Law and Regulation, Government Contracts, Government Policy and Practice, HealthCare, Indian Law, Insurance, Intellectual Property, International Law, Labor and Employment, Litigation and Dispute Resolution, Mergers and Acquisitions, Products Liability Defense, Public Finance, Real Estate, Retail Law, Securities, Taxation and Estates, Trade Associations.

FIRM PROFILE: Dykema Gossett PLLC represents the interests of domestic and foreign-based companies and institutions on a broad array of matters. Our diversified practice and Midwest work ethic have long made Dykema the choice of Fortune 100 companies, privately-held businesses, entrepreneurial enterprises and emerging businesses. With offices in Michigan, California, Illinois and Washington, D.C., Dykema has expanded beyond its original Michigan roots to become one of the largest firms in the United States. Our recent merger with Rooks Pitts in Illinois, effective April 1, 2004, is a significant milestone in our continued growth in the Midwest. We are proud to be recognized by area businesses as a corporate leader, and our broad-based litigation practice is routinely chosen by clients and peers alike as one of the best in the nation. Dykema is equally well known for our experienced government relations specialists, whose experience at the national, state and local levels is unrivalled. From manufacturers amd automotive suppliers to financial institutions, from patent and trademark disputes to complex class action defense, from startups to large multinational corporations, our clients repeatedly look to Dykema to help them navigate through an ever-increasing stream of complex litigation and changing business environments.

MEMBERS OF FIRM

DAVID J. BRESSLER, born Milwaukee, Wisconsin, September 5, 1957; admitted to bar, 1982, Illinois and U.S. District Court, Central and Northern Districts of Illinois including Trial Bar; 1991, U.S. Court of Appeals, Seventh Circuit. *Education:* University of Minnesota (B.A., 1979); Loyola University, Chicago (J.D., 1982). Listed as "Illinois Super Lawyer," 2005, 2006. ***PRACTICE AREAS:*** Corporate Law; Litigation; Labor and Employment Law. ***Email:*** dbressler@dykema.com

THOMAS B. CASSIDY, born Chicago, Illinois, August 4, 1944; admitted to bar, 1969, Illinois. *Education:* Loyola University, Chicago (B.S., 1966; J.D., 1969). Phi Alpha Delta. ***PRACTICE AREAS:*** Finance; Banking; Mergers and Acquisitions. ***Email:*** tcassidy@dykema.com

GEORGE N. GILKERSON, JR., born Tucson, Arizona, September 8, 1945; admitted to bar, 1970, Illinois; 1982, U.S. District Court, Northern District of Illinois including Trial Bar. *Education:* University of Illinois (B.S., Accounting, 1967; J.D., 1970). ***PRACTICE AREAS:*** Business Law; Commercial Law; Real Estate; Asset Based Finance; Estate Planning. ***Email:*** ggilkerson@dykema.com

BRUCE L. GOLDSMITH, born Aurora, Illinois, December 21, 1945; admitted to bar, 1971, Illinois and U.S. District Court, Northern District of Illinois; 1975, U.S. Court of Appeals, Seventh Circuit; 1981, U.S. Supreme Court. *Education:* Northwestern University (B.A., summa cum laude, 1968); University of Chicago (J.D., 1971). Phi Beta Kappa. ***PRACTICE AREAS:*** Commercial Real Estate Law; Corporate Law; Labor and Employment; Commercial Litigation; Zoning, Planning and Land Use. ***Email:*** bgoldsmith@dykema.com

(This Listing Continued)

SCOTT M. HARDEK, born Chicago, Illinois, February 7, 1964; admitted to bar, 1990, Illinois and U.S. District Court, Northern District of Illinois. *Education:* University of Notre Dame (B.A., 1986; J.D., 1990). *Member:* DuPage County Bar Association. ***PRACTICE AREAS:*** Insurance Defense; Medical Malpractice Defense; Employment Law; Commercial Litigation; Contract Litigation; Municipal Law; Creditors Rights; Real Estate Litigation. ***Email:*** shardek@dykema.com

JOHN J. MANGAN, born Chicago, Illinois, May 26, 1951; admitted to bar, 1976, Illinois; 1982, U.S. District Court, Northern District of Illinois including Trial Bar; U.S. Court of Appeals, 7th Circuit and U.S. Tax Court. *Education:* University of Kansas (B.A., 1973); John Marshall Law School (J.D., with distinction, 1976). *Member:* DuPage County, Illinois State and American Bar Associations; American Health Lawyers Association; Society of Trial Lawyers. ***PRACTICE AREAS:*** Business Law; Corporate Law; Health Care; Litigation; Commercial Law. ***Email:*** jmangan@dykema.com

OF COUNSEL

RICHARD L. WILLIAMS, born Savannah, Georgia, September 22, 1970; admitted to bar, 1995, Illinois and U.S. District Court, Northern District of Illinois. *Education:* University of Illinois (B.A., with high distinction, 1992); Northern Illinois University, (J.D., cum laude, 1995). ***PRACTICE AREAS:*** Real Estate; Zoning, Planning and Land Use; Corporate Law; Litigation. ***Email:*** rwilliams@dykema.com

ASSOCIATES

JERROLD L. CHERWIN, JR., born Chicago, Illinois, December 1, 1976; admitted to bar, 2001, Illinois. *Education:* University of Iowa (B.S., 1998); University of Kansas (J.D., 2001). *Member:* Illinois State Bar Association. ***PRACTICE AREAS:*** Commercial Real Estate; Zoning, Planning and Land Use. ***Email:*** jcherwin@dykema.com

KIMBERLY D. FAHRBACH, born June 23, 1971; admitted to bar, 1996, Illinois and U.S. District Court, Northern, Southern, and Central Districts of Illinois, including Trial Bar. *Education:* Elmhurst College (B.S., 1993); Chicago-Kent College of Law, Illinois Institute of Technology (J.D., 1996). *Member:* Chicago, Illinois State and American Bar Associations. ***PRACTICE AREAS:*** Medical Malpractice; Labor and Employment; Municipal Law. ***Email:*** kfahrbach@dykema.com

GREGORY L. LACEY, born April 28, 1967; admitted to bar, 1993, New York and New Jersey; 1997, Illinois and U.S. District Court, Northern District of Illinois; 2000, U.S. District Court, Eastern District of New York; 2002, U.S. District Court, Eastern District of Louisiana. *Education:* Washington University (B.A., Political Science, 1989); University of Iowa School of Law (J.D., 1992). ***PRACTICE AREAS:*** Professional Malpractice; Labor and Employment; Commercial Litigation. ***Email:*** glacey@dykema.com

DENNIS P. LINDELL, born June 9, 1973; admitted to bar, 2001, Illinois and U.S. District Court, Northern District of Illinois. *Education:* Purdue University (B.A., 1996); Valparaiso University School of Law (J.D., 1999). ***PRACTICE AREAS:*** Real Estate; Corporate; Zoning. ***Email:*** dlindell@dykema.com

DANIEL J. PETERS, born Somerset, New Jersey, February 6, 1969; admitted to bar, 2000, Illinois; U.S. District Court, Central District of Illinois; U.S. District Court, Northern District of Illinois. *Education:* Michigan State University (B.S., 1993); Chicago-Kent College of Law (J.D., 2000). ***PRACTICE AREAS:*** Litigation. ***Email:*** dpeters@dykema.com

HINSHAW & CULBERTSON LLP

Hinshaw & Culbertson LLP is an Illinois registered limited liability partnership that has elected to be governed by the Illinois Uniform Partnership Act (1997)

Established in 1934

4343 COMMERCE COURT, SUITE 415
LISLE, ILLINOIS 60532-1099
Telephone: 630-505-0010
Facsimile: 630-505-0959
Telex: 880248
Email: kfox@hinshawlaw.com
URL: http://www.hinshawlaw.com

Other Office Locations: Chicago, Illinois; Appleton, Wisconsin; Belleville, Illinois; Boston, Massachusetts; Champaign, Illinois; Crystal Lake, Illinois; Edwardsville, Illinois; Fort Lauderdale, Florida; Jacksonville, Florida; Joliet, Illinois; Los Angeles, California; Miami, Florida; Milwaukee, Wisconsin; Minneapolis, Minnesota; New York, New York; Peoria, Illinois; Phoenix, Arizona; Portland, Oregon; Providence, Rhode Island; Rockford, Illinois; St. Louis, Missouri; San Francisco, California; Schererville, Indiana; Springfield, Illinois; Tampa, Florida; Waukegan, Illinois.

Appellate, Banking & Financing, Bankruptcy & Creditors' Rights, Class Action Litigation, Civil Rights Defense, Commercial Litigation, Corporate, Construction Law, Director & Officer Liability, Employee Benefits, Environmental, Fidelity & Surety, General Liability Litigation, Government, Health Care, Insurance Coverage, Insurance and Reinsurance, Labor & Employment, Legal Malpractice, Medical Malpractice, Mergers & Acquisitions, Municipal Liability, Personal Injury Defense, Public Law, Products Liability Litigation, Professional Liability, Regulatory, Real Estate, School Law, Securities, Taxation, Transportation, White Collar Crime and Workers' Compensation Defense.

FIRM PROFILE: Hinshaw & Culbertson LLP is a national AMLaw 200 firm with 425 lawyers in 27 offices coast-to-coast. The firm offers a full-service practice, with an emphasis in commercial and defense litigation, corporate, environmental, employment and construction law, as well as the representation of professionals in their liability and risk management matters.

Hinshaw provides services to a range of clients in financial services, construction, health care, not-for-profit, insurance, legal, manufacturing, real estate, transportation and other industries. Firm clients also include government agencies, municipalities and schools.

(This Listing Continued)

Hinshaw was founded in 1934. The firm is headquartered in Chicago, and maintains offices in 12 states: Arizona, California, Florida, Illinois, Indiana, Massachusetts, Minnesota, Missouri, New York, Oregon, Rhode Island and Wisconsin.

PARTNERS

LEO J. ATHAS, born Chicago, Illinois, August 18, 1943; admitted to bar, 1973, Illinois and U.S. District Court, Northern District of Illinois; 1978, U.S. Court of Appeals, Seventh Circuit. *Education:* University of Illinois (B.S., 1964); Illinois Institute of Technology, Chicago-Kent College of Law (J.D., 1969). General Counsel/Legal Advisor: Office of Superintendent of Public Education, 1973-1974; Illinois State Board of Education, 1974-1975. *Member:* Chicago and Illinois State (Chairman, School Law Committee, 1977-1978) Bar Associations. (Also at Chicago, Illinois Office). ***PRACTICE AREAS:*** School Law. ***Email:*** lathas@hinshawlaw.com

ANTHONY FICARELLI, born Chicago, Illinois, September 7, 1952; admitted to bar, 1978, Illinois, U.S. District Court, Northern District of Illinois and U.S. Court of Appeals, Seventh Circuit. *Education:* Regis College (B.S., 1974); Georgetown University (J.D., 1978). Outstanding Civil Division Attorney, 1986. Adjunct Professor, Business Finance Science Department, College of DuPage. Associate Professor, Ph.D. Education Department, Lewis University. Member, 1985-1990 and Deputy Chief, Civil Division, DuPage County State Attorney's Office. Recognized as one of the leading lawyers in School Law by the Leading Lawyers Network. *Member:* DuPage County and Illinois State Bar Associations; Illinois Association of School Attorneys; National Association of School Attorneys; Illinois Association of School Business Officials. ***PRACTICE AREAS:*** School Law; Collective Bargaining; Student Discipline Matters; Employment Law; Employment/Personnel Matters; Public Finance; Corporate and Business Law; Real Estate. ***Email:*** aficarelli@hinshawlaw.com

JAMES M. "MARC" FORKINS, JR., born Chicago, Illinois, September 22, 1951; admitted to bar, 1985, Illinois and U.S. District Court, Northern District of Illinois; 1990, U.S. District Court, Central District of Illinois; 1991, U.S. Court of Appeals, Seventh Circuit; 2003, U.S. Supreme Court. *Education:* University of Kansas (B.A., 1977); University of Chicago (R.R.T. Registered Respiratory Therapist, 1979); Loyola University of Chicago (J.D., 1985). *Member:* Illinois State Bar Association; Illinois Association of Defense Trial Counsel. ***PRACTICE AREAS:*** Labor and Employment Law; Health Care; Civil Litigation. ***Email:*** mforkins@hinshawlaw.com

ALICE K. KUSH, born Oconto, Wisconsin, January 1, 1951; admitted to bar, 1981, Illinois and U.S. District Court, Northern District of Illinois. *Education:* University of Wisconsin (B.S.N., with high honors, 1974); IIT/Chicago-Kent College of Law (J.D., with high honors, 1981). Sigma Theta Tau. Member, Chicago-Kent Law Review, 1980-1981. Registered Nurse: Wisconsin, 1974; Illinois, 1975. *Member:* DuPage County Bar Association; Illinois State Bar Association; American Bar Association; Illinois Association of Healthcare Attorneys; American Healthcare Lawyers Association; NIC Executive Circle; Illinois Home Care Council; Illinois Health Care Association; Life Services Network; Assisted Living Federation of America. ***PRACTICE AREAS:*** Medical Malpractice Defense; Risk Management; Health Care; Continuing Care Retirement Communities; Health Care Liability; Health Care Litigation; Health Care Regulation; Health Law; Home Health Care; Long Term Care; Nursing Home Liability; Nursing Home Litigation; Nursing Home Negligence; Nursing Law; Nursing Home Regulation; Health Care Contracts. ***Email:*** akush@hinshawlaw.com

JOSEPH H. McMAHON, born Elgin, Illinois, August 30, 1966; admitted to bar, 1992, Illinois and U.S. District Court, Northern District of Illinois; 2001, U.S. Supreme Court; U.S. District Court, Central District of Illinois; 2002, Capital Litigation Trial Bar. *Education:* University of Iowa (B.B.A., 1988); John Marshall Law School (J.D., 1992). Criminal Division Chief, Kane County State's Attorney Office, 1992-2000. Deputy Chief, Criminal Prosecutions, Illinois Attorney General's Office, 2000-2002. *Member:* American (Member, Health Care Section), Illinois State (Chair: Corrections & Sentencing Committee; Corporate Law Departments Section) and Kane County Bar Associations. ***PRACTICE AREAS:*** Healthcare Fraud and Abuse; White Collar Criminal Defense; Commercial Litigation. ***Email:*** jmcmahon@hinshawlaw.com

MARK C. METZGER, born Belleville, Illinois, May 30, 1964; admitted to bar, 1989, Illinois and U.S. District Court, Northern District of Illinois; 2001, U.S. District Court, Central District of Illinois; 2002, U.S. Court of Appeals, Eighth Circuit. *Education:* Illinois Wesleyan University (B.A., 1986); Southern Illinois University (J.D., 1989). Order of the Barristers. Lincoln's Inn of Court. Author and Presenter: "Legal Implications of Computer-Aided Medical Diagnosis," J. Legal Medicine, Vol. 9, No. 2, p.213 (June 1988); Computer Legal Issues, Mt. Vernon Conference IX, May 1990; "Technology Transfer," Physician Insurers Association of America, Aspen Colorado, October 1997; "Discovery of Computer-Generated Evidence," paper and presentation delivered to Illinois Association of Defense Counsel's Defense Tactics Seminar, February 1998; "The Legal Implications of the Year 2000 Problems," COMDEX (Spring, 1998); "The Year 2000 in the Law Office," ATLA Mutual Advisor (Fall, 1998); "Emergency Services Year 2000 Liability," Every Second Counts, April 1999; "Legal Issues in Data Security," Mealey's Litigation Advisor, 1999; Chair, Mealey's Electronic Evidence Conference, 2001; Program Chair IICLE Seminar on Electronic Evidence, 2002. Member, Board of Education, Indian Prairie School District 1991—; Member, Illinois Association of School Boards Board of Directors, 2001—. Member, Rush-Copley Medical Center Board of Directors, 1997—. Appointed Member, Illinois Joint House-Senate Task Force on Mold in Environments, 2004. *Member:* American Bar Association; Illinois Association of Defense Trial Counsel; Defense Research Institute; Computer Law Association. ***REPORTED CASES:*** Sampson v. Hansen, 108 F.3d 1379, 1997 WL 117261 (7 Cir. 1997); Southwest Whey, Inc. v. Nutrition 101, Inc., 126 F.Supp.2d 1143 (C.D. Ill. 2001); Southwest Whey, Inc. v. Nutrition 101, Inc., 155F.Supp.2d 1003 (C.D. Ill. 2001); Southwest Whey, Inc. v. Nutrition 101, Inc., 188 F.Supp.2d 986 (C.D. Ill. 2002); Infinity Products, Inc. v. Premier Plastics, LLC, 93 Fed. Appx. 90, 2004 WL 487724 (8th Cir. 2004). ***PRACTICE AREAS:*** School Law; Information Technology; Commercial Litigation. ***Email:*** mmetzger@hinshawlaw.com

DANIEL M. PURDOM, born Melrose Park, Illinois, August 21, 1952; admitted to bar, 1978, Illinois and U.S. District Court, Southern and Central Districts of Illinois; 1980, U.S. District Court, Northern District of Illinois and U.S. Court of Appeals, Seventh Circuit; 1990, U.S. Court of Appeals, Eleventh Circuit; U.S. District Court, Eastern District of Wisconsin. *Education:* Illinois State University (B.S., 1974); Southern Illinois University (J.D., with highest honors, 1978). Articles Editor, Southern Illinois University Law Journal, 1977-1978. Law Clerk, U.S. District Judge James L. Foreman, Southern District of Illinois, 1978-1980. Assistant U.S. Attorney, Northern District of Illinois 1980-1986. Trial Advocacy Institute Instructor, Department of Justice Advocacy Institute. National Trial Advocacy Institute Instructor, Loyola University and Northwestern University. Named "Leading Lawyers" 2004, 2005. Named "Illinois Super Lawyers" 2005. *Member:* DuPage County, Illinois State and American Bar Associations; Association of Defense Trial Attorneys; National Association of Criminal Defense; American Health Lawyers Association. ***PRACTICE AREAS:*** White Collar Crime; Health Care Fraud and Abuse; Corporate Compliance; Commercial Litigation. ***Email:*** dpurdom@hinshawlaw.com

MAUREEN LENNON ZEEB, born Chicago, Illinois, November 1964; admitted to bar, 1990, Illinois and U.S. District Court, Northern District of Illinois. *Education:* John Carroll University (B.A., History, 1986); John Marshall Law School (J.D., 1990). ***PRACTICE AREAS:*** Professional Liability Litigation; Legal Malpractice; Legal Ethics and Professional Responsbility; Medical Malpractice. ***Email:*** mlzeeb@hinshawlaw.com

ASSOCIATES

SUZANNE M. BONDS, born Trenton, Michigan, 1950; admitted to bar, 1994, Illinois and U.S. District Court, Northern District of Illinois. *Education:* University of Illinois at Chicago (B.A., 1990); Chicago Kent College of Law (J.D., 1994). Phi Beta Kappa, High Honors in Criminal Justice; Phi Kappa Phi; Golden Key National Honor Society, University of Illinios at Chicago, 1990. Semi-Finalist, Moot Court Competition, IIT Chicago Kent College of Law, 1994. Contributing Author: "Bar None: 125 Years of Women Lawyers in Illinois," highlighting biographies of 36 of the first 100 women lawyers in Illinois. *Member:* DuPage County Bar Association; Illinois State Bar Association. ***PRACTICE AREAS:*** Personal Injury; Medical Malpractice; Products Liability. ***Email:*** sbonds@hinshawlaw.com

CHRISTY L. HOOP, born Chicago, Illinois, February 14, 1970; admitted to bar, 1995, Illinois and U.S. District Court, Northern District of Illinois; 1996, Indiana and U.S. District Court, Northern and Southern Districts of Indiana. *Education:* Indiana University (B.A., 1992); DePaul University (J.D., 1995). Member, Illinois Association of School Boards. *Member:* Illinois State Bar Association. ***PRACTICE AREAS:*** School Law; Employee Discipline; Commercial Litigation; Labor and Employment; Healthcare. ***Email:*** choop@hinshawlaw.com

MANKUS & MARCHAN, LTD.

Established in 1986

5950-E. LINCOLN AVENUE, SUITE 500
LISLE, ILLINOIS 60532
Telephone: 630-960-0500
Fax: 630-960-0601
Email: tman@irstax.com
URL: http://www.irstax.com

Tax Controversies, Bankruptcy, Social Security Disability, Real Estate, Family Law.

FIRM PROFILE: We counsel and defend individuals and businesses against the full range of IRS' Actions, including audits collection activities and criminal investigations.

TONY MANKUS, born Plunge, Lithuania, April 10, 1939; admitted to bar, 1986, Illinois. *Education:* Fairleigh Dickinson University (B.A., 1968); John Marshall Law School (J.D., 1985). *Member:* Du-Page County and Chicago Bar Associations; Lithuanian-American Bar Association; National Lawyers' Association. ***LANGUAGES:*** Lithuanian, Spanish. ***PRACTICE AREAS:*** Tax Controversies; Bankruptcy. ***Email:*** tman@irstax.com

MARGARITA MARCHAN-MANKUS, born 1945; admitted to bar, 1970, Puerto Rico; 1990, Illinois. *Education:* University of Puerto Rico (B.S., 1966; J.D., 1969). ***LANGUAGES:*** Spanish. ***PRACTICE AREAS:*** Social Security Disability (80%, 150); Real Estate (10%, 75); Family Law (10%, 50).

Languages: Spanish and Lithuanian.

SWANSON, MARTIN & BELL

Established in 1992

2525 CABOT DRIVE, SUITE 204
LISLE, ILLINOIS 60532
Telephone: 630-799-6900
Fax: 630-799-6901
URL: http://www.smbtrials.com

Chicago, Illinois Office: 330 North Wabash, Suite 3300, 60611. Telephone: 312-321-9100. Fax: 312-321-0990.

Lake County, Illinois Office: 1860 West Winchester Road, Suite 201, Libertyville, Illinois, 60048. Telephone: 847-949-0025. Fax: 847-247-0555.

Waukegan, Illinois Office: 415 Washington Street, Suite 1B, Waukegan, Illinois, 60085. Telephone: 847-949-0025. Fax: 847-247-0555.

Class Action Lawsuits, Commercial Litigation, Construction Litigation/Disputes, Consumer and Warranty Law, Creditor's Rights, Drugs & Medical Devices, Employment Litigation, Environmental Law, Equipment Leasing, General Tort Liability, Healthcare, Insurance Coverage, Intellectual Property, Medical Negligence, Municipal Law, Product Liability, Professional Negligence, Real Estate Development/Zoning, Real Estate Litigation, Toxic and Mass Tort Litigation, and White Collar Criminal Defense.

PARTNERS

DAVID J. CAHILL, born Chicago, Illinois, August 5, 1955; admitted to bar, 1981, Illinois. *Education:* University of Illinois (B.A., magna, cum laude, 1977); Illinois Institute

(This Listing Continued)

SWANSON, MARTIN & BELL, Lisle—Continued

of Technology/Chicago-Kent College of Law (J.D., with high honors, 1981). Phi Beta Kappa; Phi Kappa Phi. ***PRACTICE AREAS:*** Insurance Coverage; Personal Injury; Litigation; Products Liability; Medical Malpractice. ***Email:*** dcahill@smbtrials.com

MATTHEW D. JACOBSON, born Iowa City, Iowa, February 17, 1968; admitted to bar, 1993, Illinois and U.S. District Court, Northern District of Illinois. *Education:* University of Iowa (B.S., 1990; J.D., 1993). *Member:* DuPage County, Illinois State and American Bar Associations. Defense Research Institute. ***PRACTICE AREAS:*** Products Liability; Medical Malpractice; Commercial Litigation; Insurance Defense; Insurance Coverage; Civil Litigation. ***Email:*** mjacobso@smbtrials.com

BRUCE S. TERLEP, born Elkhart, Indiana, October 29, 1958; admitted to bar, 1985, Illinois and U.S. District Court, Northern District of Illinois. *Education:* DePauw University (B.A., magna cum laude, 1981); University of Notre Dame (J.D., 1985). Phi Beta Kappa. *Member:* Du Page County and Illinois State Bar Associations. ***PRACTICE AREAS:*** Civil Litigation; Product Liability; Consumer Law; Civil Fraud; Automobile Warranty Law; Insurance Defense. ***Email:*** bterlep@smbtrials.com

ASSOCIATES

ROSS W. BARTOLOTTA, born Evergreen Park, Illinois, October 24, 1969; admitted to bar, 1994 Illinois, and U.S. District Court, Northern District of Illinois. *Education:* University of Illinois at Urbana-Champaign (B.A., 1991); Northern Illinois University (J.D., 1994). Dean's List. *Member:* Kane County and DuPage County Bar Associations; Justinian Society of Italian-American Lawyers. ***PRACTICE AREAS:*** Insurance Defense; Insurance Coverage; Medical Malpractice; Products Liability; Automobile Warranty Law; Civil Litigation; Construction Litigation; Mold Litigation. ***Email:*** rbartolo@smbtrials.com

SUZANNE M. FITCH, born Elgin, Illinois, August 9, 1975; admitted to bar, 2001, Illinois; U.S. District Court, Northern District of Illinois. *Education:* University of Illinois Urbana-Champaign (B.S., 1998); Northern Illinois University (J.D., magna cum laude, 2001). Member, Northern Illinois University Mock Trial Team. Lead Articles Editor, Northern Illinois University Law Review. *Member:* DuPage, Chicago and Illinois State Bar Associations. ***PRACTICE AREAS:*** Tort Liability; Automotive Warranty Law; Civil Litigation; Products Liability; Municipal Law. ***Email:*** sfitch@smbtrials.com

TIMOTHY G. GLEASON, born 1972; admitted to bar, 2001, Illinois and U.S. District Court, Northern District of Illinois. *Education:* University of Illinois (B.S., 1993); Northwestern University School of Law (J.D., 2001). ***Email:*** tgleason@smbtrials.com

AMY R. MILLER, born Joliet, Illinois, August 5, 1974; admitted to bar, 1999, Illinois and U.S. District Court, Northern District of Illinois. *Education:* Millikin University (B.A., cum laude, 1996); University of Illinois College of Law (J.D., magna cum laude, 1999). Recipient, Rickert Award for Oral Advocacy, 1999. *Member:* DuPage County and Illinois State Bar Associations. ***PRACTICE AREAS:*** Insurance Coverage; Medical Malpractice; Warranty Law; Products Liability; Commercial Litigation. ***Email:*** amiller@smbtrials.com

DAVID J. RISKI, born Crestwood, Illinois, November 24, 1975; admitted to bar, 2000, Illinois; 2001, U.S. District Court, Northern District of Illinois; U.S. District Court, Eastern District of Michigan. *Education:* Northern Illinois University (B.S., 1997); DePaul University (J.D., 2000). ***PRACTICE AREAS:*** Civil Litigation; Warranty Law; Products Liability; Insurance Defense.

CHRISTIAN A. SULLIVAN, born Urbana, Illinois, November 30, 1974; admitted to bar, 2002, Illinois and U.S. District Court, Northern District of Illinois. *Education:* University of Illinois, Urbana-Champaign (B.A., 1999); Northern Illinois University College of Law (J.D., magna cum laude, 2002). Research Editor, Northern Illinois University Law Review. Extern, Philip G. Reinhard, United States District Court, Western District Illinois. Author: "Juvenile Delinquency in the Twenty-First Century: Is Blended Sentencing the Middle-Road Solution for Today's Violent Kids?", 21 N. Ill. U.L. Rev. 483, 2001. *Member:* DuPage County, Chicago and Illinois State Bar Associations. ***PRACTICE AREAS:*** Automobile Warranty Law; Insurance Defense; Products Liability; Appellate Litigation; Medical Malpractice Defense. ***Email:*** csulliva@smbtrials.com

OF COUNSEL

LENARD C. SWANSON, born Oak Park, Illinois, April 5, 1937; admitted to bar, 1967, Illinois. *Education:* University of Illinois (B.S., 1963; J.D., 1967). Order of the Coif. *Member:* Du Page County, Illinois State and American Bar Associations; Society of Trial Lawyers; Illinois Defense Counsel; Defense Research Institute; The Law Club of Chicago. Fellow, American College of Trial Lawyers. ***PRACTICE AREAS:*** Products Liability; Professional Liability; Medical Malpractice; Insurance Defense. ***Email:*** lswanson@smbtrials.com

EDWARD T. BUTT, JR., born Chicago, Illinois, October 27, 1947; admitted to bar, 1971, Illinois; 1975, Wisconsin; 1997, Michigan; U.S. District Court, Northern District of Illinois including Trial Bar; U.S. Court of Appeals, Sixth and Seventh Circuits; U.S. Claims Court; U.S. District Court, Eastern District of Wisconsin. *Education:* Lawrence University (B.A., 1968); University of Michigan (J.D., 1971). Recipient, American Jurisprudence Book Award in Land Finance Law. *Member:* Seventh Circuit and American (Member, Sections on: Litigation; Tort and Insurance Practice) Bar Associations; State Bar of Wisconsin (Member, Litigation and Non-Resident Lawyers Section); Defense Research Institute (Products Liability and Insurance Coverage Sections); State Bar of Michigan. ***PRACTICE AREAS:*** Product Liability; Insurance Coverage. ***Email:*** etbjrpc@aol.com

(For biographical data on all personnel, see professional biographies at Chicago, Illinois)

WILDMAN, HARROLD, ALLEN & DIXON LLP

Established in 1967

2300 CABOT DRIVE, SUITE 455
LISLE, ILLINOIS 60532
Telephone: 630-955-0555
Fax: 630-955-0662
Email: info@wildmanharrold.com
URL: http://www.wildmanharrold.com

Chicago, Illinois Office: 225 West Wacker Drive, Suite 3000. Telephone: 312-201-2000. Fax: 312-201-2155.

General Civil, Trial and Appellate Practice, Commercial Litigation, Corporate and Business Law, Government, Medical Malpractice, Municipal Finance, Probate and Estate Planning, Real Estate, Tax, Telecommunications.

PARTNERS

JAMES B. DURKIN, born Chicago, Illinois, January 28, 1961; admitted to bar, 1990, Illinois. *Education:* Illinois State University (B.S., 1984); The John Marshall Law School (J.D., 1989). Cook County State's Attorney; Illinois Attorney General; Member: Illinois House of Representatives, 1995—2002; Misericordia-Heart of Mercy Home Board of Advisors, 1996—; 2002 Republican Nominee for United States Senate. *Member:* Chicago Bar Association. ***PRACTICE AREAS:*** Government Affairs. ***Email:*** durkin@wildmanharrold.com

DAVID H. HIGHT, born Peoria, Illinois, August 5, 1955; admitted to bar, 1985, Illinois. *Education:* Millikin University (B.A., summa cum laude, 1976); Eastern Illinois University (M.A., 1980); DePaul University (J.D., with honors, 1985). Recipient, American Jurisprudence Award. Member, DePaul Law Review, 1982-1985. *Member:* Illinois State and American Bar Associations. ***PRACTICE AREAS:*** Corporate Law; Banking Law; Real Estate Law. ***Email:*** hight@wildmanharrold.com

RICHARD C. JOHNSON, born Chicago, Illinois, February 28, 1957; admitted to bar, 1982, Illinois. *Education:* DePaul University (B.A., 1979); John Marshall Law School (J.D., 1982). *Member:* DuPage County Bar Association; DuPage County Estate Planning Council. ***PRACTICE AREAS:*** Estate Planning; Probate; Family Law; Real Estate Law. ***Email:*** johnson@wildmanharrold.com

DEAN J. LEFFELMAN, born Amboy, Illinois, June 23, 1953; admitted to bar, 1980, Illinois. *Education:* Northern Illinois University (B.S., 1976); John Marshall Law School (J.D., with distinction, 1979). Member: Order of John Marshall; John Marshall Law Review, 1978-1979. Author: "Avoiding Recognition of Income on Debt Cancellation," The Tax Advisor, February, 1980; "Planning Opportunities on Incorporation," Illinois Bar Journal, April, 1986; "Controlling A Corporation With Less Than Fifty-One Percent Ownership," Du Page Bar Journal, December, 1990. Past President, Fox Valley Estate Planning Council. Instructor of Business Law, Aurora University, 1981-1989. *Member:* Du Page County and Illinois State Bar Associations. ***PRACTICE AREAS:*** Business Law; Real Estate Law; Estate Planning and Administration. ***Email:*** leffelma@wildmanharrold.com

BART T. MURPHY, born Chicago, Illinois, January 28, 1956; admitted to bar, 1981, Illinois and U. S. District Court, Northern District of Illinois including Trial Bar; 1982, U.S. Court of Appeals, 7th Circuit; 1987, U.S. Supreme Court; 1990, U.S. District Court, Central District of Illinois; 1998, U.S. District Court, Eastern District of Wisconsin and U.S. Court of International Trade; 1999, U.S. Tax Court. *Education:* St. Mary's College of Minnesota (B.A., 1978); Loyola University (J.D., 1981). Assistant State's Attorney, Cook County, 1982. Assistant Attorney General 1982-1991. Director, Catholic Lawyers Guild of Chicago. Director, Greater Illinois Chapter Cystic Fibrosis Foundation. *Member:* Chicago, DuPage County, Illinois State and American Bar Associations. ***REPORTED CASES:*** Chicago Dist. Council of Carpenters Pension Fund, et al. v. R.G. Construction Services, Inc., No 01 C 3976, 2002 U.S. Dist LEXIS 21001 (USDC ND IL 10/28/02); Construction Consulting v. Gersten Financial & Insurance, No. 02 C 3322, 2002 U.S. Dist LEXIS 11669 (USDC ND IL 6/27/02); Market Street Securities v. Racing Champions, No. 00 C 3267, 2000 U.S. Dist LEXIS 19103 (USDC ND IL 11/20/00). ***PRACTICE AREAS:*** Litigation. ***Email:*** murphy@wildmanharrold.com

MICHAEL M. ROTH, born Joliet, Illinois, January 15, 1954; admitted to bar, 1980, Illinois; 1981, U.S. District Court, Northern District of California. *Education:* University of Illinois at Champaign (B.S., 1976); The John Marshall Law School (J.D., 1980). Phi Delta Phi. Assistant State's Attorney, Cook County, 1980-1981. *Member:* Chicago, Illinois State and American Bar Associations; Illinois Trial Lawyers Association. ***PRACTICE AREAS:*** Local Government; Cable Communications; Telecommunications; Zoning and Land Development. ***Email:*** roth@wildmanharrold.com

ERIC L. SINGER, born Pittsburgh, Pennsylvania, August 20, 1964; admitted to bar, 1988, Illinois. *Education:* University of Illinois (B.A., with distinction in Sociology, magna cum laude, 1985); University of Chicago (J.D., 1988). Phi Beta Kappa. ***PRACTICE AREAS:*** Construction and Design Law; Complex Litigation; Mechanics Liens.

JAMES M. SNYDER, born Lorain, Ohio, November 21, 1959; admitted to bar, 1987, Illinois. *Education:* Ohio State University (B.S., 1982; J.D., cum laude, 1986). Order of the Coif. *Member:* National Association of Bond Lawyers. ***PRACTICE AREAS:*** Municipal Finance; Taxation. ***Email:*** snyderj@wildmanharrold.com

ASSOCIATES

DAVID J. CHROUST, born Berwyn, Illinois, December 22, 1955; admitted to bar, 1980, Illinois; 1981, U.S. District Court, Northern District of Illinois; 1982, U.S. Court of Appeals, Seventh Circuit. *Education:* Grinnell College (B.A., 1980); Columbia University (J.D., 1980). Phi Beta Kappa; Phi Delta Phi. *Member:* Illinois State Bar Association. ***PRACTICE AREAS:*** Appellate; Civil Litigation; Financial Services and Creditors' Rights. ***Email:*** chroust@wildmanharrold.com

ELIZABETH A. McKILLIP, admitted to bar, 2004, Illinois. *Education:* University of Illinois (B.A., Philosophy, 2001); Loyola University Chicago School of Law (J.D., magna

(This Listing Continued)

cum laude, 2004). *Member:* DuPage County and Illinois State Bar Associations. ***PRACTICE AREAS:*** Estate Planning; Probate; Family Law. ***Email:*** mckillip@wildmanharrold.com

LAURIE M. MILLER, born Chicago, Illinois, April 6, 1968; admitted to bar, 1995, Illinois. *Education:* University of Wisconsin (B.A., Political Science, 1990); Chicago-Kent College of Law (J.D., with honors, 1995). *Member:* American Corporate Counsel Association. ***PRACTICE AREAS:*** Corporate. ***Email:*** millerl@wildmanharrold.com

JENEE M. STRAUB, born St. Charles, Illinois, May 17, 1973; admitted to bar, 1999, Illinois; 2000, U.S. District Court, Northern District of Illinois. *Education:* Bradley University (B.S., 1996); Northern Illinois University College of Law (J.D., cum laude, 1999). ***PRACTICE AREAS:*** Commercial Litigation; Mechanics Liens Litigation; Employment Law. ***Email:*** straub@wildmanharrold.com

CORRIE E. VALROSE, admitted to bar, 2000, Illinois. *Education:* Ball State University, College of Architecture and Planning (B.L.A., 1993); Chicago-Kent College of Law, Illinois Institute of Technology (J.D., 2000). Member, DePaul Environmental Law Journal. *Member:* Chicago and Illinois Bar Associations; American Institute of Architects (AIA); American Society of Landscape Architects (ASLA). ***PRACTICE AREAS:*** Litigation; Breach of Contract; Consumer Fraud; Truth in Lending; Mechanics Liens; Breach of Warranty; Design Professionals Liability; Contracts. ***Email:*** schafer@wildmanharrold.com

OF COUNSEL

LOUIS P. VITULLO, born Chicago, Illinois, October 15, 1944; admitted to bar, 1969, Illinois. *Education:* John Carroll University (B.A., 1966); Loyola University (J.D., 1969). Assistant and Counsel to the Governor of Illinois, 1974-1976. *Member:* Chicago and Illinois State Bar Associations. (Also at Chicago Office). ***PRACTICE AREAS:*** Commercial Litigation; Corporate, Securities, Tax; Governmental Practices; Real Estate. ***Email:*** vitullo@wildmanharrold.com

(For complete biographical information on all personnel, see Professional Biographies at Chicago, Illinois)

THERESA M. MALYSA

LOCKPORT, ILLINOIS

(See Orland Park)

Family Law, Divorce, Tax Considerations, Retirement Benefits, Child Custody, Parenting Time, Visitation, Child Support, Domestic Violence, Paternity, Matrimonial Litigation, Premarital Agreements.

PRATO & ASSOCIATES, P.C.

LOMBARD, ILLINOIS

(See Oak Brook)

Real Estate Transactions, Bankruptcy, Small Businesses, Corporate, Criminal, DUI, Personal Injury and Immigration Law.

PRICE TUNNEY REITER

A PROFESSIONAL CORPORATION

LOMBARD, ILLINOIS

(See Chicago)

Trial and Appellate Practice in State and Federal Courts. Alternative Dispute Resolution, Litigation Prevention, Health Care Professionals Liability, Legal Malpractice, Accountant's Malpractice, Hospital Litigation, Products Liability, Premises Liability, Commercial Litigation, Fraud, Real Estate Broker and Insurance Agent Errors and Omissions, Nursing Home Litigation, Insurance Coverage Disputes, Breach of Lease, Toxic Tort Litigation, Contract Disputes, Environmental Litigation.

A. TRAUB & CÁDIZ

LOMBARD, ILLINOIS

(See Schaumburg)

General Practice, Litigation, Family Law, Adoption, Child Custody/Support, Divorce, Estate Planning, Wills and Probate, Landlord and Tenant, Bankruptcy, Real Estate: Residential, Guardianship, Traffic.

PINZUR, COHEN & KERR, LTD.

Established in 1994

4180 RFD ROUTE 83
SUITE 208
LONG GROVE, ILLINOIS 60047
Telephone: 847-821-5290
Fax: 847-821-5293
Email: info@pckltdlaw.com
URL: http://www.pinzurcohenkerr.com

Administrative Matters, Adoption Law, Annexation, Appellate Practice, Arbitration, Asset Acquisitions and Sales, Banking and Loan Documentation, Banking Law, Business Law, Business Litigation, Business Planning and Formation, Business Successions, Buying and Selling of Businesses, Child Custody, Child Support, Civil Litigation in State and Federal Courts, Civil Rights, Class Actions, Closings, Collections, Commercial and Residential Development, Commercial Litigation, Commercial Real Estate, Community Association Law, Condemnation, Condominium Law, Contractual Disputes, Construction Law, Construction Arbitration, Construction Defects, Construction Litigation, Consumer Law, Contested Wills, Contracts, Cooperative Housing Law, Copyrights, Corporate Law, Corporations, Creditors Rights, Debtor and Creditor, Developer Disputes, Discrimination, Divorce, Domestic Violence, Elder Law, Employment Agreements, Employment Law, Entrepreneurial Ventures, Environmental Law, Equipment Leasing, Equitable and Injunctive Remedies, Estate Planning, Family Law, Family Business Law, Forcible Eviction Law, Foreclosures, Franchise Law, General Practice, Guardianship, Harassment, Homeowner's Association Law, Incorporation, Institutional Lending, Insurance Regulations, Workouts, Insurance, Land Development and Zoning, Landlord and Tenant Law, Leases and Leasing, Limited Liability Companies, Litigation, Matrimonial Law, Mechanics Liens, Mergers and Acquisitions, Mortgages, Municipal, Partnership Law, Personal Injury, Premarital Agreements, Probate Law, Real Estate, Real Estate Finance, Real Estate Litigation, Real Estate Tax Appeals, Real Estate Tax Assessment, Residential Real Estate, Sales Acquisitions, School Law, Secured Transactions, Small Business Law, Social Security, Spousal Support, Stock Acquisitions and Sales, Trademarks, Trusts and Estates, Uniform Commercial Code, Wills, Zoning, Planning and Land Use.

FIRM PROFILE: Pinzur, Cohen & Kerr, Ltd. was founded by Robert Pinzur in December 1994. The Firm handles civil litigation in State and Federal Courts as well as other matters in Lake County, Cook County, McHenry County and DuPage County and other Chicago area collar counties. We care about all of our clients and believe each client deserves individualized personal attention. The lights are burning nearly every night at PCK to insure we successfully, thoroughly and aggressively represent all of our clients in preparation, analysis, negotiation and litigation.

ROBERT S. PINZUR, born Chicago, Illinois, July 28, 1953; admitted to bar, 1978, Illinois, U.S. District Court, Northern District of Illinois; 1982, U.S. District Court, Eastern District of Michigan; 1990, U.S. Supreme Court. *Education:* University of Illinois (B.A., cum laude, 1975); Northwestern University (J.D., 1978). Author: "Insurable Interest: A Search For Consistency," Insurance Counsel Journal, Vol. 46, No. 1, January 1979. Instructor, Business Law, Keller Graduate School of Management, 1991-1992. Trustee: Kildeer Countryside School District 96, 1993-2001; North Suburban Mass Transit District, 1981-1984. *Member:* Chicago, Lake County and Illinois State Bar Associations; Northwest Suburban Bar Association; North Suburban Bar Association. ***LANGUAGES:*** English. ***REPORTED CASES:*** Lynch, Incorporated v. Samata Mason, N.D. IL (2002); In re Garelick, 168 Ill.App.3d 321, 522 N.E.2d 738; 119 Ill. Dec. 76 (First District 1988). ***PRACTICE AREAS:*** Business Law; Civil Rights; Contracts; Debtor and Creditor; Employment Discrimination; Employment Law; Estate Planning; Family Law; General Practice; Harassment; Insurance; Personal Injury; Real Estate; Transactional; Wrongful Termination. ***Email:*** rpinzur@pckltdlaw.com

LAURA E. COHEN, born Skokie, Illinois, March 20, 1964; admitted to bar, 1996, Illinois. *Education:* University of Illinois (B.S., 1986); Loyola University, Chicago (J.D., 1996). *Member:* Lake County Bar Association; Northwest Suburban Bar Association; North Suburban Bar Association. ***LANGUAGES:*** English. ***PRACTICE AREAS:*** Business Law; Contracts; Debtor and Creditor; Discrimination; Employment Law; Personal Injury; Social Security; Real Estate. ***Email:*** lcohen@pckltdlaw.com

MEGAN LAURA KERR, born Pinckneyville, Illinois, August 29, 1973; admitted to bar, 1998, Illinois. *Education:* University of Illinois, Urbana-Champaign (B.A., 1995); DePaul University School of Law (J.D., 1998). *Member:* Lake County, Chicago and Illinois State Bar Associations; Northwest Suburban Bar Association; North Suburban Bar Association. ***LANGUAGES:*** English. ***PRACTICE AREAS:*** Divorce; Employment Law; Real Estate. ***Email:*** mkerr@pckltdlaw.com

---

BRIAN S. BREWER, born St. Joseph, Michigan, December 31, 1975; admitted to bar, 2001, Illinois and U.S. District Court, Northern District of Illinois. *Education:* Elmhurst College (B.A., 1998); John Marshall Law School (J.D., 2001). *Member:* Illinois State, Northwest Bar Associations. ***LANGUAGES:*** English. ***PRACTICE AREAS:*** Constitutional Law; Divorce; Estate Planning; Personal Injury; Probate. ***Email:*** bbrewer@pckltdlaw.com

BRIAN R. MERFELD, born Baltimore, Maryland, June 22, 1978; admitted to bar, 2003, Illinois, U.S. District Court, District of Illinois. *Education:* University of Maryland (B.A., with honors, Government and Politics, 2000); DePaul University (J.D., 2003). Member, National Society of Collegiate Scholars; College Park Scholars in Public Leadership. Recipient: Presidential Scholarship of University of Maryland. Former Law Clerk, Katz, Friedman, Eagle, Eisenstein and Johnson. Internship with Senator Richard Durbin, Illinois. ***LANGUAGES:*** English. ***PRACTICE AREAS:*** Real Estate; Employment Law; Collections; Local Government Law; Personal Injury; Contracts. ***Email:*** bmerfeld@pckltdlaw.com

Languages: English.

REPRESENTATIVE CLIENTS: Furnished Upon Request.

HARTZELL, GLIDDEN, TUCKER AND HARTZELL

Established in 1852

OLD BAILEY HOUSE
100 SOUTH CAMPBELL STREET
MACOMB, ILLINOIS 61455
Telephone: 309-833-3121
Email: firm@adams.net

Carthage, Illinois Office: Williams Building. Telephone: 217-357-3121. FAX: 217-357-2027.

General Civil Trial and Appellate Practice in all State and Federal Courts. Real Estate, Estate Planning and Probate, Banking Law, Taxation, Personal Injury and Family Law.

(For complete biographical data on all personnel, see Professional Biographies at Carthage, Illinois)

(This Listing Continued)

WESTERVELT, JOHNSON, NICOLL & KELLER, LLC

Established in 1865

MIDAMERICA BANKING CENTER
130 NORTH SIDE SQUARE, SUITE 202
MACOMB, ILLINOIS 61435
Telephone: 309-836-2900
Fax: 309-836-2844
URL: http://www.wjnklaw.com

Peoria, Illinois Office: 14th Floor, 411 Hamilton Boulevard, 61602; Telephone: 309-671-3550. Fax: 309-671-3588.

General Civil Trial and Appellate Practice in State and Federal Courts, Insurance Defense, Health and Health Care, Labor Relations, Employment Discrimination and Affirmative Action, Products Liability Litigation, ERISA and Benefits Plans, Corporate, Agricultural, Bankruptcy, Creditors' Rights, Banking, Real Estate, State and Federal Taxation, Estate Planning, Trusts and Probate, Workers Compensation, Environmental, Commercial.

A. ANTHONY ASHENHURST, born Macomb, Illinois, May 2, 1954; admitted to bar, 1980, Georgia and U.S. District Court, Central District of Illinois; 1982, Illinois; 1991, U.S. Court of Appeals, Seventh Circuit and U.S. Supreme Court. *Education:* Western Illinois University (B.A., 1977); Drake University (J.D., 1979). Author: Revision, "Right of Way Reservations, Nichols on Eminent Domain," Matthew Bender & Co., Inc., 1994; Revision, "Builder Extractions: Dedication of Land or Payment of Fees in Lieu Thereof, Zoning and Land Use Controls," Matthew Bender & Co., Inc., 1994; "Appellate Procedures, Nichols on Eminent Domain," Matthew Bender & Co., Inc., 1994; "Taking Procedures: Nichols on Eminent Domain," Matthew Bender & Company, Inc., 1992; "Case Note, Group Life and Health Insurance v. Royal Drug," 28 Drake Law Review 977, December 1979. Instructor, Western Illinois University, 1983-1998. Special Assistant Attorney General, Illinois, 1983—. *Member:* Chicago, McDonough County, Illinois State and American Bar Associations; State Bar of Georgia; Illinois Association of Healthcare Attorneys. ***REPORTED CASES:*** Lee v. Canuteson, 214 Ill.App.3d 137, 157 Ill.Dec. 900, 573 N.E.2d 318 (1991); Department of Transportation v. First Galesburg National Bank & Trust, 141 Ill.2d 462, 566 N.E.2d 254, 152 Ill.Dec. 567 (1990). ***PRACTICE AREAS:*** Healthcare; Labor and Employment; Corporate Law; Eminent Domain. ***Email:*** aashenhurst@westerveltlaw.com

REPRESENTATIVE CLIENTS: Amerex Industries, Inc.; Benetech Inc.; Farm King Supply, Inc.; Lamoine Valley Clinic S.C.; Laverdiere Construction Inc.; McDonough District Hospital; McDonaugh Physician Hospital Organization; Mid America Natiional Bank; Sarah D. Culbertson Memorial Hospital; Vermont Foundry Company; Benetech Gmbh (Germany); Servicious Benetech, C.A. (Venezuela).

DAVID MacTAVISH

8N341 THOMAS ROAD
MAPLE PARK, ILLINOIS 60151
Telephone: 630-365-2613
Fax: 630-365-9012
Email: david@mactavish-law.com
URL: http://www.mactavish-law.com

Copyrights, Trademarks, Trade Names, Entertainment Law, Art Law, Internet, Cyberspace, Cyberpiracy, Domain Names, Idea Protection, Licensing, Trade Secrets, Unfair Competition, Computer Law.

DAVID MacTAVISH, admitted to bar, 1999, Illinois, U.S. District Court, Northern District of Illinois and U.S. Court of Appeals, Seventh Circuit. *Education:* DePaul University (B.A., Political Science, 1995); John Marshall Law School (J.D., 1999). Author: "Analysis of Canadian Copyright Act and Its Effect on United States Photographers," David MacTavish, www.ASMP.org, 1999. Co-Author: with Michal Heron, "Pricing Photography," Allworth Press, 1993, 1997, rev. 2001; with John Scott Hoff, ed., "Things That Go Bump in the Flight: In Flight Turbulence Injuries," 13 Air & Space Lawyer 1, A.B.A., 1998; with John Scott Hoff, "Things That Go Bump in the Flight: In Flight Turbulence Injuries," 20 Lawyer-Pilots Bar Association Journal 8, 1998. ***PRACTICE AREAS:*** Copyrights; Trademarks; Trade Names; Entertainment Law; Art Law; Internet; Cyberspace; Cyberpiracy; Domain Names; Idea Protection; Licensing; Trade Secrets; Unfair Competition; Computer Law.

THE LAW FIRM OF FRANKS, GERKIN & McKENNA, P.C.

Established in 1972

19333 EAST GRANT HIGHWAY
P.O. BOX 5
MARENGO, ILLINOIS 60152-0005
Telephone: 815-923-2107
Fax: 815-923-2114
Email: franklaw@mc.net
URL: http://www.famlaw.com

General, Civil & Criminal Trial Practice, Banking, Business Law, Commercial Real Estate, Corporate Law, Criminal Law, Debt Collections, Family Law, Personal Injury, Real Estate, Trusts & Estates, Immigration, Wills, Workers Compensation, Municipal Law, Traffic, Zoning, Planning and Land Use.

FIRM PROFILE: Franks, Gerkin & McKenna was founded in 1972 by Herbert H. Franks. He was joined by Peggy D. Gerkin in 1990, Terrence J. McKenna in 1992 and Jack D. Franks in 1993. The firm now consists of eight lawyers who serve both individuals and business clients. Since its formation, the firm has provided its clients with the high level of legal expertise and

(This Listing Continued)

experience typically associated with large firms, but with the cost-effectiveness and personal attention found in smaller firms. The firm's continuous growth reflects their clients' satisfaction with the quality of professional service they receive.

HERBERT H. FRANKS, born Joliet, Illinois, January 25, 1934; admitted to bar, 1961, Illinois and U.S. District Court, Northern District of Illinois; 1967, U.S. Supreme Court. *Education:* Roosevelt University (B.S., 1954); Washington College of Law, (of American University) (J.D., 1961). Author: "Law of Partition," Florida Law & Practice, 1960. Special Assistant Attorney General, 1963-1970; 1983-1993. Director, Illinois Bar Foundation, 1993-2000. President, Illinois State Bar Association 2000-2001 and Chairman, Illinois State Bar Association, Mutual Insurance Company. *Member:* McHenry County and Illinois State Bar Associations; Illinois Trial Lawyers Association (Member, Board of Managers; State Treasurer, 1985-1986; Member, Illinois Courts Commission, 2002-2003); The Association of Trial Lawyers of America. ***PRACTICE AREAS:*** Personal Injury; Worker's Compensation; Banking Law; Commercial Law. ***Email:*** hfranks@fgmlaw.com

PEGGY D. GERKIN, born Peoria, Illinois, January 30, 1962; admitted to bar, 1988, Illinois; 1990, U.S. District Court, Northern District of Illinois. *Education:* Illinois State University (B.S., 1984); Northern Illinois University (J.D., 1988). Member, National Moot Court Society. Listed in Who's Who Among American Colleges and Universities. *Member:* Boone County (President, 1995), McHenry County and Illinois State Bar Associations. ***PRACTICE AREAS:*** Criminal Law; Family Law; Personal Injury. ***Email:*** franklaw@mc.net

TERRENCE J. McKENNA, born Evergreen Park, Illinois, November 27, 1964; admitted to bar, 1989, Illinois and U.S. District Court, Northern and Eastern Districts of Illinois. *Education:* Northern Illinois University, DeKalb (B.S., 1986); DePaul University College of Law (J.D., 1989). *Member:* McHenry County and Illinois State Bar Associations. ***PRACTICE AREAS:*** Business; Business Transactions; Real Estate; Corporate Law; Trusts and Estates; Wills. ***Email:*** mckenna@fgmlaw.com

JACK D. FRANKS, born Belvidere, Illinois, October 2, 1963; admitted to bar, 1989, Illinois and U.S. District Court, Northern District of Illinois; 1990, District of Columbia; 1991, U.S. District Court, District of Columbia and U.S. District Court, Eastern District of Michigan; 1992, U.S. Supreme Court. *Education:* London School of Economics, London, England; University of Wisconsin-Madison (B.A., honors program, 1985); American University, Washington College of Law (J.D., cum laude, 1989). Articles Editor, Administrative Law Journal. State Representative, 63rd District, representing McHenry County in Illinois State Legislature, 1998. *Member:* Illinois State Bar Association ((Member, Attorney Registration and Disciplinary Committee); Illinois Trial Lawyers Association. ***LANGUAGES:*** Portuguese and Spanish. ***PRACTICE AREAS:*** Litigation; Personal Injury; Commercial Law. ***Email:*** franklaw@mc.net

ASSOCIATES

STEPHANIE A. KASTEN, born Harvard, Illinois, January 16, 1975; admitted to bar, 2000, Illinois. *Education:* Grinnell College (B.A., 1997); Northern Illinois (J.D., with honors, 2000). Phi Delta Phi. Recipient, Moot Court Award. Editor, Northern Illinois Law Review. *Member:* McHenry County, Illinois State and American Bar Associations. ***LANGUAGES:*** German, Spanish. ***PRACTICE AREAS:*** Family Law; Divorce; Child Custody; Visitation Rights; Adoption Law; Guardianship; Probate; Real Estate; General Practice; Debtor and Creditor Collections. ***Email:*** skasten@fgmlaw.com

DAVID N. RECHENBERG, born Chicago, Illinois, May 18, 1961; admitted to bar, 1987, Illinois and U.S. District Court, Northern District of Illinois; 1997, Missouri. *Education:* Northern Illinois University (B.S., Finance, 1983; J.D., 1987). *Member:* McHenry County and Illinois State Bar Associations. ***PRACTICE AREAS:*** Personal Injury; Workers Compensation; Employment Discrimination. ***Email:*** drechenberg@fgmlaw.com

MICHELLE J. COURIER, born Belvidere, Illinois, February 1, 1973; admitted to bar, 1998, Illinois and U.S. District Court, Northern District of Illinois. *Education:* University of Illinois, Urbana-Champaign (B.S., 1995); Northern Illinois University College of Law (J.D., 1998). *Member:* McHenry County, Boone County and Illinois State Bar Associations. ***PRACTICE AREAS:*** Civil Litigation; Commercial Litigation; Real Estate; Probate. ***Email:*** mcourier@fgmlaw.com

JUAN J. DEL GRANADO, born Cochabamba, Bolivia; admitted to bar, 1994, Bolivia; 1995, Illinois. *Education:* University of Chicago (B.A., Political Science, 1989; B.A., Economics, 1989); Northwestern University School of Law (J.D., 1992); Universidad Mayor De San Simon, Cochabamba, Bolivia (D.U.J., 1994). John Olin Fellow and Lloyd M. Robins Fellow, University of California, Berkeley, Boalt Hall School of Law, 1998-2000. Adjunct Professor of Law, Chicago-Kent College of Law, 2001-2004. Law Professor, Universidad Iberoamericana, La Paz, and El Alto, Bolivia, 1994-1997. *Member:* Illinois State Bar Association; Hispanic Lawyers Association of Illinois; American Immigration Lawyers Association; Ilustre Colegio De Abogados De La Pas. ***LANGUAGES:*** Spanish. ***PRACTICE AREAS:*** Immigration and Naturalization; International Business Transactions. ***Email:*** granado@fgmlaw.com

Languages: Spanish.

REPRESENTATIVE CLIENTS: First National Bank of Marengo; Wonder Lake State Bank; Castle Bank, State Bank of Richmond; Greenwood Township; Hartland Township; Chicago Midwest Credit Service; The Bricton Goup, Inc.; CitiFinancial; Marengo Foundary.

POLLOCK, MEYERS, EICKSTEADT & PULAK, LTD.

Established in 1965

100 WEST WASHINGTON STREET
MARENGO, ILLINOIS 60152
Telephone: 815-568-8071
FAX: 815-568-0003
URL: http://www.lawyers.com/pollockmeyerseicksteadt
Email: law@marengolaw.com
URL: http://www.marengolawfim.com

General Trial Practice, Appellate Practice, Estate Planning, Probate Law, Trust Law, Real Estate, Banking Law, Bankruptcy Law, Personal Injury, Workers Compensation, Administrative Law, Corporate Law, Contracts, Civil Litigation, Trusts and Estates, Real Estate Law.

FIRM PROFILE: Pollock, Meyers, Eicksteadt & Pulak, Ltd. was founded in 1965 by Norman J. Pollock and Harvey A. Meyers, formerly high school and college classmates and graduates of Chicago-Kent College of Law. Richard W. Eicksteadt, also a high school and law school classmate joined the firm in 1966. The firms practices in McHenry, Boone, DeKalb, Kane, Lake and Winnebago Counties. The firm encourages continuing professional development, and all partners and associates participate in continuing legal education, seminars, professional association activities and civic affairs. The practice includes General Civil Practice, Probate, Real Estate, Personal Injury, Family, Bankruptcy, Municipal and Corporate Law.

NORMAN J. POLLOCK, born Huntley, Illinois, August 30, 1935; admitted to bar, 1965, Illinois; 1965, U.S. District Court, Northern District of Illinois; 1973, U.S. Supreme Court. *Education:* Iowa State University and Northern Illinois University (B.S., 1960); Chicago-Kent College of Law (J.D., 1965). Phi Delta Phi. *Member:* McHenry County (President, 1978-1979) and Illinois State Bar Associations; Illinois Trial Lawyers Association; Attorneys Title Guaranty Fund of Illinois (President and Chairman of the Board, 1990-1992); Board of Directors of Attorneys Title Guaranty Fund of Colorado, Utah and Minnesota, 1989-1992. [With U.S. Army, 1954-1956]. ***PRACTICE AREAS:*** Estate Planning; Probate Law; Trust Law; Real Estate. ***Email:*** njpollock@marengolaw.com

HARVEY A. MEYERS, born Elgin, Illinois, July 21, 1934; admitted to bar, 1965, Illinois; 1965, U.S. District Court, Northern District of Illinois; 1973, U.S. Supreme Court. *Education:* Northern Illinois University (B.S., 1961); Chicago-Kent College of Law (J.D., 1965). Phi Delta Phi. Assistant States Attorney, McHenry County, 1967-1973. *Member:* McHenry County (President, 1987-1988) and Illinois State (Assembly Member, 1990-1991) Bar Associations; Attorneys Title Guaranty Fund of Illinois. [With U.S. Army, 1955-1957]. ***PRACTICE AREAS:*** Real Estate; Banking Law; Corporate Law; Bankruptcy Law. ***Email:*** hameyers@marengolaw.com

RICHARD W. EICKSTEADT, born Belvidere, Illinois, July 31, 1935; admitted to bar, 1966, Illinois and U.S. District Court, Northern District of Illinois; 1973, U.S. Supreme Court; 1994, U.S. Court of Appeals, 7th Circuit. *Education:* Central Missouri State College and University of Illinois (B.S., 1961); Chicago-Kent College of Law (J.D., 1966). Phi Delta Phi. City Attorney: Marengo, Illinois, 1966-1978; Harvard, Illinois, 1973-1978; Capron, Illinois, 1979-1981. Assistant States Attorney, McHenry County, 1968-1973. *Member:* McHenry County (Chairman, Administrative Law Committee, 1973-1980; Lawyer/clients relations, 1994—), Illinois State and American Bar Associations; Attorneys Title Guaranty Fund of Illinois. [With U.S. Air Force, 1954-1958]. ***REPORTED CASES:*** Pyne v. Witmer, 543 N.E. 2d 1304; Sauers v. City of Woodstock, 446 N.E. 2d 896. ***PRACTICE AREAS:*** Personal Injury; Workers Compensation; General Trial Practice; Appellate Practice; Administrative Law.

ASSOCIATES

TIMOTHY J. CONKLIN, admitted to bar, 2004, Illinois; 2005, U.S. District Court, Northern District of Illinois. *Education:* Northern Illinois University (B.S., Political Science, 1995; M.A., Business Administration, 2004; J.D., magna cum laude, 2004). ***PRACTICE AREAS:*** Criminal Trial; Civil Trial Practice; Estate Planning; Probate; Trust Administration; Real Estate; Family Law.

PATRICE E. KOCH, admitted to bar, 2005, Illinois. *Education:* Kishwaukee College (A.A.S., Nursing, 1994); Judson College (B.A., 2002); Northern Illinois University College of Law (J.D., cum laude, 2005). ***PRACTICE AREAS:*** Trial Practice; Personal Injury; Workers Compensation.

KIMBERLY A. MEYERS, admitted to bar, 2005, Illinois. *Education:* University of Illinois (B.S., Finance, 1995); Northern Illinois University College of Law (J.D., cum laude, 2005). ***PRACTICE AREAS:*** Trial Practice; Estate Planning; Probate; Trust Administration; Real Estate.

REPRESENTATIVE CLIENTS: Harris Bank/Marengo; Harris Bank/Woodstock; Woodstone Co.; Marengo Steel Co.; Marengo Disposal Co.; Key Development Co.; Agrinetics, Inc.; Compost Enterprises; McGill Metal Products Co.; School District #8 (1970-1990); Marengo Fire Protection District (1966-1995); Marengo Township (1972-1980); Cardinal Savings and Loan Association; Riley Township (1969-1995); Dunham Township (1993—); Prairie State Bank; Laing Management & Construction Co.

ARMSTRONG & GREEN

400 NORTH MARKET STREET
MARION, ILLINOIS 62959
Telephone: 618-993-6072
Fax: 618-993-1194
Email: sgreen@midamer.net

Insurance Defense, Personal Injury, School Law, Municipal Law, Workers Compensation, Commercial Law.

OF COUNSEL

WILLIAM A. ARMSTRONG (Retired)

(This Listing Continued)

MEMBER OF FIRM

STEPHEN R. GREEN, born Jacksonville, Florida, May 16, 1963; admitted to bar, 1989, Illinois; 1992, U.S. District Court, Southern District of Illinois; 1994, U.S. Court of Appeals, 7th Circuit. *Education:* Southern Illinois University (B.S., 1985; J.D., 1989). Member, Order of Barristers, National Moot Court Team. *Member:* Illinois State and American Bar Associations; National Association of School Lawyers. ***PRACTICE AREAS:*** Insurance Defense; Premise Liability Law; Personal Injury Law; Divorce; School Law. ***Email:*** sgreen@midamer.net

BLEYER AND BLEYER

Established in 1986

601 WEST JACKSON STREET
P.O. BOX 487
MARION, ILLINOIS 62959-0487
Telephone: 618-997-1331
FAX: 618-997-6559
Email: bleyer@bleyerlaw.com
URL: http://www.lawyers.com/josephbleyer

General and Trial Practice. Insurance Defense, Workers Compensation and Local Government Torts and Civil Rights.

FIRM PROFILE: Members of the firm have concentrated in the practice of insurance defense litigation since 1955, and serve the entire Southern Illinois area in both State and Federal Courts.

JAMES B. BLEYER, born Carterville, Illinois, October 5, 1928; admitted to bar, 1955, Illinois. *Education:* Southern Illinois University (B.A., 1951); University of Notre Dame (J.D., 1954). *Member:* Williamson County (President, 1959-1960) and Illinois State Bar Associations; Illinois Association of Defense Trial Council; Defense Research Institute. Fellow, American College of Trial Lawyers. ***REPORTED CASES:*** Calloway v. Kinkelaar, 168 Ill.2d 312, 672 N.E.2d 1.322; Gouge v. Central Illinois Public Service Co., 144 Ill.2d. 535, 582 N.E.2d 108; Farley v. Marion Power Shovel Co., Inc., 60 Ill.2d 432, 328 N.E.2d 318; Bivin v. Wright, 275 Ill.App.3d 899, 659 N.E.2d 1121; City of Carbondale v. City of Marion, 210 Ill.App.3d 870, 569 N.E.2d 290; Parker v. Universal Packaging Corp., 200 Ill.App.3d 882, 558 N.E.2d 203; Chamness v. Fairtrace, 158 Ill.App.3d 325, 511 N.E.2d 839; Magnotti v. Hughes, 57 Ill.App.3d 1000, 373 N.E.2D 801; Dapkunas v. Cagle, 42 Ill.App.3d 644, 356 N.E.2d 575. ***PRACTICE AREAS:*** Insurance Defense; Municipal Liability; Workers Compensation Defense. ***Email:*** jbbleyer@bleyerlaw.com

JOSEPH A. BLEYER, born Marion, Illinois, April 30, 1961; admitted to bar, 1986, Illinois and U.S. District Court, Southern District of Illinois. *Education:* Southern Illinois University (B.S., 1983; J.D., 1986). Phi Alpha Delta (Treasurer, 1985); Beta Alpha Psi. *Member:* Williamson County, Illinois State and American Bar Associations; Illinois Association of Defense Trial Council. ***REPORTED CASES:*** Vaughn v. West Frankfort, 166 Ill.2d 155, 651 N.E.2d 1115; Brown v. Baker, 284 Ill.App.3d 401, 672 N.E.2d 69; Maxton v. Garegnani, 255 Ill.App.3d 291, 627 N.E.2d 723; Smith v. Donna, 243 Ill.App.3d 961, 612 N.E.2d 1045. ***PRACTICE AREAS:*** Insurance Defense; Government Tort Liability; Civil Rights Defense; Workers Compensation Defense. ***Email:*** jableyer@bleyerlaw.com

KNUTE ROCKNE BLEYER, born Duquoin, Illinois, May 1, 1953; admitted to bar, 1997, Illinois; 1998, U.S. District Court, Southern District of Illinois. *Education:* Southern Illinois University (B.S., 1994; J.D., 1997). ***PRACTICE AREAS:*** Insurance Defense. ***Email:*** krbleyer@bleyerlaw.com

REPRESENTATIVE CLIENTS: Country Mutual Insurance Co.; Farmers Insurance Group of Cos.; Cincinnati Insurance Co.; Pekin Insurance Co.; Grange Mutual Casualty Co.; Bliss-McKnight /GIE; Illinois Municipal League Risk-Mgt.; Southern Illinois Insurance Trust; Martin Boyer Co.; Safeco; Allstate Inc. Co.; American International; Illinois Casualty Co.; Travelers/St. Paul; Cincinnati Insurance Co.; Unitrin; American International Group; Ameren CIPS; Ford Motor Co.; Crawford & Co.; Scottsdale Insurance Co.; Lake of Egypt Water; GEICO; State Auto Insurance; Columbia Insurance; OneBeacon Ins.; Church Mutual; Brotherhood Mutual.
REFERENCE: Bank of Marion, Marion, Illinois.

BRYANT & KAUTZ, PC

Established in 1990

4501 WEST DE YOUNG, SUITE B-2
MARION, ILLINOIS 62959
Telephone: 618-993-1468
Fax: 618-993-1329

Paducah, Kentucky Office: 601 Washington Street, P.O. Box 1876, 42002-1876. Telephone: 270-442-1422. Fax: 270-443-8788.
Metropolis, Illinois Office: 222 Ferry Street, 62960. Telephone: 618-524-5671. Fax: 618-524-9671.

General Civil and Criminal Practice. Trials and Appeals, State and Federal Courts. Personal Injury, Criminal, Real Estate, Corporation, Family Law, Trusts and Estates.

(For Complete Biographical Data on all Personnel, see Professional Biographies at Paducah, Kentucky)

FEIRICH/MAGER/GREEN/RYAN

MARION, ILLINOIS

(See Carbondale)

General Trial and Appellate Litigation, Business, Probate, Trust, Real Estate, Insurance Law, Worker's Compensation, Banking and Corporation Law, Intellectual Property and Healthcare Law.

HARRIS, LAMBERT, HOWERTON & DORRIS

MARION, ILLINOIS

(See Howerton, Dorris & Stone)

HART AND HART

MARION, ILLINOIS

(See Benton)

General Trial and Appellate Practice in State and Federal Courts. Probate, Trust, Real Estate Deeds and Title Insurance, Bankruptcy (Creditors), Traffic, Banking, Business, Commercial and Corporation Law and Creditor Collections, Employment Law.

HOWERTON, DORRIS & STONE

Established in 1932

300 WEST MAIN STREET
MARION, ILLINOIS 62959
Telephone: 618-993-2616
Fax: 618-997-1845
URL: http://www.hdsplaw.lawoffice.com
Email: hds@neondsl.com
URL: http://www.lawyers.com/hlh&d

Plaintiff's Personal Injury, Workers Compensation Law, Insurance Bad Faith, Breach of Contract, Criminal Defense, Medical Malpractice, General Civil and Trial Practice.

FIRM PROFILE: Howerton, Dorris & Stone was originally established 70 years ago. The firm primarily practices in Southern Illinois in the areas of personal injury, workers compensation and unfair insurance practices including bad faith, insurance coverage and stacking. Howerton, Dorris & Stone is listed in the Bar Register of Preeminent Lawyers.

Significant cases handled by the firm: Brown v. Baker (1996), 284 Ill.App.3d 401, 672 N.E.2d 69; Bruder v. Country Mutual Ins. Co., 156 Ill2d 179, 620 N.E.2d 355, appealed therefrom from Illinois Appellate Court 232 Ill.App.3d 221, 596 N.E.2d 875; Murphy v. State Farm Mutual Auto. Ins. Co. (1992), 234 Ill.App.3d 222, 599 N.E.2d 446; Gibbs v. Madison Mutual Inc. Co. (1993), 242 Ill.App.3d 147, 610 N.E.2d 143; Fearheiley v. Summers (1993), 246 Ill.App.3d 86, 614 N.E.2d 1377; Emerson v. American Bankers Ins. Co. of Florida (1992), 223 Ill.App.3d 929, 585 N.R.2d 1315; Lane v. Hardees (7th Cir. 1999), 184 F.3d 705; Howat v. Donelson (1999), 305 Ill.App.3d 183, 711 N.E.2d 440.

MEMBERS OF FIRM

ROBERT H. HOWERTON, born Carbondale, Illinois, July 27, 1943; admitted to bar, 1968, Illinois; U.S. District Court, Southern District of Illinois; U.S. Court of Appeals, Seventh Circuit and U.S. Supreme Court. *Education:* Southern Illinois University (B.A., 1965); Northwestern University (J.D., 1968). Phi Eta Sigma. Williamson County State's Attorney (1972-1979). Trial Judge, First Circuit (1979-1988). Justice, Illinois Appellate Court, Fifth District (1988-1992). Author: Civil Trial Guide, Matthew Bender, 1991; "Show and Tell," Litigation Magazine, 1986; "Capstar," Litigation Magazine, 1987. Instructor: Southern Illinois University School of Law, 1985-1996; Trial Advocacy Program, Emory University School of Law, 1992-1997; State's Attorney's Legal Training Commission, 1978-1991. Member, National Institute of Trial Advocacy-National Session, Boulder, Colorado, Midwest Regional, Northwestern University Central Regional, St. Paul, Minnesota. Lifetime Member: Laborers' International Union; Who's Who; Leading Lawyers of America. Ford Foundation Fellow. Master Lawyer, Southern Illinois Inns of Court. *Member:* Williamson County and Illinois State Bar Associations; Illinois Judges Association; Association of Trial Lawyers of America; Illinois Trial Lawyers Association (Member, Board of Managers). ***REPORTED CASES:*** Baggett v. Industrial Commission, 201 Ill.2d 187, 775 N.E.2d 908 (2002); Janes v. Western States Insurance Co., et al, 335 Ill. App. 3d 1109, 783 N.E.2d 37 (2001); Bonnie Owen Realty, Inc. v. Cincinnati Insurance Company (1996), 283 Ill.App.3d 812, 670 N.E.2d 1182; McKenzie v. S K Hand Tool Corporation (1995), 272 Ill.App.3d 1, 650 N.E.2d 612; Coriasco v. Hutchcraft (1993), 245 Ill.App.3d 969, 615 N.E.2d 64; Garrison v. Gould Inc. (1994 Seventh Circuit). 36 F.3d 588; Pasquino v. Prather (1994 Seventh Circuit), 13 F.3d 1049. ***PRACTICE AREAS:*** Plaintiff's Personal Injury; Workers Compensation; Insurance Bad Faith. ***Email:*** rhunter@neondsl.com

DOUGLAS N. DORRIS, born Tacoma, Washington, December 22, 1954; admitted to bar, 1981, Illinois; U.S. District Court, Southern District of Illinois, U.S. Court of Appeals, Seventh Circuit and U.S. Supreme Court. *Education:* Southern Illinois University at Carbondale (B.S., 1977; J.D., 1981). President's Scholar. Editor, Notes and Comments, Southern Illinois University Law Journal, 1980-1981. Legal Intern, Franklin County State Attorney's Office, 1979-1980. ***REPORTED CASES:*** Howat v. Donelson (1999), 305 Ill.App.3d 183, 711 N.E.2d 440; Emerson v. American Bankers Insurance Company of Florida (1992), 223 Ill.App.3d 929, 585 N.E.2d 1315; Economy Fire & Cas. Co. v. Bassett, 170 Ill. App.3d 765, 525 N.E.2d 539; Stricklin v. Chapman, 197 Ill. App. 3d 385, 554 N.E.2d 658 (1990); Southeastern Illinois Elec. Co-Op v. Ill. Human Rights Comm., 162 Ill. App. 3d 806, 516 N.E.2d 825 (1987). ***PRACTICE AREAS:*** Plaintiff's Personal Injury; Workers Compensation; Unfair Insurance Practice.

STEPHEN W. STONE, born Decatur, Illinois, August 17, 1965; admitted to bar, 1990, Illinois; 1991 Missouri; U.S. District Court, Southern District of Illinois; U.S. Court of Appeals, Seventh Circuit. *Education:* Southern Illinois University (B.A., 1987; J.D., 1990). Pi Sigma Delta. Order of Barrister. Recipient: Newman-O'Brien Scholarship; American Jurisprudence Award. American Bar Association Courtroom Advocacy Champion. Adjunct Professor of Law, Southern Illinois University School of Law. *Member:* The Missouri Bar; Association of Trial Lawyers of America; Illinois Trial Lawyers Association. ***REPORTED CASES:*** Halverson v. Stamm (2002), 329 Ill.App.3d 1206, 769 N.E.2d 1076; Simpson v. Matthews (2003), 339 Ill.App.3d 322, 790 N.E.2d 401; Kost v. Farmers Auto Insurance Association (2002), 328 Ill.App.3d 649, 766 N.E.2d 676; Hall v. General Casualty (2002), 328 Ill.App.3d 655, 766 N.E.2d 680. ***PRACTICE AREAS:*** Personal Injury; Workers Compensation; Unfair Insurance Practices; Employment Discrimination Discharge. ***Email:*** sstone@neondsl.com

(This Listing Continued)

ASSOCIATE

GREGORY E. GUSTAVSON, born Bloomington, Illinois, February 26, 1946; admitted to bar, 1988, Illinois. *Education:* University of Arizona (B.S., 1970); Stetson University (J.D., 1974). Registered Nurse, 1982. [E-5, U.S. Army, 1975-1978]. ***PRACTICE AREAS:*** Personal Injury; Medical Malpractice; Workers Compensation.

LEGAL SUPPORT PERSONNEL

SAM L. JORDAN. *Education:* Southern Illinois University (B.S., 1977; Masters of Science of Ed., 1998); Northwestern University, School of Police Staff and Command Northwestern Traffic Institute (Graduate, Summer, 1977); FBI National Academy Quantico, Virginia (170th Session, Summer, 1992);. Private Investigator, Illinois, 2004. *Member:* FBI National Academy (President and Vice President, Illinois Chapter and Sub-Chapter); Illinois Association of Chiefs of Police. (Private Investigator). ***Email:*** sjordan@neondsl.com

PAMELA N. REHBEIN. *Education:* St. Louis Community College (A.A.S., 1983). (Paralegal)

JELLIFFE, FERRELL, MORRIS & DOERGE

MARION, ILLINOIS

(See Harrisburg)

Insurance Law, Negligence and Personal Injury, Litigation, Workers' Compensation Law, and Employment Law. Commercial Collection and DUI's. General Civil Practice in State and Federal Courts. Trials and Appeals.

MITCHELL & MITCHELL

Established in 1949

404 NORTH MONROE
P.O. BOX 488
MARION, ILLINOIS 62959-2328
Telephone: 618-993-2134
Telecopier: 618-993-8702
Email: mail@mitchell-lawfirm.com
URL: http://www.lawyers.com/mmb

General Trial and Appellate Practice. Insurance, Personal Injury, Medical Malpractice, Products Liability, Commercial Law, Litigation and Divorce.

J. C. MITCHELL, born Marion, Illinois, February 2, 1925; admitted to bar, 1949, Illinois. *Education:* Northwestern University; University of Illinois (LL.B., 1949). Phi Alpha Delta. *Member:* Williamson County (President, 1961), Illinois State (Member, Committees on: Aeronautics, 1958-1968; President, Southern District, First Federation, 1965-1966) and American Bar Associations. Fellow, American College of Trial Lawyers. ***PRACTICE AREAS:*** Plaintiffs Personal Injury; Age Discrimination; Product Liability; Insurance Defense; Dramshop; Divorce. ***Email:*** mail@mitchell-lawfirm.com

BRUCE W. MITCHELL, born Carbondale, Illinois, December 1, 1950; admitted to bar, 1982, Illinois; 1985, U.S. District Court, Eastern District of Illinois; 1988, U.S. Court of Appeals, Seventh Circuit. *Education:* Southern Illinois University (B.A., 1979); Tulsa University (J.D., 1982). Phi Delta Phi. *Member:* Williamson County, Illinois State and American Bar Associations. [Illinois National Guard, 1970-1976, Spec. 4]. ***PRACTICE AREAS:*** Personal Injury; Medical Malpractice; Insurance Defense; Automobile Liability; Product Liability Law; Dramshop; Divorce. ***Email:*** mail@mitchell-lawfirm.com

OF COUNSEL

JOHN E. BRADLEY, born Harrisburg, Illinois, May 10, 1971; admitted to bar, 1996, Illinois, 1997, U.S. District Court, Southern District of Illinois. *Education:* Southeastern Illinois College (A.A./A.S., 1991); University of Texas at Austin (B.A., 1993); University of Illinois (J.D., cum laude, 1996). Phi Delta Phi. Commencement Speaker, University of Illinois. *Member:* Illinois State Bar Association. ***PRACTICE AREAS:*** Business; Personal Injury; Litigation; Family; Criminal; Divorce; Child Custody. ***Email:*** mail@mitchell-lawfirm.com

REPRESENTATIVE CLIENTS: St. Paul Fire & Casualty Insurance Company; Liberty Mutual Insurance Company; Wal-Mart Stores, Inc.; Illinois State Medical Insurance Exchange; Atlantic Casualty Company; Shelter Insurance Company; Preferred Risk Insurance Company; Iowa Mutual Insurance Company; Jefferson Insurance Company; Waite Hill Insurance Company; Horace Mann Insurance; Great West Casualty Company; Indiana Lumbermens Insurance; Hinz Claim Mangement; Werner Enterprises; Kentucky Farm Bureau; United Security Life Insurance; Coregis; Illinois Guaranty Fund; Lake States Insurance; Penn America; Baldwin Lyons Insurance; National States Insurance; Unison Insurance Company; CIGNA; Amerisure; AIG Specialty Auto Claims; Illinois National Insurance Company; Indiana Lumbermen's Insurance; Atofina Chemicals; Capitol Indemnity Corporation; Ecoverage; GuideOne Insurance Group; Harleysville Insurance; Lloyds London; Maxson-Young; CMI (Claims Management Inc.); Laidlaw Transit, Inc.; Superior Insurance.

SAM C. MITCHELL & ASSOCIATES

MARION, ILLINOIS

(See West Frankfort)

Plaintiff Personal Injury and Workers Compensation cases only.

WINTERS, BREWSTER, CROSBY AND SCHAFER LLC

Established in 1976
111 WEST MAIN
P.O. BOX 700
MARION, ILLINOIS 62959
Telephone: 618-997-5611
Fax: 618-997-6522
Email: winlaw@winterslaw.com
URL: http://www.lawyers.com/winlaw

General Practice. Trials in State and Federal Courts. Plaintiffs Personal Injury, Workers' Compensation. Probate, Estate Planning, Real Estate, Corporation, Environmental Law, Wills, Trusts, Estates, Probate and Class Actions.

FIRM PROFILE: Developed from the general local practice of Charles D. Winters, now deceased, the firm focuses on plaintiff's personal injury litigation, worker's compensation, commercial litigation and commercial transactions doing referral work for other firms throughout the Southern Illinois area. The firm attempts to utilize the latest technology and encourages the continuing professional development of all partners, associates and staff in legal, professional and civic affairs.

MEMBERS OF FIRM

CHARLES D. WINTERS (1917-1992)

JOHN S. BREWSTER, born St. Louis, Missouri, August 25, 1950; admitted to bar, 1976, Illinois, U.S. District Court, Southern District of Illinois and U.S. Court of Appeals, Seventh Circuit. *Education:* Syracuse University (B.A., 1971); University of Illinois (M.B.A., 1973); Southern Illinois University (J.D., 1976). Instructor, Southern Illinois University, 1979-1989. *Member:* Williamson County (Vice-President, 1979-1982; President, 1983-1985), Illinois State (Chairman, Section Council, State Taxation, 1983; Member: Real Estate Section Council; Law Office Economics Section Council) and American Bar Associations; Illinois Trial Lawyers Association; The Association of Trial Lawyers of America. ***PRACTICE AREAS:*** Real Estate; Corporations; Real Estate Taxation; Probate. ***Email:*** jbrewster@winterslaw.com

THOMAS F. CROSBY, III, born Cleveland, Ohio, July 11, 1953; admitted to bar, 1981, Illinois and U.S. District Court, Southern District of Illinois; U.S. Court of Appeals, Seventh Circuit. *Education:* Southern Illinois University (B.A., 1976; J.D., 1981). Editor, Southern Illinois University Law Review, 1980-1981. Assistant Attorney General, State of Illinois, 1982-1983. *Member:* Illinois State Bar Association; Illinois Trial Lawyers Association; The Association of Trial Lawyers of America. ***PRACTICE AREAS:*** Civil Trial Litigation; Workers Compensation Law. ***Email:*** tcrosby@winterslaw.com

PAUL JASON SCHAFER, born Marion, Illinois, December 21, 1967; admitted to bar, 1994, Illinois and U.S. District Court, Southern District of Illinois. *Education:* Southern Illinois University (B.S., 1990; J.D., 1994). *Member:* Williamson County (Officer); Illinois State and American Bar Associations; The Association of Trial Lawyers of America; Illinois Trial Lawyers Association; Million Dollar Advocates Forum. ***PRACTICE AREAS:*** Personal Injury; Workers Compensation; Retaliatory Discharge; Insurance; Litigation; Medical Malpractice; Nursing Home Abuse. ***Email:*** PaulJSchafer@aol.com

ASSOCIATE

LINDA J. BRAME, born St. Louis, Missouri, August 12, 1976; admitted to bar, 2002, Illinois. *Education:* St. Louis University (B.A., 1998); Southern Illinois University School of Law (J.D., 2002). *Member:* Illinois State and American Bar Associations; Illinois Trial Lawyers Association; The Association of Trial Lawyers of America; Bar Association of Metropolitan St. Louis. ***PRACTICE AREAS:*** Civil Trial Practice; Personal Injury; Plaintiffs Personal Injury; Workers Compensation; Employment Law. ***Email:*** lbrame@winterslaw.com

REPRESENTATIVE CLIENTS: Banterra Bank of Marion; South Pointe Bank, Marion, IL; Southern Illinois Power Cooperative; Union Planters; Plumbers & Pipefitters Local 551 & Local 160; Marion Pepsi-Cola; Harrisburg Medical Center, Harrisburg, Ill.
GENERAL COUNSEL FOR: Banterra Bank of Marion, Marion, Ill.; Southern Illinois Power Cooperative.
LOCAL COUNSEL FOR: Community Media Group, Inc.
REFERENCES: The Bank of Herrin, Herrin, Ill.; Banterra Bank of Marion.

MARAMBA & ASSOCIATES, LLC

MARKHAM, ILLINOIS

(See Arlington Heights)

Business Law, Chancery Practice, Corporate Litigation, Civil Litigation, Complex Litigation, Defense Litigation, Federal Litigation, Administrative Litigation, Business Enterprises, Business Litigation, Closely Held Business Law, Real Estate Litigation, Veterans Rights, Military Law, Wills, Commercial Collections, Post Judgment Collections, Closely Held Corporations.

BENNETT, SCHROEDER & WIECK

Established in 1951
517 LOCUST STREET
P.O. BOX 98
MARSHALL, ILLINOIS 62441
Telephone: 217-826-8051
Fax: 217-826-5011
URL: http://www.lawyers.com/bennettschroederwieck

General Civil and Criminal Trial Practice. Personal Injury, Workers Compensation, Domestic Relations, Family, Probate, Business/Contract, Wills/Estate Planning, Income Tax, Social Security Disability, Real Estate, Bankruptcy Law, Collections and Traffic.

(This Listing Continued)

FIRM PROFILE: Bennett, Schroeder and Wieck was originally founded by Grendel F. Bennett and his brother Caslon Bennett in 1951. Serving clients in Clark, Crawford, Edgar, Coles, Cumberland, and surrounding counties, Bennett, Schroeder and Wieck is a full service firm.

MEMBERS OF FIRM

GRENDEL F. BENNETT (1900-1987)

JOSEPH R. SCHROEDER, born Terre Haute, Indiana, March 8, 1950; admitted to bar, 1975, Illinois and Indiana. *Education:* Indiana University (A.B., 1972); John Marshall Law School (J.D., 1975). Deputy Prosecutor, Vigo County, Indiana, 1976. City Attorney, Marshall, Illinois, 1976. *Member:* Clark County (President, 1978, 1998), Illinois State, Indiana State and American (Member, General Practice Section) Bar Associations; The Association of Trial Lawyers of America; Illinois Trial Lawyer's Association. ***PRACTICE AREAS:*** Probate; Personal Injury; Workmen's Compensation; Business/Contract; Real Estate; Bankruptcy; Income Tax; Estate Planning; Wills; Trust Law. ***Email:*** jschroeder@joink.com

PAUL E. WIECK, born Morris, Illinois, September 2, 1956; admitted to bar, 1981, Wisconsin; 1982, Illinois. *Education:* University of Illinois (B.A., 1978); Illinois Institute of Technology/Chicago-Kent College of Law (J.D., 1981). Member, International Moot Court Team. Special Assistant to Attorney General, 1986-1987. *Member:* Clark County (President, 1984, 1990, Treasurer, 1998—) and Illinois State (Member, Sections on: General Practice; Family Law) Bar Associations; The Association of Trial Lawyers of America; Illinois Trial Lawyer's Association. ***REPORTED CASES:*** Allen v. Storer, 235 Ill.App. 3d 5, 175 Ill.Dec. 805, 600 N.E. 2d 1263. ***PRACTICE AREAS:*** Social Security Disability; Domestic Relations; Family; Criminal; Traffic; Personal Injury; Income Tax; Business/Contracts; Workers Compensation; Bankruptcy; Divorce; Child Custody; DUI. ***Email:*** pwieck@joink.com

COUNSEL FOR: Marshall Fire Protection District; Marshall Ambulance District; Townships of Douglas, Dolson, Auburn, Orange and Wabash; Multitownship Assessment District; Marshall Mutual County Fire Insurance Co.; Clark County Park District; Lincoln Trail Chrysler Jeep Dodge; Forsythe Land Company, Inc.; First Bank & Trust s.b.; Lincoln Trial Ford Mercury, Inc.; Forsythe Family Farm, Inc.

THE BRAINARD LAW OFFICES

MARSHALL, ILLINOIS

(See Charleston)

General Practice. Insurance Defense, Personal Injury, Products Liability, Probate, Trusts, Real Estate, Taxation, Municipal, Family and Health Law. Trials in all State and Federal Courts.

HELLER, HOLMES & ASSOCIATES, P.C.

MARSHALL, ILLINOIS

(See Mattoon)

General Civil and Trial Practice in all State, Federal and Appellate Courts. Personal Injury, Medical Negligence, Criminal Defense, Insurance, Litigation, Probate, Workers Compensation, Corporation, Commercial, Family Law, Oil and Gas.

LAW OFFICES OF GRAY & IDRIS, P.C.

MATTESON, ILLINOIS

(See Joilet)

General Practice.

ARMSTRONG & GROVE

Established in 1996
1400 CHARLESTON AVENUE
P.O. BOX 1425
MATTOON, ILLINOIS 61938
Telephone: 217-234-2872
Fax: 217-234-2533
Email: aglaw@armstronggrove.com
URL: http://www.armstronggrovelaw.com

Estate Planning, Probate, Trusts, Wills, Mineral Law, Drainage and Levee Law.

MEMBERS OF FIRM

JOHN H. ARMSTRONG, born Champaign, Illinois, January 30, 1934; admitted to bar, 1960, Illinois. *Education:* University of Illinois (B.A., 1958; J.D., 1960). Phi Delta Phi. Author: "Coal Leasing—Rights of Parties," Chapter 9b, Oil, Gas and Coal Law, Illinois Institute for Continuing Legal Education, 1978; "Mineral Rights," Chapter 15, Advising Farmers, Illinois Institute for Continuing Legal Education, 1987. Co-Author: with James M. Dion, "Coal: Leasing and Purchase of Mineral Interests," Chapter 8, Mineral Law, Illinois Institute for Continuing Legal Education, 1994; "A Fractional Mineral Interest? 'Danger UXB'," 65 Chicago Bar Record 20, July-August, 1983. Co-Author: with Kenneth D. Peters: "Enhanced Recovery of Oil," 5 Eastern Min. L. Inst. 13-1, 1984; Co-Author: with James M. Dion, "Fiduciary Relationships and Their Impact on Oil and Gas Operations," 11 Eastern Min. L. Inst. 15-1, 1990. Member, Board of Library Directors, City of Mattoon, 1968-1985. Member, 1996— and Secretary, 1996—, Tarble Arts Center Advisory Board, Eastern Illinois University. Member, 1983—, Trustee, 1986— and Assistant Treasurer, 1994-1995, Energy and Mineral Law Foundation. *Member:* Coles-Cumberland County (President, 1976-1977) and Illinois State (Member, 1966-1971 and Chairman, 1968-1969, Drainage and Levee Law Section Council; Member, Environmental Control Law Section Council, 1974-1976; Chairman, Mineral Law Subcommittee, 1982, Real Estate Section;

(This Listing Continued)

ARMSTRONG & GROVE, Mattoon—Continued

Member, 1984— and Chairman, 1987-1988, Mineral Law Section Council) and American Bar Associations. Fellow, American College of Trust and Estate Counsel. ***PRACTICE AREAS:*** Estate Planning; Probate; Business Law; Mineral Law; Drainage and Levee. ***Email:*** aglaw@armstronggrove.com

JANET L. GROVE, born Pittsburgh, Pennsylvania, March 20, 1955; admitted to bar, 1985, Illinois. *Education:* Purdue University (B.S., 1976; M.S., 1979); Indiana University (J.D., 1985). Author: "Estate Planning for Non-Traditional Relationships," Illinois State Bar Association LawEd Series, 2004; "Estate Planning Basics," Illinois State Bar Association Mid-Year Meeting, 2004; "Estate Planning for 21st Century Families," 91 Illinois Bar Journal 631, Dec. 2003; "Ethics in Illinois and the New Tax Law-Where are You?" Illinois State Bar Association LawEd Series, 2001. Co-Author with Shannon Delamar, "Post-Death Administration of a Revocable Trust," Illinois State Bar Association LawEd Series, 2000. Member, Estate Planning Short Course Planning Committee, Illinois Institute for Continuing Legal Education, 1998-2000. *Member:* Coles-Cumberland County (Secretary and Treasurer, 1990-1997), Illinois State (Member, Trust and Estate Section Council, 2000-2003) and American Bar Associations. ***PRACTICE AREAS:*** Estate Planning; Probate; Elder Law; Real Estate; Fiduciary Law. ***Email:*** aglaw@armstronggrove.com

THE BRAINARD LAW OFFICES

MATTOON, ILLINOIS

(See Charleston)

General Practice. Insurance Defense, Personal Injury, Products Liability, Probate, Trusts, Real Estate, Taxation, Municipal, Family and Health Law. Trials in all State and Federal Courts.

CRAIG & CRAIG

Established in 1868

1807 BROADWAY

P.O. BOX 689

MATTOON, ILLINOIS 61938-0689

Telephone: 217-234-6481

Telecopier: 217-234-6486; 258-8292

Email: mattoon@craiglaw.net

URL: http://www.lawyers.com/craig&craiglawoffices

Mount Vernon, Illinois Office: 115 North 7th Street. Telephone: 618-244-7511. Telecopier: 618-244-7628. Email: mtvernon@craiglaw.net.

General Practice in State and Federal Courts. Coal, Oil, Gas, Mining, Oil and Gas Transportation, Insurance, Drainage and Levee Law, Environmental, Corporation, Labor Relations, Workers Compensation and Real Estate Law. Estate Planning, Probate and Bankruptcy Law. Trials and Appeals.

FIRM PROFILE: The firm was founded in 1868 and has been practicing continuously since then at the same location in Mattoon. The Mt. Vernon office was opened in 1986. Although its practice is concentrated in Central and Southern Illinois, the firm handles business throughout the entire State including Cook County. Over the decades, the firm has played a significant part in developing the law of drainage districts; oil, gas, coal and other minerals; real property; and personal injury and insurance in Illinois.

The firm's philosophy is to provide the highest standard of professional service consistent with the greatest economy for the client. This includes pursuit of alternative dispute resolution procedures whenever feasible. The management and handling of each matter or case is assigned according to the specialty of the individual partner and matters delegated to associates are under the active supervision of partners.

Three partners are Fellows of the American College of Trial Lawyers. Partners in the firm have been extremely active over the decades in writing and lecturing for continuing legal education organizations in the State and nationally.

Most of the litigation partners in the firm are members of DRI and the Illinois Association of Defense Trial Counsel and have served as members of the Board of Directors, as officers and have been active in writing and lecturing for IDC.

Management of the firm is shared among the partners.

MEMBERS OF FIRM

RICHARD F. RECORD, JR., born Mattoon, Illinois, December 20, 1937; admitted to bar, 1963, Illinois and District of Columbia. *Education:* Georgetown University (B.S., 1959); George Washington University (LL.B., 1963). Author: "Medical Malpractice," Practising Law Institute, 1972; "Remedies for Backlog in the Appellate Court of Illinois," 62 Illinois Bar Journal 82, 1973; "The Federal Rules of Evidence—Origins, Analysis and Impact," 24 Defense Law Journal 111, 1975; "Introduction to Third Party Practice," Third Party Practice, Illinois Institute for Continuing Legal Education, Chapter 1, 1992; "Res Ipsa Loquitor," Representing Defendants in Medical Negligence Cases, Illinois Institute for Continuing Legal Education, Chapter 3, 1987. Member, Illinois Supreme Court Committee on Rules of Evidence, 1975-1979. Chancellor of Episcopal Diocese of Springfield, 1989-1995. *Member:* Coles-Cumberland Bar Association (President, 1982-1983); Illinois State Bar Association; Appellate Lawyers Association (President, 1979-1980); American Academy of Appellate Lawyers; Illinois Association of Defense Trial Counsel; National Association of Railroad Trial Counsel. Fellow, American College of Trial Lawyers. ***PRACTICE AREAS:*** Civil Trials and Appeals (State and Federal Courts). ***Email:*** rfr@craiglaw.net

STEPHEN L. CORN, born Danville, Illinois, June 12, 1944; admitted to bar, 1969, Illinois. *Education:* University of Illinois (B.A., 1966; J.D., 1969). Author: "Settlement," Illinois Civil Practice Before Trial, Illinois Institute for Continuing Legal Education, Chapter 3, 1992. Member, Lawyers Trust Fund of Illinois Implementation Commission, 1983-1984. Board of Directors, Lawyers Trust Fund of Illinois, 1991-1994; Secretary/Treasurer, 1994-1995. *Member:* Coles-Cumberland Bar Association (President, 1986-1987); Illinois State (Member of Council, Young Lawyers Section, 1971-1979; Chairman, 1978-1979; Chairman, Long Range Planning Committee, 1984-1985; Insurance Law Section, 1999—; Special Committee on Ethics, 2000, 1999—; Special Committee on Federal Practice, 2000—; Special Committee on Future of Courts, 2000—; Supreme Court of Illinois Special Committee on Judicial Practice, 2000—) and American Bar Associations; Illinois Association of Defense Trial Counsel (Member, Board of Directors, 1984-1992; President, 1991-1992); Defense Research Institute. American College of Trial Lawyers. ***PRACTICE AREAS:*** Medical Law; Hospital Liability; General Civil. ***Email:*** slc@craiglaw.net

ROBERT G. GRIERSON, born St. Louis, Missouri, August 17, 1950; admitted to bar, 1975, Illinois. *Education:* Bradley University (B.S., 1972); University of Illinois (J.D., 1975). *Member:* Coles-Cumberland Bar Association (President, 1994-1995); Illinois State (Member, Drainage and Levee Law Committee, Real Estate Law Section, 1982—) and American Bar Associations. ***PRACTICE AREAS:*** Banking Law; Commercial Law; Bankruptcy; Real Estate Law; Drainage Law; Estate Planning; Probate; Estates. ***Email:*** rgg@craiglaw.net

GREGORY C. RAY, born Freeport, Illinois, July 17, 1952; admitted to bar, 1976, Illinois. *Education:* Southern Illinois University (B.S., with honors, 1973); University of Illinois (J.D., 1976). Author: "Commercial and Professional Liability Insurance," published by Illinois Institute for Continuing Legal Education, Chapter 5, 2002; "Third Party Practice," published by Illinois Institute for Continuing Legal Education, Chapter 1, 2000; "Supreme Court Watch," published by IDC Quarterly (Columnist, 1992-2000). *Member:* Coles-Cumberland, Illinois State (Member, Insurance Law Section Council, 1980-1982) and American Bar Associations; Illinois Appellate Lawyers Association; Illinois Association of Defense Trial Counsel (Vice-President, 2000-2001; President, 2001-2002); Defense Research Institute. ***PRACTICE AREAS:*** Employment Law; Civil Trials and Appeals; Workers Compensation Law. ***Email:*** gcr@craiglaw.net

PAUL R. LYNCH, born Chicago, Illinois, August 12, 1952; admitted to bar, 1977, Illinois. *Education:* Loyola University (B.A., magna cum laude, 1974); University of Illinois (J.D., 1977). Alpha Sigma Nu; Blue Key. Author: "Jurisdiction of Courts Other Than District Courts," Federal Civil Practice in Illinois, Illinois Institute for Continuing Legal Education, Chapter 2, 1992 (Supplement 1996). *Member:* Seventh Circuit, Jefferson County and Illinois State Bar Associations; Appellate Lawyers Association; Illinois Association of Defense Trial Counsel. (Resident, Mount Vernon Office). ***PRACTICE AREAS:*** Civil Trials and Appeals (State and Federal Courts). ***Email:*** prl@craiglaw.net

KENNETH F. WERTS, born Champaign, Illinois, February 27, 1957; admitted to bar, 1984, Illinois. *Education:* University of Illinois (B.A., 1979); Southern Illinois University (J.D., 1984). Phi Sigma Alpha. Co-Author: "Kotecki v. Cyclops Welding and its Progeny," Third-Party Practice, Illinois Institute for Continuing Legal Education, Chapter 8, 2004. Co-Author: "Settlement," Illinois Civil Practice Before Trial, Illinois Institute for Continuing Legal Education, Chapter 3, 2003; "The IDC Monograph: The Normal Daily Activity Exception to Workers' Compensation Claims," IDC Quarterly, Third Quarter 2004, Volume 14, Number 3. *Member:* Jefferson County, Illinois State (Chairman, Worker's Compensation Law Section Council, 1997-1998; ISBA Assembly, 2004—) and American (Member, Workers' Compensation and Employers' Liability Law Committee, 2001—) Bar Associations; Illinois Association of Defense Trial Counsel (Member, Board of Directors, 2001—; Chair, Employment Law Committee, 2001-2003; Chair, Workers' Compensation Committee, 2003—); National Association of Railroad Trial Counsel. (Resident, Mount Vernon Office). ***PRACTICE AREAS:*** Workers Compensation Law; Black Lung; Occupational Disease Law; Personal Injury Litigation. ***Email:*** kfw@craiglaw.net

JOHN L. BARGER, born Mattoon, Illinois, August 1, 1958; admitted to bar, 1984, Illinois and U.S. District Court, Central and Southern Districts of Illinois, U.S. Court of Appeals, Seventh Circuit. *Education:* Eastern Illinois University (B.A., 1980); University of Arkansas (J.D., 1983). Phi Alpha Delta. *Member:* Coles-Cumberland County, Illinois State and American Bar Associations; The Seventh Circuit Bar Association; Illinois Association of Defense Trial Counsel; Bar Association for the Central and Southern Districts of Illinois. ***PRACTICE AREAS:*** Workers Compensation Law; Probate; Guardianship; Elder Law; Real Estate; Estate Planning; Personal Injury Litigation; Civil Litigation; Appellate Practice. ***Email:*** jlb@craiglaw.net

JULIE A. WEBB, born Paducah, Kentucky, November 29, 1971; admitted to bar, 1996, Illinois. *Education:* University of Illinois, Champaign-Urbana (B.S., with honors, 1993); Southern Illinois University (J.D., 1996). Author: "Kotecki v. Cyclops Welding and its Progency," Third-Party Practice, IICLE, Chapter 8, 2004. Co-Author: "Settlement," Illinois Civil Practice Before Trial, IICLE, Chapter 3, 2003. *Member:* Jefferson County, Illinois State and American Bar Associations; Illinois Association of Defense Trial Counsel. (Resident, Mount Vernon Office). ***PRACTICE AREAS:*** Workers Compensation; Civil Litigation. ***Email:*** jaw@craiglaw.net

JOHN F. WATSON, born Oak Lawn, Illinois, July 7, 1967; admitted to bar, 1993, Illinois. *Education:* Bradley University (B.S., Mechanical Engineering, 1990); John Marshall Law School (J.D., with honors, 1993). Member, 1991-1993; Associate Leads Editor, 1992-1993, John Marshall Law Review. John Marshall Moot Court Saul Lefkowitz Trademark Competition, 1993. Author: "The Cause, Effect and Constitutional Consequence of Unequal Funding: Public Education in Illinois," 26 J. Marshall Law Rev. 399, 1993; "Illinois Tort Law Update," Illinois Defense Counsel Seminar, Fall 2001. *Member:* Coles-Cumberland (Secretary-Treasurer, 2001—), Illinois State and American Bar Associations; Illinois Defense Counsel; The Bar Association of the Central and Southern Federal Districts of Illinois (Member, Communications Committee, 2002—). ***PRACTICE AREAS:*** Civil Litigation; Insurance Coverage Litigation; Intellectual Property; Criminal Litigation. ***Email:*** jfw@craiglaw.net

R. SEAN HOCKING, born Honolulu, Hawaii, February 6, 1973; admitted to bar, 1999, Illinois. *Education:* University of Illinois (B.S., 1995); Southern Illinois University (J.D., 1999). *Member:* Coles-Cumberland Counties, Illinois State and American Bar Associations; Illinois Association of Defense Counsel. ***PRACTICE AREAS:*** General Practice; Products Liability. ***Email:*** rsh@craiglaw.net

(This Listing Continued)

ASSOCIATES

SARAH D. MOSKOWITZ, born Moline, Illinois, December 1, 1976; admitted to bar, 2002, Illinois. *Education:* University of Iowa (B.A., 1999); Southern Illinois University (J.D., 2002). *Member:* Coles-Cumberland Counties, Illinois State and American Bar Associations. ***Email:*** sdm@craiglaw.net

SARAH B. HOLSAPPLE-MILLER, born Mattoon, Illinois, July 12, 1980; admitted to bar, 2004, Illinois. *Education:* Eastern Illinois University (B.A., 2001); Southern Illinois University (J.D., 2004). Phi Alpha Delta. Articles Editor, Southern Illinois University Law Journal, 2003-2004. *Member:* Coles-Cumberland and Illinois State Bar Associations. ***Email:*** sbh@craiglaw.net

J. PATRICK LEE, born Springfield, Illinois, May 4, 1974; admitted to bar, 2002, Illinois. *Education:* Eastern Illinois University (B.A., 1996); University of Illinois (J.D., 2002). Former Associate: Sunderland, Spenn, Johnson & Thompson, Ltd.; Dilks, Rodeen & Gibson, Ltd., 2002-2004. Assistant Public Defender, Iroquois Co. ***PRACTICE AREAS:*** General Practice. ***Email:*** jpl@craiglaw.com

OF COUNSEL

JOHN P. EWART, born Effingham, Illinois, April 18, 1936; admitted to bar, 1961, Illinois. *Education:* University of Illinois (J.D., 1960). *Member:* Coles-Cumberland County (President, 1979-1980); Illinois State Bar Association; Illinois Association of Defense Trial Counsel (Member, Board of Directors, 1971-1979 and President, 1978-1979); Appellate Lawyers Association; American College of Trial Lawyers. (Retired). ***PRACTICE AREAS:*** Trials and Appeals (State and Federal Courts); Insurance Law; Labor and Employment Law; Oil and Gas Transportation. ***Email:*** jpe@craiglaw.net

REPRESENTATIVE CLIENTS: Freeman United Coal Mining Co.; Marathon Oil Company; Mattoon Enterprise Park, L.L.C.; Howell Paving, Inc.; CN/ICRR; First Federal Savings and Loan Association of Mattoon, Illinois; Illinois Consolidated Telephone Co., Consolidated Communications; R. R. Donnelley & Sons Co.; Kal Kan Foods, Inc.; Continental General Tire, Inc.; D-CO, Inc.; Illinois Municipal League Risk Management Association; Crawford & Company; The Medical Protective Company; The Doctors' Company; Carle Risk Management; ProNational Ins. Co.; TIG Insurance Company; ESIS, Inc.; Kemper Insurance Co.; Indiana Insurance Co.; St. Paul Insurance Co.; Cincinnati Insurance Co.; Rockford Mutual; EMC Insurance Companies; Lake Land College; Scattering Fork Drainage District of Douglas County, Illinois; Mattoon Township Park District of Coles County, Illinois; Humboldt Township of Coles County, Illinois; CNA Encompass Insurance; Central Insurance Co.; Gallagher Bassett; APSpecialty Insurance Corp.; First Mid-Illinois Bank & Trust, Mattoon, IL; Travlers Insurance, Fremont Compensation Insurance Group; ITT Hartford.

DILSAVER & NELSON

Established in 1924

1500 BROADWAY
P.O. BOX 649
MATTOON, ILLINOIS 61938-0649
Telephone: 217-235-5651
Telecopier: 217-235-5255
Email: dnelson@dilsaver-nelson.com
URL: http://www.dilsaver-nelson.com

Banking and Finance, Bankruptcy, Business Law, Criminal, Family Law, Litigation, Personal Injury, Real Estate, Trusts and Estates, Wills and Probate.

FIRM PROFILE: Since its establishment, the firm has maintained a general civil practice. The firm primarily represents corporations, small businesses and individuals throughout the state of Illinois.

MEMBERS OF FIRM

JEWELL I. DILSAVER (1902-1991)

DAVID C. NELSON, born Bridgeport, Connecticut, September 4, 1946; admitted to bar, 1972, Illinois; U.S. District Court, Central District of Illinois; U.S. Tax Court. *Education:* Northern Illinois University (B.S., 1968); Illinois Institute of Technology, Chicago-Kent College of Law (J.D., with distinction, 1972). Delta Theta Phi. Special Assistant to William J. Scott, Attorney General, State of Illinois, 1975-1978. *Member:* Coles-Cumberland (President, 1988) and Illinois State Bar Associations. ***PRACTICE AREAS:*** Banking Law; Finance; Bankruptcy; Business Law; Criminal Law; Family Law; Litigation; Personal Injury; Real Estate; Trusts and Estates; Wills; Probate. ***Email:*** dnelson@dilsaver-nelson.com

ASSOCIATE

ERNEST LEE WAITE, II, born Taylorville, Illinois, October 3, 1973; admitted to bar, 2000, Illinois; 2001, U.S. District Court, Central District of Illinois; 2002, U.S. District Court, Southern District of Illinois. *Education:* Southern Illinois University at Carbondale (B.S., 1996); Southern Illinois University School of Law (J.D., 2000). *Member:* Illinois State Bar Association. ***PRACTICE AREAS:*** Bankruptcy; Criminal Law; Family Law; General Practice; Personal Injury. ***Email:*** leewaite@dilsaver-nelson.com

REPRESENTATIVE CLIENTS: First Mid-Illinois Bank & Trust; Allstate Insurance Co.; Rural King Supply, Inc.; B&M Construction; Curry Construction; Unique Home Properties; Heritage Builders; Anamet Electrical, Inc.; Parrish Carpets; Wells Fargo Bank.

HELLER, HOLMES & ASSOCIATES, P.C.

1101 BROADWAY
P.O. BOX 889
MATTOON, ILLINOIS 61938-0889
Telephone: 217-235-2700
FAX: 217-235-0743
Email: hhlawoff@aol.com
URL: http://www.hhlawoff.com

General Civil and Trial Practice in all State, Federal and Appellate Courts. Personal Injury, Medical Negligence, Criminal Defense, Insurance, Litigation, Probate, Workers Compensation, Corporation, Commercial, Family Law, Oil and Gas.

(This Listing Continued)

FIRM PROFILE: Heller, Holmes & Associates, P.C. is an extremely strong litigation firm with a reputation which affords the firm clients throughout the entire state of Illinois.

One partner is a fellow in the American College of Trial Lawyers and all partners and associates are extremely active in both professional and civic organizations.

HARLAN HELLER, born Bloomington, Illinois, June 14, 1928; admitted to bar, 1951, Illinois. *Education:* Illinois State Normal University and University of Illinois (B.S., 1951); University of Illinois (J.D., 1952). Phi Alpha Delta. Recipient, Laureate, Academy of Illinois Lawyers; Distinguished Graduate, University of Illinois College of Law. Member, Illinois Supreme Court Committee on Jury Instruction, 1973-1995. Former Chairman, Rules Committee, Federal Court, Central District. Member, Civil Justice Reform Act Committee, Central District. Member: U.S. Senate Nominating Commission for Central District of Illinois; Supreme Court Committee on Character and Fitness. *Member:* Coles-Cumberland County, Illinois State and American Bar Associations. Fellow: American College of Trial Lawyers; Society of Trial Lawyers. ***PRACTICE AREAS:*** Litigation. ***Email:*** HH@HHlawoff.com

BRENT D. HOLMES, born Villa Grove, Illinois, September 12, 1953; admitted to bar, 1978, Illinois. *Education:* University of Illinois (B.S., 1975; J.D., magna cum laude, 1978). Order of the Coif. Editorial Board, Illinois Bar Journal, 1995—, Secretary, 2001. Associate Editor, 2002-2004 and Editor-in-Chief, 2004—, Illinois Bar Journal. Author, "Opening Statements: A Plaintiffs' Lawyer's Guide," 83 Ill.B.J. 91 (1995). Member, Board of Managers, Illinois Trial Lawyers Association, 1989—. *Member:* Coles-Cumberland County (President, 2000) and Illinois State Bar Associations; Association of Trial Lawyers of America. ***PRACTICE AREAS:*** Civil Litigation; Malpractice; Workers Compensation; Family Law; Appellate Practice. ***Email:*** Brent@HHlawoff.com

H. KENT HELLER, born Bloomington, Illinois, March 30, 1952; admitted to bar, 1977, Illinois; 1978, U.S. Tax Court, U.S. District Court, Northern District of Illinois including Trial Bar and U.S. District Court, Southern District of Wisconsin, U.S. District Court, Central and Southern Districts of Illinois; U.S. District Court, Northern District of Indiana; 1991, U.S. Supreme Court, U.S. Court of Appeals, Seventh Circuit. *Education:* University of Illinois (B.S., 1974; J.D., 1977). Certified Public Accountant, Illinois, 1974. Appointed, 1996— and Chairman, 2005, Illinois Supreme Court Committee on Jury Instruction. *Member:* Coles-Cumberland County, Illinois State and American Bar Associations; Association of Trial Lawyers of America; Illinois Trial Lawyers Association (Member, Board of Advocates); American Bar Foundation (Fellow). ***PRACTICE AREAS:*** Civil Trial Practice; Criminal Defense; Civil Rights; Federal Trial Practice; Personal Injury; Malpractice. ***Email:*** Kent@HHlawoff.com

DAVID STEVENS, born Buffalo, New York, June 22, 1947; admitted to bar, 1993, Illinois; 1994, U.S. District Court, Northern District of Illinois and U.S. Court of Appeals, Seventh Circuit; 1995, U.S. District Court, Central and Southern Districts of Illinois; 1999, U.S. Supreme Court. *Education:* Michigan State University (B.A., 1969); Kent State University (M.A., 1970); Bowling Green State University (Ph.D., 1973); Southern Illinois University (J.D., magna cum laude, 1993). Phi Delta Phi. Author: "Negligence Liability for Transfusion-Associated AIDS Transmission," 12 J. Legal Medicine 221 (1991); "Challenging Sentencing After a Guilty Plea," 81 Ill. Bar J. 151 (1993); "Extended Term Sentencing and Attempt Crimes," 82 Ill. Bar J. 41 (1994); "Mandatory Consecutive Sentencing," 83 Ill. bar J. 526 (1995); "Abolishing Permissive Inference of Guilt of Burglary," 84 Ill. Bar J. 583 (1996). *Member:* Coles-Cumberland, Illinois State and American (National Student Director, Appellate Advocacy Competition, 1992-1993) Bar Associations; Illinois Trial Lawyers Association; American Trial Lawyers Association. ***LANGUAGES:*** Spanish. ***PRACTICE AREAS:*** Plaintiff's Personal Injury Litigation; Criminal Defense; Family Law; Real Estate; Appellate Practice. ***Email:*** DavidStevens@HHlawoff.com

FRED JOHNSON, born Chicago, Illinois, July 19, 1956; admitted to bar, 1981, Illinois; 1982, U.S. Court of Appeals, Seventh Circuit and U.S. District Court, Southern District of Illinois; 1987, U.S. Supreme Court; 1992, U.S. District Court, Central District of Illinois. *Education:* Augustana College (B.A., 1978); Southern Illinois University (J.D., 1981). Author: "The Downsizing, Then Supersizing of Medicare's Super Lien," 92 I.B.J. 1, 2004. Public Defender, Effingham County, Illinois, 1990-1991. Member, Supreme Court Committee on Character & Fitness. *Member:* Coles-Cumberland, Crawford County and Southeastern Illinois (Secretary, 1988) Bar Associations. ***PRACTICE AREAS:*** Civil Trial Practice; Criminal Defense; Family Law. ***Email:*** Fred@HHlawoff.com

JASON M. CROWDER, born Hinsdale, Illinois, May 5, 1970; admitted to bar, 1996, Illinois; U.S. District Court, Northern, Central and Southern Districts of Illinois; U.S. Court of Appeals, Seventh Circuit; U.S. Bankruptcy Court. *Education:* Purdue University (B.A., 1992); Loyola University (J.D., 1996). *Member:* Coles-Cumberland, Illinois State and American Bar Associations; Illinois Trial Lawyers Association; American Trial Lawyers Association. ***PRACTICE AREAS:*** Civil Litigation; Medical Malpractice; Products Liability; Bankruptcy; Creditors Rights; Probate. ***Email:*** Jason@HHlawoff.com

MARK E. BOVARD, born Effingham, Illinois, August 20, 1972; admitted to bar, 1997, Illinois and U.S. District Court, Central and Southern Districts of Illinois; 1998, U.S. Court of Appeals, Seventh Circuit. *Education:* Eastern Illinois University (B.A., cum laude, 1994); Indiana University (J.D., 1997). *Member:* Coles-Cumberland County and Illinois State Bar Associations; Illinois Trial Lawyers Association. ***PRACTICE AREAS:*** Civil Litigation; Malpractice; Civil Rights; Family Law. ***Email:*** Mbovard@HHlawoff.com

GINA R. VONDERHEIDE, born Effingham, Illinois, October 2, 1976; admitted to bar, 2004, Illinois. *Education:* Millikin University (B.S., cum laude, 1998); St. Louis University (J.D., 2004). *Member:* Coles-Cumberland and Illinois State Bar Associations. ***Email:*** gina@hhlawoff.com

REFERENCES: First National Bank, Mattoon; First Federal Savings and Loan, Mattoon.

RYAN, BENNETT & RADLOFF

300 RICHMOND EAST
P.O. BOX 629
MATTOON, ILLINOIS 61938-0629
Telephone: 217-234-2000
Fax: 217-234-2001
URL: http://www.lawyers.com/rbrkolaw

General, Civil and Criminal Practice. Trials in all Courts. Insurance Defense, Workers Compensation, Negligence, Corporation, Probate, Estate Planning, Bankruptcy, Taxation and Oil and Gas Law. Domestic Relations, Divorce, Child Custody and Adoption Law.

FIRM PROFILE: Since the firm's establishment, the firm has represented small businesses, individuals and corporations throughout the counties of Coles, Cumberland, Effingham, Shelby, Clark, Douglas, Macon and Jasper. The firm maintains a general, civil and criminal practice with an emphasis on litigation, personal injury, workers compensation, bankruptcy and estate planning.

MEMBERS OF FIRM

WILLIS P. RYAN (1911-1983)

JAMES A. BENNETT, born Wheaton, Kansas, November 10, 1940; admitted to bar, 1965, Kansas; 1967, Illinois; 1971, U.S. Tax Court; 1972, U.S. Supreme Court. *Education:* St. Benedict's College (B.A., 1962); Catholic University of America (J.D., 1965). Internal Revenue Estate Tax Examiner, U.S. Treasury Department, 1965-1967. *Member:* Coles-Cumberland County (President, 1986-1987) and Illinois State Bar Associations; Commercial Law League of America; American Bankruptcy Institute. ***PRACTICE AREAS:*** Commercial Law; Bankruptcy; Real Estate Law; Contracts; Probate. ***Email:*** bennett.rbrkolaw@advant.net

STEPHEN R. RYAN, born Mattoon, Illinois, November 2, 1946; admitted to bar, 1974, Illinois and Iowa. *Education:* Northwestern University and Illinois State University (B.S., 1972); University of Iowa (J.D., 1974). *Member:* Coles-Cumberland County, Illinois State and Iowa State Bar Associations; Illinois Trial Lawyers Association; The Association of Trial Lawyers of America; National Association of Criminal Defense Lawyers. ***PRACTICE AREAS:*** Family Law; Criminal Law; Civil Practice; Personal Injury; Litigation. ***Email:*** sryan.rbrkolaw@advant.net

MICHAEL D. RYAN, born Mattoon, Illinois, December 19, 1950; admitted to bar, 1976, Illinois. *Education:* Denison University (A.B., 1973); John Marshall Law School (J.D., with distinction, 1976). *Member:* Coles-Cumberland County and Illinois State Bar Associations; Worker's Compensation Lawyers Association; Illinois Association of Defense Trial Counsel; Defense Research Institute. ***PRACTICE AREAS:*** Personal Injury Litigation; Insurance Defense; Negligence; Premises Liability. ***Email:*** mryan.rbrkolaw@advant.net

MICHAEL K. RADLOFF, born Charleston, Illinois, October 11, 1954; admitted to bar, 1983, Illinois. *Education:* Eastern Illinois University (B.A., 1977; M.A., 1978); University of Illinois (J.D., 1983). *Member:* Coles-Cumberland County, Illinois State and American Bar Associations; Illinois Association of Defense Trial Counsel. ***PRACTICE AREAS:*** Personal Injury Litigation; Criminal Law; Insurance Defense; Family Law; Insurance. ***Email:*** radloff.rbrolaw@advant.net

COUNSEL FOR: Auto-Owners Insurance Co.; State Farm Insurance Cos.; Country Cos.; Bituminous Insurance Cos.; Millers Mutual Insurance; Horace Mann Insurance Co.; Western States Insurance Co.; Pekin Insurance.
REFERENCE: First Mid-Illinois Bank & Trust, Mattoon, Ill.

LAW OFFICES OF
WINTER-BLACK & LIVESAY

201 NORTH LOGAN STREET
P.O. BOX 835
MATTOON, ILLINOIS 61938
Telephone: 217-235-3400
Fax: 217-235-3402
URL: http://winter-blacklivesaylaw.com

Toledo, Illinois Office: 102 S. Meridian, 62468. Telephone: 217-849-2700. Fax: 217-849-2569.

Family Law, Foreclosures, Collections, Probate and Wills, Real Estate Contracts and Closings, Estate Planning, Bankruptcy, Appellate Practice.

MEMBERS OF FIRM

JANETT S. WINTER-BLACK, born Olney, Illinois, March 1, 1954; admitted to bar, 1979, Illinois; U.S. District Court, Central District of Illinois and U.S. Tax Court. *Education:* Eastern Illinois University (B.A., with high honors, 1975); Southern Illinois University (J.D., 1979). Phi Alpha Eta; Pi Sigma Alpha; Phi Alpha Delta. Instructor, Substantive Criminal Law, Lakeland Junior College, Mattoon, Illinois, 1985-1986. Coles County Law Librarian, 1985-1987. *Member:* Coles-Cumberland County (President, 2003—), Illinois State and American Bar Associations; Illinois Trial Lawyers Association. ***PRACTICE AREAS:*** Family Law; Foreclosures; Collections; Probate; Wills; Real Estate Contracts. ***Email:*** jswblaw1@consolidated.net

JUDY TORBECK-LIVESAY, *born Vandalia, Illinois, October 26, 1952; admitted to* bar, 1992, Illinois. *Education:* Eastern Illinois University (B.A., 1974); Southern Illinois University (J.D., 1991). *Member:* Coles-Cumberland and Illinois State Bar Associations. ***PRACTICE AREAS:*** Family Law; Probate; Estate Planning; Collections; Bankruptcy; Appellate Practice; Real Estate. ***Email:*** jt.jswblaw1@consolidated.net

MITCHELL HOFFMAN & WOLF LLC

MAYWOOD, ILLINOIS

(See Chicago)

Plaintiffs Personal Injury, Automobile Accidents, Wrongful Death, Medical Malpractice, Construction Accidents, Premises Liability.

WEAVER LAW GROUP, LLC

MAYWOOD, ILLINOIS

(See Chicago)

Regulatory and Administrative Practice to the Food, Drug, Cosmetic, Device and Dietary Supplement Industry. Trademark and Copyright Practice, Direct Sales, Telemarketing, Network Marketing, US Customs, Federal Trade Commission, Civil Litigation and Business Transactions.

THE LAW FIRM OF
FRANKS, GERKIN & McKENNA, P.C.

McHENRY, ILLINOIS

(See Marengo)

General, Civil & Criminal Trial Practice, Banking, Business Law, Commercial Real Estate, Corporate Law, Criminal Law, Debt Collections, Family Law, Personal Injury, Real Estate, Trusts & Estates, Immigration, Wills, Workers Compensation, Municipal Law, Traffic, Zoning, Planning and Land Use.

MICHLING HOFMANN VINTON
PLAZA & WICK, P.C.

McHENRY, ILLINOIS

(See Woodstock)

Personal Injury, Workers Compensation, Criminal Law, Family Law, Civil Litigation, Corporate Law, Residential Real Estate, Commercial Real Estate, Landlord and Tenant Law, Wills and Trusts, Land Use and Development, Zoning, Appellate Practice.

LAW OFFICES OF
THOMAS J. POPOVICH, P.C.

Established in 1997

3416 WEST ELM STREET
McHENRY, ILLINOIS 60050
Telephone: 815-344-3797
Fax: 815-344-5280
Email: tkpopovich@aol.com
URL: http://www.popovichlaw.com

Catastrophic Personal Injury including Wrongful Death, Medical Malpractice including Birth Injuries, Cancer, Failure to Diagnose or Misdiagnosis, Obstetric, Surgical, Cardiac, Orthopedic and Nursing Malpractice, Automobile Accidents and Injuries, Head, Brain, Back and Neck Injuries, Motorcycle Accidents and Injuries, Construction Accidents and Injuries, Product Liability, Unsafe Product Injuries, Workers Compensation.

FIRM PROFILE: Mr. Popovich began his career representing insurance companies in one of the largest and most prestigious downtown Chicago law firms. Five years later he was recruited into one of the city's most respected plaintiff practices.

After a productive and successful time at that firm he decided to return to his hometown in McHenry County. His goal was to establish one of the first law firms in the county devoted exclusively to representing the interests of personal injury victims. The vast majority of clients are referred by other lawyers and past clients.

THOMAS J. POPOVICH, born Indianapolis, Indiana, March 9, 1964; admitted to bar, 1990, Illinois. *Education:* Illinois State University (B.S., 1986); DePaul University Law School (J.D., 1990). *Member:* Chicago, Lake County, McHenry County, Illinois State and American Bar Associations; Illinois Trial Lawyers Association; Association of Trial Lawyers of America. ***PRACTICE AREAS:*** Personal Injury; Medical Malpractice; Nursing Home Negligence; Workers Compensation. ***Email:*** tkpopovich@aol.com

---

KIMBERLY A. POPOVICH, born Alabama, May 4, 1968; admitted to bar, 1993, Wisconsin and Indiana; 1997, Illinois. *Education:* Carthage College (B.A., 1989); Marquette University (J.D., cum laude, 1993). *Member:* State Bar of Wisconsin; Lake County, Illinois State, Indiana State and American Bar Associations; American Trial Lawyers Association; Illinois Trial Lawyers Association. ***PRACTICE AREAS:*** Personal Injury; Wrongful Death; Medical Malpractice; Workers Compensation. ***Email:*** tkpopovich@aol.com

HANS A. MAST, born Evanston, Illinois, November 4, 1962; admitted to bar, 1991, Illinois and U.S. District Court, Northern District of Illinois; 1993, U.S. District Court, Eastern District of Wisconsin. *Education:* McHenry County College (A.A.S., 1984) Illinois State University (B.S., 1986); Illinois Institute of Technology (J.D., 1991). Alpha Phi Gamma. *Member:* Winnebago County and Illinois Bar Associations; Illinois Trial Lawyers Association. ***PRACTICE AREAS:*** Personal Injury Defense Law. ***Email:*** hansmast@sbcglobal.net

JOHN A. KORNAK, born Chicago, Illinois, July 8, 1956; admitted to bar, 1986, Illinois; 1994, U.S. District Court, Northern District of Illinois including Trial Bar; 1995, Wis-

(This Listing Continued)

consin and Illinois Trial Bar, Northern District. *Education:* University of Illinois (A.B., 1983); Valparaiso University College of Law (J.D., 1986). Phi Alpha Delta. Former Assistant States Attorney, Lake County. Former Chief Drug Pros Division. *Member:* Lake County and Illinois State Bar Associations; Illinois Trial Lawyers Association; Association of Trial Lawyers of America (Member, Traumatic Brain Injury Litigation Group); Brain Injury Association of Illinois; National Crime Victims Bar Association; Trial Lawyers for Public Justice. ***PRACTICE AREAS:*** Catastrophic Personal Injury; Wrongful Death; Medical Malpractice; Brain Injury. ***Email:*** kanrok@aol.com

JAY R. ORLOWSKI, born Chicago, Illinois, October 13, 1961; admitted to bar, 1987, Illinois; 1996, Wisconsin. *Education:* Loyola University (B.B.A., cum laude, 1983; J.D., cum laude, 1987). Certified Public Accountant, Illinois, 1983; Certified in Principals of Life Insurance by Life Office Management Association, 1983. *Member:* McHenry, Chicago, Lake County, Illinois State and American Bar Associations; Illinois Defense Council. ***PRACTICE AREAS:*** Personal Injury; Wrongful Death; Medical Malpractice. ***Email:*** orlowskijr@aol.com

SCOTT A. HIERA, born Chicago, Illinois, March 23, 1963; admitted to bar, 2003, Illinois; 2004, U.S. District Court, Northern District of Illinois. *Education:* Southern Illinois University (B.S., 1997); Chicago-Kent College of Law (J.D., 2002). [Second Petty Officer, U.S. Navy, 1982-1986]. ***PRACTICE AREAS:*** Personal Injury; Medical Malpractice; Wrongful Death; Workers Compensation. ***Email:*** shiera@prodigy.net

HART AND HART

McLEANSBORO, ILLINOIS

(See Benton)

General Trial and Appellate Practice in State and Federal Courts. Probate, Trust, Real Estate Deeds and Title Insurance, Bankruptcy (Creditors), Traffic, Banking, Business, Commercial and Corporation Law and Creditor Collections, Employment Law.

JELLIFFE, FERRELL, MORRIS & DOERGE

McLEANSBORO, ILLINOIS

(See Harrisburg)

Insurance Law, Negligence and Personal Injury, Litigation, Workers' Compensation Law, and Employment Law. Commercial Collection and DUI's. General Civil Practice in State and Federal Courts. Trials and Appeals.

LAW OFFICES OF LEYNAUD & LEYNAUD

A PROFESSIONAL CORPORATION

MENDOTA, ILLINOIS

(See Peru)

General Civil and Trial Practice, Personal Injury, Mediation, Worker's Compensation, Real Estate, Criminal, Landlord/Tenant and Family Law. Business/Banking Litigation, DUI and Traffic. Insurance, General Practice, Medical Malpractice, Zoning and Land Use. Bad Faith, Drug Crimes, Juvenile Crimes, White Collar, Adoptions, Child Custody, Divorce, Child Support, Visitation Rights, Domestic Violence. Auto Accidents, Dog Bites, Slip and Fall, Wrongful Death, Buying and Selling, Wills and Probate.

BRYANT & KAUTZ, PC

Established in 1990

222 FERRY STREET

METROPOLIS, ILLINOIS 62960

Telephone: 618-524-5671

Fax: 618-524-9671

Paducah, Kentucky Office: Bryant & Kautz, PC, 601 Washington Street, P.O. Box 1876, 42002-1876. Telephone: 270-442-1422. Fax: 270-443-8788.

Marion, Illinois Office: 4501 West De Young, Suite B-2, 62959. Telephone: 618-993-1468. Fax: 618-993-1329.

General Civil and Criminal Practice. Trials and Appeals, State and Federal Courts. Personal Injury, Criminal, Real Estate, Corporation, Family Law, Trusts and Estates.

(For Complete Biographical Data on all Personnel, see Professional Biographies at Paducah, Kentucky)

KRUGER, HENRY & HUNTER

110 WEST 5TH

P.O. BOX 568

METROPOLIS, ILLINOIS 62960

Telephone: 618-524-9302

Fax: 618-524-9305

URL: http://www.lawyers.com/khhlaw

Civil and Criminal Trial and Appellate Practice. Negligence, Product Liability, Wrongful Death, Workman's Compensation, Criminal, Family, Real Estate, Corporate, Probate, Bankruptcy, Divorce, Driving While Intoxicated.

FIRM PROFILE: Kruger, Henry & Hunter was founded over 25 years ago by Richard Kruger in the same location as today. The firm is unique in the region since the partners possess over 60 years combined experience in an assortment of areas. The firm, which is located across from the courthouse, handles matters in the lower ten counties of Illinois.

(This Listing Continued)

MEMBERS OF FIRM

RICHARD KRUGER, born Carbondale, Illinois, October 20, 1945; admitted to bar, 1971, Illinois; 1972, U.S. District Court, Southern District of Illinois. *Education:* University of Illinois (A.B., 1967; J.D., 1971). *Member:* Massac County (President, 1974-1981), Illinois State (Member, General Practice Section Council, 1974-1976), Southern Six (Vice President, 1976-1978) and American Bar Associations. [With U.S. Army, 1969-1971]. ***PRACTICE AREAS:*** Real Estate; Probate and Estate Planning; Corporation Law; Divorce; Bankruptcy; Wills; Trust Law.

PAUL F. HENRY, born Des Moines, Iowa, November 15, 1950; admitted to bar, 1979, Illinois; 1980, U.S. District Court, Southern District of Illinois; 1985, U.S. Court of Appeals, Seventh Circuit; 1988, U.S. Supreme Court. *Education:* Southern Illinois University (B.A., 1974; J.D., 1979). City Attorney, 1985-1989. *Member:* Massac County (President, 1985-1989) and Illinois State Bar Associations; Illinois Trial Lawyers Association; The Association of Trial Lawyers of America. ***PRACTICE AREAS:*** Personal Injury; Workers Compensation; Criminal Law; Divorce; Child Custody; Driving While Intoxicated.

MARK C. HUNTER, born Marion, Illinois, June 27, 1958; admitted to bar, 1983, Illinois; 1984, U.S. District Court, Southern District of Illinois; 1994, U.S. Court of Appeals, Seventh Circuit. *Education:* University of Illinois (B.A., 1980); St. Louis University (J.D., cum laude, 1982). Massac County State's Attorney, 1986-1992. *Member:* Massac County (President, 1990-1990) and Illinois State Bar Association. ***PRACTICE AREAS:*** Personal Injury; Family Law; Criminal Law; Driving While Intoxicated; Divorce; Child Custody; Automobile Accidents.

OF COUNSEL

RICK W. ABELL, born Paducah, Kentucky, September 28, 1959; admitted to bar, 1984, Illinois. *Education:* University of Illinois (B.S., 1981); Southern Illinois University (J.D., 1984). *Member:* Illinois State and American Bar Associations; Association of Trial Lawyers of America.

REPRESENTATIVE CLIENTS: Mermet Grain Co.; Metropolis Builder's Supply; J.M. Walters & Sons, Inc. (Electrical Contractor); Village of Joppa; Southgate Health Care, Inc.; Mid-South Towing Co.; American States Insurance Co.
APPROVED ATTORNEYS FOR: Attorney's Title Guaranty Fund, Inc.; St. Paul Title Insurance Co.; Farmer's Home Administration.
REFERENCES: City National Bank, Metropolis, Illinois; National State Bank, Metropolis, Illinois.

THE NEELY LAW FIRM

Established in 1976

P.O. BOX 428

METROPOLIS, ILLINOIS 62960-0428

Telephone: 618-524-2642

Fax: 618-524-2433

Email: jjn@hcis.net

URL: http://www.lawyers.com/neelylaw

General Trial and Appellate Practice. Probate, Real Estate, Family, Corporate, Personal Injury, Municipal and Criminal Law.

MEMBER OF FIRM

JOSEPH J. NEELY, born St. Louis, Missouri, January 10, 1950; admitted to bar, 1976, Illinois; 1977, U.S. District Court, Southern and Eastern Districts of Illinois; 1985, U.S. Court of Appeals, Seventh Circuit and U.S. Supreme Court; 1987, Kentucky and U.S. District Court, Western District of Kentucky; 1989, U.S. Court of Appeals, Sixth Circuit. *Education:* Southern Illinois University (B.S., 1972); The John Marshall School of Law (J.D., with distinction, 1976). Assistant State's Attorney, Massac County, Illinois, 1976-1977. City Attorney: City of Brookport, 1976-1982; 1986-1993; City of Metropolis, 1980-1981; 1989-2001. Attorney, Village of New Grand Chain, 1990—; Village of Karnak, 1986—. Former Chairman, Illinois Community College Board. *Member:* Massac County (Secretary, 1978-1981; President, 1981-1985), Illinois State and Kentucky Bar Associations. ***PRACTICE AREAS:*** Corporate Law; Criminal Law; Family Law; Municipal Law; Personal Injury; Real Estate; Probate. ***Email:*** neelylaw@djklink.net

REPRESENTATIVE CLIENTS: MidCountry Bank of Metropolis; Massac County Housing Authority; United Cities Gas Co.; Massac County Jail Commission; Lafarge Corporation; Massac County Mental Health and Family Counseling Center; MAP Training Center.
APPROVED ATTORNEYS FOR: Farmers Home Administration; Chicago Title & Trust Co.; Veterans Administration.
LOCAL COUNSEL FOR: Peoples First National Bank and Trust.
REFERENCE: MidCountry Bank, Metropolis, Illinois.

THERESA M. MALYSA

MOKENA, ILLINOIS

(See Orland Park)

Family Law, Divorce, Tax Considerations, Retirement Benefits, Child Custody, Parenting Time, Visitation, Child Support, Domestic Violence, Paternity, Matrimonial Litigation, Premarital Agreements.

ANDICH & ANDICH

MOLINE, ILLINOIS

(See Rock Island)

Commercial Law, Business Litigation, Consumer Litigation, Creditor's Rights, Media, Bankruptcy, Employment, Domestic Relations, Real Estate, Probate, Civil Trial and Appeals, Wills, Estates, Family Law, Divorce, Child Custody, Child Support, Adoption.

BOZEMAN, NEIGHBOUR, PATTON & NOE, LLP

Established in 1946

1630 5TH AVENUE
P.O. BOX 659
MOLINE, ILLINOIS 61266-0659
Telephone: 309-797-0850
Fax: 309-764-1371
URL: http://www.bnpn.com

Davenport, Iowa Office: 4300 E. 53rd Street, Suite 103, 52807. Telephone: 563-449-1037. Fax: 309-764-1371.

General Practice in State and Federal Courts. Appellate Practice, Bankruptcy, Banks and Banking, Business Law, Civil Practice, Civil Rights, Commercial Law, Commercial Real Estate, Constitutional Law, Construction Law, Contracts, Corporate Law, Debtor and Creditor, Disabilities, Employee Benefits, Environmental Law, Family Law, Fidelity and Surety, Finance, Guardianship and Conservatorship, Health Care, Hospital Law, Housing Law, Insurance, Insurance Defense, Labor and Employment, Leases and Leasing, Legal Ethics and Professional Responsibility, Litigation, Medical Malpractice, Mergers, Acquisitions and Divestitures, Mortgages, Municipal Law, Negligence, Personal Injury, Probate, Products Liability, Professional Liability, Real Estate, Taxation, Torts, Trusts and Estates, Wills, Workers' Compensation.

JOHN V. PATTON (1922-1993)

MEMBERS OF FIRM

ROBERT J. NOE, born Rock Island, Illinois, March 1, 1939; admitted to bar, 1963, Illinois. *Education:* St. Ambrose University (B.A., 1960); University of Notre Dame (J.D., 1963). Listed: Leading Lawyers of Illinois; Super Lawyers, 2005. *Member:* Rock Island County (President, 1995-1997), Illinois State (Assembly of Delegates, 1972-1978) and American Bar Associations; International Association of Insurance Counsel; Defense Research Institute. Fellow, American College of Trial Lawyers.

JAMES D. MOWEN, born Grand Rapids, Michigan, April 22, 1943; admitted to bar, 1968, Illinois. *Education:* University of Iowa (B.S., 1965); Loyola University (J.D., 1968). *Member:* Chicago, Rock Island County, Illinois State and American Bar Associations; Illinois Workers' Compensation Lawyers Association.

RICHARD M. BATCHER, born Waterloo, Iowa, August 9, 1941; admitted to bar, 1967, Iowa; 1968, Illinois. *Education:* Iowa State University (B.S.M.E., 1963); University of Iowa (J.D., 1967). Named, "Illinois Super Lawyer" by Chicago Magazine, 2005. *Member:* Rock Island County, Scott County, Illinois State, Iowa State and American Bar Associations. (Also at Davenport, Iowa Office)

JOHN P. HARRIS, born Normal, Illinois, March 2, 1955; admitted to bar, 1980, Iowa and Illinois. *Education:* Hope College; University of Iowa (B.A., 1977; J.D., 1980). *Member:* Rock Island County, Scott County, Illinois State and Iowa State Bar Associations. (Also at Davenport, Iowa Office)

GARY L. SISSEL, born Davenport, Iowa, April 23, 1948; admitted to bar, 1973, Iowa; 1986, California; 1988, Illinois. *Education:* University of Iowa (B.A., 1970; J.D., with honors, 1973). *Member:* Rock Island County, Scott County (Member, Executive Council, 1982-1987), Illinois State, Iowa State and American Bar Associations; State Bar of California. (Also at Davenport, Iowa Office)

JAMES R. PATTON, born Moline, Illinois, December 30, 1954; admitted to bar, 1984, Illinois. *Education:* Augustana College (B.A., 1978); Northern Illinois University (J.D., 1984). *Member:* Rock Island County, Illinois State and American Bar Associations; Illinois Association of Defense Trial Counsel.

MARK R. McLAUGHLIN, born Davenport, Iowa, February 20, 1960; admitted to bar, 1988, Illinois. *Education:* University of Iowa (B.A., 1982); St. Louis University (J.D., 1987). *Member:* Rock Island County, Illinois State and American Bar Associations; Defense Research Institute, Inc.

WILLIAM L. CLEAVER, born Harrisburg, Pennsylvania, December 7, 1949; admitted to bar, 1974, Iowa; 1975, Illinois. *Education:* Augustana College (B.A., 1971); University of Iowa (J.D., 1974). *Member:* Rock Island County, Scott County, Illinois State (Assembly of Delegates, 2002—; Elder Law Section Council, 1994—; Standing Committee on Military Affairs, 2002—; Standing Committee on the Delivery of Legal Services, 1993-1999), Iowa State (Member, Real Estate Section Council, 2002—) and American Bar Associations. (Also at Davenport Office)

J. SUE MYATT, born Marshalltown, Iowa, July 10, 1963; admitted to bar, 1989, Iowa; 1990, Illinois. *Education:* University of Northern Iowa (B.A., 1986); University of Iowa (J.D., with high distinction, 1989). Law Clerk, Seventh Judicial District Court of Iowa, 1989-1990. *Member:* Rock Island County, Scott County, Illinois State, Iowa State and American Bar Associations.

WILLIAM P. RECTOR, born Davenport, Iowa, January 6, 1962; admitted to bar, 1987, Illinois; 1999, Iowa. *Education:* Wake Forest University (B.A., cum laude, 1984); University of Iowa (J.D., with distinction, 1987). *Member:* Rock Island County, Iowa State and American Bar Associations; Professional Liability Underwriting Society. (Also at Davenport, Iowa Office)

JEFFREY D. MARTENS, born Moline, Illinois, October 18, 1969; admitted to bar, 1994, Wisconsin, Iowa and Illinois. *Education:* Augustana College (B.A., cum laude, 1991); University of Wisconsin-Madison (J.D., 1994). *Member:* Rock Island County, Scott County, Illinois State, Iowa State and American Bar Associations; State Bar of Wisconsin.

MARK A. TARNOW, born South Bend, Indiana, September 30, 1959; admitted to bar, 1984, Iowa; 1985, Illinois. *Education:* Western Illinois University (B.A., with high honors; 1981); University of Iowa (J.D., with distinction, 1984). *Member:* Rock Island County, Scott County, Illinois State and Iowa State Bar Associations.

(This Listing Continued)

ASSOCIATES

BENJAMIN J. SAMUELSON, born Davenport, Iowa, July 5, 1974; admitted to bar, 2000, Illinois; 2001, Iowa. *Education:* University of Iowa (B.A., 1997); Loyola University, Chicago (J.D., 2000). *Member:* Rock Island County, Scott County, Illinois State and Iowa State Bar Associations.

HEATHER G. ROULEAU, born Moline, Illinois, July 19, 1976; admitted to bar, 2001, Illinois, U.S. District Court, Central District of Illinois, U.S. Court of Appeals, Fifth, Sixth and Seventh Circuits. *Education:* University of Illinois, Springfield (B.A., 1998); Northern Illinois University (J.D., magna cum laude, 2001). Notes and Comments Editor, Northern Illinois University Law Review. Law Clerk to Hon. Richard Mills, U.S. District Court, Central District of Illinois. *Member:* Rock Island, Illinois State and American Bar Associations.

OF COUNSEL

VIRGIL BOZEMAN, born Fort Smith, Arkansas, June 6, 1912; admitted to bar, 1937, Illinois. *Education:* University of Illinois; Southern Methodist University (LL.B., 1937).

HUBBARD B. NEIGHBOUR, born Moline, Illinois, March 26, 1925; admitted to bar, 1950, Illinois. *Education:* Northwestern University (B.S.M.E., 1945; J.D., 1950). *Member:* Rock Island County (President, 1976-1978), Illinois State and American Bar Associations.

DANIEL P. ELLARD, born Gainesville, Georgia, September 6, 1955; admitted to bar, 1980, Georgia; 1986, Iowa and Illinois. *Education:* Vanderbilt University (B.S., 1977); University of Georgia (J.D., 1980); New York University (LL.M., Taxation, 1983). *Member:* Rock Island County, Scott County, Illinois State, Iowa State (Chairman and Co-Chairman, Governing Tax Council, 1994-1997; Estate Planning and Gift Tax Committee) and American Bar Associations; State Bar of Georgia. (Also practicing individually)

REPRESENTATIVE CLIENTS: Deere & Company; City of Moline; Southeast National Bank; Central Bank of Geneseo; Chip King Industries, Inc.; General Grind and Machine; Iowa Masonic Facilities; East Moline Metal Products Co.; Ryder Systems, Inc.; McLaughlin Body Co.; Jancy Engineering Co.; The Lamar Corp.; Olsen Engineering, LP; One Solution Staffing, Inc.; Alleman High School; John Deere Health Care, Inc.; United Distributors, Inc. *Insurance Companies:* AIG; AP Capital/APA; Arrowhead Claims Management; Auto-Owners Insurance Co.; Capital Indemnity Corp.; The Cincinnati Insurance Co.; Country Insurance & Financial Services; Crawford Co.; Cumis Insurance Society; Design Professionals Insurance Co.; EMC Insurance Co.; EMC Insurance Society; Farmers Insurance Group; General Casualty Cos.; Horace Mann Insurance Co.; Illinois Casualty Co.; Illinois Providers Trust; Illinois State Medical Inter-Insurance Exchange; Iowa Mutual Insurance Co.; ISBA Mutual Insurance Co.; Madison Mutual Insurance Co.; Markel Insurance Company; Met-Life Auto & Home Insurance Co.; OneBeacon Insurance Group; Pharmacist Mutual Insurance Company; Rockford Mutual Insurance Co.; Royal Insurance Co.; Safeco Property & Casualty; St. Paul Insurance Co.; Sentry Insurance Co.; Special Risk Services; TIG Insurance; United States Liability Insurance Group.

CALIFF & HARPER, P.C.

Established in 1870

6TH FLOOR FIRST MIDWEST BANK BUILDING
506 FIFTEENTH STREET
P.O. BOX 719
MOLINE, ILLINOIS 61266-0719
Telephone: 309-764-8361
Facsimile: 309-764-8394
URL: http://www.califf.com

Wheaton, Illinois Office: 123 West Front Street, Suite 200, 60187. Telephone: 800-764-4999. Facsimile: 630-871-1347.

Corporate, Commercial, Civil Litigation in all State and Federal Courts, Labor, Employment, Banking, Governmental, School, Administrative (including N.L.R.B.), Products Liability, Insurance, Taxation, Estate Planning and Probate Law, Real Estate, Land Development and Zoning, Business Enterprises, Closely Held Business, Limited Liability Companies, Partnerships, Small Business, Buying or Selling a Business, Collections, Employee Benefits, Employment Contracts, Human Resources, Contracts, Business Lawsuits, Internet Law, E-Commerce, Commercial Leasing, Landlord and Tenant; Buying or Selling a Home; Tax Planning and Asset Protection.

FIRM PROFILE: Califf & Harper, P.C. and its predecessor partnerships have been meeting the legal needs of the Western Illinois and Eastern Iowa bi-state area for over 130 years. The firm offers a wide range of legal services to clients in private sector industries, including construction, development, and manufacturing, and to municipalities and public sector special districts, including districts for schools, entertainment, and transportation. The firm serves clients in state and federal courts in both Illinois and Iowa. In addition, the firm has extensive experience in administrative law proceedings before state and federal agencies involving employee and labor relations matters, and substantial arbitration practice before the American Arbitration Association and the Federal Mediation and Conciliation Service.

ROBERT P. BOEYE, born Evanston, Illinois, June 14, 1934; admitted to bar, 1959, Iowa; 1960, Illinois; 1964, U.S. District Court, Central District of Illinois, U.S. District Court, Southern District of Iowa and U.S. Court Appeals, Seventh Circuit. *Education:* Lawrence University (B.A., 1956); University of Iowa (J.D., 1959). Member, Quad City Industrial Relations Society. *Member:* Rock Island County, Illinois State, Iowa State and American (Member, Labor Law Section) Bar Associations. **PRACTICE AREAS:** Employment and Labor Law. **Email:** rboeye@califf.com

DENNIS R. FOX, born Watseka, Illinois, November 9, 1939; admitted to bar, 1965, Illinois. *Education:* University of Illinois (B.S., 1961); Northwestern University (J.D., 1964). *Member:* Rock Island County (President, 1988-1989) and Illinois State Bar Associations. **PRACTICE AREAS:** Litigation and Insurance Law. **Email:** dfox@califf.com

JOHN A. SLOVER, JR., born Moline, Illinois, September 28, 1944; admitted to bar, 1969, Illinois. *Education:* Black Hawk College (A.A., 1964); University of Illinois (B.A., 1966; J.D., 1969). *Member:* Rock Island County, Illinois State, Iowa State and American

(This Listing Continued)

Bar Associations; Quad City Estate Planning Council (President, 2002-2003). ***PRACTICE AREAS:*** Advanced Estate Planning; Taxation; Business Entities; Charitable Organizations Law. ***Email:*** jslover@califf.com

THOMAS A. HARPER, born Moline, Illinois, April 5, 1950; admitted to bar, 1976, Illinois; 1985, Iowa and U.S. District Court, Central District of Illinois; 1986, U.S. Court of Appeals, Seventh Circuit. *Education:* Drake University (B.S., 1972; J.D., 1976). *Member:* Rock Island County, Illinois State and American Bar Associations. ***PRACTICE AREAS:*** Probate; Estate Planning; Banking; Real Estate; Elder Law. ***Email:*** tharper@califf.com

JEFFREY B. MOORHOUSE, born Fairfield, Iowa, June 24, 1945; admitted to bar, 1972, Iowa, U.S. District Court, Northern District of Iowa and U.S. Tax Court; 1980, Illinois; 1987, U.S. District Court, Central District of Illinois. *Education:* University of Iowa (B.B.A., 1967; J.D., 1972). Phi Delta Phi. *Member:* Rock Island County, Illinois State, Iowa State and American Bar Associations. ***PRACTICE AREAS:*** Corporation; Banking; Construction Law; Tax Law and Litigation. ***Email:*** jmoorhouse@califf.com

ROGER L. STRANDLUND, born Moline, Illinois, June 1, 1955; admitted to bar, 1981, Illinois and U.S. District Court, Central District of Illinois; 1982, Iowa and U.S. Court of Appeals, Seventh Circuit; 1992, U.S. Tax Court; 1995, U.S. District Court, Northern District of Illinois, including Trial Bar; 1996, U.S. Court of Appeals, Sixth Circuit; 1998, U.S. Supreme Court. *Education:* Iowa State University (B.S., magna cum laude, 1977); University of Iowa (J.D., 1981). Member: Rock Island County Building Board of Appeals, 1986—; Moline Planning Commission, 1989—. *Member:* Rock Island County, Scott County, Illinois State, Iowa State and American Bar Associations. ***PRACTICE AREAS:*** Litigation; Municipal Law; Construction Law. ***Email:*** strandlaw@califf.com

ARTHUR W. EGGERS, born Clinton, Iowa, August 1, 1952; admitted to bar, 1977, Nebraska and U.S. District Court, District of Nebraska; 1978, Iowa, Illinois and U.S. District Court, Southern District of Illinois; 1990, U.S. Court of Appeals, Eighth Circuit. *Education:* University of Iowa (B.B.A., 1974); Creighton Law School (J.D., 1977). *Member:* Rock Island County, Illinois State, Iowa State and American (Member, Labor Law Section) Bar Associations. ***PRACTICE AREAS:*** Employment and Labor Law. ***Email:*** aeggers@califf.com

HARVEY A. LEVIN, born Chicago, Illinois, May 14, 1943; admitted to bar, 1971, Illinois; 1972, U.S. Tax Court. *Education:* Michigan State University (B.A., with high honors, 1965); Northwestern University (J.D., 1968). Certified Public Accountant, Illinois, 1967. Senior Vice President, Chief Financial Officer, and General Counsel of Moline Paint Manufacturing, 1982-1994. *Member:* Rock Island and Illinois State Bar Associations; Airports Council International-N.A. Legal Committee (Chairman, 1990). ***PRACTICE AREAS:*** Corporate Law; Estate Planning; Taxation; Airport; Business Planning; Mergers and Acquisitions Law. ***Email:*** hlevin@califf.com

JAMES S. ZMUDA, born Moline, Illinois, September 29, 1964; admitted to bar, 1989, Illinois; 1990, Iowa. *Education:* University of Iowa (B.B.A., 1986); Northern Illinois University (J.D., cum laude, 1989). Recipient, American Jurisprudence Award in Civil Procedure. Lead Articles Editor, Northern Illinois University Law Review, 1988-1989. Author: Note, "Beyond Mite--CTS v. Dynamics: Has Management Won the Fight in the Battle Against the Tender Offer and What Injury Has the Individual Shareholder Suffered?" 9 N. Ill. U.L. Rev. 187 (1988). *Member:* Illinois State (Chairman, Committee on Federal Income Taxation), Iowa State and American Bar Associations. ***PRACTICE AREAS:*** Taxation; Business Planning; Estate Litigation. ***Email:*** jzmuda@califf.com

JONATHON C. FOX, born Moline, Illinois, February 7, 1969; admitted to bar, 1996, Illinois and U.S. District Court, Central District of Illinois; 1997, Iowa. *Education:* Indiana University (B.A., 1991); Salmon P. Chase College of Law, Northern Kentucky University (J.D., 1996). Recipient, CALI Excellence Award for Achievement in the Study of Bankruptcy, 1995. *Member:* Rock Island County, Illinois State, Iowa State and American Bar Associations. ***PRACTICE AREAS:*** Litigation; Banking Law; Creditor Rights. ***Email:*** jfox@califf.com

FRANKLIN S. MITVALSKY, born Cedar Rapids, Iowa, July 17, 1972; admitted to bar, 1998, Illinois; 1999, Iowa. *Education:* Northwestern University (B.A., 1995); University of Iowa (J.D., with distinction, 1998). Member, Journal of Corporation Law, 1996-1998. *Member:* Rock Island County, Illinois State and Iowa State Bar Associations; Quad City Estate Planning Council. ***PRACTICE AREAS:*** Corporate Law; Business Planning; Estate Planning; Estate Administration; Litigation. ***Email:*** fmitvalsky@califf.com

---

KARLA C. STEELE, born March 22, 1970; admitted to bar, 2002, Illinois; 2003, Iowa and U.S. District Court, Central District of Illinois. *Education:* San Diego State University (B.A., cum laude, Phi Beta Kappa, 1997); University of Iowa (J.D./M.B.A., 2002). *Member:* Rock Island County, Scott County, Illinois State, Iowa State and American Bar Associations. ***LANGUAGES:*** Spanish. ***PRACTICE AREAS:*** Real Estate; Business Law; Estate Planning; Labor and Employment; Landlord and Tenant Law; Creditors Rights. ***Email:*** ksteele@califf.com

OF COUNSEL

JAMES A. HARPER, born Moline, Illinois, June 28, 1917; admitted to bar, 1942, Illinois. *Education:* University of Michigan (A.B., 1939; J.D., 1942). *Member:* Rock Island County (President, 1980-1981) and Illinois State Bar Associations.

REPRESENTATIVE CLIENTS: *CORPORATE:* Deere & Company; Mid-American Energy; Mel Foster Co.; Murphy Bros., Inc.; H.C. Duke & Son, Inc.; Thoms-Proestler Co., Inc.; The Marthens Co.; Terrace Holding Co.; Serv-A-Lite Products, Inc.; Hiland Auto Sales, Inc.; Fort Dearborn Company; Trinity Medical Center; Parr Instrument Company; Packaging Technologies. *REAL ESTATE, CONSTRUCTION AND DEVELOPMENT:* Contracting Corp. of Illinois; Renew Moline, Inc.; L & S Real Estate, Inc.; Axiom Properties, Inc.; Heritage Realty Management, Inc.; Revitalize and Develop East Moline,Inc. *LABOR LAW AND EMPLOYMENT:* Associated Employers of the Quad Cities; RiverStoneGroup, Inc.; Norcross Footwear, Inc.; Krieder Services, Inc.; Rock Island County, Illinois; Scott County, Iowa; Warren County, Illinois; Mercer County, Illinois; City of Moline, Illinois; City of East Moline, Illinois; City of Rock Island, Illinois. *FINANCIAL INSTITUTIONS:* First Midwest Bank, N.A.; I.H. Mississippi Valley Credit Union; Valley Bank, Metrobank. *SCHOOLS:* East Moline Public School District; Rockridge School District; Augustana College (Planned Giving). *PUBLIC LAW:* MidAmerican Energy Company; Metropolitan Airport Authority of Rock Island County; Illinois Quad City Civic Center Authority; Mercer County Public Building Commission. *INSURANCE:* Travelers Insurance Co.; Chubb Group of Insurance Cos.; Sentry Insurance; CNA Insurance Co.; Fireman's Fund Insurance Co.; Continental Western Insurance Group.

(This Listing Continued)

CHURCHILL & CHURCHILL, P.C.

Established in 1886

1610 FIFTH AVENUE

MOLINE, ILLINOIS 61265

Telephone: 309-762-3643; 762-3644

FAX: 309-762-4690

Email: cclaw@churchillfirm.com

URL: http://www.churchilllawfirm.com

General Civil Trial Practice in State and Federal Courts. Corporation, Business Law, Commercial, Banking, Real Estate, Probate and Bankruptcy Law, Trusts and Estates, Wills, Estate Planning, Taxation.

FIRM PROFILE: In 1886, J.B. Oakleaf, a member of a well regarded Moline family, started his practice of law and was joined in future years by his son, J.L. Oakleaf, Cyrus Churchill and Daniel Churchill. The firm today offers general legal services with concentration in business clients, real estate, estate planning and representation of financial institutions.

MEMBERS OF FIRM

J. B. OAKLEAF (1886-1930)

J. L. OAKLEAF (1905-1958)

CYRUS CHURCHILL (1903-1999)

DANIEL CHURCHILL, born Davenport, Iowa, March 3, 1943; admitted to bar, 1969, Illinois and Iowa. *Education:* Augustana College (B.A., 1965); University of Illinois (J.D., 1968). *Member:* Rock Island County, Illinois State, Iowa State and American Bar Associations. (President). ***PRACTICE AREAS:*** Litigation; Banking; Corporate; Commercial Law.

MARK D. CHURCHILL, born Moline, Illinois, June 10, 1977; admitted to bar, 2002, Illinois. *Education:* Butler University (B.S., 1999); University of Illinois (J.D., 2002). *Member:* Illinois State, Rock Island County and American Bar Associations. ***PRACTICE AREAS:*** Banking Law; Litigation; Corporate Law; Commercial Law.

LEGAL SUPPORT PERSONNEL

LYNN A. DOY, born Moline, Illinois, December 18, 1951. *Education:* Northern Illinois University (B.S., 1973). (Accountant/CPA). ***PRACTICE AREAS:*** Accounting and Tax Preparation.

PARALEGALS

ANNE MARIE MERRICK, born Dubuque, Iowa, May 6, 1960. *Education:* Black Hawk College (A.A.S., 1980). ***PRACTICE AREAS:*** Litigation Documentation; General Secretarial Responsibilities.

DEBBRA NORDQUIST, born Moline, Illinois, March 28, 1953. *Education:* Black Hawk College. ***PRACTICE AREAS:*** Real Estate Documentation; General Secretarial Responsibilities.

NANCY J. VAN VOLTENBURG, born Milwaukee, Wisconsin, June 24, 1957. *Education:* Black Hawk College (A.A.S., 1976). Recipient, 1984 Professional Legal Secretary Certificate from National Association of Legal Secretaries (International). Member, Rock Island Legal Secretaries Association, 1978-1987. ***PRACTICE AREAS:*** Estate Planning; Probate; Commercial Business Documentation.

REPRESENTATIVE CLIENTS: Bank One, N.A.; Southeast National Bank of Moline; 1st Community Bank; Moline Dispatch Publishing Co.; Roofing Technology, Inc.; Crippen, Reid & Bowen, CPA; Builders Sales & Service Co.; Western Structural Co.; Johnson Contracting Company, Inc.; Estes Company; Green Chevrolet, Inc.; Key Buick-Pontiac-AMC, Inc.; Kimberly Chrysler-Plymouth, Inc.; Moline Board of Education; Sherrard Community School District 200; Saelens Beverages, Inc.
REFERENCES: Bank One, N.A.; Southeast National Bank of Moline.

GOSMA, TARBOX & ASSOCIATES, P.L.C.

MOLINE, ILLINOIS

(See Davenport, Iowa)

General Civil Practice, including Business and Corporate Organization and Transactions, Banking, Real Estate, Estate Planning, Elder Law, Trust and Estate Administration, and Personal Injury, Business and Probate Litigation, Medical Malpractice, Business Enterprises, Slip and Fall, Personal Injury, Automobile Accidents, Wrongful Death, Buying and Selling, Zoning and Land Use, Construction, Asset Protection, Guardianships, Banking and Finance, Closely Held Business, Corporate, Franchise, Limited Liability, Small Business, Partnerships, Buying and Selling of Businesses, Creditors Rights, Contracts, Business Planning, Law Suites, Insurance, Commercial Leasing, Business Start-Ups.

STEVE HANNA
ATTORNEY AT LAW

Established in 1995

418 SIXTEENTH STREET

MOLINE, ILLINOIS 61265

Telephone: 309-797-9000

Fax: 309-762-0177

Email: steve@hanna-law.com

URL: http://www.hanna-law.com

Criminal Law, Driving While Intoxicated, Drug Crimes, Juvenile Criminal Law, Parole and Probation, Traffic Violations. Illinois, Iowa, Federal Practice.

(This Listing Continued)

STEVE HANNA ATTORNEY AT LAW, Moline—Continued

FIRM PROFILE: Illinois, Iowa, State and Federal Courts

Drug Cases - Many cases have resulted in dismissals due to the suppression of evidence. Over 3000 lbs. of drugs have been suppressed from introduction into evidence.

DUI - Hundreds of DUI cases have resulted in dismissals, favorable verdicts, suppression of test results, and minimum sentences.

Driving While Revoked or Suspended - Outcomes have included dismissals, favorable verdicts, and probable cause hearings where police were found to have violated constitutional rights. In many cases, jail sentences are avoided.

Theft - Many cases resulted in dismissals, acquittals, and reduction of charges. In some, states evidence was excluded due to illegal searches.

Drivers License Reinstatement - Hundreds of clients have had their drivers licenses returned after it has been revoked or suspended for years.

Sex Crimes - Results have been dismissals and minimum sentences, which have allowed clients to avoid the requirement to register as a sex offender for 10 years.

Traffic Case - Thousands of clients avoided suspension and revocation of drivers licenses through dismissals, acquittals, and minimum sentences. In addition, clients have avoided mandatory minimum jail sentences.

STEVE HANNA, born Moline, Illinois, August 4, 1954; admitted to bar, 1990, Iowa and Illinois; U.S. District Court, Central District of Illinois. *Education:* St. Ambrose College (B.A., 1986); University of Iowa College of Law; St. Louis University School of Law (J.D., 1990). *Member:* Rock Island County, Illinois and Iowa State Bar Associations; Bar Association of the Central and Southern Federal Districts of Illinois; Illinois Association of Criminal Defense Lawyers.

KATZ, HUNTOON & FIEWEGER, P.C.

Established in 1909

1000 36TH AVENUE

MOLINE, ILLINOIS 61265-7126

Telephone: 309-797-3000

Facsimile: 309-797-3330

Email: attorneys@katzlawfirm.com

URL: http://www.katzlawfirm.com

Civil Trial and Appellate Practice. Personal Injury, Insurance, Commercial, Banking, Bank and Savings and Loan Failures, Bankruptcy, Corporation, Probate, Real Estate, Labor Relations, Taxation, Professional Malpractice, Products Liability, Workers Compensation, Employment, Administrative, Public, School and Municipal Law and Business Crimes.

FIRM PROFILE: Katz, Huntoon & Fieweger, P.C., was founded in 1909. The firm's attorneys offer extensive experience and expertise in a variety of areas of law with licensed attorneys in both Illinois and Iowa. Its litigation and appellate lawyers have successfully handled cases at all levels of the judicial system, including oral arguments in the United States Supreme Court. Since its inception, the firm has maintained a tradition of providing quality legal services with a commitment of accessibility and responsiveness to its clients.

ISADOR I. KATZ (1905-1996)

MARTIN H. KATZ, born Moline, Illinois, May 7, 1937; admitted to bar, 1962, Illinois and U.S. District Court, Central District of Illinois; 1980, U.S. Court of Appeals, Seventh Circuit. *Education:* Augustana College (B.A., magna cum laude, 1959); Northwestern University (J.D., 1962). Phi Delta Phi; Phi Beta Kappa. Member, Review Board, Attorneys Registration and Discipline Commission, 1991—. *Member:* Rock Island County and Illinois State Bar Associations; Illinois Defense Counsel. Fellow: American College of Trial Lawyers; Illinois Bar Foundation. ***PRACTICE AREAS:*** Civil Trials and Appeals; Products Liability Law; Medical Malpractice; Insurance Law; Business Litigation. ***Email:*** attorneys@katzlawfirm.com

PETER C. FIEWEGER, born Davenport, Iowa, December 23, 1934; admitted to bar, 1962, Illinois, Iowa and U.S. District Court, Central District of Illinois; 1971, U.S. Court of Appeals, Seventh Circuit. *Education:* University of Notre Dame (B.S., cum laude, 1956); Northwestern University School of Law (J.D., 1962). Adjunct Faculty Member. Instructor, Health Law, College of St. Francis, 1989-1992. Assistant State's Attorney, Rock Island County, Illinois, 1965. Arbitrator, American Arbitrators Association. *Member:* Rock Island County (Vice President, 1984-1985; President, 1986-1987) and Illinois State Bar Associations. ***PRACTICE AREAS:*** Civil Trials and Appeals; Personal Injury Law; Medical Malpractice; Employment and Labor Law. ***Email:*** attorneys@katzlawfirm.com

FRANK R. EDWARDS, born Rock Island, Illinois, September 15, 1931; admitted to bar, 1958, Illinois and U.S. District Court, Central District of Illinois. *Education:* University of Notre Dame (B.A., cum laude, 1953); University of Illinois (LL.B., 1958). Phi Delta Phi. *Member:* Rock Island County (Vice President, 1992-1993; President, 1994-1995) and Illinois State Bar Associations. ***PRACTICE AREAS:*** Real Estate Law; Probate Law; Estate Planning Law. ***Email:*** attorneys@katzlawfirm.com

H. KARL HUNTOON, born Davenport, Iowa, December 19, 1949; admitted to bar, 1975, Illinois and U.S. District Court, Central District of Illinois; 1976, U.S. Tax Court; 1992, Iowa. *Education:* University of Illinois (B.S., with honors, 1972; J.D., 1975). *Member:* Rock Island County (Secretary-Treasurer, 1988-1989; Vice President, 1990-1991; President, 1992-1993), *Scott County, Illinois State (Member, Real Estate Section Council,* 1992-1999) and Iowa State Bar Associations. (Resident). ***PRACTICE AREAS:*** Real Estate Law; Business Law; Probate; Estate Planning. ***Email:*** khuntoon@katzlawfirm.com

DALE G. HAAKE, born Wauconda, Illinois, May 14, 1952; admitted to bar, 1979, Illinois and U.S. District Court, Central District of Illinois; 1983, U.S. Court of Appeals, Seventh Circuit; 1991, Iowa. *Education:* Sorbonne University, Paris, France (Diplôme, 1973); Augustana College (B.A., cum laude, 1974); University of Illinois (J.D., 1979). Co-Recipient, Harry A. Blackmun *Pro Bono Award,* 1988. Member, Legal Service, Commission of the European Communities, 1980. Instructor, European Community Law, Augustana College, 1981. Member, Board of Directors, 1989—, Prairie State Legal Services, Inc. Member, 1989—and President, 1992-1994, Iowa-Illinois International Trade Association. *Member:* Rock Island County, Illinois State and American Bar Associations; International Association of Young Lawyers. ***LANGUAGES:*** French and Spanish. ***PRACTICE AREAS:*** Bankruptcy Law; Commercial Law; International Law; Immigration Law; Thrift Institution Law. ***Email:*** dhaake@katzlawfirm.com

FRANK L. NOWINSKI, born Chicago, Illinois, June 5, 1955; admitted to bar, 1980, Illinois; 1982, U.S. District Court, Central District of Illinois, 1986, Iowa. *Education:* Augustana College (B.A., cum laude, 1977); Loyola University (J.D., 1980). *Member:* Rock Island County, Scott County, Illinois State and Iowa State Bar Associations. (Resident). ***PRACTICE AREAS:*** Real Estate Law; Business Law; Bankruptcy. ***Email:*** fnowinski@katzlawfirm.com

BRIAN S. NELSON, born Harvey, Illinois, May 22, 1961; admitted to bar, 1986, Illinois; 1987, U.S. District Court, Central District of Illinois; 1990, U.S. Court of Appeals, Seventh Circuit. *Education:* Augustana College (B.A., 1983); Valparaiso University (J.D., 1986). *Member:* Rock Island County, Illinois State and American Bar Associations; Illinois Trial Lawyers Association; The Association of Trial Lawyers of America. ***PRACTICE AREAS:*** Civil Trials and Appeals; Civil Rights Litigation; Municipal Law; Law Enforcement Litigation; Criminal Law. ***Email:*** bnelson@katzlawfirm.com

STEPHEN T. FIEWEGER, born Chicago, Illinois, December 16, 1961; admitted to bar, 1987, Illinois; 1988, U.S. District Court, Central District of Illinois; 1989, Iowa and U.S. Court of Appeals, Seventh Circuit. *Education:* University of Notre Dame (B.B.A., 1984); Northern Illinois University (J.D., cum laude, 1987). Staff Member, Northern Illinois University Law Review, 1986-1987. *Member:* Rock Island County, Scott County, Illinois State, Iowa State and American Bar Associations. ***PRACTICE AREAS:*** Civil Trials and Appeals Law; Personal Injury Law; Employment Law; Civil Rights Litigation. ***Email:*** sfieweger@katzlawfirm.com

JOHN F. DOAK, born Urbana, Illinois, May 21, 1965; admitted to bar, 1990, Illinois and U.S. District Court, Central District of Illinois; 1991, Iowa; 1992, U.S. Court of Appeals, Seventh Circuit. *Education:* Augustana College (B.A., cum laude, 1987); University of Illinois (J.D., cum laude, 1990). *Member:* Rock Island County, Scott County, Illinois State and Iowa State Bar Associations; Illinois Defense Counsel; Illinois Trial Lawyers Association. ***PRACTICE AREAS:*** Civil Trials and Appeals; Personal Injury Law; Environmental Law; Employment Law; Product Liability Law; Construction Litigation; Real Estate Litigation. ***Email:*** jdoak@katzlawfirm.com

THOMAS E. CADY, born Rock Island, Illinois, October 16, 1965; admitted to bar, 1996, Illinois; 1997, Iowa and U.S. District Court, Central District of Illinois. *Education:* Western Illinois University (B.S., Law Enforcement Administration, 1987); Northern Illinois University (J.D., 1996). Northern Illinois University Law Review, 1994-1996. ***PRACTICE AREAS:*** General Litigation; Workers Compensation. ***Email:*** tcady@katzlawfirm.com

CHRISTINE A. GEUTHER, born Cincinnati, Ohio, July 14, 1971; admitted to bar, 1996, Illinois and U.S. District Court, Central District of Illinois; 1997, Iowa. *Education:* University of Iowa (B.A., 1993); Northern Illinois University (J.D., 1996). *Member:* Rock Island County, Illinois State and Iowa State Bar Associations. (Resident). ***PRACTICE AREAS:*** Real Estate Law; Business Law; Family Law. ***Email:*** cgeuther@katzlawfirm.com

ATTORNEYS FOR: Augustana College; Bethany Home; Illinois Hospital; Swords Veneer; Economy Roofing and Insulating Co.
LOCAL ATTORNEYS FOR: International Truck and Engine Corp.; Maryland Casualty Co.; Liberty Mutual Insurance Co.; General Casualty Co. of Wisconsin; Pekin Insurance, Pekin, Ill.; Country Mutual Insurance Co.; CIGNA Cos.; Farmers Insurance Group; The Home Insurance Co.; Medical Protective Assn.; Fireman's Fund; West Bend Insurance; St. Paul Insurance; Clark Equipment Co.; Navistar International; Illinois Municipal League Risk Management Assn.; Essex; Indiana Lumbermens Mutual; Rockford Mutual Insurance.

PHILIP E. KOENIG

MOLINE, ILLINOIS

(See Rock Island)

Wills and Probate, Estate Planning, Real Estate, Business Organization, Tax, Bankruptcy, Commercial Real Estate, Commercial Bankruptcy, Trusts and Estates and General Civil Practice, including Trials and Appeals.

LAREAU LAW OFFICE

3551 7TH STREET, SUITE 206

MOLINE, ILLINOIS 61265

Telephone: 309-764-0775

Fax: 309-764-0975

URL: http://www.lareaulaw.com

HECTOR L. LAREAU, born Dekalb, Illinois, December 23, 1963; admitted to bar, 1993, Iowa; 1994, Illinois. *Education:* Parkland College; University of Illinois (B.A., 1989); Drake University (J.D., with honors, 1993). Delta Theta Phi. Author, "Rights of Surface Owners on Federally Patented Lands," 10 U. Ky. J. Natural Resources & Environ. L 13 (1995). Arbitrator, 14th Judicial Circuit. Member, Catholic Charities Community Advisory Board. Member, 1996-1998 and Chairman, 1998-1999, OSF St. Anthony's Continuing Care Center Foundation Council. Member, 1994 and Member, Board of Directors, 1998-2000, Rock Island Noon Kiwanis. *Member:* Rock Island County, Scott County, Iowa State and Illinois State (Council Member, Education Law Section, 2003) Bar Associations; Illinois Council of School Attorneys (Member, Executive Committee, 2002-2003). ***PRACTICE AREAS:*** Education Law; Commercial Litigation; Labor and Employment Law.

(This Listing Continued)

REPRESENTATIVE CLIENTS: Rock Island-Milan School District; Moline School District; Quad City Bank & Trust Co.; Miller Container Corporation; FKI Industries; QC Bankard.

McCARTHY, CALLAS, FUHR & ELLISON, P.C.

MOLINE, ILLINOIS

(See Rock Island)

Divorce, Commercial and Residential Real Estate, Labor Law, Labor Relations, Labor Arbitration, Commercial Litigation, Criminal Defense, Probate and Probate Administration, Inheritance, Dram Shop Law, Liquor Liability, Casualty Insurance, Medical Negligence, Debtor/Creditor Bankruptcy, ERISA, Personal Injury, Wrongful Death, Maritime Accidents, Products Liability, Traffic Violations.

PAPPAS & SCHNELL, P.C.

MOLINE, ILLINOIS

(See Rock Island)

Labor and Employment, Litigation, Trusts and Estates, Probate, Taxation, Corporate, Business Law, Real Estate, Education.

SHARON L. PULSIFER

3325 AVENUE OF THE CITIUS
MOLINE, ILLINOIS 61265
Telephone: 309-762-6831
Fax: 309-736-3034
Email: slpattorney@sbcglobal.net
URL: http://www.attorneypulsifer.com

Family Law, Bankruptcy, Adoptions, Child Custody, Child Support, Divorce, Domestic Violence, Visitation Rights, Divorce, Real Estate, Wills and Probate.

SHARON L. PULSIFER, admitted to bar, 1980, Illinois. *Education:* St. Ambrose College (B.A., 1975); University of Illinois (J.D., 1979). Alpha Chi. Formerly with Jackson, Pulsifer & Jackson. ***PRACTICE AREAS:*** Family Law; Bankruptcy.

SNYDER, PARK & NELSON, P.C.

MOLINE, ILLINOIS

(See Rock Island)

Banking, Bankruptcy, Commercial, Corporation, General Civil Litigation in all State and Federal Courts, Insurance, Labor Law, Probate, Real Estate, Taxation, Estate Planning, Trials, Employment Law, Workers Compensation, Construction and Commercial Litigation and Administrative Law.

STANLEY, LANDE & HUNTER

A PROFESSIONAL CORPORATION

MOLINE, ILLINOIS

(See Davenport, Iowa)

General Civil and Trial Practice. Corporation, Business, Banking, Taxation, Securities, Tax-Exempt Financing, Labor, Employment Discrimination, Administrative, Creditor Bankruptcy and Agricultural Law, Insurance Defense, Personal Injury and Property Damage Law, Pension and Profit-Sharing, Real Estate, Probate, Estate Planning and Charitable Trusts and Foundations Law.

WINSTEIN, KAVENSKY & WALLACE

MOLINE, ILLINOIS

(See Rock Island)

General Civil Practice in all State and Federal Courts. Trial and Appellate Practice. Personal Injury, Products Liability, Labor, Workers Compensation, Matrimonial, Criminal, Bankruptcy, Probate, Real Estate and Commercial Litigation Law.

TINA M. OLTON

114 N. DIXIE STREET
P.O. BOX 39
MOMENCE, ILLINOIS 60954
Telephone: 815-472-2417
Fax: 815-472-2477
Email: oltonlaw@aol.com
URL: http://www.tinaolton.com

Real Estate, Social Security Disability, Family Law, Divorce, Child Custody, Bankruptcy, Wills, Probate.

TINA M. OLTON, born East Chicago, Indiana, March 31, 1956; admitted to bar, 1981, Illinois. *Education:* Ball State University (B.S., 1978); Indiana University (J.D., 1981). *Member:* Kankakee County, Illinois State and American Bar Associations.

BEAL, PRATT & PRATT

57 SOUTHEAST PUBLIC SQUARE
P.O. BOX 200
MONMOUTH, ILLINOIS 61462-0200
Telephone: 309-734-3193
Telecopier: 309-734-7279
Email: attys@bealprattlaw.com

General Civil and Trial Practice. Probate, Estate Planning, Real Estate, Insurance, Personal Injury, Corporation and Municipal Law.

FIRM PROFILE: Beal, Pratt & Pratt serves clients throughout Warren, Henderson, Knox, McDonough, Mercer and surrounding counties. The firm is a general practice firm with a focus on Estate, Probate, Real Estate and Civil Trial work.

MEMBERS OF FIRM

EDWARD B. LOVE (1906-1972)

MARION L. BEAL (1922-1999)

CHANNING L. PRATT, born Monmouth, Illinois, March 17, 1929; admitted to bar, 1954, Indiana; 1958, Illinois. *Education:* Monmouth College (A.B., 1951); Indiana University (J.D., 1954). Phi Delta Phi. Monmouth College, Senate, 1991—; President, Warren County, Y.M.C.A., 1963-1964. State's Attorney, 1964-1968. Assistant Attorney General, 1972-1975. Counsel, City of Monmouth, 1973-1981. *Member:* Warren County (President, 1965-1966; 1982-1983), and American Bar Associations. ***PRACTICE AREAS:*** Corporate Organization Law; Civil Litigation; Trusts and Estates Law.

JANE HARTLEY PRATT, born Kankakee, Illinois, May 19, 1930; admitted to bar, 1955, Indiana; 1957, Illinois. *Education:* Franklin College of Indiana (A.B., cum laude, 1952); Indiana University (J.D., 1955). Author: "Independent Administration" Chapter in Illinois Estate Administration, Illinois Institute for Continuing Education, 1993. Instructor, Business Law, Monmouth College, 1973-1979. Member, Board of Directors, Security Savings Bank, 1979-2002. *Member:* Warren County (President, 1967-1968 and 1986-1987), Illinois State (Secretary, Trusts and Estate Council, 1961-1965; 1997, 1998; Chair, 2000-2001) and American Bar Associations. Fellow, American College of Trust and Estate Counsel. ***PRACTICE AREAS:*** Trusts and Estates Law; Charitable Trusts and Foundations; Real Estate.

REPRESENTATIVE CLIENTS: Village of Roseville; Alexis and Biggsville Fire Protection Districts; Wells Fargo Bank, Monmouth.
REFERENCES: Midwest Bank of Western Illinois, Monmouth; Wells Fargo Bank, Monmouth; Community National Bank, Monmouth; Security Savings Bank, Monmouth.

STANSELL, WHITMAN & BABER

Established in 1919

203 EAST BROADWAY
P.O. BOX 408
MONMOUTH, ILLINOIS 61462
Telephone: 309-734-7926
Fax: 309-734-7929
Email: swb@lawyer.com
URL: http://www.lawyers.com/swb

Personal Injury, Banking, Bankruptcy, Collections, Criminal, Divorce, Probate and Wills, Real Estate, Workers Compensation Law. Civil Litigation.

FIRM PROFILE: Stansell, Whitman & Baber was originally founded by John Kritzer in 1919, Serving Clients throughout Warren, Knox, Henderson, Mercer, McDonough and surrounding counties. The firm has general practice with sub specialties that the members of the firm maintain expertise in.

MEMBERS OF FIRM

THEODORE L. STANSELL (Retired 2002)

KENNETH E. CRITSER (1928-1983)

MR. RICHARD L. WHITMAN, SR., born Peoria, Illinois, January 11, 1947; admitted to bar, 1972, Illinois. *Education:* Eastern Illinois University (B.A., 1969); Northwestern University (J.D., cum laude, 1972). Valedictorian, E.I.U., 1969. Order of the Coif. Editor, Northwestern Law Review, 1971-1972. Author: "Implied Warranty in Sale of New Home," Illinois Trial Lawyer Journal, Fall, 1979; "Warranties in the Purchase of a New Residence," Illinois Trial Lawyers Journal, Fall, 1979; "Actions in Accounting," a chapter in Equitable Remedies in Chancery, Illinois Institute for Continuing Legal Education, 1978, 1982, 1989, 1992 and 2001. Instructor, Business Law, Monmouth College, 1978—. Mediator. Member, National Arbitration Forum. *Member:* Warren County (President, 1977-1978) and Illinois State Bar Associations; Illinois Trial Lawyers Association. ***LANGUAGES:*** Spanish. ***PRACTICE AREAS:*** Civil Litigation; Bankruptcy; Real Estate; Probate; Corporate Law; School Law; Estate Planning; Family Law; Noncompetition Law; Criminal Defense; Personal Injury; Medical Malpractice. ***Email:*** swb@lawyer.com

MR. JAMES G. BABER, born Freeport, Illinois, September 11, 1961; admitted to bar, 1986, Illinois. *Education:* Highland Community College; Southern Illinois University (B.A., 1983; J.D., 1986). Author and Editor, Southern Illinois Law Journal, 1984-1986. Law Clerk, Illinois Appellate Court, Third District, 1987-1992. Member, Monmouth Planning Commission, 1987-1994. Member, Board of Directors, West Central Illinois Legal Assistance, 1990-1994. Member Monmouth Noon Lion's Club, 1992—. *Member:* Warren County (President, 1990-1991), Illinois State and American Bar Associations. ***PRACTICE AREAS:*** Personal Injury; Workers Compensation; Criminal Defense Law; Family Law; Collections. ***Email:*** swb@lawyer.com

(This Listing Continued)

STANSELL, WHITMAN & BABER, Monmouth—Continued

MR. THOMAS R. SIEGEL, born Chicago, Illinois, November 4, 1977; admitted to bar, 2003, Illinois. *Education:* Monmouth College (B.A., cum laude, 1999); Northern Illinois University (J.D., cum laude, 2002). Instructor, Constitutional Law, Monmouth College, Spring 2004. *Member:* Warren County (Treasurer, 2004-2005) and Illinois State Bar Associations. ***PRACTICE AREAS:*** Civil Litigation; Bankruptcy; Real Estate; Personal Injury; Collections; Criminal Defense; Civil Appeals; Criminal Appeals. ***Email:*** swb@lawyer.com

REPRESENTATIVE CLIENTS: Midwest Bank of Western Illinois; Monmouth Feed Service, Inc.; Monmouth Grain and Dryer; Riverland F.S.; Liberty Publishing; Warren School District; Monmouth School District; Swan, Coldbrook and Monmouth Townships; Monmouth College; Monmouth Park District; Warren County Housing Authority; Alexis Heights Finance; Warren County Public Library; Tompkins State Bank.
REFERENCES: Midwest Bank of Western Illinois; Marquette Bank; Community Security Savings Bank, all of Monmouth, Ill.

BECKETT & WEBBER, P.C.

MONTICELLO, ILLINOIS

(See Urbana)

General, Trial, Appellate and Federal Practice, Criminal, Personal Injury, Family, Probate and Estate Planning Law, DWI, Traffic Violations, Wills, Child Support, Divorce, Child Custody, Adoption, Workers Compensation, Real Estate, Elder Law.

MEYER CAPEL

A PROFESSIONAL CORPORATION

MONTICELLO, ILLINOIS

(See Champaign)

General Civil Litigation, Corporate Law, Business Law, Estate Planning, Estate Administration, Real Estate, Tax, Telecommunications and Public Utility, Intellectual Property Law, Labor and Employment Law (Management), Municipal Law, Family Law, Health Care Law, Personal Injury, Products Liability Law, Criminal Law, Social Security Disability, Software Licensing, Education Law.

SHONKWILER, AYERS & RHOADES

114 SOUTH CHARTER STREET
MONTICELLO, ILLINOIS 61856
Telephone: 217-762-3661
Fax: 217-762-8199
Email: ayers@prairienet.net
URL: http://www.lawyers.com/sarlaw

General Civil Trial Practice. Probate, Real Estate, Tax, Estate Planning, Corporate and Family Law.

MEMBERS OF FIRM

JAMES L. AYERS, born Decatur, Illinois, January 13, 1948; admitted to bar, 1972, Oklahoma; 1973, Illinois. *Education:* University of Illinois (B.S., 1970); University of Tulsa (J.D., 1972). Mayor, City of Monticello, 1993-2001. *Member:* Piatt County, Oklahoma, Illinois State and American Bar Associations. [With U.S. Air Force, 1972-1976]. ***PRACTICE AREAS:*** Probate; Wills; Trusts; Trial Practice.

DANA RHOADES, born Leavenworth, Kansas, July 21, 1970; admitted to bar, 1995, Illinois. *Education:* Illinois State University (B.S., 1992); Loyola University (J.D., 1995). *Member:* Piatt County, Illinois State and American Bar Association. ***PRACTICE AREAS:*** Real Estate; Estate Planning; Criminal Law; Probate.

REPRESENTATIVE CLIENTS: Bank One of Monticello; First State Bank of Monticello; Hammond State Bank; State Bank of Bement; Central Illinois Manfacturing Co.

BRENNER, FORD, MONROE & SCOTT, LTD.

MORRIS, ILLINOIS

(See Chicago)

Insurance Defense, Personal Injury, Medical Malpractice, Construction Law, Product Liability, Uninsured/Underinsured Motorist Arbitrations and Litigation of Contested Coverage Issues.

FABRIZIO, HANSON, PEYLA & KAWINSKI, P.C.

MORRIS, ILLINOIS

(See Joliet)

General Civil and Trial Practice. Insurance Defense, Personal Injury, Automobile Accidents, Products Liability, Wrongful Death, Construction Accidents, Workers Compensation, Corporate, Business, Probate, Real Estate, Health Care and Construction Litigation.

LAW OFFICES OF LEYNAUD & LEYNAUD

A PROFESSIONAL CORPORATION

MORRIS, ILLINOIS

(See Peru)

General Civil and Trial Practice, Personal Injury, Mediation, Worker's Compensation, Real Estate, Criminal, Landlord/Tenant and Family Law. Business/Banking Litigation, DUI and Traffic. Insurance, General Practice, Medical Malpractice, Zoning and Land Use. Bad Faith, Drug Crimes, Juvenile Crimes, White Collar, Adoptions, Child Custody, Divorce, Child Support, Visitation Rights, Domestic Violence. Auto Accidents, Dog Bites, Slip and Fall, Wrongful Death, Buying and Selling, Wills and Probate.

LAW OFFICES OF HAROLD L. TURNER

MORRISON, ILLINOIS

(See Rockford)

Personal Injury including Automobile Accidents and Injuries, Head, Neck and Back Injuries, Medical Malpractice including Misdiagnosis and Failure to Diagnose, Birth Injuries, Cancer, Obstetric, Surgical, Cardiac, Orthopedic and Nursing Malpractice, Nursing Home Abuse and Neglect including Bedsores, Malnutrition, Dehydration, Wandering, Falls, Fractures, Physical, Verbal and Sexual Abuse and Assault, Legal Ethics and Professional Responsibility including Professional Malpractice, Legal Malpractice, Mediation and Arbitration.

CUTLER & ASSOCIATES, LTD.

MORTON GROVE, ILLINOIS

(See Skokie)

Bankruptcy, Consumer Bankruptcy, Bankruptcy Chapter 7, Foreclosures, Small Business, Buying and Selling of Businesses, Family Business, Limited Liability, Partnership, Corporate, Contract, Breach of Contract, General Practice, Debtor and Creditor, Collections, Creditors, Rights and Civil Litigation.

JAY A. SLUTZKY

MORTON GROVE, ILLINOIS

(See Niles)

Wills, Living Trusts, Estate Planning, Residential Real Estate, Commercial Real Estate, Divorce, Personal Injury, Bankruptcy Law, Elder Law, DUI, DWI, Business Law, Commercial Law, Commercial Litigation, Business Organization, Business Transactions, Business Counseling, Business Advice, Real Estate Law, Real Estate Litigation, Commercial Transactions, Contracts, Construction Law, Litigation, Motor Vehicle Accidents, Personal Injury Defense, Plaintiffs Personal Injury, Probate, Estate Administration, Trusts, By-Pass Trusts, Credit Shelter Trusts, Special Needs Trusts, Testamentary Trusts, Ancillar Administration, Durable Powers of Attorney, Medical Powers of Attorney, Living Wills, Pour-Over Wills, Marital Deduction Trusts, Beneficiary Designations, Irrevocable Life Insurance Trusts, Split Dollar Purchase Agreements, Crummey Trusts, Workers Compensation, Civil Litigation, Criminal Defense, Pre-Marital Agreements, Planning for Disabled Spouses, Planning for Disabled Children, Estate Tax Return Preparation, Second Marriage Issues, Contested Wills and Trusts, Partnerships, Corporations, Limited Liability Companies.

KRUGER, HENRY & HUNTER

MOUND CITY, ILLINOIS

(See Metropolis)

Civil and Criminal Trial and Appellate Practice. Negligence, Product Liability, Wrongful Death, Workman's Compensation, Criminal, Family, Real Estate, Corporate, Probate, Bankruptcy, Divorce, Driving While Intoxicated.

RHINE, ERNEST & VARGO

Established in 1979

631 MARKET STREET
MOUNT CARMEL, ILLINOIS 62863-1489
Telephone: 618-262-8611
Fax: 618-262-7145
Email: information@rhinelaw.com
URL: http://www.rhinelaw.com

Evansville, Indiana Office: Old National Place, One Main Street, Suite 600, 47708. Telephone: 812-759-0600. Fax: 812-759-0601.

Coal, Oil and Gas Law, Real Estate, Corporate, Civil Trial Practice, Wills and Estates, Environmental Law.

MEMBERS OF FIRM

JOHN E. RHINE, born Eldorado, Illinois, November 12, 1952; admitted to bar, 1977, Illinois; 1979, U.S. District Court, Southern District of Illinois; 1985, U.S. Court of Appeals, Seventh Circuit. *Education:* Southern Illinois University (B.A., 1974); University of Illinois (J.D., magna cum laude, 1977). Order of the Coif. Law Clerk to Justice Robert C. Underwood, Illinois Supreme Court, 1977-1978. Special Assistant Attorney General, 1980-1983. Chairman, Voices for Illinois Children, 1993-1996. Visiting Professor of Law, Moscow State Institute for International Relations (MGIMO), 1993, 1995. *Member:* Illi-

(This Listing Continued)

nois State Bar Association (Member, Mineral Law Section Council, 1993—, Chairman, 1999-2000). *PRACTICE AREAS:* Coal; Oil and Gas Law; Real Estate; Corporate Finance; Commercial Litigation. **Email:** jrhine@rhinelaw.com

STANTON D. ERNEST, born Salem, Illinois, January 19, 1950; admitted to bar, 1977, Illinois; 1978, U.S. District Court, Southern District of Illinois; 1991, U.S. Supreme Court; 1993, U.S. District Court, Southern District of Indiana; 1999, Kentucky; 2004, Indiana. *Education:* University of Illinois (B.S., 1974); Hamline University (J.D., cum laude, 1976). *Member:* Illinois State Bar Association (Member, Mineral Law Section Council, 2000—). [With: U.S. Army, 1969-1971; Judge Advocate General's Corps., U.S. Naval Reserve, 1983—]. *PRACTICE AREAS:* Estate Planning; Business Planning; Estate and Trust Administration; Civil Litigation; Coal, Oil and Gas Law. **Email:** ernestsd@rhinelaw.com

JOSEPH F. VARGO, born Cincinnati, Ohio, September 24, 1954; admitted to bar, 1989, Illinois. *Education:* University of Kentucky (B.S.C.E., Mining Option, 1976); Southern Illinois University (J.D., 1988). Tau Beta Pi; Chi Epsilon; Phi Alpha Delta. Recipient, American Jurisprudence Award in Agricultural Law. *Member:* Wabash County and Illinois State Bar Associations. *PRACTICE AREAS:* Coal; Oil and Gas Law; Real Estate; Civil Litigation; Adoption; Family Law. **Email:** jvargo@rhinelaw.com

WILLIAM C. ILLINGWORTH, born Greencastle, Indiana, January 16, 1973; admitted to bar, 1999, Illinois, Indiana, U.S. District Courts, Northern and Southern Districts of Indiana and U.S. District Court, Southern District of Illinois; 2004, U.S. Court of Appeals, Sixth Circuit. *Education:* University of Southern Indiana (B.S., 1996); University of North Dakota (J.D., with distinction, 1999). Order of the Coif. *Member:* Wabash County (President), Indiana State and Illinois State Bar Associations. *PRACTICE AREAS:* Civil Litigation; Coal, Oil and Gas Law; Real Estate; Estate Planning. **Email:** illingworth@rhinelaw.com

ASSOCIATES

WILLIAM EASTON, JR., born Gillespie, Illinois, September 7, 1964; admitted to bar, 2002, Illinois. *Education:* Southern Illinois University (B.S., 1986); University of Illinois (M.Ed., 1989); University of North Dakota (J.D., 2001). Order of Barristers. Member, North Dakota Law Review. *Member:* Wabash County (Secretary) Bar Association; The American Trial Lawyers Association. *PRACTICE AREAS:* Civil Litigation; Family Law. **Email:** easton@rhinelaw.com

BRANDON S. RENNER, born Springfield, Illinois, September 1, 1974; admitted to bar, 2004, Indiana and U.S. District Court, Northern and Southern Districts of Indiana; 2005, Illinois. *Education:* Southern Illinois University (B.A., cum laude, 2000); The John Marshall Law School (J.D., 2003). Phi Kappa Phi. *Member:* Indianapolis, Evansville, Indiana State and American Bar Associations. [U.S. Navy, 1993-1997]. *PRACTICE AREAS:* Civil Litigation; Coal, Oil and Gas Law; Estate Planning. **Email:** brenner@rhinelaw.com

SHANNON L. PRICE, born Edwardsville, Illinois, February 24, 1979; admitted to bar, 2004, Illinois. *Education:* Grinnell College (B.A., 2001); University of Illinois College of Law (J.D., 2004). *Member:* Wabash County and Illinois State Bar Associations. *PRACTICE AREAS:* Civil Litigation; Coal, Oil and Gas Law. **Email:** slprice@rhinelaw.com

CHRISTINE ST. JOHN, born Wheeling, West Virginia, August 8, 1956; admitted to bar, 1991, Ohio; 1992, West Virginia; 2001, Illinois. *Education:* Wheeling Jesuit College (B.S.B.A., summa cum laude, 1988); West Virginia University (J.D., cum laude, 1991). Member: Order of the Coif, Trial Advocacy; West Virginia Mineral Law Foundation. Licensed Mediator, State of Ohio. *PRACTICE AREAS:* Coal; Oil and Gas Law; Mineral Rights; Property Rights; Real Estate Title; Mediation; Employment Practices Liability Insurance; Business Law. **Email:** cstjohn@rhinelaw.com

MELISSA J. GREENLEE, born Olney, Illinois, January 1, 1978; admitted to bar, 2004, Indiana and U.S. District Court, Northern and Southern Districts of Indiana (Not admitted in Illinois). *Education:* University of Illinois, Urbana-Champaign (B.S., 2000); Indiana University School of Law (J.D., 2004). *Member:* Evansville and Indiana State Bar Associations. *PRACTICE AREAS:* Civil Litigation; Coal, Oil and Gas Law. **Email:** mgreenlee@rhinelaw.com

REPRESENTATIVE CLIENTS: Foundation Coal Company; Southern Illinois Land Company; Sahara Coal Trust; Sahara Enterprises; Cline Resources and Development; Kieffer Bros. Construction Company; Royal Talon; Old National Bank; Ayrshire Land Company; Vigo Coal Company; Wabash Mine Holding Company; Delta Mine Holding Company; Ameren Energy Fuels; Wabash Community Unit School District #348; Arclar Company; Peabody Coal Company, Friendsville Mine, LLC; Black Beauty Coal Company; Pond River Coal Company.

THE LAW OFFICES OF THOMAS GLASGOW, LTD.

MOUNT PROSPECT, ILLINOIS

(See Schaumburg)

Criminal, Federal, State, Felony, Misdemeanor, DUI, Traffic, Drunk Driving, Revoked and Suspended License, Murder, Drug Offense, Weapons Charge, Civil, Contracts Litigation, Administrative, Divorce, Family Law.

DANIEL K. ROBIN, LTD

MOUNT PROSPECT, ILLINOIS

(See Arlington Heights)

Bankruptcy, Chapter 7, Chapter 13, Divorce, Family Law, Child Support, Separation, Prenuptial Agreements, Equitable Distribution, Driving While Intoxicated, Traffic Violations, Criminal Law, Wills and Trusts, Estate Planning, Asset Protection.

SAUL R. SODOS

300 WEST GOLF ROAD, SUITE 201
MOUNT PROSPECT, ILLINOIS 60056
Telephone: 847-398-3052
Fax: 847-398-3054
Email: TXMAVN@aol.com
URL: http://www.lawyers.com/sodos

Taxation, Trusts and Estate Planning, Wills and Probate, Residential and Commercial Real Estate, Consumer Bankruptcy, Consumer Law, Contracts, Corporations, Light Trespass.

SAUL R. SODOS, born Milwaukee, Wisconsin, June 1, 1957; admitted to bar, 1984, Minnesota; 1995, Illinois. *Education:* University of Wisconsin-Eau Claire (B.B.A., 1980); Drake Law School (J.D., 1983).

LAW OFFICES OF ROGER W. STELK

MOUNT PROSPECT, ILLINOIS

(See Arlington Heights)

Family Law, Divorce, Real Estate, Buying and Selling a Home, Civil Litigation.

CAMPBELL, BLACK, CARNINE, HEDIN, BALLARD & McDONALD, P.C.

Established in 1977
108 SOUTH NINTH STREET
P.O. DRAWER C
MOUNT VERNON, ILLINOIS 62864
Telephone: 618-242-3310
Fax: 618-242-3735
Email: frontdesk@illinoisfirm.com
URL: http://www.illinoisfirm.com

General Civil Practice in State and Federal Courts. Mining, Oil and Gas, Insurance, Workers Compensation, Corporation, Family, Probate, Real Estate and Trust Law. Trials and Appeals.

FIRM PROFILE: The law firm of Campbell, Black, Carnine, Hedin, Ballard & McDonald, P.C. originally began practicing law in Mt. Vernon, Illinois in 1938 as a separate office of a Central Illinois law firm. In 1977 the Mt. Vernon office became a separate firm named Campbell, Furnall, Moore & Jacobsen. In 1988, the name was again changed to Campbell, Black, Carnine & Hedin, P.C., to reflect the names of the active senior principals. The firm initially concentrated in oil, gas and coal law and soon added defense of civil liability claims, including negligence, products liability and medical malpractice, as a major concentration. Presently the firm has members concentrating in most major fields of civil practice including domestic relations, general litigation, real estate, banking, bankruptcy, general business, corporate and estate planning as well as insurance defense and coal, oil and gas law. The firm has active cases across the entire southern third of Illinois, in both state and federal courts.

DAVID A. CAMPBELL, born Mt. Vernon, Illinois, January 3, 1944; admitted to bar, 1969, Illinois. *Education:* Westminster College (A.B., 1966); University of Illinois (J.D., 1969). Delta Theta Phi. *Member:* Jefferson County and Illinois State (Member, Family Law Section) Bar Associations. Fellow, Illinois Bar Foundation. *PRACTICE AREAS:* Domestic Relations Cases. **Email:** dcampbell@illinoisfirm.com

TERRY R. BLACK, born Evansville, Indiana, August 4, 1945; admitted to bar, 1970, Illinois; 1971, U.S. District Court, Southern District of Illinois; 1988, U.S. Court of Appeals, Seventh Circuit. *Education:* Illinois Wesleyan University (B.A., 1967); Duke University (J.D., 1970). Phi Alpha Delta. Author: "Surface Owner Issues," Special Institute on Subsidence, Eastern Mineral Law Foundation, 1989. Speaker: Various institutes for Eastern Mineral Law Foundation and Illinois Institute for Continuing Education. *Member:* Jefferson County and Illinois State (Member, Mineral Law Subcommittee, Real Estate Section, 1983) Bar Associations; Illinois Oil and Gas Association; Eastern Mineral Law Foundation. Fellow, Illinois Bar Foundation. *PRACTICE AREAS:* Real Estate Law; Business Litigation; Mineral Law; Commercial and Banking Litigation. **Email:** tblack@illinoisfirm.com

ROY L. CARNINE, born Mattoon, Illinois, April 1, 1949; admitted to bar, 1973, Mississippi; 1974, Illinois. *Education:* Eastern Illinois University (B.S. in Business, 1971); University of Mississippi (J.D., 1973). Member, Moot Court. *Member:* Jefferson County and Illinois State Bar Associations; Association of Defense Trial Attorneys; Illinois Association of Defense Trial Counsel; Defense Research Institute; Southern Illinois Inn of Court; American Board of Trial Advocates. *PRACTICE AREAS:* Defense of Civil Litigation; Negligence; Products Liability; Insurance Defense. **Email:** rcarnine@illinoisfirm.com

CRAIG R. HEDIN, born Petaluma, California, January 12, 1950; admitted to bar, 1975, Illinois and Oklahoma. *Education:* DePauw University (B.A., 1972); University of Tulsa (J.D., 1975). Member, Order of the Curule Chair. Author: "Oil and Gas: Titles and Leasing Procedures, 1994, Chapter 6, Mineral Law, IICLE; "Title Examination", Special Institute on Mineral Titles, Eastern Mineral Law Foundation, 1985. *Member:* Jefferson County and Illinois State Bar Associations (Member, Mineral Law Section Council); Illinois Oil and Gas Association (Director; General Counsel); Eastern Mineral Law Foundation. *PRACTICE AREAS:* Real Estate Law; Mineral Law; Title Insurance; General Civil Practice. **Email:** chedin@illinoisfirm.com

MARK J. BALLARD, born Mt. Carmel, Illinois, August 29, 1953; admitted to bar, 1978, Illinois. *Education:* University of Illinois (B.A., 1975; J.D., 1978). Phi Eta Sigma. Notes Editor, Recent Decisions Section, Illinois Bar Journal, 1977-1978. *Member:* Jefferson County and Illinois State Bar Associations. *PRACTICE AREAS:* Estate and Trust

(This Listing Continued)

CAMPBELL, BLACK, CARNINE, HEDIN, BALLARD & McDONALD, P.C., Mount Vernon—Continued

Planning and Administration; General Corporate Representation; Real Estate Law; Workmen's Compensation Defense; General Civil Practice. ***Email:*** mballard@illinoisfirm.com

JEROME E. McDONALD, born Chicago, Illinois, July 21, 1955; admitted to bar, 1980, Illinois. *Education:* Drake University (B.A., summa cum laude, 1977); University of Illinois (J.D., 1980). Phi Beta Kappa; Phi Delta Phi. *Member:* Jefferson County, Illinois State and American Bar Associations; Illinois Association of Defense Trial Counsel; Defense Research Institute. ***PRACTICE AREAS:*** Defense of Civil Liability Claims; Insurance Law; Employment Law; Insurance Defense. ***Email:*** jmcdonald@illinoisfirm.com

HOWARD W. CAMPBELL (1911-1980)

JOHN E. JACOBSEN (1922-1985)

GLENN E. MOORE (1911-1991)

DAVID E. FURNALL (1905-1993)

FRED R. MANN, born Palestine, Illinois, October 23, 1952; admitted to bar, 1985, Illinois. *Education:* University of Illinois (B.S., 1974); Southern Illinois University (J.D., 1985). *Member:* Jefferson County and Illinois State Bar Associations. ***PRACTICE AREAS:*** Real Estate Law; Mineral Law; Civil Practice. ***Email:*** fmann@illinoisfirm.com

AARON S. CARNINE, born Champaign, Illinois, December 22, 1969; admitted to bar, 1998, Illinois. *Education:* University of Illinois (B.A., 1993); Southern Illinois University School of Law (J.D., 1997). *Member:* Jefferson County (Secretary/Treasurer, 2003) and Illinois State Bar Associations. ***PRACTICE AREAS:*** General Practice; Civil Litigation; Insurance Law; Technology Law; Traffic Violations; Driving While Intoxicated. ***Email:*** acarnine@illinoisfirm.com

C. STEPHEN SWOFFORD, born Carbondale, Illinois, May 28, 1952; admitted to bar, 1977, Illinois and U.S. District Court, Southern District of Illinois; 1994, Missouri. *Education:* Southern Illinois University (B.S., 1974; J.D., 1977). Phi Alpha Delta. States Attorney, Wayne County, 1984-1988. *Member:* Jefferson County and Illinois State Bar Associations. ***PRACTICE AREAS:*** Family Law; Civil Litigation; Insurance. ***Email:*** sswofford@illinoisfirm.com

SHANE M. CARNINE, born Mt. Vernon, Illinois, February 22, 1977; admitted to bar, 2003, Illinois; 2004, U.S. District Court, Southern District of Illinois. *Education:* Eastern Illinois University (B.A., Political Science, 1999); Southern Illinois University School of Law (J.D., 2003). Phi Delta Phi. Recipient, CALI Awards in Evidence and Corporations. *Member:* Jefferson County, Illinois State and American Bar Associations. ***Email:*** scarninr@illinoisfirm.com

REPRESENTATIVE CLIENTS: Marathon Ashland Petroleum, LLC; Collins Brothers Oil Co.; Consolidation Coal Co.; Rend Lake Conservancy District; Southern Illinois Stone Co.; Southern Illinois Asphalt Co., Inc.; Country Mutual Insurance Co.; Employers Insurance of Wausau; Kemper Insurance Cos.; Travelers Insurance; State Farm Insurance; Illinois Founders Insurance Co.; Pekin Insurance Co.; Employers Casualty Co.; St. Paul Insurance Cos.; Milwaukee Mutual Insurance Co.; Indiana Lumbermens Mutual Insurance Co.; Millers Mutual Insurance Co.; Exxon Coal U.S.A.; Freeman United Coal Co.; Underwriters at Lloyds, London; Union Insurance Group; American International Group; Northland Insurance Companies; Indiana Insurance Co.; Shelter Insurance Co.; Continental Western Insurance Co.; Countrymark Cooperative, Inc.; Rockford Mutual Ins. Co.; The American Coal Company; Peoples National Bank; Monterey Coal Company.

CRAIG & CRAIG

Established in 1868

115 NORTH 7TH STREET

P.O. BOX 1545

MOUNT VERNON, ILLINOIS 62864

Telephone: 618-244-7511

Telecopier: 618-244-7628

Email: mtvernon@craiglaw.net

URL: http://www.lawyers.com/craig&craiglawoffices

Mattoon, Illinois Office: 1807 Broadway. Telephone: 217-234-6481. Telecopier: 217-234-6486. Email: mattoon@craiglaw.net

General Practice in State and Federal Courts. Coal, Oil, Gas, Mining, Insurance, Drainage and Levee Law, Environmental, Corporation, Labor Relations, Workers Compensation and Real Estate Law. Estate Planning and Probate. Trials and Appeals.

FIRM PROFILE: The firm was founded in 1868 and has been practicing continuously since then at the same location in Mattoon. The Mt. Vernon office was opened in 1986. Although its practice is concentrated in Central and Southern Illinois, the firm handles business throughout the entire State including Cook County. Over the decades, the firm has played a significant part in developing the law of drainage districts; oil, gas, coal and other minerals; real property; and personal injury and insurance in Illinois.

The firm's philosophy is to provide the highest standard of professional service consistent with the greatest economy for the client. This includes pursuit of alternative dispute resolution procedures whenever feasible. The management and handling of each matter or case is assigned according to the specialty of the individual partner and matters delegated to associates are under the active supervision of partners.

Three partners are Fellows of the American College of Trial Lawyers. Partners in the firm have been extremely active over the decades in writing and lecturing for continuing legal education organizations in the State and nationally.

Management of the firm is shared among the partners.

(This Listing Continued)

RESIDENT PERSONNEL

PAUL R. LYNCH, born Chicago, Illinois, August 12, 1952; admitted to bar, 1977, Illinois. *Education:* Loyola University (B.A., magna cum laude, 1974); University of Illinois (J.D., 1977). Alpha Sigma Nu; Blue Key. Author: "Jurisdiction of Courts Other Than District Courts," Federal Civil Practice in Illinois, Illinois Institute for Continuing Legal Education, Chapter 2, 1992 (Supplement 1996). *Member:* Seventh Circuit, Jefferson County and Illinois State Bar Associations; Appellate Lawyers Association; Illinois Association of Defense Trial Counsel. (Resident). ***PRACTICE AREAS:*** Civil Trials and Appeals (State and Federal Courts); Mineral Law. ***Email:*** prl@craiglaw.net

KENNETH F. WERTS, born Champaign, Illinois, February 27, 1957; admitted to bar, 1984, Illinois. *Education:* University of Illinois (B.A., 1979); Southern Illinois University (J.D., 1984). Phi Sigma Alpha. Co-Author: "Kotecki v. Cyclops Welding and its Progeny," Third-Party Practice, Illinois Institute for Continuing Legal Education, Chapter 8, 2004. Co-Author: "Settlement," Illinois Civil Practice Before Trial, Illinois Institute for Continuing Legal Education, Chapter 3, 2003; "The IDC Monograph: The Normal Daily Activity Exception to Workers' Compensation Claims," IDC Quarterly, Third Quarter 2004, Volume 14, Number 3. *Member:* Jefferson County, Illinois State (Chairman, Worker's Compensation Law Section Council, 1997-1998; ISBA Assembly, 2004—) and American (Member, Workers' Compensation and Employers' Liability Law Committee, 2001—) Bar Associations; Illinois Association of Defense Trial Counsel (Member, Board of Directors, 2001—; Chair, Employment Law Committee, 2001-2003; Chair, Workers' Compensation Committee, 2003—); National Association of Railroad Trial Counsel. (Resident). ***PRACTICE AREAS:*** Workers Compensation Law; Black Lung; Occupational Disease Law; Personal Injury Litigation. ***Email:*** kfw@craiglaw.net

JULIE A. WEBB, born Paducah, Kentucky, November 29, 1971; admitted to bar, 1996, Illinois. *Education:* University of Illinois, Champaign-Urbana (B.S., with honors, 1993); Southern Illinois University (J.D., 1996). Author: "Kotecki v. Cyclops Welding and its Progency," Third-Party Practice, IICLE, Chapter 8, 2004. Co-Author: "Settlement," Illinois Civil Practice Before Trial, IICLE, Chapter 3, 2003. *Member:* Jefferson County, Illinois State and American Bar Associations; Illinois Association of Defense Trial Counsel. (Resident). ***PRACTICE AREAS:*** Workers Compensation; Civil Litigation. ***Email:*** jaw@craiglaw.net

(For Other Personnel, see Professional Biographies at Mattoon, Illinois)

HART AND HART

MOUNT VERNON, ILLINOIS

(See Benton)

General Trial and Appellate Practice in State and Federal Courts. Probate, Trust, Real Estate Deeds and Title Insurance, Bankruptcy (Creditors), Traffic, Banking, Business, Commercial and Corporation Law and Creditor Collections, Employment Law.

LAW OFFICES OF HARVEY & BRADLEY

Established in 1985

2029 BROADWAY

MOUNT VERNON, ILLINOIS 62864

Telephone: 618-244-9544

Fax: 618-244-9344

Email: lhlaw@mvn.net

URL: http://www.lawyers.com/morrisharvey

Litigation. Negligence, Personal Injury, Domestic Relations, Insurance Law, Oil and Gas. Trials and Appeals.

FIRM PROFILE: The Law Offices of Morris Harvey opened in 1985 for the purpose of providing competent and professional representation to the residents of Southeastern Illinois across the broad range of civil litigation. Mr. Harvey began the practice of law in April, 1975 and has, since that time, limited his practice to litigation matters in state and federal trial courts of the first, second and fourth judicial circuits of Illinois as well as the U.S. District Court for the Southern District of Illinois. In addition, the office has an extensive practice in the Illinois Appellate and Supreme Courts in the areas of oil and gas, negligence and personal injury, including product liability, as well as domestic relations. Mr. Harvey and Josh Bradley formed the Law Offices of Harvey and Bradley, LLC, effective January 2004. The office's professional objective is to continue to provide quality legal representation to the people of Southeastern Illinois. The current partnership will continue this tradition of excellence.

MORRIS LANE HARVEY, born Madisonville, Kentucky, April 22, 1950; admitted to bar, 1975, Illinois. *Education:* Murray State University (B.S., 1972); University of Kentucky (J.D., 1974). *Member:* Jefferson County, Illinois State and American Bar Associations; Illinois Trial Lawyers Association; The Association of Trial Lawyers of America. ***REPORTED CASES:*** Bell v. Lincoln Elec. Co., 258 Ill.App. 3rd 842, 630 N.E.2d 514, 196 Ill. Dec. 579, Prod. Liab. Rep. (CCH) P 13,896 (Ill.App. 5 Dist., Mar 10, 1994) (No. 5-91-0335); In re Marriage of Weiler, 258 Ill.App. 3d 454, 629 N.E.2d 1216, 196 Ill. Dec. 372 (Ill.App. 5 Dist., Mar 02, 1994) (No. 5-92-0307); In re Estate of King, 245 Ill.App.3d 1088, 614 N.E.2d 1348, 185 Ill. Dec. 663 (Ill.App. 5 Dist., June 10, 1993) (No. 5-91-0612); In re Marriage of Hazel, 219 Ill.App.3d 920, 579 N.E.2d 1265, 162 Ill. Dec. 451 (Ill.App. 5 Dist., Oct. 08, 1991) (No. 5-90-0186); Bank of Illinois in Mt. Vernon v. Bill's King City Stationery, Inc., 198 Ill.App.3d 434, 555 N.E.2d 1133, 144 Ill. Dec. 614 (Ill.App. 5 Dist., May 24, 1990) (No. 5-89-0014); Hickox v. Bell, 195 Ill.App.3d 976, 552 N.E.2d 1133, 142 Ill. Dec. 392 (Ill.App. 5 Dist., Mar 16, 1990) (No. 5-87-0648); Holden v. Nevergall, 172 Ill.App.3d 700, 526 N.E.2d 928, 122 Ill. Dec. 535 (Ill.App. 5 Dist., Jul 26, 1988) (No. 5-87-0201); In re Marriage of Hawkins, 160 Ill.App.3d 71, 513 N.E.2d 143, 111 Ill. Dec. 897 (Ill.App. 5 Dist., Sep 02, 1987) (No. 5-86-0299); Cali v. Demattei, 121 Ill.App.3d 623, 460 N.E.2d 121, 77 Ill. Dec. 262 (Ill.App. 5 Dist., Feb 09, 1984) (No. 5-83-0556); Bell v. Reid, 118 Ill.App.3d 310, 454 N.E.2d 1117, 73 Ill. Dec. 868 (Ill.App. 5 Dist., Sep 23, 1983) (No. 83-142); Frye v. Massis, 115 Ill.App.3d 48, 450 N.E.2d 411, 70 Ill. Dec. 938 (Ill.App. 5

(This Listing Continued)

Dist., May 11, 1983) (No. 82-464); Bagwell v. Industrial Comm., 94 Ill.2d 101, 445 N.E.2d 773, 68 Ill. Dec. 129 (Ill., Feb 04, 1983) (No. 56135); Giamanco v. Giamanco, 111 Ill.App.3d 1017, 444 N.E.2d 1090, 67 Ill. Dec. 606 (Ill.App. 5 Dist., Dec 13, 1982) (No. 82-256); Inland Steel Coal Co. v. Industrial Commission, 81 Ill. 2d 61, 405 N.E.2d 781, 39 Ill. Dec. 802 (Ill., May 22, 1980) (No. 52593); Meeker v. Beeson, 76 Ill.App.3d 940, 395 N.E.2d 698, 32 Ill. Dec. 468 (Ill.App. 5 Dist., Sep 26, 1979) (No. 79-151); Venturi, Inc. v. Austin Co., 681 F.Supp. 584 (S.D. Ill., Mar 08, 1988) (No. Civ. 87-4373); Feltmeier v. Feltmeier, (333 Ill.App.3d 1167, 777 N.E. 2d 1032, 268 Ill. Dec. 109), affirmed 207 Ill.2d 263, 798 N.E.2d 75, 278 Ill. Dec. 228 (2003); Hileman v. Maze, 367 F.3d 694 (May 10, 2004). ***PRACTICE AREAS:*** Family Law; Litigation; Personal Injury; Torts. ***Email:*** lharvey@harvey-bradley.com

JOSHUA M. BRADLEY, born Harrisburg, Illinois, May 28, 1974; admitted to bar, 1999, Illinois. *Education:* University of Mississippi (B.A., 1996); Southern Illinois University (J.D., 1999). *Member:* Jefferson County and Illinois State Bar Associations; The Central and Southern Federal Districts of Illinois Bar Association; The Association of Trial Lawyers of America; Southern Illinois Inn of Court. ***PRACTICE AREAS:*** Family Law; Litigation. ***Email:*** jbradley@harvey-bradley.com

ASSOCIATE

RHONDA K. BLADES, born August 13, 1971; admitted to bar, 2001, Illinois. *Education:* Southern Illinois University, Carbondale (B.S.Ed., 1995; J.D., 2001). ***PRACTICE AREAS:*** Family Law; Litigation. ***Email:*** rblades@harvey-bradley.com

HASSAKIS & HASSAKIS, P.C.

Established in 1950

SUITE 201, BOSTON BUILDING
206 SOUTH NINTH STREET
P.O. BOX 706
MOUNT VERNON, ILLINOIS 62864-0706
Telephone: 618-244-5335
Telefax: 618-244-5330
Email: mhass@hassakislaw.com
URL: http://www.hassakislaw.com

Concentrated in Civil Trial Practice, Negligence, Workers Compensation, Insurance, Medical and Nursing Home Malpractice.

MARK D. HASSAKIS, born Mt. Vernon, Illinois, October 5, 1951; admitted to bar, 1976, Illinois. *Education:* Northwestern University (B.A., 1973); St. Louis University (J.D., 1976). *Member:* Chicago, Jefferson County, Illinois State and American Bar Associations; Illinois Trial Lawyers Association; The Association of Trial Lawyers of America; Hellenic Bar Association of Illinois; Illinois Bar Foundation. ***PRACTICE AREAS:*** Personal Injury; Workers' Compensation; Medical Malpractice. ***Email:*** mhass@hassakislaw.com

REFERENCES: Fifth Third Bank, Effingham, Illinois; Bank of America, Mt. Vernon, Illinois.

HOWARD, LEGGANS, PIERCY & HOWARD, LLP

Established in 1959

1008 MAIN
P.O. DRAWER U
MOUNT VERNON, ILLINOIS 62864
Telephone: 618-242-6594
Fax: 618-244-7197
URL: http://www.lawyers.com/hlph

General Practice in all Courts. Probate and Estate Planning. Tax, Corporation, Municipal and Real Estate Law.

FIRM PROFILE: Howard, Leggans, Piercy & Howard is a small personal firm dedicated to the specific needs of each individual client. Serving Central and Southern Illinois since 1932 when George W. Howard, Jr. began his practice, our partners have concentrated their efforts in the areas of Probate and Estate Planning, Tax, Corporate and Real Estate Law.

MEMBERS OF FIRM

GEORGE W. HOWARD, JR. (1907-1994)

G. W. HOWARD, III, born Mt. Vernon, Illinois, January 7, 1935; admitted to bar, 1959, Illinois; 1962, U.S. District Court, Southern District of Illinois; 1986, U.S. Court of Appeals, Seventh Circuit. *Education:* University of Illinois (A.B., 1956; J.D., 1959). Phi Beta Kappa; Phi Kappa Phi; Phi Eta Sigma; Phi Delta Phi; Order of the Coif. City Attorney, 1961-1983. Corporation Counsel, 1983—. Special Assistant Attorney General, 1964-1970. Member, Board of Trustees, University of Illinois, 1970-1988. Fellow, American College of Trust and Estate Counsel. *Member:* Jefferson County and Illinois State Bar Associations. [Captain, U.S. Army Reserve, 1957-1965]. ***PRACTICE AREAS:*** Trusts and Estates; Municipal Law; Taxation. ***Email:*** gwh@mvn.net

DAVID R. LEGGANS, born Carbondale, Illinois, April 21, 1955; admitted to bar, 1979, Illinois. *Education:* Shawnee College (A.S., 1974); Southern Illinois University (B.A., with highest honors, 1976); University of Illinois (J.D., cum laude, 1979). Phi Kappa Phi. City Attorney, 1983—. Special Assistant Attorney General, 1984-1990. *Member:* Jefferson County, Illinois State and American Bar Associations. ***PRACTICE AREAS:*** Municipal Law; Family Law; Real Estate Law. ***Email:*** drl@mvn.net

DAVID L. PIERCY, born Champaign, Illinois, July 14, 1957; admitted to bar, 1982, Illinois; 1983, U.S. District Court, Southern District of Illinois; 1986, U.S. Court of Appeals, Seventh Circuit. *Education:* University of Illinois (B.A., summa cum laude, 1979; J.D., magna cum laude, 1982). Phi Beta Kappa; Phi Kappa Phi; Phi Eta Sigma; Order of the Coif. *Member:* Jefferson County, Illinois State and American Bar Associations. ***PRACTICE AREAS:*** Banking Law; Corporate Law; Estates Law; Commercial Law. ***Email:*** dlp@mvn.net

(This Listing Continued)

JEFFREY G. HOWARD, born Mount Vernon, Illinois, September 10, 1963; admitted to bar, 1990, Illinois; 1991, New Jersey. *Education:* University of Illinois (B.A., 1985; J.D., magna cum laude, 1990). *Member:* Jefferson County and Illinois State Bar Associations. ***PRACTICE AREAS:*** Trusts and Estates; Commercial Law; Real Estate. ***Email:*** jgh@mvn.net

COUNSEL FOR: Integra Bank, N.A.; First State Bank of Dix; Tri-County Electric Cooperative; Hamilton County Telephone Co-op.; Jefferson County Fire Protection District; City of Mt. Vernon; E. F. Wielt Plumbing, Inc.; Mt. Vernon Township; Shiloh Township; Texico State Bank.

LAW OFFICE OF KERLEY & ASSOCIATES, P.C.

MOUNT VERNON, ILLINOIS

(See Springfield)

Collections, Estate Planning, Probate, Employment, Contested Estates, Business Advise, Financial Planning, Commercial Litigation, Insurance Coverage, Insurance Defense, Business Law, Commercial Law, Insurance, Real Estate Agents and Brokers Errors and Omissions, Personal Injury, Real Estate.

McMAHON, BERGER, HANNA, LINIHAN, CODY & McCARTHY

A PROFESSIONAL CORPORATION

MOUNT VERNON, ILLINOIS

(See Collinsville)

Labor Relations, Civil Rights and Administrative Law, Employment Litigation in all Courts.

MITCHELL LAW OFFICE, P.C.

2020 BROADWAY
P.O. BOX 1088
MOUNT VERNON, ILLINOIS 62864
Telephone: 618-242-0705
Fax: 618-242-4820
Email: abenlaw@charter.net

General Civil Practice.

A. BEN MITCHELL, born Mt. Vernon, Illinois, June 15, 1941; admitted to bar, 1966, Illinois; U.S. District Court, Central and Southern Districts of Illinois; U.S. Court of Appeals, Seventh Circuit. *Education:* University of Tulsa (B.S., Business Administration, 1963); University of Illinois (J.D., 1966). Phi Delta Phi. Author: "Plugging Responsibilities: The Deep Pocket Theory," 9th Eastern Mineral Law Institute, 1989; "Responsibilities Attendant to Well Abandonment," Eastern Mineral Law Special Institute, 1991. Co-Author: "Release, Abandonment, and Plugging," IICLE Mineral Law, 1994; "Well Plugging Abandonment & Restoration," IOGA, 1996; "Well Plugging Responsibilities," Interstate Oil & Gas Compact Commission, 2002. *Member:* Jefferson County (President, 1970-1971), Central Federal District of Illinois, Southern Federal District of Illinois, Illinois State (Member, Committees on: Unauthorized Practice of Law, 1968-1971; Agricultural Law, 1983-1991; Oil and Gas Securities Sub-Committee, Securities Advisory, 1987-1993) and American Bar Associations; Energy and Mineral Law Foundation; Illinois Oil and Gas Association (Director, 2000-2003). ***PRACTICE AREAS:*** Commercial Law; Commercial Litigation; Corporate Law; Trust Law; Wills; Estate Planning; Trust Administration; Probate; Oil and Gas Law; Real Estate.

MEAGAN N. CARNINE, born West Frankfort, Illinois, August 16, 1979; admitted to bar, 2004, Illinois; 2005, U.S. District Court, Southern District of Illinois. *Education:* Southern Illinois University, Carbondale (B.S., magna cum laude, 2000; J.D., 2004). Phi Delta Phi, Legal Fraternity, 2001-2004. Staff Member, 2003 and Articles Editor, 2004, Southern Illinois University Law Journal. *Member:* Illinois State Bar Association. ***Email:*** abenlaw@charter.net

REPRESENTATIVE CLIENTS: South Pointe Bank; Lampley Oil; Stewart Producers, Inc.; Auto Credit of Southern Illinois; Mt. Vernon City Schools District #80; Independent Boat Builders, Inc. (IBBI); Mid-Central Production Corporation.

THOMAS J. NOONAN, P.C.

MOUNT VERNON, ILLINOIS

(See St. Louis, Missouri)

Asbestos Litigation, Bankruptcy Litigation, Civil Litigation, Commercial Bankruptcy, Creditor Bankruptcy, Foreclosures, General Liability Defense, Insurance, Insurance Defense, Insurance Litigation, Litigation, Personal Injury, Personal Injury Defense, Products Liability, Mold Litigation, Motor Carrier Defense, Real Estate Bankruptcy, Real Estate Foreclosure, Tort Defense, Workers Compensation Defense.

LAW OFFICE OF TERRY SHARP, P.C.

Established in 1973

1115 HARRISON STREET
P.O. BOX 906
MOUNT VERNON, ILLINOIS 62864
Telephone: 618-242-0246
Fax: 618-242-1170
Email: law@lotsharp.com
URL: http://www.lawyers.com/tsharp

Benton, Illinois Office: 105 North Main Street. Telephone: 618-435-5109. FAX: 618-242-1170.

Bankruptcy, Creditor's Rights, Commercial, Banking, Real Estate, Corporate, Probate and Estate Planning Law. No small collections.

FIRM PROFILE: The firm has extensive experience in creditor's remedies, inside and outside of bankruptcy, has represented most of the bankruptcy trustees who serve in the Southern District of Illinois, and has also represented a large number of debtors. In addition to bankruptcy law, the firm also practices in the areas of commercial, banking, real estate, corporate, probate and estate planning law throughout its geographic area. Firm is issuing agent for 4 title insurance companies and has a staff of abstractors providing real estate title searches throughout Southern Illinois. The firm maintains its main office in Mt. Vernon with a branch office in Benton. The firm's central location allows easy access to all bankruptcy and circuit courts in the Southern District of Illinois. Terry Sharp, senior attorney, has lectured at numerous professional and trade seminars, has published several articles dealing with bankruptcy and accounting issues.

TERRELL LEE SHARP, born Mt. Vernon, Illinois, July 28, 1944; admitted to bar, 1973, Illinois and U.S. District Court, Southern District of Illinois; 1986, U.S. Court of Appeals, Seventh Circuit; 1991, U.S. Supreme Court. *Education:* University of Illinois (B.S., 1970; J.D., 1973). Certified Public Accountant, Illinois, 1969. Certified Fraud Examiner, 1993. Author: "Bridging the Gap," Illinois Institute for Continuing Legal Education, 1978; "The Chapter 12 Trustee," Agricultural Bankruptcy Practice. . . A Field of Transition, 1987, Illinois Institute of Continuing Legal Education; "Ten Reasons to Lessen the Fears of Ag Lenders About Chapter 12 Bankruptcy," The Journal of Commercial Bank Lending, August, 1987; "Do You Need Bankruptcy Advice?," Northwest Oil World, May, 1987; "Make My Day: Ten Reasons Why a Banker Should Not Necessarily Fear a Chapter 12 Bankruptcy Proceeding," Norton Bankruptcy Law Advisor, June, 1987; "Defining Value," The Journal of Commercial Lending, January 1996. Planning Chairman, Secured Transaction Procedures in Illinois, Basic and Advanced Course, I.I.C.L.E., 1988. Lecturer, Commercial Bankruptcy and Banking Seminar, IICLE, 1989. Editor, Southern Illinois Bankruptcy Institute, 1991—. *Member:* Jefferson County (President, 1975), Illinois State Bar Associations; Illinois Trial Lawyers Association. ***REPORTED CASES:*** In re Atchison, 925 F.2d 209 (7th Cir. 1991), US Cert. Den. 112 S.Ct. 178; In re Tomer, 128 B.R. 746 (Bankr. S.D. Ill. 1991); In re McDowell, 87 B.R. 554 (Bankr. S.D. Ill. 1988); Veath vs. Specialty Grains, Inc., 190 Ill.App.3d 787, 137 Ill.Dec. 892, 546 N.E.2d 1005 (5th Dist. 1989); Home Federal Sav. & Loan Ass'n. of Centralia vs. Cook, 170 Ill.App.3d 720, 121 Ill.Dec. 345. 525 N.E.2d 151 (5th Dist. 1988); Anna National Bank vs. Prater, 154 Ill.App.3d 6, 107 Ill.Dec. 26, 506 N.E.2d 769 (5th Dist. 1987); In re Tomer, 147 B.R. 461 (S.D.Ill. 1992); In re Chenoweth, 132 B.R. 161 (Bankr. S.D.Ill. 1991), aff'd 143 B.R. 527 (S.D.Ill. 1992), aff'd 3 F.3d 1111 (7th Cir. 1993); Deason vs. Gutzler, 622 N.E.2d 1276 (Ill.App. 5th Dist. 1993); Farm Credit Bank of St. Louis vs. Dorr, 620 N.E.2d 549 (Ill. App. 5th Dist. 1993); Knight's Prairie Hunting Club, Inc. vs. Holmes, 636 N.E. 2d 29 (Ill.App. 5th Dist. 1994). ***PRACTICE AREAS:*** Bankruptcy (30%); Creditor; Real Estate (8%); Real Estate Title Insurance (20%); Banks and Banking (15%); Foreclosure Law (15%); Litigation (5%); Collections (5%); Estate Planning (2%). ***Email:*** law@lotsharp.com

JOHN T. HUNDLEY, born Abilene, Kansas, October 13, 1948; admitted to bar, 1979, Illinois and U.S. District Court, Northern District of Illinois, including Trial Bar; 1980, U.S. Court of Appeals, Seventh Circuit; 1981, U.S. District Court, Northern District of California; 1983, U.S. District Court, Central District of Illinois; 2001, U.S. District Court, Southern District of Illinois. *Education:* University of Illinois (B.S., with honors, 1970); DePaul University (J.D., with honors, 1979). Author: "'Inadvertent Waiver' of Evidentiary Privileges: Can Reformulating the Question Lead to More Sensible Decisions?" 19 S. Illinois Univ. L. J. 263 (1995); "Business Expansion Through Asset Acquisition: Some Problems Posed By Product Liability Doctrines," 77 Ill. B. J. 492 (1989); "White Knights, Pre-Nuptial Confidences, and the Morning After: The Effect of Transaction-Related Disclosures on the Attorney-Client and Related Privileges," 5 DePaul Bus. L. J. 59 (1992-1993); "Waiver of Evidentiary Privilege by Inadvertent Disclosure-State Law," 51 A.L.R. 5th 603 (1997); "Waiver of Evidentiary Privilege by Inadvertent Disclosure-Federal Law," 159 A.L.R. Fed. 153 (2000); "Long Arms and Foreign Pockets: Can Multinational Financial Organizations Be Used To Subject Alien Defendants to the Enforcement of Illinois Judgments?" Chi. Bar Assn. Record 24 (Sept. 1990); "Assignments of Wages in Illinois: Pitfalls for Employer Businesses," 14 DePaul Bus. L.J. 21 (2001). Lecturer: Pretrial Civil Litigation, DePaul University College of Law (1990-91); Debt Collection in Illinois, National Business Institute, Schaumburg, IL (2004). Partner, 1986-1990; Associate, 1979-1986, Mayer, Brown & Platt. *Member:* Illinois State and American Bar Associations; American Trial Lawyers Association. ***REPORTED CASES:*** Noyola v. Board of Ed. of City of Chicago, 179 Ill.2d 121, 688 N.E.2d 81 (1997); In re Fine Paper Antitrust Litigation, 685 F.2d 810 (3rd Cir. 1983); Grant v. Board of Ed. of City of Chicago, 282 Ill.App.3d 1011, 668 N.E.2d 1188 (1996); Stewart v. EGNEP (Pty) Limited, 581 F.Supp. 788 (C.D.Ill. 1983); Ford Motor Credit Co. v. Aaron Lincoln-Mercury, Inc., 563 F.Supp. 1108 (N.D.Ill. 1983); Ford Motor Credit Co. v. Aaron Lincoln-Mercury, Inc., 563 F.Supp. 1118 (N.D.Ill. 1983); In re Torres, 191 B.R. 735 (Bankr. N.D.Ill. 1996). ***PRACTICE AREAS:*** Civil Litigation (75%); Business Law; Collections; Commercial Law; Contracts; Chancery and Equity. ***Email:*** jhundley@lotsharp.com

REPRESENTATIVE CLIENTS: Housing Authority of the City of Mt. Vernon; N.E. Mt. Vernon Water Co.; Peoples National Bank; South Pointe Bank; Centrue Bank, First Financial Bank.

(This Listing Continued)

LOCAL COUNSEL FOR: Ag Lease or Loan, LLC; Farm Credit Leasing; States Resources Corp.

SHAW & MARTIN, P.C.

U.S. BANK BUILDING
123 SOUTH TENTH STREET, SUITE 302
P.O. BOX 1789
MOUNT VERNON, ILLINOIS 62864
Telephone: 618-244-1788
Fax: 618-244-2588
URL: http://www.shawmartin.com
Email: shawmartin@mvn.net
URL: http://www.lawyers.com/shaw&martin

Banking, Commercial Law, Creditors Rights, Wills, Trusts and Estates, Real Estate, Family Law, Civil Trials and Appeals.

ROBERT E. SHAW, born Kansas City, Missouri, March 4, 1943; admitted to bar, 1979, Illinois and U.S. District Court, Southern District of Illinois; 1980, U.S. District Court, Central District of Illinois; 1991, U.S. Court of Appeals, Seventh Circuit. *Education:* University of Missouri at Columbia (B.S. in Industrial Engineering, 1965); Southern Illinois University (J.D., 1979). *Member:* Jefferson County, Illinois State (Member, General Practice Section Council, 1988-1992) and American Bar Associations; American Bankruptcy Institute. ***PRACTICE AREAS:*** Banking; Creditors Rights; Real Estate; Probate; Business Transfers; Wills and Trusts; Qualified Domestic Relations Orders (QDROs); Civil Litigation. ***Email:*** shawmartin@mvn.net

CURTIS W. MARTIN, born Mount Vernon, Illinois, July 18, 1964; admitted to bar, 1989, Illinois; 1990, Missouri and U.S. District Court, Southern District of Illinois; 1991, U.S. Court of Appeals, Seventh Circuit. *Education:* University of Illinois (B.S., with honors, 1986); Southern Illinois University (J.D., 1989). *Member:* Jefferson County (President, 1993-1994) and Illinois State Bar Associations. ***PRACTICE AREAS:*** Adoption Law; Business Law; Civil Litigation; Collections; Commercial Law; Construction Law; Contracts; Corporate Law; Creditor Bankruptcy; Creditor Rights; Family Law; Guardianship and Conservatorship; Landlord and Tenant Law; Real Estate; Trusts and Estate; Wills. ***Email:*** shawmartin@mvn.net

WHAM & WHAM

MOUNT VERNON, ILLINOIS

(See Centralia)

General Trial and Appellate Practice. Insurance Defense including Medical Malpractice, Automobile Accidents, Premises Liability, Products Liability, Personal Injury, Probate, Wrongful Discharge from Employment.

RICHARD A. ANDERSON

MUNDELEIN, ILLINOIS

(See Grayslake)

Criminal Law, Driving While Intoxicated, Misdemeanors, Felonies, Real Estate, Buying and Selling of Businesses, Juvenile Criminal Law.

LAW OFFICES OF RANDIE BRUNO

MUNDELEIN, ILLINOIS

(See Waukegan)

Criminal Law, Driving While Intoxicated, Drug Crimes, Felonies, Homicide, Juvenile, Misdemeanors, Parole and Probation, Sexual Assault, Traffic Violations, Family Law, Divorce, Child Custody, Child Support, Domestic Violence, Spousal Support.

LAW OFFICES OF ELMAN & ELMAN

700 N. LAKE STREET, SUITE 205
MUNDELEIN, ILLINOIS 60060
Telephone: 847-949-8182
847-949-8185
Email: elmanlaw@aol.com
URL: http://www.elmanlaw.com

Bankruptcy, Personal Injury, Workers Compensation, Health Care, Litigation.

MEMBERS OF FIRM

FRED W. ELMAN, born 1937; admitted to bar, 1962, Illinois. *Education:* DePaul University (LL.B.). ***PRACTICE AREAS:*** Bankruptcy; Personal Injury Law. ***Email:*** elms24@aol.com

ANTHONY R. ELMAN, born 1966; admitted to bar, 1992, Illinois. *Education:* University of Michigan (B.A., 1988); Tulane University of Louisiana (J.D., 1992); DePaul University (LL.M. in Health Care, 1994). ***PRACTICE AREAS:*** Personal Injury; Workers Compensation; Health Care; Litigation.

BOGDAN MARTINOVICH

MUNDELEIN, ILLINOIS

(See Libertyville)

Personal Injury, Automobile Accidents, Dog Bites, Nursing Home Abuse, Slip and Fall, Products Liability, Wrongful Death, Medical Malpractice, Head and Spinal Injuries, Commercial Litigation.

HOWERTON, DORRIS & STONE

MURPHYSBORO, ILLINOIS

(See Marion)

Plaintiff's Personal Injury, Workers Compensation Law, Insurance Bad Faith, Breach of Contract, Criminal Defense, Medical Malpractice, General Civil and Trial Practice.

MAURICE J. McCANN

Established in 1988

1331 WALNUT STREET
MURPHYSBORO, ILLINOIS 62966-2026
Telephone: 618-684-5242
Email: mjmccann@globaleyes.net

Criminal Law, DUI, Probate, Personal Injury, Divorce.

MAURICE J. McCANN, born St. Louis, Missouri, July 26, 1950; admitted to bar, 1986, Illinois; 1987, Missouri and U.S. District Court, Eastern District of Missouri; 1988, U.S. District Court, Southern District of Illinois; 1998, U.S. Court of Appeals, Seventh Circuit. *Education:* Southern Illinois University (Ph.D., 1976; J.D., 1986). ***PRACTICE AREAS:*** Criminal Law (30%); DUI (10%); Probate (30%); Personal Injury (10%); Divorce (10%).

AMBROSE & CUSHING, P.C.

NAPERVILLE, ILLINOIS

(See Chicago)

Personal Injury, Medical Malpractice, Products Liability, Workers Compensation, Medical Negligence, Premises Liability, Automobile Accidents and Injuries, Slip and Fall, Spinal Injury, Wrongful Death, Construction Accidents and Commercial Litigation, Real Estate Law.

ANDERSON & ASSOCIATES, P.C.

NAPERVILLE, ILLINOIS

(See Schaumburg)

Family Law, Bankruptcy, Real Estate Litigation and Transactions, Estate Planning and Probate.

THEA ARMSTRONG

232 N. WASHINGTON STREET
NAPERVILLE, ILLINOIS 60540
Telephone: 630-355-7680
Fax: 630-355-7684
Email: thea@theaarmstrong.com
URL: http://www.theaarmstronglaw.com

Criminal Defense, Criminal Law, Driving While Intoxicated, Drug Crimes, Felonies, Homicide, Juvenile Law, Misdemeanors, Parole and Probation, Sexual Assault, Traffic Violations, Elder Law, Family Law, Adoptions, Child Custody, Child Support, Divorce, Domestic Violence, Premarital Agreements, Spousal Support, Visitation Rights, Commercial Real Estate, Residential Real Estate, Wills and Probate, Guardianship and Conservatorship, Business Formation, Buying and Selling Businesses, Small Business Law, Commercial Leasing.

THEA ARMSTRONG, born Madison, South Dakota, March 31, 1941; admitted to bar, 1986, Illinois and U.S. District Court, Northern District of Illinois. *Education:* South Dakota State University (B.S., 1963); John Marshall Law School (J.D., 1986). Member, Order of John Marshall Law Review. ***PRACTICE AREAS:*** Criminal Defense; Divorce; Real Estate; Probate; Traffic Violations.

BANIAK PINE & GANNON

NAPERVILLE, ILLINOIS

(See Chicago)

Intellectual Property, Patent, Trademark, Copyright and Trade Secret Law, Litigation, Licensing.

BROIDA AND TULLIS, LTD.

Established in 1990

NAPERVILLE CORPORATE CENTER, SUITE 108
1250 EAST DIEHL ROAD
NAPERVILLE, ILLINOIS 60563
Telephone: 630-245-1515
Fax: 630-245-1565
Email: broidatullis@aol.com

Civil Trial and Appellate Practice in State and Federal Courts, including Business and Commercial, Employment Discrimination, Labor, Corporate and Real Estate Litigation, Divorce and Family Law, Personal Injury, Municipal Representation, Arbitration and Mediation, General and Transactional Practice.

MEMBERS OF FIRM

RONALD J. BROIDA, born Louisville, Kentucky, March 30, 1943; admitted to bar, 1969, Illinois and U.S. District Court, Northern District of Illinois and Trial Bar; 1982, U.S. Court of Appeals, Seventh Circuit and U.S. Supreme Court. *Education:* University of Illinois (B.A., 1966; J.D., 1969). Phi Delta Phi. Author: Lincoln Award Winning Article, the "History of the Development of the Remedy of 'Piercing the Corporate Veil,'" Illinois Bar Journal, April, 1977; "Recent Developments in Practice and Procedure or What Real Estate Lawyers Should Be Aware of Before Going to Court," Illinois State Bar Association Real Property Newsletter, March, 1987. Co-Author: "Tortious Interference With Contract and Prospective Advantage in Illinois," DePaul Law Review, Winter, 1983; "When Can a Divorce Be Appealed?" DuPage County Bar Association Brief, November, 1993; "The Trial Court Always Loses Jurisdiction After a Notice of Appeal is Filed-Not," DuPage County Bar Association Brief, June, 1995; "ADA Update," DuPage County Bar Association Brief, November, 1999. Fire Commissioner, Darien-Woodridge Fire Protection District, 1994-1995. Senior Counsel, The College of Master Advocates and Barristers. *Member:* Chicago, DuPage County (Chair, Appellate Law and Practice Committee, 1992-1993; Editor of the Brief, 2000; Director, 2001—), Will County, Illinois State (Member, Civil Practice and Procedure Section Council, 1988-1991) and American Bar Associations; West Suburban Bar Association (President, 1979 and 1980). ***PRACTICE AREAS:*** Commercial Litigation; Business Litigation; Real Estate Litigation; Labor and Employment Litigation; Divorce; Family Law; Personal Injury; Municipal Law; Appellate Practice; General Practice; Business Transactions; Arbitration; Mediation. ***Email:*** broidatullis@aol.com

JEFFREY A. TULLIS, born Berwyn, Illinois, August 23, 1971; admitted to bar, 1997, Illinois and U.S. District Court, Northern District of Illinois and Trial Bar. *Education:* Loyola University (B.A., cum laude, 1994); John Marshall Law School (J.D., 1997). Author, "Textbook Examples of Defense to Title VII Employment Harassment Cases," DuPage County Bar Association Brief, September 2000. *Member:* Chicago, DuPage County (Chair, Labor and Employment Committee, 2004-2005), Will County, Illinois State and American (Member, Employment Law Section) Bar Associations. ***PRACTICE AREAS:*** Labor and Employment; ERISA; Employment Defense; Discrimination Litigation; Civil Litigation; Divorce; Family Law; Personal Injury; Real Estate Litigation; Appellate Practice; Municipal Law. ***Email:*** broidatullis@aol.com

ASSOCIATE

JOSEPH K. NICHELE, born Lockport, Illinois, March 19, 1980; admitted to bar, 2005, Illinois. *Education:* Purdue University (B.S., 2002); Valparaiso University School of Law (J.D., 2005). Associate Editor of Law Review. Former Judicial Extern to the Honorable Lee Preston, Circuit Court of Cook County, Illinois; Former Judicial Extern to the Honorable William Alexa, Porter County Superior Court.

OF COUNSEL

FREDRIC J. GROSSMAN, born Chicago, Illinois, August 28, 1932; admitted to bar, 1956, Kentucky; 1957, Illinois and U.S. Court of Military Appeals; 1963, U.S. District Court, Northern District of Illinois including Trial Bar. *Education:* Northwestern University (B.S.L., 1954; LL.B., 1956). Phi Delta Phi. Formerly with Clausen Miller P.C. [U.S. Army, JAGC]. ***PRACTICE AREAS:*** Medical Malpractice; Construction Law; Products Liability; General Tort Litigation; Arbitration; Mediation. ***Email:*** broidatullis@aol.com

BROOKS, ADAMS AND TARULIS

Established in 1957

101 NORTH WASHINGTON STREET
NAPERVILLE, ILLINOIS 60540
Telephone: 630-355-2101
FAX: 630-355-7843
Email: info@napervillelaw.com
URL: http://www.napervillelaw.com

General Practice including Trial and Appellate Litigation. General Business, Business/Commercial Litigation, Employment, Corporation, Municipal, School, Park, Condemnation, Real Estate, Environmental, Land Developments, Zoning, Probate, Wills, Trusts, Special Needs Trusts, Adoptions, Estate Planning, Banking, Commercial, Personal Injury, Condominium Law and Civil Rights Law, Consumer Protection, Consumer Fraud, Consumer Litigation, Family Law, Divorce, Matrimonial Law, Criminal/Traffic Defense, Juvenile Representation and School Law Matters.

FIRM PROFILE: The firm was founded in 1957 by Harris W. Fawell, U.S. Congressman from the Illinois 13th Congressional District. The firm was known as Fawell, James and Brooks from 1974 until January 1, 1990. The firm's partners and associates continue their professional leadership by active participation in continuing legal education seminars, professional education activities and state and local civic affairs.

MEMBERS OF FIRM

GERALD J. BROOKS, born Evergreen Park, Illinois, September 10, 1937; admitted to bar, 1966, Illinois; 1983, U.S. District Court, Northern District of Illinois including Trial Bar. *Education:* Southern Illinois University (B.A., 1960); Loyola University (J.D., 1966). Member and Secretary, Board of Education, DuPage District 201, 1967-1982. City Attorney, Wheaton, Illinois, 1971-1973. Village Attorney, Clarendon Hills, 1975-1999. Incorporator and President, Blackhawk Heights Sanitary District . *Member:* DuPage County (Chairman, Local Government Committee, 1979-1980, 1990-1991), Illinois State and American Bar Associations; Illinois Institute of Local Government Law. ***REPORTED CASES:*** Tyska by Tyska v. Bd. of Education, 117 Ill App 3d 917, 453 NE 2d 1344 (1st Dist 1983); Anderson v. City of Wheaton, 25 Ill App 3d 100, 323 NE 2d 129 (2nd Dist. 1975); Linhart v. Glatfelter, 584 F.Supp 1369, 771 F2d 1004 (7th Cir. 1985); People Ex Rel. Hopf v. Barger, 30 Ill. App. 3d 525 332 NE 2d 649 (2nd Dist. 1975); Winfield Fire Protection Dist v. City of Wheaton, 29 Ill App 3d 630, 332 NE 2d 43 (2nd Dist. 1975). ***PRACTICE AREAS:*** Chancery Practice; General Civil Practice; Local Government Law; Zoning and Development Law. ***Email:*** gbrooks@napervillelaw.com

STEVEN B. ADAMS, born Omaha, Nebraska, October 13, 1959; admitted to bar, 1984, Illinois and U.S. District Court, Northern District of Illinois. *Education:* Indiana University (B.A., 1981; J.D., 1984). Elected 84th Precinct Committeeman, Lisle Township Republican Organization. Board of Directors, Naperville Chamber of Commerce, 1995-1999.

(This Listing Continued)

BROOKS, ADAMS AND TARULIS, Naperville—Continued

Chairman, Legislative Committee, Naperville Chamber of Commerce 1993-1996. Member: East-West Corporate Corridor Association, 1992-1994; Illinois Fire and Police Commissioner's Association. Appointed, Naperville Board of Fire and Police Commissioners, 1997-2003. *Member:* DuPage County (Member, Local Government Law Committee), Illinois State and American Bar Associations; Illinois Institute of Local Government Law. ***PRACTICE AREAS:*** Civil Litigation; Real Estate; Local Government Law; School Law; Eminent Domain; Zoning and Development Law; Construction Law. ***Email:*** sadams@napervillelaw.com

RICHARD J. TARULIS, born Chicago, Illinois, July 27, 1958; admitted to bar, 1987, Illinois and U.S. District Court, Northern District of Illinois. *Education:* Southern Illinois University (B.S., 1983); Northern Illinois University (J.D., 1987). Phi Alpha Delta (Treasurer, 1985-1987). Member, Moot Court. Member, SSC Citizens Mitigation Advisory Task Force, 1988. Local Counsel, Cantigny War Museum, 1988—. Treasurer, Naperville Veterans Memorial Wall Committee, 1989—. Extended Member, DuPage County Board of Review, 1990-1991. Member, Finance Committee, Illinois Senator Chris Lauzen, 1993—. Elected Lisle Township Republican Precinct Committeeman, 1994—. Treasurer, Illinois Rep. Cowlishaw Campaign Committee, 1995—. Parliamentarian, Lisle Township Republican Organization, 1996—. Trustee, Lisle Township, 2000-2002. Lisle Township Clerk, 2002—. *Member:* DuPage County (Member: Local Government Committee, 1988—, Chairman, 1995-1996; Probate Law Committee, 1989-1992, Secretary, 1990), Illinois State and American (Member, Land Use Committee, State and Local Tax Committee) Bar Associations; Illinois Township Attorneys Association. [Sgt., USMC, 1976-1983]. ***REPORTED CASES:*** Ceres One Corp. v. Naperville Township Road District, _Ill.App.3d_, 278 Ill.Dec. 179, 797 N.E.2d 1097 (2nd Dist. 2003); ABN Ambro Services, Inc. v. Naperville Park District, 325 Ill.App.3d 7, 258 Ill.Dec.463, 756 N.E.2d 445 (2nd Dist. 2001); Board of Library Trustees of the Village of Westmont v. Cinco Construction, 276 Ill.App.3d 417, 213 Ill.Dec. 3, 658 N.E.2d 473 (1st Dist. 1995); Forest Preserve District of DuPage County v. Department of Revenue, 266 Ill.App.3d 264, 203 Ill.Dec 566, 639 N.E.2d 1385 (2nd Dist. 1994). ***PRACTICE AREAS:*** Civil Litigation; Condemnation Law; Park District Law; Estate Planning; Probate Law; Special Needs Trusts. ***Email:*** rtarulis@napervillelaw.com

DAVID G. WENTZ, born Elmhurst, Illinois, February 4, 1963; admitted to bar, 1989, Illinois and U.S. District Court, Northern and Central Districts of Illinois. *Education:* Augustana College (B.A., 1985); University of Illinois (J.D., 1989). Recipient: American Jurisprudence Award, International Law and World Politics, 1988; DuPage County Bar Association Scholarship, 1986. Elected Naperville Township Republican Precinct Committeeman, 1994 (Chairman, Ways and Means Committee, 1997-1998). Elected Naperville Exchange Club Secretary, 1996-1997, Board of Directors, 1996— and President, 2001-2003. Member, National Exchange Club Jurisprudence and Laws Committee, 2003-2004. Member, DuPage County Workforce Development Board, (Chairman, Membership Committee, 1999). Appointed Special Appellate Public Defender, 1995. Naperville Chamber of Commerce (Chairman, Legislative Committee) 1997-1999. *Member:* DuPage County (Member, Civil Practice, Business Law, Children's Rights, and Appellate Law Committees; Arbitrator Mandatory Arbitration Program, 1993—) and Illinois State (Member, Commercial Litigation and General Practice Committees) Bar Associations. ***REPORTED CASES:*** Galvin v. Olysaw, 212 Ill.App.3d 399 (5th Dist 1991); Illinois Municipal League Risk Management Associaton v. Seibert, 223 Ill.App.3d 864, (4th Dist. 1992). ***PRACTICE AREAS:*** Civil Litigation; Commercial Litigation; Consumer Fraud; Employment Law; Zoning; Condemnation and Eminent Domain; Insurance Defense; Insurance Coverage; Collections; Personal Injury; Business/Corporate Law; Real Estate; Adoptions; Professional Malpractice; Appeals. ***Email:*** dwentz@napervillelaw.com

ASSOCIATES

JOHN RAYMOND WIESER, born Chicago, Illinois, March 29, 1963; admitted to bar, 1992, Illinois. *Education:* North Central College (B.A., History and Political Science, 1989); Illinois Institute of Technology, Chicago-Kent College of Law (J.D., 1992). Recipient, Edmund W. Burke Award. Moot Court Honor Society, 1990-1992. Mock Trial Judge, Midwest Regionals, 1996—. Legal Writing Teaching Assistant, 1991-1992. Best Oral Advocate, National Moot Court Competition, Region 8, 1991. Assistant State's Attorney, DuPage County, 1991-1996. Special Assistant Attorney General, 1998-2002. Hearing Officer, Illinois Department of Financial Institutions, 1999-2002. Attorney Coach, North Central College Mock Trial Team, 1996—. Member, Exchange Club of Naperville, 1997—. Richter Fellow, Joint Ventures in China, 1998-1989. *Member:* DuPage County (Member, Children's Advocacy Committee and Criminal Law Section). ***LANGUAGES:*** German. ***REPORTED CASES:*** Schillerstrom Homes, Inc. v. City of Naperville, 198 Ill.2d 281, 762 N.E.2d 494, 260 Ill.Dec. 835 (2001); People v. McKenna, 328 Ill.App.3d 396, 765 N.E. 2d 1219, 262 Ill.Dec. 611 (2nd Dist. 2002). ***PRACTICE AREAS:*** Civil Litigation; Criminal Defense; Divorce Reconciliation; Juvenile Law; Traffic; DUI; Drivers License Reinstatement; Custody and Visitation; Child Support; Emergency Restraining Orders; Adoption and D.C.F.S. Matters; Real Estate Transactions; Civil Appeals; Criminal Appeals. ***Email:*** jwieser@napervillelaw.com

DOUGLAS C. TIBBLE, born Joliet, Illinois, May 26, 1952; admitted to bar, 1977, Illinois. *Education:* DePaul University (B.A., with honors, 1974); Syracuse University (J.D., summa cum laude, 1977). Order of the Coif. President, Justinian Honor Society, 1976-1977. Member, Syracuse Law Review, 1975-1976. *Member:* Chicago, DuPage County, Illinois State and American Bar Associations. ***PRACTICE AREAS:*** Litigation; Commercial Law; Real Estate. ***Email:*** dtibble@napervillelaw.com

TIMOTHY J. HOPPA, born West Allis, Wisconsin, March 26, 1978; admitted to bar, 2003, Illinois. *Education:* Carroll College (B.S., 2000); Northern Illinois University (J.D., 2003). ***PRACTICE AREAS:*** Municipal; Construction; Civil Litigation. ***Email:*** thoppa@napervillelaw.com

NICOLE L. KARAS, born Paoli, Pennsylvania, October 7, 1970; admitted to bar, 2004, Illinois; 2005, U.S. District Court, Northern District of Illinois. *Education:* Valparaiso University (B.A., cum laude, International Relations, 1992); DePaul University College of Law (J.D., summa cum laude, 2004). Dean's List; Order of the Coif. Recipient: Excellence for Future Award in Advanced Legal Research and Constitutional Law II, Computer Assisted Learning Institute; "Top Scholar" Scholarship, 2002. Associate Editor of Articles, Notes and Comments, DePaul Law Review, 2003-2004. Author: "EEOC v. Luce & the Mandatory Arbitration Agreement," 53 DePaul L. Rev. 67, 2003. *Member:* Chicago, Du Page County and Illinois State Bar Associations. ***PRACTICE AREAS:*** Business Law; Corporate Law; Local Government Law; Real Estate. ***Email:*** nkaras@napervillelaw.com

OF COUNSEL

DAVID N. SCHAFFER, born Chicago, Illinois, December 20, 1958; admitted to bar, 1984, Illinois and U.S. District Court, Northern District of Illinois; 1995, U.S. Supreme Court. *Education:* University of Illinois, Urbana (B.A., 1981); Indiana University School of Law, Bloomington (J.D., 1984). Author: Review of *Don't Settle for Less,* Chicago Bar Association Record Magazine, October 1994; "Review of Bankruptcy Reform Act as Applicable to Matrimonial Law," Chicago Daily Law Bulletin (CDLB), November 11, 1994 and Briefcase (ABA General Practice Section) Newsletter, Vol. 5 No. 1; "An Analysis of the Legitimacy of 750 ILCS 5/505(a)(5)" (percentage child support orders), Chicago Daily Law Bulletin, January 23, 1995 and Illinois Family Law Report, March 1995; "Amended Supreme Court Discovery Rules as Seen Through the Eyes of a Matrimonial Lawyer," Illinois Family Law Report, November 1995; "Child, Spousal Support Laws Work in Tandem (Most of the Time)" (UIFSA and URESA compared), Chicago Daily Law Bulletin, October 23, 1996; "The Use of Revenue Rulings in Marital Appraisals," DuPage County Bar Association Brief Magazine, November 1996; "State Law on Grandparent Visitation Needs Revision", Chicago Daily Law Bulletin, June 20, 2000; "Expert Testimony in Child Custody Cases," Family Law Up-date, Aspen Publishers, 2001; "Troxel and Lulay-Two High Courts Speak on Grandparent Visitation Rights," Illinois Bar Journal, Vol. 89, # 2, February, 2001, "When DCFS Knocks: Representing a Client Accused of Child Abuse or Neglect," Illinois Bar Journal, Vol. 92, #1, January 2004. Cited in four "Dear Abby" advice columns and two "All That Zazz" advice columns. Lecturer: Illinois State Bar Association Family Law Updates: "The New Supreme Court Discovery Rules," Chicago, Winter 1995; "Presenting an Effective Pre-trial," Chicago, Fall 1996; "Handling Custody Cases When the Expert Sides Against You," St. Louis MO, Summer 1998; "Grandparent Visitation Rights After Troxel and Lulay," Chicago, Winter, 2000; "Caselaw Update-Grandparent Visitation Rights," Lake Geneva WI, Summer, 2002; "DCFS is at the Door, What to Do - Advising Clients from Start to Appeal," Chicago, Winter 2002; "Grandparent Rights: Visitation, No; Guardianship, Maybe," Law Vegas NV, Winter 2003; "Removal of Children From the State," Chicago, Spring 2004; "The Nuts and Bolts of Contempt Proceedings," Lake Geneva WI, Summer 2004. Illinois Institute for Continuing Legal Education: "The 'Shrinking' of Child Custody Cases: The Use of Mental Health Experts— Experts and Preparing For Trial," 1996. Noted cases: "Appellate Court Will Not Second Guess Close Custody Case," Illinois Family Law Report, June 1996; "Mother's Credibility Evaporates, Unstable Environment Disqualifies Her As Custodian," Illinois Trial Court Divorce Digest May 1995; "Support Tripled," Illinois Trial Court Divorce Digest, January, 1994. Member, Anti-Defamation League Speakers Bureau and Civil Rights Committee. 1991-1993. Public Office: Trustee, Village of Lombard (DuPage County) Board of Trustees, 1997-2001, (Chair, Finance Committee), 1999-2001. Chair, DuPage County Community Development Commission, 2000-2001. Member/Instructor, American Academy of Matrimonial Lawyers Institute for Training New Associates. *Member:* Du Page County (Member, Family Law Committee), Illinois State (Appointed, Family Law Section Council Secretary, Chair, Legislative Sub-Committee; Elected-General Assembly and Agenda Committee, 1998-2001) and American (Member, Family Law Committee) Bar Associations. Fellow, American Academy of Matrimonial Lawyers. Fellow, International Academy of Matrimonial Lawyers. ***PRACTICE AREAS:*** Family Law; Complex Domestic Relations Issues; Divorce/Dissolution of Marriage; Prenuptial Agreements; Premarital Agreements; Child Custody and Visitation; Spousal Support; Alimony; Maintenance; Matrimonial Law; Matrimonial Litigation; Appeals; Marital Settlement Agreements; Separation Agreements; Property Rights; Financial Discovery and Analysis Related to Divorce; Tax Considerations Related to Divorce. ***Email:*** schaffer@napervillelaw.com

COUNSEL FOR: *Park Districts:* Bartlett, Bloomingdale, Downers Grove, Glen Ellyn, LaGrange Park, Naperville and Wards Creek; *School Districts:* Downers Grove 58; Naperville 203; *Library Boards:* Westmont; Naperville Township; South East Association for Special Parks and Recreation; Western DuPage Special Recreation Assn.; Naperville Township Highway Commissioner; Lisle Township Assessor.
REPRESENTATIVE CLIENTS: MCI Telecommunications Corporation; Browning-Ferris Industries; Monarch Life Insurance; Crampton, Inc.; Harris Bank Naperville; Mid-America Development Corp.; Meritor Academies; A.A. Rose Construction; Waste Management, Inc.

GREGORY J. BUECHE

NAPERVILLE, ILLINOIS

(See Warrenville)

MICHAEL T. BYRNE

NAPERVILLE, ILLINOIS

(See Clarendon Hills)

Criminal Law, Driving While Intoxicated, Drug Crimes, Felonies, Homicide, Sexual Assault, Traffic Violations and Probation Violations.

MARY DENISE CAHILL

1155 SOUTH WASHINGTON STREET
NAPERVILLE, ILLINOIS 60540
Telephone: 630-778-6500
Fax: 630-778-0722
Email: mdcahill@sbcglobal.net

Representing families with special needs children. Attention Deficit, Hyperactivity Disorder, Developmental Disabilities and Learning Disabilities. Family Law, School Law, Special Education, School Equal Protection, Disabled Rights, Class Action Defense, Employment Law, and Estate Planning Law, Mediation.

(This Listing Continued)

MARY DENISE CAHILL, born Chicago, Illinois; admitted to bar, 1976, Illinois; 1986, Arizona. *Education:* Loyola University (B.A., 1968; J.D., 1976).

CALABRESE ASSOCIATES

A PROFESSIONAL CORPORATION

NAPERVILLE, ILLINOIS

(See Wheaton)

Family Law including Divorce Law, Child Custody, Visitation Rights, Support, Adoption Law, Paternity, Prenuptial Agreements and Appeals.

CASSIDAY, SCHADE & GLOOR, LLP

1230 EAST DIEHL ROAD, SUITE 202
NAPERVILLE, ILLINOIS 60563-9362
Telephone: 630-328-2970
Fax: 630-328-2979
URL: http://www.cassiday.com

Chicago, Illinois Office: 20 North Wacker Drive, Suite 1040, 60606-2903. Telephone: 312-641-3100. Fax: 312-444-1669.
Libertyville, Illinois Office: 1870 West Winchester Road, Suite 148, 60048-5353. Telephone: 847-932-6922. Fax: 847-932-6947.
Rockford, Illinois Office: 120 West State Street, Suite 401, 61101-1159. Telephone: 815-962-8301. Fax: 815-962-8401.

General Practice. Civil Trial Practice, Civil Appellate Practice, Insurance Coverage, Environmental, Medical and Professional Malpractice, Products Liability, Structural Work Act, Railroad, Employment, Corporate and Health Care Law, Commercial Litigation, Construction, Workers Compensation, Intellectual Property, Municipalities, Transportation, Patent Law, Intellectual Property.

FIRM PROFILE: Serving Cook, DuPage, Kane, Kankakee, LaSalle and Will Counties and counties in Northern Indiana.

The firm also has an established Quality Control Department.

MEMBERS OF FIRM

BRIAN J. HICKEY, born Oak Park, Illinois, November 8, 1963; admitted to bar, 1988, Illinois, U.S. District Court, Northern District of Indiana and Northern District of Illinois including Trial Bar. *Education:* University of Illinois, Champaign/Urbana (B.S., 1985); DePaul University (J.D., 1988). *Member:* Chicago Bar Association. ***PRACTICE AREAS:*** Personal Injury Defense; Professional Liability Defense. ***Email:*** bjh@cs-g.com

THERESE S. SEELEY, born Grand Rapids, Michigan, November 26, 1955; admitted to bar, 1982, Illinois; 1983, U.S. District Court, Northern District of Illinois including Trial Bar. *Education:* University of Notre Dame (B.B.A., 1977); DePaul University (J.D., 1982). Arbitrator, DuPage County Circuit Court. *Member:* DuPage County and Illinois State Bar Associations; Defense Research Institute. ***PRACTICE AREAS:*** Insurance Defense; Professional Liability Defense. ***Email:*** tss@cs-g.com

DOUGLAS S. STROHM, born Fort Collins, Colorado, November 15, 1964; admitted to bar, 1991, Illinois. *Education:* University of Iowa (B.S., 1987; J.D., 1990). *Member:* DuPage County Bar Association; Illinois Association of Defense Trial Counsel. ***PRACTICE AREAS:*** Insurance Defense; Municipal Entities; Public Entities. ***Email:*** dss@cs-g.com

ASSOCIATES

JENNIFER A. BOLLOW, born Darien, Illinois, July 25, 1973; admitted to bar, 1998, Illinois. *Education:* Illinois State University (B.S., 1995); Loyola University (J.D., cum laude, 1998). ***Email:*** jab@cs-g.com

BROOK M. CAREY, born Elgin, Illinois, 1978; admitted to bar, 2003, Illinois. *Education:* Lewis University (B.A., with highest honors, 2000); Loyola University (J.D., cum laude, 2003). ***Email:*** bmc@cs-g.com

JONATHAN P. MINCIELI, born Brooklyn, New York, February 6, 1971; admitted to bar, 1997, New York; 2000, New Jersey; 2001, Illinois. *Education:* State University of New York at Oswego (B.A., 1993); St. John's University (J.D., cum laude, 1996). ***Email:*** jpm@cs-g.com

MARK A. SANSONE, born Evergreen Park, Illinois, April 27, 1975; admitted to bar, 2000, Illinois. *Education:* St. Joseph's College (B.S., 1997); Valparaiso University School of Law (J.D., 2000). ***Email:*** mas@cs-g.com

(For complete biographical data on all personnel, see Professional Biographies at Chicago, Illinois)

LAW OFFICES OF SUSAN G. CASTAGNOLI, P.C.

Established in 1991

1119 NORTH WASHINGTON STREET
NAPERVILLE, ILLINOIS 60563
Telephone: 630-717-1594; TT4-630-566-5222
Fax: 630-717-1596
Email: susancastagnoli@scastagnolilaw.com
URL: http://www.castagnolilaw.com

Kane County Office: 1444 North Farnsworth Avenue, Suite 107, Aurora, Illinois, 60505. Telephone: 630-717-1594. Fax: 630-717-1596.

(This Listing Continued)

Bankruptcy, Commercial Bankruptcy, Consumer Bankruptcy, Foreclosures, Debt Management, Family, Divorce, Divorce Planning, Premarital Agreements, Custody, Adoptions, Child Support, Real Estate, Financial Planning, Wills and Probate, Estate Planning, Trusts and Estates, Equine Law.

FIRM PROFILE: 26 Years of personal attention to the needs of the client are the benchmark of the firm. All clients meet personally with attorney Susan G. Castagnoli.

SUSAN G. CASTAGNOLI, born Aurora, Illinois, October 2, 1953; admitted to bar, 1979, Illinois and U.S. Court of Appeals, Seventh Circuit. *Education:* Monmouth College (B.A., 1974); Northern Illinois University (J.D., 1978). Justinian Honor Society, 1974. Real Estate Broker (GRI, 1987). Certified Divorce Planner. Instructor, Aurora University, Criminal Law, 1988-1994. *Member:* Du Page County Bar Association (Bankruptcy Chairman, 2000-2002; Chairman, Law Office Economics Committee, 1988-1989). ***LANGUAGES:*** Sign Language. ***PRACTICE AREAS:*** Bankruptcy; Divorce; Real Estate; Equine Law; Bankruptcy Chapter 13.

Languages: Sign Language.

CETINA & JACQUES, P.C.

NAPERVILLE, ILLINOIS

(See Oakbrook Terrace)

Personal Injury, Personal Injury Appeals, Personal Injury Arbitration, Personal Injury Defense, Personal Injury Mediation, Plaintiffs Personal Injury, Medical Malpractice, Nursing Home Abuse and Neglect, Driving While Intoxicated, Drug Crimes, Traffic Violations.

CHICAGO INTERNET ATTORNEYS

NAPERVILLE, ILLINOIS

(See Chicago)

Personal Injury, Spinal Cord Injury, Automobile Accidents, Wrongful Death, Products Liability, Medical Malpractice, Corporate, Business, Real Estate, Criminal and Civil Litigation.

CHRISTENSEN & EHRET, LLP

NAPERVILLE, ILLINOIS

(See Chicago)

Admiralty and Maritime Law, Appellate Practice, Commercial Litigation, Construction Liability, Excess and Reinsurance, Insurance Coverage, Products Liability, Professional Malpractice, Transportation, Trial Practice.

CIRIGNANI HELLER HARMAN & LYNCH LLP

NAPERVILLE, ILLINOIS

(See Chicago)

Medical Malpractice, Wrongful Death, Cerebral Palsy, ERBS Palsy, Brain Damage, Anesthesia Injury, Improper Medication, Operating Room Death, Misdiagnosis, Birth Injuries, Retardation, Surgical Error, Medical Product Failure, Nursing Errors, Hospital Negligence, Head and Spinal Injuries, Automobile Accidents, Truck Accidents, Construction Accidents, Product Liability, Labor and Employment Litigation, Commercial Litigation, Insurance Coverage, Torts. Litigation.

CREMER, KOPON, SHAUGHNESSY & SPINA, LLC

NAPERVILLE, ILLINOIS

(See Chicago)

Complex Civil Litigation Defense, including Product Liability, Construction Law, Insurance Coverage, Commercial Litigation, Drug and Medical Device Litigation, Employment Law, Toxic Torts, Commercial Real Estate, University and College Law and all aspects of Trial and Appellate work in both State and Federal Courts.

DOMMERMUTH, BRESTAL, COBINE AND WEST, LTD.

Established in 1983

123 WATER STREET
P.O. BOX 565
NAPERVILLE, ILLINOIS 60566-0565
Telephone: 630-355-5800; 355-6001
Fax: 630-355-5976
Email: PLP@DBCW.com

Aurora, Illinois Office: Old Second National Bank Building, 111 West Downer Place, Suite 300. Telephone: 630-892-5700.

General Civil Practice. Personal Injury, Worker's Compensation, Corporate, Banking, Municipal, Zoning and Development, Real Estate, Family and Probate Law, Litigation, Federal and State Taxation, Commercial Collection.

ALBIN DOMMERMUTH (1910-1998)

WILLARD F. BRESTAL, born Belleville, Illinois, June 17, 1941; admitted to bar, 1968, Illinois. *Education:* University of Illinois (B.S., 1964); Loyola University of Chicago (J.D., 1968). *Member:* Will County, DuPage County, Illinois State and American Bar Associations. ***PRACTICE AREAS:*** Municipal Law; Zoning Law; Land Development; Contracts; General Practice. ***Email:*** wfd@dbcw.com

(This Listing Continued)

DOMMERMUTH, BRESTAL, COBINE AND WEST, LTD., Naperville—Continued

CRAIG J. COBINE, born Chicago, Illinois, January 3, 1948; admitted to bar, 1972, Illinois, U.S. District Court, Eastern District of Illinois and U.S. Court of Appeals, Seventh Circuit. *Education:* Loyola University (B.A., 1969); Northwestern University (J.D., cum laude, 1972). Member, Board of Editors, Criminal Law Journal, Northwestern University Law School, 1971-1972. Author: "Elements of Liability and Actual Damages in Rule 106-5 Actions," Illinois Law Forum, 1972. ***PRACTICE AREAS:*** Commercial Real Estate; Condemnation; Business Law; Corporate Law; Contracts; General Practice. ***Email:*** cjc@dbcw.com

KATHLEEN C. WEST, born Evergreen Park, Illinois, January 28, 1951; admitted to bar, 1981, Illinois and U.S. District Court, Northern District of Illinois. *Education:* University of Illinois (B.U.P., 1973); Loyola University of Chicago Law School (J.D., 1981). *Member:* DuPage County and Illinois State Bar Associations. ***PRACTICE AREAS:*** Municipal Law; Zoning Law; Land Development; Contracts; General Practice. ***Email:*** kcw@dbcw.com

ROBERT G. GIBSON, born Yonkers, New York, June 4, 1958; admitted to bar, 1983, Illinois. *Education:* Notre Dame University (B.A., 1980); University of Illinois (J.D., 1983). Rickert Award for Excellence in Moot Court, 1982-1983. National Moot Court Team, 1982-1983. *Member:* DuPage County Bar Association; Association of Trial Lawyers of America. ***PRACTICE AREAS:*** Residential Real Estate; Personal Injury; Debtor and Creditor Collections; General Practice. ***Email:*** rgg@dbcw.com

EDWARD J. WELCH, born Aurora, Illinois, October 13, 1947; admitted to bar, 1972, Indiana and U.S. District Court, Northern District of Indiana; 1975, Illinois; 1979, Alaska; 1985, U.S. District Court, Northern District of Illinois. *Education:* University of Notre Dame (A.B., 1969; J.D., 1972). Assistant District Attorney, Anchorage, Alaska, 1983-1984. Member, Board of Directors, Alaska Legal Services, 1982-1984. *Member:* DuPage County and Alaska Bar Associations. ***PRACTICE AREAS:*** Municipal Law; Zoning Law; Land Use; Labor and Employment; Residential Real Estate; Family Law; General Practice. ***Email:*** ejw@dbcw.com

KEVIN M. GENSLER, born Chicago, Illinois, December 8, 1957; admitted to bar, 1985, Illinois. *Education:* Michigan State University (B.A., 1980); John Marshall Law School (J.D., 1985). Member, Moot Court Executive Board, 1983-1984. *Member:* Du Page County, Illinois State and American Bar Associations. ***PRACTICE AREAS:*** Residential Real Estate; Corporate Law; Business Law; Trusts and Estates; Wills; Probate; Contracts; General Practice. ***Email:*** kmg@dbcw.com

JOHN F. PHILIPCHUCK, born Aurora, Illinois, September 11, 1946; admitted to bar, 1978, Illinois and U.S. District Court, Northern District of Illinois. *Education:* University of Wisconsin-Stevens Point (B.S., 1969); John Marshall Law School (J.D., 1978). *Member:* Kane County, Illinois State and American Bar Associations; American Planning Association. ***PRACTICE AREAS:*** Municipal Law; Zoning Law; Land Use; General Practice. ***Email:*** jfp@dbcw.com

---

KEVIN M. GALLAHER, born Elmhurst, Illinois, June 1, 1963; admitted to bar, 1988, Illinois. *Education:* St John's University (B.A., 1985); DePaul University College of Law (J.D., 1988). ***PRACTICE AREAS:*** Zoning Law; Land Use; Real Estate; Estate Planning; Probate. ***Email:*** kmg1@dbcw.com

CHARLES J. CORRIGAN, born Cleveland, Ohio, September 26, 1960; admitted to bar, 1987, Illinois and U.S. District Court, Northern District of Illinois; 1991, U.S. Supreme Court and U.S. Court of Appeals, Seventh Circuit. *Education:* Georgetown University (B.A., 1983); John Marshall Law School (J.D., cum laude, 1987). Member, Order of John Marshall. Associate Editor, The John Marshall Law Review, 1986-1987. Author: Comment, "Justice Brennan's Philosophy of Federalism," 20 John Marshall Law Review 149, 1987. *Member:* Chicago, DuPage County, Illinois State and American Bar Associations; American Counsel Association; The Association of Trial Lawyers of America; The National Employment Lawyers Association. ***REPORTED CASES:*** Robert T. Wozniak v. Bradley J. Martin 91L-9204 Tried Jan. 11-31, 1996. ***PRACTICE AREAS:*** Civil Litigation; Employment Law; Small Business; Estate Planning. ***Email:*** cjc1@dbcw.com

RUSSELL G. WHITAKER, born St. Charles, Illinois, February 9, 1978; admitted to bar, 2004, Illinois. *Education:* North Central College (B.A., 2000); DePaul College of Law (J.D., 2004). ***PRACTICE AREAS:*** Zoning Law; Land Use; Real Estate; Estate Planning; Probate. ***Email:*** rgw@dbcw.com

JAMES R. SETHNA, born Chicago, Illinois, December 2, 1974; admitted to bar, 2001, Illinois. *Education:* DePaul University (B.A., Political Science, 1998); The John Marshall Law School (J.D., cum laude, 2001). Phi Delta Phi (Board Member, 2000; President, 2001). ***PRACTICE AREAS:*** Commercial Litigation; Civil Litigation; Real Estate. ***Email:*** jrs@dbcw.com

PATTI A. BERNHARD, born Chicago, Illinois, November 5, 1954; admitted to bar, 1998, Illinois. *Education:* Bradley University (B.S., 1976); The John Marshall Law School (J.D., 1998). Member, The John Marshall Law Review. ***PRACTICE AREAS:*** Land Use; Zoning Law. ***Email:*** pab@dbcw.com

VINCENT M. ROSANOVA, born Winfield, Illinois, July 15, 1977; admitted to bar, 2005, Illinois. *Education:* Lewis University (B.A., Business, 2002); Northern Illinois University College of Law (J.D., 2005). Phi Delta Phi, 2003-2005. Recipient, Brewster Parker Prize, Outstanding Achievement in Property, Real Estate & Land Use Law. Instructor, Teaching Graduate Assistantship, Contracts, Northern Illinois University College of Law, 2004-2005. ***PRACTICE AREAS:*** Government; Zoning, Planning and Land Use; Contracts. ***Email:*** vmr@dbcn.com

REPRESENTATIVE CLIENTS: DuPage Precision Products, Inc.; North Central College; Naperville Fire Protection District; Macom Corp.; Mid America Federal Savings and Loan Association; Beidelman-Kunsch Funeral Home; Engineering Equipment Co.; Shell Oil Co.; Phillips 66 Co.; Amoco Oil Co.; Mobil Oil Co.; Pulte Home Corp.; Prime Group; Catholic Diocese of Joliet; Our Savior Lutheran Church; Hawthorne Credit Union; Home Builders of Illinois; Wiseman-Hughes Enterprises, Inc.; Lakewood Homes, Inc.; Pep Boys; McDonald's Corp.; Walsh, Higgins & Co.; Crestview Builders, Inc.; Inland Realty; Central DuPage Health System; Edward Hospital; Moser Enterprises; MAF Corporation; Meijer, Inc.; Ocean Atlantic Woodland Corporation; Security Bank of DuPage; DePaul University; Cambridge Homes, Inc.; Allied Waste North America, Inc.

(This Listing Continued)

DREYER, FOOTE, STREIT, FURGASON AND SLOCUM

A PROFESSIONAL ASSOCIATION

NAPERVILLE, ILLINOIS

(See Aurora, Illinois)

Civil and Criminal Trial and Appellate Practice in all State and Federal Courts. Business Planning, Commercial, Corporate, Estate Planning, Wills, Probate, Trusts and Estates, Elder Law, Family Law, Healthcare, Insurance and Insurance Defense, Labor, Municipal, Personal Injury, Probate, Real Estate, State and Federal Taxation, Adoption, Child Support, Child Custody, Divorce, Domestic Violence, DWI, Automobile Accidents, Wrongful Death, Buying and Selling a Home, Landlord/Tenant, Construction, Bankruptcy, Guardianships, Collections, Buying and Selling a Business, Business Enterprises, Franchise, Closely Held Business, Limited Liability, Partnerships, Small Business, Contracts, Lawsuits, Starting a Business, Zoning.

THE LAW OFFICE OF RANDALL T. ERICKSON, PC

NAPERVILLE, ILLINOIS

(See Wheaton)

Intellectual Property, Patents, Patent Prosecution, Trade Secrets, Trademarks, Trademark Prosecution, Unfair Competition.

FAWELL & FAWELL, LTD.

NAPERVILLE, ILLINOIS

(See Wheaton)

Family Law, Divorce Law, Child Custody, Child Support, Domestic Violence, Spousal Support, Premarital Agreements, Mediation and Adoptions.

ELIZABETH M. FEELY, P.C.

NAPERVILLE, ILLINOIS

(See Chicago)

Family Law.

FEWKES WENTZ & STRAYER

A Law Partnership of Professional Corporations

Established in 1989

184 SHUMAN BOULEVARD
SUITE 250
NAPERVILLE, ILLINOIS 60563
Telephone: 630-527-8552
Fax: 630-527-8636
URL: http://www.businesslegalexperts.com

Business, Corporate, Mergers and Acquisitions, Commercial Real Estate and Antitrust Law.

FIRM PROFILE: FWS sets itself apart from the traditional corporate law firm with emphasis on helping businesses and business owners develop practical plans and strategies to achieve their business objectives. FWS works with clients to reduce legal risks, advance clients' business interests and provide greater value for legal services rendered.

MEMBERS OF FIRM

DAVID A. FEWKES (Retired)

WILLIAM H. WENTZ, born 1945; admitted to bar, 1970, Pennsylvania; 1973, District of Columbia; 1987, Illinois. *Education:* Brown University (A.B., 1967); University of Pennsylvania (J.D., 1970); University of Chicago (M.B.A., 1988). Recipient: Small Business Leader Award, Oak Brook Association of Commerce & Industry, 1999; Founder's Award, DuPage Area Association, 1994. Author: "Mobility Factors in Antitrust Cases: Assessing Market Power in Light of Conditions Affecting Entry and Fringe Expansion," University of Michigan Law Review, 1982; "An Antitrust Primer," and " Federal Pre-Emption of State Law," Antitrust in the Healthcare Field, 1979. Associate General Counsel, Civil Aeronautics Board, 1981-1984. Attorney Advisor to Chairman, Federal Trade Commission, 1971-1973. Coordinator, Entrepreneurial Roundtable, University of Chicago Graduate School of Business. Director, Midwest Business Brokers and Intermediaries, 1996-2001. *Member:* Chicago, DuPage County and American Bar Associations. ***PRACTICE AREAS:*** Antitrust Law; Business Law; Mergers and Acquisitions. ***Email:*** billwentz@businesslegalexperts.com

JAY B. STRAYER, born Kansas City, Missouri, March 11, 1942; admitted to bar, 1970, Kansas; 1972, Illinois and U.S. District Court, Northern District of Illinois and District of Kansas. *Education:* University of Kansas (B.A., 1964; M.B.A., 1971; J.D., 1969). Phi Delta Phi. Vice President/General Counsel/Secretary, The Jepson Corporation (NYSE), 1987-1992. General Counsel/Secretary, Atcor, Inc. (NASDAQ), 1985-1986. Assistant General Counsel, McGraw-Edison Company (NYSE), 1980-1985. Trustee, Village of Glen Ellyn, Illinois, 1999-2003. Plan Commission, Village of Glen Ellyn, 2005—. *Member:* DuPage County and American Bar Associations. [Comdr., Supply Corps, USNR (Retired)].

(This Listing Continued)

PRACTICE AREAS: Corporate Law; Estate Planning; Business Transactions. ***Email:*** jaystrayer@businesslegalexperts.com

LAW OFFICES OF
EDWARD P. GRAHAM, LTD.

Established in 1995

1112 SOUTH WASHINGTON STREET, SUITE 212
NAPERVILLE, ILLINOIS 60540
Telephone: 630-357-2333
Fax: 630-357-2393
Email: counselors@graham-law.com
URL: http://www.graham-law.com

Adoptions, Bankruptcy, Business Formation and General Counsel, Collections, Criminal Defense, Divorce, Estate Planning, Wills and Trusts, General Litigation, Juvenile, Landlord - Tenant Relations, Municipal Law, Zoning and Land Use, Personal Injury, Workers Compensation, Probate and Guardianship, Real Estate Transactions, Traffic Prosecution and Defense.

FIRM PROFILE: In 2004 the Law Offices of Edward P. Grahan, Ltd. enters its tenth year with a continuing commitment to its original mission of conscientiously serving the professional legal needs of it current and future clients through its dedicated and experienced lawyers and staff.

EDWARD P. GRAHAM, born Chicago, Illinois, October 30, 1961; admitted to bar, 1987, Illinois. *Education:* University of Notre Dame (B.A., 1983); Ohio Northern University (J.D., 1987). Recipient, American Jurisprudence Award, Estates. Member, Law Review. *Member:* Will County, DuPage County and Illinois State Bar Associations; Illinois Trial Lawyers Association; Institute for Municipal Government; Illinois Institute for Local Government Law. ***PRACTICE AREAS:*** Civil Litigation; Real Estate; Municipal Law; Juvenile Law. ***Email:*** epgraham@graham-law.com

ASSOCIATE

MELISSA A. GRAHONYA, born Chicago, Illinois, July 10, 1977; admitted to bar, 2002, Illinois. *Education:* University of Illinois (B.A., 1999; J.D., 2002). *Member:* DuPage and Illinois State Bar Associations; Will County Women's Bar Association. ***PRACTICE AREAS:*** Estate Planning; Real Estate; Juvenile Law; Municipal Law; Civil Litigation. ***Email:*** magrahonya@graham-law.com

LAW OFFICES OF
GRAY & IDRIS, P.C.

NAPERVILLE, ILLINOIS

(See Joilet)

General Practice.

THE LAW FIRM OF
DANYA A. GRUNYK, P.C.

5TH AVENUE STATION
200 EAST FIFTH AVENUE, SUITE 118
NAPERVILLE, ILLINOIS 60563
Telephone: 630-428-3300
Fax: 630-428-3313
Email: dgrunyk@aol.com
URL: http://www.lawyers.com/grunyklaw

Divorce, Family Law, Litigation, Collaborative Law, Mediation, Child Custody, Child Support, Adoptions, Guardianship, Paternity.

DANYA A. GRUNYK, born Detroit, Michigan, December 11, 1955; admitted to bar, 1987, New Jersey; 2000, Illinois. *Education:* University of Michigan (B.A., 1977); University of Detroit (M.B.A., 1981); DePaul University and Seton Hall University (J.D., 1987); Rutgers University, Conflict Management Program/Divorce Mediation (1996). Mediator, Guardian ad Litem and Child Representative, DuPage County. Adjunct Professor, John Marshall Law School (2002—). Certified Collaborative Law Professional, 2003; Certified by the Supreme Court of New Jersey as a Matrimonial Attorney, 1999-2005. Author: "The Kiddie QDRO: Federal Law Now Protects Children's Medical Benefits After Divorce," New Jersey Family Lawyer, Vol. XVI, No. 4, May/June 1996; "The British Inns of Court Concept Comes to Family Law," New Jersey Family Lawyer Vol. XV, No. 4, July, 1995; "Mechanisms to Insure that Children are Heard," New Jersey Family Lawyer, Vol. XIV, No. 8, November, 1994; "Marriage, Divorce and Separation," Editorial Assistance, West Publishing Company, New Jersey Practice, 1991 Pamphlet Editions. Lecturer: 2005, DuPage County: Case Law Update, Guardian ad Litem/Child Representative Training Program; 1997 Family Law Symposium; 1996 Family Law Summer Institute, ICLE; "The Pit-Bull Deposition - A Demonstration," American Bar Association Convention, Washington, D.C., April, 1995; "Financial Aspects of Divorce and the Equitable Distribution of Property," New Jersey State Bar Foundation, June, 1994; "Rights and Values: What Guides You," The National Conference of Christians and Jews, May, 1994. Panelist, Morris and Somerset County Matrimonial Early Settlement Panels. Graduate, Arthur T. Vanderbilt Chapter, Essex Inns of Court, 1990-1992. Corporate Management Experience, Product Management, Marketing and Business Development within the U.S.A. and Internationally, 1976-1988. Selected by Rotary International Foundation as Member of Group-Study Exchange Program in Austria, April-May, 1995. *Member:* DuPage, Will and Cook Counties, Illinois State and New Jersey State (Member, Executive Committee, Family Law Section, 1993) Bar Associations; Ukrainian-American Bar Association; New Jersey Family Law Inns of Court (Member, Executive Committees, 1993-1996). Fellow, Illinois Collaborative Law Institute, International Academy of Collaborative Professionals. ***LANGUAGES:*** Ukrainian, Portuguese. ***PRACTICE AREAS:*** Litigation; Divorce Mediation; Collaborative Law; Family Law; Adoption Law; Child Custody; Child Support; Paternity; Visitation Rights. ***Email:*** dgrunyk@aol.com

(This Listing Continued)

THE LAW OFFICE OF
JAMES W. HANAUER

NAPERVILLE, ILLINOIS

(See Wheaton)

RICHARD L. HIRSH & ASSOCIATES, P.C.

NAPERVILLE, ILLINOIS

(See Hinsdale)

Bankruptcy, Personal Bankruptcy, Debtor and Creditor, Foreclosures and Buy-Sell Agreements.

SHERYL Y. HOLLOWAY

NAPERVILLE, ILLINOIS

(See Chicago)

Real Estate Closings, Evictions, Divorces, Wills, Personal Injury, Guardianships, Expungements.

KNELL & POULOS

A PROFESSIONAL CORPORATION

NAPERVILLE, ILLINOIS

(See Chicago)

Workers Compensation Defense, Insurance Defense, Employment Defense.

STEVEN B. LEVY, LTD.

Established in 1984

650 EAST DIEHL ROAD
SUITE 121
NAPERVILLE, ILLINOIS 60563
Telephone: 630-416-6300
Telefax: 630-245-0930
URL: http://www.lawyers.com/stevenblevy
Email: slevy@sblevyltdlaw.com
URL: http://www.sblevyltdlaw.com

Plaintiff's Personal Injury, Wrongful Death, Medical Malpractice, Automobile Accidents, Truck Accidents, Products Liability and Premises Liability Law.

FIRM PROFILE: Mr. Levy practices exclusively in the areas of bodily injury and wrongful death claims. He negotiates settlements and litigates bodily injury and wrongful death claims of various kinds and complexity including vehicle collision injuries, medical malpractice, defective product/service injuries and unsafe property injuries. He represents injured persons seeking reasonable compensation for legitimate injuries.

The firm's practice is devoted to providing personal attention and professional advocacy for individuals and their families who have been injured or who have suffered wrongful death due to the carelessness of others. The firm strives to do its best in all ways for each and every client because members of the firm believe that word of mouth referrals based on client satisfaction is, and always will be, the best advertisement of a professional's success.

STEVEN B. LEVY, born Chicago, Illinois, September 3, 1954; admitted to bar, 1979, Illinois, U.S. District Court, Northern District of Illinois and U.S. Court of Appeals, 7th Circuit; 1980, Florida, U.S. District Court, Southern and Middle Districts of Florida and U.S. Court of Appeals, Tenth and Eleventh Circuits; 1993, Supreme Court. *Education:* University of Illinois (B.A., 1975); Illinois Institute of Technology (J.D., 1978). Founding Member, Du Page County Chapter, American Inns of Court. Recipient: Du Page County Bar Association's 2nd Annual Elbert H. Gary Award for Professional Excellence in recognition of Outstanding Personality, Leadership and Professionalism; Du Page County Bar Association's 20th Annual "Lawyer of the Year" Award in Recognition of Distinguished Leadership and Meritorious Services Rendered; "A Pillar of the Profession"- Illinois Bar Foundation, 2005; "A Top Personal Injury Lawyer," "A Top Medical Malpractice Lawyer," 2005, 2004, 2003 Chicago Daily Law Bulletin, Peer Survey. Co-Editor and Chapter Author of 2005 Illinois Continuing Legal Education Medical Malpractice Guidebook; Speaker: Tort Law Seminar, Illinois State Bar Association, 2005, 2004, 2003, 2002 and 2001; Insurance Law Seminar, Illinois State Bar Association, 2000; Civil Practice and Procedure Seminar, Illinois State Bar Association, 1999. Member: Illinois Supreme Court Rules Committee, Appointed by Illinois Supreme Court, 1998-2001; Illinois Supreme Court Committee on Professional Responsibility, Appointed by Illinois Supreme Court, 1996-1998. *Member:* Du Page County (Editor-in-Chief, Bar Journal, 1995-1999) and Illinois State (Member: Editorial Board, Bar Journal, 1996—; Standing Committee on Continuing Legal Education, 1997—. ***REPORTED CASES:*** Boyd vs. Traveler's Insurance Company, 166 Ill. 2d 188, 652 N.E. 2d 267, 1995. Established a negligence cause of action in Illinois for spoliation of evidence. The case involved a product liability claim in which Traveler's Insurance Company lost the evidence (the alleged defective product) essential to Boyd's pursuit of his claim. The Illinois Supreme Court, ruling in favor of the plaintiff, held: "A defendant owes a duty of due care to preserve evidence if a reasonable person in the defendant's position should have foreseen that the evidence was material to a potential civil action," 166 Ill. 2d

(This Listing Continued)

STEVEN B. LEVY, LTD., Naperville—Continued

193. ***PRACTICE AREAS:*** Plaintiffs Personal Injury; Wrongful Death; Medical Malpractice; Automobile Accidents; Truck Accidents; Products Liability; Premises Liability Law. ***Email:*** slevy@sblevyltdlaw.com

---

ALLYSON B. HARRIS, born Chicago, Illinois, April 5, 1963; admitted to bar, 1994, Illinois. *Education:* DePaul University (B.A., 1987); Chicago-Kent College of Law, Illinois Institute of Technology (J.D., 1994). Order of the Coif. Notes and Comments Editor, Chicago-Kent College of Law Review, 1993-1994. Law Clerk to: Honorable Judge Robin Pierce, Northern District of Indiana, 1994-1995; Honorable Robert D. McLaren, 2nd District Appellate Court, Illinois, 1995-2005. *Member:* Illinois State and DuPage County Bar Associations. ***REPORTED CASES:*** Assisted in writing: Mull v. Kane County Forest Preserve Dist., 337 Ill. App.3d 589, 786 N.E.2d 236, 2003; Lowe Excavating Co. v. International Union of Operating Engineers Local No. 150, 327 Ill. App.3d 711, 765 N.E.2d 21, 2002; Pancott v. Mayes, 304 Ill. App.3d 108, 709 N.E.2d 287, 1999; Pekin Ins. Co. v. Willett, 301 Ill. App.3d 1034, 704 N.E.2d 923, 1998; Schanowitz v. State Farm Mut. Auto. Ins. Co., 299 Ill. App.3d 843, 702 N.E.2d 629, 1998; Fuller's Car Wash, Inc. v. Liberty Mut. Ins. Co., 298 Ill. App.3d 167, 698 N.E.2d 237, 1998; Johnson v. St. Therese Medical Center, 296 Ill. App.3d 341, 694 N.E.2d. 3694 N.E.2d 1088, 1998; American Country Ins. Co. v. Bruhn, 298 Ill. App.3d 241, 682 N.E.2d 366, 1997; City of Harvard v. Gaut, 277 Ill. App.3d 1, 660, N.E.2d 259, 1996; Exline v. Exline, 277 Ill. App.3d 10, 659 N.E.2d 407, 1995. ***PRACTICE AREAS:*** Plaintiffs Personal Injury; Wrongful Death; Civil Appeals; Medical Malpractice; Automobile Accidents and Injuries; Truck Accidents; Products Liability; Premises Liability.

Languages: Spanish.

DAVID H. McCARTHY, III

Established in 1989

1155 SOUTH WASHINGTON STREET, SUITE 102
NAPERVILLE, ILLINOIS 60540
Telephone: 630-357-4520
Fax: 630-355-5949
Email: dhm1649@aol.com
URL: http://www.lawyers.com/dhmlaw

Personal Injury, Divorce and Family Law, Corporate and Employment Law, Elder Law and Probate, Real Estate.

DAVID H. McCARTHY, III, born Springfield, Illinois, January 6, 1949; admitted to bar, 1979, Illinois and U.S. District Court, Northern District of Illinois. *Education:* University of Notre Dame (B.A., 1971); John Marshall Law School (J.D., with distinction, 1979). Member, Order of John Marshall. Member, 1977-1979 and Associate Editor, 1978-1979, John Marshall Law Review. Recipient, Distinguished Service Award, Chicago Volunteer Legal Services Foundation, 1994 and 1995. Author: "Pre-trial Dismissal Based On Other Affirmative Matter: An Open Invitation Has Its Limits, Too," DCBA Brief, July 2005. *Member:* Chicago, DuPage County (Member, Publication Board, DCBA Brief, 2005—) and Illinois State Bar Associations.

McJOYNT & KRISTUFEK, P.C.

NAPERVILLE, ILLINOIS

(See Downers Grove)

General Civil Practice, Litigation, Criminal, Matrimonial, DUI, Real Estate, Probate, Estate Planning, Corporate and Transactional and Small Business Law.

DENISE B. MOLINE

1212 SOUTH NAPER BOULEVARD, SUITE 119-215
NAPERVILLE, ILLINOIS 60540
Telephone: 630-753-0112
Facsimile: 630-753-0137
Email: dbmoline@wowway.com

Telecommunications Law, Mass Media, Wireless, Satellite.

DENISE B. MOLINE, born Fall River, Massachusetts, January 11, 1948; admitted to bar, 1983, Florida and District of Columbia; 1985, U.S. Court of Appeals for the District of Columbia Circuit; 1991, Virginia; 1993, U.S. Supreme Court (Not admitted in Illinois). *Education:* Rivier College (B.A., 1969); Florida State University (J.D., 1982); American University. Order of the Barristers. Member, Appellate Moot Court Team. Legal Writing Instructor, FSU, 1980-1981. *Member:* The District of Columbia Bar; The Florida Bar (inactive); Virginia State Bar (inactive); Federal Communications Bar Association. ***PRACTICE AREAS:*** Communications Law.

GARY M. MOORE

Established in 1994

535 SOUTH WASHINGTON STREET
NAPERVILLE, ILLINOIS 60540-6662
Telephone: 630-357-6966
Fax: 630-357-1210; 630-839-3007
Email: garymoore@naperlaw.com
URL: http://www.naperlaw.com

Real Estate, Trusts and Estates, Estate Planning, Bankruptcy, Taxation, Wills and Probate, Small Business, Corporate.

(This Listing Continued)

FIRM PROFILE: Sole practitioner, concentrating in residential real estate, business purchases and sales, estate planning, including wills, living trusts and powers of attorney, probate, and bankruptcy. Over 25 years in practice in the Chicago area, 10 as a sole practitioner. Works on matters in DuPage, Will, Cook, Kane and Kendall Counties, Illinois. Mr. Moore works to give his clients personal attention and to be sure they understand what their options are and what is being done for them. He does not attempt to be the least expensive provider of services, but to charge at rates, both fixed and hourly, that are fair for his clients and for him.

GARY M. MOORE, born Oak Park, Illinois, December 28, 1952; admitted to bar, 1978, Illinois. *Education:* University of Illinois (B.A., 1975; J.D., 1978). *Member:* Illinois State Bar Association; DuPage County Bar Association.

LAW OFFICE OF BRENDA L. MURZYN

1300 IROQUOIS AVENUE, SUITE 125
NAPERVILLE, ILLINOIS 60563
Telephone: 630-961-1058
Fax: 630-961-1333
Email: brendamurzynlaw@ameritech.net
URL: http://www.lawyers.com/murzyn

Chicago Office: 1255 North State Parkway, 60610. Telephone: 312-330-3458. Fax: 312-266-5967.

Real Estate Closings, For Sale By Owner Investment Property, Foreclosure, Probate, Wills, Residential Real Estate, Commercial Real Estate, Real Estate Investment, Land Trusts, Land Sales, Real Estate Acquisitions, Real Estate Contracts.

BRENDA L. MURZYN, born Evansville, Indiana, October 10, 1954; admitted to bar, 1983, Illinois and U.S. District Court, Northern and Southern Districts of Indiana. *Education:* Indiana University (B.S., 1976); Northern Illinois University (J.D., 1982). Recipient, American Jurisprudence Award. *Member:* Kane County, DuPage County, Illinois State, Indiana State and American Bar Associations; Illinois Real Estate Lawyers Association.

ASSOCIATE

EDWARD F. STETTER, born 1979; admitted to bar, 2004, Illinois. *Education:* University of Notre Dame (B.B.A., cum laude, 2001); Illinois Institute of Technology; Chicago Kent College of Law (J.D., 2004). *Member:* Kane County, DuPage County and Illinois State Bar Associations. ***PRACTICE AREAS:*** Real Estate; Landlord and Tenant Law; Evictions; Wills.

THE LAW OFFICE OF PHILIP R. NATHE

552 S. WASHINGTON, SUITE 104
NAPERVILLE, ILLINOIS 60540
Telephone: 630-416-7600
Fax: 630-357-1922
Email: prnathe@aol.com
URL: http://www.law-shack.com

Criminal Defense, Criminal Law, DUI, Traffic Violations, Juvenile Law, Civil Litigation.

FIRM PROFILE: Since 1981, Phil Nathe has played a role within the Du Page County Court System. While attending law school, he served as an Assistant Circuit Court Clerk and Probation Officer in Du Page County, Illinois. Upon his graduation from law school, he served as an Assistant State's Attorney under Jim Ryan for more than two years. Since then he has dedicated his practice to representing adults and juveniles who have been charged with committing criminal offenses, including but not limited to felonies, misdemeanors and in particular DUI. His experience within the Du Page County Court System makes him uniquely qualified to handle matters in the same jurisdiction. He also represents individuals in Kane, Will and Cook County.

PHILIP R. NATHE, born Chicago, Illinois, September 9, 1959; admitted to bar, 1988, Illinois and U.S. District Court, Northern District of Illinois. *Education:* Western Illinois University (B.A., Political Science, with honors, 1981); John Marshall Law School (J.D., 1988). DuPage County Probation Officer, 1984-1988. Assistant States Attorney, DuPage County States Attorney Office, 1988-1990. Instructor, Criminal Justice, College of DuPage, 1989-1984. *Member:* DuPage County and Illinois State Bar Associations. ***PRACTICE AREAS:*** Criminal Defense (95%); Civil Litigation (5%).

LAW OFFICE OF BRENT E. OHLMANN, P.C.

1730 PARK STREET, SUITE 210
NAPERVILLE, ILLINOIS 60563
Telephone: 630-355-8008
Fax: 630-355-8068
Email: beo@beohlmann.com
URL: http://www.beohlmann.com

Trademarks, Copyrights, Business Transactions, S-Corporation and LLC Issues, Entertainment Contracts, Software Licensing, Confidentiality Agreements, Strategic Alliances, Business Succession Planning, Internet Law.

FIRM PROFILE: Law Office of Brent E. Ohlmann, P.C. is a boutique firm offering a wide variety of intellectual property and business law experience for clients in consulting, technology, retail, entertainment and manufacturing.

(This Listing Continued)

BRENT E. OHLMANN, born Sioux Falls, South Dakota, March 6, 1964; admitted to bar, 1990, Illinois. *Education:* Indiana University at Bloomington (B.A., 1986); Northern Illinois University (J.D., 1989). Associate Editor, NIU Law Review, 1988-1989. Author: "Protecting Computer Databases After Feist and Corsearch"--DuPage County Bar Association Brief, July/August 1993. *Member:* Illinois State Bar Association. ***PRACTICE AREAS:*** Trademarks; Copyrights; Internet Law; Business Transactions; Software Licensing; Confidentiality Agreements; Strategic Alliances; Business Succession Planning. ***Email:*** beo@beohlmann.com

ANTHONY PERRELLI

NAPERVILLE, ILLINOIS

(See Deerfield)

Business Corporate, Small Business, Contracts, Business Planning, Real Estate, Commercial Litigation and Taxation.

KEVIN R. PETERS

NAPERVILLE, ILLINOIS

(See Chicago)

Driving While Intoxicated, Drug Crimes, Felonies, Homicide, Misdemeanors, Sexual Assault, Traffic Violations, Police Misconduct, Civil Rights.

LAW OFFICES OF STEPHEN S. PHALEN LLC

NAPERVILLE, ILLINOIS

(See Chicago)

Personal Injury, Wrongful Death, Automobile Accidents, Boating Accidents, Motorcycle Accidents, Trucking Accidents, Bus Accidents, Train Accidents, Construction Accidents, Medical Malpractice, Head Trauma, Spinal Injuries.

PRATO & ASSOCIATES, P.C.

NAPERVILLE, ILLINOIS

(See Oak Brook)

Real Estate Transactions, Bankruptcy, Small Businesses, Corporate, Criminal, DUI, Personal Injury and Immigration Law.

LAW OFFICES OF ROGERS & COYNE, LLC

1700 PARK STREET, SUITE 102
NAPERVILLE, ILLINOIS 60563-2902
Telephone: 630-579-0635
Fax: 630-579-0638
Email: susanrrogers616B@aol.com
URL: http://www.lawyers.com/rogerslawfirm

Estate Planning, Trust and Estate Administration, Residential and Commercial Real Estate.

FIRM PROFILE: The Law Office of Rogers & Coyne, LLC prides itself by being attentive and accessible to its clients. Our clients reside all over Chicago and the collar counties. Our clientele is diverse and ranges from high net worth individuals with complex estate planning needs to the recent college graduate buying their first home.

We are particularly attentive to the needs of our seniors. We routinely travel to meet with clients when their traveling to our office would be inconvenient. We also schedule appointments outside of business hours when it is difficult for the client to meet during the workday. We will always do what is necessary to meet the needs of our clients.

Our firm practices in the areas of wills and trusts, estate planning, estate taxation, trust and estate administration, residential and commercial real estate, and business planning. We are also proud members of the Naperville Chamber of Commerce. We can be reached toll free at (800) 583 0025.

SUSAN R. ROGERS, born Bronx, New York, July 20, 1961; admitted to bar, 1991, Illinois. *Education:* Wheaton College (B.A., 1983); College for Financial Planning (CFP, 1987); Northern Illinois University (J.D., 1991). *Member:* Illinois State Bar Association.

KEVIN M. COYNE, born Chicago, Illinois, September 4, 1975. *Education:* University of Iowa (B.B.A., 1997); DePaul University (J.D., 2000). Member, Naperville Chamber of Commerce. *Member:* DuPage County and Illinois State Bar Associations. ***PRACTICE AREAS:*** Residential Real Estate; Commercial Real Estate; Estate Planning; Estate Administration; Business Planning; Business Litigation. ***Email:*** kevcoy1@aol.com

LAW OFFICES OF GLENN W. SEBESTA, P.C.

2503 BAR HARBOR COURT
NAPERVILLE, ILLINOIS 60564
Telephone: 630-922-5400
Fax: 630-922-5408
Email: sebestalawoffices@sbcglobal.net
URL: http://www.sebestalawoffices.com

Healthcare Provider Professional Rights, Healthcare Provider Defense in Licensing/Privileging Actions.

(This Listing Continued)

GLENN W. SEBESTA, born LaGrange, Illinois; admitted to bar, 1991, Illinois. *Education:* Illinois Wesleyan University (B.A., 1985); University of Illinois College of Law (J.D., 1991). Healthcare Peer Review Hearing Officer. *Member:* Illinois State Bar Association; American Health Lawyers Association. ***PRACTICE AREAS:*** Health Care; Health Care Licensing. ***Email:*** sebestalawoffices@sbcglobal.net

SHAW GUSSIS FISHMAN GLANTZ WOLFSON & TOWBIN LLC

NAPERVILLE, ILLINOIS

(See Chicago)

Bankruptcy and Insolvency Law, Creditors Rights, Real Estate and related services, Land Use and Zoning, Commercial Litigation, and Secured Lending.

STOCK, CARLSON, FLYNN & ASSOCIATES

NAPERVILLE, ILLINOIS

(See Wheaton)

Business Organizations, Divorce, Elder Law, Estate Planning, Real Estate.

KATHLEEN VAUGHT, P.C.

NAPERVILLE, ILLINOIS

(See Wheaton)

Bankruptcy, Consumer Bankruptcy, Business Bankruptcy, Financial Planning, Litigation, Tort Litigation, Contract Litigation, Real Estate, Divorce, Family, Estate Planning, Probate Law, Arbitration, Mediation, Alternative Dispute Resolution, Debt Relief Agent.

WALLENSTEIN WAGNER & ROCKEY, LTD.

NAPERVILLE, ILLINOIS

(See Chicago)

Intellectual Property and Technology Related Law including Protection and Licensing of United States and International Patent, Trademark, Copyright Trade Secret and Unfair Competition Matters and Related Litigation in the Courts and United States International Trade Commission.

WALTON LAW OFFICES, LLC

608 S. WASHINGTON STREET
SUITE 207
NAPERVILLE, ILLINOIS 60540
Telephone: 888-432-7792
Fax: 630-893-3586

Divorce Law.

ERNEST J. WALTON, born Washington, D.C., August 26, 1957; admitted to bar, 1987, Illinois. *Education:* Trinity College (B.A., Philosophy, 1980); DePaul University (J.D., 1987). *Member:* Illinois State Bar Association. ***PRACTICE AREAS:*** Divorce Law. ***Email:*** ewalton@divorcejustice.com

RUSSEL G. WINICK & ASSOCIATES, P.C.

Established in 1998

1220 IROQUOIS AVENUE, SUITE 100
NAPERVILLE, ILLINOIS 60563
Telephone: 630-548-5800
Fax: 630-548-5568
Email: russwinlaw@sbcglobal.net
URL: http://www.winicklaw.com

Business Law, Business Development, Business Formation, Business Litigation, Business Organization, Business Planning, Business Start-Ups, Business Transactions, Business Transfers, Buy-Sell Agreements, Buying and Selling of Businesses, Closely Held Business Law, Complex Business Litigation, Emerging Business Law, Entrepreneurial Business Law, Joint Ventures, Limited Liability Company Law, Small Business Law.

FIRM PROFILE: Russel G. Winick & Associates, P.C. adds value to its business clients. We view our clients as partners, and offer creative, cost-effective solutions for achieving goals and tackling problems. From start-up companies to large corporations, with transactions or litigation, you'll get the expert and responsive service that you deserve.

RUSSEL G. WINICK, born Chicago, Illinois, May 12, 1955; admitted to bar, 1983, Illinois and U.S. District Court, Northern District of Illinois. *Education:* Grinnell College (B.A., 1978); University of Oregon (J.D., 1983). Author: "When Can A Landlord Legally Retain A Security Deposit ?", Northwest Suburban Bar Association Journal, March, 1985. *Member:* DuPage County (Past Chairman, Business Law and Practice Committee), Illinois State and American Bar Associations. ***REPORTED CASES:*** Nassau Terrace Condo v. Silverstein, 182 Ill. App. 3d 221, 537 N.E. 2d 998 (1989); Applegate Apts. v. Commercial Coin Laundry, 276 Ill. App. 3d 433, 657 N.E.2d 1172 (1995). ***PRACTICE AREAS:*** Business Law; Corporate Law; Business Transactions; Commercial Litigation. ***Email:*** russwinlaw@sbcglobal.net

(This Listing Continued)

RUSSEL G. WINICK & ASSOCIATES, P.C., Naperville—Continued

ROBERT KOBACK, born Chelsea, Michigan, December 22, 1955; admitted to bar, 1998, Illinois and U.S. District Court, Northern District of Illinois; 1999, Michigan. *Education:* Michigan State University; Wayne State University (B.S., 1980); The University of Michigan (M.S., 1986); The John Marshall Law School (J.D., 1998). Recipient, Awarded INPO Fellowship for Graduate Studies in Health Physics. *Member:* Chicago, Illinois State and American Bar Associations; State Bar of Michigan. ***PRACTICE AREAS:*** Business Law; Commercial Law; Business Litigation; Estate Planning; Probate; Intellectual Property Licensing. ***Email:*** russwinlaw@sbcglobal.net

LEGAL SUPPORT PERSONNEL

MICHELLE A. BUHLE, born Taylorville, Illinois, October 28, 1968. *Education:* Western Illinois University (B.B., 1990). (Paralegal). ***Email:*** russwinlaw@sbcglobal.net

ARLEESIA L. McDONALD, born Summit-Argo, Illinois, January 3, 1977. *Education:* University of Illinois (B.F.A., 1999); The Ohio State University (J.D., 2002). Delta Theta Phi. (Paralegal). ***Email:*** russwinlaw@sbcglobal.net

MARY A. MARTIN, born Bolings AFB, Washington, D.C. (Paralegal). ***Email:*** russwinlaw@sbcglobal.net

REPRESENTATIVE CLIENTS: Acrotech Industries, Inc.; Advanced Casting Technologies, L.L.C.; Air I Wireless, Inc.; Belusa Volleyball Club, Ltd.; Blue Kangaroo Laundromats; Bluetek Digital Printing, Inc.; Burhan Industrial Supply Co.; Chicagoland Barbecue, Inc.; Coinmach Corporation; Commercial Coin Laundry Systems; Compsearch Software Services, Inc.; Conventions Psychiatry & Counseling, P.C.; Creative Cakes, L.L.C.; DMC Security Services, Inc.; Doreen Schweitzer Interiors, Ltd.; Family Pride Laundries; First Impressions Marketing, Inc.; Impact Sales, Inc.; J&N Electric, Inc.; JMC Healthcare Associates, Corp.; M&M Tax Services, Inc.; Michigan Steel, Inc.; Midwest Sales and Merchandising, Inc.; One-2-One Computer Assistance, Inc.; Prairie Business Credit; Prime Telecommunications, Inc.; Throwback Sports, Ltd.; Twin Anchors, Inc.; Universal Medical Exposure, Inc.

CASEY WOODRUFF & ASSOCIATES

NAPERVILLE, ILLINOIS

(See Chicago)

Workers Compensation, Personal Injury, Automobile Accidents, Social Security, Medical Malpractice, Products Liability.

KATHLEEN T. ZELLNER & ASSOCIATES

1717 NORTH NAPER BOULEVARD
SUITE 203
NAPERVILLE, ILLINOIS 60563
Telephone: 630-955-1212
Facsimile: 630-955-1111
URL: http://www.kathleent.zellner.com
Email: k21234@aol.com
URL: http://www.lawyers.com/zellnerlaw

Medical Malpractice, Civil Rights, Premises Liability, Trials and Appeals in State and Federal Courts.

KATHLEEN T. ZELLNER, born Midland, Texas, May 7, 1956; admitted to bar, 1983, Illinois; U.S. Court of Appeals, Seventh Circuit; U.S. District Court, Northern District of Illinois; U.S. Supreme Court. *Education:* Concordia University (B.A., with honors, 1974); Northern Illinois University (J.D., 1983). Corpus Juris Secundum Award, 1980, 1981. Editor-in-Chief, Northern Illinois University Law Review, 1980-1981. *Member:* Chicago, DuPage County, Illinois State and American Bar Associations; Million Dollar Advocate Forum.

DOUGLAS H. JOHNSON, born Detroit, Michigan, April 2, 1964; admitted to bar, 1991, Illinois and U.S. District Court, Northern District of Illinois; 1993, U.S. Court of Appeals, Seventh Circuit. *Education:* University of Michigan (B.S., 1986); Loyola University (J.D., 1991). ***PRACTICE AREAS:*** Medical Malpractice; Civil Rights; Premises Liability. ***Email:*** boblo6766@aol.com

BROWN & ASSOCIATES

NASHVILLE, ILLINOIS

(See Belleville)

Civil Litigation, Personal Injury, Medical Malpractice, Products Liability, Admiralty Law, Railroad Law and Commercial Law.

FEHSEKE & ESCHMAN LAW OFFICES

NAUVOO, ILLINOIS

(See Fort Madison, Iowa)

General Civil Practice including Trials and Appeals, Personal Injury, Probate, Real Estate, Workers Compensation Law, Maritime Law, Medical Malpractice, Products Liability, Trusts and Estates, Estate Planning, and Elder Law.

COX, PHILLIPS, WEBER, TEDFORD & HEAP, P.C.

NEWTON, ILLINOIS

(See Robinson)

General Civil, Trial and Appellate Practice. Probate, Real Estate, Title Insurance, Municipal, Taxation, Corporation, Estate Planning, Workers Compensation, Oil and Gas Law, Collections, and Matrimonial Law.

THE LAW OFFICES OF MARC L. BROWN

NILES, ILLINOIS

(See Park Ridge)

Elder Law, Real Estate, Trusts and Estates, Wills, Probate, Living Trusts, Guardianship, Nursing Home Abuse and Neglect, Health Care.

CUTLER & ASSOCIATES, LTD.

NILES, ILLINOIS

(See Skokie)

Bankruptcy, Consumer Bankruptcy, Bankruptcy Chapter 7, Foreclosures, Small Business, Buying and Selling of Businesses, Family Business, Limited Liability, Partnership, Corporate, Contract, Breach of Contract, General Practice, Debtor and Creditor, Collections, Creditors, Rights and Civil Litigation.

THE LAW OFFICES OF ANTHONY B. FERRARO

NILES, ILLINOIS

(See Rosemont)

Wills, Trusts, Estates, Estate Planning, Estate Taxation, Probate and Trust Administration, Medicaid, Guardianship, Elder Law, and Trust and Estate-Related Commercial Transactions including Business Acquisitions and Real Estate, Commercial Arbitration.

PTASINSKI & SMITH, P.C.

Established in 1975

241 GOLF MILL PROFESSIONAL BUILDING
SUITE 800
NILES, ILLINOIS 60714
Telephone: 847-296-6631
Fax: 847-296-7503
URL: http://www.ptasinskismith.com
URL: http://www.lawyers.com/ptasinski-smith

Probate, Estate Planning and Administration, Trusts and Estates, Wills, Elder Law, Real Estate, Business Law, Divorce.

FIRM PROFILE: A Law Firm dedicated to client service and legal excellence.

LAWRENCE J. PTASINSKI, born Chicago, Illinois, September 17, 1949; admitted to bar, 1975, U.S. District Court, Northern District of Illinois; 1979, Illinois; 1980, U.S. Supreme Court. *Education:* University of Notre Dame (B.B.A, 1971); John Marshall Law School (J.D., 1975). *Member:* Chicago, Illinois State, Northwest Suburban and American Bar Associations; Northwest Suburban Estate Planning Council; Illinois Real Estate Lawyers Association; Attorneys' Title Guaranty Fund. ***PRACTICE AREAS:*** Estate Planning; Estate Administration; Trusts and Estates; Wills; Probate; Estate and Gift Taxation; Real Estate; Business Law. ***Email:*** ljp@ptasinskismith.com

DONALD A. SMITH, born Chicago, Illinois, February 21, 1958; admitted to bar, 1984, Illinois. *Education:* University of Notre Dame (B.A., 1980); Loyola University of Chicago (J.D., 1984). Des Plaines City Alderman. *Member:* Chicago, Northwest Suburban and Illinois State Bar Associations; Northwestern Suburban Estate Planning Council; Illinois Real Estate Lawyers Association; Attorneys' Title Guaranty Fund. ***PRACTICE AREAS:*** Real Estate Law; Real Estate Sales; Trusts and Estates; Estate Planning; Elder Law; Divorce; Guardianship; Probate; Wills. ***Email:*** dsmith@ptasinskismith.com

JAY A. SLUTZKY

7749 NORTH MILWAUKEE AVENUE
NILES, ILLINOIS 60714
Telephone: 847-967-7979
Fax: 847-967-7984
Email: jayslutzky@yahoo.com

Wills, Living Trusts, Estate Planning, Residential Real Estate, Commercial Real Estate, Divorce, Personal Injury, Bankruptcy Law, Elder Law, DUI, DWI, Business Law, Commercial Law, Commercial Litigation, Business Organization, Business Transactions, Business Counseling, Business Advice, Real Estate Law, Real Estate Litigation, Commercial Transactions, Contracts, Construction Law, Litigation, Motor Vehicle Accidents, Personal Injury Defense, Plaintiffs Personal Injury, Probate, Estate Administration, Trusts, By-Pass Trusts, Credit Shelter Trusts, Special Needs Trusts, Testamentary Trusts, Ancillar Administration, Durable Powers of Attorney, Medical Powers of Attorney, Living Wills, Pour-Over Wills, Marital Deduction Trusts, Beneficiary Designations, Irrevocable Life Insurance Trusts, Split Dollar Purchase Agreements, Crummey Trusts, Workers Compensation, Civil Litigation, Criminal Defense, Pre-

(This Listing Continued)

Marital Agreements, Planning for Disabled Spouses, Planning for Disabled Children, Estate Tax Return Preparation, Second Marriage Issues, Contested Wills and Trusts, Partnerships, Corporations, Limited Liability Companies.

JAY A. SLUTZKY, born Chicago, Illinois, 1948; admitted to bar, 1974, Illinois and U.S. District Court, Northern District of Illinois. *Education:* DePaul University (B.A., 1970; J.D., 1974). ***PRACTICE AREAS:*** Estate Planning; Real Estate; Estate Administration; Litigation; Family Law; Business Law; Bankruptcy; Criminal Law.

THE PRIOR LAW FIRM, P.C.

NORMAL, ILLINOIS

(See Bloomington)

Criminal Defense, Driving While Intoxicated, Traffic Violations, Juvenile Law, Family Law, Personal Injury, Collections and Insurance Subrogation.

MICHAEL V. FAVIA

NORRIDGE, ILLINOIS

(See Chicago)

Civil Litigation, Personal Injuries, Automobile Accidents, Medical Malpractice, Products Liability, Work Injuries, Health Law, Medicare and Medicaid Fraud, Medical and Health Related Regulatory Issues, Professional Licensure Matters.

THE LAW OFFICES OF ANTHONY B. FERRARO

NORRIDGE, ILLINOIS

(See Rosemont)

Wills, Trusts, Estates, Estate Planning, Estate Taxation, Probate and Trust Administration, Medicaid, Guardianship, Elder Law, and Trust and Estate-Related Commercial Transactions including Business Acquisitions and Real Estate, Commercial Arbitration.

BERLIN & BRAUDE

SUITE 456
650 DUNDEE ROAD
NORTHBROOK, ILLINOIS 60062
Telephone: 847-412-1300
Telecopier: 847-412-1314

Civil Practice in all State and Federal Courts. Commercial Real Estate Transactions, Corporations, Taxation, Employee Benefits, Labor and Employment, Estate Planning and Probate.

ARTHUR E. BERLIN (Retired)

MICHAEL E. BRAUDE, born Chicago, Illinois, October 1, 1940; admitted to bar, 1965, Illinois; U.S. District Court, Northern District of Illinois including Trial Bar, U.S. District Court, Central District of Illinois and U.S. Court of Appeals, Seventh Circuit. *Education:* Wharton School of Finance and Commerce, University of Pennsylvania (B.S., 1962); University of Chicago (J.D., 1965). Attorney, Federal Trade Commission, 1965-1969. *Member:* Chicago (Member: Antitrust Committee, 1976—; Employee Benefits Committee, 1983-2002; Federal Tax Committee, 2002—), Federal (Director, 1970—, President, 1987-1988, Member, 1987— and Chair, 1999—, Judicial Selection Committee, Chicago Chapter; Vice President for the Seventh Circuit, 1991-2005) and American Bar Associations.

LOUISE S. GREENFIELD, born Chicago, Illinois, January 20, 1951; admitted to bar, 1977, Illinois; U.S. District Court, Northern District of Illinois including Trial Bar. *Education:* University of Illinois (B.A., 1972; J.D., 1977). Co-Author, "Dealing With Neuropsychological Evidence," 31 For The Defense 7, 1989. Majority Counsel, Illinois House of Representatives Judiciary I Committee, 1977-1981. Instructor, University of California at Berkeley Law School, 1981-1983. *Member:* Chicago (Member: Real Property Law Committee, 1985—; Probate Practice, 1987-1998 and 2000—; Trust Law Committee, 1994—; Federal Tax Committee, 2000—) and Illinois State (Editor-in-Chief, Recent Decisions Section, Illinois Bar Journal, 1976-1977) Bar Associations.

MICHAEL R. GOLDFEIN, born Chicago, Illinois, January 6, 1951; admitted to bar, 1980, Illinois and U.S. District Court, Northern District of Illinois including Trial Bar; 1985, U.S. Claims Court. *Education:* University of Illinois (B.S., with high honors, 1972); Northwestern University; Loyola University (J.D., 1980). Member, 1978-1979 and Lead Articles Editor, 1979-1980, Loyola Law Journal. Author: "Finding the Key to the Deductibility of Rental Payments Under a Gift and Leaseback," 10 Loyola University of Chicago Law Journal 767, 1979. Law Clerk to Hon. Thomas J. Moran, Justice, Illinois Supreme Court, 1980-1982. *Member:* Chicago (Member, Corporate Law Committee, 1994—; Labor and Employment Law Committee, 1992—) and Federal Bar Associations.

LAW OFFICES OF BRADFORD E. BLOCK

Established in 1981
1935 SHERMER ROAD, SUITE 350
NORTHBROOK, ILLINOIS 60062
Telephone: 847-559-0860
Fax: 847-509-8523
URL: http://www.blocklawoffices.com

Business Formation, Corporate Finance, Mergers and Acquisitions, Asset Based Finance, Securities Offerings, Corporate Contracts, Technology Contracts, Equipment Leasing, Computer Law.

(This Listing Continued)

FIRM PROFILE: The Law Offices of Bradford E. Block serves both business and individual clients with an emphasis in the following areas: business formation; corporate finance; mergers and acquisitions; asset base finance; securities offerings; corporate contracts; technology contracts; equipment leasing; computer law; federal income tax; estate planning and residential real estate.

BRADFORD E. BLOCK, born June 2, 1946; admitted to bar, 1975, Illinois, U.S. District Court, Northern District of Illinois and U.S. Tax Court. *Education:* University of Pennsylvania, Wharton School of Finance and Commerce (B.S., 1968); DePaul University College of Law (J.D., summa cum laude, 1975). Editor-in-chief of DePaul Law Review, 1975. Certified Public Accountant, California, 1969. Lecturer, Business Planning, Accounting and the Law, and Partnerships, DePaul University College of Law. ***PRACTICE AREAS:*** Business Formation; Corporate Finance; Mergers and Acquisitions; Asset Based Finance; Securities Offerings; Corporate Contracts; Technology Contracts; Equipment Leasing; Computer Law.

REPRESENTATIVE CLIENTS: Bryant & Stratton Business Institute, Inc.; Egg Harbor Restaurants; LaSalle Systems Leasing, Inc.; Meridian Leasing Corporation; First Eagle National Bank; Chile Today-Hot Tamale, Inc.; Alexander Capital Vendor Finance, Inc.; BNY Midwest Trust Co.

LEONARD J. BRENNER, LTD.

Established in 1999
555 SKOKIE BOULEVARD, SUITE 500
NORTHBROOK, ILLINOIS 60062
Telephone: 847-480-1020
Fax: 847-480-0034
Email: ljbrenner@brennerlegal.com
URL: http://www.leonardbrenner.com

Business and Corporate Law, Tax Controversies, Estate Planning and Probate.

FIRM PROFILE: Leonard J. Brenner concentrates his practice in corporate and business matters, contracts, business transactions, mergers and acquisitions, real estate, tax controversies, not-for-profit organizations, estate planning and probate. Mr. Brenner is licensed to practice law in both Illinois and Wisconsin and is a Certified Public Accountant. Mr. Brenner graduated from the University of San Diego School of Law in 1984, from Northern Illinois University in 1979 with a degree in accounting, and practiced in public accounting before attending law school. Mr. Brenner is admitted to practice before the United States Tax Court and the United States District Court for the Northern District of Illinois.

LEONARD J. BRENNER, born Chicago, Illinois, August 15, 1957; admitted to bar, 1985, Illinois; 1987, U.S. District Court, Northern District of Illinois; 2000, Wisconsin. *Education:* Northern Illinois University (B.S., 1979); University of San Diego (J.D., 1984). Certified Public Accountant, Illinois, 1981. *Member:* Illinois State and American Bar Associations; American Association of Attorney-Certified Public Accountants. ***Email:*** ljbrenner@brennerlegal.com

CAROL DI GIACOMO & KATHRYN SOMERS, L.L.C.

NORTHBROOK, ILLINOIS

(See Northfield)

Family Law, Divorce, Collaborative Law, Child Custody, Child Support, Spousal Support, Visitation, Adoption, Mediation and Complex Family Law relating to Valuation and Tax Considerations, Estate Planning, Real Estate, Contract and Bankruptcy Law.

ELIZER & MEYERSON, L.L.C.

900 SKOKIE BOULEVARD, SUITE 208
NORTHBROOK, ILLINOIS 60062-4031
Telephone: 847-513-6600
Fax: 847-513-6692
URL: http://emlegal.lawoffice.com

Criminal Law, Felonies and Misdemeanors, DUI, DWI, Traffic Violations, Personal Injury, Automobile Accidents, Wrongful Death.

FIRM PROFILE: For nearly twenty years, Mr. Meyerson has prosecuted and defended hundreds of DUIs, traffic violations, and felony and misdemeanor criminal offenses in the Chicagoland area. Practices criminal, DUI and traffic defense extensively in Northern and Northwest Suburban Cook County, Lake County and Chicago. Free consultations. Promptly returns telephone calls and messages.

STEVEN H. ELIZER, born Chicago, Illinois, 1957; admitted to bar, 1983, Illinois; 1983, U.S. District Court, Northern District of Illinois; 1985, Florida. *Education:* Washington University (B.A., 1979; J.D., 1983). Order of the Coif. Senior Editor, Washington University Law Quarterly, 1982-1983. Former Member, Rudnick & Wolfe (now Piper, Marbury, Kudnick & Wolfe). Former Associate, Smith & Levenstein, P.A. *Member:* American Bar Association; Chicago Surety Claims Association. ***Email:*** selizer@emlegal.com

DAVID S. MEYERSON, born Chicago, Illinois, 1963; admitted to bar, 1989, Illinois; 1994, U.S. District Court, Northern District of Illinois and U.S. Court of Appeals, Seventh Circuit. *Education:* University of Illinois (B.A., 1986); University of Tulsa College of Law (J.D., 1989). Former Cook County Assistant States Attorney. Member, Civil Actions Bureau. Commercial Litigator, Barnard & McCollam, Ltd. ***Email:*** dmeyerson@emlegal.com

LAW OFFICES OF
ERIC S. FREIBRUN, LTD.

630 DUNDEE ROAD, SUITE 120
NORTHBROOK, ILLINOIS 60062-2749
Telephone: 847-562-0099
Fax: 847-562-0033
URL: http://www.freibrun.com
Email: efreibrun@msn.com
URL: http://www.lawyers.com/freibrun

Intellectual Property, Intellectual Property Licensing, Intellectual Property Litigation, Internet Intellectual Property, Internet Law, Trademark Law, Proprietary Rights, Computers and Software, Computer Contracts, Computer Law, Computer Security, Computer Software Law, Information Technology, Information Technology Contracts, Information Technology Licensing, International Computer Law, Software Copyright, Software Licensing, Software Protection, Software Publishing Technology, E-commerce.

ERIC S. FREIBRUN, admitted to bar, 1983, Illinois and U.S. District Court, Northern District of Illinois. *Education:* University of Illinois (B.S., 1980); University of Lund, Lund, Sweden; Washington University (J.D., 1983). Washington University Law Quarterly Review, 1981-1983.

GIGNILLIAT & HYMEN, P.C.

Established in 1936

500 SKOKIE BOULEVARD, SUITE 530
NORTHBROOK, ILLINOIS 60062
Telephone: 847-564-7880
Fax: 847-564-7890
Email: gnh@earthlink.net
URL: http://www.lawyers.com/g&hlaw

Corporate, Estate Planning, Trusts and Estates, Wills and Probate, Taxation and Real Estate Law, Commercial Real Estate.

FIRM PROFILE: General business/corporate matters, Real Estate, Estate Planning, Taxation.

LEIGH R. GIGNILLIAT, III (1928-2005)

ROGER J. HYMEN, born Chicago, Illinois, January 6, 1951; admitted to bar, 1975, Illinois and U.S. District Court, Northern District of Illinois; 1979, U.S. Court of Appeals, 7th Circuit. *Education:* University of Illinois (B.A., cum laude, 1972); Loyola University (J.D., 1975). *Member:* Chicago and American Bar Associations. ***PRACTICE AREAS:*** Real Estate Law; Corporate Law; Taxation Law; Estate Planning; Business Formation; Business Transactions; Buying and Selling of Businesses; Limited Liability Company Law; Commercial Real Estate; Commercial Contracts; Business Acquisitions; Business Divestitures; Charitable Trusts and Foundations; Commercial Leasing; Probate; Condominium Development; Real Estate Acquisitions; Real Estate Sales; Trusts and Estates; Wills. ***Email:*** gnh@earthlink.net

---

GRANT AND GRANT

PROFESSIONAL CORPORATION

Established in 1943

707 SKOKIE BOULEVARD, SUITE 600
NORTHBROOK, ILLINOIS 60062
Telephone: 847-291-4343
Email: info@grantandgrant.com
URL: http://www.lawyers.com/grantandgrantlaw

Chicago, Illinois Office: 30 North La Salle Street, 29th Floor, 60602. Telephone: 312-641-3600. Fax: 312-641-2723.

Complex Family Law including Divorce, Dissolution of Marriage, Marital Property Distribution including Retirement Benefits, Spousal Support, Alimony, Maintenance, Child Custody, Visitation, Child Support, Domestic Violence, Paternity, all phases of Matrimonial Litigation, Post Divorce Modification, Premarital Agreements, Separation Agreements, Marital Settlement Agreements, Postmarital Agreements and Appeals.

FIRM PROFILE: Grant and Grant, established in 1943 by Louis Z. Grant, is considered one of the oldest matrimonial law firms in the State of Illinois. The firm has represented prominent men and women and is responsible for higher court decisions that have helped to shape Illinois matrimonial law. The principals, Burton F. Grant and Joan C. Grant, a unique and dynamic husband and wife team recognized as experts in matrimonial law, have extensive trial experience, and are frequently called upon to lecture for the major bar associations. Mr. Grant has been called upon as an expert witness in matrimonial litigation. Mrs. Grant is frequently appointed by the Court to represent children in highly contested custody matters and is appointed to bar association committees and special task forces. Both have authored numerous family law publications.

(For complete biographical data on all personnel, see Professional Biographies at Chicago, Illinois)

THE FIRM OF
PER K. HANSON ASSOCIATED

NORTHBROOK, ILLINOIS

(See Glenview)

Estate Planning, Trusts, Asset Protection, Charitable Giving, Guardianship and Conservatorship, Wills and Probate, Corporate, Real Estate, Business Law, and Collections.

MARC H. HEISLER

NORTHBROOK, ILLINOIS

(See Evanston)

Real Estate, Residential Real Estate, Buying and Selling a Home, Commercial Real Estate, Condominium Law and Mortgages. Business, Small Business, Partnership, Family Business and Buying and Selling a Business. Probate and Wills. Adoption Law. Civil Litigation, Chancery Practice, Collections, Personal Injury and Automobile Accidents.

THE HILL FIRM

666 DUNDEE ROAD, SUITE 1201
NORTHBROOK, ILLINOIS 60062
Telephone: 847-509-0250
Fax: 847-509-0255
Email: dagross@hillfirm.com

Intellectual Property Law, Patent, Copyright, Trade Secrets, Unfair Competition, Trademark and Technology Agreements.

MEMBER OF FIRM

DENNIS A. GROSS, born Evanston, Illinois, June 13, 1940; admitted to bar, 1966, Illinois, U.S. District Court, Northern District of Illinois including Trial Bar, U.S. Supreme Court and U.S. Court of Appeals for the Federal Circuit; registered to practice before U.S. and Canadian Patent and Trademark Offices. *Education:* Georgetown University and College of St. Thomas (B.A., 1962); Northwestern University (J.D., 1965). Phi Alpha Delta. *Member:* Illinois State and American Bar Associations; Intellectual Property Law Association of Chicago. ***PRACTICE AREAS:*** Patents; Trademarks; Copyrights. ***Email:*** dagross@hillfirm.com

LEGAL SUPPORT PERSONNEL

CATE LARSON, (Paralegal)

HORWOOD MARCUS & BERK

CHARTERED

NORTHBROOK, ILLINOIS

(See Chicago)

Corporate, Federal and State Taxation, Real Estate, Trust and Estate Planning and Probate Law. Commercial and Tax Litigation.

LEVUN, GOODMAN & COHEN, LLP

Comprised of Professional Corporations

500 SKOKIE BOULEVARD
SUITE 650
NORTHBROOK, ILLINOIS 60062
Telephone: 847-509-7700
Fax: 847-509-7709
Email: lgc@lgclaw.com
URL: http://www.lgclaw.com

Chicago, Illinois Office: One North LaSalle Street, Suite 1920. Telephone: 312-263-4661.

General Business and Tax Practice including Federal and State Taxation, Corporate Law, Partnership Law, Employee Benefits and Executive Compensation, Real Estate, Estate Planning, Estate and Trust Administration, and Commercial Litigation.

LAWRENCE S. GOODMAN, LTD., born Chicago, Illinois, 1942; admitted to bar, 1967, Illinois, U.S. District Court, Northern District of Illinois, U.S. Tax Court and U.S. Court of Appeals, Seventh Circuit. *Education:* University of Wisconsin (B.B.A., 1964); University of Illinois (J.D., 1967). *Member:* Chicago (Member, Federal Taxation Committee, 1968—; Chair, Estate and Gift Tax Division, 1981-1982; Member, Executive Council, 1979-1982; Member, 1970— and Chair, 1976-1977, Employee Benefits Committee), Illinois State (Member: Corporate Law Department Section Council, 1968-1970; Employee Benefits Section Council, 1981-1983; Federal Taxation Section Council 1987-1989) and American Bar Associations. ***PRACTICE AREAS:*** Federal Taxation; Business Planning; Wealth Preservation; Estate Planning; Trusts and Estates; Employee Benefits; Executive Compensation. ***Email:*** lsgoodman@lgclaw.com

CHARLES R. LEVUN, LTD., born Asbury Park, New Jersey, 1944; admitted to bar, 1970, Illinois, U.S. Tax Court and U.S. Claims Court. *Education:* University of Illinois (B.S., 1966); University of Chicago (J.D., 1970). Beta Gamma Sigma; Beta Alpha Psi. Certified Public Accountant, Illinois, 1966. Adjunct Professor, Graduate Program in Taxation, IIT/Chicago-Kent College of Law, 1985—. Consultant to the CCH Incorporated Partnership Tax Planning and Practice Guide, 1986—. Author of the Guide's Monthly Partner's Perspective Column, 1988—. Editor-in-Chief, Journal of Passthrough Entities, 1998—. Creator and Chair of the Faculty for the nationwide annual Partnership, LLC & S Corporation Tax Planning Forums, 1987— and for the nationwide annual "Back to Basics" Partnership, LLC & S Corporation Seminars, 1996—. *Member:* Chicago (Member, 1971—and Chair, 1993-1994, Committee on Federal Taxation; Member, Executive Committee, 1978-1983, 1989—), Illinois State (Member, 1979—, Chair, 1984-1985, Federal Taxation Section Council) and American (Member, 1979—, Chair, 1998-2000, Committee on Partnerships and LLC's, Taxation Section) Bar Associations; Fellow, American College of Tax Counsel. ***PRACTICE AREAS:*** Taxation; Corporate Law; Partnership Law; Estate Planning. ***Email:*** crlevun@lgclaw.com

MICHAEL J. COHEN, LTD., born Chicago, Illinois, 1954; admitted to bar, 1981, Illinois and U.S. District Court, Northern District of Illinois. *Education:* University of Pennsylvania, Wharton School of Finance and Commerce (B.S., 1975); DePaul University

(This Listing Continued)

(M.B.A., 1981); IIT/Chicago-Kent College of Law (J.D., with high honors, 1981; LL.M. in Taxation, 1984). Notes and Comments Editor, Chicago-Kent Law Review, 1980-1981. Certified Public Accountant, Illinois. Co-Creator and Faculty Member for the nationwide annual Partnership, LLC & S Corporation Tax Planning Forums, 1987— and for the nationwide annual "Back to Basics" Partnership, LLC & S Corporation Seminars, 1996—. Co-Author: Monthly Partner's Perspective Column to the CCH Incorporated Partnership Tax Planning and Practice Guide, 1988—. Associate Editor-in-Chief, Journal of Passthrough Entities, 1998—. *Member:* Chicago and American Bar Associations. ***PRACTICE AREAS:*** Taxation; Corporate Law; Partnership Law; Trusts and Estates. ***Email:*** mjcohen@lgclaw.com

GARY B. SHULMAN, LTD., born Chicago, Illinois, 1955; admitted to bar, 1980, Illinois and U.S. District Court, Northern District of Illinois. *Education:* University of Illinois at Chicago-Circle (B.A., with honors, 1976); The John Marshall Law School (J.D., with distinction, 1980). *Member:* Chicago and Illinois State Bar Associations. ***PRACTICE AREAS:*** Litigation; Real Estate; Corporate Law; Labor and Employment. ***Email:*** gbshulman@lgclaw.com

JEFFERY S. TAYLOR, LTD., born Nashville, Indiana, 1956; admitted to bar, 1981, Illinois and U.S. District Court, Northern District of Illinois. *Education:* Indiana University (B.A., 1978); The John Marshall Law School (J.D., 1981); IIT/Chicago Kent College of Law (LL.M., in Taxation, 1991). Author: "The Charitable Remainder Trust: A Unique Planning Technique," Taxes Magazine, February, 1991. *Member:* Chicago Bar Association. ***PRACTICE AREAS:*** Taxation; Estate Planning; Partnership Law; Corporate Law. ***Email:*** jstaylor@lgclaw.com

LEE A. ARBUS, LTD., born Chicago, Illinois, 1953; admitted to bar, 1978, Illinois and U.S. District Court, Northern District of Illinois. *Education:* University of Illinois (B.S., 1975); Chicago-Kent College of Law (J.D., 1978). Certified Public Accountant, Illinois, 1979. *Member:* Chicago and Illinois State Bar Associations; Illinois Certified Public Accountant Society; American Institute of Certified Public Accountants. ***PRACTICE AREAS:*** Estate Planning; Estate Administration; Trust Administration; Corporate Law; Federal Income Taxation; Commercial Real Estate. ***Email:*** laarbus@lgclaw.com

ASSOCIATES

SUSAN J. BERKUN, born Chicago, Illinois, 1955; admitted to bar, 1980, Illinois and U.S. District Court, Northern District of Illinois. *Education:* Indiana University and University of Illinois (B.A., with highest honors, 1977); Loyola University of Chicago (J.D., 1980). Certified Public Accountant, Illinois, 1977. *Member:* American Bar Association. ***PRACTICE AREAS:*** Taxation; Estate Planning; Probate; Real Estate; Corporate Law. ***Email:*** sjberkun@lgclaw.com

SUSAN H. BOOKER, born Brooklyn, New York, 1960; admitted to bar, 1985, Illinois and U.S. District Court, Northern District of Illinois including Trial Bar. *Education:* Rutgers University (B.A., 1982); Washington College of Law (J.D., 1985). Recipient, U.S. Attorney General's Outstanding Achievement Award, 1992, 1995, 1997. Adjunct Professor, Legal Writing Professor, John Marshall Law School. Trial Attorney, U.S. Department of Justice, Antitrust Division, 1989-1999. Arbitrator, Circuit Courts of Cook and Lake Counties. *Member:* Chicago Bar Association. ***PRACTICE AREAS:*** Litigation. ***Email:*** shbooker@lgclaw.com

VASILI D. RUSSIS, born Park Ridge, Illinois, 1966; admitted to bar, 1995, Illinois. *Education:* University of Illinois (B.S., 1989); Chicago-Kent College of Law (J.D., 1995). Certified Public Accountant, Illinois, 1990. *Member:* Chicago and Illinois State Bar Associations. ***LANGUAGES:*** Greek. ***PRACTICE AREAS:*** Taxation; Estate Planning; Probate; Real Estate; Litigation. ***Email:*** vdrussis@lgclaw.com

OF COUNSEL

ROBERT D. GORMAN, born Detroit, Michigan, August 28, 1962; admitted to bar, 1987, Michigan; 2002, Illinois. *Education:* Michigan State University (B.A., 1984); DePaul University (J.D., 1987). Author, "Hospital Liability and AIDS Treatments: the Need for a National Standard of Care," 20 University of California at Davis Law Review, 441, (1987), reprinted in the Personal Injury Review - 1988, 226 (1988). *Member:* Illinois State Bar Association; State Bar of Michigan. ***PRACTICE AREAS:*** Technology Law; Closely Held Business Law; Contracts; Mergers and Acquisitions; Commercial Real Estate Transactions. ***Email:*** rdgorman@lgclaw.com

CHARLES L. MERVIS, born Pensacola, Florida, 1941; admitted to bar, 1967, Illinois and U.S. District Court, Northern District of Illinois. *Education:* Amherst College (B.A., 1963); Loyola University School of Law, Chicago (J.D., cum laude, 1967). Associate Editor, Loyola Law Journal, 1966-1967. *Member:* Chicago Bar Association. ***PRACTICE AREAS:*** Real Estate; Trusts and Estates; Probate. ***Email:*** clmervis@lgclaw.com

LEWINTHAL, SKLAMBERG & ASSOCIATES

633 SKOKIE BOULEVARD, SUITE 410
NORTHBROOK, ILLINOIS 60062
Telephone: 847-480-0110
Fax: 847-480-0156
Email: lewinthal@comcast.net
URL: http://www.adignifieddivorce.com

Family Law, Divorce, Child Custody, Child Support, Spousal Support, Domestic Relations, Alimony, Matrimonial, Palimony, Paternity, Premarital Agreements and Separation Agreements, Divorce Tax Considerations.

FIRM PROFILE: Working towards a Dignified Divorce even when Litigation is necessary.

MEMBERS OF FIRM

ROBERT A. LEWINTHAL, born Chicago, Illinois, July 20, 1951; admitted to bar, 1976, Illinois; 1977, U.S. District Court, Northern District of Illinois. *Education:* University of Denver (B.A., 1973); Chicago-Kent College of Law, Illinois Institute of Technology (J.D., 1976); John Marshall Law School (LL.M. in Taxation, 1981). *Member:* Illinois State Bar Association. ***PRACTICE AREAS:*** Matrimonial Law; Dissolution; Child Custody; Complex Family Law; Business Valuation; Complex Tax; Family Law; Divorce; Child Support; Spousal Support; Domestic Relations; Alimony; Paternity; Palimony; Premarital Agreements; Separation Agreements. ***Email:*** lewinthal@comcast.net

(This Listing Continued)

SANDRA H. SKLAMBERG, born Chicago, Illinois, September 20, 1953; admitted to bar, 1981, Illinois. *Education:* University of Illinois (B.A., 1975); Chicago-Kent College of Law, Illinois Institute of Technology (J.D., 1981). Speaker, Landlord & Tenant Law, Local Municipalities, 2001—. Instructor, Paralegal Courses, Mallinckrodt College. ***PRACTICE AREAS:*** Family Law; Divorce; Child Custody; Child Support; Spousal Support; Domestic Relations; Matrimonial Law; Premarital Agreements; Separation Agreements; Real Estate; Landlord and Tenant Law; Evictions. ***Email:*** lewinthal@comcast.net

BARRY LOCKE & ASSOCIATES, LTD.

NORTHBROOK, ILLINOIS

(See Chicago)

Family Law, Divorce, Child Custody, Child Support, Paternity, Parentage, Visitation Rights.

O'HALLORAN, KOSOFF, GEITNER & COOK, P.C.

EDENS CORPORATE CENTER, FOURTH FLOOR
650 DUNDEE ROAD
NORTHBROOK, ILLINOIS 60062
Telephone: 847-291-0200
Fax: 847-291-9230
URL: http://www.okgc.com

Civil Trial and Appellate Practice in Federal and State Courts. Complex and Multi-District Litigation, Civil Rights and Government Tort Liability, Municipal Liability Defense, Construction, Insurance, Product Liability Defense, Securities, Estate Planning, Real Estate, Corporate, Commercial Transactions and Business Law.

JAMES E. O'HALLORAN, JR., born Pawtucket, Rhode Island, June 13, 1938; admitted to bar, 1965, Illinois; U.S. District Court, Northern District of Illinois; U.S. Court of Appeals, Seventh Circuit. *Education:* Colgate University (A.B., 1962); Northwestern University (J.D., summa cum laude, 1965). Member, Board of Editors, Northwestern University Law Review, 1964-1965. *Member:* Law Club of Chicago; Legal Club of Chicago. ***PRACTICE AREAS:*** Litigation. ***Email:*** johalloran@okgc.com

CLIFFORD G. KOSOFF, born New York, N.Y., January 12, 1954; admitted to bar, 1978, Illinois and U.S. District Court, Northern District of Illinois; 1980, Florida; 1991, U.S. District Court, Eastern District of Wisconsin; 1997, U.S. District Court, Central District of Illinois; 1998, U.S. District Court, Southern District of Illinois. *Education:* University of Maryland (B.A., 1975); John Marshall Law School (J.D., 1978). Phi Delta Phi. *Member:* The Florida Bar; Bar Associations of the Central and Southern Districts of Illinois; Defense Research Institute. ***PRACTICE AREAS:*** Litigation; Insurance Coverage and Defense; Civil Rights; Municipal Liability Defense. ***Email:*** ckosoff@okgc.com

NEAL P. GEITNER, born Highland Park, Illinois, December 27, 1955; admitted to bar, 1982, Georgia; 1983, Illinois. *Education:* Southern Illinois University (B.S. with highest honors, 1977); University of Georgia (J.D., 1981). *Member:* State Bar of Georgia; Illinois State Bar Association. ***PRACTICE AREAS:*** Estate Planning; Business Law. ***Email:*** ngeitner@okgc.com

GERARD W. COOK, born Chicago, Illinois, May 17, 1953; admitted to bar, 1978, Wisconsin and U.S. District Court, Western District of Wisconsin; 1979, Illinois; 1980, Florida and U.S. District Court, Northern, Central and Southern Districts of Illinois. *Education:* Northwestern University (B.A., 1975); John Marshall Law School (J.D., 1978). Phi Delta Phi. *Member:* State Bar of Wisconsin; The Florida Bar; Illinois Association of Defense Trial Counsel; Defense Research Institute. ***PRACTICE AREAS:*** Insurance Defense; Product Liability Defense; Government Tort Liability. ***Email:*** gcook@okgc.com

MARK M. ANDERSON, born Chicago, Illinois, June 1, 1951; admitted to bar, 1976, Illinois and U.S. District Court, Northern District of Illinois. *Education:* Duke University (A.B., 1973); DePaul University (J.D., 1976); John Marshall Law School (LL.M. in Taxation, 1983). *Member:* Illinois State and American Bar Associations. ***PRACTICE AREAS:*** Corporate; Real Estate; Commercial Transactions; Business Law. ***Email:*** manderson@okgc.com

JULIE A. BRUCH, born Evanston, Illinois, May 6, 1967; admitted to bar, 1993, Illinois; U.S. District Court, Northern, Central and Southern Districts of Illinois. *Education:* Northwestern University (B.A. 1989); Loyola University, Chicago (J.D., 1993). Student Articles Editor, Loyola Law Journal. *Member:* Chicago and American Bar Associations; Defense Research Institute; Illinois Association of Defense Trial Counsel; Bar Associations of the Central and Southern Districts of Illinois. ***PRACTICE AREAS:*** Employment Law; Civil Rights; Municipal Liability; Municipal Defense. ***Email:*** jbruch@okgc.com

GEORGE J. CASSON, JR., born Evergreen Park, Illinois, August 23, 1947; admitted to bar, 1972, Illinois; U.S. District Court, Northern, Central and Southern Districts of Illinois; U.S. Court of Appeals, Seventh Circuit. *Education:* Georgetown University (B.S.F.S., 1969); University of Chicago (J.D., 1972). *Member:* American Bar Association. ***PRACTICE AREAS:*** Litigation. ***Email:*** gcasson@okgc.com

SALLY O. JOYCE, born Evanston, Illinois, October 24, 1964; admitted to bar, 1994, Illinois. *Education:* Marquette University (B.S., 1986); Loyola University (J.D., magna cum laude, 1994). Phi Alpha Delta. Member, Loyola Law Journal, 1992-1993. Certified Public Accountant, Illinois, 1987. *Member:* Illinois State and American Bar Associations. ***PRACTICE AREAS:*** Business Transactions; Commercial Real Estate; Estate Planning; Tax. ***Email:*** sjoyce@okgc.com

JANE M. MAY, born Chicago, Illinois, May 15, 1966; admitted to bar, 1991, Illinois; U.S. District Court, Northern, Central and Southern Districts of Illinois. *Education:* Uni-

(This Listing Continued)

O'HALLORAN, KOSOFF, GEITNER & COOK, P.C., Northbrook—Continued

versity of Chicago (B.A., 1988); Boston College (J.D., 1991). *Member:* Defense Research Institute. ***PRACTICE AREAS:*** Employment; Civil Litigation; Governmental Liability; Products Liability. ***Email:*** jmay@okgc.com

STACY M. OVERBY, born New York, New York, September 27, 1965; admitted to bar, 1990, Georgia; 1994, Texas; 2000, Illinois. *Education:* Emory University (B.B.A., 1987); University of Pennsylvania, Law School (J.D., 1990). Comment Editor, Comparative Labor Law Journal. *Member:* Illinois Bar Association; State Bar of Georgia; State Bar of Texas. ***PRACTICE AREAS:*** Corporate Law; Real Estate Law; Estate Planning. ***Email:*** soverby@okgc.com

GREGORY J. MELGARES, born Colorado Springs, Colorado, September 30, 1966; admitted to bar, 1996, Illinois. *Education:* Creighton University (B.S., 1989); Loyola University, Chicago (J.D., 1996). Certified Public Accountant, Illinois, 1991. *Member:* Chicago, Illinois State and American Bar Associations. ***PRACTICE AREAS:*** Estate Planning; Tax Planning; Business Transactions. ***Email:*** gmelgares@okgc.com

ELISHA S. ROSENBLUM, born Rockford, Illinois, March 13, 1969; admitted to bar, 1994, Illinois; 1995, U.S. Court of Appeals, Seventh Circuit; 1996, U.S. District Court, Northern District of Illinois. *Education:* Loyola University (B.B.A., 1991); Chicago-Kent College of Law (J.D., 1994). Corporation Counsel, Torts Division, City of Chicago, 1996-1998. *Member:* Chicago Bar Association. ***LANGUAGES:*** Hebrew. ***REPORTED CASES:*** People v. Siuek,— 671 N.E.2d 358; People v. Grano,— 676 N.E.2d 248. ***PRACTICE AREAS:*** Tort Defense; Construction Litigation; Products Liability; Medical Malpractice; Employment Discrimination; Premises Liability. ***Email:*** erosenblum@okgc.com

REPRESENTATIVE CLIENTS: American National Bank and Trust Company of Chicago; Ceisel Masonry, Inc.; CNA Insurance Company; Gotham Insurance Company; Great American Insurance Companies; Illinois Counties Risk Management Trust; Lutheran General Hospital; Motorola Inc.; Mutual Marine Insurance Company; New York Marine & General Insurance Company; Northland Insurance Companies; Power Packaging, Inc.; Rex Electric Inc. Assurance Agency Ltd.; The Private Bank and Trust Company; Utilities, Inc.; Willis Corporation; Whitehall North Convalescent and Nursing Home; Wine Sergi & Co., LLC.

ANTHONY PERRELLI

NORTHBROOK, ILLINOIS

(See Deerfield)

Business Corporate, Small Business, Contracts, Business Planning, Real Estate, Commercial Litigation and Taxation.

LAW OFFICES OF DAVID L. PINSEL, P.C.

NORTHBROOK, ILLINOIS

(See Rolling Meadows)

Divorce, Family, Child Custody, Child Support, Visitation Rights, Paternity, Real Estate, Landlord and Tenant Law, Commercial Collections, Debtor and Creditor Law.

PIONEER PATENT, LLC

1334 SHERMER ROAD, SUITE 220
NORTHBROOK, ILLINOIS 60062
Telephone: 847-412-0073
Fax: 847-412-0074
URL: http://www.Pioneer-Patent.com
Email: NEBOLSKY@Pioneer-Patent.com
URL: http://www.lawyers.com/pioneerpatent

Mailing Address: P.O. Box 128, Northbrook, IL 60065-0128

Intellectual Property, Patent, Trademark, Copyright, Licensing Agreements and Trade Secrets. Entertainment Law.

SHANNON L. NEBOLSKY, born January 1, 1965; admitted to bar, 1996, Illinois and U.S. District Court, Northern District of Illinois; registered to practice before U.S. Patent and Trademark Office. *Education:* University of Illinois (B.Sc., in Chem., with highest distinction, 1987); University of Newcastle-Upon-Tyne, Newcastle, England (1985-1986); Northwestern University (M.Sc., 1989; Ph.D., 1995; J.D., 1996). Phi Lambda Upsilon (Secretary, 1988-1989; President, 1989-1990). Co-Author: Journal of the American Chemical Society 44:11401-11407, 1998; Journal of Inorganic Biochemistry 51:171, 1993. *Member:* Chicago and American (Member: Intellectual Property Section; Science and Technology Division) Bar Associations; American Chemical Society (Member: Division of Chemistry and the Law); Licensing Executives Society. ***PRACTICE AREAS:*** Intellectual Property; Patents; Trademarks. ***Email:*** Nebolsky@Pioneer-Patent.com

LAW OFFICES OF STEVEN I. RAPAPORT

630 DUNDEE ROAD, SUITE 120
NORTHBROOK, ILLINOIS 60062-9280
Telephone: 847-559-9270
Fax: 847-559-9280
Email: raplaw@ameritech.net

Workers Compensation, Personal Injury, Automobile Accidents, Construction Accidents, Criminal Law, Traffic Violations, DWI, Insurance, Legal Malpractice, Estate Planning.

(This Listing Continued)

STEVEN I. RAPAPORT, born Chicago, Illinois, July 31, 1958; admitted to bar, 1984, Missouri; 1985, Illinois. *Education:* Duke University (A.B., 1980); Washington University (J.D., 1984). *Member:* Chicago, Lake County, Illinois State, and Federal Bar Association; The Missouri Bar. ***PRACTICE AREAS:*** Workers Compensation; Personal Injury; Automobile Accidents; Wrongful Death; Driving Under the Influence; Insurance; Construction; Estate Planning.

STEVEN HERZBERG, born Rapid City South Dakota, November 12, 1957; admitted to bar, 2001, Illinois. *Education:* Northwestern University (B.A., 1995); John Marshall Law School, Chicago (J.D., with honors, 2001). Board Member, Moot Court Honors Society. Recipient, Corpus Juris Secundum Award for Excellence in Criminal Law. Referee, Illinois High School Basketball. Board President, Condominium Association. *Member:* Chicago and Illinois State Bar Associations; Illinois Trial Lawyers Association. ***PRACTICE AREAS:*** Criminal Defense; Driving Under the Influence; Driving While Intoxicated; Traffic Violations; Workers Compensation; Personal Injury; Civil Practice. ***Email:*** herzlaw@ameritech.net

LAW OFFICES OF CAREY S. ROSEMARIN, P.C.

500 SKOKIE BOULEVARD, SUITE 510
NORTHBROOK, ILLINOIS 60062
Telephone: 847-897-8000
Fax: 312-896-5786
Email: csr@rosemarinlaw.com
URL: http://www.rosemarinlaw.com

Environmental Law.

CAREY S. ROSEMARIN, born Englewood, New Jersey, August 19, 1950; admitted to bar, 1978, Tennessee and U.S. District Court, Eastern District of Tennessee; 1982, Illinois; U.S. District Court, Northern District of Illinois. *Education:* University of Michigan (B.S., 1972); Pennsylvania State University (M.S., 1974); University of Tennessee (J.D., 1978). Formerly with: U.S. Environmental Protection Agency, 1980-1986; Katten Muchin & Zavis, 1986-1990; Jenner & Block, 1990-1999. *Member:* Chicago (Vice Chairman, 1984—and Chairman, 1985-1986, Environmental Law Committee), Tennessee and American Bar Associations; Environmental Law Institute. ***PRACTICE AREAS:*** Environmental Law.

LAW OFFICES OF DAVID M. SHULTS

555 SKOKIE BOULEVARD, SUITE 500
NORTHBROOK, ILLINOIS 60062
Telephone: 847-480-1020
Fax: 847-480-7859
Email: lawdms@yahoo.com

Commercial Law, Civil Litigation, Real Estate, and Family Law.

DAVID M. SHULTS, born Elgin, Illinois, January 24, 1973; admitted to bar, 2003, Illinois and U.S. District Court, Northern District of Illinois. *Education:* DePaul University (B.S., 1996; J.D., 2003). *Member:* Chicago, Illinois State and American Bar Associations. ***PRACTICE AREAS:*** Commercial Law; Civil Litigation; Real Estate; Buying and Selling a Home; Commercial Real Estate; Wills; Probate; Business Law.

SNOW & SNOW, LTD.

NORTHBROOK, ILLINOIS

(See Chicago)

Estate Planning, Asset Protection, Wills and Probate, Trusts and Estates, Guardianships, Elder Law, Trust, Taxation, Small Closely Held Business Law, Business Succession Planning, Estate Planning, General Practice, Real Estate, Buying and Selling a Home, Buying and Selling a Business and IRS Audits.

STONE, McGUIRE & SIEGEL

801 SKOKIE BOULEVARD, SUITE 200
NORTHBROOK, ILLINOIS 60062
Telephone: 847-239-7555
FAX: 847-239-7556
URL: http://www.stonemcguire.com

Federal and State Taxation, IRS Circular 230, Administrative Law, General Corporate and Commercial Law, Healthcare, Business Acquisitions and Dispositions, General Securities, Computer Fraud and Employee Embezzlement Law, Probate, Not-For-Profit Governance, Criminal Tax Law, Criminal and Civil Trial and Appellate Practice in all State and Federal Courts.

MEMBERS OF FIRM

HOWARD L. STONE, born Chicago, Illinois, September 16, 1941; admitted to bar, 1972, Illinois, U.S. District Court, Northern District of Illinois and U.S. Court of Appeals, Seventh Circuit; 1977, U.S. Tax Court; 1981, U.S. Supreme Court. *Education:* University of Illinois; Roosevelt University (B.S.B.A., 1963); DePaul University (J.D., 1972). Author: "Defending the Federal Tax Case: What To Do When the IRS Steps In," Illinois Institute of Continuing Legal Education, 1978; "Income Taxation for Attorneys," General Practice Handbook (Chapter Author), Illinois Institute of Continuing Legal Education, 1981. Co-Author and Co-Editor, textbook, "Handling Criminal Tax Cases: A Lawyers Guide," Illinois Institute of Continuing Legal Education, 1982. Co-author: "Federal Civil Tax Practice, Administrative Summons," Illinois Institute of Continuing Legal Education, 1983; "Client Tax Fraud—A Practical Guide to Protecting Your Rights," Illinois CPA Foundation, 1984; "IRS to Audit Lifestyle Not Tax Returns," CPA, Insight Magazine, 1996; "When the IRS

(This Listing Continued)

Agent Peeks Under the Mattress," New York Times, 1996; "IICLE Health Care Fraud and Compliance Plans," 2002; "ILLCPA Foundation Criminal Fraud," 2002; "New Lifestyle Audits is IRS' Reality Check," San Diego Union-Tribune, 1997; "Health Care Fraud and Compliance", Insight Magazine, 1998. Resident Lecturer: Tax Fraud and the C.P.A., Illinois C.P.A. Foundation, 1976-2004; IRS Restructuring—Has The IRS Changed, ICPA, 1999; Tax Fraud, ICPA, 1999; Tax Fraud, IAAI, 2000; Long Term Health Care Compliance, ICPA, 1999; Health Care Compliance & Fraud Conference Chair, ICPA, 1999-2005; IRS Circular 230, ICPA 2005. Adjunct Professor, University of Illinois, Chicago. Internal Revenue Agent, of Internal Revenue Service, 1964-1972. Special Assistant, U.S. Attorney, U.S. Department of Justice, 1972-1976. Chief Financial Auditor and Investigator, Northern District of Illinois, U.S. Attorneys Office, 1972-1976. *Member:* Chicago (Member, Committees on: Federal Taxation, 1981—; Criminal Law, 1981—; Elder Law, 2000—), Illinois State (Member, Federal Taxation Committee, 1976—), Federal and American (Member, Committees on: Complex White Collar Crimes, 1981—; Federal Civil and Criminal Tax Penalties, 1981—; Corporate General Counsel, 1981—; HCCO Healthcare Compliance Officer, 2000—) Bar Associations; Decalogue Society of Lawyers; American Institute of Certified Public Accountants; Illinois C.P.A. Foundation; National Association Certified Fraud Examiners; American Health Lawyers Association. ***Email:*** howard.stone@stonemcguire.com

DAVID A. McGUIRE, born Chicago, Illinois, December 30, 1946; admitted to bar, 1974, Illinois and U.S. District Court, Northern District of Illinois; 1974, U.S. Court of Appeals, Seventh Circuit; 1975, U.S. Tax Court. *Education:* Roosevelt University (B.S.B.A., 1968); DePaul University (J.D., 1974). Beta Gamma Sigma. Author: "Handling Criminal Tax Cases, Protecting the Evidence; Constitutional and Procedural Rights," Illinois Institute of Continuing Legal Education, 1980 and 1982. Co-author, "Client Tax Fraud—A Practical Guide to Protecting Your Rights," Illinois CPA Foundation, 1984. Faculty Member, Trial Bar Skills for Practicing Attorneys, 1983. Instructor, Advanced Income Tax for Experienced Revenue Agents, Internal Revenue Service, 1972. Lecturer, Client Tax Fraud, AAA-CPA Mid-Year Meeting, 1984. Internal Revenue Agent, 1968-1969, 1971-1974. Assistant United States Attorney, Northern District of Illinois, 1974-1976. *Member:* American Bar Association. ***Email:*** david.mcguire@stonemcguire.com

MICHAEL L. SIEGEL, born Chicago, Illinois, April 12, 1950; admitted to bar, 1975, Illinois and U.S. District Court, Southern District of Illinois; 1977, U.S. Court of Appeals, Seventh Circuit; 1982, U.S. District Court, Northern District of Illinois. *Education:* Grinnell College (B.A., 1972); University of Singapore, Singapore; University of Illinois (J.D., with honors, 1975). Phi Beta Kappa. Finalist, Frederick Green Moot Court Competition. Co-Author, "Curbside Consultation: An Informal Communication in Medical Practice," 1996. Teaching Assistant: Legal Writing, University of Illinois, 1974-1975; Adjunct Professor, Appellate Advocacy, John Marshall School of Law, 1980. Adjunct Professor, Appellate Advocacy, Loyola University, 1989-2000. Chairperson, Local School Council, Abraham Lincoln Elementary School 1989-1997. Member, Local School Council, Lincoln Park High School, 1998-2000. Law Clerk to Judge Harlington Wood, Jr., U.S. District Court, Southern District of Illinois, Southern Division, 1975-1976 and U.S. Court of Appeals, Seventh Circuit, 1976-1977. Assistant U.S. Attorney, U.S. Attorney's Office, Chicago, 1977-1983. *Member:* Chicago and American Bar Associations. ***PRACTICE AREAS:*** Criminal Law; Entertainment Law; Healthcare Law; Business Litigation. ***Email:*** michael.siegel@stonemcguire.com

CARL E. POLI, born Lucca, Italy, July 7, 1952; admitted to bar, 1978, Illinois and U.S. District Court, Northern District of Illinois; 1979, U.S. Court of Appeals, 5th and 7th Circuits; 1980, U.S. Tax Court; 1986, U.S. Supreme Court; 2002, U.S. Court of Appeals, 4th Circuit. *Education:* Loyola University (A.B., magna cum laude, 1974); Loyola University, Rome, Italy; DePaul University (J.D., with honors, 1978). Chair qualified arbitrator, Circuit Court of Cook County Mandatory Arbitration Program, 1997. Author: "1977-1978 Staff Assistant I. Goldstein & F. Lane, Trial Technique," Callaghan & Co., 2d Ed. 1969. Co-Author: "Corporate Counsel, Corporate Officers and Corporate Conflict: The Attorney Client Privilege in the Corporate Context," Illinois CPA Foundation, 1991. Lecturer: Limited Liability Companies and Limited Liability Partnerships, Structure & Taxation, 1996 Federal Tax Seminar, Homewood, Illinois, Winter 1996; Lecturer, OSHA Structure and OSHA Penalties, An Overview for Accountants, Success Institute Seminar for Certified Public Accountants, Rosemont, Illinois, Fall 1992; Lecturer, Copyright Litigation from Complaint to Appeal, DePaul University College of Law, Fall 1989. Legislative Assistant, Illinois General Assembly, 1973-1975. Member, DePaul University Endowment Board, 1979. Member, Board of Directors, Retinitis Pigmentosa Foundation Fighting Blindness Chapter, 1986. *Member:* Chicago Bar Association. ***LANGUAGES:*** Co-ordinate bilingual, English & Italian. ***Email:*** carl.poli@stonemcguire.com

(For Complete Biographical Data on all Personnel, see Chicago, Illinois Professional Biographies)

STRAUSS & MALK LLP

A Limited Liability Partnership including Professional Corporations

Established in 1994

135 REVERE DRIVE

NORTHBROOK, ILLINOIS 60062

Telephone: 847-562-1400
Chicago: 312-441-0900
Fax: 847-562-1422
Email: straussmalk@straussmalk.com
URL: http://www.straussmalk.com

Estate Planning, Wealth Preservation, Probate, Business Succession Planning, Corporate Law, Business Acquisitions and Sales, Real Estate Acquisition and Development, Business and Real Estate Financing, ERISA, Executive Compensation, Professional Service Businesses, Tax Law, Litigation including Commercial, Business Transactions, Real Estate, Trusts and Estates and Torts.

ARNOLD B. MALK, born Chicago, Illinois, April 25, 1947; admitted to bar, 1972, Illinois, U.S. District Court, Northern District of Illinois and U.S. Tax Court. *Education:* University of Illinois (B.A., 1969); DePaul University (J.D., 1972). Staff Member, De Paul Law Review. *Member:* Illinois State Bar Association. ***PRACTICE AREAS:*** Purchases and Sales of Businesses; Health Care Practices; Commercial Real Estate; Real Estate Development; Commercial Borrowing and Lending; Corporate; Partnerships and LLCs; General Business; Employee Contracting; Transactional Practice. ***Email:*** amalk@straussmalk.com

BENTON C. STRAUSS, born Chicago, Illinois, March 20, 1947; admitted to bar, 1972, Illinois; 1987, Wisconsin. *Education:* University of Illinois (B.A., 1968); Loyola University (J.D., 1972). Author: 1994-2001, Co-Author, 2002—, *Estate and Gift Planning for the Business Owner,* Research Institute of America, 1994—; *Legal Checklists, Life Insurance Arrangements* West Group, 1986—. Co-Author: 2005 Supplement to Post Mortem Tax Planning by Jerry A. Kasner. Lecturer and Author: Illinois Institute for Continuing Legal Education, 1985-1986; Minnesota Society of Certified Public Accountants, 1990-1991; Illinois CPA Society, 1994. *Member:* Chicago (Editor-in-Chief, Young Lawyer's Journal, 1974-1975; Member, 1975— and Chairman, 1991-1992, Trust Law Committee), Illinois State and American Bar Associations; State Bar of Wisconsin (Board of Governors, 2001-2004 and President, Nonresident Lawyers Division, 2002-2003). Fellow, American College of Trust and Estate Counsel (1995—). ***PRACTICE AREAS:*** Estate Planning; Probate; Wealth Preservation; Business Succession Planning; Business Representation; ERISA; Tax Law; Trusts and Estates; Asset Protection. ***Email:*** bstrauss@straussmalk.com

JOYCE A. LEVY, born Chicago, Illinois, February 24, 1955; admitted to bar, 1981, Illinois; 1982, U.S. District Court, Northern District of Illinois; 1983, U.S. Tax Court. *Education:* Yale University (B.A., 1976); Vanderbilt University (J.D., 1981); New York University (LL.M., Taxation, 1983). Office of District Counsel, Internal Revenue Service, 1983. Attorney Advisor, U.S. Tax Court, 1984-1985. *Member:* Chicago and American (Member, Taxation Section) Bar Associations. ***PRACTICE AREAS:*** Federal Taxation; Estate Planning; Probate; Business Succession Planning. ***Email:*** jlevy@straussmalk.com

KENNETH A. KOSKY, born Evanston, Illinois, September 29, 1958; admitted to bar, 1985, Illinois. *Education:* University of Illinois (B.A., 1980); John Marshall Law School (J.D., 1985). Licensed Real Estate Broker, Illinois. Former Instructor: Real Estate Courses at Wright College; Century 21 Real Estate. *Member:* Lake County and Chicago Bar Associations. ***PRACTICE AREAS:*** Commercial Real Estate; Commercial Borrowing and Lending; Business Transactions; Corporate Law; Partnership Law; Limited Liability Company Law; Employment Contracts; Business Sales; Business Acquisitions. ***Email:*** kkosky@straussmalk.com

BRAD S. GRAYSON, born Chicago, Illinois, November 11, 1960; admitted to bar, 1987, Illinois and U.S. District Court, Northern District of Illinois including Trial Bar; 1989, U.S. District Court, Central District of Illinois; 1991, U.S. Court of Appeals, Seventh Circuit. *Education:* University of Michigan (B.A., 1981); University of Chicago (M.A., 1984); Loyola University (J.D., 1987). Recipient, American Jurisprudence Award (Civil Procedure), 1985. Executive Editor, Loyola University of Chicago Law Journal, 1986-87. Author: "Problems in Defining 'Tender Offer': The decision in Hanson Trust PLC v. SCM Corp.," 17 Loyola University Law Journal 693 (1986). Editor: "Development of Legal Theories and Causes of Action," Chapter 2, Business and Commercial Litigation Handbook, Illinois Institute for Continuous Legal Education, 1999. ***PRACTICE AREAS:*** Litigation. ***Email:*** bgrayson@straussmalk.com

MICHAEL S. STRAUSS, born Skokie, Illinois, June 12, 1970; admitted to bar, 1998, Illinois and U.S. District Court, Northern District of Illinois. *Education:* University of Wisconsin-Madison (B.S., 1992); DePaul University (M.B.A., 1994); Chicago-Kent College of Law (J.D., with high honors, 1998). Member, Order of the Coif. Author: *Legal Checklists, Checklist 10-5, Life Insurance Arrangements,* West Group, 2000—. Co-Author: *Estate and Gift Planning for the Business Owner,* Research Institute of America, 2002—; 2005 Supplement to Post Mortem Tax Planning by Jerry A. Kasner. *Member:* Chicago and American Bar Associations. ***PRACTICE AREAS:*** Estate and Trust Planning; Tax; Business Transactions. ***Email:*** mstrauss@straussmalk.com

H. JAY GLAUBINGER, born Fredericksburg, Virginia, March 8, 1970; admitted to bar, 1999, Missouri; 2000, Illinois. *Education:* Indiana University (B.S., 1992); Washington University (J.D., 1999). Certified Public Accountant, Illinois, 1992 and Missouri, 1999. *Member:* Chicago, Illinois State and American Bar Associations; The Missouri Bar. ***PRACTICE AREAS:*** Tax Planning; Estate Planning; Trust Planning; Corporate Law; Business Transactions. ***Email:*** jglaubinger@straussmalk.com

MICHELLE H. GOOZE-MILLER, born Chicago, Illinois, April 19, 1971; admitted to bar, 1997, Illinois. *Education:* Northwestern University (B.A., with honors, 1993); University of Chicago (J.D., with honors, 1997). Phi Betta Kappa. *Member:* Chicago Bar Association; Greater North Shore Estate Planning Council. ***PRACTICE AREAS:*** Estate Planning; Probate; Taxation; Corporate Law. ***Email:*** mgooze@straussmalk.com

JEREMY J. KRAMER, born Hammond, Indiana, June 3, 1971; admitted to bar, 1996, Illinois and U.S. District Court, Northern District of Illinois. *Education:* Indiana University (B.A., 1993); John Marshall Law School (J.D., 1996). ***PRACTICE AREAS:*** Commercial Litigation. ***Email:*** jkramer@straussmalk.com

OF COUNSEL

ROBERT O. ROSENMAN, born Chicago, Illinois, June 6, 1931; admitted to bar, 1956, Illinois; 1988, U.S. Tax Court. *Education:* University of Michigan (B.B.A., 1953; M.B.A., 1956; J.D., 1956). Phi Alpha Delta; Phi Eta Sigma. Case Club Quarter Finalist and Judge, 1955. Recipient, American Jurisprudence Award in Administrative Law. *Member:* Chicago (Member, Probate Practice Committee, 1973—; Chairman, Division III, 1979-1980; Member, State and Local Tax Committee, 1988—), Illinois State and American (Member: Committees on Administration and Distribution of Decedents' Estates and Estate and Trust Litigation, Section of Real Property, Probate and Trust Law, 1972—; Forum Committee on Air and Space Law, 1988—) Bar Associations; Chicago Council of Lawyers. ***PRACTICE AREAS:*** Estate Planning; Probate; Aviation Law; Taxation; Real Estate Tax. ***Email:*** rrosenman@straussmalk.com

HAROLD R. BURNSTEIN, admitted to bar, 1950, Illinois; 1951 U.S. Tax Court. *Education:* Northwestern University (B.S. 1940); DePaul University College of Law (J.D.

(This Listing Continued)

STRAUSS & MALK LLP, Northbrook—Continued

1950). *Member:* Chicago and American Bar Associations; Illinois Society of Certified Public Accountants; American Institute of Certified Public Accountants. ***PRACTICE AREAS:*** State Taxation; Federal Taxation; Corporate Transaction; Business Successions; Estate Planning; Wealth Preservation; Probate Administration; Trust Administration. ***Email:*** hburnstein@straussmalk.com

WEIL & ASSOCIATES

60 REVERE DRIVE, SUITE 888
NORTHBROOK, ILLINOIS 60062
Telephone: 847-509-0015
Fax: 847-509-0021
Email: weil@weilassoc.com
URL: http://www.weilassociates.com

Family Law, Divorce, Collaborative Law, Adoptions, Child Custody, Child Support, Divorce, Domestic Violence, Premarital Agreements, Spousal Support.

SANDRA M. WEIL, born Omaha, Nebraska, December 15, 1944; admitted to bar, 1979, Illinois and U.S. District Court, Northern District of Illinois including Trial Bar. *Education:* University of Missouri, Kansas City (B.A., 1977; J.D., 1978). *Member:* Academy of Collaborative Professionals; Collaborative Law Institute of Illinois. ***PRACTICE AREAS:*** Family Law; Trusts and Estates; Civil Litigation; Business Litigation. ***Email:*** weil@weilassoc.com

ASSOCIATE

LLEWELLYN KENNEDY, born Anchorage, Alaska, July 13, 1968; admitted to bar, 1998, Illinois. *Education:* Whittier College (B.A., 1991); Chicago-Kent College of Law (J.D., 1998). *Member:* Academy of Collaborative Professionals; Collaborative Law Institute of Illinois. ***PRACTICE AREAS:*** Family Law; Civil Litigation; Business Litigation. ***Email:*** weil@weilassoc.com

LAW OFFICES OF STEVEN C. WEISS

ONE NORTHBROOK PLACE
5 REVERE DRIVE, SUITE 200
NORTHBROOK, ILLINOIS 60062
Telephone: 312-782-3415
Fax: 312-782-3421
Email: scweiss@msn.com
URL: http://www.lawyers.com/weisslawfirm

Logistics and Supply Chains, Third Party Supplier Contracting, Freight Forwarding, Freight Brokers, Admiralty and Maritime Law, Business Transactions, Corporate Law, Inland Marine Law, Marine Cargo, Air Cargo, Freight Loss and Damage, Insurance Coverage Disputes, Interstate Commerce, Motor Carrier Defense, Motor Carrier Liability, Shipping Regulation, Surface Transportation.

STEVEN C. WEISS, born Chicago, Illinois, February 4, 1956; admitted to bar, 1979, Illinois and U.S. District Court, Northern District of Illinois; 1980, U.S. Court of Appeals, Seventh Circuit; 1982, U.S. Supreme Court and U.S. Court of International Trade; 1983, U.S. District Court, Eastern District of Wisconsin; 1985, U.S. Court of Appeals, Eighth Circuit; 1988, U.S. Court of Appeals, District of Columbia Circuit; 1999, U.S. Court of Appeals, Sixth Circuit. *Education:* Illinois Institute of Technology (B.S., with Honors, 1976); Chicago-Kent College of Law (J.D., with Honors, 1979); Kellogg School of Management, Northwestern University (M.B.A., 2005). Named: 2005 Illinois Super Lawyer, Illinois Super Lawyers Magazine, 2005; Chicago Magazine, May, 2005. Author: "Loss and Damage Considerations in International Shipments Between Canada and the United States", Gestion Logistique, 1998; "Loss and Damage Considerations in the Sale and Transportation of Goods", Air Cargo World, 1998; "The Transportation Equity Act for the 21st Century and You", Lifting and Transportation International, 1998; "Extra Care Shipments, Food, Drugs, Cosmetics", Traffic World, 1997; "Freight Loss and Damage Claim Tips", 1997 and "Trucking Freight Charge Issues: An Overview of the New Laws", 1996, The Illinois Manufacturers Association. "Backbilling-Your Rights Under the New Transportation Laws," The Illinois Manufacturer, November/December 1995. Co-Author: Chapter entitled "Commercial Bribery," The Illinois Institute for Continuing Legal Education (IICLE) volume on Antitrust and Unfair Competition, 1996, chapter update, 1998. Contributing Legal Editor, Intermodal Age International, 1988-1991. Conference Speaker, Canadian Intermodal 2004, September 2004. Speaker, Regional Seminar, Transportation Lawyers Association, 2000. Faculty Member/Panelist, Cargo Loss and Damage Claims, Continuing Legal Education Satellite Network, April, 1990. *Member:* Association for Transportation Law, Logistics and Policy (Chair, Committee on Litigation in the Courts, 1993-1999, Committee on Programs, 1995). ***REPORTED CASES:*** Federal Insurance Company, a/s/o Heyman Corporation v. Mitsui O.S.K. Lines, Ltd., Urie Transportation Management, Inc. et. al. 2001 U.S. Dist. LEXIS 18209 (N.D., IL 2001). ***PRACTICE AREAS:*** Administrative Law; Administrative Agency Practice; Logistics; Admiralty and Maritime Law; Business Transactions; Corporate Law; Inland Marine Law; Marine Cargo; Air Cargo; Bills of Lading; Freight Claims; Freight Loss and Damage; Insurance Coverage Disputes; International Shipping; Interstate Commerce; Motor Carrier Defense; Motor Carrier Liability; Motor Carrier Regulation; Shipping; Shipping Regulation; Surface Transportation.

OF COUNSEL

LAWRENCE E. RISSMAN, born Chicago, Illinois, December 16, 1954; admitted to bar, 1979, Illinois. *Education:* Yale University (B.S., cum laude, 1976); University of Michigan (J.D., cum laude, 1979). Co-Author: "Advising Illinois Banks on Checks," Chapter in Advising Illinois Financial Institutions, IICLE, 2002. *Member:* Chicago, Illinois State and American (Member: Banking Law and Uniform Comm. Code Committees; Business Law Section) Bar Associations. ***PRACTICE AREAS:*** Banking Law; Banking Regulation; Check Fraud; Electronic Banking; Negotiable Instruments; Uniform Commercial Code; Commercial Transactions; Secured Transactions; Commercial Contracts. ***Email:*** lrissman@worldnet.att.net

LASKY & RIFKIND, LTD.

NORTH CHICAGO, ILLINOIS
(See Chicago)

Litigation Practice including Securities, Business, Commercial, Class Actions, Professional Malpractice and Appellate Practice.

MANDELL MENKES LLC

NORTH CHICAGO, ILLINOIS
(See Chicago)

General Civil Practice, Class Action Defense, Consumer Finance and Banking, Corporate, Commercial Litigation, Employment, Media, Entertainment and Intellectual Property Law including Copyright and Trademark Law, Computer and Technology Law, Health Care, Captive Insurance and Purchasing and Risk Retention Groups and Insurance Coverage, Directors and Officers Liability, Professional Liability, Casualty, Life, Health and Disability.

PAUL B. NOVAK

NORTH CHICAGO, ILLINOIS
(See Waukegan)

Criminal Law, Juvenile Law, Family Law.

DAVID M. STERNBERG

NORTH CHICAGO, ILLINOIS
(See Chicago)

Automobile Accidents and Injuries, Slip and Fall, Wrongful Death, Personal Injury and Workers Compensation Law.

LAW OFFICES OF PAUL CHATZKY

790 WEST FRONTAGE ROAD, SUITE 212
NORTHFIELD, ILLINOIS 60093
Telephone: 847-441-4288
Fax: 847-441-4289
Email: pc@chatzkylaw.com
URL: http://www.chatzkylaw.com

General Practice, Divorce, Family Law, Criminal Defense, Felonies, Driving While Intoxicated, Real Estate, Business Law, Estate Planning, Wills, Personal Injury and Civil Litigation.

FIRM PROFILE: Paul Chatzky represents individual and commercial clients throughout Cook, Lake, Dupage, and McHenry Counties. The firm commits to provide cost effective legal services without compromise to the highest ethical and professional standards of practice.

PAUL CHATZKY, born Havana, Cuba, June 25, 1958; admitted to bar, 1983, Illinois, U.S. District Court, Northern District of Illinois and U.S. Supreme Court. *Education:* University of Florida (B.A., with high honors, 1980; J.D., 1982). Phi Beta Kappa; Phi Kappa Phi; Golden Key National Honors Society. Member, Board of Directors: Bridgeview Chamber of Commerce and Industry, 1985; Congregation B'nai Shalom, 1994-1997; Tourette Syndrome Association, Inc. of Illinois, 1998—. *Member:* Chicago, Lake County and Illinois State Bar Associations. ***LANGUAGES:*** Spanish. ***SPECIAL AGENCIES:*** Approved attorney agent for Attorneys' National Title Network, Inc. ***PRACTICE AREAS:*** Divorce; Family Law; Criminal Defense; Felonies; Driving While Intoxicated; Real Estate; Business Law; Estate Planning; Wills; Personal Injury; Civil Litigation.

CAROL DI GIACOMO & KATHRYN SOMERS, L.L.C.

211 WAUKEGAN ROAD, SUITE 105
NORTHFIELD, ILLINOIS 60093
Telephone: 847-784-8900
Fax: 847-784-8929
URL: http://www.digiacomo-somersllc.com

Family Law, Divorce, Collaborative Law, Child Custody, Child Support, Spousal Support, Visitation, Adoption, Mediation and Complex Family Law relating to Valuation and Tax Considerations, Estate Planning, Real Estate, Contract and Bankruptcy Law.

CAROL A. DI GIACOMO, born Chicago, Illinois, March 29, 1952; admitted to bar, 1982, Illinois. *Education:* University of Illinois (B.A., 1973); University of Barcelona; Illinois Institute of Technology/Chicago-Kent College of Law (J.D., 1982). Member, Part-Time Teaching Staff, Oakton Community College and DuPage Community College. *Member:* Chicago, Illinois State and Northwest Suburban Bar Associations; Northwest Suburban Estate Planning Council. ***LANGUAGES:*** Spanish. ***PRACTICE AREAS:*** Family; Divorce; Child Custody; Adoption; Child Support; Visitation; Collaborative Law; Estate Planning; Real Estate; Contract; Bankruptcy. ***Email:*** carol@digiacomo-somers.com

KATHRYN M. SOMERS, born Chicago, Illinois, November 10, 1953; admitted to bar, 1981, Illinois; 1994, U.S. District Court, Northern District of Illinois including Trial Bar. *Education:* Northwestern University (B.A., 1975); Northeastern Illinois University (M.A., 1976); DePaul University (J.D., 1980). Board Member, Mediation Council of Illinois, 1992-2002. Former host of Law Talk. *Member:* Chicago (Chairperson, Alternative

(This Listing Continued)

Dispute Resolution Committee, 1983), Illinois State, North Suburban and Lake County Bar Associations; Lake County Arbitration Panel. Fellow, Collaborative Law Institute of Illinois. ***PRACTICE AREAS:*** Family; Divorce; Child Custody; Adoption; Child Support; Visitation; Mediation; Collaborative Law; Estate Planning; Real Estate; Contract; Bankruptcy. ***Email:*** kathryn@digiacomo-somers.com

LAW OFFICES OF CHRISTOPHER DWYER

788 W. FRONTAGE ROAD
SUITE 109
NORTHFIELD, ILLINOIS 60093
Telephone: 847-784-8606
Fax: 847-919-3821
Email: christopher_dwyer@yahoo.com

Estate Planning, Estate Administration, Business Succession Planning, Income Tax Planning and Retirement Planning.

CHRISTOPHER D. DWYER, born Indianapolis, Indiana, March 22, 1967; admitted to bar, 1992, Connecticut; 1993, New York; 1998, Illinois. *Education:* Providence College (B.A., 1989); Case Western Reserve University (J.D., 1992); New York University (LL.M., Taxation, 1993). Omicron Delta Epsilon. Articles Editor, Case Western Reserve Journal of International Law, 1991-1992. Co-Author: "Making Most of the New Illinois Perspectives Statute," Illinois Bar Journal, November 1999. Associate, 1997-2000 and Partner, 2001-2004, Jenner & Block LLP. *Member:* Chicago and Illinois State Bar Associations. ***PRACTICE AREAS:*** Estate Planning; Estate Administration; Business Succession Planning; Income Tax Planning; Retirement Planning.

MARIA J. JAFFE

1 NORTHFIELD PLAZA, SUITE 300
NORTHFIELD, ILLINOIS 60093
Telephone: 847-441-1814
URL: http://www.mariajaffelawfirm.com

Chicago, Illinois Office: 8 South Michigan Avenue, Suite 3200, 60603. Telephone: 312-641-1052. Fax: 312-641-1052.

Adoption, Child Support, Criminal Law, Custody and Visitation, Debtor/Creditor, Divorce, Family Law, Immigration Law, Landlord/Tenant, Mediation, Medical Malpractice, Motor Vehicle Accidents, Plaintiff Personal Injury, Real Estate.

(For complete biographical data on all personnel, see Professional Biographies at Chicago, Illinois)

KAPLAN & GREENSWAG LLC

181 WAUKEGAN ROAD, SUITE 205
NORTHFIELD, ILLINOIS 60093
Telephone: 847-501-5300
Fax: 847-501-5325
Email: firm@kaplangreenswag.com
URL: http://www.kaplangreenswag.com

Chicago Office: 600 W. Jackson Boulevard, Suite 200, 60661.

Commercial Litigation, Trial Practice, Dispute Resolution, Franchise Law, Bankruptcy Litigation, Business Law, Contracts, Unfair Competition, Covenants Not to Compete, Noncompetition and Non-Solicitation Agreements, Restrictive Covenants, Business Fraud, Deceptive Trade Practices, Trade Secrets, Estate Planning, Commercial Real Estate.

DANIEL S. KAPLAN, born 1958; admitted to bar, 1990, Illinois, U.S. District Court, Northern and Central Districts of Illinois and U.S. Court of Appeals, Seventh Circuit. *Education:* Arizona State University (B.S., with honors, 1980); George Washington University (M.B.A., with honors, 1982); Loyola University of Chicago (J.D., cum laude, 1990). Author: "Protecting the Franchisor's Interests When a Franchisee Files for Bankruptcy Protection," Franchise Law Journal, Vol. 21, Fall 2001; "Resolving Disputes with Troubled Franchisees," IFA, June 2001; "Enforcing Agreements to Arbitrate Franchise Related Issues in the Forum Selected," Leaders Publications, Winter 2000; "Illinois Law Survey - Labor Law Survey," Loyola University of Chicago Law Journal, Volume 21, Number 2, Winter 1990. Former General Counsel, Moran Industries, Inc. Former Shareholder: Jenkens & Gilchrist, P.C.; Former Shareholder, Becker & Kaplan, LLC; Former Associate, Wildman, Harrold, Allen & Dixon. *Member:* Chicago, Illinois State and American (Member: Forum on Franchising; Business Law Section) Bar Associations; International Franchise Association (Past Co-chair, Chicago Franchise Business Network); American Association of Franchisees and Dealers Supplier. ***PRACTICE AREAS:*** Litigation; Business Law; Franchises and Franchising; Restaurant Law; Employment Law; Alternative Dispute Resolution; Bankruptcy Litigation. ***Email:*** dkaplan@kaplangreenswag.com

RICHARD A. GREENSWAG, born 1954; admitted to bar, 1979, Illinois. *Education:* Colgate University (B.A., 1976); University of Iowa (J.D., with honors, 1979). Former Shareholder, Chandler & Greenswag, P.C. Shareholder, Richard A. Greenswag, P.C. *Member:* Chicago, Illinois State and American Bar Associations. ***PRACTICE AREAS:*** Business Law; Business Transactions; Closely Held Business Law; Business Acquisitions; Employment Law; Contracts; Real Estate; Estate Planning; Probate; Commercial Loans. ***Email:*** rgreenswag@kaplangreenswag.com

JORDON S. STEINWAY, born March 14, 1979; admitted to bar, 2004, Illinois. *Education:* Boston University (B.A. Psychology, magna cum laude, 2001); Loyola University School of Law (J.D., 2004). *Member:* Chicago, Illinois State and American Bar Associations. ***PRACTICE AREAS:*** Corporate Law; Commercial Litigation; Franchise Law; Business Transactions; Employment Law. ***Email:*** jsteinway@kaplangreenswag.com

(This Listing Continued)

LEVENFELD PEARLSTEIN, LLC

Established in 1999
211 WAUKEGAN ROAD, SUITE 300
NORTHFIELD, ILLINOIS 60093
Telephone: 847-441-7676
Facsimile: 847-441-9976
Email: lplegal@lplegal.com
URL: http://www.lplegal.com

Chicago Office: 2 North LaSalle Street, Suite 1300, 60602. Telephone: 312-346-8380. Facsimile: 312-346-8434.

Corporate Law, Mergers, Acquisitions and Divestitures, Banks and Banking, Financial Institutions Law, Finance, Secured Lending, Federal Taxation, State Taxation, Securities, Bankruptcy, Workouts, Estate Planning, Employment Law.

(For complete biographical data on all personnel, see Professional Biographies at Chicago)

NEAL & McDEVITT

Established in 1998
1776 ASH STREET
NORTHFIELD, ILLINOIS 60093
Telephone: 847-441-9100
Fax: 847-441-0911
Email: info@nealmcdevitt.com
URL: http://www.lawyers.com/nealmcdevitt

Intellectual Property Practice (including Trademarks, Copyrights, Unfair Competition, Licensing and Litigation).

FIRM PROFILE: Neal & McDevitt is an Intellectual Property law firm founded in 1998 by experienced attorneys who have specialized in Intellectual Property law throughout their careers. The firm represents a wide range of industrial, financial and commercial enterprises, including large corporations, small and medium-sized businesses and individuals.

MEMBERS OF FIRM

SUSAN SOMERS NEAL, born November 11, 1949; admitted to bar, 1982, Illinois and U.S. District Court, Northern District of Illinois; 1984, Trial Bar; 1985, U.S. Court of Appeals, Eleventh Circuit; 1987, U.S. Court of Appeals, Third Circuit; 1989, U.S. Court of Appeals, Seventh Circuit; 1990, U.S. District Court, Western District of Texas; 1991, U.S. Court of Appeals, Ninth Circuit; 1994, U.S. Supreme Court; 1996, U.S. District Court, Central District of Illinois; 1997, District of Columbia. *Education:* Southern Illinois University (A.A., 1969); DePaul University (B.A., 1979; J.D., 1982). Adjunct Professor, Advanced Trademark Law, DePaul University College of Law. Instructor: Copyright and Trademark Law, Mallinckrodt College, Wilmette, Illinois; Trademark Law, The John Marshall Law School. *Member:* American Bar Association; International Trademark Association; Copyright Society of the United States. ***PRACTICE AREAS:*** Trademarks; Copyrights; Unfair Competition; Counselling; Prosecution; Licensing; Litigation. ***Email:*** sneal@nealmcdevitt.com

KEVIN J. McDEVITT, born August 27, 1965; admitted to bar, 1990, Illinois and U.S. District Court, Northern District of Illinois; 1993, District of Columbia; 1996, U.S. Court of Appeals, Seventh Circuit, U.S. District Court, District of Arizona and U.S. District Court, Central District of Illinois; 1997, U.S. District Court, Western District of Texas; 2000, U.S. District Court, Western District of Wisconsin; 2001, U.S. District Court, Eastern District of Michigan and U.S. Supreme Court. *Education:* Purdue University (B.A., 1987); Syracuse University (J.D., 1990). Publications: Contributing Author: J. Gilson, Trademark Protection and Practice (Matthew Bender & Co.) A.J. Sternstein et al, Designing An Effective Intellectual Property Compliance Program (Clark Boardman Callaghan); Rabkin & Johnson, Current Legal Forms With Tax Analysis (Trademark Section) (Matthew Bender & Co.). Associate Editor for Licensing Law and Business Report (Clark Boardman Callaghan, 1991-1994. *Member:* International Trademark Association. ***PRACTICE AREAS:*** Trademarks; Copyrights; Unfair Competition; Licensing; Litigation. ***Email:*** kmcdevitt@nealmcdevitt.com

LISA A. IVERSON, born Madison, Wisconsin, March 14, 1963; admitted to bar, 1988, Illinois. *Education:* University of Wisconsin-Madison (B.A., 1985; J.D., cum laude, 1988); John Marshall Law School (LL.M., 1998). ***PRACTICE AREAS:*** Intellectual Property; Trademark; Copyright. ***Email:*** lisa.iverson@nealmcdevitt.com

RICHARD B. BIAGI, born Melrose Park, Illinois, July 23, 1970; admitted to bar, 2001, Illinois and U.S. District Court, Northern District of Illinois. *Education:* University of Illinois (B.M., 1992); DePaul University (J.D., with honors, 2001). Order of the Coif. Author: "The Intersection of First Amendment Commercial Speech Analysis and The Federal Trademark Dilution Act: A Jurisprudential Roadmap," The Trademark Reporter, Vol. 91, No. 4, Pg. 867. *Member:* American Bar Association; International Trademark Association; Computer Law Association. ***PRACTICE AREAS:*** Trademark; Copyright; Unfair Competition. ***Email:*** rbiagi@nealmcdevitt.com

OF COUNSEL

ANDREA E. FRIEDMAN, born Chicago, Illinois, March 16, 1957; admitted to bar, 1985, Illinois. *Education:* University of Illinois at Urbana (B.A., 1979); University of Chicago (J.D., 1985). Recipient, American Jurisprudence Award in Torts. ***PRACTICE AREAS:*** Intellectual Property; Advertising Law; Marketing Law; Commercial Contracts.

LAW OFFICES OF MARGARET A. BENNETT, P.C.

Established in 1983

1200 HARGER ROAD, SUITE 718
OAK BROOK, ILLINOIS 60523-1908
Telephone: 630-573-8800
Fax: 630-573-9810
Email: mbennetlaw@aol.com
URL: http://www.lawyers.com/mabennett

Family Law, Divorce, Domestic Relations, Marital Property Law, Child Custody, Child Support, Visitation Rights, Alimony, Spousal Support, Legal Separation, Equitable Distribution, Marital Agreements, Marital Property Settlements, Separation Agreements, Matrimonial Law, Post Divorce, Real Property.

MARGARET A. BENNETT, born San Francisco, California; admitted to bar, 1976, Illinois, 1977, U.S. District Court, Northern District of Illinois; 1983, U.S. Court of Appeals, Seventh Circuit; 2002, Colorado; 2005, England and Wales. *Education:* University of California at Berkeley (A.B., cum laude, 1972); University of San Francisco; Loyola University of Chicago (J.D., 1976). Recipient: Illinois State Bar Association Certificate of Appreciation, 1990; DuPage County Bar Association Certificate of Appreciation, 1989; Board of Directors Award, 1998; President's Award, Realtor Association of the Western Suburbs, 1995. Author: "Legal Practice Tips," Illinois Bar Journal, Volume 88, December, 2000; "The Real Estate Lawyer's Divorce Primer (and the Divorce Lawyer's Guide to Real Estate)", Illinois Bar Journal, September 1998; "Mandatory Matrimonial Fee Arbitration," DuPage County Bar Brief, November 1997, DuPage County Blue Ribbon Committee on People with Disabilities. *Member:* DuPage County Bar Association (Chairperson, Real Estate Law Committee, 1994-1995; Chairperson, Professional Responsibility Committee, 1996-1997; Chairperson, Matrimonial Law Committee, 1997-1998; Member, Family Court Task Force Committee, 1997-2001); Illinois State Bar Association (Assembly, 1986-1990 and 1994-2000; Real Property Section Council, 1996-2002; Standing Committee on Judicial Evaluations, 1997—; Chairman, Northern Illinois Real Estate Law Committee, 1994-1997); DuPage Association of Women Lawyers. ***PRACTICE AREAS:*** Family Law. ***Email:*** mbennetlaw@aol.com

---

ANNE V. SWANSON, born Elmhurst, Illinois, October 10, 1954; admitted to bar, 1981, Illinois; 1982, U.S. District Court, Northern District of Illinois; 1984, U.S. Court of Appeals, Seventh Circuit. *Education:* Augustana College (B.A., 1976); John Marshall Law School (J.D., with distinction, 1981). Order of John Marshall; Illinois Bar Foundation Research Assistant Fellowship. Member, The John Marshall Law Review, 1980-1981. Author: "A Comparative Analysis of Three Lemon Laws: the Magnuson-Moss Warranty Act, Uniform Commercial Code and the Illinois New Car Buyer Protection Act," 75 Illinois Bar Journal, 436, 1987; "Comment, Illinois Independent Administration of Decedents' Estates: A Will Without Probate," 14 J. Mar. L. Rev. 519, 1981. Co-Author: with Judge Ann B. Jorgensen, "A Review of Mandatory Arbitration in Illinois," 83 Illinois Bar Journal, 364, 1995. Co-Editor and Author: Alternative Dispute Resolution, Chapter 8, Court-Annexed Mandatory Arbitration, Illinois Institute for Continuing Legal Education, 2001. Instructor: Arbitrator Training Program, 1993-1998; "Presentation of an Arbitration Case," DuPage Association of Legal Secretaries, 1994; "How to Present an Arbitration Case," DuPage County Bar Association New Lawyers Seminar, 1994-1996. *Member:* Dupage County (Certificate of Appreciation, 1994) and Illinois State Bar Associations; DuPage Association of Women Lawyers (Director, 1993-1995; Secretary, 1995-1999; Newsletter Editor, 1999-2002; Certificate of Appreciation, 1995-2002). ***REPORTED CASES:*** In re Marriage of Hartney 355 Ill App. 3d 1088 (2005). ***PRACTICE AREAS:*** Collection Law; Corporate Law.

RICHARD G. RIUS, JR., born June 4, 1978; admitted to bar, 2004, Illinois; 2005, U.S. District Court, District of Illinois. *Education:* Illinois Wesleyan University (B.A., 2000); Case Western Reserve University (J.D., 2004). Recipient, American Academy of Matrimonial Lawyers Award. *Member:* DuPage County and Illinois State Bar Associations. ***PRACTICE AREAS:*** Family Law. ***Email:*** richard.rius@lawbennett.com

REPRESENTATIVE CLIENTS: McDonald's Corporation, Oak Brook, Illinois; County of DuPage, Wheaton, Illinois; Stromwater Management Committee; DuPage County Fair and Exposition Authority; DuPage Department of Transportation.

BISHOP, ROSSI & SCARLATI, LTD.

OAK BROOK, ILLINOIS

(See Oakbrook Terrace)

Federal and State Taxation, Commercial Litigation and Personal Injury, Business Law, Corporate Law, Real Estate Law, Commercial Transactions, Private Charitable Foundation Law, Trusts and Estates, Probate Law and Banking.

LAW OFFICE OF JAMES X. BORMES, P.C.

OAK BROOK, ILLINOIS

(See Chicago)

Construction Law, Construction Defects, Mechanics Liens, Consumer Law, Consumer Fraud, Business Law, Business Litigation, Breach of Contract, Employment Contracts, Landlord and Tenant Law, Securities Fraud.

BOTTI, MARINACCIO & DeLONGIS, LTD.

720 ENTERPRISE DRIVE
OAK BROOK, ILLINOIS 60523
Telephone: 630-573-8585
Fax: 630-573-8586
URL: http://www.lawyers.com/bottimaridellaw

Wheaton, Illinois Office: Suite 402 The Ticor Title Building, 330 Naperville Road. Telephone: 630-653-2100.

Trial and Appellate Practice in State and Federal Courts, Civil, Criminal, Personal Injury, Family, Zoning, Corporation, Probate, Commercial and Government Litigation.

ALDO E. BOTTI, born Brooklyn, N.Y., December 27, 1936; admitted to bar, 1966, Illinois and U.S. District Court, Northern District of Illinois, including Trial Bar; U.S. Court of Appeals, Seventh Circuit. *Education:* Rockhurst College (A.B., 1962); St. Louis University (J.D., 1965). Assistant State's Attorney, 1969-1971. Special Assistant State's Attorney, 1987. Elected DuPage County Board Chairman, 1990-1994. Deputy Public Defender, 1971-1972. Member, DuPage County Law Enforcement Commission, 1972-1973. Chairman, Mandatory Arbitration Program, 18th Judicial Circuit. General Counsel, Illinois State Crime Commission. Illinois Super Lawyers, 2005. *Member:* Chicago, DuPage County (General Counsel, 1988-1990), Illinois State and American Bar Associations; Illinois Trial Lawyers Association; The Association of Trial Lawyers of America; American Judicature Society; Chicago Justinian Society; DuPage County Justinian Society; National Association of Criminal Defense Lawyers; Capital Litigation Trial Bar. [With U.S. Army, 1955-1958]. ***PRACTICE AREAS:*** Civil Practice; Commercial Litigation; Criminal Law; Family Law; Medical Malpractice; Personal Injury; Products Liability; Toxic Torts. ***Email:*** aeb@botti-law.com

LEE A. MARINACCIO, born Buffalo, New York, August 24, 1944; admitted to bar, 1971, Illinois and U.S. District Court, Northern District of Illinois, U.S. Supreme Court. *Education:* Elmhurst College (B.A., 1967); Loyola University (J.D., 1971). Assistant State's Attorney, DuPage County, 1971-1972. Assistant U.S. Attorney, U.S. Department of Justice, 1972-1975. 1st Assistant States Attorney, Kane County, 1975. Recognized as Outstanding Attorney by Leading Illinois Attorney's Publication and the National Registry of Who's Who. Recognized as an Illinois Super Lawyer. Former Member, The Association of Trial Lawyers of America. *Member:* DuPage County (Matrimonial Law Committee), Kane County, Illinois State (Family Law Section) and American (Family Law Section) Bar Associations; DuPage County Family Court Special Task Force; DuPage County Justinian Society. ***PRACTICE AREAS:*** Family Law; Contested Litigation. ***Email:*** lam@botti-law.com

STEPHEN R. BOTTI, born Brooklyn, New York, March 18, 1954; admitted to bar, 1980, Illinois and U.S. District Court, Northern District of Illinois. *Education:* University of Richmond (B.S., 1976; J.D., 1979). Assistant States Attorney, Cook County, 1981-1984. Illinois Super Lawyers, 2005; Leading Lawyers of America, 2005. *Member:* DuPage County (Member, Matrimonial Law Committee) and Illinois State Bar Associations; Justinian Society of Lawyers. ***PRACTICE AREAS:*** Family Law. ***Email:*** srb@botti-law.com

PETER M. DeLONGIS, born Chicago, Illinois, March 7, 1956; admitted to bar, 1982, Illinois and U.S. District Court, Northern District of Illinois. *Education:* Northern Illinois University (B.S., Finance, cum laude, 1978); Illinois Institute of Technology/Chicago-Kent College of Law (J.D., with high honors, 1982). Member, IIT/Chicago-Kent Law Review, 1981-1982. Cook County Assistant States Attorney, Felony Trial Division, 1982-1988. *Member:* Du Page County, Illinois State and American Bar Associations; Justinian Society of Lawyers. ***PRACTICE AREAS:*** Civil Practice; Commercial Litigation; Criminal Law; Medical Malpractice; Personal Injury; Products Liability; Toxic Torts. ***Email:*** pmd@botti-law.com

JEAN LASICS-WESSELS, born East Chicago, Indiana, January 31, 1968; admitted to bar, 1995, Illinois and U.S. District Court, Northern District of Illinois. *Education:* Valparaiso University (B.A., 1990); Thomas M. Cooley Law School (J.D., 1995). Member, Thomas M. Cooley Law Review, 1994-1995. *Member:* DuPage County and Illinois State Bar Associations. ***PRACTICE AREAS:*** Civil Practice; Medical Malpractice; Commercial Litigation; Personal Injury; Products Liability; Real Estate. ***Email:*** jml@botti-law.com

---

CARLA LABUNSKI, born Kansas City, Missouri; admitted to bar, 2002, Illinois and U.S. District Court, Northern District of Illinois. *Education:* Northwestern University (B.S.J., cum laude, 1998); Loyola University (J.D., 2002). Kappa Tau Alpha. Author: "Seeking and Avoiding Rule 137 Sanctions," Illinois Bar Journal August 2004. *Member:* Chicago, DuPage County and Illinois State Bar Associations; The Association of Trial Lawyers of America. ***PRACTICE AREAS:*** Civil Litigation; Commercial Litigation. ***Email:*** cll@botti-law.com

PAIGE M. McCLELLAND-THEOBALD, born Peoria, Illinois, February 8, 1976; admitted to bar, 2004, Illinois. *Education:* Drake University (B.A., 1999); Northern Illinois University (J.D., 2003). Phi Alpha Delta. Trial Advocacy, 2003-2004. Member, Public Interest Law Society, 2002-2004. *Member:* DuPage County and Illinois State Bar Associations. ***PRACTICE AREAS:*** Family Law; Civil Law; Criminal Law. ***Email:*** pmt@botti-law.com

JAMIE LYNN RYAN, born Chicago, Illinois, September 18, 1977; admitted to bar, 2002, Illinois. *Education:* University of Illinois, Urbana-Champaign (B.S. in Psychology, 1999); Chicago Kent College of Law-Illinois Instute of Technology (J.D., 2002). ***PRACTICE AREAS:*** Family Law. ***Email:*** jlr@botti-law.com

DASPIN & AUMENT, LLP

210 W. 22ND STREET, SUITE 102
OAK BROOK, ILLINOIS 60523
Telephone: 630-928-0430
Fax: 630-928-0392

Chicago Office: 10 South Riverside Plaza, Suite 1220, 60606. Telephone: 312-258-1600. Fax: 312-258-1955.

Real Estate, Commercial Real Estate Development, Estate Planning, Business Succession Planning, Tax Planning, Trust Administration, Estate Administration, Corporate Law and Financial Services Law. Intellectual Property including Patents, Trademarks, Copyrights and Computer Law.

(For complete biographical data on all personnel, see Professional Biographies at Chicago, Illinois)

FEWKES WENTZ & STRAYER

OAK BROOK, ILLINOIS

(See Naperville)

Business, Corporate, Mergers and Acquisitions, Commercial Real Estate and Antitrust Law.

GAROFALO, SCHREIBER, HART & STORM

CHARTERED

OAK BROOK, ILLINOIS

(See Chicago)

Insurance Defense Law, Employers' Liability, Workers Compensation-Defense, State and Federal, Trials and Appeals.

JEFFREY M. HUCEK

1900 SPRING ROAD
SUITE 200
OAK BROOK, ILLINOIS 60523
Telephone: 630-586-9600
Fax: 630-586-9610
Email: huceklaw@aol.com
URL: http://www.lawyers.com/huceklaw

Estate Planning, Family Wealth Transfers, Wills, Trusts and Estates, Estate and Gift Taxation, Charitable Gift Planning, Contested Trusts and Estates, Premarital Agreements, Real Estate.

JEFFREY M. HUCEK, born Chicago, Illinois, April 8, 1955; admitted to bar, 1983, Minnesota; 1984, U.S. Tax Court; 1989, Illinois; 1999, Colorado. *Education:* University of Virginia (B.S.C., Accounting, with distinction, 1977); University of Minnesota (J.D., cum laude, 1983). Beta Gamma Sigma. Certified Public Accountant, Illinois, 1977. Co-Author: "Minnesota Legal Forms: Probate," Butterworth Legal Publishers, 1983-1991. Senior Auditor, Arthur Andersen & Co., 1977-1980. Tax and Probate Research Assistant, Dean Robert A. Stein, 1981-1983. Attorney, Arthur, Chapman & McDonough, P.A., Minneapolis, 1983-1988. Attorney, Winston & Strawn, Chicago, 1988-1993. *Member:* Chicago Bar Association. (Also Of Counsel to Masuda, Funai, Eifert & Mitchell, Ltd., Chicago). ***PRACTICE AREAS:*** Estate Planning; Family Wealth Transfers; Wills; Trusts and Estates; Estate and Gift Taxation; Charitable Gift Planning; Contested Trusts and Estates; Premarital Agreements; Real Estate.

WILLIAM F. KNEE, LTD.

1900 SPRING ROAD, SUITE 204
OAK BROOK, ILLINOIS 60523
Telephone: 630-571-7777
Fax: 630-954-1984
URL: http://www.kneelawoffice.com
URL: http://www.williamfknee.com

Family Law and Child Custody Law.

FIRM PROFILE: Our firm has been representing clients in family law cases, including divorce, separation, child custody and child support for 10 years. We represent clients in DuPage, Cook, Will and McHenry Counties. Other practice areas include general civil litigation, real estate transactions, wills and trusts and criminal defense. We take pride in our utuilization of the latest practice management technology to deliver timely, cost effective legal services to our clients.

WILLIAM F. KNEE, admitted to bar, 1995, Illinois. *Education:* University of Colorado at Boulder (B.A., 1991); Northern Illinois University (J.D., 1995). Winner, Pro Bono Service Award, 2002-2003. Co-Editor, Monthly Illinois Supreme Court Caselaw Update, DuPage County, 2004-2005. Court-Approved Child's Representative and Guardian ad Litem, DuPage County. *Member:* DuPage County Bar Association (Chairman, Legal Aid Committee, 2005-2006; Member: Family Law Committee; Publications Board); Illinois State Bar Association. ***PRACTICE AREAS:*** Family Law; Child Custody. ***Email:*** bknee@kneelawoffice.com

J. RICHARD KULERSKI, P.C.

Established in 1963

1200 HARGER ROAD, SUITE 320
OAK BROOK, ILLINOIS 60523
Telephone: 630-928-0600
Fax: 630-928-0670
Email: rk@familylawdupage.com
URL: http://www.illinoisdivorceinfo.com

Divorce, Mediation, Custody, Collaborative Divorce, Family Law, Alimony.

FIRM PROFILE: Practice limited to divorce law.

J. RICHARD KULERSKI, born Chicago, Illinois, January 1, 1940; admitted to bar, 1963, Illinois; 1971, U.S. Supreme Court. *Education:* Benedictine College; Loyola University; DePaul University (J.D., 1963). Mediator: American Academy of Family Mediators; The Mediation Council of Illinois. Advanced Mediation Training: Harvard Law School, 2000; Pepperdine Law School, 2000; Negotiation Training, Harvard Law School, 1999; Advanced Negotiation Training, Harvard Law School, 2001; JDS Mediation Training Institute, Chicago, Illinois, 1998. Listed, The National Registry of Who's Who, 2001. Former Member: Chicago (Domestic Relations Panel of the Lawyers Referral Service and Matrimonial Law Committee), Will County (Family Law Committee), West Suburban and Southwest (Family Law Committee) Bar Associations. Former Appointee, Chicago Bar Relations Subcommittee of the Domestic Relations Advisory Committee, Attorney for the Child or Guardian Ad Litem, in Custody and Visitation matters, Domestic Relations Division of Circuit Court of Cook County, IL. Member, International Academy of Collaborative Professionals, 2002. Fellow, Collaborative Law Institute of Illinois, 2002-2003. *Member:* DuPage County (Matrimonial Trial Advocacy Workshop, 2000; Member, Family Law and Alternate Dispute Resolution Committees), Illinois State (Trained, L.A.P. Volunteer, 1999; Member, Family Law Committee) and American (Member, Family Law and Alternative Dispute Resolution Sections) Bar Associations; The Mediation Council of Illinois (Member, Board of Directors, 2000-2001); Association for Conflict Resolution. ***PRACTICE AREAS:*** Divorce; Mediation; Child Custody; Collaborative Family Law; Family Law; Alimony. ***Email:*** rk@familylawdupage.com

KARI L. CORNELISON, born Chicago, Illinois, May 27, 1971; admitted to bar, 1996, Illinois; 1997, Florida. *Education:* Michigan State University (B.A., 1993); John Marshall Law School (J.D., 1996). ***PRACTICE AREAS:*** Family Law; Real Estate.

MATTHEW M. WILLIAMS, admitted to bar, 2003, Illinois. *Education:* Northeastern Illinois University (B.A., 1995); Northern Illinois University College of Law (J.D., 2003).

IRWIN E. LEITER

1301 W. 22ND STREET, SUITE 210
OAK BROOK, ILLINOIS 60523
Telephone: 630-571-7767
Fax: 630-573-0460
Email: lionelir@sbcglobal.net

Real Estate Development, Condominium Law, Estate Planning.

IRWIN E. LEITER, born Chicago, Illinois, August 27, 1949; admitted to bar, 1977, Illinois and U.S. District Court, Northern District of Illinois. *Education:* University of Illinois (B.A. in History with honors, 1971); IIT/Chicago-Kent College of Law (J.D., with honors, 1977). Recipient, Bar and Gavel Award. Advisory Editor, Chicago-Kent Law Review, 1976-1977. Author: Comment, "The Enforcement of HUD Mortgage Foreclosure Guidelines: Possible Illinois Court Interpretations," 52 Chicago-Kent Law Review 645, 1976; Note, "Eminent Domain: *United States v. 58.16 Acres of Land,*" 51 Chicago-Kent Law Review, 1974; "How To Buy A Condominium or Townhouse," Sourcebooks, 1997. Real Estate Lecturer, Roosevelt University's Lawyers Assistant Program, 1984-1988. Vice President and Lecturer, Institute for Advanced Paralegal Studies, 1987—. *Member:* Chicago (Chairman: Unauthorized Practice Committee, 1987—; Real Property Committee, 1977-2005; Condominium Subcommittee, 1979-2005; Mechanics Lien-Condominiums Special Subcommittee, 1985; Land Trust, 1985), Illinois State (Member, Real Property, Probate and Trusts Sections) and American (Member, Real Property Condemnation Subcommittee, 1976) Bar Associations; Home Builders Association of Greater Chicago (Member, Legislative and Hospitality Committees). ***PRACTICE AREAS:*** Real Estate Development; Condominium Law; Estate Planning.

REPRESENTATIVE CLIENTS: Terrestris Development Corporation; Draper and Kramer; Mortgage Corporation; US Home Corporation and Kenar, L.L.C.

BARRY LOCKE & ASSOCIATES, LTD.

OAK BROOK, ILLINOIS

(See Chicago)

Family Law, Divorce, Child Custody, Child Support, Paternity, Parentage, Visitation Rights.

MARTIN, CRAIG, CHESTER & SONNENSCHEIN

Established in 1953

2215 YORK ROAD, SUITE 550
OAK BROOK, ILLINOIS 60523
Telephone: 630-472-3400
Fax: 630-472-0048
Email: firm@mccslaw.com
URL: http://www.mccslaw.com

General Practice including: business organization and operations, acquisitions and divestitures, federal, state and local taxation, real estate and real estate finance, employee benefits, employment law, labor relations, not-for-profit and charitable organizations, municipal law, administrative proceedings, estate planning, probate and trust, family foundations and environmental law.

FIRM PROFILE: Martin, Craig, Chester & Sonnenschein provides a broad base of general business, and personal legal services. Founded in 1953 by Jacob Martin and Sydney Craig, the firm has steadily built upon the foundation of the original partners to establish a law practice of diverse capabilities.

The firm provides a full spectrum of services to meet the legal needs of business. Martin, Craig, Chester & Sonnenschein has served a varied clientele that includes manufacturing and service companies, financial institutions, not-for-profit organizations, municipalities, and real estate businesses.

MEMBERS OF FIRM

W. B. MARTIN GROSS, born Chicago, Illinois September 9, 1936; admitted to bar, 1961, Illinois. *Education:* Amherst College (B.A., 1958); Harvard Law School (LL.B., 1961). Village Prosecutor, Village of La Grange Park, 1964-1968. Village Attorney, Village of La Grange Park, 1969—. Special Assistant Attorney General, Illinois, 1968-1969. Special Assistant, Vice President of the U.S., 1967-1969. Trustee, 1981-1985 and President, 1989-1993, Village of Hinsdale, Illinois. Member, 1971-1976 and President, 1977-1980, School District 181, Hinsdale, Illinois. *Member:* Chicago (Member, Committees on: Probate Practice, 1963-1965; Trust Law, 1963-1970; Municipal Law, 1970-1976), Du Page County, Illinois State and American Bar Associations; Legal Club of Chicago. ***PRACTICE AREAS:*** Probate Law; Estate Planning; Corporate Law.

NORMAN V. CHIMENTI, born Chicago, Illinois, September 18, 1940; admitted to bar, 1967, Illinois. *Education:* Yale University (B.A., 1962; LL.B., 1967). Member: National Tank Truck Carriers Association, 1984—; Hinsdale, Illinois Plan Commission, 1990-1995 (Chairman, 1993-1995); Hinsdale Community House (Trustee, Board of Trustees), 1996—; Wayland Academy, Beaver Dam, Wisconsin (Trustee, Board of Trustees), 1985-2000; Yale Club of Chicago (Director), 1993-1999; Wellness House, Hinsdale, Illinois (Trustee, Board of Trustees), 1998-2000; Illinois EPA, Small Business Assistance Task Force, 1993—. Special Assistant Illinois Attorney General, 1995—. *Member:* Chicago (Member: Labor and Employment Law Committee; Environmental Law Committee), Du Page County (Member: Environmental Law Committee; Labor and Employment Law Committee) and Illinois State Bar Associations. [Sgt., USMC, 1963-1968]. ***PRACTICE AREAS:*** Environmental; Labor; Employment Law; Land Use; Corporate. ***Email:*** nvc@mccslaw.com

CATHLEEN M. KEATING, born Chicago, Illinois, April 12, 1955; admitted to bar, 1980, Illinois. *Education:* University of Illinois (B.A., 1977), James Scholar; University of Illinois College of Law (J.D., 1980). Instructor, Legal Research, Mallinckrodt College, 1982. Author: "Post Judgment Collection Proceedings: How Associations Should Respond," Illinois Reporter, Vol. 6, no. 5; "Fiduciary Misappropriation," 72 Illinois Bar Journal 298. Member: School District 102, LaGrange, Illinois, 1991-1995; LaGrange Park Zoning Board of Appeals, 1995-1997. *Member:* Du Page County and Illinois State Bar Associations. ***PRACTICE AREAS:*** Real Estate; Land Use; Financial Institutions; Estate Planning; Probate. ***Email:*** cmk@mccslaw.com

MARK D. TOLJANIC, born Robbins A.F.B., Georgia, February 3, 1961; admitted to bar, 1986, Illinois. *Education:* Indiana University (B.S., with distinction, 1983); University of Michigan (J.D., 1986). Certified Public Accountant, Illinois, 1986. Village Prosecutor, Village of La Grange Park, 1993—. Director, Arlington Heights Youth Athletic Association, 1993—. Member, Arlington Heights Environmental Control Commission, 1996-1999. Director, United Way of Arlington Heights, 1997-1999; Trustee Village of Arlington Heights, 1999—. *Member:* Chicago and American Bar Associations. ***PRACTICE AREAS:*** Corporate/Business Law; Individual Income Tax. ***Email:*** mdt@mccslaw.com

STEPHEN R. PAUL, admitted to bar, 1993, Illinois. *Education:* Cornell University (B.S., 1990); Northern Illinois University, College of Law (J.D., 1993); Marshall Law School (L.L.M., Taxation, Estate Planning and Employee Benefits, with honors, 2003). Dean's List.*Member:* Illinois State and American Bar Associations. ***PRACTICE AREAS:*** Estate Planning; Estate Administration; Probate; Taxation; Financial Institutions. ***Email:*** spaul@mccslaw.com

REFERENCES: Harris Trust & Savings Bank; The Northern Trust Co.

OLDFIELD & FOX, P.C.

Established in 1987

SUITE 201
2021 MIDWEST ROAD
OAK BROOK, ILLINOIS 60523
Telephone: 630-495-3377
Facsimile: 630-495-2774
URL: http://www.oldfieldfox.com
Email: eloesq@oldfieldfox.com
URL: http://www.lawyers.com/eloesq

Chicago, Illinois Office: 30 North La Salle Street, Suite 1524, 60602. Telephone: 312-782-0933. Fax: 312-782-4474.

(This Listing Continued)

Inverness, Illinois Office: 1622 Colonial Parkway, Suite 201, 60067. Telephone: 847-358-5757. Fax: 847-358-7706.

General Civil Litigation. Commercial Transactions, Business Law, Family Law, Real Estate, Personal Injury, Probate, Wills and Trusts, Misdemeanor Criminal, Mediation, Arbitration and Livestock Insurance Defense.

FIRM PROFILE: A general practice law firm engaged in civil and criminal litigation and transactional law, including business formation and representation, real estate, estate planning, personal injury and family law.

We have an "of counsel" relationship with The Law Offices of Michael R. Panter in Chicago and The Law Offices of Robert J. Ross, in Inverness. In addition to the outlying offices and the legal personnel, the main office in Oak Brook has two paralegals.

E. LAWRENCE OLDFIELD, born Lake Forest, Illinois, December 21, 1944; admitted to bar, 1973, Illinois and U.S. District Court, Northern District of Illinois; 1974, U.S. Court of Appeals, Seventh Circuit; 1979, U.S. Supreme Court; 1983, Federal Trial Bar; 1985, U.S. Court of Appeals, Third Circuit; 1986, U.S. Court of Appeals, Tenth Circuit; 1990, U.S. District Court, Western District of Wisconsin and U.S. Court of Appeals, Eighth Circuit; 1991, U.S. District Court, District of Nebraska; 1994, U.S. District Court, Eastern District of Oklahoma. *Education:* Long Island University; Wheaton College; Near East School of Archaeology, Jordan; Northern Illinois University (B.A., 1969); DePaul University (J.D., 1973). Pi Sigma Alpha, National Political Science Honorary Society; Tau Kappa Epsilon. Federal Agent, DHUD, 1969-1970. General Counsel, Livestock Department, Hartford Fire Insurance Company, 1977-1987. Trustee, Village of Glen Ellyn, 1981-1985. Member, District 41 Board of Education, 1991-1995. President, Breakfast Club of Oak Brook, 1999-2001. *Member:* Chicago, West Suburban, DuPage County, Illinois State and American Bar Associations; Illinois Trial Lawyers Association; Federal Trial Bar; The Association of Trial Lawyers of America. [With U.S. Army, 1964-1967]. ***PRACTICE AREAS:*** Business Law; Commercial Litigation; Creditors Rights; Personal Injury; Real Estate; Trusts and Estates; Wills; Probate; Criminal; Mediation; Arbitration; Livestock Insurance Defense. ***Email:*** eloesq@oldfieldfox.com

JONATHAN J. FOX, born Chicago, Illinois, March 19, 1964; admitted to bar, 1995, Illinois. *Education:* Southern Illinois University (B.A., 1987); John Marshall Law School (J.D., 1995). Recipient, College of Communications Award for High Achievement. *Member:* Cook County, DuPage County (Board Member, Publication), Illinois State and American Bar Associations. ***PRACTICE AREAS:*** Family Law; Business Law; Commercial Law; Real Estate; Civil Litigation. ***Email:*** foxesquire@oldfieldfox.com

OF COUNSEL

MICHAEL R. PANTER, born Chicago, Illinois, August 10, 1952; admitted to bar, 1978, Illinois; 1979, Florida and U.S. Court of Appeals, Seventh Circuit; 1982, U.S. District Court, Northern District of Illinois; 1984, U.S. Supreme Court. *Education:* St. John's College; University of Wisconsin-Madison (B.A., 1975); DePaul University (J.D., 1978). Writing Staff, De Paul Law Review, 1978. Author: "Why Shareholders have the Right to Accept Tender Offers," Chicago Bar Record, May, June, Volume 61, No. 6, 1980. *Member:* Chicago (Member, Tort Litigation Committee), Illinois State and American Bar Associations; The Florida Bar; Illinois Trial Lawyers Association; Decalogue Society. (Resident, Chicago Office; Also Practicing Individually, Chicago, Illinois). ***PRACTICE AREAS:*** Plaintiff's Tort Litigation. ***Email:*** panterm@mrpanter.com

ROBERT J. ROSS, born Chicago, Illinois, May 12, 1956; admitted to bar, 1980, Illinois; 1984, U.S. District Court, Northern District of Illinois. *Education:* Triton College (A.D., with honor, 1975); University of Illinois (B.A., with honor, 1977); DePaul University (J.D., with honor, 1980). Phi Alpha Delta; Phi Kappa Phi. James Scholar. Lead Articles Administrator, De Paul Law Review, 1979-1980. Author: "Government Appeal from Defendant's Successful Motion to Dismiss not Barred by the Double Jeopardy Clause—United States v. Scott," 28 De Paul Law Review 485-501, 1979. *Member:* Chicago, Northwest Suburban and Illinois State Bar Associations; National Lawyers Association. Christian Legal Society. (Resident at Inverness Office; Also Practicing Individually, Inverness, Illinois). ***PRACTICE AREAS:*** Commercial Law; Business Law; Real Estate Law; Estate Planning; Estate Administration. ***Email:*** bobrosslaw@aol.com

REPRESENTATIVE CLIENTS: Mid-Way Supply, Inc.; Medical Applications Specialists, Inc.; Energy Associates, Inc.; National Cattlemen's Beef Association; Leo Construction, Inc.; Earthwise Environmental, Inc.; Dupage Credit Union; Liquid Dynamics Corporation; Hartford Fire Insurance Co.; Fireman's Fund; Star Insurance Company.

PRATO & ASSOCIATES, P.C.

2725 35TH STREET
OAK BROOK, ILLINOIS 60523
Telephone: 630-570-5299
Fax: 630-570-5298
URL: http://members.aol.com/PRATOLAW/index.html
Email: pratolaw@aol.com
URL: http://www.lawyers.com/pratolaw

Real Estate Transactions, Bankruptcy, Small Businesses, Corporate, Criminal, DUI, Personal Injury and Immigration Law.

JACK VINCENT PRATO, born Chicago, Illinois, July 2, 1954; admitted to bar, 1995, Illinois, Florida and U.S District Court, Seventh Circuit. *Education:* DePaul University (B.A., 1992; J.D., 1995). Board Member, Girl Scouts of America. Member, ARAG Group (Prepaid Legal Services) Network Attorney, Des Moines, Iowa. *Member:* Illinois State Bar Association; The Florida Bar. ***PRACTICE AREAS:*** Real Estate; Bankruptcy; Criminal Defense; Corporate Law; Immigration. **Email:** pratolaw@aol.com

Languages: Spanish and Italian.

TITLE POLICY ISSUING AGENT FOR: Chicago Title & Trust Company.

SKOKOS LAW GROUP, LLC

1100 JORIE BOULEVARD, SUITE 220
OAK BROOK, ILLINOIS 60523
Telephone: 630-368-1699
Fax: 630-368-3586
URL: http://www.skokoslawgroup.com
Email: sskokos@aol.com
URL: http://www.soulaskokoslawfirm.com

Intellectual Property, Patents, Trademarks, Copyrights.

SOULA SKOKOS, admitted to bar, 2002, Illinois. *Education:* Northwestern University (B.S., Biomedical Engineering, 1997) Loyola University (J.D., 2002; M.B.A., 2002). ***LANGUAGES:*** Greek. ***PRACTICE AREAS:*** Intellectual Property; Patents; Trademarks; Copyrights. ***Email:*** sskokos@aol.com

---

LAW OFFICES OF SULLIVAN HINCKS & CONWAY

A Partnership of Professional Corporations
Established in 1970

122 WEST 22ND STREET, SUITE 100
OAK BROOK, ILLINOIS 60523
Telephone: 630-573-5021
Fax: 630-573-5130
URL: http://www.shlawfirm.com
Email: dansullivan@shlawfirm.com
URL: http://www.lawyers.com/sullivan&hincks

Corporate and Business Law, Civil Litigation, Real Estate, Logistics, Transportation, Taxation, Administrative, Environmental, Employment and Related Litigation, Insurance Coverage, Insurance Regulatory Matters, Commercial Law, Equine Law.

FIRM PROFILE: Representation emphasizes business law including real estate, commercial transactions, transportation, logistics, Federal and State taxation, civil litigation, criminal, equine law, commercial collections and general representation of privately held companies. Representation has included real estate syndications, insurance companies, oil companies, manufacturing companies, trucking companies, surface and air freight forwarders, transportation brokers, logistics companies, railroads, commercial shippers of freight, and vending companies.

DANIEL C. SULLIVAN, admitted to bar, 1967, Kansas and U.S. District Court, District of Kansas; 1970, Illinois and U.S. District Court, Northern District of Illinois; U.S. Supreme Court; U.S. Court of Appeals for the District of Columbia, Third, Fifth, Seventh, Eighth, Ninth, Tenth Circuits and U.S. Court of Federal Claims. *Education:* Kansas State University (A.B., 1962); Washburn University of Topeka (J.D., 1967). Member, Washburn Law Journal. Assistant County Attorney, Shawnee County, Kansas, 1967-1968. Assistant General Counsel, State Corporation Commission of Kansas, 1968-1970. Associate General Counsel, Allied Van Lines, Inc., 1970, present firm, 1970—. *Member:* Illinois State Bar Association; Transportation Lawyers Association; Association For Transportation Law, Logistics and Policy. ***PRACTICE AREAS:*** Corporate Law; Commercial Real Estate; Nonpublic Transactions; Administrative Litigation; Tax Litigation; Civil Litigation; Transportation; Logistics; Equine Law. ***Email:*** dansullivan@shlawfirm.com

PATRICK M. HINCKS, born April 10, 1964; admitted to bar, 1989, Illinois and U.S. District Court, Northern District of Illinois. *Education:* St. Mary's University, MN (B.A., magna cum laude, 1986); Loyola University School of Law (J.D., 1989). Tax Attorney, Ernst & Young, Chicago, Illinois. Associate, Sullivan & Associates, Ltd., 1992-1995. Partner, Sullivan & Hincks, 1995—. *Member:* Chicago, DuPage County and Illinois State Bar Associations. ***PRACTICE AREAS:*** Corporate Law; Business Transactions; Insurance Regulatory; Insurance Liquidation Litigation; Civil Litigation; Commercial Leasing; Residential and Commercial Real Estate; Securities Law; NASD Arbitration; ERISA-COBRA; Environmental Law; Federal and State Tax Law; Sports and Entertainment; Limited Liability Companies. ***Email:*** pathincks@shlaw.com

JOHN J. CONWAY, born Chicago, Illinois, 1961; admitted to bar, 1993, Illinois, U.S. District Court, Northern District of Illinois and U.S. Court of Appeals, Seventh Circuit. *Education:* Illinois State University (B.S., 1985); DePaul University College of Law (J.D., 1993). Certified Public Accountant, Illinois, 1985. Tactical Officer/Investigator, Chicago Police Department, 1987-1994. *Member:* Chicago and Illinois State Bar Associations. ***PRACTICE AREAS:*** Civil Litigation; Corporate Law; Real Estate; Health Care (HIPPA); Franchising (PMPA). ***Email:*** johnconway@shlawfirm.com

ASSOCIATES

JOHN P. CALLAHAN, JR., born 1963; admitted to bar, 1988, Illinois and U.S. District Court, Northern District of Illinois. *Education:* Marquette University (B.S., Accounting, 1985); Illinois Institute of Technology, Chicago-Kent College of Law (J.D., 1988). Tax Attorney, Price Waterhouse & Company, Chicago, Illinois, 1988-1989. Assistant State's Attorney, Cook County State's Attorney, Chicago, Illinois, 1989-1996. *Member:* Chicago and Illinois State Bar Associations. ***PRACTICE AREAS:*** Criminal Law; Residential and Commercial Real Estate; Commercial Collections; Tax Law; Civil Litigation; Business Transactions. ***Email:*** jackcallahan@shlawfirm.com

DESMOND PATRICK CURRAN, born Chicago, Illinois, 1967; admitted to bar, 1992, Illinois; 1993, U.S. District Court, Northern District of Illinois; 1999, U.S. District Court, Northern District of Indiana. *Education:* University of Notre Dame (B.A., 1989; J.D., 1992). Associate: William M. Smith & Associates, 1993-1994; Pretzel & Stouffer, Chartered, 1994-1999; Sullivan Hincks & Conway, 1999—. *Member:* Illinois State Bar Association. ***PRACTICE AREAS:*** Civil Litigation; Insurance Coverage; Administrative Compliance; Real Estate. ***Email:*** desmondcurran@shlawfirm.com

(This Listing Continued)

MATTHEW P. BARRETTE, born Indianapolis, Indiana, March 30, 1976; admitted to bar, 2001, Illinois and U.S. District Court, Northern District of Illinois; 2003, U.S. Court of Appeals, Tenth Circuit and U.S. District Court, Eastern District of Wisconsin; 2005, U.S. District Court, Central District of Illinois. *Education:* University of Notre Dame (B.A., cum laude, 1998); University of Notre Dame Law School (J.D., cum laude, 2001). *Member:* Transportation Lawyers Association. ***PRACTICE AREAS:*** Commercial Litigation; Transportation; Residential Real Estate. ***Email:*** mattbarrette@shlawfirm.com

MATTHEW B. SPEISER, born Maywood, Illinois, January 16, 1977; admitted to bar, 2002, Illinois and U.S. District Court, Northern District of Illinois; 2005, U.S. District Court, Central District of Illinois. *Education:* Illinois Wesleyan University (B.A., Business Administration, 1999); DePaul University College of Law (J.D., 2002). Associate attorney, Jenner & Block, LLC, 2002-2003. *Member:* Chicago, Illinois State and American Bar Associations. ***PRACTICE AREAS:*** Corporate Law; Business Transactions; Civil Litigation; Commercial Litigation; Residential Real Estate. ***Email:*** mattspeiser@shlawfirm.com

REPRESENTATIVE CLIENTS: Schneider National, Inc.; United Armored Services; Olds Products Co. of Illinois; Fitzpatrick Bros., Inc.; Bellair Expediting Service Co., Inc.; Environmental Protection Industries, Inc.; Texor Petroleum Company; Premium Armored Services, Inc.; Anchor Mechanical, Inc.

MASARU K. TAKIGUCHI

1415 WEST 22ND STREET, TOWER FLOOR
OAK BROOK, ILLINOIS 60523
Telephone: 630-645-3833
Fax: 630-645-3834
URL: http://www.mastakiguchilaw.com

Real Estate, Probate and Estate Planning, Civil Litigation, Commercial Transactions.

MASARU K. TAKIGUCHI, born Chicago, Illinois, January 25, 1955; admitted to bar, 1986, Illinois. *Education:* Loyola University at Chicago (B.A., 1982); John Marshall Law School, Chicago (J.D., 1986). Real Estate Broker License, Illinois, 2001—. Commissioner, 1976-2004 and Chairman, 2000-2004, Village of Oak Park Housing Authority. *Member:* DuPage County and American Bar Associations. ***PRACTICE AREAS:*** Real Estate; Probate; Estate Planning; Civil Litigation; Commercial Transactions.

LAW OFFICES OF MARTIN D. TASCH, P.C.

Established in 1996

1200 JORIE BOULEVARD, SUITE 329
OAK BROOK, ILLINOIS 60523
Telephone: 630-571-9000
Fax: 630-571-9009
Email: mtasch@taschlaw.com
URL: http://www.taschlaw.com

Commercial Litigation, Contract Disputes, Collection, Construction Disputes, Mechanics Lien Disputes, Real Estate Litigation, Business, Corporate, Mergers and Acquisitions, Arbitration, Mediation, Franchise Disputes, Negligence, Partnership Disputes, Shareholders Disputes, Mortgage Foreclosures, Collections.

MARTIN D. TASCH, born Oak Park, Illinois, November 1, 1960; admitted to bar, 1985, Illinois and U.S. District Court, Northern District of Illinois. *Education:* Western Illinois University (B. Bus. with high honors, 1982); Northwestern University; University of Illinois (J.D., 1985). Phi Kappa Phi; Omicron Delta Epsilon; Beta Gamma Sigma. Member, Board of Education, Lake Park High School District 108. Certified Arbitrator, Cook County and DuPage County.*Member:* Chicago, American and DuPage County Bar Associations. ***Email:*** mtasch@taschlaw.com

LEGAL SUPPORT PERSONNEL

Elena Rodriguez

REPRESENTATIVE CLIENTS: First American Bank; Kone Inc.; Mount Prospect National Bank.

FRANK P. TIGHE III

OAK BROOK, ILLINOIS

(See Chicago)

Trials and Appeals in Federal and State Courts.

TROTT NELSON, P.C.

1550 SPRING ROAD, SUITE 225
OAK BROOK, ILLINOIS 60523
Telephone: 630-530-4161
Fax: 630-214-5351
Email: alan@trottnelson.com
URL: http://www.trottnelson.com

Construction Law, Mechanics Lien, Construction Contracts, Construction Litigation.

GREGORY K. TROTT, born Chicopee, Massachusetts, 1968; admitted to bar, 1996, Illinois. *Education:* Ohio University (B.S.A.S., 1991); Capital University (J.D., 1996). *Member:* Chicago, Illinois State and American Bar Associations. ***PRACTICE AREAS:*** Construction Law; Mechanics Liens; Construction Contracts; Construction Litigation. ***Email:*** greg@trottnelson.com

ALAN H. NELSON, born Chicago, Illinois; admitted to bar, 1995, Illinois. *Education:* University of Illinois (B.S.C.E., 1976); Illinois Institute of Technology Chicago Kent Col-

(This Listing Continued)

TROTT NELSON, P.C., Oak Brook—Continued

lege of Law (J.D., 1995). Licensed Professional Engineer of Illinois, 1977. *Member:* Chicago and Illinois State Bar Associations; Illinois Society of Professional Engineers. ***PRACTICE AREAS:*** Construction Law; Mechanics Liens; Construction Contracts; Construction Litigation. ***Email:*** alan@trottnelson.com

BISHOP, ROSSI & SCARLATI, LTD.

TWO TRANSAM PLAZA, SUITE 200
OAKBROOK TERRACE, ILLINOIS 60181
Telephone: 630-916-0123
Telecopier: 630-916-0567
Email: brs@bishoprossi.com

Federal and State Taxation, Commercial Litigation and Personal Injury, Business Law, Corporate Law, Real Estate Law, Commercial Transactions, Private Charitable Foundation Law, Trusts and Estates, Probate Law and Banking.

FIRM PROFILE: The firm offers a full range of legal services in the areas of civil litigation, business law and tax planning, of entity selection and formation, general counsel, ownership succession, reorganizations and asset transactions. For individuals, our services are also available with respect to lifetime and testamentary transfers of property in connection with trust and will drafting, dispositions of business interests, financial planning and probate law.

Trial and appellate litigation and dispute resolution are substantial portions of our practice. Our litigation attorneys have extensive experience in Federal and State courts in the areas of contract, business and tax litigation. The firm also has extensive experience in employment disputes, construction and personal injury litigation, land development and zoning.

RAYMOND E. ROSSI, born Chicago Heights, Illinois, August 1, 1953; admitted to bar, 1980, Illinois and U.S. District Court, Northern District of Illinois including Trial Bar; 1987, U.S. Court of Appeals, 7th Circuit; 1993, U.S. Court of Federal Claims. *Education:* North Central College (B.A., 1975); DePaul University (M.B.A., 1977); John Marshall School of Law (J.D., 1980). Associate Editor, Young Lawyers Journal, 1982. Mayor, Frankfort, Illinois, 1993—. Chairperson, South Suburban Tollway Authority. Adjunct Professor, Graduate School of Management, Lewis University, 1987-1989. Listed in Who's Who in American Law for numerous editions and national registries. *Member:* Illinois State Bar Association (Member, Judicial Evaluation Committee). ***PRACTICE AREAS:*** Commercial Law; Business Law; Personal Injury; Litigation; Real Estate. ***Email:*** rrossi@bishoprossi.com

FRANK S. SCARLATI JR., born Oak Park, Illinois, June 1, 1961; admitted to bar, 1987, Illinois and U.S. District Court, Northern District of Illinois; 1992, U.S. Tax Court; 1993, U.S. Court of Federal Claims. *Education:* DePaul University (B.S.C., cum laude, 1983); Northern Illinois University (J.D., cum laude, 1987). Delta Theta Phi. Certified Public Accountant, Illinois, 1984. *Member:* Illinois State and American Bar Associations; Illinois Certified Public Accountant Society. ***PRACTICE AREAS:*** Taxation; Commercial Transactions.

ROBERT A. HALL, born Chicago, Illinois, June 10, 1942; admitted to bar, 1973, Illinois; 1975, U.S. District Court, Northern District of Illinois, U.S. Tax Court and U.S. Court of Appeals, Seventh Circuit. *Education:* Illinois Wesleyan University (B.A., 1964); John Marshall Law School (J.D., with honors, 1973; LL.M., in Taxation, 1982). Certified Public Accountant, Illinois, 1967. ***PRACTICE AREAS:*** Trusts and Estates; Commercial Transactions; Taxation. ***Email:*** rhall@bishoprossi.com

GEORGE F. LaFORTE, JR., born Oak Lawn, Illinois, December 15, 1970; admitted to bar, 1996, Illinois and U.S. District Court, Northern District of Illinois; 1999, U.S. Court of Appeals, 7th Circuit. *Education:* Northern Illinois University (B.S., 1992); The John Marshall Law School (J.D., 1996). *Member:* DuPage County and Illinois State Bar Associations. ***PRACTICE AREAS:*** Civil Litigation; Complex Litigation; Plaintiffs Personal Injury. ***Email:*** glafortejr@bishoprossi.com

OF COUNSEL

LESLIE R. BISHOP (1928-1997)

LUCY M. BISHOP, born Chicago, Illinois, July 27, 1934; admitted to bar, 1958, Illinois. (Retired)

RICHARD C. ERNST, (LTD.) (1935-2004)

CETINA & JACQUES, P.C.

1S450 SUMMIT AVENUE
SUITE 140
OAKBROOK TERRACE, ILLINOIS 60181
Telephone: 630-953-8200
Fax: 630-953-0866
Email: mcetina@cetina-jacques.com
URL: http://www.cetinaandjacquespc.com

Personal Injury, Personal Injury Appeals, Personal Injury Arbitration, Personal Injury Defense, Personal Injury Mediation, Plaintiffs Personal Injury, Medical Malpractice, Nursing Home Abuse and Neglect, Driving While Intoxicated, Drug Crimes, Traffic Violations.

MICHAEL S. CETINA, born Chicago, Illinois, May 27, 1960; admitted to bar, 1985, Illinois. *Education:* Grinnell College (B.A., 1982); Washington University (J.D., 1985). Life Member, Who's Who National Registry. *Member:* DuPage County Bar Association; The Association of Trial Lawyers of America; Illinois Trial Lawyers Association. ***PRACTICE AREAS:*** Plaintiffs Personal Injury; Medical Malpractice; Nursing Home Abuse and Neglect; Driving While Intoxicated; Drug Crimes; Traffic Violations. ***Email:*** mcetina@cetina-jacques.com

(This Listing Continued)

CHARLES T. JACQUES, born Chicago, Illinois, June 13, 1959; admitted to bar, 1988, Illinois and U.S. District Court, Northern District of Illinois. *Education:* Tulane University (B.A., 1981); The John Marshall Law School (J.D., 1988). Assistant States Attorney, DuPage, 1989-1993. *Member:* DuPage, Will County and Illinois State Bar Associations. ***PRACTICE AREAS:*** Plaintiffs Personal Injury; Medical Malpractice; Nursing Home Abuse and Neglect; Driving While Intoxicated; Drug Crimes; Traffic Violations. ***Email:*** cjacques@cetina-jacques.com

HOLLAND & KNIGHT LLP

SUITE 1000
ONE MID AMERICA PLAZA
OAKBROOK TERRACE, ILLINOIS 60181
Telephone: 630-954-2100
Fax: 630-954-2112
URL: http://www.hklaw.com

Annapolis, Maryland Office: State Circle Building, 47 State Circle, Suite 400, 21401. Telephone: 410-263-7800. Fax: 410-263-3768.

Atlanta, Georgia Office: One Atlantic Center, 1201 West Peachtree Street, N.E., Suite 2000, 30309. Telephone: 404-817-8500. Fax: 404-881-0470.

Beijing, China Office: No. 33, 14th Floor, IBM Tower, Pacific Century Place, 2 A Workers Stadium Road North, Chaoyang District, 100027. Telephone: 86-10-653-91232. Fax: 86-10-653-91060.

Bethesda, Maryland Office: 3 Bethesda Metro Center, Suite 800, 20814. Telephone: 301-654-7800. Fax: 301-656-3978.

Boston, Massachusetts Office: 10 St. James Avenue, 11th Floor, 02116. Telephone: 617-523-2700. Fax: 617-523-6850.

Bradenton, Florida Office: Bradenton Financial Center, 1401 West Manatee Avenue, Suite 1200, 34205. Telephone: 941-748-7076. Fax: 941-747-9774.

Chicago, Illinois Office: 131 South Dearborn Street, 30th Floor, 60603. Telephone: 312-263-3600. Fax: 312-578-6666.

Fort Lauderdale, Florida Office: One East Broward Boulevard, Suite 1300, 33301. Telephone: 954-525-1000. Fax: 954-463-2030.

Jacksonville, Florida Office: 50 North Laura Street, Suite 3900, 32202. Telephone: 904-353-2000. Fax: 904-358-1872.

Lakeland, Florida Office: 92 Lake Wire Drive, 33815. Telephone: 863-682-1161. Fax: 863-688-1186.

Los Angeles, California Office: 633 West Fifth Street, 21st Floor, 90071. Telephone: 213-896-2400. Fax: 213-896-2450.

Mexico City, Mexico Office: Holland & Knight - Gallastegui y Lozano, S.C., Edificio Arcos Bosques Corporativo, Paseo de los Tamarindos 400-B, Piso 2, Delegación Cuajimalpa, Bosques de las Lomas, 05120. Telephone: 525-55-261-1866. Fax: 525-55-261-1867.

Miami, Florida Office: 701 Brickell Avenue, Suite 3000, 33131. Telephone: 305-374-8500. Fax: 305-789-7799.

New York, New York Office: 195 Broadway, 24th Floor, 10007. Telephone: 212-513-3200. Fax: 212-385-9010.

Northern Virginia: 1600 Tysons Boulevard, Suite 700, McLean, Virginia, 22102. Telephone: 703-720-8600. Fax: 703-720-8610.

Orlando, Florida Office: SunTrust Building, Suite 2600, 200 South Orange Avenue, 32801. Telephone: 407-425-8500. Fax: 407-244-5288.

Portland, Oregon Office: 2300 U.S. Bancorp Tower, 111 Southwest Fifth Avenue, 97204. Telephone: 503-243-2300. Fax: 503-241-8014.

Providence, Rhode Island Office: One Financial Plaza, Suite 1800, 02903. Telephone: 401-751-8500. Fax: 401-553-6850.

Rancho Santa Fe, California Office: 6050 El Tordo, 92067. Telephone: 858-756-4410. Fax: 858-756-4386.

Sacramento, California Office: 1215 K Street, 17th Floor, 95814. Telephone: 916-503-1695. Fax: 916-503-2401.

San Antonio, Texas Office: 112 East Pecan Street, Suite 2700, 78205. Telephone: 210-229-3000. Fax: 210-229-1194.

San Francisco, California Office: 50 California Street, Suite 2800, 94111. Telephone: 415-743-6900. Fax: 415-743-6910.

Seattle, Washington Office: 2600 Pike Tower, 520 Pike Street, 98101. Telephone: 206-340-1825. Fax: 206-623-4363.

St. Petersburg, Florida Office: 200 Central Avenue, Suite 1600, 33701. Telephone: 727-896-7171. Fax: 727-822-8048.

Tallahassee, Florida Office: 315 South Calhoun Street, Suite 600, 32301. Telephone: 850-224-7000. Fax: 850-224-8832.

Tampa, Florida Office: 100 North Tampa Street, Suite 4100, 33602. Telephone: 813-227-8500. Fax: 813-229-0134.

Tokyo, Japan Office: Akasaka Tokyu Building, 7th Floor, 2-14-3 Nagatacho, Chiyoda-Ku, Tokyo, 100-0014. Telephone: 03-3539-5881. Fax: 03-3503-1033.

Washington, D.C. Office: 2099 Pennsylvania Avenue, N.W., Suite 100, 20006. Telephone: 202-955-3000. Fax: 202-955-5564.

West Palm Beach, Florida Office: 222 Lakeview Avenue, Suite 1000, 33401. Telephone: 561-833-2000. Fax: 561-650-8399.

Representative Offices:

Caracas, Venezuela Office: Tinoco, Travieso, Planchart & Núñez, Avenida Francisco De Miranda, Torre Country Club, Pisos 1 y 2, Chacaito, 1050. Telephone: 582-12-952-9033 (Master). Fax: 582-12-953-1053/8365/7583.

Helsinki, Finland Office: Holland & Knight Oy, Pohjoisesplanadi 33, FIN-00100. Telephone: 358-9-684-1520. Fax: 358-9-6841-5252.

Tel Aviv, Israel Office: Haim Samet, Steinmetz, Haring & Co. Advocates, 23 Begin Road, 66814. Telephone: 972-3-567-0100. Fax: 972-3-567-01010.

Litigation, Government Law, Business Law, Real Estate Law and Private Wealth Services.

(This Listing Continued)

FIRM PROFILE: At Holland & Knight we leverage the talents and resources of our entire firm to provide effective advocacy and comprehensive, integrated solutions in virtually all areas of the law, across the U.S., and around the world. The firm's infrastructure, along with its collaborative approach, enables clients to benefit fully from the size of our team, the depth of our experience and our extensive geographic footprint.

Holland & Knight's "one firm" structure allows the firm to support the most complex matters at all levels. The firm is organized into five practice Sections—Litigation, Government, Business, Real Estate and Private Wealth Services. Through integrated practice groups and industry-based teams, we can provide efficient and responsive legal representation anywhere in the world. We serve clients on the basis of their needs, not merely location. Holland & Knight's interdisciplinary approach assures that clients have access to the lawyers with the most appropriate experience.

OAKBROOK TERRACE MEMBER

CARL A. NEUMANN, admitted to bar, 1968, Wisconsin; 1974, Illinois. *Education:* University of Wisconsin-Milwaukee (B.A., 1964); Northwestern University (M.A., 1966); University of Wisconsin-Madison (J.D., 1968). Attorney, Chicago Regional Office, Securities and Exchange Commission, 1968-1969. *Member:* DuPage County Bar Association. (Also at Chicago Office). ***PRACTICE AREAS:*** Corporate Law; Mergers and Acquisitions; Banking Law; Family Business; Estate Planning; Employee Stock Ownership Plans. ***Email:*** carl.neumann@hklaw.com

ASSOCIATE

JAMES P. CHIVILO, born Park Ridge, Illinois, February 10, 1975; admitted to bar, 2000, Illinois. *Education:* Illinois Benedictine College (B.A., 1997); John Marshall Law School (J.D., 2000). (Also at Chicago Office). ***PRACTICE AREAS:*** Litigation; Construction Law; Insurance Law; General Commerical Litigation. ***Email:*** james.chivilo@hklaw.com

(For Biographical Data of other firm Personnel, see Professional Biographies at other offices indicated in the heading of this card).

KUBIESA, SPIROFF, GOSSELAR & ACKER, P.C.

OAKBROOK TERRACE, ILLINOIS

(See Elmhurst)

Municipal Law, Business Law, General Civil and Trial Practice in all Courts, Public Finance, Land Use Law, Administrative Law, Employment Law, Corporate Law, Civil Litigation, Appeals, Real Estate, General Practice, Criminal Law, Eminent Domain.

PETER S. LUBIN

17 W-220 22ND STREET, SUITE 200
OAKBROOK TERRACE, ILLINOIS 60181
Telephone: 630-333-0000
Facsimile: 630-333-0333
Email: psl@ditommasolaw.com
URL: http://www.lawyers.com/peterslubin

General Business Lawsuits, Small Business Lawsuits, Employment Law, Employment Discrimination, Sexual Harassment, Wrongful Termination, Consumer, Consumer Fraud, Unsafe Products, Warranties, Class Actions, Consumer Class Actions, Legal Malpractice, Franchises, Business Law, Business Litigation, Business Fraud.

PETER S. LUBIN, born Chicago, Illinois, December 3, 1957; admitted to bar, 1983, Illinois; 1984, U.S. District Court, Northern and Central Districts of Illinois; 1993, U.S. Court of Appeals, Second, Third, Fifth, Seventh, Tenth, Eleventh and District of Columbia Circuits and U.S. Supreme Court. *Education:* Dartmouth College (A.B., 1980); University of Chicago (J.D., 1983). *Member:* Chicago, Illinois State, DuPage and American Bar Associations; American Inns of Court (Markey-Wigmore Chapter); Chicago Council of Lawyers. ***PRACTICE AREAS:*** Business Law; Business Litigation; Employment Law; Employment Discrimination; Sexual Harassment; Wrongful Termination; Consumer; Consumer Fraud; Unsafe Products; Warranties; Class Actions; Consumer Class Actions; Legal Malpractice; Franchises.

McBRIDE BAKER & COLES

OAKBROOK TERRACE, ILLINOIS

(See Holland & Knight LLC)

IAN McMILLAN

1 S 376 SUMMIT AVENUE, UNIT C
OAKBROOK TERRACE, ILLINOIS 60181
Telephone: 630-620-5990
Fax: 630-932-0758

Contracts, Trusts, Estates, Wills, Probate, Guardianship.

IAN McMILLAN, born Chicago, Illinois, May 5, 1935; admitted to bar, 1966, Illinois; 1966, U.S. District Court, Northern District of Illinois; 1967, U.S. Court of Appeals, 7th Circuit and U.S. Supreme Court. *Education:* Valparaiso University (B.A., 1960; J.D., 1964).

REPRESENTATIVE CLIENTS: A.O. Smith Corp.; English District of the Lutheran Church - Missouri Synod.
REFERENCES: Chicago Title & Trust Co.; Northern Trust Co.

FORST LAW OFFICES

9150 SOUTH CICERO AVENUE, SUITE 204
OAK LAWN, ILLINOIS 60453
Telephone: 708-499-2560
Fax: 708-499-2560
Email: forstlaw@sbcglobal.net

Divorce, Debtor Bankruptcy.

RICHARD J. FORST, born Oak Park, Illinois, March 18, 1958; admitted to bar, 1983, Illinois. *Education:* Loyola University (B.A., 1980); Chicago-Kent College of Law (J.D., 1983). *Member:* Chicago, Illinois State and American State Bar Associations; Southwest Suburban Bar Association.

THOMAS W. LYNCH, P.C.

Established in 1991

9231 S. ROBERTS ROAD
OAK LAWN, ILLINOIS 60457
Telephone: 708-598-5999
Fax: 708-598-6299
Email: twlpc@worldnet.att.net
URL: http://www.thomaswlynchpc.com

Federal Taxation, IRS and State Representation including Collections Division, Audits, Appeals, Tax Court and State or US District Court, State Taxation, Tax Appeals and Real Estate.

FIRM PROFILE: This Firm has been providing quality legal services since 1991. Our attorneys have extensive experience in dealing with Debt, Bankruptcy, Federal and State Tax Problems, Real Estate Transactions and Criminal Matters, including Traffic, Corporate Litigation and Probate. Visit us at our website www.thomaswlynchpc.com.

This firm has represented hundreds of Individuals and Businesses who have found themselves in conflict with government agencies which enforce the law.

THOMAS W. LYNCH, born 1955; admitted to bar, 1987, Illinois, U.S. District Court, Northern District of Illinois, U.S. Court of Appeals, Seventh Circuit and U.S. Tax Court. *Education:* DePaul University (B.S., 1979); John Marshall Law School (J.D., 1986). ***PRACTICE AREAS:*** Federal Taxation; Federal Income Tax; Income Tax; State Taxation; Tax Appeals. ***Email:*** twlpc@worldnet.att.net

LAW OFFICE OF JAMES J. SIWEK

OAK LAWN, ILLINOIS

(See Worth)

Bankruptcy - Chapters 7 and 13, Consumer Fraud, Criminal Law, Misdemeanors and Felonies, Driving While Intoxicated, Drug Crimes, Juvenile Law, Parole and Probation, Family Law, Adoptions, Child Custody, Child Support, Divorce, Domestic Violence, Visitation Rights, General Practice, Real Estate, Buying or Selling a Home, Construction, Landlord and Tenant, Trusts and Estates, Land Trusts, Living Trusts, Guardianships, Powers of Attorney, Wills and Probate.

ASH, ANOS, FREEDMAN & LOGAN, L.L.C.

OAK PARK, ILLINOIS

(See Chicago)

General Trial Practice. Products Liability, Malpractice, Probate, Corporate, Zoning, Municipal, Real Estate and Condominium Law.

CHITTENDEN, MURDAY & NOVOTNY, LLC

OAK PARK, ILLINOIS

(See Chicago)

Appellate Practice, Business and Commercial Litigation, Business and Corporate Law, Class Action Defense, Employee Benefits Law, Employment and Labor Law, Insurance Tax Litigation, Life, Health & Disability Insurance Law, Managed Health Care Law, Medical Malpractice Defense, Product Liability Law, Securities Litigation and Arbitration.

GABRIELLE S. DAVIS, P.C.

1011 LAKE STREET, SUITE 424
OAK PARK, ILLINOIS 60301
Telephone: 708-660-9164
Fax: 708-358-1335
URL: http://www.gabrielledavislaw.com

Family Law.

GABRIELLE S. DAVIS, born Houston, Texas, November 7, 1955; admitted to bar, 1983, Illinois. *Education:* Knox College (B.A., 1977); Chicago-Kent College of Law, Illinois Institute of Technology (J.D., 1983). Volunteer, Energy & Environment Commission, Village of Oak Park. *Member:* Chicago (Member, Matrimonial Law Committee and Legislative Sub-Committee), Illinois State and American Bar Associations. ***LANGUAGES:*** French. ***REPORTED CASES:*** Snover vs. McGraw, Illinois Supreme Court. ***PRACTICE AREAS:*** Matrimonial Law; Mediation. ***Email:*** gabrielle@gabrielledavis.com

DOWELL BAKER

229 RANDOLPH STREET
OAK PARK, ILLINOIS 60302
Telephone: 708-660-1413
Fax: 312-873-4466

Lafayette, Indiana Office: 1001 Main Street, 47901. Telephone: 765-429-4004. Telephone: 765-429-4114.

General Practice.

MEMBER OF FIRM

GEOFFREY A. BAKER, born New York, N.Y., July 15, 1965; admitted to bar, 1996, Wisconsin, Illinois, U.S. District Court, Western District of Wisconsin, U.S. District Court, Northern District of Illinois including Trial Bar, U.S. District Court, District of Colorado and U.S. Court of Appeals for the Federal Circuit; registered to practice before U.S. Patent and Trademark Office. *Education:* University of Pennsylvania (B.S.E., 1987); University of Wisconsin, Madison (J.D., 1996). Recipient: Salmon W. Dalberg Award, Outstanding Member of Graduating Class; American Jurisprudence Award, Criminal Law. ***LANGUAGES:*** French, Italian, Spanish and Portuguese. ***PRACTICE AREAS:*** Litigation; Intellectual Property Law.

GOEDERT, HUNTINGTON & DEBOER

Established in 1971
1011 LAKE STREET
SUITE 303
OAK PARK, ILLINOIS 60301-1138
Telephone: 708-848-6066
Fax: 708-848-6067
URL: http://www.ghdlaw.com
Email: ghd@ameritech.net
URL: http://www.lawyers.com/gh&dlaw

Business Law, Corporate Law, Mergers and Acquisitions, Contracts, Employee Benefits, Taxation, Trusts and Estates, Wills, Decedents Estates, Probate, Elder Law, Nonprofit and Charitable Organizations, Real Estate.

FIRM PROFILE: The firm was founded in 1971 by John P. Goedert. Mr. Huntington joined the firm in 1976 and Mr. DeBoer joined the firm in 1986. Our practice has focused on a wide range of business advice and transactions, business succession planning, estate planning, decedent's estates, and federal and state taxation and tax matter resolution. Our attorneys are committed to providing superior service and personal attention to all of our clients.

MEMBERS OF FIRM

ROBERT A. HUNTINGTON, born New York, N.Y., March 22, 1946; admitted to bar, 1972, Wisconsin; 1976, Illinois; 1981, U.S. Tax Court. *Education:* Marquette University (B.S. in Accounting, 1968; J.D., 1972); New York University (LL.M. in Taxation, 1974). *Member:* Chicago (Member, Corporation Law Committee, 1980—; Division Chairman, 1983-1987), Illinois State (Member, Sections on: Estate Planning, Probate and Trust; Financial Planning), West Suburban and American (Member, Real Property, Probate and Trust Law Section) Bar Associations; State Bar of Wisconsin. ***PRACTICE AREAS:*** Business Law; Corporate Law; Taxation; Trusts and Estates; Nonprofit and Charitable Organizations; Mergers and Acquisitions; Contracts; Employee Benefits; Wills; Decedents Estates; Probate; Elder Law; Real Estate. ***Email:*** rhuntington@ameritech.net

MICHAEL J. DEBOER, born LaGrange, Illinois, September 30, 1958; admitted to bar, 1986, Illinois. *Education:* Calvin College; University of Denver (B.S., Accounting, 1980); IIT/Chicago-Kent College of Law (J.D., with honors, 1986). *Member:* Chicago, Illinois State and American (Member: Sections on: Real Property, Probate and Trust Law and Business Law) Bar Associations. ***PRACTICE AREAS:*** Business Law; Trusts and Estates; Probate; Nonprofit and Charitable Organizations; Real Estate; Corporate Law; Mergers and Acquisitions; Contracts; Employee Benefits; Taxation; Wills; Decedents Estates; Elder Law. ***Email:*** mdeboer@ameritech.net

HUGHES SOCOL PIERS RESNICK & DYM, LTD.

OAK PARK, ILLINOIS
(See Chicago)

General Civil and Litigation Practice in all Courts. Insurance and Reinsurance. Personal Injury, Immigration, Civil Rights, Class Actions, Labor and Employment, Commercial, Professional Liability, Litigation.

THE LAW OFFICES OF PHILIP A. IGOE

OAK PARK, ILLINOIS
(See Chicago)

Bankruptcy Law, Criminal Law, DUI/DWI, Traffic Violations, Transportation Law, White Collar Crimes.

JAMES L. KOPECKY, P.C.

OAK PARK, ILLINOIS
(See Chicago)

Securities, Securities Fraud, Securities Arbitration and Litigation, Shareholder Disputes, Business and Contract Litigation, General Civil Litigation and Personal Injury.

OAK PARK LEGAL CLINIC

114 CHICAGO AVENUE, 2ND FLOOR
OAK PARK, ILLINOIS 60304
Telephone: 708-524-1181
Fax: 708-524-1346
URL: http://www.lawyers.com/oakparklegal

Bankruptcy, Real Estate, Criminal Law, Divorce, Accidents, Social Security.

MEMBER OF FIRM

ROBERT RATTLER, admitted to bar, 1987, Illinois. *Education:* Elmhurst College (B.S., 1983); Chicago-Kent College of Law (J.D., 1987). ***Email:*** oakpklegal.1@netzero.net

CHARLES RIECK

100 FOREST PLACE, SUITE 405
OAK PARK, ILLINOIS 60301
Telephone: 630-399-7751
Fax: 708-386-3728
Email: mitstnfnd@aol.com

Computer, Electronics and Software Patents, Patent Applications, Patent Infringement, Patent Prosecution. Intellectual Property Law, Licensing Agreements.

CHARLES RIECK, born Chicago, Illinois; admitted to bar, 1978, Illinois; registered to practice before U.S. Patent and Trademark Office. *Education:* University of Notre Dame (B.A., magna cum laude); Massachusetts Institute of Technology (Ph.D., E.E./Physics, 1973); Stanford University (J.D., 1978). Editor, Stanford Law Review, 1977-1978.

R.M. STEPHENSON, LLC

801 SOUTH BOULEVARD, SUITE 3
OAK PARK, ILLINOIS 60302
Telephone: 708-434-1267
Fax: 708-434-0784
Email: info@rmstephenson.com
URL: http://www.rmstephenson.com

Appellate Practice, Criminal Defense, Family Law, Wills, Trusts and Estates, Civil Litigation, Business Law, Real Estate Law.

ROBERT STEPHENSON, born Atlanta, Georgia, 1971; admitted to bar, 2002, Illinois. *Education:* The Ohio State University Law School (J.D.). Former Assistant Defender, Office of the State of Illinois Appellate Defender, 7th Circuit; Former Judicial Law Clerk to the Honorable Peggy Bryant, 10th District Court of Appeals. *Member:* Chicago, Illinois State and American Bar Associations. ***PRACTICE AREAS:*** Appellate Practice; Criminal Defense; Family Law; Wills; Trusts and Estates; Civil Litigation; Business Law; Real Estate. ***Email:*** info@rmstephenson.com

MASARU K. TAKIGUCHI

OAK PARK, ILLINOIS
(See Oak Brook)

Real Estate, Probate and Estate Planning, Civil Litigation, Commercial Transactions.

TAMARI & BLUMENTHAL, LLC

OAK PARK, ILLINOIS
(See Chicago)

Commercial Litigation, Consumer Litigation, Corporate Law, Personal Injury Litigation, Business Litigation, Landlord Tenant Litigation.

STEPHEN L. TYMA, P.C.

OAK PARK, ILLINOIS
(See Chicago)

Federal and State Litigation, Trial and Appellate Practice, Business Law, Commercial Law, Construction Law, Contracts, Corporate Law, Environmental Law, Family Law, Divorce, Partnership Law, Probate, Professional Liability, Real Estate, RICO, General Practice.

COX, PHILLIPS, WEBER, TEDFORD & HEAP, P.C.

OBLONG, ILLINOIS
(See Robinson)

General Civil, Trial and Appellate Practice. Probate, Real Estate, Title Insurance, Municipal, Taxation, Corporation, Estate Planning, Workers Compensation, Oil and Gas Law, Collections, and Matrimonial Law.

TIMOTHY S. WILTSIE

O'FALLON, ILLINOIS
(See Belleville)

Civil Trial and Appellate Practice, Family Law, Divorce, Child Support, Child Custody, Business Litigation, Business Transactions, Real Estate, Personal Injury, Wills, Trusts and Estates.

HART BELL LLC

OLNEY, ILLINOIS

(See Vincennes, Indiana)

General Practice. Litigation, Insurance, Banking, Corporate, Employment, Probate and Estate Planning, State and Federal Tax Law, Real Estate, Construction, Commercial, Business, Elder, Creditors Rights, Personal Injury, Family Law and Criminal Defense.

HELLER, HOLMES & ASSOCIATES, P.C.

OLNEY, ILLINOIS

(See Mattoon)

General Civil and Trial Practice in all State, Federal and Appellate Courts. Personal Injury, Medical Negligence, Criminal Defense, Insurance, Litigation, Probate, Workers Compensation, Corporation, Commercial, Family Law, Oil and Gas.

STANSELL, WHITMAN & BABER

OQUAWKA, ILLINOIS

(See Monmouth)

Personal Injury, Banking, Bankruptcy, Collections, Criminal, Divorce, Probate and Wills, Real Estate, Workers Compensation Law. Civil Litigation.

BOYLE, CORDES, WITHEFT & BROWN, LLC

OREGON, ILLINOIS

(See De Kalb)

General Civil Trial Practice in State and Federal Courts. Probate, Corporate, Trust and Estate Planning, Real Estate, Zoning and Planning, Secured Lending.

DANIEL A. CWYNAR

OREGON, ILLINOIS

(See Rockford)

Bankruptcy including individual and small business, foreclosures, repossessions, chapter 7, chapter 13; Residential and Commercial Real Estate, Buying and Selling, Contracts, Criminal Defense, DUI, Traffic, Misdemeanors.

JOHN GILBERT

OREGON, ILLINOIS

(See Rockford)

Criminal Law, DUI/DWI, Drug Crimes, Parole and Probation, Juvenile Law, Traffic Violations, Bankruptcy, Real Estate, Criminal Leasing, Residential, Family Law, Child Custody, Child Support, Divorce, Visitation Rights, Domestic Violence, Adoption, Wills and Probate, Trusts and Estates, Estate Planning, Business Law, Business Planning, Contracts, Business Litigation, Business Enterprises.

WILLIAMS & McCARTHY

A PROFESSIONAL CORPORATION

607 WASHINGTON STREET
P.O. BOX 339
OREGON, ILLINOIS 61061
Telephone: 815-732-2101
Fax: 815-732-2289

Rockford, Illinois Office: 321 West State Street, P.O. Box 219. Telephone: 815-987-8900. Fax: 815-968-0019.

General Civil and Trial Practice. Administrative Law, Advertising and Media Law, Banking, Bankruptcy and Commercial Work Outs, Business Litigation, Closely-held Business, Commercial Lending, Condemnation and Zoning, Construction Law, Education Law, Employee Benefits, Employers' Liability, Environmental Law, Family Law, Health Care and Hospital Law, Insurance Coverage, Insurance Defense, International Law, Labor and Employment (Management), Municipal Finance, Probate, Trust Law and Estate Planning, Products Liability, Real Estate, Taxation, Unfair Competition, Workers' Compensation (Management).

Kim D. Krahenbuhl **Clayton L. Lindsey**
Wendy S. Howarter

REPRESENTATIVE CLIENTS: *Financial:* Alpine Bank of Illinois; Amcore Bank, N.A.; National City Bank; Associated Bank; Forreston State Bank; Lena State Bank; Navistar Financial Corp; State Bank of Pearl City; Firstar Bank.
HEALTH CARE: Alpine Fireside Health Center; Benefit Administrative Service; Janet Wattles Center; Lundholm Surgical Group, LTD; Milestone, Inc.; Northern Illinois Blood Bank; Wesley Willows; Orthopedic & Arthritis Clinic; Pediatric Associates of Rockford; Peoria Urological Associates, Inc.; Riverside Medical Clinic; Rockford Clinic; Rockford Health System; Rockford Health Plans; Rockford Memorial Hospital; Rockford Orthopedic Associates; Rockford Surgical Services; Rosecrance Health Network; Visiting Nurses Association.
EDUCATIONAL: Rockford School District 205; Harlem Education Foundation; Forrestville Valley Community School District; Oregon School District; Rockford Business School; Rockford College; Rock Valley College Foundation; Swank Educational Enterprises, Inc.; Community Foundation Northern Illinois.
INSURANCE: Cincinnati Insurance Co.; Country Companies; Employers Mutual Insurance Co.; Gallagher Bassett Insurance Co.; The Hartford; Kemper Group; Liberty Mutual Insurance Co.; Springfield Fire & Casualty Co.; The St. Paul Companies; Shelby Insurance Co.; The Travelers Companies; Wausau Insurance Companies; West Bend Mutual Insurance Co.; Williams-Manny.

(This Listing Continued)

MANUFACTURING: DaimlerChrysler Corp.; Advance Dial Co.; Advanced Machine & Engineering; Aircraft Gear Corp.; Anderson Packaging, Inc.; Arachnid, Inc.; Atwood Mobile Products; Behr Machinery & Equipment Corp.; Dean Foods, Co.; DeKalb Genetics Corp.; Etynre International, LTD.; Hydraforce, Inc.; Ingersoll Milling Machine Co.; Haldex Hydraulics Corp.; Joseph Behr & Sons, Inc.; Martin Automatic, Inc.; Miller Engineering Co.; Niigata Machinery (USA) Co.; Pacsci Motion, Control, Inc.; Pegard Products, Inc.; Roper-Whitney of Rockford; Southern Imperial, Inc.; Stickle Enterprises, LTD.; Terra Industries; The Valvoline Company; W.A. Whitney Co.; Zenith Cutter Co.
MUNICIPAL: Boone County; City of Byron; Cherry Valley Library District; North Suburban Library District; City of Oregon; Oregon Park District; City of Rockford; Rockford Mass Transit District; Rockford Park District; Rockford Metro Authority; Rockford Police Pension Fund; Village of Lena; Winnebago County.
REAL ESTATE, REAL ESTATE DEVELOPMENT & CONSTRUCTION: Landis Reality; Mid-Northern Management; Ringland-Johnson, Inc.; Hillcrest Development, Inc.; Sproule Construction Co.; Star Development, LLC; Stock Lumber Co.
COMMUNICATIONS: Aero Computing, LTD; Airplay Broadcasting Co.; Pride Communications, LLC; Radio Works, Inc.; R World Communications; Segueway Broadcasting Corp.; WTVO Television.
RETAIL/SERVICE: Accent on Travel; Cal Cars, Inc; Golf Shack, LLC; Kelley-Williamson Company; Lawyers Title Insurance Corp.; Premium Oil Co.; Rock River Ford, Inc.; Title Underwriters Agency, Inc.; Viking Distributors, Inc.; Vista Marketing Group, LTD.

(For Complete Biographical Data on all Personnel, see Professional Biographies at Rockford, Illinois)

THE LAW OFFICES OF DAVID DAUDELL

ORLAND PARK, ILLINOIS

(See Chicago)

Adoption Law, Bankruptcy, Business Organization, Contracts, Criminal Law, Driving While Intoxicated, Divorce, Family Law, Gaming Law, Landlord and Tenant Law, Medical Malpractice, Motor Vehicle Accidents and Injuries, Personal Injury, Probate, Estate Administration, Real Estate, White Collar Crime, Wills, Litigation.

JAMES F. DUNNEBACK, P.C.

14535 JOHN HUMPHREY DRIVE, SUITE 101
ORLAND PARK, ILLINOIS 60462
Telephone: 708-460-4000
Fax: 708-460-6967
Email: jdunneback@dunnebacklaw.com
URL: http://www.lawyers.com/dunnebacklaw

Corporate, Business, Contracts, Estate Planning, Probate, Probate Litigation, Real Estate and Real Estate Development.

JAMES F. DUNNEBACK, born Chicago, Illinois, June 1, 1949; admitted to bar, 1975, Illinois, U.S. District Court, Northern District of Illinois and U.S. Court of Appeals, Seventh Circuit. *Education:* DePaul University (B.A., 1971; J.D., 1975). *Member:* Illinois State Bar Association. **PRACTICE AREAS:** Corporate Law; Probate; Real Estate; Trusts and Estates. **Email:** jdunneback@dunnebacklaw.com

ANNE M. KELLY, admitted to bar, 1982, Illinois. *Education:* Illinois State University (B.S., 1979); Chicago-Kent College of Law (J.D., 1982); Saint Xavier University, Graham School of Management (M.B.A., Finance, 1991). Adjunct Faculty Member, Introduction to Financial Management, Saint Xavier University, Graham School of Management, 1992). Vice President and Trust Officer: Founders Bank, Worth, Illinois, 1998-2000; Marquette National Bank, Chicago, Illinois, 1987-1991. Trust Officer, First National Bank of Evergreen Park, Evergreen Park, Illinois, 1996-1998. Sole Practitioner, Anne M. Kelly Attorney at Law, 1991-1996. *Member:* Chicago and Illinois State Bar Associations. **Email:** akelly@dunnebacklaw.com

JOHN M. GALICH, born Chicago, Illinois, July 2, 1963; admitted to bar, 1988, Illinois and U.S. District Court, Northern District of Illinois; 1991, U.S. Court of Appeals, Seventh Circuit. *Education:* University of Denver (B.A., 1985); DePaul University (J.D., 1988). Former Associate, Charles Brusso & Associates. **PRACTICE AREAS:** Collections; Real Estate; Civil Litigation. **Email:** jgalich@dunnebacklaw.com

THOMAS W. LYNCH, P.C.

ORLAND PARK, ILLINOIS

(See Oak Lawn)

Federal Taxation, IRS and State Representation including Collections Division, Audits, Appeals, Tax Court and State or US District Court, State Taxation, Tax Appeals and Real Estate.

THERESA M. MALYSA

LANDMARK ATRIUM BUILDING, SUITE 303
9501 WEST 144TH PLACE
ORLAND PARK, ILLINOIS 60462
Telephone: 708-403-1550
Fax: 708-403-1556
Email: ldyloyr@prodigy.net
URL: http://www.lawyers.com/idyloyr

Family Law, Divorce, Tax Considerations, Retirement Benefits, Child Custody, Parenting Time, Visitation, Child Support, Domestic Violence, Paternity, Matrimonial Litigation, Premarital Agreements.

THERESA M. MALYSA, born New York, N.Y., March 7, 1942; admitted to bar, 1984, Illinois; 1986, Florida, U.S. District Court, Northern District of Illinois and U.S. Supreme Court. *Education:* University of Miami (B.A., 1963); John Marshall Law School (J.D.,

(This Listing Continued)

THERESA M. MALYSA, Orland Park—Continued

1984). *Member:* Chicago and Illinois State Bar Associations; Women's Southwest Suburban Bar Association (Member, Family Law Committee, 1998—); Will County Women's Bar Association. ***PRACTICE AREAS:*** Divorce; Family Law; Child Support; Child Custody.

DREYER, FOOTE, STREIT, FURGASON AND SLOCUM

A PROFESSIONAL ASSOCIATION

OSWEGO, ILLINOIS

(See Aurora, Illinois)

Civil and Criminal Trial and Appellate Practice in all State and Federal Courts. Business Planning, Commercial, Corporate, Estate Planning, Wills, Probate, Trusts and Estates, Elder Law, Family Law, Healthcare, Insurance and Insurance Defense, Labor, Municipal, Personal Injury, Probate, Real Estate, State and Federal Taxation, Adoption, Child Support, Child Custody, Divorce, Domestic Violence, DWI, Automobile Accidents, Wrongful Death, Buying and Selling a Home, Landlord/Tenant, Construction, Bankruptcy, Guardianships, Collections, Buying and Selling a Business, Business Enterprises, Franchise, Closely Held Business, Limited Liability, Partnerships, Small Business, Contracts, Lawsuits, Starting a Business, Zoning.

MAHONEY, SILVERMAN & CROSS, LTD.

OSWEGO, ILLINOIS

(See Joliet)

Administrative Law; Appellate Practice; Banking Law; Business Law, including Business Formation, Maintenance and Planning, Financing, Acquisitions, Licensing and Business Transactions; Civil Litigation in State and Federal Courts, including Commercial, Construction, Personal Injury, Eminent Domain, Alternative Dispute Resolution, Zoning and Land Use; Construction Law; Land Use Law, including Zoning, Planning and Land Development; Local Governmental Law, including cities, villages, townships, fire protection, library and park districts, and governmental financing including tax increment financing districts; Real Estate Law; Tax Law; Traffic Law; Estate Planning; Trust Administration; Estate Administration; Contested Trusts and Estates; Elder Law; Gift, Estate and Income Tax Law.

ARMSTRONG & SURIN

724 COLUMBUS STREET
OTTAWA, ILLINOIS 61350
Telephone: 815-431-1234
Fax: 815-434-5338
URL: http://www.lawyers.com/armstrongsurinandassociates
Email: aslaw@mchsi.com
URL: http://www.armstrongsurin.com

Personal Injury, Workers Compensation, Corporation, Probate, Real Estate, Negligence, Family Law, Bankruptcy, Criminal, Traffic, Wills and Trusts.

MEMBERS OF FIRM

CRAIG M. ARMSTRONG (1927-1996)

WILLIAM T. SURIN, born Chicago, Illinois, July 23, 1949; admitted to bar, 1975, Illinois. *Education:* Eastern Illinois University and University of Illinois at Chicago Circle (B.A., 1971); Illinois Institute of Technology, Chicago Kent College of Law (J.D., 1975). Phi Alpha Delta. Assistant Public Defender, La Salle County, 1975-1979. Member, Illinois Defender Project, 1975-1981. *Member:* La Salle County and Illinois State Bar Associations; The Association of Trial Lawyers of America. ***PRACTICE AREAS:*** Probate; Corporations.

GENERAL COUNSEL FOR: Orbit Transportation, Inc.; The Peltier Glass Co.; Black Marine, Inc.; First Federal Savings Bank.
REFERENCES: First National Bank of Ottawa, Illinois; Union Bank/Ottawa.

HERBOLSHEIMER, LANNON, HENSON, DUNCAN AND REAGAN, P.C.

Established in 1916

FIRST FEDERAL SAVINGS BUILDING
633 LA SALLE STREET, SUITE 409
OTTAWA, ILLINOIS 61350
Telephone: 815-434-1400
Fax: 815-434-2423

La Salle, Illinois Office: State Bank Building, Suite 400, 654 First Street, P.O. Box 539. Telephone: 815-223-0111. FAX: 815-223-5829.

General Civil Practice and Trials in all Courts. Insurance, Real Estate, Probate, Corporation, Federal, Tax and School Law.

FIRM PROFILE: Herbolsheimer, Lannon, Henson, Duncan and Reagan was founded by J.E. Malone in 1916. Serving clients throughout North Central Illinois inclusive of LaSalle, Bureau, Grundy, DeKalb, Livingston and Lee counties. The firm is a General Practice with a focus on Insurance Defense.

(For Complete Biographical Data on all Personnel, see Professional Biographies at La Salle, Illinois)

LAW OFFICES OF LEYNAUD & LEYNAUD

A PROFESSIONAL CORPORATION

OTTAWA, ILLINOIS

(See Peru)

General Civil and Trial Practice, Personal Injury, Mediation, Worker's Compensation, Real Estate, Criminal, Landlord/Tenant and Family Law. Business/Banking Litigation, DUI and Traffic. Insurance, General Practice, Medical Malpractice, Zoning and Land Use. Bad Faith, Drug Crimes, Juvenile Crimes, White Collar, Adoptions, Child Custody, Divorce, Child Support, Visitation Rights, Domestic Violence. Auto Accidents, Dog Bites, Slip and Fall, Wrongful Death, Buying and Selling, Wills and Probate.

MYERS, BERRY, O'CONOR & KUZMA, LTD.

Established in 1948

130 EAST MADISON STREET
OTTAWA, ILLINOIS 61350
Telephone: 815-434-6206
Fax: 815-434-6203

Streator, Illinois Office: 7 Northpoint Drive, 61364. Telephone: 815-672-3116. Fax: 815-672-0738.

General Civil and Trial Practice in all Courts. Banking, Commercial and Corporate Law, Government and School Law, Estate Planning and Probate, Real Estate, Health Care Law.

FIRM PROFILE: The firm serves clients throughout Northern Central Illinois in the practice areas noted.

JOHN A. BERRY (1912-1986)

ANDREW J. O'CONOR (1919-1998)

STEPHEN C. MYERS, born Streator, Illinois, October 20, 1946; admitted to bar, 1971, Illinois. *Education:* University of Notre Dame (A.B., cum laude, 1968); Northwestern University (J.D., 1971). Member, Northwestern University Law Review, 1969-1971. *Member:* La Salle County and Illinois State Bar Associations. ***PRACTICE AREAS:*** Corporate Law; Government Law; School Law; Litigation. **Email:** scm@mdbok.com

RICHARD J. BERRY, born Bloomington, Illinois, April 16, 1952; admitted to bar, 1977, Illinois. *Education:* Vanderbilt University (B.A., magna cum laude, 1974); University of Notre Dame (J.D., 1977). Phi Eta Sigma. *Member:* La Salle County, Illinois State (Member: Commercial, Banking and Bankruptcy Law Section Council, 1983-1987; Health Care Section Council, 1990-1992) and American Bar Associations; American Academy of Hospital Attorneys; Illinois Bankers Association (Member, Committee on Bank Counsel, 1986—; Chairman, 1988). ***PRACTICE AREAS:*** Banking Law; Commercial Law; Health Care Law; Civil Litigation; Appellate Practice. **Email:** rberry@mdbok.com

SHERYL H. KUZMA, born Chicago, Illinois, December 31, 1965; admitted to bar, 1990, Illinois, U.S. District Court, Northern District of Illinois and Western District of Wisconsin. *Education:* Northern Illinois University (B.A., magna cum laude, 1987); University of Wisconsin (J.D., 1990). Member, Moot Court, National Team. *Member:* Chicago, LaSalle County and Illinois State Bar Associations. ***PRACTICE AREAS:*** Litigation; Government Law. **Email:** shk@mdbok.com

REPRESENTATIVE CLIENTS: Streator Elem. School Dist. #44; Union Bancorp, Inc.; Union Bank; First State Bank; Auto Owners Ins. Co.; St. Mary's Hosp.; Streator Township H.S. Dist. 40; Allied Ins.; Ottawa Elem. School Dist. No. 141; City of Streator; Farmers Union Cooperative Ins. Co.; Iowa Mutual Insurance.

POOL, LEIGH & FABRICIUS

An Association of Professional Corporations

CENTRAL LIFE BUILDING
628 COLUMBUS STREET, SUITE 208
OTTAWA, ILLINOIS 61350
Telephone: 815-434-0097
Fax: 815-434-0270
Email: plflaw@theramp.net

General Civil Trial and Appellate Practice in all Courts, Insurance, Real Estate and Family Law.

MEMBER OF FIRM

RAYMOND P. FABRICIUS, (P.C.), born Chicago, Illinois, January 22, 1959; admitted to bar, 1988, Illinois, U.S. District Court, Northern District of Illinois and U.S. Court of Appeals, Seventh Circuit. *Education:* DePaul University (B.S., 1983); John Marshall Law School (J.D., 1987). *Member:* La Salle County Bar Association; Illinois Association of Defense Trial Counsel; The Association of Trial Lawyers of America (Associate Member). ***PRACTICE AREAS:*** Insurance Defense; Insurance Coverage; Litigation; Appeals. **Email:** plflaw@theramp.net

---

JENNIFER H. KOENIG, born Carroll, Iowa, July 21, 1971; admitted to bar, 1998, Illinois. *Education:* University of Michigan (B.A., with distinction, 1993); Depaul University (J.D., 1998).

JAMES R. LINDIG, born Peoria, Illinois, August 21, 1961; admitted to bar, 1990, Illinois; 1991, U.S. District Court, Northern District of Illinois; 1992, U.S. Court of Appeals, Seventh Circuit; 1994, U.S. District Court, Central District of Illinois. *Education:* Northern Illinois University, DeKalb (B.S., History, 1987; J.D., 1990). [Second Lieutenant, Illinois

(This Listing Continued)

Army National Guard, 1983-1990]. ***LANGUAGES:*** English. ***PRACTICE AREAS:*** Personal Injury; Litigation; Family Law; Misdemeanors; Civil Litigation; Probate; Bankruptcy; Real Estate.

LEGAL SUPPORT PERSONNEL

Sheila Parrott ***Shannon Lowman***
Laureve Callison

REPRESENTATIVE CLIENTS: State Farm Insurance Co.; Allstate Insurance Co.; Country Companies; Shelby Insurance Co.; Union Insurance Group; Westfield Companies; Central Insurance Co.; Progressive Insurance Co.; Badger Insurance.

ANTHONY C. RACCUGLIA & ASSOCIATES, P.C.

Established in 1959

633 LA SALLE STREET
OTTAWA, ILLINOIS 61350
Telephone: 815-434-2003
Email: raccuglialaw@insightbb.com

Peru, Illinois Office: 1200 Maple Drive. Telephone: 815-223-0230.

General Civil and Trial Practice in all State and Federal Courts. Personal Injury, Medical Malpractice, Products Liability, Workers Compensation, Probate, Real Estate, Construction Accidents, Structural Work Cases, Business Litigation.

FIRM PROFILE: Anthony C. Raccuglia founded the firm in 1959. He has served clients in LaSalle, Bureau, Grundy, Lee, DeKalb, McLean, Will and surrounding counties for the past 38 years. The firm concentrates on plaintiff personal injury and death in medical malpractice, vehicular collision, product liability and construction cases.

ANTHONY C. RACCUGLIA, born La Salle, Illinois, September 4, 1933; admitted to bar, 1959, Illinois. *Education:* University of Illinois (B.S., 1957); John Marshall Law School (J.D., 1959). Order of John Marshall. Selected by Leading Lawyers as one of the top Illinois lawyers in personal injury law, 2004-2005. First Assistant States Attorney, La Salle County, 1960-1968. City Attorney, La Salle, Illinois, 1989—. Laureate, Academy of Illinois Lawyers, ISBA, 2003. *Member:* La Salle-Peru-Oglesby, La Salle County (President, 1976-1977), Illinois State (Member, Board of Governors, 1975-1981; Laureate, Academy of Illinois Lawyers, 2003) and American Bar Associations; Illinois Trial Lawyers Association (Member, Board of Governors, 1986-1989); The Association of Trial Lawyers of America (Member, Board of Governors, 1986-1989). ***PRACTICE AREAS:*** Personal Injury Law; Medical Malpractice; Products Liability Law; Construction Accidents; Structural Work Cases.

REFERENCES: La Salle National Bank; Citizens First National Bank of Peru, Illinois.

(For complete biographical data on all personnel, see Professional Biographies at Peru, Illinois)

WHITE, MARSH, ANDERSON, MARTIN, VICKERS, DEOBLER & GOODE

Established in 1966

511 EAST ETNA ROAD
OTTAWA, ILLINOIS 61350
Telephone: 815-434-2000
Fax: 815-434-0564
Email: wmavd@aol.com
URL: http://www.wmavd.com

Earlville, Illinois Office: 201 S. Ottawa Street. Telephone: 815-246-8121.

General Civil and Trial Practice, Automobile Accidents, Wrongful Death, Personal Injury, Workers Compensation, Insurance Defense, Probate, Estate Planning, Wills and Trusts, Real Estate, Zoning Law, Municipal Law, Corporate Law, Banking, Commercial, Criminal and Appellate Practice.

FIRM PROFILE: The firm was founded by Robert E. White in 1966 and is the successor to Anderson and Anderson established by Thomas M. Anderson, Sr. in 1937. Serving clients for over 50 years throughout LaSalle, DeKalb, Kendall and Grundy Counties, the firm has a general practice with lawyers who focus in certain areas of law. The firm is a member of the Ottawa Chamber of Commerce.

THOMAS M. ANDERSON, JR. (1934-1988)
THOMAS M. ANDERSON, SR. (1904-1989)

MEMBERS OF FIRM

ROBERT E. WHITE (1933-2004). ***REPORTED CASES:*** Talty v. Talty, 166 Ill.2nd 232.

ALAN B. MARSH, born Chicago, Illinois, August 3, 1939; admitted to bar, 1966, Illinois; 1982, U.S. Supreme Court and U.S. District Court, Northern District of Illinois including Trial Bar. *Education:* Knox College (A.B., 1961); University of Illinois; John Marshall Law School (J.D., 1965) and The Lawyers Institute. Board Member, Community Hospital of Ottawa, 1992-1998. *Member:* Chicago, La Salle County and Illinois State Bar Associations; Illinois Trial Lawyer's Association (Member, Amicus Curiae Committee, 1982); Appellate Lawyers Association of Illinois. ***REPORTED CASES:*** Farmers State Bank of Somonauk v. National Bank of Earlville, 230 Ill. App.3d 881; Board of Ed. of Serena Community Unit School Dist. No. 2, LaSalle County v. Regional Bd. of School Trustees of LaSalle County, 85 Ill.App. 3d 394. ***PRACTICE AREAS:*** Commercial Litigation; Probate; Trusts; Real Estate.

PAUL V. MARTIN, born Ottawa, Illinois, September 17, 1943; admitted to bar, 1973, Illinois. *Education:* Northern Illinois University (B.S., 1967); John Marshall Law School (J.D., 1973). Special Assistant Illinois Attorney General, 1983-1995. Village Attorney: Sheridan, Illinois, 1988-1996; Naplate, Illinois, 1997—. Township Attorney: Mission, Meriden, Fall River, Serena, Manlius, 1997—. *Member:* LaSalle County and Illinois State Bar Associations; Defense Research Institute; Illinois Defense Trial Counsel. ***PRACTICE AREAS:*** Trial Practice; Appellate Practice; Real Estate; Government; Zoning Law; Insurance; Probate; Estate Planning. ***Email:*** mart-law@udnet.net

JOHN F. VICKERS, born Chicago, Illinois, June 14, 1947; admitted to bar, 1978, Illinois and U.S. District Court, Northern District of Illinois. *Education:* University of Dayton (B.A., 1969); Loyola University (J.D., 1978). Instructor, Business Law, Illinois Valley Community College, 1982-1988. *Member:* LaSalle County and Illinois State Bar Associations. [1st Lieut., U.S. Army, 1969-1971]. ***PRACTICE AREAS:*** Divorce; Collections; Insurance; Government; Negligence; Criminal Law; Personal Injury; Workers Compensation. ***Email:*** wmavd@aol.com

ERIC B. DEOBLER, born East Peoria, Illinois, September 24, 1945; admitted to bar, 1972, Illinois; 1973, U.S. District Court, Eastern and Central Districts of Illinois; 1990, U.S. District Court, Northern District of Illinois. *Education:* University of Illinois (B.A., 1967; J.D., 1972). *Member:* LaSalle County and Illinois State Bar Associations. ***REPORTED CASES:*** City of Marseilles v. Radke, 287 Ill.App.3d 757, 679 N.E.2d 125, 223 Ill.Dec. 181 (Ill.Ap.3 Dist., Apr 23, 1997, No. 3-96-0187); Paukovitz v. Imperial Homes, Inc., 271 Ill.App.3d 1037, 649 N.E.2d 473, 208 Ill.Dec. 417, Ill.App.3 Dist., Apr 06, 1995, No. 3-94-0715; Osborne v. Sprowls, 83 Ill.App.3d 968, 404 N.E.2d 1065, 39 Ill.Dec. 474, Ill. App.3 Dist., May 07, 1980, affm'd 84 Ill.2d 390, 419 N.E.2d 913, 50 Ill.Dec. 645, Ill., March 31, 1981, No. 79-507; Mid-City Architectural Iron Co. v. Industrial Commission, 83 Ill.2d 34, 413 N.E.2d 1248, 46 Ill.Dec. 135, Ill. Dec. 01, 1980; No. 53400; Lee v. Industrial Commission, 82 Ill.2d 496, 413 N.E.2d 425, 45 Ill. Dec. 947, Ill., Nov. 18, 1980; Rutgens distrubutors, Inc. v. U.S. Fidelity and Guaranty Co., 94 Ill.App.3d 753, 419 N.E.2d 59, Ill.Dec. 192, Ill.App.3 dist., Mar 27, 1981, No. 80-235. ***PRACTICE AREAS:*** Corporate Law; Real Estate Law; Tax Law; Construction Contracts; Probate; Litigation; Appellate Practice. ***Email:*** wmavd@aol.com

MARK E. ANDERSON, born Sandwich, Illinois, March 1, 1963; admitted to bar, 1994, Illinois and U.S. District Court, Northern District of Illinois. *Education:* Aurora University (B.A., 1985); John Marshall Law School (J.D., 1994). *Member:* LaSalle County and Illinois State Bar Associations. ***PRACTICE AREAS:*** General Litigation; Negligence; Family; Collections; Criminal Law; Real Estate. ***Email:*** wmavd@aol.com

GINA E. GOODE, born Ottawa, Illinois, May 4, 1967; admitted to bar, 1996, Illinois and U.S. District Court, Northern District of Illinois. *Education:* College of St. Francis (B.A., 1990); John Marshall Law School (J.D., 1996). *Member:* LaSalle County Bar Association; Illinois State Bar Association; American Bar Association; Business and Professional Women's Club; Starved Rock Kennel Club. ***PRACTICE AREAS:*** Family Law; Real Estate; Equine Law; Litigation. ***Email:*** wmavd@aol.com

REPRESENTATIVE CLIENTS: First National Bank of Grand Ridge, IL; National Bank of Earlville, Earlville, IL; Housing Authority LaSalle County; City of Leland; Rutland School District #230; Reading and Leland Fire Protection District; Allstate Ins.; Constitutional Casualty; Capital Indemnity; State Farm Auto; LaSalle County Farm Supply Corp.; Rockford Mutual Insurance Co.; Utica Mutual Insurance Co.; Countryside Development; CNA Holdings, Inc.; Golden Rule Lumber Co.
LOCAL COUNSEL FOR: Hyatt Legal Services; Castle Bank, N.A.
REFERENCES: National Bank of Earlville; First National Bank of Grand Ridge, Illinois; First National Bank of Ottawa; UnionBank, Ottawa, Illinois.

(This Listing Continued)

ADLER LAW OFFICES, LTD.

PALATINE, ILLINOIS

(See Arlington Heights)

Personal Injury, Automobile Accidents, Medical Malpractice, Products Liability, Wrongful Death.

ANGELINA & PALMER, P.C.

PALATINE, ILLINOIS

(See Inverness)

Family Law, including Divorce, Child Support, Child Custody, Alimony/Maintenance, Division of Property and Debt, Parentage, Grandparents' Rights, Visitation, Post Decree/Post Divorce Disputes, Separation, Uncontested Divorce, Divorce Settlements. Commercial Real Estate and Residential Real Estate Transactions, including Contract Drafting and Negotiation, Real Estate Closings, Real Estate and Construction Litigation, Zoning, Commercial and Residential Landlord/Tenant, Evictions, Commercial Lease Negotiation and Drafting. Business Law, including Formation of Corporations, Limited Liability Companies (LLC), and Limited Liability Partnerships (LLP). Advice for Business Legal Problems and Business Litigation. Employment Law, Executive Employment Agreements, Buy-Sell Agreements, Operating Agreements, Partnership Agreements, Asset Sales, Sales of Business.Estate Planning, including Wills, Trusts, Power of Attorney, Health Care Power of Attorney, Living Will, Special Needs Trust, Tax Avoidance Trust, Irrevocable Trust, Codicil, Probate.Criminal Law, including Criminal Defense, Felony, including Unlawful Use of Weapons, Battery, Theft, Burglary, Assault, DUI, Driving Under the Influence, Drug Possession, Drug Manufacture, Misdemeanor, Traffic, Ordinance Violation. Personal Injury for Serious Injuries and Wrongful Death.

FAVARO & GORMAN, LTD.

835 STERLING AVENUE, SUITE 100
PALATINE, ILLINOIS 60067
Telephone: 847-934-0060
Fax: 847-934-6899
URL: http://www.favarogorman.com

Crystal Lake, Illinois Office: 9510 Turnberry Trail, 60014. Telephone: 815-477-1110. Fax: 815-477-1165.

(This Listing Continued)

FAVARO & GORMAN, LTD., Palatine—Continued

Employment Law, Civil Litigation, Business Law, Commercial Litigation.

DENNIS R. FAVARO, born Kankakee, Illinois, February 18, 1961; admitted to bar, 1986, Illinois; 1987, U.S. District Court, Northern District of Illinois, including Trial Bar; 1987, U.S. Court of Appeals, Seventh Circuit. *Education:* Illinois Wesleyan University (B.A., 1983); Valparaiso University (J.D., 1986). *Member:* Northwest Suburban Bar Association (Co-Founder and Past Chair, Employment Law Committee; Treasurer, Vice President, Executive Vice President and President); McHenry County Bar Association (Past Chair, Employment Law Committee); National Employment Lawyers Association. ***PRACTICE AREAS:*** Employment Law; Discrimination Law; Sexual Harassment; Retaliatory Discharge; Whistleblower Litigation; Wrongful Termination; Civil Litigation. ***Email:*** Dfavaro@fbgltd.com

PATRICK J. GORMAN, born Aurora, Illinois, August 5, 1958; admitted to bar, 1983, Illinois and U.S. District Court, Northern District of Illinois including Trial Bar; 1984, U.S. Court of Appeals for the Seventh Circuit; 1998, U.S. District Court, District of Colorado; 1999, Colorado; 2000, U.S. District Court, Central District of Illinois. *Education:* St. John's University (B.A., 1979); Loyola University (J.D., 1983). *Member:* Northwest Suburban Bar Association (Member, Employment Law Committee). (Also at Broomfield, Colorado Office). ***PRACTICE AREAS:*** Trial Practice; Covenants Not To Compete; Trade Secrets; Employment Law; Business Law. ***Email:*** Pgorman@fbgltd.com

SUSAN R. BAUER, born Chicago, Illinois, October 24, 1957; admitted to bar, 1985, Illinois. *Education:* Northern Illinois University (B.A., 1981); John Marshall Law School (J.D., 1985). Executive Comments Editor and Associate Lead Articles Editor, John Marshall Law Review, 1984-1985. *Member:* Chicago, Illinois State and American Bar Associations; National Employment Lawyers Association. ***PRACTICE AREAS:*** Employment Law; Sexual Harassment; Sex Discrimination; Race Discrimination; Appellate Practice. ***Email:*** Sbauer@fbgltd.com

ANDREW H. HABER, born Chicago, Illinois, May 6, 1954; admitted to bar, 1988, Illinois; 1989, U.S. District Court, Northern District of Illinois including Trial Bar and U.S. Court of Appeals, Seventh Circuit. *Education:* Millikin University (B.M., 1976); University of Illinois (M.B.A., 1988; J.D., 1988). *Member:* Northwest Suburban (Association Attorney, 2004—; Co-Chair, Employment Law Committee, 2001—), Chicago and Illinois State Bar Associations. ***PRACTICE AREAS:*** Employment Law; Age Discrimination; Race Discrimination; Sex Discrimination; ERISA Litigation; Shareholder Agreements. ***Email:*** Pjochum@fbgltd.com

---

PATRICIA L. JOCHUM, born Elgin, Illinois, April 22, 1965; admitted to bar, 1991, Illinois and U.S. District Court, Northern District of Illinois; 2002, U.S. Court of Appeals, Seventh Circuit. *Education:* University of Illinois (B.A., 1989); John Marshall Law School (J.D., 1991). *Member:* Northwest Suburban Bar Association (Member, Employment Law Committee). ***PRACTICE AREAS:*** Employment Law; Employment Discrimination; Sexual Harassment; Americans with Disabilities Act; Family and Medical Leave Act; Wrongful Death; Defamation. ***Email:*** Pjochum@fbgltd.com

RODNEY E. DRISCOLL, born Holton, Kansas, April 6, 1965; admitted to bar, 1997, Illinois and U.S. District Court, Northern District of Illinois. *Education:* Kansas State University (B.S., magna cum laude; B.S.I.E., magna cum laude, 1988); John Marshall Law School (J.D., 1997; LL.M., Employee Benefits, with honors, 2002). Phi Kappa Phi; Tau Beta Pi. *Member:* Illinois State (Member, Employee Benefits Section Council) and Northwest Suburban (Member, Employment Law Committee) Bar Associations. ***PRACTICE AREAS:*** ERISA; Executive Compensation; Retirement Benefit Plans; Pension and Profit Sharing Plans; Health Benefits; Employment Agreements; Unemployment Compensation.

NEIL H. GOOD

800 E. NORTHWEST HIGHWAY, SUITE 814
PALATINE, ILLINOIS 60074
Telephone: 847-577-4476
Fax: 847-934-7292
Email: neil@neilgood.com
URL: http://www.neilgoodlawfirm.com

Chicago, Illinois Office: 30 N. La Salle, Suite 3400, 60602. Telephone: 312-629-1212.

Social Security Disability, Personal Injury, Medical Malpractice, Plaintiffs Personal Injury.

NEIL H. GOOD, born Chicago, Illinois, August 27, 1960; admitted to bar, 1986, Illinois; 1988, U.S. Court of Appeals, Seventh Circuit and U.S. District Court, Northern District of Illinois. *Education:* Northern Illinois University (B.S., Finance, 1982); Chicago-Kent College of Law, Illinois Institute of Technology (J.D., 1985). Chairman, Civil Litigation Committee. Author: Northwest Suburban Bar Association, Newsletter: "Pleading & Practice - The Verified Complaint," October, 1993; "When a Dog's Bite is Worse Than It's Bark," November, 1993; "Plaintiff's Recovery Under the Structural Work Act," December, 1993; "Personal Injuries and the Minor Child," January, 1994. Lecturer, Real Estate Contracts, 1989 and Moderator, Deposition Seminar, 1994, Northwest Suburban Bar Association. Chairman, Board of Directors, Listening Angels of McHenry County, CASA, 1999. *Member:* Chicago, Illinois State and American Bar Associations; The Volunteer Center (Member, Board of Directors); Northwestern Suburban Bar Association (Member: Board of Governors, 1998; Real Estate Committee, 1988-1991; Real Estate Contract Committee, *1988-1990; Civil Litigation Committee, 1992— Civil Litigation Chairman, 1993-1994,* 1997-1998; Judicial Screening Committee, 1998—); NOSSCAR; Association of Trial Lawyers of America; Illinois Trial Lawyers Association; Pro-Bono Advocates; Volunteer Association of NW Chicago (Member, Board of Directors). ***PRACTICE AREAS:*** Social Security Disability; Personal Injury; Medical Malpractice; Plaintiffs Personal Injury.

THE LAW OFFICES OF ROBERTA K. KANABAY

PALATINE, ILLINOIS

(See Schaumburg)

Family, Divorce, Child Custody, Child Support, Criminal, Driving While Intoxicated, Traffic and Commercial Litigation.

KLEST LAW FIRM

PALATINE, ILLINOIS

(See Schaumburg)

Personal Injury, Medical Malpractice, Products Liability, Legal Malpractice, Construction Accidents, Airplane Crash Litigation, Insurance Bad Faith, Automobile Accidents, Motorcycle Accidents, Birth Trauma, Sexual Abuse, Child Abuse and Neglect, Slip and Fall, Wrongful Death, Dog Bites, Railroad Accidents and Injuries, Automobile Products, Liability and Drug and Medical Device Litigation, Trial Practice.

PINDERSKI & PINDERSKI, LTD.

Established in 1906
115 WEST COLFAX
PALATINE, ILLINOIS 60067-5086
Telephone: 847-358-5220
FAX: 847-358-4506
Email: PinderLaw@aol.com
URL: http://www.pinderski.com

General Practice. Litigation. Corporate and Business Transactions, Securities, Estate Planning, Probate, Real Estate Development, Bankruptcy, Intellectual Property, Immigration, Family Law.

LOUIS PINDERSKI (1883-1943)

JEROME W. PINDERSKI (1925-1993)

PAUL C. PINDERSKI, born Chicago, Illinois, December 12, 1959; admitted to bar, 1984, Illinois. *Education:* Eastern Illinois University (B.A., 1980); John Marshall Law School (J.D., 1983). *Member:* International Trademark Association. ***PRACTICE AREAS:*** Intellectual Property; Litigation; Real Estate; Corporate Law. ***Email:*** paul@pinderski.com

JEROME W. PINDERSKI, JR., admitted to bar, 1981, Illinois and U.S. District Court, Northern District of Illinois; 1990, District of Columbia, U.S. Court of Appeals, Seventh Circuit, U.S. Court of International Trade and U.S. Supreme Court. *Education:* Marquette University (B.A., 1978); Loyola University (J.D., 1981). Listed in: Who's Who in America; Who's Who in American Law. *Member:* Illinois State and American Bar Associations; International Bar Association (London). ***PRACTICE AREAS:*** Corporate Law; Business Law; Estate Planning Law; Litigation; Real Estate Development; Securities; Family Law. ***Email:*** jerome@pinderski.com

POLLY J. PINDERSKI, born Chicago, Illinois, July 6, 1967; admitted to bar, 1992, Illinois and U.S. District Court, Northern District of Illinois. *Education:* University of Illinois (B.A., 1989); DePaul University (J.D., 1992). Member, Chicago Inn of Court. Recipient, American Jurisprudence Award for Trial Advocacy; John Powers Crowley Scholarship for Excellence in Trial Advocacy. ***PRACTICE AREAS:*** General Civil Practice. ***Email:*** polly@pinderski.com

REPRESENTATIVE CLIENTS: Clean Air Engineering; Total Marketing Associates; Royal American Bank; IL & P Enterprises; Harris Bank Palatine, N.A.
REFERENCES: Royal American Bank; Harris Bank Palatine, N.A.

LINDA K. SCHNEIDER AND ASSOCIATES

1627 COLONIAL PARKWAY, SUITE 204
PALATINE, ILLINOIS 60067
Telephone: 847-359-9202
Fax: 847-359-9605
URL: http://www.lindakschneider.com

Adoption, Child Support, Custody and Visitation, Divorce, Family Law.

LINDA K. SCHNEIDER, born Pittsburgh, Pennsylvania, July 18, 1948; admitted to bar, 1987, Illinois. *Education:* Millersville State College (B.S., 1970); Northeastern Illinois University (M.A., 1976); ITT/Chicago-Kent College of Law (J.D., 1987). *Member:* Chicago (Member, Matrimonial Committee, 1989), Illinois State and American Bar Associations. ***PRACTICE AREAS:*** Matrimonial.

LAW OFFICES OF ROGER W. STELK

PALATINE, ILLINOIS

(See Arlington Heights)

Family Law, Divorce, Real Estate, Buying and Selling a Home, Civil Litigation.

THOMAS YOUNG LAW FIRM

350 N. ERIC DRIVE
PALATINE, ILLINOIS 60067
Telephone: 847-359-8999
Fax: 847-359-9234
Email: thomascyou@aol.com
URL: http://www.thomasyounglaw.com

Real Estate, Civil Practice.

(This Listing Continued)

THOMAS C. YOUNG, born Chicago, Illinois, May 22, 1943; admitted to bar, 1979, Illinois, U.S. Court of Appeals, 7th Circuit and U.S. District Court, Northern District of Illinois. *Education:* DePaul University (B.A., 1969); Northern Illinois University Law School (J.D., 1979). *Member:* American Bar Association; American Trial Lawyers Association.

LAW OFFICE OF JAMES J. SIWEK

PALOS HEIGHTS, ILLINOIS

(See Worth)

Bankruptcy - Chapters 7 and 13, Consumer Fraud, Criminal Law, Misdemeanors and Felonies, Driving While Intoxicated, Drug Crimes, Juvenile Law, Parole and Probation, Family Law, Adoptions, Child Custody, Child Support, Divorce, Domestic Violence, Visitation Rights, General Practice, Real Estate, Buying or Selling a Home, Construction, Landlord and Tenant, Trusts and Estates, Land Trusts, Living Trusts, Guardianships, Powers of Attorney, Wills and Probate.

LAW OFFICE OF JAMES J. SIWEK

PALOS HILLS, ILLINOIS

(See Worth)

Bankruptcy - Chapters 7 and 13, Consumer Fraud, Criminal Law, Misdemeanors and Felonies, Driving While Intoxicated, Drug Crimes, Juvenile Law, Parole and Probation, Family Law, Adoptions, Child Custody, Child Support, Divorce, Domestic Violence, Visitation Rights, General Practice, Real Estate, Buying or Selling a Home, Construction, Landlord and Tenant, Trusts and Estates, Land Trusts, Living Trusts, Guardianships, Powers of Attorney, Wills and Probate.

MICHAEL D. WALSH PC

10001 SOUTH ROBERTS ROAD
PALOS HILLS, ILLINOIS 60465
Telephone: 708-599-7500
Email: mdwalsh53@netscape.net
URL: http://www.lawyers.com/michaelwalshlawfirm

Family Law, Divorce, Personal Injury, Workers Compensation, Real Estate, Child Custody, Child Support, Premarital Agreements, Spousal Support, Visitation Rights, Automobile Accidents, Medical Malpractice, Dog Bites, Head and Spinal Injuries, Nursing Home Litigation, Railroad Accidents, Sexual Abuse, Slip and Fall, Truck Accidents, Wrongful Death, Traffic Violations, Driving While Intoxicated, Commercial Leasing, Zoning and Land Use, Eminent Domain, Union Contractor Benefit Contributions.

MICHAEL D. WALSH, born 1953; admitted to bar, 1977, Illinois and U.S. District Court, Northern District of Illinois. *Education:* Loyola University, Chicago (B.A., 1976); DePaul University (J.D., 1977). *Member:* Illinois Trial Lawyers Association; Southwestern Bar Association. ***Email:*** mdwalsh53@netscape.net

THERESA M. MALYSA

PALOS PARK, ILLINOIS

(See Orland Park)

Family Law, Divorce, Tax Considerations, Retirement Benefits, Child Custody, Parenting Time, Visitation, Child Support, Domestic Violence, Paternity, Matrimonial Litigation, Premarital Agreements.

ASHER, SMITH & ISAF

236 WEST COURT STREET
P.O. BOX 340
PARIS, ILLINOIS 61944-0340
Telephone: 217-465-6444
Fax: 217-463-2486
URL: http://www.asilaw.net

General Practice in all Courts. Trials and Probate Law. Corporation, Insurance and Commercial Banking Law and Workers Compensation Law, Personal Injury and Negligence Litigation. Divorce, Child Custody, Child Support.

FIRM PROFILE: Asher, Smith & Isaf was founded by Mr. Ward E. Dillavou in 1932. Serving clients in Central and Southern Illinois, Asher, Smith & Isaf is a full service firm with partners concentrating in specific areas of law.

MEMBERS OF FIRM

WARD E. DILLAVOU (1909-1987)

JACK O'HAIR ASHER, born Paris, Illinois, May 21, 1930; admitted to bar, 1957, Louisiana; 1959, Alaska; 1967, Illinois. *Education:* University of Illinois (B.S., 1954); Tulane University of Louisiana (J.D., 1957). District Attorney, State of Alaska, 1st Judicial District, 1960-1967. Member, 1973-1983 and Chairman, 1981-1983, Illinois Committee on Professional Ethics. Member, Professional Inquiry and Hearing Panels, 1984—. Illinois Attorney Registration and Disciplinary Commission. *Member:* Edgar County, Alaska, Louisiana State and Illinois State Bar Associations. ***PRACTICE AREAS:*** Banking; Real Estate Law; Probate; Corporate Law. ***Email:*** joa@aol.com

S. CRAIG SMITH, born Lexington, Kentucky, May 3, 1949; admitted to bar, 1976, Illinois. *Education:* University of Alabama (B.S., 1971); Cumberland School of Law of Samford University (J.D., 1975). Phi Delta Phi. Lecturer: Illinois Institute of Continuing Legal Education, 1988, 1989, 1990, 1994, 1996 and 1998, Illinois Workers' Compensation

(This Listing Continued)

(Third Party Practice & Subrogation); University of Illinois at Chicago 1990, 1991 and 1992, Litigation Preparation: The Physician on the witness stand; Rehabilitation Institute of Chicago, 1989, 1990-1994. Professional Education System, 1988, Illinois Workers Compensation. Public Defender for Edgar and Clark Counties, 1976-1979. *Member:* Edgar County, Illinois State (Assembly Member, 1984-1998; Member, Workers' Compensation Committee, 1990-1992) and American (First Vice-President, Law Student Division, 1974-1975) Bar Associations; Illinois Trial Lawyers Association (Member, Committee on Workmen's Compensation, 1980-1986); Illinois Association of Defense Trial Lawyers; The Association of Trial Lawyers of America. ***PRACTICE AREAS:*** Workers Compensation Law; Civil Litigation. ***Email:*** CSmith@tigerpaw.com

MARK R. ISAF, born Cortland, New York, May 20, 1963; admitted to bar, 1991, Illinois; 1992, U.S. District Court, Central District of Illinois. *Education:* Hamilton College (B.A., 1985); Northern Illinois University at DeKalb (J.D., 1991). Special Assistant Attorney General, Land Condemnation, 2000—. Chairman, Illinois Workers Compensation Advisory Board, 1998—. *Member:* Edgar County, Illinois State and American Bar Associations; Illinois Trial Lawyers Association (Member, Workers Compensation Committee, 1997—); Illinois Association of Defense Trial Counsel. ***PRACTICE AREAS:*** Workers Compensation Law; Civil Litigation; Family Law; Eminent Domain. ***Email:*** MIsaf@tigerpaw.com

OF COUNSEL

RALPH S. PEARMAN, born Paris, Illinois, August 7, 1929; admitted to bar, 1953, Illinois. *Education:* University of Illinois (B.S., 1951; J.D., 1953). State Attorney, Edgar County, Illinois, 1960-1964. Circuit Judge, Fifth Judicial Circuit, 1971-1998. Chief Judge, 1976-1996. [1st Lt., U.S. Army, 1953-1955]. ***PRACTICE AREAS:*** Personal Injury; Estate Planning; Probate; Real Estate.

REPRESENTATIVE CLIENTS: Kansas State Bank; Edgar County Bank & Trust Co., Paris, Illinois; Citizens National Bank of Paris; The Morgan Co.; Illinois Insurance Co.; Liberty Mutual Insurance Co.; American States Insurance Co.; Zurich Insurance Co.; Allstate Insurance Co.; Continental Cos.; Crawford & Co.; Trailmobile, Inc.; Neal Machinery Erectors, Inc., Paris; First National Bank of Georgetown; Gallagher Bassett; CNA; American Adjusting Co.; Indiana Insurance; CIGNA Insurance.

THE BRAINARD LAW OFFICES

PARIS, ILLINOIS

(See Charleston)

General Practice. Insurance Defense, Personal Injury, Products Liability, Probate, Trusts, Real Estate, Taxation, Municipal, Family and Health Law. Trials in all State and Federal Courts.

FRUIN, GARST & KASH

Established in 1941
129 NORTH CENTRAL AVENUE
PARIS, ILLINOIS 61944-1783
Telephone: 217-465-4196
Fax: 217-466-1213
Email: fgk@comwares.net
URL: http://www.fruingarstkash.com

General Practice, Probate and Estates, Trusts, Taxation, Elder and Family Law, Corporations, Criminal Law, Trials, DWI, Drug Crimes, Elder Abuse, Bankruptcy, Municipal, Drainage, Adoption, Divorce, Custody, Child Support, Visitation.

FIRM PROFILE: Roger J. Fruin and Paul Lauher founded the firm in 1941. The present lawyers have been together since 1987. Fruin Garst & Kash serves clients in Edgar, Vermilion, Clark, Coles and Douglas Counties, and has a general practice with a focus on Probate, Estate Planning, Real Estate and Domestic Relations.

MEMBERS OF FIRM

STEVEN L. GARST, born Normal, Illinois, December 21, 1949; admitted to bar, 1974, Illinois; 1978, U.S. District Court of Illinois, Central and Southern District of Illinois. *Education:* Illinois State University (B.A., 1971); University of Illinois (J.D., 1974). Phi Delta Phi. Public Defender, Edgar County and Clark County, 1981-1988. *Member:* Edgar County and Illinois State Bar Associations. ***PRACTICE AREAS:*** Real Estate; Elder Law; Estate Planning Law.

RICHARD M. KASH, JR., born Fort Monmouth, New Jersey, January 29, 1953; admitted to bar, 1978, Illinois; 1982, U.S. District Court, Central and Southern Districts of Illinois. *Education:* University of Illinois (B.S., 1975; J.D., 1978). Assistant State's Attorney, Edgar & Clark Counties, 1980-1986. Senior Law Clerk, Presiding Justice at 4th Appellate District of Illinois, 1986-1991. Public Defender, Edgar and Clark Counties, 1991-1997. *Member:* Edgar County (President, 1984), Clark County and Illinois State Bar Associations. ***PRACTICE AREAS:*** General Litigation; Criminal Defense Law; Criminal Appeals; Civil Appeals; Family Law; Bankruptcy Law; Commercial Law.

ROGER J. FRUIN (1915-2002)

REPRESENTATIVE CLIENTS: Mooney Motors, Inc.; Mike Mooney, Inc.; Tim Mooney, Inc.; EnerStar Power Corp.; City Attorneys, City of Paris; Englum Grain Co.; Human Resources Center of Edgar & Clark Counties, Clark-Edgar Water District.
REFERENCES: Edgar County Bank & Trust Co.; The Citizens National Bank of Paris; State Bank of Chrisman; First National Bank of Chrisman; Kansas State Bank of Kansas; First Bank & Trust, S.B., of Paris.

LAW OFFICES OF SCOTT M. ANNES

Established in 1992

2 WEST TALCOTT
PARK RIDGE, ILLINOIS 60068
Telephone: 847-292-0105
Fax: 847-292-0113
Email: smalaw@aol.com
URL: http://www.scottannesattorney.com

Commercial Litigation with focus on Small Business Law, Small Business Litigation, Family Business Law, Partnership Law, Breach of Contract, Employment Law and Wrongful Termination, Elder Law and Real Estate.

SCOTT M. ANNES, born Chicago, Illinois, December 9, 1963; admitted to bar, 1991, Illinois. *Education:* University of Illinois (B.S., 1986); De Paul University (J.D., 1990). *Member:* Chicago, Illinois State and American Bar Associations. ***PRACTICE AREAS:*** Commercial Litigation.

JOHN F. BRENNAN, P.C.

422 N. NORTHWEST HIGHWAY, SUITE B2
PARK RIDGE, ILLINOIS 60068-3272
Telephone: 847-292-0032
Fax: 847-292-0153
Email: jbrennanlaw@sbcglobal.net

Civil Litigation, Insurance Defense, Insurance Coverage, First Property, Reinsurance, Subrogation.

JOHN F. BRENNAN, born Shenandoah, Pennsylvania, May 5, 1947; admitted to bar, 1973, Illinois; 1980, Pennsylvania; U.S. District Court, Central and Northern Districts of Illinois including Trial Bar. *Education:* St. Joseph's University (B.S., 1969); Northwestern University School of Law (J.D., 1973). *Member:* Chicago, Illinois State and American (Member, Tort and Insurance Practice Section) Bar Associations; Illinois Trial Lawyer's Association; International Association of Arson Investigators. ***Email:*** jbrennanlaw@sbcglobal.net

THE LAW OFFICES OF MARC L. BROWN

422 N. NORTHWEST HIGHWAY
PARK RIDGE, ILLINOIS 60068
Telephone: 847-825-1900
Fax: 847-825-1979
Email: marclbrown@sbcglobal.net

Elder Law, Real Estate, Trusts and Estates, Wills, Probate, Living Trusts, Guardianship, Nursing Home Abuse and Neglect, Health Care.

MARC L. BROWN, born Princeton, Illinois, February 7, 1952; admitted to bar, 1986, Illinois; 1995, Illinois and U.S. District Court, Northern District of Illinois. *Education:* Illinois Wesleyan University (B.S., with honors, 1974); Chicago-Kent College of Law (J.D., 1986); DePaul University (LL.M., Taxation, 1991). Certified Public Accountant, Illinois, 1979. *Member:* Chicago, Northwest Suburban, Illinois State and American Bar Associations. Fellow, National Academy of Elder Law Attorneys. ***PRACTICE AREAS:*** Elder Law; Real Estate; Trusts and Estates; Wills; Probate; Living Trusts; Guardianship; Nursing Home Abuse and Neglect; Health Care.

CUTLER & ASSOCIATES, LTD.

PARK RIDGE, ILLINOIS

(See Skokie)

Bankruptcy, Consumer Bankruptcy, Bankruptcy Chapter 7, Foreclosures, Small Business, Buying and Selling of Businesses, Family Business, Limited Liability, Partnership, Corporate, Contract, Breach of Contract, General Practice, Debtor and Creditor, Collections, Creditors, Rights and Civil Litigation.

DI FRANCO & ASSOCIATES, P.C.

617 DEVON AVENUE
PARK RIDGE, ILLINOIS 60068
Telephone: 847-825-7744
Fax: 847-825-7746
Email: difrancolaw@aol.com
URL: http://www.difrancolaw.com

Criminal Defense, Civil Litigation.

FRANK R. DI FRANCO, born Park Ridge, Illinois, July 15, 1961; admitted to bar, 1988, Illinois. *Education:* Loyola University (B.A., 1984); Chicago-Kent Law School (J.D., 1987). *Member:* Northwest Suburban Bar Association. ***REPORTED CASES:*** Bojalad v. Parliament Enterprises; S. Prado v. City of Evanston; People v. Edward Glasier; Meadors v. Borg Warner, Protective Services Corp.; Floss v. Fagiano; People v. Lisa Palomo. ***PRACTICE AREAS:*** Criminal Defense; Civil Litigation; Personal Injury; DUI/DWI; Traffic Violations. ***Email:*** difrancolaw@aol.com

LAWRENCE M. LYKOWSKI, born Chicago, Illinois; admitted to bar, 1976, Illinois. *Education:* University of Colorado at Boulder (B.A., 1972); Chicago-Kent College of Law (J.D., 1976). Former, Cook County Assistant State's Attorney, 25 years; Personally Prosecuted 45 Felony Jury Trials; Former Trial Supervisor and NITA Instructor. *Member:* Northwest Suburban (Member, Criminal Law Committee, 2000-2005) Bar Association; State of Illinois Capital Litigation Trial Bar. ***PRACTICE AREAS:*** Criminal Defense; Driving While Intoxicated; Personal Injury Litigation.

KATRINA M. MAGLAYA, born Chicago, Illinois, May 18, 1975; admitted to bar, 2001, Illinois. *Education:* DePaul University (B.A., 1997; J.D., 2000). ***PRACTICE AREAS:*** Real Estate; Civil Litigation; Family Law.

JOHN A. LEWERT, born 1977; admitted to bar, 2002, Illinois. *Education:* Illinois Wesleyan University (B.A., 1999); DePaul University (J.D., 2002). ***PRACTICE AREAS:*** Civil Litigation; Personal Injury; Family Law; Probate.

BRYAN L. BLACK, born May 10, 1975; admitted to bar, 2000, Illinois. *Education:* University of St. Francis (B.B.A., 1997); Washburn University of Topeka (J.D., 2000). *Member:* DuPage County and Will County Bar Associations. ***PRACTICE AREAS:*** Criminal Law; Family Law.

DI MONTE & LIZAK

216 WEST HIGGINS ROAD
PARK RIDGE, ILLINOIS 60068
Telephone: 847-698-9600
Fax: 847-698-9623
Email: firm@dimonteandlizak.com

Construction and Real Estate Development (Zoning, Mechanics' Lien, etc.), Banking, Bankruptcy and Insolvency, Corporate Law, Estate Planning, Probate and Trust Litigation, Employment Law, Health Care Law, Civil Litigation Trials and Appeals.

FIRM PROFILE: DiMonte & Lizak is a Chicago suburban law firm which practices in various areas of law and seeks to meet the needs of its diverse clientele. We specialize in the needs of the construction industry and real estate developers and emphasize land use planning, zoning, and environmental law; construction and joint venture contracts; condominium developments and disputes; real estate loans and loan documentation; real estate sales; commercial and mechanics' lien collection law. In addition, we engage in all aspects of employment law, banking, bankruptcy and insolvency. Transactional matters relating to estate planning, probate and corporate work, particular mergers, acquisitions and sales, are a large part of our practice. Each of our partners has a specialized field of practice and work together to provide our clients with a full-service firm to attend to all of their legal needs. Our office is on the "L" line to Downtown within 10 minutes of O'Hare Field. Our litigators appear regularly in the various Trial and Appellate Courts of Cook County, as well as Lake, Du Page, McHenry and Kane Counties.

MEMBERS OF FIRM

MARGHERITA M. ALBARELLO, born Chicago, Illinois, August 23, 1957; admitted to bar, 1984, Illinois. *Education:* University of Illinois-Urbana (B.S., 1979); IIT/Chicago-Kent College of Law (J.D., with high honors, 1984). *Member:* National Employment Lawyers Association. ***PRACTICE AREAS:*** Employment Law; Immigration Law; Commercial Law. ***Email:*** malbarello@dimonteandlizak.com

DAVID T. ARENA, born East Orange, New Jersey, March 5, 1968; admitted to bar, 1996, Illinois. *Education:* Loyola University (B.A., 1993); Cleveland Marshall College of Law (J.D., cum laude, 1996). ***PRACTICE AREAS:*** Commercial Litigation; Construction Litigation; Civil Litigation. ***Email:*** darena@dimonteandlizak.com

ABRAHAM E. BRUSTEIN, born Bridgeport, Connecticut, January 2, 1950; admitted to bar, 1976, Illinois and U.S. District Court, Northern District of Illinois including Trial Bar; 1977, U.S. Court of Appeals, Seventh Circuit; 1984, U.S. Supreme Court. *Education:* Northwestern University (B.A., 1971); DePaul University (J.D., 1976). ***PRACTICE AREAS:*** Debtor and Creditor; Commercial Litigation; Business Transactions.

EUGENE A. DI MONTE, born Chicago, Illinois, September 2, 1936; admitted to bar, 1961, Illinois and U.S. District Court, Northern District of Illinois. *Education:* DePaul University (B.S.C., 1958; J.D., 1961). Director, Barrington Area Development Council, 1970-1980. Plan Commission Member, Village of South Barrington, 1973 and 1974. *Member:* Chicago and Illinois State Bar Associations; Justinian Society of Lawyers. ***REPORTED CASES:*** Hines Lumber Co. v. Dell Corp., 49 Ill. App. 3d 873, 7 Ill. Dec. 207 Ill. Dec. 20, 364 N.E.2d 368; Goggin v. Fox Valley Const. Corp., 8 Ill. Dec. 271 Dec. 27, 365 N.E.2d 509, 48 Ill. App. 3d 103. ***PRACTICE AREAS:*** Construction Law; Real Estate; Commercial Litigation; Zoning; Corporate; Banking. ***Email:*** edimonte@dimonteandlizak.com

RICCARDO A. DI MONTE, born Oak Park, Illinois, June 11, 1960; admitted to bar, 1985, Illinois; 1986, U.S. District Court, Northern District of Illinois. *Education:* Southern Illinois University (B.S., 1982); DePaul University (J.D., 1985). Member, Justinian Society. Recipient, American Jurisprudence Award in Debtor-Creditor-Bankruptcy Law. Arbitrator, Cook County Mandatory Arbitration Program. *Member:* Chicago, Illinois State and American Bar Associations. ***REPORTED CASES:*** Fisher vs. Harris Trust, 506 N.E.2d 418, 154 Ill. App. 3d 79 (1987); Wilmette Partners vs. Hamel, 594 N.E.2d 1177 (1992). ***PRACTICE AREAS:*** Civil Trials and Appeals; Commercial Banking Law; Bankruptcy Law. ***Email:*** rdimonte@dimonteandlizak.com

PAUL A. GRECO, born Trenton, New Jersey, November 30, 1969; admitted to bar, 1995, Illinois; 1996, New Jersey; 1999, New York. *Education:* St. Lawrence University (B.A., 1992); Chicago-Kent College of Law (J.D., 1995). ***Email:*** pgreco@dimonteandlizak.com

LINSCOTT R. HANSON, born Evanston, Illinois, October 4, 1937; admitted to bar, 1961, Illinois; U.S. District Court, Northern District of Illinois. *Education:* University of Michigan (B.A., 1959; J.D., 1961). Author: "Professional Corporations," Illinois Bar Journal, November, 1970; "Committee Billing," The Audio Lawyer, ALI/ABA, 1986; "Effectively Counseling Family Owned Business," Illinois Institute of Continuing Legal Education, 1990; "Illinois Limited Liability Company System," 1994. Co-Author, "Illinois Corporation System," 6th Edition, IL Forms, Inc., 2001. Chair, Secretary of State's Committee on Business Laws. *Member:* Illinois State Bar Association (Chairman, Law Office Man-

(This Listing Continued)

agement & Technology Committee, 1978-1979; Chairman, Business Advice and Financial Planning, 1989-1990). ***PRACTICE AREAS:*** Corporation Law; Estates and Estate Planning; Limited Liability Company Law. ***Email:*** lhanson27@aol.com

CHESTER A. LIZAK, born Chicago, Illinois, September 29, 1936; admitted to bar, 1963, Illinois and U.S. District Court, Northern District of Illinois; 1964, U.S. Court of Appeals, Seventh Circuit; 1994, U.S. Supreme Court. *Education:* DePaul University (B.S., 1961; J.D., 1963). Phi Alpha Delta (President, 1962). Editor, De Paul Law Review, 1962-1963. Lecturer: Illinois State Bar Association's Seminar, 1968; on "Criminal Jury Trials," National Advocate Society's 1981 National Convention on "Civil Litigation Systems." Member, 1965— and President, 1979, Advocate Society. *Member:* Chicago (Chairman, Defense of Prisoners Committee, 1969-1970) and Illinois State Bar Associations; Illinois Trial Lawyers Association. ***REPORTED CASES:*** People v. Ellsworth Brown, 99 Ill.App.2d 281; Nandorf, Inc. v. CNA Insurance Companies, 134 Ill.App.3d 134; Harden v. Desideri, 2 Ill.App.3d 590; Geise v. Phoenix, 159 Ill.2d 50 - All cases of first impression. ***PRACTICE AREAS:*** Commercial Litigation; Insurance Coverage; Personal Injury; Appeals. ***Email:*** clizak@dimonteandlizak.com

JEFFREY S. McDONALD, born LaGrange, Illinois, September 28, 1958; admitted to bar, 1987, Illinois; U.S. Court of Appeals, 7th Circuit; U.S. Tax Court and U.S. Claims Court. *Education:* University of Notre Dame (B.S., Accounting, 1980); The John Marshall Law School (J.D., 1987); DePaul University (M.S., Taxation, 1988). Co-Author, "Illinois Corporation System," 5th Edition, Illinois Institute for Continuing Legal Education, July 1996. Certified Public Accountant, Illinois. ***PRACTICE AREAS:*** Commercial Transactions; Taxation; Estate Planning. ***Email:*** jmcdonald@dimonteandlizak.com

ROBERT S. MINETZ, born Chicago, Illinois, December 24, 1946; admitted to bar, 1973, Illinois and U.S. District Court, Northern District of Illinois. *Education:* DePaul University (B.A., 1968); University of Illinois (J.D., with honors, 1973). Order of the Coif. Author: "The Quandary Facing a Deponent Who Erred at His or Her Deposition," Illinois State Bar Journal, April 2000; "Liability for Retaliatory Discharge and Your Employee's 'Secret File'," Council on Education in Management, Personnel Law Update, 1996; "Arbitration-An Alternative to Litigation," The Business Edge, a publication of Blackman, Kallick & Bartelstein, April 1, 1990; "Does An Illinois Entrepreneur Have A Duty To Provide A Reasonably Safe Means of Ingress and Egress To Its Business Premises Or Has This Well-Established Rule of Law Become a Mere Exception?", DePaul L. Rev. 403 (Winter, 1981); "Recent Illinois Supreme Court Decisions Concerning The Authority of Home Rule Units to Control Local Environment Problems," 26 DePaul L.Rev. 306 (1977); "May a 'Wrongdoer' Recover a Deficiency Judgment, Or Is Section 9-5-7 (1) A Debtor's Exclusive Remedy?", 6 U.C.C.L.J. 344 (1974); "Zoning Ordinances Which Restrict the Definition of a Family and Constitutional Considerations," 62 Ill.B.J. 38 (1973); "An Examination of The Rule Which Forbids A Trustee to Offset His Investment Losses Against His Investment Gains," 1972 U.Ill.L.F. 784. Editor: "Court Handbook for Chicago Lawyers," Chicago Bar Association (1978). *Member:* Chicago Bar Association (Chairman, Circuit Court Committee). [Army, 1968-1970, Specialist 5]. ***REPORTED CASES:*** Schaffner v. 514 West Grant Place Condo Ass'n, 258 Ill. Dec. 580, 756 N.E.2d 854 (1st Dist. 2001); Spencer v. Riordan, 240 Ill. App. 3d 938, 181 Ill. Dec. 359, 608 N.E.2d 432 (1st Dist. 1992); Derby Meadows Util v. Inter-Continental, Camelot Homes, 202 Ill. App. 3d 345, 147 Ill. Dec. 646, 559 N.E.2d 986 (1st Dist. 1990); Robinson v. Industrial Com'n., 96 Ill. 2d 87, 70 Ill. Dec. 232, 449 N.E.2d 106 (1983); People ex rel. Fahner v. Carriage Way West, Inc., Sportsman's Country Club, 88 Ill. App. 3d 297, 43 Ill. Dec. 384, 410 N.E.2d 384 (1st Dist. 1980), rev'd 88 Ill, 2d 300, 58 Ill. Dec. 754, 430 N.E. 2d 1005 (1981). ***PRACTICE AREAS:*** Civil Litigation; Appellate Practice. ***Email:*** rminetz@dimonteandlizak.com

JANE KAMINSKI SIMERS, born Chicago, Illinois, May 26, 1954; admitted to bar, 1985, Illinois. *Education:* University of Illinois (James Scholar); Northern Illinois University (B.S., 1976); DePaul University, College of Law (J.D., with honors, 1985). *Member:* Chicago and Illinois State Bar Associations; National Academy of Elder Law Attorneys; Chicago and National Advocates Societies. ***PRACTICE AREAS:*** Estate Planning; Probate. ***Email:*** jsimers@dimonteandlizak.com

ALAN L. STEFANIAK, born Chicago, Illinois, February 9, 1947; admitted to bar, 1973, Illinois and U.S. District Court, Northern District of Illinois. *Education:* Northwestern University (B.A., with honors, 1969); University of Illinois (J.D., 1973). Author: "Conditional Rezoning in Illinois," Illinois Bar Journal, Vol. 63, No. 3, November 1974. Member, Zoning Board of Appeals, Village of Palatine, Illinois, 1976-1980. Member and Chairman, Plan Commission, Village of Kildeer, Illinois, 1985-1993. Trustee, Village of Kildeer, 1995-2001. Village President, Village of Kildeer, 2001—. *Member:* Chicago and Illinois State Bar Associations. ***REPORTED CASES:*** Chicago Title & Trust Company, Trustee, Trust No. 1091974 v. Village of Iverness, 249 Ill. Dec 82, 735 NE 2d 686 (2000); O.T. Pickell Builders Inc. v. Witowski, WL 664949 (N.D.Ill., 1998). ***PRACTICE AREAS:*** Construction Law and Construction Litigation; Zoning and Land Use Development; Real Estate Law. ***Email:*** alslawr@aol.com

ASSOCIATES

FRANCIS J. FERRARO, IV, born Arlington Heights, Illinois, August 9, 1978; admitted to bar, 2003, Illinois. *Education:* Indiana University (B.A., 1999); DePaul University (J.D., cum laude, 2003). Author: "When Athletics Engulfs Academics: A Study of the Violations Committed by the University of Minnesota Men's Basketball Program," 1 De Paul Journal of Sports Law and Contemporary Problems (January 2004). *Member:* American Bar Association. ***PRACTICE AREAS:*** Estate Planning; Real Estate; Uniform Commercial Code. ***Email:*** fferraro@dimonteandlizak.com

JULIA E. JENSEN, born Chicago, Illinois, August 25, 1975; admitted to bar, 2000, Illinois. *Education:* University of Illinois at Chicago (B.A., 1997); Loyola University (J.D., 2000). Phi Alpha Delta. ***PRACTICE AREAS:*** Commercial Litigation; Civil Litigation; Bankruptcy. ***Email:*** jjensen@dimonteandlizak.com

SARAH LAPPIN, born Jerusalem, Israel, November 7, 1977; admitted to bar, 2002, Illinois. *Education:* Illinois State University (B.S., 1999); DePaul College of Law (J.D., 2002). *Member:* Chicago Bar Association. ***PRACTICE AREAS:*** Litigation. ***Email:*** slappin@dimonteandlizak.com

RICHARD W. LAUBENSTEIN, born Chicago, Illinois, December 27, 1960; admitted to bar, 1986, Illinois and U.S. District Court, Northern District of Illinois. *Education:* Concordia College (B.A., cum laude, 1983); Illinois Institute of Technology/Chicago-Kent College of Law (J.D., cum laude, 1986). Member, International Law Moot Court Team, 1984-1986. Recipient, American Jurisprudence Award in Accounting. Lecturer, Lake County Bar Association Seminar on Mechanic's Liens, 1994. Lake and Cook County Arbitrator. *Member:* Lake County and Illinois State Bar Associations. ***PRACTICE AREAS:*** Real Estate; Commercial Law; Mechanic; Construction Disputes; Civil Litigation. ***Email:*** rlaubenstein@dimonteandlizak.com

REPRESENTATIVE CLIENTS: American National Bank; Armed Forces Insurance Co.; Austin Bank of Chicago; Beck's Book Stores; Campanelli Bros.; Charter National Bank; Chicago Trust Co.; Cole-Taylor Bank; Edward Hines Lumber Co.; Bank One; Firstar Bank; Gatwood Crane Service, Inc.; General Electric Co.; Glidden Paint Co.; Global CFS; Hyde Park Bank; Illinois Instrummments, Inc.; International Electric; LaSalle Bank, N.A. M.G. Electric; Marathon Oil; Marchris Engineering Ltd.; NBD Woodfield Bank; Northern Trust Co.; Occidental Fire & Casualty Co.; Olson Oil Company, Inc.; Oxford Bank; P. I. Products, Inc.; Racconto Imports; Rosemont Building Supply Co.; Sherwin Williams Co.; St. Paul Federal Bank for Savings Swirlon International.

(This Listing Continued)

THE LAW OFFICES OF ANTHONY B. FERRARO

PARK RIDGE, ILLINOIS

(See Rosemont)

Wills, Trusts, Estates, Estate Planning, Estate Taxation, Probate and Trust Administration, Medicaid, Guardianship, Elder Law, and Trust and Estate-Related Commercial Transactions including Business Acquisitions and Real Estate, Commercial Arbitration.

HARRIS KESSLER & GOLDSTEIN LLC

PARK RIDGE, ILLINOIS

(See Chicago)

General Business Practice including Litigation, Secured Lending, Real Estate, Health Care and Estate Planning.

ROBERT K. LOCK, JR.

PARK RIDGE, ILLINOIS

(See Chicago)

Complex Corporate Litigation and Negotiation, Credit Collection, Complex Class Action Litigation.

MARAMBA & ASSOCIATES, LLC

PARK RIDGE, ILLINOIS

(See Arlington Heights)

Business Law, Chancery Practice, Corporate Litigation, Civil Litigation, Complex Litigation, Defense Litigation, Federal Litigation, Administrative Litigation, Business Enterprises, Business Litigation, Closely Held Business Law, Real Estate Litigation, Veterans Rights, Military Law, Wills, Commercial Collections, Post Judgment Collections, Closely Held Corporations.

MINER, BARNHILL & GALLAND, P.C.

PARK RIDGE, ILLINOIS

(See Chicago)

General Practice, Trial and Appellate Litigation, Commercial, Employment, Employee Benefits, Civil Rights and Securities Litigation, Banking Law, Single and Multi-Family Housing Finance and Development, Non-Profit Corporations.

OWENS, OWENS & RINN, LTD.

Established in 1923
444 N. NORTHWEST HIGHWAY
P.O. BOX 578
PARK RIDGE, ILLINOIS 60068
Telephone: 847-825-2128; Chicago: 773-693-3565
Fax: 773-693-3567
Email: office@owensowensrinn.com
URL: http://www.owensowensrinn.com

Estate Planning, Probate, Taxation, Real Estate, Zoning, and Corporate Law. General Civil Trial and Appellate Practice in Federal and State Courts.

JOHN E. OWENS, SR. (1894-1966)
THOMAS L. OWENS (1898-1948)
VINCENT G. RINN (1905-1996)
SAMUEL W. MILLER (1907-1979)

JOHN E. OWENS, born Chicago, Illinois, June 6, 1936; admitted to bar, 1962, Illinois; 1970, U.S. Supreme Court. *Education:* Loyola University (B.S.C., 1958); University of Vienna, Vienna, Austria; DePaul University (J.D., 1962). Delta Theta Phi (Chancellor, 1975-1977). *Member:* Chicago (Member: Committee on Immigration, 1977-1983; Chairman, 1980-1981; Committee on Suburban Liaison, 1974-1976), Northwest Suburban (Member, Board of Governors, 1970-1976; President, 1974-1975; Member, Probate and Practice Committee), Illinois State (Chairman, 1968-1969; Member of Council, 1966-1971, Section on International Law; Chairman, 1977-1978, Committee on Member Relations and Activities) and American (Member, Committees on: Law Practice Management ; Business Law; Real Property, Probate and Trust; Senior Lawyers Division) Bar Associations; Northwest

(This Listing Continued)

OWENS, OWENS & RINN, LTD., Park Ridge—Continued

Suburban Estate Planning Council. ***LANGUAGES:*** German and Spanish. ***PRACTICE AREAS:*** Estate Planning; Real Estate; Zoning; Corporate; General Civil. ***Email:*** johneowens@owensowensrinn.com

DENIS J. OWENS, born Chicago, Illinois, January 1, 1940; admitted to bar, 1964, Illinois and U.S. Court of Appeals. *Education:* University of Notre Dame (B.B.A., 1961); DePaul University (J.D., 1964). Delta Theta Phi (Tribune, Chicago Alumni, 1969-1973; District Chancellor, 1972-1975; Board of Governors, 1976-1984; Vice Dean, 1974; Dean, 1975). *Member:* Northwest Suburban (Member, Committees on: Membership, 1977; Social, 1972; Finance, 1971-1975; Real Estate, 1976-1977; Chairman: Probate Practice Committee, 1977-1979, 1984-1985; Public Service Committee, 1977; Budget Committee, 1978-1984; Member, Board of Governors, 1977-1983), Chicago, Illinois State and American (Member, Committee on Taxation, 1970—) Bar Associations; Catholic Lawyers Guild of Chicago; Northwest Suburban Estate Planning Council. [Capt., Judge Advocate General, U.S. Army, 1968-1971]. ***PRACTICE AREAS:*** Taxation; Probate; Estate Planning; Real Estate; Corporate. ***Email:*** denisjowens@owensowensrinn.com

PATRICK D. OWENS, born Chicago, Illinois, March 17, 1971; admitted to bar, 1996, Illinois and U.S. District Court, Northern District of Illinois. *Education:* University of Notre Dame (B.B.A., 1993); DePaul University (J.D., 1996); The John Marshall Law School (LL.M., Taxation, with honors, 2002). Recipient, Chicago Volunteer Legal Services Distinguished Service Award, 1998, 2002. Member, Chicago Volunteer Legal Services. *Member:* Chicago, Illinois State and American (Member, Committees on: Real Property, Probate and Trust, Taxation, Trusts and Estates) Bar Associations; Northwest Suburban Estate Planning Council (Board Member, 1999-2005; President, 2005). ***PRACTICE AREAS:*** Estate Planning; Estate Administration; Individual Taxation; Estate and Gift Taxation; Probate; Real Estate. ***Email:*** patrickdowens@owensowensrinn.com

---

URSULA SZCZEPANSKI, born Chicago, Illinois, April 18, 1975; admitted to bar, 2001, Illinois. *Education:* Rosary College (B.A., 1997); John Marshall Law School (J.D., 2001). *Member:* Chicago, Illinois State and American Bar Associations. ***LANGUAGES:*** Polish. ***PRACTICE AREAS:*** Real Estate; Corporate Law; General Practice. ***Email:*** ursula@owensowensrinn.com

OF COUNSEL

JOHN V. OWENS, born Evanston, Illinois, November 6, 1962; admitted to bar, 1987, Illinois. *Education:* University of Notre Dame (J.D., 1987). Delta Theta Phi. *Member:* Chicago Bar Association. (currently on leave with Chemonics International Inc. serving as Chief of Party of the United States Agency of International Development's Microenterprise Access to Banking Services in Mindanao Project based in Manila, Philippines; previously served in Jamaica and Bolivia). ***LANGUAGES:*** Italian and Spanish. ***Email:*** johnvowens@owensowensrinn.com

REFERENCES: Northern Trust Co./Park Ridge and Chicago; The National Bank & Trust Company of Sycamore, Sycamore, Illinois; National City Bank of Michigan/Illinois.

PEMBROKE, BIELSKI AND ASSOCIATES, LLC

A Limited Liability Company of Attorneys

Established in 1992

SUITE 150
422 NORTH NORTHWEST HIGHWAY
PARK RIDGE, ILLINOIS 60068
Telephone: 847-696-0060; 847-825-1900
Facsimile: 847-696-0950
URL: http://www.pembrokelaw.com

Corporate Law, Federal and State Income, Estate and Gift Tax, Commercial Litigation, Wills, Trusts, Estate Planning, General Commercial Law, Elder Law, Probate, Real Estate and Financial Planning.

JOHN J. PEMBROKE, born Evergreen Park, Illinois, May 27, 1950; admitted to bar, 1979, Illinois and U.S. District Court, Northern District of Illinois; 1980, U.S. Court of Appeals, Seventh Circuit; 1981, U.S. Tax Court; 1986, U.S. Claims Court. *Education:* University of Illinois at Chicago Circle (B.S., with honors and distinction in Accounting, 1975); Northwestern University (J.D., 1979). Beta Gamma Sigma. Certified Public Accountant, Illinois, 1976. Personal Financial Planner, 2002. *Member:* Chicago, Illinois State and American (Member, Section on Taxation) Bar Associations. ***Email:*** jjpembroke@aol.com

JOHN N. BIELSKI II, born Winfield, Illinois, March 10, 1972; admitted to bar, 1997, Illinois. *Education:* Illinois Benedictine College (B.A., Accounting, cum laude, 1994); De Paul University College of Law (J.D., 1997); Kellstadt Graduate School of Business, DePaul University (M.B.A., Concentration in Finance, 1997). Certified Public Accountant. *Member:* DuPage County, Kane County and Illinois State Bar Associations.

PTASINSKI & SMITH, P.C.

PARK RIDGE, ILLINOIS

(See Niles)

Probate, Estate Planning and Administration, Trusts and Estates, Wills, Elder Law, Real Estate, Business Law, Divorce.

RAYSA & ZIMMERMANN, LLC

22 SOUTH WASHINGTON AVENUE
PARK RIDGE, ILLINOIS 60068
Telephone: 847-268-8600
Fax: 847-268-8614

Local Government Law, Zoning, Real Estate, Probate, Trusts, Wills, Estate Planning, General Civil Trial Practice, Insurance Defense and Subrogation.

JOHN J. ZIMMERMANN, born Chicago, Illinois, April 30, 1939; admitted to bar, 1967, Illinois. *Education:* DePaul University (A.B., 1962; J.D., 1967). President, International Municipal Lawyers Association, 2001-2002. ***PRACTICE AREAS:*** Local Government Law; Zoning; Real Estate; Corporation; Estate Planning. ***Email:*** jjzimm@rzllc.com

MICHAEL F. ZIMMERMANN, born Chicago, Illinois, October 5, 1969; admitted to bar, 1994, Illinois. *Education:* Marquette University (B.A., 1991); DePaul University (J.D., 1994). ***PRACTICE AREAS:*** Commercial Litigation; Civil Litigation; Local Government Law; Land Use; Zoning. ***Email:*** mfzimm@rzllc.com

WILLIAM G. RAYSA, born 1945; admitted to bar, 1975, Illinois. *Education:* Hamline University (B.A., 1971); Loyola University (J.D., 1974). ***PRACTICE AREAS:*** Local Government Law; Zoning Law; Real Estate; Probate; Estates. ***Email:*** wraysa@rzllc.com

RUSSELL MARC BARNETT, born Queens, New York, January 10, 1969; admitted to bar, 1994, Illinois and U.S. District Court, Northern District of Illinois; U.S. Supreme Court. *Education:* University of Illinois, Urbana-Champaign (B.A., 1991); DePaul University (J.D., 1994). *Member:* Chicago, Illinois State and American Bar Associations; Association of Trial Lawyers of America. ***PRACTICE AREAS:*** Civil Litigation; Personal Injury; Real Estate; Subrogation; Commercial Litigation. ***Email:*** rbarnett@rzllc.com

DANIEL P. BLONDIN, born Oak Park, Illinois, December 23, 1952; admitted to bar, 1981, Illinois. *Education:* Elmhurst College (B.A., 1976); Northern Illinois University (J.D., 1980). ***PRACTICE AREAS:*** Local Government Law; Zoning Law; Real Estate; Eminent Domain; Civil Litigation; Employment. ***Email:*** dblondin@rzllc.com

---

CAROLYN VICTORIA J. LEES, born Mayfield Heights, Ohio, October 9, 1978; admitted to bar, 2003, California; 2004, Illinois and U.S. District Court, Northern District of Illinois. *Education:* University of Chicago (B.A., 2000); Santa Clara University (J.D., 2003). *Member:* Chicago and Illinois State Bar Associations; State Bar of California. ***PRACTICE AREAS:*** Local Government Law; Civil Litigation; Commercial Litigation. ***Email:*** clees@rzllc.com

JAY A. SLUTZKY

PARK RIDGE, ILLINOIS

(See Niles)

Wills, Living Trusts, Estate Planning, Residential Real Estate, Commercial Real Estate, Divorce, Personal Injury, Bankruptcy Law, Elder Law, DUI, DWI, Business Law, Commercial Law, Commercial Litigation, Business Organization, Business Transactions, Business Counseling, Business Advice, Real Estate Law, Real Estate Litigation, Commercial Transactions, Contracts, Construction Law, Litigation, Motor Vehicle Accidents, Personal Injury Defense, Plaintiffs Personal Injury, Probate, Estate Administration, Trusts, By-Pass Trusts, Credit Shelter Trusts, Special Needs Trusts, Testamentary Trusts, Ancillar Administration, Durable Powers of Attorney, Medical Powers of Attorney, Living Wills, Pour-Over Wills, Marital Deduction Trusts, Beneficiary Designations, Irrevocable Life Insurance Trusts, Split Dollar Purchase Agreements, Crummey Trusts, Workers Compensation, Civil Litigation, Criminal Defense, Pre-Marital Agreements, Planning for Disabled Spouses, Planning for Disabled Children, Estate Tax Return Preparation, Second Marriage Issues, Contested Wills and Trusts, Partnerships, Corporations, Limited Liability Companies.

LAW OFFICES OF JEFF SMITH

PARK RIDGE, ILLINOIS

(See Evanston)

Computer Law, Internet Law, Business Law, E-Commerce, Contract Litigation, Intellectual Property, Estate Planning, Domestic Relations, Municipal Law, Employment Law and Real Estate.

TUTTLE, VEDRAL & COLLINS PC

PARK RIDGE, ILLINOIS

(See Des Plaines)

Residential and Commercial Real Estate, Foreclosures, Banking Law, Trust and Estate Planning, Probate, Family Law, Divorce, Equitable Distribution, Corporate Law.

DALE STROUGH
ATTORNEY AT LAW

PAXTON, ILLINOIS

(See Watseka)

Bankruptcy, Family, Divorce, Adoption, Visitation Rights, Criminal, DWI, Drug Crimes, Juvenile Crimes, Traffic Violations, White Collar Crimes, Domestic Violence, Personal Injury, Medical Malpractice, Wrongful Death, Trusts and Estates, Estate Planning and Wills and Probate Law. General Practice.

ELLIFF, KEYSER, OBERLE & DANCEY, P.C.

109 SOUTH FOURTH STREET
P.O. BOX 873
PEKIN, ILLINOIS 61554
Telephone: 309-346-4148
Fax: 309-346-0633

General Practice. Business, Estate Planning, Probate, Banking, Municipal and Real Estate Law, Civil Trial and Appellate Practice, No Collections under $3000.00.

JOHN T. ELLIFF (1872-1960)
NATHAN T. ELLIFF (1905-1993)

PATRICK E. OBERLE, born Pekin, Illinois, November 28, 1946; admitted to bar, 1975, Illinois. *Education:* Drake University (B.S.B.A., 1968; J.D., 1975). Order of the Coif. Staff Member, Drake University Law Review, 1973-1975. *Member:* Tazewell County, Illinois State and American Bar Associations. [Capt., USAF, 1968-1972]. ***PRACTICE AREAS:*** Business Law; Tax; Real Estate Law; Probate Law; Banking Law.

BURT L. DANCEY, born Pekin, Illinois, June 20, 1948; admitted to bar, 1977, Illinois. *Education:* Dartmouth College (B.A., 1970); University of Illinois (M.A., 1971); Northeastern University (J.D., 1977). *Member:* Peoria County Bar Association. ***PRACTICE AREAS:*** Appellate Law; Real Estate Law; Family Law; School Law.

WILLIAM P. STREETER, born Burbank, California, December 20, 1962; admitted to bar, 1989, California; 1992, Illinois. *Education:* Stanford University (B.S., 1984); University of California at Los Angeles (J.D., 1989). ***PRACTICE AREAS:*** Business Law; Municipal Law; Real Estate; Banking Law.

RONALD L. KEYSER, born Peoria, Illinois, October 22, 1933; admitted to bar, 1957, Illinois; 1985, Arizona. *Education:* Bradley University; University of Illinois (J.D., 1957). Phi Delta Phi. *Member:* Tazewell County, Illinois State and American Bar Associations; State Bar of Arizona. (Retired)

ASSOCIATE

SUSAN BOSICH, born Peoria, Illinois, July 14, 1953; admitted to bar, 1996, Connecticut; 1997, New York; 2003, Illinois. *Education:* University of Connecticut (B.S., 1993); Pace Law School (J.D., 1996). *Member:* New York State, Connecticut, and Illinois State Bar Associations.

REPRESENTATIVE CLIENTS: Heartland Bank of Pekin; First American Title Co.; Missouri-Pacific Lumber Co.; Morton Buildings, Inc.; Spring Lake School Dist.; Ray Dennison Chevrolet, Inc.; Velde Ford; Velde Oldsmobile-Cadillac-GMC Truck, Inc.; Velde Lincoln Mercury, Inc.; Peoria Rivermen; Pekin Hospital; City of Pekin; Central Illinois Dock.
LOCAL COUNSEL FOR: Pekin Hospital.
REFERENCES: Herget National Bank; Commerce Bank.

KUHFUSS & PROEHL, P.C.

Established in 1936
342 ELIZABETH STREET
P.O. BOX 1068
PEKIN, ILLINOIS 61555-1068
Telephone: 309-347-4164
Fax: 309-347-7872

General Civil Practice in all Courts. Trials, Probate and Real Estate Law, Banking.

MEMBERS OF FIRM

HAROLD H. KUHFUSS (1909-1993)

W. THAD KUHFUSS, born Peoria, Illinois, February 27, 1945; admitted to bar, 1972, Illinois. *Education:* University of Illinois (B.S., 1967); Washington University (J.D., 1972). *Member:* Tazewell County and Illinois State Bar Associations. ***PRACTICE AREAS:*** Banking Law; Estate Planning; Probate; Real Estate.

JASON W. PROEHL, born Peoria, Illinois, March 4, 1976; admitted to bar, 2003, Illinois. *Education:* University of Illinois, Urbana-Champaign (B.S., 2000); Northern Illinois University (J.D., 2003). *Member:* Tazewell County, Illinois State and American Bar Associations. ***PRACTICE AREAS:*** Agriculture Law; Estate Planning; Real Estate; Banking Law; Insurance Law. ***Email:*** jasonproehl@grics.net

ATTORNEYS FOR: Pekin National Bank; First Farmers State Bank of Minier; Pekin Savings Bank; First Federal Savings and Loan Association of Pekin.
GENERAL COUNSEL FOR: Pekin Insurance Cos.
REFERENCES: Herget National Bank, Pekin; Pekin Savings Bank, Pekin; Pekin National Bank.

LYNCH AND BLOOM, P.C.

PEKIN, ILLINOIS
(See Peoria)

Matrimonial and Family Law, Divorce, Adoptions, Child Support, Child Custody, General Civil Litigation. Personal Injury Law.

NICOARA & STEAGALL

PEKIN, ILLINOIS
(See Peoria)

General Civil Trial and Appellate Practice in State and Federal Courts. Personal Injury and Insurance Law, Civil Rights Litigation, Employment Discrimination, Auto Accidents, Aviation Law, Legal Malpractice, Medical Malpractice, Products Liability, Sex Offenses. Arbitration and Mediation Services.

PRUSAK, WINNE & GORMAN, LTD.

PEKIN, ILLINOIS
(See Peoria)

General Practice. Trial, Insurance, Workers Compensation, Personal Injury, Probate, Corporate, Construction Litigation, Fire Loss, Professional Liability, Real Estate Law, Automobile Liability Defense, Insurance Coverage, Uninsured and Underinsured Motorists Arbitration, Products Liability Defense, Professional Liability Defense.

ROBERT C. STRODEL, LTD.

PEKIN, ILLINOIS
(See Peoria)

General Practice. Personal Injury Claims, with specialty in Medical Malpractice.

RICHARD W. ZUCKERMAN

PEKIN, ILLINOIS
(See Peoria)

Family Law, Divorce, Post-Divorce, Mediation, Appeals, Paternity, Child Custody, Child Support, Visitation Rights, Adoption Law.

LAW OFFICES OF HALL ADAMS LLC

PEORIA, ILLINOIS
(See Chicago)

Trial Practice, State and Federal Courts, Personal Injury, Catastrophic Injury, Automobile Accidents, Premise Liability, Professional Negligence, Wrongful Death, Consumer Fraud, Business Litigation.

BAKER, BAKER & KRAJEWSKI, LLC

PEORIA, ILLINOIS
(See Springfield)

Labor and Employment Discrimination Law. General Civil, Trial and Appellate Practice before State and Federal Courts and Administrative Agencies. Estate Planning, Probate, Real Estate, Corporate, Tax, Railroad Law, Labor Relations, Healthcare Compliance Law.

BENASSI & BENASSI, P.C.

Established in 1980
300 NORTHEAST PERRY
PEORIA, ILLINOIS 61603
Telephone: 309-674-3556
FAX: 309-674-7989
URL: http://www.benassi.com
Email: lawfirm@benassi.com
URL: http://www.lawyers.com/benassi&benassi

Civil and Trial Practice. Administrative, Personal Injury, Workers Compensation, Family, Employment Discrimination, Civil Rights, Labor and Employee Benefits Law, Divorce, Child Custody.

FIRM PROFILE: Benassi & Benassi, P.C. was founded by A. Lou Benassi and Patricia C. Benassi in 1980. Both lawyers have been practicing law in Peoria for over 30 years. The firm serves clients throughout Central Illinois and focuses its practice in litigation with an emphasis on Employment, Civil Rights, Personal Injury, Workers Compensation and Family Law.

A. LOU BENASSI, born Litchfield, Illinois, April 12, 1942; admitted to bar, 1968, Illinois. *Education:* University of Illinois (B.S., with high honors, 1964); University of California at Berkeley (J.D., 1968). Author, Chapter 1, "Practical and Legal Considerations," Vol. 1, Family Law, Illinois Institute of Continuing Legal Education, 1978—. Fellow: American Academy of Matrimonial Lawyers, 1976—; Marital Arbitrator, 1990—. Member, Illinois Institute for Continuing Legal Education's Committee for Continuing Education in Family Law. *Member:* Peoria County (Chairman, Family Law Committee, 1977-1978), Illinois State (Chairman, Family Law Committee, 1975-1976; Special Committee on Legislation, 1975, 1976-1977; Standing Committee on Professional Ethics, 1977-1979) and American (Member, Family Law Section) Bar Associations; American Trial Lawyers Association; Illinois Trial Lawyers Association. ***REPORTED CASES:*** Sutton, 136 Ill. 2d 441 (1990); Sutton, 178 Ill.App.3d 928 (1989); Clark v. Clark, 237 Ill.App.3d 492 (1992); Grossweiler v. Brinkman, et al., 301 Ill.App.3d 1104 (3rd Dist.) (1988) (Decision not published); Binder Plumbing & Heating, Inc. v. Plumbers & Pipefitters Local Union, 99, 253 Ill.App.3d. 972. ***PRACTICE AREAS:*** Family Law; Personal Injury Law; Employee Benefits; Workers Compensation.

PATRICIA C. BENASSI, born Chicago, Illinois, May 28, 1943; admitted to bar, 1969, Illinois. *Education:* University of Heidelberg, Heidelberg, Germany and California State University at Northridge (B.A., with high honors, 1964); University of Illinois and University of California at Berkeley (J.D., 1969). Instructor, National Labor Relations Board litigation schools, 1977-1979. Trial Specialist, National Labor Relations Board, 1969-1976. Supervisory Attorney, National Labor Relations Board, 1976-1979. *Member:* Peoria County and Illinois State (Member, Labor Law Section Council, 1980—; Chairman, 1985—) and American Bar Associations; American Trial Lawyers Association; Illinois Trial Lawyers Association. Abraham Lincoln Inns of Court (Master, 1988—); National Employment Lawyers Association. ***REPORTED CASES:*** Knapp v. Whitaker, 757 F.2d

(This Listing Continued)

BENASSI & BENASSI, P.C., Peoria—Continued

827 (7th Cir. 1985); Volk v. Coler, 845 F.2d 1422 (7th Cir. 1988); International Union of Operating Engineers, Local Union 965-965A-965B-965C-965RA v. Associated General Contractors of Illinois, 845 n.2d 704 (7th Cir. 1988); Isaacs v. Caterpillar, 765 F.Supp. 1359 (1991); Zorzi v. County of Putnam, 30 F.3d 885 (7th Cir. 1994); Wright v. Illinois Dept. of Children and Family Services, 40 F.3d 1492 (7th Cir. 1994); Sutton v. Overcash, 623 N.E.2d 820 (Ill.App. 3rd Dist. 1993); Piquard & Duran v. City of East Peoria and Board of Trustees of the City of East Peoria Police Pension Fund, 887 F.Supp. 1106; Taylor v. Canteen, 69 F.3d 773 (7th Cir. 1995); Lead co-counsel for Plaintiffs in Linda Evans, et al. v. Mitsubishi Motor Manufacturing of America, Inc., Case No. 94-1545, United States District Court for the Central District of Illinois.; Ryan v. Illinois Dept. of Children and Family Services, 185 F.3rd 751 (7th Cir. 1999); David v. Caterpillar, 324 F.3d 851 (7th Cir. 2003). ***PRACTICE AREAS:*** Employment Discrimination Law; Civil Rights Law; Labor Law; General Employment Law. ***Email:*** Patricia@Benassi.com

---

ATHENA M. PAPACHRONIS HERMAN, born East Chicago, Indiana, July 29, 1972; admitted to bar, 1997, Illinois; U.S. District Court, Central and Northern Districts of Illinois; 2002, U.S. Court of Appeals, Seventh Circuit. *Education:* Bradley University (B.S., summa cum laude, 1994); University of Illinois (J.D., magna cum laude, 1997). Phi Kappa Phi; Pi Kappa Delta; Phi Delta Phi. Harnow Fellow. Recipient, John C. McAndrews Pro Bono Service Award, Illinois State Bar Association, 2001. Author, "Raising an Affirmative Defense to Constructive Discharge in Hostile Work Environment Cases," Illinois Bar Journal, Feb. 2005. Adjunct Faculty, "Legal Advocacy", Bradley University. *Member:* Peoria County and Illinois State Bar Associations; National Employment Lawyers Association; The Association of Trial Lawyers of America. ***REPORTED CASES:*** David v. Caterpillar, 324 F.3d 851 (7th Cir. 2003); Palmer v. Combined Ins. Co. of Am., 217 F.R.D. 430 (N.D. Ill. 2003). ***PRACTICE AREAS:*** Employment Discrimination; Civil Rights; Employment; Family Law; Personal Injury. ***Email:*** athena@benassi.com

JOEL E. BROWN, ATTORNEY AT LAW

416 MAIN STREET, SUITE 625
PEORIA, ILLINOIS 61602
Telephone: 309-673-4357
Fax: 309-673-6119
Email: jebrownlaw@aol.com
URL: http://www.jebrownlaw.com

Personal Injury, Medical Malpractice, Criminal Law.

JOEL E. BROWN, born Peoria, Illinois, April 26, 1965; admitted to bar, 1992, Missouri; 1993, Illinois. *Education:* Washington University (A.B., 1987); St. Louis University (J.D., 1992). ***PRACTICE AREAS:*** Personal Injury; Medical Malpractice; Criminal Law.

CARTER LAW OFFICES

COMMERCE BANK BUILDING, SUITE 529
PEORIA, ILLINOIS 61602
Telephone: 309-673-3517
Facsimile: 309-673-3318
URL: http://www.jcarterlaw.com
Email: jcarter@jcarterlaw.com
URL: http://www.lawyers.com/carterlaw

Products Litigation including Asbestos and Toxic Tort Litigation, Medical Malpractice, Appellate Law, Wrongful Death, Birth Trauma. Tort Litigation, Insurance, Employment and Civil Rights Litigation. Commercial Litigation.

FIRM PROFILE: The firm concentrates in Wrongful Death and Catastrophic, Personal Injury, Complex Products cases including tread separation and bead failures, and Toxic Tort Litigation, Medical Malpractice including Birth Trauma, Commercial Litigation, and serves clients throughout Illinois and The United States.

MEMBER OF FIRM

JAMES R. CARTER, born Alton, Illinois, November 6, 1953; admitted to bar, 1978, Illinois; 1981, U.S. District Court, Central District of Illinois; 1984, U.S. Court of Appeals, Seventh Circuit; 1985, U.S. Supreme Court; 1988, U.S. District Court, Northern District of Illinois Trial Bar; 1993, U.S. District Court, Southern District of Illinois. *Education:* Tulane University of Louisiana; Indiana University (B.A., 1975); John Marshall Law School (J.D., 1978). Master, The Abraham Lincoln Inn of Court. *Member:* Peoria County, Illinois State and American Bar Associations; Illinois Trial Lawyers Association; The Association of Trial Lawyers of America; Defense Research Institute. ***PRACTICE AREAS:*** Civil Trial Practice; Civil Appeals; Medical Malpractice; Products Liability; Asbestos Litigation; Toxic Torts Litigation; Complex Torts; Commercial Litigation. ***Email:*** jcarter@jcarterlaw.com

ASSOCIATES

LAURA OSTROWSKI, born Aurora, Illinois, June 1, 1973; admitted to bar, 2000, Illinois. *Education:* Northern Illinois University (B.A., with honors, 1995; J.D., cum laude, 1999). Phi Alpha Delta. Instructor, Legal Research, 2001 and Business Law, 2001—, Illinois Central College. *Member:* Peoria County and Illinois State Bar Associations. ***PRACTICE AREAS:*** Civil Litigation; Asbestos Litigation. ***Email:*** lostrowski@jcarterlaw.com

BRIAN ALLEN KUEHN, born Saginaw, Michigan, February 27, 1953; admitted to bar, 1980, Illinois. *Education:* Western Michigan University (B.A., cum laude, 1976); University of Illinois (J.D., 1980). Phi Alpha Delta. *Member:* Peoria County, Illinois State and American Bar Associations.

CASSIDY & MUELLER

Established in 1921
323 COMMERCE BANK BUILDING
416 MAIN STREET
PEORIA, ILLINOIS 61602
Telephone: 309-676-0591
Fax: 309-676-8036
Email: c_m@mtco.com
URL: http://www.cassidymueller.com

General, Civil, Trial and Appellate Practice. Product Liability, Asbestos, Medical Malpractice, Drug and Medical Device and Commercial, Employment, Federal Civil Rights and Insurance Litigation. Banking, Business, Insurance, Officers, Directors and Professional Liability, Probate, Real Estate and Worker's Compensation Law.

FIRM PROFILE: The firm was founded in 1921 by John E. Cassidy, Sr. Since that time, the emphasis of its practice has been in the area of commercial, federal civil rights and tort litigation at both the trial and appellate levels. The firm is active in both the state and federal systems throughout Illinois and the eastern part of Iowa, with its members having appeared before the United States Supreme Court, the Seventh and Eighth Circuit Courts of Appeal, the Illinois Supreme Court and numerous trial and intermediate appellate courts. Lawyers with the firm are also active in continuing legal education, having participated frequently as lecturers and authors.

MEMBERS OF FIRM

JOHN E. CASSIDY, SR. (1896-1984)

JOHN E. CASSIDY, JR. (1924-2003)

DAVID B. MUELLER, born Denver, Colorado, July 28, 1941; admitted to bar, 1966, Illinois. *Education:* University of Oklahoma (B.A., 1963); University of Michigan (LL.B., 1966). Phi Delta Phi. Editor, Tort Trends Newsletter, 1976-1979. Author: "Liability to the Public Servant-A Dividend Approach To Duty," 1980 Issue of the Illinois Bar Journal; "Timely Disclosure of Expert Witnesses-Analysis of Supreme Court Rule 220," July, 1986 Issue of the Illinois Bar Journal; "The New Discovery Rules: Reshaping the Landscape for Illinois Litigators," December 1995 Issue of the Illinois Bar Journal; "Comparative Fault in Strict Liability Cases Under Section 2-1116 of the Code of Civil Procedure," IDC Quarterly, 4th Quarter 1992; "Has the General Assembly Expanded the Concept of 'Contributory Fault' in Strict Tort Liability Actions? A Defendant's Perspective," ISBA Trial Briefs, December 1992; "Complexities In Construction Negligence Litigation," IDC Quarterly 2003, Vol. 13, No. 3; "Developments In Product Liability Law," IDC Quarterly 2003, Vol. 14, No. 2; "Recent Developments In Construction Negligence," IDC Quarterly 2003, Vol. 14, No. 2; "Ins and Outs Of Amended Section 2-1117, presented IDC Trial Tactics Seminar, Feb. 2004; "Spoliation Of Evidence An Intellectual Quagmire," IDC Newsletter, December, 2002; Chapter, IICLE "Revised Federal Discovery Rules and Related Practice in the Central District of Illinois," 1995; Chapter, IICLE "Winning Pretrial Preparation in the New World of Illinois Civil Litigation," 1995; Chapter IICLE 2002 Liability Insurance, "Duty to Settle-Exhaustion," IICLE Effective Illinois Jury Selection, Spring 2003 "Observations On Jury Selection From The Defense Perspective,"; Co-Chairman, Supreme Court Committee to Revise the Rules of Discovery, 1983-1993. Advisory Member on Discovery Rules, Illinois Judicial Conference, 1993—. Member: Joint Judicial Conference and Illinois Rules Committee, 1995; Special Discovery Rules Drafting Committee, 1995; Illinois Supreme Court Committee on Jury Instructions in Civil Cases, 1995—. Master and Secretary, 1989-1990, Counselor, 1990-1991, President, 1991-1992, Abraham Lincoln Inns of Court. Chairman, Civil Justice Reform Act Advisory Committee for the Central District of Illinois, 1991—. *Member:* Peoria County (First Vice President, 2000-2001), Illinois State (Secretary, Tort Law Section, 1977-1979; Member, Standing Committee on Legal Education, Admission and Competence, 1984-1987; Associate Member, Civil Practice and Procedure Council, 1985—) and American Bar Associations. Fellow, Illinois State Bar Foundation. ***REPORTED CASES:*** Coney v. JLG Industries, Inc., 97 Ill.2d 104 (1983); Prewein v. Caterpillar Tractor Co., 108 Ill.2d 141 (1985); J.L. Simmons Co., Inc. ex rel. Hartford v. Firestone Tire & Rubber Co., 108 Ill.2d 106 (1985); Clarkson v. Wright, 108 Ill.2d 129 (1985); Dukes v. J.L. Case Co., 118 Ill.2d 447 (1987); Kirk v. Michael Reese Hospital, et al., 117 Ill.2d 507 (1987); Dunn v. B & O Railroad Co., 127 Ill.2d 350 (1989); Wilsey v. Eddingfield, 780 F.2d 614 (7th Cir. 1986); Hartford Insurance Group v. Gulf Insurance, 837 F.2d 767 (7th Cir. 1988); Kraciun, et al. v. Garlock Inc., et al., 895 F.2d 444 (8th Cir. 1990); Massachusetts Mutual Life Insurance Co. v. O'Brien, 5 F. 3d 1117 (7th Cir. 1993); Schrock v. Shoemaker, 159 Ill.2d 533 (1994); N.C. Illinois Trut Co. v. Firt Illini Bancorp, 323 Ill.App.3d 254 (2001). ***PRACTICE AREAS:*** Civil Tort Litigation; Liability Insurance Coverage Litigation; Product Liability Litigation; Medical Malpractice Litigation; Construction Related Injury Litigation; Estate and Trust Litigation; Drug and Medical Device Litigation; State and Federal Appellate Practice.

JOHN E. CASSIDY, III, born Peoria, Illinois, July 23, 1954; admitted to bar, 1983, Illinois, U.S. District Court, Central and Northern Districts of Illinois and U.S. Court of Appeals, Seventh Circuit. *Education:* Regis College (B.S., 1976); St. Louis University (J.D., 1982). *Member:* Peoria County, Illinois State and American Bar Associations; Abraham Lincoln Inns of Court; Assembly of Illinois State Bar Association. ***REPORTED CASES:*** Hill v. Shelander, 924 F.2d 1370 (7th Cir. 1991); Hill v. Shelander, 992 F.2d 714 (7th Cir. 1993). ***PRACTICE AREAS:*** Corporate Law; Commercial Law; Business Planning Law; Commercial Litigation; Bankruptcy Litigation; Estate Planning Law; Tort Litigation; Construction Related Injury Litigation; Product Liability Litigation; Civil Rights Litigation; State and Federal Trial and Appellate Practice.

TIMOTHY J. CASSIDY, born Peoria, Illinois, June 24, 1955; admitted to bar, 1983, Illinois and U.S. District Court, Northern and Central District of Illinois; U.S. Court of Appeals, Seventh Circuit. *Education:* Regis College (B.S., 1977); St. Louis University (J.D., magna cum laude, 1983). Author: "Termination of Parental Rights; The Substantive Due Process Issue," St. Louis University Law Journal, 1984. Certified Public Accountant, 1978. President, Pleasure Driveway and Park District of Peoria. Vice-President, Illinois Association of Park Districts. Member, City of Peoria Riverfront Development Commission. *Mem-*

(This Listing Continued)

ber: Peoria County, Illinois State and American Bar Associations. ***PRACTICE AREAS:*** Commercial Law; Commercial Litigation; Bankruptcy Litigation; Civil Tort Litigation; Construction Related Injury Litigation; Product Liability Litigation; Workers' Compensation Practice.

ANDREW D. CASSIDY, born Peoria, Illinois, November 1, 1961; admitted to bar, 1989, Illinois and U.S. District Court, Central District of Illinois and U.S. Court of Appeals, Seventh Circuit. *Education:* Regis College; Marquette University (B.S., 1984); Northern Illinois University (J.D., 1989). *Member:* Peoria County and Illinois State Bar Associations; Abraham Lincoln Inns of Court. ***REPORTED CASES:*** Scott v. Cleaver, 261 Ill.App.3d 993, 634 N.E.2d 1232 (1994). ***PRACTICE AREAS:*** Real Estate Law; Commercial Law; Business Planning Law; Commercial Litigation; Civil Trial Practice; Corporate Law; Probate; Workers' Compensation.

CHRISTOPHER F. CASSIDY, born Peoria, Illinois, December 25, 1956; admitted to bar, 1994, Illinois and U.S. District Court, Central District of Illinois. *Education:* Illinois State University (B.S., 1991); Southern Illinois University (J.D., 1993). *Member:* Peoria County, Illinois State and American Bar Associations; Abraham Lincoln Inns of Court. ***PRACTICE AREAS:*** Civil Trial Practice; Real Estate Law; Business Planning; Trust and Estate Planning; Probate; Workers Compensation.

GAY NELL G. GERMAN, born Freeport, Texas, February 14, 1969; admitted to bar, 1996, Colorado; 2001, Illinois. *Education:* University of Illinois (B.A., 1991); University of Colorado at Boulder (J.D., 1995). *Member:* Peoria County, Illinois State and American Bar Associations. ***PRACTICE AREAS:*** Civil Trial Practice; Trusts and Estate Planning; Probate.

JENNIFER L. WOLFE, born Aberdeen, Maryland, October 29, 1974; admitted to bar, 1999, Illinois. *Education:* University of Illinois (B.A., 1996); Northern Illinois University (J.D., 1999). *Member:* Peoria County and Illinois State Bar Associations. ***PRACTICE AREAS:*** Civil Trial Practice; Trusts and Estate Planning; Probate.

REPRESENTATIVE CLIENTS: Archer Daniels Midland Company; Atchison, Topeka & Santa Fe Railroad Co.; Briggs Mfg. Co.; Caterpillar, Inc.; Central Insurance Co.; Chicago Motor Club Ins. Co.; Chrysler Corp.; Commercial Union Assurance Co.; Consolidated Coal Company; Continental Oil Company; CPC International; Dow Corning, Inc.; E.I. DuPont-DeNemours & Company; Economy Fire & Casualty Co.; First of America Bank-Peoria; Gates-McDonald Co.; Grinnell Mutual Group; Hartford Accident & Indemnity Company; Hartford Fire Insurance Co.; Hinz Claims Management; Illinois-American Water Company; John Deere Ins. Co.; John P. Pearl & Associates, Ltd.; Lake States Insurance Company; Liberty Mutual Insurance Co.; Med Marc; Meridian Insurance Co.; Merrell Dow Pharmaceuticals, Inc.; Nationwide Insurance Co.; Occidental Petroleum Company; Parke Davis & Company; Pekin Energy Co.; Rockford Mutual Insurance Company; Santa Fe Southern Pacific Corporation; Scotsdale Insurance Company; Squibb & Sons, Inc.; St. Paul Fire and Casualty Company; The Travelers Insurance Co.; Underwriters Adjusting Co.; United Fire and Casualty Company; United Heartland Insurance; University of Illinois; The Upjohn Company; Warner-Lambert Company.
REFERENCES: Commerce Bank; Bank One; First of America Bank-Peoria; First Financial Savings Bank.

DAVIS & CAMPBELL L.L.C.

401 MAIN STREET, SUITE 1600
PEORIA, ILLINOIS 61602-1241
Telephone: 309-673-1681
Fax: 309-673-1690
Email: info@dcamplaw.com
URL: http://www.dcamplaw.com

Chicago, Illinois Office: 161 N. Clark, Suite 4700, 60601. Telephone: 312-523-2120. Fax: 312-523-2121.
Washington, D.C. Office: 1828 L Street N.W., Suite 660. Telephone: 202-293-5690. Fax: 202-296-5706.

Management Labor Law, Corporate Law, Trial Practice, Employee Benefits, Mergers and Acquisitions, Employer Rights, Local Government Rights, Employment Law, Commercial Law, Commercial Litigation, Complex Litigation, Intellectual Property, Securities Regulation, Antitrust, Immigration and Naturalization, Real Estate, Zoning Planning and Land Use, Tax Law, Estate Planning, Probate.

ROY G. DAVIS, born Peoria, Illinois, October 31, 1948; admitted to bar, 1973, Illinois and District of Columbia. *Education:* Bradley University (B.S., 1970); George Washington University (J.D., with honors, 1973). *Member:* American Bar Association. ***PRACTICE AREAS:*** Management Labor Law; Employer Rights; Trial Practice; Local Government Law. ***Email:*** rgdavis@dcamplaw.com

WILLIAM H. CAMPBELL, born Pittsburgh, Pennsylvania, September 18, 1951; admitted to bar, 1976, Pennsylvania; 1977, Illinois. *Education:* Lehigh University (B.S., 1973); University of Pittsburgh (J.D., 1976). Certified Public Accountant, Illinois, 1979. ***PRACTICE AREAS:*** Corporate Law; Tax Law; Employee Benefits; Mergers and Acquisitions. ***Email:*** whcampbell@dcamplaw.com

J. REED ROESLER, born Decatur, Illinois, February 2, 1954; admitted to bar, 1979, Illinois. *Education:* Colorado State University (B.A., 1976); University of Illinois (J.D., 1979). Phi Beta Kappa. Recipient, Illinois State Bar Association Board of Governors Award, 1990-1991. *Member:* Peoria County (Secretary/Treasurer, 1994-1997; Vice President, 1997-1999; President, 1999-2000), Illinois State (Chair, Committee on Public Relations, 1989-1990) and American Bar Associations. Fellow, Illinois Bar Foundation. ***PRACTICE AREAS:*** Management Labor Law; Employer Rights; Trial Practice. ***Email:*** jrroesler@dcamplaw.com

KEITH J. BRASKICH, born Evergreen Park, Illinois, April 18, 1956; admitted to bar, 1981, Illinois. *Education:* University of Dayton (B.A., cum laude, 1977); DePaul University (J.D., with honors, 1981). *Member:* Illinois State and American Bar Associations. ***PRACTICE AREAS:*** Management Labor Law; Employer Rights; Local Government Law. ***Email:*** kbraskich@dcamplaw.com

DAVID G. LUBBEN, born Gilman, Illinois, October 5, 1963; admitted to bar, 1990, Illinois; 1991, California. *Education:* University of Illinois at Urbana (B.A., magna cum laude, 1985); Stanford University (J.D., with distinction, 1988). Recipient: Department of Justice Special Achievement Award, 1991. Member, Vol. 39 and Sr. Editor, Vol. 40, Stanford Law Review. Law Clerk, Hon. Myron H. Thompson (M.D. Ala.) 1988-1989; Hon. Paul

(This Listing Continued)

Roney (11th Cir.) 1989-1990; Hon. John C. Godbold (11th Cir.) 1990. Adjunct Professor, Disability Law and Legal Process, Bradley University, 1997—. ***PRACTICE AREAS:*** Complex Litigation; Employer Rights; Commercial Litigation. ***Email:*** dglubben@dcamplaw.com

ROBERT J. COLETTA, born Peoria, Illinois, March 28, 1960; admitted to bar, 1985, Illinois and U.S. District Court, Central District of Illinois. *Education:* Colorado State University (B.A., 1982); Washburn University of Topeka (J.D., with honors, 1985). Phi Kappa Phi; Phi Delta Phi. *Member:* Peoria County Bar Association. ***PRACTICE AREAS:*** Corporate Law; Real Estate; Zoning, Planning and Land Use; Commercial Law; Estate Planning. ***Email:*** rjcoletta@dcamplaw.com

---

JANET L. JANNUSCH, born Kankakee, Illinois, January 11, 1951; admitted to bar, 1976, Indiana; 1978, Illinois. *Education:* Northern Illinois University (B.A., magna cum laude, 1973); Valparaiso University (J.D., 1976). Assistant Instructor, Legal Problems, Valparaiso University, 1975-1976. ***PRACTICE AREAS:*** Trial Practice; Employer Rights; Criminal Defense. ***Email:*** jljannusch@dcamplaw.com

JAMES R. JORGENSEN, born Sacramento, California, December 4, 1968; admitted to bar, 1997, Illinois. *Education:* Purdue University (B.S., 1991); Bradley University (M.B.A., with distinction, 1994); DePaul University College of Law (J.D., 1997). Articles and Note Editor, DePaul Business Law Journal. Certified Public Accountant, Illinois, 1993. Certified Management Accountant, 1995. *Member:* Peoria County, Illinois State and American Bar Associations. ***PRACTICE AREAS:*** Corporate Law; Tax Law; Real Estate; Estate Planning; Probate. ***Email:*** jrjorgensen@dcamplaw.com

NANCY L. BARNHART, born Peoria, Illinois, July 6, 1972; admitted to bar, 1997, Illinois. *Education:* Spoon River College (A.A., 1992); Knox College (B.A., 1994); John Marshall Law School (J.D., 1997). *Member:* Chicago, Illinois State and American Bar Associations. ***PRACTICE AREAS:*** Labor and Employment; Employer Rights; Bankruptcy. ***Email:*** nlbarnhart@dcamplaw.com

RICHARD A. RUSSO, born Rock Island, Illinois, July 3, 1978; admitted to bar, 2003, Illinois. *Education:* Augustana College (B.A., cum laude, 2000); University of Illinois, Urbana-Champaign (J.D., magna cum laude, 2003). Harno Scholar. *Member:* Peoria County, Illinois State and American Bar Associations. ***PRACTICE AREAS:*** Labor and Employment Litigation; Civil Litigation. ***Email:*** rarusso@dcamplaw.com

JEREMY M. PELPHREY, born Peoria, Illinois, April 30, 1976; admitted to bar, 2004, Illinois. *Education:* Eastern Illinois University (B.A., 1999); John Jay College of Criminal Justice, City University of New York (M.A., 2000); Dickinson School of Law of the Pennsylvania State University (J.D., 2004). Psi Chi; Delta Theta Phi (Treasurer, 2002-2003). Member, American Psychological Association, 1999-2001. Adjunct Lecturer, John Jay College of Criminal Justice, 2000-2001. *Member:* Illinois State and American Bar Associations. ***PRACTICE AREAS:*** Employee Benefits; Tax Law; Mergers and Acquisitions; Employee Stock Ownership Plans; Corporate Law. ***Email:*** jmpelphrey@dcamplaw.com

OF COUNSEL

CARLOS M. RECIO, born Fairmont, West Virginia, August 10, 1952; admitted to bar, 1977, Maryland; 1981, California; 1982, District of Columbia; 1985, Virginia (Not admitted in Illinois). *Education:* Seton Hall University (B.A., 1974); Georgetown University (J.D., 1977); Harvard University (LL.M., 1978). Editor, American Criminal Law Review, 1975-1977. Law Clerk to Damon J. Keith, U.S. Court of Appeals, Sixth Circuit, 1978-1981. Assistant Professor of Law, The Detroit College of Law, Detroit, Michigan 1980-1981. *Member:* The District of Columbia Bar; Virginia State Bar; Maryland State and American Bar Associations. (Also Of Counsel, Bowytz Savit Szymkowicz, LLP, Bethesda, Maryland). ***PRACTICE AREAS:*** Immigration and Naturalization; Complex Litigation; Commercial Law. ***Email:*** CRecio@erols.com

JONATHAN G. BUNGE, born La Crosse, Wisconsin, October 20, 1936; admitted to bar, 1961, Illinois. *Education:* Princeton University (A.B., cum laude, 1958); Harvard University (J.D., 1961). Listed in, Who's Who in American Law. Professor, John Marshall Law School, 1968-1973. Formerly with: Lees & Bunge, 1961-1962; Keck, Mahin & Cate, 1964-1995; Ross & Hardies, 1995-2000. *Member:* Chicago, Judicial 7th Circuit and American Bar Associations; Maritime Law Association of the United States; Economic Club of Chicago. (Also Practicing Individually, Chicago, Illinois). ***PRACTICE AREAS:*** Commercial Litigation; Complex Litigation; Antitrust and Trade Regulation; Intellectual Property Litigation; Securities Litigation. ***Email:*** jgbunge@dcamplaw.com

ELIAS, MEGINNES, RIFFLE & SEGHETTI, P.C.

Established in 1996

416 MAIN STREET, SUITE 1400
PEORIA, ILLINOIS 61602
Telephone: 309-637-6000
Facsimile: 309-637-8514
URL: http://www.emrslaw.com

Tax, Corporate, Real Estate, Litigation, Environmental, Intellectual Property, Municipal, Estate Planning, Probate, Health Care.

JOHN S. ELIAS, born Lawrence, Massachusetts, May 2, 1951; admitted to bar, 1979, Illinois; 1980, Ohio; 1981, New York; 1982, Massachusetts. *Education:* Dartmouth College (A.B., summa cum laude, 1973, Phi Beta Kappa, Rufus Choate Scholar, Dartmouth General Fellowship); Oxford University, Oxford, England (M.A., 1975, Reynolds Scholar); Harvard University (J.D., 1979); New York University (LL.M., in Taxation, 1982). Recipient, Reynolds Memorial Scholarship. Clerk to Justice William B. Brown, Ohio Supreme Court, 1979-1981. Lecturer: Illinois Institute of Continuing Legal Education, 1984-1988; U.S. League of Savings Institutions 1987 Attorneys Clinic; New York University Tax Institute, 1988; Illinois State Bar Association Law Ed. Series, 1989-1992. Author: "Preferred Stock Recapitalization: Income, Estate and Gift Tax Issues," 13 J. Corp. Taxation 332 (Winter 1987); "The Partnerships Capital Freeze: A Path Through the Maze," 40 Tax Lawyer 45

(This Listing Continued)

ELIAS, MEGINNES, RIFFLE & SEGHETTI, P.C., Peoria—Continued

(Fall 1986); "Below-Market Loans After the Tax Reform Act of 1984," 73 Ill. Bar Journal 554 (June 1985); "Tax Reform Act of 1986: Provisions of Interest to Financial Institutions," Legal Bulletin (January 1987). *Member:* Peoria County, Illinois State (Vice Chairman, 1989 and Chairman, 1990, Federal Tax Section Council) and American Bar Associations. ***PRACTICE AREAS:*** Tax Law; Corporate Law; Real Estate Law; Estate Planning. ***Email:*** jelias@emrslaw.com

BRIAN J. MEGINNES, born Peoria, Illinois, April 17, 1953; admitted to bar, 1978, Illinois. *Education:* University of Notre Dame (B.A., magna cum laude, 1975); University of Illinois (J.D., magna cum laude, 1978). Phi Beta Kappa; Order of the Coif; Pi Sigma Alpha. Member, Board of Education, Dunlap School District No. 323. *Member:* Illinois State and American Bar Associations; American Health Lawyers Association; Association of University Technology Managers, Inc. ***PRACTICE AREAS:*** Corporate Law; Environmental Law; Intellectual Property Law; Healthcare Law. ***Email:*** bmeginnes@emrslaw.com

ROBERT M. RIFFLE, born Decatur, Illinois, January 19, 1959; admitted to bar, 1985, Illinois, U.S. District Court, Central and Southern Districts of Illinois and U.S. Court of Appeals, Sixth and Seventh Circuits; U.S. District Court, Western District of Michigan. *Education:* University of Illinois (B.S., 1980); University of Utah (J.D., 1985). Staff Member, Utah Law Review, 1984-1985. Judicial Clerk, Presiding Justice Joseph R. Spitz, Illinois Appellate Court, Fourth District, November, 1985-February 1988. *Member:* Illinois State and American Bar Associations. ***REPORTED CASES:*** Keach v. U.S. Trust Co., N.A., 245 F. Supp. 20 941 (C.D. Ill. 2003); Waldschmidt v. Amoco Oil Co., 924 F. Supp. 88 (C.D. Ill. 1996); Onsite Engineering and Management, Inc. v. Illinois Tool Works, 319 Ill. App.3d 362, 744 N.E.2d 928 (Ill. App.1st Dist. 2001); First of America Trust Co. v. Armstead, 269 Ill.App.2d.432, 646 N.E.2d. 302, 206 Ill.Dec. 935 (Ill. 1996); Ransburg v. Haase, 224 Ill.App.3d. 681, 586 N.E.2d 1295, 167 Ill.Dec. 23 (Ill.App. 3 Dist., Jan. 24, 1992)(NO. 3-90-0889, 3-91-0174); Whalen v. Whalen, 217 Ill.App.3d 557, 577 N.E.2d. 859, 160 Ill-.Dec. 534 (Ill.App. 3 Dist., Aug. 23, 1991)(NO. 3-91-0092). ***PRACTICE AREAS:*** Litigation; Environmental; ERISA. ***Email:*** rriffle@emrslaw.com

MICHAEL R. SEGHETTI, born Peoria, Illinois, December 8, 1961; admitted to bar, 1986, Illinois, U.S. District Court, Central District of Illinois, U.S. Court of Appeals, Seventh Circuit. *Education:* University of Illinois (B.S., with honors, 1983); University of Notre Dame (J.D., with honors, 1986). Member, 1984-1985 and Notes Editor, 1985-1986, Notre Dame Law Review. Certified Public Accountant, Illinois, 1983. President, Peoria Public Library Board of Trustees, 1994-1996. *Member:* Peoria County, Illinois State and American Bar Associations. ***PRACTICE AREAS:*** Real Estate Law; Municipal Law; Corporate Law. ***Email:*** mseghetti@emrslaw.com

TROY N. PUDIK, born Peoria, Illinois, July 17, 1968; admitted to bar, 1993, Illinois, U.S. District Court, Central District of Illinois and U.S. Tax Court. *Education:* University of Illinois (A.B., 1990); Drake University (M.B.A., 1993; J.D., with honors, 1993). *Member:* American Intellectual Property Law Association; Peoria County, Illinois State and American Bar Associations. ***PRACTICE AREAS:*** Corporate Law; Real Estate Law; Intellectual Property Law; Healthcare Law. ***Email:*** tpudik@emrslaw.com

---

DAVID N. SCHELLENBERG, born Peoria, Illinois, March 20, 1961; admitted to bar, 1990, Illinois. *Education:* Bradley University (B.S. in Political Science, 1983); Southern Illinois University (J.D., 1989); University of Miami (LL.M., in Estate Planning, 1990). Recipient, Best Editor Award, Staff Member, 1987-1988, and Lead Articles Editor, 1988-1989, Southern Illinois University Law Journal. ***PRACTICE AREAS:*** Employee Benefits; Corporate Law; Tax Law; Estate Planning. ***Email:*** dschellenberg@emrslaw.com

JANAKI NAIR, born Highland Park, Illinois, November 16, 1978; admitted to bar, 2002, Illinois and U.S. District Court, Central District of Illinois. *Education:* University of Chicago (B.A., with special honors, 1999); University of Illinois (J.D., cum laude, 2002). *Member:* Peoria County and American Bar Associations. ***REPORTED CASES:*** Health Professionals, Ltd. v. Johnson, 339 Ill.App.3d 1021, 791 N.E.2d 1179, 274 Ill. Dec. 768 (Ill. App.3 Dist. June 4, 2003). ***PRACTICE AREAS:*** Litigation; Corporate Law. ***Email:*** jnair@emrslaw.com

SONYA A. PASQUINI, born Peoria, Illinois, November 28, 1977; admitted to bar, 2002, Illinois; 2003, U.S. District Court, Central District of Illinois. *Education:* Washington University (B.A., with honors, 1999); University of Illinois (J.D., magna cum laude, 2002). Order of the Coif. Editor, Illinois Law Review. Clerk to Judge Michael M. Mihm, Federal District Court for Central District of Illinois, 2002-2003. *Member:* Peoria County Bar Association. ***Email:*** spasquini@emrslaw.com

OF COUNSEL

CYNTHIA LEE ELIAS, born Zanesville, Ohio, October 16, 1953; admitted to bar, 1978, Illinois; 1981, Ohio; 1982, Massachusetts; 1999, U.S. District Court, Central District of Illinois; 2000, U.S. Tax Court. *Education:* Miami University (A.B., summa cum laude, 1975); Harvard University (J.D., 1978); Illinois State University, Normal, Illinois (Ph.D. Psychology, 1999). Phi Kappa Phi Scholarship. Recipient, Mortar Board, SPERS, Ohio Fellow. Member, American Psychological Association, 1997—. Member, Society for Research in Child Development, 1997-1999. Certified School Psychologist, 1997—. Author: "The School Psychologist as an Expert Witness: Strategies And Issues in the Courtroom," 28 School Psychology Review 44, 1999. *Member:* Peoria County and Illinois State Bar Association. ***PRACTICE AREAS:*** Civil Litigation. ***Email:*** celias@emrslaw.com

HALLIHAN INTELLECTUAL PROPERTY LAW, LTD.

PEORIA, ILLINOIS

(See Chicago)

Litigation, Intellectual Property Law, Patents, Trademarks, Copyrights, Trade Secrets and Entertainment Law.

RONALD L. HAMM

415 HAMILTON BOULEVARD
PEORIA, ILLINOIS 61602
Telephone: 309-671-9701
Fax: 309-637-5788
Email: rhamm@cfgolaw.com

Personal Injury, Criminal Law, Workers Compensation.

RONALD L. HAMM, born Peoria, Illinois, November 25, 1941; admitted to bar, 1968, Illinois. *Education:* Monmouth College and Bradley University; John Marshall Law School (J.D., 1968). Delta Theta Phi. Member, John Marshall Journal of Law and Procedure, 1967-1968. Licensed Real Estate Broker, Illinois, 1975. Assistant State's Attorney, Peoria County, Illinois, 1968-1971. Assistant Public Defender, 1971-1972. *Member:* Peoria County, Fulton County, Illinois State and American Bar Associations; The Association of Trial Lawyers of America; Illinois Trial Lawyers Association; Illinois Attorneys for Criminal Justice. American Inns of Court. ***PRACTICE AREAS:*** Personal Injury; Criminal Law; Workers Compensation.

HAMM & HANNA, LTD.

A PROFESSIONAL CORPORATION

Established in 1977

411 HAMILTON BOULEVARD
SUITE 1004
PEORIA, ILLINOIS 61602
Telephone: 309-676-3608
Fax: 309-676-3219
Email: hammhanna@sbcglobal.net
URL: http://www.hammhanna.com

General Civil Trial and Appellate Practice. Workers Compensation, Personal Injury, Airplane Crash Litigation, Products Liability, Medical Malpractice, Criminal Law, Driving Under the Influence. Practice in State and Federal Courts.

FIRM PROFILE: Collectively, the law firm of Hamm & Hanna, LTD. has been practicing law in Peoria for nearly 40 years. Serving clients throughout Tazewell, McLean, Peoria, Fulton, Knox, Mason, Cass, Schuyler, Woodford and surrounding counties. A general practice with individuals concentrating in certain areas of law.

RONALD HANNA, born Berwyn, Illinois, September 17, 1946; admitted to bar, 1972, Illinois. *Education:* Illinois State University (B.S., 1968); University of Illinois (J.D., 1972). Assistant Attorney General, 1972-1973. First Assistant State's Attorney, Peoria County, Illinois, 1973-1975. *Member:* Peoria County, Fulton County, Illinois State and American Bar Associations; The Association of Trial Lawyers of America; Illinois Trial Lawyers Association; Illinois Attorneys for Criminal Justice; National Association of Criminal Defense Lawyers. [1st Lt., Illinois National Guard, 1969-1976]. ***PRACTICE AREAS:*** Personal Injury; Criminal Law; Workers Compensation; Medical Negligence. ***Email:*** ronhanna@sbcglobal.net

---

RONALD LEN HANNA, born Peoria, Illinois, January 10, 1976; admitted to bar, 2001, Illinois, U.S. District Court, Central District of Illinois and U.S. Court of Appeals, 7th Circuit. *Education:* University of Illinois, Urbana-Champaign (B.A., 1998); Southern Illinois University (J.D., cum laude, 2001). Phi Alpha Delta. National Order of Barristers. Lead Articles Editor, Law Journal, Southern Illinois University School of Law. *Member:* Peoria County, Illinois State and American Bar Associations. ***PRACTICE AREAS:*** Criminal Law; Personal Injury; Workers Compensation; Wrongful Death. ***Email:*** lenhanna@sbcglobal.net

LEGAL SUPPORT PERSONNEL

DIANE McPHERSON

HASSELBERG, ROCK, BELL & KUPPLER LLP

SUITE 200, ASSOCIATED BANK BUILDING
4600 NORTH BRANDYWINE DRIVE
PEORIA, ILLINOIS 61614
Telephone: 309-688-9400
Fax: 309-688-9430
URL: http://www.hrbklaw.com

General Civil and Trial Practice. Corporate, Business, Real Estate and Development, Estate Planning, Trusts and Probate, Taxation, Municipal, Construction, Landlord and Tenant Law, Debtor and Creditor, Replevin, Employment and Family Law. Commercial and Civil Litigation, Personal Injury and Workers' Compensation.

(This Listing Continued)

MEMBERS OF FIRM

ERIC E. HASSELBERG, born Peoria, Illinois, October 27, 1950; admitted to bar, 1975, Iowa; 1976, Illinois; 1977, U.S. District Court, Central District of Illinois. *Education:* University of Iowa (B.A., 1972; J.D., with high distinction, 1975). Research Attorney, Iowa Supreme Court, 1975-1976. *Member:* Peoria County (Past Chairman, Real Property Committee), Illinois State, Iowa State and American Bar Associations; Central Illinois Estate Planning Council. ***PRACTICE AREAS:*** Elder Law; Probate; Estate Planning; Federal Income Tax; Estate and Gift Taxation; Real Estate. ***Email:*** ehasselberg@hrbklaw.com

JEFFREY B. ROCK, born Princeville, Illinois, October 30, 1952; admitted to bar, 1977, Illinois and U.S. District Court, Central District of Illinois; 1983, U.S. Court of Appeals, Seventh Circuit. *Education:* University of Illinois (B.A., 1974); Washington University (J.D., 1977). Edmund J. James Scholar. Illinois Attorney General Special Assistant, 1983-1991. Master of the Bench, Abraham Lincoln Inn of Court. Civil Mediator. *Member:* Peoria County, Illinois State and American Bar Associations. ***PRACTICE AREAS:*** Commercial Litigation; Professional Contract Litigation; Personal Injury Litigation; Workers' Compensation; Alternative Dispute Resolution. ***Email:*** jrock@hrbklaw.com

CHARLES M. ROCK, born Peoria, Illinois, September 18, 1954; admitted to bar, 1980, Illinois. *Education:* University of Illinois (B.S., 1976); Washington University (J.D., 1980). Author: "Securing Free and Clear Title: Basic Real Estate Law in Illinois," National Business Institute, 1991. Member, Abraham Lincoln Inn of Court. *Member:* Peoria County (Past Chairman, Real Property Committee) and Illinois State Bar Associations. ***PRACTICE AREAS:*** Real Estate; Business Formations; Contracts; Corporate Law; Construction Litigation; Mechanics Liens; Commercial Litigation. ***Email:*** c.rock@hrbklaw.com

GREGORY S. BELL, born Lincoln, Nebraska, May 7, 1948; admitted to bar, 1975, Illinois; 1977, U.S. District Court, Central District of Illinois; 1980, U.S. Court of Appeals, Seventh Circuit. *Education:* University of Illinois (B.A., high honors, 1970; J.D., honors, 1975). Edmund J. James Scholar. Phi Beta Kappa; Phi Eta Sigma. Notes and Comments Editor, University of Illinois Law Review, 1974-1975. Law Clerk to Chief Justice Robert C. Underwood, Illinois Supreme Court, 1975-1976. Village Attorney, Germantown Hills, 1982—. Master of the Bench, Abraham Lincoln Inn of Court (President, 2004-2005). *Member:* Peoria County, Illinois State and American Bar Associations. ***PRACTICE AREAS:*** Commercial Litigation; Construction Law; Municipal Law. ***Email:*** gbell@hrbklaw.com

KARL B. KUPPLER, born Nuremberg, Germany, July 10, 1956; admitted to bar, 1981, Illinois and U.S. District Court, Northern District of Illinois; 1984, U.S. Tax Court; 1987, U.S. District Court, Central District of Illinois. *Education:* North Central College (B.A., summa cum laude, 1978); University of Illinois (J.D., magna cum laude, 1981). Order of the Coif. Member, 1979-1980 and Editor, 1980-1981, University of Illinois Law Review. Co-Author: "Annual Survey of Illinois Law"; "Buying and Selling Businesses," Illinois Institute for Continuing Legal Education. *Member:* Peoria County, Illinois State (Member, Estate Planning, Probate and Trust Section Council, 1988-1994) and American (Vice Chairman, Tax Committee, General Practice Section, 1989-1991) Bar Associations; Central Illinois Estate Planning Council (President, 1989-1990). ***PRACTICE AREAS:*** Federal Income Tax; Estate and Gift Taxation; Estate Planning; Real Estate; Corporate Law; Business Law. ***Email:*** kkuppler@hrbklaw.com

JULIE L. GALASSI, born Decatur, Illinois, November 27, 1959; admitted to bar, 1988, Illinois, U.S. District Court, Central District of Illinois and U.S. Court of Appeals, Seventh Circuit. *Education:* Illinois State University (B.S., 1982); Northern Illinois University (J.D., 1987). Member, Northern Illinois Law Review, 1986-1987. Master of the Bench, Abraham Lincoln Inn of Court. *Member:* Peoria County, Illinois State and American Bar Associations. ***PRACTICE AREAS:*** Family Law; Labor and Employment Law; Civil Litigation; Family Mediation. ***Email:*** jgalassi@hrbklaw.com

DANNY L. SCHROEDER, JR., born Peoria, Illinois, February 1, 1956; admitted to bar, 1982, Illinois and U.S. District Court, Central District of Illinois; 1994, U.S. Court of Appeals, Seventh Circuit; 1999, Iowa; 2005, U.S. District Court, Northern and Southern Districts of Illinois. *Education:* Illinois Wesleyan University (B.A., magna cum laude, 1978); Southern Illinois University (J.D., 1981). Phi Alpha Delta. *Member:* Peoria County and Illinois State Bar Associations. ***PRACTICE AREAS:*** Landlord-Tenant; Debtor-Creditor; Replevin; Family Law; Corporate Law; Estate Planning; Estate Administration. ***Email:*** dschroeder@hrbklaw.com

ASSOCIATE

MARCI M. SHOFF, born Peoria, Illinois, July 1, 1977; admitted to bar, 2002, Illinois and U.S. District Court, Central District of Illinois; 2005, U.S. District Court, Northern and Southern Districts of Illinois. *Education:* University of Illinois (B.S., high honors, 1999; J.D., honors, 2002). Beta Gamma Sigma; Alpha Lambda Delta; Phi Eta Sigma. *Member:* Peoria County, Illinois State and American Bar Associations. ***PRACTICE AREAS:*** Civil Litigation; Probate; Guardianship; Family Law. ***Email:*** mshoff@hrbklaw.com

HASSELBERG, WILLIAMS, GREBE, SNODGRASS & BIRDSALL

BANK ONE BUILDING, SUITE 360
124 S.W. ADAMS STREET
PEORIA, ILLINOIS 61602-1320
Telephone: 309-637-1400
Telecopier: 309-637-1500
URL: http://www.hwgsb.com

General Practice, Litigation, Wills, Trusts and Estates, Probate, Elder Law, Estate Planning, Federal Taxation, Insurance, Insurance Defense, Real Estate, Personal Injury, Workers Compensation, Agricultural Law, Corporate Law, Governmental Law, Administrative Law, Commercial Law, Criminal Law, Driving While Intoxicated, Traffic Violations, Labor and Employment, Family Law, Adoption Law, Bankruptcy, Zoning, Planning and Land Use and Real Estate Title Insurance.

(This Listing Continued)

FIRM PROFILE: Hasselberg, Williams, Grebe, Snodgrass & Birdsall is a full service law firm with individual lawyers concentrating in particular areas of the law. The firm serves clients throughout the State with a focus on Central and Southern Illinois.

MICHAEL R. HASSELBERG, admitted to bar, 1975, Illinois. *Education:* University of Illinois (B.A., 1968; M.A., 1972); John Marshall Law School (J.D., 1975). President, Abraham Lincoln Inn of the American Inns of Court, 1997-1998. Fellow, American Academy of Matrimonial Lawyers since 1990, Recertified, 1995 and 2000. *Member:* Peoria County (Member, Board of Directors, 1996—; Chairman, Family Law Committee, 1988 and 1994; Chairman Continuing Legal Education Committee, 2000) and Illinois State Bar Associations. ***PRACTICE AREAS:*** Family Law. ***Email:*** mhasselberg@hwgsb.com

RAYMOND C. WILLIAMS, admitted to bar, 1980, Illinois. *Education:* Millikin University (B.M.E., 1966); University of Miami (M.M., 1973); University of Illinois (J.D., 1980). *Member:* Peoria County and Illinois State Bar Associations; Central Illinois Estate Planning Council; National Academy of Elder Law Attorneys. ***PRACTICE AREAS:*** Wills; Trusts and Estates; Probate; Real Estate; Elder Law; Workers Compensation Defense; Corporate Law; Governmental Law. ***Email:*** rwilliams@hwgsb.com

JAMES R. GREBE, admitted to bar, 1980, Illinois. *Education:* Concordia University (B.A., 1977); University of Illinois (J.D., 1980). *Member:* Peoria County (Member, Board of Directors, 2001-2002; Chairman, Real Property Committee, 2001-2002) and Illinois State (Vice Chairman, Agricultural Law Section Council, 2002-2003) Bar Associations; Christian Legal Society; Central Illinois Estate Planning Council; National Academy of Elder Law Attorneys; American Agricultural Law Association. ***PRACTICE AREAS:*** Agricultural Law; Corporate Law; Wills; Trusts and Estates; Probate; Elder Law; Federal Taxation; Real Estate; Commercial Law. ***Email:*** jgrebe@hwgsb.com

KENNETH M. SNODGRASS, JR., admitted to bar, 1981, Illinois. *Education:* University of Illinois (B.A., 1978; J.D., 1981). *Member:* Peoria County and Illinois State Bar Associations; Illinois Trial Lawyers' Association. ***PRACTICE AREAS:*** Civil Litigation; Labor and Employment; Personal Injury; Insurance Defense; Workers Compensation; Agricultural Law. ***Email:*** ksnodgrass@hwgsb.com

CHARLES J. URBAN, admitted to bar, 1989, Illinois. *Education:* University of Illinois (B.S., 1985); Southern Illinois University (J.D., 1988). *Member:* Peoria County (Chairman, Family Law Committee, 2001-2002), Illinois State Bar Associations. ***PRACTICE AREAS:*** Family Law; Labor and Employment; Civil Litigation; Insurance Defense; Real Estate; Administrative Law; Bankruptcy; Personal Injury. ***Email:*** curban@hwgsb.com

SANDRA J. BIRDSALL, admitted to bar, 1982, Illinois. *Education:* Western Illinois University (B.S., 1964); Illinois Institute of Technology, Chicago-Kent College of Law (J.D., with high honors, 1982). Member, Chicago Kent Law Review, 1981-1982. Mayor, Village of Roselle, Illinois, 1979-1988. President, DuPage Mayors and Managers Conference, 1984. Chairman, City of Peoria Planning Commission, 1989-1994. Member, YWCA Board of Directors, 1990-1994; President, 1993-1994. Peoria Area Chamber of Commerce Board of Directors, 1995—, Chairman, 2001-2003; Nature Conservancy Regional Board, 1999—. *Member:* Peoria County and Illinois State (Member, Real Estate Section Council, 1995-2000; 2002—) Bar Associations. ***PRACTICE AREAS:*** Real Estate; Zoning and Land Use; Corporate; Municipal Law. ***Email:*** sbirdsall@hwgsb.com

DAVID L. WENTWORTH, II, admitted to bar, 1993, Illinois. *Education:* Albion College (B.A., 1989); University of Detroit School of Law (J.D., 1993). Member, University of Detroit Law Review, 1992-1993. *Member:* Peoria County, Illinois State and American Bar Associations; State Bar of Michigan. ***PRACTICE AREAS:*** Commercial Litigation; Agricultural Law; Insurance; Wills; Trusts and Estates; Bankruptcy. ***Email:*** dwentworth@hwgsb.com

ASSOCIATES

KENNETH E. DAVIES, admitted to bar, 1997, Illinois. *Education:* College of Wooster (B.A., 1991); Southern Illinois University School of Law (J.D., cum laude, 1997). Author: Southern Illinois University Law Journal, Volume 21, Page 149, 1996. *Member:* Peoria County Bar Association. ***PRACTICE AREAS:*** Corporate Law; Real Estate; Zoning and Land Use; Probate; Wills; Trusts and Estates. ***Email:*** kdavies@hwgsb.com

ALISON E. McLAUGHLIN, admitted to bar, 1998, Illinois; 2000, New York. *Education:* State University of New York at Albany (B.A., 1995); Hofstra University School of Law (J.D., 1998). ***PRACTICE AREAS:*** Bankruptcy; Family Law; Personal Injury. ***Email:*** amclaughlin@hwgsb.com

BOYD O. ROBERTS, III, admitted to bar, 1997, Illinois and U.S. District Court, Central District of Illinois. *Education:* University of Illinois (B.A., 1994); DePaul University College of Law (J.D., 1997). ***PRACTICE AREAS:*** Workers Compensation; Commercial Litigation; Insurance Defense Litigation; Family Law; Criminal Defense. ***Email:*** broberts@hwgsb.com

MEGAN R. RUSSO, admitted to bar, 2002, Illinois. *Education:* Ball State University (B.A., 1999); University of Illinois College of Law (J.D., magna cum laude, 2002). ***PRACTICE AREAS:*** Real Estate; Business Organization; Probate; Estate Administration; Commercial Litigation. ***Email:*** mrusso@hwgsb.com

LISA R. BARBEE, born Peoria, Illinois; admitted to bar, 2003, Illinois. *Education:* Augustana College (B.A., cum laude, 1998); Case Western Reserve University (J.D., cum laude, 2003). *Member:* Peoria County and Illinois State Bar Associations. ***LANGUAGES:*** Spanish. ***PRACTICE AREAS:*** Probate; Tax; Real Estate; Business. ***Email:*** lbarbee@hwgsb.com

HEIPLE LAW OFFICES

Established in 1994

9121 N. INDUSTRIAL ROAD, SUITE A

PEORIA, ILLINOIS 61615-1549

Telephone: 309-691-7263
Fax: 309-691-7266
URL: http://www.heiple.com
Email: heiple@earthlink.net
URL: http://www.lawyers.com/heiplelaw

Christian firm with diverse General Civil Trial and Appellate Practice including: Workers' Compensation, Personal Injury, Guardianship, Advance Directives, Business and Corporate, Real Estate, Wills and Trust/Estate Planning, and Probate.

FIRM PROFILE: Heiple Law Offices practices from a distinctly Christian perspective, using Biblical principles and guidelines wherever possible both in counseling its clients and in operating the firm. Heiple Law Offices enjoys a statewide practice for its appellate and workers" compensation clientele, and the other aspects of its diverse general civil practice are concentrated in the 9th, 10th and 11th Judicial Circuits in Central Illinois.

MEMBERS OF FIRM

JEREMY H. HEIPLE, born Peoria, Illinois, January 4, 1962; admitted to bar, 1987, Illinois. *Education:* Albion College (B.A., summa cum laude, 1984); University of Illinois (J.D., 1987). Phi Beta Kappa. Named Volunteer Lawyer of the Year, Peoria County Bar Association, 2004. Law Clerk to Honorable Roger A. Sommer, Chief Justice, Illinois Court of Claims, 1993-1999. Author and Lecturer, "Workers' Compensation in Illinois" (1999) and "Advanced Workers' Compensation in Illinois" (2000), National Business Institute. *Member:* Peoria County, Tazewell County, Illinois State and American Bar Associations; National Lawyers Association; Illinois Trial Lawyers Association; National Guardianship Association, Illinois Guardianship Association. ***PRACTICE AREAS:*** Guardianship and Advance Directives; General Litigation; Workers Compensation; Civil Practice; Guardian Ad Litem; Insurance Defense; Probate; Real Estate; Trusts and Estates; Wills.

JONATHAN J. HEIPLE, born Peoria, Illinois, June 24, 1964; admitted to bar, 1992, Illinois; 1995, Missouri; 1996, Iowa. *Education:* Albion College (A.B., 1985); Indiana University (M.B.A., 1987); University of Virginia (J.D., 1992). Phi Beta Kappa; Beta Gamma Sigma; Phi Delta Phi. Notes Editor, Managing Board, Journal of Law & Politics, University of Virginia, 1991-1992. Law Clerk to Honorable Richard Mills, U.S. District Court, Central District of Illinois, 1992-1994 and Honorable Duane Benton, Missouri Supreme Court, 1994-1995. Author, "Fiscal Policy Reform," Journal of Law & Politics, Winter 1992. *Member:* Peoria County and Illinois State Bar Associations. ***PRACTICE AREAS:*** Civil Practice; Appellate Practice; Municipal Law.

OF COUNSEL

JOHN A. SCHELLENBERG, born Peoria, Illinois, July 3, 1965; admitted to bar, 1990, Illinois. *Education:* Bradley University (B.S., cum laude, 1987); Southern Illinois University (J.D., 1990). Author and Lecturer: "Collection Law in Illinois," Lorman Education Services, Inc., 1995. Co-Author: "The Basic Agreement," (Real Estate), Illinois Institute for Continuing Legal Education, 1995. Intermittent Hearings Referee, Illinois Department of Employment Security, 1995—. Instructor: Wills, Trusts and Estates, Illinois Central College, 1998-2002. *Member:* Peoria County and Illinois State Bar Associations. ***PRACTICE AREAS:*** Estate Planning; Probate Administration; Real Estate; Corporate.

HEYL, ROYSTER, VOELKER & ALLEN

PROFESSIONAL CORPORATION

SUITE 600, CHASE BUILDING
124 S.W. ADAMS

PEORIA, ILLINOIS 61602

Telephone: 309-676-0400
Telecopier: 309-676-3374
Email: firm@hrva.com
URL: http://www.hrva.com

Springfield, Illinois Office: Suite 575, National City Center, P.O. Box 1687, 62705. Telephone: 217-522-8822. Telecopier: 217-523-3902.

Urbana, Illinois Office: Suite 300, 102 East Main Street, P.O. Box 129, 61803-0129. Telephone: 217-344-0060. Telecopier: 217-344-9295.

Rockford, Illinois Office: Second Floor, National City Bank Building, 120 West State Street, P.O. Box 1288, 61105-1288. Telephone: 815-963-4454. Telecopier: 815-963-0399.

Edwardsville, Illinois Office: Suite 100, Mark Twain Plaza II, 103 West Vandalia Street, P.O. Box 467, 62025. Telephone: 618-656-4646. Telecopier: 618-656-7940.

General Civil Trial and Appellate Practice in all Courts, Insurance Defense, Workers' Compensation Defense, Professional Liability Defense, Truck Accidents, Construction Law, Railroad Accidents and Injuries, Insurance Coverage, Self Insured Defense, Products Liability Defense, Civil Rights, Asbestos Defense, Class Action Defense, Corporate Law, Health Care, Banking, Government, Employment, Environmental, Probate, Elder Law, Agribusiness, Immigration, Religious Institutions, Nonprofit and Charitable Organizations, College and University Law, and Real Estate.

MANAGING PARTNER

ROBERT V. DEWEY, JR., born September 15, 1944; admitted to bar, 1969, Minnesota; 1972, Illinois. *Education:* Brown University (B.A., 1966); University of Wisconsin (J.D., 1969). Fellow, American College of Trial Lawyers. *Member:* Peoria County Bar Association (President, 1997-1998); Federation of Defense and Corporate Counsel (President, 2002-2003); DRI (Board of Directors, 2001-2004); Lawyers for Civil Justice (Board of Directors, 2002-2004); Illinois Association of Defense Trial Counsel (President, 1987-1988); Illinois Institute for Continuing Legal Education (Chair, Board of Directors, 1998-1999); National Association of Railroad Trial Counsel; Society of Trial Lawyers (Illinois). ***PRACTICE AREAS:*** Products Liability Defense; Transportation Liability Defense; Professional Liability Defense; Insurance Defense. ***Email:*** rdewey@hrva.com

PARTNERS

BRENT H. GWILLIM, born July 28, 1946; admitted to bar, 1971, Illinois; 1985, U.S. Tax Court. *Education:* Bradley University (B.A., 1968); University of Missouri (J.D., 1971). Member, Illinois Secretary of State Business Act Advisory Committee. *Member:* Illinois State Bar Association (Chair: Corporation, Securities and Business Law Section Council; Past Chair: Task Force on Limited Liability of Attorneys); Illinois Association of Hospital Attorneys. ***PRACTICE AREAS:*** Business Planning; Business Acquisitions; Probate Administration; Estate Planning; Real Property Acquisitions. ***Email:*** bgwillim@hrva.com

REX K. LINDER, born January 15, 1948; admitted to bar, 1974, Illinois. *Education:* Bradley University (B.S., 1969); Washburn University Law School (J.D., 1973). Fellow, American College of Trial Lawyers. *Member:* Peoria County (President, 2005—) and Seventh Circuit (Liaison, Illinois Central District) Bar Association; International Association of Defense Counsel (President, 1998-1999); DRI (Member, Board of Directors, 1997-2000); Lawyers For Civil Justice (President, 2002-2003); Illinois Association of Defense Trial Counsel (Past Chair, Product Liability Committee); Bar Association of Central and Southern Federal Districts of Illinois (Treasurer, 2001—); Society of Trial Lawyers (Illinois). ***PRACTICE AREAS:*** Products Liability Defense; Professional Liability Defense; Federal Litigation. ***Email:*** rlinder@hrva.com

TIMOTHY L. BERTSCHY, born November 12, 1952; admitted to bar, 1977, Illinois. *Education:* University of Illinois (B.A., magna cum laude, 1974); George Washington University (J.D., 1977). Fellow: Illinois State Bar Foundation (Past Director); American Bar Foundation. *Member:* Peoria County (Immediate Past Chair, Diversity Committee), Illinois State (President, 1998-1999) and American (Member, House of Delegates, 1995—; Co-Chair, Section of Litigation Business Torts Committee; Member, Board of Governors 2004—) Bar Associations; American Judicature Society; Illinois Lawyers' Assistance Program (Past President); Illinois Equal Justice Foundation (President); Bar Association of the Central and Southern Districts (Illinois) Rules and Practices (Co-Chair); Illinois Coalition for Equal Justice (President, 2000-2003); Illinois Township Attorneys Association (President, 1989-1993; Member, Board of Directors, 2002—); United States District Court Advisory Committee on Local Rules, Central District of Illinois (Chair). ***PRACTICE AREAS:*** Commercial Litigation; Governmental Law; Religious Nonprofit Corporation Law. ***Email:*** tbertschy@hrva.com

GARY D. NELSON, born October 18, 1950; admitted to bar, 1977, Illinois. *Education:* University of Illinois (B.A., 1972; J.D., 1977). *Member:* Illinois State (Past Chair, Insurance Section Council) and American (Past Chair, Self Insurers and Risk Managers Committee) Bar Associations; DRI; Illinois Association of Defense Trial Counsel (Past Chair, Insurance Coverage Committee); Trucking Industry Defense Association; Federation of Defense and Corporate Counsel. ***PRACTICE AREAS:*** Insurance Coverage; Construction; Motor Carrier Defense; Professional Liability Defense. ***Email:*** gnelson@hrva.com

DAVID R. SINN, born July 28, 1950; admitted to bar, 1976, Illinois; 1993, Washington. *Education:* Western Illinois University (B.S., 1973); University of Tennessee (J.D., 1976). *Member:* Illinois Association of Defense Trial Counsel; DRI; American Society of Law and Medicine. ***PRACTICE AREAS:*** Medical Malpractice Defense; Drug and Medical Device Defense; Legal Malpractice Defense. ***Email:*** dsinn@hrva.com

ROGER R. CLAYTON, born April 6, 1953; admitted to bar, 1978, Illinois. *Education:* Bradley University (B.A., magna cum laude, 1975); Southern Illinois University (J.D., 1978). *Member:* American Society of Law, Medicine and Ethics; DRI; Illinois Association of Defense Trial Counsel (IDC Quarterly Health Law Columnist); American Health Lawyers Association; Illinois Association of Healthcare Attorneys (Secretary-Treasurer, Board Member, Planning Committee, Annual Health Law Symposium); Illinois Society of Healthcare Risk Management (Past President, 2003-2004 and Board Member). Inns of Court (Chapter President, 2000-2001). ***PRACTICE AREAS:*** Health Care; Medical Malpractice Defense; Professional Liability Defense; Hospital Law. ***Email:*** rclayton@hrva.com

BRADFORD B. INGRAM, born April 12, 1954; admitted to bar, 1980, Illinois. *Education:* Drake University (B.A., 1976; J.D., 1980). *Member:* American Bar Association (Past Chair, Workers' Compensation Employer Liability Law Committee; Past Chair, Governmental Liability Committee); DRI (Past Chair, Workers' Compensation Committee, 2000—; Program Chair, Employment Law Committee, 2003; Editor, DRI Employment Law Newsletter); International Association of Defense Counsel (Editor, IADC Employment Law Committee Newsletter); National Association of College and University Attorneys. ***PRACTICE AREAS:*** Employment Law; Workers Compensation Defense; Civil Rights Discrimination; College and University Law. ***Email:*** bingram@hrva.com

NICHOLAS J. BERTSCHY, born October 24, 1956; admitted to bar, 1981, Illinois, Wisconsin. *Education:* University of Illinois (B.S., magna cum laude, 1978); University of Wisconsin (J.D., with honors, 1981). *Member:* Illinois Association of Defense Trial Counsel; Illinois Bar Foundation (First Pillar of the Profession; Member, Board of Directors, 1996-2005). ***PRACTICE AREAS:*** Medical Malpractice Defense; Products Liability Defense; Dram Shop Liability. ***Email:*** nbertschy@hrva.com

STEPHEN J. HEINE, born November 23, 1955; admitted to bar, 1981, Illinois. *Education:* Illinois State University (B.S., 1978); Southern Illinois University (J.D., cum laude, 1981). *Member:* American Bar Association (Past Chair, Commercial Transportation Litigation Committee); Bar Association of The Seventh Federal Circuit; DRI (State Representative, Illinois 2004—); Illinois Appellate Lawyers Association; Illinois Association of Defense Trial Counsel (President, 2004-2005); National Association of Railroad Trial Counsel; Association of Defense Trial Attorneys. ***PRACTICE AREAS:*** Railroad Litigation; Products Liability Defense; First Party Insurance Defense; Construction Insurance Defense. ***Email:*** sheine@hrva.com

KAREN L. KENDALL, born February 5, 1945; admitted to bar, 1981, Illinois. *Education:* Southern Illinois University (B.A., 1967; M.A., 1976; J.D., cum laude, 1981).

(This Listing Continued)

Southern Illinois University Law School Alumnus of the Year, 1996. Editor-in-Chief, Appellate Law Review, 1992-1996. Law Clerk to: Honorable Howard C. Ryan, Chief Justice, Illinois Supreme Court, 1981-1982; Honorable Jay J. Alloy, Illinois Appellate Court, 1984, Third District. Illinois Supreme Court Civil Jury Instruction Committee, 1987-1996). Fellow, American Bar Foundation. *Member:* Peoria County (Secretary-Treasurer, 2005—); Illinois State (Special Committee on Appellate Practice, 2001-2002) and American (Past Chair, Appellate Advocacy Committee) Bar Associations; American Academy of Appellate Lawyers (Director 2003—); Illinois Appellate Lawyers Association (President, 1994-1995); Illinois Association of Defense Trial Counsel (Past Chair, Amicus Committee); Association of Defense Trial Attorneys; Bar Association of the Seventh Federal Circuit; DRI (Member, Appellate Advocacy Steering Committee); Inns of Court (Chapter President, 2003-2004); Scribes, American Society of Writers on Legal Subjects. ***PRACTICE AREAS:*** Appellate Practice; Nonprofit Organizations Law; Contract Litigation; Local Government Liability. ***Email:*** kkendall@hrva.com

CRAIG S. YOUNG, born July 19, 1960; admitted to bar, 1985, Illinois. *Education:* Bradley University (B.A., summa cum laude, 1982); University of Illinois (J.D., 1985). *Member:* American Immigration Lawyers Association. ***PRACTICE AREAS:*** Employment Law; Immigration Law; Workers Compensation Defense; Self Insured Defense. ***Email:*** cyoung@hrva.com

WILLIAM I. COVEY, born November 21, 1957; admitted to bar, 1983, Illinois. *Education:* University of Illinois (B.S., Accountancy Honors, 1980); Southern Illinois University (J.D., summa cum laude, 1983). Certified Public Accountant, Illinois, 1983. *Member:* National Council of Farm Cooperatives. ***PRACTICE AREAS:*** Business Organization; Buying and Selling of Businesses; Agricultural Cooperatives; Corporate Contracts. ***Email:*** wcovey@hrva.com

CHRISTOPHER P. LARSON, born March 4, 1959; admitted to bar, 1984, Illinois. *Education:* Bradley University (B.A., 1981); University of Illinois (J.D., 1984). *Member:* DRI; Illinois Association of Defense Trial Counsel. ***PRACTICE AREAS:*** Complex and Multi-District Litigation; Asbestos Litigation Defense; Toxic Tort Defense. ***Email:*** clarson@hrva.com

JAMES M. VOELKER, born February 1, 1961; admitted to bar, 1986, Illinois. *Education:* University of Illinois (B.S., cum laude, 1983); University of Iowa (J.D., with distinction, 1986). ***PRACTICE AREAS:*** Workers Compensation Defense; Asbestos Litigation Defense; Computer Software Litigation. ***Email:*** jvoelker@hrva.com

JOSEPH G. FEEHAN, born June 26, 1961; admitted to bar, 1988, Illinois. *Education:* Illinois State University (B.S., 1983); Northern Illinois University (J.D., cum laude, 1988). *Member:* Illinois State Bar Association (Member: Tort Law Section Council); Illinois Association of Defense Trial Counsel (Co-Chair, Young Lawyers Committee; Associate Editor, IDC Quarterly). ***PRACTICE AREAS:*** Products Liability Defense; Motor Carrier Defense; Commercial Litigation. ***Email:*** jfeehan@hrva.com

MATTHEW S. HEFFLEFINGER, born February 10, 1962; admitted to bar, 1989, Illinois. *Education:* Bradley University (B.S., magna cum laude, 1984); Southern Illinois University (M.B.A., 1989; J.D., 1989). *Member:* Illinois Association of Defense Trial Counsel; Inns of Court (Chapter President, 2005-2006). ***PRACTICE AREAS:*** Transportation Liability Defense; Construction Litigation Defense; Aviation Liability Defense; Commercial Litigation. ***Email:*** mhefflefinger@hrva.com

DAVID A. PERKINS, born March 26, 1957; admitted to bar, 1987, Illinois. *Education:* University of Illinois at Springfield (B.A., with honors, 1985); University of Iowa (J.D., 1987). *Member:* Illinois Association of Defense Trial Counsel (Columnist, IDC Quarterly). ***PRACTICE AREAS:*** Constitutional Law; Police Liability Defense; Municipal Liability Defense; Civil Rights Defense; Arson and Insurance Fraud. ***Email:*** dperkins@hrva.com

LISA A. LACONTE, born April 24, 1964; admitted to bar, 1988, Illinois; 1989, Missouri. *Education:* University of Illinois (B.S., 1985); Washington University (J.D., 1988); St. Louis University (LL.M., Health Law, 2002). *Member:* American Health Lawyers Association. ***PRACTICE AREAS:*** Toxic Tort Defense; Asbestos Litigation Defense; Professional Liability Defense; Health Care; Hospital Law. ***Email:*** llaconte@hrva.com

BRAD A. ELWARD, born September 6, 1964; admitted to bar, 1989, Illinois. *Education:* University of Illinois (B.S., 1986); Southern Illinois University (J.D., magna cum laude, 1989). *Member:* Illinois Appellate Lawyers Association (Board of Directors, 1997-1999; Chairman, Rules Committee, 1998-2000); Illinois Association of Defense Trial Counsel (Columnist, IDC Quarterly). ***PRACTICE AREAS:*** Appellate Practice; Workers Compensation Appeals; Administrative Hearings and Appeals. ***Email:*** belward@hrva.com

JAMES J. MANNING, born October 11, 1967; admitted to bar, 1992, Illinois. *Education:* University of Notre Dame (B.B.A., 1989); St. Louis University (J.D., 1992). ***PRACTICE AREAS:*** Residential Real Estate; Workers Compensation Defense; Civil Litigation Defense. ***Email:*** jmanning@hrva.com

TIMOTHY W. KIRK, born October 24, 1956; admitted to bar, 1981, Illinois. *Education:* Illinois State University (B.S., 1978); Drake University (J.D., 1981). Order of the Coif. General Counsel, Central Illinois Light Co., 1995-1997. Vice President and General Counsel, ROHN Industries Inc., 1997-1998. *Member:* National Academy of Elder Law Attorneys. ***PRACTICE AREAS:*** Corporate Law; Public Utility Law; Contract Law; Real Estate Planning; Elder Law. ***Email:*** tkirk@hrva.com

MARK D. HANSEN, born September 11, 1969; admitted to bar, 1994, Illinois. *Education:* Northern Illinois University (B.S., cum laude, 1991); University of Illinois (J.D., cum laude, 1994). *Member:* Illinois State Bar Association (Member, Civil Practice and Procedure Section Council, 1999-2003; Co-Editor, Trial Briefs, 1999—); Illinois Association of Defense Trial Counsel (Co-Chair, Young Lawyers Committee; Chair, 2004 Rookie Seminar; Co-Chair, 2005 Spring Defense Tactics Seminar); DRI. ***PRACTICE AREAS:*** Civil Litigation Defense; Commercial Litigation; Utility Law; Professional Liability Defense. ***Email:*** mhansen@hrva.com

DEBRA L. STEGALL, born September 21, 1955; admitted to bar, 1991, Illinois. *Education:* University of Illinois (B.A., 1988); Southern Illinois University (J.D., 1991). In-House Counsel: Roadmaster Industries, Inc., 1991-1996; Bicycle's Division, Brunswick Corporation, 1997-1999. *Member:* DRI (Member, Employment Law Section); Illinois Association of Healthcare Attorneys; American Health Lawyers Association; Illinois Feed and Grain Association. ***PRACTICE AREAS:*** Employment Law; Agricultural Cooperatives; Administrative Agency Practice; Mergers and Acquisitions; Business Law. ***Email:*** dstegall@hrva.com

CRAIG L. UNRATH, born July 25, 1955; admitted to bar, 1991, Illinois. *Education:* Shimer College (Mount Carroll)(B.A., 1978); University of Illinois (J.D., 1991). *Member:* Illinois Appellate Lawyers Association (Board Secretary, 2005—); DRI. ***PRACTICE AREAS:*** Appellate Practice. ***Email:*** cunrath@hrva.com

ASSOCIATES

Robert M. Bennett	***Carol J. Perkins***
Tobin J. Taylor	***Adam J. Lagocki***
Mark A. Ludolph	***Gregory J. Rastatter***
Thomas J. Dluski	***Maureen R. De Armond***
Andrew J. Keyt	***John M. Redlingshafer***
John K. Kim	

RETIRED OF COUNSEL

Lyle W. Allen	***Richard N. Molchan***
Duncan B. Cooper III	***Gary M. Peplow***
Clarence W. Heyl (1884-1968)	***John H. Royster*** (1907-1985)
William J. Voelker, Jr. (1917-1993)	

Our lawyers are members of the American, state and local bar associations and, in many cases, are members of the local American Inn of Court chapters; where applicable, leadership positions in these organizations are listed.

REPRESENTATIVE CLIENTS: Abbott Laboratories; Ace USA; Allied Insurance; Ameren Corporation; APCapital; Ashland Oil; Auto Owners Insurance Co.; Bechtel Corporation; BP Amoco; Bradley University; Burlington Northern Santa Fe Railway; Carle Clinic Assn.; Carle Foundation Hospital; Caterpillar Inc.; Catholic Diocese of Peoria; Catholic Charities; CertainTeed Corporation; CGU Insurance; CIGNA; Cincinnati Insurance Co.; CNA; Continental Western Group; Country Insurance & Financial Services; Dana Corporation; XL Design Professionals; Dow Chemical; Eastern Illinois University; Erie Insurance Group; Galesburg Cottage Hospital; Gateway, Inc.; GE Medical Protective Co.; General Casualty Cos.; Great West Casualty; GROWMARK, Inc.; GuideOne Insurance; Hartford Life; Illinois Mutual Life & Casualty Co.; Iowa Mutual Insurance Co.; ISMIE Mutual Ins. Co.; Johnson & Johnson; Liberty Mutual Ins. Co.; Maremont Corporation; Methodist Medical Center of Illinois; MetLife Auto & Home; Mitsubishi Motor Manufacturing; OHIC Ins. Co.; Ohio Casualty Group; Parker-Hannifen Corporation; Pearl Companies.; Proctor Hospital; Prudential Property and Casualty; Riley Stoker Corporation; Risk Enterprise Management; Saint Gobain; Schering-Plough Corporation; Southern Illinois University School of Medicine; State Farm Mutual Automobile Insurance Company; St. Paul Companies, Inc.; T.H. Agriculture and Nutrition; Travelers Insurance Co.; Union Carbide; University of Illinois; U.S. Aviation Underwriters; Zurich North America.

(For Other Biographical Information, see Professional Biographies at Edwardsville, Rockford, Springfield and Urbana).

HINSHAW & CULBERTSON LLP

Hinshaw & Culbertson LLP is an Illinois registered limited liability partnership that has elected to be governed by the Illinois Uniform Partnership Act (1997)

Established in 1934

456 FULTON STREET
SUITE 298
PEORIA, ILLINOIS 61602-1220
Telephone: 309-674-1025
Facsimile: 309-674-9328
Telex: 880248
Email: kfox@hinshawlaw.com
URL: http://www.hinshawlaw.com

Other Office Locations: Chicago, Illinois; Appleton, Wisconsin; Belleville, Illinois; Boston, Massachusetts; Champaign, Illinois; Crystal Lake, Illinois; Edwardsville, Illinois; Fort Lauderdale, Florida; Jacksonville, Florida; Joliet, Illinois; Lisle, Illinois; Los Angeles, California; Miami, Florida; Milwaukee, Wisconsin; Minneapolis, Minnesota; New York, New York; Phoenix, Arizona; Portland, Oregon; Providence, Rhode Island; Rockford, Illinois; St. Louis, Missouri; San Francisco, California; Schererville, Indiana; Springfield, Illinois; Tampa, Florida; Waukegan, Illinois.

Appellate, Banking & Financing, Bankruptcy & Creditors' Rights, Class Action Litigation, Civil Rights Defense, Commercial Litigation, Corporate, Construction Law, Director & Officer Liability, Employee Benefits, Environmental, Fidelity & Surety, General Liability Litigation, Government, Health Care, Insurance Coverage, Insurance and Reinsurance, Labor & Employment, Legal Malpractice, Medical Malpractice, Mergers & Acquisitions, Municipal Liability, Personal Injury Defense, Public Law, Products Liability Litigation, Professional Liability, Regulatory, Real Estate, School Law, Securities, Taxation, Transportation, White Collar Crime and Workers' Compensation Defense.

FIRM PROFILE: Hinshaw & Culbertson LLP is a national AMLaw 200 firm with 425 lawyers in 27 offices coast-to-coast. The firm offers a full-service practice, with an emphasis in commercial and defense litigation, corporate, environmental, employment and construction law, as well as the representation of professionals in their liability and risk management matters.

Hinshaw provides services to a range of clients in financial services, construction, health care, not-for-profit, insurance, legal, manufacturing, real estate, transportation and other industries. Firm clients also include government agencies, municipalities and schools.

Hinshaw was founded in 1934. The firm is headquartered in Chicago, and maintains offices in 12 states: Arizona, California, Florida, Illinois, Indiana, Massachusetts, Minnesota, Missouri, New York, Oregon, Rhode Island and Wisconsin.

PARTNERS

PAUL C. ESTES, born Waukegan, Illinois, March 1, 1955; admitted to bar, 1980, Illinois. *Education:* Eastern Illinois University (B.A. with high honors, 1977); University of

(This Listing Continued)

HINSHAW & CULBERTSON LLP, Peoria—Continued

Virginia (J.D., 1980). *Member:* Peoria County and Illinois State Bar Associations; Illinois Trial Lawyers Association; Defense Research Institute; Illinois Association of Hospital Attorneys; Illinois Defense Counsel. ***PRACTICE AREAS:*** Professional Liability Litigation; Medical Malpractice; Products Liability Litigation; Personal Injury Litigation. ***Email:*** pestes@hinshawlaw.com

RHONDA J. FERRERO-PATTEN, born Peoria, Illinois, January 23, 1965; admitted to bar, 1992, Illinois and U.S. District Court, Central District of Illinois; 2001, U.S. Court of Appeals, Seventh Circuit. *Education:* Illinois Central College (A.D.N., 1985); Illinois State University (B.S., cum laude, 1988); Northern Illinois University (J.D., magna cum laude, 1992). Delta Theta Phi. Editor, Revisions, Northern Illinois University Law Review, 1991-1992. Registered Professional Nurse, Illinois, 1985. Author, "Collective Bargaining Units in the Health Care Industry," 12 N.I.U. Law Review 135, 1991. Member, Womens Law Caucus. Member of Supreme Court Committee on Civil Jury Instructions 2000—. *Member:* Illinois State Bar Association. ***PRACTICE AREAS:*** Tort Insurance Defense; Professional Negligence; Construction Accidents; Medical Malpractice Defense. ***Email:*** rferrero-patten@hinshawlaw.com

DAVID E. JONES, born Wichita, Kansas, August 17, 1947; admitted to bar, 1980, Illinois and U.S. District Court, Central District of Illinois; 1989, U.S. Court of Appeals, Seventh Circuit. *Education:* Baylor University (B.M., cum laude, 1969); University of Cincinnati (M.M., 1972); University of Illinois (J.D., 1980). Phi Eta Sigma; Phi Mu Alpha. Member, Illinois Supreme Court Committee on Civil Jury Instructions. *Member:* Peoria County, Illinois State and American Bar Associations; National Association of Railroad Trial Counsel; Abraham Lincoln Inn of Court; Illinois Association of Defense Trial Counsel (Co-Chair, Professional Liability Committee). ***PRACTICE AREAS:*** Insurance Defense; Product Liability; Legal Malpractice; Accountants Malpractice; Architects and Engineers Malpractice. ***Email:*** djones@hinshawlaw.com

DOUGLASS A. MARSHALL, born Bloomington, Indiana, September 19, 1948; admitted to bar, 1982, Illinois and U.S. District Court, Northern District of Illinois; 1984, U.S. District Court, Central District of Illinois. *Education:* Western Illinois University (B.A., 1970); St. Louis University (M.H.A., 1980; J.D., 1982). Managing Editor, St. Louis University Law Journal, Vol. 26, 1981-1982. *Member:* Peoria County and Illinois State Bar Associations; Illinois Association of Healthcare Attorneys (Immediate Past President, Board of Directors); American Academy of Hospital Attorneys; American College of Healthcare Executives (Diplomate). ***PRACTICE AREAS:*** Healthcare Law; Employment Law; Computer Law; Business Law; Corporate Law. ***Email:*** dmarshall@hinshawlaw.com

L. LEE SMITH, born April 28, 1953; admitted to bar, 1978, Illinois; 1980, U.S. District Court, Central District of Illinois and U.S. Court of Appeals, Seventh Circuit; 1991, U.S. District Court, Northern and Southern Districts of Illinois; 2004, U.S. Supreme Court. *Education:* University of Illinois (B.A., English, 1975); Southern Illinois University (J.D., magna cum laude, 1978). ***PRACTICE AREAS:*** White Collar Crime; Employment Litigation; Commercial Litigation; ERISA Litigation. ***Email:*** lsmith@hinshawlaw.com

ASSOCIATES

ALLEN L. DeVARY, born Normal, Illinois, January 30, 1971; admitted to bar, 1999, Illinois and U.S. District Court, Central District of Illinois; 2000, Missouri. *Education:* Illinois State University (B.S., Accounting-Financial Sequence, 1994); Southern Illinois University School of Law (J.D., 1999). Phi Delta Phi. Certified Public Accountant, 1995. *Member:* East St. Louis, St. Clair County, Illinois State (Member, Law Student and Young Lawyers Divisions) and American (Member, Law Student Division and Attorney Membership Section) Bar Associations; The Missouri Bar. ***PRACTICE AREAS:*** Medical Malpractice Defense; Products Liability Defense; Health Care Reimbursement. ***Email:*** adevary@hinshawlaw.com

DANIELLE A. GROH, born Arlington Heights, Illinois, October 29, 1979; admitted to bar, 2005, Illinois. *Education:* Eastern Illinois University (B.A., History, 2000); Ohio Northern University (J.D., with high distinction, 2004). Phi Alpha Delta. Member, Ohio Northern University Law Review. Author, "State v. Doe" and "State v. Fischer," Ohio Northern Law University Law Review. *Member:* Peoria County and Illinois State Bar Associations. ***PRACTICE AREAS:*** Employment Litigation; Professional Liability Litigation; Medical Malpractice Defense; Insurance Litigation. ***Email:*** dgroh@hinshawlaw.com

JAMES LeFANTE, born New Brunswick, New Jersey, 1971; admitted to bar, 1996, Illinois and U.S. District Court, Northern District of Illinois; 1998, New York; 2001, U.S. District Court, Central District of Illinois. *Education:* Western Illinois University (B.A., Political Science, 1992); The John Marshall Law School (J.D., 1996). ***PRACTICE AREAS:*** Medical Malpractice; General Liability Litigation; Collections. ***Email:*** jlefante@hinshawlaw.com

GARTH C. K. MADISON, born Tampa, Florida, 1977; admitted to bar, 2002, Virginia, District of Columbia and U.S. District Court, Eastern and Western Districts of Virginia; 2004, Illinois and U.S. District Court, Northern and Central Districts of Illinois. *Education:* Duke University (B.S., 1998; J.D., 2001). *Member:* American Bar Association (Member, Litigation Section); Virginia State Bar; District of Columbia Bar; Illinois State Bar Association; Peoria County Bar Association. ***PRACTICE AREAS:*** Labor and Employment; Litigation; Federal Litigation. ***Email:*** gmadison@hinshawlaw.com

PATRICIA J. NAYLOR, born August 3, 1978; admitted to bar, 2003, Illinois. *Education:* University of Illinois (B.A., 1999); Northern Illinois University (J.D., cum laude, 2003). *Member:* Peoria County and Illinois State Bar Associations. ***PRACTICE AREAS:*** Professional Liability Litigation; Commercial Litigation. ***Email:*** pnaylor@hinshawlaw.com

TIMOTHY J. NEWLIN, born Peoria, Illinois, December 2, 1952; admitted to bar, 1978, Illinois; 1980, U.S. District Court, Central District of Illinois; 1986, U.S. Court of Appeals, Seventh Circuit and U.S. Supreme Court; 2003, U.S. Court of Federal Claims. *Education:* Southern Methodist University (B.A., 1974; J.D., 1977). Assistant State's Attorney, Peoria County, 1981-1983. Assistant Attorney General, 1983-1985. Member and President, Greater Peoria Claims Association, 1991. Instructor, Law and Banking, Illinois Central College, 1985. *Member:* Peoria County and Illinois State Bar Associations; Abraham Lincoln Inns of Court. ***REPORTED CASES:*** Neuswanger v. Ikegai American Corp., 582 N.E.2d 192 (Ill.App.3rd 1991). ***PRACTICE AREAS:*** Business Planning Law; Workers Compensation; Tort Litigation; Asbestos Litigation; Family Law; Real Estate Law. ***Email:*** tnewlin@hinshawlaw.com

TAMARA A. PAUL-REEFF, born November 14, 1974; admitted to bar, 2004, New York; 2005, Illinois and U.S. District Court, Central District of Illinois. *Education:* Illinois State University (B.S., Sociology/Political Science, with honors, 2000); Syracuse University (J.D., 2003). Member, Golden Key National Honor Society. Dean's List, 2001-2002. *Member:* Peoria County, Illinois State and New York State Bar Associations. ***PRACTICE AREAS:*** Employment Litigation; Commercial Litigation; Medical Malpractice. ***Email:*** tpaul-reeff@hinshawlaw.com

CHRISTOPHER J. SPANOS, born Spring Valley, Illinois, July 11, 1963; admitted to bar, 1995, Illinois; 1997, U.S. District Court, Central District of Illinois. *Education:* Illinois State University (B.S., Finance, 1990); Valparaiso University (J.D., magna cum laude, 1995). Member, Law Review, 1993-1994. Member, Moot Court, 1994-1995. Chartered Property & Casualty Underwriter (CPCU), 2004. *Member:* Peoria County and Illinois State Bar Associations; Illinois Association of Defense Trial Counsel; National Society of CPCU; The Greater Peoria Claims Association. [United States Navy, 1983-1988]. ***PRACTICE AREAS:*** General Liability Litigation; Toxic Tort Defense; Insurance Coverage; Product Liability Litigation; Professional Liability Litigation; Employment Litigation. ***Email:*** cspanos@hinshawlaw.com

OF COUNSEL

RICHARD E. EAGLETON, born Peoria, Illinois, June 29, 1930; admitted to bar, 1958, Illinois; 1959, U.S. District Court, Southern District of Illinois; 1962, U.S. Court of Appeals, Seventh Circuit; 1965, U.S. Supreme Court; 1968, U.S. Court of Military Appeals. *Education:* Yale University (B.A., 1952); University of Illinois (J.D., 1958). Phi Delta Phi. Member, Illinois Supreme Court Committees: Pattern Criminal Jury Instructions, 1982-1991; Criminal Justice Programs, 1970-1982; Judicial Information Systems, 1980-1982 and Subcommittee on Judicial Education, 1978-1981. Assistant U.S. Attorney, Southern District of Illinois, 1961-1964. First Assistant States Attorney, Peoria County, Illinois, 1964-1965. U.S. Attorney, Southern District of Illinois, 1965-1969. Chief Judge, 1979-1981 and Circuit Judge, 1970-1990, Tenth Judicial Circuit of Illinois. Illinois Governor's Criminal Justice Award, 1972. Member: Illinois Law Enforcement Commission, 1973-1977; Illinois Criminal Justice Information Authority, 1983-1985. Director: Southside Bank of Peoria, 1991—; Children's Home Association of Illinois, 1991—. *Member:* Peoria County (Secretary/Treasurer, 1961-1965), Illinois State (Member, 1965-1971 and Chairman, 1969-1970, Criminal Law Section Council; Member, 1971-1976 and Chairman, 1974-1975, Judicial Administrative Council) and American (Director, Crime Control Project, 1969-1970) Bar Associations; Clarence Darrow Inn of Court (President, 1990); National Association of Former U.S. Attorneys (Board of Directors, 2004—). [Ret. Capt., USNR, JAGC, 1990 (active duty, 1952-1955)]. ***PRACTICE AREAS:*** General Trial Practice. ***Email:*** reagleton@hinshawlaw.com

JEROLD I. HORN

Established in 1970

124 S.W. ADAMS STREET, SUITE 515
PEORIA, ILLINOIS 61602-1355
Telephone: 309-676-2778
Fax: 309-676-2779
Email: JIHORN@AOL.COM

Estate Planning, Trusts and Estates, Taxation, Business Law and Real Estate.

FIRM PROFILE: Jerold I. Horn serves clients nationwide with a focus in Central Illinois.

JEROLD I. HORN, born January 25, 1941; admitted to bar, 1966, Pennsylvania; 1970, Illinois and U.S. Supreme Court. *Education:* Princeton University (A.B., summa cum laude, 1963); Yale University (J.D., 1966). Phi Beta Kappa. Author (partial list): "Flexible Trusts and Estates for Uncertain Times," ALI-ABA, 2nd ed., 2005; "Planning and Drafting for the Generation-Skipping Transfer Tax," ALI-ABA, 2nd ed. 1994; "Avoiding and Attracting Grantor Trust Treatment," 24 ACTEC Notes 204, Winter 1998; "Transferring Control of Family Businesses with Discounts in Value for Lack of Control," 24 ACTEC Notes 157, Fall 1998; "Prudent Investor Rule, Modern Portfolio Theory, and Private Trusts: Drafting and Administration Including the 'Give-Me-Five' Unitrust," 33 Real Property Probate and Trust Journal 1, Spring 1998; "Limited Partnerships: Some Thoughts and Theories About Key Issues," 23 ACTEC Notes 36, Summer 1997; "Section 2703 and Buy-Sell Agreements: Modifying Grandfathered Agreements and Drafting New Agreements (with Form)," 1 ALI-ABA Estate Planning Course Materials Journal 19, June 1995; "Using Insurance Proceeds Not Included in Insured's Gross Estate to Provide Liquidity," CLU Journal, October 1979; "Whom Do You Trust: Planning, Drafting and Administering Self and Beneficiary - Trusteed Trusts," 20 University of Miami Institute on Estate Planning, 1986. Co-Author: "Drafting Wills and Trust Agreements," Illinois Institute for CLE, 1990. Visiting Adjunct Professor, University of Miami Law School, 1984-1986. Associated with Reed Smith Shaw & McClay, Pittsburgh, Pennsylvania, 1966-1970. *Member:* International Academy of Estate and Trust Law; American Law Institute; American College of Trust and Estate Counsel (President, 1997-1998); American College of Tax Counsel. ***PRACTICE AREAS:*** Estate Planning; Trusts and Estates; Taxation; Business Law; Real Estate.

REFERENCE: National City Bank

HOWARD, HABECKER & MORRIS, LLC

456 FULTON STREET, SUITE 398
PEORIA, ILLINOIS 61602
Telephone: 309-671-4555
Fax: 309-671-4556
URL: http://www.hhmlaw.com

Insurance Defense, Civil Litigation, Workers Compensation, Torts.

(This Listing Continued)

(This Listing Continued)

MEMBERS OF FIRM

JOHN W. HOWARD, born Peoria, Illinois, April 22, 1949; admitted to bar, 1974, Washington; 1976, Illinois; 1977, U.S. District Court, Central District of Illinois. *Education:* Wabash College; Stanford University (B.A., 1971); University of Illinois (J.D., 1974). *Member:* Peoria County and Illinois State Bar Associations. ***PRACTICE AREAS:*** Banking Law; Residential Real Estate; Commercial Real Estate; Business Acquisitions; Estate Planning; Probate. ***Email:*** jhoward@hhmlaw.net

EDWARD T. HABECKER, born Peoria, Illinois, March 9, 1953; admitted to bar, 1981, Illinois; U.S. District Court, Central District of Illinois. *Education:* University of Mississippi (B.A., 1975); Hamline University (J.D., 1981). Sigma Nu Phi. *Member:* Peoria County, Tazewell County and Illinois State Bar Associations; Illinois Association of Defense Trial Counsel; Abraham Lincoln Inn of Court, DRI. ***PRACTICE AREAS:*** Insurance Defense; Litigation; Civil Litigation; Business Litigation. ***Email:*** ehabecker@hhmlaw.net

STEPHEN M. MORRIS, born Peoria, Illinois, May 8, 1971; admitted to bar, 1996, Illinois, U.S. District Court, Central and Northern Districts of Illinois and U.S. Court of Appeals, Seventh Circuit. *Education:* Creighton University (B.A., 1993; J.D., 1996). *Member:* Peoria County and Illinois State Bar Associations; Illinois Association of Defense Trial Counsel. ***PRACTICE AREAS:*** Personal Injury Defense; Family Law; Collections; Commercial Litigation. ***Email:*** smorris@hhmlaw.net

---

KATHY CHAMBERLAIN, born Tiskilwa, Illinois, September 8, 1975; admitted to bar, 2000, Illinois; 2001, U.S. District Court, Central District of Illinois; 2002, U.S. District Court, Southern District of Illinois. *Education:* University of Illinois, Urbana/Champaign (B.A.); Chicago-Kent College of Law, Illinois Institute of Technology (J.D.). ***PRACTICE AREAS:*** Insurance Defense; Insurance Coverage; Landlord and Tenant Law; Guardianship. ***Email:*** kchamberlain@hhmlaw.net

---

HOWARD & HOWARD ATTORNEYS, P.C.

Established in 1869

ONE TECHNOLOGY PLAZA, SUITE 600
211 FULTON STREET
PEORIA, ILLINOIS 61602-1350
Telephone: 309-672-1483
Fax: 309-672-1568
URL: http://www.h2law.com

Kalamazoo, Michigan Office: Comerica Building, Suite 800, 151 Rose Street. Telephone: 269-382-1483. Telecopier: 269-382-1568.
Bloomfield Hills, Michigan Office: The Pinehurst Office Center, Suite 101, 39400 Woodward Avenue. Telephone: 248-645-1483. Telecopier: 248-645-1568.
Ann Arbor, Michigan Office: One North Main, Suite 300, 101 North Main Street. Telephone: 734-222-1483. Fax: 734-761-5957.

Administrative, Business, Commercial, Corporate, Creditors Rights, Education, Employee Benefits, Environmental, Financial Institutions, Government Relations, Immigration, Intellectual Property (Patents, Trademarks, Copyrights, and Gaming), Labor and Employment, Litigation, Probate, Public Finance, Real Estate, Securities, Taxation (Federal, State and Local), Trusts and Estates.

FIRM PROFILE: Founded in 1869, Howard & Howard is a full service law firm providing national and international legal services from our five offices in Michigan and Illinois. Our distinguished clientele consist of organizations from the manufacturing, distribution, service and public sectors including automotive, retail, real estate, healthcare, high technology, financial services, and public/private finance, as well as governmental entities. Our attorneys are dedicated to our philosophy of providing high quality legal services, on time, at a reasonable price which meet or exceed our clients' expectations, and to our Strongly Held Beliefs. Our success stems in part from our corporate form of governance, which allows us to deliver more efficient service, and our commitment to constant communication internally and externally with our clients.

THEODORE L. EISSFELDT, born Sycamore, Illinois, February 28, 1950; admitted to bar, 1976, Illinois and U.S. District Court, Northern District of Illinois; 1982, U.S. District Court, Central District of Illinois. *Education:* University of Illinois (B.S., 1972; M.S., 1973; J.D., 1976). Articles Editor, University of Illinois Law Review, 1975-1976. *Member:* Peoria, Chicago, Illinois State (Secretary, 1982, Vice-Chairman, 1983 and Chairman, 1984-1985, Corporation and Securities Law Section) and American (Vice Chairman, 1985-1987 and Chairman, 1988-1991, Business and Commercial Law Committee, General Practice Section; Member, Committee on Banking Law, Business Law Section) Bar Associations. ***PRACTICE AREAS:*** Corporate Law; Securities; Banking Law; Mergers and Acquisitions; Financial Institutions Law. ***Email:*** TEissfeldt@howardandhoward.com

JON S. FALETTO, born Peru, Illinois, April 4, 1956; admitted to bar, 1983, Illinois and U.S. District Court, Northern District of Illinois; 1991, Missouri; 1994, Michigan; U.S. District Court, Central District of Illinois; 1997, Indiana, U.S. District Court, Northern and Southern Districts of Indiana and U.S. Court of Appeals, Seventh Circuit; 1999, U.S. Court of Appeals, District of Columbia Circuit. *Education:* University of Illinois (B.S., 1978); Tulane University, 1978-1980, Environmental Post Graduate Studies; I.I.T. Chicago-Kent College of Law (J.D., cum laude, 1983). Recipient: American Jurisprudence Award for Administrative Law. Author: "NSR Reform - Keep Holding Your Breath," FindLaw Corporate Counsel Section, August 2003; "Negotiating Resolution of Environmental Enforcement Actions," Northern Illinois University Law Review, Summer, 1998. "Enhanced Clean Air Act Enforcement," *Metal Finishing,* May, 1997. *Member:* Illinois State, Indiana State and American (Member, Natural Resources, Energy and Environmental Law) Bar Associations; The Missouri Bar; State Bar of Michigan; Air and Waste Management Association; Clean Air Information Network. ***SPECIAL AGENCIES:*** Former Assistant Regional Counsel, U.S. Environmental Protection Agency, Region V, Chicago, Il. ***PRACTICE AREAS:*** Environmental Law; Administrative Law; Energy Law; Environmental Litigation; Clean Air Act. ***Email:*** JSF@H2Law.com

TIMOTHY J. HOWARD, born Princeton, Illinois, May 27, 1950; admitted to bar, 1976, Illinois and U.S. District Court, Central District of Illinois; 1981, U.S. Court of Appeals, Seventh Circuit; 1987, U.S. District Court, Northern District of Illinois; 1991, Michigan; 1995, U.S. Supreme Court; 1997, U.S. District Court, Southern District of Indiana; 1998, U.S. District Court, Southern District of Illinois. *Education:* Princeton University (A.B., 1972); University of Notre Dame (J.D., 1976). Elected Office: Peoria County Board, 1982-1992 (Vice Chairman, 1988-1992). Appointed Office: Greater Peoria Sanitary District, 1996—, President, 1998—. *Member:* Peoria County, Illinois State (Member, Sections on: Commercial, Banking and Bankruptcy Law; Federal Civil Practice) and American (Member, Sections on: Litigation; Business Law; Member: Business Bankruptcy Committee; Commercial and Banking Litigation Committee; Bankruptcy and Insolvency Litigation Committee) Bar Associations; State Bar of Michigan; American Bankruptcy Institute; American Agricultural Law Association. ***REPORTED CASES:*** Frost Nat'l Bank v. Midwest Autohaus, Inc., 241 F3d 862 (7th Cir. 2001). ***PRACTICE AREAS:*** Business Litigation; Commercial Litigation; Trust Litigation; Real Estate Litigation; Bankruptcy; Creditors Rights Law. ***Email:*** THoward@howardandhoward.com

FRANK W. IERULLI, born Peoria, Illinois, May 1966; admitted to bar, 1992, Illinois; 1999, U.S. District Court, Central District of Illinois; 2004, U.S. District Court, Northern and Southern Districts of Illinois and U.S. Court of Appeals, Seventh Circuit. *Education:* Loyola University (B.A., 1988); Creighton University (J.D., 1992). *Member:* Peoria County and Illinois State Bar Associations; Illinois Capital Litigation Trial Bar. [U.S. Army Reserves]. ***PRACTICE AREAS:*** Municipal Law; Litigation. ***Email:*** fierulli@howardandhoward.com

DIANA M. JAGIELLA, born Chicago, Illinois, September 16, 1959; admitted to bar, 1987, Illinois. *Education:* Purdue University (B.A., 1983); DePaul University (J.D., 1987). Author: "Environmental Due Diligence in Transactions," Environmental Law for Transactional Attorneys, Illinois Institute for Continuing Legal Education, 2001; "Release Reporting Requirements," Environmental Law in Illinois, Illinois Institute for Continuing Legal Education, 2001; "The Emergency Planning and Community Right-to-Know Act," Environmental Law in Illinois, Illinois Institute for Continuing Legal Education, 2001. Member: Lakeview Museum Board of Directors; YWCA Board of Directors; Crittenton Board of Directors. *Member:* Peoria County and Illinois State (Vice Chair, 1999-2000; Chair, 2000-2001, Environmental Law Section Council) Bar Associations; Air and Waste Management Association (Chair, 2003-2004 and Member, Lake Michigan Section). ***PRACTICE AREAS:*** Environmental Law; Real Estate Law. ***Email:*** DJagiella@howardandhoward.com

MICHAEL ROBERT LIED, born Offenbach A/M, Germany, 1953; admitted to bar, 1983, Michigan and U.S. District Court, Eastern District of Michigan; 1985, U.S. Court of Appeals, Sixth Circuit; 1987, U.S. District Court, Central District of Illinois and U.S. Supreme Court; 1988, Illinois and U.S. District Court, Northern District of Illinois; 1990, U.S. Claims Court; 1992, U.S. Court of Appeals, Seventh Circuit; 1995, U.S. District Court, Southern District of Illinois; 2002, U.S. District Court, Northern District of Indiana. *Education:* University of Illinois (B.S., 1975; M.A., 1977); University of Michigan (J.D., 1983). Author: "The Lawyer-Employer: A Hiring Primer," Vol. 86, Ill Bar J. (May 1998); "Plant Closings or Layoffs: How to 'WARN' Your Client," Vol. 81, Ill. Bar.J. (Aug. 1993); numerous other articles in professional or trade publications. Co-Author: "The Family and Medical Leave Act: Employee Rights and Employer Responsibilities," Vol. 83, Ill. Bar J. (Sept. 1995). *Member:* Peoria County, Illinois State (Member and Newsletter Editor; Chair, 1994-1995, Labor and Employment Law Section Council) and American Bar Associations; State Bar of Michigan; Bar Associations of the Central and Southern Federal Districts of Illinois; The Association of Trial Lawyers of America; American Immigration Lawyers Association. ***PRACTICE AREAS:*** Labor and Employment; Immigration and Naturalization; Litigation. ***Email:*** MLied@howardandhoward.com

TRACY C. LITZINGER, born St. Louis, Missouri, January 16, 1967; admitted to bar, 1994, Illinois; 1998, U.S. District Court, Central District of Illinois; 2000, U.S. District Court, Northern and Southern Districts of Illinois; 2003, U.S. Court of Appeals, Seventh Circuit. *Education:* University of Missouri at St. Louis (B.S., 1990); Saint Louis University (J.D., 1994). Law Clerk to the Hon. Michael M. Mihm, U.S. District Judge, Central District, Illinois, 1994-1996. *Member:* Peoria County, Central Federal District, Southern Federal District and Illinois State Bar Associations. ***PRACTICE AREAS:*** Labor and Employment; Commercial Litigation. ***Email:*** Tlitzinger@howardandhoward.com

JANICE M. POWELL, born Rockford, Illinois, 1958; admitted to bar, 1983, Illinois and U.S. District Court, Northern District of Illinois; 1999, Minnesota; U.S. District Court, Central District of Illinois; 2000, U.S. Court of Appeals, Tenth Circuit; 2001, U.S. Court of Appeals, Seventh Circuit. *Education:* University of Illinois (B.A., 1980; J.D., magna cum laude, 1983). Order of the Coif. Member, University of Illinois Law Review, 1981-1983. *Member:* Peoria County and American Bar Associations. ***PRACTICE AREAS:*** Creditors Rights; Business Law; Securities; Public Finance; Structured Finance. ***Email:*** JPowell@howardandhoward.com

LEONARD W. SACHS, born Waukegan, Illinois, May 27, 1964; admitted to bar, 1989, Illinois; 1990, U.S. District Court, Central District of Illinois; 1992, U.S. Court of Appeals, Seventh Circuit; 1995, U.S. Court of Federal Claims; 1999, U.S. District Court, Eastern District of Michigan and Southern District of Illinois. *Education:* College of Lake County (A.A., 1982); Northwestern University (B.S., 1986); University of Illinois (J.D., 1989). Phi Theta Kappa. Emeritus Member, Abraham Lincoln Inn of the American Inns of Courts. *Member:* Peoria County and Illinois State (Member, Sections on: Civil Litigation; Labor and Employment) Bar Associations. ***PRACTICE AREAS:*** Labor and Employment; Family and Medical Leave Act; Labor Relations; Employment Litigation; Class Actions. ***Email:*** LSachs@howardandhoward.com

MICHAEL S. SENECA, born Peoria, Illinois, 1975; admitted to bar, 2000, Illinois and U.S. District Court, Northern and Central Districts of Illinois. *Education:* Southern Illinois University (B.S., Accounting, 1997; J.D., 2000). Editor, Southern Illinois Law Journal. Associate, 2000-2003 and Summer Clerk, 1999, Heyl, Royster, Voelker & Allen. Summer Clerk, Chambers of Chief Judge Michael M. Mihm, 1998. Certified Public Accountant,

(This Listing Continued)

HOWARD & HOWARD ATTORNEYS, P.C., Peoria—Continued

1998. Externship with PricewaterhouseCoopers, 1997. Past Member, Illinois Certified Public Accountants. *Member:* Illinois State and American Bar Associations. ***PRACTICE AREAS:*** Bankruptcy; Litigation; Class Actions. ***Email:*** MSeneca@howardandhoward.com

JEFFREY G. SORENSON, born Oak Park, Illinois, 1964; admitted to bar, 1989, Illinois; 1990, U.S. District Court, Central District of Illinois; 1996, U.S. District Court, Northern District of Illinois. *Education:* Miami University (B.A., cum laude, 1986); University of Illinois (J.D., 1989). Phi Beta Kappa. *Member:* Peoria County and Illinois State Bar Associations. ***PRACTICE AREAS:*** Commercial Litigation; Insurance Coverage; Creditors Rights Law. ***Email:*** JSorenson@howardandhoward.com

SANDRA M. TRAICOFF, born O'Neill, Nebraska, 1944; admitted to bar, 1978, Illinois; 1990, Michigan. *Education:* University of Kansas (B.A., 1967); University of Illinois, Champaign/Urbana Illinois (M.S., 1970); DePaul University (J.D., 1978). *Member:* Peoria County and Illinois State (Member, Sections on: Commercial Banking and Bankruptcy and Corporation, Securities and Business Law) Bar Associations; State Bar of Michigan. ***PRACTICE AREAS:*** Banks and Banking; Banking Regulation; Bank Mergers and Acquisitions; Consumer Banking; Bank Holding Company Law. ***Email:*** STraicoff@howardandhoward.com

REPRESENTATIVE CLIENTS: Caterpillar, Inc.; Marion Memorial Hospital; Greater Peoria Airport Authority; DaimlerChrysler Corporation; Occidental Chemical; Champion International; AmerenCILCO.; Archer-Daniels-Midland Co.; Princeton National Bancorp, Inc.; MidAmerica National Bank; Methodist Medical Center of Illinois; Pekin Insurance Company; City of Peoria; Bloomington Housing Authority; Illinois Development Finance Authority; Morton Buildings, Inc.; Kellogg Company; Indian Head Industries; Jabil Circuit, Inc.; FabriSteel Products, Inc.; Semco Energy, Inc.; The Trammell Crow Company; ExxonMobil Oil Corporation. Financial Institutions: National City Bank of Michigan/Illinois; Main Street Trust, Inc.; Fifth Third Bancorp; Citizens Banking Corporation. Construction Industries: Clark Industries; Walbridge Aldinger Co. Manufacturing: A.M.Todd Company; Amsted Industries; GKN Automotive; Stryker Corp. Municipalities, Schools and Exempt Organizations: City of Detroit; City of Kalamazoo; State Building Authority of Michigan. Health Care: United Memorial Hospital; . State Tax Counsel For: Dow Chemical Corp.; Catalina Marketing. International Counsel For: F.X. Coughlin Co.

HUSCH & EPPENBERGER, LLC

401 MAIN STREET, SUITE 1400
PEORIA, ILLINOIS 61602-1241
Telephone: 309-637-4900
FAX: 309-637-4928
URL: http://www.husch.com

Jefferson City, Missouri Office: 235 East High Street, Monroe House, Suite 300, P.O. Box 1251. Telephone: 573-635-9118. FAX: 573-634-7854.
Kansas City, Missouri Office: 1200 Main, Suite 2300. Telephone: 816-421-4800. FAX: 816-421-0596.
St. Louis, Missouri Office: 190 Carondelet Plaza, Suite 600. Telephone: 314-480-1500. FAX: 314-480-1505.
Springfield, Missouri Office: 1949 E. Sunshine Street, Suite 2-300. Telephone: 417-862-6726. FAX: 417-862-6948.
Chattanooga, Tennessee Office: 736 Georgia Avenue, Suite 300. Telephone: 423-266-5500. FAX: 423-266-5499.
Memphis, Tennessee Office: One Memphis Place, 200 Jefferson Avenue, Suite 1450, 38103. Telephone: 901-523-1123. FAX: 901-523-7472.
Nashville, Tennessee Office: 2525 West End Avenue, Suite 1400, 37203. Telephone: 615-963-2200. FAX: 615-963-3611.

Administrative Law, Agricultural Law, Alternative Dispute Resolution, Antitrust, Appellate Practice, Asset Protection, Bankruptcy, Banks and Banking, Business Law, Casinos and Gambling, Children, Civil Practice, Class Action, Commercial Law, Commercial Real Estate, Communications and Media, Complex and Multi District Litigation, Computers and Software, Constitutional Law, Construction Law, Consumer Law, Contracts, Copyrights, Corporate Finance, Corporate Law, Debtor and Creditor, Education Law, Election, Campaign and Political Law, Eminent Domain, Employee Benefits, Entertainment Law, Environmental Law, Estate Planning, Family Law, Fidelity and Surety, Finance, Government, Guardianship and Conservatorship, Health Care, Hospital Law, Immigration and Naturalization, Insurance, Insurance Defense, Intellectual Property, International Law, International Trade, Investments, Labor and Employment, Litigation, Medical Malpractice, Mergers, Acquisitions and Divestitures, Municipal Law, Nonprofit and Charitable Organizations, Occupational Safety and Health, Partnership Law, Patents, Probate, Products Liability, Property Law, Real Estate, Securities, Taxation, Technology and Science, Torts, Toxic Torts, Trade Secrets, Trademarks, Trusts and Estates, Wills, Worker's Compensation, Zoning, Planning and Land Use.

LAW FIRM ALLIANCES/ASSOCIATIONS: ***TERRALEX, THE WORLDWIDE NETWORK OF INDEPENDENT LAW FIRMS***

MEMBERS OF FIRM

SUEANN SAGE BILLIMACK, born Champaign, Illinois; admitted to bar, 1994, Illinois; U.S. District Court, Northern, Central and Southern Districts of Illinois; U.S. Court of Appeals, Seventh Circuit. *Education:* Knox College (B.A., Biology, magna cum laude, 1987); University of Illinois (J.D., magna cum laude, 1994). Phi Beta Kappa; Order of the Coif; Harno Fellow; Mortar Board. Recipient, Rickert Award. Executive Administrative Editor, University of Illinois Law Review. Author, "Reliance on an Official Interpretation of the Law: The Defense's Appropriate Dimensions," Volume 1993, Number 3, University of Illinois Law Review. *Member:* Peoria County, Illinois State and American Bar Associations. ***PRACTICE AREAS:*** Labor and Employment. ***Email:*** sueann.billimack@husch.com

STEPHEN M. BUCK, born Clayton, Missouri, 1966; admitted to bar, 1992, Illinois; 1993, Missouri; U.S. District Court, Central and Southern Districts of Illinois; U.S. Court of Appeals, Seventh Circuit. *Education:* St. Louis University (B.A., Criminal Justice, magna cum laude, 1989; J.D., magna cum laude, 1992). Alpha Sigma Nu; Phi Beta Kappa. Order of the Woolsack. Staff Member, St. Louis University Public Law Review, 1992. *Member:* Peoria County and Illinois State Bar Associations; American Inns of Court. ***PRACTICE AREAS:*** Business Litigation; Intellectual Property Litigation. ***Email:*** stephen.buck@husch.com

KENNETH R. EATHINGTON, born Avon, Illinois, 1961; admitted to bar, 1991, Illinois; U.S. District Court, Northern and Central Districts of Illinois; U.S. Tax Court. *Education:* University of Illinois (B.S., Agricultural Economics, highest honors, 1983; J.D., summa cum laude, 1991). Phi Alpha Delta. Order of the Coif. Harno Fellow. Bronze Tablet. Recipient, Rickert Award for Academic Achievement. Associate Editor, University of Illinois Law Review. Awards: Peoria Area Association of Realtors Affiliate of the Year, 2004; Peoria County Bar Association Pro Bono Lawyer of the Year, 2001. Member, Peoria Chamber of Commerce Small Business Committee, 2000-2002. Dunlap Biddy Basketball Coach and Supervisor. Dunlap Little League Baseball Coach. United Way Campaign, Account Volunteer, 2002-2004. *Member:* Peoria County, Illinois State (Member, Agricultural Law Section Council) and American Bar Associations; American Agricultural Law Association; Estate Planning Council of Central Illinois (Board Member). ***SPECIAL AGENCIES:*** Illinois Department of Agriculture; Pollution Control Board; Illinois Environmental Protection Agency; Property Tax Appeal Board. ***PRACTICE AREAS:*** Corporate Law; Real Estate; Banks and Banking; Insolvency. ***Email:*** kenny.eathington@husch.com

DAVID L. HIGGS, born Canton, Illinois, 1951; admitted to bar, 1981, Illinois; 1983, U.S. Tax Court; U.S. District Court, Central District of Illinois; U.S. Court of Appeals, Seventh Circuit. *Education:* Western Illinois University (B.S., Mathematics, with high honors, 1972); Southern Illinois University (J.D., Valedictorian, summa cum laude, 1981). Phi Kappa Phi. Research Editor, Southern Illinois University Law Journal, 1981. Author, "The Simplified Retirement Plan Alternative," 81 Illinois Bar Journal 88. Recipient: Judge James O. Monroe Award for excellence in legal writing and research; John S. Rendelman Award for outstanding senior law student. *Member:* Peoria County, Illinois State (Past chair, Employee Benefits Section; Council, Professional Conduct Section Council) and American Bar Associations. ***PRACTICE AREAS:*** Trusts and Estates; Federal Income Tax; Employee Benefits; Taxation. ***Email:*** david.higgs@husch.com

ANDREW A. HONEGGER, admitted to bar, 1994, Massachusetts (inactive); 1995, Illinois; U.S. District Court, Central and Northern Districts of Illinois; U.S. Court of Appeals, First Circuit. *Education:* University of Illinois (B.A., Political Science, 1991); Boston University School of Law (J.D., cum laude, 1994). University of Illinois: Atius-Sachem Honorary; Student Alumni Association; and the Senior 100 Honorary, recognizing the 100 most distinguished graduating seniors of 1991. Boston University: Winner, Homer Albers Moot Court Competition; Boston University National Moot Court Team; Editor, American Journal of Law and Medicine. Member: Morton, Illinois Rotary Club; Morton, Illinois Chamber of Commerce. *Member:* Peoria County and Illinois State Bar Associations; The Abraham Lincoln American Inn of Court. ***PRACTICE AREAS:*** Banking Law; Commercial Litigation; Business Transactions. ***Email:*** andrew.honegger@husch.com

CHRISTOPHER A. NICHOLS, born South Bend, Indiana, 1962; admitted to bar, 1988, Illinois; 1994, Indiana; U.S. District Court, Northern and Central Districts of Illinois; U.S. District Court, Northern and Southern Districts of Indiana; U.S. District Court, Western District of Michigan; U.S. Court of Appeals, Seventh Circuit. *Education:* DePauw University (B.A., Political Science, cum laude, 1985); Indiana University School of Law (J.D., cum laude, 1988). Member, Indiana University Law Journal, 1986-1988. *Member:* Peoria County, Illinois State, Indiana State and American Bar Associations; Bar Association of the Central and Southern Federal Districts of Illinois. ***PRACTICE AREAS:*** Labor and Employment; Commercial Litigation; Intellectual Property. ***Email:*** chris.nichols@husch.com

BRIAN W. RUDDELL, born Palestine, Illinois, 1949; admitted to bar, 1974, Indiana (inactive) and Illinois; U.S. District Court, Central District of Illinois; U.S. Court of Appeals, Seventh Circuit; U.S. Court of Military Appeals; U.S. Supreme Court. *Education:* University of Illinois (B.S., Economics, with high honors, 1971); University of Notre Dame (J.D., magna cum laude, 1974). Bronze Tablet, University of Illinois. Author: Case Comment, "S & E Contractors, Inc. v. United States," 48 Notre Dame Lawyer, 1972; Chapter: "Arbitration," volume on "Construction Litigation," published by Illinois Institute for Continuing Legal Education, 1983. Speaker on Employee Benefits and Tax-exempt Organizations and related topics at seminars sponsored by Husch, accounting firms, and Lorman Business Seminars. Member, Board of Directors, Central Illinois Chapter of the American Red Cross. Member, Board of Trustees, Peoria Public Library. Past President, Kiwanis Club of Peoria. Trustee, Charitable Endowment Trust of the Kiwanis Club of Peoria. Member, Pillars Society of the Heart of Illinois United Way. Member, Klystron Society of WTVP Channel 47. Member, Tower Society of WCBU Public Radio. *Member:* Peoria County, Illinois State and American Bar Associations; American Health Lawyers Association. ***PRACTICE AREAS:*** Employee Benefits; Health Care; Corporate Law. ***Email:*** brian.ruddell@husch.com

JEFFREY A. RYVA, born Chicago, Illinois, 1955; admitted to bar, 1980, Illinois. *Education:* University of Illinois (B.A., Finance, with distinction, 1977); John Marshall Law School (J.D., with high distinction, 1980). Editor-in-Chief, John Marshall Law Review, 1979-1980. ***PRACTICE AREAS:*** Appellate Practice; Commercial Litigation; Bankruptcy Litigation; Trademark Litigation; Family Law. ***Email:*** jeff.ryva@husch.com

CHARLES H. YOUNG, born Galesburg, Illinois, 1948; admitted to bar, 1973, Illinois. *Education:* Augustana College (A.B., History, 1970); University of Illinois (J.D., 1973). Order of the Coif. Notes and Comments Editor, University of Illinois Law Forum, 1972-1973. *Member:* Peoria County and American Bar Associations. ***PRACTICE AREAS:*** Corporate Law; Commercial Law; Trademarks; Copyrights. ***Email:*** charles.young@husch.com

ASSOCIATES

DAVID A. CHAMBERS, admitted to bar, 2002, Illinois; 2003, Missouri; registered to practice before U.S. Patent and Trademark Office. *Education:* Bradley University (B.S., Manufacturing, cum laude, 1995); University of Illinois (J.D., cum laude, 2002). Author: "Using Copyright to Protect Your Website," eBusiness Update (June, 2001). Speaker, "Festo Corp. vs. Shoketsu Kinzoku Kabushiki Co., Ltd.," Summer Intellectual Property Retreat (2001). *Member:* Peoria County, Illinois State and American Bar Associations. ***PRACTICE AREAS:*** Intellectual Property. ***Email:*** david.chambers@husch.com

(This Listing Continued)

TYLER PETERSEN, admitted to bar, 1999, Illinois. *Education:* University of Illinois (B.S., Finance, 1996; J.D., magna cum laude, 1999). Phi Delta Phi. Co-Author: Chapter, "Formation of Illinois Corporations," Illinois Business Law Series, January, 2005. Author: "Your Employee Files for Bankruptcy—Can You Terminate Employment?" Hoosier Banker, 2003; "Formation of Illinois Corporations," supplement to Illinois Continuing Legal Education Practice Handbook, 2002; "Effective 'Click-Wrap' and 'Shrink-Wrap' Agreements," Business to Business, 2000. Co-Author: "New Powers For Illinois Banks," Commercial Banking & Bankruptcy Law, Illinois State Bar Association Newsletter, 2000. *Member:* Peoria County and Illinois State Bar Associations. ***PRACTICE AREAS:*** Corporate Law. ***Email:*** tyler.petersen@husch.com

KIMBERLY A. SUTTON SARFF, admitted to bar, 2001, Indiana; 2002, Illinois. *Education:* Murray State University (B.A., summa cum laude, 1997); Southern Illinois University (J.D., magna cum laude, 2001). Phi Alpha Delta (President). Moot Court Board, Appellate Division. Casenote/Comment Editor, Southern Illinois University Law Journal. Author: "Illinois' Proposed Mediation Privilege," 25 S. Ill. U. L. J. 179, 2000. First-Vice President, Student Bar Association. *Member:* Peoria County, Illinois State, Indiana State and American Bar Associations. ***PRACTICE AREAS:*** Business Litigation. ***Email:*** kim.sarff@husch.com

REPRESENTATIVE CLIENTS: Advanced Technology Services, Inc.; Ameren CIPS; Associated Anesthesiologists, S.C.; Associated Surgical Group, S.C.; Avanti's, Inc.; Cast Technologies, Inc.; Commerce Bank, N.A.; Dick Blick Company; Federal Warehouse Co.; Fleming Publishing Company, LLC; Freesen, Inc.; Granite City Broadcasting; Health Professionals, Ltd.; Hicks Oils and Hicksgas, Inc.; Illinois Valley Paving Co.; Kewanee Hospital; Lincoln Office, LLC; Morton Buildings, Inc.; Morton Community Bank; Morton Industrial Group, Inc.; Morton Park District; Peoria Charter Coach Company; Peoria Pulmonary Associates, Ltd.; Peoria Surgical Group, Ltd.; Phillips Swager Associates, Inc.; Police Pension Fund of Peoria; Rapp Technologies, Inc.; RenalCare Associates, S.C.; Rowe Construction Co.; Sonopress Produktionsgesellschaft fuer Ton- und Informationstraeger mbH, a subsidiary of Bertelsmann AG; The Wilton Mortuary, Inc.; United Contractors Midwest, Inc.; United Ready Mix, Inc.; Utilities Service Corp.; Vaughan & Bushnell Manufacturing Company.

(For Biographical data on Jefferson City, Kansas City, Springfield and St. Louis, Missouri; Chattanooga, Memphis and Nashville, Tennessee Lawyers, see Professional biographies at Jefferson City, Kansas City, Springfield and St. Louis, Missouri; Chattanooga, Memphis and Nashville, Tennessee)

JANSSEN LAW CENTER

JANSSEN BUILDING
MAIN AND JEFFERSON
333 MAIN STREET
PEORIA, ILLINOIS 61602
Telephone: 309-676-2341
Fax: 309-676-7678
URL: http://www.jjlaw.com
Email: jay@jjlaw.com
URL: http://www.lawyers.com/janssen

Personal Injury, Automobile Accidents, Dog Bites, Sexual Abuse, Slip and Fall, Wrongful Death, Airplane Crashes, Maritime Injuries, Nursing Home Abuse, Unsafe Products, Products Liability, Litigation, Medical Malpractice, Pharmaceutical Malpractice, Workers Compensation, Health, Civil Rights.

FIRM PROFILE: The firm carries the highest legal ability rating in Martindale-Hubbell.

JAY H. JANSSEN, born Peoria, Illinois, October 20, 1937; admitted to bar, 1961, Illinois, U.S. District Court, Central District of Illinois and U.S. Supreme Court; 1970, U.S. Court of Appeals, Seventh Circuit; 1995, Illinois. *Education:* Bradley University (B.S., cum laude, Political Science, 1959); University of Illinois (J.D., 1961). Chairman, Attorney Registration & Disciplinary Commission of Illinois, by Appointment of the Supreme Court of Illinois, 1998-2000. *Member:* Illinois State Bar Association. ***PRACTICE AREAS:*** Personal Injury; Products Liability; Litigation. ***Email:*** jay@jjlaw.com

---

RALPH D. DAVIS, born Canton, Illinois, July 3, 1949; admitted to bar, 1987, Illinois; U.S. District Court, Northern District of Indiana; U.S. District Court, Northern District of Illinois and U.S. Court of Appeals, Seventh Circuit; U.S. District Court, Central District of Illinois; U.S. Supreme Court. *Education:* University of Chicago (A.B., 1971; M.B.A., 1972) Northwestern University School of Law (J.D., 1987). Numerous Publications including: Contemporary Business Law and the Legal Environment (5th Ed. McGraw Hill). *Member:* Chicago, Fulton County, Peoria County and Illinois State Bar Associations; Association of Trial Lawyers of America; Illinois Trial Lawyers Association; Seventh Circuit Bar Association; American Inns of Court. ***PRACTICE AREAS:*** Personal Injury; Workers Compensation; Medical Malpractice; Products Liability; Litigation. ***Email:*** rdavis@jjlaw.com

CHRISTOPHER R. DOSCOTCH, born Hinsdale, Illinois, August 17, 1969; admitted to bar, 1994, Illinois; 1995, U.S. District Court, Central District of Illinois; 2000, U.S. District Court, Northern Dustrict of Indiana. *Education:* Knox College (B.A., 1991); Southern Illinois University School of Law (J.D., 1994). Phi Gamma Delta. *Member:* Illinois State Bar Association (Member, Workers Compensation Section). [Infantry, Illinois National Guard, 1990-1998]. ***PRACTICE AREAS:*** Plaintiffs Personal Injury; Litigation; Workers Compensation; Products Liability; Medical Malpractice.

JOSEPH W. DUNN, born Owensboro, Kentucky, March 11, 1965; admitted to bar, 1995, Illinois; 1996, U.S. District Court, Central District of Illinois. *Education:* University of Illinois (B.S., 1992); Southern Illinois University (J.D., 1995). Phi Delta Phi. *Member:* Peoria County, Illinois State and American Bar Associations; Illinois Trial Lawyers Association; American Trial Lawyers Association. [U.S. Navy, 1983-1987]. ***PRACTICE AREAS:*** Plaintiffs Personal Injury (100%).

DONOVAN W. GAEDE, born Daytona Beach, Florida, April 17, 1968; admitted to bar, 1994, Illinois. *Education:* Northwestern University (B.A., English, 1990); Southern Illinois University School of Law (J.D., cum laude, 1994). Recipient: American Jurisprudence Award, Torts Law; Order of the Barristers Award. Articles Editor, Southern Illinois University Law Journal, 1993-1994. Comment, Constitutional Law-Policing the Obscene: Modern Obscenity Doctrine Re-Evaluated and Casenote, Constitutional Law-Why the Supreme Court Hates Hate-Crime Ordinances. R.A.V. v. St. Paul, 112 S. Ct. 2538 (1992), Southern Illinois L.J. Vol. 18, Winter, 1994. Member, Midwest Regional Champion ABA Moot Court Team, 1992-1993. ***PRACTICE AREAS:*** Personal Injury (40%, 65); Workers Compensation (60%, 45).

PATRICK S. OSHAUGHNESSY, born Peoria, Illinois, October 17, 1971; admitted to bar, 1996, Illinois; 1997, U.S. District Court, Central District of Illinois. *Education:* Bradley University (B.S., 1993); Northwestern University School of Law (J.D., 1996). ***PRACTICE AREAS:*** Plaintiffs Personal Injury; Medical Malpractice; Litigation. ***Email:*** patricko@jjlaw.com

(This Listing Continued)

JOHNSON, BUNCE & NOBLE, P.C.

EXECUTIVE OFFICES - PARKWAY PLAZA
7800 N. SOMMER STREET, SUITE 425
PEORIA, ILLINOIS 61615-1994
Telephone: 309-691-9650
Fax: 309-691-9651
Email: info@peorialawyers.com
URL: http://www.peorialawyers.com

General Civil and Trial Practice in all Courts. Corporation, Banking, Municipal, Commercial, Probate, Taxation, Real Estate, Estate Planning, Collections, Eminent Domain, Family Law, Title Insurance.

FIRM PROFILE: Johnson, Bunce & Noble, P.C. was established in Peoria, Illinois in 1946. Serving clients in Peoria, Woodford, Tazewell, Fulton, Stark, Marshall and surrounding counties. The firm engages in a general civil practice.

JAMES H. BUNCE, born Aurora, Illinois, August 20, 1940; admitted to bar, 1966, Illinois. *Education:* Bradley University (B.A., with honors, 1962); Georgetown University (J.D., 1965). Editor-in-Chief, Res Ipsa Loquitur, 1964-1965. Instructor, Real Estate Law, Illinois Central College, 1991-1997. *Member:* Peoria County Bar Association (Board of Directors, 1977-1978, 1985-1986, and 1991-1992). ***PRACTICE AREAS:*** Real Estate Law; Corporate/Business Law.

KENT A. NOBLE, born Wichita, Kansas, August 8, 1943; admitted to bar, 1968, Illinois. *Education:* University of Illinois (B.S., 1965; J.D., 1968). Selected for inclusion in the 1996 first edition of the Illinois Consumer Guidebook to Law & Leading Attorneys. President: Prairie State Legal Services, Inc., 1977-1978; Central Illinois Legal Aid Society, Inc.; Greater Peoria Legal Aid Society, 1975-1976. *Member:* Peoria County Bar Association (President, 1986-1987). ***PRACTICE AREAS:*** Trust and Estate Planning Law; Taxation Law.

FREDERICK A. JOHNSON, born Peoria, Illinois, June 1, 1944; admitted to bar, 1968, Illinois. *Education:* University of Illinois (B.S., 1966; J.D., 1968). ***PRACTICE AREAS:*** Real Estate Law; Corporate Law; Local Government Law; Mortgage Foreclosure Law; Title Insurance.

JAMES P. JOHNSON, born Peoria, Illinois, May 21, 1953; admitted to bar, 1978, Illinois. *Education:* University of Illinois (A.B., 1975; J.D., 1978); University of Denver (LL.M., in Taxation, 1980). Special Assistant, Illinois Attorney General, Land Acquisition (1983-1999). ***PRACTICE AREAS:*** Taxation; Real Estate Law; Eminent Domain.

MATTHEW P. JONES, born Pekin, Illinois, September 30, 1965; admitted to bar, 1991, Illinois; 2000, U.S. District Court, Central and Northern Districts of Illinois. *Education:* Illinois Central College (A.A., 1985); University of Illinois (B.S., 1988; J.D., 1991). Assistant State Attorney, 1991-1996. Legal Counsel, Illinois Senate Majority, 1996-1999. Committee, Supreme Court Rules, 1999. *Member:* Peoria County (Board of Directors, 2001-2003) and Sangamon County Bar Associations. ***PRACTICE AREAS:*** Legislative Practice; Family Law; Litigation; Property Tax Appeals.

LESTER W. VICARY, JR., born Peoria, Illinois, December 5, 1952; admitted to bar, 1978, Illinois. *Education:* Illinois College (B.S., 1975); Southern Illinois University (J.D., 1978). *Member:* Peoria County Bar Association. ***PRACTICE AREAS:*** Real Estate Law; Corporate Law.

REPRESENTATIVE CLIENTS: Brimfield Bank; Pioneer Industrial Park, Inc.; Traders Realty Corp.; Greater Peoria Sanitary District; Traders Development Corp.; Northern Border Pipeline Co.; Neenah Springs, Inc.; Illinois Crane, Inc.; Mitchel Aerial Application, Inc.; Peoria Central Warehouse, Inc.; Wilton Mortuary; Vision Care Associates; Austin Engineering Co., Inc.; Peoria-Tazewell Pathology Group, S.C.; Advanced Medical Transport; Thornridge Development Company, Ltd.; Transmission Repair Co.

KINGERY DURREE WAKEMAN & RYAN, ASSOC.

COMMERCE BANK BUILDING
416 MAIN STREET, SUITE 915
PEORIA, ILLINOIS 61602
Telephone: 309-676-3612
FAX: 309-676-1329
URL: http://www.kdwrlaw.com
Email: KDWRyan@sbcglobal.net
URL: http://www.lawyers.com/kingerydurree

General Civil and Trial Practice, Products Liability, Workers Compensation, Personal Injury, Medical and Professional Malpractice Law, Automobile Accidents, Wrongful Death, Dog Bites, Slip and Fall.

FIRM PROFILE: Kingery Durree Wakeman & Ryan, Assoc. serves clients throughout all of central Illinois. The firm engages in a general litigation practice with a focus in Medical and Professional Malpractice, Workers Compensation and Personal Injury Law. The firm is included in the Bar Register of Preeminent Lawyers.

(This Listing Continued)

KINGERY DURREE WAKEMAN & RYAN, ASSOC., Peoria—Continued

ARTHUR R. KINGERY, born Montrose, Illinois, January 20, 1942; admitted to bar, 1966, Illinois and U.S. District Court, Central District of Illinois; 1969, U.S. Court of Appeals, Seventh Circuit; 1977, U.S. Supreme Court. *Education:* University of Illinois (B.S., 1963; J.D., 1966). Phi Delta Phi. *Member:* Peoria County, Illinois State and American Bar Associations; Illinois Trial Lawyers Association; The Association of Trial Lawyers of America; Illinois Association of Defense Trial Counsel; Worker's Compensation Lawyers Association. [United States Army, Armor, Captain, 1967-1969]. ***PRACTICE AREAS:*** General Tort Law; Workers Compensation Law; Personal Injury Law; Products Liability Law.

EDWARD R. DURREE, born Streator, Illinois, June 2, 1949; admitted to bar, 1975, Illinois and U.S. District Court, Central District of Illinois; 1979, U.S. Supreme Court; 1986, U.S. Court of Appeals, Seventh Circuit. *Education:* Augustana College and University of Illinois (B.A., with honors, 1971); Drake University (J.D., with honors, 1975). Member, Drake Law Review, 1973-1975. Author: "Iowa Rule of Civil Procedure 8: Recent Developments," Drake Law Review, January 1975. *Member:* Peoria County (President, 1994-1995) and Illinois State Bar Associations; American College of Trial Lawyers; Illinois Trial Lawyers Association; The Association of Trial Lawyers of America; American Inns of Court, Abraham Lincoln Chapter (Master Emeritus). ***PRACTICE AREAS:*** Personal Injury Law; Medical and Professional Malpractice Law.

STEVEN A. WAKEMAN, born Peoria, Illinois, June 16, 1953; admitted to bar, 1977, Illinois; 1980, U.S. Court of Appeals, Seventh Circuit. *Education:* Bradley University (B.A., summa cum laude, 1974); University of Illinois (J.D., cum laude, 1977). Phi Kappa Phi. Member, National Moot Court Team. Law Clerk, U.S. District Court for the Southern District of Illinois, Northern Division, 1977-1978. *Member:* Peoria County and Illinois State Bar Associations; Illinois Trial Lawyers Association; The Association of Trial Lawyers of America; American Inns of Court, Abraham Lincoln Chapter (Emeritus). ***PRACTICE AREAS:*** Personal Injury Law; Medical Malpractice; Product Liability Law; Divorce; Business Litigation; Family Law.

CHRISTOPHER P. RYAN, born Chicago, Illinois, October 24, 1959; admitted to bar, 1984, Illinois; 1985, U.S. District Court, Central District of Illinois and U.S. Court of Appeals, Seventh Circuit. *Education:* University of Illinois (B.A., 1981; J.D., 1984). *Member:* Peoria County, Illinois State and American Bar Associations; Illinois Trial Lawyers Association; The Association of Trial Lawyers of America; National Panel of Consumer Arbitrators (BBB). ***PRACTICE AREAS:*** Personal Injury Law; Medical and Professional Malpractice; Business Litigation; Family Law.

PHILIP M. O'DONNELL, born Peoria, Illinois, July 23, 1969; admitted to bar, 1994, Illinois and U.S. District Court, Central District of Illinois; U.S. Court of Appeals, Seventh Circuit. *Education:* University of Illinois (B.S., magna cum laude, 1991); University of Kansas (J.D., 1994). *Member:* Peoria County and Illinois State Bar Associations; Illinois Trial Lawyers Association; The Association of Trial Lawyers of America. ***PRACTICE AREAS:*** General Tort Law; General Practice; Estate Law.

JAMES P. LAWSON, born Peoria, Illinois, November 2, 1970; admitted to bar, 1995, Illinois and U.S. District Court, Central District of Illinois. *Education:* University of Illinois (B.S., 1992); Southern Illinois University (J.D., 1995; M.B.A., 1995). *Member:* Peoria County and Illinois State Bar Associations; Illinois Trial Lawyers Association; The Association of Trial Lawyers of America. ***PRACTICE AREAS:*** Personal Injury; Divorce Law; General Practice.

MICHAEL S. McKINLEY, born Peoria, Illinois, January 22, 1968; admitted to bar, 1993, Illinois; 1994, U.S. District Court, Central District of Illinois. *Education:* Spring Hill College (B.S., cum laude, 1990); Southern Illinois University School of Law (J.D., 1993). Omicron Delta Epsilon. *Member:* Peoria County, Illinois State and American Bar Associations; Illinois Trial Lawyers Association; The Association of Trial Lawyers of America. ***PRACTICE AREAS:*** Personal Injury; Medical Malpractice; Products Liability; Professional Malpractice.

REFERENCE: Commerce Bank of Peoria.

KNELL & KELLY, L.L.C.

504 FAYETTE
PEORIA, ILLINOIS 61603
Telephone: 309-655-1530
Fax: 309-655-1535
Email: law@knell-kelly.com
URL: http://www.lawyers.com/knellkelly

General Practice.

MEMBERS OF FIRM

CHARLES D. KNELL, born Urbana, Illinois, January 10, 1950; admitted to bar, 1976, Illinois and U.S. District Court, Central District of Illinois; U.S. Court of Appeals, Seventh Circuit. *Education:* University of Illinois (B.A., 1973); Southern Methodist University (J.D., 1975). Lecturer: Peoria County Continuing Legal Education Committee; Illinois Institute of Continuing Legal Education; Central Illinois RIMD Association; Employers Association of Illinois; Lorman Education Services; National Business Institute, Inc. Workers' Compensation Self-Insured Trust and Illinois School District Agency Property Casualty Programs; Council on Education in Management. Listed in Who's Who in American Lawyers. Member: Rules Committee Illinois Industrial Commission; St. Jude Midwest Affiliate Board of Directors, 1978-1990, President, 1988-1990. *Member:* Chicago, Peoria County, Illinois State and American Bar Associations; Greater Peoria Claims Association; Illinois Association of Defense Trial Counsel; Defense Research Institute; Workers' Compensation Association; Illinois Trial Lawyers Association; Abraham Lincoln Inns of Court (Master). ***REPORTED CASES:*** Gallianetti vs. Industrial Commission, 734 N.E.2d 482, 2000; McCuen v. Peoria Park District, 643 NE2d 778, S.Ct., 1994; Kerker v. Elbert, 634 NE2d 482, 1994; Wolland v. Industrial Commission, 434 NE2d 1132, S.Ct., 1982; R.A. Cullinan & Sons, Inc. v. Industrial Commission, 549 NE2d 805, 1990; Village of Oreana v. Industrial Commission, 289 Ill.App.3d, 682 NE2d 1158, 1997; Maskel v. Industrial Commission, 3rd District, April 11, 1996 unpublished; Blake v. Industrial Commission, 4th District January 25, 1990 unpublished; Cook v. Industrial Commission, 596 NE2d 746, 1992; R.A. Cullinan & Sons, Inc. v. Industrial Commission, 575 NE2d 1240, 1991. ***PRACTICE AREAS:*** Workers Compensation Law; Employment Law; Automobile Liability; Trucking Law; Government; Municipal Law; Premises Liability; Civil Rights; Appellate Practice; State Government Law; Federal Government Law. ***Email:*** deathknell@knell-kelly.com

STEPHEN P. KELLY, born Peoria, Illinois, July 21, 1964; admitted to bar, 1990, Illinois; U.S. District Court, Central District of Illinois. *Education:* St. Ambrose University (B.A., 1987); John Marshall Law School (J.D., 1990). Lecturer: Central Illinois Employers Association; Illinois Nursing Home Association; Nursing Home Risk Management Association; Illinois Groceries Association. Assistant Professor: Illinois Central College; Lorman Education Services. Lecture Topics: Americans with Disability Act; Illinois Workers' Compensation Act; Fraud Cases in the Workers' Compensation Act. Workers' Compensation Fraud Prosecution: Participated in the first successful indictment and conviction in Sangamon County of a petitioner in a fraud case in front of the Illinois Industrial Commission. The case resulted in a Class II felony against the petitioner. *Member:* Chicago, Peoria County, Sangamon County, Illinois State and American Bar Associations; Illinois Association of Defense Trial Counsel; Sangamon Claims Association; Greater Peoria Claims Association; Association of Trial Lawyers of America; Illinois Workers' Compensation Claims Association. ***REPORTED CASES:*** E.R. Carpenter v. Illinois Industrial Commission, (4th District, April 1992 unpublished); Lascody Trucking v. Illinois Industrial Commission, (3rd District, June 1992 unpublished); Woodrum v. Bunn-O-Matic, (4th District, January 24, 2003, 783 N.E. 2d 1072); Morton CUSD v. Illinois Industrial Commission, (3rd District, August 2003 unpublished); Health Staff v. Illinois Industrial Commission, (4th District). ***PRACTICE AREAS:*** Trial Practice; Workers Compensation; Employment Law; Automobile Negligence; Appellate Practice; State Government Law; Federal Government Law. ***Email:*** skelly@knell-kelly.com

---

ANDREW S. DE BLANK, born Pekin, Illinois, May 24, 1964; admitted to bar, 1989, Florida; 1993, Illinois; U.S. District Court, Central District of Illinois. *Education:* Boston University (B.A., magna cum laude, 1986); Florida State University (J.D., with honors, 1989); Purdue University (M.B.A., Finance, 1992). Recipient, American Jurisprudence Awards, Real Estate Transactions. Lecturer: Central Illinois Employers Association; Nursing Home Risk Management Association. *Member:* Peoria County, Chicago and Illinois State Bar Associations; The Florida Bar. ***PRACTICE AREAS:*** Trial Practice; Workers Compensation; Civil Liability. ***Email:*** adeblank@knell-kelly.com

DARCY K. GIBSON, born March 16, 1977; admitted to bar, 2002, Illinois; U.S. District Court, Central District of Illinois. *Education:* University of Illinois, Urbana-Champaign (B.S. 1999); Southern Illinois University School of Law (J.D. 2002). *Member:* Peoria County and Illinois State Bar Associations. ***PRACTICE AREAS:*** Workers Compensation; Civil Practice; Federal Practice; Insurance Defense; Trial Practice.

REPRESENTATIVE CLIENTS: Bituminous Insurance; Central Insurance Co.; Citizens Management, Inc.; CNA Insurance; Country Cos.; ESIS, Inc.; Employer's Security Insurance; Fireman's Fund; Harleysville Insurance; Hinz Claim Management, Inc.; Illinois Insurance Guaranty Fund; Liberty Mutual Insurance Co.; Midwest Insurance Co.; Pearl Cos.; Risk Enterprise Management, Inc.; St. Paul Insurance Cos.; Travelers Property and Casualty; Universal Underwriters; Westfield Group; Zurich North America; Ace USA; Attenta; Berkley Risk Enterprises; Brentwood Services; Broadspire; Cambridge Integrated Services, Inc.; Cannon Cochran Management Services, Inc.; Claims One; Crawford & Co.; Gallagher Bassett Services, Inc.; HCR Manor Care; Martin Boyer Co., Inc.; Sedgwick CMS; American Buildings, Inc.; Carhartt, Inc.; City of Galesburg; City of Pekin; County of Peoria; Heico Cos.; Illinois Municipal League Risk Management Assn.; Interstate Brands Cos.; Komatsy America Corp.; L.R. Nelson, Inc.; Methode Electronics, Inc.; Methodist Medical Center; Midwest Truckers Group; NTN Bower; Peoria Journal Star; Peoria Rivermen, Inc.; R.A. Cullinan & Son, Inc.; River City Construction; Rowe Construction Co.; TI Automotive; United Contractors Midwest.

KOEPKE & HILTABRAND, P.C.

PEORIA, ILLINOIS

(See Springfield)

General Civil Trial and Appellate Practice in all Courts, Insurance Defense, Workers' Compensation Defense, Professional Liability Defense, Insurance Coverage, Self Insured Defense, Employment/Discrimination Defense.

J. PHILLIP KRAJEWSKI

PEORIA, ILLINOIS

(See Baker, Baker & Krajewski, LLC)

LYNCH AND BLOOM, P.C.

Established in 1978

411 HAMILTON BOULEVARD, SUITE 1300
PEORIA, ILLINOIS 61602
Telephone: 309-673-7415
Fax: 309-673-3189
Email: dlynch4780@aol.com
URL: http://www.lynchbloom.com

Matrimonial and Family Law, Divorce, Adoptions, Child Support, Child Custody, General Civil Litigation. Personal Injury Law.

FIRM PROFILE: Lynch and Bloom was established in 1978 by David M. Lynch and the late Prescott E. Bloom. Serving clients throughout Central Illinois, engaging in a focus on Domestic Relations Law.

(This Listing Continued)

DAVID M. LYNCH, born Peoria, Illinois, October 31, 1947; admitted to bar, 1974, Illinois and U.S. District Court, Southern District of Illinois. *Education:* Monmouth College (B.A., 1969); University of Illinois (J.D., 1974). Phi Alpha Delta (President, 1974). *Member:* Peoria County (Chairman, Domestic Relations Committee, 1981-1984, 1986-1988, 1998-1999; At Large Member, Board of Directors, 1983-1986; Second Vice President, 1987; President, 1989) and Illinois State (Member, Young Lawyers Division, 1978-1981; Associate Member, Family Law Committee) Bar Associations. [With U.S. Army, 1969-1971]. ***PRACTICE AREAS:*** Family Law; Civil Litigation; Probate Law. ***Email:*** dlynch4780@aol.com

PRESCOTT E. BLOOM (1942-1986)

MICHAEL T. MAHONEY, LTD.

Established in 1984

414 HAMILTON BOULEVARD, SUITE 300
PEORIA, ILLINOIS 61602
Telephone: 309-673-0375
Fax: 309-274-5405
Email: mahoney@mchsi.com
URL: http://www.mahoneyltd.com

Chillicothe Office: 1011 North Second Street, 61523. Telephone: 309-274-5451.

Civil Litigation, Wills and Probate, Trusts and Estates, Estate Planning, Family Law, Personal Injury, Juvenile Law, DUI, Divorce, Adoptions, Child Support and Custody, Visitation Rights, Automobile Accidents, Dog Bites, Slip and Fall, Wrongful Death, Real Estate, Buying and Selling, Construction Law, Workers Compensation, Title and Insurance, Domestic Relations.

(For complete biographical data on all personnel, see Professional Biographies at Chillicothe, Illinois)

MILLER, HALL & TRIGGS

416 MAIN STREET, SUITE 1125
PEORIA, ILLINOIS 61602
Telephone: 309-671-9600
Fax: 309-671-9616
URL: http://www.mhtlaw.com

General Civil Practice, School and Local Government, Real Estate, Corporations, Probate, Labor, Banking, Taxation, Litigation and Title Insurance (ATGF).

ROBERT C. HALL, born Peoria, Illinois, May 21, 1948; admitted to bar, 1973, Illinois and Florida. *Education:* Bradley University (B.S., magna cum laude, 1970); University of Illinois (J.D. with honors, 1973). Order of the Coif. *Member:* Peoria County and Illinois State Bar Associations; The Florida Bar. ***PRACTICE AREAS:*** Real Estate; Estate Planning and Administration; Land Use and Zoning; Taxation. ***Email:*** robert.hall@mhtlaw.com

DENNIS R. TRIGGS, born Peoria, Illinois, December 9, 1944; admitted to bar, 1970, District of Columbia; 1976, Illinois. *Education:* United States Air Force Academy (B.S., 1967); Georgetown University (J.D., 1970); George Washington University (LL.M., 1972). *Member:* Peoria County and Illinois State (Member, School and Local Government Law Section) Bar Associations; Illinois Council of School Attorneys; National Council of School Attorneys. [With JAGC, USAF, 1970-1975]. ***PRACTICE AREAS:*** School and Local Government. ***Email:*** dennis.triggs@mhtlaw.com

WILLIAM R. KOHLHASE, born Chicago, Illinois, May 27, 1950; admitted to bar, 1975, Illinois, U.S. District Court for the Central District of Illinois and U.S. Court of Appeals, Seventh Circuit; 1987, U.S. Tax Court. *Education:* University of Wisconsin-Madison (B.A., 1972); George Washington University (J.D., 1975). Order of the Coif. Member, George Washington University Law Review. *Member:* Peoria County, Illinois State and American Bar Associations. ***PRACTICE AREAS:*** Business and Commercial Law; Litigation. ***Email:*** william.kohlhase@mhtlaw.com

PATRICK A. MURPHEY, born Princeton, Illinois, September 21, 1950; admitted to bar, 1977, Illinois; U.S. District Court, Central District of Illinois; U.S. Court of Appeals, Seventh Circuit. *Education:* Doane College (B.A., 1972); Valparaiso University (J.D. with high honors, 1977). *Member:* Peoria County, Illinois State and American Bar Associations. ***PRACTICE AREAS:*** Labor Relations; Employment; Civil Rights; School and Local Government. ***Email:*** patrick.murphey@mhtlaw.com

MICHAEL J. TIBBS, born Pekin, Illinois, April 25, 1949; admitted to bar, 1975, Illinois; 1976, U.S. District Court, Central District of Illinois; U.S. Court of Appeals, Seventh Circuit. *Education:* University of Illinois (B.S., 1971); St. Louis University (J.D., 1975). *Member:* Peoria County and Illinois State Bar Associations; Illinois Council of School Attorneys; National Council of School Attorneys. ***PRACTICE AREAS:*** School and Local Government; Finance; Real Estate. ***Email:*** michael.tibbs@mhtlaw.com

RICHARD M. JOSEPH, born Peoria, Illinois, August 22, 1960; admitted to bar, 1985, Wisconsin, Illinois and U.S. District Court, Eastern District of Wisconsin; 1988, U.S. Tax Court; 1989, U.S. District Court, Central District of Illinois. *Education:* University of Notre Dame (B.B.A., 1982); Marquette University (J.D., cum laude, 1985). Thomas More Scholar. Member, Marquette Law Review. *Member:* Peoria County and Illinois State Bar Associations; State Bar of Wisconsin. ***PRACTICE AREAS:*** Real Estate; Banking; Municipal Law; Municipal Finance; Local Government Law. ***Email:*** richard.joseph@mhtlaw.com

THOMAS R. DAVIS, born Peoria, Illinois, May 28, 1952; admitted to bar, 1986, Illinois; U.S. District Court, Northern, Central and Southern Districts of Illinois; U.S. Court of Appeals, Seventh Circuit. *Education:* University of Illinois (B.S., 1974); DePaul University (J.D. with honors, 1986). Member, DePaul University Law Review. *Member:* Peoria County and Illinois State Bar Associations. ***PRACTICE AREAS:*** Civil Litigation; Civil Appeals; Civil Rights; Employment Law; Commercial Litigation; Bankruptcy; Real Estate; Land Use; Zoning Law; School Law; Local Government Law. ***Email:*** thomas.davis@mhtlaw.com

(This Listing Continued)

NATHAN R. MILLER, born Peoria, Illinois, February 10, 1957; admitted to bar, 1982, Illinois; 1984, U.S. District Court, Central District of Illinois and U.S. Court of Appeals, Seventh Circuit. *Education:* University of Illinois (B.A., 1979; J.D., 1982). *Member:* Peoria County, Illinois State and American Bar Associations. ***PRACTICE AREAS:*** Estate Planning and Administration; Real Estate; General Business. ***Email:*** nathan.miller@mhtlaw.com

JAY E. GREENING, born Beaufort, South Carolina, September 13, 1968; admitted to bar, 1995, Illinois. *Education:* Bradley University (B.S., 1991); Northern Illinois University (J.D., magna cum laude, 1995). *Member:* Peoria County and Illinois State Bar Associations. ***PRACTICE AREAS:*** School and Local Government; Labor and Employment; General Business. ***Email:*** jaygreening@hotmail.com

SCOTT A. BRUNTON, born Seattle, Washington, July 26, 1963; admitted to bar, 1992, Illinois; U.S. District Court, Northern and Central Districts of Illinois; U.S. Court of Appeals, Seventh Circuit; U.S. Supreme Court. *Education:* Purdue University (B.S.M.E., 1985); University of Illinois (J.D., magna cum laude, 1992). States Attorney, Woodford County, 1997-1998. *Member:* Peoria County, Woodford County, Illinois State and American Bar Associations; Illinois Council of School Attorneys; National Council of School Attorneys. ***PRACTICE AREAS:*** Municipal Law; School Law; Governmental Law; Labor Law. ***Email:*** scott.brunton@mhtlaw.com

DOUGLAS G. GRIFFIN, born Peoria, Illinois, April 28, 1966; admitted to bar, 1991, Illinois; 1998, Florida. *Education:* Illinois State University (B.S., 1988); Southern Illinois University (J.D., 1991). ***PRACTICE AREAS:*** School Law; Municipal Law; Labor and Employment; Contracts; Civil Litigation. ***Email:*** douglas.griffin@mhtlaw.com

JEFFREY E. KRUMPE, born Peoria, Illinois, November 4, 1968; admitted to bar, 1995, Illinois; U.S. District Court, Northern and Central Districts of Illinois. *Education:* Wabash College (B.A., magna cum laude, 1991); University of London, London, England (M.A., 1992); University of Illinois (J.D., cum laude, 1995). Phi Beta Kappa. *Member:* Peoria County, Illinois State and American Bar Associations; Abraham Lincoln Inns of Court. ***PRACTICE AREAS:*** Civil Litigation; Commercial Litigation; Municipal Law; Appellate Practice. ***Email:*** jeffrey.krumpe@mhtlaw.com

M. CURT RICHARDSON, born Champaign, Illinois, October 16, 1977; admitted to bar, 2002, Illinois; U.S. District Court, Central District of Illinois. *Education:* Eastern Illinois University (B.A., 1998); Southern Illinois University School of Law (J.D., 2002). Member, Law Journal. Phi Alpha Delta. *Member:* Peoria County, Illinois State and American Bar Associations; Illinois and National Council of School Attorneys. ***PRACTICE AREAS:*** Municipal Law; Education Law. ***Email:*** m.curt.richardson@mhtlaw.com

JAMISON J. ALLEN, born Jasper, Indiana, July 15, 1974; admitted to bar, 2002, Illinois. *Education:* Indiana State University (B.S., 1996); University of Illinois (J.D., 2002). Member: Moot Court; Law Journal. *Member:* Peoria County, Illinois State and American Bar Associations. ***PRACTICE AREAS:*** Real Estate; Municipal Law; Education Law; Litigation. ***Email:*** jamison.j.allen.@mhtlaw.com

ALLISON R. KEERS-SANCHEZ, born Joliet, Illinois, September 28, 1974; admitted to bar, 2004, Illinois. *Education:* Illinois Wesleyan University (B.A., 1996); Southern Illinois University (J.D., 2004). Phi Kappa Phi. Author, Mandatory Provision of Foreign Language Interpreters in Health Care Services, 24 Journal of Legal Medicine 557-578 Dec. 2003. *Member:* Peoria County and Illinois State Bar Associations. [Ssg and (E-5) United States Air Force, 1996-2001]. ***LANGUAGES:*** German. ***PRACTICE AREAS:*** Real Estate; Municipal Law. ***Email:*** allison.sanchez@mhtlaw.com

REPRESENTATIVE CLIENTS: *Communications:* Glasford Telephone Co.; Thompson Electronics Co.; Affina, Inc.; Clear Channel Communications; Illinois Valley Public Telecommunications Corporation (WTVP). *Contractors:* D. Joseph Construction & Development; Midwest Foundation Corp. *Dealers:* Aldi, Inc.; Neal Auto Parts, Inc.; Mac's Convenience Food Stores; Action Mobility; American TV and Appliance. *Financial:* First Bank, F.S.B.; Morton Community Bank; Eagle Mortgage Co.; Stern Brothers & Co. *Manufacturing:* Quality Metal Products, Inc.; Pro-Fab, Inc.; Alcast Co.; Illinois Valley Plastics, Inc.; Cast Technologies, Inc.; *Municipal:* Fondulac Park District; Village of Roanoke; City of Eureka; City of Minonk; City of East Peoria; Washington Park District; County of Peoria; City of Henry; Village of Metamora; Ogle County Intergovernmental Agency. *Professional:* Midwest Orthopaedic Center, S.C.; Architectural Research & Design, P.C.; Peoria Ear, Nose and Throat Group, S.C. *Real Estate:* Simon Property Group; Edward Rose & Sons; Maloof Commercial Real Estate Co.; Cullinan Companies; Wald/Land Corp.; Cohen Development Co.; D. Joseph Sons & Associates; Wisdom Development Group; Jorgenson Real Estate Group. *Schools:* Bradley University; Byron Community Unit School District No. 226; Morton Unit School District; Pekin High School District; Tazewell-Mason Counties Special Education; McLean County Unit District No. 5. *Wholesalers:* Westmont Interior Supply House, Inc.; Dove Equipment Co., Inc.; Crawford Door Co. of Peoria, Inc. *Others:* Bo-Jac Seed Co.

NICOARA & STEAGALL

Established in 1980

COMMERCE BANK BUILDING
416 MAIN STREET, SUITE 815
PEORIA, ILLINOIS 61602-1103
Telephone: 309-674-6085
Fax: 309-674-6032
URL: http://www.nicoara.com
Email: nicsteag@mtco.com
URL: http://www.lawyers.com/nicoaralaw

Affiliated With: Katz, Friedman, Eagle, Eisenstein & Johnson. 77 W. Washington Street, 20th Floor, Chicago, Illinois, 60602. Telephone: 312-263-6330.

General Civil Trial and Appellate Practice in State and Federal Courts. Personal Injury and Insurance Law, Civil Rights Litigation, Employment Discrimination, Auto Accidents, Aviation Law, Legal Malpractice, Medical Malpractice, Products Liability, Sex Offenses. Arbitration and Mediation Services.

FIRM PROFILE: Nicoara & Steagall has over 50 years of combined experience practicing law in Peoria, Illinois. Serving clients throughout central Illinois inclusive of Peoria, Tazewell, Woodford, McLean, Knox, Marshall, Stark, Fulton, McDonough and LaSalle counties and the

(This Listing Continued)

NICOARA & STEAGALL, Peoria—Continued

U.S. District Court for the Central District of Illinois and other federal courts. Engaged in personal injury litigation, federal civil rights, discrimination, and other complex litigation matters.

MEMBERS OF FIRM

JOHN P. NICOARA, born Gary, Indiana, July 24, 1948; admitted to bar, 1975, Illinois; 1976, U.S. District Court, Central District of Illinois; 1982, U.S. Court of Appeals, Seventh Circuit; 1984, U.S. Supreme Court. *Education:* University of Michigan (A.B., 1970); University of Illinois (J.D., 1975). Notes and Comments Editor, University of Illinois Law Review, 1974-1975. Assistant States Attorney, Woodford County, 1975-1978. Master and Executive Committee Member, Abraham Lincoln Inn of Court, 1988-1992; Emeritus Member, 1993—. Former Board Member and Secretary, Illinois Lawyers' Assistance Program. Member: Illinois Supreme Court Rules Committee; Supreme Court of Illinois Committee on Judicial Performance Evaluation; Judicial Vacancy Advisory Screening Committee; Federal Civil Justice Reform Act Advisory Committee. *Member:* Peoria County (Director, 1982—; President, 1996-1997), Woodford County, Illinois State and American Bar Associations; Illinois Trial Lawyer's Association; Illinois Defense Counsel; Defense Research and Trial Lawyers Association. [With U.S. Army, 1971-1973]. ***LANGUAGES:*** Romanian. ***REPORTED CASES:*** Canopy v. Hentz, 2004 WL 119383; R.A.N. Consultants, Inc., vs. Peacock, 201 111.App.3d 67, 559 N.E.2d 283 (3rd Dist. 1990); Holley v. Badgerow, 162 111.App.3d 572, 515 N.E.2d 1257 (3rd Dist. 1987); Arkansas Best Freight System, Inc., vs. Illinois News Service, Inc., 159 Ill.App.3d 775, 512 N.E.2d 1063 (3rd Dist. 1987); Smith v. McNeil Corp., 74 Ill.App.3d 356, 392 N.E.2d 1376 (3rd Dist. 1979); Allison v. Davies, 64 Ill.App.3d 900, 381 N.E..2d 1034 (3rd Dist. 1978); National Bank of Bloomington vs. Podgogski, 57 Ill.App.3d 256, 373 N.E.2d 82 (3rd Dist. 1978). ***PRACTICE AREAS:*** Products Liability; Professional Malpractice; Insurance; Negligence Law. ***Email:*** nicoara@mtco.com

RICHARD L. STEAGALL, born Indianapolis, Indiana, June 30, 1953; admitted to bar, 1977, Florida; 1978, Illinois, U.S. District Court, Central District of Illinois and U.S. Court of Appeals, Seventh Circuit; 1982, U.S. Supreme Court and U.S. District Court, Middle District of Florida; 1986, U.S. District Court, Northern District of Illinois; 1995, U.S. District Court, Northern District of Ohio; 2000, U.S. Court of Appeals, Tenth Circuit. *Education:* Illinois Wesleyan University (B.A., cum laude, 1975); Stetson University; University of Georgia (J.D., 1977). Sigma Nu Phi. Author: "Illinois Adopts Comparative Assumption of Risk and Misuse in Strict Products Liability Cases," Illinois Bar Journal (May 1984); "Loss of Chance of Survival in Medical Malpractice Cases," Ill. Bar J. (October, 1991). Barrister, 1988-1992; Master, 1993-1996; Program Chairman, Executive Committee Member, 1994-1995 and Emeritus, 1996—, Abraham Lincoln Inn of Court. Member, Leading Lawyers Network, Civil Rights, Constitutional Law, 2003. *Member:* Peoria County, Illinois State and American Bar Associations; The Florida Bar; Illinois Trial Lawyers Association; The Association of Trial Lawyers of America. ***REPORTED CASES:*** Massey v. Helman, 196 F.3d 727 (7th Cir. 1999); Corley v. Rosewood Care Center, Inc. of Peoria, 142 F.3d 1041 (7th Cir. 1998); Cooper v. Wal-Mart Stores, Inc., 106 F.3d (7th Cir. 1997); Thompson v. Boggs, 33 F.3d 847 (7th Cir. 1994), cert. denied, 514 V.S.1063 (1994); In Re Agent Orange Product Liability Litigation, 818 F.2d 145 (2d Cir. 1986), cert. denied, Pickney v. Dow Chemical Co., 484 U.S. 1004 (1988); Ricker v. Fulton County Soil and Water Conservation Dist., 800 F.Supp. 636 (C.D.Ill. 1992); Coney v. J.L.G. Industries, Inc., 97 Ill.2d 104, 454 N.E.2d 197, 73 Ill.Dec. 337 (1983); Zinser v. Rose, 245 Ill.App.3d 881, 614 N.E.2d 1259, 185 Ill.Dec. 574 (3d Dist. 1993); Carrigan v. New World Enterprises, Ltd., 112 Ill.App.3d 970, 446 N.E.2d 265, 68 Ill.Dec. 531 (3d Dist. 1983). 43500. ***PRACTICE AREAS:*** Civil Rights; Constitutional Law; Employment Discrimination; Personal Injury; Negligence Law. ***Email:*** steagall@mtco.com

Languages: Romanian.

REPRESENTATIVE CLIENTS: Founders Insurance Co.; American Service Insurance Co.; Illinois Casualty Insurance Co.
REFERENCE: Commerce Bank.

PRUSAK, WINNE & GORMAN, LTD.

Established in 1983

403 N.E. JEFFERSON STREET
PEORIA, ILLINOIS 61603-3725
Telephone: 309-674-4222
Fax: 309-674-9701
Email: mprusak@mtco.com
URL: http://www.lawyers.com/prusak&winne

General Practice. Trial, Insurance, Workers Compensation, Personal Injury, Probate, Corporate, Construction Litigation, Fire Loss, Professional Liability, Real Estate Law, Automobile Liability Defense, Insurance Coverage, Uninsured and Underinsured Motorists Arbitration, Products Liability Defense, Professional Liability Defense.

FIRM PROFILE: Maximilian M. Prusak and Joseph E. Winne first began practicing together in 1978 at the firm of Golsworthy, Fifield & Prusak. In 1980 they formed a law firm called Nicol, Newell, Prusak & Winne, where they were principals until 1983 when they formed a professional corporation called Prusak & Winne, Ltd. Katherine S. Gorman joined the firm in September of 1993. While focusing on areas of litigation, the firm offers a full range of legal services to its client in a courteous, competent and cost effective manner.

MAXIMILIAN M. PRUSAK, born Granite City, Illinois, March 22, 1943; admitted to bar, 1968, Illinois. *Education:* University of Illinois (B.S., 1965; J.D., 1968). Phi Delta Phi. *Member:* Peoria County and Illinois State Bar Associations; Illinois Association of Defense Trial Counsel; Defense Research Institute. *[Capt., Judge Advocate, USAF, 1969-1973].* ***PRACTICE AREAS:*** Insurance Defense; Civil Practice; Products Liability; Construction Litigation; Fire Loss; Professional Liability; Premises Liability; Arbitration; Mediation; Insurance Law. ***Email:*** mprusak@mtco.com

(This Listing Continued)

JOSEPH E. WINNE, born Peoria, Illinois, December 13, 1949; admitted to bar, 1976, Illinois; U.S. Supreme Court. *Education:* St. Ambrose College (B.A., 1972); Hamline University (J.D., with honors, 1976). *Member:* Peoria County and Illinois State Bar Associations. ***PRACTICE AREAS:*** Insurance Defense; Civil Practice; Workers Compensation; Insurance; Products Liability; Construction Litigation; Fire Loss; Insurance Coverage; Professional Liability. ***Email:*** jwinne@mtco.com

KATHERINE GORMAN HUBLER, born April 14, 1968; admitted to bar, 1993, Illinois. *Education:* University of Illinois (B.S., 1990); Southern Illinois University (J.D., 1993). Phi Delta Phi. *Member:* Peoria County and Illinois State Bar Associations. ***PRACTICE AREAS:*** Insurance Defense; Civil Practice; Workers Compensation; Insurance; Products Liability. ***Email:*** kgorman@mtco.com

BLAKE E. DUNLAP, born White Hall, Illinois, February 4, 1976; admitted to bar, 2001, Illinois. *Education:* Blackburn College (B.A., 1998); Southern Illinois University (J.D., 2001). *Member:* Illinois State and American Bar Associations; Illinois Association of Defense Trial Counsel; Inns of Court. ***PRACTICE AREAS:*** Insurance Defense; Civil Practice; Workers Compensation; Products Liability. ***Email:*** bedunlap@mtco.com

LEGAL SUPPORT PERSONNEL

MICHELLE WEGHORST (Paralegal)
ROBYN MOORE-PATINO, (Paralegal)

REPRESENTATIVE CLIENTS: *Corporate and Business Clients:* Central Illinois Light Company; Lacon Manufacturing; *Insurance Company-Defense Clients:* TIG Holdings, Inc. (formerly Transamerica); Martin Boyer Company; Blue Cross-Blue Shield of Illinois; National Farmers Union Insurance Company; Milwaukee Insurance Co.; Pekin Insurance Company; Indiana Insurance Company; Western States Insurance Company; Iowa Mutual Insurance Company; Casualty Insurance Company; Cuna Insurance Co.; Atlanta Casualty Company; Prudential Insurance Company; Viking Insurance Company; Ohio Farmers Insurance Company; Superior Insurance Co.; State-Auto Insurance Co.; Kemper Insurance Co.; Lake States Insurance Co.; Grange Insurance; The Cincinnati Insurance Companies; Goodville Mutual Casualty Company; Great West Casualty Company; Kemper National Insurance Companies; Erie Insurance Company; American Family Mutual Insurance Company; OneBeacon Insurance Co.; Hastings Insurance Co.; Standard Mutual Insurance Company; Victoria Insurance Co.; Meridian Insurance Co.; Chubb Group of Insurance Companies; Founders Insurance Company; Great Central Insurance Company; GEICO Insurance; Gulf Insurance Group; Jackson National Life Insurance Company; Essex Insurance Company; Shelter Insurance.

QUINN, JOHNSTON, HENDERSON & PRETORIUS

CHARTERED

Established in 1946

(Formerly McConnell, Kennedy, Quinn & Johnston)

227 N. E. JEFFERSON STREET
PEORIA, ILLINOIS 61602
Telephone: 309-674-1133
Telecopier: 309-674-6503
Email: quinnlaw@qjhp.com
URL: http://www.qjhp.com

Springfield, Illinois Office: 205 South Fifth Street, Suite 900, 62701. Telephone: 217-753-1133. Fax: 217-753-1180.

Trial Practice in all Courts. Personal Injury, Professional Negligence, Admiralty, Insurance Law, Workers Compensation Law, Banking, Commercial and Bankruptcy Law. Real Estate, Corporate and Probate Law.

FIRM PROFILE: Founded in 1946 by Lowell and Golden McConnell and Tom Kennedy, the firm presently consists of 16 partners and 7 associates assisted by four paralegals and three Nurse/Legal Consultants. This general practice firm provides top quality legal service to a broad base of clients across Central Illinois, from the Indiana to the Iowa borders. A majority of the lawyers engage in insurance defense trial work.

LOWELL R. McCONNELL (1911-1971)
GOLDEN A. McCONNELL (1914-1974)
JOSEPH A. LEIMKUEHLER (1931-1974)
THOMAS B. KENNEDY, SR. (1912-1988)
RICHARD E. QUINN (1928-2000)

R. MICHAEL HENDERSON, born Gillespie, Illinois, August 9, 1944; admitted to bar, 1969, Illinois, U.S. District Court, Central and Northern Districts of Illinois, U.S. Court of Appeals, Seventh Circuit and U.S. Supreme Court. *Education:* University of Illinois (B.S., 1966); Loyola University (J.D., 1969). Phi Alpha Delta. Recipient, Award for Distinguished Service to Law and Society, Illinois Bar Foundation, 2002. Listed in: Strathmore's Who's Who, 2003; The Contemporary Who's Who, 2003. Co-Chairman, Committee to Redraft Local Rules of Federal District Court, Central District of Illinois, 1986. Member, Local Federal Rules Committee, 1995-2004. Member, Board of Directors, Illinois Client Security Fund, 1992-1994. Member, Board of Directors, 1994-2000 and President, 1997-1999, Lawyers Trust Fund of Illinois. Selected as one of: Leading Illinois Lawyers, American Research Corporation, 1997; Leading Illinois Attorneys by Leading Lawyers Network, 2003. Recipient, Illinois Bar Foundation Award, Distinguished Service to Law and Society, 2002. Chair, Illinois Coalition for Equal Justice, 2004. *Member:* Peoria County (Member, Board of Directors, 1978, 1989, 1992-1997; Second Vice President, 1993-1994; President Elect, 1994-1995; President, 1995-1996; Chairman, Courts and Procedure Committee, 1978, 1989; Chairman Professional Standards Committee, 1992-1993) and Illinois State (Member, Board of Governors, 1988-1994; Secretary, 1993-1994; Council Member, Civil Practice and Procedure Section, 1977-1983, 1994-1997; Council Member, Insurance Law Section, 1994-1999, Secretary, 1995-1996, Vice Chair, 1996-1997 and Chairman, 1997-1998; Standing Committee on Judicial Appointments, 1995-2000; Assemblyman, 1982—; Member, Section on Tort Law, Committee on Aeration/Space Law, 1982-1983; Council Member, Tort Law Section Council, 1984-1987, 1998—; Board of Governors, 1988-1994; Secretary, 1993-1994; Chairman, Committee to Review Client Security Fund, 1990-1993; Member: Media Law Section, 1990-1994; Budget and Finance Committee, 1993-1994,

(This Listing Continued)

1998-2000; Long Range Planning Committee, 1993-1995; Task Force on Governance, 1995-1996; Legislation, 1996—; Agenda/Program Committee, 1996-1997; Judicial Evaluation Committee, 1995—; Downstate Chairperson, 2000-2003; Judicial Discipline Committee, 1996-1997; Membership and Bar Activities, 1999—; Committee on Funding of the Courts, 2001—; Examiners Committee on Character & Fitness, 2002) Bar Associations; Defense Research Institute; Illinois Association of Defense Trial Counsel (Member, Board of Directors, 1980—; Secretary-Treasurer, 1984-1986; Vice-President, 1986-1989; President, 1989-1990); International Association of Defense Counsel; Federal Inns of Court (Master Emeritus, Abraham Lincoln Chapter); American Law Firm Association; ALFA International. American Bar Foundation; Illinois Bar Foundation (Charter Member, The Fellows; Gold Stalwart Fellow, Member, Board of Directors, 1989-2000). Fellow: American Board of Trial Advocates; American College of Trial Lawyers; Society of Trial Lawyers; American College of Barristers. ***PRACTICE AREAS:*** Products Liability; Professional Malpractice; Commercial Litigation; Negligence; Libel and Defamation. ***Email:*** mickhenderson@qjhp.com

MURVEL PRETORIUS, JR., born Evanston, Illinois, July 23, 1946; admitted to bar, 1971, Illinois and U.S. District Court, Central District of Illinois; 1986, U.S. Supreme Court and U.S. Court of Appeals, Seventh Circuit. *Education:* Knox College (B.A., 1968); University of Illinois (J.D., 1971). Lecturer: Peoria County Continuing Legal Education Program. Downstate Chairman, State of Illinois, 2001-2003. *Member:* Peoria County and Illinois State Bar Associations; Defense Research Institute; Illinois Association of Defense Trial Counsel; International Association of Defense Counsel; Greater Peoria Claims Association; Illinois Association of Hospital Attorneys; Illinois Appellate Lawyers Association. Master Emeritus, American Inns of Court; American College of Trial Lawyers. ***PRACTICE AREAS:*** Healthcare Law; Medical Malpractice; Professional Negligence. ***Email:*** mpretorius@qjhp.com

BRADLEY W. DUNHAM, born Jacksonville, Illinois, June 18, 1944; admitted to bar, 1969, Illinois; 1973, U.S. District Court, Central District of Illinois; 1983, U.S. Supreme Court. *Education:* Black Hawk College (A.A., 1964); University of Illinois (B.A., 1966; J.D., 1969). Staff Attorney, Illinois Legislative Reference Bureau, Springfield, Illinois, 1969-1971. *Member:* Peoria County and Illinois State Bar Associations; National Lawyers Association; Illinois Appellate Lawyers Association; Illinois Association of Defense Trial Counsel; Defense Research Institute; American Law Firm Association; Christian Legal Society; Greater Peoria Claims Association. ***PRACTICE AREAS:*** Product Liability; Municipal Law; Premises Liability; Insurance Coverage; Negligence. ***Email:*** bdunham@qjhp.com

ROBERT H. JENNETTEN, born Belleville, Illinois, January 13, 1945; admitted to bar, 1972, Illinois and U.S. District Court, Central District of Illinois. *Education:* Quincy College (B.A., 1967); University of Illinois (J.D., 1972). *Member:* Peoria County (Member, Civil Practice and Procedure and Pro Bono Committees; President, 2004) and Illinois State Bar Associations; Illinois Association of Defense Trial Counsel (Member, Insurance Law and Employment Law Committees); Defense Research Institute; Greater Peoria Claims Association. Master Emeritus, Abraham Lincoln Chapter, Inns of Court. ***PRACTICE AREAS:*** Workers Compensation; Negligence; Insurance Coverage. ***Email:*** bjennetten@qjhp.com

GREGORY A. CERULO, born St. Louis, Missouri, June 28, 1954; admitted to bar, 1979, Illinois and U.S. District Court, Central District of Illinois; 1989, U.S. Supreme Court and U.S. Court of Appeals, Seventh Circuit; 1991, U.S. District Court, Northern District of Illinois; 2001, U.S. District Court, Southern District of Illinois. *Education:* Purdue University; University of Missouri (B.A., 1975); University of Illinois (J.D., 1979). Past Lecturer: Peoria County Legal Education Program; Illinois State Bar Association. *Member:* Peoria County, Illinois State and American Bar Associations; Defense Research Institute; Illinois Association of Defense Trial Lawyers Association; International Association of Defense Counsel; American Arbitration Association. ***PRACTICE AREAS:*** Products Liability; Alternative Dispute Resolution; Professional Malpractice; Fire Loss; Construction Litigation; Insurance Coverage Litigation. ***Email:*** gcerulo@qjhp.com

PAUL P. GILFILLAN, born Northridge, California, March 31, 1957; admitted to bar, 1982, Illinois and U.S. District Court, Central District of Illinois. *Education:* Illinois State University (B.S., 1979); Valparaiso University School of Law (J.D., 1982). *Member:* Peoria County (Member, Board of Directors, 1993) and Illinois State Bar Associations; Illinois Association of Defense Trial Counsel; Defense Research Institute; Greater Peoria Claims Association (Officer, 1992-1997). ***PRACTICE AREAS:*** Municipal Liability; Insurance Defense Litigation; Malpractice Defense; Family Law. ***Email:*** pgilfillan@qjhp.com

LAURIE M. JUDD, born Peoria, Illinois, February 12, 1952; admitted to bar, 1983, Illinois; 1984, U.S. District Court, Central District of Illinois; 1985, U.S. Court of Appeals, Seventh Circuit. *Education:* University of Illinois (B.A., 1974); Southern Illinois University (J.D., cum laude, 1983). Editor-in-Chief, Southern Illinois University Law Journal, 1982-1983. Co-Author: "Financing the Dealer", Advising Illinois Financial Institutions, IICLE, 1987 and 1989. Author: "Lender Procedures for Commercial Mortgages," Advising Illinois Financial Institutions, Supp., 1997. Clerk to Chief Justice Howard C. Ryan, Illinois Supreme Court, 1983-1984. *Member:* Peoria County (Member, Board of Directors, 1989-1991; Real Property Committee, 1995-1996) and Illinois State (Member: Commercial, Banking and Bankruptcy Law Section; Local Government Law; Real Property) Bar Associations; The Bar Association of the Central and Southern Districts of Illinois. ***PRACTICE AREAS:*** Commercial Law; Bankruptcy Law; Real Estate Law; Governmental Law. ***Email:*** ljudd@qjhp.com

DAVID BLAIR COLLINS, born Clinton, Iowa, December 27, 1960; admitted to bar, 1989, Illinois; 1991, U.S. District Court, Central District of Illinois; 2001, U.S. District Court, Southern District of Illinois. *Education:* University of Iowa (B.A., 1983); Northern Illinois University (J.D., cum laude, 1989). Editor-in-Chief, Northern Illinois University Law Review, 1988-1989. Judicial Clerkship with Illinois Appellate Court Justices William B. Wombacher (Deceased), 1989-1990 and John A. Gorman, 1990-1991. *Member:* Peoria County and Illinois State Bar Associations; Appellate Lawyers Association; Defense Research Institute; Illinois Association of Defense Trial Counsel; Abraham Lincoln Inns of Court (Barrister). ***PRACTICE AREAS:*** Product Liability Law; Municipal Tort Liability; Negligence Law. ***Email:*** dcollins@qjhp.com

(This Listing Continued)

JOHN F. KAMIN, born Peoria, Illinois, October 1, 1965; admitted to bar, 1990, Missouri; 1991, Illinois and U.S. District Court, Central District of Illinois. *Education:* Bradley University (B.S., 1987); Southern Illinois University School of Law (J.D., summa cum laude, 1990). Phi Kappa Phi; Phi Delta Phi. President, Moot Court Board. Lead Articles Editor, Southern Illinois University Law Journal. Author: Note, "The Extension of Implied Warranty Protection to Employees of a Purchaser," 14 S. Ill. U.L.J. 123 (1989). *Member:* Peoria County, Illinois State (Member, Workers Compensation Section Council, 1996-1999) and American Bar Associations; The Missouri Bar; Illinois Association of Defense Trial Counsel; Defense Research Institute; Master, Abraham Lincoln Inns of Court. ***PRACTICE AREAS:*** Workers Compensation; Civil Litigation; Insurance Law. ***Email:*** jkamin@qjhp.com

MATTHEW B. SMITH, born Peoria, Illinois, November 7, 1967; admitted to bar, 1993, Illinois and U.S. District Court, Central District of Illinois; 1997, U.S. Court of Appeals, Seventh Circuit; 2001, U.S. Supreme Court. *Education:* University of Illinois (B.S., with high honors, 1990; J.D., 1993). Member, Chicago Moot Court Team. Staff Editor, University of Illinois Law Review, 1992-1993. Author: Note, "Defining Property in the Post-lucas World," 1994 U. Ill. L. Rev. 443. *Member:* Peoria County and Illinois State Bar Associations; Defense Research Institute; Illinois Association of Defense Trial Counsel. ***PRACTICE AREAS:*** Civil Defense Litigation; Medical Malpractice; Personal Injury; Products Liability; Employment Discrimination; Municipal Liability; Appellate Practice. ***Email:*** msmith@qjhp.com

PETER R. JENNETTEN, born Burlington, Iowa, October 4, 1969; admitted to bar, 1996, Illinois and U.S. District Court, Central District of Illinois; 1997, U.S. Court of Appeals, Seventh Circuit; 2002, U.S. District Court, Southern District of Illinois. *Education:* University of Illinois (B.S., cum laude, with distinction, 1991; M.S., 1993); Georgetown University Law Center (J.D., cum laude, 1996). Phi Beta Kappa; Phi Alpha Delta. Recipient, Illinois State Bar Association Young Lawyer of the Year, 2003. Senior Articles Editor, Georgetown International Environmental Law Review, 1995-1996. Co-author: with R.H. Jennetten and M.D. Pretorius, "Defenses to Third Party Actions in Tort," in Third Party Practice (IICLE 2000). Author: "State Environmental Agreements with Foreign Powers: The Compact Clause and the Foreign Affairs Power of the States," 8 Georgetown International Environmental Law Review 141, 1995. ISBA Young Lawyer of the Year, Downstate, 2003: 40 Leaders Under 40, Peoria, 2002. *Member:* Peoria County, Illinois State and American Bar Associations; Illinois Association of Defense Trial Counsel (Co-Chair, Young Lawyers Committee, 2000-2004); Defense Research Institute; Abraham Lincoln Inns of Court; American Inns of Court. ***PRACTICE AREAS:*** Civil Rights; Municipal Liability; Insurance Defense; Litigation; Appellate Practice; Insurance Coverage. ***Email:*** peter@qjhp.com

MICHAEL A. KRAFT, born Peoria, Illinois, October 13, 1968; admitted to bar, 1993, Illinois; 1994, U.S. District Court, Central District of Illinois; 1995, Indiana; U.S. District Court, Northern District of Illinois. *Education:* University of Illinois (A.B., Phi Beta Kappa, 1990; J.D., magna cum laude, 1993). Phi Beta Kappa. Co-Author with R. Michael Henderson, "Real Estate Malpractice," Illinois Causes of Action, Illinois Institute of Continuing Legal Education, 2002. Instructor, Business Law, Illinois Central College, 1994-1995. Member, Board of Directors, Alzheimer's Association Central Illinois Chapter, 2000—. *Member:* Peoria County and Illinois State Bar Associations. ***PRACTICE AREAS:*** Business and Employment Law; Commercial Litigation; Real Estate; Probate. ***Email:*** mkraft@qjhp.com

JONATHAN A. STUMP, born Minneapolis, Minnesota, December 30, 1970; admitted to bar, 1996, Michigan; 1997, Illinois. *Education:* Oakland University (B.A., 1993) Departmental Honors, N.C.A.A. Academic All American; University of Illinois (J.D., 1996). Moot Court Honors, Trial Advocacy Honors. *Member:* Grand Rapids, Peoria County and Illinois State Bar Associations; State Bar of Michigan; Defense Research Institute,. ***PRACTICE AREAS:*** Insurance Defense Litigation; Insurance Coverage; Auto Negligence; Premises Liability; Medical Malpractice; Construction Law. ***Email:*** jstump@qjhp.com

LAURA A. PETERSEN, born Evanston, Illinois, June 10, 1973; admitted to bar, 1998, Illinois; 2000, U.S. District Court, Central District of Illinois. *Education:* University of Illinois (B.S., summa cum laude, 1995; J.D., magna cum laude, 1998). Phi Delta Phi. Member, Moot Court. *Member:* Peoria County and Illinois State Bar Associations; Illinois Association of Defense Trial Counsel; Defense Research Institute; Illinois Association of Healthcare Attorneys. ***PRACTICE AREAS:*** Health Care Law; Professional Malpractice; Employment Discrimination; Automobile Negligence; Premises Liability; Municipal Liability. ***Email:*** lpetersen@qjhp.com

JO TEWES WETHERILL, born Hartley, Iowa, October 16, 1971; admitted to bar, 1997, Illinois and U.S. District Court, Central District of Illinois. *Education:* University of Iowa (B.S., with distinction, 1993; J.D., with distinction, 1997). Phi Delta Phi. Law Clerk to Hon. Mary McDade, 2001-2002. *Member:* Peoria County and Illinois State Bar Associations; Illinois Association of Defense Trial Counsel; Defense Research Institute. ***PRACTICE AREAS:*** Insurance Law; Malpractice. ***Email:*** jwetherill@qjhp.com

ADAM P. CHADDOCK, born Peoria, Illinois, May 26, 1976; admitted to bar, 2001, Illinois and U.S. District Court, Central and Southern Districts of Illinois. *Education:* University of Illinois (B.A., History, 1998; J.D., 2001). Member, Frederick Green Moot Court Board/Chicago Team. *Member:* Peoria County and Illinois State Bar Associations; Illinois Association of Defense Trial Counsel; Defense Research Institute. ***PRACTICE AREAS:*** Insurance Defense. ***Email:*** achaddock@qjhp.com

ALLISON N. BELL, born Des Moines, Iowa, June 21, 1971; admitted to bar, 1997, Illinois. *Education:* Grinnell College (B.A., 1994); University of Iowa (J.D., 1997). *Member:* Peoria County and Illinois State Bar Associations; Abraham Lincoln Inn of Courts. ***PRACTICE AREAS:*** Insurance Defense Litigation. ***Email:*** abell@qjhp.com

MELINDA ROWE, born LaSalle, Illinois, June 3, 1971; admitted to bar, 2003, Illinois and U.S. District Court, Central District of Illinois. *Education:* Northern Illinois University (B.S., cum laude, 1995; J.D., cum laude, 2003); Lewis University (M.B.A., 1997). Phi Delta Phi (Treasurer, 2001-2002). Recipient, Graduate School of Management Academic Achievement Award. *Member:* Peoria County, Illinois State and American Bar Associations; Illinois Association of Defense Trial Counsel. ***PRACTICE AREAS:*** Civil Litigation. ***Email:*** mrowe@qjhp.com

(This Listing Continued)

QUINN, JOHNSTON, HENDERSON & PRETORIUS, CHARTERED, Peoria—Continued

OF COUNSEL

W. THOMAS JOHNSTON, born Chicago, Illinois, September 29, 1941; admitted to bar, 1966, Illinois, U.S. District Court, Central District of Illinois and U.S. Court of Appeals, Seventh Circuit. *Education:* Western Illinois University (B.A., 1963); University of Illinois (J.D., 1966). Lecturer, Peoria County Continuing Legal Education Seminars, 1980-1984. Member, National Panel of Arbitrators, American Arbitration Association. Member, Supreme Court Committee on Civil Jury Instructions, 1996-1999. *Member:* Peoria County and Illinois State Bar Associations; Illinois Association of Defense Trial Counsel; Defense Research Institute; Master, Abraham Lincoln Federal Inns of Court. ***PRACTICE AREAS:*** Products Liability; Professional Malpractice; Municipal Tort Liability; Negligence; Structural Work Act; State and Federal Appellate Courts. ***Email:*** tjohnston@qjhp.com

REPRESENTATIVE INSURERS, CLAIM ADMINISTRATORS AND SELF-INSURED CLIENTS: Allstate Insurance Co.; American International Insurance Co.; American Isuzu Motors, Inc.; Amerisure; Asplundh Tree Expert Co.; Auto Owners Insurance Co.; Autozone, Inc.; Bituminous Casualty Corp.; Bridgestone/Firestone Tire & Rubber Co.; Bromenn Healthcare; Browning Ferris Industries; Cambridge Integrated Services; CCMSI; CIGNA Cos.; City of Bloomington; City of Canton; City of Galesburg; CNA Insurance; Commercial Union Insurance Co.; Columbia Insurance; Continental Insurance; Country Mutual Insurance Company; Crawford & Co; Cunningham-Lindsey; Crum & Forster; E. C. Fackler Co.; Farmers Automobile Insurance Association; Fremont Compensation; Gallagher Basset Services, Inc.; General Casualty; General Motors; Grinnell Mutual Reinsurance Co.; Guide One Insurance Co.; Harleysville Insurance; Illinois Grocers Risk Management Association; Illinois Municipal League Risk Management Association; Illinois Provider Trust; Illinois State Ambulance Risk Management Association; Illinois State Bar Association Mutual; Illinois State Medical Insurance Services, Inc.; Insurance Company of North America; ITT/Hartford; John Warner Hospital; Kemper Group; Liberty Mutual; McDonough District Hospital; Methodist Medical Center; MSI Insurance Companies; Navistar International Corp.; New Hampshire International Corp.; Newmar Corporation; Nissan Motor Corp.; Nursing Homes Risk Management Association; Pekin Insurance; Pekin Memorial Hospital/Progressive Health Systems; Peoria Area Chamber of Commerce Trust; RMR Group; Royal Insurance Co.; SAFECO/American States; St. Paul Insurance Co./USFĞ Security Insurance Group; Selective Insurance; State Farm Fire & Casualty; Statesman Insurance Co.; Travelers Insurance; United Capitol Insurance; United Heartland; Westfield Insurance Co.; Western States; Zurich International; Zurich-U.S.
REPRESENTATIVE CORPORATE, FINANCIAL AND GOVERNMENTAL CLIENTS: Anderson State Bank; Baumgarten Distributing Company, Inc.; BDC Wine, Inc.; Brewers Distributing Company; Cargill, Incorporated; Citizens Equity First Credit Union; City of Galesburg, IL; City of Peoria, IL; Consumers Gas Company; Cookies By Design of Peoria, Inc.; Illinois Gas Company; Insurance Car Rentals, Inc.; Inventory Technology, Inc.; Kickapoo Corporation; Marquette Bank-Illinois; Par-A-Dice; Peoria Journal Star, Inc.; Village of Princeville, IL; Village of Southern View, IL.

DAVID B. RADLEY, P.C.

700 COMMERCE BANK BUILDING
416 MAIN STREET, SUITE 700
PEORIA, ILLINOIS 61602-1180
Telephone: 309-674-8125
Fax: 309-674-8149
Email: Radleydb@prodigy.net

General Civil Practice, Appellate Practice, State and Federal Commercial and Civil Litigation, Real Estate, Probate, Arbitration, Securities Fraud, Trusts and Estates, Construction, Buying and Selling a Home, Commercial Real Estate, Buying and Selling of Businesses, Commercial Leasing, Business Law, Contracts, Lawsuits, Small Business Law, Personal Injury, Automobile Accidents, Wills and Probate, Estate Planning.

DAVID B. RADLEY, born Peoria, Illinois, 1941; admitted to bar, 1966, Illinois; 1967, U.S. District Court, Eastern District of Illinois; 1968, U.S. District Court, Central District of Illinois; 1981, U.S. Court of Appeals, Seventh Circuit; 1996, U.S. Supreme Court. *Education:* University of Colorado (B.A., 1963); University of Illinois (J.D., 1966). Author: "Attorney Disqualification: A Review," Illinois Bar Journal, P. 255, January, 1989. *Member:* Peoria County (President, 1990-1991), Illinois State (Member: Assembly; Real Estate Law Section Council, 1983-1989) and Federal District Bar Associations; Appellate Lawyers Association of Illinois. ***Email:*** Radleydb@prodigy.net

LAW OFFICE OF TROY I. ROBERTS, PC

PEORIA PROFESSIONAL BUILDING
207 MAIN STREET, SUITE 500
PEORIA, ILLINOIS 61602
Telephone: 309-655-3003
Fax: 309-672-2201
Email: troyroberts@ameritech.net

Family Law, Civil Litigation, Civil Appeals, Personal Injury Law, Workers Compensation, Criminal Law.

TROY I. ROBERTS, born Canton, Illinois, October 23, 1962; admitted to bar, 1993, Illinois and U.S. District Court, Northern and Central Districts of Illinois. *Education:* University of Illinois (B.A., 1989); Indiana University (J.D., cum laude, 1993). Order of the Coif. Member, Chicago Bar Association Moot Court. *Member:* Peoria County, Illinois State and American Bar Associations; The Association of Trial Lawyers of America. ***PRACTICE AREAS:*** Family Law; Civil Litigation; Civil Appeals; Personal Injury Law; Workers Compensation; Criminal Law. ***Email:*** troyroberts@ameritech.net

SORLING, NORTHRUP, HANNA, CULLEN AND COCHRAN, LTD.

Established in 1944
Formerly Sorling, Catron and Hardin
401 S.W. WATER STREET
SUITE 301
PEORIA, ILLINOIS 61602
Telephone: 309-674-1144
Telecopier: 309-671-4368
Email: businessdevelopment@sorlinglaw.com
URL: http://www.sorlinglaw.com

Springfield Office: 800 Illinois Building, 607 East Adams Street, P.O. Box 5131, 62705. Telephone: 217-544-1144. Telecopier: 217-522-3173.

General Civil Practice including Administrative Law, Agricultural Law, State and Federal Appellate Practice, Banking and Finance, Banking, Bankruptcy, Business Law, Civil Rights Defense, Commercial Law, Communications, Construction Law, Contract Preparation and Litigation, Corporate Law, Education Law, Elder Law, Election Law, Employee Benefits, Energy Law including Public Utilities, Environmental Law, Family Law, Illinois Governmental Advocacy and Representation, Health and Hospital Law, Insurance Regulation and Defense; Intellectual Property Rights, Labor and Employment Law, General State and Federal Litigation, News Media Representation, Mergers and Acquisitions, Municipal and Local Governmental Law, Natural Resources, Not for Profit Organizations, Personal Injury and Torts, Probate, Estate and Trust, Professional Liability and Disciplinary Defense, Products Liability, Real Estate, Securities, Taxation, Telecommunications, Trade and Professional Association Representation, Transportation Law, Workers Compensation, Zoning Planning and Land Use.

FIRM PROFILE: The firm was founded by Carl A. Sorling in 1944. It is the largest private practice law firm in Springfield, Illinois. There are 19 active shareholders, 8 associates and 4 attorneys with an of counsel relationship.

The firm has a diversified general and specialty practice in Springfield and Illinois in general. The practice includes substantial work in the corporate, civil litigation, financial institution, insurance regulation and defense, utility, family law, employment, health care, construction, local, state and federal tax, estate planning, probate, environmental, municipal, public finance, real estate, legislative advocacy and administrative law areas. The firm represents a growing number of local private and public corporations, as well as professional trade associations. The firm also serves a diversified national clientele as regional or local counsel in commercial, regulatory and litigation matters.

The firm has developed a large governmental practice, and is active in all aspects of government relations, including trade association representation, vendor assistance, and all state regulatory matters. In addition, the firm represents clients with national and state-wide interests in both the legislative and executive branch processes.

The firm stresses development and retention of lawyers with individual skills designed to offer creative and cost efficient legal and business solutions for clients. The goal is always to bring a responsive and personal approach to the practice of law.

JAMES D. BROADWAY, born De Ridder, Louisiana, December 26, 1944; admitted to bar, 1968, Texas; 1969, Illinois. *Education:* Tulane University (B.A., 1965); Southern Methodist University (J.D., 1968). *Member:* Peoria County, Illinois State and American Bar Associations; State Bar of Texas; American Academy of Hospital Attorneys. (Also at Springfield Office). ***PRACTICE AREAS:*** Hospital Law; Health Care Law; Corporate Law; Real Estate Law. ***Email:*** jdbroadway@sorlinglaw.com

COUNSEL FOR: Advanced Orthopedics, P.C.; Associates in Obstetrics & Gynecology, S.C.; BroMenn Regional Medical Center; CLG Foundation; Callahan Construction Services, Inc.; Camp Street Crossing, LLC; David Vaughn Investments, Inc.; Fayette Companies; Galesburg Orthopedic Services, Ltd.; Goodwill Industries of Central Illinois, Inc.; Human Service Center; Human Service Center Foundation; John B. Dale, D.M.D., M.S., P.C.; John Bearce Ford, Inc.; LaSalle Bank; Memorial Health System; Memorial Medical Center; Planned Parenthood Heart of Illinois; Riverfront Automart, Inc.; SMF, Inc.; The Illinois Critical Access Hospital Network; The Iona Group, Inc.; The Woodyard Club, Inc.; World Gym Peoria, Inc.

ROBERT C. STRODEL, LTD.

Established in 1959
927 COMMERCE BANK BUILDING
PEORIA, ILLINOIS 61602
Telephone: 309-676-4500
Fax: 309-676-4566
URL: http://www.attorneylocate.com
Email: stro927@aol.com
URL: http://www.lawyers.com/strodellaw

General Practice. Personal Injury Claims, with specialty in Medical Malpractice.

FIRM PROFILE: Robert C. Strodel, Ltd. has over 49 years of experience practicing law in Peoria, Illinois. He serves clients throughout all of Central Illinois with his vast experience in the entire spectrum of law, concentrating on Personal Injury, Litigation, Medical Malpractice and General Practice. Mr. Strodel is listed in the Bar Register of Preeminent Lawyers.

ROBERT C. STRODEL, born Evanston, Illinois, August 12, 1930; admitted to bar, 1955, Illinois; U.S. Supreme Court; U.S. Court of Appeals, Seventh Circuit; U.S. District Court, Northern and Central Districts of Illinois. *Education:* Northwestern University (B.S., 1952); University of Michigan (J.D., 1955). Phi Alpha Delta. A Winner of the Illinois State Bar "Lincoln Award" for Legal Writing in 1961, 1963 and 1965. Author: "Traumatic Arthritis—An Occupational Disease," Illinois Bar Journal, February 1961; "Illinois Scaffold Act in Perspective," Illinois Bar Journal, March 1966; "Illinois Structural Work Act," University of Illinois Law Forum, Spring 1967; "Structural Work Liability," Trial & Tort

(This Listing Continued)

Trends, 1969; "Medical Malpractice: Anesthesia-Halothane Toxic Hepatitis," American Trial Lawyers Association Convention Proceedings Transcript, Anderson, 1971; "Preservation of Physicians' Records in Original Form," Examination of Medical Experts, Volume II, Matthew Bender, 1973; "Medical Malpractice—Radical Mastoidectomy Ear Surgery," Trial and Tort Trends, Coiner, 1973; General Editor and Contributor: "Medical Evidence," 1976, 1980, 1984, 1987, 1997 and 2000, Illinois Institute for Continuing Legal Education; "Medical Malpractice—A Primer for Attorneys," Medical Trial Technique Quarterly, Vol. XXIV, No. 2, Callaghan & Co., Fall 1977; "Medical Malpractice Litigation—Triumph & Tribulation," Personal Injury Annual, Matthew Bender Co., 1977; ATLA Bar News, January 1977; "Medical-Legal Relationships: A Physician's Patient is the Same as an Attorney's Client," Legal Aspects of Medical Practice, March 1978; Chapter Contributor: "Plaintiff Medical Malpractice," 1981, 1984, 1985 and 1986, Illinois Institute for Continuing Legal Education; Chapter Contributor: Forensic Sciences, Wecht, Matthew Bender Co., 1981; "Medical Expert Witnesses—The Cornerstone of Malpractice Cases," TRIAL, June 1982; Video Cassette Contributor: "Trying Medical Malpractice Cases," Matthew Bender Co., 1982; "Malpractice: Final Argument in Rural Setting," Personal Injury Annual, Matthew Bender Co., 1982; Contributor, "Art of Advocacy Series: Cross-Examination of Medical Experts," Houts, Matthew Bender Co., 1982; Author: "Securing and Using Medical Evidence in Personal Injury and Health Care Cases," Prentice-Hall, Inc., 1988; "Medical Evidence: Acquisition and Use," Lawyers and Judges Publishing Co. (2001); Chapter Contributor: "Medical Malpractice," Zaremski and Goldstein, Callaghan & Co., 1988; Chapter Contributor: "Assessment of Fetal Well-Being," Eden and Boehm, Appleton-Century-Crofts, 1988; "The Impaired Physician," Medical Trial Technique Quarterly, Vol. XXIV, No. 4, Callaghan & Co., Winter, 1981; "Handling Rural Juries," Personal Injury Annual, Matthew Bender Co., 1980. Panelist: 1980 Governor's Conference on Sports Injuries in Illinois High Schools; University of Wyoming Health Law Forum, 1983. Lecturer, Nationally for ATLA, State Trial Lawyers Associations and other groups on Medical-Legal Subjects and Trial Practice. Assistant States Attorney, Peoria County, 1961. Member, Illinois Dangerous Drugs Advisory Council, 1971-1973. Trustee, The Melvin Belli Society, 1982—. *Member:* Peoria County, Illinois State and American Bar Associations; Illinois Trial Lawyers Association (Member, Board of Managers, 1984—; Executive Committee 1999-2000); The Association of Trial Lawyers of America (Vice Chairman, Tort Section, 1980; Member, Board of Governors, 1987-1996); Roscoe Pound Institute; Illinois Bar Foundation (Founding Fellow); Civil Justice Foundation (Founding Sponsor and President, 1998-2000). Certified Diplomate: American Board of Professional Liability Attorneys; American Board of Forensic Examiners (Law Division); Academy of Experts in Traumatic Stress. Certified as a Civil Trial Advocate by the National Board of Trial Advocacy, 1980-2000. ***PRACTICE AREAS:*** Personal Injury Law; Medical Malpractice Law; Litigation; General Practice. ***Email:*** stro927@aol.com

LAW OFFICE OF JOSEPH B. VANFLEET, L.L.C.

Established in 1998

PEORIA PROFESSIONAL BUILDING
207 MAIN STREET, SUITE 500
PEORIA, ILLINOIS 61602
Telephone: 309-672-2200
Facsimile: 309-672-2201
Email: jvanfleet@vanfleetlaw.com
URL: http://www.lawyers.com/vanfleet

Commercial Litigation, Corporate Investigations, White Collar Criminal Defense, Real Estate Litigation, Real Estate Development, Real Estate Disputes, Alternative Dispute Resolution, Business Law.

FIRM PROFILE: Founded by Joseph B. VanFleet in 1998 after practicing for several years with a large national law firm in Chicago, Mr. VanFleet has established a sophisticated practice to personally serve the needs and concerns of clients on local, state and national levels. In 2000, Mr. VanFleet was honored by Law Bulletin Publishing Company as one of its inaugural "40 Lawyers Under the Age of 40 to Watch in Illinois.".

MEMBER OF FIRM

JOSEPH B. VANFLEET, born Galesburg, Illinois, December 14, 1964; admitted to bar, 1990, Illinois and U.S. District Court, Northern District of Illinois; 1996, U.S. District Court, Central District of Illinois. *Education:* University of Illinois (B.S., high honors, Finance, 1987; J.D., 1990). Edmund J. James Scholar. Harno Scholar. Administrative Editor, University of Illinois Law Review, 1989-1990. Professor of Business Law, Eureka College, 1997-2000. Named "One of 40 Lawyers Under the Age of 40 to Watch in Illinois." *Member:* Peoria County, Illinois State and American Bar Associations; American Inns of Court. ***PRACTICE AREAS:*** Commercial Litigation; Corporate Investigations; White Collar Criminal Defense; Real Estate Litigation; Real Estate Development; Real Estate Disputes; Alternative Dispute Resolution. ***Email:*** jvanfleet@vanfleetlaw.com

ASSOCIATE

JOHN G. DUNDAS, born Chicago Heights, Illinois, April 22, 1974; admitted to bar, 2000, Illinois; 2001, U.S. District Court, Central District of Illinois. *Education:* University of Illinois (B.S., 1997; J.D., 2000). Former Member: Cassidy & Mueller; Quinn, Johnston, Henderson & Pretorious. *Member:* Peoria County and Illinois State Bar Associations. ***PRACTICE AREAS:*** Commercial Litigation; Corporate Investigations; Real Estate Litigation; Real Estate Development; White Collar Crime Defense; Employment Law. ***Email:*** jdundas@vanfleetlaw.com

C. EDWIN WALKER & ASSOCIATES

411 HAMILTON, SUITE 1710
PEORIA, ILLINOIS 61602
Telephone: 309-674-3740
Fax: 309-674-3743
Email: ewalker627@aol.com
URL: http://www.lawyers.com/walker

General Civil Practice, Commercial Law, Collections, Credit Law, Bankruptcy and Construction Law.

C. EDWIN WALKER, born Coronado, California, July 7, 1955; admitted to bar, 1982, Illinois and U.S. District Court, District of Illinois. *Education:* Southern Illinois University (B.A., with honors, 1978); University of Illinois (J.D., 1982). *Member:* Peoria County and Illinois State Bar Associations; Commercial Law League of America; Illinois Creditor Bar Association. ***PRACTICE AREAS:*** Collections; Commercial Litigation; Bankruptcy; Construction; Consumer; General Practice.

ASSOCIATE

BARBARA G. PHELPS, born Canton, Illinois, June 4, 1956; admitted to bar, 2002, Washington; 2004, Illinois. *Education:* University of Illinois (B.A., magna cum laude, 1998); University of Tulsa (J.D., 2001). *Member:* Peoria County, Illinois State and Washington State Bar Associations; Illinois Creditors Bar. ***PRACTICE AREAS:*** Civil Practice; Commercial Law; Collections; Credit Law; Bankruptcy; Construction Law. ***Email:*** barbaraphelps627@aol.com

WESTERVELT, JOHNSON, NICOLL & KELLER, LLC

Established in 1865

14TH FLOOR
411 HAMILTON BOULEVARD
PEORIA, ILLINOIS 61602
Telephone: 309-671-3550
Fax: 309-671-3588
URL: http://www.wjnklaw.com

Macomb, Illinois Office: MidAmerica Banking Center, 130 North Side Square, Suite 202, 61435. Telephone: 309-836-2900. Fax: 309-836-2844.

General Civil Trial and Appellate Practice in State and Federal Courts, Insurance Defense, Health and Health Care, Labor Relations, Employment Discrimination and Affirmative Action, Products Liability Litigation, ERISA and Benefits Plans, Corporate, Agricultural, Bankruptcy, Creditors' Rights, Banking, Real Estate, State and Federal Taxation, Estate Planning, Trusts and Probate, Workers Compensation, Environmental, Commercial.

MEMBERS OF FIRM

FRANK T. MILLER (1873-1948)

O. P. WESTERVELT (1887-1970)

EUGENE R. JOHNSON (1899-1981)

DAVID A. NICOLL (1913-1993)

HOMER W. KELLER, born Peoria, Illinois, July 8, 1917; admitted to bar, 1943, Illinois. *Education:* University of Idaho (B.S., 1940); University of Illinois (LL.B., 1943). *Member:* Peoria County (President, 1971-1972), Illinois State and American Bar Associations. Fellow, The College of Labor and Employment Lawyers. ***PRACTICE AREAS:*** Labor and Employment Law.

ROSS E. CANTERBURY, born Chicago, Illinois, February 24, 1942; admitted to bar, 1968, Illinois. *Education:* Yale University (B.A., 1964; J.D., 1967). *Member:* Peoria County, Illinois State and American Bar Associations. ***PRACTICE AREAS:*** Labor and Employment Law; Employment Discrimination; Estate Planning.

THOMAS G. HARVEL, born Peoria, Illinois, September 10, 1946; admitted to bar, 1972, Iowa and Illinois. *Education:* Bradley University (B.A., with honors, 1968); Drake University (J.D., with honors, 1972). Order of the Coif. *Member:* Peoria County, Iowa State, Illinois State and American Bar Associations. ***PRACTICE AREAS:*** Labor and Employment Law; Civil Rights Law; Employment Discrimination Law. ***Email:*** tharvel@westerveltlaw.com

ROGER E. HOLZGRAFE, born Quincy, Illinois, April 9, 1948; admitted to bar, 1973, Illinois. *Education:* University of Notre Dame (B.A., 1970); Georgetown University (J.D., 1973). *Member:* Peoria County, Illinois State and American Bar Associations. ***PRACTICE AREAS:*** Corporate Law; Probate and Estate Administration; Real Estate Transfers; Hospital and Health Care Law. ***Email:*** rholzgrafe@westerveltlaw.com

DANIEL L. JOHNS, born Mt. Carmel, Illinois, October 15, 1946; admitted to bar, 1971, Illinois. *Education:* University of Illinois (B.A., high honors, 1968; J.D., 1971). Member, Board of Editors, Illinois Law Forum, 1970-1971. *Member:* Peoria County, Illinois State and American Bar Associations; Abraham Lincoln Inns of Court; Illinois Defense Counsel. [JAGC, USN, 1971-1975]. ***PRACTICE AREAS:*** Products Liability; Medical Malpractice; Insurance Defense; Insurance Law. ***Email:*** djohns@westerveltlaw.com

KEVIN D. SCHNEIDER, born Peoria, Illinois, December 3, 1953; admitted to bar, 1983, Illinois. *Education:* Bradley University (B.A., 1979); Drake University (J.D., with honors, 1982). *Member:* Peoria County, Illinois State and American Bar Associations; Abraham Lincoln Inn of Court. ***PRACTICE AREAS:*** Banking and Financial Institutions Law; Bankruptcy Creditors' Rights; Commercial Law; Intellectual Property Law. ***Email:*** kschneider@westerveltlaw.com

JAMES R. MORRISON, born San Clemente Island, California, August 23, 1945; admitted to bar, 1971, Illinois. *Education:* University of Iowa (B.A., 1968); University of Il-

(This Listing Continued)

WESTERVELT, JOHNSON, NICOLL & KELLER, LLC, Peoria—Continued

linois (J.D., 1971). *Member:* Peoria County and Illinois State Bar Associations; Illinois Trial Lawyers Association; The Association of Trial Lawyers of America; Illinois Association of Defense Trial Counsel; Defense Research Institute. ***PRACTICE AREAS:*** Trials and Appeals in all Courts; Insurance Defense; Litigation; Insurance Law. ***Email:*** jmorrison@westerveltlaw.com

THOMAS W. O'NEAL, born New Castle, Pennsylvania, March 20, 1955; admitted to bar, 1980, Illinois. *Education:* Knox College (B.A., cum laude, 1977); Southern Methodist University (J.D., 1980). Assistant Attorney General for Agricultural Law, Office of Illinois Attorney general, 1985-1986. *Member:* Peoria County, Illinois State (Member, Agricultural Law Section Council, 1990-1998) and American Bar Associations; American Bankruptcy Institute; Abraham Lincoln Inns of Court. ***PRACTICE AREAS:*** Bankruptcy; Commercial Litigation; Agricultural Law; Employment Law. ***Email:*** toneal@westerveltlaw.com

CHARLES COURI, born Peoria, Illinois, January 30, 1956; admitted to bar, 1982, Illinois. *Education:* Illinois State University (B.S., 1978); Southern Illinois University (J.D., cum laude, 1982). Certified Public Accountant, Illinois, 1979. *Member:* Peoria County, Illinois State and American Bar Associations. ***PRACTICE AREAS:*** Employee Benefits Law; Estate Planning; Taxation; Corporate Law; Probate and Estate Administration. ***Email:*** ccouri@westerveltlaw.com

THOMAS A. McCONNAUGHAY, born Geneva, Illinois, November 8, 1960; admitted to bar, 1986, Massachusetts; 1993, Illinois. *Education:* University of Illinois (A.B., summa cum laude, with highest distinction in Political Science, 1981; J.D., magna cum laude, 1986); Harvard Law School. Bronze Tablet. *Member:* Peoria County, Illinois State and American Bar Associations. ***PRACTICE AREAS:*** Real Estate Law; Corporate Law; Land Use; Commercial Law. ***Email:*** tmcconnaughay@westerveltlaw.com

ASSOCIATES

MICHELE A. MILLER, born Valparaiso, Indiana, May 10, 1969; admitted to bar, 2000, Illinois. *Education:* Illinois State University (B.S., 1991); Southern Illinois University (J.D., magna cum laude, 2000). *Member:* Peoria County, Illinois State and American Bar Associations; Abraham Lincoln Inns of Court. ***PRACTICE AREAS:*** Employment Law; Insurance Defense; Litigation; Trusts and Estates. ***Email:*** mamiller@westerveltlaw.com

JUDITH A. SERRITELLA, born Peoria, Illinois, August 11, 1976; admitted to bar, 2001, Illinois. *Education:* University of Illinois (B.A., 1998); Southern Illinois University (J.D., 2001). Formerly with Peoria County States Attorney Office. *Member:* Peoria, Illinois State and American Bar Associations. ***PRACTICE AREAS:*** Driving While Intoxicated; Insurance Defense; Criminal Law; Divorce; Litigation. ***Email:*** jserritella@westerveltlaw.com

RONALD W. HASINGER, born Indiana, Pennsylvania, December 30, 1966; admitted to bar, 2003, Illinois. *Education:* Indiana University of Pennsylvania (B.A., 1992); North Carolina State University (M.P.A., 1997); University of Illinois (J.D., 2003). *Member:* Peoria County, Illinois State and American Bar Associations. ***PRACTICE AREAS:*** Labor and Employment; Employment Litigation; Employment Discrimination. ***Email:*** rhasinger@westerveltlaw.com

OF COUNSEL

WILLIAM L. BLAKE, born Chicago, Illinois, April 5, 1938; admitted to bar, 1966, Illinois and Virginia. *Education:* University of Illinois (B.S., 1960); Georgetown University (LL.B., 1966). Director, Illinois Division of Aeronautics, 1992-1999. *Member:* Peoria County, Illinois State and American Bar Associations; Virginia State Bar. [Lt., U.S. Army, 1960-1963]. ***PRACTICE AREAS:*** Aviation Law; Banking Law; Financial Institutions Law; Real Estate; Estate Planning. ***Email:*** wblake@westerveltlaw.com

REPRESENTATIVE CLIENTS: A. Miller & Co., Inc.; Air-Land Transport Service, Inc.; Allstate Ins. Cos.; Amerex Industries, Inc.; American Family Insurance Group; Aventine Renewable Energy, Inc.; Benetech, Inc.; B.F. Goodrich; Bituminous Insurance Companies; BroMenn Healthcare Central; Caterpillar Inc.; Central Illinois Pathology SC; Centre State International Truck, Inc.; Citizens Equity First Credit Union; Citizens Savings Bank; City of Peoria; City of Princeton; Country Companies Insurance Group; Country Mutual Insurance Co.; Deere and Co.; Employers Reinsurance Corp.; Eureka College; Farm King Supply Inc.; Green Chevrolet, Inc.; Hertz Corporation; Human Service Center; Illinois Agricultural Association and Affiliated Companies; Illinois Power Co.; J.H. Benedict Co., Inc.; John P. Pearl & Associates, Ltd.; Kemper Insurance Group; Lamoine Valley Clinic S.C.; Laverdiere Construction, Inc.; Madison Mutual Insurance Co.; Mason District Hospital; Massachusetts Mutual Life Ins. Co.; McDonough District Hospital; McDonough Physician Hospital Organization; McDonough Service Organization Inc.; Metropolitan Life Ins. Co.; Mid-America National Bank; Mutual of America Life Ins. Co.; Peoria and Pekin Union Ry. Co.; Peoria Disposal Co.; Peoria Castle Lodge (Torrey Park, LLC); Peoria NEXT; Perry Memorial Hospital; The Prudential Ins. Co. of America; Salem Children's Home; Sam Leman Dodge City, Inc.; Sarah D. Culbertson Memorial Hospital; Sentry Insurance Co.; Shelter Insurance Co.; State Farm Fire Insurance Co.; State Farm Mutual Automobile Insurance Co.; Supervalu Inc.; Tazewell Machine Works, Inc.; United Facilities, Inc.; Vermont Foundary Company; Versa Press, Inc.; Westminster Village, Inc.

RICHARD W. ZUCKERMAN

415 HAMILTON BOULEVARD
PEORIA, ILLINOIS 61602
Telephone: 309-637-3732
Fax: 309-637-5788
Email: rwzuckermanesq@insightbb.com

Family Law, Divorce, Post-Divorce, Mediation, Appeals, Paternity, Child Custody, Child Support, Visitation Rights, Adoption Law.

RICHARD W. ZUCKERMAN, born 1951; admitted to bar, 1976, Illinois; 1977, U.S. District Court, Central District of Illinois and U.S. Court of Appeals, Seventh Circuit. *Education:* Bradley University (B.S., 1973); John Marshall Law School (J.D., 1976); Aurora University (Mediation Certification, 1999). Author: "Dissipation of Marital Assets," Vol. 91, No. 9, Illinois Bar Journal; "Enforcement of Child Support," *Family Law Handbook*, Illinois State Bar Association, 1994; "Child Support and Your Driver's License," Family Law Newsletter, March 1996; "Illinois Supreme Court Limits Modifiability of Maintenance," Family Law Newsletter, December 1990. Commissioner, Peoria Housing Authority, 1996-2002; Chair, 2002—; Vice Chair, 1999-2002. Member: Citizens Utility Board, 18th Congressional District, 1995-2003; Child Support Advisory Task Force, 1990-1993, 1998-2002. Member, Inquiry Panel, Attorney Registration and Disciplinary Commission, 1993-1997; Hearing Panel, 1997—; Chair, 1999—. *Member:* Peoria County (Member: Board of Directors, 1993-1995, 1996-2000; Family Law Committee, 1982-1992, 1994—, Chair, 1992-1994); Illinois State (Treasurer, 2004-2005; Member: Board of Governors, 2000—; Assembly, 1984-1990, 1995-2000; Task Force on Allocation of Judges, 1998-1999; Task Force on Parental Responsibilities Act, Co-Chair, 2004; Family Law Section Council, 1988-1992, 1993-2001, Secretary, 1996-1997, Vice-Chair, 1997-1998; Chair, 1998-1999; Newsletter Co-Editor, 2000-2001; Legislation Committee, 1995-2002; Delivery of Legal Services Committee, 1993-2004; Supreme Court Rules Committee, 1994-2003; ARDC Committee, 1999—; Reduction of Costs, Delays and Involvement, 1983-1984; Alternative Forum of Dispute Resolution, 1981-1983, Chair, 1982-1983; Arbitration of Disputes, 1981-1982) and American (Member: Alimony, Maintenance and Child Support Committee, 1993-1995; Federal Legislation and Procedures Committee, 1993-1995; Custody Committee, 1993-1995) Bar Associations; Abraham Lincoln Inns of Court (Master; Secretary/Treasurer, 2000-2001; Vice President, 2001-2002; President, 2002-2003). Fellow, American Academy of Matrimonial Lawyers (President, Illinois Chapter, 2004; Vice-President, Illinois Chapter, 1998-2003; Board of Managers, 1996—). ***REPORTED CASES:*** Wickham v. Byrne, 99 Ill. 2nd 309; Marriage of Shaddle, 317 Il. Ap 3rd 959.

HERBOLSHEIMER, LANNON, HENSON, DUNCAN AND REAGAN, P.C.

PERU, ILLINOIS
(See La Salle)

Corporate Law, Business Law, Criminal Law, DWI/DUI, Juvenile Law, Employment Law, Administrative Law, Employment Termination, Sexual Harassment, Estate Planning, Probate, Tax Planning, Wills and Trusts, Family Law, Divorce, Adoption, Prenuptial Agreements, Health Care, Civil Litigation, Insurance Defense, Products Liability, Insurance, Subrogation, Real Estate, Boundary Disputes, Easements.

LAW OFFICES OF LEYNAUD & LEYNAUD

A PROFESSIONAL CORPORATION
1200 38TH STREET
PERU, ILLINOIS 61354-2005
Telephone: 815-224-4700
Fax: 815-224-4703
URL: http://www.leynaudlaw.com
Email: george@leynaudlaw.com
URL: http://www.lawyers.com/leynaud&leynaud

General Civil and Trial Practice, Personal Injury, Mediation, Worker's Compensation, Real Estate, Criminal, Landlord/Tenant and Family Law. Business/Banking Litigation, DUI and Traffic. Insurance, General Practice, Medical Malpractice, Zoning and Land Use. Bad Faith, Drug Crimes, Juvenile Crimes, White Collar, Adoptions, Child Custody, Divorce, Child Support, Visitation Rights, Domestic Violence. Auto Accidents, Dog Bites, Slip and Fall, Wrongful Death, Buying and Selling, Wills and Probate.

FIRM PROFILE: The firm is dedicated to meeting individual and business clients' needs and rights in a society wherein litigation is a fact of life. Since its inception, the firm provides aggressive and thorough legal representation on behalf of its clients. Serving La Salle, Bureau, Putnam, Marshall, Lee, DeKalb, McLean, Peoria, Grundy Counties, Illinois.

GEORGE G. LEYNAUD, born Peru, Illinois, April 28, 1958; admitted to bar, 1983, Illinois and U.S. District Court, Central and Northern Districts of Illinois including Trial Bar. *Education:* Marquette University; Bradley University (B.S., 1980); Thomas M. Cooley School of Law (J.D., 1983); Pepperdine University, School of Law, Strauss Institute for Dispute Resolution (Mediation Training Program, 2005). Listed in: Who's Who in American Law, 1991; America's Leading Lawyers, 1993. Lecturer, Housing Law, Illinois Association of Housing Authorities. Author: "Is an Excluded Driver Really Excluded?" Illinois State Bar Association, Tort Trends, Dec. 2002, Vol. 38, No. 2. Lecturer: "Void Provisions of Insurance Policies," Illinois State Bar Association Annual Meeting, June 2003; "Anatomy of an Automobile Case, Defense of Complicity," Law Ed series, May 2004. Member, LaSalle County (Secretary-Treasurer, 1984-1986; President, Elect, 1986-1987; President, 1987-1988; Secretary, 1995). Member, Board of Education, District 120, LaSalle-Peru Township High School, 1995-1997 and Vice-President. *Member:* Illinois State (Member: Capital Counsel Team, Grass Roots Lobbying, Insurance Law Section; Tort Law Section; Insurance Law Section Council, 2000—; Secretary, Charman, June 2005—;Tort Law Section Counsel, 2002—; Assembly Member, 13th Judicial Circuit, 2001—; Member, Election Committee, 2004—; and American Bar Associations; The Association of Trial Lawyers of America. Illinois Bar Foundation. ***REPORTED CASES:*** People v. Finley, 568 N.E.2d 412, 154 Ill-.Dec. 412, 209 Ill. App.3d 968 (1991); In re: The Marriage of Hall, 215 ILL. Dec. 419, 633 N.E. 2d 430 (1996). ***PRACTICE AREAS:*** Personal Injury; Mediation; Uninsured and Underinsured Motorists; Workers Compensation; Criminal Felony; Divorce; DUI; Traffic; Real Estate; Business Litigation; Insurance; Medical Malpractice; Zoning Law; Land Use. ***Email:*** george@leynaudlaw.com

REBECCA M. LEYNAUD, born Peru, Illinois, May 14, 1965; admitted to bar, 1990, Illinois. *Education:* Bradley University (B.S., 1987); Northern Illinois University College of Law (J.D., 1990). Member, Judicial Screening Committee, 2001. Mediation Certificate, Family and Divorce, De Paul University, March 2003. Lecturer, "In re: The Marriage of Davis," 341 Ill. App.3d, 792 N.E.2d 391, 275 Ill.Dec. 160 (2003)," Illinois State Bar As-

(This Listing Continued)

sociation Family Law, March 2004. *Member:* LaSalle County (President-Elect, 1992-1993; President, 1993-1994; Treasurer, 1994—), Illinois State (Member, Continuing Education Committee, Family Law Section Council, 1999-2005) and American Bar Associations. Fellow, Illinois Bar Foundation. **REPORTED CASES:** People v. Finley, 568 N.E.2d 412, 154 Ill.Dec. 412, 209 Ill. App.3d 968 (1991); In re: The Marriage of Hall, 215 ILL. Dec. 419, 633 N.E. 2d 430 (1996); In re: The Marriage of Davis, 341 Ill. App.3d, 792 N.E.2d 391, 275 Ill.Dec. 160 (2003). **PRACTICE AREAS:** Divorce; Family Law; Custody; Uniform Child Custody Jurisdiction Act; Landlord and Tenant Law; Adoptions; Real Estate. **Email:** rebecca@leynaudlaw.com

REFERENCES: Peru Federal Savings & Loan Association, Peru; Union Bank, Peru; La Salle National Bank, La Salle, Illinois; Amcore Bank; First State Bank.

ANTHONY C. RACCUGLIA & ASSOCIATES, P.C.

Established in 1959

1200 MAPLE DRIVE

PERU, ILLINOIS 61354

Telephone: 815-223-0230

Email: raccuglialaw@insightbb.com

URL: http://raccuglialawoffice.lawoffice

Ottawa, Illinois Office: 633 La Salle Street. Telephone: 815-434-2003.

General Civil and Trial Practice in all State and Federal Courts. Personal Injury, Medical Malpractice, Products Liability, Workers Compensation, Probate, Real Estate, Construction Accidents, Structural Work Cases, Business Litigation.

FIRM PROFILE: Anthony C. Raccuglia founded the firm in 1959. He has served clients in LaSalle, Bureau, Grundy, Lee, DeKalb, McLean, Will and surrounding counties for the past 38 years. The firm concentrates on plaintiff personal injury and death in medical malpractice, vehicular collision, product liability and construction cases.

ANTHONY C. RACCUGLIA, born La Salle, Illinois, September 4, 1933; admitted to bar, 1959, Illinois. *Education:* University of Illinois (B.S., 1957); John Marshall Law School (J.D., 1959). Order of John Marshall. Selected by Leading Lawyers as one of the top Illinois lawyers in personal injury law, 2004-2005. First Assistant States Attorney, La Salle County, 1960-1968. City Attorney, La Salle, Illinois, 1989—. Laureate, Academy of Illinois Lawyers, ISBA, 2003. *Member:* La Salle-Peru-Oglesby, La Salle County (President, 1976-1977), Illinois State (Member, Board of Governors, 1975-1981; Laureate, Academy of Illinois Lawyers, 2003) and American Bar Associations; Illinois Trial Lawyers Association (Member, Board of Governors, 1986-1989); The Association of Trial Lawyers of America (Member, Board of Governors, 1986-1989). **PRACTICE AREAS:** Personal Injury Law; Medical Malpractice; Products Liability Law; Construction Accidents; Structural Work Cases.

ASSOCIATES

JAMES A. McPHEDRAN, born LaSalle, Illinois, March 27, 1950; admitted to bar, 1975, Illinois. *Education:* Illinois Valley Community College (A.A., magna cum laude, 1970); Northern Illinois University (B.S., summa cum laude, 1972); John Marshall Law School (J.D., with distinction, 1975). Phi Theta Kappa; Beta Alpha Psi; Beta Gamma Sigma. Member, John Marshall Law School National Moot Court Team, 1974. Member, John Marshall Law Review, 1974-1975. Certified Public Accountant, Illinois, 1977. *Member:* LaSalle County, Illinois State and American (Member, Sections on: Taxation; Real Property, Probate and Trust Law) Bar Associations; Illinois Certified Public Accountants Society; Illinois Trial Lawyers Association. **PRACTICE AREAS:** Business Litigation; Workmen's Compensation; Construction Accidents; Structural Work Cases.

BRAD POPURELLA, born Lasalle, Illinois, June 10, 1976; admitted to bar, 2001, Illinois; 2002, Wisconsin. *Education:* University of Illinois (B.A., History, 1998); Northern Illinois University (J.D., 2001). Member, Lasalle County States Attorney Office. *Member:* Illinois State Bar Association; State Bar of Wisconsin. **PRACTICE AREAS:** Personal Injury; Medical Malpractice; Products Liability.

REFERENCES: La Salle National Bank; Citizens First National Bank of Peru, Illinois.

LAW OFFICES OF NOLAN LIPSKY

106 EAST JACKSON STREET

PETERSBURG, ILLINOIS 62675

Telephone: 217-632-2612

Toll Free: 888-662-2612

Fax: 217-632-2450

URL: http://www.nolanlipsky.com

Springfield Office: 1100 South 5th Street, 62703. Telephone: 217-789-1607.

Family Law, Divorce, Custody, Paternity, Personal Injury, Criminal.

NOLAN LIPSKY, born Chicago, Illinois, August 3, 1944; admitted to bar, 1969, Illinois and U.S. District Court, Northern and Southern Districts of Illinois; 1972, U.S. District Court, Central District of Illinois; 1988, U.S. Court of Appeals, Seventh Circuit. *Education:* University of Illinois (B.S., 1966); Chicago-Kent College of Law (J.D., 1969). Phi Alpha Delta. Author: "The Function of Attorney General Legal Opinions," Northwestern University Law Review, 1973. Assistant Attorney General, State of Illinois, 1972-1974. States Attorney, Menard County, 1976-1984. *Member:* Sangamon County, Menard County and Illinois State Bar Associations; Illinois Trial Lawyers Association; Lincoln-Douglas Inns of Court. **PRACTICE AREAS:** Family Law; Divorce; Child Custody; Criminal Law; Personal Injury; Paternity.

HART AND HART

PINCKNEYVILLE, ILLINOIS

(See Benton)

General Trial and Appellate Practice in State and Federal Courts. Probate, Trust, Real Estate Deeds and Title Insurance, Bankruptcy (Creditors), Traffic, Banking, Business, Commercial and Corporation Law and Creditor Collections, Employment Law.

JOHNSON, SEIBERT & BIGHAM

ONE NORTH MAIN

P.O. BOX 467

PINCKNEYVILLE, ILLINOIS 62274

Telephone: 618-357-2178

Fax: 618-357-3314

Email: jsbattorneys@midamer.net

URL: http://www.lawyers.com/js&b

General Civil Practice, Probate, Trust, Estate Planning, Real Estate, Oil and Gas and Coal Law, Federal and State Taxation, Banking, Corporate, Negligence, Municipal, School and Family Law, Trial and Appellate Practice.

MEMBERS OF FIRM

DON E. JOHNSON, born Decatur, Illinois, January 29, 1939; admitted to bar, 1961, Illinois. *Education:* Millikin University (A.B., 1959); University of Illinois (LL.B., 1961). City Attorney: Du Quoin, 1965-1968; Pinckneyville, 1984-2003. Perry County State's Attorney, 1968-1972. *Member:* Perry County, Illinois State (Federal Taxation Section Council, Chairman, 1983-1984; Mineral Law Section Council Chairman, 1984-1986; 1994-1995; 1996-1997) and American Bar Associations; The Association of Trial Lawyers of America. Fellow, Illinois State Bar Foundation. Fellow, American College of Trust and Estate Counsel; Trustee, Eastern Mineral Law Foundation.

ROGER H. SEIBERT, born Omaha, Nebraska, January 4, 1946; admitted to bar, 1974, Illinois. *Education:* Valparaiso University (B.A., 1969; J.D., 1974). *Member:* Perry County, Illinois State and American Bar Associations; The Association of Trial Lawyers of America; Illinois Trial Lawyers Association.

DONALD BIGHAM, born Du Quoin, Illinois, November 13, 1953; admitted to bar, 1978, Illinois. *Education:* Southern Illinois University (B.A., 1975); University of Illinois (J.D., 1978). *Member:* Perry County, Illinois State (Real Estate Section, 1985-1989; Assembly Member, 1998—) and American Bar Associations; Illinois Trial Lawyers Association.

COUNSEL FOR: Oakdale State Bank; Murphy-Wall State Bank & Trust Co. of Pinckneyville; First National Bank of Pinckneyville; Consolidation Coal Co.; Amax Coal Co.; Zeigler Coal Co.; Old Ben Coal Co.

JERRY A. FOGELMAN

13122 MERGANSER COVE

PLAINFIELD, ILLINOIS 60544

Telephone: 815-685-3538

Fax: 815-254-6917

Email: jerryfogelman@att.net

URL: http://www.fogelmanlawoffice.com

Litigation, Business Law, Corporate Law, Family Law, Divorce, Child Custody, Personal Injury and Medical Malpractice, Real Estate, General Practice.

JERRY A. FOGELMAN, born Gary, Indiana, November 30, 1956; admitted to bar, 1981, Indiana and Illinois; 1982, U.S., District Court, Northern District of Indiana; 1988, U.S. District Court, Northern District of Illinois and Trial Bar. *Education:* Indiana University (B.S., with distinction, 1978; J.D., 1981). Beta Gamma Sigma; Phi Delta Phi. Associate, Indiana Law Journal, 1979-1980. *Member:* Will County and Illinois State Bar Associations. **PRACTICE AREAS:** Bankruptcy; Business Law; Child Custody; Visitation Rights; Corporate Law; Family Law; Divorce; Post Divorce Modification; Premarital Agreements; Guardianship; Health Care Fraud; Hospital Negligence; Medical Malpractice; Medicare Fraud and Abuse; Personal Injury; Real Estate; Wrongful Death.

LAW OFFICE OF PATRICK A. MESZAROS

PLAINFIELD, ILLINOIS

(See Joliet)

Personal Injury, Automobile Accidents and Injuries, Slip and Fall and Real Estate Law.

JOHNSON & TAYLOR

Established in 1837

Formerly Ortman, Johnson & Taylor

109 NORTH MILL STREET

P.O. BOX 497

PONTIAC, ILLINOIS 61764-0497

Telephone: 815-844-7151

Fax: 815-844-7539

General Practice. Probate, Estate Planning, Tax and Real Estate Law.

(This Listing Continued)

JOHNSON & TAYLOR, Pontiac—Continued

FIRM PROFILE: Johnson & Taylor was founded in 1837. The present lawyers have been practicing law in Pontiac, Illinois since 1970. Serving clients in Livingston, McLean, Woodford, La Salle, Grundy, and Ford counties. The firm has a General Practice with a focus on Probate, Tax and Real Estate Law.

MEMBERS OF FIRM

F. A. ORTMAN (1882-1955)

J. KENNETH JOHNSON (1912-2000)

PARTNERS

JOHN A. TAYLOR, born Pontiac, Illinois, January 19, 1925; admitted to bar, 1950, Illinois and U.S. Tax Court. *Education:* University of Texas and Northwestern University (B.S., 1947); Northwestern University (J.D., 1950). State's Attorney, Livingston County, 1952-1956. *Member:* Livingston County (President, 1972-1973) and Illinois State Bar Associations. ***PRACTICE AREAS:*** Probate and Estate Planning; Real Estate; Federal Taxation.

TAYLOR F. JOHNSON, born Pontiac, Illinois, July 24, 1947; admitted to bar, 1972, Illinois; 1976, U.S. Tax Court. *Education:* Northwestern University (B.A., 1969); University of Illinois (J.D., 1972). *Member:* Livingston County (President, 2004), Illinois State and American Bar Associations. ***PRACTICE AREAS:*** Probate and Estate Planning; Real Estate; Federal Taxation. ***Email:*** taylor@adcomnet.net

ATTORNEY FOR: Flanagan State Bank; Good Samaritan Home of Flanagan; Villages of Flanagan and Long Point; Flanagan-Graymont and Reddick and Long Point Fire Districts; CAPS and Flanagan Park Districts; Evenglow Lodge; Oliver Trusts; Matin Scholarship Trust.

LAW OFFICES OF LEYNAUD & LEYNAUD

A PROFESSIONAL CORPORATION

PRINCETON, ILLINOIS

(See Peru)

General Civil and Trial Practice, Personal Injury, Mediation, Worker's Compensation, Real Estate, Criminal, Landlord/Tenant and Family Law. Business/Banking Litigation, DUI and Traffic. Insurance, General Practice, Medical Malpractice, Zoning and Land Use. Bad Faith, Drug Crimes, Juvenile Crimes, White Collar, Adoptions, Child Custody, Divorce, Child Support, Visitation Rights, Domestic Violence. Auto Accidents, Dog Bites, Slip and Fall, Wrongful Death, Buying and Selling, Wills and Probate.

ANTHONY C. RACCUGLIA & ASSOCIATES, P.C.

PRINCETON, ILLINOIS

(See Peru)

General Civil and Trial Practice in all State and Federal Courts. Personal Injury, Medical Malpractice, Products Liability, Workers Compensation, Probate, Real Estate, Construction Accidents, Structural Work Cases, Business Litigation.

RUSSELL, ENGLISH, SCOMA & BENEKE, P.C.

(Formerly, Johnson, Martin, Russell, English, Scoma & Beneke, P.C.)

TEN PARK AVENUE WEST
PRINCETON, ILLINOIS 61356
Telephone: 815-875-4555
Fax: 815-875-2211
Email: tenpark@theramp.net

General Civil, Trial and Appellate Practice. Probate, Real Estate, Insurance, Corporation, Governmental, Taxation, Employment and Family Law.

FIRM PROFILE: Russell, English, Scoma & Beneke, P.C. was founded over 150 years ago. Serving clients throughout Bureau, La Salle, Henry, Marshall, Putnam, Lee and surrounding counties, the firm is in general practice with individual lawyers focusing in specific areas of law.

DANIEL K. RUSSELL, born Princeton, Illinois, April 27, 1944; admitted to bar, 1969, Illinois. *Education:* Western Illinois University (B.A., 1966); University of Illinois (J.D., 1969). Pi Gamma Mu. *Member:* Bureau County (President, 1990-1992) and Illinois State Bar Associations; Illinois Association of Defense Trial Counsel. ***PRACTICE AREAS:*** Insurance Defense Law; Plaintiffs Civil Litigation; Appeals.

ROBERT F. RUSSELL, born Princeton, Illinois, January 10, 1948; admitted to bar, 1974, Illinois; 1975, U.S. District Court, Southern District of Illinois. *Education:* Stanford University (A.B., 1970); University of Illinois (J.D., 1973). Director: Attorneys Title Guaranty Fund, Inc., 1995—; Amcore Bank North Central, N.A., 1985-2000; Perry Memorial Hospital, 1996-2003. *Member:* Bureau County and Illinois State (Member, Real Estate Section Council, 1988-1992; School Law Section Council, 1993-1995) Bar Associations; Illinois Township Attorneys Association; National Academy for Elder Law Attorneys. ***PRACTICE AREAS:*** Local Government Law; Zoning Law; Estate Planning; Real Estate Law; Probate Law. ***Email:*** *rfr@theramp.net*

MICHAEL L. ENGLISH, born Huron, South Dakota, August 15, 1953; admitted to bar, 1978, Wisconsin; 1980, Illinois. *Education:* Indiana University (B.A., 1975); University of Minnesota (J.D., cum laude, 1978). Phi Beta Kappa; Gamma Eta Gamma. *Member:* Bureau County, Illinois State (Member, Corporation and Securities Law Section Council, 1985-1989; Federal Taxation Section Council, 1992-2003; Chairman, 2001-2002 and Member, 1995-2003, Trusts and Estates Section Council; Member, Real Estate Law Section Council, 2002—) and American Bar Associations; State Bar of Wisconsin. ***PRACTICE AREAS:*** Taxation Law; Estate Planning Law; Real Estate Law; Probate Law; Corporate Business Law.

PAUL M. SCOMA, born LaSalle, Illinois, November 14, 1952; admitted to bar, 1982, Illinois. *Education:* Northern Illinois University (B.A., magna cum laude, 1974); Loyola University of Chicago (J.D., 1982). Omicron Delta Kappa. Recipient, American Jurisprudence Awards, 1980-1982. Board of Directors, 1986-1996 and Chairman, 1991-1995, Perry Memorial Hospital. *Member:* Bureau County and Illinois State Bar Associations; Illinois Association of Defense Trial Counsel. ***PRACTICE AREAS:*** General Civil Litigation; Civil Appeals; Personal Injury Law; Insurance Defense Law; Family Law. ***Email:*** pscoma@theramp.net

WILLIAM S. BENEKE, born Fort Dodge, Iowa, January 10, 1953; admitted to bar, 1979, Iowa; 1982, Illinois. *Education:* Cornell College (B.A., 1975); University of Oklahoma (J.D., 1978). Member, Board of Trustees, 1993— and President, 1999-2004, Matson Public Library. *Member:* Bureau County, Illinois State and Iowa State Bar Associations. ***PRACTICE AREAS:*** Estate Planning Law; Probate Law; Real Estate Law; Taxation Law; Drainage and Levee Law.

DANIEL C. ANDERSON, born San Diego, California, August 31, 1978; admitted to bar, 2004, Illinois. *Education:* Western Illinois University (B.A., 2000); Southern Illinois University (J.D., 2003). Phi Delta Phi (2002—). Member, Southern Illinois University Law Journal, 2001-2003. *Member:* Bureau County and Illinois State Bar Associations. ***PRACTICE AREAS:*** Civil Litigation; Insurance Defense; Family Law; Real Estate; Probate. ***Email:*** danderson@theramp.net

OF COUNSEL

DONALD C. MARTIN, born Omaha, Nebraska, January 26, 1925; admitted to bar, 1952, Iowa; 1953, Illinois. *Education:* University of Missouri (A.B., 1948); University of Iowa (LL.B., 1952).

GENERAL COUNSEL FOR: Walnut Sand and Gravel Co.; Mineral Fire Protection District; Princeton Fire Protection District; LaMoille Fire Protection District; Advanced Asphalt Co.; Princeton Township; Princeton Park District; LaSalle County Asphalt Co.; Beck Oil Company of Illinois; Faber Motors, Inc.; First State Bank of Van Orin; Union Special Drainage District; Mineral Marsh Drainage District; Michlig Agricenter, Inc.
LOCAL INSURANCE COUNSEL FOR: Country Mutual Ins. Co.; Farmer's Insurance Group; General Casualty Co.; Hartford Insurance Co.; Kemper Insurance Group; Transamerica Insurance Group; Colonial Penn Insurance; Home Insurance Co.; Transport Indemnity Co.; Travelers Insurance Co.; Ohio Casualty Insurance Co.; Great Central Insurance Co.; Auto Owners Insurance Co.; Rockford Mutual Insurance Co.; Grinnell Mutual Insurance Co.; Cincinnati Insurance Co.

JOHN V. BOSHARDY & ASSOCIATES, P.C.

QUINCY, ILLINOIS

(See Springfield)

Workers Compensation, Personal Injury, On the Job Injuries, Automobile Accidents, Medical Malpractice, Wrongful Death.

ANTHONY B. CAMERON

529 HAMPSHIRE, SUITE 511
QUINCY, ILLINOIS 62301
Telephone: 217-228-8669
Fax: 217-228-2225
Email: dacamara@adams.net
URL: http://www.abclawoffice.com

Professional Discipline. Employment, Environmental Litigation. Administrative Law (State and Federal). Civil Litigation. Licensing. Municipal Law.

ANTHONY B. CAMERON, born Evanston, Illinois, December 27, 1942; admitted to bar, 1973, Illinois and Arkansas. *Education:* University of Illinois (B.A., 1970); University of Iowa (J.D., 1972). Phi Alpha Delta. Public Defender, 1978-1980, Adams County State's Attorney, 1980-1984. Faculty Advisor, National College District Attorneys 1983, Quincy City Attorney, Special Assistant Attorney General. *Member:* Adams County, Illinois State and Arkansas Bar Associations.

SCHMIEDESKAMP, ROBERTSON, NEU & MITCHELL

Established in 1914

525 JERSEY
P.O. BOX 1069
QUINCY, ILLINOIS 62306
Telephone: 217-223-3030
Fax: 217-223-1005
Email: srnm@srnm.com
URL: http://www.srnm.com

General Practice. General Civil and Appellate Practice. Corporate, Mergers and Acquisitions, Federal Taxation, Banking and Insurance Law, Real Estate, Commercial, Bankruptcy, Estate Planning and Probate, Employment and Labor Law, Education Law.

(This Listing Continued)

FIRM PROFILE: The firm of Schmiedeskamp, Robertson, Neu & Mitchell was established in 1914, and has continuously provided quality legal representation in Central and West Central Illinois, and now also provides legal representation in Northeast Missouri. In addition, the firm represents multiple animal feed companies and other corporate clients on a nationwide basis.

The firm consists of thirteen partners and three associates, some who serve as legal instructors at national, state and local programs, Chairpersons of legal councils and committees, and are Fellows of both the American College of Trial Lawyers and the International Society of Barristers. The firm also has a rich tradition of community service and strives to continually promote the legal profession.

The firm has a diversified general and specialty practice which includes antitrust; corporate; commercial; mergers and acquisitions; estate planning; probate; taxation; banking; bankruptcy and debt collection; education law; health care; real estate; and civil litigation, including commercial, product liability, professional malpractice and personal injury, both defense and complex plaintiff cases.

MEMBERS OF FIRM

GEORGE H. WILSON (1866-1949)

RICHARD W.S. NEU (1905-1951)

CARL G. SCHMIEDESKAMP (1898-1987)

SAM G. JENKINS (1907-1989)

JOHN T. ROBERTSON (1916-1995)

THEODORE GRANT HOUSE (1930-1980)

RICHARD B. NEU (Retired)

DELMER R. MITCHELL, JR., born West Frankfort, Illinois, September 21, 1941; admitted to bar, 1966, Illinois; 1978, U.S. Supreme Court; U.S. District Court, Central and Southern Districts of Illinois. *Education:* Southern Illinois University (A.B., 1963); University of Illinois (J.D., 1966). Phi Alpha Delta. Instructor: National Institute for Trial Advocacy, Boulder, Colorado, Chicago, Illinois and Hempstead, New York, 1977—; Emory Trial Techniques Program, Atlanta, Georgia, 1984-1990; Harvard Trial Techniques Program, 1990-1995; Pace University, 1994. Member, Rules Committee, Federal District Court, Central District of Illinois, 1994—. Member, Illinois Supreme Court Rules Committee, 1986-1996. *Member:* Adams County, Illinois State (Member, 1973— and Chairman, 1977-1978, Tort Section Council) and American Bar Associations; Defense Research Institute; International Association of Defense Counsel; Bar Association of Central and Southern Federal Districts of Illinois. Fellow: International Society of Barristers; American College of Trial Lawyers; The American Bar Foundation. ***PRACTICE AREAS:*** Civil Litigation; Corporate Law; Mergers and Acquisitions; Employment Law. ***Email:*** dmitchell@srnm.com

DENNIS W. GORMAN, born St. Louis, Missouri, June 16, 1942; admitted to bar, 1967, Illinois. *Education:* University of Illinois (B.A., 1964; J.D., 1967). Omicron Delta Kappa; Phi Delta Phi. Adjunct Faculty, Education Law, Graduate School of Education, Quincy University. Past President, Adams County Bar Association. *Member:* Adams County, Illinois State and American Bar Associations; Illinois Council of School Attorneys. ***PRACTICE AREAS:*** Education Law; Probate and Trust Law; Real Estate and Banking Law. ***Email:*** dgorman@srnm.com

JERRY L. BRENNAN, born Moberly, Missouri, January 7, 1936; admitted to bar, 1967, Illinois. *Education:* University of Missouri (B.S., Engineering, 1957); University of Illinois (J.D., 1967). Phi Alpha Delta. *Member:* Adams County (President, 1985) and Illinois State Bar Associations; Illinois Trial Lawyers Association. [Capt., U.S. Air Force, 1958-1960]. ***PRACTICE AREAS:*** Medical Malpractice Defense Litigation; Insurance Defense Litigation. ***Email:*** jbrennan@srnm.com

WILLIAM G. KELLER, JR., born Quincy, Illinois, January 12, 1949; admitted to bar, 1974, Illinois; 1978, U.S. Supreme Court. *Education:* University of Illinois (B.S., 1971); Valparaiso University (J.D., 1974). Member, Illinois Supreme Court Character and Fitness Committee, 1995-2004. *Member:* Adams County (President, 1993), Illinois State and American Bar Associations. ***PRACTICE AREAS:*** Corporate Law; Mergers and Acquisitions; Estate Planning and Probate Law; Banking Law; Health Care Law. ***Email:*** wkeller@srnm.com

WILLIAM M. McCLEERY, JR., born Quincy, Illinois, September 17, 1955; admitted to bar, 1981, Illinois and U.S. District Court, Central District of Illinois. *Education:* Vanderbilt University (B.A., magna cum laude, 1977); Georgetown University (J.D., 1981). Phi Eta Sigma; Phi Beta Kappa. Member, Illinois Supreme Court Character and Fitness Committee, 2004—. *Member:* Adams County (President, 2002) and Illinois State (Member, Commercial, Banking and Bankruptcy Law Section Council, 1990-1997, Chairman, 1995-1996) Bar Associations. ***PRACTICE AREAS:*** Banking Law; Real Estate Law; Bankruptcy; Mergers and Acquisitions. ***Email:*** wmccleery@srnm.com

TED M. NIEMANN, born Quincy, Illinois, September 24, 1957; admitted to bar, 1983, Illinois. *Education:* University of Illinois (B.A., 1980); DePaul University (J.D., 1983). Phi Alpha Delta. Author: "Material Changes in Illinois' Uniform Commercial Code Secured Transactions," 47, No. 1 Illinois State Bar Association Real Property 7, Oct. 2001; "Insurance," Residential Real Estate (IICLE, 2003 and 2005 Supplement). *Member:* Adams County (President, 2003-2004) and Illinois State (Vice-Chairman, Real Estate Law Section Council, 2005—) Bar Associations. ***PRACTICE AREAS:*** Real Estate; Commercial Law; Corporate/Partnership; Banking; Collections; Estate Planning. ***Email:*** tniemann@srnm.com

GENA J. AWERKAMP, born Keokuk, Iowa, January 21, 1947; admitted to bar, 1982, Missouri; 1988, Illinois. *Education:* University of Missouri-Columbia (B.S.Ed., cum laude, 1969; J.D., cum laude, 1982). Order of the Coif. Member, Missouri Law Review, 1981-1982. Member, Capital Litigation Trial Bar Screening Committee, Fourth District, 2001—. Author: "Article 9 Governs Assignment of Vendor's Rights Under an Installment Land Contract as Security for a Debt," 47 Missouri Law Review 328, 1982. Member, Illinois Supreme Court Rules Committee, 1996—. *Member:* Adams County and Illinois State Bar Associations; The Missouri Bar. ***PRACTICE AREAS:*** Medical Malpractice Law; Insurance Defense; Employment Law; Health Care Law. ***Email:*** gawerkamp@srnm.com

BRETT K. GORMAN, born Champaign, Illinois, November 30, 1966; admitted to bar, 1992, Illinois and U.S. District Court, Northern District of Illinois; 1996, U.S. District Court, Central District of Illinois; 1999, Missouri. *Education:* University of Illinois, Champaign-Urbana (B.A., 1989; J.D., 1992). Phi Beta Kappa. *Member:* Chicago, Adams County and Illinois State Bar Associations; The Missouri Bar; Defense Research Institute; Illinois Association of Defense Trial Counsel. ***PRACTICE AREAS:*** Corporate Litigation; Personal Injury Defense Litigation; Professional Malpractice; Products Liability; Insurance Law; Appellate Practice. ***Email:*** bgorman@srnm.com

HAROLD B. OAKLEY, born Quincy, Illinois, April 25, 1968; admitted to bar, 1993, Missouri; 1994, Illinois. *Education:* Westminster College (B.A., cum laude, 1990); Albert-Ludwig Universität, Germany; University of Missouri, Columbia (J.D., 1993). Phi Alpha Theta; Alpha Mu Gamma; Alpha Chi; Omicron Delta Kappa; Order of the Coif. Lead Articles Editor, Missouri Law Review. Author: Note, "Promises of Confidentiality: Do Reporters Really Have to Keep Their Word?" 57, Missouri Law Review, 955, 1992. *Member:* Bar Association of Metropolitan St. Louis; Adams County, Illinois State and American Bar Associations; The Missouri Bar; American Health Lawyers Association; Illinois Association of Healthcare Attorneys. ***PRACTICE AREAS:*** Corporate Law; Mergers and Acquisitions; Health Care Law; Education Law; Estate Planning. ***Email:*** hoakley@srnm.com

MICHAEL A. BICKHAUS, born Quincy, Illinois, March 3, 1968; admitted to bar, 1994, Illinois; 1995, Missouri. *Education:* Quincy College (B.A., Accounting, 1990); University of Missouri-Columbia (J.D., 1994). *Member:* Adams County, Illinois State and American Bar Associations; The Missouri Bar. ***PRACTICE AREAS:*** Corporate Law; Banking Law; Elder Law; Estate Planning; Probate Law; Real Estate Law; Tax Law. ***Email:*** mbickhaus@srnm.com

DAVID G. PENN, born Lexington, Kentucky, September 25, 1969; admitted to bar, 1994, Illinois and U.S. District Court, Northern District of Illinois; 1997, U.S. District Court, Central District of Illinois. *Education:* Boston College (B.A., magna cum laude, 1991; J.D., cum laude, 1994). Assistant State's Attorney, Felony Division, Sangamon County, Illinois, 1996-1999. . *Member:* Adams County, Illinois State and American Bar Associations. ***PRACTICE AREAS:*** Professional Malpractice; Product Liability; Agribusiness Litigation; Insurance Coverage; Corporate Litigation; Employment Law; Education Law. ***Email:*** dpenn@srnm.com

JAMES A. HANSEN, born Royal Oak, Michigan, September 10, 1970; admitted to bar, 1997, Missouri and U.S. District Court, Eastern District of Missouri; 1998, Illinois and U.S. District Court, Southern District of Illinois; 2002, U.S. District Court, Central District of Illinois. *Education:* Western Illinois University (B.B., 1991; M.B.A., 1993) St. Louis University (J.D., 1997). Member, National Moot Court Team, Saint Louis University. Author: "The Statutory Employee Defense: Have You Tried It Lately?" Missouri Organization of Defense Lawyers Newsletter, Fall 2001. *Member:* Adams County and Illinois State Bar Associations; The Missouri Bar; Defense Research Institute. ***PRACTICE AREAS:*** Civil Litigation; Commercial Litigation; Products Liability; Construction Litigation. ***Email:*** jhansen@srnm.com

GREGORY A. PRATT, born Quincy, Illinois, January 27, 1972; admitted to bar, 1999, Illinois; 2000, U.S. District Court, Central District of Illinois. *Education:* Quincy University (B.A., cum laude, 1995); University of Illinois College of Law (J.D., 1999). Phi Delta Phi. *Member:* Adams County and Illinois State Bar Associations. ***PRACTICE AREAS:*** Corporate Law; Partnership Law; Real Estate; Commercial Transactions; Mergers and Acquisitions. ***Email:*** gpratt@srnm.com

BABETTE L. BRENNAN, born Quincy, Illinois, May 15, 1961; admitted to bar, 1988, Illinois; 1989, Missouri; U.S. District Court, Central District of Illinois; U.S. District Court, Eastern District of Missouri. *Education:* University of Missouri (B.S., Business Administration, 1982); St. Louis University (J.D., 1988). Author: "Supreme Court Rule 219(e)-Plaintiff Beware: Defendant Too!!," General Practice, Solo & Small Firm Newsletter, Vol. 27, No. 7, March 1999; "Food for Thought: Estate Planning for Subsequent Marriages," General Practice, Solo & Small Firm Newsletter, Vol. 27, No. 7, March 1999; "Practice Reminder: Simple Wills—Tricky Issues," General Practice, Solo & Small Firm Newsletter, Vol. 29, No. 2, September 2000; "Disclose Your Opinion Witness even when Your Opponent Doesn't Ask," General Practice Solo & Small Firm Newsletter, Vol. 29, No. 8, June 2001. *Member:* Adams County, Illinois State (Member: General Practice, Solo and Small Firm Section Council, 1999-2002; Illinois Bar Journal Editorial Board, 2001-2002) and American Bar Associations; The Missouri Bar. ***PRACTICE AREAS:*** Insurance Defense Litigation; Estate Planning. ***Email:*** bbrennan@srnm.com

ANDREW K. CASHMAN, born Quincy, Illinois, March 10, 1974; admitted to bar, 1999, Missouri; 2002, Minnesota; 2003, Illinois; 2005, U.S. District Court, Central District of Illinois. *Education:* University of Illinois (B.S., 1996); University of Kansas (J.D., 1999); Georgetown University Law Center (LL.M., with highest distinction, 2000). *Member:* Adams County and Illinois State Bar Associations; The Missouri Bar; Minnesota Bar Association. ***PRACTICE AREAS:*** Taxation; Corporate Law; Business Organization; Estate Planning; Real Estate; Banking Law; Mergers and Acquisitions; Health Care Law. ***Email:*** acashman@srnm.com

MELINDA S. MADISON, born Quincy, Illinois, August 1, 1964; admitted to bar, 1999, New York; 2000, Illinois and U.S. District Court, Central and Southern Districts of Illinois. *Education:* Quincy College (B.S., summa cum laude, 1991); Southern Illinois University School of Law (J.D., 1998). Phi Delta Phi. *Member:* Adams County and Illinois State Bar Associations. ***PRACTICE AREAS:*** Litigation; Appellate Practice. ***Email:*** mmadison@srnm.com

REPRESENTATIVE CLIENTS: *Banking:* Bank of Quincy; Better Bank Group; Brown County State Bank; Gaither Tool Co.; Golden State Bank; ITR, Inc.; Kinderhook State Bank; Knapheide Equipment Co.; Knapheide Truck Equipment Co.; Marine Bank and Trust; Memphis Bancshares, Inc.; Mercantile Bancorp, Inc.; Mercantile Trust & Savings Bank; Perry State Bank; Security St. Bank of Hamilton; State Bank of Augusta; State Street Bank and Trust Company; Community Bank of Memphis. *Corporate:* Archer Daniels Midland Company; Area Distributors, Inc.; Awerkamp Machine Co.; Brahler's Truckers Supply, Inc.; Broadcast

(This Listing Continued)

SCHMIEDESKAMP, ROBERTSON, NEU & MITCHELL, Quincy—Continued

Electronics, Inc.; Central Stone Company; Gardner-Denver, Inc.; Glenayre Electronics; Harborstone Group, L.L.C.; Illinois Ayers Oil Company; J.M. Huber Corp.; Knapheide Manufacturing Company; Manna Pro Corporation; Mississippi Valley Council, Boy Scouts of America; Niemann Foods, Inc.; Norfolk & Western R.R.; Prince Agri Products; Prince Mfg. Co.; Quincy Mack Sales & Service; Resource Land Holdings, LLC; Seminole Feed; S.E.M. Minerals, Inc.; Sharkey Transportation, Inc.; Titan International, Inc.; Ursa Farmers Co-Operative Co.; Richard McNay, Inc.; Denman Services, Inc.; Farm & Home Supply. *Health Care:* Blessing Corporate Services, Inc.; Blessing Hospital; Illini Community Hospital; Quincy Medical Group. *Insurance:* Aetna Casualty & Surety Co.; Allied Mutual Insurance Co.; Allied Property & Casualty Insurance Co.; Allstate Insurance Co.; American Agri-Business Insurance Company; American Continental Insurance Company; American Feed Industry Insurance Company; Beneficial Insurance Group; Bituminous Casualty Corp.; CIGNA/INA; Cincinnati Insurance Company; CNA Insurance; Continental Insurance Cos.; Economy Fire & Casualty Co.; Employers-Commercial Union Cos.; Essex Insurance Company; Firemen's Fund Insurance Co.; General Accident and Liability Assurance Corp., Ltd.; General Casualty Insurance; Golden Rule Insurance Co.; Grinnell Mutual Reinsurance Co.; Hartford Accident & Indemnity Co.; Hawkeye Security Insurance Co.; Home Insurance Co.; Illinois Farmers Insurance Co.; Illinois State Medical Insurance Services, Inc.; John Hancock Mutual Life Insurance Co.; Liberty Mutual Insurance Co.; New Hampshire Insurance Group; OHIC Insurance; Prudential Insurance Co.; St. Paul Insurance Cos.; Sentry Insurance; Shelter Insurance Company; State Farm Insurance Company; Travelers Insurance Co.; Underwriters Adjusting Co. *Schools:* Camp Point Public Schools; Quincy Public Schools; Culver-Stockton College; Liberty Public Schools; Quincy University Foundation.

SCHOLZ, LOOS, PALMER, SIEBERS & DUESTERHAUS

625 VERMONT STREET
QUINCY, ILLINOIS 62301
Telephone: 217-223-3444
Fax: 217-223-3450
Email: slpsd@rnet.com
URL: http://www.slpsd.com

General Civil and Trial Practice in all Courts. Probate, Real Estate, Banking, Insurance Defense and Corporation Law, Tax, Bankruptcy, Commercial Law and Employment Law, Wills and Trusts.

MEMBERS OF FIRM

RICHARD F. SCHOLZ, SR. (1901-1975)

DELBERT LOOS (1909-1993)

CHARLES A. SCHOLZ, born Murphysboro, Illinois, October 29, 1926; admitted to bar, 1950, Illinois; 1975, U.S. Supreme Court. *Education:* Mercer University (LL.B., 1949); University of South Carolina. Phi Alpha Delta; Blue Key. Assistant States Attorney, Adams County, Illinois, 1952-1956. Field Assistant Attorney General, State of Illinois, 1961-1969. *Member:* Adams County (President, 1966-1967), Illinois State (Member, 1950—, and Chairman, 1982-1983, Legal Education and Admission to Bar Committee) and American Bar Associations; The Missouri Bar. ***PRACTICE AREAS:*** Estate Planning; Probate; Corporate. ***Email:*** cascholz@slpsd.com

JAMES L. PALMER, born Herrin, Illinois, January 28, 1948; admitted to bar, 1973, Illinois; 1979, U.S. Supreme Court; 1991, Missouri; U.S. District Court, Central District of Illinois and Eastern District of Missouri; U.S. Court of Appeals, Seventh and Eighth Circuits. *Education:* Quincy University (B.A. and B.A., both with high honors, 1970); University of Illinois (J.D., 1973). National Institute for Trial Advocacy (1979). Phi Alpha Theta. Author: "Fair Compensation for Representation of Indigent Defendants," 68 Illinois Bar Journal 458, 1980. Law Clerk, Judge James C. Craven, Illinois Appellate Court, Fourth District, 1973-1974. Public Defender, Adams County, 1978-1979. Assistant State's Attorney, Adams County, 1980-1984. Corporation Counsel, City of Quincy, 1985. Member, Inquiry Board, 1976-1984 and Hearing Board, 1984-2003, Attorney Registration and Disciplinary Commission. *Member:* Adams County, Illinois State, and American Bar Associations; The Missouri Bar; The Defense Research Institute; American Health Lawyers Association; Illinois Association of Healthcare Attorneys; Illinois Association of Defense Trial Counsel; Illinois Trial Lawyers Association; Association of Trial Lawyers of America (Associate Member); Association of Defense Trial Attorneys; National Institute of Trial Advocacy. ***PRACTICE AREAS:*** Civil Litigation; Employment; Insurance Defense; Workers Compensation. ***Email:*** jpalmer@slpsd.com

STEVEN E. SIEBERS, born Quincy, Illinois, August 8, 1954; admitted to bar, 1979, Illinois; 1980, Missouri; U.S. Court of Appeals, Seventh Circuit; U.S. District Court, Eastern District of Missouri and Central District of Illinois. *Education:* Western Illinois University (B.B., high honors, 1976); University of Illinois (J.D., magna cum laude, 1979). Order of the Coif. Certified Public Accountant Certificate, 1976. *Member:* Adams County, Illinois State and American Bar Associations; The Missouri Bar. ***PRACTICE AREAS:*** Corporate; Banking; Real Estate; Probate; Tax; Bankruptcy; Civil Litigation. ***Email:*** ssiebers@slpsd.com

JOSEPH A. DUESTERHAUS, born Quincy, Illinois, August 20, 1953; admitted to bar, 1983, Illinois; 1991, Missouri, U.S. District Court, Central District of Illinois and Eastern District of Missouri, and U.S. Court of Appeals, Seventh Circuit. *Education:* Grinnell College (B.A., 1980); University of Iowa (J.D., with distinction, 1983). Phi Beta Kappa. *Member:* Adams County, Illinois State and American Bar Associations; The Missouri Bar. ***PRACTICE AREAS:*** Corporate; Banking; Real Estate; Commercial Litigation; Bankruptcy. ***Email:*** jduesterhaus@slpsd.com

CHRISTOPHER G. SCHOLZ, born Quincy, Illinois, October 29, 1957; admitted to bar, 1987, Illinois; 1988, U.S. District Court, Central District of Illinois; 1992, U.S. Supreme Court; 2003, Missouri. *Education:* Western Illinois University (B.A., with high honors, 1984); Mercer University (J.D., 1987). Phi Kappa Phi; Phi Alpha Delta. Assistant Attorney General, Illinois, 1987-1989. Assistant State's Attorney, Adams County, 1989-1993. Assistant Corporation Counsel, City of Quincy, Illinois, 1993-2001. Corporation Counsel, City of Quincy Illinois, 2001—. *Member:* Adams County and Illinois State Bar Associations; The Missouri Bar. ***PRACTICE AREAS:*** Real Estate; Probate; Family Law; Wills; Estate Planning; Civil Litigation. ***Email:*** cgscholz@slpsd.com

JENNIFER A. WINKING, born Quincy, Illinois, October 11, 1966; admitted to bar, 1996, Illinois; 1997, Missouri, U.S. District Court, Central District of Illinois, U.S. District Court, Eastern District of Missouri and U.S. Court of Appeals, Seventh Circuit. *Education:* Quincy University (B.A., Political Science & History, summa cum laude, 1993); University of Missouri (J.D., 1996). Phi Kappa Phi; Phi Alpha Delta; Phi Alpha Theta. Order of the Coif. Member, 1994-1996 and Managing Editor, 1995-1996, Missouri Law Review. Author: Eleventh Amendment: "A Move Toward Simplicity in the Test For Immunity," 60 Mo. L.Rev. 953, 1995. *Member:* Adams County, Illinois State and American Bar Associations; The Missouri Bar; Illinois Association of Defense Trial Counsel. ***PRACTICE AREAS:*** Civil Litigation; Employment; Workers Compensation; Insurance Defense. ***Email:*** jwinking@slpsd.com

WILLIAM L. SIEBERS, born Quincy, Illinois, August 29, 1971; admitted to bar, 1996, Illinois and U.S. District Court, Central and Northern District of Illinois; 2004, Missouri and U.S. Supreme Court. *Education:* Quincy University (B.S., cum laude, 1993); Valparaiso University (J.D., summa cum laude, 1996). Moot Court, 1995-1996. Law Clerk, Judge Robert W. Cook, Illinois Appellate Court, Fourth District, 1999-2001. *Member:* Adams County, Illinois State and American Bar Associations; The Missouri Bar; National Academy of Elder Law Attorneys. ***PRACTICE AREAS:*** Civil Litigation; Civil Appeals; Corporate; Estate Planning; Personal Injury Litigation; Insurance Defense; Elder Law. ***Email:*** wsiebers@slpsd.com

REPRESENTATIVE CLIENTS: Heintz Electric Co.; Niemann Foods, Inc.; Sunset Home; Quincy Notre Dame Foundation; Mother Dennis Foundation; Municipal Insurance Cooperative Assoc.; First Bankers Trust Company, N.A.; Quincy Newspapers, Inc.; Quincy Broadcasting Co.; Nutrition 101, Inc.; United State Bank; Quincy Public Library; Bank of America, National Association; First Federal Bank; Marlboro Wire, Ltd.; Exact Packaging, Inc.; Family Medicine Associates of Quincy, Chartered; N. Kohl Grocer Company; T.F. Ehrhart Co.; JB Automatic, Inc.
LOCAL COUNSEL: Associates Commercial Corp.; Firemen's Fund Insurance; Ohio Casualty Insurance Co.; Sentry Insurance Co.; Travelers Insurance Co.; Mutual Life Insurance Company of New York; Gallagher-Bassett Services, Inc.; Crum and Forster Commercial Insurance Group; Western Heritage Insurance Co.; Lexington Insurance Co.; Federated Insurance Co.; Safeco/American States Insurance Company; Auto-Owners Insurance Co.; Argonaut Great Central Insurance Co.; Allied Group Insurance; Continental Grain Company; Progressive Insurance Companies; The Frank Gates Service Company; Cannon Cochran Management Services, Inc.; Royal & SunAlliance.
REFERENCES: First Bankers Trust Company, N.A.; Bank of America, National Association.

ALLEN & KORKOWSKI & ASSOCIATES

123 NORTH GARRARD STREET
RANTOUL, ILLINOIS 61866
Telephone: 217-893-1401
Fax: 217-893-4788
URL: http://www.ak-lawoffice.com
Email: bscott@mchsi.com
URL: http://www.aklaw.com

Business Law, Real Estate, Estate Planning, Administrative Law, Family Law, Bankruptcy and Commercial Collections.

MEMBERS OF THE FIRM

WILLIAM R. SCOTT, born Evergreen Park, Illinois, November 3, 1950; admitted to bar, 1975, Illinois, U.S. District Court, Central District of Illinois, U.S. Court of Appeals, Seventh Circuit and U.S. Supreme Court. *Education:* University of Illinois (B.A., 1972; J.D., 1975). Phi Beta Kappa. *Member:* Champaign County and Illinois State Bar Associations. ***PRACTICE AREAS:*** Estate Administration; Estate Planning; Real Estate. ***Email:*** bscott@mchsi.com

CRAIG R. HUNT, born Paxton, Illinois, January 21, 1958; admitted to bar, 1983, Illinois. *Education:* Eastern Illinois University (B.S., 1980); John Marshall Law School (J.D., 1983). ***PRACTICE AREAS:*** Real Estate Law; Divorce Law; Bankruptcy Law. ***Email:*** chunt@mchsi.com

REPRESENTATIVE CLIENTS: Bank of Rantoul; Hicks Oils; Hicksgas, Inc.; Rantoul First Bank; Rantoul Park District.
REFERENCES: Bank of Rantoul, Rantoul, Illinois.

MEYER CAPEL

A PROFESSIONAL CORPORATION

RANTOUL, ILLINOIS

(See Champaign)

General Civil Litigation, Corporate Law, Business Law, Estate Planning, Estate Administration, Real Estate, Tax, Telecommunications and Public Utility, Intellectual Property Law, Labor and Employment Law (Management), Municipal Law, Family Law, Health Care Law, Personal Injury, Products Liability Law, Criminal Law, Social Security Disability, Software Licensing, Education Law.

BROWN & ASSOCIATES

RED BUD, ILLINOIS

(See Belleville)

Civil Litigation, Personal Injury, Medical Malpractice, Products Liability, Admiralty Law, Railroad Law and Commercial Law.

(This Listing Continued)

JAMES L. KOPECKY, P.C.

RIVER FOREST, ILLINOIS

(See Chicago)

Securities, Securities Fraud, Securities Arbitration and Litigation, Shareholder Disputes, Business and Contract Litigation, General Civil Litigation and Personal Injury.

FREDERICK C. NIEMI

362 EAST BURLINGTON
RIVERSIDE, ILLINOIS 60546
Telephone: 708-442-0635
Fax: 708-442-6884
Email: niemiatlaw@sbcglobal.net
URL: http://www.niemilaw.com

Wills and Probate, Real Estate, Trusts and Estates, Guardianships, Alternatives to Probate.

FREDERICK C. NIEMI, born Chicago, Illinois, October 10, 1938; admitted to bar, 1964, Illinois. *Education:* University of Illinois (B.A., 1961); Chicago-Kent College of Law (J.D., 1964). Honorary Counsel, Finland-Illinois. ***PRACTICE AREAS:*** Wills; Probate; Real Estate; Trusts and Estates; Guardianship.

THE BRAINARD LAW OFFICES

ROBINSON, ILLINOIS

(See Charleston)

General Practice. Insurance Defense, Personal Injury, Products Liability, Probate, Trusts, Real Estate, Taxation, Municipal, Family and Health Law. Trials in all State and Federal Courts.

COX, PHILLIPS, WEBER, TEDFORD & HEAP, P.C.

216 SOUTH CROSS STREET
P.O. BOX 250
ROBINSON, ILLINOIS 62454-0250
Telephone: 618-544-8661
Fax: 618-544-3003
Email: cpwth@midwest.net

General Civil, Trial and Appellate Practice. Probate, Real Estate, Title Insurance, Municipal, Taxation, Corporation, Estate Planning, Workers Compensation, Oil and Gas Law, Collections, and Matrimonial Law.

M.E. COX (1880-1958)

CARROLL T. COX (1912-1976)

FRANK J. WEBER, born Olney, Illinois, June 15, 1944; admitted to bar, 1969, Illinois. *Education:* Eastern Illinois University (B.S., Education, 1966); University of Illinois (J.D., 1969). City Attorney: Robinson, 1973—; Newton, 1974-1977. ***PRACTICE AREAS:*** Civil Practice; Trial Practice; Appellate Practice; Probate; Real Estate; Municipal Law; Estate Planning; Oil and Gas Law.

MAX L. TEDFORD, born Lawrenceville, Illinois, November 18, 1952; admitted to bar, 1977, Illinois. *Education:* Eastern Illinois University (B.A., 1974); Southern Illinois University (J.D., 1977). City Attorney, Newton, Illinois. ***PRACTICE AREAS:*** Civil Trial Practice; Appellate Practice; Probate; Real Estate; Title Insurance; Municipal Law; Taxation; Corporate Law; Estate Planning; Oil and Gas Law; Collections; Matrimonial Law.

WILLIAM G. HEAP, born Sullivan, Indiana, April 30, 1948; admitted to bar, 1979, Illinois. *Education:* Indiana University; Indiana State University (B.S., 1971); John Marshall Law School (J.D., 1979). Delta Theta Phi; Order of John Marshall. ***PRACTICE AREAS:*** Civil Trial Practice; Appellate Practice; Probate; Real Estate; Title Insurance; Municipal Law; Corporate Law; Estate Planning; Oil and Gas Law; Collections; Matrimonial Law.

THOMAS R. WISEMAN, born Chicago, Illinois, September 25, 1962; admitted to bar, 1987, Illinois. *Education:* University of Illinois (B.A., 1984); Southern Illinois University (J.D., 1987). ***PRACTICE AREAS:*** Civil Trial Practice; Appellate Practice; Probate; Real Estate; Title Insurance; Municipal Law; Taxation; Corporate Law; Workers Compensation; Oil and Gas Law; Collections; Matrimonial Law.

CHRISTOPHER L. WEBER, born Olney, Illinois, October 13, 1969; admitted to bar, 1994, Illinois. *Education:* University of Illinois (B.S., 1991; J.D., 1994). ***PRACTICE AREAS:*** Civil Trial Practice; Appellate Practice; Probate; Real Estate; Title Insurance; Municipal Law; Taxation; Corporate Law; Estate Planning; Oil and Gas Law; Collections; Matrimonial Law.

CRAIG O. WEBER, born Olney, Illinois, March 17, 1972; admitted to bar, 1997, Illinois; 1998, Indiana. *Education:* University of Illinois (B.S., with honors, 1994); Southern Illinois University (J.D., cum laude, 1997). Certificate of Certified Public Accountant, 1994. ***PRACTICE AREAS:*** Civil Trial Practice; Appellate Practice; Probate; Real Estate; Title Insurance; Municipal Law; Taxation; Corporate Law; Estate Planning; Oil and Gas Law; Collections; Matrimonial Law.

OF COUNSEL

G. KENT PHILLIPS, born Memphis, Tennessee, December 15, 1913; admitted to bar, 1957, Illinois. *Education:* University of Illinois; Eastern Illinois State Teachers College; private study.

(This Listing Continued)

REPRESENTATIVE CLIENTS: Regions Bank; First National Bank Olney; First Robinson Savings Bank; Peoples State Bank-Newton; First Community Bank, N.A.; Robinson Daily News; Robinson-Palestine Water Commission; Oblong School District No. 4; City of Robinson; City of Newton; Crawford Memorial Hospital; United Methodist Village.
AUTHORIZED ATTORNEYS FOR: Attorneys Title Guaranty Fund; TICOR Title.

HELLER, HOLMES & ASSOCIATES, P.C.

ROBINSON, ILLINOIS

(See Mattoon)

General Civil and Trial Practice in all State, Federal and Appellate Courts. Personal Injury, Medical Negligence, Criminal Defense, Insurance, Litigation, Probate, Workers Compensation, Corporation, Commercial, Family Law, Oil and Gas.

LAW OFFICES OF JAMES D. STOUT

309 SOUTH JEFFERSON
P.O. BOX 714
ROBINSON, ILLINOIS 62454
Telephone: 618-546-5404
Fax: 618-544-3659
Email: jds1@shawneelink.net
URL: http://www.lawyers.com/stoutholtzhouser
Bridgeport, Illinois Office: 324 North Main Street. Telephone: 618-945-2911. Fax: 618-945-3941.

General Civil Practice. Trials. Corporation, Real Estate, Oil and Gas, Probate and Estate Planning Law, Family Law, Creditor Bankruptcy.

JAMES D. STOUT, admitted to bar, 1974, Texas; 1978, Illinois. *Education:* Southern Illinois University (B.A., 1969); University of Illinois (J.D., 1974). *Member:* Crawford County, Lawrence County and Illinois State Bar Associations; State Bar of Texas.

ASSOCIATE

LINDSEY D. FLOYD, admitted to bar, 2003, Illinois. *Education:* University of Evansville (B.S., 2000); Southern Illinois University, Carbondale (J.D., 2003). *Member:* Illinois State Bar Association. (Resident, Bridgeport Office)

§§.

ABATE & SMITH

6072 BRYNWOOD DRIVE, SUITE 201
ROCKFORD, ILLINOIS 61114
Telephone: 815-282-8228
Fax: 815-282-6620
URL: http://www.abatateandsmith.com

Family Law including Divorce, Child Custody, Child Support, Spousal Support, Alimony, Visitation Rights, Distribution of Property, Paternity, Adoption Law, Personal Injury including Automobile Accidents and Injuries, Real Estate, Contracts.

ALEX M. ABATE, born Rockford, Illinois, May 21, 1947; admitted to bar, 1974, Illinois; 1975, U. S. District Court, Northern District of Illinois. *Education:* University of Illinois (B.S., 1969; J.D., 1974). Phi Delta Phi. Lecturer: Family Law, Illinois Institute for Continuing Legal Education, 1985—; Illinois State Bar Association Family Law Council, 1985—. *Member:* Winnebago County (Treasurer, Younger Members Section, 1977), Illinois State (Member, Council on Family Law Section, 1979-1984) and American (Member, Family Section Council, Committee for Continuing Education, 1984-1986) Bar Associations; Illinois Trial Lawyers Association; American Academy of Matrimonial Lawyers. ***PRACTICE AREAS:*** Domestic Relations Law.

MICHAEL J. SMITH, born Rockford, Illinois, October 2, 1955; admitted to bar, 1980, Illinois; 1982, U.S. District Court, Northern District of Illinois. *Education:* Western Illinois University (B.A., with honors, 1977); Southern Illinois University (J.D., cum laude, 1980). Sigma Tau Delta; Phi Kappa Phi; Kappa Delta Pi. *Member:* Winnebago County (Secretary, 1994-1995; President, Young Lawyers; Director, 1990-1991; Member, Sections on: Family Law, Real Estate and Criminal Law) and American Bar Associations; State Bar of Michigan (Member, Sections on: Family Law, Real Estate and Criminal Law); Leading Lawyers Network Family Law. ***PRACTICE AREAS:*** Domestic Relations Law; General Practice. ***Email:*** AttorneyMJSmith@aol.com

BARRETT & GILBERT LLP

1645 TEMPLE LANE
ROCKFORD, ILLINOIS 61112
Telephone: 815-332-9600
Fax: 815-332-9646
Email: gbarrett@barrettandgilbert.com
Email: dtbarrett@barrettandgilbert.com
URL: http://www.barrettandgilbert.com

Medical Malpractice, Catastrophic Personal Injury, Law Enforcement Litigation, Products Liability, Commercial Motor Vehicle Safety, General Litigation, Transportation, Automobile Accidents, Dog Bites, Slip and Fall, Wrongful Death, International Law.

MEMBERS OF FIRM

GREGORY E. BARRETT, born Mason City, Iowa, November 27, 1949; admitted to bar, 1974, Nebraska, U.S. District Court, District of Nebraska and Illinois; 1975, U.S. District Court, Northern District of Illinois; 1982, U.S. Court of Appeals, Seventh Circuit. *Edu-*

(This Listing Continued)

BARRETT & GILBERT LLP, Rockford—Continued

cation: Trinity College (B.A., cum laude, 1971); University of Nebraska (J.D., 1974). *Member:* Winnebago County (Treasurer, 1980; Chairman: Lawyer Referral Committee, 1977; Continuing Legal Education Committee, 1979; Trial Section, 1986; Federal Section, 1989), Illinois State and American Bar Associations; Illinois State Trial Lawyers Association; Association of Trial Lawyers of America. [1st Lt. U.S. Army Reserves, AG Branch, 1973-1979]. ***PRACTICE AREAS:*** Personal Injury Law; Medical Malpractice; Products Liability; Litigation.

DANIEL T. GILBERT, born Rockford, Illinois, December 25, 1954; admitted to bar, 1980, Illinois; 1981, U.S. District Court, Northern District of Illinois; 1985, Wisconsin; 1987, U.S. District Court, Eastern District of Wisconsin; 2001, U.S. District Court for the District of Columbia. *Education:* Rockford College (B.S., magna cum laude, 1976); The John Marshall Law School (J.D., 1980); F.B.I. Academy National Law Institute. Author: with R.R. Blackburn, two legal treatises for National Academy of Sciences, 1995; with contributing author M. Cohen, chapter, "Photographic enforcement of traffic laws," *NCHRP Project 20-5,* Topic 22-1, Syntheses 219, National Academy of Sciences, Transportation Research Board, 1995-1996; with N. Emerson, chapter, "Double jeopardy and administrative license revocation, and several other revisions," *Apprehending and prosecuting the drunk driver,* University of Wisconsin Law School, 1996; chapter, "Photographic enforcement of traffic laws, a study of all traffic and case law regarding the use of photographic technology in the enforcement of traffic laws," *NCHRP No. 38,* National Academy of Sciences, December 1995. Professor of Law, Rockford College, 1981—. Instructor of Law, Northwestern University, Traffic Institute, 1989-1999. *Member:* Winnebago County and Illinois State Bar Associations; State Bar of Wisconsin; The Association of Trial Lawyers of America; Illinois Trial Lawyer's Association (Former Executive Director and Legal Advisor, National Committee on Uniform Traffic Laws and Ordinances, 1990-1995; Member, National Committee on Uniform Traffic Control Devices, 1990-1995). ***REPORTED CASES:*** Kurt Carlson et al. v. The Islamic Republic of Iran, Civil Action No. 00-1309, before the D.C. Federal Court, April 2002. ***PRACTICE AREAS:*** Medical Malpractice; Catastrophic Injury; Personal Injury; Transportation.

SUSAN M. BRAZAS, born Lafayette, Indiana, September 15, 1959; admitted to bar, 1990, Illinois. *Education:* Bradley University (B.S., magna cum laude, 1981; M.B.A., 1983); University of Illinois (J.D., magna cum laude, 1990). Law Clerk to Hon. P. Michael Mahoney and to Hon Hon. Stanley J. Roszkowski, U.S. District Court, Northern District of Illinois, 1989-1991. *Member:* Winnebago County (Chair, Federal Section, 1998-1999; Federal and Boone County Civil Jury Reporter; Editor and Member, Editorial Board, "The Lawyer," 1995-2000; Chair, Membership Committee, 1995-1996; Member, Judicial Liaison Committee, 1997-2000), Illinois State (Secretary, 1998-1999; Vice-Chair, 1999-2000; Chair-Elect, 2000-2001) and American Bar Associations; Winnebago County Womens Bar (President, 1995-1997). ***PRACTICE AREAS:*** Medical Malpractice; Professional Liability; Personal Injury; Civil Practice; Hospital Law.

BARRICK, SWITZER, LONG, BALSLEY & VAN EVERA

Established in 1938

6833 STALTER DRIVE, FIRST FLOOR
ROCKFORD, ILLINOIS 61108
Telephone: 815-962-6611
Facsimile: 815-962-0687
Email: info@bslbv.com

Insurance Defense Litigation: Products Liability, Environmental Law, Premises Liability, Age Discrimination in Employment, Sex Discrimination, Race Discrimination, Dram Shop Liability, Professional Malpractice, Automobile, Construction and Fire, Business Law, Real Estate, Family Law, Probate, Civil Trial in All State and Federal Courts.

FIRM PROFILE: Barrick, Switzer, Long, Balsley, & Van Evera has served Northern Illinois as a general practice law firm for over 60 years. The law firm is result oriented. Various members of the firm focus their practice on insurance defense, banking, bankruptcy, criminal law, commercial law, personal injury, worker compensation, domestic relations, estate planning and municipal law.

MEMBERS OF FIRM

STEPHEN G. BALSLEY, born Beloit, Wisconsin, January 14, 1947; admitted to bar, 1972, Illinois. *Education:* University of Wisconsin (B.S., with honors, 1969); University of Illinois (J.D., with honors, 1972). Order of the Coif. Member, 1970-1972 and Note and Comment Editor, 1971-1972, University of Illinois Law Forum. Member of Panel, U.S. Interim Bankruptcy Trustees for Northern District of Illinois, 1979—. *Member:* Winnebago County (Secretary, 1986-1987), Illinois State and American Bar Associations. ***PRACTICE AREAS:*** Commercial Law; Real Estate Law; Bankruptcy Law. ***Email:*** sbalsley@bslbv.com

RICHARD K. VAN EVERA, born Hinsdale, Illinois, May 1, 1948; admitted to bar, 1978, Illinois. *Education:* Coe College (B.A., 1970); Cumberland School of Law Samford University (J.D., 1978). *Member:* Winnebago County, Illinois State and American Bar Associations; Illinois Association of Defense Trial Counsel. [Capt., USAF, 1970-1974]. ***PRACTICE AREAS:*** Civil Trial Law; Personal Injury; Insurance Defense; Insurance Coverage Litigation; Workers' Compensation Claims; Workers' Compensation Defense. ***Email:*** rvanevera@bslbv.com

JAMES E. STEVENS, born Belvidere, Illinois, July 28, 1954; admitted to bar, 1980, Illinois. *Education:* Rock Valley Junior College (A.A., 1974); University of Illinois (B.A., 1976); Gonzaga University (J.D., 1979). Law Clerk to the Honorable Richard N. DeGunther, U.S. Bankruptcy Judge, Northern District of Illinois, Western Division, 1979-1981. Member of Panel, U.S. Interim Bankruptcy Trustees for Northern District of Illinois. *Member:* Winnebago County, Illinois State and American Bar Associations. ***PRACTICE AREAS:*** Commercial Law; Bankruptcy Law; Municipal Law; Real Estate. ***Email:*** jstevens@bslbv.com

(This Listing Continued)

THOMAS A. GREEN, born Rockford, Illinois, September 20, 1957; admitted to bar, 1984, Illinois and U.S. District Court, Northern District of Illinois. *Education:* University of Wisconsin-Eau Claire (B.A., 1980); Northern Illinois University (J.D., 1984). Law Clerk to the Honorable Richard DeGunther, Bankruptcy Judge, Northern District of Illinois, Western Division, 1984-1985. *Member:* Winnebago County, Illinois State and American Bar Associations; Bar Association of the Seventh Circuit Court of Appeals. ***PRACTICE AREAS:*** Commercial Law; Bankruptcy Law; Municipal Law. ***Email:*** tgreen@bslbv.com

ROBERT C. POTTINGER, born Belvidere, Illinois, October 26, 1966; admitted to bar, 1990, Illinois and U.S. District Court, Northern District of Illinois including Trial Bar; U.S. Court of Appeals, Seventh Circuit. *Education:* Baylor University (B.A., 1987); Chicago-Kent College of Law (J.D., 1989). *Member:* Winnebago County, Illinois State and American Bar Associations; Illinois Association of Defense Trial Counsel. ***PRACTICE AREAS:*** Civil Litigation; Real Estate Law; Municipal Law. ***Email:*** rcpottinger@bslbv.com

JASON H. ROCK, born Princeton, New Jersey, August 22, 1969; admitted to bar, 1994, Illinois, U.S. District Court, Northern District of Illinois and U.S. Court of Appeals, Seventh Circuit. *Education:* Clemson University (B.A., 1991); Drake University Law School (J.D., 1994). Omicron Delta Upsilon. *Member:* Winnebago County and Illinois State Bar Associations. ***PRACTICE AREAS:*** Bankruptcy; Construction Litigation; Debtor and Creditor; Mechanics Liens; Traffic Violations. ***Email:*** jrock@bslbv.com

DOUGLAS R. HENRY, born St. Joseph, Michigan, March 11, 1961; admitted to bar, 1995, Illinois; 1996, District of Columbia. *Education:* University of Michigan at Ann Arbor (B.A., 1983); University of Toledo (J.D., 1995). *Member:* Winnebago County and Illinois State Bar Associations; District of Columbia Bar. ***PRACTICE AREAS:*** Civil Litigation; Criminal Defense; Collections; Municipal Law; Insurance Defense. ***Email:*** dhenry@bslbv.com

---

TYLER A. MOORE, born Monmouth, Illinois, July 16, 1976; admitted to bar, 2001, Illinois; U.S. District Court, Northern District of Illinois. *Education:* Augustana College (B.A., 1998); Northern Illinois University (J.D., 2001). *Member:* Winnebago County, Illinois State and American Bar Associations. ***PRACTICE AREAS:*** Bankruptcy; Commercial Law; Civil Litigation. ***Email:*** tmoore@bslbv.com

LAURA A. BALUCH, born Rockford, Illinois, May 21, 1977; admitted to bar, 2003, Illinois. *Education:* Northern Illinois University, De Kalb (B.S., 1999); Thomas M. Cooley Law School (J.D., magna cum laude, 2003). Member, Cooley Law Journal. *Member:* Winnebago County, Illinois State and American Bar Associations; Illinois Trial Lawyers Association. ***PRACTICE AREAS:*** Family Law; Civil Litigation; Workers Compensation. ***Email:*** lalauch@bslbv.com

STACY K. SHELLY, born Freeport, Illinois, November 18, 1978; admitted to bar, 2003, Illinois. *Education:* Lawrence University (B.A., cum laude, 2000); University of Michigan, Ann Arbor (J.D., 2003). ***PRACTICE AREAS:*** Civil Litigation; Municipal Law; Estate Planning.

ADAM S. LONG, born Rockford, Illinois, October 17, 1979; admitted to bar, 2004, Illinois. *Education:* University of Illinois, Urbana-Champaign (B.A., Economics, 2001); University of Kentucky (J.D., 2004). Dean's List (1998-2001). ***PRACTICE AREAS:*** Civil Litigation; Commercial Litigation; Creditors Rights; Bankruptcy. ***Email:*** along@bslbv.com

CHARLOTTE A. LeCLERCQ, born Aurora, Illinois, February 17, 1970; admitted to bar, 2004, Illinois. *Education:* Grinnell College (B.A., 1992); Northern Illinois University Law School, DeKalb (J.D., summa cum laude, 2004). ***PRACTICE AREAS:*** Civil Litigation; Municipal Law; Estate Planning. ***Email:*** cleclercq@bslbv.com

OF COUNSEL

WILLIAM H. BARRICK (1916-2003)

PETER S. SWITZER, born West Milwaukee, Wisconsin, May 12, 1938; admitted to bar, 1963, Illinois. *Education:* Lawrence College (B.A., 1960); University of Wisconsin (LL.B., 1963).

JOSEPH L. LONG, born Princeton, Illinois, June 15, 1936; admitted to bar, 1963, Illinois. *Education:* University of Illinois (B.S., 1958; LL.B., 1963). Phi Delta Phi. *Member:* Winnebago County, Illinois State and American Bar Associations. [Lt., U.S. Naval Reserve Active Duty, 1958-1960]. ***PRACTICE AREAS:*** Probate Law; Municipal Law; Real Estate Law.

ARMOUR T. BECKSTRAND, born Rockford, Illinois, February 7, 1928; admitted to bar, 1956, Texas; 1957, 1964, Illinois. *Education:* Carthage College; Washington & Lee University (LL.B., 1955). Member, Board of Trustees: Swedish-American Hospital Association, 1978-1990; Chairman, City of Rockford Zoning Commission, 1974. [Pharmacist Mate III Class, U.S. Navy, 1945-1946]. ***Email:*** abeckstrand@bslbv.com

REPRESENTATIVE CLIENTS: St. Paul Insurance Companies; State Farm Insurance Company; Allied Insurance Company; Metropolitan Life Insurance Company; William Charles, Ltd.; Alpine Bank, NA; Three Hammer Construction Company; Belvidere National Bank & Trust Company; J. Rubin & Company; United Mercantile Agencies, Inc.; Dickerson Nieman Realtors; Auto Owners Insurance Company; Progressive Steel, Inc.; Rockford Structures Construction Company; Pella Products, Inc.; USBancorp; Stillman BancCORP, NA; First Bank, BC; Bergstrom, Inc.; Village of Machesney Park; Village of Capron; Village of Pacatonia and Village of Cherry Valley.
REFERENCE: Bank One, Rockford, N.A.

LAW OFFICE OF TOMIKO L. BUCHANAN

555 N. COURT STREET, SUITE 10
ROCKFORD, ILLINOIS 61103-6898
Telephone: 815-961-8760
Email: Tomikolaw@sbcglobal.net
URL: http://www.tomikolaw.com

Criminal Law, Expungements, DWI, Juvenile Law, Personal Injury, Automobile Accidents, Child Support, Expungements.

TOMIKO L. BUCHANAN, born 1972; admitted to bar, 1997, Illinois and U.S. District Court, Northern District of Illinois. *Education:* Northern Illinois University (B.S., 1994); Valparaiso University (J.D., 1997). *Member:* Illinois State Bar Association; Association of Trial Lawyers of America. ***PRACTICE AREAS:*** Criminal Law; Driving While Intoxicated; Juvenile Law; Personal Injury; Automobile Accidents and Injuries; Child Support; Expungements.

CASSIDAY, SCHADE & GLOOR, LLP

120 WEST STATE STREET, SUITE 401
ROCKFORD, ILLINOIS 61101-1159
Telephone: 815-962-8301
Fax: 815-962-8401
URL: http://www.cassiday.com

Chicago, Illinois Office: 20 North Wacker Drive, Suite 1040, 60606-2903. Telephone: 312-641-3100. Fax: 312-444-1669.
Libertyville, Illinois Office: 1870 West Winchester Road, Suite 148, 60048-5353. Telephone: 847-932-6922. Fax: 847-932-6947.
Naperville, Illinois Office: 1230 East Diehl Road, Suite 202, 60563-9362. Telephone: 630-328-2970. Fax: 630-328-2979.

General Practice. Civil Trial Practice, Civil Appellate Practice, Insurance Coverage, Environmental, Medical and Professional Malpractice, Products Liability, Structural Work Act, Railroad, Employment, Corporate and Health Care Law, Commercial Litigation, Construction, Workers Compensation, Intellectual Property, Municipalities, Transportation, Patent Law.

FIRM PROFILE: Cassiday Schade & Gloor, LLP was founded in 1979. The firm specializes in civil trial litigation, representing corporations, hospitals, and insurers. It maintains offices in Chicago, Libertyville, Naperville, and Rockford, Illinois. The firm has expertise in virtually all areas of civil litigation, including health care litigation, product liability, construction law, insurance law, environmental and toxic injury litigation, employment practices, workers compensation, intellectual property, municipalities, patent law and intellectual property.

The firm also has an established Quality Control Department.

MEMBERS OF FIRM

MARC F. BENJOYA, born Chicago, Illinois, July 3, 1958; admitted to bar, 1983, Illinois including Federal Trial Bar, U.S. District Court, Northern District of Illinois and Wisconsin; 1999, U.S. District Court, Southern District of Indiana. *Education:* Northern Illinois University (B.A., cum laude, 1980); IIT/Chicago-Kent College of Law (J.D., 1983). *Member:* Lake County, Illinois State and Wisconsin State Bar Associations; Illinois Association of Hospital Attorneys; Illinois Association of Defense Trial Counsel. (Also at Libertyville). ***PRACTICE AREAS:*** Professional Negligence; Professional Liability Defense; Insurance Defense. ***Email:*** mfb@cs-g.com

WILLIAM W. RANARD, born Helena, Montana, November 7, 1966; admitted to bar, 1992, Illinois; 1993, Missouri; 1995, Illinois; 2000, Wisconsin. *Education:* Northwestern University (B.A., 1989); University of Missouri (J.D., 1992). Treasurer, Grievance Committee and Chair, Faculty Appointments Committee, University of Missouri. Board Member, Harbor Light Salvation Army, 1993-1994. *Member:* Winnebago County and Illinois State Bar Associations; The Missouri Bar; State Bar of Wisconsin. (Also at Chicago Office). ***PRACTICE AREAS:*** Insurance; Medical Malpractice; Personal Injury; Civil Rights Defense; Medical Malpractice Defense. ***Email:*** wwr@cs-g.com

SALLY J. ZIMMERMAN, born East Liverpool, Ohio, April 29, 1954; admitted to bar, 1991, Illinois; U.S. District Court, Northern District of Illinois. *Education:* Bethesda Hospital School of Nursing (Nsg., 1975); Illinois Benedictine College (B.S.N., 1986); Northern Illinois University (J.D., 1991). Registered Nurse, Illinois. *Member:* Illinois State Bar Association. (Also at Chicago Office). ***PRACTICE AREAS:*** Medical Malpractice Defense; Professional Liability Defense. ***Email:*** sjz@cs-g.com

ASSOCIATE

RONALD D. FIET, born Rockford, Illinois, March 17, 1966; admitted to bar, 1996, Illinois. *Education:* Augustana College (B.A., 1988); Valparaiso University (J.D., 1995). *Member:* Winnebago County (Treasurer, Young Lawyers Division, 1998-1999), Illinois State and American Bar Associations. (Also at Chicago Office). ***Email:*** rdf@cs-g.com

A list of Representative Clients will be made available upon request.

CICERO & FRANCE, A PROFESSIONAL CORPORATION

6323 EAST RIVERSIDE BOULEVARD
ROCKFORD, ILLINOIS 61114
Telephone: 815-226-7700
Fax: 815-226-7701
URL: http://www.cicerofrancelaw.com

Insurance Defense, First and Third Party Insurance Defense, Property and Casualty Defense, Automobile Insurance Defense, Business Law and Litigation including Family Owned Businesses, Fraud, Contracts, Employment Agreements, Business Sales and Acquisitions, Commercial Litigation, Family Law including Divorce, Child Custody, Child Support, Spousal Support, Alimony, Adoptions, Visitation Rights, Separation Agreements and Parenting Plans.

PAUL R. CICERO, born Rockford, Illinois, January 21, 1949; admitted to bar, 1974, Illinois; 1975, U.S. District Court, Northern District of Illinois including Trial Bar; 1985, U.S. Court of Appeals, 7th Circuit. *Education:* University of Illinois (B.A., 1970); Washington University (J.D., 1974). Fellow, Illinois Bar Foundation. Assistant Public Defender, Winnebago County, Illinois, 1974-1978. Member, Board of Trustees, University of Illinois, 1988-1989. *Member:* Winnebago County (Member, Board of Governors, 1985-1988) and Illinois State (Member, ISBA Assembly, 1984-1988; Member, Unauthorized Practice of Law Committee, 1986-1990. Fellow, 1987—) Bar Associations. ***PRACTICE AREAS:*** Family Law; Business Law; Corporate Law; Estates.

JOHN W. FRANCE, born Chicago, Illinois, January 12, 1946; admitted to bar, 1975, Illinois; 1975, U.S. District Court, Northern District of Illinois; 1987, U.S. Court of Appeals, 7th Circuit and Federal Trial Bar. *Education:* University of Wisconsin (B.S., 1968); Illinois Institute of Technology, Chicago-Kent-College of Law (J.D., 1975). Phi Alpha Delta. Attorney for Rockford Area Substance Abuse Committee, 1988-1994. *Member:* Winnebago County (Chairman, Legal-Medical Committee, 1980-1981; Member: Professional Responsibility Committee, 1985-1986; Continuing Legal Education Committee, 1988-1989; Board of Directors, 1990-1993; Chairman, Trial Section, 1990-1991; President, 1997-1998), Illinois State (Member, Workers Compensation Section, 1980-1983; Assembly, 1988-1994) and American Bar Associations; Illinois Association of Defense Trial Counsel; Defense Research Institute. ***PRACTICE AREAS:*** Civil Litigation; Professional Liability; First and Third Party Insurance Defense.

RONALD A. BARCH, born Chicago, Illinois, August 20, 1964; admitted to bar, 1992, Illinois; U.S. District Court, Northern District of Illinois. *Education:* Western Illinois University (B.S., 1986); The John Marshall Law School (J.D., 1992). *Member:* Winnebago County, Illinois State and American Bar Associations; Illinois Association of Defense Trial Counsel. ***PRACTICE AREAS:*** Civil Litigation; Commercial Litigation; Insurance Defense; Personal Injury. ***Email:*** rb@cicerofrance.com

CHARLES P. ALEXANDER, born Rockford, Illinois, March 27, 1969; admitted to bar, 1993, Illinois and U.S. District Court, Northern District of Illinois. *Education:* University of Illinois (B.S., 1990); Northern Illinois University (J.D., cum laude, 1993). Assistant City Attorney, 1994-1998. *Member:* Winnebago County (Chair, Family Law Section, 2003-2004; Member, Board of Directors, 2001-2004) and Illinois State Bar Associations. ***PRACTICE AREAS:*** Family Law; Divorce; Child Custody; Child Support; Civil Litigation; General Practice. ***Email:*** cpa@cicerofrance.com

CONDE KILLOREN BUESCHEL & CALGARO

120 WEST STATE STREET, SUITE 400
ROCKFORD, ILLINOIS 61101
Telephone: 815-987-4000
Fax: 815-987-9889

Estate Planning including Probate, Trusts, Charitable Giving, Business Succession Planning, Wealth Preservation, Taxation, Commercial Law, Corporate Law, Business Law and Litigation, School Law, Residential and Commercial Real Estate, Contracts, Leases, Land Use, Zoning.

MEMBERS OF FIRM

DALE F. CONDE, born Rockford, Illinois, June 17, 1922; admitted to bar, 1948, Illinois. *Education:* University of Illinois; Washington University; Northwestern University (J.D., 1948). Order of the Coif. Assistant States Attorney, Winnebago County, 1948-1952. Attorney: Loves Park Civil Service Commission, 1955-1960; Rock River Fire Protection District, 1952-1964; Rockford School District, 1964—. Member, Rockford Zoning Commission, 1961-1964. *Member:* Winnebago County (President, 1975-1976), Illinois State (Member, Federal Judiciary and Related Appointments Committee, 1976-1984) and American Bar Associations; Council of School Attorneys of the National School Board Association. [With U.S. Armed Services, 1942-1945]. ***PRACTICE AREAS:*** Estate Planning Law; Probate Law; Commercial Law.

THOMAS A. KILLOREN, born Oak Park, Illinois, February 16, 1931; admitted to bar, 1959, Illinois. *Education:* University of Illinois (B.A., in Acc., with University honors, 1952; J.D., 1959). Phi Alpha Delta; Beta Gamma Sigma. Member, Bronze Tablet. Certified Public Accountant, Illinois, 1957. Attorney, Rochelle School District, 1982-1985. *Member:* Chicago (Chairman, Employee Benefits Committee, 1973-1974), Winnebago County, Illinois State and American (Member, Taxation Section) Bar Associations. [Officer, U.S. Navy, 1952-1956]. ***PRACTICE AREAS:*** Estate Planning Law; Taxation Law; Corporate Law.

THOMAS A. BUESCHEL, born Rockford, Illinois, January 18, 1952; admitted to bar, 1978, Illinois. *Education:* Bradley University (B.S., 1974); Gonzaga University (M.S., 1976; J.D., 1978). *Member:* Winnebago County Bar Association (Member, Young Lawyers Section); National Council of School Board Attorneys; Illinois Council of School Attorneys. ***PRACTICE AREAS:*** School Law; General Civil Litigation; Appellate Practice.

ROBERT A. CALGARO, born Rockford, Illinois, April 20, 1954; admitted to bar, 1978, Illinois. *Education:* Northwestern University (B.A., 1975); University of Illinois (J.D., 1978). Member, Order of the Coif. *Member:* Winnebago County Bar Association. ***PRACTICE AREAS:*** General Civil Litigation; Business Law; Corporate Law; Appellate Practice; Real Estate; Commercial Real Estate; Residential Real Estate. ***Email:*** dwoodsq@aol.com

(This Listing Continued)

DANIEL A. CWYNAR

ONE COURT PLACE, SUITE 100
ROCKFORD, ILLINOIS 61101
Telephone: 815-964-4601
Fax: 815-964-3932
Email: dac53golf@aol.com
URL: http://www.rockfordbankruptcylaw.com

Bankruptcy including individual and small business, foreclosures, repossessions, chapter 7, chapter 13; Residential and Commercial Real Estate, Buying and Selling, Contracts, Criminal Defense, DUI, Traffic, Misdemeanors.

DANIEL A. CWYNAR, born Rockford, Illinois, December 14, 1953; admitted to bar, 1979, Illinois, U.S. District Court, Northern District of Illinois. *Education:* DePaul University (J.D., 1979). *Member:* Winnebago County Bar Association. ***PRACTICE AREAS:*** Bankruptcy; Real Estate; Probate; Traffic Violations; Misdemeanors.

KEITH FRANTZ

401 WEST STATE STREET, SUITE 200
ROCKFORD, ILLINOIS 61101
Telephone: 815-987-9820
Fax: 815-987-9869
Email: Keith_Frantz@msn.com
Email: KeithFrantz@aol.com

Intellectual Property Law including Patents, Trademarks, Trade Secrets, Trade Dress, Unfair Competition, Franchise Matters, Computer Law and related litigation and licensing matters with an emphasis in the Electrical, Mechanical, Chemical, Pharmaceutical and Biotechnology areas.

KEITH FRANTZ, born Fort Madison, Iowa, July 23, 1955; admitted to bar, 1993, Illinois; 1994, registered to practice before U.S. Patent and Trademark Office. *Education:* Iowa State University (B.S.M.E., 1981); University of Illinois (M.S., Theoretical & Applied Mechanics, 1990); Northern Illinois University (J.D., 1993). ***PRACTICE AREAS:*** Patents; Trademarks; Intellectual Property.

PAUL E. GAZIANO

311 SEVENTH STREET
ROCKFORD, ILLINOIS 61104
Telephone: 815-964-7933
Fax: 815-964-6189

Criminal Litigation. Criminal Appeals in Federal and State Courts, Traffic, DUI, Juvenile.

PAUL E. GAZIANO, born Rockford, Illinois, April 13, 1949; admitted to bar, 1975, Illinois, U.S. District Court, Northern District of Illinois and U.S. Court of Appeals, Seventh Circuit. *Education:* College of St. Thomas (B.A., 1971); William Mitchell College of Law (J.D., cum laude, 1975). Assistant Public Defender, Winnebago County, Illinois, 1976-1979. Appointed Special Prosecutor, Stephenson County, Illinois, 1985. Winnebago County Volunteer Lawyer of the Year, 1987-1988. Instructor, Business Law, Rock Valley College, 1977-1988. *Member:* Winnebago (Treasurer, 1980-1981; Chairman, Family Law Section, 1980-1981; Chairman, Criminal Law Section, 1983-1984, 1985-1986, 1988-1989; Member, Board of Directors, 1990, 1991, 1992 and 1993) and Illinois State (Member, Sections of: Juvenile Law Justice; Criminal Law) Bar Associations; Illinois Association of Criminal Defense Lawyers (Board of Directors, 2000—). ***REPORTED CASES:*** People v. Brownell, 96 Ill. 2d 167; 449 NE2d 1318; People v. Hepler, 132 Ill. App.3d. 705; 477 NE2d 768; Hough v. Webster, et al, 202 Ill. App.3d 674; 560 NE2d 5; People v. Freeman, 167 Ill. App.3d 740; 521 NE2d 1191.

GEISSLER LAW OFFICE, P.C.

6845 WEAVER ROAD, SUITE 100
ROCKFORD, ILLINOIS 61114
Telephone: 815-633-2500
Fax: 815-633-2516
Email: geissler@geisslerlaw.com

Business Law and Litigation including corporate, Limited Liability Companies (LLC's), Partnerships, Mergers, Acquisitions, Dissolutions, Contracts, Business Formation, Employment Agreement, Real Estate Law including, Contracts, Leases, Like-Kind Exchanges, Estate Planning including Gift and Estate Tax Advisement, Simple and Complex Trusts, Charitable Gift Planning, Business Succession Planning, Probate and Trust Administration.

BURKHARD GEISSLER, admitted to bar, 1969, Illinois. *Education:* University of Illinois (B.A., 1966); University of Iowa (J.D., 1969); DePaul University (LL.M., Taxation, 1990). ***LANGUAGES:*** German. ***PRACTICE AREAS:*** Business Law (30%); Wills (40%); Taxation (10%); Corporate Law (20%). ***Email:*** geissler@geisslerlaw.com

JOHN GILBERT

202 WEST STATE STREET
ROCKFORD, ILLINOIS 61101
Telephone: 815-877-2500
Fax: 815-877-2300
Email: attygilb1@aol.com
URL: http://www.jgilbertlawfirm.com

Criminal Law, DUI/DWI, Drug Crimes, Parole and Probation, Juvenile Law, Traffic Violations, Bankruptcy, Real Estate, Criminal Leasing, Residential, Family Law, Child Custody, Child Support, Divorce, Visitation Rights, Domestic Violence, Adoption, Wills and Probate, Trusts and Estates, Estate Planning, Business Law, Business Planning, Contracts, Business Litigation, Business Enterprises.

(This Listing Continued)

JOHN GILBERT, born Rockford, Illinois; admitted to bar, 1995, Illinois. *Education:* Western Illinois University (B.A., 1986); Thomas M. Cooley Law School (J.D., 1995). ***PRACTICE AREAS:*** Real Estate; Corporate; Business; Bankruptcy; Criminal.

GUYER & ENICHEN, P.C.

Established in 1928

2601 REID FARM ROAD, SUITE B
ROCKFORD, ILLINOIS 61114
Telephone: 815-636-9600
Fax: 815-636-9666
URL: http://www.guyerlaw.com
Email: guyer@guyerlaw.com
URL: http://www.guyerlawfirm.com

Real Estate Law and Litigation including Land Use and Zoning, Real Estate Valuation, Commercial and Residential Real Estate, Property Assessment Challenge, Land Development, Municipal Law, Estate Planning, Wealth Preservation, Charitable Giving, Business Succession Planning, Trusts, Estate, Taxation, Probate, Probate Litigation, Business, Corporate, Environmental Law, Commercial Litigation, Creditors Rights, Bankruptcy, Mechanics Liens, Private and Agency Adoptions.

FIRM PROFILE: Guyer & Enichen, P.C. was founded by Stanley H. Guyer in 1928. The present lawyers have a combined experience of over 100 years practicing law in the area. Serving clients throughout Winnebago, Ogle, Boone, Stephenson, Lake, McHenry, Jo Daviess, Lee (Illinois) and Rock, Walworth, Green, Dane and Milwaukee (Wisconsin) counties. The firm has a general practice with a focus on Estate Planning, Land Use Development, and Real Estate Law.

STANLEY H. GUYER (1903-1986)

EDWARD J. ENICHEN, born Dixon, Illinois, October 14, 1929; admitted to bar, 1954, Illinois; 1999, Wisconsin. *Education:* Coe College (B.A., 1951); University of Illinois (J.D., 1954). Phi Delta Phi. *Member:* Winnebago County (President, 1985-1986), Illinois State and American Bar Associations; State Bar of Wisconsin; National Network of Estate Planning Attorneys (Founding Member). ***PRACTICE AREAS:*** Estate Planning Law; Wealth Preservation. ***Email:*** enichen@guyerlaw.com

G. MICHAEL SCHEURICH, born Chicago, Illinois, October 30, 1947; admitted to bar, 1972, Illinois; 1973, Wisconsin. *Education:* St. Mary's University of Minnesota; Loyola University (A.B., 1969); Northwestern University (J.D., cum laude, 1972). Member: Editorial Board, Journal of Criminal Law, Criminology and Police Science, 1970-1972. *Member:* Winnebago County and Illinois State Bar Associations; State Bar of Wisconsin (Staff Assistant, 1972-1974); National Network of Estate Planning Attorneys. ***PRACTICE AREAS:*** Municipal Law; Real Estate; Taxation Law; Probate; Estate Planning Law. ***Email:*** scheurich@guyerlaw.com

JAMES E. TUNEBERG, born Rockford, Illinois, June 29, 1958; admitted to bar, 1984, Illinois. *Education:* Rock Valley College (A.A., 1978); Rockford College (B.S., 1981); Drake University (J.D., 1984). Phi Alpha Delta. Former Elected Member, Winnebago County Board. *Member:* Winnebago County, Illinois State and American Bar Associations; Northern Illinois Estate Planning Council. ***PRACTICE AREAS:*** Zoning and Land Development; Property Assessment; Valuation Litigation; Real Estate; Municipal Law; Commercial Litigation; Personal Injury Litigation. ***Email:*** jet@guyerlaw.com

EDWARD M. MAHER, born Monroe, Wisconsin, February 11, 1949; admitted to bar, 1975, Illinois; 1991, Wisconsin. *Education:* University of Wisconsin-Madison (B.A., 1972); Loyola University, Chicago (J.D., 1975). Member: Annexed Mediation Panel, 17th Judicial Circuit Court; Panel of Arbitrators, American Arbitration Association. *Member:* Winnebago County, Illinois State and American (Member, Sections on: Litigation; Tort and Insurance Practice) Bar Associations; State Bar of Wisconsin. ***PRACTICE AREAS:*** Civil Litigation; Appeals; Environmental Law. ***Email:*** emaher@guyerlaw.com

SHAWN C. FULBRIGHT, born Niles, Michigan, January 5, 1970; admitted to bar, 1996, Illinois. *Education:* Michigan State University (B.S., 1992); Drake University (J.D., 1996). *Member:* Winnebago County, Illinois State and American Bar Associations. ***PRACTICE AREAS:*** Corporate; Estate Planning; Civil Litigation; Commercial Litigation. ***Email:*** scf@guyerlaw.com

---

MELISSA S. OULAVONG, born Nam Keung Mai, Laos, Ocober 22, 1978; admitted to bar, 2003, Illinois and U.S. District Court, Northern District of Illinois. *Education:* Northwestern University (B.A., English, with honors, 2000); University of California at Los Angeles School of Law (J.D., 2003). *Member:* Winnebago County, Illinois State and American Bar Associations; National Asian Pacific Bar Association. ***LANGUAGES:*** Lao and Spanish. ***PRACTICE AREAS:*** Civil Litigation; Adoption; Real Estate. ***Email:*** moulavong@guyerlaw.com

THOMAS R. JAKEWAY, born Rockford, July 20, 1978; admitted to bar, 2004, Illinois. *Education:* Northern Illinois University (B.S., 2000; J.D., magna cum laude, 2004). *Member:* Winnebago County, Illinois State and American Bar Associations; Commercial Law League of America. ***PRACTICE AREAS:*** Commercial Litigation; Civil Litigation. ***Email:*** jakeway@guyerlaw.com

TIMOTHY A. MULDOWNEY, born Rockford, Illinois, August 10, 1955; admitted to bar, 1997, Illinois, U.S. District Court, Northern District of Illinois; 1999, Kansas, U.S. District Court, Northern District of Kansas. *Education:* University of Wisconsin (B.S., 1977); University of Missouri, Kansas City (J.D., 1997); Baker University, Kansas (M.S., Management). ***PRACTICE AREAS:*** Personal Injury; Insurance Defense; Medical Malpractice. ***Email:*** muldowney@guyerlaw.com

REFERENCE: Alpine Bank Illinois.

GEORGE P. HAMPILOS

308 WEST STATE STREET
SUITE 210
ROCKFORD, ILLINOIS 61101
Telephone: 815-962-0044
Fax: 815-962-6250
URL: http://www.lawyers.com/sm&h
Email: GEORGEHAMP@AOL.COM
URL: http://www.smhlawoffice.com

Commercial Collections and Creditors Rights.

GEORGE P. HAMPILOS, born Chicago, Illinois, July 12, 1967; admitted to bar, 1992, Illinois and U.S. District Court, Northern District of Illinois. *Education:* Southern Illinois University (B.A., 1989); Syracuse University Maxwell School of Citizenship and Public Affairs (M.P.A., 1992); Syracuse University College of Law (J.D., cum laude, 1992). Extern, U.S. Bankruptcy Court, Northern District of New York, 1991-1992. (Also Member, Schirger, Monteleone & Hampilos, P.C.). ***LANGUAGES:*** Greek. ***PRACTICE AREAS:*** Commercial Collections; Creditors Rights Law; Business Law; Corporate Law; Contracts; Bankruptcy; Family Law; Divorce; Personal Injury; Automobile Accidents and Injuries; Child Custody; Child Support; Medical Malpractice.

HEYL, ROYSTER, VOELKER & ALLEN

PROFESSIONAL CORPORATION
SECOND FLOOR, NATIONAL CITY BANK BUILDING
120 WEST STATE STREET
P.O. BOX 1288
ROCKFORD, ILLINOIS 61105-1288
Telephone: 815-963-4454
Telecopier: 815-963-0399
Email: firm@hrva.com
URL: http://www.hrva.com

Peoria, Illinois Office: Suite 600, Chase Building, 124 S.W. Adams, 61602. Telephone: 309-676-0400. Telecopier: 309-676-3374.

Springfield, Illinois Office: Suite 575, National City Center, P.O. Box 1687, 62705. Telephone: 217-522-8822. Telecopier: 217-523-3902.

Urbana, Illinois Office: Suite 300, 102 East Main Street, P.O. Box 129, 61803-0129. Telephone: 217-344-0060. Telecopier: 217-344-9295.

Edwardsville, Illinois Office: Suite 100, Mark Twain Plaza II, 103 West Vandalia Street, P.O. Box 467, 62025. Telephone: 618-656-4646. Telecopier: 618-656-7940.

General Civil Trial and Appellate Practice in all Courts, Insurance Defense, Workers' Compensation Defense, Professional Liability Defense, Truck Accidents, Construction Law, Railroad Accidents and Injuries, Insurance Coverage, Self Insured Defense, Products Liability Defense, Civil Rights, Asbestos Defense, Class Action Defense, Corporate Law, Health Care, Banking, Government, Employment, Environmental, Probate, Elder Law, Agribusiness, Immigration, Religious Institutions, Nonprofit and Charitable Organizations, College and University Law, and Real Estate.

PARTNERS

DOUGLAS J. POMATTO, born April 22, 1952; admitted to bar, 1977, Illinois. *Education:* Bradley University, Rhodes Scholar Candidate (B.S., 1974); Cumberland School of Law of Samford University (J.D., 1977). Certified Mediator, Winnebago County Court-Annexed Mediation Program. *Member:* Illinois Association of Defense Trial Counsel (President, 1998-1999); DRI (State Representative, Illinois, 1999-2000); Society of Trial Lawyers (Illinois). ***PRACTICE AREAS:*** Medical Malpractice Defense; Professional Liability Defense; Products Liability Defense; Insurance Defense. **Email:** dpomatto@hrva.com

KEVIN J. LUTHER, born January 23, 1959; admitted to bar, 1984, Illinois; 1994, Wisconsin. *Education:* Blackburn College (B.A., summa cum laude, 1981); Washington University at St. Louis (J.D., 1984). *Member:* Illinois Association of Defense Trial Counsel (Board of Directors, 2002-). ***PRACTICE AREAS:*** Workers Compensation Defense; Civil Rights; Labor and Employment; Professional Liability Defense. **Email:** kluther@hrva.com

MARK J. McCLENATHAN, born September 3, 1962; admitted to bar, 1987, Illinois. *Education:* University of Wisconsin-Eau Claire (B.A., magna cum laude, 1984); Hamline University (J.D., 1987). *Member:* Illinois Association of Defense Trial Counsel; DRI; Illinois Municipal League. ***PRACTICE AREAS:*** Construction Law; Professional Liability Defense; Products Liability Defense; Municipal Law; Commercial Law. **Email:** mmcclenathan@hrva.com

OF COUNSEL

BRENT A. SWANSON, born August 11, 1952; admitted to bar, 1977, Illinois; 1998, Wisconsin. *Education:* Valparaiso University (B.A., 1974; J.D., 1977). ***PRACTICE AREAS:*** Medical Malpractice Defense; Civil Litigation Defense; ERISA; Life and Health Insurance Claims. **Email:** bswanson@hrva.com

SCOTT G. SALEMI, born September 26, 1966; admitted to bar, 1992, Illinois; 1998, North Carolina. *Education:* DePauw University (B.A., 1989); Northern Illinois University (J.D., 1992). *Member:* Illinois Association of Defense Trial Counsel. ***PRACTICE AREAS:*** Medical Malpractice Defense; Insurance Defense; White Collar Fraud Defense. **Email:** ssalemi@hrva.com

KATHLEEN M. STOCKWELL, born May 29, 1968; admitted to bar, 1993, Illinois. *Education:* University of Illinois (B.A., 1990; J.D., 1993). *Member:* Illinois Association of Defense Trial Counsel. ***PRACTICE AREAS:*** Medical Malpractice Defense. **Email:** kstockwell@hrva.com

(This Listing Continued)

CHARLES E. TIMMERWILKE, born June 4, 1966; admitted to bar, 1991, Illinois. *Education:* Carthage College (B.A., summa cum laude, 1988); Valparaiso University (J.D., magna cum laude, 1991). ***PRACTICE AREAS:*** Civil Litigation; Professional Liability; Motor Carrier Defense. **Email:** ctimmerwilke@hrva.com

ASSOCIATES

Jill I. Rogers-Manning	***Andrew J. Roth***
Brad A. Antonacci	***Lori E. McGirk***
Thomas P. Crowley	***Jana L. Brady***
Michael J. Denning	***Lynsey A. Crowell***

Our lawyers are members of the American, state and local bar associations and, in many cases, are members of the local American Inn of Court chapters; where applicable, leadership positions in these organizations are listed.

(For Other Biographical Information, see Professional Biographies at Peoria, Edwardsville, Springfield and Urbana)

HINSHAW & CULBERTSON LLP

Hinshaw & Culbertson LLP is an Illinois registered limited liability partnership that has elected to be governed by the Illinois Uniform Partnership Act (1997)

Established in 1934
100 PARK AVENUE
P.O. BOX 1389
ROCKFORD, ILLINOIS 61105-1389
Telephone: 815-490-4900
Facsimile: 815-490-4901
Telex: 880248
Email: kfox@hinshawlaw.com
URL: http://www.hinshawlaw.com

Other Office Locations: Chicago, Illinois; Appleton, Wisconsin; Belleville, Illinois; Boston, Massachusetts; Champaign, Illinois; Crystal Lake, Illinois; Edwardsville, Illinois; Fort Lauderdale, Florida; Jacksonville, Florida; Joliet, Illinois; Lisle, Illinois; Los Angeles, California; Miami, Florida; Milwaukee, Wisconsin; Minneapolis, Minnesota; New York, New York; Peoria, Illinois; Phoenix, Arizona; Portland, Oregon; Providence, Rhode Island; St. Louis, Missouri; San Francisco, California; Schererville, Indiana; Springfield, Illinois; Tampa, Florida; Waukegan, Illinois.

Appellate, Banking & Financing, Bankruptcy & Creditors' Rights, Class Action Litigation, Civil Rights Defense, Commercial Litigation, Corporate, Construction Law, Director & Officer Liability, Employee Benefits, Environmental, Fidelity & Surety, General Liability Litigation, Government, Health Care, Insurance Coverage, Insurance and Reinsurance, Labor & Employment, Legal Malpractice, Medical Malpractice, Mergers & Acquisitions, Municipal Liability, Personal Injury Defense, Public Law, Products Liability Litigation, Professional Liability, Regulatory, Real Estate, School Law, Securities, Taxation, Transportation, White Collar Crime and Workers' Compensation Defense.

FIRM PROFILE: Hinshaw & Culbertson LLP is a national AMLaw 200 firm with 425 lawyers in 27 offices coast-to-coast. The firm offers a full-service practice, with an emphasis in commercial and defense litigation, corporate, environmental, employment and construction law, as well as the representation of professionals in their liability and risk management matters.

Hinshaw provides services to a range of clients in financial services, construction, health care, not-for-profit, insurance, legal, manufacturing, real estate, transportation and other industries. Firm clients also include government agencies, municipalities and schools.

Hinshaw was founded in 1934. The firm is headquartered in Chicago, and maintains offices in 12 states; Arizona, California, Florida, Illinois, Indiana, Massachusetts, Minnesota, Missouri, New York, Oregon, Rhode Island and Wisconsin.

PARTNERS

JAMES M. ALLEN, born Rockford, Illinois, December 8, 1972; admitted to bar, 1999, Illinois and U.S. District Court, Northern District of Illinois. *Education:* Illinois State University (B.S., 1995); The John Marshall Law School (J.D., cum laude, 1999). *Member:* Winnebago County and American Bar Associations. ***PRACTICE AREAS:*** Commercial Litigation; Construction Litigation; Bankruptcy and Creditors' Rights; Real Estate. **Email:** jallen@hinshawlaw.com

JERROD L. BARENBAUM, born Chicago, Illinois, July 22, 1969; admitted to bar, 1994, Illinois and U.S. District Court, Northern District of Illinois. *Education:* Lake Forest College (B.A., 1991); DePaul University (J.D., 1994). *Member:* Winnebago County Bar Association; Illinois Association of Defense Trial Counsel; Defense Research Institute. ***PRACTICE AREAS:*** Medical Malpractice; Litigation; Torts; Premises Liability. **Email:** jbarenbaum@hinshawlaw.com

THOMAS H. BOSWELL, born Harrisburg, Illinois, July 24, 1950; admitted to bar, 1980, Illinois and U.S. District Court, Southern District of Illinois; 1986, U.S. Court of Appeals, Seventh Circuit; 1988, U.S. District Court, Northern (Western Division) and Central Districts of Illinois. *Education:* United States Military Academy at West Point (B.S., 1972); Southern Illinois University (J.D., 1980). *Member:* Winnebago County and Illinois State Bar Associations; Defense Research Institute. [Capt., U.S. Army, 1972-1977]. ***PRACTICE AREAS:*** Commercial Litigation; General Liability Litigation; Insurance Coverage; Bad Faith; Professional Liability Litigation. **Email:** tboswell@hinshawlaw.com

PAMELA S. FOX, born Rockford, Illinois, January 9, 1951; admitted to bar, 1977, Illinois. *Education:* University of Colorado (B.A., 1974; J.D., 1977). Chairman: Governance Committee, Rockford Health System Board of Trustees; Council of 100 (Economic Development) Board of Directors. Member, Executive Committee, University of Illinois College of Medicine at Rockford Advisory Council. *Member:* Winnebago County, Illinois State and American Bar Associations. ***PRACTICE AREAS:*** Banking; Finance; Employment Law; Estate Planning; Estate Administration. **Email:** pfox@hinshawlaw.com

(This Listing Continued)

HINSHAW & CULBERTSON LLP, Rockford—Continued

VICTORIA R. GLIDDEN, born Fairmont, Minnesota, July 17, 1957; admitted to bar, 1988, Indiana and U.S. District Court, Northern and Southern Districts of Indiana; 1989, Illinois and U.S. District Court, Northern District of Illinois; 1998, U.S. District Court, Central and Southern Districts of Illinois and U.S. District Court, Eastern and Western Districts of Wisconsin. *Education:* Indiana University (B.A., 1979; J.D., cum laude, 1988). Phi Beta Kappa. Advisory Board Member, Leading Lawyers Network. *Member:* Winnebago County Bar Association. ***PRACTICE AREAS:*** Health Care Reimbursement; Debtor-Creditor Rights; Bankruptcy Law. ***Email:*** vglidden@hinshawlaw.com

MARY LINN GREEN, born Rockford, Illinois, February 24, 1952; admitted to bar, 1992, Illinois and U.S. District Court, Northern District of Illinois. *Education:* College of St. Teresa (B.S., Nursing, 1974); Loyola University (M.S., Nursing, 1978); Northern Illinois University (J.D., cum laude, 1992). Sigma Theta Tau. Registered Professional Nurse, Illinois, 1974. Chapter Author, "Legal and Ethical Issues," Critical Care Nursing, Philadelphia, W.B. Saunders Co., 1999; "The Nurse in the Community," Nurses & The Law, Philadelphia, W.B. Saunders Co., 2001. *Member:* Winnebago County and Illinois State Bar Associations; American Association of Nurse Attorneys. ***PRACTICE AREAS:*** Medical Malpractice; Health Law.

CHARLES F. HELSTEN, born Rockford, Illinois, December 30, 1950; admitted to bar, 1979, Iowa; 1980, U.S. District Court, Northern and Southern Districts of Iowa and U.S. Court of Appeals, Eighth Circuit; 1984, Illinois and U.S. District Court, Northern District of Illinois; 1985, U.S. Tax Court. *Education:* Eureka College (B.A., magna cum laude, 1974); Drake University (J.D., with distinction, 1979). Phi Alpha Delta. *Member:* Winnebago County (Member, Environmental Law Committee), Illinois State (Member, Section on Environmental Control Laws) and Iowa State Bar Associations; Iowa Trial Lawyers Association; Defense Research Institute (Member, Environmental Law Committee); Illinois Association of Defense Trial Counsel (Member, Environmental Law Group); Iowa Defense Counsel. ***PRACTICE AREAS:*** Environmental Law; Environmental Litigation; Audits, Due Diligence and Regulatory Compliance; Real Estate, Brownfields and Site Remediation. ***Email:*** chelsten@hinshawlaw.com

MATTHEW M. HEVRIN, born 1973; admitted to bar, 1998, Illinois and U.S. District Court, Northern District of Illinois. *Education:* University of Illinois (B.S., 1995); Northern Illinois University (J.D., cum laude, 1998). *Member:* Winnebago County Bar Association. ***PRACTICE AREAS:*** Commercial Litigation; Employment Law; Real Estate; Banking. ***Email:*** mhevrin@hinshawlaw.com

LORI L. HOADLEY, born Chicago, Illinois, August 22, 1962; admitted to bar, 1999, Illinois, U.S. District Court, Northern and Central Districts of Illinois; 2002, U.S. Court of Appeals, Seventh Circuit. *Education:* Northern Illinois University (B.A., 1984; M.A., 1992; J.D., cum laude, 1999). Member, Omicron Delta Kappa National Leadership Honor Society. Member and Recipient, Best Brief Award, Chicago Bar Association Moot Court Team. Recipient, Outstanding Woman Leadership Award. Member, NIU Law Review. *Member:* Winnebago County, Illinois State and American Bar Associations. ***PRACTICE AREAS:*** Employment Law; Employment Litigation; Labor Union Matters; School Law. ***Email:*** lhoadley@hinshawlaw.com

GARY R. KARDELL, born Rockford, Illinois, September 12, 1947; admitted to bar, 1973, Illinois; 1976, U.S. District Court, Northern District of Illinois. *Education:* Southern Illinois University; University of Illinois (B.S., 1971; J.D., 1973). *Member:* Winnebago County and Illinois State Bar Associations. ***PRACTICE AREAS:*** Insurance Litigation; Personal Injury. ***Email:*** gkardell@hinshawlaw.com

JAMES W. KEELING, born Iowa City, Iowa, August 26, 1948; admitted to bar, 1974, Illinois and U.S. District Court, Northern District of Illinois; 1977, U.S. Court of Appeals, Seventh Circuit. *Education:* Lawrence University (B.A., 1970); University of Colorado (J.D., with honors, 1974). Order of the Coif. Managing Editor, University of Colorado Law Review, 1973-1974. *Member:* Winnebago County, Illinois State and American Bar Associations; International Association of Financial Planners. ***PRACTICE AREAS:*** Business Law; Real Estate; Estate and Financial Planning. ***Email:*** jkeeling@hinshawlaw.com

PENELOPE M. LECHTENBERG, born Des Plaines, Illinois; admitted to bar, 1993, Illinois and U.S. District Court, Northern and Central Districts of Illinois. *Education:* Duke University (A.B., 1990); Chicago-Kent College of Law (J.D., 1993). *Member:* Winnebago County and Illinois State Bar Associations; American Immigration Lawyers Association. ***PRACTICE AREAS:*** Labor and Employment; Employment Litigation; Employment Law; Labor Relations; Collective Bargaining; Immigration Law. ***Email:*** plechtenberg@hinshawlaw.com

THOMAS J. LESTER, born Evergreen Park, Illinois, January 27, 1953; admitted to bar, 1985, Illinois and U.S. District Court, Northern District of Illinois, including Trial Bar. *Education:* University of Dayton (B.S., 1975); Keller Graduate School of Management (M.B.A., 1980); John Marshall Law School (J.D., with distinction, 1985). Member, Order of John Marshall. Justice, Moot Court Executive Board, 1984. Law Clerk, Chief Judge Robert L. Eisen, U.S. Bankruptcy Court, Northern District of Illinois, 1985-1987. *Member:* Winnebago County, Illinois State and American Bar Associations. ***PRACTICE AREAS:*** Commercial Litigation; Debtor/Creditor; Bankruptcy; Creditors Rights; School Law. ***Email:*** tlester@hinshawlaw.com

FRANK P. MAGGIO, born Rockford, Illinois, April 13, 1937; admitted to bar, 1963, Illinois and Indiana. *Education:* Regis College (A.B., 1960); University of Notre Dame (J.D., 1963). Associate Editor, Notre Dame Law Review, 1962-1963. *Member:* Winnebago County, Illinois State and American Bar Associations. ***PRACTICE AREAS:*** Corporate; Business Transactions; Banking; Finance; Estate Planning. ***Email:*** fmaggio@hinshawlaw.com

STEPHEN T. MOORE, born Murphysboro, Illinois, June 30, 1949; admitted to bar, 1974, Iowa; 1975, Illinois; 1976, U.S. District Court, Northern District of Illinois. *Education:* Western Illinois University (B.S., 1971); Drake University (J.D., with honors, 1973). Law Clerk to Chief Justice C. Edwin Moore, Iowa Supreme Court, 1974-1975. Assistant Attorney General, Iowa, 1974-1975. *Member:* Winnebago County Bar Association (Chair, Business Law Section, 1990-1991); American Health Lawyers Association; Illinois Association of Healthcare Attorneys (Director, 1990-1993; Secretary, 1993). (Co-Chair, Health Care Specialty Practice Group). ***PRACTICE AREAS:*** Corporate Healthcare; Compliance Counseling; Regulatory Law; Health Planning; Joint Ventures; Banking and Financing; Mergers and Acquisitions; Real Estate. ***Email:*** smoore@hinshawlaw.com

MARCIA L. MUELLER, born St. Louis, Missouri, October 20, 1953; admitted to bar, 1978, Illinois; 1979, U.S. District Court, Northern District of Illinois. *Education:* University of Missouri (B.A., 1975); John Marshall Law School (J.D., 1978). Phi Delta Phi; Order of John Marshall; The Gavel Society. *Member:* Winnebago County Bar Association; Illinois State Bar Association; American Bar Association. ***PRACTICE AREAS:*** Estate Planning; Financial Planning; Qualified Employee Benefit Plans; Trusts and Estates; Employee Benefits; Taxation; Trusts and Estates Taxation; Corporate Income Tax; Corporate Organization. ***Email:*** mmueller@hinshawlaw.com

JAMES R. PIRAGES, born Rockford, Illinois, October 12, 1955; admitted to bar, 1980, Illinois. *Education:* Rockford College (B.A., magna cum laude, 1977); Southern Illinois University (J.D., 1980). Phi Beta Kappa. Notes and Comments Editor, Southern Illinois University Law Journal, 1979-1980. *Member:* Winnebago County and Illinois State (Member, Labor Law Section) Bar Associations. ***PRACTICE AREAS:*** Labor Relations (Management) Law; Employment Law. ***Email:*** jpirages@hinshawlaw.com

RICHARD S. PORTER, born Springfield, Illinois, September 10, 1966; admitted to bar, 1992, Illinois and U.S. District Court, Northern District of Illinois. *Education:* Illinois State University (B.S., 1988); Southern Illinois University (J.D., cum laude, 1992). Member, National Honor Society of the Financial Management Association. Managing Editor, Southern Illinois University Law Journal, 1992. Team Captain, Environmental Law Moot Court Team, 1992. Author: "Extraterritorial Application of Title VII," 15 So. Ill. U.L.J. 645 (1991); "Does the Responsible Corporate Officer Doctrine Apply to the Resource Conservation and Recovery Act?" Vol. 16 So. Ill. U.L.J. (1992). *Member:* Winnebago County Bar Association. ***PRACTICE AREAS:*** Environmental Law; Environmental Litigation; Regulatory; Commercial Litigation; Appellate Law; Administrative Law; Land Use Law and Litigation. ***Email:*** rporter@hinshawlaw.com

RICHARD M. SCHILLING, born Green Bay, Wisconsin, June 15, 1937; admitted to bar, 1962, Illinois; 1963, U.S. District Court, Northern District of Illinois. *Education:* University of Wisconsin-Madison (B.S., 1959); Harvard University (LL.B., 1962). Phi Beta Kappa; Phi Kappa Phi. *Member:* Winnebago County Bar Association; Machinery and Allied Products Institute. ***PRACTICE AREAS:*** Business Communications; Corporate Governance; Corporate Compliance Programs; Corporate Ethics; Securities. ***Email:*** rschilling@hinshawlaw.com

D. RENEÉ SCHROEDER, born Kankakee, Illinois, March 7, 1960; admitted to bar, 1985, Illinois; 1986, U.S. District Court, Northern District of Illinois. *Education:* Illinois State University (B.S., summa cum laude, 1982); Northern Illinois University College of Law (J.D., magna cum laude, 1985). Alpha Phi Sigma; Delta Theta Phi. Bone Scholar. Member, Red Tassel Mortar Board. Recipient, Moot Court Best Brief Award, Oral Finalist. Member, Editorial Board Staff, Northern Illinois University Law Review, 1984-1985. Member, Board of Directors: Rosecrance Foundation; March of Dimes. *Member:* Winnebago County, Illinois State and American Bar Associations; Illinois Trial Lawyers Association; Association of Trial Lawyers of America. ***PRACTICE AREAS:*** Corporate Law; Business Law; Municipal Law; Mergers and Acquisitions; Commercial Litigation; Workers Compensation Defense. ***Email:*** dschroeder@hinshawlaw.com

JEFFRY S. SPEARS, born Belvidere, Illinois, November 29, 1956; admitted to bar, 1981, Illinois and U.S. District Court, Northern District of Illinois; 1982, U.S. Court of Appeals, Seventh Circuit; 1990, U.S. District Court, Eastern District of Wisconsin. *Education:* Western Illinois University (B.A., 1978); University of Illinois (J.D., magna cum laude, 1981). Phi Delta Phi; Order of the Coif. Editor, University of Illinois Law Review, 1980-1981. Recipient, Rickert Award. *Member:* Winnebago County Bar Association (Federal Section: Chairman, 1987-1988; Vice Chairman, 1986-1987; Judicial Liaison Committee, 1988-1989); Defense Research Institute; National Health Lawyers Association/American Academy of Hospital Attorneys; Illinois Association of Healthcare Attorneys; Illinois Association of Defense Trial Counsel. ***PRACTICE AREAS:*** Medical Defense; Hospital Defense; Insurance Defense; Health Care Law; General Litigation. ***Email:*** jspears@hinshawlaw.com

CHARLES F. THOMAS, born Rockford, Illinois, June 26, 1934; admitted to bar, 1960, Illinois and U.S. District Court, Northern District of Illinois; 1970, U.S. Supreme Court; 1979, U.S. Court of Appeals, Seventh Circuit; 1990, Wisconsin. *Education:* Georgetown University (B.S., 1957; J.D., 1960). *Member:* Winnebago County and Illinois State Bar Associations; Wisconsin State Bar; National Association of Hospital Attorneys; Society of Attorneys of the American Hospital Association; Illinois State Bankers Association; National Catholic Conference of Diocesan Attorneys. ***PRACTICE AREAS:*** Corporate Law; Business Law; Mergers and Acquisitions; Corporate Health Care; Banking; Finance. ***Email:*** cthomas@hinshawlaw.com

ASSOCIATES

MAUREEN FLANAGAN, born Chicago, Illinois, January 12, 1945; admitted to bar, 1999, Oregon; 2004, Illinois. *Education:* Concordia College (B.S., Management and Communication, 1992); Lewis and Clark College (J.D., 1998). *Member:* Winnebago County, Illinois State and American Bar Associations. ***PRACTICE AREAS:*** Commercial Real Estate; Commercial Conveyancing; Commercial Real Estate Acquisitions; Commercial Real Estate Contracts; Commercial Loans. ***Email:*** mflanagan@hinshawlaw.com

SHERRY L. HARLAN, born Green Bay, Wisconsin, September 2, 1961; admitted to bar, 1987, Illinois, Wisconsin, U.S. District Court, Northern District of Illinois and U.S. District Court, Western District of Wisconsin. *Education:* Illinois Wesleyan University (B.A., 1983); University of Wisconsin-Madison (J.D., 1987). *Member:* Winnebago County Bar Association; State Bar of Wisconsin. ***PRACTICE AREAS:*** Commercial Real Estate; Contracts; Corporate Law; Leases and Leasing. **Email:** sharlan@hinshawlaw.com

KENYA A. JENKINS, born May 16, 1978; admitted to bar, 2003, Illinois. *Education:* Valparaiso University (B.A., 2000); Northern Illinois University School of Law (J.D., 2003). Author: "Shaming Penalties and the Sexual Offender: A Dangerous Combination," Northern Illinois University Law Review, 2002. Past President, Black Law Student Asso-

(This Listing Continued)

ciation; Past Treasurer, Latino Law Students Association. Member, ACLU. ***PRACTICE AREAS:*** Medical Malpractice; Professional Liability; Professional Liability Litigation. ***Email:*** kjenkins@hinshawlaw.com

ERIK W. LINDBERG, born Rockford, Illinois, February 14, 1974; admitted to bar, 2001, Illinois and U.S. District Court, Northern District of Illinois. *Education:* Miami University (B.S., Business Administration, 1997); St. Louis University School of Law (J.D., 2000). *Member:* Chicago (Co-Chair, Corporate Practice Committee, Young Lawyers Section, 2002-2004) and Winnebago County Bar Associations. ***PRACTICE AREAS:*** Corporate and Business Law; Real Estate; Commercial Litigation; Mergers and Acquisitions; Corporate Organization and Governance. ***Email:*** elindberg@hinshawlaw.com

TIMOTHY J. LEAKE, born Decorah, Iowa, May 25, 1977; admitted to bar, 2002, Illinois and U.S District Court, Northern District of Illinois; 2003, U.S. Court of Appeals, Seventh Circuit. *Education:* Luther College (B.A., cum laude, 1999); John Marshall Law School (J.D., cum laude, 2002). Member, John Marshall Law Review, 2000-2001. Staff Editor, Review of Intellectual Property Law, 2001-2002. Externship, Securities and Exchange Commission, Spring 2001; the Honorable George W. Lindberg, Northern District of Illinois, Fall 2001. *Member:* Winnebago County, Illinois State and American Bar Associations. ***PRACTICE AREAS:*** Corporate Law; Business Law; Commercial Litigation; Corporate Organization; Corporate Governance; Estate Planning; Financial Planning. ***Email:*** tleake@hinshawlaw.com

CAROL A. LOCKWOOD, born Belvidere, Illinois, December 11, 1962; admitted to bar, 2001, Illinois. *Education:* Northwestern University (B.A., 1985); University of Sussex, England (M.A., 1987; Ph.D., 1991); University of Illinois (J.D., cum laude, 2001). Member, Dean's List. Rickert Award for Excellence in Legal Writing. *Member:* Illinois State and American Bar Associations. ***PRACTICE AREAS:*** Business Law; Real Estate. ***Email:*** clockwood@hinshawlaw.com

LISA R. MUNCH, admitted to bar, 1999, Illinois and U.S. District Court, Northern District of Illinois. *Education:* University of South Carolina (B.S., 1990); Northern Illinois University (J.D., cum laude, 1999). *Member:* Winnebago County (Treasurer 2003-2004) and Illinois State Bar Associations. [U.S. Army, 1984-1987]. ***PRACTICE AREAS:*** Professional Liability Litigation; Health Care Litigation. ***Email:*** lmunch@hinshawlaw.com

ALYSON R. RUMSHAS, born Hammond, Indiana, November 2, 1973; admitted to bar, 2005, Illinois. *Education:* University of Central Florida (B.A., magna cum laude, Legal Studies, 2000); DePaul University College of Law (J.D., 2004). Recipient, CALI Award, Illinois Civil Procedure. [Paralegal and Weather Observer, U.S. Air Force, 1992-1998]. ***PRACTICE AREAS:*** Labor and Employment; Employment Litigation; Labor Relations; Collective Bargaining; Occupational Safety and Health; Employee Benefits.

HOLMSTROM & KENNEDY, P.C.

Established in 1923
800 NORTH CHURCH STREET
P.O. BOX 589
ROCKFORD, ILLINOIS 61105
Telephone: 815-962-7071
Fax: 815-962-7181
Email: mail@holmstromlaw.com
URL: http://www.holmstromlaw.com

General Civil, Trial and Appellate Practice in State and Federal Courts, Complex Litigation, Administrative, Professional Malpractice Defense, Creditor's Rights and Bankruptcy, Health Care, Labor and Employment, Corporate and Business, Tax, Technology, Computer and Telecommunications, Real Estate, Estate Planning and Probate, Mediation and Arbitration.

FIRM PROFILE: For over 80 years Holmstrom & Kennedy has provided a full range of legal services throughout Northern Illinois. Clients range from major commercial, financial and health care institutions to closely held entrepreneurial enterprises and individuals. The firm is committed to strong, ethical advocacy. The firm has an active litigation practice in State and Federal courts and often serves as local counsel to national law firms in complex litigation.

JOHN HOLMSTROM, JR., born Rockford, Illinois, December 19, 1920; admitted to bar, 1948, Illinois. *Education:* University of Illinois (B.S., 1942; J.D., 1948). Recipient, Illinois State Bar Association Award of Merit, 1977. *Member:* Winnebago County (President, 1971-1972), Illinois State (Member, Board of Governors, 1975-1976) and American Bar Associations. Fellow, Illinois Bar Foundation. Laureate, Academy of Illinois Lawyers. ***PRACTICE AREAS:*** Estate Planning; Probate; General Corporate.

RICHARD D. GAINES, born Elgin, Illinois, July 15, 1944; admitted to bar, 1969, Illinois; 1973, U.S. District Court, Northern District of Illinois; 1981, U.S. Court of Appeals, Seventh Circuit; 1984, U.S. Supreme Court. *Education:* DePauw University (B.A., 1966); University of Illinois (J.D., 1969). Co-Author: "Court-Annexed Mediation," Alternative Dispute Resolution, Illinois Institute for Continuing Legal Education, 2001. Member, 1982-1988 and Member, Executive Committee, 1985-1988, Illinois Institute for Continuing Legal Education Board. Certified Mediator, 17th Judicial Circuit, Illinois and U.S. District Court, Northern District of Illinois. "Leading Lawyer," Illinois. *Member:* Winnebago County (President, 1986-1987), Illinois State (Chairman, Young Lawyers Section, 1979-1980; Member, Board of Governors, 1980-1982; Member, Assembly, 1980-1988, 1990-1994) and American (Delegate to Young Lawyers Assembly, 1975-1980) Bar Associations; Association of Defense Trial Attorneys. Fellow, American College of Trial Lawyers. ***PRACTICE AREAS:*** General Civil Litigation; Medical Malpractice Defense; Mediation; Arbitration. ***Email:*** rgaines@holmstromlaw.com

PHILIP R. FRANKFORT, born Franklin, Virginia, April 16, 1948; admitted to bar, 1974, Illinois; 1978, Virginia; 1994, Arizona. *Education:* University of Virginia and University of Arizona (B.S., 1970); University of Arizona (J.D., 1974). Member, Order of the Coif. Author: Casenote, 14 Arizona Law Review 543, 1972. *Member:* Winnebago County, Illinois State (Member of Health Care Section Council, 1986-1990) and American Bar Associations; Virginia State Bar; State Bar of Arizona; American Health Lawyers Association; Illinois Association of Healthcare Attorneys. ***PRACTICE AREAS:*** Health Care Law; Estate Planning; General Corporate. ***Email:*** pfrankfort@holmstromlaw.com

(This Listing Continued)

DONALD L. MOORE, born Murphysboro, Illinois, January 9, 1948; admitted to bar, 1974, Colorado; 1977, U.S. District Court, Northern District of Illinois, U.S. Supreme Court and Illinois. *Education:* Western Illinois University (B.A., 1970); University of Illinois (J.D., 1973); DePaul University (Mediation Certificate Training and Advanced Certificate Training, 2000). Member, Association for Conflict Resolution, Chicago Area Chapter. *Member:* Winnebago County (Past President; Member, Sections on: Real Estate and Business Law; Past Chairman, Real Estate and Business Law Sections) and Illinois State Bar Associations. Past Fellow, Winnebago County Bar Foundation (Past President). [Capt., JAGC, U.S. Army, 1974-1977]. ***PRACTICE AREAS:*** Commercial Real Estate Law; Business Transactions; Mediation; Estate Planning; Estate Administration; Wills; Probate. ***Email:*** dmoore@holmstromlaw.com

BRADLEY T. KOCH, born Savanna, Illinois, September 16, 1951; admitted to bar, 1976, Minnesota; 1978, Illinois; 1979, U.S. District Court, Northern District of Illinois; 1981, U.S. Court of Appeals, Seventh Circuit; 1988, U.S. District Court, District of Minnesota and U.S. Court of Appeals, Eighth Circuit. *Education:* University of Iowa (B.A., 1973); Creighton University (J.D., cum laude, 1976). Student Articles Editor, Creighton Law Review, 1975-1976. Author: Casenote, 8 Creighton Law Review 555, 1974. Law Clerk to Justice John J. Todd, Minnesota Supreme Court, 1976-1977. *Member:* Winnebago County, Illinois State (Member, Editorial Board, 1982-1989 and Editor-in-Chief, 1987-1988, Illinois Bar Journal; Member, Section Council, Commercial, Banking and Bankruptcy Law, 1982-1983) and American Bar Associations. ***PRACTICE AREAS:*** Bankruptcy, Commercial and Secured Transactions; Commercial Litigation; Mediation. ***Email:*** bkoch@holmstromlaw.com

KIM M. CASEY, born Watertown, New York, June 1, 1957; admitted to bar, 1981, Illinois; 1982, U.S. Court of Appeals, Seventh Circuit and U.S. District Court, Northern District of Illinois, Trial Bar, 1991. *Education:* Illinois State University (B.S., with high honors, 1978); University of Illinois (J.D., 1981). Past Member, McHenry County Bar Association (Member, Board of Governors, 1983-1985). *Member:* Winnebago County (Director, 2004-2007; Past Chairman, Federal Section; Chairman, Real Estate Section, 2003-2004), Illinois State (Member, Standing Committee on Bar Publications, 2002-2004) and American (Member, Litigation Section) Bar Associations; American Health Lawyers Association. Fellow, Winnebago County Bar Foundation (Past Vice President). ***PRACTICE AREAS:*** Debtor/Creditor; Real Estate and Commercial Litigation. ***Email:*** kcasey@holmstromlaw.com

ROBERTA L. HOLZWARTH, born Toledo, Ohio, March 19, 1958; admitted to bar, 1983, Illinois; 1984, U.S. District Court, Northern District of Illinois; 1989, U.S. Court of Appeals, Seventh Circuit. *Education:* Stanford University (B.A., 1980); University of Illinois (J.D., cum laude, 1983). Certified Mediator: 17th Judicial Circuit, Illinois, 1996; U.S. District Court, Northern District of Illinois, 2003. Member, Board of Directors, U.S. Office of Compliance, 2000—. *Member:* Winnebago County (President, 1999-2000), Illinois State and American (Member, Labor and Employment Law Section) Bar Associations. ***PRACTICE AREAS:*** Labor and Employment Law (Management). ***Email:*** rholzwarth@holmstromlaw.com

MICHAEL J. SCHAPPERT, born Chicago, Illinois, December 22, 1955; admitted to bar, 1980, Illinois and Wisconsin. *Education:* University of Notre Dame (B.B.A., 1977); Marquette University (J.D., 1980). Phi Alpha Delta. *Member:* Winnebago County (Chairman, Estate Section, 1991-1992 and 2003-2004) and Illinois State Bar Associations; State Bar of Wisconsin; Northern Illinois Estate Planning Council (Director, 1995-1996). ***PRACTICE AREAS:*** Trusts and Estates; Wills; Probate; Business Law. ***Email:*** mschappert@holmstromlaw.com

MICHAEL JON SHALBRACK, born LaFayette, Indiana, August 12, 1959; admitted to bar, 1984, Illinois and U.S. District Court, Northern District of Illinois; 1988, U.S. Tax Court. *Education:* University of Wisconsin-Madison (B.B.A., 1981); DePaul University (J.D., 1984; LL.M., Taxation, 1990). *Member:* Winnebago County (Member, Sections on: Business (Chairman, 1995-1996; Real Estate; Estate and Trust; Treasurer, 1994-1995), Illinois State and American Bar Associations. Fellow, Winnebago County Bar Foundation (Past Secretary). ***PRACTICE AREAS:*** General Corporate; Business Transactions; Taxation; Estate Planning and Administration; Probate; Real Estate. ***Email:*** mshalbrack@holmstromlaw.com

EUGENE G. DOHERTY, born Fort Wayne, Indiana, May 18, 1961; admitted to bar, 1989, Illinois, U.S. District Court, Northern District of Illinois including Trial Bar and U.S. Court of Appeals, Seventh Circuit. *Education:* Northern Illinois University (B.S., 1983; J.D., summa cum laude, 1989). Member, Northern Illinois Law Review, 1988-1989. Author: "Priority of the Subrogation Interest in the Insured's Personal Injury Recovery," 80 Ill. Bar J. 224 (March 1992); "Section 2-1117: Several Liability's Effect on Settlement and Contribution," 79 Ill. Bar J. 122, (March 1991); "Equal Protection Under the Fifth and Fourteenth Amendment: Patterns of Congruence, Divergence, and Judicial Deference," 16 Ohio Northern Law Review 591, 1989. Law Clerk, Illinois Appellate Court Justice Philip G. Reinhard, 1990-1991. *Member:* Winnebago County and Illinois State Bar Associations; Appellate Lawyers Bar Association; Illinois Association of Defense Trial Counsel. ***PRACTICE AREAS:*** Civil Litigation; Medical Malpractice Defense; Civil Appeals. ***Email:*** edoherty@holmstromlaw.com

ALEXANDER J. MEZNY, born Chicago, Illinois, July 8, 1967; admitted to bar, 1992, Illinois; U.S. District Court, Northern District of Illinois including Trial Bar; 1995, U.S. Court of Appeals, Seventh Circuit. *Education:* Yale University (B.A., with distinction, 1989); University of Illinois College of Law (J.D., 1992). *Member:* Winnebago County and Illinois State Bar Associations. ***PRACTICE AREAS:*** Labor and Employment Law (Management); Employee Benefit Litigation; Business Litigation; Commercial Litigation. ***Email:*** amezny@holmstromlaw.com

AARON W. BROOKS, born Litchfield, Illinois, July 24, 1969; admitted to bar, 1996, Illinois. *Education:* Christopher Newport College (B.A., cum laude, 1993); University of Illinois (J.D., magna cum laude, 1996). Author: "The Effect of HIPAA's Privacy Regulations on Employers and Group Health Plans," 91 IBJ 192, 2003; "The Law of Privacy: Past, Present and Future," ISBA Intellectual Property Newsletter, Vol. 42, No. 1, October 2002; "From Ink to e-sign: A Conceptual History of the Electronic Signature," ISBA Intellectual Property Newsletter, Vol. 40, No. 2, February 2001; "A Brief History of the UDRP," ISBA Intellectual Property Newsletter, Vol. 39, No. 3, May 2000; "Domain-Marks: The Cautious

(This Listing Continued)

HOLMSTROM & KENNEDY, P.C., Rockford—Continued

Interplay Between Trademarks and Internet Domain Names," 74 IBJ 88, February, 2000 (Winner, First Place Lincoln Writing Award); "The Business Attorney's Guide to Trade Names," 87 IBJ 526, October 1999 (Winner, Third Place Lincoln Writing Award); "How to Protect Your Client's Web Site," 86 IBJ 70, February 1998, (Winner, First Place Lincoln Writing Award); "The Trustee's Balancing Act: Impartiality When a Beneficiary Goes Bad," 86 IBJ 22, January 1998; "Chuck the Box: Proposed Entity Classification Regulations Bring Bad Policy," 70 Tax Notes 1669, 1996. Co-Author: with Megan G. Heeg, "The Gramm-Leach Bliley Act: Does it Apply to You?" 90 IBJ 412, August 2002. *Member:* Winnebago County and Illinois State (Chairman, IP Section Council, 2004-2005) Bar Associations. ***PRACTICE AREAS:*** Intellectual Property; Technology; Privacy Law; Business Transactions; Health Insurance Portability and Accountability Act (HIPAA). ***Email:*** abrooks@holmstromlaw.com

KRISTINE PIHL YOUMAN, born Rockford, Illinois, April 13, 1971; admitted to bar, 1997, Illinois. *Education:* University of Illinois (B.A., 1993; J.D., magna cum laude, and M.B.A., 1997). Author: "Minority Shareholders Must Only Prove Defendant's Statutory Misconduct to Receive Forced Buyout of Shares," 85 Illinois Bar Journal (April 1997). *Member:* Winnebago County (Secretary, 2002-2003; Treasurer, Young Lawyers Division, 2003-2004) and Illinois State Bar Associations. ***PRACTICE AREAS:*** Health Care; Business Law; Contracts; Corporate Law; Mergers and Acquisitions; Real Estate; Trusts and Estates; Wills; Probate. ***Email:*** kyouman@holmstromlaw.com

---

SUZANNE R. LUKAS, born Berwyn, Illinois, July 7, 1973; admitted to bar, 1998, Illinois and U.S. District Court, Northern District of Illinois. *Education:* DePaul University (B.A., cum laude, 1995); University of Illinois (J.D., cum laude, 1998). *Member:* Chicago, Winnebago County and Illinois State Bar Associations. ***LANGUAGES:*** Spanish. ***PRACTICE AREAS:*** Commercial Litigation; Medical Malpractice Defense; Banking Litigation. ***Email:*** slukas@holmstromlaw.com

JAMES C. LUKAS, born Milwaukee, Wisconsin, November 20, 1968; admitted to bar, 1997, Illinois. *Education:* University of Wisconsin-Madison (B.B.A., 1991); University of Illinois (J.D., 1997). *Member:* Chicago, Winnebago County and Illinois State Bar Associations. ***PRACTICE AREAS:*** Corporate; Business Transactions; Real Estate; Banking; Estate Planning; Estate Administration; Health Care. ***Email:*** jlukas@holmstromlaw.com

ANGELA CONNELLY BRESNAHAN, born Morrison, Illinois, July 17, 1976; admitted to bar, 2001, Illinois. *Education:* Northern Illinois University (B.S., magna cum laude, 1998); University of Illinois (J.D., cum laude, 2001). *Member:* Winnebago County, Chicago and Illinois State Bar Associations. ***PRACTICE AREAS:*** Commercial Litigation; Civil Litigation; Labor and Employment; Medical Malpractice Defense. ***Email:*** abresnahan@holmstromlaw.com

ERIN E. WALSH, born Evergreen Park, Illinois, April 22, 1978; admitted to bar, 2003, Wisconsin, Illinois and U.S. District, Eastern and Western Districts of Wisconsin. *Education:* University of Iowa (B.B.A., 2000); Marquette University (J.D., cum laude, 2003). Board Member, Moot Court. Recipient, CALI Award Winner, Employment, Discrimination, Legal Writing and Juvenile Law. *Member:* Chicago, Winnebago County and Illinois State Bar Associations; State Bar of Wisconsin. ***PRACTICE AREAS:*** Labor and Employment Law (Management); Estate Planning; Civil Litigation. ***Email:*** ewalsh@holmstromlaw.com

REPRESENTATIVE CLIENTS: SwedishAmerican Health System; Rockford Health System; Rochelle Community Hospital; Grinnell Mutual Reinsurance Company; TIG Insurance, CNA Insurance; The Doctors' Company; St. Paul Insurance; LaSalle Bank; Associated Bank; U.S. Bank; Cornerstone Credit Union; Stewart Title Insurance Co.; Rockford Police Pension Board; Pacific Bearing; Rockford Manufacturing Group; Viking Chemical Company; Header Die & Tool Company; Stenstrom General Contractor-Design/Build Group; Schmeling Construction Company; Universal Technical Systems; ARC Design Resources; Trekk Design; KMK Media Group, Inc.; Barrington Broadcasting Co.; Rockford Gastroenterology Associates; Rockford Radiology Associates; Northern Illinois Nephrology; Orthopedic Associates of Northern Illinois.

HYZER, HYZER & JACOBS

855 NORTH MADISON STREET
ROCKFORD, ILLINOIS 61107-3095
Telephone: 815-965-3600
Fax: 815-965-3636
Email: hyzerlawfirm@ameritech.net

Residential Real Estate, Commercial Real Estate, Condominium Development, Business Law, Corporate Law, Trusts and Estates, Civil Litigation and Appellate Practice.

FIRM PROFILE: Hyzer, Hyzer & Jacobs was founded in 1976 by Keith Hyzer. Serving clients throughout Winnebago, Boone, Ogle and Stephenson Countries, the firm engages in a General Practice with an emphasis on Real Estate.

KEITH HYZER, born Lewistown, Illinois, September 24, 1931; admitted to bar, 1958, Illinois. *Education:* Knox College (B.A., 1953); University of Illinois (J.D., 1958). Order of the Coif. Member, Board of Editors, Illinois Law Forum, 1957-1958. Adjunct Professor, Real Estate Law, Northern Illinois University College of Law, 1992. General Counsel, Rockford Area Association of Realtors, 1980—. *Member:* Winnebago County (President, 1981-1982) and Illinois State (Member, Real Estate Law Section Council, 1978-1983) Bar Associations. ***PRACTICE AREAS:*** Residential Real Estate; Commercial Real Estate; Business Law; Corporate Law; Trusts and Estates.

NANCY HYZER, born Rockford, Illinois, January 29, 1939; admitted to bar, 1984, Illinois. *Education:* University of Wisconsin (B.S., 1961); Northern Illinois University (J.D., cum laude, 1984). Casenote and Comment Editor, Northern Illinois University Law Review, 1983-1984. Author: "Recent Changes to the Residential Real Property Disclosure Act," Ill. Bar Journal, 1998. *Member:* Winnebago County (Member, Board of Directors, 1996-1999; Second and First Vice-President, President, 2002-2003) and Illinois State (Member, Real Estate Law Section Council, 1992-1996; Newsletter Author and Associate Editor, 1994-1998; Standing Committee on Bar Publications Board, 2000-2002) Bar Associations; Illinois Real Estate Lawyers Association; Winnebago County Bar Foundation (Past President). ***PRACTICE AREAS:*** Residential Real Estate; Commercial Real Estate; Condominium Development; Business Law; Corporate Law; Trusts and Estates.

(This Listing Continued)

ERIK K. JACOBS, born Detroit, Michigan, February 28, 1965; admitted to bar, 1991, Illinois; U.S. District Court, Northern District of Illinois. *Education:* University of Iowa (B.B.A., Finance, 1987); Northern Illinois University College of Law (J.D., cum laude, 1991). Delta Theta Phi. Member, National Moot Court Team. Member, Northern Illinois University Law Review, 1990-1991. Research Assistant to Dean Leonard P. Strickman. Law Clerk to the Honorable Philip G. Reinhard, U.S. District Court, Northern District of Illinois, 1991-1993. *Member:* Winnebago County and Illinois State Bar Associations; The Association of Trial Lawyers of America. ***REPORTED CASES:*** B. Sanfield, Inc. v. Finlay Fine Jewelry Corp., 258 F.3d 578, 2001-2 Trade Cases P73, 347, U.S.P.Q.2d 1377 (7th Cir., 2001); B. Sanfield, Inc. v. Finlay Fine Jewelry Corp., 168 F.3d 967, 1999-1 Trade Cases P72, 453, 49 U.S.P.Q.2d 1831 (7th Cir., 1999); Lanxon v. Magnus, 296 Ill. App.3d 377, 694 N.E.2d 610, 230 Ill. Dec. 641 (Ill. App.3 Dist., 1998); Wingo by Wingo v. Rockford Memorial Hosp., 292 Ill. App.3d 896, 686 N.E. 2d 722, 226 Ill. Dec. 939 (Ill. App.2 Dist., 1997); Yu v. Kobayashi, 281 Ill. App.3d 489, 667 N.E. 2d 106, 217 Ill. Dec. 313 (Ill. App.2 Dist., 1996); Dalton v. Community General Hosp., 275 Ill. App.3d 73, 655 N.E. 2d 462, 211 Ill. Dec. 433 (Ill. App.3 Dist, 1995); Dewey v. Zach, 272 Ill. App.3d 742, 651 N.E. 2d 643, 209 Ill. Dec. 465 (Ill. App.2 Dist., 1995); Zalazar v. Vercimak, 261 Ill. App.3d 250, 633 N.E. 2d 1223, 199 Ill. Dec. 232 (Ill. App.3 Dist., 1993). ***PRACTICE AREAS:*** Civil Litigation; Insurance Defense; Personal Injury; Appellate Practice; Real Estate Law; Corporate Law. ***Email:*** ejacobs@ameritech.net

REPRESENTATIVE CLIENTS: Bank One Trust Company, N.A.; Leading Edge Hydraulics, Inc.; Clinkenbeard & Associates, Inc.; Jerhen Industries, Inc.; North American Clutch and Driveline, Inc.; All American Escrow & Title Services, Inc.; Lawyers Title Insurance Corporation; MetLife Auto & Home; Unitrin Property & Casualty Ins. Co.; Peterson Office Service, Inc. d/b/a Peterson Computer Technologies, Inc.; R.K. Johnson & Associates, Inc., Land Surveyors and Engineers; Rockford Area Association of Realtors.

LEYDIG, VOIT & MAYER, LTD.

6815 WEAVER ROAD, SUITE 300
ROCKFORD, ILLINOIS 61114-8018
Telephone: 815-963-7661
Telecopier: 815-963-7664
Email: mail@leydig.com
URL: http://www.leydig.com

Chicago, Illinois Office: Two Prudential Plaza, 180 North Stetson Avenue, Suite 4900. Telephone: 312-616-5600. Telecopier: 312-616-5700.
Washington, D.C. Office: Leydig, Voit & Mayer, 700 Thirteenth Street, N.W., Suite 300. Telephone: 202-737-6776. Telecopier: 202-737-6776.
Seattle, Washington Office: 1420 Fifth Avenue, Suite 2200. Telephone: 206-521-5985. Telecopier: 206-224-3557.

Patent, Trademark, Copyright, Unfair Competition and Related Antitrust and International Trade Law. Trials and Appeals.

ASSOCIATE

JOHN T. BRETSCHER, born Valparaiso, Indiana, 1958; admitted to bar, 1999, Illinois; U.S. District Court, Northern District of Illinois. *Education:* University of Chicago (B.A., Physics, 1981); Chicago-Kent College of Law, Illinois Institute of Technology (J.D., 1999). ***LANGUAGES:*** German. ***Email:*** jbretscher@leydig.com

OF COUNSEL

CHARLES S. OSLAKOVIC, born Chicago, Illinois, 1941; admitted to bar, 1973, Illinois; U.S. Court of Appeals for the Federal Circuit; U.S. District Court, Northern District of Illinois, including Trial Bar; registered to practice before U.S. Patent and Trademark Office. *Education:* Illinois Institute of Technology (B.S.E.E., 1966); DePaul University (J.D., 1973). (Resident). ***Email:*** coslakovic@leydig.com

---

NORMAN LINDSTEDT

ONE COURT PLACE, SUITE 300
ROCKFORD, ILLINOIS 61101
Telephone: 815-965-4412
Fax: 815-967-0783

Family Law, Complex Domestic Relations Issues, Divorce, Dissolution of Marriage, Prenuptial Agreements, Premarital Agreements, Child Custody, Visitation Rights, Spousal Support, Alimony, Maintenance, Matrimonial Law, Litigation, Mediation, Marital Settlement Agreements, Separation Agreements, Property Rights, Financial Discovery and Analysis Related to Divorce, Tax Consideration related to Divorce.

FIRM PROFILE: Prior to establishing his own practice, Mr. Lindstedt had been a partner at one of Rockford's largest and most respected law firms. He is the only attorney in Rockford to be listed in the Family Law Section of the Martindale-Hubbell Bar Register of Pre-eminent Attorneys.

NORMAN LINDSTEDT, born Moline, Illinois, September 5, 1942; admitted to bar, 1969, Illinois. *Education:* Valparaiso University (B.A., 1964; J.D., 1967). Phi Alpha Delta. Special Assistant Attorney General, State of Illinois, 1975-1979. *Member:* Winnebago County (President, 1992-1993; President, Younger Members Section, 1976-1977; Chairman, Family Law Section, 1987, 1990), Illinois State and American (Member, Family Law Section, 1994) Bar Associations. ***PRACTICE AREAS:*** Civil Litigation; Family Law.

MARAMBA & ASSOCIATES, LLC

ROCKFORD, ILLINOIS

(See Arlington Heights)

Business Law, Chancery Practice, Corporate Litigation, Civil Litigation, Complex Litigation, Defense Litigation, Federal Litigation, Administrative Litigation, Business Enterprises, Business Litigation, Closely Held Business Law, Real Estate Litigation, Veterans Rights, Military Law, Wills, Commercial Collections, Post Judgment Collections, Closely Held Corporations.

MATEER & ASSOCIATES

401 WEST STATE STREET, SUITE 400
ROCKFORD, ILLINOIS 61101
Telephone: 815-965-7745
Fax: 815-965-7749

Insurance Defense including Automobile Casualty and Fire, Products Liability and Professional Malpractice.

FIRM PROFILE: The firm's focus is primarily insurance defense. However the firm will accept select catastrophic plaintiff injury cases as long as they do not conflict with our defense clientele.

MEMBER OF FIRM

DON M. MATEER, born Evanston, Illinois, July 29, 1945; admitted to bar, 1971, Illinois; 1972, U.S. District Court, Northern District of Illinois; 1974, U.S. Court of Appeals, 7th Circuit; 1981, U.S. Supreme Court. *Education:* University of Michigan (B.A., 1967); University of Illinois (J.D., 1971). Fellow, American College of Trial Lawyers. Leading Lawyer, Illinois. Member, Panel of Arbitrators, American Arbitration Association. Mediator and Arbitrator, Winnebago County. *Member:* Winnebago County (Chairman, Judicial Liaison Committee, 1986-1987; Chairman, Professional Responsibility Committee, 1997-1998), Illinois State (Assembly Rep., 1988-1990) and American (Vice Chairman, Trial Techniques Committee, Tort and Insurance Practice Section, 1987-1988) Bar Associations; Illinois Association of Defense Trial Counsel; Defense Research Institute. ***PRACTICE AREAS:*** Personal Injury; Insurance. ***Email:*** dmateer@mateerlawfirm.com

ASSOCIATES

WILLIAM M. GOFF, born Rockford, Illinois, March 16, 1956; admitted to bar, 1984, Iowa and Illinois. *Education:* Western Illinois University (B.A., 1978); Drake University (J.D., with honors, 1984). *Member:* Winnebago County, Illinois State and American Bar Associations. ***PRACTICE AREAS:*** Insurance Defense. ***Email:*** wgoff@mateerlawfirm.com

DAWN HALLSTEN, born Fort Leonard Wood, Missouri, December 23, 1951; admitted to bar, 1993, Wisconsin and Illinois. *Education:* Rockford College (B.A., summa cum laude, 1973); University of Wisconsin (J.D., cum laude, 1993). Phi Beta Kappa. Member, County Board, Winnebago County, 1982-1990. *Member:* Winnebago County, Illinois State and American (Member, Sections on: Law Practice Management; Family Law; Tort and Insurance Practice; Urban, State and Local Government Law; Litigation) Bar Associations; State Bar of Wisconsin. ***PRACTICE AREAS:*** Family Law; Divorce; Real Estate. ***Email:*** dhallsen@mateerlawfirm.com

DONNA R. HONZEL, born Columbia, Missouri, April 9, 1965; admitted to bar, 1991, Illinois. *Education:* Central Missouri State University (B.S., 1988); University of Illinois (J.D., 1991). Assistant States Attorney, Illinois, 1991-1995. *Member:* American, Winnebago County and Illinois State Bar Associations. ***PRACTICE AREAS:*** Insurance Defense; Personal Injury; Criminal Defense; White Collar Criminal Defense. ***Email:*** dhonzel@mateerlawfirm.com

REPRESENTATIVE CLIENTS: American States; The Andover Cos.; AVCO Group; Calvert Fire Insurance Co.; Church Mutual Insurance Co.; Colonial Penn; Commonwealth Edison Co.; Continental Insurance Cos.; CNA; Dairyland Insurance Co.; Drake Insurance Co.; Empire Fire & Marine Insurance Co.; Hanover Insurance Co.; The Hartford; Hertz; Horace Mann Insurance Co.; Metropolitan Insurance Co.; Michigan Mutual Insurance Co.; Millers Mutual Insurance Co.; Montgomery Wards Insurance; NCI Insurance Co.; New Hampshire Group; Pekin Insurance Co.; Preferred Risk Mutual; Progressive Casualty Insurance Co.; Royal-Globe Insurance Co.; Sentry Insurance Co.; Signal Insurance Co.; State Farm Fire & Casualty Co.; State Farm Mutual Automobile Insurance Co.; Time Insurance Co.; U.S.F.& G.; Western States Insurance Co.; Zurich Insurance Co.; CUNA Mutual Insurance Group; J C Penny Casualty Co.; Economy Fire & Gas Co.; West Bend Insurance Co.; General Casualty; NCMIC Insurance Co.; ISBA Mutual Insurance Co.

LESLIE V. MATLAW, P.C.

ROCKFORD, ILLINOIS

(See Chicago)

Housing Discrimination, Fair Housing Law.

McGREEVY • WILLIAMS, P.C.

Established in 1967
6735 VISTAGREEN WAY
P.O. BOX 2903
ROCKFORD, ILLINOIS 61132-2903
Telephone: 815-639-3700
Fax: 815-639-9400

General Civil, Trial and Appellate Practice in all Courts. Business Litigation, Insurance, Real Estate, Corporation, Tax, Commercial, Environmental, Bankruptcy, Collection, Family Law, Probate and Estate Planning.

MICHAEL T. McGREEVY (1930-1993)
RAYMOND E. JOHNSON (1939-2001)

(This Listing Continued)

DANIEL T. WILLIAMS, JR., born Evergreen Park, Illinois, December 21, 1946; admitted to bar, 1971, Illinois. *Education:* University of Illinois (B.A., 1968; J.D., 1971). Member, Illinois Supreme Court Committee on Pattern Jury Instructions (Civil), 1979-1981. Reporter, Chicago Bar Association's Young Lawyers Section to American Bar Association Joint Study on Implementation in Illinois of A.B.A. Standard for Criminal Justice, Trial by Jury, 1973. Special Assistant State's Attorney, Winnebago County, 1978. Mediator, U.S. District Court, Northern District of Illinois, Western Division. *Member:* Winnebago County, Illinois State and American Bar Associations. ***PRACTICE AREAS:*** Employment Discrimination Defense Law; Family Law; Personal Injury Law; Municipal Civil Rights Defense. ***Email:*** dtw@mjwpc.com

MICHAEL F. O'BRIEN, born Rio de Janeiro, Brazil, September 25, 1944; admitted to bar, 1969, Pennsylvania; 1973, Illinois. *Education:* DePauw University (B.A., 1966); Duke University (J.D., 1969). Order of the Coif. Recent Developments Editor and Member, Executive Committee, Duke Law Journal, 1968-1969. Assistant District Attorney, 1970-1972 and Chief Public Defender, 1972-1973, Bucks County, Pennsylvania. Assistant U.S. Attorney, Northern District of Illinois, 1973-1976. *Member:* Winnebago County (President, 1994-1995), Illinois State, Pennsylvania, Seventh Circuit and American Bar Associations. ***PRACTICE AREAS:*** Business Litigation. ***Email:*** mobrien@mjwpc.com

BRUCE ROSS-SHANNON, born Gary, Indiana, August 4, 1951; admitted to bar, 1977, California; 1978, Illinois. *Education:* Stanford University (B.A., 1973); University of Southern California (J.D., 1977). Phi Beta Kappa. Commissioner, Illinois Nature Preserves Commission, 2002-2005. *Member:* Winnebago County (President, 2004-2005), Illinois State and American Bar Associations; State Bar of California. ***PRACTICE AREAS:*** Real Estate Law. ***Email:*** brs@mjwpc.com

DANIEL M. DONAHUE, born Freeport, Illinois, September 25, 1951; admitted to bar, 1979, Illinois. *Education:* University of Illinois (B.A., 1974; M.A. in Mathematics, 1976; J.D., cum laude, 1979). Member, University of Illinois Law Forum, 1978. Summer Intern, Antitrust Division, Department of Justice, 1978. Member, Panel of U.S. Bankruptcy Trustees, Northern District of Illinois, 1985-2005. *Member:* Winnebago County, Illinois State and American Bar Associations. ***PRACTICE AREAS:*** Business Law; Bankruptcy Law; Creditors Rights Law. ***Email:*** ddonahue@mjwpc.com

WILLIAM A. REILLY II, born Evergreen Park, Illinois, May 11, 1958; admitted to bar, 1983, Iowa and Illinois. *Education:* Loras College (B.S., magna cum laude, 1980); University of Iowa (J.D., with distinction, 1983). Author: "Debt Collection Practices: Iowa Remedies for Abuse of Debtors' Rights," 68 Iowa Law Review 753, 1983. Arbitrator, Illinois Supreme Court Mandatory Court Annexed Arbitration Project, 1988—. *Member:* Winnebago County, Illinois State, Iowa State and American Bar Associations. ***PRACTICE AREAS:*** Business Law; Commercial Transactions; Creditors Rights Law. ***Email:*** wreilly@mjwpc.com

DONALD Q. MANNING, born Chicago, Illinois, January 27, 1961; admitted to bar, 1987, Illinois; U.S. District Court, Northern District of Illinois; U.S. Court of Appeals, Seventh Circuit; U.S. District Court, Eastern and Western Districts of Wisconsin. *Education:* University of Wisconsin-Madison (B.S., 1983); John Marshall Law School (J.D., 1987). John Marshall Law Review, 1986-1987. *Member:* Winnebago County and Illinois State Bar Associations. ***PRACTICE AREAS:*** Commercial Litigation; Real Estate Litigation; Employment Litigation; Municipal Litigation; Civil Appeals. ***Email:*** dqm@mjwpc.com

ANN MARIE DITTMAR, born Freeport, Illinois, October 13, 1958; admitted to bar, 1989, Illinois, U.S. Court of Appeals, Seventh Circuit, and U.S. District Court, Northern District of Illinois. *Education:* Northern Illinois University (B.S., 1982; M.S., 1984); University of Illinois (J.D., 1989). Sigma Iota Epsilon; Beta Gamma Sigma. Recipient, Rockford Area Personnel Association Scholarship. Judicial Clerk, U.S. District Court, Northern District of Illinois, Western Division. Arbitrator for the 17th Judicial Circuit. *Member:* Winnebago County (Vice-Chair, 1991-1992 and Chair, 1992-1993, Federal Section; Board of Directors, 1994-1997; Vice-Chair, 1997-1998 and Chair, 1998-1999, Family Law Section), Illinois State, Federal and American Bar Associations; Women's Bar Association (President, 2000-2001). ***REPORTED CASES:*** Snider v. Belvidere Township, 216 F.3d 616 (7th Cir. 2000); Perkins v. Civil Constructors of Ill., Inc., 163 F3d 1027 (7th Cir. 1998); Stykel v. City of Freeport, 318 Ill.App.3d 839 (2nd Dist. 2001); IRMO: Marriott, 264 Ill.App.3d 23 (2nd Dist. 1994); IRMO: Wonderlick, 259 Ill.App.3d 692 (2nd Dist. 1994). ***PRACTICE AREAS:*** Labor and Employment; Family Law; Civil Trial; General Practice. ***Email:*** adittmar@mjwpc.com

CHRISTOPHER J. COCOMA, born Rockford, Illinois, April 26, 1968; admitted to bar, 1993, Illinois; 1994, U.S. District Court, Northern District of Illinois; 1998, U.S. Court of Appeals, Seventh Circuit. *Education:* Beloit College (B.A., with departmental honors, 1990); Vermont Law School (J.D., 1993). *Member:* Winnebago County and Illinois State Bar Associations. ***REPORTED CASES:*** Miller vs. Civil Constructors, Inc., 272 Ill. App.3d 263, 651 N.E.2d 239, 209 Ill. Dec. 311 (2nd Dist. 1995); Liebovich vs. Advance Iron Works, Inc., 353 Ill. App. 3d 311, 818 N.E. 2d 895, 288 Ill. Dec. 960 (2nd Dist. 2004). ***PRACTICE AREAS:*** Litigation. ***Email:*** cjc@mjwpc.com

NANCY L. DOEPKE, born Ann Arbor, Michigan, December 12, 1966; admitted to bar, 1994, Georgia and Illinois; 1997, U.S. District Court, Northern District of Illinois. *Education:* Central Michigan University (B.A., cum laude, 1989); Thomas M. Cooley Law School (J.D., 1993). *Member:* Winnebago County (Secretary, 1999-2000; President, Young Lawyer's Division, 1998-1999), Illinois State and American Bar Associations. ***LANGUAGES:*** French and Spanish. ***PRACTICE AREAS:*** Business Law; Family Law. ***Email:*** ndoepke@mjwpc.com

BARBARA L. HUFFMAN, born Harrisburg, Pennsylvania, March 20, 1953; admitted to bar, 1991, Illinois and U.S. District Court, Northern District of Illinois. *Education:* Allegheny College (B.A., in English, 1975); Northern Illinois University (J.D., 1990). *Member:* Winnebago County (Chairperson, Estate Section, 1994), Illinois State and American Bar Associations; Women's Bar Association (Treasurer/Secretary 1995; Vice-President 1996). ***PRACTICE AREAS:*** Estate Planning; Probate; Guardianship. ***Email:*** bhuffman@mjwpc.com

CHRISTOPHER T. LOGLI, born Des Moines, Iowa, September 13, 1977; admitted to bar, 2003, Illinois and U.S. District Court, Northern District of Illinois. *Education:* Uni-

(This Listing Continued)

McGREEVY • WILLIAMS, P.C., Rockford—Continued

versity of Iowa (B.A., with highest distinction, 2000; J.D., 2003). Phi Beta Kappa. *Member:* Winnebago County, Illinois State and American Bar Associations. ***PRACTICE AREAS:*** Real Estate; Business Law; General Practice. ***Email:*** ctl@mjwpc.com

SCOTT P. ROBINSON, born Woodstock, Illinois, April 24, 1976; admitted to bar, 2003, Illinois and U.S. District Court, Northern District of Illinois. *Education:* Northern Illinois University, DeKalb (B.A., magna cum laude, 1999); University of Illinois (J.D., cum laude, 2003). Kappa Tau Alpha, National Journalism Honors Society (1999). Voted Outstanding Senior, Department of Communications, Northern Illinois University (1999). Commencement Speaker, College of Liberal Arts and Sciences, Northern Illinois University (1999). *Member:* Winnebago County, Illinois State and American Bar Associations. ***PRACTICE AREAS:*** General Practice; Litigation. ***Email:*** spr@mjwpc.com

JEFFREY P. ORDUNO, born Aurora, Colorado, December 7, 1970; admitted to bar, 2004, Illinois. *Education:* Rockford College (B.A., 1994); John Marshall Law School (J.D., 2004). Member: Moot Court; Order of John Marshall. *Member:* Winnebago County, Illinois State and American Bar Associations. ***PRACTICE AREAS:*** Litigation; Business Law; Real Estate. ***Email:*** jpo@mjwpc.com

REPRESENTATIVE CLIENTS: Financial: Alpine Bank; Amcore Investment Group; Associated Bank of Illinois, N.A.; First Northern Credit Union; Heritage Credit Union; MembersAlliance Credit Union; Rock Valley Federal Credit Union; Stillman BancCorp, N.A.; U.S. Bank National Association.
MANUFACTURING: Action Tool & Manufacturing, Inc.; Bi-State Cash Register Corp.; Liebovich Bros., Inc.; Invensys Building Systems, Inc. (formerly Barber-Coleman Co.); Paperchine, Inc.; Precision Dose, Inc.; Rockford Oil Company.
CONSTRUCTION AND DEVELOPMENT: Contry Homes; Cord Construction Co.; Eagle Ridge Realty, Inc.; Erickson & Associates, Inc.; Gambino, Inc.; Hallmark Homes, L.L.C.; Home Builders Association of Rockford; Landmark Development, Inc.; Lobdell & Hall, Inc.; Midwest Construction, Inc.; Oakridge Development Group, Inc.; Premier-Coldwell Banker; Rubloff Development Group, Inc.; William Charles, Ltd.
SERVICES: Cruises International, Inc.; John H. Camlin Co.; S & H Spherion Staffing Co.
NOT-FOR-PROFIT: Burpee Museum of Natural History; Girl Scouts, Rock River Valley Council.

NETZEL & ASSOCIATES, P.C.

ROCKFORD, ILLINOIS

(See Chicago)

Whistle Blower, Qui Tam Litigation/Whistleblower Litigation, Health Care Fraud, Employment Retaliation, Class Action Litigation, Commercial Litigation.

O'BRIEN, HEALY & ZUBA

6067 STRATHMOOR
ROCKFORD, ILLINOIS 61107
Telephone: 815-397-7000
Fax: 815-397-1834
URL: http://www.zubalaw.com

Family Law including Divorce, Child Custody, Child Support, Visitation Rights, Spousal Support, Alimony, Paternity, Adoption Law, Qualified, Domestic Orders, QDRO's, Criminal Defense including White Collar, Criminal Defense, Felonies, Fraud, Litigation.

FIRM PROFILE: Prior to joining the practice, Mr. Zuba spent twelve years as an assistant United States Attorney. The firm emphasis is now with assisting individuals through divorce. In addition, Mr. Zuba does handle a few select felony criminal defense matters.

MEMBERS OF FIRM

JAMES T. ZUBA, born Chicago, Illinois, July 20, 1958; admitted to bar, 1986, Illinois, U.S. District Court, Northern District of Illinois; 1987, U.S. Court of Appeals, Seventh Circuit. *Education:* Rock Valley College (A.A., 1978); Arizona State University (B.S., magna cum laude, 1980); DePaul University (J.D., magna cum laude, 1986). Certified Public Accountant, 1980. Instructor, U.S. Department of Justice Criminal Trial Advocacy Course. Assistant United States Attorney, 1986-1998. *Member:* Winnebago County, Illinois State and American Bar Associations; Association of Trial Lawyers of America. ***PRACTICE AREAS:*** Criminal Law; Family Law.

LINDA M. ZUBA, born Bogota, Colombia, April 25, 1959; admitted to bar, 2001, Wisconsin; 2002, Illinois. *Education:* Arizona State University (B.S., Nursing, 1981); Loyola University, Illinois (Masters in Nursing, 1986); University of Wisconsin at Madison (J.D., 2000). *Member:* Winnebago County and Illinois State Bar Associations. ***LANGUAGES:*** Spanish. ***PRACTICE AREAS:*** Personal Injury; Health Law; General Practice. ***Email:*** lmzuba@aol.com

ASSOCIATE

DANIEL A. LEWANDOWSKI, born Rockford, Illinois, December 6, 1972; admitted to bar, 2000, Illinois. *Education:* Augustana College (B.A., 1995); The John Marshall Law School (J.D., 1999). *Member:* Winnebago County Bar Association. ***PRACTICE AREAS:*** Family Law; Criminal Defense; Wills.

MARY ALICE ODLING

401 WEST STATE STREET, SUITE 201
ROCKFORD, ILLINOIS 61101
Telephone: 815-961-2663
Fax: 815-965-2601
Email: maodling@yahoo.com
URL: http://www.odlinglaw.com

Family Law, Child Custody, Divorce, Juvenile Law, Traffic Violations, Probate, Adoption, Child Support, Spousal Support, Visitation Rights, Domestic Violence.

(This Listing Continued)

MARY ALICE ODLING, born Evergreen Park, Illinois, April 16, 1952; admitted to bar, 1993, Illinois. *Education:* University of Illinois (B.A.B.S., 1974); Rockford College (M.A., 1980); Northern Illinois University (J.D., 1993). Court Appointed Special Advocate, 1995—. Board Member, Boys and Girls Club of America, 1999—. *Member:* Winnebago, Illinois State and American Bar Associations; Winnebago Women's Bar Association.

O'HAGAN, SMITH & AMUNDSEN

STEWART SQUARE
308 WEST STATE STREET, SUITE 320
ROCKFORD, ILLINOIS 61101-1140
Telephone: 815-987-0441
Fax: 815-987-9891
URL: http://www.osalaw.com

Chicago, Illinois Office: 150 North Michigan Avenue, Suite 3300, 60601. Telephone: 312-894-3200. Fax: 312-894-3210.
St. Charles, Illinois Office: 3815 E. Main Street, Suite A-1, 60174-2488. Telephone: 630-587-7910. Fax: 630-587-7960.
Waukegan, Illinois Office: 415 West Washington Street, Suite 204, 60079-0410. Telephone: 847-599-9503. Fax: 847-599-9525.
Woodstock, Illinois Office: 666 Russel Court, 60098. Telephone: 815-337-4900. Fax: 815-337-4910.
Milwaukee, Wisconsin Office: 4811 South 76th Street, Suite 305, 53220. Suite 117, 53406-3770. Telephone: 414-282-7103. Fax: 414-282-1830.

Commercial; Commercial Transportation; Appellate; Complex Litigation; Construction; Corporate Transactions; Employment; Extra-Contractual/Insurance Litigation; Healthcare; Insurance Coverage; Personal Lines; Product Liability; Professional Liability; Property Litigation.

MEMBER OF FIRM

RUTH E. ROBINSON, admitted to bar, 1991, Illinois. *Education:* Northern Illinois University (B.S., 1984); Illinois Institute of Technology Chicago Kent College of Law (J.D., 1991). *Member:* Winnebago County, Illinois State and American Bar Associations; American Association of Nurse Attorneys. ***PRACTICE AREAS:*** Personal Injury Litigation; Medical Malpractice; Health Care. ***Email:*** rrobinson@osalaw.com

ASSOCIATE

BRETTE E. FREEDLE, admitted to bar, 1998, Illinois. *Education:* Northwestern University (B.A., 1994); John Marshall Law School (J.D., 1998). ***Email:*** bfreedle@osalaw.com

(For complete biographical data on other personnel, see Professional Biographies at other cities)

OLIVER, CLOSE, WORDEN, WINKLER & GREENWALD LLC

Established in 1908
SUITE 300, WATERSIDE CENTER
124 NORTH WATER STREET
P.O. BOX 4749
ROCKFORD, ILLINOIS 61110-4749
Telephone: 815-968-7591
Facsimile: 815-968-7507
Email: attorneys@rockfordlaw.com
URL: http://www.rockfordlaw.com

Business Transactions, Corporate and Commercial Real Estate, Banking, Labor and Employment, Probate and Estate Planning, Civil Trial and Appellate Practice in all State, Federal, and Bankruptcy Courts, and General Practice.

FIRM PROFILE: The firm, which is Rockford's oldest continuous law firm, traces its beginning to 1908. It has been in its current location in the Waterside Center since May of 1983. The firm also maintains offices in Lake Geneva, Wisconsin. Most of the attorneys are licensed in both Illinois and Wisconsin.

MEMBERS OF FIRM

ROBERT J. OLIVER, born Rockford, Illinois, March 11, 1932; admitted to bar, 1956, Illinois; 1989, Wisconsin. *Education:* Northwestern University (B.S., 1953; J.D., 1956). Phi Delta Phi. Secretary to Appellate Court Justice, 1965-1971 and Supreme Court Justice, State of Illinois, 1971-1975. Attorney, Department of Justice, Antitrust Division, 1956-1958. *Member:* Winnebago County, Illinois State and American Bar Associations; State Bar of Wisconsin. ***PRACTICE AREAS:*** Commercial Law; Corporate Law; General Business Law; Estate Planning. ***Email:*** rjodco@aol.com

CURTIS D. WORDEN, born Racine, Wisconsin, April 22, 1936; admitted to bar, 1961, Wisconsin; 1962, Illinois. *Education:* University of Wisconsin (B.S., 1959; J.D., 1961). Special Assistant Attorney General, State of Illinois, 1969-1973. Lecturer, Northern Illinois University School of Law, 1983-1987. Commissioner, Greater Rockford Airport Authority (Chairman, 1994-1996). Member, Board of Directors: Rockford Health System; Rockford Memorial Hospital; Rockford Clinic; Rockford Health Plans (Chairman, 2000-2002); YMCA of Rockford (Past President). *Member:* Winnebago County, Illinois State and American Bar Associations; State Bar of Wisconsin. ***PRACTICE AREAS:*** Business Transactions; Corporate Law; Commercial Real Estate; Estate Planning; Probate.

KARL F. WINKLER, born Oak Park, Illinois, January 15, 1942; admitted to bar, 1969, Illinois; U.S. District Court, Northern District of Illinois; U.S. Court of Appeals, Seventh Circuit. *Education:* Dartmouth College (A.B., 1964); University of Illinois (J.D., 1967). Frederick Green Moot Court Competition Finalist. Author, "Libel in the Soviet Press: The

(This Listing Continued)

New Civil Remedy in Theory and Practice," 41 Tulane Law Review 55, 1966. Co-author: "Local Rules of Practice," Winnebago County Bar, 1985. Instructor, Business Law, Rock Valley College, 1974-1978. Certified Mediator, Major Civil Litigation, 17th Judicial Circuit State of Illinois. External Mediator, U.S. Postal Service. Airplane Owners and Pilots Association Legal Panel Member. Chairman, 1974-1976 and Vice Chairman, 1975-1976, City of Rockford Human Rights Commission. Chairman, Winnebago County Building Board of Appeals, 1976-1982. Chicago Area Representative Dartmouth Alumni Council, 1988-1991. Member and 2nd Vice President, Board of Directors, United Way, 1990-1997. *Member:* Winnebago County (President, 2000-2001), Illinois State and American Bar Associations. [Captain, Air Defense Artillery, active duty, 1967-1969]. ***PRACTICE AREAS:*** Civil Litigation; Business Law; Corporate Law. ***Email:*** karlw@rockfordlaw.com

THOMAS E. GREENWALD, born Milwaukee, Wisconsin, July 25, 1945; admitted to bar, 1970, Wisconsin; 1975, Illinois. *Education:* Dominican College (B.A., 1967); Marquette University (J.D., 1970). Delta Theta Phi. Lead Article Editor, Marquette Law Review, 1969-1970. Author: "Examination of the Basis of the Uninsured Motorist Endorsement," 53 Marquette Law Review 320, 1970. Co-author: "Legal and Practical Problems Arising from Subrogation Clauses," 54 Marquette Law Review, 255, 1971. *Member:* Walworth County, Winnebago County and Illinois State Bar Associations; State Bar of Wisconsin. ***PRACTICE AREAS:*** Personal Injury Law; Civil Litigation. ***Email:*** greenwald@rockfordlaw.com

JOHN REARDEN, JR., born Reading, Pennsylvania, October 5, 1956; admitted to bar, 1984, Georgia; 1985, Illinois; 1991, U.S. Supreme Court; 1995, Wisconsin. *Education:* Eastern Illinois University (B.A., with high honors, 1978); University of Illinois (M.S., 1980; Ph.D., 1985); Emory University (J.D., with distinction, 1984). Order of the Coif. Law Clerk to Judge E. Grady Jolly, U.S. Court of Appeals, Fifth Circuit, 1985-1986. Lecturer, Labor and Employment Law For National Business Institute and Lorman Education Services, 1992—. *Member:* Winnebago County and Illinois State (Member, and Labor Law Section Council, 1990-1998, Vice-Chair, 1995; Chair, 1996-1997) Bar Associations; State Bar of Georgia (inactive). ***PRACTICE AREAS:*** Civil Litigation; Labor Law; Employment Relations (Management) Law. ***Email:*** rearden@rockfordlaw.com

ANN T. DEMPSEY, born Rockford, Illinois, December 5, 1965; admitted to bar, 1990, Wisconsin; 1991, Illinois; 1992, U.S. Court of Appeals, Seventh Circuit; 1993, U.S. Supreme Court. *Education:* University of Illinois (B.A., 1987; J.D., 1990). *Member:* Winnebago County, Illinois State and American Bar Associations; State Bar of Wisconsin. ***PRACTICE AREAS:*** Corporate Law; Real Estate; Civil Litigation; Debt Collection. ***Email:*** adempsey@rockfordlaw.com

TIMOTHY A. MILLER, born Freeport, Illinois, May 23, 1961; admitted to bar, 1988, Illinois, New York, U.S. District Court, Western District of New York and U.S. District Court, Northern District of Illinois; 1999, Wisconsin. *Education:* Loras College (B.A., cum laude, 1983); University of Alabama (J.D., 1987). Lecturer, Commercial Litigation, Lorman Education Services. *Member:* Winnebago County, Illinois State and American Bar Associations; State Bar of Wisconsin; Crusader Central Clinic Association (Former Member, Board of Directors). ***PRACTICE AREAS:*** Corporate Law; Business Law; Banking Law; Creditor Bankruptcy; Real Estate; Estate Planning; Probate; Civil Litigation. ***Email:*** miller@rockfordlaw.com

DEBRA A. DELIA, born Rockford, Illinois, October 8, 1962; admitted to bar, 1987, Illinois. *Education:* Marquette University (B.A., Honors, cum laude, 1984); University of Illinois (J.D., 1987). Lecturer, Lorman Education Services. Illinois Assistant Attorney General, 1987-1989. Member, Board of Directors, YWCA of Rockford. *Member:* Winnebago County, Illinois State and American Bar Associations. ***PRACTICE AREAS:*** Corporate Law; Business Law; Banking Law; Creditors Bankruptcy; Real Estate; Estate Planning; Probate; Civil Litigation. ***Email:*** debd@rockfordlaw.com

OF COUNSEL

HENRY J. CLOSE, born Washington, D.C., March 4, 1936; admitted to bar, 1961, Illinois; 1991, U.S. Supreme Court. *Education:* Regis College (A.B., 1958); Loyola University (J.D., 1961). Chapter Author: "The Labor Law Handbook," Illinois Institute for Continuing Legal Education, 1980-2001. Lecturer, "Labor and Employment Law," National Business Institute, 1987-2001. Council on Education in Management, 1994-1996. *Member:* Winnebago County (Secretary, 1970-1971), Illinois State (Member, Labor Law Section Council, 1973-1978; Chairman, 1976-1977) and American Bar Associations. ***PRACTICE AREAS:*** Labor and Employment Relations (Management) Law; General Business Law; Corporate Law; Estate Planning; Probate. ***Email:*** hjc@rockfordlaw.com

ASSOCIATE

BRADLEY A. RIGHTNOWAR, born Mount Vernon, Illinois, June 28, 1974; admitted to bar, 2004, Illinois and U.S. District Court, Northern District of Illinois. *Education:* University of Illinois, Urbana-Champaign (B.S., 1996; M.P.A., 2002); Northern Illinois University (J.D., 2004). Boone County Board Member, 2004—. *Member:* Boone County, Winnebago County, Illinois State and American Bar Associations. ***PRACTICE AREAS:*** Corporate Law; Business Law; Civil Litigation; Real Estate; Estate Planning. ***Email:*** rightnowar@rockfordlaw.com

REPRESENTATIVE CLIENTS: Bank One, Illinois, NA; Aqua-Aerobics Systems, Inc.; Seiberling Associates, Inc.; Bourn & Koch Inc.; Rockford Public Library; Quality Metal Finishing Co.; Smith Oil Corp.; Great American Insurance Companies; Commercial Mortgage & Finance Company; Dasco Pro, Inc.; Dial Machine, Inc.; Rochelle Travel Plaza; Northwest Bank of Illinois; First National Bank of Beloit; FTI International, Inc.; Nelson Carlson Mechanical Contractors Co.; Pierce Biotechnology, Inc.

LOCAL COUNSEL FOR: Melvin Simon & Associates; Laidlaw Environmental Services, Inc.; Casio, Inc.; America Online, Inc.; CBL (Cherryvale Regional Shopping Center); Kasper Trucking; Rockford Health System; Rockford Memorial Hospital; YMCA of the Rock River Valley.

REPRESENTATIVE LABOR/EMPLOYMENT CLIENTS: Streator Dependable Manufacturing Co.; Wahl Clipper Corp.; Modern Metal Products Co.; Zion Development Corp.

PAVALON, GIFFORD, LAATSCH & MARINO

ROCKFORD, ILLINOIS

(See Chicago)

Civil Trial and Appellate Practice in all Courts. Personal Injury, Wrongful Death, Railroad Injuries, (F.E.L.A.), Medical Malpractice, Products Liability, Aviation Law, Complex Commercial Litigation and Class Actions.

PICHA & SALISBURY

Established in 1992

EDGEBROOK COURT BUILDING

1639 NORTH ALPINE, SUITE 300

ROCKFORD, ILLINOIS 61107-1449

Telephone: 815-227-4300

Fax: 815-227-4330

URL: http://www.pichasal.com

Workers Compensation Defense, Civil Trial, Employers Liability, Insurance Defense, Labor and Employment (Management); Environmental Law, Real Estate.

FIRM PROFILE: Picha & Salisbury was founded in 1992. Our attorneys have protected the interests of clients throughout all of Northern Illinois and have served the community for over 35 years.

MEMBERS OF FIRM

GEORGE J. PICHA, born Oak Park, Illinois, January 13, 1938; admitted to bar, 1963, Illinois and U.S. District Court, Northern District of Illinois. *Education:* North Central College (B.A., 1959); Northwestern University (J.D., 1962). Recipient: Outstanding Alumnus Award, North Central College, 1994; Paul Revere Award for Business Advocacy, Rockford Regional Chamber of Commerce, 1997. Author: "Procedure Appeals and Special Remedies," Chapter 5 of Workers' Compensation Handbook, Illinois Institute for Continuing Legal Education, 1972—. Lecturer: Courses on Workers Compensation Law; Illinois Institute for Continuing Legal Education; and Illinois State Bar Association. Member: Leading Lawyers Network; Governmental Affairs Council, Rockford Regional Chamber of Commerce; Illinois Manufacturer's Association; Workers' Compensation Lawyers Association; Defense Research Institute; Illinois Self Insurers Association. *Member:* Winnebago County, Illinois State and American Bar Associations. Charter Fellow, Illinois Bar Foundation. ***PRACTICE AREAS:*** Workers Compensation Defense; Employers Liability. ***Email:*** gpicha@pichasal.com

JEFFREY L. SALISBURY, born Rockford, Illinois, October 14, 1953; admitted to bar, 1983, Illinois. *Education:* University of Maryland (B.A., 1979); University of Illinois (J.D., 1983). Lecturer, Courses on Workers' Compensation Law, Employers Association of Illinois and Winnebago County Bar Association. Member: Leading Lawyers Network. *Member:* Winnebago County, Illinois State and American Bar Associations; Workers' Compensation Lawyers Association; Illinois Self Insurers Association. [U.S. Air Force, 1973-1980]. ***PRACTICE AREAS:*** Workers Compensation Defense; Employer Liability; Management Employment Law; Management Labor Law. ***Email:*** jsalisbury@pichasal.com

LLOYD R. McCUMBER, born Peoria, Illinois, April 18, 1963; admitted to bar, 1988, Illinois. *Education:* Southern Illinois University (B.A., with honors, 1985); Northern Illinois University (J.D., 1988). Lecturer, Courses on Workers Compensation and Employer's Liability issues: Employers' Association of Illinois; American Society of Safety Engineers; Workers' Compensation Claims Association; National Business Institute; Winnebago County Bar Association. *Member:* Winnebago County, Illinois State and American Bar Associations; Workers' Compensation Lawyers Association. ***PRACTICE AREAS:*** Litigation; Workers Compensation Defense; Employment Law; Automobile Negligence; Premises Liability; Construction Accidents; Appellate Practice. ***Email:*** lmccumber@pichasal.com

ROBERT M. O'CONNELL, born Chicago, Illinois, December 2, 1945; admitted to bar, 1971, Illinois; 1987, Texas and U.S District Court, Northern District of Illinois including Trial Bar. *Education:* Loyola University (B.A., 1968); University of Houston (J.D., 1970). Associate Editor, Houston Law Review. *Member:* State Bar of Texas (Member Litigation Section); American Bar Association. (Board Certified, Labor and Employment Law, Texas Board of Legal Specialization). ***PRACTICE AREAS:*** Labor and Employment; Civil Litigation. ***Email:*** roconnell@pichasal.com

LAURA A. O'CONNELL, born Chicago, Illinois, May 21, 1945; admitted to bar, 1983, Illinois; 1987, Texas; U.S. District Court, Northern District of Illinois including Trial Bar. *Education:* Loyola University (B.S., 1968); Chicago-Kent College of Law (J.D., with highest honors, 1983); University of Houston (LL.M., Environmental and Energy Law, 1994). Notes and Comments Editor, Chicago-Kent Law Review, 1982-1983. Law Clerk to the Honorable John A. Nordberg, U.S. District Court, Northern District of Illinois, 1983-1985. *Member:* Illinois State and American (Employee Rights and Responsibilities Committee) Bar Associations. ***PRACTICE AREAS:*** Business Litigation; Environmental Litigation; Employment Law. ***Email:*** loconnell@pichasal.com

ASSOCIATES

CAROL A. HARTLINE, born Sycamore, Illinois, June, 24, 1972; admitted to bar, 1999, Illinois. *Education:* University of Illinois (B.A., 1994); Northern Illinois University College of Law (J.D., magna cum laude, 1999). Member: Law Review; Moot Court. *Member:* Winnebago County, Illinois State and American Bar Associations. ***PRACTICE AREAS:*** Workers Compensation Defense; Civil Litigation; Labor and Employment. ***Email:*** chartline@pichasal.com

MICHAEL P. WILLIAMS, born Rockford, Illinois, January 24, 1973; admitted to bar, 1998, Illinois. *Education:* Beloit College (B.A., 1995); The John Marshall Law School (J.D., 1998). Lecturer, Workers' Compensation, Lorman Education Services. *Member:*

(This Listing Continued)

PICHA & SALISBURY, Rockford—Continued

Winnebago County, Illinois State and American Bar Associations. ***LANGUAGES:*** Spanish. ***PRACTICE AREAS:*** Workers Compensation Defense; Real Estate; Commercial Litigation. ***Email:*** mwilliams@pichasal.com

MICHELLE L. LANDON, born Hinsdale, Illinois, February 28, 1979; admitted to bar, 2004, Ohio; 2005, Illinois. *Education:* Northwestern University (B.A., 2001); The Ohio State University Moritz College of Law (J.D., cum laude, 2004). Member: Ohio State Law Journal. ***PRACTICE AREAS:*** Civil Litigation; Labor and Employment. ***Email:*** mlandon@pichasal.com

LEGAL SUPPORT PERSONNEL

MARICLARE VAULMAN, born Chicago, Illinois, July 20, 1959. *Education:* Harper College (A.A., 1994; Legal Technology Certificate, 1994). Phi Theta Kappa Society. *Member:* Illinois Paralegal Association; National Federation of Paralegal Associations. ***Email:*** mvaulman@pichasal.com

REPRESENTATIVE CLIENTS: Clarcor; DaimlerChrysler AG; Dura Automotive; Estwing Manufacturing Co.; Etnyre International Ltd.; Ingersoll Cutting Tools; Hamilton Sundstrand Corp., Div. of United Technologies Corp.; Rockford Board of Education; Rockford Health System; Rockford Products; SwedishAmerican Hospital; Taylor Co., Div. of United Technologies Corp.; William Charles Risk Management Group; Woodward Governor Co.
INSURANCE CARRIERS: American Family Insurance Group; American International Group; Capitol Indemnity Company; General Casualty Company; Grinnell Mutual Reinsurance Company; ITT Hartford Insurance Co.; Liberty Mutual Insurance Co.; NHRMA Mutual; Sentry Claim Service; United Heartland Insurance Company; St. Paul Travelers; West Bend Mutual Insurance Co.; Westfield Companies; Zurich American Insurance Co.

REINHART BOERNER VAN DEUREN S.C.

Established in 1894

SUITE 7
483 NORTH MULFORD ROAD
ROCKFORD, ILLINOIS 61107-5191
Telephone: 815-484-1900
Fax: 815-484-1032
URL: http://www.reinhartlaw.com

Milwaukee, Wisconsin Office: 1000 North Water Street, P.O. Box 2965, 53201-2965. Telephone: 414-298-1000. Facsimile: 414-298-8097.
Madison, Wisconsin Office: 22 East Mifflin Street, P.O. Box 2018, 53701-2018. Telephone: 608-229-2200. Fax: 608-229-2100.
Greenwood Village, Colorado Office: 8400 Prentice Avenue, The Penthouse, 80111. Telephone: 303-843-6042. Fax: 303-721-1083.
Waukesha, Wisconsin Office: W233 N2080 Ridgeview Parkway, P.O. Box 2265. Telephone: 262-951-4500. Fax: 262-951-4690.

General Practice. Litigation, Corporation, Securities, Real Estate, Taxation, Banking, Bankruptcy, Estate Planning, Probate, Labor/Employment, Admiralty, Employee Benefits, Environmental Law, Health Care, Intellectual Property, International Law, Patent Trademark, Copyright Law and related Litigation, OSHA, Telecommunications and Energy, Insurance.

FIRM PROFILE: Reinhart Boerner Van Deuren s.c. serves business needs with innovation, focus and commitment. With offices in Milwaukee, Madison and Waukesha, Wisconsin, the firm's attorneys are dedicated to providing service efficiently and cost-effectively. Teams of attorneys respected for their focus and experience assemble across disciplines to offer a legal edge. Founded in 1894, the firm's total commitment to clients and to innovation has allowed it to grow to nearly 200 attorneys in three cities in the state. Reinhart offers in-depth knowledge, serving as attorneys and business counselors to public and privately held corporations, financial institutions, family-owned businesses, retirement plans, exempt organizations and individuals. Combining this client-focused philosophy with the capabilities of a major national law firm assures the needs of a business are met on an individual basis with legal expertise.

LAW FIRM ALLIANCES/ASSOCIATIONS: **INTERLAW**

LAWRENCE E. CROWE, admitted to bar, 1997, Illinois. *Education:* University of Illinois (B.S., 1978); John Marshall Law School (J.D., 1997). ***PRACTICE AREAS:*** Intellectual Property. ***Email:*** lcrowe@reinhartlaw.com

ANDREW J. HEINISCH, admitted to bar, 1997, Illinois. *Education:* University of Illinois (B.S., 1994; J.D., 1997). ***PRACTICE AREAS:*** Intellectual Property. ***Email:*** aheinisc@reinhartlaw.com

JEFFERY J. MAKEEVER, admitted to bar, 1997, North Carolina and Illinois; U.S. District Court, Northern District of Illinois; registered to practice before U.S. Patent and Trademark Office. *Education:* Ohio Northern University (B.S.E.E., 1987); The John Marshall Law School (J.D., magna cum laude, 1997). Tau Beta Phi. Member, The Order of John Marshall. Recipient, Chicago Bar Foundation Scholarship. Member, Law Review. *Member:* North Carolina and American Bar Associations. ***Email:*** jmakeeve@reinhartlaw.com

KEVIN L. WINGATE, admitted to bar, 1998, Illinois. *Education:* University of Illinois (B.S., 1986; M.S., 1990); John Marshall Law School (J.D., 1998). *Member:* Institute of Electrical and Electronics Engineers; American Intellectual Property Law Association. ***PRACTICE AREAS:*** Intellectual Property; Patents; Trademarks; Copyrights; Licensing. ***Email:*** kwingate@reinhartlaw.com

---

WILLIAM H. DIETRICH, admitted to bar, 1997, South Dakota; 2001, Wisconsin (Not admitted in Illinois). *Education:* South Dakota School of Mines and Technology (B.S., 1994); University of South Dakota School of Law (J.D., 1997); University of Wisconsin-Milwaukee (B.S., 2004). ***PRACTICE AREAS:*** Intellectual Property. ***Email:*** wdietric@reinhartlaw.com

(For complete biographical data on all personnel, see Professional Biographies at Milwaukee, Wisconsin)

RENO & ZAHM LLP

Established in 1923

2902 MCFARLAND ROAD, SUITE 400
ROCKFORD, ILLINOIS 61107
Telephone: 815-987-4050
Fax: 815-987-4092
URL: http://www.renozahm.com

General Civil and Trial Practice. Corporation, Banking, Creditors' Rights, Real Estate, Insurance, Taxation, Labor, Employee Benefits, Estate Planning, Probate, Workers Compensation, Trusts and Estates.

SHELBY L. LARGE (1911-1960)
GUY B. RENO (1917-1972)
RALPH S. ZAHM (1935-1984)
H. EMMETT FOLGATE (1954-1993)
WILLIAM B. POWELL (1913-2003)

WESLEY E. LINDBERG, born Beloit, Wisconsin, May 2, 1934; admitted to bar, 1959, Illinois. *Education:* University of Illinois (B.S. in M.E., 1956; LL.B., 1959). Tau Beta Pi; Phi Kappa Phi. *Member:* Winnebago County and Illinois State Bar Associations. ***PRACTICE AREAS:*** Corporation Law; Commercial Law; Real Estate Law; Estate Planning.

R. JEROME PFISTER, born Monroe, Wisconsin, June 20, 1936; admitted to bar, 1961, Colorado; 1967, Illinois. *Education:* Augustana College (B.A., magna cum laude, 1958); University of Illinois (J.D., with high honors, 1961). Order of the Coif; Phi Beta Kappa; Phi Delta Phi. Editor-in-Chief, University of Illinois Law Forum, 1960-1961. Instructor, University of Wisconsin Law School, 1962-1963. *Member:* Winnebago County and Illinois State Bar Associations. ***PRACTICE AREAS:*** Business Acquisitions; Business Law; Real Estate; Estate Planning; Trusts and Estates.

ROBERT A. FREDRICKSON, born Rockford, Illinois, June 1, 1945; admitted to bar, 1971, Wisconsin, Illinois and U.S. District Court, Western District of Wisconsin and Northern District of Illinois including Trial Bar; 1983, U.S. Supreme Court. *Education:* Miami University; University of Wisconsin-Madison (B.B.A., with honors, 1967; J.D., with honors, 1971). Arbitrator, American Arbitration Association. Certified Mediator, 17th Judicial Circuit, Major Civil Case Program. Certified Member, Panel of Mediators for U.S. District Court, Northern District of Illinois. Selected Trial Attorney by *Law & Leading Attorneys. Member:* Winnebago County (Treasurer, 1991-1992; Judicial Liaison, Federal Section) and American Bar Associations; State Bar of Wisconsin; Illinois Trial Lawyers Association; The Association of Trial Lawyers of America. ***PRACTICE AREAS:*** Civil Litigation; Commercial Litigation; Personal Injury; Business Law; Business Transactions; Mediation; Arbitration; Trusts and Estates.

JACK D. WARD, born Blue Island, Illinois, August 14, 1952; admitted to bar, 1978, Illinois; 1983, U.S. Supreme Court; U.S. District Court, Northern District of Illinois including Trial Bar. *Education:* Brigham Young University (B.S., summa cum laude, 1975; J.D., cum laude, 1978). Beta Gamma Sigma. Speaker, Federal Jurisdiction; Section 1111(b) elections, Bankruptcy Rules & Creditor Strategies, Federal and Bankruptcy Seminars, Northern Illinois, April 22, 1985, October 25, 1987 and June 1, 1989 and September 5, 1991. Mediator, 17th Circuit Major Cases Program. *Member:* Winnebago County (Membership Chairman, 1981; Judicial Liaison, 1983-1985; Professional Responsibility Committee, 1989-1992; Vice Chairman, Trial Section, 1990-1991; Chairman: Federal Section, 1985-1986; Member, Continuing Legal Education Committee, 1986-1993; Vice-Chairman, 1987-1989; Chairman, Trial Section, 1991-1992; Chairman, Bankruptcy Section, 1992-1993; Chairman and Moderator, Bankruptcy Seminar, March 24, 1993; Vice Chairman, Professional Responsibility Committee, 1993-1994; Chairman, Unauthorized Practice of Law Committee, 1993-1994; Chairman, Professional Responsibility Committee, 1994-1995), Illinois State Bar Association; Winnebago County Arbitration (Panelist); American Bankruptcy Institute. ***PRACTICE AREAS:*** Bankruptcy Law; Civil and Commercial Litigation; Corporation Law; Dispute Resolution. ***Email:*** jdw@renozahm.com

JAN H. OHLANDER, born Rockford, Illinois, July 10, 1954; admitted to bar, 1979, Wisconsin and Illinois; U.S. Supreme Court; U.S. Court of Appeals, Seventh Circuit; U.S. District Court, Northern District of Illinois including Trial Bar; U.S. District Court, Western and Eastern Districts of Wisconsin. *Education:* University of Illinois (B.S., 1976); Marquette University (J.D., 1979). Member, Marquette Law Review, 1977-1979. Mediator, 17th Circuit Major Cases Program. Chair, Winnebago County Alternate Dispute Resolution Committee, 1996-1997. Leading Lawyers Network: Commercial Litigation, ADR Commercial Litigation, ADR Personal Injury, Professional Malpractice Defense. *Member:* Winnebago County, Illinois State and American Bar Associations; State Bar of Wisconsin; The Association of Trial Lawyers of America; Illinois Trial Lawyers Association. ***PRACTICE AREAS:*** Federal and State Trial Practice; Dispute Resolution; Personal Injury; Commercial; Real Estate; Trusts and Estates. ***Email:*** jho@renozahm.com

JOHN H. YOUNG, born Augsburg, Germany, June 1, 1960; admitted to bar, 1985, Iowa, Illinois, U.S. Tax Court and U.S. District Court, Northern District of Illinois. *Education:* Judson College (B.A., with distinction, 1982); Drake University (J.D., with honors, 1985). Elected Board Member, Boone County Board, 1996-2002. *Member:* Winnebago County, Boone County, Illinois State and Iowa State Bar Associations. ***PRACTICE AREAS:*** Litigation; Personal Injury; Workers' Compensation; Real Estate; Trusts and Estates. ***Email:*** jhy@renozahm.com

JAMIE J. SWENSON CASSEL, born Camp Pendleton, California, May 20, 1960; admitted to bar, 1986, Utah and U.S. District Court, District of Utah; 1989, Illinois and U.S. District Court, Northern District of Illinois. *Education:* University of Wyoming (B.S., 1982; J.D., 1986). Speaker: "Collecting Judgements in Illinois," June 11, 1992. Moderator: Bankruptcy Seminar, March 1994; Illinois State Bar Association Basic Commercial Law, "Attachment, Perfection & Priorities," 1995. Author, "Dischargeability of Debt v. Denial of Discharge," Winnebago County Bar Journal, April 1993. Named to *Law & Leading Attorneys*, Bankruptcy. *Member:* Winnebago County (Chairman: Bankruptcy Section, 1993-1994; Federal Section, 1995-1996; Member, Board of Directors) and Illinois State (Mem-

(This Listing Continued)

ber, Sections on: Trial Practice; Commercial Law; Health Care) Bar Associations; Utah State Bar; American Bankruptcy Institute. ***PRACTICE AREAS:*** Bankruptcy; Business Law; Uniform Commercial Code; Civil Litigation; Commercial Litigation. **Email:** jsc@renozahm.com

CRAIG P. THOMAS, born North Tarrytown, New York, April 4, 1964; admitted to bar, 1989, Illinois; 1990, U.S. District Court, Northern District of Illinois; 1991, U.S. Court of Appeals, Seventh Circuit. *Education:* Beloit College (B.A., 1986); University of Illinois (J.D., 1989). Certified Mediator, United States District Court, Western Division, Northern District of Illinois. *Member:* Winnebago County (Chairman, Federal Section, 1999-2000; Unauthorized Market Law, 2002-2003) and Illinois State Bar Associations. ***PRACTICE AREAS:*** Employee Benefits; Labor and Employment; Estate Planning; Dispute Resolution; Business Law; Business Acquisitions. **Email:** cpt@renozahm.com

ARTHUR G. KIELTY, born Moorhead, Minnesota, June 23, 1966; admitted to bar, 1991, Illinois and U.S. District Court, Northern District of Illinois. *Education:* University of Illinois (A.B., 1988; J.D., 1991). Member, University of Illinois Law Review, 1990-1991. Adjunct Faculty, Rock Valley College. *Member:* Winnebago County and Illinois State Bar Associations. ***PRACTICE AREAS:*** Federal and State Trial Practice; Personal Injury; Business Law; Real Estate; Estate Planning. **Email:** agk@renozahm.com

ASSOCIATES

NANCY GRIMME SCHILLING, born Monroe, Wisconsin, November 2, 1969; admitted to bar, 1997, Illinois and Wisconsin; U.S. District Court, Northern District of Illinois and U.S. District Court, Western District of Wisconsin. *Education:* Beloit College (B.A., cum laude, 1992); University of Wisconsin at Madison (J.D., 1997). *Member:* Winnebago County, Illinois State and American Bar Associations; State Bar of Wisconsin. ***PRACTICE AREAS:*** Corporate Law; Business Litigation; Estate Planning; Mergers and Acquisitions; Real Estate. **Email:** ngs@renozahm.com

RODNEY W. KLEITSCH, born Manchester, Iowa, June 30, 1976; admitted to bar, 2001, Illinois. *Education:* University of Iowa (B.A., 1998; J.D. with distinction, 2001). Phi Delta Phi. *Member:* Winnebago County and Illinois State Bar Associations. ***PRACTICE AREAS:*** Personal Injury; Commercial Law; Immigration Law. **Email:** rwk@renozahm.com

IAN K. LINNABARY, born Rockford, Illinois, July 31, 1973; admitted to bar, 2002, Illinois. *Education:* University of Illinois at Springfield (B.A., 1996); Northern Illinois University College of Law (J.D., cum laude, 2002). Phi Delta Phi; Pi Sigma Alpha, National Political Science Honor Society. Adjunct Professor, Rock Valley College. *Member:* Winnebago, Illinois State and American Bar Associations. ***PRACTICE AREAS:*** Business Law; Transactions; Civil Litigation; Commercial Litigation; Bankruptcy; Real Estate; Election Law. **Email:** ikl@renozahm.com

STACEY M. GAMM, born Leavenworth, Kansas, January 15, 1974; admitted to bar, 2001, Illinois. *Education:* University of Missouri (B.S.Ed., 1996); Northern Illinois University (J.D., 2001). Associate, Tess & Redington, Rochelle, Illinois, 2001-2003. *Member:* Winnebago County and Illinois State Bar Associations. ***PRACTICE AREAS:*** Family Law; Real Estate; Employment Law; Business Law; Civil Litigation.

ERIN E. KASTBERG, born Red Wing, Minnesota; admitted to bar, 2004, Illinois. *Education:* Iowa State University (B.S., with honors, with distinction, 2001); University of Iowa (J.D., 2004). Phi Kappa Phi; Golden Key National Honor Society. *Member:* Winnebago County, Illinois State and American Bar Association. ***PRACTICE AREAS:*** General Practice; Family Law; Estate Planning; Real Estate; Business Law. **Email:** eek@renozahm.com

JEFFREY M. GLAZER, admitted to bar, 2004, Illinois; 2005, U.S. District Court, Northern District of Illinois. *Education:* University of Toledo (B.B.A., 1997); Chicago-Kent College of Law (J.D., 2004). *Member:* Winnebago County and Illinois State Bar Associations. ***PRACTICE AREAS:*** Business Law; Corporate Law; Trademarks; Copyrights. **Email:** jmg@renozahm.com

COUNSEL

ROGER RENO, born Rockford, Illinois, May 16, 1924; admitted to bar, 1950, Illinois. *Education:* Kenyon College; University of Wisconsin; Carleton College (A.B., 1947); Yale University (LL.B., 1950). *Member:* Winnebago County (President, 1979), Illinois State and American Bar Associations. (Practicing Individually at: Suite 500, Amcore Financial Plaza, 501 7th Street, P.O. Box 4353, Rockford, Illinois 61110). ***PRACTICE AREAS:*** Trusts.

EDWARD J. FAHY, born Toluca, Illinois, March 26, 1911; admitted to bar, 1936, District of Columbia; 1937, Illinois; 1956, U.S. Supreme Court. *Education:* Georgetown University (A.B., 1933; J.D., 1937). *Member:* Winnebago County (Member, Executive Committee, 1965-1967), Illinois State (Chairman, Labor Law Section, 1951-1953) and American (Member: Labor and Employment Law Section; Committee on Development of Law under NLRA) Bar Associations. ***PRACTICE AREAS:*** Labor Relations (Management) Law; Corporation Law.

RITZ & LAUGHLIN, LTD.

728 NORTH COURT STREET
ROCKFORD, ILLINOIS 61103
Telephone: 815-968-1807
Fax: 815-961-1917
Email: kenritz@aol.com

Commercial Law, emphasizing Creditors Rights, Commercial Collections and Bankruptcy Law, in the U.S. District Court in Rockford, Illinois and in State Courts throughout Northwestern Illinois.

FIRM PROFILE: Ritz & Laughlin, LTD. was established in 1966. Serving clients for over 30 years throughout Winnebago, Boone, Stephenson, Ogle, and McHenry counties. The firm's focus is on commercial and bankruptcy law.

(This Listing Continued)

KENNETH F. RITZ, born Venice, Illinois, April 1, 1935; admitted to bar, 1959, Illinois; 1965, U.S. Court of Appeals, 7th Circuit and U.S. District Court, Northern District of Illinois including Trial Bar. *Education:* University of Toledo (B.B.A., 1957); University of Illinois (LL.B., 1959). Member, Board of Editors, University of Illinois Law Review, 1958-1959. Author and Lecturer: "Creditor's Rights in Illinois," IICLE, 1968; "Bankruptcy Practice, Representing the Creditor with a Secured Claim," IICLE, 1981; "Legal Issues of Problem Collections," National Business Institute, 1991; "Foreclosure and Repossession," National Business Institute, 1993; "Chapter 11, A Practical Guide for Creditors and Debtors", published by The Durand Corporation, 1994. *Member:* Winnebago County, Illinois State (Board Member, Commercial, Banking and Bankruptcy Section, 1967-1976) and American Bar Associations. ***PRACTICE AREAS:*** Commercial Law; Commercial Collections; Creditors Rights Law; Bankruptcy Law. **Email:** KENRITZ@AOL.COM

THOMAS E. LAUGHLIN, born Freeport, Illinois, July 4, 1947; admitted to bar, 1972, Illinois. *Education:* University of Iowa (B.A., 1969); University of Illinois (J.D., 1972). Listed in 6th Edition of Who's Who in American Law. Assistant Attorney General, State of Illinois, 1972-1973. Law Clerk to Illinois Supreme Court Justice Charles H. Davis, 1973-1975. Adjunct Professor, Northern Illinois University, Chapter 11 Bankruptcy Reorganization, 2001-2003. *Member:* Winnebago County Bar Association. ***PRACTICE AREAS:*** Civil Litigation; Corporate Bankruptcy Law. **Email:** tloff@aol.com

MARK ROULEAU

5301 E. STATE STREET
SUITE 215D
ROCKFORD, ILLINOIS 61108-2392
Telephone: 815-229-7246
Fax: 815-229-7251
Email: rouleau-law@afo.net
URL: http://www.rouleaulaw.com

Catastrophic Personal Injury including Wrongful Death, Automobile Accidents and Injuries, Motorcycle Accidents, Trucking Accidents. Medical Malpractice including Surgical Malpractice, Failure to Diagnose/Misdiagnosis, Hospital Malpractice, Nursing Malpractice, Pharmaceutical Malpractice.

MARK ROULEAU, born Frankfurt, West Germany, June 3, 1958; admitted to bar, 1983, Illinois and U.S. District Court, Northern District of Illinois; 1995, U.S. Supreme Court. *Education:* Southern Illinois University (B.A., Economics, Political Science 1980) President's Scholar; DePaul University (J.D., 1983). ***REPORTED CASES:*** People v. Joseph Spiezer, (2nd Dist. 2000), 316 Ill.App.3d 75, 735 N.E.2d 1017, 249 Ill.Dec. 192; Hills v. Bridgeview Little League Ass'n, (Ill.App. 1 Dist. 1999) 713 N.E.2d 616, 306 Ill.App.3d 13, (Amicus brief of counsel, for the Illinois Trial Lawyers Association); People v. Quigley, (Ill. 1998) 697 N.E.2d 735, 183 Ill.2d 1, (trial and appellate counsel); People v. Lavariega, (Ill. 1997) 676 N.E.2d 643, 175 Ill.2d 153, (trial and appellate counsel); City of Rockford v. Xayasouk, (Ill.App. 2 Dist. 1998) 705 N.E.2d 110, 301 Ill.App.3d 663, (trial and appellate counsel); Krivitskie v. Cramlett, (Ill.App. 2 Dist. 1998) 704 N.E.2d 957, 301 Ill.App.3d 705, (trial and appellate counsel); People v. Crabbe, (Ill.App. 2 Dist. 1990) 552 N.E.2d 19, 195 Ill.App.3d 163, (trial and appellate counsel); Application of County Collector, (Ill.App. 2 Dist. 1988) 530 N.E.2d 598, 175 Ill.App.3d 985, (trial and appellate counsel). ***PRACTICE AREAS:*** Personal Injury; Accidents; Automobile Accidents and Injuries; Automobile Negligence; Bicycle Accidents; Boating Accidents; Bodily Injury; Brain Injury; Catastrophic Injury; Commercial Vehicle Liability; Head Injury; Motor Vehicle Accidents and Injuries; Motorcycle Accidents; Neurolaw; Pedestrian Injuries; Personal Injury Appeals; Personal Injury Arbitration; Plaintiffs Personal Injury; Personal Injury Mediation; School Bus Accidents; Severe Burns; Spinal Injury; Vehicular Homicide; Wrongful Death; Freedom of Religion; Accident Insurance; Automobile Insurance; Automobile Insurance Coverage; Automobile Liability; General Liability; Insurance Bad Faith; Malpractice; Uninsured and Underinsured Motorists; Uninsured and Underinsured Motorists' Arbitration; Libel, Slander and Defamation; Defamation; Libel and Slander; Medical Malpractice; Medical Liability; Birth Trauma; Medical Negligence; Nursing Malpractice; Nursing Negligence; Obstetric Malpractice; Pharmacists Liability; Products Liability; Automotive Crashworthiness; Automotive Design Liability; Automotive Products Liability; Automotive Restraints; Bicycle Products Liability; Biomedical Products Liability; Chemical Products Liability; Dalkon Shield Litigation; Motorcycle Products Liability; Product Defects; Product Failure; Product Safety; Product Warning Labels; Recreational Products Liability; Toxic Torts; Chemical Exposure; Toxic Exposure.

SODERBERG & ASSOCIATES, P.C.

1330 EAST STATE STREET
ROCKFORD, ILLINOIS 61104
Telephone: 815-964-0100
Fax: 815-964-6151
Email: DSoderberg@htslawyers.com
URL: http://www.soderberglaw.com

Medical Malpractice including Wrongful Death, Birth Injuries, Failure to Diagnose or Misdiagnosis, Obstetric, Surgical, Cardiac, Orthopedic and Nursing Malpractice.

FIRM PROFILE: Soderberg & Associates, P.C. serves clients throughout Winnebago, DeKalb, Ogle, and Boone Counties. The firm focuses its practice in the area of Civil Litigation, with concentration in medical malpractice and personal injury claims.

DARLENE D. SODERBERG, R.N., born Chicago, Illinois, December 17, 1948; admitted to bar, 1995, Illinois, U.S. District Court, Northern District of Illinois, U.S. Claims Court, U.S. Court of Appeals, Seventh Circuit. *Education:* Rockford Valley College (R.N., 1982); Rockford College (B.S.N., magna cum laude, 1985); Northern Illinois University (J.D., 1995). Delta Theta Phi. Registered Nurse, Illinois, 1982. *Member:* Winnebago, Illinois State and American Bar Associations; Illinois Trial Lawyers Association; The Asso-

(This Listing Continued)

SODERBERG & ASSOCIATES, P.C., Rockford—Continued

ciation of Trial Lawyers of America. ***PRACTICE AREAS:*** State and Federal Civil Trial Law; Medical Malpractice; Personal Injury Law; Torts. ***Email:*** DSoderberg@htslawyers.com

MICHAEL J. HEDEEN, born Austin, Texas, February 20, 1953; admitted to bar, 1988, Missouri; 1989, Illinois; U.S. District Court, Northern District of Illinois; U.S. District Court, Eastern District of Missouri; U.S. Court of Appeals, Eighth Circuit and U.S. Court of Appeals, Seventh Circuit. *Education:* Southern Illinois University (B.S., 1975; J.D., magna cum laude, 1988). Phi Kappa Phi. Recipient, American Jurisprudence Awards. Writing Program Editor, Southern Illinois Law Journal, 1987-1988. Author: "Substantive Due Process: Closing The Curtain on Fundamental Rights To Privacy," 11 Southern Illinois Law Journal 1305. *Member:* Illinois State and American Bar Associations; The Missouri Bar. ***REPORTED CASES:*** Holden v. Rockford Memorial Hospital, 287 Ill. App.3d 320 (2nd Dist. 1997); Draper v. Frontier Insurance Co., 265 Ill. App.3d 739 (2nd Dist. 1994). ***PRACTICE AREAS:*** Civil Litigation; Personal Injury; Product Liability; Worker's Compensation. ***Email:*** hedeen7943@aol.com

SREENAN & CAIN, P.C.

SUITE 700
321 WEST STATE STREET
ROCKFORD, ILLINOIS 61101
Telephone: 815-962-5490
Telefax: 815-962-2755
Email: dcain@sreenan-cain.com
URL: http://www.sreenan-cain.com

Criminal and Civil Trial Practice in Federal and State Courts, Felonies, Misdemeanors, DUI, Traffic, Family, Negligence, General Practice. Personal Injury, Workers Compensation, Medical Malpractice.

PATRICK H. SREENAN (1930-1994)

DANIEL J. CAIN, born Chicago, Illinois, September 19, 1948; admitted to bar, 1975, Illinois; 1978, ; 1991, Florida; 2000, U.S. District Court, Eastern District of Wisconsin. *Education:* University of Illinois (B.S., 1972); Illinois Institute of Technology, Chicago-Kent College of Law (J.D., 1975). Assistant State's Attorney, Winnebago County, Illinois, 1976-1978. *Member:* Winnebago County, Illinois State and American Bar Associations; The Florida Bar; Illinois Trial Lawyers Association; Capital Litigation Trial Bar. ***PRACTICE AREAS:*** Administrative Law; Administrative Hearings and Appeals; Alternative Dispute Resolution; Arbitration; Mediation; Police Misconduct; First Amendment Law; Criminal Law; White Collar Crime; Domestic Violence; Juvenile Law; Medical Malpractice.

RANDY WILT, born Greenville, Ohio, February 28, 1956; admitted to bar, 1980, Illinois; 1981, U.S. District Court, Northern District of Illinois and U.S. Court of Appeals, Seventh Circuit. *Education:* The Ohio State University (B.A., 1977); Loyola University of Chicago (J.D., 1980). Listed in, Who's Who in American Law, 1998-1999. Assistant Public Defender, 1985-1996. President, Y's Men Service Club, 1981-1990. Associate, Miller, Hickey & DeBruyne Ltd., 1980-1982; Partner, Swanson & Wilt, 1982-1985; Felony Attorney, Winnebago County Public Defender's Office, 1985-1996. *Member:* Winnebago County (Member: Editorial Committee; Criminal Committee), Illinois State and American Bar Associations; National Association of Criminal Defense Lawyers; Capital Litigation Trial Bar. ***PRACTICE AREAS:*** Criminal Law; Municipal Law; Felonies; Employment Law; Commercial Collections; Civil Litigation; Personal Injury; Medical Malpractice; Contracts. ***Email:*** rwilt@sreenan-cain.com

DEBRA D. SCHAFER, born DeKalb, Illinois, July 24, 1966; admitted to bar, 1991, Illinois; 1999, U.S. District Court, Northern District of Illinois. *Education:* Illinois State University (B.S., 1988); University of Illinois (J.D., 1991). Assistant State's Attorney, Winnebago County State's Attorney's Office, 1991-1996. *Member:* Winnebago County and Illinois State Bar Associations; Capital Litigation Trial Bar. ***PRACTICE AREAS:*** Felonies; Misdemeanors; Traffic Violations; Juvenile Law; Appellate Practice; Criminal Law. ***Email:*** dschafer@sreenan-cain.com

CHRISTOPHER A. DERANGO, born Bloomington, Illinois, September 9, 1964; admitted to bar, 1994, Illinois; 2000, U.S. District Court, Northern District of Illinois. *Education:* Northern Illinois University (B.A., 1989; J.D., 1994). Assistant State's Attorney, Winnebago County State's Attorney, 1993-1995. Associate, Vella, Sparkman, Wheeler & Lund, 1995-1999. ***PRACTICE AREAS:*** Criminal Law; Felonies; Misdemeanors; Driving While Intoxicated; Traffic Violations. ***Email:*** cderango@sreenen-cain.com

PETER B. NOLTE, born Brooklyn, New York, August 8, 1949; admitted to bar, 1974, Illinois, U.S. District Court, Northern District of Illinois; 1979, Supreme Court. *Education:* Kent State University (B.A., 1971); Chicago-Kent College of Law (J.D., 1974). *Member:* Illinois State and American Bar Associations. ***PRACTICE AREAS:*** Appellate Practice; Plaintiffs Personal Injury. ***Email:*** mail@sreenen-cain.com

ANNE M. VECCHIO, born Rockford, Illinois, 1980; admitted to bar, 2004, Illinois; 2005, Arizona; U.S. District Court, Northern District of Illinois. *Education:* University of Illinois at Urbana-Champaign (B.A., 2001); Arizona State University, College of Law (J.D., 2004). Kappa Kappa Gamma. Recipient, Jeremy Grovekar Scholarship, 2001-2004. *Member:* Winnebago County Bar Association.

SWANSON, MARTIN & BELL

ROCKFORD, ILLINOIS

(See Chicago)

Asbestos Litigation, Class Action Lawsuits, Commercial Litigation, Construction Litigation/Disputes, Consumer and Warranty Law, Creditor's Rights, Drugs & Medical Devices, Employment Litigation, Environmental Law, Equipment Leasing, General Tort Liability, Healthcare, Insurance Coverage, Intellectual Property, Medical Negligence, Municipal Law, Product Liability, Professional Negligence, Real Estate Development/Zoning, Real Estate Litigation, Toxic and Mass Tort Litigation and White Collar Criminal Defense.

SWEET & MAIER, S.C.

ROCKFORD, ILLINOIS

(See Elkhorn, Wisconsin)

Real Estate, Condominium, Corporate, Business, Civil Litigation, Probate, Estate Planning, Taxation and Collections, Zoning, Planning and Land Use.

THE SZYMANSKI KOROLL LITIGATION GROUP

Established in 2004
ONE COURT PLACE, SUITE 102
ROCKFORD, ILLINOIS 61101-1007
Telephone: 815-639-9000
Fax: 815-639-9066
Email: sklg@sklg.com
URL: http://www.szymanskikoroll.com

Lake Worth, Florida Office: 6894 Lake Worth Road, Suite 203, 33467. Telephone: 561-686-9444. Fax: 561-968-7988.

Personal Injury, Wrongful Death, Medical Malpractice including Birth Injuries, Cancer, Failure to Diagnose and Misdiagnosis, Bar iatric Weight Loss Surgery, Obstetric, Surgical, Cardiac, Orthopedic, Nursing Malpractice, Nursing Home Abuse and Neglect including Bedsores, Malnutrition, Falls, Physical Abuse, Medication Errors, Automobile Accidents and Injuries, Head, Neck and Back Injuries, Burns.

KARL A. SZYMANSKI, born Rochester, New York, October 16, 1952; admitted to bar, 1982, Florida; 1990, U.S. District Court, Southern District of Florida; 2000, Illinois; 2002, U.S. District Court, Northern District of Illinois, including Trial Bar. *Education:* Slippery Rock State College (1971); Florida State University (B.S., 1974); University of Florida (J.D., 1982). Phi Delta Phi. Team Member, National Mock Trial Competition, 1982. Member, Million Dollar Advocates Forum, 1989. *Member:* Palm Beach County Bar Association; Academy of Florida Trial Lawyers; The Association of Trial Lawyers of America; Winnebago County Bar Association; Illinois Trial Lawyers Association. ***LANGUAGES:*** English. ***PRACTICE AREAS:*** Medical Malpractice (50%, 25); Personal Injury (30%, 1000); Nursing Home Negligence (20%, 15). ***Email:*** kasattyatlaw@aol.com

CYNTHIA J. SZYMANSKI KOROLL, born Huntington, New York, December 28, 1959; admitted to bar, 2001, Illinois; U.S. District Court, Northern District of Illinois, including Trial Bar. *Education:* Northern Illinois University (B.S.N., 1988; M.S., Nursing, 1994; J.D., 2001). Sigma Theta Tau. Professional Registered Nurse, Illinois, 1986—. Member, Million Dollar Advocates Forum, 2004*Member:* Winnebago County Bar Association; Association of Trial Lawyers of America; Illinois Trial Lawyers of Association. [Capt., USAR, U.S. Army Nurse Corp Reserves, 1986-2004]. ***LANGUAGES:*** English. ***PRACTICE AREAS:*** Medical Malpractice (85%); Nursing Home Negligence (10%); Personal Injury (5%). ***Email:*** cindi@kslg.com

LAW OFFICE OF MARIO J. TARARA, P.C.

3600 EAST STATE STREET
SUITE 315
ROCKFORD, ILLINOIS 61108
Telephone: 815-399-6090
Facsimile: 815-397-2907
Email: mjtarara@sbcglobal.net
URL: http://www.tararalaw.com

Real Estate, Real Estate Development, Zoning and Land Use, Construction Disputes, Business Law, Corporate Law and Contracts, Mechanics Liens.

MARIO J. TARARA, admitted to bar, 1998, Wisconsin and U.S. District Court, Eastern District of Wisconsin; 2000, Illinois. *Education:* University of Illinois (B.A., 1995); University of Michigan (J.D., 1998). *Member:* Chicago, Illinois State and American Bar Associations; State Bar of Wisconsin. ***PRACTICE AREAS:*** Buy-Sell Agreements; Eminent Domain; Landlord and Tenant Law; Commercial Leasing.

LAW OFFICES OF HAROLD L. TURNER

1330 EAST STATE STREET
P.O. BOX 4504
ROCKFORD, ILLINOIS 61110-4504
Telephone: 815-964-0100
Fax: 815-964-6151
Email: hturner@htslawyers.com
URL: http://www.haroldturnerlaw.com

Personal Injury including Automobile Accidents and Injuries, Head, Neck and Back Injuries, Medical Malpractice including Misdiagnosis and Failure to Diagnose, Birth Injuries, Cancer, Obstetric, Surgical, Cardiac, Orthopedic and Nursing Malpractice, Nursing Home Abuse and Neglect including Bedsores, Malnutrition, Dehydration, Wandering, Falls, Fractures, Physical, Verbal and Sexual Abuse and Assault, Legal Ethics and Professional Responsibility including Professional Malpractice, Legal Malpractice, Mediation and Arbitration.

(This Listing Continued)

FIRM PROFILE: The Law Offices of Harold L. Turner serves clients throughout Winnebago, Whiteside, DeKalb, Ogle, Boone, Kane, JoDaviess, Rock Island and surrounding counties in Wisconsin. The firm focuses its practice in the area of Civil Litigation with concentration in medical malpractice and personal injury claims. Mr. Turner is one of the few attorneys listed in Rockford in The Bar Register of Pre-eminent Attorneys in the field of personal injury.

HAROLD L. TURNER, born Moline, Illinois, February 3, 1943; admitted to bar, 1967, Illinois; 1971, U.S. Court of Appeals, Seventh Circuit; 1974, U.S. District Court, Northern District of Illinois including Trial Bar; 1996, U.S. Claims Court; 2000, Wisconsin. *Education:* Blackhawk College (A.A., 1963); University of Iowa; University of Illinois (J.D., 1967). Member, Mandatory Arbitration Panel, 17th Judicial Circuit. Assistant State's Attorney, Champaign County, 1968. Assistant State's Attorney, Ogle County, 1970. Mediator, Illinois Supreme Court A.D.R. 17th Judicial Circuit Court Pilot Program. *Member:* Winnebago County, Illinois State, Federal and American Bar Associations; State Bar of Wisconsin; Illinois Trial Lawyers Association; Wisconsin Academy of Trial Lawyers; The Association of Trial Lawyers of America; American Arbitration Association. [With U.S. Army, 1968-1970]

WILLIAMS & McCARTHY

A PROFESSIONAL CORPORATION

321 WEST STATE STREET

P.O. BOX 219

ROCKFORD, ILLINOIS 61105-0219

Telephone: 815-987-8900

Fax: 815-968-0019

Email: mail@wilmac.com

URL: http://www.wilmac.com

Oregon, Illinois Office: 607 Washington Street. P.O. Box 339. Telephone: 815-732-2101. Fax: 815-732-2289.

General Civil and Trial Practice. Administrative Law, Advertising and Media Law, Banking, Bankruptcy and Commercial Work Outs, Business Litigation, Closely-held Business, Commercial Lending, Condemnation and Zoning, Construction Law, Education Law, Employee Benefits, Employers' Liability, Environmental Law, Family Law, Health Care and Hospital Law, Insurance Coverage, Insurance Defense, International Law, Labor and Employment (management), Municipal Finance, Probate, Trust Law and Estate Planning, Products Liability, Real Estate, Taxation, Unfair Competition, Workers' Compensation (management).

FIRM PROFILE: Since its beginning over 70 years ago, Williams & McCarthy has grown to become one of the largest full service firms in Illinois outside of Chicago. We are a Regional firm that represent a broad cross section of business, industrial, governmental, health care, financial, insurance and individual interests. Our business clients, many of whom operate on a regional, national and international level, include such industries as agriculture, automotive, banking and financial, computers and technology, construction, engineering, health care, hotels and hospitality, insurance, machine tool, manufacturing, media, petroleum marketing, real estate development, retail, personal service, telecommunications and transportation.

While a substantial portion of our client base is made up of institutional and corporate clients, the firm represents a significant number of small businesses and individuals. Our work for individual clients includes such matters as probate, complex estate planning and tax services, family law, real estate transactions, incorporation, litigation and general legal counseling.

A full service law firm, Williams & McCarthy's core departments are designated Business Law, Litigation, Employment Law (management), Real Estate, Trusts & Estates, Creditor's Rights and Health Care. Within the Business Law group several of our members concentrate in mergers and acquisitions. The firm maintains a large litigation practice with an emphasis on complex commercial litigation, unfair competition, employers' liability, insurance defense, and workers compensation (management). Members of the litigation group practice in the state courts of Illinois and Wisconsin, as well as all federal courts and routinely act as co-counsel with national law firms in complex disputes, including commercial litigation. From its core groups, Williams & McCarthy lawyers have developed expertise in a variety of areas of concentration which allows the Firm to meet the increasingly sophisticated needs of its clients.

State of the art technology and support systems allow us to meet our clients' needs on a timely cost-efficient fashion. We recruit highly capable personnel and require continuing professional education and development. We encourage our members to become active in the community and are pleased that our lawyers routinely serve in leadership positions of organizations that serve our region.

In addition to our principal office in Rockford, we also maintain a regional office in Oregon, Illinois to serve several adjacent counties southwest of Rockford.

THOMAS S. JOHNSON, born Rockford, Illinois, 1942; admitted to bar, 1967, Illinois. *Education:* Rockford College (A.B., 1964); Harvard University (LL.B., 1967); Rockford College (L.H.D., Hon., 1989). Phi Beta Kappa. Trustee, 1979-1991 and Chairman, 1986-1989, Rockford College. Member, Board of Governors, Regents College, London, England, 1984-1989. Trustee, Eastern Illinois University, 1996-2000. Member, Board of Directors, 1981-1987 and Chairman, 1985-1986, Illinois Institute for Continuing Legal Education. Treasurer, Lawyers Trust Fund of Illinois, 1983-1986. Trustee, Clients Security Fund of Illinois, 1983-1986. Chancellor, Illinois Academy of Lawyers, 1999-2000. *Member:* Winnebago County (President, 1990-1991), Illinois State (Secretary, 1980-1981; Member, Board of Governors, 1976-1982) and American (Member, House of Delegates, 1982-1989; Chairman, 1975-1976, Committee on the Delivery of Legal Services; Member, 1975-1982 and 1985-1988 and Chairman, 1976-1979, Consortium on Legal Services and the Public; Chairman, Lawyers Referral Committee, 1979-1982; Member, 1984-1988 and Chairman, 1985-1988, Commission on Advertising) Bar Associations; American Judicature Society (Member, Board of Directors, 1986-1990). Life Fellow: American Bar Foundation; Illinois Bar Foundation. Fellow, American College of Trust and Estate Council. ***PRACTICE AREAS:*** Estate Planning and Administration. ***Email:*** tjohnson@wilmac.com

RUSSELL D. ANDERSON, born Paxton, Illinois, 1946; admitted to bar, 1971, Illinois. *Education:* University of Illinois (B.A., 1968; J.D., with honors, 1971). Order of the Coif. Projects Editor, University of Illinois Law Forum, 1971. Law Clerk to Chief Justice Robert C. Underwood, Illinois Supreme Court, 1971-1972. *Member:* Winnebago County (Member, Board of Directors, 1987-1990), Illinois State (Member, 1978-1984, 1986—; Chairman, Insurance Program Committee, 1982-1983) and American Bar Associations; American Judicature Society. ***PRACTICE AREAS:*** Corporate Law; Real Estate Law; Business Law; Environmental Law; Estate Planning; Estate Administration. ***Email:*** randerson@wilmac.com

JOHN E. PFAU, born Rockford, Illinois, 1948; admitted to bar, 1973, Illinois. *Education:* University of Illinois (B.S., 1970; J.D., 1973). Certified Public Accountant, Illinois, 1972. *Member:* Winnebago County (Treasurer, 1977), Illinois State (Member, Federal Taxation Section Council, 1981-1984) and American Bar Associations. ***PRACTICE AREAS:*** Employee Benefits Law; Taxation. ***Email:*** jpfau@wilmac.com

RICHARD A. BERMAN, born Chicago, Illinois, 1944; admitted to bar, 1974, Illinois. *Education:* Illinois Wesleyan University (B.A., 1966); Northern Illinois University (M.S. in Ed., 1971); Valparaiso University (J.D., 1974). Note Editor, Valparaiso University Law Review, 1973-1974. Faculty Member: Illinois Institute for Continuing Legal Education, Workers Compensation Seminars; Law Ed Series, Workers' Compensation Seminars; National Business Institute, Workers Compensation Seminars. Member, Board of Directors, 1984— and President, 1988-1989, Janet Wattles Mental Health Center. *Member:* Winnebago County, Illinois State and American Bar Associations; Workers Compensation Lawyers Association. ***PRACTICE AREAS:*** Workers Compensation Law. ***Email:*** rberman@wilmac.com

JOHN L. SHEPHERD, born Pontiac, Illinois, 1947; admitted to bar, 1975, Illinois. *Education:* University of Illinois (B.A., 1969); John Marshall Law School (J.D., 1975). Faculty Member: Illinois Institute for the Continuing Legal Education, Workers Compensation Seminar, 1989; National Business Institute, Workers' Comp. Seminars, 1989, 1990 and 1993; Illinois State Bar Association, Workers Compensation Seminar Speaker, 1990—. *Member:* Winnebago County (Chairman, Workers Compensation Section), Illinois State (Member, Workers Compensation Section Council) and American Bar Associations; Workers Compensation Lawyers Association (Member, Board of Directors, 1991). Fellow, Illinois Bar Foundation; Winnebago County Bar Foundation (President). ***PRACTICE AREAS:*** Workers Compensation Law. ***Email:*** jshepherd@wilmac.com

TERRY D. ANDERSON, born Rockford, Illinois, 1945; admitted to bar, 1976, Illinois. *Education:* Rockford College (B.A., summa cum laude, 1971); University of Illinois (J.D., with honors, 1976). Phi Beta Kappa; Order of the Coif. Chairman, 2003-2005, Member, Illinois Secretary of State Business Laws Advisory Committee, 1991—. *Member:* Winnebago County, Illinois State (Member, Section Council, Corporate and Securities Law, 1986-1987) and American Bar Associations; American Judicature Society; Illinois Association of Healthcare Attorneys (Member, Board of Directors, 1978-1985 and President, 1984-1985). ***PRACTICE AREAS:*** Mergers and Acquisitions; Corporate; Health Care. ***Email:*** tanderson@wilmac.com

KIM D. KRAHENBUHL, born Dixon, Illinois, 1950; admitted to bar, 1975, Illinois; 1977, U.S. District Court, Northern District of Illinois. *Education:* Southern Methodist University (B.B.A., 1972; J.D., 1975). *Member:* Ogle County, Illinois State and American Bar Associations. (Resident Partner, Oregon, Illinois Office). ***PRACTICE AREAS:*** Probate Law; Real Estate Law; Civil Litigation. ***Email:*** kkrahenbuhl@wilmac.com

SCOTT C. SULLIVAN, born Hanover, Illinois, 1954; admitted to bar, 1979, Illinois; 1980, U.S. District Court, Northern District of Illinois including Trial Bar and U.S. Court of Appeals, Seventh Circuit; 1997, U.S. Supreme Court. *Education:* University of Notre Dame (B.B.A., summa cum laude, 1976; J.D., cum laude, 1979). *Member:* Winnebago County (Secretary, 1983-1984; Chairman, Mandatory Arbitration Committee, 1988-1989), Illinois Court Certified Mediator. *Member:* Illinois State (Member Sections on: Civil Practice; Corporate and Securities; Banking Law; Insurance Law) and American (Member, Sections on: Litigation, Health Care and Business Law) Bar Associations; Illinois State Bankers Association; Illinois Leading Lawyers Network; The Notre Dame Law Association (Director, 1998—); Certified Mediator, U.S. District Court of Northern Illinois. ***PRACTICE AREAS:*** Commercial Litigation; Corporate Law; Shareholder Litigation; Mediation; Unfair Competition. ***Email:*** ssullivan@wilmac.com

CAROL N. BAILEY, born Portsmouth, Virginia, 1953; admitted to bar, 1977, Illinois and U.S. District Court, Southern District of Illinois; 1982, U.S. District Court, Northern District of Illinois. *Education:* DePaul University (B.S., 1974); St. Louis University (J.D., 1976). Recipient, YWCA Leadership Luncheon Alta Hulett Award for Women in the Professions, 1989. Instructor: Rock Valley College Adult Education Course on Women's Legal Rights, 1978-1981; Northern Illinois University School of Nursing, Nursing Law, 1981-1985. Founding Member, President, 1980-1983 and Former Legal Counsel, Family Advocate, Inc. Founder and First Chairperson, Illinois Department of Children and Family Services, Rockford Regional Advisory Committee, 1981. Current, Volunteer Expert Panel Member, Winnebago County Child Protection Association, Member, Family Abuse Consultation Team. Member, Carrie Lynn Expert Advisory Panel. Named, Person of the Year, National Association of Social Services. Certified Mediator. Former Assistant Attorney General. Named, First Woman appointed Assistant State Attorney, Winnebago County. *Member:* Winnebago County, Illinois State and American (Member, Family Law Section and Women Rainmakers) Bar Associations; Winnebago County Women's Bar Association of Illinois (Founder and First President); Association of Conflict Resolution. ***PRACTICE AREAS:*** Domestic Law; Family Law; Litigation. ***Email:*** cbailey@wilmac.com

JAMES P. DEVINE, born Evergreen Park, Illinois, 1956; admitted to bar, 1981, Illinois; 1984, U.S. District Court, Northern District of Illinois. *Education:* Eastern Illinois University (B.A., 1978); University of Illinois (J.D., 1981). Assistant State's Attorney, 1981-1984. *Member:* Winnebago County, Illinois State (Member, Sections on: Civil Practice and Procedure and Insurance Law Section) and American Bar Associations; Illinois Association of Defense Trial Counsel. ***PRACTICE AREAS:*** Litigation; Criminal Law. ***Email:*** jdevine@wilmac.com

(This Listing Continued)

WILLIAMS & McCARTHY, A PROFESSIONAL CORPORATION, Rockford—Continued

JOHN J. HOLEVAS, born Elgin, Illinois, 1961; admitted to bar, 1986, Illinois; 1987, U.S. District Court, Northern District of Illinois. *Education:* University of Iowa (B.A., 1983); Valparaiso University (J.D., 1986). *Member:* Winnebago, Illinois State and American Bar Associations; The Association of Trial Lawyers of America. ***LANGUAGES:*** Greek. ***PRACTICE AREAS:*** Litigation. ***Email:*** jholevas@wilmac.com

TIMOTHY J. ROLLINS, born Mendota, Illinois, 1959; admitted to bar, 1985, Illinois; 1986, U.S. Court of Military Review; 1990, U.S. District Court, Northern District of Illinois. *Education:* University of Illinois (B.A., magna cum laude, 1982); Harvard University (J.D., magna cum laude, 1985). Phi Beta Kappa. Member, Harvard Law Review, 1984-1985. Author: "Standing-Injury in Fact Requirements," 98 Harvard Law Review 236 (1984); A Contract Lawyer's Guide to the Requirement for Meaningful Discussions in Negotiated Procurements," 122 Mil. L. Rev. 221, 1988; "Processing GAO Bid Protests," The Army Lawyer, May 1988. *Member:* Winnebago County, Illinois State and American Bar Associations. [Capt., Judge Advocate General's Corps, U.S. Army, 1986-1990]. ***PRACTICE AREAS:*** Corporate Law; Employment Law; Health Care Law. ***Email:*** trollins@wilmac.com

CLAYTON L. LINDSEY, born Quincy, Illinois, 1959; admitted to bar, 1984, Illinois; 1985, U.S. District Court, Northern District of Illinois, including Trial Bar; 1991, Wisconsin. *Education:* Illinois State University (B.S., with honors, 1981); John Marshall Law School (J.D., with distinction, 1984). Executive Lead Articles Editor, John Marshall Law Review, 1983-1984. Author: "Breaching the Duty of Fair Representation: The Union's Responsibility," John Marshall Law Review, 1984. *Member:* Ogle County, Winnebago County, Illinois State and American Bar Associations; State Bar of Wisconsin; The Association of Trial Lawyers of America. (Resident Partner, Oregon, Illinois Office). ***PRACTICE AREAS:*** Commercial and Civil Litigation; Personal Injury; Employment Law; Family and Juvenile Law. ***Email:*** clindsey@wilmac.com

STEPHEN E. BALOGH, born Casablanca, Morocco, 1956; admitted to bar, 1987, Illinois; 1988, U.S. District Court, Northern District of Illinois; 1990, U.S. Court of Appeals, Seventh Circuit and U.S. Supreme Court; 2002, Wisconsin and U.S. District Court, Eastern and Western Districts of Wisconsin. *Education:* University of Maryland (B.S., summa cum laude, 1983); University of Illinois (J.D., cum laude, 1987). Phi Kappa Phi; Phi Delta Phi. *Member:* Winnebago County (Member, Board of Directors, 1998-2001; First Vice-President, 2005-2006), Illinois State (Section Council, Labor and Employment Law Section; Member, Federal and Litigation Sections), Seventh Circuit and American (Member, Litigation and Labor and Employment Law Sections) Bar Associations; Wisconsin State Bar (Member, Non-Resident Division, Labor & Employment Law Section); Winnebago County Bar Foundation (President, Board of Directors, 1993-1994); Defense Research Institute. [With U.S. Marine Corps, 1977-1980]. ***PRACTICE AREAS:*** Employment; Labor Law; Civil Rights; Commercial Litigation. ***Email:*** sbalogh@wilmac.com

MARC C. GRAVINO, born Galesburg, Illinois, 1962; admitted to bar, 1988, Wisconsin, Illinois and U.S. District Court, Western District of Wisconsin; 1989, U.S. District Court, Northern District of Illinois; 1999, U.S. Court of Appeals, 7th Circuit. *Education:* University of Illinois; Northern Illinois University (B.G.S., cum laude, 1985); University of Wisconsin (J.D., 1988). *Member:* Winnebago County, Illinois State and American Bar Associations; State Bar of Wisconsin. ***PRACTICE AREAS:*** Commercial Litigation; Insurance Coverage. ***Email:*** mgravino@wilmac.com

THOMAS P. SANDQUIST, born Chicago, Illinois, 1963; admitted to bar, 1988, Illinois and U.S. District Court, Northern District of Illinois; 1995, Wisconsin. *Education:* Rockford College (B.A., cum laude, 1985); University of Illinois (J.D., cum laude, 1988). *Member:* Winnebago County (Chairman, Real Estate Section, 1993), Illinois State (Member and Newsletter Editor, Commercial, Banking and Bankruptcy Section Council, 1992—; Chairman, 1999-2000) and American Bar Associations; State Bar of Wisconsin. ***PRACTICE AREAS:*** Corporate Law; Real Estate; Debtor Creditor Law; Bankruptcy. ***Email:*** tsandquist@wilmac.com

CARL A. ECKLUND, born Rockford, Illinois, 1964; admitted to bar, 1990, Illinois; Wisconsin and U.S. District Court, Western District of Wisconsin and Northern District of Illinois. *Education:* Wheaton College (B.A., cum laude 1987); University of Wisconsin (J.D., cum laude 1990). *Member:* Winnebago County, Illinois State and American Bar Associations; State Bar of Wisconsin. ***PRACTICE AREAS:*** Corporate; Real Estate. ***Email:*** cecklund@wilmac.com

WENDY S. HOWARTER, born Chicago, Illinois, 1966; admitted to bar, 1991, Illinois. *Education:* University of Illinois (B.S., 1988; J.D., 1991). Delta Theta Phi. *Member:* Ogle County (Secretary-Treasurer, 1993-1996), Illinois State and American Bar Associations. (Resident Partner, Oregon, Illinois Office). ***PRACTICE AREAS:*** Civil Litigation; Municipal Law; Family Law; Insurance Defense. ***Email:*** whowarter@wilmac.com

MICHAEL T. CYRS, born Wausau, Wisconsin, 1969; admitted to bar, 1994, Wisconsin and Illinois. *Education:* University of Notre Dame (B.B.A., 1991); Marquette University (M.B.A., 1994; J.D., 1994). Certified Financial Planner, 2000. *Member:* Winnebago County (Treasurer and Director, 2001-2002; Chairman, Tax Section, 2000), Illinois State and American Bar Associations; State Bar of Wisconsin; Northern Illinois Estate Planning Council. ***PRACTICE AREAS:*** Estate Planning; Estate Administration; Tax Exempt Organizations; Charitable Giving; Elder Law; Corporate Law. ***Email:*** mcyrs@wilmac.com

TROY E. HAGGESTAD, born Willmar, Minnesota, 1968; admitted to bar, 1995, Illinois. *Education:* Nothern Illinois University (B.S., 1991); University of Notre Dame Law School (J.D., 1995). *Member:* Winnebago County, Illinois State and American Bar Associations. ***PRACTICE AREAS:*** Commercial Litigation; Employment Law; Insurance Coverage. ***Email:*** thaggestad@wilmac.com

BRENDAN A. MAHER, born Washington, D.C.,1970; admitted to bar, 1997, Illinois and U.S. District Court, Northern District of Illinois. *Education:* Augustana College (B.A., cum laude, 1992); Valparaiso University (J.D., summa cum laude, 1997). *Member:* Winnebago County, Illinois State and American Bar Associations; Defense Research Institute. ***PRACTICE AREAS:*** Civil Litigation; Employment Law; Employment Litigation; Insurance Defense; Insurance Coverage. ***Email:*** bmaher@wilmac.com

(This Listing Continued)

BENJAMIN W. BERNSTEN, born Madison, Wisconsin, 1975; admitted to bar, 2002, Wisconsin, Illinois, U.S. District Court, Northern District of Illinois and U.S. District Court, Eastern District of Wisconsin. *Education:* Lawrence University (B.A., 1997); University of Wisconsin (J.D., 2002). *Member:* Winnebago County, Illinois State and American Bar Associations; State Bar of Wisconsin. ***PRACTICE AREAS:*** Real Estate Law; Business Transactional Law.

JACOB M. CARPENTER, admitted to bar, 2003, Illinois. *Education:* DePauw University (B.A., cum laude, 1999); Mercer University, Walter F. George School of Law (J.D., cum laude, 2002). Recipient, Mercer University's Woodruff Scholarship. Member, Mercer Law Review.

KARL C. WILLIAMS (1934-1984)

EDWARD R. TELLING, III (1970-2004)

REPRESENTATIVE CLIENTS: *Financial:* Alpine Bank of Illinois; Amcore Bank, N.A.; National City Bank; Associated Bank; Forreston State Bank; Lena State Bank; Navistar Financial Corp; State Bank of Pearl City; Firstar Bank.
HEALTH CARE: Alpine Fireside Health Center; Benefit Administrative Service; Janet Wattles Center; Lundholm Surgical Group, LTD; Milestone, Inc.; Rock River Valley Blood Center; Wesley Willows; Orthopedic & Arthritis Clinic; Pediatric Associates of Rockford; Riverside Medical Clinic; Rockford Clinic; Rockford Health System; Rockford Health Plans; Rockford Memorial Hospital; Rockford Orthopedic Associates; Rockford Surgical Services; Rosecrance Health Network; Visiting Nurses Association.
EDUCATIONAL: Rockford School District 205; Harlem Education Foundation; Forrestville Valley Community School District; Oregon School District; Rockford College; Rock Valley College Foundation; Community Foundation Northern Illinois.
INSURANCE: Cincinnati Insurance Co.; Country Companies; Employers Mutual Insurance Co.; Gallagher Bassett Insurance Co.; The Hartford; Kemper Group; Liberty Mutual Insurance Co.; Springfield Fire & Casualty Co.; The St. Paul Companies; Shelby Insurance Co.; The Travelers Companies; Wausau Insurance Companies; West Bend Mutual Insurance Co.; Williams-Manny.
MANUFACTURING: DaimlerChrysler Corp.; Advanced Machine & Engineering; Aircraft Gear Corp.; Arachnid, Inc.; Behr Machinery & Equipment Corp.; Dean Foods, Co.; DeKalb Genetics Corp.; Etynre International, LTD.; Hydraforce, Inc.; Ingersoll Milling Machine Co.; Haldex Hydraulics Corp.; Joseph Behr & Sons, Inc.; Martin Automatic, Inc.; Miller Engineering Co.; Pacsci Motion, Control, Inc.; Pegard Products, Inc.; Roper-Whitney of Rockford; Southern Imperial, Inc.; Stickle Enterprises, LTD.; Terra Industries; The Valvoline Company; W.A. Whitney Co.; Zenith Cutter Co.
MUNICIPAL: Boone County; City of Byron; Cherry Valley Library District; North Suburban Library District; City of Oregon; Oregon Park District; City of Rockford; Rockford Mass Transit District; Rockford Park District; Rockford Metro Authority; Rockford Police Pension Fund; Village of Lena; Winnebago County.
REAL ESTATE, REAL ESTATE DEVELOPMENT & CONSTRUCTION: Landis Reality; Mid-Northern Management; Ringland-Johnson, Inc.; Hillcrest Development, Inc.; Spring Creek Development Company; Sproule Construction Co.; Star Development, LLC; Stock Lumber Co.
COMMUNICATIONS: Airplay Broadcasting Co.; Pride Communications, LLC; Radio Works, Inc.; R World Communications; Segueway Broadcasting Corp.; WTVO Television.
RETAIL/SERVICE: Cal Cars, Inc; Golf Shack, LLC; Kelley-Williamson Company; Lawyers Title Insurance Corp.; Premium Oil Co.; Title Underwriters Agency, Inc.; Viking Distributors, Inc.; Vista Marketing Group, LTD.

ANDICH & ANDICH

SAFETY BUILDING, SUITE 404
1800 THIRD AVENUE
ROCK ISLAND, ILLINOIS 61201
Telephone: 309-788-9337
Facsimile: 309-788-9332
URL: http://www.andichlaw.com

Commercial Law, Business Litigation, Consumer Litigation, Creditor's Rights, Media, Bankruptcy, Employment, Domestic Relations, Real Estate, Probate, Civil Trial and Appeals, Wills, Estates, Family Law, Divorce, Child Custody, Child Support, Adoption.

MEMBERS OF FIRM

DAVID W. ANDICH, born Davenport, Iowa, October 1, 1947; admitted to bar, 1975, Illinois and U.S. District Court, Northern District of Illinois; 1978, U.S. Court of Appeals, Seventh Circuit; 1981, U.S. Court of Appeals, Fifth Circuit; 1982, U.S. Supreme Court; 1990, U. S. District Court, Central District of Illinois. *Education:* Northern Illinois University (B.S., 1969; M.B.A., 1971); The John Marshall Law School (J.D., 1975). Member, Order of John Marshall. Associate Editor, The John Marshall Journal of Practice & Procedure, 1974-1975. Author: "The Freedom of Information Act, a Challenge to the Executive and Judiciary," The John Marshall Journal of Practice & Procedure, Vol. 7, No. 2, 1974. Instructor, Appellate Practice, Research and Writing, The John Marshall Law School, 1975-1979. Young Lawyers Federal Trial Bar Advocacy Course, Chicago Bar Association, 1984-1985; Law Clerk, Appellate Court of Illinois, Judge Charles R. Barrett, 1975-1976. Member and Secretary of Board of Commissioners of Office of State Appellate Defender, 1997—. President, Illinois Board of Admissions to the Bar, 2001—. President, Rock Island Community Foundation, 2003—. *Member:* Chicago (Member, 1984-1989 and Vice Chairman, 1988-1989, Communications Law Committee), Rock Island County and Illinois State Bar Associations. ***PRACTICE AREAS:*** Commercial Litigation; Media Law; Defamation and Privacy Law; Family Law; Appellate Practice; Probate; Employment Law. ***Email:*** dandich@qconline.com

STEPHEN G. ANDICH, born Rock Island, Illinois, February 8, 1949; admitted to bar, 1975, Illinois; 1977, U.S. District Court, Central District of Illinois; 1993, U.S. Court of Appeals, Seventh Circuit; 1995, U.S. Supreme Court. *Education:* Northern Illinois University (B.S., 1971); The John Marshall Law School (J.D., 1975). Assistant States Attorney, Rock Island County, 1975-1976. Special City Prosecutor, City of East Moline, 1976—. *Member:* Rock Island County (Secretary-Treasurer, 1999-2003; Vice President, 2004—) and Illinois State Bar Associations; Commercial Law League. ***PRACTICE AREAS:*** Debtor and Creditor; Probate; Real Estate; Bankruptcy; Wills; Estates; Commercial Litigation; Consumer Litigation; Creditors Rights. ***Email:*** sandich@qconline.com

OF COUNSEL

Marvin S. Andich

BETTY, NEUMAN & McMAHON

ROCK ISLAND, ILLINOIS

(See Davenport, Iowa)

General Civil Practice in State and Federal Courts, Trials and Appeals, Insurance Defense, Estate Planning, Trusts and Probate, Real Estate, Family, Taxation, Business and Corporation Law.

BOZEMAN, NEIGHBOUR, PATTON & NOE, LLP

ROCK ISLAND, ILLINOIS

(See Moline)

General Practice in State and Federal Courts. Appellate Practice, Bankruptcy, Banks and Banking, Business Law, Civil Practice, Civil Rights, Commercial Law, Commercial Real Estate, Constitutional Law, Construction Law, Contracts, Corporate Law, Debtor and Creditor, Disabilities, Employee Benefits, Environmental Law, Family Law, Fidelity and Surety, Finance, Guardianship and Conservatorship, Health Care, Hospital Law, Housing Law, Insurance, Insurance Defense, Labor and Employment, Leases and Leasing, Legal Ethics and Professional Responsibility, Litigation, Medical Malpractice, Mergers, Acquisitions and Divestitures, Mortgages, Municipal Law, Negligence, Personal Injury, Probate, Products Liability, Professional Liability, Real Estate, Taxation, Torts, Trusts and Estates, Wills, Workers' Compensation.

BROOKS & TRINRUD

A PROFESSIONAL CORPORATION

Established in 1990

3725 BLACKHAWK ROAD
P.O. BOX 3487
ROCK ISLAND, ILLINOIS 61204-3487
Telephone: 309-786-4900
Fax: 309-786-4940
Email: info@btlawpc.com
URL: http://www.BTLawPC.com

Davenport, Iowa Office: 220 Emerson Place, 52801. Telephone: 563-326-4900. Fax: 563-326-4944.

General Practice, Civil Litigation, Workers Compensation, Bankruptcy, Estate Planning, Trusts and Probate, Business Law (including Corporations, Partnerships), Family Law, Commercial Collections, Real Estate Foreclosure, Real Estate, Commercial Real Estate.

JACK L. BROOKS, born Maysville, Kentucky, August 21, 1950; admitted to bar, 1975, Iowa, Illinois and U.S. District Court, Central District of Illinois. *Education:* Dartmouth College (B.A., cum laude, 1972); Drake University (J.D., with honors, 1974). Order of the Coif. Certified Mediator and Arbitrator, 14th Judicial Circuit, Illinois. *Member:* Iowa State Bar Association and American Arbitration Association; Illinois Association of Defense Trial Counsel; Defense Research Institute. ***PRACTICE AREAS:*** Medical Malpractice; Personal Injury; Insurance Defense; Commercial Law; Banking Law; Construction Litigation. ***Email:*** jbrooks@btlawpc.com

RICHARD J. TRINRUD, born Decorah, Iowa, April 15, 1950; admitted to bar, 1981, Illinois; 1983, U.S. District Court, Central District of Illinois; 1991, Iowa; 1997, U.S. Supreme Court; 2001, U.S. District Court, Northern District of Illinois including Trial Bar. *Education:* St. Olaf College (B.A., 1972); Hamline University (J.D., cum laude, 1981). *Member:* Iowa State Bar Association; Illinois Association of Defense Trial Counsel; Iowa Defense Counsel Association; Defense Research Institute. ***PRACTICE AREAS:*** Medical Malpractice; Personal Injury; Insurance Defense. ***Email:*** rtrinrud@btlawpc.com

JEFFREY C. McDANIEL, born Davenport, Iowa, February 17, 1968; admitted to bar, 1993, Iowa, Illinois; 1994, U.S. District Court, Central District of Illinois; 2001, U.S. District Court, Northern District of Illinois; 2002, U.S. District Court, Southern District of Illinois. *Education:* University of Iowa (B.A., 1990; J.D., 1993). *Member:* Illinois State Bar Association; Illinois Association of Defense Trial Counsel; Iowa Defense Counsel Association; Defense Research Institute; American Bankruptcy Institute. ***PRACTICE AREAS:*** Insurance Defense; Personal Injury; Commercial Litigation; Bankruptcy; Real Estate Foreclosure; Disability Law. ***Email:*** jcm@btlawpc.com

BERNARD J. HOFMANN, born Davenport, Iowa, February 19, 1966; admitted to bar, 1993, Iowa; 1994, Illinois and U.S. District Court, Central District of Illinois. *Education:* University of Iowa (B.A., 1989); Drake University (J.D., 1993). *Member:* Iowa State and American Bar Associations. ***PRACTICE AREAS:*** Real Estate; Estate Planning; Corporate Law; Business Law; Probate. ***Email:*** bjh@btlawpc.com

JEFFREY D. BERT, born Moline, Illinois, May 8, 1967; admitted to bar, 1992, Iowa; 1993, Illinois; 1994, U.S. District Court, Central District of Illinois. *Education:* Iowa State University (B.A., 1989); University of Iowa (J.D., with distinction, 1992). *Member:* Iowa State Bar Association; Iowa Defense Counsel Association. ***PRACTICE AREAS:*** Insurance Defense; Workers Compensation; Commercial Litigation; Medical Malpractice; Real Estate; Construction Litigation; Personal Injury. ***Email:*** jdb@btlawpc.com

MILISSA K. HOFMANN, born Dubuque, Iowa, April 17, 1968; admitted to bar, 1993, Iowa; 1994, Illinois. *Education:* Cornell College; Augustana College (B.A., 1990); Drake University (J.D., 1993). Member, Iowa Supreme Court Probate Rules Committee, 1995—. *Member:* Scott County, Rock Island County, Iowa State (Member: Real Estate; Agricultural Sections, 1994—), Illinois State and American Bar Associations. ***PRACTICE AREAS:*** Real Estate; Commercial Law; Business Law; Corporate Law; Estate Planning; Probate. ***Email:*** mkh@btlawpc.com

(This Listing Continued)

DEREK G. JONES, born Davenport, Iowa, May 2, 1972; admitted to bar, 1997, Iowa; 1998, Illinois; 2000, U.S. District Court, Central District of Illinois. *Education:* University of Iowa (B.A., 1994; J.D., 1997). ***PRACTICE AREAS:*** Insurance Defense; Civil Litigation; Bankruptcy; Real Estate Foreclosure; Disability Law; Criminal Law; Appellate Practice. ***Email:*** dgj@btlawpc.com

KATHLEEN E. MESICH, born Moline, Illinois, June 20, 1976; admitted to bar, 2002, Illinois and U.S. District Court, Northern and Central Districts of Illinois; 2003, Iowa; 2004, U.S. District Court, Southern District of Iowa, U.S. District Court, Eastern District of Missouri. *Education:* University of Illinois (B.S., 1998); Southern Illinois University (J.D., 2002). *Member:* Illinois State Bar Association. ***PRACTICE AREAS:*** Commercial Litigation; Real Estate Foreclosure; Creditor Bankruptcy; Collections; Landlord and Tenant Law. ***Email:*** kem@btlawpc.com

HENRY W. LATHAM, II, born Davenport, Iowa, September 1, 1964; admitted to bar, 1991, Iowa (Not admitted in Illinois). *Education:* St. Ambrose College (B.A., 1986); University of Iowa (J.D., 1989). *Member:* Scott County (Past President, Executive Counsel, 2003-2004) and Iowa State Bar Associations; American Inns of Court. ***PRACTICE AREAS:*** Real Estate; Family Law; Criminal Law; Corporate Law; Business Law. ***Email:*** hwl@btlawpc.com

BRIAN T. FAIRFIELD, born Huron, South Dakota, June 24, 1969; admitted to bar, 1994, Iowa; 2000, U.S. District Court, Southern District of Iowa; 2004, Illinois. *Education:* Creighton University (B.A., 1991; J.D., 1994). *Member:* Rock Island County, Scott County, Iowa State and Illinois State Bar Associations. ***PRACTICE AREAS:*** Insurance Defense; Personal Injury; Workers Compensation; Commercial Litigation. ***Email:*** btf@btlawpc.com

ALLISON E. BARTSH, born Rochester, Minnesota, February 13, 1978; admitted to bar, 2003, Illinois; 2004, Iowa. *Education:* University of Notre Dame (B.A., 2000); University of Iowa (J.D., 2003). *Member:* Iowa State and Illinois State Bar Associations. ***PRACTICE AREAS:*** Estate Planning; Probate; Real Estate; Bankruptcy; Corporate. ***Email:*** aeb@btlawpc.com

JASON P. BUTT, born Clinton, Iowa, June 28, 1975; admitted to bar, 2001, Nevada; 2003, Iowa. *Education:* University of Iowa (B.A., 1997); Arizona State University (J.D., 2001). *Member:* Iowa Bar Association. ***PRACTICE AREAS:*** Civil Litigation; Insurance Defense; Personal Injury; Workers Compensation. ***Email:*** jpb@btlawpc.com

PARALEGALS

Lisa Gibson
Anne Resetich
Rhoda Staker

REPRESENTATIVE CLIENTS: Alcoa Employees and Community Credit Union; Acuity; ANPAC; Auto Owners Insurance; Bank Orion; Cincinnati Insurance; US Bank, N.A.; First City Mortgage Corp.; Illinois Casualty Co.; Illinois State Medical Insurance Society; IMT Insurance Co.; John Deere Harvester Works of Deere & Co.; John Deere Insurance Co.; John Deere Parts Distribution Center of Deere & Co.; Metlife Auto and Home; Midwest Medical Insurance Company; Nuvell Financial; Progressive Insurance; Quad City Bank and Trust Company; RIA Federal Credit Union; State Farm Insurance Co.; The National Bank; The St. Paul Companies; Wells Fargo Financial Acceptance.

CALIFF & HARPER, P.C.

ROCK ISLAND, ILLINOIS

(See Moline)

Corporate, Commercial, Civil Litigation in all State and Federal Courts, Labor, Employment, Banking, Governmental, School, Administrative (including N.L.R.B.), Products Liability, Insurance, Taxation, Estate Planning and Probate Law, Real Estate, Land Development and Zoning, Business Enterprises, Closely Held Business, Limited Liability Companies, Partnerships, Small Business, Buying or Selling a Business, Collections, Employee Benefits, Employment Contracts, Human Resources, Contracts, Business Lawsuits, Internet Law, E-Commerce, Commercial Leasing, Landlord and Tenant; Buying or Selling a Home; Tax Planning and Asset Protection.

CHURCHILL & CHURCHILL, P.C.

ROCK ISLAND, ILLINOIS

(See Moline)

General Civil Trial Practice in State and Federal Courts. Corporation, Business Law, Commercial, Banking, Real Estate, Probate and Bankruptcy Law, Trusts and Estates, Wills, Estate Planning, Taxation.

GOSMA, TARBOX & ASSOCIATES, P.L.C.

ROCK ISLAND, ILLINOIS

(See Davenport, Iowa)

General Civil Practice, including Business and Corporate Organization and Transactions, Banking, Real Estate, Estate Planning, Elder Law, Trust and Estate Administration, and Personal Injury, Business and Probate Litigation, Medical Malpractice, Business Enterprises, Slip and Fall, Personal Injury, Automobile Accidents, Wrongful Death, Buying and Selling, Zoning and Land Use, Construction, Asset Protection, Guardianships, Banking and Finance, Closely Held Business, Corporate, Franchise, Limited Liability, Small Business, Partnerships, Buying and Selling of Businesses, Creditors Rights, Contracts, Business Planning, Law Suites, Insurance, Commercial Leasing, Business Start-Ups.

LAW OFFICE OF JAY R. HAMILTON, PLC

ROCK ISLAND, ILLINOIS

(See Davenport, Iowa)

Member: Patent Prosecution and Licensing, Intellectual Property, Trademarks, Copyrights, Trade Secrets, Consumer Fraud.

STEVE HANNA ATTORNEY AT LAW

ROCK ISLAND, ILLINOIS

(See Moline)

Criminal Law, Driving While Intoxicated, Drug Crimes, Juvenile Criminal Law, Parole and Probation, Traffic Violations. Illinois, Iowa, Federal Practice.

HENINGER AND HENINGER

PROFESSIONAL CORPORATION

ROCK ISLAND, ILLINOIS

(See Davenport, Iowa)

General Practice. Business Law, Probate, Real Estate, Health Care, Labor and Employment, Personal Injury, Estate Planning, Medical Malpractice, Professional Liability, Trial Practice.

KATZ, HUNTOON & FIEWEGER, P.C.

ROCK ISLAND, ILLINOIS

(See Moline)

Civil Trial and Appellate Practice. Personal Injury, Insurance, Commercial, Banking, Bank and Savings and Loan Failures, Bankruptcy, Corporation, Probate, Real Estate, Labor Relations, Taxation, Professional Malpractice, Products Liability, Workers Compensation, Employment, Administrative, Public, School and Municipal Law and Business Crimes.

PHILIP E. KOENIG

1515 FOURTH AVENUE
ROCK ISLAND, ILLINOIS 61201
Telephone: 309-786-3313
Fax: 309-786-0061
Email: pkoenig@qconline.com
URL: http://www.lawyers.com/koeniglaw

Wills and Probate, Estate Planning, Real Estate, Business Organization, Tax, Bankruptcy, Commercial Real Estate, Commercial Bankruptcy, Trusts and Estates and General Civil Practice, including Trials and Appeals.

PHILIP E. KOENIG, born Berwyn, Illinois, July 29, 1949; admitted to bar, 1975, Illinois and U.S. District Court, Central District of Illinois; 1995, U.S. Tax Court. *Education:* Southern Illinois University (B.A., 1972); Southwestern University (J.D., 1975). Delta Theta Phi. Author: "Survey of Illinois Law - Real Estate Finance," 12 Southern Illinois University Law Journal 1157, 1988. *Member:* Rock Island County, Illinois State (Member: Trusts and Estates Section Council, 1999—; Illinois Real Estate Law Section Council, 1979-1985, 1990-1999; Chair, 1996-1997; Member, Commercial, Banking and Bankruptcy Section Council, 1986-1989) and American Bar Associations; Illinois Bar Foundation (Charter Member); Quad City Estate Planning Council.

REPRESENTATIVE CLIENTS: Buffalo Prairie State Bank; Joy State Bank; Trinity Health Care Foundation; State Bank of Toulon; Country Bank.

LANE & WATERMAN LLP

224 18TH STREET, SUITE 500
ROCK ISLAND, ILLINOIS 61201
Telephone: 309-786-1600
Fax: 309-786-1794
URL: http://www.l-wlaw.com

Davenport, Iowa Office: 220 North Main Street, Suite 600. Telephone: 563-324-3246. Fax: 563-324-1616.

General Civil Practice.

MEMBERS OF FIRM

CHARLES E. MILLER, born June 13, 1945; admitted to bar, 1973, Iowa; 1989, Illinois. *Education:* Phillips Exeter Academy and Northwestern University (A.B., 1966); University of Iowa (J.D., with distinction, 1973). Phi Delta Phi. Member, Dillon Inn of Court (Treasurer, 1993-1995). Member: Iowa Supreme Court Advisory Committee on the Rules of Civil Procedure, 1993-1998; Iowa Uniform Court Instructions Committee, 1983-1986. *Member:* Iowa Academy of Trial Lawyers; Iowa Defense Counsel Association (President, 1995-1996); International Association of Defense Counsel. [CDR, U.S. Navy, 1966-1969]. ***PRACTICE AREAS:*** Labor and Employment Law; Defense Litigation; Malpractice Defense. ***Email:*** cmiller@l-wlaw.com

DANA M. CRAIG, born June 12, 1950; admitted to bar, 1975, Iowa; 1989, Illinois. *Education:* Iowa State University (B.S., with distinction, 1972); University of Michigan (J.D., 1975). *Member:* Iowa Defense Counsel Association; Propane Gas Defense Association; American Intellectual Property Association. ***PRACTICE AREAS:*** Litigation; Product Liability Law; Construction Law; Computer Law; Trademark, Copyright and Unfair Competition. ***Email:*** dcraig@l-wlaw.com

ROBERT V. P. WATERMAN, JR., born November 20, 1955; admitted to bar, 1981, Iowa; 1983, Illinois. *Education:* Northwestern University (B.A., 1978); University of Iowa (J.D., 1981). Fellow: American College of Trial Lawyers; Iowa Academy of Trial Lawyers; Iowa Defense Counsel Association; Illinois Association of Defense Trial Counsel; Quad City Claims Association (President, 1987-1988). ***PRACTICE AREAS:*** Litigation; Insurance Law; Environmental Coverage Litigation. ***Email:*** bwaterman@l-wlaw.com

PETER J. BENSON, born March 7, 1957; admitted to bar, 1982, Iowa; 1983, Illinois. *Education:* Northwestern University (B.A., 1979); University of Iowa (J.D., with high distinction, 1982). Order of the Coif. *Member:* Iowa Society of Hospital Attorneys (President, 1997-1998); American Health Lawyers' Association. ***PRACTICE AREAS:*** Health (Health Care) and Hospital Law; Corporate Law. ***Email:*** pbenson@l-wlaw.com

JOHN D. TELLEEN, born April 26, 1958; admitted to bar, 1984, Iowa; 1985, Illinois. *Education:* Augustana College (B.A., cum laude, 1980); University of Iowa (J.D., with distinction, 1984). *Member:* Iowa Defense Counsel Association; Illinois Association of Defense Trial Counsel. ***PRACTICE AREAS:*** Civil Litigation; Insurance Law; Environmental Coverage Litigation. ***Email:*** jtelleen@l-wlaw.com

RICHARD A. DAVIDSON, born September 12, 1959; admitted to bar, 1984, Iowa; 1986, Illinois. *Education:* Drake University (B.S.B.A., magna cum laude, 1981; J.D., with honors, 1984). Beta Alpha Psi; Order of the Coif. Law Clerk, Fifth Judicial District of Iowa, 1984-1985. ***PRACTICE AREAS:*** Real Estate; Commercial Law; Bankruptcy Law; Probate Law. ***Email:*** rdavidson@l-wlaw.com

JASON J. O'ROURKE, born March 24, 1973; admitted to bar, 1998, Iowa; 1999, Illinois. *Education:* Creighton University (B.A., cum laude, 1995; J.D., magna cum laude, 1998). ***PRACTICE AREAS:*** Products Liability; Construction Law; Insurance Defense. ***Email:*** jo'rourke@l-wlaw.com

COURTNEY M. KAY-DECKER, born May 7, 1973; admitted to bar, 1997, Iowa; 1998, Illinois. *Education:* Northwestern University (B.A., 1994); University of Iowa (J.D., with distinction, 1997). *Member:* Iowa State Board of Tax Review. ***PRACTICE AREAS:*** Corporate; Estate Planning. ***Email:*** ckay-decker@l-wlaw.com

DIANE M. REINSCH, born September 14, 1958; admitted to bar, 1996, Iowa and Illinois. *Education:* Iowa State University (B.A., with high distinction, 1984); University of Iowa (M.A., 1989; J.D., with high distinction, 1995). ***PRACTICE AREAS:*** Civil Litigation; Insurance Defense. ***Email:*** dreinsch@l-wlaw.com

ASSOCIATES

ALISSA D. KLEIN, born April 23, 1978; admitted to bar, 2004, Iowa; 2005, Illinois. *Education:* University of Northern Iowa (B.A., summa cum laude, 2000; B.A., summa cum laude, 2001); University of Iowa (J.D., with distinction, 2004; M.H.A., 2005). ***Email:*** aklein@l-wlaw.com

JENNIFER L. HAMILTON, born 1975; admitted to bar, 2002, Illinois. *Education:* University of Texas at Austin (B.B.A., 1997); University of Iowa (J.D., 2002). ***Email:*** jkoger@l-wlaw.com

All attorneys are members of the Illinois State and Rock Island County Bar Associations.

(For Complete Biographical Data on all Personnel, see Professional Biographies at Davenport, Iowa).

McCARTHY, CALLAS, FUHR & ELLISON, P.C.

Established in 1997

THE LAW CENTRE
329 18TH STREET
ROCK ISLAND, ILLINOIS 61201
Telephone: 309-788-2800
Fax: 309-793-4090
Email: mcfe@thelawcentre.com
URL: http://www.mcfe-law.com

Divorce, Commercial and Residential Real Estate, Labor Law, Labor Relations, Labor Arbitration, Commercial Litigation, Criminal Defense, Probate and Probate Administration, Inheritance, Dram Shop Law, Liquor Liability, Casualty Insurance, Medical Negligence, Debtor/ Creditor Bankruptcy, ERISA, Personal Injury, Wrongful Death, Maritime Accidents, Products Liability, Traffic Violations.

FIRM PROFILE: The law firm of McCarthy, Callas, Fuhr & Ellison, P.C. practices throughout Illinois and Iowa. The firm is committed to provide quality legal representation, our practice reflects high standards, diligence, experience and integrity.

RICHARD W. McCARTHY, born Rock Island, Illinois, December 17, 1922; admitted to bar, 1949, Illinois; 1950, U.S. District Court, Central District of Illinois; 1985, Iowa. *Education:* St. Ambrose College; DePaul University (J.D., 1949). Phi Alpha Delta. Assistant State's Attorney, Rock Island County, 1950-1954. Assistant Attorney General, State of Illinois, 1965. *Member:* Rock Island County, Illinois State, Iowa State and American Bar Associations. ***PRACTICE AREAS:*** Probate Administration; Divorce; Residential Real Estate; Labor Relations; Inheritance.

JOHN S. CALLAS, born Moline, Illinois, August 27, 1957; admitted to bar, 1982, Illinois and U.S. District Court, Central District of Illinois; 1990, U.S. Court of Appeals, Seventh Circuit. *Education:* University of Illinois (B.A., 1979); Illinois Institute of Technology Chicago-Kent College of Law (J.D., 1982). Commissioner: Metropolitan Airport Authority, 1989-1995; Rock Island County Merit Commission, 2000—; Board of Directors, Fidlar-Doubleday & Brelsh Holdings; Director, Skills Vocational and Rehabilitation Services, 1997-2002. Bono of Directors, Illinois Casuality Company, 2004—. *Member:* Rock Island County (Board of Managers, 1992-1993), Illinois State (Employee Benefit Section Council, 2003—) and American Bar Associations; Federal Bar Association (Central and South-

(This Listing Continued)

ern Districts of Illinois); The Association of Trial Lawyers of America; Illinois Trial Lawyers Association; American Inns of Court; Matrimonial Lawyers of Rock Island County (President and Charter Member). ***PRACTICE AREAS:*** ERISA; Family Law; General Practice; Commercial Litigation; Labor. ***Email:*** JCallas@mcfe-law.com

FRANK R. FUHR, born Aledo, Illinois, September 20, 1955; admitted to bar, 1980, Illinois; 1985, U.S. District Court, Central District of Illinois; 1986, Iowa; 1996, U.S. District Court, Southern District of Iowa. *Education:* Southern Illinois University (B.A., 1976); University of Wisconsin (J.D., cum laude, 1980). Assistant States Attorney, Rock Island County, 1980-1984. Assistant Public Defender, Rock Island County, 1984-1985. *Member:* Rock Island County, Scott County, Illinois State and Iowa State Bar Associations. ***PRACTICE AREAS:*** Personal Injury; Wrongful Death; Maritime Accidents; Dram Shop Law; Commercial Litigation; Real Estate; Probate; Products Liability. ***Email:*** FFuhr@mcfe-law.com

PETER W. CHURCH, born Red Oak, Iowa, September 27, 1967; admitted to bar, 1993, Iowa and U.S. District Court, Southern District of Iowa; 1994, Illinois and U.S. District Court, Central District of Illinois. *Education:* Iowa State University (B.A., with distinction, 1990); University of Iowa (J.D., with distinction, 1993). Member, National Moot Court Team, 1993. Member, Iowa Law Review. *Member:* Scott County, Rock Island County, Iowa State and American Bar Associations. ***PRACTICE AREAS:*** Family Law; Criminal Defense; Traffic Violations; General Practice. ***Email:*** pchurch@mcfe-law.com

TIMOTHY M. FEENEY, born Davenport, Iowa, April 30, 1967; admitted to bar, 1993, Illinois and Iowa; 1994, U.S. District Court, Central and Northern Districts of Illinois and Southern and Northern Districts of Iowa. *Education:* University of Iowa (B.S., 1989; J.D., with distinction, 1992). Law Clerk, Hon. Lee M. Jackwig, Chief U.S. Bankruptcy Judge, U.S. District Court, Southern District of Iowa, 1993-1994. Assistant Director, Client Counseling, University of Iowa Law School, 1992. Member: Board of Directors, Big Brothers/Big Sisters, Quad Cities, Inc., 1996-2000; Board of Directors Quad City Claims Association, 1996-2004. *Member:* Scott County, Rock Island County, Iowa State (Member, U.P.L. Commission) and Illinois State Bar Associations; Federal Bar Association; American Bankruptcy Institute; Defense Research Institute. ***PRACTICE AREAS:*** Personal Injury; Bankruptcy; Debtor and Creditor; Dram Shop Liability; Commercial Litigation; Workers Compensation; Insurance Defense. ***Email:*** tfeeney.mcfe@thelawcentre.com

---

PAMELA J. KENNERLY, born Carbondale, Illinois, August 29, 1969; admitted to bar, 1997, Illinois; 2002, U.S. District Court, Central District of Illinois. *Education:* Monmouth College (B.A., 1992); Southern Illinois University School of Law (J.D., 1997). Assistant States Attorney, Macon County, 1997-2001. *Member:* Illinois State Bar Association. ***PRACTICE AREAS:*** Domestic Relations; Family Law; Criminal Law; Traffic Violations; General Practice. ***Email:*** pkennerly@mcfe-law.com

OF COUNSEL

PETER H. LOUSBERG, born Des Moines, Iowa, August 19, 1931; admitted to bar, 1956, Illinois; 1961, U.S. District Court, Central District of Illinois; 1972, Florida; 1973, U.S. Court of Appeals, Seventh Circuit; 1983, U.S. District Court, Northern District of Illinois; 1985, Iowa. *Education:* Yale University (B.A., 1953); Notre Dame Law School (J.D., cum laude, 1956). President and Chairman of Board, 1993-1994, Illinois State Bar Association Mutual Insurance Co. Member, Board of Directors, 1983-1987 and Vice-President, 1987, Lawyers Trust Fund of Illinois. *Member:* Illinois State (President, 1992-1993; Chair, Special Committee on Professionalism, 1986-1987) and American (Assembly Member, 1989-1994) Bar Associations; The Florida Bar (Chairman, Out-of-State Practitioners Committee, 1985-1986); Illinois Trial Lawyers Association (Member, Board of Managers, 1974-1978); American Law Institute; American Judicature Society; National Legal Aid and Defenders Association. Fellow: Illinois Bar Foundation (Charter Member, 1983; Chairman, Board of Directors, 1987-1991); American Bar Foundation; American College of Trial Lawyers. [U.S. Marine Corps, J.A.G., certified, 1957-1958]. ***PRACTICE AREAS:*** Civil Trials; Malpractice; Damage Law; Personal Injury.

ATTORNEYS FOR: Illinois Casualty Co.; US Liability Insurance Co.; Employers Mutual Companies; Employer's Reinsurance Corp.; Merchants Mutual Bonding Co.; Kendall Insurance Co.; Home Insurance Co.; Aul Life Insurance Co.; International Brotherhood of Teamsters & Chauffeurs, Local 371; Plumbers & Steamfitters, Local 25; International Union of Operating Engineers, Local #150; International Brotherhood of Electrical Workers, Local 145; Bricklayers, Local #6; Rock Island Structural and Ornamental Iron Workers, Local 111; Millwright & Technical Engineers, Local No. 2158; Sheet Metal Workers Local #91; North Point Ins. Co.; Continental Western Ins. Co.; County of Rock Island; Cement Masons Local #18; Quad City Foundation for Fair Contracting; Service Plus Credit Union; U.S. Federal Credit Union; E.T. Video, Inc.; North Pointe, Insurance Co.; Millennium Waste Inc.; Quad City Garage Policy Group; Moline Housing Authority; Illinois Department of Children and Family Services.

PAPPAS & SCHNELL, P.C.

Established in 1996

PADDOCK BUILDING
1617-2ND AVENUE, SUITE 300
P.O. BOX 5408
ROCK ISLAND, ILLINOIS 61204-5408
Telephone: 309-788-7110
Fax: 309-788-2773
Email: pslaw@pappasandschnell.com
URL: http://www.pappasandschnell.com

Labor and Employment, Litigation, Trusts and Estates, Probate, Taxation, Corporate, Business Law, Real Estate, Education.

MATTHEW P. PAPPAS, born Davenport, Iowa, July 25, 1962; admitted to bar, 1988, Illinois; 2001, Iowa; U.S. District Court, Northern and Central Districts of Illinois and U.S. District Court, Southern District of Iowa; U.S. Court of Appeals, Seventh and Eighth Circuits. *Education:* University of Illinois (B.A., 1985); Valparaiso University (J.D., 1988). Editorial Review Board, The Illinois Labor Letter. *Member:* Rock Island County; Illinois State (Member, Section Council: Labor and Employment, 1995-1999) and American (Member, Sections on: Labor and Employment Law; Individual Rights and Responsibilities) Bar Associations; American Employment Law Council; Society for Human Resource Management; Great River Human Resources Association (President, 1998, Vice-President, 1997, Legislative Chair, 1999-2000, 2003); Iowa State Council for the Society for Human Resource Management (1999). ***PRACTICE AREAS:*** Management Labor Law; Employment Law; Litigation. ***Email:*** mpappas@pappasandschnell.com

MOLLY O'MEARA SCHNELL, born Elkader, Iowa, April 5, 1964; admitted to bar, 1989, Iowa and Illinois; U.S. District Court, Southern District of Iowa. *Education:* University of Iowa (B.B.A., 1986; J.D., with distinction, 1989). Member, Quad City Estate Planning Council. *Member:* Scott County, Rock Island County, Iowa State (Member, Sections on: Probate and Trust Law; Taxation; Real Estate and Title Law); Illinois State (Member, Sections on: Federal Taxation; Trusts and Estates) and American (Member, Sections on: Probate; Real Property; Federal Taxation; Law Practice Management) Bar Associations. ***PRACTICE AREAS:*** Corporate; Trusts and Estates; Real Estate; Taxation; Business; Probate. ***Email:*** mschnell@pappasandschnell.com

PATRICK J. FLYNN, born Davenport, Iowa, March 7, 1948; admitted to bar, 1974, Tennessee; 1976, U.S. Court of Appeals for the Armed Forces; 1979, Minnesota; 1980, Iowa; 1992, Illinois; U.S. District Court, Central District of Illinois, U.S. District Court, Northern and Southern Districts of Iowa and U.S. District Court, District of Minnesota. *Education:* Denison University (B.A., 1970); Vanderbilt University (J.D., 1974). Adjunct Faculty/Instructor, Black Hawk College Paralegal Program, Real Estate Law, 2001. *Member:* Rock Island County, Scott County, Tennessee, Minnesota State, Iowa State (Member: Probate and Trust Law and Corporation, Banking and Business Law Sections), Illinois State and American (Member, Sections on: Real Property; Probate; Trust) Bar Associations. [Judge Advocate, USMC, 1974-1979; Judge Advocate General Corps, U.S. Navy Reserve, 1980-2002; Certified Military Judge, 1996]. ***PRACTICE AREAS:*** Real Estate; Trusts and Estates; Probate; Corporate Law. ***Email:*** pflynn@pappasandschnell.com

TERRI L. MARTIN, born Fort Sam Houston, Texas, September 24, 1952; admitted to bar, 1999, Illinois; 2000, Iowa, U.S. District Court, Central and Southern Districts of Illinois and U.S. Court of Appeals, Eighth Circuit; U.S. Court of Appeals, Seventh Circuit. *Education:* Kansas State University (B.S., 1993); John Marshall Law School (J.D., cum laude, 1999). Phi Delta Phi; Order of John Marshall. Leads Article Editor, John Marshall Law Review. Author, "Retaliatory Discharge for Attorney-Employees in Private Practice," 33 John Marshall L. Rev., (383, Winter 2000). Adjunct Faculty/Assistant Professor, Black Hawk College, Litigation Support and Legal Research and Writing, 1991-2001. *Member:* Bar Association of the Central and Southern Federal Districts of Illinois; Rock Island County, Scott County, Illinois State (Member, Employment and Labor Law and Litigation Sections), Iowa State and American (Member, Employment and Labor Law and Litigation Sections) Bar Associations; Illinois Association of Defense Trial Counsel. ***PRACTICE AREAS:*** Management Employment Law; Litigation. ***Email:*** tmartin@pappasandschnell.com

OF COUNSEL

ROY W. VANDER KAMP, born Pella, Iowa, January 22, 1919; admitted to bar, 1943, Iowa; 1944, Ohio; 1958, U.S. Supreme Court, 1960, Illinois. *Education:* Central College, Pella, Iowa (B.A., 1941); University of Iowa (J.D., with distinction, 1943). Member, 1964-1973 and Chair, 1967-1978, Board of Directors, University of Dubuque, Dubuque, Iowa. *Member:* Scott County (Iowa), Rock Island County (Illinois), Illinois State, Iowa State (Member, Special Corporation Committee, 1956-1959; Member, Probate Committee, 1991) and American (Chair, 2032A Sub-Committee, 1981-1982; Agricultural Tax Committee, 1979—; Sections on: Real Property and Probate and Taxation) Bar Associations. Fellow, Illinois Bar Foundation (Charter Member). Fellow, Iowa Bar Foundation. Fellow, The American College of Trust and Estate Counsel. ***PRACTICE AREAS:*** Probate; Trust and Estates; Tax; Corporate Organization; Business Organization; Business Law. ***Email:*** rvanderkamp@pappasandschnel.com

STUART R. LEFSTEIN, born Rock Island, Illinois, January 7, 1934; admitted to bar, 1958, Illinois, U.S. Supreme Court, U.S. Tax Court, U.S. Court of Appeals, Seventh, Eighth and Federal Circuits, U.S. District Court, Northern and Central Districts of Illinois and U.S. District Court, Southern District of Iowa. *Education:* Augustana College (B.A., 1955); University of Michigan (J.D., 1958). Named, Illinois Super Lawyer in Chicago Magazine, 2005. Author: "Wrongful Death: More Than Survivors Survive," Illinois Defense Counsel, February 1975; "The Flag is Not Sacred - How Can It be Desecrated?" Chicago Tribune, July 4, 1989; "It's Not Too Late for the Crucible," ABA Journal, May 1992; "The Truth Must Out In Hill-Thomas Affair," The National Law Journal, November 9, 1992. Hearing Examiner, Illinois Fair Employment Practices Commission, 1971-1975. Trustee, Black Hawk College, 1970-1974. Member, Review Board of Attorney Registration and Disciplinary Commission of Illinois Supreme Court. Member, 1993-2004 and Chair, 1996-2004, Advisory Committee on Rules to U.S. Courts in Central District of Illinois. Member, 1998-2003 and Chair, 2000-2002, Illinois Supreme Court Third District Character and Fitness Committee for Bar Admissions. Certified, Mediation Training, CAADRS. *Member:* Illinois Appellate Lawyers Association (Director, 1978-1980). Fellow, American College of Trial Lawyers (Chair, Downstate Illinois Committee, 1990-1991). ***REPORTED CASES:*** Christianson v. Colt, 486 U.S. 800 (1988). ***PRACTICE AREAS:*** Trials and Appeals; Personal Injury; Professional Malpractice; Mediation and Arbitration. ***Email:*** slefstein@pappasandschnell.com

---

KAREN J. BARROWS, born Davenport, Iowa, October 21, 1969; admitted to bar, 2001, Iowa; 2002, Illinois; U.S. District Court, Central District of Illinois. *Education:* University of Iowa (B.S., 1992); St. Ambrose University (M.C.J., Criminal Justice, 1997); Drake University (J.D., honors, 2001). Adjunct Instructor, Business Law, Western Illinois University, 2003-2005. *Member:* Scott County, Iowa State and Illinois State and American (Member, Employment and Labor Law Section) Bar Associations. ***PRACTICE AREAS:*** Management Employment Law; Management Labor Law. ***Email:*** kbarrows@pappasandschnell.com

(This Listing Continued)

PAPPAS & SCHNELL, P.C., Rock Island—Continued

MELISSA A. HANCOCK, born 1976; admitted to bar, 2002, Iowa; 2003, Wisconsin; 2005, Illinois. *Education:* Loras College (B.A., 1998); University of Iowa (J.D., 2002). *Member:* Iowa State Bar Association (Member, Sections on: Business Law; Probate and Trust Law; Real Estate and Title Law); American Bar Association (Member, Sections on: Business Law; Real Property; Probate and Trust Law). ***PRACTICE AREAS:*** Corporate Law; Trusts and Estates; Business Law. ***Email:*** mhancock@pappasandschnell.com

POOL, LEIGH & FABRICIUS

ROCK ISLAND, ILLINOIS

(See Ottawa)

General Civil Trial and Appellate Practice in all Courts, Insurance, Real Estate and Family Law.

SHARON L. PULSIFER

ROCK ISLAND, ILLINOIS

(See Moline)

Family Law, Bankruptcy, Adoptions, Child Custody, Child Support, Divorce, Domestic Violence, Visitation Rights, Divorce, Real Estate, Wills and Probate.

SNYDER, PARK & NELSON, P.C.

Established in 1983

1600 FOURTH AVENUE, SUITE 200
P.O. BOX 3700
ROCK ISLAND, ILLINOIS 61204-3700
Telephone: 309-786-8497
Telefax: 309-786-0463
Email: lawfirm@snyderpark.com
URL: http://www.snyderpark.com

Banking, Bankruptcy, Commercial, Corporation, General Civil Litigation in all State and Federal Courts, Insurance, Labor Law, Probate, Real Estate, Taxation, Estate Planning, Trials, Employment Law, Workers Compensation, Construction and Commercial Litigation and Administrative Law.

FIRM PROFILE: Snyder, Park & Nelson, P.C. engages in the general practice of law with a concentration on commercial and business transactions and civil litigation in the States of Illinois and Iowa. The firm has been in existence since March 1, 1983.

WILLIAM J. SNYDER, born Walters, Oklahoma, October 17, 1942; admitted to bar, 1967, Iowa and Illinois. *Education:* St. Ambrose College and University of Iowa (B.A., 1964; J.D., 1967). Phi Alpha Delta. Member, Board of Editors, Iowa Law Review, 1966-1967. Member, Board of Directors, American Red Cross, 1984-1991. Director, YMCA, 1984-1986. Member, Board of Directors, Eagle Food Centers, Inc., 1989-2004. *Member:* Scott County (Iowa), Rock Island County (Illinois), Illinois State and Iowa State Bar Associations. ***Email:*** wsnyder@snyderpark.com

ROBERT T. PARK, born Rock Island, Illinois, December 13, 1946; admitted to bar, 1973, Illinois and U.S. District Court, Central District of Illinois; 1977, U.S. Court of Appeals, Seventh Circuit and U.S. Supreme Court; 1984, Iowa. *Education:* University of Illinois (B.A., 1968; J.D., 1973). Editor-in-Chief, Illinois Defense Counsel Quarterly, 2003-2004. *Member:* Rock Island County, Scott County, Illinois State (Member, Assembly, 1994-2001) and Iowa State Bar Associations; Defense Research Institute; Illinois Defense Counsel (Director, 1993—); Quad Cities Claims Association. ***PRACTICE AREAS:*** Civil Trial Law; Insurance Law. ***Email:*** rpark@snyderpark.com

STEVEN L. NELSON, born Davenport, Iowa, December 31, 1948; admitted to bar, 1977, Iowa and Illinois. *Education:* Black Hawk Junior College; Western Illinois University (B.A., 1970); Drake University (J.D., 1976). *Member:* Rock Island County, Scott County, Illinois State and Iowa State Bar Associations; Workers Compensation Lawyers Association, Ltd; American Bankruptcy Institute. ***PRACTICE AREAS:*** Bankruptcy; Workers Compensation; Commercial Litigation. ***Email:*** snelson@snyderpark.com

DEE ANN RUNNELS, born Clinton, Iowa, March 30, 1950; admitted to bar, 1980, Iowa; 1981, Illinois. *Education:* Luther College (B.A., magna cum laude, 1972); University of Iowa College of Law (J.D., with distinction, 1980). Law Clerk to Iowa District Court, Scott County, 1980-1981. *Member:* Rock Island County (Illinois), Scott County (Iowa), Iowa State and Illinois State Bar Associations. ***Email:*** drunnels@snyderpark.com

JOSEPH N. VAN VOOREN, born Atkinson, Illinois, January 10, 1970; admitted to bar, 1996, Illinois; 2002, Iowa. *Education:* Illinois State University (B.S., 1992); Northern Illinois University (J.D., magna cum laude, 1996). ***PRACTICE AREAS:*** Litigation; Insurance Defense; Employment Law. ***Email:*** jvanvooren@snyderpark.com

---

AMY LYNN KEYS, born Madison, Wisconsin, March 26, 1975; admitted to bar, 2000, Iowa; 2001, Illinois. *Education:* Bradley University (B.S., summa cum laude, 1997); University of Iowa College of Law (J.D., with distinction, 2000). Phi Delta Phi (Treasurer, Spring 1999). Staff Member, Journal of Corporation Law. Law Clerk, Iowa District Court, Scott County, 2000-2001. *Member:* Rock Island County (Illinois), Scott County (Iowa), Iowa State and Illinois State Bar Associations. ***Email:*** akeys@snyderpark.com

OF COUNSEL

PAMELA M. ANDERSON, born Kansas City, Kansas, November 8, 1949; admitted to bar, 1980, Iowa and Illinois. *Education:* University of Kansas; University of Texas (B.A., 1973); University of Colorado; University of Iowa (J.D., with high honors, 1980). *Member:* Scott County, Rock Island County, Iowa State and Illinois State Bar Associations. ***Email:*** panderson@snyderpark.com

REPRESENTATIVE CLIENTS: Eagle Food Centers, Inc.; Bituminous Casualty Corp.; Blackhawk Foundry and Machine Co.; Modern Woodmen of America; American Bank & Trust Co.; Cincinnati Insurance Co.; CIGNA Corp.; CNA Insurance Co.; General Reinsurance Corp.; Hillebrand Construction Co.; Trinity Medical Center; Meridian Insurance Company; AAA Chicago Motor Club Insurance Company; Roemer Machine Co.; Royal Neighbors of America; Quad-City Botanical Center; National Chiropractic Mutual Insurance Company; Alcoa Employees & Community Credit Union; Bank One; City of East Moline; Country Insurance; County of Rock Island; Deere & Company Credit Union; Deere Harvester Credit Union; Fairlane Credit; First Midwest Bank; First National Bank; Ford Motor Credit Co.; John Deere Harvester Works; John Deere Parts Distribution Center; John Deere Seeding Group; Kia Financial Services; Mazda American Credit; MidAmerican Energy Co.; Museum of Art Foundation; Nancy's Pies, Inc.; Safeco Insurance Co.; Sentry Insurance Co.; Specialty Claims, Inc.; St. Paul Insurance Co.; Toyota Motor Credit Corp.; Trinity Regional Health Systems; Unitrin Specialty Lines Insurance Co.; Wells Fargo; National City Bank; Valley Construction Co.; Work Fitness Center, Inc.; Midwest Property Group, Ltd.

STANLEY, LANDE & HUNTER

A PROFESSIONAL CORPORATION

ROCK ISLAND, ILLINOIS

(See Davenport, Iowa)

General Civil and Trial Practice. Corporation, Business, Banking, Taxation, Securities, Tax-Exempt Financing, Labor, Employment Discrimination, Administrative, Creditor Bankruptcy and Agricultural Law, Insurance Defense, Personal Injury and Property Damage Law, Pension and Profit-Sharing, Real Estate, Probate, Estate Planning and Charitable Trusts and Foundations Law.

MICHAEL J. WARNER & ASSOCIATES

1600 4TH AVENUE, SUITE 410
P.O. BOX 3544
ROCK ISLAND, ILLINOIS 61204-3544
Telephone: 309-794-1660
Fax: 309-794-1454
Email: warner@mjwlaw.com
URL: http://www.mjwlaw.com

Personal Injury, Wrongful Death, Medical Malpractice, Products Liability, Workers Compensation.

MICHAEL J. WARNER, born Chicago, Illinois, November 9, 1945; admitted to bar, 1971, Illinois and U.S. District Court, Northern District of Illinois; 1973, U.S. District Court, Central District of Illinois; U.S. District Court, Southern District of Iowa. *Education:* University of Illinois (B.S., 1968); Illinois Institute of Technology, Chicago-Kent College of Law (J.D., 1971). Speaker: "Liens & Subrogation Interests," ITLA Seminar, 1997; "Plaintiff's Trial Strategies," IPT Risk Management Meeting, 1998. Member, Illinois Pattern Jury Instructions (Civil) Committee, 2001—. *Member:* Rock Island County and Illinois State (Assembly Member, 1981-1988; Professional Conduct Committee 1978-1991, Vice Chairman 1988-1990 and Chairman 1990-1991; Standing Committee on Judicial Appointments Committee, 1991—) Bar Associations; Illinois Trial Lawyers Association (Member, Board of Managers, 1983-2003; Parliamentarian, 1997-1998; Secretary, 1998-1999); The Association of Trial Lawyers of America; Mississippi Valley Alzheimer Association (Board of Directors, 1997-2001). ***PRACTICE AREAS:*** Personal Injury; Wrongful Death; Medical Malpractice; Products Liability. ***Email:*** warner@mjwlaw.com

ASSOCIATE

THERESA L. SOSALLA, born Sac City, Iowa, July 22, 1962; admitted to bar, 1994, Iowa, Illinois and U.S. District Court, Central District of Illinois. *Education:* Coe College (B.A., 1987); University of Iowa College of Law (J.D., with distinction, 1993). Trustee, City of LeClaire Library Board of Trustees, 2000-2002. *Member:* Illinois and Iowa State Bar Associations. ***PRACTICE AREAS:*** Personal Injury; Wrongful Death; Medical Malpractice; Civil Appeals; Workers Compensation. ***Email:*** tsosalla@mjwlaw.com

WINSTEIN, KAVENSKY & WALLACE

4TH FLOOR, U.S. BANK BUILDING
224 18TH STREET
P.O. BOX 4298
ROCK ISLAND, ILLINOIS 61201
Telephone: 309-794-1515; 800-747-1527
Fax: 309-794-9929
URL: http://www.wkwlawyers.com

General Civil Practice in all State and Federal Courts. Trial and Appellate Practice. Personal Injury, Products Liability, Labor, Workers Compensation, Matrimonial, Criminal, Bankruptcy, Probate, Real Estate and Commercial Litigation Law.

FIRM PROFILE: Winstein, Kavensky & Wallace have been serving the community for over 50 years, with clients throughout Rock Island, Henry, Mercer, Whiteside and surrounding counties. This is a full service firm with individuals focusing on specific areas of law.

MEMBERS OF FIRM

STEWART R. WINSTEIN, born Viola, Illinois, May 28, 1914; admitted to bar, 1939, Illinois. *Education:* Augustana College and Theological Seminary (B.S., 1935); University of Chicago (J.D., 1938). Author: "Obtaining Valid Judgment or Decree and Enforcement of Divorce Decrees in Foreign State," Volume 61, September, 1972; "Antenuptial Agreement—What the Law Now Says," 1974, Illinois Bar Journal; "Chapter 11—Procedure Under the Illinois Revised Reciprocal Enforcement of Support Act," Illinois Family Law I,

(This Listing Continued)

Institute on Continuing Education of the Illinois Bar, 1974 and 1984. Public Administrator, Rock Island County, Illinois, 1961-1965; 1974-1978. Board Chairman, 1976-1978; 1986-1987 and Member, 1980—, Metropolitan Airport Authority. *Member:* Rock Island, Chicago, Illinois State and American Bar Associations; The Association of Trial Lawyers of America. ***PRACTICE AREAS:*** Labor Law; Matrimonial Law; Commercial Law.

HARRISON H. KAVENSKY, born Rock Island, Illinois, July 16, 1928; admitted to bar, 1952, Illinois and U.S. District Court, Central District of Illinois. *Education:* University of Illinois (B.S.L., 1950; J.D., 1952). *Member:* Rock Island County (Member, Board of Governors, 1965-1971), Illinois State and American Bar Associations; Illinois Trial Lawyers Association (Member, Negligence Committee, 1982-1984; Workers Compensation Committee, 1996-1998); The Association of Trial Lawyers of America; Illinois Workers Compensation Lawyers Association. ***PRACTICE AREAS:*** Personal Injury Law; Workers Compensation Law; Products Liability Law.

FRANKLIN S. WALLACE, born New York, N.Y., November 24, 1927; admitted to bar, 1953, Illinois. *Education:* University of Wisconsin; United States Merchant Marine Academy (B.S., cum laude, 1950); University of Michigan (J.D., 1953). Frederick L. Leckie Scholar. Phi Delta Sigma. Assistant States Attorney, Rock Island County, 1967-1969. *Member:* Rock Island County, Illinois State (Secretary, 1978-1979 and Chairman, 1980-1981, Illinois Judicial Polls) and American Bar Associations; Illinois Trial Lawyers Association; The Association of Trial Lawyers of America; National Association of Criminal Defense Lawyers. ***PRACTICE AREAS:*** Labor Law; Matrimonial Law; Criminal Law; General Civil Litigation; Appellate Practice.

CRAIG L. KAVENSKY, born Davenport, Iowa, September 12, 1957; admitted to bar, 1982, Illinois and U.S. District Court, Central District of Illinois. *Education:* University of Illinois (B.S., with high honors, 1979); Illinois Institute of Technology/Chicago-Kent College of Law (J.D., with high honors, 1982). *Member:* Chicago, Rock Island County, Illinois State and American Bar Associations; Illinois Trial Lawyers Association; Illinois Workers Compensation Lawyers Association. ***PRACTICE AREAS:*** Personal Injury Law; Workers Compensation Law; Products Liability Law. ***Email:*** ckavensky@wkwlaw.com

ARTHUR R. WINSTEIN, born Moline, Illinois, June 24, 1963; admitted to bar, 1988, Illinois and U.S. District Court, Central District of Illinois; 1988, U.S. Tax Court; 1989, U.S. Court of Appeals for the Federal Circuit. *Education:* St. Ambrose University; University of Iowa (B.G.S., 1985); Washington University School of Law (J.D., 1988). Phi Delta Phi (Clerk, 1987-1988). Order of the Barristers. *Member:* Rock Island County, Illinois State and American Bar Associations; American Intellectual Property Lawyers Association. ***PRACTICE AREAS:*** Domestic Relations Law; General Civil Law; Criminal Litigation. ***Email:*** awinstein@wkwlaw.com

DAVID L. CUNNINGHAM, born Escondido, California, May 23, 1962; admitted to bar, 1989, Iowa; 1991, Illinois. *Education:* Drake University (B.A., 1985; M.P.A., 1989; J.D., 1989). Phi Delta Phi. Finalist, C. Edwin Moore Moot Court Competition. Second Place, Iowa Supreme Court Sesquicentennial Brief Writing Competition. Author: "Insurance Coverage for Environmental Claims: Defense and Liability Coverage for Hazardous Releases," Iowa State Bar Association Continuing Legal Education, 1989. Assistant County Attorney, Scott County, Iowa, 1990-1991. *Member:* Scott County, Polk County, Iowa State and American Bar Associations. ***PRACTICE AREAS:*** Criminal Litigation; General Civil Law; Domestic Relations; Appellate Practice. ***Email:*** dcunningham@wkwlaw.com

ROBERT KELLY LEYSHON, born Cambridge, Ohio, March 29, 1969; admitted to bar, 1994, Iowa, Illinois, U.S. District Court, Northern and Southern Districts of Iowa, U.S. District Court, Central District of Illinois and U.S. Court of Appeals, Seventh Circuit. *Education:* University of Iowa (B.A., with distinction, 1991; J.D., 1993). Phi Beta Kappa. *Member:* Iowa State (Member: Labor and Employment and Young Lawyer Division Sections; Young Lawyer Division Sub Committee on Americans with Disabilities Act; Young Lawyer Division Human Needs Committee, 1995—), Illinois State and American (Member: Labor and Employment and Young Lawyer Division Sections) Bar Associations; Iowa Trial Lawyers Association; The Association of Trial Lawyers of America. ***LANGUAGES:*** Spanish. ***PRACTICE AREAS:*** Civil Rights; Workers' Compensation; Personal Injury. ***Email:*** rleyshon@netexpress.net

BARBARA K. WALLACE, born Davenport, Iowa, April 1, 1970; admitted to bar, 1997, Iowa; 1998, Illinois and U.S. District Court, Central District of Illinois. *Education:* Augustana College (B.A., with honors, 1993); University of Iowa (J.D., with distinction, 1997). Member, Dillon Inn of Court. *Member:* Scott County, Iowa State and American Bar Associations; Iowa Trial Lawyers Association. ***PRACTICE AREAS:*** Family Law; Criminal Law; Traffic Violations; Litigation. ***Email:*** bwallace@wkwlaw.com

ASSOCIATES

ERIC RYAN, born Mt. Olive, Illinois, May 12, 1975; admitted to bar, 2001, Illinois; 2003, U.S. District Court, Central District Illinois; 2004, Iowa. *Education:* University of Illinois (B.S., 1998); Northern Illinois University (J.D., summa cum laude, 2001). Law Review Articles Editor, Northern Illinois University, 2000-2001. Co-author, Chapter 9 "Guardians and Receivers" IICLE Chancery and Special Remedies Upcoming Ed". Associate, Third District Illinois Appellate Court. *Member:* Rock Island County, Illinois State and American Bar Associations. ***PRACTICE AREAS:*** Personal Injury (60%); Civil Litigation (19%); Workers Compensation (18%); Appellate Practice (3%). ***Email:*** eryan@wkwlaw.com

MATTHEW G. GRUSHON, born St. Louis, Missouri, June 20, 1975; admitted to bar, 2003, Iowa; 2004, U.S. District Court, Southern and Northern Districts of Illinois (Not admitted in Illinois). *Education:* Ohio University (B.S., 1999); Ohio State University (J.D., 2003). Associate, Gomez, May, Cartee, Schutte and Yeggy. ***PRACTICE AREAS:*** Real Estate (50%); Bankruptcy (40%); Corporate Law (10%). ***Email:*** mgrushon@wkwlaw.com

LOCAL REGIONAL COUNSEL FOR: United Auto Workers.
REPRESENTATIVE CLIENTS: United Auto Workers, UAW Local 1442 (Red Jacket); International Association of Machinists; United Rubber Workers: Motion Picture Machine Operators, International Brotherhood of Electrical Workers; United Food and Commercial Workers; Case-International Harvester, East Moline Works Local; Deer & Co.-Harvester, Plow Planter, foundry, distribution and warehouse locals; Independent Construction Equipment Builders Union; American Postal Worker's Union; Bettendorf Police Dept.; Bettendorf Fire Dept., International Assn. of Firefighters Local 3190; Davenport Police, Davenport Union of Professional Police; East Moline Firefighters, The International Assn. of Firefighters Local #929; International Assn. of Tool Craftsman Local No. 1; Moline Firefighters, The International Association of Firefighters Local #581; Rock Island Firefighters, The International Assn. of Firefighters Local #26; Scott County Deputy Sheriff's Assn.
REFERENCE: U.S. Bank.

(This Listing Continued)

ANGELINA & PALMER, P.C.

ROLLING MEADOWS, ILLINOIS

(See Palatine)

Family Law, including Divorce, Child Support, Child Custody, Alimony/Maintenance, Division of Property and Debt, Parentage, Grandparents' Rights, Visitation, Post Decree/Post Divorce Disputes, Separation, Uncontested Divorce, Divorce Settlements. Commercial Real Estate and Residential Real Estate Transactions, including Contract Drafting and Negotiation, Real Estate Closings, Real Estate and Construction Litigation, Zoning, Commercial and Residential Landlord/Tenant, Evictions, Commercial Lease Negotiation and Drafting. Business Law, including Formation of Corporations, Limited Liability Companies (LLC), and Limited Liability Partnerships (LLP). Advice for Business Legal Problems and Business Litigation. Employment Law, Executive Employment Agreements, Buy-Sell Agreements, Operating Agreements, Partnership Agreements, Asset Sales, Sales of Business.Estate Planning, including Wills, Trusts, Power of Attorney, Health Care Power of Attorney, Living Will, Special Needs Trust, Tax Avoidance Trust, Irrevocable Trust, Codicil, Probate.Criminal Law, including Criminal Defense, Felony, including Unlawful Use of Weapons, Battery, Theft, Burglary, Assault, DUI, Driving Under the Influence, Drug Possession, Drug Manufacture, Misdemeanor, Traffic, Ordinance Violation. Personal Injury for Serious Injuries and Wrongful Death.

CHRISTOPHER M. COSLEY

1931 ROHLWING ROAD, SUITE C
ROLLING MEADOWS, ILLINOIS 60008
Telephone: 847-809-0625
Fax: 847-253-3434
URL: http://www.cosleylawfirm.com

Criminal Law, Divorce, Real Estate, Bankruptcy, Driving While Intoxicated, Drug Crimes, Traffic Violation, Misdemeanors, Felonies, Juvenile Crimes, Parole and Probation.

CHRISTOPHER M. COSLEY, born Arlington Heights, Illinois, September 26, 1971; admitted to bar, 1999, Illinois. *Education:* Knox College (B.A., 1993); Chicago-Kent College of Law (J.D., 1998). (Also with O' Donnell & Associates). ***PRACTICE AREAS:*** Criminal Law; Divorce; Real Estate; Bankruptcy; Personal Injury.

THE LAW OFFICES OF THOMAS GLASGOW, LTD.

ROLLING MEADOWS, ILLINOIS

(See Schaumburg)

Criminal, Federal, State, Felony, Misdemeanor, DUI, Traffic, Drunk Driving, Revoked and Suspended License, Murder, Drug Offense, Weapons Charge, Civil, Contracts Litigation, Administrative, Divorce, Family Law.

GLEASON & MACMASTER, LLC

ROLLING MEADOWS, ILLINOIS

(See Chicago)

Bankruptcy, Divorce, Real Estate, Driving While Intoxicated (DUI).

KLEST LAW FIRM

ROLLING MEADOWS, ILLINOIS

(See Schaumburg)

Personal Injury, Medical Malpractice, Products Liability, Legal Malpractice, Construction Accidents, Airplane Crash Litigation, Insurance Bad Faith, Automobile Accidents, Motorcycle Accidents, Birth Trauma, Sexual Abuse, Child Abuse and Neglect, Slip and Fall, Wrongful Death, Dog Bites, Railroad Accidents and Injuries, Automobile Products, Liability and Drug and Medical Device Litigation, Trial Practice.

MARAMBA & ASSOCIATES, LLC

ROLLING MEADOWS, ILLINOIS

(See Arlington Heights)

Business Law, Chancery Practice, Corporate Litigation, Civil Litigation, Complex Litigation, Defense Litigation, Federal Litigation, Administrative Litigation, Business Enterprises, Business Litigation, Closely Held Business Law, Real Estate Litigation, Veterans Rights, Military Law, Wills, Commercial Collections, Post Judgment Collections, Closely Held Corporations.

THE LAW OFFICES OF BRUCE D. PAYNTER

ROLLING MEADOWS, ILLINOIS

(See Arlington Heights)

Criminal Law, Felonies, Misdemeanors, Drug Offenses, Driving While Intoxicated, Assaults, Weapons Charges, Drivers License Suspension, Traffic Violations, Sex Offenses, Personal Injury, Automobile Accidents, Motorcycle Accidents, Trucking Accidents, Wrongful Death, Real Estate Transactions, Buying and Selling Real Estate.

LAW OFFICES OF DAVID L. PINSEL, P.C.

3701 ALGONQUIN ROAD, SUITE 750
ROLLING MEADOWS, ILLINOIS 60008
Telephone: 847-818-8700
Fax: 847-818-8226
Email: dpinsel@aol.com
URL: http://www.lawyers.com/pinsel

Divorce, Family, Child Custody, Child Support, Visitation Rights, Paternity, Real Estate, Landlord and Tenant Law, Commercial Collections, Debtor and Creditor Law.

DAVID L. PINSEL, born Chicago, Illinois, December 4, 1959; admitted to bar, 1985, Illinois and U.S. District Court, Northern District of Illinois; 1992, Indiana and U.S. District Court, Northern and Southern Districts of Indiana. *Education:* University of Illinois (B.S., with honors, 1982; J.D., 1985). Lecturer and Author for National Business Institute, Inc. Qualified Mediator (Family Law-IN). *Member:* Illinois State and American Bar Associations; Association of Trial Lawyers of America; Northwest Suburban Bar Association. ***PRACTICE AREAS:*** Divorce; Family Law; Child Custody; Child Support; Paternity; Real Estate; Landlord and Tenant Law; Commercial Collections; Debtor and Creditor.

THE SULLIVAN FIRM, LTD.

Established in 1981
THE MEADOWS CORPORATE CENTER-EAST TOWER
2550 WEST GOLF ROAD, SUITE 101
ROLLING MEADOWS, ILLINOIS 60008-4501
Telephone: 847-228-1100
Fax: 847-228-5199
Email: thesullivanfirm@aol.com
URL: http://www.lawyers.com/thesullivanfirm

Litigation, Criminal Law, Family Law, Employment Law, Business Law, DWI and Real Estate.

TERRY SULLIVAN, born 1943; admitted to bar, 1968, Illinois. *Education:* St. Josephs College (B.S., 1965); Loyola University (J.D., 1968). (Also Of Counsel, Martin J. Healy, Jr. & Associates, Chicago, Il). ***PRACTICE AREAS:*** Litigation; Criminal Law; Corporate Law. ***Email:*** thesullivanfirm@aol.com

MICHAEL D. SULLIVAN, born Chicago, Illinois, February 16, 1940; admitted to bar, 1965, Illinois. *Education:* University of Notre Dame (B.B.A., cum laude, 1962; J.D., 1965). *Member:* Chicago (Federal Tax Committee, 1967-1981; Employee Benefit Committee, 1974-1981), Illinois State (Member, Sections on: Corporate Law; Securities Law; Public Utilities and Transportation) and American (Member, Sections on: Public Utilities Commission and Transportation Law; Taxation Law) Bar Associations. ***PRACTICE AREAS:*** Business Law; Transportation; Contracts. ***Email:*** thesullivanfirm@aol.com

NANCY J. NICOL, born Middletown, Ohio, August 1, 1949; admitted to bar, 1978, Illinois. *Education:* University of Dayton (B.S., 1971); DePaul University (J.D., 1978). ***PRACTICE AREAS:*** Civil Litigation; Appellate Practice; General Practice. ***Email:*** NJN96@aol.com

JUDY CHESSICK, born New York, N. Y., February 18, 1948; admitted to bar, 1983, Illinois. *Education:* University of Illinois (B.A., 1969); Northeastern University (M.ED., 1973); University of Florida (J.D., 1983). *Member:* Northwest Suburban and Illinois State Bar Associations; Illinois Real Estate Lawyers Association (IRELA). ***PRACTICE AREAS:*** Real Estate; Family Law; Wills. ***Email:*** thesullivanfirm@aol.com

LAW OFFICE OF PATRICK A. MESZAROS

ROMEOVILLE, ILLINOIS

(See Joliet)

Personal Injury, Automobile Accidents and Injuries, Slip and Fall and Real Estate Law.

GAILAN & NAJERA, P.C.

ROSELLE, ILLINOIS

(See Addison)

Criminal Defense, Family Law, Divorce, Child Custody, Adoption, Grandparents Rights, Domestic Violence, Visitation Rights, Child Support, Criminal Law, Driving While Intoxicated, Drug Crimes, Juvenile Crimes, Parole and Probation, Traffic Violations, White Collar Crimes.

LAW OFFICE OF GREGORY J. MARTUCCI, P.C.

Established in 1983
1150 W. LAKE STREET, SUITE B
ROSELLE, ILLINOIS 60172
Telephone: 630-980-8333
Fax: 630-980-8404
URL: http://www.martuccilaw.com

Bankruptcy, Criminal Law, Driving While Intoxicated, Juvenile Criminal Law, Traffic Violations, Domestic Violence, Personal Injury, Automobile Accidents and Injuries, Slip and Fall, Workers Compensation.

FIRM PROFILE: Experience that yields results for our clients - concentrating in Bankruptcy, Criminal/Traffic Defense and Personal Injury/Workers Compensation.

(This Listing Continued)

GREGORY J. MARTUCCI, born Chicago, Illinois, July 25, 1957; admitted to bar, 1983, Illinois; 1985, U.S. District Court, Northern District of Illinois. *Education:* Elmhurst College (B.A., 1980); John Marshall School of Law (J.D., 1983). Chair-Qualified Arbitrator, DuPage County Circuit Court. *Member:* Illinois State and DuPage County Bar Associations. ***PRACTICE AREAS:*** Bankruptcy; Criminal Law; Driving While Intoxicated; Drug Crimes; Juvenile Criminal Law; Traffic Violations; Domestic Violence; Personal Injury; Automobile Accidents and Injuries; Slip and Fall; Workers Compensation.

CUTLER & ASSOCIATES, LTD.

ROSEMONT, ILLINOIS

(See Skokie)

Bankruptcy, Consumer Bankruptcy, Bankruptcy Chapter 7, Foreclosures, Small Business, Buying and Selling of Businesses, Family Business, Limited Liability, Partnership, Corporate, Contract, Breach of Contract, General Practice, Debtor and Creditor, Collections, Creditors, Rights and Civil Litigation.

THE LAW OFFICES OF ANTHONY B. FERRARO

5600 NORTH RIVER ROAD
SUITE 764
ROSEMONT, ILLINOIS 60018
Telephone: 847-292-1220
Fax: 847-292-1221
Email: abfcpalaw@aol.com
URL: http://www.lawyers.com/ferraro

Wills, Trusts, Estates, Estate Planning, Estate Taxation, Probate and Trust Administration, Medicaid, Guardianship, Elder Law, and Trust and Estate-Related Commercial Transactions including Business Acquisitions and Real Estate, Commercial Arbitration.

ANTHONY B. FERRARO, born Chicago, Illinois, November 28, 1951; admitted to bar, 1983, Illinois and U.S. District Court, Northern District of Illinois. *Education:* DePaul University (B.S., Accountancy, 1973; M.S., Taxation, 1976; J.D., 1983). Certified Public Accountant, Illinois, 1977.

STORINO, RAMELLO & DURKIN

9501 WEST DEVON AVENUE, EIGHTH FLOOR
ROSEMONT, ILLINOIS 60018
Telephone: 847-318-9500
Telecopier: 847-318-9509
URL: http://www.srd-law.com

General Civil Trial and Appellate Practice. Real Estate, Corporation, Tort and Commercial Litigation, Municipal Law and Revenue Bonds.

FIRM PROFILE: Storino, Ramello & Durkin is engaged in the general practice of law. The firm maintains a practice which services the needs of municipalities, school districts, financial institutions, national corporations, local businesses as well as individuals. Its lawyers regularly appear in the various courts located in Cook, DuPage, Lake, Kane and McHenry Counties. The firm's lawyers also appear before governmental bodies in the areas of real estate taxation, land use planning and zoning. The firm's transactional practice concentrates in the areas of corporate acquisitions, mergers and sales, commercial leasing, real estate development, tax increment financing, and construction contracts. Our offices are conveniently located in northwest suburban Cook County adjacent to O'Hare Airport.

MEMBERS OF FIRM

DONALD J. STORINO, born Oak Park, Illinois, February 1, 1947; admitted to bar, 1973, Illinois; 1980, U.S. Supreme Court. *Education:* St. Benedict's College and University of Notre Dame (A.B., cum laude, 1969); DePaul University (J.D., 1973). Omicron Delta Epsilon. Special Assistant Attorney General, 1976-1982. Village Attorney, Villages of: Glendale Heights, 1980—; Village of South Barrington, 1997—; Village of Franklin Park, 1997—. Special Assistant Attorney General, 1993. Member, Governor Blagojevich's Legal Transition Team. Member, Cook County Sheriff's Merit Board, 1999—. Judge, Illinois Court of Claims, 2004—. *Member:* Chicago, Illinois State and American (Member, Sections on: Local Government; Real Estate) Bar Associations. ***PRACTICE AREAS:*** Municipal Law; Real Estate Law; Corporate Law; Revenue Law; General Obligation Bonds Law; Probate Law.

MICHAEL K. DURKIN, born Chicago, Illinois, April 14, 1953; admitted to bar, 1978, Illinois. *Education:* University of Illinois (B.A., 1975); Chicago-Kent College of Law (J.D., 1978). Village Prosecutor, Village of Elmwood Park, 1980—. Village Prosecutor, Village of Rosemont, 1979—. Village Attorney: Village of Elmwood Park, 1985—; Village of Streamwood, 1996—. Attorney, Wheeling Township School Trustees, 1984-1997. Attorney, School District 16, 1984-1986. Attorney, School District 81, 1992—. Special Assistant Attorney General, 1993—. *Member:* Illinois State and Northwest Suburban (Member, Broker-Lawyer Accord Committee, 1982-1984) Bar Associations. ***PRACTICE AREAS:*** Municipal Law; Civil Litigation; Labor Law; Employment Relations Law; Domestic Relations Law; Corporate Law.

RICHARD J. RAMELLO, born Oak Park, Illinois, June 23, 1954; admitted to bar, 1979, Illinois. *Education:* Bradley University (B.S., in Construction, 1976); DePaul University (J.D., 1979). Village Prosecutor, Village of Glendale Heights, 1980-1985. Village Attorney, Village of Brookfield, 1993-2001. *Member:* Northwest Suburban, Illinois State and American Bar Associations; Illinois Trial Lawyers Association; The Association of Trial Lawyers of America. ***PRACTICE AREAS:*** Construction Law; Personal Injury Law; Municipal Law; Real Estate Law.

(This Listing Continued)

NICHOLAS S. PEPPERS, born Bowling Green, Ohio, January 11, 1960; admitted to bar, 1985, Illinois. *Education:* Carleton College (B.A., 1982); DePaul University (J.D., 1985). ***PRACTICE AREAS:*** Commercial Real Estate; Finance; Land Development.

DONALD M. ROSE

THOMAS M. BASTIAN

ANGELO F. DELMARTO

JAMES E. MACHOLL

MARY K. CONNOLLY

BRIAN W. BAUGH

MELISSA A. MIROBALLI

PETER A. PACIONE

ANTHONY J. CASALE, admitted to bar, 1980, Illinois. *Education:* DePaul University (B.S., 1976); Lewis University (J.D., 1979). ***PRACTICE AREAS:*** General Practice (100%, 200).

OF COUNSEL

JOSEPH G. KUSPER, born Chicago, Illinois, June 3, 1954; admitted to bar, 1979, Illinois. *Education:* University of Notre Dame (B.B.A., 1976); Northern Illinois University (J.D., 1979); John Marshall Law School (LL.M., 1986). Certified Public Accountant, Illinois, 1983. ***PRACTICE AREAS:*** Tax Law; Corporate Law; Real Estate Law; Revenue Law; General Obligation Bonds Law; Estate Planning Law; Probate Law.

MARK R. STEPHENS

BRYAN J. BERRY

DONALD J. STORINO II

LEONARD P. DIORIO

REPRESENTATIVE CLIENTS: Villages of Rosemont, Elmwood Park, Glendale Heights, Streamwood, Franklin Park, South Barrington, Rolling Meadows, Hanover Park and Forest Park; School District 81; Lake Park High School District 108; Northwest Community Hospital; Westex, Inc.; Western Piece Dyers and Finishers, Inc.; Taubman Textiles Co.; Burbank Financial Corp.; Unitex, Inc.; W.M. Plastics, Inc.; Archer Wire International Co.; American Wire and Stamping Co.; Capron Manufacturing Co.; Wire Sales Co.; Duraco Products, Co.; Re-Mi Foods, Inc.; MGI Industries; Rockwell International; Sysco Corp.; Quantum Corp.; Laidlaw Waste Systems.; Village Bank & Trust.
REFERENCE: U.S. Bank, Rosemont.

RICHARD A. ANDERSON

ROUND LAKE, ILLINOIS

(See Grayslake)

Criminal Law, Driving While Intoxicated, Misdemeanors, Felonies, Real Estate, Buying and Selling of Businesses, Juvenile Criminal Law.

LAW OFFICE OF PAUL R. IDLAS

ROUND LAKE, ILLINOIS

(See Grayslake)

Bankruptcy, Real Estate, Chapter 7 Bankruptcy, Real Estate Closings.

STEPHEN A. BRUNDAGE

ST. CHARLES, ILLINOIS

(See Wheaton)

Criminal Law, Driving While Intoxicated, Drug Crimes, Felonies, Homicide, Juvenile Law, Misdemeanors, Parole and Probation, Sexual Assault, Traffic Violations, Assault and Battery, Burglary, Criminal Defense, Drivers License Suspension, Forgery, Manslaughter, Search and Seizure, Sex Crimes, Theft, Juvenile Law, Family Law, Divorce, Child Custody, Child Support, Domestic Violence, Premarital Agreements, Spousal Support, Martial Agreements, Marital Property Distribution, Martial Property Law, Marital Property Settlements, Matrimonial Law, Paternity, Post Divorce Modification, Real Estate, Real Estate Sales, Residential Real Estate, Residential Real Estate Sales, Personal Injury, Automobile Accidents and Injuries, Dog Bites, Sexual Abuse, Slip and Fall and Wrongful Death Law.

CASEY, BRANNEN & ROMAG

A Partnership of Professional Corporations

TIMBERS PROFESSIONAL CENTER

240 W. RIVER DRIVE

ST. CHARLES, ILLINOIS 60174-5535

Telephone: 630-513-0066

Fax: 630-513-0109

Email: caseylaw@lawyers.com

URL: http://www.cbrlaw.net

Personal Injury Litigation, Truck Accidents, Motorcycle Accidents, Boat Accidents, Construction Accidents, Aircraft Accidents, and other Major Accidents and Injuries, Medical Malpractice, Nursing Home Negligence, Wrongful Death, Products Liability, Premises Liability, Dram Shop Liability, Insurance Defense, Insurance Coverage Law, Uninsured and Underinsured Motorists.

(This Listing Continued)

FIRM PROFILE: Casey and Brannen was founded in 1989 by two of the areas most prominent litigators, James J. Romag joined the firm, 1994. The firm handles significant litigation and injury claims and its attorneys have handled jury trials in both Federal and State courts in the following Chicago area counties: Kane, DuPage, DeKalb, Cook, McHenry, Will, Kendall, Winnebago & LaSalle.

MEMBERS OF FIRM

ROBERT F. CASEY, (P.C.), born Borton, Illinois, September 25, 1921; admitted to bar, 1949, Illinois. *Education:* University of Illinois (B.S., 1946; LL.B., 1948). State Representative, Illinois, 1957-1961; 1979-1980. Special State's Attorney, Kane County, 1976-1977. Interim State's Attorney, Kane County, 1988. Special Prosecutor, Kane County State's Attorney, 1989. ***PRACTICE AREAS:*** Litigation; Personal Injury; Real Estate.

GEORGE W. BRANNEN, (P.C.), born Evanston, Illinois, December 2, 1940; admitted to bar, 1968, Illinois. *Education:* Dartmouth College (B.A., 1962); Duke University (J.D., 1968). ***PRACTICE AREAS:*** Accidents; Personal Injury; Wrongful Death; Spinal Injury; Brain Injury; Business Litigation; Labor Law; Medical Malpractice; Legal Malpractice Defense; Insurance Litigation; Insurance Coverage; Appellate Practice. ***Email:*** georgebrannen@lawyers.com

JAMES J. ROMAG, born Oak Park, Illinois, June 14, 1964; admitted to bar, 1991, Illinois. *Education:* Northern Illinois University (B.S., cum laude, 1988; J.D., cum laude, 1991). Member, Northern Illinois Law Review, 1990-1991. ***PRACTICE AREAS:*** Personal Injury; Accidents; Uninsured and Underinsured Motorists; Medical Malpractice; Motorcycle Accidents; Medical Law; Products Liability Defense. ***Email:*** jamesromag@lawyers.com

REPRESENTATIVE CLIENTS: City of Elgin; ESIS, Inc.; Farmers Insurance Group; Pride Petroleum Company, Inc.; Vandermolen Disposal Co.; Waste Management of Illinois, Inc.
REFERENCES: State Bank of Geneva; Old Kent Bank.

CLANCY LAW OFFICES

7 SOUTH SECOND AVENUE

ST. CHARLES, ILLINOIS 60174

Telephone: 630-584-7666

Fax: 630-584-1649

URL: http://www.clancylaw.com

Personal Injury, Medical Malpractice, Professional Malpractice, Catastrophic Injury, Products Liability, Business Transactions, Partnership Law.

WENDELL W. CLANCY, (P.C.), born Chicago, Illinois, March 27, 1938; admitted to bar, 1963, Illinois; 1980, Wisconsin (inactive). *Education:* Duke University (B.A., 1959); University of Chicago (J.D., 1962). Member, 1995— and Chair, 1996-1998, Illinois Supreme Court Committee on Jury Instructions in Civil Cases. *Member:* Kane County (Secretary, 1965-1966; President, 1983-1984), DuPage County, Illinois State and American Bar Associations; American Board of Trial Advocates (Vice President, Illinois Chapter); Association of Trial Lawyers of America. Fellow, American Bar Foundation. ***PRACTICE AREAS:*** Automobile Accidents and Injuries; Truck Accidents; Construction Accidents; Medical Malpractice; Professional Malpractice; Products Liability; Catastrophic Injury. ***Email:*** wclancy@clancylaw.com

MICHAEL W. CLANCY, born Durham, North Carolina, June 29, 1959; admitted to bar, 1985, Massachusetts, U.S. District Court, District of Massachusette and U.S. Coaurt of Appeals, First Circuit; 1992, Illinois, U.S. District Court, Northern District of Illinois including Trial Bar and U.S Court of Appeals, Seventh Circuit; 1998, Wisconsin and U.S. District Court, Eastern District of Wisconsin and Central District of Illinois. *Education:* Amherst College (B.A. cum laude, 1981); Boston College School of Law (J.D., 1984). Member, National Moot Court Team, 1983-1984. Member, American Board of Trial Advocates. Certified, Civil Trial National Board of Trial Advocacy, 1995, recertified 2000. Examiner, National Board of Trial Advocacy, 1997—. *Member:* Kane County, DuPage County, Illinois State (Member, Board of Governors, 1999-2002), Massachusetts and American Bar Associations; State Bar of Wisconsin; The Association of Trial Lawyers of America; Illinois Trial Lawyers Association. Fellow: Illinois Bar Foundation; Kane County Bar Foundation (Member, Board of Governors, 2003-2006); Million Dollar Advocates Forum. ***PRACTICE AREAS:*** Medical Malpractice; Professional Malpractice; Products Liability; Catastrophic Injury; Automobile Accidents and Injuries; Truck Accidents; Construction Accidents. ***Email:*** mclancy@clancylaw.com

SUSAN CLANCY BOLES, born Winfield, Illinois, April 9, 1965; admitted to bar, 1990, Illinois; 1991, U.S. District Court, Northern District of Illinois and U.S. Court of Appeals, Seventh Circuit. *Education:* Vanderbilt University (B.A., 1987); Valparaiso University (J.D., with high distinction, 1990). *Member:* Kane County and American Bar Associations; The Associations of Trial Lawyers of America. ***PRACTICE AREAS:*** Automobile Accidents and Injuries; Medical Malpractice; Professional Malpractice; Catastrophic Injury; Products Liability. ***Email:*** sboles@clancylaw.com

---

DENKER & MUSCARELLO, LLC

Established in 2003

4N701 SCHOOL ROAD

ST. CHARLES, ILLINOIS 60175

Telephone: 630-513-9191

Fax: 630-524-9146

Email: info@denkermuscarello.com

URL: http://www.denkermuscarello.com

Business Law, Business and Commercial Litigation, Corporate Law, Commercial Law, Information Technology Law, Computer and Internet Law, Intellectual Property Law, Health Care Law, Real Estate Law, Family Law.

(This Listing Continued)

DENKER & MUSCARELLO, LLC, St. Charles—Continued

FIRM PROFILE: Denker & Muscarello, LLC was formed in 2003 with a specific goal in mind - to provide sophisticated legal counsel in a small firm setting to the expanding business population in the Chicagoland area. Its attorneys are experienced in a broad spectrum of disciplines and have practiced in both large firm and small firm environments in the City of Chicago - as well as in varying sized practices in the Chicago suburbs - representing entities ranging in size from small, family businesses to Fortune 500 companies. As a result, Denker & Muscarello provides its clients with seasoned, well-rounded counsel irrespective of the size, complexity, or nature of the particular organization or underlying transaction or dispute.

MICHAEL J. DENKER, born Oak Park, Illinois, September 15, 1970; admitted to bar, 1995, Illinois and U.S. District Court, Northern District of Illinois. *Education:* University of Southern California (B.A., magna cum laude, 1992); Northwestern University (J.D., 1995). Phi Beta Kappa; Phi Kappa Phi; Mortar Board. *Member:* Kane County, Illinois State and American Bar Associations; Computer Law Association. ***PRACTICE AREAS:*** Business Law; Corporate Law; Commercial Law; Technology Law; Business Litigation; Commercial Litigation; Intellectual Property Law; Health Care Law. ***Email:*** mjd@denkermuscarello.com

CHARLES V. MUSCARELLO, born Park Ridge, Illinois, October 17, 1970; admitted to bar, 1995, Illinois; U.S. District Court, Northern District of Illinois. *Education:* Miami University (B.S., 1992); Washington University School of Law (J.D., 1995). Certified Public Accountant, 1997. *Member:* Kane County and Illinois State Bar Associations. ***PRACTICE AREAS:*** Business Law; Corporate Law; Commercial Law; Technology Law; Business Litigation; Commercial Litigation; Real Estate Law; Family Law. ***Email:*** cvm@denkermuscarello.com

---

GRIFFIN & HOSKINS LLC

40W320 LAFOX ROAD
SUITE E
ST. CHARLES, ILLINOIS 60175
Telephone: 630-584-6327
Fax: 630-584-6403
URL: http://www.griffinhoskinsbrizuela.com

Real Estate Sales and Acquisitions, Development and Zoning, Buying and Selling a Home, Buying and Selling of Businesses, Corporate, Business Planning and Litigation, Municipal Law, General Civil Litigation, Appeals in State and Federal Courts.

FIRM PROFILE: Griffin & Hoskins specializes in representing clients with a wide array of real estate needs, including sales, acquisitions, zoning and development. The firm represents numerous development entities and homeowners associations in and around the western suburbs of Chicago.

MEMBERS OF FIRM

PATRICK M. GRIFFIN, born Melbourne, Florida, October 8, 1968; admitted to bar, 1995, Illinois; 1996, U.S. District Court, Northern District of Illinois. *Education:* University of Illinois at Urbana-Champaign (B.S., 1991); Northern Illinois University College of Law (J.D., 1995). Editor-in-Chief, Northern Illinois University Law Review, 1994-1995. Staff Sergeant, Illinois Army National Guard, 1986-1994. *Member:* Kane County, Illinois State and American Bar Associations. ***PRACTICE AREAS:*** Real Estate Sales; Real Estate Acquisitions; Real Estate Development; Zoning, Planning and Land Use; Municipal Law. ***Email:*** pmgriffin@justice.com

GREGORY W. HOSKINS, born Ft. Madison, Iowa, August 12, 1963; admitted to bar, 1995, Illinois and U.S. District Court, Northern District of Illinois. *Education:* University of Iowa (B.B.A., 1985); Northern Illinois University College of Law (J.D., 1995). Research Editor, Northern Illinois University Law Review, 1994-1995. Law Clerk to Illinois Supreme Court Justice John L. Nickels, 1995-1998. Author, "Violent Crimes at ATMs: Analysis of the Liability of Banks and the Regulation of Protective Measures," Northern Illinois University Law Review, Vol. 14 No. 3, Summer 1994. Editor-in-Chief, KSBA Bar Briefs, 2004—. *member:* Kane County and Illinois State Bar Associations. ***PRACTICE AREAS:*** Civil Litigation; Business Law; Real Estate; Appellate Practice. ***Email:*** gwhoskins@justice.com

ASSOCIATES

KENNETH L. KAERGARD, born Chicago, Illinois, December 22, 1950; admitted to bar, 1977, Illinois and U.S. District Court, Northern District of Illinois; 1979, U.S. Court of Appeals, Seventh Circuit. *Education:* Illinois Institute of Technology (B.S., 1972); John Marshall Law School (J.D., 1977). Judicial Law Clerk, Illinois Appellate Court, 1977-1980. Instructor, Business Law, College of DuPage, 1980-2000. *Member:* Kane County and Illinois State Bar Associations. ***PRACTICE AREAS:*** Real Estate; Business; Corporate Law.

M. CAROLINE BRIZUELA, born St. Charles, Illinois, April 7, 1968; admitted to bar, 1993, Illinois. *Education:* University of Illinois (B.A., 1990); Northern Illinois University College of Law (J.D., 1993). *Member:* Kane County and Illinois State Bar Associations. ***PRACTICE AREAS:*** Real Estate; Corporate; Business.

REPRESENTATIVE CLIENTS: B & B Enterprises Land Developers; Fox Mill Homeowners Association; GRH Development, Inc.; Pacific Midwest Homes; Heron Creek Homeowners Association; Blackberry Creek Homeowners Association; Prairie Lakes Homeowners Association; Westwoods of St. Charles Community Association; Valley Community Bank; Kane County Fair; Taut Incorporated; Coilform Company; The Windings of Ferson Creek Homeowners Association.

HOSCHEIT, McGUIRK, McCRACKEN & CUSCADEN, P.C.

Established in 1991

1001 EAST MAIN STREET, SUITE G
ST. CHARLES, ILLINOIS 60174
Telephone: 630-513-8700
630-513-8799
Email: johnm@hmcpc.com
URL: http://www.hmcpc.com

General Civil Practice including, Personal Injury, Workers Compensation, Real Estate, Corporate, Commercial Litigation, Estate Planning and Criminal Law, Construction, Buying and Selling, Landlord Tenant, Zoning and Land Use, DWI, Traffic, Drug Crimes, Juvenile Law, White Collar, Family, Divorce, Child Custody, Child Support, Adoptions, Commercial Leasing, Business Law, Franchise, Limited Liability, Contracts, Starting a Business, Auto, Dog Bites, Slip and fall, Wrongful Death.

FIRM PROFILE: Hoscheit, McGuirk, McCracken & Cuscaden, P.C. provides legal services throughout the Chicagoland area including Kane, DuPage, DeKalb, Kendall, McHenry and Cook Counties.

JOHN J. HOSCHEIT, born Oak Park, Illinois, February 5, 1959; admitted to bar, 1984, Illinois. *Education:* University of Illinois (B.S., high honors, 1981; J.D., 1984). Certified Public Accountant, 1981. *Member:* Kane County, Illinois State and American Bar Associations. (Arbitrator). ***PRACTICE AREAS:*** General Civil Litigation; Personal Injury; Commercial Transactions; Corporations; Real Estate; Zoning; Estate Planning. ***Email:*** johnh@hmcpc.com

JOHN M. McGUIRK, born Johnstown, Pennsylvania, December 27, 1948; admitted to bar, 1975, Illinois. *Education:* University of Dayton (B.A., 1970); DePaul University (J.D., cum laude, 1975). *Member:* Kane County (General Counsel), DuPage County, Illinois State and American Bar Associations. (Arbitrator). ***PRACTICE AREAS:*** General Civil Litigation; Personal Injury; Commercial Transactions; Corporations; Real Estate; Estate Planning; Estate Administration. ***Email:*** johnm@hmcpc.com

KATE L. McCRACKEN, born Aurora, Illinois, April 28, 1959; admitted to bar, 1986, Washington; 1989, Illinois; U.S. District Court, Northern District of Illinois. *Education:* University of Wisconsin-Madison (B.A., 1981); Seattle University School of Law (J.D., 1985). *Member:* Kane County and Illinois State (Arbitrator) Bar Associations; Illinois Real Estate Lawyers Association. ***PRACTICE AREAS:*** Real Estate; Real Estate Development; Zoning; Commercial Transactions. ***Email:*** kate@hmcpc.com

DOUGLAS R. CUSCADEN, born Chicago, Illinois, June 7, 1961; admitted to bar, 1988, Illinois. *Education:* Elmhurst College (B.A., with high honors, 1983); John Marshall Law School (J.D., 1988). *Member:* Kane County and Illinois State Bar Associations. (Arbitrator). ***PRACTICE AREAS:*** Family Law; Real Estate; Civil Litigation; Criminal Defense. ***Email:*** doug@hmcpc.com

REPRESENTATIVE CLIENTS: Chicago Title; Bernat Development Company; Institutional Funds & Services, Inc.; Randall Arch, Inc.; Microplastics, Inc.; Racetrack Graphics, Inc.; Health Tech Systems, Ltd.; Harris Trust & Savings; Taralan; Midwest Custom Homes, Inc.; Avondale Custom Homes, Inc.; McFarlane Construction, Inc.; Brother Custom Concrete Inc; Westway Carpentry, Inc.; Walnut Street Partners, LLC; Private Bank & Trust Co.; J & B Builders Inc.; EPS Bank.
AGENTS FOR: Chicago Title; Attorneys Title Guaranty Fund; First American Title.

O'HAGAN, SMITH & AMUNDSEN

3815 E. MAIN STREET, SUITE A-1
ST. CHARLES, ILLINOIS 60174-2488
Telephone: 630-587-7910
Fax: 630-587-7960
Email: choffice@osalaw.com
URL: http://www.osalaw.com

Chicago, Illinois Office: 150 North Michigan Avenue, Suite 3300, 60601. Telephone: 312-894-3200. Fax: 312-894-3210.
Rockford, Illinois Office: Stewart Square, 308 West State Street, Suite 320, 61101-1140. Telephone: 815-987-0441. Fax: 815-987-9891.
Waukegan, Illinois Office: 415 West Washington Street, Suite 204, 60079-0410. Telephone: 847-599-9503. Fax: 847-599-9525.
Woodstock, Illinois Office: 666 Russell Court, 60098. Telephone: 815-337-4900. Fax: 815-337-4910.
Milwaukee, Wisconsin Office: 4811 South 76th Street, Suite 305, 53220. Telephone: 414-282-7103. Fax: 414-282-1830.

Commercial; Commercial Transportation; Appellate; Complex Litigation; Construction; Corporate Transactions; Employment; Extra-Contractual/Insurance Litigation; Healthcare; Insurance Coverage; Personal Lines; Product Liability; Professional Liability; Property Litigation.

MEMBERS OF FIRM

RITA LOWERY GITCHELL, admitted to bar, 1985, Illinois and U.S. District Court, Northern District of Illinois; 1989, Michigan; 1997, U.S. Supreme Court. *Education:* Illinois State University (B.S., 1977); University of Illinois (M.A., 1979); Chicago-Kent College of Law, Illinois Institute of Technology (J.D., with honors, 1985). Phi Alpha Delta. Recipient: ABA/LSD Bar and Gavel Award, 1985; NLA President's Recognition, 1988. *Member:* Chicago, DuPage County (ADR Committee) and Illinois State Bar Associations; State Bar of Michigan; National Lawyers Association (Board of Directors, 1999; Chairperson, Litigation Committee, 1997-1998; Secretary, 1996-1997); Illinois Association of Defense Trial Counsel; Defense Research Institute. ***PRACTICE AREAS:*** Medical Malpractice; Dental Malpractice; Mediation; Professional Liability; Civil Litigation. ***Email:*** rgitchell@osalaw.com

(This Listing Continued)

ELLEN L. GREEN, admitted to bar, 1988, Illinois; 1989, U.S. District Court, Northern District of Illinois; 1990, U.S. Court of Appeals, Seventh Circuit. *Education:* Linfield College (B.A., magna cum laude, 1982); University of Illinois College of Law (J.D., 1988). *Member:* Chicago, Illinois State and American Bar Associations. ***PRACTICE AREAS:*** Insurance Coverage; Litigation; Appellate Practice. ***Email:*** egreen@osalaw.com

JAMIE SEAN LANE, admitted to bar, 1991, Illinois and U.S. District Court, Northern District of Illinois. *Education:* DePaul University (B.S., 1988; J.D., 1991). *Member:* DuPage County and Illinois State Bar Association. ***PRACTICE AREAS:*** Civil Litigation; Insurance Defense; Personal Injury; Property Law. ***Email:*** jlane@osalaw.com

MICHAEL J. PAVLISIN, admitted to bar, 1982, Illinois and U.S. District Court, Northern District of Illinois; 1987, U.S. Federal Trial Bar and U.S. District Court, Northern District of Illinois. *Education:* Western Illinois University (B.B., 1978; M.B.A., 1979); John Marshall Law School (J.D., 1982). *Member:* DuPage County, Kane County, Illinois State and American (Co-Chair, Commercial Transportation Litigation Committee, former Rail and Motor Carrier Law Committee, 1995—) Bar Associations; Transportation Lawyers Association (TLA); Loss Executives Association (LEA); Trucking Industry Defense Association (TIDA); Illinois Defense Counsel; International Association of Arson Investigators (General Counsel, 1993—; Assistant General Counsel, 1992; Attorney Advisory Committee; Standing Committee on Constitution and By Laws; General Counsel, Illinois Chapter of IAAI, 1992—); IAAI Educational Foundation (General Counsel, 1993—; Assistant General Counsel, 1992). ***PRACTICE AREAS:*** Property Coverage; Arson and Insurance Fraud; Transportation Law; Trucking Accidents; Insurance Defense; Products Liability; General Liability; Construction Accidents. ***Email:*** mpavlisin@osalaw.com

THOMAS P. SCHERSCHEL, admitted to bar, 1983, Illinois and U.S. District Court, Northern District of Illinois. *Education:* Southern Illinois University (B.S., 1972); IIT/Chicago-Kent College of Law (J.D., with high honors, 1983). Past Member, Review Board, Illinois Attorneys Registration and Disciplinary Commission. *Member:* DuPage County and Illinois State Bar Associations. ***PRACTICE AREAS:*** Professional Liability; Automobile; Construction; Medical Malpractice Litigation. ***Email:*** tscherschel@osalaw.com

H. EVAN WILLIAMS, IV, admitted to bar, 1976, Illinois and U.S. District Court, Northern District of Illinois; 1995, U.S. District Court, Central District of Illinois. *Education:* University of Illinois (B.S.M.E., 1972); Illinois Institute of Technology (J.D., 1976). Member, Illinois Society of Professional Engineers. *Member:* Chicago, DuPage County and Illinois State Bar Associations; Defense Research Institute. ***PRACTICE AREAS:*** Construction Litigation; Architectural Malpractice; Engineer Malpractice; Insurance Law Litigation; Commercial Litigation; Business Litigation. ***Email:*** hwilliams@osalaw.com

ASSOCIATES

KARL E. BAYER, admitted to bar, 1996, Illinois. *Education:* Knox College (B.A., 1992); John Marshall Law School (J.D., 1996). ***Email:*** kbayer@osalaw.com

WILLIAM B. CRANE, admitted to bar, 2002, Illinois. *Education:* Loyola University (B.A., 1999); DePaul University (J.D., 2002). ***Email:*** wcrane@osalaw.com

GAIL A. GALANTE, admitted to bar, 1984, Illinois. *Education:* Northwestern University (B.A., 1976); Loyola University (J.D., 1984). ***Email:*** ggalante@osalaw.com

GERALD C. HUANG, admitted to bar, 2000, Illinois. *Education:* University of Illinois (B.S., Economics, 1997; J.D., 2000). ***Email:*** ghuang@osalaw.com

KEITH A. JOHNSON, admitted to bar, 1995, Illinois and U.S. District Court, Northern District of Illinois. *Education:* University of Illinois (B.A., 1992); Northern Illinois University (J.D., cum laude, 1995). ***Email:*** kjohnson@osalaw.com

TONDA LEE, admitted to bar, 2003, Illinois. *Education:* The College of Wooster (B.A., cum laude, 2000); Chicago-Kent College of Law, Illinois Institute of Technology (J.D., 2003). ***Email:*** tlee@osalaw.com

BRADLEY G. RAUSA, admitted to bar, 1998, Illinois. *Education:* Northwestern University (B.A., 1995); Boston University School of Law (J.D., 1998). ***Email:*** brausa@osalaw.com

JENNIFER ANNE SEIDLER, admitted to bar, 1998, Illinois and U.S. District Court, Northern and Central Districts of Illinois. *Education:* Millikin University (B.F.A., summa cum laude, 1992); DePaul University (J.D., 1998). ***Email:*** jseidler@osalaw.com

WARREN WILKOSZ, admitted to bar, 2004, Illinois. *Education:* Marquette University (B.S., 2001); University of Illinois (J.D., 2004). ***Email:*** wwilkosz@osalaw.com

(For complete biographical data on other personnel, see Professional Biographies at other cities)

JOHN M. QUINN & ASSOCIATES, LTD.

ST. CHARLES, ILLINOIS

(See Bloomingdale)

Drivers License Suspension, Administrative Hearings, Driving While Intoxicated, Criminal Law, Traffic Violations, Criminal Defense, Misdemeanors.

RINELLA AND RINELLA, LTD.

ST. CHARLES, ILLINOIS

(See Chicago)

Practice Limited to Family Law and Divorce including the areas of Legal Separation, Negotiating and Drafting Premarital and Postnuptial Agreements, Judgment Enforcement, Child Custody and Child Support Actions, Domestic Violence, Spousal Support, Appeals, Adoption, Parentage Actions and Interstate Support Enforcement.

SHEARER & AGRELLA

Established in 1929 as Hempstead & Green

4N701 SCHOOL ROAD
ST. CHARLES, ILLINOIS 60175
Telephone: 630-584-3142
Fax: 630-584-4198
URL: http://www.shearerandagrella.com
URL: http://www.lawyers.com/shearer&agrella

General Practice, Civil Litigation, Probate, Estate Planning, Real Estate, Corporate Litigation, Personal Injury, Family Law, Construction Litigation.

MEMBERS OF FIRM

RICHARD SHEARER (1916-1994)

RAYMOND F. AGRELLA, born Negaunee, Michigan, September 24, 1937; admitted to bar, 1967, Illinois; 1968, U.S. District Court, Northern District of Illinois; 1974, U.S. Supreme Court. *Education:* Lake Forest College (B.A., 1959); Loyola University at Chicago (J.D., 1967). Special Assistant Attorney General, 1971-1975. Director, Harris Bank, St. Charles, 1984—. *Member:* Kane County and Illinois State Bar Associations. [Lieut., U.S. Coast Guard Reserve, active duty, 1960-1963]. ***PRACTICE AREAS:*** Personal Injury; Family Law; Corporate Law; Civil Litigation; Estate Planning; Commercial Litigation; Construction Litigation. ***Email:*** rfa@shearerandagrella.com

JOSEPH P. SAUBER, JR., born St. Charles, Illinois, January 27, 1960; admitted to bar, 1985, Illinois; U.S. District Court, Northern District of Illinois; registered to practice before U.S. Patent and Trademark Office. *Education:* Elgin Community College; University of Illinois (B.S., 1982); Chicago-Kent College of Law (J.D., 1985). *Member:* Kane County, DuPage County and DeKalb County Bar Associations. ***PRACTICE AREAS:*** Complex Civil Litigation; Commercial Litigation; Construction Litigation; Mechanics Liens; Family Law; Personal Injury. ***Email:*** jsauber@shearerandagrella.com

MARY AGRELLA FITZPATRICK, born San Diego, California, April 19, 1963; admitted to bar, 1988, Illinois including Trial Bar; 1989, U.S. District Court, Northern District of Illinois. *Education:* University of Illinois (B.A., 1985); Northern Illinois University (J.D., magna cum laude, 1988). Phi Alpha Delta. Assistant Editor, Northern Illinois University Law Review, 1987-1988. *Member:* Kane County and Illinois State Bar Associations. ***PRACTICE AREAS:*** Civil Litigation; Family Law; Corporate Law; Probate; Bankruptcy; Real Estate; Estate Planning. ***Email:*** maf@shearerandagrella.com

ASSOCIATE

JEROME L. BETTAG, born Illinois, September 17, 1962; admitted to bar, 1994, Illinois and U.S. District Court, Northern District of Illinois. *Education:* Illinois Benedictine College (B.A., 1985); Northern Illinois University (J.D., 1994). Delta Theta Phi. ***PRACTICE AREAS:*** Corporate Law; Real Estate; Zoning Law; Municipal Law. ***Email:*** lbettag@shearerandagrella.com

REPRESENTATIVE CLIENTS: Harris Bank, St. Charles; ShoDeen, Inc.; St. Charles Sanitary District; St. Charles Township.; Gen. Press Colors, Ltd.; Coleman Management Company; 5th Avenue Electric, Inc.; Tek-Pac, Inc.; American Guardian Warranty Services, Inc.; St. Charles Insurance Company.

WESSELS & PAUTSCH, P.C.

DUNHAM CENTER
2035 FOXFIELD DRIVE
ST. CHARLES, ILLINOIS 60174
Telephone: 630-377-1554
Fax: 630-377-1653
Email: wessels@stch.w-p.com
URL: http://www.w-p.com

Milwaukee, Wisconsin Office: Two Plaza East, 330 East Kilbourn Avenue, Suite 1475. Telephone: 414-291-0600. Fax: 414-291-0200.
Chicago, Illinois Office: Chicago Bar Association Building, 321 South Plymouth Court, Suite 900. Telephone: 312-461-0500. Fax: 312-461-0595.
Davenport, Iowa Office: Northwest Bank Building, 101 W. Second Street, Suite 307. Telephone: 563-333-9102. Fax: 563-333-9105.
Minneapolis, Minnesota Office: MoneyGram Tower, 1550 Utica Avenue South, Suite 450. Telephone: 952-746-1700. Fax: 952-746-1704.
Indianapolis, Indiana Office: Market Tower, 10 West Market Street, Suite 1770. Telephone: 317-656-8800. Fax: 317-656-8855.

Representing Employers in Labor and Employment Law Matters. NLRA, RLA, all Federal and State Employment Discrimination Laws, Federal and State Disability Laws, Wrongful Discharge, Employment Contracts, Collective Bargaining Negotiations and Arbitrations, Employee Substance Abuse, Safety and Health, Unemployment Insurance, Benefits Law, Wage and Hour, and Employment-Based Immigration Matters. Litigation before all Federal and State Courts and Agencies, Trial and Appellate Practice.

FIRM PROFILE: Wessels & Pautsch, P.C.'s six offices in the Midwest serve a practice that is nationwide in scope. The firm's maxim "we run through walls for our clients" reflects its aggressive advocacy of its clients' positions coupled with its broad knowledge of its clients' businesses. The firm's aim is to provide cost-effective service together with personalized attention to matters assigned to it.

RICHARD H. WESSELS, born Geneva, Illinois, June 29, 1939; admitted to bar, 1967, Illinois; 1972, U.S. District Court, Northern District of Illinois; 1989, Wisconsin; 1994, Iowa; U.S. Court of Appeals, Seventh Circuit. *Education:* Knox College (B.A., 1961); DePaul University (J.D., 1967). *Member:* Chicago, DuPage County, Kane County, Illinois State, Iowa State and American Bar Associations; State Bar of Wisconsin. ***Email:*** riwessels@stch.w-p.com

(This Listing Continued)

WESSELS & PAUTSCH, P.C., St. Charles—Continued

EARL P. BAILEY, born Amherst, Ohio, July 28, 1942; admitted to bar, 1971, Ohio (Not admitted in Illinois). *Education:* Ohio University (B.B.A., 1964); Cleveland-Marshall College of Law (J.D., 1971). *Member:* Chicago, Ohio State and American Bar Associations. ***Email:*** eabailey@stch.w-p.com

NANCY E. JOERG, born Brooklyn, New York, May 24, 1945; admitted to bar, 1985, Illinois; U.S. District Court, Northern District of Illinois. *Education:* University of Sheffield, England; William Smith College (B.A. with honors, 1967); Northern Illinois University (J.D. with honors, 1985). Recipient, American Jurisprudence Award in Constitutional Law. Author, *Welcome to the World of Independent Contractors and Other Contingent Workers*, CCH, 1996. *Member:* Chicago, Kane County (Chair, Labor and Employment Law Committee, 1989-1994 and 2002-2003), Illinois State and American Bar Associations. ***Email:*** najoerg@stch.w-p.com

SENIOR ATTORNEYS

ANTHONY J. CARUSO, JR., born Daytona Beach, Florida, August 29, 1947; admitted to bar, 1975, Illinois; U.S. District Court, Northern District of Illinois. *Education:* Central Missouri State University (B.S., 1969); University of Tennessee, College of Law (J.D., 1974). Phi Alpha Delta. *Member:* Kane County Bar Association; Workers' Compensation Lawyers Association. ***Email:*** ancaruso@stch.w-p.com

JEFFREY A. RISCH, born Cincinnati, Ohio, January 7, 1972; admitted to bar, 1998, Oklahoma; 2000, Illinois; U.S. District Court, Northern District of Illinois. *Education:* Illinois State University (B.S., 1994); University of Tulsa (J.D. highest honors, 1998). Delta Theta Phi; Order of the Curule Chair. Member, Moot Court Board. Production Editor, Tulsa Law Journal, 1997-1998. Recipient: Merit Scholar; CALI Award for Legal Writing, Philosophy of Law and Advocacy; 2004 "Outstanding Speaker," Award for Lorman Educational Services. Contributing Author: "Conducting the Employment Practices Audit," IICLE's 2004 Ed. Member: VIA Human Resources Association; Oak Brook Human Resources Association. Chairman, Employment Law and Litigation Committee, Illinois Chamber of Commerce, 2003—. *Member:* Oklahoma and Illinois State Bar Associations. ***Email:*** jerisch@stch.w-p.com

LAURA M. NEWMAN, born Janesville, Wisconsin, April 17, 1968; admitted to bar, 1995, Illinois and U.S. District Court, Northern and Central Districts of Illinois, U.S. District Court, District of Arizona and U.S. Court of Appeals, Seventh Circuit. *Education:* University of Illinois-Champaign (B.S., Marketing, high honors, 1990); Chicago-Kent College of Law (J.D., 1995). Moot Court Honor Society. *Member:* Chicago, Kane County and Illinois State Bar Associations. ***Email:*** lanewman@stch.w-p.com

---

JULIE PROSCIA, born Park Ridge, Illinois, October 24, 1975; admitted to bar, 2003, Illinois and U.S. District Court, Northern District of Illinois. *Education:* Eastern Illinois University (M.A., 1998); Northern Illinois University (J.D., 2003). ***Email:*** juproscia@stch.w-p.com

REPRESENTATIVE CLIENTS: Ace Hardware Corp.; Alexander Lumber Company; Aronson Furniture & Appliances; Atlantis Plastics, Inc.; Best-Tronics, Inc.; Bowne of Chicago, Inc.; Brad Foote Gear Works, Inc.; Briggs Industries, Inc.; Champion Parts, Inc.; Chicago Messenger Service, Inc.; Chicago Paperboard Corp.; City of St. Charles; Claire's Stores, Inc.; Consolidated Grain & Barge Ent.; Cornell Forge; Darvin Furniture & Appliances; Davenport Lutheran Home; DuKane Corp.; Eldercare, Inc.; Florist Transworld Delivery, Inc.; Four Fountains Convalescent Center; Fox River Foods; Gold Standard Liquors, Inc.; Haegar Industries, Inc.; Heart of America Restaurants & Inns, Inc.; Hill-Behan Lumber Co.; Edward Hines Lumber Co.; Hu-Friedy Mfg. Co.; Illinois Crane, Inc.; Ingersoll Cutting Tools; Insurance Corp. of Hannover; Jays Foods, LLC; John B. Sanfilippo & Sons; Krones, Inc.; Lyon Metal Products, LLC; Medallion Kitchens; Miner Enterprises, Inc.; National Metal Fabricators; Newly Weds Foods, Inc.; Pace Industries, Inc.; Patten Industries, Inc.; Plunkett Furniture; Power Packaging Inc.; Processed Plastics Co.; Rinn Corp.; Rollex Corp.; Rubschlager Baking Corporation; Schnadig Corp.; Senior Flexonics, Inc.; Shopko Stores, Inc.; Sullivan-Schein Dental Co.; Sun Chemical Corp.; Swords Veneer & Lumber Co.; Tractor Supply Co.; Superior Services, Inc.; Valley Pride Pack, Inc.; Varco-Pruden Buildings, Inc.; Village of Summitt; Wisconsin Retail Lumber Association.

(For complete biographical data on other personnel, see Professional Biographies at Chicago, Illinois; Milwaukee, Wisconsin; Davenport, Iowa; Minneapolis, Minnesota and Indianapolis, Indiana)

CAMPBELL, BLACK, CARNINE, HEDIN, BALLARD & McDONALD, P.C.

SALEM, ILLINOIS

(See Mount Vernon)

General Civil Practice in State and Federal Courts. Mining, Oil and Gas, Insurance, Workers Compensation, Corporation, Family, Probate, Real Estate and Trust Law. Trials and Appeals.

CRAIG & CRAIG

SALEM, ILLINOIS

(See Mount Vernon)

General Practice in State and Federal Courts. Coal, Oil, Gas, Mining, Insurance, Drainage and Levee Law, Environmental, Corporation, Labor Relations, Workers Compensation and Real Estate Law. Estate Planning and Probate. Trials and Appeals.

WHAM & WHAM

SALEM, ILLINOIS

(See Centralia)

General Trial and Appellate Practice. Insurance Defense including Medical Malpractice, Automobile Accidents, Premises Liability, Products Liability, Personal Injury, Probate, Wrongful Discharge from Employment.

ANDERSON & ASSOCIATES, P.C.

1701 EAST WOODFIELD ROAD, SUITE 1050
SCHAUMBURG, ILLINOIS 60173
Telephone: 847-995-9999
Fax: 847-995-0117
URL: http://www.andersonandassociatespc.com

Chicago Office: 166 W. Washington Street, Suite 640. Telephone: 312-236-5599.
Wheaton Office: 400 S. County Farm Road, Suite 120. Telephone: 630-653-9400. Fax: 630-653-9450.

Family Law, Bankruptcy, Real Estate Litigation and Transactions, Estate Planning and Probate.

JONATHAN G. ANDERSON, born Joliet, Illinois, June 16, 1953; admitted to bar, 1981, Florida, Illinois and U.S. District Court, Northern District of Illinois. *Education:* University of Wisconsin-Madison (B.A., 1975); University of Florida (J.D., 1980). *Member:* Du Puge County Bar Association (Family Law Section); Northwest Suburban Bar Association (Family Law Section). ***PRACTICE AREAS:*** Family Law; Bankruptcy; Real Estate Litigation; Estate Planning; Probate. ***Email:*** andrsnlaw@aol.com

---

ROBIN M. ZANDRI, born New York, N.Y., August 10, 1956; admitted to bar, 1997, Illinois; 2001, U.S. District Court, Northern District of Illinois. *Education:* University of Illinois at Chicago (B.S., 1993); Northern Illinois University (J.D., 1997). *Member:* Northwest Suburban Bar Association. ***PRACTICE AREAS:*** Family Law; Bankruptcy. ***Email:*** andrsnlaw@aol.com

ANDREA C. LAWRENCE, born Oak Lawn, Illinois, February 13, 1972; admitted to bar, 1997, Illinois and U.S. District Court, Northern District of Illinois. *Education:* Northern Illinois University (B.A., 1994); DePaul University (J.D., 1997). *Member:* Du Page County Bar Association. ***PRACTICE AREAS:*** Family Law; Bankruptcy; Real Estate. ***Email:*** andrsnlaw@aol.com

CHRISTOPHER J. MAURER, born Park Ridge, Illinois, August 5, 1972; admitted to bar, 1997, Illinois. *Education:* University of Illinois at Urbana-Champaign (B.S., 1994); Loyola University, Chicago (J.D., 1997). ***PRACTICE AREAS:*** Family Law; Plaintiffs Personal Injury. ***Email:*** andrsnlaw@aol.com

MIA DO, born Seoul, South Korea; admitted to bar, 2004, Illinois. *Education:* University of Illinois (B.A., 1999); University of Chicago (M.M., 2001); Chicago-Kent College of Law (J.D., 2004). *Member:* Christian Legal Society; Asian Pacific American Law Student Association. ***LANGUAGES:*** Korean. ***PRACTICE AREAS:*** Family Law; Immigration. ***Email:*** andrsnlaw@aol.com

ANGELINA & PALMER, P.C.

SCHAUMBURG, ILLINOIS

(See Inverness)

Family Law, including Divorce, Child Support, Child Custody, Alimony/Maintenance, Division of Property and Debt, Parentage, Grandparents' Rights, Visitation, Post Decree/Post Divorce Disputes, Separation, Uncontested Divorce, Divorce Settlements. Commercial Real Estate and Residential Real Estate Transactions, including Contract Drafting and Negotiation, Real Estate Closings, Real Estate and Construction Litigation, Zoning, Commercial and Residential Landlord/Tenant, Evictions, Commercial Lease Negotiation and Drafting. Business Law, including Formation of Corporations, Limited Liability Companies (LLC), and Limited Liability Partnerships (LLP). Advice for Business Legal Problems and Business Litigation. Employment Law, Executive Employment Agreements, Buy-Sell Agreements, Operating Agreements, Partnership Agreements, Asset Sales, Sales of Business.Estate Planning, including Wills, Trusts, Power of Attorney, Health Care Power of Attorney, Living Will, Special Needs Trust, Tax Avoidance Trust, Irrevocable Trust, Codicil, Probate.Criminal Law, including Criminal Defense, Felony, including Unlawful Use of Weapons, Battery, Theft, Burglary, Assault, DUI, Driving Under the Influence, Drug Possession, Drug Manufacture, Misdemeanor, Traffic, Ordinance Violation. Personal Injury for Serious Injuries and Wrongful Death.

BARRETT & GILBERT LLP

SCHAUMBURG, ILLINOIS

(See Rockford)

Medical Malpractice, Catastrophic Personal Injury, Law Enforcement Litigation, Products Liability, Commercial Motor Vehicle Safety, General Litigation, Transportation, Automobile Accidents, Dog Bites, Slip and Fall, Wrongful Death, International Law.

LAURENCE J. BOLON

SCHAUMBURG, ILLINOIS

(See Chicago)

Family Law, Divorce, Child Custody, Child Support, Visitation Rights, Criminal Law, Federal Criminal Law, White Collar Crime, Bank Fraud, Electronic Fraud, Felonies, Drug Offenses, Driving While Intoxicated, Civil Litigation, Business and Probate Litigation.

WARREN J. BRESLIN LAW OFFICES

10 N. MARTINGALE ROAD, SUITE 400
SCHAUMBURG, ILLINOIS 60173-2418
Telephone: 847-934-7070
Fax: 847-934-5551
URL: http://www.breslinlaw.com
Email: warren@breslinlaw.com
URL: http://www.lawyers.com/breslin

Criminal Law (All Felonies & Misdemeanors); DUI & All Traffic Violations (Major & Minor); Revoked & Suspended Licenses, Driver's License Reinstatement; Petitions for Executive Clemency (Governor Pardons); Expungements (Clearing Criminal & Traffic Arrest Records).

FIRM PROFILE: Warren J. Breslin is an experienced trial attorney having successfully defended clients in virtually every type of felony and misdemeanor case, including criminal law, felonies, misdemeanors, traffic violations, driving while intoxicated, driving while suspended or revoked, drug crimes, guns, weapons, homicide, domestic violence, assault and battery, sexual assault, sexual abuse, arson, robbery, burglary, fraud, theft, parole and probation, juvenile crimes, juvenile law, constitutional law, civil rights, internet law, litigation, appellate practice, administrative hearings, license hearings, criminal and traffic defense.

Warren Breslin is honored to be listed in the Martindale-Hubbell Bar Register of Pre-Eminent Lawyers.

WARREN J. BRESLIN, born Chicago, Illinois, April 25, 1949; admitted to bar, 1979, Illinois; 1980, U.S. Court of Appeals, Seventh Circuit; 1982, U.S. Supreme Court; 1988, Colorado, District of Columbia and Wisconsin; 1991, Florida. *Education:* DePaul University (B.A., 1971; M.S., Valedictorian, 1975); Loyola University (J.D., Valedictorian, 1979). Essay Finalist, Howard Schwab Memorial Award, American Bar Association, 1978. Author: "Police Intervention in Domestic Confrontations, Northwestern University School of Law / IACP," Journal of Police Science and Administration, Volume 6, No. 3, September 1978; "A Study in the Organization, Administration & Management of Municipal Police Departments," Masters of Science Thesis, 1975. Former Associate, Chapman and Cutler. Former Assistant State's Attorney/Prosecutor, Special Task Force on Political and Organized Crime, Cook County State's Attorney's Office. Former Analyst/Liaison Officer, Superintendent of Police, Chicago Police Department. Past Membership: Chicago; Illinois State and Northwest Suburban Bar Associations; Association of Trial Lawyers of America; Illinois Attorneys for Criminal Justice; National Association of Criminal Defense Lawyers.

LAW OFFICES OF HERBERT BUETOW

11 E. SCHAUMBURG ROAD, 2ND FLOOR
SCHAUMBURG, ILLINOIS 60194
Telephone: 847-584-2264
Fax: 847-584-2258
Email: hbuetow@msn.com

Bankruptcy, Real Estate, Civil Litigation.

HERBERT R. BUETOW, born Chicago, Illinois, December 7, 1955; admitted to bar, 1988, Illinois. *Education:* Northeastern Illinois University (B.A., 1978); George Williams College (M.S.W., 1982); Chicago-Kent College of Law, Illinois Institute of Technology (J.D., 1988). ***PRACTICE AREAS:*** Bankruptcy; Real Estate; Civil Litigation.

MALINI M. BYANNA, LLC

869 EAST SCHAUMBURG ROAD, # 352
SCHAUMBURG, ILLINOIS 60194
Telephone: 847-923-1706
Facsimile: 847-923-1707
Email: malini@creativefamilylaw.com
URL: http://www.creativefamilylaw.com

Domestic Relations, Mediation, Collaborative Law, Family Law, Divorce, Guardianship, Child Custody, Child Support, Visitation Rights, Domestic Violence.

MALINI M. BYANNA, born Bangalore, India, 1968; admitted to bar, 2003, Illinois. *Education:* University of Illinois, Chicago (B.A., Psychology, 1992); Chicago-Kent College of Law, Illinois Institute of Technology (J.D., 2003). Recipient, CALI Award for Excellence in Advanced Research and Writing and Criminal Procedure, Chicago-Kent College of Law. Columnist, "Crisis and Crossroads" at India Tribune (www.indiatribune.com). President, Lotus Rising Foundation (www.lotusrisingfoundation.org). Member: Family Violence Coordinating Council, Third Municipal District, Circuit Court, Cook County, Illinois; Mediation Council of Illinois; Collaborative Law Institute of Illinois; Association of American University Women. *Member:* Chicago, Illinois State and American Bar Associations; Northwest Suburban Bar Association; Asian American Bar Association (Member, Judicial Evaluation Committee); Women's Bar Association of Illinois. ***PRACTICE AREAS:*** Domestic Relations; Mediation; Collaborative Law; Family Law; Divorce; Guardianship; Child Custody; Child Support; Visitation Rights; Domestic Violence. ***Email:*** malini@creativefamilylaw.com

CHRISTOPHER M. COSLEY

SCHAUMBURG, ILLINOIS

(See Rolling Meadows)

Criminal Law, Divorce, Real Estate, Bankruptcy, Driving While Intoxicated, Drug Crimes, Traffic Violation, Misdemeanors, Felonies, Juvenile Crimes, Parole and Probation.

JOSEPH P. DOYLE

105 S. ROSELLE ROAD, SUITE 203
SCHAUMBURG, ILLINOIS 60193
Telephone: 847-985-1100
Fax: 847-985-1126
URL: http://www.joedoylelaw.com

Bankruptcy.

JOSEPH P. DOYLE, born 1976; admitted to bar, 2003, Illinois. *Education:* Loyola University (B.S., 1996); Ohio Northern University (J.D., 2001). ***PRACTICE AREAS:*** Bankruptcy.

LAW OFFICES OF CARYL JACOBS GABE & ASSOCIATES, INC.

SCHAUMBURG, ILLINOIS

(See South Barrington)

Family, Divorce, Paternity, Mediation, Child Custody, Child Support, Matrimonial Law, Domestic Relations, Orders of Protection, Prenuptial Agreements, Adoptions, and Injunctions.

THE LAW OFFICES OF THOMAS GLASGOW, LTD.

Established in 1999

1834 WALDEN OFFICE SQUARE, SUITE 500
SCHAUMBURG, ILLINOIS 60173
Telephone: 847-654-0650
Fax: 847-654-0520
Email: glasgowlaw_TG@hotmail.com
URL: http://www.glasgowlaw.net

Criminal, Federal, State, Felony, Misdemeanor, DUI, Traffic, Drunk Driving, Revoked and Suspended License, Murder, Drug Offense, Weapons Charge, Civil, Contracts Litigation, Administrative, Divorce, Family Law.

THOMAS T. GLASGOW, admitted to bar, 1994, Illinois, U.S. District Court, Northern District of Illinois, Federal Trial Bar, Northern District of Illinois and U.S. Court of Appeals, Seventh Circuit; 1997, U.S. Supreme Court. *Education:* University of Mississippi (B.A., 1990); Chicago-Kent College of Law (J.D., 1994). Dean's List. Member, National Trial Competition Team. Recipient, Jacob and Yolanda Van Emden Scholarship, Dean's Advisory Council. Instructor, Health Care Investigator training, Illinois Department of Professional Regulation. Past Member: United States Department of Justice, Central District of Illinois Health Care Fraud Committee; Northwest Community Hospital Foundation; Felony Review, 1997-1998; Narcotics Division, 1995-1997; Juvenile Division, 1994; Traffic Division, 1994. Judge, Chicago Kent Regional Trial Competition. Commissioner, Cook County Northwest Water Commission. Chairman, Arlington Heights Zoning Board of Appeals. Chief, Medical Division, Illinois Department of Professional Regulation, 1998-1999. Cook County State's Attorney, Chicago, Illinois, 1994-1998. ***PRACTICE AREAS:*** Criminal Law; Administrative Law; Civil Litigation. ***Email:*** glasgowlaw_TG@hotmail.com

ASSOCIATES

NICHOLE M. WALTZ, admitted to bar, 2001, Illinois. *Education:* University of Iowa (B.A., 1998); DePaul University (J.D., 2001). Participant: International Criminal Law Seminar, Sicily, 2001; Family Law, Chicago, Illinois, 2003; Criminal Trial Lawyers Course, Northwestern University School of Law, 2004. *Member:* Chicago and Northwest Suburban Bar Associations. ***PRACTICE AREAS:*** Criminal Law; Family Law; Civil Law. ***Email:*** glasgowlaw_NMW@hotmail.com

JACQUELINE LACY, born Aurora, Illinois; admitted to bar, 2003, Illinois. *Education:* Western Illinois University (B.S., cum laude, 1999); John Marshall Law School (J.D., 2002). Phi Alpha Delta. *Member:* Illinois State Bar Association; DuPage Association of Women Lawyers (Member, Board of Directors, 2005-2006). ***PRACTICE AREAS:*** Criminal Defense; Civil Practice.

LEGAL SUPPORT PERSONNEL

LUISA M. LUCE, born Chicago, Illinois. *Education:* University of Illinois (B.S., 2001). ***LANGUAGES:*** Spanish, Portuguese. ***PRACTICE AREAS:*** Administrative. ***Email:*** glasgowlaw_LLM@hotmail.com

JOHN C. GRIESMAIER, born Arlington Heights, Illinois. *Education:* Columbia College, Chicago (1998-2000). ***Email:*** glasgowlaw_JCG@hotmail.com

Languages: Spanish, German and Portuguese.

GRAFT & JORDAN

Established in 1996

1900 EAST GOLF ROAD, SUITE 600
SCHAUMBURG, ILLINOIS 60173-5006
Telephone: 847-330-2423
Fax: 847-330-1652
Email: law@graftjordan.com
URL: http://www.lawyers.com/graftjordan

Burr Ridge Office: (By Appointment) 7420 County Line Road, 80527. Telephone: 630-325-2255.

(This Listing Continued)

GRAFT & JORDAN, Schaumburg—Continued

Land Use Entitlement and Zoning, Commercial Real Estate, Mergers and Acquisitions, Complex Corporate Planning, Corporate Law and Commercial Loan Documentation.

FIRM PROFILE: Graft & Jordan provides sophisticated legal services to its business clients in an effective, efficient and timely basis. The firm's managing partner is a former partner of a large law firm who serves as counsel to a prestigious local, national and international clientele, including public and private companies, banks and financial institutions, and entrepreneurial business entities. The firm's sophisticated legal work includes corporate and business law matters, land use entitlement and zoning, mergers and acquisitions, commercial real estate, complex corporate and business planning, corporate and business law and commercial loan documentation. Graft & Jordan believes that its daily implementation of best practices and high standards provides reliable, outstanding results for its clients. The firm carries the highest legal ability rating in Martindale-Hubbell.

MEMBERS OF FIRM

WILLIAM C. GRAFT, born Barrington, Illinois, August 22, 1961; admitted to bar, 1986, Illinois. *Education:* Creighton University (B.A. in Philosophy, 1982); DePaul University College of Law (J.D., 1986). Member, 1984-1986 and Editor of Articles and Notes, 1985-1986, De Paul Law Review. President, 1985-1986 and Vice President, 1984-1985, De Paul Student Bar Association. Member, De Paul University Law Alumni Board, 1986-1990. Author: "Copyright Protection of Computer Software: A Statutory Proposal," 35 DePaul L. Rev. 951 (1985); "The Pleasures of Pro Bono," Chicago Bar Association Record, May, 1992. Director, 1996—, Barrington Bank and Trust Company. Director, Wintrust Financial Corporation (NASDAQ Symbol: WTFC), 1997-2003. President, Barrington Area Arts Council. Board Member, Good Shepherd Hospital. Chairman, 2004— and Director, 1999-2004, Advocate Charitable Foundation. Director, Halquist Company, 1998—. Educational Foundation Board Member, Harper College, 2003—. Included in: Who's Who in American Law (1994-1998); Who's Who in the Midwest (1998-1999). *Member:* Illinois State (Member, Real Estate, Corporate, Zoning and Business Law Sections) Bar Association. (Also Of Counsel, Thiedmann & Edler, Chicago, Illinois). ***PRACTICE AREAS:*** Land Use; Business Law; Commercial Law; Real Estate; Mergers and Acquisitions. ***Email:*** wcg@graftjordan.com

THOMAS E. JORDAN, born Oak Park, Illinois, October 28, 1964; admitted to bar, 1996, Illinois and U.S. District Court, Northern District of Illinois. *Education:* University of Illinois (B.S., 1986; M.B.A., 1990); Chicago-Kent College of Law (J.D., with honors, 1996). Real Estate Salesperson License, Illinois, 1986. *Member:* Illinois State Bar Association. ***PRACTICE AREAS:*** Land Use; Real Estate; Employment Law; Mergers and Acquisitions; Corporate Law; Commercial Law; Finance. ***Email:*** tej@graftjordan.com

Languages: English and Mandarin (Chinese).

REPRESENTATIVE CLIENTS: Advocate Health Care; Bank One; Northern Trust Bank, LaSalle Bank; Wintrust Financial Corporation; Sunrise Assisted Living.

GRECO AND TARALLO L.L.P.
ATTORNEYS AND COUNSELLORS AT LAW

Established in 1987

MB FINANCIAL BANK BUILDING
200 WEST HIGGINS ROAD, SUITE 300
SCHAUMBURG, ILLINOIS 60195-3718
Telephone: 847-843-8850
Fax: 847-843-2583
Email: gretarlaw@aol.com
URL: http://www.lawyers.com/greco&tarallo

Corporate and Transactional Law. Commercial and Residential Real Estate. Civil Trial and Appellate Practice in all State and Federal Courts. Family, Divorce, Matrimonial and Estate Planning Law. Employment and Civil Rights Litigation.

MEMBERS OF FIRM

JOSEPH F. GRECO, born Chicago, Illinois, September 4, 1941; admitted to bar, 1970, Illinois and U.S. District Court, Northern District of Illinois including Trial Bar; 1978, U.S. Supreme Court; 1983, U.S. Court of Appeals, Seventh Circuit. *Education:* De-Paul University (B.A., 1964; J.D., 1970). Special Assistant Illinois Attorney General, Consumer Fraud Division, 1970-1979. Prosecuting Attorney, Village of University Park, Illinois, 1972-1988. Advisor, Illinois Citizenship Experience, 1979-1993. Arbitrator, Cook County Mandatory Arbitration Program. *Member:* Northwest Suburban and Illinois State Bar Associations; Illinois Real Estate Lawyers Association. [1st Lt., U.S. Army, 1964-1966]. ***PRACTICE AREAS:*** Employment/Labor Relations Law; Corporate Law; Real Estate Law; Estate Planning; Criminal Misdemeanor; Civil Litigation. ***Email:*** gretarlaw@aol.com

PHILLIP S. TARALLO, born Chicago, Illinois, August 24, 1960; admitted to bar, 1985, Illinois and U.S. District Court, Northern District of Illinois. *Education:* Northern Illinois University; DePaul University (B.A., 1982; J.D., 1985). Recipient, American Jurisprudence Award. *Member:* Du Page County, Northwest Suburban and Illinois State Bar Associations; Illinois Real Estate Lawyers Association. ***PRACTICE AREAS:*** Real Estate Law; Family Law; Civil Litigation; Criminal Misdemeanor; Commercial Litigation. ***Email:*** gretarlaw@aol.com

OF COUNSEL

DAVID E. RUEDLIN, born Toledo, Ohio, September 29, 1943; admitted to bar, 1969, Illinois; 1970, U.S District Court, Northern District of Illinois. *Education:* Bradley University (B.S., 1966); University of Toledo (J.D., 1969). Phi Alpha Delta; Pi Kappa Delta. Member, University of Toledo Law Review and Casenote published in University of Toledo Law Journal, Spring, 1968 - Volume 1, Number 3; Research Editor, University of Toledo Law Review, 1968-1969; Member, Board of Editors, University of Toledo Law Review, 1968-1969. Previously with: Forrest and Ruedlin, 1972-1975; Ruedlin and Clery, 1976-1980; Ruedlin, Clery and Clery, 1980-1983. *Member:* Chicago and Illinois State Bar Associations; Attorneys Title Guaranty Fund (Northwest Suburban Advisory Board Member, 1993-1997); Illinois Real Estate Lawyers Association. ***PRACTICE AREAS:*** Real Estate Law; Business Formation; Corporate Law; Estate Planning. ***Email:*** druedlin@msn.com

(This Listing Continued)

REPRESENTATIVE CLIENTS: Lucid Dreams Software; Technicool Corp; Southwestern Bell; Sears Roebuck & Co.; American Cellular Communications, Inc.; Pumps & Process Equipment, Inc.; Kean's Baking Co., Inc.; Solidyne Inc.; Temperature Service Corporation; J.D. Brown Co., Inc.; Wolf Electric Co., Inc.; Cutrona Insurance, Inc.; Midwest Automotive, Inc.; Vanguard Heating & Air Conditioning, Inc.; Aria Architects, Inc.; Port to Port, Inc.; A & T Trucking, Inc.; Acorn Tire, Inc.; Crescent City Iron, Inc.; Sam's of Arlington, Inc.; Fastenal, Inc.

LAW OFFICES OF
ELLIOT HEIDELBERGER

SCHAUMBURG, ILLINOIS

(See Hanover Park)

Family Law, Divorce, Child Custody, Child Support, Premarital Agreements, Spousal Support, Parentage, Real Estate Closings.

LAW OFFICES OF THADDEUS HUNT

SCHAUMBURG, ILLINOIS

(See Chicago)

Bankruptcy, Consumer Bankruptcy, Commercial Bankruptcy, Foreclosures, Libel, Slander and Defamation, Consumer Fraud, Automobile Accidents, Dog Bites, Slip and Fall, Condominium Law, Homeowners Association Law, Landlord and Tenant Law, Residential Real Estate, Buying and Selling a Home, Business Law, Mechanics Liens, Breach of Contract, Identity Theft, Commercial Transactions, Civil Litigation, Federal Litigation, Trial Practice.

THE LAW OFFICES OF
ROBERTA K. KANABAY

1920 THOREAU DRIVE, SUITE 171
SCHAUMBURG, ILLINOIS 60173
Telephone: 847-925-1007
Fax: 847-925-1012
Email: kanabaylaw@sbcglobal.net
URL: http://www.lawyers.com/kanabay

Family, Divorce, Child Custody, Child Support, Criminal, Driving While Intoxicated, Traffic and Commercial Litigation.

ROBERTA K. KANABAY, born Chicago, Illinois, June 26, 1953; admitted to bar, 1997, Illinois. *Education:* DePaul University (B.A., Communication, 1994); Chicago-Kent College of Law, Illinois Institute of Technology (J.D., 1997).

KLEST LAW FIRM

1701 EAST WOODFIELD ROAD, SUITE 909
SCHAUMBURG, ILLINOIS 60173-5137
Telephone: 847-969-9510
Fax: 847-969-9514
URL: http://www.lawyers.com/klest
Email: info@josephklest.com
URL: http://www.chicagotriallaw.com

Personal Injury, Medical Malpractice, Products Liability, Legal Malpractice, Construction Accidents, Airplane Crash Litigation, Insurance Bad Faith, Automobile Accidents, Motorcycle Accidents, Birth Trauma, Sexual Abuse, Child Abuse and Neglect, Slip and Fall, Wrongful Death, Dog Bites, Railroad Accidents and Injuries, Automobile Products, Liability and Drug and Medical Device Litigation, Trial Practice.

JOSEPH G. KLEST, born Chicago, Illinois, April 18, 1953; admitted to bar, 1982, Illinois, U.S. District Court, Northern District of Illinois; 1991, Federal Trial Bar. *Education:* Northeastern Illinois University; John Marshall Law School (J.D., 1982). Arbitrator, Circuit Court of Cook County, 1990—. *Member:* Chicago Bar Associations; Illinois Trial Lawyers Association (Member, Medical Malpractice, Civil Practice, Rules and Amicus Committees); Association of Trial Lawyers of America (Member, Committee on Child Sexual Abuse Litigation Group); Northwest Suburban Bar Association; The National Crime Victim Bar Association. ***REPORTED CASES:*** Clay v. Kuhl, Illinois Supreme Court, 189 Ill.2d 603, 727 N.E.2d 217, 244 Ill.Dec. 918 (2000).

LAW OFFICE OF
GREGORY J. MARTUCCI, P.C.

SCHAUMBURG, ILLINOIS

(See Roselle)

Bankruptcy, Criminal Law, Driving While Intoxicated, Juvenile Criminal Law, Traffic Violations, Domestic Violence, Personal Injury, Automobile Accidents and Injuries, Slip and Fall, Workers Compensation.

MELTZER, PURTILL & STELLE LLC

SECOND FLOOR
1515 EAST WOODFIELD ROAD
SCHAUMBURG, ILLINOIS 60173-5431
Telephone: 847-330-2400
Fax: 847-330-1231
Email: mps@mpslaw.com

Business and commercial transactions, real estate transactions, commercial finance, financial institution regulatory matters and commercial litigation, with emphasis in asset-based and construction lending, sales and purchases of business, representation of land developers and builders, and general business representation.

MEMBERS OF FIRM

DEBORAH S. BUSSERT, admitted to bar, 1984, Illinois, U.S. District Court, Northern and Central Districts of Illinois including Trial Bar, U.S. District Court, Eastern District of Wisconsin; 1990, U.S. Supreme Court, U.S. Court of Appeals, Seventh Circuit. *Education:* Loyola University (B.B.A., Economics, summa cum laude, 1981); Northwestern University (J.D., cum laude, 1984). Beta Gamma Sigma; Alpha Sigma Nu; Order of the Coif. Articles Editor, Journal of Criminal Law and Criminology, 1983-1984. Certified Arbitrator and Mediator. *Member:* Chicago, Illinois State and American Bar Associations. ***PRACTICE AREAS:*** Business Law; Corporate Law; Commercial Litigation; Mediation; Arbitration; Employment Law. ***Email:*** dbussert@mpslaw.com

WILLIAM J. GRINDE, born Madison, Wisconsin, April 6, 1947; admitted to bar, 1975, California; 1992, Illinois. *Education:* University of Wisconsin at Madison (B.B.A., with honors, 1969); Stanford University (J.D., 1974). *Member:* Chicago, Illinois State and American Bar Associations; State Bar of California; American Institute of Certified Public Accountants; Illinois CPA Society; Northwest Suburban Bar Association; Northwest Suburban Estate Planning Council. ***PRACTICE AREAS:*** Employee Benefits (25%); Estate Planning (40%); Taxation (35%). ***Email:*** wgrinde@mpslaw.com

SCOTT D. GUDMUNDSON, born Mount Holly, New Jersey, March 23, 1958; admitted to bar, 1985, Illinois. *Education:* University of Chicago (B.A., 1982); Loyola University (J.D., 1985). *Member:* Chicago Bar Association. ***PRACTICE AREAS:*** Real Estate Finance; Real Estate Development; Secured Lending. ***Email:*** sgudmundson@mpslaw.com

SAMUEL G. HARROD IV, born Bloomington, Illinois, November 5, 1965; admitted to bar, 1991, Illinois. *Education:* Eureka College (B.A., summa cum laude, 1988); University of Illinois (J.D., magna cum laude, 1991). Associate Editor, University of Illinois Law Review, 1990-1991. *Member:* Chicago and Illinois State Bar Associations. ***PRACTICE AREAS:*** Litigation; Employment Law. ***Email:*** sharrod@mpslaw.com

RAYMOND J. HORN III, born Chicago, Illinois, June 30, 1967; admitted to bar, 1992, Illinois. *Education:* Drake University (B.A., summa cum laude, 1989); University of Illinois (J.D., summa cum laude, 1992). Phi Beta Kappa; Order of the Coif; Omnicorn Delta Kappa. Recipient, Rickert Award. ***PRACTICE AREAS:*** Corporate Law; Banking Law. ***Email:*** rhorn@mpslaw.com

TERENCE P. KENNEDY, born New York, N.Y., April 1, 1953; admitted to bar, 1984, Illinois. *Education:* University of Notre Dame (B.A., 1975); Virginia Commonwealth University (M.F.A., 1977); Fordham University (J.D., 1984). Editor, Fordham Urban Law Journal, 1983-1984. ***PRACTICE AREAS:*** Mergers and Acquisitions; Securities; Corporate Law. ***Email:*** tkennedy@mpslaw.com

RANDALL S. KULAT, born Galesburg, Illinois, March 18, 1955; admitted to bar, 1980, Illinois. *Education:* University of Illinois (B.A., with high distinction in History, 1977; J.D., 1980). Phi Beta Kappa. *Member:* Chicago and Illinois State Bar Associations. ***PRACTICE AREAS:*** Banking Law; Tax Exempt Finance; Business Law; Corporate Law. ***Email:*** rkulat@mpslaw.com

BRIAN MELTZER, born Chicago, Illinois, April 15, 1944; admitted to bar, 1969, Illinois. *Education:* Cornell University (A.B., 1966); Harvard University (J.D., 1969). ***PRACTICE AREAS:*** Real Estate; Construction Lending Law; Condominium Development; Planned Unit Development Law. ***Email:*** bmeltzer@mpslaw.com

WILLIAM J. MITCHELL, born Indiana, Pennsylvania, December 23, 1962; admitted to bar, 1988, Illinois. *Education:* St. Vincent College (B.A., 1984); Chicago-Kent College of Law, Illinois Institute of Technology (J.D., 1988). *Member:* Illinois State Bar Association. ***PRACTICE AREAS:*** Real Estate Finance; Real Estate Development; Planned Unit Development Law; Construction Law; Secured Lending; Condominium Conversions. ***Email:*** wmitchell@mpslaw.com

THOMAS R. PALMER, born Chicago, Illinois, February 28, 1953; admitted to bar, 1979, Illinois; 1980, U.S District Court, Northern District of Illinois and U.S. Court of Appeals, Seventh Circuit. *Education:* DePaul University (B.A., with highest honors, 1975; J.D., 1979). Author, "Evaluating the Enforceability of Non Compete Agreements," DuPage County Bar Association Journal, July 1991. Lecturer: "Hiring and Firing," 1984 and "Wage and Hour Review," 1985, Illinois State Chamber of Commerce Seminars. "Employee Confidentiality and Non-Compete Agreements," 1989, 1996, "What a Person Needs to Know Before Starting a Business," 1991, 1992 and "When and How an Individual May Be Hired as an Independent Contractor Rather Than an Employee," 1993, "Limited Liability Companies," 1999, "Shareholder Agreements," 2002, Northwest Suburban Bar Association Seminars. *Member:* Chicago, Northwest Suburban (Chairman: Employment Law Committee, 1991-1993, 1996; Corporate/Business Law Committee, 1997; Member, Continuing Legal Education, 1996; Legal Counsel, 2004), Illinois State and American (Member, Sections on: Labor and Employment Law; Business Law) Bar Associations. ***PRACTICE AREAS:*** Labor and Employment; Corporate Law; Business Transactions; Asset Protection; Estate Planning. ***Email:*** tpalmer@mpslaw.com

JOHN F. PURTILL, born Chicago, Illinois, May 11, 1950; admitted to bar, 1976, Illinois. *Education:* Northwestern University (B.A., 1972); Loyola University (J.D., 1976); John Marshall Law School (LL.M., Taxation, 1985). *Member:* Illinois State Bar Association. ***PRACTICE AREAS:*** Banking Law; Corporate Law; Real Estate. ***Email:*** jpurtill@mpslaw.com

(This Listing Continued)

MARK R. RAYMOND, born Des Plaines, Illinois, October 9, 1964; admitted to bar, 1991, Illinois. *Education:* Northern Michigan University (B.S., 1986); Loyola University, Chicago (J.D., 1991). *Member:* Illinois State Bar Association. ***PRACTICE AREAS:*** Business Law; Corporate Law; Employee Benefits; Executive Compensation; Retirement Planning; Estate Planning; Labor and Employment Law; Taxation. ***Email:*** mraymond@mpslaw.com

ROGER T. STELLE, born Springfield, Illinois, September 19, 1944; admitted to bar, 1970, Indiana and Illinois. *Education:* Northwestern University (B.S., 1966; M.B.A., 1967); Indiana University School of Law (J.D., 1970); John Marshall Law School (LL.M., 1975). *Member:* Chicago and Illinois State Bar Associations. [LTC, JAGC, USAR Ret.]. ***PRACTICE AREAS:*** Mergers and Acquisitions; Corporate Law; Banking Law. ***Email:*** rstelle@mpslaw.com

MICHAEL J. WOLFE, born Michigan City, Indiana, November 15, 1960; admitted to bar, 1986, Illinois and U.S. District Court, Northern District of Illinois. *Education:* University of Dayton (B.A., cum laude, 1983); Cleveland-Marshall College of Law (J.D., 1986). Editor-in-Chief, Journal of Law and Health, 1985-1986. *Member:* Illinois State and American (Member, Sections on: Real Estate; Banking; Business Law) Bar Associations; National Association of Corporate Real Estate Executives. ***PRACTICE AREAS:*** Commercial Real Estate; Corporate Law; Business Law; Secured Lending. ***Email:*** mwolfe@mpslaw.com

ASSOCIATES

ALLEN C. BALK, admitted to bar, 1996, Illinois. *Education:* Loyola University of Chicago (B.B.A. in Finance, 1986); Chicago-Kent College of Law (J.D., 1996). *Member:* Chicago and Illinois Bar Associations. ***PRACTICE AREAS:*** Real Estate; Commercial Finance Law; Restructurings. ***Email:*** abalk@mpslaw.com

VICTORIA C. BRESNAHAN, born Chicago, Illinois, November 13, 1970; admitted to bar, 1995, Illinois. *Education:* University of Illinois (B.A., 1992); John Marshall Law School (J.D., 1995). *Member:* Chicago and Illinois State Bar Associations. ***PRACTICE AREAS:*** Real Estate Law; Condominium Law; Planned Unit Development Law. ***Email:*** vbresnahan@mpslaw.com

KEVIN J. JOYCE, born Chicago, Illinois, April 7, 1970; admitted to bar, 1998, Illinois. *Education:* University of Wisconsin at Madison (B.A., History and Psychology, 1993); South Texas College of Law (J.D., 1997). *Member:* Illinois State and American Bar Associations; Northwest Suburban Bar Association (Chairperson, Civil Practice Division). ***PRACTICE AREAS:*** Civil Litigation. ***Email:*** kjoyce@mpslaw.com

SHANNON R. SILVERMAN, born Grand Rapids, Michigan, April 1, 1971; admitted to bar, 1997, Illinois. *Education:* University of Michigan (B.A., 1993); Wayne State University (J.D., 1997). Associate Editor, Wayne Law Review, 1996. *Member:* Chicago and Illinois State Bar Associations. ***PRACTICE AREAS:*** Business Law; Corporate Law. ***Email:*** ssilverman@mpslaw.com

LEGAL SUPPORT PERSONNEL

KATHY ABELL, born Chicago, Illinois, July 28, 1950. *Education:* Northern Illinois University (B.S., 1972). Licensed Real Estate Broker, 1990—. (Paralegal). ***PRACTICE AREAS:*** Real Estate. ***Email:*** kabell@mpslaw.com

TANYA M. BALDRIDGE, born St. Charles, Illinois, May 4, 1965. *Education:* University of Iowa (1987); Elgin Community College (A.A.S., Paralegal certificate, 1997); Northern Illinois University (2003). ***PRACTICE AREAS:*** Real Estate; Secured Lending.

AMY DEAN, born Evanston, Illinois, February 16, 1960. *Education:* William Rainey Harper College (A.A.S., 1980); Paralegal Certificate (1983). ***PRACTICE AREAS:*** Business Law; Corporate Law. ***Email:*** adean@mpslaw.com

ELLEN SEPKE, born Chicago, Illinois, December 27, 1963. *Education:* Harper College (A.A., 1985). ***PRACTICE AREAS:*** Condominium Law; Real Estate; Business; Corporate Law. ***Email:*** esepke@mpslaw.com

IRENE SCHULTE, born Chicago, Illinois, May 14, 1952. *Education:* Wright Junior College (1972); MacCormac College (1981). (Paralegal). ***PRACTICE AREAS:*** Real Estate Law; Commercial Lending. ***Email:*** ischulte@mpslaw.com

MEGAN ZIECH, born Oak Park, Illinois, December 19, 1967. *Education:* Triton College (1988); Western Kentucky University (1989). (Paralegal). ***PRACTICE AREAS:*** Litigation.

OF COUNSEL

PAMELA L. McLEAN, born New York, N.Y., July 2, 1966; admitted to bar, 1992, Illinois. *Education:* University of Virginia (B.A., 1988); University of Notre Dame (J.D., cum laude, 1992). Legal Writing Teaching Assistant, University of Notre Dame, 1991-1992. ***PRACTICE AREAS:*** Real Estate Law; Real Estate Finance; Commercial Real Estate Development; Residential Real Estate Development; Secured Lending. ***Email:*** pmclean@mpslaw.com

JOY S. GOLDMAN, born Chicago, Illinois, November 16, 1952; admitted to bar, 1977, Illinois. *Education:* Northwestern University (B.A., 1974; J.D., 1977). *Member:* Illinois State Bar Association. ***PRACTICE AREAS:*** Real Estate; Real Estate Finance; Commercial Real Estate Development; Residential Real Estate Development; Secured Lending. ***Email:*** jgoldman@mpslaw.com

STEPHEN E. GOODMAN, born Bridgeport, Connecticut, November 17, 1944; admitted to bar, 1969, Missouri; 1975, Illinois. *Education:* University of Illinois (B.S., 1966; J.D., 1969). Order of the Coif. Assistant Editor, University of Illinois Law Review, 1968-1969. *Member:* Illinois State and American Bar Associations. ***PRACTICE AREAS:*** Business Law; Corporate Law; Securities. ***Email:*** sgoodman@mpslaw.com

MICHAEL T. NORRIS, LTD. & JOHN W. CALLAHAN, LTD.

ONE WOODFIELD PLACE
1701 E. WOODFIELD ROAD, SUITE 1101
SCHAUMBURG, ILLINOIS 60173
Telephone: 1-877-FELONY-3; 1-877-335-6693
Fax: 847-605-0440
Email: callahanjw@sbcglobal.net
URL: http://www.chicagofelonylaw.com

Murder, Rape, Armed Robbery, Bank Robbery, Burglary, Predatory Criminal Sexual Assault, Aggravated Criminal Sexual Abuse, Aggravated Criminal Sexual Assault, Child Pornography, Delivery of a Controlled Substance, All Narcotics Offenses, including multi-kilo possession and delivery charges. Aggravated Battery, Unlawful Restraint, White Collar Crimes, Aggravated Felony, DUI, Reckless Homicide, Aggravated Driving While License Revoked. DWI, Traffic Violations, Drivers License Issues, Formal and Informal Secretary of State Hearings.

JOHN W. CALLAHAN, born Chicago, Illinois, 1970; admitted to bar, 1997, Illinois; 2001, U.S. District Court, Central District of Illinois; 2002, U.S. District Court, Northern District of Illinois; 2002, U.S. District Court, Northern District of Illinois Trial Bar. *Education:* University of Illinois (B.S., 1992); DePaul University College of Law (J.D., 1997). Phi Kappa Psi. Member, MENSA. *Member:* Chicago and Du Page County Bar Associations; Northwest Suburban Bar Association. ***PRACTICE AREAS:*** Murder; Rape; Armed Robbery; Bank Robbery; Burglary; Predatory Criminal Sexual Assault; Aggravated Criminal Sexual Abuse; Child Pornography; Delivery of A Controlled Substance; Narcotics; Aggravated Battery; Unlawful Restraint; White Collar Crime; Aggravated Felony; DUI; Reckless Homicide; Driving While License Revoked; Driving While Intoxicated; Traffic Violations; Drivers License Issues.

MICHAEL T. NORRIS, born Chicago, Illinois, 1944; admitted to bar, 1971, Illinois; U.S. District Court, Central and Northern Districts of Illinois; U.S. District Court, District of Minnesota; 1990, U.S. District Court, Eastern District of Wisconsin; 1991, U.S. Court of Appeals, 7th Circuit; U.S. Supreme Court. *Education:* DePaul University (B.A.; J.D., 1971). Formerly, Lead Counsel in major criminal cases in both the State and Federal Courts in the following jurisdictions: Washington D.C.; Atlanta, GA; Columbus, OH; Las Vegas, NV. ***PRACTICE AREAS:*** Murder; Rape; Armed Robbery; Bank Robbery; Burglary; Predatory Criminal Sexual Assault; Aggravated Criminal Sexual Abuse; Child Pornography; Delivery of A Controlled Substance; Narcotics; Aggravated Battery; Unlawful Restraint; White Collar Crime; Aggravated Felony; DUI; Reckless Homicide; Driving While License Revoked; Driving While Intoxicated; Traffic Violations; Drivers License Issues.

THE LAW OFFICES OF BRUCE D. PAYNTER

SCHAUMBURG, ILLINOIS

(See Arlington Heights)

Criminal Law, Felonies, Misdemeanors, Drug Offenses, Driving While Intoxicated, Assaults, Weapons Charges, Drivers License Suspension, Traffic Violations, Sex Offenses, Personal Injury, Automobile Accidents, Motorcycle Accidents, Trucking Accidents, Wrongful Death, Real Estate Transactions, Buying and Selling Real Estate.

Y. JACQUELINE PERKINS

SCHAUMBURG, ILLINOIS

(See Arlington Heights)

Family Law, Criminal, Murder, Homicide, Drug Crimes, Wrongful Felonies, Misdemeanors, Sex Assault, Police Misconduct, Divorce, Child Support, Domestic Violence.

ANTHONY PERRELLI

SCHAUMBURG, ILLINOIS

(See Deerfield)

Business Corporate, Small Business, Contracts, Business Planning, Real Estate, Commercial Litigation and Taxation.

KEVIN R. PETERS

SCHAUMBURG, ILLINOIS

(See Chicago)

Driving While Intoxicated, Drug Crimes, Felonies, Homicide, Misdemeanors, Sexual Assault, Traffic Violations, Police Misconduct, Civil Rights.

DANIEL K. ROBIN, LTD

SCHAUMBURG, ILLINOIS

(See Arlington Heights)

Bankruptcy, Chapter 7, Chapter 13, Divorce, Family Law, Child Support, Separation, Prenuptial Agreements, Equitable Distribution, Driving While Intoxicated, Traffic Violations, Criminal Law, Wills and Trusts, Estate Planning, Asset Protection.

ROSENFELD HAFRON SHAPIRO & FARMER

Established in 1972
SUITE 570
1111 PLAZA DRIVE
SCHAUMBURG, ILLINOIS 60173
Telephone: 847-330-9800
Fax: 847-330-0600
Email: ed@shapiro-lawyers.com
URL: http://www.lawyers.com/shapiro-lawyers

Chicago, Illinois Office: 221 North La Salle Street, Suite 1763. Telephone: 312-372-6058. Fax: 312-641-3139.

Commercial and Civil Litigation. Real Estate, Mortgages, Business, Contracts, Corporate, Partnership, Family, Divorce, Child Custody, Child Support and Matrimonial Litigation. Personal Injury.

RESIDENT PARTNER

EDWIN H. SHAPIRO, born Chicago, Illinois, March 12, 1938; admitted to bar, 1963, Illinois. *Education:* University of Illinois (B.S., 1959); Northwestern University (J.D., 1963). Certified Public Accountant, Illinois, 1962. *Member:* Northwest Suburban (President, 1985-1987), Illinois State and American Bar Associations. ***PRACTICE AREAS:*** Civil Litigation; Matrimonial Law; Automobile Accidents and Injuries; Residential Real Estate; Commercial Real Estate.

THE SULLIVAN FIRM, LTD.

SCHAUMBURG, ILLINOIS

(See Rolling Meadows)

Litigation, Criminal Law, Family Law, Employment Law, Business Law, DWI and Real Estate.

A. TRAUB & CÁDIZ

Established in 2001
1305 REMINGTON ROAD SUITE O
SCHAUMBURG, ILLINOIS 60173
Telephone: 847-839-4590
Fax: 847-839-4591
Email: atraub@atclaw.com
URL: http://www.atclaw.com

General Practice, Litigation, Family Law, Adoption, Child Custody/Support, Divorce, Estate Planning, Wills and Probate, Landlord and Tenant, Bankruptcy, Real Estate: Residential, Guardianship, Traffic.

FIRM PROFILE: Practicing throughout DuPage, Cook, and Kane County.

ANGEL M. TRAUB, born July 22, 1971; admitted to bar, 2001, Illinois and U.S. District Court, Northern District of Illinois. *Education:* Northern Illinois University (B.A., summa cum laude, honors, 1998); John Marshall Law School (J.D., cum laude, Distinguished Scholar, 2001). Published in "The John Marshall Law Review," Fall 2000. *Member:* DuPage Association of Women Lawyers (Board Member). ***PRACTICE AREAS:*** Child Custody; Child Support; Divorce; Estate Planning; Wills; Probate; Landlord and Tenant Law; Real Estate; Guardianship; Children; Family Law; Contracts. ***Email:*** Atraub@sbcglobal.net

CAROL CÁDIZ, born 1970; admitted to bar, 1996, Illinois; U.S. District Court, Northern District of Illinois. *Education:* University of Illinois (B.S., 1992); DePaul University (J.D., 1996). ***LANGUAGES:*** Spanish. ***PRACTICE AREAS:*** Real Estate; Divorce; Family Law; Child Support; Landlord and Tenant Law; Estate Planning; Wills; Contracts. ***Email:*** carol@atclaw.com

Language: Spanish.

WALLENSTEIN WAGNER & ROCKEY, LTD.

SCHAUMBURG, ILLINOIS

(See Chicago)

Intellectual Property and Technology Related Law including Protection and Licensing of United States and International Patent, Trademark, Copyright Trade Secret and Unfair Competition Matters and Related Litigation in the Courts and United States International Trade Commission.

LAW OFFICES OF WILLIAM H. WISE & ASSOCIATES

1821 WALDEN OFFICE SQUARE, 4TH FLOOR
SCHAUMBURG, ILLINOIS 60173
Telephone: 847-397-1112
Fax: 847-272-4255
Email: wise4444@aol.com
URL: http://www.wiseattorneys.net

Chicago, Illinois Office: 134 North LaSalle Street, Suite 1515, 60602. Telephone: 312-346-4555. Fax: 847-272-4255.

Criminal Law, Driving While Intoxicated, Traffic Violations, Juvenile Law, Expungement, Parole and Probation, Drug Crimes, Felonies, Homicide, Misdemeanors, Secretary of State Drivers License Revocation, White Collar Crime, Personal Injury, Automobile Accidents, Constitutional Law and Workers Compensation.

(This Listing Continued)

WILLIAM H. WISE, born Chicago, Illinois, October 17, 1940; admitted to bar, 1965, Illinois; 1976, Colorado. *Education:* Roosevelt University (A.B., 1963); John Marshall Law School (J.D., 1965). Circuit Court Judge, State of Illinois, Criminal Division, 1995-1999. *Member:* Chicago, Northwest Suburban, North Suburban and Illinois State Bar Associations; American Academy of Trial Lawyers; National Association of Criminal Defense Lawyers; American Judicature Society; Decalogue Society of Lawyers. ***PRACTICE AREAS:*** Criminal Law; Driving While Intoxicated; Traffic Violations; Juvenile Law; Expungements; Parole and Probation; Drug Crimes; Felonies; Homicide; Misdemeanors; White Collar Crime; Personal Injury; Automobile Accidents; Constitutional Law; Workers Compensation.

ASSOCIATE

HOWARD J. WISE, born Des Plaines, Illinois, July 29, 1968; admitted to bar, 1997, Illinois. *Education:* University of Arizona (B.F.A., 1991); Thomas M. Cooley Law School (J.D., 1996). Assistant State Attorney, Cook County: Criminal Division, 2000-2001; Traffic Division, 1999-2000. Approved Bar Attorney, Chicago Bar Association. ***PRACTICE AREAS:*** Criminal Defense; Felonies; Misdemeanors; Traffic Violations; DUI; Drug Crimes; Juvenile Law; Expungements; Personal Injury; Workers Compensation. ***Email:*** hof444444@aol.com

THOMAS YOUNG LAW FIRM

SCHAUMBURG, ILLINOIS

(See Palatine)

JELLIFFE, FERRELL, MORRIS & DOERGE

SHAWNEETOWN, ILLINOIS

(See Harrisburg)

Insurance Law, Negligence and Personal Injury, Litigation, Workers' Compensation Law, and Employment Law. Commercial Collection and DUI's. General Civil Practice in State and Federal Courts. Trials and Appeals.

THE BRAINARD LAW OFFICES

SHELBYVILLE, ILLINOIS

(See Charleston)

General Practice. Insurance Defense, Personal Injury, Products Liability, Probate, Trusts, Real Estate, Taxation, Municipal, Family and Health Law. Trials in all State and Federal Courts.

CHRISTOPHER M. TIETZ

SHELBYVILLE, ILLINOIS

(See Decatur)

Civil Litigation. Business Transactions, Real Estate, Corporate, Commercial, International, Employment, Construction, Technology, Insurance Defense, Products Liability, Professional Liability, Estate Planning, Trust and Probate Law.

McKEOWN, FITZGERALD, ZOLLNER, BUCK, HUTCHISON & RUTTLE

SHOREWOOD, ILLINOIS

(See Joliet)

General Civil, Trial and Appellate Practice. Corporate, Business, Municipal, Probate, Estate Planning, Real Estate, Taxation, Employment, Healthcare, School and Personal Injury.

LAW OFFICES OF RANDIE BRUNO

SKOKIE, ILLINOIS

(See Waukegan)

Criminal Law, Driving While Intoxicated, Drug Crimes, Felonies, Homicide, Juvenile, Misdemeanors, Parole and Probation, Sexual Assault, Traffic Violations, Family Law, Divorce, Child Custody, Child Support, Domestic Violence, Spousal Support.

FRANK CECE, JR.

SKOKIE, ILLINOIS

(See Chicago)

Criminal Defense, Federal Crimes, Felonies, Misdemeanors and Traffic including DUI, Battery, Domestic, Drugs, Possession, Theft, Forgery, Burglary, Robbery, Criminal Sexual Assault, Reckless Homicide, Murder, Probation Violations, Bond Hearings, Preliminary Hearings, Personal Injury, Automobile Accidents, Wrongful Death, Construction Accidents, Truck Accidents.

LAW OFFICES OF PAUL CHATZKY

SKOKIE, ILLINOIS

(See Northfield)

General Practice, Divorce, Family Law, Criminal Defense, Felonies, Driving While Intoxicated, Real Estate, Business Law, Estate Planning, Wills, Personal Injury and Civil Litigation.

CIRIGNANI HELLER HARMAN & LYNCH LLP

SKOKIE, ILLINOIS

(See Chicago)

Medical Malpractice, Wrongful Death, Cerebral Palsy, ERBS Palsy, Brain Damage, Anesthesia Injury, Improper Medication, Operating Room Death, Misdiagnosis, Birth Injuries, Retardation, Surgical Error, Medical Product Failure, Nursing Errors, Hospital Negligence, Head and Spinal Injuries, Automobile Accidents, Truck Accidents, Construction Accidents, Product Liability, Labor and Employment Litigation, Commercial Litigation, Insurance Coverage, Torts. Litigation.

CUTLER & ASSOCIATES, LTD.

5550 W. TOUHY AVENUE, 4TH FLOOR
SKOKIE, ILLINOIS 60077
Telephone: 847-673-8600
Fax: 847-673-8636
Email: David@CutlerLtd.com
URL: http://www.dhclegal.com

Bankruptcy, Consumer Bankruptcy, Bankruptcy Chapter 7, Foreclosures, Small Business, Buying and Selling of Businesses, Family Business, Limited Liability, Partnership, Corporate, Contract, Breach of Contract, General Practice, Debtor and Creditor, Collections, Creditors, Rights and Civil Litigation.

FIRM PROFILE: Practicing throughout Northern Cook County.

DAVID H. CUTLER, born Chicago, Illinois, June 11, 1964; admitted to bar, 1990, Illinois and U.S. District Court, Northern District of Illinois including Trial Bar. *Education:* Touro College (B.S.,1986); University of Miami (J.D., 1990). ***PRACTICE AREAS:*** Bankruptcy; Business Law; Corporate Law; Contracts; Collections; Civil Litigation.

LAW OFFICES OF JULIE T. EMERICK, LTD.

SKOKIE, ILLINOIS

(See Chicago)

Immigration and Naturalization Law.

EVANSTON MAIN LAW OFFICE

SKOKIE, ILLINOIS

(See Evanston)

Bankruptcy, Consumer Bankruptcy, Family, Divorce, Child Custody, Child Support, Premarital Agreements, Spousal Support, Corporate, Business, Contract, Wills, Trusts, Estate Planning, Probate, Criminal, Driving While Intoxicated, Traffic Violations, Misdemeanors, Felonies and Civil Litigation Practice.

STUART A. FELDMAN

SKOKIE, ILLINOIS

(See Wilmette)

Wills and Probate, Estate Planning, Trusts and Estates, Guardianships, Tax Planning, Taxation, IRS Audits, Business Planning, Small Business, General Business and Real Estate.

MICHAEL S. FROMAN

SUITE 322, WESTMORELAND BUILDING
9933 LAWLER AVENUE
SKOKIE, ILLINOIS 60077-3703
Telephone: 847-677-1555
Fax: 847-677-1080
Email: mfromanlaw@aol.com
URL: http://www.lawyers.com/michaelsfroman

Insurance Defense, General Liability Claims Defense, Subrogation, Workers Compensation Defense, Personal Injury. Arbitration and Alternative Dispute Resolution. Corporate and Business Litigation. Probate and Estate Planning. Legal Audit and Claims Review Services.

FIRM PROFILE: We are pleased to provide high quality affordable legal services to our valued friends and clients since 1979 from our offices in Skokie, Illinois, just north of Chicago. We serve the entire Chicago area in all State and Federal Courts.

We are readily available to provide answers, suggestions, counsel and assistance to our clients. Claims personnel and individuals and business clients often call us to discuss questions of all kinds, seek guidance, and prevent problems before they arise. We value such interchanges as they add to our understanding and depth of knowledge of issues concerning our clients. As a small firm, we are proud of the excellent relationships we enjoy with our clients.

Our practical perspectives are grounded in a combination of strong legal skills, understanding of our local court systems, and the economic realities of litigation. All this enables us to help achieve favorable results efficiently and at a reasonable cost. We apply these valuable elements to litigation and legal auditing and claims review.

We welcome the opportunity to work with you.

MICHAEL S. FROMAN, born Chicago, Illinois, August 3, 1950; admitted to bar, 1976, Illinois and U.S. District Court, Northern District of Illinois. *Education:* University

(This Listing Continued)

MICHAEL S. FROMAN, Skokie—Continued

of Illinois (B.A., with high honors, 1972); DePaul University (J.D., 1975). Member, Panel of Arbitrators, American Arbitration Association. *Member:* Chicago, Northwest Suburban, Lake County and Illinois State (Member, Insurance and Trial Sections) Bar Associations; Defense Research Institute; National Academy of Elder Law Attorneys. ***PRACTICE AREAS:*** Insurance Defense Law; Personal Injury; Civil Litigation; Business Litigation.

REPRESENTATIVE CLIENTS: Chubb Group of Insurance Cos.; Aetna Casualty and Surety Co.; GAB Business Services, Inc.; CIGNA, Corp.; McDonald's Corp.; Great American Insurance Cos.; Kemper Group; Allstate Insurance Co.; Independent Insurance Services.
REFERENCE: Citibank, N.A., Skokie, Illinois.

SHERYL RAE GHEZZI

SKOKIE, ILLINOIS

(See Lincolnwood)

Civil Litigation, Family Law, Child Custody, Divorce, Premarital Agreements, D.U.I., Drug Crimes, Juvenile Crimes, Misdemeanors, Traffic, DUI Defense, Immigration, Wills and Probate, Divorce, Child Support, Visitation Interference, Visitation Abuse, Personal Injury Defense, Property Damage Defense, Estate Planning, Real Estate Litigation.

MARC H. HEISLER

SKOKIE, ILLINOIS

(See Evanston)

Real Estate, Residential Real Estate, Buying and Selling a Home, Commercial Real Estate, Condominium Law and Mortgages. Business, Small Business, Partnership, Family Business and Buying and Selling a Business. Probate and Wills. Adoption Law. Civil Litigation, Chancery Practice, Collections, Personal Injury and Automobile Accidents.

JAMES L. KOPECKY, P.C.

SKOKIE, ILLINOIS

(See Chicago)

Securities, Securities Fraud, Securities Arbitration and Litigation, Shareholder Disputes, Business and Contract Litigation, General Civil Litigation and Personal Injury.

BARRY MICHAEL LEWIS

SKOKIE, ILLINOIS

(See Chicago)

Personal Injury, Medical Malpractice, Product Liability, Criminal, DUI, DWI, Traffic Violations, Felonies, Serious Misdemeanors, Drug Cases.

BARBARA E. LUSKY

SUITE 322, WESTMORELAND BUILDING
9933 LAWLER AVENUE
SKOKIE, ILLINOIS 60077-3703
Telephone: 847-676-2575
Fax: 847-677-1080
Email: luskylaw@sbcglobal.net
URL: http://www.lawyers.com/luskylaw

Concentration in Family Law, Divorce, Child Custody, Child Support. Also available to practice in Probate, Estate Planning, Civil Litigation.

BARBARA E. LUSKY, born November 12, 1953; admitted to bar, 1982, Illinois. *Education:* Indiana University (B.A., 1975); John Marshall Law School (J.D., 1982). *Member:* North Suburban Bar Association; Illinois State Bar Association. ***PRACTICE AREAS:*** Workers Compensation Law; Probate Law; Estate Planning Law; Family Law; Divorce Law; Child Custody Law; Child Support Law; Alimony; Annulment; Cohabitation Agreements; Domestic Partnerships; Domestic Violence; Marital Agreements; Marital Property Law; Marital Property Settlements; Non-Traditional Family Law; Paternity; Post Divorce Modification; Postnuptial Agreements; Premarital Agreements; Restraining Orders; Guardianship and Conservatorship; Adult Guardianship; Advance Directives.

MANDELL MENKES LLC

SKOKIE, ILLINOIS

(See Chicago)

General Civil Practice, Class Action Defense, Consumer Finance and Banking, Corporate, Commercial Litigation, Employment, Media, Entertainment and Intellectual Property Law including Copyright and Trademark Law, Computer and Technology Law, Health Care, Captive Insurance and Purchasing and Risk Retention Groups and Insurance Coverage, Directors and Officers Liability, Professional Liability, Casualty, Life, Health and Disability.

MARAMBA & ASSOCIATES, LLC

SKOKIE, ILLINOIS

(See Arlington Heights)

Business Law, Chancery Practice, Corporate Litigation, Civil Litigation, Complex Litigation, Defense Litigation, Federal Litigation, Administrative Litigation, Business Enterprises, Business Litigation, Closely Held Business Law, Real Estate Litigation, Veterans Rights, Military Law, Wills, Commercial Collections, Post Judgment Collections, Closely Held Corporations.

MATEK LAW OFFICES, P.C.

SKOKIE, ILLINOIS

(See Chicago)

Subrogation, Collections, Commercial Litigation, Bankruptcy, Commercial Law.

AZITA M. MOJARAD

SKOKIE, ILLINOIS

(See Chicago)

Collections, Contracts, Family Law, Immigration and Naturalization and Real Estate.

PATTON & RYAN LLC

SKOKIE, ILLINOIS

(See Chicago)

Tort Litigation, Commercial Litigation, Product Liability Law, Environmental Law, Construction Law, Insurance Coverage, Civil Litigation, Insurance Defense, Professional Liability, Medical Malpractice.

LAW OFFICES OF DAVID L. PINSEL, P.C.

SKOKIE, ILLINOIS

(See Rolling Meadows)

Divorce, Family, Child Custody, Child Support, Visitation Rights, Paternity, Real Estate, Landlord and Tenant Law, Commercial Collections, Debtor and Creditor Law.

PAUL W. PLOTNICK ATTORNEY AT LAW

Established in 1974
9933 LAWLER AVENUE
SUITE 312
SKOKIE, ILLINOIS 60077
Telephone: 847-675-2660
Fax: 847-675-2661
Email: 9933212@SBCGlobal.net
Email: lawfun@msn.com
URL: http://www.lawyers.com/plotnicklaw

Real Estate, Real Estate Litigation, Family Law, Divorce, Criminal Law, Driving While Intoxicated, Felonies, Business Law, Corporate Law, Personal Injury.

FIRM PROFILE: The attorney carries the highest legal ability rating in Martindale Hubbell. Paul W. Plotnick was a Chicago Public School Teacher. He served as an Assistant Public Defender and tried numerous jury cases including murder cases. In 1979 he left the Public Defender's Office and established his own firm. The firm is still involved in sophisticated litigation.

PAUL W. PLOTNICK, born Chicago, Illinois, 1947; admitted to bar, 1974, Illinois, U.S. District Court, Northern District of Illinois and U.S. Court of Appeals, Seventh Circuit; 1975, U.S. Tax Court; 1977, U.S. Supreme Court. *Education:* Southern Illinois University (B.A., 1969); DePaul University College of Law (J.D., 1974). Phi Kappa Phi National Honor Society. Recipient: Ruby Pin Award Kiwanis; Distinguished Service Award, Chicago Volunteer Legal Services, 1995; Distinguished President and Secretary Skokie Valley Kiwanis; Layperson of the Year Division 7 Kiwanis; Leaning Tower YMCA Recognition Award for Volunteer Services; Certificate for 20 Years Service Skokie Chamber of Commerce. Listed, Who's Who in American Law. Certified School Teacher, State of Illinois. Certified Real Estate Broker. Former Member, Board of the Midwest Federation of Men's Club. Assistant Public Defender, Cook County Public Defenders Office, Chicago, 1975-1979. Former Hearing Officer, Illinois Secretary of State. Arbitrator, Circuit Court of Cook County. Candidate For Judge of the Circuit Court. Past President, Beth Hillel Mens Club. Board of Directors, North Suburban Bar. Past Member, Board of Directors, The Congregation Board Beth Hillel. Life Member, Hadassah Associate. Member, The American Legion. *Member:* Chicago, Illinois State and American Bar Associations; Northwest Suburban Bar Association; North Suburban Bar Association; Decalogue Society. [Staff Sergeant, U.S. Army Reserve, 1969-1975]

Language: Romanian.

SCHOENBERG, FISHER, NEWMAN & ROSENBERG, LTD.

SKOKIE, ILLINOIS

(See Chicago)

General Business Practice, including Corporate, Litigation, Trade Associations, Independent Manufacturers Representatives, Labor Law, Employee Benefits, Federal, State and Real Estate Taxation, Estate Planning, Probate, Real Estate, Environmental Law, Mergers and Acquisitions, Securities, Banking, Intellectual Property, Bankruptcy, Family Law, Unfair Trade Practices, Legal Ethics and Professional Responsibility.

SHAW GUSSIS FISHMAN GLANTZ WOLFSON & TOWBIN LLC

SKOKIE, ILLINOIS

(See Chicago)

Bankruptcy and Insolvency Law, Creditors Rights, Real Estate and related services, Land Use and Zoning, Commercial Litigation, and Secured Lending.

SIMON, LAPIDOS & SIMON, LLC

4709 WEST GOLF ROAD, SUITE 475
SKOKIE, ILLINOIS 60076
Telephone: 847-329-7878
Facsimile: 847-329-9450
Email: earlsimon44@hotmail.com
URL: http://www.lawyers.com/simonlapidos&simonllc

Commercial Litigation, Residential and Commercial Real Estate, Business Transactions including Acquisitions and Mergers, Contracts, Taxation, Probate, Estate Planning including Guardianship and Elder Law, Landlord and Tenant Law, General Practice, Corporate Debtor and Creditor Reorganization and Bankruptcy, Pension and Profit Sharing Plans.

FIRM PROFILE: Providing quality legal services to families and small to medium-sized businesses for over 35 years.

EARL L. SIMON, born Chicago, Illinois, October 22, 1944; admitted to bar, 1969, Illinois. *Education:* University of Illinois (B.S., Accounting, 1966); DePaul University (J.D., 1969). Certified Public Accountant, Illinois, 1966. *Member:* Chicago, Illinois State and American Bar Associations; Decalogue Society. ***LANGUAGES:*** Yiddish. ***PRACTICE AREAS:*** Business Transactions; Real Estate; Corporate Law; Estate Planning; Pension and Profit Sharing Plans; Taxation; Elder Law. ***Email:*** earlsimon44@hotmail.com

MANNY M. LAPIDOS, born Chicago, Illinois, June 9, 1945; admitted to bar, 1970, Illinois. *Education:* University of Illinois (B.S., with honors, 1967; J.D., 1970). *Member:* Illinois Real Estate Lawyers Association. ***PRACTICE AREAS:*** Real Estate Law. ***Email:*** mlapidos@yahoo.com

STEPHANIE D. SIMON, born Chicago, Illinois; admitted to bar, 1998, Wisconsin and Illinois. *Education:* University of Illinois (B.S., with honors, 1995); University of Wisconsin (J.D., cum laude, 1998; Order of the Coif). Member, Moot Court, 1996-1998. Certified Public Accountant, 1995. *Member:* Illinois State Bar Association; State Bar of Wisconsin. ***PRACTICE AREAS:*** Business Transactions; Commercial Real Estate; Residential Real Estate; Corporate Law; Estate Planning; Corporate Reorganization; Business Law; Bankruptcy; Secured Lending. ***Email:*** stephanie973@msn.com

JAY A. SLUTZKY

SKOKIE, ILLINOIS

(See Niles)

Wills, Living Trusts, Estate Planning, Residential Real Estate, Commercial Real Estate, Divorce, Personal Injury, Bankruptcy Law, Elder Law, DUI, DWI, Business Law, Commercial Law, Commercial Litigation, Business Organization, Business Transactions, Business Counseling, Business Advice, Real Estate Law, Real Estate Litigation, Commercial Transactions, Contracts, Construction Law, Litigation, Motor Vehicle Accidents, Personal Injury Defense, Plaintiffs Personal Injury, Probate, Estate Administration, Trusts, By-Pass Trusts, Credit Shelter Trusts, Special Needs Trusts, Testamentary Trusts, Ancillar Administration, Durable Powers of Attorney, Medical Powers of Attorney, Living Wills, Pour-Over Wills, Marital Deduction Trusts, Beneficiary Designations, Irrevocable Life Insurance Trusts, Split Dollar Purchase Agreements, Crummey Trusts, Workers Compensation, Civil Litigation, Criminal Defense, Pre-Marital Agreements, Planning for Disabled Spouses, Planning for Disabled Children, Estate Tax Return Preparation, Second Marriage Issues, Contested Wills and Trusts, Partnerships, Corporations, Limited Liability Companies.

DAVID M. STERNBERG

SKOKIE, ILLINOIS

(See Chicago)

Automobile Accidents and Injuries, Slip and Fall, Wrongful Death, Personal Injury and Workers Compensation Law.

LAW OFFICES OF LAURIE J. WASSERMAN

Established in 1980

WESTMORELAND BUILDING
9933 LAWLER AVENUE, SUITE 122
SKOKIE, ILLINOIS 60077-3703
Telephone: 847-674-7324
Fax: 847-674-6684
Email: ljw@webemploymentlaw.com
URL: http://www.lawyers.com/wassermanlaw

Employment, Employment Discrimination, Employee and Employer Rights, Sexual Harassment, Americans With Disabilities Act, Family and Medical Leave Act, Whistle Blower Cases, Severance Agreements, Non-Compete Agreements, Retaliation.

FIRM PROFILE: Boutique employment law practice, concentrating on the rights of employees and small businesses. Represents individuals and small businesses in resolving employment issues; negotiating and drafting executive employment contracts and separation package; litigation and/or mediation f employment relate matters: discrimination including sexual harassment, age and ADA, Family and Medical Leave Act claims, breach of contract, non-compete agreements, theft of trade secrets, defamation, and retaliation. In addition, the firm provides estate planning services.

LAURIE J. WASSERMAN, born Washington, District of Columbia; admitted to bar, 1979, Illinois and U.S. District Court, Northern District of Illinois including Trial Bar. *Education:* University of Chicago (A.B., 1970); Northwestern University (Ph.D., 1981; J.D., 1974). *Member:* Chicago Bar Association (Member, Labor and Employment Law Committee); The Association of Trial Lawyers of America; National Employment Lawyers Association. ***REPORTED CASES:*** Schulz v. CTCA, No. 99 C 8287; Bundalo v. Norwood Park/Rocco Secco, No. 01 C 8782; Hartman v. Lisle Park District, No. 01 C 1904; Haiman v. Fox Lake, No. 98 C 0158; Nieminski v. John Nuveen & Co., No. 96 C 1960; Ilyes v. John Nuveen, No. 96 C 2087; Tabora v. Gottlieb Memorial Hospital, No. 92 C 8179; Bilal v. Rotec Industries, No. 03 C 9220; Pollak v. Board of Trustees of University of Illinois, et al, No. 99 C. 710; Walters v. Central States Coca-Cola Bottling Co., 98 C 4526. ***PRACTICE AREAS:*** Employment Law; Estate Planning.

ASSOCIATE

CAROL G. SILVERMAN, born Chicago, Illinois; admitted to bar, 1985, Illinois and U.S. District Court, Northern District of Illinois. *Education:* University of Illinois (B.A., 1975); Chicago-Kent College of Law, Illinois Institute of Technology (J.D., 1984). Moot Court Nominee, Chicago-Kent College of Law. *Member:* Illinois State Bar Association; Women's Bar Association of Illinois; National Employment Lawyers Association. ***REPORTED CASES:*** Hartman v. Lisle Park District, No. 01 C 1904; Walters v. Central States Coca-Cola Bottling Co., 98 C 4526. ***PRACTICE AREAS:*** Employment Law. ***Email:*** cgs@webemploymentlaw.com

LAW OFFICES OF CARYL JACOBS GABE & ASSOCIATES, INC.

Established in 1993

33 WEST HIGGINS ROAD, SUITE 620
SOUTH BARRINGTON, ILLINOIS 60010
Telephone: 847-551-3751
Fax: 847-551-3791
Email: CGABE7129@aol.com
URL: http://www.lawyers.com/gabe

Family, Divorce, Paternity, Mediation, Child Custody, Child Support, Matrimonial Law, Domestic Relations, Orders of Protection, Prenuptial Agreements, Adoptions, and Injunctions.

CARYL JACOBS GABE, born New York, N.Y.; admitted to bar, 1976, Illinois. *Education:* Brooklyn College of the City University of New York (B.A., cum laude, 1972); John Marshall Law School (J.D., with honors, 1976). Member, Order of John Marshall; John Marshall Law Review. *Member:* Chicago (Member, Matrimonial Law Committee, 1979—); DuPage County (Member, Matrimonial Law Committee); Illinois State; American and Northwest Suburban Bar Associations.

BROWN & ASSOCIATES

SPARTA, ILLINOIS

(See Belleville)

Civil Litigation, Personal Injury, Medical Malpractice, Products Liability, Admiralty Law, Railroad Law and Commercial Law.

ARMSTRONG TEASDALE LLP

A Partnership including Professional Corporations

3201 PLEASANT RUN, SUITE A
P.O. BOX 13317
SPRINGFIELD, ILLINOIS 62791-3317
Telephone: 217-726-8200
Facsimile: 217-726-8300
Email: armstrongteasdale@armstrongteasdale.com
URL: http://www.armstrongteasdale.com

St. Louis, Missouri Office: One Metropolitan Square, Suite 2600, 63102. Telephone: 314-621-5070. Facsimile: 314-621-5065.
Kansas City, Missouri Office: 2345 Grand Boulevard, Suite 2000, 64108. Telephone: 816-221-3420. Facsimile: 816-221-9786.
Washington, D.C. Office: 1747 Pennsylvania Avenue, N.W., Suite 300, 20006. Telephone: 202-454-2800. Facsimile: 202-454-2805.
Jefferson City, Missouri Office: 3405 West Truman Blvd., Suite 210, 65109-5713. Telephone: 573-636-8394. Facsimile: 573-636-8457.
Belleville, Illinois Office: 23 South First Street, 62220. Telephone: 618-397-4411.
Overland Park, Kansas Office: 7400 West 132nd Street, Suite 200, 66213.
Edwardsville, Illinois Office: 241 North Main Street, 62025. Telephone: 618-650-7087. Facsimile: 618-655-4004.
Henderson, Nevada Office: 701 North Green Valley Parkway, Suite 200, 89074. Telephone: 702-678-5070. Facsimile: 702-990-3003.
Sydney, Australia Office: C/Clayton Utz, Level 31, No. 1 O'Connell Street, Sidney, NSW 2000, Australia. Telephone: 61-29-262-6700. Facsimile: 61-29-262-3263.
New York, New York Office: 230 Park Avenue, Suite 2300, 10169. Telephone: 212-867-9500. Facsimile: 212-599-1759.
Shanghai, China Office: 1376 Nan Jing Xi Lu, Shanghai Center - Suite 718, Shanghai 200040, P.R. China. Telephone: 011-8621-6279-8808. Facsimilie: 011-8621-6279-8866.

(This Listing Continued)

ARMSTRONG TEASDALE LLP, Springfield—Continued

General Civil Practice. Administrative Law, Agricultural Law, Alternative Dispute Resolution, Antitrust and Trade Regulation Law, Appellate Practice, Banking and Financial Services, Biotechnology/Life Sciences, Business Law, Civil Rights, Class Actions, Communications Law, Computer, Constitutional Law, Construction Law, Corporate Compliance and Governance, Corporate Law, Corporate Finance, Education Law, Eminent Domain, Employee Benefits, Employment and Labor, Energy, Entertainment & Sports, Environmental Law, Financial Restructuring, Reorganization and Bankruptcy, Distribution and Franchise, Government Contracts, Governmental Relations, Health Care, Immigration and Naturalization, Insurance Coverage/Reinsurance and Extracontractual Liability, International Law, International Trade, Internet Law, Investments, Litigation, Medical Malpractice, Mergers & Acquisitions, Natural Resources, Occupational Safety & Health Administration, Patent, Trademark and Intellectual Property, Pension and Executive Compensation, Personal Injury, Products Liability, Professional Liability, Public Law and Finance, Real Estate, Securities, Taxation, Technology and Science, Toxic Torts, Transportation, Trusts and Estates, White Collar Crime, Workers Compensation and Zoning, Planning & Land Use and Development.

FIRM PROFILE: Armstrong Teasdale LLP conducts a comprehensive nationwide civil law practice from offices in St. Louis, Kansas City and Jefferson City, Missouri; Overland Park, Kansas; Edwardsville, Belleville and Springfield, Illinois; Las Vegas, Nevada; Washington, D.C.; New York, New York; Shanghai, P.R.C.; and Sydney, Australia. The firm is the Missouri member of Lex Mundi, an international association of independent law firms, as well as State Law Resources, Inc. and United States Law Firm Group, both national networks of independent law firms.

ASSOCIATE

JOHN H. STOCKMAN, born Troy, New York, August 20, 1964; admitted to bar, 1990, New York; 1999, Illinois. *Education:* Rochester Institute of Technology (B.S., high honors, 1986); Albany Law School of Union College (J.D., 1989). *Member:* Illinois State Bar Association. (Also at Edwardsville, Illinois Office). ***PRACTICE AREAS:*** Public Law; Finance. ***Email:*** jstockman@armstrongteasdale.com

OF COUNSEL

THOMAS W. KELTY, born Springfield, Illinois, January 8, 1945; admitted to bar, 1971, Illinois; 1982, U.S. Supreme Court; 1985, Missouri and U.S. Tax Court. *Education:* Creighton University (B.A., 1967); University of Missouri at Kansas City (J.D., 1971). Phi Alpha Delta; Sigma Alpha Epsilon. Contributing Editor: "Illinois Jurisprudence - Municipal Law," Lawyers Cooperation Publishing, 1995. Author: "Special District Government in Illinois," Illinois Institute for Continuing Legal Education. *Member:* Sangamon County, Illinois State and American Bar Associations; The Missouri Bar; Illinois Trial Lawyers Association; National Association of Bond Lawyers; National Institute of Municipal Law Officers. (Also at Edwardsville, Illinois Office). ***PRACTICE AREAS:*** Municipal Law; Municipal Bonds; Municipal Finance; Corporate Finance; Corporate Law; Insurance; Workers Compensation; Estate Planning; Trusts and Estates; Wills; Probate; Commercial Real Estate; Commercial Litigation; Antitrust; Securities; Class Actions. ***Email:*** tkelly@armstrongteasdale.com

(For Biographical Data on other Personnel, see Professional Biographies at St. Louis, Kansas City and Jefferson City, Missouri; Washington, D.C.; Belleville and Edwardsville, Illinois; Henderson, Nevada; and Shanghai, China Offices)

BAKER, BAKER & KRAJEWSKI, LLC

415 SOUTH SEVENTH STREET
SPRINGFIELD, ILLINOIS 62701
Telephone: 217-522-3445
Telecopier: 217-522-8234
Email: bakerlaw@sbcglobal.net

Labor and Employment Discrimination Law. General Civil, Trial and Appellate Practice before State and Federal Courts and Administrative Agencies. Estate Planning, Probate, Real Estate, Corporate, Tax, Railroad Law, Labor Relations, Healthcare Compliance Law.

JAMES P. BAKER, born Streator, Illinois, December 15, 1945; admitted to bar, 1971, Illinois; 1972, U.S. District Court, Central District of Illinois; U.S. District Court, Southern District of Illinois; U.S. Court of Appeals, Seventh and Eighth Circuits, U.S. Supreme Court and U.S. Tax Court. *Education:* Hanover College (B.A., 1968); University of Denver (J.D., 1970). Author: Chapter on Employment Torts, Illinois Institute for Continuing Legal Education, 1994 Handbook on Employment Termination. Faculty Member, Illinois Estate Administration, 1975 and Creative Financing in Today's Real Estate Market, 1980, Illinois Institute for Continuing Legal Education. *Member:* Sangamon County, Illinois State and American (Member, Section on Labor and Employment Law) Bar Associations; Lincoln Douglas Inns of Court.

JOHN A. BAKER, born Springfield, Illinois, February 18, 1971; admitted to bar, 1998, Illinois; 1999, U.S. District Court, Central District of Illinois and U.S. Court of Appeals, Seventh Circuit. *Education:* University of Missouri (B.A., 1993); John Marshall Law School (J.D., cum laude, 1998). *Member:* Sangamon County, Illinois State and American Bar Associations; Lincoln Douglas Inns of Court.

J. PHILLIP KRAJEWSKI, born Princeton, Illinois, December 10, 1943; admitted to bar, 1969, Illinois; 1975, District of Columbia; 1977, Pennsylvania; 1979, Virginia; U.S. District Court, Northern, Central and Southern Districts of Illinois. *Education:* University of Illinois (B.A., 1966; J.D., 1969). Attorney, Criminal Division, U.S. Department of Justice, 1969-1976. Assistant U.S. Attorney: Middle District of Pennsylvania, 1976-1978; Eastern District of Virginia, 1978-1994. *Member:* Peoria County, Illinois State and American Bar Associations; American Health Lawyers Association; Abraham Lincoln Inns of Court; Lincoln Douglas Inns of Court. ***PRACTICE AREAS:*** Health Care; Compliance Planning; Employment Litigation.

(This Listing Continued)

REPRESENTATIVE CLIENTS: Homebuilders Association of Illinois; Mid America Machinery Co.; Brandt Consolidated, Inc.; Creasy Printing; Kirby Hospital; Design Ideas; Perry Hospital.
REFERENCES: US Bank of Springfield; Warren Boyton State Bank, New Berlin, Ill.

BARBER SEGATTO HOFFEE AND HINES

Formerly Barber & Barber
MONROE AT NINTH
P.O. BOX 79
SPRINGFIELD, ILLINOIS 62705-0079
Telephone: 217-544-4868
Telecopier: 217-544-5225
URL: http://www.barberlaw.com

Waverly, Illinois Office: 176 West State Street. Telephone: 217-435-7241.

Banking, Condemnation, Contract, Corporation, Estate Planning, General Civil Trial and Appellate Practice in State and Federal Courts, Media, Negligence Law, Probate, Real Estate, Taxation and Workers Compensation, Bankruptcy, Business Law, land Use and Zoning.

MEMBERS OF FIRM

JOHN A. BARBER (1870-1939)
CLAYTON J. BARBER (1879-1970)
CHARLES F. BARBER (1904-1988)
HENRY R. BARBER (1910-1991)
ALTON G. HALL (1904-1991)
BERNARD G. SEGATTO (1931-1994)

CARL O. HOFFEE, born St. Louis, Missouri, July 7, 1934; admitted to bar, 1958, Illinois. *Education:* University of Illinois (LL.B., 1958). Phi Delta Phi; Order of the Coif. Member, Board of Editors, Illinois Law Forum, 1957-1958. Legal Secretary to Justice Harry B. Hershey, Illinois Supreme Court, 1961-1962. *Member:* Sangamon County, Illinois State and American Bar Associations. ***Email:*** hoffee@barberlaw.com

BARRY O. HINES, born Springfield, Illinois, April 18, 1947; admitted to bar, 1972, Illinois; U.S. District Court, Central District of Illinois, U.S. Court of Appeals, Seventh Circuit, U.S. Tax Court and U.S. Supreme Court. *Education:* University of Illinois (B.S., 1969; J.D., 1972). Author: "Overview of Probate," IICLE, 1984; "Sales, Exchanges and Auctions of Farm Real Estate," IICLE, 1983; "Understanding and Planning for IRC 2057: It's Not Just for Farms," IICLE, 2001; "Election Law: Media and Broadcasting," IICLE, 2002; "Section 1031 Real Estate Exchanges," Lorman, 2005. Member, Leading Lawyers Network. *Member:* Sangamon County, Illinois State (Chairman, Fair Trial-Free Press Committee, 1983-1984) and American Bar Associations. ***PRACTICE AREAS:*** Estate Planning; Commercial Real Estate; Taxation; Business Planning. ***Email:*** hines@barberlaw.com

BERNARD G. SEGATTO, III, born Springfield, Illinois, February 20, 1960; admitted to bar, 1985, Illinois, U.S. District Court, Northern, Southern and Central Districts of Illinois, U.S. Court of Appeals, Seventh Circuit. *Education:* University of Notre Dame (B.A., with honors, 1982); Southern Illinois University (J.D., magna cum laude, 1985). Phi Kappa Phi; Phi Alpha Delta. Author: "Sales, Exchanges and Auctions of Farm Real Estate," IICLE, 1987. Member, Leading Lawyers Network. *Member:* Sangamon County, Illinois State and American Bar Associations. ***PRACTICE AREAS:*** Banks and Banking; Bankruptcy; Real Estate; Probate; Business Law. ***Email:*** bsegatto@barberlaw.com

R. KURT WILKE, born East Chicago, Indiana, November 12, 1959; admitted to bar, 1985, Illinois; U.S. District Court, Central District of Illinois; U.S. Court of Appeals, Seventh Circuit; U.S. Tax Court. *Education:* University of Illinois (B.S., 1981; M.B.A., 1984); Indiana University (J.D., 1985). Sigma Iota Epsilon; Delta Theta Phi. Member, Board of Editors, Indiana Law Journal, 1984-1985. Author: "Media and Broadcasting," IICLE, 2002; "Sales, Exchanges and Auctions of Farm Real Estate," IICLE, 1987. *Member:* Sangamon County, Illinois State and American Bar Associations. ***PRACTICE AREAS:*** Real Estate; Corporate; Litigation. ***Email:*** wilke@barberlaw.com

RANDALL W. SEGATTO, born Springfield, Illinois, August 24, 1961; admitted to bar, 1986, Illinois. *Education:* Beloit College (B.A., 1983); Southern Illinois University (J.D., 1986). Phi Alpha Delta. Author: "Selection Issues to Maximize Government Program Eligibility," IICLE, 2002; "Making Wills an Effective Part of Estate Planning," National Business Institute, 1999. Speaker, "Necessity of Guardianships for Disabled Persons," United Cerebral Palsy of Illinois, 1998. *Member:* Sangamon County, Illinois State and American Bar Associations. ***PRACTICE AREAS:*** Real Estate; Corporate Law; Litigation; Estate Planning; Elder Law; Wills and Trusts. ***Email:*** rsegatto@barberlaw.com

ASSOCIATES

MATTHEW J. CATE, born Silvas, Illinois, June 24, 1975; admitted to bar, 2000, Illinois and U.S. District Court, Central and Southern Districts of Illinois. *Education:* Western Illinois University (B.A., summa cum laude, 1997); Southern Illinois University (J.D., cum laude, 2000). Phi Delta Phi. Articles Editor, Southern Illinois University Law Review, 1999-2000. Author: "Physician Peer Review - Serving the Patient or the Physician," Journal of Legal Medicine, 2000. *Member:* Sangamon County, Illinois State and American Bar Associations. ***PRACTICE AREAS:*** Real Estate; Estate Planning; Bankruptcy; Corporate Law. ***Email:*** matthewcate@barberlaw.com

JOHN CHARLES MILHISER, born Hampton, Virginia, December 23, 1969; admitted to bar, 1997, Illinois, U.S. District Court, Central District of Illinois and U.S. Court of Appeals, Seventh Circuit. *Education:* James Madison University (B.S., 1992); University of Illinois (J.D., 1997). *Member:* Sangamon County Bar Association. ***Email:*** milhiser@barberlaw.com

LEGAL SUPPORT PERSONNEL

PEGGI L. WEYMOUTH, born Butler, Pennsylvania, April 4, 1952. *Education:* University of Pittsburgh (B.A., 1973). Member: American Institute of Certified Public Accoun-

(This Listing Continued)

tants and Illinois CPA Society, 1980; National Association of Certified Valuation Analysts, 1997; Sangamon Valley Estate Planning Council, Treasurer, 1986-2003; President, 2004. (Certified Public Accountant)

REPRESENTATIVE CLIENTS: J.P. Morgan Chase; Carter Bros. Lumber Co.; Casey's General Stores, Inc.; The Copley Press; Eastern American Energy Corp.; George G. Kerasotes Corp.; Giuffre Buick; Identix, Inc.; Village of Williamsville; Wanless Trusts; Navistar Financial Corp.; P.S. Deppe Construction Co.; Rochester State Bank; Singer Asset Finance Company, LLC; Wemple State Bank.

BEAVERS, GRAHAM & FINES

SPRINGFIELD, ILLINOIS

(See Taylorville)

BELLATTI, BARTON, HAMILL & COCHRAN, LLC

944 CLOCK TOWER DRIVE
SUITE A
SPRINGFIELD, ILLINOIS 62704
Telephone: 217-793-9300
Fax: 217-793-9301
Email: lawyers@bellatti-barton.com

Estate Planning, Business Planning, Agricultural Law, Wills, Probate, Trust, Real Estate and Federal Income, Estate, Gift Taxation and Environmental Law.

FIRM PROFILE: Bellatti, Barton, Hamill & Cochran, LLC is a specialized law firm which counsels with families and owners of family business, with a special emphasis on farmland owners and farm operators. The primary areas of concentration for the firm are in estate planning, income tax planning, business planning, environmental law, farm real estate, probate and trust administration. With over 50 years of legal practice, the members of the firm are experienced and qualified to assist families in achieving their business and estate planning goals and objectives.

MEMBERS OF FIRM

ROBERT M. BELLATTI (1948-2005)

MICHAEL G. BARTON, born Pittsfield, Illinois, May 24, 1955; admitted to bar, 1983, Illinois. *Education:* University of Illinois (B.S., with highest honors, 1977; M.S., 1978; J.D., with honors, 1983). Phi Alpha Delta. *Member:* Sangamon County and Illinois State Bar Associations; Sangamon Valley Estate Planning Council (Director, 1989-1990); American Agricultural Law Association. ***PRACTICE AREAS:*** Farm Law; Income Tax; Estate and Gift Taxation; Business Planning Law; Probate Law; Trust Law.

MARK S. COCHRAN, born Springfield, Illinois, August 15, 1952; admitted to bar, 1977, Indiana; 1979, Illinois. *Education:* Purdue University (B.S., with honors, 1974); Indiana University (J.D., cum laude, 1977). *Member:* Sangamon County and Illinois State Bar Associations; American Agricultural Law Association. ***PRACTICE AREAS:*** Real Estate; Environmental; Farm Law. ***Email:*** lawyers@bellatti-barton.com

THOMAS G. HAMILL, born Arlington Heights, Illinois, May 1, 1968; admitted to bar, 1993, Illinois. *Education:* University of Illinois (B.A., 1990; J.D., cum laude, 1993). Phi Beta Kappa. ***PRACTICE AREAS:*** Estate Planning; Estate Administration; Estate and Gift Taxation.

JOHN V. BOSHARDY & ASSOCIATES, P.C.

1610 SOUTH 6TH STREET
SPRINGFIELD, ILLINOIS 62703
Telephone: 217-544-8000
Fax: 217-544-8063

Workers Compensation, Personal Injury, On the Job Injuries, Automobile Accidents, Medical Malpractice, Wrongful Death.

FIRM PROFILE: If you've been injured, put the skill and reputation of John V. Boshardy & Associates, P.C. to work for you. John V. Boshardy & Associates, P.C. are respected through Central Illinois for representing injury victims. You will speak to an attorney from the beginning of your case until you recover the compensation you deserve.

Don't get lost in the crowd. Choose the law firm that values quality representation. At John Boshardy & Associates, P.C. you're not just a number, you're a person who needs help. We'll work hard for you so you'll remember us.

JOHN V. BOSHARDY, born Park Ridge, Illinois, June 2, 1965; admitted to bar, 1991, Illinois. *Education:* DePaul University (B.A.S., 1986); John Marshall Law School (J.D., 1991). *Member:* Illinois State Bar Association; Illinois Trial Lawyers Association. ***PRACTICE AREAS:*** Workers Compensation (90%, 100); Personal Injury (10%, 25). ***Email:*** jvb@boshardylaw.com

BROWN, HAY & STEPHENS, LLP

Established in 1828
205 SOUTH FIFTH STREET, SUITE 700
P.O. BOX 2459
SPRINGFIELD, ILLINOIS 62705-2459
Telephone: 217-544-8491
Fax: 217-544-9609
URL: http://www.bhslaw.com

General Civil Trial and Appellate Practice in State and Federal Courts. Health Law, Real Estate, Probate, Insurance, Banking, Environmental, Governmental, School Law, Corporation, Family Law, Administrative Proceedings, Injunctions, Public Utilities, Labor Law, Chancery Practice and Oil and Gas Law.

FIRM PROFILE: Brown, Hay & Stephens, LLP is centrally located in the capital city of Springfield, Illinois. Founded in 1828, the firm has continuously provided Springfield and its surrounding communities with expert legal representation in a variety of practice areas. Today, nineteen partners, one counsel, three senior practitioners and four associates continue this tradition.

The educational and professional background of the firm members is diverse with many of Brown, Hay & Stephens' lawyers having served in State and Federal Clerkships. The firm's attorneys are respected, active members of the Springfield Community, serving on boards of directors for numerous charitable and civic organizations as well as chairing Bar Association Committees and instructing at Legal Seminars. The firm is listed in the Bar Register of Preeminent Lawyers.

Brown, Hay & Stephens, LLP is a Meritas (fka Commercial Law Affiliates) member providing business clients legal services nationally through independent affiliated law firms.

MEMBERS OF FIRM

ROBERT A. STUART, JR., born Springfield, Illinois, September 8, 1948; admitted to bar, 1973, Illinois; 1980, U.S. Supreme Court; 1982, U.S. Tax Court. *Education:* Bowdoin College (B.A., 1970); University of Illinois (J.D., 1973). Phi Delta Phi. *Member:* Chicago, St. Louis, Sangamon County, Illinois State (Chair, Estate Planning, Probate and Trust Section, 1986-1987) and American Bar Associations; American College of Trust and Estate Counsel. Fellow, American Bar Foundation. ***PRACTICE AREAS:*** Trusts and Estates; Probate. ***Email:*** rstuart@bhslaw.com

J. PATRICK JOYCE, JR., born Chicago, Illinois, November 10, 1947; admitted to bar, 1972, Illinois. *Education:* Loyola University, Chicago (B.A., cum laude, 1969; J.D., 1972). *Member:* Sangamon County, Illinois State and American Bar Associations. ***PRACTICE AREAS:*** Real Estate; Business Law; Corporate Law; Commercial Transactions; Zoning. ***Email:*** jpjoyce@bhslaw.com

ERIC L. GRENZEBACH, born Des Moines, Iowa, December 7, 1944; admitted to bar, 1973, Illinois. *Education:* Denison University (B.A., 1967); Northwestern University (M.B.A., 1969); Loyola University, Chicago (J.D., 1973). *Member:* Sangamon County, Illinois State and American Bar Associations. ***PRACTICE AREAS:*** Education Law; Commercial Law; Labor and Employment. ***Email:*** elg@bhslaw.com

JEFFERY M. WILDAY, born Springfield, Illinois, July 13, 1952; admitted to bar, 1977, Illinois. *Education:* Yale University (B.A., 1974); Washington University, School of Law (J.D., 1977). Firm's managing partner (2000—). *Member:* Sangamon County, Illinois State and American Bar Associations. ***PRACTICE AREAS:*** Labor and Employment; Corporate Law; Banking Law. ***Email:*** jwilday@bhslaw.com

PAUL BOWN, born Winchester, Illinois, April 27, 1949; admitted to bar, 1976, Illinois; U.S. Supreme Court. *Education:* Augustana College (B.A., 1971); Southern Illinois University (J.D., summa cum laude, 1976). Editor, Southern Illinois University Law Journal, 1975-1976. Law Clerk to Hon. J. Waldo Ackerman, U.S. District Court, Central District of Illinois. *Member:* Sangamon County, Illinois State and American Bar Associations; Lincoln Douglas Inns of Court. [With U.S. Army, 1971-1973]. ***PRACTICE AREAS:*** Hospital Law; Medical Malpractice; Commercial Law; Insurance. ***Email:*** pbown@bhslaw.com

ALMON A. MANSON, JR., born Springfield, Illinois, October 28, 1949; admitted to bar, 1978, Illinois. *Education:* George Washington University (B.A., 1971); St. Louis University (M.A., 1974; J.D., 1978). Member and Editor, St. Louis University Law Journal, 1977-1978. *Member:* Sangamon County, Illinois State and American Bar Associations; Lincoln Douglas Inns of Court. ***PRACTICE AREAS:*** Litigation; Commercial Law; Corporate Law. ***Email:*** amanson@bhslaw.com

DWIGHT H. O'KEEFE, III, born Springfield, Illinois, November 27, 1943; admitted to bar, 1970, Illinois. *Education:* Southern Methodist University (B.A., 1965); University of Illinois (J.D., 1968). Phi Delta Phi. Trustee, Capital Township, 1977-1997. President, Township Officials of Illinois, 1993-1996. *Member:* Chicago, Sangamon County, Illinois State (Member, 1976-1982 and Chair, 1981; Insurance Law Section; State and Local Taxation Section, 1996-2002) and American Bar Associations; Illinois Township Attorneys Association (Board Member, 1990—; Trusts and Estates Section Council, 2003—). ***PRACTICE AREAS:*** Government; Trusts and Estates; Probate; Insurance Defense. ***Email:*** dokeefe@bhslaw.com

DONALD R. TRACY, born Urbana, Illinois, April 22, 1950; admitted to bar, 1976, Tennessee; 1977, Illinois. *Education:* Arizona State University (B.S., 1972); University of Memphis (J.D., 1976). Phi Alpha Delta. Adjunct Professor of Law, Secured Transactions, University of Memphis, 1980. Author: "Disclaiming and Limiting Liability For Commercial Damages," Commercial Law Journal, 1978; "Illinois Landlord Liens," Illinois Bar Journal, 1985; "Illinois Close Corporation Act," Illinois Bar Journal, 1992. President, Abraham Lincoln Association, 1998-2002. President, Oak Ridge Cemetery Board, 1995-1996. Chair, Illinois Secretary of State Corporate Acts Advisory Committee, 1995-1997. *Member:* Chicago, Sangamon County (President, 1996), Illinois State (Past Chair, Corporation and Securities Law Section; Past Chair, Judicial Advisory Polls Committee) and American Bar Associations. ***PRACTICE AREAS:*** Corporate and Employment Law; Business Litigation. ***Email:*** dtracy@bhslaw.com

(This Listing Continued)

BROWN, HAY & STEPHENS, LLP, Springfield—Continued

EMMET A. FAIRFIELD, born Champaign, Illinois, June 8, 1958; admitted to bar, 1981, Illinois. *Education:* Parkland College (A.S., 1976); University of Illinois (B.S. highest honors, 1978; J.D., 1981). Phi Delta Phi. Law Clerk to: Hon. James T. Londrigan, 1981-1982; Hon. Ben K. Miller, 1982-1984, Appellate Court of Illinois. *Member:* Sangamon County, Illinois State (Member, General Practice Section, 1986-1987) and American Bar Associations. ***PRACTICE AREAS:*** Bankruptcy; Debtor and Creditor; Commercial Law; Appellate Practice. ***Email:*** efairfield@bhslaw.com

DENISE M. DRUHOT, admitted to bar, 1987, Illinois. *Education:* Vanderbilt University (B.A., magna cum laude, French, 1983; Phi Beta Kappa); Southern Illinois University (J.D., 1986). Member, Board of Editors, Southern Illinois University Law Journal, 1985-1986. *Member:* Sangamon County, Illinois State and American Bar Associations. ***PRACTICE AREAS:*** Education Law; Labor and Employment; Civil Practice; Litigation; Administrative Law; Appellate Practice; Government; Estate Planning. ***Email:*** ddruhot@bhslaw.com

HARVEY M. STEPHENS, born Springfield, Illinois, February 25, 1963; admitted to bar, 1988, Illinois. *Education:* Kenyon College (A.B., 1985); Washington University, School of Law (J.D., 1988). *Member:* Sangamon County, Illinois State and American Bar Associations. ***PRACTICE AREAS:*** Business Law; Banks and Banking; Trusts and Estates; Real Estate. ***Email:*** hmstephens@bhslaw.com

JAMES W. BRUNER, born Springfield, Illinois, July 28, 1967; admitted to bar, 1994, Illinois. *Education:* Bradley University (B.S., 1989); Thomas M. Cooley Law School (J.D., 1993). *Member:* Sangamon County, Illinois State and American Bar Associations. ***PRACTICE AREAS:*** Business Law; Construction Law. ***Email:*** jbruner@bhslaw.com

LORILEA BUERKETT, born Springfield, Illinois, April 20, 1956; admitted to bar, 1993, Illinois. *Education:* University of North Dakota (E.D., 1978; J.D. with distinction, 1993). Order of the Coif. Law Clerk to the Hon. Rodney S. Webb, Chief Judge, U.S. District Court, District of North Dakota. *Member:* Sangamon County, Illinois State and American Bar Associations. ***PRACTICE AREAS:*** Labor and Employment; School Law; Real Estate; Civil Litigation. ***Email:*** lbuerkett@bhslaw.com

THOMAS R. LAMONT, born Jacksonville, Illinois, March 8, 1947; admitted to bar, 1973, Illinois; 1976, U.S. District Court, Central District of Illinois; 1983, U.S. Court of Military Appeals; 1986, U.S. Supreme Court. *Education:* Illinois State University (B.S., with honors, 1969); University of Illinois (J.D., 1972). Member: Board of Trustees, University of Illinois, 1990—; Illinois Board of Higher Education, 1996—. *Member:* Illinois State Bar Association. [Col., Illinois Army National Guard, 1981—]. ***PRACTICE AREAS:*** Government; Administrative Law; Legislative. ***Email:*** tlamont@bhslaw.com

AMY K. SCHMIDT, born Tulsa, Oklahoma, June 24, 1965; admitted to bar, 1990, Illinois and U.S. District Court, Central District of Illinois. *Education:* Oral Roberts University (B.S., magna cum laude, Accounting, 1987); University of Tulsa (J.D. with honors, 1990). Phi Alpha Delta. Member, Order of Barristers. Member, Tulsa Law Journal. Court Certified Child's Representative. *Member:* Sangamon County (President, 2002), Illinois State and American (Member, Family Law Committee) Bar Associations; Lincoln Douglas Inn of Court. Fellow, American Academy of Matrimonial Lawyers. ***PRACTICE AREAS:*** Family Law; Litigation. ***Email:*** aschmidt@bhslaw.com

SCOTT C. HELMHOLZ, born Oak Park, Illinois, August 5, 1953; admitted to bar, 1978, Missouri; 1983, Illinois, U.S. District Court, Central and Southern Districts of Illinois; 1991, U.S Court of Appeals, Seventh Circuit; 1994, U.S. Supreme Court. *Education:* Drake University (B.A., 1975); Washington University (J.D., 1978). Law Clerk to the Honorable Charles Shangler, Missouri Court of Appeals, Western District, 1979-1980. Author: "Challenges to Wills," Illinois Causes of Action-Elements, Forms and Winning Practice Tips, Chapter 36, IICLE 2002; "The Consequences of 'General Advertising' in the Context of Private Offering Exemptions," Mineral Law, Volume 15, No. 1, Illinois State Bar Association, November 1988; "The 1989 Amendments to the Illinois Securities Law: Impact on Capital Formation for Mineral Offerings," Mineral Law, Volume 16, No. 2, Illinois State Bar Association, December 1989; "Jury Instructions in Civil Fraud Actions Under Section 12.G of the Illinois Securities Law of 1953," Mineral Law, Volume 16, No. 3, Illinois State Bar Association, March 1990. Instructor, Business Law: Longview Community College, Lee's Summit, Missouri, 1982-1983; Park College, Parkville, Missouri, 1980-1982. Special Assistant Attorney General, 1985-1994. Special Labor Relations Counsel, Illinois Department of Central Management Services, 1988-1994. Member, Board of Arbitrators, National Association of Securities Dealers, 1987—. Member, Illinois Petroleum Resources Board, 2001-2004. *Member:* Illinois State (Member, Mineral Law Section Council, 1986-1996) and Federal Bar Associations; Lincoln Douglas Inns of Court. ***REPORTED CASES:*** Bracey et al. v. Monsanto, 823 SW 2d 946 (MO 1992); Kralman v. Illinois Dept. of Veterans Affairs, 23 F. 3d, 150 (7th Cir. 1994); Central Illinois Public Service Company, et al., v. Illinois Commerce Commission, et al., 206 Ill. Dec. 49, 644 N.E.2d 817 (4th Dist. 1994); Podolsky v. Alma Energy Corp., 143 F.3d 364 (7th Cir. 1998); Smith Production Co. v. Baldwin, 1997 WL 34742 (7th Cir. 1997); United States v. Rhodes, 201 F. Supp 2d 906 (C.D. Ill. 2002); Illinois Licensed Beverage Assn. v. Advanta et al, 776 N.E., 2d 255 (4th Dist. 2002); Central Illinois Public Service Company v. Illinois Commerce Commission, 342 Ill. App. 3d 617 (4th Dist. 2003). ***PRACTICE AREAS:*** Oil and Gas Law; Civil Litigation; Public Utilities; Federal Practice; Administrative Law. ***Email:*** shelmholz@bhslaw.com

THOMAS P. SCHANZLE-HASKINS, III, born Olney, Illinois, December 22, 1946; admitted to bar, 1976, Illinois and U.S. District Court, Central District of Illinois; 1979, U.S. Court of Appeals, Seventh Circuit; 1980, U.S. Supreme Court. *Education:* Southern Illinois University (B.A., 1970; J.D., 1976). Assistant Corporation Counsel, City of Springfield, Illinois, 1976-1979. Assistant U.S. Attorney, 1979-1982. *Member:* Sangamon County, Illinois State (Member, Litigation Council, Young Lawyers Division, 1983-1986; Assembly Delegate, 1988-1992) and American Bar Associations; Illinois Association of Defense Trial Counsel. [U.S. Army, Finance Corps, 1970-1973]. ***REPORTED CASES:*** Hunter v. Southworth Products Corp., 333 Ill. App. 3d 158, 775 N.E.2d 238, 266 (Ill.App. 4 Dist., Aug 14, 2002); Boulahanis v. Board of Regents and Illinois State University, 198 F.3d 633 (7th Cir. 1999); Harper v. Board of Regents and Illinois State University, 35 F. Supp.2d 1118 (D.D. Ill, 1999); Management Services of Illinois, Inc., d/b/a Management Services, Inc., v. Health Management Systems, Inc., a Corporation, Victor Kugajevsky, 907 F. Supp. 289 (C.D., Ill. 1995); U.S. v. F.J. Vollmer & Co., Inc., 1 F.3d 1511 (7th Cir. Ill. 1993); In re Leavell, 141 B.R. 393 (Bankr. S.D. Ill. 1992); U.S. v. Nevius, 792 F. Supp. 609 (C.D. Ill. 1992); Heritage House Restaurants, Inc., v. Continental Funding Group, Inc., 906 F.2d 276 (7th Cir. Ill. 1990); Moreland v. Department of Corrections, 166 Ill. App. 3d 1040 (Ill. App. 4 Dist. 1988); In re Bonnett, 73 B.R. 715 (D.D. Ill. 1987); Janssen v. City of Springfield, 79 Ill. 2d 435 (Ill. S. Ct. 1980). ***PRACTICE AREAS:*** Civil Litigation; Commercial Litigation; Administrative Litigation; Employment Litigation; Federal Criminal Defense. ***Email:*** tsh@bhslaw.com

HUGH F. DRAKE, born Springfield, Illinois, June 10, 1970; admitted to bar, 1999, Illinois. *Education:* University of Illinois (B.A., 1992; J.D., cum laude, 1999); Southern Illinois University (M.A., 1995). *Member:* Sangamon County, Illinois State and American (Fellow, Real Property, Probate and Trust Law Section, 2003-2005) Bar Associations; Sangamon Valley Estate Planning Council. ***PRACTICE AREAS:*** Trusts and Estates; Probate; Business Law. ***Email:*** hdrake@bhslaw.com

COUNSEL

ELIZABETH W. ANDERSON, born Midland, Texas, September 19, 1963; admitted to bar, 1989, Illinois and U.S. District Court, Central District of Illinois. *Education:* Southern Methodist University (B.F.A., 1985; J.D., 1988). Co-Author: "IICLE, Guardianships for Disabled Adults Practice Handbook," 2004. *Member:* Sangamon County, Illinois State and American Bar Associations; Sangamon Valley Estate Planning Council; Central Illinois Women's Bar Association. ***LANGUAGES:*** Spanish. ***PRACTICE AREAS:*** Probate; Trusts and Estates; Real Estate; Guardianship. ***Email:*** eanderson@bhslaw.com

CLAIRE A. MANNING, born Spring Valley, Illinois, December 31, 1953; admitted to bar, 1979, Illinois; 1994, U.S. Supreme Court. *Education:* Bradley University (B.A., magna cum laude, 1976); Loyola University (J.D., 1979). Chairman, Illinois Pollution Control Board, 1993-2002. Member, Illinois State Labor Relations Board, 1984-1993. Labor Relations Counsel, State of Illinois, 1980-1984. Fair Employment Practices Commission, 1977-1979. Adjunct Professor, University of Illinois Institute of Labor and Industrial Relations, Champaign-Urbana, Illinois, 1987-1991. Arbitrator/Mediator, FMCS, Iowa Public Employment Relations Board and Wisconsin Employment Relations Commission, 1986—. *Member:* Sangamon County, Illinois State (Past Chair, Administrative Law Section Council; Committee Member, Special Committee on Women and the Law; Committee Member, Environmental Law Section Council) and American Bar Associations; Government Bar Association. ***SPECIAL AGENCIES:*** Illinois Pollution Control Board; Illinois State Labor Board. ***PRACTICE AREAS:*** Environmental; Labor and Employment; Administrative; Regulatory. ***Email:*** cmanning@bhslaw.com

ASSOCIATES

ROLAND R. CROSS, born Springfield, Illinois, September 7, 1965; admitted to bar, 2001, Illinois, U.S. District Court, Central and Southern Districts of Illinois, U.S. Court of Appeals, Seventh Circuit. *Education:* Denison University (B.A., 1987); University of Missouri-Columbia (M.A., 1989; Ph.D., 1998); St. Louis University, School of Law (J.D., 2001). Research Fellow, St. Louis University School of Law, 1999-2001. *Member:* Sangamon County, Illinois State and American Bar Associations. ***PRACTICE AREAS:*** School Law; Family Law; Employment Law; Collections. ***Email:*** rcross@bhslaw.com

JAMES L. NICHELSON, born Springfield, Illinois, August 25, 1975; admitted to bar, 2001, Illinois and U.S. District Court, Central District of Illinois. *Education:* Millikin University (B.S., magna cum laude, 1998); Southern Illinois University (J.D., cum laude, 2001). *Member:* Sangamon County, Illinois State and American Bar Associations. ***PRACTICE AREAS:*** Corporate Law; Collections; Real Estate; Civil Litigation. ***Email:*** jnichelson@bhslaw.com

ROBERT M. SHUPENUS, born Springfield, Illinois, July 1, 1971; admitted to bar, 1996, Illinois and U.S. District Court, Central District of Illinois; 2004, U.S. District Court, Northern and Southern Districts of Illinois; 2005, U.S. Court of Appeals, Seventh Circuit. *Education:* DePauw University (B.A., 1993); Drake University Law School (J.D., 1996). *Member:* Sangamon County and Illinois State Bar Associations. ***PRACTICE AREAS:*** General Civil Litigation; Commercial Litigation. ***Email:*** rshupenus@bhslaw.com

DANIEL K. WRIGHT, born St. Louis, Missouri, January 16, 1979; admitted to bar, 2004, Illinois. *Education:* Illinois College (B.A., 2001); St. Louis University (J.D., 2004). Phi Delta Phi. *Member:* Illinois State and American Bar Associations. ***PRACTICE AREAS:*** Litigation; Business Organization. ***Email:*** dwright@bhslaw.com

JENNIFER L. PARKER, born Memphis, Tennessee, December 19, 1971; admitted to bar, 2005, Illinois. *Education:* Friends University (B.A., with honors, Music, Piano Performance, 1994) Presser Scholar, 1993; University of Missouri-Kansas City Conservatory of Music (Post-Graduate, 1997-2000; Master of Music, Piano Performance, 1997); Alpha Chi Honor Society, 1993; University of Missouri-Kansas City School of Law (2000-2002) Staff Member, The Urban Lawyer ABA Journal; Dean's List, Fall 2001; Valparaiso University School of Law (J.D., 2004). Class Honors, Family Law Practicum, Fall, 2003. Federal Externship, Magistrate Judge Paul Cherry, Northern District of Indiana. *Member:* Illinois State and American Bar Associations. ***Email:*** jparker@bhslaw.com

OF COUNSEL

HARVEY B. STEPHENS, born Springfield, Illinois, February 17, 1934; admitted to bar, 1960, Illinois; 1982, U.S. Supreme Court. *Education:* Bowdoin College (A.B., cum laude, 1955); University of Chicago (J.D., 1960). *Member:* Sangamon County, Illinois State and American Bar Associations; Bar Association of Seventh Circuit. Fellow, American Bar Foundation. ***PRACTICE AREAS:*** Banks and Banking; Business Law; Trusts and Estates. ***Email:*** stephenslaw@bhslaw.com

EDWARD J. CUNNINGHAM, born Chicago, Illinois, October 30, 1933; admitted to bar, 1960, Illinois. *Education:* Yale University (B.A., 1957); University of Chicago (J.D., 1960). Law Clerk to Hon. Samuel O. Smith, Illinois Appellate Court, Fourth District. Attorney for National Labor Relations Board, 1962-1965. *Member:* Sangamon County, Illinois State and American Bar Associations; American Health Lawyers Association. ***REPORTED CASES:*** Lapidot v. Memorial Medical Center, 144 Ill. App. 3d 141; Scheller v.

(This Listing Continued)

Health Care Service Corp., 138 Ill. App. 3d 219; Dugan Oil Co., Inc. v. Coalition of Area Labor, 98 Ill. App. 3d 126; Janssen v. City of Springfield, 79 Ill. App. 2d 435; Wiseman v. Law Research Service, Inc., 133 Ill. App. 2d 790. ***PRACTICE AREAS:*** Civil Litigation; Labor and Employment; White Collar Crime; Medical Malpractice; Health Law. ***Email:*** ecunningham@bhslaw.com

SIMON L. FRIEDMAN, born Springfield, Illinois, November 18, 1921; admitted to bar, 1944, Illinois; 1960, U.S. Supreme Court. *Education:* University of Illinois (A.B., 1943; J.D., 1944). Phi Delta Phi. Assistant Legal Advisor, Superintendent of Public Instruction, State of Illinois, 1958-1962. Circuit Judge, Seventh Judicial Circuit, State of Illinois, 1972-1990. *Member:* Sangamon County (President, 1970-1971) and Illinois State Bar Associations.

CHARLES A. CHAPIN, born Springfield, Ill., February 27, 1921; admitted to bar, 1950, Illinois. *Education:* Carleton College (B.A., 1942); University of Michigan (J.D. with distinction, 1949). Phi Beta Kappa. Member, Community Unit School District #5, 1968-1977. *Member:* Sangamon County, Illinois State and American Bar Associations. ***PRACTICE AREAS:*** Corporation; Real Estate; Probate; Chancery Law. ***Email:*** cchapin@bhslaw.com

SAUL J. MORSE, born New York, N.Y., January 17, 1948; admitted to bar, 1973, Illinois; 1976, U.S. District Court, Central District of Illinois; 1979, U.S. Supreme Court; 1982, U.S. Tax Court; 1983, U.S. Court of Appeals, 7th Circuit. *Education:* University of Illinois (B.A., 1969; J.D., 1972). Author: "Aids and the Law," Illinois Medical Journal, August, 1987. Adjunct Assistant Professor, Southern Illinois University School of Medicine. Adjunct Lecturer, University of Illinois-Springfield, Legal Studies. Member, State Board of Election Governor's Screening Committee, 1978. Member, Sangamon County Board, Special Committee on Zoning and Land Use Planning, 1979. Member: Governor's Commission on Election Law Reform, 1984-1985; Governor's Task Force on Nursing Home Reimbursement, 1985; Illinois Human Rights Commission, 1986-2002. Director, Illinois Comprehensive Health Insurance Plan, 1987-1991. Illinois Guardianship and Advocacy Commission, 2003—. *Member:* Sangamon County, Illinois State (Member: Special Committee on Reform of the Legislative Process, 1976-1980; Committee on The Role of the Government Attorney, 1977-1979; Special Committee on the Handicapped Lawyer, 1978-1980; Secretary, Section Council on Administrative Law, 1977-1980) and American (Member, Forum Committee on Health Law, 1979; Vice Chair, Medicine and Law Committee, Tort and Insurance Practice Section, 1986—) Bar Associations; American Society of Law and Medicine; American Health Lawyers Association. ***PRACTICE AREAS:*** Health Care (40%); Legislative Practice (10%); Corporate Insurance (35%). ***Email:*** smorse@bhslaw.com

DONALD L. WOODS, born Springfield, Illinois, February 26, 1950; admitted to bar, 1983, Illinois. *Education:* Blackburn College (B.A., 1972); Southern Illinois University (J.D., 1983). Member, Board of Editors, Southern Illinois University Law Journal. Graduate Teaching Assistant, Legal Writing and Reasoning, Southern Illinois University School of Law, 1981-1983. ***LANGUAGES:*** French. ***PRACTICE AREAS:*** Administrative Law; Public Utility Regulation. ***Email:*** dwoods@bhslaw.com

REPRESENTATIVE CLIENTS: Memorial Medical Center; Memorial Health System; Ball Chatham Community Unit School District; Springfield School District 186; Pleasant Plains School District; Lincoln Land Community College; Heartland Community College; Greenville College; Pathway Services Unlimited, Inc.; Capitol Area Association of Realtors; Fred Davey Scholarship Trust; Littler Trust Estate; DeFratis Charitable Trust; Altorfer Inc.; Barker Real Estate; Bunge Corp.; Capital Supply Co.; Central Laborers' Pension, Annuity & Welfare Funds; Dot Foods Inc.; Dot Transportation Inc.; Friendly Chevrolet; Garrett Aviation Services Co.; General Motors Acceptance Corp.; George G. Kerasotes Corp.; Hanson Professional Services; Harmon Foods Inc.; Illinois Valley Paving Co.; Isringhausen Imports, Inc.; Roland Machinery Co.; Freesen, Inc.; Lincoln Land FS, Inc.; U.S. Electric; Winchester Farmers Elevator; WNNS/WMAY/WQLZ Radio; Chatham Township; Gardner Township; Lanesville Township; Rochester Township; Township Officials of Illinois Risk Management Association; Township Officials of Illinois; Buffalo Fire Protection; Western Fire Protection District; US Bank, NA; Middletown State Bank; State Bank of Latham; United Community Bank; Warren Boynton State Bank; American Family Life Assurance Co.; CNA Insurance Co.; Hudson Insurance Co.; Illinois Association of Mutual Insurance Co.; Madison Mutual Insurance; ISBA Mutual Insurance Co.; Mental Health Centers of Illinois; Springfield Clinic, LLP; Roberts Food, Inc.; United Contractors Midwest, Inc.; Dell Computers; Illinois Department of Transportation; State of Illinois - Department of Children and Family Services; Illinois National Bank; AmerenCIPS; AmerenUE; AmerenCILCO; Petco Petroleum; Smith Production Corp.; Wells-Fargo Home Mortgage, Inc.; Pactiv; Prime Panels, Inc.; Precision Tank and Equipment; Watts Copy Systems; Midwest Trucking Association; ISMIE Mutual Insurance Co.; HÆ Construction Services, Inc.; GE/Medical Protective Co.

BRADFORD C. BUCKLIN

230 WEST CARPENTER STREET
P.O. BOX 2346
SPRINGFIELD, ILLINOIS 62705
Telephone: 217-544-5441
Toll Free: 888-646-3600
Fax: 217-789-1210
Email: bucklin@prodigy.net
URL: http://www.bucklinlaw.com

Automobile Accidents, Personal Injury, Wrongful Death, Workers Compensation, Social Security.

BRADFORD C. BUCKLIN, born Jacksonville, Illinois, July 22, 1954; admitted to bar, 1980, Illinois and U.S. District Court, Central District of Illinois. *Education:* University of Illinois (B.A., 1977); Southern Illinois University (J.D., 1980). Lecturer: Workers Compensation, National Business Institute, 1993—; Workers Compensation, Lorman Business Institute, 1997. Author: "Social Security Disability," Springfield Magazine, May 2000; "Types of Benefits," Workers' Compensation in Illinois, Lorman Educational Services December, 1999; "Securing Medical and Basic Evidence," Workers Compensation in Illinois, lorman Educational Services, December, 1998; "Vocational Rehabilitation," Workers' Compensation in Illinois, Lorman Educational Services, December 1998; "Preparation of the Injured Employee's Case," Advanced Workers' Compensation in Illinois, National Business Institute, April 1998; "Ethical Considerations," Workers' Compensation in Illinois, National Business Institute, December, 1997; "Liens and Subrogation Rights," Advanced Workers Compensation in Illinois, national Business Institute, June 1994. *Member:* Sangamon County and Illinois State Bar Associations; Illinois Trial Lawyers Association.

CRAIG & CRAIG

SPRINGFIELD, ILLINOIS
(See Mattoon)

General Practice in State and Federal Courts. Coal, Oil, Gas, Mining, Oil and Gas Transportation, Insurance, Drainage and Levee Law, Environmental, Corporation, Labor Relations, Workers Compensation and Real Estate Law. Estate Planning, Probate and Bankruptcy Law. Trials and Appeals.

DONALD M. CRAVEN, P.C.

1005 NORTH 7TH STREET
SPRINGFIELD, ILLINOIS 62702-3918
Telephone: 217-544-1777
Fax: 217-544-0713
URL: http://www.cravenlawoffice.com

Media and First Amendment, Libel Defense, Intellectual Property, Commercial Transactions, Commercial Litigation, Appellate Practice and Legislative Law.

DONALD M. CRAVEN, born Springfield, Illinois, May 16, 1956; admitted to bar, 1981, Illinois and U.S. District Court, Central and Southern Districts of Illinois; 1987, U.S. Court of Appeals, Seventh Circuit; 1988, U.S. District Court, Northern District of Illinois and U.S. Court of Appeals, Ninth Circuit. *Education:* St. Olaf College (B.A., 1978); Southern Illinois University (J.D., 1981). Department Distinction, Political Science, St. Olaf College, 1978. Hearing Officer, City of Springfield, Illinois, 1991-1994. *Member:* Sangamon County and Illinois State (Member, Media Law Committee, 1994—) Bar Associations; Illinois Trial Lawyers Association. ***PRACTICE AREAS:*** Media and First Amendment; Libel Defense; Commercial Litigation; Appellate Practice; Commercial Transactions. ***Email:*** don@cravenlawoffice.com

SCOTT B. SIEVERS, born Royal Oak, Michigan, September 7, 1968; admitted to bar, 2001, Illinois. *Education:* St. Cloud State University (B.S., 1993); University of Illinois College of Law (J.D., 2001). ***PRACTICE AREAS:*** Libel, Slander and Defamation; Media Law; General Practice; Litigation. ***Email:*** scott@cravenlawoffice.com

REPRESENTATIVE CLIENTS: Illinois Press Assoc.; Illinois Broadcasters Assoc.; Illinois News Broadcasters Assoc.; Tribune Co.; Media/Professional Insurance; Employers Reinsurance Corporation; Lee Enterprises, Inc.

DEES LAW OFFICE

1035 SOUTH SECOND STREET
SPRINGFIELD, ILLINOIS 62704
Telephone: 217-528-9226
Fax: 217-528-6837
URL: http://www.deeslawoffice.com
Email: brian@deeslawoffice.com
URL: http://www.lawyers.com/dees-law

Divorce, Family Law, Child Custody, Child Support, Bankruptcy, Workers Compensation, Driving While Intoxicated, Personal Injury.

BRIAN J. DEES, born Decatur, Illinois, February 4, 1960; admitted to bar, 1989, Illinois; 1991, U.S. District Court, Central District of Illinois; 1995, U.S. District Court, Southern District of Illinois and U.S. Court of Appeals, Seventh Circuit. *Education:* Millikin University (B.A., 1982); University of Illinois (J.D., 1989). Assistant State's Attorney, Sangamon County, 1989-1991. *Member:* Sangamon County and Illinois State Bar Associations. ***Email:*** brian@deeslawoffice.com

---

DRAKE, NARUP & MEAD, P.C.

Established in 1989
107 EAST ALLEN STREET
SPRINGFIELD, ILLINOIS 62704
Telephone: 217-528-9776
Telecopier: 217-528-9401
URL: http://www.dnmpc.com

Insurance Defense, General Civil and Trial Practice in all Courts, Professional Liability, Personal Injury, Probate, Real Estate, Legal Malpractice, Medical Malpractice Law, Arbitration and Mediation.

FIRM PROFILE: Drake, Narup & Mead, P.C. was founded in 1989 by David L. Drake, Richard H. Narup and Randall A. Mead. The firm now provides insurance defense, corporate organization and professional liability services throughout central and southern Illinois. The firm's members frequently lecture on medical-legal issues and insurance law.

DAVID L. DRAKE, born Canton, Illinois, March 21, 1948; admitted to bar, 1973, Illinois, U.S. District Court, Central District of Illinois and U.S. Court of Appeals, Seventh Circuit. *Education:* Western Illinois University (B.A., 1970); Chicago-Kent College of Law (J.D., 1973). Blue Key; Delta Theta Phi (President, 1972-1973). Adjunct Associate Professor, S.I.U. School of Medicine, 1979—. *Member:* Sangamon County and Illinois State Bar Associations; Illinois Association of Defense Trial Counsel; American Society of Law of Medicine; Adjusters Association of Central Illinois; Lincoln-Douglas Inns of Court.

(This Listing Continued)

DRAKE, NARUP & MEAD, P.C., Springfield—Continued

PRACTICE AREAS: Professional Liability Law; Personal Injury Law; Medical And Liability; Malpractice Defense Law; HMO Law; Liability Defense; Insurance Law; Mediation; Arbitration. ***Email:*** drake@dnmpc.com

RICHARD H. NARUP, born Batchtown, Illinois, September 13, 1956; admitted to bar, 1981, Illinois, U.S. District Court, Central District of Illinois and U.S. Court of Appeals, Seventh Circuit. *Education:* Blackburn College (B.A., 1978); Southern Illinois University (J.D., 1981). Administrative Law Judge, Illinois State Police, 1999-2003. *Member:* Sangamon County and Illinois State (Member, Section Council, 1988-1989) Bar Associations; Adjusters Association of Central Illinois; Defense Research Institute. ***PRACTICE AREAS:*** Insurance Defense Law; Personal Injury Law; Probate Law; Real Estate Law. ***Email:*** narup@dnmpc.com

RANDALL A. MEAD, born Bloomington, Illinois, March 26, 1956; admitted to bar, 1981, Illinois, U.S. District Court, Central District of Illinois and U.S. Court of Appeals, Seventh Circuit. *Education:* Western Illinois University (B.A., 1978); Southern Illinois University (J.D., 1981). Adjunct Associate Professor, Medical Humanities, S.I.U. School of Medicine. Editor, Adjusters Association Newsletter. Author: "The FCC Lacks the Power to Force Cable Television Systems into a Common Carrier Capacity: FCC v. Midwest Video Corporation," Southern Illinois University Law Journal, p. 125, 1980. Menard County Public Guardian and Administrator, 1991-2003. Board of Directors, Lawyers Trust Fund, 1987-1993. Member, Illinois Supreme Court Committee on Jury Instructions in Civil Cases, 1995-2003. Member, DRI, the voice of the Defense Bar. *Member:* Sangamon County Bar Association; Adjusters Association of Central Illinois. ***PRACTICE AREAS:*** Personal Injury Law; Insurance Law; Litigation; Medical Malpractice Defense; Truck Accidents; Church and State. ***Email:*** mead@dnmpc.com

KIRK W. LAUDEMAN, born Oak Park, Illinois, October 16, 1965; admitted to bar, 1990, Illinois and U.S. District Court, Northern and Central Districts of Illinois. *Education:* University of Illinois (B.A., 1987); John Marshall Law School (J.D., 1990). Administrative Law Judge, Illinois State Police, 1999-2003. *Member:* Sangamon County and Illinois State Bar Associations; Adjusters' Association of Central Illinois.; Illinois Association of Defense Trial Counsel; American Health Lawyers Association. ***REPORTED CASES:*** Towne Realty v. Shaffer, 331 516 App.3d 531 (4th Ass., 2002). ***PRACTICE AREAS:*** Insurance Defense; Medical Malpractice Defense; Health Care Law; Litigation. ***Email:*** laudeman@dnmpc.com

PAULETTE F. DOVE, born Ticonderoga, New York, September 13, 1971; admitted to bar, 1997, Illinois and U.S. District Court, Central District of Illinois; U.S. Court of Appeals, Seventh Circuit. *Education:* State University of New York at Albany (B.A., cum laude, 1992); Washington College of Law, The American University (J.D., cum laude, 1997). *Member:* Sangamon County and Illinois State Bar Associations; Adjusters' Association of Central Illinois; Women's Bar Association; Lincoln-Douglas Inn of Court. ***PRACTICE AREAS:*** Insurance Defense; Medical Malpractice Defense; Civil Litigation. ***Email:*** dove@dnmpc.com

---

CHRISTIAN D. BISWELL, born MaComb, Illinois, August 26, 1971; admitted to bar, 2001, Illinois; 2002, U.S. District Court, Central District of Illinois. *Education:* Southern Illinois University (B.A., 1995; M.A., 1997; J.D., 2001). ***PRACTICE AREAS:*** Insurance Defense; Medical Malpractice Defense; Contracts; Litigation; Subrogation; Civil Rights. ***Email:*** biswell@dnmpc.com

STEVEN C. WARD, born Jacksonville, Illinois, January 22, 1956; admitted to bar, 1983, Illinois; 1985, U.S. District Court, Northern District of Illinois; 1988, U.S. District Court, Central District of Illinois; 1989, U.S. District Court, Southern District of Illinois; 1992, U.S. Court of Appeals, Seventh Circuit. *Education:* DePauw University (B.A., 1978); Chicago-Kent College of Law (J.D., 1982). Author: "Motion Practice," Federal Civil Practice, Ch. 7, Ill. Inst. for CLE, 1989; "Entrustee's Right To Sue For Negligent Entrustment," 78 Ill. Bar J. 606, 1990; "Gibellina vs. Handley: Toward A Federal Approach To Voluntary Dismissal," 79 Ill. Bar J. 336, 1991; "One Bad Apple: Narrowing the Scope of Federal Rule 11," 80 Ill. Bar J. 342, 1992. Instructor, National Academy For Paralegal Studies, Civil Procedure and Evidence, Bankruptcy and Alternatives and Legal Analysis and Writing, 1990-1991. Seminar: "Illinois Insurance Law: Primer and Recent Developments," Lorman Business Center, Inc., 1996; "Advanced Legal Drafting for Illinois Paralegals," Institute for Paralegal Education, National Business Institute, 2004. *Member:* Sangamon County and Illinois State Bar Associations; Attorneys' Title Guaranty Fund, Inc. ***REPORTED CASES:*** Kane v. Doctors Hosp. 302 Ill.App. 3d 775 (4th Dist.1999); Kennedy v. First National Bank of Mattoon, 259 Ill. App. 560 (4th Dist.1994); Collins v. Reynard, 154 Ill.2d. 48 (1992); King vs. Petefish, 185 Ill.App. 3d 630, (4th Dist.1989). ***PRACTICE AREAS:*** Litigation. ***Email:*** ward@dnmpc.com

REPRESENTATIVE CLIENTS: State Farm Mutual Automobile Insurance Co.; State Farm Fire and Casualty Co.; Farmers Insurance; ISMIE Mutual Insurance Co.; Preferred Physicians Medical; Blessing Hospital; Illinois Provider Trust; Progressive Insurance Co.; Empire Fire & Marine Insurance Co.; Indiana Farmers Mutual Insurance Group; Brandt Fertilizer Inc.; Northland Insurance Co.; United Equitable Insurance Co.; Foremost Insurance Co.; CGR Insurance Co.; Zurich/Steadfast; Liberty Mutual Group; Eaton Electrical; The St. Paul Insurance Co.; A P Specialty Insurance Corp.; The Doctors Co.; Darwin Professional Underwriters.

FELDMAN, WASSER, DRAPER & BENSON

Established in 1987

1307 SOUTH SEVENTH STREET
P.O. BOX 2418
SPRINGFIELD, ILLINOIS 62705
Telephone: 217-544-3403
Facsimile: 217-544-1593
Email: feldwass@feldwass.com
URL: http://www.feldman-wasser.com

Administrative Law, Civil Litigation and Appeals, Civil Rights, Construction Law, Criminal Defense, Domestic Relations, General Practice.

(This Listing Continued)

FIRM PROFILE: FELDMAN, WASSER, DRAPER & BENSON provides to businesses, individuals and not-for-profit organizations a full range of legal services, with an emphasis on trial practice. Attorneys with the firm have had extensive public sector legal experience. FELDMAN, WASSER, DRAPER & BENSON offices are equipped with modern word processing equipment and with Internet and Lexis access.

MEMBERS OF FIRM

HOWARD W. FELDMAN, born Chicago, Illinois, July 18, 1946; admitted to bar, 1973, Illinois; 1975, U.S. District Court, Central District of Illinois; 1976, U.S. Court of Appeals, Seventh Circuit; 1977, U.S. Supreme Court. *Education:* Purdue University (B.S., 1968); Indiana University (J.D., 1973). Author: Illinois Institute of Continuing Legal Education Administrative Law Book, Chapters on the Illinois Court of Claims, Civil Service Commission. Instructor, Evidence, Employment Law, Sangamon State University, 1984. Assistant Attorney General, State of Illinois, 1973-1979. Chief General Law Division, Office of the Attorney General, 1978-1979. General Counsel, Illinois Capital Development Board, State of Illinois, 1979-1982. Special Assistant Attorney General, 1982-1992. *Member:* Illinois State (Member: Forum Committee on Construction Law, 1979; Family Law Section Council, 1998—; Assembly, 1996—; Chairman, Committee on Administrative Law, 1980; Member, Board of Governors, 2000—; Secretary, 2003-2004) and American Bar Associations; Illinois Development Finance Authority. Fellow, American Academy of Matrimonial Lawyers. ***PRACTICE AREAS:*** Civil Rights Section 1983; Construction Arbitration; Construction Litigation; Criminal Defense; Domestic Relations. ***Email:*** howard@feldwass.com

STANLEY N. WASSER, born Washington, D.C., July 19, 1950; admitted to bar, 1975, District of Columbia; 1976, Illinois; 1977, U.S. District Court, Central District of Illinois; 1978, U.S. Court of Appeals, Seventh Circuit; 1992, U.S. District Court, Southern District of Illinois; 1996, U.S. Court of Appeals, Second Circuit; 1999, U.S. Supreme Court. *Education:* Pennsylvania State University (B.A., 1972); Catholic University of America (J.D., 1975). Staff Counsel, Illinois Office of the Comptroller, 1975-1976. Assistant Attorney General, Illinois Attorney General's Office, 1977. Assistant/Deputy Chief Counsel, Illinois Department of Transportation, 1977-1984. General Counsel, Illinois Bureau of the Budget, 1984-1985. Chief Counsel, Illinois Department of Transportation, 1985-1986. *Member:* The District of Columbia Bar; Sangamon County, Illinois State (Council Member, Alternative Dispute Resolution Section, 2002—) and American Bar Associations. ***PRACTICE AREAS:*** Civil Litigation; Construction Litigation; Criminal Defense; Employment Law; Estate Litigation. ***Email:*** stan@feldwass.com

CARL R. DRAPER, born Springfield, Missouri, April 18, 1955; admitted to bar, 1981, Illinois and U.S. District Court, Central District of Illinois; 1982, U.S. Tax Court. *Education:* Bradley University (B.S., 1976); University of Illinois (J.D., 1981). Phi Alpha Delta. Assistant Attorney General, State of Illinois, 1982-1984. Counsel to the Governor, State of Illinois, 1984-1987. Member, State Board of Elections. *Member:* Sangamon County and Illinois State (Member, Mineral Law Section, 1988-1989; Law Office Economics Section Council, 1994—; ARDC Committee, 2002-2004; Administrative Law Section Council, 2004—; Assembly, 2002—) Bar Associations. ***REPORTED CASES:*** Chavez v. Cady, 207 F.2d 901 (7th Cir., 2000); Lucas v. Lakin, 175 Ill.2d 166 (1997). ***PRACTICE AREAS:*** Administrative Hearings and Appeals; Civil Rights Section 1983; Domestic Relations; Election Law; Personal Injury. ***Email:*** carl@feldwass.com

FREDRIC BENSON, born Chicago, Illinois, January 5, 1948; admitted to bar, 1972, Illinois; 1975, U.S. District Court, Central District of Illinois; 1981, U.S. Court of Appeals, Seventh Circuit. *Education:* University of Wisconsin-Madison (B.A., 1969); University of Illinois (J.D., 1972). Staff Attorney, Illinois Legislative Reference Bureau, 1972-1973. Assistant Attorney General, Illinois Attorney General's Office, 1973-1976. Corporation Counsel, City of Springfield, Illinois, 1976-1987. *Member:* Sangamon County, Illinois State and American Bar Associations. ***PRACTICE AREAS:*** Civil Appeals; Corporate Formation; Real Estate; Municipal Corporation Law; Personal Bankruptcy; Estate Administration. ***Email:*** fred@feldwass.com

J. RANDALL COX, born Urbana, Illinois, June 19, 1966; admitted to bar, 1991, Illinois; 1992, U.S. District Court, Central District of Illinois; 1994, U.S. Court of Appeals, Seventh Circuit; 1997, U.S. District Court, Northern District of Illinois including Trial Bar; 2003, U.S. District Court, Southern District of Illinois. *Education:* Knox College (B.A., 1988); Southern Illinois University (J.D., 1991). Instrument Rated Private Pilot. *Member:* Sangamon County and Illinois State (Member: Committee on Legal Education, Admission and Competence, 2001-2002; Standing Committee on Continuing Legal Education, 2002—) Bar Associations. ***REPORTED CASES:*** In re marriage of Self, 265 Ill.App. 3d 804 (4th Dist. 1994); Williams Bros. Constr. v. Public Bldg. Commission, 243 Ill.App. 3d 949 (2nd Dist. 1993); Jones v. White 352 Ill.App.3d 316 (4th Dist. 2004). ***PRACTICE AREAS:*** Criminal Defense; Federal Criminal Law; Creditor Bankruptcy; Foreclosures; Nursing Home Litigation. ***Email:*** randy@feldwass.com

ASSOCIATES

KELLI ELLEN HILLIS, born Springfield, Illinois, May 26, 1973; admitted to bar, 1998, Illinois. *Education:* University of Illinois (B.S., 1995); Southern Illinois University (J.D., 1998). *Member:* Sangamon County, Illinois State and American Bar Associations; Women's Bar Association (Member: Civil Practice and Procedure Section Council, 2001—; Young Lawyers Section Council, 2001—). ***PRACTICE AREAS:*** Domestic Relations; Landlord and Tenant Law; General Practice. ***Email:*** kelli@feldwass.com

MICHELLE L. BLACKBURN, born Liberty, Illinois, November 3, 1971; admitted to bar, 2001, Illinois and U.S. District Court, Central District of Illinois. *Education:* Eastern Illinois University (B.S., 1993); John Marshall Law School (J.D., 2001). Member, Executive Board, John Marshall Law Moot Court, 1999-2000. *Member:* Sangamon County, Illinois State and American Bar Associations. ***PRACTICE AREAS:*** Family Law; General Practice. ***Email:*** michelle@feldwass.com

JAMES J. RAMMELKAMP, born New York, New York, November 25, 1978; admitted to bar, 2004, Illinois. *Education:* University of Illinois, Urbana (B.A., 2001); University of Illinois, Champaign (J.D., 2004). ***PRACTICE AREAS:*** General Litigation. ***Email:*** jay@feldwass.com

(This Listing Continued)

OF COUNSEL

THOMAS J. IMMEL, born Chicago, Illinois, January 7, 1943; admitted to bar, 1968, Illinois; 1970, U.S. District Court, Central, Northern and Southern Districts of Illinois; 1972, U.S. Supreme Court. *Education:* Northwestern University (B.A., 1965); Loyola University (J.D., 1968). Formerly with Burditt & Immel. ***PRACTICE AREAS:*** Real Estate; Corporate Law; Environmental Law; Trial Practice; Appellate Practice. ***Email:*** tom@feldwass.com

REPRESENTATIVE CLIENTS: Williams Brothers Construction Co.; Kinney Contractors, Inc.; Network Knowledge; Kirlin-Egan & Butler Funeral Home, PC; Town & Country Bank; Halverson Construction Co., Inc.; Newman-Alton, Inc. Contractors; Ironhustler Excavating, Inc.; City of Springfield Police Pension Board; Bird Armour, LLC, CPA's.
REFERENCE: Town & Country Bank, Springfield, Illinois.

FREEBORN & PETERS LLP

217 E. MONROE STREET
SUITE 202
SPRINGFIELD, ILLINOIS 62701
Telephone: 217-535-1060
Fax: 217-535-1069
URL: http://www.freebornpeters.com

Chicago, Illinois Office: 311 South Wacker Drive, Suite 3000, 60606. Telephone: 312-360-6000. Fax: 312-360-6520.

Corporate Counseling and Transactions; Litigation and Alternative Dispute Resolution; Compliance with Regulations by Government Agencies.

PARTNERS

ROGER H. BICKEL, admitted to bar, 1989, Illinois a. *Education:* Indiana University (B.A., with honors, 1982); Loyola University of Chicago (J.D., 1989). Co-Author: "1991 Survey of Illinois Administrative Law," Illinois Institute for Continuing Legal Education; 1992-1996, Annual Surveys of Administrative Law. Member, Illinois Secretary of State's Corporate Acts Advisory Committee, 1991-1995. General Counsel, Illinois Secretary of State, 1991-1995. Special Assistant U.S. Attorney for the Central District of Illinois, 1992-1994. ***PRACTICE AREAS:*** Business Litigation; Administrative Law; Regulatory Compliance. ***Email:*** rbickel@freebornpeters.com

ANN M. ZWICK, admitted to bar, 1989, Illinois. *Education:* University of Illinois (B.S., with highest honors, 1986); Northwestern University (J.D., cum laude, 1989). Former Assistant Counsel with the Illinois Environmental Protection Agency. ***PRACTICE AREAS:*** Environmental, Health and Safety Law; Real Estate; Land Use; Government Relations; Regulatory Law. ***Email:*** azwick@freebornpeters.com

ASSOCIATE

JENNIFER L. MILOS, admitted to bar, 2001, Illinois. *Education:* University of Michigan (B.A., English Literature, 1998); University of Illinois (J.D., 2001). ***PRACTICE AREAS:*** Business Litigation. ***Email:*** jmilos@freebornpeters.com

(For biographical data on other personnel, see Professional Biographies at Chicago, Illinois and Denver, Colorado)

FULTZ LAW OFFICES

524 EAST CAPITOL AVENUE
SPRINGFIELD, ILLINOIS 62701
Telephone: 217-492-1560
Fax: 217-492-1562
Email: danfultz@sbcglobal.net
URL: http://www.brunsfultz.com

Criminal Defense, Family Law, Estate Planning, Real Estate, Governmental Affairs.

MEMBER OF FIRM

DANIEL L. FULTZ, born Aurora, Illinois, November 9, 1968; admitted to bar, 2004, Illinois and U.S. District Court, Central District of Illinois. *Education:* Eastern Illinois University (B.A., magna cum laude, 1993; M.A., 1995); St. Louis University (J.D., Academic Excellence Award, 2004). *Member:* Sangamon County, Illinois State and American Bar Associations. ***PRACTICE AREAS:*** Criminal Defense; Civil Litigation; General Practice. ***Email:*** danfultz@sbcglobal.net

GATES, WISE & SCHLOSSER, P.C.

1231 SOUTH 8TH STREET
SPRINGFIELD, ILLINOIS 62703
Telephone: 217-522-9010
Fax: 217-522-9020
URL: http://www.gwspc.com

Criminal Defense, Federal Criminal Law, Business Transactions, Commercial Litigation, Real Estate Transactions, Corporate Law, Personal Injury, Civil Rights, General Litigation and Appeals.

GORDON W. GATES, born Chicago Heights, Illinois, April 24, 1961; admitted to bar, 1986, Illinois and U.S. District Court, Central District of Illinois; 1988, U.S. Court of Appeals, Seventh Circuit; U.S. Supreme Court. *Education:* University of Iowa (B.B.A., 1983); Northern Illinois University (J.D., cum laude, 1986). *Member:* Sangamon County, Illinois State and American Bar Associations. ***REPORTED CASES:*** Chronister Oil Company v. Unocal, 34 F.3d 462 (7th Cir., 1994); Irvin v. Lincoln Heritage, 950 F.2d 1318 (7th Cir., 1991); Baptist v. Baptist, 598 N.E. 2d 278 (4th Dist.); Soyland Power Co-op v. Illinois Power Co., 572 N.E.2d 462 (4th Dist., 1991); Kleczel v. Jorgensen, 767 N.E.2d 913 (4th Dist. 2002). ***PRACTICE AREAS:*** Business Transactions; Corporate Law; Commercial Litigation; Real Estate Transactions; Construction Law; Appellate Practice; General Litigation; Mechanics Liens; Zoning Law. ***Email:*** gordon@gwspc.com

(This Listing Continued)

D. PETER WISE, born Springfield, Illinois, April 16, 1959; admitted to bar, 1984, Illinois and U.S. District Court, Central and Southern Districts of Illinois; 1985, U.S. Court of Appeals, Seventh Circuit; U.S. Supreme Court. *Education:* Tulane University (B.A., 1981); John Marshall Law School (J.D., with honors, 1984). AUTHOR: "A Plaintiffs Counsels' Guide to Corporate Scienter and Discovering the Basis of Punitive Damages in Products Litigation," Illinois Trial Lawyers Association Journal, Vol. 5, No. 2, Spring/Summer, 1983; "An Overview of Federal Rule of Evidence 702 in Seventh Circuit Criminal Law Decisions," Illinois Trial Lawyers Association, Spring and Summer Journal, 1986; "Operation Valkyrie: Illinois' Version of the Drug Courier Profile," Illinois Attorneys for Criminal Justice Newsletter, Vol. 3, No. 1, Winter 1989; "DCFS Code of Ethics Proves to be a Boon for Father Accused of Sexual Assault and a Bane for the Prosecution," Illinois Attorneys for Criminal Justice Newsletter, Winter/Spring 1999. LECTURER: Effective Use of Discovery in Criminal Cases, Law Ed Series, Illinois State Bar Association, 1990; Search & Seizure Symposium, University of Illinois College of Law, 1994. Illinois Association of Criminal Defense Lawyers DUI Defense Seminar, "Field Sobriety Testing: Abnormal Tests to Test Normal Faculties," June 2003; "Winning Strategies for Depositions in Capital Cases," Illinois Institute for Continuing Legal Education, Defending Illinois Death Penalty Cases in 2005. FACULTY: Illinois State Appellate Defender's Public Defender Trial Advocacy Program, Chicago-Kent IIT College of Law, 1998-2003. *Member:* Illinois Supreme Court Capital Litigation Trial Bar (Lead Counsel Designation); National Association of Criminal Defense Lawyers; Illinois Association of Criminal Defense Lawyers (Board Member, President Elect); American Civil Liberties Union; Association of Trial Lawyers of America; Illinois Trial Lawyers Association; Sangamon County Criminal Defense Bar (President, 1988-1989 and Secretary, 1987-1988); Sangamon County, Illinois State and American Bar Associations. ***REPORTED CASES:*** U.S. v. Lanterman, 76 F.3d 158 (7th Cir., 1996); U.S. v. Sablotny, 21 F.2d 747 (7th Cir., 1993); U.S. v. Beler, 20 F.3d 1428 (7th Cir., 1994); Arkebauer v. Kiley, 985 F.2d 1351 (7th Cir., 1993); Arkebauer v. Kiley, 751 F. Supp. 783 (C.D. Ill. 1990); U.S. v. Garcia, 986 F.2d 1135, 38 Fed. R. Evid. Serv. 151 (7th Cir., 1993); U.S. v. Erwin, 902 F.2d 510 (7th Cir., 1990); In the Matter of Clark, 246 Ill.App.3d 362, 615 N.E.2d 1244 (4th Dist., 1993); People v. Huisinga, 242 Ill.App.3d 418, 610 N.E.2d 168 (4th Dist., 1993); Barter v. Slayback, 235 Ill.App.3d 18, 600 N.E.2d 538 (5th Dist., 1992); People v. Harrell, 226 Ill.App.3d 866, 589 N.E.2d 943 (4th Dist., 1992); People v. Burg, 207 Ill.App.3d 67, 565 N.E.2d 306 (4th Dist., 1990); People v. Stephenson, 198 Ill.App.3d 189, 555 N.E.2d 802 (4th Dist., 1990); People v. Arkebauer, 198 Ill.App.3d 470, 555 N.E.2d 1162 (5th Dist., 1990); People v. Morgan, 307 Ill.App.3d. 707, 718 N.E.2d 206 (4th Dist., 1999); People v. Morgan 197 Ill 2d 404, 758 N.E 2d 813 (2001) (Ill. S. Ct); McCloughan v. City of Springfield, 208 F.R.D. 236 (C.D. Ill. 2002); . ***PRACTICE AREAS:*** Criminal Defense; Federal Criminal Law; Appellate Practice; Civil Rights; Capital Offenses; Criminal Conspiracy; Felonies; Grand Jury Practice; Search and Seizure; Sex Crimes; Drug Crimes; Drug Forfeiture; Criminal Fraud; Criminal Appeals; Death Penalty. ***Email:*** peter@gwspc.com

FREDERICK J. SCHLOSSER, born Springfield, Illinois, June 17, 1963; admitted to bar, 1992, Illinois; 1993, U.S. Court of Appeals, Seventh Circuit and U.S. District Court, Central and Southern Districts of Illinois. *Education:* University of Notre Dame (B.B.A., 1985); Southern Illinois University (J.D., cum laude, 1992). Member, Moot Court Team, 1991-1992. Member, Southern Illinois University Law Journal, 1991-1992. Author: Casenote, "The Fifth Amendment Right Against Self-Incrimination: An Individual's Right Versus the Government's Need for Effective Law Enforcement," 16 So. Ill. U.L.J. 197 (1991); Comment, "The Constitutionality of Police Protection Statutes," 16 So. Ill. U.L.J. 707 (1992). Co-Author: "Compilations of Motions, Recent Cases and Articles to Assist Criminal Defense Attorneys," Illinois Attorneys for Criminal Justice, Annual Meeting (1993). *Member:* Sangamon County, Illinois State and American Bar Associations; Illinois Attorneys for Criminal Justice; National Association of Criminal Defense Lawyers; Illinois Supreme Court Capital Litigation Trial Bar (Lead Counsel); Association of Trial Lawyers of America; Illinois Trial Lawyers Association. ***REPORTED CASES:*** Case v. Ahitow, 301 F.3d 605 (7th Cir. 2002); Gregory v. Weigler, 873 F.Supp. 1189 (C.D. Ill. 1995); McCloughan v. City of Springfield, 208 F.R.D. 236 (C.D. Ill. 2002); Naylor v. Kindred 250 Ill.App.3d 997, 620 N.E.2d 520 (4th District, 1993); Pope v. Shafer, 86 F.3d 90 (7th Cir., 1996). ***PRACTICE AREAS:*** Criminal Defense; Federal Criminal Law; Appellate Practice; Personal Injury; Medical Malpractice; General Litigation. ***Email:*** fred@gwspc.com

BRADLEY B. WILSON, born Columbia, Missouri, May 17, 1965; admitted to bar, 1996, Illinois; 1998, U.S. District Court, Central District of Illinois; 2001, U.S. Court of Appeals, Seventh Circuit. *Education:* University of Missouri (B.A., Political Science, 1990); Northern Illinois University (J.D., cum laude, 1996). Recipient: American Jurisprudence Award for Constitutional Law II; Dean's Scholarship, Northern Illinois University College of Law, 1994-1996. Administrative Law Judge, Illinois State Labor Relations Board, 1997-1998. Assistant Corporate Counsel, City of Springfield, Illinois, 1998-2001. *Member:* Sangamon County, Illinois State and American Bar Associations; Illinois Trial Lawyers Association; American Trial Lawyer's Association. ***REPORTED CASES:*** Kehrer v. City of Springfield et al 104 F.Supp 1001 (C.D. Ill., 2000); McGuire v. City of Springfield, 133 F.Supp. 2d 1095, 2001 WL 242582 (C.D. Ill., 2001); Howard et al v. City of Springfield 274 F. 3d 1141 (7th Cir 2001; Springfield Branch of National Association for Advancement of Colored People v. City of Springfield, Ill. 137 F. Supp. 2d 990 (C.D. Ill., 2001); Case v. Ahitow, 301 F.3d 605 (7th Cir. 2002). ***PRACTICE AREAS:*** Litigation; Personal Injury; Labor and Employment. ***Email:*** brad@gwspc.com

TODD M. GOEBEL, born Shelbyville, Illinois, November 2, 1975; admitted to bar, 2001, Illinois and U.S. District Court, Central District of Illinois; 2004, U.S. District Court, Southern District of Illinois. *Education:* University of Illinois, Urbana-Champaign (B.S., Finance, with honors, 1998); Southern Illinois University, Carbondale (J.D., cum laude, 2001). *Member:* Sangamon County, Illinois State and American Bar Associations. ***REPORTED CASES:*** People v. Gott, 346 Ill.App.3d 236, 803 N.E.2d 900, 281 Ill.Dec. 279 (5th Dist. 2004). ***PRACTICE AREAS:*** Criminal Defense; Civil Litigation; Commercial

(This Listing Continued)

GATES, WISE & SCHLOSSER, P.C., Springfield—Continued

Litigation; Business Transactions; Appellate Practice; Drivers License Suspension. ***Email:*** goebel@gwspc.com

GIFFIN, WINNING, COHEN & BODEWES, P.C.

Established in 1911

1 WEST OLD STATE CAPITOL PLAZA
SUITE 600 MYERS BUILDING
P.O. BOX 2117
SPRINGFIELD, ILLINOIS 62705
Telephone: 217-525-1571
Facsimile: 217-525-1710
Email: gifwinlaw@gifwinlaw.com
URL: http://www.gifwinlaw.com

General Civil Trial and Appellate Practice in Federal and State Courts. Corporation, Bankruptcy, Banking and Financial Institutions, Commercial Law, Employment Law, Real Estate, Taxation, Probate and Estates, Legislative Affairs and Administrative Law.

FIRM PROFILE: The law firm of Giffin, Winning, Cohen & Bodewes, P.C. was founded in 1911 and has provided quality legal Services for over 90 years. The firm counts among its former members and associates a current U.S. Senator from Illinois, congressmen, judges and prominent private and government leaders.

Giffin, Winning, Cohen & Bodewes, P.C. carries on a substantial litigation practice in Federal and State courts; legislative and governmental affairs practice; real estate development; transactional, business, commercial and banking practice; and agricultural economics practice. Clients include insurance companies, trade associations, manufacturing companies, financial institutions, business enterprises, distributors, professional and consulting firms, general contractors, health care facilities, transportation companies, real estate developers, governmental units and universities.

The firm's attorneys maintain practice in wide-ranging areas of the law. Where appropriate, the firm is able to combine the specialties of several areas of law to provide a comprehensive approach to problem solving.

One of the strongest assets of Giffin, Winning, Cohen & Bodewes, P.C. is the wide range of interests and diversity of backgrounds our attorneys bring to the firm. Members of the firm have been recruited from the ranks of governmental agencies, prosecutors and clerks for judges. Our attorneys serve on the boards of professional, cultural, educational and civic groups.

Members of the firm have written articles for West Publishing Company, numerous pieces for Association newsletters and law journals. Firm members have also conducted seminars for Illinois Institute for Continuing Legal Education and are active in both State and Local Bar Associations.

Giffin, Winning, Cohen & Bodewes, P.C. is a member of the State Capital Global Law Firm Group, a nonprofit membership association consisting of fifty independent law firm members located in or near their respective state capitals as well as international representatives. The Group was formed to share information and expertise about the practice of law before state legislative, judicial, administrative, regulatory and executive bodies in the represented capital cities. The Group facilitates communications between members to improve their ability to serve the needs of their individual clients.

There are over 4,000 attorneys in the member firms in the United States and 44 countries worldwide. Member firms of the State Capital Law Firm Group practice independently and not in a relationship for the joint practice of law.

D. LOGAN GIFFIN (1890-1980)
MONTGOMERY S. WINNING (1892-1966)
C. TERRY LINDNER (1903-1987)
ALFRED F. NEWKIRK (1904-1980)
JAMES M. WINNING (Retired)

HERMAN G. BODEWES, born St. Louis, Missouri, July 25, 1937; admitted to bar, 1964, Illinois; 1973, U.S. Supreme Court. *Education:* St. Louis University (B.S., 1961; J.D., 1964). Member, Legislative Reapportionment Commission, 1971. Law Clerk, U.S. District Court, 1964-1965. Counsel, Illinois Senate, 1967-1971. *Member:* Sangamon County, Illinois State and American Bar Associations; The District of Columbia Bar; Federation of Insurance Counsel. ***PRACTICE AREAS:*** Legislative Practice; Government Affairs; Financial Institutions Law; Business Law; Commercial Law. ***Email:*** hbodewes@gifwinlaw.com

JOHN L. SWARTZ, born Chicago, Illinois, November 26, 1945; admitted to bar, 1971, Illinois; 1975, U.S. Supreme Court; 1981, U.S. Court of Appeals, Seventh Circuit. *Education:* University of Illinois (A.B., 1968); University of Chicago (J.D., 1971). Phi Beta Kappa. Member, Staff Counsel, Illinois House of Representatives, 1971-1973. Staff Member, Illinois State Appellate Defenders Office, 1973-1977. Commissioner, Illinois Appellate Defender Commission, 1983-1990. Panel Trustee, U.S. Trustee, Central District of Illinois, 1990—. *Member:* Sangamon County and Illinois State Bar Associations; Illinois Appellate Lawyers Association; National Association of Bankruptcy Trustees. ***PRACTICE AREAS:*** Bankruptcy; Real Estate; Municipal Law. ***Email:*** jlswartz@gifwinlaw.com

R. MARK MIFFLIN, born Urbana, Illinois, November 12, 1951; admitted to bar, 1978, Illinois; 1979, U.S. Court of Appeals, Seventh Circuit; 1982, U.S. Supreme Court. *Education:* Western Illinois University (B.A., 1973); Southern Illinois University (J.D., magna cum laude, 1978). Articles Editor, Southern Illinois University Law Journal, 1977. Illinois Legislative Staff Intern, 1974-1975. Law Clerk to U.S. District Judge, Central District of Illinois, 1978-1980. Law Clerk to Illinois Supreme Court Justice, 1978. Assistant U.S. Attorney, 1980-1982. Author: "Open vs. Closed Primaries, A Dilemma in the Illinois Election Process," 1978 So. Ill. U.L.J. 210. Co-Author: "Lobbying, PAC's and Campaign Finance," 50 State Handbook, (Illinois chapter) West Group 2005 . *Member:* Sangamon County and Illinois State Bar Associations; Illinois Association of Defense Trial Counsel. ***PRACTICE AREAS:*** Litigation; Legislative Practice; Government Affairs. ***Email:*** mmifflin@gifwinlaw.com

DAVID A. HERMAN, born Springfield, Illinois, March 8, 1966; admitted to bar, 1992, Illinois and U.S. District Court, Central and Northern Districts of Illinois; 1994, U.S. Court of Appeals, Seventh Circuit; 1998, U.S. District Court, Southern District of Illinois and U.S. Supreme Court. *Education:* Illinois State University (B.S., cum laude, 1989); Northern Illinois University (J.D., magna cum laude, 1992). Recipient, American Jurisprudence Awards in Constitutional Law, Commercial Transactions and Advanced Legal Research. Lead Articles Editor, Northern Illinois University Law Review. Published "Products Liability," 50 State Handbook (Illinois Chapter) (West 1994); "Rutan vs. Republican Party of Illinois and Patronage Employment Practice: Clarification or Confusion," 11 N. Ill. U.L. Rev. 355, 1991. *Member:* Sangamon County (Member, Board of Directors; Vice President, Young Lawyers Division), Illinois State and American Bar Associations; Seventh Circuit Bar Association; Illinois Association of Defense Counsel. [Illinois Air National Guard, 183rd FG, 1986-1995]. ***PRACTICE AREAS:*** Torts; Products Liability; Labor and Employment; Insurance; Business Litigation; Commercial Law; Civil Appeals. ***Email:*** dherman1@gifwinlaw.com

MICHAEL JOSEPH MANNION, born Chicago, Illinois, July 25, 1967; admitted to bar, 1992, Illinois and U.S. District Court, Northern, Central and Southern Districts of Illinois; 1994, U.S. Court of Appeals, Seventh Circuit. *Education:* Marquette University (B.S., 1989); John Marshall Law School (J.D., 1992). Assistant Counsel to Speaker Lee A. Daniels, Illinois House of Representatives for the 89th General Assembly, 1995-1996. *Member:* Chicago, Sangamon County, Illinois State and American Bar Associations. ***REPORTED CASES:*** Davis v. McCormick, 898 F.Supp 1275 (C.D. Ill. 1995). ***PRACTICE AREAS:*** Civil Litigation; Products Liability; Personal Injury; Family Law; Legislative Practice; Government Affairs. ***Email:*** mmannon@gifwinlaw.com

DAVID O. EDWARDS, born Springfield, Illinois, March 5, 1970; admitted to bar, 1995, Illinois; 1996, U.S. District Court, Central District of Illinois; 1999, U.S. Court of Appeals, Seventh Circuit and U.S. Supreme Court. *Education:* University of Illinois (B.S., 1992; J.D., 1995). Order of the Coif. Associate Editor, University of Illinois Law Review, 1994-1995. Recipient American Jurisprudence Awards: Contracts/Sales I; Contracts/Sales II. Law Clerk to the Hon. James D. Heiple, Illinois Supreme Court, Peoria, Illinois, 1995-1996. *Member:* Sangamon County and Illinois State (Trustee Estates Section Council, 2004—) Bar Associations. ***PRACTICE AREAS:*** Appellate Practice; Tax Law; Trusts and Estates; Wills; Probate; Banking Law; Creditors Rights; Real Estate. ***Email:*** davidoedwards@gifwinlaw.com

CREIGHTON R. CASTLE, born Harvey, Illinois, May 29, 1966; admitted to bar, 1993, Illinois; 1995, District of Columbia. *Education:* Illinois State University (B.S., Accounting, 1989; M.S., 1990); John Marshall Law School (J.D., 1993); Georgetown University Law School (LL.M., Taxation, 1994). Member, Journal of Computer & Information Law Review. Author: "Note, Orthopedic & Sports Injury Clinic, et. al. v. Wang Laboratories, Inc.: Can Liability Extend to Computer Service Repair Persons Outside of the Remedies Available Within the Sellers' Maintenance Agreement?" 5 Software L.J. 653 (1992). Certified Public Accountant, 1990. Associate, Piper Marbury Rudnick & Wolfe, 2000-2002. Tax Manager, Ernst & Young, 1994-2000. Member, Motivation Foundation, 2001-2002. *Member:* Sangamon County and Illinois State Bar Associations. ***PRACTICE AREAS:*** Taxation; Business Transactions; Real Estate; Bankruptcy; General Practice. ***Email:*** crcastle@gifwinlaw.com

---

PHILIP C. KAUFMANN, born Carbondale, Illinois, December 20, 1973; admitted to bar, 2001, Illinois; 2002, U.S. District Court, Central District of Illinois and U.S. Court of Appeals, Seventh Circuit. *Education:* Illinois College (B.A., History, magna cum laude, 1998); University of Illinois College of Law (J.D., cum laude, 2001). *Member:* Sangamon County, Illinois State and American Bar Associations. ***PRACTICE AREAS:*** Civil Litigation; Traffic Violations; Criminal Law; Municipal Law; Federal Practice. ***Email:*** pkaufmann@gifwinlaw.com

KENT GRAY, born Springfield, Illinois, February 28, 1970; admitted to bar, 2002, Illinois and U.S. District Court, Central District of Illinois. *Education:* Loyola University, Chicago (B.B.A., 1997); University of Illinois (M.B.A., 2001); St. Louis University (J.D., 2002); Employment Law Certificate. Co-Author: "Lobbying, Pac's & Campaign Finance," 50-State Handbook, (Illinois Chapter) West Group 2003-2005. Trustee, Lincoln Land Community College, 1999—. *Member:* Sangamon County and Illinois State Bar Associations. ***PRACTICE AREAS:*** Business Law; Corporate Law; Election, Campaign and Political Law; Labor and Employment; Government. ***Email:*** kgray@gifwinlaw.com

CHRISTOPHER E. SHERER, born Hillsboro, Illinois, February 1, 1975; admitted to bar, 2000, Missouri; 2001, Illinois and Kansas; U.S. District Court, District of Kansas and Eastern District of Missouri; 2003, U.S. District Court, Central and Southern Districts of Illinois; U.S. Court of Appeals, 7th Circuit and U.S. Supreme Court. *Education:* Southeast Missouri State University (B.S., 1997); University of Missouri at Kansas City (J.D., 2000). Phi Delta Phi. Note and Comment Editor, UMKC Law Review. Judicial Law Clerk, Hon. Thomas H. Newton, Missouri Court of Appeals, Western District, Kansas City, Missouri, 2000-2002. Law Clerk, U.S. Department of Labor, Office of Solicitor, Kansas City, Missouri, January 1999-April 1999. Author: 68 UMKC L. Rev. 115, Fall 1999; 68 UMKC L. Rev. 263, Winter 1999; 23 Hamline J. Pub. L. & Pol'y 2, Fall 2001. Member, Hillsboro, Illinois Volunteer Fire Department. *Member:* Montgomery County, Sangamon County and Illinois State Bar Associations; The Missouri Bar; Defense Research Institute; Illinois Association of Defense Trial Counsel (Member, Business Litigation Committee); Montgomery County Young Democrats (ViceChairman). ***PRACTICE AREAS:*** Litigation; Appellate Practice; Family Law; Election; Campaign Ethics; Municipal Law; Construction Law. ***Email:*** csherer@gifwinlaw.com

ELIZABETH R. GAFFNEY, born Chicago, Illinois, August 1, 1972; admitted to bar, 2004, Illinois and U.S. District Court, Central and Southern Districts of Illinois. *Education:*

(This Listing Continued)

Smith College (B.A., 1994); Loyola University (J.D., 2004). Recipient, Certificate in Health Law, Loyola University, Chicago, 2004. *Member:* Sangamon County and Illinois State Bar Associations. ***PRACTICE AREAS:*** General Practice; Administrative Law; Health Care; Legislative Practice; Corporate Law. ***Email:*** egaffney@gifwinlaw.com

KRISTINA E. MONY, born Vicksburg, Michigan, Kalamazoo, January 18, 1972; admitted to bar, 1999, Michigan and U.S. District Court, Eastern District of Michigan; 2005, Illinois. *Education:* Kalamazoo College (B.A., Political Science and Sociology, 1994); Wayne State University (J.D., 1999). Clarence L. Remynse Scholar. National Moot Court. *Member:* Sangamon County, Illinois State and American Bar Associations; State Bar of Michigan. ***PRACTICE AREAS:*** Medical Malpractice Defense; Civil Litigation. ***Email:*** kristinamony@gifwinlaw.com

OF COUNSEL

ROBERT S. COHEN, born Pittsburgh, Pennsylvania, August 30, 1932; admitted to bar, 1959, Illinois. *Education:* University of Illinois (B.S., 1954); Washington University (J.D., 1959). Phi Delta Phi. Board Member and Treasurer, Illinois Housing Development Authority, 1972-1975. *Member:* Sangamon County and Illinois State Bar Associations. ***PRACTICE AREAS:*** Banking Law; Real Estate; Commercial Law; Administrative Law; Corporate Law. ***Email:*** rcohen@gifwinlaw.com

RONALD W. PERIARD, born Detroit, Michigan, July 13, 1943; admitted to bar, 1968, Illinois. *Education:* University of Michigan (B.S., 1965; J.D., 1968). *Member:* Christian County, Illinois State (Delegate, 1982-1988) and American Bar Associations; Illinois Trial Lawyers Association; Illinois Association of Defense Trial Counsel. Fellow, Illinois Bar Foundation. ***PRACTICE AREAS:*** Estate Planning; Probate Law; Trust Administration; Real Estate; General Practice. ***Email:*** rperiard@gifwinlaw.com

CAROLYN TAFT GROSBOLL, born Springfield, Illinois, December 3, 1961; admitted to bar, 1988, Illinois; 1991, U.S. District Court, Central District of Illinois. *Education:* Southern Illinois University (B.A., History, 1984; J.D., 1987). Director, 1995-2004 and Deputy Director/Legal Counsel, 1993-1995, Illinois Nature Preserves Commission. Staff Attorney, Legislative Reference Bureau, 1989-1993. Assistant Counsel, Illinois Secretary of State, 1987-1989. Vice President, Soujourn Shelter & Services. Director-At-Large, Illinois Audubon Society. Director, Prairie Rivers Network. President, Government Bar Association, 1993-1994. ***PRACTICE AREAS:*** Natural Resources (50%); Real Property (15%); Zoning, Planning & Land Use (15%); Government (10%); Environmental Law (10%). ***Email:*** cgrosboll@gifwinlaw.com

REPRESENTATIVE CLIENTS: Illinois League of Financial Institutions; Associated Beer Distributors of Illinois; Illinois Asphalt Paving Association; Illinois Professional Firefighter's Association; Park Superintendents Professional Association; Illinois Community Action Association; Illinois Motorcycle Dealers Association; Humane Society of Central Illinois; Central Illinois Builders of Associated General Contractors; Jones-Blythe Construction Co.; Petri-Kuhne Construction Co., Inc.; Siciliano Construction Company; Benanti Builders; Henson-Robinson Co.; Security Bank, S.B; Illinois National Bank; First National Bank of Petersburg; Town & Country Bank; Capital Community Bank; Bunn-O-Matic Co.; Bunn Capitol Co.; Genesee & Wyoming; Illinois Midland Rail Road; Capitol Healthcare, Inc.; Capitol Illini Veterinary Clinic; Agridyne, LLC; Family Video, Inc.; Meramec Specialty Co.; E.M.C. Inc.; Heritage House Restaurants; Selective Properties, Inc.; Grinnell Mutual Reinsurance Co.; Illinois Founders Insurance Company; Auto-Owners Insurance Company; Great Central Insurance Co.; Standard Mutual Insurance Co.; Ohio Casualty Group of Insurance Cos.; Atlantic Mutual Insurance Co.; Horace Mann Insurance Company; AirUSA; World Freefall Convention; City of Petersburg; Village of Jerome; WebMD; Illinois Baptist State Association.

GRAHAM AND GRAHAM, LTD.

1201 SOUTH EIGHTH STREET
SPRINGFIELD, ILLINOIS 62703
Telephone: 217-523-4569
Fax: 217-523-4656

General Civil Practice in all Courts of Record and Commissions. Health Care and Hospital Law. Probate and Real Estate Law. Trials.

JAMES M. GRAHAM (1851-1945)

JAMES J. GRAHAM (1880-1965)

HUGH J. GRAHAM (1877-1972)

HUGH J. GRAHAM, JR. (1910-1994)

HUGH J. GRAHAM, III, born 1937; admitted to bar, 1961, Illinois. *Education:* University of Illinois (A.B., 1958; LL.B., 1961). *Member:* Illinois State and American Bar Associations; American Academy of Hospital Attorneys. ***PRACTICE AREAS:*** Health Law; Hospital Law; Civil Trial Practice; General Practice; Real Estate Law.

RICHARD J. WILDERSON, born Springfield, Illinois, 1948; admitted to bar, 1978, Illinois. *Education:* St. Louis University (B.A., 1970; J.D., 1978). *Member:* Sangamon County Bar Association; Illinois Association of Defense Trial Counsel; Illinois Association of Hospital Attorneys. ***PRACTICE AREAS:*** Health Law; Hospital Law; Medical Malpractice Law; Defense Litigation.

NANCY ECKERT MARTIN, born Park Ridge, Illinois, 1960; admitted to bar, 1985, Illinois. *Education:* University of Illinois (B.S., 1982); Southern Illinois University (M.B.A., 1985; J.D., 1985). Phi Alpha Delta. *Member:* Sangamon County, Christian County and Illinois State Bar Associations. ***PRACTICE AREAS:*** Probate; Guardianship; Real Estate Law; General Practice.

BRADLEY E. HUFF, born Galesburg, Illinois, 1964; admitted to bar, 1991, Illinois. *Education:* Lincoln Land Community College (A.A., 1984); University of Illinois (A.B., 1987); Southern Illinois University (J.D., 1990). Phi Delta Phi. *Member:* Illinois State Bar Association. ***PRACTICE AREAS:*** Real Property Law; Defense Litigation; General Practice.

(This Listing Continued)

RYAN R. WILSON, born Macomb, Illinois, April 10, 1979; admitted to bar, 2004, Illinois. *Education:* Western Illinois University (B.S., 2000); Southern Illinois University (J.D., 2004). ***PRACTICE AREAS:*** Medical Malpractice Defense; Civil Litigation; Wills; Estate Planning; Business Law; Employment Law.

NATHAN L. WETZEL, born Fort Collins, Colorado, August 8, 1978; admitted to bar, 2004, Illinois. *Education:* Colorado College (B.A., 2001); Chicago Kent College of Law (J.D., 2004). *Member:* Illinois State Bar Association. ***PRACTICE AREAS:*** General Practice. ***Email:*** nlwetzel@yahoo.com

COUNSEL FOR: Hospital Sisters Health System.
REPRESENTATIVE CLIENTS: Illinois and Midland Railroad; SPCSL Railway; St. Anthony's Memorial Hospital, Effingham; St. Mary's Hospital, Decatur; St. John's Hospital, Springfield.

HART, SOUTHWORTH & WITSMAN

Established in 1985
ONE NORTH OLD STATE CAPITOL PLAZA
SUITE 501
SPRINGFIELD, ILLINOIS 62701-1323
Telephone: 217-753-0055
Telecopier: 217-753-1056

Public Finance, Municipal Bonds, Banks and Banking, Creditor Rights, Real Estate, Commercial Real Estate, Construction Law, Commercial Law, Business Law, Corporate Law, Probate, Trusts and Estates, Estate Planning, Employment Law, Insurance Law.

RICHARD E. HART, born Ottawa, Illinois, December 13, 1942; admitted to bar, 1967, Illinois; U.S. District Court, Central District of Illinois. *Education:* University of Illinois (A.B., with honors, 1964; J.D., 1967). Special Assistant Attorney General, 1972-1982. *Member:* Sangamon County, Illinois State and American Bar Associations; National Association of Bond Lawyers. ***PRACTICE AREAS:*** Estate Planning; Municipal; Corporate. ***Email:*** rhart@hswnet.com

MIKE SOUTHWORTH, born Des Moines, Iowa, December 31, 1954; admitted to bar, 1983, Illinois and U.S. District Court, Central District of Illinois. *Education:* Yale University (B.A., 1977); Washington University (J.D., 1983). Assistant Attorney General, 1983-1985. *Member:* Illinois State Bar Association; National Association of Bond Lawyers. ***PRACTICE AREAS:*** Municipal; Corporate; Real Estate; Construction Law; Insurance. ***Email:*** msouthworth@hswnet.com

SAMUEL J. WITSMAN, born Danville, Illinois, September 12, 1958; admitted to bar, 1986, Illinois and U.S. District Court, Northern District of Illinois; 1991, U.S. District Court, Central District of Illinois. *Education:* Illinois State University (B.S.; M.A., 1979); University of Illinois (J.D., 1986). ***PRACTICE AREAS:*** Corporate; Banking; Municipal; Creditors' Rights. ***Email:*** switsman@hswnet.com

TIMOTHY RIGBY, born Mexico, Missouri, February 19, 1969; admitted to bar, 1994, Illinois and U.S. District Court, Central District of Illinois. *Education:* Eastern Illinois University (B.S. Bus., 1991); Southern Illinois University (J.D., 1994). ***PRACTICE AREAS:*** Corporate; Estate Planning; Contracts; Municipal Finance; Creditors' Rights. ***Email:*** trigby@hswnet.com

ASSOCIATE

AMY D. SANDERS, born Centralia, Illinois, July 27, 1979; admitted to bar, 2004, Illinois. *Education:* University of Illinois (B.S., high honors, 2001); University of Illinois College of Law (J.D., high honors, 2004). *Member:* Illinois State Bar Association. ***PRACTICE AREAS:*** Corporate Law (20%); Estate Planning (20%); Contracts (20%); Municipal Finance (20%); Creditors Rights (20%). ***Email:*** asanders@hswnet.com

HEDINGER LAW OFFICE

2601 SOUTH FIFTH STREET
SPRINGFIELD, ILLINOIS 62703
Telephone: 217-523-2753
Facsimile: 217-523-4366
Email: hhlaw@cityscape.net
URL: http://www.lawyers.com/hedingerlaw

Environmental Law, Civil Litigation, Construction Law, Consumer Rights and Mediation.

STEPHEN F. HEDINGER, born Roaring Spring, Pennsylvania, November 27, 1959; admitted to bar, 1988, Illinois. *Education:* Southern Illinois University (B.A., 1982; J.D., summa cum laude, 1988). Phi Kappa Phi; Phi Delta Phi. Managing Editor, S.I.U. Law Journal, Vol. 12, 1987-1988. Law Clerk, U.S. District Judge Richard Mills, 1988-1990. *Member:* Sangamon County and Illinois State Bar Associations. ***Email:*** hedinger@cityscape.net

REPRESENTATIVE CLIENTS: Komatsu America, Inc.; Marathon Petroleum Company LLC; Peabody Coal Company, LLC; Peabody Energy; DTE Coal Services, Inc.; PermaTreat of Illinois, Inc.

HENNESSY & ROACH, P.C.

2501 CHATHAM ROAD, SUITE 220
SPRINGFIELD, ILLINOIS 62704
Telephone: 217-726-0037
Fax: 217-726-0137
Email: hennroach@hennessyroach.com
URL: http://www.hennessyroach.com

Chicago, Illinois Office: Marquett Building, 140 S. Dearborn, Suite 520, 60603. Telephone: 312-346-5310. Fax: 512-346-5330.

St. Louis, Missouri Office: 720 Olive Street, Suite 2222, 63101. Telephone: 314-231-0770. Fax: 314-231-0990.

(This Listing Continued)

HENNESSY & ROACH, P.C., Springfield—Continued

Workers Compensation Defense, including litigation, mediation and arbitration; Liability Defense, including insurance defense, construction accidents, post-structured work act; Employer Liability, retaliatory discharge; Premises Liability, industrial machinery, auto and truck, consumer products; Insurance Coverage, Transportation, Property Damage, Fire Loss, Motor Vehicle Accidents, Industrial Accidents; Civil, State and Federal Appeals, Industrial Commission Appeals.

MANAGING PARTNER

STEPHEN J. KLYCZEK, admitted to bar, 1990, Illinois. *Education:* Northern Illinois University (B.A., cum laude, 1986); Northern Illinois University School of Law (J.D., 1990). ***PRACTICE AREAS:*** Workers Compensation; Insurance Defense; Labor and Employment; Construction Law; General Liability. ***Email:*** sklyczek@hennessyroach.com

---

CHRISSIE L. PETERSON, admitted to bar, 2003, Illinois. *Education:* Knox College (1998); Southern Illinois University School of Law (J.D., 2003). ***PRACTICE AREAS:*** Workers Compensation; Insurance Defense; Labor and Employment; Construction Law. ***Email:*** cpeterson@hennessyroach.com

EMILIE A. MILLER, admitted to bar, 2004, Illinois. *Education:* Eastern Illinois University (1999); Southern Illinois University School of Law (J.D., 2004). ***PRACTICE AREAS:*** Workers Compensation; Insurance Defense; Labor and Employment; Construction Law. ***Email:*** emiller@hennessyroach.com

REPRESENTATIVE CLIENTS: Ace Hardware; Advance Transformer Company; Advantica/Denny's Restaurants; AmCOMP; American Home Products; Arkansas Best; Freightway, Inc.; Armstrong Tools; Autozone; Automobile Club of Southern California; Avis; Bank One; Borg Warner; Brach & Brock Confections; Brownyard Claims; Budget Rent A Car; Cambridge Integrated; Canteen Corporation; Cass Transport; Century Workers' Compensation; Chubb Insurance Company; Cherry Corporation; Celotex Corporation; City of Chicago - Department of Aviation; Clinton Electronics; CNA Insurance Company; Commonwealth Edison; Compass Group; Crawford & Company; Culligan; Cunningham Lindsey; Danville Metal Stamping; Dart Transit; Dominick's Finer Foods; Eagle Foods; Eagle Wings Industries, Inc.; ESIS; EMC Insurance Companies; Employer's Security Insurance; FCCI/Monroe Guaranty Insurance; Federal Mogul; Forest Preserve District of Cook County, Illinois; Frito-Lay, Inc.; GAB Robins; Gates McDonald; Great American Insurance; G&K Services, Inc.; Hendrickson Stamping; Interlake; Jewel Food Stores; Joslyn Corporation; Kelly Temporary Services; Kemper Insurance; Liberty International Canada; Liberty Mutual Insurance Co.; Lucent Technologies; Manufacturers Life Insurance; Company USA; Marshalls; Midwest Insurance Co.; Montgomery Ward; Nabisco; Nestle; USA, Norrell Temporary Services; Northrop Grumman; Omni Super Stores; OSI Corporation; Penske Truck Leasing; Plano Molding Corporation; Prime Trucking; Risk Enterprise; Rollins, Inc.; RSKCo.; Ryerson Tull, Inc.; SBC Ameritech; Schwan's Sales Corporation; Sedgwick CMS; Sentry Insurance; Southwest Airlines, Spartan Light Metal Products, Terminix, T.J. Maxx, Transport Corporation of America; Travelers Insurance Company; Unitrin Property & Casualty Ins.; Universal Underwriters; Walgreens; Ward North America, Inc.; Westfield Insurance Companies; White Way Sign; Witco Corporation; Yellow Freight Systems; Zenith Electronics; Zexel Corporation.

HEYL, ROYSTER, VOELKER & ALLEN

PROFESSIONAL CORPORATION

SUITE 575, NATIONAL CITY CENTER
P.O. BOX 1687
SPRINGFIELD, ILLINOIS 62705
Telephone: 217-522-8822
Telecopier: 217-523-3902
Email: firm@hrva.com
URL: http://www.hrva.com

Peoria, Illinois Office: Suite 600, Chase Building, 124 S.W. Adams, 61602. Telephone: 309-676-0400. Telecopier: 309-676-3374.
Urbana, Illinois Office: Suite 300, 102 East Main Street, P.O. Box 129, 61803-0129. Telephone: 217-344-0060. Telecopier: 217-344-9295.
Rockford, Illinois Office: Second Floor, National City Bank Building, 120 West State Street, P.O. Box 1288, 61105-1288. Telephone: 815-963-4454. Telecopier: 815-963-0399.
Edwardsville, Illinois Office: Suite 100, Mark Twain Plaza II, 103 West Vandalia Street, P.O. Box 467, 62025. Telephone: 618-656-4646. Telecopier: 618-656-7940.

General Civil Trial and Appellate Practice in all Courts, Insurance Defense, Workers' Compensation Defense, Professional Liability Defense, Truck Accidents, Construction Law, Railroad Accidents and Injuries, Insurance Coverage, Self Insured Defense, Products Liability Defense, Civil Rights, Asbestos Defense, Class Action Defense, Corporate Law, Health Care, Banking, Government, Employment, Environmental, Probate, Elder Law, Agribusiness, Immigration, Religious Institutions, Nonprofit and Charitable Organizations, College and University Law, and Real Estate.

PARTNERS

FREDERICK P. VELDE, born December 19, 1946; admitted to bar, 1972, Illinois. *Education:* DePauw University (B.A., 1969); University of Tennessee (J.D., 1972). *Member:* DRI; Federation of Defense and Corporate Counsel; Illinois Association of Defense Trial Counsel; Lawyers Trust Fund of Illinois (President, 1991-1992); Society of Trial Lawyers (Illinois). American Bar Foundation; Illinois Bar Foundation; Lincoln-Douglas Inn of Court (President, 1995-1996). ***PRACTICE AREAS:*** Professional Liability Defense; Insurance Defense; Products Liability Defense; Motor Carrier Defense. ***Email:*** fvelde@hrva.com

GARY L. BORAH, *born April 25, 1949; admitted to bar, 1975, Illinois. Education:* University of Illinois (B.S., 1971); University of Toledo (J.D., 1975). *Member:* American Society of Law, Medicine and Ethics; Illinois Appellate Lawyers Association; Illinois Workers Compensation Lawyers Association. ***PRACTICE AREAS:*** Workers Compensation Defense; Employment Law. ***Email:*** gborah@hrva.com

(This Listing Continued)

GARY S. SCHWAB, born March 10, 1956; admitted to bar, 1981, Illinois and Iowa. *Education:* Illinois Wesleyan University (B.A., summa cum laude, 1978); University of Iowa (J.D., with distinction, 1981). ***PRACTICE AREAS:*** Insurance Agents and Brokers Defense; Insurance Coverage; Civil Litigation Defense. ***Email:*** gschwab@hrva.com

ADRIAN E. HARLESS, born December 17, 1956; admitted to bar, 1982, Illinois. *Education:* University of Illinois (B.S., 1979); St. Louis University (J.D., 1982). *Member:* Illinois Association of Defense Trial Counsel; DRI; Illinois Supreme Court on Pattern Jury Instructions in Civil Cases. ***PRACTICE AREAS:*** Medical Malpractice Defense; Professional Liability Defense; Libel/Slander Defense. ***Email:*** aharless@hrva.com

SCOTT D. SPOONER, born September 28, 1952; admitted to bar, 1981, Illinois. *Education:* Western Illinois University (B.A., summa cum laude, 1977); Drake University (J.D., 1981). Assistant Attorney General, State of Illinois, 1981-1989. ***PRACTICE AREAS:*** Architects and Engineers Liability Defense; Legal Malpractice Defense; Medical Malpractice Defense; Motor Carrier Defense. ***Email:*** sspooner@hrva.com

DANIEL R. SIMMONS, born September 16, 1959; admitted to bar, 1985, Illinois. *Education:* Augustana College (B.A., magna cum laude, 1981); University of Iowa (J.D., 1984). *Member:* Lincoln-Douglas American Inn of Court (President, 2000-2001). ***PRACTICE AREAS:*** Workers Compensation Defense; Civil Litigation Defense. ***Email:*** dsimmons@hrva.com

THERESA M. POWELL, born September 1, 1969; admitted to bar, 1995, Illinois. *Education:* Eastern Illinois University (B.A., summa cum laude, 1991); Southern Illinois University (J.D., cum laude, 1995). *Member:* Illinois Association of Defense Trial Counsel. ***PRACTICE AREAS:*** Medical Malpractice Defense; Professional Liability Defense. ***Email:*** tpowell@hrva.com

OF COUNSEL

SARAH J. PRATT, born January 4, 1960; admitted to bar, 1985, Illinois. *Education:* Illinois College (B.A., summa cum laude, 1982); University of Illinois (J.D., 1985). Assistant Attorney General, State of Illinois, 1985-2003. ***PRACTICE AREAS:*** Workers Compensation Defense; Labor Law; Employment Law; Civil Rights Defense; ADR. ***Email:*** spratt@hrva.com

ASSOCIATES

April G. Troemper ***John O. Langfelder***
Matthew R. Booker ***Peter E. Naylor***

Our lawyers are members of the American, state and local bar associations and, in many cases, are members of the local American Inn of Court chapters; where applicable, leadership positions in these organizations are listed.

(For Other Biographical Information, see Professional Biographies at Peoria, Edwardsville, Rockford and Urbana).

HINSHAW & CULBERTSON LLP

Hinshaw & Culbertson LLP is an Illinois registered limited liability partnership that has elected to be governed by the Illinois Uniform Partnership Act (1997)

Established in 1934

400 SOUTH NINTH STREET, SUITE 200
SPRINGFIELD, ILLINOIS 62701-1908
Telephone: 217-528-7375
Facsimile: 217-528-0075
Telex: 880248
Email: kfox@hinshawlaw.com
URL: http://www.hinshawlaw.com

Other Office Locations: Chicago, Illinois; Appleton, Wisconsin; Belleville, Illinois; Boston, Massachusetts; Champaign, Illinois; Crystal Lake, Illinois; Edwardsville, Illinois; Fort Lauderdale, Florida; Jacksonville, Florida; Joliet, Illinois; Lisle, Illinois; Los Angeles, California; Miami, Florida; Milwaukee, Wisconsin; Minneapolis, Minnesota; New York, New York; Peoria, Illinois; Phoenix, Arizona; Portland, Oregon; Providence, Rhode Island; Rockford, Illinois; St. Louis, Missouri; San Francisco, California; Schererville, Indiana; Tampa, Florida; Waukegan, Illinois.

Appellate, Banking & Financing, Bankruptcy & Creditors' Rights, Class Action Litigation, Civil Rights Defense, Commercial Litigation, Corporate, Construction Law, Director & Officer Liability, Employee Benefits, Environmental, Fidelity & Surety, General Liability Litigation, Government, Health Care, Insurance Coverage, Insurance and Reinsurance, Labor & Employment, Legal Malpractice, Medical Malpractice, Mergers & Acquisitions, Municipal Liability, Personal Injury Defense, Public Law, Products Liability Litigation, Professional Liability, Regulatory, Real Estate, School Law, Securities, Taxation, Transportation, White Collar Crime and Workers' Compensation Defense.

FIRM PROFILE: Hinshaw & Culbertson LLP is a national AMLaw 200 firm with 425 lawyers in 27 offices coast-to-coast. The firm offers a full-service practice, with an emphasis in commercial and defense litigation, corporate, environmental, employment and construction law, as well as the representation of professionals in their liability and risk management matters.

Hinshaw provides services to a range of clients in financial services, construction, health care, not-for-profit, insurance, legal, manufacturing, real estate, transportation and other industries. Firm clients also include government agencies, municipalities and schools.

Hinshaw was founded in 1934. The firm is headquartered in Chicago, and maintains offices in 12 states: Arizona, California, Florida, Illinois, Indiana, Massachusetts, Minnesota, Missouri, New York, Oregon, Rhode Island and Wisconsin.

PARTNERS

D. BRADLEY BLODGETT, born Edwardsville, Illinois, August 9, 1937; admitted to bar, 1962, Illinois; 1972, California; 1973, U.S. District Court, Southern District of Illinois; 1975, U.S. District Court, Central District of Illinois; 1987, U.S. Court of Appeals, Seventh

(This Listing Continued)

Circuit. *Education:* University of Illinois (B.S., 1959; LL.B., 1962). Phi Delta Phi. Assistant State's Attorney, 1966-1972 and First Assistant, 1968-1972, Sangamon County. Corporation Counsel, City of Springfield, 1972-1977. Legal Advisor to President of Illinois State Senate and Assistant Senate Parliamentarian, 76th General Assembly, 1977-1978. *Member:* Sangamon County (President, 1982-1983) and Illinois State Bar Associations; State Bar of California; International Association of Railroad Trial Counsel. ***PRACTICE AREAS:*** Commercial Litigation; Construction Litigation; Personal Injury Litigation; Government Affairs; Appellate. ***Email:*** dblodgett@hinshawlaw.com

EDWARD R. GOWER, born Burlington, Iowa, September 5, 1955; admitted to bar, 1980, Illinois and U.S. District Court, Northern District of Illinois including Trial Bar; 1984, U.S. Court of Appeals, Fourth Circuit. *Education:* DePauw University (B.A., magna cum laude, 1977); University of Virginia (J.D., 1980). Phi Beta Kappa. Special Counsel to the Illinois House Minority Leader, 1986-1987. *Member:* Chicago, Sangamon County and Illinois State Bar Associations. ***PRACTICE AREAS:*** Transportation Law; Government Affairs; Highway Construction Law; Airport Construction Law; Administrative Law. ***Email:*** egower@hinshawlaw.com

EDWARD R. GREEN, born Elgin, Illinois, August 30, 1950; admitted to bar, 1975, Illinois; 1978, U.S. District Court, Central and Southern Districts of Illinois; 1986, U.S. Court of Appeals, Seventh Circuit. *Education:* Knox College (B.A., cum laude, 1972); University of Iowa (J.D., with distinction, 1975). Phi Delta Phi. Assistant Appellate Defender, 1975-1978. *Member:* Sangamon County and Illinois State Bar Associations; Appellate Lawyers Association of Illinois. ***PRACTICE AREAS:*** Government Law; Family Law; Bankruptcy and Creditors' Rights; Commercial Litigation. ***Email:*** egreen@hinshawlaw.com

WILLIAM P. HARDY, born Davenport, Iowa, July 2, 1961; admitted to bar, 1989, Illinois and U.S. District Court, Central District of Illinois; 1990, U.S. Court of Appeals, Seventh Circuit; 1991, U.S. District Court, Southern District of Illinois; 2004, U.S. District Court, Northern District of Illinois. *Education:* Sangamon State University (B.A., 1986); Southern Illinois University (J.D., cum laude, 1989). *Member:* Illinois Association of Defense Attorneys; Illinois Appellate Lawyers Association. ***PRACTICE AREAS:*** Appellate Law; Commercial Litigation; Administrative Law; Class Action Litigation; Workers Compensation Defense. ***Email:*** whardy@hinshawlaw.com

JAMES M. LESTIKOW, born Chicago Heights, Illinois, September 8, 1948; admitted to bar, 1973, Illinois and U.S. District Court, Central District of Illinois; 1978, U.S. Supreme Court. *Education:* Northern Illinois University (B.S., 1970); University of Illinois (J.D., 1973); DePaul University (Certificate, Mediation Training, 2003). Speaker, "Handling Illiquid Assets in Trusts", 48th IICLE Estate Planning Short Course (2005). General Editor, "Estate Planning for Illinois Lawyers: The Basics and Beyond," Illinois Institute for Continuing Legal Education, 2001 and 2005. Member and Past Chair, Sangamon Valley Estate Planning Council. Founding Advisory Board Member, Central Illinois Family Business Forum, 1998. Member, Standing Advisory Board for Estate Planning, IICLE. Director and Treasurer, Illinois Bar Foundation. Director and Vice Chair, Greater Springfield Chamber of Commerce. *Member:* Sangamon County, Illinois State (Member and Past Chair: Trusts and Estates Section Council; Business Advice and Financial Planning Section Council) and American (Member, Real Property, Probate and Trust Law and Alternative Dispute Resolution Sections) Bar Associations. Fellow, American College of Trust and Estate Counsel. Charter Fellow, Illinois Bar Foundation. ***PRACTICE AREAS:*** Estate Planning; Business Advice; Commercial Real Estate. ***Email:*** jlestikow@hinshawlaw.com

JOHN E. NOLAN, born 1966; admitted to bar, 1991, Illinois; 1992, U.S. District Court, Central District of Illinois; 2002, U.S. Court of Appeals, Seventh Circuit. *Education:* Southern Methodist University (B.A., 1988); St. Louis University (J.D., 1991). ***PRACTICE AREAS:*** Employment Litigation; Civil Rights Defense; Personal Injury Litigation; Toxic Tort; Administrative; Professional Liability Litigation; General Liability Litigation; Appellate. ***Email:*** jnolan@hinshawlaw.com

ANDREW M. RAMAGE, born Mattoon, Illinois, 1971; admitted to bar, 1998, Illinois and U.S. District Court, Southern, Central and Northern Districts of Illinois; 1999, U.S. Court of Appeals, Seventh Circuit; 2001, Trial Bar, U.S. District Court, Northern District of Illinois. *Education:* Eastern Illinois University (B.A., Political Science, 1993; M.A., Political Science, 1994); Southern Illinois University (J.D., 1998). Recipient, Dean's List. Member, National Trial Advocacy Team, The Association of Trial Lawyers of America. Articles Editor, Southern Illinois Law Journal, 1997-1998. Member, Association of Trial Lawyers of America, 1998-1999. Assistant Attorney General, March 1999-May 2001. Member, Board of Trustees, Lincoln Land Community College. Board Member, Springfield Parks Foundation. *Member:* Sangamon County Bar Association; Illinois State Bar Association; Federal Bar Association for the Central and Southern Districts of Illinois; American Inn of Court (Member, Lincoln-Douglas Chapter). ***REPORTED CASES:*** Walker v. Benjamin, 100 F. Supp. 2d 901 (C.D. Ill. 2000); Predmore v. Schwartz, 141 F. Supp. 2d 1150 (C.D. Ill. 2001); Stone v. Sangamon County, 168 F. Supp. 2d 925 (C.D. Ill. 2001); Hanke v. American Intern. South Ins. Co., 335 Ill. App. 3d 1164, 782 N.E.2d 328 (2002); Prairie Eye Center v. Butler, 329 Ill. App. 3d 293, 768 N.E.2d 414 (4th Dist. 2002); Bond v. Aguinaldo, 256 F. Supp. 2d 810 (N.D. Ill. 2003); Bond v. Aguinaldo, 265 F. Supp. 2d 926 (N.D. Ill. 2003). ***PRACTICE AREAS:*** Administrative and Governmental Law; Commercial Litigation; Civil Rights Defense; Class Actions; Labor and Employment; School Law. ***Email:*** aramage@hinshawlaw.com

RUSSELL L. REED, born Taylorville, Illinois, November 3, 1961; admitted to bar, 1987, Illinois and U.S. District Court, Northern, Southern and Central Districts of Illinois. *Education:* Illinois State University (B.S., 1984); Northern Illinois University (J.D., 1987). Delta Theta Phi. *Member:* Sangamon County Bar Association (President, 1997); Illinois State Bar Association; Illinois Association of Defense Counsel; Defense Research Institute (Member, Medical Liability Committee); American Business Club; Lincoln-Douglas Inn of Courts. ***PRACTICE AREAS:*** Medical Malpractice; Legal Ethics and Professional Responsibility Liability; Professional Liability; Insurance Defense; Insurance Coverage. ***Email:*** rreed@hinshawlaw.com

J. WILLIAM ROBERTS, admitted to bar, 1968, Illinois and U.S. District Court, Central District of Illinois; 1969, U.S. Court of Appeals, Seventh Circuit; 1978, U.S. Supreme Court; 2001, U.S. District Court, Northern and Southern Districts of Illinois. *Education:* Illinois Wesleyan University (B.A., 1964); Washington University (J.D., 1967). Managing Partner, Hinshaw & Culbertson LLP, 1997—. Chief Legal Counsel to Illinois Governor Jim Edgar, 1995-1997. U.S. Attorney, Central District of Illinois, 1986-1993. U.S. Attorney General's Advisory Committee of U.S. Attorneys (Chairman, 1991-1992. Senior Advisory to the Attorney General in Washington, D.C., 1991-1992. State's Attorney of Sangamon County, 1979-1986. Assistant U.S. Attorney, Central District of Illinois, 1968-1972. *Member:* Sangamon County (President, 1983) and Illinois State (Member, Board of Governors, 1994-2000; Chair, Criminal Justice Section Council, 1984-1985) Bar Associations; National District Attorneys Association (Board of Directors, 1982-1986). (Also at Chicago, Illinois Office). ***PRACTICE AREAS:*** Complex Civil and Criminal Litigation; Criminal Defense; Government Relations; Corporate Compliance Law. ***Email:*** broberts@hinshawlaw.com

CHARLES R. SCHMADEKE, born Blue Island, Illinois, November 15, 1952; admitted to bar, 1977, Illinois and U.S. District Court, Northern District of Illinois; 1984, U.S. Court of Appeals, Seventh Circuit and U.S. Supreme Court; 1988, U.S. District Court, Central District of Illinois; 1989, U.S. District Court, Southern District of Illinois. *Education:* Northern Illinois University (B.A, 1974); John Marshall Law School (J.D., 1977). Phi Delta Phi. Member, John Marshall Journal, 1975-1977. Order of John Marshall. *Member:* Illinois State and Sangamon County Bar Associations; Federal Bar Association for the Central and Southern Districts of Illinois. ***PRACTICE AREAS:*** Administrative Law; Public Law; Civil Rights Defense; Employment Litigation; Government; School Law; Commercial Litigation. ***Email:*** cschmadeke@hinshawlaw.com

ASSOCIATE

RAYLENE DeWITTE GRISCHOW, born Kewanee, Illinois, January 21, 1972; admitted to bar, 1999, Illinois and U.S. District Court, Southern District of Illinois; 2001, Colorado and U.S. District Court, District of Colorado; 2002, U.S. District Court, Central District of Illinois. *Education:* Illinois State University (B.S., 1994); Washington University School of Law, St. Louis (J.D., 1998). *Member:* Illinois State Bar Association; Colorado Bar Association; Sangamon County Bar Association (Treasurer, Young Lawyers Division); Illinois Association of Defense Trial Counsel; Central Illinois Woman's Bar Association (Vice-President). ***PRACTICE AREAS:*** Medical Malpractice; Legal Malpractice; Professional Liability Litigation; Personal Injury Litigation; Workers Compensation Defense. ***Email:*** rgrischow@hinshawlaw.com

HODGE DWYER ZEMAN

3150 ROLAND AVENUE
P.O. BOX 5776
SPRINGFIELD, ILLINOIS 62705-5776
Telephone: 217-523-4900
Facsimile: 217-523-4948
URL: http://www.hdzlaw.com

Environmental Law.

FIRM PROFILE: The focus of Hodge Dwyer Zeman's practice is to assist companies in compliance with the increasingly complex maze of environmental laws and regulations. The firm represents clients in all phases of compliance counseling, permitting including landfill sitting, and when necessary, litigation before State and Federal courts and environmental agencies.

MEMBERS OF FIRM

EDWARD W. DWYER, admitted to bar, 1988, Illinois and U.S. District Court, Central District of Illinois; 1989, U.S. District Court, Northern District of Illinois including Trial Bar and Southern District of Illinois. *Education:* University of Arizona (B.A., 1982); Southern Illinois University (J.D., 1987).

KATHERINE D. HODGE, admitted to bar, 1986, Illinois; 1991, U.S. Court of Appeals, Seventh Circuit and U.S. District Court, Central District of Illinois. *Education:* Florida State University (B.S., 1982); Southern Illinois University (J.D., 1986).

CHRISTINE G. ZEMAN, admitted to bar, 1979, Illinois and U.S. District Court, Central District of Illinois. *Education:* University of Illinois (B.A., 1974); Southern Illinois University (J.D., 1979).

N. LaDONNA DRIVER, admitted to bar, 1994, Illinois and U.S. District Court, Central District of Illinois; 1996, U.S. Court of Appeals, Seventh Circuit. *Education:* Rhodes College (B.A., 1990); Southern Illinois University (J.D., magna cum laude, 1994).

THOMAS G. SAFLEY, admitted to bar, 1995, Indiana and U.S. District Court, Northern and Southern Districts of Indiana; 1996, U.S. Court of Appeals, Seventh Circuit; 1999, U.S. District Court, Central District of Illinois; 2000, Illinois; 2001, U.S. District Court, Southern District of Illinois. *Education:* University of Missouri, Columbia (B.A., cum laude and departmental honors, 1992); University of Iowa (J.D., special honors/with distinction, 1995). Phi Beta Kappa.

ASSOCIATES

GALE W. NEWTON, admitted to bar, 2001, Delaware; 2004, Illinois. *Education:* University of Illinois at Springfield (B.A., with high honors, 1991; M.A., 1992); Cornell University Law School (J.D., 2001).

JEANNE B. HEATON, admitted to bar, 1988, Illinois. *Education:* University of Illinois, Urbana-Champaign (B.A., 1980) Phi Beta Kappa; Indiana University School of Law (J.D., cum laude, 1988).

MONICA T. RIOS, admitted to bar, 2004, Illinois. *Education:* Central Michigan University (B.S., summa cum laude, 2000); American University (J.D., cum laude, 2004).

RYAN E. MOHR, admitted to bar, 2005, Illinois. *Education:* Southern Illinois University, Carbondale (B.A., 1999); Southern Illinois University, Edwardsville (M.S., cum laude, 2003); St. Louis University School of Law (J.D., 2005).

(This Listing Continued)

HODGE DWYER ZEMAN, Springfield—Continued

OF COUNSEL

JAMES R. SCHICK, admitted to bar, 1975, Illinois. *Education:* University of Illinois, Urbana-Champaign and Chicago, IL (B.A., High Honors, 1972; J.D., 1975). Phi Beta Kappa.

HOLLEY & ROSEN

440 WEST SOUTH GRAND AVENUE
SPRINGFIELD, ILLINOIS 62704
Telephone: 217-544-3368; Toll Free: 1-888-828-9037
Fax: 217-544-5262
URL: http://www.holleyrosenlaw.com
Email: hr@holleyrosenlaw.com
URL: http://www.lawyers.com/holleyrosen

Mailing Address: P.O. Box 5036, Springfield, IL 62705

General Civil Trial and Appellate Practice in State and Federal Courts, Plaintiff Personal Injury, Insurance Defense, Plaintiffs Medical Malpractice, Employment Discrimination, Mediation/Arbitration, Workers Compensation, Automobile Accidents, Dog Bites, Slip and Fall, Wrongful Death.

MEMBERS OF FIRM

GRADY E. HOLLEY, born Springfield, Missouri, October 22, 1946; admitted to bar, 1970, Illinois and U.S. District Court, Central District of Illinois; 1973, U.S. Court of Appeals, Seventh Circuit; 1975, U.S. Supreme Court; 1989, U.S. District Court, Northern District of Illinois including Trial Bar. *Education:* University of Illinois (B.S., 1967; J.D., 1970); University of Missouri. Chairman, 1991-1995 and Member, Springfield Election Commission, 1996—, Springfield Housing Authority. *Member:* Sangamon County and Illinois State Bar Associations; The Association of Trial Lawyers of America; Illinois Trial Lawyers Association. Fellow, Illinois Bar Foundation. ***PRACTICE AREAS:*** Litigation; Civil Practice; Trial Practice; Construction Litigation; Civil Rights.

STEVEN J. ROSEN, born Chicago, Illinois, July 5, 1965; admitted to bar, 1990, Illinois; 1994, U.S. District Court, Central District of Illinois and U.S. Court of Appeals, Seventh Circuit. *Education:* University of Illinois (B.A., 1987); Washington University (J.D., 1990). Pi Sigma Alpha. Recipient, American Jurisprudence Award for UCC Article 2; Sales. *Member:* Sangamon County and Illinois State Bar Associations; The Association of Trial Lawyers of America. ***PRACTICE AREAS:*** Personal Injury; Workers Compensation; Labor and Employment; Drivers License Reinstatement.

ASSOCIATE

PETER C. BEARD, born Springfield, Illinois, February 19, 1969; admitted to bar, 1997, Illinois; 1998, U.S. District Court, Central District of Illinois; 1999, U.S. District Court, Southern District of Illinois. *Education:* Bradley University (B.A., 1991); Southern Illinois University (J.D., 1997). Assistant State's Attorney, Sangamon County, 1997-1999; Assistant Attorney General, Illinois, 1999-2000. *Member:* Sangamon County, Illinois State and American Bar Associations. ***PRACTICE AREAS:*** Personal Injury; Civil Litigation; Criminal Law; Traffic Violations; DUI.

HOWARD & HOWARD ATTORNEYS, P.C.

SPRINGFIELD, ILLINOIS

(See Peoria)

Administrative, Business, Commercial, Corporate, Creditors Rights, Education, Employee Benefits, Environmental, Financial Institutions, Government Relations, Immigration, Intellectual Property (Patents, Trademarks, Copyrights, and Gaming), Labor and Employment, Litigation, Probate, Public Finance, Real Estate, Securities, Taxation (Federal, State and Local), Trusts and Estates.

KELTY LAW OFFICES

SPRINGFIELD, ILLINOIS

(See Armstrong Teasdale LLP)

LAW OFFICE OF KERLEY & ASSOCIATES, P.C.

2131 W. WHITE OAK DRIVE, SUITE B2
SPRINGFIELD, ILLINOIS 62704
Telephone: 217-698-0007
Fax: 217-726-0006
Email: lawyerjohn@aol.com
URL: http://www.johnkerleylawfirm.com

Collections, Estate Planning, Probate, Employment, Contested Estates, Business Advise, Financial Planning, Commercial Litigation, Insurance Coverage, Insurance Defense, Business Law, Commercial Law, Insurance, Real Estate Agents and Brokers Errors and Omissions, Personal Injury, Real Estate.

JOHN E. KERLEY, born Benton, Illinois, October 8, 1960; admitted to bar, 1989, Illinois and U.S. District Court, Central District of Illinois; 1990, U.S. Court of Appeals, Seventh Circuit; 1999, U.S. District Court, Southern District of Illinois. *Education:* Southern Illinois University (B.S., 1983; J.D., cum laude, 1989). Law Review. Board of Editors, Southern Illinois University Law Journal, 1989. Author: Comment, "Future Interests-Remainders-Status of Implied Conditions of Survivorship in Illinois 12.S. ILL. U.L.J 131

(This Listing Continued)

(1998); Case Note: Constitutional Law-Christian Science Malpractice-Illinois Appellate Court Commands: "Thou Shalt Not Interfere With Faith Healers" 13.S. ILL. U. L.J. 411 (1989). *Member:* Sangamon County and Illinois State Bar Associations (Member, Insurance Law Section Council). ***PRACTICE AREAS:*** Commercial Litigation; Insurance Coverage; Insurance Defense; Business Law; Commercial Law; Insurance Agents and Brokers Errors and Omissions; Personal Injury; Estates; Probate; Real Estate. ***Email:*** lawyerjohn@aol.com

KOEPKE & HILTABRAND, P.C.

2050 WEST ILES, SUITE G
SPRINGFIELD, ILLINOIS 62704
Telephone: 217-726-8646
Fax: 217-726-8861

General Civil Trial and Appellate Practice in all Courts, Insurance Defense, Workers' Compensation Defense, Professional Liability Defense, Insurance Coverage, Self Insured Defense, Employment/Discrimination Defense.

FIRM PROFILE: The law firm of Koepke & Hiltabrand is a newly organized progressive law firm specializing in all aspects of civil litigation defense including, workers' compensation and employment law.

KURT M. KOEPKE, born Prairie du Chien, Wisconsin, July 29, 1961; admitted to bar, 1988, Illinois and U.S. District Court, Central District of Illinois; 1989, U.S. Court of Appeals, Seventh Circuit. *Education:* Western Illinois University (B.A., Political Science, 1983); Southern Illinois University School of Law (J.D., 1988). Faculty Member, Illinois Institute of Continuing Legal Education. Author: "Providing Fault in Automobile Cases: Across the Center Line," Illinois Institute for Continuing Legal Education, 2002. Presentations: Medical Disposition Preparation, Worker's Compensation Claims, Illinois Institute for Continuing Legal Education, January 14, 2004. *Member:* Sangamon County, Illinois State and American Bar Associations; Adjuster Association of Central Illinois. ***REPORTED CASES:*** SUPREME COURT: Bubb v. Springfield School District; Webster v. Hartman, Eads v. Heritage Enterprises, Inc. APPELLATE COURT: Sunderland v. Tri-City Community Unit School District 1; State Street Bank & Trust Co. of Quincy; Illinois v. INA Insurance Company of Illinois; Watson v. J.C. Penney; GTE North, Inc. v. Henkels & McCoy, Inc.; Clinton Price v. Industrial Commission. JURY TRIAL: Schwab v. Honey Bend; Camile v. Logan; Krueger v. Trader; Bishop v. Jones; Reynolds v. Killian; Vancil v. Grant; Homa v. Jordan; Hatten v. Branson; Champley v. Camatti; Bales b. Digirolamo, Voss v. Zoelzer, et al; Cavage v. Roof; Smith v. MacMurray College and Arnie Charron; Osborne v. Belcher; Goodrich v. Thornley; Burdine v. Bridgestone/Firestone; Schnapp v. Vern's Chatham 66; Rossmiller v. Hamilton; Buchanan v. Kirchner; Whitlock v. Brennan; Felchner v. Van Proyen; Sides v. Moorman; Redland Insurance v. Newingham; Pedigo v. Miller. ***PRACTICE AREAS:*** General Liability Defense; Professional Negligence; Premises Liability; Construction Litigation; Products Liability; Automobile Liability; Workers Compensation; Subrogation. ***Email:*** kkoepke@koepkelaw.net

LORI POPPE HILTABRAND, born Fairbury, Illinois, February 19, 1969; admitted to bar, 1997, Illinois and U.S. District Court, Central District of Illinois. *Education:* Illinois Wesleyan University (B.A., Political Science, 1991); Southern Illinois University School of Law (J.D., cum laude, 1997). Presentation: "Arising Out of and in the Course of Employment," Addus Healthcare Management (September 15, 2004); "How to Conduct a Deposition from a Respondent's Point of View," IICLE Seminar on Worker's Compensation Law (January 2004); "Employer's Perspective on Employment Discrimination, FMLA, ADA and Worker's Compensation," Lorman Seminar (Fall 2002). Co-Author: "Across the Center Line," ICLE Supplement on Proving Fault in Automobile Cases, Illinois Institute for Continuing Legal Education (2002). Faculty Member, Illinois Institute of Continuing Education. Vice President, Adjuster's Association of Central Illinois. *Member:* Sangamon County, Illinois State and American Bar Associations. ***REPORTED CASES:*** ARBITRATION DECISIONS: Bolin v. Dermatology Center; Mammen v. Shell Air Jiffy; Williams v. ServPro; Hagene v. Construx of Illinoise; Rodden v. Christian Farm Supply; Burdell v. Community Healthcare; Marvell Kirkwood v. Bemco Mattress; Roger Heffron v. Super Gas America; Donald Watson v. K-Bowl. JURY TRIALS: Robinson v. Standfer Lawn Care and Scaduto Properties; Glasscock v. Shop N Save; Shirly v. Trendler. FEDERAL COURT CASES: Fafoglia v. Springfield School District 186, U.S. Dist. Federsl Court, Central District of Illinois. ***PRACTICE AREAS:*** Workers Compensation Defense; Automobile Liability Defense; Employment Law; General Liability; Premises Liability Defense; Products Liability; Subrogation. ***Email:*** lhiltabrand@koepkelaw.net

---

JOSHUA J. ISHMAEL, born Taylorville, Illinois, June 14, 1978; admitted to bar, 2004, Illinois. *Education:* University of Illinois, Urbana-Champaign (B.A., 2001); Southern Illinois University, Carbondale (J.D., 2004). Member, Adjuster Association of Central Illinois. *Member:* Sangamon County and Illinois State Bar Associations. ***PRACTICE AREAS:*** Workers Compensation Defense; Automobile Liability Defense; General Liability Defense; Premises Liability Defense; Subrogation. ***Email:*** jishmael@koepkelaw.net

REPRESENTATIVE CLIENTS: A2 Transport, Inc.; Amica Mutual Insurance Company; Cincinnati Insurance; Farmers Insurance Group; Foremost Insurance Company; Hinz Claim Management, Inc.; Illinois Guaranty Fund; MetLife Auto & Home; Midwest Insurance companies; Pekin Insurance Company; Pemco Service Company; Rockford Mutual Insurance company; State Farm Mutual Automobile Insurance Company; Zenith Insurance Companies.

LAW OFFICES OF NOLAN LIPSKY

1100 S. 5TH STREET
SPRINGFIELD, ILLINOIS 62703
Telephone: 217-789-1607
Toll Free: 888-662-2612
URL: http://www.nolanlipsky.com

Petersburg Office: 106 East Jackson Street, 62675. Telephone: 217-632-2612. Fax: 217-532-2450.

(This Listing Continued)

Family Law, Divorce, Custody, Paternity, Personal Injury, Criminal.

(for comlete biographical data on personel, see Professional Biograhies at Petersburg)

LAW OFFICE OF MICHAEL J. LOGAN, LTD.

837 S. 4TH STREET
P.O. BOX 3163
SPRINGFIELD, ILLINOIS 62708
Telephone: 217-522-8880
Fax: 217-522-8887
URL: http://www.lawyers.com/mikelogan

Personal Injury, Workers Compensation, General Practice.

MICHAEL J. LOGAN, admitted to bar, 1972, Illinois. *Education:* MacMurray College (B.A., 1965); John Marshall Law School (J.D., 1971). ***PRACTICE AREAS:*** Bankruptcy; Workers Compensation Law.

LONDRIGAN, POTTER & RANDLE, P.C.

Established in 1970

1227 SOUTH 7TH STREET
P.O. BOX 399
SPRINGFIELD, ILLINOIS 62705
Telephone: 217-544-9823
Telecopier: 217-544-9826
URL: http://www.lprpc.com
Email: lpr@lprpc.com
URL: http://www.lawyers.com/lprpc

General, Trial and Appellate Practice. Insurance, Negligence, Products Liability, Medical Malpractice, Employment Discrimination, Corporation and Antitrust Law.

FIRM PROFILE: The firm was founded in 1970 by Thomas F. Londrigan and James R. Potter specializing in corporate and commercial practice and civil litigation. The firm expanded with the addition of Craig A. Randle in 1975 followed by Alexandra de Saint Phalle in 1977. In 2003, the firm merged with the law firm of Londrigan & Londrigan during which time Timothy J. Londrigan joined the firm as a partner and James T. Londrigan joined the firm as of-counsel. In 2004, Douglas J. Quivey joined the firm followed by Carissa A. Mahr. The firm concentrates its practice in primarily two areas: significant personal injury and death claims involving automobile defects and products liability, medical and other professional negligence, and the representation of commercial clients with regard to business structures and the litigation of contract and other commercial disputes.

THOMAS F. LONDRIGAN, born Springfield, Illinois, May 10, 1937; admitted to bar, 1962, Illinois. *Education:* University of Notre Dame (A.B., 1959); University of Wisconsin and University of Illinois (LL.B., 1962). Assistant U.S. Attorney, 1963-1965. Law Clerk, 4th District, Appellate Court, 1965-1966. Attorney's Information Exchange Group (Board Member, Executive Committee Member, 1980—). *Member:* Sangamon County, Illinois State (Chairman: Civil Practice Procedure Section Council, 1973-1974; Co-Chairman Uniform Circuit Court, Rules Committee, 1973-1978; Special Committee on Offer of Judgment, 1984-1985) and American (Member: Tort and Insurance Practice Section; Commission to Improve Tort Liability System, 1987-1990; Chairman, Medicine and Law Committee 1986-1987) Bar Associations; American College of Law and Medicine (Member, 1991—); Illinois Trial Lawyers Association (Member, Board of Directors, 1974-1980; President, 1983-1984); The Association of Trial Lawyers of America (Member, Board of Directors, 1986-1989); American College of Trial Lawyers (Member, 1985—). Fellow: International Academy of Trial Lawyers. ***REPORTED CASES:*** Sherman v. City of Springfield, 111 Ill.App.2d 391, 250 N.E.2d 537 (4th Dist. 1969); Churchill vs. Norfolk & Western Railway Company, 73 Ill.2d 127, 383 N.E.2d 929 (1978); Contractor Utility Sales Co., Inc. vs. Certain-Teed Corporation, 748 F.2d 1151 (1984); Ballweg vs. City of Springfield, 114 Ill.2d 107, 499 N.E.2d 1273 (1986); Miller vs. Solaglas California, Inc., 870 P.2d 559 (Colo. App. 1993); May v. Central Illinois Public Service Co., 260 Ill.App.3d 41, 633 N.E.2d 97, 198 Ill.Dec 635 (5th Dist., Nov. 4, 1994); Donaldson v. Central Illinois Public Service, Co., 191 Ill.2d 528, 738 N.E.2d 925, 250 Ill. Dec. 456 (2002). ***PRACTICE AREAS:*** Personal Injury; Product Liability; Civil Trials and Appeals; Professional Negligence. ***Email:*** tom@lprpc.com

JAMES R. POTTER, born Springfield, Illinois, March 12, 1940; admitted to bar, 1966, Illinois and Iowa. *Education:* Knox College (B.A., 1963); University of Iowa (J.D., 1966); University of Chicago (M.B.A., 1979). Phi Delta Phi. *Member:* Illinois State and American Bar Associations; Illinois Trial Lawyers Association. ***PRACTICE AREAS:*** Corporate Law; Finance; General Litigation. ***Email:*** bud@digitalgroup.net

CRAIG A. RANDLE, born Belleville, Illinois, July 18, 1949; admitted to bar, 1974, Illinois. *Education:* Southern Illinois University (B.A., 1971); University of Illinois (J.D., *1974). Phi Alpha Delta. Member:* Illinois Supreme Court Pattern Jury Instruction Committee, 1987-1996; Institute for Injury Reduction, 1991—. *Member:* Sangamon County, Illinois State and American Bar Associations; Illinois Trial Lawyers Association (Board of Managers). ***PRACTICE AREAS:*** Civil Trials and Appeals. ***Email:*** crandle@lprpc.com

ALEXANDRA DE SAINT PHALLE, born Philadelphia, Pennsylvania, August 5, 1951; admitted to bar, 1977, Illinois. *Education:* University of Chicago (B.A., cum laude, 1973; M.A., 1974); Indiana University (J.D., cum laude, 1977). Speaker, Liens, Illinois Trial Lawyers Association Seminar, 2003. *Member:* Sangamon County, Illinois State and American Bar Associations; Illinois Trial Lawyers Association; The Association of Trial Lawyers of America. ***REPORTED CASES:*** Roach v. Springfield Clinic, 157 Ill. 2d 29, 623 N.E.2d 246 (1993); Wilsey vs. Eddingfield, 780 F.2d 614, cert. den. 475 U.S.1130 (J.

(This Listing Continued)

White, Brennan and Marshall dissenting from denial of cert.); Loyd vs. Phillips Bros., 25 F3d 518 (1995). ***PRACTICE AREAS:*** Medical Malpractice; Civil Trials; Employment Discrimination. ***Email:*** alex@digitalgroup.net

TIMOTHY J. LONDRIGAN, born Springfield, Illinois, December 6, 1957; admitted to bar, 1983, Illinois and U.S. District Court, Central and Southern Districts of Illinois; U.S. Court of Appeals, Seventh Circuit; U.S. Supreme Court. *Education:* Southern Illinois University (B.S., with honors, 1980; J.D., 1983). *Member:* Sangamon County and Illinois State (Assemblyman, 1994-1997; Member, ITLA Board of Advocates, 2004—) Bar Associations; Illinois Trial Lawyers Association; American Trial Lawyers Association. ***REPORTED CASES:*** Potts v. Illinois Dept. of Registration and Educ., 128 Ill.2d 322, 538 N.E.2d 1140, 131 Ill.Dec. 584 (Ill.Apr 20, 1989) (NO. 66739); Mount Zion State Bank & Trust v. Consolidated Communications, Inc., 169 Ill.2d 110, 660 N.F.2d 863, 214 Ill.Dec. 156 (Ill. Nov 02, 1995) (NO. 78178); Nelson v. Board of Trustees of Police Pension Fund of City of Springfield, 141 Ill.App.3d 411, 490 N.E.2d 216, 95 Ill.Dec. 743 (Ill.App. 4 Dist. Mar 05, 1986) (NO. 4-85-0448). ***PRACTICE AREAS:*** Personal Injury; Products Liability; Insurance Bad Faith; Professional Negligence; Civil Appeals. ***Email:*** tim@lprpc.com

DOUGLAS J. QUIVEY, born DeKalb, Illinois, April 10, 1965; admitted to bar, 1994, Illinois; 1995, Colorado, U.S. Supreme Court, U.S. Court of Appeals, Seventh Circuit and U.S. District Court, Central, Northern and Southern Districts of Illinois. *Education:* Eastern Illinois University (B.A., 1986; M.A., 1991); University of Illinois (J.D., magna cum laude, 1994). Notes and Comments Editor, University of Illinois Law Review, 1993-1994. Law Clerk for the Honorable Richard Mills, U.S. District Court Judge, 1994-1996. Author: "Market-Oriented Approach to Determining Drug Quantity Under the Federal Sentencing Guidelines," University of Illinois Law Review, Vol. 1993, Issue 3. *Member:* Illinois State and American Bar Associations; Bar Association Central and Southern Federal Districts of Illinois; Illinois Trial Lawyers Association; The Association of Trial Lawyers of America; Reserve Officers Association. [1st Lt., U.S. Army, 1986-1990; Maj., U.S. Army Reserve 1990—]. ***REPORTED CASES:*** United States v. Coe, 220 F.3d 573 (7th Cir. 2000); Stevens v. Illinois Depatment of Transportation, 210 F.3d 732 (7th Cir. 2000); People v. Fowler, 298 Ill. App. 3d 706; 700 N.E.2d 216, 233 Ill Dec. 115 (4th Dist. 1998); Swearingen v. Industrial Commission, 298 Ill. App. 3d 666, 699 N.E.2d 237, 232 Ill. Dec.790 (5th Dist. 1998). ***PRACTICE AREAS:*** Civil Trials and Appeals; Commercial Litigation; Employment Discrimination; Personal Injury; White Collar Crime; Criminal Defense. ***Email:*** doug@lprpc.com

CARISSA A. HANING, born Canton, Illinois, September 13, 1975; admitted to bar, 2003, Illinois. *Education:* Monmouth College (B.A., 1996); Illinois University School of Law (J.D., 2000). *Member:* Sangamon County, Illinois State and American Bar Associations; Illinois Trial Lawyers Association; American Trial Lawyers Association. ***REPORTED CASES:*** Borrowman vs Prastein 356 Ill.App.3d 546; 826 N.E.2d 600; 292 Ill-.Dec. 459 (4th Dist. 2005). ***PRACTICE AREAS:*** Civil Trials; Appeals; Personal Injury. ***Email:*** carissa@lprpc.com

OF COUNSEL

JAMES T. LONDRIGAN, born Springfield, Illinois, February 23, 1925; admitted to bar, 1950, Illinois. *Education:* University of Illinois; Chicago-Kent College of Law, Illinois Institute of Technology (J.D., 1949). Phi Delta Phi. Illinois State Representative, 1969-1976. Circuit Court Judge, Illinois, 1976-1981. Justice of Illinois Appellate Court, 1981-1982. *Member:* Sangamon County and Illinois State Bar Associations. ***PRACTICE AREAS:*** Personal Injury; Negligence; Wills; Trusts and Estates.

REPRESENTATIVE CLIENTS: American Central Financial Group; CCB Credit Services, Inc.; Kerasotes Theaters, Inc.; Midwest Gland Pack, Inc.; Oil Filter Recyclers, Inc.; Prairie Analytical Systems, Inc.; American Central BanCorp, Inc.; P.H. Broughton & Sons, Inc.; Perry Broughton Trucking & Excavating, Inc.
REFERENCES: Prairie State Bank & Trust, Springfield, Illinois; Bank One, Springfield, Illinois; Springfield Marine Bank, Springfield, Illinois.

McNAMARA & EVANS

Established in 1972

931 SOUTH FOURTH STREET
P.O. BOX 5039
SPRINGFIELD, ILLINOIS 62705
Telephone: 217-528-8476
Telecopier: 217-528-8480
Email: mcnamara.evans@springnetl.com
URL: http://www.mcnamaraevens.com

Edwardsville, Illinois Office: 21 Glen-Ed Professional Park. Telephone: 618-656-3511; Telecopier: 618-656-3534.

General Civil, Trial and Appellate Practice in State and Federal Courts. Administrative Practice before Governmental Agencies. Corporation, Insurance, Probate and Real Estate Law. Administrative and Governmental Law. Computer, Environmental, Franchise and Health Law. Public Utilities, Motor Carrier and Interstate Commerce Law.

MEMBER OF FIRM

EDWARD D. McNAMARA, JR., born Springfield, Illinois, March 13, 1943; admitted to bar, 1968, Illinois; 1969, U.S. District Court, Eastern District of Illinois; 1972, U.S. Supreme Court and U.S. District Court, Southern District of Illinois. *Education:* St. Louis University (B.S., 1965); University of Illinois College of Law (J.D., 1968). Phi Delta Phi. Assistant State's Attorney of Vermilion County, Illinois, 1968-1969. Member, Illinois State Bar Association—Chicago Bar Association Joint Committee on Illinois Commerce Commission Rules of Practice, 1978-1982. *Member:* Vermilion County, Sangamon County, Illinois State (Member and Vice Chairman, 1978-1979; Chairman, 1979-1980, Section on Public Utilities and Transportation Law) and American Bar Associations; The Association of Trial Lawyers of America; Illinois Trial Lawyers Association; Motor Carrier Lawyers Association. ***PRACTICE AREAS:*** Litigation; Motor Carrier; Public Utilities Law.

(This Listing Continued)

McNAMARA & EVANS, Springfield—Continued

OF COUNSEL

VERNE H. EVANS, born Hartford City, Indiana, 1937; admitted to bar, 1963, Illinois; 1966, U.S. District Court, Northern District of Illinois; 1969, U.S. Court of Appeals, Seventh Circuit; 1984, U.S. Tax Court; 1985, U.S. District Court, Central District of Illinois; 1988, U.S. Court of Appeals for the Federal Circuit; 1991, U.S. District Court, Southern District of Illinois. *Education:* Wheaton College (B.S., 1959); Northwestern University (J.D., 1962). Phi Delta Phi. Counsel, Illinois Bureau of the Budget, 1971. General Counsel, Illinois Department of Public Aid, 1972-1979. *Member:* Sangamon County and Illinois State Bar Associations. ***PRACTICE AREAS:*** Litigation; Administrative Law; Corporation Law; Franchise Law; Health Law.

REPRESENTATIVE CLIENTS: Golden Rule Life Insurance Co.; Nussbaum Trucking, Inc. Sarti Architectural Group, Inc.; Peoria Charter Coach Co.; Care Information Systems, Inc.; Realty Executives, Inc.; Health Care Informatics, Inc.
REFERENCE: Bank One.

METNICK, CHERRY, FRAZIER & SABIN, L.L.P.

Established in 1983

SECOND FLOOR, MYERS BUILDING
1 WEST OLD STATE CAPITOL PLAZA
P.O. BOX 12140
SPRINGFIELD, ILLINOIS 62791
Telephone: 217-753-4242
Telefax: 217-753-4642
URL: http://www.springfieldlawfirm.com
Email: info@springfieldlawfirm.com
URL: http://www.lawyers.com/springfieldlawfirm

General Trial and Appellate Practice. Criminal Defense, Workers Compensation, Personal Injury, Family Law, Labor and Employment Law, Estate Planning, Business Law.

MEMBERS OF FIRM

MICHAEL B. METNICK, born Chicago, Illinois, October 25, 1947; admitted to bar, 1975, Illinois and U.S. District Court, Northern and Central Districts of Illinois; 1978, U.S. Court of Appeals, Seventh Circuit. *Education:* University of Oklahoma (B.A., 1970); John Marshall Law School (J.D., 1975). Recipient: Award of Excellence and Meritorious Achievement, Illinois Public Defenders Association, 1987; Presidents Award, Springfield Chapter, NAACP, 2003; Achievement Award, Center on Wrongful Convictions, Northwestern University School of Law, 2002. Certified Member, Capitol Litigation Trial Bar. Author: "Trial Issues," Illinois Institute of Continuing Legal Education, Defending Illinois Criminal Cases, 1988. "Expert Testimony of Battered Women's Syndrome, A New Frontier," Illinois Trial Lawyers Association, Fall and Winter Journal, 1983; Co-Author: "Available Forms of Temporary Relief Under The Illinois Marriage and Dissolution of Marriage Act," Illinois Family Law Report, 1988. Lecturer: Illinois Institute of Legal Education, 1979-1981, 1985-1997; Update and Review Seminar, Illinois Trial Lawyers Association, 1983, 1987; "Ethical Issues Facing Criminal Defense Attorneys," Law Ed Series, Illinois State Bar Association, 1996; "DNA. Frye Hearing Guide," Law Ed Series, Illinois State Bar Association, 1990; "Getting By On A Shoestring Budget," Law Ed Series, Illinois State Bar Association, 1991; Illinois Public Defender's Association, 1984, 1987; "Motions in Limine," 1997; Illinois Attorneys for Criminal Justice, "Creative Motion Practice", 1993; "Illinois Law and Practice on Jury Selection in Capital Cases," Illinois Institute for Continuing Legal Education; "Illinois Law & Practice on Jury Selection in Capital Cases," Illinois Institute for Continuing Legal Education, 2001. Faculty Member, Illinois Public Defender's Association Trial Advocacy School, 1985-1995. Member: Legal Advisory Committee, University of Illinois at Springfield, 1984-1997. Lecturer: Illinois Trial Lawyers Association, 1987, 1989, 1990; Illinois State Bar Association, 1990,1991, 1993, 1996, 1997. Lecturer: Illinois Institute for Continuing Legal Education, "Defending Illinois Death Penalty Cases: Essential Know-How for Defense Lawyers," 2001. President, Sangamon County Criminal Defense Bar, 1986-1987. *Member:* Chicago, Sangamon County, Illinois State (Secretary, 1992, Vice Chairman, 1993, Chairman, 1994 and Member, Criminal Justice Section Council; Standing Committee on Continuing Legal Education, 1990-1992) and American Bar Associations; Illinois Trial Lawyers Association (Chairman, Criminal Law Section, 1983; Co-Chairman, 1985-1986); The Association of Trial Lawyers of America; Decalogue Society of Lawyers; National Association of Criminal Defense Lawyers; Illinois Attorneys For Criminal Justice (President, 1989-1990); Lincoln Douglas Chapter, American Inns of Court. Fellow, Illinois State Bar Association. ***PRACTICE AREAS:*** Criminal Law (50%); Family Law (20%); Personal Injury (30%). ***Email:*** metnick@springfieldlawfirm.com

DIANA N. CHERRY, born Princeton, New Jersey, January 4, 1952; admitted to bar, 1976, Illinois; U.S. District Court, Central District of Illinois; U.S. Court of Appeals, Seventh Circuit. *Education:* Goucher College (B.A., 1973); Catholic University of America (J.D., 1976). Lecturer: "Modifications under the IMDMA and the Illinois Code of Civil Procedure," Law Ed. Series, Illinois State Bar Association, 2004; "Ethical Dilemmas in Family Law," Law Ed. Series, Illinois State Bar Association, 1995; Wiretap Law and Family Law, Illinois Law Ed. Series, Illinois State Bar Association, 1996. Co-Author: "Available Forms of Temporary Relief Under The Illinois Marriage and Dissolution of Marriage Act," Illinois Family Law Report, 1988. Assistant State Appellate Defender, 1977-1986. *Member:* Sangamon County, Illinois State (Member, Family Law Section; Civil Law Section) and American Bar Associations; Central Illinois Women's Bar Association (Treasurer, 1983-1984; President, 1985-1986); Illinois Attorneys For Criminal Justice; American Inns of Court. ***REPORTED CASES:*** Marriage of Eaton; 646 NE 2d 635 (4th Dist. 1995); People v. Simpkins; 697 NE2d 302 (4th Dist. 1998). ***PRACTICE AREAS:*** Family Law *(80%); Criminal Law (10%); Personal Injury Law (10%).* ***Email:*** cherry@springfieldlawfirm.com

RICHARD D. FRAZIER, born Pittsfield, Illinois, June 2, 1961; admitted to bar, 1986, Illinois; 1988, U.S. District Court, Central District of Illinois; 1989, U.S. Court of Appeals, Seventh Circuit; 1990, U.S Supreme Court; 1994, U.S. District Court, Southern District of Illinois. *Education:* Illinois College; Eastern Illinois University (B.A., summa cum laude, 1983); Southern Illinois University (J.D., 1986). Co-Author, "1991-1992 Survey of Criminal Law," Southern Illinois University Law Journal. Assistant State Appellate Defender, 1986-1989. Panel Attorney: Illinois Capital Resource Center, 1990—; Office of the State Appellate Defender, 1990—. *Member:* Sangamon County, Illinois State and American Bar Associations; Illinois Attorneys for Criminal Justice; National Association of Criminal Defense Lawyers; Sangamon County Criminal Defense Bar; National Employment Lawyers Association; American Trial Lawyers Association; Illinois Trial Lawyers Association (Member, Legislative Committee, 2002-2004). ***PRACTICE AREAS:*** Criminal Law (10%); Labor and Employment Law (10%); Personal Injury Law (30%); Civil Litigation (10%); Family Law (30%); Worker's Compensation (10%). ***Email:*** frazier@springfieldlawfirm.com

(This Listing Continued)

SCOTT A. SABIN, born Detroit, Michigan, June 18, 1967; admitted to bar, 1992, Illinois; 1993, Missouri. *Education:* University of Michigan (B.A., 1989); Washington University (J.D., 1992). Vice Chairman, Springfield Department of Community Relations. *Member:* Sangamon County (President, Young Lawyers Division, 1998; Treasurer, 1999, 2000; Secretary 2002; President-Elect, 2004), Illinois State (Member, Traffic and Courts Section Council, 2000-2001) and American Bar Associations; National Association of Criminal Defense Lawyers; Sangamon County Criminal Defense Bar; Illinois Attorneys for Criminal Justice. ***PRACTICE AREAS:*** Criminal Defense; Traffic Violations; Driving While Intoxicated; Personal Injury; Civil Litigation. ***Email:*** sabin@springfieldlawfirm.com

ASSOCIATES

RICHARD KIM, born New York, New York, November 12, 1969; admitted to bar, 1994, North Carolina; 1995, Illinois and U.S. District Court, Central District of Illinois; 1997, U.S. Court of Appeals, Seventh Circuit; 2002, U.S. District Court, Southern District of Illinois. *Education:* Wake Forest University (B.A., 1991); Wake Forest University School of Law (J.D., 1994). *Member:* Sangamon County, Illinois State Bar Association; Illinois Attorneys for Criminal Justice; National Association of Criminal Defense Lawyers. ***PRACTICE AREAS:*** Criminal Law; Personal Injury; General Practice. ***Email:*** kim@springfieldlawfirm.com

CHRISTOPHER G. PERRIN, born Pekin, Illinois, June 12, 1960; admitted to bar, 1988, Illinois and U.S. District Court, Central District of Illinois; 1986, U.S. Supreme Court. *Education:* University of Notre Dame (B.A., 1983); Southern Illinois University (J.D., 1988). Phi Delta Phi. *Member:* Sangamon County (Director, 1995-1997; President, Young Lawyers Division, 1996) and Illinois State (Member, Business Advice and Financial Planning Section Council) Bar Associations. ***PRACTICE AREAS:*** Corporate; Business Law; Commercial Transactions; Banking Law; Estate Planning; Real Estate. ***Email:*** perrin@springfieldlawfirm.com

MOHAN, ALEWELT, PRILLAMAN & ADAMI

Established in 1975

SUITE 325
1 NORTH OLD CAPITOL PLAZA
SPRINGFIELD, ILLINOIS 62701-1323
Telephone: 217-528-2517
Telecopier: 217-528-2553
URL: http://www.mohanlaw.com

General Commercial, Contract and Construction Litigation. Environmental Law. Corporation Law, Federal and State Taxes, Estate Planning and Real Estate Law and Tax. Personal Injury. Bankruptcy. Matrimonial Law.

MEMBERS

JAMES T. MOHAN (1927-2004)

FRED C. PRILLAMAN, born Springfield, Illinois, December 29, 1942; admitted to bar, 1968, Illinois. *Education:* Trinity College, Conn. (B.A., 1965); Northwestern University (J.D., 1968). Author: "Legislative Base For Environmental Law," Environmental Law in Illinois, Chap. 1 (IICLE, 1993; rev.2001). Chief, Legal Section, Air Pollution Control, Illinois Environmental Protection Agency, 1970-1972. ***PRACTICE AREAS:*** Environmental Law; Construction Litigation. ***Email:*** prillaman@mohanlaw.com

PAUL E. ADAMI, born Peoria, Illinois, October 7, 1950; admitted to bar, 1975, Illinois. *Education:* University of Illinois (B.S., 1972; J.D., 1975). Law Clerk, Southern District, Peo. Div., U.S. District Court, 1975-1976. ***PRACTICE AREAS:*** Personal Injury; Commercial Law; Construction Litigation; Matrimonial Law; Probate Litigation. ***Email:*** adami@mohanlaw.com

CHERYL S. NEAL, born Champaign, Illinois, April 23, 1953; admitted to bar, 1984, Illinois. *Education:* University of Illinois-Springfield (B.A., Accountancy, 1981); University of Illinois (J.D., 1984). ***PRACTICE AREAS:*** Civil Litigation; Estate Planning and Probate; Corporate Law; Bankruptcy. ***Email:*** neal@mohanlaw.com

PATRICK D. SHAW, born Peoria, Illinois, July 10, 1968; admitted to bar, 1993, Illinois. *Education:* University of Illinois (B.A., 1990); Tulane Law School (J.D., cum laude, 1993). Managing Editor, Tulane Environmental Law Journal, 1992-1993. Author: "Civil Penalties Under the Environmental Protection Act," 88 Ill. Bar J. 344 (June 2000); Comment, "See No Evil, Speak No Evil: Discharging CERCLA Claims in Bankruptcy Without Notice," 6 Tulane Envtl. L.J. 127 (1992). ***PRACTICE AREAS:*** Environmental Law; Civil Litigation. ***Email:*** shaw@mohanlaw.com

JOEL A. BENOIT, born Kankakee, Illinois, June 26, 1963; admitted to bar, 1992, Illinois; 1993, Missouri. *Education:* Parkland College (A.S., 1987); University of Illinois (B.S., 1989); Southern Illinois Law School (J.D., 1992). Phi Delta Phi. Lead Articles Editor, Southern Illinois University Law Journal, 1991-1992. Law Clerk to, U.S. District Court Judge William L. Beatty, 1992-1994. ***PRACTICE AREAS:*** Environmental Law; Civil Litigation; Construction Law; Real Estate; Bankruptcy. ***Email:*** benoit@mohanlaw.com

(This Listing Continued)

ASSOCIATE

CHRISTOPHER D. OSWALD, born Macomb, Illinois, April 16, 1977; admitted to bar, 2002, Illinois. *Education:* University of Illinois (B.S., Agriculture, with departmental honors, 1999); Northern Illinois University (J.D., cum laude, 2002). Phi Delta Phi (President, 2001-2002). ***PRACTICE AREAS:*** Business Law; Commercial Law; Environmental Law; Estate Planning; Probate; Civil Litigation; Real Estate. ***Email:*** oswald@mohanlaw.com

RETIRED PARTNER

EDWARD J. ALEWELT

REPRESENTATIVE CLIENTS: Briggs Industries, Inc.; BP Amoco Oil Company; Andrews Environmental Engineering, Inc.; Bemco Mattress, Inc.; Calhoun County Contracting Corp.; Capitol Ready Mix, Inc.; Central Illinois Ice Co.; Clear Lake Sand and Gravel Co.; Contractors Lumber City; Curry Ready-Mix, Inc.; Curry Ice & Coal, Inc.; Evans Construction Co.; Halverson Construction Co.; J.M. Huber Corporation; R.D. Lawrence Construction Co.; Mid-America Commodities, Inc.; Nord Farms, Inc.; Oldcastle Precast Building Systems; Pfizer, Inc.; Southern Illinois University, Edwardsville.

POSEGATE & DENES, P.C.

Established in 2000

111 NORTH 6TH STREET, SUITE 200
SPRINGFIELD, ILLINOIS 62701
Telephone: 217-522-6152
Fax: 217-522-6184
Email: jane@posegate-denes.com
URL: http://www.lawyers.com/posegate&denes

General Civil Litigation, Employment Law, Estate Planning, Taxation, Business Law, College and University Law, Administrative Law.

CAROL HANSEN POSEGATE, born Fargo, North Dakota, April 28, 1949; admitted to bar, 1973, District of Columbia; 1975, U.S. Court of Claims; 1977, Illinois; 1980, U.S. Supreme Court. *Education:* Concordia College (B.A., magna cum laude, 1970); Georgetown University (J.D., 1973). Adjunct Professor of Legal Medicine, Southern Illinois University Medical School, 1985-1997. Trial Attorney, U.S. Department of Justice, 1973-1976. Member: Illinois Bar Association 2005 Class of Academy Laureates; Illinois Supreme Court Committee on Professional Responsibility. Counsel, Illinois Commerce Commission, 1976-1978. Board Counsel, Board of Regents, Regency Universities of Illinois, 1987-1995. Board Counsel, Illinois State University Board of Trustees, 1996—. Member: Advisory Committee on Rules of Civil Procedure, Judicial Conference of the United States, 1991-1997; Advisory Board for Federal Discovery News by LRP Publications, 1996-2000; Federal Court Appointed Monitor for Class Action Discrimination Settlements; frequent lecturer on Federal Rules of Civil Procedure; Million Dollar Advocates Forum. Elected Trustee, Lincoln Land Community College, 2001—. Member, Lincoln-Douglas Inn of Court, 1991-2004. *Member:* Sangamon County, Illinois State and American Bar Associations; District of Columbia Bar; National Employment Law Association; The Association of Trial Lawyers of America. ***PRACTICE AREAS:*** Civil Litigation Law; Employment Law; College and University Law. ***Email:*** carol@posegate-denes.com

JANE N. DENES, born Springfield, Illinois, October 24, 1951; admitted to bar, 1984, Missouri; 1994, Illinois. *Education:* Smith College (B.A., 1973); Northwestern University (M.A., 1975); Washington University (J.D., 1983; LL.M., 1992). *Member:* Bar Association of Metropolitan St. Louis; Sangamon County, Illinois State and American Bar Associations; The Missouri Bar. ***PRACTICE AREAS:*** Estate Planning; Taxation; Business Law. ***Email:*** jane@posegate-denes.com

REPRESENTATIVE CLIENTS: Illinois State University Board of Trustees; Governor, State of Illinois; Brown County Mental Health Association; Lincoln Land Oil, Inc.; Illinois State Police Merit Board; Sangamon Eye Associates, P.C.; Jones-Blythe Construction Co.; Illinois National Bank; Springfield College; United Steelworkers of America.

QUINN, JOHNSTON, HENDERSON & PRETORIUS

CHARTERED

Established in 1946

(Formerly McConnell, Kennedy, Quinn & Johnston)

205 SOUTH FIFTH STREET, SUITE 900
SPRINGFIELD, ILLINOIS 62701
Telephone: 217-753-1133
Fax: 217-753-1180
Email: quinnlaw@qjhp.com
URL: http://www.qjhp.com

Peoria, Illinois Office: 227 N. E. Jefferson Street, 61602. Telephone: 309-674-1133.

Trial Practice in all Courts. Personal Injury, Professional Negligence, Admiralty, Insurance Law, Workers Compensation Law, Banking, Commercial and Bankruptcy Law. Real Estate, Corporate and Probate Law.

FIRM PROFILE: Founded in 1946 by Lowell and Golden McConnell and Tom Kennedy, the firm presently consists of 16 partners and 7 associates assisted by four paralegals and three Nurse/Legal Consultants. This general practice firm provides top quality legal service to a broad base of clients across Central Illinois, from the Indiana to the Iowa borders. A majority of the lawyers engage in insurance defense trial work.

STANLEY L. MORRIS, born De Kalb, Missouri, October 4, 1939; admitted to bar, 1971, Missouri; 1975, U.S. Supreme Court; 1983, Illinois and U.S. District Court, Central District of Illinois; 1988, U.S. Tax Court; U.S. Court of Appeals, Seventh Circuit. *Education:* Northwest Missouri State University (B.S., 1961); University of Missouri at Kansas City (J.D., 1971). *Member:* Sangamon County and Illinois State Bar Associations; The Missouri Bar; Bar Association of the Central and Southern Federal Districts of Illinois; Defense

(This Listing Continued)

Research Institute; Illinois Association of Defense Trial Counsel. ***PRACTICE AREAS:*** Municipal Law; Public Utility Law; Insurance Defense; Self-Insuring Pools. ***Email:*** smorris@qjhp.com

JAMES ANDREW BORLAND, born Middletown, Ohio, November 4, 1966; admitted to bar, 1991, Illinois, U.S. District Court, Central District of Illinois and U.S. Court of Appeals, Seventh Circuit. *Education:* Quincy College (B.A., summa cum laude, 1988); Pepperdine University School of Law (J.D., 1991). Phi Delta Phi; Phi Alpha Theta. *Member:* Sangamon County and Illinois State Bar Associations; Defense Research Institute; Illinois Association of Defense Trial Counsel; Adjustors Association of Central Illinois. ***PRACTICE AREAS:*** Insurance Defense. ***Email:*** jborland@qjhp.com

MICHAEL J. HOLT, born Blue Island, Illinois, November 8, 1962; admitted to bar, 1990, Illinois and U.S. District Court, Central District of Illinois; 1992, Missouri. *Education:* Northern Arizona University (B.S., with honors, 1984); John Marshall Law School (J.D., cum laude, 1990). Associate Editor, Lead Articles, The John Marshall Law Review, 1989-1990. Judicial Clerk: Hon. Justice Robert O. Buckley, Illinois Appellate Court, First District, 1990-1992; John M. O'Connor, Jr., 1992-1993. *Member:* Peoria County and Illinois State Bar Associations; Illinois Association of Defense Trial Counsel; Defense Research Institute. ***PRACTICE AREAS:*** Worker's Compensation; Insurance Defense. ***Email:*** mholt@qjhp.com

MATTHEW J. MADDOX, born Springfield, Illinois, December 26, 1956; admitted to bar, 1983, Illinois and U.S. District Court, Central District of Illinois; 1988, U.S. Court of Appeals, Seventh Circuit. *Education:* University of Illinois (B.S., 1978); Hamline University (J.D., 1983). *Member:* Sangamon County and Illinois State Bar Associations; Illinois Association of Defense Trial Counsel. ***PRACTICE AREAS:*** Medical Malpractice Defense; Railroad Liability; Personal Injury Defense. ***Email:*** mmaddox@qjhp.com

ASSOCIATE

JOHN A. WOLTERS, born Elmhurst, Illinois, October 7, 1955; admitted to bar, 1999, Illinois; U.S. District Court, Central District of Illinois; U.S. Court of Appeals, Seventh Circuit. *Education:* Southern Illinois University (B.A., 1981); University of Illinois (M.A., 1989); DePaul University (J.D., 1999). *Member:* Sangamon County and Illinois State Bar Associations; Lincol-Douglas Inns of Court; Defense Research Institute; Adjustors Association of Central Illinois. ***PRACTICE AREAS:*** Civil Litigation Defense. ***Email:*** jwolters@qjhp.com

REPRESENTATIVE INSURERS, CLAIM ADMINISTRATORS AND SELF-INSURED CLIENTS: Allstate Insurance Co.; American International Insurance Co.; American Isuzu Motors, Inc.; Amerisure; Asplundh Tree Expert Co.; Auto Owners Insurance Co.; Autozone, Inc.; Bituminous Casualty Corp.; Bridgestone/Firestone Tire & Rubber Co.; Bromenn Healthcare; Browning Ferris Industries; Cambridge Integrated Services; CIGNA Cos.; City of Bloomington; City of Canton; City of Galesburg; CNA Insurance; Commercial Union Insurance Co.; Columbia Insurance; Continental Insurance; Country Mutual Insurance Company; Crawford & Co; Cunningham-Lindsey; Crum & Forster; E. C. Fackler Co.; Farmers Automobile Insurance Association; Fremont Compensation; Gallagher Basset Services, Inc.; General Casualty; General Motors; Grinnell Mutual Reinsurance Co.; Guide One Insurance Co.; Harleysville Insurance; Hinz Claim Management, Inc.; Illinois Grocers Risk Management Association; Illinois Municipal League Risk Management Association; Illinois Provider Trust; Illinois State Ambulance Risk Management Association; Illinois State Bar Association Mutual; Illinois State Medical Insurance Services, Inc.; Insurance Company of North America; ITT/Hartford; John Warner Hospital; Kemper Group; Liberty Mutual; McDonough District Hospital; Methodist Medical Center; MSI Insurance Companies; Navistar International Corp.; New Hampshire International Corp.; Newmar Corporation; Nissan Motor Corp.; Nursing Homes Risk Management Association; Pekin Insurance; Pekin Memorial Hospital/Progressive Health Systems; Peoria Area Chamber of Commerce Trust; RMR Group; Royal Insurance Co.; SAFECO/American States; St. Paul Insurance Co./USFG Security Insurance Group; Selective Insurance; State Farm Fire & Casualty; Statesman Insurance Co.; Travelers Insurance; United Capitol Insurance; United Heartland; Westfield Insurance Co.; Western States; Zurich International; Zurich-U.S.
REPRESENTATIVE CORPORATE, FINANCIAL AND GOVERNMENTAL CLIENTS: Anderson State Bank; Baumgarten Distributing Company, Inc.; BDC Wine, Inc.; Brewers Distributing Company; Cargill, Incorporated; Citizens Equity First Credit Union; City of Galesburg, IL; City of Peoria, IL; Consumers Gas Company; Cookies By Design of Peoria, Inc.; Illinois Gas Company; Insurance Car Rentals, Inc.; Inventory Technology, Inc.; Kickapoo Corporation; Marquette Bank-Illinois; Par-A-Dice; Peoria Journal Star, Inc.; Village of Princeville, IL; Village of Southern View, IL.

(For Complete Biographical Data on all Personnel, See Professional Biographies at Peoria)

SAMUELS, MILLER, SCHROEDER, JACKSON & SLY, LLP

SPRINGFIELD, ILLINOIS

(See Decatur)

General Civil Trial and Appellate Practice, Personal Injury, Auto Accidents, Medical Malpractice, Workers Compensation, Corporate, Commercial, Employment, Banking, Finance, Mergers and Acquisitions, Health Care, Real Estate and Environmental, Trusts, Estates, Wills and Estates Planning.

WILLIAM NEWELL SIEBERT

SPRINGFIELD, ILLINOIS

(See Chicago)

Naturalization, Working Visas, Consular Practice, Family and Employment Based Permanent Residency Cases, PERM Labor Certification, Kennedy McCain.

SORLING, NORTHRUP, HANNA, CULLEN AND COCHRAN, LTD.

Established in 1944

Formerly Sorling, Catron and Hardin

800 ILLINOIS BUILDING
607 EAST ADAMS STREET
P.O. BOX 5131
SPRINGFIELD, ILLINOIS 62705
Telephone: 217-544-1144
Telecopier: 217-522-3173
Email: businessdevelopment@sorlinglaw.com
URL: http://www.sorlinglaw.com

Peoria Office: 401 S.W. Water Street, Suite 301, 61602. Telephone: 309-674-1144. Telecopier: 309-671-4368.

General Civil Practice including Administrative Law, Agricultural Law, State and Federal Appellate Practice, Banking and Finance, Banking, Bankruptcy, Business Law, Civil Rights Defense, Commercial Law, Communications, Construction Law, Contract Preparation and Litigation, Corporate Law, Education Law, Elder Law, Election Law, Employee Benefits, Energy Law including Public Utilities, Environmental Law, Family Law, Illinois Governmental Advocacy and Representation, Health and Hospital Law, Insurance Regulation and Defense; Intellectual Property Rights, Labor and Employment Law, General State and Federal Litigation, News Media Representation, Mergers and Acquisitions, Municipal and Local Governmental Law, Natural Resources, Not for Profit Organizations, Personal Injury and Torts, Probate, Estate and Trust, Professional Liability and Disciplinary Defense, Products Liability, Real Estate, Securities, Taxation, Telecommunications, Trade and Professional Association Representation, Transportation Law, Workers Compensation, Zoning Planning and Land Use.

FIRM PROFILE: The firm was founded by Carl A. Sorling in 1944. It is the largest private practice law firm in Springfield, Illinois. There are 19 active shareholders, 8 associates and 4 attorneys with an of counsel relationship.

The firm has a diversified general and specialty practice in Springfield and Illinois in general. The practice includes substantial work in the corporate, civil litigation, financial institution, insurance regulation and defense, utility, family law, employment, health care, construction, local, state and federal tax, estate planning, probate, environmental, municipal, public finance, real estate, legislative advocacy and administrative law areas. The firm represents a growing number of local private and public corporations, as well as professional trade associations. The firm also serves a diversified national clientele as regional or local counsel in commercial, regulatory and litigation matters.

The firm has developed a large governmental practice, and is active in all aspects of government relations, including trade association representation, vendor assistance, and all state regulatory matters. In addition, the firm represents clients with national and state-wide interests in both the legislative and executive branch processes.

The firm stresses development and retention of lawyers with individual skills designed to offer creative and cost efficient legal and business solutions for clients. The goal is always to bring a responsive and personal approach to the practice of law.

MEMBERS OF FIRM

CARL A. SORLING (1896-1991)

B. LACEY CATRON, JR. (1912-1959)

JOHN H. HARDIN (1909-1978)

GEORGE WILLIAM CULLEN (1917-1986)

THOMAS L. COCHRAN (1916-1994)

R. GERALD BARRIS, born Elwood, Indiana, January 26, 1940; admitted to bar, 1969, Missouri and Illinois. *Education:* Denison University (B.A., cum laude, 1962); Washington University (J.D., 1969). Author: "Original Process and Appearance," Illinois Civil Practice Volume 1 (Ill, Inst. for CLE, 1991, Supp. 1997). President, Lincoln-Douglas Inn of Courts, 1998-1999. *Member:* The Bar Association of Metropolitan St. Louis; Sangamon County, Illinois State (Chairman, Civil Practice and Procedure Section Council, 1984-1985) and American (Member, Sections on: Litigation) Bar Associations; The Missouri Bar; The Association of Trial Lawyers of America; Illinois Association of Defense Trial Counsel; Illinois Trial Lawyers Association. ***PRACTICE AREAS:*** Litigation; Eminent Domain; Personal Injury; Insurance Defense; Insurance Litigation; Insurance Bad Faith; Employment Litigation; Commercial Litigation; Construction Litigation; Products Liability; Health Care Litigation; Health Insurance Coverage; Administrative Litigation; Administrative Hearings and Appeals; Alternative Dispute Resolution. ***Email:*** rgbarris@sorlinglaw.com

STEPHEN A. TAGGE, born Moline, Illinois, February 1, 1944; admitted to bar, 1969, Illinois. *Education:* Knox College (B.A., 1966); University of Chicago (J.D., 1969). Co-author: "Special Types of Collateral Chapter," IICLE, 1990. Instructor, Banking Law, American Institute of Banking, 1973-1976. *Member:* Sangamon County and Illinois State Bar Associations; American Bankruptcy Institute. ***REPORTED CASES:*** Westwood Forum, Inc. et al. v. Commercial Realty Partners, Ltd. et al., Appellate Court of Illinois, 4th Dist., 261 Ill.App.3d 911; 634 N.E.2d 1154; 1994 Ill.App. Lexis 781; 199 Ill. Dec. 800, April 12, 1994; In the Matter of the Annexation of Certain Territory to the Village of Chatham, Illinois, Appellate Court of Illinois, 4th Dist., 245 Ill.App.3d 786; 614 N.E.2d 1278; 1993 Ill.App. Lexis 803; 185 Ill. Dec. 593, June 3, 1993. ***PRACTICE AREAS:*** Banks and Banking; Bankruptcy; Commercial Law; Contracts; Commercial Transactions; *Commercial Litigation; Business Law; Business Transactions; Construction Litigation;* Real Estate Development. ***Email:*** satagge@sorlinglaw.com

MICHAEL A. MYERS, born Chicago, Illinois, May 10, 1945; admitted to bar, 1970, Illinois. *Education:* Tulane University of Louisiana (B.A., 1967); Washington University (J.D., 1970). *Member:* Sangamon County and Illinois State Bar Associations. ***REPORTED CASES:*** Bossman v. Village of Riverton, 291 Ill. App. 3d 769, 684 N.E. 2d 427, (4th Dist. 1997). ***PRACTICE AREAS:*** Real Estate Law; Foreclosure Law; Commercial Litigation. ***Email:*** mamyers@sorlinglaw.com

CARL CLARK GERMANN, born Springfield, Illinois, May 31, 1945; admitted to bar, 1972, Illinois. *Education:* Springfield College (A.A., 1965); Illinois College (B.S., with honors, 1967); University of Illinois (J.D., with honors, 1972). Order of the Coif. Law Clerk to Judge Leland Simkins, Illinois Appellate Court, Fourth District, 1972-1974. Director of Research, Illinois Appellate Court, Fourth District, 1974-1975. *Member:* Sangamon County, Illinois State and American Bar Associations. ***PRACTICE AREAS:*** Corporate Law; Real Estate Law; Oil and Gas Law. ***Email:*** ccgermann@sorlinglaw.com

GARY A. BROWN, born Equality, Illinois, May 25, 1947; admitted to bar, 1977, Illinois. *Education:* Southeastern Illinois College (A.S., 1967); University of Illinois (B.S., 1970); Washington University (J.D., 1977). Phi Delta Phi (Vice President, 1977). *Member:* Sangamon County and Illinois State Bar Associations. ***REPORTED CASES:*** Central Illinois Public Service Company v. Gibbell et al., 65 IL App 3rd 890; 382 NE 2d 846; 22 IL Dec 456, 4th Dist. (1978); Rousey v. Industrial Commission, et al. Central Illinois Public Service Company, 224 IL App 3d 1096; 587 NE 2d 26; 167 IL Dec 144, 4th Dist. (1992). ***PRACTICE AREAS:*** Workers Compensation Law; Labor and Employment; Utilities; OSHA; Real Estate. ***Email:*** gabrown@sorlinglaw.com

FREDERICK B. HOFFMANN, born Springfield, Illinois, September 2, 1941; admitted to bar, 1968, Illinois. *Education:* Swarthmore College and University of Chicago (Ph.B., 1963); University of Illinois (J.D., 1967). *Member:* Sangamon County, Illinois State and American Bar Associations. ***PRACTICE AREAS:*** Wills; Trusts and Estates; Estate Planning; Probate; Real Estate; Agricultural Law. ***Email:*** fbhoffmann@sorlinglaw.com

WILLIAM R. ENLOW, born Springfield, Illinois, November 20, 1947; admitted to bar, 1979, Illinois. *Education:* University of Illinois (B.A., 1970); Chicago-Kent College of Law, Illinois Institute of Technology (J.D., 1979). Assistant to the Director, Illinois Department of State Police, 1976-1979. Senior Vice President, General Counsel and Secretary, Marine Bank of Springfield and Marine Corporation, 1979-1988. *Member:* Sangamon County, Illinois State and American Bar Associations. [With U.S. Army, 1971-1973]. ***PRACTICE AREAS:*** Banking; Trade Associations; Government Relations; Insurance Regulation. ***Email:*** wrenlow@sorlinglaw.com

MICHAEL C. CONNELLY, born Decatur, Illinois, February 19, 1957; admitted to bar, 1985, Illinois. *Education:* University of Illinois (B.S., with highest honors, 1979; J.D., magna cum laude, 1985). Order of the Coif. Author: "Wills and Trusts: Disqualifying Adopted Adult Children," 78 IBJ, 612, 1990. Contributing Author: IICLE, State and Local Taxation, 1991. *Member:* Sangamon County and Illinois State Bar Associations. ***REPORTED CASES:*** Ill. Dept. of Rev. v. Corrosion Systems, Inc., 133 Ill. Dec. 647, 185 Ill. App. 3d 580, 541 N.E.2d 858 (1989). ***PRACTICE AREAS:*** Taxation; Commercial Transactions; Trusts and Estates; Wills; Real Estate. ***Email:*** mcconnelly@sorlinglaw.com

JOHN A. KAUERAUF, born Springfield, Illinois, July 3, 1961; admitted to bar, 1986, Illinois. *Education:* Illinois Wesleyan University (B.A., cum laude, 1983); University of Illinois (J.D., 1986). Co-Author: Special Types of Collateral Chapter," IICLE, 1990, 2001. Author: IICLE Business Law Flashpoints (2002—). Special Assistant Attorney General, Illinois, 1992-1997, 2001—. *Member:* Sangamon County (Secretary-Treasurer, 1991, Vice President, 1992, President, 1993, Young Lawyers Section, Board of Directors, 1995-1996); Illinois State and American Bar Associations. ***REPORTED CASES:*** Osborne v. Kelly, 207 Ill App 3d 488, 565 NE 2d 1340, 152 Ill Dec 422, (4th Dist., 1991); Yates v. Salvation Army, 1993 ILHUM LEXIS 194,402 (1993); Kralman v. Ill. Dept. of Veterans Affairs, 23 F.3d 150 (7th Cir. 1994); Castle v. Ill. Vet. Home at Manteno, 1995 ILHUM LEXIS 751, 753 (1995); Creasey v. Phillips Brothers, Inc., 1995 ILHUM LEXIS 621 (1995); Davis v. Hardee's, 1995 ILHUM LEXIS 266,595 (1995); Legg v. Ill. Vet. Home at Manteno, 1995 ILHUM LEXIS 165 (1995); Williams v. Franklin Life Insurance Co., 1998 ILHUM LEXIS 151 (1998); Woollen v. Perkins Family Restaurant, 1999 ILHUM LEXIS 11 (1999); Marshall v. Hardee's, 2000 ILHUM LEXIS 148 (2000); Sims v. Pinnacle Limited Partnership, 2002 ILHUM LEXIS 42 (2002); Dawkins v. Ill. Comm. College Bd., 2003 ILHUM LEXIS 13 (2003); Wiley v. Ill. Dept. of Veterans' Affairs, 2004 U.S. App. LEXIS 1192 (7th Cir. 2004).. ***PRACTICE AREAS:*** Business Law; Labor and Employment Law; Health Care Law; Real Estate Taxation; Nonprofit and Tax Exempt Organizations. ***Email:*** jakauerauf@sorlinglaw.com

JAMES M. MORPHEW, born Chicago, Illinois, April 8, 1954; admitted to bar, 1983, Illinois. *Education:* Lewis University (B.A., 1975); Sangamon State University; Loyola University (J.D., 1983). Member, Moot Court Team. Author: "Structure, Function and Legal Status of Political Parties," Election Law Handbook, Illinois Institute for Continuing Legal Education, 1991. Trustee, Springfield Mass Transit District, 1991-1993. Legal Counsel to Speaker of Illinois House of Representatives, 1985-1992. *Member:* Sangamon County and Illinois State Bar Associations. ***REPORTED CASES:*** *Kluk v. Lang,* 125 Ill.2d 306, 531 N.E. 2d 790 (1988); *Rock v. Burris,* 139 Ill.2d 494, 564 N.E. 2d 1240 (1990); *Times Mirror Cable Television v. First National Bank of Springfield, et. al.,* 221 Ill.App 3d 582 N.E. 2d 216 (1991); *Bryant v. Cook County Officers Electoral Board,* 195 Ill.App.3d 556, 553 N.E. 2d 26 (1990); Medical Disposal Services, Inc. v. Environmental Protection Agency, 677 N.E. 2d 428, 222 Ill. Dec. 225 (1st Dist. 1997) (amicus curiae). ***PRACTICE AREAS:*** Government Relations; Legislative Lobbying; Environmental Law; Administrative Law; Regulatory Agency Practice. ***Email:*** jmmorphew@sorlinglaw.com

STEPHEN J. BOCHENEK, born Dayton, Ohio, November 22, 1951; admitted to bar, 1977, Illinois. *Education:* St. Louis University (A.B., 1973); The Ohio State University (J.D., 1977). *Member:* Sangamon County and Illinois State (Member, Real Estate Section Council, 1986-1994, 2002—; Chairman, 1992-1993) Bar Associations. ***PRACTICE AREAS:*** Business Law; Business Transactions; Real Estate Law; Labor and Employment Law; Trade Association Law. ***Email:*** sjbochenek@sorlinglaw.com

DAVID A. ROLF, born Decatur, Illinois, February 19, 1962; admitted to bar, 1987, Illinois. *Education:* University of Illinois (B.S., with high honors, 1984; J.D., 1987). Delta Theta Phi; Alpha Zeta. Contributing Author: *ITLA Trial Notebook,* 1989-1990 Edition. Co-Author: "Illinois Drainage Law," Cooperative Extension Service Circular 1305, December,

(This Listing Continued)

1991. *Member:* Sangamon County and Illinois State Bar Associations; American Agricultural Law Association; Illinois Trial Lawyers Association. ***REPORTED CASES:*** Lucht v. Stage 2, Inc., 239 Ill. App. 3d 679, 606 N.E. 2nd 750 (4th Dist. 1992); Midland Risk Service Illinois v. Knickman, 298 Ill. App. 3d 1111, 700 N.E. 2d 458 (4th Dist. 1998). ***PRACTICE AREAS:*** Insurance Defense; Personal Injury Law; Employment Litigation; Commercial Litigation; Construction Litigation; Appellate Practice. ***Email:*** darolf@sorlinglaw.com

MARGARET (PEGGY) J. RYAN, born Springfield, Illinois, December 18, 1961; admitted to bar, 1990, Illinois and U.S. District Court, Central District of Illinois; 1996, U.S. Court of Appeals, Seventh Circuit. *Education:* University of Missouri (B.J., 1984); Southern Illinois University (J.D., 1990). Phi Delta Phi (President, 1989-1990). Member, Magister Lesar Inn, 1989-1990. Notes and Comments Editor, Southern Illinois University Law Journal, 1989-1990. Author: "Note, The Sixth Amendment Right to Counsel: A Criminal Defendant's Right to Counsel of Choice v. The Courts' Interest in Conflict Free Representation," 14 S.I.U. Law Journal 657, 1990; "Comment, The Status of Civil Liability When Child Protection Workers Fail to Do Their Jobs," 14 S.I.U. Law Journal 573, 1990. Co-Author: "Reverse Mortgages - Tapping Equity," Illinois Banker, Nov., 1991. *Member:* Sangamon County, Illinois State and American Bar Associations. ***REPORTED CASES:*** Dunlap v. Dunlap, 690 N.E. 2d 1023 (1998); Vickery v. Jones, and Saline County Republican Central Committee, 100 F. 3d 1334 (7th Cir. 1996), Cert. Denied 137 L. Ed 2d 701) (1997). Beal v. Schewe, 291 Ill App. 3d 204, 683 N.E. 2d 1019, 225 Ill Dec. 516 (4th Dist. 1997). ***PRACTICE AREAS:*** Family Law. ***Email:*** pjryan@sorlinglaw.com

MARK K. CULLEN, born Springfield, Illinois, September 27, 1962; admitted to bar, 1988, Illinois. *Education:* Northwestern University (B.A., with honors, 1984); University of Illinois (M.B.A., 1988; J.D., 1988). MBA Scholar, University of Illinois College of Business Administration. *Member:* Sangamon County, Illinois State and American Bar Associations. ***PRACTICE AREAS:*** Corporate Law; Banking; Securities; Commercial Transactions; Mergers and Acquisitions; Municipal Law; Administrative Law; Regulatory Law. ***Email:*** mkcullen@sorlinglaw.com

THOMAS H. WILSON, born Erie, Pennsylvania, January 22, 1964; admitted to bar, 1989, Illinois. *Education:* Gannon University (B.A., magna cum laude, 1986); Southern Illinois University (J.D., summa cum laude, 1989). Law Clerk to the Hon. Richard Mills, U.S. District Judge, Central District of Illinois, 1989-1991. Editor in Chief, Southern Illinois University Law Journal, 1988-1989. Author: Comment, Real Estate Brokers, Guarantors of the Seller or Guardians of the Buyer? 13 Southern Illinois Law Journal 975, 1989; Wilson & Charlton, Survey of Illinois Law - Property, 14 Southern Illinois Law Journal 1187, 1990. *Member:* Sangamon County and Illinois State Bar Associations; Defense Research Institute. ***PRACTICE AREAS:*** Civil Rights; Insurance Litigation; Nursing Home Litigation; Commercial Litigation; Appellate Practice; Personal Injury; Bankruptcy Law; Labor and Employment Law. ***Email:*** thwilson@sorlinglaw.com

TODD MICHAEL TURNER, born Charleston, Illinois, December 12, 1965; admitted to bar, 1992, Illinois. *Education:* Western Illinois University (B.A., summa cum laude, 1988); University of Illinois College of Law (J.D., magna cum laude, 1992). Phi Kappa Phi; Phi Alpha Theta; Phi Alpha Delta. Member, Editorial Board, Essays in History Student Journal. Author: "The New Agency law in a Nutshell: The Basics of Senate Bill 1624," Illinois Realtor, Nov. 1994. Co-author: "Is your Armored Carrier Protection Safe?" Illinois Banker, Nov., 1994. Chapter Co-author: 1997 Supplement, "Residential Mortgage Lending Procedures: Application of Federal and State Laws," Advising Ill. Financial Institutions, (Ill. Institute for Continuing Legal Education); 1997 Supplement, "Tax Considerations," Basic Real Estate, (Ill. Institute for Continuing Legal Education). Former Adjunct Faculty Instructor of Real Estate Law at University of Illinois at Springfield. *Member:* Sangamon County, Illinois State and American Bar Associations. ***REPORTED CASES:*** C-Call Corp. v. Zoning Bd. of Appeals of Edwardsville, 700 NE 2d 441; 233 IL Dec. 136. ***PRACTICE AREAS:*** Commercial Law; Real Estate Law; Banking Law; Taxation; Sales and Use Tax; Business Transactions. ***Email:*** tmturner@sorlinglaw.com

R. LEE ALLEN, born Vandalia, Illinois, March 16, 1963; admitted to bar, 1994, Illinois. *Education:* University of Illinois (B.S., with honors, 1985; J.D., summa cum laude, 1994). Order of the Coif. Co-Author: Supplement Chapter 9 S. "Agricultural and Agri-Business Loans," Advising Illinois Financial Institutions, IICLE (1997); "Family Limited Partnerships in Illinois," National Business Institute (1997); Supplement Chapter 3 S. "Tax Considerations," Basic Real Estate Practice, IICLE (1998); Section 4. "Tax Considerations in Structuring the Purchase or Sale of a Business," Buying and Selling Businesses, Negotiating, Structuring and Closing the Deal, IICLE (2001). Author, "Limited Liability Companies and Limited Liability Partnerships in Illinois," National Business Institute (2002). Member, Sangamon Valley Estate Planning Council. *Member:* Sangamon County, Illinois State and American Bar Associations. ***PRACTICE AREAS:*** Trusts and Estates; Estate Planning; Closely Held Business Estate Planning; Private Foundations; Charitable Organizations Law; Business Law; Tax Law; Real Estate Law; Elder Law. ***Email:*** rlallen@sorlinglaw.com

CHARLES J. NORTHRUP, born Springfield, Illinois, March 19, 1960; admitted to bar, 1988, Illinois. *Education:* Ripon College (B.A., 1982); Southern Illinois University (J.D., 1988). Associate Editor, Southern Illinois University Law Journal, 1987-1988. Co-Author: Northrup & Layman, "Illinois' New Environmental Audit Privilege Provides Limited Protections," 83 Ill. B.J. 520 (1995); Northrup & Crain, "Issues Relating to Naturally Occurring Radioactive Materials and the Oil and Gas Industry," 22 ISBA Mineral Law 1 (Nov. 1995); Northrup & Layman, "Survey of Illinois Law: Environment," 22 S.Ill.U.L.J. 879 (1998); Northrup & Layman, "Survey of Illinois Law: Environment," 23 S. Ill.U.L.J. *1105 (1999). Author:* "Illinois' New Brownfields Law: Giving New Life to Contaminated Property," Illinois Realtor 2 (Mar. 1997); "Are Environmental Audits Obsolete," 35 Illinois Realtor 3 (May, 1998); "Unauthorized Practice of Law," Chapter 43; "Illinois Causes of Action - Elements, Forms and Winning Practice Tips: Estate, Business & Non Personal Injury Actions (Ill. Inst. for CLE 2002). Counsel, Attorney Registration and Disciplinary Commission, 1988-1990. Assistant Counsel, Illinois Environmental Protection Agency, 1990-1993. *Member:* Sangamon County, Illinois State and American Bar Associations; Association of Professional Responsibility Lawyers. ***REPORTED CASES:*** ESG Watts, Inc. v. Pollution Control Board, 282 Ill. App 3d 43, 668 N.E. 2d 1015, 218 Ill. Dec 183 (4th Dist. 1996); ESG Watts, Inc. v. Pollution Control Board and Illinois Environmental Protection Agency, 676 N.E. 2d 299, 221 Ill. Dec. 778 (3rd Dist. 1997); Medical Disposal Services, Inc. v. Environmental Protection Agency, 677 N.E. 2d 428, 222 Ill. Dec. 225 (1st Dist. 1997) (amicus curiae).; Abbasi v. Paraskevoulakos, 187 Ill.2d 386, 240 Ill Dec 700 (Ill 1999) (amicus curiae). ***PRACTICE AREAS:*** Environmental Law; Commercial Litigation; Attorney Discipline; Professional Discipline; Professional Liability; Legal Malpractice; Oil and Gas Law. ***Email:*** cjnorthrup@sorlinglaw.com

(This Listing Continued)

JAMES D. BROADWAY, born De Ridder, Louisiana, December 26, 1944; admitted to bar, 1968, Texas; 1969, Illinois. *Education:* Tulane University (B.A., 1965); Southern Methodist University (J.D., 1968). *Member:* Peoria County, Illinois State and American Bar Associations; State Bar of Texas; American Academy of Hospital Attorneys. (Also at Peoria Office). ***PRACTICE AREAS:*** Hospital Law; Health Care Law; Corporate Law; Real Estate Law. ***Email:*** jdbroadway@sorlinglaw.com

---

ELIZABETH A. URBANCE, born Springfield, Illinois, September 5, 1962; admitted to bar, 1987, Missouri; 1992, Illinois. *Education:* Western Illinois University (B.S., Cum laude, 1984); University of Missouri (J.D., 1987). Beta Gamma Sigma. *Member:* Sangamon County and Illinois State Bar Associations; The Missouri Bar. ***PRACTICE AREAS:*** Real Estate Law. ***Email:*** eaurbance@sorlinglaw.com

E. ZACHARY DINARDO, born Springfield, Illinois, July 3, 1973; admitted to bar, 1999, Illinois, U.S. District Court, Central District of Illinois and U.S. Court of Appeals; 2000, U.S. District Court, Southern District of Illinois. *Education:* University of Illinois at Springfield (B.A. with high honor, 1996); St. Louis University (J.D., magna cum laude, 1999). Order of the Woolsack. Lead Editor, Journal of Health Law, 1998-1999. Certificate in Health Law with Honors. *Member:* Sangamon County, Illinois State and American Bar Associations. ***PRACTICE AREAS:*** Business Law; Corporate Law; Commercial Litigation; Health Care Law. ***Email:*** ezdinardo@sorlinglaw.com

JAMES G. FAHEY, born Farmington, Michigan, January 1, 1961; admitted to bar, 1997, Illinois. *Education:* Illinois Benedictine College (B.A., 1984); St. Louis University (J.D., cum laude, 1996). Lincoln-Douglas Inn of Court, 1999-2000. Certificate in Employment Law. Law Clerk to Justice Sue E. Myerscough, 4th District App. Court Illinois, 1998-2000. Author, "U.S. v. NTEU: Restrictions on Free Speech of Government Employees & The Rebalancing of Pickering," 15 St. Louis U. Pub. L. Rev. 555 (1996); "Opening Doors to Equal Opportunity: In-Depth Coverage on Fair Housing Laws and Requirements for Realtors," Illinois Realtor Magazine, May, 2001; "Appeals from Plea Agreements: New Rules Clarify the Law," 88 Illinois Bar Journal II (November, 2000); "Illinois Causes of Action - Negligent Hiring and/or Retention of Employees, Chapter 22, (IICLE 2002). Director, Sangamon County Adult Court Services, Seventh Judicial Circuit, 1997-1998.*Member:* Sangamon County, Illinois State and American Bar Associations. ***PRACTICE AREAS:*** Appellate Practice; Civil Trial Practice; Labor and Employment Law. ***Email:*** jgfahey@sorlinglaw

JEFFREY R. JURGENS, born Urbana, Illinois, March 29, 1975; admitted to bar, 2000, Illinois. *Education:* Illinois State University (B.S., 1997); American University (J.D., 2000). Member, Board of Trustees of Lincoln Library, 2000—. *Member:* Sangamon County, Illinois State and American Bar Associations. ***PRACTICE AREAS:*** Family Law; Corporate Law; Trusts and Estate; Wills; Probate; Election Law. ***Email:*** jrjurgens@sorlinglaw.com

MICHAEL G. HORSTMAN, JR., born St. Louis, Missouri, May 6, 1972; admitted to bar, 1997, Illinois and U.S. District Court, Northern District of Illinois. *Education:* University of Illinois (B.A., 1994); Washington University (J.D., 1997). *Member:* Chicago, Illinois State and American Bar Associations. ***Email:*** mghorstman@sorlinglaw.com

JENNIFER M. ASCHER, born Springfield, Illinois, May 12, 1978; admitted to bar, 2003, Illinois. *Education:* University of Illinois (B.S., 1999); St. Louis University School of Law (J.D., 2003). Phi Alpha Delta. Lead Editor, Journal of Health Law. *Member:* Illinois State and American Bar Associations. ***PRACTICE AREAS:*** General Practice. ***Email:*** jmascher@sorlinglaw.com

LISA PETRILLI, born Springfield, Illinois, September 9, 1977; admitted to bar, 2003, Illinois. *Education:* University of Illinois (B.A., cum laude, 1999); The John Marshall Law School (J.D., cum laude, 2003). Member: The John Marshall Law Review; Moot Court; Order of John Marshall. Author: "Lost Chance in Illinois? That May Still Be the Case," 36 J. Marshall L. Rev. 249 (Fall 2002). *Member:* Illinois State and American Bar Associations. ***PRACTICE AREAS:*** General Practice. ***Email:*** lapetrilli@sorlinglaw.com

EMILY B. FATHAUER, born Decatur, Illinois, July 7, 1980; admitted to bar, 2005, Illinois. *Education:* Illinois Wesleyan University (B.A., cum laude, 2002); St. Louis University School of Law (J.D., 2005). *Member:* Sangamon County and Illinois State Bar Associations. ***Email:*** ebfathauer@sorlinglaw.com

OF COUNSEL

PATRICK V. REILLY, born Evanston, Illinois, February 4, 1939; admitted to bar, 1963, Illinois. *Education:* University of Notre Dame (B.B.A., cum laude, 1960); Northwestern University (J.D., 1963). *Member:* Sangamon County and Illinois State (Member, Sections on: Civil Practice; Tort Law) Bar Associations; Illinois Trial Lawyers Association (Board of Managers, 1982-1989). ***REPORTED CASES:*** Metropolitan Life Ins. Co. v. Washburn, Nos. 62513, 62575 cons., Supreme Court of Illinois, 112 Ill. 2d 486, 493 N.E.2d 1071, 98 Ill. Dec. 50 (1986); Hofferkamp v. Brehm. No. 4-93-0716, Appellate Court of Illinois, Fourth District, 273 Ill. App. 3d 263, 652 N.E.2d 1381; 1995 Ill. App. Lexis 543, 210 Ill. Dec. 405 (1995); Minnesota Mut. Life Ins. Co. v. O'Connor, No. 16764, Appellate Court of Illinois, Fourth District, 98 Ill. App. 3d 1040, 425 N.E.2d 38, 54 Ill. Dec. 526 (1981); Huber Pontiac, Inc. v. Wells, Nos. 14428, 14540 cons., Appellate Court of Illinois, Fourth District, 59 Ill. App. 3d 14, 375 N.E.2d 149, 16 Ill. Dec. 518 (1978); Keller v. Brunswick Corp., No. 13961, Appellate Court of Illinois, Fourth District, 54 Ill. App. 3d 271, 369 N.E.2d 327, 11 Ill. Dec. 873 (1977); Wilson v. Massey-Ferguson, Inc., No. 12428, Appellate Court of Illinois, Fourth District, 21 Ill. App. 3d 867, 315 N.E. 2d 580, 15 U.C.C. Rep. Serv. (Callaghan) 654 (1974); Kenney v. Churchill Truck Lines, Inc., No. 11418, Appellate Court of Illinois, Fourth District, 6 Ill. App. 3d 983, 286 N.E.2d 619 (1972); People v. Warrington, Gen. Nos. 11211, 11212 Consolidated, Appellate Court of Illinois, Fourth

(This Listing Continued)

SORLING, NORTHRUP, HANNA, CULLEN AND COCHRAN, LTD., Springfield—Continued

District, Second Division, 125 Ill. App. 2d 370, 260 N.E.2d 764 (1970). ***PRACTICE AREAS:*** Products Liability Law; Commercial Litigation; Oil and Gas Law. ***Email:*** pvreilly@sorlinglaw.com

WILLIAM S. HANLEY, born Chicago, Illinois, June 4, 1939; admitted to bar, 1964, Illinois; 1994, Maine. *Education:* University of Notre Dame (A.B., 1961); University of Chicago (J.D., 1964). Ford Foundation Fellow, Institute of Government and Public Affairs, University of Illinois, 1964-1965. Listed in Who's Who in American Law. Legislative Counsel to Governor Richard B. Ogilvie, Illinois, 1969-1972. General Counsel, Illinois Community College Board, 1981-1999. Chairman, Secretary of State's Advisory Council on Public Records and Privacy, 1992. Chairman, Greater Springfield Chamber of Commerce, 1995. *Member:* Sangamon County, Illinois State (Administrative Law Section Council Chairman, 1981-1982; Member, Sections on Administrative Law, Civil Practice), Maine State and American Bar Associations; Illinois Appellate Lawyers Association; Maine Trial Lawyers Association; Federation of Regulatory Counsel, Inc. (Insurance). (Also practicing individually, Blue Hill, Maine). ***Email:*** whanley@hypernet.com

WILLIAM B. BATES, born Lincoln, Illinois, September 27, 1954; admitted to bar, 1979, Illinois. *Education:* Westminster College (B.A., Accounting and Economics, 1976); Drake University (J.D., with honors, 1978). Order of the Coif. Recipient, American Jurisprudence Award. *Member:* Logan County, Illinois State and American Bar Associations. (Also Member, Woods & Bates, Lincoln, Illinois). ***Email:*** bilbates@ccaonline.com

MARK H. FERGUSON, born St. Louis, Missouri, December 9, 1953; admitted to bar, 1978, Illinois; 1979, U.S. Tax Court; 1982, U.S. Supreme Court. *Education:* University of Illinois (B.A., 1975; J.D., 1978). *Member:* Sangamon County, Illinois State and American Bar Associations.

RETIRED

CHARLES H. NORTHRUP, born Bloomington, Illinois, June 4, 1914; admitted to bar, 1939, Illinois. *Education:* Illinois Wesleyan University (A.B., 1936); University of Illinois at Springfield (M.A., 1980); University of Illinois (J.D., 1939). Phi Delta Phi. Adjunct Assistant Professor of Legal Studies, Sangamon State University, 1983—. *Member:* Sangamon County, Illinois State (Chairman, Real Estate Law Section, 1971-1972) and American Bar Associations. [Lt. Col., USAF, Judge Advocate, Ret.]. (Retired, 2004). ***PRACTICE AREAS:*** Real Estate Law; Municipal Law. ***Email:*** bldrew@sorlinglaw.com

PHILIP E. HANNA, born Geneseo, Illinois, May 3, 1920; admitted to bar, 1945, Illinois. *Education:* Cornell College, Mt. Vernon, Iowa (A.B., 1942); University of Michigan (LL.B., 1945). Phi Delta Phi. *Member:* Sangamon County, Illinois State (Chairman, Labor Law Section Council, 1978-1979) and American Bar Associations. (Retired, 2004). ***PRACTICE AREAS:*** Labor Law; Taxation Law; Probate Law. ***Email:*** jmflint@sorlinglaw.com

COUNSEL FOR: Ameren Services; Bank One Illinois, NA; BroMewn Regional Medical Center; Hulcher Emergency Services, Inc.; Illini Dairy Queen; WICS-TV; Bank of Springfield; Egizii Electric, Inc.; Springfield Electric Supply Company; Lincoln Land Development Company; Hilton Springfield; Phillips Brothers Printers; Federated Funeral Directors of America; Professional Independent Insurance Agents of Illinois; Illinois Baptist State Association; The Illinois Great Rivers Annual Conference of the United Methodist Church; Gas Utilities Alliance; Illinois Association of Realtors; Illinois Community College Board; Northern Illinois University; Illinois Development Finance Authority; Springfield Airport Authority; General Assembly Retirement System; Judges Retirement System; State Employees' Retirement System of Illinois; City of Springfield; City of Leland Grove; Village of Rochester; Springfield Mass Transit District; Evans Construction Company; Freesen, Inc.; Memorial Health System; Memorial Medical Center; Crete Oil Company, Inc.; Petco Petroleum; CIGNA; Aetna Life Insurance Company; Midwest Insurance Company; M. J. Kellner Company; Tom Lange Company; The Salvation Army; Land of Lincoln Goodwill Industries; Illinois Manufactured Housing Association; The Curry Companies; Springfield Service Corporation.

TURNER LAW OFFICE

1 WEST OLD STATE CAPITAL PLAZA, SUITE 810
SPRINGFIELD, ILLINOIS 62701
Telephone: 217-525-7008
Fax: 217-525-7056
URL: http://www.chadturnerlaw.com
Email: cturner@chadturnerlaw.com
URL: http://www.chadturnerlawfirm.com

Criminal Defense, Driving While Intoxicated, Driving Under the Influence, Traffic Violations, Felonies, Misdemeanors, Drug Crimes, Appeals, Forfeiture, Search and Seizure, Sex Crimes.

CHAD E. TURNER, born Jacksonville, Illinois, April 7, 1970; admitted to bar, 1998, Illinois. *Education:* Eastern Illinois University (B.S., 1993); Southern Illinois University (J.D., 1997). ***PRACTICE AREAS:*** Criminal; DUI; Personal Injury. ***Email:*** cturner@chadturnerlaw.com

ROBERT C. WALBAUM

BARRISTER BUILDING
1231 SOUTH EIGHTH STREET
SPRINGFIELD, ILLINOIS 62703
Telephone: 217-789-0911
Fax: 217-789-0913
Email: walbaumlaw@sbcglobal.net

General Civil Practice. Probate, Trusts, Wills, Estate Planning. Real Estate, Banking and Corporation Law.

ROBERT C. WALBAUM, born Springfield, Illinois, November 13, 1933; admitted to bar, 1961, Illinois; 1964, U.S. District Court, Central District of Illinois; 1973, U.S. Court of Appeals, 7th Circuit; 1989, U.S. Supreme Court. *Education:* University of Illinois (B.S., 1955); Washington University (J.D., 1960). Phi Alpha Delta. Assistant States' Attorney, Sangamon County, Illinois, 1961-1963. City Attorney, City of Springfield, 1964-1969. Attorney, Springfield Park District, 1984—. Member, 1965-1975 and Chairman, 1974, Sangamon County Board. *Member:* Sangamon County, Illinois State (Assembly Delegate, 1980-1982) and American Bar Associations. [With U.S. Army, 1955-1957]

(This Listing Continued)

REPRESENTATIVE CLIENTS: Illinois National Bank; Brandt Consolidated, Inc.; Solomon Colors, Inc.; Midstate Warehouse, Inc.; Pleasant Plains, New Berlin and Island Grove Fire Protection Districts; Springfield Plastics Inc.; Springfield Park District.
REFERENCE: Illinois National Bank.

PERRY & ASSOCIATES

3309 CARDINAL LANE
SPRING GROVE, ILLINOIS 60081
Telephone: 815-678-4920
Fax: 501-634-0943
URL: http://www.perrylaws.com
Email: perryr@core.com
URL: http://www.perryassociateslaw.com

Land Use, Zoning, Municipal Law, Government, Employment Law, Civil Rights.

ROBIN L. PERRY, born Battle Creek, Michigan, June 22, 1964; admitted to bar, 1997, Illinois and U.S. District Court, Northern District of Illinois. *Education:* De Pual University (B.S., 1992); John Marshall Law School (J.D., 1997). Director, Family Services in McHenry. *Member:* Chicago, Illinois State and American Bar Associations. ***PRACTICE AREAS:*** Land Use; Zoning Law; Municipal Law; Government; Employment Law; Civil Rights.

REPRESENTATIVE CLIENTS: County of McHenry; Algonquin Municipalities: Hebron, McHenry, Harvard, Lake in the Hills; Greenwood Municipalities: West Dundee, Woodstock, Lakewood.

HERBOLSHEIMER, LANNON, HENSON, DUNCAN AND REAGAN, P.C.

STREATOR, ILLINOIS
(See La Salle)

Corporate Law, Business Law, Criminal Law, DWI/DUI, Juvenile Law, Employment Law, Administrative Law, Employment Termination, Sexual Harassment, Estate Planning, Probate, Tax Planning, Wills and Trusts, Family Law, Divorce, Adoption, Prenuptial Agreements, Health Care, Civil Litigation, Insurance Defense, Products Liability, Insurance, Subrogation, Real Estate, Boundary Disputes, Easements.

MYERS, BERRY, O'CONOR & KUZMA, LTD.

7 NORTHPOINT DRIVE
STREATOR, ILLINOIS 61364
Telephone: 815-672-3116
Fax: 815-672-0738

Ottawa, Illinois Office: 130 East Madison Street, 61350. Telephone: 815-434-6206. Fax: 815-434-6203.

General Civil and Trial Practice in all Courts. Banking, Commercial and Corporate Law, Government and School Law, Probate, Real Estate, Health Care Law, Mediation and Arbitration.

FIRM PROFILE: The firm serves clients throughout Northern Central Illinois in the practice areas noted.

(For complete Biographical Data on all Personnel, see Professional Biographies at Ottawa, Illinois)

LAW OFFICES OF RUBEN SANMIGUEL

Established in 2002
330 N. DIVISION DRIVE, SUITE C
SUGAR GROVE, ILLINOIS 60554
Telephone: 630-466-8400
Fax: 630-466-8401
Email: rubensanmiguel@comcast.net
URL: http://www.lawsanmiguel.com

Criminal Law, Real Estate, Business Development.

FIRM PROFILE: For over a Decade I have Defended my Clients Rights and Advocated for the Best Results.

RUBEN D. SANMIGUEL, born Hinsdale, Illinois, December 27, 1959; admitted to bar, 1991, Illinois; 1994, Florida. *Education:* Loyola University, Chicago (B.A., 1982; J.D., 1990). Former, Assistant Public Defender, Cook County, Illinois. Advisor-Contractor, Department of Defense, Caribbean, 2002-2004. *Member:* Illinois State Bar Association; Kane County Bar Association; West Suburban Bar Association; Hispanic Lawyers Association of Illinois. [U.S. Navy, 1982-2002; U.S. Navy Reserve, 1981-2002; USS Kitty Hawk CV-63, 1984-1986; Officer of the Deck; Surface Warfare Officer; Joint Service Achievement Medal, 2000; Blue and Gold Officer, U.S. Naval Academy, 1991—; Navy Achievement Medal, 2002]. ***LANGUAGES:*** Spanish. ***PRACTICE AREAS:*** Criminal Law (50%); Real Estate (30%); Business Development (20%). ***Email:*** rubensanmiguel@comcast.net

LEGAL SUPPORT PERSONNEL

MELANIE BANNISTER, (admission pending)
Language: Spanish.

THE BRAINARD LAW OFFICES

SULLIVAN, ILLINOIS

(See Charleston)

General Practice. Insurance Defense, Personal Injury, Products Liability, Probate, Trusts, Real Estate, Taxation, Municipal, Family and Health Law. Trials in all State and Federal Courts.

McLAUGHLIN AND FLORINI, LTD.

16 SOUTH WASHINGTON STREET
P.O. BOX 228
SULLIVAN, ILLINOIS 61951
Telephone: 217-728-7325
Fax: 217-728-8122
Email: twignor@one-eleven.net

Probate, Real Estate, Estate Planning, Corporation and Tax Law. Trials. General Civil Practice.

JOSEPH L. McLAUGHLIN (1884-1963)

JAMES M. McLAUGHLIN (1918-2005)

JOSEPH V. FLORINI, born Shelbyville, Illinois, August 17, 1941; admitted to bar, 1965, Illinois; 1968, U.S. Court of Military Appeals. *Education:* University of Illinois (B.S., 1964; J.D., 1965). Phi Alpha Delta. *Member:* Moultrie County, Illinois State and American Bar Associations. ***PRACTICE AREAS:*** Probate; Real Estate.

REPRESENTATIVE CLIENTS: Scott State Bank, Bethany, Ill.; State Bank of Arthur, Ill.; Arthur Farm Power, Inc.; First Mid-Illinois Bank & Trust.

SCHLICHTER, BOGARD & DENTON

2661 N. ILLINOIS, SUITE 187
SWANSEA, ILLINOIS 62226
Telephone: 618-632-3329
URL: http://www.lawyers.com/sbd

St. Louis, Missouri Office: 100 South Fourth Street, Suite 900. Telephone: 314-621-6115.

Personal Injury, Railroad Personal Injury, Maritime Personal Injury, Medical Malpractice, Products Liability, Toxic Tort Law.

(For complete biographical data, see Professional Biographies at St. Louis, Missouri)

CAMIC, JOHNSON, WILSON & McCULLOCH, P.C.

Established in 1987
207 W. STATE STREET
SYCAMORE, ILLINOIS 60178
Telephone: 815-899-0155
Email: administrator@cjwm.com
URL: http://www.lawyers.com/cjwm

Criminal Trial Practice, including Assault, Batter, Burglary, Driver's License Suspension, Driving While Intoxicated (DUI), Forfeiture, Fraud, Death Penalty, Felonies, Forgery, Manslaughter, Misdemeanors, Murder, Parole and Probation, Post-Conviction Remedies, Search and Seizure, Sex Crimes, Theft, Traffic Violations, and Weapons Charges. Expungements and Secretary of State hearings. Family Practice, including Child Custody and Visitation, Divorce, Child Support and Adoption. Real Estate.

DAVID E. CAMIC, admitted to bar, 1987, Illinois; U.S. District Court, Northern and Central Districts of Illinois; 1995, New York. *Education:* Aurora University (B.A., 1982); DePaul University; John Marshall School (J.D., 1987). *Member:* Illinois State and American Bar Associations; The Association of Trial Lawyers of America. ***PRACTICE AREAS:*** Criminal Defense.

GARY V. JOHNSON, admitted to bar, 1978, Illinois. *Education:* Illinois Wesleyan University (B.A., magna cum laude, 1975); Drake University (J.D., with honors, 1978). Order of the Coif. Assistant State's Attorney, Kane County, 1978-1982. Elected Kane County State's Attorney, 1988-1992. *Member:* Kane County and Illinois State Bar Associations. ***PRACTICE AREAS:*** Criminal Law.

THOMAS O. McCULLOCH, admitted to bar, 1974, Illinois; 1976, U.S. District Court, Northern District of Illinois; 1977, U.S. Court of Appeals, Seventh Circuit and U.S. Supreme Court. *Education:* Denison University (B.A., 1967); John Marshall Law School (J.D., 1974). Assistant States Attorney, Kane County, 1974-1976. Public Defender, Kane County, 1976-1982. Criminal Defense Board Member, Illinois Attorneys for Criminal Justice. *Member:* Kane County, Illinois State and American Bar Associations. [With USN, 1967-1971; Capt., USNR, 1967—]. ***PRACTICE AREAS:*** Criminal Defense Litigation; Family Law.

Languages: Spanish.

CHARLES E. CRONAUER

1101 DEKALB AVENUE
SYCAMORE, ILLINOIS 60178
Telephone: 815-895-8585
FAX: 815-895-4070
Email: cronauerlaw@aol.com
URL: http://www.cronauerlaw.com

General Civil Trial and Appellate Practice in State and Federal Courts. Real Estate, Zoning Planning, Land Use, Business, Corporation, Commercial, Probate, Estate Planning, Trust, Personal Injury, Products Liability, Workers Compensation, Insurance, and National and International Franchising and Agricultural Law, Elder Law, Business Law, Environmental Law.

(This Listing Continued)

FIRM PROFILE: Charles E. Cronauer has been practicing law in Sycamore, Illinois for 30 years. Serving clients in De Kalb, Kane, Lee, Ogle, Winnebago and Du Page Counties. Engaging in a focus in Commercial, Real Estate, Agriculture, Will and Trusts.

CHARLES E. CRONAUER, born Johnstown, Pennsylvania, January 2, 1945; admitted to bar, 1974, Illinois and U.S. District Court, Northern District of Illinois; 1995, U.S. District Court of Nebraska; 1977, U.S. Supreme Court. *Education:* University of Notre Dame (B.A., 1967); John Marshall Law School (J.D., 1974). Assistant State's Attorney, Civil Division, De Kalb County, 1976-1982. *Member:* DeKalb County (President, 1991-1992; Vice-President, 1990-1991; Secretary-Treasurer, 1976-1977); Illinois State and American Bar Associations; Illinois Trial Lawyers Association; The Association of Trial Lawyers of America. [1st Lt., U.S. Army, 1967-1970]. ***REPORTED CASES:*** Teacher's College Board vs. Aetna Casualty, 348 N.E.2d 265 and Wolfenberger vs. Madison, 357 N.E.2d 656, 1976; The Bank of Commerce vs. Riverside Trails, 367 N.E.2d 993 and Loyd vs. Board of Education, 364 N.E.2d 977, 1977; Wielert vs. Larson, 404 N.E.2d 1111, 1980; Manning vs. Board of Education, 416 N.E.2d 381, 1981; Phillips vs. Special Hearing Board, 504 N.E.2d 1251, 1986.

APPROVED ATTORNEY FOR: Attorneys Title Guaranty Fund, Inc.
REPRESENTATIVE CLIENTS: National Bank & Trust Company of Sycamore; The Armoloy Corp.; Surftec Enterprises, Inc.; Electrolizing, Inc.; American Family Insurance; Armoloy of Illinois; Kishwaukee Country Club, Inc.; Mascal Electric, Inc.; Milner & Associates, Inc.; De Kalb Forge Co.; American Title Guaranty, Inc.; Pierce Packaging Co.; DeKalb Real Estate, Inc.; Surface Technical Systems, Inc.; Jo-Davies-Carroll Area Vocational Center; Illini Swine, Inc.; Illini Farms, Inc.
REFERENCES: National Bank & Trust Company of Sycamore; The American National Bank of DeKalb.

KINNALLY, KRENTZ, LORAN, HODGE & HERMAN, P.C.

SYCAMORE, ILLINOIS

(See Aurora)

General Practice. Civil Trial Practice, Personal Injury, Auto Accidents, Worker's Compensation, Corporate Law, Immigration and Naturalization, Business Law, Estate Planning, Trusts, Estates and Probate, Municipal and Zoning Law, Education Law, Environmental and Eminent Domain.

KLEIN, STODDARD, BUCK, WALLER & LEWIS, LLC

Established in 1978
2045 ABERDEEN COURT
SYCAMORE, ILLINOIS 60178
Telephone: 815-748-0380
Fax: 815-748-4030
Email: info@ksbwl.com
URL: http://www.ksbwl.com

General Civil and Trial Practice. Appeals, Probate, Real Estate, Bankruptcy, Banking, Corporate, Commercial, Estate Planning Law, Elder Law, Personal Injury, Divorce, Adoption, and Family Law.

FIRM PROFILE: Klein, Stoddard, Buck, Waller & Lewis, LLC has been existence in Sycamore, Illinois since its establishment in 1978. Serving clients in De Kalb, Kane, Ogle, Lee, La Salle, Boone and surrounding counties. Engaging in a General Practice with Partners who specialize in specific areas. (Notice pursuant to federal law: We are a debt relief agency. We help people file for bankruptcy relief under the Bankruptcy Code).

RONALD G. KLEIN, born Waterman, Illinois, August 25, 1939; admitted to bar, 1963, Illinois. *Education:* University of Illinois (B.S., 1961; LL.B., 1963). City Attorney, Village of Hinckley, 1967—. Public Defender, 1968-1969. Zoning Hearing Officer, 1989—. *Member:* DeKalb County (President, 1976-1977) and Illinois State Bar Associations. [Capt., U.S. Marine Corps., 1964-1966]. ***PRACTICE AREAS:*** Estate Planning Law; Real Estate Law; Tax Law. ***Email:*** rklein@ksbwl.com

JAMES A. STODDARD, born DeKalb, Illinois, July 11, 1951; admitted to bar, 1976, Illinois. *Education:* University of Illinois (B.S., 1973; J.D., 1976). *Member:* DeKalb County, Illinois State and American Bar Associations. ***PRACTICE AREAS:*** Trusts and Estates; Real Estate; Taxation; Wills; Agricultural Law; Probate. ***Email:*** jstoddard@ksbwl.com

JAMES R. BUCK, born Elgin, Illinois, March 30, 1946; admitted to bar, 1974, Illinois. *Education:* Lawrence University (B.A., magna cum laude, 1968); University of Illinois (J.D., 1974). *Member:* DeKalb County, Illinois State and American (Member, Family Law Section) Bar Associations. [U.S. Army, 1969-1970]. ***PRACTICE AREAS:*** General Trial Practice; Appeals; Personal Injury; Social Security Disability; Divorce, Family Law and Adoption. ***Email:*** jbuck@ksbwl.com

BRADLEY J. WALLER, born LaFayette, Indiana, December 18, 1961; admitted to bar, 1988, Illinois; 1989, U.S. District Court, Northern District of Illinois. *Education:* University of Cincinnati; Northern Illinois University (B.S., 1985; J.D., cum laude, 1988). Trustee, Chapter Seven Bankruptcy, Northern District of Illinois, 1992— Recipient, American Jurisprudence Award in Estate Planning. *Member:* Illinois State and American Bar Associations. ***REPORTED CASES:*** Matter of Marchiando, 13 F.3d 1111 (7th Cir. 1994); County of DeKalb v. Vidmar, 251 Ill.App.3d 419, 622 N.E.2d 667 (Ill.App. 2 Dist. 1993); In re Churchill Properties III, 197 B.R. 283 (Bankr. N.D. Ill. 1996). ***PRACTICE AREAS:*** Civil Litigation; Bankruptcy; Real Estate. ***Email:*** bwaller@ksbwl.com

JEFFREY L. LEWIS, born Galesburg, Illinois, November 6, 1969; admitted to bar, 1999, Illinois and U.S. District Court, Northern District of Illinois. *Education:* Northern Illinois University (B.S., 1990; J.D., magna cum laude, 1998). *Member:* De Kalb County Bar Assocation (Secretary and Treasurer, 2000-2003), Illinois State and American Bar As-

(This Listing Continued)

KLEIN, STODDARD, BUCK, WALLER & LEWIS, LLC, Sycamore—Continued

sociations. ***REPORTED CASES:*** Vinzenz v. Hintzsche Fertilizer, Inc., 336 Ill.App.3d 468, 783 N.E.2d 1087 (Ill.App. 2 Dist. 2003). ***PRACTICE AREAS:*** Elder Law; Probate; Estate Planning; Real Estate; Civil Litigation. ***Email:*** jlewis@ksbwl.com

REPRESENTATIVE CLIENTS: The National Bank and Trust Co.; Resource Bank; Pierce Township; Squaw Grove Township; Village of Hinckley; Union Drainage District #1 of Cortland & Pierce Townships; Union Drainage District of Squaw Grove; Cortland Community Fire Protection District; Sycamore Fire Protection District; Kishwaukee Community Hospital; Conserv FS, Inc.; DeKalb University Development Corp.; Dekalb Area Association of Realtors; Hintzsche Fertilizer, Inc.; Castle Bank, N.A.; Illinois Community Credit Union.

JEFFREY M. KRASNER

Established in 1978

407 WEST STATE STREET, SUITE 4
SYCAMORE, ILLINOIS 60178-1455
Telephone: 815-899-8436
Fax: 815-895-1700
Email: krasnerlaw2001@yahoo.com
URL: http://www.lawyers.com/krasnerlaw

General Practice. Real Estate, Estate Planning, Bankruptcy, Debtors and Creditor Rights, Business Law, Litigation, Wills, Trusts, Estates, Collections.

JEFFREY M. KRASNER, born Waukegan, Illinois, November 10, 1949; admitted to bar, 1977, Illinois. *Education:* Wabash College (A.B., 1971); Chicago-Kent College of Law, Illinois Institute of Technology (J.D., 1977). Instructor, Real Estate Transactions, Northern Illinois University, 1990. *Member:* Chicago, De Kalb County (President, 2001-2002), Illinois State and American Bar Associations. ***LANGUAGES:*** German. ***PRACTICE AREAS:*** General Practice; Real Estate; Probate; Estate Planning; Business Planning; Bankruptcy Chapter 7; Bankruptcy Chapter 13; Wills; Trusts and Estates; Collections.

Language: German.

REPRESENTATIVE CLIENTS: 1st American Title Insurance Company; Welsh Industries; Star Properties; S & H Builders; U.A.G., Inc.; T.Q.M., Inc.; Bygone Era; 407 West State Associates.

LAW OFFICES OF LEYNAUD & LEYNAUD

A PROFESSIONAL CORPORATION

SYCAMORE, ILLINOIS

(See Peru)

General Civil and Trial Practice, Personal Injury, Mediation, Worker's Compensation, Real Estate, Criminal, Landlord/Tenant and Family Law. Business/Banking Litigation, DUI and Traffic. Insurance, General Practice, Medical Malpractice, Zoning and Land Use. Bad Faith, Drug Crimes, Juvenile Crimes, White Collar, Adoptions, Child Custody, Divorce, Child Support, Visitation Rights, Domestic Violence. Auto Accidents, Dog Bites, Slip and Fall, Wrongful Death, Buying and Selling, Wills and Probate.

SMITH & TUCKER

1958 ABERDEEN COURT
SYCAMORE, ILLINOIS 60178
Telephone: 815-787-7033
Fax: 815-748-1020
URL: http://www.smithtucker.com

From its offices in Sycamore, Illinois, Smith & Tucker provides services to its clients in the following core areas: civil litigation, corporate and business law, municipal and non-profit law, real estate development (including zoning, land use, and planning), commercial and residential real estate sale and leasing transactions, employer labor law, banking practices and loan review, creditor's rights and bankruptcy, collections and mortgage foreclosures, wills and trusts, estate planning and health care directives, probate, personal injury law, employment law, civil rights law, election law and criminal litigation.

MEMBERS OF FIRM

PETER THOMAS SMITH, born Red Wing, Minnesota, February 9, 1946; admitted to bar, 1971, District of Columbia and U.S. District Court, District of Columbia; 1972, U.S. Court of Military Appeals; 1975, U.S. Court of Appeals, District of Columbia Circuit; 1977, Illinois; 1980, U.S. Supreme Court; 1983, U.S. District Court, Northern District of Illinois including Trial Bar and U.S. Court of Appeals, Seventh Circuit. *Education:* Loyola University (B.S., with honors, 1968); George Washington University (J.D., with honors, 1971). Phi Alpha Delta. Associate, Keller & Heckman, Washington, D. C., 1974-1977. Private Practice, Sycamore, Illinois, 1976-1979, 1984-1990. Partner: Minnihan & Smith, 1980-1984; Smith & Strauss, 1990-2000; Smith Strauss Tucker & Brown, 2000-2001; Smith Tucker and Brown, 2001-2005. City Attorney, City of Sycamore, 1990-2003. Treasurer, DeKalb County Republicans, 1980. Chairman: Sycamore United Givers Fund, 1985; DeKalb County Unit, American Cancer Society, 1992-1996; St. Mary's School Foundation, 1997—. President, Sycamore Kiwanis Club, 1990. *Member:* DeKalb County (President, 2002-2003), Kane County, Illinois State and American Bar Associations; The District of Columbia Bar *(inactive). [Judge Advocate,* 1971-1974 and Officer, 1968-1976 (Capt.), U.S. Marine Corps]. ***REPORTED CASES:*** Laue v. Leifheit, *105 Ill.2d 191 (1984);* Minnesota v. Cloverleaf Creamery, 449 U.S. 456 (1981); Society of the Plastics Industry v. OSHA, 589 F.2d 2362 (2nd Cir. 1975); Natick Paperboard v. Weinberger, 524 F 2d 1103 (1975); Falkner v. Hinckley Parachute, 533 N.E. 23 941 (1988); Eckhardt v. Kirts, 179 Ill.App.3d 863, 534 N.E.2d 1339 (2d Dist. 1989). ***PRACTICE AREAS:*** Civil Litigation; Business Organization; Contracts; Commercial Law; Corporate Law; Elder Law; Municipal Law; Personal Injury Law; Probate Law; Real Estate Law. ***Email:*** ptsmith@smithtucker.com

WATSON B. TUCKER, born Dobbs Ferry, New York, November 16, 1940; admitted to bar, 1965, Illinois and U.S. District Court, Northern District of Illinois; 1970, U.S. Court of Appeals, Seventh Circuit; 1971, U.S. Supreme Court; 1976, U.S. Court of Appeals, Second Circuit; 1981, U.S. Court of Appeals, Third Circuit; 1996, U.S. Court of Appeals, Ninth Circuit. *Education:* Northwestern University (B.S., Speech, 1962; J.D., magna cum laude, 1965). Partner, Mayer Brown & Platt, Chicago, Illinois, 1965-1997. Fellow, American College of Trial Lawyers, 1985. ***REPORTED CASES:*** HS Services, Inc. v. Nationwide Mutual Ins. Co., 109 F.3d 642 (9th Cir. 1997); Pierce v. F.R. Tripler & Co., 955 F.2d 820 (2d Cir. 1992); In re Nucorp Securities Litigation, 661 F. Supp. 1403 (S.D. Cal. 1987); In re Uranium Antitrust Litigation, 473 F. Supp. 393 (N.D. Ill. 1979); Teachers Ins. v. LaSalle Nat. Bank, 691 N.E. 2d 881 (Ill. App. 2d Dist 1998); FDIC v. Brants, 2 F.3d 147 (5th Cir. 1993); Brunswick Corp. v. Sheridan, 582 F.2d 175 (2d Cir. 1978); Weit v. Continental Bank, 535 F.2d 1010 (7th cir. 1976); Velle v. Sanders, 518 F.Supp. 512 (C.D. Cal. 1981); Gautreaux v. Chicago Housing Auth., 436 F.2d 306 (7th Cir. 1970). ***PRACTICE AREAS:*** Federal Litigation; State Litigation; Alternative Dispute Resolution. ***Email:*** wbtucker@smithtucker.com

ALEXANDER J. SMITH, born Washington, D.C., 1970; admitted to bar, 1998, Illinois. *Education:* Purdue University (B.A., 1992); DePaul University (J.D., 1998). Associate: Kenneth Johnson & Associates, 1998-2001; Smith & Tucker, 2001-2005. *Member:* DeKalb County, Kane County and Illinois State Bar Associations. ***PRACTICE AREAS:*** Civil Litigation; Business Organization; Foreclosures; Unlawful Detainer; Real Estate; Business Transactions; Contracts; Wills; Trust Law; Plaintiffs Personal Injury; Probate. ***Email:*** ajsmith@smithtucker.com

MICHAEL P. COGHLAN, born Chicago, Illinois, 1958; admitted to bar, 1983, Illinois; 1985, U.S. District Court, Northern District of Illinois including Trial Bar and U.S. Court of Appeals, Seventh Circuit. *Education:* University of Illinois (B.A., with distinction, 1979); IIT/Chicago-Kent College of Law (J.D., 1983). Assistant Attorney General, Illinois Attorney General's Office, 1983-1986; First Assistant State's Attorney, DeKalb County State's Attorney Office, 1986-1988; State's Attorney's Office, 1988-1996; Kane County Assistant State's Attorney, 2000-2005. Chairman, Board of Directors, Voluntary Action Center, 1995-1997. Member: DeKalb County Youth Service Providers, 1995-1997; Dekalb County Republicans, 1987-1996; Illinois State's Attorney Association, 1988-1996; Sycamore A.Y.S.O. Attorney, 2004—. Co-Chair, DeKalb County Violence Prevention Task Force, 1990-1996. Chair, Law Enforcement Sub-committee, DeKalb County Partnership for Substance Abuse Free Environment (D.C.P./S.A.F.E.), 1990-1996. ***PRACTICE AREAS:*** Land Use Law; Government Law; Civil Litigation; Personal Injury Law; Estate Litigation; Election Law.

REPRESENTATIVE CLIENTS: DeKalb County Housing Authority; DeKalb Park District; Cortland Fire Protection District; Cortland Library Board; Virgil Solid Waste Disposal District; The Daily Chronicle; The National Bank & Trust Company of Sycamore; Castle Bank; American National Bank of DeKalb County, Sycamore; Old Second Bank; Elmer Larson Inc.; L & S Venture; Shepard Construction DK, Inc.; DeKalb County Residential Development Corporation; IDEAL Industries; Sycamore Prairie Business Park; Aspen Business Condominiums; Hoffman Development; Northern Illinois Wetlands, LLC; Midlands Office Park; Algus Realty, LLC; Advantage Capital Financial Service, Inc.; Maple Terrace Subdivision; DeKalb Forge Company; Rockford Drop Forge and Machine Company; Eagle Forge and Machine Company; Algus Packaging, Inc.; Cavel International, Inc.; M&L Joint Venture; Nicomm, Inc.; Northern Illinois University Office of Technology Commercialization; DevNet, Inc.; DeKalb Clinic Chartered; Midwest Sports Medicine; The Knolls Subdivision; Northfield Farm Subdivision; Prairie Ridge Subdivision.

BEAVERS, GRAHAM & FINES

Established in 1928

221 WEST MAIN CROSS
P.O. BOX 320
TAYLORVILLE, ILLINOIS 62568
Telephone: 217-824-3341
Facsimile: 217-824-3842
URL: http://www.lawyers.com/bg&flaw

Civil Trial Law, Probate, Real Estate, Taxation, Personal Injury Defense, Insurance Law, Domestic Relations, Appellate Practice, Banking Law.

MEMBERS OF FIRM

CHARLES EVANS BLISS (1906-1986)

RICHARD G. HERSHEY (1916-1991)

JAMES O. BEAVERS, born Sullivan, Illinois, June 1, 1934; admitted to bar, 1964, Illinois; 1965, Missouri; 1979, U.S. Tax Court. *Education:* Eastern Illinois University (B.S.Ed., 1956); St. Louis University (J.D., 1963). Phi Alpha Delta. Faculty, Illinois Institute of Continuing Legal Education, 1976—. Internal Revenue Agent and Estate Tax Examiner, U.S. Treasury Department, 1956-1966. Member, Advisory Board, Illinois Department of Revenue, 1974-1976. City Attorney, Taylorville, Illinois, 1977-1986. *Member:* The Bar Association of Metropolitan St. Louis; Christian County, Illinois State and American Bar Associations; The Missouri Bar. ***PRACTICE AREAS:*** Civil Trial Law; Probate Law; Real Estate Law; Taxation Law. ***Email:*** jobeavers@ctitech.com

EDWARD T. GRAHAM, JR., born Elmhurst, Illinois, January 25, 1952; admitted to bar, 1982, Illinois; 1988, U.S. District Court, Central District of Illinois; 1992, U.S. Court of Appeals, Seventh Circuit and U.S. Supreme Court. *Education:* University of Wisconsin-LaCrosse (B.S., 1976); The John Marshall Law School (J.D., 1982). Board of Directors, 1986-1996 and President, 1991, YMCA of Christian County, Illinois. *Member:* Christian County (Secretary and Treasurer, 1985-1987; President, 1992); Illinois State (Assembly, 2001-2004; Section Council on Law Office Economics, 2004) and American Bar Associations; Illinois Association of Defense Trial Counsel (Section Council on Civil Practice and Procedure, 2004); Lincoln-Douglas American Inn of Court. ***PRACTICE AREAS:*** Personal Injury Defense; Insurance Law; Domestic Relations; Trial and Appellate Practice. ***Email:*** etgrahamjr@ctitech.com

(This Listing Continued)

DAVID R. FINES, born Springfield, Illinois, April 14, 1962; admitted to bar, 1987, Illinois; 1993, U.S. Supreme Court; 1987, U.S. District Court, Northern District of Illinois; 1991, U.S. District Court, Central District of Illinois; 1995, U.S. Tax Court. *Education:* University of Illinois (B.S., with honors, 1984; J.D., 1987). *Member:* Christian County and Illinois State Bar Associations. ***PRACTICE AREAS:*** Civil Trial Law; Corporate Law; Probate Law; Real Estate Law; Taxation Law; Banking Law. ***Email:*** davlaw@ctitech.com

BETH E. BROTHERTON, born Bloomington, Illinois, June 1, 1965; admitted to bar, 1997, Illinois. *Education:* Millikin University (B.A., Elementary Education, 1991); St. Louis University (J.D., 1996). *Member:* Illinois State and American Bar Associations. ***PRACTICE AREAS:*** General Practice; Real Estate; Domestic Relations; Appellate Practice. ***Email:*** bef@ctitech.com

MICHELLE M. COADY, born Taylorville, Illinois, August 25, 1976; admitted to bar, 2003, Illinois. *Education:* Southern Illinois University (B.S., 1999); University of Missouri, Columbia (J.D., 2002). *Member:* Illinois State and American Bar Associations. ***PRACTICE AREAS:*** Appellate Practice; Creditors Rights; Automotive Defense; Consumer Products Defense; Insurance Defense. ***Email:*** coady_michelle@hotmail.com

ATTORNEYS FOR: First National Bank of Mt. Auburn; Ayars Bank of Moweaqua; Assumption, Morrisonville and Stonington Cooperative Grain Companies; Morrisonville; Country Mutual Insurance Co.; Fort Dearborn Life Insurance Co.; Pekin Insurance; Country Casualty Insurance Company; US Life Insurance Company; Auto Owners Insurance Co; Village of Kincaid, Illinois; Village of Morrisonville; Country Life Insurance Company; Peoples Bank & Trust; First National Bank of Taylorville; First National Bank of Nokomis; UMB First State Bank of Morrisonville; U.S. Bank of Taylorville; Village of Harvel; Taylorville City Attorney.

MEYER, AUSTIN & ROMANO, P.C.

Established in 1869

210 SOUTH WASHINGTON STREET
P.O. BOX 140
TAYLORVILLE, ILLINOIS 62568-0140
Telephone: 217-824-4931
Telecopier: 217-824-8892

General Civil and Criminal Trial and Appellate Practice in State and Federal Courts. Insurance Defense, Personal Injury, Workers Compensation, Real Estate, Probate, Estate Planning, Family, Business and Municipal Law.

CLARK H. MILEY (1905-1985)

DANIEL W. AUSTIN, born Springfield, Illinois, February 24, 1949; admitted to bar, 1974, Illinois, U.S. District Court, Central District of Illinois, U.S. Court of Appeals, Seventh Circuit and U.S. Supreme Court; U.S. Tax Court. *Education:* Millikin University (B.A., 1971); Washington University (J.D., 1974). Phi Delta Phi. Member, The Order of Barristers. *Member:* Christian County, Illinois State and American Bar Associations. ***PRACTICE AREAS:*** Real Estate; Probate; Estate Planning; Business Law. ***Email:*** danaustin@ctitech.com

ROCCI L. ROMANO, born Decatur, Illinois, April 23, 1949; admitted to bar, 1974, Illinois; U.S. District Court, Central District of Illinois. *Education:* Eastern Illinois University (B.S., 1971); Washington University (J.D., 1974). Phi Delta Phi. City Attorney for Edinburg, Mt. Auburn and Palmer, Illinois. *Member:* Christian County, Illinois State and American Bar Associations; Illinois Trial Lawyers Association; Illinois Association of Defense Trial Counsel. ***PRACTICE AREAS:*** Family Law; Civil Litigation; Municipal Law; Financial Institutions; Personal Injury; Insurance Defense. ***Email:*** rocciromano@ctitech.com

WILLIAM J. MEYER, JR. (Retired)

REFERENCES: Grinnell Mutual Reinsurance Company; Taylorville Community Credit Union; Citizens Bank of Edinburg; Palmer Bank.

LAW OFFICES OF RONALD N. PRIMACK, L.L.C.

Established in 1985

18401 MAPLE CREEK DRIVE
SUITE 100
TINLEY PARK, ILLINOIS 60477
Telephone: 708-444-0277
Fax: 708-444-4149
Email: rnplaw@earthlink.net

General Practice including Banking, Real Estate, Commercial Litigation, Business and Municipal Law.

MEMBER OF FIRM

RONALD N. PRIMACK, born Gary, Indiana, August 25, 1955; admitted to bar, 1981, Illinois. *Education:* University of Wisconsin (B.S., with honors, 1978); DePaul University (J.D., 1981). *Member:* Chicago, Lansing and Illinois State Bar Associations. ***REPORTED CASES:*** Berg & Associates v. Nelsen Steel & Wire Co., 221 Ill.App.3d 526, 580 N.E.2d 1198 (1st. Dist. 1991). ***PRACTICE AREAS:*** General Practice; Banking Law; Commercial Litigation; Municipal Law; Real Estate; Probate.

ASSOCIATES

LINDA C. KLESZYNSKI, born New Haven, Connecticut; admitted to bar, 1987, Illinois. *Education:* Loyola University (B.S., 1972); Chicago-Kent College of Law, Illinois Institute of Technology (J.D., 1987). ***PRACTICE AREAS:*** General Practice; Real Estate; Estate Planning; Probate.

CAROLYN L. MOREHOUSE, born Schenectady, New York, June 1, 1974; admitted to bar, 1999, Illinois. *Education:* Vanderbilt University (B.A., 1996); Indiana University School of Law (J.D., cum laude, 1999).

(This Listing Continued)

REPRESENTATIVE CLIENTS: Centier Bank; Best Trailer; First National Bank of Illinois; Mercantile National Bank; Giovane Construction Company; Great Northern Lumber; Hosley International Trading Corporation; Land O'Frost, Inc.; Lan Oak Park District; Rohm & Haas; Fifth Third Bank; Team Athletic Goods-TAG; Spectrasite Communications, Inc.; Pro Met Steel; Armitage Industries.

THE BRAINARD LAW OFFICES

TUSCOLA, ILLINOIS

(See Charleston)

General Practice. Insurance Defense, Personal Injury, Products Liability, Probate, Trusts, Real Estate, Taxation, Municipal, Family and Health Law. Trials in all State and Federal Courts.

MEYER CAPEL

A PROFESSIONAL CORPORATION

TUSCOLA, ILLINOIS

(See Champaign)

General Civil Litigation, Corporate Law, Business Law, Estate Planning, Estate Administration, Real Estate, Tax, Telecommunications and Public Utility, Intellectual Property Law, Labor and Employment Law (Management), Municipal Law, Family Law, Health Care Law, Personal Injury, Products Liability Law, Criminal Law, Social Security Disability, Software Licensing, Education Law.

BECKETT & WEBBER, P.C.

508 SOUTH BROADWAY
P.O. BOX 17160-61803
URBANA, ILLINOIS 61801-7160
Telephone: 217-328-0263
Fax: 217-328-0290
URL: http://www.lawyers.com/beckettwebberlaw

General, Trial, Appellate and Federal Practice, Criminal, Personal Injury, Family, Probate and Estate Planning Law, DWI, Traffic Violations, Wills, Child Support, Divorce, Child Custody, Adoption, Workers Compensation, Real Estate, Elder Law.

FIRM PROFILE: Beckett & Webber, P.C. was founded in 1993 by J. Steven Beckett, graduate of the University of Illinois College of Law, who has a long-standing Champaign County practice. Mr. Beckett is a lifelong resident of Central Illinois.

ROGER B. WEBBER, born Kankakee, Illinois, June 21, 1958; admitted to bar, 1983, Illinois; U.S. Supreme Court; U.S. Court of Appeals, Seventh Circuit; U.S. District Court, Northern, Central and Southern Districts of Illinois. *Education:* Illinois State University (B.S., 1980); DePaul University (J.D., 1983). Presenter, "Free Speech, Ethics, and Restrictions on Attorney Communications," First Amendment Lawyers Association, August 2003. *Member:* Champaign County (Past Member, Board of Governors) and Illinois State (Member, Criminal Justice Section) Bar Associations; First Amendment Lawyer's Association; Champaign County Criminal Defense Lawyers. ***PRACTICE AREAS:*** Criminal Defense Law; First Amendment Litigation; Family Law; Civil Litigation. ***Email:*** roger@beckettwebber.com

CHAD S. BECKETT, born Urbana, Illinois, March 7, 1972; admitted to bar, 1998, Illinois, U.S. District Court, Central and Northern Districts of Illinois and U.S. Court of Appeals, Seventh Circuit. *Education:* University of Illinois at Urbana (B.A., with distinction, 1994); University of Illinois at Champaign (J.D., 1998). *Member:* Champaign County (Member, Family Law Committee), Illinois State and American Bar Associations. ***PRACTICE AREAS:*** Trusts and Estates; Family Law; Real Estate Transfers; Civil Litigation. ***Email:*** chad@beckettwebber.com

PETER T. BORICH, born Chicago, Illinois, November 24, 1961; admitted to bar, 1992, Illinois. *Education:* University of Illinois at Urbana-Champaign (B.S., 1984); DePaul University College of Law (J.D., 1992). Phi Alpha Delta. Editor, De Paul Journal of Art and Entertainment Law, 1991-1992. Past President, Champaign County, Criminal Defense Lawyers Association, (1996-2000); Illinois Trial Lawyers Association; Association of Trial Lawyers of America. ***PRACTICE AREAS:*** Personal Injury; Workers Compensation; Criminal Defense. ***Email:*** pete@beckettwebber.com

BRETT N. OLMSTEAD, born Jacksonville, Illinois, June 23, 1968; admitted to bar, 1994, Illinois, U.S. District Court, Central and Southern Districts of Illinois and U.S. Court of Appeals, Seventh Circuit. *Education:* University of Illinois (B.A., 1990; J.D., magna cum laude, 1994). Phi Beta Kappa; Order of the Coif. Associate Editor, University of Illinois Law Review, 1992-1994. Author: "In Search of a Drinking Companion's Complicity Under Illinois' Dramshop Act," 1994 University of Illinois Law Review 217. *Member:* Champaign County and Illinois State Bar Associations; National Association of Criminal Defense Lawyers; Champaign County Criminal Defense Lawyers Association. ***PRACTICE AREAS:*** Civil Litigation; Criminal Defense; Family Law; Civil Appeals; Criminal Appeals. ***Email:*** brett@beckettwebber.com

CAROL A. DISON, born Marksville, Louisiana, October 21, 1961; admitted to bar, 1991, Illinois, U.S. District Court, Central and Northern Districts of Illinois and U.S. Court of Appeals, Seventh Circuit. *Education:* University of Southwestern Louisiana (B.A., 1983); University of Illinois College of Law (J.D., 1991). Member, Merit Selection Panel for Reappointment of U.S. Magistrate Judge, Urbana, 2002. *Member:* Champaign County and Illinois State Bar Associations; Champaign County Criminal Defense Lawyers Association; National Association of Criminal Defense Lawyers. ***PRACTICE AREAS:*** Criminal Defense; Civil Litigation; Civil Appeals; Criminal Appeals. ***Email:*** carol@beckettwebber.com

ANDREW W. B. BEQUETTE, born Danville, Illinois, September 29, 1976; admitted to bar, 2001, Illinois, U.S. District Court, Central District of Illinois and U.S. Court of Ap-

(This Listing Continued)

BECKETT & WEBBER, P.C., Urbana—Continued

peals, Seventh Circuit. *Education:* University of Illinois (B.S., 1998; J.D., 2001). *Member:* Champaign County, Illinois State and American Bar Associations; Central Southern Federal Bar. ***PRACTICE AREAS:*** Civil Litigation; Criminal Law; General Practice. ***Email:*** andrew@beckettwebber.com

BARBRA ANN WEBBER, born Stevens Point, Wisconsin, July 4, 1972; admitted to bar, 1997, Illinois; 1998, U.S. District Court, Central District of Illinois. *Education:* Illinois Wesleyan University (B.A., summa cum laude, 1994); University of Illinois (J.D., magna cum laude, 1997). *Member:* Illinois State and American (Member, Family Law Section) Bar Associations. ***PRACTICE AREAS:*** Family Law; Adoption Law; General Practice; Civil Litigation; Civil Appeals. ***Email:*** barbra@beckettwebber.com

OF COUNSEL

J. STEVEN BECKETT, born Urbana, Illinois, June 24, 1948; admitted to bar, 1973, Illinois; U.S. Supreme Court. *Education:* University of Illinois (B.A., 1970; J.D., 1973). Recipient, Champaign County ACLU W. Ellison Chalmers Memorial Award, 1990. Author: "Illinois Joint Tenancy Bank Accounts: The Presumption of Donative Intent and the Emasculation of the Fiduciary Rule," 63 Illinois Bar Journal 706, 1975; "Massage Parlor Ordinances and Constitutional Issues," 64 Illinois Bar Journal 622, Lincoln Award, Second Place, 1976; "Obscenity: *Ward v. Illinois,* the Miller Promise Abandoned," 60 Chicago Bar Record 183, 1979. Co-Author: "Community Standards: Admitting a Public Opinion Poll into Evidence in an Obscenity Case," 84 Case and Comment 18, 1979. Author: "The 1977 Illinois Death Penalty: Individualized Focus Under the 8th and 14th Amendments," 62 Chicago Bar Record 6, 1981; "Speaking from the Grave—A Homicide Victim's Antecedent Accusatory Statements About the Defendant," 71 Illinois Bar Journal 250, 1982; "Whatever Happened to the Bill of Rights? A Criminal Lawyer's Perspective," University of Illinois Law Review, 1992. Co-Author: "Preparing for your Deposition, PMIC 1994: A Comprehensive Guide to the Deposition Process for Physicians and Other Professionals." Recipient, Illinois Public Defenders Association Award of Excellence and Meritorious Service, 1984. Coordinator and Lecturer, Trial Advocacy Program, University of Illinois College of Law, 1987—. Director of Trial Advocacy, University of Illinois College of Law, 2004—. *Member:* Champaign County, Illinois State and American Bar Associations; First Amendment Lawyers Association (President, 1980); Champaign County Criminal Defense Lawyers; National Association of Criminal Defense Lawyers; Illinois Attorneys for Criminal Justice (Director, 1986-1991). Member, Illinois Supreme Court, Committee on Professional Responsibility, (1997-2002). Fellow: American Bar Association Foundation (2002—). ***PRACTICE AREAS:*** Criminal Defense Law; Personal Injury; First Amendment Litigation. ***Email:*** steve@beckettwebber.com

CRAIG & CRAIG

URBANA, ILLINOIS

(See Mattoon)

General Practice in State and Federal Courts. Coal, Oil, Gas, Mining, Oil and Gas Transportation, Insurance, Drainage and Levee Law, Environmental, Corporation, Labor Relations, Workers Compensation and Real Estate Law. Estate Planning, Probate and Bankruptcy Law. Trials and Appeals.

DOBBINS, FRAKER, TENNANT, JOY & PERLSTEIN

A PROFESSIONAL CORPORATION

URBANA, ILLINOIS

(See Champaign)

General Practice, Trial and Appellate Practice in State and Federal Courts. Health Care, Privacy Law, Real Estate, Corporate, Estate Planning, Probate, Insurance Defense, Alternative Dispute Resolution, Family, Personal Injury, Medical Malpractice, Professional Liability, Products Liability, Commercial Litigation, Workers Compensation, Municipal and Drainage and Levee Law.

ERWIN, MARTINKUS & COLE, LTD.

URBANA, ILLINOIS

(See Champaign)

General Civil Trial and Appellate Practice. Business and Corporate Practice including Securities and Banking Law. Tort and Insurance Litigation. Medical Malpractice, Probate and Estate Planning, Real Estate, Family Law, Bankruptcy and Immigration and Naturalization.

FLYNN, PALMER & TAGUE

URBANA, ILLINOIS

(See Champaign)

General Civil Practice in State and Federal Courts. Trials and Appeals. Banking, Estate Planning and Probate, Personal Injury, Real Estate, Family and Taxation Law.

HARRINGTON & TOCK

URBANA, ILLINOIS

(See Champaign)

General Practice. Business, Partnership Law, Small Business Law, Family Business Law, Business Formation, Commercial Litigation, Probate, Tax, Corporation, Real Estate, Eminent Domain and Drainage Law, Shopping Center Law, Commercial Leasing, Commercial Landlord

(This Listing Continued)

and Tenant Law, Tax Planning, IRS Controversies, Trials, Appeals and Commercial Arbitration.

HEYL, ROYSTER, VOELKER & ALLEN

PROFESSIONAL CORPORATION

SUITE 300, 102 EAST MAIN STREET
P.O. BOX 129
URBANA, ILLINOIS 61803-0129
Telephone: 217-344-0060
Telecopier: 217-344-9295
Email: firm@hrva.com
URL: http://www.hrva.com

Peoria, Illinois Office: Suite 600, Chase Building, 124 S.W. Adams, 61602. Telephone: 309-676-0400. Telecopier: 309-676-3374.

Springfield, Illinois Office: Suite 575, National City Center, P.O. Box 1687, 62705. Telephone: 217-522-8822. Telecopier: 217-523-3902.

Rockford, Illinois Office: Second Floor, National City Bank Building, 120 West State Street, P.O. Box 1288, 61105-1288. Telephone: 815-963-4454. Telecopier: 815-963-0399.

Edwardsville, Illinois Office: Suite 100, Mark Twain Plaza II, 103 West Vandalia Street, P.O. Box 467, 62025. Telephone: 618-656-4646. Telecopier: 618-656-7940.

General Civil Trial and Appellate Practice in all Courts, Insurance Defense, Workers" Compensation Defense, Professional Liability Defense, Truck Accidents, Construction Law, Railroad Accidents and Injuries, Insurance Coverage, Self Insured Defense, Products Liability Defense, Civil Rights, Asbestos Defense, Class Action Defense, Corporate Law, Health Care, Banking, Government, Employment, Environmental, Probate, Elder Law, Agribusiness, Immigration, Religious Institutions, Nonprofit and Charitable Organizations, College and University Law, and Real Estate.

PARTNERS

JAMES C. KEARNS, born November 8, 1944; admitted to bar, 1975, Illinois. *Education:* University of Notre Dame (B.A., 1966); University of Illinois (J.D., 1975). Fellow: American College of Trial Lawyers; American Bar Foundation. *Member:* DRI; Illinois Association of Defense Trial Counsel; National Association of Railroad Trial Counsel; International Association of Defense Counsel; American Judicature Society. ***PRACTICE AREAS:*** Products Liability Defense; Medical Malpractice Defense; Professional Liability Defense; Insurance Defense. ***Email:*** jkearns@hrva.com

EDWARD M. WAGNER, born May 25, 1951; admitted to bar, 1980, Illinois. *Education:* Marquette University (B.A., 1973); Creighton University (J.D., cum laude, 1980). *Member:* Illinois Manufacturer's Association, 1993—; Illinois Supreme Court Rules Committee, 2003—; DRI; Illinois Association of Defense Trial Counsel. [U.S. Marine Corps, Captain, 1973-1977]. ***PRACTICE AREAS:*** Medical Malpractice Defense; Professional Liability Defense; Employment Law; Products Liability Defense. ***Email:*** ewagner@hrva.com

MICHAEL E. RAUB, born August 27, 1952; admitted to bar, 1977, Illinois; 1981, Florida. *Education:* Southern Illinois University (B.A., 1974; J.D., cum laude, 1977). Law Clerk to Honorable Henry S. Wise, U.S. District Court, Central District of Illinois, 1978-1982. ***PRACTICE AREAS:*** Civil Litigation Defense; Motor Carrier Defense. ***Email:*** mraub@hrva.com

BRUCE L. BONDS, born April 19, 1957; admitted to bar, 1982, Illinois. *Education:* University of Illinois (A.B., 1979); Washington University-St. Louis (J.D., 1982). Adjunct Professor of Law, University of Illinois College of Law, 1998—. *Member:* Illinois State (Chair, Workers' Compensation Law Section Council, 2003-2004) and American (Vice Chair, Workers' Compensation Employer Liability Law Committee) Bar Associations; Illinois Association of Defense Trial Counsel; Workers' Compensation Lawyers Association. ***PRACTICE AREAS:*** Workers Compensation Defense; Workers Compensation Appeals. ***Email:*** bbonds@hrva.com

JOHN D. FLODSTROM, born July 28, 1961; admitted to bar, 1986, Illinois. *Education:* University of Illinois (B.A., 1983); Northern Illinois University (J.D., with honors, 1986). ***PRACTICE AREAS:*** Workers Compensation Defense; Civil Litigation Defense. ***Email:*** jflodstrom@hrva.com

BRADFORD J. PETERSON, born April 19, 1962; admitted to bar, 1987, Illinois. *Education:* Illinois State University (B.S., with honors, 1984); Southern Illinois University (J.D., 1987). *Member:* Illinois State (Past Chair, Bench & Bar Section Council; Assembly Member, 1999-2003). ***PRACTICE AREAS:*** Products Liability Defense; Professional Liability Defense; Workers Compensation Defense. ***Email:*** bpeterson@hrva.com

KEITH E. FRUEHLING, born September 1, 1968; admitted to bar, 1993, Illinois. *Education:* University of Illinois (B.S., 1990); John Marshall Law School (J.D., 1993). *Member:* Champaign County (President, 2001-2002), Illinois State (Board of Governors, 2002—; Young Lawyer of the Year, 2002) and American (Member, House of Delegates) Bar Associations; Illinois Association of Defense Trial Counsel. ***PRACTICE AREAS:*** Products Liability Defense; Professional Liability Defense; Toxic Tort Defense. ***Email:*** kfruehling@hrva.com

ASSOCIATES

Toney J. Tomaso — ***Kingshuk K. Roy***
Jay E. Znaniecki — ***Monica H. Sholar***
Keith B. Hill — ***Joseph K. Guyette***

Our lawyers are members of the American, state and local bar associations and, in many cases, are members of the local American Inn of Court chapters; where applicable, leadership positions in these organizations are listed.

(For Other Biographical Information, see Professional Biographies at Peoria, Edwardsville, Rockford and Springfield)

LIETZ, BANNER & FORD

URBANA, ILLINOIS

(See Champaign)

Employment Law, Wills and Estates, Agricultural Law, Real Estate, General Litigation, Personal Injury, Securities.

LAW OFFICE OF SHAYLA MAATUKA

306 W. GREEN STREET
URBANA, ILLINOIS 61801
Telephone: 217-337-0700
Fax: 217-337-0707
Email: maatukalaw@insightbb.com
URL: http://www.maatukalaw.com

Real Estate: Litigation, Residential, Commercial, Contracts, Closings, Land Trusts, Landlord Tenant, Evictions, Foreclosures; Business Law including Contracts, Incorporations, LLC's, Small Business, Advertisement, Corporate; Taxation; Family Law & Divorce; Immigration.

FIRM PROFILE: Prior to establishing her firm, Ms. Shayla Maatuka was the co-owner of a local news publication, a daycare, as well as a Real Estate Company. In addition, she does have an MBA on Staff for specific questions and concerns.

SHAYLA MAATUKA, admitted to bar, 2004, Illinois. *Education:* University of Illinois, Urbana-Champaign (B.A., Speech Communication, 1995; J.D., 2003). Law MAP Scholar, University of Illinois College of Law, Summer 1994. Departmental Internship, Teaching Assistant for SpCom 101. Intern: Winnebago County State's Attorney's Office, Fall 1990; Sundstrand Corporation, Spring 1991; Pedersen & Houpt, Summer 1994; City of Urbana, 1995-1997; Land of Lincoln Legal Assistance Foundation, Inc., Summer 1996; State Farm Insurance Companies, Summer 1997. Corresponding Secretary and Editor-in-Chief of Newsletter, Black Law Student Association. Member: Student Government Association; Women Law Students; Public Interest Law Foundation. Co-Founder and Coordinator, P.O.W. Big Sister Program. Chief Financial Officer, Infinite Eight Properties, LLC, 2001—. Co-Director, Village Day Care, 1999-2004. Marketing Director, Black Thought Enterprises, Inc., 1997-2001. ***LANGUAGES:*** English and Spanish.

MEYER CAPEL

A PROFESSIONAL CORPORATION
URBANA, ILLINOIS

(See Champaign)

General Civil Litigation, Corporate Law, Business Law, Estate Planning, Estate Administration, Real Estate, Tax, Telecommunications and Public Utility, Intellectual Property Law, Labor and Employment Law (Management), Municipal Law, Family Law, Health Care Law, Personal Injury, Products Liability Law, Criminal Law, Social Security Disability, Software Licensing, Education Law.

PHEBUS & KOESTER

Established in 1895
136 WEST MAIN STREET
URBANA, ILLINOIS 61803-2797
Telephone: 217-337-1400
Telecopier: 217-337-1607
URL: http://www.phebuslaw.com
Mailing Address; P.O. Box 1008, Urbana, IL 61803-1008

Civil trial practice in all courts, including class actions, mass torts, personal injury, including products liability, medical malpractice, automobile accidents, slip and fall, and railroad.

FIRM PROFILE: Founded in 1895 by F.M. and H.I. Green, the firm's business is now primarily in claimants' civil litigation. Attorneys in the firm have served as plaintiffs' counsel in various class actions in the consumer law area. Members of the firm have been actively involved in representing persons suffering from catastrophic injuries, from defective products, automobile collisions and medical malpractice.

MEMBERS OF FIRM

JOSEPH W. PHEBUS, born Champaign, Illinois, February 13, 1940; admitted to bar, 1968, Illinois; U.S. District Court, Northern, Central and Southern Districts of Illinois; U.S. Court of Appeals, Third, Fourth, Sixth, and Eleventh Circuits. *Education:* University of Illinois (B.S. in Met. Eng., 1962; J.D., 1968). Order of the Coif. *Member:* Champaign County, Illinois State and American Bar Associations; The Association of Trial Lawyers of America; Illinois Trial Lawyers Association (Member Board of Managers). ***PRACTICE AREAS:*** Class Actions; Mass Torts; Personal Injury; Products Liability. ***Email:*** jwphebus@phebuslaw.com

THOMAS F. KOESTER, born Ridgewood, New Jersey, July 28, 1956; admitted to bar, 1982, Illinois; 1994, U.S. District Court, Central District of Illinois; 1995, U.S. Court of Appeals, Seventh Circuit; 1996, U.S. District Court, Northern District of Indiana. *Education:* University of Iowa (B.A., 1979); Drake University (J.D., 1981). *Member:* Champaign County and Illinois State Bar Associations; Illinois Trial Lawyers Association. ***PRACTICE AREAS:*** Personal Injury Law; Plaintiff's Professional Negligence; Criminal Defense. ***Email:*** tkoester@phebuslaw.com

GARY D. FORRESTER, born Decatur, Illinois, July 3, 1946; admitted to bar, 1975, Illinois; 1980, South Dakota; 1983, Oregon; 1986, Australia; U.S. District Court, Northern, Central and Southern Districts of Illinois; U.S. Court of Appeals, Eleventh Circuit; U.S. Supreme Court; Cheyenne River Sioux Tribal Court. *Education:* Eastern Illinois University (B.S., 1968; M.A., 1972); University of Illinois College of Law (J.D., 1975). Kappa Mu Epsilon. ***PRACTICE AREAS:*** Plaintiffs Personal Injury; Consumer Class Actions; Medical Malpractice; Transactional. ***Email:*** gforrester@phebuslaw.com

DANIEL J. POPE, born Chicago, Illinois, November 22, 1948; admitted to bar, 1975, Illinois and U.S. District Court, Northern District of Illinois, including Trial Bar; 1976, U.S. Court of Appeals, Seventh and Tenth Circuits; 1983, New York (inactive); 1985, U.S. Tax Court; 1989, U.S. District Court, Northern District of Texas; 1995, Texas (inactive); 1996, U.S. Supreme Court. *Education:* Loyola University (B.A., 1972); University of Chicago, Graduate School of Business (1977-1978); The John Marshall Law School (J.D., cum laude, 1975). President, Tau Kappa Epsilon. Research and Writing Instructor, John Marshall, 1976-1977. Author: "For every action, there is an equal and opposite reaction," IADC Midyear Meeting (2000); "MDPs: A Corporate Perspective," Tort Source, Vol. 2, No. 2, pp. 1, 5. (Winter 2000); "Of Mice and Men," IADC Defense Counsel Journal, Vol. 66, pp. 569-573 (Oct. 1999); "Breach of Fiduciary Duty and Punitive Damages," TIPS, Professionals', Officers' & Directors' Liability Newsletter (Spring 1999); "Breach of Fiduciary Duty and Punitive Damages," IADC Defense Counsel Journal, Vol. 65, pp. 257-265 (April 1999); "Criminal Defense Malpractice Claim: Methuselah and Beyond," IADC Professional Errors and Omissions Committee Newsletter (Dec. 1998). "Recent Developments of Interest to Corporate Counsel," TIPS Annual Survey of Law, Vol. 33, No. 2, pp. 357-373 (Winter 1998). *Member:* Chicago (Mediator, Cook County Settlement Program, 1991-1993; Member, Committee for the Evaluation of Judicial Candidates, 1981-1986; Chair, Aviation Committee, 1978-1979), Illinois State (Chair, Pro Bono Development Committee, 1991) and American (Member, Litigation Section; Chair, Criminal Law Committee, 2001-2002; Board of Editors, Litigation Ethics Newsletter, 1998-2001; Board of Editors, Professional Liability Update, 1998-2001; Chair, Corporate Counsel's Subcommittee on Law Schools, 1988-1994; Member, Trial Evidence Committee, 1975-1985; Tort and Insurance Practice Section; Member, Scope and Correlation Committee, 1999-2000; Member, Section Task Force on MDPs, 1999-2000; Chair, Corporate Counsel Committee, 1998-1999) Bar Associations; International Association of Defense Counsel (Ethics and Professionalism Articles Author, 1995-2002; Board of Editors, Defense Counsel Journal, 1995-2001; Chair, Amicus Curiae Committee, 1997-2001; Chair, Professional Errors and Omissions Committee, 1998-2001; Member, Task Force on MDPs, 1999-2000; Member, Defense Counsel Committee, 1990-2000; Member, Illinois State Membership Committee, 2004). [United States Merchant Marines, 1966-1967.]. ***REPORTED CASES:*** United States v. Commonwealth Edison; Panter v. Marshall Field & Company; In re Amoco Cadiz Scholes v. Stone, McGuire & Benjamin; In re Federated Department Stores COMPUAAD Corp; In re UNR American Stores, Inc. and Jewel Company v. The Home, et al; In re Sundstrand Cor; Evanston v. Browning Ferris, Inc.; JMB Realty Corporation, et al. v. Osler, Hoskin & Harcourt. ***PRACTICE AREAS:*** Civil Litigation; Criminal Prosecution; Banking; Securities; Professional Liability; Products Liability; Mediation. ***Email:*** dpope@phebuslaw.com

HELEN POPE, born Madison, Wisconsin; admitted to bar, 1991, Illinois and U.S. District Court, Northern District of Illinois; 1993, U.S. Court of Appeals, Seventh Circuit. *Education:* University of Illinois, Urbana-Champaign (B.A., 1986; J.D., magna cum laude, 1991). Dean's List. Harno Scholar. Rickert's Scholar. Member, 1988-1991 and Chairperson, 1990-1991, University of Illinois Prisoners' Rights Research Project. Author: "Constitutional Law/6th Amendment/Peremptory Challenges May Exclude Cognizable Groups from Jury," 79 Illinois Bar Journal 460; "Recent Decisions Note: Constitutional Law/4th and 14th Amendments/Random Drug Testing," 78 Illinois Bar Journal 516. Teacher, Legal Writing, University of Illinois, Department of English, 2004-2005. *Member:* Chicago, Illinois State (Member, Young Lawyers Division), Federal and American Bar Associations. ***PRACTICE AREAS:*** Civil Litigation; Civil Appellate Practice; Professional Malpractice; Complex and Multi-District Litigation; Civil Class Action.

REPRESENTATIVE CLIENTS: Furnished upon request.

JOHN T. PHIPPS LAW OFFICES, P.C.

URBANA, ILLINOIS

(See Champaign)

General Civil Trial Practice. Family, Personal Injury, Corporate, Banking, Paternity, Child Custody, Visitation, Divorce, Wills and Estate Planning, Domestic Relations, Probate, Elder Law, Traffic Defense, Business Fraud, White Collar Crimes, Mediation, Arbitration, Real Estate, Criminal Law, Domestic Violence, DUI.

RAWLES, O'BYRNE, STANKO & KEPLEY, P.C.

URBANA, ILLINOIS

(See Champaign)

General practice in all State and Federal Courts, Trials and Appeals, Personal Injury, Product Liability, Estate and Business Planning, Probate, Real Estate, Hospital and Health Law, Commercial Litigation, Insurance Defense, Malpractice, Criminal Law, Taxation, Domestic Relations, Employment Law, Bankruptcy, Worker's Compensation, and General Counseling.

REISMAN LAW OFFICE

212 W. GREEN STREET
P.O. BOX 395
URBANA, ILLINOIS 61803
Telephone: 217-344-1000
Fax: 217-344-1010
Email: creisman61@yahoo.com
URL: http://www.reismanlaw-firm.com

Personal Injury, Automobile Accidents, Slip and Fall, Workers Compensation, Wrongful Death.

(This Listing Continued)

REISMAN LAW OFFICE, Urbana—Continued

MEMBER OF FIRM

CARL H. REISMAN, born Rochester, New York, July 30, 1961; admitted to bar, 1996, Illinois. *Education:* University of Illinois (B.A., 1982; J.D., 1996). *Member:* Champaign County and Illinois State (Commissioner, Urbana Human Relations Commission) Bar Associations. ***PRACTICE AREAS:*** Workers Compensation; Personal Injury; Automobile Accidents and Injuries; Slip and Fall; Wrongful Death. ***Email:*** creisman61@yahoo.com

THOMAS, MAMER & HAUGHEY, LLP

URBANA, ILLINOIS

(See Champaign)

General Practice, Federal and State Trials, Probate, Trusts, Taxation, Real Estate, Business and Commercial Law, Insurance Defense, Employment and Employment Discrimination, Elder Law, Discrimination, Construction Accident, Adoptions, Premarital Agreements, Long Term Care, American with Disabilities Act, Family and Medical Leave Act, Sexual Harassment, Wrongful Termination, Medical practice, Automobile Accidents, Slip and Fall, Wrongful Death, Condominium Law, Landlord and Tenant Law, Residential Real Estate, Estate and Gift Taxation, Income Tax, Estate Litigation, Estate Planning, Guardianship and Conservatorship, Wills and Probate, Workers Compensation, Business Formation, Business Litigation, Buying and Selling of Business, Limited Liability Company Law, Partnership Law, Small Business Law, Construction Accidents, Breach of Contract, Employment Contracts, Personal Policies, Commercial Leasing, Commercial Real Estate, Landlord and Tenant Law.

TUMMELSON BRYAN & KNOX

Established in 1993

115 NORTH BROADWAY
URBANA, ILLINOIS 61801-0099
Telephone: 217-367-2500
Fax: 217-367-2555
Email: info@tbklaw.com
URL: http://www.tbklaw.com

Mailing Address: P.O. Box 99, Urbana, IL 61803-0099

General Practice in all Courts including Trials and Appeals, Insurance, Workers' Compensation, Corporation, Administrative, Probate, Banking, Real Estate, Creditor's Rights and Mortgage Law.

FIRM PROFILE: Tummelson Bryan & Knox serves clients in East Central Illinois inclusive of Champaign, Vermilion, Iroquois, Ford, Piatt, Douglas, DeWitt, McLean, Macon, Edgar, Coles, Jasper, Kankakee and Peoria counties. The firm engages in a general practice with a focus on trial, estate, and banking work. Firm attorneys have been practicing law in East Central Illinois in excess of 200 years.

PARTNERS

GEORGE G. BRYAN, born Syracuse, New York, June 28, 1939; admitted to bar, 1964, Indiana and Illinois; 1965, U.S. Tax Court. *Education:* University of Illinois and Eastern Illinois University (B.S., 1961); Indiana University (J.D., 1964); New York University (LL.M., in Taxation, 1965). Phi Delta Phi. *Member:* Champaign County, Indiana State, Illinois State and American Bar Associations; Illinois Association of Defense Trial Counsel. ***PRACTICE AREAS:*** Workers Compensation Law; Tort Law; Real Estate Law; Probate Law. ***Email:*** ggbryan@tbklaw.com

E. PHILLIPS KNOX, born Champaign, Illinois, April 23, 1946; admitted to bar, 1971, Illinois. *Education:* Miami University (B.S., with honors, 1968); University of Illinois (J.D., with honors, 1971). Order of the Coif. *Member:* Champaign County, Illinois State and American Bar Associations. ***PRACTICE AREAS:*** Estate Planning; Probate Law; Real Estate Law. ***Email:*** epknox@tbklaw.com

ALLEN E. VERCHOTA III, born Paris, Illinois, August 4, 1961; admitted to bar, 1988, Illinois. *Education:* University of Illinois (B.A., 1983); Mississippi College of Law (J.D., 1987). *Member:* Champaign County, Illinois State and American Bar Associations; Illinois Association of Defense Trial Counsel. ***PRACTICE AREAS:*** Personal Injury Defense; General Practice. ***Email:*** Allen3d@aol.com

ASSOCIATE

HELEN F. GRANDONE, born Bloomington, Illinois, June 23, 1947; admitted to bar, 1995, Illinois and U.S. District Court, Central District of Illinois. *Education:* University of Illinois (B.A., 1969; M.S.W., 1971; J.D., magna cum laude, 1995). *Member:* Champaign County, Illinois State and American Bar Associations; East Central Illinois Women Attorneys. ***PRACTICE AREAS:*** Estate Planning; Probate Law; Real Estate; Elder Law; General Practice. ***Email:*** hfgrandone@tbklaw.com

OF COUNSEL

HURSHAL C. TUMMELSON, born Champaign, Illinois, February 3, 1923; admitted to bar, 1950, Illinois. *Education:* University of Illinois (J.D., 1949). Phi Alpha Delta. *Member:* Illinois State and American Bar Associations; Federation of Insurance Counsel; Society of Trial Lawyers. Fellow, American College of Trial Lawyers. ***PRACTICE AREAS:*** Automobile Law; Personal Injury Law; Public Utility Law. ***Email:*** HTUMMELSON@aol.com

FREDERICK S. GREEN, born Urbana, Illinois, November 23, 1923; admitted to bar, 1951, Illinois. *Education:* University of Illinois, Urbana-Champaign (B.S., 1949; LL.B., 1951). Champaign County Judge, 1956-1964; Circuit Judge, 1964-1974; Appellate Judge, 1974-1998.

(This Listing Continued)

REPRESENTATIVE CLIENTS: First Busey Corp.; Busey Bank; First Busey Trust & Investment Co.; Country Insurance & Financial Services; The Equitable Life Assurance Society of the United States; Farm Bureau Insurance Co.; Grinnell Mutual Reinsurance Co.; John Hancock Mutual Life Insurance Co.; State Farm Mutual Insurance Co.; Travelers Insurance Co.; United States Fidelity and Guaranty Co.; U.S. Fire & Casualty; U.S. Insurance Group.

WEBBER & THIES, P.C.

Established in 1946

P.O. BOX 189
URBANA, ILLINOIS 61803-0189
Telephone: 217-367-1126
Fax: 217-367-3752

General, Appellate, Trial and Federal Practice, Complex Litigation, Probate, Trust, Family, Corporation, Labor/Employment (Management), Taxation, Real Estate, Zoning, Environmental, Health, Banking and Intellectual Property Law.

FIRM PROFILE: The law firm was founded in 1946 by Charles M. Webber after he had served 12 years as county judge of Champaign County. The firm has concentrated on serving the total legal needs of individual and corporate residents of central Illinois and throughout the State of Illinois. The firm and its personnel are committed to the highest standards of professional legal representation and to serving the community in a variety of civic, charitable and religious activities.

CRAIG R. WEBBER (1936-1998)

CHARLES M. WEBBER (1903-1991)

RICHARD L. THIES, born Scottsbluff, Nebraska, November 7, 1931; admitted to bar, 1955, Illinois, U.S. Supreme Court, U.S. Court of Appeals, Seventh Circuit and U.S. District Court, Central District of Illinois. *Education:* University of Illinois (B.A., 1953; J.D., 1955). *Member:* Chicago, Champaign County (Member, Board of Governors, 1965-1967), Illinois State (Board of Governors, 1967-1973; 1979-1988; Treasurer, 1971-1973; Secretary, 1982-1983; President, 1986-1987) and American (Member: House of Delegates, 1985-1997; State Delegate and Nominating Committee, 1994-2005; Board of Governors, 1988-1991; Executive Committee, 1990-1991; Constitution and Bylaws Standing Committee, 1993-1996; Retirement Association Board, 1992; President, 1997-1998) Bar Associations; Bar Association of the Seventh Federal Circuit; Bar Association Central and Southern Federal Districts of Illinois (President, 2001—); Illinois Bar Foundation; American Law Institute. Fellow, American Bar Foundation (Chair, 1993-1994). [1st Lieut., JAGC, U.S. Air Force, active duty, 1956-1958]. ***PRACTICE AREAS:*** Corporate; Taxation; Environmental; Communications; Commercial Litigation; General Practice. ***Email:*** rthies@webberthies.com

CARL M. WEBBER, born Champaign, Illinois, May 23, 1944; admitted to bar, 1974, Illinois. *Education:* Northwestern University (B.S., 1966); University of Illinois (J.D., 1973). Board of Visitors, University of Illinois College of Law, 1979—; President, 1990. Adjunct Professor, Office of Real Estate Research, University of Illinois College of Commerce, 1987-1990. *Member:* Champaign County (Secretary-Treasurer, 1978-1980; Board of Governors, 1980-1983; President, 1981-1982), Illinois State (Member, Family Law Section Council, 1977-1978; Real Estate Section Council, 1983-1988; Co-Chair, Committee to Draft Model ISBA Real Estate Contract) and American Bar Associations; Bar Association Central and Southern Federal Districts of Illinois. Fellow: Illinois Bar Foundation; American Bar Foundation. [Lt., U.S. Navy, 1966-1970]. ***PRACTICE AREAS:*** Real Estate Law; Corporate Law; Business Litigation. ***Email:*** cwebber@webberthies.com

DAVID C. THIES, born Urbana, Illinois, December 6, 1955; admitted to bar, 1980, Illinois; 1982, U.S. District Court, Central District of Illinois. *Education:* Cours de Civilisation Francaises-Sorbonne, Paris, France; University of Illinois (B.A., with distinction in Economics, 1977; J.D., 1980). *Member:* Champaign County, Illinois State and American Bar Associations; Bar Association for Central and Southern Federal District of Illinois. Fellow: Illinois Bar Foundation; American Bar Foundation. ***LANGUAGES:*** French. ***PRACTICE AREAS:*** Business Representation; General Practice. ***Email:*** dthies@webberthies.com

HOLTEN D. SUMMERS, born East St. Louis, Illinois, December 31, 1938; admitted to bar, 1983, Illinois; U.S. District Court, Central District of Illinois. *Education:* University of Maryland (B.A., 1978); University of Illinois (M.A.P.A., 1983; J.D., 1983). *Member:* Champaign County, Illinois State (Chair, 1992-1993) and American Bar Associations; Bar Association Central and Southern Federal Districts of Illinois. [CM Sgt., U.S. Air Force, 1955-1979, Ret.]. ***PRACTICE AREAS:*** General Practice; Elder Law; Estate Planning; Probate Law; Tax Law; Real Estate Law. ***Email:*** hsummers@webberthies.com

JOHN E. THIES, born Urbana, Illinois, July 16, 1962; admitted to bar, 1988, Illinois; 1989, U.S. District Court, Central District of Illinois; 1998, U.S. Supreme Court and U.S. Court of Appeals, 7th Circuit. *Education:* Indiana University (B.A., with distinction, 1984); University of Illinois (J.D., 1988). Phi Beta Kappa; Phi Alpha Delta. Co-Author, "Rethinking American Housing Policy: Defederalizing Subsidized Housing," University of Illinois Law Review, Vol. 1987, Issue, 4. *Member:* Champaign County, Illinois State (Member: Board of Governors, 2001—; Assembly, 1996—; Standing Committee on Membership and Bar Activities, 1989-1999; Secretary, 1994-1996; Vice Chair, 1996-1997; Chair, 1997-1998; Law Student Committee, 1986-1988, 1993-1994; Special Committee on Employment of New Lawyers, 1992; Standing Committee on Government Lawyers, 1999-2001; Standing Committee on Women & the Law, 1998-1999; Special Committee on Professional Fulfillment, 1998-1999; Illinois Bar Foundation Advisory Counsel, 2000—; and American Bar Associations; Bar Association for Central and Southern Federal Districts of Illinois. ***PRACTICE AREAS:*** Business Representation; Civil Litigation; Health Insurance Law; Employment Law (Management); Class Action Defense. ***Email:*** jthies@webberthies.com

PHILLIP R. VAN NESS, born Anaconda, Montana, June 11, 1946; admitted to bar, 1975, Illinois and U.S. District Court, Central District of Illinois. *Education:* University of Montana (B.S., 1968); John Marshall Law School (J.D., 1975). Phi Alpha Delta. Member, Gavel Society, John Marshall Law School, 1975. Co-Author: "Rebuttal to Construction-Permit Water Regulations Article," *Chicago Bar Record,* May-June 1981 (pp. 320-324). Co-Editor and Author: "Environmental Law of Transactional Attorneys," *Illinois Institute*

(This Listing Continued)

For Continuing Legal Education, 2001. *Member:* Government (Secretary, 1987-1998), Champaign County, Illinois State (Member, Environmental Law Section; Newsletter Editor, 2001—: Legislation Subcommittee, 2000—; Secretary, 2003—) and American Bar Associations; American Intellectual Property Bar Association; Bar Association for Central and Southern Federal Districts of Illinois. ***PRACTICE AREAS:*** Environmental Law; Real Estate; Copyrights; Trademarks; Administrative Law; General Practice. ***Email:*** pvanness@webberthies.com

REPRESENTATIVE CLIENTS: Porter Athletic Equipment Co. (Sporting Goods Mfg.); Village of Thomasboro; Illinois Crop Improvement Assoc.; GMS Management of Illinois, Inc. (Real Estate Development & Leasing); Frasca International; Heath Care Service Corporation, d/b/a Blue Cross/Blue Shield of Illinois; Regional Health Resource Center, Inc.; National Council of Teachers of English; Illinois-American Water Company; Durst Cycle; Sangamon Towship.

BURNSIDE, JOHNSTON, CHOISSER & SHEAFOR

Established in 1901

FIRST NATIONAL BANK BUILDING
VANDALIA, ILLINOIS 62471
Telephone: 618-283-3260
Fax: 618-283-2851
Email: bjcs@bjcs-law.com

General, Civil and Trial Practice in all Courts, Banking, Real Estate, Estate Planning and Probate Law, Personal Injury, Family Law, Municipal Law, Criminal Defense.

MEMBERS OF FIRM

J. G. BURNSIDE (1873-1969)

ROBERT G. BURNSIDE (1913-2005)

JACK B. JOHNSTON, born Evanston, Illinois, November 27, 1937; admitted to bar, 1962, Illinois. *Education:* DePauw University (B.A., 1959); University of Illinois (LL.B., 1962). Phi Delta Phi. Vandalia City Attorney, 1963—. Village Attorney, Village of St. Peter. *Member:* Fayette County (Secretary, 1964-1972; President, 1977-1981) and Illinois State (Member, Assembly of Delegates, 1972-1976) Bar Associations. ***PRACTICE AREAS:*** Banking; Real Estate; Civil Litigation; Estate Planning; Municipal Law; Probate. ***Email:*** bjcs@bjcs-law.com

DALE F. CHOISSER, born Eldorado, Illinois, February 11, 1953; admitted to bar, 1978, Illinois. *Education:* Vanderbilt University (B.A., 1975); John Marshall Law School (J.D., 1978). City Attorney: St. Elmo, 1981-1992; Brownstown, 2003—. Public Defender, Fayette County, 1980-1983. *Member:* Fayette County (Secretary, 1987-2002) and Illinois State Bar Associations; Illinois Trial Lawyers Association. ***PRACTICE AREAS:*** Family Law; Collections; Civil Litigation; Real Estate; Estate Planning; Probate; Personal Injury. ***Email:*** bjcs@bjcs-law.com

M. DON SHEAFOR, born Vandalia, Illinois, February 11, 1955; admitted to bar, 1981, Illinois. *Education:* Eastern Illinois University (B.A., 1977); Thomas M. Cooley School of Law (J.D., 1981). Assistant State Attorney, 1981-1983 and State Attorney, 1983-1992, Fayette County, Illinois. *Member:* Fayette County and Illinois State Bar Associations. ***PRACTICE AREAS:*** Family Law; Estate Planning; Criminal Law; Personal Injury; Civil Litigation; Real Estate; Probate. ***Email:*** bjcs@bjcs-law.com

J. MARC KELLY, born Oxford, Mississippi, September 30, 1973; admitted to bar, 2000, Illinois. *Education:* Southern Illinois University (B.A., 1996); John Marshall Law School (J.D., 2000). Assistant State's Attorney, Fayette County, May-September, 2000. Public Defender, Fayette County, 2002—. *Member:* Fayette County and Illinois State Bar Associations. ***PRACTICE AREAS:*** Criminal Law; Collections; Family Law; Personal Injury; Civil Litigation. ***Email:*** bjcs@bjcs-law.com

GENERAL COUNSEL FOR: First National Bank; First State Bank of St. Peter; Vandalia Mutual Fire Ins. Co.; Vandalia Sand and Gravel, Inc.; FAYCO Enterprises; South Central FS, Inc.; South-Central Regional Planning And Development Commission; S&S Urethane, Inc.; City of Vandalia; Brownstown Fire Protection District; Leo Brown Lumber Co.; Arthur Young, Inc.; Lotz Trucking, Inc.; National Timber & Veneer Corporation; Pine Ridge Homes, Inc.; Village of Brownstown.

TAYLOR LAW OFFICES, P.C.

VANDALIA, ILLINOIS

(See Effingham)

Trial Practice in State and Federal Courts. Insurance, Personal Injury, Trusts, Probate, Estate Planning, Commercial, Municipal, Corporate, Bankruptcy, Real Estate, Oil and Gas, Criminal Law, Family Law, Collections, Utility, Energy and Power Generation Law, Land Use Law, Water Cooperatives.

LAW OFFICE OF ROLAND A. ECKERT

VERNON HILLS, ILLINOIS

(See Lake Forest)

General Business Practice, Corporate, Contracts, Zoning, Planning and Land Use, Environmental, Hazardous Materials and Substances, Hazardous Materials Management, Hazardous Materials Transportation, Construction Defects, Mechanics Liens, Buying and Selling of Businesses, Family Business, Limited Liability Company, Partnership, Small Business, Real Estate, Commercial Real Estate, Condominium and Mortgages.

FULLIN LEGAL SERVICES LLC

VERNON HILLS, ILLINOIS

(See Libertyville)

Patents, Trademarks, Licensing, Copyrights, Trade Secrets.

RICHARDS, RALPH & SCHWAB

CHARTERED

Established in 1976

ONE HAWTHORN PLACE
175 EAST HAWTHORN PARKWAY, SUITE 345
VERNON HILLS, ILLINOIS 60061
Telephone: 847-367-9699
Fax: 847-367-9621
Email: attorney@rrs-chtd.com
URL: http://www.lawyers.com/richardandschwab

Chicago, Illinois Office: 39 South LaSalle Street, Suite 905, 60603. Telephone: 312-641-6696. Fax: 847-367-9621. Email: attorney@rrs-chtd.com.

Corporate and Business. Banking and Finance. Bankruptcy and Creditors' Rights. Real Estate. Commercial Litigation.

MICHAEL L. RALPH, SR., born Chicago, Illinois, May 15, 1947; admitted to bar, 1972, Wisconsin and U.S. District Court, Western District of Wisconsin; 1972, Illinois and U.S. District Court, Northern District of Illinois including Trial Bar. *Education:* Carthage College (B.A., 1969); Marquette University (J.D., 1972). Bankruptcy Trustee, U.S. District Court, Northern District of Illinois, Eastern Division, 1976-1980. *Member:* Chicago, Lake County (Past Chairman, Bankruptcy and Creditor's Rights Committee), Illinois State and American Bar Associations; Commercial Law League of America; American Bankruptcy Institute. ***PRACTICE AREAS:*** Bankruptcy Law; Debtor Creditor Rights Law; Workouts; Banking Law; Real Estate Law. ***Email:*** mralph@rrs-chtd.com

ALAN E. RICHARDS, born Chicago, Illinois, March 7, 1949; admitted to bar, 1976, Wisconsin, Illinois and U.S. District Court, Eastern District of Illinois. *Education:* Carthage College (B.A., 1970); Marquette University (J.D., 1976). Member, 1974-1976 and Member, Editorial Board, 1975-1976, Marquette Law Review. Author: "Grand Jury in Wisconsin," Marquette Law Review, 1976. *Member:* Lake County, Illinois State and American Bar Associations; The Association of Trial Lawyers of America. ***PRACTICE AREAS:*** Commercial Trial Practice; Real Estate Law; Business Transactions. ***Email:*** arichards@rrs-chtd.com

DAVID J. SCHWAB, born Milwaukee, Wisconsin, April 6, 1963; admitted to bar, 1990, Illinois and U.S. District Court, Northern District of Illinois. *Education:* Indiana University (B.S., 1985); DePaul University College of Law (J.D., 1990). Executive Editor, DePaul Business Law Journal Vol. II, 1989-1990. Certified Public Accountant, Illinois, 1986. Author, "Recent 7th Circuit Bankruptcy Cases," Advance Bankruptcy Seminar, Lake County Bar Association. Co-Author: "Valuation, Assignment of Rents and Related Issues," Critical Issues in Advanced Bankruptcy Practice, Commercial Law League of America, 1991. Member, Alumni Board, DePaul University College of Law, 1998-2001. *Member:* Chicago, Illinois State and American Bar Associations; American Bankruptcy Institute; Illinois Association of Certified Public Accountants; Illinois Association of Attorney-Certified Public Accountants (Member, Board of Directors, 1999—). ***PRACTICE AREAS:*** Bankruptcy; Debtor and Creditor Rights; Workouts; Business Law; Commercial Litigation. ***Email:*** dschwab@rrs-chtd.com

---

MICHAEL L. RALPH, JR., born Yuma, Arizona, October 23, 1974; admitted to bar, 1999, Illinois and U.S. District Court, Northern District of Illinois. *Education:* Indiana University, Bloomington (B.A., 1996); Chicago-Kent College of Law (J.D., with honors, 1999). Recipient, Cali Award, Bankruptcy. *Member:* Chicago, Lake County, Illinois State and American Bar Associations. ***PRACTICE AREAS:*** Real Estate; Mechanics Liens; Banking; Corporate and Business Law; Bankruptcy; Creditors Rights. ***Email:*** mlralph@rrs-chtd.com

LAUREN B. SCHREEDER, born Atlanta, Georgia, June 30, 1970; admitted to bar, 1995, Georgia; 1996, Illinois. *Education:* Emory University (B.A., 1991); Tulane University School of Law (J.D., cum laude, 1995). ***PRACTICE AREAS:*** Commercial Litigation; Real Estate Litigation. ***Email:*** lschreeder@rrs-chtd.com

REPRESENTATIVE CLIENTS: Amcore Bank, N.A.; A. E. Bancorp, Inc.; American Enterprise Bank; American Enterprise Leasing; Bank of Lincolnwood; Cambridge Bank; Des Plaines National Bank; First American Bank; Lakeland Community Bank; LaSalle Bank, N.A.; Libertyville Bank & Trust Company; Mt. Prospect National Bank; Mundelein Community Bank; National City Bank; Northside Community Bank; Lake County Partnership for Economic Development, Inc.; Midwest, Inc.; Riverside Foundation; Transamerica Small Business Capitol.
REFERENCES: American Enterprise Bank; LaSalle Bank, N.A.; Libertyville Bank & Trust Company.

GARY L. SCHLESINGER

VERNON HILLS, ILLINOIS

(See Libertyville)

Trials and Appeals of Divorce, Custody, Support, Paternity, Adoption, Family Law and Domestic Relations.

JELLIFFE, FERRELL, MORRIS & DOERGE

VIENNA, ILLINOIS

(See Harrisburg)

Insurance Law, Negligence and Personal Injury, Litigation, Workers' Compensation Law, and Employment Law. Commercial Collection and DUI's. General Civil Practice in State and Federal Courts. Trials and Appeals.

KRUGER, HENRY & HUNTER

VIENNA, ILLINOIS

(See Metropolis)

Civil and Criminal Trial and Appellate Practice. Negligence, Product Liability, Wrongful Death, Workman's Compensation, Criminal, Family, Real Estate, Corporate, Probate, Bankruptcy, Divorce, Driving While Intoxicated.

LAW OFFICE OF KIM L. MOORE

121 N. SPRINGFIELD STREET
VIRDEN, ILLINOIS 62690
Telephone: 217-965-3772
Fax: 217-965-3778
URL: http://www.kimmoorelaw.com

Family Law, Divorce, Spousal Support, Child Support, Domestic Violence, Alimony, Real Estate, Title, Contracts, Business Law, Corporate Law, Estate Planning, Litigation, Commercial.

KIM L. MOORE, born March 1, 1955; admitted to bar, 2003, Illinois. *Education:* Upper Iowa University; Northern Illinois University (J.D., 2003). *Member:* Macoupin County, Illinois State and American Bar Associations; The Association of Trial Lawyers of America.

GREGORY J. BUECHE

27475 FERRY ROAD
WARRENVILLE, ILLINOIS 60555
Telephone: 630-717-2962
Fax: 630-717-3556
Email: gbueche7035@wowway.com
URL: http://www.lawyers.com/gbueche

General Civil Litigation, Corporate and Business Law, Employment Matters, Estate Planning and Probate.

GREGORY J. BUECHE, born Flint, Michigan, November 16, 1960; admitted to bar, 1986, Illinois, U.S. District Court, Northern District of Illinois and U.S. Court of Appeals, Seventh Circuit. *Education:* University of Michigan (B.A., with distinction, 1983; J.D., cum laude, 1986). Arbitrator: Cook County Court-Annexed Mandatory Arbitration; DuPage County Court-Annexed Mandatory Arbitration. Author: "How To Handle Smoking or Non-Smoking and Employment; A Labor Law Issue," DuPage Bar Brief, Vol. 6, No. 10, p. 19 (July, 1994). *Member:* DuPage County (Member, Civil Practice Section) Bar Association.

BROWN & ASSOCIATES

WATERLOO, ILLINOIS

(See Belleville)

Civil Litigation, Personal Injury, Medical Malpractice, Products Liability, Admiralty Law, Railroad Law and Commercial Law.

CROWDER & SCOGGINS, LTD.

WATERLOO, ILLINOIS

(See Columbia)

Trial and Appellate Practice in State and Federal Courts. Personal Injury, Workers Compensation, Commercial, Banking, Municipal, Corporate, Tax, Estate Planning and Family, Criminal and Real Estate Law.

DUNHAM, BOMAN & LESKERA

WATERLOO, ILLINOIS

(See Belleville)

General Civil Trial and Appellate Practice. Negligence and Products Liability, Medical Malpractice, Probate, Insurance, Family, Real Estate, Environmental, School, Criminal and Bankruptcy Law.

STRELLIS & FIELD

CHARTERED

115 EAST MILL STREET
WATERLOO, ILLINOIS 62298
Telephone: 618-939-3404
FAX: 618-939-3402
Email: lawyers@waterloolaw.com

Belleville, Illinois Office: 216 West Washington, 62220. Telephone: 618-235-8701. Fax: 618-235-8967.

Chicago, Illinois Office: 444 North Wells Street, Suite 202, 60610. Telephone: 312-201-0000. Fax: 312-201-0007.

General, Civil Trial Practice in all Courts. Personal Injury, Wrongful Death, Workers Compensation, Products Liability, Probate and Estate Planning, Real Estate, Family Law and Adoption, Trademark, Patent, Intellectual Property.

JACK A. STRELLIS, born Chicago, Illinois, July 5, 1944; admitted to bar, 1971, Illinois and U.S. District Court, Southern, Central and Northern Districts of Illinois; 1972, U.S. Court of Appeals, Seventh Circuit; 1982, U.S. Tax Court; 1986, U.S. Court of Appeals, Eighth Circuit and U.S. Supreme Court; 1987, U.S. Claims Court; 2002, U.S. District Court, Eastern District of Missouri and U.S. District Court, Eastern District of Michigan; U.S. District Court, Southern District of Indiana. *Education:* University of Illinois (A.B., 1967); Loyola University (J.D., 1971). Assistant United States Attorney, 1971-1975. Special Assistant Attorney General of the State of Illinois, 1976-1983. Waterloo City Attorney, 1977-1979. *Member:* Chicago (Member, Committee of Tort Law and Federal Civil Practice), St. Clair County, Monroe County (President, 1983-1984), 7th Circuit (Member, Board of Governors, 1999—; Liaison to Southern District of Illinois, 1980-1999), Illinois State (Secretary, Federal Civil Practice Section; Member, Bench and Bar) and American (Vice-Chair, Judiciary Committee, General Practice Division) Bar Associations; The Bar Association of the Central and Southern Federal Districts of Illinois (Member, Board of Directors). ***PRACTICE AREAS:*** Civil Practice; Personal Injury; Wrongful Death; Workers Compensation; Products Liability. ***Email:*** jack@waterloolaw.com

DENNIS M. FIELD, born East St. Louis, Illinois, June 5, 1955; admitted to bar, 1986, Illinois and U.S. District Court, Southern District of Illinois. *Education:* Southern Illinois University-Edwardsville (B.S., 1982); Southern Illinois University-Carbondale (J.D., 1986). *Member:* St. Clair County, Monroe County, 7th Circuit and Illinois State Bar Associations. ***PRACTICE AREAS:*** General Civil Trial; Medical Malpractice; Personal Injury; Workers Compensation; Products Liability; Family Law. ***Email:*** dennis@waterloolaw.com

GREGG E. STRELLIS, born Belleville, Illinois, November 16, 1972; admitted to bar, 1998, Illinois and U.S. District Court, Southern District of Illinois; 2002, U.S. District Court, Eastern District of Michigan; 2003, U.S. District Court, Northern and Central Districts of Illinois. *Education:* University of Illinois (B.S., 1994); Indiana University, Bloomington (J.D., 1998). *Member:* St. Clair County, 7th Circuit and Illinois State Bar Associations; The Bar Association of the Central and Southern Federal Districts of Illinois; The Association of Trial Lawyers of America; Illinois Trial Lawyers Association. ***PRACTICE AREAS:*** Civil Practice; Personal Injury; Wrongful Death; Products Liability; Medical Malpractice; Workers Compensation; Animal Law. ***Email:*** gstrellis@strellislaw.com

JONATHAN ALAN ROSENFELD, born Illinois, Chicago, June 5, 1974; admitted to bar, 2001, Illinois and U.S. District Court, Northern District of Illinois. *Education:* Lehigh University (B.A., 1996); Chicago-Kent College of Law (J.D., 2001). *Member:* Illinois State Bar Association; Illinois Trial Lawyers Association. ***PRACTICE AREAS:*** Wrongful Death; Construction Accidents; Medical Negligence; Aviation Accidents; Maritime Personal Injury; Railroad Accidents and Injuries; Workers Compensation. ***Email:*** rosenfeld@strellislaw.com

KELLY J. EBERSPECHER, born Kenai, Alaska, August 8, 1968; admitted to bar, 1998, Illinois and U.S. District Court, Northern District of Illinois; 1999, U.S. District Court, Western District of Michigan; 2001, U.S. Court of Appeals, Federal Circuit; 2003, U.S. Court of Appeals, Seventh Circuit; registered to practice before U.S. Patent and Trademark Office. *Education:* University of Wyoming (B.S., 1994); Indiana University, Bloomington (J.D., 1998). Member, Sherman Minton Moot Court Board, 1997-1998. Formerly with Brinks Hofer Gilson Lione. [U.S. Navy, SEAL Team 2 (1986-1990)]. ***PRACTICE AREAS:*** Patent Litigation; Trademark Litigation; Copyright Litigation; Civil Litigation; Personal Injury. ***Email:*** eberspecher@strellislaw.com

A List of Representative Clients will be furnished upon request.
REFERENCE: First National Bank of Waterloo.

LAW OFFICES OF FRANK J. SIMUTIS, P.C.

123 SOUTH FOURTH STREET
WATSEKA, ILLINOIS 60970
Telephone: 815-432-5567
Fax: 815-432-5582
Email: fjslaw@earthlink.net

General Civil Defense Law, Probate Law, Banking Law, Municipal Law, Corporate Law, Estate Planning, Personal Injury.

FRANK J. SIMUTIS, born Chicago, Illinois, November 12, 1946; admitted to bar, 1971, Illinois; 1973, Arizona; 1982, U.S. District Court, Central District of Illinois. *Education:* University of Illinois (B.A., 1968; J.D., 1971). *Member:* Iroquois County (President, 1989-1993), Kankakee County and Illinois State Bar Associations; State Bar of Arizona; Illinois Defense Counsel. [Capt., USAF, 1971-1976]. ***PRACTICE AREAS:*** General Civil Trial Practice; Probate; Real Estate; Banking Law; Municipal Law. ***Email:*** fjslaw@earthlink.net

REPRESENTATIVE CLIENTS: Iroquois Federal Savings and Loan Association; First National Bank of Gilman; Iroquois Farmers State Bank; Farmers State Bank of Danforth; MainSource Bank; Central Bank of Ashkum; City of Gilman; Village of Crescent City; City of Watseka; Village of Papineau; Iroquois Memorial Hospital; State Farm Insurance; Country Insurance and Financial, Inc.; Columbia Insurance Group; American Family Insurance.

DALE STROUGH ATTORNEY AT LAW

Established in 1987

216 EAST WALNUT STREET
WATSEKA, ILLINOIS 60970
Telephone: 815-432-4921
Fax: 815-432-6628
URL: http://www.daslaw.com

Bankruptcy, Family, Divorce, Adoption, Visitation Rights, Criminal, DWI, Drug Crimes, Juvenile Crimes, Traffic Violations, White Collar Crimes, Domestic Violence, Personal Injury, Medical Malpractice, Wrongful Death, Trusts and Estates, Estate Planning and Wills and Probate Law. General Practice.

(This Listing Continued)

DALE A. STROUGH, born 1952; admitted to bar, 1978, Illinois. *Education:* Illinois State University (B.S.); DePaul University (J.D.). ***PRACTICE AREAS:*** General Practice; Municipal Law; Probate; Estate Planning; Family Law; Divorce; Adoption Law; Driving While Intoxicated; Medical Malpractice; Wrongful Death; Trusts and Estates; Wills; Visitation Rights.

TUNGATE LAW OFFICES, LTD.

Established in 1976

744 EAST WALNUT STREET
P.O. BOX 337
WATSEKA, ILLINOIS 60970
Telephone: 815-432-4979
Fax: 815-432-4977
Email: tungate7733@sbcglobal.net
URL: http://www.lawyers.com/tungate

Cissna Park, Illinois Office: Railroad Avenue at Third Street, P.O. Box 272, 60924. Telephone: 815-457-2723.

Onarga, Illinois Office: 109 North Chestnut Street. 60955. Telephone: 815-268-4979.

General Civil and Criminal Trial Practice in all State and Federal Courts. Personal Injury, Banking, Probate, Real Estate, Corporate, Taxation, Family, Commercial, School and Municipal Law.

JAMES L. TUNGATE, born Columbus, Ohio, September 27, 1947; admitted to bar, 1979, Illinois; 1985, U.S. Supreme Court. *Education:* Illinois Wesleyan University (B.S., with honors, 1969); Northwestern University (M.A.,1970; Ph.D., 1972); University of Illinois (J.D., 1979). Phi Alpha Delta. Assistant to the State's Attorney, Iroquois County, 1978. Member, Committee on Fitness and Character, Illinois Supreme Court. *Member:* Chicago, Iroquois County (President, 1999—), Illinois State (Member: Real Property, Probate and Trust Law Section; General Assemblyman) Bar Associations. ***PRACTICE AREAS:*** General Practice; Probate; Real Estate; Traffic Violations; Real Estate Title Insurance. ***Email:*** tungate7733@sbcglobal.net

REPRESENTATIVE CLIENTS: Sumner National Bank of Sheldon, Ill.; Cissna Park State Bank; Hicksgas; Federated Bank of Onarga; Citizens State Bank of Cropsey; Village of Onarga; Iroquois Mental Health Center.
REFERENCES: Sumner National Bank of Sheldon, Ill.; Cissna Park State Bank; Village of Cissna Park; Milford Community Consolidated School District #280; Federated Bank of Onarga; Citizens State Bank of Cropsey.

THE LAW OFFICE OF VITO P. LoVERDE

729 SADDLEWOOD DRIVE
WAUCONDA, ILLINOIS 60084
Telephone: 847-487-4909
Fax: 847-487-4822
Email: vpl@loverdelaw.com

Litigation, Corporate Law, Alternative Dispute Resolution.

VITO P. LoVERDE, admitted to bar, 1991, Illinois and U.S. District Court, Northern District of Illinois. *Education:* Northeastern Illinois University (B.S., 1983); National University, Evanston, Illinois (M.S., Management, 1985); John Marshall Law School (J.D., 1991). Author: "Naked Before the Law, John Marshall Law School Law Review, 1990. *Member:* Chicago, Illinois State and American Bar Associations. ***PRACTICE AREAS:*** Litigation; Corporate Law; Alternative Dispute Resolution.

CLAY J. MITCHELL

121 EAST LIBERTY STREET
SUITE 3
WAUCONDA, ILLINOIS 60084-1929
Telephone: 847-487-7988
Fax: 847-526-9498

General Practice, Personal Injury, Insurance Law, Criminal Defense, Traffic and DUI and Real Estate Transactions.

CLAY J. MITCHELL, born Barrington, Illinois, July 16, 1959; admitted to bar, 1989, Illinois. *Education:* University of Michigan (B.A., 1981); DePaul University (J.D., 1987).

ANTHONY G. ARGEROS, L.L.C.

WAUKEGAN, ILLINOIS

(See Chicago)

Personal Injury, Wrongful Death, Products Liability, Diesel Exposure, Toxic Mold, Automobile Accidents, Medical Malpractice, Birth Trauma, Traumatic Head Injuries, Nursing Home Litigation, Workers' Compensation, Civil Litigation, Appellate Practice.

BRENNER, FORD, MONROE & SCOTT, LTD.

WAUKEGAN, ILLINOIS

(See Chicago)

Insurance Defense, Personal Injury, Medical Malpractice, Construction Law, Product Liability, Uninsured/Underinsured Motorist Arbitrations and Litigation of Contested Coverage Issues.

LAW OFFICES OF RANDIE BRUNO

118 NORTH GENESEE STREET
WAUKEGAN, ILLINOIS 60085
Telephone: 847-244-5002
Email: olb9239@yahoo.com

Criminal Law, Driving While Intoxicated, Drug Crimes, Felonies, Homicide, Juvenile, Misdemeanors, Parole and Probation, Sexual Assault, Traffic Violations, Family Law, Divorce, Child Custody, Child Support, Domestic Violence, Spousal Support.

RANDIE BRUNO, born Chicago, Illinois; admitted to bar, 1985, Illinois. *Education:* Indiana University, Bloomington (B.A., Journalism and Political Science, 1980); John Marshall Law School, Chicago (J.D., 1985). Moot Court Justice. Recipient: Best Oralist Award, Chicago Bar Association Moot Court Competition. Participant, Craven Moot Court Competition. Member, Inns of Court. *Member:* Capital Litigation Trial Bar. ***PRACTICE AREAS:*** Criminal Law; Traffic Violations.

OF COUNSEL

LOUIS M. BRUNO, born Chicago, Illinois, September 29, 1956; admitted to bar, 1981, Illinois and U.S. District Court, Northern District of Illinois. *Education:* DePaul University (B.A., 1978; J.D., 1981). ***PRACTICE AREAS:*** Criminal Law; Domestic Relations; Family Law; Real Estate.

ERIN E. CARTWRIGHT

409 GRAND AVENUE
WAUKEGAN, ILLINOIS 60085
Telephone: 847-336-0710
Fax: 847-244-5399
Email: ecartwright@aol.com
URL: http://www.erincartwrightlaw.com

General Practice.

ERIN E. CARTWRIGHT, born 1977; admitted to bar, 2000, Illinois.

LAW OFFICES OF PAUL CHATZKY

WAUKEGAN, ILLINOIS

(See Northfield)

General Practice, Divorce, Family Law, Criminal Defense, Felonies, Driving While Intoxicated, Real Estate, Business Law, Estate Planning, Wills, Personal Injury and Civil Litigation.

CONNELLY ROBERTS & McGIVNEY LLC

WAUKEGAN, ILLINOIS

(See Chicago)

Commercial Litigation, Corporate Transactions, Mergers and Acquisitions, Securities, Technology Law, Licensing, Intellectual Property, Commercial Real Estate, Healthcare, Antitrust, Professional Liability, Product Liability, Employment Disputes, Transportation, Rail and Aviation Law, Insurance and Reinsurance Disputes, Construction Defect Litigation, Copyright and Trademark Law, and Employment Litigation.

MICHAEL J. CONWAY ATTORNEY AT LAW, L.L.C.

222 NORTH MARTIN LUTHER KING, JR. AVENUE
WAUKEGAN, ILLINOIS 60085
Telephone: 847-599-1969
Fax: 847-263-1258
Email: mjconwaylaw@ameritech.net
URL: http://www.michaelconwaylaw.com

Criminal Defense, Family Law, Parental Rights, Juvenile Law, Driving Under the Influence, Traffic Violations, Personal Injury.

MICHAEL J. CONWAY, born Colorado Springs, Colorado, October 3, 1965; admitted to bar, 1992, Illinois. *Education:* College of Lake County (A.S., 1986); University of Illinois, Urbana-Champaign (B.A., 1988); Thomas M. Cooley Law School (J.D., 1991). *Member:* Chicago, Lake County (Chairman, Juvenile Committee, 2002—) and Illinois State Bar Associations. ***PRACTICE AREAS:*** Criminal Defense; Family Law; Parental Rights; Juvenile Law; Driving Under the Influence; Traffic Violations; Personal Injury. ***Email:*** mjconwaylaw@ameritech.net

THE LAW OFFICES OF MARK C. CURRAN, JR.

235 NORTH WEST STREET
WAUKEGAN, ILLINOIS 60085
Telephone: 847-782-0200
Fax: 847-782-0600
Email: curranlaw@aol.com
URL: http://www.curran-criminallawyer.com

Criminal Defense including State and Federal, Drugs, Narcotics, Search and Seizure, Trafficking, RICO, Conspiracy, Felonies, Misdemeanors, Sexual Misconduct, Sexual Offenses, Sexual Abuse and Sexual Assault, Internet Crimes, Pornography, Weapons, Traffic Violations, Driving

(This Listing Continued)

THE LAW OFFICES OF MARK C. CURRAN, JR., Waukegan—Continued

While Intoxicated (DWI); Family Law including Divorce, Child Custody, Child Support, Visitation Rights, Spousal Support (Alimony), Personal Injury, Workers Compensation, Juvenile Matters.

MARK C. CURRAN, JR., born Pittsburgh, Pennsylvania, April 4, 1963; admitted to bar, 1990, Illinois. *Education:* Spring Hill College (B.S., Business Administration, 1985); Illinois Institute of Technology, Chicago-Kent College of Law (J.D., 1990). Lake County State's Attorney, all divisions, 1990-1998. Supervisor, Criminal Division/Civil Division of Illinois Attorney General's Office, 1998-2002. Special Assistant United States Attorney, 1999-2002; Illinois Attorney General's Office, 1998-2002. Prosecutor, Department of Child Family Services, 2004—. *Member:* Lake County Bar Association; Prosecutors Bar Association (Founding Member; Former: Member, Board of Directors; Elected Representative for the Second Judicial District). ***LANGUAGES:*** Spanish.

MICHAEL S. DANIAN, P.C.

NINE NORTH COUNTY STREET
WAUKEGAN, ILLINOIS 60085
Telephone: 847-662-8777
Fax: 847-662-8794
Email: danianmsdlaw@aol.com

General Civil, Criminal Trial and Appellate Practice. Personal Injury, Workers Compensation, Pharmaceutical, Corporation, Real Estate, Probate, Driving While Intoxicated Felonies and Family Law.

MICHAEL S. DANIAN, born Waukegan, Illinois, November 29, 1931; admitted to bar, 1974, Ohio; 1976, Illinois and U.S. District Court, Northern District of Illinois; 1989, U.S. Supreme Court. *Education:* University of Wisconsin (B.S., 1953; M.B.A., 1959; Ph.D., 1964); Salmon P. Chase College of Law of Northern Kentucky University (J.D., 1974). Order of The Curia. Editor-in-Chief, Northern Kentucky State Law Forum, 1974. Lecturer, John Marshall Law School, 1978-1985. Assistant State's Attorney, Lake County, 1976-1977. City Prosecutor, Waukegan, Illinois, 1985-1993. *Member:* Illinois State Bar Association; Illinois Trial Lawyers Association. [U.S. Army, First Lt., Medical Service Corps, 1954-1956]

DECKER & LINN, LTD.

WAUKEGAN, ILLINOIS

(See Linn & Campe, Ltd.)

THE LAW OFFICES OF DAVID R. DEL RE

A PROFESSIONAL CORPORATION
210 N. MARTIN LUTHER KING, JR. AVENUE
WAUKEGAN, ILLINOIS 60085
Telephone: 847-625-9800
Fax: 847-625-9980
URL: http://www.delrelawfirm.com
Email: drd@delrelaw.net
URL: http://www.daviddelrelaw.com

Criminal Defense, Family Law.

DAVID R. DEL RE, born Arlington Heights, Illinois, July 20, 1971; admitted to bar, 1998, Illinois. *Education:* Augustana College; University of Illinois at Chicago (B.A., 1994); University of Tulsa (J.D., 1998). Member, Jefferson Inn-An American Inn of Court. Lake County State's Attorneys Office, 1998-2000. *Member:* Lake County and Illinois State Bar Associations. ***PRACTICE AREAS:*** Criminal Defense; Family Law.

DESANTO, MORGAN & MITTELMAN

AN ASSOCIATION OF PROFESSIONAL CORPORATIONS

WAUKEGAN, ILLINOIS

(See Libertyville)

Plaintiff's Personal Injury, Automobile Accidents and Injuries, Slip and Fall, Wrongful Death, Insurance Bad Faith, Products Liability, Commercial Litigation, Employment Litigation, Discrimination, Harassment, Wrongful Termination.

DIVER, GRACH, QUADE & MASINI, LLP

Established in 1904
BANK OF WAUKEGAN BUILDING
111 NORTH COUNTY STREET
WAUKEGAN, ILLINOIS 60085
Telephone: 847-662-8611
FAX: 847-662-2960
Email: divergrach@divergrach.com
URL: http://www.divergrach.com

General Litigation and Appellate Practice, Wills and Probate, Trusts and Estates, Municipal Law, Real Estate, Taxation, Commercial Litigation, Corporate Law, Family, Criminal, Financial Institutions.

(This Listing Continued)

MEMBERS OF FIRM

CLARENCE W. DIVER (1883-1962)

THOMAS W. DIVER (1916-2000)

BRIAN S. GRACH, born Chicago, Illinois, May 29, 1945; admitted to bar, 1970, Illinois and U.S. District Court, Northern District of Illinois; 1980, U.S. Tax Court. *Education:* University of Illinois (B.S., 1967; J.D., 1970). Certified Public Accountant, Illinois, 1968. Author: "Tax Implications of Settlements," Real Property, Probate and Trust Journal, 1975. Corporation Counsel, City of Waukegan, 1977-1985 and 1993—. *Member:* Lake County (Chairman, Taxation Committee), Illinois State and American (Sub-Committee Chairman, Review of Regulations and Rulings Committee and Sub-Committee on New Developments, Domestic Tax Section, 1973) Bar Associations; Illinois Society of Certified Public Accountants; American Association of Attorneys-Certified Public Accountants; Lake County Estate Planning Council (President, 1995). ***PRACTICE AREAS:*** Trusts and Estates; Wills; Probate; Municipal Law; Taxation; Business Law. ***Email:*** bgrach@divergrach.com

DAVID R. QUADE, born Chicago, Illinois, November 16, 1941; admitted to bar, 1968, Illinois and U.S. District Court, Northern District of Illinois including Trial Bar; 1971, U.S. Court of Appeals, 7th Circuit; 1973, U.S. Supreme Court. *Education:* Bradley University (B.S., 1964); John Marshall Law School (J.D., 1968). Member, Subcommittee on Human Studies, Veterans Administration Medical Center, North Chicago, Illinois, 1988-1991 and 1993-1996. Member: Board of Trustees, Chicago Association for Research & Education in Science, Hines, Illinois, 1997-2004; Board of Directors, North Shore Research & Education Foundation, Inc., North Chicago, Illinois, 1996-1999; Board of Directors, Village Childrens' Center, Inc., Lake Bluff, Illinois, 1997-2000. Member: Society of Trial Lawyers, 1980-2002; Association of Defense Trial Attorneys, 1988-2003; International Association of Defense Counsel, 1984-2003. *Member:* Chicago, Lake County (President, 1992-1993), Illinois State and American (Member, Sections on: Tort and Insurance Practice; Litigation) Bar Associations; Illinois Association of Defense Trial Counsel (Member, Board of Directors, 1982-1985); Defense Research Institute; Lake County Trial Lawyers Association; Fellow: Illinois Bar Foundation. ***PRACTICE AREAS:*** Insurance Law; Torts; Personal Injury; Workers Compensation. ***Email:*** dquade@divergrach.com

ROBERT J. MASINI, born Highland Park, Illinois, August 21, 1951; admitted to bar, 1976, Illinois and U.S. District Court, Northern District of Illinois; 1980, U.S. Supreme Court. *Education:* University of Wisconsin (B.A., 1973); University of Illinois (J.D., 1976). Associate Corporation Counsel, City of Waukegan, 1983-1985 and 1993—. *Member:* Chicago, Lake County, Illinois State and American Bar Associations. ***PRACTICE AREAS:*** Commercial Real Estate; Residential Real Estate; Landlord and Tenant Law; Zoning, Planning and Land Use; Real Property Taxation Law; Local Government Law. ***Email:*** rmasini@divergrach.com

DAVID L. HAZAN, born Chicago, Illinois, March 23, 1951; admitted to bar, 1977, Illinois; U.S. Court of Appeals, Seventh Circuit; U.S. District Court, Northern and Central Districts of Illinois including Trial Bar. *Education:* Purdue University and Arizona State University (B.A., 1973); John Marshall Law School (J.D., with honors, 1977). Member, Order of John Marshall. Member, Panel of Commercial Arbitrators, American Arbitration Association. *Member:* Lake County, Chicago (Member: Labor and Employment Committee, 1981-1984; Consumer Credit Committee, 1984-1986; Commercial Banking and Bankruptcy Law Committee, 1984-1986) and Illinois State Bar Associations. ***PRACTICE AREAS:*** Commercial Litigation; Litigation; Financial Institutions Law; Creditor Services; Bankruptcy; Commercial Real Estate; Residential Real Estate. ***Email:*** dlhazan@divergrach.com

DONNA-JO RODDEN VORDERSTRASSE, born St. Louis, Missouri, September 25, 1956; admitted to bar, 1984, Illinois. *Education:* Valparaiso University (B.A., Highest Distinction, 1979); Washington University (J.D., 1984). *Member:* Chicago, Lake County and Illinois State Bar Associations; Association of Womens Attorneys of Lake County (Member, Board of Directors, 1995-1996, 2004-2005; Treasurer, 2000-2004; Vice President, 2005-2006). ***PRACTICE AREAS:*** Elder Law; Trusts and Estates; Wills; Probate; Real Estate; Family Law; Mediation. ***Email:*** djvord@divergrach.com

ASSOCIATES

GRETCHEN A. NEDDENRIEP, born Highland Park, Illinois, January 31, 1974; admitted to bar, 1999, Illinois. *Education:* Eastern Illinois University (B.A., magna cum laude, 1995); John Marshall Law School (J.D., cum laude, 1999). Member, Jefferson Inns of Court, 2003. *Member:* Lake County and Illinois State Bar Association; Women's Bar Association (Member, Board of Directors, 2001). ***PRACTICE AREAS:*** Criminal Law; Driving While Intoxicated; Traffic Violations; Municipal Law; Real Estate; Wills; Probate. ***Email:*** gnedden@divergrach.com

WILLIAM P. ANDERSON, born Waukegan, Illinois, July 6, 1953; admitted to bar, 1978, Illinois and U.S. District Court, Northern District of Illinois. *Education:* Western Illinois University (B.A., 1975); Southern Illinois University (J.D., 1978). Member, The Order of Barristers; Moot Court Board. Assistant Editor, Southern Illinois University Law Journal. Special Editor, "The Problem of Punitive Damages in Civil Cases Can Be Solved," IDC Monograph, 1980. Board Member: Waukegan Public Library, 1990—; Waukegan Unit School District 60, 2003—. Member, Insurance Law Committee, 1993-1994. *Member:* Lake County and Illinois State Bar Associations. ***PRACTICE AREAS:*** Municipal Law; Personal Injury; Construction Law; Civil Rights; Insurance. ***Email:*** wpanderson@divergrach.com

A list of Representative Clients will be furnished upon request.
REFERENCE: First Midwest Bank of Waukegan.

DAVID ECKBERG

WAUKEGAN, ILLINOIS

(See Chicago)

Criminal Law, Driving While Intoxicated, Drug Crimes, Juvenile Crimes, Parole and Probation, Traffic Violations, White Collar Crime, Child Custody, Child Support, Divorce, Domestic Violence, Visitation Rights, Automobile Accidents, Sexual Abuse, Wrongful Death, Condemna-

(This Listing Continued)

tion and Fast Track Demolition, Employment Law, Domestic Relations, Bankruptcy, Discrimination, Employee Benefits, Wrongful Termination.

LAW OFFICE OF ROLAND A. ECKERT

WAUKEGAN, ILLINOIS

(See Lake Forest)

General Business Practice, Corporate, Contracts, Zoning, Planning and Land Use, Environmental, Hazardous Materials and Substances, Hazardous Materials Management, Hazardous Materials Transportation, Construction Defects, Mechanics Liens, Buying and Selling of Businesses, Family Business, Limited Liability Company, Partnership, Small Business, Real Estate, Commercial Real Estate, Condominium and Mortgages.

ELIZER & MEYERSON, L.L.C.

WAUKEGAN, ILLINOIS

(See Northbrook)

Criminal Law, Felonies and Misdemeanors, DUI, DWI, Traffic Violations, Personal Injury, Automobile Accidents, Wrongful Death.

GIBSON & KOPSICK, LTD.

Established in 1993

415 WEST WASHINGTON STREET, SUITE 103
WAUKEGAN, ILLINOIS 60085
Telephone: 847-263-5100
Fax: 847-249-7588
Email: attorney@gibkop.com
URL: http://www.gibsonkopsicklaw.com

Personal Injury, Medical Malpractice, Automobile Accidents, Uninsured and Underinsured Motorist, Construction Accidents, Motorcycle Accidents, Vehicular Accidents, Lawyers Malpractice, Professional Negligence, Products Liability, Workers Compensation.

FIRM PROFILE: Gibson & Kopsick exclusively represents individuals and families, in all State and Federal Courts throughout Illinois, who have been injured by an individual, company, corporation, public government or other entity.

SCOTT B. GIBSON, born Oak Park, Illinois, June 11, 1957; admitted to bar, 1982, Illinois and U.S. District Court, Northern District of Illinois; 2000, U.S. Supreme. *Education:* University of Illinois (B.A., 1979); De Paul University (J.D., 1982). Invited to be included as a personal injury specialist in Law & Leading Attorneys, "Illinois Consumer Guidebook," American Research Corporation Survey. Certified by peers to be included in the top one percent of lawyers in Illinois, 1996. Life Member, National Registry of Who's Who. Assistant State's Attorney, Career Offender Unit and Felony Trial, Lake County, IL, 1983-1987. Treasurer & Founding Board Member, Lake County Child Advocacy Center, 1987-1989. Pro Bono Attorney. Lake County Volunteer Legal Program, 1987. Vice President, Lake County State's Attorney Alumni Association, 1987. Member, University of Dubuque, Pre-Law Committee, 1992—. Member, Lake County Judicial Civil Alternative Dispute Ad Hoc Committee, 2000—. *Member:* Lake County (Member: Civil Trial Committee, 1989—; Legal-Medical Committee, 1994—; Judicial Selection and Retention Committee, 1996—; Chairman, Civil Trial and Appeal Committee, 1998—; Ad Hoc Judicial Advisory Committee, 1999—; Officer Nominating Committee, 2001—; Civil Trial and Appeal Committee Practice Seminar, "Medical Malpractice, Tips," May 2000), Chicago (Member, Tort Practice Committee, 1003-1004) and Illinois State (Assembly Member, 1989-1994; Tort Section, 1989-1993, 1997; Chairman, Tort Section Subcommittee on Liens and Statutory Disbursements, 1991-1993; Member, Tort Section Subcommittee on Legislative Affairs, 1991-1993; Co-liaison Tort Section to ISBA and its legislative leaders regarding all proposed and pending Illinois State and Federal Legislation, 1998—) Bar Associations; Lake County Trial Lawyers Association; Illinois Trial Lawyers Association (Member, Committee on New Membership, 1988—); The Association of Trial Lawyers of America (Member, Professional Negligence Section, 1994—); Million Dollar Advocates Forum; Illinois Bar Foundation; American Inns of Court (Lincoln Inn, Waukegan, Il, 1989-1997). ***PRACTICE AREAS:*** Personal Injury; Medical Negligence; Professional Negligence; Products Liability.

RICHARD S. KOPSICK, born New York, New York, March 10, 1957; admitted to bar, 1982, Illinois; 1984, U.S. District Court, Northern District of Illinois; 2000, U.S. Supreme Court. *Education:* University of Michigan (B.A., with distinction, 1979); DePaul University (J.D., 1982). *Member:* Lake County (Second Vice President, 2001-2002; First Vice President, 2002-2003; President, 2003-2004), Chicago, Illinois State and U.S. Supreme Court Bar Associations; Illinois Trial Lawyers Association (Member, Docket Editorial Board, 2000—); Million Dollar Advocate Forum. ***PRACTICE AREAS:*** Personal Injury; Medical Negligence; Professional Negligence; Products Liability.

OF COUNSEL

MARY ELLEN (MEGAN) CHADWICK, born Peoria, Illinois, September 21, 1959; admitted to bar, 1985, Illinois; 1987, Florida and California. *Education:* Illinois State University (B.S., 1982); John Marshall Law School (J.D., 1985). Certified Public Accountant, 1982. Member, Board of Directors, Association of Women Attorneys, Lake County, Illinois, 1991-1993. *Member:* Lake County, Chicago, Illinois State and American Bar Associations. ***PRACTICE AREAS:*** Personal Injury; Medical Malpractice; Products Liability.

GRIESHEIMER & ASSOCIATES

321 GRAND AVENUE
WAUKEGAN, ILLINOIS 60085
Telephone: 847-244-3131
Fax: 847-244-0766
URL: http://www.goldenrulelaw.com

Family, Divorce, Child Custody, Personal Injury, Criminal, Driving While Intoxicated, Military, Probate, Bankruptcy and General Civil Trial Practice.

RONALD E. GRIESHEIMER, born Chicago, Illinois, January 25, 1936; admitted to bar, 1961, Texas and Illinois; 1967, U.S. District Court, Northern District of Illinois; 1971, U.S. Supreme Court. *Education:* University of Illinois; Bradley University; Southern Methodist University (LL.B., 1961). Phi Delta Phi (Founding President of Inn, 1959-1961). Chief Justice Southern Methodist University Student Court. Member of Editor's Staff, Southern Methodist University Student Casenotes and Comments, Southwestern Law Journal, 1960-1961. Lake County, Illinois Public Conservator, 1970-1971. Illinois Public Guardian for Lake County, Illinois, 1980-1984. Special Assistant Attorney General, 1971-1973. Member of Illinois General Assembly, 1972-1980. Former Associate, Hall, Meyer, Fisher, Holmberg, Snook & May, 1965-1968. *Member:* Lake County, Illinois State, The Colorado and American Bar Associations. [Major, U.S. Air Force, Judge Advocate General's Division, 1961-1978]. ***Email:*** griesheimerlaw@tds.net

CHRISTOPHER J. FEKETE, born Youngstown, Ohio, June 2, 1952; admitted to bar, 1979, Ohio (inactive); 1982, Indiana (inactive); 1983, Utah (inactive); 1986, U.S. Court of Military Appeals; 1997, Illinois and U.S. Court of Appeals, Armed Forces. *Education:* Youngstown State University (B.A., 1975); University of Akron Law School (J.D., 1979). Military Judge, 1990-1993. [Lt. Commander, JAG Corps, U.S. Navy, 1985-1997 (Ret.)]. ***LANGUAGES:*** German. ***Email:*** griesheimerlaw@tds.net

HARRIS KESSLER & GOLDSTEIN LLC

404 WATER STREET
WAUKEGAN, ILLINOIS 60085
Telephone: 847-263-1919
URL: http://www.hkgold.com

Chicago, Illinois Office: 640 North LaSalle Street, Suite 590, 60610-3731. Telephone: 312-280-0111. Fax: 312-280-8232.

General Business Practice including Litigation, Secured Lending, Real Estate, Health Care and Estate Planning.

(For Complete Biographical data on all personnel, see Professional Biographies at Chicago).

HINSHAW & CULBERTSON LLP

Hinshaw & Culbertson LLP is an Illinois registered limited liability partnership that has elected to be governed by the Illinois Uniform Partnership Act (1997)

Established in 1934

110 NORTH WEST STREET
WAUKEGAN, ILLINOIS 60085-4330
Telephone: 847-244-0551
Facsimile: 847-244-0579
Telex: 880248
Email: kfox@hinshawlaw.com
URL: http://www.hinshawlaw.com

Other Office Locations: Chicago, Illinois; Appleton, Wisconsin; Belleville, Illinois; Boston, Massachusetts; Champaign, Illinois; Crystal Lake, Illinois; Edwardsville, Illinois; Fort Lauderdale, Florida; Jacksonville, Florida; Joliet, Illinois; Lisle, Illinois; Los Angeles, California; Miami, Florida; Milwaukee, Wisconsin; Minneapolis, Minnesota; New York, New York; Peoria, Illinois; Phoenix, Arizona; Portland, Oregon; Providence, Rhode Island; Rockford, Illinois; St. Louis, Missouri; San Francisco, California; Schererville, Indiana; Springfield, Illinois; Tampa, Florida.

Appellate, Banking & Financing, Bankruptcy & Creditors' Rights, Class Action Litigation, Civil Rights Defense, Commercial Litigation, Corporate, Construction Law, Director & Officer Liability, Employee Benefits, Environmental, Fidelity & Surety, General Liability Litigation, Government, Health Care, Insurance Coverage, Insurance and Reinsurance, Labor & Employment, Legal Malpractice, Medical Malpractice, Mergers & Acquisitions, Municipal Liability, Personal Injury Defense, Public Law, Products Liability Litigation, Professional Liability, Regulatory, Real Estate, School Law, Securities, Taxation, Transportation, White Collar Crime and Workers' Compensation Defense.

FIRM PROFILE: Hinshaw & Culbertson LLP is a national AMLaw 200 firm with 425 lawyers in 27 offices coast-to-coast. The firm offers a full-service practice, with an emphasis in commercial and defense litigation, corporate, environmental, employment and construction law, as well as the representation of professionals in their liability and risk management matters.

Hinshaw provides services to a range of clients in financial services, construction, health care, not-for-profit, insurance, legal, manufacturing, real estate, transportation and other industries. Firm clients also include government agencies, municipalities and schools.

Hinshaw was founded in 1934. The firm is headquartered in Chicago, and maintains offices in 12 states: Arizona, California, Florida, Illinois, Indiana, Massachusetts, Minnesota, Missouri, New York, Oregon, Rhode Island and Wisconsin.

PARTNERS

ALLYN J. FRANKE, born Springfield, Illinois, November 20, 1918; admitted to bar, 1942, Illinois. *Education:* Springfield Junior College and University of Chicago (A.B.,

(This Listing Continued)

HINSHAW & CULBERTSON LLP, Waukegan—Continued

1941; LL.B., 1942). Phi Alpha Delta. *Member:* Illinois State Bar Association; American Judicature Society; National School Boards Association Council of School Attorneys; Illinois Council of School of Attorneys. ***PRACTICE AREAS:*** School Law; Municipal Law. ***Email:*** afranke@hinshawlaw.com

MICHAEL F. HENRICK, born Chicago, Illinois, February 29, 1948; admitted to bar, 1974, Illinois and U.S. District Court, Northern District of Illinois; 1979, U.S. Supreme Court; 1985, Wisconsin and U.S. District Court, Eastern District of Wisconsin. *Education:* Loyola University (B.S., 1971); John Marshall Law School (J.D., 1974). Phi Alpha Delta. *Member:* Lake County and Illinois State Bar Associations; State Bar of Wisconsin; International Association of Defense Counsel; Illinois Association of Defense Counsel; Jefferson American Inn of Court; American Society of Law and Medicine; Illinois Association of Hospital Attorneys; Trial Lawyers Club of Chicago; Defense Research Institute; Society of Trial Lawyers; American College of Trial Lawyers. ***PRACTICE AREAS:*** Professional Liability Litigation; Medical Malpractice; Personal Injury Litigation; Health Care. ***Email:*** mhenrick@hinshawlaw.com

THOMAS A. MORRIS, JR., born Ilion, New York, January 5, 1947; admitted to bar, 1971, Virginia; 1977, Illinois; 1978, U.S. District Court, Northern District of Illinois, including Trial Bar; 1982, U.S. Court of Appeals for the Federal Circuit; 1989, U.S. Court of Appeals, Seventh Circuit. *Education:* College of the Holy Cross (A.B., 1968); University of Virginia (J.D., 1971). Phi Delta Phi; Arbitrator, Nineteenth Judicial Circuit; Illinois Council of School Attorneys. *Member:* Lake County, Illinois State and American Bar Associations. [Col., JAGC, U.S. Army Reserves, 1971-1996]. ***PRACTICE AREAS:*** School Law; Construction Law; Contract Litigation; Environmental. ***Email:*** tmorris@hinshawlaw.com

STACEY L. SENECZKO, born Keokuk, Iowa, March 16, 1964; admitted to bar, 1989, Illinois; 1994, U.S. District Court, Northern District of Illinois; 1995, U.S. District Court, Eastern District of Wisconsin. *Education:* Southern Illinois University, Carbondale (B.S., 1986; J.D., magna cum laude, 1989). Phi Kappa Phi. Recipient, American Jurisprudence Awards in Property I, Torts II, Constitutional Law (14th Amendment) and Legal Argumentation. Law Clerk, Hon. Lawrence D. Inglis, Illinois Appellate Court, 2nd Judicial District, 1989-1991. Author: "The Effect of Mandatory Medicare Assignment on Health Care," 10 J. Legal Med. 529, 1989; "The Parental Tort Immunity Doctrine Applied to Wrongful Death Actions: A Rule Without Reason, Chamness v. Fairtrace," 158 Ill. App. 3d 325, 511 N.E. 2d 839 (5th Dist. 1987), 13 S.Ill. U.L.J. 1975, 1988. Associate, Brydes, Riseborough, Peterson, Franke & Morris, Waukegan, Illinois, 1991-1996. Partner, Hinshaw & Culbertson, Waukegan, Illinois, 1996—. *Member:* Lake County, Illinois State and American Bar Associations; Professional Liability Underwriters Society; Women's Bar Association of Illinois; National Association of Women in Construction. ***PRACTICE AREAS:*** Appellate Practice; Construction Law; Professional Liability. ***Email:*** sseneczko@hinshawlaw.com

ASSOCIATES

RICHARD S. KOLODZIEJ, born Park Ridge, Illinois, July 29, 1971; admitted to bar, 1996, Illinois. *Education:* Bradley University (B.S., Political Science, summa cum laude, 1993); DePaul University (J.D., 1996). *Member:* Lake County and Illinois State Bar Associations; Illinois Trial Lawyers Association. ***PRACTICE AREAS:*** Professional Liability; Medical Malpractice. ***Email:*** rkolodziej@hinshawlaw.com

STEPHEN A. OAKLEY, born Evanston, Illinois, April 20, 1970; admitted to bar, 1997, Illinois and U.S. District Court, Northern District of Illinois; 2005, North Carolina. *Education:* University of Illinois, Urbana-Champaign (B.A., History, 1993); The John Marshall Law School (J.D., 1997). Dean's List. Herzog Moot Court Competition Finalist. Member, Illinois Trucking Association Safety Council. *Member:* Chicago, Lake County, Illinois State and North Carolina Bar Associations; Defense Research Institute. ***PRACTICE AREAS:*** Corporate Transactions; Commercial Litigation; Construction Litigation; Products Liability Litigation; Transportation Law; Real Estate; Appellate; Estate Planning and Administration. ***Email:*** soakley@hinshawlaw.com

HUGHES SOCOL PIERS RESNICK & DYM, LTD.

WAUKEGAN, ILLINOIS

(See Chicago)

General Civil and Litigation Practice in all Courts. Insurance and Reinsurance. Personal Injury, Immigration, Civil Rights, Class Actions, Labor and Employment, Commercial, Professional Liability, Litigation.

IMMIGRATION LAW CENTER, P.C.

WAUKEGAN, ILLINOIS

(See Chicago)

Immigration Law, Visas, Work Permits, Employment Immigration, Citizenship, Business Law, Small Business Law, Family Businesses, Contracts, Civil Litigation, Consumer Bankruptcy.

JOHNSON & BELL, LTD.

Established in 1975

325 WASHINGTON STREET
SUITE 200
WAUKEGAN, ILLINOIS 60085
Telephone: 847-662-7458
Facsimile: 847-662-7366
Email: novys@jbltd.com
URL: http://www.johnsonandbell.com

Chicago, Illinois Office: Suite 4100, 55 East Monroe Street, 60603-5896. Telephone: 312-372-0770. Facsimile: 312-372-9818.

(This Listing Continued)

Highland, Indiana Office: 9000 Indianapolis Boulevard, Suite A, 46322. Telephone: 219-923-5250. Facsimile: 219-923-6170.

Trial practice in state and federal courts, including national coordinating counsel. Appellate Law, Asbestos Litigation, Automotive Product Liability Litigation, Aviation Litigation, Benefits, Business Litigation and Practice, Complex Plaintiff Litigation, Construction Litigation, Corporate Health Care, Criminal Litigation, Employment Law, ERISA, Environmental Law, Financial Crimes, Financial Institution Representation, General Negligence and Premises Liability, Gun Litigation, Hospital Law and Medical Liability, Insurance Coverage, Intellectual Property, Long Term Care/Nursing Home Liability, Mass Tort, Medical Device Liability, Mold Litigation, Municipal Liability, National Coordinating Counsel, Probate, Product Liability, Professional Liability, Railroad Litigation, Toxic Tort and Trucking and Transportation.

LAW FIRM ALLIANCES/ASSOCIATIONS: **AMERICAN LAW FIRM ASSOCIATION (ALFA):** *Johnson & Bell, Ltd. is the exclusive Chicago area law firm of ALFA, an international association of independent law firms dedicated to improving the quality, efficiency, and affordability of legal services.*

SHAREHOLDERS

STEVEN B. NOVY, born Manitowoc, Wisconsin, December 23, 1947; admitted to bar, 1973, Illinois; 1974, U.S. District Court, Northern District of Illinois including Trial Bar; 1984, Wisconsin; 1986, U.S. District Court, Eastern District of Wisconsin; 1996, U.S. District Court, Western District of Wisconsin. *Education:* University of Illinois (B.A., 1970); University of Notre Dame (J.D., 1973). ***PRACTICE AREAS:*** Transportation (55%); Tort Defense (40%); Cargo Claims (5%). ***Email:*** novys@jbltd.com

STEVE C. CANTY, admitted to bar, 1996, Illinois. *Education:* University of Illinois (B.A., 1993); DePaul University (J.D., with honors, 1996). *Member:* Lake County, McHenry County and Illinois State Bar Associations; Defense Research Institute. ***PRACTICE AREAS:*** General and Civil Litigation; Tort Litigation; Personal Injury; Premises Liability; Transportation. ***Email:*** cantys@jbltd.com

ASSOCIATES

Paul E. Brady ***Angela M. Kotsalieff***
Jason Orleans

REPRESENTATIVE CLIENTS: Advocate Health Care Systems; AIG Technical Services, Inc.; Assurant Health; Atlantic Mutual Insurance Co.; Certain Underwriters at Lloyds, London; City of Harvey; CNH America, LLC; Elliott Turbomachinery Co., Inc.; Emerson Electric Company; Essex Insurance Company; Exxon Mobil; Hilton Hotels Corporation; Illinois Provider Trust; ISBA Mutual Insurance Co.; Lynch Ford, Inc.; Provena Health; Rockville Risk Management Associates; St. Paul Travelers Companies; Volkswagen of America; Walgreen Company; Waste Management, Inc.; Western General Management, Inc.

(For complete biographical data on all personnel, see Professional Biographies at Chicago, Illinois)

KIESLER & BERMAN

WAUKEGAN, ILLINOIS

(See Chicago)

General Civil Trial and Appellate Practice. Insurance, Workers Compensation, Trucking Law, Construction Litigation, Corporation, Real Estate and Probate Law. Asbestos Litigation, Civil Rights Law, Estate Planning, Insurance Coverage, Insurance Defense Law, Medical Malpractice Law, Police Misconduct, RICO, Surety and Fidelity Bond Law, Tort Law, Toxic Substances Law and Toxic Torts, Lanham Act Litigation, Condemnation Litigation, Arbitrations.

LAW OFFICES OF KOMIE AND ASSOCIATES

WAUKEGAN, ILLINOIS

(See Chicago)

Civil and Criminal Litigation. Federal, State, International, Trial and Appellate Practice. Complex Litigation, Criminal Defense, Divorce, Family Law, Probate, Taxation, Immigration Law, International Criminal Law, Real Estate Law.

LEIBOWITZ LAW CENTER

Established in 1999

420 CLAYTON AVENUE
WAUKEGAN, ILLINOIS 60085
Telephone: 847-249-9100
Fax: 847-249-9180
URL: http://www.lawyers.com/lakelaw
Email: dpl@lakelaw.com
URL: http://www.lakelaw.com

Bankruptcy, Creditors Rights, Business and Real Estate, Litigation, Estate and Probate, Commercial Litigation, Elder Law, Consumer Protection.

FIRM PROFILE: We represent people and business in financial matters. Leibowitz Law Center is the leading bankruptcy and financial services firm in Lake County, Illinois. From its deep foundation in bankruptcy law and practice, Leibowitz Law Center has developed expertise and depth of practice in estate planning and probate, including probate litigation, business organizations and transactions, contracts and contract litigation in the Circuit Court of Lake County. Now, Leibowitz Law Center is developing a reputation as a consumer advocate in matters such as Truth-In-Lending, Lemon Law Litigation and a wide array of other consumer causes of action. Leibowitz Law Center - Serving your legal needs in Lake County.

DAVID P. LEIBOWITZ, born 1950; admitted to bar, 1974, Illinois. *Education:* Northwestern University (B.A., 1970); Loyola University (J.D., cum laude, 1974). Member, United States Trustee Panel for Northern District of Illinois, 1991—. Adjunct Professor,

(This Listing Continued)

John Marshall Law School, 1996-2001. Member and President, Highland Park Public Library Board of Trustees. Past Member and President, North Shore School District 112 Board of Education. Schwartz, Cooper, Kolb and Gaynor, Chtd., 1976-1991, Shareholder, 1980-1991. Partner, Freeborn and Peters, 1992-1999. *Member:* Chicago, Lake County, Illinois State and American Bar Associations; American Bankruptcy Institute; National Association of Bankruptcy Trustees. (Certified in Business and Consumer Bankruptcy Law by the American Board of Certification). ***LANGUAGES:*** Spanish and French. ***REPORTED CASES:*** Leibowitz v. Parkway Bank, 139 F.2d 574 (7th Cir. 1998); Kramer v. Exchange National Bank of Chicago, 118 Ill. 2d 277, 515 N.E. 2d 57, 113 Ill. Dec. 248 (1987); In re UNR Industries, Inc. 736 F.2d 1136 (7th Cir. 1984); Gabellini v. Rega, 724 F.2d 579 (7th Cir. 1984); Sparks v. Sparks, 200 B.R. 481 (Bankr. N.D. Ill. 1997); Leibowitz v. Saleh (1994 Bankr. LEXIS 29 (Bankr. N.D. Ill. 1994). ***PRACTICE AREAS:*** Bankruptcy (50%); International Bankruptcy (5%); Creditors Rights (10%); Business (15%); Real Estate (10%); Litigation (10%). ***Email:*** dpl@lakelaw.com

LAURA BARRIENTOS-DUVALL, born Fort Wayne, Indiana, May 9, 1977; admitted to bar, 2002, Illinois and U.S. District Court, Northern District of Illinois. *Education:* Saint Louis University (B.A., 1999); DePaul University (J.D., 2002). *Member:* American Bar Association; American Bankruptcy Institute. ***LANGUAGES:*** Spanish. ***PRACTICE AREAS:*** Business Law (15%); Bankruptcy (85%). ***Email:*** lbd@lakelaw.com

ASSOCIATE

CHAYA D. WILLIAMS, born Milwaukee, Wisconsin, March 25, 1977; admitted to bar, 2004, Illinois and U.S. District Court, Northern District of Illinois. *Education:* University of Illinois, Urbana-Champaign (B.S., 1999; J.D., 2003). Certified Public Accountant, Illinois, 2000. Treasurer, Shiloh Baptist Church Credit Union. *Member:* Chicago, Lake County, Illinois State and American Bar Associations; American Association of Attorney-Certified Public Accountants. ***LANGUAGES:*** Spanish. ***PRACTICE AREAS:*** Civil Litigation (10%); Estate Planning (10%); Real Estate (20%); Bankruptcy (60%). ***Email:*** cdw@lakelaw.com

OF COUNSEL

ALLAN G. SWEIG, born Chicago, Illinois, 1935; admitted to bar, 1960, Illinois. *Education:* Northwestern University (B.S.B.A., 1957; J.D., 1960). Tau Epsilon Rho. Order of the Coif. Contributing Editor, Collier Bankruptcy Guide, 1981, 1984, 1987, 1990 and 1995. Adjunct Professor of Law, Northwestern University School of Law, 1984-1986. *Member:* Chicago and Illinois State Bar Associations. ***PRACTICE AREAS:*** Bankruptcy; Business Organization; Civil Litigation; Estate Planning; Probate; Real Estate. ***Email:*** ags@lakelaw.com

Languages: Spanish and French.

LINN & CAMPE, LTD.

215 N. MARTIN LUTHER KING, JR. AVENUE
WAUKEGAN, ILLINOIS 60085
Telephone: 847-249-4600
Fax: 847-249-9927

Plaintiff's Catastrophic Personal Injury, Construction Litigation, Professional Negligence, Automobile Accidents and Injuries, Wrongful Death Litigation, Workers' Compensation.

CRAIG M. LINN, born Minneapolis, Minnesota, September 20, 1947; admitted to bar, 1976, Illinois. *Education:* St. Olaf College (B.A., 1971); John Marshall Law School (J.D., with distinction, 1976). Lecturer, Moderator and Writer for Illinois State Bar Association Workers' Compensation Seminars and Illinois Trial Lawyers Association Seminars. *Member:* Lake County (Past Chair, Workers' Compensation Committee) and Illinois State (Past Delagate, Assembly; Past Chair, Workers' Compensation Section Council) Bar Associations; Illinois Trial Lawyers Association (Past Downstate Chair, Workers' Compensation Committee); Workers' Compensation Lawyers Association (Past Member, Board of Directors). ***PRACTICE AREAS:*** Workers Compensation; Plaintiffs Personal Injury; Catastrophic Injury; Construction Litigation; Professional Negligence; Automobile Accidents and Injuries; Wrongful Death Litigation.

THOMAS D. CAMPE, JR., born Arlington Heights, Illinois, August 23, 1963; admitted to bar, 1989, Illinois. *Education:* University of Illinois (B.S., 1985; J.D., magna cum laude, 1989). Assistant State's Attorney, Lake County, Illinois, August 1990-February, 1992. Lecturer and Moderator, Illinois State Bar Association seminars and Lake County Bar Association seminars. *Member:* Illinois State Bar Association (Board of Governors, 1997-2001, Tort Section Council, 1993-2003); Illinois Trial Lawyers Association (Board of Managers, 1996—; Board of Advocates, 1993-1996); Association of Trial Lawyers of America. ***PRACTICE AREAS:*** Plaintiff's Catastrophic Personal Injury; Automobile Accidents; Professional Negligence; Construction Litigation; Wrongful Death Litigation.

JOHN J. RIZZO, born Blue Island, Illinois, June 6, 1968; admitted to bar, 1994, Illinois. *Education:* Loyola University (B.A., 1990); Creighton University (J.D., 1994). *Member:* Lake County (Chair, Workers' Compensation Committee) and Illinois State Bar Associations; Illinois Trial Lawyers Association; Illinois Workers Compensation Lawyers Association. ***PRACTICE AREAS:*** Workers Compensation; Plaintiffs Personal Injury; Catastrophic Injury; Construction Litigation; Professional Negligence; Automobile Accidents and Injuries; Wrongful Death Litigation.

LARRY A. APPELBAUM, born Chicago, Illinois, September 26, 1962; admitted to bar, 1987, Illinois. *Education:* University of Illinois (B.A., 1984); Chicago Kent College of Law, Illinois Institute of Technology (J.D., 1987). American Jurisprudence Award, Insurance Law, Spring 1987. Assistant Public Defender, Lake County, Illinois, August 1988-November 1991. Staff Council: Merit Insurance Co., November 1991-November 1995; CNA Insurance Co., November 1995-November 1998. Published: "Application of Section 414, Restatement (Second) of Torts in Construction Negligence Cases", Tort Trends, Vol. 36, No. 2, November 2000; "Serving the Uncooperative Defendant", Tort Trends, Vol. 37, No. 2, May 2002. *Member:* Lake County and Illinois State (Tort Section Council, 2000-2002; Civil Practice and Procedure Section Council, 2003-2004) Bar Associations; Illinois Trial Lawyers Association. ***PRACTICE AREAS:*** Plaintiffs Catastrophic Personal Injury; Construction Litigation; Professional Negligence; Automobile Accidents; Wrongful Death Litigation. ***Email:*** lappelbaum@mcleodusa.net

MARAMBA & ASSOCIATES, LLC

WAUKEGAN, ILLINOIS

(See Arlington Heights)

Business Law, Chancery Practice, Corporate Litigation, Civil Litigation, Complex Litigation, Defense Litigation, Federal Litigation, Administrative Litigation, Business Enterprises, Business Litigation, Closely Held Business Law, Real Estate Litigation, Veterans Rights, Military Law, Wills, Commercial Collections, Post Judgment Collections, Closely Held Corporations.

MAY & BUEGE

33 NORTH COUNTY, SUITE 500
WAUKEGAN, ILLINOIS 60085-4388
Telephone: 847-244-9100
Fax: 847-244-9298
Email: maybuegelaw@earthlink.net

Personal Injury, Workers Compensation and Insurance Law. Litigation.

CHARLES M. MAY (1924-1987)

ROBERT M. BUEGE, born Chicago, Illinois, August 12, 1947; admitted to bar, 1983, Illinois, U.S. District Court, Northern District of Illinois, U.S. Court of Appeals, Seventh Circuit including Trial Bar. *Education:* Northern Illinois University (B.S., 1970); College of Lake County (A.A.S., 1975); John Marshall Law School (J.D., with high distinction, 1983). Phi Theta Kappa. *Member:* Chicago, Lake County, Illinois State and American Bar Associations; Illinois Trial Lawyers Association; The Association of Trial Lawyers of America; Illinois Workers Compensation Lawyers Association; Jefferson Inn (American Inn of Court). ***PRACTICE AREAS:*** Personal Injury; Workers Compensation; Insurance; Litigation.

JOSEPH P. McCAFFERY
ATTORNEY AT LAW

WAUKEGAN, ILLINOIS

(See Aurora)

Criminal Litigation, White Collar, Felonies, Misdemeanors, Civil Defense, Legal Malpractice Defense, Insurance Defense, Medical Malpractice, Personal Injury, Divorce, Wills and Trusts, Real Estate Transactions, Banking, Securities, Corporate and Commercial Litigation.

LAW OFFICES OF
STEVEN P. McCOLLUM, P.C.

Established in 1995
415 WASHINGTON STREET, SUITE 103
WAUKEGAN, ILLINOIS 60085-5564
Telephone: 847-662-2474
Fax: 847-249-7588
URL: http://www.stevenmccollum.com
Email: stevenpmccollum@aol.com
URL: http://www.lawyers.com/smccollumlaw

Criminal Law, Felonies, White Collar Crime, Juvenile Law, Termination of Parental Rights, Misdemeanors, Driving While Intoxicated, Drug Crimes, Homicide, Parole and Probation, Sexual Assault, Traffic Violations, Domestic Violence, Assault and Battery, Grand Jury Practice, Capital Offences, Construction Accidents, Personal Injury, Products Liability, Wrongful Death, Automobile Accidents and Injuries, Sexual Abuse. General Practice.

STEVEN P. McCOLLUM, born Harlingen, Texas, October 6, 1953; admitted to bar, 1978, Illinois. *Education:* University of Illinois (B.A., 1975; J.D., 1978); Rutgers University. Speaker, Criminal Law, Lake County Bar Association Seminar, 1999, 2002. Assistant States Attorney, Peoria County, 1979-1981. Lake County States Attorney Office: Chief Deputy State's Attorney, 1990-1995; Chief of Felony Review Division, 1987-1990; Chief of Misdemeanor and Traffic Division, 1984-1987; Chief of Juvenile Trial Division, 1983-1984; Felony Trial Attorney, 1982-1983 and Assistant States Attorney, 1981-1982. Member, Domestic Violence Council, 1992-1995. Member, Board of Safe Place Domestic Violence Center, 1988-1994. *Member:* Lake County Bar Association (Chair, Criminal Law Committee, 1997-1998; 1999-2002; Member, Judicial Selection and Retention Committee, 1994—); 19th Judicial Circuit Bar Association (Member, Capital Litigation Trial Bar Screening Committee, 2001—); Illinois State Bar Association. ***PRACTICE AREAS:*** Criminal Law; Juvenile Law; Driving While Intoxicated; Traffic Violations; Homicide; Felonies; Misdemeanors; Drug Crimes; Civil Litigation. ***Email:*** stevenpmccollum@aol.com

McKENNA STORER

Established in 1954
33 NORTH COUNTY STREET
6TH FLOOR
WAUKEGAN, ILLINOIS 60085-4343
Telephone: 847-249-1620
Fax: 847-249-8457
Email: postmaster-@mckenna-law.com
URL: http://www.mckenna-law.com

Chicago, Illinois Office: 33 N. LaSalle Street, 14th Floor, 60602-2610. Telephone: 312-558-3900. Fax: 312-558-8348.

(This Listing Continued)

McKENNA STORER, Waukegan—Continued

Woodstock, Illinois Office: 666 Russel Court, Suite 303, 60098-2672. Telephone: 815-334-9690. Fax: 815-334-9697.

Administrative Hearings, Appellate, Banking and Lending, Bankruptcy, Civil Rights, Commercial, Construction, Employment, Estate Planning, Fidelity, Insurance Coverage, Legal Malpractice, Mediation Services, Medical Malpractice, National Coordination, Personal Injury, Products Liability, Professional Liability, Surety, Tax and Toxic Tort.

FIRM PROFILE: McKenna Storer celebrated its 50th Anniversary in 2004. The Firm has a history and reputation for providing quality legal services to its clients. Our clients are individuals, corporations and insurance companies. We serve local, national and international clients from our offices in the Chicago, Illinois metropolitan area.

Client focused and service driven, the Firm is committed to cost-effective client services that are effective, personal and timely. Whether retained for litigation or consultation, McKenna Storer's philosophy is to consider traditional and creative solutions to our clients' legal needs.

RESIDENT PARTNER

RICHARD M. CLARK, admitted to bar, 1975, Illinois. *Education:* College of the Holy Cross (B.A., 1972); Stanford University (J.D., 1975). ***Email:*** rclark@mckenna-law.com

(For complete biographical data on other personnel, see Professional Biographies at Chicago, Illinois)

MINER, BARNHILL & GALLAND, P.C.

WAUKEGAN, ILLINOIS

(See Chicago)

General Practice, Trial and Appellate Litigation, Commercial, Employment, Employee Benefits, Civil Rights and Securities Litigation, Banking Law, Single and Multi-Family Housing Finance and Development, Non-Profit Corporations.

THE LAW FIRM OF WENDY R. MORGAN

WAUKEGAN, ILLINOIS

(See Arlington Heights)

Family Law, Divorce, Child Custody, Interstate Custody, Adoptions, Child Support, Paternity, Premarital Agreements, Domestic Violence, Visitation Rights, Adoption Law, Domestic Violence, Visitation Rights.

NADLER, PRITIKIN & MIRABELLI, L.L.C.

WAUKEGAN, ILLINOIS

(See Chicago)

Family Law and Domestic Relations Law including Dissolution of Marriage, Division and Valuation of Marital and Non-Marital Property, Maintenance and Support, Custody and Visitation, Domestic Violence, Establishment of Paternity, Prenuptial and Postnuptial Agreements and, When Necessary, Litigation of Cases and the Prosecution and Defense of Appeals. Mediation and Arbitration.

NOONAN, PERILLO, POLENZANI, LTD.

Established in 1969

25 NORTH COUNTY STREET
WAUKEGAN, ILLINOIS 60085-4342
Telephone: 847-244-0111
FAX: 847-244-0513
URL: http://www.sullivansmithlaw.com
URL: http://www.lawyers.com/sulsmi

General Trial and Appellate Practice in State and Federal Courts. Negligence and Insurance Law. Workers Compensation, Commercial, Banking, Domestic Relations and Municipal Defense, Military Law, Civil Rights, Product Liability, Criminal Law and Traffic Law, Nursing Home Negligence.

MICHAEL K. NOONAN, born Lansing, Michigan, March 3, 1946; admitted to bar, 1974, Illinois and U.S. District Court, Northern District of Illinois including Trial Bar; 1979, U.S. Supreme Court. *Education:* Northern Illinois University (B.A., 1968); University of Michigan (J.D., 1973). Pi Sigma Alpha (President, 1967-1968). Guest Lecturer: Physical Therapist and the Law, University of Health Sciences/Chicago Medical School, 1983-1987. Elected Member, Board of Education, District 68, Lake County, IL. Arbitrator, 19th Judicial Circuit, 1991—. *Member:* Lake County (Chairman, Judiciary and Court Rules Committee, 1987—), Illinois State (Guest Lecturer, 1992 and 1993; Appointed Member, Ad Hoc Committee on Discovery) and American Bar Associations; Illinois Association of Defense Counsel; Lake County Trial Lawyers Association; Jefferson Inn, American Inns of Court. [U.S. Army1969-1971]. ***PRACTICE AREAS:*** Personal Injury Defense; Litigation; Municipal Defense; Civil Rights; Construction Litigation; Commercial Litigation; Sexual Harassment Litigation. ***Email:*** mnoonan@sullivansmithlaw.com

MICHAEL J. PERILLO, JR., born Brooklyn, N.Y., February 11, 1955; admitted to bar, 1983, New York and U.S. District Court, Southern and Eastern Districts of New York; 1988, Illinois and U.S. District Court, Northern District of Illinois. *Education:* Drew University (B.A., 1977); New York Law School (J.D., cum laude, 1983). Senior Assistant Public Defender, 1988-1990 and Senior Assistant State's Attorney, 1990-1992, Lake County, IL. *Member:* Lake County and Illinois State Bar Associations. [Lt., JAGC, US Navy, 1983-1987]. ***PRACTICE AREAS:*** Personal Injury; Criminal Law; Military Law; Civil Litigation; Nursing Home Negligence. ***Email:*** mperillo@sullivansmithlaw.com

JOSEPH E. POLENZANI, born Chicago, Illinois, May 21, 1960; admitted to bar, 1987, Illinois. *Education:* Illinois State University (B.A., 1982); John Marshall Law School (J.D., 1987). Senior Assistant State's Attorney, Lake County, IL, 1987-1992. *Member:* Lake County, Illinois State and American Bar Associations. ***PRACTICE AREAS:*** Personal Injury; Criminal Defense; Workers Compensation; Traffic. ***Email:*** jpolenzani@sullivansmithlaw.com

ASSOCIATE

JASON S. MARKS, born Highland Park, Illinois, February 8, 1976; admitted to bar, 2001, Illinois. *Education:* University of Iowa (B.B.A., with honors, 1998); DePaul University (J.D., with honors, 2001). *Member:* Lake County and Illinois State Bar Associations. ***PRACTICE AREAS:*** Personal Injury; Criminal Defense; Workers Compensation; Family Law; Civil Litigation.

OF COUNSEL

LEO J. SULLIVAN, III, born St. Louis, Missouri, August 16, 1934; admitted to bar, 1958, Illinois and Missouri. *Education:* St. Louis University (J.D., 1958). Phi Delta Phi. *Member:* Lake County (President, 1983-1984), Illinois State (Assembly Member, 1992-1996; Board Member, ISBA Mutual Insurance Company, 1992—; Member, Claims Committee) and American Bar Associations; Appellate Lawyers Association; Jefferson Inn, American Inns of Court; Lake County Trial Lawyers Association. ***PRACTICE AREAS:*** Personal Injury Defense; Civil Litigation. ***Email:*** lsullivan@sullivansmithlaw.com

RICHARD J. SMITH, born Freeport, Illinois, July 10, 1939; admitted to bar, 1966, Illinois. *Education:* Augustana College (B.A., cum laude, 1961); Purdue University (M.S., 1964); University of Michigan (J.D., 1966). Phi Beta Kappa. Member, Inquiry Panel of Attorney's Registration and Disciplinary Commission of Illinois Supreme Court, 1973-1983 and Member, Hearing Panel, 1980-1983. *Member:* Lake County and Illinois State (Chairman, New Members Committee, 1971-1972) Bar Associations; The Association of Trial Lawyers of America; National Lawyers Association; Lake County Trial Lawyers Association. ***PRACTICE AREAS:*** Personal Injury; Civil Litigation; Appellate Practice. ***Email:*** bvasilius@sullivansmithlaw.com

REPRESENTATIVE CLIENTS: Allstate Insurance Co.; Northbrook Excess and Surplus Insurance Co.; New Hampshire Insurance Co.; Inland National Insurance Co.; Country Mutual Insurance; Farmers Insurance Group.; Abbott Laboratories; Illinois National Insurance Co.; New Hampshire Indemnity Co.; Country Cos.; Milwaukee Insurance Co.; City of North Chicago; American States Insurance Co.; City of Waukegan; City of Highland Park.
REFERENCE: First Midwest Bank of Waukegan.

PAUL B. NOVAK

210 NORTH MARTIN LUTHER KING JR. AVENUE
WAUKEGAN, ILLINOIS 60085
Telephone: 847-244-1399
Fax: 847-625-9980
Email: paul@novaklaw.net
URL: http://www.paulnovaklaw.com

Criminal Law, Juvenile Law, Family Law.

PAUL B. NOVAK, born Chicago, Illinois, February 2, 1971; admitted to bar, 1996, Illinois. *Education:* Illinois State University (B.S., Criminal Justice, 1993); John Marshall Law School (J.D., 1996). *Member:* Chicago, Illinois State and American Bar Associations. ***PRACTICE AREAS:*** Criminal Law; Juvenile Law; Family Law.

O'HAGAN, SMITH & AMUNDSEN

415 WEST WASHINGTON STREET, SUITE 204
WAUKEGAN, ILLINOIS 60079-0410
Telephone: 847-599-9503
Fax: 847-599-9525
URL: http://www.osalaw.com

Chicago, Illinois Office: 150 North Michigan Avenue, Suite 3300, 60601. Telephone: 312-894-3200. Fax: 312-894-3210.

Rockford, Illinois Office: Stewart Square, 308 West State Street, Suite 320, 61101-1140. Telephone: 815-987-0441. Fax: 815-987-9891.

St. Charles, Illinois Office: 3815 E. Main Street, Suite A-1, 60174-2488. Telephone: 630-587-7910. Fax: 630-587-7960.

Woodstock, Illinois Office: 666 Russel Court, 60098. Telephone: 815-337-4900. Fax: 815-337-4910.

Milwaukee, Wisconsin Office: 4811 South 76th Street, Suite 305, 53220. Suite 117, 53406-3770. Telephone: 414-282-7103. Fax: 414-282-1830.

Commercial; Commercial Transportation; Appellate; Complex Litigation; Construction; Corporate Transactions; Employment; Extra-Contractual/Insurance Litigation; Healthcare; Insurance Coverage; Personal Lines; Product Liability; Professional Liability; Property Litigation.

MEMBER OF FIRM

MARK P. BRODERICK, admitted to bar, 1995, Wisconsin; 1996, Illinois. *Education:* University of Notre Dame (B.A., 1985); Thomas M. Cooley Law School (J.D., 1995). Assistant Editor, Thomas M. Cooley Law Review, 1994-1995. Recipient, American Jurisprudence Awards in Legal Research and Writing, Evidence, Lawyering Before Trial and Comparative Procedure. Member, Moot Court. Law Clerk, Kenosha County Circuit Court, 1995-1996. *Member:* State Bar of Wisconsin; Illinois State and American Bar Associations. ***PRACTICE AREAS:*** Insurance Defense; Civil Litigation. ***Email:*** mbroderick@osalaw.com

(This Listing Continued)

ASSOCIATE

BRIAN S. EBENER, admitted to bar, 1987, Illinois. *Education:* University of Wisconsin-Parkside (B.A., magna cum laude, 1984); Northern Illinois University (J.D., cum laude, 1987). **Email:** bebener@osalaw.com

(For complete biographical data on other personnel, see Professional Biographies at other cities)

PAUL F. O'KEEFE, P.C.

Established in 2000

32 N. WEST STREET, SECOND FLOOR
WAUKEGAN, ILLINOIS 60085
Telephone: 847-263-9262
Email: okeefelaw@msn.com
URL: http://www.okeefelawoffice.com

Chicago, Illinois Office: 20 North Clark Street, Suite 2550. 60602. Telephone: 312-263-9200. Fax: 312-263-6245.

Arbitration, Business Law, Business Litigation, Complex Business Litigation, Federal Civil Practice, Commercial Law, Complex Commercial Litigation, Contracts, Breach of Contracts, Contract Litigation, Corporate Law, Corporate Litigation, Criminal law, Criminal Defense, Governmental Law, Labor and Employment, Employment Breach of Contract, Litigation, Civil Litigation, Complex Litigation, Defense Litigation, Federal Litigation, Trial Practice, Medical Malpractice, Personal Injury, Probate, Ancillary Probate, Probate Administration, Probate Litigation, Criminal Taxation, Trusts and Estates, Contested Trusts and Estates, Decedents Estates, Estate Litigation, Estate Settlements, White Collar Crimes, White Collar Criminal Defense, Wills, Contested Wills, Inheritance, Decedents Estates, Estate Administration, Estate Litigation, Estate Planning, Internet Crimes, Felonies.

FIRM PROFILE: We are dedicated to our clients.

Languages: Spanish.

(For biographical data on all personnel, see Professional Biographies, Chicago, Illinois)

LAW OFFICES OF GARRY A. PAYTON

325 WASHINGTON STREET, SUITE 201
WAUKEGAN, ILLINOIS 60085
Telephone: 847-625-9900
Fax: 847-625-8880
Email: payton@attorneygarrypayton.com
URL: http://www.lawyers.com/gapayton

Criminal Defense, Personal Injury, Medical Malpractice, Products Liability, Automobile Accidents, Wrongful Death, Construction Site Accidents, Driving While Intoxicated, Drug Crimes, Felonies, Homicide, Juvenile, Misdemeanors, Sexual Assault and Traffic Violations.

GARRY A. PAYTON, born Cairo, Illinois, September 13, 1958; admitted to bar, 1987, Illinois; 2002, U.S. Court of Appeals, 7th Circuit. *Education:* Southern Illinois University (B.A., Arts, 1982); University of Minnesota Law School (J.D., 1985). Assistant Prosecutor, Cook County State Attorneys Office, 1989-1994. *Member:* Illinois State Bar Association. **PRACTICE AREAS:** Criminal Law; Personal Injury; Business Law; Medical Malpractice; Real Estate.

PINZUR, COHEN & KERR, LTD.

WAUKEGAN, ILLINOIS

(See Long Grove)

Administrative Matters, Adoption Law, Annexation, Appellate Practice, Arbitration, Asset Acquisitions and Sales, Banking and Loan Documentation, Banking Law, Business Law, Business Litigation, Business Planning and Formation, Business Successions, Buying and Selling of Businesses, Child Custody, Child Support, Civil Litigation in State and Federal Courts, Civil Rights, Class Actions, Closings, Collections, Commercial and Residential Development, Commercial Litigation, Commercial Real Estate, Community Association Law, Condemnation, Condominium Law, Contractual Disputes, Construction Law, Construction Arbitration, Construction Defects, Construction Litigation, Consumer Law, Contested Wills, Contracts, Cooperative Housing Law, Copyrights, Corporate Law, Corporations, Creditors Rights, Debtor and Creditor, Developer Disputes, Discrimination, Divorce, Domestic Violence, Elder Law, Employment Agreements, Employment Law, Entrepreneurial Ventures, Environmental Law, Equipment Leasing, Equitable and Injunctive Remedies, Estate Planning, Family Law, Family Business Law, Forcible Eviction Law, Foreclosures, Franchise Law, General Practice, Guardianship, Harassment, Homeowner's Association Law, Incorporation, Institutional Lending, Insurance Regulations, Workouts, Insurance, Land Development and Zoning, Landlord and Tenant Law, Leases and Leasing, Limited Liability Companies, Litigation, Matrimonial Law, Mechanics Liens, Mergers and Acquisitions, Mortgages, Municipal, Partnership Law, Personal Injury, Premarital Agreements, Probate Law, Real Estate, Real Estate Finance, Real Estate Litigation, Real Estate Tax Appeals, Real Estate Tax Assessment, Residential Real Estate, Sales Acquisitions, School Law, Secured Transactions, Small Business Law, Social Security, Spousal Support, Stock Acquisitions and Sales, Trademarks, Trusts and Estates, Uniform Commercial Code, Wills, Zoning, Planning and Land Use.

QUERREY & HARROW, LTD.

Established in 1939

SUITE 205
415 WEST WASHINGTON STREET
WAUKEGAN, ILLINOIS 60085
Telephone: 847-249-4440
Fax: 847-249-4932
Email: tburke@querrey.com
URL: http://www.querrey.com

Chicago, Illinois Office: 175 West Jackson Boulevard, Suite 1600. Telephone: 312-540-7000. Fax: 312-540-0578.
Crystal Lake, Illinois Office: 651 West Terra Cotta Avenue, Suite 221. Telephone: 815-479-1929. Fax: 815-479-1978.
Joliet, Illinois Office: 2 Rialto Square, Suite 401, 116 North Chicago Street. Telephone: 815-726-1600. Fax: 815-726-1674.
Wheaton, Illinois Office: 310 South County Farm Road, Third Floor. Telephone: 630-653-2600. Fax: 630-653-0178.
Merrillville, Indiana Office: 8585 Broadway, Suite 510. Telephone: 219-738-1820. Fax: 219-738-1821.
New York, N.Y. Office: 120 Broadway, Suite 2800. Telephone: 212-233-0130. Fax: 212-233-0172.
London, England Office: 141-142 Fenchurch Street, Fifth Floor. Telephone: 207-929-6670. Fax: 207-929-6671.

General Practice and Trial Practice.

THOMAS P. BURKE, admitted to bar, 1984, Illinois. *Education:* St. Vincent College (B.A., high honors, 1976); Southern Illinois University (M.A., 1978); Loyola of Chicago (J.D., 1984). (Resident). **PRACTICE AREAS:** Litigation; Transportation; Construction Injuries; Employment.

ELLEN E. GIBSON, admitted to bar, 1991, Illinois. *Education:* University of Michigan (B.A., 1986); University of Illinois (J.D., Honors, 1991). (Resident). **PRACTICE AREAS:** Litigation; Construction; Product Liability; Insurance Coverage. **Email:** egibson@querrey.com

---

NICHOLAS JOHNSON, admitted to bar, 2005, Illinois. *Education:* University of Wisconsin (B.A., 2003); Thomas M. Cooley Law School (J.D., magna cum laude, 2005). **PRACTICE AREAS:** Litigation. **Email:** njohnson@querrey.com

LAWRENCE A. STEINGOLD, admitted to bar, 2003, Illinois. *Education:* Indiana University (B.S., 1996); Chicago-Kent College of Law (J.D., 2002). (Resident). **PRACTICE AREAS:** Litigation. **Email:** lsteingold@querrey.com

(For complete biographical data on all personnel, see Professional Biographies at Chicago, Illinois)

RICHARDS, RALPH & SCHWAB

CHARTERED

WAUKEGAN, ILLINOIS

(See Vernon Hills)

Corporate and Business. Banking and Finance. Bankruptcy and Creditors' Rights. Real Estate. Commercial Litigation.

RINELLA AND RINELLA, LTD.

WAUKEGAN, ILLINOIS

(See Chicago)

Practice Limited to Family Law and Divorce including the areas of Legal Separation, Negotiating and Drafting Premarital and Postnuptial Agreements, Judgment Enforcement, Child Custody and Child Support Actions, Domestic Violence, Spousal Support, Appeals, Adoption, Parentage Actions and Interstate Support Enforcement.

RYAN AND RYAN

WAUKEGAN, ILLINOIS

(See Chicago)

Eminent Domain, Condemnation.

SALVI, ROSKAM & MAHER, L.L.C.

325 WASHINGTON STREET, SUITE 302
WAUKEGAN, ILLINOIS 60085
Telephone: 847-662-3303
Fax: 847-662-3453
Email: srmtms@sbcglobal.net
URL: http://www.salvi-law.com

Personal Injury, Automobile Accidents and Injuries, Slips and Falls, Dog Bites, Construction Accidents, Wrongful Death, Medical Malpractice, Workers Compensation and Legal Malpractice.

MEMBERS OF FIRM

ALBERT J. SALVI, born Evanston, Illinois, April 25, 1960; admitted to bar, 1985, Illinois; 1987, California. *Education:* Sophia University, Tokyo, Japan; University of Notre Dame (B.A., 1982); University of Illinois (J.D., 1985). **LANGUAGES:** Japanese.

(This Listing Continued)

SALVI, ROSKAM & MAHER, L.L.C., Waukegan—Continued

PETER J. ROSKAM, born Hinsdale, Illinois, September 13, 1961; admitted to bar, 1989, Illinois. *Education:* University of Minnesota; University of Illinois (B.A., 1983); Catholic University of America; Illinois Institute of Technology (J.D., 1989). (Resident, Wheaton Office)

MICHAEL E. MAHER, born Gardner, Illinois, October 9, 1960; admitted to bar, 1985, Illinois. *Education:* Loras College (B.A., 1982); DePaul University (J.D., 1985).

SALVI, SCHOSTOK & PRITCHARD P.C.

Established in 1999

Established 1982 as Law Offices of Patrick A. Salvi, P.C.

218 NORTH MARTIN LUTHER KING JR. AVENUE
WAUKEGAN, ILLINOIS 60085
Telephone: 847-249-1227
Facsimile: 847-249-0138
Email: psalvi@salvilaw.com
URL: http://www.salvilaw.com

Chicago, Illinois Office: 181 West Madison, Suite 3800, 60602. Telephone: 312-372-1227. Telefax: 312-372-3720.

Concentration in representing Plaintiffs in personal injury, medical malpractice, wrongful death, transportation liability, aviation, product liability and commercial litigation.

FIRM PROFILE: Salvi, Schostok & Pritchard P.C. is proud of the reputation it has built over the years by representing victims of negligence. For over 23 years, the Firm has been dedicated to helping families recover both emotionally and economically by providing the highest professional and ethical legal representation. Since 1987, SS&P has successfully won 110 separate verdicts or settlements of $1 million or more totaling over $335 million. All the Firm's attorneys are active participants in numerous legal associations. Patrick A. Salvi was recently named one of The Best Lawyers of America by Woodward/White, Inc. and is a Past President of the Illinois Trial Lawyers Association (ITLA). Michael P. Schostok is also a Past President of ITLA and David J. Prichard was recently elected to the Board of Directors for the Illinois Society of Trial Lawyers.

PATRICK A. SALVI, born Evanston, Illinois, February 10, 1953; admitted to bar, 1978, Illinois and U.S. District Court, Northern District of Illinois including Federal Trial Bar; 1979, Florida; 1985, Wisconsin and U.S. District Court, Eastern District of Wisconsin; U.S. Court of Appeals, Seventh Circuit. *Education:* St. Mary's University of Minnesota (B.A., cum laude, 1975; Doctor of Laws, honoris causa, 1999); University of Notre Dame (J.D., 1978). Ratings: "Leading American Attorneys of Illinois" by the Consumer Law Guidebook; "Top 5% of all Lawyers in Illinois" by the Leading Lawyers Network; "Best Lawyers in America" by Woodward/White, Inc. Cited in Countless Legal Publications and Gives Keynote Speeches Across the Country. Guest Lecturer at: University of Notre Dame; Harvard University; Northwestern University. *Member:* International Academy of Trial Lawyers; Illinois Trial Lawyers Association (Past President); Association of Trial Lawyers of America; Lake County, Cook County, Illinois State and American Bar Associations; State Bar of Wisconsin; The Florida Bar. ***REPORTED CASES:*** Skonieczny v.Gardner et al., 98 L 4578 (2001) Jury Verdict $13, 298, 052; Stelton v. Merchandise Mart et al., 91 L 14568 (1996) Settlement $12,560,000; Cunningham v. Undisclosed Medical Facility (2003) Settlement $12,500,000; Lay v. Good Samaritan, et al., 98 L 65 (2002) Jury Verdict $11,024,371.31; Wingo v. Rockford Memorial, et al., 92 L 345 (1996) Jury Verdict $10,232,523. ***PRACTICE AREAS:*** Catastrophic Personal Injury; Wrongful Death; Medical Malpractice; Birth Injuries; Nursing Home Negligence; Transportation Liability; Aviation Litigation; Commercial Litigation. ***Email:*** psalvi@salvilaw.com

MICHAEL P. SCHOSTOK, born Oak Park, Illinois, March 8, 1961; admitted to bar, 1986, Illinois; 1995, U.S. District Court, Northern District of Illinois including Federal Trial Bar. *Education:* Miami University (B.A., 1983); Capital University (J.D., 1986). Ratings: "Top 5% of all Lawyers in Illinois" by the Leading Lawyers Network. Cited in Countless Legal Publications and Gives Keynote Speeches Across the State. *Member:* Illinois Trial Lawyers Association (Past President); Lake County and Illinois State Bar Associations. ***REPORTED CASES:*** Skonieczny v.Gardner et al., 98 L 4578 (2001) Jury Verdict $13, 298, 052; Stelton v. Merchandise Mart et al., 91 L 14568 (1996) Settlement $12,560,000; Lay v. Good Samaritan, et al., 98 L 65 (2002) Jury Verdict $11,024,371.31; Miroballi v. Estate of A. Locascio, et al., 88 L 11751 (1992) Jury Verdict $7,148,775; Hoffman v. Dey Laboratories, et al., 98 L 09673 (2002) Settlement $4,500,000. ***PRACTICE AREAS:*** Catastrophic Personal Injury; Wrongful Death; Medical Malpractice. ***Email:*** mschostok@salvilaw.com

DAVID J. PRITCHARD, born Evanston, Illinois, August 15, 1952; admitted to bar, 1977, Illinois and U.S. District Court, Northern District of Illinois including Trial Bar; 1980, U.S. Court of Appeals, Seventh Circuit. *Education:* Loyola University (B.B.A., Economics, Alpha Sigma Nu, 1974; M.A., Theology, 1992); DePaul University (J.D., 1977). Ratings: "Top 5% of all Lawyers in Illinois" by the Leading Lawyers Network. Past President, Board of Directors, Legal Assistance Foundation, Chicago, 1985-1998. Member: Ethics Advisory Board, The Children's Memorial Hospital of Chicago, 1992-1999; Board of Directors, Gastro-Intestinal Research Foundation of the University of Chicago Hospitals, 1993-1995. Past Board President, Legal Assistance Foundation of Chicago. Currently Serves on Boards of United Cerebral Palsy of greater Chicago as well as Friends Without A Border, which founded Angkor Children's Hospital in Cambodia. *Member:* Illinois Trial Lawyers Association; Chicago Bar Association; Society of Trial Lawyers. (Resident, Chicago Office). ***REPORTED CASES:*** Cunningham v. Undisclosed Medical Facility et al., (2003) Settlement $12,500,000; Grant v. SSM Regional Health, et al., 00 L 6788 (2004) Settlement $10,000,000; Ball v. Undisclosed Medical Facility et al., (2004) Settlement $8,550,000; Arredondo v. Westlake Hospital, et al., 00 L 13977 (2004) Settlement $8,300,000; McDonald v. Freeport Memorial Hospital, et al., 99 L 17 (2002) Settlement $5,500,000. ***PRACTICE AREAS:*** Catastrophic Injury; Wrongful Death; Medical Malpractice; Birth Injuries. ***Email:*** dpritchard@salvilaw.com

(This Listing Continued)

DAVID G. PRIBYL, born Milwaukee, Wisconsin, April 10, 1961; admitted to bar, 1988, Illinois; 1989, U.S. District Court, Northern District of Illinois; 1995, Wisconsin. *Education:* University of Wisconsin (B.A., 1983); John Marshall Law School (J.D., 1988). Member of the Judicial Selection & Retention Committee for the Circuit Court of the 9th Judicial Circuit, Lake County, Il, 2000—. Elected, Partner of Salvi, Schostok & Pritchard P.C., January 2003. *Member:* McHenry County and Illinois State Bar Associations; State Bar of Wisconsin. ***REPORTED CASES:*** Eddy v. OSF Healthcare System, et al., 99 L 379 (2001) Settlement $3,000,000; Green v. Northwest Community, et al., 99 L 669 (2003) Settlement $3,000,000; Hall v. Curry Ready Mix, et al., 00 L 167 (2004) Settlement $2,750,000; Christoffer v. Quincy Physicians, et al., 99 L 41 (2003) Settlement $2,250,000; Schlapper v. U.S. Express, et al., 99 L 159 (2001) Settlement $1,000,000. ***PRACTICE AREAS:*** Medical Malpractice; Products Liability; Automobile Accidents and Injuries; Aviation Law. ***Email:*** dpribyl@salvilaw.com

DONALD R. McGARRAH, born Norfolk, Virginia, July 5, 1953; admitted to bar, 1978, Missouri; 1979, Illinois and Trial Bar, U.S. District Court, Northern District of Illinois. *Education:* Spring Hill College (B.A., 1975); St. Louis University School of Law (J.D., 1978). Recipient, Everett Hulverson Award for Excellence in Trial Practice, St. Louis University School of Law, Spring 1978. Author: "When It's Not the Real Thing: The Sale of Counterfeit Sporting Goods Costs Trademark Owners and Retailers Millions of Dollars A Year, Here's How to Fight Back," NSGA Retail Focus (August, 1993); "Partnership Within the Law: Developing Legal Issues Among Manufacturers Agents and Retailers," Presentation to NSGA Management Conference (May 1993); "A Guide to the Cross-Examination of a Plaintiff's Economic Expert," Product Liability Advisory Council, April 1995; "Issues Regarding "Other Accident" Evidence," presentation at ABA Automobile Law Committee (August 1995). Panel Speaker: "Management of Catastrophic Damages," Trial Tactics Breakout Group, DRI Annual Product Liability Conference, Beverly Hills, CA, February 2002. Author and Speaker: "Management of Other Occurrence Evidence," DRI National Product Liability Meeting, New Orleans, LA, February 1998. Sustaining Member, Product Liability Advisory Council, 1990—. *Member:* Chicago, Illinois State and American (Member, Section of Litigation) Bar Associations; The Missouri Bar. (Resident, Chicago Office). ***PRACTICE AREAS:*** Medical Malpractice; Products Liability; Personal Injury; Wrongful Death; Aviation Law. ***Email:*** dmcgarrah@salvilaw.com

MARK N. SENAK, born Gary, Indiana, October 15, 1961; admitted to bar, 1987, Illinois and U.S. District Court, Northern District of Illinois, 1992, Trial Bar; 1992, U.S. District Court, Central District of Illinois and U.S. Court of Appeals, Seventh Circuit; 1994, U.S. District Court, Western District of Michigan; 1996, U.S. District Court, Southern District of Illinois; 1997, U.S. District Court, Southern District of Indiana. *Education:* Indiana University (B.A., English and Psychology, 1983); DePaul University College of Law (J.D., 1987). Member, Law Review, 1983-1987. Author: "Factual Investigation from the Insurer's Viewpoint," 1998 ed. of Property Insurance, Illinois Institute of Continuing Legal Education. Associate Instructor, Legal Writing, DePaul College of Law, 1984. *Member:* Chicago, Illinois State and American Bar Associations. (Resident, Chicago Office). ***PRACTICE AREAS:*** Commercial Litigation; Insurance Coverage; Property Subrogation; Employment Discrimination. ***Email:*** msenak@salvilaw.com

---

SCOTT R. CLEWIS, born Chicago, Illinois, March 4, 1965; admitted to bar, 2000, Illinois. *Education:* University of Illinois, Champaign - Urbana (B.A., 1987); ITT/Chicago-Kent College of Law (J.D., 1998). *Member:* Chicago, Lake County and Illinois State Bar Associations; American Trial Lawyers Association; Illinois Trial Lawyers Association. ***PRACTICE AREAS:*** Personal Injury; Wrongful Death; Medical Malpractice; Product Liability. ***Email:*** sclewis@salvilaw.com

KATHLEEN A. McGINTY, born Chicago, Illinois, 1963; admitted to bar, 1997, Illinois. *Education:* University of Illinois College of Nursing (B.S.N., with honors, 1982); Loyola University School of Law (J.D., 1997). *Member:* Illinois State Bar Association; Illinois Trial Lawyers Association; American Trial Lawyers Association. (Resident, Chicago Office). ***PRACTICE AREAS:*** Medical Malpractice; Personal Injury; Wrongful Death. ***Email:*** kmcginty@salvilaw.com

MATTHEW L. WILLIAMS, born Libertyville, Illinois, June 10, 1973; admitted to bar, 1998, Illinois. *Education:* University of Illinois (B.A., History, 1995); DePaul University (J.D., 1998). Staff Writer, De Paul Law Review. Recipient, CALI Award, Business Organization. *Member:* Lake County and Illinois State Bar Associations. ***PRACTICE AREAS:*** Medical Malpractice; Personal Injury; Wrongful Death; Automobile Accidents; Products Liability. ***Email:*** mwilliams@salvilaw.com

JOHN S. MUIR, born White Plains, New York, March 5, 1965; admitted to bar, 1993, Illinois, U.S. Court of Appeals, Seventh Circuit and U.S. Supreme Court. *Education:* Texas Christian University (B.S., 1988); John Marshall law School (J.D., with honors, 1993). Phi Delta Phi. Order of John Marshall. *Member:* Chicago Bar Association; Illinois Trial Lawyers Association. (Resident, Chicago Office). ***PRACTICE AREAS:*** Medical Malpractice; Wrongful Death; Personal Injury; Criminal Law. ***Email:*** jmuir@salvilaw.com

TARA R. PLEWE, born Princeton, New Jersey, April 6, 1978; admitted to bar, 2003, Wisconsin and Illinois. *Education:* University of Illinois (B.A., 2000); Marquette Law School (J.D., 2003). Phi Alpha Delta. *Member:* Chicago, Illinois State and American Bar Associations; State Bar of Wisconsin. ***PRACTICE AREAS:*** Personal Injury; Medical Malpractice; Insurance Coverage; Wrongful Death. ***Email:*** tplewe@salvilaw.com

STEVEN H. LEECH, born Winthrop Harbor, Illinois, December 11, 1980; admitted to bar, 2004, Illinois. *Education:* University of Chicago (B.A., 2001); Notre Dame Law School (J.D., 2004). *Member:* Chicago, Lake County, and Illinois State Bar Associations. ***PRACTICE AREAS:*** Commercial Litigation; Personal Injury; Wrongful Death; Medical Malpractice. ***Email:*** sleech@salvilaw.com

OF COUNSEL

JAMES H. CANEL, born Chicago, Illinois, February 26, 1944; admitted to bar, 1968, Illinois; 1969, U.S. District Court, Northern District of Illinois including Trial Bar; 1973, U.S. Court of Appeals, Seventh Circuit; 1974, U.S. Supreme Court. *Education:* Boston University; Washington University (B.A., 1964); DePaul University (J.D., 1968). Author, "The Standard of Care Instruction," Illinois Tort Report, Vol. 1, No. 3. Associate-in-Law, Ameri-

(This Listing Continued)

can College of Legal Medicine, 1980. Director, The Society of Trial Lawyers, 1991-1993. *Member:* Chicago (Member: Hearing Division, Judicial Candidate Evaluation Committee, 1976-1978; Investigative Division, 1982-1984; Medical Legal Relations Committee; Secretary, 1978-1979; Vice-Chairman, 1979-1980; Chairman, 1980-1981), Illinois State (Member: House of Delegates, 1978-1981; Sections on: Civil Practice; Tort Law; Civil Practice and Procedure) and American (Member, Sections on: Litigation; Tort and Insurance Practice; Vice-Chair, Committee on Medicine and Law, 1987-1988) Bar Associations; Illinois Trial Lawyers Association (Member, Board of Managers, 1985-1996); The Association of Trial Lawyers of America. (Also practicing individually, Chicago, Illinois). ***PRACTICE AREAS:*** Medical Malpractice; Personal Injury; Wrongful Death.

THOMAS F. LOIZZO, born Kenosha, Wisconsin, June 8, 1950; admitted to bar, 1976, Illinois; 1978, U.S. District Court, Northern District of Illinois; 1979, U.S. Court of Appeals, Seventh Circuit; 1982, U.S. Supreme Court; 1984, Wisconsin. *Education:* University of Wisconsin-Madison (B.S., 1971); John Marshall Law School (J.D., 1976). Assistant State's Attorney, McHenry County, Illinois, 1976-1978. *Member:* McHenry County, Illinois State and American Bar Associations; Illinois Trial Lawyers Association. (Also practicing individually in Woodstock). ***PRACTICE AREAS:*** Litigation; Family and Marital Matters; Criminal Defense Law; Personal Injury-Plaintiff Law.

REFERENCES: First Midwest Bank, Waukegan, Illinois; Northern Trust Bank, Lake Forest, Illinois; Commercial Litigation Clients; Anderson Consulting, LLP.; Baxter Healthcare; Brunswick Corporation, Lake Forest, Illinois.

GARY L. SCHLESINGER

WAUKEGAN, ILLINOIS

(See Libertyville)

Trials and Appeals of Divorce, Custody, Support, Paternity, Adoption, Family Law and Domestic Relations.

LAW OFFICE OF SHERBY DIANNE SCURTO, P.C.

Established in 2004

222 WASHINGTON STREET
WAUKEGAN, ILLINOIS 60085
Telephone: 847-336-9755
Fax: 847-336-9765

URL: http://www.sherbyscurto.com

Discrimination, Sexual Harassment, Wrongful Discharge, Civil Rights, Gay and Lesbian Rights, Criminal Records, Real Estate Closing, Buyer and Seller, Personal Injury.

SHERBY DIANNE SCURTO, admitted to bar, 2004, Illinois. *Education:* Elmhurst College (B.S. Chemistry; M.A., Industrial/Organizational Psychology); John Marshall Law School (J.D.). *Member:* Chicago, DuPage, Lake County and American Bar Associations; American Chemical Society. [VietNam-Era Veteran, U.S. Army]. ***PRACTICE AREAS:*** Divorce; Family Law; Military Divorce; Paternity; Uncontested Divorce; Real Estate; Personal Injury; Criminal Law; Discrimination; Sexual Harassment; Wrongful Termination; Civil Rights; Buy-Sell Agreements; Domestic Violence; Marital Property Distribution; Marital Property Settlements; Name Changes; Qualified Domestic Relations Orders (QDROs); Restraining Orders; Separation Agreements; Spousal Support; Consumer Law; Consumer Fraud; Consumer Rights; Consumer Litigation. ***Email:*** sds@sherbyslaw.com

---

STEIN, RAY & HARRIS LLP

WAUKEGAN, ILLINOIS

(See Chicago)

Construction and Design Law, Mechanics Liens, Government Contracts, Insurance, Complex Litigation and Construction Related Insurance Bankruptcy.

STONE & ASSOCIATES L.L.C.

415 WASHINGTON STREET, SUITE 107
WAUKEGAN, ILLINOIS 60085
Telephone: 847-336-7888; 312-943-7881
Fax: 847-336-0733
Email: jstone@jedstone.com

Practice limited to Criminal Law including White Collar Crime, Capital Offenses, Narcotics and Drugs, Death Penalty, Murder, Homicide and Federal Criminal Law.

FIRM PROFILE: Stone & Associates L.L.C. has acquired a nationwide reputation for vigorous advocacy on behalf of persons accused of serious crimes in state and federal courts. Mr. Stone has been invited to appear on such well known shows as Primetime, 20/20, Dateline, Unsolved Mysteries, American Justice and Hardcopy as well as a legal consultant for MSNBC-News.

JED STONE, born Chicago, Illinois, September 30, 1949; admitted to bar, 1976, Illinois and U.S. District Court, Northern District of Illinois; 1983, U.S. Court of Appeals, Seventh Circuit; 1984, U.S. Supreme Court; 1985, U.S. Court of Appeals, Fifth Circuit; 1986, U.S. Court of Appeals, Eleventh Circuit; 1989, U.S. District Court, Central District of Illinois. *Education:* Lake Forest College (B.A., with honors, 1971); University of Chicago; Illinois Institute of Technology/Chicago-Kent College of Law (J.D., 1975). Author: "Preserving the Record," *Defending Illinois Criminal Cases;* "A Lawyer's Reflection on Death," *The Chicago Bar Record,* Chicago Bar Association, October, 1992; *Illinois Criminal Defense Motions,* West Publishing, 1995. Adjunct Professor, Northwestern University School of Law, 1997-1999; Visiting Professor of American Studies, Weinberg College of Art & Sciences, Northwestern University, 1999—; Instructor, Department of Politics, Lake Forest College, 1999—. *Member:* Chicago, Lake County (Chair, Criminal Law Committee, 1984-1986), Illinois State and American Bar Associations; National Association of Criminal Defense Lawyers; Illinois Attorneys for Criminal Justice (President, 1995; Member, Board of Directors, 1986—); National Criminal Defense College (Faculty, 1994—); Texas Criminal Defense Lawyers Association (Honorary Member, 1994); The Bar Association of St. Petersburg, Russia (Honorary Member, 1995). Fellow, American Board of Criminal Lawyers. ***PRACTICE AREAS:*** Criminal Trial Practice; Appellate Law. ***Email:*** jstone@jedstone.com

JOHN CURNYN, born Moline, Illinois, May 26, 1970; admitted to bar, 1998, Illinois and U.S. District Court, Northern District of Illinois. *Education:* Augustana College (B.A., 1992); Emporia State University (M.S., 1994); Illinois Institute of Technology/Chicago-Kent College of Law (J.D., 1997). Member, Human Rights Committee, Little City Foundation. *Member:* Chicago and Illinois State Bar Associations; National Association of Criminal Defense Lawyers. ***PRACTICE AREAS:*** Criminal Law; Civil Rights Section 1983; Appellate Law; Criminal Defense. ***Email:*** jpcurnyn@jedstone.com

---

SWANSON, MARTIN & BELL

Established in 1992

415 WASHINGTON STREET
SUITE 1B
WAUKEGAN, ILLINOIS 60085
Telephone: 847-949-0025
847-247-0555

URL: http://www.smbtrials.com

Chicago, Illinois Office: 330 North Wabash, Suite 3300. Telephone: 312-321-9100. Fax: 312-321-0990.

DuPage County, Illinois Office: 2525 Cabot Drive, Lisle, Illinois, 60532. Telephone: 630-799-6900. Fax: 630-799-6901.

Libertyville, Illinois Office: 1860 West Winchester Road, Suite 201. Telephone: 847-949-0025. Fax: 847-247-0555.

Class Action Lawsuits, Commercial Litigation, Construction Litigation/Disputes, Consumer and Warranty Law, Creditor's Rights, Drugs & Medical Devices, Employment Litigation, Environmental Law, Equipment Leasing, General Tort Liability, Healthcare, Insurance Coverage, Intellectual Property, Medical Negligence, Municipal Law, Product Liability, Professional Negligence, Real Estate Development/Zoning, Real Estate Litigation, Toxic and Mass Tort Litigation, and White Collar Criminal Defense.

PARTNERS

STEVEN L. LARSON, born Elgin, Illinois, December 31, 1952; admitted to bar, 1977, Illinois and U.S. District Court, Northern District of Illinois. *Education:* University of Illinois (B.A., 1973); Washington University (J.D., 1977). Associate Notes and Comments Editor, Washington University Law Quarterly, 1976-1977; Author, Comment, "Prohibition of Religious Snakehandling," Washington University Law Quarterly, Volume 1976, Number 2. *Member:* Lake County and Illinois State Bar Associations; Illinois Association of Defense Trial Counsel; American Board of Trial Advocates; Illinois Society of Trial Lawyers. ***PRACTICE AREAS:*** Insurance Industry; Product Liability; Medical Malpractice; Trial Practice; Recreational Products; Commercial Litigation. ***Email:*** slarson@smbtrials.com

DAVID F. PARDYS, born Chicago, Illinois, September 1, 1957; admitted to bar, 1982, Illinois and U.S. District Court, Northern District of Illinois; 1986, U.S. Court of Appeals, Seventh Circuit and U.S. District Court, Eastern District of Wisconsin, U.S. District Court, Southern District of Indiana. *Education:* University of Illinois (B.A., 1979); IIT/Chicago Kent College of Law (J.D., with honors, 1982). *Member:* Lake County Bar Association. ***PRACTICE AREAS:*** Appellate; Health Care; Insurance Industry; Municipal; Product Liability; Trial. ***Email:*** dpardys@smbtrials.com

LINDA E. SPRING, born Bellefonte, Pennsylvania, September 17, 1945; admitted to bar, 1983, Illinois. *Education:* University of Minnesota (B.S., 1967; M.S., 1970); Loyola University (J.D., 1983). Law Clerk to Appellate Court Justice Hon. Glenn K. Seidenfeld, 1983-1984. *Member:* Lake County, Illinois State and American Bar Associations; Association of Women Attorneys of Lake County, Appellate Lawyers Association. ***PRACTICE AREAS:*** Medical Malpractice; Trial Practice; Appellate Practice; Governmental. ***Email:*** lspring@smbtrials.com

JOHN A. TERSELIC, born LaSalle, Illinois, September 29, 1967; admitted to bar, 1992, Illinois. *Education:* Southern Illinois University (B.A., 1989); DePaul University (J.D., 1992). Law Clerk to Senior Judge Kenneth R. Harkins, U.S. Court of Federal Claims, 1992-1993. *Member:* Chicago, Lake County and Illinois State Bar Associations; U.S. Court of Federal Claims Bar Association. ***PRACTICE AREAS:*** Insurance Defense; Medical Malpractice Defense. ***Email:*** jterseli@smbtrials.com

ASSOCIATES

DAVID S. GOLES, born Melrose Park, Illinois, May 7, 1972; admitted to bar, 1998, Illinois. *Education:* American University (B.A., 1994); Northern Illinois University (J.D., cum laude, 1998). Member, Law Review Editorial Board. Author: Smith v. Fair Employment and Housing Commission: Religious Freedom and Anti-Discrimination Laws Square Off in the Landlord/Tenant Setting, Northern Illinois University Law Review Vol. 18, Issue Number 1. *Member:* Lake County and Illinois State Bar Associations; Christian Legal Society. ***PRACTICE AREAS:*** Civil Litigation; Municipal; General Practice. ***Email:*** dgoles@smbtrials.com

MICHONE J. KUHLMAN, born Ames, Iowa, September 26, 1967; admitted to bar, 1996, Illinois; U.S. District Court, Northern District of Illinois and U.S. District Court, Southern District of Indiana. *Education:* Iowa State University (B.S., 1989); Georgia State University, College of Law (J.D., 1996). ***PRACTICE AREAS:*** Insurance Defense; Medical Malpractice Defense; Corporate Law. ***Email:*** mkuhlman@smbtrials.com

JOY I. PADNOS, born Chicago, Illinois, June 15, 1974; admitted to bar, 2000, Illinois, U.S. District Court, Northern District of Illinois. *Education:* Pitzer College (B.A., 1996);

(This Listing Continued)

SWANSON, MARTIN & BELL, Waukegan—Continued

John Marshall Law School (J.D., cum laude, 2000). ***PRACTICE AREAS:*** Civil Litigation; Municipal Law; Insurance Defense; General Practice. ***Email:*** jpadnos@smbtrials.com

WEINSTEIN & DOUGLAS, P.C.

325 WASHINGTON STREET, SUITE 301
WAUKEGAN, ILLINOIS 60085-5572
Telephone: 847-336-4343
Fax: 847-336-4916
Email: contactus@weinsteinanddouglas.com
URL: http://www.lawyers.com/weinsteinanddouglas

Criminal Defense, Family Law, Divorce, Adoptions, Child Custody, Child Support, Domestic Violence, Premarital Agreements, Spousal Support, Paternity, Juvenile Law, Personal Injury, Automobile Accidents, Traffic Violations, Driving While Intoxicated, Drug Crimes, Felonies, Homicide and Sexual Assault.

DAVID S. WEINSTEIN, born Chicago, Illinois, August 29, 1965; admitted to bar, 1991, Illinois and U.S. District Court, Northern District of Illinois including Trial Bar. *Education:* Indiana University (B.A., Political Science, 1988); University of Miami (J.D., 1991). Certified Arbitrator, Nineteenth Judicial Circuit. *Member:* Lake County and Illinois State Bar Associations; Illinois Capital Litigation Trial Bar. ***PRACTICE AREAS:*** Criminal Law; Personal Injury.

DWAYNE DOUGLAS, born Des Plaines, Illinois, 1965; admitted to bar, 1991, Illinois and U.S. District Court, Northern District of Illinois including Trial Bar. *Education:* Northern Illinois University (B.A., Psychology, 1987); Chicago-Kent College of Law (J.D., 1990). Certified Arbitrator, Nineteenth Judicial Circuit. Certified for Appointment as a child representative. *Member:* Lake County and Illinois State Bar Associations. ***PRACTICE AREAS:*** Family Law; Divorce; Child Support; Child Custody.

JOSEPH WROBEL, LTD.

WAUKEGAN, ILLINOIS

(See Chicago)

Bankruptcy including Personal Bankruptcy, Business Bankruptcy, Chapter 7, Chapter 11, Chapter 13, Foreclosures and Garnishments and Business Dissolutions.

LAW OFFICES OF PHILIP P. YANEZ

WAUKEGAN, ILLINOIS

(See Chicago)

Family Law, Criminal Law, Traffic, D.U.I., Residential Real Estate, Consumer Bankruptcy, Personal Injury, Slip and Fall, Auto Accidents, Dog Bites.

JUERGENSMEYER AND ASSOCIATES

WEST DUNDEE, ILLINOIS

(See Elgin)

General, Civil Trial and Appellate Practice. Personal Injury, Governmental, Real Estate, Family, Workers Compensation Law, Municipal, Divorce, Chancery, Commercial, Insurance, Banking, Corporation, Trust and Probate Law.

HART AND HART

WEST FRANKFORT, ILLINOIS

(See Benton)

General Trial and Appellate Practice in State and Federal Courts. Probate, Trust, Real Estate Deeds and Title Insurance, Bankruptcy (Creditors), Traffic, Banking, Business, Commercial and Corporation Law and Creditor Collections, Employment Law.

SAM C. MITCHELL & ASSOCIATES

Established in 1968

115 1/2 EAST MAIN STREET
P.O. BOX 280
WEST FRANKFORT, ILLINOIS 62896
Telephone: 618-932-2772; 937-2662
Telecopier: 618-932-3456
URL: http://www.lawyers.com/samcmitchell

Plaintiff Personal Injury and Workers Compensation cases only.

SAM C. MITCHELL, born Benton, Illinois, October 30, 1939; admitted to bar, 1968, Illinois; 1969, U.S. District Court, Eastern District of Illinois. *Education:* Southern Illinois University (B.S., 1964); Loyola University (J.D., 1967). *Member:* Franklin County (President, 1973), Illinois State and American Bar Associations; Illinois Trial Lawyers Association (Member, Board of Governors, 1974-1980; 1989-1991); American Arbitration Association; The Association of Trial Lawyers of America; American Judicature Society; World Association of Lawyers; International Association of Law Enforcement Instructors; American Society of Law Enforcement Trainers; Illinois Tactical Officers Association. ***PRACTICE AREAS:*** Personal Injury; Wrongful Death; Workers Compensation.

(This Listing Continued)

ASSOCIATES

BRUCE D. IRISH, born Kendallville, Indiana, August 19, 1942; admitted to bar, 1973, Illinois; 1975, U.S. Court of Appeals, Seventh Circuit; 1976, U.S. District Court, Eastern District of Illinois and U.S. Supreme Court. *Education:* University of Chicago; Washington University (B.S.B.A., with honors, 1969; J.D., 1972). Adjunct Professor of Law, St. Louis University School of Law, 1976. Lecturer: Illinois State's Attorney's Association Annual Conferences, 1974-1978; Illinois Judicial Conference, 1979-1989. Instructor, State's Attorney's Legal Training Committee, 1979-1980. Research Director, Illinois Fifth District Appellate Court, 1972-1974; Deputy Director, Illinois Fifth Judicial District, Illinois State's Attorney's Appellate Service Commission, 1974-1978. Associate Judge, Illinois Second Judicial Circuit, 1978-1991. Governor's Task Force on Judicial Merit Selection, 1987. Business Manager, Washington University Law Quarterly. *Member:* Franklin County Bar Association; Illinois Trial Lawyers Association; Illinois Tactical Officers Association. [U.S. Army, 1964-1967]. ***REPORTED CASES:*** People vs. Nicholls, 359 N.E. 2d 1095, 374 N.E. 2d 194; Payne vs. Country Mutual Insurance, 553 N.E. 2d 52; Bank of Illinois vs. Bill's King City Stationery, 555 N.E. 2d 1133; Scot Lad Foods vs. 1st Bank & Trust Co., 546 N.E. 2d 1168; Beck vs. IL Dept. of Revenue, 460 N.E. 2d 24; Skidmore v. Throgmorton, 751 N.E. 2d 637; Hall v. General Casualty, 766 N.E. 2d 680; Szczeblewski v. Gossett, 795 N.E. 2d 368. ***PRACTICE AREAS:*** Personal Injury; Workers Compensation.

WILLIAM A. ALEXANDER, born Bloomington, Illinois, December 28, 1943; admitted to bar, 1973, Illinois; 1974, U.S. District Court, Southern District of Illinois. *Education:* University of Illinois (B.S., 1967; J.D., 1973). Associate Circuit Judge, 1975-1978. *Member:* Franklin County (President, 1979-1980) and Illinois State Bar Associations. ***PRACTICE AREAS:*** Personal Injury; Wrongful Death; Workers Compensation.

LANCE P. BROWN, born Eldorado, Illinois, February 15, 1977; admitted to bar, 2003, Illinois. *Education:* Southern Illinois University (B.S., with honors, Minor in Accounting, 2000; J.D., 2003; M.B.A., 2003). *Member:* Illinois State Bar Association; Illinois Trial Lawyers Association. ***PRACTICE AREAS:*** Personal Injury; Wrongful Death; Workers Compensation.

BRITT W. SOWLE, born Springfield, Illinois, June 22, 1974; (admission pending). *Education:* University of Illinois (B.A., 1997); Southern Illinois University School of Law (J.D., 2004). Member, Southern Illinois University School of Law Alumni Association. *Member:* Illinois State Bar Association; Christian Legal Society. ***PRACTICE AREAS:*** Personal Injury; Wrongful Death; Workers Compensation.

LAW OFFICE OF THERESA V. JOHNSON

Established in 1999

200 EAST CHICAGO AVENUE, SUITE 200
WESTMONT, ILLINOIS 60559
Telephone: 630-321-1330
Fax: 630-321-1185
Email: theresavjohnson@prodigy.net
URL: http://www.theresavjohnson.com

Foreign and Domestic Intellectual Property (IP) including Patents, Trademarks, Trade Secrets, Copyrights, Unfair Competition, Licensing, International IP Arbitration and Mediation, IP Litigation, Madrid Protocol Trademark Filing and Consultation, Patent Cooperation Treaty and Paris Convention Filing, International Law, Immigration, Entertainment Law, Defamation, Title VII Discrimination/Retaliation, Family Medical Leave Act (FMLA), Americans with Disabilities Act (ADA), Personal Injury, Mechanics Liens, Replevin/Recovery of Engagement Ring, Probate, Estates.

FIRM PROFILE: Law Office of Theresa V. Johnson founded by Theresa V. Johnson, a former Intellectual Property Manager for AT&T Corporation, is a one-stop, full service, no-nonsense law office with the emphasis in foreign and domestic intellectual property, international law, immigration, entertainment law and general litigation servicing individuals, businesses, organizations and international clients. Our firm offers well rounded legal advice due to Ms. Johnson's extensive corporate business experience and invaluable international and domestic law education. We provide simple every day English explanations of legal concepts and issues, personal and friendly service, reasonable rates, hourly and flat rate fees (if appropriate), no bureaucracy, no politics, no being shuffled around to lower level attorneys, convenient suburban location, weekend and evening hours by appointment, and free parking. We welcome solo inventors, artists and entrepreneurs.

THERESA V. JOHNSON, born Chicago, Illinois, April 26, 1951; admitted to bar, 1996, Illinois and U.S. District Court, Northern District of Illinois. *Education:* Barat College for English Majors, Oxford, England (B.A., 1972); University of Chicago (M.A.T., 1975); Georgetown University Summer Law Program, Florence, Italy (1991); Duke University Summer Institute in Transnational Law, Brussels, Belgium (1993); Chicago-Kent College of Law, Illinois Institute of Technology (J.D., Certificate in International and Comparative Law, 1994). Certificate in: Domain Name Dispute Resolution, 2004; WIPO Arbitration, 2004, World Intellectual Property Organization (WIPO), Geneva, Switzerland. Listed, WIPO's List of Neutrals, 2004—. *Member:* Chicago, DuPage and Illinois State Bar Associations; American Intellectual Property Law Association. ***PRACTICE AREAS:*** Intellectual Property; Patents; Trademarks; Trade Secrets; Copyrights; Unfair Competition; Intellectual Property Licensing; International Intellectual Property; International Mediation; Intellectual Property Litigation; International Law; Immigration Law; Entertainment Law; Defamation; Title VII Discrimination; Family and Medical Leave Act; Americans with Disabilities Act; Personal Injury; Mechanics Liens; Probate; Estate Planning.

LAW OFFICE OF SHERBY DIANNE SCURTO, P.C.

WESTMONT, ILLINOIS

(See Waukegan)

Discrimination, Sexual Harassment, Wrongful Discharge, Civil Rights, Gay and Lesbian Rights, Criminal Records, Real Estate Closing, Buyer and Seller, Personal Injury.

ANDERSON & ASSOCIATES, P.C.

400 S. COUNTY FARM ROAD, SUITE 120
WHEATON, ILLINOIS 60187
Telephone: 630-653-9400
Fax: 630-653-9450

Chicago Office: 166 W. Washington Street, Suite 640. Telephone: 312-236-5599.
Schaumburg Office: 1701 East Woodfield Road, Suite 1050. Telephone: 847-995-9999. Fax: 847-995-0117.

Family Law, Bankruptcy, Real Estate Litigation and Transactions, Estate Planning and Probate.

JONATHAN G. ANDERSON, born Joliet, Illinois, June 16, 1953; admitted to bar, 1981, Florida, Illinois and U.S. District Court, Northern District of Illinois. *Education:* University of Wisconsin-Madison (B.A., 1975); University of Florida (J.D., 1980). *Member:* Du Puge County Bar Association (Family Law Section); Northwest Suburban Bar Association (Family Law Section). ***PRACTICE AREAS:*** Family Law; Bankruptcy; Real Estate Litigation; Estate Planning; Probate. ***Email:*** andrsnlaw@aol.com

---

ROBIN M. ZANDRI, born New York, N.Y., August 10, 1956; admitted to bar, 1997, Illinois; 2001, U.S. District Court, Northern District of Illinois. *Education:* University of Illinois at Chicago (B.S., 1993); Northern Illinois University (J.D., 1997). *Member:* Northwest Suburban Bar Association. ***PRACTICE AREAS:*** Family Law; Bankruptcy. ***Email:*** andrsnlaw@aol.com

ANDREA C. LAWRENCE, born Oak Lawn, Illinois, February 13, 1972; admitted to bar, 1997, Illinois and U.S. District Court, Northern District of Illinois. *Education:* Northern Illinois University (B.A., 1994); DePaul University (J.D., 1997). *Member:* Du Page County Bar Association. ***PRACTICE AREAS:*** Family Law; Bankruptcy; Real Estate. ***Email:*** andrsnlaw@aol.com

CHRISTOPHER J. MAURER, born Park Ridge, Illinois, August 5, 1972; admitted to bar, 1997, Illinois. *Education:* University of Illinois at Urbana-Champaign (B.S., 1994); Loyola University, Chicago (J.D., 1997). ***PRACTICE AREAS:*** Family Law; Plaintiffs Personal Injury. ***Email:*** andrsnlaw@aol.com

MIA DO, born Seoul, South Korea; admitted to bar, 2004, Illinois. *Education:* University of Illinois (B.A., 1999); University of Chicago (M.M., 2001); Chicago-Kent College of Law (J.D., 2004). *Member:* Christian Legal Society; Asian Pacific American Law Student Association. ***LANGUAGES:*** Korean. ***PRACTICE AREAS:*** Family Law; Immigration. ***Email:*** andrsnlaw@aol.com

---

BAILEY & BAILEY

WHEATON, ILLINOIS

(See Chicago)

Civil Litigation and Appellate Practice, Business Litigation, Breach of Contract, Labor and Employment, Employment Discrimination, Sexual Harassment, Wrongful Termination, Civil Rights, Pension and Profit Sharing, Insurance Law, Personal Injury, Automobile Accidents, Libel, Slander and Defamation, Consumer Law Defense.

BECK, HOULIHAN & SCOTT, P.C.

Established in 2001
534 WEST ROOSEVELT ROAD
WHEATON, ILLINOIS 60187
Telephone: 630-933-9220
Fax: 630-933-0220
Email: lawyers@bhsatlaw.com
URL: http://www.lawyers.com/bhsatlaw

Trial Practice. Domestic Relations, Real Estate, General Practice, Criminal and Commercial Law, Bankruptcy, Estate Planning, Family Law Mediation.

WILLIAM J. SCOTT, JR., born Aurora, Illinois, August 1, 1948; admitted to bar, 1973, Illinois and U.S. District Court, Northern District of Illinois; 1977, U.S. Court of Appeals, Seventh Circuit. *Education:* St. Louis University (A.B., 1970); DePaul University (J.D., 1973). Chief, Grand Jury and Preliminary Hearing Division, 1974-1975 and Felony Trial Attorney, 1975-1977, DuPage County State's Attorneys Office. *Member:* DuPage County (Chairman: Entertainment Committee, 1978-1980; Matrimonial Committee, 1984-1985; Member: Criminal Law Committee, 1978-1985; Matrimonial Committee, 1980—; Member, Board of Directors, 1980-1987; President, 1989-1991) and Illinois State (Assembly Member, 1983-1986) Bar Associations. Fellow, American Academy of Matrimonial Lawyers (President, Illinois Chapter). ***PRACTICE AREAS:*** Divorce; Family; Matrimonial; Domestic Relations. ***Email:*** wscott@bhsatlaw.com

JOSEPH M. BECK, born Chicago, Illinois, February 4, 1959; admitted to bar, 1985, Illinois. *Education:* University of Illinois (B.S., 1981); John Marshall Law School (J.D., 1984). *Member:* DuPage County (Chairman: Law Day Committee, 1986-1987; Family Law and Practice Committee, 1991-1992; Admission and Membership Committee, 1993; Legal Aid Committee, 2000-2001) and Illinois State Bar Associations; Collaborative Law Institute of Illinois. ***PRACTICE AREAS:*** Divorce; Family; Matrimonial; Domestic Relations; Real Estate Law; Family Law Mediator; Collaborative Law. ***Email:*** jbeck@bhsatlaw.com

(This Listing Continued)

JOHN P. HOULIHAN, born Columbus, Ohio, June 11, 1961; admitted to bar, 1986, Illinois; 1987, U.S. District Court, Northern District of Illinois. *Education:* Grinnell College (B.A., 1983); Drake University (J.D., 1986). Member, Drake University Law Review. *Member:* DuPage County (Co-Chairman: Younger Members Committee, 1988-1989; Civil Law Committee, 1987-1988; Criminal Law Committee, 1989—; Vice Chairman, 1990-1991; Chairman, 1991-1992; Chairman, Membership Committee, 2000-2001) and Illinois State Bar Associations. ***PRACTICE AREAS:*** Criminal Law; Real Estate; Bankruptcy; Civil Litigation. ***Email:*** jhoulihan@bhsatlaw.com

PATRICIA A. FOX, born Evergreen Park, Illinois, January 20, 1962; admitted to bar, 1990, Illinois and U.S. District Court, Northern District of Illinois. *Education:* Illinois State University (B.S., 1984); John Marshall Law School (J.D., 1989). *Member:* DuPage County and Illinois State Bar Associations. ***PRACTICE AREAS:*** Divorce; Family; Personal Injury; Collections. ***Email:*** pfox@bhsatlaw.com

---

BOTTI, MARINACCIO & DELONGIS, LTD.

SUITE 402 TICOR TITLE BUILDING
330 NAPERVILLE ROAD
WHEATON, ILLINOIS 60187
Telephone: 630-653-2100
URL: http://www.lawyers.com/bottimaridellaw

Oak Brook, Illinois Office: 720 Enterprise Drive. Telephone: 630-573-8585. Fax: 630-573-8586.

Trial and Appellate Practice in State and Federal Courts, Civil, Criminal, Personal Injury, Family, Zoning, Corporation, Probate Law, Commercial and Government Litigation.

(For complete biographical data on all personnel, see Professional Biographies at Oak Brook)

BRENNER, FORD, MONROE & SCOTT, LTD.

WHEATON, ILLINOIS

(See Chicago)

Insurance Defense, Personal Injury, Medical Malpractice, Construction Law, Product Liability, Uninsured/Underinsured Motorist Arbitrations and Litigation of Contested Coverage Issues.

BRODSKY & ODEH

WHEATON, ILLINOIS

(See Chicago)

Criminal Defense, Commercial Litigation, Immigration Law, Family Law and Real Estate Law.

STEPHEN A. BRUNDAGE

1749 SOUTH NAPERVILLE ROAD, SUITE 105
WHEATON, ILLINOIS 60187
Telephone: 630-260-9647
Fax: 630-462-3767
Email: Sablaw@aol.com
URL: http://www.lawyers.com/brundagelaw

Criminal Law, Driving While Intoxicated, Drug Crimes, Felonies, Homicide, Juvenile Law, Misdemeanors, Parole and Probation, Sexual Assault, Traffic Violations, Assault and Battery, Burglary, Criminal Defense, Drivers License Suspension, Forgery, Manslaughter, Search and Seizure, Sex Crimes, Theft, Juvenile Law, Family Law, Divorce, Child Custody, Child Support, Domestic Violence, Premarital Agreements, Spousal Support, Martial Agreements, Marital Property Distribution, Martial Property Law, Marital Property Settlements, Matrimonial Law, Paternity, Post Divorce Modification, Real Estate, Real Estate Sales, Residential Real Estate, Residential Real Estate Sales, Personal Injury, Automobile Accidents and Injuries, Dog Bites, Sexual Abuse, Slip and Fall and Wrongful Death Law.

STEPHEN A. BRUNDAGE, born Oak Park, Illinois, June 2, 1958; admitted to bar, 1990, Illinois; 1991, U.S. District Court, Northern District of Illinois. *Education:* Triton College (A.S., 1978); Lewis University (B.A., 1987); DePaul University College of Law (J.D., 1990). Recipient, American Jurisprudence Award in Legal Writing II. Author: "Consensual" Searches and Seizures: Does 'Yes' Really Mean 'Yes?' " DuPage County Bar Association Brief, August 1998; "Fighting Words and the 1st Amendment," DuPage County Bar Association Brief, September 1992. Instructor: Criminal Justice, College of DuPage, 1992—; Criminal Law, Arrest, Search, & Seizure, Suburban Law Enforcement Academy, 1992. Police Commissioner, Village of Winfield, 1996-2000. Police Officer, City of Wheaton, 1979-1987. *Member:* DuPage County (Member, Committees on: Criminal Law; Judiciary, Law Day, Professional Responsibility), Illinois State and American Bar Associations; National Association of Criminal Defense Lawyers.

CATHERINE M. BYRNE

WHEATON, ILLINOIS

(See Chicago)

Family Law including Child Custody, Child Support, Divorce, Domestic Violence, Premarital Agreement, Removal, Orders of Protection and Spousal Support.

MICHAEL T. BYRNE

WHEATON, ILLINOIS

(See Clarendon Hills)

Criminal Law, Driving While Intoxicated, Drug Crimes, Felonies, Homicide, Sexual Assault, Traffic Violations and Probation Violations.

CALABRESE ASSOCIATES

A PROFESSIONAL CORPORATION

310 SOUTH COUNTY FARM ROAD, SUITE H

WHEATON, ILLINOIS 60187

Telephone: 630-588-8010

Fax: 630-588-8070

Email: calabreseassoc@aol.com

URL: http://www.lawyers.com/calabreseassociates

Family Law including Divorce Law, Child Custody, Visitation Rights, Support, Adoption Law, Paternity, Prenuptial Agreements and Appeals.

MICHAEL J. CALABRESE, born Chicago, Illinois, May 31, 1969; admitted to bar, 1993, Illinois and U.S. District Court, Northern District of Illinois. *Education:* Dominican University (B.A., cum laude, 1990); DePaul University (J.D., with honors, 1993). Order of the Coif. DePaul University Law Review, 1992-1993. *Member:* DuPage County (Member, Family Law Committee), Illinois State (Member, Family Law Section) and American (Member, Family Law Section) Bar Associations. ***LANGUAGES:*** Spanish. ***PRACTICE AREAS:*** Family Law; Divorce; Child Custody; Child Support.

CALIFF & HARPER, P.C.

Established in 1870

123 WEST FRONT STREET, SUITE 200

WHEATON, ILLINOIS 60187

Telephone: 800-764-4999

Facsimile: 630-871-1347

URL: http://www.califf.com

Moline, Illinois Office: 6th Floor First Midwest Bank Building, 506 Fifteenth Street, P.O. Box 719. Telephone: 309-764-8361. Facsimile: 309-764-8394.

Corporate, Commercial, Civil Litigation in all State and Federal Courts, Labor, Employment, Banking, Governmental, School, Administrative (including N.L.R.B.), Products Liability, Insurance, Taxation, Estate Planning and Probate Law, Real Estate, Land Development and Zoning.

FIRM PROFILE: Califf & Harper, P.C. and its predecessor partnerships have been meeting the legal needs of the Western Illinois and Eastern Iowa bi-state area for over 130 years. The firm offers a wide range of legal services to clients in private sector industries, including construction, development, and manufacturing, and to municipalities and public sector special districts, including districts for schools, entertainment, and transportation. The firm serves clients in state and federal courts in both Illinois and Iowa. In addition, the firm has extensive experience in administrative law proceedings before state and federal agencies involving employee and labor relations matters, and substantial arbitration practice before the American Arbitration Association and the Federal Mediation and Conciliation Service.

REPRESENTATIVE CLIENTS: *CORPORATE:* Deere & Company; Mid-American Energy; Mel Foster Co.; Murphy Bros., Inc.; H.C. Duke & Son, Inc.; Thoms-Proestler Co., Inc.; The Marthens Co.; Terrace Holding Co.; Serv-A-Lite Products, Inc.; Hiland Auto Sales, Inc.; Fort Dearborn Company; Trinity Medical Center; Parr Instrument Company; Packaging Technologies. *REAL ESTATE, CONSTRUCTION AND DEVELOPMENT:* Contracting Corp. of Illinois; Renew Moline, Inc.; L & S Real Estate, Inc.; Axiom Properties, Inc.; Heritage Realty Management, Inc.; Revitalize and Develop East Moline,Inc. *LABOR LAW AND EMPLOYMENT:* Associated Employers of the Quad Cities; RiverStoneGroup, Inc.; Norcross Footwear, Inc.; Krieder Services, Inc.; Rock Island County, Illinois; Scott County, Iowa; Warren County, Illinois; Mercer County, Illinois; City of Moline, Illinois; City of East Moline, Illinois; City of Rock Island, Illinois. *FINANCIAL INSTITUTIONS:* First Midwest Bank, N.A.; I.H. Mississippi Valley Credit Union; Valley Bank, Metrobank. *SCHOOLS:* East Moline Public School District; Rockridge School District; Augustana College (Planned Giving). *PUBLIC LAW:* MidAmerican Energy Company; Metropolitan Airport Authority of Rock Island County; Illinois Quad City Civic Center Authority; Mercer County Public Building Commission. *INSURANCE:* Travelers Insurance Co.; Chubb Group of Insurance Cos.; Sentry Insurance; CNA Insurance Co.; Fireman's Fund Insurance Co.; Continental Western Insurance Group.

(For complete biographical data on all personnel, see Professional Biographies at Moline, Illinois)

CETINA & JACQUES, P.C.

WHEATON, ILLINOIS

(See Oakbrook Terrace)

Personal Injury, Personal Injury Appeals, Personal Injury Arbitration, Personal Injury Defense, Personal Injury Mediation, Plaintiffs Personal Injury, Medical Malpractice, Nursing Home Abuse and Neglect, Driving While Intoxicated, Drug Crimes, Traffic Violations.

CHICAGO INTERNET ATTORNEYS

WHEATON, ILLINOIS

(See Chicago)

Personal Injury, Spinal Cord Injury, Automobile Accidents, Wrongful Death, Products Liability, Medical Malpractice, Corporate, Business, Real Estate, Criminal and Civil Litigation.

WILLIAM G. CLARK, JR. & ASSOCIATES, LTD.

WHEATON, ILLINOIS

(See Chicago)

Family Law, Divorce, Support, Custody, Prenuptial Agreements.

CLAUSEN MILLER P.C.

BUILDING C, SUITE 1700

2100 MANCHESTER ROAD

WHEATON, ILLINOIS 60187-2402

Telephone: 630-668-9100

Fax: 630-668-9169

Email: info@clausen.com

URL: http://www.clausen.com

Chicago, Illinois Office: 10 South LaSalle Street, Suite 1600, 60603-1098. Telephone: 312-855-1010. Fax: 312-606-7777. Internet Email: clientservices@clausen.com.

European Affiliated Law Firm—Clausen Miller Europe: Tetaud-Lambard-Jami & Associés, 83, boulevard Raspail, 75006, Paris, France. Telephone: +33.1.45.48.62.63. Fax: +33.1.45.48.42.57. Studio Legale Corapi, Via Flaminia, 318 00196- Roma. Telephone: 39.06.32.18.563. Fax: 39.06.32.00.992. van Cutsem-Wittamer-Marnef & Partners, Avenue Louise 137/1, B-1050 Brussels, Belgium. Telephone: +32-2-543-02-00. Fax: +32-2-538-13-78.

European Affiliated Law Firm—Clausen Miller, L.L.P.: 148 Leadenhall Street, London, EC3V 4QT England. Telephone: +44.20.7648.8460. Fax: +44.20.7648.8461.

New York, N.Y. Office: One Chase Manhattan Plaza, 10005. Telephone: 212-805-3900. Fax: 212-805-3939.

Newark, New Jersey Office: One Gateway Center, Suite 2600, 07102-5397. Telephone: 973-645-0564. Fax: 973-622-3423.

Irvine, California Office: 2040 Main Street, Suite 500, 92614. Telephone: 949-474-3100. Fax: 949-474-3190.

General Civil Practice. Insurance, Corporations.

FIRM PROFILE: Clausen Miller P.C., a full-service civil litigation and general practice firm with more than 175 proven trial attorneys nationwide, is headquartered in the heart of the business, financial and legal district of downtown Chicago. Clausen Miller's five additional offices span from coast to coast, with affiliate offices in England, France and Italy.

During our 70-year history, we've built a solid reputation as an insurance defense firm, while expanding our practice areas to include everything from admiralty to corporate transactions and litigation to Intellectual Property. This expansion has allowed us to better serve the needs of our diverse client base. To enhance client relationships, our attorneys participate in various community projects and professional activities as well as sponsoring industry conferences.

We at Clausen Miller have always stressed the important role our clients play in the success of the firm. This spirit of partnership is the basis for our creative and hard-working legal style. Because many of our lawyers and paralegals have additional degrees, they are able to understand the industries our clients are working in and provide fast, effective solutions. This strong legal scholarship allows us to provide proven results in or out of the courtroom.

At Clausen Miller, the needs of the client dictate the direction we take.

THOMAS H. RYERSON, born Evanston, Illinois, May 2, 1951; admitted to bar, 1976, Illinois. *Education:* Northwestern University (B.A., 1973); Loyola University, Chicago School of Law (J.D., 1976). Editor, Loyola University Law Journal, 1976. Member, National Moot Court Team, 1975. Chairman, Moot Court Board, 1976. Author: "Illinois Fitness for Trial: Processes, Paradoxes and Proposals," 6 Loyola University Law Journal 678, 1975. President, Glen Ellyn Public Library Board of Trustees, 1989-1991. *Member:* DuPage County (Chairman, Civil Law and Practice Committee, 1987-1989), Kane County, Illinois State and American Bar Associations; Defense Research Institute; Chicago Casualty Adjusters Association (Counsel, 1987—). ***PRACTICE AREAS:*** Insurance; Business Litigation; Commercial Litigation; Construction Litigation; Insurance Coverage; Medical Malpractice; Health Care; Premises Liability; Products Liability; Professional Liability; Casualty Insurance Defense. ***Email:*** tryerson@clausen.com

MICHAEL L. VITTORI, born Oak Park, Illinois, November 17, 1957; admitted to bar, 1986, Illinois. *Education:* University of Illinois (B.A., 1982); John Marshall Law School (J.D., with distinction, 1986). *Member:* Illinois Trial Lawyers Association. ***PRACTICE AREAS:*** Admiralty and Maritime Law; Medical Malpractice; Health Care; Business; Commercial Litigation; Insurance Coverage; Premises Liability; Products Liability; Liability Insurance Coverage; Casualty/Liability Defense. ***Email:*** mvittori@clausen.com

MICHAEL E. ZIDEK, born Oak Park, Illinois, April 11, 1961; admitted to bar, 1987, Illinois. *Education:* John Carroll University (B.S., 1983); Creighton University School of Law (J.D., 1987). Member, Moot Court Board. *Member:* DuPage, Illinois State (Member, Insurance Law Section) and American (Member, Litigation Section) Bar Associations. ***PRACTICE AREAS:*** Admiralty and Maritime; Medical Malpractice; Health Care; Premises Liability; Professional Liability; Casualty Insurance Defense. ***Email:*** mzidek@clausen.com

---

DENIS K. SHEEHAN, born Evergreen Park, Illinois, November 5, 1963; admitted to bar, 1989, Illinois; 1990, U.S. District Court, Northern District of Illinois; 1999, U.S. Court of Appeals, Seventh Circuit; 2000, U.S. Supreme Court. *Education:* Dartmouth College (B.A., 1985); Loyola University, Chicago (J.D., 1989). *Member:* Illinois State Bar Associa-

(This Listing Continued)

tion. **PRACTICE AREAS:** Medical Malpractice; Health Care; Premises Liability; Professional Liability; Municipal Defense; Casualty; Liability Defense. **Email:** dsheehan@clausen.com

REFERENCES: The First National Bank of Chicago; La Salle National Bank.

(For complete biographical data on all personnel, see Professional Biographies at Chicago, Illinois)

CLINGEN CALLOW & McLEAN, LLC

Established in 1995

2100 MANCHESTER ROAD
SUITE 1750
WHEATON, ILLINOIS 60187
Telephone: 630-871-2600
Fax: 630-871-9869
URL: http://www.ccmlawyer.com

Banking, Commercial Litigation, Corporate, Employment Law, Estate Planning, Real Estate, Business Planning.

KENNETH W. CLINGEN, born La Grange, Illinois, August 23, 1960; admitted to bar, 1987, Illinois; 1988, U.S. District Court, Northern District of Illinois. *Education:* University of Notre Dame (B.B.A., 1982; J.D., 1987). Certified Public Accountant, Illinois, 1982. Member, ESOP Association. *Member:* American Bar Association (Member, Sections on: Taxation and Business Law). ***PRACTICE AREAS:*** Corporate; Mergers and Acquisitions; Taxation; Estate and Succession Planning. ***Email:*** clingen@ccmlawyer.com

MARY E. CALLOW, born Chicago, Illinois, August 29, 1945; admitted to bar, 1985, Illinois and U.S. District Court, Northern District of Illinois. *Education:* Dominican University, Formerly Rosary College (B.A., 1967); John Marshall Law School (J.D., 1985). *Member:* DuPage County Bar Association; DuPage County Estate Planning Council. ***PRACTICE AREAS:*** Estate Planning; Probate; General Business. ***Email:*** callow@ccmlawyer.com

TIMOTHY M. McLEAN, born Rochester, New York, March 12, 1961; admitted to bar, 1988, Illinois, U.S. District Court, Northern District of Illinois including Trial Bar; 1991, U.S. Court of Appeals, Seventh Circuit. *Education:* Notre Dame University (B.A., magna cum laude, 1983; J.D., cum laude, 1988). Member, Board of Directors, Notre Dame Law School Association. Trustee, Marmiom Academy, Aurora, Illinois. *Member:* DuPage County Bar Association (Member, Civil Litigation and Business Law Committees). ***PRACTICE AREAS:*** Commercial Litigation; Business Counseling. ***Email:*** mclean@ccmlawyer.com

PAUL M. FULLERTON, born Winchester, Massachusetts, September 4, 1958; admitted to bar, 1990, Illinois and U.S. District Court, Northern District of Illinois, 1999, Trial Bar; 1991, U.S. District Court, Central District of Illinois; 1999, U.S. Court of Appeals, Seventh Circuit. *Education:* Northern Illinois University (B.S., 1981); The John Marshall Law School (J.D., cum laude, 1990). Arbitrator, DuPage County. Commissioner, Wheaton Park District. *Member:* DuPage County and Illinois State Bar Associations. ***PRACTICE AREAS:*** Commercial Litigation; Intellectual Property; General Business Counseling. ***Email:*** fullerton@ccmlawyer.com

ROSS I. MOLHO, born Elkhart, Indiana, August 6, 1968; admitted to bar, 1993, Ohio; 1996, Illinois, U.S. District Court, Northern District of Illinois, including Trial Bar and Northern and Central Districts of Ohio and U.S. Court of Appeals, Sixth and Seventh Circuits. *Education:* Macalester College (B.A., magna cum laude, 1990); Case Western Reserve University (J.D., cum laude, 1993). Phi Beta Kappa. Member, Case Western Law Review, 1991-1992. Arbitrator, Cook and DuPage Counties. Senior Professional in Human Resources (SPHR), 2002. *Member:* Illinois State Bar Association. ***SPECIAL AGENCIES:*** EEOC; NLRB; Illinois Department of Human Rights. ***PRACTICE AREAS:*** Employment Law; Labor Law; Insurance Coverage; Commercial Litigation. ***Email:*** molho@ccmlawyer.com

KENNETH J. VANKO, born Joliet, Illinois, May 22, 1972; admitted to bar, 1997, Illinois. *Education:* The Ohio State University (B.S.B.A., 1994); University of Illinois (J.D., magna cum laude, 1997). Associate Editor, University of Illinois Law Review. ***PRACTICE AREAS:*** Business Law; Commercial Litigation; Employment Law; Unfair Competition Law; Corporate Law. ***Email:*** vanko@ccmlawyer.com

ASSOCIATES

DEANNA M. QUINN-McCOLLIAN, born Chicago, Illinois, July 15, 1968; admitted to bar, 1998, Illinois. *Education:* Concordia University (B.A., 1995); Northern Illinois University (J.D., cum laude, 1997). *Member:* Illinois State Bar Association; DuPage Association of Women Lawyers; Illinois Real Estate Lawyer's Association. ***PRACTICE AREAS:*** Real Estate; Corporate Law. ***Email:*** quinn@ccmlawyer.com

DEVEN S. KANE, born Naperville, Illinois, April 29, 1975; admitted to bar, 2000, Illinois. *Education:* Texas A & M. University (B.B.A., 1997); University of Illinois, Urbana-Champaign (J.D., cum laude, 2000). Recipient: Lechner Fellowship; Harno Scholarship. ***LANGUAGES:*** Hindi and Marathi. ***PRACTICE AREAS:*** Corporate Law; Mergers and Acquisitions; Banking Law; Taxation; Securities. ***Email:*** kane@ccmlawyer.com

OF COUNSEL

DELROSE ANN KOCH, born Maquoketa, Iowa, August 7, 1956; admitted to bar, 1981, Illinois. *Education:* Loras College (B.A., maxima cum laude, 1978); University of Iowa College of Law (J.D., special honors with high distinction, 1981). *Member:* Illinois State Bar Association; DuPage County Estate Planning Council. ***PRACTICE AREAS:*** Estate Planning; Trusts; Probate. ***Email:*** koch@ccmlawyer.com

CONNELLY ROBERTS & McGIVNEY LLC

WHEATON, ILLINOIS

(See Chicago)

Commercial Litigation, Corporate Transactions, Mergers and Acquisitions, Securities, Technology Law, Licensing, Intellectual Property, Commercial Real Estate, Healthcare, Antitrust, Professional Liability, Product Liability, Employment Disputes, Transportation, Rail and Aviation Law, Insurance and Reinsurance Disputes, Construction Defect Litigation, Copyright and Trademark Law, and Employment Litigation.

DOMMERMUTH, BRESTAL, COBINE AND WEST, LTD.

WHEATON, ILLINOIS

(See Naperville)

General Civil Practice. Personal Injury, Worker's Compensation, Corporate, Banking, Municipal, Zoning and Development, Real Estate, Family and Probate Law, Litigation, Federal and State Taxation, Commercial Collection.

JOSEPH P. DOYLE

WHEATON, ILLINOIS

(See Schaumburg)

Bankruptcy.

DRUNKEN DRIVING DEFENSE LAWYERS OF ILLINOIS, LTD.

WHEATON, ILLINOIS

(See Chicago)

Practice Limited to Criminal Defense, Driving While Intoxicated (DWI) and Other Offenses Arising Out of Operation of Motor Vehicles, Drug Crimes, Felonies, Homicide, Misdemeanors, Parole and Probation and Traffic Violations.

ECKHOFF & MASSARELLI, P.C.

330 SOUTH NAPERVILLE ROAD
SUITE 408
WHEATON, ILLINOIS 60187
Telephone: 630-510-0660
Fax: 630-682-4938
URL: http://www.lawyers.com/gelawoffices
Email: lawyers@gelawoffices.com
URL: http://www.gelawoffices.com

Civil Litigation including but not limited to Divorce, Collections, Personal Injury, Domestic Violence, Slip and Fall, Trucking and Automobile Accidents, Real Estate, Shareholders Disputes, Creditors Bankruptcy, Wills, Probate, Check Fraud, Corporate Litigation.

GRANT ECKHOFF, born Chicago Heights, September 14, 1959; admitted to bar, 1985, Illinois. *Education:* Michigan State University (B.S., 1981); Chicago-Kent College of Law, Illinois Institute of Technology (J.D., with honors, 1985). Member, Wheaton City Council, 1989-2002. Commissioner, DuPage County Board, 2002—. *Member:* DuPage County, Kane County and Illinois State Bar Associations. ***PRACTICE AREAS:*** Family Law; Divorce; Collections; Real Estate; Civil Litigation; Wills; Trust Law. ***Email:*** lawyers@gelawoffices.com

CATHERINE M. MASSARELLI, born Chicago, Illinois, April 13, 1963; admitted to bar, 1990, Illinois. *Education:* University of Iowa (B.S., 1985); Chicago-Kent College of Law, Illinois Institute of Technology (J.D., 1990). *Member:* DuPage County and Illinois State Bar Associations. ***PRACTICE AREAS:*** Civil Litigation; Personal Injury; Corporate Litigation; Divorce; Real Estate; Collections; Wills; Probate. ***Email:*** lawyers@gelawoffices.com

THE LAW OFFICE OF RANDALL T. ERICKSON, PC

Established in 2004

425 W. WESLEY STREET, SUITE 1
WHEATON, ILLINOIS 60187
Telephone: 630-665-9404
Fax: 630-665-9414
Email: randallerickson@sbcglobal.net
URL: http://www.lawyers.com/randallericksonlaw

Intellectual Property, Patents, Patent Prosecution, Trade Secrets, Trademarks, Trademark Prosecution, Unfair Competition.

FIRM PROFILE: Randall T. Erickson has recently founded his own solo practice having been a partner at a prominent Chicago intellectual property law firm. He has sixteen years of intellectual property law experience primarily preparing and prosecuting patent and trademark applications, client counseling and preparing patent validity and infringement opinions. Mr. Erickson has patent experience in diverse fields such as utility vehicles and farm equipment, electronic and electrical components, packaging machinery, household appliances, consumer electronics and plastic injection molding machines.

(This Listing Continued)

THE LAW OFFICE OF RANDALL T. ERICKSON, PC, Wheaton—Continued

RANDALL T. ERICKSON, born Elgin, Illinois, July 11, 1957; admitted to bar, 1989, Illinois and U.S. District Court, Northern District of Illinois; U.S. Court of Appeals for the Federal Circuit; registered to practice before U.S. Patent and Trademark Office. *Education:* University of Illinois, Chicago (B.S.M.E., 1980); Loyola University (J.D., 1989). Licensed Professional Engineer, Illinois, 1988. *Member:* DuPage County and Illinois State Bar Associations; Intellectual Property Association of Chicago. ***PRACTICE AREAS:*** Intellectual Property; Patents; Patent Prosecution; Trade Secrets; Trademarks; Trademark Prosecution; Unfair Competition. ***Email:*** randallerickson@sbcglobal.net

FAWELL & FAWELL, LTD.

2100 MANCHESTER ROAD, SUITE 945
WHEATON, ILLINOIS 60187
Telephone: 630-871-2400
Fax: 630-871-2404
Email: tflaw622@aol.com
URL: http://www.fawelllaw.com

Family Law, Divorce Law, Child Custody, Child Support, Domestic Violence, Spousal Support, Premarital Agreements, Mediation and Adoptions.

TERRY FAWELL, born Hammond, Indiana, June 22, 1950; admitted to bar, 1975, Illinois and U.S. District Court, Northern District of Illinois. *Education:* Michigan State University (B.A., cum laude, 1972); DePaul University (J.D., 1975). Omicron Delta Epsilon. Author: "Spousal Health Insurance Rights Act", Du Page County Bar Association Law Journal; "Drafting an Enforceable Antenuptial Agreement", Du Page County Bar Association Brief. Co-Author: Chapter, "Section 2-1401 Proceedings", Illinois Family Law Volume, published by Illinois Institute of Continuing Legal Education, 1994. Public Defender, Du Page County, Illinois, 1975-1980. Chairperson, Du Page County Mandatory Arbitration Program, 1989—. Family Law Moderator, Illinois Institute of Continuing Legal Education, 1984. *Member:* DuPage County (Member, Family Law Committee) and Illinois State Bar Associations. Lawyers Association. ***PRACTICE AREAS:*** Family Law; Personal Injury Law; Civil Litigation.

MICHAEL W. FLEMING
ATTORNEY AT LAW

WHEATON, ILLINOIS

(See Elmhurst)

Criminal Defense Litigation, Felonies, Misdemeanors, DUI and Juvenile Law.

FORAN GLENNON PALANDECH & PONZI PC

WHEATON, ILLINOIS

(See Chicago)

Civil Litigation, Property Insurance, Design Professional Liability, Construction Litigation, Products, Professional and Employment Liability, Bad Faith, Insurance Coverage Defense, Excess and Reinsurance, Subrogation and Liability Coverage.

FUCHS & ROSELLI, LTD.

WHEATON, ILLINOIS

(See Chicago)

General Civil and Trial Appellate Practice. Corporation, Federal, State and Local Tax, Real Estate, Labor, Bankruptcy, Probate, Construction, Employee Benefits, Employment and Administrative Agency Law.

KENT A. GAERTNER, P.C.

400 SOUTH COUNTRY FARM ROAD, SUITE 330
WHEATON, ILLINOIS 60187
Telephone: 630-510-0000
Fax: 630-510-0004
URL: http://www.lawyers.com/gaertnerlaw

Bankruptcy, Business Reorganization, Business Formation and Real Estate Law, Bankruptcy Litigation.

KENT A. GAERTNER, born Blue Island, Illinois, July 15, 1952; admitted to bar, 1977, Florida; 1978, Illinois. *Education:* Carthage College (B.A., 1974); Nova University Law Center (J.D., 1977). Phi Alpha Delta. Author, "A Chapter 11 Fairy Tale," Dupage County Bar Association Brief Magazine. Member: Kiwanis Club, 1979-1982; Jaycees, 1977-1978 and 1988-1990; Y Indian Guides, 1988-1992 (Nation Chief, Lombard, Illinois, 1993); Lombard YMCA Board of Directors, 1992-1993. Coach, Lombard Boys Baseball, 1995. Council Member, Holy Trinity Lutheran Church, 1994. Member, Board of Directors, Chicago Central Suburban Men's Senior Baseball League, 1997-1998. *Member:* DuPage County Bar Association (Board of Directors, 2001—; Committee Chair, New Member Committee, 1986-1987; Committee Chair, Bankruptcy Committee, 1992-1993 and 1999-2000); Illinois State Bar Association; The Florida Bar; American Bankruptcy Institute. *(Also Member, Springer, Brown, Covey, Gaertner and Davis, L.L.C.).* ***PRACTICE AREAS:*** Personal Bankruptcy; Commercial Bankruptcy; Bankruptcy Litigation; Pre-Bankruptcy Workouts; Business Reorganization; Business Formation; Real Estate Contracts; Business Enterprises; Closely Held Business Law; Corporate Law; Franchise Law; Limited Liability Company Law; Partnership Law; Small Business Law; Buying and Selling of Businesses; Business Law; Business Planning; Contracts.

(This Listing Continued)

GAILAN & NAJERA, P.C.

WHEATON, ILLINOIS

(See Addison)

Criminal Defense, Family Law, Divorce, Child Custody, Adoption, Grandparents Rights, Domestic Violence, Visitation Rights, Child Support, Criminal Law, Driving While Intoxicated, Drug Crimes, Juvenile Crimes, Parole and Probation, Traffic Violations, White Collar Crimes.

LAW OFFICES OF
EDWARD P. GRAHAM, LTD.

WHEATON, ILLINOIS

(See Naperville)

Adoptions, Bankruptcy, Business Formation and General Counsel, Collections, Criminal Defense, Divorce, Estate Planning, Wills and Trusts, General Litigation, Juvenile, Landlord - Tenant Relations, Municipal Law, Zoning and Land Use, Personal Injury, Workers Compensation, Probate and Guardianship, Real Estate Transactions, Traffic Prosecution and Defense.

THE LAW FIRM OF
DANYA A. GRUNYK, P.C.

WHEATON, ILLINOIS

(See Naperville)

Divorce, Family Law, Litigation, Collaborative Law, Mediation, Child Custody, Child Support, Adoptions, Guardianship, Paternity.

GUERARD, KALINA & BUTKUS

100 WEST ROOSEVELT ROAD, SUITE A-1
WHEATON, ILLINOIS 60187
Telephone: 630-665-9033
Telecopier: 630-690-9652

Real Estate Construction and Development, Banking and Commercial Finance, Mechanic Liens, Personal Injury, Workers Compensation, Creditor's Rights, Financial Services, Corporate and Commercial Law, Zoning and Land Use, Estate Planning and Probate, General Civil and Trial Practice.

MEMBERS OF FIRM

J. STEVEN BUTKUS, born Cincinnati, Ohio, June 1, 1957; admitted to bar, 1982, Illinois and U.S. District Court, Northern District of Illinois. *Education:* Drake University (B.A., cum laude, 1979); De Paul University (J.D., 1982). ***PRACTICE AREAS:*** Banking; Commercial Law; Real Estate; Corporate; Construction and Development; Zoning and Land Use; Mechanics Liens; Commercial Civil Litigation; General Civil Litigation.

RICHARD M. GUERARD, born Philadelphia, Pennsylvania, July 22, 1947; admitted to bar, 1975, Illinois; 1976, U.S. Court of Appeals, Seventh Circuit and U.S. District Court, Northern District of Illinois including Trial Bar; 1983, U.S. Supreme Court. *Education:* Northern Illinois University (B.S., 1969); John Marshall Law School (J.D., with honors, 1975). ***PRACTICE AREAS:*** Real Estate; Real Estate Development; Construction Law.

MARK F. KALINA, born Chicago, Illinois, August 11, 1954; admitted to bar, 1981, Illinois and U.S. District Court, Northern District of Illinois; 1983, U.S. Court of Appeals, Seventh Circuit and U.S. Tax Court; 1984, U.S. Supreme Court. *Education:* Northern Illinois University (B.S., 1976); DePaul University (J.D., 1981). Certified Public Accountant, Illinois, 1977. Real Estate Broker, Illinois, 1984. Instructor: Department of Finance, Northern Illinois University, DeKalb, Illinois, 1982-1989; Bank Compliance School, Illinois Bankers Association, 1988. *Member:* DuPage County (Member, Tax Law Committee, 1982-1987 and Chairman, 1986-1987; Member, Scholarship Committee, 1988) and Illinois State (Member, Federal Taxation Section Council, 1985) Bar Associations. ***PRACTICE AREAS:*** Banking and Commercial Law; Real Estate; Estate Planning; Franchise Law.

MARY KRASNER, born Chicago, Illinois, February 24, 1952; admitted to bar, 1979, Illinois and U.S. District Court, Northern District of Illinois; 1983, U.S. Court of Appeals, Seventh Circuit. *Education:* St. Mary's College (B.A. summa cum laude, 1974); DePaul University (J.D., 1979). ***PRACTICE AREAS:*** Real Estate Construction and Development; Zoning and Land Use; Banking.

JOHN J. PCOLINSKI, JR., born Norristown, Pennsylvania, August 1, 1960; admitted to bar, 1986, Arizona and U.S. District Court, District of Arizona; 1987, Illinois; 1988, U.S. District Court, Northern District of Illinois. *Education:* North Central College (B.A., magna cum laude, 1983); University of Illinois (J.D., 1986). Adjunct Professor, Business Law, North Central College and North Central College Graduate School of Business, 1987—. Arbitrator, 18th Judicial Circuit, Dupage County Illinois, 1990—; Panel Chairperson, 1992—. Member, Board of Directors, Junior Achievement of DuPage County, 1990-1993. *Member:* Du Page County (Chair: Young Members Committee, 1993-1994; Appellate Law Committee, 1998-1999; Associate Editor, Editor, Editorial Board, DCBA Brief, 1995—) and Illinois State (Vice President, Student Chapter University of Illinois College of Law, 1984-1985, 1985-1986; Member, Committee on Admissions Competence, 1984-1985, 1985-1986, 2002—; Assembly Member, 1988-1994, 1996-2000) Bar Associations; State Bar of Arizona. ***PRACTICE AREAS:*** Commercial and General Civil Litigation; General Practice; Appellate Law.

MARK G. PATRICOSKI, born Wilmington, Delaware, September 6, 1961; admitted to bar, 1989, Illinois and U.S. Tax Court; 1990, District of Columbia and U.S. Court of Appeals, Seventh Circuit. *Education:* Florida Southern College (B.S., 1984); Illinois Bene-

(This Listing Continued)

dictine University (M.B.A., 1986); John Marshall Law School (J.D., 1989). *Member:* DuPage County, Illinois State and American Bar Associations; Illinois Trial Lawyers Association. ***PRACTICE AREAS:*** Personal Injury; Worker's Compensation; Insurance Coverage; Litigation; Accidents; Serious Injuries. ***Email:*** mgpatricoski@ameritech.net

ASSOCIATE

MARK J. CARROLL, born Naperville, Illinois, April 12, 1974; admitted to bar, 2001, Illinois; U.S. District Court, Northern District of Illinois. *Education:* Hillsdale College (B.A., cum laude, 1996); Northern Illinois University (J.D., cum laude, 2001). *Member:* DuPage County, Illinois State and American Bar Associations. ***PRACTICE AREAS:*** Civil Litigation; Insurance Coverage; Real Estate; Real Estate Development; Estate Planning; Zoning Law; Land Use.

REPRESENTATIVE CLIENTS: Amalgamated Bank of Chicago; U.S. Bank, N.A.; Cole Taylor Bank; West Suburban Bank; Harris Banks; Hinsdale Bank & Trust Company; The Private Bank and Trust Company; Mid America Savings Bank; American Chartered Bank; Hinsbrook Bank and Trust; Bank One, N.A.; First United Bank; Dairy Queen of Northeastern Illinois; Lisle Savings Bank; First Midwest Bank; First Oakbrook Bancshares; GMAC Mortgage Corp; Servicemaster Acceptance Company, L.P.; Inland Real Estate Group; Chicago Block & Brick Co.; R.A. Faganel Builders, Inc.; Edward Hines Lumber Co.; Wyndham-Deerpoint Homes.

THE LAW OFFICE OF JAMES W. HANAUER

Established in 2005

600 W. ROOSEVELT ROAD
SUITE B1
WHEATON, ILLINOIS 60187
Telephone: 630-784-1800
Fax: 630-784-1806
Email: jameshanauerlaw@aol.com
URL: http://www.jameshanauerlaw.com

Family Law, Divorce, Child Custody, Child Support, Real Estate and Personal Injury Law.

JAMES W. HANAUER, born Milwaukee, Wisconsin, October 29, 1964; admitted to bar, 1996, Illinois and U.S. District Court, Northern District of Illinois. *Education:* Aurora College (B.A., 1990); John Marshall Law School (J.D., 1993). *Member:* DuPage County, Illinois State and American Bar Associations. ***PRACTICE AREAS:*** Family Law; Divorce; Child Custody; Child Support; Real Estate; Personal Injury.

HANDLER, THAYER & DUGGAN, LLC

WHEATON, ILLINOIS

(See Chicago)

Transactional Practice, Business, Finance, Estate Planning, Tax, Real Estate, Sports and Entertainment.

HARRISON LAW OFFICES, P.C.

WHEATON, ILLINOIS

(See Woodstock)

Concentrating in Employment Law and Civil Rights, Employment Discrimination, Sexual Harassment, Disability, Gender, Race, Religion, Age, Civil Rights, Unemployment Compensation, Employers' Policy Manuals, Privacy Rights, Severance Agreements, Wrongful Discharge and Retaliatory Discharge, Employment Contracts, Restrictive Covenants, Non-competition Agreements, Wage and Hour Claims, Government Law, Pension Claims, Employment Handbooks, Employer/Employee Rights, Labor Unions, State and Federal Appeals, Professional License-holder Defense.

DENNIS W. HOORNSTRA ATTORNEY

100 W. ROOSEVELT ROAD, UNIT B-8
WHEATON, ILLINOIS 60187
Telephone: 630-462-8100
Fax: 630-462-8127
URL: http://www.hoornstralaw.com

Real Estate, Dissolution of Marriage Law.

DENNIS W. HOORNSTRA. PRACTICE AREAS: Real Estate Law; Dissolution of Marriage Law.

HUCK BOUMA PC

Established in 1980

1755 S. NAPERVILLE ROAD, SUITE 200
WHEATON, ILLINOIS 60187-8144
Telephone: 630-221-1755
Fax: 630-221-1756
URL: http://www.wp.com/HuckLaw/
Email: hucklaw@ix.netcom.com
URL: http://www.huckbouma.com

Corporate Law, Business Law, Commercial Real Estate, Estate Planning, Taxation, Land Use, Civil Litigation, Business Litigation, Personal Injury, Estate Settlements, Banking.

(This Listing Continued)

FIRM PROFILE: Huck Bouma PC provides comprehensive legal services to closely held companies, individuals, and fiduciaries and beneficiaries of estates and trusts. With office in DuPage and Kane Counties, Huck Bouma has earned a reputation as the premier law firm in Chicago's western suburbs by consistently providing the highest quality legal representation.

Huck Bouma PC was founded by Ralph R. Bouma, Jr. and John P. Martin in the fall of 1980 when they established their offices in Wheaton, Illinois. In 1988, James M. Huck, Jr. joined the firm as a shareholder. Jim Huck has practiced law in DuPage County since 1963 and has extensive experience in the areas of corporate and business transactions, commercial real estate, and estate planning. The firm continued its rapid growth through the late 1980s and 1990s, during which time George M. Bradshaw joined the firm as a shareholder. George Bradshaw has over thirty years of experience, mostly in DuPage County, and he is the lead counsel in sales of businesses, mergers and acquisitions, family business planning, and bank loan documentation and workouts. In 1999, Robert E. Jones joined the firm as a litigation shareholder. Bob Jones has extensive experience in business litigation and trial work, serious personal injury, contested estate litigation, and alternative dispute resolution.

In 2002, C. William Pollard returned to the practice of law and business consulting by becoming of counsel for Huck Bouma, after 25 years with ServiceMaster, including serving as its chief executive officer and chairman of its board.

JAMES M. HUCK, JR., born Evanston, Illinois, December 5, 1938; admitted to bar, 1963, Illinois. *Education:* University of Illinois (B.S., 1960; LL.B., 1963). Phi Delta Phi. *Member:* DuPage County and Illinois State Bar Associations; American Society of Hospital Attorneys. ***PRACTICE AREAS:*** Corporate Law; Business Law; Commercial Real Estate Law; Estate Planning. ***Email:*** jhuck@huckbouma.com

RALPH R. BOUMA, JR., born 1942; admitted to bar, 1968, Washington; 1969, Illinois. *Education:* Knox College (B.A., 1964); University of Illinois (J.D., 1967); De Palul University (LL.M., Taxation, 1982). ***PRACTICE AREAS:*** Estate Planning (80%); Taxation (20%). ***Email:*** rbouma@huckbouma.com

JOHN P. MARTIN, admitted to bar, 1972, Illinois. *Education:* University of Illinois (B.A., 1969); University of Minnesota (J.D., 1972). ***PRACTICE AREAS:*** Commercial Real Estate Law; Land Use. ***Email:*** jmartin@huckbouma.com

ROBERT E. JONES, born Oakland, California, March 21, 1949; admitted to bar, 1974, Illinois. *Education:* Wheaton College (B.A., with honors, 1971); Vanderbilt University (J.D., 1974). Author: "Failure to Warn in Products Liability," Du Page County Bar News, June/July, 1985. *Member:* Chicago, Du Page County, Illinois State and American Bar Associations; Du Page County Trial Lawyers Association; Illinois Trial Lawyers Association. ***PRACTICE AREAS:*** Civil Litigation; Business Litigation; Personal Injury; Estate Settlements. ***Email:*** rjones@huckbouma.com

GEORGE M. BRADSHAW, admitted to bar, 1972, Illinois. *Education:* Elmhurst College (B.A., 1969); John Marshall Law School (J.D., 1972). ***PRACTICE AREAS:*** Corporate (50%); Banking Law (20%); Commercial Real Estate (30%). ***Email:*** gbradshaw@huckbouma.com

PATRICK B. HURLEY, born Boston, Massachusetts, March 31, 1968; admitted to bar, 1993, Massachusetts; 1999, Illinois. *Education:* Boston College (B.A., 1990; J.D., 1993). ***PRACTICE AREAS:*** Civil Litigation. ***Email:*** phurley@huckbouma.com

KATHLEEN R. RYDING, born Evergreen Park, Illinois, October 16, 1956; admitted to bar, 1981, Illinois; 1986, Pennsylvania. *Education:* University of Illinois (B.S., with high honors, 1978; J.D., with honors, 1981). *Member:* Allegheny County and American Bar Associations. ***PRACTICE AREAS:*** Business Litigation; Estate Litigation; Personal Injury Litigation. ***Email:*** kryding@huckbouma.com

LAWRENCE A. STEIN, born Baltimore, Maryland, March 18, 1965; admitted to bar, 1993, Illinois; 1994, Maryland; 1997, U.S. Supreme Court. *Education:* University of Chicago (A.B., 1988); Northern Illinois University (J.D., 1993). *Member:* DuPage County, Illinois State and American Bar Associations. ***PRACTICE AREAS:*** Trial Practice; Appeals. ***Email:*** lstein@huckbouma.com

WILLIAM J. STRONS, born Westminster, California, December 11, 1967; admitted to bar, 1993, Illinois. *Education:* University of Illinois (B.A., Finance, 1990); DePaul University (J.D., 1993). *Member:* Illinois State and DuPage County Bar Associations. ***PRACTICE AREAS:*** Mergers and Acquisitions; Corporate Law; Joint Ventures; Business Law; Wealth Preservation. ***Email:*** wstrons@huckbouma.com

HUGHES SOCOL PIERS RESNICK & DYM, LTD.

WHEATON, ILLINOIS

(See Chicago)

General Civil and Litigation Practice in all Courts. Insurance and Reinsurance. Personal Injury, Immigration, Civil Rights, Class Actions, Labor and Employment, Commercial, Professional Liability, Litigation.

THE LAW OFFICE OF CYNTHIA HAYES HUTCHINS, P.C.

620 WEST ROOSEVELT ROAD, SUITE C-1
WHEATON, ILLINOIS 60187
Telephone: 630-510-0600
Fax: 630-510-0618
Email: chhutchins@aol.com
URL: http://www.lawyers.com/hutchins

Estate Planning, Trust Law, Wills and Probate, Estate and Gift Taxation, Probate Administration, Probate Litigation, Contested Trusts and Estates, Guardianship, Elder Law.

(This Listing Continued)

THE LAW OFFICE OF CYNTHIA HAYES HUTCHINS, P.C., Wheaton—Continued

CYNTHIA HAYES HUTCHINS, born Detroit, Michigan, February 11, 1958; admitted to bar, 1987, Illinois. *Education:* University of Michigan (B.A., 1980); Northwestern University (J.D., cum laude, 1987). *Member:* Du Page County (Chair, Estate Planning and Probate Committee, 1998-1999), Illinois State and American Bar Associations. ***REPORTED CASES:*** In re Estate of Ann L. Cuneo, Deceased, 334 Ill. App. 3d 594, 780 N.E. 2d. 325, 269 Ill. Dec. 140 (2nd Dist., 2002). ***Email:*** chhutchins@aol.com

IWAN CRAY HUBER HORSTMAN & VANAUSDAL LLC

WHEATON, ILLINOIS

(See Chicago)

Litigation Practice. Product Liability, Insurance Coverage, E-Commerce, Commercial, Professional Liability, Medical Malpractice, Transportation Liability, Premises Liability, Hospital Liability, Toxic Tort, Environmental Litigation and Civil Appeals in State and Federal Courts.

KINZY & ASSOCIATES, P.C.

WHEATON, ILLINOIS

(See Chicago)

Immigration, Deportation, Real Estate, Business Law, Asset Protection, Estate Planning.

WILLIAM F. KNEE, LTD.

WHEATON, ILLINOIS

(See Oak Brook)

LAW OFFICES OF KOMIE AND ASSOCIATES

WHEATON, ILLINOIS

(See Chicago)

Civil and Criminal Litigation. Federal, State, International, Trial and Appellate Practice. Complex Litigation, Criminal Defense, Divorce, Family Law, Probate, Taxation, Immigration Law, International Criminal Law, Real Estate Law.

LARAIA & HUBBARD, P.C.

1761 S. NAPERVILLE ROAD
SUITE 203
WHEATON, ILLINOIS 60187
Telephone: 630-690-6800
Fax: 630-690-0196
Email: laraiahubbardpc@ameritech.net
URL: http://www.lawyers.com/laraia&hubbardpc

Criminal Law, General Civil and Chancery Litigation, Personal Injury, Divorce and General Trial Practice.

JOSEPH M. LARAIA, born Melrose Park, Illinois, May 4, 1937; admitted to bar, 1962, Illinois; 1963, U.S. District Court, Northern District of Illinois. *Education:* DePauw University; Northwestern University (B.A., 1959; J.D., 1962). Phi Alpha Delta. Assistant State's Attorney, Du Page County, 1966-1973. *Member:* Du Page County (President, 1980; Chairman, Criminal Law Committee, 1978; Man of the Year Award in 1981) and Illinois State Bar Associations; Illinois Trial Lawyers Association; National Criminal Defense Association; Du Page County Criminal Law Association (President, 1982); Illinois Auto Dealer's Association; American College of Trial Lawyers. [With USAF National Guard Reserve, 1962-1967]. ***PRACTICE AREAS:*** Business Law; Civil Litigation; Criminal; DWI; Felonies; Juvenile Criminal Law; Misdemeanors; Personal Injury; Auto Accidents; Slip and Fall; Wrongful Death; Divorce; Domestic Violence; Child Custody; Premarital Agreements; General Trial Practice. ***Email:*** laraiahubbardpc@hotmail.com

KENNETH D. HUBBARD, born Oak Park, Illinois, September 1, 1954; admitted to bar, 1986, Illinois and U.S. District Court, Northern District of Illinois. *Education:* Southern Illinois University (B.S., 1977); DePaul University (M.A., with distinction, 1982); John Marshall Law School (J.D., with distinction, 1986). *Member:* Du Page County (Member, Matrimonial Committee) and Illinois State Bar Associations; DuPage County Criminal Defense Lawyer's Association; Illinois Trial Lawyer's Association. ***PRACTICE AREAS:*** Criminal; DWI; Felonies; Misdemeanors; Juvenile Law; Personal Injury; Auto Accidents; Slip and Fall; Wrongful Death; Matrimonial Law; Divorce; Domestic Violence; Child Custody; Premarital Agreements; Order of Protection; General Trial Practice. ***Email:*** laraiahubbardpc@hotmail.com

---

JAMES J. LARAIA, born La Grange, Illinois, November 14, 1974; admitted to bar, 2001, Illinois. *Education:* Illinois Benedictine College (B.A., 1997); Northern Illinois University (J.D., 2001). Participant, Mock Trial Team, Northern Illinois University. Vice President, Justinian Society, 2000-2001. Assistant States Attorney, DuPage County, Illinois, 2002. *Member:* DuPage County and Illinois State Bar Associations. ***PRACTICE AREAS:*** Fraud; Lemon Law; Misdemeanors; Traffic Violations; Personal Injury; Divorce; Family Law; Trial Practice; Business Law; Civil Litigation. ***Email:*** laraiahubbardpc@hotmail.com

(This Listing Continued)

DENNIS A. HARRISON, born Baraboo, Wisconsin, September 25, 1950; admitted to bar, 1986, Illinois and U.S. District Court, Northern District of Illinois. *Education:* DePaul University (B.A., 1972); John Marshall Law School (J.D., with distinction, 1986). Formerly with Harrison & Byrne. Assistant States Attorney, Du Page County, Illinois, 1999-2002. *Member:* Du Page County, Illinois State and National Bar Associations; Criminal Defense Association. ***PRACTICE AREAS:*** Criminal Law; Family Law; Driving While Intoxicated; Felonies; Juvenile Criminal Law; Misdemeanors; Divorce; Personal Injury; Trial Practice. ***Email:*** laraiahubbardpc@hotmail.com

STEVEN B. LEVY, LTD.

WHEATON, ILLINOIS

(See Naperville)

Plaintiff's Personal Injury, Wrongful Death, Medical Malpractice, Automobile Accidents, Truck Accidents, Products Liability and Premises Liability Law.

THE LINCOLN LAW GROUP

CARLTON SENTRE
300 SOUTH CARLTON AVENUE
SUITE 130
WHEATON, ILLINOIS 60187
Telephone: 630-933-8400
Fax: 630-933-8432
Email: migloreatlaw@yahoo.com
URL: http://www.lawyers.com/lincolnlawgroup

Criminal Law, Felonies, Traffic Violations, Appeals, Driving While Intoxicated, Divorce, Family, Child Custody, Litigation, Commercial Litigation, Real Estate, Insurance Defense, Insurance Coverage and Estate Planning Law.

FIRM PROFILE: The firm practices throughout Cook, DuPage, Kane and DeKalb Counties. The firm carries the highest legal ability rating given by Martindale-Hubbell.

SALVATORE C. MIGLORE, born Chicago, Illinois, February 13, 1953; admitted to bar, 1981, Illinois, U.S. District Court, Northern District of Illinois, U.S. Court of Appeals, Seventh Circuit, Trial Bar and U.S. Supreme Court. *Education:* Lewis University (B.A., 1975; M.S., 1977); DePaul University (J.D., 1981). Member, Cook County Mandatory Arbitration Program. *Member:* Chicago, DuPage County, Illinois State and American Bar Associations; The Association of Trial Lawyers of America; National Association of Criminal Defense Lawyers; Dupage County Criminal Defense Lawyers Association. (Also Of Counsel, Karchmar and Stone, Chicago, Illinois). ***PRACTICE AREAS:*** Criminal Law; DUI; Divorce; Custody; Litigation; Commercial Litigation; Real Estate; Insurance/Coverage Defense; Estate Planning.

Languages: English, Spanish, Polish and Italian.

MARAMBA & ASSOCIATES, LLC

WHEATON, ILLINOIS

(See Arlington Heights)

Business Law, Chancery Practice, Corporate Litigation, Civil Litigation, Complex Litigation, Defense Litigation, Federal Litigation, Administrative Litigation, Business Enterprises, Business Litigation, Closely Held Business Law, Real Estate Litigation, Veterans Rights, Military Law, Wills, Commercial Collections, Post Judgment Collections, Closely Held Corporations.

MIRABELLA & KINCAID, P.C.

Established in 1956
1776 SOUTH NAPERVILLE ROAD,
P.O. BOX 1029
WHEATON, ILLINOIS 60187
Telephone: 630-665-7300
Fax: 630-665-7609
Email: mkpclaw@aol.com
URL: http://www.mirabellakincaid.com

Trial Practice. Domestic Relations, Appellate Practice, Personal Injury, Real Estate, General Practice, Commercial Law, Mediation.

JOSEPH F. MIRABELLA, JR., born Oak Park, Illinois, May 22, 1935; admitted to bar, 1964, Illinois and Illinois Supreme Court; 1974, U.S. Supreme Court. *Education:* University of Illinois (A.B., 1958); Chicago-Kent College of Law (LL.B., 1964). *Member:* DuPage County (President, 1984-1985) and Illinois State (Member, Family Law Council, 1989-1991) Bar Associations. ***PRACTICE AREAS:*** Divorce; Family; Matrimonial; Domestic Relations. ***Email:*** mkpclaw@aol.com

JOHN B. KINCAID, born Chicago, Illinois, August 25, 1938; admitted to bar, 1963, Illinois; 1973, U.S. Supreme Court. *Education:* Northern Illinois University (B.S., 1961); Chicago-Kent College of Law (J.D., 1963). Board Member, 1986-2000 and President, 1996-1998, Illinois Bar Foundation. Panel Member, Inquiry Division, Illinois Attorneys Registration and Disciplinary Commission, 1986-1990. *Member:* DuPage County (President, 1991-1992; General Counsel, 1986-1989; Chairman, Professional Responsibility Committee, 1980-1985) and Illinois State (Member, Illinois Tort Council, 1984-1986; Civil Practice Committee, 1999—; Judicial Evaluation Committee, 1999—) Bar Associations; Illinois Trial Lawyers Association; The Association of Trial Lawyers of America. ***PRACTICE AREAS:*** Trial Law; Commercial Litigation; Probate Litigation; Personal Injury Appeals; Mediation. ***Email:*** mkpclaw@aol.com

(This Listing Continued)

GEORGE S. FREDERICK, born Evanston, Illinois, February 15, 1965; admitted to bar, 1998, Illinois. *Education:* Arizona State University (B.S., Accounting, 1993); Northern Illinois University (J.D., summa cum laude, 1998). *Member:* DuPage County and Illinois State Bar Associations. ***PRACTICE AREAS:*** Divorce; Family; Employment Law; Civil Litigation. ***Email:*** cre8law@aol.com

LYNN M. MIRABELLA, born Oak Park, Illinois, February 11, 1962; admitted to bar, 1987, Illinois; 1995, U.S. District Court, Northern District of Illinois. *Education:* University of Illinois (L.A.S., 1984); Illinois Institute of Technnology,Chicago-Kent College of Law (J.D., 1987). Chairman, World and National Events Committee, 1987-1989 and Member, 1987-1990, Kane County Bar Association. *Member:* Du Page County (Vice-Chair, Law Day Committee, 1996-1997) and Illinois State Bar Associations. ***PRACTICE AREAS:*** Real Estate; Family Law. ***Email:*** lynnmira211@aol.com

List of Clients furnished upon request.

MOMKUS McCLUSKEY MOLTZEN MONROE MARSH & SPYRATOS, LLC

WHEATON, ILLINOIS

(See Downers Grove)

General Civil Practice, Corporate Practice with particular expertise in Corporate and Transactional Law, Civil Litigation, Commercial Litigation, Product Liability Defense, Insurance Defense and Coverage, Personal Injury and Property Damage, Appeals, Mediation, Arbitration, Commercial and Residential Real Estate, Tax-Based Transactions, Employment Law, Environmental Law, Construction, Collections, Financing, Estate Planning, Catastrophic Injuries, Intellectual Property and Covenants Not to Compete, Premises Liability, Injunctive Remedies, and Real Property Owner Disputes.

THE LAW FIRM OF WENDY R. MORGAN

WHEATON, ILLINOIS

(See Arlington Heights)

Family Law, Divorce, Child Custody, Interstate Custody, Adoptions, Child Support, Paternity, Premarital Agreements, Domestic Violence, Visitation Rights, Adoption Law, Domestic Violence, Visitation Rights.

MOSS AND BLOOMBERG, LTD.

WHEATON, ILLINOIS

(See Tressler, Soderstrom, Maloney & Priess)

MULHERIN, REHFELDT & VARCHETTO, P.C.

211 SOUTH WHEATON AVENUE
WHEATON, ILLINOIS 60187
Telephone: 630-653-9300
Fax: 630-653-9316; 630-653-0776
Email: mrv@mrvlaw.com
URL: http://www.mrvlaw.com

Commercial and Business Transactions, Health Care, Estate Planning, Litigation, Business, Tax, Employment, Insurance Defense, Medical Malpractice Defense and Employment Litigation.

JOHN M. MULHERIN, born Evergreen Park, Illinois, June 12, 1942; admitted to bar, 1967, Illinois and U.S. District Court, Northern District of Illinois; 1981, U.S. Tax Court. *Education:* University of Illinois (A.B., 1964); Northwestern University (J.D., 1967). Adjunct Assistant Professor, Lewis University School of Law, 1975-1978. *Member:* DuPage County (Editor, Bar Brief, 1988-1995) and Illinois State Bar Associations. ***PRACTICE AREAS:*** Health Care Law; Business Organization; Real Estate. ***Email:*** jmulherin@mrvlaw.com

LOUIS A. VARCHETTO, born Chicago, Illinois, December 11, 1954; admitted to bar, 1979, Illinois and U.S. District Court, Northern District of Illinois; 1983, U.S. District Court, Northern District of Illinois, Trial Bar; 1986, U.S. Court of Appeals, Seventh Circuit and U.S. Supreme Court; 2002, Missouri. *Education:* University of Illinois (B.A., 1976); John Marshall Law School (J.D., with distinction, 1979). *Member:* DuPage County (Chairman, Law Day Committee, 1982-1983; Young Lawyers Committee, 1983-1984; Co-Chairman, Civil Practice Committee, 1984-1986; Director, 1986-1989), Illinois State and American Bar Associations. ***PRACTICE AREAS:*** Medical Malpractice Defense; Insurance Coverage; Insurance Defense. ***Email:*** lvarchetto@mrvlaw.com

STEPHEN A. REHFELDT, admitted to bar, 1974, Illinois, U.S. Supreme Court and U.S. Court of Appeals, Seventh Circuit. *Education:* Purdue University (B.S.); University of Illinois (J.D.). *Member:* DuPage County and Illinois State Bar Association; Illinois Appellate Lawyers Association; U.S. Supreme Court Historical Society. ***PRACTICE AREAS:*** Real Estate; Tax; Corporate; Probate; Appellate Practice; Estate Planning. ***Email:*** srehfeldt@mrvlaw.com

JOSEPH G. SKRYD, born Hinsdale, Illinois, January 19, 1963; admitted to bar, 1988, Illinois; 1989, U.S. District Court, Northern District of Illinois. *Education:* Purdue University (B.S., 1985); John Marshall Law School (J.D., 1988). *Member:* Chicago, DuPage County, Illinois State and American Bar Associations; Defense Research Institute. ***PRACTICE AREAS:*** Insurance Defense; Professional Liability Defense; Construction Insurance Defense; Transportation Liability. ***Email:*** jskryd@mrvlaw.com

RAY H. RITTENHOUSE, born 1953; admitted to bar, 1981, Illinois and U.S. District Court, Northern District of Illinois. *Education:* DePaul University (B.A., 1976; J.D., 1981).

(This Listing Continued)

Member: Chicago and Illinois State Bar Associations; Illinois Defense Trial Counsel; Defense Research Institute. ***PRACTICE AREAS:*** Insurance Defense; Insurance Law; Chancery Practice; Professional Liability Law; Employment Law. ***Email:*** rhritt@mrvlaw.com

JAMES P. MORAN, born Alamogordo, New Mexico, September 22, 1957; admitted to bar, 1982, Illinois and U.S. District Court, Northern District of Illinois. *Education:* University of Notre Dame (B.B.A., 1979); IIT/Chicago-Kent College of Law (J.D., with high honors, 1982). Co-Author: "Illinois Construction Lien and Bond Law," Fifty State Construction Lien and Bond Law, Wiley Law Publications; "Complying with The Illinois Mechanics' Lien By Furnishing Lienable Materials Or Services," 1992; "Common Pitfalls On Requests For Changes And Extras," 1991. Author: "Technical Defenses To A Mechanics' Lien Claim," 1993; "New Construction Contracts From the Purchaser's Perspective," 1993. Guest Speaker for the American Bar Association and the Chicago Bar Association on issues involving mechanics' liens and real estate transactions, and for industry trade associations. *Member:* Chicago (Vice-Chairman, Subcommittee on Mechanics' Liens) and American Bar Associations. ***PRACTICE AREAS:*** Civil Litigation; Insurance Defense. ***Email:*** jmoran@mrvlaw.com

WILLIAM J. ULRICH, JR., born Elmhurst, Illinois, April 6, 1949; admitted to bar, 1980, Illinois, U.S. District Court, Northern District of Illinois and U.S. Court of Appeals, Seventh Circuit; 1986, U.S. Supreme Court. *Education:* Robert Morris College (A.B.A., 1969); Northern Illinois University (B.S., 1971); DePaul University (J.D., 1979). Instructor, Business Law, North Central College, 1988. Criminal Justice Instructor, College of DuPage, 1989. Executive Board Member, DuPage Area Council of Boy Scouts of America, 1988—. Arbitration Judge, DuPage County, 1989—. *Member:* DuPage County and Illinois State Bar Associations; Illinois Trial Lawyers Association; The Arab American Bar Association. ***PRACTICE AREAS:*** Commercial Real Estate; Commercial Transactions; Corporate Law; Civil Litigation. ***Email:*** wulrich@mrvlaw.com

PATRICIA L. ARGENTATI, born Milwaukee, Wisconsin, July 4, 1953; admitted to bar, 1982, Illinois; U.S. District Court, Northern District of Illinois; U.S. Court of Appeals, Seventh Circuit. *Education:* Marquette University (B.A., 1975); Chicago-Kent College of Law (J.D., 1982). *Member:* DuPage County, Illinois State and American Bar Associations; Illinois Trial Lawyers Association; Du Page Association of Women Lawyers; Illinois Association of Defense Trial Counsel. ***PRACTICE AREAS:*** Trial Practice; Malpractice; Civil Rights; Employment Law; Municipal Litigation. ***Email:*** pargentati@mrvlaw.com

THOMAS B. CAHILL, born Chicago, Illinois, March 12, 1957; admitted to bar, 1983, Illinois and U.S. District Court, Northern District of Illinois; 1986, U.S. Supreme Court. *Education:* Illinois Benedictine College (B.A., 1979); Northern Illinois University, College of Law, DeKalb (J.D. cum laude, 1983). Adjunct Professor of Law, Chicago-Kent College of Law, 1987—. Prior Employment: Lundgren & Associates, Mt. Prospect, IL, 1983-1984; Guerard & Drenk, Wheaton, IL, 1984-1987; Sears, Roebuck and Co., Hoffman Estates, IL; Kritzer & Levick, Schaumburg, IL. Member: International Council of Shopping Centers. *Member:* Illinois State and American (Member, Remedies and Miscellaneous Clauses Committee) Bar Associations. ***PRACTICE AREAS:*** Commercial Real Estate; Commercial Transactions. ***Email:*** tcahill@mrvlaw.com

---

ANDREW R. POYTON, born Berkeley, California, September 2, 1970; admitted to bar, 1996, Illinois and U.S. District Court, Northern District of Illinois. *Education:* University of Colorado at Boulder (B.A., Economics, 1992); DePaul University (J.D., 1996). *Member:* DuPage County, Illinois State and American Bar Associations. ***PRACTICE AREAS:*** Commercial Litigation; Corporate Law; Business Organization; Real Property; Probate. ***Email:*** apoyton@mrvlaw.com

MARCELLINE DEFALCO, born 1970; admitted to bar, 1997, Illinois. *Education:* Northeastern Illinois University (B.A.); John Marshall Law School (J.D.). Order of John Marshall. Dean's List. Recipient: West Publishing Juris Secundum Award for Excellence in Torts; DuPage County Justinian Society of Lawyers Scholarship. *Member:* DuPage County, Illinois State and American Bar Associations; DuPage Association of Women Lawyers. ***PRACTICE AREAS:*** Civil Litigation; Medical Malpractice; Insurance Defense; Subrogation. ***Email:*** mdefalco@mrvlaw.com

WILLIAM J. HOFFMANN, born Chicago, Illinois, March 20, 1967; admitted to bar, 1993, Illinois. *Education:* Lake Forest College (B.A., 1989); John Marshall Law School (J.D., 1993). *Member:* DuPage County Bar Association (Member, Ethics Committee, 1994-1995); Illinois Trial Lawyers Association; National Association of Subrogation Professionals. ***PRACTICE AREAS:*** Insurance Defense Litigation; Insurance Coverage; Subrogation. ***Email:*** whoffmann@mrvlaw.com

KATHLEEN A. REID, born Oak Park, Illinois, April 14, 1973; admitted to bar, 1998, Illinois and U.S. District Court, Northern and Central Districts of Illinois. *Education:* University of Illinois, Champaign-Urbana (B.A., 1995); John Marshall Law School (J.D., 1998). *Member:* DuPage County, Illinois State and American Bar Associations. ***PRACTICE AREAS:*** Civil Litigation; Insurance Defense; Medical Malpractice Defense; Subrogation. ***Email:*** kreid@mrvlaw.com

CHRISTINE C. PERAKIS, born Evanston, Illinois, June 28, 1974; admitted to bar, 2000, Illinois and U.S. District Court, Northern District of Illinois. *Education:* Northern Illinois University (B.S., 1996); John Marshall Law School (J.D., 2000). *Member:* Chicago, Hellenic, DuPage, Illinois State and American Bar Associations. ***PRACTICE AREAS:*** Civil Litigation; Insurance Defense; Subrogation. ***Email:*** cperakis@mrvlaw.com

WILLIAM R. BRODZINSKI, born Elkhart, Indiana, August 17, 1973; admitted to bar, 1999, Illinois and U.S. District Court, Northern District of Illinois. *Education:* Purdue University (B.S., Management, 1995); Chicago-Kent College of Law, Illinois Institute of Technology (J.D., with honors, 1999). Vice-President, Chicago-Kent Moot Court Honor Society, 1998-1999. *Member:* DuPage County, Chicago and Illinois State Bar Associations. ***PRACTICE AREAS:*** Commercial Litigation; Corporate Law; Real Estate; Probate. ***Email:*** wbrodzinski@mrvlaw.com

NADLER, PRITIKIN & MIRABELLI, L.L.C.

WHEATON, ILLINOIS

(See Chicago)

Family Law and Domestic Relations Law including Dissolution of Marriage, Division and Valuation of Marital and Non-Marital Property, Maintenance and Support, Custody and Visitation, Domestic Violence, Establishment of Paternity, Prenuptial and Postnuptial Agreements and, When Necessary, Litigation of Cases and the Prosecution and Defense of Appeals. Mediation and Arbitration.

CAROL A. NOLAN

620 WEST ROOSEVELT ROAD
SUITE C-1
WHEATON, ILLINOIS 60187
Telephone: 630-668-6600
Fax: 630-510-0618
Email: canolanlaw@aol.com
URL: http://www.lawyers.com/canolan

Elder Law, Medicaid Planning, Estate Planning, Special Needs Trusts, Probate, Wills, Trust Law, Living Trusts, Guardianship, Contested Trusts and Estates, Powers of Attorney.

CAROL A. NOLAN, born New York City, N.Y., August 3, 1951; admitted to bar, 1996, Illinois and U.S. District Court, Northern District of Illinois. *Education:* Northern Illinois University (B.A., magna cum laude, 1992; J.D., 1995). *Member:* DuPage County (Member, Probate Committee) and Illinois State Bar Associations; National Academy of Elder Law Attorneys; Dupage Association of Women Lawyers; Association of Senior Service Providers.

NORTON, MANCINI, WEILER & DeANO

109 NORTH HALE STREET
P.O. BOX 846
WHEATON, ILLINOIS 60189-0846
Telephone: 630-668-9440
Fax: 630-668-9489
Email: firm@nortonmancini.com

Chicago, Illinois Office: 111 West Washington Street, Suite 835. Telephone: 312-807-4999. Fax: 312-807-4998.

Trial Practice. Personal Injury, Malpractice, Products Liability, Environmental Law, Corporate Litigation, Commercial Litigation, Municipal Litigation, Insurance and Probate Law, Medical Malpractice.

JOHN E. NORTON, born Rockford, Illinois, August 14, 1949; admitted to bar, 1975, Illinois. *Education:* University of Notre Dame (A.B., 1971); DePaul University (J.D., 1975). *Member:* Chicago, DuPage County (Member, Board of Directors, 1987-1989), Illinois State and American Bar Associations; The Society of Trial Lawyers; The American Board of Trial Advocates; Illinois Association of Defense Trial Counsel. ***PRACTICE AREAS:*** Trial Practice; Corporate Litigation; Malpractice; Products Liability; Environmental Litigation; Medical Malpractice. ***Email:*** jnorton@nortonmancini.com

LORENZO A. MANCINI, born Mola Di Bari, Italy, July 15, 1946; admitted to bar, 1977, Illinois. *Education:* St. Mary's College (B.A., 1968); DePaul University (J.D., summa cum laude, 1977). *Member:* Chicago, Du Page County, Illinois State and American Bar Associations; Illinois Association of Defense Trial Counsel. ***PRACTICE AREAS:*** Trial Practice; Insurance Law; Malpractice; Products Liability; Environmental Litigation; Medical Malpractice; Automobile Liability. ***Email:*** lmancini@nortonmancini.com

THOMAS R. WEILER, born Chicago, Illinois, November 11, 1958; admitted to bar, 1983, Illinois. *Education:* University of Notre Dame (B.B.A., 1980); Loyola University of Chicago (J.D., 1983). *Member:* Chicago, Du Page County, Illinois State and American Bar Associations; Illinois Trial Lawyers Association; The Association of Trial Lawyers of America. ***PRACTICE AREAS:*** Trial Practice; Civil Rights; Employment Litigation; Commercial Litigation; Insurance Defense. ***Email:*** tweiler@nortonmancini.com

JAMES L. DeANO, born Chicago, Illinois, October 28, 1956; admitted to bar, 1981, Illinois. *Education:* Western Illinois University (B.A., 1978); John Marshall Law School (J.D., with honors, 1981). Order of John Marshall. Member, John Marshall Law Review, 1980-1981. *Member:* Illinois State and American Bar Associations. ***PRACTICE AREAS:*** Trial Practice; Municipal Law; Products Liability. ***Email:*** jdeano@nortonmancini.com

THOMAS J. LONG, born Bangor, Maine, October 4, 1958; admitted to bar, 1983, Illinois. *Education:* University of Notre Dame (B.A., 1980); Loyola University (J.D., 1983). *Member:* Du Page County and Illinois State Bar Associations. ***PRACTICE AREAS:*** Trial Practice; Insurance; Legal Malpractice; Personal Injury. ***Email:*** tlong@nortonmancini.com

W. ANTHONY ANDREWS, born Folkston, Georgia, December 9, 1966; admitted to bar, 1993, Illinois; 1995, U.S. District Court, Northern District of Illinois. *Education:* Lewis University (B.A., 1990); DePaul University (J.D., 1993). *Member:* Dupage and Chicago Bar Associations. ***PRACTICE AREAS:*** Insurance Defense; Insurance Coverage; Municipal; Civil Rights Defense; Automobile Liability. ***Email:*** wandrews@nortonmancini.com

---

KENNETH C. YUEN, born 1970; admitted to bar, 1995, Illinois. *Education:* University of Chicago (B.A., 1992; M.A., 1992); Chicago-Kent College of Law, Illinois Institute of Technology (J.D., 1995). Certified Arbitrator, Personal Injury. Arbitrator, Cook County Mandatory Arbitration System. ***PRACTICE AREAS:*** Insurance Defense; Personal Injury; Products Liability. ***Email:*** kyuen@nortonmancini.com

(This Listing Continued)

KARA N. LUNDY, born Stillwater, Minnesota, August 1, 1977; admitted to bar, 2002, Illinois. *Education:* St. Mary's College of Maryland (B.A., 1999); University of Minnesota (J.D., 2002). Member, Order of the Coif. Member, Minnesota Law Review, 2000-2002. Author: "Juror Questioning of Witnesses: Questioning the United States Justice System Criminal Justice System," 85 Minn. L.R. 2001. ***Email:*** klundy@nortonmancini.com

MARY T. YONG, born Chicago, Illinois, April 2, 1976; admitted to bar, 2001, Illinois. *Education:* North Central College (B.A., 1998); John Marshall law School (J.D., 2001). Recipient, John Marshall Law School Dean's Scholarship, Fall Semester, 1998. ***PRACTICE AREAS:*** Insurance Defense; Civil Litigation. ***Email:*** myong@nortonmancini.com

SCOTT L. GINSBURG, born Louisville, Kentucky, June 16, 1979; admitted to bar, 2004, Illinois. *Education:* DePauw University (B.A., 2001); Washington University (J.D., 2004). Member: Washington University Journal of Law and Policy; Moot Court. *Member:* Illinois State and American Bar Associations. ***PRACTICE AREAS:*** Insurance Defense; Municipal Law; Trial Practice; Employment Law. ***Email:*** sginsburg@nortonmancini.com

OF COUNSEL

ADRIANNA K. LIBER, born Paterson, New Jersey, June 24, 1959; admitted to bar, 1986, Illinois. *Education:* University of Chicago (B.A., 1981); DePaul University (J.D., 1986). *Member:* Chicago, Illinois State and American Bar Associations.

REPRESENTATIVE CLIENTS: Allstate Insurance Company; American Family Insurance Group; Auto-Owners Insurance; Chicago Hospital Risk Pooling Program; County of DuPage; CNA Insurance Company; Custard Claims Management Service, Inc.; Gallagher Bassett Insurance Service; Gordon Food Ser vice Inc.; Great American Insurance Company; Illinois State Medical Insurance Services, Inc.; Intergovernmental Risk Management Agency; ISBA Mutual Insurance Company; McLarens Toplis North America, Inc.; Multi Systems Agency, Inc.; Ophthalmic Mutual Insurance Company; Oshkosh Truck Corporation; Parker Hannifin Corporation; Park District Risk Management Agency (PDRMA); St. Paul Travelers Insurance Company; Sentry Insurance Company; SRS Specialty Risk Services (Hartford); State Farm Insurance Company; Trammel Crow.

THOMAS V. O'CONNOR

SUITE 300, TICOR TITLE BUILDING
330 SOUTH NAPERVILLE ROAD
WHEATON, ILLINOIS 60187-5442
Telephone: 630-665-9400
Fax: 630-665-3011

General Trial Practice. Negligence Litigation, including Personal Injury, Real Estate, Contract and Family Law.

FIRM PROFILE: By Referral Only.

THOMAS V. O'CONNOR, born Chicago, Illinois, September 16, 1941; admitted to bar, 1965, Illinois. *Education:* University of Notre Dame (B.B.A., 1964; J.D., 1965). *Member:* DuPage County, Illinois State and American Bar Associations; Illinois Trial Lawyers Association. ***PRACTICE AREAS:*** General Trial Practice; Negligence Litigation; including Personal Injury Law; Real Estate Law; Contract Law; Family Law.

O'HAGAN, SMITH & AMUNDSEN

WHEATON, ILLINOIS

(See St. Charles)

Commercial; Commercial Transportation; Appellate; Complex Litigation; Construction; Corporate Transactions; Employment; Extra-Contractual/Insurance Litigation; Healthcare; Insurance Coverage; Personal Lines; Product Liability; Professional Liability; Property Litigation.

JOHN J. O'LEARY

WHEATON, ILLINOIS

(See Chicago)

Construction Law and Commercial and Residential Real Estate Law, Lending Law.

OTTOSEN TREVARTHEN BRITZ KELLY & COOPER, LTD.

Established in 1992

300 SOUTH COUNTY FARM ROAD, THIRD FLOOR
WHEATON, ILLINOIS 60187
Telephone: 630-682-0085
Facsimile: 630-682-0788
URL: http://www.otbkc.com

Elburn, Illinois Office: 303 North Main Street, 60119. Telephone: 630-365-6441. Fax: 630-365-6451.

Joliet, Illinois Office: Crystal Square Building, 81 North Chicago Street, Suite 204, 60432. Telephone: 815-723-0601. Fax: 815-723-2599.

Fire Protection Districts, Local Government Law, Municipal Law, Education Law, School Law, Public Finance, Public Pensions, Labor and Employment, Election Law, Estate Planning, Probate, Insurance Defense, Family Law, Commercial Litigation, Business Law, Real Estate, Administrative Law, Zoning Law. Civil Practice.

ROBERT J. BRITZ, born Chicago, Illinois, 1949; admitted to bar, 1978, Illinois. *Education:* University of Illinois, Chicago (B.A., 1974); Northern Illinois University, DeKalb (J.D., 1978). (Resident, Elburn Office). ***PRACTICE AREAS:*** Probate; Estate Planning; Local Government; Real Estate; Business. ***Email:*** rbritz@otbkc.com

(This Listing Continued)

G. ROBB COOPER, born Fort Lewis, Washington, August 2, 1951; admitted to bar, 1987, Illinois. *Education:* Oregon State University (B.S., 1973); Edinburgh University, Edinburgh, Scotland (M.S.C., 1979); Loyola University (J.D., 1986; Ph.D., 1987). ***PRACTICE AREAS:*** Education Law. ***Email:*** profrobb@aol.com

THOMAS J. GILBERT, born Chicago, Illinois, September 9, 1949; admitted to bar, 1974, Illinois, U.S. Court of Appeals, Seventh Circuit; 1980, Florida. *Education:* University of Michigan (B.A., 1971); Loyola University (J.D., 1974). ***PRACTICE AREAS:*** Municipal Law; Commercial Litigation; Real Estate Law; General Practice. ***Email:*** tgilbert@otbkc.com

JOHN H. KELLY, born Evanston, Illinois, November 16, 1951; admitted to bar, 1982, Illinois. *Education:* Northwestern University (B.A., 1973); John Marshall Law School (J.D., 1982). Commissioner, Lake Zurich Fire & Police Commission, 1994—. ***PRACTICE AREAS:*** Government Law; Administrative Law; Real Estate. ***Email:*** jkelly@otbkc.com

KARL R. OTTOSEN, born Freeport, Illinois, May 1, 1960; admitted to bar, 1984, Illinois. *Education:* Western Illinois University (B.S. with high honors, 1981); University of Illinois (J.D., 1984). ***LANGUAGES:*** Sign Language. ***PRACTICE AREAS:*** Local Government; Labor and Employment Law; School Law. ***Email:*** kottosen@otbkc.com

THE PAPE LAW FIRM

100 WEST ROOSEVELT ROAD, BUILDING A-3, SUITE 102
WHEATON, ILLINOIS 60187-5260
Telephone: 630-933-9300
Fax: 630-933-9301
Email: apape@papelaw.com
URL: http://www.papelaw.com

Real Estate Law, Construction Law.

ARTHUR E. PAPE, born Hartford, Connecticut, October 30, 1939; admitted to bar, 1965, Ohio; 1975, Illinois. *Education:* Ohio Wesleyan University; University of Pittsburgh (B.A., 1963); Harvard University (LL.B., 1965). Adjunct Professor in the Master of Real Estate Law Program of John Marshall Law School, Chicago. *Member:* DuPage, Chicago, Illinois State and American Bar Associations; American College of Real Estate Lawyers. Lambda Alpha. ***PRACTICE AREAS:*** Real Estate Law; Construction Law. ***Email:*** apape@papelaw.com

PEREGRINE, STIME, NEWMAN, RITZMAN & BRUCKNER, LTD.

Established in 1959
221 EAST ILLINOIS STREET
P.O. BOX 564
WHEATON, ILLINOIS 60189
Telephone: 630-665-1900
Fax: 630-665-0407
Email: law@psnrb.com
URL: http://www.psnrb.com

General Civil Practice. Commercial Litigation, Corporations, Estate Planning, Trusts and Estates, Probate, Real Estate, Family Law, Personal Injury, Insurance, Worker's Compensation, Municipal Law, Banking Law, Library Law, Collections, Trials and Appeals, Condemnations.

HARTMAN E. STIME (1927-1991)

ROY I. PEREGRINE, born Oak Park, Illinois, July 8, 1928; admitted to bar, 1956, Illinois; 1966, U.S. Supreme Court and U.S. District Court, Northern District of Illinois including Trial Bar. *Education:* Carleton College (B.A., 1950); Chicago-Kent College of Law (J.D., 1956). Phi Delta Phi. Member, Hearing Board, Attorney Registration and Disciplinary Commission, 1974-1987. Commissioner, Character and Fitness Committee of Illinois Board of Law Examiners, 1980-1996. Court Certified Mediator. *Member:* Chicago, DuPage County and Illinois State Bar Associations; Illinois Defense Counsel. ***PRACTICE AREAS:*** Personal Injury Law; Corporate Law; Probate; Estate Planning; Trusts and Estates; Real Estate Law. ***Email:*** rperegrine@psnrb.com

THOMAS M. NEWMAN, born Hinsdale, Illinois, May 15, 1945; admitted to bar, 1971, Illinois. *Education:* DePauw University (B.A., 1967); Indiana University (J.D., 1971). Phi Delta Phi. *Member:* DuPage County (Chairman, Legal Aid Committee, 1975-1976; Member, Judiciary Committee) and Illinois State Bar Associations; The Association of Trial Lawyers of America. ***PRACTICE AREAS:*** Family Law; Trial Practice; Personal Injury Law. ***Email:*** tnewman@psnrb.com

ROGER A. RITZMAN, born De Kalb, Illinois, August 30, 1951; admitted to bar, 1976, Illinois. *Education:* University of Michigan (B.A., with distinction, 1973); University of Illinois (J.D., 1976). Special Assistant State's Attorney, DuPage County (Civil Matters). *Member:* DuPage County and Illinois State Bar Associations. ***PRACTICE AREAS:*** Municipal Law; Corporate Law; Eminent Domain. ***Email:*** rritzman@psnrb.com

DALE W. BRUCKNER, born Berwyn, Illinois, May 31, 1952; admitted to bar, 1977, Illinois. *Education:* University of Wisconsin-Madison (B.A., 1974); University of Kentucky (J.D., 1977). Member, Order of the Coif. Member, Kentucky Law Journal, 1975-1977. Court Appointed Civil Mediator. *Member:* DuPage County and Illinois State Bar Associations; The Association of Trial Lawyers of America. ***PRACTICE AREAS:*** Workers Compensation Law; Trial Practice; Appellate Practice; Personal Injury Law; Real Estate Law. ***Email:*** dbruckner@psnrb.com

ROBERT T. C. KAY, born Geneva, Illinois, February 9, 1961; admitted to bar, 1986, Illinois and U.S. District Court, Northern District of Illinois. *Education:* Wheaton College (B.A., 1983); DePaul University (J.D., 1986). *Member:* DuPage County and Illinois State Bar Associations. ***PRACTICE AREAS:*** Real Estate Law; Land Use Law; Municipal Law; Estate Planning; Probate; Trusts and Estates. ***Email:*** rkay@psnrb.com

(This Listing Continued)

DAVID W. CLARK, born South Bend, Indiana, May 2, 1966; admitted to bar, 1992, Illinois and U.S. District Court, Northern District of Illinois; 1998, Federal Trial Bar. *Education:* Indiana University (B.A., English and Speech Communication, with honors, 1989); Loyola University (J.D, 1992). *Member:* DuPage County and Illinois State Bar Associations; Defense Research Institute; Illinois Trial Lawyers Association. ***REPORTED CASES:*** Greenberg v. Orthosport, 282 Ill.App.3d 830, 668 N.E.2d 1012 (1996); Monti v. Silvercross Hospital, 262 Ill.App.3d 503, 637 N.E.2d 427 (1994). ***PRACTICE AREAS:*** Insurance Defense; Personal Injury; Commercial Litigation; Workers Compensation. ***Email:*** dclark@psnrb.com

DANIEL B. MAIDLOW, born Toledo, Ohio, September 24, 1973; admitted to bar, 2000, Illinois. *Education:* Ohio University (B.A., 1996); University of Toledo College of Law (J.D., 1999). *Member:* Chicago, DuPage County, Illinois State and American Bar Associations. ***PRACTICE AREAS:*** Real Estate Law; Corporate Law; Municipal Law. ***Email:*** dmaidlow@psnrb.com

ELIZABETH P. SCHAFFER, born Deerfield, Illinois, September 28, 1958; admitted to bar, 1984, Illinois and U.S. District Court, Northern District of Illinois. *Education:* Vanderbilt University (B.A., 1980); Chicago-Kent College of Law, Illinois Institute of Technology (J.D., 1984). *Member:* DuPage County and Illinois State Bar Associations. ***PRACTICE AREAS:*** Civil Litigation; Insurance Defense; Personal Injury; Insurance Coverage; Trial Practice. ***Email:*** eschaffer@psnrb.com

REPRESENTATIVE CLIENTS: The Hartford Insurance Cos.; Naperville Public Library; Winnetka Public Library District; The Order of Franciscan Sisters; York Center Community Cooperative, Inc.; Wheaton Sanitary District; General Adjustment Bureau; Gallagher Bassett Services, Inc.; Neumann Homes, Inc.; City of Wheaton (Worker's Compensation only); Murphy Builders, Inc.; American Slide-Chart Corporation; Allured Publishing Co.; Metals & Services Co.; Oswego Public Library District.

PERKINS & ZAYED, P.C.

1751 SOUTH NAPERVILLE ROAD, SUITE 203
WHEATON, ILLINOIS 60187
Telephone: 630-665-2300
Toll Free: 1-877-TRUST.50
Facsimile: 630-665-4343
Email: pzlaw@att.net
URL: http://www.lawyers.com/p&z

Estate Planning Law, Tax Planning, Business Succession Planning, Wealth Preservation, Asset Protection and Charitable Planning.

MARK D. PERKINS, born Shirley, Massachusetts, January 29, 1965; admitted to bar, 1990, Illinois. *Education:* Elmhurst College (B.S., 1987); Illinois Institute of Technology (J.D., 1990). Member, Student Senate and Moot Court Team. Guest Speaker, Estate Planning, "Money Talks" (AM 1530) Radio Program. *Member:* DuPage County Bar Association (Past-Chair: Estate Planning Committee; Tax Law Committee). ***LANGUAGES:*** German. ***PRACTICE AREAS:*** Estate Planning; Trusts; Business Succession Planning; Wealth Preservation. ***Email:*** mperkins@att.net

DEAN K. ZAYED, born Chicago, Illinois, November 8, 1972; admitted to bar, 1997, Illinois. *Education:* Northwestern University (B.A., 1994; J.D., 1997); Chicago-Kent College of Law (LL.M., 2003). Omicron Delta Epsilon. *Member:* Chicago, Du Page County (Past-Chair: Estate Planning Committee; Tax Law Committee), Illinois State and American Bar Associations; Illinois Forum of Estate Planning Attorneys. (Managing Partner). ***PRACTICE AREAS:*** Estate Planning; Tax Planning; Wealth Preservation; Asset Protection; Charitable Planning. ***Email:*** dzayed@att.net

ANTHONY PERRELLI

WHEATON, ILLINOIS

(See Deerfield)

Business Corporate, Small Business, Contracts, Business Planning, Real Estate, Commercial Litigation and Taxation.

PESCH LAW OFFICE

310 S. COUNTY FARM ROAD, SUITE H
WHEATON, ILLINOIS 60187-2409
Telephone: 630-462-9300
Fax: 630-462-0422
Email: peschlaw@aol.com
URL: http://www.lawyers.com/peschlawoffice

Family, Divorce, Child Custody, Child Support, College Expenses, Post-Decree issues, Mediation, Child Representative, Guardian Ad Litem, Adoption, Guardianship, Name Change.

SUSAN MARIE PESCH, admitted to bar, 1991, Illinois. *Education:* Northern Illinois (B.S., with honors, 1988); Loyola University (J.D., 1991). Legal Teaching Position, Kane County Divorce Education "KIDS" Program Presenter, 1993—. *Member:* DuPage County (Committees on Family Law; Alternative Dispute Resolution; Children Advocacy) and Illinois State Bar Associations. ***PRACTICE AREAS:*** Family Law; Divorce; Child Custody; Child Support; Mediation; Guardian Ad Litem; Adoption Law; Guardianship; Name Changes; Child Advocacy; Grandparents Custody; Post Divorce Modification; Paternity; Premarital Agreements; Day Care; Cohabitation Agreements.

PICCIONE, KEELEY & ASSOCIATES LTD.

Established in 1982

122 S. COUNTY FARM ROAD

WHEATON, ILLINOIS 60187-4594

Telephone: 630-653-8000

Fax: 630-653-8029

Email: info@pkalaw.com

URL: http://pkalaw.lawoffice.com

Civil Trial and Appellate Practice, Business Law and Complex Litigation, Mergers and Acquisitions, Negligence, Product and Aviation Litigation, Securities Law, Family Law, Real Estate, Probate Law, Zoning and Eminent Domain Law.

FIRM PROFILE: The Firm was founded in 1982 by John J. Piccione and Patrick C. Keeley and is located in a firm-owned office building across from the DuPage County Governmental Complex. The practice includes a broad spectrum of legal services provided throughout the entire Chicago metropolitan area and internationally, with a concentration in complex transactions and litigation. The firm combines the traditional expertise of large firms with the personal involvement found in smaller boutique practices.

JOHN J. PICCIONE, born Chicago, Illinois, October 6, 1942; admitted to bar, 1967, Illinois and U.S. District Court, Northern District of Illinois; 1973, U.S. Supreme Court; 1982, U.S. Court of Appeals, Seventh Circuit and U.S. District Court, Northern District of Illinois including Trial Bar. *Education:* University of Illinois (B.S., 1964); Loyola University (J.D., 1967). *Member:* Chicago, DuPage County, Illinois State and American Bar Associations; Illinois Trial Lawyers Association; Association of Trial Lawyers of America. Commercial Licensed Pilot. ***PRACTICE AREAS:*** Civil Litigation and Appeals; Personal Injury, Plaintiff and Defense; Family Law; Custody. ***Email:*** jpiccione@pkalaw.com

PATRICK C. KEELEY, born Chicago, Illinois, July 15, 1952; admitted to bar, 1979, Illinois and U.S. District Court, Northern District of Illinois including Trial Bar; 1982, U.S. Court of Appeals, Seventh Circuit; 1982, U.S. Supreme Court. *Education:* University of Illinois (B.S., 1974; M.B.A., 1976); Loyola University (J.D., 1979). Phi Beta Kappa; Phi Kappa Phi. Recipient, Honors Day Convocation Award, University of Illinois, 1970-1974. *Member:* Chicago, DuPage County, Illinois State and American Bar Associations; Association of Trial Lawyers of America; Illinois Trial Lawyers Association. Illinois Licensed Real Estate Broker. ***SPECIAL AGENCIES:*** Special Assistant Attorney General for the State of Illinois. ***TRANSACTIONS:*** Acquisition of LPC, Inc. by Pitney Bowes Corporation; Franchise of College Craft Enterprises, Ltd. Redemption of Travelers Insurance Group, Inc. shares by Resource Information Management Systems, Inc.; Recapitalization of Natural Golf Corporation; Acquisition of Sysdraw Software Company by Visio Corp. ***PRACTICE AREAS:*** Complex Litigation; Civil Litigation and Appeals; Business and Commercial Law; Transactional Practice; Mergers and Acquisitions; Eminent Domain Litigation; Real Estate Development; Employment Disputes. ***Email:*** pkeeley@pkalaw.com

MARK W. TADER, born Minneapolis, Minnesota, January 27, 1960; admitted to bar, 1985, Illinois and U.S. District Court, Central District of Illinois; 1987, U.S. District Court, Northern District of Illinois including Trial Bar. *Education:* Wheaton College (B.A., with honors, 1981); University of Michigan; University of Illinois (J.D., 1985). National Merit Scholar. Author: "Reallocating Western Water: Beneficial Use, Property and Politics," 1986 University of Illinois Law Review 277. Law Clerk to: Honorable Donald W. Morthland, Appellate Court, Fourth District, 1985-1986; Honorable James A. Knecht, Appellate Court, Fourth District, 1986-1987. *Member:* DuPage County, Illinois State and American Bar Associations. ***PRACTICE AREAS:*** Civil Litigation and Appeals; Mechanics Liens; General Practice. ***Email:*** mtader@pkalaw.com

LYNN R. CONRAD, born Shreveport, Louisiana, May 22, 1958; admitted to bar, 1986, Illinois; 1988, U.S. District Court, Northern District of Illinois. *Education:* Louisiana Tech University (B.S., 1981); Loyola University of Chicago (J.D., 1986). *Member:* DuPage County and Illinois State Bar Associations. ***PRACTICE AREAS:*** Commercial Transactions; Estate Planning; Probate. ***Email:*** lconrad@pkalaw.com

ALISON S. FRANKLIN, born Springfield, Illinois, December 2, 1960; admitted to bar, 1988, Illinois; 1989, U.S. District Court, Northern District of Illinois and U.S. Court of Appeals, Seventh Circuit. *Education:* University of Illinois (B.S., 1982; J.D., cum laude, 1988). ***PRACTICE AREAS:*** Civil Litigation; Commercial Transactions; Employment Disputes. ***Email:*** afranklin@pkalaw.com

THOMAS A. JACKSON, born Chicago, Illinois, November 20, 1967; admitted to bar, 1992, Illinois and U.S. District Court, Northern District of Illinois. *Education:* University of Illinois (B.A., 1989; J.D., 1992). Phi Kappa Phi. *Member:* DuPage County and Illinois State Bar Associations. ***PRACTICE AREAS:*** Civil Litigation; Family Law. ***Email:*** tjackson@pkalaw.com

ASSOCIATE

JASON SINGLETON, born Kansas City, Missouri, November 10, 1975; admitted to bar, 2001, Illinois. *Education:* University of Missouri at Columbia (B.S.B.A., 1997; J.D., 2001). *Member:* DuPage County and Illinois State Bar Associations. ***Email:*** jsingleton@pkalaw.com

REPRESENTATIVE CLIENTS: Resource Information Management Systems, Inc.; American Family Insurance Company; Board of Library Trustees, Village of Carol Stream; West Chicago Public Library District; Illinois Department of Transportation; Corporate Concepts, Inc.; United Recycling Industries, Inc.; College Craft Enterprises, Ltd.; Natural Golf Corporation; Konica U.S.A.; Central Soya Co., Inc.; OAS Software Corp.; 3D Exhibits, Inc.; SR Art Plus Associates, Inc.
APPROVED ATTORNEYS FOR: Attorneys' Title Guaranty Fund, Inc.
REFERENCES: All clients listed above, specifically: Resource Information Management Systems, Inc., Naperville, IL; United Recycling Industries, Inc., Franklin Park, IL.

QUERREY & HARROW, LTD.

Established in 1939

310 SOUTH COUNTY FARM ROAD, THIRD FLOOR

WHEATON, ILLINOIS 60187-5473

Telephone: 630-653-2600

Fax: 630-653-0178

Email: jjendryk@querrey.com

URL: http://www.querrey.com

Chicago, Illinois Office: 175 West Jackson Boulevard, Suite 1600. Telephone: 312-540-7000. Fax: 312-540-0578.

Crystal Lake, Illinois Office: 651 West Terra Cotta Avenue, Suite 221. Telephone: 815-479-1929. Fax: 815-479-1978.

Joliet, Illinois Office: 2 Rialto Square, Suite 401, 116 North Chicago Street. Telephone: 815-726-1600. Fax: 815-726-1674.

Waukegan, Illinois Office: 415 West Washington Street, Suite 205. Telephone: 847-249-4440. Fax: 847-249-4932.

Merrillville, Indiana Office: 8585 Broadway, Suite 510. Telephone: 219-738-1820. Fax: 219-738-1821.

New York, N.Y. Office: 120 Broadway, Suite 2800. Telephone: 212-233-0130. Fax: 212-233-0172.

London, England Office: 141-142 Fenchurch Street, Fifth Floor. Telephone: 207-929-6670. Fax: 207-929-6671.

General Practice and Trial Practice.

JAMES S. JENDRYK, admitted to bar, 1975, Illinois. *Education:* University of Notre Dame (B.B.A., 1972); John Marshall Law School (J.D., 1975). ***PRACTICE AREAS:*** Litigation.

LISSA L. HAMER, admitted to bar, 1987, Illinois. *Education:* Marquette University (B.S., 1981); Northern Illinois University (J.D., 1987). Medical Technologist, 1981. (Resident). ***PRACTICE AREAS:*** Litigation. ***Email:*** lhamer@querrey.com

---

CYNTHIA D. TRAYNOR, admitted to bar, 1988, Illinois. *Education:* Ripon College (A.B., 1981); The John Marshall Law School (J.D., 1988). ***PRACTICE AREAS:*** Litigation. ***Email:*** ctraynor@querrey.com

(For complete biographical data on all personnel, see Professional Biographies at Chicago, Illinois)

QUINLAN & CARROLL, LTD.

WHEATON, ILLINOIS

(See Chicago)

JOHN M. QUINN & ASSOCIATES, LTD.

WHEATON, ILLINOIS

(See Bloomingdale)

Drivers License Suspension, Administrative Hearings, Driving While Intoxicated, Criminal Law, Traffic Violations, Criminal Defense, Misdemeanors.

RATHJE & WOODWARD

Established in 1938

300 EAST ROOSEVELT ROAD, SUITE 300

WHEATON, ILLINOIS 60187

Telephone: 630-668-8500

Fax: 630-668-7350

Email: info@rathjewoodward.com

URL: http://www.rathjewoodward.com

General Civil and Appellate Practice. Commercial, Industrial and Residential Real Estate, Municipal, Zoning, Insurance, Probate, Estate Planning, Environmental, Eminent Domain, Corporate, Trademarks, Unfair Competition, Copyright, Family Law, Personal Injury, and Business Law.

FIRM PROFILE: Rathje & Woodward has served clients from across the United States in matters pending in the Chicago Metropolitan area and north and north central Illinois for six decades. The firm is pleased to serve businesses and residents in the region in a full-service capacity in federal and state courts and before various local, state and federal authorities.

MEMBERS OF FIRM

R. TERENCE KALINA, born Oak Park, Illinois, September 30, 1947; admitted to bar, 1972, Illinois. *Education:* St. Procopius College (B.A., 1969); University of London, London, England; University of Notre Dame (J.D., 1972). Blue Key. *Member:* Du Page County and Illinois State Bar Associations. ***PRACTICE AREAS:*** Estate Planning; Probate; Banking; Contracts. ***Email:*** rtkalina@rathjewoodward.com

HENRY S. STILLWELL, III, born Urbana, Illinois, January 9, 1948; admitted to bar, 1975, Illinois. *Education:* University of Illinois (B.S., 1971); John Marshall Law School (J.D., 1975). Phi Alpha Delta. *Member:* DuPage County, Illinois State and American Bar Associations. ***PRACTICE AREAS:*** Real Estate; Zoning, Planning and Land Use. ***Email:*** hstillwell@rathjewoodward.com

GARY L. TAYLOR, born Berwyn, Illinois, December 4, 1951; admitted to bar, 1976, Illinois. *Education:* University of Illinois (B.A., 1973); John Marshall Law School (J.D., with distinction, 1976). Staff Member, John Marshall Journal of Practice and Procedure,

(This Listing Continued)

1974-1976. *Member:* DuPage County, Illinois State and American Bar Associations. ***PRACTICE AREAS:*** Real Estate; Litigation; Zoning, Planning and Land Use. ***Email:*** gtaylor@rathjewoodward.com

JOHN F. GARROW, born Elmhurst, Illinois, May 20, 1953; admitted to bar, 1979, Illinois. *Education:* Western Illinois University (B.A., 1976); Drake University (J.D., 1979). Managing Editor, Drake Law Review, 1978-1979. Author: "Metro. Hous. Dev. Corp. v. Village of Arlington Heights," 27 Drake Law Review 166, 1978. *Member:* DuPage County, Illinois State and American Bar Associations. ***PRACTICE AREAS:*** Real Estate; Family Law; Divorce. ***Email:*** jgarrow@rathjewoodward.com

REESE J. PECK, born Washington, D.C., May 18, 1953; admitted to bar, 1982, Illinois, U.S. District Court, Northern District of Illinois including Trial Bar. *Education:* Iowa Wesleyan College (B.A., 1976); Drake University Law School (J.D., 1981). *Member:* DuPage County, Illinois State and American Bar Associations; Illinois Trial Lawyers Association; The Association of Trial Lawyers of America; Federal Trial Lawyers Bar. ***PRACTICE AREAS:*** Litigation; Real Estate; Construction Liability; Contracts; Commercial Litigation. ***Email:*** rpeck@rathjewoodward.com

TRACY D. KASSON, born La Grange Park, Illinois, October 29, 1961; admitted to bar, 1987, Illinois. *Education:* University of Illinois (B.A., 1983); Loyola University (J.D., 1987; M.A., 1988). Pi Sigma Alpha. Articles Editor, Loyola Law Journal, 1986-1987. Author: "Election Redistricting: A Call For Reform," 17 Loyola University of Chicago Law Journal 659, 1986. *Member:* DuPage County, Illinois State and American Bar Associations; Appellate Lawyers Association. ***PRACTICE AREAS:*** Zoning, Planning and Land Use; Civil Litigation; Appellate Practice; Eminent Domain. ***Email:*** tkasson@rathjewoodward.com

MARK W. DANIEL, born Normal, Illinois, April 22, 1968; admitted to bar, 1994, Ohio; 1995, Illinois and U.S. District Court, Southern District of Ohio; 1996, U.S. District Court, Northern District of Illinois including Trial Bar; 2001, U.S. Supreme Court. *Education:* University of Illinois (B.S., 1990); John Marshall Law School (J.D., magna cum laude, 1994). Moot Court. Associate Editor, Law Review. Author: "Protecting Copyright in Building Plans and Structures," Builder Architect Magazine, Oct.-Dec. 1995. Co-Author: Lisle, Illinois Zoning Hearings, "The Big Box and Fair Process," Int'l Mun.L. Assn., Sept. 2001. Lecturer, "Zoning and Land Use in Illinois," Continuing Legal Education Seminars, 2003—. Speaker, Chicago Bar and DuPage Bar Associations, 1999—. *Member:* DuPage County, Chicago, Illinois State and American Bar Associations; Association of Trial Lawyers of America; American Planning Association. ***PRACTICE AREAS:*** Federal Litigation; Civil Litigation; Appellate Practice; Trademark; Government; Copyrights; Environmental; Business Law; Constitutional Law; Complex Litigation; Zoning, Planning and Land Use. ***Email:*** mdaniel@rathjewoodward.com

JOHN R. ZEMENAK, born Mount Holly, New Jersey, April 10, 1968; admitted to bar, 1994, Illinois and U.S. District Court, Northern District of Illinois. *Education:* Miami University of Ohio (B.A., 1990); John Marshall Law School (J.D., 1994). John Marshall Journal of Computer and Information Law. Co-Author: Lisle, Illinois Zoning Hearings, "The Big Box and Fair Process," Int'l Mun.L. Ass'n, Sept. 2001. *Member:* Chicago, DuPage County and Illinois State Bar Associations. ***PRACTICE AREAS:*** Civil Litigation; Municipal Law; Zoning, Planning and Land Use; Corporate Law. ***Email:*** jzemenak@rathjewoodward.com

SCOTT E. POINTNER, born Chicago, Illinois, November 1, 1967; admitted to bar, 1996, Illinois; 1997, U.S. District Court, Northern District of Illinois including Trial Bar; 2001, U.S. Supreme Court. *Education:* Indiana University (B.S., 1990); Southwestern University School of Law (J.D., 1996). Member, Board of Governors, Moot Court Honor Society, 1995-1996. Lecturer, "Zoning and Land Use in Illinois," Continuing Legal Education Seminar, February 25, 2003. *Member:* DuPage County, Illinois State and American Bar Associations. ***PRACTICE AREAS:*** Civil Litigation; Real Estate; Zoning, Planning and Land Use; Eminent Domain; Municipal Law; Corporate Law; Contracts; Appellate Practice. ***Email:*** spointner@rathjewoodward.com

ASSOCIATES

CAROL ANNE WATKISS, born Chicago, Illinois, April 25, 1967; admitted to bar, 2000, Illinois. *Education:* Illinois State University (B.A., 1989; M.A., 1991); Northern Illinois University (J.D., 2000). *Member:* Chicago, DuPage County, Illinois State and American Bar Associations. ***PRACTICE AREAS:*** Family Law; Divorce; Real Estate; Civil Litigation; Appellate Practice. ***Email:*** cwatkiss@rathjewoodward.com

KEVIN M. CARRARA, born Naperville, Illinois, December 2, 1969; admitted to bar, 2001, Illinois and U.S. District Court, Northern District of Illinois. *Education:* Northern Illinois University (B.S., Finance, 1994); The John Marshall Law School (J.D., 2001). *Member:* DuPage, Illinois State and American Bar Associations. ***PRACTICE AREAS:*** Zoning, Planning and Land Use; Civil Litigation; Municipal Law; Business Law; Construction Litigation. ***Email:*** kcarrara@rathjewoodward.com

OF COUNSEL

ELIZABETH ANNE HAMBRICK-STOWE, born Tientsin, China, December 3, 1948; admitted to bar, 1984, Maryland; 1985, Pennsylvania; 1994, U.S. Supreme Court; 1997, U.S. District Court, Eastern District of Pennsylvania; 1998, U.S. Court of Appeals, Third Circuit; 2004, Illinois. *Education:* Wellesley College (B.A., honors, 1970) Phi Beta Kappa; Pacific School of Religion (M.A., M.Div., 1973); University of Baltimore School of Law (J.D., summa cum laude, 1983). Member, Heuisler Honor Society. Articles Editor, University of Baltimore Law Review, 1983. Author: "Abandoning Nonconforming Use: The Land Use Equivalent of Jumbo Shrimp?" PBA Municipal Law Section Newsletter, Vol. 20, No. 3-4, p.1, Summer/Fall 2003; "Between the Rock of Regulation and the Hard Place of Temporary Taking Relief from the Supreme Court," Fall 1999, Vol. 16, No.3, pp.5-6. Lecturer, "Performance Reviews," Employment Law Institute, Pennsylvania Bar Association, 2002; "How to Initiate the Probate Process and Handle Claims Against the Probate Estate," 1996, 1998, 2001; "Estate Planning for the Elderly," 1997, 1999; "How to Prepare the Federal Estate Tax Return," 1999; "Estate Planning for Life: Principles and Practice," Community College of Allegheny College, 2004; "Employment Law Basics," 2003; "Appeals of Land Use Cases," Lancaster County Bar Association; "Condemnation," 2002. *Member:* Illinois State, Pennsylvania and Maryland State Bar Associations; DuPage County Estate Planning Council. ***PRACTICE AREAS:*** Estate Planning; Probate; Business Law; Commercial Law; Employment Law.

TIMOTHY D. ELLIOTT, born Oak Park, Illinois, 1971; admitted to bar, 1996, Illinois and U.S. District Court, Northern District of Illinois; 1998, U.S. District Court, District of Arizona; 1999, U.S. District Court, District of Colorado; 2001, U.S. District Court, Western District of Michigan; 2002, Trial Bar for Northern District of Illinois; 2003, U.S. Court of Appeals, Third and Seventh Circuits; 2004, U.S. Court of Appeals, Fifth Circuit. *Education:* Miami University (B.A., magna cum laude, 1992); Harvard Law School (J.D., cum laude, 1996). Phi Beta Kappa; Phi Alpha Theta. Adjunct Faculty, Loyola University School of Law, 2004—. ***PRACTICE AREAS:*** Commercial Litigation; Bankruptcy Reorganization. ***Email:*** telliott@rathjewoodward.com

ATTORNEYS FOR: Airhart Construction; Burnside Construction Company; Citizens Utilities; Cog Hill Golf & Country Club, Inc.; Cook Golf Properties; DuPage County Fair Association; Faganel Builders; Gladstone Builders & Developers; Glenwoodie Golf & Country Club, Inc.; Highland Management; Image Base; Industrial Chimney Engineers; J.B. Architecture Group, Inc.; Joe Keim Enters.; Kennedy Transportation; Krughoff Homes; Michael S.Was Enterprises; Neslund & Associates; Northern Illinois Home Builders Association; Northwest Construction; Pine Meadow Golf Club, Inc.; Roake & Assoc. Engineers; St. Andrews Golf & Country Club, Inc.; Village of Westmont; Wiseman-Hughes Enters.
LOCAL ATTORNEYS FOR: AT&T; Amica Insurance Co.; Bankers United Life; Central Security Insurance; Commonwealth Edison; Ferrari Financial Services; Girl Scouts of DuPage County Council; Home Depot; Homestead Village; McDonalds; Metro Storage, L.L.C.; The Northern Trust Co.; Perkins Insurance; Prudential Insurance; The Ryland Group; State Farm Insurance; Studio Plus; Target Stores; Town & Country Homes; Village of Diamond; Walgreen's; Wheaton Town Square.
REAL ESTATE ATTORNEYS FOR: Albertson's; The Daly Group; Equity Growth Group; Home Depot; Homestead Village; McDonalds; The Ryland Group; Studio Plus; Town & Country Homes; Trammell-Crow; Wiseman-Hughes Enters.

RINELLA AND RINELLA, LTD.

WHEATON, ILLINOIS

(See Chicago)

Practice Limited to Family Law and Divorce including the areas of Legal Separation, Negotiating and Drafting Premarital and Postnuptial Agreements, Judgment Enforcement, Child Custody and Child Support Actions, Domestic Violence, Spousal Support, Appeals, Adoption, Parentage Actions and Interstate Support Enforcement.

ROBERTS AND ASSOCIATES, P.C.

Established in 1979

104 EAST ROOSEVELT ROAD, SUITE 202
WHEATON, ILLINOIS 60187
Telephone: 630-668-4211
Fax: 630-668-2076
URL: http://www.robertsandassoc.com

Litigation, Family Law.

KEITH E. (CHUCK) ROBERTS, JR., born Golconda, Illinois, September 22, 1955; admitted to bar, 1983, Illinois; 1984, U.S. District Court, Northern District of Illinois, including Trial Bar. *Education:* Rose-Hulman Institute of Technology (B.S.M.E., 1977); Northern Illinois University (J.D., 1983). *Member:* DuPage County (President, 2005-2006) and Illinois State Bar Associations. ***PRACTICE AREAS:*** Litigation; Family Law. ***Email:*** chuckroberts@mindspring.com

OF COUNSEL

KEITH E. ROBERTS, SR., born White Hall, Illinois, April 27, 1928; admitted to bar, 1953, Illinois. *Education:* Western Illinois University, George Washington University and University of Illinois (B.S., 1951); University of Illinois (J.D., 1953). Phi Delta Phi. Student Editor-in-Chief, University of Illinois Law Forum, 1952-1953. Assistant Attorney General, 1966-1969. *Member:* DuPage County and Illinois State Bar Associations; International Society of Barristers. ***PRACTICE AREAS:*** Litigation.

ROSEMARIE FRONTZAK, born Chicago, Illinois, October 12, 1963; admitted to bar, 1988, Illinois. *Education:* Loyola University (B.A., 1985); Chicago-Kent College of Law, Illinois Institute of Technology (J.D., 1988). *Member:* DuPage County and Illinois State Bar Associations. ***PRACTICE AREAS:*** Appellate Practice; Real Estate.

MARIE F. LEACH, born Chicago, Illinois, June 26, 1945; admitted to bar, 1982, Ohio; 1985, Illinois; U.S. District Court, Northern District of Ohio, U.S. District Court, Northern District of Illinois, including Trial Bar and U.S. Court of Appeals, 6th Circuit. *Education:* Knox College (B.A., 1972); Northern Illinois University (J.D., 1982). *Member:* DuPage County and Illinois State Bar Associations. ***PRACTICE AREAS:*** Litigation; Family Law.

ROBERT S. MARCOTT, born Oak Park, Illinois, August 9, 1951; admitted to bar, 1981, Montana; 1987, U.S. Court of Appeals, Ninth Circuit; 1990, Illinois and U.S. District Court, Northern District of Illinois, including Trial Bar, 1998. *Education:* Western Illinois University (B.A., 1974); University of Montana (J.D., with honors, 1981). University of Montana Law Review, 42 Mont. L. Rev. 315; Dean's Award for Outstanding Leadership, University of Montana Law School, 1981. Law Clerk to U.S. District Judge Russell E. Smith, District of Montana, 1981-1983. Adjunct Lecturer, School of Law, University of Montana, 1983-1988. *Member:* DuPage County and Illinois State Bar Associations. ***PRACTICE AREAS:*** Commercial Law; Litigation; Civil Practice; Business Law; Probate.

DANIELLE M. JAESCHKE, born Wisconsin; admitted to bar, 1987, Illinois and U.S. District Court, Northern District of Illinois. *Education:* Miami University (B.S., 1984); De Paul University (J.D., cum laude, 1987). Member, De Paul Law Review. Recipient of seven

(This Listing Continued)

ROBERTS AND ASSOCIATES, P.C., Wheaton—Continued

American Jurisprudence Awards and a Lex Legio Scholarship. Graduated first in her class. *Member:* DuPage County and Illinois State Bar Associations. ***PRACTICE AREAS:*** Family Law; Probate; Civil Litigation.

KATE M. ROXAS, born Milwaukee, Wisconsin; admitted to bar, 1999, Illinois. *Education:* University of Wisconsin-Madison (B.A., 1995); John Marshall Law School (J.D., 1999). Semi-Finalist, ATLA Trial Competition, 1998. Seminar, Prairie State College, South Suburban Bar Association, 2001. *Member:* DuPage County and Illinois State Bar Associations. ***PRACTICE AREAS:*** Domestic Relations; Child Custody; Divorce; Paternity.

LAW OFFICES OF ROGERS & COYNE, LLC

WHEATON, ILLINOIS

(See Naperville)

Estate Planning, Trust and Estate Administration, Residential and Commercial Real Estate.

ROLEWICK & GUTZKE, P.C.

Established in 1981

DANADA WEST PROFESSIONAL CENTER
1776 SOUTH NAPERVILLE ROAD, SUITE 104A
WHEATON, ILLINOIS 60187-8133
Telephone: 630-653-1577
Fax: 630-653-1579
Email: rg@rglawfirm.com
URL: http://www.rglawfirm.com

General Practice with an emphasis on Estate Planning, Tax Planning, Real Estate, Business Law and Commercial Litigation.

DAVID F. ROLEWICK, born Riverside, Illinois, May 11, 1946; admitted to bar, 1971, Illinois and U.S. District Court, Northern District of Illinois including Trial Bar; 1978, U.S. Court of Appeals, Seventh Circuit; 1984, U.S. Supreme Court. *Education:* Loyola University (B.S., 1968; J.D., 1971). Alpha Sigma Nu. Staff Member, 1969-1970 and Notes Editor, 1970-1971, Loyola University Law Journal. Author: "A Short History of the Illinois Judicial Systems," Illinois Bar Foundation, 1968; "Unconscionability Under the Uniform Commercial Code," 1 Loyola University Law Journal 313, 1971; "Voir Dire Examination of Jurors," 25 DePaul Law Review 50, 1975. Special Assistant Attorney General, State of Illinois, 1974-1999. Member, Inquiry Board, Attorney Registration and Disciplinary Commission of the Supreme Court of Illinois, 1990-1994; Hearing Panel Chairman, 1994—. *Member:* DuPage County (Chairman, Committee on Corporation Law, 1982-1983), Illinois State (Member, Corporations/Securities Law Section Council, 1989—; Chairman, 1994-1995) and American Bar Associations; The Association of Trial Lawyers of America; DuPage County Estate Planning Council (Secretary and Member, Board of Directors, 1982-1983; Member, Board of Directors, 1980-1986; Vice President, 1984-1985; President, 1985-1986). [Captain, U.S. Army, active duty, 1972]. ***PRACTICE AREAS:*** Corporations; Commercial Litigation; Shareholder Litigation; Estate Planning Law; Trusts and Estates; Mergers, Acquisitions and Divestitures; Employment Law. ***Email:*** davidr@rglawfirm.com

JOHN D. GUTZKE, born Madison, Wisconsin, August 3, 1958; admitted to bar, 1984, Illinois; 1987, U.S. District Court, Northern District of Illinois. *Education:* Franklin College, Lugano, Switzerland (A.A., 1978); University of Illinois (B.A., 1981; J.D., 1984). Member, DuPage County Estate Planning Council, 1988—. *Member:* DuPage County (Member: Real Estate Committee, 1986; Corporate Law Committee, 1985) and Illinois State (Member, Trusts & Estates Section Council, 1992—) Bar Associations. ***PRACTICE AREAS:*** Real Estate; Estate Planning; Corporate Law; Business Law; Contracts; Trusts and Estates; Employment Law. ***Email:*** johng@rglawfirm.com

JUSTIN J. KARUBAS

RYAN AND RYAN

WHEATON, ILLINOIS

(See Chicago)

Eminent Domain, Condemnation.

LAWRENCE K. RYNNING

WHEATON OFFICE CENTER
310 SOUTH COUNTY FARM ROAD
WHEATON, ILLINOIS 60187
Telephone: 630-682-9500
Fax: 630-682-8107
Email: lkrlaw@ameritech.net

Insurance Coverage, Civil Litigation, General Civil Practice.

LAWRENCE K. RYNNING, born Marinette, Wisconsin, March 23, 1955; admitted to bar, 1980, Illinois and U.S. District Court, Northern District of Illinois; 1981, U.S. District Court, Northern District of Indiana; 1989, U.S. District Court, Eastern District of Wisconsin; 1992, U.S. District Court, Western District of Michigan; 2001, U.S. District Court, Southern District of Illinois. *Education:* Carroll College (B.S., 1977); University of North Carolina at Chapel Hill (J.D., with honors, 1980). *Member:* American, Illinois State and Du Page County Bar Associations. ***PRACTICE AREAS:*** Insurance Coverage; Civil Litigation; Civil Practice.

(This Listing Continued)

SCHILLER, DUCANTO AND FLECK

Established in 1981

311 SOUTH COUNTY FARM ROAD, SUITE G
WHEATON, ILLINOIS 60187
Telephone: 630-665-5800
Fax: 630-665-6082
Email: schillerducantoandfleck@sdflaw.com
URL: http://www.sdflaw.com

Chicago, Illinois Office: 200 North La Salle Street, 30th Floor. Telephone: 312-641-5560. Fax: 312-641-6361.

Lake Forest, Illinois Office: Suite 300, 207 East Westminster Avenue. Telephone: 847-615-8300. Fax: 847-615-8284.

Family Law, Complex Domestic Relations Issues, Divorce/Dissolution of Marriage, Prenuptial Agreements/Premarital Agreements, Child Custody and Visitation, Spousal Support/Alimony/Maintenance, Matrimonial Law and Litigation, Appeals, Mediation-Family/ Divorce, Marital Settlement Agreements, Separation Agreements, Property Rights, Financial Discovery and Analysis Related to Divorce, and Tax Considerations Related to Divorce.

FIRM PROFILE: Schiller, DuCanto and Fleck is the largest law firm in the country to devote its practice exclusively to matrimonial law. The firm was founded in 1981 by Chicago attorneys Donald C. Schiller and Joseph N. DuCanto. Charles J. Fleck, former presiding judge of the Cook County Domestic Relations Division, joined in 1982. Firm members are nationally recognized experts in all aspects of matrimonial law, and many are current and past leaders of local, state and national bar associations. The biographies listed below contain specific references to articles authored, memberships and offices held by our attorneys within the last seven years. A more complete list can be found in the extended biographies listed on the firm's web page.

MEMBERS

TIMOTHY M. DAW, born Chicago, Illinois, December 31, 1959; admitted to bar, 1985, Illinois. *Education:* University of Illinois (B.S., 1982); DePaul University (J.D., with distinction, 1985). Listed: Illinois Super Lawyers (Family Law) 2004—. Member, Leading Lawyers Network 2004—. Author: "Sifting Through the Tax Return," Illinois Institute for Continuing Legal Education, 1990, and Financial Planning and Tax Considerations of Divorce, Illinois CPA Society, 1995; "The Possible Interjection of the New Spouse's Finances Into Post-Decree Dissolution of Marriage Proceedings," DuPage County Bar Association Brief, Volume 13, Issue 6, February 2001; "Revisiting Transmutation 20 Years Later: Still Untamed?", DuPage County Bar Association Brief, Volume 15, Issue 8, April 2, 2003; "Client Management & Education"; Illinois Family Law Series Volume I, IICLE, 2003; "The Modification of Judgments for Dissolution of Marriage," Family Law Conference, IICLE, Spring 2004. Author & Lecturer, sections of "Family Law Litigation," National Business Institute, 1996; "QDRO's: What Can and Can't Be Done," ABA Family Law Section, Spring CLE Meeting, April 2002; "Cross-Examination, Anybody Can Do It!", ABA Family Law Section Fall CLE Meeting, November 2002; "The Modification of Judgments for Dissolution of Marriage", Family Law Conference, IICLE, Spring 2004. Retired Member, Committee on Character and Fitness, Supreme Court of Illinois, 1991-2000. *Member:* DuPage County (Member and Former Chairman, Family Law Committee; Member, Judicial Evaluation Committee), Will County, and Illinois State (Member, Family Law Section) and American (Member, Family Law Section) Bar Associations. ***Email:*** tdaw@sdflaw.com

MICHAEL R. GALASSO, born Chicago, Illinois, April 29, 1936; admitted to bar, 1961, Illinois; 1963, U.S. District Court; 1965, U.S. Supreme Court. *Education:* Elmhurst College (B.S.B.A., 1958); Illinois Institute of Technology, Chicago-Kent College of Law (J.D., 1961). Illinois Super Lawyers (Family Law) 2004—. Member, Leading Lawyers Network, 2004—. Judge, 18th Judicial Circuit, 1984-1999; Chief Judge Matrimonial Law Division, 1988-1995; Chief Judge, 18th Judicial Circuit, 1995-1999; Justice of Illinois Appellate Court, Second District, 1999-2000. *Member:* DuPage County and Illinois State Bar Associations. ***Email:*** mgalasso@sdflaw.com

DAVID A. KING, born Minneapolis, Minnesota, December 17, 1965; admitted to bar, 1993, Illinois. *Education:* University of Illinois (B.S., with honors, 1988); DePaul University (J.D., 1993). Illinois Super Lawyers (Family Law) 2004—. Member, Leading Lawyers Network 2004—. Speaker: "Trial Practice, DCBA Law Day Seminar; "Trusts and Estate Planning Relative to Divorcing Parents," Single Parents Advocates of Illinois; "Grandparents Rights," American Association of Retired Persons. Arbitrator, Expedited Matrimonial Arbitration Program for the Circuit Court of the Eighteenth Judicial Circuit, DuPage County, Illinois. Lead Articles Editor, DuPage Bar Brief. *Member:* American Bar Association; Illinois State Bar Association (Member, Family Law Section; Chair, Committee on Child Support); Dupage County Bar Association (Chair, Publication Board; Editor, Law Journal). ***Email:*** dking@sdflaw.com

ASSOCIATES

DEBORAH A. CARDER, born Evergreen Park, Illinois, November 28, 1970; admitted to bar, 1995, Illinois. *Education:* University of Illinois (B.A., 1992); DePaul University (J.D., 1995). Member, Family Law Committee, Womens Bar Association of Illinois, 1999-2000. Member, Family Law Committee, Lake County Bar Association, 1998-2000. *Member:* DuPage County (Member, Family Law Committee), Illinois State and American Bar Associations. ***REPORTED CASES:*** People of the State of Illinois v. Juan Falcon, 292 Ill.App.3d 538 685 N.E.2d 962 (1997). ***Email:*** dcarder@sdflaw.com

ABIGAIL M. CHIESA, born Summit, New Jersey, July 26, 1968; admitted to bar, 1993, Maryland; 1996, District of Columbia; 2003, Illinois. *Education:* Southwestern University (B.A., magna cum laude, 1990); George Washington University Law School (J.D., 1993); Judge Advocate General's School, U.S. Army (Distinguished Graduate, 1996). Re-

(This Listing Continued)

cipient, American Bar Association Award for Professional Merit, 1996. *Member:* DuPage County, Illinois State and American Bar Associations. [JAGC, U.S. Army]. ***LANGUAGES:*** Spanish. **Email:** achiesa@sdflaw.com

OF COUNSEL

HAROLD G. FIELD, born Chicago, Illinois, February 27, 1923; admitted to bar, 1952, Illinois. *Education:* Arizona State College (B.S., 1948); Chicago-Kent College of Law (J.D., 1952). Listed: Best Lawyers in America by Neifeh & Smith, 1983-2000; Leading Attorneys in Illinois, 2000. Contributor to: Professional Responsibility/A.R.D.C. Seminar, 1996. Moderator: Illinois Chapter American Academy of Matrimonial Lawyers Seminar, DuPage County, 1994 & 1996. Speaker: ISBA Seminar 1999 DuPage County Trial Advocate Training-Evaluation-2000. Life Member of National Registry of Who's Who. *Member:* DuPage County (President, 1977-1978), Illinois State (Member, Board of Governors, 1982-1987) and American Bar Associations (Member, Family Law Section, 1981-1995); American Academy of Matrimonial Lawyers (Member, Board of Governors (Nationally), 1983-1989; Vice President, 1989-1994; President of Illinois Chapter, 1985-1986); International Academy of Matrimonial Lawyers (Member, Board of Governors, 1990-1993; Attorney, 1992-1996). **Email:** hfield@sdflaw.com

SCOTT, HALSTED & BABETCH, P.C.

WHEATON, ILLINOIS

(See Chicago)

Civil Litigation, Trials, Defense Litigation, Appeals, Personal Injury, Automobile, Premises Liability, Uninsured, Underinsured Motorists, Negligence, Strict Liability Law, Construction, Commercial and Insurance Law.

SHERIDAN & LASS, P.C.

315 NAPERVILLE ROAD
P.O. BOX 572
WHEATON, ILLINOIS 60189-0572
Telephone: 630-665-3900
Fax: 630-665-3912
Email: sheridanlaw@prodigy.net
URL: http://www.lawyers.com/sheridanlass

Business Law, Contracts, Collections, Bankruptcy, Civil Practice, Corporate Law, Litigation, Commercial Real Estate, Probate, Real Estate, Trusts and Estates, Wills.

FIRM PROFILE: Sheridan & Lass, P.C. provides legal services to businesses and individuals throughout the Chicago Metropolitan area, principally in Du Page and Kane counties. Since 1971, the firm has represented businesses in litigation and transactional matters. It represents secured creditors in bankruptcy, replevin and forcible entry and detainer. The firm also represents individuals in litigation, bankruptcy, mortgage foreclosures, probate and real estate.

GERALD M. SHERIDAN, JR., born Freeport, Illinois, August 21, 1931; admitted to bar, 1960, Illinois. *Education:* DePaul University (B.S., in Com., 1953; J.D., 1960). Editor-in-Chief, De Paul Law Review, 1960. General Counsel: Wheaton Chamber of Commerce, 1997, 1998; Fox Valley Airport Authority, 1979-1986; St. Charles Savings & Loan Association, 1981-1990. Airport Counsel, Village of Prospect Heights Palwaukee Airport, 1984. Airport Litigation Counsel, Cities of Batavia, Geneva, St. Charles (DuPage Airport), 1988-1990. *Member:* The Lawyers Club of Chicago; Appellate Lawyers Association of Illinois.

CHRISTINA M. L. LASS, born Chicago, Illinois, May 9, 1967; admitted to bar, 1992, Illinois; 1993, Missouri; 2003, U.S. Supreme Court. *Education:* University of Chicago (A.B., 1989); Valparaiso University (J.D., 1992). Articles Editor, Valparaiso University Law Review, 1991-1992. *Member:* Du Page County and Illinois State Bar Associations.

SKOKOS LAW GROUP, LLC

WHEATON, ILLINOIS

(See Oak Brook)

Intellectual Property, Patents, Trademarks, Copyrights.

STEIN, RAY & HARRIS LLP

WHEATON, ILLINOIS

(See Chicago)

Construction and Design Law, Mechanics Liens, Government Contracts, Insurance, Complex Litigation and Construction Related Insurance Bankruptcy.

STOCK, CARLSON, FLYNN & ASSOCIATES

124 S. COUNTY FARM ROAD
WHEATON, ILLINOIS 60187
Telephone: 630-665-2500
Fax: 630-665-9427
URL: http://www.scfalaw.com
URL: http://www.dupagebusinesslaw.com

Business Organizations, Divorce, Elder Law, Estate Planning, Real Estate.

JOHN P. STOCK, III, born Duluth, Minnesota, February 9, 1946; admitted to bar, 1975, Illinois. *Education:* Monmouth College (B.A., 1969); DePaul University (J.D., 1975). Lecturer, Real Estate Law 1984, 1st United Richport Real Estate School. *Member:* Chicago (Director, Young Lawyers Section, 1979-1981), DuPage County, Illinois State and American Bar Associations. ***PRACTICE AREAS:*** Family Law (30%); Civil Litigation (15%); Real Estate (25%); Corporate; Business Litigation (10%); Divorce. **Email:** stock@scflaw.com

(This Listing Continued)

KURT A. CARLSON, admitted to bar, 1971, Illinois. *Education:* DePaul University (J.D., 1971). ***PRACTICE AREAS:*** Civil Litigation; Real Estate; Estate Planning; Business Law. **Email:** carlson@scflaw.com

JOHN W. FLYNN, born 1940; admitted to bar, 1968, Illinois. *Education:* Southern Illinois University (B.S., 1964); DePaul University (J.D., 1968). ***PRACTICE AREAS:*** Divorce Law; Real Estate; Small Corporations; Discrimination; Consumer Fraud. **Email:** flynn@scflaw.com

REPRESENTATIVE CLIENTS: West Chicago State Bank; The Conservative Baptist Foreign Mission Society; DuPage County School Districts No. 20; West Chicago Park District; Wheaton College; MAP International; Investors Real Estate; Compost Supply, Inc.

SULLIVAN TAYLOR AND GUMINA

1749 SOUTH NAPERVILLE ROAD
SUITE 106
WHEATON, ILLINOIS 60187-8192
Telephone: 630-665-7676
Fax: 630-665-8630
Email: lawyers@stglaw.com
URL: http://www.lawyers.com/sullivantaylor

Family Law including Divorce, Child Custody, Child Support, Visitation Rights, Adoption Law, Paternity, Prenuptial Agreements and Mediation, Collaborative Law, Appellate Practice.

FIRM PROFILE: The firm provides legal representation to clients undergoing change in family and personal relationships. A team approach is utilized in order to include the expertise of professionals, accountants, financial planners, and medical and mental health care providers to prepare for complex litigation and collaborative law.

MAUREEN SULLIVAN TAYLOR, born Chicago, Illinois; admitted to bar, 1982, Illinois, U.S. District Court, Northern District of Illinois and U.S. Supreme Court. *Education:* Marycrest College (B.A., 1963); Northern Illinois University (J.D., 1982); Divorce Mediation Institute (1991). Staff Member, Northern Illinois University Law Review. Recipient, American Jurisprudence Award for Outstanding Achievement in Matrimonial Law. Mediator, Mandatory Family Law Mediation Program, DuPage County. Arbitrator and Chairperson, Mandatory Court-Annexed Arbitration Program, DuPage County, 1989—. *Member:* DuPage County (Member, Committees on: Family Law, Alternative Dispute Resolution; Professional Responsibility), Illinois State and American Bar Associations; DuPage Association of Women Lawyers; The Association of Trial Lawyers of America. Fellow: Collaborative Institute of Illinois; International Academy of Collaborative Professionals. ***LANGUAGES:*** French. ***PRACTICE AREAS:*** Family Law; Divorce; Child Custody; Visitation Rights; Adoption Law; Paternity; Prenuptial Agreements; Mediation; Collaborative Law.

JULI A. GUMINA, born Waukesha, Wisconsin; admitted to bar, 1995, Illinois and U.S. District Court, Northern District of Illinois. *Education:* Loyola University (B.A., cum laude, 1991); Chicago-Kent College of Law, Illinois Institute of Technology (J.D., 1995). Member, Chicago Kent Bart Gavel Society. Recipient, Pro Bono Service Award, DuPage County Bar Association. Listed in Strathmore's Who's Who's. *Member:* DuPage County (Member: Lawyer Referral Committee; Family Law Committee; Chair, Legal Aid Committee), Illinois State and American Bar Associations. ***PRACTICE AREAS:*** Family Law; Divorce; Child Custody; Visitation Rights; Probate; Guardianship; Adoption Law; Paternity; Premarital Agreements; Mediation. **Email:** lawyers@stglaw.com

---

EMILY R. CARRARA, born Philadelphia, Pennsylvania, September 9, 1971; admitted to bar, 2001, Illinois, U.S. District Court, Northern District of Illinois and U.S. Supreme Court. *Education:* Boston University (B.A., 1993); John Marshall Law School (J.D., with honors, 2001) Dean's List. *Member:* DuPage County (Member, Family Law Committee; Chair, New Lawyers Committee), Illinois State and American Bar Associations; DuPage Association of Women Lawyers. ***PRACTICE AREAS:*** Family Law; Divorce; Child Custody; Visitation Rights; Adoption Law; Paternity; Premarital Agreements.

KELLY MARIE MOORE, born Elmhurst, Illinois, January 13, 1978; admitted to bar, 2004, Illinois and U.S. District Court, Northern District of Illinois. *Education:* University of Illinois, Urbana-Champaign (B.A., 2000); The John Marshall Law School, Chicago (J.D., 2004). *Member:* DuPage County, Illinois State and American Bar Associations. ***PRACTICE AREAS:*** Family Law; Divorce; Child Custody. **Email:** lawyer@stglaw.com

TRESSLER, SODERSTROM, MALONEY & PRIESS

2100 MANCHESTER ROAD, SUITE 950
WHEATON, ILLINOIS 60187-4532
Telephone: 630-668-2800
Telecopier: 630-668-3003
URL: http://www.tsmp.com

Chicago, Illinois Office: 233 Wacker Drive, Sears Tower, 22nd Floor, 60606. Telephone: 312-627-4000. Fax: 312-627-1717.

Bolingbrook, Illinois Office: 305 West Briarcliff Road, Suite 201, 60440-0858. Telephone: 630-759-0800. FAX: 630-759-8504.

Newark, New Jersey Office: 744 Broad Street, Suite 1510, 07102. Telephone: 973-848-2900. Fax: 973-623-0405.

Los Angeles, California Office: 1901 Avenue of the Stars, Suite 450, 90067. Telephone: 310-203-4800. Fax: 310-203-4850.

Costa Mesa, California Office: 3070 Bristol Street, Suite 450, 92626. Telephone: 714-429-2900. Fax: 714-429-2901.

(This Listing Continued)

TRESSLER, SODERSTROM, MALONEY & PRIESS, Wheaton—Continued

General Civil Litigation and Trial Practice, Insurance, Reinsurance, Litigation, Insurance Bad Faith, Appellate Practice, Business Litigation, Business Transactions, Class Action Defense, Commercial Litigation, Complex Litigation, Directors and Officers Liability, Construction Law, Architects and Engineers, Fidelity and Surety, Real Estate Litigation and Transactions, Alternative Dispute Resolution, Product Liability, Intellectual Property, Internet Law, Electronic Commerce, Environmental Law, Asbestos Litigation, Health Care, ERISA, Labor and Employment, Technology Law, Securities Litigation, Health Care, Bankruptcy, Advertising Law, Personal Injury, Trusts and Estates, Contracts, Professional Liability, Regulatory, White Collar Crime, Corporate Law, Mergers and Acquisitions, Commodities, Condominium and Common Interest Community Law, Municipal Law.

LAW FIRM ALLIANCES/ASSOCIATIONS: **HARMONIE GROUP**

MEMBERS

WILLIAM A. KINDORF, III, born St. Louis, Missouri, March 21, 1952; admitted to bar, 1977, Illinois. *Education:* University of Illinois (B.S., 1974); University of Michigan (J.D., 1976). (Also at Chicago Office). ***PRACTICE AREAS:*** Business Law; Health Care; Estate Planning; Real Estate; Corporate Law. ***Email:*** bkindorf@tsmp.com

MICHAEL J. POLACHEK, born Chicago, Illinois, October 22, 1950; admitted to bar, 1976, Illinois. *Education:* University of Illinois at Urbana-Champaign (B.A., 1973); Chicago-Kent College of Law (J.D., 1976). ***PRACTICE AREAS:*** Closely Held Business Law; Business Acquisitions; Business Divestitures; Commercial Real Estate; Zoning Law; Estate Planning. ***Email:*** mpolachek@tsmp.com

HARRY E. BARTOSIAK, born Hinsdale, Illinois, May 20, 1966; admitted to bar, 1992, Illinois. *Education:* Loyola University, Chicago (B.A., 1989; J.D., 1992). (Resident). ***PRACTICE AREAS:*** Corporate Law; Business Transactions; Health Care; Real Estate; HIPAA Compliance. ***Email:*** hbartosiak@tsmp.com

OF COUNSEL

C. JACKSON DARNALL, born Waukegan, Illinois, January 14, 1934; admitted to bar, 1960, Illinois. *Education:* Northwestern University (B.A., 1957; J.D., 1960). ***PRACTICE AREAS:*** Real Estate; Estate Planning; Closely Held Business Law; Credit Union Law. ***Email:*** cjdarnall@tsmp.com

RESIDENT ASSOCIATE

BURKE J. NIHILL, born Agana, Guam, July 9, 1978; admitted to bar, 2003, Illinois. *Education:* Illinois Wesleyan University (B.A., 2000); Chicago-Kent College of Law, Illinois Institute of Technology (J.D., 2003). ***Email:*** bnihill@tsmp.com

(For Complete Biographical Data on all Personnel, see Professional Biographies at Chicago, Illinois)

KATHLEEN VAUGHT, P.C.

600 WEST ROOSEVELT ROAD, SUITE B-1
WHEATON, ILLINOIS 60187
Telephone: 630-871-9100
Fax: 630-871-9200
URL: http://www.kathleenvaught.com

Bankruptcy, Consumer Bankruptcy, Business Bankruptcy, Financial Planning, Litigation, Tort Litigation, Contract Litigation, Real Estate, Divorce, Family, Estate Planning, Probate Law, Arbitration, Mediation, Alternative Dispute Resolution, Debt Relief Agent.

KATHLEEN VAUGHT, born Chicago, Illinois, March 1, 1948; admitted to bar, 1977, Illinois; 1978, U.S. District Court, Southern and Central Districts of Illinois; 1981, U.S. Court of Appeals, Seventh Circuit; 1991, U.S. District Court, Northern District of Illinois. *Education:* Santa Clara University (B.A., Economics, 1970); Southern Illinois University (J.D., 1976). Author: "Protecting a Co-Debtor in a Chapter 13 Bankruptcy," DuPage County Bar Association Brief, March 1994. Advanced Negotiation and Mediation Training, National Institute of Trial Advocacy. Illinois State Real Estate Broker. Member: Economic Development Commission, City of Fairview Heights, 1988-1990; Panel of Arbitrators, American Arbitration Association, 1987—;. Chair Qualified Arbitrator: DuPage County; Cook County. ***PRACTICE AREAS:*** Bankruptcy; Creditor's Rights; Estate Planning; Debt Relief Agent.

HENRY B. VESS III, P.C.

Established in 2003
2100 MANCHESTER ROAD, SUITE C1640
WHEATON, ILLINOIS 60187
Telephone: 630-510-8220
Fax: 630-510-8250
Email: henry@vesslawfirm.com
URL: http://www.vesslawfirm.com

Civil Trial Practice, Real Estate Litigation, Eminent Domain, Commercial Litigation, Personal Injury.

FIRM PROFILE: Litigation and trial of select civil cases in State and Federal courts in DuPage and surrounding counties in practice areas including eminent domain, real estate, business, commercial, and tort including personal injury.

HENRY B. VESS, III, born Boston, Massachusetts, November 2, 1947; admitted to bar, 1972, Illinois and U.S. District Court, Northern District of Illinois, including Trial Bar; 1980, U.S. Court of Appeals, Seventh Circuit. *Education:* Kenyon College (B.A., cum laude, 1969); Northwestern University (J.D., 1972). Author: "Liens Upon Illinois Tort Actions," IICLE, (1993, 2d Ed. 1995, 3rd Ed. 2002); "Walking a Tightrope: A Survey of Limitations on the Prosecutor's Closing Arguments," 64 Journal of Criminal Law and Criminology 22, 1973. Member, Board of Directors: Legal Assistance Foundation of Chicago, 1987-1990; Legal Clinic for the Disabled, Inc., 1987-1989; Public Interest Law Internship, 1985-1987. Member, Panel of Arbitrators, American Arbitration Association. *Member:* Chicago (Board of Managers, 1985-1987; Chair, Medico-Legal Relations Committee, 1988-1989), DuPage County and Illinois State Bar Associations; Illinois Trial Lawyers Association; The Association of Trial Lawyers of America. ***PRACTICE AREAS:*** Litigation; Eminent Domain; Real Estate Litigation; Business Litigation; Personal Injury. ***Email:*** henry@vesslawfirm.com

(This Listing Continued)

WALSH, KNIPPEN, KNIGHT & POLLOCK

CHARTERED
Established in 1980
601 WEST LIBERTY DRIVE
WHEATON, ILLINOIS 60187
Telephone: 630-462-1980
Fax: 630-462-1984
Email: lawyers@wkkplaw.com
URL: http://www.wkkplaw.com

Trial Practice concentrated in representing plaintiffs in complex damage cases, including claims for wrongful death & personal injury arising out of transportation, medical negligence, legal negligence and product liability cases.

FIRM PROFILE: Walsh, Knippen, Knight & Pollock, Chartered is a trial lawyer firm whose practice is limited to representing plaintiffs in complex damage cases involving personal injury, wrongful death and medical malpractice claims. The firm limits itself to a select group of clients in order to provide the highest quality and most sophisticated legal expertise possible.

Ed Walsh founded the firm in 1980. He and his partners, Jim Knippen and Tom Knight, have tried to verdict more than 350 jury and non-jury cases having a duration of three (3) days to six (6) weeks each.

Ed Walsh, Jim Knippen and the firm hold the highest rating, provided by the prestigious and highly selective Martindale-Hubbell National Law Directory. The members of the firm regularly attend and speak at seminars and continuing legal education programs in their specialty area of trial law and practice.

The skilled use of state of the art computerization, paralegals, and professionally organized mock trials/focus groups has enabled the firm's attorneys to consistently secure multi-million dollar awards for its needy clients.

EDWARD J. WALSH, born February 25, 1948; admitted to bar, 1973, Illinois. *Education:* Coe College (B.A., cum laude, 1970); Loyola University (J.D., 1973). Member, 1971-1973 and Associate Editor, 1973, Loyola University Law Journal. Law Clerk to Justice William L. Guild, Illinois Appellate Court, Second District, 1973-1974. Member, by appointment of the Illinois Supreme Court, Committees on Character and Fitness and Professionalism. *Member:* DuPage County (Associate and General Counsel, 1988-1996), Illinois State and American Bar Associations; The Association of Trial Lawyers of America; Illinois Trial Lawyers Association (Member, Board of Managers). ***PRACTICE AREAS:*** Catastrophic Injury; Medical Malpractice; Legal Malpractice. ***Email:*** ed@wkkdlaw.com

JAMES H. KNIPPEN II, born Geneva, Illinois, December 27, 1952; admitted to bar, 1979, Illinois; U.S. District Court, Northern District of Illinois and U.S. Court of Appeals, Seventh Circuit. *Education:* St. Norbert College (B.A., magna cum laude, 1975); University of Illinois (J.D., 1979). Delta Epsilon Sigma. *Member:* Du Page County and Illinois State Bar Associations; The Association of Trial Lawyers of America (ATLA). ***PRACTICE AREAS:*** Complex Commercial Litigation; Municipal Law; Malpractice Litigation; Personal Injury Litigation. ***Email:*** jim@wkkdlaw.com

THOMAS L. KNIGHT, born Cleveland, Ohio, June 24, 1945; admitted to bar, 1970, Illinois; 1985, U.S. District Court, Northern District Court including Trial Bar; 1972, U.S. Court of Appeals, Seventh Circuit. *Education:* MacMurray College (B.A., Psychology, 1967); University of Illinois (J.D., 1970). Phi Delta Phi. Private civil trial practice, 1990—. U.S. Department of Justice, Northern District of Illinois, 1985-1990. DuPage County State's Attorney Office, 1976-1984. Champaign County State's Attorney Office, 1970-1976. *Member:* DuPage County and American Bar Associations; The Association of Trial Lawyers of America; Illinois Trial Lawyers Association. ***PRACTICE AREAS:*** Medical Malpractice Litigation; Personal Injury; Defamation; Complex Litigation. ***Email:*** tom@wkkdlaw.com

BRADLEY N. POLLOCK, born St. Charles, Illinois, September 23, 1970; admitted to bar, 1995, Illinois and U.S. District Court, Northern District of Illinois. *Education:* University of Illinois (B.A., with distinction in Speech Communication, 1992); Loyola University (J.D., 1995). Phi Alpha Delta. Recipient, American Jurisprudence Award in the Study of Appellate Practice, 1994. *Member:* DuPage County and Illinois State Bar Associations; The Association of Trial Lawyers of America; Illinois Trial Lawyers Association. ***PRACTICE AREAS:*** Catastrophic Injury; Medical Malpractice Litigation. ***Email:*** brad@wkkdlaw.com

ASSOCIATE

ADAM C. KRUSE, born Norborne, Missouri, May 19, 1979; admitted to bar, 2004, Illinois. *Education:* University of Missouri at Columbia (A.B., summa cum laude, 2001; J.D., 2004). *Member:* Illinois State Bar Association; Chicago Bar Association; Illinois Trial Lawyers Association. ***PRACTICE AREAS:*** Catastrophic Injury; Medical Malpractice; Municipal Law. ***Email:*** adam@wkkdlaw.com

REFERENCES: City of Wheaton, Illinois; Village of Roselle, Illinois; Northern Trust Bank, Naperville, Illinois.

WIEDNER & McAULIFFE, LTD.

WHEATON, ILLINOIS

(See Chicago)

Workers' Compensation, Wrongful Discharge, ADA, Sexual Harassment and Human Rights Claims, Product Liability and Personal Injury Law. General Civil, Trial and Appellate Practice in both State and Federal Courts.

RUSSEL G. WINICK & ASSOCIATES, P.C.

WHEATON, ILLINOIS

(See Naperville)

Business Law, Business Development, Business Formation, Business Litigation, Business Organization, Business Planning, Business Start-Ups, Business Transactions, Business Transfers, Buy-Sell Agreements, Buying and Selling of Businesses, Closely Held Business Law, Complex Business Litigation, Emerging Business Law, Entrepreneurial Business Law, Joint Ventures, Limited Liability Company Law, Small Business Law.

GEORGE M. ZUGANELIS ATTORNEY AT LAW, P.C.

WHEATON, ILLINOIS

(See Chicago)

Criminal Defense, Real Estate, Personal Injury, Adoption, Workers Compensation.

ADLER LAW OFFICES, LTD.

WHEELING, ILLINOIS

(See Arlington Heights)

Personal Injury, Automobile Accidents, Medical Malpractice, Products Liability, Wrongful Death.

LOIS KULINSKY & ASSOCIATES, LTD.

Established in 1983

395 E. DUNDEE ROAD, SUITE 200
WHEELING, ILLINOIS 60090
Telephone: 847-459-4448
Fax: 847-459-8548
Email: lois@kulinskylaw.com
URL: http://www.lawyers.com/kulinskylaw

Family Law, Divorce, Adoptions, Child Custody, Child Support, Real Estate, Domestic Violence, Visitation Rights, Buying or Selling a Home, Trusts and Estates, Estate Planning, Wills and Probate, Incorporation.

FIRM PROFILE: Established 22 years ago, this firm services Cook, Lake, DuPage, McHenry and Kane Counties.

LOIS KULINSKY, admitted to bar, 1980, Illinois. *Education:* University of Minnesota (B.S., 1967); University of Chicago (M.A.T., 1970); Illinois Institute of Technology (J.D., with high distinction, 1980). Teaching Assistant, Legal Writing Professor, Illinois Institute of Technology, Chicago-Kent College of Law. Assisted Professor Sheldon Nahmod in writing a chapter for a book on section 1983 civil rights. Approved as a GAL and Attorney Representative for Children in Family Law Cases in the Circuit Court of Cook County. Teacher and Lecturer, Ethics a they relate to Family Law and Tax Aspects of Maintenance of Divorces, National Business Institute. *Member:* Chicago, Lake County and Illinois Bar Associations. ***REPORTED CASES:*** In RE Marriage of Brooks, case affirmed by IL Supreme Court on issue of whether property acquired after separation of the parties is marital property. IL Law was amended thereafter to reflect the case decision. ***PRACTICE AREAS:*** Family Law; Real Estate; Corporate; Estate Planning. ***Email:*** lois@kulinskylaw.com

STAFF ATTORNEY

ELEANOR M. PROCTOR, born 1951; admitted to bar, 1991, Illinois. *Education:* Northern Illinois University (B.S., 1988); John Marshall Law School (J.D., 1991). *Member:* Illinois State Bar Association. ***PRACTICE AREAS:*** Family Law.

DANIEL K. ROBIN, LTD

WHEELING, ILLINOIS

(See Arlington Heights)

Bankruptcy, Chapter 7, Chapter 13, Divorce, Family Law, Child Support, Separation, Prenuptial Agreements, Equitable Distribution, Driving While Intoxicated, Traffic Violations, Criminal Law, Wills and Trusts, Estate Planning, Asset Protection.

PATRICK W. WALSH

625 PLAINFIELD ROAD
WILLOWBROOK, ILLINOIS 60527
Telephone: 630-794-0300
Email: docs@walshdocs.com
URL: http://www.walshdocs.com

Criminal Law.

(This Listing Continued)

PATRICK W. WALSH, born Joliet, Illinois, August 20, 1963; admitted to bar, 1989, Illinois; 1990, California; 1998, Texas. *Education:* Indiana University (B.S., Public Administration, 1985); John Marshall School of Law (J.D., 1989). Law Enforcement Instructor, Illinois Law Enforcement Training and Standards Board. *Member:* DuPage County, Chicago, Illinois State and American Bar Associations; The Seventh Circuit Bar Association; State Bar of Texas American College of Mortgage Attorneys.

STUART A. FELDMAN

811 WESTWOOD LANE
WILMETTE, ILLINOIS 60091-2162
Telephone: 847-256-9800
Fax: 847-256-5191
Email: sfeldman@northshore.net
URL: http://www.stuartfeldmanlaw.com

Wills and Probate, Estate Planning, Trusts and Estates, Guardianships, Tax Planning, Taxation, IRS Audits, Business Planning, Small Business, General Business and Real Estate.

STUART A. FELDMAN, born Chicago, Illinois, December 12, 1951; admitted to bar, 1976, Illinois and U.S. District Court, Northern District of Illinois; 1978, U.S. Tax Court. *Education:* University of Wisconsin-Madison (B.B.A., with distinction, 1972); Georgetown University (J.D., 1976). Certified Public Accountant, Illinois, 1973. *Member:* Chicago Bar Association; Chicago Estate Planning Council.

MARC H. HEISLER

WILMETTE, ILLINOIS

(See Evanston)

Real Estate, Residential Real Estate, Buying and Selling a Home, Commercial Real Estate, Condominium Law and Mortgages. Business, Small Business, Partnership, Family Business and Buying and Selling a Business. Probate and Wills, Adoption Law. Civil Litigation, Chancery Practice, Collections, Personal Injury and Automobile Accidents.

S. RANDOLPH KRETCHMAR

1170 MICHIGAN AVENUE
WILMETTE, ILLINOIS 60091
Telephone: 847-853-8106
Fax: 847-853-0114
Email: s_randolph@earthlink.net

Mental Health Law, Right to Refuse Psychiatry.

S. RANDOLPH KRETCHMAR, born Ann Arbor, Michigan, February 14, 1952; admitted to bar, 2001, Illinois. *Education:* Northwestern University (B.A., magna cum laude, 1998); DePaul University (J.D., 2001). Phi Beta Kappa. ***PRACTICE AREAS:*** Mental Health Law; School Law; Civil Rights.

NEAL & McDEVITT

WILMETTE, ILLINOIS

(See Evanston)

Intellectual Property Practice (including Trademarks, Copyrights, Unfair Competition, Licensing and Litigation).

MARILEE ROBERG

121 6TH STREET
WILMETTE, ILLINOIS 60091-3435
Telephone: 847-853-1208
Fax: 847-853-9425
Email: mroberg@ameritech.net

Appellate Practice, Arbitration and Alternative Dispute Resolution.

MARILEE ROBERG, admitted to bar, 1977, Illinois and U.S. District Court, Northern District of Illinois; 1979, U.S. Court of Appeals, 7th Circuit; 1993, U. S. Court of Appeals, Third Circuit; 1994, U.S. Supreme Court; 1998, U.S. Court of Appeals, Fourth Circuit. *Education:* Swarthmore College (B.A., with honors, 1973); Case Western Reserve University (J.D., 1977). Preservation Commission, City of Evanston, 1988-1992, Co-Chair, 1990-1992; Swarthmore College Alumni Council, 1992-1995; 1998—; Swarthmore College Alumni Association, Chair, Chicago Chapter, 1998—; Board of Directors, Public Interest Law Initiative, 1991-1993; Board of Directors, Swedish Covenant Hospital, 1992-2000; 2001—; Institutional Review Board, Swedish Covenant Hospital, 1979—; Board of Directors, Covenant Ministries of Benevolence, 1993-1998, 2000-2005, Chair, 1997-1998. *Member:* Chicago (Member, Board of Managers, 1991-1993; Chair, Federal Civil Procedure Committee, 1989-1990; Co-Chair, Alternative Dispute Resolution Committee, 2001-2002; Young Lawyers Section: Director, 1983-1985; Chair, Architecture and the Law Committee, 1981-1983; Recipient, David C. Hilliard Award for Outstanding Committee Service to the Legal Profession and Community, 1983; Editor, The Practical Guide to Illinois Preservation Law), Illinois State and American (Member, Dispute Resolution Section) Bar Associations; Women's Bar Association of Illinois; Appellate Lawyers Association; Commercial and Securities Arbitration Panels, American Arbitration Association; NASD Dispute Resolution (Arbitrator). ***PRACTICE AREAS:*** Appellate Practice; Arbitration; Alternative Dispute Resolution; Mediation.

COURI & COURI

Established in 1965

552 LINCOLN AVENUE
WINNETKA, ILLINOIS 60093
Telephone: 847-446-7372
Fax: 847-501-4858

Civil Trial Practice. Civil Liability, Corporate, Banking, Probate, Estate Planning, Commercial Real Estate, Residential Real Estate, Family and Tax Law.

MEMBERS OF FIRM

PHILLIP E. COURI, born Peoria, Illinois, May 6, 1937; admitted to bar, 1962, Illinois; U.S. District Court, Northern District of Illinois and U.S. Court of Appeals, Seventh Circuit. *Education:* Marquette University (B.S., 1959); DePaul University (J.D., 1962). Phi Alpha Delta. *Member:* Chicago, Illinois State, American and Arab-American Bar Associations. ***Email:*** peccouri@attglobal.net

DAVID G. BURDEN, born Evanston, Illinois, October 8, 1936; admitted to bar, 1962, Illinois. *Education:* Loyola University (B.S., with honors, 1959); DePaul University (J.D., 1962). Phi Alpha Delta. ***Email:*** dgburden@aol.com

PHILLIP A. COURI, born Evanston, Illinois, February 19, 1969; admitted to bar, 1995, Illinois, U.S. District Court, Northern District of Illinois and U.S. Court of Appeals, Seventh Circuit. *Education:* University of Notre Dame (B.A., 1991); Loyola University (J.D., 1995). Member, American Inns of Court, 1995—. *Member:* Chicago, Illinois State and American Bar Associations; Arab-American Bar Association. ***Email:*** paccouri@attglobal.net

GEORGE L. PLUMB (1936-1992)

REFERENCES: Bank One, Winnetka; Harris Bank, Glencoe; Harris Bank, Winnetka.

MARC H. HEISLER

WINNETKA, ILLINOIS

(See Evanston)

Real Estate, Residential Real Estate, Buying and Selling a Home, Commercial Real Estate, Condominium Law and Mortgages. Business, Small Business, Partnership, Family Business and Buying and Selling a Business. Probate and Wills. Adoption Law. Civil Litigation, Chancery Practice, Collections, Personal Injury and Automobile Accidents.

PADGITT, PADGITT & PEPPEY LTD.

Established in 1978

SUITE 100, 560 GREEN BAY ROAD
WINNETKA, ILLINOIS 60093-2260
Telephone: 847-446-2900
Facsimile: 847-446-2908
Email: info@ppp-ltd.com

General Practice. Corporate, Real Estate, Probate and Estate Planning Law.

FIRM PROFILE: Since 1978 the firm has provided legal counseling and transactional services for closely held and family corporations, other business enterprises, health care entities and individuals. In addition, the firm is continuously engaged in estate planning, trust administration, probate and real estate matters.

DONALD L. PADGITT, born Chicago, Illinois, July 3, 1930; admitted to bar, 1959, Illinois; 1961, U.S. District Court, Northern District of Illinois; 1965, U.S. Tax Court; 1981, U.S. Court of Appeals, Seventh Circuit. *Education:* Knox College (A.B., 1954); University of Chicago (J.D., 1958). Phi Delta Phi. *Member:* Illinois State Bar Association; American Health Lawyers Association; National Academy of Elder Law Attorneys. ***PRACTICE AREAS:*** Business Law; Corporate Law; Probate; Estate Planning. ***Email:*** donpadgitt@ppp-ltd.com

D. LEE PADGITT, born Oak Park, Illinois, December 22, 1960; admitted to bar, 1990, Utah; 1991, Illinois and U.S. District Court, Northern District of Illinois. *Education:* University of Oregon (B.S., 1983); University of Utah (J.D., 1989). *Member:* Chicago and Illinois State Bar Associations; Utah State Bar; National Academy of Elder Law Attorneys. ***PRACTICE AREAS:*** Residential Real Estate; Commercial Real Estate; Probate; Estate Planning; Business Law; Corporate Law; Intellectual Property; Zoning Law. ***Email:*** lpadgitt@ppp-ltd.com

BROOKE L. B. PEPPEY, born Milwaukee, Wisconsin, October 4, 1962; admitted to bar, 1989, Illinois and U.S. District Court, Northern District of Illinois. *Education:* University of Wisconsin-Madison (B.S., with honors, 1985); New York University (J.D., 1989). Phi Beta Kappa. *Member:* Chicago, Illinois State and American Bar Associations; National Academy of Elder Law Attorneys. ***PRACTICE AREAS:*** Probate and Estate Planning Law; Taxation; Trusts and Estates; Trust Law; Family Limited Partnerships; Guardianship and Conservatorship; Business Successions; Premarital Agreements. ***Email:*** bpeppey@aol.com

---

MICHAEL MELANDER, admitted to bar, 2003, Illinois; 2004, Iowa, U.S. District Court, Central District of Illinois. *Education:* Ohio University, Tutorial College (B.A., with honors, 1995); University of Illinois, Urbana-Champaign (J.D., 2002). *Member:* Illinois State and Iowa State Bar Associations. ***PRACTICE AREAS:*** Estate Planning; Trusts and Estates; Probate; Business Law; Contracts; Partnership Law; Elder Law; Social Security; Medicare and Medicaid; Guardianship and Conservatorship; Premarital Agreements; Real Estate; Zoning, Planning and Land Use; Taxation; Litigation. ***Email:*** mmelander@ppp-ltd.com

ANA M. MENCINI

Established in 2004

345 GEORGETOWN SQUARE, SUITE 206
WOOD DALE, ILLINOIS 60191
Telephone: 630-616-3900
Fax: 630-616-3913
Email: amencini@mencinilaw.com
URL: http://www.mencinilaw.com

Real Estate (Residential and Commercial), Landlord/Tenant, Business Law, Family Law, Estate Planning, Wills, Trusts, Powers of Attorney, Probate, Immigration.

ANA M. MENCINI, born Poughkeepsie, New York, August 15, 1969; admitted to bar, 2001, Illinois and U.S. District Court, Northern District of Illinois. *Education:* Lake Forest College (B.A., English, 1990); DePaul University (M.A., Writing, 1993); Chicago-Kent College of Law, Illinois Institute of Technology (J.D., 2001). Co-Author: "Internet Road Shows: Oral or Written Prospectus Under the Securities Act of 1993," Illinois Bar Journal, January 2002. Author: "New Technology Raises a New Question: What is the Definition of a Broker-Dealer?" Corporation, Securities and Business Law Forum, March 2003. Former Vice President, Documentation, Training and Quality Assurance, SunGard Futures Systems, Chicago. *Member:* Chicago, DuPage County, Illinois State and American Bar Associations. ***PRACTICE AREAS:*** Real Estate; Residential Real Estate; Commercial Real Estate; Business Law; Family Law; Estate Planning; Wills; Trust Law; Powers of Attorney; Probate; Immigration Law.

RICHARD L. HIRSH & ASSOCIATES, P.C.

WOODRIDGE, ILLINOIS

(See Hinsdale)

Bankruptcy, Personal Bankruptcy, Debtor and Creditor, Foreclosures and Buy-Sell Agreements.

LAW OFFICES OF
JOHN J. LYNCH

3590 HOBSON ROAD, SUITE 103
WOODRIDGE, ILLINOIS 60517
Telephone: 630-253-2900
Fax: 630-968-5540
URL: http://www.johnjlynch.net
Email: jlynch@johnjlynchesq.com
URL: http://www.johnjlynchesq.com

Bankruptcy, Wills and Trusts, Probate, Real Estate, Business Law.

JOHN J. LYNCH, born Union City, New Jersey, August 31, 1958; admitted to bar, 1999, Illinois. *Education:* Florida International University (B.A., 1993); Nova Southeastern University (J.D., 1998). *Member:* DuPage County and Illinois State Bar Associations; American Bankruptcy Institute. ***PRACTICE AREAS:*** Real Estate; Estate Planning; Bankruptcy; Business Law; Asset Protection; Construction Law; Probate; Wills; Trusts and Estates.

STEVEN R. MERICAN, P.C.

3840 VARDON COURT
SUITE 200
WOODRIDGE, ILLINOIS 60517
Telephone: 630-579-6460
Fax: 630-579-6461
URL: http://www.lawyers.com/localcounsel
Email: merican@illinoislocalcounsel.com
URL: http://www.illinoislocalcounsel.com

Appellate Practice, Civil Appeals, Criminal Appeals, Products Liability, Toxic Torts, Toxic Exposure, Commercial Litigation, Commercial Torts, Breach of Contract, Contract Litigation, Personal Rights, Election Law, Civil Litigation.

STEVEN R. MERICAN, admitted to bar, 1982, Illinois. *Education:* Trenton State College (B.A., cum laude, 1978); Chicago-Kent College of Law (J.D., 1982). ***PRACTICE AREAS:*** Appellate Practice; Civil Appeals; Criminal Appeals; Products Liability; Toxic Torts; Toxic Exposure; Commercial Litigation; Commercial Torts; Breach of Contract; Contract Litigation; Personal Rights; Election Law; Civil Litigation.

THE LAKIN LAW FIRM, P.C.

Established in 1980

300 EVANS AVENUE
P.O. BOX 229
WOOD RIVER, ILLINOIS 62095-0027
Telephone: 618-254-1127
Telecopier: 618-254-0193
Email: lakinlaw@com
URL: http://www.lakinlaw.com

St. Louis, Missouri Office: 1015 Locust Street, Suite 800. Telephone: 314-231-3138.

General Trial Practice. Admiralty, Federal Employers Liability Act (FELA), Personal Injury and Workers Compensation.

(This Listing Continued)

L. THOMAS LAKIN, born Wood River, Illinois, May 21, 1940; admitted to bar, 1970, Illinois; 1972, U.S. District Court, Southern District of Illinois. *Education:* Southern Illinois University (B.S., 1964); University of Louisville (J.D., 1969). *Member:* Madison County, Wood River and Illinois State Bar Associations; Illinois Trial Lawyers Association; The Association of Trial Lawyers of America (Chairman, Young Lawyers Section, 1973); Lawyer-Pilots Bar Association; Worker's Compensation Lawyers Association. ***PRACTICE AREAS:*** Admiralty Law; Federal Employers Liability Act (FELA); Personal Injury Law. ***Email:*** toml@lakinlaw.com

BRADLEY M. LAKIN, born Alton, Illinois, October 9, 1970; admitted to bar, 1997, Illinois; 1998, U.S. District Court, Southern District of Illinois. *Education:* University of Illinois (B.S., 1995); Northern Illinois University (J.D., 1997). ***PRACTICE AREAS:*** Maritime Law; Personal Injury; Federal Employers Liability Act (FELA); Nursing Home Regulation. ***Email:*** bradl@lakinlaw.com

ASSOCIATES

ROY C. DRIPPS, born St. Louis, Missouri, July 19, 1956; admitted to bar, 1982, Missouri and Illinois; 1985, U.S. District Court, Eastern District of Missouri and U.S. Court of Appeals, Eighth Circuit; 1986, U.S. District Court, Southern District of Illinois; 1990, U.S. Claims Court; 1991, U.S. Court of Appeals, Seventh Circuit; 1992, U.S. Court of Appeals, Tenth Circuit; 1999, U.S. District Court, Eastern and Western Districts of Arkansas, U.S. District Court, District of Nebraska and U.S. Supreme Court. *Education:* St. Louis University (A.B., 1978; J.D., cum laude, 1981). Law Clerk: Justice Moses W. Harrison, 1981-1983; Justice James Mejda, 1983-1984. Instructor, Legal Research and Writing, St. Louis University School of Law, 1980-1981. Adjunct Professor, Trial Advocacy, St. Louis University Law School, 1997-1998. *Member:* The Bar Association of Metropolitan St. Louis; Alton-Wood River and Illinois State Bar Associations; The Missouri Bar; Illinois Trial Lawyers Association; The Association of Trial Lawyers of America; Missouri Association of Trial Attorneys. ***REPORTED CASES:*** Lewis v. Lewis & Clark Marine, Inc., 531 U.S. 438, 121 S. Ct. 993, 148 L.Ed.2d 931 (2001); Hearn v. Beelman Trucking Co., 507 N.E.2d 1295 (Ill.App. 1987); Bland v. Norfolk & Western Railway Co., 506 N.E.2d 1291 (Ill. 1987); Lane v. City of Harvey, 533 N.E.2d 75 (Ill.App. 1988); In re Apex Oil Co., 884 F.2d 343 (8th Cir. 1989); Little v. IGA, 544 N.E.2d 28 (Ill.App. 1989); Redmon v. Austin, 543 N.E.2d 1351 (Ill.App. 1989); Wood v. Procter & Gamble Mfg. Co., 787 S.W.2d 816 (Mo.App. 1990); Sheary v. State Farm Mutual Automobile Insurance Co., 566 N.E.2d 794 (Ill.App. 1991); Karr v. Noel, 571 N.E.2d 271 (Ill.App. 1991); Elberg v. Mobil Oil Corp., 967 F.2d 1146 (7th Cir. 1992); Williams v. Missouri Pacific Railroad Co., 11 F.3d 132, 39 Fed.R.Evid.Serv. 1381 (10th Cir. 1993); Gilbert's Ethan Allen Gallery v. Ethan Allen, Inc., 642 N.E.2d 470 (Ill. 1994); May v. Wood River Township Hospital, 629 N.E.2d 170 (Ill.App. 1994); Environmental Control Systems v. Pollution Control Board, 630 N.E.2d 554 (Ill.App. 1994); Walker v. American River Transportation Co., 660 N.E.2d 550 (Ill.App. 1996); In re Marriage of Lakin, 662 N.E.2d 617, 278 (Ill.App.1996); Lakin v. Board of Election Commissioners, 676 N.E.2d 637 (111.1996); In re Complaint of McCarthy Brothers, Inc., 83 F.3d 821 (7th Cir. 1996); Allen v. Norman Brothers, Inc., 678 N.E.2d 317, 286 (Ill.App.1997); Johnson v. ADM-Growmark River Systems, Inc., 295 Ill.App.3d 463, 693 N.E.2d 477 (1998); Hearn v. American River Transportation Co., 303 Ill.App.3d 619, 707 N.E.2d 1283 (1999); Morrison v. Wagner, 191 Ill.2d 162, 729 N.E.2d 486 (2000) (amicus brief supporting plaintiff); Hanks v. Luhr Bros., Inc., 303 N.E.2d 661, 707 N.E.2d 1266 (1999), certiorari denied, U.S., 145 L.Ed. 314, 120 S.Ct. 402 (1999); Niepotter v. Central Illinois Public Service Co., 303 Ill.App.3d 632, 707 N.E.2d 1278 (1999); Norfolk & Southern Railway v. Guthrie, —F.3d— (7th Cir. 2000); Boxdorfer v. DaimlerChrysler Corp., —Ill.App.3d—, —N.E.2d—, 2003 WL 21003724 (Ill.App.5 Dist. 2003); Morton v. Madison County Nursing Home Auxiliary, 198 Ill.2d 183, 761 N.E.2d 145, 260 Ill.Dec. 301 (2001); Callis, Papa, Jackstadt & Halloran, P.C. v. Norfolk and Western Ry. Co., 195 Ill.2d 356, 748 N.E.2d 153, 254 Ill.Dec. 707, 167 L.R.R.M. (BNA) 2507 (Ill. 2001) (amicus curiae counsel); Norfolk Southern Railway Co. v. Guthrie, 233 F.3d 532, 142 Lab. Cas. P 10,889 (7th Cir. 2000); Johnson v. Daggett, Van Dover, Donovan & Perry, PLLC 99 F.Supp.2d 1008 (E.D.Ark. 2000). ***PRACTICE AREAS:*** Admiralty and Maritime Law; Railroad Law; Products Liability; Personal Injury; Appellate Practice. ***Email:*** royd@lakinlaw.com

RICHARD J. BURKE, JR., born Passaic, New Jersey, July 10, 1953; admitted to bar, 1978, Missouri; 1983, U.S. District Court, Eastern District of Missouri and U.S. Court of Appeals, Eighth Circuit; 1998, Illinois, U.S. District Court, Southern District of Illinois and U.S. Court of Appeals, Seventh Circuit; 1999, U.S. Supreme Court. *Education:* Knox College (B.A., cum laude, 1975); Washington University (J.D., 1978). With St. Louis City Public Defender's Office, 1978-1982. Faculty Member, Missouri Public Defender Association. *Member:* The Bar Association of Metropolitan St. Louis; The Missouri Bar; Illinois State and American Bar Associations (Tort & Insurance Practice and Medicine & Law Committee); Lawyers Association of St. Louis; Missouri Association of Criminal Defense Lawyers; Missouri Association of Trial Attorneys; The Association of Trial Lawyers of America; Illinois Trial Lawyers Association. ***PRACTICE AREAS:*** Products Liability Law; Personal Injury Law; Federal Criminal Law; Railroad Law; Negligence and Malpractice Law; Class Actions. ***Email:*** richardb@lakinlaw.com

MARC W. PARKER, born Belleville, Illinois, July 19, 1965; admitted to bar, 1990, Illinois and U.S. District Court, Central and Southern Districts of Illinois. *Education:* Belleville Area College; Southern Illinois University at Edwardsville (B.S., with honors, 1987); St. Louis University (J.D., cum laude, 1990). Order of the Woolsack. Law Clerk: Illinois Appellate Court Justice Charles W. Chapman, 1990-1991; Illinois Supreme Court Justice Moses W. Harrison, 1992-1993. Chief Civil Assistant States Attorney, St. Clair County, Illinois, 1991-1992. *Member:* Illinois Trial Lawyers Association; American Trial Lawyers Association; Association of Trial Lawyers of America. ***PRACTICE AREAS:*** Admiralty Law; Personal Injury; Workers Compensation. ***Email:*** marcp@lakinlaw.com

CRAIG J. JENSEN, born Chicago, Illinois, August 8, 1959; admitted to bar, 1988, Illinois; 1996, U.S. District Court, Southern District of Illinois. *Education:* Loyola University (B.S., 1982); John Marshall Law School (J.D., 1987). *Member:* Alton-Wood River, Madison County and Illinois State Bar Associations; Illinois Trial Lawyers Association. ***PRACTICE AREAS:*** Personal Injury; Admiralty and Maritime Law. ***Email:*** craigj@lakinlaw.com

(This Listing Continued)

CHARLES W. ARMBRUSTER, III, born St. Louis, Missouri, December 25, 1966; admitted to bar, 1992, Missouri; 1993, Illinois; 1999, West Virginia. *Education:* University of Michigan (B.A., 1989); Washington University (J.D., 1992). ***PRACTICE AREAS:*** FELA; Personal Injury. ***Email:*** charlesa@lakinlaw.com

GAIL RENSHAW, born St. Louis, Missouri; admitted to bar, 1976, Missouri; 1981, U.S. Supreme Court; 1992, Illinois, U.S. Court of Appeals, Sixth, Seventh, Eighth and Tenth Circuits, U.S. District Court, Eastern District of Missouri and U.S. District Court, Southern District of Illinois. *Education:* University of Missouri at St. Louis (B.A., magna cum laude, 1972); Georgetown University (J.D., 1976). Recipient, Whitehall Foundation Scholarship. Member, Illinois Bar Journal Editorial Board, 1997-2002. Law Clerk, Justice John Kelly, Jr., Missouri Court of Appeals, 1978-1979. *Member:* Bar Association of Metropolitan St. Louis; Illinois State Bar Association; The Missouri Bar; Illinois Trial Lawyers Association; The Association of Trial Lawyers of America; Women's Caucus Illinois State Association; Women's Caucus State Liaison; Illinois Appellate Attorneys Association; Women Lawyers Association. ***LANGUAGES:*** French. ***REPORTED CASES:*** William D. Heldenbrand v. Roadmaster Corporation, 277 Ill.App.3d 664, 660 N.E.2d 854; Ronnie W. Walker v. American River Transportation, 277 Ill.App.2d 87, 660 N.E.2d 550; Hartman v. Pittsburgh Corning Corp., 199 Ill.Dec. 779, 634 N.E.2d 1133, appeal denied, 205 Ill.Dec. 162, 645 N.E.2d 1279 (1994); Turner v. Jarden, 275 Ill.App.2d 890, 656 N.E.2d 1125, 212 Ill.Dec. 291 (Ill.App. 1995); Bazzell v. Bazzell, 907 S.W.2d 328 (Mo.App. E.D. 1995); Ross v. Union Pacific R.R.Co., 906 S.W.2d 711 (Mo. 1995); Mamer v. Apex R.E.&T., 59 F.3d 780 (8th Cir. Mo. 1995); Ross v. Union Pacific R.Co., 1995 WL 15466 (Mo.App.E.D. 1995); Mike Schlemer, Inc. v. Pulizos, 267 Ill.App.3d 393, 642 N.E.2d 200, 204 Ill.Dec. 738 (Ill.App. 1994); Weathers v. Bean Dredging Corp., 26 F.3d 70 (8th Cir. Ark. 1994); In re Marriage of Parks, 258 Ill.App.3d 479, 630 N.E.2d 509, 196 Ill.Dec. 574 (Ill.App. 1994); Martz v. MacMurray College, 255 Ill.App.3d 749, 627 N.E.2d 1133, 194 Ill.Dec. 491, 89 Ed.Law.Rep. 186 (Ill.App. 1993); Williams v. Missouri Pacific R.R.Co., II F.3d 132, 39 Fed.R.Evid.Serv. 1381 (10th Cir. Okla. 1993); Graham v. Hildebrand, 248 Ill.App.3d 742, 618 N.E.2d 1259, 188 Ill.Dec. 689 (Ill.App. 1993); Piper v. Missouri Pacific R.Co., 847 S.W.2d 907 (Mo.App.E.D. 1993); Rutledge v. Scott Chotin, Inc., 972 F.2d 820 (7th Cir. Ill. 1992); Johnson v. Norfolk & Western R.Co., 836 S.W.2d 83 (Mo.App.E.D. 1992); Elberg v. Oil Corp., 967 F.2d 1146, 1993 A.M.C. 328 (7th Cir. Ill. 1992); Rogers v. Illinois Cent. R.Co., 833 S.W.2d 426 (Mo.App.E.D. 1992); Paul v. Missouri Pacific R.Co., 963 F.2d 1058 (8th Cir. Ark. 1992); Lloyd v. Missouri Pacific R.Co., 832 S.W.2d 310 (Mo.App.E.D. 1992); Alexander v. Missouri Pacific R.Co., 827 S.W.2d 757 (Mo.App.E.D. 1992); Green v. Groose, 959 F.2d 708 (8th Cir. Mo. 1992); Gardocki v. Gardocki, 682 S.W.2d 496 (Mo.App.E.D. 1984); Trapani v. Trapani, 684 S.W.2d 500 (Mo.App.E.D. 1984); Berger v. City of University City, 676 S.W.2d 39 (Mo.App.E.D. 1984); State v. Robinson, 670 S.W.2d 541 (Mo.App.E.D. 1984); Thomas v. State, 665 S.W.2d 621 (Mo.App.E.D. 1983); Adail v. Wyrick, 711 F.2d 99 (8th Cir. Mo. 1983); State v. Clark, 652 S.W.2d 123 (Mo. 1983); Adams v. Kerr, 655 S.W.2d 49 (Mo.App.E.D. 1983); Ware v. Ware, 647 S.W.2d 582 (Mo.App.E.D. 1983); Vaughn v. Sears Roebuck & Co., 643 S.W.2d 30 (Mo.App.E.D. 1982); Villanueva v. State, 636 S.W.2d 103 (Mo.App.E.D. 1982); Adail v. Wyrick, 671 F.2d 1218 (8th Cir. Mo. 1982); State v. Taylor, 626 S.W. 647 (Mo.App.E.D. 1981); U.S. v. Cabbell, 662 F.2d 477 (8th Cir. Iowa 1981); Bonner v. Wyrick, 650 F.2d 150 (8th Cir. Mo. 1981); Hollis v. Capritta, 612 S.W.2d 816 (Mo.App.E.D. 1981); Delay v. Delay, 612 S.W.2d 391 (Mo.App.E.D. 1981); Cabbell v. U.S., 636 F.2d 246 (8th Cir. Iowa 1980); In re Marriage of Biancardi, 611 S.W.2d 250 (Mo.App.E.D. 1980); State ex rel. Bullington v. Mason, 593 S.W.2d 224 (Mo.1980); State ex rel. Westfall v. Mason, 594 S.W.2d 908 (Mo.1980); State v. Fultz, 598 S.W.2d 478 (Mo.App.E.D. 1980); Herring v. State, 590 S.W.2d (Mo.App.E.D. 1979). ***PRACTICE AREAS:*** Appellate Practice; Torts; Admiralty Law; Class Actions. ***Email:*** gailr@lakinlaw.com

JOHN E. WINTERSCHEIDT, born Seneca, Kansas, March 25, 1964; admitted to bar, 1990, Missouri; 1991, Illinois; 1996, Kansas. *Education:* Augustana College (B.A., History, 1986); Washington University (J.D., 1990). Formerly with, Valentine & Rouse. *Member:* Illinois State and Kansas Bar Associations; The Missouri Bar. ***PRACTICE AREAS:*** Workers Compensation. ***Email:*** johnw@lakinlaw.com

DANIEL J. COHEN, born St. Louis, Missouri, January 16, 1967; admitted to bar, 1992, Missouri; 1993, Illinois; 1995, U.S. District Court, Eastern District of Missouri; 1997, U.S. Court of Appeals, Fifth Circuit. *Education:* Washington University (B.A., 1989; J.D., 1992). *Member:* Association of Trial Lawyers of America; Missouri Association of Trial Attorneys. ***PRACTICE AREAS:*** Class Actions; Federal Employers Liability Act (FELA); Personal Injury; Negligence; Product Liability; Premises Liability; Motor Vehicle Accidents and Injuries. ***Email:*** danc@lakinlaw.com

JEFFREY A.J. MILLAR, born Toronto, Ontario, Canada, September 24, 1973; admitted to bar, 1999, Missouri; 2000, Illinois, U.S. Court of Appeals, Seventh Circuit, U.S. District Court, Southern District of Illinois and U.S. District Court, Northern and Eastern Districts of Oklahoma. *Education:* University of Detroit Mercy (J.D., 1999); University of Windsor (LL.B., 1999). *Member:* Illinois State and American Bar Associations; The Missouri Bar; The Association of Trial Lawyers of America. ***PRACTICE AREAS:*** Complex Litigation; Class Actions; Personal Injury; Workers Compensation. ***Email:*** jeffm@lakinlaw.com

THOMAS G. MAAG, born Fort Campbell, Kentucky, September 8, 1975; admitted to bar, 2000, Illinois; 2001, U.S. District Court, Southern District of Illinois and U.S. Court of Appeals, Seventh and Eighth Circuits. *Education:* University of Mississippi (B.P.A., 1997); Southern Illinois University (J.D, 2000). Phi Delta Phi. Law Clerk to the Honorable G. Patrick Murphy, Chief Judge, U.S. District Court, Southern District of Illinois, 2001-2002. *Member:* Illinois State Bar Association; Illinois Trial Lawyers Association. ***PRACTICE AREAS:*** Class Actions; Consumer Fraud; Personal Injury; Workers Compensation. ***Email:*** tomm@lakinlaw.com

PAUL A. MARKS, born Alton, Illinois; admitted to bar, 1999, Missouri and Illinois. *Education:* Illinois State University (B.S., Political Science and History, 1988); St. Louis University (J.D., 1999). Law Clerk to Justice Thomas M. Welch, Illinois Court of Appeals, Fifth District. *Member:* Bar Association of Metropolitan St. Louis; Tri-City Bar Association; Madison County, Illinois State and American Bar Associations; The Missouri Bar. ***PRACTICE AREAS:*** Class Actions Litigation. ***Email:*** paulm@lakinlaw.com

MICHAEL T. BLOTEVOGEL, born Waverly, Missouri, March 23, 1972; admitted to bar, 2003, Missouri and U.S. District Court, District of Missouri; 2004, Illinois and U.S.

(This Listing Continued)

THE LAKIN LAW FIRM, P.C., Wood River—Continued

District Court, Southern District of Illinois; U.S. District Court, Northern and Eastern Districts of Oklahoma. *Education:* Truman State University (B.A., B.S., magna cum laude, 1995); Washington University (J.D., 2003); University of Minnesota (M.A., 1997). Order of the Coif; Phi Kappa Phi; Pi Sigma Alpha. Notes Editor, Washington University Law Quarterly. Author: "Testing Title VII'S Patience? The Need for Better Remedies when State 'Teacher Testing' Requirements Have a Disparate Impact on Employment Opportunities for Minority Populations," Washington University Law Quarterly, Summer 2003. *Member:* Metropolitan, St. Louis and American Bar Associations; American Trial Lawyers Association. ***PRACTICE AREAS:*** Railroad Law; Federal Employers Liability Act (FELA); Nursing Home Negligence; Civil Litigation; Personal Injury. ***Email:*** mikeb@lakinlaw.com

GARY E. PEEL, born East St. Louis, Illinois, March 15, 1944; admitted to bar, 1968, Illinois; 1971, U.S. District Court, Southern District of Illinois; 1974, U.S. Court of Appeals, Seventh Circuit; 1975, U.S. Supreme Court; 1979, Arizona; 1980, U.S. Court of Appeals, Eighth Circuit; 1981, Missouri; 1982, U.S. District Court, Eastern District of Missouri. *Education:* Southern Illinois University (B.A., 1966); University of Arkansas (J.D., 1968). Adjunct Associate Professor, Trial Advocacy, St. Louis University School of Law, 1996. Coordinator on matters of Specialization, NBTA State, Illinois, 1991—. Chief Judge, James L. Foreman. Circuit Judges, William D. Stiehl and William L. Beatty. Formerly with: Reed, Armstrong, Gorman & Coffey, 1969-1974; Chapman & Chapman, 1974-1978; Lakin, Herndon & Peel, P.C., 1978-1983; Law Offices of Gary E. Peel, 1983-1993; Peel, Beatty & Walters, 1993-1996; Peel, Beatty, Motil & Walters, Peel, Beatty & Motil, 1996-2003. Member, American Board of Professional Liability Attorneys (Certified as a Diplomat). Member, Merit Selection Panel to Select a part-time Federal Magistrate for the United States District Court for the Southern District of Illinois, 1990. *Member:* Tri-City (Secretary, 1978-1979), Madison County (President, 1983-1984; Vice President, 1982-1983; Secretary, 1972-1973), Illinois State (Member, Standing Committee of Continuing Legal Education; Appointed, 1995-1996; Re-Appointed, 1996-1997) and American (Member, General Practice Section, Vice Chairman: Insurance and Tort Committee, 1987-1989; Litigation Committee, 1989-1992; Specialization and Certification Committee, 1992-1993) Bar Associations; State Bar of Arizona; The Missouri Bar; Illinois Trial Lawyers Association; The Association of Trial Lawyers of America. (Board Certified, Civil Trial Advocacy by the National Board of Trial Advocacy). ***REPORTED CASES:*** Gary E. Peel v. Attorney Registration and Disciplinary Commission of Illinois (1990) 110 S.Ct. 2281, 496 U.S. 91. ***PRACTICE AREAS:*** Class Actions; Legal Malpractice; Plaintiffs Personal Injury; Nursing Home Litigation.

GERALD R. WALTERS, born Granite City, Illinois, May 16, 1947; admitted to bar, 1974, Illinois and U.S. District Court, Southern District of Illinois; 2003, Missouri. *Education:* University of Illinois (B.A., 1969; J.D., 1974). [U.S. Army, 1970-1972]. ***PRACTICE AREAS:*** Class Actions; Consumer Fraud; Personal Injury. ***Email:*** geraldw@lakinlaw.com

ELIZABETH A. PARKER, born Alton, Illinois, December 28, 1951; admitted to bar, 2001, North Carolina and U.S. District Court, Middle District of North Carolina; 2003, Missouri and U.S. District Court, Southern District of Illinois; 2004, Illinois and U.S. Court of Appeals, Seventh Circuit. *Education:* Western Michigan University (B.S., 1996); Arizona State University (J.D., 2000). Phi Alpha Delta. Registered Respiratory Therapist, 1983. *Member, Alton-Woodriver and Illinois State Bar Associations; The Missouri Bar.* ***PRACTICE AREAS:*** Nursing Home Regulation; Personal Injury; Workers Compensation. ***Email:*** lizp@lakinlaw.com

DENNIS J. BARTON, III, born Indianapolis, Indiana, July 14, 1973; admitted to bar, 2003, Missouri. *Education:* Indiana University (B.S., 1996; B.A., 1996); Washington University (J.D., 2003). Recipient, William M. Pomecantz Trial Prize. ***PRACTICE AREAS:*** Consumer Class Actions; Personal Injury; Employment Law; Contract Litigation. ***Email:*** dennisb@lakinlaw.com

RODNEY D. CAFFEY, born Alton, Illinois; admitted to bar, 2003, Illinois and U.S. District Court, Southern District of Illinois and Missouri. *Education:* Illinois State University (B.S., 1992); Oklahoma City University (J.D., 2002). Phi Delta Phi. International Legal Fraternity, 2002—. *Member:* American Trial Lawyers Association; Illinois Trial Lawyers Association. ***PRACTICE AREAS:*** Personal Injury; Maritime Law; Products Liability; Railroad Law; Federal Employers Liability Act (FELA); Nursing Home Litigation. ***Email:*** rodneyc@lakinlaw.com

ROBERT W. SCHMIEDER, II, born Belleville, Illinois, September 7, 1971; admitted to bar, 1996, Missouri; 1997, Illinois, U.S. District Court, Southern District of Illinois and U.S. District Court, Eastern District of Missouri; U.S. District Court, Central District of Illinois; U.S. Court of Appeals, Seventh and Eighth Circuits. *Education:* Northwestern University (B.A., 1993); Southern Illinois University (J.D., cum laude, 1996). Order of Barristers. Member: National Health Law Moot Court; Moot Court Board. Board of Editors, Southern Illinois University Law Journal. Recipient: Best Comment Award; CALI Award for Excellence-Commercial Law I. Author: "Stuck on the Tracks: The FELA Engine vs. The Ethical Caboose," 20 S. Ill. U. L.J. 331, 1996; "Workers' Compensation and Contribution in Illinois: Punching a Hole in the Kotecki Ceiling," 20 S. Ill. U. L.J. 651, 1996; "Health Care Lawyer," Illinois State Bar Association, vol. 11, nos. 1-4, vol. 12, nos. 1-4. *Member:* The Missouri Bar; Illinois State and American Bar Associations. ***PRACTICE AREAS:*** Litigation; Insurance; Products Liability; Torts. ***Email:*** robs@lakinlaw.com

OF COUNSEL

BENJAMIN B. ALLEN, born St. Louis, Missouri, July 2, 1940; admitted to bar, 1969, Illinois and U.S. District Court, Southern District of Illinois; 1980, U.S. Court of Appeals, Seventh Circuit. *Education:* Southern Illinois University (B.S., 1964); University of Oklahoma (J.D., 1968). Phi Delta Phi. President, 1965-1968. Assistant State Attorney, Madison County, Illinois, 1969-1973. *Member:* Illinois State Bar Association; American Trial Lawyers Association. ***PRACTICE AREAS:*** Felonies; Personal Injury; Workers Compensation. ***Email:*** bena@lakinlaw.com

CHARLES W. CHAPMAN, born 1942; admitted to bar, 1967, Illinois and U.S. District Court, Southern District of Illinois; 1969, U.S. Court of Appeals, Seventh Circuit; 1979, U.S. Supreme Court. *Education:* Southern Illinois University (B.A., 1963); St. Louis University (J.D., 1967); University of Virginia (LL.M., 1992). Adjunct Professor, Judicial Seminars in Product Liability, Professional Negligence, Law and Literature, Judicial Management of Civil Jury Trials, Evidences, St. Louis University of Law School, 1984-2001. Author: "Product Liability Law in Illinois," Chicago Daily Law Bulletin Publication, 1992; "Illinois Objections," Trial Butterworth Publication, Co., 1992; "Bright, Carlson, O'Brien and Chapman, Illinois Objections at Trial," Butterworth Publishing Company, 1992; "Jaws XVI": The Exceptions That Ate Rule 220," 26 John Marshall Law Review, Winter 1993; "An Appellate Judge Looks at Recent Rule 220,"" Chapman, 82 Illinois Bar Journal 478, 1994. ***REPORTED CASES:*** Thomas Bailey v. Dow Chemical, 407 F.2d 680, CA Ill. 1969; Brewer v. Norfolk and Western Railway Company, 4Ill.App.3d 118, 280 NE 2d 249; Hahn v. Norfolk and Weatern Railway Company, 241 Ill. App.3d 97, 608 NE 2d 683, 181 Ill.Dec. 610 1993. ***PRACTICE AREAS:*** Plaintiffs Personal Injury; Class Actions. ***Email:*** cchapman@lakinlaw.com

JAY HOFFMAN, admitted to bar, 1986, Illinois; 1987, Missouri. *Education:* Illinois State University (B.S., Finance, 1983); St. Louis University (J.D., 1986). Assistant State's Attorney, St. Clair County State's Attorney's Office. Assistant State's Attorney, Madison County. Director of Probation and Court Services, Illinois Twentieth Judicial Circuit. Illinois State Representative, 1990—. Chairman, House Transportation Committee. Majority Floor Leader. Member, Judiciary Committee. *Member:* St. Clair County and Illinois State Bar Associations; Illinois Trial Lawyers Association. ***PRACTICE AREAS:*** Personal Injury. ***Email:*** jayh@lakinlaw.com

LEGAL SUPPORT PERSONNEL

LEGAL INVESTIGATORS

HOWARD L. PEDERSON. *Education:* Drake University (B.A., 1970). Owner, Attorney's Service of Montana, 1971-1989. Certified Legal Investigator, NALI, 1993. *Member:* National Association of Legal Investigators. [Special Agent, Intelligence, U.S. Army, 1966-1969]. ***PRACTICE AREAS:*** Personal Injury; Railroad; Products Liability; Arson. ***Email:*** howardp@lakinlaw.com

GLORIA J. WENDLE. *Education:* Lewis and Clark Community College, 1978-1979, 1985. *Member:* National Association of Legal Investigators. (Maritime Investigator). ***PRACTICE AREAS:*** Admiralty and Maritime Law. ***Email:*** gloriaw@lakinlaw.com

GLEN BROWN, Formerly with: Missouri Pacific Union Pacific Risk Management, 1974-1993; Investigation for plaintiff law firms, 1994—. *Member:* National Association of Railroad Safety Consultants and Investigators. ***PRACTICE AREAS:*** Railroad Accident Investigation. ***Email:*** glenb@lakinlaw.com

MARK JOHNSEY. *Education:* Southern Illinois University (B.S., 1986). Faculty Member, Department of Environmental Pathology, St. Louis University School of Medicine. Board Certified Senior Crime Analyst, International Association for Identification. Member, American Academy of Forensic Sciences. Retired Master Sergeant, Illinois State Police, Division of Forensic Services. Crime Scene Investigator and Forensic Anthropologist. ***PRACTICE AREAS:*** Nursing Home Liability. ***Email:*** markj@lakinlaw.com

RON HOOVER. *Education:* Southern Illinois University (B.A., History and Government). Employed by State Farm Auto as Claims Specialist for 31 years, 2 years independent investigations. Testifies as expert in insurance company bad faith cases. ***LANGUAGES:*** Hungarian. ***PRACTICE AREAS:*** Personal Injury. ***Email:*** ronh@lakinlaw.com

---

M. MARGARET BRADSHAW, P.C.

454 WEST JACKSON STREET
WOODSTOCK, ILLINOIS 60098
Telephone: 877-SSD-ATTY or 815-206-2908
Fax: 877-773-9889
Email: margaret@SSDAtty.com
URL: http://www.SSDAtty.com

Social Security, Social Security Disability.

MARGARET MURRAY-BRADSHAW, born Bloomington, Indiana, October 18, 1967; admitted to bar, 1994, New York and U.S. District Court, Western District of New York; 1999, Illinois. *Education:* Indiana University (B.S. Public Affairs, 1990); Albany Law School of Union University (J.D., 1993). Lecturer: Social Security Disability Claims Process, National Alliance for the Mentally Ill, Kane County, 2002; Arthritis Foundation, Fibromyalgia Group, Willowbrook, 2003. Member, Woodstock Illinois Plan Commission, 2000-2004. *Member:* McHenry County, Kane County and Illinois State Bar Associations; National Organization of Social Security Claimants' Representatives. ***REPORTED CASES:*** Co-Authored Appellate Briefs: In re Marriage of Brackett, 242 Ill.Dec. 798 (2d Dist. 1999); Israel v. Israel, 663 N.Y.S.2d 460 (4th Dept. 1997); Baumgart v. Baumgart, 605 N.Y.S.2d 610 (4th Dept. 1993); People v. David, 152 Misc.2d 66 (Monroe County 1991). ***PRACTICE AREAS:*** Social Security Disability.

CALDWELL, BERNER & CALDWELL

Established in 1915
100 1/2 CASS STREET
P.O. BOX 1289
WOODSTOCK, ILLINOIS 60098
Telephone: 815-338-3300
Fax: 815-338-0015
Email: caldwell1@ameritech.net

General Practice. Appellate, Insurance, Real Property, Zoning Law, Estate Planning, Probate, Administrative Law, Litigation. Agricultural Law. Negligence, Personal Injury, Products Liability, Family and Criminal Law, Business and Commercial Law.

(This Listing Continued)

MEMBERS OF FIRM

WILLIAM I. CALDWELL (1908-1971)

JAMES E. BERNER, born Woodstock, Illinois, December 29, 1930; admitted to bar, 1957, Illinois; 1959, U.S. District Court, Northern District of Illinois; 1970, U.S. Court of Appeals, Seventh Circuit; 1971, U.S. Supreme Court; 1974, U.S. District Court, Eastern District of Wisconsin; 1975, U.S. District Court, Northern and Southern Districts of Florida; 1976, U.S. Court of Appeals, Fifth Circuit; 1982, Wisconsin. *Education:* DePaul University (Ph.B., 1955; J.D., 1957). Attorney, Dorr Township, 1962—. *Member:* Chicago, McHenry County (President, 1965-1966), Illinois State and American Bar Associations; State Bar of Wisconsin. ***PRACTICE AREAS:*** Probate; Real Estate; Estate Planning. ***Email:*** JEBerner@aol.com

WILLIAM I. CALDWELL, JR., born Chicago, Illinois, September 10, 1942; admitted to bar, 1967, Illinois; 1969, U.S. District Court, Northern District of Illinois; 1970, U.S. Court of Appeals, Seventh Circuit; 1971, U.S. Supreme Court; 1984, Wisconsin and U.S. District Court, Eastern District of Wisconsin. *Education:* Marquette University (B.A., 1964); Loyola University (J.D., 1967). Delta Theta Phi; Blue Key. *Member:* Chicago, McHenry County (President, 1983-1984) and Illinois State Bar Associations; State Bar of Wisconsin; Illinois Trial Lawyers Association; Defense Research Institute. ***PRACTICE AREAS:*** Litigation; Commercial Law; Real Estate; Domestic Relations. ***Email:*** caldwell1@ameritech.net

JEFFREY A. ROUHANDEH, born Manhattan, Kansas, September 16, 1958; admitted to bar, 1985, Illinois; 1990, U.S. District Court, Northern District of Illinois. *Education:* Southern Illinois University (B.A., 1980; J.D., 1985). *Member:* Chicago, McHenry County, Illinois State (Section Council Law Office Economics and Judicial Evaluations Outside Cook County)and American Bar Associations. ***PRACTICE AREAS:*** Civil Litigation; Criminal Law; Domestic Relations. ***Email:*** caldwell1@ameritech.net

SANDRA S. KERRICK, born Terre Haute, Indiana, January 31, 1948; admitted to bar, 1974, Illinois and U.S. District Court, Northern District of Illinois; 1987, U.S. Supreme Court; 2002, U.S. Court of Appeals, Seventh Circuit. *Education:* University of Illinois (A.B., 1970); The Ohio State University (J.D., 1974). Licensed Real Estate Broker, Illinois, 1987. Author: "Estates Under 425,000: Is the Residuary Trust Practical for Any But the Elderly?" Illinois Bar Journal, September 1979; "Who Needs A Residuary Trust?", Case and Comment, March-April 1980, Vol. 85, No. 2 and Estate Planning, The National Underwriter Co., May 1981, Sec. 51, 89, re-publication. President, McHenry County Estate Planning Council, 1980. Commissioner, Illinois Supreme Court. Hearing Board Member, ARDC, 1985-1987. Inquiry Board Member, ARDC, 1979-1985. Member, Crystal Lake Economic Development Commission, 1995-1996. *Member:* McHenry County, Illinois State and American Bar Associations. ***PRACTICE AREAS:*** Commercial Real Estate; Zoning Law; Commercial Transactions; Estate Planning. ***Email:*** caldwell1@ameritech.net

CYNTHIA A. SCHAUPP, born Skokie, Illinois, December 2, 1971; admitted to bar, 1997, Illinois; 2001, U.S. District Court, Northern District of Illinois. *Education:* University of Iowa (B.A., 1994); John Marshall Law School (J.D., 1997). Phi Alpha Delta. Member, Executive Branch, John Marshall Moot Court. *Member:* Mc Henry County and Illinois State (Member, Young Lawyers Division) Bar Associations. ***PRACTICE AREAS:*** Civil Litigation; Criminal Law; Domestic Relations. ***Email:*** caldwell1@ameritech.net

LOCAL COUNSEL FOR: Capitol Indemnity Corp.; Milwaukee Insurance Co.; Sentry Insurance Co.; Dorr Township; American Home Insurance Groups.

CAMPION, CURRAN, DUNLOP & LAMB, P.C.

WOODSTOCK, ILLINOIS

(See Crystal Lake)

General Practice, Corporate Law, Trusts and Estate, Real Estate Law, Zoning, Planning and Land Use, Criminal Law, Appellate Practice, Insurance, Family Law, Labor and Employment, Administrative Law, Environmental Law, Personal Injury, Workers Compensation.

CARROLL & CARROLL

107 DEAN STREET
WOODSTOCK, ILLINOIS 60098
Telephone: 815-337-4259
Fax: 815-337-2006
Email: pfcarrolllaw@sbcglobal.net
URL: http://www.peterfcarroll.com

Divorce, Custody, Paternity, Real Estate, Traffic, Criminal, Wills, Estate Planning, Probate.

PETER F. CARROLL, born Woodstock, Illinois, November 5, 1953; admitted to bar, 1983, Illinois; 1984, U.S. District Court, Northern District of Illinois including Trial Bar. *Education:* University of Illinois (B.S., 1977; M. Music, 1979); John Marshall Law School (J.D., with distinction, 1983). *Member:* McHenry County and Illinois State Bar Associations. ***Email:*** pfcarrolllaw@sbcglobal.net

---

LAW OFFICE OF
MICHAEL J. FLECK, P.C.

WOODSTOCK, ILLINOIS

(See Huntley)

Real Estate, Estate Planning, Estate Administration, Wills, Probate Law, Trusts and Estates, Corporate Law, Business Law, General Practice.

THE LAW FIRM OF
FRANKS, GERKIN & McKENNA, P.C.

WOODSTOCK, ILLINOIS

(See Marengo)

General, Civil & Criminal Trial Practice, Banking, Business Law, Commercial Real Estate, Corporate Law, Criminal Law, Debt Collections, Family Law, Personal Injury, Real Estate, Trusts & Estates, Immigration, Wills, Workers Compensation, Municipal Law, Traffic, Zoning, Planning and Land Use.

THE GITLIN LAW FIRM

663 EAST CALHOUN STREET
WOODSTOCK, ILLINOIS 60098-4262
Telephone: 815-338-9401
Fax: 815-338-9403
Email: susan@gitlinlawfirm.com
URL: http://www.gitlinlawfirm.com

Family Law, Divorce, Child Custody, Child Support and Matrimonial Law.

FIRM PROFILE: The Gitlin Law Firm of Woodstock, Illinois exclusively handles family law cases in McHenry County, Kane County and Lake County. Areas include custody, divorce, paternity, premarital agreements and adoption.

GUNNAR J. GITLIN, born Woodstock, Illinois, 1962; admitted to bar, 1987, Illinois. *Education:* Kenyon College (B.A., 1984); Loyola University (J.D., 1987). Recipient: one of five Illinois Family Lawyers for Illinois Institute for Continuing Legal Education Master Teacher Project for the 21st Century; Selected by peers for Leading Lawyers Network in Illinois. Developed, *Gitlin on Divorce Online Research System* online database of every significant Illinois Family Law Case since January 1, 1987. Frequent author including chapter author, "Business Valuation" for IICLE's Family Law Handbook. Lecturer: American Academy of Matrimonial Lawyers (state and national); American Bar Association Family Law Section (state and national); Law Education Institute, Inc.; Illinois Institute for Continuing Legal Education (IICLE); Northwest Suburban, DuPage County, Kane County and McHenry County Bar Associations. Associate: Schiller, DuCanto and Fleck, 1987-1988; Gitlin and Burns, 1988-1991. Partner, Gitlin & Gitlin, Woodstock, Illinois, 1991-2002. Board of Directors, 1997-2003 and Chairman, 1997-1998; 2001-2002 New Case Law Committee, Illinois Chapter of AAML. *Member:* McHenry County (Chairman, Legal Aid Committee, 1993-1996), Lake County, Kane County, Illinois State and American (Co-editor, Family Law Sections' Fax News Update, 1999-2003) Bar Associations; American Academy of Matrimonial Lawyers (Co-chair, Lawyer's Institute for Training New Lawyers, 1999-2002). Fellow, American Academy of Matrimonial Lawyers. ***REPORTED CASES:*** IRMO Brackett 722 N.E.2d 287 (1999). ***PRACTICE AREAS:*** Family Law. ***Email:*** susan@gitlinlawfirm.com

PAULETTE M. GRAY, born Chicago, Illinois, 1969; admitted to bar, 1996, Illinois and U. S. District Court, Northern District of Illinois. *Education:* University of Minnesota (B.A., 1991); John Marshall Law School (J.D., 1996). Moot Court National Finalist, 1996. Author: "Negotiating Child Custody Disputes," 2000 IICLE Book- Child Custody Litigation; "Useful Tips for Negotiating a Child Custody Dispute," Illinois Family Report, Vol. XXI, No. 9. Co-Author: "Negotiating Child Custody Disputes," 1998 IICLE Book- Child Custody Litigation. Contributing Author: "Gitlin on Divorce, Case Reports," 1994-2002. *Member:* McHenry County (President, Family Law Section, 2000-2001; Secretary-Treasurer, 1999-2000; Member, Board of Governors, 2001—) and Illinois State (Member, Family Law Section Council, 2000—) Bar Associations; Illinois Appellate Lawyers Association. ***REPORTED CASES:*** IRMO Lindsey-Robinson (2002). ***PRACTICE AREAS:*** Family Law.

ASSOCIATE

ERICKA B. PAVEY, born Lawrenceburg, Indiana, December 22, 1973; admitted to bar, 1999, Illinois; 2000, U.S. District Court, Southern and Central Districts of Illinois. *Education:* Eastern Illinois University (B.A., 1996; B.S., 1996); John Marshall Law School (J.D., 1999). Sigma Iota Lambda (President, 1994-1996); Delta Theta Phi (President, 1998-1999). Associate Justice, Moot Court. Member, Mock Trial Team. Instructor, Child Custody, Illinois Continuing Legal Education, 2003. *Member:* McHenry County Bar Association (President, Family Law Section, 2004—). ***PRACTICE AREAS:*** Family Law. ***Email:*** bree@gitlinlawfirm.com

---

GUMMERSON & RAUSCH

101 S. BENTON STREET, SUITE 201
WOODSTOCK, ILLINOIS 60098
Telephone: 815-337-7700
Fax: 815-337-7990
URL: http://www.lawgr.com

Criminal Defense, Workers Compensation, Commercial Litigation, Family Law, Personal Injury, Medical Malpractice Defense, Zoning, Trusts and Estates, Corporate Law.

R. MARK GUMMERSON, born Woodstock, Illinois, October 15, 1955; admitted to bar, 1980, Illinois and U.S. District Court, Northern District of Illinois. *Education:* Loras College (B.A., cum laude, 1977); Drake University (J.D., 1979). Phi Alpha Delta. Commissioner, Woodstock Site Plan Review, Illinois, 1985-1991. *Member:* McHenry County (Member, Board of Governors, 1981-1984; Treasurer, 1984-1985; Secretary, 1985-1986; Second Vice President, 1986-1987; First Vice President, 1987-1988; President, 1988-1989) and Illinois State Bar Associations. ***PRACTICE AREAS:*** Criminal Defense; Workers Compensation; Commercial Litigation; Family Law.

TOM E. RAUSCH, born Neenah, Wisconsin, June 6, 1950; admitted to bar, 1976, Illinois; 1979, U.S. District Court, Northern District of Illinois; 1981, U.S. Court of Appeals,

(This Listing Continued)

GUMMERSON & RAUSCH, Woodstock—Continued

Seventh Circuit. *Education:* University of Wisconsin-Green Bay and Vanderbilt University (B.A., 1972); John Marshall Law School (J.D., with honors, 1976). Assistant State's Attorney, Moultrie County, Illinois, 1976-1977. *Member:* McHenry County (President, 1984-1985), Illinois State (Assemblyman, 19th Judicial District, 1982-1988) and American Bar Associations; Illinois Trial Lawyers Association. ***PRACTICE AREAS:*** Personal Injury; Medical Malpractice Defense; Zoning, Planning and Land Use Law.

ASSOCIATES

PHILIP E. WAND, born Evanston, Illinois, September 1, 1970; admitted to bar, 1995, Minnesota; 1998, Illinois; 1999, U.S. District Court, Northern District of Illinois including Trial Bar; 2001, U.S. Court of Appeals, Seventh Circuit. *Education:* Northern Illinois University (B.A., summa cum laude, 1992); University of Minnesota (J.D., cum laude, 1995). *Member:* Chicago, Illinois State and Minnesota State Bar Associations. [U.S. Navy Judge Advocate General's Corps, 1995-1998]. ***PRACTICE AREAS:*** Civil Litigation; Medical Malpractice Defense; Insurance Defense; Construction Law; Military Law. ***Email:*** ewand@lawgr.com

ROBERT L. GRAY, born Naperville, Illinois, December 7, 1968; admitted to bar, 1994, Illinois; 2003, U.S. District Court, Northern District of Illinois. *Education:* Illinois State University (B.A., 1991); DePaul University (J.D., 1994). *Member:* McHenry County Bar Association. ***PRACTICE AREAS:*** Personal Injury; Family Law; Real Estate; Commercial Law. ***Email:*** rgray@lawgr.com

JAMIE RAE WOMBACHER, born Cedar Rapids, Iowa, April 17, 1978; admitted to bar, 2003, Illinois and U.S. District Court, Northern District of Illinois. *Education:* University of Iowa (B.A., 1999; J.D., 2003). *Member:* Chicago, McHenry County and Illinois State Bar Associations. ***PRACTICE AREAS:*** Criminal Law; Civil Litigation; Family Law. ***Email:*** jwombacher@lawgr.com

CHRISTOPHER M. KERN, born Cuba City, Wisconsin, December 19, 1971; admitted to bar, 2001, Illinois. *Education:* University of Wisconsin-Platteville (B.A., 1994); Syracuse University (J.D., 2000). Author, Syracuse Journal of International, Child Labor Laws and the Corporate Impact. *Member:* McHenry County Bar Association. ***PRACTICE AREAS:*** Real Estate; Estate Planning; Corporate Transactions; Family Law; Civil Litigation. ***Email:*** ckern@lawgr.com

HARRISON LAW OFFICES, P.C.

684 S. EASTWOOD DRIVE (RT. 47)
WOODSTOCK, ILLINOIS 60098
Telephone: 815-338-7773
Fax: 815-338-7738
Email: jharrison@harrisonlawoffices.com
URL: http://www.harrisonlawoffices.com

Concentrating in Employment Law and Civil Rights, Employment Discrimination, Sexual Harassment, Disability, Gender, Race, Religion, Age, Civil Rights, Unemployment Compensation, Employers' Policy Manuals, Privacy Rights, Severance Agreements, Wrongful Discharge and Retaliatory Discharge, Employment Contracts, Restrictive Covenants, Non-competition Agreements, Wage and Hour Claims, Government Law, Pension Claims, Employment Handbooks, Employer/Employee Rights, Labor Unions, State and Federal Appeals, Professional License-holder Defense.

JAMES T. HARRISON, born McHenry, Illinois, March 8, 1958; admitted to bar, 1991, Illinois, U.S. Supreme Court and U.S. District Court, Northern District of Illinois, including Trial Bar; 1996, U.S. Court of Appeals, Eastern District of Wisconsin. *Education:* John Marshall Law School (J.D., 1991). ***PRACTICE AREAS:*** Employment Law; Civil Rights; Employment Discrimination: Sexual Harassment, Disability, Gender, Race, Religion, Age; Unemployment Compensation; Employer Rights/Employee; Privacy Law/Rights; Severance Agreements; Wrongful Termination; Retaliatory Discharge; Employment Contracts; Restrictive Covenants; Noncompetition Agreements and Non-Solicitation Agreements; Wage and Hour Law; Pension Plans; Government Law; Labor Law; Union Labor Law; Appellate Practice; Professional License-Holder Defense; Personal Injury.

McKENNA STORER

Established in 1954
666 RUSSEL COURT
SUITE 303
WOODSTOCK, ILLINOIS 60098-2672
Telephone: 815-334-9690
Fax: 815-334-9697
Email: postmaster@mckenna-law.com
URL: http://www.mckenna-law.com

Chicago, Illinois Office: 33 N. LaSalle Street, 14th Floor, 60602-2610. Telephone: 312-558-3900. Fax: 312-558-8348.
Waukegan, Illinois Office: 33 North Country Street, 6th Floor, 60085-4343. Telephone: 847-249-1620. Fax: 847-249-8457.

Administrative Hearings, Appellate, Banking and Lending, Bankruptcy, Civil Rights, Commercial, Construction, Employment, Estate Planning, Fidelity, Insurance Coverage, Legal Malpractice, Mediation Services, Medical Malpractice, National Coordination, Personal Injury, Products Liability, Professional Liability, Surety, Tax and Toxic Tort.

FIRM PROFILE: McKenna Storer celebrated its 50th Anniversary in 2004. The Firm has a history and reputation for providing quality legal services to its clients. Our clients are individuals, corporations and insurance companies. We serve local, national and international clients from our offices in the Chicago, Illinois metropolitan area.

(This Listing Continued)

Client focused and service driven, the Firm is committed to cost-effective client services that are effective, personal and timely. Whether retained for litigation or consultation, McKenna Storer's philosophy is to consider traditional and creative solutions to our clients' legal needs.

RESIDENT PARTNER

SARA E. COOK, admitted to bar, 1980, Illinois. *Education:* University of Iowa (B.A., 1975); Loyola University (J.D., 1980). ***Email:*** scook@mckenna-law.com

ASSOCIATE

PATRICIA C. KRAFT, admitted to bar, 1985, Illinois. *Education:* Northern Illinois University (B.S., 1982); Loyola University, Chicago (J.D., 1985). ***Email:*** pkraft@mckenna-law.com

(For complete biographical data on other personnel, see Professional Biographies at Chicago, Illinois)

MICHLING HOFMANN VINTON PLAZA & WICK, P.C.

101 N. THROOP STREET
WOODSTOCK, ILLINOIS 60098
Telephone: 815-338-9600
Fax: 815-337-4005; 337-3611

Personal Injury, Workers Compensation, Criminal Law, Family Law, Civil Litigation, Corporate Law, Residential Real Estate, Commercial Real Estate, Landlord and Tenant Law, Wills and Trusts, Land Use and Development, Zoning, Appellate Practice.

PETER D. MICHLING, born Chicago, Illinois, May 16, 1954; admitted to bar, 1982, Illinois and U.S. District Court, Northern District of Illinois. *Education:* South Dakota State University (B.S., 1976); Western State College of Colorado (M.A., 1979); John Marshall Law School (J.D., 1982). *Member:* McHenry County (Treasurer, 1988-1989; Secretary, 1989-1990; Past President, 1992-1993), Illinois State and American Bar Associations; Illinois Trial Lawyers Association. ***PRACTICE AREAS:*** Family Law; Civil Litigation; Appellate Practice; Collections; Personal Injury; Workers Compensation. ***Email:*** pmichling@woodstocklawpros.com

DANIEL T. HOFMANN, born Chicago, Illinois, November 24, 1954; admitted to bar, 1980, Illinois; 1989, U.S. District Court, Northern District of Illinois. *Education:* Southern Illinois University, Carbondale (B.S., 1976); John Marshall Law School (J.D., 1980). *Member:* McHenry County and Illinois State Bar Associations; Illinois Association of Criminal Defense Lawyers; National Association of Criminal Defense Lawyers. ***PRACTICE AREAS:*** Criminal Law (100%). ***Email:*** dhofmann@woodstocklawpros.com

NORMAN D. VINTON, born Toledo, Ohio, October 4, 1958; admitted to bar, 1989, Wisconsin; 1990, Illinois. *Education:* Jackson Community College; Northern Michigan University (B.S., cum laude, 1982); DePaul University (J.D., 1989). *Member:* Milwaukee County Bar, Illinois State and American Bar Associations; State Bar of Wisconsin; American Society of Industrial Security. [Staff Sergeant (E-5), U.S.A.F., 1978-1982]. ***PRACTICE AREAS:*** Litigation (60%); Corporate Law (20%); Landlord and Tenant Law (10%); Wills (10%). ***Email:*** nvinton@woodstocklawpros.com

EDWIN M. PLAZA, born Chicago, Illinois, February 2, 1953; admitted to bar, 1978, Illinois; 1979, U.S. District Court, Northern District of Illinois. *Education:* Marquette University (B.A., 1974): Illinois Institute of Technology, Chicago-Kent College of Law (J.D., 1978). *Member:* McHenry County and Illinois State Bar Associations. ***PRACTICE AREAS:*** Personal Injury (90%); Workers Compensation (10%). ***Email:*** eplaza@woodstocklawpros.com

MELISSA A. WICK, born Elgin, Illinois, January 17, 1963; admitted to bar, 1994, Illinois; 1996, U.S. District Court, Northern District of Illinois. *Education:* Mundelein College (B.A., 1990); DePaul University (J.D., 1994). *Member:* McHenry County and Illinois State Bar Associations. ***PRACTICE AREAS:*** Residential Real Estate; Commercial Real Estate; Civil Litigation; Collections; Wills; Trust Law; Probate. ***Email:*** mwick@woodstocklawpros.com

ANGELA C. THUMA, born Jacksonville, Florida, August 13, 1971; admitted to bar, 1996, Illinois and U.S. District Court, Northern District of Illinois. *Education:* University of Illinois (B.S., 1993); Northern Illinois University (J.D., magna cum laude, 1996). *Member:* McHenry County, Illinois State and American Bar Associations. ***PRACTICE AREAS:*** Family Law (80%); Estate Planning (15%); Probate (5%). ***Email:*** athuma@woodstocklawpros.com

PAIGE D. HOYT, born November 29, 1963; admitted to bar, 2003, Illinois. *Education:* Iowa State University (B.A., 1987); Northern Illinois University (J.D., 2003). *Member:* Illinois State Bar Association; McHenry County Bar Association. ***PRACTICE AREAS:*** Family Law; Civil; Real Estate.

JENÉT GONZÁLEZ PEQUEÑO, born December 28, 1978; admitted to bar, 2004, Illinois. *Education:* Northern Illinois University (B.A., 2001); University of Miami (J.D., 2004). *Member:* American Bar Association; McHenry County Bar Association. ***LANGUAGES:*** English and Spanish. ***PRACTICE AREAS:*** Criminal; Traffic Violations; Family; Real Estate; Civil Practice.

MILITELLO, ZANCK & COEN, P.C.

WOODSTOCK, ILLINOIS

(See Crystal Lake)

Trial Practice in all State and Federal Courts, Banking, Business Acquisitions, Corporation and Partnership, Employment Law, Environmental, Insurance Defense, Probate and Guardianship, Real Estate, Wills and Trusts and Zoning and Land Planning.

O'HAGAN, SMITH & AMUNDSEN

666 RUSSEL COURT
WOODSTOCK, ILLINOIS 60098
Telephone: 815-337-4900
Fax: 815-337-4910
URL: http://www.osalaw.com

Chicago, Illinois Office: 150 North Michigan Avenue, Suite 3300, 60601. Telephone: 312-894-3200. Fax: 312-894-3210.
Rockford, Illinois Office: Stewart Square, 308 West State Street, Suite 320, 61101-1140. Telephone: 815-987-0441. Fax: 815-987-9891.
St. Charles, Illinois Office: 3815 E. Main Street, Suite A-1, 60174-2488. Telephone: 630-587-7910. Fax: 630-587-7960.
Waukegan, Illinois Office: 415 West Washington Street, Suite 204, 60079-0410. Telephone: 847-599-9503. Fax: 847-599-9525.
Milwaukee, Wisconsin Office: 4811 South 76th Street, Suite 305, 53220. Suite 117, 53406-3770. Telephone: 414-282-7103. Fax: 414-282-1830.

Commercial; Commercial Transportation; Appellate; Complex Litigation; Construction; Corporate Transactions; Employment; Extra-Contractual/Insurance Litigation; Healthcare; Insurance Coverage; Personal Lines; Product Liability; Professional Liability; Property Litigation.

MEMBERS OF FIRM

JOYCE E. KRAEGER, admitted to bar, 1995, Illinois. *Education:* University of Illinois (B.A., 1990); Loyola University (J.D., 1995). ***Email:*** jkraeger@osalaw.com

HEATHER E. SHEA, admitted to bar, 1994, Illinois. *Education:* Valparaiso University (B.A., 1990); John Marshall Law School (J.D., 1994). Staff Editor, Software Law Journal, John Marshall Law School, 1994. *Member:* McHenry County and Illinois State Bar Associations. ***PRACTICE AREAS:*** General Practice. ***Email:*** hshea@osalaw.com

ELIZABETH FELT WAKEMAN, admitted to bar, 1993, Illinois and U.S. District Court, Northern District of Illinois. *Education:* University of Illinois (B.S., with honors, 1987); DePaul University College of Law (J.D., 1993). Recipient, American Jurisprudence Award in Product Liability. Vice Chair, Parks & Recreation Board, Lake in the Hills, 1996—. *Member:* Illinois State Bar Association. ***PRACTICE AREAS:*** Insurance Defense. ***Email:*** ewakeman@osalaw.com

(For complete biographical data on other personnel, see Professional Biographies at other cities)

LAW OFFICE OF THEODORE A. E. POEHLMANN, P.C.

202 WEST SOUTH STREET
P.O. BOX 271
WOODSTOCK, ILLINOIS 60098-0271
Telephone: 815-337-3337
Fax: 815-337-3340

General Civil and Trial Practice. Probate, Real Estate, Family, Corporation, Negligence and Zoning Law, Personal Injury.

THEODORE A. E. POEHLMANN, born Chicago, Illinois, May 15, 1931; admitted to bar, 1962, Illinois; 1963, U.S. District Court, Northern District of Illinois. *Education:* University of Illinois (B.A., 1953); Northwestern University (J.D., 1959). Phi Delta Phi. *Member:* McHenry County, Lake County, Illinois State and American Bar Associations; Lake County Trial Lawyers Association. Fellow: Illinois Bar Foundation; American Judicature Society; International Association of Defense Counsel. ***PRACTICE AREAS:*** General Civil Law; Trial Practice; Probate Law; Real Estate Law; Family Law; Corporation Law; Negligence Law; Zoning Law.

PHILIP A. PROSSNITZ, born Evanston, Illinois, December 27, 1955; admitted to bar, 1980, Louisiana; 1983, Illinois. *Education:* Duke University (A.B., cum laude, 1976); Tulane University (J.D., 1980). Assistant States Attorney McHenry Co., 1988-1992. Chief Assistant States Attorney McHenry Co., 1992-2000. ***PRACTICE AREAS:*** Criminal Defense; Trial Practice; Personal Injury; Insurance Defense Litigation; Real Estate Practice.

REPRESENTATIVE CLIENTS: Country Mutual Insurance Co.; Liberty Mutual Insurance Co.; State Farm Mutual Automobile Insurance Co.; Rockford Mutual Insurance Company.
REFERENCE: Harris Bank Woodstock.

POLLOCK, MEYERS, EICKSTEADT & PULAK, LTD.

WOODSTOCK, ILLINOIS

(See Marengo)

General Trial Practice, Appellate Practice, Estate Planning, Probate Law, Trust Law, Real Estate, Banking Law, Bankruptcy Law, Personal Injury, Workers Compensation, Administrative Law, Corporate Law, Contracts, Civil Litigation, Trusts and Estates, Real Estate Law.

RINELLA AND RINELLA, LTD.

WOODSTOCK, ILLINOIS

(See Chicago)

Practice Limited to Family Law and Divorce including the areas of Legal Separation, Negotiating and Drafting Premarital and Postnuptial Agreements, Judgment Enforcement, Child Custody and Child Support Actions, Domestic Violence, Spousal Support, Appeals, Adoption, Parentage Actions and Interstate Support Enforcement.

SWANSON, MARTIN & BELL

WOODSTOCK, ILLINOIS

(See Chicago)

Asbestos Litigation, Class Action Lawsuits, Commercial Litigation, Construction Litigation/Disputes, Consumer and Warranty Law, Creditor's Rights, Drugs & Medical Devices, Employment Litigation, Environmental Law, Equipment Leasing, General Tort Liability, Healthcare, Insurance Coverage, Intellectual Property, Medical Negligence, Municipal Law, Product Liability, Professional Negligence, Real Estate Development/Zoning, Real Estate Litigation, Toxic and Mass Tort Litigation and White Collar Criminal Defense.

WEISZ BOTTO & GILBERT, P.C.

2030 NORTH SEMINARY AVENUE (ROUTE 47)
WOODSTOCK, ILLINOIS 60098
Telephone: 815-338-3838
Fax: 815-338-7817
Email: complaw@mc.net
URL: http://www.weiszbottogilbert.com

Personal Injury, Workers Compensation, Family, Criminal Trial, Residential, Industrial and Commercial Real Estate, Zoning and Real Estate Development Law. Civil Litigation and Appellate Practice.

MITCHELL R. WEISZ, born Chicago, Illinois, March 18, 1957; admitted to bar, 1981, Illinois and U.S. District Court, Northern District of Illinois. *Education:* Northwestern University (B.A., 1978); ITT/Chicago-Kent College of Law (J.D., 1981). *Member:* McHenry County and Illinois State Bar Associations; Illinois Trial Lawyers Association; Workers Compensation Lawyers Association; American Trial Lawyers Association. ***PRACTICE AREAS:*** Workers Compensation Law (100%).

FRANCISCO J. BOTTO, born 1960; admitted to bar, 1993, Illinois. *Education:* Amherst College (B.A, cum laude, 1989); Northwestern University (J.D., 1992). Executive Editor, Journal of Criminal Law & Criminology. Member, McHenry County Latino Coalition. *Member:* McHenry County Bar Association; Illinois Association of Criminal Defense Lawyers; National Association of Criminal Defense Attorneys. ***LANGUAGES:*** Portuguese and Spanish. ***PRACTICE AREAS:*** Personal Injury (20%); Criminal (80%). ***Email:*** fbotto@wbglawonline.com

THEODORE A. GILBERT, born Chicago, Illinois, May 11, 1948; admitted to bar, 1975, Illinois. *Education:* Northern Illinois University (B.A., 1970); John Marshall Law School (J.D., 1975). Tau Epsilon Rho. *Member:* Illinois Trial Lawyers Association; The Association of Trial Lawyers of America; Workmen's Compensation Lawyers Association. ***LANGUAGES:*** Spanish. ***PRACTICE AREAS:*** Personal Injury (90%); Workers Compensation (10%). ***Email:*** tgilbert@wbglawonline.com

JAMES H. ANDRLE, III, born Elmhurst, Illinois, July 9, 1969; admitted to bar, 1999, Illinois and U.S. District Court, Northern District of Illinois. *Education:* Northern Illinois University (B.S., Political Science-Public Law, 1992); University of Wisconsin at Madison; Quinnipiac College School of Law (J.D., 1998). Phi Delta Phi. Legal Honor's Fraternity. Burn's Inn. Recipient: Superior Classroom Performance Award; Service to the Law School Award; Service to the Community Award. Executive Business Editor, Quinnipiac Health Law Journal, 1997-1998. Academic Tutor, Student Support Services, Quinnipiac College, 1997-1998. President, Criminal Law Society, 1995-1998. Coordinator, L.E.A.P., 1995-1998. *Member:* Chicago and DuPage County Bar Associations. ***LANGUAGES:*** Spanish. ***PRACTICE AREAS:*** Family Law (50%); Criminal Defense (50%). ***Email:*** jandrle@wbglawonline.com

CAROLINA A. RECH, born Porto Alecre, Brazil, March 2, 1977; admitted to bar, 2002, Illinois. *Education:* University of Illinois (B.S., Economics, 1999; J.D., 2002). *Member:* Hispanic Lawyers Association of Illinois. ***LANGUAGES:*** Spanish and Portuguese. ***PRACTICE AREAS:*** Criminal Defense; Traffic; Family Law. ***Email:*** crech@wbglawonline.com

EDWARD J. JANUSZKIEWICZ, admitted to bar, 2003, Illinois. *Education:* Loyola University (B.A., Political Science, 1998); John Marshall Law School (J.D., 2002). ***LANGUAGES:*** Spanish. ***PRACTICE AREAS:*** Criminal Defense; Traffic Defense; Family Law.

KELLY L. LANCASTER, born Rochester, Minnesota, February 28, 1978; admitted to bar, 2003, Illinois. *Education:* Carthage College (B.A., History & Political Science, 2000); New England School of Law (J.D., 2003). Member, New England Law Review, 2001-2003. New England Scholar, 2000-2003. Author, "Felony Drinking & Driving Convictions as Crimes of Violence," New England Law Review, Vol. 37. *Member:* McHenry County Bar Association; Illinois Trial Lawyers Association. ***PRACTICE AREAS:*** Personal Injury; Family Law.

JOSE ANTONIO RENTERIA, born Guadalajara, Mexico, March 24, 1967; admitted to bar, 2000, Illinois. *Education:* Governor's State University (B.A., 1996); University of Illinois (J.D., 2000). Assistant State's Attorney, Winnebago County, Illinois, 2000-2004. *Member:* Illinois State Bar Association. ***LANGUAGES:*** Spanish. ***PRACTICE AREAS:*** Criminal Law (50%); Personal Injury (25%); Workers Compensation (25%). ***Email:*** jrenteria@wbglawonline.com

ZUKOWSKI, ROGERS, FLOOD & McARDLE

WOODSTOCK, ILLINOIS

(See Crystal Lake)

General Practice, Banking and Finance, Bankruptcy, Commercial, Construction, Corporation, Environmental, Family, Government, Insurance, Labor and Employment, Litigation, Personal Injury and Torts, Probate, Trust and Estate, Real Property, Vehicle Warranty, Fraud Litigation.

LAW OFFICE OF JAMES J. SIWEK

6657 W. 111TH STREET
P.O. BOX 367
WORTH, ILLINOIS 60482
Telephone: 708-448-5210; 708-429-3420
Fax: 708-448-7428
Email: siweklaw@comcast.net

Bankruptcy - Chapters 7 and 13, Consumer Fraud, Criminal Law, Misdemeanors and Felonies, Driving While Intoxicated, Drug Crimes, Juvenile Law, Parole and Probation, Family Law, Adoptions, Child Custody, Child Support, Divorce, Domestic Violence, Visitation Rights, General Practice, Real Estate, Buying or Selling a Home, Construction, Landlord and Tenant, Trusts and Estates, Land Trusts, Living Trusts, Guardianships, Powers of Attorney, Wills and Probate.

JAMES J. SIWEK, born Oak Park, Illinois, November 15, 1953; admitted to bar, 1987, Illinois. *Education:* Drake University (B.S., 1974); Northern Illinois University (J.D., 1987). ***PRACTICE AREAS:*** Bankruptcy Chapter 7; Bankruptcy Chapter 13; Consumer Fraud; Criminal Law; Misdemeanors; Felonies; Driving While Intoxicated; Drug Crimes; Juvenile Law; Parole and Probation; Family Law; Adoption Law; Child Custody; Child Support; Divorce; Domestic Violence; Visitation Rights; General Practice; Real Estate;

(This Listing Continued)

Real Estate Acquisitions; Real Estate Sales; Construction Law; Landlord and Tenant Law; Trusts and Estates; Land Trusts; Living Trusts; Guardianship; Powers of Attorney; Wills; Probate.

DREYER, FOOTE, STREIT, FURGASON AND SLOCUM

A PROFESSIONAL ASSOCIATION

YORKVILLE, ILLINOIS

(See Aurora, Illinois)

Civil and Criminal Trial and Appellate Practice in all State and Federal Courts. Business Planning, Commercial, Corporate, Estate Planning, Wills, Probate, Trusts and Estates, Elder Law, Family Law, Healthcare, Insurance and Insurance Defense, Labor, Municipal, Personal Injury, Probate, Real Estate, State and Federal Taxation, Adoption, Child Support, Child Custody, Divorce, Domestic Violence, DWI, Automobile Accidents, Wrongful Death, Buying and Selling a Home, Landlord/Tenant, Construction, Bankruptcy, Guardianships, Collections, Buying and Selling a Business, Business Enterprises, Franchise, Closely Held Business, Limited Liability, Partnerships, Small Business, Contracts, Lawsuits, Starting a Business, Zoning.

KINNALLY, KRENTZ, LORAN, HODGE & HERMAN, P.C.

YORKVILLE, ILLINOIS

(See Aurora)

General Practice. Civil Trial Practice, Personal Injury, Auto Accidents, Worker's Compensation, Corporate Law, Immigration and Naturalization, Business Law, Estate Planning, Trusts, Estates and Probate, Municipal and Zoning Law, Education Law, Environmental and Eminent Domain.

JAMES O. ANDERSON

Established in 1980
800 MAIN STREET
SUITE 210
ANDERSON, INDIANA 46016
Telephone: 765-643-3100
Fax: 765-643-0609
Email: jamand@indy.net
URL: http://www.lawyers.com/janderson

Wills, Probate, Trusts and Estates, Estate Planning, Asset Protection, Guardianships, Banking, Real Estate, Estate Administration, Business Law, Business Planning, Contracts, Lawsuits, Debtor and Creditor, Collections, Entrepreneurial Business Law, Partnerships, Corporate Law, Limited Liability Company Law, Small Business, Real Estate Litigation, Probate Litigation, Taxation Law and Civil Trials in all Courts.

JAMES O. ANDERSON, born Anderson, Indiana, 1955; admitted to bar, 1980, Indiana. *Education:* Indiana University (J.D., 1980). Probate Civil Magistrate, Madison Superior Court, 1985-1989; 1998—. *Member:* Madison County (President, 2002-2003) and Indiana State Bar Associations. ***LANGUAGES:*** Italian.

REFERENCES: Community Bank; National City Bank.

BINGHAM, FARRER & WILSON, A PROFESSIONAL CORPORATION

ANDERSON, INDIANA

(See Elwood)

General Practice, Banking and Finance, Bankruptcy, Business Planning, Sales and Acquisitions, Consumer and Commercial Law, Consumer and Commercial Collections, Transactions and Litigation, Contracts, Corporate Law, Creditors Rights, Debtor-Creditor Law, Elder Law, Family Law, Domestic Relations, Adoption Law, Child Support, Custody, Dissolution/Divorce, Separation and Visitation, Government Relations, Zoning, Planning and Land Use, Municipal Law, Probate, Guardianship, Estate Planning, Wills and Trusts, Real Estate, Foreclosures, Mechanics Liens.

BUSBY, AUSTIN, COOPER & FARR

Established in 1966
800 MAIN STREET, SUITE 200
ANDERSON, INDIANA 46016-1564
Telephone: 765-644-2891
Fax: 765-644-2894
URL: http://www.bacf.com

General Civil, Trial and Appellate Practice. Real Estate, Wills and Probate and Estate Planning, Trusts and Estates, Asset Protection, Guardianships, Corporation, Banking, Creditors Rights, Business Litigation, Business Planning, Business Law, Contracts, Lawsuits, Business Enterprises, Partnerships, Limited Liability Companies, Starting a Business, Buying and Selling a Business, Debt and Credit, Creditor Rights, Collections, Banking and Finance, Mediation.

MEMBERS OF FIRM

LAWRENCE M. BUSBY (1898-1983)

JOHN A. FARR, JR. (1926-1990)

RALPH E. SIPES, born Frankfort, Indiana, December 25, 1953; admitted to bar, 1984, Indiana and U.S. District Court, Southern District of Indiana; 1985, U.S. District Court, Northern District of Indiana; 1989, U.S. Supreme Court. *Education:* Ball State University (B.S., magna cum laude, 1980); Indiana University (J.D., 1983). Law Clerk to Chief Justice Richard M. Givan, Indiana Supreme Court, 1983-1984. Chief Deputy to Indiana Supreme Court Reporter, 1982-1983. Bailiff, Marion County Superior Court, 1981-1982. *Member:* Madison County, Indiana State and American Bar Associations; Indiana Trial Lawyers Association; The Association of American Trial Lawyers; Indiana Bar Foundation. ***PRACTICE AREAS:*** Civil Trial and Appellate Practice; Insurance Defense Law; Commercial Litigation; Banking Law; Creditors Rights in Bankruptcy. ***Email:*** sipes@bacf.com

D. ERIC HALL, born Anderson, Indiana, September 3, 1952; admitted to bar, 1977, Indiana and U.S. District Court, Southern District of Indiana. *Education:* Anderson University (B.A., cum laude, 1974); Indiana University School of Law (J.D., 1977). Director of East Central Indiana Legal Services Program, 1977-1981. Madison County Deputy Prosecutor, 1981-1982. *Member:* Madison County, Indiana State and American Bar Associations. ***PRACTICE AREAS:*** Commercial Law; Family Law; Mediation; Estate Planning and Probate; Civil Trial. ***Email:*** hall@bacf.com

ASSOCIATE

KATHERINE S. BROWN, born Anderson, Indiana, March 14, 1975; admitted to bar, 2001, Indiana and U.S. District Court, Northern and Southern Districts of Indiana. *Education:* Indiana State University (B.S., magna cum laude, 1997); Indiana University School of Law (J.D., cum laude, 2001). Articles Editor, Indiana Law Review, 2000-2001. Law Alumni Scholar, Indiana University School of Law Alumni Association, 1998-1999. *Member:* Indiana State Bar Association. ***PRACTICE AREAS:*** Civil Practice; Appellate Practice; Mediation. ***Email:*** brown@bacf.com

OF COUNSEL

ROBERT L. AUSTIN, born Anderson, Indiana, July 13, 1918; admitted to bar, 1942, Indiana; 1947, U.S. Supreme Court. *Education:* Indiana University (A.B., 1939; J.D., 1942). Phi Delta Phi. Faculty Member, University of Kansas, March to September, 1946.

(This Listing Continued)

Assistant to the Dean and Member of the Law Faculty, Indiana University Law School, 1946-1947. Judge, Anderson City Court, 1952-1955. *Member:* Madison County, Indiana State and American Bar Associations. Fellow: American College of Trust and Estate Counsel; Indiana Bar Foundation. ***PRACTICE AREAS:*** Probate and Estate Planning; Corporations; Real Estate.

PHILIP S. COOPER, born Greenfield, Indiana, June 15, 1919; admitted to bar, 1948, Indiana; 1980, U.S. Supreme Court. *Education:* Indiana University (B.S., with distinction in Finance and Banking, 1941; J.D., with distinction, 1948). Order of the Coif; Phi Delta Phi. *Member:* Madison County (President, 1956), Indiana State (Chairman, Probate, Trust and Real Property Section, 1963-1964; Member, Board of Managers, 1974-1976) and American Bar Associations. Former Fellow and State Chairman, American College of Probate and Trust. Fellow: American College of Trust and Estate Counsel; American Bar Foundation; Indiana Bar Foundation. ***PRACTICE AREAS:*** Estate Planning and Probate.

GENERAL COUNSEL FOR: Executive Council of the Church of God, Inc.; Saint John's Health System; Saint John's Medical Center; Mid-America Surgery Center; Anderson Tool and Engineering Co., Inc.; Perfecto Tool and Engineering Co., Inc.; M.K. Betts Engineering & Contracting, Inc.; Reflectix, Inc.; Ram Graphics, Inc.; Kennedy Machine & Tool Inc.; Klelnhenn Co., Inc.; S & S Steel Co., Inc.
LOCAL COUNSEL FOR: National City Bank of Indiana; Bank One Trust Co.; Western Union Financial Services, Inc.; Key Trust Company of Indiana, N.A.; CIGNA Companies; The Continental Insurance Cos.; Commercial Union Insurance Co.; CUNA Mutual Insurance Co.; K & K Insurance Group, Inc.; Pekin Insurance Company; Philadelphia Indemnity Insurance Company; Farm Bureau Insurance Cos.; Viking Insurance Co. of Wisconsin; Public Service Company of Indiana, Inc.; National Insurance Association; Indiana Power and Light Company; Brockway Glass Co.; Indiana Gas Company, Inc.; Grange Insurance; Continental Western Insurance Company.
APPROVED COUNSEL FOR: Prudential Home Mortage Co., Inc.; Merrill Lynch Credit Corporation.

JAMES E. DAVIS ATTORNEY AT LAW

ANDERSON, INDIANA

(See Greenfield)

Personal Injury, Social Security Disability, Wrongful Death, Medical Malpractice, Wills and Probate Law, Automobile Accidents and Injuries, Head Injury, Spinal Injury, Slip and Fall, Trucking Accidents, Construction Accidents, Railroad Accidents, Nursing Home and Abuse and Neglect.

DEFUR VORAN LLP

ANDERSON, INDIANA

(See Muncie)

General Civil Practice. Business Organizations, Personal Planning, Education, Health, Personnel and Employment, Banking, Real Estate, Taxation, Employee Benefit/Retirement Plans, Creditor's Rights, Civil Litigation, Mediation, Intellectual Property, Family.

JILL A. GONZALEZ, ATTORNEY AT LAW

ANDERSON, INDIANA

(See Muncie)

Family Law, Personal Injury, Criminal Law, Divorce.

THEODORE F. SMITH, JR.

Established in 1976
215 HISTORIC WEST 8TH
ANDERSON, INDIANA 46016-1374
Telephone: 765-644-8410; 800-296-2290
Fax: 765-643-8613
URL: http://www.tedsmithlaw.com
Email: tsmith@tedsmithlaw.com
URL: http://www.lawyers.com/tedsmithlaw

Social Security Disability, Personal Injury, Wrongful Death.

THEODORE F. SMITH, JR., born Anderson, Indiana, October 19, 1951; admitted to bar, 1976, Indiana and U.S. District Court, Southern District of Indiana; 2005, U.S. District Court, Northern District of Indiana. *Education:* University of Notre Dame (B.A, 1973; J.D., 1976). Listed in: Indiana Super Lawyer, 2004 and 2005; Best Lawyers in America, 2005. Member, Rules of Practice and Procedure Committee, Indiana Supreme Court, 2003—. *Member:* Indiana Trial Lawyers Association (President, 2000-2001). ***PRACTICE AREAS:*** Social Security Disability; Personal Injury; Wrongful Death.

CRAIG T. BENSON

109 SOUTH MARTHA STREET
ANGOLA, INDIANA 46703
Telephone: 260-665-6111
Fax: Available Upon Request

General Civil Practice. Estate Planning, Probate and Real Estate Law. Trials.

CRAIG T. BENSON, born Angola, Indiana, November 5, 1947; admitted to bar, 1972, Indiana. *Education:* Tulane University of Louisiana (B.A., cum laude, 1969); University of Texas School of Law (J.D., 1972). Prosecuting Attorney, 1975-1978 and 1983-1986.

REPRESENTATIVE CLIENTS: Steuben County Board of Aviation Commissioners; Swager Communications, Inc.; EMF Corp.

JAMES W. BURNS

213 W. MAUMEE STREET
ANGOLA, INDIANA 46703-1424
Telephone: 260-665-6611
Fax: 260-665-2887
Email: burnsjw@hotmail.com

Criminal Law, Domestic Relations, Divorce, Civil Litigation and Probate, Business and Corporate Law.

JAMES W. BURNS, born 1954; admitted to bar, 1979, Indiana. *Education:* Indiana University (A.B., 1976; J.D., 1979). ***PRACTICE AREAS:*** Criminal Law; Domestic Relations; Divorce; Civil Litigation; Probate; Business; Corporation.

DAVID L. HENRY

Established in 1976

1275 N. 290 WEST
ANGOLA, INDIANA 46703-9004
Telephone: 260-668-8868
Fax: 260-668-8868
Email: angolahenry@hotmail.com
URL: http://www.dhenrylaw.com

Business Law, Corporate Law, Real Estate Law, Business litigation, Contracts, Wills and Probate, Elder Law, Trusts and Estates, Estate Planning, Social Security Disability, Civil Litigation.

DAVID L. HENRY, born Fort Wayne, Indiana, November 6, 1948; admitted to bar, 1975, Indiana and U.S. District Court, Southern District of Indiana; 1976, U.S. District Court, Northern District of Indiana. *Education:* University of Indianapolis (B.A., 1971); Indiana University School of Law (J.D., 1975). Prosecuting Attorney, Steuben County, 1979-1982. Prosecuting Attorney, Perry County, 1991-1998. Deputy Prosecuting Attorney, 1985-1986, 1999—. ***PRACTICE AREAS:*** Business Law; Corporate Law; Real Estate; Business Litigation; Contracts; Wills; Probate; Elder Law; Trusts and Estates; Estate Planning; Social Security Disability; Civil Litigation.

ROEBUCK & ASSOCIATES, P.C.

ANGOLA, INDIANA

(See Ft. Wayne)

Personal Injury, Automobile Accidents, Boat Accidents, Motorcycle Accidents, Truck Accidents, Slip and Fall, Dog Bites, Medical Malpractice, Head Injuries, Nursing Home Abuse and Neglect, Products Liability, Insurance, Social Security, Social Security Disability, and Wrongful Death.

STOUT, WHEELER & ZABONA

118 W. MAUMEE STREET
ANGOLA, INDIANA 46703
Telephone: 260-665-5717
Fax: 260-665-1122
URL: http://www.swzlaw.com

General Practice, DUI, Driving While Intoxicated, Drug Crimes, Juvenile Crimes, Parole and Probation, Traffic Violations, White Collar Crime, Criminal Law, Domestic Violence, Adoptions, Child Custody, Child Support, Divorce, Domestic Violence, Visitation Rights, Prenuptial Agreements, Unmarried Couples, Guardianships, Automobile Accidents, Dog Bites, Head and Spinal Injuries, Nursing Home Abuse, Sexual Abuse, Slip and Fall, Trucking Accidents, Wrongful Death, Class Actions, Construction Accidents, Personal Injury, Railroad Accidents, Natural Disasters, Business Enterprises, General Business, Starting a Business, Buying or Selling a Home, Construction, Eminent Domain, Environmental, Landlord and Tenant, Zoning and Land Use, Neighbors and Pets, Natural Disasters, Asset Protection, Estate Planning, Wills and Probate.

MEMBERS OF FIRM

ALLEN R. STOUT, born Vincennes, Indiana, December 21, 1944; admitted to bar, 1981, Indiana. *Education:* Tri-State University (B.A., 1978); Thomas M. Cooley Law School (J.D., 1981). *Member:* Steuben County Bar Association (Chair, Steuben County Public Defender's Board, 2004—); Indiana Public Defenders Council; American Trial Lawyers Association; Indiana Trial Lawyers Association. ***PRACTICE AREAS:*** Personal Injury; Family Law; Criminal Defense.

CHRISTOPHER J. WHEELER, born Huntington, Indiana, March 30, 1967; admitted to bar, 1995, Indiana and U.S. District Court, Northern and Southern Districts of Indiana; 1998, U.S. Supreme Court. *Education:* Indiana University (B.S., Criminal Justice, 1989); Indiana University School of Law, Indianapolis (1995, J.D.). Board Member, Steuben County Community Foundation. *Member:* American Trial Lawyers Association; Indiana Trial Lawyers Association; Indiana Public Defenders Council. ***PRACTICE AREAS:*** Appellate Practice; Family Law; Criminal Law; Wills; Probate; Trusts and Estates; Business Law; Real Estate; Personal Injury.

LINDA ANN ZABONA, born 1967; admitted to bar, 2000, Indiana. *Education:* Ball State University (B.S., 1990); Thomas M.Cooley Law School (J.D., 2000). Formerly Litigation Paralegal, *1995 - 2000;* Pro Bono participant, Indiana State Bar Association. *Member:* Indiana State Bar Association (Member; Family Law Section); American Trial Lawyers Association; Indiana Trial Lawyers Association; Indiana Public Defender Association. ***PRACTICE AREAS:*** General Practice; Family Law.

THOMAS E. WILSON

109 SOUTH MARTHA STREET
ANGOLA, INDIANA 46703-1916
Telephone: 260-665-5715
Fax: Available Upon Request

Probate and Estate Planning, and Real Estate Law.

THOMAS E. WILSON, born Sturgis, Michigan, March 12, 1948; admitted to bar, 1973, Indiana. *Education:* Hanover College (B.A., 1970); Indiana University (J.D., 1973). Prosecuting Attorney, 1991—. ***PRACTICE AREAS:*** Probate Law; Estate Planning Law; Real Estate Law.

REPRESENTATIVE CLIENT: First Federal Savings & Bank of Angola.
REFERENCE: First Federal Savings & Bank of Angola.

BLACKBURN & GREEN

ATTICA, INDIANA

(See Fort Wayne)

Litigation, Personal Injury Law.

BLACKBURN & GREEN

AUBURN, INDIANA

(See Fort Wayne)

Litigation, Personal Injury Law.

JAMES P. McCANNA

1320 SOUTH GRANDSTAFF
P.O. BOX 543
AUBURN, INDIANA 46706
Telephone: 260-925-3787
FAX: 260-925-4884
Email: jpmccanna123@mchsi.com

Wills, Trusts and Estates, Real Estate, Banks and Banking, Corporate, Commercial, Elder Law, Civil and Family Mediation.

FIRM PROFILE: James P. McCanna began his solo practice in 1994, following 20 years of legal experience with other local law firms. Mr. McCanna offers legal services throughout Northeastern Indiana with an emphases on DeKalb County. Forecast areas of concentration include estate planning, business planning and Municipal Law. Mr. McCanna also maintains community involvement and is a past president of the DeKalb Memorial Hospital, Board of Directors, as well as past president of the Auburn Chamber of Commerce.

JAMES P. McCANNA, born Detroit, Michigan, March 10, 1947; admitted to bar, 1974, Indiana and U.S. District Court, Southern District of Indiana; 1975, U.S. District Court, Northern District of Indiana. *Education:* Georgetown University (A.B., 1969); Indiana University (J.D., cum laude, 1974). Law Clerk to Hon. Dixon W. Prentice, Indiana Supreme Court, 1973-1975. DeKalb Count Attorney, 2004—. Member, Indiana Supreme Court Committee on Character and Fitness, 1988—. Registered Mediator, 1999. *Member:* DeKalb County (President, 1982-1984) and Indiana State Bar Associations.

REPRESENTATIVE CLIENTS: DeKalb Financial Credit Union; DeKalb Memorial Hospital; Ralph E. Sechler & Son, Inc.; Foley Pattern Corp.; Bridgewater Golf Club, Inc.; Bridgewater Development Group, Inc.; DeKalb County Government (County Board of Commissioners and County Council); DeKalb County Government and DeKalb County Redevelopment Commission; Auburn Professional Village, Inc.

MEFFORD AND WEBER, P.C.

Established in 1918

130 EAST SEVENTH STREET
AUBURN, INDIANA 46706-1839
Telephone: 260-925-2300
Facsimile: 260-925-2610
URL: http://www.lawmw.com

Personal Injury, Trial and Civil Practice. Banking, Commercial, Corporation, Probate and Estate Planning, Elder Law, Taxation, Real Estate, Environmental, Municipal and Zoning Law, Domestic Relations, Civil and Domestic Relations Mediation.

FIRM PROFILE: The firm of Mefford and Weber, P.C. started in 1918 with a sole practitioner, Oak Husselman. Later, his son William H. Husselman joined him in the practice. Since that time the firm has expanded its personnel and its geographic scope to serve throughout northeast Indiana. The firm currently offers combined legal experience of more than 70 years. All of the attorneys maintain active roles in the Auburn community and surrounding areas, both in local government and non-governmental activities.

DONALD T. MEFFORD, born Auburn, Indiana, February 10, 1929; admitted to bar, 1956, Indiana and U.S. District Court, Northern and Southern Districts of Indiana; 1972, U.S. Court of Appeals, Seventh Circuit and U.S. Supreme Court; 1983, U.S. Tax Court. *Education:* Wabash College (B.A., 1951); Indiana University (J.D., 1956). Attorney: DeKalb County Central United School District, 1962-1972, 1978-2000; City of Auburn, 1964-1975, 1992-1994; Town of Ashley, 1980-1994. *Member:* DeKalb County (President, 1961-1962, 1973) and Indiana State Bar Associations; National Academy of Elder Law Attorneys; Indiana Bar Foundation. ***PRACTICE AREAS:*** Banking; Commercial; Estate Planning and Administration; Real Estate Law; Corporate Law.

(This Listing Continued)

W. ERIK WEBER, born Bloomington, Indiana, June 13, 1971; admitted to bar, 1998, Indiana and U.S. District Court, Northern and Southern Districts of Indiana; U.S. Court of Appeals, Seventh Circuit; 2003, U.S. Supreme Court. *Education:* St. Joseph's College, Indiana (B.S., cum laude, 1994); John Marshall Law School (J.D., 1998). Assistant City Attorney, Auburn, Indiana, 1998-2003. City Attorney, Auburn Indiana, 2003—. DeKalb County Central United School District, 2003—. DeKalb County Division of Family and Children, 2003—. Deputy Prosecutor, DeKalb County, 2000-2004. Attorney, Union Township Trustee, 2001—. *Member:* DeKalb County and Indiana State Bar Associations; Association of Trial Lawyers of America. ***PRACTICE AREAS:*** Personal Injury Law; Dissolution; Bankruptcy; Civil Litigation; Municipal Law; Juvenile Law. ***Email:*** Erik@lawmw.com

NEAL R. BLYTHE, born Fort Wayne, Indiana, July 1, 1977; admitted to bar, 2003, Indiana and U.S. District Court, Northern and Southern Districts of Indiana. *Education:* Indiana University, Bloomington (B.A., 2000); Indiana University School of Law (J.D., 2003). Deputy Prosecutor, DeKalb County, 2003—. *Member:* DeKalb County, Indianapolis and Indiana State Bar Associations; National Association of Elder Law Attorneys. ***PRACTICE AREAS:*** Financial Planning; Estate Administration; Elder Law; Real Estate; Family Law; Civil Litigation. ***Email:*** neal@lawmw.com

GENERAL COUNSEL FOR: City of Auburn, Indiana; DeKalb County Office, Division of Family and Children; DeKalb County Central United School District.
APPROVED ATTORNEYS FOR: Ticor Title Insurance Company; Title Insurance Company of Minnesota; Stewart Title Guaranty Co.; American Title Insurance Co.

ROEBUCK & ASSOCIATES, P.C.

AUBURN, INDIANA

(See Ft. Wayne)

Personal Injury, Automobile Accidents, Boat Accidents, Motorcycle Accidents, Truck Accidents, Slip and Fall, Dog Bites, Medical Malpractice, Head Injuries, Nursing Home Abuse and Neglect, Products Liability, Insurance, Social Security, Social Security Disability, and Wrongful Death.

STOUT, WHEELER & ZABONA

AUBURN, INDIANA

(See Angola)

General Practice, DUI, Driving While Intoxicated, Drug Crimes, Juvenile Crimes, Parole and Probation, Traffic Violations, White Collar Crime, Criminal Law, Domestic Violence, Adoptions, Child Custody, Child Support, Divorce, Domestic Violence, Visitation Rights, Prenuptial Agreements, Unmarried Couples, Guardianships, Automobile Accidents, Dog Bites, Head and Spinal Injuries, Nursing Home Abuse, Sexual Abuse, Slip and Fall, Trucking Accidents, Wrongful Death, Class Actions, Construction Accidents, Personal Injury, Railroad Accidents, Natural Disasters, Business Enterprises, General Business, Starting a Business, Buying or Selling a Home, Construction, Eminent Domain, Environmental, Landlord and Tenant, Zoning and Land Use, Neighbors and Pets, Natural Disasters, Asset Protection, Estate Planning, Wills and Probate.

TROTTER LAW OFFICE

AUBURN, INDIANA

(See Fort Wayne)

Family Law, Bankruptcy, Personal Injury, Traffic Violations, Misdemeanors, Child Custody.

CHAPMAN & NELSON, P.C.

BEDFORD, INDIANA

(See Bloomington)

Criminal Law, Driving While Intoxicated, Traffic Violations, Personal Injury, Litigation, Family Law, Dissolutions of Marriage, Adoption Law, Guardianship, Modification of Support and Visitation, Name Changes.

HENDERSON & HENDERSON

Established in 1939

P.O. BOX 909

BEDFORD, INDIANA 47421-0909

Telephone: 812-275-5644

Fax: 812-279-0423

Email: donaldghenderson@msn.com

Business Law, Commercial Transactions, Property Law, Probate and Estates.

FIRM PROFILE: The Firm was founded in 1939 by Gordon R. Henderson.

MEMBERS OF FIRM

GORDON R. HENDERSON (1911-1995)

DONALD G. HENDERSON, born Bedford, Indiana, January 20, 1945; admitted to bar, 1971, Indiana; 1972, U.S. Tax Court. *Education:* Indiana University (B.S., 1968; J.D., 1971). Phi Alpha Delta. Public Defender, Lawrence County, Indiana, 1974-1976. Member, Board of Governors, 1976-1988, 1999— and Chairman, 1979-1986, Dunn Memorial Hospital. Member, Lawrence County Election Board, 1978—. Federal Bankruptcy Trustee, 1979—. *Member:* Lawrence County (President, 1973-1974); Indiana State and American Bar Associations. [Legal Assistance Officer, JAGC, U.S. Army, 1971-1973]. ***PRACTICE AREAS:*** Business Law; Commercial Transactions; Property Law; Probate; Estates.

(This Listing Continued)

REPRESENTATIVE CLIENTS: The Stone City Bank of Bedford; Peoples Trust Company of Linton, Indiana; Indiana Limestone Co., Inc.; Architectural Stone Sales, Inc.; Elliott Stone Co., Inc.; Aztec Aviation, Inc.; Board of Aviation Commissioners; Monroe-Lawrence Farm Bureau Co-op.
REFERENCES: The Stone City Bank of Bedford; NBD Bank, N.A.

MALLOR CLENDENING GRODNER & BOHRER LLP

BEDFORD, INDIANA

(See Bloomington)

Civil Litigation, Insurance Defense, Business Law, Wills, Trusts and Estates, Family Law, Personal Injury, Taxation, Corporate Law, Real Estate, Probate, Labor and Employment.

BARNHART, STURGEON & SPENCER

Established in 1935

313 NORTH LINCOLN

P.O. BOX 1234

BLOOMINGTON, INDIANA 47402-1234

Telephone: 812-332-9476

Fax: 812-331-8819

General Civil Practice. Corporation, Probate and Estate Planning, Construction, Real Estate, Criminal Law, Guardianship, Municipal and Zoning Law, Trials and Personal Injury, Guardianship and Probate.

FIRM PROFILE: The firm traces its roots back to 1935 when the firm was established by Alfred Evens and Leroy Baker and was known as Evens & Baker. Frank A. Barnhart later joined the firm and it has evolved over the years to the current law firm. The firm has maintained a general practice and represents clients primarily throughout Greene, Owen, Lawrence, Brown, Monroe and Morgan Counties but is not limited to those areas. The firm renders services at a reasonable charge and has extensive experience in real estate development law, landlord tenant, and estate planning areas.

MEMBERS OF FIRM

ALFRED EVENS (1881-1949)

LEROY BAKER (1903-1989)

FRANK A. BARNHART, born Morgantown, West Virginia, December 6, 1929; admitted to bar, 1957, Indiana. *Education:* Indiana University (B.S., 1952; J.D., 1957). Phi Delta Phi. Town Attorney, Town of Nashville, 1972-1983. *Member:* Monroe County (President, 1975) and Indiana State Bar Associations. ***PRACTICE AREAS:*** Estates Law; Real Estate Development; Construction; Business Law.

SUZANNE STURGEON, born Indianapolis, Indiana, January 8, 1950; admitted to bar, 1983, Indiana. *Education:* Indiana State University (B.A., cum laude, 1972); Indiana University (M.A.T., 1977; J.D., cum laude, 1983). Alpha Lambda Delta; Pi Lambda Delta. Part-time Referee, Owen Circuit Court, 1992-2002. *Member:* Monroe County, Indiana State and American Bar Associations. ***PRACTICE AREAS:*** Probate; Guardianships; Estate Planning; Personal Injury.

MICHAEL J. SPENCER, born Caracas, Venezuela, January 21, 1949; admitted to bar, 1973, Indiana. *Education:* Indiana University (B.S., 1970; J.D., 1973). Deputy Public Defender for Monroe County, 1991—. Town Attorney for Town of Ellettsville, 1984—. *Member:* Monroe County, Indiana State and American Bar Associations. ***PRACTICE AREAS:*** Criminal Law; Municipal Law; Probate Law; Business Law.

LOCAL ATTORNEYS FOR: The Peoples State Bank, Ellettsville, Indiana; CBS Corp.; Monroe County Hospital Authority; Neidigh Construction Co.; Hyde Park Development Corp.; Park 48, Inc.; Park 37, Inc.; Century Suites, Inc.; Town of Ellettsville; Bloomington Township; Van Buren Township; Washington Township; Corporate Medical Services, Inc. Indiana Home Health Care, Inc.; Hallmark Rentals & Management, Inc.; Coppertree Homeowners Association; Sycamore Village Homeowners Association; Sherwood Green Homeowners Association; Greene County Board of Realtors; Bedford Board of Realtors; Timbersmith, Inc.; Sims & Pedigo, Inc.; Saint Remy Homeowners Association; Star Quarries, Inc.; Star Stone Co., Inc.; Framemakers, Inc.; Winding Brook Homeowners Association; Urban Homes, Inc.; Hidden Hills Golf Course; KDK Financial Services, Inc.; Danhechar, LLC; L.D. Construction, Inc.; Winding Brook Homeowners Assoc.; Woodridge Homeowners Assoc.; Windemere Homeowners Assoc.; Tempo Properties, Inc.; Indiana Live Steamers, Inc.; CRM Enterprises, Inc.; Neufeld, LLC; Silver Creek Homeowners Assoc.; Bayberry Homeowners Assoc.; Barrington Place Homeowners Assoc.; Stone Belt ARC, Inc.; Sherwood Hills Homeowners Assn.; Regency Associates; Waters Edge Homeowners Assn.; Eastland Plaza, Inc.; Barrington Place Homeowners Assn.; Revere's Run Homeowner's Assn.; Viacom, Inc.; Regency Associates, Inc.; Bloomington Auto Tech, Inc.; Monroe Co. Towing & Recovery, Inc.; Machango Construction; Maps of the Past, Inc.
APPROVED ATTORNEYS FOR: Lawyers Title Insurance Corp.; Prudential Insurance Co. (Mortgage Loan Department); Veterans Administration (Mortgage Loans); Monroe Bank; GMAC; Norwest Mortgage Co.; Peoples State Bank; Indiana University Employees Federal Credit Union; Bloomfield State Bank; Irwin Union Bank & Trust Co.; Owen County Bank; Fifth Third Bank; Bank One Mortgage; Old National Bank; United Commerce Bank; Union Planters Bank; Jackson County Bank; Farmers & Mechanics Savings & Loan Assn.; Peoples Trust Co.

BERRY & DOMER

701 NORTH WALNUT STREET

BLOOMINGTON, INDIANA 47404

Telephone: 812-336-8300

Fax: 812-336-2343

URL: http://www.tomberry.com

Email: lawyer@tomberry.com

URL: http://www.berry-law.com

General Civil and Business Litigation. Personal Injury, Criminal Defense, Family Law and Estates.

(This Listing Continued)

BERRY & DOMER, Bloomington—Continued

THOMAS A. BERRY, born Columbus, Ohio, March 30, 1939; admitted to bar, 1965, Indiana and U.S. District Court, Southern District of Indiana; 1969, U.S. Supreme Court. *Education:* Ohio State University (B.S., in accounting, 1962); Indiana University (J.D., 1965). Deputy Prosecuting Attorney, 1965-1966 and Prosecuting Attorney, 1967-1973, 10th Judicial Circuit, Indiana. *Member:* Monroe County, Indiana State (Chair, Litigation Section, 1995) and American Bar Associations.

MICHELLE BERRY DOMER, born Bloomington, Indiana, May 9, 1967; admitted to bar, 1992, Indiana. *Education:* University of Wisconsin (B.A., 1989); Indiana University (J.D., 1992). Certified Family Law Mediator. *Member:* Monroe County and Indiana State Bar Associations. (Certified as a Family Law Specialist by the National Board of Trial Advocacy). ***Email:*** michelle@tomberry.com

ASSOCIATE

DEBRA TRAYLOR DAVIS, born Indianapolis, Indiana, May 27, 1955; admitted to bar, 2004, Indiana. *Education:* Indiana University, Bloomington (B.A., 2001; J.D., 2003). *Member:* Monroe County, Indiana State and American Bar Associations. ***Email:*** debra@tomberry.com

A List of Representative Clients and References furnished upon request.

BUNGER & ROBERTSON

Established in 1949

226 SOUTH COLLEGE SQUARE
P.O. BOX 910
BLOOMINGTON, INDIANA 47402-0910
Telephone: 812-332-9295
Fax: 812-331-8808
Email: br@lawbr.com
URL: http://www.lawbr.com

General Practice, Civil Practice, Trial Practice, Corporate Law, Business Law, Banking Law, Wills and Probate, Trusts and Estates, Guardianships, Elder Law, Estate Planning, Insurance, Hospital Law, Health Care, Education Law, School Law, Real Estate, Land Use, Contracts, Lawsuits, Business Planning, Business Enterprises, Limited Liability Companies, Partnerships, Small Business.

FIRM PROFILE: Bunger & Robertson traces its origin to 1949. Our firm has grown in size and in the variety of legal services offered. Our attorneys concentrate in specific practice areas to best serve our clients' needs.

MEMBERS OF FIRM

LEN E. BUNGER, JR. (1921-1993)

DON M. ROBERTSON, born Seymour, Indiana, January 1, 1938; admitted to bar, 1965, Indiana, U.S. District Court, Southern District of Indiana and U.S. Supreme Court. *Education:* Purdue University (B.S., 1960); Indiana University (J.D., 1965). *Member:* Monroe County, Indiana State and American Bar Associations. (Of Counsel). ***Email:*** rob@lawbr.com

THOMAS BUNGER, born Bloomington, Indiana, April 29, 1951; admitted to bar, 1976, Indiana and U.S. District Court, Southern District of Indiana. *Education:* Indiana University (B.S., 1973; J.D., 1976). Phi Delta Phi. *Member:* Monroe County, Indiana State and American Bar Associations; National School Boards Association, Council of School Attorneys. ***PRACTICE AREAS:*** Real Estate; Estate Administration; Estate Planning; School Law; Trust Administration; Elder Law. ***Email:*** tbunger@lawbr.com

JOSEPH D. O'CONNOR, born Chicago, Illinois, September 13, 1953; admitted to bar, 1978, Indiana and U.S. District Court, Southern District of Indiana; 1986, U.S. District Court, Northern District of Indiana; 1989, U.S. Court of Appeals, Seventh Circuit. *Education:* Purdue University (B.S., 1975); Indiana University (J.D., cum laude, 1978). Certified Mediator. *Member:* Monroe County, Indiana State (President, 1994-1995; President Elect, 1993-1994; Vice President, 1992-1993; Member, Board of Managers, 1990-1992; Secretary, 1989-1990; Treasurer, 1987-1988; Chairman, Young Lawyers Section, 1986-1987) and American (Member, Board of Governors, 1998-2001; Executive Committee, 2000-2001; Chair, Standing Committee on Meetings and Travel, 1997-1998; Member, House of Delegates, 1986-2001; Delegate-At-Large, 2002-2005) Bar Associations; Defense Trial Counsel of Indiana. Fellow: American Bar Foundation; Indiana Bar Foundation. ***PRACTICE AREAS:*** Insurance Defense; Mediation; Commercial Litigation; Domestic Relations; General Practice. ***Email:*** joc@lawbr.com

JAMES L. WHITLATCH, born Dayton, Ohio, May 10, 1958; admitted to bar, 1984, Indiana and U.S. District Court, Southern and Northern Districts of Indiana. *Education:* DePauw University (B.A., magna cum laude, 1980); Indiana University (J.D., cum laude, 1984). Phi Beta Kappa. Certified Mediator. Administrative Editor and Associate Member, Indiana Law Journal, 1982-1984. Adjunct Faculty, "Legal Aspects of Healthcare," Indiana University, 1989—. *Member:* Monroe County, Indiana State (Chair, Health Law Section, 2004-2005; Chairman, General Practice Section, 1989-1990) and American Bar Associations; American Health Lawyers Association (Panel Member, National Arbitration Forum). ***PRACTICE AREAS:*** Hospital Law; Health Care; Civil Litigation; Business Law; Corporate Law; Medical Malpractice; Labor and Employment. ***Email:*** jwhit@lawbr.com

SAMUEL R. ARDERY, born Indianapolis, Indiana, January 15, 1958; admitted to bar, 1984, Indiana and U.S. District Court, Southern, Northern Districts of Indiana. *Education:* DePauw University (B.A., cum laude, 1980); Indiana University (J.D., 1983). Member, Society of Professionals in Dispute Resolution. Co-Author: "Commercial Litigation in Indiana." Guest Lecturer, Trial Techniques, Indiana School of Law. Advanced Certification, Civil Mediator. Family Mediator Certification. Faculty Trainer, Assistant Faculty for Advanced Mediation Certification. Chair, Advisory Board, Community Mediation Project. Deputy Prosecutor, Shelby County, Indiana, 1984-1985. *Member:* Monroe County, Indiana State and American Bar Associations; Indiana Trial Lawyers Association; The Association of Trial Lawyers of America; Indiana Association of Mediators; American Arbitration Association; Association of Conflict Resolution. ***PRACTICE AREAS:*** Civil Practice; Personal Injury; Commercial Litigation; Mediation; Facilitation; Arbitration. ***Email:*** sardery@lawbr.com

MARGARET M. FRISBIE, born Chicago, Illinois, April 21, 1950; admitted to bar, 1984, Kentucky and U.S. Court of Appeals, Sixth Circuit; 1985, Illinois and U.S. District Court, Northern District of Illinois; 1991, Indiana and U.S. District Court, Southern District of Indiana. *Education:* Northwestern University (B.S., 1971); University of Kentucky (J.D., summa cum laude, 1983). Order of the Coif. Editor-in-Chief, Kentucky Law Journal, 1982-1983. Clerk, Chief Judge Pierce Lively, U.S. Sixth Circuit Court of Appeals, 1983-1984. Visiting Assistant Professor of Law (1990-1991) and Adjunct Lecturer in Law (1994), Indiana University School of Law, Indianapolis. Faculty Member, The Fund Raising School. Senior Research Fellow, Center on Philanthropy, Indiana University, 1991-1997. *Member:* Indiana State and American Bar Associations; Hoosier Hills Estate Planning Council (Director and Past President). ***PRACTICE AREAS:*** Charitable Organizations; Estate Planning; Trust Administration; Probate Administration; Business Planning; Elder Law. ***Email:*** mfrisbie@lawbr.com

WILLIAM J. BEGGS, born Bloomington, Indiana, January 24, 1967; admitted to bar, 1992, Indiana and U.S. District Court, Southern and Northern Districts of Indiana. *Education:* DePauw University (B.A., 1989); Valparaiso University (J.D., 1992). Delta Theta Phi. Member, Valparaiso Moot Court Board, 1991-1992. *Member:* Monroe County (President, 2002), Indiana State (Member, House of Delegates) and American Bar Associations; Defense Trial Counsel of Indiana. ***PRACTICE AREAS:*** Civil Litigation; Hospital Law; Health Care; Corporate Law; Insurance Defense; Zoning, Planning and Land Use. ***Email:*** wjbeggs@lawbr.com

JOHN W. RICHARDS, born Bloomington, Indiana, March 28, 1964; admitted to bar, 1992, Indiana and U.S. District Court, Southern and Northern Districts of Indiana. *Education:* Indiana University (B.S., 1988; J.D., 1992; M.B.A., 1992). *Member:* Monroe County, Indiana State and American Bar Associations; Defense Trial Counsel of Indiana. ***PRACTICE AREAS:*** General Practice; Civil Litigation; Insurance Defense; Criminal Defense. ***Email:*** jwr@lawbr.com

STEVEN K. EMERY, born Bedford, Indiana, July 11, 1960; admitted to bar, 1987, Indiana; 1988, U.S. Tax Court; U.S. District Court, Southern and Northern Districts of Indiana. *Education:* Indiana University (B.S., cum laude, 1982; J.D., cum laude, 1987). *Member:* Monroe County and Indiana State Bar Associations. ***PRACTICE AREAS:*** Real Estate; Real Estate Title Insurance; Real Estate Development; Business Transactions; Business Organization; Business Transfers; Zoning, Planning and Land Use. ***Email:*** semery@lawbr.com

---

HOLLY M. HARVEY, born Kokomo, Indiana, September 16, 1971; admitted to bar, 1997, Indiana and U.S. District Court, Southern and Northern Districts of Indiana. *Education:* Indiana University (B.A., High Distinction, 1994; J.D., 1997). Phi Beta Kappa. Senior Managing Editor, Indiana Journal of Global Legal Studies. Certified Domestic Relations Mediator. *Member:* Monroe County, Indiana State (District Representative, Young Lawyers Section Council, 1998—) and American Bar Associations. ***PRACTICE AREAS:*** Civil Litigation; Family Law; Adoption Law; Insurance Defense; Real Estate. ***Email:*** hmharvey@lawbr.com

SUZETTE VANDIVIER SIMS, born Indianapolis, Indiana, November 29, 1963; admitted to bar, 1989, Indiana and U.S. District Court, Northern and Southern Districts of Indiana. *Education:* Indiana University (B.A., with honors, 1986); Indiana University School of Law (J.D., 1989). Deputy Attorney General, State of Indiana, 1993-1994. *Member:* Monroe County, Indiana State and American Bar Associations; Defense Trial Counsel of Indiana. ***PRACTICE AREAS:*** Civil Litigation; Negligence; Toxic Tort; Agricultural Law; Motor Vehicle Accidents and Injuries; Premises Liability; Employment Law; Civil Rights; Worker's Compensation; Insurance Coverage. ***Email:*** ssims@lawbr.com

KEVIN A. HALLORAN, born Dearborn, Michigan, March 23, 1966; admitted to bar, 1992, Indiana and U.S. District Court, Northern and Southern Districts of Indiana; 2000, Illinois. *Education:* Indiana University (B.A., 1988); Indiana University School of Law (J.D., 1992). Certified Public Accountant, Indiana, 1999. Formerly with Ernst & Young, LLP. *Member:* Indiana State Bar Association; Indiana CPA Society; American Institute of Certified Public Accountants. ***PRACTICE AREAS:*** Corporate Taxation; Partnership Taxation; Closely Held Business Law; Business Succession Planning; Bankruptcy Reorganization. ***Email:*** khalloran@lawbr.com

MARYANNE PELIC, born Trenton, New Jersey, November 19, 1960; admitted to bar, 1986, New Jersey. *Education:* Indiana University, Bloomington (B.S., 1983); Indiana University School of Law - Bloomington (J.D., 1986). Deputy Prosecutor, Monroe County, Indiana, 1987-2004. *Member:* Monroe County, Indiana State and American Bar Associations. ***PRACTICE AREAS:*** Child Welfare; Civil Litigation; Public Policy. ***Email:*** mpelic@lawbr.com

LARA CUTSHALL, born Indianapolis, Indiana, November 18, 1976; admitted to bar, 2004, Indiana and U.S. District Court, Northern and Southern Districts of Indiana. *Education:* Miami University (B.A., 1999); Indiana University (J.D., 2004). *Member:* Monroe County, Indiana State and American Bar Associations. ***PRACTICE AREAS:*** General Practice; Civil Litigation; Health Care; Employment; Business Law.

GENERAL COUNSEL FOR: B.G. Hoadley Quarries, Inc.; Agency for Instructional Technology (AIT); Bloomington Hospital. Curry-Buick-Cadillac-Pontiac-GMC Truck, Inc.; Monroe County Community School Corp.; Monroe County Public Library; Brown County Public Library; Southern Indiana Radiological Assn.; Southern Indiana Pediatrics, LLC; Bloomington Cardiology, P.C.; Eastern Greene County Community School Corporation; Children's Organ Transplant Association; Full-0-Pep Appliances, Inc.; Southern Indiana Medical Group; Owens, Bryan & Reed Realtors; Pritchett Brothers, Inc.; Bloomfield State Bank; Lone Star Investments, Inc.; Smith Neubecker & Associates, Inc.; Rubeck & Co., Inc.
DISTRICT COUNSEL FOR: State Farm Mutual Automobile Insurance Co.; Lowes Home Centers.; Stephens Olds-Honda; Trueblood Oil Co.; Bynum Fanyo, Inc.
LOCAL COUNSEL FOR: American International Group; Auto Owners; CNA Insurance Co.; Cigna Group; Commercial Union Group; Electric Mutual Insurance Co.; Fireman's Fund Insurance Co.; GAB Business Services, Indianapolis; GRE America; Gulf Insurance; Hawkeye-Security Insurance Co.; INAPRO; Indiana Farmers Insurance Group; Liberty Mutual; Medical Protective Co.; Motorists Mutual Insurance Co.; OHIC Insurance Co.; Prudential

(This Listing Continued)

Insurance Company of America; Reliance Insurance Co.; Ranger Insurance Co.; Shelter Insurance Co.; Underwriter's Adjusting Co.; Westfield Insurance Cos.; Western Reserve Mutual Ins. Co.; AIG Insurance Companies; Bank One; Union Planters Bank; Indiana University, Voluntary Hospitals of America.
APPROVED ATTORNEYS FOR: TICOR Title Insurance Company (formerly Pioneer National Title Insurance Co.); American General Finance, Inc.; Chicago Title Insurance Co.; Union Planters Bank.

CARSON BOXBERGER LLP

3100 JOHN HINKLE PLACE, SUITE 106
BLOOMINGTON, INDIANA 47408
Telephone: 812-333-1225
Fax: 812-333-1925
URL: http://www.carsonboxberger.com

Fort Wayne, Indiana Office: 1400 One Summit Square. Telephone: 260-423-9411. Telecopier: 260-423-4329.

General Civil Trial and Appellate Practice in all State and Federal Courts. Corporate, Business Transactions, Financial Institutions, Health Care, Probate and Estate Planning, Family Law, Transportation Law and Administration, Civil Rights, Real Estate, Labor, Insurance, Medical and Professional Malpractice, Products Liability, Workers' Compensation, Commercial, Creditors Rights and Bankruptcy Law, Mediation, Municipal.

MEMBERS OF FIRM

EDWARD J. LIPTAK, born 1954; admitted to bar, 1979, Indiana; U.S. District Court, Northern and Southern District of Indiana; U.S. Court of Appeals, Seventh Circuit. *Education:* Boston College (A.B., magna cum laude, 1976); Indiana University (J.D., cum laude, 1979). Managing Editor, Indiana Law Journal, 1978-1979. *Member:* Monroe County, Indiana State and American Bar Associations; Defense Trial Counsel of Indiana; Defense Research Institute. ***PRACTICE AREAS:*** Civil Litigation; Personal Injury Defense; Medical Malpractice Defense; Workers Compensation Defense; Product Liability Defense; Municipal Defense; Civil Rights Defense; Mediation. ***Email:*** ejl@carsonboxberger.com

DOUGLAS A. HOFFMAN, born 1965; admitted to bar, 1990, Indiana and U.S. District Court, Northern and Southern Districts of Indiana; U.S. Court of Appeals, Seventh Circuit. *Education:* Wittenberg University (B.A., cum laude, 1987); Indiana University (J.D., cum laude, 1990). *Member:* Allen County (Member: Young Lawyers Section; Litigation Section), Indiana State and American Bar Associations. ***PRACTICE AREAS:*** Civil Litigation; Workers Compensation; Insurance Defense. ***Email:*** dah@carsonboxberger.com

JEREMY M. DILTS, born 1975; admitted to bar, 2000, Indiana and U.S. District Court, Northern and Southern Districts of Indiana. *Education:* Indiana University (B.A., 1996; J.D., 2000). *Member:* Indiana State Bar Association. ***PRACTICE AREAS:*** Civil Rights Defense; Medical Malpractice Defense; Insurance Defense; Subrogation. ***Email:*** jmd@carsonboxberger

REPRESENTATIVE CORPORATE AND FINANCIAL CLIENTS: Advanced Machine & Tool Corporation; American Electric Power Company; Ashland Chemical Co.; Anthony Wayne Services; Bank One, Indiana, N.A.; BMA Medical; CB Richard Ellis Sturges; City of Fort Wayne; Ear Nose & Throat Associates; Flickinger Industries; Fort Wayne Dermatology; Fort Wayne Redevelopment Commission; Hayes Lemmerz International; Irmscher, Inc.; JobWorks; Lutheran Hospital of Indiana; National City Bank; Perfection Bakeries, Inc.; Professional Federal Credit Union; Quorum Health; Schust Engineering, Inc.; Speidell Homes Development, Inc.; Spine Technonlogy and Rehabilitation, P.C.; Sweetwater Sound, Inc.; Three Rivers Ambulance Authority; Vera Bradley Designs, Inc.; Wal-Mart Stores, Inc.
REPRESENTATIVE INSURANCE CLIENTS: American International Group; Allstate Insurance Company; Bituminous Insurance Company; Cincinnati Insurance Companies; Continental Western Insurance Company; Employer's Mutual Company; Fremont Compensation Insurance Company; GAB Robins North America; Gallagher Bassett Services; Governmental Insurance Exchange; Hamilton Mutual Insurance Company; Hastings Mutual Insurance Company; Indiana Farmers Mutual Insurance Group; Liberty Mutual Insurance Co.; Medical Assurance of Indiana; OHIC Insurance Company; ProAssurance; Progressive Insurance Group; ProNational Insurance Group; Reliance National Insurance Company; RLI Insurance Company; Rockwood Insurance Company; SAFECO Insurance Companies; St. Paul Companies; United Fire & Casualty Company; Universal Underwriters Insurance Company; Wausau Insurance Company.

(For Complete Biographical Data on all Personnel see Professional Biographies at Fort Wayne, Indiana)

CHAPMAN & NELSON, P.C.

Established in 2000
GRAHAM PLAZA
P.O. BOX 521
BLOOMINGTON, INDIANA 47404
Telephone: 812-333-9900
Fax: 812-333-9902
Email: shn@cnbloomington.com
URL: http://www.cnbloomington.com

Criminal Law, Driving While Intoxicated, Traffic Violations, Personal Injury, Litigation, Family Law, Dissolutions of Marriage, Adoption Law, Guardianship, Modification of Support and Visitation, Name Changes.

MEMBERS OF FIRM

RONALD L. CHAPMAN, born Anderson, Indiana, December 11, 1942; admitted to bar, 1971, Indiana. *Education:* Rose-Hulman Institute of Technology (B.S.E.E., 1965); Indiana University School of Law (J.D., 1971). Articles and Book Review Editor, Indiana Law Journal, 1970-1971. Lecturer, Indiana University School of Law, 1974-1977. Member, Indiana Public Defender's Council. *Member:* Monroe County and Indiana State Bar Associations; National Association of Criminal Defense Lawyers; Indiana Defense Lawyers Association. ***PRACTICE AREAS:*** Criminal Law; Personal Injury; Litigation. ***Email:*** rlc@cnbloomington.com

(This Listing Continued)

SUSAN H. NELSON, born Kansas City, Missouri, March 8, 1948; admitted to bar, 1975, Indiana. *Education:* Valparaiso University (B.A., 1970; J.D., 1975). Lecturer, Indiana University School of Business, 1992-1994. *Member:* Monroe County Bar Association (President, 1999-2000; Secretary, 2003—). ***PRACTICE AREAS:*** Family Law; Divorce; Guardianship; Adoption Law; Mediation. ***Email:*** shn@cnbloomington.com

GREENE & SCHULTZ TRIAL LAWYERS

320 W. 8TH STREET, SUITE 100
BLOOMINGTON, INDIANA 47401
Telephone: 812-336-4357
Fax: 812-336-5615
URL: http://www.greeneschultztriallawyers.com

Personal Injury, Automobile Negligence, Products Liability, Wrongful Death, Premises Liability, Wrongful Denial of Insurance, Tort Law, Insurance Disputes.

MEMBERS OF FIRM

BETSY K. GREENE, born Indianapolis, Indiana, July 20, 1957; admitted to bar, 1982, Indiana and U.S. District Court, Southern District of Indiana; 1989, U.S. Court of Appeals, Seventh Circuit and U.S. Supreme Court; 1998, U.S. Court of Appeals, Sixth Circuit; 2000, U.S. District Court, Northern District of Indiana. *Education:* Indiana University (B.A., 1975); Indiana University School of Law (J.D.,1982). Deputy Prosecuting Attorney, 1983 and Chief Deputy Prosecutor, Morgan County, 1985-1988. Member, Indiana Supreme Court Committee on Character and Fitness, 1993—. *Member:* Monroe County (President, 2005—), Morgan County, Indiana State and Seventh Circuit Bar Associations; Indiana Trial Lawyers Association (Member, Board of Directors, Advocacy, 1992—and Executive Committee, 1994—President-Elect, 2005—); Association of Trial Lawyers of America; American Board of Trial Advocates (President). Fellow, Indiana Trial Lawyers Association College. (Board Certified Civil Trial Advocate by the National Board of Trial Advocacy). ***REPORTED CASES:*** Davidson, by Floyd v. Davidson, 558 N.E.2d 849 (Ind.Ct.App. 1990); Inman v. Farm Bureau Insurance, 584 N.E.2d 567 (Ind.Ct.App. 1992); Pafco General Ins. Co. v. Providence Washington Ins. Co., 587 N.E.2d 728 (Ind.Ct.App. 1992); Meridian Mutual Ins. Co. v. Auto-Owners Ins. Co., 698 N.E.2d 770 (Ind. 1998); American Economy Ins. Co. v. Motorist Mut. Ins., 605 N.E.2d 162 (Ind. 1992); Indiana Limestone Co. v. Staggs, 672 N.E.2d 1377 (Ind.Ct.App. 1996). ***PRACTICE AREAS:*** Personal Injury; Automobile Negligence; Products Liability; Wrongful Death; Premises Liability; Wrongful Denial of Insurance. ***Email:*** bkgreene@kiva.net

FRED SCHULTZ, born Akron, Ohio, December 19, 1969; admitted to bar, 1996, Indiana and U.S. District Court, Southern and Northern Districts of Indiana. *Education:* Butler University (B.S., Economics, 1992); Indiana University School of Law (J.D., 1996). *Member:* Indiana State Bar Association; Association of Trial Lawyers of America (Member, Board of Governors, 2004-2006); Indiana Trial Lawyers Association (Member, Board of Directors, 2004—); American Board of Trial Advocates. ***PRACTICE AREAS:*** Personal Injury; Tort Law; Products Liability; Automobile Negligence; Premises Liability; Insurance Disputes. ***Email:*** fschultz@kiva.net

JONES, McGLASSON & BENCKART, P.C.

205 SOUTH WALNUT STREET
P.O. BOX 279
BLOOMINGTON, INDIANA 47402
Telephone: 812-332-4431
Fax: 812-332-0554
Email: jmbattys@bloomington.in.us
URL: http://www.jmbattys.com

General Civil and Trial Practice. Probate and Estate Planning and Administration, Real Estate, Title Insurance, Corporation, Commercial, Business, Creditors Rights, Bankruptcy, Taxation, Contracts, Construction Law, Banking, Personal Injury, Insurance, Non-profit Corporations and Motor Carrier Law.

FIRM PROFILE: The firm traces its roots back to 1947 with the establishment of the firm formerly known as Rogers & Rogers by David Rogers and Donald Rogers. Later on, Robert Delano Jones joined the firm. Over the years, the name has changed; however, the practice has remained the same as a General Civil and Trial Practice with an emphasis on Real Estate, Business, Personal Injury, Trust, Probate, Estate Planning and General Litigation. The firm primarily represents individuals, small and large corporations, businesses and banks in Monroe County and the surrounding counties but is not limited to those areas. The firm is listed in the Bar Register of Preeminent Lawyers.

ROBERT DELANO JONES, born Vevay, Indiana, December 29, 1942; admitted to bar, 1968, Indiana, U.S. District Court, Southern District of Indiana and U.S. Court of Military Appeals; 1972, U.S. Supreme Court. *Education:* Indiana University (A.B., 1965); Indiana University School of Law at Bloomington (J.D., 1968). Deputy Prosecuting Attorney, 1973. *Member:* Monroe County (President, 1994), Indiana State and American Bar Associations. [Assistant Judge Advocate, U.S. Army, 1968-1972]. ***PRACTICE AREAS:*** Litigation; Banking Law; Real Estate Law; Business Organization; Probate; Personal Injury. ***Email:*** rdjones@bloomington.in.us

THOMAS M. McGLASSON, born Martinsville, Indiana, May 17, 1943; admitted to bar, 1968, Indiana and U.S. District Court, Southern District of Indiana; 1987, U.S. Tax Court. *Education:* Indiana University (A.B., 1965; J.D., 1968). Adjunct Associate Professor of Law, Indiana University School of Law, 1984-1994. General Counsel, Indiana University Foundation, 1970-1993. *Member:* Monroe County (President, 1992), Indiana State (Chairman, Young Lawyers Section, 1975; Chairman, Taxation Section, 1994) and American Bar Associations. ***PRACTICE AREAS:*** Estate Planning; Probate; Business Organizations; Non-Profit and Charitable Organizations; Taxation. ***Email:*** tmmatt@bloomington.in.us

(This Listing Continued)

JONES, McGLASSON & BENCKART, P.C., Bloomington—Continued

JANET C. STAVROPOULOS, born Chicago, Illinois, December 5, 1946; admitted to bar, 1995, Indiana. *Education:* Gettysburg College (B.A., with distinction, 1967); Indiana University (M.A., 1971; Ph.D., 1978); Indiana University School of Law (J.D., 1994). Phi Beta Kappa. *Member:* Monroe County and Indiana State Bar Associations; American Immigration Lawyers Association; National Academy of Elder Law Attorneys. ***LANGUAGES:*** French. ***PRACTICE AREAS:*** Elder Law; Medicaid Planning; Wills; Trusts; Estate Planning; Estate Administration; Immigration Law. ***Email:*** jmbattys@bloomington.in.us

MARGUERITE R. SHREVE, born Cohasset, Massachusetts, September 28, 1946; admitted to bar, 1971, Massachusetts; 1976, Vermont, U.S. District Court, District of Vermont and District of Massachusetts and U.S. Court of Appeals, First Circuit; 1979, U.S. Supreme Court; 1985, New York; 1988, U.S. Tax Court; 1989, Indiana and U.S. District Court, Southern District of Indiana. *Education:* Mount Holyoke College (A.B., with honor and distinction, 1968); Oxford University; Boston University (J.D., 1971); New York University (LL.M., in Taxation, 1988). Adjunct Professor of Law, Indiana University, 1989—. Member: Monroe County Redevelopment Authority, 1994—; Indiana Board of Bar Examiners, Character and Fitness Committee, 1995—. *Member:* Monroe County, Massachusetts, Vermont, New York State, Indiana State and American Bar Associations. ***PRACTICE AREAS:*** Estate Planning; Estate Administration; Trust Administration; Taxation; Business Organization; Nonprofit and Charitable Organizations. ***Email:*** jmbattys@bloomington.in.us

LYNDSAY A. HALLER, born Indianapolis, Indiana, 1978; admitted to bar, 2004, Indiana and U.S. District Court, Northern and Southern Districts of Indiana. *Education:* Indiana University, Bloomington (B.A., 2001); Hamline University School of Law (J.D., 2004). *Member:* Monroe County, Indiana State and American Bar Associations; Indiana Trial Lawyers Association. ***PRACTICE AREAS:*** Banking Law; Finance; Business Law; Commercial Law; Real Estate; Probate; Estate Administration; Business Organization. ***Email:*** jmbattys@bloomington.in.us

OF COUNSEL

JUDITH CORCORAN BENCKART, born South Bend, Indiana, June 1, 1956; admitted to bar, 1985, Indiana and U.S. District Court, Southern District of Indiana. *Education:* Ball State University (B.S., 1978); Indiana University School of Law (J.D., 1985). Phi Delta Phi. *Member:* Monroe County, Indiana State and American Bar Associations; Transportation Lawyers Association; Indiana Motor Truck Association. ***PRACTICE AREAS:*** Motor Carrier Law; Creditors Rights; Bankruptcy; Real Estate Law; Business Formation; Business Sales; Business Transfers; Buying and Selling of Business; Small Business Law; Contracts; Real Estate Foreclosure; Real Estate Leasing; Real Estate Sales; Real Estate Title; Mortgage Banking Law; Business Organizations; Motor Carrier Regulation; Commercial Collections; Garnishments.

DAVID ROGERS, born Bloomington, Indiana, July 18, 1928; admitted to bar, 1955, Indiana. *Education:* Indiana University (A.B. with high honors, 1950; J.D. with high distinction, 1955). Phi Delta Phi; Phi Beta Kappa; Order of the Coif. State Senator, 1956-1972. Senate Minority Leader, 1969-1972. *Member:* Monroe County, Indiana State and American Bar Associations.

REPRESENTATIVE CLIENTS: Monroe Bank; Demshar Construction Co.; Woolery Stone Co., Inc.; BMB Heating & Cooling, Inc.; Maxwell's Business Machines, Inc.; Stone Belt Freight Lines, Inc.; Indiana University Foundation; Indiana University Alumni Association; Rogers Group Investment, Inc.; Best Way Express, Inc.; Independent Limestone Co.; Indiana MRI, LLC.
APPROVED ATTORNEYS FOR: Old Republic National Title Insurance Co.
REFERENCE: Monroe Bank.

KELLEY, BELCHER & BROWN

A PROFESSIONAL CORPORATION

Established in 1993

301 WEST SEVENTH STREET
P.O. BOX 3250
BLOOMINGTON, INDIANA 47402-3250
Telephone: 812-336-9963
Telecopier: 812-336-4588

General Civil and Insurance, Personal Injury, Corporate, Banking and Probate Law.

WILLIAM H. KELLEY, born Bloomington, Indiana, January 25, 1946; admitted to bar, 1971, Indiana and U.S. District Court, Southern and Northern Districts of Indiana; U.S. Court of Appeals, Seventh Circuit. *Education:* Indiana University (A.B., 1968; J.D., 1971). First Recipient: Indiana Defense Lawyer of the Year, 1989. Deputy Prosecuting Attorney, Monroe County, 1969-1971. Panelist: "Auto Accidents - Non-driver Liability," ICLEF, 1986; "The Nuts and Bolts of an Automobile Negligence Case," ICLEF, 1987; "Basic Insurance Law," ICLEF, 1990; "Trial Objections," ICLEF, 1993. Registered Mediator. *Member:* Monroe County, Indiana State and American Bar Associations; Indiana Defense Lawyers Association. ***REPORTED CASES:*** Roggow vs. Mineral Processing Corp., 894 F 2nd 246, S.D. IND. 1989; Wathen vs. Greencasre Skate Place, Inc. 606 NE 2nd 887 IND. Appra, 1 Dist 1993. ***PRACTICE AREAS:*** Civil Litigation; Insurance Defense; Product Liability; Personal Injury; Appellate Practice; Mediation.

THOMAS J. BELCHER, born Bloomington, Indiana, August 16, 1952; admitted to bar, 1980, Indiana and U.S. District Court, Southern District of Indiana; U.S. Court of Appeals, Seventh Circuit. *Education:* Indiana University (B.A., 1977; J.D., 1980). Registered Mediator. *Member:* Monroe County, Indiana State and American Bar Associations; Indiana Defense Lawyers Association. ***PRACTICE AREAS:*** Civil Litigation; Insurance Defense; Personal Injury; Banking; Probate; Mediation.

(This Listing Continued)

DARLA SUE BROWN, born Indianapolis, Indiana, May 16, 1963; admitted to bar, 1988, Indiana and U.S. District Court, Northern and Southern Districts of Indiana; U.S. Court of Appeals, Seventh Circuit; U.S. Supreme Court. *Education:* Indiana University (B.A., 1985; J.D., 1988). Alpha Lambda Delta; Golden Key; Order of the Barristers. Registered Mediator. *Member:* Morgan County, Monroe County and Indiana State Bar Associations; Defense Trial Counsel of Indiana. ***PRACTICE AREAS:*** Civil Litigation; Insurance Defense; Product Liability; Personal Injury; Appellate Practice.

SHANNON L. ROBINSON, born Washington, Indiana, May 8, 1962; admitted to bar, 1990, Florida, Indiana and U.S. District Court, Northern and Southern Districts of Indiana; U.S. Court of Appeals, Seventh Circuit; U.S. Supreme Court. *Education:* University of Evansville, School of Business (B.S., 1984); Indiana University (J.D., 1989). Recipient: American Jurisprudence Award in Advanced Torts. Registered Mediator. *Member:* Monroe County, Indiana State and American Bar Associations; The Florida Bar; Indiana Defense Lawyers Association; Indiana Trial Lawyers Association. ***PRACTICE AREAS:*** Criminal; Civil; Insurance; Personal Injury; Appellate Practice; Mediation.

THADDEUS CRAIG KELLEY, born Bloomington, Indiana, September 13, 1973; admitted to bar, 2000, Indiana. *Education:* Hanover College (B.A., 1996); University of Louisville, Louis D. Brandeis School of Law (J.D., 1999). ***PRACTICE AREAS:*** Insurance Defense; Personal Injury; Property Damage; Wills; Trusts and Estates. ***Email:*** tkelley@kelleybelcherbrown.com

REPRESENTATIVE CLIENTS: Bank One Indiana, N.A.; Bloomfield State Bank; Aetna Casualty & Surety Co.; American Family Insurance Co.; General Casualty Insurance Co.; Hoosier Insurance Co.; Grange Mutual Casualty Co.; Indiana Insurance Co.; Liberty Mutual Insurance Co.; State Farm Fire & Casualty Co.; Monroe Guaranty Ins.

MALLOR CLENDENING GRODNER & BOHRER LLP

511 WOODSCREST DRIVE
P.O. BOX 5787
BLOOMINGTON, INDIANA 47407-5787
Telephone: 812-336-0200
Fax: 812-333-0083
Email: info@mcgb.com
URL: http://www.mcgb.com

Indianapolis, Indiana Office: Suite 770 Market Square Center, 151 N. Delaware Street, 46204. Telephone: 317-453-2000. Fax: 812-333-0083.

Civil Litigation, Insurance Defense, Business Law, Wills, Trusts and Estates, Family Law, Personal Injury, Taxation, Corporate Law, Real Estate, Probate, Labor and Employment.

FIRM PROFILE: At Mallor Clendening Grodner & Bohrer LLP, we take great pride in our team of lawyers, legal assistants and staff. Each member of our team is committed to providing quality legal services and personal attention to the needs of our clients. To assure the professionalism of our services, we are divided into four primary departments-Business, Litigation, Family Law, and Estate Planning and Probate.

PARTNERS OF FIRM

ANDREW C. MALLOR, born Newark, New Jersey, January 19, 1949; admitted to bar, 1974, Indiana and U.S. District Court, Southern District of Indiana; 1981, U.S. Supreme Court and U.S. Tax Court. *Education:* Indiana University (A.B., 1971; J.D., 1974). Certified Family Law Mediator. Fellow, American Academy of Matrimonial Lawyers. Certified, Family Law Specialist. ***PRACTICE AREAS:*** Family Law; Domestic Relations; Estate Planning; Pre-Marital Agreements; Civil Litigation. ***Email:*** acmallor@mcgb.com

GARY J. CLENDENING, born Fresno, California, January 16, 1944; admitted to bar, 1968, Indiana; U.S. District Court, Southern District of Indiana. *Education:* DePauw University; Indiana University (A.B., with distinction, 1965; J.D., 1968). Certified Civil Mediator. Fellow, American College of Trial Lawyers. ***PRACTICE AREAS:*** Insurance Defense; Civil Litigation; Medical Malpractice Defense; Legal Malpractice Defense; Environmental Litigation; Toxic Tort Defense. ***Email:*** gjclende@mcgb.com

GEOFFREY M. GRODNER, born Houston, Texas, August 22, 1950; admitted to bar, 1975, Indiana and U.S. District Court, Southern District of Indiana; 1978, U.S. Court of Appeals, Seventh Circuit; 1998, U.S. Supreme Court. *Education:* Indiana University (A.B., 1972; J.D., cum laude, 1975). Certified Civil Mediator. ***PRACTICE AREAS:*** Civil Litigation; Criminal Defense; Automotive Franchises and Dealerships; Environmental Law; Environmental Litigation; Business Law; Corporate Law. ***Email:*** gmgrodne@mcgb.com

JAMES F. BOHRER, born New Albany, Indiana, June 14, 1957; admitted to bar, 1982, Indiana and U.S. District Court, Southern District of Indiana; 1985, U.S. Tax Court. *Education:* Indiana University (B.S., 1979; J.D., magna cum laude, 1982). *Member:* Indiana Certified Public Accountant Society (Associate Member); Monroe County Building Association. ***PRACTICE AREAS:*** Real Estate Development; Estate Planning; Business Law; Corporate Law; Probate; Taxation. ***Email:*** jfbohrer@mcgb.com

KENDRA GOWDY GJERDINGEN, born Marshalltown, Iowa, July 20, 1950; admitted to bar, 1978, Minnesota; 1993, Indiana and U.S. District Court, Southern District of Indiana; 1994, U.S. Court of Appeals, Seventh Circuit; 1998, U.S. Supreme Court. *Education:* University of Iowa (B.A., 1972); William Mitchell College of Law (J.D., cum laude, 1978) Indiana University (M.B.A., 1990). Phi Beta Kappa. Certified Family Law Mediator. Certified Family Law Specialist. ***PRACTICE AREAS:*** Corporate Law; Family Law; Domestic Relations; Interstate Support; Interstate Child Custody; Insurance Defense; Appellate Practice. ***Email:*** kggjerdi@mcgb.com

CARYL M. BOWERS, born New York, New York, January 15, 1954; admitted to bar, 1990, Indiana. *Education:* The Ohio State University (B.S., 1974); Indiana University (J.D., 1989). Certified Family Mediator. ***PRACTICE AREAS:*** Family Law; Domestic Relations; Adoption Law. ***Email:*** cmbowers@mcgb.com

(This Listing Continued)

LANCE D. LIKE, born Vincennes, Indiana, December 10, 1964; admitted to bar, 1990, Colorado and U.S. District Court, District of Colorado; 1991, Indiana. *Education:* University of Evansville (B.S., 1987); Indiana University School of Law (J.D., cum laude, 1990). Delta Theta Phi. ***PRACTICE AREAS:*** Estate Planning; Probate; Real Estate; Corporate Law. ***Email:*** ldlike@mcgb.com

LONNIE D. JOHNSON, born Elnora, Indiana, May 11, 1957; admitted to bar, 1992, Indiana, U.S. District Court, Northern and Southern Districts of Indiana. *Education:* Indiana University (B.A., summa cum laude, 1989; J.D., cum laude, 1992). Phi Beta Kappa. ***PRACTICE AREAS:*** Civil Litigation; Insurance Defense; Business Law. ***Email:*** ljohnson@mcgb.com

ASSOCIATES

CARRIE L. BATALON, born Milwaukee, Wisconsin, June 21, 1971; admitted to bar, 1998, Indiana and U.S. District Court, Southern District of Indiana. *Education:* Indiana University (B.S., 1993; J.D., 1998). ***PRACTICE AREAS:*** Civil Litigation; Business Litigation; Taxation; Family Law. ***Email:*** cbatalon@mcgb.com

GARRY L. FOUNDS, born Columbus, Ohio, April 16, 1967; admitted to bar, 2000, Indiana and U.S. District Court, Northern and Southern Districts of Indiana. *Education:* Anderson University (B.A., 1989); Indiana University School of Law - Bloomington (J.D., magna cum laude, 1999). Order of the Coif. ***PRACTICE AREAS:*** Business Law; Family Law; Financial Law; Estate Planning. ***Email:*** gfounds@mcgb.com

D. MICHAEL ALLEN, born Kankakee, Illinois, April 16, 1975; admitted to bar, 2000, Indiana and U.S. District Court, Southern and Northern Districts of Indiana; 2004, California and U.S. District Court, Central District of California. *Education:* Indiana University (B.A., 1997; J.D., 2000). ***PRACTICE AREAS:*** Civil Litigation; Insurance Defense. ***Email:*** dmallen@mcgb.com

JANICE L. STERLING, born Oak Lawn, Illinois, December 8, 1972; admitted to bar, 2001, Indiana and U.S. District Court, Southern District of Indiana. *Education:* College of St. Francis (B.A., summa cum laude, 1995); DePaul Law School (J.D., with honors, 2001). Order of the Coif. ***PRACTICE AREAS:*** Employment; Civil Litigation; Insurance Defense. ***Email:*** jsterling@mcgb.com

STACY F. THOMPSON, born Peoria, Illinois, August 17, 1977; admitted to bar, 2002, Indiana and U.S. District Court, Northern and Southern Districts of Indiana. *Education:* Indiana University (B.S., 1999; J.D., 2002). ***PRACTICE AREAS:*** Insurance Defense; Medical Malpractice Defense; Civil Litigation; Business Law. ***Email:*** sthompso@mcgb.com

ANTHONY J. YORIO, JR., born Brooklyn, New York, July 1, 1972; admitted to bar, 2002, Pennsylvania and New Jersey; 2003, Indiana and U.S. District Courts, Northern and Southern Districts of Indiana; 2005, Connecticut. *Education:* Western Connecticut State University (B.A., 1997); Indiana University (J.D., 2002). Order of the Barristers. ***PRACTICE AREAS:*** Civil Litigation; Criminal Law; Business Organization. ***Email:*** ayorio@mcgb.com

PATRICK OMILIAN, born Buffalo, New York, July 19, 1973; admitted to bar, 2003, Indiana and U.S. District Court, Southern and Northern Districts of Indiana. *Education:* Cornell University (B.S., 1995); Indiana University (J.D., 2002). ***PRACTICE AREAS:*** Environmental Law; Water Law; Civil Litigation. ***Email:*** pomilian@mcgb.com

REPRESENTATIVE CLIENTS: Bill C. Brown Associates; Nick's English Hut, Inc.; United Commerce Bank; Indiana University Employees Federal Credit Union; ISU/The May Agency, Inc.; Rogers Group, Inc.; City of Bloomington, Indiana; Bloomington Utilities Service Board; Royal Auto Group; Community Chrysler Plymouth Dodge Jeep, Inc.; Poynter Chevrolet-Oldsmobile, Inc.; Bloomington Ford Inc.; Wilson Oldsmobile Cadillac, Inc.; Marco Plastics, Inc.; Wininger/Stolberg Group; Rumpke of Indiana, Inc.; Steele-Beard Electric, Inc.; Gentry Development Company; Winslow Farm Development Company, Inc.; Monroe County Building Association; The Cincinnati Insurance Co.; The Medical Protective Co.; General Casualty Co.; American Family Insurance Co.; American Standard, Inc.
REFERENCES: Monroe County Bank; United Commerce Bank.

TIMOTHY J. VRANA LLC

BLOOMINGTON, INDIANA

(See Columbus)

Social Security Disability, Civil Litigation, Civil Appeals.

ROEBUCK & ASSOCIATES, P.C.

BLUFFTON, INDIANA

(See Ft. Wayne)

Personal Injury, Automobile Accidents, Boat Accidents, Motorcycle Accidents, Truck Accidents, Slip and Fall, Dog Bites, Medical Malpractice, Head Injuries, Nursing Home Abuse and Neglect, Products Liability, Insurance, Social Security, Social Security Disability, and Wrongful Death.

BAMBERGER, FOREMAN, OSWALD AND HAHN, LLP

BOONVILLE, INDIANA

(See Evansville)

Administrative Law, Antitrust Law, Appellate Practice, Arbitration, Banking Law, Bankruptcy Law, Business Law, Civil Rights, Civil Trial Practice, Commercial Law, Commercial Litigation, Communications Law, Construction Law, Corporate Law, Creditors' Rights, Elder Law, Energy Law, Environmental Law, Health Care Law, Insurance Defense, Intellectual Property Law, Labor and Employment Law, Land Use Law, Medical Malpractice, Mergers and Acquisitions, Product Liability Law, Public Utilities Law, Real Estate Law, Trademark, Copyright and Unfair Competition, Trusts and Estates, Wills and Probate.

KAHN, DEES, DONOVAN & KAHN, LLP

BOONVILLE, INDIANA

(See Evansville)

General Civil Practice including Litigation, Environmental, Labor Management, Corporate, Pension, Banking, Hospital, Insurance Defense, Real Estate, Workers' Compensation, Tax, Construction, Immigration and General Civil Law.

RUDOLPH, FINE, PORTER & JOHNSON LLP

BOONVILLE, INDIANA

(See Evansville)

General Corporate Practice. Health Care Law, Commercial Litigation, Insurance Defense, Real Estate, Zoning and Land Use Law, Mediation and Arbitration, Bankruptcy Law, Mergers and Acquisitions. Probate and Estate Planning, Tax, Employment Law, Appeals, Banking. Trials in all State and Federal Courts.

TERRELL, BAUGH, SALMON & BORN, LLP

BOONVILLE, INDIANA

(See Evansville)

General Civil Trial and Appellate Practice in State and Federal Courts. Insurance Defense, Commercial Transactions, Business Organizations, Employment, Construction, Bankruptcy, Probate and Estate Planning and Administration, Real Estate, Personal Injury, Environmental, Mediation, Zoning, Shopping Center Development and Leasing.

WILKINSON, GOELLER, MODESITT, WILKINSON & DRUMMY

BRAZIL, INDIANA

(See Terre Haute)

General Civil Practice in all Courts. Taxation, Corporation, Trust, Probate, Estate Planning, Insurance Law, Health Law, Municipal Law, Bankruptcy, and Creditors Rights. Insurance Defense, Business Litigation, Mediation and Arbitration.

THOMPSON LAW OFFICE

BROOKVILLE, INDIANA

(See Connersville)

Personal Injury, Debt Collection, Estate Planning, Criminal Law, Appellate Practice, Bankruptcy, Environmental Law, Family Law.

DONNA J. BAYS

BROWNSBURG, INDIANA

(See Indianapolis)

Family Law, Divorce, Child Custody, Paternity, Premarital Agreements.

TUCKER LAW OFFICES

61 RIDGEWAY DRIVE
BROWNSBURG, INDIANA 46112-1004
Telephone: 317-852-3291
Fax: 317-852-7537
Email: mtuckeresq@aol.com

Intellectual Property, Patent and Trademark Law.

FIRM PROFILE: The Tucker Law Offices offer over 25 years of experience in all facets of intellectual property law, including patents, trademarks, trade secrets, validity and infringement opinions, design and implementation of IP strategy, asset evaluation, licensing, intellectual property management, expert witnesses and mediation services.

MARY ANN TUCKER, admitted to bar, 1973, Indiana, U.S. District Court, Southern District of Indiana and U.S. Court of Appeals, Seventh Circuit; 1980, U.S. Supreme Court; 1990, New York; 1992, Ohio; registered to practice before U.S. Patent and Trademark Office. *Education:* North Dakota State University (B.S., Chem., 1961); Iowa State University (M.S., Physical Chemistry, 1965); Indiana University (J.D., summa cum laude, 1973; M.B.A., Finance, 1981). Beta Gamma Sigma. Assistant Patent Counsel, Eli Lilly and Company, 1973-1989. Staff Vice President and Chief Patent Counsel, Bausch & Lomb, 1989-1990; Vice President and Associate General Counsel, B.F. Goodrich Company, 1991-1998. Member, 1994— President, 1997-1998, National Inventors Hall of Fame. Member, Commerce Department International Advisory Committee on Intellectual Property and Trade, 1984-1998. *Member:* Indiana State Bar Association; Cleveland Intellectual Property Law Association (President, 1995); American Intellectual Property Law Association; Association of Corporate Patent Counsel (Director, 1997-1998). ***PRACTICE AREAS:*** Intellectual Property.

CAMPBELL KYLE PROFFITT LLP

Established in 1915

11595 N. MERIDIAN, SUITE 701
CARMEL, INDIANA 46032
Telephone: 317-846-6514
FAX: 317-843-8097
Email: ckplaw@ckplaw.com
URL: http://www.ckplaw.com

Noblesville Office: 198 South Ninth Street, P.O. Box 2020. Telephone: 317-773-2090. Fax: 317-776-5051.

Civil Practice. State and Federal Courts and Administrative Agencies, Domestic Relations, Family Law, Divorce, Adoptions, Personal Injury, Corporation, Business Law, Utility Law, Insurance, Wills and Probate, Trusts and Estates, Estate Planning and Elder Law, Real Estate, Zoning, Employment Law, Criminal Law. Contracts, Taxation, Real Estate, Commercial Litigation.

FIRM PROFILE: Campbell Kyle Proffitt LLP has provided legal services to clients in central Indiana since 1915. The firm serves individuals, partnerships, corporations and various municipal and other public entities. While we are a general practice firm, the members of the firm concentrate their respective work within a few areas of the law. For complex matters it is not unusual for two or more members of the firm to become involved. Our touchstone is prompt personal attention to our clients' needs.

MEMBERS OF FIRM

JOHN D. PROFFITT, born Lebanon, Indiana, 1932; admitted to bar, 1959, Missouri; 1963, Indiana. *Education:* Wabash College (A.B., 1954); University of Chicago (J.D., 1959). *Member:* Hamilton County, Indiana State (Treasurer, 1991-1992; Vice President, 1993-1994; President, 1995-1996) and American Bar Associations; Fellow: American College of Trial Lawyers; American Academy of Matrimonial Lawyers; American Bar Foundation; Indiana State Bar Foundation. ***PRACTICE AREAS:*** Civil Practice; Personal Injury; Business Litigation; Family Law; Domestic Relations. ***Email:*** jproffitt@ckplaw.com

DEBORAH L. FARMER, born Indianapolis, Indiana, 1954; admitted to bar, 1983, Indiana. *Education:* Butler University (B.S., cum laude, 1976); Indiana University School of Law (J.D., magna cum laude, 1983). Certified Family Law Specialist. Author, "Survey of Recent Developments in Family Law," Indiana Law Review, Vol. 29, Nov. 3, 1991. *Member:* Hamilton County and Indiana State (Member, Board of Managers, 1990-1992; Counsel to the President, 1993; Chair, Family and Juvenile Law Section, 1995-1997) Bar Associations. American Academy of Matrimonial Lawyers; Fellow, Indiana Bar Foundation (President, 1998-2000). ***PRACTICE AREAS:*** Domestic Relations; Mediation. ***Email:*** dfarmer@ckplaw.com

WILLIAM E. WENDLING, JR., born Kendallville, Indiana, 1950; admitted to bar, 1983, Indiana. *Education:* Texas A. & I. University (B.A., 1973); Indiana University School of Law (J.D., 1983). Law Clerk to the Hon. James E. Noland, Chief Judge, U.S. District Court, Southern District of Indiana, 1983-1984. Member, Indiana Education Employment Relations Board, 1989—. Treasurer, Indiana Bar Foundation. *Member:* Hamilton County and Indiana State Bar Associations. ***PRACTICE AREAS:*** Civil Practice; Real Estate; Zoning Law; Family Law; Domestic Relations; Personal Injury; Criminal Law; Business Litigation. ***Email:*** wwendling@ckplaw.com

ANNE HENSLEY POINDEXTER, born Salina, Kansas, 1962; admitted to bar, 1988, Indiana. *Education:* Ball State University (B.S., 1984); Indiana University School of Law (J.D., cum laude, 1988). Registered Mediator. Tax Analyst, Supervisor, 1985-1987 and Administrator, 1987-1988, Inheritance Tax Division, Indiana Department of Revenue. *Member:* Hamilton County (President, 1996-1998), Indiana State and American Bar Associations. ***PRACTICE AREAS:*** Civil Practice; Probate; Estate Planning; Domestic Relations; Mediation; Public Utility Law. ***Email:*** apoindexter@ckplaw.com

MICHAEL A. CASATI, born Milwaukee, Wisconsin, 1959; admitted to bar, 1992, Indiana. *Education:* Indiana University (B.A., with distinction, 1982; J.D., cum laude, 1992). Indiana University Police Academy, 1981. Indiana State Police Academy, 1983. Certified Family Law Specialist. *Member:* Hamilton County and Indiana State Bar Associations. Fellow, Indiana Bar Foundation. ***PRACTICE AREAS:*** Family Law; Civil Litigation; Criminal Litigation. ***Email:*** mcasati@ckplaw.com

RODNEY T. SARKOVICS, born Buffalo, New York, 1970; admitted to bar, 1996, Indiana. *Education:* Canisius College (B.S., 1992); Ohio Northern University (J.D. with distinction, 1996). Phi Kappa Phi; American Inns of Court. Editor, Ohio Northern Law Review. Author: "How Loud Is Too Loud," Indiana State Bar Association Young Lawyer's Section Network, Fall, 1999; Case Summaries: Family Matters, 1999—. *Member:* Hamilton County, Indiana State and American Bar Associations. ***PRACTICE AREAS:*** Family Law; Criminal Law; Civil Litigation. ***Email:*** rsarkovics@ckplaw.com

ASSOCIATES

SCOTT P. WYATT, born Dubuque, Iowa, 1970; admitted to bar, 1998, Indiana. *Education:* Northeast Missouri State University (B.A., 1993); Indiana University (J.D., 1998). Phi Delta Phi. Past Deputy Proscuetor, Marion County Prosecutors Office, 1998-2001. *Member:* Indiana and American Bar Associations. ***PRACTICE AREAS:*** Criminal Law; Family Law; Civil Litigation; Utilities. ***Email:*** swyatt@ckplaw.com

AMY E. HIGDON, born Marion, Indiana, 1975; admitted to bar, 1999, Indiana. *Education:* Ball State University (B.S., summa cum laude, 1996); Indiana University School of Law-Indianapolis (J.D., cum laude, 1999). Phi Delta Phi. Law Clerk to the Hon. Margret G. Robb, Indiana Court of Appeals, 1999-2001. *Member:* Hamilton County, Indiana State (Member, Family Law Section) and American Bar Associations. ***PRACTICE AREAS:*** Family Law. ***Email:*** ahigdon@ckplaw.com

N. SCOTT SMITH, born Benton Harbor, Michigan, 1976; admitted to bar, 2005, Indiana. *Education:* Purdue University (B.A., 1999); Indiana University School of Law (J.D, 2004). Runner Up, Moot Court Barrister Championship. Recipient, John J. Dillon Scholarship. Realtor, 2001. ***LANGUAGES:*** Spanish. ***Email:*** ssmith@ckplaw.com

(This Listing Continued)

GENERAL COUNSEL FOR: Clay Township Regional Waste District; Lake Santee Regional Waste District; Industrial Dielectrics, Inc.; Beck's Superior Hybrids, Inc.; Underwriters Surety, Inc.; Carmel Clay Public Library; Advanced Marketing Technologies, Inc.; Lake Santee Property Owners Association.
REPRESENTATIVE CLIENTS: PSI Energy, Inc.; Mobil Oil Corp.; Minnesota Mining & Manufacturing Co.; Conseco Insurance Companies; Metro Plastics Technology, Inc; Inland Paperboard and Packaging, Inc.; Mohawk Industries, Inc..

(For Complete Personnel and Biographical Data, see Professional Biographies at Noblesville, Indiana)

DANIEL R. CARROLL

CARMEL, INDIANA

(See Indianapolis)

Business Law, Contracts, Litigation, Insurance, Debtor and Creditor, Collections, Business Enterprises, Corporate Law, Partnerships, Real Estate, Commercial Litigation, Commercial Leasing, Buy-Sell Agreements, Employment Law, Noncompete Litigation, Wrongful Termination, Trade Secrets, Personal Injury, Automobile Accidents, Slip and Fall, Wrongful Death, Bankruptcy, Arbitration, Mediation.

CHURCH, CHURCH, HITTLE & ANTRIM

CARMEL, INDIANA

(See Noblesville)

General Civil Trial Practice in all State and Federal Courts. Appellate and Federal Practice, Personal Injury, Automobile Accidents, Wrongful Death, Family Law, Adoption Law, Child Custody, Child Support, Divorce, Visitation Rights, Municipal and Governmental Regulations, Real Estate, Zoning Law, Land Use, Commercial Leasing, Wills, Probate, Trusts and Estates, Estate Planning, Asset Protection, Guardianship Law, Estate Administration and Litigation, Tax Planning, Tax Controversies, Business Law, Contracts, Litigation, Business Enterprises, Business Transactions, Corporate Formation, Corporate Litigation, School Law, Commercial Litigation, Professional License Defense, Medical Malpractice, Bankruptcy, Criminal Law, Driving While Intoxicated, Drug Crimes, Felonies, Misdemeanors, Mediation.

COOTS, HENKE & WHEELER

PROFESSIONAL CORPORATION

Established in 1978

255 EAST CARMEL DRIVE
CARMEL, INDIANA 46032
Telephone: 317-844-4693
Fax: 317-573-5385
URL: http://www.lawyers.com/chwlaw

General Civil and Criminal Practice. Litigation in all Courts. Corporate, Insurance, Probate and Estate Planning, Taxation, Real Estate and Zoning and Planning Law. Business Law, Personal Injury, Insurance Defense, Tort and Family Law, Divorce Law, Criminal Law, Domestic Relations.

FIRM PROFILE: Coots, Henke & Wheeler established in 1978 primarily serves the Northern suburbs of Indianapolis in many General Practice areas with an emphasis on Business, Real Estate, Personal Injury and Corporate Law. We are committed to providing quality cost effective legal services to meet the needs of our diverse client base.

E. DAVIS COOTS, born Jeffersonville, Indiana, January 24, 1944; admitted to bar, 1969, Indiana and U.S. District Court, Southern District of Indiana; 1971, U.S. Court of Appeals, 7th Circuit; 1993, U.S. Supreme Court. *Education:* Monmouth College (B.A., 1965); Indiana University (J.D., 1969). Member, 1976-1980 and President, 1979, Carmel City Council. Member, 1976-1980 and President, 1977-1980, Carmel Planning Commission. Carmel City Attorney, 1982-1983. *Member:* Indianapolis (Member, Board of Managers, 1975-1978; 1996-1997), Hamilton County, Indiana State and American Bar Associations. ***PRACTICE AREAS:*** Litigation; Business Law; Planning and Zoning Law; Mediation. ***Email:*** dcoots@chwlaw.com

JAMES K. WHEELER, born Shelbyville, Indiana, April 12, 1945; admitted to bar, 1971, Indiana and U.S. District Court, Northern and Southern Districts of Indiana; 1977, U.S. Court of Appeals, 7th Circuit. *Education:* Purdue University (B.S.M.E., 1967); Indiana University (J.D., 1971). *Member:* Indianapolis, Hamilton County, Indiana State and American (Member, Sections on: Corporation, Banking and Business Law; Tort and Insurance Practice) Bar Associations; American Board of Trial Advocates. ***PRACTICE AREAS:*** General Practice; Litigation; Corporate Law; Product Liability Mediation. ***Email:*** jwheeler@chwlaw.com

JAY CURTS, born Inglewood, California, February 19, 1963; admitted to bar, 1988, Indiana and U.S. District Court, Northern and Southern Districts of Indiana. *Education:* Indiana University-Bloomington (B.S., Finance, 1985); Indiana University-Indianapolis (J.D., 1988). *Member:* Indianapolis, Hamilton County, Indiana State and American Bar Associations. ***PRACTICE AREAS:*** Probate Administration Law; Estate Planning Law; Business Organizations and Transactions; Real Estate. ***Email:*** jcurts@chwlaw.com

JAMES D. CRUM, born Columbus, Ohio, February 8, 1961; admitted to bar, 1989, Indiana and U.S. District Court, Southern and Northern Districts of Indiana. *Education:* Ohio State University (B.A., 1983); Indiana University-Indianapolis (J.D., 1989). Phi Delta Phi. *Member:* Hamilton County, Indiana State and American Bar Associations; Defense Research Institute. ***PRACTICE AREAS:*** Criminal Defense; Criminal Law; Insurance Defense Law; Appeals; Municipal Liability; Municipal Defense. ***Email:*** jcrum@chwlaw.com

JEFFREY S. ZIPES, born Durham, North Carolina, May 31, 1965; admitted to bar, 1990, Indiana, U.S. District Court, Northern and Southern Districts of Indiana, U.S. Court of Appeals, Seventh Circuit and U.S. Supreme Court. *Education:* Tulane University (B.A., 1987); Indiana University-Indianapolis (J.D., 1990). *Member:* Indianapolis, Hamilton

(This Listing Continued)

County, Indiana State and American Bar Associations; Indiana Defense Lawyers Association. ***PRACTICE AREAS:*** Mass Torts; Insurance Defense; Family Law; Collections; Mediation; Personal Injury; General Litigation. ***Email:*** jzipes@chwlaw.com

ELIZABETH I. VAN TASSEL, born Hammond, Indiana, December 28, 1959; admitted to bar, 1991, Indiana and U.S. District Court, Northern and Southern Districts of Indiana. *Education:* Indiana University School of Nursing (A.D., 1982); College of St. Francis (B.S., 1987); Indiana University (J.D., magna cum laude, 1991). Cale J. Holder Merit Scholar. Note Development Editor, Indiana Law Review, 1990-1991. *Member:* Indianapolis, Hamilton County, Indiana State and American Bar Associations. ***PRACTICE AREAS:*** General Civil Practice; Medical Malpractice; Family Law; Estate Planning Law. ***Email:*** lvantassel@chwlaw.com

MATTHEW L. HINKLE, born Brownsburg, Indiana, September 22, 1970; admitted to bar, 1996, Indiana, U.S. District Court, Northern and Southern District of Indiana, U.S. Court of Appeals, Seventh Circuit and U.S. Supreme Court. *Education:* Indiana University (B.A., 1993; J.D., summa cum laude, 1996). Cale J. Holder Merit Scholar. F. Emerson Boyd Trial Advocacy Award. *Member:* Indianapolis, Hamilton County, Lake County, Indiana State and American Bar Associations; Defense Trial Counsel of Indiana; Defense Research Institute. ***PRACTICE AREAS:*** Insurance Defense; Product Liability; Municipal Defense; General Litigation. ***Email:*** mhinkle@chwlaw.com

J. KATHRYN JENKINS, born Indianapolis, Indiana, July 28, 1944; admitted to bar, 1994, Indiana and U.S. District Court, Southern and Northern Districts of Indiana. *Education:* Purdue University (B.S., 1966); Indiana University (J.D., 1994). Phi Alpha Delta. *Member:* Indianapolis, Hamilton County, Indiana State and American Bar Associations. ***LANGUAGES:*** Spanish. ***PRACTICE AREAS:*** Civil Practice; Family Law; Estate Planning. ***Email:*** kjenkins@chwlaw.com

DANIEL E. COOTS, born Indianapolis, Indiana, July 21, 1972; admitted to bar, 1999, Indiana and U.S. District Court, Northern and Southern Districts of Indiana. *Education:* Indiana University-Bloomington (B.S. Marketing, 1995; J.D., 1998). *Member:* Indianapolis, Hamilton County, Indiana State and American Bar Associations. ***PRACTICE AREAS:*** Civil Litigation; Business Organizations; Business Transactions; Estate Planning; Real Estate. ***Email:*** dancoots@chwlaw.com

RYAN H. CASSMAN, born Indianapolis, Indiana, September 21, 1975; admitted to bar, 2002, Indiana and U.S. District Court, Northern and Southern Districts of Indiana. *Education:* Indiana University (B.A., 1997); Indiana University School of Law (J.D., 2002). Phi Delta Phi, 1999-2002. *Member:* Indianapolis, Hamilton County and Indiana State Bar Associations. ***PRACTICE AREAS:*** Litigation; Domestic Relations; Education Law. ***Email:*** rcassman@chwlaw.com

LAURA E. TRULOCK, born Indianapolis, Indiana, June 19, 1978; admitted to bar, 2003, Indiana and U.S. District Court, Northern and Southern Districts of Indiana. *Education:* Indiana University (B.A., 2000; J.D., 2003). Note Development Editor, Indiana Law Review, 2002-2003. *Member:* Hamilton County, Indianapolis, Indiana State and American Bar Associations. ***PRACTICE AREAS:*** General Practice; Criminal Defense; Municipal Defense. ***Email:*** ltrulock@chwlaw.com

ERIN MALOY, born Milwaukee, Wisconsin, May 22, 1978; admitted to bar, 2004, Indiana. *Education:* Indiana University (B.A., 2000; J.D., 2004). *Member:* Indianapolis and American Bar Associations. ***PRACTICE AREAS:*** Litigation; Family Law; Criminal Law. ***Email:*** emaloy@chwlaw.com

OF COUNSEL

STEVEN H. HENKE, born Evansville, Indiana, April 24, 1951; admitted to bar, 1977, Indiana and U.S. District Court, Southern District of Indiana. *Education:* Indiana University (B.S., magna cum laude, 1973; J.D., cum laude, 1977). Beta Gamma Sigma. *Member:* Indianapolis, Hamilton County, Indiana State and American Bar Associations. ***PRACTICE AREAS:*** Corporate Law; Real Estate Law; Personal Injury Law.

REPRESENTATIVE CLIENTS: Alliance Insurance Company; Conseco, Incorporated; Municipal Insurance Alliance; Tutwiler Cadillac; Toyota Motor Corporation; Freightliner Corporation; Volvo-GM Heavy Truck Corporation; Landmark Development Corporation; Thomas & Skinner, Incorporated; Wheeler Corporation; Bultmann Maschenbau; Pearson Ford, Incorporated; Indianapolis Signworks, Inc.; Kroger Corporation; Central Indiana Restaurants, Incorporated; Avalon Wealth Advisors, L.L.C.; IBM; Dow Chemical Company; Automotive Group, Inc.; Ritz Charles, Inc.; Domino's Pizza/LiLiCo., Inc.; Lo Carb USA; Delello & Sons Asphalt Paving, Inc.; Affco Machine Sales, Inc.; Diversified Communications Group, Inc.; Exterior Home Improvements, Inc.; The Fineberg Group, LLC; G&S Research, Inc.; Tank & Piping Contractors, Inc.; Assurance Partners Bank; Community Development, Inc.; Carmax, Inc.; Indiana Members Credit Union; Carmel-Clay Veterans Memorial, Inc.; Caterpillar Corp.; Kimball International; Network Adjusters, Inc.; Irwin Union Bank & Trust; Superior Roofing Services, Inc.; Buckaroo Boat Compan; Valeo Financial Advisors, Inc.
REFERENCES: Huntington National Bank of Indiana; KeyBank, Indiana; Bank One, Indianapolis, N.A.; First Indiana National Bank.

DELANEY & DELANEY LLC

CARMEL, INDIANA

(See Indianapolis)

Employment Litigation, Litigation, Products Liability, International Law, Media Law, Election Law, Business Law, Fraud, Breach of Contract, Securities, Estate Administration, First Amendment Law.

DREWRY SIMMONS VORNEHM, LLP

CARMEL, INDIANA

(See Indianapolis)

Business, Construction, Government Contracts, Surety, Commercial and related Arbitration and Litigation, Securities, Estate Planning, Trusts, Taxation, Construction and Public Contracts law, Surety, Civil Litigation, Mediation and Arbitration, Corporations, Business and Securities Law, Estate Planning and Administration, Commercial Real Estate Transactions, Land Use Planning and Zoning, Labor and Employment Law, Adoption.

DUTTON & ASSOCIATES, L.L.C.

CARMEL, INDIANA

(See Indianapolis)

Bankruptcy Law.

EICHHORN & EICHHORN

9640 NORTH AUGUSTA DRIVE
SUITE 412
CARMEL, INDIANA 46032
Telephone: 317-228-9670
Telecopier: 317-228-9569

Hammond, Indiana Office: 200 Russell Street, P.O. Box 6328, 46325. Telephone: 219-931-0560. Fax: 219-931-5370.

General Practice, Litigation in State and Federal Courts. Public Utility, Banking, Corporation, Health Care, Insurance, Commercial Transactions, Labor and Employment Law, Real Estate, Professional Liability and Tort Law. Mediation.

(For complete biographical data on all personnel, see Professional Biographies at Hammond, Indiana)

HARRISON & MOBERLY, LLP

Established in 1950
11611 NORTH MERIDIAN STREET
SUITE 150
CARMEL, INDIANA 46032
Telephone: 317-639-4511
Fax: 317-574-6055
Email: attorneys@h-mlaw.com
URL: http://www.harrisonmoberly.com

Marion Office: 315 South Adams Street, 3rd Floor, Marion, Indiana, 46952. Telephone: 765-673-6499.

FIRM PROFILE: Harrison & Moberly is a comprehensive, full-service law firm located at the crossroads of America, with offices in Indianapolis, Carmel, and Marion, Indiana. The firm has a long history and tradition, going all the way back to its founding in 1950. Although the firm's headquarters are in the Midwest, Harrison & Moberly serves its clients' needs locally, nationally and internationally.

(For Complete Biographical Data on all Personnel, see Biographies at Indianapolis, Indiana)

HOLT, FLECK & ROMINE

CARMEL, INDIANA

(See Noblesville)

Civil and Criminal Trials in all Courts, Criminal Law, Drug Crimes, Driving While Intoxicated, Parole and Probation, Traffic Violations, Wills and Probate, Trusts and Estate, Guardianships, Asset Protection, Estate Planning, Business, Contracts, Business Planning, Lawsuits, Business Enterprises, Closely Held Business, Corporate, Partnerships, Limited Liability Companies, Small Business, Real Estate, Buying and Selling Real Estate, Commercial Leasing, Family Law, Adoptions, Child Custody, Child Support, Divorce, Visitations Rights, Domestic Violence, Domestic Relation, Personal Injury, Automobile Accidents, Slip and Fall, Wrongful Death, Medical Malpractice, Unsafe Products, Bankruptcy, Elder Law.

KNOWLES & ASSOCIATES, LLC

811 SOUTH RANGE LINE ROAD
CARMEL, INDIANA 46032
Telephone: 317-848-4360
Telecopier: 317-848-4363
Email: Firm@KnowlesAssociatesLLC.com
URL: http://www.lawyers.com/knowles

Practice limited to Wills and Probate, Business Law, Business Planning, Starting a Business, Buying and Selling a Business, Elder Law, Estate Planning, Litigation, Trusts and Estates, Tax Planning, Medicaid Planning.

FIRM PROFILE: Knowles & Associates, LLC has been in service to individuals throughout the state of Indiana for over 70 years. The firm was established in 1934 by Hugh J. Baker, Esquire, and focuses on estate and business planning. The firm offers a team approach to legal services.

WILLIAM W. KNOWLES, born Indianapolis, Indiana; admitted to bar, 1969, Indiana and U.S. District Court, Southern District of Indiana; 1970, U.S. Court of Appeals, Seventh Circuit; 1971, U.S. Tax Court; 1972, U.S. District Court, Northern District of Ohio; 1976, U.S. Supreme Court; 1996, U.S. District Court, Northern District of Indiana. *Education:* Indiana University (A.B., 1963; J.D., 1969). Phi Delta Phi. Trust Officer, Indiana National Bank, 1964-1968, Merchants National Bank, 1969. Deputy Prosecutor, Marion County, 1970. Assistant U.S. Attorney, Southern District of Indiana, 1970-1971. Hearing Officer, Public Service Commission of Indiana, 1971. City Attorney, Carmel, Indiana, 1979. *Member:* Indianapolis (Member, Legal Ethics Committee, 1969-1971; 1977; Chair, Small Firm Practice Section, 1995), Hamilton County (Member, Court Liaison Committee, 1976-1978), Indiana State (Delegate, ISBA House of Delegates, 1992) and Federal Bar Associations; Indiana Trial Lawyers Association; Indianapolis Estate Planning Council; Na-

(This Listing Continued)

KNOWLES & ASSOCIATES, LLC, Carmel—Continued

tional Academy of Elder Law Attorneys; Christian Legal Society; Rotary Club of Indianapolis. ***PRACTICE AREAS:*** Elder Law; Estate Planning; Litigation; Civil Appeals; Criminal Appeals; Probate Administration; Trust Administration; Business Law. ***Email:*** firm@knowlesassociatesllc.com

MILLICENT E. HATCH, born Dayton, Ohio; admitted to bar, 1978, Indiana and U.S. District Court, Southern District of Indiana. *Education:* Université Laval, Quebec City, Quebec, Canada (1969); Anderson University (B.A., 1971); Ball State University (M.A., 1974); Indiana University School of Law (J.D., 1978). Associate Editor, Indiana Law Review; Listed in Who's Who in American Colleges & Universities. Research Assistant, Indiana Judicial Center, 1976-1977. Madison County Prosecutor's Office intern, 1978. Instructor, Business Communications and Business Law, Indiana Wesleyan University, 1997-1998. ***PRACTICE AREAS:*** Business Law; Contracts; Elder Law; Estate Planning; Litigation; Criminal Appeals; Civil Appeals; Probate; Trust Administration. ***Email:*** m.hatch@knowlesassociatesllc.com

---

SHAWN M. SCOTT, born Indianapolis, Indiana; admitted to bar, 2004, Illinois; 2005, Indiana. *Education:* Hanover College (B.A., Political Science, 2000); John Marshall Law School (J.D., 2005; LL.M., Intellectual Property, 2005). Previously with Carroll and Wall, Chicago, Illinois. *Member:* Chicago, Indianapolis, Illinois State, Indiana State and American Bar Associations. ***PRACTICE AREAS:*** Estate Planning; Probate; Trust Litigation. ***Email:*** sscott@knowlesassociatesllc.com

DANIEL K. DILLEY, born Muncie, Indiana; admitted to bar, 2001, Indiana, U.S. District Court, Northern and Southern Districts of Indiana. *Education:* Liberty University (B.S., 1996); Indiana University School of Law (J.D., 2000). *Member:* Indianapolis Bar Association; Indiana State Bar Association (Member, Young Lawyers Section). ***PRACTICE AREAS:*** Estate Planning; Medicaid Planning; Litigation; Business Law. ***Email:*** d.dilley@knowlesassociatesllc.com

KRIEG DeVAULT LLP

Established in 1870

12800 NORTH MERIDIAN STREET, SUITE 300
CARMEL, INDIANA 46032
Telephone: 317-566-1110
Fax: 317-636-1507
Email: contact@kdlegal.com
URL: http://www.kriegdevault.com

Indianapolis, Indiana Office: One Indiana Square, Suite 2800, 46204. Telephone: 317-636-4341. Fax: 317-636-1507.
Fort Wayne, Indiana Office: Krieg DeVault Lundy LLP, 825 Anthony Wayne Building, 203 East Berry Street, 46802. Telephone: 260-422-1534. Fax: 260-423-1590.
Hammond, Indiana Office: Krieg DeVault Galvin LLP, 5231 Hohman Avenue, 46320. Telephone: 219-933-0380. Fax: 219-933-0471.

Acquisitions, Divestitures and Mergers, Antitrust, Appeals, Banking, Bankruptcy, Business and Commercial, Copyright, Corporations, Creditors' Rights, Employee Benefits, Energy, Environmental, ERISA, Estate Planning and Probate, Family/Domestic Relations, Federal and State Taxation, Government Relations, Health Care, Hospital Law, Intellectual Property, Insurance, International, Labor and Employment, Legislative, Litigation, Patent, Public Finance, Public Utilities, Products Liability, Real Estate, Securities Law, Tax-Exempt and Nonprofit Organizations, Technology and E-Commerce, Trademark.

LAW FIRM ALLIANCES/ASSOCIATIONS: ***MERITAS:*** *Members of Meritas, serving the needs of clients in more than 145 markets worldwide.*

PARTNERS

BRADLEY S. FUSON, born Terre Haute, Indiana, December 16, 1959; admitted to bar, 1986, Indiana. *Education:* DePauw University (B.A., cum laude, 1982); Indiana University (M.B.A., 1985); Indiana University School of Law - Indianapolis (J.D., summa cum laude, 1985). *Member:* Indianapolis, Indiana State and American Bar Associations. Fellow, Indianapolis Bar Foundation. ***PRACTICE AREAS:*** Asset-Based Lending; Commercial Real Estate Finance; Real Estate; Commercial Leasing and Property Dispositions; Business and Corporate Law; Acquisitions, Divestitures and Mergers. ***Email:*** bfuson@kdlegal.com

JEFFREY C. McDERMOTT, born Cleveland, Ohio, August 16, 1961; admitted to bar, 1986, Indiana, U.S. District Court, Southern and Northern Districts of Indiana and U.S. Court of Appeals, Seventh Circuit. *Education:* Purdue University (B.A., with highest distinction, 1983); University of Notre Dame Law School (J.D., 1986). *Member:* Indianapolis, Indiana State and Seventh Circuit Bar Associations. ***PRACTICE AREAS:*** Litigation; Products Liability; Toxic Torts; RICO Litigation; Securities Fraud; Personal Injury; Wrongful Death. ***Email:*** jmcdermott@kdlegal.com

FRANK A. HOFFMAN, born Evansville, Indiana, September 1, 1957; admitted to bar, 1983, Indiana. *Education:* DePauw University (B.A., 1979); Indiana University School of Law - Indianapolis (J.D., 1982). *Member:* Indianapolis, Indiana State and American Bar Associations. ***PRACTICE AREAS:*** Real Estate; Health Care; Emerging Business Law; Business and Corporate Law; Federal and State Taxation; Securities; Commercial Finance. ***Email:*** fhoffman@kdlegal.com

ERIC A. MANTERFIELD, born New York, N.Y., October 2, 1947; admitted to bar, 1972, Indiana and U.S. District Court, Southern and Northern Districts of Indiana. *Education:* Denison University (B.A., magna cum laude, 1969); University of Michigan Law School (J.D., 1972). Author, "Critical Elements of Estate Planning With Forms," (EAM Publisher) 2002. *Member:* Indianapolis, Indiana State and American Bar Associations. Fellow, American College of Trust and Estate Counsel. ***PRACTICE AREAS:*** Family Business Successions; Estate Planning; Estate Administration; Estate Litigation; Trust Litigation. ***Email:*** emanterfield@kdlegal.com

(This Listing Continued)

ANDREW B. BUROKER, born Marion, Indiana, September 2, 1961; admitted to bar, 1990, Indiana and U.S. District Court, Southern and Northern Districts of Indiana; 2001, U.S. Supreme Court. *Education:* DePauw University (B.A., 1984); University of London, England (1988); Indiana University School of Law - Bloomington (J.D., cum laude, 1989). *Member:* Indianapolis, Indiana State and American Bar Associations. ***PRACTICE AREAS:*** Real Estate; Environmental Law; Municipal Law; Commercial Finance; Real Estate Finance; Financial Institutions; Securities; Business Law. ***Email:*** aburoker@kdlegal.com

GLENN T. TROYER, born Chicago, Illinois, April 5, 1944; admitted to bar, 1975, Indiana and Ohio. *Education:* Wittenberg University (B.A., 1967); Indiana University (M.H.A., 1971); Capital University Law School (J.D., cum laude, 1975). ***PRACTICE AREAS:*** Health Care and Hospital Law. ***Email:*** gtroyer@kdlegal.com

THE HONORABLE JERRY M. BARR, born Noblesville, Indiana, November 22, 1941; admitted to bar, 1967, Indiana and U.S. District Court, Southern District of Indiana; 1979, U.S. Supreme Court. *Education:* Yale University (A.B., 1964); University of Chicago Law School (J.D., 1967); Indiana Judicial College (1985). *Member:* Indiana State and American Bar Associations; American Judicature Society. Fellow, Indiana Bar Foundation (Master). ***PRACTICE AREAS:*** Alternative Dispute Resolution; Arbitration; Private Judging. ***Email:*** jbarr@kdlegal.com

SUSAN E. ZIEL, born Pittsburgh, Pennsylvania, June 16, 1951; admitted to bar, 1991, South Carolina; 1998, Indiana. *Education:* Madonna University (B.S.N., 1980); University of Michigan (M.P.H., 1984); University of South Carolina School of Law (J.D., 1991). Registered Nurse License, Indiana, 1998—, South Carolina, 1983-1998 and Michigan, 1974-1983. Adjunct Professor, Health Care Law, University of South Carolina School of Law, 1994-1997. Adjunct Professor, Indiana University School of Nursing, 1998—. *Member:* Indiana State and American Bar Associations; American Health Lawyers Association. ***PRACTICE AREAS:*** Health and Hospital Law; Administrative Law. ***Email:*** sziel@kdlegal.com

CHARLES S. COLEMAN, II, born Knoxville, Tennessee, August 22, 1971; admitted to bar, 1996, Alabama; 1999, Indiana. *Education:* University of Notre Dame (B.B.A., 1993); University of Alabama School of Law (J.D., 1996). *Member:* Indianapolis, Indiana State and American Bar Associations; Alabama State Bar. ***PRACTICE AREAS:*** Business and Corporate Law; Securities Regulation; Public Finance; Business Succession Planning. ***Email:*** ccoleman@kdlegal.com

OF COUNSEL

EDWARD R. SCHMIDT, born Philadelphia, Pennsylvania, August 21, 1947; admitted to bar, 1972, Pennsylvania and U.S. District Court, Eastern District of Pennsylvania; 1974, Michigan and U.S. District Court, Western District of Michigan; 1983, Indiana and U.S. District Court, Southern District of Indiana; U.S. Supreme Court; U.S. Court of Appeals, Third and Seventh Circuits. *Education:* Susquehanna University (B.S., 1969); University of Notre Dame Law School (J.D., 1972). *Member:* Indianapolis, Indiana State and American Bar Associations; State Bar of Michigan. ***PRACTICE AREAS:*** Nonprofit and Charitable Organizations; Tax Exempt Organizations; Business and Corporate Law. ***Email:*** eschmidt@kdlegal.com

ASSOCIATES

RODNEY S. RETZNER, born Sunman, Indiana, August 30, 1968; admitted to bar, 1998, Indiana and U.S. District Court, Southern and Northern Districts of Indiana. *Education:* Rose-Hulman Institute of Technology (B.S.M.E., 1990); University of Cincinnati College of Law (J.D., 1998). *Member:* Indianapolis, Indiana State and American Bar Associations. [Lt. Commander, U.S. Navy, USS Alabama, SSBN 731G, 1989-1995]. ***PRACTICE AREAS:*** Estate Planning; Estate and Gift Taxation; Probate; Business Succession Planning; Nonprofit and Charitable Organizations; Taxation; Business Law; Commercial Law. ***Email:*** rretzner@kdlegal.com

ROBERT S. SCHEIN, born Indianapolis, Indiana, January 30, 1970; admitted to bar, 1997, Indiana and U.S. District Court, Southern and Northern Districts of Indiana; Indiana Supreme Court. *Education:* Indiana University (B.A., 1992); Indiana University School of Law - Indianapolis (J.D., 1997). *Member:* Indianapolis, Boone County, Hamilton County, Indiana State and American Bar Associations. ***PRACTICE AREAS:*** Construction Law; Creditors Rights; Bankruptcy; Workouts; Real Estate; Litigation. ***Email:*** rschein@kdlegal.com

STEPHAN H. GEISLER, born Indianapolis, Indiana, September 10, 1961; admitted to bar, 1988, New York; 1995, U.S. Court of Appeals for the Armed Forces; 2002, Indiana. *Education:* University of Michigan (B.A., 1983); Georgetown University (M.B.A., 1987); Georgetown University School of Law (J.D., 1987). *Member:* Indianapolis and Indiana State Bar Associations. ***PRACTICE AREAS:*** Corporate Law; Financial Institutions; Securities. ***Email:*** sgeisler@kdlegal.com

MATTHEW R. STRZYNSKI, born Lawrenceburg, Indiana, August 16, 1976; admitted to bar, 2002, Indiana and U.S. District Court, Southern and Northern Districts of Indiana. *Education:* Indiana University (B.A., 1998); University of Cincinnati College of Law (J.D., 2002). *Member:* Indianapolis, Indiana State and American Bar Associations. ***PRACTICE AREAS:*** Creditors Rights; Bankruptcy; Litigation; Real Estate. ***Email:*** mstrzynski@kdlegal.com

MATTHEW E. CONRAD, born Berne, Indiana, September 10, 1978; admitted to bar, 2003, Indiana and U.S. District Court, Southern and Northern Districts of Indiana; 2004, Florida. *Education:* Taylor University (B.S., magna cum laude, 2000); Indiana University School of Law - Bloomington (J.D., cum laude, 2003). *Member:* Indianapolis, Indiana State and American Bar Associations; The Florida Bar; American Institute of Certified Public Accountants. ***PRACTICE AREAS:*** Mergers and Acquisitions; Corporate Taxation; Partnership Taxation; Corporate Finance; Real Estate. ***Email:*** mconrad@kdlegal.com

KELLY J. GREEN, born Muncie, Indiana, June 20, 1969; admitted to bar, 2004, Indiana and U.S. District Court, Southern and Northern Districts of Indiana. *Education:* Ball State University (B.S., 1995); Indiana University School of Law - Indianapolis (J.D., magna cum laude, 2004). *Member:* Indianapolis, Indiana State and American Bar Associations. ***PRACTICE AREAS:*** Health Care. ***Email:*** kgreen@kdlegal.com

(This Listing Continued)

ANGELA L. HAMM, born South Bend, Indiana, March 19, 1974; admitted to bar, 1999, Indiana and U.S. District Court, Southern and Northern Districts of Indiana; U.S. Court of Appeals, Seventh Circuit. *Education:* Indiana University (B.A., 1996); Indiana University School of Law - Indianapolis (J.D., 1999). *Member:* Indianapolis, Indiana State and American Bar Associations. ***PRACTICE AREAS:*** Complex and Multi-District Litigation; Environmental Law; Products Liability; Toxic Torts; Appellate Practice. ***Email:*** ahamm@kdlegal.com

NIGEL J. RIGGINS, born Chicago, Illinois, April 7, 1978; admitted to bar, 2005, Indiana. *Education:* DePauw University (B.A., 2000); Indiana University School of Law - Indianapolis (J.D., 2005). ***PRACTICE AREAS:*** Creditors Rights; Business Law; Real Estate; Litigation. ***Email:*** nriggins@kdlegal.com

SHEILA A. MARSHALL

320 S. RANGELINE ROAD
CARMEL, INDIANA 46032
Telephone: 317-575-0320
Fax: 317-575-9570
Email: sam@mandmlawyers.com
URL: http://www.smarshalllaw.com

Family Law, Divorce, Child Custody, Visitation Issues, Child Support, Prenuptial Agreements, Mediation.

SHEILA A. MARSHALL, born Shelbyville, Indiana, November 1, 1956; admitted to bar, 1986, Indiana and U.S. District Court, Southern and Northern Districts of Indiana. *Education:* Indiana University; Franklin College of Indiana (B.A., magna cum laude, 1978); Indiana University (J.D., 1986). Certified Family Law Mediator, 1990—. *Member:* Indianapolis, Hamilton County (President, 1994-1995), Indiana State and American Bar Associations. ***PRACTICE AREAS:*** Family Law; Divorce; Child Custody; Visitation Rights; Child Support; Premarital Agreements; Domestic Relations; Mediation.

MAURER RIFKIN & HILL, P.C.

11550 NORTH MERIDIAN STREET, SUITE 115
CARMEL, INDIANA 46032
Telephone: 317-844-8372
Fax: 317-573-5564
Email: rrifkin@mrhlaw.com
URL: http://www.maurerrifkinandhill.com

Labor and Employment Law, Disability Accommodation, Discrimination, Employee Benefits, Wrongful Termination, Sexual Harassment, Civil Rights, Business Law, Business Planning, Contracts, Business Litigation, Business Enterprises, Small Business, Partnerships, Limited Liability Companies, Buying and Selling a Business, Starting a Business, Corporate Law, Family Law, Adoptions, Child Custody, Child Support, Divorce, Wills, Probate, Trusts and Estates, Estate Planning.

ROBERT S. RIFKIN, born Hammond, Indiana, March 19, 1944; admitted to bar, 1972, Indiana and U.S. District Court, Southern District of Indiana; 1976, U.S. Court of Appeals, Seventh Circuit. *Education:* University of Illinois (B.A., 1965; M.A., Labor and Industrial Relations, 1967); Indiana University School of Law (J.D., 1972). ***Email:*** rrifkin@mrhlaw.com

SHERWOOD P. HILL, born Buffalo, New York, June 30, 1935; admitted to bar, 1970, Indiana and U.S. District Court, Southern District of Indiana; 1976, U.S. Supreme Court. *Education:* Indiana University (B.S., 1966; J.D., 1970). Supervisor, Marion County Prosecutors Office Felony Courts, 1974-1977. ***Email:*** shill@mrhlaw.com

---

CLINTON E. BLANCK, born Lebanon, Indiana, June 16, 1971; admitted to bar, 1996, Indiana and U.S. District Court, Southern and Northern Districts of Indiana. *Education:* Indiana University (B.A., 1993); Indiana University School of Law (J.D., 1996). ***Email:*** cblanck@mrhlaw.com

STEPHANIE J. FAIRFIELD, born Indianapolis, Indiana, 1965; admitted to bar, 2000, Indiana. *Education:* Indiana University (B.S., 1993); Indiana University School of Law - Indianapolis (J.D., 2000). *Member:* Indianapolis, Indiana and American Bar Associations. ***Email:*** sfairfield@mrhlaw.com

IDA C. LAMBERTI, born Clare, Iowa, 1939; admitted to bar, 1992, Indiana; U.S. District Court, Southern and Northern Districts of Indiana; U.S. Court of Appeals, Seventh Circuit. *Education:* Creighton University (B.A., English, 1962); California State University (M.A., English, 1969); Indiana University School of Law (J.D., 1992). *Member:* Indiana Employment Lawyers Association. ***Email:*** iclamberti@mrhlaw.com

THOMAS M. JOHNSTON, born Battle Creek, Michigan, January 13, 1948; admitted to bar, 1974, Indiana. *Education:* Indiana University (B.S., 1970; J.D., summa cum laude, 1974).

MEYER LAW OFFICE

CARMEL, INDIANA
(See Indianapolis)

Wills, Trusts and Estates, Probate Law, Charitable Giving, Non-profit Organizations, Small Business, Business Law, Real Estate, Income Tax, Estate and Gift Taxation and Wealth Preservation Law.

NEWTON BECKER BOUWKAMP

CARMEL, INDIANA
(See Indianapolis)

General Practice. Business Law, Estate Planning, Family Law, Insurance Coverage Law, Litigation, Manufactured Housing and Recreational Vehicles Law, Mediation and Arbitration, Not-for-Profit Law and Real Estate Law.

STEVEN SAMS

CARMEL, INDIANA
(See Indianapolis)

Employment Law, Wrongful Termination, Disability Accomodation, Employee Benefits, Sexual Harassment, Workers Compensation, Civil Rights, Discrimination, Sexual Harassment, Family Law, Adoptions, Divorce, Child Custody, Child Support, Visitation Rights, Wills, Probate, Trusts and Estates, Estate Planning, Guardianship, Personal Injury, Automobile Accidents, Medical Malpractice, Business Law, Contracts, Commercial Leasing, Business Enterprise, Business Formation, Buying and Selling of Businesses, Mold Litigation, State, Federal and Appellate Courts.

SCHULTZ & POGUE, LLP

Established in 2000
11611 NORTH MERIDIAN STREET
SUITE 706
CARMEL, INDIANA 46032
Telephone: 317-569-2570
Fax: 317-569-2580
URL: http://www.schultzpoguelaw.com

Insurance Defense, Personal Injury, Medical Malpractice, Pharmacy Law, Drugs and Medical Devices, Health Care, Administrative Law, Appellate Practice, Government Liability, Products Liability, Construction Law, Labor and Employment.

THOMAS R. SCHULTZ, born Wausau, Wisconsin, May 21, 1962; admitted to bar, 1987, Indiana. *Education:* Indiana University (B.A., 1984; J.D., 1987). *Member:* Indianapolis and Indiana State Bar Associations; American Board of Trial Advocates; Defense Research Institute (Member, Sections on: Trial Tactics; Governmental Liability); Defense Trial Counsel of Indiana (Treasurer, Legislative Committee; Member, Sections on: Products Liability and Business Litigation); International Association of Defense Counsel. ***PRACTICE AREAS:*** Negligence Defense; Products Liability; Medical Malpractice; Governmental Liability; Commercial Law; Employment Law; Construction Law. ***Email:*** tschultz@schultzpoguelaw.com

PETER H. POGUE, born Cynthiana, Kentucky, September 1, 1961; admitted to bar, 1989, Indiana. *Education:* DePauw University (B.A., 1983); Valparaiso University (J.D., 1989). Note Editor, Law Review, Valparasio University. *Member:* Indianapolis and Indiana State Bar Associations; Defense Research Institute (Member, Sections on: Medical Liability; Drug and Medical Devices); Defense Trial Counsel of Indiana (Chair, Health Law Litigation Section, 2001-2002). ***PRACTICE AREAS:*** Medical Malpractice; Drugs and Medical Devices; Pharmacy Law; Class Actions Defense; Multi-District Litigation; Administrative Law. ***Email:*** ppogue@schultzpoguelaw.com

JON M. PINNICK, born New Albany, Indiana, October 29, 1964; admitted to bar, 1990, Indiana. *Education:* Hanover College (B.A., 1987); Indiana University, School of Law (J.D., 1990). *Member:* Indianapolis and Indiana State Bar Associations; Defense Research Institute; Defense Trial Counsel of Indiana. ***PRACTICE AREAS:*** Medical Malpractice; Litigation; Health Care. ***Email:*** jpinnick@schultzpoguelaw.com

DONALD B. KITE, SR., born Kokomo, Indiana, November 22, 1960; admitted to bar, 1987, Indiana. *Education:* Loyola College (B.A., 1982); Indiana University, School of Law (J.D., 1986). Law Clerk for Federal Magistrate Judge Kennard P. Foster, 1988-1990; Senior District Judge James E. Noland, 1990-1992; Senior District Judge, William E. Steckler, 1992-1995. *Member:* Indianapolis, Seventh Circuit, Indiana State and Federal Bar Associations; Defense Research Institute (Member, Governmental Liability Section); Defense Trial Counsel of Indiana (Former Chair, Insurance Coverage Section; Member, Amicus Committee). ***PRACTICE AREAS:*** Civil Litigation; Civil Rights Defense; Products Liability; Insurance Coverage; Appellate Practice. ***Email:*** dkite@schultzpoguelaw.com

---

JILL M. EMERSON, born Noblesville, Indiana, November 28, 1967; admitted to bar, 1995, Indiana and U.S. District Court, Northern and Southern Districts of Indiana; 1997, U.S. Court of Appeals, Seventh Circuit. *Education:* Purdue University (B.A., 1990); Indiana University (J.D., cum laude, 1995). *Member:* Indianapolis and Indiana State Bar Associations; Defense Trial Counsel of Indiana. ***PRACTICE AREAS:*** Litigation; Medical Malpractice; Labor and Employment. ***Email:*** jemerson@schultzpoguelaw.com

DAVID G. FIELD, born East Chicago, Indiana, September 7, 1971; admitted to bar, 1997, Indiana and U.S. District Court, Northern and Southern Districts of Indiana. *Education:* Indiana University (B.S., 1993; J.D., 1997). *Member:* Indianapolis, Indiana State and American Bar Associations. ***PRACTICE AREAS:*** Medical Malpractice; Insurance Defense; Business Litigation. ***Email:*** dfield@schultzpoguelaw.com

CATHERINE L. KYLE, born Ann Arbor, Michigan, 1971; admitted to bar, 1996, Indiana and U.S. District Court, Southern District of Indiana; 2001, U.S. Court of Appeals, Seventh Circuit; 2002, U.S. District Court, Northern District of Indiana. *Education:* University of North Carolina at Chapel Hill (B.A., 1993); Indiana University School of Law - Bloomington (J.D., magna cum laude, 1996). Order of the Coif. Managing Editor, and Note Author, Indiana Law Journal, Vol. 71. *Member:* Evansville, Indianapolis, Indiana State and American Bar Associations; Defense Trial Counsel of Indiana; Defense Research Institute. ***PRACTICE AREAS:*** Medical Malpractice; Litigation; Employment Law.

(This Listing Continued)

SCHULTZ & POGUE, LLP, Carmel—Continued

JEFFREY L. LUND, born Bay City, Michigan, February 5, 1973; admitted to bar, 2000, Indiana, U.S. District Court, Northern and Southern Districts of Indiana and U.S. Court of Appeals, Seventh Circuit. *Education:* Kalamazoo College (B.A., 1995); Freie Universität Berlin (Hanns-Seidel Fellow, 1995-1997); Valparaiso University (J.D., cum laude, 2000). Executive Member, Valparaiso University Moot Court Society. Participant: ABA National Moot Court Competition, Washington, D.C.; National First Amendment Moot Court Competition, Vanderbilt University. *Member:* Indianapolis and Indiana State Bar Associations; Defense Research Institute; Defense Trial Counsel of Indiana. ***PRACTICE AREAS:*** Medical Malpractice; Insurance Defense; Litigation; Labor and Employment; Wrongful Termination Defense; Employment Defense; Commercial Law; Landlord and Tenant Law. ***Email:*** jlund@schultzpoguelaw.com

CHARLES S. SMITH, born Champaign, Illinois, June 22, 1972; admitted to bar, 2001, Indiana; U.S. District Court, Southern and Northern Districts of Indiana. *Education:* Ball State University (B.S., magna cum laude, 1994); University of Georgia (M.P.A., 1996; J.D., cum laude, 2001). *Member:* Indianapolis, Indiana State and American Bar Associations. ***PRACTICE AREAS:*** Medical Malpractice; Insurance Defense. ***Email:*** csmith@schultzpoguelaw.com

OF COUNSEL

CARLA V. GARINO, born Terre Haute, Indiana, April 11, 1973; admitted to bar, 1998, Indiana and U.S. District Court, Northern and Southern Districts of Indiana. *Education:* Butler University (B.A., 1995); Indiana University-Bloomington (J.D., 1998). *Member:* Indianapolis Bar Association. ***PRACTICE AREAS:*** Medical Malpractice; Drug and Medical Device Defense; Employment Law; Commercial Law. ***Email:*** cgarino@schultzpoguelaw.com

ANGELA L. SOUTHERN, born Inglewood, California; admitted to bar, 1988, Indiana and U.S. District Court, Southern District of Indiana. *Education:* DePauw University (B.A., 1985); Indiana University (J.D., 1988). *Member:* Indianapolis Bar Association. ***PRACTICE AREAS:*** Medical Malpractice; Commercial Insurance Defense; General Liability Defense; Professional Liability Defense. ***Email:*** asouthern@schultzpoguelaw.com

REPRESENTATIVE CLIENTS: Advanced Physical Therapy, P.C.; American Airlines; Bestfoods, Inc.; CVS; Gallagher Bassett Services, Inc.; Genzyme Corp.; ProAssurance; FCCI Insurance Group; NCMIC Group; Specialty Risk Services; The Hartford; The Kroger Co.; The GE Medical Protective Co.; Gulf Insurance Co.; Reid Hospital and Health Care Services; The Travelers; Interstate Insurance Group; Jefferson Insurance Co.; Garage Doors of Indianapolis, Inc.; Citizens Insurance Company of America; Erie Insurance Company; Rogers Group, Inc.; Heritage Property Investment Trust, Inc.

WAGNER REESE & CROSSEN, LLP

Established in 2000

11939 NORTH MERIDIAN
CARMEL, INDIANA 46032
Telephone: 317-569-0000; 800-792-0332
Fax: 317-569-8088
URL: http://www.InjuryAttorneys.com
Email: WRC@InjuryAttorneys.com
URL: http://www.lawyers.com/wrclaw

Personal Injury, Wrongful Death, Premises Liability, Construction Accidents, Medical Malpractice, Legal Malpractice, Workers Compensation, Insurance Claims, Civil Rights, Class Actions.

FIRM PROFILE: Personal injury law firm. Our injury attorneys handle medical malpractice, wrongful death and worker's compensation claims throughout Indiana and nationwide.

STEPHEN M. WAGNER, born Indianapolis, Indiana, June 3, 1969; admitted to bar, 1994, Indiana and U.S. District Court, Northern and Southern Districts of Indiana. *Education:* University of Notre Dame (B.A., cum laude, 1991); Indiana University-Bloomington (J.D., cum laude, 1994). Phi Alpha Delta. Member, National Moot Court Team, 1994. Recipient, Best Brief Award, Sherman Minton Moot Court Competition, 1993. Selected to Department of Justice, Attorney General's Honor Program, 1994. Graduated with honors, Federal Law Enforcement Training Academy, 1994. Presenter, "Workers Compensation in Indiana," National Business Institute Seminar, 2001, 2002. Named an "Indiana Super Lawyer" by Indianapolis Monthly Magazine for 2004. *Member:* Indianapolis, Indiana State and American Bar Associations; Indiana Trial Lawyers Association (Sustaining Member); The Association of Trial Lawyers of America. ***PRACTICE AREAS:*** Personal Injury; Products Liability; Civil Rights; Class Actions; Medical Malpractice; Workers Compensation. ***Email:*** swagner@InjuryAttorneys.com

JASON R. REESE, born Davenport, Iowa, December 31, 1971; admitted to bar, 1997, Indiana and U.S. District Court, Northern and Southern Districts of Indiana. *Education:* University of Arizona (B.A., magna cum laude, 1994); Indiana University - Bloomington (J.D., 1997). Phi Alpha Delta. Team Captain: NITA Trial Competition, 1997; ATLA Trial Competition, 1996. National Moot Court Competition. Part-time Federal Public Defender, 1997-1998. Recipient, "Outstanding Young Lawyer of the Year," Indiana State Bar Association, 2002-2003. Named: an "Indiana Super Lawyer" by Indianapolis Monthly Magazine for 2004; IBJ's 40 Under 40, 2005. *Member:* Indianapolis and Indiana State Bar Associations; Indiana Trial Lawyers Association (Sustaining Member and Board of Directors); The Association of Trial Lawyers of America (Member, Board of Governors, New Lawyers Division); Sagamore American Inn of Court (Barrister, 1999—). ***PRACTICE AREAS:*** Personal Injury; Products Liability; Medical Malpractice; Professional Liability; Legal Malpractice. ***Email:*** jreese@InjuryAttorneys.com

TREVOR J. CROSSEN, born San Antonio, Texas, January 19, 1969; admitted to bar, 1995, Indiana, U.S. District Court, Southern and Northern Districts of Indiana and U.S. Court of Appeals, Seventh Circuit. *Education:* Princeton University (A.B., 1991); Indiana University (J.D., 1995). Member: ABA National Moot Court Competition, 1994; National Health Law Moot Court Competition 1995. Presenter: "Does it Pay to Represent an Injured Worker?," Advanced Worker's Compensation Seminar 2002; "Issues to Consider When Handling the Catastrophic Worker's Compensation Claim," ITLA Lifetime Achievement Seminar 2004. *Member:* Indianapolis, Indiana State (Council Member at Large) and American Bar Associations; Indiana Trial Lawyers Association; The Association of Trial Lawyers of America; Sagamore American Inn of Court (Barrister 2002—). ***REPORTED CASES:*** Duhamell v. P.T. Barnum's Night Club, 766 N.E. 2d 729 (Ind. Ct. App. 2002), trans. denied. ***PRACTICE AREAS:*** Personal Injury; Premises Liability; Medical Malpractice; Workers Compensation. ***Email:*** tcrossen@InjuryAttorneys.com

ASSOCIATE

JUDY W. PIPPIN, born Muncie, Indiana, November 6, 1965; admitted to bar, 1992, Indiana and U.S. District Court, Northern and Southern Districts of Indiana. *Education:* Ball State University (B.S., 1988); Indiana University (J.D., 1992); American Paralegal School (1994-1997). Articles Editor, Indiana International Law Review, 1991-1992. Author: "The Ancient Chinese Secret: A Comparison of Chinese & American Mediation," Ind. Int'l and Comp. Law Rev. 300, 1992; "A Review of Indiana Worker's Compensation," Ind. Law Review, 1997. *Member:* Indianapolis and Indiana Bar Associations; Defense Research Institute; National Society of Professional Insurance Investigators; Defense Trial Counsel. ***PRACTICE AREAS:*** Workers Compensation; Personal Injury.

MICHAEL S. WALSH, P.C.

11350 NORTH MERIDIAN STREET
SUITE 420
CARMEL, INDIANA 46032-4528
Telephone: 317-575-5700
Fax: 317-575-5704
Email: msw@mwalshprofcorp.com

General Civil Practice. Commercial, Corporate, Trusts and Estates, Estate Planning and Administration, Real Estate, Civil Litigation, Business Law and Closely Held Business Law.

FIRM PROFILE: Michael S. Walsh began his sole practice in 1984. Chief areas of concentration and expertise include closely-held business and estate administration.

MICHAEL S. WALSH, born Indianapolis, Indiana, May 20, 1950; admitted to bar, 1975, Indiana. *Education:* University of Notre Dame (B.B.A., with highest honors, 1972); Duke University (J.D., 1975). Beta Gamma Sigma.

REPRESENTATIVE CLIENTS: Herff Jones, Inc.; Superb Sound, Inc.

BOSE McKINNEY & EVANS LLP

Established in 1955

P.O. BOX 957
CHESTERTON, INDIANA 46304
Telephone: 219-983-1552
Facsimile: 219-983-1741
URL: http://www.boselaw.com

Indianapolis, Indiana Office: 2700 First Indiana Plaza, 135 North Pennsylvania Street, 46204. Telephone: 317-684-5000. Facsimile: 317-684-5173.
Indianapolis, Indiana North Office: 600 East 96th Street, Suite 500 46240. Telephone: 317-684-5300. Facsimile: 317-684-5316.
Washington, D.C. Office: 700 North One Lafayette Centre, 1120 20th Street, N.W., 20036. Telephone: 202-973-1229. Fax: 202-973-1212.
Crown Point, Indiana Office: 3577 West Lakeshore Drive, 46307. Telephone: 219-663-2968. Fax: 219-663-2969.
West Lafayette, Indiana Office: 3000 Kent Avenue. Telephone: 765-464-3200. Fax: 765-464-3225.

General Civil Practice in all Courts including Agricultural Law, Antitrust, Appellate Practice, Capital Strategies, Civil Rights, Commercial Law, Communications and Media, Constitutional Law, Corporate Law, Creditors Rights, Creditors Rights in Bankruptcy, Debtor Bankruptcy, Education Law, Employee Benefits, Entertainment and the Arts, Entrepreneurial Services, Environmental Law, Finance, Financial Institutions Law, Government Contracts, Government Relations, High Technology, Insurance, Intellectual Property, International Law, Labor and Employment, Legislative Practice, Litigation, Mergers and Acquisitions, Municipal Finance, Municipal Law, Planning and Land Use, Probate, Real Estate, Regulated Industries, Regulatory Agency Practice, Securities, Taxation, Trusts and Estates, Utility Law, Wills and Zoning.

MONICA J. CONRAD, born Mishawaka, Indiana, July 21, 1964; admitted to bar, 1994, Illinois and Indiana; U.S. District Court, Northern District of Indiana, U.S. District Court, Northern District of Illinois and U.S. Court of Appeals, Seventh Circuit. *Education:* Indiana State University (B.S., 1986; M.A., 1994); Valparaiso University (J.D., 1993). Frequent Author and Speaker, including, "Developing Legally and Educationally Defensible Programs for Children with Autism Spectrum Disorder," Indiana Council of Special Education Administrators, April 2001; "Student Violence & Discipline - School Security Concerns," Professional Development Network, February, 2001; "Discipline of Special Education Students," Indiana School Boards Association, November, 2000; "Legal Issues with the Medically Fragile Child," Lorman Education Services; "Current Issues in Special Education," Indiana State University School of Educations School Law Conference, April, 2000; "IDEA '97," Indiana State University School Law Conference, April 1999. ***PRACTICE AREAS:*** Education Law; Employment Law. ***Email:*** mconrad@boselaw.com

BRAJE & NELSON, LLP

Established in 1976

1100 S. CALUMET ROAD, SUITE 3-C
CHESTERTON, INDIANA 46304
Telephone: 219-728-0100
Fax: 219-728-0123

Michigan City, Indiana Office: 126 West Fourth Street, P.O. Box 1006, 46361. Telephone: 219-872-2100. Fax: 219-873-9163.

(This Listing Continued)

General Civil and Criminal Trial Practice. Commercial, Real Estate, Family, Domestic Relations, Personal Injury Law, Estate Planning, Probate and Bankruptcy.

MEMBERS OF FIRM

CRAIG V. BRAJE, born Melrose Park, Illinois, October 21, 1949; admitted to bar, 1974, Indiana and Illinois. *Education:* Western Illinois University (B.A., 1971); Valparaiso University (J.D., 1974). Recipient, American Jurisprudence Award, 1972. Corporation Counsel, City of Michigan City, Indiana, 1976-1979. LaPorte County Deputy Prosecutor, 1979-1987. LaPorte County Public Defender, 1994—. *Member:* La Porte County, Porter County, Indiana State, Illinois State and American Bar Associations; Indiana Trial Lawyers Association; American Trial Lawyers Association; National Association of Criminal Defense Lawyers. ***PRACTICE AREAS:*** Civil and Criminal Litigation; Personal Injury; Commercial Law; Real Estate Law; Family Law; Domestic Relations Law; Medical Malpractice. **Email:** cvb@adsnet.com

WILLIAM J. NELSON, JR., born La Porte, Indiana, January 8, 1965; admitted to bar, 1992, Indiana. *Education:* Taylor University (B.A., 1987); Valparaiso University (J.D., 1992). LaPorte County Deputy Public Defender, 1994—. Counsel, Michigan City Sanitary District. *Member:* La Porte County, Porter County, Indiana State and American Bar Associations; National Association of Criminal Defense Lawyers; American Trial Lawyers Association. ***PRACTICE AREAS:*** Civil and Criminal Trial Practice; Domestic Law; Personal Injury Law; Real Estate Law; Products Liability. **Email:** wjn@adsnet.com

KURT R. EARNST, born Knoxville, Illinois, October 6, 1970; admitted to bar, 1996, Indiana, Illinois and U.S. District Court, Northern and Southern Districts of Indiana. *Education:* Purdue University (B.A., 1992); Valparaiso University (J.D., 1996). *Member:* La Porte County, Porter County, Indiana State, Illinois State and American Bar Associations; The Association of Trial Lawyers of America; National Association of Criminal Defense Lawyers. ***PRACTICE AREAS:*** Civil Litigation; Criminal Litigation; Family Law; Domestic Relations; Adoption Law; Bankruptcy; Real Estate; Personal Injury; Traffic Law. **Email:** kre@adsnet.com

ELIZABETH ANN FLYNN, born Valparaiso, Indiana, March 22, 1970; admitted to bar, 1995, Illinois; 1998, Indiana. *Education:* University of Evansville (B.A., cum laude, 1992); Valparaiso University (J. D., cum laude, 1995). States Attorney's Office, Chicago, Illinois, 1995-1999. *Member:* LaPorte County, Porter County, Indiana State, Illinois State and American Bar Associations. ***PRACTICE AREAS:*** Civil Litigation; Criminal Litigation; Traffic Law; Domestic Relations; Personal Injury; Medical Malpractice. **Email:** eaf@adsnet.com

---

CHRISTOPHER L. WILLOUGHBY, born Michigan City, Indiana, July 17, 1970; admitted to bar, 2002, Indiana and U.S. District Court, Northern and Southern Districts of Indiana. *Education:* North Central College (B.A., 1994); Valparaiso University (J.D., 2001). Phi Delta Phi. *Member:* LaPorte County, Porter County, Indiana State and American Bar Associations. ***PRACTICE AREAS:*** Estate Planning; Probate; Business Law; Real Estate; Bankruptcy; Debtor and Creditor Rights. **Email:** clw@adsnet.com

CARRI N. CRIDER, born Greenfield, Indiana, April 4, 1974; admitted to bar, 1999, Indiana. *Education:* Indiana University (B.A., 1996); Valparaiso University (J.D., 1999). Member, Moot Court Society, 1997-1999. Formerly with Austgon, Decker & Phillips, P.C. *Member:* Lake County, LaPorte County, Porter County and Indiana State Bar Associations. ***LANGUAGES:*** German. ***REPORTED CASES:*** Bursuk v. Town of St. John, 820 N.E.2d 118 (Ind. 2005); Gary Bd. of Zoning Appeals v. Eldridge, 774 N.E.2d 579 (End Gr. App. 2002). ***PRACTICE AREAS:*** Civil Litigation; Criminal Law; Municipal Law; Real Estate; Land Use; Land Development; Employment Law; Labor Law; Appellate Practice. **Email:** cnc@adsnet.com

RETIRED

C. T. KITOWSKI, born Michigan City, Indiana, 1925; admitted to bar, 1952, Indiana. *Education:* Valparaiso University (J.D., 1952). Former LaPorte County Chief Deputy Prosecuting Attorney. *Member:* Porter County, Indiana State and American Bar Associations.

REPRESENTATIVE CLIENTS: B & E Marine, Inc.; Delco, Inc.; LaPorte County Hospital Authority; Commercial Investment Transactions, Inc.; Northern Indiana Education Foundation; Frech USA; Automated Data Systems, Inc.; Concrete Specialists, Inc.; R.L. Roofing, Inc.; Dominiack Mechanical, Inc.; Sanitary District of Michigan City; Members Advantage Credit Union; Moore Surgical Associates, P.C.; Library Board of Michigan City; Michigan City Housing Authority; Boys and Girls Club of Michigan City; Wiesemann Plumbing and HVAC, Inc.
REFERENCE: Bank One, N.A.

(For complete biographical data on all personnel, see Professional Biographies at Michigan City, Indiana)

HARRIS, WELSH & LUKMANN

107 BROADWAY
CHESTERTON, INDIANA 46304
Telephone: 219-926-2114
Fax: 219-926-1503
Email: hwl@hwllaw.com
URL: http://www.hwllaw.com

General Civil Practice in all State and Federal Courts. Corporation, Wills and Probate, Trusts and Estates, Estate Planning, Personal Injury, Automobile Accidents, Wrongful Death, Insurance, Real Property, Eminent Domain, Banking and Municipal Law. Trials.

MEMBERS OF FIRM

MICHAEL C. HARRIS, born Evanston, Illinois, February 22, 1938; admitted to bar, 1964, Indiana. *Education:* University of Colorado and Indiana University (B.S., 1960); Indiana University (J.D., 1964). Phi Delta Phi. *Member:* Porter County (President, 1969), Indiana State and American Bar Associations. **Email:** mharris@hwllaw.com

(This Listing Continued)

ROBERT A. WELSH, born Paterson, New Jersey, December 25, 1943; admitted to bar, 1968, Indiana. *Education:* Indiana University (A.B., 1965; J.D., 1968). Porter County Attorney, 1977-1995. *Member:* Porter County (Vice President, 1973; President, 1975), Indiana State and American Bar Associations. **Email:** bwelsh@hwllaw.com

L. CHARLES LUKMANN, III, born Hammond, Indiana, March 31, 1953; admitted to bar, 1979, Indiana. *Education:* University of Notre Dame (B.A., with honors, 1975); Indiana University (J.D., cum laude, 1979). Deputy Prosecuting Attorney, Eighth Judicial Circuit, Indiana, 1978. Deputy Attorney General, Indiana, 1979. *Member:* Porter County (President, 1993), Indiana State and American Bar Associations. **Email:** clukmann@hwllaw.com

CHARLES F. G. PARKINSON, born Canton, Ohio, June 4, 1964; admitted to bar, 1998, Indiana and U.S. District Court, Northern and Southern Districts of Indiana. *Education:* Grand Valley State University (B.S., 1987); Western Michigan University (M.A., 1991); Valparaiso University (J.D., cum laude, 1998). Moot Court Society. Associate Editor, Valparaiso University Law Review, 1997-1998. *Member:* Porter County, Indiana State and American Bar Associations. **Email:** cparkinson@hwllaw.com

REPRESENTATIVE CLIENTS: Northern Indiana Commuter Transportation District; Duneland School Corp.; Town of Burns Harbor, Indiana; Town of Chesterton; Porter Memorial Hospital; Paulson Oil Company; Steel & Machinery Transport, Inc.; Centier Bank; Rediehs Transit Line, Inc.; Oak Management Company.

HERBERT S. LASSER & ASSOCIATES, P.C.

CHESTERTON, INDIANA

(See Merrillville)

Personal Injury, Wrongful Death, Automobile and All Accidents, Construction Law, Family Law, Divorce, Child Custody, Child Support, Domestic Violence, Visitation Rights, Work Accidents, Trials and Appeals, Business Law, Business Planning, Contracts, Law Suits, Insurance, Business Enterprises, Closely Held Business, Corporate, Limited Liability Companies, Partnerships, Small Business, Franchises, Buying and Selling A Business, Debt and Credit, Collections, Creditors Rights, Banking and Finance, Venture Capital, Employee Benefits, Employment Contracts, Human Resources, Discrimination, Sexual Harassment, Workers Compensation, Wrongful Termination, Real Estate, Buying or Selling, Commercial Leasing, Environmental, Landlord and Tenant, Zoning and Land Use, Starting a Business, Strategic Alliances, Joint Ventures, Mergers, Civil Rights, Consumer Law, Consumer Fraud, Unsafe Products, Criminal Law, Drunk Driving, Misdemeanors, Drug Crimes, Juvenile Crimes, Parole and Probation, Traffic Violations, Medical Malpractice, Legal Malpractice, Products Liability, Slip and Fall, Wills and Probate, Trusts and Estates, Asset Protection, Estate Planning, General Civil and Criminal Practice, General Practice, Trademark Patent Litigation.

ANDREW W. LEVENFELD & ASSOCIATES, LTD.

CHESTERTON, INDIANA

(See Chicago, Illinois)

Civil Litigation, Trial Practice, Commercial and Residential Real Estate, Buying and Selling a Home, Condominium Law, Cooperative Housing Law, Homeowners Association Law, Land Acquisitions, Sales, Trusts, Real Estate Arbitration, Real Estate Development, Real Estate Development, Real Estate Leasing, Real Estate Mediation, Real Estate Tax Liens, Construction Law, Trusts and Estates, Elder Law, Estate Administration, Estate Planning, Estate Litigation, Family Trust, Powers of Attorney, Trust Litigation, Wealth Preservation, Probate Litigation, Asset Protection, Guardianship, Tax Litigation, Wills, Probate, Employment Discrimination, Sex Discrimination, Age Discrimination, Conservatorship, Corporate Law, Nonprofit Organization Law, Corporate Litigation, S Corporations, Small Business Corporations, Litigation, Consumer Fraud.

LAW OFFICE OF BART COLOMB

CLARKSVILLE, INDIANA

(See New Albany)

Social Security, Workers Compensation and Family Law.

MATTOX MATTOX & WILSON

CLARKSVILLE, INDIANA

(See New Albany)

Civil Trial Litigation. Personal Injury and Wrongful Death, Products Liability, Medical Malpractice, Insurance Law, Corporate Law, Business Torts, Family Law, Aviation Law, Labor and Employment Law, Health Care Regulations.

BLACKBURN & GREEN

COLUMBIA CITY, INDIANA

(See Fort Wayne)

Litigation, Personal Injury Law.

ROEBUCK & ASSOCIATES, P.C.

COLUMBIA CITY, INDIANA

(See Ft. Wayne)

Personal Injury, Automobile Accidents, Boat Accidents, Motorcycle Accidents, Truck Accidents, Slip and Fall, Dog Bites, Medical Malpractice, Head Injuries, Nursing Home Abuse and Neglect, Products Liability, Insurance, Social Security, Social Security Disability, and Wrongful Death.

ROTHBERG LOGAN & WARSCO LLP

COLUMBIA CITY, INDIANA

(See Fort Wayne)

General Civil Litigation in all Courts. Corporate, Banking, Bankruptcy, Commercial, Insurance, Labor and Employment Law, Municipal Law, Municipal Finance, Securities, Real Estate, Construction, Probate and Estate Planning, Transportation, Tax, Creditors' Rights, Agricultural Law, Family/Domestic Relations, Health Care Law.

DEPPE FREDBECK & BOLL

225 WASHINGTON STREET
COLUMBUS, INDIANA 47202
Telephone: 812-378-5137
Fax: 812-378-5256

Franklin, Indiana Office: Nine East Court, 46131. Telephone: 317-736-5138. Fax: 317-736-8268.

General, Civil, Criminal and Trial Practice. Probate and Estate Planning, Elder Law, Corporation and Real Property, Labor Relations, School, Health Care and Commercial Law.

(For Biographical data on all Personnel, see Professional Biographies at Franklin, Indiana)

GREENE & SCHULTZ TRIAL LAWYERS

COLUMBUS, INDIANA

(See Bloomington)

Personal Injury, Automobile Negligence, Products Liability, Wrongful Death, Premises Liability, Wrongful Denial of Insurance, Tort Law, Insurance Disputes.

JEWELL, CRUMP, ANGERMEIER & PRALL

Established in 1972
1325 WASHINGTON STREET
P.O. BOX 1061
COLUMBUS, INDIANA 47202-1061
Telephone: 812-376-9751
Fax: 812-372-6384
Email: fjc@iquest.net
URL: http://www.jcalaw.com

General Civil and Criminal Trial Practice. Driving While Intoxicated, Drug Crimes, Juvenile Law, Parole and Probation, Traffic Violations, Personal Injury, Automobile Accidents, Slip and Fall, Wrongful Death, Wills and Probate, Trusts and Estates, Estate Planning, Taxation, Business Organizations, Commercial Law, Business Law, Business Litigation, Business Planning, Contracts, Buying and Selling a Business, Business Start-Ups, Debtor and Creditor, Collections, Business Enterprises, Corporate, Limited Liability Companies, Small Business, Partnerships, Family/Domestic Relations, Child Custody, Child Support, Divorce, Visitation Rights, Adoptions, Insurance Defense, Real Estate and Title Insurance Law.

FIRM PROFILE: On the 14th day of February 1972, the law firm of Crump and Angermeier was formed on the second floor of the old First National Bank Building by the principal partners of this firm. Ralph L. Jewell was admitted as a general partner on the 21st day of July 1975, after being in solo practice for several years; on the same date the partnership moved into its present building which was constructed especially for the needs of the firm.

Ralph L. Jewell retired from the active practice of law on the 30th day of June 1988. Jerry E. Prall joined the firm as an associate in 1990.

The firm serves Bartholomew County and the surrounding counties in the general practice of law. The firm strives daily to give its clients good quality and cost effective service.

MEMBERS OF FIRM

GERALD G. ANGERMEIER (1940-2005). ***PRACTICE AREAS:*** Personal Injury; Criminal Law; Family Law; Probate; Insurance Defense.

F. JEFFERSON CRUMP, III, born Alexandria, Virginia, December 4, 1942; admitted to bar, 1967, Indiana. *Education:* Virginia Military Institute (B.S., 1964); Indiana University (J.D., 1967). Phi Alpha Delta. *Member:* Bartholomew County (President, 1983-1984; Treasurer and Board of Directors, 2001—) and Indiana State Bar Associations. ***REPORTED CASES:*** Estate of Von Wendesse v. Hoffman 618 NE2d 1332 (Ind. Ct. App. 1993). ***PRACTICE AREAS:*** Probate; Trusts and Estates; Wills; Taxation; Real Estate; Partnership Law; Business Law; Collections; Business Acquisitions. **Email:** fjc@iquest.net

JERRY E. PRALL, born Martinsville, Indiana, July 20, 1956; admitted to bar, 1984, Indiana. *Education:* Indiana University (B.S., Business Administration, with highest distinction, 1978; J.D., cum laude, 1984). Beta Gamma Sigma; Phi Alpha Delta. Member, Order of the Coif. Deputy Prosecuting Attorney, Brown County, Indiana, 1987-1990. *Member:* Bartholomew County and Indiana State Bar Associations. ***PRACTICE AREAS:*** Family Law; Workers Compensation; Social Security Disability; Criminal Law; Personal Injury.

RETIRED

RALPH L. JEWELL, born Columbus, Indiana, August 17, 1930; admitted to bar, 1957, Indiana. *Education:* Indiana University (A.B., 1951; J.D., 1957). Deputy Prosecuting Attorney, Bartholomew County, 1960-1962. *Member:* Bartholomew County and Indiana State Bar Associations. [Col. (JAG) U.S. Air Force Reserve 1953-1983]. (Retired). **Email:** rjewell1@juno.com

(This Listing Continued)

LEGAL SUPPORT PERSONNEL

LINDA G. KAUFMAN

ANGELA J. HOOVER

JENNIFER L. NEWLAND

REPRESENTATIVE CLIENTS: Imperial Casualty & Indemnity Co.; Mahan Leasing Co., Inc.; Beckemeyer Insurance Agency, Inc.; Arnett and Associates Insurance, Inc.; First National Corporation; American General Finance, Inc.; Alan Industries; GoAmerica Ins. Co.; Business & Industrial Federal Credit Union; Central Sheet Metal, Inc.; Continental Western Insurance Co.; Hessit Works, Inc.; Hastings Mutual Ins. Co.; Indiana Conservation Officers; Shoe Biz, Inc.; Unizan Bank (Ohio); Geoby Children's Products, Inc.; Seneca Insurance Co.
REFERENCES: Home Federal Savings Bank, Columbus, Indiana; National Attorney's Title Assurance Fund, Inc.

LAW OFFICE OF BENJAMIN LOHEIDE

421 WASHINGTON STREET
COLUMBUS, INDIANA 47201
Telephone: 812-376-8135
Fax: 812-376-9286
Email: loheidelaw@sbcglobal.net
URL: http://www.loheidelaw.com

Criminal Law, Family Law, Divorce, Bankruptcy.

BENJAMIN LOHEIDE, born Indianapolis, Indiana, June 20, 1974; admitted to bar, 2004, Indiana and U.S. District Court, Northern and Southern Districts of Indiana. *Education:* Indiana University, Bloomington (B.S., 1997); Indiana University School of Law-Bloomington (J.D., 2003). Public Defender, Jennings County, Indiana, 2004-2005. *Member:* Bartholomew County and Indiana State Bar Associations. ***PRACTICE AREAS:*** Criminal Law; Family Law; Divorce; Bankruptcy.

SHARPNACK BIGLEY STROH & WASHBURN LLP

Established in 1824
321 WASHINGTON STREET
P.O. BOX 310
COLUMBUS, INDIANA 47202-0310
Telephone: 812-372-1553
Fax: 812-372-1567
Email: sbsw@sbswlaw.com

Trials. Business, Corporation, Probate and Estate Planning, Elder Law, Real Estate, Family/Domestic Relations, Banking. General Practice.

MEMBERS OF FIRM

THOMAS C. BIGLEY, JR., born Indianapolis, Indiana, August 4, 1939; admitted to bar, 1963, Indiana; U.S. Supreme Court. *Education:* Stanford University and Indiana University (A.B., 1960; J.D., 1963). Member, Board of Editors, Indiana Law Journal, 1962-1963. *Member:* Indiana State and American Bar Associations. Fellow, American College of Trust and Estate Counsel. [Capt., J.A.G.C., U.S. Army, 1963-1966]. ***PRACTICE AREAS:*** Estate Planning Law; Business Law; Trial Practice; Elder Law.

JOHN A. STROH, born Muncie, Indiana, May 30, 1946; admitted to bar, 1982, Indiana. *Education:* Ohio Wesleyan University (B.A., 1968); Butler University (M.S., 1974); Indiana University (J.D. cum laude, 1982). *Member:* Indiana State and American Bar Associations. ***PRACTICE AREAS:*** Litigation; Family Law; Elder Law.

JEFFREY S. WASHBURN, born Indianapolis, Indiana, December 14, 1957; admitted to bar, 1983, Indiana. *Education:* Hanover College (B.A., cum laude, 1980); Indiana University (J.D., 1983). *Member:* Bartholomew County, Indiana State and American Bar Associations; American Agricultural Law Association. ***PRACTICE AREAS:*** Business Law; Probate; Estate Planning; Elder Law.

LISA HENSLEY ANDERSON, born Batesville, Indiana, October 2, 1973; admitted to bar, 2000, Indiana and U.S. District Court, Southern and Northern Districts of Indiana. *Education:* Indiana University (B.A., 1996); Indiana University School of Law - Indianapolis (J.D., 2000). *Member:* Bartholomew County, Indiana State and American Bar Associations. ***PRACTICE AREAS:*** Litigation; Family Law.

JASON H. GUTHRIE, born Columbus, Indiana, March 24, 1971; admitted to bar, 1997, Indiana and U.S. District Court, Southern and Northern Districts of Indiana. *Education:* Ball State University (B.S., 1993); Indiana University School of Law-Indianapolis (J.D., 1997). *Member:* Bartholomew County, Indiana State and American Bar Associations. ***PRACTICE AREAS:*** Litigation; Estate Planning; Business Law.

REPRESENTATIVE CLIENTS: State Farm Mutual Insurance Cos.; American Family Insurance; Irwin Union Bank and Trust Co.; Centra Credit Union; Home News Enterprises; Columbus Area Chamber of Commerce; Heritage Fund of Bartholomew County; Product Engineering Co., Inc.; Golden Foundry, Inc.; Taylor Brothers Construction, Co.; Columbus Radiology, Inc.; Farm Credit Services, Inc.; Pardieck Development Co.; Worldwide Properties, Inc.; Northeast Lakewood Shopping Center, Houston, Texas; 25th Street Shopping Center, Columbus, IN; Richards Elevator, Inc.; Glick Farms, Inc.; Bartholomew County Library; Instant Products of America, Inc.; Lees Inns of America, Inc.; Louisville & Indiana Railroad.

TIMOTHY J. VRANA LLC

636 3RD STREET
P.O. BOX 527
COLUMBUS, INDIANA 47202
Telephone: 812-375-9306
Toll-Free: 1-866-788-8270
Fax: 812-375-9304
Email: tim@timvrana.com
URL: http://www.timvrana.com

Social Security Disability, Civil Litigation, Civil Appeals.

TIMOTHY J. VRANA, born Seward, Nebraska, March 4, 1952; admitted to bar, 1982, Indiana; 1984, U.S. Court of Appeals, Seventh Circuit. *Education:* University of Nebraska; Duke University (A.B., magna cum laude, with distinction in Political Science, 1973); Indiana University (J.D., cum laude, 1982). Commissioner, 1982-1985 and Chairman, 1984-1985, Columbus Human Rights Commission. *Member:* Bartholomew County, Indiana State (Member, Governing Council, Appellate Practice Section, 2001—) and American Bar Associations; Defense Trial Counsel of Indiana (Member, Board of Directors, 1992-2001); National Organization of Social Security Claimant's Representatives. ***PRACTICE AREAS:*** Civil Litigation; Social Security Disability; Civil Appeals. ***Email:*** tim@timvrana.com

CLARKSON & GULDE, P.C.

CONNERSVILLE, INDIANA

(See Rushville)

Accidents and Personal Injury, Family Law, Criminal Law, Probate, General Trial Practice.

THOMPSON LAW OFFICE

705 WEST 30TH STREET
CONNERSVILLE, INDIANA 47331
Telephone: 765-827-3082
Fax: 765-827-6500
Email: info@tomthompsonlaw.com
URL: http://www.tomthompsonlaw.com

Personal Injury, Debt Collection, Estate Planning, Criminal Law, Appellate Practice, Bankruptcy, Environmental Law, Family Law.

FIRM PROFILE: Thompson Law Office has developed a client service plan utilizing technology in all facets of our practice to provide our clients with cutting edge, large firm resources and the accessibility of a small town firm.

MEMBERS AND ASSOCIATES

THOMAS M. THOMPSON, born Connersville, Indiana; admitted to bar, 1993, Indiana. *Education:* University of Notre Dame (B.A., 1990); Indiana University School of Law (J.D., 1993). Editorial Staff, Indiana Law Journal, 1991-1993. City Attorney, Connersville, 2000-2003. County Attorney, Union County, 2001—. *Member:* Fayette County Bar Association (Treasurer, 1994-2003; Vice President, 2004—); Indiana Trial Lawyers Association; Indiana Municipal Lawyers Association. ***REPORTED CASES:*** Ritz v. Franklin Co. Area Plan Comission, 698 N.E. 2d 386 (Ind. Ct. App.1998); Davis v. State, 749 NE. 2d 552 (Ind. Ct. App. 2001); In Re: The Custody of A.N.W., 798 N.E. 2d 556 (Ind. Ct. App. 2003); (numerous other published opinions furnished upon request). ***PRACTICE AREAS:*** Personal Injury; Collections; Estate Planning; Criminal Law; Appellate Practice. ***Email:*** tthompson@tomthompsonlaw.com

THOMAS T. WELLMAN, born Connersville, Indiana, September 28, 1975; admitted to bar, 2003, Indiana and U.S. District Court, Southern District of Indiana. *Education:* Ball State University (B.S., 1998); Indiana University-Indianapolis (J.D., 2003). *Member:* Hamilton County, Fayette County and Indiana State Bar Associations. ***PRACTICE AREAS:*** Bankruptcy; Family Law; Criminal Law; Personal Injury; Civil Litigation.

REPRESENTATIVE CLIENTS: Connersville Utilities; Connersville Credit Bureau; Connersville Department of Stormwater Management; Union County Health Department; Union County Area Plan Commission.

MATTOX MATTOX & WILSON

CORYDON, INDIANA

(See New Albany)

Civil Trial Litigation. Personal Injury and Wrongful Death, Products Liability, Medical Malpractice, Insurance Law, Corporate Law, Business Torts, Family Law, Aviation Law, Labor and Employment Law, Health Care Regulations.

MERKLEY LAW OFFICE

CORYDON, INDIANA

(See Jeffersonville)

Family Law, Criminal Law, Estates and Wills, Personal Injury, Municipal Law.

CHARLES R. MURPHY

CORYDON, INDIANA

(See New Albany)

Real Estate, Elder Law, Business Law, Buying or Selling a Home, Eminent Domain, Landlord and Tenant Law, Zoning and Land Use, Tax Deferred Exchanges, Business Start-Ups, Buying or Selling a Business, Business Enterprises, Limited Liability Company Law, Corporations, Partnerships, Small Business Law.

CAPPER, TULLEY & REIMONDO

Established in 1907
131 NORTH GREEN STREET
P.O. BOX 429
CRAWFORDSVILLE, INDIANA 47933
Telephone: 765-362-7340
Fax: 765-362-5023
Email: bctatty@sbcglobal.net

General Civil and Probate Practice. Agricultural Law, Business Law and Litigation, Construction Law, Corporation, Real Estate, Family, Municipal, Environmental Law, Real Estate Development, Planning and Zoning Law, and Personal Injury Law. Trials.

FIRM PROFILE: Originally established in 1907, today's Capper, Tulley and Reimondo offers over 80 combined years of legal expertise. Providing a general practice of law to Montgomery and surrounding counties, the firm's emphasis includes Personal Injury, Probate, Estate Planning, Corporation, Municipal, and Family/Domestic relations law.

ANDREW N. FOLEY (1877-1963)

JOHN R. BERRY (1907-1986)

RICHARD G. TULLEY, born Marion County, Indiana, December 5, 1932; admitted to bar, 1962, Indiana and U.S. District Court, Southern District of Indiana; 1973, U.S. Supreme Court. *Education:* Wabash College (B.A., 1955); Indiana University (J.D., 1962). Phi Alpha Delta. Member of Staff, Indiana Law Journal, 1961-1962. Prosecuting Attorney, Montgomery County, 1971-1974. City Attorney, City of Crawfordsville, Indiana, 1988-2003. *Member:* Montgomery County (President, 1964-1965), The Indiana State and American Bar Associations. ***PRACTICE AREAS:*** Probate Law; Real Estate Law; Litigation.

JOHN S. CAPPER, IV, born Winamac, Indiana, July 14, 1949; admitted to bar, 1974, Indiana, U.S. District Court, Southern District of Indiana, U.S. Claims Court; U.S. Court of Appeals, Seventh Circuit and for the Federal Circuit and U.S. Supreme Court. *Education:* Ball State University (B.S., 1971); Indiana University (J.D., 1974). Assistant City Attorney, City of Crawfordsville, 1988-2003. *Member:* Montgomery County (President, 1978-1979), The Indiana State and American Bar Associations. ***PRACTICE AREAS:*** Personal Injury Law; Litigation; Family Law; Municipal Law.

ROBERT N. REIMONDO, born Galion, Ohio, December 31, 1970; admitted to bar, 1997, Indiana and U.S District Court, Southern and Northern Districts of Indiana. *Education:* Wabash College (B.A., 1993); Indiana University (J.D., 1997). *Member:* Montgomery County and Indiana State Bar Associations.

REPRESENTATIVE CLIENTS: Linden State Bank; Farmers State Bank; Raybestos Products Co.; Pohlmann Hog Farms; Superior Moving & Storage; Physician Associates of Crawfordsville, Inc.; Davis Realty; Deckard Engineering & Surveying; Athens Medical Group, Inc.; Crawfordsville Pediatric Association, Inc.; Kraft Foods Inc.; Hazlett Enterprises Inc.; Clifton & Quigg Fertilizer Service Inc.; Crawfordsville Ear, Nose & Throat LLC; McCormick-Metsker Agency, Inc.; Women's Health Specialists, LLC; J'ville Properties, Inc., Holiday Inn; RPM Print & Copy Service, Inc.; Allen Monument Co.; Vertical Air Support, Inc.; Comfort Inn; Central Indiana Juvenile Attention Center, Inc.; Toner Tek; Thrifty Wholesale Supply, Inc.; Magic Light-Neon Sign Co.; S&S Enterprises; Airmedia LLC; Natural Pork II; PWD Enterprises LLC (Sears); B&R Fire Protection, Inc.; Walden Warehousing and Recycling; Sugar Creek Eyecare, Inc.

ELIZABETH A. JUSTICE

506 EAST MARKET STREET
CRAWFORDSVILLE, INDIANA 47933-1817
Telephone: 765-364-1111
Facsimile: 765-364-1430
URL: http://www.justice-law.com
Email: elizabeth@justice-law.com
URL: http://www.ejusticelaw.com

Estate Planning, Wills and Probate, Trusts and Estates, Guardianships, Real Estate, Business Law, Contracts, Family Law, Divorce, Child Support, Personal Injury and Litigation.

ELIZABETH A. JUSTICE, born Logansport, Indiana, 1958; admitted to bar, 1983, California (inactive); 1987, Indiana; 1989, U.S. Supreme Court; U.S. District Court, Northern and Eastern Disitrcts of California and Northern and Southern Districts of Indiana. *Education:* Radcliffe College, Harvard University (A.B., 1980); Indiana University School of Law (J.D., 1983). Member, Indiana University Moot Court Board and National Moot Court Team. *Member:* Montgomery County and Indiana State Bar Associations; State Bar of California.

DANIEL W. KELLY

CRAWFORDSVILLE, INDIANA

(See Terre Haut)

Personal Injury, Family Law, Wills, Estate Administration, Bankruptcy.

WERNLE, RISTINE & AYERS, L.P.C.

Established in 1836
309 DUBOIS AVENUE
CRAWFORDSVILLE, INDIANA 47933
Telephone: 765-362-2640
Fax: 765-339-7852

General Civil Practice. Corporation, Construction, Contracts, Domestic Relations, Real Estate, Negligence, Insurance, Probate and Estate Planning. Trials.

FIRM PROFILE: The firm dates from 1836 when Ben Taylor Ristine began the practice of law in Crawfordsville. The firm offers a wide range of legal services, and its members are active in civic and community affairs.

(This Listing Continued)

WERNLE, RISTINE & AYERS, L.P.C., Crawfordsville—Continued

RETIRED

ROBERT F. WERNLE (1914-2005)

RICHARD O. RISTINE, born Indianapolis, Indiana; admitted to bar, 1944, New York and Indiana. *Education:* Wabash College (A.B., 1941); Columbia Law School (LL.B., 1944). Phi Beta Kappa. Emeritus Trustee, Wabash College. Lieut. Governor, State of Indiana, 1961-1965.

MEMBER OF FIRM

JAMES E. AYERS, born Russiaville, Indiana; admitted to bar, 1966, Indiana; U.S. District Court, Northern and Southern Districts of Indiana; U.S. District Court, District of Colorado; U.S. Court of Appeals, Seventh Circuit; 2002, Colorado; U.S. Supreme Court. *Education:* Wabash College (A.B., 1963); Harvard University (LL.B., 1966). Phi Beta Kappa. *Member:* The Association of Trial Lawyers of America. [Capt., JAG, U.S. Army, 1967-1971]. ***LANGUAGES:*** German. ***REPORTED CASES:*** Richardson et al v. County of Montgomery and State of Indiana et al, 653 N.E.2d 136, 726 N.E.2d 888; Spears v. Blackwell, 666 N.E.2d 974; Shell Oil Company v. The Lovold Company, 687 N.E.2d 383; MSP Collaborative Developers v. Fidelity & Deposit Co., 596 F.2d 247. ***PRACTICE AREAS:*** Civil Litigation; Construction; Corporations; Contracts; Negligence; Insurance; School Law; Social Security; Workers Compensation.

ASSOCIATE

JAMES R. STYTLE, born Angola, Indiana; (admission pending). *Education:* Wabash College (A.B., 1996); Community College of the Air Force (A.A.S., 1998); Indiana University School of Law, Indianapolis (J.D., 2005). [Indiana Air National Guard, 1992-1998, SSGT]. ***PRACTICE AREAS:*** Civil Litigation.

OF COUNSEL

GWYNETH A.E. AYERS, born El Paso, Texas, 1968; admitted to bar, 1997, Colorado; 1999, U.S. District Court, Northern and Southern Districts of Indiana; 2000, Indiana. *Education:* Indiana University (B.S., 1993); University of Colorado at Boulder (J.D., 1997). Editor, Amicus, 1995-1997. Law Clerk to the Hon. William L. West, District Court Judge, 20th Judicial District of Colorado, 1997-1998. *Member:* Boulder and Colorado Bar Associations; The Association of Trial Lawyers of America; Colorado Trial Lawyers Association; American Civil Liberties Union. ***PRACTICE AREAS:*** Appellate Practice; Civil Rights; Negligence; Employment Law.

LEGAL SUPPORT PERSONNEL

TROY D. DECKARD, born Crawfordsville, Indiana. *Education:* Cedarville College (B.A., 1991). (Legal Assistant). ***PRACTICE AREAS:*** Workers Compensation; Social Security.

REPRESENTATIVE CLIENTS: Montgomery County North Ridge Development, Inc; SPI Binding, Inc.; Masonic Temple Association; McKeown Engineering; Tip Scott Architect; Crawfordsville District Public Library; Safety National Casualty Corporation.
REFERENCES: National City Bank; Crawfordsville, Indiana; Tri-County Bank & Trust Co., Roachdale, Indiana.

ABRAHAMSON & REED

CROWN POINT, INDIANA

(See Hammond)

General Civil Practice in all State and Federal Courts. Trials and Appeals.

HERMAN L. BARBER, JR.

130 NORTH MAIN STREET
CROWN POINT, INDIANA 46307
Telephone: 219-663-5600
Fax: 219-662-3519
Email: hbarber@austgenlaw.com
URL: http://www.hbarberlaw.com

Real Estate, Wills and Probate, Trusts and Estates, Estate Planning, Asset Protection, Guardianship, Elder Law, Family Law, Adoption, Child Custody, Child Support, Divorce, Visitation Rights.

HERMAN L. BARBER, JR., born Sharon, Pennsylvania, February 16, 1941; admitted to bar, 1966, Indiana. *Education:* DePauw University (B.A., 1963); Valparaiso University (J.D., 1966). City Judge, Crown Point, 1976-2003. *Member:* Indiana State Bar Association. ***PRACTICE AREAS:*** Real Estate; Probate; Family Law; Elder Law.

BECKMAN, KELLY & SMITH

CROWN POINT, INDIANA

(See Hammond)

General Practice, Commercial, Corporation, Transportation and Trucking, Products and Professional Liability Defense, Elder Law, Estate and Trust Planning and Administration, Franchising, Real Estate, Employment, Taxation and Environmental Law, Trials and Appeals in all Courts, Medical Malpractice Defense and Workers Compensation Defense.

BOSE McKINNEY & EVANS LLP

Established in 1955

3557 WEST LAKESHORE DRIVE
CROWN POINT, INDIANA 46307
Telephone: 219-663-2968
Facsimile: 219-663-2969
URL: http://www.boselaw.com

Indianapolis, Indiana Office: 2700 First Indiana Plaza, 135 North Pennsylvania Street, 46204. Telephone: 317-684-5000. Facsimile: 317-684-5173.
Indianapolis, Indiana North Office: 600 East 96th Street, Suite 500 46240. Telephone: 317-684-5300. Facsimile: 317-684-5316.
Washington, D.C. Office: 700 North One Lafayette Centre, 1120 20th Street, N.W., 20036. Telephone: 202-973-1229. Fax: 202-973-1212.
Chesterton, Indiana Office: P.O. Box 957, 46304. Telephone: 219-983-1552. Fax: 219-983-1741.
West Lafayette, Indiana Office: 3000 Kent Avenue. Telephone: 765-464-3200. Fax: 765-464-3225.

General Civil Practice in all Courts including Agricultural Law, Antitrust, Appellate Practice, Capital Strategies, Civil Rights, Commercial Law, Communications and Media, Constitutional Law, Corporate Law, Creditors Rights, Creditors Rights in Bankruptcy, Debtor Bankruptcy, Education Law, Employee Benefits, Entertainment and the Arts, Entrepreneurial Services, Environmental Law, Finance, Financial Institutions Law, Government Contracts, Government Relations, High Technology, Insurance, Intellectual Property, International Law, Labor and Employment, Legislative Practice, Litigation, Mergers and Acquisitions, Municipal Finance, Municipal Law, Planning and Land Use, Probate, Real Estate, Regulated Industries, Regulatory Agency Practice, Securities, Taxation, Trusts and Estates, Utility Law, Wills and Zoning.

OF COUNSEL

PETER LYNN GOERGES, born Evansville, Indiana, July 7, 1944; admitted to bar, 1969, Indiana and U.S. District Court, Southern District of Indiana. *Education:* University of Evansville (B.A., 1966); Indiana University (J.D., 1969). Phi Alpha Delta. *Member:* Indiana State and American (Member, Labor Law Section) Bar Associations. ***PRACTICE AREAS:*** Employment Law; Education Law; Municipal Law. ***Email:*** pgoerges@boselaw.com

---

MARCE GONZALEZ, JR.

CROWN POINT, INDIANA

(See Merrillville)

Criminal Defense, Drug Crimes, Driving While Intoxicated, Juvenile Law, Felonies and Misdemeanors, Appellate, Traffic Violations, Personal Injury, Automobile Accidents, Slip and Fall, Dog Bites, Wrongful Death, Attorney Discipline Defense.

THOMAS M. GREENBERG, P.C.

CROWN POINT, INDIANA

(See Merrillville)

General Practice, Trusts and Estates, Estate Planning, Probate, Real Estate, Real Estate Transactions, Employment Law, Employee Benefits, Business Law, Business Formation, Business Enterprises, Limited Liability Company Law, Commercial Law, Professional Practices, Tax Exempt Organizations, Health Law, Mental Health Law, Local Government Law, General Civil Litigation.

EDWARD P. GRIMMER

603 N. MAIN STREET
CROWN POINT, INDIANA 46307-3233
Telephone: 219-662-1661
Fax: 219-663-4151
Email: ed@grimmerlaw.com
URL: http://www.grimmerlaw.com

Civil Litigation in all Courts. Commercial Litigation, Probate and Estate Planning, Trusts and Estates, Guardianship, Asset Protection, Real Estate, Corporate and Business, Contracts, Business Planning, Business Enterprises, Partnership Law, Limited Liability Company Law, Real Estate, Municipal and Zoning, Utility Law.

EDWARD P. GRIMMER, born Fort Wayne, Indiana, 1950; admitted to bar, 1976, Indiana, District of Columbia and U.S. District Court, Southern District of Indiana; 1979, U.S. District Court, Northern District of Indiana. *Education:* University of Notre Dame (A.B., 1972; J.D., 1976). Trial Attorney, Federal Trade Commission, 1976-1979. *Member:* Indiana State and Lake County (Treasurer, 1989-1990) Bar Associations; District of Columbia Bar.

REPRESENTATIVE CLIENTS: Furnished Upon Request.

HODGES & DAVIS, P.C.

CROWN POINT, INDIANA

(See Merrillville)

General Civil Practice in all State and Federal Courts, Trials and Appeals, Insurance Defense, Corporation, Health and Hospital, Municipal and Zoning Law, Criminal, Driving While Intoxicated, Financing, Tax and Administrative Law. EEOC, Negligence, Products Liability, Environmental, Wills and Probate, Trusts and Estates, Estate Planning, Real Estate and Foreclosure Law. Consumer and Commercial Collections, Business Law, Business Planning, Business

(This Listing Continued)

Litigation, Business Enterprises, Corporate, Partnerships, Small Business, Buying and Selling a Business, Business Start-Ups.

HOEPPNER WAGNER & EVANS LLP

CROWN POINT, INDIANA

(See Valparaiso)

General Practice. Trials and Appeals in State, Federal and Tax Courts. Bankruptcy, Commercial and Banking, Corporate, Creditors' Rights, Probate and Estate Planning, Estate Administration, Financial Resources Planning, Insurance Defense, Municipal Bonds, Municipal and Zoning, Personal Injury, Product Liability, Professional Malpractice, Real Estate, Taxation, Workers Compensation, Labor and Employment. Mediation, OSHA, Employee Benefits Law.

KENT A. JEFFIRS

104 WEST CLARK STREET
CROWN POINT, INDIANA 46307
Telephone: 219-663-7781
Fax: 219-663-7820
Email: kent@jeffirslawoffice.com
URL: http://www.jeffirslawoffice.com

Wills and Probate, Trusts and Estates, Estate Planning, Guardianship, Civil Litigation, Real Estate, Family Law, Adoptions.

KENT A. JEFFIRS, born Plymouth, Indiana, January 23, 1967; admitted to bar, 1992, Indiana and U.S. District Court, Northern and Southern Districts of Indiana. *Education:* University of Notre Dame (B.A., with honors, 1989); Indiana University (J.D., magna cum laude, 1992). Associate Editor, 1991-1992 and Member, Indiana Law Journal, 1990-1992. Judge, City of Crown Point, 2004—. *Member:* Lake County (President, 2005—), Indiana State and American Bar Associations.

JOHNSON & RAPPA, LLC

CROWN POINT, INDIANA

(See Merrillville)

Trial, Appellate, Personal Injury, Automobile Accidents, Slip and Fall, Wrongful Death, and Defense Practice in State and Federal Courts. Insurance, Civil Rights, Labor and Employment, Wrongful Termination, Employment Contracts, Mediation and Arbitration, Class Actions, Construction, Administrative, Products Liability and Transportation Law.

TIMOTHY F. KELLY AND ASSOCIATES

CROWN POINT, INDIANA

(See Dyer)

General Practice, Commercial, Business Law, Business Planning, Contracts, Business Litigation, Business Enterprises, Wills and Probate, Trusts and Estates, Asset Protection, Guardianships, Estate Planning, Corporation, Real Estate, Labor and Employment, Trials and Appeals in all Courts, Insurance Defense, Automobile Accidents, Slip and Fall, Wrongful Death, Products Liability, Professional Liability and Medical Malpractice.

KOPKA, PINKUS, DOLIN & EADS

5240 FOUNTAIN DRIVE
CROWN POINT, INDIANA 46307-1000
Telephone: 219-794-1888
Fax: 219-794-1892
URL: http://www.kpdlawfirm.com
Email: gapkinkus@kopkalaw.com
URL: http://www.kopkalaw.com

South Bend, Indiana Office: 227 South Main Street, Suite 200, 46601-2624. Telephone: 574-288-3270. Fax: 574-288-3280.
Farmington Hills, Michigan Office: 32605 West Twelve Mile Road, Suite 200, 48334-3339. Telephone: 248-324-2620. Fax: 248-324-2610.
Chicago, Illinois Office: 200 North LaSalle Street, Suite 2850, 60601. Telephone: 312-782-9920. Fax: 312-782-9965.
Buffalo Grove, Illinois Office: 100 Lexington Drive, Suite 100, 60089-6937. Telephone: 847-549-9611. Fax: 847-549-9636.
Indianapolis, Indiana Office: 10333 N. Meridian Street, Suite 475, 46290. Telephone: 317-818-1360. Fax: 317-818-1390.

Insurance Defense, Product Liability, Professional Liability, Insurance Fraud, Workers Compensation, Transportation, Toxic Tort and Environmental Liability.

FIRM PROFILE: A firm of over 50 attorneys, Kopka, Pinkus, Dolin & Eads is a law firm dedicated to the defense of litigated matters on behalf of insurance companies, their insured and self-insured corporations. We decline representation of individuals as plaintiffs in tort actions and claimants in workers' compensation cases. We maintain a network of six offices in Illinois, Indiana and Michigan, each of which has strong local roots but all of which share our philosophy of service and responsiveness to clients. The centralized structure of our multi-state partnership combines the advantages of extensive resources, expertise and technology while maintaining personal services. For a more complete overview of our firm and all of our attorneys, please visit our website.

GENE A. PINKUS, admitted to bar, 1989, Ohio; 1990, Indiana and Illinois. *Education:* University of Toledo (B.A., 1986; J.D., 1989). ***Email:*** gapinkus@kpdlawfirm.com

(This Listing Continued)

MARK L. DOLIN, admitted to bar, 1991, Michigan; 1992, Illinois (Not admitted in Indiana). *Education:* University of Toledo (B.S., 1987; J.D., 1991). ***Email:*** mldolin@kopkalaw.com

JOHN T. EADS, III, admitted to bar, 1990, Michigan (Not admitted in Indiana). *Education:* Hillsdale College (B.A., 1987); University of Richmond Law School (J.D., 1990). *Member:* Oakland County and American Bar Associations; State Bar of Michigan. ***PRACTICE AREAS:*** Insurance Defense; Automobile Negligence Defense; Commercial Vehicle Defense; Premises Liability Defense. ***Email:*** jteads@kopkalaw.com

JAMES E. O'GALLAGHER, admitted to bar, 1990, Indiana. *Education:* Marquette University (B.A., 1987); Indiana University at Bloomington (J.D., 1990). ***Email:*** jeogallagher@kpdlawfirm.com

MICHAEL LAMBERT

CROWN POINT, INDIANA

(Merrillville)

Criminal Law, Drug Crimes, Driving While Intoxicated, Parole and Probation, Juvenile Crimes, Traffic Violations, Family Law, Adoption, Divorce, Child Custody, Child Support, Domestic Violence, Visitation Rights, Employment Law, Wrongful Termination, Sexual Harassment, Civil Rights, Discrimination, Personal Injury, Automobile Accidents, Slip and Fall, Wrongful Death, Bankruptcy, Wills and Probate, Guardianships, Business Law, Contracts, Lawsuits, Business Enterprises.

LUCAS, HOLCOMB & MEDREA LLP

CROWN POINT, INDIANA

(See Merrillville)

General Practice, State and Federal Courts. Trials and Appeals. Corporate, Business, Business Litigation, Contracts, Business Planning, Business Enterprises, Commercial, Employment, Wrongful Termination, Banking, Tax, Wills and Probate, Trusts and Estates and Estate Planning, Insurance, Bankruptcy, Personal Injury, Automobile Accidents, Wrongful Death, Products Liability, Family/Domestic Relations, Adoptions, Child Custody, Child Support, Divorce, Visitation Rights, Hospital, Real Estate, Municipal and Zoning Law, Consumer and Commercial Collection Law, Construction Litigation.

GEORGE C. PATRICK & ASSOCIATES

706 MERRILLVILLE ROAD
CROWN POINT, INDIANA 46307
Telephone: 219-662-7959
Fax: 219-226-9061
Email: george@georgepatrick.com
URL: http://www.georgepatrick.com

Plaintiffs Worker's Compensation Litigation, Government Practice, Litigation.

GEORGE C. PATRICK, admitted to bar, 1992, Indiana, U.S. District Court, Northern and Southern Districts of Indiana and U.S. Court of Appeals, Seventh Circuit; U.S. Supreme Court. *Education:* Northwestern University (B.A., 1989); Valparaiso University (J.D., 1992). Admitted to the Worker's Compensation Board of the State of Indiana. President, Student Bar, 1991-1992. Member: Indiana Work Compensation Institute; National Board of Directors, Workplace Injury Litigation Group, 1999—; Lake Board of Directors Bar Association, 1997-1999. Life Member, Indiana Horse Council. *Member:* The Association of Trial Lawyers of America; Indiana State Bar Association; Lake County Bar Association; Inns of Court of America. ***REPORTED CASES:*** 58 FSUP P2d 935 655NE2d 1243 659NE2d684 679NE2d882.; Rivera, Joseph v. USX Corp, et al., 45A03-9502-CV-00028; Cooper Industries v. Edward Jones, 93A02-9460-EX-00325; Rueth, Claudia A/K/A Firrek, C.v. Quinn, Kathleen and John, 45A04-9502-CV-00034; United States Steel Corp. v. Spence, William, 93A02-9504-EX-00183; Two Market Square Association v. Tax Commissioners, 49T10-9404-TA-00119; Two Market Square Association v. Tax Commissioners, 49S10-9603-TA-001199; Little, Richard & Little, Gerald v. Little, Alan Richard, et al.; Lake County Board of Commissioners v. VanRunden, James, 45A04-9706-CV-00243; Board of Commissioners of Lake County v. State Board of Tax, 45T10-9803-TA-00028; Lake Superior Court v. Lake County Board of Commissioners, 45S00-9803-MF-00174; Hickory Hills Development Co., et al. v. Coffman, Daniel, et al., 45A03-9704-CV-00174; Lake County Plan Commission v. Bunce, Henrietta, 45A03-9806-CV-0025; Lake County Juvenile Detention Center v. McNair, Tiyi-Kitan, 93A02-9903-EX-00203; State of Indiana Ex. Rel. v. Lake County Superior Court, et. al., 45S00-9911-OR-00641; State of Indiana Ex. Rel. v. Lake County Superior Court, et al., 45S00-9911-OR-00642; Ameritech Disability Service Center v. Szarkowicz, Allen, 93A02-0011-EX-00700; Havlin, Patricia v. Wabash National Corporation, 93A02-0205-EX-00388; Lake County Board of Commissioners v. Grey, Richard, 93A02-0211-EX-00983; Lake County C & D Development v. Lake County Plan Commission, 45A03-0212-CV-00437; Carson Pirie Scott & Co. v. Mathis, Laura, 93A02-0303-EX-00264; Lake County Health Department v. CRD Enterprises, Inc., et al., 45A03-0401-CV-00018; Kozlowski, Sue v. Lake County Plan Commission, et. al., 45A05-0006-CV-00253; State of Indiana Ex. Rel. the Attorney General v. Lake County Superior Court, 45S00-0405-OR-00224; Governor of State of Indiana v. Miller Citezens Corporation, 45S00-0405-CV-00224; Prentoski, Krste v. Five Star Painting, 93A02-0410-EX-00815; Sanchez, Karen v. Lake County Nursing, 93A02-0410-EX-00815; Storey, Julia v. Pro Golf Distributors, 93A02-0411-EX-01001; Kozlowski, Sue v. Drodieski, Dordia, 45A05-0502-CV-00086; Harvey, Sally v. Fountainview Place, 93A02-0503-EX-00214; Prewitt, Shawn v. Lange Roofing, 93A02-0507-EX-00606; Phillips, Ray Alonzo v. Vanguard Services, 93A02-0507-EX-00607. ***PRACTICE AREAS:*** Plaintiffs Workers Compensation; Government; Litigation; Civil Practice; Federal Civil Practice; Civil Rights; Civil Liberties.

PINKERTON AND FRIEDMAN

PROFESSIONAL CORPORATION

CROWN POINT, INDIANA

(See Munster)

Federal Income and State Taxation, Probate and Estate Planning, Estate Administration, Trusts, Wills, Real Estate, Partnership, Business and Corporate Law. Municipal and Zoning Law, Employee Benefits, Business Litigation, Real Estate, Health Care Law.

SPANGLER, JENNINGS & DOUGHERTY, P.C.

CROWN POINT, INDIANA

(See Merrillville)

General Trial and Appellate Practice. Administrative, Banking, Bankruptcy, Business Reorganizations, Business Transactions, Civil Rights, Commercial, Construction, Corporate, Creditors' Rights, Criminal Litigation, Family/Domestic Relations, Drug and Device, Eminent Domain, Environmental, ERISA and Employee Benefits, Probate and Estate Planning and Administration, Fire/Arson, Guardianships, Health Care, Insurance, Labor and Employment, Municipal and Zoning, Personal Injury, Product Liability, Professional Liability, Medical Malpractice Defense, Real Estate, School, Federal, State and Local Taxation, Toxic Torts, Transportation, Workers Compensation, Land Development.

JOSEPH STALMACK & ASSOCIATES, P.C.

CROWN POINT, INDIANA

(See Hammond)

General Practice. Trials and Appeals. Insurance, Products Liability, Probate and Estate Planning, Transportation, Asbestos Litigation, Automobile, Common Carrier, Complex and Multi-District Litigation, Computer, Construction, Environmental and Industrial Disease, Environmental, Fire Insurance, Hazardous Materials, Legal Malpractice, Medical Malpractice, Mediation Services, Professional Malpractice, Subrogation, Toxic Substances and Toxic Torts Law, Personal Injury.

HINKLE & GIBBS

Established in 1962

35 WEST MARION STREET

DANVILLE, INDIANA 46122

Telephone: 317-745-5441

Fax: 317-745-0490

URL: http://www.h-glaw.com

Email: khinkle105@aol.com

URL: http://www.lawyers.com/hinkle&gibbslaw

Civil and Criminal Trial Practice in all State and Federal Courts, Litigation, Bankruptcy, Personal Injury, Corporate, Probate and Estate Planning, Real Estate, Family, Domestic Relations and Banking Law.

FIRM PROFILE: The firm is successor to Palmer & Hinkle founded in 1962. The firm serves businessmen, bankers, farmers and corporations in the Indianapolis area and has an extensive probate practice. Firm members are active in civic organizations and serve as board members of various organizations.

MEMBERS OF FIRM

HARLAN H. HINKLE, born Knox County, Indiana, May 24, 1932; admitted to bar, 1962, Indiana and U.S. District Court, Southern District of Indiana; 1968, U.S. Supreme Court; 1971, U.S. Court of Appeals, Seventh Circuit. *Education:* Vincennes University (A.A., 1952); Indiana University (B.S., 1954; J.D., 1961); ICLEF Seminar, Probate Litigation (1997). Author: "Failure of a Trust," Res Gestae, 1960. Faculty Member: ICLEF Seminar, "Probate Administration for Indiana Practitioners," 1983—; Hendricks County Probate Practice Seminar, 1988—; Probate Litigation Seminar, 1997. Chief Deputy Prosecuting Attorney, 55th Judicial Circuit, 1963-1970. Member, House of Delegates, 1980-1989. *Member:* Hendricks County and Indiana State Bar Associations (Member, Probate Council, 1980-1989; Vice-President, 1991-1994, Probate, Trust and Real Property Section). [U.S. Army Intelligence (Japan) 1956-1958]. ***PRACTICE AREAS:*** Probate; Trusts; Real Property. ***Email:*** harlan@h-glaw.com

KEVIN J. HINKLE, born Sagamihara, Japan, May 26, 1956; admitted to bar, 1981, Indiana and U.S. District Court, Southern District of Indiana. *Education:* Indiana University (B.A., 1978; J.D., 1981). Order of the Barristers. Certified Mediator, 1995—. Member, Hendricks County Council, 1984-1989, Prosecuting Attorney, Hendricks County, 1990-1994. Member, Board of Directors, Association of Indiana Prosecuting Attorneys, 1994. *Member:* Hendricks County (Chairman, Continuing Legal Education Committee, 1987-1991) and Indiana State Bar Associations; Indiana Trial Lawyers Association; Association of Trial Lawyers of America. ***REPORTED CASES:*** PSI Energy, Inc. v. Home Ins. Co., 801 N.E. 2d 705. ***PRACTICE AREAS:*** Personal Injury; Business Litigation; Criminal; Real Estate. ***Email:*** khinkle@h-glaw.com

J. GORDON GIBBS, JR., born La Porte, Indiana, April 13, 1939; admitted to bar, 1968, Indiana and U.S. District Court, Southern District of Indiana; 1980, U.S. Supreme Court. *Education:* Wabash College (B.A., 1961); Indiana University School of Law (J.D., 1968). Chief Counsel, Office of the Attorney General, 1977-1992. *Member:* Hendricks County Bar Association. [U.S. Army 1962-1964 SP4]. ***REPORTED CASES:*** ISHKON v. Bowen; Indiana State Fair Board v. Hockey Corp. of America. ***PRACTICE AREAS:*** Contract Law; Constitutional Law; Domestic Relations; Tort; Real Estate; Eminent Domain; Criminal.

(This Listing Continued)

ASSOCIATE

JEREMY P. GOOCH, born Bloomington, Indiana, March 21, 1974; admitted to bar, 2001, Indiana. *Education:* Indiana University - Bloomington (B.A., 1996); Indiana University School of Law - Indianapolis (J.D., cum laude, 2001). Golden Key Honor Society. Member, Civil Town of Speedway Board of Zoning Appeals, 2002-2003. *Member:* Indiana State and American Bar Associations. ***PRACTICE AREAS:*** Wills; Trusts and Estates; Civil Litigation; Domestic Relations; Collections; Landlord and Tenant Law. ***Email:*** jeremy@h-glaw.com

REPRESENTATIVE CLIENTS: ENT Group, LLC.; The North Salem State Bank; Hendricks County Bank and Trust Co.; Kiefer & Associates, Inc.; Preston Realtors; Dayton Enterprises, Inc.; Century 21 Axiom Realtors, Commercial Union Insurance; National City Bank, Indiana; Walnut Equipment Leasing, Inc; Nucor Steel SBQ, LLC; One Beacon Insurance Group; Lloyds London; London Market Insurance Companies (MGP litigation).
REFERENCES: Hendricks County Bank and Trust Co.; The North Salem State Bank.

KENDALL, WOOD, LOWRY & KESSINGER

1 SOUTH WASHINGTON STREET

P.O. BOX 8

DANVILLE, INDIANA 46122

Telephone: 317-745-4408

Fax: 317-745-0390

General Trial Practice in all Courts. Probate and Estate Planning, Personal Injury, Real Estate, School, Family, Domestic Relations and Criminal Defense Law.

MEMBERS OF FIRM

JOHN A. KENDALL (1907-1993)

ROBERT A. WOOD, born Terre Haute, Indiana, September 4, 1948; admitted to bar, 1974, Indiana and U.S. District Court, Southern District of Indiana; 1978, U.S. Supreme Court. *Education:* Indiana State University (A.B., 1970); Indianapolis Law School of Indiana and Purdue Universities (J.D., cum laude, 1974). Phi Delta Phi. Deputy Prosecuting Attorney, Hendricks County, 1974-1975, 1983-1985. *Member:* Hendricks County (President, 1979) and Indiana State Bar Associations. ***PRACTICE AREAS:*** Domestic Relations; Real Estate; Tort; School Law; Probate; General Practice; Litigation.

JAMES L. LOWRY, born Carbondale, Illinois, November 20, 1939; admitted to bar, 1966, Indiana and U.S. District Court, Southern District of Indiana; 1982, U.S. Court of Appeals, 7th Circuit. *Education:* Butler University (B.A., 1962); Indiana University (J.D., 1966). Deputy Prosecuting Attorney, 1966 and Prosecuting Attorney, 1967-1971, Rush County. President, Rush County Mental Health Association, 1967. Chairman, Rush County March of Dimes Association, 1969-1970. Chairman, Hendricks County United Way, 1977-1978. *Member:* Rush County (President, 1968), Hendricks County (President, 1972-1994) and Indiana State (Member: House of Delegates, 1966-1982; Board of Managers, 1980, 1982; Treasurer, 1981-1982) Bar Associations; Indiana Trial Lawyers Association; National Lawyers Association. [Indiana National Guard, 1957-1961]. ***PRACTICE AREAS:*** Domestic Relations; Trials and Tort; Will Contests; Personal Injury; Criminal. ***Email:*** lowryj@iquest.net

TERRY M. KESSINGER, born Hillsboro, Illinois, September 25, 1948; admitted to bar, 1976, Indiana and U.S. District Court, Southern District of Indiana; 1980, U.S. Supreme Court. *Education:* Western Illinois University; University of Tennessee at Knoxville (B.S., 1971); Indiana University (J.D., 1976). Chief Deputy Prosecutor, Hendricks County, Indiana, 1979-1990. *Member:* Hendricks County (President, 1984-1985), Indiana State and American Bar Associations. ***PRACTICE AREAS:*** Criminal Defense; Domestic Relations; General Civil Litigation.

REPRESENTATIVE CLIENTS: Danville, Plainfield and Mill Creek Community School Corp.; Northwest Hendricks School Corp.; Town of Coatesville.
LOCAL COUNSEL FOR: Public Service Co. of Indiana, Inc.; Indiana Insurance Co; Prudential Life Insurance Co.; Indiana Bell Telephone Co.

RUPPERT & SCHAEFER, P.C.

DANVILLE, INDIANA

(See Indianapolis)

Family Law, Divorce, Pre-marital Agreements, Child Custody, Child Support, Paternity, Visitation Rights, Step Parent Adoptions.

BLACKBURN & GREEN

DECATUR, INDIANA

(See Fort Wayne)

Litigation, Personal Injury Law.

ROEBUCK & ASSOCIATES, P.C.

DECATUR, INDIANA

(See Ft. Wayne)

Personal Injury, Automobile Accidents, Boat Accidents, Motorcycle Accidents, Truck Accidents, Slip and Fall, Dog Bites, Medical Malpractice, Head Injuries, Nursing Home Abuse and Neglect, Products Liability, Insurance, Social Security, Social Security Disability, and Wrongful Death.

BLACKBURN & GREEN

DELPHI, INDIANA

(See Fort Wayne)

Litigation, Personal Injury Law.

HERBERT S. LASSER & ASSOCIATES, P.C.

DEMOTTE, INDIANA

(See Merrillville)

Personal Injury, Wrongful Death, Automobile and All Accidents, Construction Law, Family Law, Divorce, Child Custody, Child Support, Domestic Violence, Visitation Rights, Work Accidents, Trials and Appeals, Business Law, Business Planning, Contracts, Law Suits, Insurance, Business Enterprises, Closely Held Business, Corporate, Limited Liability Companies, Partnerships, Small Business, Franchises, Buying and Selling A Business, Debt and Credit, Collections, Creditors Rights, Banking and Finance, Venture Capital, Employee Benefits, Employment Contracts, Human Resources, Discrimination, Sexual Harassment, Workers Compensation, Wrongful Termination, Real Estate, Buying or Selling, Commercial Leasing, Environmental, Landlord and Tenant, Zoning and Land Use, Starting a Business, Strategic Alliances, Joint Ventures, Mergers, Civil Rights, Consumer Law, Consumer Fraud, Unsafe Products, Criminal Law, Drunk Driving, Misdemeanors, Drug Crimes, Juvenile Crimes, Parole and Probation, Traffic Violations, Medical Malpractice, Legal Malpractice, Products Liability, Slip and Fall, Wills and Probate, Trusts and Estates, Asset Protection, Estate Planning, General Civil and Criminal Practice, General Practice, Trademark Patent Litigation.

TIMOTHY F. KELLY AND ASSOCIATES

202 JOLIET STREET
SUITE 2A
DYER, INDIANA 46311
Telephone: 219-322-0606
Fax: 219-322-0707
Email: tfklaw@tfklaw.net
URL: http://www.tfklaw.net

General Practice, Commercial, Business Law, Business Planning, Contracts, Business Litigation, Business Enterprises, Wills and Probate, Trusts and Estates, Asset Protection, Guardianships, Estate Planning, Corporation, Real Estate, Labor and Employment, Trials and Appeals in all Courts, Insurance Defense, Automobile Accidents, Slip and Fall, Wrongful Death, Products Liability, Professional Liability and Medical Malpractice.

FIRM PROFILE: Timothy F. Kelly is listed in the Bar Register of Preeminent Lawyers in the areas of general practice, insurance defense, labor and employment law, civil trial practice, product liability law, personal injury, and medical malpractice. His firm utilizes an experienced legal support staff to provide strong services to its clients.

MEMBERS OF FIRM

TIMOTHY F. KELLY, born Hammond, Indiana, February 22, 1947; admitted to bar, 1972, Indiana. *Education:* St. John's University (B.A., 1969); University of Minnesota (J.D., 1972). *Member:* Hammond, Lake County, Indiana State, American and Seventh Circuit Bar Associations; Association of Trial Lawyers of America; Indiana Trial Lawyers Association; American Judicature Society; Indiana Defense Lawyers Association; Defense Research Institute. Fellow, Indiana Bar Foundation. ***PRACTICE AREAS:*** Personal Injury; Commercial Litigation; Contract Litigation. ***Email:*** tfk@tfklaw.net

KARL K. VANZO, born Hammond, Indiana, June 29, 1957; admitted to bar, 1982, Indiana. *Education:* University of Notre Dame (B.A., with high honors, 1979); Indiana University at Bloomington (J.D., cum laude, 1982). *Member:* Hammond, Lake County, Indiana State and American Bar Associations. ***PRACTICE AREAS:*** Insurance Law; Commercial Law; Medical Malpractice. ***Email:*** kkv@tfklaw.net

ASSOCIATES

MICHAEL P. MASSUCCI, born Chicago, Illinois, June 15, 1977; admitted to bar, 2002, Wisconsin and U.S. District Court, Eastern District of Wisconsin; 2003, Indiana. *Education:* Marquette University (B.A., 1999; J.D., 2002). ***PRACTICE AREAS:*** Civil Litigation; Estate Planning; Business Law; Contracts; Professional Sports Law; Amateur Sports Law. ***Email:*** mpm@tfklaw.net

BETH L. BROWN, born Valparaiso, Indiana, November 8, 1977; admitted to bar, 2003, Indiana. *Education:* Valparaiso University (B.A., 2000; J.D., 2003). *Member:* Indiana State Bar Association; Indiana Trial Lawyers Association; Association of Trial Lawyers of America. ***Email:*** blb@tfklaw.net

DANIEL STEPHENS, admitted to bar, 2000, Indiana. *Education:* Valparaiso University (B.A., 1997; J.D., 1999). *Member:* Indiana State Bar Association. ***PRACTICE AREAS:*** Personal Injury; Medical Malpractice; Nursing Home Abuse and Neglect. ***Email:*** dbs@tfklaw.net

LEGAL SUPPORT PERSONNEL

PARALEGALS

KERRY E. KELLY, born Stuttgart, Germany, June 14, 1971. *Education:* Northern Arizona University (B.A., 1996); Roosevelt University (Civil Litigation, 1996). Member: American Trial Lawyers Association - Paralegal Division; National Association of Legal Assistants. (Legal Assistant). ***PRACTICE AREAS:*** Litigation Support. ***Email:*** kek@tfklaw.net

LYNN M. SHIVELY, born Hammond, Indiana, November 25, 1967. *Education:* Sawyer Business College (1991). Member: National Association of Legal Assistants; Indiana Paralegal Association. (Legal Assistant). ***PRACTICE AREAS:*** Litigation Support; Probate; Real Estate; Estate Planning. ***Email:*** lms@tfklaw.net

REPRESENTATIVE CLIENTS: Acuity Insurance Co.; Baldwin and Lyons; Broadwest Comprehensive Medical Partnership; Crown Corr, Inc.

BECKMAN, KELLY & SMITH

EAST CHICAGO, INDIANA

(See Hammond)

General Practice, Commercial, Corporation, Transportation and Trucking, Products and Professional Liability Defense, Elder Law, Estate and Trust Planning and Administration, Franchising, Real Estate, Employment, Taxation and Environmental Law, Trials and Appeals in all Courts, Medical Malpractice Defense and Workers Compensation Defense.

BAKER & DANIELS LLP

Established in 1863
317 WEST FRANKLIN STREET
P.O. BOX 507
ELKHART, INDIANA 46515-0507
Telephone: 574-296-6000
Fax: 574-296-6001
URL: http://www.bakerdaniels.com

Indianapolis, Indiana Office: 300 North Meridian Street, Suite 2700, 46204. Telephone: 317-237-0300. Fax: 317-237-1000.
South Bend, Indiana Office: First Bank Building, 205 West Jefferson Boulevard, Suite 250, 46601. Telephone: 574-234-4149. Fax: 574-239-1900.
Fort Wayne, Indiana Office: 111 East Wayne Street, Suite 800, 46802. Telephone: 260-424-8000. Fax: 260-460-1700.
Indianapolis-96th Street, Indiana Office: Parkwood Six, 600 East 96th Street, Suite 600, 46240. Telephone: 317-569-9600. Fax: 317-569-4800.
Washington, D.C. Office: 805 15th Street, N.W., Suite 700, 20005. Telephone: 202-312-7440. Fax: 202-312-7460.
Qingdao, China Office: 4/F, Office Tower, Crowne Plaza Qingdao, No. 76 Hong Kong Middle Road, 266071. Telephone: +011-86-532-575-1051. Fax: +011-86-532-575-1055.
Beijing, China Office: Room 1919, Tower 2, China World Trade Center, No. 1 JianGuoMenWai Avenue, 100004. Telephone: +86-10-6505-7733. Fax: +86-10-6505-8730.

Antitrust, Bankruptcy, Business Planning, Commercial, Corporate Finance, Creditors Rights, Employee Benefits, Employment, Environment, Estate and Probate, Family, Financial, Food and Drug, Government Affairs, Health Care, Insurance, Intellectual Property, International, Legislative, Litigation, Medical Technology Regulation, Municipal, Nonprofit, Product Liability, Real Estate, Securities, Sports, Tax, Transportation, Utilities, Year 2000, Zoning and Land Use Law.

FIRM PROFILE: Since 1863 we have been helping clients do business throughout Indiana, across the country and around the world. From Fortune 500 corporations to regional businesses, local governments and individuals, clients look to Baker & Daniels LLP for excellence in all areas of legal practice, for a creative and individualized approach to solving client problems, and for a deep understanding of business, law and government. More than 350 Baker and Daniels' professionals serve clients from the firm's seven offices in Indiana, Washington, D.C. and China (we are one of only 31 U.S. law firms licensed to practice in China). Our service to clients is enhanced by our Washington, D.C. government affairs consulting subsidiary, Sagamore Associates, and our exclusive Indiana membership in Lex Mundi, an association of more than 158 independent law firms around the world.

LAW FIRM ALLIANCES/ASSOCIATIONS: **TAGLAW (The Appleton Group Legal Network):** *The Firm is a member of TAGLaw, an international association of prominent law firms and an exclusive Indiana Member of Lex Mundi.*

MEMBERS OF FIRM

JAMES R. BROTHERSON, born 1952; admitted to bar, 1978, Indiana and Michigan. *Education:* Duke University (B.A., 1974); Indiana University School of Law (J.D., 1978). Assistant Dean for Alumni Relations and Operations, 1996; Past President, Indiana University School of Law, Bloomington, Alumni Association; Past Member, Indiana University School of Law, Bloomington, Board of Visitors and Alumni Board of Directors; Deputy Prosecuting Attorney, 1983. *Member:* Elkhart City, Monroe County, Indiana State and American Bar Associations; State Bar of Michigan. ***PRACTICE AREAS:*** Business Law; Commercial Transactions; Bankruptcy; Estate Planning; Real Estate; Employment. ***Email:*** james.brotherson@bakerd.com

GLENN E. KILLOREN, born 1958; admitted to bar, 1983, Indiana; 1987, Illinois; 1984, U.S. Tax Court. *Education:* University of Notre Dame (B.B.A., 1980; J.D., 1983). Deputy Prosecuting Attorney, 1986, 1989-1990. Certified as Civil Mediator, Indiana, 1993. *Member:* Elkhart City, Illinois State, Indiana State and American Bar Associations. ***PRACTICE AREAS:*** Business; Corporate; Real Estate. ***Email:*** glenn.killoren@bakerd.com

KENNARD R. WEAVER, born 1940; admitted to bar, 1965, Indiana; 1973, U.S. Supreme Court; 1976, Michigan. *Education:* Michigan State University (B.A., 1962); Harvard University (J.D., 1965). Phi Kappa Phi. Chairman, Lawyers Committee, Manufactured Housing Institute, 1990—. *Member:* Elkhart City, Elkhart County, Indiana State (Chairman, Corporation, Banking and Business Law Section, 1985-1986) and American Bar Associations; State Bar of Michigan. (Resident). ***PRACTICE AREAS:*** Business Law; Securities; Estate Planning; Probate; Litigation; Taxation. ***Email:*** ken.weaver@bakerd.com

ROBERT C. WHIPPO, born 1965; admitted to bar, 1991, U.S. District Court, Northern and Southern Districts of Indiana; 1992, Indiana. *Education:* Valparaiso University (B.A., 1988; J.D., cum laude, 1991). *Member:* Elkhart City, Indiana State and American Bar Associations. ***PRACTICE AREAS:*** Corporate; Commercial Transactions; Appellate Practice; Civil Litigation; Employment Law. ***Email:*** robert.whippo@bakerd.com

OF COUNSEL

ROBERT A. PFAFF, born 1933; admitted to bar, 1961, Indiana and Michigan. *Education:* Washington & Lee University (A.B., 1955); University of Michigan (J.D., 1961).

(This Listing Continued)

BAKER & DANIELS LLP, Elkhart—Continued

Member, Character and Fitness Committee, Indiana State Board of Law Examiners, 1965—. Certified Civil Mediator, Indiana, 1993; Family Law Mediator, 1995. *Member:* Elkhart City (President, 1985), Indiana State and American Bar Associations; State Bar of Michigan. Master Fellow, Indiana Bar Foundation. ***PRACTICE AREAS:*** Real Estate; Land Use; Business Planning. ***Email:*** robert.pfaff@bakerd.com

ASSOCIATES

JENNIFER ELAINE GREENE, admitted to bar, 2005, Indiana. *Education:* Purdue University (B.A., cum laude, 2002); Washington University (J.D., 2005). ***PRACTICE AREAS:*** Strategic Business Services. ***Email:*** jennifer.greene@bakerd.com

JEREMY D. PFISTER, admitted to bar, 2003, Indiana. *Education:* University of Wisconsin (B.A., cum laude, 2000); Indiana University School of Law (J.D., 2003). ***PRACTICE AREAS:*** Litigation. ***Email:*** jeremy.pfister@bakerd.com

CHRISTOPHER J. SPATARO, born 1971; admitted to bar, 1996, Indiana and Michigan. *Education:* New York University (B.A., cum laude, 1993); Notre Dame Law School (J.D., 1996). Certified Mediator. *Member:* Elkhart City and Indiana State Bar Associations. ***LANGUAGES:*** Italian. ***PRACTICE AREAS:*** Civil Litigation; Commercial Collections; Employment; Creditors Rights. ***Email:*** christopher.spataro@bakerd.com

KRISTA J. ZIMMERMAN, admitted to bar, 2001, Indiana. *Education:* Goshen College (B.A., 1997); University of Notre Dame (J.D., 2001). ***PRACTICE AREAS:*** Labor and Employment Law; Business Planning. ***Email:*** krista.zimmerman@bakerd.com

REPRESENTATIVE CLIENTS: 1st Source Bank; American Commercial Lines, Inc.; American General Finance, Inc.; American Trans Air, Inc.; Amoco, Inc.; Anthem Insurance Companies, Inc.; ARAMark Corp.; Arvin-Meritor, Inc.; AT&T Corp.; Auburn Foundry, Inc.; Ball Corporation; Bank One, Indianapolis, NA; Bindley Western Industries, Inc.; Borg-Warner Corporation; Brightpoint Inc.; Browning Investments, Inc.; Browning-Ferris Industries, Inc.; Central Soya Company, Inc.; Chevron Chemical Company; Chubb Group of Insurance Companies; Cinergy Corporation; Citizens Gas & Coke Utility; City of Elkhart; City of Fort Wayne; City of Indianapolis; City of South Bend; Clarian Health Partners; Conseco, Inc.; CSX Transportation, Inc.; Cummins Engine Company, Inc.; Delco Electronics Corporation; Denison, Inc.; DePauw University; Dow AgroSciences LLC; Dow Brands, L.P.; DowElanco; EFP Corporation; EIG Operating Partnership; Eli Lilly and Company; Emmis Communications; Enkei America, Inc.; Ernest & Julio Gallo Winery; Essex Group, Inc.; Farm Credit Services of Mid-America; Fort Wayne News-Sentinel; Fujitsu TEN; General Electric Capital Corp.; General Electric Company/Motor Business Group; General Motors Acceptance Corporation; General Motors Corporation; Golden Rule Insurance Company; Grumman Allied Industries; Guardian Industries, Inc.; Guidant Corporation; Heartland Steel, Inc.; Heritage Environmental Services, Inc.; Hill-Rom; Hillenbrand Industries, Inc.; Hill's Pet Nutrition; Hudson Institute, Inc.; Hughes Aircraft Co.; Hughes Technical; Hurco Co., Inc.; Indiana Bond Bank; Indiana Constructors, Inc.; Indiana Dental Association; Indiana Michigan Power Company; Indiana University; Indianapolis Life Insurance Company; Indianapolis Public Schools; Inland Paperboard and Packaging, Inc.; Ispat Inland Inc.; ITT Corporation (Aerospace/Optical Division); IWC Resources Corporation; Jayco, Inc.; Jewel Cos., Inc./Osco Drug, Inc.; John Hancock Mutual Life Insurance Co.; Key Bank; Kimball International; Kraft Foods, Inc.; Lilly Endowment, Inc.; McDonald's Corporation; McDonald & Company Securities, Inc.; Meridian Financial Corporation; Meridian Mutual Insurance; Metropolitan Life Insurance Company; Miller Brewing Company; Minnesota Mining & Manufacturing; Modernfold, Inc.; MSA Realty Corporation; National City Bank; National Enterprises, Inc.; National Retail Hardware Association; National Starch & Chemical Company; New Bern Transport Corporation; NOLHGA; North American Van Lines, Inc.; Olive B. Cole Foundation, Inc.; Olive LLP; Paul Harris Stores, Inc.; Philip Morris Company; PSI Energy, Inc.; Quality Dining, Inc.; Quantum Chemical Corporation; Quorum Health Group of Indiana; R.R. Donnelley & Sons Co.; Raffensperger, Hughes & Co., Inc.; Ralston Purina Company; Rand McNally & Company; Rea Magnet Wire, Inc.; Red Ball Corporation; Roche Diagnostic Systems, Inc.; Rockwell International Corporation; Rose Acre Farms, Inc.; Saint John's Medical Center; Schult Homes Corporation; Seyfert Foods, Inc.; Shambaugh & Son, Inc.; Shoe Carnival; Simon & Schuster; Simon Property Group, Inc.; Sisters of St. Francis Health Services, Inc.; Slater Steels Corporation; Society Corporation; South Bend Community Schools Corporation; St. John's Health System; Steel Dynamics Inc.; Subaru-Isuzu; Tecumseh Compressor; Tenaska, Inc.; The Lutheran Hospital of Indiana, Inc.; The Prudential Insurance Company of America; Trammell Crow Company; Tranex Credit Corporation; U.S. Gymnastics Federation; United Airlines; Wabash College; Wal-Mart Stores, Inc.; Weaver Popcorn, Inc.; Westinghouse Electric Corporation; Wells Fargo; WSBT, Inc.; York International Corporation; Zimmer, Inc.

(For complete biographical data on other Members of Firm, Of Counsel and Associates, See Professional Biographies at Indianapolis, Fort Wayne, South Bend, Indiana, Washington, D.C., Qingdao and Beijing, China)

BARNES & THORNBURG LLP

121 WEST FRANKLIN STREET, SUITE 200
ELKHART, INDIANA 46516
Telephone: 574-293-0681
FAX: 574-296-2535
URL: http://www.btlaw.com

Indianapolis, Indiana Office: 11 South Meridian Street, 46204. Telephone: 317-236-1313. FAX: 317-231-7433.

Fort Wayne, Indiana Office: 600 One Summit Square, 46802. Telephone: 260-423-9440. FAX: 260-424-8316.

South Bend, Indiana Office: 600 1st Source Bank Center, 100 North Michigan, 46601-1632. Telephone: 574-233-1171. FAX: 574-237-1125.

Chicago, Illinois Office: One North Wacker Drive, Suite 4400, 60606-2833. Telephone: 312-357-1313. FAX: 312-759-5646.

Washington, D.C. Office: Suite 900, 750 17th Street, N.W., 20006. Telephone: 202-289-1313. FAX: 202-289-1330.

Grand Rapids, Michigan Office: 300 Ottawa Avenue, N.W., Suite 500, 49503. Telephone: 616-742-3930. FAX: 616-742-3999.

Acquisitions and Divestitures, Ad Valorem Tax, Administrative Law, Affirmative Action, Agriculture Law, Americans with Disabilities Act, Antidumping, Antitrust, Antitrust and Trade Regulation, Appellate Practice, Attorney Grievances, Automotive Warranty Law, Aviation and Aerospace, Aviation Law, Banking Law, Banking Regulations, Bankruptcy, Bankruptcy Reorganization, Banks and Banking, Biochemical Patents, Biomedical Products Liability, Biomedical Technology, Biotechnology Patent Prosecution, Bond Law, Brain Injury, Breach of Warranty, Brown Fields Redevelopment, Business Immigration, Business Law, Business Litigation, Business Planning, Business Regulatory and Administrative, Business Start-ups, Business Suc-

(This Listing Continued)

cession Planning, Business Taxation, Business Torts, Business Transactions, Business Transfers, Buying and Selling of Businesses, Cable TV, Cargo Claims, Charitable Trusts and Foundations, Chemical Intellectual Property, Chemical Patent Prosecution, Chemical Patents, Chemical Products Liability, Civil Appeals, Civil Litigation, Civil Practice, Civil RICO, Class Action Defense, Clean Air Act, Clean Water Act, Closely Held Business Estate Planning, Closely Held Businesses, Closely Held Business Law, Closely Held Corporations, Collective Bargaining, Commercial Bankruptcy, Commercial Finance Law, Commercial Law, Commercial Leasing and Financing, Commercial Litigation, Commercial Conveyancing, Commercial Real Estate, Commercial Real Estate Acquisition, Commercial Real Estate Development, Commercial Real Estate Finance, Commercial Transactions, Commodities Fraud, Communications and Media, Complex Commercial Litigation, Complex Litigation, Computer and Software Patents, Computer Law, Computers and Software, Conflicts of Interest, Construction Labor Law, Construction Law, Consumer Credit, Contract Litigation, Cooperatives, Copyrights, Corporate Finance, Corporate Formation, Corporate Law, Corporate Taxation, Corporate Tax Planning, Countervailing Duties, Covenants Not To Compete, Creditors Rights, Creditors Rights in Bankruptcy, Criminal Defense, Criminal Law, Criminal Tax Audits, Customs Law, Dealer and Distributor Termination, Debt and Equity Finance, Decedents Estates, Defense Litigation, Design Patents, Disability Insurance Defense, Discrimination, Distribution, Drug and Medical Device Defense, Economic Development, Education Law, Elder Law, Election, Campaign and Political Law, Electric Power, Electric Utilities, Electrical Intellectual Property, Electrical Patents, Electro-mechanical Patents, Electronic Commerce, Electronic Patents, Eminent Domain, Employee Benefits, Employee Stock Ownership Plans, Employment Defense, Employment Discrimination, Employment Law, Employment Litigation, Energy, Energy Contracts, Energy Regulation, Environmental Administrative Law, Environmental Cleanup, Environmental Compliance, Environmental Criminal Defense, Environmental Law, Environmental Litigation, Environmental Permitting, Environmental Real Estate, Environmental Regulation, Environmental Risk Management, Equal Employment Opportunity Law, ERISA Litigation, Estate Administration, Estate and Gift Taxation, Estate Planning, Estate Planning and Taxation, Estate Planning and Administration, Estate Planning and Probate, Estate Planning for Parents of Handicapped Children, Estate Planning for Unmarried Individuals, Executive Compensation, Executive Severance Contracts, Export Regulation, Fair Employment Practices, Family and Medical Leave Act, Family Business Successions, Family Wealth Transfer, Federal and State Administrative Regulatory Practice, Federal and State Legislative Practice, Federal Civil Litigation, Federal Civil Practice, Federal Criminal Law, Federal Estate and Gift Taxation, Federal Litigation, Federal Tax Controversies, Federal Taxation, Fiduciary Income Tax, Finance, Financial Transactions, First Party Insurance, Foreign Investment in the United States, Freight Claims, Freight Loss and Damage, Gaming Law, Gaming Licensing, Gas Utilities, General Litigation, Government, Government Affairs, Government Agency Practice, Government Contracts, Government Investigations, Government Relations, Groundwater Contamination, Hazardous Materials and Substances, Hazardous Waste, Hazardous Waste Liability, Head Injury, Health Care, Health Care Corporate Law, Health Care Contracts, Health Care Fraud, Health Care Licensing, Health Care Litigation, Health Care Mergers and Acquisitions, Health Care Regulation, Health Care Reimbursement, Health Law, Heavy Equipment Products Liability, Immigration Law, Industrial Revenue Bond Law, Inheritance Tax, Initial Public Offerings, Insurance, Insurance Bad Faith, Insurance Coverage, Insurance Litigation, Insurance Regulation, Integrated Health Care Delivery Systems, Intellectual Property, Intellectual Property General Prosecution, Intellectual Property Infringement, Intellectual Property Licensing, Intellectual Property Litigation, Intellectual Property Procurement, Intellectual Property Protection, Intellectual Property Rights, International Business Law, International Intellectual Property, International Law, International Patents, International Trade, International Transportation Law, Internet Law, Internet Trademark Law, Joint Ventures, Labor and Employment, Labor Arbitration, Labor Law, Labor Relations, Land Use, Lease Law, Leasing, Legal Ethics and Professional Responsibility, Legal Malpractice Defense, Legislative Practice, Licensing, Life Insurance Defense, Limited Liability Company Law, Limited Partnerships, Liquor Licensing, Litigation, Loans, Lobbying, Local Government Law, Logistics, Long Term Care, Managed Care, Managed Care Contracts, Management Employment Law, Management Labor Law, Manufacturers Liability, Maritime Regulations, Mechanical Intellectual Property, Mechanical Patents, Media Law, Mediation, Medical Antitrust, Medical Intellectual Property, Medical Patents, Mental Health Law, Mergers, Acquisitions and Divestitures, Mergers and Acquisitions, Mineral Taxation, Molecular Biology Patents, Motor Carrier Law, Motor Carrier Regulation, Multi-Employer Pensions, Municipal Bonds, Municipal Bonds Taxation, Municipal Finance, Municipal Law, Municipal Leasing, Municipal Redevelopment, Municipal Securities, Municipal Taxation, National Labor Relations Act, Neurolaw, Nonprofit and Charitable Organizations, Nonprofit Organizations Law, North American Free Trade Agreement, Occupational Safety and Health, OSHA, Partnership Law, Partnership Taxation, Patent Infringement, Patent Interference Practice, Patent Litigation, Patent Prosecution, Patents, PCT Legal Export, Personal Injury, Personal Injury Defense, Pesticide Litigation, Pharmaceutical Intellectual Property, Pharmaceutical Patents, Physician Contracts, Physician Practices, Planning and Land Use, Power Line Contact Injury, Probate, Probate Litigation, Products Liability, Products Liability Defense, Professional Liability, Property Law, Property Tax, Property Tax Abatement, Property Tax Appeals, Psychological Injury, Public Finance, Public Sector Labor Relations, Public Utility Law, Railroad Law, Real Estate, Real Estate Acquisitions, Real Estate Contracts, Real Estate Development, Real Estate Finance, Real Estate Licensing, Real Estate Secured Lending, Real Estate Title Insurance, Real Property, Real Property Acquisitions, Real Property Finance, Reorganizations, Resource Conservation and Recovery Act (RCRA), Retirement Benefit Plans, School Law, Securities, Securities Litigation, Securitization, Semiconductor Technology, Sexual Harassment, Small Business Corporations, State Government Law, State Tax Controversies, State Taxation, Structured Finance, Succession Planning, Superfund, Tax Controversies, Tax Exempt Finance, Tax Exempt Organizations, Tax Increment Finance, Tax Law, Tax Litigation, Taxation, Technology and Science, Technology Law, Technology Licensing, Technology Transfers, Telecommunications Competition, Telecommunications Law, Theft of Trade Secrets, Title VII Discrimination, Title IX Discrimination, Tort Defense, Toxic Exposure, Toxic Tort Class Actions, Toxic Torts, Toxic Tort Defense, Trade Dress, Trade Secrets, Trademark Litigation, Trademarks, Trademark Prosecution, Trademark Protection, Trademark Registration, Transportation, Transportation Safety, Trial Practice, Trusts and Estates, Unfair Competition, Unfair Trade, Uniform Commercial Codes, Union Contract Negotiations, Union Elections, Utilities, Utility Law, Wage and Hour Law, WARN Act, Water Pollution, Water Quality, Water Utilities, Wetland Regulation,

(This Listing Continued)

White Collar Crime, White Collar Criminal Defense, Wills, Workers Compensation, Workouts, World Trade Organization, Wrongful Death, Wrongful Termination, Wrongful Termination Defense, Zoning, Planning and Land Use.

FIRM PROFILE: Quality. Service. Efficiency. Communication. These are the cornerstones of the firm's culture and the keys to its success.

Established on January 1, 1982, Barnes & Thornburg LLP is relatively young; however, its founding date belies the firm's rich history. The firm's roots can be traced to two cities, South Bend and Indianapolis. Our northern Indiana presence began in 1926 with the establishment of Seebirt Oare & Omacht, and later grew when they merged with an Elkhart firm, Cawley and Harman. In Indianapolis, four partners opened Barnes Hickam Pantzer & Boyd on September 13, 1940. They began the firm with 13 people in an office of 13 rooms on the 13th floor of the Merchants Bank Building, the tallest in Indiana at that time. The number 13 has proven to be a lucky number for Barnes & Thornburg LLP.

Since 1982, the firm has opened offices in Chicago, Fort Wayne, Washington, D.C., Grand Rapids and merged with Jenkins, Coffey, Hyland, Badger & Conard, an intellectual property firm; Roberts, Ryder, Rogers & Scism, a labor and employment law firm; Church, Nilsson & Paulen of Elkhart; Roemer & Mintz, LLP, of South Bend and, most recently, Lee, Mann, Smith, McWilliams, Sweeney & Ohlson of Chicago. The firm has also been joined by Gallucci, Hopkins & Theisen, P.C., a Fort Wayne firm with an extensive labor and employment practice, and Johnson Lawhead Buth & Pope, P.C., an Indianapolis firm with a concentration in estate planning. Today Barnes & Thornburg LLP is the largest law firm in Indiana and one of the largest in the Midwest. More than 390 attorneys provide legal services to more than 11,000 international, national, regional and local clients.

With offices in Indianapolis, Fort Wayne, South Bend, Elkhart, Chicago, Washington, D.C., and Grand Rapids, we are a business-minded law firm serving clients ranging from Fortune 100 companies and governmental entities to individuals and nonprofit organizations. We represent the interests of businesses in our primary practices: business, tax and real estate, creditors' rights, energy, telecommunications and utilities, environmental law, governmental services and finance, healthcare, intellectual property, labor and employment law, litigation, appellate, business and technology, construction law, e-commerce, economic development, entrepreneurial services, financial institutions, international, media, pension and benefits litigation, property tax, transportation and white collar crime. Each of our offices offers a unique blend of services which collectively make Barnes & Thornburg LLP a diverse and dynamic legal resource for our clients and communities.

We have lawyers involved at city, state and national levels of the legal profession as officers, chairpersons and committee members in legal organizations. Others are authors, presenters and drafters of legislation. Most of our lawyers are active in their communities and provide civic leadership. Each office sponsors, contributes to, and often leads, an array of community activities.

LAW FIRM ALLIANCES/ASSOCIATIONS: ***TECHLAW GROUP***

TERRALEX, THE WORLDWIDE NETWORK OF INDEPENDENT LAW FIRMS

PARTNERS

GEOFFREY K. CHURCH, admitted to bar, 1971, Indiana. *Education:* Dartmouth College (B.A., 1968); Indiana University School of Law (J.D., 1971). ***PRACTICE AREAS:*** Creditors Rights; Bankruptcy; Commercial Law; Commercial Workouts; Business Law; Buying and Selling of Businesses. ***Email:*** geoffrey.church@btlaw.com

SAMUEL S. THOMPSON, admitted to bar, 1974, Indiana. *Education:* Purdue University (B.S., 1971); Indiana University (J.D., magna cum laude, 1974). ***PRACTICE AREAS:*** Corporate Law; Federal Taxation. ***Email:*** samuel.thompson@btlaw.com

RAND W. NILSSON, admitted to bar, 1974, Indiana. *Education:* Wabash College (B.A., magna cum laude, 1967); Duke University (J.D., with honors, 1974). Phi Beta Kappa. Woodrow Wilson Fellow, Johns Hopkins University, 1967-1968. [U.S. Army, 1968-1971]. ***PRACTICE AREAS:*** Real Estate; Health Care; Business Law. ***Email:*** rand.nilsson@btlaw.com

RICHARD W. PAULEN, admitted to bar, 1974, Indiana. *Education:* University of Evansville (B.A., 1968); University of Louisville (M.S., 1971); Valparaiso University (J.D., 1974). President, Elkhart County Estate Planning Council, 1979-1980. ***PRACTICE AREAS:*** Environmental Law; Environmental Compliance; Environmental Permitting; Superfund; Wetlands Regulation; Real Estate. ***Email:*** richard.paulen@btlaw.com

J. SCOTT TROEGER, admitted to bar, 1981, Illinois; 1985, Indiana. *Education:* DePauw University (A.B., 1978); Indiana University (J.D., cum laude, 1981). ***PRACTICE AREAS:*** Business Law; Corporate Law; Securities; Mergers, Acquisitions and Divestitures; Real Estate. ***Email:*** scott.troeger@btlaw.com

BRIAN J. CLARK, admitted to bar, 1984, Indiana. *Education:* Indiana University (B.S., 1981); Valparaiso University (J.D., 1984). *Member:* Elkhart City and Indiana State (Tax and Probate-Real Property Sections) Bar Associations. ***PRACTICE AREAS:*** Federal Taxation; Estate Planning; Business Law; Corporate Law; Employee Benefits. ***Email:*** brian.clark@btlaw.com

ERIC H. J. STAHLHUT, admitted to bar, 1992, Indiana and U.S. District Court, Northern and Southern Districts of Indiana. *Education:* Bowdoin College (B.A., magna cum laude, James Bowdoin Scholar, 1987); St. Louis University (J.D., cum laude, 1991); Georgetown University Law Center (L.L.M., in labor, with distinction, 1992). Member, St. Louis Law Journal, 1990-1991. Recipient, American Jurisprudence Awards. ***PRACTICE AREAS:*** Labor and Employment; Employment Discrimination; Labor Relations. ***Email:*** eric.stahlhut@btlaw.com

OF COUNSEL

ROBERT G. DEVETSKI, admitted to bar, 1988, Indiana and Illinois; 1993, U.S. Court of Appeals, Seventh Circuit. *Education:* University of Notre Dame; Indiana University (B.A., Biology, 1983; J.D., 1987). *Member:* Elkhart City, Laporte County, St. Joseph County, Indiana State (Board of Governors 2002-2004, Litigation Section Vice-President 2005-2006 and Business Law Section) Bar Associations; Robert A. Grant American Inn of Court (President 2003-2005); Defense Research Institute, Inc.; Defense Trial Counsel of Indiana; Indiana Bar Foundation. ***PRACTICE AREAS:*** Business Litigation; Insurance Coverage; Bad Faith; Employment Law; Products Liability; Mediation. ***Email:*** robert.devetski@btlaw.com

TIMOTHY A. WEAVER, admitted to bar, 1990, Illinois; 1991, U.S. Court of Appeals, Seveth Circuit; 1993, New York; 1996, Indiana. *Education:* DePauw University (B.A., magna cum laude, 1987); Northwestern University School of Law (J.D., cum laude, 1990). Law Clerk to Judge Kenneth F. Ripple, U.S. Court of Appeals for the 7th Circuit, 1990-1991. *Member:* Indiana State Bar Association. ***PRACTICE AREAS:*** Corporate; Estates and Trusts; Elder Law. ***Email:*** timothy.weaver@btlaw.com

ASSOCIATES

CHRISTOPHER RILEY, admitted to bar, 2001, Indiana. *Education:* University of Redlands (B.A., magna cum laude, 1996); California State University San Bernardino (M.A., 1998); University of Notre Dame (J.D., cum laude, 2001). *Member:* Indiana State Bar Association. ***PRACTICE AREAS:*** Bankruptcy; Commercial Litigation; Construction Law; Labor Litigation; Privacy Litigation; Products Liability; Personal Injury; Secured Lending; Warranty Litigation; Zoning; Election Law. ***Email:*** christopher.riley@btlaw.com

ANDREW M. HICKS, admitted to bar, 2002, Indiana; U.S. District Court, Northern and Southern Districts of Indiana. *Education:* Saint Joseph's College (B.S., Math-Physics, magna cum laude, 1998); Notre Dame Law School (J.D., 2002). *Member:* Elkhart City Bar Association; Indiana State Bar Association. ***PRACTICE AREAS:*** Business Law; Agricultural Law; Litigation; Commercial Law; Corporate Law. ***Email:*** andrew.hicks@btlaw.com

ANDREW G. HELFRICH, born Fort Wayne, Indiana; admitted to bar, 2004, Indiana and U.S. District Court, Northern and Southern Districts of Indiana. *Education:* Manchester College (B.A., cum laude, 2001); Valparaiso University School of Law (J.D., cum laude, 2004). Jurist Scholarship; Associate Editor, Valparaiso University Law Review, 2003-2004. *Member:* Elkhart and Indiana State Bar Associations. ***PRACTICE AREAS:*** Business Law; Corporate Law; Estate Planning; Real Estate; Taxation. ***Email:*** andrew.helfrich@btlaw.com

REPRESENTATIVE CLIENTS: Airco Industrial Gases; American Electric Power; American Electronic Components, Inc.; Ameritech; Amoco Oil Company; Atwood Mobile Products Corp.; Bank One; Barger Packaging, Inc.; Beck Industries; Champion Enterprises, Inc.; Damon Corporation; Dometic Sales Corp.; Elkhart Community Schools; Elkhart Container, Inc.; Elkhart General Hospital Inc.; Elixir Industries, Inc.; Fisher-Calo RDRA Superfund Group; F.M. Properties Corporation; Geocel Corp.; Godfrey Marine Corporation; Goshen General Hospital, Inc.; Heywood Williams Group, PLC; Himco Waste-Away Service, Inc.; Izuzu Motors America; KeyBank National Association; Kinro, Inc.; Klink Trucking, Inc. Lakehead Pipeline Company, Inc.; LaSalle Bristol Corporation; Mast Construction, LLC; Monaco Coach Corporation; New Venture Gear, Inc.; NIBCO, Inc.; Nishikawa Standard Company; Partners National Health Plans of Indiana, Inc.; Pathfinder Communications Corporation; REA Magnet Wire Company, Inc.; Rieth-Riley Construction Co., Inc.; Skyline Corporation; Starcraft Corporation; Steel Suppliers, Inc.; Tecumseh Products Co.; Toyota Motor Sales; Truth Publishing Company, Inc.; United Musical Instruments USA, Inc.; Utilimaster Corporation; Vector Pipeline; Wagner Land Development Co., Inc.; Warrick Industries; Wells Cargo, Inc.; Whirlpool Corporation.

BECKMAN, KELLY & SMITH

ELKHART, INDIANA

(See Hammond)

General Practice, Commercial, Corporation, Transportation and Trucking, Products and Professional Liability Defense, Elder Law, Estate and Trust Planning and Administration, Franchising, Real Estate, Employment, Taxation and Environmental Law, Trials and Appeals in all Courts, Medical Malpractice Defense and Workers Compensation Defense.

CHESTER LAW OFFICE

Established in 1980

230 N. MAIN, SUITE 2

P.O. BOX 1768

ELKHART, INDIANA 46515

Telephone: 574-296-1515

Fax: 574-295-9316

Email: ed@chesterlawoffice.com

Personal Injury, Civil Trials and Appeals in State and Federal Courts, including Employment and Commercial Litigation, Wrongful Death.

EDWARD J. CHESTER, born Elkhart, Indiana, January 29, 1953; admitted to bar, 1980, Indiana. *Education:* Indiana University (B.A., 1975; J.D., cum laude, 1980). Deputy Prosecuting Attorney, 1980-1983 and Public Defender, 1983-1984, Elkhart County. *Member:* Elkhart City, Indiana State and American Bar Associations; Indiana Trial Lawyers Association (Director, 2005); The Association of Trial Lawyers of America. ***REPORTED CASES:*** H.B. v. State, 713 N.E.2d 300 (Ind.Ct.App. 1999); Landis v. Landis, 664 N.E.2d 754 (Ind. Ct.App. 1996); Captain & Co., Inc., v. Stenberg, 505 N.E.2d 88 (Ind. Ct.App. 1987); Santini v. Consolidated Rail Corp., 505 N.E.2d 832 (Ind. Ct.App. 1987). ***PRACTICE AREAS:*** Civil Trials; Appellate Practice; Personal Injury; Wrongful Death; Employment Discrimination. ***Email:*** ed@chesterlawoffice.com

ASSOCIATE

LAURA L. EZZELL, born Louisville, Kentucky, August 21, 1964; admitted to bar, 2003, Indiana and U.S. District Courts, Northern and Southern Districts of Indiana. *Education:* Purdue University (B.A., 1986); Valparaiso University (J.D., 2002). *Member:* Elkhart City, Indiana State and American Bar Associations; Indiana Trial Lawyers Association; The Association of Trial Lawyers of America. ***PRACTICE AREAS:*** Personal In-

(This Listing Continued)

CHESTER LAW OFFICE, Elkhart—Continued

jury; Civil Litigation; Estate Administration; Business Associations Law. ***Email:*** laura@chesterlawoffice.com

DORAN • BLACKMOND LLP

ELKHART, INDIANA

(See South Bend)

Civil Trial and Appellate Practice in Federal and State Courts, Insurance Defense and Coverage Questions, Special Investigation, Personal Injury, Product Liability, Architect and Engineer Liability, Legal Malpractice, Worker's Compensation, Construction Law, Commercial, Creditor's Rights, Bankruptcy and Reorganization, Mediation and Arbitration.

BERNARD KATZ

Established in 1964

421 SOUTH SECOND STREET, SUITE 300
ELKHART, INDIANA 46516
Telephone: 574-293-3597
Fax: 574-294-7224

General Civil Trial Practice in all Courts. Corporate, Business, Real Estate, Children, Family, Domestic Relations, Adoptions, Divorce, Child Custody, Child Support, Parenting Time Rights, Paternity, Personal Injury, Automobile Accidents, Slip and Fall, Wrongful Death, Trusts, Wills, Probate and Estate Planning Law.

BERNARD KATZ, born St. Louis, Missouri, January 18, 1935; admitted to bar, 1964, Illinois, Indiana and U.S. District Court, Northern District of Indiana; 2002, U.S. Supreme Court. *Education:* Bradley University (B.S., cum laude, 1957); University of Notre Dame (J.D., 1964). Omicron Delta Kappa; Pi Kappa Delta; Zeta Pi. Member, Federation of Bradley Scholars. Listed in Who's Who Among Students in American Universities and Colleges. *Member:* Elkhart(President, 1984), Elkhart County, Indiana State (Member, Sections on: Corporate Counsel; Family and Juvenile Law; Probate, Trust and Real Property) and American (Member, Sections on: Corporation, Banking and Business Law; Family Law) Bar Associations.

Representative Clients and Bank References furnished upon request.

KONOPA, REAGAN & AIGOTTI, P.C.

ELKHART, INDIANA

(See South Bend)

General Civil Practice. Personal Injury, Automobile Accidents, Products Liability, Brain Injury, Truck Accidents, Nursing Home Negligence, Wrongful Death, Insurance (Personal and Commercial Lines), and Commercial Law. Business Law, Contracts, Litigation, Trial and Appellate Practice in all State and Federal Courts. Mediations and Arbitrations.

JAY LAUER

ELKHART, INDIANA

(See South Bend)

General Civil Practice in All State and Federal Courts. Criminal Law, Driving While Intoxicated, Drug Crimes, Juvenile Law, Parole and Probation, Traffic Violations, White Collar Crime, Labor, Employment Discrimination, Sexual Harassment, Wrongful Termination, Medical Malpractice, Personal Injury, Automobile Accidents and Injuries, Slip and Fall, Wrongful Death, Product Liability, Social Security Disability, Workers Compensation, Bankruptcies, Investment Fraud, Municipal Law, Real Estate, Wills, Probate, Trusts and Estates, Estate Planning, Asset Protection, Guardianships, Domestic Relations, Family Law, Adoptions, Child Custody, Child Support, Divorce, Domestic Violence, Visitation Rights.

MAY OBERFELL LORBER

ELKHART, INDIANA

(See Mishawaka)

Corporate and Commercial Transactions, Litigation, Environmental Law, Real Estate, Labor and Employment, Banking and Bank Related Matters, Estate Planning, Municipal and Administration Law, Products Liability, Alternative Dispute Resolution, Health Care, Medical Malpractice Defense, Insurance Litigation, Trademark and Copyright, Tax, Plaintiff's Litigation, General Civil and Appellate Practice in State and Federal Courts.

McCASLIN & McCASLIN

Established in 1963

228 WEST HIGH STREET
ELKHART, INDIANA 46516
Telephone: 574-293-6033
Fax: 574-293-7012
URL: http://www.mccaslin-law.com
Email: jlmnam@aol.com
URL: http://www.mccaslinlaw.com

Civil Trial Litigation and Appellate Practice in all State Courts. Wills and Probate, Trusts and Estates, Estate Planning, Elder Law, Corporate, Real Estate, Commercial, Family Law, Adoptions, Divorce.

(This Listing Continued)

FIRM PROFILE: The law firm of McCaslin & McCaslin consists of husband and wife team James L. McCaslin and Nancy A. McCaslin. The firm concentrates their legal expertise in Elkhart County.

JAMES L. McCASLIN, born Anderson, Indiana, June 9, 1937; admitted to bar, 1963, Indiana and U.S. District Court, Northern, Southern Districts of Indiana. *Education:* Indiana University (B.A., 1959; LL.B., 1963). Phi Delta Phi. Assistant City Attorney, 1976-1979, City Attorney, 1980, Elkhart, Indiana. *Member:* Elkhart City (Former President; Vice President; Secretary), Indiana State (Member, Sections on: Probate; Corporations; Family Law; Member, House of Delegates, 1972-1981) and American Bar Associations. ***PRACTICE AREAS:*** Real Estate; Trusts and Estates; Probate; Estate Planning; Corporate; Business Law; Elder Law. ***Email:*** jlmnam@aol.com

NANCY A. McCASLIN, born Elwood, Indiana, November 26, 1941; admitted to bar, 1981, Indiana and U.S. District Court, Northern and Southern Districts of Indiana. *Education:* Indiana University (B.S., 1963); Ball State University (M.A., 1970); Valparaiso University (J.D., 1981). Deputy Prosecuting Attorney, Elkhart, Indiana. 1981-1982. Author: "Collecting Assets," *Indiana Estate Planning and Probate Practice,* (Matthew Bender); "Unrelated Third-Party Visitation," Res Gestae. *Member:* Indiana State Bar Association (Member: Education Citizenship Advisory Committee; Written Publication Committee; Appellate Practice Section). ***PRACTICE AREAS:*** Commercial Law; Civil Appeals; Criminal Appeals. ***Email:*** jlmnam@aol.com

REFERENCE: BankOne.
ATTORNEYS FOR: Elkhart County Board of Realtors; Elkhart County Multiple Listing Service.

PFAFF, BROTHERSON & KILLOREN, LLP

ELKHART, INDIANA

(See Baker & Daniels LLP)

LAW OFFICES ROWE & ROWE

ELKHART, INDIANA

(See South Bend)

Insurance Defense. Trials and Appeals in State and Federal Courts. Personal Injury, Automobile Accidents, Truck Accidents, Slip and Fall, Traumatic Brain Injury, Wrongful Death, Unsafe Products, Medical Malpractice, Legal Malpractice.

SANDERS • PIANOWSKI, LLP

Established in 1966

300 RIVERWALK DRIVE
ELKHART, INDIANA 46516
Telephone: 574-294-1499
Fax: 574-294-7277
Email: lawyers@riverwalklaw.com
URL: http://www.riverwalklaw.com

General Practice, Corporate, Business Law, Civil Litigation, Insurance, Bank Collection and Foreclosure, Commercial Litigation, Labor and Employment, Mergers and Acquisitions, Real Estate, Estate Planning, Trusts and Estates, Probate, Wills and Estate Administration, Environmental, Family Law, Adoption, Child Custody, Child Support, Divorce, Visitation Rights.

MEMBERS OF FIRM

PHILIP E. BYRON, JR. (1911-1977)

ROBERT C. DANIELS (1928-1995)

ROBERT T. SANDERS, III, born Ft. Wayne, Indiana, 1949; admitted to bar, 1973, Indiana. *Education:* Indiana University (B.S., 1970); Indiana University School of Law (J.D., cum laude, 1973). Beta Gamma Sigma. *Member:* Elkhart City, Indiana State and American Bar Associations. ***PRACTICE AREAS:*** Appellate Practice; Civil Litigation; Insurance Defense; Insurance Coverage; Labor and Employment. ***Email:*** rsanders@riverwalklaw.com

MICHAEL A. PIANOWSKI, born South Bend, Indiana, 1947; admitted to bar, 1979, Indiana. *Education:* Ball State University (B.S., 1969; M.B.A., 1970); Valparaiso University (J.D., 1978). *Member:* Elkhart City and Indiana State Bar Associations. ***PRACTICE AREAS:*** Corporate; Estate Planning; Mergers and Acquisitions. ***Email:*** mpianowski@riverwalklaw.com

JAMES L. TODD, born Dayton, Ohio, 1947; admitted to bar, 1979, Ohio; 1986, Indiana. *Education:* United States Naval Academy (B.S., 1969); Valparaiso University (J.D., 1978). Associate Editor, Valparaiso University Law Review, 1977-1978. *Member:* Elkhart City, Ohio State and Indiana State Bar Associations. [Capt., U.S. Marine Corps, 1969-1976]. ***PRACTICE AREAS:*** Corporate; Estate Administration; Estate Planning; Real Estate; Mergers and Acquisitions. ***Email:*** jtodd@riverwalklaw.com

MATTHEW A. YEAKEY, born Elkhart, Indiana, 1964; admitted to bar, 1990, Indiana. *Education:* University of Notre Dame (B.A., cum laude, 1987); Indiana University School of Law (J.D., 1990). *Member:* Elkhart City, Indiana State and American Bar Associations. ***PRACTICE AREAS:*** Civil Litigation; Insurance Defense; Debt Collection; Estate Administration; Personal Injury; Family Law. ***Email:*** myeakey@riverwalklaw.com

P. SHAWN LEWIS, born South Hill, Virginia, 1967; admitted to bar, 1992, Indiana; 1993, Michigan. *Education:* Purdue University (B.S., 1989); Capital University Law School (J.D., Order of the Curia, 1992). Delta Theta Phi. *Member:* Elkhart City, Indiana State and Michigan State Bar Associations. ***PRACTICE AREAS:*** Corporate; Real Estate; Probate and Estate Administration; Mergers and Acquisitions; Labor and Employment. ***Email:*** slewis@riverwalklaw.com

(This Listing Continued)

DANIEL G. AREAUX, born Coldwater, Michigan, 1955; admitted to bar, 1981, Indiana and U.S. District Court, Southern and Northern Districts of Indiana. *Education:* Indiana University (B.S., with high honors, 1978; J.D., magna cum laude, 1981). Phi Alpha Delta. Beta Gamma Sigma. Member: Elkhart Estate Planning Council; Elkhart Historical Preservation Council. *Member:* Elkhart and Indiana State Bar Associations. ***PRACTICE AREAS:*** Estate Planning; Estate Administration; Business Succession Planning; Domestic Relations. ***Email:*** dareaux@riverwalklaw.com

ASSOCIATES

JASON G. WARD, born Lafayette, Indiana; admitted to bar, 1997, Indiana; 1998, Michigan. *Education:* Indiana University (B.A., 1993; J.D., 1997). *Member:* Elkhart City and Indiana State Bar Associations State Bar of Michigan. ***PRACTICE AREAS:*** Corporate; Estate Administration; Creditors Rights; Estate Planning. ***Email:*** jward@riverwalklaw.com

PENNY J. MEYERS, born Sturgis, Michigan, 1969; admitted to bar, 2000, Indiana and U.S. District Court, Northern and Southern Districts of Indiana; 2002, Michigan. *Education:* Hillsdale College (B.A., 1991); Valparaiso University School of Law (J.D., magna cum laude, 2000). Symposium Editor, Valparaiso University Law Review, 1999-2000. *Member:* Elkhart City, Indiana State and American Bar Associations. ***PRACTICE AREAS:*** Corporate; Real Estate; Estate Planning; Probate Administration; Estate Administration; General Litigation. ***Email:*** pmeyers@riverwalklaw.com

COURTNEY G. WILLIAMS, born Birmingham, Alabama, 1972; admitted to bar, 2001, Indiana; 2002, Illinois. *Education:* Davidson College (B.A., 1994); Valparaiso University (J.D., with honors, 2001). ***PRACTICE AREAS:*** Litigation; Corporate Law; Commercial Litigation; Insurance Defense; Domestic Relations. ***Email:*** cwilliams@riverwalklaw.com

REPRESENTATIVE CLIENTS: Franger Gas Co., Inc.; Tom Naquin Chevrolet, Inc.; WKJG-TV; WSJV-TV; M & M Fabricators Corp.; Cincinnati Insurance Cos.; Ascot Enterprises, Inc.; Voyager Products; KeyBank National Association; Brookwood Golf Course; Midwest Plastic Engineering, Inc.; Carriage, Inc.; United Expressline, Inc.; Monroe Guaranty Insurance Co.; Bank One, N.A.; Elk Enterprises, Inc.; Vitco, Inc.; Yoder Oil Company, Inc.; Foreclosure Management Co.; ARC, LP; Wise-TV; Bennington Marine, LLP; Royal Cargo Trailers, Inc.; Cardinal Buses, Inc.; North American Forest Products, Inc.; Duncan Systems, Inc.; Rotational Solutions Corp.; TruPay Corporation; L.E. Technologies, LLC; Vitco, LLC; Vintage Trailers, Ltd.
REFERENCES: KeyBank National Association; Bank One; 1st Source Bank.

STUTSMAN, MULVANEY & DeBOER

Established in 1977
1300 CASSOPOLIS STREET
P.O. BOX 1337
ELKHART, INDIANA 46515-1337
Telephone: 574-266-8500
1-800-867-5907
Fax: 574-206-9215
URL: http://www.smdlawfirm.com

General Civil and Appellate Practice in all State and Federal Courts. Personal Injury, Automobile Accidents, Slip and Fall, Wrongful Death, Workers Compensation, Medical Malpractice, Corporate, Wills and Probate, Trusts and Estates, Asset Protection, Guardianships, Estate Planning, Real Estate, Internet Law.

FIRM PROFILE: The law firm of Stutsman, Mulvaney & DeBoer has been representing injured people in the Elkhart area for more than fifteen years. Partners David T. Stutsman, Douglas A. Mulvaney, David L. DeBoer handle Personal Injury, Worker's Compensation, Products Liability, and Medical Malpractice. They are members of the Elkhart City Bar Association, Indiana State Bar Association, American Bar Association, The Indiana Trial Lawyers Association and The Association of Trial Lawyers of America.

DAVID T. STUTSMAN, born Bristol, Indiana, 1940; admitted to bar, 1971, Indiana and U.S. District Court, Southern District of Indiana; 1972, U.S. Court of Appeals, Seventh Circuit; 1977, U.S. District Court, Northern District of Indiana. *Education:* Ball State University; Western Michigan University (B.A., 1967); Indiana University (J.D., 1970). Recipient, American Jurisprudence Award. Law Clerk for the Honorable S. Hugh Dillin, U.S. District Court, Southern District of Indiana, 1970-1973. Public Defender, Elkhart Superior Court II, Elkhart County, Indiana, 1977-1979. Elkhart City Attorney, 1980-1981. Assistant City Attorney, 1981-1983. *Member:* Elkhart City, Elkhart County, Indiana State and American Bar Associations; The Association of Trial Lawyers of America; Indiana Trial Lawyers Association (Director, 1994—). ***PRACTICE AREAS:*** Personal Injury; Workers Compensation; Civil Litigation; Probate and Estate Planning; Corporate. ***Email:*** stutsmanmulvaney.deboer@verizon.net

DOUGLAS A. MULVANEY, born Cobleskill, New York, 1957; admitted to bar, 1983, Indiana and U.S. District Court, Northern and Southern Districts of Indiana. *Education:* Hope College (B.A., 1980); Vermont Law School (J.D., 1983). Phi Delta Phi (Clerk, 1982-1983). Recipient, American Jurisprudence Award. *Member:* Elkhart City, Elkhart County, Indiana State and American Bar Associations; The Association of Trial Lawyers of America; Indiana Trial Lawyers Association. ***PRACTICE AREAS:*** Personal Injury; Workers Compensation. ***Email:*** stutsmanmulvaney.deboer@verizon.net

DAVID L. DeBOER, born Grand Rapids, Michigan, 1950; admitted to bar, 1975, Indiana. *Education:* Calvin College (B.A., 1972); Valparaiso University (J.D., cum laude, 1975). Phi Alpha Delta. Associate Editor, Valparaiso University Law Review, 1974-1975. Valparaiso City Attorney, 1991-1999. *Member:* Porter County (President, 1989-1990), Indiana State and American Bar Associations; Indiana Trial Lawyers Association; The Association of Trial Lawyers of America. ***PRACTICE AREAS:*** Personal Injury Law; Civil Litigation; Medical Malpractice Law; Product Liability. ***Email:*** stutsmanmulvaney.deboer@verizon.net

REFERENCE: Bankone, Elkhart, Ind.

THORNE • GRODNIK, LLP

Established in 1963
228 WEST HIGH STREET
ELKHART, INDIANA 46516-3176
Telephone: 574-294-7473
FAX: 574-294-5390
Email: firm@tglaw.us
URL: http://www.tglaw.us

Mishawaka, Indiana Office: 420 Lincoln Way West, P.O. Box 1210, 46544. Telephone: 574-256-5660. FAX: 574-674-6835.

Commercial and Civil Litigation, Creditors Rights, Bankruptcy, Banking and Bank Related Matters, Corporate and Commercial Transactions, Insurance Defense, Personal Injury, Automobile Accidents, Slip and Fall, Wrongful Death, Real Estate and Zoning, Wills and Probate, Trusts and Estates, Estate Planning, School Law and Family Law, Adoptions, Divorce, Child Custody, Child Support, Visitation Rights, Mediation.

FIRM PROFILE: The firm of Thorne • Grodnik, LLP traces its roots to 1963. The core of the firm's practice remains Litigation, Business Matters and Civil Mediation.

MEMBERS OF FIRM

WILLIAM A. THORNE (Retired)

CHARLES H. GRODNIK, born Minneapolis, Minnesota, September 7, 1944; admitted to bar, 1970, Indiana. *Education:* University of Minnesota (B.A., 1966; J.D., 1969). Member, Elkhart County Election Board, 1984-1986. Judge, Elkhart City Court, 1992—. Certified in Mediation. *Member:* Elkhart City (Secretary, 1977; Treasurer 1987-1991; President, 1994), Elkhart County and Indiana State (Member, Family Law Section) Bar Associations; The Association of Trial Lawyers of America. ***PRACTICE AREAS:*** Personal Injury; Zoning and Land Use; Family/Domestic Relations; Mediation Law; Real Estate. ***Email:*** chgrodnik@tglaw.us

J. RICHARD RANSEL, born South Bend, Indiana, September 11, 1947; admitted to bar, 1974, Indiana. *Education:* Miami University, Oxford, Ohio (B.A., 1969); University of Notre Dame (J.D., 1974). Adjunct Professor, Creditors Rights and Bankruptcy, University of Notre Dame Law School, 1979-1981. U.S. Bankruptcy Trustee, Northern District of Indiana, 1979—. *Member:* Elkhart City, Elkhart County and Indiana State (Member, Creditors Rights Section) Bar Associations; American Bankruptcy Institute; National Association of Bankruptcy Trustees. ***PRACTICE AREAS:*** Business Bankruptcy; Secured Transactions; Banking. ***Email:*** jransel@tglaw.us

GLENN L. DUNCAN, born Louisville, Kentucky, February 2, 1949; admitted to bar, 1975, Indiana. *Education:* Indiana University (B.A., 1971; J.D., cum laude, 1975). Attorney for Osolo Township, 1985—. Member, Elkhart County-City Planning Advisory Committee, 1987. Bristol Town Attorney, 1986—. Member, Elkhart School Board of Trustees, 1990—. *Member:* Elkhart City, Elkhart County, Indiana State (Member, Creditors Rights Section) and American Bar Associations. ***PRACTICE AREAS:*** Warranty Law; Products Liability; Labor and Employment; Corporate Litigation; Commercial Litigation; Bankruptcy; Probate; Estate Planning; Probate Administration; Probate Litigation; Probate Taxation; Ancillary Probate. ***Email:*** glduncan@tglaw.us

STEVEN L. HOSTETLER, born Kokomo, Indiana, July 12, 1958; admitted to bar, 1983, Indiana. *Education:* Olivet Nazarene University (B.S., magna cum laude, 1980); Indiana University (J.D., cum laude, 1983). Author: "Farm Reorganizations Under Chapter 12 of the Bankruptcy Code," Res Gestae, Indiana State Bar Association Journal, November, 1987; "Doing Business with Bankrupt Companies," Indiana Business Magazine, April, 1992. *Member:* St. Joseph County and Indiana State Bar Associations. (Resident, Mishawaka Office). ***PRACTICE AREAS:*** Bankruptcy; Creditors Rights; Commercial Litigation; Real Estate; Corporations. ***Email:*** slhostetler@tglaw.us

MICHAEL A. TRIPPEL, born Mishawaka, Indiana, June 17, 1963; admitted to bar, 1992, Indiana. *Education:* Indiana University (B.S., 1985); Valparaiso University (J.D., cum laude, 1992). Mishawaka Common Council Attorney, 2004—. *Member:* St. Joseph County and Indiana State Bar Associations; Robert A. Grant Inn of Court. (Resident, Mishawaka Office). ***PRACTICE AREAS:*** Civil Litigation; Corporate; Real Estate; Banking Law; Probate Administration. ***Email:*** mtrippel@tglaw.us

ASSOCIATES

JACOB S. FROST, born South Bend, Indiana, September 21, 1970; admitted to bar, 1996, Indiana and U.S. District Court, Northern and Southern Districts of Indiana; 1998, Michigan and U.S. District Court, Eastern and Western Districts of Michigan. *Education:* Notre Dame University (B.A., 1993); Indiana University School of Law, Indianapolis (J.D., cum laude, 1996). Order of Barristers, Moot Court. Member, Indiana Law Review. Law Clerk, Honorable Robert H. Staton, Indiana Court of Appeals, 1996-1998. *Member:* Elkhart County and Indiana State Bar Associations; State Bar of Michigan. ***REPORTED CASES:*** Lowry v. Lanning, 712 N.E. 2d 1000 (Ind. Ct. App. 1998); Troyer v. Cowels Products Company, 732 N.E.2d 246 (Ind.Ct.App. 2000); GKC Indiana Theatres, Inc. v. Elk Retail Investors, LLC, 764 N.E.2d 647 (Ind.Ct.App. 2002); F.B.I. Farms, Inc. v. Moore, 769 N.E.2d 688 (Ind.Ct.App. 2002); The Estate of Samuel J. Dellinger, Sr., 771 N.E.2d 1271 (Ind.Ct.App. 2002). ***PRACTICE AREAS:*** Civil Appeals; Civil Litigation. ***Email:*** jsfrost@tglaw.us

JAMIE C. WOODS, born Mishawaka, Indiana, March 4, 1974; admitted to bar, 1999, Indiana and U.S. District Court, Northern and Southern Districts of Indiana. *Education:* Manchester College (B.S., 1996); Indiana University (J.D., 1999). Attorney, Town of Osceola, Indiana. Member, Penn-Harris-Madison School Boad of Trustees. Author and Presenter: "Mastering the Trial Notebook in Indiana," Institute for Paralegal Education Seminar, June 2004; "Arbitration of Construction Disputes," St. Joseph Valley Association of Plumbing-Heating-Cooling Contractors, Inc., March, 2004; "Construction Payment Remedies," St. Joseph Valley Association of Plumbing-Heating-Cooling Contractors, Inc., October, 2002; "An Overview of Preferential Transfers and Debtor in Possession Accounts," The Michigan Credit Management Association, November, 2002. *Member:* St. Joseph

(This Listing Continued)

THORNE • GRODNIK, LLP, Elkhart—Continued

County and Indiana State Bar Associations. (Resident, Mishawaka Office). ***PRACTICE AREAS:*** Creditors Rights; Construction Law; Civil Litigation. ***Email:*** jwoods@tglaw.us

JORDAN P. WILLIAMS, born Valparaiso, Indiana, August 1, 1976; admitted to bar, 2001, Indiana. *Education:* DePauw University (B.A., 1998); Valparaiso University (J.D., 2001). *Member:* Elkhart City, Indiana State and American Bar Associations. ***PRACTICE AREAS:*** Civil Litigation; Bankruptcy; Insurance Defense. ***Email:*** jpwilliams@tglaw.us

OF COUNSEL

JOSEPH C. ZAKAS, born November 7, 1950; admitted to bar, 1980, Indiana and U.S. District Court, Northern District of Indiana. *Education:* University of Illinois (B.A., 1972); University of Notre Dame (M.B.A., 1980; J.D., 1980). Indiana State Senator, 1982—. *Member:* St. Joseph County and Indiana State Bar Associations.

COUNSEL FOR: National City Bank; Forest River, Inc.; MFB Financial; Lake City Bank; International Wood, Inc.; AAA Associates, Inc.; Office Interiors, Inc.; Schafer Gear Works, Inc; Builders Enterprise Corp.; Star Tire Corp.; Elpaco Coatings Corp.; Newmar Corp.; MOR/Ryde Inc.; United Tool & Stamping, Inc.; Godfrey Conveyer Co.; Inc.; Dynasty Boats, Inc.; Laidig Industrial Systems, Inc.; Maron Products, Inc.; Impressions, Inc.; Sunnybrook RV, Inc.; Duo Form Plastics, Inc.

TUESLEY & HALL, LLP

ELKHART, INDIANA

(See South Bend)

Corporate and Business Law, Business Litigation, Business Formation, Mergers, Buying and Selling a Business, Commercial Transactions, Taxation and Estate Planning, Probate, Commercial Litigation, Real Estate, Land Use, and Construction Law, Personal Injury and Defense Litigation, Automobile Accidents, Wrongful Death, Health Care Law, General Civil and Trial Practice in State and Federal Courts.

WARRICK & BOYN, L.L.P.

SUITE 400, 121 WEST FRANKLIN STREET
ELKHART, INDIANA 46516-3278
Telephone: 574-294-7491
Fax: 574-294-7284
Email: thefirm@warrickandboyn.com
URL: http://www.warrickandboyn.com

General Civil Practice in all Courts. Corporation, Litigation, Real Estate, Environmental, Securities, Labor and Employment, EEOC, Bond Counsel, Probate and Estate Planning, Bankruptcy, Municipal and Zoning Law, and Banking Law. Federal Taxation, Elder Law, School Law.

MEMBERS OF FIRM

THOMAS E. WARRICK, born South Bend, Indiana, May 29, 1932; admitted to bar, 1960, Illinois; 1970, Indiana. *Education:* Indiana University (B.A., 1954); University of Michigan (LL.B., 1960). Mentor in Estate Planning, 1965-1970 and Instructor in Federal Estate and Gift Tax, 1968-1970, John Marshall Law School. *Member:* Elkhart City, Elkhart County and Indiana State Bar Associations. ***PRACTICE AREAS:*** Estate Planning; Corporate Law; School Law; Probate Law. ***Email:*** twarrick@warickandboyn.com

GARY D. BOYN, born Princeton, Minnesota, August 9, 1945; admitted to bar, 1972, Indiana; 1974, Michigan. *Education:* Concordia College (B.A., 1967); Valparaiso University (J.D., 1972). Interim Trustee in Bankruptcy, 1978—. Special Counsel, 1980-1981 and Corporate Counsel, 1981-1983, City of Elkhart. *Member:* Elkhart City, Elkhart County, Indiana State and American Bar Associations; State Bar of Michigan. [With U.S. Army, 1968-1970]. ***PRACTICE AREAS:*** Bankruptcy Practice and Litigation; Corporate; Employment Law; Municipal Law; Commercial Law; Litigation; Mediation. ***Email:*** gboyn@warrickandboyn.com

JAMES V. WOODSMALL, born Kansas City, Missouri, July 23, 1950; admitted to bar, 1978, Indiana; 1979, Michigan. *Education:* San Diego Mesa College and Northwestern University (B.A., 1975); Northwestern University (J.D., 1978). *Member:* Elkhart City, Elkhart County and Indiana State Bar Associations; State Bar of Michigan. ***PRACTICE AREAS:*** Corporate; Environmental; Securities; Mergers and Acquisitions. ***Email:*** jwoodsmall@warrickandboyn.com

CYNTHIA SCHAEFER GILLARD, born Oak Park, Illinois, July 25, 1954; admitted to bar, 1982, Indiana; 1983, Michigan. *Education:* Kalamazoo College (B.A., 1976); Indiana University; University of Notre Dame (J.D., 1982). *Member:* Elkhart City, Elkhart County, St. Joseph County (Michigan), Indiana State and American Bar Associations; State Bar of Michigan (Member, Corporation, Business and Finance Law Section); Indiana State Board of Law Examiners (President, 2005—; Member: Foreign License Committee; Professional Corporation Committee). ***PRACTICE AREAS:*** Corporate Law; Merger/Acquisition Law; Securities; Commercial Litigation; Employment Law; Real Estate Law. ***Email:*** cgillard@warrickandboyn.com

RANDALL G. HESSER, born Nuremberg, Germany, September 17, 1958; admitted to bar, 1983, Indiana; 1984, Michigan. *Education:* Indiana University (B.A., 1980); Boston College (J.D., cum laude, 1983). *Member:* Elkhart City, Elkhart County, Indiana State and American Bar Associations; State Bar of Michigan. ***PRACTICE AREAS:*** Corporate Law; Employment Law; Commercial Litigation; Estate Planning. ***Email:*** rhesser@warrickandboyn.com

TIMOTHY S. SHELLY, born Indianapolis, Indiana, March 3, 1960; admitted to bar, 1985, Indiana; 1986, Michigan. *Education:* DePauw University (B.A., cum laude, 1982); College of William & Mary (J.D., 1985). Pi Sigma Alpha; Gold Key. *Member:* Elkhart City, Elkhart County, Indiana State and American Bar Associations; State Bar of Michigan; Defense Research Institute; Defense Trial Counsel of Indiana. ***PRACTICE AREAS:*** Commercial Litigation; School Law. ***Email:*** tshelly@warrickandboyn.com

(This Listing Continued)

WILLIAM D. HAUT, born Elkhart, Indiana, January 16, 1961; admitted to bar, 1986, Indiana; 1987, Michigan; U.S. District Court, Northern and Southern Districts of Indiana. *Education:* Purdue University (B.S., 1983); Washburn University of Topeka (J.D., 1986). *Member:* Elkhart City, Elkhart County and Indiana State Bar Associations; State Bar of Michigan. ***PRACTICE AREAS:*** Corporate Law; Employment Law; Employee Benefits Law. ***Email:*** whaut@warrickandboyn.com

ASSOCIATES

DEAN E. LEAZENBY, born Winamac, Indiana, February 19, 1972; admitted to bar, 1998, Indiana; 1999, Michigan. *Education:* Purdue University (B.A., 1994); Indiana School of Law (J.D., 1998). Phi Beta Kappa. *Member:* Elkhart City, Elkhart County and Indiana State Bar Associations; State Bar of Michigan. ***PRACTICE AREAS:*** Corporate Law; Litigation; Employment Law. ***Email:*** dleazenby@warrickandboyn.com

WILLIAM L. LAW, III, born Pittsburgh, Pennsylvania, May 6, 1978; admitted to bar, 2003, Indiana. *Education:* University of Central Florida (B.A., cum laude, 2000); University of Notre Dame (J.D., cum laude, 2003). Article Editor, Notre Dame Law Review. *Member:* Elkhart City and Indiana State Bar Associations. ***Email:*** wlaw@warrickandboyn.com

REPRESENTATIVE CLIENTS: Axis Products, Inc.; Bristol Fire Dept. Corp.; Buchanan Metal Forming, Inc.; Carlton Manufacturing, Inc.; C&B Custom Modular, Inc.; Centurion Vehicles, Inc.; City of Elkhart; Concord Community Schools; E.W. Marine, Inc.; Elkhart Brass Manufacturing Co., Inc.; Elkhart Plastics, Inc.; Flexible Concepts, Inc.; FM/CM, Inc.; Fairfield Community Schools; Flexsteel Industries, Inc.; Graphix Unlimited, Inc.; Indiana Building Systems, LLC; Johnson Corporation; Lakeside Anestesiologists, PC; Middlebury Community Schools; Noble Composites, Inc.; Odyssey Group, LLC; Pace American, Inc.; Patriot Homes, Inc.; Patrick Industries, Inc.; Pleasant Street Homes, Inc.; Prime Transport, Inc.; Quality Metal Products, Inc.; River Oaks OB/GYN Associates, PC; R&R Trailers, Inc.; River Park, Inc.; Russell Products, Inc.; West Side OB/GYN Associates, PC.

YODER, AINLAY, ULMER & BUCKINGHAM, LLP

ELKHART, INDIANA

(See Goshen)

General Litigation and Appellate Practice in State and Federal Courts. Corporation, Mergers and Acquisitions, Governmental, Employment, Environmental, Insurance, Probate and Estate Planning, Trust, Negligence, Taxation, Banking and Real Estate Law.

BINGHAM, FARRER & WILSON, A PROFESSIONAL CORPORATION

1601 SOUTH ANDERSON STREET
P.O. BOX 494
ELWOOD, INDIANA 46036
Telephone: 765-552-9878
Fax: 765-552-5496
URL: http://www.bfwlawyers.com

General Practice, Banking and Finance, Bankruptcy, Business Planning, Sales and Acquisitions, Consumer and Commercial Law, Consumer and Commercial Collections, Transactions and Litigation, Contracts, Corporate Law, Creditors Rights, Debtor-Creditor Law, Elder Law, Family Law, Domestic Relations, Adoption Law, Child Support, Custody, Dissolution/Divorce, Separation and Visitation, Government Relations, Zoning, Planning and Land Use, Municipal Law, Probate, Guardianship, Estate Planning, Wills and Trusts, Real Estate, Foreclosures, Mechanics Liens.

FIRM PROFILE: Bingham, Farrer & Wilson was formed in January 1982 from a predecessor firm established in Elwood, Indiana in 1976. Although a local firm, Bingham, Farrer & Wilson serves individuals and business clients throughout north central Indiana.

Over the years, Bingham, Farrer & Wilson, has maintained its small town roots while developing an expanding regional practice in debtor-creditor relations and bankruptcy matters throughout central Indiana.

We are a general practice firm that emphasizes a broad spectrum of professional services, utilizing a team concept to serve clients in all areas of the law.

MICHAEL E. FARRER, admitted to bar, 1975, Indiana; U.S. District Court, Southern and Northern Districts of Indiana and U.S. Court of Appeals, Seventh Circuit. *Education:* Indiana State University (B.S., 1967); Indiana University School of Law (J.D., 1975). *Member:* Madison County and Indiana State Bar Associations. ***PRACTICE AREAS:*** Bankruptcy; Commercial Law; Consumer Collections; Consumer Litigation; Commercial Collections; Commercial Transactions; Commercial Litigation; Creditors Rights; Real Estate. ***Email:*** mfarrer@bfwlawyers.com

JAMES W. WILSON, admitted to bar, 1976, Indiana; U.S. District Court, Southern and Northern Districts of Indiana and U.S. Court of Appeals, Seventh Circuit. *Education:* Ball State University (B.S., with honors, 1972); Creighton University (J.D., 1976). Deputy Prosecutor, Madison County, 1976-1982, 1998-2000. Judge, Elwood City Court, 1984-1996. City of Alexandria General Counsel, 2000—, Madison County General Counsel, 2005—, Madison County Council General Counsel, 1998—. *Member:* Madison County and Indiana State Bar Associations. ***PRACTICE AREAS:*** Business Planning; Mergers and Acquisitions; Elder Law; Estate Planning; Government Relations; Guardianship; Probate; Wills; Trust Law. ***Email:*** jwilson@bfwlawyers.com

REPRESENTATIVE CLIENTS: Alexandria Housing and Economic Development Corp.; Ball State Federal Credit Union; City of Alexandria, Indiana; Elwood Community Development Corp.; Executive Escrow Company; Finance Center Federal Credit Union; First County Federal Credit Union; First Farmers Bank & Trust Co.; Madison County; Madison County Council; Perfect Wireless, Inc.; Star Financial Bank; Title Guaranty Abstract Co.

ALLYN & GIVENS

EVANSVILLE, INDIANA

(See Mt. Vernon)

General Civil and Criminal Practice in all State and Federal Courts. Probate, Trusts, Real Estate and Natural Resources Law.

BAMBERGER, FOREMAN, OSWALD AND HAHN, LLP

Established in 1959

20 NW FOURTH STREET, SUITE 708
EVANSVILLE, INDIANA 47708
Telephone: 812-425-1591
Fax: 812-421-4936
URL: http://www.bamberger.com

Indianapolis, Indiana Office: Market Tower, Suite 2950, 10 West Market Street, 46204. Telephone: 317-464-1591. Fax: 317-464-1592. Toll Free: 888-994-7976.

Mt. Vernon, Indiana Office: 309 Main Street, 47620. Telephone: 812-838-4495. Fax: 812-838-9445.

Poseyville, Indiana Office: 178 South Lockwood, 47633. Telephone: 812-874-3365. Fax: 812-874-3366.

Princeton, Indiana Office: 302 N. Prince Street, 47670. Telephone: 812-386-6482. Fax: 812-386-6480.

Administrative Law, Antitrust Law, Appellate Practice, Arbitration, Banking Law, Bankruptcy Law, Business Law, Civil Rights, Civil Trial Practice, Commercial Law, Commercial Litigation, Communications Law, Construction Law, Corporate Law, Creditors' Rights, Elder Law, Energy Law, Environmental Law, Health Care Law, Insurance Defense, Intellectual Property Law, Labor and Employment Law, Land Use Law, Medical Malpractice, Mergers and Acquisitions, Product Liability Law, Public Utilities Law, Real Estate Law, Trademark, Copyright and Unfair Competition, Trusts and Estates, Wills and Probate.

MEMBERS OF FIRM

ROBERT H. HAHN (1925-2004)

ROBERT M. BECKER, born Evansville, Indiana, 1946; admitted to bar, 1971, Indiana. *Education:* Indiana University (A.B., 1968); University of Michigan (J.D., 1971). *Member:* Evansville Estate and Financial Planning Council (President, 1994-1995; Director, 1988-1995). Fellow: American College of Trust and Estate Counsel. ***PRACTICE AREAS:*** Estate Planning; Probate; Business Law. ***Email:*** bbecker@bamberger.com

FRED S. WHITE, born Mattoon, Illinois, September 15, 1940; admitted to bar, 1972, Indiana. *Education:* Purdue University (B.S., 1966); Indiana University School of Law (J.D., summa cum laude, 1972). Law Clerk, Indiana Supreme Court, 1971-1972. ***PRACTICE AREAS:*** Insurance Defense; Products Liability; Medical Malpractice Defense. ***Email:*** fwhite@bamberger.com

R. THOMAS BODKIN, born Anderson, Indiana, 1945; admitted to bar, 1973, Indiana. *Education:* Indiana University (B.S., 1967; J.D., cum laude, 1973). Law Clerk, U.S. District Court, Southern District of Indiana, 1973-1975. Adjunct Faculty, University of Southern Indiana, School of Nursing and Health Professions. Town Attorney, Town of Newburgh, Indiana, 1984—. *Member:* Defense Research Institute; Defense Trial Counsel of Indiana (Director, 1981-1984, 1999—; Secretary, 1983; Diplomat); Indiana Municipal Lawyers Association (Director, 1986-1988); American Health Lawyers Association; Association of Defense Trial Attorneys; International Right of Way Association. Fellow: American College of Trial Lawyers. ***PRACTICE AREAS:*** Health Care; Personal Injury; Medical Malpractice; Products Liability; Municipal Law; Zoning Law; Subdivisions. ***Email:*** tbodkin@bamberger.com

TERRY G. FARMER, born Tiffin, Ohio, 1957; admitted to bar, 1981, Ohio; 1982, Indiana; 2002, Illinois. *Education:* Indiana University (B.S., with highest distinction, 1978; J.D., cum laude, 1980). ***PRACTICE AREAS:*** Mergers and Acquisitions; Commercial Law; Banking Law; Bankruptcy; Creditors Rights. ***Email:*** tfarmer@bamberger.com

HENRY C. HUDSON, born Scottsburg, Indiana, 1941; admitted to bar, 1966, Indiana. *Education:* Indiana University (A.B., 1963; J.D., 1966). Certified Civil Mediator. Town Attorney, New Harmony, 1969-1971 and 1974. City Attorney, Mount Vernon, 1971-1988. County Attorney, 1986—. ***PRACTICE AREAS:*** Municipal Law; Real Estate; Probate and Estate Planning; Business Law. ***Email:*** hhudson@bamberger.com

JERRY D. STILWELL, born Oakland City, Indiana, 1944; admitted to bar, 1972, Indiana. *Education:* Oakland City College (A.B., 1966); Indiana University (J.D., 1972). City Attorney, Princeton, 1976-1979, 1984-1986. County Attorney, Gibson County, 1977; 2000, 2003 —. *Member:* Indiana Trial Lawyers Association; Association of Trial Lawyers of America. ***PRACTICE AREAS:*** Personal Injury; Municipal Law; Business Planning; Estate Planning; Family Law; Civil Litigation. ***Email:*** jstilwell@bamberger.com

THOMAS J. KIMPEL, born Cincinnati, Ohio, 1950; admitted to bar, 1976, Ohio; 1978, Indiana. *Education:* Butler University (B.A., 1972); John Marshall Law School (J.D., 1976). ***PRACTICE AREAS:*** Business Law; Health Care; Real Estate; Estate Planning. ***Email:*** tkimpel@bamberger.com

DONALD J. FUCHS, born Evansville, Indiana, 1954; admitted to bar, 1979, Indiana. *Education:* Wabash College (B.S., magna cum laude, 1976); Indiana University (J.D., 1979). Phi Beta Kappa. ***PRACTICE AREAS:*** Real Estate; Banking Law; Creditors Rights. ***Email:*** dfuchs@bamberger.com

MICHELE S. BRYANT, born Martinsville, Indiana, 1963; admitted to bar, 1989, Indiana. *Education:* DePauw University (B.A., 1986); Indiana University (J.D., 1988). *Member:* Defense Trial Counsel of Indiana; Defense Research Institute. ***PRACTICE AREAS:*** Litigation; Medical Malpractice Defense; Health Care. ***Email:*** mbryant@bamberger.com

MARC E. HAWLEY, born Fort Wayne, Indiana, 1951; admitted to bar, 1981, Indiana. *Education:* Purdue University (B.S.E.E., 1973; B.A., 1977); Indiana University (J.D., 1981). Contributing Author: "Mineral Law," Indiana ICLEF. ***PRACTICE AREAS:*** Real Estate; Mineral Law; Probate and Estate Planning. ***Email:*** mhawley@bamberger.com

JOHN P. BROADHEAD, born Evansville, Indiana, 1956; admitted to bar, 1981, Indiana. *Education:* University of Evansville (B.S., with honors, 1978); Indiana University (J.D., summa cum laude, 1981). Member: Evansville Estate and Financial Planning Council, Inc., 1988—; National Academy of Elder Law Attorneys, 2001—. ***PRACTICE AREAS:*** Probate; Elder Law; Real Estate; Agricultural Law; Business Law. ***Email:*** jbroadhead@bamberger.com

J. HERBERT DAVIS, born Hymera, Indiana, 1966; admitted to bar, 1991, Indiana. *Education:* Indiana University (B.A., 1988; J.D., cum laude, 1991). Phi Beta Kappa. ***PRACTICE AREAS:*** Public Utility Law; Real Estate; Business Law; Employment Law. ***Email:*** hdavis@bamberger.com

MARJORIE M. BLALOCK, born Evansville, Indiana, 1966; admitted to bar, 1991, Indiana; 1998, Illinois. *Education:* DePauw University (B.A., magna cum laude, 1988); Indiana University (J.D., 1991). Phi Beta Kappa. ***PRACTICE AREAS:*** Real Estate; Banking Law; Bankruptcy. ***Email:*** mmeeks@bamberger.com

CATHERINE A. NESTRICK, born Evansville, Indiana, 1967; admitted to bar, 1993, Indiana; 1994, Kentucky. *Education:* Hanover College (B.A., 1990); Indiana University (J.D., 1993). ***PRACTICE AREAS:*** Commercial Litigation; Lender Liability Defense; Creditors' Rights Law; Civil Litigation. ***Email:*** cnestrick@bamberger.com

M. BETH BURGER, born Jasper, Indiana, 1967; admitted to bar, 1993, Indiana. *Education:* University of Evansville (B.S., summa cum laude, 1990); Indiana University (J.D., cum laude, 1993). Phi Kappa Phi; Order of the Coif. ***PRACTICE AREAS:*** Estate Planning; Probate; Elder Law; Business Law. ***Email:*** bburger@bamberger.com

JASON P. LUEKING, born Bloomington, Indiana, 1968; admitted to bar, 1993, Indiana; 1994, Kentucky. *Education:* Rose-Hulman Institute of Technology (B.S.C.E., cum laude, 1990); Indiana University (J.D., 1993). Member: American Society of Civil Engineers; International Right of Way Association; Indiana Land Title Association. ***PRACTICE AREAS:*** Real Estate; Commercial Law; Banking Law. ***Email:*** jlueking@bamberger.com

DOUGLAS A. WELP, born Princeton, Indiana, 1969; admitted to bar, 1994, Indiana; 1999, Kentucky. *Education:* Wabash College (B.A., magna cum laude, 1991); Indiana University (J.D., cum laude, 1994). Town Attorney, Town of Darmstadt, 1997—. County Attorney, Warrick County, 2005—. *Member:* Defense Research Institute; Defense Trial Counsel of Indiana; Indiana Municipal Lawyers Association. ***PRACTICE AREAS:*** Commercial Litigation; Municipal Law; Corporate Law. ***Email:*** dwelp@bamberger.com

LORI YARBOR YOUNG, born Seymour, Indiana, 1970; admitted to bar, 1995, Indiana; 2003, Kentucky. *Education:* Purdue University (B.S., with honors, 1992); Indiana University (J.D., 1995). Phi Beta Kappa. ***PRACTICE AREAS:*** Mergers and Acquisitions; Commercial Transactions; Banking Law. ***Email:*** lyoung@bamberger.com

LAURA A. SCOTT, born Vincennes, Indiana, 1970; admitted to bar, 1995, Indiana; 2003, Kentucky. *Education:* Indiana University (B.S., with highest distinction, 1992; J.D., 1995). ***PRACTICE AREAS:*** Banking Law; Commercial Law; Commercial Litigation; Business Acquisitions. ***Email:*** lscott@bamberger.com

ANDREW C. OZETE, born Bloomington, Indiana, 1970; admitted to bar, 1996, Indiana; 1998, Illinois. *Education:* Indiana University (B.A., 1992; J.D., 1996). ***LANGUAGES:*** Spanish. ***PRACTICE AREAS:*** Commercial Law; Banking Law; Creditor's Rights. ***Email:*** aozete@bamberger.com

CHRISTOPHER C. WISCHER, born Evansville, Indiana, 1970; admitted to bar, 1996, Kentucky; 1997, Indiana. *Education:* Transylvania University (B.A., 1993); University of Kentucky (J.D., 1996). ***PRACTICE AREAS:*** Real Estate; Zoning and Land Use; Title Insurance; General Corporate Practice. ***Email:*** cwischer@bamberger.com

ASSOCIATES

MICHAEL G. SMITH, born Salt Lake City, Utah, 1968; admitted to bar, 2001, Indiana. *Education:* University of Utah (B.S., 1997); Indiana University School of Law (J.D., 2001). ***PRACTICE AREAS:*** Medical Malpractice Defense; Employment; Litigation. ***Email:*** msmith@bamberger.com

HEATHER H. LACY, born Evansville, Indiana, 1968; admitted to bar, 2003, Indiana. *Education:* University of Evansville (B.S., 1990); Indiana University (J.D., 2002). *Member:* Defense Trial Counsel of Indiana. ***PRACTICE AREAS:*** Litigation; Insurance Defense; Family Law. ***Email:*** hlacy@bamberger.com

SHAWN ROUNTREE, born Mount Vernon, Illinois; admitted to bar, 2003, Indiana; 2004, Illinois. *Education:* Illinois College (B.A., 2000); Southern Illinois University (J.D., 2003). ***PRACTICE AREAS:*** Banking Law; Commercial Law; Corporate Law. ***Email:*** srountree@bamberger.com

D. ANDREW NESTRICK, born Evansville, Indiana; admitted to bar, 2003, Indiana; 2004, Kentucky. *Education:* University of Kentucky (B.S., 2000); Valparaiso University (J.D., cum laude, 2003). ***PRACTICE AREAS:*** Estate Planning; Probate; Real Estate; Business Planning. ***Email:*** anestrick@bamberger.com

JAMES E. GENTRY, JR., born Henderson, Kentucky; admitted to bar, 2003, Indiana; 2004, Illinois and Kentucky. *Education:* University of Kentucky (B.S., 2000); Southern Illinois University (J.D., 2003). Member, American Health Lawyers Association. ***PRACTICE AREAS:*** Health Care; Litigation. ***Email:*** jgentry@bamberger.com

ADAM J. FARRAR, born Evansville, Indiana; admitted to bar, 2004, Indiana. *Education:* Indiana University (B.A., 2001; J.D., 2004). ***PRACTICE AREAS:*** Real Estate; Estate Planning. ***Email:*** afarrar@bamberger.com

JAMES C. HALL, born Dothan, Alabama; admitted to bar, 2004, Indiana. *Education:* Freed-Hardeman University (B.S., 1999); University of Toledo (J.D., 2004). ***PRACTICE AREAS:*** Banking Law; Commercial Law; Corporate Law. ***Email:*** jhall@bamberger.com

JENNIFER A. ELSTON, born Jasper, Indiana; admitted to bar, 2004, Indiana. *Education:* University of Evansville (B.S., 2001); Indiana University (J.D., 2004). ***PRACTICE AREAS:*** Civil Litigation; Family Law. ***Email:*** jelston@bamberger.com

(This Listing Continued)

BAMBERGER, FOREMAN, OSWALD AND HAHN, LLP, Evansville—Continued

SENIOR COUNSEL

CHARLES E. OSWALD, JR., born Evansville, Indiana, 1922; admitted to bar, 1948, Indiana. *Education:* Indiana University (B.S., 1943; J.D., 1943). ***PRACTICE AREAS:*** Real Estate; Business Law; Coal Mining; Oil and Gas Law.

K. RICHARD HAWLEY, born South Bend, Indiana, 1927; admitted to bar, 1951, Indiana. *Education:* Indiana University (B.S., 1949; J.D., with distinction, 1951). Prosecuting Attorney, Posey County, Indiana, 1953-1959. ***PRACTICE AREAS:*** Probate and Estate Planning; Trusts; Elder Law; Mineral Law; Real Estate Law. ***Email:*** dhawley@bamberger.com

PAULL MICHAEL MITCHELL, born Toledo, Ohio, 1936; admitted to bar, 1964, Indiana and Kentucky. *Education:* Yale University (A.B., 1959); Indiana University (LL.B., 1964). Fellow: Indiana Bar Foundation. ***PRACTICE AREAS:*** Estate Planning; Probate; Business Organization; Real Estate. ***Email:*** mmitchell@bamberger.com

OF COUNSEL

GERALD H. EVANS, born New Brunswick, New Jersey, 1937; admitted to bar, 1962, Missouri; 1968, Indiana. *Education:* Wabash College (B.A., 1959); University of Chicago (J.D., 1962). Special Tax Counsel, Indiana Department of Revenue, 1971-1988. Past President, Evansville Estate Planning Council, 1989. ***PRACTICE AREAS:*** Taxation; Probate and Estate Planning; Business Planning; Health Care Law. ***Email:*** jevans@bamberger.com

JOHN STUFF STASER, born Evansville, Indiana, 1945; admitted to bar, 1971, Indiana. *Education:* Indiana University (A.B., 1967; J.D., 1971). Assistant City Attorney, 1972-1975; City Attorney, 1976-1980. ***PRACTICE AREAS:*** Estate Planning; Financial Planning; Business Law. ***Email:*** sstaser@bamberger.com

MICHAEL J. CORK, born Elgin, Illinois, 1950; admitted to bar, 1977, Illinois; 1982, Texas; 1987, Indiana. *Education:* Carthage College (B.A., cum laude, 1972); Valparaiso University (J.D., 1976). Staff Attorney, Norwich-Eaton Pharmaceuticals, 1978-1979. Associate Counsel, Alcon Laboratories, Inc., 1979-1982. Corporate Counsel, Boehringer Mannheim Corporation, 1982-1987. Registered Indiana Civil Mediator. ***PRACTICE AREAS:*** Employment; Litigation. ***Email:*** mcork@bamberger.com

W. TRENT VAN HAAFTEN, born Evansville, Indiana, 1964; admitted to bar, 1990, Indiana. *Education:* Lake Forest College (B.A., 1987); Drake University Law School (J.D., 1990). Posey County Prosecuting Attorney (1995-2003). State Representative, District 76, Indiana General Assembly (2004—). ***PRACTICE AREAS:*** Litigation; Government Relations. ***Email:*** tvanhaaften@bamberger.com

KAREN T. POULTON, born Akron, Ohio, 1949; admitted to bar, 1991, Kansas; 2000, Nebraska and Massachusetts; 2004, Indiana. *Education:* Ohio State University (B.S., 1972; M.A., 1975); University of Florida (Ph.D., 1981); Washburn University (J.D., cum laude, 1991). Author: "Employment Discrimination: Subjective Employment Practices Under the Disparate Impact Theory: Merging Evidentiary Standards?" 28 Wash. L.J. 456, 1988. ***PRACTICE AREAS:*** Employment; Municipal.

REPRESENTATIVE CLIENTS: Available Upon Request.

BARBER, SHOULDERS & SIESKY, LLP

123 N.W. FOURTH STREET, SUITE 402
EVANSVILLE, INDIANA 47708
Telephone: 812-425-9211
Fax: 812-425-9216
Email: mail@barlegal.net
URL: http://www.barlegal.net

General Practice, Estates and Wills, Personal Injury, Social Security Claims, Business Law, Corporate Law, Family Law, Divorce, Insurance Claims, Criminal Defense.

STEVE BARBER, born Evansville, Indiana, April 13, 1948; admitted to bar, 1974, Indiana; 1975, U.S. Court of Appeals, Seventh Circuit; 1983, U.S. Court of Appeals for the Federal Circuit. *Education:* Indiana University (A.B., cum laude, 1970); Indiana University (J.D., 1974). Phi Beta Kappa; Order of the Coif. Note Editor, Indiana Law Journal, 1973-1974. Author: Note, 48 Indiana Law Journal, Page 452, 1973; "Is This Any Way to Treat a Guest?" Indiana Continuing Legal Education Foundation, 1980; "(Cost) Effective Use of Expert Witnesses," Indiana Continuing Legal Education Foundation, 1986; "Legal Writing For Paralegals," South-Western Publishing Co., 1993. "Legal Research," Lawyers Cooperative Publishing, 1996. ***PRACTICE AREAS:*** Civil Litigation; Commercial Law; Corporate Litigation; Construction Law; Real Estate; Divorce; Family Law.

JEFFREY T. SHOULDERS, born Evansville, Indiana, July 4, 1967; admitted to bar, 1992, Indiana and U.S. District Court, Southern District of Indiana. *Education:* Indiana University (B.A., 1989); University of Dayton (J.D., 1992). *Member:* Evansville and Indiana State Bar Association. ***PRACTICE AREAS:*** Social Security; Personal Injury; Civil Litigation.

LANE C. SIESKY, born Evansville, Indiana, August 26, 1972; admitted to bar, 1998, Indiana; 1999, Illinois. *Education:* Indiana University (B.S., 1995; J.D., 1998). Phi Beta Kappa. ***PRACTICE AREAS:*** Civil Litigation; Personal Injury; Medical Malpractice; Social Security.

A list of Representative Clients furnished upon request.

BARRETT LAW OFFICES, P.C.

915 MAIN STREET, SUITE 205
P.O. BOX 3052
EVANSVILLE, INDIANA 47730
Telephone: 812-424-4878; 800-380-4878
Fax: 812-424-8875
Email: bbarrettlaw@aol.com
URL: http://www.bbarrettlaw.com

Personal Injury, Medical Malpractice, Wrongful Death, Wills, Trusts, Estates, Medicaid Planning.

BARBARA S. BARRETT, born Evansville, Indiana, 1950; admitted to bar, 1990, Missouri; 1991, Indiana and Illinois. *Education:* University of Evansville (B.A., 1972); Indiana University (M.A.T., 1979); St. Louis University (J.D., 1990). *Member:* Evansville (Board Member) and Indiana State Bar Associations; American Judicature Society. ***PRACTICE AREAS:*** Personal Injury; Medical Malpractice; Wrongful Death; Wills; Trusts and Estates; Medicaid Planning.

DIANE L. BENDER

111 SOUTHEAST THIRD STREET, SUITE 402
P.O. BOX 1536
EVANSVILLE, INDIANA 47706-1536
Telephone: 812-423-8558
Fax: 812-423-8559

General Civil Practice including Probate and Estate Planning Law.

DIANE L. (WOLF) BENDER, born Evansville, Indiana, October 21, 1955; admitted to bar, 1980, Indiana; 1990, U.S. Supreme Court. *Education:* University of Notre Dame (B.B.A., with highest honors, 1977; J.D., cum laude, 1980). Beta Gamma Sigma; Beta Alpha Psi. Member, Board of Editors, Notre Dame Lawyer, 1979-1980. Certified Public Accountant, Illinois, 1980. Member, Indiana Probate Code Study Commission, 1992-2004. Member, Indiana Supreme Court Disciplinary Commission, 1999-2004, Vice Chair, 2004. *Member:* Evansville (President, 1992-1993), Indiana State (Chair, Probate, Trust and Real Property Section, 1996-1997) and American Bar Associations. Fellow, American College of Trust and Estate Counsel.

REFERENCE: Old National Bank in Evansville, Evansville, Indiana.

BERGER AND BERGER

Established in 1946
313 MAIN STREET
EVANSVILLE, INDIANA 47708-1485
Telephone: 812-425-8101
Toll Free: 800-327-0182
Fax: 812-421-5909
Email: berger@bergerlaw.com
URL: http://www.bergerlaw.com

Personal Injury, Admiralty, Labor and Employment, Municipal, Family Law, Probate, Business Law, Trials. General Civil in all State and Federal Courts.

FIRM PROFILE: The firm was established in 1946 by Sydney L. Berger. The firm has maintained a General Practice with an emphasis on Personal Injury and Labor Law. The firm primarily represents individuals throughout Southwestern Indiana and Southeastern Illinois but is not limited to those areas. The firm is listed in the Bar Register of Preeminent Lawyers under Labor and Employment Law, Civil Trial Practice, Personal Injury and Product Liability Law.

MEMBERS OF FIRM

SYDNEY L. BERGER (1917-1988)

CHARLES L. BERGER, born Evansville, Indiana, October 14, 1947; admitted to bar, 1972, Indiana, U.S. District Court, Southern District of Indiana and U.S. Court of Appeals, Seventh Circuit; 1975, U.S. Court of Appeals, District of Columbia Circuit; 1977, U.S. Supreme Court; 1981, U.S. District Court, Western District of Kentucky; 1984, U.S. Court of Appeals, Sixth Circuit. *Education:* Indiana University; University of Evansville (B.A., 1969); Indiana University School of Law (J.D., cum laude, 1972). Phi Kappa Phi. Adjunct Professor in Constitutional Law, 1998—. Recipient: James Bethel Gresham Award. Director, Indiana Lawyers' Commission, 1973-1977. *Member:* Evansville, Indiana State (Chairman, Trial Lawyers Section, 1982-1983) and American Bar Associations; Indiana Trial Lawyers Association (Director, 1977—; Treasurer, 1982-1983; Vice President, 1984-1985); American Board of Trial Advocates; The Association of Trial Lawyers of America (State Committeeman, 1975-1979); Bar Association of the Seventh Federal Circuit; Indiana Judicial Nominating Commission. Fellow: Indiana Bar Foundation; American Inns of Court Foundation (President Elect, 1990-1991; Treasurer, Brooks Inns of Court Chapter, 1988-1989); Indiana Supreme Court Rules Committee. ***PRACTICE AREAS:*** Personal Injury; Civil Litigation; Labor and Employment. ***Email:*** cberger@bergerlaw.com

SHEILA M. CORCORAN, born Evansville, Indiana, November 21, 1950; admitted to bar, 1979, Indiana and U.S. District Court, Southern District of Indiana. *Education:* University of Evansville (B.A., cum laude, 1972); Indiana University School of Law (J.D., cum laude, 1979). Phi Delta Phi; Phi Kappa Phi. Adjunct Instructor, University of Evansville, Paralegal Program, 1989-1996. General Counsel, Hospital Authority of Evansville, 1983—. Brooks American Inns of Court, 1988—. Member, Board of Law Examiners, State of Indiana, 1998—. *Member:* Evansville (Director, 1987-1989; Officer, 1993-1998; President, 1997-1998; Chairman, Continuing Legal Education Committee, 1988; Member, Probate, Women in the Law and Private Adoption Committees); and Indiana State (Member, Sections on: Probate; Family Law; Member, House of Delegates, 1997-2002; Board of

(This Listing Continued)

Governors, 2002-2004; Chair, Women in the Law Committee, 1997-1999) Bar Associations. ***PRACTICE AREAS:*** Probate; Family Law; Business Law; Social Security Disability. ***Email:*** corcoran@bergerlaw.com

MARK W. RIETMAN, born Evansville, Indiana, August 31, 1951; admitted to bar, 1976, Indiana and U.S. District Court, Southern District of Indiana; 1980, U.S. Court of Appeals, 7th Circuit and U.S. Supreme Court. *Education:* Indiana University (A.B., 1973); Indiana University School of Law (J.D., cum laude, 1976). Adjunct Instructor, Constitutional Law, University of Southern Indiana, 2000—. *Member:* Evansville and Indiana State Bar Associations; Indiana Trial Lawyers Association. ***PRACTICE AREAS:*** Personal Injury; Municipal Law. ***Email:*** berger@bergerlaw.com

ASSOCIATE

JENNIFER ULRICH-KEPPLER, born Evansville, Indiana, July 17, 1976; admitted to bar, 2001, Indiana and U.S. District Court, Southern and Northern Districts of Indiana; U.S. Court of Appeals, Sixth and Seventh Circuits and U.S. Supreme Court. *Education:* Indiana University (B.A., 1997; J.D., 1999). Phi Beta Kappa. Volunteer: Court Appointed Special Advocates; Albion Fellows Bacon Center. Chair, Young Lawyers Committee. Member, Board of Directors, Evansville Bar Association. *Member:* Indiana State Bar Association. ***PRACTICE AREAS:*** Personal Injury; Civil Litigation; Labor and Employment; Family Law. ***Email:*** ulrich@bergerlaw.com

OF COUNSEL

WILLIAM J. BRUNE, born 1928; admitted to bar, 1962, Indiana and U.S. District Court, Southern District of Indiana; 1967, U.S. Court of Appeals, Seventh Circuit; 1988, U.S. Supreme Court. *Education:* University of Evansville (A.B.); Indiana University School of Law (LL.B.). President, Vanderburgh County Council, 1969-1980. Prosecuting Attorney, 1971-1976. Judge, Vanderburgh County Superior Court, 1977-1999.

REFERENCES: Old National Bank, Evansville; Integra Bank, Evansville.

BOWERS HARRISON, LLP

25 N.W. RIVERSIDE DRIVE
P.O. BOX 1287
EVANSVILLE, INDIANA 47706-1287
Telephone: 812-426-1231
Fax: 812-464-3676
Email: web@bowersharrison.com
URL: http://www.bowersharrison.com

General Civil Practice and Litigation in all Courts, Banking, Corporation and other Business Entities, Railroad, Mineral, Environmental, Probate and Estate Planning, Real Estate, Taxation, Labor and Employment, Bankruptcy, Patent and Trademark.

FIRM PROFILE: One of Southern Indiana's largest and perhaps oldest continuously practicing law firm. It originally commenced practice as Hynes and Gilchrist in 1873.

All attorneys are members of the local and state bar associations of their respective bar admissions.

EQUITY PARTNERS

JOSEPH H. HARRISON, admitted to bar, 1953, Indiana and District of Columbia; 1955, U.S. District Court, Southern District of Indiana; 1968, U.S. Court of Appeals, Seventh Circuit and U.S. Tax Court. *Education:* University of Notre Dame (A.B., 1952; J.D., cum laude, 1953). Note Editor, Notre Dame Law Review, 1953. Director, 1958-1968 and President, 1964-1966, Vanderburgh County Legal Aid Society. Commissioner: Ohio River Valley Water Sanitation Commission (ORSANCO), 1982— (Chairman, 1986-1987); Evansville Economic Development Commission, 1991— (President, 1996-2001); Vanderburgh County Convention & Visitors Bureau, 1998-2001. ***PRACTICE AREAS:*** Taxation; Real Estate; Banking Law; Business Law; Mineral Law; Estate Planning. ***Email:*** jhh@bowersharrison.com

PAUL E. BLACK, born 1945; admitted to bar, 1970, Indiana, U.S. District Court, Southern District of Indiana, U.S. Court of Appeals, Seventh Circuit and U.S. Court of Appeals for the Armed Forces. *Education:* University of Evansville (B.A., 1967); Indiana University School of Law (J.D., 1970). Phi Alpha Delta. Member, 1979-1991 and President, 1990-1991, Vanderburgh County Election Board. President, Evansville Bar Association, 1999-2000. Commissioner, 1978—, and Chairman, 1996—, Indiana Commission on Proprietary Education. *Member:* National Association of Railroad Trial Counsel (Member and Secretary, National Executive Committee); Brooks Inns of Court. [Lt., USNR, JAGC, 1970-1974]. ***PRACTICE AREAS:*** Litigation; Banking Law; Medical Law; Social Security; Railroad Law. ***Email:*** peb@bowersharrison.com

ARTHUR D. RUTKOWSKI, born 1942; admitted to bar, 1967, Indiana and U.S. District Court, Southern District of Indiana; 1976, U.S. Court of Appeals, Seventh Circuit; 1991, U.S. Supreme Court. *Education:* Indiana University (B.S., 1964; J.D., 1967). Publisher, Health Employment Law Update and Employment Law Update, Newsletters, 1985—. Member, Committee on ADR in Labor and Employment Law. ***PRACTICE AREAS:*** Labor Law; Employment Law. ***Email:*** adr@bowersharrison.com

PAUL J. WALLACE, admitted to bar, 1979, Indiana and U.S. District Court, Southern District of Indiana; 1981, U.S. Court of Appeals, Seventh Circuit; 1984, U.S. Tax Court and U.S. Supreme Court. *Education:* Indiana University (B.S., 1975; M.B.A., 1979; J.D., 1979). Attorney, Evansville Airport Authority District, 2004—. *Member:* Indiana State Bar Association (Chair, Taxation Section, 1996-1997; Member: Ethics and Aviation Law Committees; 8th District Representative Council, Business Law Section, 2002—). ***PRACTICE AREAS:*** Corporate Law; Health Care Law; Taxation; Estate Planning; Business Litigation; Tax Litigation. ***Email:*** pjw@bowersharrison.com

DAVID L. JONES, born Elkton, Maryland; admitted to bar, 1976, Indiana and U.S. District Court, Southern District of Indiana; 1982, U.S. Court of Appeals, Seventh Circuit; 1997, U.S. Supreme Court. *Education:* U.S. Merchant Marine Academy, Lincoln University; University of Evansville (B.A., cum laude, 1972); Indiana University (J.D., 1975). Listed, Indiana Super Lawyers, 2004. Member, 1991—, Judge Advocate and Board of Directors, Veterans Council of Vanderburgh County. County Attorney, Vanderburgh County, Indiana, 1981-1986. Attorney to Vanderburgh County Council, 1978-1986. Adjunct Faculty Instructor, American Institute of Banking, University of Evansville, 1979-1984. Court Commissioner, Vanderburgh Circuit Court, 1976-1977. Corporation Counsel, City of Evansville, 2004—. Member, Board of Directors, John Sanders Memorial Evansville Bar Foundation. Member, Board of Directors, Vanderburgh Law Library Foundation. [With U.S.N.R.; With U.S. Merchant Marine Academy, 1965-1966; With U.S. Marine Corps, 1966-1968; Service in Vietnam, 1966-1968]. ***PRACTICE AREAS:*** Civil Litigation; Insurance Defense; Law Enforcement Liability; Civil Rights; Municipal Law; Personal Injury; Product Liability. ***Email:*** dlj@bowersharrison.com

DAVID E. GRAY, born 1951; admitted to bar, 1978, Indiana and U.S. District Court, Southern District of Indiana; 1981, U.S. Court of Appeals, Seventh Circuit; 1986, U.S. Tax Court. *Education:* Indiana State University (B.S., magna cum laude, 1974); Indiana University (J.D., magna cum laude, 1977). Associate Editor, Indiana Law Review, 1976-1977. [USMC, 1970-1972]. ***PRACTICE AREAS:*** Estate Planning; Probate; Appellate Practice; Taxation. ***Email:*** deg@bowersharrison.com

THOMAS A. MASSEY, born 1959; admitted to bar, 1984, Indiana and U.S. District Court, Northern and Southern Districts of Indiana; 1989, U.S. Supreme Court. *Education:* Purdue University (B.S.M., 1981); Valparaiso University (J.D., 1984). Law Review, 1982-1984. Police Merit Commissioner, City of Evansville, 1999-2004. Member, ICLEF Board of Directors, 1999—. Member, Vanderburgh County Election Board, 1994-1996. Board Member, Indiana Equal Justice Fund, 1998—. Certified Mediator Family Law Mediator, 1992—. Master, American Inn of Court No. 36. ***PRACTICE AREAS:*** Family Law; Litigation. ***Email:*** tam@bowersharrison.com

KEITH E. ROUNDER, born Evansville, Indiana, August 23, 1959; admitted to bar, 1987, Indiana and U.S. District Court, Southern and Northern Districts of Indiana; U.S. Cout of Appeals, Seventh Circuit. *Education:* University of Evansville (B.A., 1981); Indiana University (J.D., 1987). Vanderburgh County Attorney, 1993-1996. ***PRACTICE AREAS:*** Banking Law; Commercial Litigation; Real Estate Law; Lender Liability Law; Corporate Law. ***Email:*** ker@bowersharrison.com

NON-EQUITY PARTNERS

GREG A. GRANGER, born 1956; admitted to bar, 1983, Indiana; U.S. District Court, Northern and Southern Districts of Indiana; U.S. Court of Appeals, Seventh Circuit. *Education:* Indiana University (B.A., 1978; J.D., 1983). Certified: NBPA Player Agent, 1999—; NFLPA Contract Advisor, 1997-2000. Warrick County Council Attorney, 2001. *Member:* Sports Lawyers Association. ***PRACTICE AREAS:*** Commercial Litigation; Business Litigation; Sports Law. ***Email:*** gag@bowersharrison.com

JOSEPH H. HARRISON, JR., born Evansville, Indiana, 1959; admitted to bar, 1985, Indiana; U.S. District Court, Southern and Northern Districts of Indiana. *Education:* DePauw University (B.A., 1981); Indiana University School of Law (J.D., 1984). Evansville City Attorney, 2002—. Evansville-Vanderburgh County Building Authority Attorney, 2002—. Area Plan Commission Attorney, 2002—. Vanderburgh County Attorney, 1997-2000. ***PRACTICE AREAS:*** Municipal Law; Litigation; Commercial Law. ***Email:*** jhj@bowersharrison.com

CHRISTOPHER L. LUCAS, born 1961; admitted to bar, 1987, Indiana and U.S. District Court, Southern District of Indiana. *Education:* Indiana State University (B.S., 1984); Indiana University (J.D., 1987). ***PRACTICE AREAS:*** Real Estate Law; Construction and Development Law; Business Law; Corporate Law; Estate Planning; Probate; Estate Administration. ***Email:*** cll@bowersharrison.com

GARY K. PRICE, born Evansville, Indiana, November 4, 1956; admitted to bar, 1990, Indiana; registered to practice before U.S. Patent and Trademark Office. *Education:* Chaminade University of Waikiki, Hawaii (B.S., Computer Science, 1981); University of Louisville (J.D., 1989). Adjunct Professor, Computer Science, University of Evansville and University of Southern Indiana, 1983—. ***PRACTICE AREAS:*** Intellectual Property; Patents; Trademarks; Copyrights; Corporate Law; Business Law; Unfair Competition. ***Email:*** gkp@bowersharrison.com

JAY A. ZIEMER, born 1965; admitted to bar, 1991, Indiana and Illinois; U.S. District Court, Northern, Central and Southern Districts of Illinois; U.S. District Court, Southern District of Indiana and U.S. Court of Appeals, Seventh Circuit. *Education:* Marquette University (B.A., 1987); Indiana University (J.D., cum laude, 1991). Articles Editor, Indiana Law Review, 1990-1991. Assistant Vanderburgh County Attorney, 2001—. ***PRACTICE AREAS:*** Business Litigation; Commercial Litigation; Construction Litigation; Criminal Litigation; Litigation; Municipal Law; Personal Injury; Employment Litigation. ***Email:*** jaz@bowersharrison.com

SARA HARRISON ZEIDLER, born 1965; admitted to bar, 1992, Indiana and U.S. District Court, Southern District of Indiana. *Education:* St. Mary's College (B.A., 1987); Indiana University (J.D., 1992). ***LANGUAGES:*** Italian. ***PRACTICE AREAS:*** Title Insurance; Real Estate. ***Email:*** shz@bowersharrison.com

ASSOCIATES

KELLY A. LONNBERG, born 1963; admitted to bar, 1988, Indiana and U.S. District Court, Southern District of Indiana; U.S. Court of Appeals, Sixth and Seventh Circuits. *Education:* University of Illinois (B.A.B.S., 1985); Southern Illinois University School of Law (J.D., 1988). Certified Family Law Specialist. Family Law Mediator. Board Member, Legal Aid Society. Member, Brooks Inn of Court. ***PRACTICE AREAS:*** Family Law; Civil Litigation; Mediation; Insurance Defense; Personal Injury. ***Email:*** kal@bowersharrison.com

MARK F. WARZECHA, born Jersey City, New Jersey; admitted to bar, 1994, New York; U.S. District Court, Eastern District of New York; 1995, New Jersey and U.S. District Court, District of New Jersey; 2002, Indiana and U.S. District Court, Northern and Southern Districts of Indiana. *Education:* Rutgers University (B.S., 1991); California Western School of Law (J.D., 1994). ***PRACTICE AREAS:*** Intellectual Property; Entertainment Law; Corporate Law; Real Estate. ***Email:*** mfw@bowersharrison.com

(This Listing Continued)

BOWERS HARRISON, LLP, Evansville—Continued

CORY A. KUHLENSCHMIDT, born Evansville, Indiana; admitted to bar, 2001, Indiana and U.S. District Court, Northern and Southern Districts of Indiana. *Education:* Indiana University at Bloomington (B.A., 1998); T.C. Williams School of Law (J.D., 2001). ***PRACTICE AREAS:*** Litigation; Corporate Law. ***Email:*** cak@bowersharrison.com

OF COUNSEL

F. WESLEY BOWERS, admitted to bar, 1951, Indiana and U.S. District Court, Southern District of Indiana; 1967, U.S. Court of Appeals, Seventh Circuit; 1994, U.S. District Court, Southern District of Illinois. *Education:* Indiana University (A.B., cum laude, 1948; J.D., 1951). Phi Beta Kappa. State Senator, 1962-1966. Certified Mediator, Indiana, 1992. NASD Arbitrator Panel. *Member:* National Association of Railroad Trial Counsel (Director, 1981-1991; American Board of Trial Advocates (President, Indiana Chapter, 1995). ***PRACTICE AREAS:*** Litigation; Railroad Law; Civil Mediation; Arbitration. ***Email:*** fwb@bowersharrison.com

KEITH M. WALLACE, born Evansville, Indiana, April 2, 1956; admitted to bar, 1983, Indiana and U.S. District Court, Northern and Southern Districts of Indiana; 1984, Kentucky; 1985, U.S. Court of Appeals, Seventh Circuit; 1997, U.S. Supreme Court. *Education:* University of Tennessee at Knoxville; Indiana University (B.A., 1978); Valparaiso University (J.D., 1983). Hearing Officer, City of Evansville Department of Code Enforcement, 1992-1999. Assistant City Attorney, City of Evansville, 1984-1990. Foreign Expert, Peking University, Beijing, PRC, 1990-1991. *Member:* American Academy of Adoption Attorneys; American Immigration Lawyers Association; Christian Legal Society. ***PRACTICE AREAS:*** Utility Law; Workers Compensation; Civil Litigation; Commercial Law; Administrative Law; Environmental Law. ***Email:*** kmw@bowersharrison.com

GEORGE A. PORCH, born Evansville, Indiana, August 20, 1943; admitted to bar, 1968, Indiana; U.S. Court of Appeals, 7th Circuit and District of Columbia Circuit; U.S. Supreme Court. *Education:* Evansville College (B.A., 1965); Indiana University (J.D., 1968). Recipient: Bronze Star, U.S. Army; Evansville Bar Association Perdue Service Award, 2001; Advocacy Award. Secretary, Vanderburgh County Government Study Commission. Town Attorney, Town of New Harmony, 1972-1974. Assistant City Attorney, City of Evansville, 2004—. General Counsel, Southern Indiana Gas and Electric Company, 1980-2001. Chief Litigator, Deputy Indiana Consumer Counselor, 2001-2002. *Member:* Evansville (President, 1990) and Indiana State (Member, Board of Managers, 1992-1994; Founder and President, Utility Law Section) Bar Associations. Fellow and Trustee, Indiana Bar Foundation. [U.S. Army, 1968-1970]. ***PRACTICE AREAS:*** Civil Litigation; Insurance Defense; Utility Law; Workers Compensation; Municipal Law; Administrative Law. ***Email:*** gporch@bamberger.com

REPRESENTATIVE CLIENTS: ADM/Growmark; American Family Insurance Co.; American General Finance, Inc.; Ameritech Corp.; Bank of Evansville; Bernardin, Lochmueller & Associates, Inc.; Castle Properties and Construction; Commonwealth Land Title Insurance Co.; Deaconess Womens' Hospital; Evansville Surgery Center; Dunn Hospitality Group; GMAC Insurance Group; Hardee's Restaurants; Harding Shymanski & Co.; Hartford Insurance Group; Integra Bank, N.A.; Kenny Kent Toyota; Midwestern Pet Foods, Inc.; Meisler Companies; Norfolk Southern Railway Co.; Peabody Development Co.; Regency Commercial Associates; Romain Buick, Inc.; United Fidelity Bank; WFIE-TV.
REPRESENTATIVE LABOR CLIENTS: Amealth, Inc.; Citiy of Flora, Illinois; Dollar General Corporation (Indiana); Marion Pepsi-Cola Bottling Co.; Peabody Coal Co; Regional Medical Center of Madisonville, Kentucky; Vincent Industrial Plastics, Inc.; Whirlpool Corporation.
REFERENCES: Integra Bank N.A.; Old National.

LLOYD D. BRIGHT

2321 WEST DELAWARE STREET
EVANSVILLE, INDIANA 47712
Telephone: 812-423-6885
Fax: 812-423-6893
Email: ldbrightatty@sigecom.net
Mailing Address: P.O. Box 6388, Evansville, IN 47719

Oil and Gas, Coal, Real Estate, Title, Regulatory, Business and Probate.

LLOYD D. BRIGHT, born Louisville, Kentucky, April 15, 1948; admitted to bar, 1980, Kentucky; 1983, Illinois; 1984, Indiana. *Education:* University of Kentucky (B.G.S., 1976; J.D., 1979). *Member:* Kentucky and Illinois State Bar Associations. ***PRACTICE AREAS:*** Oil and Gas Law.

BRINKERHOFF RILEY LLC

Established in 2004
400 COURT STREET
EVANSVILLE, INDIANA 47708
Telephone: 812-464-3966
Fax: 812-464-3968
Email: ssbrinkerhoff@yahoo.com
URL: http://www.brinkerhoffrileylaw.com

Family Law, Child Custody, Divorce, Juvenile Matters, Criminal Defense, Felonies, Misdemeanors, Probation Violations, Small Claims, Contract Disputes, Medical Malpractice and Employment Law.

STEPHANIE BRINKERHOFF RILEY, born Danville, Illinois, August 12, 1972; admitted to bar, 2001, Indiana; 2002, U.S. District Court, Northern District of Illinois and U.S. District Court, Northern District of Indiana; 2005, U.S. District Court, Southern District of Indiana. *Education:* University of Evansville (B.S., Environmental Administrative, minor in Pol. Sci., cum laude, 1996); Indiana University School of Law - Bloomington (J.D., 1999). *Member:* Indianapolis, Evansville and Indiana State Bar Associations. ***PRACTICE AREAS:*** Family Law; Criminal Law; Medical Malpractice; Employment Law; Contracts. ***Email:*** ssbrinkerhoff@yahoo.com

LAW OFFICES OF RANDALL K. CRAIG

Established in 1989
5000 EAST VIRGINIA STREET, SUITE 1
EVANSVILLE, INDIANA 47715
Telephone: 812-477-3337
Telefax: 812-477-3658
Email: rkcraig@dynasty.net
URL: http://www.rkcraiglaw.com

Taxation, Probate, Estate Planning, Elder, Corporate, Business and Real Estate Law.

FIRM PROFILE: Mr. Craig, who has achieved Martindale-Hubbell's highest rating for ethical standards and legal ability is Certified as an Elder Law Attorney by The National Elder Law Foundation.

RANDALL K. CRAIG, born Evansville, Indiana, March 15, 1950; admitted to bar, 1975, Indiana and U.S. Tax Court. *Education:* Indiana University (B.S., with distinction, 1972; J.D., cum laude, 1975). Beta Gamma Sigma. Recipient, F. J. Feeney Tax Award. Licensed Real Estate Broker, Indiana, 1973. Author: "Some Observations on the Use of Life Insurance In Estate Planning," Res Gestae, April, 1977. Contributing Author: "Estate Planning and Probate in Indiana," National Business Institute, 1988. Co-Author: with Amelia E. Pohl, J.D., "A Will is not Enough in Indiana," 2004, Eagle Publishing. Adjunct Professor, in areas of Income Taxation, Estate Planning and Administration and Real Estate, University of Evansville, 1976-1979. *Member:* Evansville (Treasurer, 1982-1985; Chairman, Probate Committee, 1982; Chairman, Bar Services Committee, 1993; Chairman, Elder Law Committee, 1996; Member, Board of Directors, 1985-1986; Probate Committee, 1989) and Indiana State (Member, Sections on: Taxation and Real Property; Probate and Trust Law) Bar Associations; National Academy of Elder Law Attorneys (Member, Tax and Trusts Special Interest Groups). Southwestern Indiana Regional Council on Aging Foundation (Member, Board of Directors); Vanderburgh County Council on Aging (Former President; Vice President and Member, Board of Directors); Southwestern Indiana Regional Council on Aging, Inc. (President, Former Vice President and Member, Board of Directors); Christian Legal Society; Sagamore of the Wabash.

EARLY, ARNOLD & ZIEMER, LLP

EVANSVILLE, INDIANA

(See Ziemer, Stayman, Weitzel & Shoulders, LLP)

FINE & HATFIELD

A PROFESSIONAL CORPORATION
Established in 1921
520 N.W. SECOND STREET
P.O. BOX 779
EVANSVILLE, INDIANA 47705-0779
Telephone: 812-425-3592
Telecopier: 812-421-4269
Email: Fine@Fine-Hatfield.com
URL: http://www.Fine-Hatfield.com

Bankruptcy, Commercial, Corporate and Business, Environmental, Health Care Law, Insurance, Labor and Employment, Probate and Estate Planning, Real Estate, Land Use, Federal Securities Litigation and Taxation Law. Defense of Professional Malpractice including Medical, Legal, Architects and Accounting, Products Liability, Trials in State and Federal Courts.

FIRM PROFILE: Fine & Hatfield has a diversified practice of a sophisticated nature. Its clientele includes regional representation of insurance companies, large national and multinational corporations, businesses and individuals in Indiana, southern Illinois and western Kentucky.

ISADORE J. FINE (1897-1975)
JOE S. HATFIELD (1908-1993)
JAMES E. MARCHAND (1931-1999)

THOMAS H. BRYAN, born Evansville, Indiana, September 14, 1944; admitted to bar, 1969, Indiana and U.S. District Court, Southern District of Indiana; 1971, Illinois and U.S. District Court, Northern District of Illinois; 1984, U.S. Supreme Court. *Education:* Purdue University (B.S.M.E., 1966); Indiana University (J.D., 1969). *Member:* Evansville and Indiana State Bar Associations; Indiana Defense Lawyers Association. ***PRACTICE AREAS:*** Product Liability Defense Law; Medical Malpractice Defense; Civil Trials; Construction Law. ***Email:*** thb@fine-hatfield.com

THOMAS R. FITZSIMMONS, born Indianapolis, Indiana, May 27, 1950; admitted to bar, 1975, Indiana and U.S. District Court, Southern District of Indiana; 1990, U.S. Supreme Court. *Education:* Northwestern University (B.A., 1972); Indiana University (J.D., magna cum laude, 1975). Delta Theta Phi. *Member:* Evansville and Indiana State Bar Associations; American Society of Law, Medicine and Ethics. ***PRACTICE AREAS:*** Acquisitions, Divestitures and Mergers; Health Care Law; Estate Planning Law; Taxation Law; Contract Law; Business Law. ***Email:*** trf@fine-hatfield.com

DANNY E. GLASS, born Muncie, Indiana, November 11, 1950; admitted to bar, 1977, Indiana and U.S. District Court, Southern District of Indiana; 1994, Illinois, U.S. District Court, Southern District of Illinois and U.S. Court of Appeals, Seventh Circuit; 1995, Kentucky. *Education:* Hanover College (B.A., 1973); Indiana University (J.D., 1976). Phi Eta Sigma. *Member:* Evansville, Kentucky and Indiana State Bar Associations; Indiana Defense Lawyers Association. Fellow, American College of Trial Lawyers. ***PRACTICE AREAS:*** Commercial Litigation; Professional Liability Defense Law; Business Litigation; Civil Litigation; Unfair Competition Law. ***Email:*** deg@fine-hatfield.com

(This Listing Continued)

TODD I. GLASS, born Muncie, Indiana, October 19, 1961; admitted to bar, 1988, Indiana and U.S. District Court, Northern and Southern Districts of Indiana; 1990, U.S. Court of Appeals, Seventh Circuit. *Education:* Wabash College (A.B., 1984); University of Dayton School of Law (J.D., 1988). *Member:* Indiana State and Evansville Bar Associations. ***PRACTICE AREAS:*** Wills; Trusts and Estates; Probate; Business Law; Private Adoption. ***Email:*** tig@fine-hatfield.com

JOHN J. KREIGHBAUM, born Elgin, Illinois, June 28, 1952; admitted to bar, 1994, Indiana and U.S. District Courts, Northern and Southern Districts of Indiana; 1997, U.S. Court of Appeals, Seventh Circuit. *Education:* State University of New York (B.S., 1989); Indiana University School of Law, Indianapolis (J.D., cum laude, 1994). *Member:* Evansville and Indiana State Bar Associations. [E 6, U.S. Navy, 1970-1979]. ***PRACTICE AREAS:*** Civil Litigation; Insurance Defense; Medical Malpractice. ***Email:*** jjk@fine-hatfield.com

DAVID D. SANDERS, born Linton, Indiana, February 27, 1962; admitted to bar, 1997, Indiana and U.S. District Court, Southern District of Indiana. *Education:* University of Arizona (B.S., 1993); Indiana University (J.D., 1997). *Member:* Evansville and Indiana State Bar Associations. ***PRACTICE AREAS:*** Business Law; Trust Planning; Estate Planning; Trust Administration; Estate Administration; Real Estate. ***Email:*** dds@fine-hatfield.com

H. LINWOOD SHANNON, III, born Henderson, Kentucky, January 16, 1970; admitted to bar, 1995, Indiana and Kentucky. *Education:* Centre College of Kentucky (B.A., 1992); University of Louisville (J.D., 1995). *Member:* Evansville, Henderson, Indiana and Kentucky Bar Associations. ***PRACTICE AREAS:*** Labor and Employment; Wrongful Termination Defense; Wage and Hour Law; Workers Compensation Defense Law. ***Email:*** hls@fine-hatfield.com

---

JESSICA A. McCARTHY, born Evansville, Indiana, October 22, 1976; admitted to bar, 2003, Indiana and U.S. District Court, Southern and Northern Districts of Indiana; 2004, Kentucky. *Education:* University of Southern Indiana (B.A., magna cum laude, 1999); Valparaiso University School of Law (J.D., magna cum laude, 2003). *Member:* Evansville and Indiana State Bar Associations. ***PRACTICE AREAS:*** Civil Litigation; Insurance Defense. ***Email:*** jam@fine-hatfield.com

DANIEL B. GEARHART, born Evansville, Indiana, April 9, 1975; admitted to bar, 2003, Indiana and U.S. District Court, Northern and Southern Districts of Indiana. *Education:* Indiana University (B.S., Business, 1997); Indiana University School of Law (J.D., magna cum laude, 2003). *Member:* Evansville and Indiana State Bar Associations. ***PRACTICE AREAS:*** Employment Law; Labor Law; Civil Practice; Workers Compensation Defense; Divorce. ***Email:*** dbg@fine-hatfield.com

JAMES D. JONES, born Hopkinsville, Kentucky, July 19, 1973; admitted to bar, 2000, New York; 2004, Indiana. *Education:* Ball State University (B.S., Accounting, 1995); University of Virginia School of Law (J.D., 1998); New York University School of Law (LL.M., Taxation, 2001). Certified Public Accountant, Maryland, 1999; Indiana, 2004. *Member:* Evansville and Indiana State Bar Associations. ***PRACTICE AREAS:*** Mergers, Acquisitions and Divestitures; Taxation; Business Law; Estate Planning; Bankruptcy. ***Email:*** jdj@fine-hatfield.com

JULIA A. CONDICT, born Troy, Ohio, November 3, 1978; admitted to bar, 2004, Indiana and U.S. District Court, Northern and Southern Districts of Indiana. *Education:* Taylor University (B.S., International Business, 2001); Indiana University School of Law - Indianapolis (J.D., 2004). *Member:* Evansville and Indiana State Bar Associations. ***PRACTICE AREAS:*** Insurance Defense; Medical Malpractice Defense; Civil Litigation. ***Email:*** jac@fine-hatfield.com

OF COUNSEL

RONALD R. ALLEN, born Evansville, Indiana, June 1, 1938; admitted to bar, 1965, Indiana, U.S. District Court, Southern District of Indiana and U.S. Court of Appeals, Sixth and Seventh Circuits. *Education:* University of Evansville (A.B., 1961); Indiana University (LL.B., 1965). ***PRACTICE AREAS:*** Labor Relations Law; Employer Law; Discrimination Law. ***Email:*** rra@fine-hatfield.com

A List of Representative Clients Furnished Upon Request.

FOSTER, MONTGOMERY & O'DANIEL, LLP

Established in 2000

3820 OAK HILL ROAD
EVANSVILLE, INDIANA 47711
Telephone: 812-424-8101 Toll Free: 888-280-8101
Fax: 812-437-8364
Email: tstatz@fmolaw.com
URL: http://www.fmolaw.com

Criminal Defense, DWI, Bankruptcy, Family and Domestic Relations, Probate and Estates. Practice in all State and Federal Courts.

MARK A. FOSTER, born Franklin, Kentucky, May 16, 1958; admitted to bar, 1983, Indiana and the U.S. District Court, Southern District of Indiana; 1992, U.S. Court of Appeals, Seventh Circuit; 1994, U.S. Supreme Court. *Education:* Indiana State University (B.S., 1980); Indiana University (J.D., 1983). Phi Delta Phi. Certified Field Sobriety Testing, NHTSA; Certified Bac Datamaster Operator, NPAS. Contributing Author and Lecturer: "Defense Techniques for DWI Clients," Indiana Continuing Legal Education Forum, 1989; "DWI Dram Shop," (ICLEF), 1990; "Criminal Law," (ICLEF), 1990; "Planning Your First Criminal Defense," ICLEF, 1997; "DWI," ICLEF, 1998; "What Every Lawyer Should Know about DWI," ICLEF, 1998; "DWI," ICLEF, 1999; "DWI & HTV-Quebec City, Quebec" ICLEF, 1999; "Traffic Law School" ICLEF, 2000; "Criminal Law-Las Vegas" ISBA & ICLEF, 2001; "The Best of DWI" ICLEF, 2001; "Civil and Criminal Evidence" ICLEF, 2001; "DUI Defense" ICLEF, 2002; "Misdemeanor Court" Legal Aid Society, 2002; "Traffic Law School" ICLEF, 2002; "DWI Experts, Technology and Equipment," ICLEF, 2003; "Hot Topics-DWI," EBA, 2003; "Traffic School for Lawyers," ICLEF, 2004. Instructor,

(This Listing Continued)

Criminal Law and Procedure, University of Evansville, 1984-1992. Deputy Prosecutor, Vanderburgh County, 1983-1985. Referee, Vanderburgh Superior Court, Misdemeanor/Traffic Division, 1985-1987. *Member:* Evansville (Chairman, Criminal Law Committee, 1989-1990), Gibson County and Indiana State Bar Associations; Indiana Trial Lawyers Association; The Association of Trial Lawyers of America; National Association of Criminal Defense Lawyers (Life Member); Evansville Association of Criminal Defense Lawyers (Founding President); National College for DUI Defense. ***PRACTICE AREAS:*** Criminal Defense Law; DWI. ***Email:*** mfoster@fmolaw.com

THOMAS L. MONTGOMERY, born Evansville, Indiana, August 13, 1963; admitted to bar, 1990, Indiana and U.S. District Court, Southern and Northern Districts of Indiana. *Education:* University of Evansville (B.S., 1985); Indiana University (J.D., 1989). Delta Theta Phi. Public Defender, Vanderburgh Superior Court, Evansville, Indiana, 1988—. *Member:* Evansville, Gibson County and Indiana State Bar Associations; National Association of Criminal Defense Lawyers; Evansville Association of Criminal Defense Lawyers; Brooks Inns of Court. ***PRACTICE AREAS:*** Criminal Defense; Wills & Estates; General Civil; Personal Injury; Bankruptcy. ***Email:*** tmontgomery@fmolaw.com

CONOR M. O'DANIEL, born Terre Haute, Indiana, July 30, 1971; admitted to bar, 1996, Indiana, U.S. District Court, Southern District of Indiana and U.S. Court of Appeals, 7th Circuit. *Education:* Wabash College (A.B., 1993); Indiana University (J.D., 1996). Phi Delta Phi. Deputy Prosecuting Attorney, 1996-2000. Public Defender: Vanderburgh Superior Court, 2000; Circuit Court, 2001—. Contributing Member and Lecturer, "Dual Experts, Technology and Equipment," CLEF, 2003; "Traffic School for Lawyers," ICLEF, 2004. *Member:* Evansville and Gibson County Bar Associations; National Association of Criminal Defense Lawyers; Brooks Inns of Court; Evansville Association of Criminal Defense Lawyers (Vice President). ***PRACTICE AREAS:*** Criminal; Family; Estates; Paternity. ***Email:*** odaniel@fmolaw.com

---

FRICK POWELL WHINREY CRAVENS & SCHMITT, LLP

Established in 1987

223 S.E. SECOND STREET
P.O. BOX 1200
EVANSVILLE, INDIANA 47706
Telephone: 812-425-4687
Fax: 812-425-4690
URL: http://www.fpwcs.com

General Civil Practice in all Courts. Corporate, Probate and Estate Planning, Family/Domestic Relations, Real Estate and Litigation in all State and Federal Courts.

MEMBERS OF FIRM

BERNARD A. FRICK (1910-1967)

WILLIAM D. POWELL (1927-1987)

JOHN B. WHINREY, born Indianapolis, Indiana, September 25, 1941; admitted to bar, 1966, Indiana. *Education:* Northwestern University; College of Wooster (B.A., 1963); University of Michigan (J.D., 1966). *Member:* Evansville (President, 1986-1987), Indiana State and American Bar Associations. ***PRACTICE AREAS:*** Corporate Law; Probate and Estate Planning Law. ***Email:*** johnw@fpwcs.com

GARLAND W. CRAVENS, JR., born Clarksville, Indiana, April 9, 1953; admitted to bar, 1982, Indiana. *Education:* Indiana University (B.A., 1976); Indiana University (J.D., 1982). Phi Alpha Delta. *Member:* Evansville, Indiana State (Member, Sections on: Trust and Real Property Law; Family Law) and American Bar Associations. ***REPORTED CASES:*** Graves v. Kelly, 625 N.E.2d 493. ***PRACTICE AREAS:*** Real Estate Law; Corporate Law; Family Law; Probate. ***Email:*** garlandc@fpwcs.com

REED S. SCHMITT, born Albuquerque, New Mexico, July 20, 1959; admitted to bar, 1984, Indiana; 1987, U.S. Tax Court. *Education:* Purdue University (B.A., 1981); Indiana University (J.D., 1984). Phi Delta Theta; Pi Sigma Alpha; Phi Delta Phi. *Member:* Evansville (President, 1998-1999), Indiana State Bar Association (Member, Sections on: Probate, Trust and Real Property Law; Taxation); Brooks American Inns of Court. ***REPORTED CASES:*** Koch v. James, 616 N.E.2d 759; Koch v. James 670 N.E. 2d 113; Hydraulic Exchange v. K.M. Specialty, 690 N.E. 2d 782; Kelly v. Estate of Johnson, 788 N.E.2d 933. ***PRACTICE AREAS:*** Corporate Law; Probate and Estate Planning Law; Litigation. ***Email:*** reeds@fpwcs.com

DAVID G. HARRIS, born Lafayette Indiana, September 11, 1970; admitted to bar, 1996, Indiana. *Education:* Indiana State University (B.S., 1993); Indiana University at Indianapolis (J.D., 1996). *Member:* Evansville, Indiana State and American Bar Associations. ***PRACTICE AREAS:*** Corporate Law; Probate and Estate Planning Law. ***Email:*** davidh@fpwcs.com

REPRESENTATIVE CLIENTS: Center Heights Lumber Co., Inc.; Crescent City Security, Inc.; Deters, Inc.; Evansville Blueprint Co.; Evansville Wallpaper Co., Inc.; The Good Samaritan Home, Inc.; Ice Products, Inc.; K M Specialty Pumps, Inc.; Lefler Body Shop, Inc.; Mills-Wallace & Associates, Inc.; Midwest Equipment & Supply Co., Inc.; Ohio Valley Pathologists, P.C.; Scheller Woodruff & Associates, Inc.; The State Group Industrial (USA), Ltd.; Talley Medical-Surgical Eye Care Associates, P.C.; Reddinger Constructors, Inc.; Techcon Design, Inc.; Wilhite Supply Co., Inc.
APPROVED ATTORNEYS FOR: Commonwealth Land Title Insurance Corp.; National Attorneys Title Assurance Fund.
REFERENCES: Integra Bank; Old National Bank in Evansville; Fifth Third Bank.

GERLING LAW OFFICES

PROFESSIONAL CORPORATION

Established in 1963

519 MAIN STREET
P.O. BOX 3203
EVANSVILLE, INDIANA 47731
Telephone: 812-423-5251
Fax: 812-423-9928
Email: info@gerlinglaw.com
URL: http://www.gerlinglaw.com

Personal Injury, Wrongful Death, Negligence, Products Liability, Mediation, Arbitration, Medical Malpractice, Social Security Disability, Commercial Litigation and Workers Compensation Law. (Plaintiffs Only).

GAYLE GERLING PETTINGA, born 1961; admitted to bar, 1987, Indiana. *Education:* Smith College (A.B., cum laude, 1984); Indiana University (J.D., magna cum laude, 1987). ***Email:*** info@gerlinglaw.com

EDWARD B. ANDERSON, born 1950; admitted to bar, 1977, Indiana. *Education:* Indiana State University (B.S., 1974); University of San Fernando Valley (J.D., 1977). ***Email:*** info@gerlinglaw.com

DAVID G. HATFIELD, born 1954; admitted to bar, 1980, Indiana; 1989, Kentucky. *Education:* University of Evansville (B.A., cum laude, 1977); Indiana University (J.D., 1980). ***Email:*** info@gerlinglaw.com

STEPHEN HENSLEIGH THOMAS, born 1951; admitted to bar, 1976, Indiana; 1988, Kentucky; 1998, Illinois. *Education:* Southern Illinois University (B.A., 1972); Southern Illinois University (J.D., 1976). Certified as Civil Mediator, American Board of Trial Advocates. ***Email:*** info@gerlinglaw.com

DANIEL A. BARFIELD, born 1970; admitted to bar, 1995, Indiana and Illinois. *Education:* Purdue University (B.A., 1991); Valparaiso University (J.D., summa cum laude, 1995). ***Email:*** info@gerlinglaw.com

OF COUNSEL

GARY L. GERLING, born 1937; admitted to bar, 1963, Indiana. *Education:* University of Evansville (B.S., 1960); Indiana University (J.D., 1963). Order of the Coif. Advocate, American Board of Trial Advocates. ***Email:*** info@gerlinglaw.com

All Attorneys are Members of Evansville, Indiana State, The Association of Trial Lawyers of America, and the Indiana Trial Lawyers Association.

JOHN ANDREW GOODRIDGE LAW OFFICE

1904 E. MULBERRY
EVANSVILLE, INDIANA 47714
Telephone: 812-426-0482
Fax: 812-426-2211
URL: http://www.jaglofirm.com
Email: jgoodridge@jaglo.com
URL: http://www.jaglo.com

Bankruptcy and Federal Criminal Law.

JOHN ANDREW GOODRIDGE, born Evansville, Indiana, December 11, 1970; admitted to bar, 1996, Indiana and U.S. District Court, Northern and Southern Districts of Indiana; 2003, U.S. Court of Appeals, Seventh Circuit. *Education:* Wabash College (B.A., 1993); Valparaiso University School of Law (J.D., 1996). *Member:* Evansville Bar Association; Inns of Court. **PRACTICE AREAS:** Bankruptcy; Federal Criminal Law.

GLENN A. GRAMPP

115 S.E. 4TH STREET
P.O. BOX 3401
EVANSVILLE, INDIANA 47733
Telephone: 812-464-8800
Fax: 812-422-8832
URL: http://www.gramplaw.com
URL: http://www.lawyers.com/gramplaw

Civil and Criminal Trial Practice in all Courts. Personal Injury Litigation and Family/Domestic Relations.

GLENN A. GRAMPP, born Evansville, Indiana, January 11, 1948; admitted to bar, 1973, Indiana and U.S. District Court, Southern District of Indiana; 1985, U.S. Court of Appeals, Seventh Circuit; 1986, U.S. Supreme Court. *Education:* Indiana State University (B.S., 1970); Indiana University (J.D., 1973). *Member:* Evansville, Indiana State and American Bar Associations; Indiana Trial Lawyers Association; Indiana Association of Criminal Defense Lawyers; National Association of Criminal Defense Lawyers. **PRACTICE AREAS:** Personal Injury Litigation; Criminal Law; Civil Trial; Family Law.

REFERENCE: Citizens National Bank.

HALL, PARTENHEIMER & KINKLE

EVANSVILLE, INDIANA

(See Princeton)

General Civil Practice. Personal Injury, Probate and Estate Planning, Real Estate, Mining, Oil and Gas and Corporate Law, Municipal Law, Trials.

JOHNSON, CARROLL, NORTON, KENT & STRAUS, P.C.

Established in 1952

2230 WEST FRANKLIN STREET
P.O. BOX 6016
EVANSVILLE, INDIANA 47719-0016
Telephone: 812-425-4466
Telecopier: 812-425-4233
URL: http://www.jcglaw.com

General Civil and Trial Practice. Personal Injury, Condemnation, Probate and Estate Planning, Real Estate, Intellectual Property, Corporation and Mineral Law, Family Law, Divorce.

FIRM PROFILE: The law firm of Johnson, Carroll, Norton, Kent & Straus, P.C. was established in 1952 as a General Practice with emphasis on Elder Law, Estate Planning, Corporation, Family Law and Litigation. These experienced attorneys are dedicated to providing quality personalized service with great concern for clients' needs, while maintaining a sensitivity to the cost of legal services. A highly-trained legal support staff and state-of-the-art computer research and data recovery resources are utilized to enable the firm to handle a broad spectrum of litigation needs. The practice is concentrated in Vanderburgh County.

EDWIN W. JOHNSON (1922-2002)

EDWARD W. JOHNSON, born Evansville, Indiana, October 23, 1944; admitted to bar, 1970, Indiana. *Education:* Indiana University (B.S., 1966; J.D., 1969). Adjunct Faculty, Para-Legal Instruction, University of Evansville, 1975-1979. Assistant State Attorney General, 1970-1973. Registered Domestic Relations Mediator. *Member:* Evansville (President, 1989-1990), Indiana State and American Bar Associations. **PRACTICE AREAS:** Mediation; Probate Law; Real Estate Law; General Litigation; Family Law.

BRIAN K. CARROLL, born Evansville, Indiana, October 26, 1956; admitted to bar, 1982, Indiana. *Education:* Harlaxton Study Center, Grantham, England; Indiana University (B.S., 1978; J.D., cum laude, 1982). Certified Elder Law Attorney, National Elder Law Foundation. Publications: ICLEF, Mineral Law of Indiana 1984 - Indiana Dormant Minerals Act; ICLEF, Out of Country Seminar 1988 - Real Estate Litigation; ICLEF Practice Skills 1991, 1992, Real Estate (Co-Chair, 1992). Co-Author: "Avoiding the Will Contest," Res Gestae, May 1994, Probate and Property, May/June 1994; ICLEF, Basic Will Drafting (and other planning), Drafting to Avoid the Will Contest and Other Estate Litigation, 1994; "Yours, Mine and Ours, Estate Planning for Previously Married Couples," Res Gestae, June 1997; ICLEF, Planning Your First Probate Estate Administration - Recovery of Estate Assets, 1997; ICLEF, Untrust-Worthy Non-Probate Transfer - Creditor's Rights, 1998; ICLEF, Will and Trust Drafting Institute, Simple Will Drafting, 1999; ICLEF, Disclaimers and Post Mortem Planning, Administrative Decisions-Revising Documents, 1999; ICLEF, The Process of Probate Practice, Co-Chair, 2001. Hearing Officer, City of Evansville Department of Code Enforcement, 1999-2003. Past President: Rotary Club of Evansville; Harlexton Society of the University of Evansville. *Member:* Evansville (Director, 1996-2000; Chair, Probate Committee, 1997-1998; Chair, Elder Law Committee, 2000-2001), Indiana State (Director, Young Lawyers Section, 1984-1993; Chair, 1991-1992; Chair, General Practice Section, 1993-1994; Director, Chair, Specialization Committee, Real Property, Probate and Trust Section, 1996—; Delegate, House of Delegates, 1998) and American Bar Associations; Evansville Estate Planning Council; National Academy of Elder Law Attorneys. Fellow, Indiana Bar Foundation. **PRACTICE AREAS:** Wills; Trust Administration; Estate Administration; Estate Planning; Elder Law; Business Planning; Litigation. ***Email:*** bcarroll@jcglaw.com

THOMAS P. NORTON, born Evansville, Indiana, January 9, 1952; admitted to bar, 1977, Indiana and U.S. District Court, Southern District of Indiana. *Education:* Centre College of Kentucky (B.A., 1974); Cumberland School of Law of Samford University (J.D., 1977). Phi Alpha Delta. Assistant City Attorney, 1979. Board of Directors, ECHO Housing Corp. President, Visiting Nurse Plus, Inc., 1982—. *Member:* Evansville, Indiana State and American Bar Associations; Bar Association of the U.S. Court of Appeals, 7th Circuit; International Law Society. **PRACTICE AREAS:** Corporate and Commercial; Health Care; Family; Real Estate; Estate Planning and Administration.

DAVID W. KENT, born Evansville, Indiana, May 15, 1966; admitted to bar, 1992, Indiana and U.S. District Court, Southern District of Indiana. *Education:* University of Southern Indiana (B.S., 1988); Thomas M. Cooley Law School (J.D., 1991). Phi Alpha Delta. Board of Directors, Legal Aid Society, 2002—. Recipient, Doran E. Perdue Evansville Bar Association Service Award, 2002. Lecturer, "Planning Your First Divorce," ICLEF, 1997; "Ethical Issues in Family Law," ICLEF, Evansville Bar Association, 2000; "Everyday Ethics and Civility," ICLEF, Evansville Bar Association, 2001. *Member:* Evansville (Board of Directors, 1994; Chairman, Grievance Committee, 1999-2003), and Indiana State Bar Associations. **PRACTICE AREAS:** Litigation; Family Law; Criminal Defense. ***Email:*** dkent@jcglaw.com

J. AUGUST STRAUS, born Evansville, Indiana, August 13, 1974; admitted to bar, 2000, Indiana and U.S. District Court, Southern District of Indiana. *Education:* Arizona State University (B.A., summa cum laude, 1997); University of Memphis (J.D., 2000). Phi Alpha Delta. Recipient, Dean's Distinguished Service Award and CALI/Dean's Academic Excellence Award for ADR-Mediation. *Member:* Evansville (Chair: Mock Trials, 2002-2003; Young Lawyers, 2004) and Indiana State Bar Associations. **PRACTICE AREAS:** Civil Litigation; Criminal Defense; Personal Injury; Family Law. ***Email:*** astraus@jcglaw.com

RETIRED

JOHN L. CARROLL, born Chicago, Illinois, April 6, 1922; admitted to bar, 1948, Indiana; 1961, U.S. Supreme Court and U.S. Court of Appeals, Seventh Circuit. *Education:* Indiana University (A.B., 1946; J.D., 1948). Phi Delta Phi; Order of the Coif. Lecturer, Products Liability, Indiana University, 1969. Author: "Inverse Condemnation," Res Gestae, May, 1969. Co-Author: "The Primer on Indiana Rules of Procedure," Indiana State Bar Association, 1971; "Avoiding the Will Contest," Res Gestae, 1979; "Will Contests," Indiana Continuing Legal Education, 1980. *Member:* Evansville (President, 1970), Indiana

(This Listing Continued)

State (Treasurer, 1976-1977; Chairman, Public Relations Committee, 1977; Member, Board of Managers, 1978-1980; President, 1983-1984) and American Bar Associations; American Judicature Society. Fellow: American Bar Foundation; Indiana Bar Foundation. (Retired)

CHARLES C. GRIFFITH, born Evansville, Indiana, February 18, 1939; admitted to bar, 1966, Indiana. *Education:* Purdue University (B.S., 1960); Indiana University (J.D., 1966). Phi Delta Phi. Member, Adjunct Faculty, University of Evansville, 1978-1992. Member of Faculty, Indiana Trial Advocacy Skills Workshop, 1985—. *Member:* Evansville and Indiana State Bar Associations; Indiana Trial Lawyers Association (Member, Board of Directors, 1985-1993); The Association of Trial Lawyers of America. Fellow, American College of Trial Lawyers. [Lt. Supply Corps, U.S. Navy, 1960-1963]. (Retired). ***LANGUAGES:*** French. ***PRACTICE AREAS:*** Litigation; Family Law; Social Security Disability; Workers Compensation.

COUNSEL FOR: QADCO; Lensing Wholesale, Inc.; Black Beauty Resources, Inc.; Black Beauty Coal Company; Wannemuehler Oil Co.; Tri-State Communications, Inc.; Arc Construction Co., Inc.; Lloyds Old Fashioned Ice Cream, Inc.; Donut Bank, Inc.; MidWest Roofing & Sheetmetal, Inc.; Curran Miller Auction & Realty, Inc.; Paint and Carpet Depot; Hamrick's Recovery Service; Alfab Metals Corporation; G.T. Engineering, Inc.; Ansul, Inc. Ohio Valley Plastics, Inc.; Multi Seal, Inc.; University of Evansville; Visiting Nurse Association of Southwestern Indiana; Walgrove Corporation.
REFERENCES: First Federal Savings Bank; Old National Bank in Evansville.
AGENT FOR: National Attorneys Title Assurance Ford, Inc.

KAHN, DEES, DONOVAN & KAHN, LLP

Established in 1908

FIFTH MAIN FINANCIAL PLAZA, SUITE 305
P.O. BOX 3646
EVANSVILLE, INDIANA 47735-3646
Telephone: 812-423-3183
Fax: 812-423-3841
Email: evvlaw@k2d2.com
URL: http://www.k2d2.com

General Civil Practice including Litigation, Environmental, Labor Management, Corporate, Pension, Banking, Hospital, Insurance Defense, Real Estate, Workers' Compensation, Tax, Construction, Immigration and General Civil Law.

FIRM PROFILE: We are a member of Meritas (formerly Commercial Law Affiliates), a worldwide affiliation of independent business and litigation law firms.

MEMBERS OF FIRM

ISIDOR KAHN (1887-1963)

HARRY P. DEES (1912-2004)

ARTHUR R. DONOVAN (1910-2000)

ROBERT KAHN (1918-1999)

ALAN N. SHOVERS, born Racine, Wisconsin, 1939; admitted to bar, 1964, Wisconsin, Illinois; 1968, Indiana. *Education:* University of Wisconsin (B.B.A., 1961; J.D., 1964). Order of the Coif. Member, Board of Editors, Wisconsin Law Review, 1963-1964. Certified Public Accountant, Wisconsin, 1967 and Indiana, 1968. ***PRACTICE AREAS:*** Federal Income; Estate Planning; Gift Estate Taxation; Business; Healthcare. ***Email:*** alanshovers@k2d2.com

THOMAS O. MAGAN, born Evansville, Indiana, 1942; admitted to bar, 1970, Indiana. *Education:* DePauw University (A.B., 1964); Indiana University (J.D., cum laude, 1970). Staff Member, Indiana University Law Journal, 1969-1970. ***PRACTICE AREAS:*** Labor and Employment (Management) Law; College and University Law; Litigation. ***Email:*** tommagan@k2d2.com

LARRY R. DOWNS, born Michigan City, Indiana, 1948; admitted to bar, 1974, Indiana. *Education:* DePauw University (B.A., 1970); Indiana University (J.D., 1974). ***PRACTICE AREAS:*** Employment Discrimination Law; Labor and Employment (Management) Law; Municipal Law. ***Email:*** larrydowns@k2d2.com

JON D. GOLDMAN, born Evansville, Indiana, 1951; admitted to bar, 1977, Indiana. *Education:* Indiana University (B.A., 1973); Brown University (1974); Illinois Institute of Technology, Chicago-Kent College of Law (J.D., 1977). ***PRACTICE AREAS:*** Employment Litigation; Management Labor Law; Employment Discrimination; Regulatory Compliance; Union Elections. ***Email:*** jongoldman@k2d2.com

BRIAN P. WILLIAMS, born Evansville, Indiana, 1956; admitted to bar, 1981, Indiana. *Education:* Indiana University (A.B., 1978; J.D., 1981). *Member:* Evansville Bar Association (President, 2004-2005; Board Member, 1997-2005). ***PRACTICE AREAS:*** Federal Practice; Contract Law; Litigation; Employment Litigation; Economic Development. ***Email:*** brianwilliams@k2d2.com

G. MICHAEL SCHOPMEYER, born Terre Haute, Indiana, 1958; admitted to bar, 1983, Indiana. *Education:* University of Evansville (B.S., 1980); Indiana University (J.D., 1983). Chairperson, Metro. Evansville Chamber of Commerce, 2005. *Member:* Indiana State Bar Association (Past Chairman, Environmental Law Section, 2002). ***PRACTICE AREAS:*** Alternative Dispute Resolution; Commercial Transactions; Construction; Environmental; Property Tax; Real Property; Intellectual Property. ***Email:*** mikeschopmeyer@k2d2.com

JOHN E. HEGEMAN, born St. Louis, Missouri, 1948; admitted to bar, 1985, Indiana. *Education:* St. Louis University (A.B., 1972); Indiana University (J.D., 1985). ***PRACTICE AREAS:*** Estate Planning, Probate and Trusts; Business; Taxation; Independent Adoption; General Civil Practice; Healthcare Law. ***Email:*** johnhegeman@k2d2.com

JEFFREY K. HELFRICH, born Evansville, Indiana, 1959; admitted to bar, 1985, Indiana; 1992, Kentucky. *Education:* Indiana University (B.S., 1982; J.D., cum laude, 1985). ***PRACTICE AREAS:*** Mergers and Acquisitions; Business Law; Real Estate; Banking; Corporate Law; Healthcare. ***Email:*** jeffhelfrich@k2d2.com

(This Listing Continued)

JEFFREY W. AHLERS, born Tulsa, Oklahoma, 1962; admitted to bar, 1987, Indiana. *Education:* DePauw University (B.A., 1984); Valparaiso University (J.D., 1987). Delta Theta Phi. Mock Trial Team. Attorney for Vanderburgh county Council, 1997—. ***PRACTICE AREAS:*** Commercial Litigation; Insurance Defense; Personal Injury; Products Liability; Negligence Litigation; Employment Litigation; Environmental Litigation. ***Email:*** ahlers@k2d2.com

KENT A. BRASSEALE II, born Dayton, Ohio, 1967; admitted to bar, 1993, Indiana. *Education:* Purdue University (B.S., 1990); Indiana University (J.D., 1993). ***PRACTICE AREAS:*** Environmental Law; Real Estate Law; Construction Law; Business Corporate Law; Trademark Law; Copyright Law. ***Email:*** kentbrasseale@k2d2.com

CHRISTOPHER D. LEE, born Bedford, Indiana, October 20, 1966; admitted to bar, 1993, Indiana. *Education:* DePauw University (B.A., 1989); Indiana University (J.D., 1993). *Member:* Defense Trial Counsel of Indiana; Defense Research Institute (Asbestos, Mass tort, Automotive and Product Liability Practice Sections); National Institute of Trial Advocacy. ***PRACTICE AREAS:*** Product Liability; Toxic Tort Litigation; Complex Litigation; Mass Tort Litigation; Civil Litigation; Insurance Defense. ***Email:*** chrislee@k2d2.com

MARK S. SAMILA, born Mexico, Missouri, July 28, 1964; admitted to bar, 1989, Missouri; 1990, Illinois; 1998, Indiana. *Education:* University of Missouri (B.S., Accounting, with honors, 1986; J.D., 1989). Certified Public Accountant Missouri. ***PRACTICE AREAS:*** Business Law; Commercial Transactions; Bankruptcy; Creditors Rights; Taxation; Employee Benefits; Estate Planning. ***Email:*** marksamila@k2d2.com

ROBERT F. "TED" BARRON II, born Evansville, Indiana, September 17, 1957; admitted to bar, 1997, Indiana and Kentucky. *Education:* Indiana University (B.A., 1979; J.D., cum laude, 1996); University of Missouri (M.B.A., 1990). Assistant Editor, Indiana Law Journal, 1996. ***LANGUAGES:*** Spanish and Portuguese. ***PRACTICE AREAS:*** Healthcare; Employment; Business Law. ***Email:*** tedbarron@k2d2.com

ALLISON K. COMSTOCK, born Evansville, Indiana, March 12, 1970; admitted to bar, 1994, Indiana. *Education:* Azusa Pacific University (B.A., magna cum laude, 1991); Southwestern University School of Law (J.D., cum laude, 1993). ***PRACTICE AREAS:*** Real Estate; Estate Planning; Commercial Transactions; Probate; Trusts. ***Email:*** allisoncomstock@k2d2.com

STEVEN S. HOAR, born West Point, Nebraska, April 3, 1972; admitted to bar, 1997, Indiana. *Education:* DePauw University (B.A., cum laude, 1994); Indiana University (J.D., 1997). Recipient, CALI Award for Trial Process. ***PRACTICE AREAS:*** Commercial Litigation; Construction Litigation; Creditors Rights; Consumer Litigation; Bankruptcy Litigation; Real Estate Litigation. ***Email:*** stevehoar@k2d2.com

TODD C. BARSUMIAN, born Pittsburgh, Pennsylvania, August 24, 1973; admitted to bar, 1998, Indiana; 2001, Kentucky. *Education:* Hanover College (B.A., 1995); Drake University Law School (J.D., with honors, 1998). Member, 1997-1998, Drake Law Review. Recipient, CALI Award for Constitutional Law. ***Email:*** toddbarsumian@k2d2.com

ASSOCIATES

MARIA TALBERT WORTHINGTON, born Bloomington, Indiana, August 5, 1971; admitted to bar, 1997, Indiana. *Education:* University of Evansville (B.S., 1994; B.A., 1994); Indiana University (J.D., 1997). ***LANGUAGES:*** Spanish. ***Email:*** mariaworthington@k2d2.com

AMY E. STEINHART, born Wyandotte, Michigan, July 2, 1972; admitted to bar, 1997, Indiana. *Education:* Indiana University (B.A., 1994; J.D., 1997). ***Email:*** amysteinhart@k2d2.com

KRISTI PRUTOW CIRIGNANO, born Bartlesville, Oklahoma, August 8, 1975; admitted to bar, 2000, Indiana. *Education:* John Brown University (B.A., 1997); Indiana University, Bloomington (J.D., 2000). Member, Order of the Barristers. Recipient: CALI Award, Constitutional Litigation. *Member:* Defense Trial Counsel of Indiana. ***Email:*** kristicirignano@k2d2.com

MONICA E. EDWARDS, born Ft. Bragg, North Carolina, August 2, 1972; admitted to bar, 2000, Indiana. *Education:* Southern Methodist University (B.S., Chemistry, 1994; M.S., Environmental, 1996); University of Louisville (J.D., 2000). ***Email:*** monicaedwards@k2d2.com

MICHAEL E. DiRIENZO, born Cleveland, Ohio, October 9, 1973; admitted to bar, 2001, Indiana. *Education:* Franciscan University of Steubenville (B.A., 1997); University of Notre Dame (J.D., 2001). ***Email:*** mikedirienzo@k2d2.com

GREG J. FREYBERGER, born Jasper, Indiana, April 20, 1976; admitted to bar, 2001, Indiana. *Education:* Indiana State University (B.S., 1998); Indiana University (J.D., 2001). ***Email:*** gregfreyberger@k2d2.com

JACOB R. FULCHER, born Bloomington, Indiana, October 24, 1976; admitted to bar, 2002, Indiana. *Education:* University of Southern Indiana (B.S., 1999); California Western School of Law (J.D., 2001). Pro Bono Honors Society, California Western School of Law. ***Email:*** jakefulcher@k2d2.com

ELIZABETH A. BROWNING, born Manchester, Kentucky, April 5, 1974; admitted to bar, 2002, Indiana. *Education:* University of Kentucky (B.A., 1999); Indiana University, Bloomington (J.D., cum laude, 2002). Phi Delta Phi, 1999—. ***Email:*** bethbrowning@k2d2.com

KEVIN R. MARTIN, born Evansville, Indiana, May 24, 1976; admitted to bar, 2001, Indiana. *Education:* Indiana University, Kelley School of Business (B.S., Accounting, 1998); Indiana University School of Law (J.D., 2001). ***Email:*** kevinmartin@k2d2.com

ROBIN MICHELLE EVERNHAM, born Fort Thomas, Kentucky, April 30, 1978; admitted to bar, 2003, Indiana. *Education:* University of Kentucky (B.A., 2000); University of Louisville (J.D., 2003). ***Email:*** robinevernham@k2d2.com

CARRIE M. ROELLE, born October 20, 1972; admitted to bar, 2001, Colorado; 2004, Indiana. *Education:* Indiana University (B.S., Kinesiology, 1995); University of Denver College of Law (J.D., 2001). ***PRACTICE AREAS:*** Ski Area Liability. ***Email:*** carrieroelle@k2d2.com

(This Listing Continued)

KAHN, DEES, DONOVAN & KAHN, LLP, Evansville—Continued

COUNSEL FOR: Deaconess Hospital, Inc.; Wabash General Hospital; The Rehabilitation Center, Inc.; University of Southern Indiana; AIG/American General Financial Group; AK Steel Corporation; Anchor Industries, Inc.; Buchta Leasing, Inc.; Card Management Corporation; Champion Laboratories, Inc. div of United Component Parts; Crescent Plastics, Inc.; Cresline Plastic Pipe Co., Inc.; DSM Engineering Plastics, Inc.; Fifth Third Bank; Integra Bank; J.H. Rudolph & Co., Inc.; George Koch Sons, Inc.; Keller Crescent Company, Inc.; Lewis Bakeries, Inc.; Mulzer Companies; Princeton Mining Company, Inc.; Raben Tire Co., Inc.; Red Spot Paint & Varnish Co., Inc.; rsc THE QUALITY MEASUREMENT COMPANY; Sterling Boiler & Mechanical Inc.; Toyota Motor Corporate Services of North America, Inc.; Wabash Plastics, Inc.
REPRESENTATIVE LABOR CLIENTS: Airtex Products; Frontier-Kemper Constructors, Inc.; Gibbs Die Casting Aluminum Corporation; Holm Industries, Inc.; Ideal-American Dairy; Jasper Chair Company; JOFCO, Inc.; Lancaster Colony; Lear Corporation; Mid-State Rubber Products, Inc.; Modern Welding Company, Inc.; Quality Manufacturing, Inc.; Refreshment Services, Inc.; Springfield Pepsi-Cola Bottling Company; Tyco Electronics Corporation; UniFirst Corporation; University of Evansville; West Irving Die Casting of Kentucky, Inc.; Young Manufacturing Co., Inc.
REPRESENTATIVE INSURANCE CLIENTS: AFLAC, Inc.; Allstate Insurance Co.; Kemper Insurance Companies; London Market Insurers; The St. Paul Travelers Insurance Company; Country Mutual Insurance Companies; Grocers Insurance Company; Kentucky Farm Bureau; State Farm Insurance Companies.

KECK & FOLZ

420 MAIN STREET, SUITE 1402
P.O. BOX 3437
EVANSVILLE, INDIANA 47733-3437
Telephone: 812-424-5558
Fax: 812-428-6617
Email: keckfolz@evansville.net

General Civil Practice in all State and Federal Courts. Probate Administration and Estate Planning, Corporation, Real Estate, Trials, Tax, Commercial and Administrative Law, General Litigation, Mediation, Labor and Employment.

MEMBERS OF FIRM

DAVID M. KECK (1934-2002)

FREDERICK R. FOLZ, born Evansville, Indiana, September 13, 1951; admitted to bar, 1976, Indiana. *Education:* Vanderbilt University (B.A., with honors, 1973); Indiana University School of Law (J.D., with honors, 1976). Associate Editor, IUSTITIA, Indiana University, 1975-1976. Law Clerk to Hon. Cale J. Holder, Judge, U.S. District Court for the Southern District of Indiana, 1976-1978. Certified Mediator. *Member:* Evansville and Indiana State Bar Associations. ***PRACTICE AREAS:*** Probate Administration; Trusts; Real Estate; Civil Practice; Mediation; Corporate Law; Estate Planning.

ASSOCIATE

ANDREW S. WARD, born St. Johnsbury, Vermont, July 24, 1961; admitted to bar, 1988, Illinois; 1990, U.S. District Court, Southern District of Indiana; 1991, Indiana, U.S. District Court, Northern District of Indiana, U.S. Court of Appeals, Seventh Circuit. *Education:* University of Vermont (B.A., 1983); Indiana University School of Law (J.D., 1988). Law Clerk to Judge William G. Hussmann, Jr., U.S. Magistrate, Southern District of Indiana, 1988-1991. Licensed Vermont Real Estate Broker, 1982—. National Association of Realtors, 1982-1985. Member, Indiana Worker's Compensation Board, Indianapolis, Indiana, 1997—. *Member:* Illinois State, Indiana State and American (Member, Labor Law Section) Bar Associations. ***PRACTICE AREAS:*** Labor and Employment; Probate Administration; Civil Practice.

REFERENCES: Old National Bank in Evansville; Fifth Third Bank (Evansville); Integra Bank.

KIGHTLINGER & GRAY, LLP

7311 EAGLE CREST BLVD.
EVANSVILLE, INDIANA 47715
Telephone: 812-474-4400
Telecopier: 812-474-4414
Email: info@k-glaw.com
URL: http://www.k-glaw.com

Indianapolis, Indiana Office: Market Square Center, Suite 600, 151 North Delaware Street, 46204. Telephone: 317-638-4521. Telecopier: 317-636-5917.
New Albany, Indiana Office: One Commerce Square, 4106 Charlestown Road, 47150. Telephone: 812-949-2300. Telecopier: 812-949-8556.

Civil Litigation, Commercial and Business Litigation, Drug and Medical Device Litigation, Environmental and Toxic Tort Litigation, Casualty, Surety and Life Insurance Law, General Litigation, Malpractice Litigation (Pharmacy, Medical, Legal, Architects and Engineers, Accountants, Insurance Agents, Real Estate Agents and School Boards), Products Liability Law, Trucking Defense Litigation, Construction Law, ICC Regulatory Law, Appeals (State and Federal), Worker's Compensation, Maritime Law, Civil Rights and Wrongful Discharge Law, All areas of Government Liability, including Law Enforcement Liability Litigation, Class Actions, Labor Law, Securities Litigation.

RESIDENT PARTNERS

BRENT R. WEIL, born Evansville, Indiana, June 5, 1960; admitted to bar, 1985, Indiana and Michigan; U.S. District Court, Northern and Southern Districts of Indiana; U.S. Court of Appeals, Seventh Circuit; U.S. Supreme Court. *Education:* Purdue University (B.S., 1982); Valparaiso University (J.D., 1985). Phi Alpha Delta; Alpha Chi Sigma. Selected by Law & Politics magazine as an "Indiana Super Lawyer," 2004 and 2005. Deputy Prosecuting Attorney, First Judicial Court, 1991—. Member: Board of Directors, Albion Fellows Bacon Domestic Violence Center, 1992—; Purdue University Alumni Association. *Member:* Evansville and Indiana State Bar Associations; State Bar of Michigan; Defense Trial Counsel of Indiana (named Diplomat, 2004); Defense Research Institute; Indiana Bar Foundation (Master Fellow); Brooks American Inns of Court (Master). ***PRACTICE***

(This Listing Continued)

AREAS: General Liability Litigation; Toxic Exposure; Construction Accident Litigation; Police Liability Law; Professional Malpractice Litigation; Alternative Dispute Resolution; Insurance Defense; Insurance Bad Faith Defense; Arson and Insurance Fraud; Automobile Insurance Defense; Automobile Insurance Fraud Defense; Automobile Liability Defense; Casualty Insurance Defense; Disability Insurance Defense; Fire Insurance Defense; First and Third Party Insurance Defense; General Liability Defense; Insurance Coverage Defense; Insurance Defense Subrogation; Personal Liability Defense; Property Damage Defense; Property Insurance Defense; Business Law; Business Litigation; Civil Rights; Civil Rights Defense; Commercial Law; Commercial Litigation; Real Estate; Condominium Law; Construction Law; Construction Insurance Defense; Construction Insurance; Construction Liability; Construction Litigation; Election Law; Estate Planning; Estate Litigation; Trust Litigation; Trust Law; Probate; Probate Litigation; Guardianship; Civil Litigation; Complex Litigation; Defense Litigation; Federal Civil Litigation; Trial Practice; U.S. Supreme Court Litigation; Medical Malpractice; Medical Malpractice Defense; Nonprofit and Charitable Organizations; Nonprofit Organizations Law; Occupational Safety and Health; OSHA; Personal Injury; Personal Injury Defense; Products Liability; Products Liability Defense; Products Liability Insurance Coverage; Products Liability Subrogation; Toxic Torts; Transportation; Common Carrier Liability Law; Motor Carrier Defense; Motor Carrier Liability; Transportation Liability; Truck Accidents; Trucking Law; Trucking Liability; Law Enforcement Liability; Law Enforcement Officers Rights; Police Liability; Police Liability Defense; Law Enforcement. ***Email:*** bweil@k-glaw.com

RICHARD O. HAWLEY, JR., born Pittsburg, Kansas, 1965; admitted to bar, 1991, Indiana; U.S. District Court, Northern and Southern Districts of Indiana. *Education:* DePauw University (B.A., cum laude, 1988); Ohio State University (J.D., with honors, 1991). Fellowship, University of Chicago Graduate School of Business, 1987. Assistant to Vanderburgh County Attorney, 1991-1993. Tell City-Troy Township School Board Attorney, 1992-1994. Speaker: Environmental Law Update Seminar, 1994-1997; Commercial Law Affiliates Annual Conference, 1997. Volunteer: Leadership Evansville; Signature School Intern Program; National Forensic League Judge; Big Brothers/Big Sisters, Counsel for United Caring Shelters. *Member:* Evansville and Indiana State (Member, Litigation Section) Bar Associations; Defense Research Institute. ***PRACTICE AREAS:*** Commercial Litigation; Civil Litigation; Eminent Domain; Insurance Defense; Insurance Coverage Defense; Litigation; Complex Litigation; Personal Injury; Personal Injury Defense; Products Liability; Products Liability Defense; Transportation; Common Carrier Liability Law; Motor Carrier Defense; Motor Carrier Liability; Transportation Liability; Truck Accidents; Trucking Law; Trucking Liability. ***Email:*** rhawley@k-glaw.com

RESIDENT ASSOCIATES

SACHA L. ARMSTRONG, born Hays, Kansas, January 18, 1975; admitted to bar, 2003, Kentucky; 2004, Indiana. *Education:* University of Maryland (B.A., 1999); University of Louisville (J.D., 2003). Staff Member, 2001-2002 and Editor, 2002-2003, Brandeis Law Journal. Law Clerk to: Charles F. Merz & Associates, 2001-2002; Vaughn & Pride, PLLC, 2002. Paralegal, Merle F. Maffei, P.A., 2000. Russian Translator and Training Manager for the U.S. Navy, National Security Agency. Member, Kentucky Legal Aid Society, Louisville, Kentucky, 2001-2002. *Member:* Evansville, Henderson County, Kentucky and Indiana State Bar Associations; Defense Research Institute; Kentucky Young Lawyers' Association. ***LANGUAGES:*** Russian, French. ***PRACTICE AREAS:*** Civil Practice; Litigation; Civil Litigation; Federal Civil Litigation; Defense Litigation; Federal Litigation; Trial Practice; Workers Compensation; Workers Compensation Defense. ***Email:*** sarmstrong@k-glaw.com

CURTIS D. CONDICT, born Evansville, Indiana, May 26, 1978; admitted to bar, 2003, Indiana; U.S. District Court, Northern and Southern Districts of Indiana. *Education:* DePauw University (B.A., 2000); Indiana University School of Law (J.D., 2003). Former Board Member, Youth Services Bureau. *Member:* Indiana State and American Bar Associations. ***PRACTICE AREAS:*** Collections; Commercial Collections; Commercial Litigation; Contracts; Contract Litigation; Criminal Law; Criminal Defense; Labor and Employment; Employment Defense; Employment Law; Labor Law; Insurance Defense; Arson and Insurance Fraud; Fire Insurance Defense; First and Third Party Insurance Defense; Insurance Coverage Defense; Insurance Defense Subrogation; Defense Litigation; Trial Practice; Complex Litigation; Medical Malpractice; Medical Malpractice Defense; Personal Injury; Personal Injury Defense; Products Liability; Products Liability Subrogation; Products Liability Defense; Products Liability Insurance Coverage. ***Email:*** ccondict@k-glaw.com

CHAD M. SMITH, born Vincennes, Indiana, November 11, 1976; admitted to bar, 2002, Indiana; U.S. District Court, Northern and Southern Districts of Indiana. *Education:* Indiana University (B.S., Finance, 1999); Indiana University School of Law at Indianapolis (J.D., 2002). *Member:* Indianapolis (Member, Sections on: Litigation; Young Lawyers), Indiana State (Member, Sections on: Litigation; Young Lawyers) and American (Member, Sections on: Labor and Employment; Litigation; Tort and Insurance Practice; Young Lawyers) Bar Associations; Defense Research Institute; Defense Trial Counsel of Indiana (Member, Sections on: Medical Malpractice; Insurance Coverage; Employment Law; Business Litigation). ***PRACTICE AREAS:*** Insurance Defense; First and Third Party Insurance Defense; Litigation; Complex Litigation; Defense Litigation; Trial Practice; Personal Injury; Personal Injury Defense; Products Liability; Products Liability Defense; Civil Litigation; Federal Civil Litigation; Federal Litigation. ***Email:*** csmith@k-glaw.com

(For complete biographical data on Indianapolis, Indiana and New Albany, Indiana personnel, see Professional Biographies at those locations)

LOCKYEAR KORNBLUM & MACER LLP

555 SYCAMORE STREET
P.O. BOX 3515
EVANSVILLE, INDIANA 47734
Telephone: 812-422-1199
Fax: 812-426-0779
Email: info@lockyear-kornblum.com
URL: http://www.lockyear-kornblum.com

Personal Injury Law and Trials. Class Actions. General Civil Practice in all State and Federal Courts. Appellate Practice.

(This Listing Continued)

MEMBERS OF FIRM

THEODORE LOCKYEAR (1929-2004)

JAMES A. KORNBLUM, born Evansville, Indiana, August 3, 1951; admitted to bar, 1977, Indiana and U.S. District Court, Southern District of Indiana; 1978, U.S. Court of Appeals, Seventh Circuit; U.S. Supreme Court. *Education:* Ball State University and University of Evansville (B.A., 1973); Indiana University (J.D., 1977). Certified Civil Mediator. *Member:* Indiana State Bar Association (Chair, Litigation Section, 1996-1997); The Association of Trial Lawyers of America; Indiana Trial Lawyers Association; First Amendment Lawyers Association; Evansville Association of Criminal Defense Attorneys. Brooks Inns of Court. ***PRACTICE AREAS:*** Automobile Accidents and Injuries; Wrongful Death; Labor and Employment; Criminal Law; Divorce. ***Email:*** jkornblum@lockyear-kornblum.com

B. MICHAEL MACER, born Evansville, Indiana, July 28, 1972; admitted to bar, 1997, Indiana, U.S. District Court, Northern and Southern Districts of Indiana. *Education:* University of Evansville (B.S., 1994); Indiana University School of Law (J.D., 1997). *Member:* Evansville and Indiana State Bar Associations; The Association of Trial Lawyers of America; Indiana Trial Lawyers Association. Brooks Inns of Court. ***PRACTICE AREAS:*** Automobile Accidents and Injuries; Employment Discrimination; Divorce; Probate; Civil Litigation. ***Email:*** mmacer@lockyear-kornblum.com

MILLER & ASSOCIATES

915 MAIN STREET
SUITE 408
P.O. BOX 3009
EVANSVILLE, INDIANA 47730-3009
Telephone: 812-425-1490 Toll Free: 1-888-279-0947
Fax: 812-425-3493
URL: http://www.indianalawonline.com

General Litigation, Small Business, Labor and Employment Law, Real Estate, Taxation, Collections, Debtor and Creditor Law, Federal Practice, Commercial Law, Personal Injury, Family Law, Estate Planning.

FIRM PROFILE: Miller & Associates is dedicated to providing complete efficient and effective legal representation to businesses and individuals throughout southwestern Indiana. The firm enjoys strong community ties and is active in civic affairs.

MARK E. MILLER, born Evansville, Indiana, August 8, 1957; admitted to bar, 1984, Connecticut and U.S. District Court, District of Connecticut; 1985, Indiana and U.S. District Court, Northern and Southern Districts of Indiana; 1990, U.S. Supreme Court; 1991, U.S. Court of Appeals, 7th Circuit. *Education:* Wesleyan University (B.A., cum laude, with honors, 1979); University of Connecticut (J.D., 1984). Publication: "An Analysis of Tort Reform In Indiana," Vol. 17, Verdict 3, 10. Member: Citizens Commission for the Future of Indiana Courts, 1996-2000; Juries for the 21st Century, 1998-2000. Board of Directors: National Issues Forms Institute, Washington, D.C., 1995-1999; Indiana Civil Liberties Union, Indianapolis, Indiana, 1999—. *Member:* Evansville and Indiana State Bar Associations; Brooks American Inn of Court #36 (Master). ***LANGUAGES:*** French. ***REPORTED CASES:*** 7th Circuit 160 Federal 3rd 409; 7th Circuit 969 F.2d 585. ***PRACTICE AREAS:*** General Litigation; Small Business; Commercial Law; Labor and Employment; Real Estate; Estate Planning; Collections; Debtor and Creditor; Family Law; Personal Injury. ***Email:*** mmiller@indianalawonline.com

ASSOCIATE

DOUGLAS S. WALTON, born Evansville, Indiana, September 30, 1973; admitted to bar, 2000, Indiana and U.S. District Court, Northern and Southern Districts of Indiana. *Education:* University of Southern Indiana (B.A., 1996); Valparaiso University (J.D., 2000). *Member:* Evansville Bar Association. ***LANGUAGES:*** Spanish. ***PRACTICE AREAS:*** Criminal Defense; Civil Litigation; Personal Injury; Probate. ***Email:*** dwalton@indianalawonline.com

OLSEN, WHITE & HAMBIDGE, LLP

123 LOCUST STREET
EVANSVILLE, INDIANA 47708-1488
Telephone: 812-423-3143
Fax: 812-429-0448
URL: http://www.thelawteam.net

Probate, Business Law, Family Law, Wills, Personal Injury, Criminal Law, Real Estate.

MEMBERS OF FIRM

OLE J. OLSEN, JR., born 1937; admitted to bar, 1961, Indiana. *Education:* University of Evansville (B.S., 1958); Vanderbilt University (J.D., 1961). *Member:* Evansville and Indiana State Bar Associations. ***PRACTICE AREAS:*** Probate (45%); Business Law (17%); Family Law (16%); Wills (22%). ***Email:*** ojo@thelawteam.net

TERRY A. WHITE, born Princeton, Indiana, April 23, 1953; admitted to bar, 1978, Indiana and U.S. District Court, Southern District of Indiana. *Education:* University of Evansville (B.A., cum laude, 1975); Indiana University (J.D., 1978). Phi Alpha Delta (Vice-Justice, 1978); Blue Key. Member, Indiana Law Review, 1977-1978. Deputy Prosecutor, 1979—. *Member:* Evansville and American Bar Associations. ***PRACTICE AREAS:*** Personal Injury (25%); Criminal Law (21%); Family Law (13%); Probate Law (4%). ***Email:*** taw@thelawteam.net

TIMOTHY J. HAMBIDGE, born South Bend, Indiana, January 18, 1957; admitted to bar, 1982, Indiana, U.S. District Court, Northern and Southern Districts of Indiana and U.S. Court of Appeals, Seventh Circuit; 2003, U.S. Supreme Court. *Education:* Purdue University (B.A., 1979); Indiana University (J.D., 1982). Phi Delta Phi. Hearing Officer, Indiana State Employee's Appeal Commission, 1980-1982. *Member:* Evansville and Indiana State Bar Associations; Bar Association for the Seventh Circuit; Indiana Trial Lawyers Association; Brooks American Inns of Court (Charter Member, 1987-1992). ***PRACTICE AREAS:*** Personal Injury (36%); Business Law (16%); Family Law (25%); Probate; Real Estate (3%). ***Email:*** tjh@thelawteam.net

(This Listing Continued)

JILL DEWIG WESCH, born Evansville, Indiana, April 27, 1977; admitted to bar, 2004, Indiana, U.S. District Court, Southern District of Indiana. *Education:* University of Southern Indiana (B.S., 2000); Valparaiso University School of Law (J.D., 2004). Phi Alpha Delta (Justice, 2003). *Member:* Evansville, Gibson County, Indiana State and American Bar Associations; Indiana Trial Lawyers Association. ***PRACTICE AREAS:*** Personal Injury (35%); Family Law (34%); Bankruptcy (10%); Probate (5%).

RHINE, ERNEST & VARGO

Established in 1979

OLD NATIONAL PLACE
ONE MAIN STREET, SUITE 600
EVANSVILLE, INDIANA 47708
Telephone: 812-759-0600
Fax: 812-759-0601
Email: information@rhinelaw.com

Mount Carmel, Illinois Office: 631 Market Street, 62863-1489. Telephone: 618-262-8611. Fax: 618-262-7145. URL: http://www.rhinelaw.com.

Coal, Oil and Gas Law, Real Estate, Corporate, Civil Trial Practice, Wills and Estates, Environmental Law.

REPRESENTATIVE CLIENTS: Foundation Coal Co.; Southern Illinois Land Co.; Sahara Coal Trust; Sahara Enterprises; Cline Resources and Development; Kieffer Bros. Construction Co.; Royal Talon; Old National Bank; Ayrshire Land Company; Vigo Coal Company; Wabash Mine Holding Company; Delta Mine Holding Company; Ameren Energy Fuels; Wabash Community District-348; Arclar Company; Peabody Coal Company, Friendsville Mine, LLC; Black Beauty Coal Company; Koester Companies; Pond River Coal Company.

(For complete biographical data on all personnel, see Professional Biographies at Mount Carmel, Illinois)

RUDOLPH, FINE, PORTER & JOHNSON LLP

Established in 1987

221 N.W. FIFTH STREET
P.O. BOX 1507
EVANSVILLE, INDIANA 47706
Telephone: 812-422-9444
Fax: 812-421-7459
Email: rfpj@rfpj.com
URL: http://www.rfpj.com

General Corporate Practice. Health Care Law, Commercial Litigation, Insurance Defense, Real Estate, Zoning and Land Use Law, Mediation and Arbitration, Bankruptcy Law, Mergers and Acquisitions. Probate and Estate Planning, Tax, Employment Law, Appeals, Banking. Trials in all State and Federal Courts.

FIRM PROFILE: Rudolph, Fine, Porter & Johnson LLP was established in 1987 and is dedicated to providing clients high quality and cost effective representation. Our attorneys and staff utilize a team approach to serving clients and the latest technological legal research tools and support systems allow the firm to provide clients with reliable legal advice in a prompt and efficient manner. The firm divides its professional services between a litigation department, which includes formal court proceedings, mediation and arbitration, and a corporate department, which includes all matters of business, real estate, tax, banking, employment and labor law. The firm provides title insurance and closing services for its real estate clients. Lawyers of the firm participate as speakers in seminars and regularly serve on boards of both legal and community associations. The firm is a medium sized firm for its geographic region and well suited to provide quality legal services to local and regional corporate and business clients, and to meet the litigation needs of many regional and national insurance and publicly owned companies.

This firm is included in the Bar Register of Preeminent Lawyers and in A.M. Best's Directory of Recommended Insurance Attorneys.

This firm is a member of Netlink Legal Alliance, a global alliance of independent law firms.

MEMBERS OF FIRM

ROSS E. RUDOLPH, born Evansville, Indiana, May 31, 1955; admitted to bar, 1980, Indiana and U.S. District Court, Southern District of Indiana. *Education:* Miami University, Oxford, Ohio (B.A., cum laude, 1977); Indiana University (J.D., 1980). Phi Beta Kappa; Phi Delta Phi. Indiana Certification in Alternative Dispute Resolution Civil Mediation, August 1992, re-certified 1996 and 2001. Seminar Chair, " Drafting Injunctions: A Desk Reference," Indiana Continuing Legal Education Forum, April 2001. Co-Seminar Chair, "60 Things You Need to Know About Taking Your Case to Mediation," Indiana Continuing Legal Education Forum, November 1998. Author/Instructor: "The Injunctions Kit," Indiana Continuing Legal Education Forum Seminar, May, 1995; "Uninsured and Underinsured Motorist Coverage," Indiana Continuing Legal Education Forum Seminar, March 1991. *Member:* Evansville Bar Association (Chairman, Diversity Task Force, 2004—); Indiana State Bar Association; Defense Research Institute; Defense Trial Counsel of Indiana; Brooks American Inns of Court (President, 1998-2000); Vanderburgh County Public Defender Board (Secretary, 1999-2003; President, 2003—); Association of Trial Lawyers of America (Associate Member, 2001—); Vanderburgh County Community Corrections Board (1998-2000). Fellow, Indiana Bar Foundation. ***REPORTED CASES:*** Ackerman v. Northwestern Mutual Life Insurance Company, 172 F.2d 467; Northwestern Mutual Life Insurance Company v. Stinnett, 698 N.E.2d 1236; Citizens National Bank of Evansville vs., Foster 668 N.E. 2d. 1236; Meyers v. Furrow Building Materials, 659 N.E.2d 1147; Koenig v. Bedell and Aetna Insurance Company, 601 N.E. 2d 453; Aetna Casualty & Surety Com-

(This Listing Continued)

RUDOLPH, FINE, PORTER & JOHNSON LLP, Evansville—Continued

pany v. Crafton, 551 N.E. 2d 893; Johnson v. Payne and National Insurance Association, 549 N.E. 2d 48. ***PRACTICE AREAS:*** Mediation; Insurance Defense Law; Arbitration; Products Liability; Commercial Litigation. ***Email:*** rer@rfpj.com

MARC D. FINE, born Evansville, Indiana, July 23, 1959; admitted to bar, 1984, Indiana, Florida and U.S. District Court, Southern and Northern Districts of Indiana. *Education:* Indiana University (B.S. with distinction, 1981); University of Illinois (J.D., 1984). Beta Gamma Sigma; Phi Alpha Delta. Author/Instructor: "Differences Between Living Trusts, Wills, and Wills with Testamentary Trusts," Indiana Continuing Legal Education Forum, March, 1997. *Member:* Evansville and Indiana State Bar Associations; The Florida Bar; Evansville Estate and Financial Planning Council. ***PRACTICE AREAS:*** Corporate and Business Law; Real Estate Law; Probate and Estate Planning; Trust Administration; Banking Law. ***Email:*** mdf@rfpj.com

L. MONTGOMERY PORTER, born Evansville, Indiana, February 22, 1961; admitted to bar, 1986, Indiana and U.S. District Court, Southern and Northern Districts of Indiana. *Education:* University of Evansville (B.S., summa cum laude, 1983); Indiana University (J.D., cum laude, 1986). Phi Kappa Phi. *Member:* Evansville and Indiana State Bar Associations; National Health Lawyers Association. ***PRACTICE AREAS:*** Corporate and Business Law; Business Acquisitions Law; Health Care; Contract Law. ***Email:*** lmp@rfpj.com

JAMES D. JOHNSON, born Evansville, Indiana, April 6, 1960; admitted to bar, 1987, Indiana. *Education:* Florida State University (B.S. with honors, 1984); Indiana University (J.D., cum laude, 1987). Associate Editor, Indiana Law Review, 1986-1987. *Member:* Evansville, Indiana State and American Bar Associations; Defense Research Institute; Defense Trial Counsel of Indiana; Brooks American Inns of Court. ***PRACTICE AREAS:*** Commercial Litigation; Trade Secrets; Products Liability; Appeals. ***Email:*** jdj@rfpj.com

KRISTA B. LOCKYEAR, born Evansville, Indiana, December 19, 1966; admitted to bar, 1992, Indiana and U.S. District Court, Southern District of Indiana. *Education:* Indiana University (B.A., Political Science, 1989; J.D., cum laude, 1992). Agent: Chicago Title Insurance Company, Attorney, Title Guaranty Fund, Inc. *Member:* Evansville and Indiana State Bar Associations; National Academy of Elder Law Attorneys. ***PRACTICE AREAS:*** Real Estate Law; Zoning and Land Use; Real Estate Title Insurance; Environmental Law; Business Law; Probate And Estate Planning; Elder Law. ***Email:*** kbl@rfpj.com

KEITH A. SERMERSHEIM, born Huntingburg, Indiana, December 20, 1965; admitted to bar, 1994, Indiana, U.S. District Court, Southern District of Indiana and U.S. Court of Appeals, Seventh Circuit. *Education:* Purdue University (B.A., 1991); Indiana University (J.D., 1994). Phi Beta Kappa; Phi Kappa Phi.*Member:* Evansville and Indiana Bar Associations; Indiana Defense Lawyers Association; Defense Research Institute. ***REPORTED CASES:*** Fellows v. Board of Trustees of Welborn Clinic, 63 F Supp. 2d 942 (S.D. Ind. 1998); Tweedall v. Fritz, et. al 987 F. Supp. 1126 (S.D. Ind. 1997); Foster v. Ivy Tech State College, 1997 WL 907910 (S.D. Ind. 1997). ***PRACTICE AREAS:*** Labor and Employment Law; Employment Discrimination Law; Employee Benefits Law; Contract Law; Corporate and Business Law. ***Email:*** kas@rfpj.com

JEFFREY W. HENNING, born Evansville, Indiana, March 9, 1968; admitted to bar, 1993, Indiana; 1999, Illinois, U.S District Court, Southern and Northern Districts of Indiana, U.S. District Court, Southern District of Illinois. *Education:* Indiana University (B.S., 1990); St. Louis University School of Law (J.D., 1993). Recipient, American Jurisprudence Award in Secured Transactions. Graduate, National Institute of Trial Advocacy. *Member:* Evansville, Illinois State and Indiana State Bar Associations. ***REPORTED CASES:*** Bosecker v. Westfield Ins. Co., 699 N.E. 2d 769 (Ind.App. 1998); Benton v. City of Oakland City, 684 N.E. 2d 251 (Ind.App. 1997); Myers v. Furrow Building Material, 659 N.E. 2d 1147 (Ind.App. 1996). ***PRACTICE AREAS:*** Commercial Litigation; Employment Litigation; Trade Secrets. ***Email:*** jwh@rfpj.com

ANGELA L. FREEL, born Elkhart, Indiana, February 9, 1973; admitted to bar, 1998, Indiana. *Education:* Indiana University (B.S. with high distinction, 1995); Indiana University School of Law (J.D., 1998). *Member:* Evansville and Indiana State Bar Associations; Defense Research Institute; Defense Trial Counsel of Indiana; Brooks American Inns of Court. ***PRACTICE AREAS:*** Insurance Defense; Commercial Litigation; Family Law. ***Email:*** alf@rfpj.com

ASSOCIATES

STACY K. HARRIS, born Detroit, Michigan, August 16, 1971; admitted to bar, 1996, Indiana and U.S. District Court, Southern and Northern Districts of Indiana; 1999, U.S. Court of Appeals, Seventh Circuit. *Education:* Purdue University (B.A., 1993); Indiana University School of Law- Indianapolis (J.D., summa cum laude, 1996). *Member:* Evansville and Indiana State Bar Associations; Brooks Inns of Court. ***PRACTICE AREAS:*** Employment Discrimination; Municipal Law; Insurance Defense; Commercial Litigation. ***Email:*** skh@rfpj.com

BRIAN E. TOWNSEND, born Marion, Indiana, September 5, 1968; admitted to bar, 1999, Indiana and U.S. District Court, Southern and Northern Districts of Indiana. *Education:* Indiana University (B.A., 1991; J.D., 1999). Phi Delta Phi. *Member:* Evansville, Indiana State and American Bar Associations. ***PRACTICE AREAS:*** Corporate Law; Business Law; Real Estate Law; Contract Law; Banking Law. ***Email:*** bet@rfpj.com

KELLY J. JACKSON, born Tell City, Indiana, March 3, 1975; admitted to bar, 2000, Indiana and U.S. District Court, Southern and Northern Districts of Indiana. *Education:* Western Kentucky University (B.A., summa cum laude, 1997); Indiana University School of Law (J.D., cum laude, 2000). Phi Kappa Phi. Golden Key National Honor Society. *Member:* Evansville and Indiana State Bar Associations. ***PRACTICE AREAS:*** Corporate Law; Business Law; Health Care Law; Contract Law. ***Email:*** kjj@rfpj.com

ABIGAIL BROWN-COX, born Vincennes, Indiana, September 26, 1975; admitted to bar, 2001, Indiana. *Education:* University of Evansville (B.S., 1998); Capital University Law School (J.D., 2001). *Member:* Evansville and Indiana State Bar Associations; Defense Research Institute; Defense Trial Counsel of Indiana. ***PRACTICE AREAS:*** Insurance Defense; Commercial Litigation; Domestic Relations; Family Law; Collections. ***Email:*** adb@rfpj.com

MAX E. FIESTER, born Princeton, Indiana, March 16, 1977; admitted to bar, 2002, Indiana. *Education:* Indiana University (B.A., 1999; J.D., 2002). *Member:* Indiana State and Evansville Bar Associations; Brooks Inns of Court; Defense Trial Counsel of Indiana; Transportation Lawyers Association. ***PRACTICE AREAS:*** Insurance Defense; Commercial Litigation. ***Email:*** mef@rfpj.com

TED C. ZIEMER, IV, born Evansville, Indiana, April 7, 1977; admitted to bar, 2003, Indiana. *Education:* Indiana University (B.A., 1999; J.D., 2002). *Evansville, Indiana State Bar Associations.* ***PRACTICE AREAS:*** Commercial Law; Corporate Law; Real Estate. ***Email:*** tcz@rfpj.com

OF COUNSEL

R. STEVEN KROHN, born Evansville, Indiana, August 28, 1945; admitted to bar, 1970, Indiana, U.S. District Court, Southern District of Indiana and U.S. Court of Military Appeals; 1973, U. S. Supreme Court; 1979, U.S. Court of Appeals, Seventh Circuit. *Education:* Indiana University (B.S., 1967; J.D., 1970). Assistant City Attorney, Evansville, Indiana, 1975-1978. *Member:* Evansville (Secretary, 1979-1981; Director, 1989-1991 and 2000-2003) and Indiana State (Member, Sections on: Corporate and Banking Law, Probate, Trust and Real Property Law) Bar Associations. [Capt., U.S. Army JAGC, 1970-1974]. ***PRACTICE AREAS:*** Business Law; Commercial Transactions; Real Estate; Decedents' Estates. ***Email:*** rsk@rfpj.com

REPRESENTATIVE INSURANCE CLIENTS: AIG Specialty Auto; Airborne Express; Airgas, Inc.; American United Life Insurance Company; Archer Daniels Midland Company; Asplundh Tree Expert Company; Anthem-Blue Cross; Automobile Club Insurance Company; The Budd Company; Burlington Air Express; CUNA Mutual; Chrysler Insurance Company; Chubb Group of Insurance Companies; Church Mutual Insurance Company; Cincinnati Insurance Companies; Courtaulds Coating, Inc.; Emro Marketing Company; Erie Insurance Group; Federated Insurance Company; Fidelity & Deposit Company of Maryland; Go America Insurance Group; GRE Insurance Group; General Accident Insurance Company; Hartford Insurance Company; Hertz Claim Management; Highlands Insurance Company; Holiday Foods & Groceries; Hurst Manufacturing; ITT Hartford; Inland Container Corporation; Jefferson Pilot Corporation; Monroe Guaranty Insurance Company; Motorists Mutual Insurance Group; National Gypsum Company; Northwestern Mutual Life; Olsten Corporation; Omni Insurance Company; Progressive Casualty Company; Rockwell Mutual Insurance Company; Schering-Plough Corporation; Sentry Insurance; Sumitomo Marine Management; Sunbeam Corporation; TIG Insurance, Transamerica Group; Western Reserve Mutual Casualty Company; Western-Southern Life Insurance Company; Westfield Companies; Westingtonhouse Electric Corporation; Whirlpool Corporation.
REPRESENTATIVE CLIENTS: Action Pest Control, Inc.; Advanced Pain Care Clinic; American Enviro Services, Inc.; Bank of Evansville; Basden RV Center, Inc.; Berry Plastics Corporation; Bradley David Productions, Inc.; Bootz Manufacturing Co.; Carbolite Foods, Inc.; Carver Community Organization, Inc.; Edgewater Grille; Emergency Room Associates, Inc.; Evansville Pavilion, LLC; Evansville Sheet Metal Works, Inc.; Gribbins Insulation Company, Inc.; Gus Doerner Sports, Inc.; Hebron Pediatrics; Heritage Petroleum, LLC; Oral Surgery Group of Evansville, Inc.; Physicians Health Group, LLC; Ohio Valley Eye Institute, P.C.; Ohio Valley Heartcare, Inc.; Premier Properties USA, Inc.; Princeton Cancer Center, LLC; Riverbend Capital Resources Corp.; Riverside Prostheties & Orthotics, Inc.; Therapy Associates, Inc.; Tri-State Neurosurgical, Inc.; Tri-State Gastroenterology Associates, P.C.; Tri-State Orthopedic Surgeons, Inc.
REFERENCES: Old National Bank; Bank of Evansville.

CHARLES A. SPAETTI

5011 WASHINGTON AVENUE, SUITE 103
EVANSVILLE, INDIANA 47715
Telephone: 812-477-6483
Fax: 812-477-1836

General Civil Practice including Bankruptcy, Collections and Insurance Law.

CHARLES A. SPAETTI, born 1948; admitted to bar, 1972, Indiana. *Education:* Indiana University (A.B., 1970); Indiana University School of Law (J.D., 1972). Deputy Prosecuting Attorney, Vanderburgh County, 1979—. ***PRACTICE AREAS:*** Collections; Bankruptcy Law.

STATHAM ALLEGA & JESSEN, LLP

915 MAIN STREET, SUITE 202
P.O. BOX 3567
EVANSVILLE, INDIANA 47734-3567
Telephone: 812-425-5223
Facsimile: 812-421-4238
Email: sajr@statham-ajr.com
URL: http://www.statham-ajr.com

Civil and Commercial Litigation, Insurance Law, Product Liability Law, Malpractice Defense, Trials.

MEMBERS OF FIRM

WILLIAM E. STATHAM, admitted to bar, 1956, Indiana. *Education:* Evansville College (A.B., 1953); Indiana University (J.D., with distinction, 1956). Order of the Coif. *Member:* Evansville, Indiana State (Member, Board of Managers, 1972-1974; Presidential Citation, 1974) and American Bar Associations; American Board of Trial Advocates (Advocate Member). Master Fellow, Indiana Bar Foundation; Defense Research Institute; Defense Trial Counsel of Indiana. ***PRACTICE AREAS:*** Litigation; Medical Malpractice Defense; Products Liability; Insurance Defense.

GERALD F. ALLEGA, admitted to bar, 1977, Indiana. *Education:* Indiana State University (B.S., magna cum laude, 1974); Indiana University (J.D., magna cum laude, 1977). Order of the Coif. *Member:* Evansville and Indiana State Bar Associations; Defense Trial Counsel of Indiana; American Board of Trial Advocates. ***PRACTICE AREAS:*** Litigation; Insurance Defense; Medical Malpractice Defense; Contracts.

(This Listing Continued)

DOUGLAS V. JESSEN, admitted to bar, 1981, Indiana. *Education:* Iowa State University (B.S., 1969); Indiana University (J.D., cum laude, 1980). *Member:* Evansville and Indiana State Bar Associations. **PRACTICE AREAS:** Medical Malpractice Defense; Products Liability.

REPRESENTATIVE LITIGATION AND INSURANCE CLIENTS: American Family Insurance Group; Acuity Insurance; Clark County Memorial Hospital; Safeco Ins.; CNA; Cincinnati Insurance Co.; Commercial Union; Crawford & Co.; Deaconess Hospital, Inc.; Fireman's Fund; Good Samaritan Hospital; General Motors Corp.; Hartford Insurance Group; Indiana Insurance Cos.; Indiana Farmer's Insurance; Indiana Insurance Guaranty Association; Kraft Foods North America, Inc.; Medical Assurance Company; Medical Protective Insurance Co.; Meridian Mutual Insurance; Monroe Guaranty; National Chiropractic Mutual; National Indemnity; Ohio Casualty; Royal Insurance; Star Insurance Company; St. Paul Insurance Cos.; Shelter Insurance; State Auto Ins; WBH, Inc.

TERRELL, BAUGH, SALMON & BORN, LLP

Established in 1969

700 S. GREEN RIVER ROAD, SUITE 2000
EVANSVILLE, INDIANA 47715
Telephone: 812-479-8721
Fax: 812-474-6059
Email: bsalmon@tbsblaw.com

General Civil Trial and Appellate Practice in State and Federal Courts. Insurance Defense, Commercial Transactions, Business Organizations, Employment, Construction, Bankruptcy, Probate and Estate Planning and Administration, Real Estate, Personal Injury, Environmental, Mediation, Zoning, Shopping Center Development and Leasing.

MEMBERS OF FIRM

THOMAS H. TERRELL, born Evansville, Indiana, December 5, 1938; admitted to bar, 1968, Indiana. *Education:* Indiana University (B.S., 1960; J.D., 1968). *Member:* Evansville and Indiana State Bar Associations. **PRACTICE AREAS:** Commercial Transactions; Real Estate; Employment Law; Corporations; Probate and Estate Planning; Environmental Law; Shopping Center Development; Shopping Center Leasing. **Email:** tterrell@tbsblaw.com

BRADLEY J. SALMON, born Lincoln, Nebraska, July 10, 1958; admitted to bar, 1983, Indiana; 2003, U.S. Supreme Court. *Education:* Indiana State University (B.S., cum laude, 1980); Valparaiso University (J.D., 1983). *Member:* Evansville, Indiana State and American Bar Associations; Evansville Estate and Financial Planning Council. **PRACTICE AREAS:** Business Law; Real Estate; Family Law; Estate Planning; Probate; Elder Law; Litigation. **Email:** bsalmon@tbsblaw.com

D. TIMOTHY BORN, born Evansville, Indiana, May 28, 1955; admitted to bar, 1981, California; 1987, Indiana and U.S. District Court, Southern District of Indiana; 1994, U.S. Court of Appeals, Seventh Circuit; 1998, U.S. Supreme Court. *Education:* Indiana State University (B.S., 1977); Pepperdine University (J.D., 1980). *Member:* Evansville (President) and Indiana State Bar Associations; State Bar of California; Defense Trial Counsel of Indiana; Brooks American Inn of Court. **PRACTICE AREAS:** Civil Trials; Insurance Defense Law; Professional Liability Defense Law; Insurance Coverage Issues; Medical Law; Zoning Law. **Email:** tborn@tbsblaw.com

PATRICIA KAY WOODRING, born Hilltop, Kentucky, April 1, 1951; admitted to bar, 1987, Indiana and U.S. District Court, Southern and Northern Districts of Indiana. *Education:* Ball State University (B.S., 1984); Indiana University (J.D., 1987). Registered Mediator. *Member:* Evansville, Indiana State and American Bar Associations; Defense Trial Counsel of Indiana; Brooks American Inns of Court. **PRACTICE AREAS:** Civil Trials; Insurance Defense Law; Employment Discrimination; Medical Malpractice Defense; Professional Liability Defense. **Email:** pwoodring@tbsblaw.com

SHAWN M. SULLIVAN, born Orange, California, December 5, 1968; admitted to bar, 1994, Indiana; 1996, U.S. Court of Appeals, Seventh Circuit; 1998, U.S. Supreme Court. *Education:* University of California at Davis (B.S., summa cum laude, 1991); Indiana University (J.D., cum laude, 1994). Article and Seminar Speaker, "The Admissibility of Collateral Source Payments in Negligence Cases," ICLEF Seminar, April 1998. *Member:* Evansville and Indiana State Bar Associations; Defense Trial Counsel of Indiana; Brooks American Inn of Court. **PRACTICE AREAS:** Insurance Defense Law; Commercial Transactions; Workers Compensation; Zoning Law; Civil Trials and Appeals. **Email:** ssullivan@tbsblaw.com

DANIEL J. KING, born Evansville, Indiana, June 17, 1969; admitted to bar, 1994, Indiana. *Education:* Tulane University (B.A., cum laude, 1991; J.D., cum laude, 1994). *Member:* Evansville and Indiana State Bar Associations. **PRACTICE AREAS:** Estate Planning; Probate; Elder Law; Real Estate; Commercial Transactions; Corporate Law; Business Law. **Email:** dking@tbsblaw.com

RETIRED

JERRY P. BAUGH

REPRESENTATIVE CLIENTS: Auto-Owners Insurance Company; Cincinnati Insurance Company; CSX Transportation, Inc.; Guaranty National Insurance Company; Regency Property Management, Inc.; Eades Properties; Shoe Carnival, Inc.; Environmental Testing and Consulting, Inc.; Hahn Realty Corporation; Titan Group; Reliance Ins. Group; Sterling Boiler & Mechanical, Inc.; American States; A Safeco, Company; Allstate Insurance Co.; Federated Insurance; Leader National; St. Paul Fire and Marine Insurance Co.; Progressive Insurance; Farmers Insurance Group; Phico Insurance Co; Lincoln Land Mortgage Brokers.
APPROVED ATTORNEYS FOR: Chicago Title Insurance Co.; Lawyers Title Co.; Commonwealth Land Title Insurance Company.
REFERENCE: Old National Bank in Evansville.

WRIGHT AND DALY

Established in 1981

425 MAIN STREET
EVANSVILLE, INDIANA 47708
Telephone: 812-424-3300
Fax: 812-421-5588
Email: WED-MainSt@MSN.Com
URL: http://www.wrightdaly.com

General Civil Litigation, Civil Litigation, including Trials and Appeals in State and Federal Courts. Construction Law, Family Law, Insurance Law, including Automobile, Commercial, Life and Health, Liability and Property Law. Personal Injury Claims and Litigation. Products Liability Claims and Litigation. Social Security, Wills, Estates and Probate Law, including Litigation and Worker's Compensation.

MEMBERS OF FIRM

CLAUDE B. LYNN (Retired)

DONALD R. WRIGHT, born Muncie, Indiana, October 6, 1937; admitted to bar, 1961, Indiana and U.S. District Court, Southern District of Indiana; 1970, U.S. Court of Appeals, Seventh Circuit; 1972, U.S. Supreme Court. *Education:* Indiana University (B.S., 1959); Indiana University School of Law (J.D., 1961). Phi Delta Phi. *Member:* Evansville (President, 1978-1979), Seventh Circuit, Indiana State and American Bar Associations; Defense Research Institute; Indiana Defense Lawyers Association. Fellow, Indiana Bar Foundation. **REPORTED CASES:** Peyronnin Const. Co. vs. Weiss, 1965, Appellate Court of Indiana, 137 Ind. App. 417, 208 N.E.2d 489; Wallace vs. Woods, 1971, Court of Appeals of Indiana, 149 Ind. App. 257, 271 N.E.2d 487; Rodgers vs. Hembd, 1988, Court of Appeals of Indiana, 518 N.E.2d 1120; City of Tell City vs. Noble, 1986, Court of Appeals of Indiana 489 N.E.2d 958; Madison vs. Hawkins, 1994, Court of Appeals of Indiana, 644 N.E.2d 184. **PRACTICE AREAS:** Civil Trials and Appeals; Negligence; Personal Injury; Products Liability; Commercial Litigation; Insurance Litigation; Probate; Wills and Estates; Workers' Compensation. **Email:** donald.wright@wrightdaly.com

R. LAWRENCE DALY, born Chicago, Illinois, April 5, 1941; admitted to bar, 1971, Indiana and U.S. District Court, Southern District of Indiana. *Education:* Vanderbilt University (B.A., 1963); Indiana University School of Law (J.D., cum laude, 1971). Phi Alpha Delta; Order of the Coif. Member, Indiana University Law Journal, 1970-1971. President, Vanderburgh County Legal Aid Society, 1974-1975. Member, Adjunct Faculty, Paralegal Program, University of Evansville, 1975—. *Member:* Evansville, Indiana State and American Bar Associations. **PRACTICE AREAS:** Litigation; Insurance Law; Products Liability; Negligence; Personal Injury; Commercial Law; Creditors Rights; Domestic Relations; Probate; Wills and Estates. **Email:** lawrence.daly@wrightdaly.com

REPRESENTATIVE CORPORATE CLIENTS: Jerry David Enterprises Co., Inc.; Marsch Plumbing Co., Inc.; Truck Clean, Inc.; Servicemaster of Evansville, Inc.; Shore and Roth, Inc.; Friends of Angel Mounds, Inc.; D.P.F., Inc.; F&F Concrete Co. Inc.; Hayden Development Corp.; Jeff's Plumbing & Boiler, Inc.; Miller Motors, Inc.; St. Joe Inn, Inc.; Sunburst Jewelers, Inc.; Sunridge Condominiums; JK, LLC.
REPRESENTATIVE INSURANCE CLIENTS: Allstate Insurance Co.; Canal Insurance Co.; Church Mutual Insurance Co.; Employer Security Insurance; Erie Insurance Company; Liberty Mutual Insurance Companies; Helmsman Management Services, Inc.; Wausau Insurance Company; Underwriters Safety & Claims; National Life & Accident Insurance Co.; America Insurance Co.; Go America Insurance Co.; Indiana Insurance Co.; Toyota Motor Insurance Co.

ZIEMER, STAYMAN, WEITZEL & SHOULDERS, LLP

Established in 1940

(Formerly Early, Arnold & Ziemer)

ONE RIVERFRONT PLACE
20 N.W. FIRST STREET
9TH FLOOR
P.O. BOX 916
EVANSVILLE, INDIANA 47706-0916
Telephone: 812-424-7575
Telecopier: 812-421-5089 (9th Fl.); 812-421-5076 (7th Fl.)
URL: http://www.zsws.com

General Civil Practice. Litigation in Federal and State Courts. Banking, Bankruptcy and Business Reorganization, Business and Commercial Transactions, Construction, Corporation, Creditors Rights, Environmental Law, Hospital and Medical, Insurance, Negligence and Products Liability, Labor and Employment Discrimination, Oil and Gas and Mining, Probate, Estate Planning and Administration, Mergers and Acquisitions, Real Estate, and Workers Compensation. Environmental Law.

MEMBERS OF FIRM

JOHN E. EARLY (1912-1983)

TED C. ZIEMER, JR., born Evansville, Indiana, February 21, 1935; admitted to bar, 1962, Indiana. *Education:* St. Louis University (B.S., 1956); Indiana University (LL.B., 1962). Delta Theta Phi. *Member:* Evansville, Indiana State (Member: Board of Managers and House of Delegates, 1970-1972; Chairman, Young Lawyers Section, 1970-1972) and American Bar Associations. **PRACTICE AREAS:** Health Care Law; Probate Law; Corporation Law; Real Estate Law. **Email:** tziemer@zsws.com

ROBERT F. STAYMAN, born Chicago, Illinois, March 30, 1946; admitted to bar, 1973, Indiana; 1980, U.S. Court of Appeals, Seventh Circuit. *Education:* DePauw University (B.A., 1968); University of Michigan (J.D., 1973). *Member:* Evansville (President, 1988-1989), Indiana State and American Bar Associations. Fellow, Indiana Bar Foundation. **PRACTICE AREAS:** Banking Law; Construction Law; Litigation. **Email:** rstayman@zsws.com

(This Listing Continued)

ZIEMER, STAYMAN, WEITZEL & SHOULDERS, LLP, Evansville—Continued

STEPHAN E. WEITZEL, born Princeton, Indiana, June 20, 1949; admitted to bar, 1975, Indiana. *Education:* DePauw University (B.A., cum laude, 1971); University of Freiburg, Freiburg, Germany; University of Exeter, Exeter, England and Emory University (J.D., 1975). Phi Delta Phi. Member: Board of Editors, Emory Law Journal, 1974-1975; Indiana Probate Code Study Commission, 1990-1992, Director, 1985-1993, President, 1992-1994, Legal Aid Society of Evansville. *Member:* Evansville, Indiana State (Director, Young Lawyers Section, 1979-1981) and American Bar Associations. ***PRACTICE AREAS:*** Corporation Law; Business and Commercial Transactions; Mergers and Acquisitions; Estate Planning and Probate. ***Email:*** sweitzel@zsws.com

PATRICK A. SHOULDERS, born Evansville, Indiana, 1953; admitted to bar, 1978, Indiana and U.S. District Court, Southern District of Indiana; 1979, U.S. Court of Appeals, Seventh Circuit; 1985, U.S. Supreme Court; 1986, Kentucky; 1987, U.S. District Court, Western District of Kentucky. *Education:* Indiana University (B.A., 1975; J.D., magna cum laude, 1978). Member, Local Rules Committee, U.S. District Court, Southern District of Indiana. Trustee, Indiana University, 2002. Co-chair, Indiana Trial Advocacy College. *Member:* Evansville (President, 1985-1986), Seventh Circuit, Indiana State (Chairman, 1991-1992, Litigation Section; Member, Board of Governors, 1998-2000), Kentucky State and American (Member, Trial Practice Committee, 1984-1986, Litigation Section) Bar Associations; Federation of Insurance and Corporate Counsel. Fellow, American College of Trial Lawyers; American Board of Trial Advocates; American Bar Foundation. Master Fellow, Indiana Bar Foundation. ***PRACTICE AREAS:*** Litigation; Employment Law. ***Email:*** pshoulders@zsws.com

DAVID V. MILLER, born Evansville, Indiana, March 20, 1943; admitted to bar, 1969, Indiana, U.S. Supreme Court, U.S. Court of Appeals, Seventh Circuit, U.S. Tax Court and U.S. District Court, Southern District of Indiana; 1992, U.S. District Court, District of Arizona. *Education:* University of Michigan (A.B., 1965); Indiana University (J.D., 1969). Law Clerk, Indiana Supreme Court, 1967-1969. Editor-in-Chief, Indiana Legal Forum, 1968. Certified Civil Mediator, Indiana, 1992. Deputy Prosecutor, 1970-1975. U.S. Magistrate, 1976-1985. Attorney, Vanderburgh County, 1981-1991. ***PRACTICE AREAS:*** Business Litigation; Banking Litigation; Employment Law; Litigation; Appellate Practice; Civil Mediation; Intellectual Property; International Adoption; Healthcare; Medicare. ***Email:*** dmiller@zsws.com

WM. MICHAEL SCHIFF, born Alton, Illinois, 1953; admitted to bar, 1979, Indiana and U.S. District Court, Southern District of Indiana; 1980, U.S. Court of Appeals, Seventh Circuit; 1986, U.S. Court of Appeals, Sixth Circuit; 1989, Kentucky; 1991, U.S. District Court, Western District of Kentucky. *Education:* University of Southern Indiana (B.A., 1975); Indiana University (J.D., 1979). Associate Editor, Indiana Law Review, 1978-1979. Author, Indiana Unemployment Compensation Handbook, 3rd Ed. 2003. *Member:* Evansville (Director, 1996-1997), Indiana State, Kentucky and American (Member, Labor and Employment Law Sections) Bar Associations. Fellow, Indiana Bar Foundation. ***PRACTICE AREAS:*** Employment Discrimination Law; Labor; Employment; Management Employment Law; Unemployment Compensation Law. ***Email:*** mschiff@zsws.com

MARCO L. DeLUCIO, born Richmond, Indiana, February 13, 1959; admitted to bar, 1984, Indiana. *Education:* University of Freiburg, Freiburg, West Germany; DePauw University (B.A., 1981); Drake University; Indiana University-Indianapolis (J.D., summa cum laude, 1984). President, Vanderburgh County Law Library Foundation, 1993-1994. Vice-Chairman, Governmental and Administrative Affairs, Metropolitan Evansville Chamber of Commerce, 1997-1999. *Member:* Evansville (President, 1995-1996), Indiana State and American Bar Associations. ***PRACTICE AREAS:*** Bankruptcy Law; Creditors' Rights; Real Estate Law; Commercial Transactions; Environmental Law. ***Email:*** mdelucio@zsws.com

STEVEN K. HAHN, born Evansville, Indiana, August 6, 1956; admitted to bar, 1981, Indiana and U.S. District Court, Southern District of Indiana. *Education:* Indiana University (B.A., 1978; J.D., 1981). Law Clerk to the Hon. William E. Steckler, Chief Judge, U.S. District Court, Southern District of Indiana, 1981-1983. Member, American Judicature Society. Director, Legal Aid Society of Evansville, Inc., 1994—. *Member:* Evansville, Indiana State and American Bar Associations; Indiana Defense Lawyers Association. ***PRACTICE AREAS:*** Civil Litigation; Healthcare; Commercial Litigation; Insurance Law. ***Email:*** shahn@zsws.com

JAMES P. CASEY, born Chicago, Illinois, 1954; admitted to bar, 1980, Indiana and U.S. District Court, Southern District of Indiana; 1982, U.S., Court of Appeals, Seventh Circuit; 1990, U.S. Supreme Court. *Education:* Indiana University (B.S., 1977; J.D., 1980). Member, Board of Directors, Indiana Continuing Legal Education Forum, 1987-1995. Author: ABA Recognition Award Topic Author, "How Arbitration Works," Elkouri, 4th Ed. Certified Civil Mediator, 1992; Referee, Duke University Private Adjudication CTR. *Member:* Evansville (President, 1993-1994), Indiana State and American (Member: Labor and Employment Law Section; Equal Opportunity Committee). ***REPORTED CASES:*** Reed v. Shepard, 939 F.2d 484 (7th Cir. 1991); Indiana Civil Rights Comm. v. Southern Indiana Gas and Electric Co., 553 N.E.2d 840, (Ind. 1990). ***PRACTICE AREAS:*** Labor Law; Employment Law; Discrimination Law; Civil Rights. ***Email:*** jcasey@zsws.com

TIMOTHY J. HUBERT, born Evansville, Indiana, January 16, 1953; admitted to bar, 1979, Indiana and U.S. District Court, Southern District of Indiana. *Education:* Indiana University (A.B., 1975; J.D., 1979). President, Evansville Fire Merit Commission. *Member:* American Academy of Adoption Attorneys; National Diocesan Attorneys Association. ***PRACTICE AREAS:*** Commercial Law; Estate Planning; Probate Administration; Adoptions; Elder Law; Real Estate. ***Email:*** thubert@zsws.com

MARY LEE SCHIFF, born Cincinnati, Ohio, 1964; admitted to bar, 1989, Ohio, Indiana and U.S. District Court, Northern and Southern Districts of Indiana; 1990, U.S. Court of Appeals, Seventh Circuit; 1992, U.S. District Court, Western District of Kentucky. *Education:* Xavier University (B.S.B.A., Economics/Marketing, 1986); University of Cincinnati (J.D., 1989). Moot Court Board. *Member:* Evansville, Indiana State and Ohio State Bar Associations; Brooks American Inns of Court. ***PRACTICE AREAS:*** Employment Law (Management); Civil Rights Litigation. ***Email:*** lschiff@zsws.com

(This Listing Continued)

DAVID A. GUERRETTAZ, born Indianapolis, Indiana, January 14, 1966; admitted to bar, 1991, Indiana and U.S. District Court, Southern and Northern Districts of Indiana; U.S. Supreme Court and U.S. Court of Appeals, Seventh Circuit. *Education:* Marian College (B.A., summa cum laude, 1988); Syracuse University (M.A., International Relations, J.D., 1991). Director, Indiana Legal Services, Inc. and Legal Aid Society of Evansville, Inc. *Member:* Evansville, Indiana State and American Bar Associations; American Immigration Lawyers' Association. ***PRACTICE AREAS:*** Civil Litigation; Employment Law; Construction Law; Family Law; Immigration Law. ***Email:*** dguerrettaz@zsws.com

ROBERT L. BURKART, born Fort Thomas, Kentucky, November 26, 1965; admitted to bar, 1992, Indiana and U.S. District Court, Southern and Northern Districts of Indiana. *Education:* Trinity College, Carmarthen, Wales; Hanover College (B.A., cum laude, 1988) ; Mortar Board; Emory University (J.D., 1992). Assistant Evansville City Attorney, 200-2003. *Member:* Evansville, Indiana State and American Bar Associations. ***PRACTICE AREAS:*** Civil Litigation; Commercial Law; Appellate Practice. ***Email:*** rburkart@zsws.com

CHARLES A. COMPTON, born Evansville, Indiana, September 23, 1966; admitted to bar, 1992, Indiana. *Education:* DePauw University (B.A., cum laude, 1989); Vanderbilt University (J.D., 1992). Golden Key; Phi Eta Sigma; Alpha Lambda Delta; Phi Delta Phi. *Member:* Evansville, Indiana State and American Bar Associations. ***PRACTICE AREAS:*** Corporate Law; Business and Commercial Transactions; Mergers and Acquisitions; Taxation Law; Municipal Finance. ***Email:*** ccompton@zsws.com

SARAH LINK HARDY, born Henderson, Kentucky, December 10, 1962; admitted to bar, 1988, Georgia; 2003, Indiana. *Education:* Centre College of Kentucky (B.A., 1984); Owen Graduate School of Management (M.B.A., 1988); Vanderbilt University (J.D., 1988). *Member:* State Bar of Georgia; Indiana State Bar; American Bar Association (Member: Business Law and Health Care Sections). ***PRACTICE AREAS:*** Mergers and Acquisitions; Corporate Law; Business Transactions; Commercial Transactions. ***Email:*** shardy@zsws.com

DIRCK H. STAHL, born Evansville, Indiana, September 5, 1968; admitted to bar, 1993, Indiana and U.S. District Court, Southern District of Indiana; U.S. Court of Appeals, Seventh Circuit and U.S. Supreme Court. *Education:* Wabash College (A.B., 1990); Indiana University School of Law (J.D., 1993). Associate Editor, Adelphia Law Journal, 1992. Adjunct Faculty, University of Evansville. Member, University of Evansville Legal Studies Advisory Board. *Member:* Evansville (Director, Officer, 1998-2001), Indiana State (Young Lawyers Council, 1998—; Chair-Elect, 2004-2005; Litigation Section Chair, 2004-2005) and American (Member, Sections on: Tort Trial; Insurance Practice) Bar Associations; Defense Trial Counsel of Indiana; Defense Research Institute; Brooks American Inn of Court; Evansville Bar Foundation (Charter Board Member). ***PRACTICE AREAS:*** Civil Litigation; Commercial Law; Insurance Law; Construction Law; Labor and Employment; Employment Discrimination; Probate. ***Email:*** dstahl@zsws.com

CHAD J. SULLIVAN, born Centralia, Illinois, August 18, 1972; admitted to bar, 1997, Missouri and U.S. District Court, Eastern District of Missouri; 1998, Illinois and U.S. District Court, Central District of Illinois; 1999, Indiana and U.S. District Court, Southern District of Indiana. *Education:* University of Missouri (B.S.B.A., 1994); Washington University (J.D., 1997). Associate Editor, Washington University Law Review. *Member:* Evansville, Indiana State, Illinois State and American Bar Associations; The Missouri Bar. ***PRACTICE AREAS:*** Employment Discrimination; Litigation; Labor and Employment; Management Labor Law; Management Employment Law; Civil Litigation. ***Email:*** csullivan@zsws.com

KEITH WILLIAM VONDERAHE, born Evansville, Indiana, November 10, 1971; admitted to bar, 1999, Indiana and U.S. District Court, Southern District of Indiana. *Education:* University of Evansville (B.S., 1994); University of Tulsa College of Law (J.D., 1999). Phi Delta Phi. *Member:* Evansville, Indiana State and American Bar Associations; The Association of Trial Lawyers of America; Indiana Trial Lawyers Association. ***PRACTICE AREAS:*** Civil Litigation; Labor and Employment; Commercial Litigation; Family Law; Municipal Law. ***Email:*** kvonderahe@zsws.com

ASSOCIATES

NICK J. CIRIGNANO, born Huntingdon, Pennsylvania, December 19, 1971; admitted to bar, 2001, Indiana and U.S. District Court, Northern and Southern Districts of Indiana. *Education:* Haverford College (B.A., Economics, 1994); Indiana University School of Law at Bloomington (J.D., 2001). Recipient: CALI Excellence for the Future Award for Excellence in the Study of Secured Transactions. Adjunct Faculty, University of Evansville. *Member:* Evansville, Indiana State and American Bar Associations. ***PRACTICE AREAS:*** Health Law; Corporate Law; Commercial Law; Bankruptcy. ***Email:*** ncirignano@zsws.com

ALLYSON R. BREEDON, born Evansville, Indiana, October 21,1975; admitted to bar, 2001, Indiana and U.S. District Court, Northern and Southern Districts of Indiana. *Education:* Indiana University (B.S., 1998); Indiana University School of Law (J.D., 2001). Executive Articles Editor, Indiana International and Comparative Law Review. Recipient: Judge Betty Barteau Scholarship; The Stephen W. Kellams Memorial Scholarship; Honorable Cale J. Holder Scholarship. Author: "Federal removal jurisdiction and its effect on plaintiff win-rates," Res Gestae September 2002; "The pitfalls of relying on the Indiana Trade Secrets Act for protection of trade secrets," The Workplace Lawyer, Fall 2002. *Member:* Indiana (Member, Sections on: Employment Law; Labor Law), Evansville and Hamilton County Bar Associations. ***Email:*** abreeden@zsws.com

JEAN M. BLANTON, born Wilkes Barre, Pennsylvania, August 16, 1978; admitted to bar, 2004, Indiana and U.S. District Courts, Northern and Southern Districts of Indiana. *Education:* University of Southern Indiana (B.S., 2001); University of Cincinnati (J.D., 2004). *Member:* Indiana, Evansville and American Bar Associations. ***PRACTICE AREAS:*** Civil Litigation; Commercial Litigation; Family Law; Labor and Employment. ***Email:*** jblanton@zsws.com

KATHRYN D. SCHYMIK, born Asheville, North Carolina, May 28, 1979; admitted to bar, 2004, Indiana and U.S. District Courts, Northern and Southern Districts of Indiana.

(This Listing Continued)

Education: Purdue University (B.A., Communication, 2001); Indiana University School of Law (J.D., 2004). *Member:* Indiana, Evansville and American Bar Associations. ***PRACTICE AREAS:*** Corporate Law; Estate Planning. ***Email:*** kschymik@zsws.com

GENERAL COUNSEL FOR: Old National Bank; Old National Bancorp; St. Mary's Medical Health System; Black Beauty Coal Company; Industrial Contractors, Inc.; Evansville Board of Realtors; Evansville-Vanderburgh School Corporation; Transitional Services, Inc.; St. Mary's; St. Elizabeth Ann Seton Hospital; Jasper Engine & Transmission Exchange.
REPRESENTATIVE CLIENTS: ABB Flakt, Inc.; Accuride Corporation; Alstom Power, Inc.; American Electric Power; Ameriqual Foods; American Fabricating Co.; Aztar Indiana Gaming; Azteca Milling, L.L.P.; Bristol-Meyers U.S. Pharmaceutical and Nutritional Group; Black Beauty Resources, Inc.; Catholic Diocese of Evansville; Central Industries of Indiana; Cissell Construction, Inc.; Citizens State Bank of Petersburg; Complete Lumber, Inc.; D-Patrick Motoplex; Diversified Healthcare, Inc.; The Evansville Courier; Evansville Drywall Supply, Inc.; F.C. Tucker/Huber, Realtors; Ford Motor Co.; Ford Motor Credit Co.; German American Bancorp; Hamilton Clinic, PC; HealthPrime, Inc.; Highway Machine Company; Jasper Rubber Products, Inc.; Kimball International, Inc.; Mid-America Distillations, Inc.; Midwestern Engineers, Inc.; Miller Block Co., Inc.; Miller Plating & Metal Finishing, Inc.; Ohio Valley Heartcare, P.C.; Omni Plastics, LLC; Perfection Hydraulics; PPG Industries, Inc.; Raben Tire Co., Inc.; Redline Media; Schnucks Markets; Sport Service Corp.; Stagg Safety Equipment, Inc.; Toyota Motor Credit Corp.; Vectren Corp.; Warehousing, Inc.
REPRESENTATIVE INSURANCE CLIENTS: Aetna Casualty & Surety Company; Auto-Owners Insurance Company; Chubb Group of Insurance Companies; Clarendon Insurance Company; General Accident Insurance Co.; Motorist Mutual Insurance Co.; Utica Mutual Insurance Co.
LABOR COUNSEL: Adco Corp.; The American Red Cross; Argosy Casino: Big Rivers ElectricCorporation; Bootz Manufacturing; Bristol-Meyers Squibb, Inc.; Buehler Foods, Inc.; Casey's Inc.; Corn Island Shipyard; Daughters of Charity of St. Vincent de Paul of Indiana, Inc.; East Gibson School Corp; Evansville Courier; Evansville Metal Products; Eyemart; Farm Boy Meats; Faultless Caster Corporation; Futaba Indiana of America Corp.; Graham Farms, Inc.; Grain Processing Corp.; Hoosier Energy REC, Inc.; Hoosier Stamping & Mfg. Co.; Koch Originals, Inc.; Memorial Hospital and Health Center; NASCO, Inc.; North Gibson School Corp.; Orion Electric (America), Inc.; Pyrotek, Inc.; Rexam Closures, Inc.; South Gibson School corp.; Streicher Construction, Inc.; Tell City-Troy Township School Corp.; Visiting Nurse Association of Southwestern Indiana, Inc.; Visiting Nurse Plus, Inc.; Walt's Drive-A-Way Service, Inc.; Yager Materials, Inc.
APPROVED ATTORNEYS FOR: Lawyers Title Insurance Corp.; Ticor Title Insurance Co.; Chicago Title Insurance Co.; American Title Insurance Co.
REFERENCE: Old National Bank.

DONNA J. BAYS

FISHERS, INDIANA

(See Indianapolis)

Family Law, Divorce, Child Custody, Paternity, Premarital Agreements.

CAMPBELL KYLE PROFFITT LLP

FISHERS, INDIANA

(See Noblesville)

Civil Practice. State and Federal Courts and Administrative Agencies, Domestic Relations, Family Law, Divorce, Adoptions, Personal Injury, Corporation, Business Law, Utility Law, Insurance, Wills and Probate, Trusts and Estates, Estate Planning and Elder Law, Real Estate, Zoning, Employment Law, Criminal Law. Contracts, Taxation, Real Estate, Commercial Litigation.

DANIEL R. CARROLL

FISHERS, INDIANA

(See Indianapolis)

Business Law, Contracts, Litigation, Insurance, Debtor and Creditor, Collections, Business Enterprises, Corporate Law, Partnerships, Real Estate, Commercial Litigation, Commercial Leasing, Buy-Sell Agreements, Employment Law, Noncompete Litigation, Wrongful Termination, Trade Secrets, Personal Injury, Automobile Accidents, Slip and Fall, Wrongful Death, Bankruptcy, Arbitration, Mediation.

CHURCH, CHURCH, HITTLE & ANTRIM

FISHERS, INDIANA

(See Noblesville)

General Civil Trial Practice in all State and Federal Courts. Appellate and Federal Practice, Personal Injury, Automobile Accidents, Wrongful Death, Family Law, Adoption Law, Child Custody, Child Support, Divorce, Visitation Rights, Municipal and Governmental Regulations, Real Estate, Zoning Law, Land Use, Commercial Leasing, Wills, Probate, Trusts and Estates, Estate Planning, Asset Protection, Guardianship Law, Estate Administration and Litigation, Tax Planning, Tax Controversies, Business Law, Contracts, Litigation, Business Enterprises, Business Transactions, Corporate Formation, Corporate Litigation, School Law, Commercial Litigation, Professional License Defense, Medical Malpractice, Bankruptcy, Criminal Law, Driving While Intoxicated, Drug Crimes, Felonies, Misdemeanors, Mediation.

SEAN M. CLAPP, LLC

8766 SOUTH STREET, SUITE 220
FISHERS, INDIANA 46038
Telephone: 317-578-9966
Fax: 317-578-9967
Email: sean@seanmclapp.com
URL: http://www.clapplawfirm.com

Commercial Real Estate, Residential Real Estate, Title Claims, Foreclosures, Landlord and Tenant Law, Mortgages, Eminent Domain, Real Estate Tax Law, Commercial Leasing, Construction Law, Business Litigation, Copyright and Trademark Law, Internet Law, Business Enterprises, Limited Liability Company Law, Professional Practices, Small Business Law,

(This Listing Continued)

Closely Held Business, Corporate Law, Partnerships, Buying and Selling of Businesses, Collections, Creditor's Rights, Business Law, Business Planning, Contracts, Intellectual Property, Trade Secrets, Business Start-Ups.

SEAN M. CLAPP, born Gary, Indiana, October 14, 1962; admitted to bar, 1988, Indiana and U.S. District Court, Northern and Southern Districts of Indiana. *Education:* Valparaiso University (B.A., high distinction, 1985); Indiana University-Bloomington (J.D., magna cum laude, 1988). Pi Sigma Alpha; Order of The Coif. Member, Mortar Board. Member, Editorial Staff, Indiana Law Journal, 1987-1988. Recipient, American Jurisprudence Awards: Wills and Trusts; Corporations; Advanced Bankruptcy. *Member:* Indianapolis, Indiana State and American Bar Associations. ***PRACTICE AREAS:*** Real Estate Law; Litigation; Construction Law. ***Email:*** sean@seanmclapp.com

DEFUR VORAN LLP

Established in 1906
8409 FISHERS CENTRE DRIVE
FISHERS, INDIANA 46038
Telephone: 317-585-8085
Telecopier: 317-585-8858
Email: "atty's first initial, last name"@defur.com
URL: http://www.defur.com

Muncie, Indiana Office: 201 East Jackson Street, Suite 400, 47305. Telephone: 765-288-3651. Telecopier: 765-288-7068.

General Civil Practice. Business Organizations, Personal Planning, Education, Health, Personnel and Employment, Banking, Real Estate, Taxation, Employee Benefit/Retirement Plans, Creditor's Rights, Civil Litigation, Mediation, Intellectual Property, Family.

FIRM PROFILE: East Central Indiana's leading law firm, DeFur Voran LLP has been in existence for nearly a century, providing a broad range of legal services for individual, corporate and institutional clients.

The Fishers office opened in 2003 to provide a broader continuum of services to its existing clients and to expand its legal services to central Indiana.

WILLIAM H. LUTZ, born Ann Arbor, Michigan, September 7, 1959; admitted to bar, 1991, Missouri; 1992, Indiana. *Education:* Valparaiso University (B.S.W., 1981); Indiana University (M.S.B.A., 1986); St. Louis University (J.D., cum laude, 1991). Recipient: Academic Achievement Award in Administrative Law, St. Louis University. Articles Editor, St. Louis University Public Law Review, 1990-1991. Law Clerk to Hon. William Crandall, Missouri Court of Appeals, 1991-1992. Author: "The House Rich But Cash Poor Elderly: A Solution For First Time Home Buyers," St. Louis University Public Law Review, Vol. X, No. 2, p. 531, 1990. *Member:* Muncie, Indiana State and American Bar Associations; The Missouri Bar; National Academy of Elder Law Attorneys. ***PRACTICE AREAS:*** Elder Law; Estate Planning; Estate Administration. ***Email:*** wlutz@defur.com

GREGORY J. CAGNASSOLA, born Plainfield, New Jersey, August 11, 1962; admitted to bar, 1992, Indiana. *Education:* Purdue University (B.S., 1984); Indiana University (J.D., 1992). Certified Public Accountant, Indiana, 1989 (Inactive). Associate Counsel and Corporate Counsel, Inland Paperboard and Packaging, Inc., 1993-2003. ***PRACTICE AREAS:*** Tax Law; Estate Planning and Administration; Corporate Law; Business Transactions; Real Estate. ***Email:*** gcagnassola@defur.com

MICHELLE L. COOPER, born Muncie, Indiana, May 5, 1973; admitted to bar, 1999, Indiana, U.S. District Court, Northern and Southern Districts of Indiana. *Education:* Ball State University (B.S., 1995); Indiana University (J.D., cum laude, 1999). Executive Note Development Editor, Indiana International and Comparative Law Review. Law Clerk to the Honorable Patricia Riley, Indiana Court of Appeals, 1998. *Member:* Hamilton County, Indianapolis, Indiana State and American Bar Associations. ***PRACTICE AREAS:*** Labor and Employment; Litigation; Intellectual Property. ***Email:*** mcooper@defur.com

HOLLY J. WANZER, born Fort Wayne, Indiana, January 14, 1973; admitted to bar, 1999, Indiana, U.S. District Court, Northern and Southern Districts of Indiana. *Education:* Ball State University (B.S., magna cum laude, 1995); Indiana University School of Law (J.D., summa cum laude, 1999). Note Development Editor, Indiana University Law Review, 1998-1999. Law Clerk to the Honorable Theodore Boehm, Indiana Supreme Court, 1997. Member: Indianapolis, Indiana State and American Bar Associations. ***PRACTICE AREAS:*** Family Law; Litigation. ***Email:*** hwanzer@defur.com

OF COUNSEL

LESTER H. COHEN, born New York, New York, June 15, 1944; admitted to bar, 1988, Indiana; 1995, U.S. Supreme Court. *Education:* University of California at Los Angeles (B.A., 1966); Yale University (M.Phil., 1972; Ph.D., 1974); Indiana University (J.D., 1988). Former Professor, Purdue University, Intellectual History and American Studies. *Member:* Indiana State Bar Association; Indiana Trial Lawyers Association; Seventh Circuit Bar Association. ***REPORTED CASES:*** Carr v. Allison Gas Turbine Div. 32 F.3rd 1007 (7th Cir. 1994); Watson v. Amedco Steel, Inc., 29 F.3d 274 (7th Cir. 1994); Lenoir v. Roll Coater, Inc., 13 F.3d 1130 (7th Cir 1994); Harvest Life Ins. Co. v. Getche, 701 N.E.2d 871 (Ind. App. 1998); Campbell v. Criterion Group, 605 N.E.2d 150 (Ind. 1992). ***PRACTICE AREAS:*** Labor and Employment; Litigation; Civil Mediation. ***Email:*** lcohen@defur.com

GENERAL COUNSEL FOR: Ball State University; Cardinal Health System, Inc.; Ball Memorial Hospital, Inc.; First Merchants Bank, N.A.; Mount Pleasant Township Community Schools; Muncie Housing Authority; AGBEST, LLC; Westminster Village Muncie, Inc.; Muncie Power Products, Inc.; Ball Brothers Foundation; Complete Masonry Services, Inc.; Delaware Community School Corp.; Blackford County Schools; The Community Foundation of Muncie and Delaware County, Inc.; Muncie Aviation Co.; Gale Tschuor Company, Inc.; Mid-West Metal Products Co., Inc.; Gate City Steel, Inc.; Youth Opportunity Center, Inc.; City Machine Tool & Die Co., Inc.

(This Listing Continued)

DEFUR VORAN LLP, Fishers—Continued

REPRESENTATIVE CLIENTS: Delaware Advancement Corporation; Cardinal Greenway, Inc.; LifeStream Services, Inc.; Muncie Family YMCA; Performance Dynamics, Inc.; Park One/332; Sanyo-Verbatim CD Company, LLC; Old National Bank; Old National Trust; Integra Health Services, LLC.

(For biographical data on all personnel, see Professional Biographies at Muncie)

HOLT, FLECK & ROMINE

FISHERS, INDIANA

(See Noblesville)

Civil and Criminal Trials in all Courts, Criminal Law, Drug Crimes, Driving While Intoxicated, Parole and Probation, Traffic Violations, Wills and Probate, Trusts and Estate, Guardianships, Asset Protection, Estate Planning, Business, Contracts, Business Planning, Lawsuits, Business Enterprises, Closely Held Business, Corporate, Partnerships, Limited Liability Companies, Small Business, Real Estate, Buying and Selling Real Estate, Commercial Leasing, Family Law, Adoptions, Child Custody, Child Support, Divorce, Visitations Rights, Domestic Violence, Domestic Relation, Personal Injury, Automobile Accidents, Slip and Fall, Wrongful Death, Medical Malpractice, Unsafe Products, Bankruptcy, Elder Law.

MADDOX HARGETT & CARUSO, P.C.

10100 LANTERN ROAD, SUITE 150
FISHERS, INDIANA 46037
Telephone: 317-598-2040
Telefax: 317-598-2050
URL: http://www.investorprotection.com

New York, N.Y. Office: 80 Broad Street, 5th Floor, 10004. Telephone: 212-837-7908. Telefax: 212-837-7998.

Mediation, Securities Arbitration, Securities Litigation.

MARK E. MADDOX, born Indianapolis, Indiana, January 22, 1961; admitted to bar, 1986, Indiana; 1995, U.S. Supreme Court; 2000, Illinois. *Education:* Wabash College (B.A., magna cum laude, 1983); Vanderbilt University (J.D., 1986). Phi Beta Kappa. Indiana Securities Commissioner, 1989-1991. Public Member, Panel of Arbitrators For: The New York Stock Exchange; Former Director, Public Investor Arbitration Bar Association, 1993-2002, Past President, 1999-2000. Member: NASD, National Arbitration and Mediation Committee, 1996-1998, 2003-2005, Chairman, 2004-2005. *Member:* Indianapolis and Indiana State (Past President, State Securities Committee) Bar Associations. ***LANGUAGES:*** French. ***PRACTICE AREAS:*** Securities Arbitration and Litigation; Securities Regulation Law; Securities Mediation; Consumer Class Actions. ***Email:*** mmaddox@mhclaw.com

THOMAS A. HARGETT, born Atlantic City, New Jersey, August 11, 1958; admitted to bar, 1994, Indiana and U.S. District Court, Northern and Southern Districts of Indiana. *Education:* Indiana University (B.A., 1980; J.D., 1994); Northwestern University; Kellogg Graduate School of Management (Master of Business Administration, 1983). Member, Public Investor Arbitration Bar Association. *Member:* Indianapolis, Indiana State and American Bar Associations. ***PRACTICE AREAS:*** Securities Arbitration; Securities Litigation; Securities Mediation; Class Action Litigation. ***Email:*** tahargett@mhclaw.com

STEVEN B. CARUSO, born New York, N.Y., January 10, 1956; admitted to bar, 1981, New York, U.S. District Court, Southern and Eastern Districts of New York, U.S. Tax Court and U.S. Court of Appeals, Second Circuit; U.S. Supreme Court. *Education:* American University (B.A., 1977); Hofstra University Law School (J.D., 1980). Author: "NASD Arbitration Discovery Procedures: Knowing Your Customer From the Securities Professional Perspective," American Bar Association, Section of Litigation, Committee on Securities Litigation, August 1995; "On-Line Trading - The New Frontier," Practicing Law Institute, Securities Arbitration, July 1999; "Examination of the Adverse Broker: Unimpeachable Questions with an Internet Twist," Practicing Law Institute, Securities Arbitration, August 2001; "Ethical Considerations in Settlement Agreements," Association of the Bar of the City of New York, June 2004; "Model Arbitrator Instructions: Luxury of Emerging Necessity," Practicing Law Institute, Securities Arbitration, August 2004; "Discovery Objections Which are Irrelevant, Unduly Burdensome and are Reasonably Calculated to Lead to the Concealment of Admissible Evidence," New York State Bar Association, Securities Arbitration 2004, October 2004; "Arbitrator Training in the Securities Dispute Arena," The Review of Securities and Commodities Regulation, January 2005. *Member:* The Association of the Bar of the City of New York; American Bar Association (Member, Sections on: Business Law; Litigation, Securities Litigation Subcommittee); Public Investors Arbitration Bar Association (Director). (Resident, New York, N.Y. Office). ***PRACTICE AREAS:*** Securities Arbitration; Securities Litigation. ***Email:*** scaruso@mhclaw.com

---

THOMAS K. CALDWELL, born Lansing, Michigan, October 21, 1963; admitted to bar, 1989, Michigan; 1990, U.S. District Court, Eastern and Western Districts of Michigan; 1991, Indiana and U.S. District Court, Northern and Southern Districts of Indiana. *Education:* Michigan State University (B.A., 1986); Indiana University School of Law (J.D., 1989). Law Clerk to Hon. Lawrence P. Zatkoff, U.S. District Court, Eastern District of Michigan, 1989-1991. Deputy Attorney General, State of Indiana, 1992-1993. *Member:* Indianapolis and Indiana State Bar Associations; State Bar of Michigan. ***PRACTICE AREAS:*** Civil Litigation; Securities Litigation; Securities Arbitration; Class Actions. ***Email:*** tkcaldwell@mhclaw.com

KEITH L. GRIFFIN, born Elkhart, Indiana, February 8, 1973; admitted to bar, 2000, Indiana and U.S. District Court, Southern and Northern Districts of Indiana. *Education:* Indiana University (B.A., 1996; J.D., 2000). Secretary of State, Securities Division, 2000-2003; Member, Public Investors Arbitration Bar Association. *Member:* Indiana State and American Bar Associations. ***PRACTICE AREAS:*** Securities Arbitration; Securities Litigation; Blue Sky Law; Securities Regulation. ***Email:*** klgriffin@mhclaw.com

(This Listing Continued)

BARBARA QUINN SMITH, born Cleveland, Ohio, December 30, 1964; admitted to bar, 1991, Ohio and U.S. District Court, Northern District of Ohio; 2002, U.S. Court of Appeals, Sixth Circuit (Not admitted in Indiana). *Education:* John Carroll University (B.A., 1987); Case Western Reserve University (J.D., 1991). *Member:* Ohio State Bar Association. ***REPORTED CASES:*** Walters v. The Enrichment Center of Wishing Well, Inc., 78 Ohio St.3d 118 (1997); Gary Phillips & Assoc. v. Ameritech Corp., 144 Ohio App. 3d 149 (10th Dist. 2001); Walker v. Firelands Community Hosp., 2003 WL 21299923 (6th Dist. 2003); Gomez v. Towne Bancorp, Inc., 217 F.Supp.2d 829 (N.D. Ohio 2002); Dalahunt v. Cytodyne Technologies, 241 F. Supp. 2d 827 (S.D. Ohio 2003). ***PRACTICE AREAS:*** Class Actions Litigation; Securities Litigation. ***Email:*** bqses@aol.com

REFERENCE: Bank One, Indianapolis.

THE MARCUS LAW FIRM

11978 FISHERS CROSSING DRIVE
FISHERS, INDIANA 46038
Telephone: 317-845-4444
Fax: 317-284-0266
Email: cmarcus@marcus-law.com
URL: http://www.marcus-lawfirm.com

Healthcare Law, Elder Law, Personal Injury, Automobile Accidents, Slip and Fall, Wrongful Death, Legal Malpractice, Consumer Law, Medical Malpractice, Unsafe Products, Civil Rights, Employment law, Wrongful Termination, Discrimination, Harassment, Trial Practice, Family Law, Adoptions, Child Custody, Child Support, Divorce, Visitation Rights, Real Estate, Wills and Probate, Trusts and Estates, Estate Planning, Guardianships, Asset Protection, Business Law, Business Planning, Contracts, Lawsuits, Business Enterprises, Corporate, Limited Liability Companies, Partnerships, Buying and Selling a Business.

CYNTHIA A. MARCUS, born Corona, California, April 15, 1954; admitted to bar, 1995, Indiana. *Education:* Ball State University (B.S., Nursing, 1991); Indiana University (J.D., 1994). Sigma Theta. *Member:* Indiana State Bar Association; Indiana Trial Lawyers Association; American Trial Lawyers Association. [USAF 1976-1978; USAR 1985-1992]. ***REPORTED CASES:*** Miller v. Ryan, 706 N.E.2d 244, Ind. Ct. App. 1999. ***PRACTICE AREAS:*** Health Care; Trial Practice; Medical Malpractice; Family Law; Civil Rights. ***Email:*** cmarcus@marcus-law.com

ASSOCIATE

AMBER L. SMALL, born Valparaiso, Indiana, January 11, 1976; admitted to bar, 2003, Indiana. *Education:* Indiana University (B.S. 1999); Valparaiso University (J.D., 2002). Phi Delta Phi. *Member:* Indianapolis and Indiana State Bar Associations. ***PRACTICE AREAS:*** Family Law; Personal Injury; Medical Malpractice; Probate. ***Email:*** asmall@marcus-law.com

MEYER LAW OFFICE

FISHERS, INDIANA

(See Indianapolis)

Wills, Trusts and Estates, Probate Law, Charitable Giving, Non-profit Organizations, Small Business, Business Law, Real Estate, Income Tax, Estate and Gift Taxation and Wealth Preservation Law.

MITCHELL & ASSOCIATES

FISHERS, INDIANA

(See Indianapolis)

Mitchell & Associates is an association of attorneys who offer services in all areas of family law, including but not limited to divorce and post-divorce modification; domestic litigation; family mediation; qualified domestic relations orders (QDROS); antenuptial agreements; child custody and support; visitation rights; paternity; adoption; domestic violence; guardianships; grandparent's visitation rights; simple wills and trusts and other related matters.

JEFFERY B. RISINGER, P.C.

12985 LANTERN ROAD
FISHERS, INDIANA 46038
Telephone: 317-578-1801
Fax: 317-578-1480
Email: jbrfinlaw@aol.com
URL: http://www.lawyers.com/risinger

Business Law, Finance, Securities and Investments, Business Enterprises, Closely Held Business Law, Corporate, Franchises, Limited Liability Companies, Partnership Law, Small Business Law, Buying and Selling of Businesses, Business Planning, Contracts, Real Estate, Commercial Leasing, Business Start-Ups, Strategic Alliances, Joint Ventures, Mergers, Taxation, Tax Planning, Water Law, Sewer Utilities.

JEFFERY B. RISINGER, born Charlestown, Indiana, January 15, 1956; admitted to bar, 1981, Indiana. *Education:* Indiana University School of Business (B.S., with highest distinction/honors program, Beta Gamma Sigma, 1978); University of Chicago Law School (J.D., 1981). Adjunct Professor of Business Law, Butler University, 1999-2001. Partner, Leagre & Barnes, 1984-1992. *Member:* Indiana State Bar Association. ***Email:*** jbrfinlaw@aol.com

ARATA LAW FIRM

LINCOLN TOWER - 14TH FLOOR
116 E. BERRY STREET
FORT WAYNE, INDIANA 46802
Telephone: 260-424-1010
Fax: 260-420-1406
Email: patarata@aol.com
URL: http://www.thearatalawfirm.com

Civil and Criminal Litigation, Driving While Intoxicated, Personal Injury.

PATRICK J. ARATA, born Fort Wayne, Indiana, February 28, 1953; admitted to bar, 1979, California and U.S. District Court, Eastern District of California; 1980, Indiana; 1981, U.S. District Court, Southern and Northern Districts of Indiana, U.S. Court of Appeals, 7th Circuit and U.S. Tax Court; 1985, U.S. Supreme Court. *Education:* Indiana University (B.A., 1976); McGeorge College of Law (J.D., 1979). Deputy Public Defender, Allen County, 1987-1992. Member: National College for DUI Defense, Sustaining Member; American Inns of Court, (Master) Benjamin Harrison Chapter. *Member:* Allen County (Chairman, Criminal Defense Attorney's Section, 2000—) and Indiana State Bar Associations; National Association of Criminal Defense Lawyers (Life Member); Indiana Association of Criminal Defense Lawyers; Association of Federal Attorneys; Indiana Trial Lawyers Association (ITLA); Association of Trial Lawyers of America (ATLA). ***PRACTICE AREAS:*** Criminal Law; DUI Defense; Personal Injury; Civil Litigation. ***Email:*** parata@aratalawfirm.com

---

ROBERT W. GEVERS, born Fort Wayne, Indiana, March 26, 1960; admitted to bar, 1985, Indiana and U.S. District Courts, Northern District of Indiana and Western District of Michigan; 1992, U.S. Court of Appeals, Seventh Circuit. *Education:* Northwestern University (B.A., cum laude, 1982); Indiana University (J.D., cum laude, 1985). Adjunct Professor, Criminal Justice Program, School of Public and Environmental Affairs, Indiana-Purdue University, 1991-1994. Associate Member, International Association of Forensic Nurses. Prosecuting Attorney, Allen County, Indiana, 1995-2002. Assistant U.S. Attorney, Northern District of Indiana, 1990-1993. *Member:* Allen County Bar Association; National College for DUI Defense; National Association of Criminal Defense Lawyers. ***PRACTICE AREAS:*** Criminal Law; Driving While Intoxicated; Personal Injury; Trial Practice; White Collar Crime. ***Email:*** rgevers@aratalawfirm.com

ALBERT ANZINI, III, born Portsmouth, Virginia, January 11, 1961; admitted to bar, 1990, Virginia; 2000, Indiana; 2003, U.S. District Court, Northern District of Indiana. *Education:* Indiana-Purdue University Fort Wayne (B.A., 1987); Marshall-Wythe at the College of William & Mary (J.D., 1990). *Member:* National College for DUI Defense; American Inns of Court (Benjamin Harrison Chapter). [U.S. Army, SP5 1981-1985, Cpt.1991-1999]. ***PRACTICE AREAS:*** Criminal Law; Driving While Intoxicated; Drugs and Narcotics; Personal Injury. ***Email:*** al@aratalawfirm.com

---

BAKER & DANIELS LLP

Established in 1863
111 EAST WAYNE STREET, SUITE 800
FORT WAYNE, INDIANA 46802
Telephone: 260-424-8000
Fax: 260-460-1700
URL: http://www.bakerdaniels.com

Indianapolis, Indiana Office: 300 North Meridian Street, Suite 2700, 46204. Telephone: 317-237-0300. Fax: 317-237-1000.
South Bend, Indiana Office: First Bank Building, 205 West Jefferson Boulevard, Suite 250, 46601. Telephone: 574-234-4149. Fax: 574-239-1900.
Elkhart, Indiana Office: 317 West Franklin Street, Suite 507, P.O. Box 507, 46515-0507. Telephone: 574-296-6000. Fax: 574-296-6001.
Indianapolis-96th Street, Indiana Office: Parkwood Six, 600 East 96th Street, Suite 600, 46240. Telephone: 317-569-9600. Fax: 317-569-4800.
Washington, D.C. Office: 805 15th Street, N.W., Suite 700, 20005. Telephone: 202-312-7440. Fax: 202-312-7460.
Qingdao, China Office: 4/F, Office Tower, Crowne Plaza Qingdao, No. 76 Hong Kong Middle Road, 266071. Telephone: +011-86-532-575-1051. Fax: +011-86-532-575-1055.
Beijing, China Office: Room 1919, Tower 2, China World Trade Center, No. 1 JianGuoMenWai Avenue, 100004. Telephone: +86-10-6505-7733. Fax: +86-10-6505-8730.

Antitrust, Bankruptcy, Business Planning, Commercial, Corporate Finance, Creditors Rights, Employee Benefits, Employment, Environment, Estate and Probate, Family, Financial, Food and Drug, Government Affairs, Health Care, Insurance, Intellectual Property, International, Legislative, Litigation, Medical Technology Regulation, Municipal, Nonprofit, Product Liability, Real Estate, Securities, Sports, Tax, Transportation, Utilities, Year 2000, Zoning and Land Use Law.

FIRM PROFILE: Since 1863 we have been helping clients do business throughout Indiana, across the country and around the world. From Fortune 500 corporations to regional businesses, local governments and individuals, clients look to Baker & Daniels LLP for excellence in all areas of legal practice, for a creative and individualized approach to solving client problems, and for a deep understanding of business, law and government. More than 350 Baker and Daniels' professionals serve clients from the firm's seven offices in Indiana, Washington, D.C. and China (we are one of only 31 U.S. law firms licensed to practice in China). Our service to clients is enhanced by our Washington, D.C. government affairs consulting subsidiary, Sagamore Associates, and our exclusive Indiana membership in Lex Mundi, an association of more than 158 independent law firms around the world.

(This Listing Continued)

LAW FIRM ALLIANCES/ASSOCIATIONS: ***TAGLAW (The Appleton Group Legal Network):*** *The Firm is a member of TAGLaw, an international association of prominent law firms and an exclusive Indiana Member of Lex Mundi.*

MEMBERS OF FIRM

J. STEPHEN BENNETT, born 1969; admitted to bar, 1995, Illinois; 2000, U.S. District Court, Central District of Illinois (Not admitted in Indiana). *Education:* University of Illinois (B.A., 1991); George Washington University (J.D., 1994). *Member:* Defense Research Institute. ***PRACTICE AREAS:*** Product Liability; Litigation. ***Email:*** stephen.bennett@bakerd.com

JON A. BOMBERGER, born 1959; admitted to bar, 1984, Indiana. *Education:* Western Michigan University (B.A., cum laude, 1981); University of Notre Dame (J.D., 1984). Contributing Author: "Advanced Real Estate Law in Indiana," NBI, Inc., 1993; "Residential Leasing 201," ICLEF, 1994; "Commercial Loan Documentation," ICLEF, 1995. *Member:* Allen County and Indiana State Bar Associations. ***PRACTICE AREAS:*** Commercial Real Estate Acquisitions; Commercial Real Estate Development; Commercial Real Estate Finance; Zoning, Planning and Land Use. ***Email:*** jon.bomberger@bakerd.com

JOHN R. BURNS, III, born 1949; admitted to bar, 1974, Ohio; 1976, Indiana; 1990, U.S. Supreme Court. *Education:* Ball State University (A.B., 1971); University of Notre Dame Law School (J.D., 1974). Blue Key. Executive Editor, Notre Dame Law Review, 1973-1974. Contributing Author: "Bankruptcy 1986," ICLEF, 1986; "Mortgage Foreclosures in Indiana," ICLEF, 1987; "Basic Bankruptcy in Indiana: Creditors, Debtors and the Estate," National Business Institute, 1987; "Business, Banks, Borrowers and the Environment," ICLEF, 1991; "Annual Bankruptcy Institute," ICLEF, 1993, 1994 and 1998; "Rats, Rodents and Rosenbloom: Journal Gazette v. Bandido's," Res Gestae, Vol. 45, No. 1, July/August 2001; "Suing the Foreign Business Entity: An Introduction to the Commercial Activities Exception to the Foreign Sovereign Immunities Act ("FSIA")," Commercial and Business Litigation Journal, ABA, Section of Litigation, Commercial and Business Litigation Committee, Winter 2001-2002; "Service of Process upon the Foreign Individual or Business Entity: An Introduction to the Application of FRCP 4(f)," Commercial and Business Litigation Journal, ABA, Section of Litigation, Commercial and Business Litigation Committee, Spring 2002; "Effective Deposition Preparation," Commercial and Business Litigation Journal, ABA, Section of Litigation, Winter 2002-2003. *Member:* Allen County (Chairman, Bankruptcy Section, 1990-1992), Indiana State (Chair, Bankruptcy Section, 2001-2002) and American (Litigation Section, Programs Co-chair, Business and Commercial Litigation Committee) Bar Associations; American Inns of Court (Master). [Lt.,USNR, JAG, 1971-1978]. ***REPORTED CASES:*** In re Consolidated Industries Corp., 279 BR 831 (DC ND IN, 2002); Kaghann's Korner, Inc. v. Brown & Sons Fuel Company, Inc., 711 NE2d 1286 (IN App, 1999); Reed v. Central Soya Company, Inc., 644 NE2d 84 (SC IN, 1994); In the Matter of Gould, 977 F2d 1038 (7th Cir., 1992); Mars Steel Corporation v. Continental Bank N.A., 880 F2d 928 (7th Cir., 1989, amicus curiae for Ind. State Bar Assoc.). ***PRACTICE AREAS:*** Bankruptcy; Commercial Litigation; Media Law. ***Email:*** john.burns@bakerd.com

TIMOTHY J. HAFFNER, born 1959; admitted to bar, 1985, Indiana. *Education:* Wabash College (B.A., summa cum laude, 1982); Indiana University (J.D., 1985). Phi Beta Kappa. Member, National Moot Court Board. *Member:* Allen County and Indiana State Bar Associations. ***PRACTICE AREAS:*** Corporate Law. ***Email:*** tim.haffner@bakerd.com

STEVEN H. HAZELRIGG, born 1952; admitted to bar, 1977, Indiana. *Education:* DePauw University (B.A., with honors, 1974); Indiana University (J.D., cum laude, 1977). Phi Delta Theta. Managing Editor, Indiana Law Journal, 1976-1977. ***PRACTICE AREAS:*** Corporate Law; Securities; Banking Law; Employee Benefits. ***Email:*** steven.hazelrigg@bakerd.com

JOHN F. HOFFMAN, born 1947; admitted to bar, 1972, Virginia; 1977, Indiana; registered to practice before U.S. Patent and Trademark Office. *Education:* University of Notre Dame (B.S. in Elec. Engr., 1969); George Washington University (J.D., with honors, 1972). *Member:* Indiana State Bar Association (Chairman, Patent Section, 1981-1982); American Intellectual Property Law Association. ***PRACTICE AREAS:*** Intellectual Property. ***Email:*** john.hoffman@bakerd.com

DAVID P. IRMSCHER, born 1956; admitted to bar, 1982, Texas and U.S. District Court, Northern District of Texas; 1983, U.S. Court of Appeals, Fifth Circuit; 1989, Indiana; 1990, U.S. District Court, Northern District of Indiana; U.S. Court of Appeals, Federal Circuit. *Education:* Dartmouth College (A.B., cum laude, 1979); University of Michigan at Ann Arbor (J.D., 1982). *Member:* Allen County, Indiana State and American Bar Associations; American Intellectual Property Law Association. ***PRACTICE AREAS:*** Intellectual Property. ***Email:*** david.irmscher@bakerd.com

STEVEN L. JACKSON, born 1951; admitted to bar, 1978, Indiana and U.S. District Court, Northern and Southern Districts of Indiana; 1981, U.S. District Court, Eastern District of Illinois; 1982, U.S. Supreme Court; 1984, U.S. Court of Appeals, Seventh Circuit; 1989, U.S. Court of Appeals, Federal Circuit; 2003, U.S. Court of Appeals, Third Circuit. *Education:* Purdue University (B.A., with honors, 1973); Indiana University (J.D., magna cum laude, 1977). President, Moot Court Board, 1977. Instructor, Commercial Law, Indiana University-Purdue University at Fort Wayne, 1978-1983. Faculty: Seminar on Civil Litigation in Federal Courts, 1997—; Masters Class in Federal Litigation, 2002; The Trial of a Sex Harassment Case, 2002. Benjamin Harrison American Inn of Court: Vice President, 2000; President 2001; Counselor to the Inn 2003. *Member:* Allen County, Indiana State and Seventh Circuit Bar Associations. ***PRACTICE AREAS:*** Health Care; Employment Law; Civil Litigation. ***Email:*** steven.jackson@bakerd.com

MICHAEL L. JAMES, born 1951; admitted to bar, 1977, Minnesota; 1982, Indiana. *Education:* University of Evansville (B.A., cum laude, 1974); Indiana University (J.D., 1977). Authorized Mediator, Indiana Alternative Dispute Resolution Rules. *Member:* Allen County, Indiana State and American (Member, Litigation Section and Construction Litigation and Products Liability Subcommittees) Bar Associations. ***PRACTICE AREAS:*** General Civil Litigation; Construction Law; Trademarks; Products Liability; Commercial Sales; Distribution. ***Email:*** michael.james@bakerd.com

JOSEPH W. KIMMELL, II, born 1947; admitted to bar, 1972, Indiana; 1981, U.S. Tax Court; U.S. District Court, Northern and Southern Districts of Indiana; 2000, Indiana; 2001, District of Columbia. *Education:* Duke University (B.A., 1969); University of Michi-

(This Listing Continued)

BAKER & DANIELS LLP, Fort Wayne—Continued

gan (J.D., 1972). Member, Board of Directors, Indiana Lawyer's Commission, Inc., 1977-1978. Corporation Counsel, City of Fort Wayne, 2002—. Chairman, International and China Practice, 2000—. Visiting Professor, Qingdao University Law School, Qingdao, China, 2000. *Member:* Indiana State Bar Association; District of Columbia Bar. (Also at Washington, D.C. and Peoples Republic of China Offices). ***PRACTICE AREAS:*** International Transactions; Mergers and Acquisitions; Municipal Law. ***Email:*** joseph.kimmell@bakerd.com

DAVID J. KUKER, born 1967; admitted to bar, 1995, Indiana and U.S. District Court, Northern District of Indiana. *Education:* University of Chicago (A.B., with honors, 1989); Valparaiso University (J.D., summa cum laude, 1995). *Member:* Allen County, Indiana State and American Bar Associations. ***PRACTICE AREAS:*** Business Planning; Corporate Law; Franchises; Commercial Real Estate. ***Email:*** dave.kuker@bakerd.com

JEANNE E. LONGSWORTH, born 1956; admitted to bar, 1987, Indiana; U.S. District Court, Northern and Southern Districts of Indiana. *Education:* Indiana University (B.S., 1984); Valparaiso University (J.D., 1987). Certified Public Accountant, Indiana, 2000. *Member:* Allen County, Indiana State and American Bar Associations; Indiana CPA Society. ***PRACTICE AREAS:*** Estate Planning; Estate Administration; Taxation Law. ***Email:*** jeanne.longsworth@bakerd.com

ROBERT D. MORELAND, born 1962; admitted to bar, 1988, Indiana. *Education:* Anderson College (B.A., cum laude, 1984); Indiana University (J.D., cum laude, 1988). Senior Managing Editor, Indiana Law Journal, Vol. 63. *Member:* Allen County, DeKalb County and Indiana State Bar Associations. ***PRACTICE AREAS:*** Commercial Litigation; Employment Litigation; Intellectual Property Litigation. ***Email:*** rob.moreland@bakerd.com

MICHAEL J. NADER, born 1962; admitted to bar, 1988, Indiana. *Education:* University of Michigan (B.A., 1985); Wayne State University (J.D., cum laude, 1988). Chairman, Lex Mundi Employee Benefits Committee, 1991-1994. ***PRACTICE AREAS:*** Employee Benefits. ***Email:*** michael.nader@bakerd.com

ANTHONY NIEWYK, born 1941; admitted to bar, 1973, Michigan; 1985, Indiana; 1987, U.S. District Court, Northern District of Indiana; registered to practice before U.S. Patent and Trademark Office. *Education:* Calvin College (B.S., 1963); University of Michigan (B.S.E.E., 1963; M.S.E.E., 1964); George Washington University (J.D., with honors, 1972). Tau Beta Pi; Eta Kappa Nu. ***PRACTICE AREAS:*** Intellectual Property. ***Email:*** anthony.niewyk@bakerd.com

LAURA C. O'DONNELL, born 1971; admitted to bar, 1996, Indiana, U.S. District Courts, Northern and Southern Districts of Indiana and U.S. Court of Appeals, Seventh Circuit. *Education:* Michigan State University (B.A., cum laude, 1993); Indiana University School of Law (J.D., cum laude, 1996). Order of the Barristers. Recipient, Sherman Minton Moot Court Best Brief and Best Oralist Award. Senior Notes Editor, Federal Communications Law Journal. (Also at Indianapolis office). ***PRACTICE AREAS:*** Labor Relations; Employment Relations. ***Email:*** laura.o'donnell@bakerd.com

MACLYN T. PARKER, born 1929; admitted to bar, 1954, Michigan and Indiana. *Education:* DePauw University (A.B., 1951); University of London; University of Michigan (J.D., 1954); University of California at Berkeley. Awarded LL.D., Purdue University, 2000. Chairman, Greater Ft. Wayne Chamber of Commerce, 1976-1977; 1990-1991. ***PRACTICE AREAS:*** Probate Law; Estate Planning Law; Tax Exempt Organizations. ***Email:*** maclyn.parker@bakerd.com

DOUGLAS DORMIRE POWERS, born 1953; admitted to bar, 1983, Indiana. *Education:* Oberlin College (A.B., 1977); University of Toledo (J.D., 1983). Note and Comment Editor, University of Toledo Law Review, 1982-1983. Law Clerk to: Magistrate James G. Carr, U.S. District Court, Northern District of Ohio, 1985; Hon. Don J. Young, U.S. District Court, Northern District of Ohio, 1985-1986; Hon. William C. Lee, U.S. District Court, Northern District of Indiana, 1986-1987. *Member:* Allen County (Chair, Trial Lawyers Section, 1992-1994), Indiana State, American and Seventh Circuit Bar Associations. ***REPORTED CASES:*** Lincoln Nat. Life Ins. Co. v. Donaldson, Lufkin & Jenrette Sec. Corp., 9 F. Supp.2d 994 (N.D. Ind. 1998); Bollenbacher v. Helena Chemical Co., 934 F. Supp. 1015 (N.D. Ind. 1996); Newton v. Van Otterloo, 756 F. Supp. 1121 (N.D. Ind. 1991). ***PRACTICE AREAS:*** Litigation; Employee Benefits. ***Email:*** doug.powers@bakerd.com

DAVID A. SCOTT, born 1947; admitted to bar, 1972, Indiana. *Education:* Miami University (A.B., 1969); Indiana University (J.D., cum laude, 1972). *Member:* Allen County, Indiana State and American Bar Associations. ***PRACTICE AREAS:*** Real Estate; Commercial Law; Estate Planning Law. ***Email:*** david.scott@bakerd.com

LAWRENCE E. SHINE, born 1947; admitted to bar, 1973, Indiana. *Education:* Indiana University (B.A., 1969; M.A., 1970; J.D., 1973); University of St. Francis (M.B.A., 1978). *Member:* Allen County, Indiana State and American Bar Associations. ***PRACTICE AREAS:*** Corporate Law; Securities; Municipal Finance. ***Email:*** lawrence.shine@bakerd.com

THOMAS M. SHOAFF, born 1941; admitted to bar, 1968, Illinois; 1969, Indiana. *Education:* Williams College (B.A., 1964); Vanderbilt University (LL.B., 1967). Associate Editor, Vanderbilt Law Review, 1963-1964. *Member:* Allen County, Indiana State and American Bar Associations. ***PRACTICE AREAS:*** Corporate Law; Mergers and Acquisitions; Administrative Law; Business Litigation. ***Email:*** thomas.shoaff@bakerd.com

N. REED SILLIMAN, born 1946; admitted to bar, 1973, Indiana. *Education:* Hanover College (B.A., 1968); University of Louisville (J.D., magna cum laude, 1973). Phi Kappa Phi; Omicron Delta Kappa; Delta Theta Phi. Notes Editor, Journal of Family Law, 1972-1973. *Member:* Allen County, Indiana State and American Bar Associations; National Health Lawyers Association. ***PRACTICE AREAS:*** Corporate Law; Estate Planning; Health Care. ***Email:*** reed.silliman@bakerd.com

KEITH E. WHITE, admitted to bar, 1983, Indiana and U.S. District Court, Southern District of Indiana; 1987, U.S. Court of Appeals, Seventh Circuit; 1997, U.S. District Court, Northern District of Indiana. *Education:* Hanover College (B.A., magna cum laude, 1980); Indiana University School of Law - Bloomington (J.D., 1983). *Member:* Indianapolis (Past

(This Listing Continued)

Chair, Labor Law Section), Indiana State (Past Chair, Corporate Counsel Section) and American (Committee on ADR in Labor and Employment Law) Bar Associations. ***PRACTICE AREAS:*** Labor and Employment. ***Email:*** keith.white@bakerd.com

COUNSEL

KAREN T. MOSES, born 1960; admitted to bar, 1985, Indiana and Illinois. *Education:* Northwestern University (B.A., 1982); Indiana University (J.D., 1985). ***PRACTICE AREAS:*** Commercial Litigation. ***Email:*** karen.moses@bakerd.com

RESIDENT ASSOCIATES

THOMAS R. BIEHL, JR., admitted to bar, 1996, Ohio (Not admitted in Indiana). *Education:* The Ohio State University (B.A., 1993); University of Toledo College of Law (J.D., 1996). Director, Labor and Industrial Relations, Superior Essex, Fort Wayne, Indiana. Staff Attorney, Montgomery County Public Defender's Office, Dayton, Ohio. ***PRACTICE AREAS:*** Labor and Employment. ***Email:*** thomas.biehl@bakerd.com

BETSY M. BROOKS, admitted to bar, 2005, Indiana. *Education:* Arizona State University (B.A., 2002); University of Toledo (J.D., 2005). ***PRACTICE AREAS:*** Labor and Employment. ***Email:*** betsy.brooks@bakerd.com

MICHAEL S. BURNS, admitted to bar, 2001, Indiana. *Education:* Wabash College (A.B., 1998); Indiana University School of Law - Indianapolis (J.D., 2001). ***PRACTICE AREAS:*** Labor and Employment. ***Email:*** michael.burns@bakerd.com

SCOTT C. BURNS, born Boise, Idaho, May 13, 1976; admitted to bar, 2001, California; 2004, Tennessee (Not admitted in Indiana). *Education:* University of Washington (B.A., 1997); Vanderbilt University School of Law (J.D., 2001). Member: Moot Court Board, 1999-2001; Moot Court Board Associate Justice, 2000-2001. *Member:* Los Angeles County and American Bar Associations. ***PRACTICE AREAS:*** Employee Benefits; Executive Compensation; Labor and Employment. ***Email:*** scott.burns@bakerd.com

ABIGAIL MARIE BUTLER, born 1975; admitted to bar, 2000, Indiana. *Education:* Hillsdale College (B.S., Chemistry, 1997); Michigan State University (J.D., magna cum laude, 2000). ***PRACTICE AREAS:*** Intellectual Property; Products Liability. ***Email:*** abigail.butler@bakerd.com

CYNTHIA M. CORMANY, born 1965; admitted to bar, 1990, Indiana; U.S. District Court, Northern and Southern Districts of Indiana. *Education:* Indiana University (B.A., with highest distinction, 1987; J.D., magna cum laude, 1990). Phi Beta Kappa; Order of the Coif. ***PRACTICE AREAS:*** Litigation; Product Liability. ***Email:*** cynthia.cormany@bakerd.com

ADAM F. COX, born 1974; admitted to bar, 1999, Indiana, U.S. District Court, Northern and Southern Districts of Indiana; registered to practice before U.S. Patent and Trademark Office. *Education:* Miami University (B.S., Chemistry, 1996); Indiana University (J.D., magna cum laude, 1999). ***PRACTICE AREAS:*** Intellectual Property. ***Email:*** adam.cox@bakerd.com

DAVID P. DURM, born 1970; admitted to bar, 1998, Indiana. *Education:* Indiana University (B.S., 1992); Indiana University, Bloomington, School of Law (J.D., 1998). Order of the Barristers. ***PRACTICE AREAS:*** Real Estate; Business Planning; Health Care. ***Email:*** david.durm@bakerd.com

BRIAN THOMAS GEISLER, born Pittsburgh, Pennsylvania; admitted to bar, 2003, Ohio; registered to practice before U.S. Patent and Trademark Office (Not admitted in Indiana). *Education:* Youngstown State University (B.E. magna cum laude, 1997; M.S., 1999); University of Akron (J.D., magna cum laude, 2003). *Member:* Ohio State and American Bar Associations. ***PRACTICE AREAS:*** Intellectual Property. ***Email:*** brian.geisler@bakerd.com

JEFFREY V. GERY, born 1967; admitted to bar, 1994, Indiana; U.S. District Court, Northern and Southern Districts of Indiana. *Education:* Indiana University (B.A., 1990; J.D., 1994). *Member:* Allen County, Indiana State and American Bar Associations; Securities Industry Association (Member, Compliance and Legal Division). ***PRACTICE AREAS:*** Securities Litigation; Securities Arbitration; Commercial Litigation; Class Action Litigation; Product Liability Litigation. ***Email:*** jeffrey.gery@bakerd.com

JEFFREY A. GOEGLEIN, admitted to bar, 2004, Indiana and U.S. District Court, Northern and Southern Districts of Indiana. *Education:* Indiana University (B.S., 1997; M.B.A., 2004); Indiana University School of Law - Bloomington (J.D., 2004). *Member:* Allen County and Indiana State Bar Associations; American Institute of Certified Public Accountants. ***PRACTICE AREAS:*** Business Planning.

SHELLIE L. GOETZ, born 1970; admitted to bar, 2004, Indiana. *Education:* Vincennes University (A.S., 1990); Indiana University-Purdue University, Ft. Wayne (B.A., with highest distinction, 2000); Indiana University School of Law (J.D., 2004). Senior Business Manager, Federal Communications Law Journal, 2003-2004; National Telecommunications Moot Court Team Coach, Federal Communications Law Journal, 2003-2004; Sherman Minton Moot Court, 2002. *Member:* Indiana State and American Bar Associations. ***PRACTICE AREAS:*** Employment. ***Email:*** shellie.goetz@bakerd.com

DAMIAN GOSHEFF, admitted to bar, 2005, Indiana. *Education:* Indiana University (B.S., 2001); University of Toledo (J.D., 2005). Author, "Brown's Unfulfilled Promise: Educational Finance Reform and the Separate But Equal Effect of State Education Clause Remedies - New York as a Model," 35 U. Tol. L. Rev. 889 (2004). ***LANGUAGES:*** Macedonian and Bulgarian. ***PRACTICE AREAS:*** Trusts and Estates. ***Email:*** damian.gosheff@bakerd.com

JEROME BYRON HAYES, admitted to bar, 2005, Indiana. *Education:* Hanover College (B.A., cum laude, 2001); Indiana University - Purdue University (M.S., 2002); Indiana University School of Law - Bloomington (J.D., 2005). ***PRACTICE AREAS:*** Products Liability. ***Email:*** jerome.hayes@bakerd.com

JULIE ANNETTE HOFFMAN, born 1974; admitted to bar, 2002, Ilinois; 2004, Indiana. *Education:* Hanover College (B.A., cum laude, 1996); University of Notre Dame (J.D., summa cum laude, 2002). Federal Courts, Practice and Procedure Editor, Notre Dame Law Review, 2000-2002. Recipient, Notre Dame Law School Furahaugh Prize for High

(This Listing Continued)

Scholarship, 2002. Judicial Clerk to Judge Richard S. Arnold, Eighth Circuit Court of Appeals, 2003-2004. *Member:* Illinois State and American Bar Associations. **Email:** julie.hoffman@bakerd.com

JASON A. HOUSER, born 1977; admitted to bar, 2004, Indiana; registered to practice before U.S. Patent and Trademark Office. *Education:* Purdue University (B.S.E.E., 2000); Manchester College (B.S., 2000); Valparaiso University School of Law (J.D., 2004). Eta Kappa Nu; Tau Beta Pi. ***PRACTICE AREAS:*** Intellectual Property. **Email:** jason.houser@bakerd.com

MARK F. JUBA, born 1976; admitted to bar, 2003, Indiana and U.S. District Court, Northern and Southern Districts of Indiana. *Education:* University of Notre Dame (J.D., 2003). Member, National Appellate Moot Court Team and Board, Notre Dame Law School, 2002-2003. Recipient, A. Harold Weber Moot Court Award for Excellence in Oral Advocacy, Notre Dame Law School, 2003. *Member:* Indiana State and American (Member, Litigation Division) Bar Associations. ***PRACTICE AREAS:*** Litigation. **Email:** mark.juba@bakerd.com

THOMAS C. KUS, born 1963; admitted to bar, 1989, Indiana; 1998, U.S. Court of Appeals, Seventh Circuit. *Education:* University of Michigan (B.A., with distinction, 1986); Indiana University (J.D., 1989). Dean's Honors. Recipient, Indiana University School of Law Fellowship. *Member:* Allen County, Indiana State and American Bar Associations. ***PRACTICE AREAS:*** Products Liability Litigation; Environmental Litigation; Commercial Litigation; Patent and Trademark Litigation. **Email:** thomas.kus@bakerd.com

MARTHA M. LEMERT, born 1967; admitted to bar, 1993, Ohio; 1994, U.S. District Court, Northern District of Ohio; 1998, Indiana and U.S. District Court, Northern and Southern Districts of Indiana. *Education:* Vassar College (A.B., cum laude, 1989); Case Western Reserve University (J.D., 1993). Recipient, American Jurisprudence Award, Contracts. Articles Editor, Case Western Reserve Law Review 1992-1993. *Member:* Allen County, Indiana State and American Bar Associations. ***LANGUAGES:*** Mandarin Chinese. ***PRACTICE AREAS:*** Labor and Employment Law; Disabilities; Education Law; Litigation. **Email:** martha.lemert@bakerd.com

JON L. LINDBERG, born 1978; admitted to bar, 2003, Ohio (Not admitted in Indiana). *Education:* College of Wooster (B.A., 2000); University of Akron (J.D., 2003). Assistant Editor, University of Akron Law Review, 2002-2003. Judicial Clerk, Allen Superior Court, 2003-2004. *Member:* Ohio State Bar Association.

SHANNON K. REED, born 1975; admitted to bar, 2000, Indiana and U.S. District Court, Northern and Southern Districts of Indiana. *Education:* University of Wisconsin-Whitewater (B.A., 1997); Valparaiso University (J.D., 2000). Member, 1998-2000 and Associate Justice, 1999-2000, Moot Court. ***PRACTICE AREAS:*** Health Care Law. **Email:** shannon.reed@bakerd.com

PATRICK A. SCHEIDERER, born 1974; admitted to bar, 2000, Indiana. *Education:* Purdue University (B.S., with distinction, 1997); Indiana University School of Law, Indianapolis (J.D., summa cum laude, 2000). Beta Gamma Sigma. Judge Forest Jump Scholar. ***PRACTICE AREAS:*** Corporate Law; Real Estate. **Email:** patrick.scheiderer@bakerd.com

MICHAEL D. SCHWARTZ, born 1972; admitted to bar, 1998, Michigan and U.S. District Court, Western District of Michigan; 1999, Indiana and U.S. District Court, Northern and Southern Districts of Indiana; registered to practice before the U.S. Patent and Trademark Office. *Education:* Michigan State University (B.S.C.E., 1995); Indiana University-Bloomington (J.D., 1998). *Member:* American Bar Association; American Intellectual Property Law Association. ***PRACTICE AREAS:*** Intellectual Property. **Email:** michael.schwartz@bakerd.com

MATTHEW B. SKAGGS, admitted to bar, 2005, Indiana. *Education:* Indiana University (B.A., 2002); Indiana University School of Law - Bloomington (J.D., 2005). ***PRACTICE AREAS:*** Intellectual Property. **Email:** matthew.skaggs@bakerd.com

DAVID D. STOREY, admitted to bar, 2002, Indiana. *Education:* Indiana University-Fort Wayne (B.S., with distinction, 1998); Indiana University (J.D., cum laude, 2002). Beta Gamma Sigma. Semi-Finalist, Sherman Minton Moot Court Competition. Notes and Comments Editor, Indiana Law Journal. Author, Note: "The Amendment of Section 527: Eliminating Stealth PACs and Providing a Model for Future Campaign Finance Reform," 77 Ind.L.J. 167 (2002). *Member:* Indianapolis, Indiana State and American Bar Associations. ***PRACTICE AREAS:*** Litigation; Health Care Corporate Law. **Email:** david.storey@bakerd.com

ANDREW J. WELBORN, born 1971; admitted to bar, 1998, Indiana and U.S. District Court, Northern District of Indiana. *Education:* Wabash College (Phil., 1993); Indiana University, Bloomington (J.D., cum laude, 1998). ***LANGUAGES:*** Hungarian. ***PRACTICE AREAS:*** Corporate Law; Mergers and Acquisitions; Real Estate. **Email:** andrew.welborn@bakerd.com

MARK A. WERLING, born 1970; admitted to bar, 1997, Indiana. *Education:* Indiana University (B.S., with high distinction, 1993; J.D., magna cum laude, 1997). Order of the Coif; Order of the Barristers. ***PRACTICE AREAS:*** Commercial Litigation; Bankruptcy. **Email:** mark.werling@bakerd.com

(For complete biographical data on other Members of Firm, Of Counsel and Associates, See Professional Biographies at Indianapolis, South Bend, Elkhart, Indiana, Washington, D.C., Qingdao and Beijing, China)

BARNES & THORNBURG LLP

600 ONE SUMMIT SQUARE
FORT WAYNE, INDIANA 46802
Telephone: 260-423-9440
FAX: 260-424-8316
URL: http://www.btlaw.com

Indianapolis, Indiana Office: 11 South Meridian Street, 46204. Telephone: 317-236-1313. FAX: 317-231-7433.

(This Listing Continued)

South Bend, Indiana Office: 600 1st Source Bank Center, 100 North Michigan, 46601-1632. Telephone: 574-233-1171. FAX: 574-237-1125.

Elkhart, Indiana Office: 121 West Franklin Street, Suite 200, 46516. Telephone: 574-293-0681. FAX: 574-296-2535.

Chicago, Illinois Office: One North Wacker Drive, Suite 4400, 60606-2833. Telephone: 312-357-1313. FAX: 312-759-5646.

Washington, D.C. Office: Suite 900, 750 17th Street, N.W., 20006. Telephone: 202-289-1313. FAX: 202-289-1330.

Grand Rapids, Michigan Office: 300 Ottawa Avenue, N.W., Suite 500, 49503. Telephone: 616-742-3930. FAX: 616-742-3999.

Acquisitions and Divestitures, Ad Valorem Tax, Administrative Law, Affirmative Action, Agriculture Law, Americans with Disabilities Act, Antidumping, Antitrust, Antitrust and Trade Regulation, Appellate Practice, Attorney Grievances, Automotive Warranty Law, Aviation and Aerospace, Aviation Law, Banking Law, Banking Regulations, Bankruptcy, Bankruptcy Reorganization, Banks and Banking, Biochemical Patents, Biomedical Products Liability, Biomedical Technology, Biotechnology Patent Prosecution, Bond Law, Brain Injury, Breach of Warranty, Brown Fields Redevelopment, Business Immigration, Business Law, Business Litigation, Business Planning, Business Regulatory and Administrative, Business Start-ups, Business Succession Planning, Business Taxation, Business Torts, Business Transactions, Business Transfers, Buying and Selling of Businesses, Cable TV, Cargo Claims, Charitable Trusts and Foundations, Chemical Intellectual Property, Chemical Patent Prosecution, Chemical Patents, Chemical Products Liability, Civil Appeals, Civil Litigation, Civil Practice, Civil RICO, Class Action Defense, Clean Air Act, Clean Water Act, Closely Held Business Estate Planning, Closely Held Businesses, Closely Held Business Law, Closely Held Corporations, Collective Bargaining, Commercial Bankruptcy, Commercial Finance Law, Commercial Law, Commercial Leasing and Financing, Commercial Litigation, Commercial Conveyancing, Commercial Real Estate, Commercial Real Estate Acquisition, Commercial Real Estate Development, Commercial Real Estate Finance, Commercial Transactions, Commodities Fraud, Communications and Media, Complex Commercial Litigation, Complex Litigation, Computer and Software Patents, Computer Law, Computers and Software, Conflicts of Interest, Construction Labor Law, Construction Law, Consumer Credit, Contract Litigation, Cooperatives, Copyrights, Corporate Finance, Corporate Formation, Corporate Law, Corporate Taxation, Corporate Tax Planning, Countervailing Duties, Covenants Not To Compete, Creditors Rights, Creditors Rights in Bankruptcy, Criminal Defense, Criminal Law, Criminal Tax Audits, Customs Law, Dealer and Distributor Termination, Debt and Equity Finance, Decedents Estates, Defense Litigation, Design Patents, Disability Insurance Defense, Discrimination, Distribution, Drug and Medical Device Defense, Economic Development, Education Law, Elder Law, Election, Campaign and Political Law, Electric Power, Electric Utilities, Electrical Intellectual Property, Electrical Patents, Electro-mechanical Patents, Electronic Commerce, Electronic Patents, Eminent Domain, Employee Benefits, Employee Stock Ownership Plans, Employment Defense, Employment Discrimination, Employment Law, Employment Litigation, Energy, Energy Contracts, Energy Regulation, Environmental Administrative Law, Environmental Cleanup, Environmental Compliance, Environmental Criminal Defense, Environmental Law, Environmental Litigation, Environmental Permitting, Environmental Real Estate, Environmental Regulation, Environmental Risk Management, Equal Employment Opportunity Law, ERISA Litigation, Estate Administration, Estate and Gift Taxation, Estate Planning, Estate Planning and Taxation, Estate Planning and Administration, Estate Planning and Probate, Estate Planning for Parents of Handicapped Children, Estate Planning for Unmarried Individuals, Executive Compensation, Executive Severance Contracts, Export Regulation, Fair Employment Practices, Family and Medical Leave Act, Family Business Successions, Family Wealth Transfer, Federal and State Administrative Regulatory Practice, Federal and State Legislative Practice, Federal Civil Litigation, Federal Civil Practice, Federal Criminal Law, Federal Estate and Gift Taxation, Federal Litigation, Federal Tax Controversies, Federal Taxation, Fiduciary Income Tax, Finance, Financial Transactions, First Party Insurance, Foreign Investment in the United States, Freight Claims, Freight Loss and Damage, Gaming Law, Gaming Licensing, Gas Utilities, General Litigation, Government, Government Affairs, Government Agency Practice, Government Contracts, Government Investigations, Government Relations, Groundwater Contamination, Hazardous Materials and Substances, Hazardous Waste, Hazardous Waste Liability, Head Injury, Health Care, Health Care Corporate Law, Health Care Contracts, Health Care Fraud, Health Care Licensing, Health Care Litigation, Health Care Mergers and Acquisitions, Health Care Regulation, Health Care Reimbursement, Health Law, Heavy Equipment Products Liability, Immigration Law, Industrial Revenue Bond Law, Inheritance Tax, Initial Public Offerings, Insurance, Insurance Bad Faith, Insurance Coverage, Insurance Litigation, Insurance Regulation, Integrated Health Care Delivery Systems, Intellectual Property, Intellectual Property General Prosecution, Intellectual Property Infringement, Intellectual Property Licensing, Intellectual Property Litigation, Intellectual Property Procurement, Intellectual Property Protection, Intellectual Property Rights, International Business Law, International Intellectual Property, International Law, International Patents, International Trade, International Transportation Law, Internet Law, Internet Trademark Law, Joint Ventures, Labor and Employment, Labor Arbitration, Labor Law, Labor Relations, Land Use, Lease Law, Leasing, Legal Ethics and Professional Responsibility, Legal Malpractice Defense, Legislative Practice, Licensing, Life Insurance Defense, Limited Liability Company Law, Limited Partnerships, Liquor Licensing, Litigation, Loans, Lobbying, Local Government Law, Logistics, Long Term Care, Managed Care, Managed Care Contracts, Management Employment Law, Management Labor Law, Manufacturers Liability, Maritime Regulations, Mechanical Intellectual Property, Mechanical Patents, Media Law, Mediation, Medical Antitrust, Medical Intellectual Property, Medical Patents, Mental Health Law, Mergers, Acquisitions and Divestitures, Mergers and Acquisitions, Mineral Taxation, Molecular Biology Patents, Motor Carrier Law, Motor Carrier Regulation, Multi-Employer Pensions, Municipal Bonds, Municipal Bonds Taxation, Municipal Finance, Municipal Law, Municipal Leasing, Municipal Redevelopment, Municipal Securities, Municipal Taxation, National Labor Relations Act, Neurolaw, Nonprofit and Charitable Organizations, Nonprofit Organizations Law, North American Free Trade Agreement, Occupational Safety and Health, OSHA, Partnership Law, Partnership Taxation, Patent Infringement, Patent Interference Practice, Patent Litigation, Patent Prosecution, Patents, PCT Legal Export, Personal Injury, Personal Injury Defense, Pesticide Litigation, Pharmaceutical Intellectual Property, Pharmaceutical Patents, Physician Contracts, Physician Practices, Planning and Land Use, Power Line Contact Injury, Probate, Probate Litigation, Products Liability, Products Liability Defense, Professional Liability, Property Law, Property Tax, Property Tax Abatement, Property Tax Appeals, Psychological Injury, Public Finance, Public Sector Labor Relations, Public Utility Law, Railroad Law, Real Estate, Real

(This Listing Continued)

BARNES & THORNBURG LLP, Fort Wayne—Continued

Estate Acquisitions, Real Estate Contracts, Real Estate Development, Real Estate Finance, Real Estate Licensing, Real Estate Secured Lending, Real Estate Title Insurance, Real Property, Real Property Acquisitions, Real Property Finance, Reorganizations, Resource Conservation and Recovery Act (RCRA), Retirement Benefit Plans, School Law, Securities, Securities Litigation, Securitization, Semiconductor Technology, Sexual Harassment, Small Business Corporations, State Government Law, State Tax Controversies, State Taxation, Structured Finance, Succession Planning, Superfund, Tax Controversies, Tax Exempt Finance, Tax Exempt Organizations, Tax Increment Finance, Tax Law, Tax Litigation, Taxation, Technology and Science, Technology Law, Technology Licensing, Technology Transfers, Telecommunications Competition, Telecommunications Law, Theft of Trade Secrets, Title VII Discrimination, Title IX Discrimination, Tort Defense, Toxic Exposure, Toxic Tort Class Actions, Toxic Torts, Toxic Tort Defense, Trade Dress, Trade Secrets, Trademark Litigation, Trademarks, Trademark Prosecution, Trademark Protection, Trademark Registration, Transportation, Transportation Safety, Trial Practice, Trusts and Estates, Unfair Competition, Unfair Trade, Uniform Commercial Codes, Union Contract Negotiations, Union Elections, Utilities, Utility Law, Wage and Hour Law, WARN Act, Water Pollution, Water Quality, Water Utilities, Wetland Regulation, White Collar Crime, White Collar Criminal Defense, Wills, Workers Compensation, Workouts, World Trade Organization, Wrongful Death, Wrongful Termination, Wrongful Termination Defense, Zoning, Planning and Land Use.

FIRM PROFILE: Quality. Service. Efficiency. Communication. These are the cornerstones of the firm's culture and the keys to its success.

Established on January 1, 1982, Barnes & Thornburg LLP is relatively young; however, its founding date belies the firm's rich history. The firm's roots can be traced to two cities, South Bend and Indianapolis. Our northern Indiana presence began in 1926 with the establishment of Seebirt Oare & Omacht, and later grew when they merged with an Elkhart firm, Cawley and Harman. In Indianapolis, four partners opened Barnes Hickam Pantzer & Boyd on September 13, 1940. They began the firm with 13 people in an office of 13 rooms on the 13th floor of the Merchants Bank Building, the tallest in Indiana at that time. The number 13 has proven to be a lucky number for Barnes & Thornburg LLP.

Since 1982, the firm has opened offices in Chicago, Fort Wayne, Washington, D.C., Grand Rapids and merged with Jenkins, Coffey, Hyland, Badger & Conard, an intellectual property firm; Roberts, Ryder, Rogers & Scism, a labor and employment law firm; Church, Nilsson & Paulen of Elkhart; Roemer & Mintz, LLP, of South Bend and, most recently, Lee, Mann, Smith, McWilliams, Sweeney & Ohlson of Chicago. The firm has also been joined by Gallucci, Hopkins & Theisen, P.C., a Fort Wayne firm with an extensive labor and employment practice, and Johnson Lawhead Buth & Pope, P.C., an Indianapolis firm with a concentration in estate planning. Today Barnes & Thornburg LLP is the largest law firm in Indiana and one of the largest in the Midwest. More than 390 attorneys provide legal services to more than 11,000 international, national, regional and local clients.

With offices in Indianapolis, Fort Wayne, South Bend, Elkhart, Chicago, Washington, D.C., and Grand Rapids, we are a business-minded law firm serving clients ranging from Fortune 100 companies and governmental entities to individuals and nonprofit organizations. We represent the interests of businesses in our primary practices: business, tax and real estate, creditors' rights, energy, telecommunications and utilities, environmental law, governmental services and finance, healthcare, intellectual property, labor and employment law, litigation, appellate, business and technology, construction law, e-commerce, economic development, entrepreneurial services, financial institutions, international, media, pension and benefits litigation, property tax, transportation and white collar crime. Each of our offices offers a unique blend of services which collectively make Barnes & Thornburg LLP a diverse and dynamic legal resource for our clients and communities.

We have lawyers involved at city, state and national levels of the legal profession as officers, chairpersons and committee members in legal organizations. Others are authors, presenters and drafters of legislation. Most of our lawyers are active in their communities and provide civic leadership. Each office sponsors, contributes to, and often leads, an array of community activities.

LAW FIRM ALLIANCES/ASSOCIATIONS: **TECHLAW GROUP**

TERRALEX, THE WORLDWIDE NETWORK OF INDEPENDENT LAW FIRMS

PARTNERS

MICHAEL A. SCHEER, admitted to bar, 1976, Indiana and U.S. District Court, Southern District of Indiana; 1983, U.S. District Court, Northern District of Indiana; 1987, Michigan and U.S. District Court, Western District of Michigan. *Education:* Indiana University (A.B., 1969; J.D., 1976). ***PRACTICE AREAS:*** Union Contract Negotiations; Labor Arbitration; Affirmative Action; WARN Act; Title VII Discrimination; Management Labor Law. ***Email:*** michael.scheer@btlaw.com

WILLIAM T. (TUCK) HOPKINS, JR., admitted to bar, 1977, Indiana; 1992, Ohio; 1997, U.S. Supreme Court; 2000, Illinois. *Education:* University of Notre Dame (B.S.E.E., 1974); St. Louis University (J.D., 1977). ***PRACTICE AREAS:*** Labor Law; Employment Litigation; Collective Bargaining; Public Sector Labor Relations; Construction Labor Law; School Law. ***Email:*** tuck.hopkins@btlaw.com

DENNIS C. BECKER, admitted to bar, 1979, Indiana and U.S. District Court, Northern and Southern Districts of Indiana; 1982, U.S. Tax Court. *Education:* Indiana University (B.S., 1973); Georgetown University Law Center (J.D., 1979). *Member:* Allen County, Indiana State and American Bar Associations. ***PRACTICE AREAS:*** Non Profit and Charitable Organizations; Taxation; Closely Held Business Law; Health Law; Estate Planning. ***Email:*** dennis.becker@btlaw.com

BOBBY B. GILLENWATER, admitted to bar, 1983, District of Columbia; 1987, Indiana; registered to practice before U.S. Patent and Trademark Office. *Education:* University of Tennessee at Knoxville (B.S.E.E., 1973); Massachusetts Institute of Technology (M.S., 1980); Boston College Law School (J.D., 1983). *Member:* Indiana State and American Bar Associations; American Intellectual Property Law Association; Patent Office Society. ***PRACTICE AREAS:*** Intellectual Property; Patents; Trademarks; Copyrights. ***Email:*** bobby.gillenwater@btlaw.com

M. SCOTT HALL, admitted to bar, 1986, Indiana, U.S. District Court, Northern and Southern Districts of Indiana and U.S. Court of Appeals, Seventh Circuit. *Education:* New College of California (B.A., 1977); Indiana University at Indianapolis (J.D., 1985). ***PRACTICE AREAS:*** Labor and Employment. ***Email:*** scott.hall@btlaw.com

STEPHEN L. FINK, admitted to bar, 1988, Indiana. *Education:* Purdue University (B.S., 1983); Indiana University (J.D., 1988). *Member:* Allen County (Board of Directors, 1995-1998) and Indiana State (Bankruptcy and Creditors Rights Section) Bar Associations; Commercial Law League of America; American Bankruptcy Institute. ***PRACTICE AREAS:*** Bankruptcy; Creditors Rights; Real Estate; Zoning Law; Construction Law. ***Email:*** stephen.fink@btlaw.com

D. RANDALL BROWN, admitted to bar, 1990, Indiana, U.S. District Court, Northern and Southern Districts of Indiana and U.S. Court of Appeals, Seventh Circuit; 1994, U.S. Court of Appeals for the Federal Circuit. *Education:* Manchester College (B.S., 1987); Indiana University (J.D., magna cum laude, 1990). *Member:* Allen County, Indiana State and American Bar Associations. ***PRACTICE AREAS:*** Patent Litigation; Business Litigation; Commercial Litigation; Contract Litigation; Class Actions; Trade Secrets; Products Liability. ***Email:*** randy.brown@btlaw.com

KATHLEEN M. ANDERSON, admitted to bar, 1992, Indiana and U.S. District Court, Northern and Southern Districts of Indiana; 1994, U.S. Court of Appeals, Seventh Circuit; 2001, Ohio. *Education:* Hanover College (B.A., summa cum laude, 1989); Indiana University (J.D., magna cum laude, 1992). Order of the Coif. Recipient, Henry C. Long Citation for Citizenship and Academic Excellence. Member, Board of Editors, Indiana Law Journal, 1991-1992. *Member:* Allen County (Member, Board of Directors), Indiana State and American Bar Associations. ***PRACTICE AREAS:*** Civil Litigation; Complex Litigation; Labor and Employment; ERISA; Products Liability; Tort Defense. ***Email:*** kathleen.anderson@btlaw.com

MARK S. KITTAKA, admitted to bar, 1992, Indiana and U.S. District Court, Northern and Southern Districts of Indiana; 2000, U.S. Court of Appeals, Eleventh Circuit; 2002, U.S. Court of Appeals, Seventh Circuit. *Education:* Indiana University (Double B.A., 1989); Washington University (J.D., 1992). *Member:* Allen County, Indiana State and American (Member, Labor and Employment Sections) Bar Associations. ***PRACTICE AREAS:*** Labor and Employment; Employment Litigation; Americans with Disabilities Act; Family and Medical Leave Act; National Labor Relations Act; OSHA; Title VII Discrimination; WARN Act; Harassment; Noncompetition and Non-Solicitation; Employment Discrimination; Management Employment Law. ***Email:*** mark.kittaka@btlaw.com

DAWN R. ROSEMOND, admitted to bar, 1996, Indiana. *Education:* Indiana University (B.A., 1993); University of Illinois (J.D., 1996). ***PRACTICE AREAS:*** Intellectual Property Litigation; Commercial Litigation; Employment Litigation. ***Email:*** dawn.rosemond@btlaw.com

GARY C. FURST, born Grand Rapids, Michigan; admitted to bar, 1996, Indiana; 2005, Michigan. *Education:* Huntington College (B.A., summa cum laude, 1993); Valparaiso University (J.D., summa cum laude, 1996). Symposium Editor, Valparaiso University Law Review, 1995-1996. *Member:* Indiana State Bar Association; State Bar of Michigan. ***PRACTICE AREAS:*** Litigation; Patent Litigation; Commercial Litigation. ***Email:*** gary.furst@btlaw.com

SHAUN E. GRAHAM, admitted to bar, 1995, Indiana, U.S. District Court, Northern and Southern Districts of Indiana. *Education:* University of Notre Dame (B.A., 1992); Indiana University (J.D., 1995). *Member:* Indiana State and American Bar Associations. ***PRACTICE AREAS:*** Employment Law; Labor Law; Civil Litigation. ***Email:*** shaun.graham@btlaw.com

ASSOCIATES

MATTHEW M. HOHMAN, admitted to bar, 1998, Indiana. *Education:* Huntington College (B.S., magna cum laude, 1993); University of Minnesota (J.D., cum laude, 1998); Indiana University (M.A.T., high honors, 1998). Managing Editor, Minnesota Law Review, 1997-1998. *Member: Member:* Allen County and Indiana State Bar Associations. ***PRACTICE AREAS:*** Creditors Rights; Bankruptcy; Commercial Litigation. ***Email:*** matt.hohman@btlaw.com

GREGORY S. COOPER, admitted to bar, 1998, Indiana; registered to practice before U.S. Patent and Trademark Office. *Education:* Purdue University (B.S., Material Science Engineering, 1992); Duquesne University (D.J.P., 1998). ***PRACTICE AREAS:*** Intellectual Property; Mechanical Patent Prosecution; Technology Protection; Patent Prosecution; Intellectual Property Infringement; Intellectual Property Litigation. ***Email:*** greg.cooper@btlaw.com

MARK D. SCUDDER, admitted to bar, 2002, Indiana. *Education:* Indiana University (B.A., highest honors, 1999); Indiana University School of Law - Bloomington (J.D., 2001). Octofinalist, Sherman Minton Moot Court Competition, 1999-2000. Member, Sherman Minton Moot Court Board's External Team, 2000-2001. Note Editor, Federal Communications Law Journal. ***PRACTICE AREAS:*** Labor and Employment. ***Email:*** mark.scudder@btlaw.com

DANEL MICHELLE NICKELS, admitted to bar, 2002, Indiana. *Education:* Manchester College (B.A., magna cum laude, 1998); Indiana University School of Law - Indianapolis (J.D., 2001). *Member:* Allen County, Indiana State and American Bar Associations. ***PRACTICE AREAS:*** Commercial Law; Torts; Intellectual Property. ***Email:*** danel.nickels@btlaw.com

TIFFANY L. GOODEN, admitted to bar, 2003, Indiana and U.S. District Court, Northern and Southern Districts of Indiana. *Education:* University of Iowa (B.A., with honors; J.D., 2003); Pepperdine University School of Law (Certificate in Dispute Resolution). Research Assistant for University of Iowa's General Counsel. Member, Executive Board: Iowa Student Bar Association; Phi Alpha Delta Fraternity, Inc. Member, Journal of Gender Race and Justice; Member, Black Law Student Association. Certified Player Agent: National

(This Listing Continued)

Basketball Players Association; Women's National Basketball Players Association. *Member:* Allen County (Young Lawyers Section) and Indiana State Bar Associations. ***PRACTICE AREAS:*** Labor and Employment; School Law; Sports and Entertainment. ***Email:*** tiffany.gooden@btlaw.com

JASON T. CLAGG, admitted to bar, 2003, Indiana and U.S. District Court, Northern and Southern Districts of Indiana; 2004, U.S. Court of Appeals, Seventh Circuit. *Education:* Purdue University (B.S., 1999); Indiana University School of Law (J.D., cum laude, 2003). *Member:* Allen County, Indiana State and American Bar Associations. ***PRACTICE AREAS:*** Employment Defense; Employment Law; Employment Civil Rights; Employment Contracts; Employment Litigation. ***Email:*** jason.clagg@btlaw.com

CHRISTOPHER M. FORREST, admitted to bar, 2002, Indiana. *Education:* Manchester College (B.A., 1998); Indiana University School of Law, Bloomington (J.D., cum laude, 2002). *Member:* Allen County (Member, New Lawyers Section), Indiana State and American Bar Associations; Indiana Trial Lawyers Association. ***REPORTED CASES:*** SMDfund, Inc. v. Fort Wayne-Allen County Airport Authority, 831 N.E.2d 725 (Ind. 2005); Glander v. Mutual of Omaha Ins. Co., 347 F.Supp.2d 604 (N.D. Ind. 2004). ***PRACTICE AREAS:*** Commercial Litigation; Business Law; Real Estate; Creditors Rights. ***Email:*** christopher.forrest@btlaw.com

ROBERT R. VASS, admitted to bar, 2004, Indiana and U.S. District Court, Northern and Southern Districts of Indiana. *Education:* Wabash College (B.A., 1999); Indiana University School of Law, Indianapolis (J.D., 2004); Indiana University Kelley School of Business (M.B.A., Finance, 2004). *Member:* Allen County and Indiana State Bar Associations; Wabash College Society of Class Agents. ***PRACTICE AREAS:*** Business Law; Real Estate Law; Tax Law. ***Email:*** robert.vass@btlaw.com

REPRESENTATIVE CLIENTS: Aeroquip Vickers Corporation; Aetna Life Insurance Company; American Electric Power Company; Consolidated Freightways, Inc.; Cooper Tire & Rubber Company; Deister Machine Company, Inc.; Do it Best Corp.; EP Graphics, Inc.; Equifax Services, Inc.; Fort Wayne Medical Education Program; Fort Wayne Newspapers, Inc.; Fort Wayne Wire Die, Inc.; Frick Services, Inc.; General Motors Corporation; Goodyear Tire & Rubber Company; Hagerman Construction; Halderman Farm Management Services, Inc.; Hiler Industries, Inc.; Keltsch Bros., Inc.; Liberty Homes, Inc.; Lincoln National Corporation; Lydall, Inc.; North Indiana Conference of United Methodist Church; Square D Company; Starcraft Corporation; Travelers Insurance Group; Wells Fargo and Company.

BARRETT & McNAGNY LLP

Established in 1876

215 EAST BERRY STREET
P.O. BOX 2263
FORT WAYNE, INDIANA 46801-2263
Telephone: 260-423-9551
Telecopier: 260-423-8920
URL: http://www.barrettlaw.com

Administrative, Alternative Dispute Resolution, Antitrust, Appellate, Business and Commercial, Commercial and Business Litigation, Computer, Copyright, Corporate, Creditors' Rights and Bankruptcy, E-Commerce; Employee Benefits, Environmental, ERISA and ERISA Litigation, Estate Planning and Administration, Federal and State Tax, Financial Institutions, Franchising and Licensing, Governmental Relations, Guardianship; Health Care and Hospital, Insurance, Labor and Employment, Media, Medical and Professional Malpractice, Mergers and Acquisitions, Mortgage Banking, Municipal Finance, Products Liability, Railroad, Real Estate, Securities, School Administration, Tax Exempt Organizations, Trademark, Worker's Compensation and Zoning and Land Use Law.

FIRM PROFILE: Founded in 1876, Barrett & McNagny LLP is among the largest northeastern Indiana law firms and one of the oldest law partnerships in the state. The firm's roots trace back to when James M. Barrett, a law graduate of the University of Michigan, arrived in Fort Wayne to form a practice with Charles H. Aldrich. The two young attorneys quickly became known for their competence and professionalism. In 1925, Phil McNagny joined the firm, which then became known as Aldrich, Barrett & McNagny. In 1986, the firm officially became Barrett & McNagny. Barrett & McNagny steadily grew, attracting legal talent in many different fields.

Today, the firm provides international, national, regional, and local business clients of various sizes with comprehensive counsel and representation. Included among the firm's client base are national banks, one of the largest mortgage companies in the United States, utilities, major manufacturing concerns, service providers, several transportation companies, insurance companies, and many small and intermediate size businesses.

To better serve such a diverse clientele, Barrett & McNagny is divided into specialty sections according to its general areas of legal practice. This structure enables its attorneys to practice efficiently, develop in-depth expertise, and promptly assemble teams of attorneys with combined legal talents to handle matters that require expertise in several areas of law.

PARTNERS

WILLIAM F. McNAGNY (Retired)
JAMES M. BARRETT, III (Retired)
TED S. MILLER (Retired)
J. MICHAEL O'HARA (Retired)

JOHN M. CLIFTON, JR., born Indianapolis, Indiana, June 1, 1937; admitted to bar, 1963, Indiana; 1982, U.S. Supreme Court. *Education:* Indiana University (B.S., 1959; J.D., 1963). Phi Delta Phi. Assistant Instructor in Business Law, Indiana University School of Business, 1962-1963. Member of Faculty, Indiana, National Institute of Trial Advocacy, 1984-1985. Listed in Best Lawyers in America, 1987—. Member, Rules of Evidence Committee, Indiana Supreme Court, 1993 and 1994. *Member:* Allen County, Indiana State (Member: Trial Lawyers Section) and American (Member: Section on Tort and Insurance Practice; Trial Techniques Committee, 1977—) Bar Associations. Fellow, Indiana Bar Foundation. ***PRACTICE AREAS:*** Medical Malpractice; Litigation; Insurance Defense; Professional Liability Law; ERISA Litigation. ***Email:*** jmc@barrettlaw.com

(This Listing Continued)

ROBERT S. WALTERS, born New York, N.Y., May 28, 1941; admitted to bar, 1966, Indiana. *Education:* University of Michigan (A.B., 1963); Harvard University (LL.B., 1966). Phi Beta Kappa. *Member:* Allen County, Indiana State and American (Member, Antitrust and Business Law Sections) Bar Associations. ***PRACTICE AREAS:*** Business Law; Securities Law; Antitrust Law. ***Email:*** rsw@barrettlaw.com

JOHN F. LYONS, born Bloomington, Indiana, June 20, 1944; admitted to bar, 1969, Indiana. *Education:* Indiana University (B.S., 1966; J.D., 1969). Beta Gamma Sigma; Order of the Coif; Phi Alpha Delta. *Member:* Allen County, Indiana State (Member, Trial Lawyers Section) and American Bar Associations. Indiana Bar Foundation. Registered Mediator. ***PRACTICE AREAS:*** Litigation; Commercial Litigation; Insurance Defense; Alternative Dispute Resolution; Trial Practice; Insurance Coverage. ***Email:*** jfl@barrettlaw.com

N. THOMAS HORTON, II, born Tucson, Arizona, January 2, 1944; admitted to bar, 1970, Arizona; 1971, Indiana. *Education:* Indiana University (A.B., 1966); University of Michigan (J.D., 1969). Law Clerk to Hon. Frederick C. Struckmeyer, Jr., Chief Justice, Supreme Court of Arizona, 1970-1971. *Member:* Allen County, Indiana State and American Bar Associations; State Bar of Arizona. ***PRACTICE AREAS:*** ERISA; Professional Corporations Law; Employee Benefits; Deferred Compensation; Pension and Profit Sharing Plans. ***Email:*** nth@barrettlaw.com

RICHARD D. ROBINSON, born Fort Wayne, Indiana, May 28, 1946; admitted to bar, 1971, Indiana. *Education:* Indiana University (A.B., 1968; J.D., 1971). Blue Key. Adjunct Assistant Professor of Medicine, Fort Wayne Center for Medical Education, 1995—. Chairman, Midwest Alliance for Health Education, 1999—. Chairman, Human Rights Committee, Fort Wayne Developmental Center. *Member:* Allen County (Chairman, Health Care Committee), and Indiana State Bar Associations; National Health Lawyers Association; Indiana Hospital Attorney Association. ***PRACTICE AREAS:*** Health Care Law; Business Law; Medicare and Medicaid. ***Email:*** rdr@barrettlaw.com

PATRICK G. MICHAELS, born Washington, D.C., July 5, 1946; admitted to bar, 1973, Indiana; U.S. District Court, Northern and Southern Districts of Indiana; U.S. Court of Appeals, Seventh Circuit; 1976, U.S. Tax Court. *Education:* University of Notre Dame (B.B.A., 1968); Georgetown University (J.D., 1973). Beta Alpha Psi; Delta Theta Phi. Certified Public Accountant, Indiana, 1980. *Member:* Allen County (Treasurer, 1977-1978), Indiana State (Member, Corporation, Banking and Business Law Section) and American (Member, Business Law and Taxation Section) Bar Associations; Indiana Association of Certified Public Accountants; Indiana Banker's Association. Fellow, Indiana Bar Foundation. ***PRACTICE AREAS:*** Banking Law; Securities Law; Corporate Law; Mergers and Acquisitions. ***Email:*** pgm@barrettlaw.com

THOMAS M. FINK, born Huntington, Indiana, October 6, 1947; admitted to bar, 1973, Indiana. *Education:* Notre Dame University (B.B.A., 1970); Northwestern University (J.D., 1973). Beta Gamma Sigma. *Member:* Allen County and Indiana State Bar Associations; National Committee on Planned Giving; Northeast Indiana Planned Giving Council; Fort Wayne Estate Planning Council. Fellow, American College of Trust and Estate Counsel. ***PRACTICE AREAS:*** Probate; Trusts and Estates; Nonprofit and Charitable Organizations; Wills. ***Email:*** tmf@barrettlaw.com

RICHARD E. FOX, born Fort Wayne, Indiana, October 4, 1948; admitted to bar, 1973, Indiana. *Education:* Northwestern University (B.S., 1970); Indiana University (J.D., cum laude, 1973). Note Editor, Indiana Law Journal, 1972-1973. *Member:* Allen County, Indiana State and American Bar Associations; National Association of Bond Lawyers. ***PRACTICE AREAS:*** Corporate Law; Municipal Finance Law; Banking Law. ***Email:*** ref@barrettlaw.com

JOHN P. MARTIN, born Fort Wayne, Indiana, August 10, 1953; admitted to bar, 1978, Indiana. *Education:* Indiana University (A.B., 1975; J.D., magna cum laude, 1978). Phi Beta Kappa; Order of the Coif. *Member:* Allen County (Chairman, Taxation Section, 1986; Chairman, Business and Labor Section, 1988-1989), Indiana State and American (Member, Sections on: Taxation Law; Corporation, Banking and Business Law; Real Property, Probate and Trust Law) Bar Associations. ***PRACTICE AREAS:*** Corporate Law; Taxation Law; Real Estate Law; Partnership Law; Commercial Law. ***Email:*** jpm@barrettlaw.com

THOMAS P. YODER, born Pullman, Washington, April 8, 1952; admitted to bar, 1977, Indiana and U.S. District Court, Northern and Southern Districts of Indiana; 1985, U.S. Court of Appeals, 7th Circuit. *Education:* Hanover College (B.A., cum laude, 1974); Indiana University (J.D., 1977). Lecturer, American Bankruptcy Institute, National Business Institute, ICLEF and the Legal Education Institute. Co-Author: "Bankruptcy A Survival Guide for Lenders," American Bankruptcy Institute, 1997. Member, Board of Visitors, Indiana University School of Law, Bloomington, 1998-2000 and Indianapolis, 1998-2000. Honored, Sagamore of the Wabash, 2000. *Member:* Allen County (Member: Board of Directors, Bankruptcy Section, 2005—), Indiana State (President, 1999-2000; President, 1999-2000; President-Elect, 1998-1999, Vice President, 1997-1998, Chair, Membership Committee, 1997-1998; Member: Membership Committee, 1995-1996; Board of Governors, 1993-1995, 1997-2001; Board of Managers, 1988-1989; Accelerated Dispute Resolution Committee, 1987-1992; Nominating Committee, 1991-1992; Young Lawyers Section-Executive Council, 1985-1986; Secretary-Treasurer, 1986-1987; Chair-Elect, 1987-1988; Chair, 1988-1989; Member, Bankruptcy Section) and American (Corporation, Banking and Business Law Section; Young Lawyers Division-Executive Committee, 1987-1988; Vice-Chair, 1988-1989, Debtor-Creditor Relations Committee; Vice-Chair, 1988-1989, Alternative Dispute Resolution Committee) Bar Associations; Seventh Circuit Bar Association (Indiana Chair, Bankruptcy Committee, 1991- 2004; Member, Bankruptcy Appellate Panel Study Committee, 1995); Indiana Continuing Legal Education Forum (President, 1998-1999, President-Elect, 1997-1998); Great Plains Bankruptcy Conference (Member, Board of Directors, 1992-1995); Central States Bankruptcy Conference (Member, Advisory Board, 1997-2004); American Bankruptcy Institute (Member: Board of Directors, 1994-2000; Membership Committee, 1992-1999; Co-Chair, 1994-1999). Indiana Bar Foundation (Member, Board of Directors, 1998-1999; Projects Committee, 1990-1991, 1993-1994). Fellow, American College of Banruptcy, 2003. ***PRACTICE AREAS:*** Bankruptcy; Commercial Law. ***Email:*** tpy@barrettlaw.com

THOMAS M. KIMBROUGH, born Fort Wayne, Indiana, December 21, 1954; admitted to bar, 1980, Indiana and U.S. District Court, Northern and Southern Districts of Indiana. *Education:* Indiana University (B.A., 1977; J.D., magna cum laude, 1980). Law Clerk to Honorable Phil M. McNagny, Jr., U.S. District Court for the Northern District of Indiana,

(This Listing Continued)

BARRETT & McNAGNY LLP, Fort Wayne—Continued

1980-1981. *Member:* Allen County (Labor and Employment and Trial Lawyers Section, Secretary, Board of Directors, 1983-1985), Indiana State (Labor and Employment Law Section) and American (Member at County, State and National Levels of Labor and Employment Section, Trial Lawyers Section) Bar Associations; Defense Trial Counsel of Indiana (Board Member; Chair, Employment Law Committee). ***PRACTICE AREAS:*** Labor and Employment; Insurance Defense. ***Email:*** tmk@barrettlaw.com

RONALD J. EHINGER, born Fort Wayne, Indiana, December 16, 1956; admitted to bar, 1982, Indiana and U.S. District Court, Northern and Southern Districts of Indiana; 1983, Ohio. *Education:* Tri-State University (B.S., 1979); University of Notre Dame (J.D., summa cum laude, 1982). Associate Editor, Notre Dame Lawyer, 1980-1982. Recipient, Farabaugh Prize, 1982. *Member:* Allen County, Indiana State, Ohio State and American (Member, Sections on: Business Law; Real Property, Probate and Trust Law and Intellectual Property Law) Bar Associations. ***PRACTICE AREAS:*** Commercial Law; Consumer Law; Real Estate; Trademarks and Copyrights. ***Email:*** rje@barrettlaw.com

STEPHEN L. CHAPMAN, born Chicago, Illinois, November 13, 1955; admitted to bar, 1981, Indiana; U.S. District Court, Northern and Southern Districts of Indiana. *Education:* DePauw University (B.A., 1978); Indiana University-Indianapolis (J.D., 1981). *Member:* Allen County and Indiana State Bar Associations. ***PRACTICE AREAS:*** Real Estate Law; Mortgage Banking Law; Creditors Rights. ***Email:*** slc@barrettlaw.com

THOMAS A. HERR, born Chicago Heights, Illinois, June 10, 1956; admitted to bar, 1982, Iowa; 1984, Indiana and U.S. District Court, Northern and Southern Districts of Indiana; U.S. Court of Appeals, Seventh Circuit. *Education:* Simpson College (B.A., cum laude, 1978); University of Athens Law School, Athens, Greece; Drake University Law School (J.D., 1982). Law Clerk to United States Magistrate, Gene B. Lee, Northern District of Indiana, 1982-1984. *Member:* Allen County, Iowa State, Indiana State and American Bar Associations; Indiana Defense Lawyers Association. Accredited Mediator. ***REPORTED CASES:*** Jones v. General Electric Co, 87F. 3d 209 (7th Cir. 1996); OmniSource Corp. v. CNA/Transcontinental Insurance Co., 949 F. Supp. 681 (N.D. Ind 1996); Mountz v. Carroll 542 N.E. 2d 243 (Ind. App. 1989). ***PRACTICE AREAS:*** Commercial Litigation; Copyright Litigation; Probate; Real Estate Litigation. ***Email:*** tah@barrettlaw.com

THOMAS J. MARKLE, born Kendallville, Indiana, February 12, 1960; admitted to bar, 1986, Indiana and U.S. District Court, Northern District of Indiana; U.S. Court of Appeals, Sixth and Seventh Circuits. *Education:* Indiana University (B.S., with high distinction, 1982; M.S.B.A., 1986; J.D., cum laude, 1986). *Member:* Allen County, Indiana State and American Bar Associations. ***REPORTED CASES:*** Lions Volunteer Blinds v. Automated Group Administration, Inc., 195 F.3d 803 (6th Cir.1999). ***PRACTICE AREAS:*** Employee Benefits; Employee Benefits Litigation; COBRA; Employee Health Benefits; Flexible Benefit Plans; Pension and Profit Sharing Plans. ***Email:*** tjm@barrettlaw.com

MICHAEL P. O'HARA, born Fort Wayne, Indiana, November 21, 1960; admitted to bar, 1986, Indiana and U.S. District Court, Northern and Southern Districts of Indiana. *Education:* University of Notre Dame (B.A, 1983); DePaul University (J.D., 1986). *Member:* Allen County, Indiana State and American Bar Associations; American Bankruptcy Institute. ***PRACTICE AREAS:*** Commercial Insolvency; Workouts; Bankruptcy; Mergers and Acquisitions; Closely Held Businesses; Real Estate; Finance; E-Commerce; Business Law. ***Email:*** mpo@barrettlaw.com

THOMAS M. NIEZER, born Fort Wayne, Indiana, September 24, 1959; admitted to bar, 1986, Indiana and U.S. District Court, Northern and Southern Districts of Indiana. *Education:* Wabash College (B.A., 1982); University of Dayton (J.D., 1986). *Member:* Allen County, Indiana State (Member, Zoning and Land Use Regulation Section) and American (Member, Real Property, Probate and Trust Section) Bar Associations; National Health Lawyers Association. ***PRACTICE AREAS:*** Real Estate Law; Zoning, Planning and Land Use Law; Real Estate Development Law; Real Estate Finance Law. ***Email:*** tmn@barrettlaw.com

ANTHONY M. STITES, born Defiance, Ohio, June 26, 1963; admitted to bar, 1988, Indiana and U.S. District Court, Northern and Southern Districts of Indiana; 1989, Ohio; 1991, U.S. Court of Appeals, Seventh Circuit. *Education:* University of Toledo (B.B.A., 1985); University of Notre Dame (J.D., 1988). Alternative Dispute Resolution, Accredited Mediator. Selected "Indiana Super Lawyer" 2005. *Member:* Allen County, Indiana State, Ohio State and American Bar Associations; Indiana Defense Lawyers Association; American Inns of Court. ***REPORTED CASES:*** Diaz v. Ft. Wayne Foundry 131 fd 3d 711. ***PRACTICE AREAS:*** Labor and Employment Law; Transportation Law. ***Email:*** ams@barrettlaw.com

DAVID R. STEINER, born Bluffton, Ohio, September 20, 1963; admitted to bar, 1989, Indiana and U.S. District Court, Northern and Southern Districts of Indiana. *Education:* Taylor University (B.S., summa cum laude, 1986); Indiana University (J.D., cum laude, 1989). Moot Court. *Member:* Allen County, Indiana State (Member, Business Law, Corporate Counsel and Environmental Law Sections) and American (Member: Section of Natural Resources, Energy and Environmental Law) Bar Associations; Christian Legal Society. ***PRACTICE AREAS:*** Real Estate Law; Environmental Law; Business and Corporate Law. ***Email:*** drs@barrettlaw.com

JOHN C. BARCE, born July 10, 1964; admitted to bar, 1989, Indiana, U.S. District Court, Northern and Southern Districts of Indiana; U.S. Tax Court. *Education:* Indiana University School of Business (B.S., with high distinction, 1986); Indiana University School of Law (J.D., cum laude, 1989). Co-Author: "Defending Against the Service's Renewed Audit Emphasis on Accumulated Earnings Tax," Journal of Taxation, Dec., 1992; Panelist: "Family Limited Partnerships and Limited Liability Companies — Effective Use in Estate and Succession Planning," ICLEF Seminar, April, 1996; Speaker: "Planning with Single-Owner Entities," ICLEF Seminar, Dec. 1998. *Member:* Allen County, Indiana State (Member, Sections on: Tax, 1989—; Business and Corporate; Member, Tax Council, 1997—; Past Chair, 2004) and American (Member, Sections on: Taxation; Real Property, Probate and Trust) Bar Associations. ***PRACTICE AREAS:*** Mergers and Acquisitions; Federal Taxation; Partnership Taxation; Estate and Gift Taxation; Trusts and Estates. ***Email:*** jcb@barrettlaw.com

(This Listing Continued)

KEVIN K. FITZHARRIS, born Richmond, Indiana, April 23, 1965; admitted to bar, 1990, Indiana, U.S. Court of Appeals, Seventh Circuit and U.S. District Court, Northern and Southern Districts of Indiana. *Education:* Purdue University (B.A., 1987); Notre Dame (J.D., 1990). Phi Beta Kappa. *Member:* Allen County, Indiana State and American Bar Associations; Defense Research Institute; Defense Trial Counsel of Indiana; Christian Legal Society. ***REPORTED CASES:*** *Logan v. Schafer,* 567 N.E. 2d 855 (Ind. App. 3 Dist., 1991); *Scott V. Hagerman Construction Co.,* 741 N.E. 2d 390 (Ind. App. 2000); Ritchie v. Glidden Co., et al, 242 F.3d 713 (7th Cir. 2001). ***PRACTICE AREAS:*** Insurance Defense; Commercial Litigation; Workers Compensation; Media Law; Collections Law; Alternative Dispute Resolution; Civil Practice; Communications and Media; Eminent Domain; Administrative Law. ***Email:*** kkf@barrettlaw.com

CATHLEEN M. SHRADER, born Fort Wayne, Indiana, March 13, 1969; admitted to bar, 1994, Indiana, U.S. District Court, Northern and Southern Districts of Indiana; 1995, U.S. Court of Appeals, Seventh Circuit; 2000, U.S. Court of Appeals, Eleventh Circuit; 2003, U.S. District Court, Western District of Michigan. *Education:* Indiana University (B.S., cum laude, 1990); Duke University (J.D., 1994). Beta Gamma Sigma. Research Editor, Duke Law Journal. Co-Author: Construction Law, *Indiana Real Estate Transactions.* Co-Author: Abuse of Process, False Imprisonment and Malicious Persecution, *Indiana Personal Injury and Torts.* Speaker, *The Seven Deadly Sins of Appellate Practice,* 2005. *Member:* Allen County (Vice Chair, Appellate Practice Section), Indiana State (Vice Chair, Appellate Practice Section) and American Bar Associations. ***REPORTED CASES:*** Journal Gazette Co., Inc. v. Bandido's, Inc. 712 N.E. 2d 446 (Ind. 1999); Bader v. Johnson, 732 N.E.2d 1212 (Ind. 2000); Mullins v. Parkview Hosp., Inc., 830 N.E.2d 45 (Ind. Ct. App. 2005); Pathfinder Communications Corp. v. Macy, 795 N.E.2d 1103 (Ind. Ct. App. 2003); Ahmad v. Duncan, 732 N.E.2d 862 (Ind. Ct. App. 2000); Weston v. Buckley, 677 N.E.2d 1089 (Ind. Ct. App. 1997); Yin v. Society Nat'l Bank of Indiana 665 N.E. 2d 5831 U.C.C., Rep Serv 2d (Callaghan) 168 (Ind. Ct. App 1996); Kamphuis Pipeline Co. v. Lake George Regional Sewer District, 273 F.3d 732 (7th Cir. 2001); Omni Source Corp. v. CNA/Transcontinental Insurance Co., 949 F. Supp. 681 (N.D. Ind. 1996). ***PRACTICE AREAS:*** Commercial Litigation; Appellate Practice; Estate Litigation. ***Email:*** cms@barrettlaw.com

DAWN SNOW MATTOX, born Fort Wayne, Indiana, October 6, 1966; admitted to bar, 1992, Indiana and U.S. District Court, Northern and Southern Districts of Indiana; U.S. Tax Court. *Education:* Miami University (B.A., 1989); Indiana University School of Law at Indianapolis (J.D., cum laude, 1992). *Member:* Allen County, Indiana State and American Bar Associations; National Health Lawyers Association; Women's Business Law Network. ***PRACTICE AREAS:*** Health Care Law; Business Law. ***Email:*** dsm@barrettlaw.com

SAMUEL J. TALARICO, JR., born Fort Wayne, Indiana, January 7, 1968; admitted to bar, 1996, Indiana and U.S. District Court, Southern and Northern Districts of Indiana. *Education:* Butler University (B.S., 1990); Indiana University (J.D., 1995). Certified Public Accountant, 1994, Indiana. Elected Member of Fort Wayne City Council. Member, Fort Wayne - Allen County Economic Development Alliance. *Member:* Allen County (Former Chair, Business Section), Indiana State and American Bar Associations; Indiana Society of Certified Public Accountants. ***PRACTICE AREAS:*** Mergers, Acquisitions and Divestitures; Securities. ***Email:*** sjt@barrettlaw.com

H. JOSEPH COHEN, born Indianapolis, Indiana, June 5, 1970; admitted to bar, 1996, Indiana, U.S. Court of Appeals, Sixth Circuit, Seventh Circuit and U.S. District Court, Northern and Southern Districts of Indiana. *Education:* Indiana University (B.S., 1992; J.D., 1996). Pi Alpha Alpha. Associate Editor, Indiana Law Review, 1994-1996. *Member:* Allen County, Indiana State and American Bar Associations; Defense Trial Counsel of Indiana; Defense Research Institute; American Inns of Court. ***PRACTICE AREAS:*** Employment Law; Labor Law; Insurance Defense; Litigation. ***Email:*** hjc@barrettlaw.com

TRISHA J. PAUL, born Fort Wayne, Indiana, March 29, 1971; admitted to bar, 1996, Indiana and U.S. District Court, Northern and Southern Districts of Indiana. *Education:* St. Francis College (B.S., 1993); University of Toledo College of Law (J.D., 1996). *Member:* Allen County and Indiana State Bar Associations; Estate Planning Council; Planned Giving Council of Northeast Indiana. ***PRACTICE AREAS:*** Estate Planning; Estate Administration; Guardianship Law; Federal Estate and Gift Taxation. ***Email:*** tjp@barrettlaw.com

PATRICK G. MURPHY, born Lansing, Michigan, August 30, 1970; admitted to bar, 1996, Indiana and U.S. District Court, Northern and Southern Districts of Indiana. *Education:* Indiana University (B.S., Business, 1993); Indiana University School of Law (J.D., 1996). Prosecuting Attorney, Allen County Office. Adjunct Professor, in Evidence, Indiana University Fort Wayne. Co-Author: "Trying the Soft Tissue Injury Cases in Indiana," National Business Institute, 2001. *Member:* Allen County, Indiana State and American Bar Associations; Defense Research Institute; Defense Trial Counsel of Indiana. ***PRACTICE AREAS:*** Insurance Defense; Commercial Litigation; Criminal Defense. ***Email:*** pat@barrettlaw.com

OF COUNSEL

Howard L. Chapman (Retired)

ASSOCIATES

RENEE L. RIECKE, born Columbia City, Indiana, August 2, 1959; admitted to bar, 1985, Illinois; 1990, Indiana. *Education:* Indiana University (B.S., magna cum laude, 1981; J.D., 1984). Alpha Lambda Delta; Pi Alpha Alpha. Editor, *Mertens Law of Federal Income Taxation,*Callaghan & Company, 1985-1986. *Member:* Allen County and Indiana State Bar Associations. ***PRACTICE AREAS:*** Wills; Trusts and Probate. ***Email:*** rlr@barrettlaw.com

ANNE E. SIMERMAN, born Fort Wayne, Indiana, March 11, 1961; admitted to bar, 1995, Indiana and U.S. District Court, Northern and Southern Districts of Indiana. *Education:* Indiana University (B.S., summa cum laude, 1984); University of Louisville (J.D., cum laude, 1995). Beta Gamma Sigma; Phi Kappa Phi. Author: "The Right of Cohabitants To Recover in Tort," Journal of Family Law Vol. 32 No. 2. Speaker, "Revised Article 9-A Primer for Estate Administration," Indiana Continuing Legal Education Foundation, 2001. *Member:* Allen County, Indiana State and American (Member, Consumer Financial Services Subcommittee) Bar Associations. ***PRACTICE AREAS:*** Bankruptcy; Finance; Consumer Law; Commercial Law; Contracts. ***Email:*** aes@barrettlaw.com

(This Listing Continued)

HENRY P. NAJDESKI, born Fort Wayne, Indiana, April 2, 1971; admitted to bar, 1997, Indiana and U.S. District Court, Northern and Southern Districts of Indiana. *Education:* DePauw University (B.A., 1993); The John Marshall Law School (J.D., 1997). *Member:* Allen County (Member, Sections on: Young Lawyers; Real Estate), Indiana State and American Bar Associations. ***PRACTICE AREAS:*** Real Estate Law; Business Law; Zoning, Planning and Land Use. ***Email:*** hpn@barrettlaw.com

TINA M. BELL, born Albuquerque, New Mexico, May 22, 1974; admitted to bar, 1998, Indiana and U.S. District Court, Northern and Southern Districts of Indiana. *Education:* Eureka College (B.A., magna cum laude, 1995); Indiana University School of Law (J.D., cum laude, 1998). *Member:* Allen County, Indiana State and American Bar Associations. ***PRACTICE AREAS:*** Medical Malpractice Defense; Eminent Domain; Litigation. ***Email:*** tmb@barrettlaw.com

MICHAEL H. MICHMERHUIZEN, born Holland, Michigan, February 19, 1973; admitted to bar, 1999, Indiana and U.S. District Court, Northern and Southern Districts of Indiana. *Education:* Grand Valley State University (B.B.A., magna cum laude, 1995); University of Michigan (J.D., cum laude, 1999). ***REPORTED CASES:*** Blasko v. Menard, Inc., 831 N.E.2d 271 (Ind. Ct. App. 2005); Witte v. Mundy et al. Mundy, 820 N.E.2d 128 (Ind. 2005); Taylor v. Federal Nat. Mortgage Association, 374 F.3d 529 (7th Cir. 2004); Bailey v. Skipperliner Industries, Inc. et al., 278 F.Supp.2d 945 (N.D.Ind. 2003); Pathfinder Communications Corp. v. Macy, 795 N.E.2d 1103 (Ind. Ct. App. 2003); Luong ex rel. Luong v. Chung King Express, 781 N.E.2d 1181 (Ind. Ct. App. 2003); Wedgewood Community Association, Inc. v. Nash, 781 N.E.2d 1172 (Ind. Ct. App. 2003); GYN-OB Consultants, LLC v. Schopp, 780 N.E.2d 1206 (Ind. Ct. App. 2003); State Farm Mutual Automobile Insurance Co. v. Leybman, 777 N.E.2d 763 (Ind. Ct. App. 2002); Del Signore v. Asphalt Drum Mixers, 182 F. Supp.2d 730 (N.D.Ind. 2002). ***PRACTICE AREAS:*** Litigation; Commercial Law. ***Email:*** mhm@barrettlaw.com

JEFFREY M. WOENKER, born December 7, 1970; admitted to bar, 2000, Indiana; U.S. District Court, Northern and Southern Districts of Indiana. *Education:* Indiana University (B.S., 1993; J.D., cum laude, 2000). Certified Public Accountant, Indiana, 1997. *Member:* Allen County and Indiana State Bar Associations. ***PRACTICE AREAS:*** Tax; Business. ***Email:*** jmw@barrettlaw.com

JAMES J. O'CONNOR, JR., born New Orleans, Louisiana, August 27, 1975; admitted to bar, 2001, Indiana and U.S. District Court, Northern and Southern Districts of Indiana. *Education:* Emory University (B.A., 1997) Loyola University at New Orleans (J.D., 2001). Chairman, Moot Court Board, 2000-2001; Order of Barristers, 2001. *Member:* Indiana State Bar Association; Defense Research Institute; Defense Trial Counsel of Indiana; Inn of Court, Benjamin Harrison Chapters. ***PRACTICE AREAS:*** Litigation; Commercial; Insurance Defense; Workers Compensation. ***Email:*** jjo@barrettlaw.com

JOSHUA C. NEAL, born April 15, 1977; admitted to bar, 2002, Indiana and U.S. District Court, Northern and Southern Districts of Indiana. *Education:* University of Indianapolis (B.A., cum laude, 1999); Indiana University School of Law (J.D. magna cum laude, 2002). *Member:* Allen County, Indiana State and American Bar Associations. ***PRACTICE AREAS:*** Real Estate; Zoning, Planning and Land Use; Business Law; Corporate Law. ***Email:*** jcn@barrettlaw.com

JANELL M. SPRINKLE, born Fort Wayne, Indiana, May 11, 1972; admitted to bar, 2001, Indiana and U.S. District Court, Northern and Southern Districts of Indiana. *Education:* Texas Christian University (B.S., 1994); Indiana University (J.D., 2001). *Member:* Allen County, Indiana State and American Bar Associations. ***PRACTICE AREAS:*** Business Law; Charter School Law. ***Email:*** jms@barrettlaw.com

CHARLES C. DUBES, born Lafayette, Indiana, October 19, 1977; admitted to bar, 2003, Indiana. *Education:* DePauw University (B.A., 2000); Indiana University (J.D., 2003). *Member:* Indiana State and American Bar Associations; Inns of Court. ***PRACTICE AREAS:*** Insurance Defense; Medical Malpractice; Litigation. ***Email:*** ccd@barrettlaw.com

ZACHARY E. KLUTZ, born Fort Wayne, Indiana, January 18, 1978; admitted to bar, 2005, Indiana. *Education:* Indiana University (B.A., 2002); Indiana University, Indianapolis (J.D., 2005). ***PRACTICE AREAS:*** Litigation; Insurance Defense. ***Email:*** zek@barrettlaw.com

ALISA L. PEARSON, born Fort Wayne, Indiana, December 11, 1979; admitted to bar, 2005, Indiana and U.S. District Court, Northern and Southern Districts of Indiana. *Education:* Tennessee State University (B.B.A., 2002); University of Tennessee College of Law (J.D., 2005). ***PRACTICE AREAS:*** Business Law. ***Email:*** alp@barrettlaw.com

REPRESENTATIVE CLIENTS: Al-Fe Heat Treating, Inc.; Attorneys Title Guaranty Fund, Inc.; Biomet, Inc.; Brooks Construction Co., Inc.; City of Fort Wayne; Colwell/General, Inc.; Congress Financial Corp.; Dana Corp.; Do It Best Corp.; Dynamic Resource Group; Fifth Third Bank; Financial Federal Credit Corp.; Finova Capital Corp.; Fort Wayne Foundry Corp.; Franklin Electric Co., Inc.; Gate City Steel, Inc.; General Motors Co.; Grabill Bank; Group Dekko Services, LLC; Hagerman Construction Corp.; Headwaters Park Alliance, Inc.; Home Loan & Investment Bank; H.R. America, Inc.; Iron Dynamics, Inc.; J.O. Mory, Inc.; K-Mart Corp.; Lake City Bank; Leggett & Platt, Inc.; Liberty Homes, Inc.; Lincoln Foodservice Products, Inc.; Lincoln National Corp.; Lutheran Foundation; Masco Corp.; McCoy Bolt Works, Inc.; Menard, Inc.; National City Bank of Indiana; National On-Site Personnel Service; Northern Indiana Public Service Co.; Nowak Supply Co.; Oakmont Development Co.; OmniSource Corp.; Overnite Transport Co.; Park Center Community Mental Health Center; Parkview Health System; PAWS, Inc.; Perfection Bakeries, Inc.; Precision Plastics; Rieke Corp.; Schenkel Shultz, Inc.; Societe Generale; Star Financial Group, Inc.; Steel Dynamics, Inc.; Tippman & Dumas, LLC; T.J. Nowak Supply Co., Inc.; The Journal-Gazette; Tower Financial Corp.; Towne Air Freight LLC; Union Federal Bank of Indianapolis; Uniroyal Goodrich Tire Co.; University of St. Francis; Volvo Commercial Finance, The Americas, LLC; Waterfield Financial Corp.; Waterfield Mortgage Co., Inc.; Weigand Construction; YMCA of Greater Fort Wayne.

INSURANCE DISTRICT OR AREA COUNSEL FOR: Acordia of Indiana, LLC; Allstate Insurance Co.; AMICA Insurance Co.; Atlanta Casualty Insurance; Auto Owners Insurance Co.; Brotherhood Mutual Insurance Co.; Buckeye Mutual Insurance Co.; Central Mutual Insurance Co.; Chicago Motor Club Insurance Co.; Church Mutual Insurance Co.; Cincinnati Insurance Co.; Citizens Insurance Co. of America; Colonial Insurance Co.; Extendicare Health Services, Inc.; Federated Insurance Co.; GEICO Insurance Co.; GE Medical Protective Co.; General Casualty Insurance Co.; Hoosier Insurance; Indiana Insurance Guaranty Association; The John Hancock Mutual Life Insurance Co.; Lancer Insurance Co.; Metropolitan Insurance Co.; Nationwide Insurance Co.; Prudential Insurance Company of America; Prudential Property & Casualty Insurance Co.; Metlife Insurance Co.; SAFECO-American States Insurance Co.; Shand Morahan & Co., Inc.; State Farm Insurance Cos.; Symons International Group, Inc.; United National Group; Westfield Insurance Co.

BECKMAN LAWSON, LLP

Established in 1984

800 STANDARD FEDERAL PLAZA

FORT WAYNE, INDIANA 46802

Telephone: 260-422-0800

Facsimile: 260-420-1013

URL: http://www.beckmanlawson.com

General Civil and Criminal Trial and Appellate Practice in all Federal and State Courts. Corporate, Bankruptcy, Family, Real Estate, Planning and Zoning, Probate and Estate Planning, Administrative, Health and Hospital, Personal Injury, Environmental, Employment and Labor Law, School Law.

FIRM PROFILE: Our controlled and aggressive growth has resulted in a firm currently of over 20 lawyers with offices in Fort Wayne. The growth is a result of continued referrals from clients and attorneys who recognize the firm as being able to handle a myriad of legal problems promptly and efficiently. We pride ourselves on a reputation that has resulted in the addition of talented and seasoned lawyers to service our growing number of clients. The firm has a diverse practice and its members are widely recognized in their respective areas of specialization.

The firm also maintains one of the most technologically advanced offices in Indiana. There is a commitment to the use of computer and communications resources to best serve the increasingly complex needs of the firm's clients. This technological capability has enhanced the firm's reputation as an efficient and timely provider of legal services.

The firm's ability to respond to urgent and complex needs of referring attorneys continues to be one of its strong points and part of its vitality. We welcome challenges and can provide leadership or support at a reasonable cost under any circumstances.

PARTNERS

JACK W. LAWSON, admitted to bar, 1961, Indiana, U.S. District Court, Northern and Southern Districts of Indiana and U.S. Court of Appeals, Seventh Circuit; 1970, U.S. Supreme Court. *Education:* Purdue University; Valparaiso University (B.A., 1958; J.D., 1961). Phi Alpha Delta. Guest Lecturer of Law, Valparaiso University, 1981—. *Member:* Allen County (Secretary, 1964-1966) and Indiana State (Seminar Chairman, Indiana Continuing Legal Education Forum, 1981—) Bar Associations; American College of Real Estate Lawyers; National Health Lawyers Association (Seminar Speaker, 1986—); The Best Lawyers in America (2001—). ***PRACTICE AREAS:*** Corporate and Securities Law; Real Estate Law; Planning and Zoning Law; Health Care Law; Environmental Law. ***Email:*** jwl@beckmanlawson.com

HOWARD B. SANDLER, admitted to bar, 1972, Indiana, U.S. District Court, Northern and Southern Districts of Indiana and U.S. Court of Appeals, Seventh Circuit; 1987, U.S. Supreme Court. *Education:* Indiana University (B.S., Accounting, 1966; J.D., magna cum laude, 1972). Order of the Coif. Associate Editor, Indiana Law Journal. Certified Civil Mediator. *Member:* American Bankruptcy Institute (Certified in Business Bankruptcy Law); The Best Lawyers in America (2001—). [1st Lieut., U.S. Army, Finance Corps, 1966-1969]. ***PRACTICE AREAS:*** Business Law; Insolvency; Bankruptcy Law; Commercial Law; Mergers and Acquisitions; Litigation. ***Email:*** hbs@beckmanlawson.com

JOHN H. BRANDT, admitted to bar, 1978, Indiana. *Education:* Indiana University (B.S., 1971); University of Toledo (J.D., 1978). President, Metro Business Group (2000-2001). Allen County Court Appointed Special Advocate, 1986-2002. President, Fort Wayne Municipal Corporations (2000—). Board of Directors, 1999—, President, 2002-2004, Fort Wayne Museum of Art. *Member:* Allen County Bar Association (Past Chair, Family Law Section, 1995-1997); Indiana Association of Mediators (Judicial Nominating Commission, Allen Superior Court, 2000-2003). ***PRACTICE AREAS:*** Family Law; Mediation. ***Email:*** jhb@beckmanlawson.com

ROBERT L. NICHOLSON, admitted to bar, 1986, Texas; 1991, Indiana. *Education:* Baylor University (B.A., 1982); Texas Tech University (J.D., cum laude, 1986); Boston University (LL.M., 1990); Georgetown University (LL.M., Taxation, with distinction, 2000). Phi Kappa Phi. Order of the Coif. Note Editor, Texas Tech Law Review, 1985-1986. (Certified in Business Bankruptcy Law by the American Board of Certification). ***PRACTICE AREAS:*** Taxation; Commercial Law; Insolvency Law. ***Email:*** rln@beckmanlawson.com

CRAIG R. PATTERSON, admitted to bar, 1992, Ohio, U.S. District Court, Northern District of Ohio and U.S. Court of Appeals, Sixth Circuit; 1994, Indiana, U.S. District Court, Northern District of Indiana and U.S. Court of Appeals, Seventh Circuit; 1998, U.S. District Court, Southern District of Indiana. *Education:* Indiana University (B.A., 1988; J.D., cum laude, 1992). *Member:* Defense Trial Counsel of Indiana. ***PRACTICE AREAS:*** Employment Law Litigation; Civil Litigation; Insurance Defense. ***Email:*** crp@beckmanlawson.com

WENDY W. DAVIS, admitted to bar, 1991, Texas; 1998, Indiana and U.S. District Court, Northern District of Indiana and U.S. District Court, Northern District of Ohio; U.S. District Court, Western District of Texas; U.S. Court of Appeals, Seventh Circuit. *Education:* Wheaton College (B.A., 1988); Valparaiso University (J.D., 1991). *Member:* San Antonio and Indiana State Bar Associations; American Health Lawyers Association. ***PRACTICE AREAS:*** Labor Law; Employment Law; Federal Litigation; Health Law; Health Law Litigation; Corporate Defense; Civil Litigation. ***Email:*** wwd@beckmanlawson.com

EDWARD J. ORMSBY, admitted to bar, 1994, Indiana; U.S. District Court, Northern and Southern Districts of Indiana; U.S. Court of Appeals, Seventh Circuit; U.S. Court of Appeals, Federal Circuit; U.S. Supreme Court. *Education:* Indiana State University (B.S., 1991); Georgetown University (J.D., 1994). Beta Gamma Sigma; Phi Kappa Phi. *Member:* Million Dollar Advocates Forum; American Inns of Court. ***PRACTICE AREAS:*** Business Litigation; Commercial Law; Bankruptcy; Closely Held Business Law; Shareholders Litigation. ***Email:*** ejo@beckmanlawson.com

PATRICK R. HESS, admitted to bar, 1996, Indiana. *Education:* Indiana University (B.S., 1984); University of Cincinnati (J.D., 1996). Secretary, Land Use and Zoning Section, Indiana State Bar Association. ***PRACTICE AREAS:*** Zoning; Real Estate. ***Email:*** prh@beckmanlawson.com

(This Listing Continued)

BECKMAN LAWSON, LLP, Fort Wayne—Continued

MARK E. WITMER, admitted to bar, 1992, Indiana and U.S. District Court, Northern and Southern Districts of Indiana. *Education:* Indiana University (B.A., cum laude, 1989; J.D., cum laude, 1992). Phi Beta Kappa. Associate: Miller, Carson, Boxberger & Murphy, Fort Wayne, IN, 1992-1994; North American Van Lines, Inc. (Associate Counsel, 1994-1997; Senior Counsel, 1997-2002). ***PRACTICE AREAS:*** Estate Planning; Bankruptcy; Construction Law; Transportation; Business Law. ***Email:*** mew@beckmanlawson.com

MATTHEW J. ELLIOTT, admitted to bar, 1998, Indiana; U.S. District Court, Northern District of Indiana; U.S. Court of Appeals, Seventh Circuit. *Education:* University of Michigan (A.B., summa cum laude, 1992); Harvard University (J.D., magna cum laude, 1998). Law Clerk to the Hon. Jerome Farris, Ninth Circuit United States Court of Appeals, 1998-1999. ***PRACTICE AREAS:*** Litigation; Employment Law. ***Email:*** mje@beckmanlawson.com

ASSOCIATES

BRIAN C. HECK, admitted to bar, 1999, Minnesota; 2000, Indiana; 2001, Wisconsin. *Education:* University of Minnesota, Minneapolis (B.S., 1996); Indiana University School of Law - Bloomington (J.D., 1999). ***PRACTICE AREAS:*** Commercial Litigation; Business Litigation. ***Email:*** bch@beckmanlawson.com

MARK E. BLOOM, admitted to bar, 2001, Indiana. *Education:* Purdue University (B.A., 1994); Indiana University School of Law (J.D., 2001). ***PRACTICE AREAS:*** Employment Law; Labor Law. ***Email:*** mcb@beckman-lawson.com

MICHAEL D. STORY, admitted to bar, 2002, Indiana; U.S. District Court, Northern and Southern Districts of Indiana; U.S. Supreme Court. *Education:* Bowling Green State University (B.A., Sports Management and Marketing, 1996); Valparaiso University School of Law (J.D., 2002). Client Manager, International Management Group. ***PRACTICE AREAS:*** Commercial Law; Commercial Litigation. ***Email:*** mds@beckmanlawson.com

ANDREA R. DICK, admitted to bar, 2003, Indiana. *Education:* St. Joseph's College (B.S., 1999); Indiana University School of Law - Bloomington (J.D., 2003). ***Email:*** ard@beckmanlawson.com

JEREMY L. REIDY, admitted to bar, 2004, Indiana. *Education:* Indiana University-Purdue University (B.S., 2000); University of Dayton School of Law (J.D., 2004). Editor, University of Dayton Law Review. ***PRACTICE AREAS:*** Business Law; Real Estate Law. ***Email:*** jlr@beckmanlawson.com

OF COUNSEL

WILLIAM L. SWEET, JR., admitted to bar, 1972, Indiana; 1996, Michigan. *Education:* Wabash College (A.B., 1969); University of Michigan (J.D., cum laude, 1972). Recipient, Prentice Hall Award, Federal Income Tax. Research Assistant, Wright & Miller, Federal Practice and Procedure. Director: Drug Emporium, Inc.; Buckeye State Mutual Insurance Company. Fellow, Indiana Bar Foundation; The Best Lawyers in America (2001—). ***PRACTICE AREAS:*** Labor Law; School Law; Commercial Litigation. ***Email:*** wls@beckmanlawson.com

GARY D. JOHNSON, admitted to bar, 1991, Indiana; U.S. District Court, Northern and Southern Districts of Indiana; U.S. Court of Appeals, Seventh Circuit. *Education:* Indiana University (B.S., 1988; J.D., 1991). Member, 1989-1991 and Associate Editor, 1990-1991, Indiana Law Journal. Author: "Sexual Harassment in the Workplace," Business People Magazine, March 1992. Contributing Author: "Indiana Employment Law Handbook." Associate Professor, Personnel Law, Purdue University, 1996-1998. ***PRACTICE AREAS:*** Labor and Employment Law; Litigation. ***Email:*** gdj@beckmanlawson.com

FREDERICK A. BECKMAN, admitted to bar, 1950, Indiana. *Education:* St. Joseph's College (A.B., cum laude, 1947); Indiana University (J.D., 1949). Sigma Delta Kappa. Deputy Prosecuting Attorney, Allen County, 1960-1963. ***PRACTICE AREAS:*** Estate Planning; Estate and Trust Administration; Civil Mediation. ***Email:*** fab@beckmanlawson.com

DOUGLAS E. MILLER, admitted to bar, 1965, Iowa; 1967, Indiana. *Education:* Iowa State University (B.S., 1964); University of Iowa (J.D., 1965). Phi Alpha Delta. Assistant Attorney General, State of Iowa, 1965-1967. Listed in: The Best Lawyers in America (2001—). ***PRACTICE AREAS:*** Real Estate Law; Partnership Law; Business Law. ***Email:*** dem@beckmanlawson.com

REPRESENTATIVE CLIENTS: *Education:* Fort Wayne Community Schools; Marion Community Schools; Taylor Community Schools. *Finance:* Farm Credit Services of Mid-America, ACA; Philips Electronics Federal Credit Union; Fifth Third Bank; Arlington Capital, LLC.; Citizens Financial Services. *Insurance:* Aetna Casualty & Surety Co.; Buckeye State Mutual Insurance Co.; Guaranty Mutual Life Co.; National Casualty Co. *Manufacturing:* CFM Majestic Corp.; Red Gold, Inc.; Carson Industries, LLC; Therma Tru Corporation; Best Lock Corporation a/b/a Best Access Systems; Kelly Box & Packaging Corporation; Valbruna Slater Stainless; Norwood Promotional Products; Paragon Medical, Inc. *Health Care:* Miller's Health System; QHG of Indiana, Inc., d/b/a Lutheran Hospital; Emergency Medicine of Indiana. *Retail:* National Oil & Gas, Inc. *Real Estate Development:* Ringenberger Development; RED Development. *Transportation:* Allied Worldwide, Inc.; Allied Van Lines, Inc.; North American Van Lines, Inc. *Municipal:* City of Fort Wayne; Hessen Utilities; Zionsville, Indiana Board of Zoning and Planning. *Entrepreneurial:* Northeast Indiana Innovation Center; Renaissance Investors, LLC; Ruffolo Benson, LLC Partners.

BEERS MALLERS BACKS & SALIN, LLP

Established in 1901

110 WEST BERRY STREET, SUITE 1100
FORT WAYNE, INDIANA 46802
Telephone: 260-426-9706
Fax: 260-420-1314
URL: http://www.beersmallers.com

LaGrange, Indiana Office: 108 West Michigan Street. Telephone: 260-463-4949. FAX: 260-463-4905.

(This Listing Continued)

General Trial and Appellate Practice in all State and Federal Courts. Administrative Law, Bankruptcy, Banks and Banking, Business Law, Civil Rights, Collections, Commercial Law, Computers and Software, Construction Law, Contracts, Copyrights, Corporate Law, Debtor and Creditor, Elder Law, Environmental Law, Estate Planning and Administration, Franchising and Licensing, Government, Health Care, Insurance, Litigation, Mergers, Acquisitions and Divestitures, Municipal Law, Personal Injury, Probate, Products Liability, Public and Private Sector Labor and Employment (Management), Public Finance, Real Estate, Securities, Trademarks, Trusts and Estates, Zoning, Planning and Land Use.

FIRM PROFILE: Beers Mallers Backs & Salin, LLP is a law firm with vast experience handling the diverse legal needs of businesses and individuals. With offices located in Fort Wayne and LaGrange, the firm practices not only throughout northeastern Indiana, but also statewide, as well as in Ohio and Michigan. Many of the firm's attorneys frequently appear before state and federal courts and agencies in Indianapolis.

The Firm represents many of the leading institutions in the region, including county and municipal governments, television stations, a major health care system, several leading manufacturers and industrial concerns, financial institutions, construction companies, builders and real estate developers.

The Firm also has a strong commitment to the local community. Its members serve on the boards of many of the leading non-profit and charitable entities.

The Firm has recently developed a special niche in meeting the legal needs of businesses. The Firm is uniquely qualified to provide businesses with a full range of legal services, including: site selection, acquisition and zoning; environmental counseling and litigation; labor and employment representation; the handling and/or management of litigation involving products liability, insurance coverage and intellectual property; as well as general corporate and business representation.

MEMBERS OF FIRM

VINCENT J. BACKS, born Fort Wayne, Indiana, August 8, 1940; admitted to bar, 1965, Indiana; U.S. District Court, Northern and Southern Districts of Indiana. *Education:* Indiana University (A.B., 1962; J.D., 1965). Phi Eta Sigma. Member, Indiana Law Journal. *Member:* Allen County and Indiana State Bar Associations; Indiana Trial Lawyers Association; The Association of Trial Lawyers of America. ***PRACTICE AREAS:*** Franchises and Franchising; Corporate Law; Business Law; Estate Planning; Commercial Litigation. ***Email:*** vjbacks@beersmallers.com

STEPHEN W. ADAIR, born Hillsdale, Michigan, December 9, 1942; admitted to bar, 1967, Indiana; U.S. District Court, Northern and Southern Districts of Indiana; U.S. Court of Appeals, Seventh Circuit. *Education:* Indiana University (A.B., 1964; J.D., 1967). Certified Elder Law Attorney by the National Elder Law Foundation. *Member:* Allen County and Indiana State Bar Associations. ***PRACTICE AREAS:*** Estate Planning; Probate; Elder Law. ***Email:*** swadair@beersmallers.com

G. WILLIAM FISHERING, born Fort Wayne, Indiana, August 7, 1950; admitted to bar, 1975, Indiana; U.S. District Court, Northern and Southern Districts of Indiana; U.S. Court of Appeals, Seventh Circuit. *Education:* Hillsdale College (B.A., magna cum laude, 1972); Indiana University, School of Law (J.D., cum laude, 1975). *Member:* Allen County, Indiana State and American Bar Associations. ***PRACTICE AREAS:*** Labor and Employment; Municipal Finance Law; Construction Law. ***Email:*** gwfishering@beersmallers.com

RICHARD E. BEERS, born Fort Wayne, Indiana, July 31, 1950; admitted to bar, 1976, Indiana; U.S. District Court, Northern and Southern Districts of Indiana; U.S. Court of Appeals, Seventh Circuit. *Education:* Indiana University (B.S., 1972; J.D., 1976). *Member:* Allen County and Indiana State Bar Associations; Indiana Trial Lawyers Association. ***PRACTICE AREAS:*** Commercial Litigation; Commercial Real Estate; Personal Injury; Public Sector Employment Law. ***Email:*** rebeers@beersmallers.com

PETER G. MALLERS, born Fort Wayne, Indiana, January 8, 1951; admitted to bar, 1976, Indiana; U.S. District Court, Northern and Southern Districts of Indiana; U.S. Court of Appeals, Seventh Circuit. *Education:* Wabash College (B.A., 1973); Valparaiso University (J.D., 1976). *Member:* Allen County and Indiana State Bar Associations. ***PRACTICE AREAS:*** Business Law; Commercial Law; Franchises and Franchising; Real Estate Development; Zoning and Land Use Law; Estate Planning; Estate Administration. ***Email:*** pgmallers@beersmallers.com

JAMES P. POSEY, born Milan, Indiana, August 7, 1954; admitted to bar, 1981, Indiana; U.S. District Court, Southern District of Indiana. *Education:* Indiana University (B.A., 1977; J.D., 1981). Phi Beta Kappa. *Member:* Allen County and Indiana State Bar Associations. ***PRACTICE AREAS:*** Employment Litigation; Commercial Litigation; Personal Injury; Labor and Employment. ***Email:*** jpposey@beersmallers.com

KURT RUSSELL BACHMAN, born LaGrange, Indiana, May 31, 1964; admitted to bar, 1989, Indiana; U.S. District Court, Northern and Southern Districts of Indiana. *Education:* Manchester College (B.S., 1986); Indiana University, School of Law (J.D., 1989). Publication: "Waiting for the Hammer to Fall: A General Overview of Auction Law" 2002. *Member:* Fort Wayne Estate Planning Council, LaGrange County (Secretary/Treasurer, 1993; Vice President, 1994; President, 1995-1996), Indiana State and American Bar Associations; National Association of Bond Lawyers. ***PRACTICE AREAS:*** Corporate Law; Real Estate; Estate Planning Law; Municipal Law; Taxation; Auction Law. ***Email:*** krbachman@beersmallers.com

ROY F. KIPLINGER, born Detroit, Michigan, January 1, 1965; admitted to bar, 1991, Ohio; 1995, Indiana; U.S. District Court, Northern and Southern Districts of Ohio and Indiana; U.S. Court of Appeals, Seventh Circuit. *Education:* University of Michigan (B.A. with high honors, 1987; J.D., 1991). Phi Beta Kappa. Rotary Foundation Scholar. *Member:* Allen County, Indiana State and Ohio State Bar Associations. ***PRACTICE AREAS:*** Creditors Rights; Bankruptcy; Business Law; Commercial Law; Litigation. ***Email:*** rfkiplinger@beersmallers.com

KEVIN P. BRUNS, born Ft. Wayne, Indiana, April 16, 1966; admitted to bar, 1993, Indiana; U.S. District Court, Northern District of Indiana. *Education:* Indiana University

(This Listing Continued)

(B.A., 1989); Cleveland-Marshall College of Law (J.D., 1992). *Member:* LaGrange County and Indiana State Bar Associations. ***PRACTICE AREAS:*** Estate Administration; Business Law; Real Estate. ***Email:*** kpbruns@beersmallers.com

JOHN B. BENTZ, born Indianapolis, Indiana, August 5, 1969; admitted to bar, 1994, Indiana and U.S. District Court, Northern and Southern Districts of Indiana. *Education:* University of Notre Dame (B.S., 1991); Indiana University, School of Law (J.D., cum laude, 1994). *Member:* Allen County and Indiana State Bar Associations. ***PRACTICE AREAS:*** Real Estate; Zoning, Planning and Land Use; Business Law; Corporate Law. ***Email:*** jbbentz@beersmallers.com

CHARLES W. BACKS, born Fort Wayne, Indiana, July 22, 1970; admitted to bar, 1996, Indiana; 2005, Michigan. *Education:* Indiana University (B.A., Chemistry, 1993); Valparaiso University (J.D., 1996). *Member:* Allen County and Indiana State Bar Associations; State Bar of Michigan; National Academy of Elder Law Attorneys. ***PRACTICE AREAS:*** Business Law; Corporate Law; Elder Law; Estate Administration; Trust Administration; Medicaid Planning; Estate Planning; Guardianships; Real Estate. ***Email:*** cwbacks@beersmallers.com

LAURA L. MASER, born Marysville, Ohio, April 23, 1969; admitted to bar, 1997, Indiana, U.S. District Court, Northern and Southern Districts of Indiana and U.S. Court of Appeals, Seventh Circuit; 2004, U.S. Supreme Court. *Education:* University of Toledo (B.A., cum laude, 1991; J.D., magna cum laude, 1997). Order of the Coif. ***PRACTICE AREAS:*** Litigation; Employment Discrimination; Municipal Law. ***Email:*** llmaser@beersmallers.com

ASSOCIATES

HEIDI BIEBERICH ADAIR, born Fort Wayne, Indiana, May 27, 1969; admitted to bar, 1994, Indiana, U.S. District Court, Northern and Southern Districts of Indiana and U.S. Court of Appeals, Seventh Circuit. *Education:* Indiana University, Bloomington (B.A., 1991; J.D., 1994). *Member:* Allen County and Indiana State Bar Associations; Fort Wayne Estate Planning Council. ***PRACTICE AREAS:*** Estate Planning; Elder Law; Estate Administration; Medicaid Planning; Guardianships. ***Email:*** hbadair@beersmallers.com

LISA M. BOWEN-SLAVEN, born Seattle, Washington, July 20, 1967; admitted to bar, 1993, Indiana and U.S. District Court, Northern District of Indiana. *Education:* Purdue University (B.S., 1990); Valparaiso University (J.D., 1993). *Member:* La Grange County and Indiana State Bar Associations; American Academy of Adoption Attorneys. ***PRACTICE AREAS:*** Adoption Law; Medicaid Planning; Guardianships; Elder Law. ***Email:*** lbslaven@beersmallers.com

JOSHUA A. BURKHARDT, born Cincinnati, Ohio; admitted to bar, 2001, Indiana and U.S. District Court, Northern and Southern Districts of Indiana. *Education:* Northern Kentucky University (B.A., cum laude, 1998); Ohio Northern University, Pettit College of Law (J.D. with high distinction, 2001). Alpha Phi Sigma; Phi Kappa Phi; Golden Key. Member, Willis Society. Federal Judicial Clerkship with Hon. David F. Hamilton and Hon. John D. Tinder, U.S. District Court, Southern District of Indiana, 2001-2002. *Member:* Allen County and Indiana State Bar Associations; Defense Trial Counsel of Indiana; American Inns of Court. ***PRACTICE AREAS:*** Commercial Litigation; Appellate Practice; Business Law. ***Email:*** jaburkhardt@beersmallers.com

JONATHAN H. NUSBAUM, born Columbus, Ohio, January 20, 1971; admitted to bar, 1997, Indiana. *Education:* Trinity College (B.A., 1993); University of Toledo (J.D., cum laude, 1997). ***PRACTICE AREAS:*** Litigation. ***Email:*** jhnusbaum@beersmallers.com

STACY K. SOMERS, born Marion, Ohio, December 13, 1969; admitted to bar, 2004, Indiana. *Education:* Hanover College (B.A., 1992); Indiana University (J.D., 2004). ***Email:*** sksomers@beermallers.com

OF COUNSEL

DANIEL K. LEININGER, born Fort Wayne, Indiana, January 5, 1951; admitted to bar, 1976, Indiana; U.S. District Court, Norhtern and Southern Districts of Indiana; U.S. Court of Appeals, Fifth and Seventh Circuits. *Education:* Hanover College; Indiana University (A.B. with highest distinction, 1973; J.D., cum laude, 1976). Phi Beta Kappa; Phi Eta Sigma. Member, Board of Directors, Indiana University, School of Law Alumni Association (President, 2000-2001). *Member:* Allen County, Kosciusko County and Indiana State (Member, Commission on Lawyer's Discipline) Bar Associations. ***PRACTICE AREAS:*** Commercial Litigation; Products Liability Litigation; Civil Litigation.

REPRESENTATIVE CLIENTS: Allen County, Indiana; Allen County Public Library; Angola Public Library; Cole Hardwood Co., Inc.; Construction Control, Inc.; D.O. McComb & Sons, Inc.; Economy Co.; Electrolux; Estate Securities General Insurance Agency, Inc.; First Union Corp.; Fort Wayne Patrolman's Benevolent Association, Inc.; Fraternal Order of Police Lodge #14; F.W. Toenges Orthotics, Inc.; Town of Fremont; Fremont Public Library; Granite Broadcasting Corp. (WPTA-TV); Herdrich Petroleum; Howe Military School; Humphries Developments of Northern Indiana, Inc.; Indiana Custom Tracks, LLC; Indiana Dimension, Inc.; LaGrange County, Indiana; LaGrange County Public Library; LaGrange County REMC; LIN Television Corp. (WANE-TV); Millennium Development, Inc.; Mid-America Management; National Serv-All, Inc.; Oberlin-Jackson Marketing Co.; Pac-Tec, Inc.; Parkview Health System, Inc.; PHD, Inc.; Preferred Automotive Group, Inc.; Republic Services, Inc.; Salin Bancshares, Inc.; Salin Bank & Trust Co.; The Town of Shipshewana, Indiana; Shorewood Packaging Corp.; STAR Financial Bank; Steuben County EMS, Indiana; SUPERVALU, INC.; Time Services, Inc.; Tri-State Sports Corp.; Wabash Valley Refuse Removal Co.; Wheat First Union: Winn-Dixie; Wright-Moore Corp.

BEWLEY & KODAY, LLP

Established in 1987

110 WEST BERRY

SUITE 2006

FORT WAYNE, INDIANA 46802

Telephone: 260-424-0566

Fax: 260-423-1325

Email: bewleykoday@bewleykoday.com

URL: http://www.bewleykoday.com

Probate and Estate Planning, Tax, Mediation, Employee Benefits and Corporate Law.

(This Listing Continued)

GEORGE N. BEWLEY, JR., born Hammond, Indiana, August 19, 1947; admitted to bar, 1973, Indiana; 1977, U.S. Tax Court. *Education:* Indiana University (A.B., 1969; J.D., 1973). Phi Alpha Delta. Chartered Financial Consultant, 1981. Certified Financial Planner, 1987. Director, Indiana Continuing Legal Education Forum, 2001—. *Member:* Allen County (Chair, Probate and Trust Section, 1987 and 1993), Indiana State (Member, Sections on: Real Property, Probate and Trust Law, Council Member, 1991—, Chair, 1999; Corporation, Banking and Business Law, Council Member, 1984-1991) and American (Member, Sections on: Real Property, Probate and Trust Law; Taxation) Bar Associations; Fort Wayne Estate Planning Council (President, 1986); American College of Trust and Estate Counsel. ***PRACTICE AREAS:*** Probate and Estate Planning; Employee Benefits Law; Mediation. ***Email:*** gbewley@bewleykoday.com

JAMES KODAY, born Donora, Pennsylvania, June 25, 1951; admitted to bar, 1976, Indiana; 1984, U.S. Tax Court; 1986, Florida. *Education:* Indiana University (A.B., 1973; J.D., cum laude, 1976). Director, Indiana Continuing Legal Education Forum, 1995-2001; Indiana Bar Foundation, 2003—. *Member:* Allen County (Chairman, Taxation Section, 1985), Indiana State (Council Member, Probate, Trust and Real Property Section, 1984-1991) and American (Member, Sections on: Real Property, Probate and Trust Law) Bar Associations; The Florida Bar; Fort Wayne Estate Planning Council (Director, 1989-1992). American College of Trust and Estate Counsel. ***PRACTICE AREAS:*** Probate and Estate Planning; Corporate Law; Mediation. ***Email:*** jkoday@bewleykoday.com

BLACKBURN & GREEN

3344 MALLARD COVE LANE

FORT WAYNE, INDIANA 46804

Telephone: 260-422-4400; 800-444-1112

Telecopier: 260-436-4404

URL: http://www.lawyers.com/blackburn-green

Litigation, Personal Injury Law.

MEMBERS OF FIRM

THOMAS D. BLACKBURN, born Middlesboro, Kentucky, November 11, 1951; admitted to bar, 1977, Indiana. *Education:* Indiana University (B.S., 1974); Indiana University School of Law (J.D., 1977). *Member:* St. Joseph County, Indiana State and American Bar Associations. ***PRACTICE AREAS:*** Litigation.

RAYMOND T. GREEN, born Madison, Indiana, February 8, 1952; admitted to bar, 1977, Indiana and U.S. District Court, Southern District of Indiana. *Education:* Indiana State University (B.S., Business Management, cum laude, 1974); Indiana University at Indianapolis (J.D., cum laude, 1977). Judge: Bartholomew County Court, 1980-1982; Bartholomew Circuit Court, 1982-1985. Clerk for the Hon. Patrick D. Sullivan, Indiana Court of Appeals, 1976-1977. *Member:* Indianapolis, Indiana State and American Bar Associations; Indiana Trial Lawyers Association; The Association of Trial Lawyers of America. ***PRACTICE AREAS:*** Personal Injury Law. ***Email:*** rtgreen@blackburn-green.com

BURT, BLEE, DIXON, SUTTON & BLOOM, LLP

200 EAST MAIN STREET, SUITE 1000

FORT WAYNE, INDIANA 46802

Telephone: 260-426-1300

Fax: 260-422-2722

Email: info@burtblee.com

Mailing Address: P.O. Box 10810, Ft. Wayne, IN 46854-0810

Appellate Practice, Banking, Bankruptcy and Creditor Rights, Business Law and Business Litigation, Commercial and Agricultural Financing, Corporate, Elder Law, Probate and Estate Planning, Family Law and Domestic Relations, Personal Injury Litigation and Product Liability, Real Estate, Interstate Adoptions, Taxation, Estate and Gift Tax.

FIRM PROFILE: This firm, founded in 1978, renders legal services in all aspects of civil law. It has an extensive and varied practice in state and federal courts, with an emphasis on banking issues, creditor rights, commercial liability, contract, construction, employment, personal injury and domestic relations litigation matters. The firm also specializes in elder law, estate planning and estate administration. The firm's transactional practice covers real estate, finance, banking, commercial and general business services necessary to successfully protect and defend business in today's litigious society. The firm specializes in representing management in all aspects of labor and employment law, advising clients how to best avoid employee claims and lawsuits.

MEMBERS OF FIRM

ALTON DALE BLOOM, born Fort Wayne, Indiana, February 27, 1946; admitted to bar, 1971, Indiana. *Education:* Indiana University (B.S., 1968); Valparaiso University (J.D., 1971). *Member:* Allen County and Indiana State Bar Associations. ***PRACTICE AREAS:*** Banking Law; Real Estate Law; Commercial Transaction Law; Estate Planning. ***Email:*** bloom@burtblee.com

J. PHILIP BURT, born Muncie, Indiana, December 14, 1935; admitted to bar, 1961, Indiana. *Education:* University of Michigan (B.A., 1958; LL.B., 1961). Member: American College of Mortgage Attorneys, Inc. ***PRACTICE AREAS:*** Banking; Mortgage Law; Commercial Lending; Real Estate. ***Email:*** burt@burtblee.com

JEFFREY A. CLARK, born Knightstown, Indiana, March 17, 1965; admitted to bar, 1995, Indiana and U.S. District Court, Northern and Southern Districts of Indiana. *Education:* Indiana University (B.A., 1987; J.D., 1995). *Member:* Allen County, Indiana State and American Bar Associations. ***PRACTICE AREAS:*** Civil Litigation; Criminal Litigation; Personal Injury; Creditors Rights. ***Email:*** clark@burtblee.com

TIMOTHY L. CLAXTON, born Columbia City, Indiana, March 14, 1964; admitted to bar, 1989, Indiana and U.S. District Court, Northern and Southern Districts of Indiana. *Edu-*

(This Listing Continued)

BURT, BLEE, DIXON, SUTTON & BLOOM, LLP, Fort Wayne—Continued

cation: Indiana University (B.S., 1986; J.D., 1989). *Member:* Allen County, Indiana State and American Bar Associations. ***PRACTICE AREAS:*** Real Estate; Creditors' Rights; Business Law. ***Email:*** claxton@burtblee.com

GREGORY MARTIN COLE, born Bluffton, Indiana, September 11, 1961; admitted to bar, 1986, Indiana. *Education:* Ball State University (B.A., magna cum laude, 1983); Indiana University (J.D., 1986). Lambda Iota Tau. Member, Moot Court Society, 1984. Associate Editor, Indiana Law Review, 1985-1986. *Member:* Allen County, Indiana State and American Bar Associations; Indiana Trial Lawyers Association; The Association of Trial Lawyers of America; Public Investors Arbitration Bar Association. ***PRACTICE AREAS:*** Litigation; Banking Law; Insurance; Securities and Commodities Law. ***Email:*** cole@burtblee.com

ROBERT E. DOELLING, JR., born Fort Wayne, Indiana, June 12, 1963; admitted to bar, 1989, Indiana. *Education:* Purdue University (B.S., 1985); Valparaiso University (J.D., 1988). Executive Managing Editor, Valparaiso University Law Review, 1987-1988. ***PRACTICE AREAS:*** Business Law; Real Estate Law; Corporate Law. ***Email:*** doelling@burtblee.com

W. MICHAEL HORTON, born Hugo, Oklahoma, August 20, 1945; admitted to bar, 1973, Idaho; 1974, Indiana. *Education:* Indiana University (B.A., 1967; J.D., 1972). *Member:* Allen County and Indiana State Bar Associations. ***PRACTICE AREAS:*** Corporate; Estate Planning; Probate. ***Email:*** horton@burtblee.com

JOHN T. MENZIE, born Gary, Indiana, August 6, 1945; admitted to bar, 1981, Illinois; 1982, U.S. District Court, Northern District of Indiana; 1983, Indiana and U.S. District Court, Southern District of Indiana; 1985, U.S. Court of Appeals, Seventh Circuit. *Education:* Valparaiso University (B.A., with high distinction, 1968; J.D., 1981). Blue Key. Law Clerk, Hon. William C. Lee, Chief Judge, U.S. District Court, Northern District of Indiana, 1981-1983. *Member:* American Bar Association (Member, Labor and Employment Law Section). ***PRACTICE AREAS:*** Labor and Employment. ***Email:*** menzie@burtblee.com

MICHAEL C. MOELLERING, born Fort Wayne, Indiana, June 9, 1964; admitted to bar, 1992, Indiana. *Education:* Taylor University (B.A., 1987); Valparaiso University (J.D., 1992). Chief Justice, Moot Court Society, 1991-1992. Recipient, Corpus Juris Secundum Award, 1992. Adjunct Professor, Business Law, Taylor University, 1999—. ***PRACTICE AREAS:*** Business Law; Corporate; Employment Law. ***Email:*** moellering@burtblee.com

CAROL BENNETT RHODES, born Frankfort, Michigan, May 19, 1945; admitted to bar, 1994, Indiana; U.S. District Court, Northern and Southern Districts of Indiana. *Education:* Drake University (B.A., magna cum laude, 1966); Northwestern University (M.A., 1969); Indiana University (J.D., 1993). Phi Beta Kappa. *Member:* Allen County and Indiana State Bar Associations. ***PRACTICE AREAS:*** Family Law. ***Email:*** rhodes@burtblee.com

SUZAN L. RUTZ, born Fort Wayne, Indiana, January 9, 1962; admitted to bar, 1987, Indiana. *Education:* Indiana University (B.A., 1984); Valparaiso University (J.D., 1987). *Member:* Allen County and Indiana State Bar Associations. ***PRACTICE AREAS:*** Estate Administration; Family and Matrimonial Law; Banking Law. ***Email:*** rutz@burtblee.com

WESLEY N. STEURY, born Decatur, Indiana, July 21, 1950; admitted to bar, 1979, Indiana. *Education:* Taylor University (A.B., summa cum laude, 1972); University of Michigan (J.D., 1979). ***PRACTICE AREAS:*** Bankruptcy; Mortgage Foreclosure; Creditors Rights. ***Email:*** steury@burtblee.com

DENNIS D. SUTTON, born Hamilton, Indiana, October 1, 1947; admitted to bar, 1974, Indiana. *Education:* Tulane University and Indiana University (B.A., 1969); Indiana University (J.D., 1974). ***PRACTICE AREAS:*** Adoption Law; Interstate Adoptions; Business Law; Corporate; Estate Planning; Probate; Real Estate. ***Email:*** sutton@burtblee.com

ASSOCIATES

RENEE S. BLOOM, born Fort Wayne, Indiana, September 30, 1975; admitted to bar, 2002, Indiana. *Education:* Indiana University (B.A., 1998); Ohio Northern University (J.D., 2002). ***PRACTICE AREAS:*** Real Estate; Foreclosures; Contracts; Leases and Leasing; Estate Planning; Collections. ***Email:*** reneebloom@burtblee.com

ROBERT C. KRUGER, born Wolcottville, Indiana, August 5, 1972; admitted to bar, 2001, Indiana and U.S. District Court, Northern and Southern Districts of Indiana. *Education:* Purdue University (B.A., 1998); Indiana University School of Law-Bloomington (J.D., 2000). Member, Federal Communications Law Journal, 1999-2000. *Member:* Allen County and Indiana State Bar Associations. ***PRACTICE AREAS:*** Banking; Business Law; Real Estate; Environmental; Litigation. ***Email:*** kruger@burtblee.com

WILLIAM C. BUTLER, born Lansing, Michigan, June 16, 1974; admitted to bar, 2000, Indiana and U.S. District Court, Northern and Southern Districts of Indiana. *Education:* Michigan State University (B.A., Criminal Justice, with honors, 1996); Detroit College of Law at Michigan State University (J.D., magna cum laude, 2000). ***PRACTICE AREAS:*** Creditors Rights; Civil Litigation; Criminal Law. ***Email:*** butler@burtblee.com

SHANE C. MULHOLLAND, born Kendallville, Indiana, July 17, 1969; admitted to bar, 1998, Indiana and U.S. District Court, Northern and Southern Districts of Indiana; 2000, U.S. District Court, Western District of Michigan and U.S. Court of Appeals, 7th Circuit. *Education:* Ball State University (B.A., Political Science, 1990; M.A., Political Science, 1991); Thomas M. Cooley Law School (J.D., 1998). *Member:* Allen County (President, Labor and Employment Law Section, 2004—), Indiana State and American (Member, Labor and Employment Law Section) Bar Associations; American Inns of Court. ***PRACTICE AREAS:*** Labor and Employment Law; Civil Litigation. ***Email:*** scm@burtblee.com

JEREMY J. GROGG, born Auburn, Indiana, August 19, 1977; admitted to bar, 2003, Indiana and U.S. District Court, Southern and Northern Districts of Indiana. *Education:* Purdue University (B.A., 1999); Indiana University School of Law - Indianapolis (J.D., cum laude, 2003). *Member:* Allen County, Indiana State and American Bar Associations. ***PRACTICE AREAS:*** Civil Litigation; Commercial Litigation; Collections; Business Law; Environmental Law. ***Email:*** grogg@burtblee.com

(This Listing Continued)

EMILY S. PATTERSON, born Fort Wayne, Indiana, August 23, 1978; admitted to bar, 2003, Indiana. *Education:* Saint Francis University (B.S., with honors.; B.A.A., with honors, 2000); Indiana University School of Law - Indianapolis (J.D., 2003). *Member:* Allen County, Indiana State and American Bar Associations. ***PRACTICE AREAS:*** Corporate Law; Estate Planning; Real Estate. ***Email:*** patterson@burtblee.com

STEPHEN J. SHUMLAS, born Grand Rapids, Michigan, November 9, 1978; admitted to bar, 2004, Indiana and U.S. District Court, Northern and Southern Districts of Indiana. *Education:* Michigan State University (B.A., 2001); Indiana University School of Law - Indianapolis (J.D., 2004). *Member:* Allen County, Indiana State and American Bar Associations. ***PRACTICE AREAS:*** Business Law (50%); Creditors Rights (25%); Bankruptcy (15%); Real Estate (10%). ***Email:*** shumlas@burtblee.com

OF COUNSEL

THOMAS J. BLEE, born Fort Wayne, Indiana, January 29, 1930; admitted to bar, 1975, Indiana. *Education:* Indiana University (A.B., cum laude, 1951; J.D., summa cum laude, 1975). Phi Beta Kappa; Blue Key; Associate Editor, Indiana Law Review, 1974-1975. ***PRACTICE AREAS:*** Corporate; Estate Planning; Real Estate Development. ***Email:*** blee@burtblee.com

ALLAN E. BLOOM, born Fort Wayne, Indiana, October 16, 1932; admitted to bar, 1956, Indiana. *Education:* Valparaiso University (A.B., 1954; J.D., 1956). State Representative, 1961-1962. State Senator, 1962-1970. Fort Wayne Police Commissioner, 1970-1971. Chairman, Fort Wayne Police Commission, 1976-1981. *Member:* Allen County and Indiana State Bar Associations. [With United States Marine Corps, 1956-1958; Lt. Col., USMCR]. ***PRACTICE AREAS:*** Corporations Law; Wills; Estates.

THOMAS J. DIXON, born Chicago, Illinois, September 11, 1929; admitted to bar, 1959, Indiana. *Education:* St. Ambrose University (B.A., 1951); University of Notre Dame (LL.B., 1959; J.D., 1969). Member: National Academy of Elder Law Attorneys. ***PRACTICE AREAS:*** Business Law; Elder Care; Estate Planning; Real Estate; Probate Administration. ***Email:*** dixon@burtblee.com

REPRESENTATIVE CLIENTS: Standard Federal Bank; North Central Enterprises, Inc.; Better Business Bureau of Northeastern Indiana; Midwest Pipe & Steel, Inc.; Our Sunday Visitor, Inc.; Pretzels, Inc.; Harding, Dahm & Co., Inc.; North Eastern Construction Co., Inc.; Paragon Tube Corp.; Pizza Hut of Fort Wayne, Inc.; Zollner Credit Union; Woodburn Diamond Die, Inc.; D & L Communications, Inc.; Indiana Marine Products, Inc.; QC Onics, Inc.; Weigand Construction Company, Inc.; General Credit Union; Community Mortgage Corp.; Freedom Financial Mortgage Corp.; Liechty Homes, Inc.; E.E. Brandenberger Construction, Inc.; First Quality Homes, Inc.; Bob Labis Homes, Inc.; Attorneys Title Group, Inc.; Project Renew; Fort Wayne Neighborhood Housing Partnership.
REFERENCES: Standard Federal Bank; Tower Bank; Bank One; Ossian State Bank.

CARSON BOXBERGER LLP

Established in 1945

1400 ONE SUMMIT SQUARE
FORT WAYNE, INDIANA 46802-3173
Telephone: 260-423-9411
Telecopier: 260-423-4329
URL: http://www.carsonboxberger.com

Bloomington, Indiana Office: 3100 John Hinkle Place, Suite 106. Telephone: 812-333-1225. Fax: 812-333-1925.

General Civil Trial and Appellate Practice in all State and Federal Courts. Corporate, Business Transactions, Financial Institutions, Health Care, Probate and Estate Planning, Family Law, Transportation Law and Administration, Civil Rights, Real Estate, Labor, Insurance, Medical and Professional Malpractice, Products Liability, Workers' Compensation, Commercial, Creditors Rights and Bankruptcy Law, Mediation, Municipal.

FIRM PROFILE: For over 55 years Carson Boxberger LLP, has represented a variety of business enterprises, corporations, banks, governmental entities and individual entrepreneurs. In addition to its corporate work, the firm represents a wide variety of insurance companies in its highly sophisticated insurance defense practice. The firm has a state-wide presence with branch offices in Bloomington and South Bend; attorneys licensed to practice in Indiana, Illinois and Michigan.

MEMBERS OF FIRM

PHILIP L. CARSON, born 1942; admitted to bar, 1967, Indiana; U.S. District Court, Northern and Southern Districts of Indiana. *Education:* DePauw University (B.A., with distinction, 1964); Indiana University (J.D., cum laude, 1967). Order of the Coif. Member, Board of Editors, Indiana Law Journal, 1965-1967. *Member:* Allen County, Indiana State and American Bar Associations. ***PRACTICE AREAS:*** Corporate Law; Labor Law; Employment Law; Commercial Law; Real Estate. ***Email:*** plc@carsonboxberger.com

BRUCE O. BOXBERGER, born 1948; admitted to bar, 1974, Indiana and U.S. District Court, Northern and Southern Districts of Indiana; U.S. Tax Court; U.S. Supreme Court. *Education:* George Washington University; Indiana University (B.A., with honors, 1971; J.D., magna cum laude, 1973). Editor, Indiana Law Review, 1973. Corporation Counsel, The City of Fort Wayne, 1981-1987. *Member:* Allen County, Indiana State and American Bar Associations; American Labor Law Institute; Indiana Association of City Law Officers; National Association of Municipal Law Officers. ***PRACTICE AREAS:*** Corporate Law; Tax Law; Labor Law; Commercial Law; International Law. ***Email:*** bob@carsonboxberger.com

PAUL B. McNELLIS, admitted to bar, 1962, Indiana. *Education:* College of the Holy Cross (B.S., 1959); University of Notre Dame (LL.B., 1962). Public Defender, Allen County, Indiana, 1969. Associate City Attorney, Fort Wayne, Indiana, 1970-1971. Assistant County Attorney, Allen County, Indiana, 1974-1990. *Member:* Allen County, Indiana State and American Bar Associations; Indiana Trial Lawyers Association; The Association of Trial Lawyers of America. [JAGC, U.S. Air Force, 1962-1965; Capt., U.S. Air Force Reserve]. ***PRACTICE AREAS:*** Business Law. ***Email:*** pbm@carsonboxberger.com

(This Listing Continued)

JOHN J. WERNET, born 1950; admitted to bar, 1975, Indiana, Arizona and California; U.S. District Court, Northern District of Indiana; U.S. Tax Court. *Education:* Indiana University (B.S., 1972); John Marshall Law School (J.D., 1975). Associate City Attorney, City of Fort Wayne (Counsel for Redevelopment Commission, 1983—). *Member:* Allen County, Indiana State and American Bar Associations. ***PRACTICE AREAS:*** Corporate Law; Commercial Law; Zoning Law; Estate Planning; Estate Administration. ***Email:*** jjw@carsonboxberger.com

RICHARD P. SAMEK, born 1951; admitted to bar, 1976, Indiana; U.S. District Court, Northern and Southern Districts of Indiana; U.S. Court of Appeals, Seventh Circuit. *Education:* Indiana University (B.S., cum laude, 1973; J.D., summa cum laude, 1976). Associate Editor, Indiana Law Review, 1975-1976. *Member:* Allen County, Indiana State and American Bar Associations; Indiana Defense Lawyers Association; Defense Research Institute, Inc. ***PRACTICE AREAS:*** Civil Litigation; Insurance Defense; Commercial Litigation; Corporate Law; Property Law. ***Email:*** rps@carsonboxberger.com

PHILLIP A. RENZ, born 1950; admitted to bar, 1978, Indiana and U.S. District Court, Northern and Southern Districts of Indiana; U.S. Court of Appeals, 7th Circuit; U.S. Supreme Court. *Education:* St. Francis College (B.A., with honors, 1973); Indiana University (J.D., 1978). Deputy Prosecutor, Hancock County, 1977-1978. *Member:* Allen County, Indiana State and American Bar Associations. ***PRACTICE AREAS:*** Civil Litigation; Insurance Defense; Family Law; Real Estate; Workers Compensation; Mediation. ***Email:*** par@carsonboxberger.com

EDWARD J. LIPTAK, born 1954; admitted to bar, 1979, Indiana; U.S. District Court, Northern and Southern Districts of Indiana; U.S. Court of Appeals, Seventh Circuit. *Education:* Boston College (A.B., magna cum laude, 1976); Indiana University (J.D., cum laude, 1979). Managing Editor, Indiana Law Journal, 1978-1979. *Member:* Monroe County, Indiana State and American Bar Associations; Defense Trial Counsel of Indiana; Defense Research Institute. (Resident, Bloomington, Indiana Office). ***PRACTICE AREAS:*** Civil Litigation; Personal Injury Defense; Medical Malpractice Defense; Workers Compensation Defense; Product Liability Defense; Municipal Defense; Civil Rights Defense; Mediation. ***Email:*** ejl@carsonboxberger.com

ROBERT T. KEEN, JR., born 1957; admitted to bar, 1982, Indiana; U.S. District Court, Northern and Southern Districts of Indiana; U.S. Court of Appeals, Seventh Circuit; U.S. Supreme Court. *Education:* University of Notre Dame (B.A., cum laude, 1979; J.D., 1982). Author: "Handbook on Municipal Liability." *Member:* Allen County, Indiana State and American Bar Associations; Defense Trial Counsel of Indiana; Defense Research Institute; Federation of Insurance and Corporate Counsel; Master and Past President, American Inns of Court. ***PRACTICE AREAS:*** Civil Litigation; Commercial Litigation; Insurance Defense; Premises Liability Defense; Civil Rights Law; Products Liability; Employment Litigation. ***Email:*** rtk@carsonboxberger.com

JON A. BRAGALONE, born 1952; admitted to bar, 1981, Indiana and U.S. District Court, Northern and Southern Districts of Indiana; U.S. Court of Appeals, Fifth and Seventh Circuits. *Education:* Indiana University (B.S., 1975); Drake University (J.D., 1981). *Member:* Allen County, Indiana State and American Bar Associations. ***PRACTICE AREAS:*** Business Law; Corporate Law; Commercial Litigation; Products Liability Defense. ***Email:*** jab@carsonboxberger.com

LARRY L. BARNARD, born 1962; admitted to bar, 1987, Indiana and U.S. District Court, Northern and Southern Districts of Indiana; U.S. Court of Appeals, Seventh Circuit; U.S. Supreme Court. *Education:* Indiana University-Bloomington (B.S., 1984); Indiana University-Indianapolis (J.D., summa cum laude, 1987). *Member:* Allen County, Indiana State and American Bar Associations; Defense Research Institute; Defense Trial Counsel of Indiana. ***PRACTICE AREAS:*** Commercial Litigation; Insurance Defense; Civil Rights; Employment Litigation; Appellate Practice. ***Email:*** llb@carsonboxberger.com

ARTHUR E. MANDELBAUM, born 1964; admitted to bar, 1989, Indiana and U.S. District Court, Northern and Southern District of Indiana. *Education:* Indiana University (B.S., 1986; J.D., 1989). *Member:* Allen County, Indiana State and American Bar Associations. ***PRACTICE AREAS:*** Corporation Law; Commercial Law; Employment Law; Estate Planning. ***Email:*** aem@carsonboxberger.com

DIANA C. BAUER, born 1960; admitted to bar, 1987, Indiana and U.S. District Court, Northern and Southern Districts of Indiana; U.S. Court of Appeals, Seventh Circuit; U.S. Supreme Court. *Education:* Valparaiso University (B.A., with distinction, 1982; J.D., 1987). Law Clerk to the Honorable Gene B. Lee, U.S. Magistrate, U.S. District Court, Northern District of Indiana. *Member:* Allen County, Seventh Circuit, Indiana State and American Bar Associations; Defense Trial Counsel of Indiana; Defense Research Institute; American Judicature Society. ***PRACTICE AREAS:*** Civil Litigation; Insurance Defense; Medical Malpractice Defense; Civil Rights; Appellate Practice. ***Email:*** dcb@carsonboxberger.com

JAMES P. BUCHHOLZ, born 1963; admitted to bar, 1988, Illinois, U.S. District Court, Northern and Central Districts of Illinois, Indiana and U.S. District Court, Northern and Southern Districts of Indiana. *Education:* Wittenberg University (B.A., 1985); Indiana University (J.D., 1988). *Member:* Chicago, Allen County, Indiana State and American Bar Associations. ***PRACTICE AREAS:*** Commercial Litigation; Insurance Defense; Personal Injury; Litigation; Workers Compensation; Employment Law. ***Email:*** jpb@carsonboxberger.com

DOUGLAS A. HOFFMAN, born 1965; admitted to bar, 1990, Indiana and U.S. District Court, Northern and Southern Districts of Indiana; U.S. Court of Appeals, Seventh Circuit. *Education:* Wittenberg University (B.A., cum laude, 1987); Indiana University (J.D., cum laude, 1990). *Member:* Monroe County, Indiana State and American Bar Associations. (Resident, Bloomington Office). ***PRACTICE AREAS:*** Civil Litigation; Workers Compensation; Insurance Defense. ***Email:*** dah@carsonboxberger.com

KARL J. VERACCO, born 1966; admitted to bar, 1992, Indiana and U.S. District Court, Northern and Southern Districts of Indiana; U.S. Court of Appeals, Seventh Circuit. *Education:* Purdue University (B.A., 1988); Indiana University (J.D., M.P.A., 1992). Adjunct Professor, Law and Public Policy, Indiana University School of Public and Environmental Affairs, 1991. *Member:* Allen County, Indiana State and American Bar Associations. ***PRACTICE AREAS:*** Civil Litigation; Workers Compensation; Insurance Defense. ***Email:*** kjv@carsonboxberger.com

(This Listing Continued)

M. RANDALL SPENCER, born 1961; admitted to bar, 1991, Indiana and U.S. District Court, Northern District of Indiana. *Education:* Ball State University (B.A., summa cum laude, 1983); Notre Dame University (J.D., magna cum laude, 1991). *Member:* Allen County and Indiana State Bar Associations. ***PRACTICE AREAS:*** Corporate Law; Health Care. ***Email:*** mrs@carsonboxberger.com

TIMOTHY M. PAPE, born 1968; admitted to bar, 1995, Indiana and U.S. District Court, Northern and Southern Districts of Indiana. *Education:* Georgetown University (B.A., 1991); Indiana University (J.D., 1995). Associate Justice, Moot Court Board. Fort Wayne City Councilman. *Member:* Allen County, Indiana State and American Bar Associations; Defense Trial Counsel of Indiana. ***PRACTICE AREAS:*** Family Law; Civil Litigation; Business Law. ***Email:*** tmp@carsonboxberger.com

BRETT A. CARLILE, born 1971; admitted to bar, 1999, Indiana and U.S. District Court, Northern and Southern Districts of Indiana. *Education:* Indiana University (B.S., 1996; J.D., 1999). *Member:* Allen County, Indiana State and American Bar Associations. ***PRACTICE AREAS:*** Corporate Law; Commercial Transactions; Estate Planning; Estate Administration; Creditors Rights; Zoning, Planning and Land Use. ***Email:*** bac@carsonboxberger.com

GRANT A. LISTON, born 1972; admitted to bar, 2000, Indiana and U.S. District Court, Northern and Southern Districts of Indiana. *Education:* Indiana University (B.S., with distinction, 1996; J.D., 2000). *Member:* Allen County, Indiana State and American Bar Associations. ***PRACTICE AREAS:*** Insurance Defense. ***Email:*** gal@carsonboxberger.com

JEREMY M. DILTS, born 1975; admitted to bar, 2000, Indiana and U.S. District Court, Northern and Southern Districts of Indiana. *Education:* Indiana University (B.A., 1996; J.D., 2000). *Member:* Indiana State Bar Association. (Resident, Bloomington Office). ***PRACTICE AREAS:*** Civil Rights Defense; Medical Malpractice Defense; Insurance Defense; Subrogation. ***Email:*** jmd@carsonboxberger.com

BENJAMIN ICE, born 1976; admitted to bar, 2001, Indiana and U.S. District Court, Northern and Southern Districts of Indiana. *Education:* Ball State University (B.S., cum laude, 1998); Indiana University (J.D., 2001). *Member:* Allen County, Indiana State and American Bar Associations. ***PRACTICE AREAS:*** Civil Litigation. ***Email:*** bdi@carsonboxberger.com

JEREMY V. SENK, born 1974; admitted to bar, 2001, Indiana and U.S. District Court, Northern and Southern Districts of Indiana. *Education:* Purdue University (B.S., cum laude, 1996); Indiana University (J.D., 2001). *Member:* Allen County, Indiana State and American Bar Associations. ***PRACTICE AREAS:*** Creditors Rights; Bankruptcy Law; Commercial Transactions; Estate Planning; Estate Administration. ***Email:*** jvs@carsonboxberger.com

MARCIA M. YODER, born 1979; admitted to bar, 2004, Indiana; U.S. District Court, Northern and Southern Districts of Indiana. *Education:* Indiana University (B.S., Psychology, 2001; J.D., 2004). *Member:* Indianapolis, Allen County, Indiana State and American Bar Associations. ***PRACTICE AREAS:*** Civil Litigation; Employment Law; Civil Rights. ***Email:*** mmy@carsonboxberger.com

KEVIN P. PODLASKI, born 1960; admitted to bar, 1990, New Jersey and U.S. District Court, District of New Jersey; 1991, U.S. District Court, Eastern District of North Carolina; 1995, U.S. Supreme Court; 2004, Indiana. *Education:* University of Scranton (B.S., cum laude, 1982); Seton Hall University (J.D., 1990); University of Virginia/U.S. Army Legal Center and School (LL.M., 1996). *Member:* Allen County and American Bar Associations. ***PRACTICE AREAS:*** Litigation; Insurance Defense; Products Liability; Military Law; Security Clearances; Veterans Appeals; Military Criminal Law. ***Email:*** kpp@carsonboxberger.com

REPRESENTATIVE CORPORATE AND FINANCIAL CLIENTS: Advanced Machine & Tool Corporation; American Electric Power Company; Ashland Chemical Co.; Anthony Wayne Services; Bank One, Indiana, N.A.; BMA Medical; CB Richard Ellis Sturges; City of Fort Wayne; Ear Nose & Throat Associates; Flickinger Industries; Fort Wayne Dermatology; Fort Wayne Redevelopment Commission; Hayes Lemmerz International; Irmscher, Inc.; JobWorks; Lutheran Hospital of Indiana; National City Bank; Perfection Bakeries, Inc.; Professional Federal Credit Union; Quorum Health; Schust Engineering, Inc.; Speidell Homes Development, Inc.; Spine Technonogy and Rehabilitation, P.C.; Sweetwater Sound, Inc.; Three Rivers Ambulance Authority; Vera Bradley Designs, Inc.; Wal-Mart Stores, Inc.; SGT Development Corp.; Stulges Development Group LLC; MSKTD & Assoc., Inc.
REPRESENTATIVE INSURANCE CLIENTS: American International Group; Allstate Insurance Company; Bituminous Insurance Company; Cincinnati Insurance Companies; Continental Western Insurance Company; Employer's Mutual Company; Fremont Compensation Insurance Company; GAB Robins North America; Gallagher Bassett Services; Governmental Insurance Exchange; Hamilton Mutual Insurance Company; Hastings Mutual Insurance Company; Indiana Farmers Mutual Insurance Group; Liberty Mutual Insurance Co.; OHIC Insurance Company; ProAssurance; Progressive Insurance Group; ProNational Insurance Group; Reliance National Insurance Company; RLI Insurance Company; Rockwood Insurance Company; SAFECO Insurance Companies; St. Paul Companies; United Fire & Casualty Company; Universal Underwriters Insurance Company; Wausau Insurance Company.

DAHM & ELVIN, LLP

9604 COLDWATER ROAD, SUITE 201
FORT WAYNE, INDIANA 46825
Telephone: 260-497-6000
Fax: 260-497-6019
URL: http://www.dahmelvin.com

Chicago, Illinois Office: 161 North Clark Street, Suite 1750, 60601. Phone: 312-683-3900. Fax: 312-683-3911.

Drug & Medical Device Litigation, Product Liability, Class Action Defense, Federal Civil Litigation, Complex and Multi-District Litigation, Business Litigation.

ALBERT J. DAHM, born 1958; admitted to bar, 1983, Indiana and U.S. District Court, Northern and Southern Districts of Indiana; 1986, Arizona and U.S. District Court, District of Arizona; 1989, California and U.S. District Court, Central, Eastern, Northern and Southern Districts of California; 1997, U.S. Court of Appeals, Third Circuit; 1998, U.S. Court of Appeals, Fourth Circuit; 2005, U.S. Court of Appeals, Ninth Circuit. *Education:* Xavier University (B.S.B.A., magna cum laude, 1980); Indiana University School of Law (J.D., 1983). Associate Editor, Indiana Law Review, 1982-1983. New York Bar National Moot

(This Listing Continued)

DAHM & ELVIN, LLP, Fort Wayne—Continued

Court Team. *Member:* Allen County, Indiana State and American Bar Associations; Product Liability Advisory Council; Defense Research Institute (Member, Medical Device Committee). ***PRACTICE AREAS:*** Drug and Medical Device Defense; Product Liability; Complex & Multi District Litigation; Federal Civil Litigation; Commercial Litigation; Business Litigation. ***Email:*** bert.dahm@dahmelvin.com

MICHAEL S. ELVIN, born 1963; admitted to bar, 1988, Illinois and U.S. District Court, Northern District of Illinois; 1991, U.S. Court of Appeals, Seventh Circuit; 1998, Indiana and U.S. District Court, Northern District of Indiana; 2002, U.S. Court of Appeals, Fifth Circuit. *Education:* Bucknell University (B.S.B.A., 1985); Northwestern University (J.D., 1988). ***PRACTICE AREAS:*** Drug and Medical Device Defense; Product Liability; Complex and Multi-District Litigation; Federal Civil Litigation; Commercial Litigation; Business Litigation. ***Email:*** michael.elvin@dahmelvin.com

MATTHEW S. ELVIN, born Abington, Pennsylvania, September 27, 1967; admitted to bar, 1992, Illinois and U.S. District Court, Northern District of Illinois; 1996, U.S. Court of Appeals, Seventh Circuit; 2004, U.S. District Court, Eastern and Western Districts of Wisconsin (Not admitted in Indiana). *Education:* Bucknell University (B.A., 1989); The Dickinson School of Law of the Pennsylvania State University (J.D., cum laude, 1992). *Member:* Chicago, Illinois State and American Bar Associations. ***PRACTICE AREAS:*** Product Liability Litigation; Civil Litigation; Federal Civil Litigation; Insurance Litigation. ***Email:*** matthew.elvin@dahmelvin.com

JAMES A. BUTZ, born 1961; admitted to bar, 1986, Ohio; 1992, Indiana. *Education:* Indiana University (B.S., 1983); Case Western Reserve School of Law (J.D., 1986). Staff Member, Journal of International Law, 1983. Author: "Selling or Buying a Business," Indiana Business Magazine, Jan. 2002. In-House Counsel, NBD Bank, N.A., 1992-1994. Presenter, Counseling the Small Business Client in Indiana, National Business Institute, 2003. *Member:* Allen County, Indiana State, Ohio State and American Bar Associations. ***PRACTICE AREAS:*** Business Law; Corporate Law; Mergers and Acquisitions; Securities; Real Estate; Intellectual Property; Commercial Finance; Business Successions; Trusts and Estates; Estate Planning. ***Email:*** jim.butz@dahmelvin.com

---

SANDY L. MORRIS, born 1974; admitted to bar, 1999, Illinois; 2001, U.S. District Court, Northern District of Illinois; 2003, U.S. District Court, Southern District of Illinois (Not admitted in Indiana). *Education:* Syracuse University (B.A., 1995); University of Chicago Law School (J.D., 1999). National Merit Scholar; Chancellor's Scholar. *Member:* Chicago, Illinois State and American Bar Associations; National Association of Women Lawyers. ***PRACTICE AREAS:*** Products Liability; Litigation; Civil Litigation; Federal Civil Litigation; Insurance Litigation. ***Email:*** sandy.morris@dahmelvin.com

MATTHEW R. SHIPMAN, born Logan, Utah, May 15, 1972; admitted to bar, 1998, Indiana and U.S. District Court, Northern and Southern Districts of Indiana; 2002, Virgin Islands and U.S. District Court, District of the Virgin Islands. *Education:* Indiana University, Bloomington (B.A., 1994);Indiana University School of Law, Indianapolis (J.D., 1998). Member, Indiana International and Comparative Law Review, 1997-1998. *Member:* Indianapolis and Virgin Islands Bar Associations; Defense Research Institute. ***PRACTICE AREAS:*** Litigation; Medical Device Litigation; Commercial Litigation; Business Litigation; Employment Litigation; Insurance Litigation.

EILBACHER FLETCHER LLP

803 SOUTH CALHOUN STREET, SUITE 400
FORT WAYNE, INDIANA 46802
Telephone: 260-425-9777
Fax: 260-424-9177
Email: admin@eflawyers.com
URL: http://www.eflawyers.com

Business Litigation, Commercial Litigation, Securities Law, Litigation and Arbitration, Insurance Law, Civil Mediation and Commercial Arbitration.

MEMBERS OF FIRM

MARTIN T. FLETCHER, SR., born Long Beach, California, December 9, 1943; admitted to bar, 1969, Indiana. *Education:* Drake University (B.A., summa cum laude, 1966); Indiana University (J.D., summa cum laude, 1969). Phi Eta Sigma; Phi Beta Kappa; Order of the Coif. Associate Editor, Indiana University Law Journal, 1968-1969. Registered Civil Mediator. Listed in "Best Lawyers in America," Business Litigation. *Member:* Allen County and Indiana State Bar Associations; Benjamin Harrison Chapter of American Inns of Court (Master). ***PRACTICE AREAS:*** Securities Law; Litigation; Insurance Law; Mediation; Arbitration. ***Email:*** fletcher@eflawyers.com

DANIEL G. McNAMARA, born Huntington, Indiana, September 23, 1962; admitted to bar, 1991, Indiana and U.S. District Court, Southern and Northern Districts of Indiana; U.S. Court of Appeals, Seventh Circuit. *Education:* University of Notre Dame (B.A., 1985); Indiana University (J.D., 1990). *Member:* American, Allen County and Indiana State Bar Associations; Indiana Trial Lawyers Association; The Association of Trial Lawyers of America; Benjamin Harrison Chapter, American Inns of Court. ***PRACTICE AREAS:*** Civil Litigation; Commercial Litigation; Insurance. ***Email:*** mcnamara@eflawyers.com

DAVID E. BAILEY, born Columbus, Ohio, October 20, 1973; admitted to bar, 1999, Indiana and U.S. District Court, Northern and Southern Districts of Indiana and U.S. Court of Appeals, Seventh Circuit. *Education:* Miami University (B.S., magna cum laude, 1996); Indiana University, Bloomington (J.D., magna cum laude, 1999). Order of the Coif. Member, Indiana Law Journal. *Member:* Allen County, Indiana State and American Bar Associations; Indiana Trial Lawyers Association; Benjamin Harrison Chapter of American Inns of Court. ***PRACTICE AREAS:*** Civil Litigation; Employment Litigation; Commercial Litigation. ***Email:*** bailey@eflawyers.com

LEONARD E. EILBACHER, born Coffeyville, Kansas, October 9, 1934; admitted to bar, 1965, Indiana, U.S. District Court, Northern and Southern Districts of Indiana, U.S. Court of Appeals, Seventh Circuit and U.S. Supreme Court. *Education:* Indiana University (B.S., 1962; J.D., with distinction, 1965). Order of the Coif; Phi Delta Phi. Listed in *The Best Lawyers in America*, for business litigation and personal injury litigation. Author: "Comparative Fault and the Nonparty Tortfeasor," 17 Indiana Law Review 903, 1984; "Nonparty Tortfeasors in Indiana: The Early Cases," 21 Indiana Law Review 381, 1988. *Member:* Allen County (President, 1988), Indiana State (Chairman, Legal Ethics Committee, 1993-1995) and American Bar Associations; Defense Research Institute; Indiana Defense Lawyers Association (Diplomate, 1992). Fellow, American College of Trial Lawyers (State Chairman, 1990-1992). ***PRACTICE AREAS:*** Civil Litigation; Self Insured Defense; Mediation. ***Email:*** eilbacher@eflawyers.com

ALAN VerPLANCK, born Lansing, Michigan, May 1, 1950; admitted to bar, 1978, Indiana; 1985, U.S. Supreme Court. *Education:* Michigan State University (B.A., with high honors, 1972); Oxford University (1972-1975); University of Michigan (J.D., 1978). Phi Beta Kappa. Member, American Association of Rhodes Scholars, 1972-1975; Indiana and Missouri Selection Committee, Rhodes Scholarship Trust. Listed in *The Best Lawyers in America*, business litigation. Author: Land Use and Zoning, *Indiana Real Estate Transactions;* False Imprisonment, Abuse of Process, and Malicious Prosecution; *Indiana Personal Injury and Torts*. Adjunct Professor, Division of Labor Studies, Indiana University-Purdue University, Fort Wayne. *Member:* Indiana State and American (Member, Litigation Section) Bar Associations; Indiana Defense Lawyers Association; American Inns of Court. ***PRACTICE AREAS:*** Employment Law; Environmental Law; Corporate Litigation; ERISA Litigation. ***Email:*** verplanck@eflawyers.com

JAMES P. FENTON, born Cork, Ireland, August 13, 1949; admitted to bar, 1976, Illinois and Indiana; 1985, U.S. Supreme Court, U.S. Court of Appeals, Seventh and Eighth Circuits and U.S. District Court, Northern and Southern Districts of Indiana. *Education:* Columbia College (A.B., 1971); Indiana University (J.D., magna cum laude, 1976). Order of the Coif. Editor-in-Chief, Indiana Law Journal, 1975-1976. Law Clerk to the Hon. Jesse E. Eschbach, Chief Judge, U.S. District Court, Northern District of Indiana, 1976-1977. Listed in *The Best Lawyers in America*, Business Litigation. Author: Land Use and Zoning, *Indiana Real Estate Transactions;* False Imprisonment, Abuse of Process, and Malicious Prosecution, *Indiana Personal Injury and Torts* . Adjunct Professor, Communications Law, Indiana University-Purdue University, Fort Wayne. *Member:* Allen County, Indiana State, Illinois State and American Bar Associations; Americans Inns of Court. ***PRACTICE AREAS:*** Commercial Litigation; Environmental Litigation. ***Email:*** fenton@eflawyers.com

PATRICK L. PROCTOR, born Honolulu, Hawaii, September 2, 1967; admitted to bar, 1993, Indiana and U.S. District Court, Northern and Southern Districts of Indiana; U.S. Court of Appeals, Seventh Circuit and U.S. Supreme Court. *Education:* University of Kansas (B.A., 1990); Ohio Northern University Pettit College of Law (J.D., with distinction, 1993). Intern to Chief Justice Moyer, Ohio Supreme Court. *Member:* Allen County (Former Treasurer; Former Chair, Employment and Labor Section) and Indiana State (Member, Executive Board, Employment and Labor Section) Bar Associations; National Employment Lawyers Association; Indiana Municipal Lawyers Association; American Inns of Court. ***PRACTICE AREAS:*** Labor and Employment; Municipal Law; Civil Litigation. ***Email:*** proctor@eflawyers.com

FEDEROFF LAW FIRM, LLP

904 SOUTH CALHOUN STREET
FORT WAYNE, INDIANA 46802
Telephone: 260-407-0920
Fax: 260-407-7005
URL: http://www.federoff-law.com

Commercial and Residential Real Estate Transactions and Development, Land Use and Zoning, Business Organizations and Transactions, Business and Commercial Litigation, Real Estate and Construction Litigation, Probate Litigation, Trademark and Copyright Law.

JAMES A. FEDEROFF, born Detroit, Michigan, December 6, 1947; admitted to bar, 1975, Indiana, U.S. District Court, Southern and Northern Districts of Indiana and U.S. Court of Appeals, Seventh Circuit; 1988, U.S. Supreme Court. *Education:* Wayne State University (B.A., with distinction, 1969; J.D., 1975). Chairman and Faculty Member, ICLEF and NBI land use and real estate seminars. Allen County Plan Commission Attorney, 1983-1989. Associate Member, International Council of Shopping Centers. *Member:* Allen County (Member, 1986-1991 and President, 1989-1992, Board of Directors), Indiana State (Past Chairman, Land Use and Zoning Section, 1990-1992) and American Bar Associations. ***PRACTICE AREAS:*** Land Use; Zoning Law; Real Estate Development; Real Estate Transactions; Business Organizations; Commercial Transactions. ***Email:*** james.federoff@federoff-law.com

SCOTT M. FEDEROFF, born Warren, Michigan, November 17, 1971; admitted to bar, 1997, South Carolina; 2003, Indiana. *Education:* Indiana University (BAJ/B.A., 1994); Wake Forest University School of Law (J.D., 1997). Law Faculty Scholar. President, Phi Delta Phi, 1996-1997. *Member:* Hilton Head Island (Treasurer, 1998-1999; Secretary, 1999-2000), Allen County (Chairman, Real Estate Section), Indiana State and American Bar Associations; South Carolina Bar. ***PRACTICE AREAS:*** Real Estate Development; Real Estate Transactions; Land Use; Zoning Law; Business Organizations; Business Transactions; Trademark Law; Copyright Law. ***Email:*** smf@federoff-law.com

JASON M. KUCHMAY, born Farmington, Michigan, April 27, 1971; admitted to bar, 1998, Indiana and U.S. District Court, Northern and Southern Districts of Indiana; 2001, U.S. Court of Appeals, Seventh Circuit; U.S. Court of Appeals, Federal Circuit. *Education:* Michigan State University (B.A., 1993); University of Toledo, College of Law (J.D., magna cum laude, 1998). Order of the Coif. *Member:* Allen County, Indiana State and American Bar Associations; The Association of Trial Lawyers of America. ***PRACTICE AREAS:*** Business Litigation; Commercial Litigation; Real Estate Litigation; Construction Litigation; Probate Litigation. ***Email:*** jmk@federoff-law.com

RONALD K. GEHRING

SUITE 321 METRO BUILDING
202 WEST BERRY STREET
FORT WAYNE, INDIANA 46802-2242
Telephone: 260-422-6912
Fax: 260-422-6764

General Civil Trial Practice in all Courts. Personal Injury, Commercial, Corporate, Business, Probate, Bankruptcy, Real Estate and Family Law. Probate, Wills, Trusts and Estates.

RONALD K. GEHRING, born Ft. Wayne, Indiana, February 5, 1941; admitted to bar, 1967, Indiana and U.S. District Court, Northern and Southern Districts of Indiana; 1975, U.S. Court of Appeals, Seventh Circuit. *Education:* Indiana University (A.B., 1963; J.D., 1967). Phi Delta Phi. *Member:* Allen County (Member, 1978-1980 and Chairman, 1979-1980, Grievance Committee: Member, Board of Directors, 1980-1982; Member, Legal Ethics Committee, 1985-1991; Chairman: Member, Bankruptcy Committee; Member, Family Law Committee; Legal forms committee, Chairman, 1991-1996, Indiana State and American Bar Associations; Indiana Trial Lawyers Association; Commercial Law League of America.

REPRESENTATIVE CLIENTS: Forsite Service Bureau, Inc. (Placement Service); Hughes Properties; Concordia Cemetery Association, Inc.; Byall Homes, Inc.; Hughes Property Management; Schwarz Bros, Inc. (Automotive); GSK, Inc. (Automotive); General Construction of Indiana, Inc.; Summit Painting Co., Inc.; The Indiana District of the Lutheran Church - Missouri Synod, Inc.; Acres, Inc.
REFERENCES: Bank One; National City Bank.

GROSSMAN & LITCHIN LLP

1600 LINCOLN TOWER
FORT WAYNE, INDIANA 46802
Telephone: 260-422-4706
Fax: 260-422-4708
URL: http://www.gllawfirm.com

General Civil Practice. Personal Injury, Probate, Family/Domestic Relations, Real Estate, Bankruptcy, Creditor's Rights.

MEMBERS OF FIRM

JAMES R. GROSSMAN, born Fort Wayne, Indiana, February 20, 1927; admitted to bar, 1952, Indiana. *Education:* Indiana University (A.B., 1950; J.D., 1952). Recipient, Trial Lawyer of the Year Award, Indiana Trial Lawyers Association, 1991. *Member:* Allen County (President, 1974) and Indiana State Bar Associations; Indiana Trial Lawyers Association. Fellow, Indiana Bar Foundation. **PRACTICE AREAS:** Personal Injury; Civil Litigation; Civil Mediation; Probate and Estates; Divorce Law. **Email:** jrg1@glmlaw.net

KENT C. LITCHIN, born Fort Wayne, Indiana, February 28, 1958; admitted to bar, 1985, California; 1986, Indiana and U.S. District Court, Northern and Southern Districts of Indiana; 1985, U.S. District Court, Southern District of California. *Education:* Indiana University (B.S., 1980); California Western School of Law (J.D., 1985). Phi Alpha Delta. *Member:* Allen County and Indiana State Bar Associations; State Bar of California; Indiana Trial Lawyers Association. **PRACTICE AREAS:** Civil Litigation; Personal Injury; Probate Law; Bankruptcy; Creditors Rights; Wills; Real Estate Law. **Email:** kcl1@glmlaw.net

GRUNDEN LAW OFFICE

BUILDING 3
10355 DAWSON'S CREEK BOULEVARD, SUITE C
FORT WAYNE, INDIANA 46825
Telephone: 260-969-1177
Fax: 260-497-9747
URL: http://www.grundenlaw.com

Estate Planning, Guardianship, Business Planning, Family Law, General Litigation.

APRIL S. GRUNDEN, born Bluffton, Indiana, June 22, 1969; admitted to bar, 1997, Indiana and U.S. District Court, Northern District of Indiana. *Education:* Indiana University (B.S., 1994); Valparaiso University (J.D., 1997). *Member:* Allen County and Indiana State (Member, Family Law and Trusts and Estates Sections) Bar Associations. **PRACTICE AREAS:** Estate Planning; Estate Administration; Probate; Guardianship; Business Planning; Business Formation; Litigation.

HALLER & COLVIN, P.C.

Established in 1960
444 EAST MAIN STREET
FORT WAYNE, INDIANA 46802
Telephone: 260-426-0444
Telefax: 260-422-0274
URL: http://www.hallercolvin.com

Civil and Commercial Litigation in Federal and State Courts. Personal Injury, Wrongful Death, Products Liability, Land Use and Zoning, Domestic Relations, Employment Law, Real Estate Transactions, Taxation, Estate Planning and Administration, Hospital and Health Care, General Corporate Law, and Environmental Law, Bankruptcy and Creditor Rights.

ROBERT W. HALLER, born Fort Wayne, Indiana; admitted to bar, 1954, Indiana; 1957, U.S. Court of Military Appeals; 1961, U.S. Supreme Court. *Education:* Indiana University (A.B., 1950; J.D., 1954). Instructor, Commercial and Real Estate Law, Indiana University, 1960-1975. *Member:* Allen County (President, 1986-1987) Indiana State (Chairman, House of Delegates 1991-1992) and American Bar Associations; Lawyer-Pilots Bar Association; National Transportation Safety Board Bar Association. [Colonel, USAF Reserve (Ret.).]. **PRACTICE AREAS:** Real Estate; Estate Planning; Estate Administration; Corporate. **Email:** rhaller@hallercolvin.com

SHERRILL WM. COLVIN, born Jeffersonville, Indiana; admitted to bar, 1965, Indiana; 1968, U.S. Supreme Court. *Education:* Wabash College (A.B., 1960); Indiana University (J.D., 1965). Member of Faculty, National Institute for Trial Advocacy. Chair, Disciplinary Commission of Supreme Court, 1995-1996. *Member:* Allen County, Indiana State (President, 2003-2004) and American Bar Associations; Indiana Trial Lawyers Association (President, 1991-1992); The Association of Trial Lawyers of America. Fellow, American College of Trial Lawyers. Certified as a Civil Trial Advocate by the National Board of Trial Advocacy. **PRACTICE AREAS:** Personal Injury Litigation; Products Liability Litigation; Medical Malpractice; Professional Licensing; Commercial Litigation. **Email:** scolvin@hallercolvin.com

STEPHEN E. LEWIS, born Fort Wayne, Indiana; admitted to bar, 1969, Indiana; 1996, United States Supreme Court. *Education:* Valparaiso University (B.A., 1966; J.D., 1969). Note Editor and Member, Editorial Board, Valparaiso Law Review, 1968-1969. *Member:* Allen County and Indiana State Bar Associations. **PRACTICE AREAS:** Creditors Rights; Bankruptcy Law; Commercial Transactions; Estate Planning; Estate Administration. **Email:** slewis@hallercolvin.com

VINCENT J. HEINY, born Fort Wayne, Indiana; admitted to bar, 1976, Indiana. *Education:* Indiana University (A.B., 1973; J.D., cum laude, 1976). Member, Indiana Probate Study Commission. *Member:* Allen County, Indiana State (Member, Probate Section) and American (Member, Section of Taxation) Bar Associations. **PRACTICE AREAS:** Corporate; Estate Planning; Estate Administration; Health Care; Commercial Real Estate Development; Residential Real Estate Development; Zoning Law; Construction Law. **Email:** vheiny@hallercolvin.com

JOHN O. FEIGHNER, born Marion, Indiana; admitted to bar, 1976, Indiana. *Education:* Culver Military Academy (1969); Brown University (A.B., 1973); Indiana University (J.D., cum laude, 1976). Member, National Moot Court Team. Assistant Allen County Attorney, 1977—. Member, Indiana Judicial Qualifications and Nominating Commission, 2003-2005. *Member:* Allen County and Indiana State Bar Associations; Indiana Trial Lawyers Association (Member, Executive Committee, Board Member, 1995—); The Association of Trial Lawyers of America; President, Benjamin Harrison Chapter of the American Inns of Court, 1996-1997. Fellow, American College of Trial Lawyers. (Certified as a Civil Trial Advocate by the National Board of Trial Advocacy). **PRACTICE AREAS:** Personal Injury Litigation; Products Liability; Civil Rights and Employment Litigation. **Email:** jfeighner@hallercolvin.com

MARK E. GIAQUINTA, born Fort Wayne, Indiana; admitted to bar, 1979, Indiana. *Education:* Indiana University (A.B., with highest distinction, 1976; Phi Beta Kappa; J.D., 1978). *Member:* Allen County, Indiana State and American Bar Associations; Indiana Trial Lawyers Association. **PRACTICE AREAS:** Zoning Law; Environmental Law; Health Care; Government Law; Civil Litigation. **Email:** mgiaquinta@hallercolvin.com

MARK C. CHAMBERS, born Fort Wayne, Indiana; admitted to bar, 1975, Indiana. *Education:* Ball State University (B.S.); St. Francis College (M.S., cum laude, 1971); Tulane University of Louisiana (J.D., 1975). Lambda Iota Tau. Editor, Law Journal News. *Member:* Allen County (President, 1990-1991; Chairman, Family Law Section, 1992; Member, Judicial Nominating Board, 1990), Indiana State and American Bar Associations. **PRACTICE AREAS:** Corporate; Domestic; Commercial. **Email:** mchambers@hallercolvin.com

GEORGE SISTEVARIS, born Kastoria, Greece; admitted to bar, 1987, Indiana and U.S. District Court, Northern and Southern Districts of Indiana; U.S. Court of Appeals, Seventh Circuit. *Education:* Indiana University (B.S., 1984; J.D., 1987). Law Clerk to the Honorable Vern E. Sheldon, Allen Superior Court, Allen County, Indiana, 1987-1988; Listed in Who's Who in American Law. *Member:* Allen County, Indiana State and American Bar Associations; Indiana Trial Lawyers Association; The Association of Trial Lawyers of America. **PRACTICE AREAS:** Personal Injury; Products Liability; Civil Appeals and Litigation; Commercial Litigation; Landlord and Tenant Law; Civil Rights. **Email:** gsistevaris@hallercolvin.com

CYNTHIA P. ROCKWELL, born Gary Indiana; admitted to bar, 1988, Indiana. *Education:* Indiana University (B.A., 1974); Valparaiso University (J.D., with high distinction, 1988). Clerk to the Honorable William C. Lee, Judge, U.S. District Court, Northern District of Indiana, Fort Wayne Division, 1988-1990. Member, Board of Directors, Allen County League for the Blind and Disabled. *Member:* Allen County and Indiana State (Member, Executive Committee, State Employment and Labor Law Section) Bar Associations; Member, National Employment Lawyers Association; Founder and Co-Chair of NELA Indiana (1995—); Indiana Trial Lawyers Association. **PRACTICE AREAS:** Employment and Labor Law; Civil Rights Litigation. **Email:** crockwell@hallercolvin.com

ROBERT W. EHERENMAN, born Plymouth, Indiana; admitted to bar, 1992, Indiana and U.S. District Courts, Northern and Southern Districts of Indiana; U.S. Court of Appeals, Seventh Circuit. *Education:* DePauw University (B.A., magna cum laude, 1988) Phi Beta Kappa; Indiana University (J.D., cum laude, 1992). Attorney, Allen County Plan Commission and Allen County Board of Zoning Appeals. *Member:* Allen County and Indiana State (Section Chair, Land Use and Zoning Section, 2001-2002) Associations. **PRACTICE AREAS:** Real Estate; Land Use; Zoning Law; Environmental Law; Civil Litigation; Commercial Litigation. **Email:** rwe@hallercolvin.com

SUZANNE HAMPTON WAGNER, born Lansing, Michigan; admitted to bar, 1988, Indiana and U.S. District Court, Northern and Southern Districts of Indiana. *Education:* Central Michigan University (B.S., 1984); Thomas M. Cooley Law School (J.D., 1987). Editor: "Domestic Help," Allen County Family Law Newsletter; "Family Matters," Indiana State Family Law Newsletter. Representative, Third District, Indiana Family Law Section. Certified Family Law Specialist and Registered Family Law Mediator. *Member:* Allen County (Member, Executive Committee, Family Law Section); Indiana State and American Bar Associations. **PRACTICE AREAS:** Domestic Relations; Criminal Law; Civil Litigation. **Email:** shw@hallercolvin.com

CHARLES J. HEINY, born Fort Wayne, Indiana; admitted to bar, 1990, Indiana and U.S. District Court, Northern and Southern Districts of Indiana and U.S. Tax Court. *Edu-*

(This Listing Continued)

HALLER & COLVIN, P.C., Fort Wayne—Continued

cation: Indiana University (B.S., with high distinction, 1984); Indiana University School of Law (J.D., magna cum laude, 1990). Certified Public Accountant, Indiana, 1988. *Member:* Allen County, Indiana State and American Bar Associations; Indiana Certified Public Accountants Society. ***PRACTICE AREAS:*** Corporate Law; Mergers and Acquisitions; Health Care Law; Taxation; Estate Planning; Estate Administration; Creditor's Rights and Bankruptcy; Real Estate; Construction Law. ***Email:*** cheiny@hallercolvin.com

MARTIN E. SEIFERT, born Ireland, Indiana; admitted to bar, 1992, Indiana and U.S. District Court, Northern and Southern Districts of Indiana; 1993, U.S. Court of Appeals, Seventh Circuit; 1999, U.S. District Court, Western District of Michigan; 2001, U.S. District Court, Central District of Illinois. *Education:* University of Notre Dame (B.A., 1989); University of Innsbruck, Innsbruck, Austria; University of Notre Dame (J.D., magna cum laude, 1992). Phi Alpha Delta. Law Clerk, The Honorable Robert E. Grant, U.S. Bankruptcy Court, Northern District of Indiana, Fort Wayne Division, 1992-1994. Trustee, Chapter 7 Bankruptcy, 2002—. *Member:* Allen County (President, 2003-2004), Indiana State (Member, Bankruptcy and Creditors' Rights Section) and Seventh Circuit Bar Associations; American Judicature Society. ***LANGUAGES:*** German. ***PRACTICE AREAS:*** Bankruptcy Law; Creditors' Rights; Commercial Litigation; Business Transactions. ***Email:*** mseifert@hallercolvin.com

MELANIE L. FARR, born Hicksville, Ohio; admitted to bar, 1998, Indiana, U.S. District Court, Northern and Southern Districts of Indiana and U.S. District Court, Northern District of Ohio; 1999, Supreme Court of Ohio. *Education:* The Defiance College (B.S., summa cum laude, 1995); University of Toledo (J.D., magna cum laude, 1998). Order of the Coif. Member and Technical Editor, University of Toledo Law Review, 1997-1998. Attorney, Village of Antwerp, Ohio. Author: Note, "Wright v. Metro Health Medical Center: Anti-Nepotism Policies Carve a Slice in the Fundamental Right to Marry - Is this the Wright or Wrong Decision?", Toledo Law Review, Vol. 28, p. 841, Summer 1997. Member, Ft. Wayne Estate Planning Council. *Member:* Allen County (Member, Probate, Tax and Trust Section), Indiana State and Ohio State Bar Associations. ***PRACTICE AREAS:*** Estate Planning; Estate Administration; Commercial Litigation; Civil Litigation; Appellate Practice; Municipal Law. ***Email:*** mfarr@hallercolvin.com

---

LORI W. JANSEN, born Kendallville, Indiana; admitted to bar, 1996, Indiana and U.S. District Court, Northern and Southern Districts of Indiana; 1997, U.S. Court of Appeals, Seventh Circuit. *Education:* Purdue University (B.S., 1978); Valparaiso University (J.D., 1996). Attorney, Kendallville, Indiana Plan Commission and Board of Zoning Appeals. *Member:* Allen County, Indiana State and American Bar Associations; National Employment Lawyers Association; Indiana Trial Lawyers Association; Benjamin Harrison Chapter of American Inns of Court. ***PRACTICE AREAS:*** Civil Litigation; Labor and Employment; Civil Rights Litigation; Medical Malpractice. ***Email:*** ljansen@hallercolvin.com

DUANE J. SNOW, born Indianapolis, Indiana; admitted to bar, 2000, Indiana. *Education:* Indiana University (B.A., 1997); Indiana University School of Law (J.D., 2000). Phi Delta Phi. *Member:* Allen County, Indiana State and American Bar Associations; Indiana Trial Lawyers Association. ***PRACTICE AREAS:*** Domestic Relations; Commercial Law; Civil Litigation; Nonprofit Law; Corporate. ***Email:*** dsnow@hallercolvin.com

Languages: Spanish, German.

HAMPSHIRE & ASSOCIATES, P.C.

803 SOUTH CALHOUN, SUITE 201
FORT WAYNE, INDIANA 46802
Telephone: 260-423-3637
Fax: 260-420-1182

Family Law, Domestic Relations, Child Custody.

SHERIE L. HAMPSHIRE, born Kendallville, Indiana, August 23, 1957; admitted to bar, 1982, Indiana and U.S. District Court, Northern and Southern Districts of Indiana. *Education:* Ball State University (B.A., magna cum laude, 1979); Valparaiso University (J.D., 1982). Fellow, American Academy of Matrimonial Lawyers, 1989—. Recipient: Charles Vaughn Trial Advocacy Award. Listed, *Indiana 2004-2005 Super Lawyers* by Indianapolis Monthly and Law and Politics. Listed, *The Best Lawyers in America,* in Family Law, 1999-2006. Lecturer, Indiana Continuing Legal Education Forum. Registered Family Law Mediator. Registered AAML Family Law Arbitrator. Indiana Certified Family Law Specialist. Member, 1992-2004 and Chair, 1998-2004, Indiana State Ethics Commission. *Member:* Indiana State and Allen County (Family Law Executive Committee, 1992—Chair, 1997-1998; Co-Chair, Allen County Legal Ethics Committee, 2001) Bar Associations. ***PRACTICE AREAS:*** Family Law; Divorce; Child Custody; Premarital Agreements.

REFERENCE: Wells Fargo Bank.

HAYES & HAYES

Established in 1913

THIRD FLOOR, EIGHT TEN BUILDING
810 SOUTH CALHOUN STREET
FORT WAYNE, INDIANA 46802
Telephone: 260-420-1800
Facsimile: 260-420-1809
Email: hayesneil@aol.com
URL: http://www.hayesandhayeslaw.com

Family Law (all areas), Divorce, Dissolution of Marriage, Civil Trial Practice in all State and Federal Courts. General Practice.

FIRM PROFILE: Attorney Hayes who has achieved Martindale-Hubbell's highest rating for ethical standards and legal ability is dedicated to providing the finest in legal service to all his clients.

(This Listing Continued)

C. BYRON HAYES (1891-1975)

J. BYRON HAYES (1920-1986)

CORNELIUS B. (NEIL) HAYES, born Fort Wayne, Indiana, January 6, 1952; admitted to bar, 1980, Indiana and U.S. Federal District Court, Southern District of Indiana; 1981, U.S. Federal District Court, Northern District of Indiana; 1982, U.S. Tax Court; 1986, U.S. Supreme Court. *Education:* Indiana University School of Business (B.S., 1974); Thomas M. Cooley Law School (J.D., 1979). Certified Fellow, American Academy of Matrimonial Lawyers; Indiana Registered Family Mediator. Indiana Certified Family Law Specialist. Board Member, Independent Certification for Family Law Specialist, State of Indiana. Author and Lecturer: Indiana Continuing Education Forum (I.C.L.E.F.) 1990—; Indiana Family Law Institute. Selected: *The Best Lawyers in America,* all editions, 1995— (Family Law); Indiana Super Lawyer, 2004, 2005. Legal Counsel/Legal Deputy, Allen County Sheriffs Department. Member, Board of Directors, 1986-1991, Past Chairman/Vice Chairman, Fort Wayne Public Transportation Corporation. Board Member, Fort Wayne/Allen County Airport Authority, 2002. President, Allen County Public Defender Board. *Member:* Allen County (Member, Family Law Section, Past Chairman, Executive Committee, 1992—) and Indiana State (Member, Sections on: Family Law; Litigation) Bar Associations. ***PRACTICE AREAS:*** Family Law; Domestic Relations; Matrimonial Law; Divorce; Premarital Agreements; Dissolution. ***Email:*** hayesneil@aol.com

HELMKE, BEAMS, BOYER & WAGNER

Established in 1945

202 W. BERRY STREET, SUITE 300
FORT WAYNE, INDIANA 46802-2242
Telephone: 260-422-7422
Telecopier: 260-422-6764
URL: http://www.hbbwlaw.com

General Civil and Trial Practice. Indiana and Federal Courts, Corporate, Commercial, Insurance, Real Estate, Probate and Estate Planning, Insolvency and Municipal Law.

FIRM PROFILE: HELMKE, BEAMS, BOYER & WAGNER started when Walter E. Helmke began practice in 1925 as a solo practitioner. In 1945, returning veterans Paul W. Philips and Glen J. Beams became associated with Mr. Helmke and established a law firm. From its beginnings the practice has had a strong commitment to public service with members active in civic and charitable organizations. Its members are also active in continuing legal education seminars, professional activities and civic affairs.

MEMBERS OF FIRM

WALTER E. HELMKE (1901-1976)

WALTER P. HELMKE, born Fort Wayne, Indiana, December 28, 1927; admitted to bar, 1952, Indiana; 1969, U.S. Supreme Court. *Education:* Indiana University (A.B., 1950); Valparaiso University (J.D., 1952). Phi Alpha Delta. Deputy Prosecuting Attorney, 1955-58. Allen County Prosecuting Attorney, 1963-1970. State Senator, 1971-1974. *Member:* Allen County (President, 1982-1983), Indiana State (Chairman, Legislation Committee, 1976-1990) and American Bar Associations. ***PRACTICE AREAS:*** Corporation Law; Probate Law; Trust Law; General Business Law. ***Email:*** walterhelmke@hbbwlaw.com

R. DAVID BOYER, born Marion, Indiana, October 31, 1938; admitted to bar, 1964, Indiana; 1969, U.S. Court of Appeals, 7th Circuit. *Education:* Taylor University (A.B., cum laude, 1961); University of Pennsylvania (J.D., cum laude, 1964). Chi Alpha Omega. Law Clerk, Indiana Supreme Court, 1964-1965. Deputy Prosecuting Attorney, Allen County, 1965-1970. Associate City Attorney, City of Fort Wayne, 1988-1999. U.S. Bankruptcy Trustee, 1987—. *Member:* Allen County (Director, 1973-1975), Indiana State and American Bar Associations; National Association of Bankruptcy Trustees; American Bankruptcy Institute. ***PRACTICE AREAS:*** Estate Law; Corporation Law; Estate Planning Law; Insolvency Law. ***Email:*** daveboyer1@hbbwlaw.com

ROBERT A. WAGNER, born Kendallville, Indiana, December 18, 1939; admitted to bar, 1965, Indiana. *Education:* Valparaiso University (B.A., 1961); Indiana University (LL.B., 1964). Pi Sigma Alpha; Phi Delta Phi. Deputy Prosecuting Attorney, 1967 and 1971-1972; Chief Trial Deputy Prosecuting Attorney, 1973-1977 for Allen County. *Member:* Allen County, Indiana State and American Bar Associations. ***PRACTICE AREAS:*** Estate Planning; Probate and Trust Law; Taxation Law; Small Business Law. ***Email:*** robertwagner@hbbwlaw.com

J. TIMOTHY McCAULAY, born Indianapolis, Indiana, March 6, 1949; admitted to bar, 1975, Indiana; 1983, U.S. Court of Appeals, 7th Circuit. *Education:* Davidson College (A.B., 1971); Indiana University (J.D., cum laude, 1975). Associate Editor, Indiana Law Journal, 1974-1975. Staff Attorney, Indiana Governor's Commission on Individual Privacy, 1975-1977. Attorney for Fort Wayne/Allen County Board of Health, 1980-1987. Corporation Counsel, Fort Wayne, IN., 1988-1999. *Member:* Allen County, Indiana State and American Bar Associations. ***PRACTICE AREAS:*** Litigation; Municipal Law. ***Email:*** jtimmccaulay@hbbwlaw.com

DANIEL J. BORGMANN, born Fort Wayne, Indiana, October 30, 1950; admitted to bar, 1976, Indiana; 1978, U.S. Tax Court; 1987, Colorado. *Education:* Miami University (A.B., 1973); Ohio Northern University (J.D., 1976). Phi Delta Phi; Order of Barristers. Deputy Prosecuting Trial Attorney, 1981-1984. Attorney for Fort Wayne-Allen County Board Of Public Health, 1988—. *Member:* Allen County and Indiana State Bar Associations. Indiana Trial Lawyers Association; Indiana Defense Lawyers Association. ***PRACTICE AREAS:*** Litigation; Corporation Law; Taxation Law; Domestic Relations Law; Condemnation; Divorce; Child Custody. ***Email:*** djb@hbbwlaw.com

TRINA GLUSENKAMP GOULD, born Fort Wayne, Indiana, March 27, 1957; admitted to bar, 1982, Indiana; 1987, U.S. Court of Appeals, 7th Circuit. *Education:* Valparaiso University (B.A., 1979; J.D., 1982). Recipient, Trial Lawyer of the Year Award, Indiana Trial Lawyers Association, 1991. President, Mental Health Association of Allen County, 1991-1993. Associate City Attorney, City of Fort Wayne, 1993-1999. *Member:* Allen County (Treasurer, 1989-1993), Indiana State and American Bar Associations.

(This Listing Continued)

PRACTICE AREAS: Litigation; Domestic Relations Law; Business Law; General Practice; Divorce; Child Custody; Elder Law; Estate Administration. ***Email:*** trinagould@hbbwlaw.com

ASSOCIATES

R. DAVID BOYER, II, born Fort Wayne, Indiana, August 21, 1972; admitted to bar, 1998, Indiana and U.S. District Court, Northern and Southern Districts of Indiana. *Education:* Taylor University at Upland (B.A., 1995); Indiana University School of Law (J.D., 1998). Listed, Who's Who Among American Law Students. *Member:* Allen County, Indiana State and American Bar Associations; American Arbitration Institute. ***PRACTICE AREAS:*** Litigation; Corporation Law; Estate Law; Insolvency Law; General Practice. ***Email:*** daveboyer2@hbbwlaw.com

DONALD J. FREW, born 1964; admitted to bar, 1992, Indiana. *Education:* Ball State University (B.S., 1988); Ohio Northern University (J.D., 1992). ***PRACTICE AREAS:*** Civil Litigation; Family Law; Criminal Defense. ***Email:*** donfrew@hbbwlaw.com

OF COUNSEL

Glen J. Beams ***William A. Berning***
Paul Helmke

REPRESENTATIVE CLIENTS: Aalco Distributing Co., Inc.; Air-O-Mat, Inc.; Anchor Roon, Inc.; Brotherhood Mutual Insurance Co.; Carlos O'Kelly's Covington Memorial Gardens, Inc. Freemont Community Schools; Korte Electric, Inc.; Leo Distributors, Inc.; Poorman's Heating & Air Conditioning Services, Inc.; Ft. Wayne Urban Enterprise Assn.; Foellinger Foundations, Inc.; Indiana Institute of Technology; East Allen Community Schools.
REFERENCE: Tower Bank.

HUNT SUEDHOFF KALAMAROS LLP

803 SOUTH CALHOUN STREET, NINTH FLOOR
P.O. BOX 11489
FORT WAYNE, INDIANA 46858-1489
Telephone: 260-423-1311
Fax: 260-424-5396
URL: http://www.hsk-law.com

South Bend, Indiana Office: 120 West LaSalle Avenue, Twelfth Floor, P.O. Box 4156, 46634-4156. Telephone: 574-232-4801. Fax: 574-232-9736.

Indianapolis, Indiana Office: 6323 S. East Street, 46227. Telephone: 317-784-4966. Fax: 317-784-5566.

St. Joseph, Michigan Office: 608 S. Pleasant Street, P.O. Box 46, 49085-0046. Telephone: 269-983-4405. Fax: 269-983-5645.

General Civil Trial and Appellate Practice. Insurance Defense Litigation. Commercial Real Estate Financing and Transactions. Corporate and Commercial Law. Probate and Estate Planning.

FIRM PROFILE: Hunt Suedhoff, LLP was founded in 1950 by the late Leigh L. Hunt, a noted trial lawyer. Kalamaros and Associates was founded in 1960 by the late Edward N. Kalamaros, a noted worker's compensation lawyer. Recently, the two firms with so much in common joined forces. This solidified Hunt Suedhoff Kalamaros LLP as the premier law firm with the largest litigation practice in Northern Indiana. The firm presently serves the casualty insurance industry, as well as many regional and national corporations.

The lawyers of the firm are recognized by their peers as specialists in their fields, and frequently are called upon to participate in the training of other lawyers in various workshops and seminars sponsored by the National Institute for Trial Advocacy, the National Business Institute and the Indiana Continuing Legal Education Forum.

MEMBERS OF FIRM

P. MICHAEL MILLER, born Gary, Indiana, March 31, 1938; admitted to bar, 1965, Indiana and U.S. District Court, Northern and Southern Districts of Indiana; U.S. Court of Appeals, Seventh Circuit. *Education:* Indiana University (A.B., 1960; J.D., 1965). Order of the Coif. Member, Student Staff, Indiana Law Journal, 1964. Certified Mediator, Indiana. *Member:* Allen County, Indiana State and American Bar Associations; Indiana Defense Lawyers Association; Defense Research Institute; American Inns of Court. ***PRACTICE AREAS:*** Personal Injury; Business; Litigation; Insurance Law.

ROBERT E. KABISCH, born Fort Wayne, Indiana, October 14, 1942; admitted to bar, 1968, Indiana; U.S. District Court, Northern and Southern Districts of Indiana; U.S. Supreme Court. *Education:* Purdue University (B.A., 1965); Indiana University (J.D., 1968). Phi Delta Phi. *Member:* Allen County, Indiana State and American Bar Associations. ***PRACTICE AREAS:*** Insurance Litigation; Real Estate Law; Probate Law; Mediation.

DAVID A. STEWART, born Bronxville, New York, March 5, 1943; admitted to bar, 1968, Indiana. *Education:* University of Virginia (B.A., 1965); Indiana University (J.D., 1968). Phi Delta Phi. *Member:* Allen County, Indiana State and American Bar Associations. [JAGC, U.S. Navy, 1968-1972]. ***PRACTICE AREAS:*** Probate; Estate Planning; Real Estate Law; Health Care.

ARTHUR G. SURGUINE, JR., born Nashville, Tennessee, March 3, 1944; admitted to bar, 1973, Indiana; U.S. District Court, Northern and Southern Districts of Indiana; U.S. Court of Appeals, Seventh Circuit; U.S. Supreme Court. *Education:* Indiana University (B.A., 1971; J.D., 1973). Member of Faculty, National Institute for Trial Advocacy, 1984—. *Member:* Allen County and Indiana State Bar Associations; Indiana Defense Lawyers Association (President, 2000); Defense Research Institute. Fellow, American College of Trial Lawyers. ***PRACTICE AREAS:*** Insurance Law; Product Liability Law; Defense Litigation; Professional Malpractice.

THOMAS C. EWING, born Marion, Indiana, September 17, 1950; admitted to bar, 1975, Indiana and U.S. District Court, Southern and Northern Districts of Indiana; U.S. Court of Appeals, Seventh Circuit; U.S. Supreme Court. *Education:* Purdue University

(This Listing Continued)

(B.S., with distinction, 1972); Indiana University (J.D., cum laude, 1975). Beta Gamma Sigma; Phi Kappa Phi. *Member:* Allen County and Indiana State Bar Associations; Indiana Defense Lawyers Association. ***PRACTICE AREAS:*** Insurance Litigation.

MICHAEL D. MUSTARD, born Fort Wayne, Indiana, August 26, 1951; admitted to bar, 1978, Indiana and U.S. District Court, Northern and Southern Districts of Indiana; 1979, Florida. *Education:* University of Notre Dame (B.A., 1973; J.D., cum laude, 1978). Counsel for: Fort Wayne Community Development Corporation, 1978—; Fort Wayne Allen County Airport Authority, 1984-1989. *Member:* Allen County, Indiana State and American Bar Associations. ***PRACTICE AREAS:*** Corporation Law; Real Estate Law; Business Law.

BRANCH R. LEW, born Adrian, Michigan, January 24, 1957; admitted to bar, 1982, Indiana and U.S. District Court, Northern and Southern Districts of Indiana; U.S. Court of Appeals, Seventh Circuit. *Education:* Indiana University (B.S., with highest distinction, 1979; J.D., cum laude, 1982). Phi Eta Sigma; Beta Gamma Sigma; Phi Alpha Delta. *Member:* Allen County, Indiana State and American Bar Associations. ***PRACTICE AREAS:*** Insurance Law; Commercial Litigation; Transportation Law.

JAMES J. SHEA, SR., born Suffern, New York, November 30, 1959; admitted to bar, 1984, Indiana, U.S. District Court, Northern and Southern Districts of Indiana and U.S. Court of Appeals, Seventh Circuit. *Education:* King's College (B.A., magna cum laude, 1981); Valparaiso University (J.D., 1984). Phi Alpha Theta; Delta Epsilon Sigma; Phi Alpha Delta. Note Editor, Valparaiso University Law Review, 1983-1984. Volunteer, Deputy Prosecutor, Allen County. *Member:* Allen County and Seventh Circuit Bar Associations; Defense Research Institute; Indiana Defense Lawyers Association; Civil Rights Defense of Law Enforcement Officials. ***PRACTICE AREAS:*** General Insurance Litigation.

SCOTT L. BUNNELL, born Dearborn, Michigan, August 30, 1954; admitted to bar, 1983, Indiana; 1983, U.S. District Court, Northern and Southern Districts of Indiana. *Education:* Michigan State University (B.A., 1979); Thomas M. Cooley Law School (J.D., cum laude, 1983). Phi Alpha Delta. Law Clerk, Allen Superior Court, 1983. Probate Commissioner of Allen County, Indiana, 1984. *Member:* Allen County (Chair, Trial Lawyers Section, 1995), Indiana State and American Bar Associations. ***PRACTICE AREAS:*** Insurance Litigation; Probate Law.

DANE L. TUBERGEN, born Coldwater, Michigan, November 14, 1945; admitted to bar, 1970, Indiana. *Education:* Purdue University (B.A., 1967); Indiana University (J.D.; 1970). Certified Mediator, Indiana. Judge of Steuben Circuit Court, 1979-1993; Angola City Court, 1976-1978. *Member:* Allen County, Steuben County and Indiana State Bar Associations; Defense Trial Counsel of Indiana. ***PRACTICE AREAS:*** Insurance Litigation; Arbitration; Mediation.

CAROLYN M. TRIER, born Fort Wayne, Indiana, December 14, 1964; admitted to bar, 1990, Indiana and U.S. District Court, Southern and Northern Districts of Indiana. *Education:* Vanderbilt University (B.A., 1987); Valparaiso University (J.D., with high distinction, 1990). Phi Delta Phi. Note Editor, Valparaiso University Law Review, 1989-1990. Author: "Indiana's Criminal Treatment of Abusive Parents: Problems In Need of Solutions," 24 Val. U.L. Rev. 553 Spring 1990. *Member:* Allen County and Indiana State Bar Associations. ***PRACTICE AREAS:*** Insurance Defense; Insurance Coverage; Civil Rights Litigation; Employment Law.

KATHLEEN A. KILAR, born Detroit, Michigan, October 30, 1962; admitted to bar, 1987, Illinois; 1990, Indiana. *Education:* University of Michigan (B.A., cum laude, 1984); University of Detroit (J.D., cum laude, 1987). Phi Alpha Delta. *Member:* Allen County, Indiana State and American Bar Associations. ***PRACTICE AREAS:*** Corporate Law; Commercial Law; Health Care Law; Medical Malpractice Defense.

N. JEAN SCHENDEL, born Lackey, Kentucky, January 7, 1956; admitted to bar, 1995, Indiana and U.S. District Court, Southern and Northern Districts of Indiana. *Education:* Purdue University (B.S., in Nursing, 1990); Valparaiso University (J.D., magna cum laude, 1994). Sigma Theta Tau. Note Editor, Valparaiso University Law Review, 1993-1994. Registered Nurse, Indiana, 1977—. Adjunct Assistant Professor of Medicine, Fort Wayne Center for Medical Education, 2001— *Member:* Allen County, Indiana State and American (Member, Health Law Section) Bar Associations; American Health Lawyers Association; The American Association of Nurse Attorneys (President, Indiana Chapter, 1997-2000); Defense Trial Counsel of Indiana. ***PRACTICE AREAS:*** Medical Malpractice Defense; Health Care Law.

TIMOTHY W. DeGROOTE, born La Porte, Indiana, March 14, 1969; admitted to bar, 1995, Indiana. *Education:* Marquette University (B.A., 1991); Valparaiso University (J.D., 1995). *Member:* Allen County (Member, Steering Committee, Young Lawyers Section) and Indiana State Bar Associations; Indiana Defense Lawyers Association. ***PRACTICE AREAS:*** Insurance Defense Litigation; Corporate.

STEPHEN E. DEVER, born Fort Wayne, Indiana, June 27, 1967; admitted to bar, 1995, Indiana. *Education:* Indiana University (B.S., 1989; J.D., 1995). *Member:* Indianapolis, Allen County and Indiana State Bar Associations; Defense Research Institute; Indiana Defense Lawyers Association. ***PRACTICE AREAS:*** Insurance Defense Litigation; Workers Compensation; Business Litigation.

LINDA A. POLLEY, born Fort Wayne, Indiana, December 11, 1959; admitted to bar, 1985, Indiana; U.S. District Court, Northern and Southern Districts of Indiana; U.S. Court of Appeals, Seventh Circuit; U.S. Supreme Court. *Education:* Indiana University (B.A., 1982); University of Dayton (J.D., 1985). *Member:* Allen County and Indiana State Bar Associations.

DANIEL J. PALMER, born Michigan City, Indiana, March 9, 1966; admitted to bar, 1991, Indiana. *Education:* Butler University (B.S., cum laude, Chemistry, 1988); Indiana University (J.D., cum laude, 1991). Recipient, Willard Eason Chemistry Scholarship. *Member:* Allen County and Indiana State Bar Associations; Indiana Defense Lawyers Association. ***PRACTICE AREAS:*** Insurance Defense; Insurance Litigation.

ASSOCIATES

JASON C. CUSTER, born Decatur, Indiana, January 13, 1972; admitted to bar, 1997, Indiana and U.S. District Court, Northern and Southern Districts of Indiana. *Education:* Indiana University (B.A., 1994); Valparaiso University (J.D., 1997). *Member:* Indiana State and American Bar Association. ***PRACTICE AREAS:*** Insurance Defense.

(This Listing Continued)

HUNT SUEDHOFF KALAMAROS LLP, Fort Wayne—Continued

ORFEJ PETAR NAJDESKI, born Resen, Macedonia, October 28, 1968; admitted to bar, 1999, Indiana. *Education:* Purdue University (B.A., 1992); John Marshall Law School, Chicago (J.D., 1999). Law Clerk: Hon. Daniel G. Heath; Hon. Nancy Eshcoff, Boyer Allen Superior Court, Fort Wayne, Indiana; 1999-2000. *Member:* Indiana State Bar Association. ***PRACTICE AREAS:*** Litigation.

MELISSA GARLAND HAWK, born St. Joseph, Michigan, August 19, 1975; admitted to bar, 2001, Indiana and U.S. District Court, Northern and Southern Districts of Indiana. *Education:* Western Michigan University (B.A., cum laude, Political Science, Criminal Justice, 1997); Valparaiso University (J.D., 2001). *Member:* Allen County and Indiana State Bar Associations. ***PRACTICE AREAS:*** Civil Litigation; Medical Malpractice; Insurance Defense; Family Law.

ANDREW S. WILLIAMS, born Marion, Indiana; admitted to bar, 2002, Texas, Indiana and U.S. District Court, Northern and Southern Districts of Indiana. *Education:* Ball State University (B.S., cum laude, 1995); Baylor University (J.D., 2001). Barrister, Moot Court, 2000-2001. Senior Editor, Baylor Law Review, 2000-2001. ***PRACTICE AREAS:*** Insurance Defense; Insurance Litigation.

STEVEN S. HAND, born Fort Wayne, Indiana, May 29, 1972; admitted to bar, 2002, Indiana and U.S. District Court, Northern and Southern Districts of Indiana. *Education:* Indiana University (B.A., History, 1996); Valparaiso University School of Law (J.D., 2002). ***PRACTICE AREAS:*** Insurance Defense; Business Law; Commercial Law.

RICHARD W. KARCHER, born North Tonawanda, New York, April 16, 1965; admitted to bar, 1999, Indiana and U.S. District Court, Northern and Southern Districts of Indiana. *Education:* Indiana University, South Bend (B.S., 1994); Thomas M. Cooley Law School (J.D., cum laude, 1999). [Sgt., U.S. Air Force, 1985-1989]. ***PRACTICE AREAS:*** Litigation.

REPRESENTATIVE CLIENTS: AIG; Allied Group; American Family; Amerisure; Auto Owners; CGU; Chubb; Cincinnati; CMI (Claims Management Inst.); CNA; Crawford & Company; Crum & Forster; Dana Risk Management; E&O Professionals; EBI/Orion; ERC; Erie Insurance; Essex Insurance; Fireman's Fund; Frankenmuth; Gallagher Basset; Grange; GRE Indiana; Great West; Indiana Farmers; Indiana Insurance; ITT Hartford; ITT Specialty Risk; Kemper; Liberty Mutual; Medical Group of Ft. Wayne; Medical Protective; Meridian; Monroe Guaranty; Nationwide; Phico Group; REM f/k/a Home Ins.; RSKCO; Safeco/American States; Scottsdale; Secura; Sentry; Shelby; South Bend Medical Foundation; St. Paul/Met Life; Travelers; United Farm Bureau; Verizon Communications Inc.; Westfield; Zurich.

MARK A. KING
ATTORNEY AT LAW

FORT WAYNE, INDIANA

(See Indianapolis)

Criminal Law, Driving Under Influence, Felonies, Homicide, Family Law, Child Custody, Child Support, Business Law, Social Security, Social Security Disability, Personal Injury.

KOS & ASSOCIATE

Established in 1996

110 WEST BERRY STREET
SUITE 1904
FORT WAYNE, INDIANA 46802-2374
Telephone: 260-424-2790
Fax: 260-424-1872
Email: ekos@ekoslaw.com
URL: http://www.lawyers.com/ekoslaw

Bankruptcy, Creditors' Rights, Banking Law, Foreclosures, Collections, Commercial Litigation, Commercial Transactions, Corporate Law, Real Estate and Secured Transactions.

FIRM PROFILE: Kos & Associate initiated its practice in February 1996, when Edmund P. Kos formed the firm to implement a concentrated practice in the areas of bankruptcy, creditors' rights, commercial litigation and transactions, corporate law, real estate and secured transactions. Kos & Associate's primary client base is in Fort Wayne and surrounding communities, it also maintains a state-wide practice with clients in major population centers as well as in outlying areas. The firm serves a diverse client base, including manufacturers and service industries ranging in size and scope from small in-state businesses to multi-state banking companies to international corporations, as well as individuals. To expand the firm's capacity to serve its clients, Mr. Kos is licensed to practice in New York.

The firm's goal is to provide expert, timely, cost-effective and result-oriented legal advice and representation to their clients. To assist in achieving this goal, Kos & Associate utilizes degreed paralegal personnel and state-of-the-art technology.

EDMUND P. KOS, born Schenectady, New York, November 20, 1958; admitted to bar, 1984, New York and U.S. Army Court of Military Review; 1986, Indiana and U.S. District Court, Northern and Southern Districts of Indiana; 1990, U.S. Court of Appeals, Seventh Circuit; 1999, U.S. District Court, Western District of Michigan; 2001, U.S. District Court, Central District of Illinois. *Education:* Siena College (B.A., cum laude, 1980); Albany Law School of Union University (J.D., 1983). Editor: Indiana State Bar Association Bankruptcy Newsletter, 1988-1992; Allen County Bar Association Bankruptcy Newsletter, 1988-1995. *Member:* Indianapolis (Member, Creditors' Rights Section), Allen County (Member, Bankruptcy Section), Indiana State (Member, Bankruptcy and Creditors' Rights Section, Delegate, 1999-2003), Seventh Circuit and American (Member, Business Law and General Practice; Bankruptcy Committee Vice-Chairman; Newsletter Editor, 1996-2001) Bar Associations; American Bankruptcy Institute; National Association of Chapter 13 Trustees (Associate Member); Indiana Bankers Association; American Agricultural Law Association; Northeast Indiana Credit Union Association; Risk Management Association (Associate Member). [Capt., JAGC, U.S. Army, 1984-1988]. ***PRACTICE AREAS:*** Bankruptcy Law; Commercial Litigation; Commercial Transactions; Creditors' Rights; Banking Law; Real Estate; Secured Transactions. ***Email:*** ekos@ekoslaw.com

(This Listing Continued)

ASSOCIATE

STEVEN J. BRADFORD, born Tachikawa AFB, Japan; admitted to bar, 2001, Indiana, U.S. District Court, Northern and Southern Districts of Indiana. *Education:* Minot State University (B.A., cum laude, 1997); Valparaiso University School of Law (J.D., cum laude, 2001). Law Clerk, Allen Superior Court, Allen County, Indiana. *Member:* Allen County (Law Library Committee; Bankruptcy and Creditors' Rights Section), Indiana State and American Bar Associations; Benjamin Harrison American Inn of Court (Associate). ***PRACTICE AREAS:*** Bankruptcy; Creditors Rights; Corporate Law; Real Estate; Collections; Commercial Litigation; Secured Transactions. ***Email:*** sbradford@ekoslaw.com

REPRESENTATIVE CLIENTS: Bank One; Novartis, Inc.; Syngenta, Inc.; First Federal Bank of the Midwest; Farmers State Bank; Marquette National Bank; Pyrotek, Inc.; Edd's Supplies, Inc.; Tower Bank; Community First Bank; Salin Bank and Trust Company; Three Rivers Federal Credit Union; Financial Partners Federal Credit Union; Brooks Construction Co., Inc.; Bippus State Bank; First Bank of Berne; Grabill Bank; Icon Exhibits; Berne Apparel; Tricom Inc. of Milwaukee; Star Financial Bank; Terex, Inc.; Edon State Bank; Fifth Third Bank; SBC Capital Services, Inc.; Mill Supply, Inc.; Central Supply, Inc.; Farmers and Merchants Bank; Zions First National Bank.

KRIEG DeVAULT LUNDY LLP

Established in 1870

825 ANTHONY WAYNE BUILDING
203 EAST BERRY STREET
FORT WAYNE, INDIANA 46802
Telephone: 260-422-1534
Fax: 260-423-1590
Email: contact@kdlegal.com
URL: http://www.kriegdevault.com

Indianapolis, Indiana Office: Krieg DeVault LLP, One Indiana Square, Suite 2800, 46204. Telephone: 317-636-4341. Fax: 317-636-1507.
Indianapolis Northside Office: 12800 North Meridian Street, Suite 300, Carmel, Indiana 46032. Telephone: 317-566-1110. Fax: 317-636-1507.
Hammond, Indiana Office: Krieg DeVault Galvin LLP, 5231 Hohman Avenue, 46320. Telephone: 219-933-0380. Fax: 219-933-0471.

Acquisitions, Divestitures and Mergers, Antitrust, Appeals, Banking, Bankruptcy, Business and Commercial, Copyright, Corporations, Creditors' Rights, Employee Benefits, Energy, Environmental, ERISA, Estate Planning and Probate, Family/Domestic Relations, Federal and State Taxation, Government Relations, Health Care, Hospital Law, Intellectual Property, Insurance, International, Labor and Employment, Legislative, Litigation, Patent, Public Finance, Public Utilities, Products Liability, Real Estate, Securities Law, Tax-Exempt and Nonprofit Organizations, Technology and E-Commerce, Trademark.

LAW FIRM ALLIANCES/ASSOCIATIONS: ***MERITAS:*** *Members of Meritas, serving the needs of clients in more than 145 markets worldwide.*

PARTNER

DAVID A. LUNDY, born Boston, Massachusetts, December 26, 1934; admitted to bar, 1963, Indiana and U.S. District Court, Southern and Northern Districts of Indiana; 1982, U.S. Court of Appeals, Seventh and Tenth Circuits; 1984, U.S. Court of Appeals, Federal Circuit; 1990, U.S. Court of Appeals, Sixth Circuit; 1994, U.S. Supreme Court; registered to practice before U.S. Patent and Trademark Office, 1964. *Education:* University of Michigan (B.S., 1957; M.S., 1958); University of Michigan Law School (J.D., 1963). *Member:* Allen County and Indiana State Bar Associations. ***PRACTICE AREAS:*** Intellectual Property; Patents; Trademarks; Copyright; Unfair Competition; Trade Secrets; Franchise; Licensing; Business Law; Entertainment Law; Technology and E-Commerce; Computer Law; Litigation. ***Email:*** dlundy@kdlegal.com

JOHN R. LEAL

METRO BUILDING, SUITE 710
202 WEST BERRY STREET
FORT WAYNE, INDIANA 46802
Telephone: 260-424-3104
Fax: 260-426-3360

Probate and Estate Planning, Estate Administration, Trusts, Wills, Elder Law, Real Estate, Guardianships, Corporate Law, Immigration Law.

JOHN R. LEAL, born East Chicago, Indiana, June 19, 1929; admitted to bar, 1961, Indiana. *Education:* Valparaiso University (A.B., 1956; J.D., 1961); Northwestern University (A.M., 1958). Delta Theta Phi. Law Clerk to Chief Justice Harold E. Achor, Indiana Supreme Court, 1961-1962. President, Fort Wayne Estate Planning Council, 1969-1970. Governor, District 654, Rotary International, 1988-1989. *Member:* Allen County (Member, Board of Directors, 1976-1978), Indiana State and American Bar Associations. Fellow, Indiana Bar Foundation. ***LANGUAGES:*** Spanish. ***PRACTICE AREAS:*** Estate Planning; Administrative Law; Probate; Trust Law; Wills; Real Estate; Guardianship; Corporate Law; Immigration Law.

REFERENCES: Bankone, NA; National City Bank; Wells Fargo Bank; Tower Bank.

THOMAS S. LOCKE

Established in 1971

520 SOUTH CALHOUN STREET
FORT WAYNE, INDIANA 46802-1290
Telephone: 260-424-1333
Fax: 260-422-5242
Email: tslockeesq@aol.com

Civil Trial Practice in all State Courts. Personal Injury including Wrongful Death, Probate, Estate Planning and Administration, Elder Law, Business, Real Estate Law, Adoption.

FIRM PROFILE: Thomas S. Locke began serving the legal needs of the Fort Wayne community in 1971. In the ensuing 25 years, the practice has evolved to a preeminent level of expertise in many areas of law with a concentration on Business Law, Probate and Estate Planning.

THOMAS S. LOCKE, born Fort Wayne, Indiana, August 8, 1945; admitted to bar, 1971, Indiana and U.S. District Courts, Northern and Southern Districts of Indiana. *Education:* University of Notre Dame (B.B.A., 1967); Valparaiso University (J.D., 1971). *Member:* Allen County (Former Board Member; Chairman: Real Property Section, 1983-1984; Probate, Tax and Trust Section, 1990-1992), Indiana State and American Bar Associations.

ASSOCIATE

ZACHARY A. WITTE, born Fort Wayne, Indiana; admitted to bar, 2003, Indiana. *Education:* Indiana University (B.A., 1999); John Marshall Law School (J.D., 2003). *Member:* Allen County, Indiana State and American Bar Associations. **PRACTICE AREAS:** Civil Practice; Personal Injury; Wrongful Death; Business Law; Real Estate; Criminal Law; Family Law; Adoption. **Email:** zwitte14@MSN.com

REPRESENTATIVE CLIENTS: General Credit Union.
REFERENCE: Bank One.

THE McLEMORE FIRM

206 COURTSIDE BUILDING
803 SOUTH CALHOUN STREET
P.O. BOX 15606
FORT WAYNE, INDIANA 46885-5606
Telephone: 260-426-4451
Fax: 260-422-7469
Email: dmclemore@fortwaynelawyer.com

General, Trial and Appellate Practice. Federal and State Courts. Business, Commercial, Corporate, Criminal and Personal Injury Law.

DOYAL E. McLEMORE, JR., born Panama Canal Zone, Panama, March 23, 1952; admitted to bar, 1977, Indiana; 1982, Georgia; U.S. District Court, Northern and Southern Districts of Indiana; U.S. Court of Appeals, Fifth, Seventh and Eleventh Circuits; U.S. Supreme Court. *Education:* Indiana University (A.B., with high distinction, 1974; J.D., 1977); University of Southern California (M.P.A., Certificate of Merit, 1989). Note Editor, Indiana Law Journal, 1976-1977. Author: " Appellate Delay Reduction: An Organized Approach," 33 The Judges' J. 28 (Spring, 1994); "Punitive Damages and Double Jeopardy: A Critical Perspective of the Taber Rule," 56 Indiana Law Journal 71, 1980. Supervisory Staff Counsel, U.S. Eleventh Circuit Court of Appeals, 1983-1984. Staff Counsel, U.S. Fifth and Eleventh Circuit Courts of Appeals, 1980-1983. *Member:* Allen County Bar Association; State Bar of Georgia. **REPORTED CASES:** United States v. Suggs, 374 F.3d 508 (7th Cir. 2004); Skywalker Communications of Indiana, Inc. v. Skywalker Communications, Inc., 333 F.3d 829 (7th Cir. 2003); United States v. Taylor, 272 F.3d 980 (7th Cir. 2001); United States v. Martin, 147 F.3d 529 (7th Cir. 1998); United States v. Jester, 139 F.3d 1168 (7th Cir. 1998). **PRACTICE AREAS:** Appellate Practice; Business Law; Commercial Law; Corporate Law; Criminal Law; Personal Injury. **Email:** dmclemore@fortwaynelawyer.com

MILLER MURPHY & MILLER, L.L.P.

110 WEST BERRY STREET, SUITE 1500
FORT WAYNE, INDIANA 46802
Telephone: 260-423-1500
Fax: 260-458-8191
Email: info@millermurphymiller.com
URL: http://www.millermurphymiller.com

Appellate Practice, Alternative Dispute Resolution, Administrative Law, Civil Practice, Civil Rights, Commercial Law, Construction Law, Contracts, Corporate Law, Eminent Domain, Energy, General Practice, Government, Health Care, Insurance Defense, Labor and Employment, Leases and Leasing, Environmental Litigation, Employment Law, Civil Rights Litigation, , Medical, Accountant and Attorney Malpractice Defense, Personal Injury, Premises Liability, Utility Law and Workers Compensation.

MILFORD M. MILLER, JR., born Evansville, Indiana; admitted to bar, 1962, Indiana, U.S. District Court, Northern and Southern Districts of Indiana, U.S. Court of Appeals, 7th Circuit and U.S. Supreme Court. *Education:* Dartmouth College (A.B., 1959); Indiana University (J.D., with distinction, 1962). Order of the Coif. Member, Board of Editors, Indiana Law Journal, 1961-1962. *Member:* Allen County, Indiana State and American Bar Associations; Defense Research Institute. Fellow, American College of Trial Lawyers; Indiana Bar Foundation. **PRACTICE AREAS:** Health Law; Business Litigation; Construction Litigation; Employment Law; Mediation. **Email:** mmm@millermurphymiller.com

EDWARD L. MURPHY, JR., born 1943; admitted to bar, 1968, Indiana, U.S. District Court, Northern and Southern Districts of Indiana, U.S. Court of Appeals, 7th Circuit and U.S. Supreme Court. *Education:* Indiana University (B.S., 1965; J.D., 1968). Law Clerk to Justice Norman F. Arterburn, Indiana Supreme Court, 1968-1969. *Member:* Allen County, Seventh Circuit, Indiana State and American Bar Associations; Defense Research Institute, Inc. **PRACTICE AREAS:** Civil Litigation; Insurance Defense; Medical Malpractice Defense; Products Liability. **Email:** elm@millermurphymiller.com

CALVERT S. MILLER, born 1967; admitted to bar, 1994, Indiana and U.S. District Court, Northern and Southern Districts of Indiana. *Education:* Indiana University (B.S., 1990; J.D., 1994). Elected Council Member, Allen County's fiscal body providing annual oversight for the County's $70,000,000 general fund. *Member:* Allen County, Indiana State and American Bar Associations; Defense Trial Counsel of Indiana; Defense Research Institute. **PRACTICE AREAS:** Insurance Defense; Medical Malpractice Defense; Products Liability; Commercial Litigation; Construction Litigation; Business Litigation; Civil Practice; Federal Civil Practice; Contracts; Construction Law; Construction Accidents; Construction Insurance Defense; Leases and Leasing; Wrongful Death; Personal Injury; Premises Liability; Workers Compensation Defense; Automobile Liability Defense. **Email:** csm@millermurphymiller.com

STEPHEN J. HARANTS, born 1969; admitted to bar, 1994, Indiana and U.S. District Court, Northern and Southern Districts of Indiana. *Education:* Franklin College of Indiana (B.A., cum laude, 1991); Indiana University School of Law (J.D., 1994). *Member:* Allen County, Indiana State and American Bar Associations; Defense Trial Counsel of Indiana. **PRACTICE AREAS:** Civil Litigation; Commercial Litigation; Insurance Defense; Products Liability; Construction Litigation. **Email:** sjh@millermurphymiller.com

ASSOCIATES

JASON A. SCHEELE, born 1976; admitted to bar, 2001, Indiana and U.S. District Court, Northern and Southern Districts of Indiana. *Education:* Franklin College of Indiana (B.A., magna cum laude, 1998); Indiana University (J.D., cum laude, 2001). *Member:* Allen County, Indiana State and American Bar Associations. **PRACTICE AREAS:** Insurance Defense; Medical Malpractice Defense; Commercial Litigation; Products Liability. **Email:** jas@millermurphymiller.com

JONATHAN R. HUFFMAN, born Indianapolis, Indiana, 1978; admitted to bar, 2005, Indiana. *Education:* Valparaiso University (B.S., Business Administration, summa cum laude, 2001); University of Miami (M.B.A., 2002); Indiana University (J.D., cum laude, 2005). Student Legal Intern to the Hon. Kennard P. Foster, U.S. Magistrate Judge, Southern District of Indiana, 2004. *Member:* American Bar Association. **LANGUAGES:** Spanish. **PRACTICE AREAS:** Civil Litigation; Insurance Defense; General Liability Defense; Medical Malpractice Defense. **Email:** jrh@millermurphymiller.com

MICHAEL A. BARRANDA, born St. Augustine, Florida, 1978; admitted to bar, 2005, Indiana. *Education:* University of Notre Dame (B.A., with honors, 2001); Loyola University (J.D., 2004). Phi Alpha Delta (Justice, 2003-2004). Participant, 2003 and Student-Coach, 2004, Willem C. Vis International Commercial Arbitration Moot Court. Judicial Law Clerk to the Hon. Stanley A. Levine and the Hon. Daniel G. Heath, Allen Superior Court, 2004-2005. *Member:* Allen County and Indiana State Bar Associations. **PRACTICE AREAS:** Civil Litigation; Insurance Defense; Medical Malpractice. **Email:** mab@millermurphymiller.com

REPRESENTATIVE CLIENTS: AIG; Wausau Insurance; Culligan International; The Medical Protective Company; Kemper Insurance; Zurich Insurance; St. Paul Travelers Insurance; Lear Corporation; American Electric Power; ProAssurance; Pro National Insurance; Bituminous Insurance; Elkhart Clinic; The Doctor's Company; OHIC; Elevator's Mutual Insurance; Harris Kayot, Inc.; Ash Brokerage Company; American Sealants; Shambaugh & Son, Inc.; K and K Insurance; Certified Ad Placements, Inc.; Warner Brothers; Lloyds of London; Kraft Foods Global; Lexington Insurance; Lowe's, Inc.; York Claims Service; Citizens Trust Mortgage; Ash Brokerage Company; Meijer's, Inc.

MORE, MILLER, YATES & TRACEY

116 EAST BERRY STREET
SUITE 610
FORT WAYNE, INDIANA 46802-2786
Telephone: 260-424-2200
Fax: 260-420-0655
Email: mmyt@centralnet.net
URL: http://www.mmytlawfirm.com

General Practice in all State and Federal Courts. Corporation, Business, Bankruptcy, Reorganization, Collection, Family and Matrimonial Law. Trials.

FIRM PROFILE: More, Miller, Yates & Tracey is a small firm located in downtown Fort Wayne which prides itself in personal client service. Our practice includes family and elder law, civil litigation, labor and employment law, business law, collections, bankruptcy, collaborative law, and general practice.

MEMBERS OF FIRM

JAMES M. MORE, born Fort Wayne, Indiana, February 2, 1946; admitted to bar, 1974, Indiana. *Education:* Hillsdale College (B.S., 1968); Indiana University (J.D., 1973). Omicron Delta Kappa. *Member:* Allen County and Indiana State Bar Associations. [With U.S. Army, 1968-1970]. **PRACTICE AREAS:** Matrimonial Law; Collaborative Law; Cooperative Association Law; Civil Litigation; Collections; Wills. **Email:** jmm@centralnet.net

MICHAEL T. YATES, born Indianapolis, Indiana, April 5, 1948; admitted to bar, 1974, Indiana and U.S. District Court, Northern and Southern Districts of Indiana. *Education:* Indiana University (B.A., 1970; J.D., 1973). Instructor of Business Law, International Business College, 1977-1985. Registered Family Law Mediator. *Member:* Allen County, Indiana State and American Bar Associations. **PRACTICE AREAS:** Civil Litigation; Commercial Law; Family Law; Business Law; Family Mediation. **Email:** myates1751@aol.com

J. BRIAN TRACEY, born Angola, Indiana, February 28, 1955; admitted to bar, 1991, Indiana. *Education:* Indiana University (B.S., honors, 1981); Indiana University School of Law (J.D., 1991). *Member:* Allen County and Indiana State Bar Associations. **PRACTICE AREAS:** Labor and Employment; Corporate Law; Creditors Rights; Collections; Civil Litigation; General Practice; White Collar Criminal Defense; Personal Injury. **Email:** jbt@centralnet.net

(This Listing Continued)

MORE, MILLER, YATES & TRACEY, Fort Wayne—Continued

ASSOCIATE

ANGELA N. SNYDER, born Biloxi, Mississippi, October 7, 1972; admitted to bar, 1998, Mississippi; 2005, Indiana. *Education:* University of Tennessee at Knoxville (B.A., 1994; J.D., 1998). *Member:* Allen County and Indiana State Bar Associations. ***PRACTICE AREAS:*** Civil Litigation; Family Law; Bankruptcy; General Practice. ***Email:*** mmyt@centralnet.net

REPRESENTATIVE CLIENTS: Trinity Wholesale Distributors, Inc.; Automotive Color & Supply Co.; Brueggemann Lumber and Builders Supply, Inc.; Bank of Geneva; State Bank & Trust; Decatur Bank & Trust.

MOSS & HARRIS, LLP

Established in 1926

110 WEST BERRY STREET, SUITE 1800
P.O. BOX 10839
FORT WAYNE, INDIANA 46854-0839
Telephone: 260-422-1589
Facsimile: 260-422-1594
Email: pmoss@mossharris.com
URL: http://www.mossharris.com

General Civil Practice in all State and Federal Courts. Personal Injury, Estate Planning, Family, Real Estate and Probate Law, Corporation, Litigation, Collection and Insurance Subrogation Law, Bankruptcy. Trial and Appellate Practice, Social Security Disability.

MEMBERS OF FIRM

LINDY G. MOSS, born Hobart, Indiana, July 21, 1926; admitted to bar, 1955, Indiana. *Education:* Indiana University (B.S., 1949; A.B., 1950; LL.B., 1952). Phi Delta Phi. Special Agent, Federal Bureau of Investigation, 1952-1956. President, Indiana University School of Law Alumni Association, 1967-1969. *Member:* Allen County (President, 1970-1971), Indiana State (Member, Sections on: Corporation, Probate and Taxation) Bar Associations. Fellow, American College of Trust and Estate Counsel. ***PRACTICE AREAS:*** Tax and Estate Planning; Trusts and Estates; Elder Law; Business Law; Corporate Law. ***Email:*** lmoss@mossharris.com

WILLIAM E. HARRIS, born Sturgis, Michigan, April 4, 1938; admitted to bar, 1963, Indiana. *Education:* DePauw University (B.A., 1960); University of Michigan (J.D., 1963). Phi Beta Kappa; Phi Delta Phi. Deputy Prosecuting Attorney, 1965-1966. *Member:* Allen County and Indiana State (Member, Section of Probate, Trust and Real Property Law) Bar Associations; National Organization of Social Security Claimants Representatives. ***PRACTICE AREAS:*** Real Estate; Business Law; Trusts and Estates; Collection; Social Security Disability; Civil Mediation. ***Email:*** bharris@mossharris.com

KIRBY G. MOSS, born Elizabeth City, North Carolina, July 8, 1954; admitted to bar, 1979, Indiana and U.S. District Court, Northern and Southern Districts of Indiana; 1982, U.S. Supreme Court. *Education:* Indiana University (B.S., 1976; J.D., 1979). Phi Delta Phi. Deputy Prosecuting Attorney, Allen County, 1981-1982. *Member:* Allen County and Indiana State Bar Associations; The Indiana Trial Lawyers Association; The Association of Trial Lawyers of America; National Association of Consumer Bankruptcy Attorneys. ***REPORTED CASES:*** Curler vs City of Fort Wayne, DC Ind 1985 591F Supp 327; DeLesstine vs Fort Wayne State Hospital and Developmental Center, 1982 CA Ind 682F2d 130 cert den; Ackerman vs DeLesstine 103 SCt 378, 459 US1017, 74 LEd2d 511. ***PRACTICE AREAS:*** Personal Injury; Bankruptcy; Business Litigation; Family Law. ***Email:*** kmoss@mossharris.com

PARKER L. MOSS, born Fort Wayne, Indiana, May 6, 1959; admitted to bar, 1984, Indiana and U.S. District Court, Northern District of Indiana. *Education:* Indiana University (A.B., 1981; J.D., 1984). Counsel for Allen County Police Merit Board. Charter Member, National Association of Subrogation Professionals. *Member:* Allen County (Chairman: Young Lawyers Section, 1986; Lawyer Referral Services, 1988-1989) and Indiana State Bar Associations; Indiana Trial Lawyers Association; National Association of Subrogation Professionals; National Association of Retail Collection Attorneys; Commercial Law League. ***PRACTICE AREAS:*** Insurance Subrogation; Collections; Personal Injury; Commercial Law. ***Email:*** pmoss@mossharris.com

NIETER & GOEGLEIN

Established in 1982

SUITE 420 METRO BUILDING
202 WEST BERRY
FORT WAYNE, INDIANA 46802
Telephone: 260-426-2244
Fax: 260-424-1774
Email: ng@nietergoeglein.com
URL: http://www.lawyers.com/nieter&goeglein

Estate Planning, Estate Administration, Probate, Business Law, Credit Union, Real Estate, Civil Practice, Adoption.

ANDREW M. GOEGLEIN, born Fort Wayne, Indiana, April 22, 1956; admitted to bar, 1982, Indiana and U.S. District Court, Northern District of Indiana. *Education:* Indiana University (B.S., with highest distinction, 1978; J.D., magna cum laude, 1982). *Member:* Allen County and Indiana State Bar Associations. ***PRACTICE AREAS:*** Business Law; Credit Union; Real Estate Law; Civil Practice; Adoption. ***Email:*** agoeglein@nietergoeglein.com

DANIEL P. NIETER, born Fort Wayne, Indiana, November 1, 1957; admitted to bar, 1983, Indiana and U.S. District Court, Northern District of Indiana. *Education:* Valparaiso University (B.S., with distinction, 1980; J.D., 1983). Member, Mortar Board. *Member:* Allen County and Indiana State Bar Associations. ***PRACTICE AREAS:*** Estate Planning; Estate Administration; Business Law; Probate; Wills; Trusts. ***Email:*** dann@nietergoeglein.com

REPRESENTATIVE CLIENTS: Lutheran Homes, Inc.; MacDonald Machinery Co., Inc.; Three Rivers Federal Credit Union.
REFERENCE: National City Bank.

PERRY LAW OFFICE P.C.

Established in 2001

1010 MEMORIAL WAY, SUITE 102
FORT WAYNE, INDIANA 46805
Telephone: 260-483-3110
Fax: 260-483-3220
Email: info@perryoffice.net
URL: http://www.perryoffice.net

Collections, Social Security Disability, Creditors Rights.

FIRM PROFILE: Perry Law Office, P.C. was established in 2001. The firm has two main areas of practice: Collections and Social Security Disability.

R. SCOTT PERRY, JR., born Fort Wayne, Indiana, March 13, 1954; admitted to bar, 1980, Indiana and U.S. District Court, Northern and Southern Districts of Indiana; U.S. Court of Appeals, Seventh Circuit; U.S. Claims Court. *Education:* Purdue University (B.A., 1976); Indiana University (J.D., 1980). *Member:* Allen County, Steuben County and Indiana State Bar Associations; National Association of Retail Collection Attorneys (NARCA); Commercial Law League of America (CLLA); American Collectors Association (Member, Member Attorney Program - MAP). ***PRACTICE AREAS:*** Retail Collections; Commercial Collections; Creditors Rights Law; Social Security Disability. ***Email:*** scott@perryoffice.net

THOMAS J. KNIGHT, born Marion, Indiana, October 2, 1954; admitted to bar, 1980, Indiana; U.S. District Court, Southern and Northern Districts of Indiana. *Education:* Ball State University (B.S., 1977); Indiana University School of Law (J.D., 1980). Administrative Law Judge, Indiana Department of Workforce Development, Division of Unemployment Compensation Appeals, 1981-2001. *Member:* Allen County Bar Association (Member, Social Security Section); National Organization of Social Security Claimants' Representatives. ***PRACTICE AREAS:*** Social Security Disability; Collections. ***Email:*** tom@perryoffice.net

JOHANNA J. CAMPBELL, born Fort Wayne, Indiana, 1970; admitted to bar, 2004, Indiana; U.S. District Court, Northern and Southern Districts of Indiana. *Education:* Ivy Tech State College (A.S., magna cum laude, 1999); Concordia University (B.A., magna cum laude, 2001); Thomas M. Cooley Law School (J.D., cum laude, 2004). Recipient, Ivy Tech Distinguished Alumni Award, 2005. Adjunct Instructor, Paralegal Program, Ivy Tech State College. *Member:* Allen County and Indiana State Bar Associations. ***PRACTICE AREAS:*** Social Security Disability; Social Security Disability Insurance; Supplemental Security Income; Collections; Commercial Collections; Garnishments; Post Judgment Collections; Professional Collections; Retail Collections; Secured Collections; Unsecured Collections; Commercial Litigation; Commercial Law; Creditors Rights; Creditors Rights in Bankruptcy. ***Email:*** johanna@perryoffice.net

REPRESENTATIVE CLIENTS: Star Financial Bank, N.A.; Centennial Wireless; Ameritech SBC; Salin Bank & Trust Co.; Xerox Corp.; Glenbrook Dodge Hyundai; Evans Motors, Inc.; Professional Federal Credit Union; Komet Hockey Club; Midwest American Federal Credit Union; HILCO Receivables, LLC; Waterfield Insurance Agency, Inc.; Idigital Telecom; The Collection Co.; Pekin Insurance Cos.; Gene B. Glick Management Co.; Fort Wayne Housing Authority; Hoosier Propane; KASTCO Credit Union; Instant Furniture Rental; Sentry Management Co; Central Insurance Company.

PLEWS SHADLEY RACHER & BRAUN

FORT WAYNE, INDIANA

(See Indianapolis)

Environmental Litigation, Environmental Insurance Coverage, Environmental Cost Recovery, Complex Commercial Litigation, Environmental Corporate and Transaction Law, Environmental Administrative Law, Environmental Permitting, Superfund, Solid and Hazardous Waste, Underground Storage Tanks, Clean Air Act, Clean Water Act, Environmental Business Law, Intellectual Property, Commercial Real Estate and Land Use, Surface Coal Mining and Reclamation Act.

ROBY HOOD & MANGES

Established in 1983

200 EAST MAIN STREET, SUITE 520
FORT WAYNE, INDIANA 46802
Telephone: 260-423-3366
Fax: 260-423-3367

Personal Injury, Products Liability, Medical Malpractice, Nursing Home Liability and Trial and Appellate Practice.

FIRM PROFILE: Roby Hood & Manges Law Firm was founded in 1983 by Daniel A. Roby and G. Stanley Hood, each of whom was admitted to practice in 1966. The firm limits its practice solely to plaintiffs' personal injury litigation and appellate practice.

MEMBERS OF FIRM

DANIEL A. ROBY, born Anderson, Indiana, August 16, 1941; admitted to bar, 1966, Indiana, U.S. District Court, Northern and Southern Districts of Indiana, U.S. Court of Appeals, Seventh Circuit and U.S. Supreme Court. *Education:* Indiana University (B.A., with honors, 1963; J.D., 1966). Certified Civil Mediator. Listed in: Who's Who in American Law; Martindale-Hubbell Bar Register of Preeminent Lawyers; The Best Lawyers in

(This Listing Continued)

America. Lecturer at numerous Indiana Continuing Legal Education Programs and Indiana Trial Lawyers Association. Member: Allen County Judicial Nominating Commission, 1983-1991; Indiana Judicial Nominating and Qualifications Commission, 1997-2000. Indiana Trial Lawyer of the Year, 1986. Faculty Member, Indiana Continuing Legal Education Forum, 1981, 1983-1986, 1988. *Member:* Allen County (Member, Board of Directors, 1983-1985) and Indiana State Bar Associations; The Association of Trial Lawyers of America; Indiana Trial Lawyers Association (Executive Committee, Board of Directors, 1980—; President, 1993; Recipient, Lifetime Achievement Award, 2004). ***PRACTICE AREAS:*** Personal Injury Law; Products Liability Law; Professional Malpractice. ***Email:*** droby@robyhood.com

G. STANLEY HOOD, born Fort Wayne, Indiana, April 23, 1938; admitted to bar, 1966, Indiana and U.S. District Court, Northern District of Indiana; U.S. Supreme Court. *Education:* Indiana University (B.S., 1960; J.D., 1966). Phi Delta Phi. Certified Civil Mediator. Lecturer and Author: "Maximizing Wrongful Death Damages for the Elderly Decedent With No Dependents," ITLA Lifetime Achievement Award Seminar, 1989; "How to Apportion Policy Limits Among Several Plaintiffs," ITLA Lifetime Achievement Award Seminar, 1990; "Would You Rather Talk About the Chicago Cubs, IU Basketball or Have a Good Pre-Trial Conference," ITLA Lifetime Achievement Award Seminar, 1991; " 'When Policy Limits' Might Not Be Policy Limits," ITLA Lifetime Achievement Award Seminar, 1992; "The First Client Interview and Beyond," ITLA Lifetime Achievement Award Seminar, 1993. Founder and Moderator, Peoples Law School of Northeastern Indiana, 1988-1998. Public Defender, Allen County, 1968-1969. Associate City Attorney, Fort Wayne, Indiana, 1969-1970. Deputy Prosecuting Attorney, Allen County, Indiana, 1970-1972. *Member:* Allen County, Indiana State and American Bar Associations; Indiana Trial Lawyers Association (Member, Board of Directors, 1982—); The Association of Trial Lawyers of America. ***PRACTICE AREAS:*** Personal Injury Law; Products Liability Law. ***Email:*** shood@robyhood.com

THOMAS A. MANGES, born Fort Wayne, Indiana, October 7, 1966; admitted to bar, 1992, Indiana and U.S. District Court, Northern District of Indiana. *Education:* Hanover College (B.A., 1989); Indiana University (J.D., 1992). Lecturer and Author: "Is It 'Medical Malpractice' or 'Negligence'?", Verdict Magazine, 2005; "Admissibility of Amendments to Depositions," Verdict Magazine, 2003; "Controlling Medical Litigation Costs," ITLA Institute, 2000; "Recent Changes to Indiana's Wrongful Death Law," ACBA Seminar, 1999; "Proactive Discovery to Avoid Surprises at Trial," ICLEF Seminar, 1999; "Recent Developments in Auto Insurance Law and Practice," PESI Seminar, 1998; "Discoverability of Medical and Mental Health Records," ICLEF Seminar, 1997; ITLA Lifetime Achievement Seminars: "Dealing with Unfair Arbitration Clauses in UM/UIM Policies," 1997; "What Are Necessary Medical Expenses," 1997; "Mediation Motions: Getting the Horses to Water," 1996. Lecturer, People's Law School of Northeast Indiana, 1996. *Member:* Allen County, Indiana State and American Bar Associations; Indiana Trial Lawyers Association (Member, Board of Directors, 2004); The Association of Trial Lawyers of America. ***PRACTICE AREAS:*** Personal Injury Law; Professional Malpractice; Medical Malpractice; Products Liability Law; Nursing Home Abuse and Neglect. ***Email:*** tmanges@robyhood.com

REFERENCES: Wells Fargo Bank; Bank One.

ROEBUCK & ASSOCIATES, P.C.

Established in 1999
127 WEST BERRY, SUITE 700
FORT WAYNE, INDIANA 46802
Telephone: 260-426-4444
Fax: 260-424-6006
Email: rroeb@earthlink.net
URL: http://www.roebuckassociates.com

Personal Injury, Automobile Accidents, Boat Accidents, Motorcycle Accidents, Truck Accidents, Slip and Fall, Dog Bites, Medical Malpractice, Head Injuries, Nursing Home Abuse and Neglect, Products Liability, Insurance, Social Security, Social Security Disability, and Wrongful Death.

FIRM PROFILE: At Roebuck & Associates, personal injury law in Indiana is our business. We have been helping victims throughout the state and are proud of our achievements on behalf of our clients, which include Personal Injury, Automobile Collisions, Truck Collisions, Motorcycle Collisions, Boat Collisions, Dog Bites, Slip and Falls, Nursing Home Negligence, Medical Malpractice, Social Security Claims, Head Injuries, Wrongful Death, Products Liability, General Negligence.

We are aggressive in our pursuit of personal injury claims and maintain open communication with our clients (24 hours a day, 7 days a week). Roebuck & Associates' ultimate goal is to provide the very best legal representation to our clients. We are committed to serving our clients best interests. We take pride in the fact that our firm does not represent insurance companies, hospitals, or other corporations. We have limited our law practice to the representation of injured people. Contact our office in Fort Wayne, and schedule a free consultation with a member of our highly trained staff.

RANDOLPH L. ROEBUCK, born New York, N.Y., October 26, 1951; admitted to bar, 1988, Illinois; 1989, Indiana and U.S. District Court, Northern District of Illinois; 1991, U.S. District Court, Northern and Southern Districts of Indiana and U.S. Court of Appeals, Seventh Circuit. *Education:* Purdue University (B.S., 1976); Notre Dame College-London, England; University of Dayton (J.D., 1988). *Member:* Illinois State, Indiana State and American Bar Associations; Indiana Trial Lawyers Association; The Association of Trial Lawyers of America; Allen County Bar Association. ***PRACTICE AREAS:*** Personal Injury; Automobile Accidents; Slip and Fall; Dog Bites; Medical Malpractice; Social Security; Health Insurance; Nursing Home Abuse and Neglect; Insurance; Social Security Disability; Wrongful Death. ***Email:*** rroeb@earthlink.net

LEGAL SUPPORT PERSONNEL

CRYSTAL D. PULLEY

ROTHBERG LOGAN & WARSCO LLP

Established in 1952
2100 NATIONAL CITY CENTER
110 WEST BERRY STREET
P.O. BOX 11647
FORT WAYNE, INDIANA 46859-1647
Telephone: 260-422-9454
Telefax: 260-422-1622
Email: law@rlwlawfirm.com
URL: http://www.rlwlawfirm.com

Warsaw, Indiana Office: 212 North Buffalo Street, 46580. Telephone: 574-267-8802. Telefax: 574-267-0605.

General Civil Litigation in all Courts. Corporate, Banking, Bankruptcy, Commercial, Insurance, Labor and Employment Law, Municipal Law, Municipal Finance, Securities, Real Estate, Construction, Probate and Estate Planning, Transportation, Tax, Creditors' Rights, Agricultural Law, Family/Domestic Relations, Health Care Law.

FIRM PROFILE: Rothberg Logan & Warsco LLP was founded in 1952 by Sol Rothberg, Thomas A. Gallmeyer, and Richard T. Doermer. In 2000, the firm merged with Warsco Brogan and in 2002, the firm opened a Warsaw, Indiana office. The firm has developed a wide-ranging practice serving many of the region's leading banks and businesses as well as its international airport and community transit system.

MEMBERS OF FIRM

SOL ROTHBERG (1910-1993)

THOMAS A. GALLMEYER (1922-1981)

GEORGE E. FRUECHTENICHT (1925-1996)

F. L. DENNIS LOGAN, born Fort Wayne, Indiana, December 21, 1951; admitted to bar, 1977, Indiana. *Education:* DePauw University (B.A., with honors, 1974); Valparaiso University (J.D., 1977). Member, American Association of Airport Executives. *Member:* Allen County, The Indiana State and American Bar Associations. ***PRACTICE AREAS:*** Commercial Financing Law; Corporate Law; Real Estate Law; Public Transportation Law; Probate and Estate Planning. ***Email:*** dlogan@rlwlawfirm.com

MARK A. WARSCO, born St. Joseph, Michigan, August 28, 1955; admitted to bar, 1980, Indiana, U.S. Court of Appeals, Seventh Circuit, U.S. District Court, Northern and Southern Districts of Indiana and U.S. Tax Court. *Education:* Indiana University (B.A., 1977; J.D., cum laude, 1980). Presentation: "Collection Tools," Building Contractors Association, 3-5-98. Contributing Author: "Protection of Secured Interests in Bankruptcy in Indiana," October 23, 1992, Seminar, National Business Institute, Inc.; "Basic Bankruptcy," September 12, 1991, Seminar, National Business Institute, Inc.; "Representing the Business Creditor," April 13, 1993, Seminar, Indiana Continuing Legal Education Forum; "Asset Protection Planning in Indiana," May 3, 1994, Seminar, National Business Institute, Inc. *Member:* Allen County (Chairman, Bankruptcy Section, 1993-1994) and Indiana State (President, Bankruptcy and Creditors' Rights Section, 1993-1994; Member, Building Contractors Association) Bar Associations; National Association of Bankruptcy Trustees; American Bankruptcy Institute. ***PRACTICE AREAS:*** Banking; Creditors Rights; Bankruptcy; Construction Law; Litigation; Real Estate; Probate; Estate Planning. ***Email:*** mwarsco@rlwlawfirm.com

KATHRYN A. BROGAN, born Fort Wayne, Indiana, July 30, 1953; admitted to bar, 1980, Indiana and U.S. District Court, Southern District of Indiana; 1999, U.S. District Court, Northern District of Indiana, U.S. Court of Appeals, Seventh Circuit; 2000, U.S. Supreme Court. *Education:* Indiana University (B.A., with high distinction, 1976; J.D., summa cum laude, 1980). Order of the Coif. Law Clerk for the Honorable James B. Young, Indiana Court of Appeals, 1980-1981. Lecturer, Department of Veterans Affairs Sexual Harassment Training Seminar, 1993; Council on Education in Management Personnel Law Update, Mental and Invisible Disabilities In the Workplace, 1998, 2001, 2002; Council on Education in Management Seminar FMLA Update, 2001-2003. Associate Counsel for K & K Insurance Group, Inc., 1989-1992. President, 2001-2003 and Member, Indiana Board of Law Examinees. *Member:* Allen County (Chairperson, Business and Labor Section, 1996; Labor Law Section; Co-Chairperson, Women Lawyer's Section, 1998-1999) and Indiana State Bar Associations. ***REPORTED CASES:*** Fyfe. City of Fort Wayne, 241 F. 3rd 597 (7th Cir. 2001); Rice v. Sunrise Express, 217 F.3rd. 492 (7th Cir. 2000); Rice v. Sunrise Express, 209 F.3rd 108 (7th Cir. 2000); Block v. Art Iron, Inc., 866 F. Supp. 380 (N.D. Ind. 1994). ***PRACTICE AREAS:*** Employment Law; Labor Law; Insurance; Litigation. ***Email:*** kbrogan@rlwlawfirm.com

MARK W. BAEVERSTAD, born Denver, Colorado, April 16 1956; admitted to bar, 1981, Indiana; U.S. District Court, Northern and Southern Districts of Indiana; U.S. Court of Appeals, Seventh Circuit. *Education:* Hope College (B.A., English, Political Science, 1978); Syracuse University (J.D., magna cum laude, 1981). Order of the Coif. Certified Mediator, Indiana. Author: "Social Choices and Contributory Negligence," Loyola University of Chicago Law Journal, February, 1982. Instructor, Legal Writing, Syracuse University, 1980-1981. *Member:* Allen County and Indiana State Bar Associations; Indiana Defense Lawyers Association; American Board of Trial Advocates (ABOTA). ***PRACTICE AREAS:*** Commercial Litigation; Medical Malpractice Defense; Mediation. ***Email:*** mbaeverstad@rlwlawfirm.com

DAVID R. SMELKO, born Gary, Indiana, August 31, 1956; admitted to bar, 1982, Indiana. *Education:* Indiana University (B.A., 1978); Valparaiso University (J.D., 1982). Associate Editor Valparaiso University Law Review, 1981-1982. *Member:* Allen County, Indiana State and American Bar Associations; National Association of Bond Lawyers; Commercial Law League of America. ***PRACTICE AREAS:*** Municipal Finance Law; Creditors' Rights Law; Consumer and Commercial Financing Law; Corporate Law. ***Email:*** dsmelko@rlwlawfirm.com

DENNIS F. DYKHUIZEN, born Fort Wayne, Indiana, April 26, 1955; admitted to bar, 1980, Indiana; U.S. District Court, Northern and Southern Districts of Indiana; U.S. Tax Court. *Education:* Indiana University (B.S., in Accounting, with distinction, 1977; J.D.,

(This Listing Continued)

ROTHBERG LOGAN & WARSCO LLP, Fort Wayne—Continued

1980). Beta Gamma Sigma. *Member:* Allen County and Indiana State Bar Associations; American Health Lawyers Association; National Association of Bond Lawyers. ***REPORTED CASES:*** National Insurance Association v. Parkview Memorial Hospital, 590 N.E. 2d. 1141 (Ind. Ct. App. 1992); Stephens v. Parkview Hosp., Inc., 745 N.E.2d. 262 (Ind. Ct. App. 2001); Wayne Twp. v. Parkview Mem. Hosp., Inc., 580 N.E. 2d. 958 (Ind. 1991). ***PRACTICE AREAS:*** Health Care Law; Banking Law; Taxation Law; Corporate Law. ***Email:*** ddykhuizen@rlwlawfirm.com

ANNE CARNEY, born Somerville, New Jersey; admitted to bar, 1987, Indiana. *Education:* Indiana University (B.A., 1984); University of Notre Dame (J.D., 1987). Phi Beta Kappa. Phi Alpha Delta. Board Member: Indiana Breast Cancer Awareness Trust; Allen County Volunteer Lawyers Program. *Member:* Allen County, Indiana State and American Bar Associations. ***PRACTICE AREAS:*** Domestic Relations. ***Email:*** acarney@rlwlawfirm.com

MICHAEL T. DEAM, born Bluffton, Indiana, November 11, 1964; admitted to bar, 1989, Indiana. *Education:* Indiana University (B.S., with high distinction, 1987; J.D., 1989). *Member:* Allen County, Indiana State and American Bar Associations; American Association of Airport Executives; Airports Council International. ***PRACTICE AREAS:*** Corporation Law; Commercial Financing Law; Real Estate Law; Transportation Law; Municipal Law. ***Email:*** mdeam@rlwlawfirm.com

J. RICKARD DONOVAN, born Fort Wayne, Indiana, March 27, 1968; admitted to bar, 1993, Indiana and U.S. District Court, Northern and Southern Districts of Indiana. *Education:* Butler University (B.A., 1990); Valparaiso University (J.D., 1993). Delta Theta Phi. *Member:* Allen County and Indiana State Bar Associations. ***PRACTICE AREAS:*** Commercial Banking and Finance; Corporate and Business Law; Real Estate Law; Estate Planning. ***Email:*** rdonovan@rlwlawfirm.com

THEODORE T. STORER, born Richmond, Indiana, August 9, 1968; admitted to bar, 1993, Indiana and U.S. District Court, Northern and Southern Districts of Indiana; U.S. Court of Appeals, Seventh Circuit. *Education:* Indiana University, Bloomington (B.A., 1990); Ohio Northern University (J.D., with distinction, 1993). Ohio Northern University Law Review, 1992-1993. Phi Kappa Phi. *Member:* Allen County (Vice-Chair New Lawyers' Section, 1995-1996; Chair, Trial Lawyers Section, 2001-2002), and Indiana State Bar Associations; Indiana Trial Lawyers Association. ***PRACTICE AREAS:*** Civil Litigation; Construction Litigation; Personal Injury. ***Email:*** tstorer@rlwlawfirm.com

CHRISTINE M. STACH, born Knoxville, Tennessee, May 11, 1970; admitted to bar, 1995, Indiana; U.S. District Court, Northern and Southern Districts of Indiana; U.S. Court of Appeals, Seventh Circuit. *Education:* Ball State University (B.S., 1992); Valparaiso University (J.D., magna cum laude, 1995). *Member:* Allen County (Chair, Appellate Section, 2002-2003), Indiana State and American Bar Associations; Benjamin Harrison Chapter of American Inns of Court (1999-2002). ***REPORTED CASES:*** Tankersley v. Parkview Hosp., Inc., 791 N.E.2d 201 (Ind. 2003); Halls Drive Inns., Inc. v. City of Fort Wayne, 773 N.E.2d 255 (Ind. 2002) and 773 N.E.2d 259 (Ind. 2002); Parkview Hosp., Inc. v. Reese, 750 N.E.2d 384 (Ind. Ct. App. 2001), trans. denied; Stephens v. Parkview Hosp., Inc., 745 N.E.2d 262 (Ind. Ct. App. 2001). ***PRACTICE AREAS:*** Civil Litigation; Civil Appeals. ***Email:*** cstach@rlwlawfirm.com

ASSOCIATES

CINDY ANN WOLFER, born Cincinnati, Ohio, September 14, 1957; admitted to bar, 1991, Indiana and Ohio. *Education:* Wittenberg University (B.A., 1979); University of Cincinnati (J.D., 1991). Order of the Coif. University of Cincinnati Law Review, 1989-1990. Certified Public Accountant, Ohio, 1981. Author: "The Uniform Trust Code," Res Gestae, January, 2001. Co-author, "Guidelines on Actuary Tables in Proposed Regs.," Estate Planning, 1994. *Member:* Allen County, Indiana State (Tax, Probate Sections) and American (Tax, Real Property, Probate and Trust Law Sections) Bar Associations. ***PRACTICE AREAS:*** Estate Planning; Estate Administration; Real Property; Guardianship; Business Law; Taxation. ***Email:*** cwolfer@rlwlawfirm.com

SUSAN E. TRENT, born New Britain, Connecticut; admitted to bar, 1998, Indiana and U.S. District Court, Northern and Southern Districts of Indiana. *Education:* Indiana University (B.A., summa cum laude, 1994); University of North Carolina (J.D., 1998). Phi Beta Kappa. *Member:* Allen County and Indiana State Bar Associations. ***PRACTICE AREAS:*** Commercial Financing Law; Corporate Law. ***Email:*** strent@rlwlawfirm.com

PEGGY A. CARLILE, born Athens, Georgia, 1974; admitted to bar, 2000, Indiana and U.S. District Court, Northern and Southern Districts of Indiana. *Education:* University of Missouri at Columbia (B.A., 1997); Valparaiso University School of Law (J.D., 2000). ***Email:*** pcarlile@rlwlawfirm.com

THOMAS B. TRENT, born Fort Wayne, Indiana, July 24, 1976; admitted to bar, 2001, Indiana. *Education:* Indiana University (B.S., 1998); Tulane University (J.D., 2001). ***PRACTICE AREAS:*** Commercial Law; Financial Law; Real Estate Law. ***Email:*** ttrent@rlwlawfirm.com

OF COUNSEL

THOMAS D. LOGAN, born Fort Wayne, Indiana, April 6, 1929; admitted to bar, 1953, Indiana. *Education:* University of Notre Dame (B.S., cum laude, 1951); Indiana University (LL.B., with distinction, 1953). Phi Delta Phi; Order of the Coif. *Member:* Allen County (President, 1979-1980), The Indiana State (Member, Board of Managers, 1979-1983) and American Bar Associations; American Health Lawyers Association; Airports Council International; National Association of Bond Lawyers. ***PRACTICE AREAS:*** Banking Law; Corporation Law; Health Care Law; Municipal Law. ***Email:*** tlogan@rlwlawfirm.com

JOHN H. HEINEY, born Huntington, Indiana, January 15, 1934; admitted to bar, 1958, Indiana. *Education:* Indiana University (A.B., 1955; J.D., 1958). Phi Delta Phi. *Member:* Allen County, The Indiana State and American Bar Associations. ***PRACTICE AREAS:*** Litigation; Insurance Law; Corporate Law. ***Email:*** jheiney@rlwlawfirm.com

APPROVED ATTORNEYS FOR: Ameriquest Mortgage Company; Aon Corporation; Avis Industrial Corp.; Bank One, N.A.; Busak + Shamban, Inc.; Cameron Memorial Community Hospital; Construction Management Engineering, Inc.; City of Fort Wayne; Dell Computer Corp.; Farm Credit Services of Mid-America, ASA; Fifth Third Bank; Fort Wayne-Allen County Airport Authority; Fort Wayne Public Transportation Corporation, d/b/a Citilink; ; K & K Insurance Group, Inc.; Lake City Bank; National City Bank of Indiana; Parkview Health System; R.E. Crosby & Sons, Inc.; Slater Fort Wayne Federal Credit Union; Tower Bank; Weigand Construction Co., Inc.; Wells Fargo Bank Indiana, N.A.; Wells Fargo Home Mortgage Company; Wolf Corporation.

(For complete biographical data on all personnel, see Professional Biographies at Warsaw, Indiana)

PERRY D. SHILTS

10311 DAWSON'S CREEK BOULEVARD, SUITE C
FORT WAYNE, INDIANA 46825
Telephone: 206-489-0700
Fax: 260-497-8954
Email: perry@shiltslaw.com

Domestic Relations, Divorce, Family Law, Personal Injury and Commercial Litigation.

PERRY D. SHILTS, born Perth, Australia, March 8, 1953; admitted to bar, 1978, Indiana. *Education:* Indiana University (B.A., with honors, 1975; J.D., cum laude, 1978). Editor: "Domestic Help," Allen County Family Law Newsletter; "Family Matters," State Family Law Newsletter. Certified Family Law Specialist, 2003—. *Member:* Allen County (Member, 1992-1999 and Chairman, 1998-1999, Executive Committee, Family Law Section) and Indiana State (Representative for Indiana's Third District, northern one-third of Indiana, Family Law Section, 1996-1999) Bar Associations; Indiana Trial Lawyers Association. ***PRACTICE AREAS:*** Divorce; Family Law; Domestic Relations; Personal Injury; Commercial Litigation.

SHIPLEY & ASSOCIATES

Established in 1992

233 WEST BAKER STREET
FORT WAYNE, INDIANA 46802-3413
Telephone: 260-422-2700
Fax: 260-424-2960
URL: http://www.gshipley.com
URL: http://www.lawyers.com/shipleylaw

Bankruptcy other than consumer bankruptcy, Commercial Law, Commercial Litigation.

GRANT F. SHIPLEY, born Indianapolis, Indiana, August 22, 1945; admitted to bar, 1975, Indiana and U.S. District Court, Northern and Southern Districts of Indiana; 1976, U.S. Court of Appeals, Seventh Circuit; 1979, U.S. Supreme Court. *Education:* Brown University (A.B., 1968); Indiana University School of Law (J.D., magna cum laude, 1975). Order of the Coif. Managing Editor, Indiana Law Journal, 1974-1975. Law Clerk to Judge Jesse E. Eschbach, Chief Judge, United States District Court for the Northern District of Indiana, 1975-1976. *Member:* Allen County (Member and Chairman, Bankruptcy and Creditors' Rights Section, 1994-1995) and Indiana State (Member and Chairman, Section on Bankruptcy and Creditors' Rights, 1991-1992) Bar Associations; Seventh Circuit Bar Association; American Judicature Society; American Bankruptcy Institute. ***LANGUAGES:*** German. ***TRANSACTIONS:*** Counsel for Creditors' Committee, Mallard Coach Co. Bankruptcy, Debtor's Counsel, Parrot Packing Co. Bankruptcy. ***PRACTICE AREAS:*** Bankruptcy Law; Commercial Litigation. ***Email:*** gfs@gshipley.com

ASSOCIATE

DAWN M. OETTING, born Decatur, Indiana, August 26, 1960; admitted to bar, 2004, Indiana and U.S. District Court, Northern and Southern Districts of Indiana. *Education:* Indiana University (B.G.S., highest distinction, 2001); Valparaiso University (J.D., magna cum laude, 2004). *Member:* Allen County, Indiana State and American Bar Associations; American Bankruptcy Institute. ***PRACTICE AREAS:*** Bankruptcy; Creditors Rights. ***Email:*** dmo@gshipley.com

LEGAL SUPPORT PERSONNEL

VICKI M. BOWERS, (Paralegal)

REPRESENTATIVE CLIENTS: Bank One, Indiana, N.A.; Tower Bank & Trust Co.; Fleet Capital Corp.; Comerica Bank; Creditors Committee, Fibrex, Inc. Bankruptcy; Fort Financial Federal Credit Union; Petroleum Traders Corp.; C & M Fine Pack, Inc.; Neff Engineering, Inc.; Shelby County Bank; Grant County State Bank.

SKEKLOFF, ADELSPERGER & KLEVEN, LLP

Established in 2001

927 SOUTH HARRISON STREET
FORT WAYNE, INDIANA 46802
Telephone: 260-407-7000
Fax: 260-407-7137
URL: http://www.sak-law.com
Email: firm@adelspergerkleven.com
URL: http://www.lawyers.com/adelspergerkleven

Bankruptcy, Creditors' Rights, Insolvency, and related Commercial Litigation and Transactions.

FIRM PROFILE: Skekloff, Adelsperger & Kleven, LLP was formed to provide quality legal services in the commercial and insolvency areas. As such, its professionals are highly trained and well qualified in the areas of bankruptcy, creditors' rights, commercial and secured transactions, commercial litigation and insolvency law. The services of Skekloff,, Adelsperger & Kleven, LLP are available to both debtors and creditors, including businesses, corporations, individuals, entrepreneurs, farmers, and bankruptcy trustees. The firm strives to provide excellent, cost-effective legal services to its clients. The attorneys, each of whom limit their re-

(This Listing Continued)

spective practices and continued training to the above-listed areas, are supported by well-trained paralegals and state-of-the-art technology. The attorneys of Skekloff, Adelsperger & Kleven, LLP are especially proud of their fine reputation as commercial and insolvency practitioners, not only in Northeast Indiana, but also around the State.

DANIEL J. SKEKLOFF, born Fort Wayne, Indiana, November 28, 1953; admitted to bar, 1979, Indiana, U.S. District Court, Northern and Southern Districts of Indiana and U.S. Court of Appeals, Seventh Circuit. *Education:* Indiana University (B.A., with distinction, 1976; J.D., 1979). Member, American Bankruptcy Institute, 1997-1998. *Member:* Allen County (Member, Bankruptcy and Creditors' Rights Section, Section Chairman, 1997-1998), Indiana State and American Bar Associations. ***PRACTICE AREAS:*** Bankruptcy; Business Reorganization; Debtor and Creditor Rights; Commercial Real Estate. **Email:** djs@sak-law.com

DOUGLAS R. ADELSPERGER, born Richmond, Indiana, November 26, 1962; admitted to bar, 1988, Indiana and U.S. District Court, Northern and Southern Districts of Indiana; 1989, U.S. Court of Appeals, Seventh Circuit; 1992, U.S. Supreme Court. *Education:* University of Indianapolis; Indiana University (B.S., in Finance, 1985); Indiana University School of Law (J.D., 1988). Delta Theta Phi. Judicial Law Clerk to the Honorable Robert E. Grant, Judge, U.S. Bankruptcy Court, Northern District of Indiana, Fort Wayne Division, 1988-1990. Past Instructor, Indiana Institute of Technology in Business Law. Mediator, U.S. Bankruptcy Court, Northern District of Indiana, Fort Wayne Division, and Indiana State Courts. *Member:* Allen County (Past President, Director and Member, Bankruptcy Section), Indiana State (Member, Bankruptcy and Creditors' Rights Section) and American Bar Associations; American Bankruptcy Institute; Commercial Law League of America. (Certified in Business Bankruptcy Law by the American Board of Certification). ***REPORTED CASES:*** Matter of Smith, 966 F2d 1527 (7th cir. 1992). ***PRACTICE AREAS:*** Commercial Law; Litigation; Insolvency Law; Bankruptcy Law; Debtor and Creditor Rights; Mediation. **Email:** dra@sak-law.com

YVETTE GAFF KLEVEN, born Fort Wayne, Indiana, April 12, 1958; admitted to bar, 1983, Indiana and U.S. District Court, Northern and Southern Districts of Indiana; 1985, Illinois. *Education:* University of Michigan (B.A., in Political Science, 1980); Indiana University (J.D., 1983). Past Instructor, Business Law: University of Saint Francis; International Business College; Ivy Tech State College. *Member:* Allen County (Past President, Director and Member, Bankruptcy Section) and Indiana State (Member, Sections on: Bankruptcy; Creditor's Rights) Bar Associations. ***PRACTICE AREAS:*** Bankruptcy; Debtor and Creditor Rights. **Email:** ygk@sak-law.com

SCOT T. SKEKLOFF, born Hicksville, Ohio, June 23, 1966; admitted to bar, 1991, Indiana. *Education:* Indiana University (B.A., with highest distinction, 1988; J.D., cum laude, 1991). Phi Beta Kappa. *Member:* Allen County (Member: Bankruptcy Section; Liaison Committee) and Indiana State (Member, Bankruptcy and Creditors' Rights Section) Bar Associations; Commercial Law League of America; American Bankruptcy Institute. ***REPORTED CASES:*** Matter of Penrod; Matter of Willows of Coventry, Ltd. Partnership 154 B.R. 959. ***PRACTICE AREAS:*** Corporate Reorganization; Workouts; Debtor and Creditor Bankruptcy. **Email:** sts@sak-law.com

ASSOCIATE

CATHY T. SERRANO, born Bardstown, Kentucky, June 16, 1956; admitted to bar, 2003, Indiana. *Education:* Indiana University (B.A., 1991); Thomas M. Cooley Law School (J.D., 2002). *Member:* Allen County and Indiana State Bar Associations. ***PRACTICE AREAS:*** Bankruptcy; Consumer Law; Litigation. **Email:** cts@sak-law.com

SNYDER BIRCH CORNWELL & MORGAN LLP

904 SOUTH CALHOUN STREET
FORT WAYNE, INDIANA 46802
Telephone: 260-407-0915
Fax: 260-407-7005
URL: http://www.sbcmlaw.com

Syracuse, Indiana Office: 200 West Main Street, 46567. Telephone: 574-457-5727. Fax: 574-457-2056.

Business Litigation, Business Law, Zoning, Planning and Land Use, Real Estate, Civil Litigation, Estate Planning, Trust, Probate, Guardianship, Elder Law, Tax, Banking Law, Employee Benefits, ERISA.

DAVID D. CORNWELL, born 1950; admitted to bar, 1976, Indiana and U.S. District Court, Northern and Southern Districts of Indiana. *Education:* Indiana University (A.B., 1972; M.B.A. in Finance, J.D., 1976). Beta Gamma Sigma. Contributing Author: "Lending Considerations & Documenting Residential Mortgages," ICLEF, 1994; "Real Estate Skills Series," 1994; "Closing Estates," ICLEF; "Planning your First Probate Administration," 1997 and 1998. President, Fort Wayne Estate Planning Council, 2002-2003. Law and Banking Instructor, American Institute of Banking, 1978-1986. Former Vice President, and General Counsel, Summcorp and Summit Bank, Fort Wayne, Indiana, 1983-1992. *Member:* Allen County, Kosciusko County, Indiana State and American Bar Associations. ***PRACTICE AREAS:*** Estate Planning; Trust; Probate; Guardianship; Elder Law; Tax; Business Law; Banking Law; Employee Benefits; ERISA. **Email:** ddc@sbcmlaw.com

(For complete biographical data on other personnel, see Professional Biographies at Syracuse, Indiana)

KIM M. SPIELMAN

P.O. BOX 15175
FORT WAYNE, INDIANA 46885
Telephone: 260-414-6303; Toll Free: 1-800-866-6303
Fax: 260-486-1426
Email: kspielman@comcast.net

Personal Injury, Litigation, Real Estate Law, Commercial Law, Collections, Criminal Law, Felonies.

(This Listing Continued)

KIM M. SPIELMAN, born Fort Wayne, Indiana, January 1, 1953; admitted to bar, 1987, Indiana and U.S. District Court, Northern and Southern Districts of Indiana; 1990 U.S. Court of Appeals, Seventh Circuit. *Education:* Indiana University (B.S., with distinction, 1982; M.P.A., 1984); Ohio Northern University (J.D., with high distinction, 1986). Phi Delta Phi. Associate Professor, Indiana University, 1988—. Associate Editor, Ohio Northern Law Review, 1985-1986. Chief Counsel, Deputy Prosecuting Attorney, Office of the Prosecuting Attorney, 38th Judicial Circuit of Indiana, 1991-1992. Author: "Ohio's Pending Natural Death Act: Where We Are and Where We Are Going," 13 Ohio N.U.L. Rev. 495 (1987). *Member:* Allen County, Indiana State and American Bar Associations. ***PRACTICE AREAS:*** Personal Injury; Litigation; Real Estate Law; Commercial Law.

SWEENEY LAW FIRM

Established in 1984
8109 LIMA ROAD, SUITE B
FORT WAYNE, INDIANA 46818
Telephone: 260-420-3137
Fax: 260-969-0321
Toll Free: 866-793-6339
URL: http://www.sweeneylawfirm.com
Email: dlf@sweeneylawfirm.com
URL: http://www.lawyers.com/sweeneylawfirm

Personal Injury, Wrongful Death, Automobile Accidents, Trucking Accidents, Products Liability, Toxic Torts, Construction Site Injuries, Unfair Insurance Practices, Premises Liability, Nursing Home Negligence, Medical Malpractice.

MEMBERS OF FIRM

CHARLES A. SWEENEY, JR., born South Bend, Indiana, October 7, 1938; admitted to bar, 1964, Indiana and U.S. District Court, Northern District of Indiana; 1976, U,S, Supreme Court. *Education:* University of Dayton (B.S., 1961); University of Notre Dame (J.D., 1964). *Member:* St. Joseph County and Indiana State Bar Associations; Indiana Trial Lawyers Association (Board of Directors, 1994—).

DAVID L. FARNBAUCH, born Fort Wayne, Indiana, October 23, 1960; admitted to bar, 1986, Indiana and U.S. District Court, Northern and Southern Districts of Indiana. *Education:* University of Evansville (B.S., cum laude, 1983); Valparaiso University (J.D., 1986). Member, Valparaiso University Law Review, 1985-1986. Author: Note, "Pre-Impact Pain and Suffering in Aviation Accidents," Vol. 20, Valparaiso University Law Review, 219-53, Winter, 1986. *Member:* Indiana Trial Lawyers Association (Board of Directors, 1999—). (Board Certified Civil Trial Advocacy Specialist by the National Board of Trial Advocacy)

SWIFT & FINLAYSON

Established in 1956
116 E. BERRY STREET
SUITE 590
FORT WAYNE, INDIANA 46802-2486
Telephone: 260-423-4422
Fax: 260-423-4427
Email: mail@swift-finlayson.com

Affiliated Firm: Leeuw Oberlies & Campbell P.C. 320 N. Meridian Street, Suite 1006, Indianapolis, IN 46204. Telephone: 317-684-6960. Fax: 317-684-6961.

Real Estate Law, Corporate, Business Law, Trade Secrets, Business Torts, Zoning Law, Commercial Litigation, Estate Planning, Probate, Banking Law, Mediation, Litigation, Computer Law, International Law, Commercial Transactions.

MEMBERS OF FIRM

WILLIAM D. SWIFT, born Fort Wayne, Indiana, February 28, 1936; admitted to bar, 1964, Indiana and U.S. District Court, Northern District of Indiana; 1973, U.S. Court of Appeals, 7th Circuit; 1976, U.S. Tax Court; 2002, U.S. Supreme Court. *Education:* Indiana University (B.S., 1958; J.D., 1964). Approved Instructor, Indiana Real Estate Commission. ***PRACTICE AREAS:*** Real Estate Law; Business Law; Trade Secrets; Business Torts; Zoning Law; Commercial Litigation.

CRAIG R. FINLAYSON, born Decatur, Indiana, August 12, 1946; admitted to bar, 1973, Indiana. *Education:* Indiana University (B.S., 1968; J.D., magna cum laude, 1973). Assistant County Attorney, 1988—. *Member:* Fort Wayne Estate Planning Council (Member, Board of Directors and President, 1997). ***PRACTICE AREAS:*** Estate Planning; Business; Probate; Mediation; Banking Law.

ASSOCIATES

CHARLES D. BASH, born Fort Wayne, Indiana, May 20, 1949; admitted to bar, 1985, Indiana; U.S. District Court, Northern and Southern Districts of Indiana. *Education:* Michigan State University (B.S., with high honors, 1970); University of Chicago (M.A., 1972; J.D., 1975). Attorney: Dreibelbiss Title Insurance Company, Inc., 1980-1990; Crater Title Insurance Co., 1978-1980; Pioneer National Title Insurance (TICOR), 1975-1978. ***PRACTICE AREAS:*** Real Estate Law; Business and Corporate Law.

E. FRANKLIN HILL, JR., born Bloomington, Indiana, December 23, 1940; admitted to bar, 1966, Indiana; 1972, Michigan; U.S. District Court, Northern District of Indiana. *Education:* Indiana University (B.A., 1963); University of Michigan (J.D., 1966). Instructor, Commercial Law, Indiana Purdue Fort Wayne, 1987-1988. ***PRACTICE AREAS:*** Corporate Law; Real Estate; Litigation; Estate Planning.

CHARLES E. DAVIS, born Rochester, New York; admitted to bar, 1978, Florida; 1998, Indiana and U.S. District Court, Middle District of Florida; U.S. Court of Appeals, 11th Circuit; U.S. District Court, Northern District of Indiana. *Education:* U.S. Military Academy (B.S., 1970); Florida State University (J.D., with honors, 1977). *Member:* Allen

(This Listing Continued)

SWIFT & FINLAYSON, Fort Wayne—Continued

County, Indiana State and American Bar Associations; The Florida Bar; The Association of Trial Lawyers of America. [Capt. U.S. Army]. ***PRACTICE AREAS:*** Litigation; Business Law.

All Personnel are Members of the Allen County, Indiana State and American Bar Associations.

TROTTER LAW OFFICE

6079 STONEY CREEK DRIVE
FORT WAYNE, INDIANA 46825
Telephone: 260-496-8500
Fax: 260-496-8300
Email: TLO8500@aol.com

Family Law, Bankruptcy, Personal Injury, Traffic Violations, Misdemeanors, Child Custody.

MEMBER OF FIRM

STEPHEN D. TROTTER, born Wilmington, Delaware, April 20, 1944; admitted to bar, 1969, Indiana and U.S. District Court, Northern and Southern Districts of Indiana. *Education:* Indiana University (B.A., 1966); Indiana University School of Law - Bloomington (J.D., 1969). *Member:* Allen County, Indiana State and American Bar Associations; The Association of Trial Lawyers of America; Indiana Trial Lawyers. ***PRACTICE AREAS:*** Family Law; Bankruptcy; Personal Injury; Traffic Violations; Misdemeanors; Child Custody. ***Email:*** TLO8500@aol.com

BLACKBURN & GREEN

FOWLER, INDIANA

(See Fort Wayne)

Litigation, Personal Injury Law.

DUMAS, WEIST & MAHNESMITH

Established in 1946
WEIST BUILDING
P.O. BOX 101
FOWLER, INDIANA 47944
Telephone: 765-884-1840
Fax: 765-884-8450

Rensselaer, Indiana Office: 119 West Harrison Street, 47978-2811. Telephone: 219-866-4158. Fax: 219-866-2274.

General Civil and Criminal Trial Practice. Personal Injury, Wills and Probate, Trusts and Estates, Estate Planning, Corporate, Municipal and Zoning Law, Elder Law, Medicaid Planning.

MEMBERS OF FIRM

EDWARD P. DUMAS (Resident, Rensselaer, Indiana Office)

WILLIAM B. WEIST, born Lafayette, Indiana, December 23, 1938; admitted to bar, 1971, Kentucky, Indiana and U.S. District Court, Southern and Northern Districts of Indiana. *Education:* University of Notre Dame (B.B.A., 1961); University of Louisville (J.D., 1970). Deputy Prosecuting Attorney, 1973-1974 and Prosecuting Attorney, 1975-1998, Benton Circuit Court, 76th Judicial Circuit. Member, Board of Directors, Fowler State Bank, 1985—. *Member:* Benton County (President, 1976-1980) and Indiana State (Member, Specialization Committee, 1976-1980) Bar Associations; Indiana Prosecuting Attorneys Association (President, 1979; Chairman, Indiana Prosecuting Attorneys Council, 1989—; Member, Legal Ethics Committee, 1982—); National District Attorneys Association (Director). Fellow, Indiana Bar Foundation. ***PRACTICE AREAS:*** Probate and Estate Planning; Real Estate; Civil Litigation; Banking.

KENT E. MAHNESMITH (Resident, Rensselaer, Indiana Office)

REPRESENTATIVE CLIENTS: DeMotte State Bank; St. Joseph's College; Rensselaer Central Schools Corp.; Kankakee Valley School Corp.; West Central School Corp.; Jasper County Abstract Co.; Rensselaer Auto Parts; Jasper County Hospital; Jasper County Public Library; Jasper County Economic Development Commission; Jasper County Drainage Board; Fowler State Bank; Farmers & Merchant State Bank of Boswell; Commissioners of Benton County.

NED TONNER
ATTORNEY AT LAW

FOWLER, INDIANA

(See Rensselaer)

Personal Injury, Criminal Law, Estates, Trusts, Real Estate, Divorce, Family Law.

BLACKBURN & GREEN

FRANKFORT, INDIANA

(See Fort Wayne)

Litigation, Personal Injury Law.

DEPPE FREDBECK & BOLL

Established in 1957
NINE EAST COURT
FRANKLIN, INDIANA 46131
Telephone: 317-736-5138
Fax: 317-736-8268

Columbus, Indiana Office: 225 Washington Street, 47202. Telephone: 812-378-5137. Fax: 812-378-5256.

General, Civil, Criminal and Trial Practice. Probate and Estate Planning, Elder Law, Corporation and Real Property, Labor Relations, School, Health Care and Commercial Law.

MEMBERS OF FIRM

RICHARD L. LA GRANGE (1908-2001)

MELVIN N. FREDBECK (Retired)

BRIAN J. DEPPE, born Indianapolis, Indiana, September 29, 1946; admitted to bar, 1971, Indiana and U.S. District Court, Southern and Northern Districts of Indiana; 1981, U.S. Court of Appeals, Sixth Circuit. *Education:* DePauw University (B.A., 1968); University of Michigan (J.D., 1971). Phi Beta Kappa. Deputy Prosecutor, 1975. *Member:* Johnson County (President, 1989), Indiana State and American Bar Associations; Indiana Society of Hospital Attorneys (Chairman, 1985); American Academy of Hospital Attorneys; American Association of Homes for the Aging; Indiana Municipal Lawyers Association (Attorney Section). ***PRACTICE AREAS:*** Estate Planning Law; Probate Law; Health Care Law; Municipal Law. ***Email:*** bjdeppe@aol.com

ERIC W. FREDBECK, born Evanston, Illinois, December 31, 1955; admitted to bar, 1982, Indiana and U.S. District Court, Southern District of Indiana; 1991, U.S. District Court, Northern District of Indiana. *Education:* DePauw University (B.A., 1978); Indiana University School of Law (J.D., 1982). Assistant Corporation Counsel, Indianapolis, 1982-1983. *Member:* Johnson County (President, 2004), Indianapolis, Indiana State and American Bar Associations; Indiana Municipal Lawyers Association; National Academy of Elder Law Attorneys. ***PRACTICE AREAS:*** Civil Litigation; Estate Planning; Probate Law; Family Law. ***Email:*** efredbeck@earthlink.net

CYNTHIA A. BOLL, born Columbus, Indiana, June 16, 1955; admitted to bar, 1981, Indiana; U.S. District Court, Southern District of Indiana. *Education:* Indiana University (B.A., 1977); Indiana University School of Law-Indianapolis (J.D., 1981). Phi Delta Phi (Vice-Magister, 1979-1980, President, Province Seven, 1990-1993). *Member:* Bartholomew County (Secretary, Treasurer, 1982), Indiana State (Member, Healthcare and Medicine Section; Probate Code Study Commission, 1992-2002) and American (Member, Health Care Law Section) Bar Associations. (Resident, Columbus Office). ***PRACTICE AREAS:*** Civil Litigation; Health Care Law; Family Law; Planning and Zoning Law; Municipal Law. ***Email:*** dfb@iquest.net

ASSOCIATE

KATHRYN D. MOLEWYK, born Grand Haven, Michigan, July 8, 1956; admitted to bar, 1981, Indiana; U.S. Court of Appeals, Seventh Circuit; U.S. District Court, Southern District of Indiana. *Education:* Calvin College (B.A., 1977); Indiana University School of Law - Bloomington (J.D., 1981). Deputy Prosecuting Attorney, Bartholomew County, 1984-1991. Public Defender, Bartholomew Superior Court 2, 2002. *Member:* Bartholomew County and Indiana State Bar Associations. (Resident, Columbus Office). ***PRACTICE AREAS:*** Family Law; Criminal Law; Estate Litigation. ***Email:*** kmolewyk@hotmail.com

STEPHEN LEE HUDDLESTON

Established in 1974
CLARKE HOUSE
98 WEST JEFFERSON STREET
P.O. BOX 9
FRANKLIN, INDIANA 46131-0009
Telephone: 317-736-5121
Telecopier: 317-736-5137

General Civil, Trial and Appellate Practice. Banking, Corporate, Zoning, Juvenile, Family/Domestic Relations, Real Estate and Probate and Estate Planning.

STEPHEN LEE HUDDLESTON, born Indianapolis, Indiana, June 17, 1947; admitted to bar, 1974, Indiana, U.S. District Court, Southern District of Indiana, U.S. Court of Appeals, 7th Circuit and U.S. Supreme Court. *Education:* Indiana University (B.S., 1969; J.D., cum laude, 1973). Recipient, American Jurisprudence Award in Remedies. Adjunct Professor of Business, Business Law, Franklin College, Franklin, Indiana, 1974—. Attorney: Johnson County, 1977-1980, 1989-1998; Johnson County Board of Zoning Appeals and Plan Commission, 1977-1980, 1989-1998. Member, Committees on: Advisory, Local Rules; Civil Justice Reform, U.S. District Court, Southern District of Indiana. Member, Character and Fitness Committee, Indiana Supreme Court. *Member:* Johnson County (President, 1990) and Indiana State Bar Associations; Indiana Federal Community Defenders (Board of Directors).

ASSOCIATE

MARTHA E. McQUEEN, born Tacoma, Washington, April 27, 1966; admitted to bar, 1991, Indiana and U.S. District Court, Southern District of Indiana. *Education:* Indiana University (B.A., 1987; J.D., cum laude, 1991). Recipient, American Jurisprudence Award in: Torts; Constitutional Law; Family Law. *Member:* Indiana State Bar Association. ***LANGUAGES:*** Spanish.

COUNSEL FOR: Key National Bank; First United Bancorp; Johnson County Clerk; Ameritect; The Prudential Insurance Company of America; Aetna Life & Casualty Co.; Westfield Cos.; Ohio Casualty Insurance Co.; General Accident Assurance Corp.; Meridian Mutual Insurance Co.; The St. Paul Insurance Companies; Kawneer Co., Inc.; U.S. Fidelity & Guaranty;

(This Listing Continued)

Johnson County Youth Service Bureau; Shekinah Foundation, Inc.; Crossways Foundation Inc.; Franklin Senior Center Corp.; Adult & Child Mental Health Center, Inc.; Franklin Financial Corp.; Franklin Mortgage Corp.; Johnson County Election Board; Johnson County Association for Retarded Citizens, Inc.; Texas Gas Transmission Co., Inc.; Dow Chemical Company; Franklin College; KYB Industries; Mutual Hospital Insurance, Inc.; Mutual Medical Insurance, Inc.; Johnson County Treasurer; Johnson County Building Corporation; Legends of Indiana; Mann Properties, Wal-Mart, Texas Eastern Products Pipeline Company; Centex Homes.

JANICE E. SMITH
ATTORNEY AT LAW

FRANKLIN, INDIANA

(See Indianapolis)

Criminal, Family and Education Law.

VICKI BATTLE-CASHWELL & ASSOCIATES

4520 GRANT STREET
GARY, INDIANA 46408
Telephone: 219-884-7365
Fax: 219-985-0593
Email: v.batcash@prodigy.net
URL: http://www.lawyers.com/vbatcash

Criminal Law, Driving While Intoxicated, Drug Crimes, Felonies, Homicide, Juvenile Law, Misdemeanors, Parole and Probation, Sexual Assault, Traffic Violations, Family Law, Family and Civil Mediation, Adoptions, Child Custody, Child Support, Divorce, Domestic Violence, Premarital Agreements, Employment Law, Workers Compensation, Bankruptcy, Real Estate, Wills and Probate, Trusts and Estates, Personal Injury, Business Law, Contracts, Guardian Ad Litem.

VICKI BATTLE-CASHWELL, admitted to bar, 1999, Indiana; 2000, Illinois. *Education:* Fisk University (B.A., 1982); Valparaiso School of Law (J.D., 1999); Indiana University (M.P.A.).

BECKMAN, KELLY & SMITH

GARY, INDIANA

(See Hammond)

General Practice, Commercial, Corporation, Transportation and Trucking, Products and Professional Liability Defense, Elder Law, Estate and Trust Planning and Administration, Franchising, Real Estate, Employment, Taxation and Environmental Law, Trials and Appeals in all Courts, Medical Malpractice Defense and Workers Compensation Defense.

CALVIN D. HAWKINS

Established in 1992

4858 BROADWAY
P.O. BOX 64859
GARY, INDIANA 46401
Telephone: 219-887-2626
Fax: 219-887-2829
Email: chawkins@jovsm.com
URL: http://www.chawkinslaw.com

General Civil Practice in all State and Federal Courts. Bankruptcy, Family Law, Probate and Estate Planning. Personal Injury.

CALVIN D. HAWKINS, born Brooklyn, New York, June 14, 1945; admitted to bar, 1971, Indiana; 1972, District of Columbia. *Education:* Huntington College (A.B., 1967); Howard University (J.D., 1970); Wesley Theological Seminary, Washington D.C. (M.Div., 1974). Recipient, Honorary Doctorate, Huntington College, 1998. Adjunct Professor, Valparaiso University School of Law, 2001—. Member: Child Support Advisory Committee, 1992; Board of Law Examiners, 1995—; Gary, Police Civil Service Commission, 2004—. Interim Pastor, First United Presbyterian Church of Gary, 1995-1999; Community Presbyterian Church of Lake Station, 2000—. Board of Law Examiners, 1995- 2004. Member, Board of Directors, Northwest Indiana Legal Services, 1993—. Chapter 7 Trustee, U.S. Bankruptcy Court, 1983—. Administrative Law Judge, 1982—. Chief Deputy, Lake County Prosecutor, 1981-1983. Labor Arbitrator, 1980—. Member, Shropshire & Hawkins, 1985-1992. Member, Shropshire & Allen, 1974-1985. Attorney, Civil Rights Division, U.S. Department of Justice, 1971-1974. Legal Consultant, Lucille R. Madry Shoe Fund, Inc. Law Clerk: Civil Rights Division, U.S. Department of Justice, 1969-1970; Community Relations Service, U.S. Department of Justice, 1968. Assistant Coach, Calumet College of St. Joseph Basketball Team, 2004—. *Member:* Indiana State (Member, Indiana Bar Foundation, Board of Law Examiners) Bar Association (Chairman, Professional Services Committee, 1989); American Bar Association (Council Member, State, Urban and Local Government Law Section, 1988; Vice Chairman: Bankruptcy Committee, 1989; Reports of the Government Operations Committee); National Association of Bankruptcy Trustees; National Conference of Bar Examiners (Member, Technology Committee); Member, WTTW Citizens Advisory Committee, 1999—; Member, Bishop Noll Institute Foundation Board. ***LANGUAGES:*** Spanish. ***PRACTICE AREAS:*** Domestic Relations Law; Bankruptcy Law; Municipal Law; Church Law.

Language: Spanish.

REPRESENTATIVE CLIENTS: Artistic Cleaners, Inc.; Burger King; Gary Fire Fighters Credit Union; J.C. Penny's; Wabash Valley Presbytery.

GREGORY S. REISING

Established in 1968

607 SOUTH LAKE STREET, SUITE A
GARY, INDIANA 46403-2937
Telephone: 219-938-8080
Toll-Free: 877-524-0292
FAX: 219-938-8097
Email: ReisingLaw@AOL.COM

General Civil Trial Practice in all State and Federal Courts. Corporate, Small Business, Commercial and Residential Real Estate, Franchise, Probate and Estate Planning, Family Law Matters, Personal Injury, Automobile Accidents, Wrongful Death, Tort Law.

GREGORY S. REISING, born Gary, Indiana, February 13, 1942; admitted to bar, 1968, Indiana. *Education:* Indiana University (B.A., 1964); George Washington University (J.D., 1968). Former Member, Indiana Legislature. *Member:* Lake County and Indiana State Bar Associations.

REPRESENTATIVE CLIENTS: Rogge Insurance Co.; Classic Auto Insurance Co.; Kidstuff Playsytems, Inc.; Custom Imports; Lee Construction Management, Inc.; Ayers Realtors, Inc.; Vinzant, Inc.; Gary Community School Corporation; Cafe 444 LLC; Carbon Innovation LLC; Matine Management Inc.; Web M.O.

SPANGLER, JENNINGS & DOUGHERTY, P.C.

GARY, INDIANA

(See Merrillville)

General Trial and Appellate Practice. Administrative, Banking, Bankruptcy, Business Reorganizations, Business Transactions, Civil Rights, Commercial, Construction, Corporate, Creditors' Rights, Criminal Litigation, Family/Domestic Relations, Drug and Device, Eminent Domain, Environmental, ERISA and Employee Benefits, Probate and Estate Planning and Administration, Fire/Arson, Guardianships, Health Care, Insurance, Labor and Employment, Municipal and Zoning, Personal Injury, Product Liability, Professional Liability, Medical Malpractice Defense, Real Estate, School, Federal, State and Local Taxation, Toxic Torts, Transportation, Workers Compensation, Land Development.

BESSIE M. TAYLOR

26 EAST 15TH AVENUE
GARY, INDIANA 46407
Telephone: 219-883-2082
Fax: 219-883-0929
URL: http://www.taylorlaw.com
URL: http://www.bessietaylor.com

Personal Injury, Medical Malpractice, Family Law, Probate, Divorce, Adoption, Child Support, Child Custody, Domestic Disputes, Visitation Rights, Wrongful Death, Medical Malpractice, Slip and Fall, Legal Malpractice, Automobile Accidents, Brain Injury, Catastrophic Injury, Wills, Trusts and Estates, Guardianship.

BESSIE M. TAYLOR, born Gary, Indiana, October 25, 1953; admitted to bar, 1978, Indiana. *Education:* Michigan State University (B.A., 1974); Valparaiso University (J.D., 1978). ***PRACTICE AREAS:*** Personal Injury; Medical Malpractice; Family Law; Probate.

MAY OBERFELL LORBER

GOSHEN, INDIANA

(See Mishawaka)

Corporate and Commercial Transactions, Litigation, Environmental Law, Real Estate, Labor and Employment, Banking and Bank Related Matters, Estate Planning, Municipal and Administration Law, Products Liability, Alternative Dispute Resolution, Health Care, Medical Malpractice Defense, Insurance Litigation, Trademark and Copyright, Tax, Plaintiff's Litigation, General Civil and Appellate Practice in State and Federal Courts.

McCASLIN & McCASLIN

GOSHEN, INDIANA

(See Elkhart)

Civil Trial Litigation and Appellate Practice in all State Courts. Wills and Probate, Trusts and Estates, Estate Planning, Elder Law, Corporate, Real Estate, Commercial, Family Law, Adoptions, Divorce.

SANDERS • PIANOWSKI, LLP

GOSHEN, INDIANA

(See Elkhart)

General Practice, Corporate, Business Law, Civil Litigation, Insurance, Bank Collection and Foreclosure, Commercial Litigation, Labor and Employment, Mergers and Acquisitions, Real Estate, Estate Planning, Trusts and Estates, Probate, Wills and Estate Administration, Environmental, Family Law, Adoption, Child Custody, Child Support, Divorce, Visitation Rights.

STUTSMAN, MULVANEY & DeBOER

GOSHEN, INDIANA

(See Elkhart)

General Civil and Appellate Practice in all State and Federal Courts. Personal Injury, Automobile Accidents, Slip and Fall, Wrongful Death, Workers Compensation, Medical Malpractice, Corporate, Wills and Probate, Trusts and Estates, Asset Protection, Guardianships, Estate Planning, Real Estate, Internet Law.

THORNE • GRODNIK, LLP

GOSHEN, INDIANA

(See Elkhart)

Commercial and Civil Litigation, Creditors Rights, Bankruptcy, Banking and Bank Related Matters, Corporate and Commercial Transactions, Insurance Defense, Personal Injury, Automobile Accidents, Slip and Fall, Wrongful Death, Real Estate and Zoning, Wills and Probate, Trusts and Estates, Estate Planning, School Law and Family Law, Adoptions, Divorce, Child Custody, Child Support, Visitation Rights, Mediation.

YODER, AINLAY, ULMER & BUCKINGHAM, LLP

Established in 1957

130 NORTH MAIN STREET

P.O. BOX 575

GOSHEN, INDIANA 46527-0575

Telephone: 574-533-1171

Telecopier: 574-534-4174

Email: info@yaub.com

URL: http://www.yaub.com

General Litigation and Appellate Practice in State and Federal Courts. Corporation, Mergers and Acquisitions, Governmental, Employment, Environmental, Insurance, Probate and Estate Planning, Trust, Negligence, Taxation, Banking and Real Estate Law.

MEMBERS OF FIRM

GEORGE L. PEPPLE (1907-1963)

FRANK E. YODER (1917-1996)

CHARLES W. AINLAY (1919-2004)

JOHN D. ULMER, born Bluffton, Indiana, March 3, 1938; admitted to bar, 1963, Indiana. *Education:* Michigan State University (B.A., 1960); Indiana University (J.D., 1963). Beta Gamma Sigma; Order of the Coif. Member, Board of Editors, Indiana Law Journal, 1961-1963. Listed in The Best Lawyers in America for Business Litigation and Personal Injury Litigation. Author and Lecturer: Indiana Continuing Legal Education Forum, Articles: "Objections to Misconduct of Counsel" and "Objections during Closing Arguments," 1983; "Insurance and Third Party Investigation Files," 1988; "Constructive Cross Examination," 1995; "The New Law on Wrongful Death," 1999; "Hot Topics in Personal Injury Litigation," 2001; "Wrongful Death Litigation," 2004. Deputy Prosecuting Attorney, 1965-1969. Special Deputy Prosecuting Attorney, Ford-Pinto Trial, 1980. Member of Faculty, National Institute of Trial Advocacy, 1982-1983. *Member:* Goshen, Elkhart County and Indiana State (Member, Board of Managers, 1980-1982; Chairman, Civil Rights Law Committee, 1993-1994) Bar Associations; Indiana Trial Lawyers Association (Member, Board of Directors, 1987—); The Association of Trial Lawyers of America; College of Fellows. Fellow, American College of Trial Lawyers (State Chair, 1998-2000). ***REPORTED CASES:*** Robinson v. Wroblewski, 704 N.E.2d 467 (Ind. 1998); Hayden v. University of Notre Dame, 716 N.E.2d 603 (Ind.App. 1999). ***PRACTICE AREAS:*** Commercial Litigation; Personal Injury Litigation; Insurance Defense Litigation. ***Email:*** julmer@yaub.com

GREGORY A. HARTZLER, born Goshen, Indiana, August 14, 1944; admitted to bar, 1969, Indiana. *Education:* Goshen College (B.A., cum laude, 1966); Indiana University (J.D., cum laude, 1969). Order of the Coif. Writer and Note Editor, Indiana Law Journal, 1968-1969. Deputy Prosecuting Attorney, 1970-1974. *Member:* Goshen, Elkhart County and Indiana State Bar Associations. ***PRACTICE AREAS:*** Charitable Organizations Law; Corporate Law; Estate Planning; Taxation; Employee Benefits. ***Email:*** ghartzler@yaub.com

R. GORDON LORD, born Columbia, Tennessee, September 12, 1948; admitted to bar, 1973, Indiana. *Education:* Vanderbilt University (B.A., 1970); Indiana University (J.D., cum laude, 1973). Deputy Prosecuting Attorney, Elkhart County, Indiana, 1973-1977. County Attorney, Elkhart County, 1977—. *Member:* Goshen, Elkhart County, Indiana State and American Bar Associations. ***PRACTICE AREAS:*** Corporate Law; Business Law; Real Estate Law; Governmental Law; Zoning, Planning and Land Use. ***Email:*** glord@yaub.com

CRAIG M. BUCHE, born Gary, Indiana, May 1, 1960; admitted to bar, 1985, Indiana. *Education:* Wabash College (A.B., summa cum laude, 1982); Valparaiso University (J.D., with high distinction, 1985). Phi Beta Kappa. Associate Note Editor, Valparaiso University Law Review, 1984-1985. Member, Moot Court Team, Nationals, 1984-1985. Author: "State Implementation Plans Under the Clean Air Act: Continued Enforceability as Federal Law After State Court Invalidation on State Grounds," Valparaiso University Law Review, Volume 19, 1984-1985. *Member:* Goshen City, Elkhart County and Indiana State Bar Associations. ***PRACTICE AREAS:*** Corporate Law; Real Estate; Governmental Law; Environmental Law. ***Email:*** cbuche@yaub.com

MICHAEL F. DEBONI, born Morganfield, Kentucky, November 21, 1953; admitted to bar, 1980, Indiana. *Education:* Indiana University (B.A., 1976); University of Notre Dame (J.D., 1980). *Member:* Goshen City and Indiana State Bar Associations; The Association of Trial Lawyers of America. [Lt., JAGC, USNR, 1980-1985]. ***PRACTICE AREAS:*** Litigation; Employment Law; Governmental Law; Civil Rights Litigation; Creditors Rights. ***Email:*** mdeboni@yaub.com

B. DOUGLAS HAYES, born Fort Wayne, Indiana, October 8, 1961; admitted to bar, 1989, Indiana. *Education:* Fort Wayne Bible College (B.Mus., summa cum laude, 1983); University of Notre Dame (J.D., magna cum laude, 1989). *Author:* Note, "Secular Humanism in Public School Textbooks: Thou Shalt Have No Other Gods (Except Thyself)," 63 Notre Dame L. Rev. 358, 1988; Case Comment "Bankruptcy Law-The Standard for Rejecting Collective Bargaining Agreements in Bankruptcy: Labor Discovers it Ain't Necessarily So," 63 Notre Dame Law Review 79, 1988. *Member:* Goshen and Indiana State Bar Associations; Elkhart County Estate Planning Council; National Association of Elder Law Attorneys. ***PRACTICE AREAS:*** Estate Planning; Trust Planning; Probate; Elder Law; Business Law. ***Email:*** dhayes@yaub.com

(This Listing Continued)

MARK A. MATTHES, born Winona, Minnesota, June 28, 1965; admitted to bar, 1992, Indiana. *Education:* Grace College (B.S., 1987); Indiana University (J.D., 1992). *Member:* Goshen City and Indiana State (Litigation Chairman, District Three) Bar Associations; Indiana Trial Lawyers Association (Member, Board of Directors). ***PRACTICE AREAS:*** Litigation; Insurance Defense Litigation; Creditor's Rights; Personal Injury Litigation. ***Email:*** mmatthes@yaub.com

DENISE C. DAVIS, born South Bend, Indiana, January 1, 1966; admitted to bar, 1992, New York; 1994, Indiana; U.S. District Court, Northern and Southern Districts of Indiana. *Education:* University of Notre Dame (B.A., with honors, 1988; J.D., with honors, 1991). *Member:* Goshen City, Indiana State and American Bar Associations. ***PRACTICE AREAS:*** Business Law; Corporate Law; Employment Law; Real Estate Law. ***Email:*** ddavis@yaub.com

BODIE J. STEGELMANN, born Angola, Indiana, January 12, 1965; admitted to bar, 1994, Indiana. *Education:* Wabash College (A.B., 1987); Valparaiso University (J.D., 1994). Deputy Prosecuting Attorney, Elkhart County, Indiana, 1995-1998. *Member:* Goshen City and Indiana State Bar Associations. ***PRACTICE AREAS:*** Commercial Litigation; Real Estate; Appellate Practice; Business Law. ***Email:*** bstegelmann@yaub.com

DAVID E. SWIHART, born Elkhart, Indiana, May 25, 1969; admitted to bar, 1994, Indiana. *Education:* University of Notre Dame (B.A., 1991; J.D., 1994). Phi Alpha Delta. *Member:* Goshen City, Indiana State and American Bar Associations. ***PRACTICE AREAS:*** Corporate Law; Real Estate; Business Law; Creditors Rights. ***Email:*** dswihart@yaub.com

RANDALL M. JACOBS, born Salem, Ohio, November 15, 1961; admitted to bar, 1988, Indiana and U.S. District Court, Northern and Southern Districts of Indiana. *Education:* Goshen College (B.A., 1985); Indiana University School of Law (J.D., cum laude, 1988). Indiana Law Journal, 1987-1988. Member, Elkhart County Estate Planning Council. *Member:* Goshen, Indiana State (Member, House of Delegates) and American Bar Associations. ***PRACTICE AREAS:*** Estate Planning; Trust Law; Probate; Probate Litigation; Nonprofit Organizations; Real Estate; Corporate Law. ***Email:*** rjacobs@yaub.com

ASSOCIATES

NATHANIEL M. JORDAN, born Goshen, Indiana, June 9, 1977; admitted to bar, 2002, Indiana. *Education:* Goshen College (B.A., 1998); Boston College (J.D., 2002). *Member:* Goshen City, Indiana State and American Bar Associations. ***PRACTICE AREAS:*** Litigation. ***Email:*** njordan@yaub.com

SARA J. MACLAUGHLIN, born Goshen, Indiana, November 22, 1974; admitted to bar, 2004, Indiana. *Education:* Manchester College (B.A., 1997); Indiana University (J.D., cum laude, 2004). Registered Environmental Health Specialist, 2000. Author: Note, "Food for the Twenty-First Century: An Analysis of Regulations for Genetically Engineered Food in the United States, Canada, and the European Union," 14 Ind. Int'l and Comp. L. Rev. 375. *Member:* Goshen City, Indianapolis, Indiana State and American Bar Associations. ***PRACTICE AREAS:*** Corporate Law; Business Law. ***Email:*** smaclaughlin@yaub.com

OF COUNSEL

GEORGE E. BUCKINGHAM, born Albion, Indiana, May 1, 1938; admitted to bar, 1963, Indiana. *Education:* Indiana University (B.S., 1960; J.D., 1963). Phi Delta Phi. Member, Board of Editors, Indiana Law Journal, 1962-1963. Law Clerk to Chief Judge John S. Hastings, U.S. Court of Appeals, Seventh Circuit, 1963-1965. County Attorney, Elkhart County, 1966-1977. *Member:* Goshen, Elkhart County, Indiana State and American Bar Associations. Fellow, American College of Trust and Estate Counsel. ***PRACTICE AREAS:*** Estate Planning; Trust Law; Probate; Corporate Law; Business Law; Real Estate Law. ***Email:*** gbuckingham@yaub.com

ALAN L. WELDY, born South Bend, Indiana, July 2, 1961; admitted to bar, 1986, Indiana. *Education:* Goshen College (B.A., 1983); University of Notre Dame (J.D., 1986); Indiana University at South Bend (M.B.A., 2002). Associate Professor of Business, Goshen College. Registered Mediator. *Member:* Goshen, Indiana State and American Bar Associations; American Health Lawyers Association. ***PRACTICE AREAS:*** Corporate Law; Business Law; Health Law. ***Email:*** aweldy@yaub.com

COUNSEL FOR: Alpine Investors, L.P.; Anderson Silver Plating, Inc.; Ancon Construction Company, Inc.; AJP Corporation; Beer & Slabaugh, Inc.; Brunk Corp.; City of Nappanee Redevelopment Commission; Coachmen Industries, Inc.; Crystal Valley Financial Corp.; Culver Construction Corp.; D-J Construction Co., Inc.; The Dutch Corp.; Elkhart County Community Foundation; Eby Ford Sales, Inc.; Elkhart Bedding Co., Inc.; Elkhart County Farm Bureau Credit Union; Elkhart County Government; Elkhart County Redevelopment Commission; Elkhart County Solid Waste Management District; First State Bank; Flair Interiors, Inc.; Goshen College; Goshen Health System; Graduate Theological Foundation, Inc.; Greencroft, Inc.; Hertzler Systems, Inc.; HomeCrest Corporation; Innkeepers of Goshen, Inc.; Jason Industries, Inc.; Kuert Concrete, Inc.; Max Myers Motors, Inc.; Mennonite Foundation; Mennonite Mission Network; Mennonite Mutual Aid; Midwest Vans, Inc.; North Central Cooperative, Inc.; Nu-Way Construction Corp.; Oaklawn Psychiatric Center, Inc.; Pine Manor, Inc.; The Riegseckers, Inc.; Rollpak Corporation; Schrock Homes, Inc.; Showtime Conversions, Inc.; Show Havlers Trucks, Inc.; Smoker-Craft, Inc.; Starcraft Marine, L.L.C.; State Farm Insurance Cos.; Supreme Corp.; Town of Middlebury, Indiana; Town of Millersburg, Indiana; Triangle Rubber Co., Inc.; Walerko Tool & Engineering, Inc.; Wieland Designs, Inc.
REFERENCES: Bank One, Goshen, IN; Elkhart County Farm Bureau Credit Union, Goshen, IN; First State Bank, Middlebury, IN; 1st Source Bank, Goshen, IN; Goshen Community Bank.

TRACEY A. ANDERSON

52130 SOUTH LAKESHORE DRIVE
GRANGER, INDIANA 46530
Telephone: 574-276-7362
Fax: 574-273-6261
Email: tandersonlegal@aol.com
URL: http://www.tandersonlegal.com

Taxation, Tax Planning, Tax Audits, Wills and Probate, Trusts and Estates, Estate Planning, Asset Protection, Guardianships, Employment Law, Employee Benefits, Business Law, Business Planning, Contracts, Business Litigation, Business Enterprises, Corporate, Small Business Law, Partnerships, Limited Liability Companies, Buying and Selling of Businesses, Business Start-Ups.

TRACEY A. ANDERSON, born Indianapolis, Indiana, December 8, 1957; admitted to bar, 1985, Arizona; 1990, Indiana; 2001, Michigan. *Education:* University of Arizona (B.S., with high distinction, 1979; J.D., with distinction, 1984); University of Florida (LL.M., 1985). Certified Public Accountant, Arizona, 1985— and Indiana, 1990—. Lecturer, University of Illinois School of Business, 1986-1988. Associate Professor of Accounting, Division of Business and Economics, Indiana University at South Bend. *Member:* St. Joseph County and Indiana State Bar Associations; State Bar of Arizona; American Accounting Association; American Institute of Certified Public Accountants; Michiana Certified Public Accountant Society. ***PRACTICE AREAS:*** Taxation; Estate Planning; Probate Administration; Employee Benefits; Corporate Law.

EDWARD McGLONE LAW OFFICE

GREENCASTLE, INDIANA

(See Terre Haute)

Personal Injury, Automobile Accidents, Slip and Fall, Dog Bites, Wrongful Death, Criminal Law, Traffic Violations, Driving While Intoxicated, Juvenile Law, Drug Crimes, Felonies, Misdemeanors.

ALLEN • WELLMAN • McNEW

Established in 1918

FIVE COURTHOUSE PLAZA
P.O. BOX 455
GREENFIELD, INDIANA 46140
Telephone: 317-462-3455
Fax: 317-467-6109
Email: mail@awmlaw.com
URL: http://www.awmlaw.com

General Civil and Criminal Practice in all Courts. Trials, Personal Injury, Medical Malpractice, Family/Domestic Relations, Real Estate, Business Association, Trusts, Probate and Estate Planning, Commercial, Litigation, Business Law, Personal and Corporate Bankruptcy, Appeals, Zoning, Mediation.

FIRM PROFILE: In 1918, the firm presently known as Allen • Wellman • McNew was founded by the late Waldo C. Ging. Over the years, the firm has expanded both in terms of staff and in the variety of legal services offered. Allen • Wellman • McNew is a well-rounded general practice law firm with a breadth of experience that includes handling legal affairs for international companies, as well as for local individuals and businesses. The firm regularly practices in all federal, state and local courts in central and eastern Indiana.

WALDO C. GING (1892-1971)

JAMES L. BRAND (1938-1996)

MEMBERS OF FIRM

ERIC N. ALLEN, born Hammond, Indiana, January 17, 1952; admitted to bar, 1978, Indiana and U.S. District Court, Southern District of Indiana. *Education:* Purdue University (B.A., 1974); Indiana University (J.D., 1978). Phi Alpha Delta. Sugar Creek Township Attorney, 1979-1983. *Member:* Indianapolis, Hancock County (Vice President, 1984; President, 1985), Indiana State and American Bar Associations; American Bankruptcy Institute. ***PRACTICE AREAS:*** Real Estate; Estate Planning; Administrative Law; Commercial Litigation; Family Law; Bankruptcy Law; Business Law; Personal Injury; Mediation. ***Email:*** mail@awmlaw.com

DAWN E. WELLMAN, born Valparaiso, Indiana, August 14, 1949; admitted to bar, 1976, Indiana; U.S. District Court, Northern and Southern Districts of Indiana; U.S. Court of Appeals, Seventh Circuit. *Education:* Valparaiso University (B.A., with honors, 1971; J.D., with distinction, 1976). Delta Theta Phi. Articles Editor, Valparaiso University Law Review, 1975-1976. Faculty Member, National Institute of Trial Advocacy, 1985-1988. Member, Indiana Lawyers's Commission, 1985—. *Member:* Hancock County, Indianapolis, Indiana State (Member, Trial Lawyers Section) and American Bar Associations; Indiana Trial Lawyers Association; The Association of Trial Lawyers of America. ***PRACTICE AREAS:*** Personal Injury Law; Medical Malpractice; Domestic Relations Law; Litigation; Civil Rights. ***Email:*** dew@awmlaw.com

JAMES W. McNEW, born Indianapolis, Indiana, January 31, 1949; admitted to bar, 1976, Indiana and U.S. District Court, Southern District of Indiana; U.S. Court of Appeals, Seventh Circuit. *Education:* University of Kentucky (B.A., 1971); Indiana University (J.D., 1976). *Member:* Hancock County and Indiana State Bar Associations. ***PRACTICE AREAS:*** Criminal Law; Domestic Relations Law; General Civil Litigation. ***Email:*** mail@awmlaw.com

GEORGE A. LOHMEIER, born Clinton, Iowa, May 14, 1948; admitted to bar, 1978, Indiana and U.S. District Court, Southern District of Indiana. *Education:* Florida State University (B.S., 1975); Indiana University (J.D., 1978). *Member:* Indianapolis and Indiana State Bar Associations. [Petty Officer, 3rd Class, U.S. Navy, 1967-1971]. ***PRACTICE AREAS:*** Child Custody; Divorce; Interstate Child Custody; Family Law. ***Email:*** gal@awmlaw.com

(This Listing Continued)

KEVIN G. HARVEY, born Kearney, Nebraska, September 30, 1966; admitted to bar, 1994, Indiana and U.S. District Courts, Southern and Northern Districts of Indiana. *Education:* Augustana College (B.A., 1991); Indiana University School of Law (J.D., 1994). Member, Moot Court Society, 1993. Executive Production Editor, Indiana International & Comparative Law Review, 1993-1994. Author: "Diverging Child Protection Laws In The Commonwealth: A Comparison of Recent Legislation In England and New Zealand," 4 Indiana International & Comparative Law Review 103. *Member:* Indianapolis and Indiana State Bar Associations; Indiana Trial Lawyers Association. ***PRACTICE AREAS:*** Civil Practice; Litigation; Personal Injury; Business and Estate Planning; Probate. ***Email:*** mail@awmlaw.com

ASSOCIATES

JONATHAN M. BROWN, born Tucson, Arizona, November 20, 1971; admitted to bar, 1998, Indiana. *Education:* University of Arizona (B.A., 1994); Indiana University School of Law (J.D., 1997). Phi Delta Phi. Contributing Author for both *Indiana Practice and the Attorney Guide to the 7th Circuit*1998-2002. *Member:* Indianapolis and Indiana State Bar Associations; National Association of Consumer Bankruptcy Attorneys. ***PRACTICE AREAS:*** Bankruptcy; Family Law; Commercial Litigation; Real Estate; Bankruptcy Litigation; Criminal Law. ***Email:*** jmb@awmlaw.com

ANDREW E. CLARK, born Indianapolis, Indiana, September 23, 1972; admitted to bar, 2000, Indiana and U.S. District Court, Southern District of Indiana. *Education:* Franklin College (B.A., 1995); Indiana University School of Law-Indianapolis (J.D., 2000). Member: Hancock County and Indiana State Bar Associations. ***PRACTICE AREAS:*** Criminal Law; Civil Litigation. ***Email:*** mail@awmlaw.com

ANDRIA A. KERNEY, born Richmond, Indiana, March 24, 1971; admitted to bar, 1999, Indiana and U.S. District Court, Northern and Southern Districts of Indiana. *Education:* University of Indianapolis (A.S., 1991); Indiana University (B.S., 1995; J.D., 1999). *Member:* Hancock County and Indiana State Bar Associations. ***PRACTICE AREAS:*** Domestic Relations; Criminal Law; Civil Litigation. ***Email:*** mail@awmlaw.com

JANET L. MANSHIP, born Indianapolis, Indiana, January 14, 1971; admitted to bar, 1995, Indiana and U.S. District Court, Northern and Southern Districts of Indiana. *Education:* University of Southern Indiana (B.A., 1992); University of Memphis (J.D., 1995). *Member:* Hancock County and Indiana State Bar Associations. ***PRACTICE AREAS:*** Family Law; Criminal Law; Civil Litigation. ***Email:*** mail@awmlaw.com

JASON A. CHILDERS, born Louisville, Kentucky, February 26, 1974; admitted to bar, 1999, Kentucky; 2000, Indiana. *Education:* Purdue University (B.A., 1995); Vanderbilt University (J.D., 1999). Phi Beta Kappa. *Member:* Louisville, Kentucky and Indiana State Bar Associations. ***PRACTICE AREAS:*** General Litigation; Bankruptcy. ***Email:*** jac@awmlaw.com

DANIEL J. LAYDEN, born Lafayette, Indiana, January 23, 1975; admitted to bar, 2000, Indiana and U.S. District Court, Northern and Southern Districts of Indiana. *Education:* Xavier University (B.A., 1997); St. Louis University (J.D., 2000). *Member:* Tippecanoe County, Hancock County and Indiana State Bar Associations; Indiana Trial Lawyers Association. ***PRACTICE AREAS:*** Civil Litigation; Personal Injury; Probate; Estate Planning; Domestic Relations. ***Email:*** djl@awmlaw.com

AMY K. NOE, born Fort Worth, Texas, February 22, 1972; admitted to bar, 2000, Indiana. *Education:* Earlham College (B.A., 1994); Indiana University School of Law - Indianapolis (J.D., cum laude, 2000). Member, City of Richmond Planning Commission, 2005—. *Member:* Indiana State Bar Association (Member, Legal Ethics and Women in Law Section). ***LANGUAGES:*** French. ***PRACTICE AREAS:*** Family Law; Civil Litigation; Estate Planning; Appellate Practice. ***Email:*** akn@awmlaw.com

JAMES E. DAVIS ATTORNEY AT LAW

321 N. STATE STREET
P.O. BOX 950
GREENFIELD, INDIANA 46140
Telephone: 317-462-7759
Toll Free: 1-800-570-2928
Email: jimdavislaw@hrtc.net
URL: http://www.lawyers.com/jimdavislaw

Personal Injury, Social Security Disability, Wrongful Death, Medical Malpractice, Wills and Probate Law, Automobile Accidents and Injuries, Head Injury, Spinal Injury, Slip and Fall, Trucking Accidents, Construction Accidents, Railroad Accidents, Nursing Home and Abuse and Neglect.

JAMES E. DAVIS, born Indianapolis, Indiana, February 17, 1949; admitted to bar, 1975, Indiana and U.S. District Court, Southern and Northern Districts of Indiana. *Education:* DePauw University (B.A., 1971); Indiana University School of Law (J.D., cum laude, 1975). Associate Editor, Indiana Law Review, 1974-1975. *Member:* Hancock County (President, 1981-1982), Indiana State (Member, House of Delegates, 1977-1982) and American Bar Associations; Indiana Trial Lawyers Association (Sustaining Member); The Association of Trial Lawyers of America. ***PRACTICE AREAS:*** Personal Injury; Plaintiffs Personal Injury; Social Security Disability; Wrongful Death; Wills; Probate; Automobile Accidents and Injuries; Head Injury; Spinal Injury; Slip and Fall; Trucking Accidents; Construction Accidents; Railroad Accidents and Injuries; Nursing Home Abuse and Neglect.

WILLIAMS, CONE & BILLINGS

Established in 1962

222 NORTH STATE STREET
P.O. BOX 8
GREENFIELD, INDIANA 46140
Telephone: 317-462-5577
Fax: 317-462-0084
Email: tbillings@wcblaw.org
Email: tcone@wcblaw.org

General Civil and Criminal Practice, Driving While Intoxicates, Drug Crimes, Juvenile Law, all State and Federal Courts. Trials. Wills & Probate, Trusts & Estates, Estate Planning. Insurance, Municipal, Banking and Real Estate Law. Family, Domestic Relations, Adoption Law, Child Custody, Child Support, Divorce, Visitation Rights, Business Law, Contracts, Business Litigation, Business Planning, Business Enterprises, Corporate, Limited Liability Companies, Partnerships, Small Business, Buying and Selling a Business, Business Start-Ups.

MEMBERS OF FIRM

GLENN T. WILLIAMS (1906-1970)

C. THOMAS CONE, born Indianapolis, Indiana, April 7, 1938; admitted to bar, 1962, Indiana. *Education:* Indiana University (A.B., 1959; LL.B., 1962). Recipient, Bradshaw Patrick Memorial Award, Indiana University, 1962. Attorney, Hancock County, 1964-1965. *Member:* Indianapolis, Hancock County and Indiana State Bar Associations. ***PRACTICE AREAS:*** Civil; Criminal; Probate and Estates; Real Estate; Banking.

C. THOMAS BILLINGS, born Logansport, Indiana, September 6, 1942; admitted to bar, 1968, Indiana; 1982, U.S. Tax Court, U.S. Supreme Court and U.S. Court of Appeals, Seventh Circuit. *Education:* Franklin College (A.B., 1964); Indiana University (J.D., 1967). Greenfield City Attorney, 1972-1995, 2000—. *Member:* Hancock County and Indiana State Bar Associations. ***PRACTICE AREAS:*** Municipal; Probate and Estates; Real Estate; Family/Domestic Relations.

ATTORNEYS FOR: Greenfield Banking Co.; Hancock Memorial Hospital; City of Greenfield.
LOCAL COUNSEL FOR: Indiana Insurance Co.; American States Insurance Co.
REFERENCE: Greenfield Banking Company, Greenfield, Indiana.

LAW OFFICES OF STEPHEN P. ECKERT

GREENWOOD, INDIANA

(See Indianapolis)

Personal Injury, Automobile Accidents, Slip and Fall, Wrongful Death, Products Liability.

ELROD & MASCHER, P.C.

GREENWOOD, INDIANA

(See Indianapolis)

Probate, Trusts and Estates, Wills, Estate Planning, Family Law, Business Law, Corporate Law, General Practice, Guardianships and Conservatorships, Non-Profit and Charitable Organizations, Partnership Law, Personal Injury, Real Estate.

GROTKE & BEKES, P.C.

720 FRY ROAD, SUITE A
GREENWOOD, INDIANA 46142
Telephone: 317-888-1000
Fax: 317-888-1021
Email: gbpc@att.net
URL: http://www.grotkebekespc.com

Employment and Labor Defense, Labor Relations.

ALLEN E. GROTKE, born Buffalo, New York, July 10, 1941; admitted to bar, 1973, Ohio; 1990, Indiana. *Education:* Valparaiso University (B.A., 1963); Cleveland-Marshall College of Law (J.D., 1973). *Member:* Ohio State (Member, Labor Law Section) and American (Member, Sections on: Labor and Employment; Litigation) Bar Associations. ***PRACTICE AREAS:*** Labor and Employment. ***Email:*** gbpc@worldnet.att.net

GREGORY E. BEKES, born Philadelphia, Pennsylvania, February 15, 1950; admitted to bar, 1988, Indiana; 1989, Kentucky. *Education:* Glassboro State College (B.A., 1971); Southern Illinois University (M.B.A., 1978); University of Louisville (J.D., cum laude, 1988). Beta Gamma Sigma, Brandeis Society. *Member:* Indiana State, Kentucky and American Bar Associations. ***PRACTICE AREAS:*** Employment Law; Labor Defense. ***Email:*** gbpc@att.net

OF COUNSEL

JOHN R. PANICO, born New York, N.Y., June 9, 1952; admitted to bar, 1990, California; 1998, Utah; 2003, Indiana; U.S. Court of Appeals, Tenth Circuit, U.S. District Court, District of Utah and U.S. District Court, Southern District of Indiana. *Education:* State University of New York at Old Westbury (B.A., 1975); Irvine University (J.D., 1981); New York Institute of Technology (M.S., 1984). ***PRACTICE AREAS:*** Labor Relations; Labor and Employment. ***Email:*** jrpanico@att.net

REIBER LAW OFFICE

GREENWOOD, INDIANA

(See Indianapolis)

Family Law, Adoptions, Child Custody, Child Support, Divorce, Domestic Violence, Visitation Rights, Criminal Law, Driving While Intoxicated, Drug Crimes, Juvenile Crimes, Parole and Probation, Traffic Violations, Discrimination, Sexual Harassment, Insurance Defense, Personal Injury, Automobile Accidents, Slip and Fall, Wrongful Death, Dog Bites, Real Estate, Business Law, Contracts, Business Litigation, Limited Liability Companies, Partnerships, Small Business Law, Collections, Debt and Credit.

RUPPERT & SCHAEFER, P.C.

GREENWOOD, INDIANA

(See Indianapolis)

Family Law, Divorce, Pre-marital Agreements, Child Custody, Child Support, Paternity, Visitation Rights, Step Parent Adoptions.

WILLIAMS HEWITT BARRETT & WILKOWSKI

600 N. EMERSON AVENUE
GREENWOOD, INDIANA 46143
Telephone: 317-888-1121
Fax: 317-887-4069

General Civil and Trial Practice, Probate, Banking, Corporate, Real Estate, Zoning, Commercial Law, Health Care, Elder Law, School Law, Municipal Law, Labor and Employment and Mediation.

PARTNERS

JON E. WILLIAMS, born Evansville, Indiana, March 6, 1943; admitted to bar, 1976, Indiana and U.S. Tax Court. *Education:* Southern Missionary College (B.A., 1963); University of Missouri (M.A., 1964); Indiana University-Indianapolis (J.D., magna cum laude, 1976). Instructor: University of Indianapolis, 1976-1984; Indiana University-Purdue University, 1982-1984. Certified, Elder Lawyer, State of Indiana. *Member:* Indianapolis, Johnson County, Morgan County, Indiana State (Member, Real Property and Probate Law Section) and American (Member, Real Property and Probate Law Section) Bar Associations. ***PRACTICE AREAS:*** Probate; Estate Planning; Elder Law; Banking; Health Care.

BRIAN C. HEWITT, born Butler, Pennsylvania, May 26, 1958; admitted to bar, 1983, Indiana. *Education:* Purdue University (B.A., with highest distinction, 1980); Indiana University School of Law-Indianapolis (J.D., summa cum laude, 1983). *Member:* Indianapolis (Presenter, Estate Planning Section), Indiana State and American (Member, Sections on: Estate Planning; Probate, Trust and Real Property) Bar Associations; Indianapolis Estate Planning Council. ***PRACTICE AREAS:*** Probate; Estate Planning; Health Care; Elder Law; Banking; Mediation.

J. LEE ROBBINS, born Indianapolis, Indiana, October 17, 1960; admitted to bar, 1986, Indiana. *Education:* Wabash College (B.A., 1983); Indiana University (J.D., 1986). *Member:* Johnson County, Indianapolis and Indiana State Bar Associations. ***PRACTICE AREAS:*** Business; Real Estate; Municipal; Litigation; Mediation.

WILLIAM WALLACE BARRETT, born Mount Kisco, New York, October 1, 1962; admitted to bar, 1989, Ohio; 1990, Indiana; 1991, Florida. *Education:* Miami University (B.A., 1984); Indiana University (M.A., 1986; J.D., cum laude, 1989). *Member:* Cincinnati, Indianapolis, Ohio State and Indiana State Bar Associations. ***LANGUAGES:*** Spanish.

JOHN P. WILKOWSKI, born St. Petersburg, Florida, February 12, 1966; admitted to bar, 1994, Indiana. *Education:* University of Tennessee at Chattanooga (B.S., 1989); Indiana University (J.D., magna cum laude, 1994). Indiana Law Review. *Member:* American Bar Association. ***PRACTICE AREAS:*** Corporation Law; Civil Law.

ASSOCIATES

JOHN M. WHITE, born Franklin, Indiana, November 27, 1958; admitted to bar, 1987, Indiana. *Education:* Indiana State University (B.S., 1983); Indiana University (J.D., cum laude, 1987). [U.S. Army, 1977-1980]. ***PRACTICE AREAS:*** Commercial; Corporate; Labor and Employment.

STEPHEN K. WATSON, born Decatur, Indiana, October 11, 1965; admitted to bar, 1992, Indiana and U.S. District Court, Northern and Southern Districts of Indiana. *Education:* Olivet Nazarene University (B.A., Accounting, magna cum laude, 1988); Indiana University (J.D., 1992). *Member:* Indianapolis and Indiana State Bar Associations. ***PRACTICE AREAS:*** General Practice (60%); Municipal Law (25%); Corporation Law (5%); Real Estate (5%); Estate Planning (5%). ***Email:*** stwatson@iquest.net

RAYMOND J. SCHOETTLE, born Indianapolis, Indiana, July 19, 1964; admitted to bar, 1991, Indiana. *Education:* Ball State University (B.S., 1987); Indiana University (J.D., 1991). *Member:* Indianapolis (Member: Estate Planning and Administration Section; Taxation Section) and Indiana State (Member: Probate, Trust and Real Property Section; Taxation Section) Bar Associations. ***PRACTICE AREAS:*** Estate Planning; Probate Law; Trust Law; Guardianship Law; Federal Income, Estate and Gift Tax.

DANIEL J. PAUL, born Martinsville, Indiana, July 7, 1972; admitted to bar, 1998, Indiana. *Education:* Franklin College of Indiana (B.A., 1995); Indiana University School of Law (J.D., 1998). *Member:* Indiana State Bar Association; Indiana Trial Lawyers Association. ***LANGUAGES:*** Spanish. ***PRACTICE AREAS:*** Personal Injury; Medical Malpractice; Criminal Law; Workers Compensation. ***Email:*** djpaul@petrilaw.com

DAVID J. LEKSE, born Indianapolis, Indiana, September 20, 1969; admitted to bar, 2002, Indiana. *Education:* University of Indiana (B.S., 1994); University of Indiana (J.D., 2002). ***PRACTICE AREAS:*** Real Estate; Commercial Real Estate; Commercial Law. ***Email:*** dlekse@whrlaw.com

JENNIFER L. VANDERVEEN, born Flint, Michigan, December 10, 1974; admitted to bar, 1999, Indiana and U.S. District Court, Northern and Southern Districts of Indiana. *Education:* Albion College (B.A., magna cum laude, 1996); University of Michigan (J.D., 1999). Article Editor, Michigan Journal of International Law, 1998-1999. ***PRACTICE AREAS:*** Real Estate; Estate Planning; Corporate.

AMY L. SCHOETTLE, admitted to bar, 2003, Indiana. *Education:* University of Indiana (B.A., magna cum laude, 1996); Indiana University School of Law (J.D., summa cum laude, 2003). Associate Editor, Indiana Law Review, 2002-2003.

(This Listing Continued)

GENERAL COUNSEL FOR: Morgan County Rural Water Co.
REPRESENTATIVE CLIENTS: American Safe Deposit Association; Precision Propeller, Inc.; Harry A. Sharp Ford, Inc.; Tom Roush Lincoln-Mercury-Mazda, Inc.; CPC Valle Vista Hospital; Business Telephone Specialists, Inc.; Exotic Metal Treating, Inc.; Dressler Manufacturing, Inc.; Eagle Industries; Indiana Architectural Plywood, Inc.; Indianapolis Police Department Credit Union; Johnson County Land Title Company; Landes Costume Company; Wildwood Properties; Commonwealth Engineering, Inc.; Franklin Engineering Company; Healthcare Alliance, Inc.; Jasper Nursing Center, Inc.; Ohio Valley Healthcare Services, Inc.; Dietel's Inc. d/b/a; Mr. D'S Grocery Stores; St. Francis Hospital & Health Centers; Town of New Whiteland; Town of Prince's Lakes.

LAW OFFICE OF MARGE E. BRECLAW - TEELING

735 WEST GLEN PARK AVENUE
GRIFFITH, INDIANA 46319
Telephone: 219-934-9344
Fax: 219-934-9346
URL: http://www.lawyers.com/breclaw-teelinglaw

Family Law, Adoption Law, Divorce, Child Custody, Child Support, Premarital Agreements, Paternity, Driving While Intoxicated, Traffic Violations, Wills, Trusts, Probate, Mediation.

MARGE E. BRECLAW - TEELING, born Chicago, Illinois,; admitted to bar, 1998, Indiana. *Education:* Purdue University (B.S., 1994); Valparaiso University School of Law (J.D., 1998). Mediator in Family and Divorce Conflicts. *Member:* Lake County, Indiana State and American Bar Associations; Women Lawyers Association. ***PRACTICE AREAS:*** Family Law; Adoption; Divorce; Child Custody; Child Support; Premarital Agreements; Paternity; Driving While Intoxicated; Traffic Violations; Wills; Trusts.

ABRAHAMSON & REED

Established in 1973
200 RUSSELL STREET
HAMMOND, INDIANA 46320
Telephone: 219-937-1500
Fax: 219-937-3174

General Civil Practice in all State and Federal Courts. Trials and Appeals.

MEMBERS OF FIRM

HAROLD ABRAHAMSON, born Hammond, Indiana, July 4, 1934; admitted to bar, 1958, Indiana and Illinois; 1962, U.S. Supreme Court. *Education:* Indiana University; DePaul University (LL.B., 1958). Member, Lake County Judicial Nominating Commission, 1985-1993. *Member:* Hammond (President, 1974-1975), Lake County (Director, 1986), Indiana State, Federal (President, Northwest Indiana Chapter, 1982) and American (Chair, Railroad Law Committee, 1987-1988) Bar Associations; National Association of Railroad Trial Counsel (Member: National Executive Committee, 1988—; Central V.P. Region, 1994-1995); Indiana Trial Lawyers Association; Indiana Defense Lawyers Association; Life Master Calumet American Inn of Court, Lake County, Indiana. ***PRACTICE AREAS:*** Railroad and Transportation Litigation; Civil Litigation; Commercial Litigation; Insurance Defense; Labor and Employment.

KENNETH D. REED, born East Chicago, Indiana, May 8, 1937; admitted to bar, 1961, Iowa and Indiana. *Education:* Drake University (B.S. in B.A., 1961; LL.B., 1961). Phi Alpha Delta. *Member:* Hammond, Indiana State, Federal (Northwest Indiana Chapter) and American Bar Associations; American Judicature Society; Indiana Trial Lawyers Association. ***PRACTICE AREAS:*** Civil Litigation; Insurance Defense; Commercial Litigation; Labor and Employment.

ASSOCIATES

SCOTT R. BILSE, born Fond du Lac, Wisconsin, January 31, 1961; admitted to bar, 1987, Illinois; 1988, Indiana and U.S. District Court, Northern and Southern Districts of Indiana. *Education:* University of Notre Dame (B.B.A., 1983; J.D., 1986). Phi Alpha Delta. *Member:* Illinois, Indiana State and American Bar Associations. ***PRACTICE AREAS:*** Civil Litigation; Commercial Litigation; Insurance Defense; Probate and Estate Planning.

JOHN P. REED, born East Chicago, Indiana, December 29, 1970; admitted to bar, 1997, Indiana. *Education:* Indiana University (B.S., 1993); DePaul University (J.D., 1997). Alpha Lambda Delta; Phi Eta Sigma. Lead Articles Editor, De Paul Environmental Law Digest. Co-Author: "Proposed Takings Legislation Summary," De Paul Environmental Law Digest, 1996. Member, Criminal Appellate Division, 1996-1997.

REPRESENTATIVE CLIENTS: Conrail; Indiana Harbor Belt Railroad Co.; Amtrak; Elgin, Joliet and Eastern Railway Corp.; Motel 6; Aldon Builders, Inc.; American Savings, FSB; Hammond Group, Inc.; Hammond Lead Products, Inc.; Videotec Corp.; Sports Unlimited, Inc./Omni 41; Crown Corr, Inc./C.C.L., Inc.; Welding Specialties & Fabrications, Inc.; Mid-America Mailers, Inc.; Monarch Steel Co., Inc.; Norfolk Southern; CSXT.

BECKMAN, KELLY & SMITH

Established in 1899
5920 HOHMAN AVENUE
HAMMOND, INDIANA 46320
Telephone: 219-933-6200
Fax: 219-933-6201
Email: firm@bkslegal.com
URL: http://www.bkslegal.com

General Practice, Commercial, Corporation, Transportation and Trucking, Products and Professional Liability Defense, Elder Law, Estate and Trust Planning and Administration, Franchising, Real Estate, Employment, Taxation and Environmental Law, Trials and Appeals in all Courts, Medical Malpractice Defense and Workers Compensation Defense.

(This Listing Continued)

FIRM PROFILE: Beckman, Kelly & Smith is a firm whose lawyers practice individually and in teams to provide high quality services in almost all practice areas. The firm's goal is competent, creative and aggressive client service.

Whether you are looking for a firm that is sensitive to the local situation, or you are seeking counsel from an established firm such as ours, Beckman, Kelly & Smith is eager to help and responsive to your needs.

LAW FIRM ALLIANCES/ASSOCIATIONS: ***ALFA INTERNATIONAL:*** *Beckman, Kelly & Smith is a member of ALFA International, an association of more than 100 independent law firms. The objective of ALFA International is to improve the quality and efficiency of legal services and to provide the services at a reasonable cost. A unique strength of ALFA is the close personal relationship and trust existing among the member firms and partners. Beckman, Kelly & Smith clients benefit from the collective experience of all of ALFA's lawyers.*

MEMBERS OF FIRM

JOHN F. BECKMAN, JR. (1916-1996)

DANIEL F. KELLY (1914-1978)

J. B. SMITH (1944-2004)

ANDREW J. FETSCH, born East Chicago, Indiana, December 27, 1945; admitted to bar, 1975, Indiana and Colorado. *Education:* Purdue University (B.S., Industrial Management, 1968); University of Denver (J.D., 1974). *Member:* Lake County (Past Chair, Probate Section), Indiana State and American Bar Associations; National Academy of Elder Law Attorneys. ***PRACTICE AREAS:*** Commercial and Real Estate Law; Elder Law; Medicaid; Estate and Trust Planning; Probate Administration. ***Email:*** afetsch@bkslegal.com

RANDALL J. NYE, born Fostoria, Ohio, October 12, 1948; admitted to bar, 1976, Indiana, U.S. District Court, Northern and Southern Districts of Indiana, U.S. Court of Appeals, Seventh Circuit and U.S. Supreme Court. *Education:* Miami University (B.A., 1971); Indiana University at Bloomington (J.D., cum laude, 1976). Associate Editor, Indiana Law Journal, 1975-1976. *Member:* Lake County, Indiana State and American Bar Associations; Defense Trial Counsel of Indiana; Defense Research Institute. ***PRACTICE AREAS:*** Employment Law; Litigation; Products Liability; Workers Compensation Defense. ***Email:*** rnye@bkslegal.com

DANIEL W. GLAVIN, born Milwaukee, Wisconsin, July 21, 1954; admitted to bar, 1980, Indiana; 1985, U.S. Supreme Court. *Education:* Purdue University (B.A., 1976); Indiana University at Bloomington (J.D., 1980). Certified Mediator. *Member:* Lake County, Indiana State and American Bar Associations; Federation of Defense & Corporate Counsel; Defense Trial Counsel of Indiana (Member, Amicus Curiae Committee); Defense Research Institute. Fellow, Indiana Bar Foundation. ***PRACTICE AREAS:*** Litigation; Products Liability; Transportation. ***Email:*** dglavin@bkslegal.com

ERIC L. KIRSCHNER, born McKeesport, Pennsylvania, April 16, 1946; admitted to bar, 1973, Indiana and U.S. District Court, Northern and Southern Districts of Indiana; 1974, U.S. Court of Appeals, Seventh Circuit. *Education:* Indiana University at Bloomington (B.S., 1968; J.D., 1973). Law Clerk to Honorable Allen Sharp, U.S. District Judge, Northern District of Indiana, 1973-1976. Certified Mediator. *Member:* Lake County, Indiana State and American Bar Associations; Trucking Industry Defense Association; Defense Research Institute; Seventh Circuit Bar Association. ***PRACTICE AREAS:*** Transportation; Mediation Service; Product Liability; Complex Litigation; Commercial Litigation. ***Email:*** ekirschner@bkslegal.com

JULIE R. MURZYN, born Kankakee, Illinois, November 10, 1972; admitted to bar, 1997, Indiana and U.S. District Court, Northern and Southern Districts of Indiana. *Education:* Illinois State University (B.S., summa cum laude, 1993); Indiana University (J.D., cum laude, 1997). *Member:* Seventh Circuit, Indiana State and American Bar Associations. ***PRACTICE AREAS:*** Transportation; Commercial Litigation; Insurance Coverage. ***Email:*** jmurzyn@bkslegal.com

OF COUNSEL

MELANIE MORGAN DUNAJESKI, born Elkhart, Indiana, September 4, 1957; admitted to bar, 1984, Indiana; 1986, Illinois. *Education:* DePauw University (B.A., 1979); Indiana University-Indianapolis (J.D., 1984). Phi Delta Phi. SPHR Certification (Society of Human Resources Management). Faculty, Indiana Trial Advocacy College, 2002-2004. *Member:* Lake County and Indiana State (Chair: Editorial Board, 1998-1999; Vice-Chair, 1998-1999 and Chair, 1999-2000: Law Practice Management Committee, 1999-2000; Chair, Litigation Section, 2000-2001) Bar Associations; Defense Research Institute; Indiana Bar Foundation (Member, Board of Directors); The Executives Council (Board of Directors, Treasurer 2000-2004). ***PRACTICE AREAS:*** Insurance Coverage; Employment Law; Business Law. ***Email:*** mdunajeski@bkslegal.com

ASSOCIATES

STEPHEN J. SULLIVAN, born Oceanside, California, September 11, 1970; admitted to bar, 2000, Indiana and U.S. District Court, Northern and Southern District of Indiana. *Education:* Purdue University (B.S., 1994); Indiana University (J.D., cum laude, 2000). ***PRACTICE AREAS:*** Transactional Law; Commercial Law; Real Estate; Corporate Law; Internet Law. ***Email:*** ssullivan@bkslegal.com

ROBIN G. REMLEY, born Hammond, Indiana, August 6, 1970; admitted to bar, 2000, Indiana, Illinois and U.S. District Court, Northern and Southern Districts of Indiana. *Education:* Purdue University (B.A., 1992); Chicago-Kent College of Law, Illinois Institute of Technology (J.D., 2000). Phi Beta Kappa. *Member:* Chicago, Lake County, Illinois State and Indiana State Bar Associations; Indiana Trial Lawyers Association; American Trial Lawyers Association; Defense Trial Counsel of Indiana; Indiana Motor Truck Association; Hammond Area Tri Kappa. ***PRACTICE AREAS:*** Civil Litigation; Transportation. ***Email:*** rremley@bkslegal.com

LEEANNE C. FOSTER, born Merrillville, Indiana, January 29, 1977; admitted to bar, 2002, Indiana and U.S. District Court, Northern and Southern Districts of Indiana. *Education:* Indiana University-Bloomington (B.S., 1999; J.D., 2002). *Member:* Defense Trial

(This Listing Continued)

BECKMAN, KELLY & SMITH, Hammond—Continued

Counsel of Indiana. ***PRACTICE AREAS:*** Labor and Employment; Transportation; Products Liability; Elder Law; Estate Planning; Trust Planning; Probate Administration. ***Email:*** lfoster@bkslegal.com

ALISSA F. RESOP, born Valparaiso, Indiana, April 21, 1974; admitted to bar, 2000, Indiana and U.S. District Court, Northern and Southern Districts of Indiana. *Education:* University of Wisconsin-La Crosse (B.S., high honors, 1996); Valparaiso University School of Law (J.D., cum laude, 2000). Articles Editor, Valparaiso University School of Law, 1999-2000. Former Associate, Burke Costanza Cuppy. *Member:* Indiana State and American Bar Associations; Lake County Young Lawyers Bar Association. ***PRACTICE AREAS:*** Elder Law; Estate Planning; Estate Administration; Income Tax; Tax Law. ***Email:*** aresop@bkslegal.com

REPRESENTATIVE CLIENTS: AGA Gas; Bevel Granite Co., Inc.; Bombardier Recreational Products, Inc.; Cargill, Inc.; Covenant Transport, Inc.; C.R. England; Federated Insurance; Fleming & Hall Administrators; Hammond Public Library; Heartland Express, Inc.; Invacare Corp.; ITT Financial Corp.; Laidlaw Transit, Inc.; Landstar System, Inc.; The Navigators Group, Inc.; Markel Insurance; Northwest Indiana Public Broadcasting, Inc. WYIN Channel 56; Schoop's Enterprises, Inc.; Square D; Standex International Corp.; Swift Transportation; Vidimos, Inc.

BURKE COSTANZA & CUPPY LLP

HAMMOND, INDIANA

(See Merrillville, Munster and Valparaiso)

General Civil Practice in State and Federal Courts, Trials, Appeals, Civil Mediation, Administrative, Business Law, Business Planning, Contracts, Business Litigation, Business Enterprises, LLC's, Partnerships, Small Business, Corporate, Real Estate, Employee Benefits/ ERISA, Banking, Commercial, Insurance Defense, Personal Injury, Automobile Accidents, Wrongful Death, Wills and Probate, Trusts and Estates, Estate Planning, Medical Malpractice, Legal Malpractice, Family Law, Adoptions, Child Custody, Child Support, Divorce, Visitation Rights, Municipal and Zoning, Environmental.

EICHHORN & EICHHORN

200 RUSSELL STREET
P.O. BOX 6328
HAMMOND, INDIANA 46325
Telephone: 219-931-0560
FAX: 219-931-5370
URL: http://www.eichhornlaw.com

Carmel, Indiana Office: 9640 North Augusta Drive, Suite 412, 46032. Telephone: 317-228-9670. Telecopier: 317-228-9569.

General Practice, Litigation in State and Federal Courts. Public Utility, Banking, Corporation, Health Care, Insurance, Commercial Transactions, Labor and Employment Law, Real Estate, Professional Liability and Tort Law. Mediation.

PARTNERS OF FIRM

FREDERICK F. EICHHORN, JR. (Retired)

WILLIAM H. EICHHORN (Retired)

DAVID C. JENSEN, born Oak Park, Illinois; admitted to bar, 1971, Indiana; 1975, Illinois; 1983, U.S. Supreme Court. *Education:* DePauw University (B.A., 1968); University of Michigan (J.D., 1971). Phi Eta Sigma; Phi Beta Kappa. *Member:* Lake County, Indiana State, Illinois State and American Bar Associations. Fellow: American College of Trial Lawyers; International Society of Barristers. ***PRACTICE AREAS:*** Litigation. ***Email:*** djensen@eichhorn-law.com

PAUL A. RAKE, born Philadelphia, Pennsylvania; admitted to bar, 1975, Indiana; 1985, U.S. Supreme Court. *Education:* Indiana University (A.B., 1970; M.B.A., 1975; J.D., 1975). Phi Delta Phi. Adjunct Professor, Business Law, Indiana University Northwest, 1980-1995. Administrator, Court of Appeals of Indiana, 1975-1976. Law Clerk to Hon. George B. Hoffman, Jr., Court of Appeals of Indiana, 1977. *Member:* Lake County and Indiana State Bar Associations. ***PRACTICE AREAS:*** Litigation; Commercial Law. ***Email:*** prake@eichhorn-law.com

JOHN M. McCRUM, born Richmond, Indiana; admitted to bar, 1981, Indiana and U.S. District Court, Southern District of Indiana; 1983, U.S. District Court, Northern District of Indiana; 1996, U.S. Court of Appeals, Seventh Circuit. *Education:* Butler University (B.A., cum laude, 1977); Indiana University (J.D., 1981). Phi Kappa Phi; Blue Key. *Member:* Seventh Circuit and Indiana State Bar Associations; Defense Trial Counsel of Indiana; Defense Research Institute. ***PRACTICE AREAS:*** Litigation; Workers Compensation. ***Email:*** jmccrum@eichhorn-law.com

ROBERT J. FELDT, born Redwood Falls, Minnesota; admitted to bar, 1986, Illinois and U.S. District Court, Northern District of Illinois; 1987, Minnesota; 1990, U.S. District Court, Central District of Illinois; 1992, Indiana and U.S. District Court, Northern and Southern Districts of Indiana. *Education:* Northwestern University (B.A. in Music and Econ., 1983); ITT/Chicago-Kent College of Law (J.D., with honors, 1986). Recipient, American Jurisprudence Award in Evidence. ***PRACTICE AREAS:*** Litigation; Appeals.

GREGORY A. CRISMAN, born Valparaiso, Indiana; admitted to bar, 1992, Indiana and U.S. District Court, Northern and Southern Districts of Indiana. *Education:* Indiana University (B.S. in Business, with high distinction, 1986; J.D., cum laude, 1992). *Member:* Indiana State and American Bar Associations. ***PRACTICE AREAS:*** Litigation. ***Email:*** gcrisman@eichhorn-law.com

ALYSSA STAMATAKOS, born Philadelphia, Pennsylvania; admitted to bar, 1992, Indiana. *Education:* Tulane University (B.A., 1989); Indiana University (J.D., cum laude, 1992). *Member:* Lake County, Indiana State and American Bar Associations. ***PRACTICE AREAS:*** Litigation. ***Email:*** astamatakos@eichhorn-law.com

(This Listing Continued)

DAVID J. BEACH, born San Francisco, California; admitted to bar, 1995, Indiana and U.S. District Court, Northern and Southern Districts of Indiana; 1996, U.S. Court of Appeals, Seventh Circuit. *Education:* Southern Methodist University (B.A., 1991; J.D., 1995). *Member:* Lake County and Indiana State Bar Associations. ***PRACTICE AREAS:*** Litigation. ***Email:*** dbeach@eichhorn-law.com

LOUIS W. VOELKER, III, born Gary, Indiana; admitted to bar, 1995, Indiana. *Education:* Purdue University (B.A., 1991); Indiana University-Bloomington (J.D., cum laude, 1995). Delta Theta Phi; Order of the Barristers. Member, Moot Court Team. *Member:* Lake County and Indiana State Bar Associations. ***PRACTICE AREAS:*** Litigation. ***Email:*** lvoelker@eichhorn-law.com

JOHN P. TWOHY, born Brooklyn, New York; admitted to bar, 1996, Indiana and U.S. District Court, Northern and Southern Districts of Indiana; 1997, Illinois and U.S. District Court, Northern District of Illinois; 1998, U.S. Court of Appeals, Seventh Circuit. *Education:* University of Chicago (B.A., 1991); Indiana University School of Law (J.D., cum laude, 1996). Delta Theta Phi. Sherman Minton, Moot Court Board. *Member:* Lake County and Indiana State Bar Associations. ***PRACTICE AREAS:*** Litigation. ***Email:*** jtwohy@eichhorn-law.com

COUNSEL FOR: Northern Indiana Public Service Co.; NiSource; Mirant Corp.; Lee Publications, Inc.; Bank Calumet; Mercantile National Bank of Indiana; SBC Midwest, Inc.; AT&T; LaSalle Steel Co.; Medical Protective Co.; FCCI Insurance Group; ProAssurance, Inc.; Indiana Residual Malpractice Insurance Authority; Gulf Atlantic Insurance Co.; Baxter Healthcare Services; CNA Insurance; The Doctor's Co.; University of Chicago Hospitals; Constitution Services; Lancer Insurance Co.; Volkswagen; Fortis Corporate Insurance; City of Hammond.

CHARLES E. ENSLEN

HAMMOND, INDIANA

(See Merrillville)

Commercial Law, Personal Injury, Automobile Accidents, Slip and Fall, Wrongful Death, Negligence, Bankruptcy, Business Law, Contracts, Litigation, Business Planning, Business Enterprises, Corporate, Small Business, Partnerships, Limited Liability Company Law, Real Estate, Family Law, Divorce, Child Custody, Child Support, Adoption Law, Visitation Rights, Mediation.

LAW OFFICES OF EUGENE M. FEINGOLD

HAMMOND, INDIANA

(See Munster)

General Civil Trial Practice in all State and Federal Courts. Real Estate, Insurance, Corporation, Municipal and Zoning Law, Wills and Probate, Trusts and Estates, Estate Planning Law.

GREEN & KUCHEL, P.C.

5930 HOHMAN AVENUE, SUITE 102
HAMMOND, INDIANA 46320
Telephone: 219-852-6000
Fax: 219-852-6813
Email: firm@greenkuchel.com
URL: http://www.greenkuchellaw.com

Commercial Litigation, Negligence, Business, Business Planning, Contracts, Law Suits, Corporate, Real Estate, Wills and Probate, Trusts and Estates, Estate Planning, Estate Administration, Guardianships, Asset Protection, Personal Injury, Automobile Accidents, Slip and Fall, Wrongful Death, Taxation, Municipal Law, Employment Law, Wrongful Termination, Sexual Harassment, Discrimination, Disability Accommodation, Employee Benefits, Social Security Disability, Workers Compensation, Civil Rights, Family Medical Leave Act, ADEA, Litigation.

CAROL M. GREEN-FRALEY, born Chicago, Illinois, 1946; admitted to bar, 1987, Indiana, U.S. Court of Appeals, Seventh Circuit and U.S. Tax Court. *Education:* University of Illinois (B.A., with distinction, 1981); John Marshall Law School (J.D., 1984; L.L.M., 1993). Attorney: Hammond Redevelopment Commission; Hammond Economic Development Commission; Whiting Redevelopment Commission; Griffith Redevelopment Commission. Member, Board of Directors, 1991— and President, 1998-1999, John Marshall Law School. Trustee, Highland School Board, 2004—. *Member:* Lake County (Secretary; Vice-President, 1992-1993; Member, Board of Directors, 1992-1995; President, 1997-1998), Indiana State, Seventh Circuit, Federal and American Bar Associations; Indiana Municipal Lawyers Association. Fellow: Indiana Bar Foundation. ***PRACTICE AREAS:*** Estate Planning; Estate Administration; Taxation; Municipal Law; Corporate; Real Estate. ***Email:*** cgreenfraley@greenkuchel.com

GLENN W. KUCHEL, born La Porte, Indiana, 1961; admitted to bar, 1986, Indiana and Illinois. *Education:* Valparaiso University (B.S., 1983; J.D., 1986). Delta Theta Phi (Vice-President of Board of Directors, 1991—). Director, 2000 and Vice President of Long Range Planning & Fund Raising, 2001-2003, Board President, 2003—, YMCA of the Hammond Area. *Member:* Lake County, Illinois State, Indiana State and American Bar Associations. ***PRACTICE AREAS:*** Litigation; Employment Law; Employment Discrimination; Negligence. ***Email:*** gkuchel@greenkuchel.com

REPRESENTATIVE CLIENTS: U.S. Steel Corporation, Inc.; Hammond Redevelopment Commission; Hammond Economic Development Commission; Hammond Redevelopment Authority; Whiting Redevelopment Commission; Griffith Redevelopment Commission; Swanel, Inc.

HODGES & DAVIS, P.C.

HAMMOND, INDIANA

(See Merrillville)

General Civil Practice in all State and Federal Courts, Trials and Appeals, Insurance Defense, Corporation, Health and Hospital, Municipal and Zoning Law, Criminal, Driving While Intoxicated, Financing, Tax and Administrative Law. EEOC, Negligence, Products Liability, Environmental, Wills and Probate, Trusts and Estates, Estate Planning, Real Estate and Foreclosure Law. Consumer and Commercial Collections, Business Law, Business Planning, Business Litigation, Business Enterprises, Corporate, Partnerships, Small Business, Buying and Selling a Business, Business Start-Ups.

HOEPPNER WAGNER & EVANS LLP

HAMMOND, INDIANA

(See Valparaiso)

General Practice. Trials and Appeals in State, Federal and Tax Courts. Bankruptcy, Commercial and Banking, Corporate, Creditors' Rights, Probate and Estate Planning, Estate Administration, Financial Resources Planning, Insurance Defense, Municipal Bonds, Municipal and Zoning, Personal Injury, Product Liability, Professional Malpractice, Real Estate, Taxation, Workers Compensation, Labor and Employment. Mediation, OSHA, Employee Benefits Law.

JOHNSON & RAPPA, LLC

HAMMOND, INDIANA

(See Merrillville)

Trial, Appellate, Personal Injury, Automobile Accidents, Slip and Fall, Wrongful Death, and Defense Practice in State and Federal Courts. Insurance, Civil Rights, Labor and Employment, Wrongful Termination, Employment Contracts, Mediation and Arbitration, Class Actions, Construction, Administrative, Products Liability and Transportation Law.

TIMOTHY F. KELLY AND ASSOCIATES

HAMMOND, INDIANA

(See Dyer)

General Practice, Commercial, Business Law, Business Planning, Contracts, Business Litigation, Business Enterprises, Wills and Probate, Trusts and Estates, Asset Protection, Guardianships, Estate Planning, Corporation, Real Estate, Labor and Employment, Trials and Appeals in all Courts, Insurance Defense, Automobile Accidents, Slip and Fall, Wrongful Death, Products Liability, Professional Liability and Medical Malpractice.

KRIEG DEVAULT GALVIN LLP

Established in 1870

5231 HOHMAN AVENUE
HAMMOND, INDIANA 46320
Telephone: 219-933-0380
Fax: 219-933-0471
Email: contact@kdlegal.com
URL: http://www.kriegdevault.com

Indianapolis, Indiana Office: Krieg DeVault LLP, One Indiana Square, Suite 2800, 46204. Telephone: 317-636-4341. Fax: 317-636-1507.

Indianapolis Northside Office: 12800 North Meridian Street, Suite 300, Carmel, Indiana 46032. Telephone: 317-566-1110. Fax: 317-636-1507.

Fort Wayne, Indiana Office: Krieg DeVault Lundy LLP, 825 Anthony Wayne Building, 203 East Berry Street, 46802. Telephone: 260-422-1534. Fax: 260-423-1590.

Acquisitions, Divestitures and Mergers, Antitrust, Appeals, Banking, Bankruptcy, Business and Commercial, Copyright, Corporations, Creditors' Rights, Employee Benefits, Energy, Environmental, ERISA, Estate Planning and Probate, Family/Domestic Relations, Federal and State Taxation, Government Relations, Health Care, Hospital Law, Intellectual Property, Insurance, International, Labor and Employment, Legislative, Litigation, Patent, Public Finance, Public Utilities, Products Liability, Real Estate, Securities Law, Tax-Exempt and Nonprofit Organizations, Technology and E-Commerce, Trademark.

LAW FIRM ALLIANCES/ASSOCIATIONS: ***MERITAS:*** *Members of Meritas, serving the needs of clients in more than 145 markets worldwide.*

PARTNERS

JOHN E. CHEVIGNY, born Gary, Indiana, August 23, 1934; admitted to bar, 1960, Indiana, U.S. District Court, Northern District of Indiana; 1998, Illinois Supreme Court. *Education:* Illinois Benedictine University (B.A., 1956); Indiana University School of Law - Bloomington (LL.B., 1959). *Member:* Lake County, Indiana State and American Bar Associations. Fellow, Indiana State Bar Association. ***PRACTICE AREAS:*** Real Estate; Banking; Health Care. ***Email:*** jchevigny@kdlegal.com

PATRICK J. GALVIN, born Chicago, Illinois, July 2, 1939; admitted to bar, 1964, Indiana; 1965, Illinois and District of Columbia. *Education:* University of Notre Dame (B.A., 1961); Georgetown University (J.D., 1964; LL.M., Taxation, 1965). *Member:* Hammond, Lake County, Indiana State and American Bar Associations. ***PRACTICE AREAS:*** Banking; Creditors Rights; Litigation; Insurance Defense; Probate; Estate Planning; Real Estate. ***Email:*** pgalvin@kdlegal.com

W. PATRICK DOWNES, born South Bend, Indiana, July 24, 1947; admitted to bar, 1972, Indiana. *Education:* University of Notre Dame (B.A., cum laude, 1970); University of Notre Dame School of Law (J.D., 1972); DePaul University (LL.M., Health Care Law, 1999). *Member:* Lake County and Indiana State Bar Associations; American Health Lawyers Association. Fellow, Indiana Bar Foundation. ***PRACTICE AREAS:*** Health Care. ***Email:*** wdownes@kdlegal.com

ROBERT A. ANDERSON, born East Chicago, Indiana, July 13, 1963; admitted to bar, 1990, Indiana. *Education:* Indiana University Northwest (B.S., with highest distinction, 1986); University of Notre Dame Law School (J.D., magna cum laude, 1990). ***PRACTICE AREAS:*** Health Care; Litigation; Municipal Finance. ***Email:*** randerson@kdlegal.com

ASSOCIATES

JULIE A. ROSENWINKEL, born Indianapolis, Indiana, February 4, 1970; admitted to bar, 1995, Indiana, Illinois and U.S. District Court, Southern and Northern Districts of Indiana. *Education:* Indiana University (B.A., 1992); Indiana University School of Law - Bloomington (J.D., cum laude, 1994). *Member:* Lake County, Indiana State and American Bar Associations. ***PRACTICE AREAS:*** Health Care; Medical Malpractice. ***Email:*** jrosenwinkel@kdlegal.com

SHAWN D. COX, born Wurtsmith AFB, Michigan, June 13, 1972; admitted to bar, 1997, Indiana. *Education:* Wabash College (B.A., magna cum laude, 1994); Indiana University School of Law - Bloomington (J.D., 1997). *Member:* Lake County, Porter County, Indiana State and American Bar Associations. ***PRACTICE AREAS:*** Business Litigation; Professional Liability Defense; Health Care. ***Email:*** scox@kdlegal.com

JEFFREY M. MONBERG, born Hammond, Indiana, February 10, 1974; admitted to bar, 1999, Indiana and Illinois. *Education:* University of Notre Dame (B.B.A., cum laude, 1996); Indiana University School of Law - Bloomington (J.D., 1999). *Member:* Lake County and Indiana State Bar Associations. ***PRACTICE AREAS:*** Employment Law; Workers Compensation; Litigation; Health Care. ***Email:*** jmonberg@kdlegal.com

LUCAS, HOLCOMB & MEDREA LLP

HAMMOND, INDIANA

(See Merrillville)

General Practice, State and Federal Courts. Trials and Appeals. Corporate, Business, Business Litigation, Contracts, Business Planning, Business Enterprises, Commercial, Employment, Wrongful Termination, Banking, Tax, Wills and Probate, Trusts and Estates and Estate Planning, Insurance, Bankruptcy, Personal Injury, Automobile Accidents, Wrongful Death, Products Liability, Family/Domestic Relations, Adoptions, Child Custody, Child Support, Divorce, Visitation Rights, Hospital, Real Estate, Municipal and Zoning Law, Consumer and Commercial Collection Law, Construction Litigation.

PINKERTON AND FRIEDMAN

PROFESSIONAL CORPORATION

HAMMOND, INDIANA

(See Munster)

Federal Income and State Taxation, Probate and Estate Planning, Estate Administration, Trusts, Wills, Real Estate, Partnership, Business and Corporate Law. Municipal and Zoning Law, Employee Benefits, Business Litigation, Real Estate, Health Care Law.

SACHS & HESS, P.C.

5832 HOHMAN AVENUE
HAMMOND, INDIANA 46320
Telephone: 219-932-6070
Fax: 219-932-1103
URL: http://www.lawyers.com/sachs&hess

Schererville, Indiana Office: 141 W. Lincoln Highway, 2nd Floor, Peoples Bank 46375. Telephone: 219-932-6070. Fax: 219-322-1290.

Family Law, Adoptions, Child Custody, Child Support, Divorce, Visitations, Personal Injury, Criminal Law, Medical Malpractice, Products Liability, Wills, Probate, Trusts and Estates, Estate Planning, Real Estate, Bankruptcy, Corporations and Business Law.

ROBERT M. HESS, born Hammond, Indiana, 1939; admitted to bar, 1966, Indiana and Illinois. *Education:* Indiana University (B.S., 1961); Northwestern University (J.D., 1966). *Member:* Lake County and Indiana State Bar Associations. ***PRACTICE AREAS:*** General Practice; Domestic Relations; Personal Injury; Business Law; Child Custody; Child Support; Family Law; Divorce; Divorce Mediation; Family Mediation; Premarital Agreements; Accidents; Slip and Fall; Automobile Accidents and Injuries; Plaintiffs Personal Injury. ***Email:*** dcarlson@sachsandhess.com

RONALD F. LAYER, born 1943; admitted to bar, 1972, Indiana. *Education:* United States Military Academy (B.S., 1965); Indiana University School of Law (J.D., 1972). *Member:* Indiana State Bar Association; Indiana Trial Lawyers Association. ***PRACTICE AREAS:*** Personal Injury; Workers Compensation; Medical Malpractice. ***Email:*** RLayer@sachsandhess.com

THOMAS E. RUCINSKI, born Hammond, Indiana, 1949; admitted to bar, 1974, Iowa and Indiana. *Education:* Indiana University (B.S., 1971); Valparaiso University (J.D., 1974). ***PRACTICE AREAS:*** Family Law; Personal Injury; Divorce; Child Custody; Child Support; Visitation Rights; Divorce Mediation; Restraining Orders; Spousal Support; Medical Malpractice. ***Email:*** trucinski@sachsandhess.com

ANDREW R. TANZILLO, born Heidelberg, Germany, 1955; admitted to bar, 1980, Indiana and U.S. District Court, Northern and Southern Districts of Indiana. *Education:* Valparaiso University (B.A., with distinction, 1977; J.D., 1980). *Member:* Indiana State Bar Association. ***PRACTICE AREAS:*** Family Law; Criminal Law. ***Email:*** atanzillo@sachsandhess.com

LARRY D. STASSIN, born Chicago, Illinois, 1965; admitted to bar, 1990, Indiana. *Education:* Indiana University (B.A., 1987; J.D., 1990). *Member:* Indiana State Bar Asso-

(This Listing Continued)

SACHS & HESS, P.C., Hammond—Continued

ciation (Member, Committees on: Legal Ethics; Unauthorized Practice of Law). ***PRACTICE AREAS:*** Family Law; Personal Injury; Criminal Law; Bankruptcy; Divorce; Child Custody; Paternity; Felonies; Bankruptcy Chapter 7; Bankruptcy Chapter 13; Accidents. ***Email:*** lstassin@sachsandhess.com

MICHAEL D. BABCOCK, born Valparaiso, Indiana, 1968; admitted to bar, 1996, Indiana and Illinois. *Education:* Indiana University (B.S., 1991); Valparaiso University (J.D., 1996). ***PRACTICE AREAS:*** Personal Injury; Workers Compensation; Criminal Law; Medical Malpractice. ***Email:*** mbabcock@sachsandhess.com

JULIE A. DEMANGE, born Akron, Ohio, 1968; admitted to bar, 1995, Indiana and U.S. District Court, Northern District of Indiana; 1996, Illinois and U.S. District Court, Northern District of Illinois. *Education:* University of Iowa (B.B.A., 1991); Valparaiso University (J.D., 1995). ***PRACTICE AREAS:*** Family Law; Bankruptcy; Litigation; Guardian Ad Litem. ***Email:*** jdemange@sachsandhess.com

SPANGLER, JENNINGS & DOUGHERTY, P.C.

HAMMOND, INDIANA

(See Merrillville)

General Trial and Appellate Practice. Administrative, Banking, Bankruptcy, Business Reorganizations, Business Transactions, Civil Rights, Commercial, Construction, Corporate, Creditors' Rights, Criminal Litigation, Family/Domestic Relations, Drug and Device, Eminent Domain, Environmental, ERISA and Employee Benefits, Probate and Estate Planning and Administration, Fire/Arson, Guardianships, Health Care, Insurance, Labor and Employment, Municipal and Zoning, Personal Injury, Product Liability, Professional Liability, Medical Malpractice Defense, Real Estate, School, Federal, State and Local Taxation, Toxic Torts, Transportation, Workers Compensation, Land Development.

JOSEPH STALMACK & ASSOCIATES, P.C.

Established in 1974

5253 HOHMAN AVENUE

HAMMOND, INDIANA 46320

Telephone: 219-937-3700
Toll Free: 800-552-6860
Telecopier: 219-931-1677
Email: stalmack@jsalegal.com
URL: http://www.jsa.legal.com

General Practice. Trials and Appeals. Insurance, Products Liability, Probate and Estate Planning, Transportation, Asbestos Litigation, Automobile, Common Carrier, Complex and Multi-District Litigation, Computer, Construction, Environmental and Industrial Disease, Environmental, Fire Insurance, Hazardous Materials, Legal Malpractice, Medical Malpractice, Mediation Services, Professional Malpractice, Subrogation, Toxic Substances and Toxic Torts Law, Personal Injury.

FIRM PROFILE: Since 1974, the preeminent firm of Joseph Stalmack & Associates, P.C. has offered clients in the northern lake region of Indiana and in Chicago an aggressive civil trial practice in State and Federal courts. The top-rated firm handles complex civil trial matters and appeals, including products liability, legal malpractice, medical malpractice and toxic torts. In addition, the firm will represent plaintiffs in transportation and common carrier matters and environmental issues.

JOSEPH STALMACK, born Chicago, Illinois, September 1, 1949; admitted to bar, 1974, Illinois; 1975, Indiana, U.S. District Court, Northern and Southern Districts of Indiana, U.S. District Court, Northern District of Illinois and U.S. Court of Appeals, Seventh and Eighth Circuits. *Education:* Coe College (B.A., 1971); Loyola University (J.D., 1974). *Member:* Chicago, Illinois State, Indiana State, and American Bar Associations; Defense Research Institute; Indiana Defense Lawyers Association. ***PRACTICE AREAS:*** Litigation; Product Liability; Environmental; Construction; Professional Liability. ***Email:*** stalmack@jsalegal.com

STEPHEN DUANE BANNWART, born La Porte, Indiana, July 15, 1954; admitted to bar, 1993, Indiana, Illinois, U.S. District Court, Southern and Northern Districts of Indiana and U.S. Court of Appeals, Seventh Circuit. *Education:* Indiana University (B.A., 1976); Purdue University; Valparaiso University (J.D., 1993). Phi Alpha Delta. *Member:* Chicago, Illinois State, Indiana State and American Bar Associations. ***PRACTICE AREAS:*** Torts; Worker's Compensation; Product Liability; Environmental; Civil Rights.

KRISTY M. KOPACZEWSKI, born October 11, 1976, Hammond, Indiana; admitted to bar, 2003, Indiana, U.S. District Court, Northern and Southern Districts of Indiana. *Education:* Valparaiso University (B.A., magna cum laude, 1999; J.D., cum laude, 2002). *Member:* American and Indiana Bar Associations. ***PRACTICE AREAS:*** Insurance Defense; Civil Litigation. ***Email:*** stalmack@jsalegal.com

REPRESENTATIVE CLIENTS: BP Amoco Corporation; GMAC Insurance; Hertz Corp.; Liberty Mutual Insurance Co.; Safeco Insurance Co.; Wausau Insurance Cos.; United National Insurance; Briggs and Stratton; Utica Mutual Insurance; EÆ Professionals;; Consolidated Electrical Distributors; GO America Insurance; Mack Trucks; Rieth-Riley Construction Co. Inc.; The Housing Authority Risk Retention Group; National Casualty Co.; Travelcenters of America; Commercial Casualty Ins. Co. of North Carolina.

BLACKBURN & GREEN

HARTFORD CITY, INDIANA

(See Fort Wayne)

Litigation, Personal Injury Law.

DANIEL L. FREELAND & ASSOCIATES, P.C.

PORTE DE L'EAU PLAZA
2136 45TH AVENUE

HIGHLAND, INDIANA 46322

Telephone: 219-922-0800
Facsimile: 219-922-1261
Email: dlf9601@aol.com
URL: http://www.lawyers.com/dfreeland

Bankruptcy Reorganization, Workouts, Commercial and Consumer Bankruptcy, Debtor, Creditor, Trustee and Committee representation in Business and Consumer Bankruptcy cases, Workouts and Receiverships.

DANIEL L. FREELAND, born Chicago, Illinois, April 8, 1947; admitted to bar, 1971, Indiana, U.S. District Court, Northern and Southern Districts of Indiana and U.S. Court of Appeals, Seventh Circuit; U.S. District Court, Northern District of Illinois. *Education:* Valparaiso University (B.A., 1969; J.D., 1971). Board Certified, Business and Consumer Bankruptcy, Panel of Trustees, Northern District of Indiana, 1979—. Certified Civil Mediator. *Member:* Indianapolis, Lake County, Indiana State and American Bar Associations; American Bankruptcy Institute; Commercial Law League. (Certified in Business Bankruptcy Law and Consumer Bankruptcy Law by the American Board of Certification). ***PRACTICE AREAS:*** Bankruptcy Reorganization; Workouts; Commercial Bankruptcy. ***Email:*** dlf9601@aol.com

SHEILA A. RAMACCI, born Harvey, Illinois, December 31, 1970; admitted to bar, 1996, Indiana, Illinois, U.S. District Court, Northern District of Indiana and Northern District of Illinois; U.S. Court of Appeals, 7th Circuit. *Education:* Loras College (B.S., magna cum laude, 1993); Valparaiso University (J.D., 1996). Author, "A Look at the Split in Authority on the Availability of the New Value Defense to a Trustee's Preference Claim," Cracking the Code, 1998. *Member:* Lake County, Indiana State (Board of Directors and Member, Bankruptcy Section), Illinois State and American Bar Associations; American Bankruptcy Institute; National Association of Consumer Bankruptcy Attorneys. (Certified in Consumer Bankruptcy Law by the American Board of Certification). ***Email:*** sar4198@aol.com

MARSHALL J. GOLDSMITH

Established in 1965

2546 45TH STREET

HIGHLAND, INDIANA 46322

Telephone: 219-924-4101
Fax: 219-924-4104
URL: http://www.mjgoldsmithlaw.lawoffice.com
Email: goldsmithlaw@aol.com
URL: http://www.lawyers.com/goldsmithlaw

Chicago, Illinois Office: 77 West Wacker Drive, Suite 3200, 60601-1634. Telephone: 312-346-6622. Toll Free: 877-346-6622. Fax: 312-346-1566.

Corporations, Tax, Real Estate, Estate Planning, Wills, Trusts and Probate Law, Commercial Real Estate, Elder Law, Asset Protection.

MARSHALL J. GOLDSMITH, born East Chicago, Indiana, January 21, 1940; admitted to bar, 1965, Indiana, Illinois and U.S. Tax Court; 1976, U.S. Supreme Court. *Education:* Indiana University (B.A., 1962; J.D., 1965). Phi Delta Phi. *Member:* Chicago (Member, Tax Committee, 1965-1970), Illinois State, Indiana State (Member, Taxation Section) and American (Member, Taxation Section) Bar Associations.

(For Complete Personnel and Biographical Data, see Professional Biographies at, Chicago, Illinois)

GREEN & KUCHEL, P.C.

HIGHLAND, INDIANA

(See Hammond)

Commercial Litigation, Negligence, Business, Business Planning, Contracts, Law Suits, Corporate, Real Estate, Wills and Probate, Trusts and Estates, Estate Planning, Estate Administration, Guardianships, Asset Protection, Personal Injury, Automobile Accidents, Slip and Fall, Wrongful Death, Taxation, Municipal Law, Employment Law, Wrongful Termination, Sexual Harassment, Discrimination, Disability Accommodation, Employee Benefits, Social Security Disability, Workers Compensation, Civil Rights, Family Medical Leave Act, ADEA, Litigation.

JOHNSON & BELL, LTD.

Established in 1975

9000 INDIANAPOLIS BOULEVARD
SUITE A

HIGHLAND, INDIANA 46322

Telephone: 219-923-5250
Facsimile: 219-923-6170
Email: mcviskw@jbltd.com
URL: http://www.johnsonandbell.com

Chicago, Illinois Office: Suite 4100, 55 East Monroe Street, 60603-5896. Telephone: 312-372-0770. Facsimile: 312-372-9818.

Waukegan, Illinois Office: 325 Washington Street, Suite 200, 60085. Telephone: 847-662-7458. Facsimile: 847-662-7366.

(This Listing Continued)

Trial practice in state and federal courts, including national coordinating counsel. Appellate Law, Aviation Litigation, Benefits, Business Litigation and Practice, Complex/Class Litigation, Construction Litigation, Corporate Health Care, Criminal Litigation, Employment Law, ERISA, Environmental Law, Financial (White Collar) Crime, Financial Institution Representation, General Negligence and Premises Liability, Gun Litigation, Hospital Law and Medical Liability, Insurance Coverage, Intellectual Property, Medical Device Liability, Mold Litigation, Municipal Liability, National Coordinating Counsel, Pharmaceutical Liability, Premises Liability, Probate, Product Liability, Professional Liability, Railroad Litigation, Retirement Housing and Long Term Care, Title Insurance, Toxic Tort and Trucking and Transportation.

LAW FIRM ALLIANCES/ASSOCIATIONS: ***AMERICAN LAW FIRM ASSOCIATION (ALFA):*** *Johnson & Bell, Ltd. is the exclusive Chicago area law firm of ALFA, an international association of independent law firms dedicated to improving the quality, efficiency, and affordability of legal services.*

SHAREHOLDERS

EDWARD W. HEARN, born Goshen, Indiana, July 30, 1969; admitted to bar, 1995, Indiana and U.S. District Court, Northern and Southern Districts of Indiana; 2003, U.S. District Court, District of Colorado. *Education:* Purdue University (B.S., 1992); Valparaiso University School of Law (J.D., cum laude, 1995). *Member:* Defense Research Institute of Indiana; Defense Trial Counsel of Indiana. ***REPORTED CASES:*** Lovings v. Cleary, 799 N.E.2d 76 (Ind.Ct.App.2003); Thomas v. Dyer Construction Co., 698 N.E.2d 320 (Ind.Ct.App.1998); AT&T Wireless v. Town Porter, 203 F.Supp.2d 985 (N.D.Ind.2003). ***PRACTICE AREAS:*** Product Liability; Business Litigation; Transportation Law; Sports Law; Entertainment Law; Insurance Coverage. ***Email:*** hearnw@jbltd.com

WILLIAM K. McVISK, born Chicago, Illinois, October 8, 1953; admitted to bar, 1977, Illinois and U.S. District Court, Northern District of Illinois, 1986, Trial Bar; 1978, U.S. Court of Appeals, Seventh Circuit; 1999, Indiana and U.S. District Court, Northern and Southern Districts of Indiana; 2001, U.S. Court of Appeals, Tenth Circuit. *Education:* University of Illinois (B.A., History, 1974); Northwestern University (J.D., cum laude, 1977). *Member:* Illinois Association of Hospital Attorneys (President, 2001-2002); Illinois Association of Trial Defense Attorneys; Chicagoland Healthcare Risk Management Society. ***PRACTICE AREAS:*** Insurance; Health Care; Medical Malpractice; Litigation; Personal Injury; Torts. ***Email:*** mcviskw@jbltd.com

ASSOCIATES

Kurt E. Keagle; Daniel J. Zlatic.

REPRESENTATIVE CLIENTS: Advocate Health Care Systems; AIG Technical Services, Inc.; Assurant Health; Atlantic Mutual Insurance Co.; Certain Underwriters at Lloyds, London; City of Harvey; CNH America, LLC; Elliott Turbomachinery Co., Inc.; Emerson Electric Company; Essex Insurance Company; Exxon Mobil; Hilton Hotels Corporation; Illinois Provider Trust; ISBA Mutual Insurance Co.; Lynch Ford, Inc.; Provena Health; Rockville Risk Management Associates; St. Paul Travelers Companies; Volkswagen of America; Walgreen Company; Waste Management, Inc.; Western General Management, Inc.

(For complete biographical data on all personnel, see Professional Biographies at Chicago, Illinois)

JOHN MAKSIMOVICH

Established in 1980

3145 45TH AVENUE, SUITE G
HIGHLAND, INDIANA 46322
Telephone: 219-922-1441
Fax: 219-922-1492
URL: http://www.johnmaksimovich.com
Email: jm@johnmaksimovich.com
URL: http://www.lawyers.com/jmaksimovich

Criminal Law in State and Federal Courts. Driving While Intoxicated, Drug Crimes, Felonies, Homicide, Juvenile Law, Misdemeanors, Parole and Probation, Sexual Assault, Traffic Violations, White Collar Crime, Federal and State Criminal Appeals, Family Law, Divorce, Adoption, Child Custody, Child Support, Domestic Violence, Bankruptcy, Personal Injury, Automobile Accidents, Railroad Accidents, Slip and Fall, Wrongful Death.

FIRM PROFILE: John Maksimovich represents people facing a wide variety of legal problems in many areas of law. Mr. Maksimovich represents people in federal and state court at the trial and appellate court levels as well as in bankruptcy court. Mr. Maksimovich participates in Continuing Legal Education seminars, professional association activities and civic affairs.

JOHN MAKSIMOVICH, born Chicago, Illinois, February 27, 1953; admitted to bar, 1980, Indiana and U.S. District Court, Northern and Southern Districts of Indiana; 1995, U.S. Court of Appeals, Seventh Circuit; 1996, U.S. Supreme Court. *Education:* Wabash College (B.A., magna cum laude, 1975); Indiana University School of Law (J.D., 1980). *Member:* Lake County, Seventh Circuit, Indiana State and American Bar Associations; National Association of Criminal Defense Attorneys. ***REPORTED CASES:*** U.S. v. Contreras 249 F.3d 595 (7th Cir., 2001); U.S. v. Ramirez 182 F.3d 544 (7th Cir., 1999); U.S v. Elisha Rawlings, 341 F.3d 65 (7th Cir. 2003); U.S. App. LEXIS 18164; U.S. v. Dirk D. Jones, 371 F.3d 363 (7th Cir., 2004). ***PRACTICE AREAS:*** Criminal Defense; Bankruptcy Chapter 13; Family Law; Personal Injury; Wrongful Death; Probate; Wills; Trust Law.

PINKERTON AND FRIEDMAN

PROFESSIONAL CORPORATION

HIGHLAND, INDIANA

(See Munster)

Federal Income and State Taxation, Probate and Estate Planning, Estate Administration, Trusts, Wills, Real Estate, Partnership, Business and Corporate Law. Municipal and Zoning Law, Employee Benefits, Business Litigation, Real Estate, Health Care Law.

BENDALL DELANEY HARTBURG McNEELY & ROTH LLP

Established in 1870

533 WARREN STREET
P.O. BOX 269
HUNTINGTON, INDIANA 46750-0269
Telephone: 260-356-4100
Telecopier: 260-359-1000
URL: http://www.bdhmr.com

Warren, Indiana Office: 223A North Wayne Street. Telephone: 260-375-2311.
Roanoke, Indiana Office: National City Bank Building. Telephone: 260-672-2992.

General Civil Practice. Business, Government, Probate and Estate Planning. Trials. Personal Injury, Title Insurance, Real Estate, Family Law, Corporate, Elder Law.

MEMBERS OF FIRM

THEODORE L. BENDALL, born Bay City, Michigan, August 25, 1939; admitted to bar, 1964, Indiana. *Education:* Albion College (A.B., 1961); University of Michigan (J.D., 1964). Huntington, City Attorney. ***PRACTICE AREAS:*** Business; Probate and Estate Planning; Municipal; School Law.

RICHARD DELANEY, born Munster, Indiana, August 9, 1953; admitted to bar, 1978, Indiana. *Education:* Indiana University (A.B., with honors in Economics, 1975; J.D., 1978). City Attorney, 1984-1991. ***PRACTICE AREAS:*** Business Law; Employment Law; Commercial Law; Civil Litigation.

MICHAEL HARTBURG, born Bradford, Pennsylvania, May 27, 1965; admitted to bar, 1996, Indiana. *Education:* University of Pittsburg (B.A., 1991); Indiana University School of Law (J.D., 1996). Author: "Nota Bene, In re Donald McCarthy," 10 Issues in Law and Medicine 225 (1994). ***PRACTICE AREAS:*** Creditors Rights; Municipal Law.

DENNIS L. McNEELY, born Indianapolis, Indiana, August 27, 1951; admitted to bar, 1976, Indiana. *Education:* David Lipscomb University (B.A., summa cum laude, 1973); Indiana University (J. D., cum laude, 1976). ***PRACTICE AREAS:*** Plaintiff Litigation; Tax Law; Estate Planning; Estate Administration; Elder Law.

MATHEW J. ROTH, born Muskegon, Michigan, January 18, 1974; admitted to bar, 1999, Indiana. *Education:* Taylor University (B.A., 1996); Indiana University, Bloomington (J.D., 1999). President, Christian Legal Society, Indiana University, 1997-1999. *Member:* Huntington County, Indiana State and American Bar Associations. ***PRACTICE AREAS:*** Family Law; Real Estate; Contracts.

WILLIAM S. GORDON, JR., born Indianapolis, Indiana, June 23, 1942; admitted to bar, 1973, Indiana. *Education:* Ball State University (B.S., 1964); Indiana University (M.S., 1966; J.D., 1973). Phi Delta Phi. Deputy Prosecuting Attorney, 1979-2000. ***PRACTICE AREAS:*** Creditors Rights; Real Estate; Wills; Adoption Law; Guardianship; Estate Administration.

ASSOCIATE

LISA M. HUGHES, born Lafayette, Indiana, January 22, 1980; admitted to bar, 2004, Indiana. *Education:* Purdue University (B.S., 2000); Valparaiso University (J.D., 2003). ***PRACTICE AREAS:*** Probate; Estate Planning; Family Law; Tax Law.

All Attorneys of the Firm are Members of the Huntington County, Indiana State and American Bar Associations.

REPRESENTATIVE CLIENTS: Bippus State Bank; Carls Swine Enterprises, Inc.; Church of the United Brethren in Christ USA; City of Huntington; First Federal Savings Bank; Geiger Developing Inc.; Huntington College; Huntington County United Economic Development Corporation; Huntington County Y.M.C.A. Foundation; Huntington Nursery, Inc.; Huntington County Federal Credit Union; Huntington Schools Federal Credit Union; Lime City Manufacturing Co., Inc.; MarkleBank; McElhaney-Hart Funeral Home, Inc.; National City Bank; Schenkel's All Star Dairy, Inc.; Shuttleworth, Inc.; Simpson Grain Co., Inc.; Towns of Markle, Roanoke, Warren and Zanesville; United Methodist Memorial Home; Unizan Bank/Huntington Bank; W.A. Zimmer Company; WaterFurnace International, Inc.; Wabash Technologies.
APPROVED ATTORNEYS FOR: National Attorneys' Title Assurance Fund, Inc.

BLACKBURN & GREEN

HUNTINGTON, INDIANA

(See Fort Wayne)

Litigation, Personal Injury Law.

BOWERS, BREWER, GARRETT & WILEY

Established in 1899

301 WARREN STREET
HUNTINGTON, INDIANA 46750-2854
Telephone: 260-356-4800
Facsimile: 260-356-5196
Email: info@bbgw.com
URL: http://www.BBGW.com

Warren, Indiana Office: 121 North Wayne Street, 46792. Telephone: 260-375-2622.

General Practice. Corporation and Business Law, Probate and Estate Planning, Litigation, Family/Domestic Relations, Real Estate, Taxation, Criminal Law.

FRED H. BOWERS (1870-1937)
MILO N. FEIGHTNER (1873-1945)
LEE M. BOWERS (1896-1964)
ARTHUR J. PALMER (1906-1989)
JAMES W. BOWERS (1926-2003)

(This Listing Continued)

BOWERS, BREWER, GARRETT & WILEY, Huntington—Continued

MEMBERS OF FIRM

DAVID L. BREWER, born Cleveland, Ohio, November 24, 1936; admitted to bar, 1963, Indiana. *Education:* Culver-Stockton College and Indiana University (B.S., 1959); Indiana University (J.D., 1963). Deputy Prosecuting Attorney, 1963-66. Attorney: Board of Aviation Commissioners, 1967-1977; Welfare Department, 1969-1985. *Member:* Huntington County, Indiana State (Member, Probate, Trust and Real Property Section) and American Bar Associations; Indiana Bar Foundation. ***PRACTICE AREAS:*** Probate; Trusts and Estates; Taxation; Real Estate; Corporate Law. ***Email:*** dbrewer@bbgw.com

ROBERT S. GARRETT, born Bluffton, Indiana, July 13, 1947; admitted to bar, 1974, Indiana. *Education:* Indiana University (B.S., 1969); University of Tennessee at Knoxville (J.D., 1974). Attorney: Board of Aviation Commissioners, 1977-1980. Huntington County Attorney, 1987—. *Member:* Huntington County, Indiana State and American Bar Associations. ***PRACTICE AREAS:*** Domestic Relations; Government; Business Law; Civil Practice. ***Email:*** rgarrett@bbgw.com

JOSEPH K. WILEY, born Huntington, Indiana, November 8, 1953; admitted to bar, 1979, Indiana. *Education:* Purdue University (B.S., 1976); Indiana University (J.D., cum laude, 1979). *Member:* Huntington County and Indiana State (Member, Family Law Section) Bar Associations. ***PRACTICE AREAS:*** Domestic Relations; Criminal Law; Taxation; Business Law; School Law. ***Email:*** jwiley@bbgw.com

LEE M. BOWERS II, born Huntington, Indiana, November 17, 1962; admitted to bar, 1988, Indiana. *Education:* Denison University (B.A., 1985); Washington and Lee University School of Law (J.D., magna cum laude, 1988). Order of the Coif. City of Huntington Historic Review Board, 1992-1998. Member: Historic Landmarks Foundation of Indiana Preservation Law Advisory Council; Board of Directors, Legal Services of Maumee Valley, 1989—. Attorney, Huntington County Plan Commission; Board of Zoning Appeals; Health Department. *Member:* Huntington County Bar Association. ***PRACTICE AREAS:*** Domestic Relations; Trusts and Estates; Real Estate; Commercial Law; Civil Practice. ***Email:*** lbowers@bbgw.com

ASSOCIATE

MATTHEW G. GRANTHAM, born Portsmouth, Virginia, January 25, 1978; admitted to bar, 2005, Indiana. *Education:* University of Dallas (B.A., 2000); St. Louis University (M.A., 2002); University of Notre Dame Law School (J.D., 2005). *Member:* Huntington County and Indiana State Bar Associations.

COUNSEL FOR: The Bippus State Bank; Huntington Parkview Hospital, Inc.; Huntington County; Huntington County Department of Community Development; The Dan Quayle Commemorative Foundation; Farm Credit Services of Mid-America, ACA; Cinergy; National Attorneys Title Assurance Fund, Inc.; MagneTek, Inc.; Salamonie Mills, Inc.; Norfolk & Southern Railway Co.; Historic Forks of the Wabash, Inc.; Horace Mann Apartments Limited Partnership; Innovative Packaging, Inc.; Huntington County Community School Corporation.
APPROVED ATTORNEYS FOR: National Attorneys Title Assurance Fund, Inc.

MATHENY, MICHAEL, HAHN & DENMAN, L.L.P.

Established in 1876

45 WEST MARKET STREET
P.O. BOX 191
HUNTINGTON, INDIANA 46750-0191
Telephone: 260-356-7030
Fax: 260-356-7033
Email: mail@mmhdlaw.com
URL: http://www.lawyers.com/mmhblaw

General Practice, Civil Litigation, Criminal Defense, Family Law, Federal Income Tax, Corporate Law, Personal Injury, Real Estate, Trusts and Estates, Probate, Elder Law, Workers Compensation, Social Security Disability, Medical Malpractice.

MEMBERS OF FIRM

STEPHEN J. MICHAEL, born Cass County, Indiana, February 1, 1941; admitted to bar, 1967, Indiana and U.S. District Court, Northern and Southern Districts of Indiana. *Education:* Indiana University; Butler University (A.B., 1964); Indiana University (J.D., 1967). Phi Delta Phi. Deputy Prosecuting Attorney, Huntington County, 1970-1972. City Judge, 1972-1976 and City Attorney, 1976-1980, Huntington. Public Defender, 1988Æ. *Member:* Huntington County (President, 1970-1971); Indiana State and American Bar Associations. Fellow, Indiana Bar Foundation. ***PRACTICE AREAS:*** General Practice; Criminal Defense; Family Law.

WILFORD A. HAHN, born Bremen, Indiana, April 8, 1944; admitted to bar, 1973, Indiana; 1974, Colorado. *Education:* Purdue University (B.A., 1967); University of Denver (J.D., 1973). Deputy Prosecutor, Child Support, 1976-1978. *Member:* Huntington County (President, 1979-1980), Indiana State and American Bar Associations; Indiana Trial Lawyers Association; The Association of Trial Lawyers of America. ***PRACTICE AREAS:*** Civil Litigation; Probate; Personal Injury; Workers Compensation; Wrongful Death; Medical Malpractice. ***Email:*** whahn@mmhdlaw.com

JILL M. DENMAN, born Wabash, Indiana, July, 1971; admitted to bar, 1996, Indiana. *Education:* Bradley University (B.A., 1993); Indiana University School of Law-Bloomington (J.D., 1996). Pi Gamma Mu; Sigma Delta; Delta Theta Phi; Motar Board; Social Science Honor Society; English Honor Society; Political Science Honor Society. *Member:* Huntington County (Secretary, 1997; President, 1998—), Indiana State and American Bar Associations. ***REPORTED CASES:*** Shumate v. State (Ind. Ct. App. 1999) 718 N.E.2d 1133. ***PRACTICE AREAS:*** Criminal Law; Juvenile Delinquency; Family Law; Collections; Estate Planning; Business Transactions; Social Security Disability. ***Email:*** jdenman@mmhdlaw.com

(This Listing Continued)

ASSOCIATE

JEREMY K. NIX, born Huntington, Indiana, September 23, 1977; admitted to bar, 2003, Indiana and U.S. District Court, Northern and Southern Districts of Indiana. *Education:* Indiana University (B.S., 2000); Loyola University (J.D., 2003). Phi Beta Kappa. *Member:* Huntington County, Indiana State and American Bar Associations. ***PRACTICE AREAS:*** General Practice. ***Email:*** jnix@mmhdlaw.com

OF COUNSEL

STANLEY H. MATHENY, born Carthage, Illinois, September 10, 1934; admitted to bar, 1959, Indiana and U.S. District Court, Southern District of Indiana; 1960 U.S. District Court, Northern District of Indiana. *Education:* Wabash College (A.B., 1956); Indiana University (J.D., 1959). Judge, City Court, Huntington, 1963-1967. City Attorney, Huntington, 1967-1976. *Member:* Huntington County (President, 1967-1968), Indiana State and American Bar Associations. ***PRACTICE AREAS:*** Probate; Estate Planning; Elder Law; Income Tax; Business Law. ***Email:*** smatheny@mmhdlaw.com

REPRESENTATIVE CLIENTS: Pyle Industries, Inc.; United R.E.M.C.; Huntington County Farm Bureau Co-Op; Huntington County Farm Bureau Credit Union; Farmers Elevator of South Whitley; Johnson Petroleum; McDonald Oil; Johnson Convenience Stores; Pathfinder Services, Inc.; mignone Communications, Inc.; Baker & Sons Construction; Homier Distributing Co.; Art Chemical Products, Inc.; Family Practice Associates.
REFERENCES: Huntington College; Wells Fargo Bank; First Federal Savings Bank.

ROEBUCK & ASSOCIATES, P.C.

HUNTINGTON, INDIANA

(See Ft.Wayne)

Personal Injury, Automobile Accidents, Boat Accidents, Motorcycle Accidents, Truck Accidents, Slip and Fall, Dog Bites, Medical Malpractice, Head Injuries, Nursing Home Abuse and Neglect, Products Liability, Insurance, Social Security, Social Security Disability, and Wrongful Death.

ADINAMIS & ADINAMIS, P.C.

Established in 1969

8710 NORTH MERIDIAN STREET
INDIANAPOLIS, INDIANA 46260
Telephone: 317-580-9000
Fax: 317-587-0288
URL: http://www.lawyers.com/adinamislaw

Taxation, Estate Planning and Business Administration, Business Planning, Employee Benefits, and Business Law.

GEORGE P. ADINAMIS, born Evergreen Park, Illinois, December 28, 1933; admitted to bar, 1963, Illinois; 1967, Indiana, U.S. District Court, Northern and Southern Districts of Indiana, U.S. Tax Court and U.S. Supreme Court. *Education:* Northwestern University (B.S., 1956); John Marshall Law School (J.D., 1959). Alumnus, Kellogg School of Management. Special Agent, Criminal Investigation Division, U.S. Treasury, Chicago, Ill., 1960-1963. Attorney, Enforcement Division, Office of the Chief Counsel, Internal Revenue Service, Philadelphia, Pa., 1963-1965. Trial Attorney, Office of the Chief Counsel, Internal Revenue Service, Indianapolis, Ind., 1965-1967. Attorney, Kightlinger, Young, Gray & Hudson Law Firm, 1967-1969. Private practice of law, 1969—. *Member:* Indianapolis, Indiana State (Member, Tax Section, 1970-2004), Illinois State and American (Member, Tax Section, 1968-2004 Bar Associations. ***PRACTICE AREAS:*** Civil and Criminal Taxation; Estate Planning; Estate Administration; Business Planning; Employee Benefits; Business Law; Civil Mediation. ***Email:*** george@georgepadinamis.com

ADINAMIS, MICHAEL & SAUNDERS P.C.

500 E. 96TH STREET, SUITE 360
INDIANAPOLIS, INDIANA 46240
Telephone: 317-218-2600
Fax: 317-218-2601
URL: http://www.ams-law.com

Business Law, Estate Planning, Estate Administration, Trusts and Estates, Charitable Planning, Taxation.

CAROL M. ADINAMIS, born Philadelphia, Pennsylvania, March 28, 1965; admitted to bar, 1992, Indiana, U.S. District Court, Northern and Southern Districts of Indiana; 1993, U.S. Tax Court. *Education:* Indiana University (B.S., 1987; J.D., magna cum laude, 1992). Certified Public Accountant, Indiana, 1993. *Member:* Indianapolis, Indiana State (Chair, Legal Ethics Committee, 2001-2004) and American Bar Associations; American Institute of Certified Public Accountants; Indiana Certified Public Accountants' Society; American Association of Attorney-Certified Public Accountants. ***PRACTICE AREAS:*** Business Planning; Business Law; Taxation; Estate Planning. ***Email:*** carol@adinamis.com

SUSAN ADINAMIS MICHAEL, born Indianapolis, Indiana, February 14, 1967; admitted to bar, 1993, Indiana; 1995, Florida; U.S. District Court, Northern and Southern Districts of Indiana; U.S. Tax Court. *Education:* Indiana University, Bloomington (B.A., in Political Science and Criminal Justice, 1990); Valparaiso University School of Law (1990-1991); Indiana University School of Law (J.D., 1993). *Member:* Indiana State and American Bar Associations; The Florida Bar. ***PRACTICE AREAS:*** Estate Administration; Estate Planning; Business Law; Employment Law. ***Email:*** susan@adinamis.com

JEFFREY A. SAUNDERS, born Covington, Kentucky, November 25, 1963; admitted to bar, 1992, Indiana and U.S. District Court, Northern and Southern Districts of Indiana; U.S. Tax Court. *Education:* Ball State University (B.S., magna cum laude, 1986); Indiana University (J.D., cum laude, 1992). Certified Public Accountant, Indiana, 1989. Member: American Institute of Certified Public Accountants; Indiana Certified Public Accountant Society; American Institute of Attorney-Certified Public Accountants. *Member:* Indianapo-

(This Listing Continued)

lis, Indiana State and American Bar Associations. ***PRACTICE AREAS:*** Taxation; Estate Planning; Charitable Planning; Business Law. ***Email:*** jeff@adinamis.com

ALLEN • WELLMAN • MCNEW

INDIANAPOLIS, INDIANA

(See Greenfield)

General Civil and Criminal Practice in all Courts. Trials, Personal Injury, Medical Malpractice, Family/Domestic Relations, Real Estate, Business Association, Trusts, Probate and Estate Planning, Commercial, Litigation, Business Law, Personal and Corporate Bankruptcy, Appeals, Zoning, Mediation.

AVERY & CHEERVA, LLP

Established in 1989

INDIANA BAR CENTER
230 EAST OHIO, SIXTH FLOOR
INDIANAPOLIS, INDIANA 46204-2149
Telephone: 317-637-7575
Fax: 317-685-1106
URL: http://www.averycheerva.com

Family Law, Dissolution of Marriage, Custody, Paternity, Prenuptial Agreements, Domestic Appellate Practice, Mediation, and Arbitration.

FIRM PROFILE: Avery & Cheerva, LLP was founded as a result of a mutual interest in a concentrated family law practice. The firm now serves a wide range of clients in matters involving dissolution of marriage, custody, paternity, and related areas. The firm encourages continuing professional development of all partners and staff members, participates in Continuing Legal Education seminars, is active in the State and local Bar Associations and maintains a well staffed and technologically sophisticated office.

MEMBERS OF FIRM

MELISSA J. AVERY, born Columbus, Ohio, May 29, 1969; admitted to bar, 1994, Ohio; 1995, U.S. District Court, Southern District of Ohio; 1997, Indiana and U.S. District Court, Northern and Southern Districts of Indiana. *Education:* Ohio University (B.S., cum laude, 1991); Capital University (J.D., 1994). Order of the Curia. Named Indianapolis Monthly Super Lawyer, 2005. Frequent Lecturer. Participant: Indiana Trial Advocacy College, 1999; American Bar Association Family Law Trial Advocacy Institute, 2000. Member: Ohio Bar Association, 1994-1998; Columbus Bar Association, 1994-1997; Indianapolis Monthly Super Lawyer, 2005. *Member:* Indianapolis (Member: Family Law Section; Executive Committee, 1999— Chair, Executive Committee, 2002), Indiana State (Member, Family Law Section; Co-Chair, Judicial Improvement Committee, 2002-2004) and American (Member, Family Law Section, Young Lawyers Division; Vice Chair, Marital Property Committee, 2003-2004; Family Law Section Council, 2005—) Bar Associations; Sagamore American Inn of Court, Indianapolis Chapter, 2001-2002. (Board Certified, Family Law Specialist, Indiana State Bar Association, Family Law Certification Board). ***PRACTICE AREAS:*** Family Law. ***Email:*** mavery@averycheerva.com

MICHAEL CHEERVA, born Chicago, Illinois, May 14, 1960; admitted to bar, 1985, Indiana and U.S. District Court, Northern and Southern Districts of Indiana. *Education:* Wabash College (B.A., 1982); Indiana University (J.D., 1985). Named Indianapolis Monthly Super Lawyer, 2005. Frequent Lecturer and Author. Participant, American Bar Association Family Law Advocacy Institute, 2004. *Member:* Indianapolis (Member: Executive Committee, 1992-1995; Secretary-Treasurer, 1995; Chair, 1997; Family Law Section), Indiana State (Member, Law Practice Management Committee and State Legislation Committee) and American Bar Associations. ***PRACTICE AREAS:*** Family Law; Appellate Practice. ***Email:*** mcheerva@averycheerva.com

ASSOCIATE

CHRISTOPHER J. BARROWS, born Indianapolis, Indiana, February 2, 1972; admitted to bar, 1999, Indiana and U.S. District Court, Northern and Southern Districts of Indiana. *Education:* Goshen College (B.A., 1994); Indiana University School of Law (J.D., 1999). Registered Family Law Mediator, 2004. Frequent Lecturer. Participant, American Academy of Matrimonial Lawyers, Institute Family Law Associates, 2002. *Member:* Hamilton County, Indianapolis, Indiana State (Member, Civil Rights of Children Committee, 2002-2004; Member, Sections on: Family Law; Young Lawyers) and American Bar Associations. (Board Certified, Family Law Specialist, Indiana State Bar Association, Family Law Certification Board). ***PRACTICE AREAS:*** Family Law; Mediation. ***Email:*** cbarrows@averycheerva.com

AYRES CARR & SULLIVAN, P.C.

Established in 1914

(Formerly Steers Sullivan Professional Corporation; Steers, Sullivan, McNamar & Rogers; Steers, Klee, Jay & Sullivan and Fenton, Steers, Beasley & Klee)

251 EAST OHIO STREET, SUITE 500
INDIANAPOLIS, INDIANA 46204
Telephone: 317-636-3471
Fax: 317-636-6575

Noblesville, Indiana Office: 136 South Ninth Street. Telephone: 317-773-0882. Fax: 317-773-0943.

General Civil and Criminal Practice in all State and Federal Courts, including Trial and Appellate Practice. Administrative, Bankruptcy Reorganization, Consumer Bankruptcy, Collection and Subrogation, Commercial Law, Construction, Corporation and Business Organizations, Insurance, Legislation and Government Relations, Mediation and Dispute Resolution,

(This Listing Continued)

Personal Injury, Pension, Profit Sharing and Employee Benefits, Probate, Estate and Succession Planning, Real Estate, Taxation, Transportation and Motor Carrier, and Workers Compensation Law.

FIRM PROFILE: The Law Firm of Ayres Carr & Sullivan traces it roots back to 1914. Offering statewide representation, the firm strives to offer outstanding legal services to clients, large and small.

AQUILLA Q. JONES (1852-1926)
EDWIN M. S. STEERS (1881-1977)
(MR.) C. SEVERIN BUSCHMANN (1896-1980)
ARTHUR J. SULLIVAN (1909-1999)
EDWIN K. STEERS (1915-1992)
JOHN R. CARR, JR. (Retired 1919-2004)

ATTORNEYS

WILLIAM S. AYRES, born Fort Wayne, Indiana; admitted to bar, 1976, Indiana and U.S. District Court, Southern District of Indiana; 1980, U.S. Court of Appeals, Seventh Circuit and U.S. Supreme Court. *Education:* Ball State University (B.S., cum laude, 1973); Indiana University (J.D., 1976). Delta Theta Phi (Tribune, 1974-1975; Dean, 1975-1976). Certified Mediator, Indiana, 1992—. *Member:* Indianapolis, Indiana State and American Bar Associations; The Association of Trial Lawyers of America. ***PRACTICE AREAS:*** Trial Law; Corporation Law; Personal Injury Law; Arbitration/Mediation. ***Email:*** bayres@acs-law.com

JOHN R. CARR, III, born Boston, Massachusetts; admitted to bar, 1974, Indiana; U.S. District Court, Northern and Southern Districts of Indiana; U.S. Court of Appeals, Seventh Circuit; U.S. Supreme Court. *Education:* Middlebury College (A.B., Philosophy, 1969); Indiana University (J.D., 1974). Listed in Who's Who in Executives and Businesses, 1998-1999. Lecturer, Author and Panelist: American Bar Association, Indiana Continuing Legal Education Forum; Indianapolis Bar Association. *Member:* Hamilton County, Indianapolis (Business Law Section; Commercial and Bankruptcy Law Section; Chair, Liaison with Law Schools Committee, 1987; Chair Law Studies/Related Activities Committee, 1989; 11th District Representative, 1992-1993; Member, Long Range Planning Committee, 1993-1997; Member, Meetings Committee, 1999), Indiana State (Bankruptcy and Creditor's Rights Section including Member, Task Force on Indiana Exemptions, 1998—; Probate, Trust and Real Property Section; Member, House of Delegates, 1975-1979, 1981-1982 and 1986— including Chair, Committee on Draft, 1975-1976 and Parliamentarian, 1989-1996, 1998-1999; Chair, Improvements in the Judicial System Committee, 1989-1991; Member, Board of Managers, 1991-1993; Chair, Articles and By-Laws Committee, 1994-1995; Member, Certification of Specialties Committee, 1999-2000) and American (Tort and Insurance Practice Section including Chair, Employee Benefits Committee, 1994-1995, Chair, 1997-1999, Vice Chair, 2000—, National CLE Program, Satellite Seminar and Special CLE Program Subcommittee, 1997-1999; Employer-Employee Relations Committee; Member, CLE Board, 1995-1999 and Chair, Midyear CLE Meetings, 1995-1996; Coordinator, Joint Committee on Employee Benefits, 1996-1999; Real Property, Probate and Trust Law Section including Member, Workouts, Enforcement of Creditors' Rights and Bankruptcy Committee; Joint Committee on Employee Benefits including TTIPS Representative, 1993-1997, Member, National Institute Committee, 1997-1999 and TTIPS Representative, Government Invitational Conference, 2002) Bar Associations; Bar Association of the Seventh Federal Circuit; American Bankruptcy Institute (Member, Alternative Dispute Resolution Subcommittee; Member, Legislation Committee); American Judicature Society (Life Member; Indiana State Membership Chair, 1983-1989; Member, Board of Directors, 1985-1989). Distinguished Fellow, Indianapolis Bar Foundation. Charter and Life Patron Fellow, Indiana Bar Foundation (Member, Nominating Committee, 1989-1991; Member, Fund Raising Committee, 1992-1993). Fellow, American Bar Foundation (Indiana State Chair, 1997-2000). Charter Fellow, American College of Employee Benefits Counsel. ***SPECIAL AGENCIES:*** Records Management Committee, Indiana Supreme Court, 1991—; Indiana Supreme Court Task Force on Access to Court Records, 2003—; Advisory Committee on Local Bankruptcy Rules, Southern District of Indiana, 1986— and Chair, ADR Subcommittee, 1997—. ***PRACTICE AREAS:*** Bankruptcy Reorganization; Creditors Rights; Commercial Law; Corporation Law; Insurance Law; Employee Benefit Law. ***Email:*** jrciii@acs-law.com

BRET S. CLEMENT, born Milwaukee, Wisconsin; admitted to bar, 1979, Indiana. *Education:* University of Notre Dame (B.B.A. with high honors, 1976); University of Michigan (J.D., cum laude, 1979). Beta Gamma Sigma. Adjunct Assistant Professor of Law, Indiana University, 1984. ***PRACTICE AREAS:*** Federal and State Taxation Law; Estate and Business Planning Law; Corporate Law; Bankruptcy Reorganization. ***Email:*** bclement@acs-law.com

MICHAEL R. FRANCESCHINI, born Lafayette, Indiana; admitted to bar, 1975, Indiana and U.S. District Court, Southern District of Indiana; 1980, U.S. Court of Appeals, Seventh Circuit and U.S. Supreme Court; 1994, U.S. District Court, Northern District of Indiana. *Education:* Indiana University (B.S., 1970; J.D., 1975). Law Clerk for Chief Justice Richard Givan, Supreme Court of Indiana, 1973-1977; Indiana Supreme Court Committee on Character and Fitness, 1982—. *Member:* Indianapolis, Hancock County, Indiana State (Member Sections on: Litigation, Probate and Real Property) and American Bar Associations. ***PRACTICE AREAS:*** Civil Trial Law; Appellate Law; Corporation Law; Estate Planning and Probate. ***Email:*** mfran@acs-law.com

ROBERT W. LOSER, II, born Indianapolis, Indiana,; admitted to bar, 1969, Indiana and U.S. District Court, Southern District of Indiana. *Education:* Indiana University (B.S., 1962; J.D., 1969). Phi Delta Phi. *Member:* Indianapolis and Indiana State Bar Associations; Transportation Lawyers Association. [Capt. JAGC, USNR-Ret.]. ***PRACTICE AREAS:*** Motor Carrier Transportation Law; Probate Law; Corporation Law. ***Email:*** bloser@acs-law.com

RUTH E. MYER, born Indianapolis, Indiana; admitted to bar, 1970, Indiana and U.S. District Court, Southern District of Indiana. *Education:* Butler University (A.B., cum

(This Listing Continued)

AYRES CARR & SULLIVAN, P.C., Indianapolis—Continued

laude, 1963); Indiana University (J.D., cum laude, 1970). Order of the Coif. *Member:* Indianapolis Bar Association. ***PRACTICE AREAS:*** Collection Law; Insurance Subrogation Law; Mechanics Lien Law. ***Email:*** rmyer@acs-law.com

PATRICK M. O'BRIEN, born Rensselaer, Indiana; admitted to bar, 1986, Indiana and U.S. District Court, Northern and Southern Districts of Indiana; 1987, U.S. Tax Court. *Education:* University of Miami (B.B.A., 1981); Indiana State University (M.B.A., 1983); Indiana University (J.D., 1986). Adjunct Instructor, MBA Accounting, Butler University, Indianapolis, Indiana, 1986—. *Member:* Indianapolis, Indiana State and American Bar Associations. ***PRACTICE AREAS:*** State and Local Taxation Law; Personal Injury Law. ***Email:*** pobrien@acs-law.com

CHRISTOPHER D. SEIGEL, born Cambridge City, Indiana; admitted to bar, 1979, Indiana and U.S. District Court, Southern District of Indiana. *Education:* Ball State University (B.S., summa cum laude, 1976); Indiana University (J.D., 1979). Phi Delta Phi; Blue Key Honor Society. Member, Moot Court. Co-Author, Indiana Law Review, Indiana University School of Law-Indianapolis, survey issue on Constitutional Law, 1980. *Member:* Indiana State Bar Association. ***PRACTICE AREAS:*** General Practice; Real Estate; Municipal; Mediation; Civil Litigation; Workers Compensation. ***Email:*** cseigel@acs-law.com

CHARLES N. DOBERNECK, born Greensburg, Pennsylvania; admitted to bar, 1981, Indiana. *Education:* University of Notre Dame (B.A., 1969); Indiana University (J.D., magna cum laude, 1981). *Member:* Indianapolis and Indiana State (Member, Sections on: Corporation, Banking and Business Law; Probate, Trust and Real Property) Bar Associations. ***PRACTICE AREAS:*** Business Law; Estate Planning and Administration; Real Estate.

OF COUNSEL

RAYMOND M. ADLER, born Decatur, Indiana; admitted to bar, 1975, Indiana and U.S. District Court, Southern District of Indiana; 1976, U.S. Court of Appeals, Seventh Circuit and U.S. Tax Court; 1979, U.S. Supreme Court. *Education:* Purdue University (B.S., 1971); Indiana University (J.D., 1975). Mensa Society. Hamilton County Attorney, 1983-1986. Hamilton Heights School Board, 1988-1992. *Member:* Hamilton County, Indiana State and American Bar Associations; Indiana Trial Lawyers Association; Association of Trial Lawyers of America. (Resident, Noblesville Office). ***PRACTICE AREAS:*** General Civil Law; Criminal Trial Law; Estate Planning; Real Estate. ***Email:*** adleratty@aol.com

ALEXANDER L. ROGERS

REFERENCES: Bank One, Indianapolis; NBD National Bank, Indianapolis; National City Bank, Indianapolis.

JAMES DORR BABCOCK, P.C.

500 BARRISTER BUILDING
155 EAST MARKET STREET
INDIANAPOLIS, INDIANA 46204
Telephone: 317-634-0229
FAX: 317-637-1901

Probate, Wills, Trusts and Estates, Estate Planning, Guardianships, Commercial Law, Commercial and Consumer Collections, Bankruptcy Law, Family Law, Child Custody, Child Support, Business and Corporate Law, Real Estate, Foreclosures, Banking, Finance.

FIRM PROFILE: After several years experience with an Indianapolis firm, James Dorr Babcock established a sole practice with the goal of offering personal attention to clients of all sizes. Since that time, Mr. Babcock has expanded to serve throughout the Central Indiana area. Special areas of concentration include probate and estate planning, family and domestic relations law, real estate, collections, as well as business law.

After 13 years as a staff attorney with an Indianapolis bank, Steven L. Yount now offers his services to a variety of financial institutions. His practice devotes a substantial amount of time to commercial and consumer loan collections and litigation, bankruptcies, and foreclosures.

JAMES DORR BABCOCK, born Indianapolis, Indiana, February 21, 1946; admitted to bar, 1971, Indiana, U.S. District Court, Southern and Northern Districts of Indiana and U.S. Tax Court. *Education:* Indiana University (B.S., 1968); City of London College, London, England; Indiana University (J.D., 1971). Deputy Marion County Prosecuting Attorney, 1972-1975. Member, Estate Planning Council of Indiana, 1982—. *Member:* Indianapolis (Vice President, 1994; Member, Sections on: Family Law, Corporate and Business Law; Estate Planning and Administrative Law; Exec. Comm. 1992-1994; Commercial and Bankruptcy Law) and Indiana State (Delegate, State Bar Convention, 1981-2005; Member, Sections on: Family; Probate, Trust, Real Property, Elder Law, Construction and Surety Law) Bar Associations. Distinguished Fellow, Indianapolis Bar Foundation.

STEVEN L. YOUNT, born Franklin, Indiana, May 27, 1956; admitted to bar, 1983, Indiana and U.S. District Court, Southern District of Indiana; 1985, U.S. District Court, Northern District of Indiana and U.S. Court of Appeals, Seventh Circuit. *Education:* University of the South; DePauw University (B.A., summa cum laude, 1978); Indiana University (J.D., cum laude, 1982). Phi Beta Kappa. *Member:* Indianapolis and Indiana State (Member, Sections on: Commercial Law; Bankruptcy) Bar Associations; Commercial Law League of America. Distinguished Fellow: Indianapolis Bar Foundation.

REPRESENTATIVE CLIENTS: Bright Sheet Metal Co., Inc.; Central Indiana Contracting; Central Supply Company, Inc.; G.M. Supply Company Inc.; Integrated Network Systems, Inc.; M.D. Rowe Construction, Inc.; Rowe & Campbell, Inc.; Union Planters, N.A.; Wesco Distribution, Inc.; PDS Studios, Inc.; Premier Credit of North America; Forum Credit Union; First Indiana Bank, N.A.; Star Financial Bank.

BACKER & BACKER

A PROFESSIONAL CORPORATION
Established in 1974
8710 NORTH MERIDIAN STREET
INDIANAPOLIS, INDIANA 46260
Telephone: 317-571-0500
Telecopier: 317-571-0700
Email: sabacker@backerlaw.com

Real Estate, Construction Law, Business Law and Commercial Law.

FIRM PROFILE: This Bar Register listed firm traces its history to 1974, when Stephen A. Backer joined his father Herbert J. Backer in the practice of law. Backer & Backer offers special expertise in the areas of real estate, construction, business and commercial law. The firm services are utilized nationwide.

HERBERT J. BACKER (1914-1995)

STEPHEN A. BACKER, born Indianapolis, Indiana, February 28, 1946; admitted to bar, 1971, Indiana. *Education:* Indiana University (B.S., 1968; J.D., 1971). Deputy Prosecuting Attorney, 1975-1978. Member: Indiana State Criminal Justice Institute; Juvenile Justice Task Force, 1990-1991; Indiana Lottery Commission, 1990-1997; Carmel/Clay Parks and Recreation Board, 1997-1998; Indiana Gambling Impact Commission, 1998-1999; Indiana University Board of Trustees, 1998-2004. Member, Community College Policy Committee, 1999-2004. Member, National Board of Visitors to the Indiana University School of Education, 1999—. Member, 1994-1998, President, 1994-1996, and Secretary, 1997-1998, Carmel/Clay Board of Education. Member, Central Indian Community Foundation - Legacy Fund, 2003—. *Member:* Indianapolis, Indiana State and American Bar Associations. ***PRACTICE AREAS:*** Real Estate Law; Construction Law; Corporate Law; Commercial Law; Commercial Transactions. ***Email:*** sabacker@backerlaw.com

A List of Representative Clients will be furnished upon request.
REFERENCE: Bank One, Indianapolis.

LAW OFFICE OF BARBARA J. BAIRD

445 N. PENNSYLVANIA STREET, SUITE 401
INDIANAPOLIS, INDIANA 46204
Telephone: 317-637-2345
Fax: 317-637-2369
Email: bjbaird@bjbairdlaw.com

Estate Planning, Adoption Law, Business Start-Ups, Labor Law, Employment Law.

BARBARA J. BAIRD, born Pittsburgh, Pennsylvania, 1950; admitted to bar, 1977, Indiana; U.S. Supreme Court; U.S. Court of Appeals, Seventh Circuit; U.S. District Court, Southern District of Indiana. *Education:* Allegheny College (B.A., 1972); Indiana University School of Law - Bloomington (J.D., 1977). *Member:* Indianapolis and Indiana State Bar Associations. ***PRACTICE AREAS:*** Estate Planning; Adoption Law; Cohabitation Agreements; Non-Traditional Family Law; Probate Administration; Estate Planning for Unmarried Couples; Living Trusts; Powers of Attorney; Wills; Premarital Agreements; Labor and Employment; Business Start-Ups.

BAKER & DANIELS LLP

Established in 1863
300 NORTH MERIDIAN STREET, SUITE 2700
INDIANAPOLIS, INDIANA 46204
Telephone: 317-237-0300
Fax: 317-237-1000
URL: http://www.bakerdaniels.com

Fort Wayne, Indiana Office: 111 East Wayne Street, Suite 800, 46802. Telephone: 260-424-8000. Fax: 260-460-1700.
South Bend, Indiana Office: First Bank Building, 205 West Jefferson Boulevard, Suite 250, 46601. Telephone: 574-234-4149. Fax: 574-239-1900.
Elkhart, Indiana Office: 317 West Franklin Street, P.O. Box 507, 46515-0507. Telephone: 574-296-6000. Fax: 574-296-6001.
Indianapolis-96th Street, Indiana Office: Parkwood Six, 600 East 96th Street, Suite 600, 46240. Telephone: 317-569-9600. Fax: 317-569-4800.
Washington, D.C. Office: 805 15th Street, N.W., Suite 700, 20005. Telephone: 202-312-7440. Fax: 202-312-7460.
Qingdao, China Office: 4/F, Office Tower, Crowne Plaza Qingdao, No. 76 Hong Kong Middle Road, 266071. Telephone: +011-86-532-575-1051. Fax: +011-86-532-575-1055.
Beijing, China Office: Room 1919, Tower 2, China World Trade Center, No. 1 JianGuoMenWai Avenue, 100004. Telephone: +86-10-6505-7733. Fax: +86-10-6505-8730.

Antitrust, Business Planning, Commercial, Financial and Bankruptcy, Corporate Finance, Education, Employee Benefits, Environment, Family Business, Federal, State and Local Tax, Food and Drug Law, Government Affairs, Health Care, Individual/Family, Estate and Probate, Insurance and Financial Services, Intellectual Property, International, Labor and Employment, Life Sciences, Litigation, Medical Technology Regulation, Municipal Law/Tax-Exempt Finance, Nonprofit, Product Liability, Real Estate/Land Use, Transportation, and Utilities.

FIRM PROFILE: Established in 1863, Baker & Daniels LLP serves the legal and business needs of clients around the world. From Fortune 500 corporations to regional businesses, local governments and individuals, clients look to Baker & Daniels LLP for excellence in all areas of legal practice, for a creative and individualized approach to solving client problems, and for a deep understanding of business, law and government. More than 375 Baker & Daniels' professionals serve clients from the firm's seven offices in Indiana, Washington, D.C. and China

(This Listing Continued)

(we are one of less than 40 U.S. law firms licensed to practice in China) and through the Baker & Daniels LLP family of affiliated companies: B&D Sagamore, federal government affairs consulting; B&D Quorum, grassroots advocacy; B&D Navigator, human resources and business consulting and training; Aventor, medical technology consulting from concept to market.

LAW FIRM ALLIANCES/ASSOCIATIONS: **LEX MUNDI:** *The firm is the exclusive Indiana member of Lex Mundi, a global association of 150 independent law firms.*

TAGLAW (The Appleton Group Legal Network): *The Firm is a member of TAGLaw, an international association of prominent law firms.*

MEMBERS OF FIRM

IRENE T. ADAMCZYK, born 1949; admitted to bar, 1982, Indiana. *Education:* Indiana University (A.B., 1971); Indiana University-Purdue University (M.P.A., 1977); Indiana University (J.D., summa cum laude, 1982). *Member:* Indianapolis and American Bar Associations. ***PRACTICE AREAS:*** Antitrust; Employee Benefits. ***Email:*** reni.adamczyk@bakerd.com

TERRILL D. ALBRIGHT, born 1938; admitted to bar, 1965, Indiana and U.S. District Court, Southern District of Indiana; 1972, U.S. Supreme Court; 1980, U.S. District Court, Northern District of Indiana; 1981, U.S. Court of Appeals, 7th Circuit; 1982, U.S. Court of Appeals, 3rd Circuit and U.S. District Court for the District of Columbia Circuit; 1990, U.S. District Court, Northern District of Illinois. *Education:* Indiana University (A.B., 1960; J.D., 1965). Articles Editor, Indiana Law Journal, 1964-1965. Member, Board of Visitors, Indiana University Law School, 1978-1979 and 1991-1994. President, Indiana Continuing Legal Education Forum, 1992-1993. Certified AAA Arbitrator for Construction, International and Large Complex Case Program. CPR Panel of Distinguished Neutrals. Certified Indiana Mediator. Member, Indiana University Law School Academy of Law Alumni Fellows, 2001.*Member:* Indianapolis (Vice President, 1990; Member, Board of Managers, 1984-1985 and 1989-1990), Indiana State (President, 1993-1994; Chairman, Young Lawyers Section, 1971-1972; Member, Board of Managers, 1971-1972; 1983-1985, 1992-1995), American (Member: Executive Council, National Conference of Bar Presidents, 1995-1998; House of Delegates, 1993-1995) and Seventh Circuit Bar Associations. Fellow: American College of Trial Lawyers; Indiana Bar Foundation; American Bar Foundation; Indianapolis Bar Foundation. ***PRACTICE AREAS:*** Business Law; Alternative Dispute Resolution; Construction Law; Litigation. ***Email:*** terry.albright@bakerd.com

JAMES A. ASCHLEMAN, born 1944; admitted to bar, 1969, Indiana. *Education:* Manchester College (B.A., summa cum laude, 1966); Harvard University (J.D., 1969). *Member:* Indianapolis, Indiana State and American Bar Associations. Fellow, Indiana Bar Foundation. ***PRACTICE AREAS:*** Securities; Corporate Law; Mergers and Acquisitions. ***Email:*** jim.aschleman@bakerd.com

PHILLIP E. BAINBRIDGE, born 1942; admitted to bar, 1968, Indiana and U.S. District Court, Northern District of Indiana. *Education:* Indiana University (B.S., 1964; J.D., 1968). Recipient, Sagamore of the Wabash, 1972, 1981 and 1996. Instructor: Labor Law, 1973 and Business Law, 1974, Purdue University. Indiana State Representative, 1968-1978 and Speaker, Indiana House of Representatives, 1975-1976. Chairman, Lex Mundi Government Affairs Committee, 1996-1998. Honorary Consul, United Kingdom - Honorary Consulate, 2002—. ***PRACTICE AREAS:*** Government Services. ***Email:*** phillip.bainbridge@bakerd.com

LEWIS D. BECKWITH, born 1948; admitted to bar, 1973, Indiana. *Education:* Wabash College (B.A., 1970); Vanderbilt University (J.D., 1973). Order of the Coif. Articles Editor, Vanderbilt Law Review, 1972-1973. Listed in: "Who's Who in America"; "Who's Who in American Law." *Member:* Indianapolis, Indiana State (Member, Committees on Environmental Law and Labor Law) and American (Member: Section on Natural Resources Law; Labor Law-Subcommittee on Occupational Safety and Health Law) Bar Associations. ***PRACTICE AREAS:*** Environmental Law; Occupational Safety and Health; Administrative Law. ***Email:*** lew.beckwith@bakerd.com

BEN W. BLANTON, born 1956; admitted to bar, 1982, Indiana. *Education:* St. Meinrad College; Memphis State University (B.A., summa cum laude, 1979); Vanderbilt University (J.D., 1982). Order of the Coif. Founders Medalist. Law Clerk to Judge Gerald W. Heaney, U.S. Court of Appeals, Eighth Circuit, 1982-1984. ***PRACTICE AREAS:*** Nonprofit Law; Charitable Giving. ***Email:*** ben.blanton@bakerd.com

ELLEN E. BOSHKOFF, born 1960; admitted to bar, 1992, Indiana. *Education:* Swarthmore College (B.A., with high honors, 1983); Indiana University (J.D., summa cum laude, 1990). Order of the Coif; Order of the Barristers. Articles Editor, Indiana Law Journal. Law Clerk, Judge J. Clifford Wallace, U.S. Court of Appeals for the Ninth Circuit, 1990-1991. ***PRACTICE AREAS:*** Litigation; Employment Law; Products Liability. ***Email:*** ellen.boshkoff@bakerd.com

BRIAN K. BURKE, born 1948; admitted to bar, 1973, Wisconsin; 1978, Indiana. *Education:* Vanderbilt University (B.A., magna cum laude, 1970; J.D., 1973). Phi Eta Sigma; Phi Beta Kappa; Order of the Coif. Managing Editor, Vanderbilt Law Review, 1972-1973. *Member:* Indianapolis, Indiana State and American Bar Associations. [JAGC, USNR, 1974-1978]. ***PRACTICE AREAS:*** Employment Law Counseling and Litigation; Products Liability Litigation; Intellectual Property Litigation. ***Email:*** brian.burke@bakerd.com

H. PATRICK CALLAHAN, born 1947; admitted to bar, 1972, Indiana. *Education:* Indiana University (B.A., 1969); University of Michigan (J.D., 1972). *Member:* Indiana State and American (Member, Section on Corporate Law) Bar Associations. ***PRACTICE AREAS:*** Corporate Law. ***Email:*** pat.callahan@bakerd.com

JAMES M. CARR, born 1950; admitted to bar, 1975, Indiana. *Education:* Indiana University (B.A., 1972; J.D., magna cum laude, 1975). Order of the Coif. Co-Author: "A Guide for Bankers to the Bankruptcy Reform Act of 1978," 1979. Listed in: Best Lawyers in America, Bankruptcy Law Section, 1989—. *Member:* Indianapolis (Chairman, Commercial and Bankruptcy Law Section, 1987-1988), Indiana State (Chairman, Bankruptcy and Creditors Rights Section, 1986-1987) and American Bar Associations; American Bankruptcy Institute. Fellow, American College of Bankruptcy, 2003. ***PRACTICE AREAS:*** Business Bankruptcy; Reorganizations; Commercial Law; Creditors Rights; Commercial Litigation. ***Email:*** jim.carr@bakerd.com

(This Listing Continued)

AMIE PEELE CARTER, born 1970; admitted to bar, 1996, Indiana and U.S. District Court, Northern and Southern Districts of Indiana. *Education:* Millsaps College (B.A., Philosophy, magna cum laude, 1992); Emory University (J.D., 1996). Phi Beta Kappa. Member, Moot Court Society, 1996. ***PRACTICE AREAS:*** Intellectual Property. ***Email:*** amie.carter@bakerd.com

R. TREVOR CARTER, born 1968; admitted to bar, 1995, Indiana; U.S. District Court, Southern and Northern Districts of Indiana; U.S. Court of Appeals for the Federal Circuit; registered to practice before U.S. Patent and Trademark Office. *Education:* Purdue University (B.S.M.E., 1991); Indiana University School of Law (J.D., summa cum laude, 1995). Associate Editor, Indiana Law Review. Intern, The Honorable John D. Tinder, United States District Court, Southern District of Indiana. *Member:* Indianapolis, Indiana and American Bar Associations; American Intellectual Property Association. ***PRACTICE AREAS:*** Intellectual Property. ***Email:*** trevor.carter@bakerd.com

A. SCOTT CHINN, born 1968; admitted to bar, 1994, Indiana. *Education:* Indiana University (B.A., 1991); Indiana University School of Law (J.D., magna cum laude, 1994). Sagamore of the Wabash, 2005. Listed in: National Register's Who's Who, 2005-2006; Indianapolis Business Journal's Who's Who in Law, 2002; Indianapolis Business Journal "Forty Under Forty," 2003. Indiana Superlawyer, 2004, 2005. Law Clerk, Hon. David F. Hamilton, District Judge, U.S. District Court, Southern District of Indiana. Editor-in-Chief, Indiana International & Comparative Law Review, 1994. Co-Instructor, "Criminal Prosecution in America: From Salem to Starr," Indiana University School of Public and Environmental Affairs. Adjunct Legal Writing Professor, Indiana University School of Law, Indianapolis, 1999. Contributing Editor, "Discovering the Impact of the 'New Federalism' on State Policy Makers: A State Attorney General's Perspective," 32 Ind. L. Rev. 141, 1998. Author: "The Role of Indiana's State and Federal Courts in Legislative Redistricting," 1962-2003, 37 Ind. L. Rev. 643, 2004; "American Labor Law on Foreign Soil, Policies and Effects in a Smaller World," 3 Ind. Int' l & Comp. L. Rev. 291, 1993. President, Indiana Municipal Lawyers Association, 2005—. Counsel to Indianapolis Mayor Bart Peterson, 2004-2005. Corporation Counsel, City of Indianapolis, 2000-2004. Special Counsel to Attorney General of Indiana, 1997-1999. *Member:* Indianapolis, Seventh Circuit, Indiana and American Bar Associations; U.S. Supreme Court Historical Society. ***REPORTED CASES:*** Peterson v. Borst, 786 N.E.2d 668 (Ind. 2003); SGB Financial Services, Inc. v. Consolidated City of Indianapolis-Marion County, Indiana, 235 F.3d 1036 (7th Cir. 2000); Gresham v. Peterson, 225 F.3d 899 (7th Cir. 2000); City of Indianapolis v. Edmond, 531 U.S. 32 (2000); Nass v. State ex rel. Unity Team, Local 9212, International Union, United Automobile, Aerospace and Agricultural Implement Workers of America (UAW), 718 N.E.2d 757 (Ind. App. 1999); Myers v. State, 714 N.E.2d 276 (Ind. App. 1999); Martin v. Carraway, 712 N.E.2d 1055 (Ind. App. 1999); State ex rel. Indiana State Bd. of Tax Com'rs v. Indiana Chamber of Commerce, Inc., 712 N.E.2d 992 (Ind. App. 1999); Indiana State Highway Com'n v. Curtis, 704 N.E.2d 1015 (Ind. 1998); State v. Mohler, 694 N.E.2d 1129 (Ind. 1998). ***PRACTICE AREAS:*** Business Litigation. ***Email:*** scott.chin@bakerd.com

ELIZABETH KELLEY CIERZNIAK, born 1957; admitted to bar, 1995, Indiana. *Education:* Butler University (B.S., cum laude, 1979); Indiana University, Indianapolis (J.D., summa cum laude, 1995). *Member:* Indiana State Bar Association. ***PRACTICE AREAS:*** Government Affairs. ***Email:*** libby.cierzniak@bakerd.com

STEPHEN A. CLAFFEY, born 1945; admitted to bar, 1971, Indiana. *Education:* Wabash College (A.B., 1967); Washington University (J.D., 1971). Order of the Coif. Note and Comment Editor, Washington University Law Quarterly, 1970-1971. Law Clerk to Chief Justice Lewis, Indiana Supreme Court, 1968. Member, Board of Directors, Indiana Association for Corporate Renewal, 2000—. *Member:* Indianapolis, Indiana State and American Bar Associations. ***PRACTICE AREAS:*** Commercial Finance; Secured Finance; Creditors Rights; Bankruptcy; Corporate Law. ***Email:*** steve.claffey@bakerd.com

JAMES W. CLARK, born 1959; admitted to bar, 1987, Indiana. *Education:* Indiana University (B.A., 1982); University of Michigan (J.D., 1985). Associate and Contributing Editor, Michigan Law Review, 1983-1985. ***PRACTICE AREAS:*** Litigation; Environmental Law. ***Email:*** jim.clark@bakerd.com

MARY BETH CLAUS, born 1960; admitted to bar, 1986, Indiana. *Education:* University of Cincinnati (B.A., Political Science, magna cum laude, 1982); Indiana University (J.D., summa cum laude, 1986). Executive Assistant for Health & Human Services for Governor Evan Bayh, 1991-1993. *Member:* American Health Lawyers Association. ***PRACTICE AREAS:*** Health Care; Insurance; Litigation. ***Email:*** mary.claus@bakerd.com

SHAUN HEALY CLIFFORD, born 1960; admitted to bar, 1985, District of Columbia; 1995, Indiana. *Education:* University of Dayton (B.S., cum laude, 1982); Indiana University School of Law (J.D., magna cum laude, 1985). Recipient: Theodore Englehart Memorial Fellowship; Harold Woodward Fellowship. Recipient, Nathan Mendanhall Award. Articles Editor, Indiana Law Review, 1984-1985. Author: "The Alien's Burden of Proof Under Section 243(h): How Clear is Clear Probability?" Indiana Law Review, 1985. *Member:* District of Columbia Bar; American Bar Association; International Association of Insurance Receivers. ***PRACTICE AREAS:*** Insurance Insolvency; Insurance Regulation; Corporate Insurance. ***Email:*** shaun.clifford@bakerd.com

GREGORY N. DALE, born 1960; admitted to bar, 1986, Indiana, U.S. District Court, Northern and Southern Districts of Indiana and U.S. Court of Appeals, Seventh Circuit. *Education:* Indiana University (B.S., 1982; J.D., 1986). Certified Public Accountant, Indiana, 1989. ***PRACTICE AREAS:*** Employment Law. ***Email:*** gregory.dale@bakerd.com

MIRIAM SMULEVITZ DANT, born 1962; admitted to bar, 1987, Indiana. *Education:* Indiana University (B.S., with high distinction, 1984); University of Illinois (J.D., magna cum laude, 1987). Recipient, "Influential Women in Indianapolis" Award. Counsel to Secretary of State, 1990-1991. Indiana Securities Commissioner, 1991-1993. Executive Assistant to the Governor for Environmental and Utility Affairs, 1993-1997. Indianapolis Business Journal 40 under Forty. ***PRACTICE AREAS:*** Government Affairs; Government Agency Practice; Government Procurement; Environmental Law. ***Email:*** miriam.dant@bakerd.com

FRANCINA A. DLOUHY, born 1952; admitted to bar, 1977, Indiana and U.S. District Court, Southern District of Indiana. *Education:* Hiram College (B.A., summa cum laude, 1974); Indiana University (J.D., summa cum laude, 1977). Phi Beta Kappa; Order of the Coif. *Member:* Indianapolis, Indiana State and American Bar Associations. ***PRACTICE AREAS:*** Taxation; Administrative Law. ***Email:*** francina.dlouhy@bakerd.com

(This Listing Continued)

BAKER & DANIELS LLP, Indianapolis—Continued

KEVIN R. ERDMAN, born 1963; admitted to bar, 1987, California, Indiana, U.S. District Court, Northern District of Indiana, U.S. District Court, Northern District of California and U.S. Court of Appeals, Ninth Circuit; 1988, Pennsylvania; 1990, U.S. Court of Appeals, Federal Circuit; 1994, U.S. District Court, Southern District of Indiana; registered to practice before U.S. Patent and Trademark Office. *Education:* Indiana University (B.S., Computer Science, 1984); University of Pennsylvania (J.D., 1987). Member: Indiana Business Modernization and Technology Corporation, Software Technology and Artificial Intelligence Committee, 1988—; Indiana University Honors College Board of Alumni Advisors, 1989—; Dave Hefner Foundation Board, 1996—. Speaker for NBI, CLA, Indiana University Law School for Computer Law/Internet Law Classes/CLE, 1999—. *Member:* Computer Law Association; Indiana Information Technology Association (INITA). ***PRACTICE AREAS:*** Intellectual Property; Computer Law; Internet Law. ***Email:*** kevin.erdman@bakerd.com

THEODORE J. ESPING, born 1949; admitted to bar, 1975, New York; 1978, Indiana. *Education:* University of Florida (B.S., magna cum laude, 1971); Duke University (J.D., 1974); New York University (LL.M., Taxation, 1977). Certified Public Accountant, New York, 1976. *Member:* Indianapolis and Indiana State Bar Associations. ***PRACTICE AREAS:*** Federal Taxation; Municipal Law. ***Email:*** theodore.esping@bakerd.com

RICHARD T. FREIJE, JR., born 1958; admitted to bar, 1984, Indiana. *Education:* Purdue University (B.S.E., 1981); Indiana University (J.D., magna cum laude, 1984). Order of the Coif. Associate Note Editor, Indiana Law Journal, 1982-1983. Member and Secretary, Purdue Acacia Chapter Alumni Board, 1987-1992. St. Luke's United Methodist Church Board of Trustees, 1990-1992. Senior Vice President and Chief Administrative and Legal Officer, Indianapolis Life Insurance Company, 2000-2001. Board Member and Head Coach, Lawrence Township Boys Basketball League, 2003—. *Member:* Indianapolis, Indiana State and American Bar Associations. ***PRACTICE AREAS:*** Insurance Corporate Law; Insurance Regulation; Insurance Insolvency; Health Care Corporate Law; Health Care Regulation. ***Email:*** dick.freije@bakerd.com

THOMAS C. FROEHLE JR., born 1963; admitted to bar, 1988, Indiana. *Education:* Indiana University (B.A., high honors, 1985); University of Michigan (J.D., cum laude, 1988). Phi Beta Kappa. *Member:* Indianapolis, Indiana State and American Bar Associations; National Association of Bond Lawyers. ***PRACTICE AREAS:*** Business Law; Corporate Law; Municipal Finance. ***Email:*** tom.froehle@bakerd.com

CHIP GARVER, born 1968; admitted to bar, 1993, Indiana and Ohio (inactive). *Education:* Miami University (B.S., Business, 1990); University of Toledo (J.D., 1993). ***PRACTICE AREAS:*** Governmental Affairs. ***Email:*** chip.garver@bakerd.com

RONALD D. GIFFORD, born 1958; admitted to bar, 1985, California; 1986, Indiana. *Education:* University of Michigan (B.A., with distinction, 1981); Georgetown University (J.D., magna cum laude, 1985). Articles Editor, Georgetown Law Journal, 1984-1985. Indiana House of Representatives, Majority Attorney, 1991-1992, Parliamentarian, 1993-1994. Member, Indiana Code Revision Commission, 1994-1995. ***PRACTICE AREAS:*** Government Services Law. ***Email:*** ron.gifford@bakerd.com

DAVID A. GIVEN, born 1962; admitted to bar, 1987, Texas; 1991, Indiana. *Education:* University of Illinois (A.B., summa cum laude, 1984; J.D., summa cum laude, 1987). Phi Beta Kappa; Order of the Coif. Member, University of Illinois Law Review. Certified Public Accountant, Illinois, 1984. *Member:* Indianapolis, Indiana State and American and Seventh Circuit Bar Associations; State Bar of Texas; Indiana CPA Society. ***PRACTICE AREAS:*** Labor and Employment; Litigation. ***Email:*** david.given@bakerd.com

G. FREDERICK GLASS, born 1959; admitted to bar, 1984, Indiana, U.S. District Court, Northern and Southern Districts of Indiana and U.S. Court of Appeals, Seventh Circuit. *Education:* Indiana University (B.A., 1981; J.D., cum laude, 1984). Associate Editor, Indiana Law Review, 1983-1984. Law Clerk to Honorable S. Hugh Dillin, U.S. District Court, Southern District of Indiana, 1984-1986. Chairman, Baker & Daniels Management Committee, 2001-present. President, Capital Improvement Board of Managers of Marion County, 2000-present. Indianapolis Business Journal's 20 Most Influential City Leaders, 2003. Indianapolis Business Journal's Who's Who in Law, 2002. Indianapolis Star's 25 Most Influential People on Sports in Central Indiana, 2002. Chairman, Mayor-elect Peterson Transition Team, 1999-2000. Indiana Chairman, Clinton/Gore '96. Executive Assistant and Chief of Staff, Governor Evan Bayh, 1989-1993. ***PRACTICE AREAS:*** Business Law. ***Email:*** fred.glass@bakerd.com

KEVIN P. GRIFFITH, born 1961; admitted to bar, 1990, Indiana. *Education:* Purdue University (B.S.E.E., 1987); Indiana University (J.D., magna cum laude, 1990). Order of the Coif. Member, 1988-1989 and Managing Editor, 1989-1990, Indiana Law Journal. *Member:* Indiana State and American Bar Associations. ***PRACTICE AREAS:*** Insurance Insolvency; Insurance Regulation; Litigation; Mergers and Acquisitions. ***Email:*** kevin.griffith@bakerd.com

ERIC J. GROEN, born 1956; admitted to bar, 1985, Pennsylvania; 1999, Indiana and U.S. District Court, Northern District of Indiana; registered to practice before U.S. Patent and Trade mark Office. *Education:* Purdue University (B.S.M.E., 1978); Capital University (J.D., 1985). Order of the Curia. ***PRACTICE AREAS:*** Intellectual Property. ***Email:*** eric.groen@bakerd.com

PAUL LOWELL HAINES, born 1953; admitted to bar, 1990, Indiana. *Education:* Taylor University (B.A., 1975); Ball State University (M.A., 1977); Indiana University (J.D., cum laude, 1990). Partner, 1999— and Associate, 1990-1998, Baker & Daniels. Member, Board of Trustees, Taylor University, 2002—. Member, Executive Board and Board of Governors, Heartland Film Festival, 1994—. Editor-in-Chief, 1989-1990, and Member, 1988-1989, Indiana Law Journal. Vice President for Student Development, 1985-1987, Dean of Students, 1983-1985, Director of Student Programs, 1980-1983 and Residence Hall Director, 1977-1980, Taylor University. Author of numerous published articles addressing tax-exempt organization and higher education issues. Presenter at numerous seminars, conferences and meetings on topics addressing various tax exempt organization and higher education issues. Recipient, Indiana Bar Foundation Scholarship. Newsletter Editor, The Christian College Legal Counselor. Listed in: Outstanding Young Men in America, 1985; Who's Who in Religion, 1985. ***PRACTICE AREAS:*** Tax-Exempt Organizations; College and University Law. ***Email:*** lowell.haines@bakerd.com

JAMES H. HAM, III, born 1950; admitted to bar, 1975, Indiana and U.S. District Court, Southern District of Indiana; 1982, U.S. District Court, Northern District of Indiana and U.S. Court of Appeals, 7th Circuit. *Education:* Purdue University (B.S., 1972); Northwestern University (J.D., cum laude, 1975). Phi Beta Kappa. *Member:* Indianapolis, Indiana State (Sections on: Litigation; Business Law; Appellate Practice; Public Utility Law), American (Member, Sections on: Antitrust, Business Law; Litigation; Public Utility Law) and Seventh Circuit Bar Associations. Bencher, Sagamore American Inn of Court (Treasurer). ***PRACTICE AREAS:*** Litigation; Securities; Antitrust; Trademarks; Utility Law. ***Email:*** jay.ham@bakerd.com

DAVID R. HAMER, born 1945; admitted to bar, 1971, Indiana, U.S. District Court, Southern and Northern Districts of Indiana and U.S. Court of Appeals, Seventh Circuit. *Education:* Indiana University (A.B., 1967; J.D., 1971). Phi Alpha Delta. Vice President and Senior Counsel, Bank One, Indianapolis, NA, 1971-1987. Senior Vice President and General Counsel, Banc One Indiana Corporation, 1994-1996. ***PRACTICE AREAS:*** Banking Law; Creditors Rights; Bankruptcy; Commercial Litigation. ***Email:*** dave.hamer@bakerd.com

PETER L. HATTON, born 1948; admitted to bar, 1974, District of Columbia and U.S. Court of Appeals, District of Columbia Circuit; 1975, U.S. Court of Appeals, Fifth Circuit; 1980, Indiana, U.S. District Court, Northern District of Indiana and U.S. Court of Appeals, Seventh Circuit. *Education:* Wabash College (B.A., 1970); Indiana University School of Law (J.D., 1973). *Member:* Indiana State (Member, Utility Law Section) and American Bar Associations. ***PRACTICE AREAS:*** Litigation; Utility. ***Email:*** peter.hatton@bakerd.com

DAVID K. HERZOG, born 1955; admitted to bar, 1980, Indiana; U.S. District Court, Southern District of Indiana; U.S. District Court, Western District of Pennsylvania; U.S. Court of Appeals, Sixth and Seventh Circuits. *Education:* Wabash College (A.B., summa cum laude, 1977); Vanderbilt University (J.D., 1980). Phi Beta Kappa; Order of the Coif. Member, Vanderbilt Law Review. Executive Vice President, General Counsel and Secretary, Conseco, Inc., September, 2000-February, 2003. Managing Partner, Baker & Daniels, Indianapolis Office, January, 1998-August, 2000. *Member:* Indianapolis, Seventh Circuit, Indiana State and American Bar Associations. ***PRACTICE AREAS:*** Litigation. ***Email:*** david.herzog@bakerd.com

SCOTT D. HIMSEL, born 1962; admitted to bar, 1989, Indiana and U.S. District Court, Southern and Northern Districts of Indiana; 1994, U.S. Court of Appeals, Seventh Circuit. *Education:* Wabash College (A.B., summa cum laude, 1985); Northwestern University (J.D., cum laude, 1988). Phi Beta Kappa. Coordinating Articles Editor, Journal of Criminal Law and Criminology. Law Clerk, Hon. S. Hugh Dillin, U.S. District Court, Southern District of Indiana, 1988-1990. *Member:* Indianapolis, Indiana State, Seventh Circuit and American Bar Associations. ***PRACTICE AREAS:*** Litigation. ***Email:*** scott.himsel@bakerd.com

EDWARD E. HOLLIS, III, born 1972; admitted to bar, 1996, Indiana and U.S. District Court, Northern and Southern Districts of Indiana; 1997, U.S. Court of Appeals, Seventh Circuit; 2001, U.S. Supreme Court; 2002, U.S. Court of Appeals, Fourth Circuit. *Education:* Taylor University (B.A., summa cum laude, 1993); Indiana University (J.D., magna cum laude, 1996). ***PRACTICE AREAS:*** Employment. ***Email:*** edward.hollis@bakerd.com

JOHN S. KEELER, born 1949; admitted to bar, 1977, Indiana and U.S. District Court, Southern District of Indiana. *Education:* University of Arizona (B.S., Business Administration, 1971); Indiana University School of Law (J.D., cum laude, 1977). Indiana House of Representatives, 1982-1998. [Capt., U.S. Marine Corps, 1971-1974]. ***PRACTICE AREAS:*** Government Affairs. ***Email:*** john.keeler@bakerd.com

TIBOR D. KLOPFER, born 1954; admitted to bar, 1979, Indiana. *Education:* Indiana University (B.A., with distinction, 1976); University of Chicago (J.D., 1979). *Member:* Indianapolis, Indiana State and American Bar Associations. ***PRACTICE AREAS:*** Corporate Insurance; Securities; Corporate Law. ***Email:*** tibor.klopfer@bakerd.com

AMY E. KOSNOFF, born 1965; admitted to bar, 1991, Indiana. *Education:* Albion College (B.A., magna cum laude, with honors, 1988); University of Michigan (J.D., cum laude, 1991). Phi Beta Kappa. ***PRACTICE AREAS:*** Municipal Law; Tax-Exempt Finance. ***Email:*** amy.kosnof@bakerd.com

SCOTT M. KOSNOFF, born 1963; admitted to bar, 1988, Indiana. *Education:* Indiana University (B.S., with highest distinction, 1985); University of Michigan (J.D., magna cum laude, 1988). Order of the Coif. *Member:* American Bar Association (Chair, Public Regulation of Insurance Law Committee); Federation of Regulatory Counsel. ***PRACTICE AREAS:*** Insurance Corporate Law; Insurance Regulation; Insurance Insolvency. ***Email:*** scott.kosnoff@bakerd.com

THOMAS A. LADD, born 1947; admitted to bar, 1974, Michigan; 2004, Indiana; registered to practice before U.S. Patent and Trademark Office. *Education:* University of Michigan (B.S.E., 1970); University of Detroit (J.D., 1973). *Member:* American Bar Association; American Intellectual Property Association; American Chemical Society. ***PRACTICE AREAS:*** Intellectual Property. ***Email:*** thomas.ladd@bakerd.com

JON B. LARAMORE, born 1957; admitted to bar, 1984, Massachusetts; 1993, Indiana. *Education:* Princeton University (A.B., 1979); Harvard Law School (J.D., 1983). Wasserstein Fellow, Harvard Law School, 2003. Law Clerk, U.S. District Judge S. Hugh Dillin, 1983-1984. Chief Counsel, Indiana Attorney General, 1994-2001. Counsel: Governor Frank O'Bannon, 2002-2003; Governor Joseph Kernan, 2003-2005. Adjunct Professor, Indiana University School of Law, 2002—. *Member:* Indianapolis and Indiana State (Chair, Appellate Praction Section, 2001-2002) Bar Associations. ***PRACTICE AREAS:*** Business Litigation. ***Email:*** jon.laramore@bakerd.com

MARY KATHERINE LISHER, born 1950; admitted to bar, 1975, Indiana. *Education:* Vanderbilt University (B.A., cum laude, 1972); Indiana University (J.D., summa cum laude, 1975). Order of the Coif. *Member:* Indianapolis (Member, Business Law Section) and American (Member, Real Property, Probate and Trust Law Section) Bar Associations. ***PRACTICE AREAS:*** Real Estate Law. ***Email:*** mary.lisher@bakerd.com

(This Listing Continued)

JI-QING LIU, born 1956; admitted to bar, 1992, Indiana and U.S. District Court, Northern and Southern Districts of Indiana. *Education:* Shanghai Customs Academy, Shanghai, P.R. China (B.A., third in class, 1983); East China Institute of Politics and Law, P.R. China (Master of Laws, third in class, 1987); Columbia University (LL.M., 1989); Indiana University (J.D., 1992). Author: Anthology of Law Graduate Student Thesis, Vol. I, II (1984-1985, 1985-1986). (Also at 96th St., Indianapolis, Indiana, Qingdao and Beijing, China Offices). ***PRACTICE AREAS:*** International Law; Corporate Law; Immigration. ***Email:*** ji-qing.liu@bakerd.com

CHRISTINE GRAFFIS LONG, born 1970; admitted to bar, 1995, Indiana and U.S. District Court, Northern and Southern Districts of Indiana. *Education:* Washington University (B.A., with distinction, 1992); Indiana University School of Law (J.D., magna cum laude, 1995). Phi Beta Kappa; Order of the Coif. ***PRACTICE AREAS:*** Corporate; Securities. ***Email:*** christine.long@bakerd.com

HEATHER L. MACDOUGALL, born 1969; admitted to bar, 1994, Wisconsin, U.S. District Court, Eastern District of Wisconsin and U.S. Court of Appeals, Seventh Circuit; 1997, U.S. District Court, Western District of Wisconsin; 1998, Virginia; 1999, U.S. Court of Appeals, Sixth and the District of Columbia Circuits; 2000, U.S. Court of Appeals, Third Circuit and U.S. Supreme Court (Not admitted in Indiana). *Education:* University of Wisconsin (B.A., Political Science, 1991); Marquette University School of Law (J.D., 1994). Member, Marquette Law Review, Marquette University. Legal Counsel and Special Advisor to the Chairman, U.S. Occupational Safety and Health Review Commission, Washington, D.C., 2002-2003; Associate General Counsel, LPA, Inc., Washington, D.C., 1999-2002. Member, U.S. Chamber of Commerce Labor Relations Advisory Committee. *Member:* State Bar of Wisconsin (Member, Labor and Employment Law Section); Virginia Bar Association (Member, Labor Relations and Employment Law Section); American Bar Association (Member, Section on Labor and Employment Law). ***PRACTICE AREAS:*** Labor and Employment Law. ***Email:*** heather.macdougall@bakerd.com

MICHAEL J. MACLEAN, born 1965; admitted to bar, 1990, Indiana and U.S. District Court, Northern and Southern Districts of Indiana; 1991, U.S. Court of Appeals, 7th Circuit. *Education:* Purdue University (B.S., 1987); Indiana University (J.D., magna cum laude, 1990). Order of the Coif. Member, 1988-1989 and Senior Managing Editor, 1989-1990, Indiana Law Journal. Law Clerk to the Hon. Michael S. Kanne, U.S. Court of Appeals, Seventh Circuit, 1990-1991. *Member:* Indianapolis, Indiana State and American Bar Associations. ***PRACTICE AREAS:*** Employee Benefits; Labor and Employment. ***Email:*** michael.maclean@bakerd.com

MITZI HARRIS MARTIN, born 1947; admitted to bar, 1985, Indiana; 1989, U.S. Supreme Court. *Education:* Auburn University (B.S., cum laude, 1968); Indiana University (M.S., 1975; J.D., summa cum laude, 1985). Member, National Order of Barristers, 1985. Co-Author: "Sexual Harassment in the Workplace: U.S. Supreme Court's Premier Review," Res Gestae, Dec., 1986; "Survey of Recent Developments in Indiana Employment Law," Indiana Law Review, Vol. 24, Issue 3, June 1991. *Member:* Indianapolis (Member, Labor Law Section) and Indiana State Bar Associations. ***PRACTICE AREAS:*** Labor and Employment. ***Email:*** mitzi.martin@bakerd.com

BYRON K. MASON, born 1956; admitted to bar, 1982, Illinois and U.S. District Court, Northern District of Illinois; 1983, U.S. Court of Appeals, 7th Circuit; 1984, U.S. District Court, Northern District of Illinois including Trial Bar; 1988, Indiana and U.S. District Court, Southern District of Indiana. *Education:* Indiana University (B.A., 1978) Blue Key; Mortar Board (Officer); University of Iowa (J.D., 1981). Student Editor, Moot Court Board, 1980-1981. Law Clerk to Hon. John F. Grady, U.S. Federal District Court for the Northern District of Illinois, Eastern Division, 1980. *Member:* Indianapolis, Indiana State and American Bar Associations. ***PRACTICE AREAS:*** Products Liability; Commercial Litigation; Construction Litigation. ***Email:*** byron.mason@bakerd.com

ALAN L. MCLAUGHLIN, born 1957; admitted to bar, 1983, Indiana; U.S. District Court, Northern and Southern Districts of Indiana; 1984, U.S. Court of Appeals, 7th Circuit; 1994, U.S. Supreme Court. *Education:* Wabash College (A.B., summa cum laude, 1979); Vanderbilt University (J.D., 1982). Phi Beta Kappa. Patrick Wilson Scholar. Law Clerk To Judge Thomas A. Wiseman, Jr., U.S. District Court, Middle District of Tennessee, 1982-1983. *Member:* Indianapolis (Member: Litigation and Employment Law Sections), Indiana State (Past Chair, Litigation Section) and American (Member, Litigation and Employment Law Sections) Bar Associations. ***PRACTICE AREAS:*** Employment Litigation; Commercial Litigation. ***Email:*** alan.mclaughlin@bakerd.com

DAVID W. MILLER, born 1950; admitted to bar, 1977, Indiana and U.S. District Court, Southern District of Indiana; U.S. District Court, Northern District of Indiana; U.S. Court of Appeals, 4th, 5th, 6th, 7th and 10th Circuits. *Education:* Indiana University (A.B., 1971; J.D., summa cum laude, 1976). Listed in: Best Lawyers in America; Marquis' Who's Who in American Law. Field Examiner, National Labor Relations Board, Region 25, 1971-1976. ***PRACTICE AREAS:*** Employment Law. ***Email:*** david.miller@bakerd.com

JOSEPH E. MILLER, JR., born 1968; admitted to bar, 1995, Indiana and U.S. District Court, Northern and Southern Districts of Indiana. *Education:* Taylor University (B.A., summa cum laude, 1989); University of Denver (J.D., 1995). Order of St. Ives. Articles Editor, Denver University Law Review, 1994-1995. Author: "SEC v Peters: Stabilizing the Regulation of Tender Offer Insider Trading Without a Fiduciary Duty," 71 Denver University Law Review 783. ***PRACTICE AREAS:*** Nonprofit Organizations Law. ***Email:*** joseph.miller@bakerd.com

MARK S. MOORE, born 1957; admitted to bar, 1982, Indiana; 1986, District of Columbia;. *Education:* Wabash College (A.B., summa cum laude, 1979); Indiana University School of Law - Bloomington (J.D., cum laude, 1982). Director of Public Finance, State of Indiana, 2003-2005. Chairman, Indiana Transportation Finance Authority, 1990-1995; 2003-2005. Chairman, Indiana Board for Depositories, 2003-2005. Member, State Economic Development Cabinet, 1994-1995; 2003-2005. Special Liaison to Governor for Public Finance, 1990-1995. *Member:* The District of Columbia Bar; National Association of Bond Lawyers. ***PRACTICE AREAS:*** Business; Public Finance. ***Email:*** mark.moore@bakerd.com

JOHN T. NEIGHBOURS, born 1949; admitted to bar, 1974, Indiana; U.S. District Court, Northern and Southern Districts of Indiana; U.S. Court of Appeals, 7th Circuit; 1989, U.S. Supreme Court. *Education:* DePauw University (B.A., 1971); Indiana University (J.D., 1974). Editor, Indiana Law Letter, M. Lee Smith Publisher. *Member:* Indianapolis

(This Listing Continued)

(Labor Law Section), Indiana State (Labor Law Section) and American (Member, Section on Labor and Employment Law, Chair, Development of the Law Under the National Labor Relations Act Committee, 1997-1999; Management Editor-in-Chief, 1997-2000; Assistant Editor, 1995-1996 and Contributing Editor, 1989-1994, "Developing Labor Law," Labor and Employment Law Section) Bar Associations; College of Labor and Employment Law Lawyers. ***PRACTICE AREAS:*** Employment Law; Labor Law. ***Email:*** john.neighbours@bakerd.com

TIMOTHY E. NIEDNAGEL, born 1963; admitted to bar, 1989, Indiana; registered to practice before U.S. Patent and Trademark Office. *Education:* Purdue University (B.S.E.E., 1986); Indiana University School of Law (J.D., cum laude, 1989). *Member:* American Intellectual Property Law Association; TechPoint. ***PRACTICE AREAS:*** Intellectual Property. ***Email:*** tim.niednagel@bakerd.com

TODD M. NIERMAN, born 1961; admitted to bar, 1986, Indiana; U.S. District Court, Southern and Northern Districts of Indiana; U.S. Court of Appeals, 4th, 5th, 6th and 7th Circuits. *Education:* University of Michigan (B.B.A., with distinction, 1983); Vanderbilt University (J.D., 1986). Certified Public Accountant, Illinois, 1983. *Member:* American Bar Association (Member, Labor Section). ***PRACTICE AREAS:*** Employment Law. ***Email:*** todd.nierman@bakerd.com

ROBERT D. NULL, born 1965; admitted to bar, 1995, Indiana; registered to practice before U.S. Patent and Trademark Office. *Education:* Tri-State University (B.S.E.E., 1988); Valparaiso University School of Law (J.D., summa cum laude, 1995). Phi Kappa Theta (Former President). Editor-in-Chief, Valparaiso University Law Review. *Member:* Indiana State Bar Association. ***PRACTICE AREAS:*** Intellectual Property. ***Email:*** robert.null@bakerd.com

SHAUN HEALY O'BRIEN, born 1960; admitted to bar, 1985, District of Columbia; 1995, Indiana. *Education:* University of Dayton (B.S., cum laude, 1982); Indiana University at Indianapolis (J.D., magna cum laude, 1985). Articles Editor, Indiana Law Review, 1984-1985. Special Deputy Liquidator, Indiana Insurance Department, 1989-1990. ***PRACTICE AREAS:*** Insurance Insolvency; Insurance Regulation; Corporate Law. ***Email:*** shaun.obrien@bakerd.com

LAURA C. O'DONNELL, born 1971; admitted to bar, 1996, Indiana, U.S. District Courts, Northern and Southern Districts of Indiana and U.S. Court of Appeals, Seventh Circuit. *Education:* Michigan State University (B.A., cum laude, 1993); Indiana University School of Law (J.D., cum laude, 1996). Order of the Barristers. Recipient, Sherman Minton Moot Court Best Brief and Best Oralist Award. Senior Notes Editor, Federal Communications Law Journal. (Also at Fort Wayne Office). ***PRACTICE AREAS:*** Labor Relations; Employment Relations. ***Email:*** laura.o'donnell@bakerd.com

J. DANIEL OGREN, born 1952; admitted to bar, 1978, Indiana. *Education:* Oberlin College (A.B., 1975); University of Chicago (J.D., 1978). *Member:* Indianapolis, Indiana State and American Bar Associations. ***PRACTICE AREAS:*** Taxation; Administrative Law. ***Email:*** dan.ogren@bakerd.com

STEPHEN H. PAUL, born 1947; admitted to bar, 1972, Indiana and U.S. Court of Appeals, Seventh Circuit. *Education:* Indiana University (B.A., 1969; J.D., magna cum laude, 1972). Order of the Coif. Editor-in-Chief, Indiana Law Journal, 1971-1972. Listed in *Best Lawyers in America. Member:* Indianapolis, Indiana State (Member, Taxation Section) and American (Member, State and Local Tax Committee and Property Tax Subcommittee, Taxation Section, 1983-1988) Bar Associations; American Property Tax Counsel; Institute of Property Taxation. ***PRACTICE AREAS:*** Taxation; Sports Law; Corporate Law. ***Email:*** stephen.paul@bakerd.com

CARL R. PEBWORTH, born 1964; admitted to bar, 1991, Indiana. *Education:* Bowdoin College (A.B., summa cum laude, 1986); University of Michigan (J.D., 1991). Phi Beta Kappa; Phi Delta Phi. Recipient, Michigan State Bar Negligence Section Award. Member, Indianapolis Parks Foundation, 1999—. Member, Keep Indianapolis Beautiful, 1999—. Member, Mayor's Housing Taskforce, 1999—. *Member:* Indianapolis, Indiana State and American Bar Associations. ***PRACTICE AREAS:*** Commercial Litigation; Construction. ***Email:*** carl.pebworth@bakerd.com

HUDNALL A. PFEIFFER, born 1953; admitted to bar, 1983, Indiana and U.S. District Court, Northern and Southern Districts of Indiana; U.S. Supreme Court; U.S. Court of Appeals, Seventh Circuit and U.S. District Court, Eastern District of Michigan. *Education:* Indiana University (B.S., with distinction, 1976; M.S., 1979; J.D., summa cum laude, 1983). Edwards Fellowship (1982-1983). Member, 1984-1992 and President, 1989-1991, Pleasant Run Children's Home, Inc. Committee Member, Big Sisters of Indianapolis, Inc., 1993-1999. Member, Board of Directors, Training, Inc., 1994-1999. *Member:* Indianapolis (Member, Labor Section), Indiana State (Member, Labor Section) and American (Member, Labor Section) Bar Associations. ***PRACTICE AREAS:*** Employment Law; Public Sector Law. ***Email:*** hud.pfeiffer@bakerd.com

THOMAS A. PITMAN, born 1959; admitted to bar, 1985, Indiana. *Education:* Yale University (B.A., summa cum laude, 1981); Harvard University Law School (J.D., 1984). Phi Beta Kappa. Recipient, Warren Prize, Yale University, 1981. *Member:* Indianapolis, Indiana State and American Bar Associations; American Health Lawyers Association; National Association of Bond Lawyers. ***PRACTICE AREAS:*** Health Care; Tax-Exempt Finance; Municipal Law. ***Email:*** thomas.pitman@bakerd.com

JOHN W. PURCELL, born 1948; admitted to bar, 1976, Indiana. *Education:* Indiana State University (B.S., 1970); Indiana University (J.D., summa cum laude, 1976). Order of the Coif. *Member:* Indianapolis, Indiana State and American (Member: Taxation Section and Labor and Employment Section) Bar Associations. ***PRACTICE AREAS:*** Employee Benefits. ***Email:*** john.purcell@bakerd.com

ROBERTA SABIN RECKER, born 1943; admitted to bar, 1974, Pennsylvania; 1981, Indiana. *Education:* Westminster College (B.A., magna cum laude, 1964); Johns Hopkins University (M.L.A., magna cum laude, 1970); Dickinson School of Law (J.D., cum laude, 1974). ***PRACTICE AREAS:*** Employment Law; Litigation. ***Email:*** roberta.recker@bakerd.com

REBECCA A. RICHARDSON, born 1954; admitted to bar, 1982, Indiana. *Education:* Indiana University (B.A., cum laude, 1976; J.D., summa cum laude, 1982). *Member:*

(This Listing Continued)

BAKER & DANIELS LLP, Indianapolis—Continued

Indianapolis, Indiana State and American (Member, Consumer Financial Services Sub-Committee) Bar Associations. ***PRACTICE AREAS:*** Commercial Law; Commercial Finance; Consumer Finance. ***Email:*** rebecca.richardson@bakerd.com

ANDREA ROBERTS, born 1969; admitted to bar, 1995, Indiana. *Education:* Emporia State University (B.A., cum laude, 1991); University of Notre Dame (J.D., 1994). *Member:* Indianapolis, Indiana and American Bar Associations. ***PRACTICE AREAS:*** Products Liability Litigation; Commercial Litigation. ***Email:*** andrea.roberts@bakerd.com

MARK J. ROMANIUK, born 1966; admitted to bar, 1990, Indiana; 1995, U.S. Court of Appeals, Seventh Circuit; U.S. District Court, Northern and Southern Districts of Indiana. *Education:* Indiana University (B.S., 1987; J.D., cum laude, 1990). *Member:* Indianapolis, Indiana State and American Bar Associations. ***SPECIAL AGENCIES:*** Practice before all state and federal administrative agencies having jurisdiction over labor and employment matters. ***PRACTICE AREAS:*** Labor and Employment. ***Email:*** mark.romaniuk@bakerd.com

NORMAN P. ROWE, born 1938; admitted to bar, 1963, Indiana. *Education:* Wabash College (A.B., 1960); Harvard University; University of Edinburgh, Scotland; University of Michigan (LL.B., 1963). Law Clerk to Judge C. J. Holder, U.S. District Court for the Southern District of Indiana, 1963-1965. *Member:* Indianapolis, Indiana State, American and Seventh Circuit Bar Associations. ***PRACTICE AREAS:*** Civil Litigation. ***Email:*** norman.rowe@bakerd.com

CHRISTOPHER G. SCANLON, born 1945; admitted to bar, 1980, Indiana. *Education:* Columbia University (1963-1965); Indiana University (B.S., 1977; J.D., cum laude, 1980). Managing Editor, Indiana Law Journal, 1979-1980. *Member:* Indianapolis, Indiana State, American and Seventh Circuit Bar Associations. ***PRACTICE AREAS:*** Business Litigation. ***Email:*** chris.scanlon@bakerd.com

JOHN R. SCHAIBLEY, III, born 1953; admitted to bar, 1982, Illinois and U.S. District Court, Northern District of Indiana; 1983, U.S. Court of Appeals, 7th Circuit; 1985, Indiana and U.S. District Court, Southern District of Indiana; 1989, U.S. Supreme Court; 1994, U.S. Court of Appeals for the Federal Circuit. *Education:* Purdue University (B.A., 1975); Indiana University School of Law (J.D., summa cum laude, first in class, 1981). Order of the Coif; Order of Barristers. Recipient, American College of Trial Lawyers Medal for Excellence in Advocacy, National Moot Court Competition, 1981. Three Time Recipient, Hornbook Award, West Publishing Co. Four Time Recipient, American Jurisprudence Award. Executive Editor, Indiana Law Journal, 1980-1981. Law Clerk to: Justice John Paul Stevens, U.S. Supreme Court, 1983-1984; Judge Jesse E. Eschbach, Seventh Circuit Court of Appeals, 1981-1983; U.S. District Court, Northern District of Indiana, 1981. *Member:* Indiana State, Illinois State and Seventh Circuit Bar Associations; American Intellectual Property Law Association. ***PRACTICE AREAS:*** Intellectual Property Litigation; Commercial Litigation; Environmental Litigation. ***Email:*** john.schaibley@bakerd.com

FRED E. SCHLEGEL, born 1941; admitted to bar, 1966, Indiana. *Education:* Northwestern University (B.A., with honors, 1963); University of Michigan (J.D., with distinction, 1966). Order of the Coif. *Member:* Indianapolis, Indiana State, American and Federal Bar Associations. ***PRACTICE AREAS:*** Energy; Public Utility Law. ***Email:*** fred.schlegel@bakerd.com

GAYLE L. SKOLNIK, born 1956; admitted to bar, 1982, Indiana; U.S. District Court, Northern and Southern Districts of Indiana. *Education:* Indiana University (A.B., with highest distinction, 1979; J.D., summa cum laude, 1982). Order of the Coif. *Member:* Indianapolis and Indiana State Bar Associations. ***PRACTICE AREAS:*** Employee Benefits; Employment Law. ***Email:*** gayle.skolnik@bakerd.com

ANDREW Z. SOSHNICK, born 1962; admitted to bar, 1988, Indiana; U.S. District Court, Northern and Southern Districts of Indiana. *Education:* Northwestern University (B.A., with distinction, 1985; M.A., 1985; J.D., cum laude, 1988). Phi Beta Kappa; Order of the Coif. Member, Mortar Board. Listed in The Best Lawyers in America. Coordinating Note and Comment Editor, The Journal of Criminal Law and Criminology, 1987-1988. Author: "Valuing Business Goodwill in Marital Dissolution Actions: Boldly or Blindly Striving to Grab the Brass Ring from the Blue Sky?" Volume 39, Page 16, Res Gestae, 1995; "Indiana Family Law 1993: Much Ado About Some Things," Volume 27, No. 4, Indiana Law Review, 1994; "'Til Death Do Us Part...Baby, Check the Contract," Indiana State Bar Association, Family Matters, Winter 2003; "The Evolving World of Corporate Redemptions in Divorce Cases," Indiana State Bar Association, Family Matters, Winter 2001; Comment, "The Rape Shield Paradox: Complainant Protection Amidst Oscillating Trends of State Judicial Interpretation," Volume 78, Issue 3, The Journal of Criminal Law and Criminology, 1987. *Member:* Indianapolis, Indiana State and American Bar Associations; American Judicature Society. Fellow: American Academy of Matrimonial Lawyers; Indiana Bar Foundation; Indianapolis Bar Foundation. (Board Certified, Family Law Specialist, Indiana State Bar Association, Family Law Certification Board). ***PRACTICE AREAS:*** Family Law; Civil Litigation; Land Use. ***Email:*** drew.soshnick@bakerd.com

ROBERT K. STANLEY, born 1956; admitted to bar, 1981, Indiana and U.S. District Court, Southern District of Indiana; 1983, U.S. District Court, Northern District of Indiana; 1985, U.S. Court of Appeals, Seventh Circuit; 1987, U.S. Court of Appeals, Sixth Circuit; 1989, U.S. Supreme Court. *Education:* Ball State University (A.B., summa cum laude, 1978); Indiana University (J.D., summa cum laude, 1981). Order of the Coif. The Order of Barristers. Recipient: American College of Trial Lawyers Medal for Excellence in Advocacy, National Moot Court Competition, 1980-1981. *Member:* Seventh Circuit, Indiana State and American Bar Associations; Seventh Circuit Bar Association. ***PRACTICE AREAS:*** Antitrust; Trade Litigation; Trade Counseling; Trust Litigation; Estate Litigation; Business Litigation; Corporate Litigation. ***Email:*** robert.stanley@bakerd.com

THOMAS G. STAYTON, born 1948; admitted to bar, 1973, Indiana, U.S. District Court, Southern District of Indiana; 1977, U.S. Court of Appeals, Seventh Circuit; 1997, U.S. Court of Appeals, Third Circuit; 1998, U.S. Court of Appeals, Fourth Circuit. *Education:* Miami University (B.S., magna cum laude, 1970); University of Michigan (J.D., cum laude, 1973). Phi Beta Kappa; Omicron Delta Kappa; Phi Eta Sigma; Order of the Coif. Certified Mediator. *Member:* Indianapolis (Litigation Section), Indiana State (Litigation Section and Alternative Dispute Resolution Section), American (Litigation Section, Products Liability Committee) and Seventh Circuit Bar Associations; Product Liability Advisory Council. ***PRACTICE AREAS:*** Products Liability; Insurance Defense; Foreclosures; Litigation; Mediation. ***Email:*** tom.stayton@bakerd.com

JOHN B. SWARBRICK, JR., born 1954; admitted to bar, 1980, Indiana; 1982, U.S. Court of Appeals, 7th Circuit; 1984, U.S. Supreme Court; 1980, U.S. District Court, Southern District of Indiana. *Education:* University of Notre Dame (B.A., magna cum laude, 1976); Stanford University (J.D., 1980). Phi Beta Kappa. President and Chief Executive Officer, LMIV, LLC. Chairman, Indiana Sports Corporation. ***PRACTICE AREAS:*** Sports; Intellectual Property. ***Email:*** jack.swarbrick@bakerd.com

JOHN JOSEPH TANNER, born 1961; admitted to bar, 1987, Indiana and U.S. District Court, Northern and Southern Districts of Indiana; U.S. Court of Appeals, 7th Circuit. *Education:* Miami University (B.A., 1984); Indiana University School of Law - Indianapolis (J.D., summa cum laude, 1987); East China Institute of Politics and Law, Shanghai, China. Executive Editor, Indiana Law Review, 1986-1987. *Member:* Indianapolis, Indiana State, American and International Bar Associations. ***REPORTED CASES:*** Lytle v. Ford Motor Company, 814 N.E.2d 301 (Ind. Ct. App. 2004); American National Fire Ins. Co. v Rose Acre Farms, Inc., 107 F.3rd 451 (7th Cir. 1997); Hill's Pet Nutrition, Inc., v. Fru-Con Construction Corp, 101 F.3rd 63 (7th Cir. 1996). ***PRACTICE AREAS:*** Commercial Litigation; Products Liability; International Law; Insurance Coverage; Construction Law. ***Email:*** joe.tanner@bakerd.com

BRENT D. TAYLOR, born 1957; admitted to bar, 1982, Indiana. *Education:* Butler University (B.A., summa cum laude, with highest honors in Economics, 1979); Harvard University (J.D., 1982). Phi Kappa Phi. *Member:* Indianapolis (Litigation Section), Indiana State (Litigation Section) and American (Litigation Section) Bar Associations. ***PRACTICE AREAS:*** Business Litigation; Construction Litigation. ***Email:*** brent.taylor@bakerd.com

NANCY G. TINSLEY, born 1961; admitted to bar, 1990, Indiana; U.S. Court of Appeals, Seventh Circuit; registered to practice before U.S. Patent and Trademark Office. *Education:* Purdue University (B.S., 1982); Indiana University (J.D., cum laude, 1990). *Member:* Indianapolis (Member, Women in the Law Executive Committee), Indiana State (Chair, Civil Rights of Children Committee; Member, Women in the Law Committee), Seventh Circuit and American Bar Associations. ***PRACTICE AREAS:*** Litigation; Intellectual Property. ***Email:*** nancy.tinsley@bakerd.com

KEVIN M. TONER, born 1961; admitted to bar, 1986, Indiana; 2000, Arizona. *Education:* Indiana University (A.B., summa cum laude and departmental honors, 1983); Harvard Law School (J.D., 1986). Phi Beta Kappa. Assistant Editor, Harvard Environmental Law Review, 1985-1986. *Member:* American Bar Association; Seventh Circuit Bar Association; Indianapolis Bar Association; Defense Trial Counsel of Indiana; Defense Research Institute. ***PRACTICE AREAS:*** Complex and Multi-District Litigation; Litigation; Insurance; Computer Law; Internet Law. ***Email:*** kevin.toner@bakerd.com

GREGORY J. UTKEN, born 1949; admitted to bar, 1974, Indiana; 1975, Michigan; 1983, U.S. Supreme Court; U.S. Court of Appeals, 5th, 7th and District of Columbia Circuits; U.S. District Court, Northern and Southern Districts of Indiana, Eastern District of Michigan, Eastern District of Kentucky and Western and Eastern Districts of Arkansas. *Education:* Indiana University (A.B., 1971; J.D., magna cum laude, 1974). Chair, Labor and Employment Law Team. Note and Development Editor, Indiana Law Review, 1973-74. Frequent presentor of seminars on all aspects of labor and employment law for employers. President, Indiana University School of Law Indianapolis Alumni Association, 1984-1986. Former Member, Board of Visitors, Indiana University School of Law-Indianapolis. *Member:* Indiana State and American (Member, Sections on: Labor and Employment Law; Litigation) Bar Associations. ***PRACTICE AREAS:*** Labor Law; Employment Law. ***Email:*** greg.utken@bakerd.com

THOMAS A. VOGTNER, born 1949; admitted to bar, 1976, Indiana. *Education:* Spring Hill College (B.A., magna cum laude, 1971); University of Virginia (J.D., 1976). ***PRACTICE AREAS:*** Real Estate; Secured Lending; Construction Law. ***Email:*** tom.vogtner@bakerd.com

MARK A. VOIGTMANN, born 1956; admitted to bar, 1991, Indiana. *Education:* University of Missouri (B.J., 1978); Indiana University (J.D., magna cum laude, 1990). General Counsel: Control and Information Systems Integrators Association (CSIA); Indiana Subcontractors Association (ISA). *Member:* Indianapolis, Indiana State and American (Member, Forum on the Construction Industry) Bar Associations. ***PRACTICE AREAS:*** Construction Law; Construction Litigation; Real Estate Litigation; Business Litigation. ***Email:*** mark.voigtmann@bakerd.com

DAVID C. WORRELL, born 1951; admitted to bar, 1976, Indiana. *Education:* Wabash College (A.B., summa cum laude, 1973); University of Chicago (J.D., 1976). Phi Beta Kappa. "Best Lawyers in America" (Banking Law and Corporate Law). *Member:* American Bar Association. ***PRACTICE AREAS:*** Corporate Law; Securities; Financial Institutions Law. ***Email:*** david.worrell@bakerd.com

JOSEPH H. YEAGER, JR., born 1957; admitted to bar, 1983, Indiana; U.S. District Court, Northern and Southern Districts of Indiana; U.S. Court of Appeals, Seventh Circuit; U.S. Supreme Court. *Education:* Harvard University (B.A., cum laude, 1979); Indiana University (J.D., cum laude, 1983). *Member:* Indianapolis and Indiana State Bar Associations. ***PRACTICE AREAS:*** Litigation. ***Email:*** jay.yeager@bakerd.com

COUNSEL

VIRGIL L. BEELER, born 1931; admitted to bar, 1959, Indiana; U.S. District Court, Southern and Northern Districts of Indiana; U.S. Court of Appeals, Seventh Circuit; U.S. Supreme Court; U.S. Tax Court. *Education:* Indiana University (A.B., Economics, with distinction, 1953; J.D., first in class, 1959). Phi Beta Kappa; Order of the Coif. Article and Book Review Editor, Indiana Law Journal, 1958-1959. "Best Lawyers in America," 1987—(Business Litigation). Certified Indiana Mediator. *Member:* Indianapolis, Indiana State, American and Seventh Circuit Bar Associations. Fellow: Indiana Bar Foundation; American College of Trial Lawyers. ***PRACTICE AREAS:*** Business Litigation; Commercial Litigation; Governmental Regulation Litigation; Probate Litigation; Trusts; Estate Litigation. ***Email:*** virgil.beeler@bakerd.com

(This Listing Continued)

HENRY B. BLACKWELL, II, born 1928; admitted to bar, 1956, Indiana and U.S. District Court, Southern District of Indiana; 1961, U.S. Supreme Court; 1989, U.S. Court of International Trade. *Education:* University of Illinois (B.S., 1952); Indiana University (J.D., 1956). Phi Delta Phi. Listed in Who's Who in America and Who's Who in American Law. Secretary and General Counsel, Eli Lilly International Corporation, 1977-1989. Chairman, Indiana Export Finance Authority, 1989-1990. *Member:* Indianapolis (Member, International Law Section), Indiana State (Member, International Law Section; Chairman, 1989-1990) and American (Member, International Law and Practice) Bar Associations; Customs and International Trade Bar Association; Indianapolis Legal Aid Society. ***PRACTICE AREAS:*** International Law; Corporate Law. ***Email:*** henry.blackwell@bakerd.com

MARLINE R. BREECE, born 1957; admitted to bar, 1992, Indiana and U.S. District Court, Northern and Southern Districts of Indiana. *Education:* Purdue University (B.S., 1979); Indiana University (J.D., 1991). *Member:* Indianapolis, Hendricks County and Indiana State Bar Associations; Energy Bar Association. ***PRACTICE AREAS:*** Municipal Utility Law; Energy; Utility Law. ***Email:*** marline.breece@bakerd.com

JOSEPH B. CARNEY, born 1928; admitted to bar, 1953, District of Columbia and Indiana; U.S. Supreme Court. *Education:* DePauw University (A.B., with distinction, 1950); Harvard University (LL.B., cum laude, 1953). Certified Moderator, Indiana, 1991. Associate, Environmental Law Institute. *Member:* Indianapolis, Indiana State, American (Section on Natural Resources, Energy and Environmental Law) and Seventh Circuit (Member, 1977— and President, 1983-1984, Board of Governors) Bar Associations; National Center for State Courts (Member, Lawyers Committee). Fellow: Indianapolis, Indiana and American Bar Foundations. ***PRACTICE AREAS:*** Environmental Law. ***Email:*** joe.carney@bakerd.com

DANIEL F. EVANS, born 1949; admitted to bar, 1976, Indiana; 1983, U.S. Supreme Court; U.S. District Court, Southern District of Indiana; U.S. Court of Appeals, Seventh Circuit. *Education:* Indiana University (B.A., 1971); Indiana University School of Law (J.D., 1976). Who's Who in America, 1997. Who's Who in the World, 1986. Who's Who in American Law, 1985-1986. Outstanding Young Men of America, 1982. *Member:* Indianapolis and Indiana State Bar Associations. ***PRACTICE AREAS:*** Corporate; Health Care; Administrative Law. ***Email:*** daniel.evans@bakerd.com

DEBRA L. HINSHAW, born 1954; admitted to bar, 1984, Indiana. *Education:* University of Evansville (B.S., nursing, magna cum laude, 1976); Indiana University-Purdue University (M.S., nursing, 1980); Indiana University (J.D., magna cum laude, 1984). ***PRACTICE AREAS:*** Employee Benefits. ***Email:*** debra.hinshaw@bakerd.com

STEVEN L. HOUSEHOLDER, born 1953; admitted to bar, 1978, Indiana; U.S. District Court, Southern District of Indiana; U.S. Court of Appeals, Seventh Circuit. *Education:* Butler University (B.A., summa cum laude, 1975); Harvard Law School (J.D., 1978). Phi Eta Sigma. Author, "The Best Claim Is No Claim: Selecting and Contracting with a Waste Hauler," Environmental Claims Journal, Vol. 2, No. 4, Summer 1990. *Member:* Indianapolis, Indiana State and American Bar Associations; American Corporate Counsel Association. ***PRACTICE AREAS:*** Litigation. ***Email:*** steven.householder@bakerd.com

MICHAEL J. HUSTON, born 1942; admitted to bar, 1972, Indiana and U.S. District Court, Southern District of Indiana; 1975, U.S. District Court, Northern District of Indiana; 1980, U.S. Court of Appeals for the District of Columbia Circuit. *Education:* United States Military Academy (B.S., 1965); Indiana University (J.D., magna cum laude, 1972). Order of the Coif. Note Editor, Indiana Law Journal, 1971-1972. *Member:* Indianapolis, Indiana State (Master Fellow) and American Bar Associations. ***PRACTICE AREAS:*** Utility Law; Energy; Environmental Law. ***Email:*** mike.huston@bakerd.com

J. B. KING, born 1930; admitted to bar, 1954, Indiana, Michigan and U.S. Court of Appeals, Seventh Circuit. *Education:* Indiana University (A.B., 1951); University of Michigan (LL.B., 1954). Adjunct Professor of Law, State and Local Taxes, Indiana University Law School, 1977-1986. Former Vice President and General Counsel, Eli Lilly and Company, 1987-1995. Former Vice President and General Counsel, Guidant Corporation, 1995-2001. With Baker & Daniels, 1954-1987. Director, Indiana Legal Foundation, Inc., 1988—. *Member:* Indianapolis, Indiana State and American Bar Associations; Association of General Counsel. (Also Former Vice President and General Counsel, Guidant Corporation and Eli Lilly). ***Email:*** j.king@bakerd.com

SANDRA D. LEEK, born 1954; admitted to bar, 1979, Indiana and U.S. District Court, Southern District of Indiana. *Education:* Tufts University (B.A., 1976); Indiana Unversity School of Law - Bloomington (J.D., 1979). Listed in: Who's Who in American Law; Who's Who of Emerging Leaders in America; Who's Who of American Women; Who's Who of African Americans. Recipient: Sagamore of the Wabash Award; Dr. Andrew J. Brown Award for Leadership and Civil Rights; Thurgood Marshall Scholarship Fund Legacy and Leadership Award; Spirit of Justice Award. Member: Indiana Chapter, Southern Christian Worship Conference; Dr. Martin Luther King, Jr. Indiana Holiday Commission. *Member:* Indianapolis, Marion County (Past President) and Indiana State Bar Associations. ***PRACTICE AREAS:*** Employment Law. ***Email:*** sandra.leek@bakerd.com

MADONNA FRANCES McGRATH, born 1946; admitted to bar, 1989, Indiana and U.S. District Court, Northern and Southern Districts of Indiana. *Education:* Webster University (A.B., 1968); Roosevelt University (M.P.A., 1980); Indiana University (J.D., cum laude, 1989). Associate Editor, Indiana Law Review, 1988-1989. Author: "The Superfund Insurance Dilemma: Defining the Super Risks and Rights of Comprehensive General Liability Policies," 21 Indiana Law Review 735, 1988. Associate, Ice, Miller, Donadio & Ryan, Indianapolis, Indiana, 1989-1992. Senior Environmental Attorney, Aeroquip-Vickers, Inc., Maumee, Ohio, 1992-1999. Member, Board of Directors, Indianapolis Visiting Nurse Service, Inc. *Member:* Indianapolis and Indiana State (Member, Environmental Section) Bar Associations. ***PRACTICE AREAS:*** Environmental; Mergers and Acquisitions; Real Estate. ***Email:*** madonna.mcgrath@bakerd.com

VICKIE L. NORMAN, born 1954; admitted to bar, 1989, Illinois; 2001, Indiana. *Education:* Ball State University (B.S., 1977); John Marshall Law School (J.D., 1989). ***PRACTICE AREAS:*** Real Estate Taxation. ***Email:*** vickie.norman@bakerd.com

LARRY R. PRIBLE, admitted to bar, 1976, Indiana. *Education:* Indiana University (B.A., 1969); Indiana University School of Law (J.D., 1976). Honors, Sagamore of the Wabash. Past-President, Indiana Association of Life Insurance Companies. Past-State President, American Council of Life Insurance. Former Board Member, Life Office Management Association. Board Member, Habitat for Humanity International. Chairman, 500 Festival, 2001-2002. Board Member, Indianapolis Housing Task Force. Former Advisory Board Member: Indiana State University School of Business Insurance Program; Anderson University MBA Program; Indiana University Business Leaders Council. ***PRACTICE AREAS:*** Insurance; Financial Services. ***Email:*** larry.prible@bakerd.com

MARK C. SAUSSER, born 1959; admitted to bar, 1985, Massachusetts; 1988, California; 1991, Indiana. *Education:* Wabash College (A.B., summa cum laude, 1982); College of William and Mary (J.D., 1985). ***PRACTICE AREAS:*** Real Estate. ***Email:*** mark.sausser@bakerd.com

JOSEPH L. SMITH, JR., admitted to bar, 1995, Indiana. *Education:* DePauw University (B.A., 1992); Indiana University (J.D., 1995). *Member:* Indiana State and American Bar Associations. ***PRACTICE AREAS:*** Government. ***Email:*** jlsmith@bakerd.com

MERRILL S. THOMPSON, born 1930; admitted to bar, 1957, Illinois; 1980, U.S. Supreme Court; 1982, Indiana. *Education:* University of Illinois (A.B., with high honors, 1956); University of Illinois College of Law (J.D., with honors, 1957). Order of the Coif. Salutatorian, University of Illinois Law School. Who's Who in American Law (2nd Edition). Recipient, Associate Member Award for Outstanding Service to the Association of Food and Drug Officials, 1984. Editor, Illinois Law Review. Member, Institute of Food Technologists, 1990-1992. *Member:* Parke County, Indiana State, Illinois State and American (Member: Food, Drug and Cosmetic Law Committee and Agriculture Committee, Administrative Law Section; Food, Drug and Cosmetic Law Committee, Business Law Section) Bar Associations; National Conference on Weights and Measures; Industry Committee on Packaging and Labeling; Association of Food and Drug Officials; The Food and Drug Law Institute.

DOUGLAS A. YERKESON, born 1967; admitted to bar, 1994, Ohio; 1998, U.S. District Court, Southern District of Ohio and U.S. Court of Appeals for the Federal Circuit; 2002, Indiana; 2003, U.S. District Court, Southern District of Indiana; registered to practice before U.S. Patent and Trademark Office. *Education:* University of Cincinnati (B.S.M.E., magna cum laude, 1990; J.D., 1993). Pi Tau Sigma; Tau Beta Pi. Recipient, American Railway Engineering Association Student Award, 1992 and 1993. Listed in: Who's Who in America, 56th and 57th Editions; Who's Who in American Law, 12th Edition. *Member:* Indianapolis and Indiana State Bar Associations; American Intellectual Property Law Association. ***PRACTICE AREAS:*** Intellectual Property. ***Email:*** doug.yerkeson@bakerd.com

OF COUNSEL

SUZETTE BEWLEY, born 1968; admitted to bar, 1998, Indiana. *Education:* Purdue University (B.S., 1990); Indiana University School of Law (J.D., summa cum laude, 1998). Executive Managing Editor, Indiana International and Comparative Law Review. ***PRACTICE AREAS:*** Bankruptcy; Commercial Law; Sports. ***Email:*** suzette.bewley@bakerd.com

DAVID LAWTHER JOHNSON, born 1952; admitted to bar, 1980, District of Columbia and Indiana. *Education:* Harvard University (A.B., summa cum laude, 1974); New College, Oxford University, Oxford, England (B.A., Honours, 1976); Harvard University (J.D., cum laude, 1979). Phi Beta Kappa. Rhodes Scholar, Indiana, 1974. Legal Counsel and Professional Staff Member, U.S. Senate Committee on Foreign Relations, 1979-1983. *Member:* District of Columbia Bar; Indianapolis, Indiana State and American Bar Associations; National Association of Bond Lawyers. ***PRACTICE AREAS:*** Business Law; Corporate Law; Public Finance; Municipal Law. ***Email:*** david.johnson@bakerd.com

MICHAEL R. MAINE, born 1940; admitted to bar, 1964, Indiana and U.S. District Court, Southern District of Indiana; 1967, U.S. Supreme Court; 1968, U.S. Court of Appeals, Seventh Circuit; 2001, District of Columbia. *Education:* DePauw University (A.B., with high distinction, 1961); University of Michigan (J.D., with distinction, 1964). Phi Beta Kappa; Order of the Coif. Designated "Sagamore of the Wabash," by Governor Orr, 1986. Recipient, Bar Foundation Award for Excellence in the Profession, 1991. Chief Foreign Legal Advisor, Hebei Province, PR China, 1995—. Chief Legal Representative, Baker & Daniels China Office, 1998—. Member, Board, Community Hospital North, 1988-1997. Trustee, Secretary, 1997—, DePauw University, 1990—. Member, Board: Indiana Convention and Visitors Association, 1988-1994; Indiana Repertory Theatre, 1986—. President, 1999-2000, Japan-American Society of Indiana, Inc.; Board of Visitors, Indiana University Kelly School of Business, 1999—; Advisory Board, Indiana University Global Business Information Network, 2000—; Global Crossroads Foundation, Inc., 1997—. *Member:* Indianapolis (Member, Board of Managers, 1979-1982; Secretary, 1982; President-Elect, 1984; President, 1985), Indiana State (Chairman, Federal Judiciary Committee, 1986-1989), American (Member, Committee on Equal Opportunity Law and Procedure, Labor Law Section, 1972—; Chairman, Subcommittee on the Old Civil Rights Acts, 1980-1984) and Seventh Circuit Bar Associations. (Also at Qingdao, China Office). ***PRACTICE AREAS:*** International Law; Employment Law; Corporate Law. ***Email:*** mike.maine@bakerd.com

CHRISTOPHER J. WEBER, born 1944; admitted to bar, 1971, Indiana and U.S. District Court, Southern District of Indiana. *Education:* Marian College (B.A., 1966); Indiana University (J.D., 1971). Sole Practitioner, Indianapolis, IN, 1971-1975. Counsel, Indianapolis Power & Light Company, Indianapolis, IN, 1975-2001. Instructor, Paralegal Studies, Indiana University and Purdue University at Indianapolis, 1988-1999. *Member:* Indianapolis and Indiana State (Member, Utility Law Section; Chairman, Electric Division, 1999) Bar Associations. ***PRACTICE AREAS:*** Public Utility Law. ***Email:*** chris.weber@bakerd.com

ASSOCIATES

MATTHEW T. ALBAUGH, born Washington, Indiana; admitted to bar, 2001, Illinois; 2002, Indiana. *Education:* Indiana University (B.A., 1997); Indiana University School of Law - Bloomington (J.D., summa cum laude, 2001). Phi Delta Phi. Member, St, Thomas More Society. Indiana Law Alumni Scholar; Starr Scholar. Member: Dean's Tutorial Society; Career Services Advisory Board. Editor-in-Chief, Indiana Law Review, Vol. 34, 2000-2001. Law Clerk to Chief Justice Randall T. Shepard, Indiana Supreme Court, 2001-2002. Author, Introduction, "Revised Article 9 and Other Developments in Commercial & Consumer Law," 35 Indiana Law Review 1239 (2002). Symposiumn Co-Chair, "Caught in the

(This Listing Continued)

BAKER & DANIELS LLP, Indianapolis—Continued

Middle: A National Symposium on the Role of State Intermediate Appellate Courts," Indiana Court of Appeals. *Member:* Illinois State, Indiana State and American Bar Associations. ***PRACTICE AREAS:*** Business Litigation. ***Email:*** matthew.albaugh@bakerd.com

CHARLES W. ARNETT, born 1977; admitted to bar, 2002, Indiana. *Education:* Rose-Hulman Institute of Technology (B.S., cum laude, 1999); Indiana University School of Law (J.D., 2002). *Member:* Indianapolis and Indiana State Bar Associations. ***PRACTICE AREAS:*** Intellectual Property. ***Email:*** charles.arnett@bakerd.com

DAVID A. ARRENSEN, born 1958; admitted to bar, 1988, Illinois; 1990, Indiana. *Education:* Indiana University (A.B., with distinction, 1979; J.D., magna cum laude, 1987); Fordham University (M.A., 1983). Phi Beta Kappa; Order of the Coif. ***PRACTICE AREAS:*** Municipal Finance; Business Planning; Real Estate. ***Email:*** david.arrensen@bakerd.com

BRENT A. AUBERRY, born 1972; admitted to bar, 1998, Indiana. *Education:* University of Southern Indiana (B.A., 1995); Indiana University School of Law (J.D., 1998). Professor of Legal Writing, Indiana School of Law, 1999-2000. Trustee, University of Southern Indiana, 1993-1995. *Member:* Indianapolis Bar Association. ***PRACTICE AREAS:*** State Taxation. ***Email:*** brent.auberry@bakerd.com

RYAN C. BARKER, born 1976; admitted to bar, 2001, Indiana; 2004, District of Columbia; registered to practice before U.S. Patent and Trademark Office. *Education:* Duke University (B.S.E., 1998); Indiana University School of Law (J.D., 2001). ***Email:*** ryan.barker@bakerd.com

MAXWELL N. BARNES, born 1971; admitted to bar, 1997, Illinois; 2003, Indiana. *Education:* University of Michigan (B.A., 1994); Vanderbilt University (J.D., 1997). Administrative Editor, Vanderbilt Journal of Transnational Law, 1996-1997. ***PRACTICE AREAS:*** Securities; Corporate Law. ***Email:*** maxwell.barnes@bakerd.com

JEFFREY S. BECK, admitted to bar, 2004, Indiana. *Education:* Indiana State University (B.S., 1993); Indiana University School of Law (J.D., summa cum laude, 2004). Order of the Barristers; Dean's List. Executive Managing Editor, Indiana Law Review. ***PRACTICE AREAS:*** Labor and Employment. ***Email:*** jeff.beck@bakerd.com

GABRIEL BENDER, admitted to bar, 2000, Indiana. *Education:* Northwestern University (B.A., 1995); Indiana University School of Law (J.D., 2000). ***Email:*** gabriel.bender@bakerd.com

JAMES S. BIRGE, admitted to bar, 1999, Indiana; U.S. District Court, Northern and Southern Districts of Indiana. *Education:* Harvard University (B.A., cum laude, 1995); University of Michigan Law School (J.D., magna cum laude, 1998). Order of the Coif. Clarence Darrow Scholar. Editor, Michigan Law Review. *Member:* Indiana State and American Bar Associations. ***PRACTICE AREAS:*** Corporate Finance; Mergers and Acquisitions; Economic Development. ***Email:*** jim.birge@bakerd.com

AMANDA R. BLYSTONE, born Elkhart, Indiana, October 1, 1975; admitted to bar, 2001, Indiana. *Education:* Butler University (B.A., magna cum laude, 1998); Tulane University of Louisiana (J.D., cum laude, 2001). Author: "Implied Private Rights of Action: Encouraging Responsible Environmental Planning," 13 TLNELT 451 (2000). *Member:* Indianapolis, Indiana State and American Bar Associations. ***LANGUAGES:*** French. ***PRACTICE AREAS:*** Business Litigation. ***Email:*** amanda.blystone@bakerd.com

CRAIG M. BOROWSKI, born 1973; admitted to bar, 2000, Indiana, U.S. District Court, Northern and Southern Districts of Indiana. *Education:* Indiana University, Bloomington (B.S., 1995); Indiana University, Indianapolis (J.D., magna cum laude, 2000). Phi Delta Phi. Note Editor, Indiana International & Comparative Law Review. Associate Justice, Indiana University Moot Court Board. Recipient, Law Alumni Scholarship. Indiana University School of Law-Indianapolis Alumni Board of Directors. *Member:* Indianapolis, Indiana State and American Bar Associations. ***PRACTICE AREAS:*** Labor and Employment. ***Email:*** craig.borowski@bakerd.com

C. JOHN BROWN, admitted to bar, 2005, Indiana. *Education:* University of Maryland (B.S., 1992); Indiana University (M.B.A., 2001); Indiana University School of Law - Bloomington (J.D., 2005). ***PRACTICE AREAS:*** Intellectual Property. ***Email:*** john.brown@bakerd.com

KRISTIANA M. BRUGGER, admitted to bar, 2004, Indiana. *Education:* Indiana University (B.S., 2001); University of Virginia (J.D., 2004). Indiana University Science, Technology, and Research Scholar (STARS). Treasurer, Moot Court Board, 2003-2004. Recipient: Best Oralist Award, First Year Oral Arguments, University of Virginia School of Law, 2002; Indiana University Honors College Scholarship, 1997-2001; Indiana University Faculty Award, 1997-2001. Legal Researcher, Virginia Commission on Genetic Tissue Research, 2003. ***PRACTICE AREAS:*** Intellectual Property. ***Email:*** kristiana.brugger@bakerd.com

ADRIENNE F. BUSBY, born 1976; admitted to bar, 2001, Indiana. *Education:* University of Notre Dame (B.A., summa cum laude, 1998; J.D., magna cum laude, 2001). ***PRACTICE AREAS:*** Litigation. ***Email:*** adrienne.busby@bakerd.com

STUART R. BUTTRICK, born 1975; admitted to bar, 2000, Indiana; 2003, U.S. Court of Appeals, Sixth Circuit. *Education:* DePauw University (B.A., 1997); Indiana University (J.D., magna cum laude, 2000). Order of the Barristers. Member, Indiana International & Comparative Law Review. ***PRACTICE AREAS:*** Labor and Employment. ***Email:*** stuart.buttrick@bakerd.com

ANDREW L. CAMPBELL, admitted to bar, 2005, Indiana. *Education:* University of Montana (B.A., 2001; M.A., 2002); Indiana University School of Law - Bloomington (J.D., 2005). ***PRACTICE AREAS:*** Products Liability. ***Email:*** andrew.campbell@bakerd.com

CAROL WARREN COLLINS, born 1953; admitted to bar, 1983, Indiana. *Education:* Ball State University (B.S., cum laude, 1975); University of Illinois (M.A., cum laude, 1976); Indiana University School of Law-Indianapolis (J.D., cum laude, 1983). Member, Moot Court. *Member:* Indianapolis, Indiana State and American Bar Associations. ***PRACTICE AREAS:*** Government Relations. ***Email:*** carol.collins@bakerd.com

KELLEY BERTOUX CREVELING, admitted to bar, 1996, Indiana and U.S. District Court, Northern and Southern Districts of Indiana. *Education:* Indiana University, Bloomington (B.A., 1991); Indiana School of Law-Indianapolis (J.D., 1996). Order of the Barristers. Executive Production Editor, Indiana International and Comparative Law Review. *Member:* Indianapolis and Indiana State Bar Associations. ***PRACTICE AREAS:*** Labor and Employment. ***Email:*** kelley.creveling@bakerd.com

JANE A. DALL, born 1978; admitted to bar, 2003, Indiana and U.S. District Court, Northern and Southern Districts of Indiana; 2004, U.S. Court of Appeals, Seventh Circuit. *Education:* Hanover College (B.A., summa cum laude, 2000); Notre Dame Law School (J.D., summa cum laude, 2003). Recipient: Hoynes Prize; William T. Kirby Award for Excellence in Briefwriting. Executive Articles Editor, Notre Dame Law Review, 2002-2003. *Member:* Indiana State, Seventh Circuit and American Bar Associations. ***PRACTICE AREAS:*** Litigation. ***Email:*** jane.dall@bakerd.com

CEDRIC A. D'HUE, admitted to bar, 2005, Indiana. *Education:* Tufts University (B.S., 1999); Purdue University (M.S., 2002); Indiana University School of Law - Bloomington (J.D., 2005). Barrister: Moot Court; Soul Lefkowitz Moot Court Competition, 2004-2005. Participant, National Health Law Competition, 2004. President, Black Law Students Association. Member, Indiana Health Law Review. ***PRACTICE AREAS:*** Intellectual Property. ***Email:*** cedric.dhue@bakerd.com

SHAWNA M. EIKENBERRY, born 1974; admitted to bar, 1999, Indiana. *Education:* Butler University (B.A., magna cum laude, 1996); Indiana University School of Law - Bloomington (J.D., magna cum laude, 1999). Delta Theta Phi. Author: "Thou Shalt Not Sue the Church: Denying Court Access to Ministerial Employees," 74 Indiana Law Journal 269. *Member:* Indiana State and American Bar Associations. ***PRACTICE AREAS:*** Litigation. ***Email:*** shawna.eikenberry@bakerd.com

MEG A. GALLMEYER, born 1972; admitted to bar, 1998, Indiana and U.S. District Court, Northern and Southern Districts of Indiana. *Education:* Indiana University (B.A., with distinction, 1994); Vanderbilt University (J.D., 1998). Phi Beta Kappa; Phi Alpha Delta (Justice, 1997-1998). ***PRACTICE AREAS:*** Litigation. ***Email:*** meg.gallmeyer@bakerd.com

CARYN M. GLAWE, born 1979; admitted to bar, 2004, Indiana. *Education:* Butler University (B.A., cum laude, 2001); Northwestern University (J.D., 2004). Managing Editor, Journal of Criminal Law and Criminology, 2003-2004. *Member:* Indianapolis and American Bar Associations. ***Email:*** caryn.glawe@bakerd.com

KELLYE M. GORDON, born Gary, Indiana, 1969; admitted to bar, 2003, Indiana. *Education:* Indiana University (B.S., 1999); Indiana University School of Law, Indianapolis (J.D., cum laude, 2003). Symposium Editor, Indiana Law Review, 2002-2003. Chief Justice, Moot Court Society, 2002-2003. *Member:* Indianapolis, Indiana State and American Bar Associations. ***PRACTICE AREAS:*** Litigation. ***Email:*** kellye.gordon@bakerd.com

PHILIP J. GUTWEIN, II, admitted to bar, 2001, Indiana. *Education:* Wabash College (B.A., magna cum laude, 1996); Indiana University School of Law (J.D., cum laude, 2001). Governor's Fellowship, 1996-1997. Champion, Sherman Minton Moot Court Competition, 1999-2000. Notes Editor, Federal Communications Law Journal. ***PRACTICE AREAS:*** Employee Benefits. ***Email:*** philip.gutwein@bakerd.com

NATHAN J. HAGERMAN, born 1970; admitted to bar, 1996, Michigan, 2005, Indiana. *Education:* Purdue University (B.A., 1993); University of Michigan (J.D., 1996). Author: "Indiana Property Tax Update," Indianapolis Bar Association; "Property Tax Audits and Appeals," Institute of Management Accountants. *Member:* State Bar of Michigan; American Bar Association. ***PRACTICE AREAS:*** State Taxation; State Tax Controversies. ***Email:*** nathan.hagerman@bakerd.com

TERRY E. HALL, admitted to bar, 2000, Indiana. *Education:* University of Texas (B.A., magna cum laude, 1976); Indiana University School of Law (J.D., summa cum laude, 2000). *Member:* Indianapolis, Indiana State and American Bar Associations. ***PRACTICE AREAS:*** Commercial Law; Financial Law; Bankruptcy. ***Email:*** terry.hall@bakerd.com

DEREK C. HAMILTON, admitted to bar, 2003, Illinois (Not admitted in Indiana). *Education:* Ball State University (B.A., summa cum laude, 1998); Stanford University (J.D., 2003). ***PRACTICE AREAS:*** Trusts and Estates. ***Email:*** derek.hamilton@bakerd.com

NORMAN J. HEDGES, born 1971; admitted to bar, 1998, Indiana; registered to practice before U.S. Patent and Trademark Office. *Education:* Purdue University (B.S.M.E., 1995); Indiana University (J.D., 1998). Recipient: Evans Scholar, 1990-1995; National Evans Scholar of the Year for Scholarship and Leadership, 1995. Speaker: Indiana University School of Law, Patent Law, 2000-2003; Indianapolis Bar Association, Basic Intellectual Property Law, 2004. *Member:* Indianapolis, Indiana State and American Bar Associations; American Intellectual Property Law Association. ***Email:*** norman.hedges@bakerd.com

JOHN K. HENNING, IV, born 1974; admitted to bar, 2001, Arizona; 2002, U.S. District Court, District of Arizona; 2004, Indiana. *Education:* Texas Christian University (B.A., 1996); University of Virginia School of Law (J.D., 2001). Member, Ravens Society. Recipient, University of Virginia Ritter Award for Honor, Character and Integrity. Participant, Lile Moot Court Competition. Florence Immigration/Refugee Rights Project Volunteer Attorney. *Member:* State Bar of Arizona. ***PRACTICE AREAS:*** Litigation. ***Email:*** john.henning@bakerd.com

JENNETT M. HILL, born 1963; admitted to bar, 1998, Indiana. *Education:* DePauw University (B.A., 1985); Indiana University (J.D., magna cum laude, 1998). *Member:* Indiana State and American Bar Associations. ***LANGUAGES:*** German. ***PRACTICE AREAS:*** Tax Exempt Organizations; Nonprofit Organizations Law. ***Email:*** jennett.hill@bakerd.com

KAREEM A. HOWELL, born 1975; admitted to bar, 2002, Indiana; registered to practice before U.S. Patent and Trademark Office. *Education:* Norfolk State University (B.S., 1998); Indiana University (J.D., 2001). *Member:* American Bar Association. ***PRACTICE AREAS:*** Intellectual Property. ***Email:*** kareem.howell@bakerd.com

RYAN M. HURLEY, born 1977; admitted to bar, 2003, Georgia; 2004, Indiana. *Education:* Indiana University (B.A., 2000); Indiana University School of Law (J.D., magna cum laude, 2003). Order of the Coif; Phi Beta Kappa. Managing Editor, Indiana Law Journal. *Member:* American Bar Association (Member, Young Lawyers Section). ***PRACTICE AREAS:*** Litigation. ***Email:*** ryan.hurley@bakerd.com

(This Listing Continued)

SARAH M. JABBARI, born 1971; admitted to bar, 2000, Indiana; registered to practice before U.S. Patent and Trademark Office. *Education:* Indiana University-Purdue University (B.S., 1994); Indiana University School of Law (J.D., 2000). ***Email:*** sarah.jabbari@bakerd.com

BRANDON S. JUDKINS, admitted to bar, 2003, Indiana. *Education:* Butler University (B.A., 2000); Indiana University School of Law - Bloomington (J.D., 2003). ***PRACTICE AREAS:*** Litigation. ***Email:*** brandon.judkins@bakerd.com

JASON D. KIMPEL, born 1973; admitted to bar, 1999, Indiana. *Education:* DePauw University (B.A., magna cum laude, 1996); Indiana University-Bloomington (J.D., magna cum laude, 1999). Order of the Coif. Executive Notes and Comment Editor, Indiana Law Journal. Member, Board of Directors of COLAP, Inc. *Member:* Indiana State and American Bar Associations. ***PRACTICE AREAS:*** Corporate Law; Securities; Mergers and Acquisitions; Business Planning. ***Email:*** jason.kimpel@bakerd.com

SUSAN W. KLINE, admitted to bar, 2000, Indiana. *Education:* Butler University (B.S., 1980; M.B.A., 1993); Indiana University School of Law at Indianapolis (J.D., summa cum laude, 2000). Graduated, First in Class, Indiana University School of Law at Indianapolis. Recipient, Faculty Prize and Frandsen Scholarship. Chief Justice, Moot Court Society. Associate Editor, Indiana Law Review. Clerk to Indiana Supreme Court Chief Justice Randall T. Shepard, 2000-2002. Certified Public Accountant, 1983. Past Board Member, American Institute of Certified Public Accountants. Past President, Indiana CPA Society. Past Member, Marion County, Indiana, Board of Zoning Appeals III. Past Treasurer, Phoenix Theatre. Member, American Inn of Court. Past Adjunct Faculty Member, Butler University. Authored or Co-Authored, Annual Employment Law Update for Indiana Law Review, 2000 through 2003. ***PRACTICE AREAS:*** Employment Discrimination; Employee Discipline; Employment Litigation; Employment Termination; Fair Labor Standards; Family and Medical Leave Act; Personnel Policies; Sexual Harassment; Workplace Violence; Employee Drug Testing; Employee Privacy; Employment at Will. ***Email:*** susan.kline@bakerd.com

SHAUNE HAWKINS LANGSTON, admitted to bar, 2003, Indiana; U.S. District Court, Northern and Southern Districts of Indiana. *Education:* University of North Carolina (B.A., magna cum laude, 1999); Northwestern University School of Law (J.D., 2003). Phi Beta Kappa; Pi Sigma Alpha; Phi Sigma Tau. University Marshal. Recipient: Annie Moring Alexander Scholarship (Political Science Scholarship); Marion B. Rathje Scholarship (Leadership and Character Award); Minority Achievement Academic Excellence Awards. *Member:* Indianapolis and American Bar Associations. ***PRACTICE AREAS:*** Real Estate; Environmental Law. ***Email:*** shaune.langston@bakerd.com

DANIEL M. LECHLEITER, admitted to bar, 2005, Indiana. *Education:* University of Dayton (B.S., 2001); John Marshall Law School (J.D., 2005). Order of John Marshall. Recipient, Best Oralist Award and Regional Quarter Finalist, AIPLA Giles Sutherland Rich Memorial Moot Court Competition, 2005. Recipient: Francis D. and Corinne S. Morrissey Award in Professional Responsibility, 2004-2005; Dean's Scholarship, The John Marshall Law School. Participant, National Association of Criminal Defense Lawyers Cathy Bennett National Trial Competition, 2004. Managing Editior, The John Marshall Review of Intellectual Property Law, 2004-2005. *Member:* Chicago, Indianapolis, Indiana State and American Bar Associations; American Intellectual Property Law Association; American Society of Mechanical Engineers. ***PRACTICE AREAS:*** Intellectual Property. ***Email:*** daniel.lechleiter@bakerd.com

MATTHEW C. LESHER, admitted to bar, 2005, Indiana. *Education:* Indiana University (B.S., 1999); Indiana University School of Law - Bloomington (J.D., 2005). ***PRACTICE AREAS:*** State Taxation; Local Taxation. ***Email:*** matthew.lesher@bakerd.com

SUZANN WEBER LUPTON, born 1966; admitted to bar, 1991, Indiana and U.S. District Court, Northern and Southern Districts of Indiana; 1993, U.S. Court of Appeals, Seventh Circuit. *Education:* DePauw University (B.A., 1988); Indiana University School of Law (J.D., 1991). Member, Board of Editors, Indiana Law Review. Clerk, Honorable Justice Jon Krahulik, Indiana Supreme Court. Deputy Attorney General, State of Indiana, 1992-1997. *Member:* Indianapolis and Indiana State Bar Associations. ***PRACTICE AREAS:*** Healthcare; Litigation; Appellate Practice; Product Liability. ***Email:*** suzann.lupton@bakerd.com

KATHERINE E. McCANNA, admitted to bar, 2003, Indiana. *Education:* Hanover College (B.A., cum laude, 2000); Indiana University School of Law - Indianapolis (J.D., 2003). Member, Indiana Law Review. *Member:* Indianapolis Bar Association. ***Email:*** katie.mccanna@bakerd.com

JEROME P. McCLUSKEY, admitted to bar, 2002, Indiana. *Education:* Harvard University (B.A., magna cum laude, 1997); Stanford University School of Law (J.D., 2002). Designated Sagamore of the Wabash by Governor O'Bannon and Governor Kernan. ***PRACTICE AREAS:*** Corporate Law; Corporate Governance; Emerging Technology Companies; Economic Development Incentives. ***Email:*** jerome.mccluskey@bakerd.com

NICOLE L. McDONALD, admitted to bar, 2005, Indiana. *Education:* Kelley School of Business (B.S., with high distinction, 1997; M.B.A., with academic excellence, 2004); Indiana University School of Law (J.D., magna cum laude, 2004). *Member:* Indiana State Bar Association. ***PRACTICE AREAS:*** Corporate. ***Email:*** nicole.mcdonald@bakerd.com

CATHERINE A. MEEKER, born 1974; admitted to bar, 1999, Indiana. *Education:* Ball State University (B.A., summa cum laude, 1996); University of Chicago (J.D., cum laude, 1999). ***PRACTICE AREAS:*** Litigation. ***Email:*** catherine.meeker@bakerd.com

WILLIAM S. MEYERS, admitted to bar, 2002, Indiana, U.S. District Court, Southern and Northern Districts of Indiana; registered to practice before U.S. Patent and Trademark Office. *Education:* Rose-Hulman Institute of Technology (B.S., cum laude, 1992; M.S., 1994); Indiana University School of Law (J.D., cum laude, 2002). *Member:* Indianapolis and Indiana State Bar Associations; American Intellectual Property Law Association. ***PRACTICE AREAS:*** Intellectual Property. ***Email:*** bill.meyers@bakerd.com

M. SUE MICHAEL, born 1954; admitted to bar, 1983, Indiana. *Education:* Purdue University (B.A., with highest distinction, 1975); Indiana University-Purdue University (J.D., summa cum laude, 1983). Recipient, Indiana Bell Telephone Award for Top Ranking First Year Student, 1979. ***PRACTICE AREAS:*** Intellectual Property. ***Email:*** sue.michael@bakerd.com

(This Listing Continued)

CLAYTON C. MILLER, born 1965; admitted to bar, 1993, Indiana and U.S. District Court, Northern and Southern Districts of Indiana; 2000, U.S. Supreme Court. *Education:* Harvard University (A.B., 1987); Indiana University-Bloomington (J.D., 1993). *Member:* Indiana State and American Bar Associations. ***PRACTICE AREAS:*** Utility Law; Telecommunications Regulation; Energy. ***Email:*** clayton.miller@bakerd.com

JEFFREY C. NELSON, admitted to bar, 2004, Indiana. *Education:* University of Illinois (B.S., 2000; J.D., summa cum laude, 2004). Order of the Coif. Harno Scholar. Recipient: Rickert Award, 2004; Medal of Excellence, American Bankruptcy Institute; West Outstanding Scholastic Achievement Award. Associate Editor, The Elder Law Journal, 2003-2004. ***PRACTICE AREAS:*** Commercial Law; Financial Services Law; Bankruptcy; Creditors Rights. ***Email:*** jeffrey.nelson@bakerd.com

SHIV GHUMAN O'NEILL, admitted to bar, 2001, Ohio; 2002, Indiana. *Education:* Loyola University of Chicago (B.S., 1998); Indiana University School of Law (J.D., 2001). ***PRACTICE AREAS:*** Litigation. ***Email:*** shiv.o'neill@bakerd.com

APRIL L. OPPER, born 1976; admitted to bar, 2004, Ohio; 2005, Michigan (Not admitted in Indiana). *Education:* University of Michigan (B.A., with distinction, 1997); Eastern Michigan University (M.A., 2000); Ohio State University, Moritz College of Law (J.D., with honors, 2003). Order of the Coif. *Member:* Ohio State Bar Association. ***PRACTICE AREAS:*** Corporate Litigation; RP Litigation. ***Email:*** april.opper@bakred.com

KATHY L. OSBORN, born 1963; admitted to bar, 2000, Indiana and U.S. District Court, Southern District of Indiana. *Education:* University of Indiana, Bloomington (B.S., Biology, magna cum laude, B.A., Religious Studies, summa cum laude, 1987; J.D., magna cum laude, 1999). Law Clerk: Justice Frank Sullivan, Jr., Indiana Supreme Court, 1999-2000; Former Justice Myrna C. Selby, Indiana Supreme Court, 1999. *Member:* Indiana State Bar Association. ***PRACTICE AREAS:*** Commercial Litigation; Appellate Practice; Antitrust Litigation; Probate Litigation; Trust Litigation. ***Email:*** kathy.osborn@bakerd.com

SCOTT E. PECK, born 1972; admitted to bar, 1999, Indiana. *Education:* Indiana University, Bloomington (English, 1995; Mathematics, 1996; J.D., magna cum laude, 1999). Order of the Coif. *Member:* Indiana State and American Bar Associations; Indiana Economic Development Association. ***PRACTICE AREAS:*** Municipal Law; Tax Exempt Finance. ***Email:*** scott.peck@bakerd.com

LOUIS THOMAS PERRY, admitted to bar, 2005, Indiana. *Education:* University of Notre Dame (B.A., magna cum laude, 2002; J.D., 2005). ***PRACTICE AREAS:*** Bankruptcy; Commercial Law. ***Email:*** louis.perry@bakerd.com

JOSEPH C. PETTYGROVE, admitted to bar, 2005, Indiana. *Education:* Ball State University (B.S., 2002); Indiana University School of Law - Bloomington (J.D., 2005). ***Email:*** joseph.pettygrove@bakerd.com

SARA MANSKE POWELL, admitted to bar, 2002, Indiana. *Education:* Valparaiso University (B.A., summa cum laude, 1997); University of Chicago (J.D., 2002). *American Bar Association; Indiana State Bar Association.* ***PRACTICE AREAS:*** Insurance; Financial Services Law. ***Email:*** sara.powell@bakerd.com

STACY L. PRALL, born 1967; admitted to bar, 1996, Indiana and U.S. District Court, Northern and Southern Districts of Indiana; 1999, U.S. Court of Appeals, Fifth Circuit. *Education:* Indiana University (B.S., 1990; J.D., cum laude, 1996). ***PRACTICE AREAS:*** Intellectual Property Litigation; Securities Fraud; Commercial Litigation. ***Email:*** stacy.prall@bakerd.com

CHAD S. PRIEST, admitted to bar, 2005, Indiana. *Education:* Indiana University (B.S.N., with distinction, 1999); George Washington University (J.D., 2005). ***PRACTICE AREAS:*** Health Care. ***Email:*** chad.priest@bakerd.com

MICHAEL N. RED, admitted to bar, 2004, Indiana; U.S. District Court, Southern District of Indiana. *Education:* Indiana University (B.S., 1998); Ohio Northern University - Pettit College of Law, 2001-2002; Indiana University School of Law (J.D., 2004). *Member:* Indiana State and American Bar Associations. ***PRACTICE AREAS:*** Real Property Litigation. ***Email:*** michael.red@bakerd.com

ANNE K. RICCHIUTO, admitted to bar, 2005, Indiana. *Education:* Northwestern University (B.S., 2000); Indiana University School of Law - Bloomington (J.D., summa cum laude, 2005). Phi Delta Phi. Associate Justice, Moot Court Society. Mentor, Reach for Youth Teen Court. Articles Editor, Indiana Law Review. ***PRACTICE AREAS:*** Business Litigation. ***Email:*** anne.ricchiuto@bakerd.com

DANIEL ROY, born 1973; admitted to bar, 1999, Indiana. *Education:* DePauw University (B.A., 1996); Indiana University (J.D., magna cum laude, 1999). Order of the Coif. Articles Editor, Indiana Law Journal. ***PRACTICE AREAS:*** Litigation. ***Email:*** daniel.roy@bakerd.com

JASON M. SCHIESSER, born 1976; admitted to bar, 2001, Indiana and U.S. District Court, Northern and Southern Districts of Indiana. *Education:* Indiana University, Bloomington (B.S., with high distinction, 1998); Indiana University School of Law-Indianapolis (J.D., summa cum laude, 2001). Executive Articles Editor, Indiana Law Review. Judicial Intern to Chief Justice Randall T. Shepard, Indiana Supreme Court. Dean's List (every semester). Law Alumni Scholar. Recipient, NATAF Property Scholar Award. Mentor and Management Board Member (Vice Chair), Big Brothers Big Sisters of Central Indiana. Torchbearer, Camp Tecumseh YMCA. *Member:* Indianapolis Bar Association (Member, Executive Committee, Law Student Division); Indiana State Bar Association; American Bar Association. ***PRACTICE AREAS:*** Public Finance; Municipal Law; Business Law. ***Email:*** jason.schiesser@bakerd.com

RANDEE SIBUL-GELBERT, born 1953; admitted to bar, 1983, Illinois (inactive); 1990, Utah (inactive); 1996, Pennsylvania; 2003, Indiana. *Education:* University of Illinois (B.A., French, 1975); Chicago-Kent College of Law (J.D., 1983). *Member:* Illinois State, Indiana State and American Bar Associations. ***LANGUAGES:*** French. ***PRACTICE AREAS:*** Trademarks; Intellectual Property; Intellectual Property Licensing. ***Email:*** randee.gelbert@bakerd.com

CYNTHIA K. SPRINGER, born 1957; admitted to bar, 1997, Indiana; U.S. District Court, Southern and Northern Districts of Indiana; 1999, U.S. Court of Appeals, 7th Circuit. *Education:* Indiana University (B.M.E., with distinction, 1979; J.D., cum laude, 1997).

(This Listing Continued)

BAKER & DANIELS LLP, Indianapolis—Continued

Member: Indianapolis, Indiana State (Chair, Labor and Employment Law Section) and American Bar Associations. ***PRACTICE AREAS:*** Labor and Employment. ***Email:*** cynthia.springer@bakerd.com

DUSTIN D. STOHLER, born 1977; admitted to bar, 2003, Indiana. *Education:* Wabash College (B.A., 2000); Indiana University School of Law-Indianapolis (J.D., 2003). ***LANGUAGES:*** German. ***PRACTICE AREAS:*** Labor and Employment. ***Email:*** dustin.stohler@bakerd.com

KEITH J. SWEDO, born 1963; admitted to bar, 1995, Indiana, U.S. District Court, Southern District of Indiana; registered to practice before U.S. Patent and Trademark Office. *Education:* Purdue University (B.S., 1985); Indiana University (M.B.A., 1989); Indiana University School of Law-Indianapolis (J.D., 1995). Patent Law Intern, Delphi Technologies, 1994-1995. Engineer, Delphi Technologies, 1989-1996. Test Engineer, Delco Products, 1985-1987). Patent and Trademark attorney in two Indianapolis firms, 1996-2003. ***PRACTICE AREAS:*** Patents; Intellectual Property; Trademarks. ***Email:*** keith.swedo@bakerd.com

JANELLE TRANQUILLO, born 1976; admitted to bar, 2001, Illinois; 2004, Indiana. *Education:* Ball State University (B.S., summa cum laude, 1998); University of Notre Dame (J.D., magna cum laude, 2001). Articles Editor, Notre Dame Law Review, 2000-2001. *Member:* Chicago, Indianapolis, Illinois State, Indiana State and American Bar Associations. ***PRACTICE AREAS:*** Business Law; Finance. ***Email:*** janelle.tranquillo@bakerd.com

CHRISTINE A. WERNER, born 1972; admitted to bar, 1999, Michigan; 2001, Indiana. *Education:* Miami University (B.A., 1994); Indiana University (J.D., 1998). Phi Delta Phi. *Member:* Oakland County Bar Association; State Bar of Michigan. ***PRACTICE AREAS:*** Insurance Law. ***Email:*** christine.werner@bakerd.com

PAUL A. WOLFLA, born Indianapolis, Indiana, 1970; admitted to bar, 1998, Ohio; 1999, U.S. District Court, Southern District of Ohio; 2002, U.S. Court of Appeals, Sixth Circuit and U.S. Supreme Court; 2003, U.S. District Court, Southern District of Indiana; 2004, Indiana. *Education:* Indiana University (B.A., 1992); University of New Mexico (M.A., 1994); The Ohio State University (J.D., 1998). *Member:* Columbus and Ohio State Bar Associations. [U.S. Army Reserves, 1988-1996]. ***PRACTICE AREAS:*** Litigation. ***Email:*** paul.wolfla@bakerd.com

TAREEN ZAFRULLAH, admitted to bar, 2005, Indiana. *Education:* Washington University (B.S.B.A., summa cum laude, 2002); George Washington University (J.D., 2005). ***PRACTICE AREAS:*** Labor and Employment. ***Email:*** tareen.zafrullah@bakerd.com

INDIANAPOLIS - 96TH STREET, INDIANA OFFICE
MEMBERS OF FIRM

DAVID W. BARRETT, born 1971; admitted to bar, 1996, Indiana. *Education:* Wabash College (B.A., magna cum laude, 1993); Indiana University School of Law (J.D., cum laude, 1996). Author: "A Call for More Lenient Director Liability Standard for Small, Charitable Nonprofit Corporations," 71 Ind. L.J. 967. ***PRACTICE AREAS:*** Mergers and Acquisitions; Corporate; Venture Capital; Securities. ***Email:*** david.barrett@bakerd.com

DONALD P. BENNETT, born 1947; admitted to bar, 1973, Indiana. *Education:* Wabash College (A.B., 1969); University of Michigan (J.D., magna cum laude, 1973). Order of the Coif. Lecturer, Federal Income Taxation, Indiana University Law School, 1979-1980. *Member:* Indianapolis (Chairman, Tax Section, 1984), Indiana State and American Bar Associations. ***PRACTICE AREAS:*** Federal Income Tax; Partnerships; Mergers and Acquisitions; Venture Capital. ***Email:*** don.bennett@bakerd.com

DANIEL L. BOEGLIN, born 1959; admitted to bar, 1985, Indiana. *Education:* Indiana University (B.S., with highest distinction, 1982); University of Virginia (J.D., 1985). ***PRACTICE AREAS:*** Strategic Alliances; Joint Ventures; Mergers and Acquisitions; Corporate Finance; Venture Capital; Public Offerings; Private Placement. ***Email:*** daniel.boeglin@bakerd.com

J. JEFFREY BROWN, born 1960; admitted to bar, 1988, New York and Indiana. *Education:* Indiana University (B.A., 1982); Georgetown University (M.B.A., 1984); University of Virginia (J.D., 1987). Order of the Coif. ***PRACTICE AREAS:*** Acquisitions; Private Capital; Venture Capital; Securities; Corporate Law. ***Email:*** jeffrey.brown@bakerd.com

M. ANGELLA CASTILLE, born 1956; admitted to bar, 1989, Indiana; 1990, Michigan. *Education:* University of Southwestern Louisiana (B.A., 1978); Freie Universitat of Berlin, Germany; University of Notre Dame (J.D., 1988). Member, International Moot Court Team, University of Notre Dame. Author: "Going Global," Indiana Business Magazine. *Member:* Indiana State and American Bar Associations; State Bar of Michigan. (Vice-Chair, International Practice). ***LANGUAGES:*** German and French. ***PRACTICE AREAS:*** International Law. ***Email:*** angella.castille@bakerd.com

PATRICK S. CROSS, born 1963; admitted to bar, 1993, Indiana and U.S. District Court, Northern and Southern Districts of Indiana. *Education:* Indiana University (B.A., 1987; J.D., magna cum laude, 1993). Order of the Coif. Editor-in-Chief, Indiana Law Journal. *Member:* Indianapolis (Chair: Health Care Section), Indiana State (Secretary, Health-care and Medicinal Section) and American Bar Associations; American Health Lawyers Association. ***PRACTICE AREAS:*** Corporate Law; Emerging Business Law; Health Care. ***Email:*** patrick.cross@bakerd.com

ROBERT W. ELZER, born 1951; admitted to bar, 1976, Indiana. *Education:* Indiana University (B.A., with high distinction, 1973); Harvard University (J.D., cum laude, 1976). Phi Beta Kappa. Member: American College of Trust and Estate Counsel - ACTEL. *Member:* Indianapolis, Indiana State, American and Seventh Circuit Bar Associations; American College of Trust and Estate Counsel. ***PRACTICE AREAS:*** Estate Planning; Estate Administration; Business Transfers. ***Email:*** robert.elzer@bakerd.com

BRIAN S. FENNERTY, born 1961; admitted to bar, 1989, Indiana and U.S. District Court, Northern and Southern Districts of Indiana. *Education:* Indiana University (B.S., with highest distinction, 1984; J.D., summa cum laude, 1989). Associate Editor, Indiana Law Review, 1988-1989. Certified Public Accountant, Indiana, 1984. *Member:* Indiana State Bar Association (Member, Taxation Section). (Also at Qingdao, China Office). ***PRACTICE AREAS:*** Federal, State and Local Taxation; Business Transactions. ***Email:*** brian.fennerty@bakerd.com

DAVID A. FOSTER, born 1964; admitted to bar, 1990, Michigan; 1997, Indiana; U.S. District Court, Eastern and Western Districts of Michigan; U.S. District Court, Northern and Southern Districts of Indiana; U.S. Court of Appeals, Sixth Circuit. *Education:* University of Michigan (B.A., 1986); Indiana University (J.D., cum laude, 1990). Author: "What's So Super About Bankruptcy Code §1113?—Harmonizing the Disbursement of Benefits Under a Chapter 11 Debtor's Collective Bargaining Agreement with §507," 1994 Detroit College of Law Review 1247. *Member:* Indiana State and American (Member, Business Law Section) Bar Associations; State Bar of Michigan. ***PRACTICE AREAS:*** Secured Lending; Commercial Transactions; Bankruptcy; Aircraft Transactions. ***Email:*** david.foster@bakerd.com

BRANT O. GARDNER, born 1963; admitted to bar, 1988, Indiana and U.S. District Court, Southern and Northern Districts of Indiana. *Education:* Wheaton College (B.A., with highest honors, 1985); University of Virginia School of Law (J.D., 1988). Order of the Coif; Moot Court Board. Member, Editorial Board, University of Virginia Law Review, 1987-1988. ***PRACTICE AREAS:*** Estate Planning; Estate Administration. ***Email:*** brant.gardner@bakerd.com

JOHN A. GARDNER, born 1961; admitted to bar, 1986, Indiana. *Education:* Indiana University (B.S., 1983; J.D., summa cum laude, 1986). Business Editor, Indiana Law Review, 1985-1986. *Member:* Indianapolis, Indiana State and American Bar Association. ***PRACTICE AREAS:*** Estate Planning; Estate Administration. ***Email:*** john.gardner@bakerd.com

JAY JAFFE, born 1957; admitted to bar, 1982, Indiana and Kentucky; 1985, U.S. Court of Federal Claims. *Education:* Indiana University (B.A., with high distinction, 1979; J.D., cum laude, 1982). Phi Beta Kappa. Listed as one of the Best Bankruptcy Lawyers in Indianapolis in *The Best Lawyers in America and Indianapolis Monthly Magazine.* Served as a Standing Trustee, United States Bankruptcy Court, Southern District of Indiana, Indianapolis Division, 1986-1988. *Member:* Indianapolis (Chairman, Commercial and Bankruptcy Law Section, 1992; Treasurer, 2000-2001, Vice President, 2002 and 2003, and Board of Managers, 2000-2003) and Indiana State (Chairman, Bankruptcy and Creditors' Rights Section, 1999; Editor, "The Order for Relief," 1988) Bar Associations. ***PRACTICE AREAS:*** Creditors Rights; Bankruptcy. ***Email:*** jay.jaffe@bakerd.com

JERRY R. JENKINS, born 1944; admitted to bar, 1969, Indiana. *Education:* Southeast Missouri State College (B.A., first in class, 1966); Duke University (J.D., with high distinction, 1969). Order of the Coif. Member, Editorial Board, Duke Law Journal, 1968-1969. *Member:* Indianapolis, Indiana State and American (Member, Estate and Antitrust Sections) and Seventh Circuit Bar Associations; American Health Lawyers Association. ***PRACTICE AREAS:*** Estate Planning; Estate Administration; Antitrust. ***Email:*** jerry.jenkins@bakerd.com

JI-QING LIU, born 1956; admitted to bar, 1992, Indiana and U.S. District Court, Northern and Southern Districts of Indiana. *Education:* Shanghai Customs Academy, Shanghai, P.R. China (B.A., third in class, 1983); East China Institute of Politics and Law, P.R. China (Master of Laws, third in class, 1987); Columbia University (LL.M., 1989); Indiana University (J.D., 1992). Author: Anthology of Law Graduate Student Thesis, Vol. I, II (1984-1985, 1985-1986). (Also at 300 North Meridian St., Indianapolis, Indiana, Qingdao and Beijing, China Offices). ***PRACTICE AREAS:*** International Law; Corporate Law; Immigration. ***Email:*** ji-qing.liu@bakerd.com

KENT A. ROLLISON, born 1967; admitted to bar, 1993, Indiana and U.S. District Court, Northern and Southern Districts of Indiana; 1995, U.S. Court of Appeals, Seventh Circuit. *Education:* Butler University (B.A., cum laude, 1990); Indiana University School of Law (J.D., magna cum laude, 1993). Order of the Coif. Notes Research Editor, Indiana Law Journal. Law Clerk to Chief Judge Allen Sharp, U.S. District Court. *Member:* Indianapolis and Indiana State (Member, Probate, Trusts and Real Property Section) Bar Associations. ***PRACTICE AREAS:*** Estate Planning and Administration; Business Succession Planning. ***Email:*** kent.rollison@bakerd.com

JOSEPH M. SCIMIA, born 1959; admitted to bar, 1985, Arizona; 1987, Indiana. *Education:* Indiana University (B.S., high distinction, 1982; J.D., magna cum laude, 1985). Beta Gamma Sigma; Order of the Coif. ***PRACTICE AREAS:*** Real Estate; Land Use; Zoning Law. ***Email:*** joseph.scimia@bakerd.com

BRADLEY MERRILL THOMPSON, born 1961; admitted to bar, 1986, Indiana and U.S. Court of Appeals, Seventh Circuit; 1992, U.S. Supreme Court. *Education:* University of Illinois (B.A., cum laude, 1982; M.B.A., 1983); University of Michigan (J.D., cum laude, 1986). Adjunct Professor, Indiana University School of Law, 1992-1994. ***PRACTICE AREAS:*** Medicare and Medicaid; Food and Drug Law. ***Email:*** brad.thompson@bakerd.com

MARK E. WRIGHT, born 1960; admitted to bar, 1989, Indiana. *Education:* Indiana University (B.A., 1983; J.D., cum laude, 1989). *Member:* Indiana State Bar Association. ***PRACTICE AREAS:*** Real Estate. ***Email:*** mark.wright@bakerd.com

ROBERT S. WYNNE, born 1957; admitted to bar, 1985, Indiana. *Education:* DePauw University (B.A., 1979); Indiana University at Bloomington (M.B.A., 1981; J.D., magna cum laude, 1985). Order of the Coif. Co-Author, Panelist: "Uniform Commercial Code: Bulk Transfers," ICLEF, 1985; "Theories of Liability Based Upon Breach or Express or Implied Loan Commitments," ICLEF, 1987; "Avoidance of Liens and/or Obligations as Fraudulent Conveyances or Transfers," ICLEF, 1987; "The Secured Creditor Under the Comprehensive Environmental Response, Compensation, & Liability Act of 1980, as Amended by the Superfund Amendment and Reauthorization Act of 1986," National Business Institute's Commercial Lending in Seminar (1987); "Insider Guarantees After Deprizio," Indianapolis Bar Association, 1990; "Examination of a Complex Commercial Lending Transaction," National Business Institute Seminar, 1991. *Member:* Indiana State and American Bar Associations. ***PRACTICE AREAS:*** Real Estate; Creditors Rights; Secured Lending; Bankruptcy. ***Email:*** robert.wynne@bakerd.com

COUNSEL

DANIEL P. CARMICHAEL, born 1942; admitted to bar, 1968, Ohio and U.S. District Court, Southern District of Ohio; 1978, U.S. Supreme Court; 1979, Indiana. *Education:*

(This Listing Continued)

University of Cincinnati (B.S., Pharmacy, 1965; J.D., 1968). Rho Chi; Phi Delta Phi. Trustee and Member, Executive Committee, Food and Drug Law Institute, 1991—. Board of Directors and Member Executive Committee, American Society of Corporate Secretaries, 1997—. *Member:* Indianapolis, Indiana State and American (Member, Sections on: Antitrust Law; Administrative Law; Business Law; Regulatory Law; Health Law) Bar Associations; American Society for Pharmacy Law. ***Email:*** daniel.carmichael@bakerd.com

JOHN D. COCHRAN, born 1917; admitted to bar, 1942, New York and Pennsylvania; 1946, Indiana. *Education:* University of Pittsburgh (A.B., 1938); Harvard University (J.D., 1941). *Member:* Indianapolis, Indiana State and American Bar Associations. Fellow, Indiana Bar Foundation. ***PRACTICE AREAS:*** Corporate Law; Estate Planning; Trust Law; Taxation. ***Email:*** john.cochran@bakerd.com

RALPH F. HALL, born 1952; admitted to bar, 1977, Indiana; U.S. District Court, Southern District of Indiana. *Education:* Indiana University (A.B., magna cum laude, 1974); University of Michigan (J.D., cum laude, 1977). Visiting Professor, 2004-2005 and Adjunct Professor, 2000-2003, University of Minnesota Law School. Adjunct Professor, Indiana University School of Law - Indianapolis, 1988-1992. *Member:* Licensing Executives Society. ***PRACTICE AREAS:*** Health Care. ***Email:*** ralph.hall@bakerd.com

LEAH SCHLESINGER, admitted to bar, 1993, New York; 2004, Indiana. *Education:* University of Chicago (A.B., 1985; J.D., 1992). ***PRACTICE AREAS:*** Business and Finance; Mergers and Acquisitions. ***Email:*** leah.schlesinger@bakerd.com

ASSOCIATES

TREVOR JON BELDEN, born 1975; admitted to bar, 2000, Indiana. *Education:* Purdue University (B.A., 1996); University of Michigan, Ann Arbor (J.D., 2000). Phi Beta Kappa. ***PRACTICE AREAS:*** Corporate Finance; Business Planning. ***Email:*** trevor.belden@bakerd.com

JENNIFER L. DILL-McGILL, born 1972; admitted to bar, 1998, Indiana. *Education:* Ball State University (B.A., magna cum laude, 1995); Indiana University School of Law (J.D., 1998). ***PRACTICE AREAS:*** Trusts and Estates; Non-Profit. ***Email:*** jennifer.dill-mcgill@bakerd.com

TROY D. FARMER, born 1962; admitted to bar, 1998, Indiana; 2000, District of Columbia. *Education:* Ball State University (B.S., magna cum laude, 1984); Indiana University School of Law (J.D., magna cum laude, 1997). Member, Order of the Coif. Executive Notes and Comments Editor, Indiana Law Journal. Law Clerk, Hon. John D. Tinder, U.S. District Court, Southern District of Indiana, 1997-1998. *Member:* Indiana State Bar Association; District of Columbia Bar. ***PRACTICE AREAS:*** Estate Planning; Estate Administration; Business Succession Planning. ***Email:*** troy.farmer@bakerd.com

JOHN F. W. FLEMING, admitted to bar, 2003, Indiana. *Education:* Wabash College (A.B., cum laude, 2000); University of North Carolina (J.D., with honors, 2003). ***PRACTICE AREAS:*** Commercial Bankruptcy. ***Email:*** john.fleming@bakerd.com

VIRGINIA E. HO, born 1974; admitted to bar, 2001, Iowa; 2004, Indiana. *Education:* Indiana University, Bloomington (B.A., 1995; M.A., 1997); Harvard Law School (J.D., 2001). Phi Beta Kappa. Associate Editor and Book Notes Editor, Harvard International Law Journal, 1998-2001. Editor-In-Chief, Harvard Asia Quarterly, 2000. Jessup International Moot Court Competition, Regional Champion Team, 1999. Yontg K. Kim Memorial Prize, Harvard Law School, 2001. *Member:* Polk County, Iowa State, Indiana State and American Bar Associations. ***LANGUAGES:*** Mandarin Chinese, Russian and Cantonese. ***Email:*** virginia.ho@bakerd.com

LEAH R. KENDALL, admitted to bar, 2002, Indiana. *Education:* Butler University (B.S., summa cum laude, 1999); Indiana University-Bloomington (J.D., summa cum laude, 2002). *Member:* American Business Women's Association. ***PRACTICE AREAS:*** Health Care. ***Email:*** leah.kendall@bakerd.com

JENNIFER L. KREMP, born 1964; admitted to bar, 1994, Indiana. *Education:* Ball State University (B.S., summa cum laude, 1986); Indiana University (J.D., magna cum laude, 1994). Order of the Coif. Managing Editor, Indiana Law Journal. ***PRACTICE AREAS:*** Corporate Finance; Business Planning. ***Email:*** jennifer.kremp@bakerd.com

DENNIS P. LAGER, born 1961; admitted to bar, 1996, Indiana. *Education:* Luther College (B.A., cum laude, 1983); Indiana University School of Law (J.D., 1995). ***PRACTICE AREAS:*** Estate Planning; Estate Administration. ***Email:*** dennis.lager@bakerd.com

WATARU MATSUYASU, born 1971; admitted to bar, 2000, Massachusetts; 2004, Indiana. *Education:* Yale University (B.A., 1993); Georgetown University Law Center (J.D., 1999). ***PRACTICE AREAS:*** Affordable Housing; Housing Development; Finance. ***Email:*** wataru.matsuyasu@bakerd.com

APRIL J. RISK, admitted to bar, 2002, Indiana and U.S. District Court, Northern and Southern Districts of Indiana. *Education:* Indiana University (B.S., with high distinction, 1999; J.D., magna cum laude, 2002). Order of the Coif. Jump Scholar, 1999-2002. Articles Editor, Indiana Journal of Global Legal Studies, 2001. Member, Board of Trustees, Dance Kaleidoscope. Association Delegate to the Board of Directors of Lutheran High School of Indianapolis. ***PRACTICE AREAS:*** Trusts and Estates. ***Email:*** april.risk@bakerd.com

KATHRYN E. WILEY, born 1978; admitted to bar, 2004, Indiana. *Education:* Purdue University (B.A., 2001); Indiana University School of Law (J.D., 2004). Phi Beta Kappa; Phi Kappa Phi. Associate Editor, Indiana Law Review, 2003-2004. Alumni Scholarship Recipient. *Member:* Indianapolis Bar Association. ***PRACTICE AREAS:*** Business and Finance. ***Email:*** kathryn.wiley@bakerd.com

FORT WAYNE OFFICE
MEMBERS OF FIRM

J. Stephen Bennett (Not admitted in IN)
Jon A. Bomberger
John R. Burns, III
Timothy J. Haffner
Steven H. Hazelrigg
David J. Kuker
Jeanne E. Longsworth
Robert D. Moreland
Michael J. Nader
Anthony Niewyk
Maclyn T. Parker

(This Listing Continued)

FORT WAYNE OFFICE
MEMBERS OF FIRM (Continued)

John F. Hoffman
David P. Irmscher
Steven L. Jackson
Michael L. James
Joseph W. Kimmell, II (Also at Washington, D.C. and Peoples Republic of China Offices)
Douglas Dormire Powers
David A. Scott
Lawrence E. Shine
Thomas M. Shoaff
N. Reed Silliman

COUNSEL

KAREN T. MOSES. Email: karen.moses@bakerd.com

RESIDENT ASSOCIATES

Thomas R. Biehl, Jr. (Not admitted in IN)
Betsy M. Brooks
Michael S. Burns
Scott C. Burns (Not admitted in IN)
Abigail Marie Butler
Cynthia M. Cormany
Adam F. Cox
David P. Durm
Brian Thomas Geisler
Jeffrey V. Gery
M. Kristin Glazner
Jeffrey A. Goeglein
Shellie L. Goetz
Damian Gosheff
Jerome Byron Hayes
Julie Annette Hoffman
Jason A. Houser
Mark F. Juba
Thomas C. Kus
Martha M. Lemert
Jon L. Lindberg
Shannon K. Reed
Patrick A. Scheiderer
Michael D. Schwartz
Matthew B. Skaggs
David D. Storey
Andrew J. Welborn
Mark A. Werling

SOUTH BEND, INDIANA OFFICE
MEMBERS OF FIRM

Thomas J. Brunner, Jr.
Gerard T. Gallagher
Carl A. Greci
Eric J. Groen
M. Patricia Hackett
Richard L. Hill
James M. Matthews
Randolph R. Rompola
Edward A. Sullivan, III
Peter G. Trybula

COUNSEL

D. Lucetta Pope
Robert A. Wade

ASSOCIATES

Cara R. Brook
Alison G. Fox
Peter J. Gillin (Not admitted in IN)
Jeff R. Heck
RaeLee C. Hudson
Jennifer Bickley Hull
Thomas J. Mauch
Shawn E. Peterson
David R. Pruitt
Amy M. Steketee
Daniel Tychonievich

ELKHART, INDIANA OFFICE
MEMBERS OF FIRM

James R. Brotherson
Glenn E. Killoren
Kennard R. Weaver
Robert C. Whippo

OF COUNSEL

ROBERT A. PFAFF, born 1933; admitted to bar, 1961, Indiana and Michigan. *Education:* Washington & Lee University (A.B., 1955); University of Michigan (J.D., 1961). Member, Character and Fitness Committee, Indiana State Board of Law Examiners, 1965—. Certified Civil Mediator, Indiana, 1993; Family Law Mediator, 1995. *Member:* Elkhart City (President, 1985), Indiana State and American Bar Associations; State Bar of Michigan. Master Fellow, Indiana Bar Foundation. ***PRACTICE AREAS:*** Real Estate; Land Use; Business Planning. ***Email:*** robert.pfaff@bakerd.com

ASSOCIATES

Jennifer Elaine Greene
Jeremy D. Pfister
Christopher J. Spataro
Krista J. Zimmerman

WASHINGTON, D.C. OFFICE
MEMBERS OF FIRM

Scott D. Balderston
Thomas A. Jensen
Herbert V. Kerner
Joseph W. Kimmell, II (Also at Fort Wayne, Indiana and Qingdao, China Offices)
Charles T. Richardson
Frank S. Swain (Also at Qingdao, China Office)
Mark W. Weller
David R. Zook

COUNSEL

Robert J. Kabel
Ted R. Mannen

(This Listing Continued)

BAKER & DANIELS LLP, Indianapolis—Continued

OF COUNSEL

CAROLYN M. COLEMAN, admitted to bar, 1997, Indiana. *Education:* University of Kansas (B.S., with distinction, 1983); Indiana University School of Law - Bloomington (J.D., cum laude, 1997). ***PRACTICE AREAS:*** Government Affairs. ***Email:*** carolyn.coleman@bakerd.com

KERRY OWENS, born Washington, D.C.; admitted to bar, 1994, Maryland; 2001, District of Columbia; registered to practice before U.S. Patent and Trademark Office. *Education:* University of Wisconsin-Madison (B.S., 1985; B.S., Physics and Engineering, 1989); George Washington University (J.D., 1994). *Member:* The District of Columbia Bar. ***PRACTICE AREAS:*** Patents. ***Email:*** kerry.owens@bakerd.com

ASSOCIATES

Brandon Hurlbut (admission pending) ***David H. Milligan***

QINGDAO, CHINA OFFICE
MEMBERS OF FIRM

Ji-Qing Liu
Brian S. Fennerty (Also at Indianapolis - 96th Street, Indiana Office)
Thomas A. Jensen
Joseph W. Kimmell, II (Also at Washington, D.C. and Fort Wayne, Indiana Offices)
Frank S. Swain (Also at Washington, D.C. Office)

OF COUNSEL

MICHAEL R. MAINE. Email: mike.maine@bakerd.com

COUNSEL

ANDY WEI, admitted to bar, 1990, China. *Education:* Jilin University School of Law, Jilin, China (LL.B., 1983); China University of Political Science and Law, Beijing, China (LL.M., 1986); University of Washington (LL.M., 1997). ***PRACTICE AREAS:*** Business Law; Corporate Law; International Law. ***Email:*** andy.wei@bakerd.com

RESIDENT CONSULTANT

David M. T. Wang

BEIJING, CHINA OFFICE
MEMBER OF FIRM

Ji-Qing Liu

REPRESENTATIVE CLIENTS: 1st Source Bank; American Commercial Lines, Inc.; American General Finance, Inc.; American Trans Air, Inc.; Amoco, Inc.; Anthem Insurance Companies, Inc.; ARAMark Corp.; Arvin-Meritor, Inc.; AT&T Corp.; Auburn Foundry, Inc.; Ball Corporation; Bank One, Indianapolis, NA; Borg-Warner Corporation; Brightpoint Inc.; Central Soya Company, Inc.; Chevron Chemical Company; Chubb Group of Insurance Companies; Cinergy Corporation; Citizens Gas & Coke Utility; City of Elkhart; City of Fort Wayne; City of Indianapolis; City of South Bend; Clarian Health Partners; Conseco, Inc.; CSX Transportation, Inc.; Cummins Engine Company, Inc.; Delco Electronics Corporation; DePauw University; Dow AgroSciences LLC; Dow Brands, L.P.; DowElanco; EFP Corporation; Eli Lilly and Company; Emmis Communications; Enkei America, Inc.; Ernest & Julio Gallo Winery; Essex Group, Inc.; Farm Credit Services of Mid-America; Fort Wayne News-Sentinel; Fujitsu TEN; General Electric Capital Corp.; General Electric Company/Motor Business Group; General Motors Acceptance Corporation; General Motors Corporation; Golden Rule Insurance Company; Guardian Industries, Inc.; Guidant Corporation; Heartland Steel, Inc.; Heritage Environmental Services, Inc.; Hill-Rom; Hillenbrand Industries, Inc.; Indiana Bond Bank; Indiana Constructors, Inc.; Indiana Dental Association; Indiana Michigan Power Company; Indiana University; Indianapolis Life Insurance Company; Indianapolis Public Schools; Inland Paperboard and Packaging, Inc.; Ispat Inland Inc.; ITT Corporation (Aerospace/Optical Division); Jayco, Inc.; Jewel Cos., Inc./Osco Drug, Inc.; John Hancock Mutual Life Insurance Co.; Key Bank; Kimball International; Kraft Foods, Inc.; Lilly Endowment, Inc.; McDonald's Corporation; McDonald & Company Securities, Inc.; Meridian Financial Corporation; Meridian Mutual Insurance; Metropolitan Life Insurance Company; Miller Brewing Company; Minnesota Mining & Manufacturing; Modernfold, Inc.; MSA Realty Corporation; National City Bank; National Enterprises, Inc.; National Retail Hardware Association; National Starch & Chemical Company; New Bern Transport Corporation; NOLHGA; North American Van Lines, Inc.; Philip Morris Company; PSI Energy, Inc.; Quality Dining, Inc.; Quantum Chemical Corporation; Quorum Health Group of Indiana; R.R. Donnelley & Sons Co.; Raffensperger, Hughes & Co., Inc.; Ralston Purina Company; Rand McNally & Company; Rea Magnet Wire, Inc.; Red Ball Corporation; Roche Diagnostic Systems, Inc.; Saint John's Medical Center; Schult Homes Corporation; Seyfert Foods, Inc.; Shambaugh & Son, Inc.; Shoe Carnival; Simon & Schuster; Simon Property Group, Inc.; Sisters of St. Francis Health Services, Inc.; Slater Steels Corporation; Society Corporation; South Bend Community Schools Corporation; St. John's Health System; Steel Dynamics Inc.; Subaru-Isuzu; Tecumseh Compressor; Tenaska, Inc.; The Lutheran Hospital of Indiana, Inc.; The Prudential Insurance Company of America; Trammell Crow Company; Tranex Credit Corporation; U.S. Gymnastics Federation; Wabash College; Wabash National; Wal-Mart Stores, Inc.; Weaver Popcorn, Inc.; Westinghouse Electric Corporation; Wells Fargo; WSBT, Inc.; York International Corporation; Zimmer, Inc.

(For complete biographical data on other Members of Firm, Of Counsel and Associates, See Professional Biographies at Indianapolis, Fort Wayne, South Bend, Elkhart, Indiana, Washington, D.C., Qingdao and Beijing China)

BALDWIN & DAKICH

151 NORTH DELAWARE STREET, SUITE 1510
INDIANAPOLIS, INDIANA 46204
Telephone: 317-636-4529
Fax: 317-635-5370
Email: jbaldwin@iquest.net
URL: http://www.lawyers.com/baldwin&dakich

Criminal Defense, Sports Law, Telecommunications Law.

JEFFREY A. BALDWIN, born Cincinnati, Ohio, April 7, 1962; admitted to bar, 1987, Indiana. *Education:* Wabash College (B.A., cum laude, 1984); Indiana University (J.D., 1987). Marion County Deputy Prosecuting Attorney, 1987-1990. *Member:* Indianapolis, Seventh Circuit, Indiana State and American Bar Associations. ***PRACTICE AREAS:*** Criminal Defense; State Government Law; Federal Government Law. ***Email:*** jbaldwin@iquest.net

THOMAS P. DAKICH, born Gary, Indiana, July 12, 1960; admitted to bar, 1985, Indiana. *Education:* Wabash College (B.A., 1982); Indiana University (J.D., 1985). Marion County Deputy Prosecuting Attorney, 1985-1987. *Member:* Marion County, Indianapolis and Indiana State (Member, Young Lawyers Section) Bar Associations. ***PRACTICE AREAS:*** Sports Law; Telecommunications Law.

ASSOCIATE

GINNY MAXWELL, born Indianapolis, Indiana, December, 27, 1966; admitted to bar, 2000, Indiana. *Education:* Ohio University (B.A., 1989); Indiana University School of Law (M.P.A., 1999; J.D., 1999). ***PRACTICE AREAS:*** Criminal Defense. ***Email:*** gmaxwell@iquest.net

BARNES & THORNBURG LLP

11 SOUTH MERIDIAN STREET
INDIANAPOLIS, INDIANA 46204
Telephone: 317-236-1313
FAX: 317-231-7433
URL: http://www.btlaw.com

Fort Wayne, Indiana Office: 600 One Summit Square, 46802. Telephone: 260-423-9440. FAX: 260-424-8316.
South Bend, Indiana Office: 600 1st Source Bank Center, 100 North Michigan, 46601-1632. Telephone: 574-233-1171. FAX: 574-237-1125.
Elkhart, Indiana Office: 121 West Franklin Street, Suite 200, 46516. Telephone: 574-293-0681. FAX: 574-296-2535.
Chicago, Illinois Office: One North Wacker Drive, Suite 4400, 60606-2809. Telephone: 312-357-1313. FAX: 312-759-5646.
Washington, D.C. Office: 750 17th Street, N.W., Suite 900. 20006. Telephone: 202-289-1313. FAX: 202-289-1330.
Grand Rapids, Michigan Office: 300 Ottawa Avenue, N.W., Suite 500, 49503. Telephone: 616-742-3930. FAX: 616-742-3999.

Acquisitions and Divestitures, Ad Valorem Tax, Administrative Law, Affirmative Action, Agriculture Law, Americans with Disabilities Act, Antidumping, Antitrust, Antitrust and Trade Regulation, Appellate Practice, Attorney Grievances, Automotive Warranty Law, Aviation and Aerospace, Aviation Law, Banking Law, Banking Regulations, Bankruptcy, Bankruptcy Reorganization, Banks and Banking, Biochemical Patents, Biomedical Products Liability, Biomedical Technology, Biotechnology Patent Prosecution, Bond Law, Brain Injury, Breach of Warranty, Brown Fields Redevelopment, Business Immigration, Business Law, Business Litigation, Business Planning, Business Regulatory and Administrative, Business Start-ups, Business Succession Planning, Business Taxation, Business Torts, Business Transactions, Business Transfers, Buying and Selling of Businesses, Cable TV, Cargo Claims, Charitable Trusts and Foundations, Chemical Intellectual Property, Chemical Patent Prosecution, Chemical Patents, Chemical Products Liability, Civil Appeals, Civil Litigation, Civil Practice, Civil RICO, Class Action Defense, Clean Air Act, Clean Water Act, Closely Held Business Estate Planning, Closely Held Businesses, Closely Held Business Law, Closely Held Corporations, Collective Bargaining, Commercial Bankruptcy, Commercial Finance Law, Commercial Law, Commercial Leasing and Financing, Commercial Litigation, Commercial Conveyancing, Commercial Real Estate, Commercial Real Estate Acquisition, Commercial Real Estate Development, Commercial Real Estate Finance, Commercial Transactions, Commodities Fraud, Communications and Media, Complex Commercial Litigation, Complex Litigation, Computer and Software Patents, Computer Law, Computers and Software, Conflicts of Interest, Construction Labor Law, Construction Law, Consumer Credit, Contract Litigation, Cooperatives, Copyrights, Corporate Finance, Corporate Formation, Corporate Law, Corporate Taxation, Corporate Tax Planning, Countervailing Duties, Covenants Not To Compete, Creditors Rights, Creditors Rights in Bankruptcy, Criminal Defense, Criminal Law, Criminal Tax Audits, Customs Law, Dealer and Distributor Termination, Debt and Equity Finance, Decedents Estates, Defense Litigation, Design Patents, Disability Insurance Defense, Discrimination, Distribution, Drug and Medical Device Defense, Economic Development, Education Law, Elder Law, Election, Campaign and Political Law, Electric Power, Electric Utilities, Electrical Intellectual Property, Electrical Patents, Electro-mechanical Patents, Electronic Commerce, Electronic Patents, Eminent Domain, Employee Benefits, Employee Stock Ownership Plans, Employment Defense, Employment Discrimination, Employment Law, Employment Litigation, Energy, Energy Contracts, Energy Regulation, Environmental Administrative Law, Environmental Cleanup, Environmental Compliance, Environmental Criminal Defense, Environmental Law, Environmental Litigation, Environmental Permitting, Environmental Real Estate, Environmental Regulation, Environmental Risk Management, Equal Employment Opportunity Law, ERISA Litigation, Estate Administration, Estate and Gift Taxation, Estate Planning, Estate Planning and Taxation, Estate Planning and Administration, Estate Planning and Probate, Estate Planning for Parents of Handicapped Children, Estate Planning for Unmarried Individuals, Executive Compensation, Executive Severance Contracts, Export Regulation, Fair Employment Practices, Family and Medical Leave Act, Family Business Successions, Family Wealth Transfer, Federal and State Administrative Regulatory Practice, Federal and State Legislative Practice, Federal Civil Litigation, Federal Civil Practice, Federal Criminal Law, Federal Estate and Gift Taxation, Federal Litigation, Federal Tax Controversies, Federal Taxation, Fiduciary Income Tax, Finance, Financial Transactions, First Party Insurance, Foreign Investment in the United States, Freight Claims, Freight Loss and Damage, Gaming Law, Gaming Licensing, Gas Utilities, General Litigation, Government, Government Affairs, Government Agency Practice, Government Contracts, Government Investigations, Government Relations, Groundwater Contamination, Hazardous Materials and Substances, Hazardous Waste, Hazardous Waste Liability, Head Injury, Health Care, Health Care Corporate Law, Health Care Contracts, Health Care Fraud, Health Care Licensing, Health Care Litigation, Health Care Mergers and Acquisitions, Health Care Regulation, Health Care Reimbursement, Health Law, Heavy Equipment Products Liability, Immigration Law, Industrial Revenue Bond Law, Inheritance Tax, Initial Public Offerings, Insurance, Insurance Bad Faith, Insurance Coverage, In-

(This Listing Continued)

surance Litigation, Insurance Regulation, Integrated Health Care Delivery Systems, Intellectual Property, Intellectual Property General Prosecution, Intellectual Property Infringement, Intellectual Property Licensing, Intellectual Property Litigation, Intellectual Property Procurement, Intellectual Property Protection, Intellectual Property Rights, International Business Law, International Intellectual Property, International Law, International Patents, International Trade, International Transportation Law, Internet Law, Internet Trademark Law, Joint Ventures, Labor and Employment, Labor Arbitration, Labor Law, Labor Relations, Land Use, Lease Law, Leasing, Legal Ethics and Professional Responsibility, Legal Malpractice Defense, Legislative Practice, Licensing, Life Insurance Defense, Limited Liability Company Law, Limited Partnerships, Liquor Licensing, Litigation, Loans, Lobbying, Local Government Law, Logistics, Long Term Care, Managed Care, Managed Care Contracts, Management Employment Law, Management Labor Law, Manufacturers Liability, Maritime Regulations, Mechanical Intellectual Property, Mechanical Patents, Media Law, Mediation, Medical Antitrust, Medical Intellectual Property, Medical Patents, Mental Health Law, Mergers, Acquisitions and Divestitures, Mergers and Acquisitions, Mineral Taxation, Molecular Biology Patents, Motor Carrier Law, Motor Carrier Regulation, Multi-Employer Pensions, Municipal Bonds, Municipal Bonds Taxation, Municipal Finance, Municipal Law, Municipal Leasing, Municipal Redevelopment, Municipal Securities, Municipal Taxation, National Labor Relations Act, Neurolaw, Nonprofit and Charitable Organizations, Nonprofit Organizations Law, North American Free Trade Agreement, Occupational Safety and Health, OSHA, Partnership Law, Partnership Taxation, Patent Infringement, Patent Interference Practice, Patent Litigation, Patent Prosecution, Patents, PCT Legal Export, Personal Injury, Personal Injury Defense, Pesticide Litigation, Pharmaceutical Intellectual Property, Pharmaceutical Patents, Physician Contracts, Physician Practices, Planning and Land Use, Power Line Contact Injury, Probate, Probate Litigation, Products Liability, Products Liability Defense, Professional Liability, Property Law, Property Tax, Property Tax Abatement, Property Tax Appeals, Psychological Injury, Public Finance, Public Sector Labor Relations, Public Utility Law, Railroad Law, Real Estate, Real Estate Acquisitions, Real Estate Contracts, Real Estate Development, Real Estate Finance, Real Estate Licensing, Real Estate Secured Lending, Real Estate Title Insurance, Real Property, Real Property Acquisitions, Real Property Finance, Reorganizations, Resource Conservation and Recovery Act (RCRA), Retirement Benefit Plans, School Law, Securities, Securities Litigation, Securitization, Semiconductor Technology, Sexual Harassment, Small Business Corporations, State Government Law, State Tax Controversies, State Taxation, Structured Finance, Succession Planning, Superfund, Tax Controversies, Tax Exempt Finance, Tax Exempt Organizations, Tax Increment Finance, Tax Law, Tax Litigation, Taxation, Technology and Science, Technology Law, Technology Licensing, Technology Transfers, Telecommunications Competition, Telecommunications Law, Theft of Trade Secrets, Title VII Discrimination, Title IX Discrimination, Tort Defense, Toxic Exposure, Toxic Tort Class Actions, Toxic Torts, Toxic Tort Defense, Trade Dress, Trade Secrets, Trademark Litigation, Trademarks, Trademark Prosecution, Trademark Protection, Trademark Registration, Transportation, Transportation Safety, Trial Practice, Trusts and Estates, Unfair Competition, Unfair Trade, Uniform Commercial Codes, Union Contract Negotiations, Union Elections, Utilities, Utility Law, Wage and Hour Law, WARN Act, Water Pollution, Water Quality, Water Utilities, Wetland Regulation, White Collar Crime, White Collar Criminal Defense, Wills, Workers Compensation, Workouts, World Trade Organization, Wrongful Death, Wrongful Termination, Wrongful Termination Defense, Zoning, Planning and Land Use.

FIRM PROFILE: Quality. Service. Efficiency. Communication. These are the cornerstones of the firm's culture and the keys to its success.

Established on January 1, 1982, Barnes & Thornburg LLP is relatively young; however, its founding date belies the firm's rich history. The firm's roots can be traced to two cities, South Bend and Indianapolis. Our northern Indiana presence began in 1926 with the establishment of Seebirt Oare & Omacht, and later grew when they merged with an Elkhart firm, Cawley and Harman. In Indianapolis, four partners opened Barnes Hickam Pantzer & Boyd on September 13, 1940. They began the firm with 13 people in an office of 13 rooms on the 13th floor of the Merchants Bank Building, the tallest in Indiana at that time. The number 13 has proven to be a lucky number for Barnes & Thornburg LLP.

Since 1982, the firm has opened offices in Chicago, Fort Wayne, Washington, D.C., Grand Rapids and merged with Jenkins, Coffey, Hyland, Badger & Conard, an intellectual property firm; Roberts, Ryder, Rogers & Scism, a labor and employment law firm; Church, Nilsson & Paulen of Elkhart; Roemer & Mintz, LLP, of South Bend, and most recently, Lee, Mann, Smith, McWilliams, Sweeney & Ohlson of Chicago. The firm has also been joined by Gallucci, Hopkins & Theisen, P.C., a Fort Wayne firm with an extensive labor and employment practice, and Johnson Lawhead Buth & Pope, P.C., an Indianapolis firm with a concentration in estate planning. Today Barnes & Thornburg LLP is the largest law firm in Indiana and one of the largest in the Midwest. More than 390 attorneys provide legal services to more than 11,000 international, national, regional and local clients.

With offices in Indianapolis, Chicago, Elkhart, Fort Wayne, Grand Rapids, South Bend, and Washington, D.C., we are a business-minded law firm serving clients ranging from Fortune 100 companies and governmental entities to individuals and nonprofit organizations. We represent the interests of businesses in our primary practices: business, tax and real estate, creditors' rights, energy, telecommunications and utilities, environmental law, governmental services and finance, healthcare, intellectual property, labor and employment law, litigation, appellate, business and technology, construction law, e-commerce, economic development, entrepreneurial services, financial institutions, international, media, pension and benefits litigation, property tax, transportation and white collar crime. Each of our offices offers a unique blend of services which collectively make Barnes & Thornburg LLP a diverse and dynamic legal resource for our clients and communities.

We have lawyers involved at city, state and national levels of the legal profession as officers, chairpersons and committee members in legal organizations. Others are authors, presenters and drafters of legislation. Most of our lawyers are active in their communities and provide civic leadership. Each office sponsors, contributes to, and often leads, an array of community activities.

LAW FIRM ALLIANCES/ASSOCIATIONS: **TECHLAW GROUP**

TERRALEX, THE WORLDWIDE NETWORK OF INDEPENDENT LAW FIRMS

PARTNERS

STEPHEN J. DUTTON, admitted to bar, 1969, Indiana. *Education:* Illinois Institute of Technology (B.S., 1965); Indiana University (J.D., magna cum laude, 1969). Executive Secretary: Judicial Study Commission, 1968-1969; Judicial Conference of Indiana, 1968-1969. *Member:* Indianapolis, Indiana State and American (Chair, Newsletters Board, 1992-1994; Chair, Law Practice Division, 1990-1992; Chair, Computer Division, 1985-1990; Member Of Council, Law Practice Management Section, 1986-1992; Member, Coordinating Commission on Legal Technology, 1988-1990) Bar Associations. ***PRACTICE AREAS:*** Mergers, Acquisitions and Divestitures; Securities; Computers and Software. ***Email:*** stephen.dutton@btlaw.com

RICHARD L. JOHNSON, admitted to bar, 1972, Indiana. *Education:* University of North Dakota (B.A., 1965); Whittier College (M.Ed., 1968); Hastings College of Law, University of California (J.D., 1972). Phi Delta Phi. Member, Thurston Society. *Member:* Indiana State and American Bar Associations. ***PRACTICE AREAS:*** Real Estate Law; Commercial Finance Law. ***Email:*** richard.johnson@btlaw.com

MICHAEL R. FRUEHWALD, admitted to bar, 1973, Indiana. *Education:* Indiana University (A.B., 1970; J.D., magna cum laude, 1973). Phi Beta Kappa; Order of the Coif. Note Editor, Indiana Law Journal, 1972-1973. ***PRACTICE AREAS:*** Litigation. ***Email:*** mike.fruehwald@btlaw.com

HAROLD R. BICKHAM, admitted to bar, 1973, Indiana and U.S. District Court, Southern District of Indiana. *Education:* Purdue University (B.A., Political Science, 1970); Indiana University (J.D., 1973). Senior Litigation Counsel, U.S. Department of Justice, 1987-1988. Chief, Civil Division, United States Attorney's Office, 1988-2001. ***REPORTED CASES:*** Rogers v. United States, 902 F.2d 1268 (7th Cir. 1990); Ronnie v. Garrett, 896 F.2d 1057 (7th Cir. 1990); Barnhart v. United States, 884 F.2d 295 (7th Cir. 1989); Yowell v. United States Postal Service, 810 F.2d 644 (7th Cir. 1987); Skillern v. Bolger, 725 F.2d 1121 (7th Cir. 1984); United States v. Robert's Nursing Home, 710 F.2d 1275 (7th Cir. 1983); McNeil v. Califano, 614 F.2d 142 (7th Cir. 1980); Indiana Civil Rights Comm. v. Meridian Hills Country Club, 171 Ind.App. 341, 357 N.E.2d 5 (1976). ***PRACTICE AREAS:*** Labor and Employment. ***Email:*** harold.bickham@btlaw.com

DONALD E. KNEBEL, admitted to bar, 1974, Indiana. *Education:* Purdue University (B.S.E.E., with highest distinction, 1968); Harvard University (J.D., magna cum laude, 1974). ***PRACTICE AREAS:*** Intellectual Property; Intellectual Property Litigation; Patent Litigation; Federal Civil Litigation; Antitrust and Trade Regulation; Unfair Trade. ***Email:*** donald.knebel@btlaw.com

WAYNE C. KREUSCHER, admitted to bar, 1974, Indiana; U.S. Court of Appeals, 7th Circuit; U.S. Supreme Court. *Education:* University of Nebraska (B.A., 1968; J.D., with distinction, 1974). Phi Delta Phi; Order of the Coif. Editor-in-Chief, Nebraska Law Review, 1973-1974. *Member:* Indianapolis Bar Association; Defense Research Institute; Federation of Defense & Corporate Counsel. [U.S. Army]. ***PRACTICE AREAS:*** Civil Litigation; Products Liability; Products Liability Defense; Manufacturers Liability; Trial Practice. ***Email:*** wayne.kreuscher@btlaw.com

KRISTIN G. FRUEHWALD, admitted to bar, 1975, Indiana. *Education:* University of Nebraska (B.S., highest distinction, 1968); Indiana University (J.D., summa cum laude, 1975). Indiana Review Editor, Indiana Law Review, 1974-1975. President, Indianapolis Bar Foundation, 1997-1999. Member, American College of Trust and Estate Counsel. Indiana Probate Code Study Commission. *Member:* Indianapolis (President, 1993-1994; Chair, Estate Planning and Administration Section, 1982-1983) and Indiana State (President, 2001-2002; Chair, Probate, Trust and Real Property Section, 1987-1988) Bar Associations. ***PRACTICE AREAS:*** Probate; Trusts and Estates; Federal Estate and Gift Taxation; Inheritance Tax; Wills; Closely Held Business Estate Planning. ***Email:*** kris.fruehwald@btlaw.com

DANIEL W. McGILL, admitted to bar, 1975, Indiana. *Education:* University of Michigan (B.A., 1972; J.D., magna cum laude, 1974). Order of the Coif. Associate Editor, Michigan Law Review, 1973-1974. *Member:* Indiana State Bar Association (Chair: Legal Ethics Committee, 1982-1984; Utility Law Section, 2001-2002). ***PRACTICE AREAS:*** Public Utility Law; Energy; Water Utilities; Electric Utilities; Gas Utilities; Telecommunications Regulation. ***Email:*** dan.mcgill@btlaw.com

KENT E. AGNESS, admitted to bar, 1975, Indiana. *Education:* Indiana University (B.A., 1972); University of Virginia (J.D., 1975). Phi Beta Kappa. *Member:* Indiana State and American Bar Associations. ***PRACTICE AREAS:*** Business Law; Contracts; Corporate Law; Commercial Law; Mergers and Acquisitions. ***Email:*** kent.agness@btlaw.com

MICHAEL R. CONNER, admitted to bar, 1975, Indiana. *Education:* University of Notre Dame (B.A., 1972); Indiana University (J.D., summa cum laude, 1975). Order of the Coif. Associate Editor, Indiana Law Journal, 1974-1975. Fellow of the American College of Trial Lawyers; Board of Directors of the Defense Trial Counsel of Indiana, 1996-1999. ***PRACTICE AREAS:*** Products Liability; Drug and Medical Device Defense; Heavy Equipment Products Liability; Manufacturers Liability; Litigation; Biomedical Products Liability. ***Email:*** mike.conner@btlaw.com

CLAUDIA V. SWHIER, admitted to bar, 1975, Indiana. *Education:* Yale University (B.A., 1972); Harvard University (J.D., cum laude, 1975). Member, Board of Editors, Harvard Law Review, 1973-1975. ***PRACTICE AREAS:*** Banks and Banking; Securities; Initial Public Offerings; Mergers, Acquisitions and Divestitures; Corporate Finance; Corporate Law. ***Email:*** claudia.swhier@btlaw.com

CATHERINE L. BRIDGE, admitted to bar, 1976, New York; 1978, Indiana. *Education:* Fordham University (A.B., 1972); Columbia University (J.D., 1975). Phi Beta Kappa. Writing and Research Editor, Columbia Journal of Law & Social Problems, 1974-1975. ***PRACTICE AREAS:*** Mergers, Acquisitions and Divestitures; Securities; Initial Public Offerings; Corporate Law; Corporate Finance; Insurance Regulation. ***Email:*** catherine.bridge@btlaw.com

RICHARD D. CONARD, admitted to bar, 1975, Indiana. *Education:* Rose Polytechnic Institute (B.S.E.E., 1970); Indiana University (J.D., cum laude, 1974). Tau Beta Pi; Eta

(This Listing Continued)

BARNES & THORNBURG LLP, Indianapolis—Continued

Kappa Nu. ***SPECIAL AGENCIES:*** U.S. Patent and Trademark Office. ***PRACTICE AREAS:*** Electrical Patents; Electro-Mechanical Patents; Electronic Patents; Computer and Software Patents; Copyrights; Trademarks. ***Email:*** richard.conard@btlaw.com

LARRY J. STROBLE, admitted to bar, 1976, Indiana. *Education:* Indiana University (A.B., 1971; M.B.A. and J.D., magna cum laude, 1976). Phi Beta Kappa; Order of the Coif. Fellow, American College of Tax Counsel. *Member:* Indianapolis (Chair, Taxation Section, 1987-1988), Indiana State (Chair, Taxation Section Tax Court Liaison Committee, 1987—) and American (State and Local Tax Committee) Bar Associations. ***REPORTED CASES:*** Commissioner v. Indianapolis Power & Light Company. ***PRACTICE AREAS:*** Tax Law; Federal Tax Controversies; Tax Litigation; Property Tax; State Taxation; State Tax Controversies. ***Email:*** larry.stroble@btlaw.com

MICHAEL ROSIELLO, admitted to bar, 1977, California and Indiana. *Education:* Columbia University (A.B., 1973); Stanford University (J.D., 1976). Phi Beta Kappa. ***PRACTICE AREAS:*** Litigation; Appellate Practice. ***Email:*** mike.rosiello@btlaw.com

PETER J. RUSTHOVEN, admitted to bar, 1976, Indiana. *Education:* Harvard University (A.B., magna cum laude, 1973; J.D., magna cum laude, 1976). Phi Beta Kappa. Member, Board of Editors, 1974-1976, and Case Note Editor, 1975-1976, Harvard Law Review. Associate Counsel to President of United States, 1981-1985. Counsel to Presidential Commission on Space Shuttle Challenger Accident, 1986. Candidate for Republican nomination for U.S. Senator from Indiana, 1997-1998. Transition Counsel's Office, Bush-Cheney Presidential Transition, 2001. [U.S. Naval Reserve, JAG Corps, 1982-1996]. ***PRACTICE AREAS:*** Appellate Practice; Corporate Law; Gaming Licensing; Government Relations; Legislative Practice; Liquor Licensing. ***Email:*** peter.rusthoven@btlaw.com

LARRY A. MACKEY, admitted to bar, 1976, Indiana and Illinois. *Education:* University of Evansville (B.A., summa cum laude, 1973); Indiana University School of Law (J.D., magna cum laude, 1976); University of Evansville (Doctor of Humane Letters, 1999). Fellow, American College of Trial Lawyers. Recipient, Attorney General's Award for Exceptional Service as a Lead Prosecutor in Oklahoma City bombing trials. *Member:* Indianapolis, Indiana State, Seventh Circuit and Federal Bar Associations. ***REPORTED CASES:*** U.S. vs Timothy J. McVeigh & Terry L. Nichols. ***PRACTICE AREAS:*** Complex Litigation; Government Investigations; Federal Criminal Law; White Collar Criminal Defense; Antitrust. ***Email:*** larry.mackey@btlaw.com

JOHN W. BOYD, admitted to bar, 1976, Indiana. *Education:* Northwestern University (B.A., 1973); Tulane University of Louisiana and Indiana University at Indianapolis (J.D., cum laude, 1976). Managing Editor, Indiana Law Review, 1975-1976. Author: "The Reasonable Expectation of Privacy; Katz v. United States—A Post Scriptum," 9 Indiana Law Review 468, 1976; "Survey of Recent Development in Indiana Law—Taxation," 11 Indiana Law Review 292, 1978, 12 Indiana Law Review 320, 1979 and 16 Indiana Law Review 355, 1983. Law Clerk, Chief Judge William E. Steckler, U.S. District Court, Southern District of Indiana, 1976-1978. Member, IRS Commissioner's Advisory Group, 1992-1994. *Member:* Indianapolis, Seventh Circuit, Indiana State (Chairman, Tax Section, 1989; Chair, Unauthorized Practice of Law Committee, 1997), Federal and American (Member: Taxation Section; Closely Held Business Committee; Chairman, 1996-1998) Bar Associations. Fellow: American College of Tax Counsel; Indianapolis Bar Foundation. ***PRACTICE AREAS:*** Corporate Law; Mergers and Acquisitions; Federal Taxation; Gaming Law; Business Law. ***Email:*** john.boyd@btlaw.com

STEPHEN W. LEE, admitted to bar, 1977, Indiana. *Education:* Ball State University (B.S., 1971); Indiana University (J.D., summa cum laude, 1977). Order of the Coif. Editor-in-Chief, Indiana Law Journal, 1976-1977. Law Clerk to Hon. Jesse E. Eschbach. *Member:* Indianapolis and Indiana State Bar Associations. [Lt(jg), USNR, 1971-1974]. ***PRACTICE AREAS:*** Real Estate; Corporate Law; Commercial Real Estate; Construction Law; Zoning, Planning and Land Use; Eminent Domain. ***Email:*** stephen.lee@btlaw.com

STANLEY C. FICKLE, admitted to bar, 1974, Indiana; 1977, California. *Education:* Indiana University (A.B., 1966; M.B.A., 1968; J.D., summa cum laude, 1974). Law Clerk: to Hon. Jesse E. Eschbach, Judge, U.S. District Court, Northern District of Indiana, 1974-1975; to Hon. William J. Brennan, Jr., Justice, U.S. Supreme Court, 1975-1976; American Academy of Appellate Lawyers. ***PRACTICE AREAS:*** Litigation; Appellate Practice; Civil Appeals. ***Email:*** stan.fickle@btlaw.com

WILLIAM M. POPE, admitted to bar, 1977, Indiana. *Education:* University of Indianapolis (B.A., 1974); Indiana University (J.D., cum laude, 1977). Board of Editors, Indiana Law Journal. ***PRACTICE AREAS:*** Estate Planning; Taxation; Business Transactions; Closely Held Family Owned Businesses. ***Email:*** william.pope@btlaw.com

MICHAEL P. LUCAS, admitted to bar, 1978, Indiana. *Education:* University of Wisconsin (B.A., 1975); Indiana University (J.D., summa cum laude, 1978). Note and Development Editor, Indiana Law Review, 1977-1978. *Member:* National Association of Bond Lawyers. ***PRACTICE AREAS:*** Public Finance; Taxation; Municipal Bonds; Tax Exempt Finance; Economic Development; Federal Tax Controversies. ***Email:*** michael.lucas@btlaw.com

JOHN M. KYLE III, admitted to bar, 1979, Indiana. *Education:* Indiana University (A.B., 1976; J.D., with distinction, 1979). Strathmore's Who's Who, 1999-2000. *Member:* Indianapolis, Indiana State and American Bar Associations. Fellow, Indiana Bar Foundation. ***PRACTICE AREAS:*** Brownfields Redevelopment; Environmental Cleanup; Environmental Risk Management; Groundwater Contamination; Resource Conservation and Recovery Act (RCRA); Superfund. ***Email:*** john.kyle@btlaw.com

MICHAEL K. McCRORY, admitted to bar, 1979, Indiana; 1992, District of Columbia; U.S. District Court, Northern and Southern Districts of Indiana; U.S. Court of Appeals, Seventh Circuit; U.S. Supreme Court. *Education:* Indiana State University (B.S., cum laude, 1976); Indiana University (J.D., cum laude, 1979). Phi Delta Phi. Note and Development Editor, Indiana Law Review, 1978-1979. Law Clerk to Hon. James E. Noland, United States District Court for the Southern District of Indiana, 1979-1981. *Member:* Indianapolis (Chair, Commercial and Bankruptcy Section, 1996-1997), Indiana State (Chair, Corporation, Banking and Business Law Section, 1986-1987), Seventh Circuit and American Bar Associations; American Bankruptcy Institute. Master Fellow, Indiana Bar Foundation; Fellow, Indianapolis Bar Foundation. (Certified in Business Bankruptcy Law by the American Board of Certification). ***PRACTICE AREAS:*** Business Law; Mergers and Acquisitions; Creditors; Bankruptcy; Buying and Selling of Businesses; Commercial Transactions; Workouts. ***Email:*** michael.mccrory@btlaw.com

MARCUS B. CHANDLER, admitted to bar, 1979, Indiana. *Education:* DePauw University (B.A., with high honors, 1976); University of Chicago (J.D., 1979). Phi Beta Kappa. Recipient, Rector Scholarship. Member, Board of Editors, University of Chicago Law Review, 1978-1979. Listed in: Indianapolis Business Journal 40 Under 40 (top 40 Indianapolis Business People under 40). Co-Chairman, Business and Technology Practice Group. Past-Member, Midwest Entrepreneurial Education Center. Member, Venture Club of Indiana. Chairman, Indiana TechPoint Summit, 2004. Co-Founder, Indiana Growth 100. Co-Founder and Co-Chairman, Indiana CFO Roundtable. Member, Board of Directors, The Indiana Business Modernization and Technology Corporation. ***PRACTICE AREAS:*** Mergers and Acquisitions; Corporate Law; Technology Law; International Law; Corporate Finance; Private Placement; Intellectual Property; Intellectual Property, Licensing; Mergers and Acquisitions Finance; Sales and Use Tax. ***Email:*** marcus.chandler@btlaw.com

DAVID B. MILLARD, admitted to bar, 1979, Indiana. *Education:* Indiana University School of Business (B.S., with highest distinction, 1977); Indiana University School of Law (J.D., magna cum laude, 1979). Order of the Coif; Phi Eta Sigma; Sigma Iota Epsilon; Beta Gamma Sigma. Editor, Indiana Law Journal, 1979-1980. Listed, Indianapolis Business Journal Forty Under 40 (top 40 Indianapolis area business people under age 40). Chairman of the Board, Midwest Entrepreneurial Education Center; Advisory Board, Ball State University Entrepreneurship Program. Executive Council, Stanley K. Lacy Executive Leadership Series Alumni Association. Indianapolis Board of Associates, Rose Hulman Institute of Technology. Past President and Director, Entrepreneur's Alliance of Indiana, Inc. Past President and Director: Venture Club of Indiana, Inc.; Director, Indiana Training Exports, Inc.; Small Business Council, Indiana Chamber of Commerce. Advisory Board, Indianapolis Regional Small Business Development Center. Member: Entrepreneur's Alliance of Indiana, Inc.; Forum for International Professional Services, Inc.; National Health Lawyers Association; Venture Club of Indiana, Inc. ***PRACTICE AREAS:*** Business Law; Contracts; Corporate Finance; Mergers, Acquisitions and Divestitures; Securities. ***Email:*** david.millard@btlaw.com

ANNE N. DePREZ, born Indianapolis, Indiana, October 5, 1955; admitted to bar, 1981, Indiana and U.S. District Court, Southern District of Indiana; 1982, U.S. District Court, Northern District of Indiana; 1990, U.S. Court of Appeals, Seventh Circuit; 1999, U.S. District Court, Western District of Michigan; 2002, U.S. Court of Appeals, Sixth Circuit. *Education:* Smith College (B.A., 1977); Indiana University (J.D., magna cum laude, 1981). Order of the Coif. Managing Editor, Indiana Law Journal, 1980-1981. ***PRACTICE AREAS:*** Securities Litigation; Business Litigation; Commercial Litigation; Class Action Defense; Civil RICO; Commodities Litigation; Complex and Multi-District Litigation. ***Email:*** anne.deprez@btlaw.com

ROBERT D. MacGILL, admitted to bar, 1981, Indiana and U.S. District Court, Southern and Northern Districts of Indiana; U.S. Court of Appeals, Seventh and Eighth Circuits. *Education:* Indiana University (B.S., with high distinction, 1978; J.D., cum laude, 1981). Beta Gamma Sigma. Associate Editor, Indiana Law Review, 1980-1981. Chairman: Indiana Secondary Market for Education Loans, Inc.; Indianapolis Tennis Championships, Inc. Member, Board of Advisors, Indiana University-Purdue University Indianapolis. (Chairman, Litigation Department). ***PRACTICE AREAS:*** Intellectual Property Litigation; Commercial Litigation; Products Liability Defense; Insurance Coverage. ***Email:*** robert.macgill@btlaw.com

ROBERT T. GRAND, admitted to bar, 1983, Indiana. *Education:* Wabash College (A.B., 1978); Indiana University (J.D., 1982). Administrative Assistant to Gov. Robert D. Orr, 1979-1983. ***PRACTICE AREAS:*** Municipal Finance; Government Relations; Legislative Practice. ***Email:*** bob.grand@btlaw.com

MARK D. STUAAN, admitted to bar, 1981, Illinois; 1992, Indiana. *Education:* Wabash College (A.B., 1978); Southern Illinois University School of Law (J.D., 1981). ***PRACTICE AREAS:*** Trial Practice; Federal Litigation; White Collar Criminal Defense; Environmental Criminal Defense. ***Email:*** mark.stuaan@btlaw.com

LAWRENCE E. LAWHEAD, admitted to bar, 1981, Indiana. *Education:* Indiana University (B.S., High Distinction, 1976; J.D., cum laude, 1981). Beta Gamma Sigma; Beta Alpha Psi. Board of Editors, Indiana Law Review, 1980. Certified Public Accountant, Indiana, 1979 (inactive). Chartered Life Underwriter, 1993. Fellow, American College of Trust and Estate Counsel. *Member:* Indianapolis (Chairman Tax Section-1992; Chairman Estate Planning and Administration Section, 1996) and Indiana State Bar Associations; Indianapolis Estate Planning Council (Director, 1994-2001; President, 2000); Indianapolis Bar Foundation. ***PRACTICE AREAS:*** Business Succession Planning; Estate Planning; Trusts and Estates; Decedents Estates; Real Estate; Corporate Law. ***Email:*** lawrence.lawhead@btlaw.com

D. WILLIAM MOREAU, JR., admitted to bar, 1981, Indiana. *Education:* Purdue University (B.S., 1974; Gr., 1976); Georgetown University (J.D., 1981). Chief Deputy Secretary of State, Gubernatorial Transition Director, Chief of Staff and Legislative Director to Hon. Evan Bayh, 1986-1991. Trustee, Purdue University, 1991-2003. ***PRACTICE AREAS:*** Government Relations; Federal Legislative Practice; State Legislative Practice; Administrative Agency Practice; Higher Education Law. ***Email:*** bill.moreau@btlaw.com

ALAN A. LEVIN, admitted to bar, 1982, Indiana. *Education:* University of Pittsburgh; Mercyhurst College (B.A., 1975); Indiana University (J.D., magna cum laude, 1982). Order of the Coif. ***PRACTICE AREAS:*** Employee Benefits; Employee Stock Ownership Plans; Executive Compensation. ***Email:*** alan.levin@btlaw.com

KENNETH H. INSKEEP, admitted to bar, 1982, Indiana. *Education:* Franklin College (B.A., magna cum laude, 1979); Indiana University (J.D., summa cum laude, 1982). Order of the Coif. *Member:* Indiana State Bar Association. ***PRACTICE AREAS:*** Litigation; Products Liability; Drug and Medical Device Defense; Toxic Tort Defense; Legal Ethics; Legal Malpractice Defense. ***Email:*** ken.inskeep@btlaw.com

ALAN K. MILLS, admitted to bar, 1982, Indiana. *Education:* Carthage College (B.A., 1979); Indiana University (J.D., summa cum laude, 1982). Note and Development Editor, Indiana Law Review, 1980-1982. President, Marion County Bar Association, 1987-1988.

(This Listing Continued)

Chairperson: Indiana State Election Board, 1988-1992; Financial Institutions Practice Group. *Member:* American Bar Association. ***PRACTICE AREAS:*** Bankruptcy; Creditors Rights; Litigation; Commercial Law; Government Affairs; Labor and Employment. ***Email:*** alan.mills@btlaw.com

DOUGLAS J. HECKLER, admitted to bar, 1982, Indiana. *Education:* Valparaiso University (B.A., 1979); Indiana University (J.D., 1982). ***PRACTICE AREAS:*** Collective Bargaining; Labor Arbitration; Management Labor Law. ***Email:*** doug.heckler@btlaw.com

TIMOTHY J. RIFFLE, admitted to bar, 1983, Indiana. *Education:* Indiana University (B.A., 1980; J.D., magna cum laude, 1983). Order of the Coif. Listed in "Best Lawyers in America" 2001—. Co-Author, *Indiana Limited Liability Company Forms and Practice Manual*, Data Trace Publishing Company, Inc. 1996. *Member:* Indianapolis, Indiana State and American Bar Associations. ***PRACTICE AREAS:*** Corporate Taxation (20%); Partnership Taxation (30%); Federal Estate and Gift Taxation (10%); Probate Litigation (30%); Tax Exempt Organizations (10%). ***Email:*** tim.riffle@btlaw.com

STEVEN W. THORNTON, admitted to bar, 1983, Indiana. *Education:* Miami University (B.S.B., cum laude, 1980); Ohio State University (J.D., 1983). Order of the Coif. ***PRACTICE AREAS:*** Corporate Law; Securities; Mergers, Acquisitions and Divestitures; Commercial Transactions; Debt and Equity Finance; Structured Finance. ***Email:*** steve.thornton@btlaw.com

HOWARD E. KOCHELL, admitted to bar, 1983, Indiana. *Education:* Indiana University (B.S., 1980; J.D., cum laude, 1983). ***PRACTICE AREAS:*** Litigation; Insurance; Employee Benefits; ERISA Litigation; Multi-Employer Pensions. ***Email:*** howard.kochell@btlaw.com

KENNETH J. YERKES, admitted to bar, 1983, Indiana; 1987, Pennsylvania; U.S. Supreme Court; U.S. Court of Appeals, Sixth, Seventh and Eighth Circuits. *Education:* Earlham College (B.A., 1980); Indiana University School of Law (J.D., 1983). Phi Beta Kappa. Articles Editor, Indiana Law Journal. Chairman, Labor and Employment Department. Past-Chairman, Labor and Employment Law Section, Indiana State Bar Association. Chairman, Indiana State Chamber of Commerce, Labor Relations Committee. Listed in: The Best Lawyers in America, 2001—; Chambers' "Best Business Lawyers in America," 2003—. Recognized as one of Indiana's "Top 50" Lawyers in *Indianapolis Magazine's* "Super Lawyers" in 2004 and 2005. Author, *The Indiana Guide to Labor Relations*. Co-author, *The Indiana Guide to Hiring and Firing*. Editor In Chief, *Employer's Guide to Federal and Indiana Employment Law*. *Member:* Indiana State and American Bar Associations. ***REPORTED CASES:*** Rooney v. Koch Air, LLC, 410 F.3d 376 (7th Cir. 2005); Aubuchon v. Knauf Fiber Glass, GmbH, 359 F.3d 950 (7th Cir. 2004); EEOC v. Indiana Bell Telephone Co., 256 F.3d 813 (7th Cir. 2001, En Banc); Rouse v. Boehringer Mannheim Corp., 108 F.3d 859 (8th Cir. 1997); Garner v. Arvin Industries, 77 F.3d 255 (8th Cir. 1996); Russell v. Acme-Evans Co., 51 F.3d 64 (7th Cir. 1995); Hill Rom Co. v. NLRB, 957 F.2d 454 (7th Cir. 1992); Aungst v. Westinghouse Electric Corp., 937 F.2d 1216 (7th Cir. 1991). ***PRACTICE AREAS:*** Employment Law; Employment Litigation; Management Labor Law; Collective Bargaining; Union Elections; Wrongful Termination. ***Email:*** ken.yerkes@btlaw.com

NEAL W. STEINBART, admitted to bar, 1987, Indiana. *Education:* St. Olaf College (B.A., 1979); Northwestern University (J.D., 1982). Phi Beta Kappa. *Member:* National Association of Bond Lawyers. ***PRACTICE AREAS:*** Municipal Law; Municipal Bonds; Municipal Bonds Taxation; Municipal Finance; Municipal Securities; Tax Increment Finance. ***Email:*** neal.steinbart@btlaw.com

R. ANTHONY PRATHER, admitted to bar, 1983, Indiana; U.S. District Court, Southern and Northern Districts of Indiana and U.S. Court of Appeals, Seventh Circuit. *Education:* Indiana University (B.A., Forensic Studies, 1980); Indiana University School of Law - Bloomington (J.D., 1983). Deputy Prosecutor, Marion County, 1983-1986. Senior Trial Attorney and Supervisory Trial Attorney, Equal Employment Opportunity Commission Indianapolis, 1986-1991. Attorney, Indiana Bell Telephone Co., 1991-1994. Acting General Counsel, Indiana Bell Telephone Co., 1994-1995. Counsel, Ameritech Corp., 1995-1998. Division General Counsel, Firestone Building Products Company, Firestone Industrial Products Company and Firestone Polymers, 1998-2001. Partner, Barnes & Thornburg LLP, 1998—. *Member:* Indianapolis, National and American (Member, Minority Counsel Program; Member, Minority Partners in Majority Law Firms Committee) Bar Associations. ***PRACTICE AREAS:*** Labor and Employment; Litigation. ***Email:*** tony.prather@btlaw.com

RICHARD A. REZEK, admitted to bar, 1984, Indiana; registered to practice before U.S. Patent and Trademark Office. *Education:* Purdue University (B.S.M.E., 1980); Indiana University (J.D., 1984). Engineer, Xerox Corporation, Reprographics Manufacturing Group, 1980-1981. *Member:* American Intellectual Property Law Association. ***PRACTICE AREAS:*** Intellectual Property Licensing; Patent Prosecution; International Patents; Mechanical Intellectual Property; Patent Infringement; Design Patents. ***Email:*** richard.rezek@btlaw.com

LYNN C. TYLER, admitted to bar, 1984, Indiana. *Education:* University of Notre Dame (B.A., summa cum laude, 1981); University of Michigan (J.D., magna cum laude, 1984). Phi Beta Kappa; Order of the Coif. Recipient, Saul L. Nadler Memorial Award, University of Michigan Law School. Associate Editor and Associate Note Editor, Michigan Law Review, 1982-1984. Author, "Trade Secrets in Indiana: Property vs. Relationship," 31 Ind. L. Rev. 339 (1998); "Injunctions Against Threatened Patent Infringement," 4 Fed. Cir. B.J. 113 (1994). Chair, Neighborhood Christian Legal Clinic, 2001-2003; Indianapolis Civil Theater, 1999-2002. Recipient, Indianapolis Bar Association Pro Bono Award, 2002. *Member:* Indianapolis, Indiana State, Seventh Circuit and Federal Circuit Bar Associations; American Intellectual Property Law Association. ***PRACTICE AREAS:*** Intellectual Property Litigation; Patent Litigation; Trademark Litigation; Antitrust and Trade Regulation; Trade Secrets; Unfair Competition. ***Email:*** lynn.tyler@btlaw.com

BRUCE D. DONALDSON, admitted to bar, 1984, Indiana. *Education:* DePauw University (B.A., 1981); Indiana University School of Law (J.D., summa cum laude, 1984). Member, Order of the Coif. Articles Editor, Indiana Law Journal, 1983-1984. *Member:* National Association of Bond Lawyers; Indiana Municipal Lawyers Association. ***PRACTICE AREAS:*** Tax Exempt Finance; Municipal Redevelopment; Tax Increment Finance; Economic Development; Mediation. ***Email:*** bruce.donaldson@btlaw.com

(This Listing Continued)

ERIC R. MOY, admitted to bar, 1985, Indiana. *Education:* Earlham College (B.A., 1982); Columbia University (J.D., 1985). Phi Beta Kappa. Casenote and Comment Editor, Columbia Journal of Transnational Law, 1984-1985. *Member:* American Bar Association; Federal Regulation of Securities Committee. ***PRACTICE AREAS:*** Securities; Initial Public Offerings; Business Law; Entrepreneurial Business Law; Mergers, Acquisitions and Divestitures; Securitization. ***Email:*** eric.moy@btlaw.com

JAN M. CARROLL, admitted to bar, 1984, Indiana and U.S. District Court, Northern District of Indiana; 1985, U.S. District Court, Southern District of Indiana; 1989, U.S. Court of Appeals, Seventh Circuit; 1994, U.S. Court of Appeals, Eleventh Circuit, 2002, U.S. District Court, District of Colorado; 2005, U.S. Court of Appeals, Federal Circuit. *Education:* Southern Methodist University (B.F.A., magna cum laude, 1974); Indiana University (J.D., cum laude, 1984). Note and Development Editor, Indiana Law Review, 1983-1984. *Member:* Indiana State Bar Association. ***REPORTED CASES:*** Indianapolis Convention & Visitors Association v. Indianapolis Newspapers, Inc., 377 N.E.2d 208 (Ind. 1991). ***PRACTICE AREAS:*** Litigation; Media Law; Land Use. ***Email:*** jan.carroll@btlaw.com

MICHAEL G. PATON, admitted to bar, 1985, Indiana. *Education:* University of Notre Dame (B.B.A., with honors, 1982); Indiana University (J.D., magna cum laude, 1985). Order of the Coif; Beta Gamma Sigma; Beta Alpha Psi. *Member:* American Health Lawyers Association. ***PRACTICE AREAS:*** Employee Benefits; Health Care; Insurance. ***Email:*** michael.paton@btlaw.com

ANNE C. McGOWN, admitted to bar, 1987, Indiana. *Education:* Indiana University (B.S., with highest distinction, 1976; J.D., magna cum laude, 1986). Certified Public Accountant, Indiana, 1979. *Member:* Indianapolis, Morgan County and Indiana State Bar Associations. ***PRACTICE AREAS:*** Litigation; Mediation; Business Litigation; Commercial Litigation; Complex Litigation; White Collar Crime. ***Email:*** anne.mcgown@btlaw.com

JAMES M. GUTTING, admitted to bar, 1986, Indiana. *Education:* Indiana State University (B.S., 1974); Indiana University (J.D., 1985). Certified Public Accountant, Indiana, 1979. *Member:* Indiana State Bar Association; National Association of Bond Lawyers; CPA Society; Indiana Municipal Lawyers Association (Member, Board of Directors); American Institute of Certified Public Accountants. ***PRACTICE AREAS:*** Municipal Law; Public Finance; Government; Municipal Bonds; Gaming Law; Utility Law. ***Email:*** jim.gutting@btlaw.com

RICHARD C. STARKEY, admitted to bar, 1985, Indiana. *Education:* University of Cincinnati (B.A., summa cum laude, 1980); Indiana University (J.D., magna cum laude, 1985). Phi Beta Kappa; Federalist Society. *Member:* National Association of Bond Lawyers; Indiana Municipal Lawyers Association. ***PRACTICE AREAS:*** Bank Finance; Taxable Adjustable Rate Securities; Municipal Finance; Municipal Redevelopment; Tax Increment Finance; Public Finance; Industrial Revenue Bond Law; Tax Exempt Finance; Lease Law; Bond Law; Ad Valorem Tax; Low Income Housing. ***Email:*** richard.starkey@btlaw.com

DENNIS A. JOHNSON, admitted to bar, 1985, Indiana. *Education:* Indiana University (B.S., 1982; J.D., cum laude, 1985). ***PRACTICE AREAS:*** Real Estate Law; Commercial Finance Law. ***Email:*** djohnson@btlaw.com

JOHN R. MALEY, admitted to bar, 1988, Indiana; U.S. Supreme Court; U.S. Court of Appeals, Sixth Circuit; U.S. Court of Appeals, Seventh Circuit; U.S. Court of Appeals, Eighth Circuit; U.S. Court of Appeals, Eleventh Circuit. *Education:* University of Notre Dame (B.A., 1985); Indiana University (J.D., summa cum laude, 1988; M.B.A., 1994). Executive Editor, Indiana Law Review, 1987-1988. Order of Barristers. Law Clerk: to Hon. Larry J. McKinney, Judge, U.S. District Court for the South District of Indiana, 1988-1990. Author: *Appellate Handbook for Indiana Lawyers*, Lexis Law Publishers, 2d ed. 1998 and 3d ed. 2001. Chair, Local Rules Committee and Civil Justice Reform Advisory Group, U.S. District Court for the Southern District of Indiana, 1995—. Member: Local Rules Committee for the Northern District of Indiana, 1999—; Chair, Marion County Local Rules Committee, 2001—; Chair, Employment Section, Defense Trial Counsel of Indiana, 2001-2002. Chair, Barnes & Thornburg's Appellate Practice Group, Pro Bono Committee, and Technology Committee. Listed in Who's Who in American Law, Who's Who in Indianapolis Law, Chambers Leading American Business Lawyers, and 2nd highest votes in Indiana's Super Lawyers' survey. *Member:* Federal (President, 1997, Indianapolis Chapter), Indiana State (House of Delegates, 1995) and Indianapolis (President, 2002; Board of Managers, 1997-2003) Bar Associations. Indianapolis and Indiana Bar Foundations. ***REPORTED CASES:*** Omosegbon v. Indiana State University, 335 F.3d 668 (7th Cir. 2003)(affirming summary judgment for employer); Gawley v. Indiana University, 276 F.3d 301 (7th Cir. 2001)(affirming summary judgment for employer); Little v. Cox's Supermarkets, 71 F.3d (7th Cir. 1995)(affirming summary judgment for employer and sanctions against plaintiff's counsel); Ashkin v. Time Warner Cable, 52 F.3d 140 (7th Cir. 1995)(affirming judgment for employer after trial and assessing full appellate fees against plaintiff's counsel as a sanction); Tremper v. Air-Shields, Inc., 2001 U.S. Dist. LEXIS 13290 (S.D. Ind. 2001)(partial dismissal of employee's claims for procedural failings); Tom Raper, Inc. v. Safari Motor Coaches, 2001 U.S. Dist. LEXIS 10281 (S.D. Ind. 2001)(summary judgment for client commercial claim); Cox v. Preferred Technical Group, 110 F. Supp. 2d 786 (N.D. Ind. 2000)(assessing full fees against plaintiff after jury verdict for employer); Via v. Boat Sales, Inc., 1997 U.S. Dist. LEXIS 20826 (S.D. 1997)(summary judgment for employer on FLSA claim); Williamson v. Arvin Industries, 975 F. Supp. 1235 (E.D. Mo. 1997)(summary judgment for employer in harassment claim); Goodman v. Hill-Rom Co., 1996 U.S. Dist. LEXIS 17602 (M.D. Fla. 1996)(enforcing forum-selection clause for employer); Garner v. Arvin Industries, 885 F. Supp. 1254 (E.D. Mo. 1995)(summary judgment for employer in age case); Thor Electric v. Oberle & Associates, 741 N.E.2d 373 (Ind. Ct. App. 2000)(prevailing on cross appeal in construction case); George S. May Int'l Co. v. King, 629 N.E.2d 257 (Ind. Ct. App. 1994)(enforcing provisions of non-compete clause); Dell v. City of Tipton, 618 N.E.2d 1338 (Ind. Ct. App. 1993)(affirming dismissal of city police officer). ***PRACTICE AREAS:*** Federal Civil Litigation; Federal Civil Practice; Labor and Employment; Employment Litigation; Defense Litigation; Appellate Practice. ***Email:*** john.maley@btlaw.com

TERESA E. MORTON, admitted to bar, 1988, Indiana. *Education:* Butler University (B.S., 1983); Indiana University (J.D., 1987). *Member:* Indiana State (Utility Law Section Chair, 1997) and American Bar Associations; Indiana Utility Regulatory Commission

(This Listing Continued)

BARNES & THORNBURG LLP, Indianapolis—Continued

(Practice and Procedure Committee, 1997-1998). ***PRACTICE AREAS:*** Energy; Energy Contracts; Internet Law; Telecommunications Competition; Telecommunications Law; Utility Law. ***Email:*** teresa.morton@btlaw.com

BENJAMIN A. PECAR, admitted to bar, 1987, Indiana. *Education:* Northwestern University (B.A., 1984); Indiana University (J.D., magna cum laude, 1987). ***PRACTICE AREAS:*** Real Estate; Corporate; Shopping Center Law; Finance; Construction Law. ***Email:*** benjamin.pecar@btlaw.com

MICHAEL J. KAYE, admitted to bar, 1987, Indiana. *Education:* Michigan State University (B.A., with honors, 1984); Indiana University School of Law (J. D., cum laude, 1987). ***TRANSACTIONS:*** Agent's counsel in connection with a $75,000,000 syndicated multi-currency facility; Agent's counsel in connection with a $130,000,000 syndicated financing; Bank counsel in connection with a $7,000,000 asset-based financing; Agent's counsel in connection with a $75,000,000 secured syndicated ESOP financing; Bank counsel in connection with a $60,000,000 secured working capital facility; Bank counsel in connection with a $7,600,000 mortgage loan financing secured by 12 properties; Letter of Credit Bank counsel in connection with a $10,000,000 letter of credit issued in connection with a bond financing. ***PRACTICE AREAS:*** Secured Transactions; Mergers and Acquisitions; Commercial Finance; Corporate Law. ***Email:*** michael.kaye@btlaw.com

DEAN T. BARNHARD, admitted to bar, 1983, Indiana. *Education:* University of Miami (B.M., 1974; M.M., 1978); Indiana University (J.D., cum laude, 1983). *Member:* American Bar Association; Defense Research Institute. ***PRACTICE AREAS:*** Toxic Torts; Pesticide Litigation; Chemical Products Liability; Manufacturers Liability; Intellectual Property Litigation. ***Email:*** dean.barnhard@btlaw.com

DWIGHT D. LUECK, admitted to bar, 1988, Indiana. *Education:* Carleton College (B.A., cum laude, 1984); University of Minnesota (J.D., cum laude, 1988). ***PRACTICE AREAS:*** Intellectual Property; Trademarks; Copyrights; Litigation; Antitrust; Unfair Competition. ***Email:*** dwight.lueck@btlaw.com

J. MICHAEL GRUBBS, admitted to bar, 1988, Indiana. *Education:* DePauw University (B.A.); Butler University (M.B.A.); Indiana University (J.D.). *Member:* American Health Lawyers Association. ***PRACTICE AREAS:*** Health Care Litigation; Health Care Reimbursement; Health Care Licensing; Health Care Regulation; Health Care Mergers and Acquisitions; Long Term Care; Continuing Care Retirement Communities; Health Care Compliance; Physician Practices; Mental Health Law. ***Email:*** michael.grubbs@btlaw.com

ANTHONY C. SULLIVAN, admitted to bar, 1989, Indiana. *Education:* Purdue University (B.S., 1979); Indiana University (J.D., magna cum laude, 1989). Order of the Coif. ***PRACTICE AREAS:*** Environmental Law. ***Email:*** tony.sullivan@btlaw.com

JOSEPH C. CHAPELLE, admitted to bar, 1986, Illinois; 1989, Indiana. *Education:* University of Michigan (A.B., with honors, 1983); University of Notre Dame (J.D., cum laude, 1986). Law Clerk to Hon. John L. Coffey, U.S. Court of Appeals for the Seventh Circuit, 1986-1987. [Capt., U.S. Army, Judge Advocate General's Corp., 1987-1991]. ***PRACTICE AREAS:*** Litigation; Products Liability; Appellate Practice; Election, Campaign and Political Law. ***Email:*** joe.chapelle@btlaw.com

JOSEPH E. LOFTUS, admitted to bar, 1983, Indiana. *Education:* University of Delaware (B.A., 1976); Indiana University (M.P.A., 1978; J.D., 1983). Deputy Mayor, Indianapolis, 1992-1995. ***PRACTICE AREAS:*** Government Relations; Local Government Law; Legislative Practice; Economic Development. ***Email:*** joseph.loftus@btlaw.com

ANDREW J. DETHERAGE, admitted to bar, 1990, Indiana and U.S. District Court, Northern and Southern Districts of Indiana; 1993, U.S. Court of Appeals, Seventh Circuit; 2002, U.S. Court of Appeals, Fifth Circuit. *Education:* Indiana University (B.A., with highest distinction, 1987; J.D., summa cum laude, 1990). Chairman, Property and Casualty Insurance Coverage Practice Group. Phi Beta Kappa. Associate Editor, Indiana Law Review, 1989-1990. Member, Board of Directors and Past President, Big Brothers Big Sisters of Central Indiana. Member, Board of Directors and Secretary, RCA Championships. *Member:* Indianapolis and American Bar Associations. ***PRACTICE AREAS:*** Insurance Coverage; Insurance Bad Faith; Trade Secrets; Commercial Litigation; Complex Litigation; Toxic Tort Defense. ***Email:*** andy.detherage@btlaw.com

PAUL B. HUNT, admitted to bar, 1990, Indiana and Illinois; U.S. Court of Appeals for the Federal Circuit; registered to practice before U.S. Patent and Trademark Office. *Education:* University of Illinois (B.S.M.E., 1987; J.D., 1990). ***PRACTICE AREAS:*** Intellectual Property Litigation; Intellectual Property Licensing; Intellectual Property Portfolio Management; Theft of Trade Secrets. ***Email:*** paul.hunt@btlaw.com

TERRY W. DAWSON, admitted to bar, 1990, Indiana. *Education:* Indiana State University (B.S., 1987); Southern Illinois University (J.D., magna cum laude, 1990). ***PRACTICE AREAS:*** Labor and Employment; Litigation; Arbitration; Collective Bargaining. ***Email:*** terry.dawson@btlaw.com

NICHOLAS K. KILE, admitted to bar, 1990, Indiana. *Education:* Butler University (B.S., cum laude, 1987); Indiana University (J.D., summa cum laude, 1990). Law Clerk to the Hon. Jesse E. Eschbach. ***PRACTICE AREAS:*** Utilities; Local Government Law; Environmental Law; Energy; Cable TV. ***Email:*** nicholas.kile@btlaw.com

JOSEPH G. EATON, admitted to bar, 1991, Indiana. *Education:* Butler University (B.S., Business Administration, 1988); Indiana University (J.D., cum laude, 1991). Order of Barristers. Associate Editor, Indiana Law Review, 1990-1991. ***REPORTED CASES:*** Neal v. Dow AgroScience LLC, 2002 Tex.App. LEXIS 2035 (Tex.App.-Dallas March 20, 2002); Wallace v. Redman Homes, Inc., 730 N.E.2d 809 (Ind.Ct.App. 2000); Goeb v. v. Tharaldson, 615 N.W.2d 800 (Minn. 2000); National Bank of Commerce (Smits) v. The Dow Chemical Co., 338 Ark. 752 (Ark. 1999); National Bank of Commerce (Arnold) v. Dow Chemical Co., *165 F.3d 602 (8th Cir. 1999); National Bank of Commerce (Smits) v. Dow* Chemical Co., 965 F.Supp. 1490 (E.D. Ark. 1996), aff'd 133 F.3d 1132 (8th Cir. 1998). ***PRACTICE AREAS:*** Complex Commercial Litigation; Toxic Tort Defense; Products Liability; Toxic Exposure; Pesticide Litigation; Toxic Tort Class Actions. ***Email:*** joe.eaton@btlaw.com

(This Listing Continued)

JEFFERY J. QUALKINBUSH, admitted to bar, 1991, Indiana. *Education:* Wabash College (A.B., magna cum laude, 1988); University of Michigan (J.D., 1991). Phi Beta Kappa. ***PRACTICE AREAS:*** Municipal Leasing; Municipal Finance; Government. ***Email:*** jeffrey.qualkinbush@btlaw.com

DONALD E. WILLIAMS, admitted to bar, 1991, Indiana. *Education:* Indiana University (B.S., with highest distinction, 1988); Northwestern University (J.D., cum laude, 1991). ***PRACTICE AREAS:*** Real Estate; Construction Law; Commercial Real Estate; Commercial Real Estate Finance; Commercial Real Estate Development; Commercial Real Estate Acquisition. ***Email:*** don.williams@btlaw.com

MARIANA RICHMOND, admitted to bar, 1992, Indiana. *Education:* University of Bucharest (B.A., M.A., 1974); Indiana University (J.D., 1991). Board Member, Indiana University Law Alumni. Named "Indiana Super Lawyer 2004". *Member:* Indiana State Bar Association; American Immigration Lawyers Association (Board of Governors; Chair, Indiana Chapter, 1996-1998). ***LANGUAGES:*** Romanian (fluent), French, Serbian and Hungarian (working knowledge). ***PRACTICE AREAS:*** Business Immigration (100%). ***Email:*** mariana.richmond@btlaw.com

RICHARD J. HALL, admitted to bar, 1992, Indiana. *Education:* Ball State University (B.S., summa cum laude, 1989); Northwestern University (J.D., cum laude, 1992). Judicial Clerk: Hon. Michael S. Kanne, United States Court of Appeals for the Seventh Circuit. ***PRACTICE AREAS:*** Municipal Finance; Corporate Law; Government Relations. ***Email:*** richard.hall@btlaw.com

BART A. KARWATH, admitted to bar, 1991, Indiana; U.S. District Court, Northern and Southern Districts of Indiana; U.S. District Court, Eastern District of Wisconsin; U.S. District Court, Northern District of Illinois; U.S. Supreme Court; U.S. Court of Appeals, Seventh Circuit. *Education:* Indiana University (B.S., 1988; J.D., magna cum laude, 1991). Order of the Coif. Law Clerk to Hon. V. Sue Shields, Indiana Court of Appeals, 1991-1992; Law Clerk to Hon. Larry J. McKinney, United States District Court, Southern District of Indiana, 1992-1994. Author: "ERISA Health Plan Reimbursement Claims After Great-West Life Annuity Insurance Co. v. Knudson," Res Gestae, Vol. 47 No. 8, pp. 36-39 (April 2004); "The Supreme Court's Concept of Equitable Relief in Great-West v. Knudson," Probate & Property, Vol. 18, No. 4, pp. 50-53 (July/August 2004); "Recent Developments in Civil RICO Law," 27 Ind. L. Rev. 1151 (1994); "Has the Constituency of Continuity Plus Relationship Put an End to RICO's Pattern of Confusion?," 18 Am. J. Crim. L. 201 (1991). ***PRACTICE AREAS:*** ERISA Litigation; Federal Civil Litigation; Civil RICO; Insurance Litigation; Securities Litigation; Class Action Defense. ***Email:*** bart.karwath@btlaw.com

JEFFREY A. MICHAEL, admitted to bar, 1993, Indiana; registered to practice before U.S. Patent and Trademark Office. *Education:* Wayne State University (B.S.E.E., with distinction, 1983); University of Michigan (M.S.E.E., 1989); Indiana University, Bloomington (J.D., 1993). Eta Kappa Nu. ***PRACTICE AREAS:*** Patents; Computer and Software Patents; Electrical Patents; Semiconductor Technology; Mechanical Patents; Electro-Mechanical Patents. ***Email:*** jeffrey.michael@btlaw.com

PETER A. MORSE, JR., admitted to bar, 1993, Indiana. *Education:* DePauw University (B.A., with honors, 1990); Vanderbilt University (J.D., 1993). Gold Key (President); Beta Theta Pi (Board of Trustees, 1999—). Associate Editor, Vanderbilt Law Review, 1992-1993. ***PRACTICE AREAS:*** Labor and Employment; Employment Litigation; Union Elections. ***Email:*** pete.morse@btlaw.com

BRADFORD G. ADDISON, admitted to bar, 1993, District of Columbia; 1997, Indiana and U.S. District Court, Northern and Southern Districts of Indiana; registered to practice before the U.S. Patent and Trademark Office. *Education:* Indiana State University (B.S., Biology, 1983); University of Kentucky (Ph.D. Pharmacology, 1989, Design and Synthesis of Novel Oral Hypoglycemic Agents); University of Cincinnati (J.D., 1993). ***PRACTICE AREAS:*** Patent Law; Trademark Law; Copyrights. ***Email:*** bradford.addison@btlaw.com

CURT W. HIDDE, admitted to bar, 1993, Indiana and U.S. District Court, Southern and Northern Districts of Indiana. *Education:* Indiana University (B.A., 1990); University of Dayton (J.D., 1993). ***PRACTICE AREAS:*** Securities; Mergers and Acquisitions; Corporate Law. ***Email:*** curt.hidde@btlaw.com

EDWARD SEAN GRIGGS, admitted to bar, 1994, Indiana. *Education:* Rose-Hulman Institute of Technology (B.S.Ch.E., 1988); Indiana University School of Law at Indianapolis (J.D., magna cum laude, 1994). Associate Editor, Indiana Law Review. *Member:* Indianapolis, Indiana State and American Bar Associations. ***PRACTICE AREAS:*** Environmental Litigation; Environmental Law; Administrative Law; Toxic Torts; Appellate Practice. ***Email:*** sean.griggs@btlaw.com

THOMAS M. MAXWELL, admitted to bar, 1987, District of Columbia; 1994, Massachusetts; 1996, Indiana. *Education:* Indiana University (B.A., 1984; J.D., cum laude, 1987). ***PRACTICE AREAS:*** Banks and Banking; Securities; Commercial Law. ***Email:*** thomas.maxwell@btlaw.com

CHARLES P. EDWARDS, admitted to bar, 1993, Indiana. *Education:* Indiana University (B.A., 1990; J.D., magna cum laude, 1993). Phi Beta Kappa. Associate Editor, Indiana Law Review, 1992-1993. ***PRACTICE AREAS:*** Litigation; Products Liability; Insurance. ***Email:*** charles.edwards@btlaw.com

BRADLEY J. DOUGHERTY, admitted to bar, 1982, Indiana. *Education:* Indiana University, School of Business (B.S., 1979); Indiana University (J.D., 1982). *Member:* Indianapolis Estate Planning Council. ***PRACTICE AREAS:*** Trusts and Estates; Probate; Business Law; Estate Planning; Estate Administration; Business Transactions. ***Email:*** bradley.dougherty@btlaw.com

ELAINE WATERHOUSE WILSON, admitted to bar, 1994, New York; 1997, Indiana; U.S. Tax Court. *Education:* Boston University (B.A., magna cum laude, 1993; J.D., magna cum laude, 1993). Managing Editor, Probate Law Journal, 1992-1993. Associate Articles Editor, Probate & Property Magazine. *Member:* American Bar Association (Co-Chair, Real Property and Probate Section Committee on State and Local Concerns of Exempt Organizations); Internal Revenue Service Exempt Organizations Advisory Council (Great Lakes Region). ***PRACTICE AREAS:*** Estate Planning; Nonprofit and Charitable Organizations; Taxation. ***Email:*** elaine.wilson@btlaw.com

(This Listing Continued)

WILLIAM E. PADGETT, admitted to bar, 1995, Indiana. *Education:* Wabash College (A.B., magna cum laude, 1992); Indiana University (J.D., cum laude, 1995). *Member:* Indianapolis and Indiana State Bar Associations; Defense Research Institute. ***PRACTICE AREAS:*** Products Liability; Toxic Torts; Insurance Coverage; Complex Litigation; Crop Damage; Commercial Litigation. ***Email:*** william.padgett@btlaw.com

BRIAN L. BURDICK, admitted to bar, 1995, Indiana. *Education:* Wabash College (A.B., summa cum laude, 1991); Indiana University (J.D., cum laude, 1995). Phi Beta Kappa. Associate Editor, Indiana Law Review, 1994-1995. Deputy Treasurer, State of Indiana, 1991-1995. ***PRACTICE AREAS:*** Lobbying; State Government Law; Local Government Law; Financial Services Law; Investment Management. ***Email:*** brian.burdick@btlaw.com

MARK J. DINSMORE, admitted to bar, 1994, Indiana. *Education:* Wabash College (A.B., 1983); University of Toledo College of Law (J.D., magna cum laude, 1994). Phi Kappa Phi; Order of the Coif. Lead Articles Editor, University of Toledo Law Review, 1993-1994. Law Clerk: to Hon. John D. Tinder. ***PRACTICE AREAS:*** Litigation; Commercial Litigation; Construction Law. ***Email:*** mark.dinsmore@btlaw.com

THOMAS F. SHEA, admitted to bar, 1994, Indiana. *Education:* Purdue University (B.A., with distinction, 1991); Indiana University (J.D., cum laude, 1994). ***PRACTICE AREAS:*** Commercial Litigation; Product Litigation; Medical Device Litigation; Trial Practice. ***Email:*** thomas.shea@btlaw.com

TODD G. VARE, admitted to bar, 1995, Indiana and U.S. District Court, Northern and Southern Districts of Indiana; 1997, Illinois. *Education:* Miami University (B.A., 1987); Indiana University - Bloomington (M.B.A., 1989); Indiana University - Indianapolis (J.D., summa cum laude, 1994). *Member:* Indianapolis and Indiana State Bar Association; Indiana Information Technology Association; American Intellectual Property Association. ***PRACTICE AREAS:*** Intellectual Property Litigation; Patent Litigation; Computer and Software Protection. ***Email:*** todd.vare@btlaw.com

MICHAEL H. GOTTSCHLICH, admitted to bar, 1991, California and U.S. District Court, Central District of California; 1994, Illinois; 2001, Indiana and U.S. District Court, Southern District of Indiana; 2002, U.S. Court of Appeals, Eleventh Circuit. *Education:* Indiana University (B.A., 1987; J.D., 1991). Phi Alpha Delta. Member, Indiana University School of Law Moot Court Team, Barristers. *Member:* Indianapolis and American (Member, Sections on: Litigation; Antitrust) Bar Associations. ***LANGUAGES:*** German. ***PRACTICE AREAS:*** Commercial Litigation; Civil Trial Practice; Antitrust; Professional Liability. ***Email:*** michael.gottschlich@btlaw.com

PATRICIA L. OGDEN, admitted to bar, 1996, Indiana. *Education:* Ball State University (B.S.N., 1990); Indiana University (J.D., summa cum laude, 1996). ***PRACTICE AREAS:*** Labor and Employment Law; Occupational Safety and Health. ***Email:*** patricia.ogden@btlaw.com

SUSAN M. ZOELLER, admitted to bar, 1995, Illinois; 1997, Indiana. *Education:* Ball State University (B.A., summa cum laude, 1992); Indiana University School of Law - Bloomington (J.D., magna cum laude, 1995). ***PRACTICE AREAS:*** Labor and Employment; Employment Litigation. ***Email:*** susan.zoeller@btlaw.com

MICHAEL D. MOON, JR., admitted to bar, 1996, Indiana and U.S. District Court, Southern and Northern Districts of Indiana. *Education:* Indiana University (B.A., 1993; J.D., cum laude, 1996). ***REPORTED CASES:*** Wallace v. Meadow Acres Manufactured House., Inc., 730 N.E.2d 809 (Ind. Ct. App. 2000); Ray-Hayes v. Heinamann, 768 N.E.2d 899 (Ind. 2002); Deckard v. GMC, 307 F.3d 556 (7th cir. 2002); Old Town Neighborhood Ass'n v. Kauffman, 2004 U.S. Dist. LEXIS 27217 (S.D. Ind. 2004). ***PRACTICE AREAS:*** Complex Litigation; Products Liability; Toxic Torts. ***Email:*** michael.moon@btlaw.com

JAMES R. SWEENEY II, admitted to bar, 1996, Indiana and Illinois; 1999, District of Columbia; registered to practice before U.S. Patent and Trademark Office. *Education:* U.S. Naval Academy (B.S., with merit, 1983); Notre Dame Law School (J.D., magna cum laude, 1996). Editor in Chief, Notre Dame Law Review. Member, Association of Old Crows, 1986. *Member:* Indianapolis and Indiana State Bar Associations; District of Columbia Bar. [Lt. Col., U.S. Marine Corps Reserve, 1992—]. ***PRACTICE AREAS:*** Intellectual Property; Computers and Software; Business Law. ***Email:*** james.sweeney@btlaw.com

THOMAS H. ENGLE, admitted to bar, 1996, Indiana and U.S. District Court, Northern and Southern Districts of Indiana. *Education:* Ball State University (B.S., magna cum laude, 1981; B. Architecture, magna cum laude, 1981); Indiana University School of Law (J.D., cum laude, 1996). Speaker: "Annual Real Estate Institute" (ICLEF); "Basic Commercial Real Estate" (ICLEF); "Risk Management Techniques to Combat the Mold Claim Epidemic". Treasurer and Director, Indianapolis Chapter, American Institute of Architects. Member: Historic Landmarks Foundation of Indiana, Inc.; National Trust for Historic Preservation. Registered Architect: Massachusetts; Indiana. Certified Construction Specifier (CSI). Judicial Law Clerk, Indiana Court of Appeals, 1996-1998. Articles Editor, Indiana Law Review, 1995-1996. Recipient: AIA Student Gold Medal; American Jurisprudence and Corpus Juris Secundum Awards in Contracts. *Member:* Indianapolis, Indiana State and American Bar Associations; American Institute of Architects (Indianapolis and Central Indiana Chapters). ***PRACTICE AREAS:*** Real Estate; Construction Law; Zoning, Planning and Land Use; Historic Preservation; Appellate Practice; Leases and Leasing; Conservation Easements. ***Email:*** thomas.engle@btlaw.com

SHAWN D. BAUER, admitted to bar, 1995, Indiana and U.S. District Court, Southern District of Indiana; registered to practice before the U.S. Patent and Trademark Office. *Education:* Purdue University (B.S.E., 1991); Indiana University, Indianapolis (J.D., 1995). *Member:* Indiana State Bar Association (Member, Intellectual Property Section). ***PRACTICE AREAS:*** Intellectual Property; Patent Law; Trademark Law. ***Email:*** shawn.bauer@btlaw.com

RONALD S. HENDERSON, admitted to bar, 1996, Indiana; registered to practice before U.S. Patent and Trademark Office. *Education:* Purdue University (B.S.M.E., 1989; B.S.E.E., 1998); Indiana University School of Law - Indianapolis (J.D., cum laude, 1995). Recipient, Indiana Bar Foundation Scholarship. *Member:* Indiana State and American Bar Associations; American Intellectual Property Law Association. ***PRACTICE AREAS:*** Intellectual Property Procurement; Intellectual Property Rights; International Intellectual Property. ***Email:*** ronald.henderson@btlaw.com

(This Listing Continued)

OF COUNSEL

EDWARD A. KEIRN, admitted to bar, 1983, Indiana. *Education:* Indiana Wesleyan University (B.S., 1973); Ball State University (M.P.A., 1979); Indiana University (J.D., summa cum laude, 1983). Supervisor, Division of Research & Statistics, Indiana Department of Financial Institutions, 1977-1983. Special Counsel for Commercial Transactions and Consumer Financial Services, 1990—. ***PRACTICE AREAS:*** Consumer Credit; Commercial Transactions; Banking Regulation. ***Email:*** edward.keirn@btlaw.com

GUINN P. DOYLE, admitted to bar, 1992, Indiana. *Education:* Indiana University (B.A., 1972; J.D., 1992). Chief, Hazardous Waste Management Branch, Indiana Department of Environmental Management, 1985-1987. ***PRACTICE AREAS:*** Environmental Law; Hazardous Waste; OSHA; Clean Air Act; Resource Conservation and Recovery Act (RCRA); Environmental Cleanup. ***Email:*** giunn.doyle@btlaw.com

LINDA K. TODD, admitted to bar, 1984, Indiana. *Education:* University of Michigan (B.A., 1981); Indiana University (J.D., 1984). Certified Property and Casualty Underwriter (CPCU). *Member:* American Bar Association (Center for Professional Responsibility). ***PRACTICE AREAS:*** Legal Ethics and Professional Responsibility; Conflicts of Interest; Attorney Grievances. ***Email:*** linda.todd@btlaw.com

DILIP KULKARNI, admitted to bar, 1975, Indiana; 1976, New Jersey; 1982, New Delhi (India); registered to practice before U.S. Patent and Trademark Office. *Education:* Shivaji University (B.S.E., 1965); Indiana University (J.D., cum laude, 1974); University of Wisconsin (M.S.I.E., 1967); Butler University (M.B.A., 1983). ***PRACTICE AREAS:*** Intellectual Property Licensing; Patent Prosecution; Business Law. ***Email:*** dilip.kulkarni@btlaw.com

BARBARA J. MEIER, admitted to bar, 1991, Indiana. *Education:* University of Kansas (B.S.Ed., with high distinction, 1975; M.A., Microbiology, 1980); Indiana University (J.D., summa cum laude, 1991). *Member:* Indianapolis, Indiana State and American Bar Associations. ***PRACTICE AREAS:*** Defense Litigation; Products Liability; Drug and Medical Device Defense; Toxic Torts; Tort Defense; First Party Insurance. ***Email:*** barbara.meier@btlaw.com

KIRK E. GRABLE, admitted to bar, 1988, Ohio; 1992, Michigan; 1997, Indiana. *Education:* Indiana University (B.A., 1978; M.P.A., 1988; J.D., 1988). Order of the Coif. *Member:* Indiana Municipal Lawyers Association. [Captain, USMC, 1978-1984]. ***PRACTICE AREAS:*** Municipal Law; Municipal Finance; Municipal Securities; Municipal Bonds Taxation; Municipal Taxation. ***Email:*** kirk.grable@btlaw.com

DAVID R. WARSHAUER, born Fort Wayne, Indiana, 1957; admitted to bar, 1984, Indiana. *Education:* Washington University (B.A., 1980); Indiana University (J.D., magna cum laude, 1984). Order of the Coif. *Member:* American College of Real Estate Lawyers. ***PRACTICE AREAS:*** Real Estate; Zoning, Planning and Land Use. ***Email:*** david.warshauer@btlaw.com

BRYAN G. TABLER, admitted to bar, 1972, Indiana; U.S. Supreme Court; U.S. Court of Appeals for the District of Columbia Circuit; U.S. Court of Appeals, Fifth and Seventh Circuits; U.S. District Court, Southern and Northern Districts of Indiana. *Education:* Princeton University (A.B., 1969); Yale University (J.D., 1972). Author: "An Overview of Environmental Laws and Regulations," What Everyone Needs To Know About Environmental Law, Indiana Continuing Legal Education Forum, 1988; "EPA's Practice of Regulation-by-Memo," Natural Resources & Environment, Fall, 1990, with Mark Shere; "Indiana's Water Quality Standards - Rough Seas For Indiana," Outlook, Indiana Chamber of Commerce magazine; "Wetlands: The New Factor in Real Estate Purchases," Indianapolis Business Journal, August 6, 1990, with Jean Doyle; "Environmental Considerations in Sale and Purchase of Existing Projects," and "Buyer and Seller Legal Concerns Surrounding Purchase of Asbestos-Containing Buildings and Asbestos Abatement/Removal," Environmental Issues in Real Estate Development and Financing, Indiana Continuing Legal Education Forum, 1987; "A Summary of CERCLA as amended by SARA," Preventing and Defending Hazardous Waste Litigation, Indiana Continuing Legal Education Forum, 1987; "An Overview of Environmental Laws and Regulations," What Everyone Needs to Know About Environmental Law, Indiana Continuing Legal Education Forum, 1988; "Risk Management in Superfund Litigation," Hazardous Waste Litigation, Indiana Continuing Legal Education Forum, 1986; "Regulation of Environmental Pollution," Counseling Indiana Businesses, Indiana Continuing Legal Education Forum, 1981; "Environmental Law-Legislative Developments," 19 Indiana Law Review 17, 1986. Adjunct Professor, Indiana University School of Law, Indianapolis, IN, 1982. Associate, 1972-1978 and Partner, 1979-1994, Barnes & Thornburg. Senior Vice President, Secretary and General Counsel, Indianapolis Power & Light Company, 1994-2001. *Member:* Indiana State (Chairman: Corporate Counsel Section, 1980-1981; Environmental Law Division, Natural Resources Section, 1985-1989) and American (Chairman: Environmental Controls Committee, Business Law Section; Right-To-Know Committee, 1988-1990; Air Subcommittee, 1992-1995; Member: Legislation Committee, 1990-1992; Section of Natural Resources, Energy and Environmental Law; Committee on Toxic and Environmental Torts Litigation; Litigation Section) Bar Associations. [2nd Lt., 1965-1967 and 1st Lt., 1967-1968; U.S. Army Europe, 1965-1967 and 1st Infantry Div., Vietnam, 1967-1968]. ***REPORTED CASES:*** Indiana-Kentucky Elec. Corp. v. Comm'r Indiana Dept. of Envtl. Management, 820 N.E.2d 771 (Ind. Ct. App. 2005); United States v. Bethlehem Steel Corp., 38 F.3d 862 (7th Cir. 1994); United States v. AM General Corp., 808 F.Supp. 1353, aff'd 34 F.3d 472 (7th Cir. 1994); Bethlehem Steel Corp. v. Gorsuch, Adm'r U.S. EPA, 742 F.2d 1028 (7th Cir. 1984); Indiana & Michigan Elec. Co. v. U.S. EPA, 733 F.2d 489 (7th Cir. 1984); Bethlehem Steel Corp. v. U.S. EPA, 723 F.2d 1303 (7th Cir. 1983); Sierra Club v. Indiana-Kentucky Elec. Corp., 716 F.2d 1145 (7th Cir. 1983); Bethlehem Steel Corp. v. EPA, 638 F.2d 994 (7th Cir. 1980); United States v. Zimmer Paper Products, Inc., 27 Env't. rep. Cas. (BNA) 2093 (S.S. Ind. 1989). ***PRACTICE AREAS:*** Environmental; General Litigation. ***Email:*** bryan.tabler@btlaw.com

LYNNE M. McMAHAN, admitted to bar, 1981, Indiana. *Education:* Bowling Green State University (B.S., cum laude, 1976); Indiana University School of Law (J.D., cum laude, 1981); Indiana University School of Business (M.B.A., 1981). Phi Delta Phi. Author: "The Equal Opportunity Doctrine in Political Broadcasting: Proposed Modifications of the Communications Act of 1934," 12 Indiana Law Review 745, 1979. *Member:* Indianapolis

(This Listing Continued)

BARNES & THORNBURG LLP, Indianapolis—Continued

and Indiana State Bar Associations. ***PRACTICE AREAS:*** Business Law; Corporate Law; Investments; Mergers, Acquisitions and Divestitures; Nonprofit and Charitable Organizations; Securities. ***Email:*** lynne.mcmahan@btlaw.com

CLAUDIA EARLS, admitted to bar, 1984, Indiana. *Education:* Indiana University (B.A., Economics, 1980; M.B.A., 1984); Indiana University School of Law - Indianapolis (J.D., 1984). Certified Civil Mediator, Indiana, 2001. *Member:* Indianapolis and Indiana State Bar Associations. ***PRACTICE AREAS:*** Public Utility Law; Energy Regulation; Telecommunications Regulation; Telecommunications Contracts. ***Email:*** claudia.earls@btlaw.com

ELIZABETH HABER LACY, admitted to bar, 1991, Illinois and U.S. District Court, Northern District of Illinois; 2000, Indiana and U.S. District Court, Southern and Northern Districts of Indiana. *Education:* Duke University (A.B., Public Policy Studies, 1987); Case Western Reserve University (J.D., summa cum laude, 1991). Order of the Coif. Notes Editor, Law Review, 1990-1991. *Member:* Indiana State and Illinois State Bar Associations. ***PRACTICE AREAS:*** Mergers, Acquisitions and Divestitures; Venture Capital; Corporate Law. ***Email:*** elizabeth.lacy@btlaw.com

ROBERT V. KIXMILLER, admitted to bar, 1967, Indiana. *Education:* Purdue University (B.S., with distinction, 1964); Indiana University School of Law (J.D., magna cum laude, 1967). Managing Editor, Indiana Law Journal, 1966-1967. Law Clerk to Judge S. Hugh Dillin, United States District Court for the Southern District of Indiana, 1967-1968. Senior Trust Officer and Senior Vice President, The American National Bank of Vincennes, 1984-1988. Certified Mediator (Indiana). *Member:* Indiana State Bar Association. ***PRACTICE AREAS:*** Alternative Dispute Resolution; Commercial Law; Corporate Law; Leases and Leasing; Real Property. ***Email:*** robert.kixmiller@btlaw.com

JANET D. NEUENSCHWANDER, admitted to bar, 1983, Indiana. *Education:* University of California, Los Angeles, UCLA (B.A., 1972); Indiana University (M.A., 1980); Northwestern University School of Law (J.D., cum laude, 1983). Articles Editor, Journal of Criminal Law and Criminology, 1982-1983. Visiting Assistant Professor of Business Law, College of Business, The Ohio State University, 1987-1988. Lecturer, Indiana University School of Law, 1986-1987. ***PRACTICE AREAS:*** Banks and Banking; Corporate Law; Mergers, Acquisitions and Divestitures; Savings and Loans; Securities Regulations. ***Email:*** jan.neuenschwander@btlaw.com

KEVIN L. McLAREN, admitted to bar, 2004, Indiana and U.S. District Court, Northern and Southern Districts of Indiana; registered to practice before U.S. Patent and Trademark Office. *Education:* Harvey Mudd College (B.S., Chemistry, 1983); University of California, Berkeley (Ph.D., Chemistry, 1989); Indiana University School of Law - Indianapolis (J.D., summa cum laude, 2004). Sigma Xi Society. Listed in: Marquis' Who's Who in Science and Engineering; Marquis' Who's Who: American Law Students; Empire Who's Who, Honored Member; Madison Who's Who, Honored Member; American Biographical Institute, Contemporary Who's Who of Professionals. Note Development Editor, Indiana Law Review. Author: "Benzofuran and Benzothiophene Derivatives as Anti-inflammatory Agents," US 6,433,005 2002, EP 0113716 2003, WO 02/46178 A2 2002; "Preparation of Spinosyn Macrocyclic Lactone Aminodeoxyglycosides as Insecticides and Miticides," U.S. 6,001,981 1999, WO 9700265 1997; "3,4,N Trisubstituted-4,5-dihydro-1H- pyrazole-1-carboxamides and their Use as Insecticides," U.S. 5,493,024 1996; "Total Synthesis of the Cyclic Depsipeptide Leualacin," J. Org. Chem. 1995, 60, 6082-4; "3,4 Disubstituted-4,5-dihydro-1H-pyrazoles and a Method of Preparation," US 5,324,837 1994; "A Divergence Between the Enzyme-Catalyzed and Non-Catalyzed Synthesis of 3-Dehydroquinate," J. Org. Chem. 1994, 59, 2082-2085; "3,4,N Trisubstituted-4,5- dihydro-1H-pyrazole-1-carboxamides and their Use as Insecticides," US 5,250,532 1993, EP 92106270 1992, EP 508469 1992; "Hydroxy-bis-dihydroencelin, A Dimeric Eudesmanolide and Other Eudesmanolides from Montanoa Speciosa," Phytochemistry 1991, 30(10), 3293-3295, acknowledgement infra; "Exploration of the Shikimic Acid Pathway: Opportunities for the Study of Enzyme Mechanisms Through the Synthesis of Intermediates and Inhibitors," in Prospects for Amino Acid Biosynthesis Inhibitors in Crop Protection and Pharmaceutical Chemistry, L. G. Copping, Editor, Society of Chemical Industry, 1989, pp. 155-170; "Radical Cyclizations of Oxime Ethers," J. Am. Chem. Soc. 1988, 110, 1633-1634; "Synthetic Methodology to Develop Compounds of Biological Importance: radical cyclizations of oxime ethers," presented at the II Congreso Latinoamericana de Fitoquímica, 7-11 March 1988, Mexico D. F., Mexico; "Diastereoselectivity in the Alkylation of Chiral 2-Aminomethyl-1,3,2- dioxaphosphorinane-2-Oxides," Phosphorus and Sulfur 1987, 33, 1-14; "(+)-3,5-O-(R)- Benzylidene-6-deoxy-6-iodo-1,2-O-isopropylidene-alpha-D-glucofuranose," Acta Crystallographica, Sect. C. 1987, C43, 2104-2106; "Detection of the Static 1,2-Dimethyl-2-norbornyl Cation by Variable-Temperature 13C CPMAS NMR," J. Am. Chem. Soc. 1985, 107, 5294-5296; "Benzofuran and Benzothiophene Derivatives," W.O. 02/46178 A2 2002; "Pyrazoline-1-Carboxamides Bearing 4-(Substituted Heteroaryl) Substituents," presented at the 206th American Chemical Society National Meeting and Exposition, 22-27 August 1993, Chicago, IL; "I. Asymmetric Synthesis of oa-Aminophosphonic Acids. II. Radical Cyclizations of Oxime Ethers. III. Synthesis of 1-epi-3-Dehydroquinate: Mechanistic Studies of 3-Dehydroquinate Biosynthesis," Diss. Abstr. Int. B. 1990, 51(1), 215-432; "Preparation of Spinosyn Macrocyclic Lactone Aminodeoxyglycosides as Insecticides and Miticides," PCT Int. Appl. WO 9700265 A1 970103, WO 96-US10327 960613. *Member:* Indianapolis and American Bar Associations. ***LANGUAGES:*** Spanish. ***PRACTICE AREAS:*** Patents. ***Email:*** kevin.mclaren@btlaw.com

JACK L. STARK, JR., admitted to bar, 1993, Indiana; U.S. District Court, Southern District of Indiana. *Education:* Indiana University (B.A., 1988; J.D., 1992). Assistant Professional Responsibility Counsel. Recipient, American Jurisprudence Award in Corporations, 1991. Staff Attorney, 1993-1998 and Director, Trial Court Services, 1998-2004, Supreme Court of Indiana. Trustee, Catherine Peachey Fund, Inc., 1998—. *Member:* American Bar Association. ***PRACTICE AREAS:*** Legal Ethics; Professional Conduct. ***Email:*** jack.stark@btlaw.com

SAMUEL D. HODSON, admitted to bar, 1986, Indiana and U.S. District Court, Northern and Southern Districts of Indiana. *Education:* Indiana University (B.A., Political Science, 1982; J.D., 1986; M.B.A., Finance, 1990). Adjunct Professor, Indiana University School of Liberal Arts. Contributing Editor, American Bankruptcy Institute. Author and Speaker, Indiana Continuing Legal Education Forum, National Business Institute and Sterling Educational Services. Master Commissioner, Madison Superior Court, 1990. *Member:* Indianapolis (Commercial Law and Bankruptcy Section) and Indiana State (Commercial Law and Taxation Sections) Bar Associations; American Bankruptcy Institute. ***PRACTICE AREAS:*** Commercial Law; Bankruptcy; Business Transactions; Taxation. ***Email:*** samuel.hodson@btlaw.com

JAMES T. BURNS, admitted to bar, 1975, Indiana and U.S. District Court, Southern District of Indiana. *Education:* Indiana University (B.A., Political Science, 1972); Indiana University School of Law - Indianapolis (J.D., magna cum laude, 1975). Associate Editor, Indiana Law Review, 1974-1975. Former Assistant General Counsel: Eli Lilly and Company; Elanco Products Company. Former General Counsel, Elizabeth Arden Inc. *Member:* Indianapolis, Indiana State and American Bar Associations. ***PRACTICE AREAS:*** Products Liability; Pharmacy Law; Litigation; Risk Management; Business Regulation. ***Email:*** james.burns@btlaw.com

ASSOCIATES

MICHAEL T. SCANLON, admitted to bar, 1996, Indiana. *Education:* Ball State University (B.S., magna cum laude, 1981); Indiana University (J.D., summa cum laude, 1996; M.P.A., 1987). Inspector, Indianapolis Air Pollution Control Division, 1981-1984. Environmental Scientist/Solid Waste Management Planner, Indiana Department of Environmental Management, 1984-1987. Environmental Services Director, Ulrich Chemical, Inc., 1987-1996. Adjunct Instructor, School of Public and Environmental Affairs, Indiana University-Purdue University Indianapolis, 1989-1992. Associate Editor, Indiana Law Review, 1995-1996. Indiana University-Purdue University Indianapolis Chancellor's Scholar Award, 1996. Indiana University School of Law - Indianapolis Faculty Award, 1996. Certified Hazardous Materials Manager, Master Level. ***PRACTICE AREAS:*** Environmental Law; Environmental Compliance; Occupational Safety and Health. ***Email:*** michael.scanlon@btlaw.com

WENDY D. BREWER, admitted to bar, 1995, Georgia and Florida; 2001, Indiana; U.S. District Court, Middle, Southern and Northern Districts of Florida; U.S. Court of Appeals, Eleventh Circuit; U.S. District Court, Southern and Northern Districts of Indiana. *Education:* Florida State University (B.A., Criminology, magna cum laude, with honors in major, English minor, 1992; J.D., with high honors, 1995). Phi Delta Phi; Order of the Coif. Member, Golden Key. Recipient, Book Awards in: Constitutional Law; Litigation; Gratuitous Transfers; Estate and Gift Tax; Estate Planning. Member, 1993-1995 and Associate Editor, 1994-1995, Journal of Land Use & Environmental Law. *Member:* Indianapolis (Treasurer, Commercial and Bankruptcy Law Section, 2004), Indiana State and American Bar Associations; The Florida Bar; State Bar of Georgia; Tallahassee Women Lawyers (Treasurer, 2000); Florida Association of Women Lawyers; American Bankruptcy Institute. ***PRACTICE AREAS:*** Bankruptcy; Creditors Rights; Banks and Banking; Litigation. ***Email:*** wendy.brewer@btlaw.com

JEFFREY A. HOPPER, admitted to bar, 1997, Indiana. *Education:* Indiana University (B.S., 1991); DePaul University (J.D., 1997). Order of the Coif. ***PRACTICE AREAS:*** Business Law; Mergers, Acquisitions and Divestitures. ***Email:*** jeffrey.hopper@btlaw.com

RANDAL J. KALTENMARK, admitted to bar, 1996, Indiana and Illinois. *Education:* Valparaiso University (B.A., with honors, summa cum laude, 1993); Indiana University (J.D., cum laude, 1996). *Member:* Indianapolis (Former Chair, Tax Section), Indiana State (Member, Tax Section), Illinois State and American (Member, Tax Section) Bar Associations. ***PRACTICE AREAS:*** Partnership Taxation; Corporate Taxation; State Taxation; Tax Litigation. ***Email:*** randal.kaltenmark@btlaw.com

NATHAN A. BAKER, admitted to bar, 1997, Indiana; U.S. District Court, Northern and Southern Districts of Indiana; U.S. Court of Appeals, Seventh Circuit. *Education:* Wabash College (B.A., cum laude, 1994); University of Illinois (J.D., cum laude, 1997). *Member:* Indianapolis, Indiana State and American Bar Associations. ***PRACTICE AREAS:*** Labor and Employment; Litigation. ***Email:*** nathan.baker@btlaw.com

JULIE A. RUSSELL, admitted to bar, 1997, Indiana. *Education:* Butler University (B.A., cum laude, 1992); Duke University (J.D., cum laude, 1997). ***PRACTICE AREAS:*** Securities; Corporate Law; Mergers, Acquisitions and Divestitures. ***Email:*** julie.russell@btlaw.com

JOHN P. FISCHER, JR., admitted to bar, 1997, Indiana and U.S. District Court, Northern and Southern Districts of Indiana. *Education:* University of Notre Dame (B.A., cum laude, 1993); Indiana University (J.D., summa cum laude, 1997). Managing Editor, Indiana Law Journal, 1996-1997. *Member:* Indianapolis, Indiana State and American Bar Associations; Defense Research Institute. ***PRACTICE AREAS:*** Commercial Litigation; Insurance Coverage; Appellate Practice. ***Email:*** john.fischer@btlaw.com

JULIA SPOOR GARD, admitted to bar, 1997, Indiana and Illinois. *Education:* Ball State University (B.S., 1990); Valparaiso University (J.D., 1997). ***PRACTICE AREAS:*** Trademarks; Copyrights. ***Email:*** julia.gard@btlaw.com

CHRISTIAN P. JONES, admitted to bar, 2000, Indiana. *Education:* Indiana University (B.A., 1994); Boston University School of Law (J.D., 1997). ***PRACTICE AREAS:*** Civil Litigation; Insurance Coverage. ***Email:*** christian.jones@btlaw.com

JOHN B. BAXTER, admitted to bar, 1997, Indiana. *Education:* Miami University (B.A., 1994); Indiana University (J.D., cum laude, 1997). Member, Indiana University Law Review, 1995-1997. ***PRACTICE AREAS:*** Commercial Real Estate; Leases and Leasing; Real Estate Banking Law. ***Email:*** john.baxter@btlaw.com

JONATHAN D. MATTINGLY, admitted to bar, 1998, Indiana. *Education:* University of Notre Dame (B.S., 1995); Indiana University (J.D., magna cum laude, 1998). ***PRACTICE AREAS:*** Products Liability Defense; Pesticide Litigation; Intellectual Property Litigation. ***Email:*** jonathan.mattingly@btlaw.com

TERRI L. BRUKSCH, admitted to bar, 1998, Indiana. *Education:* DePauw University (B.A., 1995); Indiana University (J.D., magna cum laude, 1998). Order of the Coif. ***PRACTICE AREAS:*** Commercial Litigation; Products Liability Defense. ***Email:*** terri.bruksch@btlaw.com

DENNIS P. STOLLE, admitted to bar, 1997, Nebraska; 1998, Indiana and U.S. District Court, Southern and Northern Districts of Indiana. *Education:* Saint Louis University

(This Listing Continued)

(B.S., summa cum laude, 1993); University of Nebraska (M.A., Social Psychology, 1996; J.D., with high distinction, 1997; Ph.D., Social Psychology, 1998). Order of the Coif. Research Editor, University of Nebraska Law Review, 1995. *Member:* American Psychology Law Society; American Society of Trial Consultants. ***PRACTICE AREAS:*** Jury Research and Consulting; Civil Litigation; Defense Litigation; Commercial Litigation; Trade Secrets. ***Email:*** dennis.stolle@btlaw.com

ANDREW B. DZEGUZE, admitted to bar, 1999, California (inactive), Indiana and U.S. District Court, Southern and Northern Districts of Indiana; 2001, U.S. Court of Appeals, Federal Circuit; 2002, U.S. District Court, Eastern District of Michigan. *Education:* University of California, Berkeley (B.A., 1994); University of California, Hastings College of the Law (J.D., cum laude, 1998, Order of the Coif, Thurston Society). Author: Note, "Has the FDA Bought the Winston Cup?" 20 Hastings Comm & Ent LJ (1998). Author and Presenter: "Patent Remedies", (Really) Basic Patent Law Seminar, Indiana Continuing Legal Education Foundation (2003). ***PRACTICE AREAS:*** Intellectual Property Litigation; Antitrust; Patent Litigation. ***Email:*** andrew.dzeguze@btlaw.com

KEVIN D. BAILEY, admitted to bar, 1994, Missouri; 2000, Indiana; registered to practice before U.S. Patent and Trademark Office. *Education:* University of Miami (B.S.M.E., cum laude, 1991); Washington University (J.D., 1994). Phi Kappa Phi. Valedictorian of Mechanical Engineering Class. [Air Force, active duty, 1995-1999]. ***LANGUAGES:*** French. ***PRACTICE AREAS:*** Mechanical Intellectual Property; Intellectual Property Litigation. ***Email:*** kevin.bailey@btlaw.com

RICHARD P. WINEGARDNER, admitted to bar, 1993, Indiana; U.S. District Court, Northern and Southern Districts of Indiana and U.S. Court of Appeals, Seventh Circuit. *Education:* Ball State University (B.S., summa cum laude, 1989); University of Virginia (J.D., 1992). *Member:* Indianapolis and Indiana State Bar Associations. ***PRACTICE AREAS:*** Labor and Employment; Employment Litigation; Executive Severance Contracts. ***Email:*** richard.winegardner@btlaw.com

KAROLINE E. JACKSON, admitted to bar, 1998, Illinois; 2000, Indiana. *Education:* Ball State University (B.A., 1995); Indiana University School of Law-Bloomington (J.D., magna cum laude, 1998). Order of the Coif. Member, Indiana Law Journal, 1997-1998. Author: "The Legitimacy of Cross-Gender Searches and Surveillance in Prisons: Defining an Appropriate and Uniform Review," Indiana Law Journal, Volume 73, Number 3, 1998. ***PRACTICE AREAS:*** Securities Litigation; Commercial Litigation. ***Email:*** karoline.jackson@btlaw.com

REBECCA L. BALL, admitted to bar, 1999, Indiana; registered to practice before U.S. Patent and Trademark Office. *Education:* Texas A&M University (B.S., 1979); University of Texas at Austin (Ph.D., 1987); University of Houston Law Center (J.D., 1999). Sigma Xi. Recipient: McLaughlin Predoctoral Fellowship Award; Stephen C. Silverthorne Award; Verwey Fellowship Award. Listed in Who's Who Among Students in American Colleges and Universities. Member, American Association for the Advancement of Sciences. *Member:* Indiana State and American Bar Associations. ***PRACTICE AREAS:*** Chemical Intellectual Property; Medical Intellectual Property; Pharmaceutical Intellectual Property. ***Email:*** rebecca.ball@btlaw.com

CHRISTOPHER P. FELTS, admitted to bar, 1999, Indiana. *Education:* DePauw University (B.A., 1991); Indiana University (J.D., 1999). Phi Beta Kappa (DePauw Chapter). Governor's Fellow, Office of Ind. Gov. Evan Bayh, 1991-1992. International Trade Specialist, Indiana Dept. of Commerce, 1992-1994. Deputy Director, International Trade, Ind. Dept. of Commerce, 1995-1999. Named Sagamore of the Wabash by Gov. Joe Kernan, 2004. *Member:* Indianapolis, Indiana State and American Bar Associations. ***LANGUAGES:*** Spanish. ***PRACTICE AREAS:*** Business Law; International Business Law; Government Affairs. ***Email:*** christopher.felts@btlaw.com

P. JASON STEPHENSON, admitted to bar, 1999, Indiana. *Education:* Taylor University (B.A., 1996); Indiana University School of Law at Indianapolis (J.D., 1999). Order of the Barristers. Co-Author: with Kevin W. Betz, "An Examination of the Indiana Supreme Court Docket, Dispositions, and Voting in 2000," 34 Ind. L. Rev. 541 (2001); with Kevin W. Betz, "An Examination of the Indiana Supreme Court Docket, Dispositions, and Voting in 2001," 35 Ind. L. Rev. 1117 (2002); with Kevin W. Betz, "An Examination of the Indiana Supreme Court Docket, Dispositions, and Voting in 2002," 36 Ind. L. Rev. 919 (2003); with Kevin W. Betz and Mark Crandley, "An Examination of the Indiana Supreme Court Docket, Dispositions, and Voting in 2003," 37 Ind. L. Rev. 891 (2004). *Member:* Indiana State Bar Association (Member, Utility Law Section). ***PRACTICE AREAS:*** Utility Law; Administrative Law. ***Email:*** jason.stephenson@btlaw.com

WILLIAM A. HAHN II, admitted to bar, 2000, Indiana and U.S. District Court, Southern and Northern Districts of Indiana. *Education:* Wabash College (B.A., cum laude, 1996); University of Notre Dame Law School (J.D., magna cum laude, 1999). Member, Notre Dame Law Review. Law Clerk, Judge David F. Hamilton, U.S. District Court, Southern District of Indiana, Indianapolis Division. ***PRACTICE AREAS:*** Litigation. ***Email:*** william.hahn@btlaw.com

JOHN T. L. KOENIG, admitted to bar, 1998, Indiana. *Education:* Indiana University (B.A., 1990); Indiana University School of Law, Indianapolis (J.D., magna cum laude, 1998). ***PRACTICE AREAS:*** Labor and Employment. ***Email:*** john.koenig@btlaw.com

T. JOSEPH WENDT, admitted to bar, 1996, Indiana, U.S. Court of Appeals, Seventh Circuit and U.S. Supreme Court. *Education:* Wabash College (B.A., magna cum laude, 1993); Indiana University (J.D., magna cum laude, 1996). Phi Beta Kappa; Order of the Coif. *Member:* Indianapolis Bar Association. ***PRACTICE AREAS:*** Litigation.

ANN S. GRAYSON, admitted to bar, 1995, Minnesota; 2001, Indiana. *Education:* Miami University (B.A., cum laude, 1992); University of Minnesota (J.D., 1995). Member, National Moot Court. Director, Civil Practice Clinic, 1994-1995. Author: "Is That Your Final Answer? Are Insureds Entitled to Insurance Coverage for Trademark Infringement," Hamline Law Review, Vol. 23, No.2, 2000. *Member:* Indianapolis and Indiana State Bar Associations. ***PRACTICE AREAS:*** Civil Litigation; Negligence Defense; Drug and Medical Device Defense; Products Liability Defense; Toxic Tort Defense; Premises Liability Defense. ***Email:*** ann.grayson@btlaw.com

KEPTEN D. CARMICHAEL, admitted to bar, 1996, Indiana. *Education:* DePauw University (B.A., cum laude, 1993); Indiana University School of Law - Bloomington (J.D., magna cum laude, 1996). Order of the Coif. Notes and Comments Editor, Indiana Law Journal, 1995-1996. *Member:* Indianapolis and Indiana State Bar Associations. ***PRACTICE AREAS:*** Business Law; Corporate Law; Securities. ***Email:*** kepten.carmichael@btlaw.com

KIMBERLY WILLIAMS BLANCHET, admitted to bar, 1998, Indiana. *Education:* Indiana University (B.S., 1994; J.D., 1998). ***PRACTICE AREAS:*** Municipal Law; Finance; Government. ***Email:*** kimberly.blanchet@btlaw.com

JERIMI J. ULLOM, admitted to bar, 2000, Indiana. *Education:* DePauw University (B.A., 1993); DePaul University (J.D., 2000). ***PRACTICE AREAS:*** Municipal Bonds; Government Relations; Business Transactions. ***Email:*** jeremi.ullom@btlaw.com

ANDREA D. BONTRAGER UNZICKER, admitted to bar, 2000, Indiana. *Education:* Goshen College (B.A., Economics, 1991); Indiana University-Bloomington (J.D., cum laude, 2000). *Member:* Indianapolis and Indiana State Bar Associations. ***PRACTICE AREAS:*** Securities; Mergers and Acquisitions; International Trade. ***Email:*** andrea.unzicker@btlaw.com

MARY JANE FRISBY, admitted to bar, 2000, Indiana and U.S. District Court, Southern District of Indiana; U.S. Court of Appeals for the Federal Circuit. *Education:* Indiana University (B.A., 1994; J.D., summa cum laude, 2000). Adjunct Professor, Indiana University School of Law-Indianapolis Intellectual Property Center, 2000—, Copyright Law and Music Law. Recipient, John H. Edwards Fellowship, 1999-2000. Associate Editor, Indiana Law Review, 1999-2000. *Member:* American Bar Association. ***PRACTICE AREAS:*** Intellectual Property Litigation; Trademark Prosecution; Copyrights; Intellectual Property Licensing. ***Email:*** maryjane.frisby@btlaw.com

JEFFREY L. PAPA, admitted to bar, 2000, Indiana; 2001, U.S. District Court, Northern and Southern Districts of Indiana; 2004, U.S. Court of International Trade and U.S. Court of Appeals for the Federal Circuit. *Education:* Rose-Hulman Institute of Technology (B.S., Economics and Russian Technical Translation, 1993); Ball State University (M.A., Business Economics, 1999); Indiana University School of Law - Indianapolis (J.D., 1999). Member, Alumni Board, Rose-Hulman Institute of Technology; President, YETI, Inc. *Member:* Indianapolis, Boone County, Indiana State and American Bar Associations; American Immigration Lawyers Association (Chapter Vice-Chair). ***LANGUAGES:*** Russian and Spanish. ***PRACTICE AREAS:*** Immigration Law; Government. ***Email:*** jeff.papa@btlaw.com

JEFF M. BARRON, admitted to bar, 1999, Illinois (Not admitted in Indiana). *Education:* Indiana University (B.A., 1996); Loyola University (J.D., 1999). ***Email:*** jeff.barron@btlaw.com

MARTIN W. ZIVITZ, admitted to bar, 2000, Indiana and U.S. District Court, Northern and Southern Districts of Indiana. *Education:* Indiana University (B.A., Psychology and Political Science, 1997); Indiana University School of Law - Indianapolis (J.D., cum laude, 2000). Phi Delta Phi; Sigma Alpha Mu. Member, Golden Key National Honor Society. *Member:* Indianapolis, Indiana State and American Bar Associations. ***PRACTICE AREAS:*** Business Law; Debtor and Creditor. ***Email:*** martin.zivitz@btlaw.com

KENDALL MILLARD, admitted to bar, 1999, District of Columbia; 2001, U.S. District Court, District of Columbia; 2005, U.S. District Court, Southern District of Indiana (Not admitted in Indiana). *Education:* Morningside College (B.A., summa cum laude, 1990); University of Minnesota (M.A., 1992); Indiana University School of Law - Bloomington (J.D., magna cum laude, 1998). *Member:* The District of Columbia Bar; Bar Association of the District of Columbia; American Bar Association (Member, Antitrust Section). ***LANGUAGES:*** Japanese. ***PRACTICE AREAS:*** Antitrust; Complex Commercial Litigation; Political Asylum. ***Email:*** kendall.millard@btlaw.com

MARK J. CRANDLEY, admitted to bar, 2000, Indiana and U.S. District Court, Southern and Northern Districts of Indiana. *Education:* Indiana University, Bloomington (B.A., Journalism, high distinction, 1995; J.D., summa cum laude, 2000). *Member:* Supreme Court Historical Society. ***PRACTICE AREAS:*** Civil Appeals; Civil Rights Section 1983; Complex Litigation. ***Email:*** mark.crandley@btlaw.com

MELANIE D. PRICE, admitted to bar, 1999, Indiana. *Education:* Indiana University (B.A., Political Science and Criminal Justice, 1985); Indiana University School of Law, Indianapolis (J.D., cum laude, 1999). Order of the Barristers, 1998; Second place, National Administrative Law Moot Court Competition, 1998; Recipient, Cale Holder Memorial Scholarship. Law Clerk to the Honorable Robert Rucker, Associate Justice of Indiana Supreme Court, 1999-2000. Author, "The Privacy Paradox: The Divergent Paths of the United States Supreme Court and State Courts on Issues of Sexuality," 33 Ind. L. Rev. 863 (2000). Assistant General Counsel, Indiana Utility Regulatory Commission, 2000-2002. Member, U.S. Delegation to Albania to set up electricity regulatory regime, 2002. Presenter, "Negotiating Telecommunications Contracts in the Evolving World of Competition", 2003. Treasurer, Southeast Community Services Center. *Member:* Indianapolis and Indiana State Bar Associations. ***PRACTICE AREAS:*** Energy; Telecommunications; Utilities (100%). ***Email:*** melanie.price@btlaw.com

MICHELLE L. KOSSMANN, admitted to bar, 2001, Indiana. *Education:* Kentucky Wesleyan College (B.A., 1990); Indiana University School of Law - Indianapolis (J.D., 2001). ***PRACTICE AREAS:*** Real Estate; Corporate Law; Commercial Real Estate. ***Email:*** michelle.blank@btlaw.com

ERIN ROTH-BOHANNON, admitted to bar, 2001, Indiana. *Education:* Butler University (B.S., summa cum laude); Georgetown University Law Center (J.D.). ***PRACTICE AREAS:*** Litigation; Intellectual Property; International Trade. ***Email:*** erin.bohannon@btlaw.com

STEPHANIE A.H. BLACKMAN, admitted to bar, 2001, Indiana and U.S. District Court, Southern and Northern Districts of Indiana; 2003, U.S. Court of Appeals, Seventh Circuit and U.S. District Court, Central District of Illinois. *Education:* University of Illinois at Urbana-Champaign (B.S., 1998); Vanderbilt University School of Law (J.D., 2001). Order of the Coif; Dean's List. Senior Notes Editor, Vanderbilt Law Review. *Member:* Indianapolis, Indiana State and American Bar Associations. ***PRACTICE AREAS:*** Labor and Employment (100%). ***Email:*** stephanie.blackman@btlaw.com

(This Listing Continued)

(This Listing Continued)

BARNES & THORNBURG LLP, Indianapolis—Continued

CARLI E. STEWART, admitted to bar, 2001, Indiana; registered to practice before U.S. Patent and Trademark Office. *Education:* Purdue University (B.S.M.E., 1997); Indiana University School of Law, Indianapolis (J.D., 2001). ***PRACTICE AREAS:*** Intellectual Property Law. ***Email:*** carli.stewart@btlaw.com

MICHAEL J. HULKA, admitted to bar, 2001, Illinois and U.S. District Court, Northern District of Illinois; 2002, U.S. Court of Appeals, Seventh Circuit; 2003, Indiana and U.S. District Court, Northern and Southern Districts of Indiana. *Education:* Indiana University - Bloomington (B.A., 1997); Indiana University - Bloomington (J.D., magna cum laude, 2001). *Member:* Indiana State Bar Association. ***PRACTICE AREAS:*** Products Liability; Toxic Torts; White Collar Crime. ***Email:*** michael.hulka@btlaw.com

DENNIS S. SCHELL, admitted to bar, 2001, Indiana and U.S. District Court, Southern and Northern Districts of Indiana; registered to practice before U.S. Patent and Trademark Office. *Education:* Purdue University (B.S.E.E., 1989); Indiana University (J.D., cum laude, 2001). Control System Design Engineer, 1986-1990. Semi-Finalist, Indiana University Moot Court Competition. Editorial Staff, Federal Communications Law Journal, 1999-2001. Recipient, Aerial Achievement Medal, Combat Missions in Support of Operation Southern Watch. Top Graduate, USAF Navigator Training. Distinguished Graduate, USAF Officer Training School. Graduate, USAF Electronic Warfare Officer Training and Squadron Officer School. Officer, Indiana Wing of the Commemorative Air Force. *Member:* Indianapolis and Indiana State Bar Associations; American Intellectual Property Law Association; Institute of Electrical and Electronics Engineers; Aircraft Owners and Pilots Association; Experimental Aircraft Association; Association of Old Crows (The Electronic Warfare and Information Operators Association); National Eagle Scout Association. [Captain, USAF, F-15E Instructor Weapon Systems Officer / Electronic Warfare Officer, 1990-1998]. ***PRACTICE AREAS:*** Electrical Patent Prosecution; Electronic Patent Prosecution; Computer and Software Patent Prosecution; Electro-Mechanical Patent Prosecution; Business Methods Patent Prosecution; International Patent Prosecution; Intellectual Property Licensing; Patent Infringement Opinions. ***Email:*** dennis.schell@btlaw.com

JASON C. FARMER, admitted to bar, 2001, Indiana. *Education:* Pomona College (B.A., 1993); University of Louisville (M.B.A., 2001; J.D., 2001). *Member:* Indianapolis and Indiana State Bar Associations. ***PRACTICE AREAS:*** Corporate Law; Corporate Finance; Mergers and Acquisitions; Commercial Real Estate Transactions. ***Email:*** jason.farmer@btlaw.com

JOSHUA B. FLEMING, admitted to bar, 2000, Wisconsin and U.S. District Court, Eastern District of Wisconsin; 2001, U.S. District Court, Western District of Wisconsin; 2005 U.S. District Court, Southern and Northern Districts of Indiana; U.S. Court of Appeals, Sixth, Seventh and Eighth Circuits (Not admitted in Indiana). *Education:* Marquette University (B.S., 1996); Marquette University Law School (J.D., cum laude, 2000). Marquette University Law School, National Moot Court, 1999-2000. *Member:* State Bar of Wisconsin; American Bar Association; Defense Research Institute. ***PRACTICE AREAS:*** Litigation. ***Email:*** jfleming@btlaw.com

DAVID P. HOOPER, admitted to bar, 2001, Illinois and U.S. District Court, Northern District of Illinois; 2002, District of Columbia and U.S. Court of Appeals, District of Columbia Circuit (Not admitted in Indiana). *Education:* George Washington University (B.A., magna cum laude, 1997); Valparaiso University School of Law (J.D., magna cum laude, 2001). *Member:* The District of Columbia Bar. ***Email:*** dhooper@btlaw.com

ANGELA K. IMEL, admitted to bar, 2002, Indiana and U.S. District Court, Southern and Northern Districts of Indiana. *Education:* Indiana University - Purdue University Indianapolis (B.A., highest distinction, 1998); Indiana University School of Law, Indianapolis (J.D., summa cum laude, 2002); Indiana University Kelley School of Business (M.B.A., 2002). Senior Executive Editor, Indiana Law Review, 2001. *Member:* Indianapolis, Indiana State and American (Member, Business Law Section) Bar Associations. ***PRACTICE AREAS:*** Secured Transactions; Uniform Commercial Code; Commercial Transactions; Creditors Rights; Debtor and Creditor Workouts; Creditor Bankruptcy. ***Email:*** angela.imel@btlaw.com

PRESTON B. RAY, IV, admitted to bar, 2002, Indiana. *Education:* Indiana University (B.S., Biology, 1998); Indiana University School of Law (J.D., summa cum laude, 2002). Articles Editor, Indiana Law Review, 2000-2002. *Member:* Indianapolis, Indiana State and American Bar Associations. ***PRACTICE AREAS:*** Mergers and Acquisitions; Securities; Intellectual Property; Corporate Law. ***Email:*** preston.ray@btlaw.com

KITISRI SUKHAPINDA, admitted to bar, 2002, Indiana and U.S. District Court, Northern and Southern Districts of Indiana; registered to practice before U.S. Patent and Trademark Office. *Education:* North Carolina State University (B.S., Crop Science, with honors); Iowa State University (M.S.; Ph.D., Plant Breeding and Cytogenetics, minor in Statistics); Indiana University School of Law (J.D., 2001). Past Scientist with Biotechnology Group of Dow AgroSciences. Post-Doctoral Research Associate, ARCO Plant Cell Research Institute in Dublin, CA, and Senior Plant Breeder and Project Leader for the Field Crop Research Institute in Bangkok, Thailand. Co-Inventor of U.S. Patents Nos.: 6,717,035, 6,590,142 (Transgenic Plants Expressing Photorhabdus Toxin), 6,528,484 (Insecticidal Protein Toxins from Photorhabdus; and Patent Application Publication: WO 00/05391 (Antibody-Mediated Down Regulation of Plant Proteins). *Member:* Indianapolis Bar Association. ***LANGUAGES:*** Thai. ***PRACTICE AREAS:*** Patent Prosecution; Patent Litigation; Patent Licensing. ***Email:*** kitisri.sukhapinda@btlaw.com

PAUL L. JEFFERSON, admitted to bar, 2003, Indiana and U.S. District Court, Southern and Northern Districts of Indiana. *Education:* Wabash College (A.B., 1992); Indiana University School of Law - Indianapolis (J.D., magna cum laude, 2002). Order of the Barristers. Recipient: Harold R. Woodard Scholarship; Honorable Cale J. Holder Scholarship. Member, Executive Board, Indiana Law Review, 2002. Law Clerk to Associate Justice Theodore R. Boehm, Supreme Court of Indiana, 2002-2004. *Member:* Indianapolis, Indiana State and American Bar Associations. ***PRACTICE AREAS:*** Civil Litigation; Appellate Practice. ***Email:*** paul.jefferson@btlaw.com

JIMMIE L. McMILLIAN, admitted to bar, 2002, Indiana and U.S. District Court, Northern and Southern Districts of Indiana. *Education:* Indiana University, Bloomington (B.A., Political Science, 1998); Indiana University School of Law - Indianapolis (J.D., 2002). Certified Civil Mediator in the state of Indiana. *Member:* Marion County, Indianapolis and Indiana State Bar Associations. ***PRACTICE AREAS:*** Litigation. ***Email:*** jimmie.mcmillian@btlaw.com

JOSHUA P. HOLLINGSWORTH, admitted to bar, 2000, Indiana, U.S. District Court, Southern and Northern Districts of Indiana and U.S. Tax Court; 2001, U.S. District Court, Central District Illinois. *Education:* Miami University (A.B., with honors, 1997); Indiana University (J.D., summa cum laude, 2000). *Member:* Indianapolis, Indiana State and American (Member, Partnerships and Unincorporated Business Organizations Committee, Business Law Section) Bar Associations. ***PRACTICE AREAS:*** Entrepreneurial Business Law; Pass-Through Entities; Mergers and Acquisitions; Corporate Finance. ***Email:*** joshua.hollingsworth@btlaw.com

KRISTIN S. SHEDLOCK, born Memphis, Tennessee; admitted to bar, 2000, Illinois and U.S. District Court, Northern District of Illinois (Not admitted in Indiana). *Education:* St. Mary's College (B.A., 1997); Washington College of Law of American University (J.D., 2000). Note and Comment Editor, Washington College of Law International Law Review, 1999-2000. *Member:* Chicago and Illinois State Bar Associations. ***PRACTICE AREAS:*** Employment Law; Litigation. ***Email:*** kristin.shedlock@btlaw.com

HONGSUN YOON, admitted to bar, 2002, Indiana; 2003, District of Columbia; U.S. District Court, Southern and Northern Districts of Indiana; registered to practice before U.S. Patent and Trademark Office. *Education:* Indiana University (B.S., 1999); Indiana University School of Law - Bloomington (J.D., cum laude, 1995). Senior Articles Editor, Federal Communications Law Journal 2001-2002; Moot Court Board 2001-2002; Moot Court National Team 2001-2002. *Member:* Indianapolis, Indiana State and American (Member, Intellectual Property Law Section) Bar Associations; District of Columbia Bar; American Intellectual Property Law Association. ***LANGUAGES:*** Korean. ***PRACTICE AREAS:*** Intellectual Property; Intellectual Property Litigation; Intellectual Property Prosecution. ***Email:*** hongsun.yoon@btlaw.com

SHANNON M. SHAW, admitted to bar, 2003, Indiana and U.S. District Court, Southern and Northern Districts of Indiana. *Education:* Indiana University (B.A., 1997); Indiana University School of Law - Indianapolis (J.D., 2003). ***PRACTICE AREAS:*** Labor and Employment. ***Email:*** shannon.shaw@btlaw.com

YOLANDA D. EDWARDS, admitted to bar, 2003, Indiana and U.S. District Court, Northern and Southern Districts of Indiana. *Education:* Shorter College (B.A., 1994); Indiana University School of Law-Bloomington (J.D., 2003). Staff Editor, Federal Communications Law Journal. Member, Board of Directors, Indiana Youth Services Association, 2004—. *Member:* Indianapolis, Marion County, Indiana State (Member, Sections on: Utility Law; Business Law; Young Lawyers Division) and American Bar Associations. ***PRACTICE AREAS:*** Energy; Utility Law; Business Law; Regulatory Law. ***Email:*** yolanda.edwards@btlaw.com

SCOTT C. HOLLINGSWORTH, admitted to bar, 2003, Indiana and U.S. District Court, Northern and Southern Districts of Indiana. *Education:* St. Augustine's College (B.A., Political Science, 1998); Howard University School of Law (J.D., 2003). Kappa Alpha Psi. *Member:* Indianapolis, Marion County and American Bar Associations. ***Email:*** scott.hollingsworth@btlaw.com

RANDY L. CAMPBELL, JR., admitted to bar, 2003, Indiana and U.S. District Court, Northern and Southern Districts of Indiana; registered to practice before U.S. Patent and Trademark Office. *Education:* Purdue University (B.S.E.E., 1997; M.S.E.E., 2000); Indiana University School of Law - Indianapolis (J.D., 2003). *Member:* Indiana State Bar Association. ***PRACTICE AREAS:*** Intellectual Property. ***Email:*** randy.campbell@btlaw.com

ANGELA M. (LITTLE) BERG, admitted to bar, 2003, Indiana and U.S. District Court, Northern and Southern Districts of Indiana. *Education:* St. Mary's College, Notre Dame (B.A., summa cum laude, 2000); Notre Dame Law School (J.D., 2003). Member: Madeleva Society of Saint Mary's College; Notre Dame Alumni Association. *Member:* Indianapolis and Indiana State Bar Associations; Indiana Lawyers Alliance. ***PRACTICE AREAS:*** Estate and Gift Taxation; Nonprofit and Charitable Organization; Estate Planning and Adminsitration. ***Email:*** angela.berg@btlaw.com

MONICA R. BROWNEWELL SMITH, admitted to bar, 2003, Indiana and U.S. District Court, Northern and Southern Districts of Indiana. *Education:* DePauw University (B.A., 2000); Valparaiso University School of Law (J.D., summa cum laude, 2003). *Member:* Indiana State and American Bar Associations. ***LANGUAGES:*** American Sign Language. ***PRACTICE AREAS:*** Litigation. ***Email:*** monica.brownewell.smith@btlaw.com

DAVID R. NIJHAWAN, admitted to bar, 2004, Indiana; U.S. District Court, Northern and Southern Districts of Indiana; U.S. Court of Appeals, Seventh Circuit. *Education:* Purdue University (B.S., Management - minors in Information Systems/e-commerce, Human Resources, Marketing, 2000); Vanderbilt University Law School (J.D., 2003). Articles Editor, Vanderbilt University Law School Law Review, 2003. Law Clerk to Associate Justice Theodore R. Boehm, U.S. Supreme Court of Indiana. Associate Justice, Vanderbilt First Amendment Moot Court Competition. Brief Specialist, Jessup International Moot Court Team. Author, Note, "The Emperor Has No Clothes," Vanderbilt Law Review. Supporting Member, National Association of Women Business Owners. *Member:* Indianapolis (Member, Young Professionals of Central Indiana) and Indiana State Bar Associations; Sagamore Council of the American Inns of Court. ***LANGUAGES:*** Spanish. ***PRACTICE AREAS:*** Litigation; Entrepreneurial Services; White Collar Crime; Franchises and Franchising. ***Email:*** david.nijhawan@btlaw.com

ANIKA M. CALLOWAY, admitted to bar, 2002, Indiana and U.S. District Court, Northern and Southern Districts of Indiana. *Education:* Spelman College (B.A., 1997); Tulane University (J.D., 2002). *Member:* Indianapolis, Marion County, Indiana State, American and National Bar Associations. ***PRACTICE AREAS:*** Litigation. ***Email:*** anika.calloway@btlaw.com

HIROAKI NISHIKAWARA, admitted to bar, 2004, Indiana and U.S. District Court, Northern and Southern Districts of Indiana. *Education:* Wheaton College, Illinois (B.A., 1996); John Marshall Law School (J.D., 2004). *Member:* Indianapolis and Indiana State Bar Associations. ***LANGUAGES:*** Japanese. ***PRACTICE AREAS:*** Labor and Employment; Business Law; Immigration and Naturalization. ***Email:*** hiro.nishikawara@btlaw.com

(This Listing Continued)

HILLARY SPIKE FORDICE, admitted to bar, 2003, Illinois; 2004, Indiana. *Education:* University of California, Berkeley (B.A., with distinction, 2000); University of Michigan Law School (J.D., 2003). *Member:* Illinois State, Indiana State and American Bar Associations. ***PRACTICE AREAS:*** Corporate Law; Securities. ***Email:*** hillary.spikefordice@btlaw.com

SPENCER P. GOODSON, admitted to bar, 2004, Indiana and U.S. District Court, Southern and Northern Districts of Indiana; registered to practice before U.S. Patent and Trademark Office. *Education:* Hanover College (B.A., summa cum laude, 2001); University of Michigan Law School (J.D., cum laude, 2003). *Member:* Indianapolis and Indiana State Bar Associations. ***PRACTICE AREAS:*** Intellectual Property; Litigation. ***Email:*** spencer.goodson@btlaw.com

SCOTT M. SIMMONDS, admitted to bar, 2004, Indiana and U.S. District Court, Northern and Southern Districts of Indiana; registered to practice before U.S. Patent and Trademark Office. *Education:* Rose-Hulman Institute of Technology (B.S.M.E., 1991); University of Cincinnati (M.B.A., 1995); Indiana University School of Law - Indianapolis (J.D., 2004). *Member:* Indianapolis, Indiana State and American Bar Associations; American Intellectual Property Law Association. ***PRACTICE AREAS:*** Intellectual Property; Intellectual Property Portfolio Management; Patents; Patent Litigation; Patent Infringement; Trade Secrets; Trademarks; Unfair Competition. ***Email:*** scott.simmonds@btlaw.com

CHERYL A. GONZALEZ, admitted to bar, 2004 Indiana and U.S. District Court, Northern and Southern Districts of Indiana. *Education:* DePauw University (B.A., 1999); University of Minnesota (J.D., cum laude, 2004). *Member:* Indiana State (Member, Sections on: Environment and Government Services), Indianapolis and American Bar Associations. ***PRACTICE AREAS:*** Environmental Law; Governmental Law. ***Email:*** cheryl.gonzalez@btlaw.com

AARIKA D. MACK-BROWN, admitted to bar, 2004, Indiana and U.S. District Court, Southern and Northern Districts of Indiana. *Education:* Fisk University (B.A., summa cum laude, 2001); Georgetown University Law Center (J.D., 2004). Phi Beta Kappa. Reporter for the First Amendment Center at Vanderbilt University 2000-2001. Research Assistant for Georgetown University Law Center's Family Advocacy Clinic, 2003-2004. *Member:* Indianapolis, Marion County, Indiana State and American Bar Associations. ***PRACTICE AREAS:*** Labor and Employment. ***Email:*** aarika.mack@btlaw.com

ANTHONY H. GREEN, admitted to bar, 2004, Indiana; U.S. District Court, Southern and Northern Districts of Indiana. *Education:* United States Air Force Academy (B.S.); Indiana University School of Law - Indianapolis (J.D., cum laude). *Member:* Indianapolis and Indiana State Bar Associations; Association of Graduates. [Captain, U.S. Air Force, 1989-2000; Major, U.S. Air Force Reserves, 2000-2002 and 2004—]. ***PRACTICE AREAS:*** Intellectual Property Litigation; Litigation; White Collar Crime. ***Email:*** agreen@btlaw.com

DAVID M. HEGER, admitted to bar, 2004, Indiana. *Education:* Georgetown University (B.A., 1997); Washington University in St. Louis School of Law (J.D., 2004). *Member:* Indiana State and American Bar Associations. ***PRACTICE AREAS:*** Litigation; Environmental; Property and Casualty Insurance Coverage. ***Email:*** david.heger@btlaw.com

KEITH R. DONNELLY, admitted to bar, 2004 Indiana and U.S. District Court, Northern and Southern Districts of Indiana. *Education:* United States Military Academy, West Point (B.S., 1978); The Ohio State University (M.A., 1989); Indiana University School of Law (J.D., 2004). *Member:* Indiana State, Indianapolis and American Bar Associations. [Lt. Colonel, U.S. Army (retired) 1978-2001]. ***LANGUAGES:*** Spanish, German. ***PRACTICE AREAS:*** Intellectual Property; Patents. ***Email:*** keith.donnelly@btlaw.com

ASINA C. GANT, admitted to bar, 2004, Indiana and U.S. District Courts, Southern and Northern Districts of Indiana. *Education:* The University of Texas at Arlington (B.A., cum laude, 2000); Howard University School of Law (J.D., 2004). *Member:* National Bar Association (Member, Litigation Section); Indiana State, Indianapolis, Marion County and American Bar Associations. ***PRACTICE AREAS:*** Litigation. ***Email:*** asina.gant@btlaw.com

DAVID A. W. WONG, admitted to bar, 2004, Indiana and U.S. District Court, Northern and Southern Districts of Indiana. *Education:* Indiana State University (B.A., 1998); Indiana University (J.D., 2004). ***PRACTICE AREAS:*** Trademarks; Copyrights. ***Email:*** david.wong@btlaw.com

GLEN M. KELLETT, admitted to bar, 2005, Indiana and U.S. District Court, Northern and Southern Districts of Indiana. *Education:* Purdue University (B.S.E.E.T., 1999; M.S.E.E., 2001); Indiana University School of Law - Indianapolis (J.D., 2004). *Member:* Indianapolis and American Bar Associations. ***PRACTICE AREAS:*** Patent Prosecution. ***Email:*** glen.kellett@btlaw.com

AARON M. STASER, born Evansville, Indiana; admitted to bar, 2004, Indiana and U.S. District Court, Southern and Northern Districts of Indiana. *Education:* Indiana University, Bloomington (B.S., with distinction, 2000; J.D., magna cum laude, 2003). *Member:* Indiana State Bar Association. ***PRACTICE AREAS:*** Intellectual Property Litigation. ***Email:*** aaron.staser@btlaw.com

STAFF ATTORNEYS

HELEN K. GEIB, admitted to bar, 2000, Indiana and U.S. District Court, Southern District of Indiana; registered to practice before U.S. Patent and Trademark Office. *Education:* Drew University (B.A., Physics, magna cum laude, 1997); John Marshall Law School (J.D., summa cum laude, 2000). Valedictorian, John Marshall Law School, Class of 2000. ***PRACTICE AREAS:*** Intellectual Property Litigation. ***Email:*** helen.geib@btlaw.com

SHARLEE C. LITTLE, admitted to bar, 1993, Texas (Not admitted in Indiana). *Education:* Southern Methodist University (B.S., Economics and Finance, 1985; J.D., 1993). *Member:* State Bar of Texas. ***SPECIAL AGENCIES:*** Equal Employment Opportunity Commission; State and Local Equal Employment Opportunity agencies. ***PRACTICE AREAS:*** Labor and Employment; Litigation. ***Email:*** sharlee.little@btlaw.com

ZIAADDIN MOLLABASHY, admitted to bar, 2003, New Jersey and Pennsylvania; 2004, Indiana; U.S. District Court, Northern and Southern Districts of Indiana. *Education:* Indiana University, Bloomington (B.A., 1993); University of Pittsburgh School of Law (J.D., 2002). ***Email:*** zmollabashy@btlaw.com

(This Listing Continued)

KELLY B. SMITH, admitted to bar, 2002, Indiana and U.S. District Court, Southern and Northern Districts of Indiana; registered to practice before U.S. Patent and Trademark Office. *Education:* Purdue Universtiy (B.A., 1995; M.S. 1999); Indiana University (J.D., 2002). ***PRACTICE AREAS:*** Patent Litigation. ***Email:*** kelly.b.smith@btlaw.com

KATHERINE J. STOTLER, admitted to bar, 2002, Illinois; 2003, Indiana. *Education:* Indiana University - Bloomington (B.A., with distinction, 1999); Indiana University School of Law - Bloomington (J.D., 2002). *Member:* Indianapolis Bar Association. ***PRACTICE AREAS:*** Employment Law. ***Email:*** katherine.stotler@btlaw.com

ALEJANDRO VALLE, admitted to bar, 2001, Indiana and U.S. District Court, Southern District of Indiana; 2002, U.S. District Court, Northern District of Indiana and U.S. Court of Appeals, Seventh Circuit. *Education:* University of Virginia (B.A., 1998); Indiana University School of Law (J.D., cum laude, 2001). *Member:* Indianapolis Bar Association. ***LANGUAGES:*** Spanish. ***PRACTICE AREAS:*** Litigation; Toxic Torts; Products Liability; Commercial Law. ***Email:*** alejandro.valle@btlaw.com

REPRESENTATIVE CLIENTS: Allegiance Healthcare Corporation; Alpine Electronics Inc.; Ameritech; Anthem Insurance Companies, Inc.; ArvinMeritor; Bank One Corporation; Best Access Systems; Bethlehem Steel Corporation; Bristol-Myers Squibb Company; CMG Worldwide, Inc.; DePuy Orthopaedics, Inc.; Dow AgroSciences LLC; Eli Lilly and Company; The Fifth Third Bank; Finish Line, Inc.; General Electric Company; General Motors Corporation; Georgia-Pacific Corporation; Goldman, Sachs & Co.; Herff Jones, Inc.; Hillenbrand Industries, Inc.; Indiana-American Water Company, Inc.; Indiana University; The Indianapolis Museum of Art, Inc.; Indianapolis Power & Light Company; The Indianapolis Symphony Orchestra; Inland Paperboard and Packaging, Inc.; James Dean Foundation Trust; KeyBank, National Association; LDI, Ltd.; Lincoln National Corporation; Martin Marietta Corp.; Mercedes-Benz USA, Inc.; Merrill Lynch, Pierce, Fenner & Smith Inc.; National Steel Corporation; Nordstrom, Inc.; Purdue Research Foundation, Inc.; Roche Diagnostics Corporation; Simon Property Group, Inc.; Skyline Corporation; Subaru-Isuzu Automotive, Inc.; Toyota Motor Corporation; Union Acceptance Corporation; University of Notre Dame; The Valspar Corporation; Vectren Corporation; Whirlpool Corporation.

DONNA J. BAYS

ONE NORTH PENNSYLVANIA STREET, SUITE 905
INDIANAPOLIS, INDIANA 46204
Telephone: 317-630-3175
Fax: 317-630-3174
URL: http://www.donnabays.com

Family Law, Divorce, Child Custody, Paternity, Premarital Agreements.

DONNA J. BAYS, born Indianapolis, Indiana, July 7, 1958; admitted to bar, 1985, Indiana; U.S. District Court, Northern and Southern Districts of Indiana; 1987, U.S. Court of Appeals, Seventh Circuit and U.S. Claims Court. *Education:* Ball State University (B.S., magna cum laude, 1979); Indiana University School of Law-Indianapolis (J.D., summa cum laude, 1984). Recipient, American Jurisprudence Award for Civil Procedure II, Domestic Relations and Secured Transactions. Articles Editor, Indiana Law Review, 1983-1984. Author: "Statutory Authorization," Indiana Alternative Dispute Resolution Manual (Lawyers Cooperative, 1995); "Exclusive Juvenile Jurisdiction to Authorize Sterilization of Incompetent Minors," 16 Indiana Law Review 835, (1983). Contributing Author, "Court Summaries, Civil," The Indiana Lawyer, 1995-2002. *Member:* Indianapolis (Member, Family Law Section), Indiana State (Chair, Family and Juvenile Law Section, 2003-2005) and American (Member, Family Law Section) Bar Associations. (Board Certified, Family Law Specialist, Indiana State Bar Association, Family Law Certification Board)

BINGHAM McHALE LLP

Established in 1914
2700 MARKET TOWER BUILDING
10 WEST MARKET STREET
INDIANAPOLIS, INDIANA 46204-4900
Telephone: 317-635-8900
Telecopier: 317-236-9907
Email: firm@binghammchale.com
URL: http://www.binghammchale.com

Jasper, Indiana Office: Bingham McHale LLP, 212 West Sixth Street. Telephone: 812-482- 5500. Fax: 812-482-2017.
Noblesville, Indiana Office: Bingham McHale LLP, 970 Logan Street. Telephone: 317-776-8668. Fax: 317-776-8651.
Vincennes, Indiana Office: Bingham Mchale LLP, 112 North 7th Street. Telephone: 812-886-9970. Fax: 812-886-0776.

General Civil Practice including: Administrative Law; Agricultural Law; Alternative Dispute Resolution; Antitrust and Trade Regulation; Appeals; Appellate; Architects and Engineers Liability Defense; Banks and Banking; Bankruptcy and Reorganization; Business Law; Business Litigation; Cable Telecommunications Law; Collective Bargaining; Commercial Transactions; Construction Law; Contract Negotiation; Copyright; Corporate Finance; Complex Litigation; Class Actions; Corporate Law; Creditors' Rights; Drug and Medical Device Law; Election, Campaign Finance and Political Law; Employee Benefits; Environmental Law; Estate Planning and Administration; Family Law; Finance; Franchising and Licensing; Gaming Law; Governmental Services; Health Care; Hospital Law; Insurance; Intellectual Property; Labor and Employment; Leases and Leasing; Legal Malpractice, Discipline and Licensing; Libel, Slander and Defamation; Litigation; Lobbying; Matrimonial and Family Law; Media Law; Medicare and Medicaid Reimbursement, Medical and Dental Liability Defense and Disciplines and Licensing; Mergers and Acquisitions; Natural Resources Law; Occupational Safety and Health; Patent; Probate; Product Liability; Professional Liability Defense; Public Finance; Public Utility Law; Real Estate; Securities Law; Tax-Exempt Finance, Taxation (Controversies, Corporate Planning, Income, Gift and Estate, Individual, Partnership, Property, Nonprofit Organizations), Toxic Torts Law; Trademark; White Collar Criminal Defense; Zoning, Planning and Land Use.

FIRM PROFILE: Bingham McHale LLP was formed by the merger of Bingham Summers Welsh & Spilman and McHale Cook & Welch on January 1, 2002. Evident in the nearly 130 year combined history of both firms is the longstanding commitment to one ideal: providing

(This Listing Continued)

BINGHAM MCHALE LLP, Indianapolis—Continued

high quality legal services at an affordable cost. Both firms individually earned a reputation founded upon client service, and will continue and improve upon that tradition collectively as it provides the highest level of service to business, government, utility and land use clients and their individual owners.

MEMBERS OF FIRM

MICHAEL J. ALERDING, born Indianapolis, Indiana, 1970; admitted to bar, 1997, Indiana, U.S. District Court, Northern and Southern Districts of Indiana and U.S. Court of Appeals, Seventh Circuit. *Education:* Indiana University (B.A., 1993); Indiana University School of Law - Indianapolis (J.D., cum laude, 1997). Associate Editor, Indiana Law Review, 1996-1997. Co-Author: "'Two Party' Disputes in Chapter 11," American Bankruptcy Institute Journal, July/August, 1997. Board Member and Secretary, Talbot House. Advisory Board Member, St. Vincent's Hospice. *Member:* Indianapolis, 7th Circuit, Indiana State and American Bar Associations. ***PRACTICE AREAS:*** Bankruptcy; Debtors' and Creditors' Rights; Commercial Litigation.

ROBIN L. BABBITT, born Fort Wayne, Indiana, 1954; admitted to bar, 1980, Indiana. *Education:* University of Evansville (B.S., cum laude, 1976); Indiana University (J.D., magna cum laude, 1980). ***PRACTICE AREAS:*** Legal Malpractice; Business Litigation; Administrative Law. ***Email:*** rbabbitt@binghammchale.com

SUE A. BEESLEY, born Seymour, Indiana, 1955; admitted to bar, 1980, Indiana; 1995, U.S. Supreme Court. *Education:* DePauw University (B.A., 1977); Indiana University (J.D., 1980). Corporation Counsel, 1992-1997 and Assistant Corporation Counsel, 1984-1992, Indianapolis and Marion County. Law Clerk for the Honorable George B. Hoffman, Jr., Court of Appeals of Indiana, 1981-1984. ***PRACTICE AREAS:*** Government; Public Finance. ***Email:*** sbeesley@binghammchale.com

TIMOTHY J. BENDER, born South Bend, Indiana, 1959; admitted to bar, 1984, Indiana and U.S. Tax Court. *Education:* Purdue University (B.S., with distinction, 1981); Indiana University (J.D., magna cum laude, 1984). Certified Public Accountant, Indiana, 1990. ***PRACTICE AREAS:*** Taxation; Estate Planning; Wealth Transfer Planning; Business Law. ***Email:*** tbender@binghammchale.com

JEFFREY T. BENNETT, born Evansville, Indiana, 1963; admitted to bar, 1989, Indiana. *Education:* DePauw University (B.A., 1986); Indiana University, Bloomington (J.D., 1988). ***PRACTICE AREAS:*** Environmental Law; Real Estate; Property Tax. ***Email:*** jbennett@binghammchale.com

KEITH A. BICE, born Goshen, Indiana, 1972; admitted to bar, 1998, Indiana. *Education:* Butler University (B.A., cum laude, 1995); University of Notre Dame (J.D., cum laude, 1998). ***PRACTICE AREAS:*** Business Services; Banking; Commercial Finance. ***Email:*** kbice@binghammchale.com

DAVID G. BLACHLY, born Valparaiso, Indiana, 1958; admitted to bar, 1986, Indiana. *Education:* Villanova University (B.S., 1980); Indiana University (J.D., 1986). ***PRACTICE AREAS:*** Business Law; Mergers and Acquisitions; Technology Law; Insurance Regulatory Law. ***Email:*** dblachly@binghammchale.com

DANIEL L. BOOTS, born Indianapolis, Indiana, 1961; admitted to bar, 1987, Indiana; registered to practice before U.S. Patent and Trademark Office. *Education:* Purdue University (B.S.I.M., with Engineering Option, 1983); Indiana University (J.D., 1987). *Member:* Indianapolis Bar Association (Chair, Intellectual Property Section). ***PRACTICE AREAS:*** Intellectual Property Counseling and Litigation; Patents; Trademarks; Copyrights; Trade Secrets; Technology Transfers; Licensing; Unfair Competition; Technology and Science; Computers and Software; E-Commerce; Domain Name Protection; Dispute Resolution; Franchises; Entertainment and the Arts. ***Email:*** dboots@binghammchale.com

S. ANDREW BOWMAN, born Lafayette, Indiana, 1956; admitted to bar, 1982, Indiana. *Education:* Purdue University (B.S., with distinction and honors, 1978); Indiana University (M.B.A., 1982; J.D., magna cum laude, 1982). Certified Hazardous Materials Manager. Member, Board of Directors, 1994-1996; President-Elect, 2002; President, 2003; Indiana Society of Hazardous Materials Managers. ***PRACTICE AREAS:*** Environmental Law; Natural Resources. ***Email:*** abowman@binghammchale.com

WILLIAM M. BRAMAN, born Bedford, Indiana, 1965; admitted to bar, 1990, Indiana and U.S. District Court, Northern and Southern Districts of Indiana; 2000, U.S. Court of Appeals, Seventh Circuit. *Education:* DePauw University (B.A., magna cum laude, 1987); Indiana University (J.D., magna cum laude, 1990). ***PRACTICE AREAS:*** Litigation; Real Estate; Creditors' Rights; Banking; Commercial Law; Construction. ***Email:*** wmbraman@binghammchale.com

C. JOHN BRANNON, born Saint Joseph, Missouri, 1961; admitted to bar, 1997, Indiana. *Education:* University of Missouri-Rolla (B.S., Physics, Ceramic Engineering, 1985; B.S., Psychology, 1987; M.S. and Ph.D. in Ceramic Engineering, 1987, 1989); Chicago-Kent College of Law (J.D., 1997). Kent Legal Scholar, 1994-1995. Recipient, Lowell Thomas Merit Scholarship, 1994-1995. ***PRACTICE AREAS:*** Intellectual Property; Patent; Trademark; Copyright. ***Email:*** jbrannon@binghammchale.com

DANIEL P. BYRON, born Indianapolis, Indiana, 1937; admitted to bar, 1962, Indiana. *Education:* Indiana University (A.B., 1959; J.D., 1962). First Assistant U.S. Attorney, Southern District of Indiana, 1968-1969. *Member:* Indiana Broadcasters Association (Counsel, 2002). Fellow: Indiana Bar Foundation; Indianapolis Bar Foundation. [U.S. Army, Inf. and J.A.G., active duty, 1962-1966]. ***PRACTICE AREAS:*** Complex Litigation; Media Law; First Amendment Law. ***Email:*** dbyron@binghammchale.com

DAVID C. CAMPBELL, born Terre Haute, Indiana, 1949; admitted to bar, 1974, Indiana; 1982, U.S. Court of Appeals, Seventh Circuit; 1985, U.S. Supreme Court. *Education: Indiana State University (B.S., 1971); Indiana University (J.D., summa cum laude, 1974). Member:* International Association of Defense Counsel; Indiana Defense Trial Counsel (Diplomat and Past President); Indianapolis Legal Aid Society (Director, 1994— and President, 1996-2000). Fellow: American College of Trial Lawyers. ***PRACTICE AREAS:*** Litigation; Business Litigation. ***Email:*** dcampbell@binghammchale.com

(This Listing Continued)

DENNIS F. CANTRELL, born Detroit, Michigan, 1960; admitted to bar, 1986, Indiana. *Education:* Wabash College (A.B., 1982); Indiana University (J.D., cum laude, 1986). ***PRACTICE AREAS:*** Litigation; Environmental Insurance Coverage; Insurance Law; Bad Faith Litigation. ***Email:*** dcantrell@binghammchale.com

GRANTLAND M. CLAPACS, born Bloomington, Indiana, 1969; admitted to bar, 1995, Indiana. *Education:* Cornell University (B.A., with high distinction, 1992); Duke University (J.D., 1995). ***PRACTICE AREAS:*** Construction Law; Creditors Rights; Business Litigation; Insurance. ***Email:*** gclapacs@binghammchale.com

BRYAN J. COLLINS, born Gary, Indiana, 1959; admitted to bar, 1985, Indiana. *Education:* Indiana University (B.S., 1981; J.D., cum laude, 1985). Certified Public Accountant, Illinois, 1982. ***PRACTICE AREAS:*** Public Finance Law; Municipal Law. ***Email:*** bcollins@binghammchale.com

PAUL J. CORSARO, born Beech Grove, Indiana, 1943; admitted to bar, 1969, Indiana; 1970, U.S. Tax Court. *Education:* St. Joseph's College (B.S., cum laude, 1965); Indiana University (J.D., 1969). Certified Public Accountant, Indiana, 1968. Fellow: Indiana Bar Foundation; College of American Trusts and Estate Counsel. ***PRACTICE AREAS:*** Estate Planning; Probate; Trust Law; Federal Taxation; State Taxation; Business Succession Planning; Corporate Law; Mergers and Acquisitions; Partnership Law; Health Care Law. ***Email:*** pcorsaro@binghammchale.com

STEVEN G. CRACRAFT, born Indianapolis, Indiana, 1946; admitted to bar, 1973, Indiana; 1995, U.S. Supreme Court. *Education:* College of William & Mary (A.B., 1969); Indiana University (J.D., summa cum laude, 1973). Law Clerk to Hon. Allen Sharp, Court of Appeals, Indiana, 1971-1973. ***PRACTICE AREAS:*** Business Law; Commercial Litigation; Intellectual Property; Real Estate. ***Email:*** scracraft@binghammchale.com

ALAN J. DANSKER, born Vincennes, Indiana, 1952; admitted to bar, 1977, Indiana; 1978, U.S. Tax Court. *Education:* Indiana University (B.S., with high distinction, 1974; J.D., summa cum laude, 1977). ***PRACTICE AREAS:*** Taxation Law; Employee Benefit Law; Corporate Law; Health Care Law. ***Email:*** adansker@binghammchale.com

DUANE R. DENTON, born Honolulu, Hawaii, 1963; admitted to bar, 1988, Indiana. *Education:* Butler University (B.S., cum laude, 1985); Indiana University (J.D., 1988). *Member:* Indianapolis (Counsel to Board, 2002; Member, Board of Managers, 2000—), Indiana and Federal (President, Indianapolis Chapter, 2001—) Bar Associations. ***PRACTICE AREAS:*** Labor and Employment Law; Business Litigation. ***Email:*** rdenton@binghammchale.com

JULIA E. DIMICK, born Corvallis, Oregon, 1963; admitted to bar, 1990, New York; 1993, Indiana. *Education:* Ball State University (B.S., 1986); Georgetown University Law Center (J.D., 1989). Co-Author: "Show Me the Money! Allocation Issues in Evaluating the Environmental Insurance Claims," Midwest Environmental Claims Association, September 1997. Speaker, 1997 Indiana Defense Lawyers Association Annual Meeting, "Determining the Duty to Defend— Does the Insurer Have a Duty to Investigate Non-covered Allegations Under Recent Case Law." *Member:* Indianapolis, Indiana State and American Bar Associations; Outdoor Advertising Association of America (Attorney Member); Sagamore American Inn of Court (Barrister, 1999). ***PRACTICE AREAS:*** Business Litigation; Real Estate.

MICHAEL L. ECKERLE, born Jasper, Indiana, 1952; admitted to bar, 1977, Indiana. *Education:* Wabash College (B.A., magna cum laude, 1974); Duke University (J.D., with distinction, 1977). Phi Beta Kappa. Fellow: Indiana Bar Foundation; Indianapolis Bar Foundation (Trustee, 1999-2000). ***PRACTICE AREAS:*** Corporate Law; Business Transactions. ***Email:*** meckerle@binghammchale.com

PATRICK A. ELWARD, born Wabash, Indiana, 1956; admitted to bar, 1981, Indiana; 2003, U.S. Court of Federal Claims. *Education:* Ball State University (B.S., summa cum laude, 1978); Indiana University (J.D., cum laude, 1981). *Member:* Indiana Trial Lawyers Association. ***PRACTICE AREAS:*** Litigation; Products Liability; Subrogation; Workers' Compensation; Personal Injury. ***Email:*** pelward@binghammchale.com

DANIEL R. FAGAN, born Indianapolis, Indiana, 1952; admitted to bar, 1977, Indiana. *Education:* Indiana University (B.A., 1974; J.D., magna cum laude, 1977). ***PRACTICE AREAS:*** Litigation; Medical Malpractice; Torts. ***Email:*** dfagan@binghammchale.com

PHILLIP J. FOWLER, born Clarksville, Indiana, 1971; admitted to bar, 1997, Indiana and U.S. District Court, Northern and Southern Districts of Indiana. *Education:* Indiana University (B.S., with high distinction, 1994); Vanderbilt University (J.D., 1997). Phi Eta Sigma; Beta Gamma Sigma. Member: Moot Court. Recipient: Honors Division Scholarship; Leete Thompson Memorial Scholarship. Law Clerk for the Honorable David Wells, Tennessee Court of Criminal Appeals, 1995. ***PRACTICE AREAS:*** Business Litigation; Civil Litigation; Media Law. ***Email:*** pfowler@binghammchale.com

DONALD J. GRAHAM, born Lafayette, Indiana, 1955; admitted to bar, 1980, Indiana. *Education:* Purdue University (B.S., 1977); Indiana University (J.D., summa cum laude, 1980). ***PRACTICE AREAS:*** Construction Law; Insurance Regulatory and Administrative Law. ***Email:*** dgraham@binghammchale.com

GERARD L. GREGERSON, born Chicago Heights, Illinois, 1963; admitted to bar, 1989, Indiana. *Education:* Indiana University (B.A., 1985; J.D., cum laude, 1989). ***PRACTICE AREAS:*** Business and General Litigation; Creditors Rights; Construction Law; Banking Law. ***Email:*** ggregerson@binghammchale.com

MICHAEL RYAN HARTMAN, born Kewanee, Illinois, 1955; admitted to bar, 1980, Indiana; U.S. District Court, Northern and Southern Districts of Indiana. *Education:* University of Tennessee at Knoxville; Indiana University (A.B., 1997; J.D., cum laude, 1980). Associate Editor, Indiana Law Review, 1979-1980. Law Clerk, Indiana Supreme Court, 1980-1981. ***LANGUAGES:*** French. ***PRACTICE AREAS:*** Business Litigation; Real Estate Litigation; Products Liability; Personal Injury Defense. ***Email:*** mhartman@binghammchale.com

ROBERT B. HEBERT, born Greencastle, Indiana, 1948; admitted to bar, 1973, Indiana. *Education:* Indiana University (B.S., 1970; J.D., magna cum laude, 1973). Associate Editor, Indiana Law Review, 1971-1973. Fellow: Indianapolis Bar Foundation. [U.S. Army Reserve, 1969-1975]. ***PRACTICE AREAS:*** Business Law; Public Utility Law; Cable Telecommunications Law. ***Email:*** rhebert@binghammchale.com

(This Listing Continued)

KANDI K. HIDDE, born Cuba City, Wisconsin, 1967; admitted to bar, 1993, Florida; 1994, Indiana. *Education:* St. Norbert College (B.S., 1990); University of Dayton (J.D., 1993). Recipient, Book Award for Civil Trial Practice. ***PRACTICE AREAS:*** General Litigation; Legal Malpractice Litigation; Environmental Insurance Coverage. **Email:** khidde@binghammchale.com

JAMES M. HINSHAW, born Charleston, South Carolina, 1967; admitted to bar, 1992, Indiana. *Education:* DePauw University (B.A., magna cum laude, 1989); Indiana University (J.D., magna cum laude, 1992). Order of the Coif. ***PRACTICE AREAS:*** Business Litigation; Intellectual Property Litigation; Products Liability. **Email:** jhinshaw@binghammchale.com

JOSEPH H. HOGSETT, born Rushville, Indiana, 1956; admitted to bar, 1981, Indiana. *Education:* Indiana University (A.B., with honors, 1978), Phi Beta Kappa; Indiana University School of Law (J.D., 1981); Butler University (M.A., 1987); Christian Theological Seminary (M.T.S., magna cum laude, 1999). ***PRACTICE AREAS:*** Labor and Employment. **Email:** jhogsett@binghammchale.com

MARTHA SCHMIDT HOLLINGSWORTH, born Indianapolis, Indiana, 1944; admitted to bar, 1972, Indiana; 1973, Florida; 1979, U.S. Supreme Court. *Education:* Indiana University (A.B., 1966; J.D., magna cum laude, 1972). Recipient: Defense Lawyer of the Year, 1997. *Member:* Defense Research Institute; Indiana Defense Lawyers Association (President, 1996). ***PRACTICE AREAS:*** Environmental Litigation; Complex Litigation; Insurance Coverage. **Email:** mhollingsworth@binghammchale.com

DWAYNE C. ISAACS, born Connersville, Indiana, 1960; admitted to bar, 1989, Indiana. *Education:* Indiana University (B.S., 1983; J.D., cum laude, 1989). Certified Public Accountant, Indiana, 1986. ***PRACTICE AREAS:*** Corporate Law; Taxation; Estate Planning. **Email:** disaacs@binghammchale.com

PHIL L. ISENBARGER, born Evanston, Illinois, 1959; admitted to bar, 1984, Indiana and U.S. District Court, Northern and Southern Districts of Indiana. *Education:* Indiana University (B.S., 1981; J.D., 1984). *Member:* Indianapolis Bar Association (President, 1998). Fellow: Indianapolis Bar Foundation. ***PRACTICE AREAS:*** Business Litigation; Plaintiff and Defense Litigation; Products Liability; Premises Liability; Personal Injury; Tort Litigation; Copyright; Trademark; Fire; Environmental; Unfair Competition; Business Practices; Insurance Defense; Federal Trial Practice; State Trial Practice. **Email:** pisenbarger@binghammchale.com

WILLIAM J. KAISER, JR., born Jasper, Indiana, 1965; admitted to bar, 1990, Indiana. *Education:* Wabash College (B.A., 1987); Indiana University (J.D., cum laude, 1990). (Also Member, Jasper Office). ***LANGUAGES:*** German. ***PRACTICE AREAS:*** Corporate Law; Real Estate; Environmental Law; Zoning, Planning and Land Use. **Email:** bkaiser@binghammchale.com

LARRY J. KANE, born LaPorte, Indiana, 1945; admitted to bar, 1975, Indiana. *Education:* Purdue University (B.S.E.E., with highest distinction, 1967; M.S.E.E., 1968); Indiana University (J.D., 1975). Director, Office of Legal Counsel, Indiana Department of Environmental Management, 1988-1989. *Member:* Indiana State Bar Association (Chair, Environmental Law Section, 1997-1998). ***PRACTICE AREAS:*** Environmental Law. **Email:** lkane@binghammchale.com

JAN KEPLEY KEEFER, born Macon, Georgia, 1957; admitted to bar, 1991, Indiana. *Education:* Indiana University (B.A., 1981; J.D., cum laude, 1991). Associate Editor, Indiana Law Review. ***LANGUAGES:*** French. ***PRACTICE AREAS:*** Litigation; Government; Family Law. **Email:** jkkeefer@binghammchale.com

GARY L. KLOTZ, born Perryton, Texas, 1952; admitted to bar, 1978, Indiana. *Education:* DePauw University (B.A., with distinction, 1974); Indiana University (J.D., cum laude, 1978). ***PRACTICE AREAS:*** Corporate Law; Banking Law. **Email:** gklotz@binghammchale.com

SCOTT R. LEISZ, born Benton Harbor, Michigan, 1959; admitted to bar, 1986, Indiana. *Education:* Indiana University (B.S., with high distinction, 1983; J.D., cum laude, 1986). Beta Gamma Sigma. ***PRACTICE AREAS:*** Civil Litigation; Commercial Litigation; Bankruptcy; Creditors Rights. **Email:** sleisz@binghammchale.com

JEFFERY M. MALLAMAD, born Toledo, Ohio, 1953; admitted to bar, 1979, Ohio; 1986, Michigan and Indiana. *Education:* University of Toledo (B.A., cum laude, 1976); Case Western Reserve University (J.D., 1979). Law Review, 1977-1979. ***PRACTICE AREAS:*** Labor and Employment Law; Governmental Affairs; Executive Representation. **Email:** jmallamad@binghammchale.com

W. TOBIN McCLAMROCH, born Crawfordsville, Indiana, 1955; admitted to bar, 1980, Indiana. *Education:* DePauw University (B.A., 1977); Indiana University (J.D., 1980). Attorney for Republicans and Parliamentarian, Indiana House of Representatives, 1985-1996; Indianapolis City-County Council at Large, 1992—, Vice President and Majority Leader. ***PRACTICE AREAS:*** Business and Corporate Law; State Administrative; Legislative Representation. **Email:** tmcclamroch@binghammchale.com

DAVID T. McGIMPSEY, born Seattle, Washington, 1970; admitted to bar, 1998, Indiana. *Education:* Wabash College (B.A., magna cum laude, 1993); Indiana University (J.D., 1998). ***PRACTICE AREAS:*** Utility; Real Estate. **Email:** dtmcgimpsey@binghammchale.com

BRETT J. MILLER, born Buffalo, New York, 1958; admitted to bar, 1983, Indiana, U.S. District Court, Southern and Northern Districts of Indiana and U.S. Tax Court; 1984, Illinois. *Education:* Rochester Institute of Technology (B.S., with honors, 1980); Valparaiso University (J.D., 1983). ***PRACTICE AREAS:*** Taxation Law; Litigation; General Corporate Law; Real Estate Law. **Email:** bmiller@binghammchale.com

KARL L. MULVANEY, born 1949; admitted to bar, 1977, Indiana. *Education:* The Ohio State University (B.S., cum laude, 1972); Indiana University (J.D., cum laude, 1977). Indiana Supreme Court Administrator, 1984-1991. *Member:* American Academy of Appellate Lawyers. ***PRACTICE AREAS:*** Appellate Practice; Litigation; Disciplinary Law. **Email:** kmulvaney@binghammchale.com

MICHAEL W. PADGETT, born Indianapolis, Indiana, 1962; admitted to bar, 1991, Indiana and U.S. District Court, Northern and Southern Districts of Indiana; 2002, U.S. Court of Appeals, Seventh Circuits; 2003, U.S. Court of Appeals, Fifth Circuit and U.S.

(This Listing Continued)

Distict Court, Northern District of Oklahoma. *Education:* Purdue University (B.S., 1984); Indiana University (J.D., cum laude, 1991). ***PRACTICE AREAS:*** Labor and Employment Law. **Email:** mpadgett@binghammchale.com

DAVID R. PRECHTEL, born Evansville, Indiana, 1959; admitted to bar, 1985, Indiana. *Education:* Purdue University, Krannert School of Management (B.S., with distinction, 1982); Indiana University (J.D., cum laude, 1985);. ***PRACTICE AREAS:*** Business Law; Mergers & Acquisitions; Health Care; Securities Law; Financial Institutions Law. **Email:** dprechtel@binghammchale.com

MATTHEW M. PRICE, born Lafayette, Indiana, 1968; admitted to bar, 1993, Indiana. *Education:* Wabash College (B.A., cum laude, 1990); Indiana University (J.D., cum laude, 1993). Managing Editor, Indiana Law Journal, 1992-1993. ***PRACTICE AREAS:*** Corporate Law; Public Finance; Government; Real Estate. **Email:** mprice@binghammchale.com

NANA QUAY-SMITH, born Indianapolis, Indiana, 1962; admitted to bar, 1987, Indiana; 1990, U.S. Court of Appeals, Seventh Circuit; 2000, U.S. Supreme Court. *Education:* Butler University (B.S., cum laude, 1984); Indiana University (J.D., summa cum laude, 1987). *Member:* Indiana State Bar Association (Chair, Appellate Section, 1998-1999). ***PRACTICE AREAS:*** Appellate Law; Probate Law. **Email:** nsmith@binghammchale.com

JAMES A. REED, born Muncie, Indiana, 1956; admitted to bar, 1983, Indiana. *Education:* Indiana University (A.B., with honors, 1978; J.D., magna cum laude, 1983). Phi Beta Kappa. ***PRACTICE AREAS:*** Dissolution of Marriage; Complex Matrimonial Litigation; Premarital Agreements; Custody; Parenting Time; Cohabitation Matters; Domestic Partner Matters. **Email:** jreed@binghammchale.com

MATTHEW R. SCHANTZ, born Dayton, Ohio, 1969; admitted to bar, 1995, Indiana; U.S. District Court, Southern and Northern Districts of Indiana; registered to practice before U.S. Patent and Trademark Office. *Education:* Purdue University (B.S. in Electrical Engineering, 1991; B.S. in Mathematics, 1991); University of Chicago Law School (J.D., 1995). ***PRACTICE AREAS:*** Intellectual Property.

THOMAS C. SCHERER, born Columbus, Ohio, 1951; admitted to bar, 1977, Indiana. *Education:* The Ohio State University (B.A., cum laude, 1973); Indiana University (J.D., magna cum laude, 1977). ***PRACTICE AREAS:*** Bankruptcy; Reorganization; Creditors Rights. **Email:** tscherer@binghammchale.com

RANDOLPH L. SEGER, born Jasper, Indiana, 1948; admitted to bar, 1972, Indiana. *Education:* Indiana University (B.S., magna cum laude, 1970; J.D., magna cum laude, 1972). Beta Gamma Sigma. Member, Indiana Law Journal. Member, Utility Regulatory Commission Practice & Procedures Committee and Regulatory Law Committee, National Association of Water Companies. Fellow: Indiana Bar Foundation; Indianapolis Bar Foundation. ***PRACTICE AREAS:*** Public Utility Law; Agribusiness; Administrative Law; Finance. **Email:** rseger@binghammchale.com

KATHERINE L. SHELBY, born Danville, Illinois, 1954; admitted to bar, 1980, Indiana and Illinois; 1989, U.S. District Court, Southern District of Indiana; 1992, U.S. Court of Appeals, Seventh Circuit; 1997, Arizona and U.S. Supreme Court. *Education:* Indiana University (B.A., 1976; J.D., cum laude, 1980). ***PRACTICE AREAS:*** Environmental Law; Insurance Coverage; General Litigation; Appellate Law. **Email:** kshelby@binghammchale.com

LAURA MOENNING SMITH, born Indianapolis, Indiana, 1966; admitted to bar, 1991, Indiana. *Education:* Indiana University (B.A., 1988); George Washington University (J.D., 1991). ***PRACTICE AREAS:*** General Litigation; Business Litigation; Insurance Litigation. **Email:** lsmith@binghammchale.com

MARY ELIZABETH SOLADA, born Michigan City, Indiana, 1957; admitted to bar, 1982, Indiana. *Education:* Indiana University (B.S., with high distinction, 1978; J.D., 1982). ***PRACTICE AREAS:*** Real Estate Law; Zoning and Planning Law; Contract Law; Governmental Affairs. **Email:** msolada@binghammchale.com

HANS W. STECK, born Indianapolis, Indiana, 1951; admitted to bar, 1976, Indiana. *Education:* Wabash College (B.A., magna cum laude, 1973); Washington University (J.D., 1976). Phi Beta Kappa. (Managing Partner). ***PRACTICE AREAS:*** Public Finance; Municipal Law. **Email:** hsteck@binghammchale.com

AMY L. STEWART, born Philadelphia, Pennsylvania, 1963; admitted to bar, 1999, Indiana. *Education:* Indiana University (B.S., with high distinction, 1986; J.D., summa cum laude, 1999). ***PRACTICE AREAS:*** Matrimonial Law; Family Law. **Email:** astewart@binghammchale.com

JAMES P. STRENSKI, born Wheaton, Illinois, 1967; admitted to bar, 1994, Indiana. *Education:* Georgetown University (B.S.F.S., cum laude, 1990); Indiana University (J.D., magna cum laude, 1994). ***PRACTICE AREAS:*** Insurance Bad Faith Litigation; Insurance Coverage; Medical Malpractice; Products Liability; Personal Injury Defense; Appellate. **Email:** jstrenski@binghammchale.com

ROBERT L. TAGGART, born Ft. Wayne, Indiana, 1957; admitted to bar, 1985, Indiana. *Education:* St. Joseph's College (B.S., summa cum laude, 1979); Indiana University (J.D., cum laude, 1985). Associate Editor, Indiana Law Review, 1983-1985. ***PRACTICE AREAS:*** Finance; Banking Law; Corporate Law. **Email:** rtaggart@binghammchale.com

JOHN E. TAYLOR, born South Bend, Indiana, 1954; admitted to bar, 1980, Indiana and U.S. District Court, Southern and Northern Districts of Indiana. *Education:* Ball State University (B.S., magna cum laude, 1977); Indiana University School of Law (J.D., magna cum laude, 1980). Member, Marion County Circuit and Superior Court Rules Committee, 1998—. Member, Indiana Property Tax Replacement Legislative Study Commission, 2004—. Served as: Parliamentarian for the Indiana House of Representatives; Counsel to the Speaker of the Indiana House of Representatives. *Member:* Indianapolis, Indiana State and American Bar Associations; Association of Trial Lawyers of America; Indiana Trial Lawyers Association. ***PRACTICE AREAS:*** Business Litigation; Business Law.

JENNIFER K. THOMPSON, born Wabash, Indiana, 1968; admitted to bar, 1994, Indiana. *Education:* Indiana University (B.A., 1990); University of Dayton (J.D., 1994). University of Dayton Law Review, 1992-1993; Associate Editor, 1993-1994,. ***PRACTICE AREAS:*** Environmental Law. **Email:** jthompson@binghammchale.com

(This Listing Continued)

BINGHAM McHALE LLP, Indianapolis—Continued

DAVID O. TITTLE, born Gary, Indiana, 1942; admitted to bar, 1967, Indiana; 1968, U.S. Supreme Court. *Education:* Indiana University (B.S., 1964; J.D., cum laude, 1967). Registered Civil Mediator. *Member:* International Association of Defense Counsel; Indiana Defense Lawyers Association (President, 1981; Diplomat, 1986). Fellow, American College of Trial Lawyers. ***PRACTICE AREAS:*** Complex Litigation; Business Litigation; Class Actions; Product Liability; Toxic Torts; Professional Liability; Mediation. ***Email:*** dtittle@binghammchale.com

MATTHEW T. TROYER, born Indianapolis, Indiana, 1970; admitted to bar, 1997, Indiana. *Education:* Miami University (B.S., cum laude, 1992); Indiana University (J.D., summa cum laude, 1997). ***PRACTICE AREAS:*** Business Services; Mergers and Acquisitions; Business Planning; Entrepreneurial Business Development; General Corporate Transactions; Federal and State Taxation; Estate Planning; Real Estate Transactions. ***Email:*** mtroyer@binghammchale.com

MARY HAMILTON WATTS, born Greensburg, Indiana, 1950; admitted to bar, 1984, Indiana. *Education:* Indiana University (B.S., 1972; M.S., 1981; J.D., cum laude, 1984). ***PRACTICE AREAS:*** Litigation; Products Liability; Professional Liability Defense; Medical Malpractice; Professional Licensing Discipline; Legal Malpractice Matters. ***Email:*** mwatts@binghammchale.com

D. BRYAN WEESE, born Evansville, Indiana, 1965; admitted to bar, 1990, Indiana. *Education:* Indiana University (B.A., with distinction and honors, 1987); University of Virginia (J.D., 1990). ***PRACTICE AREAS:*** Real Estate; General Business and Transactional Law; Intellectual Property Law. ***Email:*** bweese@binghammchale.com

BRIAN W. WELCH, born Indianapolis, Indiana, 1951; admitted to bar, 1978, Indiana and U.S. District Court, Southern District of Indiana; 1980, U.S. Court of Appeals, Seventh Circuit; 1991, U.S. Supreme Court. *Education:* DePauw University (B.A., 1973); Indiana University (J.D., cum laude, 1978). ***PRACTICE AREAS:*** Business Litigation. ***Email:*** bwelch@binghammchale.com

ASSOCIATES

DAVID A. ADAMS, born Kalamazoo, Michigan, 1976; admitted to bar, 2001, Indiana and U.S. District Court, Northern and Southern Districts of Indiana. *Education:* Valparaiso University (B.A., summa cum laude, 1998); Indiana University (J.D., cum laude, 2001). Phi Delta Phi. Executive Managing Editor, Indiana International and Comparative Law Review, 2000- 2001. ***PRACTICE AREAS:*** Corporate Law; Real Estate; Commercial Law. ***Email:*** dadams@binghammchale.com

MICHAEL J. ADLER, born Terre Haute, Indiana, 1976; admitted to bar, 2001, Indiana. *Education:* Indiana University (B.S., 1998; J.D., summa cum laude, 2001). Associate Editor, Indiana Law Review, 1999-2001. ***PRACTICE AREAS:*** Litigation. ***Email:*** madler@binghammchale.com

DENISE W. CHAVIS, born St. Louis, Missouri, 1967; admitted to bar, 1998, Indiana. *Education:* Northwestern University (B.S., 1989); Indiana University (J.D., 1998). ***PRACTICE AREAS:*** Litigation; Appellate Practice. ***Email:*** dchavis@binghammchale.com

POLLY J. DOBBS, born Kokomo, Indiana, 1977; admitted to bar, 2004, Indiana and U.S. District Court, Northern and Southern Districts of Indiana. *Education:* Ball State University (B.S., History, cum laude, 1999); Kelley School of Business (M.B.A., 2004); Indiana University School of Law - Indianapolis (J.D., magna cum laude, 2004). *Member:* Indianapolis (Law Student Division, Executive Board Member), Indiana State and American Bar Associations. ***PRACTICE AREAS:*** Intellectual Property; Business Law.

STEPHEN L. DUE, born Indianapolis, Indiana, 1977; admitted to bar, 2002, Indiana. *Education:* Kelley School of Business, Indiana University, Bloomington (B.S., with high distinction, 1999); Indiana University, Bloomington (J.D., cum laude, 2002). Beta Gamma Sigma. ***PRACTICE AREAS:*** Labor and Employment Law. ***Email:*** sdue@binghammchale.com

GREG J. DUNCAN, born Lafayette, Indiana, 1973; admitted to bar, 1999, Indiana. *Education:* Purdue University (B.S., 1996); Indiana University (J.D., cum laude, 1999). Associate Editor, Indiana Law Review, 1997-1999. ***PRACTICE AREAS:*** Estate and Gift Planning; Probate Administration; Federal and State Taxation; Corporate and Partnership Organization. ***Email:*** gduncan@binghammchale.com

KELLY R. ESKEW, born Indianapolis, Indiana, 1964; admitted to bar, 2001, Indiana and U.S. District Court, Northern and Southern Districts of Indiana. *Education:* Regents College (B.A.); Indiana University (J.D., cum laude, 2001). ***PRACTICE AREAS:*** Litigation. ***Email:*** keskew@binghammchale.com

KENAN L. FARRELL, born Indianapolis, Indiana, 1978; admitted to bar, 2003, Indiana and U.S. District Court, Northern and Southern Districts of Indiana. *Education:* Indiana University, Bloomington (B.S., 2000); Indiana University School of Law - Indianapolis (J.D., 2003). ***PRACTICE AREAS:*** Intellectual Property; Technology Law. ***Email:*** kfarrell@binghammchale.com

MELISSA J. FORD, born Farmington, New Mexico, 1965; admitted to bar, 1998, Indiana. *Education:* Indiana University (B.S., with highest distinction, 1994); Indiana University School of Law - Indianapolis (J.D., cum laude, 1998). Former Board Member and Secretary, Westfield-Washington Chamber of Commerce. Former Board Member, Indiana Association of Child Care Resource and Referral. *Member:* Indianapolis, Indiana State and American Bar Associations. ***PRACTICE AREAS:*** Business Planning; Real Estate.

DANIEL J. GERRITZEN, born Evansville, Indiana, 1969; admitted to bar, 1997, Indiana and U.S. District Court, Northern and Southern Districts of Indiana; 2003, U.S. Court of Federal Claims. *Education:* Indiana University (B.S., 1991); Indiana University School of Law (J.D., 1997). ***PRACTICE AREAS:*** Litigation; Tort Law. ***Email:*** dgerritzen@binghammchale.com

LIANE GROTH, born 1979; admitted to bar, 2005, Indiana. *Education:* Indiana University (B.A., cum laude, 2001); Indiana University School of Law - Bloomington (J.D., 2005). Member, American Constitution Society for Law and Policy. ***PRACTICE AREAS:*** Business Litigation.

(This Listing Continued)

ANDREW W. GRUBER, born Cincinnati, Ohio, 1973; admitted to bar, 1999, Indiana and U.S. District Court, Northern and Southern Districts of Indiana; 2001, U.S. Court of Appeals, Seventh Circuit; 2002, U.S. District Court, Eastern Districts of Wisconsin; 2003, U.S. District Court, Northern District of Oklahoma. *Education:* The Ohio State University (B.A., 1996); University of Toledo (J.D., cum laude, 1999). ***PRACTICE AREAS:*** Labor and Employment Law. ***Email:*** agruber@binghammchale.com

BRADLEY DAVID HASLER, born Bluffton, Indiana, 1975; admitted to bar, 2000, Indiana; 2002, California. *Education:* DePauw University (B.A., summa cum laude, 1997); California Western School of Law (J.D., magna cum laude, 2000). ***PRACTICE AREAS:*** Real Estate; Business Litigation; Property Tax Appeals. ***Email:*** bdhasler@binghammchale.com

JOSEPH HAWKINS, born 1978; admitted to bar, 2005, Indiana. *Education:* Washington & Lee University (B.A., cum laude, 2000); University de Lille, Lille, France; Indiana University School of Law - Indianapolis (J.D., 2005). ***PRACTICE AREAS:*** Real Estate.

RICHARD J. HAYES, admitted to bar, 2002, Wisconsin; 2005, Indiana. *Education:* Indiana University (B.S., with distinction; 1999; M.B.A., 1999); Northwestern University (J.D., 2002). Director, Walker's Point Youth and Family Care Center, 2004. *Member:* State Bar of Wisconsin; American Bar Association; National Bond Lawyers Association.

JEREMY E. HILL, born Franklin, Indiana, 1975; admitted to bar, 1999, Indiana. *Education:* Indiana University (B.S., highest distinction, 1996; J.D., magna cum laude, 1999). Order of the Coif. ***PRACTICE AREAS:*** Business Transactions; Business Organizations; Securities Law Compliance. ***Email:*** jhill@binghammchale.com

PATRICIA A. HUGHEL, born Logansport, Indiana, 1974; admitted to bar, 2003, Indiana and U.S. District Court, Northern and Southern Districts of Indiana. *Education:* Purdue University (B.A., 1996); Barry University School of Law (J.D., 2002). ***PRACTICE AREAS:*** Intellectual Property and Technology. ***Email:*** phughel@binghammchale.com

BONNIE B. JAGODITZ, born Kokomo, Indiana, 1976; admitted to bar, 2003, Indiana and U.S. District Court, Northern and Southern Districts of Indiana. *Education:* Indiana University (B.A., 1998); Indiana University School of Law - Indianapolis (J.D., cum laude, 2003). Order of the Barristers. Executive Notes Editor, Indiana Law Review, 2002-2003. ***PRACTICE AREAS:*** Public Utility Law. ***Email:*** bjagoditz@binghammchale.com

WHITNEY J. JOHNSON, born Monterey, California, 1970; admitted to bar, 2002, Indiana. *Education:* Marymount University (B.A., 1993); Indiana University, Indianapolis (J.D., 2002). ***PRACTICE AREAS:*** Business Law; Environmental Law. ***Email:*** wjohnson@binghammchale.com

DERON S. KINTNER, born Columbus, Indiana, 1976; admitted to bar, 2001, Indiana. *Education:* Indiana University (B.S., with distinction, 1998; J.D., 2001). Beta Gamma Sigma. ***PRACTICE AREAS:*** Municipal Bonds; Public Utilities; Government Services. ***Email:*** dkintner@binghammchale.com

TONYA L. LENGAR, born Muncie, Indiana, 1977; admitted to bar, 2003, Indiana and U.S. District Court, Northern and Southern Districts of Indiana. *Education:* Purdue University (B.A., with honors, 2000); Indiana University School of Law - Bloomington (J.D., 2003). Notes Editor, Indiana Journal of Global Legal Studies, 2002-2003. ***PRACTICE AREAS:*** Business Litigation; Administrative Law; Agency Law. ***Email:*** tlengar@binghammchale.com

SUSAN J. LONG, born Indianapolis, Indiana, 1971; admitted to bar, 1998, Indiana. *Education:* Rollins College (B.A., cum laude, 1994); Indiana University (J.D., summa cum laude, 1998). ***PRACTICE AREAS:*** Health Care; Business Transactions; Corporate Law. ***Email:*** slong@binghammchale.com

BRAD R. MAURER, born Fort Wayne, Indiana, 1973; admitted to bar, 1999, Indiana and U.S. District Court, Northern and Southern Districts of Indiana. *Education:* Purdue University (B.A., with honors, 1996); Indiana University (J.D., cum laude, 1999). ***PRACTICE AREAS:*** Business Litigation; Intellectual Property; Technology. ***Email:*** bmaurer@binghammchale.com

JONNA L. McGINLEY, born Madison, Wisconsin, 1978; admitted to bar, 2003, Indiana and U.S. District Court, Northern and Southern Districts of Indiana. *Education:* DePauw University (B.A., cum laude, 2000); Indiana University School of Law - Bloomington (J.D., cum laude, 2003). Order of the Coif. Order of the Barristers. Managing Editor, Federal Communications Law Journal, 2002-2003. ***PRACTICE AREAS:*** Business Litigation; Media Law. ***Email:*** jmcginley@binghammchale.com

WHITNEY L. MOSBY, born Bluffton, Indiana, 1977; admitted to bar, 2002, Indiana. *Education:* Indiana University, Bloomington (B.A., with highest distinction, 1999); Indiana University, Indianapolis (J.D., cum laude, 2002). ***PRACTICE AREAS:*** Creditors Rights; Bankruptcy; Construction Law. ***Email:*** wmosby@binghammchale.com

ANNA MUEHLING MALLON, born Chicago, Illinois, 1974; admitted to bar, 2002, Indiana. *Education:* Miami University, Ohio (B.A., B.S., 1997); Indiana University, Indianapolis (J.D., 2002). ***PRACTICE AREAS:*** Insurance Litigation; Family Law. ***Email:*** amallon@binghammchale.com

KEVIN S. PRICE, born Indianapolis, Indiana, 1976; admitted to bar, 2003, Indiana and U.S. District Court, Northern and Southern Districts of Indiana. *Education:* Indiana University - Bloomington (B.S., with high distinction, 1998); Indiana University School of Law - Indianapolis (J.D., summa cum laude, 2003). Articles Editor, Indiana Law Review, 2001-2003. ***PRACTICE AREAS:*** Business Litigation. ***Email:*** kprice@binghammchale.com

C.W. RAINES, III, born Joplin, Missouri, 1974; admitted to bar, 2004, Indiana and U.S. District Court, Southern and Northern Districts of Indiana. *Education:* University of Evansville (B.S., cum laude, 1997); Indiana University School of Law - Indianapolis (J.D., 2003); Indiana University Kelly School of Business (M.B.A., 2003); Renmin University of China School of Law - Beijing, China. *Member:* Indianapolis, Indiana State and American Bar Associations. ***PRACTICE AREAS:*** Business Services; Mergers and Acquisitions; Business Planning; General Corporate Transactions; Taxation; Real Estate Transactions. ***Email:*** craines@binghammchale.com

(This Listing Continued)

JULIE D. REED, born Crawfordsville, Indiana, 1975; admitted to bar, 2004, Indiana. *Education:* Hanover College (B.S., 1997); Indiana University School of Law - Indianapolis (J.D., cum laude, 2004).

CANDACE L. SAGE, born Hammond, Indiana, 1945; admitted to bar, 1995, Indiana. *Education:* Indiana University (A.B., 1969; M.A., 1971; J.D., magna cum laude, 1995); Indiana Wesleyan University (M.S., Management, 1987). ***PRACTICE AREAS:*** Appellate; Litigation. ***Email:*** csage@binghammchale.com

RAFAEL A. SANCHEZ, born San Juan, Puerto Rico, 1974; admitted to bar, 2002, Indiana and U.S. District Court, Northern and Southern Districts of Indiana. *Education:* University of Puerto Rico (B.A., 1996); Indiana University, Bloomington (J.D., 2002). ***LANGUAGES:*** Spanish. ***PRACTICE AREAS:*** Business Litigation. ***Email:*** rsanchez@binghammchale.com

JASON TY SIBBITT, admitted to bar, 1998, Indiana. *Education:* Butler University (B.S., cum laude, highest honors, 1991); Indiana University School of Law (J.D., magna cum laude, 1998). *Member:* Indianapolis, Indiana State and American Bar Associations; National Association of Bond Lawyers; Indiana Municipal Lawyers Association. ***PRACTICE AREAS:*** Real Estate. ***Email:*** tsibbitt@binghammchale.com

TARA J. STAPLETON, born Lafayette, Indiana, 1974; admitted to bar, 2000, Indiana. *Education:* Indiana University (B.S., 1996; J.D. cum laude, 2000). ***PRACTICE AREAS:*** Insurance Defense Litigation; Intellectual Property Litigation. ***Email:*** tstapleton@binghammchale.com

MICHAEL O. WEEMS, born 1969; admitted to bar, 2005, Indiana. *Education:* Mercer University (B.A., 2000); University of Iowa College of Law (J.D., 2004). Kappa Alpha Psi. Recipient, University of Iowa Law Foundation Scholarship. CLEO/Thurgood Marshall Fellow. Executive Board Member, Kuaba Humanitarian Foundation. Alumni Advisory Committee, Council on Legal Education Opportunity. *Member:* Indianapolis, Marion County, Indiana State and American Bar Associations. ***PRACTICE AREAS:*** Business Law; Banks and Banking.

ISAAC WILLETT, admitted to bar, 2005, Indiana. *Education:* Indiana University - Bloomington (B.A., 2001); Indiana University School of Law (J.D., cum laude, 2004). *Member:* Indianapolis and Indiana State Bar Associations. ***PRACTICE AREAS:*** Business Law.

BRAD A. WILT, born Dayton, Ohio, 1970; admitted to bar, 1998, Nevada (inactive); 2004, Indiana. *Education:* University of Cincinnati (B.S., Construction Management, magna cum laude, 1994); Indiana University School of Law - Bloomington (J.D., 1998). CALI Award Recipient: Admiralty, Public Natural Resources, Public Understanding of Law.

CHRISTOPHER M. YORK, born York, Pennsylvania, 1963; admitted to bar, 1999, Indiana. *Education:* Indiana University (B.S., 1985; J.D., summa cum laude, 1999); University of Colorado (M.B.A., 1988). Recipient, Nathan Burkan Memorial Award, 1998. Note Development Editor, Indiana Law Review, 1998-1999. ***PRACTICE AREAS:*** Litigation; Utility Law. ***Email:*** cyork@binghammchale.com

OF COUNSEL

JOSEPH L. CHAMPION, born Fremont, Indiana, 1966; admitted to bar, 1991, Indiana; U.S. District Court, Northern and Southern Districts of Indiana. *Education:* Indiana University (B.S., 1988); University of Dayton School of Law (J.D., 1991). Law Clerk to Honorable Patricia Gifford, Marion County Superior Court, 1991-1992. Trial Instructor, State of Indiana Office of the Attorney General. Faculty Speaker: Professional Responsibility, I. D. E. A. Conference; Lorman Continuing Legal Education (DWI education). Certified Agent: National Basketball Association Players Association; National Football League Players Association. Chairman, Evansville Mayor Jonathan Weinzapfel's Transition Team, 2003-2004. Speaker of the House appointee to the Indiana Code Revision Commission, 2004. Parliamentarian to Indiana House of Representatives Speaker B. Patrick Bauer, 2003. Senior Policy Advisor/Counsel to Indiana House of Representatives Speaker John R. Gregg, 1999-2002. Responsible for crafting Indiana's Anti-Terrorism Bill - H. B. 1010, 2002. Past President, Indiana Beta Education Foundation - Sigma Phi Epsilon Fraternity. Past Member, American Inns of Court. *Member:* Indiana State Bar Association. ***PRACTICE AREAS:*** Government; Public Finance.

JOHN S. CHAPPELL, born Evansville, Indiana, 1947; admitted to bar, 1972, Indiana; 1974, U.S. Court of Appeals, Seventh Circuit and U.S. District Court, Southern District of Indiana. *Education:* Indiana University (B.S., 1969; J.D., 1972). Law Clerk to Hon. S. Hugh Dillin, U.S. District Court, Southern District of Indiana, 1972-1974. (Also Member, Jasper Office). ***PRACTICE AREAS:*** Corporate Law; Probate; Estate Planning; Real Estate. ***Email:*** jchappell@binghammchale.com

LANAE M. HARDEN, born Evansville, Indiana, 1968; admitted to bar, 1995, Indiana. *Education:* University of Texas (B.A., magna cum laude, 1991); Indiana University (J.D., magna cum laude, 1995). Golden Key Society; Phi Beta Kappa; Order of the Coif. Recipient: Isabella Cunningham Scholarship, 1990; F.E. Jump Memorial Scholarship, 1993-1995. Associate, Indiana Law Journal, 1995. ***PRACTICE AREAS:*** Matrimonial Law; Family Law.

BARBARA A. JONES, admitted to bar, 1990, Indiana; 1993, U.S. Court of Appeals, Eleventh Circuit. *Education:* Indiana University, Indianapolis (B.A., 1968; J.D., cum laude, 1990). Co-Founder, Indiana International and Comparative Law Review. Law Clerk, Honorable Stanley B. Miller, Indiana Court of Appeals, 1990-1992. ***PRACTICE AREAS:*** Environmental Insurance Coverage; Insurance Coverage; Insurance Defense; Appellate Practice. ***Email:*** bjones@binghammchale.com

LINDA NICHOLS KENNY, born Indianapolis, Indiana, 1959; admitted to bar, 1984, Indiana. *Education:* Valparaiso University (B.S., with high distinction, 1981); Indiana University (J.D., magna cum laude, 1984). ***PRACTICE AREAS:*** Employee Benefits; ERISA Law. ***Email:*** lkenny@binghammchale.com

MICHAEL R. KOHLHAAS, born Oak Park, Illinois, 1973; admitted to bar, 1998, Indiana; 2001, Florida. *Education:* Indiana University (B.A., 1995); Indiana University School of Law-Bloomington (J.D., 1998). Articles Editor, Indiana Law Journal, 1997-1998. ***PRACTICE AREAS:*** Appellate Practice; Matrimonial Law. ***Email:*** mkohlhaas@binghammchale.com

(This Listing Continued)

DENNIS P. LEE, born Indianapolis, Indiana, 1953; admitted to bar, 1986, Indiana. *Education:* Indiana University (B.A., 1975; M.A., 1978); University of Toledo (J.D., 1985). Indiana Secretary of State Office, 1989-1993. Indiana Attorney General Office, 1993-2000. ***PRACTICE AREAS:*** Government Services. ***Email:*** dlee@binghammchale.com

GERALD L. MOSS, born South Bend, Indiana, 1936; admitted to bar, 1962, Indiana. *Education:* Indiana University (B.S., 1958; J.D., with high distinction, 1962). *Member:* Indianapolis, Indiana State and American Bar Associations. Distinguished Fellow: Indianapolis Bar Foundation; Indiana State Bar Foundation. ***PRACTICE AREAS:*** Real Estate Law; Corporate Law; Health Care Law. ***Email:*** gmoss@binghammchale.com

JOHN G. SHUBAT, born Lebanon, Indiana, 1958; admitted to bar, 1988, Indiana. *Education:* Indiana University (B.S., 1980; J.D., cum laude, 1988). Note Development Editor, Indiana Law Review, 1987-1988. ***PRACTICE AREAS:*** General Litigation; Professional Liability; Insurance Defense; Local Government; School Law. ***Email:*** jshubat@binghammchale.com

A. DAVID STIPPLER, born Evansville, Indiana, 1946; admitted to bar, 1973, Indiana; 1979, U.S. Supreme Court. *Education:* St. Meinrad College (A.B., cum laude, 1968); Indiana University (J.D., cum laude, 1973). ***PRACTICE AREAS:*** Public Utility Law. ***Email:*** dstippler@binghammchale.com

WILLIAM F. WELCH, born Logansport, Indiana, 1918; admitted to bar, 1948, Indiana. *Education:* DePauw University (A.B., cum laude, 1940); University of Minnesota and University of Michigan (J.D., 1948). Life Trustee, DePauw University. *Member:* Seventh Circuit Bar Association (Member, Board of Governors, 1985—; President, 1991-1992). Fellow: Indianapolis, Indiana and American Bar Foundations. [Lt. Cmdr., U.S.N.R., active duty, 1941-1946]. ***PRACTICE AREAS:*** Corporate Law; Public Utility Law; Banking Law.

Bingham McHale LLP attorneys are members of the American, Indiana State, Indianapolis, Federal and Seventh Circuit Bar Associations.

REPRESENTATIVE CLIENTS: ADESA Corporation; Aearo Company; Albertsons, Inc.; Altrista Corporation; American Society of Composers, Authors and Publishers (ASCAP); American United Life Insurance Co.; Asphalt Materials, Inc.; Averitt Express, Inc.; Bangs Laboratories, Inc.; Bank One, Indiana, NA; Barth Electric Co., Inc.; Baxter Healthcare Corp.; Best Chairs, Inc.; BKD, LLP; Boone County; BP Products; Bremner & Wiley, Inc.; Bressler Outdoor, LLC; Buehler Foods, Inc.; Capital Improvement Board of Managers (RCA Dome, Conseco Fieldhouse & Victory Field, Indiana Convention Center); Chase Manhattan Bank; Cinergy Inc.; City of Carmel; City of Ft. Wayne; City of Greenwood; City of Indianapolis; Comcast Cablevision; Community Bankers Association of Indiana; CTI Billing Solutions; Davis Homes, Inc.; Deere Credit Services, Inc.; DePauw University; Duke Energy; Duke Realty Corp.; EDS, Inc.; Ericsson Mobile Communications; Fanimation, Inc.; Farbest Foods, Inc.; FEPCO; Fifth Third Bank of Central Indiana; First Merchants Corporation; Frontier Financial; Gatorade Trust; Hamilton Southeastern Utilities, Inc.; Heritage Environmental Services, LLC; Hoosier State Press Association; Indiana Bond Bank; Indiana Development Finance Authority; Indiana Heart Physicians; Indiana Horse Racing Commission; Indiana Manufacturers Association; Indiana State Poultry Association, Inc.; Indiana University; Indianapolis Housing Agency; Indianapolis Opthalomology; Insight Communications; Interstate Brands Corporation; Jasper Seating Company, Inc.; Jostens Inc.; Key Bank; Klipsch LLC; Knowledge Resource Group; Kocolene Marketing LLC; Lehigh Cement Company; LIN Television; Litho Press, Inc.; Marathon Oil Company; Market Square Partners; MasterBrand Cabinets, Inc.; Meridian Plastic Surgery Center; Midland Life Insurance Co.; Midwest Bankers Group, Inc.; Morgan Guaranty Trust Company of New York; National Association of Broadcasters; National City Bank, Indiana; National Collegiate Athletic Association (NCAA); Old National Bank; Pedigo Chevrolet; Pfizer Inc; Philip Morris, Inc.; Pizza King, Inc.; Provident Bank; Purdue University; Reeves Buick Pontiac; Resort Condominiums International (RCI); SAFECO; Sagamore Health Network, Inc.; Saint-Gobain Containers, Inc.; SBC Communications, Inc.; Schering Plough Corp.; Shell Oil Co.; Simon Property Group; Simon & Schuster, Inc.; State Farm Mutual Automobile Insurance Company; Subaru-Isuzu Automotive Inc.; SYM Financial Corporation; Tera Pharmaceuticals; The Medical Protective Co.; Thomson Multimedia, Inc.; Time Warner Cable; Wabash Valley Produce, Inc.; Xerox Corporation.

BLEECKER, BRODEY & ANDREWS

An Association - Not in Partnership

Established in 1980

9247 NORTH MERIDIAN STREET, SUITE 200
INDIANAPOLIS, INDIANA 46260
Telephone: 317-574-0700
Telecopier: 317-574-0770
Email: info@bbanda.com
URL: http://www.bbanda.com

Personal Injury Litigation. General Civil, Collection, Creditor's Rights, Corporate, Real Estate, Commercial Law, Probate and Mediation.

MARC A. BLEECKER (1940-1989)

RONALD B. BRODEY, (P.C.), born Indianapolis, Indiana, May 27, 1945; admitted to bar, 1970, Indiana and U.S. District Court, Southern District of Indiana. *Education:* Indiana University (B.S., 1967; J.D., 1970). Certified Court Mediator (Civil), March, 1994. Seminar, Personal Injury Cases, October, 1989. *Member:* Indianapolis and Indiana State Bar Associations; Indiana Trial Lawyers Association; The Association of Trial Lawyers of America; Indiana Association of Mediators. ***PRACTICE AREAS:*** Personal Injury; Corporate Law; Real Estate; Probate Law; Alternate Dispute Resolution. ***Email:*** rbbrodey@bbanda.com

STEPHEN K. ANDREWS, born Indianapolis, Indiana, October 4, 1948; admitted to bar, 1975, Indiana and U.S. District Court, Southern District of Indiana; 1979, U.S. Supreme Court; 1986, U.S. District Court, Northern District of Indiana. *Education:* Indiana University (A.B., 1970); John Marshall Law School (J.D., 1975). Author: Article, "Collecting Bad Debts," Indianapolis Business Journal, January, 1987. Lecturer: "How to Get Results in Collection of Delinquent Debts in Indiana," National Business Institute Seminar, Sept. 8, 1993. Seminars: Collection Law in Indiana, 1994; How to Collect Accounts in Indiana, 1993. Zoning Attorney, 1981-1984 and City Attorney, 1984-1991, City of Carmel. Chief Deputy Prosecuting Attorney, Hamilton County, 1976-1980. *Member:* Indianapolis, Hamilton County and Indiana State Bar Associations; Indiana Trial Lawyers Association. ***PRACTICE AREAS:*** Collection; Civil; Creditor's Rights; Commercial. ***Email:*** sandrews@bbanda.com

(This Listing Continued)

BLEECKER, BRODEY & ANDREWS, Indianapolis—Continued

ASSOCIATE

JULIA M. ANDREWS, born Indianapolis, Indiana, May 24, 1977; admitted to bar, 2003, Indiana and U.S. District Court, Northern and Southern Districts of Indiana. *Education:* Indiana University, Bloomington (B.A., 1999); Indiana University - Indianapolis (J.D., 2003). Certified Civil Court Mediator, 2004. *Member:* Indianapolis and Indiana State Bar Associations; Indiana Creditor's Rights Association; Indiana Creditors Bar Association. ***PRACTICE AREAS:*** Collections; Civil Litigation; Creditors Rights; Commercial Law; Alternative Dispute Resolution. ***Email:*** jandrews@bbanda.com

BOSE McKINNEY & EVANS LLP

Established in 1955

2700 FIRST INDIANA PLAZA
135 NORTH PENNSYLVANIA STREET
INDIANAPOLIS, INDIANA 46204
Telephone: 317-684-5000
Facsimile: 317-684-5173
URL: http://www.boselaw.com

Washington, D.C. Office: 700 North One Lafayette Centre, 1120 20th Street, N.W., 20036. Telephone: 202-973-1229. Fax: 202-973-1212.

Crown Point, Indiana Office: 3577 West Lakeshore Drive, 46307. Telephone: 219-663-2968. Fax: 219-663-2969.

Chesterton, Indiana Office: P.O. Box 957, 46304. Telephone: 219-983-1552. Fax: 219-983-1741.

Other Indianapolis, Indiana Office: 600 East 96th Street, Suite 500. Telephone: 317-684-5300. Fax: 317-684-5316.

West Lafayette, Indiana Office: 3000 Kent Avenue. Telephone: 765-464-3200. Fax: 765-464-3225.

General Civil Practice in all Courts including Agricultural Law, Antitrust, Appellate Practice, Capital Strategies, Civil Rights, Commercial Law, Communications and Media, Constitutional Law, Corporate Law, Creditors Rights, Creditors Rights in Bankruptcy, Debtor Bankruptcy, Education Law, Employee Benefits, Entertainment and the Arts, Entrepreneurial Services, Environmental Law, Finance, Financial Institutions Law, Government Contracts, Government Relations, High Technology, Insurance, Intellectual Property, International Law, Labor and Employment, Legislative Practice, Litigation, Mergers and Acquisitions, Municipal Finance, Municipal Law, Planning and Land Use, Probate, Real Estate, Regulated Industries, Regulatory Agency Practice, Securities, Taxation, Trusts and Estates, Utility Law, Wills and Zoning.

FIRM PROFILE: Bose McKinney & Evans LLP is committed to providing aggressive, results-oriented service to business and public sector clients of all sizes. The firm has a general civil practice, ranging from large and complicated financing and land development transactions to federal and state litigation involving constitutional and other substantial issues.

The firm has an extensive business organizations and transactions practice which includes general business services as well as a variety of specialized services including a focus on the legal needs of high tech businesses. The firm has represented hundreds of financial institutions, insurance companies and developers from across the United States in secured lending and real estate transactions and has lawyers experienced in securities issues, mergers and acquisitions, intellectual property, utilities regulation and federal and state taxation.

Bose McKinney & Evans also handles litigation and employment law matters for business clients located throughout the country. Lawyers from the firm have argued matters before the United States Supreme Court, participated as counsel for a major creditor in the largest individual bankruptcy in the state's history, and represented clients in one of the largest cases of stock churning in the nation and in commercial and constitutional litigation reported in the national news media. The firm's employment law practice involves both management labor relations and employment discrimination representation.

LAW FIRM ALLIANCES/ASSOCIATIONS: **ALFA INTERNATIONAL**

MEMBERS OF FIRM

LEWIS C. BOSE (1917-2001)
WILLIAM M. EVANS (1923-1991)
ROBERT H. McKINNEY (Retired)

THOMAS M. ATHERTON, born Alton, Illinois, August 9, 1944; admitted to bar, 1972, Illinois and U.S. District Court, Southern District of Illinois; 1982, U.S. Supreme Court; 1993, Indiana. *Education:* Doane College (B.A., 1966); University of Illinois (J.D., 1972). ***REPORTED CASES:*** Town of St. John v. State Board of Tax Comrs., 665 N.E. 2d 965 (Ind. Tax 1996); Boehm v. Town of St. John, 675 N.E. 2d 318 (Ind. 1996); Central Illinois Light Co. v. Johnson, 84 Ill.2d 275 (1981); Oregon Community Unit School v. The Property Tax Appeal Board, 285 Ill.App.3d 170 (1996). ***PRACTICE AREAS:*** Taxation. ***Email:*** tatherton@boselaw.com

JEFFREY B. BAILEY, born 1946; admitted to bar, 1978, Indiana and U.S. District Court, Southern District of Indiana. *Education:* Indiana University (B.S., Finance, 1972); Indiana University School of Law (J.D., cum laude, 1978). Board Member, Hook's Drug Foundation. *Member:* Indianapolis and American Bar Associations; National Association of Securities Dealers (Arbitrator). ***PRACTICE AREAS:*** Business Services. ***Email:*** JBBailey@boselaw.com

JON M. BAILEY, born Indianapolis, Indiana, October 24, 1948; admitted to bar, 1975, Indiana and U.S. District Court, Southern District of Indiana. *Education:* Ball State University (B.S., 1970); Indiana University (J.D., cum laude, 1975). Faculty: Indiana Department of Toxicology Breath Test School, "Preparing To Be An Effective Witness," 1983—; Chair, Marion County Public Defender Board. *Member:* Indianapolis (Member, Ad Hoc Committee on Public Defender System; Chair, Law Day Committee) and Indiana State Bar Associations; Commission on Public Defenders; National School Boards Association Council of School Attorneys; Indiana Municipal Lawyers Association. ***PRACTICE AREAS:*** Public Sector Employment Law; Municipal Law; Municipal Finance. ***Email:*** jbailey@boselaw.com

MICHAEL C. BARTOL, born York, Pennsylvania, May 23, 1962; admitted to bar, 1997, Indiana; registered to practice before U.S. Patent and Trademark Office. *Education:* Pennsylvania State University (B.S., Chemical Engineering, 1985); Indiana University (J.D., summa cum laude, 1997). Member, Indiana Law Review, 1995-1997. *Member:* Indianapolis, Indiana State and American Bar Associations; American Intellectual Property Law Association. ***PRACTICE AREAS:*** Intellectual Property; Patents; Prosecution; Litigation; Trademarks; Copyrights; Trade Secrets; Unfair Competition. ***Email:*** mbartol@boselaw.com

ALAN W. BECKER, born Hammond, Indiana, May 23, 1956; admitted to bar, 1981, Indiana. *Education:* Indiana University (B.S., with highest honor, 1978; J.D., summa cum laude, 1981). Phi Beta Kappa; Order of the Coif. Note Editor, Indiana Law Journal, 1980-1981. *Member:* Indianapolis, Indiana and American (Member, Sections on: Business Law; Law Practice Management) Bar Associations. ***PRACTICE AREAS:*** Securities; Business Organizations; Mergers and Acquisitions; Financial Institutions Law. ***Email:*** abecker@boselaw.com

DAVID M. BERRY, born Kokomo, Indiana, September 9, 1959; admitted to bar, 1988, Indiana. *Education:* University of Denver (B.A., 1981); Indiana University (J.D., 1988). Wherrett Scholar; Jump Scholar. Member, Indiana Law Review, 1987-1988. Certified Public Accountant, Colorado, 1982. ***PRACTICE AREAS:*** Estate Planning and Administration Law; Taxation Law; Business Law.

CARRIE WAGNER BOOTCHECK, born Farmland, Indiana; admitted to bar, 1997, Indiana. *Education:* Miami University (B.A., magna cum laude, 1994); Indiana University School of Law - Bloomington (J.D., cum laude, 1997). ***PRACTICE AREAS:*** Commercial Litigation; Construction Law; Mold Litigation; ERISA Litigation. ***Email:*** cbootcheck@boselaw.com

DAVID A. BUTCHER, born Indianapolis, Indiana, May 29, 1941; admitted to bar, 1966, Indiana. *Education:* DePauw University (A.B., 1963); Indiana University (J.D., 1966). Phi Beta Kappa; Phi Delta Phi; Order of the Coif. Editor, Indiana Law Journal, 1965-1966. Chairperson, Securities Law, ICLEF, 1986-1992. Former Officer and Director, Venture Club of Indiana, Inc. Member, Advisory Board: Indianapolis Regional Small Business Development Center; Rose Hulman Technical Institute. *Member:* Indianapolis, Indiana State and American (Member, Corporation, Banking and Business Law Section) Bar Associations. ***PRACTICE AREAS:*** Securities; Mergers and Acquisitions; Financial Institutions Law; Business Organizations. ***Email:*** dbutcher@boselaw.com

JAMES E. CARLBERG, born Jeffersonville, Indiana, May 3, 1950; admitted to bar, 1974, Indiana and U.S. District Court, Northern and Southern Districts of Indiana. *Education:* Indiana University (B.S., with high distinction, 1972; J.D., cum laude, 1974). *Member:* Indianapolis, Indiana State (Member, Bankruptcy and Creditors Rights Section) and American (Member, Business Law and Bankruptcy and Creditors Rights Sections) Bar Associations; American Bankruptcy Institute; Commercial Law League of America. ***PRACTICE AREAS:*** Secured Creditors Rights; Creditors Rights in Bankruptcy; Debtor Bankruptcy; Creditors Rights. ***Email:*** jcarlberg@boselaw.com

GARY L. CHAPMAN, born Noblesville, Indiana, March 8, 1959; admitted to bar, 1989, Indiana. *Education:* Purdue University (B.S., 1980); Indiana University (J.D., summa cum laude, 1989). Author: "Disclaimer of Joint Tenancy Property," Vol. 21 Indiana Law Review. *Member:* Indianapolis, Indiana and American Bar Associations. ***PRACTICE AREAS:*** Estate Planning; Probate; Business Organization; Nonprofit Corporations; Agricultural Law. ***Email:*** gchapman@boselaw.com

ROBERT B. CLEMENS, born Syracuse, New York, March 7, 1947; admitted to bar, 1982, Indiana, U.S. Court of Appeals, Seventh Circuit; 1986, U.S. Supreme Court. *Education:* Syracuse University (A.B., 1969); State University of New York at Albany (M.S., 1972); University of Notre Dame (J.D., 1982). Certified Mediator. *Member:* Indianapolis, Indiana State and American Bar Associations; American Board of Trial Advocates (Past President, Indiana Chapter); National Lawyers Association; Defense Research Institute; Defense Trial Counsel of Indiana. Fellow, American College of Trial Lawyers. (Board Certified Civil Trial Advocate by the National Board of Trial Advocacy). ***PRACTICE AREAS:*** Commercial Litigation; Personal Injury; Products Liability; Insurance. ***Email:*** rclemens@boselaw.com

JAMES A. COLES, born Columbus, Indiana, July 29, 1947; admitted to bar, 1974, Indiana; registered to practice before U.S. Patent and Trademark Office. *Education:* Rose-Hulman Institute of Technology (B.S.E.E., 1969); St. Louis University (J.D., 1974). *Member:* Indianapolis (Chairman, Patent, Trademark and Copyright Section, 1983-1984) and Indiana State (Chairman, Patent, Trademark and Copyright Section, 1980-1981) Bar Associations; American Intellectual Property Law Association. ***PRACTICE AREAS:*** Software Licensing; Patents; Trademarks; Copyrights; International Intellectual Property. ***Email:*** jcoles@boselaw.com

KENDALL C. CROOK, born Indianapolis, Indiana, October 23, 1945; admitted to bar, 1972, Indiana. *Education:* Harvard University (A.B., magna cum laude, 1967); Yale University (J.D., 1972). Phi Beta Kappa. *Member:* Indianapolis, Indiana State and American (Member, Sections on: Antitrust; Taxation; Corporation, Banking and Business Law) Bar Associations. ***PRACTICE AREAS:*** Business Organization; Mergers and Acquisitions; Communications Law; Intellectual Property; International Business Law; Antitrust; Trade Regulation Law. ***Email:*** kcrook@boselaw.com

AMY L. CUELLER, born Ft. Wayne, Indiana, September 3, 1963; admitted to bar, 1990, Indiana. *Education:* Indiana University, Fort Wayne (B.S., 1985); Indiana University, Indianapolis (J.D., 1989). *Member:* Indianapolis, Indiana State and Federal (Indianapolis Chapter) Bar Associations. ***REPORTED CASES:*** Moore v. Sitzmark, (1990) Ind. App., 555 N.E. 2d 1305; Akers v. Sebren (1994), Ind. App., 639 N.E. 2d 370. ***PRACTICE AREAS:*** Civil Litigation; Intellectual Property; Environmental; Construction Law; Commercial Litigation. ***Email:*** arankin@boselaw.com

CHRISTOPHER C. EARLE, born Indianapolis, Indiana, December 17, 1958; admitted to bar, 1986, Indiana, US. District Court, Northern and Southern Districts of Indiana.

(This Listing Continued)

Education: Vanderbilt University (B.A., 1981); Indiana University (J.D., 1986). *Member:* Indianapolis, Indiana State Bar Association (Sections on: Utility Law; Environmental Law), American (Sections on: Antitrust Law and Public Utility, Communications and Transportation) and Federal Communications Bar Associations; Electric Cooperative Bar Association. **Email:** cearle@boselaw.com

RONALD E. ELBERGER, born Newark, New Jersey, March 13, 1945; admitted to bar, 1969, Maryland; 1970, District of Columbia; 1971, Indiana. *Education:* George Washington University (A.A., 1964; B.A., 1966); American University (J.D., 1969). Member of Staff, American University Law Review. Phi Delta Phi. Research Assistant to Justice Abe Fortas, U.S. Supreme Court, 1968-1969. Member: Indiana Civil Liberties Union (President and Chairman, 1972-1977, Board of Directors, 1972-1980); Board of Directors, American Civil Liberties Union, 1972-1977; Vice-President for Litigation, Indiana Civil Liberties Union Foundation, 1979; Midwest Consumer Advisory Board to the Federal Trade Commission, 1973; Medical Licensing Board of Indiana, 1982-1998 (President, 1993); Emmis Communications Corporation, (General Counsel, 1987-1998, Vice President, 1987-2002; Litigation Counsel, 1998—); National Council for Media and Public Affairs, The George Washington University, 2000—. Assistant Secretary, Chip Ganassi Racing Teams, Inc. Fellow, Indianapolis Bar Foundation.*Member:* Indianapolis, Indiana State, Maryland State and American (Member, Litigation and Entertainment and Sports Sections) Bar Associations; District of Columbia Bar; Bar Association of the Seventh Federal Circuit; Indiana State Bar Foundation. ***PRACTICE AREAS:*** Litigation; Constitutional Law; Civil Rights; Communications Law; Entertainment Law. **Email:** relberger@boselaw.com

CATHY ELLIOTT, born Bedford, Indiana; admitted to bar, 1989, Florida and U.S. District Court, Middle District of Florida; 1993, Indiana and U.S. District Court, Southern and Northern Districts of Indiana; U.S. Court of Appeals, Seventh Circuit. *Education:* Indiana University; Towson State University (B.S., 1973); Stetson University College of Law (J.D., cum laude, 1989). *Member:* Indianapolis, Indiana State and American Bar Associations; The Florida Bar. ***PRACTICE AREAS:*** Civil Litigation; Business Litigation; Corporate Litigation; Commercial Litigation. **Email:** celliott@boselaw.com

DANIEL C. EMERSON, born Wichita Falls, Texas, September 21, 1954; admitted to bar, 1979, Indiana and U.S. District Court, Northern and Southern Districts of Indiana; 1981, U.S. Court of Appeals, Seventh Circuit; 1984, U.S. Supreme Court. *Education:* Macalester College (B.A., summa cum laude, 1976); Indiana University (J.D., cum laude, 1979). Phi Beta Kappa; Pi Sigma Alpha. Managing Editor, Indiana Law Journal, Vol. 54, 1978-1979. Adjunct Professor of Personnel Law, Indiana University, 1989-1999. *Member:* Indianapolis (Member, Labor and Employment and Litigation Sections; Past Chair, Labor and Employment Section), Indiana State (Member, Labor Law and Litigation Sections; Past Chair, Labor and Employment Section) Federal and American (Member, Labor and Employment Law Section; Chair, State Practice and Procedure Subcommittee, Litigation Section) Bar Associations; Bar Association of the Seventh Federal Circuit. ***PRACTICE AREAS:*** Sports and Entertainment; Labor and Employment; Litigation. **Email:** demerson@boselaw.com

JEFFREY R. GAITHER, born Indianapolis, Indiana, April 30, 1958; admitted to bar, 1983, Indiana, U.S. District Court, Southern and Northern Districts of Indiana and U.S. Court of Appeals, Sixth and Seventh Circuits; U.S. District Court, Eastern District of Michigan. *Education:* Indiana University (B.S., Public Affairs, 1980); Indiana University School of Law (J.D., cum laude, 1983). *Member:* Indianapolis and Indiana State Bar Associations; Indianapolis Bar Foundation (Board of Directors); Defense Research Institute (Business Litigation Section). ***PRACTICE AREAS:*** Business Litigation. **Email:** jgaither@boselaw.com

LISA McKINNEY GOLDNER, born Indianapolis, Indiana, November 22, 1966; admitted to bar, 1992, Indiana and U.S. District Court, Northern and Southern Districts of Indiana. *Education:* Southern Methodist University (B.A., with honors, 1989); Indiana University, Bloomington (J.D., 1992). Phi Alpha Delta; Newsletter Editor and Chairperson, Administrative and Government Law Section of the American Bar Association; Vice President, Environmental Section of the Indianapolis Bar Association; Appointed, Indiana University School of Law Alumni Board of Directors; Advisory Counsel and Collection Committee, Indianapolis Zoological Society; Advisory Counsel, Indianapolis Humane Society; Board Member, Trader's Point Hunt Charity Horse Show; Board Member, Girls Inc. of Indianapolis. *Member:* Indianapolis, Indiana State (Member and Treasurer, Environmental Law Section; Board Member, Alcohol Beverage Subcommittee) and American Bar Associations. ***PRACTICE AREAS:*** Environmental Law; Alcohol Beverage Law; Equine Law; Administrative Law; Agricultural Law. **Email:** lgoldner@boselaw.com

STEVEN D. GROTH, born Champaign, Illinois, October 30, 1962; admitted to bar, 1987, Illinois; 1992, U.S. Court of Appeals for the Armed Forces; 1993, Indiana; U.S. District Court, Northern District of Indiana; 1999, U.S. District Court, Southern District of Indiana; 2003, U.S. Court of Appeals, Seventh Circuit. *Education:* University of Illinois (B.S., 1984); Washington University (J.D., 1987). Member, Order of the Barristers. Certified Public Accountant, Illinois, 1984. *Member:* Indianapolis, Indiana State and Illinois State Bar Associations; Defense Research Institute; Defense Trial Counsel of Indiana; Trucking Industry Defense Association. [U.S. Navy, JAG Corps, 1989-1993]. ***PRACTICE AREAS:*** Litigation; Insurance Coverage. **Email:** sgroth@boselaw.com

KATHLEEN I. HART, born Freeport, Illinois, October 5, 1966; admitted to bar, 1995, Indiana and U.S. District Court, Northern and Southern Districts of Indiana; 1997, U.S. Court of Appeals, 7th Circuit. *Education:* Indiana University (B.A., with distinction, 1990; J.D., 1994). *Member:* Indianapolis, Indiana State and Federal Bar Associations; Sagamore American Inn of Court. ***PRACTICE AREAS:*** Civil Litigation; Commercial Litigation; Appellate Practice; Employment Law. **Email:** khart@boselaw.com

ROBERTS E. INVEISS, born Waukesha, Wisconsin, July 2, 1961; admitted to bar, 1986, Indiana. *Education:* University of Wisconsin-Madison (B.A., with distinction, 1983); University of Michigan (J.D., 1986). Contributing Editor, University of Michigan Journal of Law Reform, 1985-1986. *Member:* Indianapolis, Indiana State and American Bar Associations. Fellow, Indiana Bar Foundation. ***LANGUAGES:*** Latvian. ***PRACTICE AREAS:*** Corporate Law; Mergers and Acquisitions; Entrepreneurial Business Law; Intellectual Property. **Email:** rinveiss@boselaw.com

(This Listing Continued)

J. CHRISTOPHER JANAK, born Belleville, Illinois, March 3, 1966; admitted to bar, 1995, Indiana. *Education:* Wabash College (B.A., 1988); Indiana University (J.D., 1994). ***PRACTICE AREAS:*** Utility Law; Municipal Law; Litigation; Government. **Email:** jjanak@boselaw.com

DAVID J. JURKIEWICZ, born Royal Oak, Michigan, March 21, 1967; admitted to bar, 1994, Indiana. *Education:* Wayne State University (B.S., summa cum laude, 1990); Indiana University School of Law - Bloomington (J.D., magna cum laude, 1994). *Member:* Indianapolis and Indiana State Bar Associations. ***PRACTICE AREAS:*** Bankruptcy; Creditors' Rights; Commercial Law. **Email:** djurkiewicz@boselaw.com

ROBERT P. KASSING, born Indianapolis, Indiana, August 3, 1937; admitted to bar, 1964, Indiana. *Education:* Indiana University (B.S., 1959; J.D., 1964). Phi Delta Phi; Order of the Coif. Member, Board of Editors, Indiana Law Journal, 1963-1964. *Member:* Indianapolis and Indiana State Bar Associations; Bar Association of the Seventh Federal Circuit. ***PRACTICE AREAS:*** Business Planning; Mergers and Acquisitions; Succession Planning; Wealth Preservation. **Email:** rkassing@boselaw.com

BERNIE TOO KELLER, admitted to bar, 1998, Indiana. *Education:* University of Notre Dame (B.A., 1995; J.D., 1998). ***PRACTICE AREAS:*** Litigation. **Email:** too@boselaw.com

V. SAMUEL LAURIN III, born Muskegon, Michigan, April 6, 1960; admitted to bar, 1987, Indiana and U.S. District Court, Southern and Northern Districts of Indiana; U.S. Court of Appeals, Seventh Circuit and U.S. Supreme Court. *Education:* Dartmouth College (A.B., 1982); Indiana University-Bloomington (J.D., 1987). Managing Editor, Indiana University Law Journal, 1986-1987. ***PRACTICE AREAS:*** Construction Litigation; Commercial Litigation; Real Estate Litigation. **Email:** slaurin@boselaw.com

L. ROBERT LOWE, JR., born Indianapolis, Indiana, May 30, 1937; admitted to bar, 1967, Indiana. *Education:* Purdue University (B.S.C.E., 1959); Indiana University (LL.D, 1967). ***PRACTICE AREAS:*** Estate and Business Succession Planning. **Email:** rlowe@boselaw.com

KATHLEEN G. LUCAS, born Evansville, Indiana, February 16, 1950; admitted to bar, 1978, Indiana. *Education:* Indiana University (B.S., with high honors, 1972; J.D., 1978). Indiana Brownfields Advisory Board; Indianapolis Brownfields Redevelopment Advisory Group; Indiana State Bar Association Environmental Rolemaking Committee; Trustee, Evansville Greenway and Remediation Trust; Work group on Rulemaking for Office of Environmental Adjudication; Work groups on Voluntary Remediation and Spill Reporting of the Indiana Department of Environmental Management. Former Director, Office of Legal Affairs, Indiana State Department of Health. Former Deputy Attorney General representing IDEM, IDNR, ISDH, State Chemist and other state agencies. Frequent Speaker and Seminar Chair and was named by the Indianapolis Business Journal to its list of Who's Who in Environmental Law. *Member:* Indianapolis (Officer and Member, Executive Committee, Environmental Section) and Indiana (Past Chair, Governmental Practice Section; Member: Environmental Law Section; Agricultural Law Section, Governmental Practice Section; Alcohol and Tobacco Subcommittee) Bar Associations. ***PRACTICE AREAS:*** Environmental Law; Administrative Law; Agricultural Law; Alcohol and Tobacco Commission Law; Health Law. **Email:** klucas@boselaw.com

PAUL S. MANNWEILER, born South Bend, Indiana, July 20, 1949; admitted to bar, 1976, Indiana. *Education:* Indiana University (B.A., 1971; J.D., 1975). Member: Indiana House of Representatives, 1979-2001, Speaker, 1986-1988, 1994-1996, Co-Speaker, 1988-1990 and Minority Leader, 1991-1994, 1996-2000; Indianapolis Power and Light Company (Senior Vice President, 1996-2001); National Conference of State Legislatures (President, 1999-2000). Board of Directors: American Enterprise Life Insurance Company; Indiana Economic Development Council. Member: Board of Visitors, Indiana University Law School; IU Medical Workforce Task Force. *Member:* Indianapolis, Indiana State and American (Member, Labor and Employment Law Section) Bar Associations. ***PRACTICE AREAS:*** Legislative Practice; Employer-Employee Relations; Employment; Employment at Will; Employment Discrimination; Utilities. **Email:** pmannweiler@boselaw.com

R. J. McCONNELL, born Princeton, Indiana, March 13, 1960; admitted to bar, 1985, Indiana and U.S. District Court, Southern and Northern Districts of Indiana. *Education:* Purdue University (B.S., 1982); Indiana University (J.D., magna cum laude, 1985). Order of the Coif; Phi Delta Phi. *Member:* Indianapolis, Johnson County, Indiana State and American Bar Associations. ***PRACTICE AREAS:*** Business Organization Law; Estate Planning; Probate; Mergers and Acquisitions. **Email:** rmcconnell@boselaw.com

DANIEL P. McINERNY, born South Bend, Indiana, April 24, 1958; admitted to bar, 1984, Indiana. *Education:* Holy Cross Junior College (A.S., 1978); University of Notre Dame (B.A., 1980); Northwestern School of Law of Lewis and Clark College (J.D., Certificate in Environmental and Natural Resources Law, 1984). American Indoor Air Quality Council. *Member:* Indianapolis (Former Chair, Environmnetal Law Section) and Indiana State (Former Chair, Environmental Law Section; Member, Agricultural Law Section) Bar Associations. ***PRACTICE AREAS:*** Environmental Law; Natural Resources Law; Administrative Law. **Email:** dmcinerny@boselaw.com

ANDREW M. McNEIL, born Piqua, Ohio, March 23, 1969; admitted to bar, 1996, Indiana. *Education:* Taylor University (B.A., summa cum laude, 1992); University of Michigan (J.D., cum laude, 1995). ***PRACTICE AREAS:*** Labor and Employment; Litigation; Appellate Practice. **Email:** amcneil@boselaw.com

DONALD M. MEYER, born Indianapolis, Indiana, July 12, 1958; admitted to bar, 1983, Indiana and U.S. District Court, Southern District of Indiana. *Education:* University of Evansville (B.S. in Business, magna cum laude, 1980); Indiana University (J.D., summa cum laude, 1983). Delta Sigma Pi (Iota Sigma Chapter, Charter President). Certified Public Accountant. *Member:* Indianapolis, Indiana State and American Bar Associations. ***PRACTICE AREAS:*** Employee Benefits; ERISA; Federal Taxation; State Taxation; Local Taxation; Business Law; Nonprofit Organizations Law; Estate Planning. **Email:** dmeyer@boselaw.com

MARGARET BANNON MILLER, born Chicago, Illinois, October 4, 1944; admitted to bar, 1975, Indiana, U.S. District Court, Northern and Southern Districts of Indiana and U.S. Court of Appeals, 7th Circuit. *Education:* Mount Mary College (B.A., cum laude, 1967); Indiana University-Indianapolis (J.D., 1975). Member, Indiana Council of Administrators of Special Education, (1980—); (National School Boards Association Council of

(This Listing Continued)

BOSE McKINNEY & EVANS LLP, Indianapolis—Continued

School Attorneys, (1984—); Board of Directors, Fairbanks Hospital, (1991—); LRP Publications Special Education Board, (1993-2003). Ms. Miller speaks to numerous schools and school associations throughout Indiana on a variety of topics, including Section 504, Autism, IDEA / Articles 7, Sexual Harassment, Services to Students in Private Schools, and other school law topics. *Member:* Indianapolis (Lawyers Assistance Committee), Indiana State (Lawyer's Assistance Committee) and American Bar Associations. ***PRACTICE AREAS:*** Employment Law; Education Law. ***Email:*** mmiller@boselaw.com

JOHN A. MILLSPAUGH, born Anamosa, Iowa, August 30, 1970; admitted to bar, 1996, Indiana. *Education:* Ball State University (B.A., summa cum laude, 1993); University of Michigan (J.D., 1996). ***PRACTICE AREAS:*** Corporate; Business Transactions; Emerging Growth Companies; Mergers and Acquisitions; Securities. ***Email:*** jmillspaugh@boselaw.com

THEODORE J. NOWACKI, born South Bend, Indiana, August 15, 1946; admitted to bar, 1972, Indiana; 1989, U.S. Supreme Court and U.S. Court of Appeals, Seventh Circuit. *Education:* University of Notre Dame (B.A., maxima cum laude, 1969); University of Michigan (J.D., cum laude, 1972). Phi Alpha Delta; Phi Beta Kappa. *Member:* Indianapolis, Indiana State and American (Member, Sections on: Business Law; Litigation) Bar Associations. ***PRACTICE AREAS:*** Financial Institutions Law; Consumer Finance; Secured Creditors Rights; Litigation. ***Email:*** tnowacki@boselaw.com

TIMOTHY J. O'HARA, born South Bend, Indiana, July 20, 1949; admitted to bar, 1974, Mississippi; 1975, Indiana. *Education:* John Carroll University (A.B., 1971); University of Mississippi (J.D., 1974). Speaker and Author: "The Use of Experts to Prove or Disprove the Wishes of the Child," ICLEF Child Custody Seminar, 1999; "Use of a Private Investigator in a Custody or Asset Case, Biological Spouse Versus Non-Biological Spouse, Proof of Disparate Economic Circumstances and/or Future Earning Ability for Purpose of Property Division," ICLEF Seminar on Hot Tips from Family Law Experts, 1998; "Inheritance Must Be Considered When Determining Income for Child Support Calculations and Modifications," Res Gestae, Vol. 45, No. 2, 2001; "Rules of Evidence and Case Law Update," Indianapolis Bar Association Second Annual Seminar on Evidence for Family Law Practitioners, 2001. *Member:* Indianapolis, Indiana State and American Bar Associations; Indiana Trial Lawyers Association. Fellow, Indiana Bar Foundation. ***PRACTICE AREAS:*** Family Law; Litigation; Administrative Law. ***Email:*** tohara@boselaw.com

DENNIS H. OTTEN, born Beaufort, South Carolina, 1972; admitted to bar, 1998, Indiana. *Education:* Indiana University (B.A., 1994); Indiana University School of Law - Indianapolis (J.D., cum laude, 1998). *Member:* Indianapolis and Indiana State Bar Associations; National Association of Bond Lawyers; Indiana Municipal Lawyers Association. ***PRACTICE AREAS:*** Utility Law; Public Utility Finance.

CRAIG PINKUS, born Indianapolis, Indiana, February 8, 1943; admitted to bar, 1968, Indiana. *Education:* Butler University (A.B., magna cum laude, 1965); Harvard University (LL.B., 1968). ***PRACTICE AREAS:*** Litigation; Entertainment; Intellectual Property. ***Email:*** cpinkus@boselaw.com

L. PARVIN PRICE, born Tell City, Indiana, February 1, 1952; admitted to bar, 1977, Indiana; U.S. District Court, Southern District of Indiana; U.S. Court of Appeals, Seventh Circuit; U.S. Court of Appeals, Sixth Circuit; U.S. Supreme Court. *Education:* University of Evansville (B.A., cum laude, 1974); University of Louisville (J.D., 1976). Phi Alpha Delta (Justice, 1976); Blue Key. Alliance of Indiana Rural Water, General Counsel, 1996—. Deputy Attorney General, Indiana, 1977-1981. Indiana Utility Consumer Counselor, 1981-1985. MSD Pike Township School Board, 1990-1998. *Member:* Indianapolis and Indiana State (Member, Public Utility Law, Environmental Law and Governmental Practice Sections) Bar Associations; Electric Cooperative Bar Association; American Water Works Association; Alliance of Indiana Rural Water; Indiana Municipal Lawyers Association; Indiana Energy Association; Indiana Regional Sewer District Association. ***PRACTICE AREAS:*** Municipal Law; Utility Law; Environmental Law; Municipal Law. ***Email:*** pprice@boselaw.com

GEORGE E. PURDY, born Decatur, Indiana, August 5, 1955; admitted to bar, 1980, Indiana. *Education:* Ball State University (B.A. magna cum laude, 1977); Indiana University (J.D., cum laude, 1980). Moot Court Board of Barristers. Associate Editor, Indiana Law Review, 1978-1979. *Member:* Marion County and Indiana State Bar Associations; American Board of Trial Advocates. ***PRACTICE AREAS:*** Products Liability; Toxic Torts; Litigation; Intellectual Property Litigation; Mass Torts; Class Actions; Life Insurance. ***Email:*** gpurdy@boselaw.com

SARAH STEELE RIORDAN, born Detroit, Michigan, March 15, 1968; admitted to bar, 1993, Indiana; 1994, Michigan; 1995, Ohio. *Education:* University of Michigan (B.A., with high distinction, 1990); Indiana University (J.D., cum laude, 1993). ***PRACTICE AREAS:*** Complex Business Litigation; White Collar Criminal Defense; Professional Liability. ***Email:*** sriordan@boselaw.com

PHILIP J. RIPANI, born Chicago Heights, Illinois, May 3, 1951; admitted to bar, 1976, Indiana; 1998, Colorado. *Education:* Indiana University (B.S. with distinction, 1973; J.D., cum laude, 1976). Beta Gamma Sigma. *Member:* Indianapolis, Indiana State (Co-Chair, American Citizenship Committee) and American Bar Associations; American Immigration Lawyers Association; National Academy of Employment Mediators and Arbitrators; Fellow, Indiana Bar Foundation. ***PRACTICE AREAS:*** Labor and Employment; Employee Benefits Law; Immigration Law. ***Email:*** pripani@boselaw.com

CHARLES R. RUBRIGHT, born South Bend, Indiana, January 29, 1947; admitted to bar, 1974, Indiana. *Education:* Indiana State University (B.S., 1969); Indiana University-Bloomington (J.D., 1973). Phi Alpha Delta. Mediator and Hearing Examiner, Indiana Education Employment Relations Board, 1973-1975. *Member:* Indianapolis, Indiana State (Member, Labor Law Section) and American (Member, Labor and Employment Law Section) Bar Associations; National Council of School Attorneys; Legal Education Association; National Association of Educational Negotiators. ***PRACTICE AREAS:*** Employment Law; Education Law; Public Law. ***Email:*** crubright@boselaw.com

C. JOSEPH RUSSELL, born Indianapolis, Indiana, February 11, 1950; admitted to bar, 1980, Indiana, U.S. District Court, Southern District of Indiana and U.S. Court of Appeals, Seventh Circuit; 1981, U.S. Court of Military Appeals and U.S. Claims Court; 1997, U.S. District Court, Northern District of Indiana. *Education:* Western Kentucky University (B.A., 1973); Indiana University (J.D., 1980). Assistant U.S. Attorney, Southern District of Indiana, Organized Crime Drug Enforcement Task Force, 1983-1992. Distinguished Fellow, Indianapolis Bar Foundation. Member, Indianapolis Bar Foundation Board, 2001—. Indiana Federal Community Defender, 2000-2005. Member U.S. Magistrate Judge Selection Panel, Southern District of Indiana, 2000 and 2002. *Member:* Indianapolis (President, 1999; Member: Board of Managers, 1996—; Executive Council, Litigation Section, 1991-1995, Chair, 1995; Environmental and Criminal Sections), Hamilton County, Hendricks County, Indiana State (Delegate, House of Delegates from Indianapolis Bar Association), Seventh Federal Circuit (Indiana Programs Chair, 2002-2005; Indiana Criminal Practice Chair, 2005—), Federal and American (Member, House of Delegates, 2002—) Bar Associations; National Association of Criminal Defense Lawyers; Defense Research Institute. ***PRACTICE AREAS:*** White Collar Crime Defense; Civil Litigation. ***Email:*** crussell@boselaw.com

MICHAEL J. SCHNEIDER, born Jasper, Indiana, July 9, 1952; admitted to bar, 1977, Ohio and Indiana; 1978, U.S. Tax Court. *Education:* Indiana University (B.S., Finance, with highest distinction, 1974; J.D., 1977). Beta Gamma Sigma. Member, Venture Club of Indiana. *Member:* Indianapolis (Business Law Section, Executive Council, 1984-1986), Indiana State (Business Law Section) and American (Business Law Section, Negotiated Acquisitions Committee) Bar Associations. ***PRACTICE AREAS:*** Corporate; Mergers and Acquisitions; Securities; Taxation. ***Email:*** mschneider@boselaw.com

DANIEL B. SEITZ, born Terre Haute, Indiana, September 18, 1943; admitted to bar, 1969, Indiana. *Education:* Indiana University (A.B., 1965; J.D., 1968). Phi Alpha Delta. Member, Scabbard and Blade. Second V.P., State Relations, Lincoln National Corporation, 1978-1986. V.P., Governmental Relations, Lincoln National Corporation, 1986-1988. Governor's Commission on Organ Transplantation. Member: Health Care Professional Development Commission; Health Care Finance Commission Advisory Committee; Governmental Affairs Society of Indiana (Co-Founder and President); Indiana Chamber of Commerce Board; Indiana Fiscal Policy Institute Board; Indiana Legal Foundation Board; Executive Director and Counsel, Association of Indiana Life Insurance Companies, 2005—; Principal, BoseTreacy Associates LLC, 2000—. *Member:* Indianapolis, American and Indiana State Bar Associations; Association of Life Insurance Counsel. [Capt., Army Military Intelligence, 1968-1970]. ***PRACTICE AREAS:*** Government Relations; Legislative Practice; Governmental Law; Insurance Law. ***Email:*** dseitz@boselaw.com

MELINDA SHAPIRO, born Manhattan, New York, November 13, 1967; admitted to bar, 1994, Indiana. *Education:* Indiana University (B.A., 1991); University of Dayton (J.D., 1994). ***PRACTICE AREAS:*** Litigation; Medical Professional and Malpractice Liability Defense. ***Email:*** mshapiro@boselaw.com

J. GREGORY SHELLEY, born Madison, Indiana, January 17, 1960; admitted to bar, 1985, Indiana. *Education:* Indiana University (B.A., with honors, 1982; J.D., 1985). *Member:* Indianapolis (Estate Planning and Administration Section; Executive Council, 1992-2002, Chair, 2002) and Indiana State (Probate, Trust and Real Property Section) Bar Associations; Estate Planning Council of Indianapolis. ***PRACTICE AREAS:*** Estate and Business Succession Planning; Wills; Trusts; Estate Administration; Guardianships; Business Organization; Business Transactions. ***Email:*** gshelley@boselaw.com

NIKKI G. SHOULTZ, born Danville, Indiana, April 13, 1967; admitted to bar, 1992, Indiana. *Education:* Butler University (B.A., 1989); Indiana University School of Law (J.D., 1992). Tri Kappa; Kappa Alpha Theta. Board Member, Indy Reads. Board Member, Girls Inc. Member, Leadership Council and Leadership Series Committee, Hanover College Center for Business Preparation. *Member:* Indianapolis and Indiana State (Officer, Sections on: Utility; Telecommunications; Member, Women in the Law) Bar Associations. ***PRACTICE AREAS:*** Utility Law; Telecommunications; Water Utilities; Sewer Utilities; Energy. ***Email:*** nshoultz@boselaw.com

G. PEARSON SMITH, JR., born Indianapolis, Indiana, August 15, 1939; admitted to bar, 1964, Indiana. *Education:* Yale University (B.A., 1961); Yale Law School (LL.B., 1964). Member, Board of Editors, Yale Law Journal, 1962-1964. *Member:* Indianapolis (Taxation Section; Chairman, 1995-1996) and Indiana State Bar Associations; Indiana Pension Conference (Director, 1991-1995); Indianapolis Estate Planning Council. The American College of Trust and Estate Counsel (Member, Employee Benefits Committee). ***PRACTICE AREAS:*** Estate Planning; Trust Law; Taxation; Employee Benefits. ***Email:*** gpsmith@boselaw.com

RONALD M. SOSKIN, born Brooklyn, New York, August 8, 1948; admitted to bar, 1974, New York and U.S. District Court, Southern and Eastern Districts of New York; 1977, U.S. Supreme Court; 1978, Indiana; 1980, U.S. Court of Appeals, Fifth Circuit; 1983, U.S. Tax Court, U.S. Court of Appeals, Seventh Circuit and U.S. District Court, Northern District of Indiana. *Education:* University of Pennsylvania (B.S., 1970; J.D., 1973); New York University (LL.M. in Taxation, 1983). Beta Gamma Sigma; Pi Sigma Alpha. Associate Professor, University of Notre Dame Law School, 1981-1982. Member, Board of Directors, Indianapolis Hebrew Congregation, 1995-2003. *Member:* Indianapolis and Indiana State Bar Associations. ***PRACTICE AREAS:*** Taxation; Employee Benefits; Business Organization. ***Email:*** rsoskin@boselaw.com

NATALIE J. STUCKY, born Fort Wayne, Indiana, December 24, 1962; admitted to bar, 1989, Indiana. *Education:* Indiana University (B.A., 1985; J.D., magna cum laude, 1989). Phi Beta Kappa. Order of the Coif. *Member:* Indianapolis, Indiana State and American Bar Associations. ***PRACTICE AREAS:*** Secured Lending; Real Estate. ***Email:*** nstucky@boselaw.com

KARL R. STURBAUM, born Ravenna, Ohio, July 7, 1951; admitted to bar, 1986, Indiana. *Education:* Hanover College (B.A., 1974); Indiana University-Bloomington (J.D., cum laude, 1986). *Member:* National Association of Bond Lawyers; Indiana Association of School Business Officials; Indiana School Boards Association. ***PRACTICE AREAS:*** Municipal Finance; Securities; Municipal Law. ***Email:*** ksturbaum@boselaw.com

DAVID A. SUESS, born Indianapolis, Indiana, December 22, 1968; admitted to bar, 1997, Illinois; 2000, Indiana. *Education:* University of Chicago (B.A., 1991); Indiana University School of Law (J.D., magna cum laude, 1997). ***PRACTICE AREAS:*** Property Taxation; Business Services. ***Email:*** dsuess@boselaw.com

(This Listing Continued)

DAVID L. SWIDER, born Gary, Indiana, May 3, 1953; admitted to bar, 1978, Indiana. *Education:* Indiana University (B.S., magna cum laude, 1975; J.D., magna cum laude, 1978). Beta Gamma Sigma; Phi Delta Phi. Articles Editor, 1977-1978 and Associate Editor, 1976-1977, Indiana Law Review. *Member:* Indianapolis (Member and Former Chairman, Labor Law Section), Indiana State (Member, Labor and Employment Law Section) and American (Member, Labor and Employment Law Section) Bar Associations. ***PRACTICE AREAS:*** Labor and Employment. ***Email:*** dswider@boselaw.com

SCOTT E. TARTER, born Indianapolis, Indiana, September 23, 1962; admitted to bar, 1988, Indiana. *Education:* DePauw University (B.A., 1984); Indiana University School of Law - Bloomington (J.D., 1988). *Member:* Indianapolis, Indiana State and American Bar Associations. Fellow, Indiana Bar Foundation. ***PRACTICE AREAS:*** Corporate Law; Mergers and Acquisitions; Entrepreneurial Business Law; Health Care Law. ***Email:*** starter@boselaw.com

HARRY F. TODD, born Pittsburgh, Pennsylvania, December 15, 1958; admitted to bar, 1984, Indiana; U.S. District Court, Southern and Northern Districts of Indiana; U.S. Supreme Court. *Education:* Butler University (B.A., cum laude, 1981); Indiana University School of Law - Indianapolis (J.D., summa cum laude, 1984). Editor in Chief, Indiana Law Review, 1983-1984. General Counsel, Gibraltar Mausoleum Corporation, 1991-1996; Gibraltar Properties, Inc., 1996-2002. *Member:* Indianapolis, Indiana State and American Bar Associations. ***PRACTICE AREAS:*** Real Estate. ***Email:*** htodd@boselaw.com

ALAN S. TOWNSEND, born Hartford City, Indiana, December 13, 1963; admitted to bar, 1992, Indiana and U.S. District Court, Northern and Southern Districts of Indiana and U.S. Court of Appeals, Seventh Circuit. *Education:* Purdue University (B.S., with highest distinction, 1987);Indiana University (J.D., cum laude, 1992). Phi Delta Phi. Order of Barristers. Member, Sagamore American Inn of Court. *Member:* Indianapolis, Indiana State and American Bar Associations. ***PRACTICE AREAS:*** Civil Litigation. ***Email:*** atownsend@boselaw.com

SUSAN E. TRAYNOR, born Indianapolis, Indiana, November 22, 1961; admitted to bar, 1990, Indiana; U.S. District Court, Southern and Northern Districts of Indiana. *Education:* Indiana University (B.S., 1985; J.D., 1990). Phi Alpha Delta. Member: Ad Hoc Panel of Mediators and Fact-Finders; Indiana Education Employment Relations Board, 1987-1991. *Member:* Indianapolis (Member, Labor Law Section, Women Lawyers Division), Indiana State (Member, Young Lawyers Division) and American (Member, Labor and Employment Law Section) Bar Associations; National Association of Educational Negotiators; National School Boards Association Council of School Attorneys. ***PRACTICE AREAS:*** Employment Law; Education Law; Municipal Law; Special Education. ***Email:*** straynor@boselaw.com

MICHAEL A. TRENTADUE, born Oak Park, Illinois, June 1, 1960; admitted to bar, 1985, Indiana. *Education:* University of Notre Dame (B.S.M.E., 1982); University of Illinois College of Law (J.D., cum laude, 1985). Pi Tau Sigma; Phi Alpha Delta. Interim Chapter 7 Bankruptcy Trustee, July 1988 through May 1989. *Member:* Indianapolis and Indiana State Bar Associations. ***PRACTICE AREAS:*** Secured Creditors Law; Foreclosures; Lending Law; Litigation; Consumer Finance. ***Email:*** mtrentadue@boselaw.com

RICHARD S. VanRHEENEN, born Indianapolis, Indiana, June 23, 1955; admitted to bar, 1985, Indiana, U.S. District Court, Northern and Southern Districts of Indiana, U.S. District Court, Eastern District of Michigan and U.S. Court of Appeals, Seventh Circuit. *Education:* Hanover College (B.A., 1977); University of Kent, Canterbury, England; Indiana University (J.D., magna cum laude, 1984). ***PRACTICE AREAS:*** Environmental Law; Environmental Litigation. ***Email:*** rvanrheenen@boselaw.com

JOHN D. WALDA, born Fort Wayne, Indiana, June 14, 1950; admitted to bar, 1975, Indiana; 2003, Montana; U.S. District Court, Northern and Southern Districts of Indiana, U.S. District Court, Western District of Michigan and U.S. Court of Appeals, Sixth and Seventh Circuits. *Education:* Indiana University (A.B., 1972; J.D., 1975). Chairman: Indiana State Lottery Commission, 1989-1990; Clarian Health Board of Directors, 1996-2000. Member, 1990— and President, 1992-1993, 1994—, Indiana University Board of Trustees. *Member:* Allen County, Indiana State (Member, Executive Council, 1977-1980, Director, 1980-1981, Secretary-Treasurer, 1981-1982, Chairman Elect, 1982-1983 and Chairman, 1983-1984, Young Lawyers Section; Member, Board of Managers, 1983-1984) and American (Member: House of Delegates, 1983-1986; Litigation Section) Bar Associations; American Inns of Court (Master of the Bench). Fellow: Indiana Bar Foundation; American College of Trial Lawyers. ***PRACTICE AREAS:*** Litigation; Civil Litigation; Construction Litigation; Government Affairs. ***Email:*** jwalda@boselaw.com

DAVID L. WILLS, born Indianapolis, Indiana, March 11, 1946; admitted to bar, 1975, Indiana. *Education:* Greenville College and Purdue University (B.S., 1969; M.S., 1971); Harvard University (J.D., cum laude, 1975). Board of Trustees, Greenville College, 1977-1995. Board, 1994-1999, Secretary, 1996-1999, Habitat for Humanity of Greater Indianapolis, Inc. Board, Co-Founding Member, 1992-1999; President, 1995-1996, Community Organizations Legal Assistance Project, Inc. Board, local affiliate of National Alliance for the Mentally Ill, NAMI Indianapolis, 1999—. Advisory Board, Midtown Community Mental Health Center, 2001—. Indianapolis Bar Association Pro Bono Award, 1997. *Member:* Indianapolis, Indiana State and American (Member, Sections on: Corporation, Banking and Business Law; Real Property, Probate and Trust) Bar Associations; Christian Legal Society. ***PRACTICE AREAS:*** Business Organization; Communications Law; Entertainment Law; Mergers & Acquisitions. ***Email:*** dwills@boselaw.com

BRYAN B. WOODRUFF, born Canton, Ohio, September 27, 1971; admitted to bar, 1998, Indiana. *Education:* Purdue University (B.A., with highest distinction, 1992); Indiana University School of Law - Bloomington (J.D., summa cum laude, 1998). ***PRACTICE AREAS:*** Business Services; Real Estate. ***Email:*** bwoodruff@boselaw.com

JUDY L. WOODS, born Akron, Ohio, June 2, 1952; admitted to bar, 1987, Indiana. *Education:* Macalester College (B.A., magna cum laude, 1973); Bryn Mawr College (M.A., 1978); Indiana University (J.D., cum laude, 1987). The Order of Barristers. Cale J. Holder Distinguished Scholar. Associate Editor, Indiana Law Review, 1985-1987. Neutral: American Arbitration Association, Large Complex Case and Commercial Arbitration Panels; The National Research Exchange. *Member:* Indianapolis, Indiana State, Seventh Circuit and American Bar Associations. ***PRACTICE AREAS:*** Trial Practice; Appellate Practice; Antitrust; Class Actions; Shareholders Law; Banking Litigation; Business Litigation; RICO; UCC; Creditors. ***Email:*** jwoods@boselaw.com

(This Listing Continued)

KAREN BALL WOODS, born Ann Arbor, Michigan, July 8, 1968; admitted to bar, 1995, Indiana. *Education:* University of Michigan (B.A., 1990); Indiana University School of Law - Bloomington (J.D., summa cum laude, 1995; M.H.A., 1995). Phi Alpha Delta. Member: Moot Court Society; HealthLaw Society. Adjunct Professor, IUPUI School of Public and Environmental Affairs, 2000-2001. Judicial Law Clerk to the Hon. John G. Baker, Indiana Court of Appeals, 1995-1997. *Member:* Indianapolis, Indiana State and American Bar Associations. ***PRACTICE AREAS:*** Corporate Law; Mergers and Acquisitions; Securities. ***Email:*** kwoods@boselaw.com

BRANTLEY H. WRIGHT, born 1965; admitted to bar, 1992, Indiana; 1994, U.S. Tax Court. *Education:* Indiana University (B.S., Finance, 1988; M.B.A., 1992); Indiana University School of Law-Bloomington (J.D., cum laude, 1992). Volunteer: Race for the Cure; Leukemia Society; United Way. *Member:* Indianapolis, Indiana State and American (Member, Sections on: Business; Real Property; Health Care) Bar Associations; American Health Lawyers Association. ***PRACTICE AREAS:*** Business Services; Real Estate; Health Care. ***Email:*** bwright@boselaw.com

C. DANIEL YATES, born Indianapolis, Indiana, September 27, 1947; admitted to bar, 1973, Indiana. *Education:* Indiana University (A.B., 1969; M.B.A., 1973; J.D., 1973). Phi Alpha Delta. *Member:* Indianapolis, Indiana State and American Bar Associations; Estate Planning Council of Indianapolis; Planned Giving Group of Indiana; Fellow: Indiana Bar Foundation; American College of Trust and Estate Counsel. ***PRACTICE AREAS:*** Estate Planning; Trust Planning; Wealth Management Planning; Probate; Taxation; Charitable Trusts and Foundations. ***Email:*** dyates@boselaw.com

OF COUNSEL

JOHN V. BARNETT, JR., born Lebanon, Indiana, January 28, 1943; admitted to bar, 1968, Indiana. *Education:* DePauw University (B.A., 1965); Indiana University School of Law - Bloomington (J.D., 1968). Founding Director and Past President, Governmental Affairs Society of Indiana. Member: Columbia Club; Ulen Country Club. ***PRACTICE AREAS:*** Government. ***Email:*** jbarnett@bosetreacy.com

MICHAEL O. CHENOWETH, born Richmond, Indiana, November 27, 1943; admitted to bar, 1986, Indiana. *Education:* Amherst College (B.A., cum laude, 1966); The Wharton School, University of Pennsylvania (M.B.A., 1968); Indiana University (J.D., cum laude, 1986). Certified Public Accountant, Indiana, 1971. *Member:* Indianapolis, Indiana State and American Bar Associations; Estate Planning Council of Indianapolis. Fellow, Indiana Bar Foundation. ***PRACTICE AREAS:*** Estate Planning; Trust Planning; Wealth Management Planning; Probate; Charitable Trusts and Foundations; Taxation. ***Email:*** mchenoweth@boselaw.com

STEPHEN E. DeVOE, born Indianapolis, Indiana, August 19, 1935; admitted to bar, 1965, Indiana. *Education:* Princeton University (B.S., 1957); Indiana University School of Law - Indianapolis (J.D., 1965). Order of the Coif. Associate Editor, Indiana Law Journal, 1964-1965. Director, Professional Tennis, United States Tennis Association and Tournament Director, U.S. Open Tennis Championships, 1992-1993. *Member:* Indianapolis and Indiana State Bar Associations. ***PRACTICE AREAS:*** Corporate Law; Sports Law; Entertainment Law; Estate Planning; Probate. ***Email:*** sdevoe@boselaw.com

ANTHONY P. FILOMENA, born Washington, D.C., June 10, 1958; admitted to bar, 1998, Indiana; U.S. District Court, Northern and Southern Districts of Indiana; registered to practice before U.S. Patent and Trademark Office. *Education:* Washington University (B.S., Electrical Engineering, 1980; B.S., Computer Science, 1980); University of Pennsylvania (M.S., Computer Science, 1984); Indiana University (M.B.A., 1997; J.D., summa cum laude, 1997). *Member:* Indiana State Bar Association; American Intellectual Property Law Association. ***PRACTICE AREAS:*** Intellectual Property. ***Email:*** afilomena@boselaw.com

THOMAS E. FRUECHTENICHT, born Fort Wayne, Indiana, April 8, 1940; admitted to bar, 1965, Indiana. *Education:* Indiana University (B.S., 1962; J.D., 1965). Member: Columbia Club; Indiana Historical Society; Indianapolis Museum of Art. *Member:* Indianapolis, Indiana State (Former Chairman, Young Lawyers Section; Member, Board of Managers) and American Bar Associations; Governmental Affairs Society of Indiana. Master Fellow, Indiana Bar Foundation. ***PRACTICE AREAS:*** Government. ***Email:*** tef@bosetreacy.com

RODGER K. HENDERSHOT, born Oak Park, Illinois, August 27, 1950; admitted to bar, 1975, Indiana; U.S. Court of Appeals, Seventh Circuit and U.S. District Court, Northern and Southern Districts of Indiana. *Education:* Butler University (B.A., cum laude, 1972); Northwestern University; Indianapolis Law School (J.D., cum laude, 1975). Instructor, Business Law, Indiana University-Purdue University, Indianapolis. Certified Employee Benefits Specialist, CEBS Wharton School, University of Pennsylvania, 1980. *Member:* Indianapolis Bar Association. ***PRACTICE AREAS:*** Bankruptcy Law; Commercial Collection Law; General Practice. ***Email:*** rhendershot@boselaw.com

EUGENE L. HENDERSON, born Columbus, Indiana, July 21, 1925; admitted to bar, 1953, Indiana. *Education:* Franklin College (A.B., 1950); Harvard University (J.D., 1953). *Member:* Indianapolis, Indiana State and American Bar Associations. ***PRACTICE AREAS:*** Mergers and Acquisitions; Insurance Law; Corporate Law; Entrepreneurial Business Law. ***Email:*** ehenderson@boselaw.com

JEANNETTE EISAN HINSHAW, admitted to bar, 1982, Indiana. *Education:* DePauw University (B.A., magna cum laude, 1979); Indiana University School of Law, Bloomington (J.D., cum laude, 1982). Phi Beta Kappa. ***PRACTICE AREAS:*** Bankruptcy; Creditors Rights. ***Email:*** jhinshaw@boselaw.com

DANIEL J. KRIEGER, born Indianapolis, Indiana, December 23, 1954; admitted to bar, 1988, Illinois; 1989, U.S. District Court, Northern District of Illinois; 1991, U.S. Court of Appeals for the Federal Circuit; 2004, Indiana; registered to practice before U.S. Patent and Trademark Office. *Education:* Purdue University (B.S.E.E., 1977); Indiana University School of Law - Bloomington (J.D., 1988). Patent Counsel, 1993-1998 and Patent Attorney, 1993-1996, Xerox Corporation, Rochester, New York. Associate: Fitch, Even, Tabin & Flannery, Chicago, Illinois, 1991-1993; Neuman, Williams, Anderson & Olson, Chicago, Illinois, 1988-1991. *Member:* American Intellectual Property Law Association. ***PRACTICE AREAS:*** Intellectual Property. ***Email:*** dkrieger@boselaw.com

(This Listing Continued)

BOSE McKINNEY & EVANS LLP, Indianapolis—Continued

CARL D. OVERMAN, born Blufton, Indiana, April 2, 1925; admitted to bar, 1952, Indiana. *Education:* Indiana University (B.S., Business, with distinction, 1949); Indiana University School of Law (J.D., with distinction, 1952). Order of the Coif. *Member:* Indianapolis, Indiana State, Seventh Circuit and American (Tax and Business Law Sections) Bar Associations; ESOP Association (Legislative and Regulatory Advisory Committee); The National Center for Employee Ownership. ***PRACTICE AREAS:*** Employee Stock Ownership Plans. ***Email:*** coverman@boselaw.com

KAREN GLASSER SHARP, admitted to bar, 1989, Indiana. *Education:* University of Indianapolis (B.A., magna cum laude, 1985); Indiana University (J.D., summa cum laude, 1989). Phi Alpha Delta. Note Development Editor, Indiana Law Review, 1988-1989. Co-Chair, Dean's Tutorial Society, 1988-1989. Judge William E. Steckler Fellowship, 1989. ***PRACTICE AREAS:*** Labor and Employment; Education Law. ***Email:*** ksharp@boselaw.com

A.J. USHER IV, born Van Nuys, California, September 17, 1970; admitted to bar, 1997, Indiana; registered to practice before the Patent and Trademark Office. *Education:* Rose-Hulman Institute of Technology (B.S., Physics, cum laude, 1991); University of California, Irvine (M.S. Engineering, 1992); Indiana University (J.D., magna cum laude, 1997). Associate Editor, Indiana Journal of Global Legal Studies, 1996-1997. ***PRACTICE AREAS:*** Intellectual Property. ***Email:*** ausher@boselaw.com

ROBERT T. WILDMAN, born Indianapolis, Indiana, March 19, 1947; admitted to bar, 1972, Indiana. *Education:* Indiana University (A.B., 1969); Indiana University School of Law - Bloomington (J.D., magna cum laude, 1972). Order of the Coif; Phi Alpha Delta. *Member:* Indianapolis, Indiana State and American Bar Associations. ***PRACTICE AREAS:*** Business Law; Securities Law; Real Estate Law. ***Email:*** rwildman@boselaw.com

ASSOCIATES

ADRIAN ALLEN, admitted to bar, 2001, Indiana. *Education:* Indiana University (B.A., high distinction, 1995); Indiana University School of Law - Bloomington (J.D., cum laude, 2001). ***PRACTICE AREAS:*** Litigation; Construction Litigation. ***Email:*** aallen@boselaw.com

BRYAN H. BABB, admitted to bar, 1999, Indiana. *Education:* United States Military Academy (B.S., 1989); Boston University (M.S.B.A., 1994); Indiana University (J.D., cum laude, 1999). ***PRACTICE AREAS:*** Litigation; Appellate Practice. ***Email:*** bbabb@boselaw.com

PEYTON BERG, admitted to bar, 2002, Indiana. *Education:* University of Colorado (B.A.); Notre Dame Law School (J.D.). ***PRACTICE AREAS:*** Litigation; Appellate Practice; Sports Law. ***Email:*** pberg@boselaw.com

LEA ANN BREEDEN, admitted to bar, 2003, Indiana. *Education:* Centre College (B.A., Government); Louis D. Brandeis School of Law (J.D., cum laude). ***PRACTICE AREAS:*** Litigation. ***Email:*** lbreeden@boselaw.com

RHONDA YODER BREMAN, admitted to bar, 2002, Indiana. *Education:* University of Indianapolis (A.S., 1987); Indiana University, Indianapolis (B.A., 1995); Indiana University School of Law, Indianapolis (J.D., cum laude, 2002). ***PRACTICE AREAS:*** Litigation. ***Email:*** rbreman@boselaw.com

JENNIFER L. DAY, admitted to bar, 1998, Indiana. *Education:* Franklin College of Indiana (B.A., Political Science and Journalism, 1995); Indiana University School of Law (J.D., summa cum laude, 1998). ***PRACTICE AREAS:*** Intellectual Property. ***Email:*** jday@boselaw.com

CARINA M. DE LA TORRE, born Valparaiso, Indiana, August 13, 1979; admitted to bar, 2004, Indiana. *Education:* University of Miami (B.H.S., cum laude, 2001); Indiana University School of Law - Bloomington (J.D., cum laude, 2004). ***PRACTICE AREAS:*** Bankruptcy; Litigation. ***Email:*** cdelatorre@boselaw.com

CHRISTOPHER A. EVENS, born Indianapolis, Indiana, October 10, 1973; admitted to bar, 2000, Indiana; 2002, Illinois. *Education:* Indiana University (B.A., 1996); Indiana University School of Law - Indianapolis (J.D., cum laude, 2000). Judicial Law Clerk to the Hon. Allen Sharp, U.S. District Court, Northern District of Indiana, 2000-2002. *Member:* Indianapolis, Indiana State and American Bar Associations. ***Email:*** cevens@boselaw.com

W. JAMES HAMILTON, admitted to bar, 1997, Indiana; 1999, Illinois. *Education:* Cornell University (B.A., with distinction, 1994); Indiana University School of Law - Bloomington (J.D., cum laude, 1997); New York University Law School (LL.M. in Taxation, 1999). ***PRACTICE AREAS:*** Employee Benefits; HIPAA; Taxation. ***Email:*** jhamilton@boselaw.com

STEPHANIE FRANCO HOLTZLANDER, admitted to bar, 1993, Indiana. *Education:* Indiana University at Bloomington (B.A., 1990); Drake University (M.A., 1993; J.D., with honors, 1993). ***PRACTICE AREAS:*** Commercial Litigation; Civil Litigation; Products Liability; Health Care; Medical Malpractice. ***Email:*** sholtzlander@boselaw.com

ALEX C. INTERMILL, born San Diego, California, January 9, 1973; admitted to bar, 2005, Indiana. *Education:* Purdue University (B.A., 1995); Indiana University (B.S., 1999); Indiana University School of Law - Indianapolis (J.D., 2004). ***PRACTICE AREAS:*** Environmental Law; Real Estate. ***Email:*** aintermill@boselaw.com

BUREN E. JONES, admitted to bar, 2000, Indiana. *Education:* University of Evansville (B.S., 1984); Temple University (M.M., 1987); Indiana University School of Law (J.D., 2000). ***PRACTICE AREAS:*** Education Law. ***Email:*** bjones@boselaw.com

JEFFREY J. KIRK, II, admitted to bar, 2003, Indiana. *Education:* Miami University of Ohio (B.S., Accountancy and Finance, 1995); Indiana University School of Law - Indianapolis (J.D., 2002). ***PRACTICE AREAS:*** Business Services; Entrepreneurial Services; Mergers and Acquisitions; Securities; Venture Capital Finance; Bankruptcy; Creditors Rights. ***Email:*** jkirk@boselaw.com

(This Listing Continued)

MATTHEW R. MACALUSO, admitted to bar, 2001, Indiana. *Education:* Purdue University (B.S., 1995); Valparaiso University (J.D., cum laude, 2001). ***PRACTICE AREAS:*** Business Law; Banking Law; Securities Law; Mergers and Acquisitions. ***Email:*** mmacaluso@boselaw.com

KATHERINE MAYBERRY, admitted to bar, 2001, Illinois; 2003, Indiana. *Education:* Indiana University (B.A., with high honors, 1998); University of Michigan (J.D., cum laude, 2001). ***PRACTICE AREAS:*** Business Services; Estate Planning. ***Email:*** kmayberry@boselaw.com

MEGAN M. MULFORD, born Madison, Indiana, October 13, 1979; admitted to bar, 2005, Indiana. *Education:* DePauw University (B.S., 2002); Indiana University School of Law - Indianapolis (J.D., 2005). ***PRACTICE AREAS:*** Intellectual Property. ***Email:*** mmulford@boselaw.com

SUSAN OLIVER, born South Bend, Indiana, September 29, 1970; admitted to bar, 1999, Indiana. *Education:* Indiana University (B.S., 1993); Valparaiso University (J.D., magna cum laude, 1999). Law Clerk to Justice Frank Sullivan, Jr., Indiana Supreme Court, 1999-2001. ***PRACTICE AREAS:*** Labor and Employment. ***Email:*** soliver@boselaw.com

CHRISTINE E. M. ORICH, admitted to bar, 1998, Indiana. *Education:* Washington University (B.S., 1990); Indiana University (J.D., 1998). ***PRACTICE AREAS:*** Patents; Copyrights; Trademarks; Intellectual Property Law; Computer Law; Licensing. ***Email:*** corich@boselaw.com

SANDRA PERRY, admitted to bar, 2000, Indiana. *Education:* University of Memphis (B.A., summa cum laude,1997); Indiana University School of Law - Bloomington (J.D., magna cum laude, 2000). ***PRACTICE AREAS:*** Litigation; Labor and Employment. ***Email:*** sperry@boselaw.com

BETH L. RIGA, admitted to bar, 2002, Indiana. *Education:* Ball State University (B.A., summa cum laude, 1992; M.A. 1993); University of Notre Dame (J.D., 2002). ***PRACTICE AREAS:*** Litigation. ***Email:*** briga@boselaw.com

THERESA M. RINGLE, admitted to bar, 2000, Indiana. *Education:* Ball State University (B.Arch., 1993; B. Env. Design, 1993); Indiana University at Indianapolis (J.D., 1999). Member, Order of Barristers. Member, Indiana Law Review, 1998-1999. ***PRACTICE AREAS:*** General Practice; Construction Law. ***Email:*** tringle@boselaw.com

MICHAEL D. ROGERS, born Indianapolis, Indiana, January 30, 1980; admitted to bar, 2005, Indiana. *Education:* Morehouse College (B.S., 2002); Notre Dame University (J.D., 2005). ***PRACTICE AREAS:*** Litigation. ***Email:*** mrogers@boselaw.com

BRION G. ST.AMOUR, born East Lansing, Michigan, October 14, 1978; admitted to bar, 2004, Indiana; U.S. District Court, Northern and Southern Districts of Indiana; registered to practice before U.S. Patent and Trademark Office. *Education:* Purdue University (B.S., Mechanical Engineering, 2001); Indiana University School of Law - Indianapolis (J.D., 2004). ***PRACTICE AREAS:*** Intellectual Property; Patent Applications. ***Email:*** bstamour@boselaw.com

MARISOL SANCHEZ, admitted to bar, 2002, Indiana. *Education:* University of Puerto Rico (B.A., Business Administration, cum laude); The Indiana University School of Law (J.D.). ***PRACTICE AREAS:*** Litigation; Appellate Practice. ***Email:*** msanchez@boselaw.com

KELLY M. SCANLAN, born Indianapolis, Indiana, March 19, 1974; admitted to bar, 2005, Indiana. *Education:* Indiana University - Indianapolis (B.S.N., 1997); Indiana University School of Law - Indianapolis (J.D., 2005). ***PRACTICE AREAS:*** Civil Litigation; Medical Malpractice Defense. ***Email:*** kscanlan@boselaw.com

H. ANTONIO SETZER, admitted to bar, 2001, Indiana. *Education:* Indiana University (B.A., 1998; J.D., magna cum laude, 2001). ***PRACTICE AREAS:*** Real Estate; Business Organization; Commercial Finance; Commercial Transactions; Corporate Law. ***Email:*** tsetzer@boselaw.com

KATHERINE E. TAYLOR, born Anchorage, Alaska, May 27, 1974; admitted to bar, 2002, Indiana. *Education:* Anderson University (B.A., summa cum laude, 1996); Southern Methodist University (J.D., cum laude, 2000). ***PRACTICE AREAS:*** Labor and Employment; Litigation. ***Email:*** ktaylor@boselaw.com

JOEL W. THORP, born Fort Wayne, Indiana, June 19, 1979; admitted to bar, 2004, Indiana. *Education:* Wheaton College (B.A., 2001); Vanderbilt University (J.D., 2004). ***PRACTICE AREAS:*** Probate; Estate Planning; Corporate Law. ***Email:*** jthorp@boselaw.com

STEPHEN C. UNGER, admitted to bar, 2005, Indiana. *Education:* Butler University (B.A. in Political Science, with highest honors, 2002); Indiana University School of Law - Indianapolis (J.D., summa cum laude, 2005). ***PRACTICE AREAS:*** Utility Law; Municipal Utility Law.

PAUL D. VINK, admitted to bar, 2002, Indiana. *Education:* Northwestern College (B.A., cum laude, 1998); Indiana University School of Law - Indianapolis (J.D., summa cum laude, 2002). ***PRACTICE AREAS:*** Litigation. ***Email:*** pvink@boselaw.com

RYAN O. WHITE, born Terre Haute, Indiana, October 30, 1973; admitted to bar, 2000, Ohio; 2001, U.S. District Court, Southern District of Ohio; 2002, U.S. Court of Appeals, Sixth Circuit and U.S. Court of Appeals for the Federal Circuit; registered to practice before U.S. Patent and Trademark Office (Not admitted in Indiana). *Education:* Ball State University (B.S., 1996); University of Dayton (J.D., 2000). *Member:* Cincinnati, Ohio State and American Bar Associations. ***PRACTICE AREAS:*** Patent Prosecution; Patent Litigation; Intellectual Property; Food and Drug Law. ***Email:*** rwhite@boselaw.com

MARK J. WUELLNER, born Carol Stream, Illinois, March 11, 1980; admitted to bar, 2005, Indiana. *Education:* Butler University (B.S., 2002); Cornell University Law School (J.D., 2005). ***PRACTICE AREAS:*** Business Law; Securities; Banks and Banking. ***Email:*** mwuellner@boselaw.com

LEGAL SUPPORT PERSONNEL

STEVEN B. GRANNER, AICP (Zoning Consultant)

LYNN M. POTOSKY, (Public Finance Specialist). ***PRACTICE AREAS:*** Public Finance.

(This Listing Continued)

REPRESENTATIVE CLIENTS: BAA-Indianapolis, LLC; BP America; Association of Indiana Life Insurance Companies; BMW Constructors, Inc.; City of Indianapolis; Duke Realty Corporation.; Emmis Communications Corporation; Endress +Hauser, Inc.; Fall Creek Regional Waste District; First Indiana Bank; Hillenbrand Industries, Inc.; Indiana Community Business Credit Corporation; Indianapolis Colts, Inc.; Indiana Psychological Association; Kenra, Inc.; David Letterman Companies; Metropolitan Life Insurance Co.; Metropolitan School District of Wayne Township, Marion County, Indiana; Midwest Natural Gas Corp.; New Boston Citimark Limited Partnership; The Prudential Insurance Company of America; Personnel Management, Inc.; The Quaker Oats Company; Roche Diagnostics Corp.; TIAA/CREF; The Broadbent Company; Technuity; Thomson, Inc.; U.S. Steel Corporation; Wal-Mart Stores, Inc.

BOSE McKINNEY & EVANS LLP

Established in 1955

600 EAST 96TH STREET, SUITE 500
INDIANAPOLIS, INDIANA 46240
Telephone: 317-684-5300
Facsimile: 317-684-5316
URL: http://www.boselaw.com

Indianapolis, Indiana Office: 2700 First Indiana Plaza, 135 North Pennsylvania Street, 46204. Telephone: 317-684-5000. Facsimile: 317-684-5173.
Washington, D.C. Office: 700 North One Lafayette Centre, 1120 20th Street, N.W., 20036. Telephone: 202-973-1229. Fax: 202-973-1212.
Crown Point, Indiana Office: 3577 West Lakeshore Drive, 46307. Telephone: 219-663-2968. Fax: 219-663-2969.
Chesterton, Indiana Office: P.O. Box 957, 46304. Telephone: 219-983-1552. Fax: 219-983-1741.
West Lafayette, Indiana Office: 3000 Kent Avenue. Telephone: 765-464-3200. Fax: 765-464-3225.

General Civil Practice in all Courts including Agricultural Law, Antitrust, Appellate Practice, Capital Strategies, Civil Rights, Commercial Law, Communications and Media, Constitutional Law, Corporate Law, Creditors Rights, Creditors Rights in Bankruptcy, Debtor Bankruptcy, Education Law, Employee Benefits, Entertainment and the Arts, Entrepreneurial Services, Environmental Law, Finance, Financial Institutions Law, Government Contracts, Government Relations, High Technology, Insurance, Intellectual Property, International Law, Labor and Employment, Legislative Practice, Litigation, Mergers and Acquisitions, Municipal Finance, Municipal Law, Planning and Land Use, Probate, Real Estate, Regulated Industries, Regulatory Agency Practice, Securities, Taxation, Trusts and Estates, Utility Law, Wills and Zoning.

JOSEPH D. CALDERON, born Indianapolis, Indiana, August 30, 1960; admitted to bar, 1990, Indiana. *Education:* Indiana University (B.S., 1982; J.D., 1989). Co-Author: "Major Land Use Laws in Indiana," National Business Institute, Inc., 1991, 1995, 1996, 2004; "Land Use Law in a Slower Economy," National Business Institute, Inc., 1992; "Indiana Real Estate Titles," National Business Institute, Inc., 1996; "Indiana Property Tax: An Overview & Update," Lorman Education Services, 1998-2000, 2003. Author: "Appealing Property Tax Assessments," Indianapolis Business Journal, 1993, 1995, 1996, 1999. Contributing Author, Indiana Tax Handbook, 2003. Indiana Tax Seminar, Indiana Chamber of Commerce, 2003, 2004. *Member:* Indianapolis and Indiana State Bar Associations. ***REPORTED CASES:*** Western Select Properties v. Indiana State Board of Tax Commissioners, Indiana Tax Court, 1994; Equicor Development Inc. v. Westfield-Washington Plan Commission, Ind., 2001. ***PRACTICE AREAS:*** Real Estate; Land Use; Zoning Law; Property Tax; Corporate Law; Municipal Law.

JAMES C. CARLINO, born Indianapolis, Indiana, January 13, 1960; admitted to bar, 1985, Indiana and U.S. District Court, Northern and Southern Districts of Indiana. *Education:* DePauw University (B.A., cum laude, 1982); Austro-American Institute, Vienna, Austria; Karl Marx University, Budapest, Hungary; Indiana University (J.D., cum laude, 1985). Recipient, Indianapolis Bar Foundation Fellowship. Adjunct Professor, Butler University 1990-1992. *Member:* Indianapolis, Indiana State and American Bar Associations; American College of Mortgage Attorneys; American College of Real Estate Lawyers. ***PRACTICE AREAS:*** Real Estate; Lending Law; Construction Law; Environmental Law. ***Email:*** jcarlino@boselaw.com

TAMMY K. HANEY, born Plymouth, Indiana, July 26, 1964; admitted to bar, 1990, Indiana and U.S. District Court, Northern and Southern Districts of Indiana. *Education:* Ball State University (B.A., 1986) Alpha Lambda Delta; Indiana University (J.D., magna cum laude, 1990). ABA Moot Court Team. Speaker at numerous seminars regarding Real Estate issues. *Member:* Indianapolis and Indiana State Bar Associations; National Lawyers Association. ***PRACTICE AREAS:*** Real Estate; Secured Lending; Transactional Law. ***Email:*** thaney@boselaw.com

PHILIP A. NICELY, born La Porte, Indiana, February 1, 1942; admitted to bar, 1967, Indiana. *Education:* Northwestern University (A.B., 1964); University of Michigan (J.D., cum laude, 1967). Order of the Coif. Member, Board of Editors, Michigan Law Review, 1966-1967. Member, American College of Real Estate Lawyers. Member, Urban Land Institute, 1978—. *Member:* Indianapolis, Indiana State and American (Member, Real Property, Probate and Trust Law Section) Bar Associations. ***PRACTICE AREAS:*** Zoning Law; Land Use; Real Estate Development; Real Estate Finance. ***Email:*** pnicely@boselaw.com

ASSOCIATES

ANDREW J. HELD, born Indianapolis, Indiana, April 15, 1976; admitted to bar, 2003, Indiana and U.S. District Court, Southern District of Indiana; U.S. Distruct Court, Northern District of Indiana. *Education:* Indiana University (B.A., 1999; J.D., 2002). *Member:* Indianapolis, Indiana State and American Bar Associations. ***PRACTICE AREAS:*** Real Estate; Real Estate Title; Real Estate Leasing. ***Email:*** aheld@boselaw.com

ANGELA E. TEMPEL, born Aurora, Illinois, June 9, 1971; admitted to bar, 1998, Indiana. *Education:* Indiana University (B.S., 1994; J.D., cum laude, 1998). Advisory Board Member, Humane Society of Indianapolis. Member: Commercial Real Estate Women, Indianapolis Chapter; Builders Association of Greater Indianapolis. *Member:* Indianapolis, Indiana State and American Bar Associations. ***PRACTICE AREAS:*** Real Estate. ***Email:*** atempel@boselaw.com

(This Listing Continued)

BRATTAIN & MINNIX

An Association of Lawyers
151 NORTH DELAWARE STREET
SUITE 760
INDIANAPOLIS, INDIANA 46204
Telephone: 317-231-1750
Facsimile: 317-231-1760

Civil and Criminal Trial Practice in all Courts, Business, Corporate, Commercial, Bankruptcy, Personal Injury, Medical Malpractice, Family/Domestic Relations, Custody, Support.

BRUCE D. BRATTAIN, born Anderson, Indiana, May 25, 1950; admitted to bar, 1979, Indiana; 1983, U.S. Court of Appeals, Seventh Circuit; 2001, U.S. Supreme Court; U.S. District Court, Northern and Southern Districts of Indiana. *Education:* Ball State University (B.S., 1974); Indiana University School of Law (J.D., cum laude, 1979). Recipient: Distinguished Flying Cross; Army Commendation Medal; Vietnamese Cross of Gallantry. Assistant United States Attorney, Northern District of Indiana, 1983-1986. Civil Chief, United States Attorney's Office, Northern District of Indiana, 1984-1986. Lead Trial Counsel, Federal Deposit Insurance Corporation, Indianapolis, Indiana Consolidated Office, 1986. *Member:* Indianapolis, Indiana State and American Bar Associations. [Chief Warrant Officer, United States Army, 1968-1970]. ***PRACTICE AREAS:*** Civil and Criminal Litigation; Commercial Law; Bankruptcy Law; Appeals. ***Email:*** BATMI5@AOL.COM

LARRY A. MINNIX, born La Porte, Indiana, May 15, 1951; admitted to bar, 1978, Indiana; U.S. District Court, Southern District of Indiana. *Education:* Indiana University (B.A., 1973); Pepperdine University (J.D., 1976). *Member:* Indianapolis and Indiana State Bar Associations; Indiana Trial Lawyers Association; The Association of Trial Lawyers of America. ***PRACTICE AREAS:*** Personal Injury Law; Product Liability Defense; Domestic; General Civil Practice; Litigation; Civil Litigation; Products Liability. ***Email:*** laminnix@earthlink.net

MARIO GARCIA, born Bloomington, Indiana, May 23, 1973; admitted to bar, 1999, Indiana and U.S. District Court, Northern and Southern Districts of Indiana; 2001, U.S. Court of Appeals, Seventh Circuit. *Education:* Ball State University (B.S., 1995); Indiana University (J.D., 1999). Phi Delta Phi. Member: Order of the Barristers; Hispanic Law Society. *Member:* Indianapolis Bar Association. ***PRACTICE AREAS:*** Civil Litigation; Criminal Litigation; General Practice. ***Email:*** mariolaw@in.net

REPRESENTATIVE CLIENTS: Federal Deposit Insurance Corporation; Circle Business Credit, Inc.; Stricklease, Inc.; The Braun Corporation; Midwest CNC Service, Inc.; First Financial Bank, F.S.B.; Healthcare Reimbursement Specialists, Inc.; National Products, Inc.; National Bank of Indianapolis; Economy Fence, Inc.; Paul's Glass & Accessories, Inc.; Parks Out-Door Maintenance, Inc.; Union Federal Bank.

BRINKS HOFER GILSON & LIONE

A PROFESSIONAL CORPORATION
ONE INDIANA SQUARE, SUITE 1600
INDIANAPOLIS, INDIANA 46204-2001
Telephone: 317-636-0886
Facsimile: 317-634-6701
Email: iplaw@usebrinks.com
URL: http://www.usebrinks.com

Chicago, Illinois Office: NBC Tower, Suite 3600, 455 North Cityfront Plaza Drive. Telephone: 312-321-4200. Facsimile: 312-321-4299. Email: iplaw@usebrinks.com.
Ann Arbor, Michigan Office: 524 South Main Street, Suite 200. Telephone: 734-302-6000. Fax: 734-994-6331.
Arlington, Virginia Office: 2001 Jefferson Davis Highway, Suite 208. Telephone: 703-415-0303. Facsimile: 703-415-0304.

Patent, Trademark, Copyright, Trade Secret and Internet Work, Unfair Competition, Technology and Licensing Agreements, Intellectual Asset Management and Intellectual Property Litigation.

SHAREHOLDER

A. JAMES RICHARDSON, born Toronto, Ontario, October 14, 1943; admitted to bar, 1974, Virginia; 1981, Indiana; registered to practice before U.S. Patent and Trademark Office. *Education:* Colorado State College (A.B., 1964; M.A., 1968); Indiana State University (M.A., 1969); George Washington University (J.D., 1974). Member: Conference Faculty, Advanced Computer Law Seminar 2000, University of Dayton; Conference on Licensing Intellectual Property 2001, University of Dayton; Midwestern Intellectual Property Law Symposium 2001, I.C.L.E.F.; Member, Board of Advisors to Intellectual Property Counselor. *Member:* Virginia State and Indiana State Bar Associations; American Intellectual Property Law Association. (Managing Attorney, Indianapolis Office). ***REPORTED CASES:*** Primedia Intertec Corp. v. Technology Marketing Corp. (DC Kan) 50 USPQ2d 1079 (11/6/1998). ***PRACTICE AREAS:*** International Patent and Trademark; Licensing; Patent Prosecution; Technology Transfer; Mechanical; Industrial and Intellectual Property Law. ***Email:*** jrichardson@usebrinks.com

COUNSEL

LAWRENCE A. STEWARD, born Columbus, Ohio, May 12, 1950; admitted to bar, 1979, Ohio; 1988, Indiana, U.S. District Court, Southern and Northern Districts of Indiana, U.S. District Court, Northern District of Ohio, U.S. District Court, Eastern District of Michigan and U.S. Court of Appeals for the Federal Circuit; registered to practice before U.S. Patent and Trademark Office. *Education:* University of Toledo (B.S., 1972; J.D., 1979). *Member:* Indianapolis and Indiana State Bar Associations; American Intellectual Property

(This Listing Continued)

BRINKS HOFER GILSON & LIONE, A PROFESSIONAL CORPORATION, Indianapolis—Continued

Law Association. ***PRACTICE AREAS:*** Intellectual Property; Patent Prosecution; Patent Litigation; Biotechnology and Pharmaceuticals; Chemical. ***Email:*** lsteward@usebrinks.com

OF COUNSEL

DAVID H. BADGER, born Indianapolis, Indiana, June 16, 1931; admitted to bar, 1964, Indiana Supreme Court and U.S. District Court, Southern District of Indiana; 1964-1982, U.S. Court of Customs and Patent Appeals; 1982, U.S. Court of Appeals for the Federal Circuit; registered to practice before U.S. Patent and Trademark Office. *Education:* Rose-Hulman Institute of Technology (B.S.E.E., with honors, 1953); Indiana University (J.D., 1964). Tau Beta Pi. Member, Indiana Law Review, 1963-1964. Registered Professional Engineer, Indiana. *Member:* Indianapolis (Member, Intellectual Property Section), Indiana State (Member, Sections on: International; Patent, Trademark and Copyright) and American (Member, Section on: Patent, Trademark and Copyright Law) Bar Associations; American Intellectual Property Law Association; Licensing Executives Society; Association Internationale Pour La Protection De La Propriété Industrielle. [LCDR, U.S. Navy (Retired)]. ***PRACTICE AREAS:*** Intellectual Property Law. ***Email:*** dbadger@usebrinks.com

ASSOCIATES

SANDERS N. HILLIS, born Milwaukee, Wisconsin, September 6, 1964; admitted to bar, 1999, Indiana; U.S. District Court, Northern and Southern Districts of Indiana; registered to practice before U.S. Patent and Trademark Office. *Education:* Ohio University (B.S.E.E., cum laude, 1987); Indiana University (J.D., magna cum laude, 1999). Registered Professional Engineer in Indiana, Illinois, Ohio and Kentucky, 1993. *Member:* Indianapolis and Indiana State Bar Associations; American Intellectual Property Law Association; Licensing Executive Society. ***PRACTICE AREAS:*** Intellectual Property; Patents; Trademarks; Copyrights; Trade Secrets; Licensing; Right to Use Issues; Patent Prosecution; Internet/E-Commerce; Electrical; Software. ***Email:*** shillis@usebrinks.com

NICHOLAS M. BOIVIN, admitted to bar, 2003, Illinois; registered to practice before U.S. Patent and Trademark Office (Not admitted in Indiana). *Education:* Northwestern University (B.A., Chemistry, honors, 1996); Princeton University (M.A., Chemistry, 1998); University of Virginia School of Law (J.D., 2003). ***PRACTICE AREAS:*** Patents; Federal Litigation. ***Email:*** nboivin@usebrinks.com

MICHAEL E. WEVER, born Fort Wayne, Indiana, February 14, 1972; admitted to bar, 1997, South Carolina; registered to practice before U.S. Patent and Trademark Office (Not admitted in Indiana). *Education:* Rose-Hulman Institute of Technology (B.S., Computer Engineering, 1994); University of South Carolina (J.D., 1997). Recipient, Cali Award in Intellectual Property. First Place, University of South Carolina School of Law, Nathan Burkin Memorial Competition, 1997. Author: "Patent Law: Protecting Software," National Law Journal, May 8, 2000. Member, Intellectual Property and Unfair Trade Practices Committee, South Carolina Bar. *Member:* Carolina Patent, Trademark and Copyright Law Association. ***PRACTICE AREAS:*** Intellectual Property. ***Email:*** mwever@usebrinks.com

(For complete biographical data on all personnel, see Professional Biographies at Chicago, Illinois)

CORY BRUNDAGE, LLC

1700 ONE AMERICAN SQUARE
P.O. BOX 82053
INDIANAPOLIS, INDIANA 46282-0003
Telephone: 317-639-4875
Fax: 317-639-4882
Email: cb@brundagelaw.com
URL: http://www.corybrundagelaw.com

Civil Litigation, Trial and Appellate Practice, Commercial Litigation and Arbitration, Personal Injury and Wrongful Death, Products Liability, Risk Management and Litigation Avoidance, College and University Law, Legal Malpractice and Disciplinary Defense.

FIRM PROFILE: Cory Brundage received his J.D., magna cum laude, from Indiana University where he was an editor of the Law Journal and inducted into the Order of the Coif. He completed his legal education at Harvard Law School with an LL.M. He began his career at the Indianapolis firm of Ice Miller, where for over twenty years he was a partner in the Litigation Section and served on the Management Committee and as the Chairman of the Professional Standards Committee. Mr. Brundage represents clients in all state and federal courts in Indiana as well as the Seventh Circuit.

Named by Indianapolis Monthly as one of the best lawyers in Indianapolis, Mr. Brundage has attained Martindale-Hubbell's highest rating for legal ability and ethical standards.

CORY BRUNDAGE, born Chicago, Illinois, September 15, 1947; admitted to bar, 1973, Indiana, U.S. Court of Appeals, Seventh and Eighth Circuits and U.S. Supreme Court. *Education:* Indiana University (B.S., 1969; J.D., magna cum laude, 1972); Harvard Law School (LL.M., 1973).

REPRESENTATIVE CLIENTS: Agilent Technologies, Inc.; Allianz; Degussa AG; Goodyear Tire and Rubber Company; Hewlett-Packard Company; Indiana University; Loews Corporation; Nogginwerks; Nucor Steel Corporation; One Call Internet, Inc.; Ultra Chem, Inc.

CAMPBELL KYLE PROFFITT LLP

INDIANAPOLIS, INDIANA

(See Noblesville)

Civil Practice. State and Federal Courts and Administrative Agencies, Domestic Relations, Family Law, Divorce, Adoptions, Personal Injury, Corporation, Business Law, Utility Law, Insurance, Wills and Probate, Trusts and Estates, Estate Planning and Elder Law, Real Estate,

(This Listing Continued)

Zoning, Employment Law, Criminal Law. Contracts, Taxation, Real Estate, Commercial Litigation.

DANIEL R. CARROLL

Established in 1983
6500 E. WESTFIELD BOULEVARD
INDIANAPOLIS, INDIANA 46220-1110
Telephone: 317-259-4259
Fax: 317-475-4516
Email: dancarroll51@yahoo.com
URL: http://www.lawyers.com/dcarroll

Business Law, Contracts, Litigation, Insurance, Debtor and Creditor, Collections, Business Enterprises, Corporate Law, Partnerships, Real Estate, Commercial Litigation, Commercial Leasing, Buy-Sell Agreements, Employment Law, Noncompete Litigation, Wrongful Termination, Trade Secrets, Personal Injury, Automobile Accidents, Slip and Fall, Wrongful Death, Bankruptcy, Arbitration, Mediation.

DANIEL R. CARROLL, born Buffalo, New York, October 14, 1951; admitted to bar, 1983, Indiana. *Education:* University of Rochester (B.M., 1973); Indiana University School of Law (J.D., 1983). Registered Mediator. *Member:* Indianapolis, Indiana State and American Bar Associations; Indiana Trial Lawyers Association.

REPRESENTATIVE CLIENTS: Genesis Medical, Inc.; Public Affairs Resources, Inc.; Legislative Demographic Services, Inc.; Landmark Properties Group; Franklin Plaza, LLP; Bristol Holdings, LLC.

CHRISTOPHER & TAYLOR

1219 NORTH DELAWARE STREET
P.O. BOX 2850
INDIANAPOLIS, INDIANA 46206-2850
Telephone: 317-635-9000
Telecopier: 317-686-2200

Fowler Office: 306 East Fifth Street, P.O. Box 72. Telephone: 317-884-0810.

General Civil Practice. Trial and Appellate Litigation in all Courts. Administrative, Antitrust, Aviation, Bankruptcy, Business and Commercial, Class Actions, Construction, Corporate, Creditor Rights, Fidelity and Surety, Government Contracts, Insurance, Personal Injury and Property Damage, Products Liability, Professional Liability, School, Real Estate and Development, Zoning and Land Use, Trusts and Estates, Wills and Probate Law.

RODNEY V. TAYLOR, born Mount Vernon, Illinois, July 5, 1947; admitted to bar, 1973, Indiana; 1990, Kentucky, Illinois and Ohio; 1996, Missouri, U.S. District Court, Southern District of Indiana, Northern and Southern Districts of Illinois, District of Columbia, U.S. Court of Appeals, Sixth, Seventh and Ninth Circuits; U.S. Supreme Court. *Education:* University of Illinois (A.B., 1969); Indiana University School of Law (J.D., 1973). Editor in Chief, Indiana Law Review, 1971-1972. Author, "A New Look at Article V and the Bill of Rights," 6 Indiana Law Review 699 (1973). *Member:* Indianapolis, Indiana State, Illinois State, Ohio State, Kentucky and American Bar Associations; The Missouri Bar. ***Email:*** r_taylor@iquest.net

MICHAEL C. PEEK, born Indianapolis, Indiana, December 13, 1952; admitted to bar, 1979, Indiana. *Education:* Purdue University (B.A., 1975); Indiana University School of Law (J.D., cum laude, 1979). Registered Civil Mediator, 1998. Author, "Trial Rule 69 (E): Proceedings Supplemental to Execution," 11 Indiana Law Review 873 (1978). *Member:* Indianapolis, Indiana State and American Bar Associations. ***PRACTICE AREAS:*** Civil Mediation; Torts; Insurance; Commercial Law; Business Law; Personal Injury; Corporate Law. ***Email:*** mickpeek@iquest.net

DAVID J. THEISING, born Indianapolis, Indiana, January 16, 1954; admitted to bar, 1980, Indiana; 1996, Pennsylvania, North Carolina and District of Columbia; 1997, Maryland, Virginia, Texas, Colorado, U.S. District Court, Northern and Southern Districts of Indiana, Northern District of Illinois, Western District of Pennsylvania, District of Maryland, Eastern and Western Districts of Virginia, Eastern, Middle and Western Districts of North Carolina, District of Colorado and District of Columbia, and U.S. Court of Appeals, Third, Fourth, Fifth, Seventh, Tenth, District of Columbia and Federal Circuits; U.S. Tax Court; U.S. Court of Federal Claims; U.S. Supreme Court. *Education:* Indiana University (A.B., 1976); Indiana University School of Law (J.D., 1980). Member, Indiana Law Journal, 1978-1979. Teaching Fellow, 1974-1976 and Law Fellow, 1977-1980, Indiana University. Chairman and Editor, *Mechanics Liens,* Indiana Continuing Legal Education Forum, 1985. Author and Lecturer: "Mechanics Liens and Mortgage Foreclosures," Indiana Continuing Legal Education Forum, 1987; "Rights and Remedies of a Creditor in Bankruptcy Proceedings," Lorman Education Services, 1991, 1993; "Eleventh Amendment Immunity to Schools: Individual and School Board Liability under Section 1983," Indiana School Boards Association, 1994; "Mechanics Liens and Related Claims," Indiana Continuing Legal Education Forum, 1994; "Dismissal of Chapter 7 Bankruptcy Cases for Substantial Abuse under Section 707 (b)," Indiana Continuing Legal Education Forum, 1995; "Mechanics Lien Law and Strategies," National Business Institute, 1996, 2000, 2001, 2002, 2003, 2005; "Construction Law: Creative Strategies for Project Completion and Litigation Avoidance," Lorman Education Services, 1998; "Emerging Trends and Issues in Construction Law," Professional Education Systems, Inc., 1998; "Purchasing and Procurement Law in Indiana," Lorman Education Services, 2000; "Bankruptcy: A Creditor's Perspective," Lorman Education Services, 2000; "The Annual Bankruptcy Institute," Indiana Continuing Legal Education Forum, 2000; "The Basics of Drafting Wills and Trusts in Indiana," Lorman Education Services, 2002. Member, U.S. Panel of Bankruptcy Trustees, Southern District of Indiana, 1988—. Member, National Panel of Arbitrators, American Arbitration Association, 1990—. *Member:* Indianapolis, Hamilton County, Indiana State (Vice Chair, Construction and Surety Law Section, 2005—), Maryland State, Pennsylvania, Colorado, American (Member, Litigation Section; Public Contract Law Section; Tort Trial and Insurance Practice Section; Committee on Fidelity and Surety Law; Forum Committee on the

(This Listing Continued)

Construction Industry) and International Bar Associations; State Bar of Texas; Virginia State Bar; North Carolina State Bar; The District of Columbia Bar; Commercial Law League of America; Defense Trial Counsel of Indiana. **Email:** theising@iquest.net

RANDALL D. SMITH, born Indianapolis, Indiana, October 20, 1946; admitted to bar, 1976, New York; 1978, Indiana; 1982, California; U.S. District Court, Southern and Eastern Districts of New York, Northern and Southern Districts of Indiana and Northern District of California; U.S. Court of Appeals, Seventh Circuit; U.S. Supreme Court. *Education:* Hanover College; Butler University (B.A., 1968); Indiana University (J.D., cum laude, 1973). Editor-in-Chief, Indiana Law Review, 1972-1973. Associate Professor of Law, St. John's University School of Law, New York, N.Y., 1982-1984. Law Clerk to Chief Judge Edward J. Devitt, U.S. District Court of Minnesota, 1973-1975. Private Practice, Simpson Thacher & Bartlett, New York, N.Y., 1975-1976 and 1978-1980. Corporate Counsel, Eli Lilly and Company, Indianapolis, Ind., 1976-1978. Private Practice, Wilson, Sonsini, Goodrich & Rosati, Palo Alto, Calif., 1980-1982. Partner, Baker & Daniels, Indianapolis and Ft. Wayne, Ind., 1986-1991. Seminar Chairman, ICLEF Seminar on Federal Practice, 1986 and Products Liability, 1988. *Member:* The Association of the Bar of the City of New York; State Bar of California.

JOHN D. CONNOR, born Indianapolis, Indiana, April 28, 1953; admitted to bar, 1978, Indiana. *Education:* Indiana University (B.A., 1975); Indiana University School of Law (J.D., magna cum laude, 1978). Chartered Property Casualty Underwriter, 1994. *Member:* Indianapolis, Indiana State and American Bar Associations. ***PRACTICE AREAS:*** Insurance Defense.

MICHAEL A. BEASON, born Indianapolis, Indiana, October 22, 1963; admitted to bar, 1990, Indiana and U.S. District Court, Northern and Southern Districts of Indiana; U.S. Court of Appeals, Seventh Circuit. *Education:* Wabash College (B.A., cum laude, 1986); Indiana University (J.D., 1989). *Member:* Indianapolis, Seventh Federal Circuit, Indiana State and American Bar Associations; American Trial Lawyers Association; National Lawyers Association. **Email:** michaelab@iquest.net

OF COUNSEL

RICHARD L. CHRISTOPHER, born Otterbein, Indiana, March 4, 1933; admitted to bar, 1973, Indiana and U.S. District Court, Southern District of Indiana. *Education:* DePauw University (B.A., cum laude, 1955); Indiana University School of Law (J.D., summa cum laude, 1973). Phi Delta Phi. Member, Indiana Law Review, 1972. *Member:* Benton County, Indiana State and American Bar Associations. (Resident, Fowler Office)

REPRESENTATIVE CLIENTS: Abell Elevator International; Agency Rent-A-Car, Inc.; American Motorcyclist Association; American Productions, Inc.; Blue and White Service, Inc.; Cable Installation of Indiana, Inc.; Carbide Cutting Tools Abrasives, Inc.; Centin Corp.; Coast Asset Management Corp.; CPM Construction Planning and Management, Inc.; Electronic Communications, Inc.; Equity Properties Development Ltd.; FBO America; First Capital Insured Real Estate Limited; George A. Hormel & Company; Hercules Engine Co.; The Horace Mann Insurance Companies; Inland Container Corporation; Lopax, Inc.; Medical Business Services, Inc.; Millburn Peat Co., Inc.; Minnesota Fire & Casualty; MIC General Insurance Corp.; National Auto Credit, Inc.; National Grange Insurance Co.; National Property Development, Inc.; National Food Processors Assn.; Now Courier & Messenger, Inc.; Now Records Services, Inc.; O.E.S. Inc. of Kentucky; Oil Equipment Supply Corp.; Paden Engineering Co., Inc.; Penn-America Insurance Co.; Professional Careers Institute; RWB Communications, Inc.; Republic Claims Service; Republic Western Insurance Co.; Rodney D. Young Insurance Co.; The Rowland Associates, Inc.; The Ryland Group, Inc.; St. Clair Construction, Inc.; The St. Paul Insurance Companies; Simonds Manufacturing Corporation; Snap-On, Inc.; The Sign Group, Inc.; Stewart Title Guaranty Co.; Transcraft Corporation; Trident Marine Managers, Inc.; U-Haul Companies; U-Haul International, Inc.; Van Den Bergh Food Co.; Voest-Alpine Industries, Inc.; Wallace Grain Co., Inc.; Wesco, Inc.

CHURCH, CHURCH, HITTLE & ANTRIM

INDIANAPOLIS, INDIANA

(See Noblesville)

General Civil Trial Practice in all State and Federal Courts. Appellate and Federal Practice, Personal Injury, Automobile Accidents, Wrongful Death, Family Law, Adoption Law, Child Custody, Child Support, Divorce, Visitation Rights, Municipal and Governmental Regulations, Real Estate, Zoning Law, Land Use, Commercial Leasing, Wills, Probate, Trusts and Estates, Estate Planning, Asset Protection, Guardianship Law, Estate Administration and Litigation, Tax Planning, Tax Controversies, Business Law, Contracts, Litigation, Business Enterprises, Business Transactions, Corporate Formation, Corporate Litigation, School Law, Commercial Litigation, Professional License Defense, Medical Malpractice, Bankruptcy, Criminal Law, Driving While Intoxicated, Drug Crimes, Felonies, Misdemeanors, Mediation.

SEAN M. CLAPP, LLC

INDIANAPOLIS, INDIANA

(See Fishers)

Commercial Real Estate, Residential Real Estate, Title Claims, Foreclosures, Landlord and Tenant Law, Mortgages, Eminent Domain, Real Estate Tax Law, Commercial Leasing, Construction Law, Business Litigation, Copyright and Trademark Law, Internet Law, Business Enterprises, Limited Liability Company Law, Professional Practices, Small Business Law, Closely Held Business, Corporate Law, Partnerships, Buying and Selling of Businesses, Collections, Creditor's Rights, Business Law, Business Planning, Contracts, Intellectual Property, Trade Secrets, Business Start-Ups.

CLARK, QUINN, MOSES, SCOTT & GRAHN, LLP

Established in 1957

ONE INDIANA SQUARE, SUITE 2200
INDIANAPOLIS, INDIANA 46204-2011
Telephone: 317-637-1321
Fax: 317-687-2344
Email: lawyers@clarkquinnlaw.com
URL: http://www.clarkquinnlaw.com

General Practice and Litigation in State and Federal Courts, Real Estate, Land Use and Zoning, Corporate, Mergers and Acquisitions, Probate and Estate Planning, Public Utility, Family/Domestic Relations, Employment, Juvenile and Criminal Defense Law.

(This Listing Continued)

FIRM PROFILE: Clark Quinn is a general practice Law Firm founded in 1957 providing innovative, results-oriented yet practical solutions to local, regional and national organizations and individuals. The Firm provides quality professional legal services in a highly personalized environment with the primary objective of assisting our clients achieve their goals in the most efficient, cost effective and timely manner. The Firm has an extensive real estate, land use, business, estate and probate, public utility and litigation practice.

MEMBERS OF FIRM

JOSEPH M. HOWARD (—1964)

THOMAS M. QUINN, SR. (1909-1973)

PETER A. PAPPAS (1922-1986)

ALEX M. CLARK (1916-1991)

THOMAS MICHAEL QUINN, born Indianapolis, Indiana, February 12, 1937; admitted to bar, 1963, Indiana and U.S. District Court, Southern and Northern Districts of Indiana. *Education:* Indiana University (B.S., 1959); Columbia University (J.D., 1962). Phi Delta Phi. Chief Deputy Reporter, Indiana Supreme and Appellate Courts, 1964-1965. *Member:* Indianapolis (Member and Chairman, 1989, Land Use Section) and Indiana State Bar Associations. ***PRACTICE AREAS:*** Zoning Law; Planning Law; Land Use; Real Estate Law. **Email:** mikequinn@clarkquinnlaw.com

JOHN M. MOSES, born Charleston, West Virginia, July 6, 1950; admitted to bar, 1980, Indiana and U.S. District Court, Southern and Northern Districts of Indiana. *Education:* Boston University; University of Colorado (B.A., 1973); Indiana University (J.D., 1980). Deputy Prosecutor, Marion County, 1981-1982. *Member:* Indianapolis and Indiana State Bar Associations. ***PRACTICE AREAS:*** Criminal Law. **Email:** johnmoses@clarkquinnlaw.com

J. MURRAY CLARK, born Indianapolis, Indiana, November 3, 1957; admitted to bar, 1982, Indiana and U.S. District Court, Southern and Northern Districts of Indiana. *Education:* Kenyon College (B.A., 1979); Indiana University School of Law-Indianapolis (J.D., 1982). Indiana State Senate, 1994—. *Member:* Indianapolis (Member, Land Use Section) and Indiana State Bar Associations. ***PRACTICE AREAS:*** Real Estate Law; Zoning Law; Planning Law; Land Use; Business Law. **Email:** murrayclark@clarkquinnlaw.com

MATTHEW R. CLARK, born Indianapolis, Indiana, November 17, 1958; admitted to bar, 1985, Indiana and U.S. District Court, Southern and Northern Districts of Indiana; U.S. Tax Court; U.S. Court of Claims. *Education:* University of Wyoming (B.S., high honors, 1981); Indiana University (J.D., 1985). Assistant Attorney, Indiana State Senate Majority, 1987. *Member:* Indianapolis (Vice President-2006; Member-Land Use Section) and Indiana State Bar Associations. ***PRACTICE AREAS:*** Real Estate Law; Litigation; Business Law; Family Law. **Email:** mattclark@clarkquinnlaw.com

ROBERT B. SCOTT, born Lafayette, Indiana, 1961; admitted to bar, 1988, Indiana and U.S. District Court, Southern and Northern Districts of Indiana. *Education:* Indiana University (B.S., 1983); Valparaiso University (J.D., 1988). *Member:* Indianapolis (Member, Business Law Section), Indiana State (Chair, Water and Wastewater Division, 1994-1995, Utility Law Section) and American (Member, Business and Public Utility Sections) Bar Associations. ***PRACTICE AREAS:*** Business Law; Utility Law; Real Estate Law. **Email:** rscott@clarkquinnlaw.com

CHARLES R. GRAHN, born Indianapolis, Indiana, January 6, 1952; admitted to bar, 1977, Indiana and U.S. District Court, Southern and Northern Districts of Indiana. *Education:* Indiana University (A.B., 1974; J.D., 1977). *Member:* Indianapolis and Indiana State Bar Associations; Indianapolis Bar Foundation (Director, 2003). ***PRACTICE AREAS:*** Probate Law; Civil Litigation; Real Estate Law. **Email:** erg@clarkquinnlaw.com

ASSOCIATES

ROBERT V. CLUTTER, born Marion, Indiana, June 13, 1961; admitted to bar, 1988, Indiana and U.S. District Court, Southern and Northern Districts of Indiana. *Education:* Purdue University (B.S.I.E., 1984); Indiana University (J.D., 1988). *Member:* Indianapolis, Indiana State and American Bar Associations; The Association of Trial Lawyers of America. ***PRACTICE AREAS:*** Zoning Law; Planning Law; Land Use; Civil Litigation; Criminal Litigation. **Email:** bobclutter@clarkquinnlaw.com

FRANK D. OTTE, born Indianapolis, Indiana, 1970; admitted to bar, 1997, Indiana, Montana and U.S. District Court, Southern and Northern Districts of Indiana. *Education:* Indiana University, Bloomington (B.S., 1993; J.D., 1997). *Member:* Indianapolis and Indiana State Bar Associations. ***PRACTICE AREAS:*** Litigation; Estate Planning; Probate Law; Utility Law; Business Law. **Email:** fotte@clarkquinnlaw.com

RALPH W. STAPLES, JR., born Gary, Indiana, August 5, 1962; admitted to bar, 1987, Indiana. *Education:* Grinnell College (B.A., 1984); Indiana University (J.D., 1986). *Member:* Indianapolis Bar Association. ***PRACTICE AREAS:*** Business Law; Administrative Law; Civil Litigation; Criminal Defense. **Email:** ralphstaples@clarkquinnlaw.com

JOHN B. ("BART") HERRIMAN, born Marion, Indiana, January 14, 1969; admitted to bar, 1996, Indiana, U.S. District Court, Southern and Northern Districts of Indiana. *Education:* Indiana University (B.S., 1993); St. Louis University School of Law (J.D., 1996). Chairman, Indiana Alcohol and Tobacco Commission, 2003-2005. *Member:* Indiana State Bar Association (Member, Sections on: Land Use, Government Practice). ***PRACTICE AREAS:*** Real Estate; Zoning, Planning and Land Use; Alcoholic Beverages. **Email:** bherriman@clarkquinnlaw.com

DAVID PATRICK COYNE, born Knox, Indiana, September 1, 1973; admitted to bar, 2000, Indiana and U.S. District Court, Southern and Northern Districts of Indiana. *Education:* Ball State University (B.A., 1996); Indiana University School of Law-Indianapolis (J.D., 2000). *Member:* Indianapolis, Indiana State and American Bar Associations. ***PRACTICE AREAS:*** Real Estate Law; Business Law. **Email:** davidcoyne@clarkquinnlaw.com

JEFFREY L. STAYTE, born Indianapolis, Indiana, November 15, 1972; admitted to bar, 2002, Indiana and U.S. District Court, Southern and Northern Districts of Indiana. *Education:* Butler University (B.S., 1996); Indiana University School of Law, Indianapolis

(This Listing Continued)

CLARK, QUINN, MOSES, SCOTT & GRAHN, LLP, Indianapolis—Continued

(J.D., 2002). *Member:* Indianapolis and Indiana State Bar Associations. ***PRACTICE AREAS:*** Real Estate Law; Litigation; Business Law. ***Email:*** jeffreystayte@clarkquinnlaw.com

OF COUNSEL

JAMES C. CLARK, born Indianapolis, Indiana, April 13, 1929; admitted to bar, 1956, Indiana and U.S. District Court, Southern and Northern Districts of Indiana. *Education:* Wabash College (B.A., 1951); Indiana University (J.D., 1956). Representative to the Indiana General Assembly, 1963-1964. Member: Metropolitan Plan Commission of Marion County, 1976; Metropolitan Board of Zoning Appeals, 1975. *Member:* Indianapolis (Estate Planning Section) and Indiana State Bar Associations. ***PRACTICE AREAS:*** Probate Law; Business Law. ***Email:*** jimclark@clarkquinnlaw.com

RAYMOND J. GRAHN, born Bible Grove, Illinois, April 29, 1921; admitted to bar, 1945, Indiana and U.S. District Court, Southern and Northern Districts of Indiana. *Education:* Butler University (B.A., 1942); Indiana University (LL.B., 1945). *Member:* Indianapolis and Indiana State Bar Associations. ***PRACTICE AREAS:*** Probate Law; Real Estate Law; Civil Litigation. ***Email:*** rgrahn@clarkquinnlaw.com

REPRESENTATIVE CLIENTS: Albertson's/Osco; Amli Residential; CVS; Davis Homes LLC; Fort Harrison Reuse Authority; Gem Utilities, Inc.; Hamilton Southeastern Utilities, Inc.; Home Depot U.S.A., Inc.; Indianapolis Colts; Justus Companies; Kite Development Corp.; Kroger; Landmark Properties; Lowe's; Mallory Sonalert; Marina Limited Partnership; Meijer's; M/I Shottenstein; National Wine & Spirits Corporation; North American Capacitor; Paul I. Cripe, Inc.; Primax Properties; Sunbeam Corporation; Target Corporation; Truck Engineering Company; U-Stor Self Storage Warehouse; Verizon Wireless; Village Pantry; Walmart; Waterway Holdings.

CLEVELAND & HARVEY

an association of attorneys

Established in 2005

6910 N. SHADELAND AVENUE

SUITE 200

INDIANAPOLIS, INDIANA 46220

Telephone: 317-890-2460; Mobile 317-590-7815

Fax: 317-890-1731

URL: http://www.tharpinvest.com

Email: pcleveland@tharpinvest.com

URL: http://www.lawyers.com/petercleveland

Real Estate Development and Transactions, Zoning, Planning and Land Use and Real Estate Litigation.

FIRM PROFILE: Concentrating in Real Estate Transactions, Zoning and Land Use and Real Estate Litigation.

PETER D. CLEVELAND, born Chicago, Illinois, December 20, 1955; admitted to bar, 1981, Indiana. *Education:* University of North Carolina at Chapel Hill (B.A., 1978); Indiana University (J.D., 1981). Phi Eta Sigma. Faculty: "Land Use Litigation: The Land Use Lawyer's Toolbox," Planning and Zoning, Indiana Continuing Legal Education Forum, 1999; "Land Use Litigation," Indiana Environmental Law, Federal Publications Seminars, 1994, 1995; "Land Use Litigation," National Business Institute, 1993; "Boundary Disputes in Indiana," National Business Institute, 1992. *Member:* Indianapolis (Chair, Land Use Law Section, 1995), Indiana State and American Bar Associations. ***REPORTED CASES:*** Rieddle v. Buckner, 629 N.E. 2nd 860 (Ind. Ct.App. 1994); Town of Avon v. Harville, 718 N.E.2d 1194 (Ind.Ct.App. 1999). ***TRANSACTIONS:*** Twenty-five Million Dollar commercial property sale; Large development projects. ***PRACTICE AREAS:*** Real Estate Law; Land Use; Zoning Law; Real Estate Litigation. ***Email:*** pcleveland@tharpinvest.com

ERIC A. HARVEY, born Connersville, Indiana, June 24, 1968; admitted to bar, 2004, Indiana. *Education:* Indiana Wesleyan University (B.S., with honors, 1997); Indiana University (J.D., 2004). Real Estate License, Indiana, 2001. ***SPECIAL AGENCIES:*** Indiana Commercial Board of Realtors. ***TRANSACTIONS:*** Convenience Store and Business Asset Transactions. ***PRACTICE AREAS:*** Real Estate (80%); Real Estate Litigation (20%). ***Email:*** eharvey@tharpinvest.com

REPRESENTATIVE CLIENTS: Tharp Investments, Inc.; Capital City Ford; J.D. Restaurants, Inc.; Eckhart & Company, Inc.; Central Indiana Farm Bureau Coop, Inc.; Trammell Crow Company; Richard E. Nichols Associates, Inc.; YMCA of Greater Indianapolis; Real Property Services Corp.; Ameritech.

COHEN GARELICK & GLAZIER

A PROFESSIONAL CORPORATION

Established in 1904

SUITE 800, KEYSTONE CROSSING PLAZA

8888 KEYSTONE CROSSING BOULEVARD

INDIANAPOLIS, INDIANA 46240

Telephone: 317-573-8888

Telecopier: 317-574-3855

Email: ccohen@cgglawfirm.com

URL: http://www.cgglawfirm.com

General Civil Trial Practice in all State and Federal Courts. Business Law, Litigation, Corporate Law, Partnership Law, Commercial Law, Taxation, Divorce, Family Law, Personal Injury, Criminal Law, Creditors Rights, Bankruptcy, Probate, Wills, Trusts and Estates, Estate Planning, Real Estate, Construction Law, Civil Rights, Labor and Employment, Employee Benefits, Medical Malpractice, Patents, Trademarks, Intellectual Property, Alternative Dispute Resolution, Collections, Nonprofit and Charitable Organizations.

(This Listing Continued)

FIRM PROFILE: Cohen Garelick & Glazier traces its origins to 1904 and has a history of providing comprehensive legal services to a wide range of clients throughout Indiana and the nation. The firm is dedicated to providing clients with complete and expert attention to every facet of their legal needs.

CHARLES A. COHEN, born Greenville, Kentucky, September 17, 1941; admitted to bar, 1967, Indiana; 1969, Ohio. *Education:* Indiana University (B.S., 1963; J.D., with distinction, 1966). Beta Gamma Sigma; Order of the Coif. Symposium Editor, Indiana University Law Journal, 1965-1966. Author: "Policy and Procedure in Abstention: Is The Pullman Retention Technique Proper?" 40 Indiana Law Journal 248; "The Estate Tax Marital Deduction Revenue Procedure 64-19," 41 Indiana Law Journal 711. *Member:* Indianapolis and Indiana State Bar Associations. ***PRACTICE AREAS:*** Corporate Law; Taxation; Trusts and Estates; Estate and Gift Taxation; Wills; Business Law. ***Email:*** ccohen@cgglawfirm.com

ROBERT A. GARELICK, born Chicago, Illinois, July 28, 1941; admitted to bar, 1966, Indiana. *Education:* Indiana University (A.B., 1963; J.D. with distinction, 1966). Phi Delta Phi. Senior Writer, Indiana University Law Journal, 1965-1966. Deputy Prosecutor, Marion County, 1971. President, Indiana University (Bloomington) Law School Alumni Association, 1984-1985. Certified Mediator, State of Indiana. *Member:* Indianapolis (Vice President, 1973), Indiana State and American Bar Associations; Indiana Trial Lawyers Association; Indianapolis Lawyers Club (President, 1993, 1994). ***REPORTED CASES:*** Knauf Fiber Glass, GmbH vs. Stein (1993), Ind., 622 N.E. 2d 163; Rheem Mfg, Co. v. Phelps Heating & Air Conditioning, Inc. (2001), Ind. 746 N.E.2d 941; Valinet vs. Eskew (1991), Ind., 574 N.E.2d 283; Fogle vs. Shah (1989), Ind.App., 539 N.E.2d 500; Century Personnel, Inc. vs. Brummett (1986), Ind.App., 499 N.E.2d 1160; Kennedy vs. St Joseph Memorial Hospital of Kokomo, Indiana (1985), Ind.App., 482 N.E.2d 268; Indiana Bell Tel. Co., Inc. vs. O'Bryan (1980), Ind.App., 408 N.E.2d 178; Robinson vs. Century Personnel, Inc. (1997), Ind. App., 678 N.E.2d 1268; Lak, Inc. vs. Deer Creek Enterprises (1992), 7th Cir., 976 F.2d 328; Curry vs. U.S. (1985), 7th Cir., 774 F.2d 852. ***PRACTICE AREAS:*** Litigation; Family Law; Personal Injury; Mediation of Civil and Family Law Disputes; Divorce; Business Litigation; Commercial Litigation. ***Email:*** bgarelick@cgglawfirm.com

STEVEN J. GLAZIER, born Indianapolis, Indiana, July 16, 1956; admitted to bar, 1980, Indiana. *Education:* Indiana University (B.S., 1977; J.D., magna cum laude, 1980). Phi Delta Phi. Master Court Commissioner, Marion Superior Court, Room 7, 1982-1983. *Member:* Indianapolis Bar Association (Chairman, Family Law Section, 1984). ***PRACTICE AREAS:*** Real Estate; Litigation. ***Email:*** sglazier@cgglawfirm.com

STEVEN M. CRELL, born Fort Wayne, Indiana, February 14, 1963; admitted to bar, 1988, Indiana; 1989, U.S. Tax Court; 1990, U.S. Court of Appeals, Seventh Circuit. *Education:* Ball State University (B.S., Accounting, 1985); Indiana University (J.D., 1988). Phi Delta Phi. Recipient, Francis J. Feeny, Jr. Tax Award. *Member:* Indianapolis, Indiana and American Bar Associations; Sagamore American Inn of Court. ***REPORTED CASES:*** Roger v. American Testing & Engineering Corp., 734 N.E.2d 606 (Ind. Ct. App. 2000); Robinson v. Century Personnel, Inc.; 678 N.e.2d 1268 (Ind. Ct. App. 1997); Krauf Fiberglass, Gumgh v. Stein, 622 N.E.2d 163 (Ind. 1993); Valinet v. Eskew, 574 N.E.2d 283 (Ind. 1991). ***PRACTICE AREAS:*** Business Transactions; Corporate Law; Business Litigation; Real Estate; Business; Tax Litigation. ***Email:*** screll@cgglawfirm.com

EDWARD F. SCHRAGER, born South Bend, Indiana, April 18, 1953; admitted to bar, 1980, Indiana and U.S. District Court, Northern and Southern Districts of Indiana; U.S. Supreme Court. *Education:* Indiana University (B.A., 1976; J.D., 1980). Registered Mediator, Civil and Family Law, 1995—. Deputy Prosecutor: Greene County, 1980-1982; Monroe County, 1982-1984. Member, Judicial Nominating Committee, United Stated District Court, Southern District of Indiana, 2001. *Member:* Indianapolis, Indiana State and American Bar Associations; The Association of Trial Lawyers of America; Indiana Trial Lawyers Association. ***REPORTED CASES:*** Ingram v. State, Indiana Supreme Court, 718 N.E.2d 379, 1999 Ind.; US v. Miller, 159 F.3d 1106, 50 Fed. R. Evid. Serv. 906, 7th Cir. Ind. 1998; Parsons v. Bourff, 739 F. Supp. 1266, U.S. Dist. Ct., Southern Dist. Ind., 1989; US v. Taylor, 196 F.3d 854, U.S. Dist. Ct., 7th Cir. Ind. 1999. ***PRACTICE AREAS:*** Business Litigation; Commercial Litigation; Criminal Law; Corporate Law; Domestic Relations; Mediation. ***Email:*** eschrager@cgglawfirm.com

RUSSELL L. JONES, born East Chicago, Indiana, December 14, 1958; admitted to bar, 1985, Indiana. *Education:* Eastern Kentucky University (B.S., 1980); Indiana University (J.D., 1985). *Member:* Hamilton County, Indianapolis and Indiana State Bar Associations. ***PRACTICE AREAS:*** Real Estate; Construction Law; Civil Litigation; Commercial Litigation; Commercial Collections. ***Email:*** rjones@cgglawfirm.com

SANDRA LAZARUS ROTHBAUM, born Indianapolis, Indiana, August 29, 1944; admitted to bar, 1984, Indiana and U.S. District Court, Southern and Northern Districts of Indiana. *Education:* Harvard University (A.B., cum laude, 1966); University of Wisconsin-Madison (A.M., 1967); Indiana University (J.D., summa cum laude, 1984). Recipient, American Jurisprudence Awards in Property, Estates and Family Law; BNA Award. Associate Editor, Indiana Law Review, 1983-1984. Author: "Property, 1983 Survey of Recent Developments in Indiana Law," 17 Ind. L. Rev. 301. *Member:* Indianapolis and Indiana State Bar Associations. ***LANGUAGES:*** Spanish. ***PRACTICE AREAS:*** Probate; Trusts and Estates; Estate and Gift Taxation; Wills. ***Email:*** srothbaum@cgglawfirm.com

BRADLEY H. COHEN, born San Antonio, Texas, October 21, 1966; admitted to bar, 1991, Illinois and U.S. District Court, Northern District of Illinois; 1992, Indiana and U.S. District Court, Northern and Southern Districts of Indiana; 1993, U.S. Claims Court. *Education:* Indiana University (B.A., 1988); Boston University (J.D., with honors, 1991). *Member:* Indianapolis, Indiana State and American Bar Associations. ***PRACTICE AREAS:*** Business Law; Corporate Law; Trusts and Estates; Estate and Gift Taxation; Taxation; Wills; Probate. ***Email:*** bcohen@cgglawfirm.com

JILL E. GOLDENBERG, born Baltimore, Maryland, March 25, 1968; admitted to bar, 1993, Indiana. *Education:* Indiana University (B.S. in Business, with distinction, 1990); Boston University School of Law (J.D., 1993). *Member:* Indianapolis, Indiana State and American Bar Associations. (Board Certified, Family Law Specialist, Indiana State Bar Association, Family Law Certification Board). ***REPORTED CASES:*** Guardianship of

(This Listing Continued)

C.M.W. (2001) Ind. App., 755 N.E.2d 644; Bowles v. Bowles (1999) Ind.App., 721 N.E.2d 1247; Gorman v. Ziegler (1998) Ind. App., 690 N.E.2d 729. ***PRACTICE AREAS:*** Family Law; Mediation. **Email:** jgoldenberg@cgglawfirm.com

BRYAN S. REDDING, born Indianapolis, Indiana, January 20, 1967; admitted to bar, 1994, Indiana and U.S. District Court, Southern and Northern Districts of Indiana; registered to practice before U.S. Patent and Trademark Office. *Education:* Purdue University (B.S.M.E., 1991); Indiana University (J.D., cum laude, 1994). *Member:* Indianapolis and Indiana State Bar Associations; Indiana Trial Lawyers Association; The Association of Trial Lawyers of America. ***REPORTED CASES:*** Rheem Mfg. Co. v. Phelps Heating & Air Conditioning, Inc. (2001) Ind., 746 N.E. 2d 941; Campbell v. El Dee Apts (1998) Ind.App. 701 N.E.3d 616. ***PRACTICE AREAS:*** Patents; Trademarks; Copyrights; Intellectual Property; Civil Litigation; Real Estate; Personal Injury; Medical Malpractice; Business Law; Family Law. **Email:** bredding@cgglawfirm.com

HEATHER S. WYSONG ZAIGER, born Kokomo, Indiana, July 13, 1974; admitted to bar, 2002, Indiana and U.S. District Court, Northern and Southern Districts of Indiana. *Education:* Indiana University (B.A., Sociology, Honors Degree, 1997; J.D., 2002). Former Associate, Church Church Hittle & Antrim. *Member:* Indianapolis, Hamilton County, Indiana State and American Bar Associations; The Association of Trial Lawyers of America. ***PRACTICE AREAS:*** Domestic Relations; Family Law; Civil Litigation; Appellate Practice. **Email:** hwysong@cgglawfirm.com

OF COUNSEL

JOSEPH J. REISWERG, born Indianapolis, Indiana, June 15, 1948; admitted to bar, 1974, Indiana; 1980, U.S. Supreme Court. *Education:* Indiana University (B.S., 1970; J.D., 1974); Civil Mediation Training (1998). Deputy Attorney General, 1974-1976. Assistant Corporation Counsel, City of Indianapolis, 1977-1988. Staff Attorney, Indiana Lawyers Commission, 1976-1977. Author: "Diabetes Care in Schools: Benefits and Pitfalls of Public Law 94-142," The Diabetes Educator 17:33, Jan/Feb., 1991. *Member:* Indianapolis and Indiana State Bar Associations; Association of Trial Lawyers of America; Indiana Trial Lawyers Association. ***PRACTICE AREAS:*** Personal Injury Law; Litigation; Medical Malpractice. **Email:** jreiswerg@cgglawfirm.com

RICHARD L. DARST, born Muncie, Indiana, April 30, 1944; admitted to bar, 1969, Indiana and U.S. District Court, Southern District of Indiana; 1973, U.S. Court of Appeals, Seventh Circuit; 1979, U.S. Supreme Court. *Education:* Indiana University (A.B., 1966; J.D., 1969). Phi Alpha Delta (Vice President, 1968-1969). Member, Indiana Law Journal, 1967-1968. Attorney, U.S. Department of Justice, 1969-1970. Assistant U.S. Attorney, Southern District of Indiana, 1970-1977. Deputy Corporation Counsel, City of Indianapolis, 1977-1981. First Assistant U.S. Attorney, 1981-1984. Interim United States Attorney, 1984. Special Assistant to the U.S. Attorney, 1984. Member, Seventh Circuit Court of Appeals Advisory Committee to Study Pro Bono Appointments in Federal Civil Cases, 1981-1984, Southern District of Indiana Local Rules Advisory Committee, 1979-1981. President, Indiana Affiliate, 1998-1999. *Member:* Indianapolis, Seventh Circuit (President, 2000-2001), Indiana State and American Bar Associations; National Employment Lawyers Association. ***PRACTICE AREAS:*** Federal Litigation; Litigation; General Practice. **Email:** rdarst@cgglawfirm.com

SAMUEL J. MANTEL (1893-1978)

THOMAS D. MANTEL (Retired)

REPRESENTATIVE CLIENTS: Century Personnel; Karma Records; Williams Realty; Capitol Construction Services, Inc.; Herman & Kittle Properties; Wurster Construction Co., Inc.; Jewish Federation of Greater Indianapolis; Neodontics International, Inc.; Hunter Dental Laboratory; Repucare, Inc.; Kayak Pools Midwest; Benefit Consultants, Inc.; Bacompt Systems, Inc.; Bay Development Corp.; Gateway Contracting Services; Oncology & Hematology Associates, Inc.; CorVase M.D.'s, P.C.; Garrity Tool Company, Inc.; Specialty Risk International, Inc.; PK Partners, LLC.
REFERENCES: The National Bank of Indianapolis; HPS Office Systems, LLC; Complete Office Supply.

COHEN & MALAD, LLP

Established in 1970

ONE INDIANA SQUARE
SUITE 1400
INDIANAPOLIS, INDIANA 46204
Telephone: 317-636-6481
Fax: 317-636-2593
URL: http://www.cohenandmalad.com

General Civil Practice, State and Federal Courts. Commercial, Class Actions, Insurance, Probate and Estate Planning, Real Estate, Personal Injury, Securities Litigation and Family/Domestic Relations Law, Foreclosure and Creditor's Rights.

FIRM PROFILE: Cohen & Malad, LLP has grown from its inception in 1970 into a full-service law firm practicing extensively in all Indiana courts and in federal courts nationwide, facilitating its strong practice in commercial litigation, securities fraud and class actions. The firm services many individual clients for personal injury, family law, real estate and estate planning. Its commercial practice includes representation of banks, mortgage lenders, corporations, insurance companies in regulatory and defense matters, class actions, securities fraud, collection, aviation litigation and general civil litigation. The firm presents the capability of handling all sizes and types of cases, but with the benefits of the personal attention of a smaller firm. The firm was awarded Heartland Pro Bono Council's 2003 Law Firm Pro Bono award.

LOUIS F. COHEN (1936-1992)

RICHARD M. MALAD, born Indianapolis, Indiana, January 6, 1946; admitted to bar, 1973, Indiana; 1980, U.S. Supreme Court. *Education:* Marian College (B.S., 1968); Indiana University (J.D., cum laude, 1973). Lecturer: Lorman Education Services, Foreclosure and Repossession, 2000-2001, 2002, 2003, 2004, 2005; Lorman Education Service, Foreclosure in Indiana, 2001, 2002. Marion County Deputy Prosecutor, 1973-1974. Marion County Superior Court Commissioner, 1977-1978. *Member:* Indianapolis and Indiana State Bar Associations; Indiana Trial Lawyers Association; The Association of Trial Lawyers of America. ***PRACTICE AREAS:*** Mortgage Foreclosure; Creditor Bankruptcy; Lenders Rights; Personal Injury; Commercial Law and Litigation; Business Law and Litigation; Real Estate Law and Litigation. **Email:** rmalad@cohenandmalad.com

IRWIN B. LEVIN, born Indianapolis, Indiana, September 19, 1953; admitted to bar, 1978, Indiana. *Education:* Indiana University—Purdue University at Indianapolis (B.A., 1974); Indiana University (J.D., 1978). Marion County Circuit Court Commissioner, 1978. Judge Pro Tempore, Marion County Circuit Court, 1979. Chairman, Indiana Continuing Legal Education Forum, Class Action Seminar, 1995. Lecturer, ATLA Seminar, "Hormone Therapy Litigation: A Primer," paper presented entitled "Claims and Defenses," September 14, 2004. Recipient: Hoosier Freedom Award; Distinguished Alumni Award, Indiana University School of Law, 2002. *Member:* Indianapolis, Indiana State, Federal and Seventh Circuit Bar Associations; Indiana Trial Lawyers Association (Member, Securities Litigation Committee); The Association of Trial Lawyers of America. ***REPORTED CASES:*** In re: Holocaust Victim Assets Litigation, 105 F.Supp. 2d 139 (E.D.N.Y. 2000); In re: Bridgestone/Firestone, Inc., 128 F.Supp. 2d 1198; Shelton v. Wick, 715 N.E.2d 890 (Ind. App.1999); American Cyanamid v. Stephen, 623 N.E.2d 1065 (Ind. App. 1993); Burger-Fischer v. DeGussa Ag., 65 F. Supp. 2d 248 (D.N.J. 1999); Stansky v. Cummins Engine Co., Inc. (Fed. Sec. L. Rep., P.98.668), 51 F 1329, 63 USLW 2656 (C.A.7 1995); Gregory v. Home Insurance Co., 876 F.2d 602, Rico Bus. Disp. Guide 7 (C.A.7 1989); In re: Austrian, German Holocaust Litigation, 2001 WL 521 464 (C.A.2 N.Y., 2001); In re: Nazi Era Cases Against German Defendants Litigation, 198 F.R.D. 429 (D.N.J. 2000); Winter v. Assicurazioni, 2000 WL 1858482 (S.D.N.Y. 2000); Core Funding Group, LLC v. Young, 792 N.E.2d 547, Ind. App., July 22, 2003; Associated Medical Networks, Ltd. v. Lewis, 785 N.E. 2d 230. Ind. App., Feb 26, 2003, Time Waarner Entertainment Co., L.P. v. Whiteman, 802 N.E.2d 886 (Ind. 2004). ***PRACTICE AREAS:*** Commercial Litigation; Class Action Litigation; Securities Litigation; Insurance Law; Personal Injury Litigation; International Law; Mass Torts. **Email:** ilevin@cohenandmalad.com

RICHARD N. BELL, born Bloomington, Indiana, September 2, 1947; admitted to bar, 1975, Indiana and U.S. District Court, Southern and Northern Districts of Indiana; 1979, U.S. Tax Court; 1988, U.S. Court of Appeals, 7th and 11th Circuits. *Education:* Indiana University (B.S., 1970; J.D. 1975). Author: "How To Help Design a Retirement Plan That Best Suits Your Client," July 1982, Practical Accountant. Board Member, Indiana University at Indianapolis Law School Alumni Association, 1980-1983. *Member:* Indianapolis, Indiana State (Member, Taxation Committee, 1975), Federal, American (Member, Professional Service Corporations, Section of Taxation, 1978—) and Seventh Circuit Bar Associations; Indiana Trial Lawyers Association; The Association of Trial Lawyers of America; Indiana Certified Public Accountants Society (Chairman, Taxation Committee, 1981-1982); American Institute of Certified Public Accountants. [1st Lt., Medical Service Corps, U.S. Army Reserves, 1971-1979]. ***REPORTED CASES:*** Stransky v. Cummins Engine Co, Inc., 51F 3d 1329 (7th Cir. 1996); In re Smith, 128 B.R. 488 (S.D.Fla. Jun 19, 1991); Dudley vs. Ski World, Inc., 1989 WL 73208, Fed. Sec. L. Rep. P 94,384 (S.D.Ind., Feb 20, 1989); Dudley vs. Ski World, Inc., 1989 WL 73207, Fed. Sec. L. Rep. P 94,383 (S.D.Ind., Jan 25, 1989); Morey vs. Bravo Productions, Inc., 1987 WL 28526, Fed. Sec. L. Rep. P 93,554 (S.D.N.Y., Dec. 02, 1987); Huffman vs. Anderson, 118 F.R.D. 97, 10 Fed.R.Serv. 3d 238 (N.D.Ind., Nov 10, 1987); Greenfield vs. Greenfield, 591 N.E. 2d 1057 (Ind. App. 1 Dist., May 28, 1992). ***PRACTICE AREAS:*** Taxation Law; Pension and Profit Sharing Law; Securities and Class Action Litigation; Sports and Entertainment. **Email:** rbell@cohenandmalad.com

DAVID J. CUTSHAW, born South Bend, Indiana, August 20, 1956; admitted to bar, 1982, Indiana and U.S. District Court, Southern and Northern Districts of Indiana; U.S. Court of Appeals, Seventh Circuit. *Education:* University of Indianapolis (B.A., 1978); Indiana University (J.D., 1982). Phi Delta Phi. Consultant/Contributing Author: *Indiana Civil Trial Guide,*Mathew Bender, July 1, 1992. *Member:* Indianapolis and Indiana State Bar Associations; Seventh Circuit Bar Association; Indiana Trial Lawyers Association. ***REPORTED CASES:*** Stransky v. Cummins Engine Co., Inc., 51F3d 1329 (7th Cir. 1995); Dudley v. Ski World, Par. 94,383 84 Fed.Sec.L.Rep. (CCH S.D. Ind. 2-20-89); Gregory v. Home Ins. Co. 876 F.2d. 602 (7th Cir. 1989); Morey v. Bravo Productions, Inc., Par. 93,554 Fed.Sec.L.Rep. (cch) (S.D.N.Y. 1987); Collins v. Covenant Mutual Ins. Co., 644 N.E. 2d 116 (Ind. 1994); American Cyanamid Co. v. Stephen, 623 N.E. 2d 1065 (Ind. App. 1993); Boydston v. Chrysler Credit Corp., 511 N.E. 2d 318 (Ind. App. 1987); Kiracofe v. Reid Memorial Hospital 461 N.E.2d 1134 (Ind. App. 1984); Associated Medical Newtworks, Ltd. v. Lewis, 785 N.E.2d 230 (Ind. App. 2003); American Cyanamid v. Stephen, 600 N.E.2d 1387 (Ind.App. 1992); Huffman v. Hains, 865 F.2d 920 (C.A.7 (Ind.) 1989); Time Warner Entertainment Co. L.P. v. Whiteman, 802 N.E.2d 886 (Ind. 2004); Core Funding Group, LLC v. Young, 792 N.E.2d 547 (Ind. Ct. App. 2003); Vandeventer v. All American Life & Cos., Co., 101 S.W.3d 703 (Tex.App. 2003); Aide v. Chrysler Credit Corp., 699 N.E.2d 1177 (Ind. App. 1998); In re Greenwood Air Crash, 2873 F. Supp. 1257 (S.D. Ind. 1995). ***PRACTICE AREAS:*** Medical Malpractice; Personal Injury Law; Class Action Litigation; Securities Litigation; Aviation Litigation; Mass Torts. **Email:** dcutshaw@cohenandmalad.com

RICHARD E. SHEVITZ, born Indianapolis, Indiana, April 29, 1960; admitted to bar, 1985, Indiana and U.S. District Court, Northern and Southern Districts of Indiana; 1988, U.S. Supreme Court. *Education:* Indiana University (B.A., with honors, 1982); Ohio State University (J.D., 1985). Managing Editor, Ohio State University Journal of Alternative Dispute Resolution, 1984-1985. Law Clerk to Honorable Frank J. Otte, U.S. Bankruptcy Court, 1986-1987. *Member:* Indianapolis Bar Association. ***PRACTICE AREAS:*** Class Action Litigation; Securities Litigation; Healthcare; Consumer Law; Mass Torts. **Email:** rshevitz@cohenandmalad.com

GREGORY L. LAKER, born Lawrenceburg, Indiana, August 11, 1959; admitted to bar, 1984, Indiana and U.S. District Court, Northern and Southern Districts of Indiana. *Education:* Indiana University (B.S., 1981; J.D., 1984). Phi Delta Phi. Associate Editor, Indiana Law Review, 1981. Certified Family Law and Civil Mediator. *Member:* Indianapolis (Member, ADR Executive Committee) and Indiana State (Co-Chair, Alternative Dispute Resolution of Subcommittee of Family Law Section) Bar Associations; American Trial Lawyers Association; Indiana Trial Lawyers Association. ***REPORTED CASES:*** U.S. Metalsource Corp. v. Simpson (Ind. App. 4 Dist. 1995); 649 N.E. 2d 682 Waling v. Appel Service Co.,

(This Listing Continued)

COHEN & MALAD, LLP, Indianapolis—Continued

Inc. (Ind. App. 1 Dist. 1994), 641 N.E. 2nd 647; Simons v. Simons (Ind. App. 1 Dist. 1991), 566 N.E. 2d 551; Mehl v. Mehl (Ind. App. 1993), 619 N.E. 2d 615; Vann v. United Farm Family Mut. Ins. Co., 778 N.E. 2d 868 (Ind. App. 2002), trans. granted, 792 N.E. 2d 41 (N.E. 2d 41 (Ind. 2003), decision after remand, 790 N.E.2d 497 (Ind. App. 2003). ***PRACTICE AREAS:*** Personal Injury Litigation; Medical Malpractice; Wrongful Death; Mass Torts. ***Email:*** glaker@cohenandmalad.com

THOMAS L. BLACKBURN, born Linton, Indiana, August 29, 1958; admitted to bar, 1984, Indiana; 1985, U.S. District Court, Northern and Southern Districts of Indiana. *Education:* Indiana University (B.A., 1980; J.D., 1984). Member: The Order of Barristers; Moot Court Society. Speaker: NBI Seminar on Evidence in Trial Practice, 1991. *Member:* Indianapolis and Indiana State Bar Associations. ***REPORTED CASES:*** Indianapolis Housing Authority v. Pippin, 2000 WL 298615 (Ind. App. 2000); State v. Kevin Davis, 672 N.E. 2d 1365 (Ind. App. 1996). ***PRACTICE AREAS:*** Litigation; Commercial Litigation; Business Litigation; Trade Secrets Litigation. ***Email:*** tblackburn@cohenandmalad.com

DONALD D. LEVENHAGEN, born St. Louis, Missouri, May 22, 1959; admitted to bar, 1984, Indiana. *Education:* Creighton University (B.S.B.A., magna cum laude, 1981); Indiana University (J.D., cum laude, 1984). Beta Gamma Sigma. Member, Board of Editors, Indiana Law Journal, 1983-1984. Author: Note, "Class Actions: Judicial Control of Defense Communication With Absent Class Members," 59 Indiana Law Journal 133, 1983. *Member:* Indianapolis, Indiana State and American Bar Associations; Defense Trial Counsel of Indiana. ***REPORTED CASES:*** Lake Holiday Conservancy District v. Davison, 2004 WL 1048310 (Ind. Ct. App. 2004); Circle Centre Development Co. v. Y/G Indiana, L.P., 762 N.E.2d 176 (Ind. Ct. App. 2002); Community Action of Greater Indianapolis, Inc. v. Indiana Farmers Mutual Insurance Co., 708 N.E.2d 882 (Ind. Ct. App. 1999); Majors v. Engelbrecht, 149 F.3d 709 (7th Cir. 1998); Holman v. Koorsen Protection Services, Inc., 580 N.E.2d 984 (Ind. Ct. App. 1991); Weller v. Mack Trucks, Inc., 570 N.E.2d 1341 (Ind. Ct. App. 1991); Berns Construction Co., Inc. v. Miller, 491 N.E.2d 565 (Ind. Ct. App. 1986); Berns Construction Co., Inc. v. Miller, 516 N.E.2d 1053 (Ind. 1987). ***PRACTICE AREAS:*** Civil Litigation. ***Email:*** dlevenhagen@cohenandmalad.com

AREND J. ABEL, born 1960; admitted to bar, 1986, Indiana. *Education:* Ball State University (B.A., with honors in Telecommunications, magna cum laude, 1982); Indiana University School of Law (J.D., summa cum laude, 1986). Member, National Moot Court Team. Whitinger Scholar. Special Counsel, Indiana Attorney General Pamela Center, 1993-1996, with emphasis on appellate and United States Supreme Court practice. Member, State Board of Law Examiners. ***LANGUAGES:*** Spanish. ***PRACTICE AREAS:*** Appellate Practice; Bankruptcy; Civil Rights; Constitutional Law; Litigation. ***Email:*** aabel@cohenandmalad.com

SHOKRINA RADPOUR BEERING, born Brooklyn, New York, 1959; admitted to bar, 1986, Indiana. *Education:* Purdue University (B.A., 1981; M.S., 1983); Indiana University (J.D., 1986). Member, CREW Network. *Member:* American, Indiana State and Indianapolis Bar Associations. ***PRACTICE AREAS:*** Real Estate; Commercial Law; Financial Institutions Law; Business Law. ***Email:*** sbeering@cohenandmalad.com

BRIAN K. ZOELLER, born Tulsa, Oklahoma, January 26, 1970; admitted to bar, 1996, Indiana. *Education:* University of Indiana (B.A./B.S., cum laude with distinction, 1992); Indiana University (J.D., 1996). Author: Crime Victim's Litigation, Quarterly Vol. 2, No. #4, Nov. 95; Trial, Vol. 31 No. 6, June 1995. Certified Family Law Specialist. *Member:* Indianapolis and Indiana State Bar Associations. (Board Certified Family Law Specialist, Indiana State Bar Association, Family Law Certification Board). ***REPORTED CASES:*** Gilp v. Neville 681 N.E. 2d 1173. ***PRACTICE AREAS:*** Family Law. ***Email:*** bzoeller@cohenandmalad.com

---

MICHAEL C. ADLEY, born Hammond, Indiana, June 1, 1951; admitted to bar, 1979, Indiana, U.S. District Court, Northern and Southern Districts of Indiana and U.S. Court of Appeals, 7th Circuit. *Education:* Indiana University (B.A., 1973; J.D., cum laude, 1979). *Member:* Indiana State Bar Association. ***REPORTED CASES:*** Cochran v. CSX Transp., Inc., 112 F.Supp.2d 733 (N.D.Ind., Jun 30, 2000) (NO. 4:98 CV 57 AR); Martin v. American Nat. Can Co., 975 F.Supp. 1153 (N.D.Ind., Aug 25, 19997) (NO. 2:95-CV-168-RL); Gibbs v. National R.R. Passenger Corp., 170 F.R.D. 452 (N.D.Ind., Feb 27, 1997) (NO. 2:94CV226 JM); Reales v. Consolidated Rail Corp., 84 F.3d 993 (7th Cir.(Ind.), May 30, 1996) (NO. 95-2268); Civil City of South Bend, Ind. v. Consolidated Rail Corp., 880 F.Supp. 595 (N.D.Ind., Feb 14, 1995) (NO. 3:95-CV-29RM); Layden v. New Era Corp., 571 N.E.2d 547 (Ind.App. 3 Dist., Nov 01, 1990) (NO. 37A03-8812-CV-385); Consolidated Rail Corp. v. Travelers Ins. Companies, 466 N.E.2d 709 (Ind., Jul 26, 1984) (NO. 784 S 291); Weinstock v. Ott, 444 N.E.2d 1227 (Ind.App. 3 Dist., Feb 09, 1983) (NO. 3-581 A 122); Bigbie v. Local 142, Intern. Broth. of Teamsters, 530F.Supp. 402, 111 L.R.R.M. (BNA) 2658 (N.D.Ill., Dec 08, 1981) (NO. 81 C 4507). ***PRACTICE AREAS:*** Civil Litigation; Commercial Litigation; Insurance Defense; Labor and Employment; Litigation. ***Email:*** madley@cohenandmalad.com

LAURA C. JEFFS, born South Bend, Indiana, July 10, 1965; admitted to bar, 1990, Indiana. *Education:* Indiana University (B.A., 1987); Indiana University School of Law (J.D., 1990). Certified Family Law Mediator. *Member:* Indianapolis and Indiana State Bar Associations. ***PRACTICE AREAS:*** Class Action; General Civil Litigation. ***Email:*** ljeffs@cohenandmalad.com

SCOTT D. GILCHRIST, born Indianapolis, Indiana, October 6, 1966; admitted to bar, 1992, Indiana; 1996, Colorado. *Education:* Indiana University (B.A., 1989); Indiana University School of Law (J.D., cum laude, 1992). Staff Member, Indiana Law Journal. *Member:* Indianapolis, Indiana State and American (Member, Litigation Section, 1995—) Bar Associations; Association of Trial Lawyers of America. ***PRACTICE AREAS:*** Class Action; Complex Litigation; General Practice. ***Email:*** sgilchrist@cohenandmalad.com

ERIC S. PAVLACK, born Michigan City, Indiana, October 13, 1973; admitted to bar, 1999, Indiana. *Education:* Indiana University (B.S., Biology, 1996); Indiana University School of Law (J.D., 1999). Editor, Indiana International & Comparative Law Review. ***REPORTED CASES:*** Core Funding Group, LLC v. Young, 792 N.E.2d 547 (Ind.App. Jul 2003); Vann v. United Farm Family Mut. Ins. Co., 778 N.E.2d 868 (Ind. App. 2002), trans. granted, 792 N.E. 2d 41 (Ind. 2003), decision after remand, 790 N.E.2d 497 (Ind. App. 2003). ***PRACTICE AREAS:*** Class Action; Civil Litigation; Mass Torts. ***Email:*** epavlack@cohenandmalad.com

JEFFREY S. GIBSON, born Shelbyville, Indiana; admitted to bar, 2000, Indiana; U.S. District Court, Northern and Southern Districts of Indiana. *Education:* Indiana University (B.A., 1997); Indiana University School of Law (J.D., 2000). *Member:* Indianapolis and Indiana State Bar Associations. ***PRACTICE AREAS:*** Business Litigation; Commercial Litigation; Labor and Employment; Mass Torts. ***Email:*** jgibson@cohenandmalad.com

JULIE M. ANDREWS, born Indiana, 1967; admitted to bar, 2002, Indiana. *Education:* Indiana University (B.S., 1990); Indiana University School of Law (J.D., 2002). *Member:* Indianapolis and Indiana State Bar Associations. ***PRACTICE AREAS:*** Family Law. ***Email:*** jandrews@cohenandmalad.com

ELIZABETH J. DOEPKEN, admitted to bar, 2001, Indiana; registered to practice before U.S. Patent and Trademark Office. *Education:* Earlham College (B.A., 1993); Purdue University (M.S., 1996); Indiana University (J.D., cum laude, 2001). *Member:* American Bar Association; American Chemical Society. ***PRACTICE AREAS:*** Personal Injury; Products Liability; Mass Torts; Class Actions. ***Email:*** edoepken@cohenandmalad.com

PHILIP SEVER, born Athens, Ohio, 1970; admitted to bar, 1995, Ohio; 2005, Indiana. *Education:* Indiana University (B.A., 1992); University of Akron (J.D., 1995). *Member:* Public Investors Arbitration Bar Association. ***PRACTICE AREAS:*** Securities Arbitration; Estate Planning. ***Email:*** psever@cohenandmalad.com

KATHERINE A. HARMON, born Henryville, Indiana, June 29, 1976; admitted to bar, 2001, Indiana. *Education:* Indiana University (B.A., 1997; J.D., 2001). Member, Volunteer Protective Order Pro Bono Project. *Member:* Indianapolis and Indiana State Bar Associations. ***REPORTED CASES:*** Hughes v. Rogusta. ***PRACTICE AREAS:*** Family Law. ***Email:*** kharmon@cohenandmalad.com

LEGAL SUPPORT PERSONNEL

JERROLD ABRAMOWITZ, born Brooklyn, New York, July 15, 1953; admitted to bar, 1982, Ohio; 1990, Oklahoma (Not admitted in Indiana). *Education:* University of Connecticut (B.A., 1974); University of Denver (M.S.J.A., 1976); University of Toledo (J.D., 1981). Faculty Member, 22nd Annual Institute on Law Firm Management, Chicago, IL, July, 1993. Author: "Promoting Communications: The Role of the Retreat or Planning Event," ALA Management Encyclopedia, Association of Legal Administrators, 2002; "Loose Lips Sink Ships and Firms," ABA Lawyering Skills Bulletin, Spring, 1995; "Partner Productivity: The Measure of the 90's," Legal Administrator Network, Fall, 1993. *Member:* Oklahoma and American (Member, Labor Law and Law Practice Management Sections); Association of Legal Administrators. ***PRACTICE AREAS:*** Finance; Human Resources; Law Practice; Practice Group Management. ***Email:*** jabramowitz@cohenandmalad.com

REPRESENTATIVE CLIENTS: AAA Hoosier Motor Club; American Management, Inc.; Bank One, Merrillville, N.A.; Bank One, Plainfield, N.A.; Braun Corp.; Central Indiana Realty Management Associates; Farm Credit Services of Mid-America; A.C.A.; Great Fidelity Life Insurance Company; Imagicians Gallery; Manufacturers Transport, Inc.; Reliance Electric Co.; Simon Property Group, Inc.; Southmark Corp.; Standard Life Insurance Company of Indiana; Tanfastics, Inc.; The Universe Life Insurance Company; Woodland Group, Ltd.; Alan Henderson.
REFERENCES: First Indiana, Indianapolis, N.A.; National City Bank; Summit Bank; Union Bank & Trust Company of Greensburg; Household Finance Corporation; EMC Mortgage Corporation; United Mortgage and Loan Investment Corp.; Wilshire Credit Corporation; Bank One, N.A.

GARY L. COLASESSANO

1915 BROAD RIPPLE AVENUE
INDIANAPOLIS, INDIANA 46220
Telephone: 317-253-9150
Fax: 317-251-1941
Email: colasessanoesq@aol.com
URL: http://www.colasessanolaw.com

Criminal Law, Driving While Intoxicated, DUI, Drug Crimes, Homicide, Sex Crimes, Probation and Parole, Traffic Violations, White Collar Crime.

GARY L. COLASESSANO, born Indianapolis, Indiana, January 9, 1966; admitted to bar, 1992, Indiana and U.S. District Court, Northern and Southern Districts of Indiana. *Education:* Indiana University, Bloomington (B.A., 1988); Valparaiso University (J.D., 1992). *Member:* Indianapolis Bar Association (Member, Criminal Justice Section); National Association of Criminal Defense Lawyers. ***PRACTICE AREAS:*** Criminal Law.

CONOUR LAW FIRM, LLC

FOUR PARKWOOD CROSSING
500 EAST 96TH STREET, SUITE 150
INDIANAPOLIS, INDIANA 46240-3765
Telephone: 317-846-5550
Fax: 317-846-5552
URL:http://www.conour.com
URL: http://www.conourlaw.com

Plaintiff's Civil Trial and Appellate Practice in all State and Federal Courts. Construction Site Injury Litigation, Personal Injury Law, Products Liability Law, Traumatic Brain Injury, Nursing Home Liability, Auto/Trucking Collisions; Sports/Amusement Park Injury; Swimming/Boating Accidents.

MEMBER

WILLIAM F. CONOUR, born Indianapolis, Indiana, June 21, 1947; admitted to bar, 1974, Indiana and U.S. District Court, Southern and Northern Districts of Indiana; 1975, U.S. Court of Appeals, Seventh Circuit; 1982, U.S. Supreme Court. *Education:* Indiana University (B.A., 1970; J.D., cum laude, 1974); National College of Advocacy (1979); Ad-

(This Listing Continued)

vanced College of Advocacy (1981). Phi Delta Phi. Author: monthly article, *Res Gestae*, 1977-1990; "Damages to Coverage and Underinsurance," Verdict, 1992; "Tortious Interference," The Indiana Lawyer, March 2000; "Joint Liability Under Comparative Fault," The Indiana Lawyer, March 1999; "Construction Law," The Indiana Lawyer, May 1996; "Indiana Personal Injury and Torts," Lawyers Cooperative Publishing, 1996. Lecturer: Construction Site Tort Liability, Indiana Trial Lawyers Association, 1990; Trial Advocacy in Indiana, National Business Institute, 1990; Trying the Automobile Accident Case, National Business Institute, 1991; Representing the Intoxicated Client, Indiana Trial Lawyers Association, 1992; Underinsurance in Indiana, Indiana Trial Lawyers Association, 1992; Summary Judgments, Indiana Continuing Legal Education Forum, 1994; Fall Protection in Construction Site Litigation, Association of Trial Lawyers of America, Summer 1994; "Depositions," Advanced Trial Series, Indiana Continuing Legal Education Forum, 1994; "Litigating Workplace Issues," National College of Advocacy, 1995; "Adult Wrongful Death," Indiana Trial Lawyers Association, 1995; "Trucking Litigation," National Business Institute, July 2002; "Getting Around Worker's Comp," Indiana Trial Lawyers Association, 2002; "Advanced Personal Injury Practice in Indiana," National Business Institute, July 2001; "Look into the Future-Important Issues Pending on Appeal," Indiana Trial Lawyers Association, 2001; "Protecting Your Client From Another Attorney," Indiana Trial Lawyers Association, 2000; "Construction Site Injuries: Fall Protection," Indiana Trial Lawyers Association, 1999. Adjunct Associate Professor, Indiana University-Purdue University, Indianapolis, 1975-1989. Certified Civil Trial Mediator. President, Sagamore American Inn of Court, 1999-2001. Trustee, National Inns of Court Foundation, 2001—. Construction Outreach Trainer, Occupational Safety and Health Administration. Board of Directors: University High School, 1998-2004; Indiana University Alumni Association. Member, U.S. Dressage Federation; USA Equestrian. *Member:* Indianapolis (Member, Grievance Committee, 1984-1991); Indiana State (Member: Litigation Section, 1983— and Appellate Section, 1996—) and American (Member, Section on Litigation) Bar Associations; The Association of Trial Lawyers of America (Construction Site Accident Group); M Club; Indiana Trial Lawyers Association (Member: Board of Directors, 1992—; Rules of Evidence Committee, 1993-1994. Sustaining Member. Co-Chair: Amicus Curiae Committee, 1995—; LawPac, 1998—); American Board of Trial Advocates (Member, National Board of Directors, 1994-1998; President, Indiana Chapter, 1996); United States Olympic Committee (Indiana, 1995); Roscoe Pound Foundation (Fellow); Trial Lawyers for Public Justice (Sustaining Founder); National Safety Council; Hoosier Safety Council; American Society of Safety Engineers (Associate Member); Indiana Society of Safety Engineers; North American Brain Injury Society; International Brain Injury Association. Distinguished Fellow, Indianapolis Bar Foundation. Senior Life Fellow, Foundation of the American Board of Trial Advocates; Patron Fellow, Indiana State Bar Association. (Certified as a Civil Trial Advocacy Specialist by the National Board of Trial Advocacy). ***LANGUAGES:*** German, French. ***REPORTED CASES:*** McCullough v. Archibold (Ind. App.), 587 N.E.2d 158 (1992); Tate v. Secura (Ind.) 587 N.E.2d 665 (1992); Picadilly v. Raikos (Ind.) 582 N.E.2d 338 (1991); Barton-Malow v. Wilburn (Ind.), 556 N.E.2d 324 (1990); Picadilly, Inc. v. Colvin (Ind.), 519 N.E.2d 1217 (1988); Zimmerman v. Moore (Ind. App.) 441 N.E.2d 690 (1982); Ed Wiersma Trucking Co. v. Pfaff (Ind.) 678 N.E.2d 110 (1997); Elmer Buchta Trucking, Inc. v. Stanley, 744 N.E.2d 939 (Ind. 2001) (IT LA Amicus Brief); Rice v. Meridian Ins. Co., 751 N.E.2d 685 (Ind. App. 2001) (ITLA Amicus Brief); Stone v. Stakes, 749 N.E.2d 1277 (Ind. App. 2001) (ITLA Amicus Brief); Turner v. Richmond Power & Light, 756 N.E.2d 547 (Ind. App. 2000); Merritt v. Evansville-Vanderburgh School Corp., 735 N.E.2d 269 (Ind. App. 2000) (ITLA Amicus Brief); Ahmad v. Duncan, 732 N.E.2d 862 (Ind. App. 2000); Sims v. USF&G, 730 N.E.2d 232 (Ind. App. 2000); Erie Insurance Exchange v. Daryl Stephenson, et al., 674 N.E.2d 607 (Ind. App. 1996); Reeves v. Boyd & Sons, Inc., 654 N.E.2d 864 (Ind. App. 1995); Standard Mutual Ins. Co. v. Pleasants, 637 N.E.2d 1327 (Ind. App. 1994); McCaslin v. Ins. Co. of State of Pennsylvania, 597 N.E.2d 964 (Ind. App. 1992); Niles v. Stough, 487 N.E.2d 847 (Ind. App. 1986); Rattray v. Rattray, 482 N.E.2d 313 (Ind. App. 1985). ***PRACTICE AREAS:*** Personal Injury; Construction Accidents; Construction Safety; Wrongful Death; Products Liability. ***Email:*** wfc@tortsurfer.com

ASSOCIATES

JESSICA L. BURKS, born Wilmington, Delaware, August 6, 1977; admitted to bar, 2004, Indiana and U.S. District Court, Southern and Northern Districts of Indiana. *Education:* Indiana University, Bloomington (B.A., with distinction, 1999); Indiana University, Indianapolis (J.D., magna cum laude, 2004). Note Development Editor, Indiana Law Review, 2003-2004. *Member:* Indiana State Bar Association; The Association of Trial Lawyers of America; Indiana Trial Lawyers Association. ***LANGUAGES:*** Spanish. ***PRACTICE AREAS:*** Personal Injury; Construction Accidents; Wrongful Death; Products Liability. ***Email:*** jlb@tortsurfer.com

JOHN P. DALY, JR., born South Bend, Indiana, April 22, 1959; admitted to bar, 1987, Indiana; 1988, California; 1989, District of Columbia. *Education:* Indiana University (B.A., 1982; J.D., 1987; M.P.A., 1987). Mortar Board. Member, Sagamore Inn of Court, 2003-2005. *Member:* Indianapolis, Indiana State and American Bar Associations; State Bar of California; Indiana Trial Lawyers Association; Association of Trial Lawyers of America. [Sgt., Army National Guard, 1984-1990]. ***REPORTED CASES:*** Batteast Constr. Co., Inc. v Henry County Bd. of Com'rs, 202 F.Supp.2d 864 (S.D.Ind.2002); King v Northeast Security, Inc., MSD Washington Twsp. 790 N.E. 2d 474 (Ind. 2003); McQueen v Fayette County Schools 711 N.E. 2d 62 (Ind. App. 1999), transfer denied; Russell v Neumann-Steadman, 759 N.E.2d 234 (Ind.App.2001); Mason v TriCentral Schools, 738 N.E. 2d 341 (Ind.App.2000); Peters v Judd Drugs, Inc., 602 N.E.2d 162 (Ind.App.1992), transfer denied. ***PRACTICE AREAS:*** Personal Injury. ***Email:*** jpd@tortsurfer.com

COOTS, HENKE & WHEELER

PROFESSIONAL CORPORATION

INDIANAPOLIS, INDIANA

(See Carmel)

General Civil and Criminal Practice. Litigation in all Courts. Corporate, Insurance, Probate and Estate Planning, Taxation, Real Estate and Zoning and Planning Law. Business Law, Personal Injury, Insurance Defense, Tort and Family Law, Divorce Law, Criminal Law, Domestic Relations.

CREMER BURROUGHS & CREMER

An Association Not in Partnership

TWO MARKET SQUARE CENTER, SUITE 915
251 EAST OHIO STREET
INDIANAPOLIS, INDIANA 46204-2133
Telephone: 317-636-8182; Toll-free: 877-636-8182
Fax: 317-636-8199
Email: CMB@INDYLAW.COM
URL: http://www.indylaw.com

Estate and Trust Litigation in all State and Federal Trial and Appellate Courts. Estate Planning, Wills, Probate and Administration, Business Litigation, Business Formation, Family Law, Real Estate.

FIRM PROFILE: Cremer Burroughs & Cremer draws upon many years of combined legal experience, concentrating in the areas of Estate and Trust Litigation, Planning and Administration, Business Transactions and Litigation, with a particular emphasis on assisting other attorneys in specialized litigation, including serving as co-counsel for both plaintiffs and defendants throughout the State of Indiana.

CHARLES F. CREMER, JR. (1933-2000)

EDWARD P. MADINGER (1922-1997)

PHILIP D. BURROUGHS, born Bethlehem, Pennsylvania, February 28, 1947; admitted to bar, 1972, Indiana. *Education:* DePauw University (B.A., with honors, 1969); Indiana University School of Law (J.D., with honors, 1972). Adjunct Professor, Business Law, University of Maryland, 1974-1977. Majority Counsel, Indiana House of Representatives, 1978; Master Commissioner, Marion Superior Court, No. 2, 1982-1986. [JAG, USAF, 1972-1994, Lt. Col., Ret. JAG]. ***PRACTICE AREAS:*** Business; Estate Planning; Real Estate; Estate Administration; Civil Litigation.

JOHN A. CREMER, born Indianapolis, Indiana, July 17, 1962; admitted to bar, 1989, Indiana. *Education:* Indiana University (B.A., 1986; J.D., 1989). Author: Article, "Res Gestae - To What Extent May Non Probate Transfers Be Made to Defeat the Spousal Election Under I.C. 29-1-3-1?" Co-Chair, Probate Litigation ICLEF Seminar, May 2000 and December 2004. Contributing Editor, Henry's Indiana Probate Law and Practice. ***PRACTICE AREAS:*** Trusts and Estate Litigation; Estate Planning; Estate Administration.

JONATHAN E. PALMER, born Indianapolis, Indiana, February 15, 1953; admitted to bar, 1981, Indiana. *Education:* Butler University (B.S., 1975); Asbury Theological Seminary (1976-1978); Indiana University School of Law (J.D., magna cum laude, 1981). Phi Alpha Delta. Judge, Shelby Superior Court No. 1, 1983-1990. *Member:* Shelby County (President, 1996) and Indiana State Bar Associations. ***PRACTICE AREAS:*** Civil Litigation; Business Litigation; Estate Administration; Trust Litigation; Estate Litigation; Estate Planning.

TIMOTHY W. WITHERS, born Oak Lawn, Illinois, June 23, 1968; admitted to bar, 1998, Indiana. *Education:* Purdue University (B.S., 1990) Phi Beta Kappa; Indiana University (M.P.A., 1993); Valparaiso University (J.D., magna cum laude, 1998). *Member:* Indianapolis, Indiana State and American Bar Associations. ***PRACTICE AREAS:*** Real Estate. ***Email:*** twithers@indylaw.com

ASSOCIATES

SUZANNE E. KATT, born Ft. Wayne, Indiana, June 21, 1947; admitted to bar, 1983, Indiana and U.S. District Court, Southern District of Indiana. *Education:* Indiana University at Ft. Wayne (B.A., 1980); Indiana University School of Law at Bloomington (J.D., 1983). Mediator, Indiana Association of Mediators. *Member:* Indianapolis, Indiana State (Member, Sections on: Probate, Trust and Real Property) Bar Associations. ***PRACTICE AREAS:*** Trusts and Estates Litigation; Estate Planning; Estate Administration; Lobbying. ***Email:*** skatt@indylaw.com

MELISSA A. LINDLEY, born Orleans, Indiana, October 27, 1978; admitted to bar, 2004, Indiana. *Education:* University of Southern Indiana (B.S., magna cum laude, 2001); Indiana University School of Law (J.D., summa cum laude, 2004). *Member:* Indiana State Bar Association. ***PRACTICE AREAS:*** Business Law; Estate Planning; Real Estate; Estate Administration. ***Email:*** mlindley@indylaw.com

OF COUNSEL

DIANE L. LIPTACK, admitted to bar, 1976, Indiana. *Education:* Kent State University (B.A.); Ohio State University (M.A.); Vanderbilt University (J.D., 1975; M.B.A.). Certified Public Accountant, Indiana, 1978. *Member:* Indianapolis (Past Chairman, Estate Planning & Administration Section), Indiana State (Member Sections on: Probate, Trust and Real Property Section, Council Member, District 11) Bar Associations. ***PRACTICE AREAS:*** Estate Planning; Probate; Corporate Law.

REFERENCES: Tower Bank & Trust Co., Ft. Wayne; Fifth Third Bank, Indianapolis.

DAHM & ELVIN, LLP

INDIANAPOLIS, INDIANA

(See Fort Wayne)

Drug & Medical Device Litigation, Product Liability, Class Action Defense, Federal Civil Litigation, Complex and Multi-District Litigation, Business Litigation.

DALE & EKE

PROFESSIONAL CORPORATION

Established in 1978

9100 KEYSTONE CROSSING, SUITE 400

INDIANAPOLIS, INDIANA 46240-2100

Telephone: 317-844-7400

Fax: 317-574-9426

Computer Fax: 317-581-7436

Email: daleeke@daleeke.com

URL: http://www.daleeke.com

Corporate, Corporate Finance, Commercial, Taxation, Health Care, Probate and Estate Planning, Trust Law, Bankruptcy, Real Estate, Family/Domestic Relations, and Civil Litigation.

WILLIAM J. DALE, JR., born Salina, Kansas, October 16, 1942; admitted to bar, 1971, Indiana and U.S. District Court, Southern District of Indiana; 1973, U.S. Tax Court. *Education:* University of Oklahoma (B.B.A., 1964); Indiana University (J.D., 1971). Certified Public Accountant, Indiana, 1968. Adjunct Professor, Business and Estate Planning, Indiana University School of Law. Indiana Practice Consultant for Matthew Bender's Midwest Transaction Guide. Member, Board of Reviewers, and Contributing Author, Indiana Estate Planning and Probate Practice, Matthew Bender; Adjunct Professor of Law at the Indiana University School of Law - Indianapolis and Distinguished Fellow of the Indianapolis Bar Foundation. *Member:* Indianapolis, Indiana State and American Bar Associations; Indiana Society of Certified Public Accountants; Estate Planning Council of Indianapolis. Fellow: American College of Trust and Estate Counsel; American College of Tax Counsel. ***PRACTICE AREAS:*** Probate and Estate; Tax; Corporate; Real Estate; Trust. ***Email:*** wdale@daleeke.com

JOSEPH W. EKE, born Bicknell, Indiana, October 17, 1940; admitted to bar, 1973, Indiana; U.S. Tax Court and U.S. District Court, Southern District of Indiana. *Education:* Vincennes Junior College (A.S., 1964); Indiana University (B.S., 1966; J.D., cum laude, 1973). Phi Delta Phi. Certified Public Accountant: Virginia, 1969; Indiana, 1971. *Member:* Indianapolis, Indiana State and American Bar Associations. ***PRACTICE AREAS:*** Health Care; Retirement Benefit Plans; Corporate; Trust; Tax; Estate Planning; Family Law; Domestic Relations; Real Estate; Civil Litigation. ***Email:*** jeke@daleeke.com

DEBORAH J. CARUSO, born Chicago, Illinois, August 21, 1956; admitted to bar, 1981, Indiana and U.S. District Court, Southern District of Indiana; U.S. Court of Appeals, Seventh Circuit. *Education:* Indiana University (A.B., 1978; J.D., cum laude, 1981). Phi Delta Phi. Co-Author, Matthew Bender's, Indiana Civil Trial Guide. Trustee, Chapter 7 Bankruptcy Panel. *Member:* Indianapolis, Indiana State and American Bar Associations; The Association of Trial Lawyers of America; National Association of Bankruptcy Trustees. Distinguished Fellow, Indianapolis Bar Foundation. ***PRACTICE AREAS:*** Bankruptcy; Commercial Litigation; Civil and Business Litigation; Real Estate. ***Email:*** dcaruso@daleeke.com

GEFFREY D. RAINBOLT, born Indianapolis, Indiana, September 13, 1968; admitted to bar, 1994, Indiana and U.S. District Court, Southern District of Indiana. *Education:* University of Evansville (B.S., cum laude, 1991); Indiana University School of Law-Indianapolis (J.D., cum laude, 1994). *Member:* Indianapolis, Indiana State and American Bar Associations. ***PRACTICE AREAS:*** Estate Planning; Wills; Trust Law; Business Litigation; Business Law; Corporate Law; Real Estate. ***Email:*** grainbolt@daleeke.com

---

ERICK P. KNOBLOCK, born Aurora, Illinois, January 19, 1966; admitted to bar, 1995, Indiana and U.S. District Court, Southern District of Indiana; 1999, U.S. District Court, Northern District of Indiana. *Education:* Indiana University (B.A., 1988; J.D., 1994). *Member:* Indianapolis (Member, Commercial and Bankruptcy Law Section), Indiana State and American (Member, Business Law Section) Bar Associations. ***PRACTICE AREAS:*** Business Law; Commercial Law; Bankruptcy; Civil Litigation. ***Email:*** eknoblock@daleeke.com

DAVID D. DEETER, born 1954; admitted to bar, 1980, Indiana and U.S. District Court, Southern District of Indiana; 1986, North Carolina (inactive). *Education:* University of Innsbruck, Innsbruck, Austria; University of Notre Dame (B.A., 1976); Indiana University at Indianapolis (J.D., cum laude, 1980). Deputy Prosecutor, Marion County, 1980-1981. Public Defender, Marion County Municipal and Superior Court, 1981-1984. Commissioner, Marion Circuit Court, 1984. Estate Planning Council of Indianapolis, 2000. *Member:* Indianapolis, Indiana State and American Bar Associations. ***PRACTICE AREAS:*** Estate Planning; Probate Administration. ***Email:*** ddeeter@daleeke.com

GREGG S. GORDON, born Noblesville, Indiana, December 11, 1959; admitted to bar, 1996, Indiana and U.S. District Court, Southern and Northern District of Indiana; 1998, U.S. Court of Appeals, Seventh Circuit. *Education:* Indiana University at Indianapolis (B.S., with highest distinction, 1993); Indiana University School of Law (J.D., cum laude, 1996). *Member:* Indianapolis, Indiana State and American Bar Associations; Indiana Trial Lawyers Association; The Association of Trial Lawyers of America. [Special Agent AFOSI, USAF, 1980-1989.]. ***PRACTICE AREAS:*** Commercial Litigation; Probate Litigation. ***Email:*** ggordon@daleeke.com

DANN PECAR NEWMAN & KLEIMAN

PROFESSIONAL CORPORATION

Established in 1911

SUITE 2300

ONE AMERICAN SQUARE

INDIANAPOLIS, INDIANA 46282

Telephone: 317-632-3232; Indiana: 800-622-4799

Fax: 317-632-2962

Email: info@dannpecar.com

URL: http://www.dannpecar.com

General Federal and Indiana Civil, Trial and Appellate Practice. Administrative, Bankruptcy, Commercial, Commercial Lending, Construction, Corporate, Creditors' Rights, Economic Development Incentives, Employment, Environmental, Franchising, Gaming, Intellectual Property, Land Use, Mergers and Acquisitions, Municipal Law and Finance, Privatization, Probate and Estate Planning, Real Estate, Reorganization, Securities, Shopping Center, Sports, Taxation, Trademark and Zoning Law.

FIRM PROFILE: The Attorneys of Dann Pecar Newman & Kleiman, P.C., have established a tradition of practicing law for the protection, benefit and welfare of their clients. In 1911, Jackiel Joseph founded his law firm in Indianapolis. Theodore R. Dann, with law degrees from Indiana University and Harvard University, joined the Joseph law firm in 1931. Now, more than nine decades after its founding, Dann Pecar Newman & Kleiman continues to offer legal advice and services to a growing list of local, regional and national clients.

THEODORE R. DANN (1907-1993)

PHILIP D. PECAR (1930-2000)

JOEL YONOVER (1932-1995)

ROBERT A. ROSE (1931-2001)

NORMAN R. NEWMAN, born Indianapolis, Indiana, December 10, 1934; admitted to bar, 1960, Indiana. *Education:* Indiana University (A.B., 1957); Indiana University School of Law (LL.B., with distinction, 1960). *Member:* American College of Real Estate Lawyers. ***PRACTICE AREAS:*** Real Estate; Business Organizations; Business Transactions; Construction Law; Environmental Law; Mergers and Acquisitions; Gaming Law. ***Email:*** nnewman@dannpecar.com

DAVID H. KLEIMAN, born Kendallville, Indiana, April 2, 1934; admitted to bar, 1959, Indiana. *Education:* Purdue University (B.S., 1956); Northwestern University (J.D., 1959). *Member:* Commercial Law League of America; American Bankruptcy Institute. ***PRACTICE AREAS:*** Bankruptcy; Commercial Law; Business Reorganization; Banking Law; Commercial Litigation. ***Email:*** dkleiman@dannpecar.com

JON B. ABELS, born Indianapolis, Indiana, February 22, 1944; admitted to bar, 1970, Indiana; 1980, U.S. Supreme Court. *Education:* Wabash College; Butler University (B.A., 1966); Indiana University School of Law (J.D., 1970). *Member:* Commercial Law League of America. ***PRACTICE AREAS:*** Commercial Law; Bankruptcy; Business Reorganization. ***Email:*** jabels@dannpecar.com

MELVIN R. DANIEL, born Greencastle, Indiana, May 15, 1942; admitted to bar, 1972, Indiana; 1984, U.S. Court of Appeals, Seventh Circuit. *Education:* Indiana State University (B.S., 1967); Indiana University School of Law (J.D., 1972). *Member:* Indiana Trial Lawyers Association; The Association of Trial Lawyers of America; Indiana Municipal Lawyers Association. ***PRACTICE AREAS:*** Federal Civil Litigation; Civil Litigation; Municipal Law; Civil Practice. ***Email:*** mdaniel@dannpecar.com

LAWRENCE F. DOROCKE, born Chicago, Illinois, October 4, 1946; admitted to bar, 1973, Indiana; 1974, Iowa. *Education:* Purdue University (B.S., 1968; M.S., 1970); Indiana University School of Law (J.D., magna cum laude, 1973). ***PRACTICE AREAS:*** Corporate Law; Real Estate; Shopping Center Law; Municipal Law. ***Email:*** ldorocke@dannpecar.com

JEFFREY A. ABRAMS, born Indianapolis, Indiana, March 28, 1956; admitted to bar, 1981, Indiana. *Education:* Miami University (B.S., 1978); Indiana University School of Law (J.D., cum laude, 1981). ***PRACTICE AREAS:*** Banks and Banking; Commercial Arbitration; Real Estate; Alcoholic Beverages. ***Email:*** jabrams@dannpecar.com

JAMES H. SCHWARZ, born Hammond, Indiana, December 7, 1954; admitted to bar, 1980, Indiana; 1989, U.S. Tax Court. *Education:* Indiana University (B.S., highest distinction, 1977); Indiana University School of Law (J.D., summa cum laude, 1980). *Member:* American College of Real Estate Lawyers. ***PRACTICE AREAS:*** Corporate Law; Real Estate; Shopping Center Law; Municipal Finance. ***Email:*** jschwarz@dannpecar.com

WALTER E. WOLF, JR., born Indianapolis, Indiana, August 28, 1931; admitted to bar, 1955, Indiana. *Education:* Harvard University (A.B., 1952; LL.B., cum laude, 1955). ***PRACTICE AREAS:*** Real Estate; Business Organization; Tax Law. ***Email:*** wwolf@dannpecar.com

JAMES P. MOLOY, born Indianapolis, Indiana, October 6, 1959; admitted to bar, 1984, Indiana; 1986, U.S. Court of Appeals, Seventh Circuit; 1989, U.S. Tax Court; 1995, U.S. Court of Appeals, Fifth Circuit. *Education:* Indiana University (B.S., with high distinction, 1981); Indiana University School of Law (J.D., magna cum laude, 1984). ***PRACTICE AREAS:*** Bankruptcy; Commercial Law; Business Reorganization; Appellate Practice. ***Email:*** jmoloy@dannpecar.com

ANDREW A. KLEIMAN, born Indianapolis, Indiana, July 28, 1961; admitted to bar, 1986, Indiana. *Education:* Purdue University; Indiana University (B.S., 1983); Indiana University School of Law (J.D., 1986). ***PRACTICE AREAS:*** Real Estate; Corporate Law; Municipal Finance. ***Email:*** akleiman@dannpecar.com

RICHARD O. KISSEL, II, born Evansville, Indiana, August 30, 1958; admitted to bar, 1985, Illinois; 1989, Missouri; 1992, Indiana. *Education:* Indiana University (B.S., with distinction, 1981); Indiana University School of Law (J.D., cum laude, 1985). ***PRACTICE AREAS:*** Estate Planning; Tax Planning; Estate Administration; Probate. ***Email:*** rkissel@dannpecar.com

(This Listing Continued)

MARK R. WATERFILL, born Muncie, Indiana, March 11, 1961; admitted to bar, 1986, Indiana. *Education:* Hanover College (B.A., with honors in Political Science, magna cum laude, 1983); Indiana University School of Law (J.D., 1986). ***PRACTICE AREAS:*** Litigation; Employment Law; Utility Law. ***Email:*** mwaterfill@dannpecar.com

WILLIAM L. O'CONNOR, born Louisville, KY, May 8, 1964; admitted to bar, 1989, Indiana and U.S. District Court, Northern and Southern Districts of Indiana. *Education:* University of Notre Dame (B.A., 1986); Indiana University (J.D., cum laude, 1989). ***PRACTICE AREAS:*** Litigation; Employment Law; Creditors' Rights; Commercial Law; General Practice; Securities Fraud; Regulatory Law; Professional Liability. ***Email:*** woconnor@dannpecar.com

PETER A. SILVER, born Muncie, Indiana, April 17, 1955; admitted to bar, 1983, Indiana and Florida. *Education:* Indiana University (B.A., 1977; J.D., 1982). ***PRACTICE AREAS:*** Real Estate; Banks and Banking; Consumer Lending. ***Email:*** psilver@dannpecar.com

NEIL R. RAFFERTY, born Rockford, Illinois, January 6, 1965; admitted to bar, 1991, Illinois; 2003, Indiana. *Education:* University of Illinois (B.A., 1988); Indiana University (J.D., 1991). ***PRACTICE AREAS:*** Real Estate; Business Law. ***Email:*** nrafferty@dannpecar.com

KARIN L. VEATCH, born Minneapolis, Minnesota, February 4, 1969; admitted to bar, 1994, Ohio; 1995, Indiana. *Education:* Indiana University (B.A., 1991); University of Toledo (J.D., magna cum laude, 1994). ***PRACTICE AREAS:*** Estate Planning; Tax Planning; Probate Administration. ***Email:*** kveatch@dannpecar.com

JONATHAN G. POLAK, born Philadelphia, Pennsylvania, December 8, 1968; admitted to bar, 1994, Texas and U.S. District Court, Northern District of Texas; 2000, Indiana and U.S. District Court, Southern and Northern Districts of Indiana. *Education:* Southern Methodist University (B.S., 1991; J.D., 1994). Member, Order of Barristers. ***PRACTICE AREAS:*** Commercial Law; Litigation; Trademark Litigation; Intellectual Property Litigation; Construction Law; Real Estate Litigation; Bankruptcy Litigation. ***Email:*** jpolak@dannpecar.com

PATRICK F. MASTRIAN III, born Erie, Pennsylvania, September 30, 1968; admitted to bar, 1994, Indiana. *Education:* University of Pittsburgh (B.A., cum laude, 1991); Valparaiso University School of Law (J.D., cum laude, 1994). ***PRACTICE AREAS:*** Commercial Litigation; Employment Litigation; Insurance Coverage.

ANDRIELLE M. METZEL, born Cincinnati, Ohio, July 25, 1969; admitted to bar, 1996, Indiana, U.S. Court of Appeals, Seventh Circuit and U.S. District Court, Southern and Northern Districts of Indiana. *Education:* Franklin College of Indiana (B.A., 1991); Indiana University School of Law (J.D., 1996). Member: Order of Barristers. ***PRACTICE AREAS:*** Litigation; Employment Law; Real Estate; Zoning Law. ***Email:*** ametzel@dannpecar.com

ERIC M. HYLTON, born Indianapolis, Indiana, March 3, 1971; admitted to bar, 1997, Indiana and U.S. District Court, Southern and Northern Districts of Indiana. *Education:* Indiana University (B.S., 1993; J.D., magna cum laude, 1997). ***PRACTICE AREAS:*** Labor and Employment; Litigation. ***Email:*** ehylton@dannpecar.com

OF COUNSEL

LINDA E. CANTOR, born Dixon, Illinois, November 6, 1954; admitted to bar, 1979, Indiana. *Education:* Indiana University (A.B., 1976); Indiana University School of Law (J.D., 1979). ***PRACTICE AREAS:*** Estate Planning; Probate. ***Email:*** lcantor@dannpecar.com

RICHARD J. DARKO, born Indianapolis, Indiana, September 3, 1943; admitted to bar, 1968, Indiana and U.S. District Court, Southern and Northern Districts of Indiana; 1975, U.S. Supreme Court. *Education:* University of Notre Dame (B.A., 1965); Indiana University (J.D., 1968). Member, Indiana Gaming Commission, 1999-2002. ***PRACTICE AREAS:*** Civil Litigation; Labor Law. ***Email:*** ddarko@dannpecar.com

STEVEN M. PECAR, born Indianapolis, Indiana, July 28, 1959; admitted to bar, 1986, Indiana. *Education:* Indiana University (B.S., with distinction, 1981; J.D., cum laude, 1986); Tulane University of Louisiana. ***PRACTICE AREAS:*** Corporate Law; Real Estate; Shopping Center Law. ***Email:*** specar@dannpecar.com

CHARLES R. ROLPH, III, born Milwaukee, Wisconsin, December 13, 1950; admitted to bar, 1977, Iowa and Nebraska; 1986, Indiana and U.S. District Court, Southern District of Indiana. *Education:* University of Nebraska at Omaha (B.G.S., 1974); University of Nebraska at Lincoln (J.D., 1976); The American College, Bryn Mawr, Pennsylvania (M.S., Financial Services, 1984). ***PRACTICE AREAS:*** Employee Benefits. ***Email:*** crolph@dannpecar.com

ASSOCIATES

JAMES B. CHAPMAN II, born Michigan City, Indiana, February 19, 1968; admitted to bar, 1996, Illinois and U.S. Court of Appeals, Seventh Circuit; 2000, U.S. Supreme Court; 2005, Indiana. *Education:* Bob Jones University (B.A., cum laude, 1990); Southern Illinois University School of Law (J.D., magna cum laude, 1996). Law Clerk to the Honorable Richard Mills, U.S. District Judge, Central District of Illinois, 1996-2004. ***PRACTICE AREAS:*** Litigation; Employment Law; Appellate Practice. ***Email:*** jchapman@dannpecar.com

CYNTHIA M. KIRK, born Indianapolis, Indiana, March 8, 1971; admitted to bar, 1997, Indiana and U.S. District Court, Northern and Southern Districts of Indiana; 2000, U.S. Court of Appeals, Seventh Circuit. *Education:* Ball State University (B.S., 1993); Indiana University School of Law (J.D., 1997). Order of Barristers. ***PRACTICE AREAS:*** Litigation; Environmental Law; Utility Law; Intellectual Property. ***Email:*** ckirk@dannpecar.com

DAVID E. KRESS, born Erie, Pennsylvania, May 9, 1968; admitted to bar, 2000, Indiana. *Education:* Indiana University (B.A., 1990; J.D., 2000). ***PRACTICE AREAS:*** Commercial Law; Litigation; Employment Law. ***Email:*** dkress@dannpecar.com

(This Listing Continued)

AMY L. WRIGHT, born Harrisburg, Pennsylvania, February 8, 1973; admitted to bar, 2000, Indiana. *Education:* St. Joseph's College (B.S., 1996); Indiana University (J.D., 2000). ***PRACTICE AREAS:*** Litigation; Trademark Prosecution; Copyrights; Protection of Personality; Entertainment Law. ***Email:*** awright@dannpecar.com

LAURA J. PETERS, born Jasper, Indiana, December 3, 1974; admitted to bar, 2003, Indiana. *Education:* University of Evansville (B.S., 1996; M.S., 1998); Indiana University School of Law (J.D., 2002). ***PRACTICE AREAS:*** Estate Planning; Business Law; Real Estate. ***Email:*** lpeters@dannpecar.com

JEFFREY M. CROMER, born Indianapolis, Indiana, April 25, 1976; admitted to bar, 2003, Indiana. *Education:* Wabash College (B.A., 1998); Indiana University School of Law (J.D., 2003). ***PRACTICE AREAS:*** Labor Law; Employment Law; Litigation. ***Email:*** jcromer@dannpecar.com

HEIDI K. HUGHES, born Kirksville, Missouri, September 17, 1974; admitted to bar, 2004, Indiana. *Education:* Northwestern University (B.A., 1996; M.A., 1998); Indiana University School of Law (J.D., magna cum laude, 2004). ***PRACTICE AREAS:*** Bankruptcy; Creditors' Rights; Commercial Law. ***Email:*** hhughes@dannpecar.com

JARED A. SIMMONS, born Kokomo, Indiana, February 19, 1975; admitted to bar, 2004, Indiana. *Education:* Indiana University (B.A., 1992); Indiana University School of Law, Indianapolis (J.D., 2004). ***PRACTICE AREAS:*** Real Estate; Corporate Law; Litigation. ***Email:*** jsimmons@dannpecar.com

ATTORNEYS FOR: Aaron Ruben Nelson Meridian Hills Mortuary, Inc.; American Environmental Corporation; Auctionet USA; Bunn Excavating, Inc.; Carter-Lee Lumber Co. Inc.; Champ Car World Series LLC; Cheever Indy Racing, LLC; Chinsky Restaurant Group, Inc.; Cincinnati Insurance Company; Colliers Turley Martin Tucker; Continental Enterprises; Delco Pizza Products of Indiana, Inc.; Equicor Companies; Fifth Third Bank, Indiana; First Indiana Bank; First National Bank & Trust; First Place Bank; Flatfork Utilities, Inc.; Government Payment Services, Inc.; Greenfield Builders, Inc.; Greenfield Development Co., LLC; HDG Mansur Capital Group, LLC; Harrah's Entertainment, Inc.; Indiana Lubricants, Inc.; Indiana State Teachers Association; Indiana University; Indianapolis Private Industry Council; Indianapolis Shredding, LLC; Irwin Union Bank; K & F Industries, Inc.; JP Morgan Chase Bank; KeyBank National Association; LMH Utilities; LaSalle Bank National Assoc.; Mann Properties; Melvin Simon & Associates, Inc.; Nachi Technology, Inc.; National Bank of Indianapolis; National City Bank of Indiana; Paragon General Contractors; Pepper Construction Company of Indiana, LLC; Plainfield Board of Zoning Appeals; Plainfield Plan Commission; Plainfield Redevelopment Commission; Price Realty Corporation; R.J. Klein & Associates, Inc.; Regions Bank; Republic Bank; Salomon Brothers Realty Corp.; Scannell Properties; Simon Property Group, Inc.; The Estate of John Dillinger; The Estate of John Wayne; The Huntington National Bank; The Swiss Group, Inc.; The Trophy Club Golf Course; Town of Plainfield; Volkswagen of America, Inc.; Wabash Valley Power Association; and Williams Realty Group. REFERENCES: The Huntington National Bank; JP Morgan Chase Bank; and Regions Bank, all of Indianapolis.

JAMES E. DAVIS
ATTORNEY AT LAW

INDIANAPOLIS, INDIANA

(See Greenfield)

Personal Injury, Social Security Disability, Wrongful Death, Medical Malpractice, Wills and Probate Law, Automobile Accidents and Injuries, Head Injury, Spinal Injury, Slip and Fall, Trucking Accidents, Construction Accidents, Railroad Accidents, Nursing Home and Abuse and Neglect.

DAVID E. DEAL

255 NORTH ALABAMA STREET
INDIANAPOLIS, INDIANA 46204
Telephone: 317-916-0000
Fax: 317-955-2570
URL: http://www.daviddeallawfirm.com

Family Law, Creditors Rights, Civil Practice.

DAVID E. DEAL, born Indianapolis, Indiana, September 6, 1976; admitted to bar, 2001, Indiana; U.S. District Court, Northern and Southern Districts of Indiana; U.S. Supreme Court. *Education:* Purdue University (B.S., 1998); Indiana University School of Law (J.D., 2001). *Member:* Clinton County, Indiana State and American Bar Associations. ***PRACTICE AREAS:*** Family Law; Creditors Rights; Civil Practice.

DAVID E. DEARING

6100 NORTH KEYSTONE AVENUE
SUITE 657
INDIANAPOLIS, INDIANA 46220
Telephone: 317-920-0824
Fax: 317-920-1865
URL: http://www.dearinglawfirm.com

Environmental Law, Zoning, Civil Appellate, Administrative and General Litigation.

DAVID E. DEARING, born Louisville, Kentucky; admitted to bar, 1990, Indiana and U.S. District Court, Northern and Southern Districts of Indiana; 1996, Michigan, U.S. District Court, Southern District of Michigan. *Education:* Yale College (B.A., 1972); Cornell University (J.D., 1978; M.A., 1979). Member, Environmental Quality Control, Inc. Water Committee, 1992-1998. Author, "Regulatory Takings: Past, Present and Future," Nat'l. Bar Association Magazine Vol.18, No. 3 (May/June 1996); "Battle Continues Over Isolated Wetlands," 1 ABA Agricultural Law Newsletter 5 (1992); "Successor and Parent Corporations: Liability for CERCLA Response Costs," 20 Env. Rptr. (BNA) 1764 (1990). Adjunct Professor, Indiana University Law School at Indianapolis, 1993-1995. Trial Attorney, U.S. Department of Justice, Land and Natural Resources Division, 1978-1987. Sr. Vice-President, Wetland Training Institute, Inc., 1989—.

DeLANEY & DeLANEY LLC

Established in 2002

3640 WASHINGTON BOULEVARD
INDIANAPOLIS, INDIANA 46205
Telephone: 317-920-0400
Fax: 317-920-0404
Email: kathleen@delaneylaw.net
URL: http://www.delaneylaw.net

Employment Litigation, Litigation, Products Liability, International Law, Media Law, Election Law, Business Law, Fraud, Breach of Contract, Securities, Estate Administration, First Amendment Law.

FIRM PROFILE: DeLaney & DeLaney provides services to a wide variety of clients in nearly all types of Civil litigation. Together, the firm's lawyers have more than 60 years of trial practice experience. This includes nearly two years of actual time in front of juries; DeLaney & DeLaney has been certified as a Women's Business Enterprise (WBE) by the Women's Business Enterprise National Council (WBENC), the City of Indianapolis, and the (WBE) State of Indiana.

Certified as a Women's Business Enterprise by The Women's Business Development Center, the State of Indiana and the City of Indianapolis.

MEMBERS OF FIRM

KATHLEEN A. DeLANEY, born Monterey, California, June 7, 1968; admitted to bar, 1995, Indiana, U.S. District Court, Southern and Northern Districts of Indiana and U.S. Court of Appeals, Seventh Circuit. *Education:* Georgetown University (B.S.F.S., 1990); Indiana University School of Law at Bloomington (J.D., 1995). *Member:* Indianapolis (Member, Executive Council, Labor and Employment Section) and Indiana State Bar Associations. ***PRACTICE AREAS:*** Civil Litigation; Employment Litigation; ERISA Litigation; Contracts; Medical Negligence Litigation. ***Email:*** kathleen@delaneylaw.net

ANN M. DeLANEY, born Brooklyn, New York, October 21, 1945; admitted to bar, 1977, Indiana, U.S. District Court, Southern and Northern Districts of Indiana. *Education:* State University of New York at Binghamton (B.A., 1967); Indiana University School of Law at Bloomington (J.D., 1977). *Member:* Indianapolis Bar Association. ***PRACTICE AREAS:*** Employment; Corporate; Civil Litigation. ***Email:*** ann@delaneylaw.net

EDWARD O. DeLANEY, born Elmira, New York, April 19, 1943; admitted to bar, 1973, Indiana. *Education:* State University of New York at Binghamton (B.A., 1966); Harvard University (J.D., 1973). *Member:* Indianapolis Bar Association. ***PRACTICE AREAS:*** Civil Litigation; Securities Litigation; Probate Litigation; International Law. ***Email:*** ed@delaneylaw.net

ASSOCIATES

CYNTHIA A. BEDRICK, born Leesburg, Virginia, May 25, 1974; admitted to bar, 1999, Indiana, U.S. District Court, Southern and Northern Districts of Indiana. *Education:* Butler University (B.A., cum laude, 1996); Indiana University School of Law - Bloomington (J.D., summa cum laude, 1999). Order of the Coif. Indiana Law Journal, 1998-1999. Law Clerk: Hon. Theodore R. Boehm, Indiana Supreme Court, 1999-2001; Judge John D. Tinder, U.S. District Court, S.D., Ind., 2001-2002. *Member:* Indianapolis, Indiana State (Member, Wetten Publications Committee) and American Bar Associations. ***PRACTICE AREAS:*** Trial Practice; Appellate Practice; Business Litigation; Contracts; Medical Malpractice; Employment Litigation. ***Email:*** cindy@delaneylaw.net

MICHELE E. BROWN, born Peoria, Illinois, June 20, 1978; admitted to bar, 2003, Indiana. *Education:* Indiana University-Bloomington (B.S., 2000); Indiana University School of Law-Bloomington (J.D., 2003). *Member:* Indianapolis, Indiana State and American Bar Associations. ***PRACTICE AREAS:*** Civil Litigation; Employment Litigation; Medical Negligence Litigation; Contracts. ***Email:*** michele@delaneylaw.net

Language: Russian.

DOEHRMAN • CHAMBERLAIN

Established in 1988

THREE MERIDIAN PLAZA, SUITE 100
10333 N. MERIDIAN STREET
INDIANAPOLIS, INDIANA 46290
Telephone: 317-844-9999
Fax: 317-844-9977
Toll Free: 800-269-3443
URL: http://www.dclawfirm.com
URL: http://www.uslaws.com
Email: tcd@tbilawyer.com
URL: http://www.tortslaw.com

Plaintiff's Civil Trial and Appellate Practice in State and Federal Courts. Personal Injury, Automobile Accidents and Injuries, Wrongful Death, Slip and Fall, Unsafe Products, Product Liability, Construction Site Injury and Safety. Traumatic Brain Injury, Medical Malpractice, Nursing Home Abuse and Neglect, Trucking Accidents and Injuries.

FIRM PROFILE: Doehrman • Chamberlain was founded by Tom Doehrman and Dan Chamberlain to offer dependable and affordable legal representation to the injured. The firm concentrates its practice on traumatic brain injury and construction site injury litigation and also represents individuals who have been seriously injured or killed in all types of accidents, ranging from slip and fall and automobile collisions to medical malpractice, and product liability. The firm services the entire state of Indiana but also represents clients throughout the United States and in foreign countries.

(This Listing Continued)

MEMBERS OF FIRM

THOMAS C. DOEHRMAN, born Fort Wayne, Indiana, April 28, 1951; admitted to bar, 1976, Indiana and U.S. District Court, Southern District of Indiana; 1978, U.S. Court of Appeals, 7th Circuit; 1994, U.S. Supreme Court. *Education:* Indiana University (B.A., 1973; J.D., cum laude, 1976). Elected as the Indiana Trial Lawyer of the Year, Indiana Trial Lawyers Association, 2002. Assistant Editor, Indiana Law Review, 1975-1976. Author: "Indiana's 'Common Sense' Approach to Daubert," Indiana Lawyer, 2001; "Daubert in Indiana - There is a Difference," ATLA Lifetime Achievement Seminar, 2/2002; Note, "Redlining: Potential Sherman Act and Civil Rights Violations Raised By Lending Policies," Vol. 8, Issue 6, The Indiana Law Review, 1976; "The Non-Party Defense in Comparative Fault Cases," Res Gestae, 1988. Lecturer: Comparative Fault, Indiana Trial Lawyers Annual Seminar, December, 1987; Finding Expert Witnesses, Indiana State Bar Association, September, 1988; Handling the Non-Party Defense, Indiana Trial Lawyers Association, March, 1990; A Cause of Action for Loss of Chance, Indiana Trial Lawyers Association, March, 1992; "Handling the Non-Catastrophic Brain Injury Case," Indiana State Bar Association, February, 1993; "Proving That Medical Bills are Reasonable and Necessary," Indiana Trial Lawyers Association, March, 1993; "The Use of Requests For Admission at Trial," Indiana Trial Lawyers Association, March, 1994; "Product Liability: The Enforcement Case," Indiana Continuing Legal Education Forum, June, 1994; "Demonstrative Evidence: Types, Practiced Applications and Admissibility," Indianapolis Bar Association, November, 1994; "Suing the Sovereign," Indiana Continuing Legal Education Forum, January, 1994; "Use of 3-D Computer Animation in Litigation," Indiana Trial Lawyers Association, March, 1995; "Underinsurance from the Plaintiffs Perspective," Indianapolis Bar Association, October, 1996; "Using Computers in the Practice of Law," Indiana Trial Lawyers Association, November, 1996; "Understanding the Federal Motor Carrier Safety Regulations and Their Application," ATLA Summer Convention, 1997; "Traumatic Brain Injury Without Significant Coma," Indiana Continuing Legal Education Forum, August, 1997; "Economic Loss of Spouse in Wrongful Death Case", 1998; "Daubert Standards and TBI Litigation," Brain Injury Association of New York State, June, 2000; "Daubert and the Progeny," Nonscientific Experts," ATLA Las Vegas Seminar, March, 2001; "Traumatic Brain Injury Refresher Course," ICLEF, May 15, 2001; "Trial Proof in a Brain Injury Case," Brain Injury Association of California, Napa, California, September, 2001; "Understanding Federal Regulations in Large Truck Cases," ATLA Summer Seminar, Atlanta, GA, July 20, 2002; "Voir Dire in Traumatic Brain Injury Cases," ATLA Summer Seminar, Atlanta, GA, July 22, 2002; "Using Technology Effectively," Indiana Continuing Legal Education Forum Seminar, Indianapolis, IN, November 8, 2002; "Beware! Your Third-Party Settlement May Cut Off Workers Compensation Benefits," 15th Lifetime Achievement Seminar, ITLA, Indianapolis, IN, February 28, 2003. Moderator: Discovery, Depositions, and Other Related Topics, Annual ATLA Seminar During Jazz Fest, New Orleans, LA, May 1, 2003; "Utilizing the Federal Motor Carriers Safety Regulations in Trucking Cases," ITLA Seminar, Indianapolis, IN, May 21, 2003; "Mild Brain Injury: Is An Attorney Needed?," Annual Conference, National Association of Legal Investigators, Indianapolis, IN, June 26, 2003; "Unethical Defense Witnesses," Traumatic Brain Injury Litigation Group, ATLA Annual Convention, San Francisco, CA, 2003; "The Give and Take of Depositions: Giving, Taking and Defending," 5th Annual BIA Medical/Legal Conference, San Francisco, CA, October 10 and 11, 2003. "Recent Update of ITLA Amicus Cases," ITLA Seminar, February, 2004. Lectures and Publications: "Plaintiff"s Perspective-Filling the Empty Chair," Indianapolis Bar Association, October 1993; "Suing the Sovereign," ICLEF, January 1994.; "Demonstrative Evidence: Types, Cost Factors and Effectiveness," Indiana Continuing Legal Education Forum (ICLEF), February 1994; "Statutory Non-Party Provisions Similar to Those in Indiana Found to be unconstitutional by Montana Supreme Court," Indiana Trial Lawyers Association, April 1996; "A Look Into the Future-Important Issues Pending on Appeal," ITLA, March 2000; "Mixing Legal Issues & Medical Professionals," Brain Injury Association of Indiana; "The Day in the Life Video in the Catastrophic Brain Injury Case," North American Brain Injury Society 18th Annual Seminar, Amelia Island, September 2005. *Member:* Indianapolis, Indiana State and American Bar Associations; Indiana Trial Lawyers Association (Executive Board Member and Officer; Assistant Treasurer); The Association of Trial Lawyers of America (Executive Board Member and Chair-Elect of the Traumatic Brain Injury Litigation Group; Executive Board Member of the Interstate Trucking Litigation Group). Brain Injury Association of Indiana, Inc. (Chair, 2000-2001; Lifetime Member; Member, Board of Directors, 1982-2002). (Certified as a Civil Trial Advocacy Specialist by the National Board of Trial Advocacy). ***REPORTED CASES:*** Ingram v. Hooks Drugs, Inc., 476 N.E.2d 881 (Ind.App. 1985); Gates v. Riley, 723 N.E.2d 946 (Ind. APp. 2000); Ray Hayes v. Heinamenn, 768 N.E.2d 899 (Ind.2002); Fendley vs Ford, Ind. App., 458 N.E.2d 1167 (1984); Barton-Malow vs Wilburn, Ind., 556 N.E.2d 324 (1990); Amicus Brief for Indiana Trial Lawyers Association: Dillon vs Glover, 597 N.E.2d 971 (Ind. App., 1992); Selleck v. Westfield Insurance Company, (Ind. App.) 617 N.E.2d 968 (1993); Indiana Department of Insurance v. Linda Callaway, (Ind. App.) 609 N.E.2d 424 (1993), Transfer Denied, May, 1993; Schaffer v. Roberts, 650 N.E.2d 341 (Ind.App. 1995); Western Reserve Mutual Casualty Co. vs Gregory Holland and Marcia Holland (Ind. App.) 666 NE2d 966 (Ind. App. 1996); Amicus brief for ITLA, In re Guardianship of Wade, 711 N.E.2d 851 (Ind. App. 1999); Amicus brief for ITLA, Martin v. Dr. Richey, 711 N.E.2d 1273 (Ind. 1999); James H. Smith v. Dr. Washington, 734 N.E.2d 548 (Ind. 2000); Amicus brief for ITLA, Mendenhall v. Skinner & Broadbent Co., 728 N.E.2d 140 (Ind. 2000); Sheila Ray-Hayes v. Nissan Motor Company, et.al., 743 N.E.2d 777 (Ind. App. 2001); R.L. McCoy, Inc. v. Jack, Michael L. & Jack, Amy S. (Ind. Ct. 2002) 772 N.E.2d 987 (Ind. 2002). ***PRACTICE AREAS:*** Personal Injury Law; Brain Injury; Medical Malpractice Law; Products Liability Law. ***Email:*** tcd@tbilawyer.com

DANIEL S. CHAMBERLAIN, born South Bend, Indiana, September 11, 1966; admitted to bar, 1992, North Carolina, Indiana and U.S. District Court, Northern and Southern Districts of Indiana; 1995, U.S. Court of Appeals, Seventh Circuit. *Education:* Ball State University (B.S., cum laude, 1989); Indiana University (J.D., 1992). Recipient, Lambda Chi Alpha Educational Foundation Graduate Scholarship. Gruenewald Scholar. Note Editor, Indiana International Law Review, 1990-1992. Member, Moot Court Society. Member, Professional Association of Diving Instructors (P.A.D.I.) Divemaster, 1985. Author: "Administration Amends Driver Safety Rules," Indiana Lawyer, 2005; "Federal Trucking Rules Amendments," ATLA Newsletter, 2004; "Truck Cases: Rules of the Road," Trial Magazine, 1998; "Working with Co-Counsel," Trial Magazine, 1998; "Jury Prejudice in Civil Litigation," Indiana Lawyer, 1997; "The Professional Truck Driver," ATLA Newsletter,

(This Listing Continued)

1996; "A Practitioner's Guide to Filing a Tort Claim Against A Governmental Entity," Res Gestae, 1995; "Premises Liability Standards," Indiana Lawyer, 2000; "Trucking Litigation," Indiana Lawyer, 1999; "Seat Belt Defense," Indiana Lawyer, 1999. Real Property Broker, Indiana, 1990. Lecturer: "Pedestrian Slip Resistance Cases," Indiana Trial Lawyers Association, 1996; "Voir Dire: Overcoming Jury Bias," Indiana Trial Lawyers Association, 1997; "Premises Liability: Beyond the Basics," ICLEF, 1997; "The Use and Abuse of Expert Witnesses, Codes, Regulations, and Standards," ATLA, 1997; "Mastering Medical Litigation," Indiana CLEF, 1998; "Highway Defect and Design Cases," ATLA, 1998; "Effective Use of the Internet to Win Your Case," ATLA, 1998; "Connective Tissue Injury," ITLA, 1998; "Uninsured and Underinsured Motorist Law," NBI, 1999; "Juror Misconduct," ITLA, 1999; "Effective Expert Witnesses," NBI, 2000; "ASTM Standards," ATLA, 2000; "Medical Research," ICLEF, 2000; "Case Management," ATLA, 2000; "Trucking Litigation," ICLEF, 2001; "Trampoline Injury," ICLEF, 2001; "Nursing Home Litigation," Lorman, 2002. Member, Governor's Council on Impaired and Dangerous Driving, 2000—. "Transportation Litigation," ICLEF, 2003; "Litigating a Motor Vehicle Crash," NBI, 2004; "Litigating Truck Cases," ATLA, 2004. *Member:* Indianapolis (Chair, Litigation Section), Indiana State (Member, House of Delegates, 1995—; Co-chair Legislation Committees) and American (Member, Sections on: Litigation, Products Liability and Medical Malpractice Committees; Insurance) Bar Associations; The Association of Trial Lawyers of America (Chair, Tort Liability Litigation Section, 1997-2001); Indiana Trial Lawyers Association (Director, 1998— Co-Chair, Legislative Committee); American Society for Testing and Materials (F13, F15 Committee Member); Certified Civil Trial Mediator, 1993. Fellow, National College of Advocacy; Indiana Amputee Foundation, Inc. (Member: Board of Directors, 1995-1997); Brain Injury Association of Indiana, Inc. (Professional Member, 1997—). ***PRACTICE AREAS:*** Personal Injury; Brain Injury; Truck Accidents; Nursing Home Negligence; Products Liability; Construction Site Injury. ***Email:*** dsc@usLAWS.com

ASSOCIATE

RONALD S. TODD, born Ithaca, New York, August 7, 1964; admitted to bar, 1995, Indiana and U.S. District Court, Southern and Northern Districts of Indiana; 1996, U.S. Court of Federal Claims; U.S. Court of Appeals, Seventh Circuit. *Education:* Miami University (B.A., 1987); Purdue University (M.S.M., 1989); Notre Dame University (J.D., cum laude, 1995). President, Nora Toastmasters. Vice President, Carmel Lions Club. Past Chairman, Howard County Election Board. Member, Advisory Council, United Way Information and Referral/Volunteer Action Center. Instructor, Junior Achievement. *Member:* Indianapolis, Indiana State (Litigation and Small Firm Sections) and American (Litigation and Small Firm Sections) Bar Associations; Indiana Trial Lawyers Association; The Association of Trial Lawyers of America (Nursing Home Litigation Section). ***REPORTED CASES:*** Young v. Tri-/Etch, Inc., 790 N.E.2d 456 (Ind. 2003); Turner v. Richmond Power and Light Co., 763 N.E.2d 1005 (Ind. App. 2002); Blocher v. DeBartolo Properties Management, Inc. 760 N.E.2d 229 (Ind. App. 2001); Creasy v. Rusk, 730 N.E.2d 659 (Ind. 2000); City of Peru v. Brooks, 676 N.E.2d 393 (Ind. App. 1997); McKay v. McKay, 671 N.E.2d 194 (Ind. App. 1996). ***PRACTICE AREAS:*** Personal Injury Litigation; Motor Vehicle Injuries; Wrongful Death; Products Liability; Premises Liability. ***Email:*** rst@tbilawyer.com

OF COUNSEL

RALPH J. BRATCH, born Marion, Indiana, June 18, 1965; admitted to bar, 1990, Indiana; U.S. District Court, Northern and Southern Districts of Indiana. *Education:* Ball State University (B.S., 1987); Valparaiso University (J.D., 1990). *Member:* Indianapolis Bar Association (Member, Litigation Section); Indiana Trial Lawyer Association; The Association of Trial Lawyers of America; United States Army Reserve (Judge Advocate). ***PRACTICE AREAS:*** Personal Injury Litigation; Spinal Injury; Automobile Accidents and Injuries; Truck Accidents; Products Liability; Medical Malpractice. ***Email:*** rjb@sciinformation.com

REFERENCE: NBD Bank, N.A.

DOUGLAS LAW OFFICES, P.C.

Established in 1999

225 NORTH DELAWARE STREET
INDIANAPOLIS, INDIANA 46204
Telephone: 317-269-3422
Facsimile: 317-269-3419
Email: douglaslaw@dslindiana.net
URL: http://www.lawyers.com/douglaslawoffices

Family Law, Divorce, Child Custody, Child Support, Visitation Rights, Adoption, Third-Party Custody, Guardianships, Juvenile Delinquency, Paternity.

CHRISTINE DOUGLAS, born Indianapolis, May 21, 1968; admitted to bar, 1997, Indiana. *Education:* Purdue University (B.A., 1990); Valparaiso University (J.D., 1996). Certified Family Law Specialist, Indiana State Bar Association. Attorney: Legal Services Organization of Indiana, Inc., 1997-1999; Marion County Public Defenders Agency, Juvenile Division, 1999-2000. *Member:* American (Member, Sections on: Family Law; Law Practice Management; General Practice; Solo and Small Firm), Indiana State (Member: Family Law; Civil Rights of Children Committee) and Indianapolis (Member, Family Law Division; Women in the Law Executive Committee) Bar Associations; We the People; Project Peace; Indianapolis Legal Aid Society (Member, Family Law Executive Committee). ***PRACTICE AREAS:*** Family Law; Divorce; Child Custody; Visitation Rights; Child Support; Paternity; Adoption Law; Third Party Custody; Guardianship; Juvenile Law.

DREWRY SIMMONS VORNEHM, LLP

Established in 1996

8888 KEYSTONE CROSSING, SUITE 1200
INDIANAPOLIS, INDIANA 46240
Telephone: 317-580-4848
Telecopier: 317-580-4855
Email: info@drewrysimmons.com
URL: http://www.drewrysimmons.com

Business, Construction, Government Contracts, Surety, Commercial and related Arbitration and Litigation, Securities, Estate Planning, Trusts, Taxation, Construction and Public Contracts law, Surety, Civil Litigation, Mediation and Arbitration, Corporations, Business and Securities Law, Estate Planning and Administration, Commercial Real Estate Transactions, Land Use Planning and Zoning, Labor and Employment Law, Adoption.

FIRM PROFILE: Drewry Simmons Vornehm, LLP is one of Indiana's most notable law firms having a highly focused concentration in Construction Law and other associated commercial matters. Its lawyers have approximately 100 years combined experience in handling large and complex construction and design-related disputes through litigation, arbitration, mediation and negotiation. Clients of the firm include general contractors, subcontractors, material suppliers, public and private owners and developers, design professionals, sureties, financial institution, and insurers.

MICHAEL F. DREWRY, born New Albany, Indiana, May 14, 1952; admitted to bar, 1979, Indiana and U.S. District Court, Southern and Northern Districts of Indiana. *Education:* Purdue University (B.A., with highest distinction, 1974); University of Minnesota (M.A., 1975); Indiana University (J.D., magna cum laude, 1979). Phi Beta Kappa; Phi Alpha Theta. Bush Foundation Fellow, 1974-1975; 1975-1976. Indiana Bar Foundation Scholar, 1979. Seminar Chairman: "Construction Law Issues," Indiana Continuing Legal Education Forum (ICLEF), 2004; "Construction Claims & Liabilities Revisited," (ICLEF) 2001; "Mechanic's Lien and Related Claims," ICLEF, 1994; "Construction Law For The 90's," ICLEF, 1992. Author: "Performance Problems for the Owner: Delays Defective Work, Contract Defaults and Termination," ICLEF, 2004; "Mechanic's Lien Formalities and Priorities - General Coverage of the Mechanic's Lien Remedy," ICLEF, 2004, 2005; "Vesting and Priorities Among Competing Liens," ICLEF, 2004, 2005; "Owner Personal Liability to Remote Claimants," ICLEF, 2005; "Indiana Lien Law," CPI Lienlaw-Online.com, Construction Publications, Inc., 2001-2005; "Design Liabilities: Defective Plans and Specifications and Shop Drawing Risks," ICLEF, 2001; "Construction Delay and Impact Claims," ICLEF, 2001; "Mechanic's Liens," ICLEF, 2001 and 2005; "General Coverage of Mechanic's Lien Formalities & Priorities," ICLEF, 1999, 2003, 2004 and 2005; "Mechanic's Lien Update-House Bill 1367," ICLEF, 1999; "General Coverage of the Mechanic's Lien Remedy," ICLEF, 1990, 1994, 1998; "Acquiring and Perfecting Lien Rights," ICLEF, 1982, 1985 and 1987; "Specifications, Changes and Changed Working Conditions," ICLEF, 1983; "Construction Payment Remedies in Indiana," National Business Institute (NBI), 2005; "Indiana Construction Law (Field Changes, Differing Site Conditions, Job Delays and Delay/Impact Claims, Contractual and Statutory Payment Remedies, and Dispute Resolution)," NBI, 2000, 2002, 2003 and 2004; "Construction Law (Contract Changes, Differing Site Conditions, Delays, Surety Bonds and Payment Remedies)," NBI, 1987, 1990, 1991 and 1995; "Managing Complex Construction Law Issues in Indiana," NBI, 2005; "AIA Contracts in Indiana," Lorman Education Services ("Lorman"), 2004, 2005; "Public Contracting Codes & Competitive Bidding," Lorman, 2001; "Creative Strategies for Project Completion and Litigation Avoidance," Lorman, 1999, 2000, 2001, 2002, 2003 and 2004; "Construction Issues," Lorman, 2001; "Construction Claims (Contract Disputes, Bid Mistakes, Defective Specifications, Field Performance Claims, Defective Work, Defaults and Payment Claims)," Lorman, 1999-2002; "Construction Contracting For Public Entities in Indiana," Lorman, 1999 and 2001; "Law For Design Professionals," Lorman, 1999-2001; "Architect and Engineer Liability and Practice in Indiana," Lorman, 2000; "Construction Defect Claims," Lorman, 1999 and 2000; "Mechanic's Lien Law," Lorman, 1997, 1998, 1999, 2000, 2001 and 2005; "Construction Management/Design Build in Indiana," Lorman, 1999; "Construction Claims & Liens in Indiana," Lorman, 1995. Instructor: Supervisory Training Program, Associated General Contractors Education and Research Foundation, 1997; Indiana Department of Commerce Procurement Workshop, 2000; Purdue University Joint Transportation Research Program Road School, 2002. Speaker for Trade Association Conferences: Associated General Contractors of Indiana; Indiana Subcontractors Association; National Precast Contractors Association; Construction Advancement Foundation, Indiana Chapter; National Association of Women in Construction, Indianapolis Chapter; Indiana Fabricators Association; American Society of Professional Estimators, Indiana Chapter; Construction Financial Management Association, Indiana Chapter; Indiana CPA Society. *Member:* Indianapolis, Indiana State (Chairman, Construction and Surety Law Section) and American (Member: Public Contract Law Section: Forum Committee on the Construction Industry; Fidelity and Surety Law Subcommittee; Section of Litigation: Construction Litigation Committee; Surety Law Subcommittee) Bar Associations; Fellow, Indiana State Bar Foundation. ***PRACTICE AREAS:*** Construction Law and Litigation; Public Contract Law; Surety Law. ***Email:*** mdrewry@drewrysimmons.com

DAVID L. SIMMONS, born Marion, Indiana, May 12, 1953; admitted to bar, 1980, Indiana and U.S. District Court, Southern District of Indiana; 1983, U.S. Court of Appeals, Seventh Circuit; 1984, U.S. Supreme Court. *Education:* Indiana University (B.A., 1975; M.B.A., 1977; J.D., 1980). General Counsel: Construction League of Indiana, Inc.; Master Insulators Association, Inc. Lecturer and Author: "The Mechanic's Lien Remedy in Indiana," Indiana Continuing Legal Education, 2005; "Indiana Construction Management Summit," McGraw-Hill Construction/Dodge/Somerset, 2004; "Construction Claims in Indiana," Lorman, 1999-2003; "Creative Strategies for Project Completion and Litigation Avoidance," Lorman, 1999; "Effective Construction Dispute Avoidance and Resolution in Indiana," NBI, 2004; "Construction Payment Remedies," NBI, 1997, 1999, 2002 and 2004; "Advanced Construction Law," NBI, 1998 and 2000; "Contractual Relationships in Construction Contracting: An Overview of Express and Implied Terms in the Construction Industry," NBI, 1998; "The Mechanics Lien Remedy", NBI, 1997; "State and Local Public Works Claims," NBI, 1997; "Mechanic's Liens and Related Claims," ICLEF, 1994, 2005;

(This Listing Continued)

DREWRY SIMMONS VORNEHM, LLP, Indianapolis—Continued

"General Coverage of the Mechanics Lien Remedy," ICLEF, 1994; "Strategies for Management of Business Collections," Lorman, 1991 and 1993; "Construction Litigation: Representing the Contractor," Wiley and Sons, 1992; "Strategies for Management of Business Collections," Lorman, 1991; "Procedural Due Process in Postjudgment Garnishment Proceedings," 23 Indiana Law Review 221, 1990; "Construction Litigation: Representing the Contractor," Wiley and Sons, 1985; "Disregarding Business Entities in Indiana," ICLEF, 2002. Associate Faculty Member, Department of Construction Technology, IUPUI. Instructor, Supervisory Training Program, Associated General Contractors Education and Research Foundation, 1997. Registered Civil Mediator, Indiana Commission for Continuing Legal Education Registry of Approved Court Mediators. *Member:* Indianapolis (Member, Sections on: Commercial; Bankruptcy; Business Law), Indiana State (Member, Sections on: Construction and Surety Law; At-Large Council Member; ADR; Bankruptcy and Creditors Rights; Corporate, Banking and Business Law) and American (Member, Sections on: Public Contract Law; ADR; Member, Forum Committee on the Construction Industry; Fidelity and Surety Subcommittee) Bar Associations; Commercial Law League of America (Member, Creditors Rights Section). Fellow, Indiana State Bar Foundation. ***PRACTICE AREAS:*** Construction Law; Public Contract Law; Commercial Litigation. ***Email:*** dsimmons@drewrysimmons.com

DAVID B. VORNEHM, born Indianapolis, Indiana, May 21, 1949; admitted to bar, 1993, Indiana and U.S. District Court, Northern and Southern Districts of Indiana. *Education:* Indiana University (B.A., 1973; J.D., 1993). Recipient: Indiana Association of Cities and Towns Scholarship, 1992. Chief Engineer, Construction Division, Indiana Department of Public Works, 1984-1993. Author: Indiana Chapter: *2002 State Public Construction Law Source Book,* CCH Inc. Indiana Mechanic's Liens, 1998, 1999, 2000 and 2001; Construction Management/Design Build in Indiana, Lorman Education Services, 1999, 2000 and 2001. Author and Lecturer: "ABA Sourcebook on Construction Contracting, Indiana Chapter," (ABA, Public Contract Section, 1999); "Start-Up and Operation of the Indianapolis Ozone Disinfections Systems," Ozone Science and Engineering, 1988; "Limitations of the Iodometric Determination of Ozone," Journal of the American Water Works Association, June, 1989; Indiana Mechanic's Liens, Lorman Education Services, 1998, 1999 and 2000; Mechanic Lien Law, Lorman Education Services, 1998, 1999 and 2000; Indiana Construction Defect Claims, Lorman Education Services, 1999, 2000; Construction Management/Design Build in Indiana, Lorman Education Services, 1999, 2000; Construction Contracting For Public Entities in Indiana, Lorman Education Services, 1999, 2000; Creative Strategies for Project Completion and Litigation Avoidance, Lorman Education Services, 1999; Construction Claim (Contract Disputes, Field Performance Claims, Defective Work/Defaults and Payment Claims), Lorman Education Services, 1999, 2000. Adjunct Professor, Department of Construction Technology, Purdue School of Engineering and Technology, IUPUI. *Member:* Indianapolis, Indiana State (Member, Construction and Surety Law Section) and American (Member, Public Contract Law Section; Forum Committee on the Construction Industry; Fidelity and Surety Law Subcommittee; Construction Litigation Committee, Section of Litigation) Bar Associations. ***PRACTICE AREAS:*** Construction Law and Litigation; Public Contract Law; Surety; Environmental; Commercial Law. ***Email:*** dvornehm@drewrysimmons.com

JOSEPH M. LEONE, born Indianapolis, Indiana, October 17, 1966; admitted to bar, 1995, Indiana and U.S. District Court, Southern District of Indiana. *Education:* Purdue University (B.S., Civil Engineering, 1989); Indiana University (J.D., 1995). Lecturer: "Indiana Mechanic's Lien Law," Lorman Business Center, 1998-2005; "1997 AIA Document A201 Changes," ASPE, 1998; "Contractor's Liability for Jobsite Injuries," Evansville Contractors Association, 1998; "Construction Management/Design Build in Indiana," Lorman Education Services, 1999, 2002 and 2005; "Creative Strategies for Project Completion and Litigation Avoidance," Lorman Education Services, 1999-2002; "Mechanics Liens," National Business Institute, 2000-2005; "Purchasing and Procurement Law in Indiana," Lorman Education Services, 2000; "Sewer and Water Construction-Inspector Training," Indiana Water Pollution Control Association, 2000-2003; "Construction Litigation in Indiana," Lorman Education Services, 2001; "Construction Contracting for Public Entities," Lorman Education Services, 2001; "Construction Issues," Lorman Education Services, 2001; "Residential Construction Law," ICLEF, 2004; "Managing Risk in Business," ICLEF, 2004; "Indiana Construction Law, What do you do when...," Lorman, 2004; "Mechanic's Lien Law in Indiana," BKD Institute, Association General Contractors of Indiana, 2005; Co-Author, Indiana Chapter, *State by State Guide to Architect, Engineer, and Contractor Licensing,* Aspen Law & Business, 1999. *Member:* Indianapolis, Indiana State (Executive Counsel, Construction and Surety Law Section) and American (Member, Sections on: Construction Law; Public Contract Law; Forum Committee on the Construction Industry) Bar Associations; National Society of Professional Engineers. ***PRACTICE AREAS:*** Construction Litigation; Public Construction Law. ***Email:*** jleone@drewrysimmons.com

MICHAEL P. BISHOP, born Lakewood, Ohio, August 16, 1953; admitted to bar, 1980, Indiana; U.S. Court of Appeals, Seventh Circuit; U.S. District Court, Southern and Northern Districts of Indiana; U.S. Supreme Court. *Education:* Metropolitan State College (B.A., 1977); Indiana University School of Law (J.D., 1980). Listed, *The Best Lawyers in America,* 2006 Edition. Law Clerk to Hon. James E. Noland, U.S. District Court, Southern District of Indiana, 1981-1983. Author: Civil Mediation, Indiana Alternative Dispute Resolution Practice Guide; Faculty, Indiana Trial Advocacy College. Primary Trainer, Advanced Training for Civil Mediators in Indiana . *Member:* Indianapolis (Co-Chair, Settlement Week, 1986-1991; Chairman, Litigation Section, 1987-1988; Secretary, 1995-1997) and Indiana State (Chairman, ADR Section, 2000-2002; Secretary, Board of Governors, 1997-1998; District 11 Representative to Board of Governors, 2003—) Bar Associations. Distinguished Fellow, Indianapolis Bar Foundation. Fellow: Indiana State Bar Foundation; American Academy of Adoption Attorneys; American Academy of Civil Trial Mediators. ***PRACTICE AREAS:*** Civil Litigation; Mediation; Probate Litigation; Adoption Law. ***Email:*** mbishop@drewrysimmons.com

ROBERT J. MILFORD, born New Haven, Connecticut, October 31, 1955; admitted to bar, 1983, Indiana; U.S. District Court, Southern and Northern Districts of Indiana; U.S. Tax Court. *Education:* Butler University (B.S., 1977); Indiana University at Indianapolis (J.D., 1983). Certified Public Accountant, Indiana, 1981. *Member:* Indianapolis, Indiana

(This Listing Continued)

State and American (Member, Business Law Section) Bar Associations; Construction Financial Management Association. ***PRACTICE AREAS:*** Business Law; Construction Law; Trusts and Estates; Taxation. ***Email:*** rmilford@drewrysimmons.com

MARYELLEN K. BISHOP, born Marion, Indiana, April 28, 1957; admitted to bar, 1983, Indiana and U.S. Tax Court; U.S. District Court, Southern and Northern Districts of Indiana; U.S. Supreme Court. *Education:* Indiana University (B.S., 1979); Indiana University School of Law (J.D., 1982). Distinguished Fellow, Indianapolis Bar Foundation. Fellow, Indiana State Bar Foundation. Member, Indiana Probate Code Study Commission, Appointed by Governor; Program Chair and Presenter: "Basic Will and Trust Drafting," ICLEF, 1999-2004. Master Chair: "Probate Skills Series," ICLEF; "What's New in Estate Planning and Administration," 2002-2005. Vice Chair, Indiana University Alumni Association. *Member:* Indianapolis (Vice President and Member, Executive Committee, 1999-2000; Council Member of Estate Planning Section, 1997—), Indiana State (Co-Chair of Written Publications Committee for Res Gestae, 2001-2004) and American Bar Associations; Estate Planning Council of Indianapolis. ***PRACTICE AREAS:*** Estate Planning; Trust Planning; Estate Administration; Trust Administration; Estate Litigation; Trust Litigation. ***Email:*** mebishop@drewrysimmons.com

PAUL G. REIS, born Indianapolis, Indiana, June 28, 1954; admitted to bar, 1980, Indiana; U.S. District Court, Southern District of Indiana. *Education:* University of Notre Dame (B.S., 1976); Indiana University (J.D., 1980). *Member:* Indianapolis, Indiana State and American Bar Associations. ***PRACTICE AREAS:*** Commercial Real Estate; Zoning, Planning and Land Use; Real Estate Development; Commercial Leasing. ***Email:*** preis@drewrysimmons.com

DAVID A. TEMPLE, born Cleveland, Ohio, September 2, 1969; admitted to bar, 1994, Indiana; U.S. District Court, Northern and Southern Districts of Indiana; U.S. Court of Appeals, Seventh Circuit. *Education:* Indiana University (B.S., 1991; J.D., 1994). *Member:* Indianapolis, Indiana State and American Bar Associations; Defense Research Institute; Defense Trial Counsel of Indiana. ***PRACTICE AREAS:*** Corporate Litigation; Construction Law; Environmental Law; Coverage Litigation; Products Liability. ***Email:*** dtemple@drewrysimmons.com

THOMAS J. GRAU, born Mishawaka, Indiana, October 24, 1950; admitted to bar, 1983, Indiana; U.S. District Court, Northern and Southern Districts of Indiana; U.S. Court of Appeals, Seventh Circuit. *Education:* Ball State University (B.S., with honors, 1972); Indiana University (M.B.A., with distinction, 1978; J.D., cum laude, 1983). *Member:* Indianapolis, Indiana State and American (Vice Chair of the Construction Litigation Committee of the Litigation Section) Bar Associations; Defense Research Institute; The American Institute of Architects (Allied Member); American Council of Engineering Companies of Indiana. ***PRACTICE AREAS:*** Professional Liability; Environmental Law; Products Liability; Commercial Law; Commercial Litigation; Construction Law. ***Email:*** tgrau@drewrysimmons.com

---

PATRICK A. DREWRY, born Minneapolis, Minnesota, June 16, 1976; admitted to bar, 2001, Indiana; U.S. District Court, Southern and Northern Districts of Indiana. *Education:* Purdue University (B.A., Dean's Scholar, 1998); Indiana University (J.D., 2001). Contributing Author and Lecturer: "Construction Claims (Defective Specifications, Payment Claims)," Lorman, 2002; "Creative Strategies for Project Completion and Litigation Avoidance," Lorman, 2003-2004; "Payment Claims and Remedies," ICLEF, 2004; "Indiana Mechanic's Lien Law," Lorman, 2005; "AIA Contracts in Indiana," Lorman, 2005. *Member:* Indianapolis (Member, Litigation Section, Business Law Section, Young Lawyers Division), Indiana State (Member, Sections on: Construction and Surety Law; Litigation, Business Law, Young Lawyers) and American (Forum Committee on the Construction Industry, Public Contract Law Section, Fidelity and Surety Law Subcommittee; Section of Litigation, Construction Litigation Committee) Bar Associations; American Inns of Court. ***PRACTICE AREAS:*** Construction Law; Public Contract Law; Surety Law; Commercial Litigation. ***Email:*** pdrewry@drewrysimmons.com

TAMMY S. KOCH, born Fort Wayne, Indiana, January 19, 1973; admitted to bar, 1998, Indiana and U.S. District Court, Northern and Southern Districts of Indiana; 2004, U.S. Court of Appeals, Sixth Circuit. *Education:* Purdue University (B.A., with highest distinction, 1994); Indiana University (J.D., 1998). *Member:* Indianapolis, Indiana State and American Bar Associations. ***PRACTICE AREAS:*** Corporate Law; Mergers and Acquisitions; Civil Litigation. ***Email:*** tkoch@drewrysimmons.com

MATTHEW J. SCHAFER, born Cincinnati, Ohio, February 11, 1975; admitted to bar, 2001, Indiana and U.S. District Court, Northern and Southern Districts of Indiana. *Education:* Purdue University (B.S., 1997); Indiana University School of Law (J.D., 2001). *Member:* Indianapolis, Indiana State (Member, Construction and Surety Law and Aviation Law Committees) and American (Forum Committee on the Construction Industry; Section of Litigation, Construction Litigation Committee) Bar Associations. ***PRACTICE AREAS:*** Civil Litigation; Professional Liability; Commercial Law; Construction Law; Products Liability. ***Email:*** mschafer@drewrysimmons.com

BRIAN M. FALCON, born Beech Grove, Indiana, June 19, 1976; admitted to bar, 2003, Indiana and U.S. District Courts, Northern and Southern Districts of Indiana. *Education:* Ball State University (B.S., 1998); Indiana University School of Law - Indianapolis (J.D., 2003). *Member:* Indianapolis (Member, Young Lawyers Division), Indiana State (Member, Litigation Section, Committee on the Construction Industry, Construction and Litigation Committee) and American (Member, Construction and Surety Law Forum; Sections on: Public Contract Law; Construction Law) Bar Associations. ***PRACTICE AREAS:*** Construction Law; Public Contract Law; Commercial Litigation; Business Litigation. ***Email:*** bfalcon@drewrysimmons.com

SEAN T. DEVENNEY, born Phoenixville, Pennsylvania, July 14, 1973; admitted to bar, 1998, Pennsylvania; 1999, Indiana; U.S. District Court, Northern and Southern Districts of Indiana; U.S. Court of Appeals, Seventh Circuit. *Education:* The Pennsylvania State University (B.S., with high honors, Finance, 1995); Indiana University School of Law - Bloomington (J.D., cum laude, 1998). *Member:* Indianapolis, Indiana State (Construction and Surety Law Section) and American (Forum Committee on the Construction Industry; Section of Litigation, Construction Litigation Committee) Bar Associations; American Inns of Court. ***REPORTED CASES:*** *Narducci v. Tedrow,* 736 N.E.2d 1288 (Ind. App.

(This Listing Continued)

2000); *Butler ex rel. Estate of Butler v. Kokomo Rehabilitation Hosp., Inc.*, 744 N.E.2d 1041 (Ind. App. 2001). ***PRACTICE AREAS:*** Civil Litigation; Construction Law; Torts; Professional Malpractice; Insurance. ***Email:*** sdevenney@drewrysimmons.com

SEAN M. MAYBERRY, born Hershey, Pennsylvania, October 14, 1974; admitted to bar, 1999, Michigan; 2001, Illinois; 2003, Indiana and U.S. District Court, Northern and Southern Districts of Indiana. *Education:* Indiana University, Bloomington (B.A., 1996); Indiana University School of Law - Bloomington (J.D., 1999). *Member:* Indianapolis and Indiana State Bar Associations. (Attorney). ***PRACTICE AREAS:*** Corporate Law; Securities. ***Email:*** smayberry@drewrysimmons.com

PATRICK M. MILLER, born Waukesha, Wisconsin, November 4, 1976; admitted to bar, 2002, Illinois and Wisconsin; 2004, Indiana. *Education:* University of Wisconsin-Madison (B.A., 1999); Marquette University Law School (J.D., 2002). *Member:* Indianapolis, Chicago, Indiana State (Member, Construction and Surety Law Section), Illinois State and American (Member: Litigation Section, Construction Litigation Committee; Young Lawyers Division; Forum Committee on the Construction Industry) Bar Associations; State Bar of Wisconsin. ***PRACTICE AREAS:*** Construction Law; Construction Litigation; Public Contract Law; Surety Law; Commercial Litigation. ***Email:*** pmiller@drewrysimmons.com

ROBERT J. ORELUP, born Merrillville, Indiana, July 13, 1973; admitted to bar, 1999, Indiana and U.S. District Court, Northern and Southern Districts of Indiana. *Education:* Indiana University (B.A., general honors, with distinction, 1996) Phi Beta Kappa; Indiana University School of Law - Bloomington (J.D., cum laude, 1999). *Member:* Indianapolis, Indiana State (Member, Construction and Surety Law Section) and American (Member, Construction and Surety Law Section; Forum Committee on the Construction Industry; Section of Litigation, Construction Litigation Committee) Bar Associations; Defense Research Institute; Defense Trial Counsel of Indiana (Member: Employment and Construction Law Section). ***PRACTICE AREAS:*** Labor and Employment; Construction Law; Commercial Litigation; Torts. ***Email:*** rorelup@drewrysimmons.com

WILLIAM E. KELLEY, JR., born Elizabethtown, Kentucky, August 1, 1978; admitted to bar, 2003, Indiana, U.S. District Court, Southern and Northern Districts of Indiana. *Education:* Hanover College (B.A., 2000); Indiana University School of Law - Indianapolis (J.D., 2003). *Member:* Indianapolis and Indiana State (Member, Construction and Surety Law Section; Land Use and Zoning Section) and American (Member, Forum on the Construction Industry) Bar Associations. ***PRACTICE AREAS:*** Construction Law; Zoning, Planning and Land Use; Commercial Litigation; Real Estate Acquisitions; Real Estate Sales; Real Estate Leasing; Real Estate Development. ***Email:*** wkelley@drewrysimmons.com

DANIEL M. DREWRY, admitted to bar, 2003, Indiana. *Education:* Purdue University (B.A., 2000); University of Cincinnati College of Law (J.D., 2003). Member, University of Cincinnati Law Review. *Member:* Indiana State (Member, Construction and Surety Law Section) and American (Member: Forum Committee on the Construction Industry; Public Contract Law Section; Fidelity and Surety Law Subcommittee; Litigation Section, Construction Litigation Committee) Bar Associations. ***PRACTICE AREAS:*** Construction Law; Public Construction Law; Surety Law; Civil Litigation; Products Liability. ***Email:*** ddrewry@drewrysimmons.com

OF COUNSEL

S. DOUGLAS TROLSON (1942-2002)

DUE, DOYLE, FANNING & METZGER, LLP

Established in 1982

900 CIRCLE TOWER BUILDING
55 MONUMENT CIRCLE
INDIANAPOLIS, INDIANA 46204-5900
Telephone: 317-635-7700
Fax: 317-636-2408
Email: duedoyle@duedoyle.com
URL: http://www.duedoyle.com

Insurance Defense, Coverage, Corporate Litigation, Personal Injury, Workers Compensation, Products Liability, Toxic Torts, Asbestos, Alternative Dispute Resolution.

MEMBERS OF FIRM

DANFORD R. DUE, born Louisville, Kentucky, September 28, 1948; admitted to bar, 1973, Indiana. *Education:* Vanderbilt University (B.A., 1970); Indiana University (J.D., cum laude, 1973). *Member:* Indianapolis, Indiana State and American Bar Associations; Defense Trial Counsel of Indiana; Defense Research Institute; Law Club of Indianapolis. ***PRACTICE AREAS:*** Litigation; Insurance Defense; Personal Injury; Insurance Coverage; Arson, Fire and Explosions; Asbestos Defense. ***Email:*** ddue@duedoyle.com

ROBERT J. DOYLE, born Gary, Indiana, November 26, 1959; admitted to bar, 1985, Indiana. *Education:* DePauw University (B.A., 1982); Indiana University (J.D., 1985). Author: "Occupational Disease," Indiana continuing Legal Education Forum; Trial Advocacy in Indiana; National Business Institute, 1993; Advanced Workers Compensation in Indiana; National Business Institute, 1994-1996; Workers' Compensation and the ADA, 1995. . *Member:* Indianapolis, Indiana State and American Bar Associations; Indiana Defense Lawyers Association; Defense Research Institute. ***PRACTICE AREAS:*** Insurance Defense; Litigation; Personal Injury; Workers Compensation. ***Email:*** rdoyle@duedoyle.com

ROBERT A. FANNING, born Huntington, Indiana, January 18, 1951; admitted to bar, 1976, Indiana. *Education:* Indiana University (B.S., 1973; J.D., cum laude, 1976). Member, Worker's Compensation Committee, Indiana Chamber of Commerce. Chair, Worker's Compensation Committee, Indiana Manufacturer's Association. Executive Director, Indiana Self-Insurers Association. *Member:* Defense Trial Counsel of Indiana (Section Chair, 1994). ***PRACTICE AREAS:*** Workers Compensation; Workers Compensation Appeal; Workers Compensation Defense; Workers Compensation Subrogation. ***Email:*** rfanning@duedoyle.com

(This Listing Continued)

MARK A. METZGER, born Mattoon, Illinois, August 30, 1962; admitted to bar, 1989, Indiana and U.S. District Court, Northern and Southern Districts of Indiana; U.S. Court of Appeals, Seventh Circuit. *Education:* Indiana University (B.S., with distinction, 1985; M.P.A., 1989; J.D., cum laude, 1989). Fellow, Governors, 1985-1986. *Member:* Indianapolis, Indiana State and American (Member, Sections on: Insurance Law and Litigation Bar Associations; Indiana Defense Lawyers Association; Defense Research Institute. ***PRACTICE AREAS:*** Insurance Defense; Litigation; Personal Injury. ***Email:*** mmetzger@duedoyle.com

MICHAEL S. HUNTINE, born Ft. Wayne, Indiana, February 3, 1962; admitted to bar, 1987, Indiana and U.S. District Court, Northern and Southern Districts of Indiana. *Education:* Indiana University-Ft. Wayne (B.S., 1984); Indiana University-Indianapolis (J.D., 1987). Phi Delta Phi (Vice President, 1985-1986). *Member:* Indianapolis (Member, Sections on: Labor Law; Litigation); Indiana State (Member, Labor and Employment Law Section) and American (Member, Tort and Insurance Defense Section) Bar Associations. ***PRACTICE AREAS:*** Insurance Defense Litigation; Labor Law; Workers Compensation. ***Email:*** mhuntine@duedoyle.com

KRISTEN K. ROLLISON, born Vincennes, Indiana, March 14, 1961; admitted to bar, 1986, Indiana. *Education:* Indiana University (B.A., summa cum laude, 1983); University of San Diego (J.D., 1986). Member, Indiana Worker's Compensation Institute. *Member:* Indianapolis and Indiana State Bar Associations. ***PRACTICE AREAS:*** Worker's Compensation Law. ***Email:*** krollison@duedoyle.com

ASSOCIATES

MARY A. SCHOPPER, born Logansport, Indiana, December 18, 1960; admitted to bar, 1991, Indiana. *Education:* Indiana University (B.A., 1983; J.D., cum laude, 1991). *Member:* Indianapolis and Indiana State Bar Associations. ***PRACTICE AREAS:*** Workers Compensation. ***Email:*** mschopper@duedoyle.com

DANIEL G. FOOTE, born Rockford, Illinois, April 28, 1969; admitted to bar, 1997, Indiana. *Education:* Indiana University (B.A., 1992; J.D., 1997). Member, Mortar Board. Member, Indiana Worker's Compensation Institute. *Member:* Indiana State Bar Association. ***LANGUAGES:*** Spanish. ***PRACTICE AREAS:*** Workers Compensation. ***Email:*** dfoote@duedoyle.com

CYNTHIA E. MUSIC, born Quincy, Massachusetts, April 13, 1970; admitted to bar, 1998, Indiana and U.S. District Court, Northern and Southern Districts of Indiana. *Education:* Ball State University (B.S., cum laude, 1995); Indiana University School of Law - Bloomington (J.D., 1998). Member, Ball State University Honors College. Member, Johnson County Legal Aid Committee, 2001. *Member:* Johnson County, Indiana State and American Bar Associations. ***PRACTICE AREAS:*** Insurance Defense; Commercial Litigation; Corporate Law; Business Law; Administrative Law. ***Email:*** cmusic@duedoyle.com

LISA M. DILLON, born Indianapolis, Indiana, May 22, 1976; admitted to bar, 2001, Indiana and U.S. District Court, Southern District of Indiana. *Education:* Wittenberg University (B.A., 1998); Indiana University School of Law (J.D., 2001). ***PRACTICE AREAS:*** Workers Compensation; Insurance Defense. ***Email:*** ldillon@duedoyle.com

DANIEL L. QUIGLEY, born Tipton, Indiana, May 25, 1977; admitted to bar, 2003, Indiana. *Education:* Furman University (B.A., 1999); Indiana University School of Law (J.D., 2003). *Member:* Indianapolis and Indiana State Bar Associations. ***PRACTICE AREAS:*** Insurance Defense; Workers Compensation. ***Email:*** dquigley@duedoyle.com

REBECCA K. BROWNING, born Pittsburgh, Pennsylvania, November 22, 1965; admitted to bar, 1992, Indiana. *Education:* Miami University (B.Phil., 1987); Indiana University (J.D., 1992). Deputy Prosecutor, Marion County, 1992-1994, 2001-2002. *Member:* Indianapolis Bar Association; American Inn of Court. ***PRACTICE AREAS:*** Insurance Defense. ***Email:*** rbrowning@duedoyle.com

OF COUNSEL

JAMES E. DOWLING, born Posey County, Indiana, April 29, 1934; admitted to bar, 1961, Indiana. *Education:* Georgetown University School of Foreign Service (B.S.F.S., 1955); George Washington University; Indiana University (J.D., 1961). Member, Land Use Control Commission, Bloomington, Indiana, 1960-1961. Deputy Prosecutor, Marion County, 1963. *Member:* Indianapolis, Indiana State and American Bar Associations; American College of Mortgage Attorneys. [With U.S. Army Finance Corps, 1956-1957]. (Also Member, Lulich, Murphy, Dowling & Associates, P.C.). ***Email:*** email@duedoyle.com

REPRESENTATIVE CLIENTS: Accident Fund; AIG; Allied Ins. Group; American Electric Power; American Family Ins. Co.; American States Ins. Co.; Amerisure; Argonaut Insurance; Auto-Owners Ins. Co.; Casualty Ins. Co.; CIGNA; Cinergy; CNA; Crawford & Company; Crum & Foster; Cummins Engine Co.; Delphi Automotive; E.B.I. Ins. Companies; Employers Security Insurance (ESI); FCCI; Frank Gates; Fremont Compensation Group; GAB Robins; Gallagher Bassett; GDX Automotive; General Motors Corp.; Grange Insurance; Great American Insurance; Hoosier Ins. Co.; Illinois Farmers; Indiana Insurance; Indianapolis Power & Light Co.; Indianapolis Public Schools; International Steel Group; International Truck & Engine Co.; J.W.F. Specialty Co.; Liberty Mutual; Lumberman's Underwriting Alliance; Medical Assurance; Meridian Insurance; Nationwide Ins. Co.; Ohio Casualty Co.; Progressive Ins. Co.; Protective Ins. Co.; RSKCo; Rockwell Automation; Safeco; Secura Ins. Co.; Speedway/Super America; State Farm; St. Margaret Mercy Healthcare; The Hartford; Titan Indemnity; United Airlines; Unitrin; Wal-Mart; Wausau Ins. Co.; Zurich Ins. Co.

DUTTON & ASSOCIATES, L.L.C.

921 E. 86TH STREET, SUITE 130
INDIANAPOLIS, INDIANA 46240
Telephone: 317-254-9000
Fax: 317-254-9010
URL: http://www.duttonandassociates.com
Email: mdutton@duttonandassociates.com
URL: http://www.duttonlawfirm.com

Bankruptcy Law.

(This Listing Continued)

DUTTON & ASSOCIATES, L.L.C., Indianapolis—Continued

MARK C. DUTTON, born Indianapolis, Indiana, May 5, 1973; admitted to bar, 2001, Indiana. *Education:* Indiana University (B.A., 1998); Indiana University School of Law (J.D., 2001). *Member:* Indianapolis Bar Association; Indiana State Bar Association; American Bar Association. ***PRACTICE AREAS:*** Bankruptcy; Bankruptcy Chapter 7; Bankruptcy Chapter 13; Consumer Bankruptcy; Debtor Bankruptcy; Out of Court Debt Restructuring; Pre-Bankruptcy Workouts. ***Email:*** mdutton@duttonandassociates.com

EASTER & CAVOSIE

Established in 1996

8555 RIVER ROAD, SUITE 400

INDIANAPOLIS, INDIANA 46240

Telephone: 317-574-0828

Facsimile: 317-574-0969

URL: http://www.ec-lawfirm.com

Construction Law.

FIRM PROFILE: Easter & Cavosie represents construction industry participants in all phases of the construction process.

J. GREG EASTER, born Indianapolis, Indiana, February 17, 1959; admitted to bar, 1984, Indiana and U.S. District Court, Northern and Southern Districts of Indiana; 1985, U.S. Court of Appeals, Seventh Circuit. *Education:* Butler University (B.S., cum laude, 1981); Indiana University (J.D., cum laude, 1984). Associate Instructor, Appellate Advocacy, Indiana University, 1983-1984. Associate Professor, Argumentation, Indiana University-Purdue University, Indianapolis, 1985-1986. Associate Professor, Construction Law and Ethics, Indiana University-Purdue University, Indianapolis. Author: "Key Issues in Indiana Residential Construction Law," NBI, January 2004; "Construction Law: Collecting Through Creativity," ICLEF, July 1990; "Public Works Projects, Bidding and Bid Protests," ICLEF, February 1992; "Securing your Right to Payment: Mechanic's Liens are not the only Option," Indiana Industrial Journal, Oct. 1994; "Strategies for Avoiding Bid Problems" and "Strategies for Getting Paid," Lorman, October 1998; "Indiana's Public Works Statutes," Lorman, March 1999-2000. *Member:* Indianapolis, Indiana and American (Member, Forum on the Construction Industry) Bar Associations. ***PRACTICE AREAS:*** Construction Law. ***Email:*** geaster@ecp-law.net

J. MICHAEL CAVOSIE, born Indianapolis, Indiana, November 8, 1958; admitted to bar, 1992, Indiana and U.S. District Court, Northern and Southern Districts of Indiana; 1995, Illinois and U.S. District Court, Northern District of Illinois; U.S. Court of Appeals, Seventh Circuit. *Education:* Butler University (B.A., cum laude, 1981); Indiana University (J.D., magna cum laude, 1992). Order of the Coif. Recipient, American Jurisprudence Award. Associate and Senior Managing Editor, Indiana Law Journal. Co-Author: "Construction Contracts for Public Entities in Indiana," Lorman, 1999. *Member:* Indianapolis, Indiana State and American (Member, Forum on the Construction Industry) Bar Associations. ***PRACTICE AREAS:*** Construction Law; Labor and Employment. ***Email:*** mcavosie@ecp-law.net

DAVID A. TUCKER, born Oak Park, Illinois, February 27, 1963; admitted to bar, 1989, Indiana. *Education:* DePauw University (B.A., 1985); Indiana University (J.D., 1989). *Member:* Indianapolis, Indiana State and American (Member, Forum on the Construction Industry) Bar Associations. ***SPECIAL AGENCIES:*** Interstate Commerce Commission; U.S. Department of Transportation; Indiana Department of Transportation; Indiana Department of Revenue; Indiana Department of Environmental Management. ***PRACTICE AREAS:*** Construction Law; Motor Carrier Law. ***Email:*** dtucker@ecp-law.net

ASSOCIATES

THERESA L. SILVER, born South Bend, Indiana, March 31, 1974; admitted to bar, 2001, Indiana. *Education:* Purdue University (B.S.C.E., 1997); Valparaiso University (J.D., 2000). Fellow, Indiana Continuing Legal Education Opportunities. Participant, Giles Southerland Rich Memorial Moot Court Competition. Registered Engineering Intern, Indiana, 1997. *Member:* Indianapolis, Indiana State and American (Member: Forum on the Construction Industry; Women in the Law Committee) Bar Associations; American Society of Civil Engineers; Indiana Water Pollution Control Association; American Academy of Environmental Engineers. ***PRACTICE AREAS:*** Construction Law. ***Email:*** tsilver@ecp-law.net

DAVID E. BOSTWICK, born Centralia, Illinois, June 3, 1968; admitted to bar, 2002, Indiana. *Education:* Indiana University, Bloomington (B.A., 1991); Indiana University School of Law - Indianapolis (J.D., 2002). Order of the Barristers. Member, Board of Directors, American Concrete Institute, 1998-2000. *Member:* Indianapolis, Indiana State and American (Member, Forum on the Construction Industry) Bar Associations. ***PRACTICE AREAS:*** Construction Law. ***Email:*** dbostwick@ecp-law.net

LESLIE A. SINNOTT, born Washington, Indiana, August 9, 1951; admitted to bar, 1981, Scotland, Great Britain; 1986, Ohio; 1993, Indiana. *Education:* Indiana University; University of Edinburgh, Edinburgh, Scotland (M.A. magna cum laude, 1974; LL.B., 1979). Scottish Secondary School Teaching License, 1975-1976. Founder/President and Member, Women in the Law, Edinburgh, Scotland, 1984—. Member and Administrator, Meadows Festival Association, Edinburgh, Scotland, 1981-1984. Member, Cincinnati Women's Network, 1985—. *Member:* Cincinnati (Member: Young Lawyers Continuing Legal Education Committee; Practical Law Institute Committee; Law Office Management and Economics Committee), Ohio State and American Bar Associations; Greater Cincinnati Women Lawyers Association (President, 1986). ***LANGUAGES:*** German. ***PRACTICE AREAS:*** Commercial Real Estate; Business. ***Email:*** lsinnott@ecp-law.net

REPRESENTATIVE CLIENTS: Ace Air, Inc.; Allstate Steel Erectors; Beam Longest & Neff; Beazer Homes; Blue Haven Pools of Indiana; Builder's Concrete; Carmel Concrete; Central Tunneling; Centre Properties; CF Jones Group; Church Brothers Collision Repair; CNL American Properties Fund; C.R. Electric; Delello & Sons Asphalt; Dillon Construction Group; Duke Realty Corporation (and affiliated companies); Elliott-Williams Co.; General Steel Fabricating; Gilliatte General Contractors; Greenfield Builders; Hinshaw Roofing; Hoosier Steel; Indy Steel Erectors; IRC Roofing; K.E. Thompson; LCP Transportation; M/I Homes; Masiongale Electric-Mechanical; McCurdy Mechanical; Midwest Mole; Pauly Jail Building Co.; Peterson Architecture; Prairie Group; RMP Concrete; Rogers Group, Inc.; Ryland Homes; Shelly & Sands; Simon Property Group; The Skillman Corporation; Steel Services; Sun Communications; Sun Packaging; T.A. Kaiser Heating & Air; TRAMCO, Inc.; Trinity Homes; Universal Trucking; W.R. Kelso Roofing.

LAW OFFICES OF STEPHEN P. ECKERT

P.O. BOX 17526

INDIANAPOLIS, INDIANA 46217

Telephone: 317-885-9600

Fax: 317-885-9200

Personal Injury, Automobile Accidents, Slip and Fall, Wrongful Death, Products Liability.

STEPHEN P. ECKERT, born Fort Wayne, Indiana, January 15, 1955; admitted to bar, 1981, Indiana, U.S. District Court, Southern District of Indiana and U.S. Court of Appeals for the Armed Forces. *Education:* Indiana University (B.A., 1978; J.D., 1981). *Member:* Marion County, Johnson County, Indianapolis, Indiana State and American Bar Associations; Indiana Trial Lawyers Association; The Association of Trial Lawyers of America. ***PRACTICE AREAS:*** Personal Injury; Automobile Accidents and Injuries; Slip and Fall; Wrongful Death; Products Liability.

EICHHORN & EICHHORN

INDIANAPOLIS, INDIANA

(See Carmel)

General Practice, Litigation in State and Federal Courts. Public Utility, Banking, Corporation, Health Care, Insurance, Commercial Transactions, Labor and Employment Law, Real Estate, Professional Liability and Tort Law. Mediation.

ELROD & MASCHER, P.C.

Established in 1967

5329 S. EMERSON AVENUE, SUITE C

INDIANAPOLIS, INDIANA 46237

Telephone: 317-786-4929

Fax: 317-786-7899

URL: http://www.eandmlaw.com

Probate, Trusts and Estates, Wills, Estate Planning, Family Law, Business Law, Corporate Law, General Practice, Guardianships and Conservatorships, Non-Profit and Charitable Organizations, Partnership Law, Personal Injury, Real Estate.

FRENCH M. ELROD (1906-1985)

ROBERT G. ELROD, born Indianapolis, Indiana, February 24, 1940; admitted to bar, 1965, Indiana; 1979, U.S. Tax Court. *Education:* DePauw University (A.B., with honors, 1962); Harvard University (J.D., cum laude, 1965). Phi Eta Sigma. Assistant County Attorney, 1967-1968. County Attorney, 1969. Assistant City Attorney, Indianapolis, 1970-1971. City-County Counsel, 1972-2004. *Member:* Indianapolis, Johnson County, Indiana State and American Bar Associations; Indiana Municipal Lawyers Association. ***PRACTICE AREAS:*** Decedents Estates; Estate Administration; Estate Planning; Family Trusts; Living Trusts; Trust Administration; Trust Planning; Trusts and Estates Taxation; Business Estate Planning; Business Formation; Business Organization; Closely Held Business Law; Family Business Law; Limited Liability Company Law; Small Business Law; Corporate Formation; Eminent Domain; County Government Law; Local Government Law; Adult Guardianship; Elder Guardianship; Guardianship Administration; Hospital Law. ***Email:*** rgelrod@eandmlaw.com

GILBERT E. MASCHER, born Indianapolis, Indiana, December 17, 1945; admitted to bar, 1973, Indiana; 1980, U.S. Supreme Court. *Education:* Indiana University (B.S., 1967; J.D., 1973). Phi Delta Phi. Hearing Officer, 1971-1973 and Chief Hearing Officer, 1973-1974, Legal Division, Indiana Department of State Revenue. Assistant Corporation Counsel, City of Indianapolis, 1976-1986. *Member:* Indianapolis, Johnson County, Indiana State and American Bar Associations. [Capt., U.S. Army, 1968-1970]. ***PRACTICE AREAS:*** Divorce; Automobile Accidents and Injuries; Plaintiffs Personal Injury; Wrongful Death; Probate Administration; Real Estate Sales; Residential Real Estate Sales; Estate Planning; Decedents Estates; Estate Administration; Living Trusts; Business Formation. ***Email:*** gemascher@eandmlaw.com

JONATHAN R. ELROD, born Indianapolis, Indiana, May 3, 1977; admitted to bar, 2002, Indiana. *Education:* Xavier University (B.A., magna cum laude, 1999); Indiana University, Bloomington (J.D., cum laude, 2002). Editorial Staff, Indiana Law Journal. *Member:* Indiana State Bar Association. ***PRACTICE AREAS:*** Consumer Protection; Contracts; Premarital Agreements; Guardianship; Leases and Leasing; Landlord and Tenant Law; Municipal Law; Taxation; Accidents; Easements; Quiet Title; Income Tax; Property Tax. ***Email:*** jrelrod@eandmlaw.com

REFERENCE: National City Bank.

FEIWELL & HANNOY, P.C.

Established in 1986

251 NORTH ILLINOIS STREET, SUITE 1700

P.O. BOX 44141

INDIANAPOLIS, INDIANA 46244-0141

Telephone: 317-237-2727

Facsimile: 317-237-2722

Email: f&h@feiwellhannoy.com

URL: http://www.feiwellhannoy.com

General Civil Practice. Bankruptcy and Creditors' Rights, Real Estate and Foreclosure, Family/Domestic Relations, Administrative, General Business and Commercial Law.

(This Listing Continued)

MURRAY J. FEIWELL, born South Bend, Indiana, December 24, 1937; admitted to bar, 1963, Indiana. *Education:* University of Michigan (B.A., 1960; J.D., 1963). Indiana State Chair, National Committee of the University of Michigan Law School Fund, 1975-1980, National Class Vice-Chair, 1985-1987, National Vice-Chair, 1987-1989 and National Chair, 1989-1991. Member, Board of Directors, 1982-1985 and Treasurer, 1985-1989, University of Michigan Alumni Association. Member, Board of Associate Editors, Commercial Law Journal, 1990-1993. *Member:* Indianapolis, Indiana State and American Bar Associations; Seventh Circuit Bar Association; Commercial Law League of America; Association of Trial Lawyers of America; American Bankruptcy Institute; Mortgage Bankers Association of America; USFN (Member, Board of Directors, 1997-2004); National Home Equity Mortgage Association; National Association of Bankruptcy Trustees; REOMAC; American Foreclosure Network. ***PRACTICE AREAS:*** Bankruptcy; Creditors' Rights; Real Estate; Foreclosures; Business; Commercial. ***Email:*** mjf@feiwellhannoy.com

DOUGLAS J. HANNOY, born Union City, Indiana, December 12, 1960; admitted to bar, 1988, Indiana. *Education:* Indiana University (B.S., 1983; J.D., 1988). Lecturer and Author, "Indiana Foreclosure & Repossession," National Business Institute, 1995; "Basic Bankruptcy, Chapters 7 and 13," Indiana Continuing Legal Education Forum, 1985; "Residential Mortgages '99 Delinquency & Default Management," AIC Worldwide; "Foreclosure and Repossession in Indiana," Lorman Education Services, 1999-2003. *Member:* Indianapolis, Indiana State and Seventh Circuit Bar Associations; Commercial Law League of America; American Bankruptcy Institute; National Association of Bankruptcy Trustees; REOMAC; American Foreclosure Network; USFN. ***PRACTICE AREAS:*** Bankruptcy; Creditors' Rights; Real Estate; Foreclosures; Business; Commercial. ***Email:*** dhannoy@feiwellhannoy.com

MICHAEL J. FEIWELL, born Indianapolis, Indiana, October 15, 1969; admitted to bar, 1995, Indiana. *Education:* University of Michigan (B.A., 1992; J.D., 1995). Lecturer, "Mortgage Foreclosure in Indiana," Lohrman Education Services, 2001. *Member:* Indianapolis and Indiana State Bar Associations. ***PRACTICE AREAS:*** Creditors' Rights; Real Estate; Foreclosures; Bankruptcy; Business Law; Commercial Law. ***Email:*** mfeiwell@feiwellhannoy.com

MATTHEW S. LOVE, born Indianapolis, Indiana, May 30, 1970; admitted to bar, 1995, Indiana. *Education:* Indiana University (B.S., Business, 1992; J.D., 1995). Order of the Barristers. *Member:* Indianapolis and Indiana State Bar Associations. ***PRACTICE AREAS:*** Creditors' Rights; General Business; Real Estate; Foreclosures. ***Email:*** mlove@feiwellhannoy.com

BARRY T. BARNES, born Indianapolis, Indiana, May 30, 1969; admitted to bar, 1996, Indiana. *Education:* Indiana University (B.A., 1992); Oklahoma City University School of Law (J.D., 1996). *Member:* Indianapolis and Indiana State Bar Associations. ***PRACTICE AREAS:*** Foreclosures; Real Estate; Creditors Rights. ***Email:*** bbarnes@feiwellhannoy.com

SUSAN M. WOOLLEY, born Gary, Indiana, February 24, 1964; admitted to bar, 1989, Indiana; 1996, New Mexico. *Education:* Indiana University (B.A., 1985); Valparaiso University (J.D., 1989). *Member:* Indianapolis and Indiana State Bar Associations. ***PRACTICE AREAS:*** Real Estate; Foreclosure; Creditors Rights. ***Email:*** swoolley@feiwellhannoy.com

JERLYN S. SOUTHWICK, born Indianapolis, Indiana, July 12, 1950; admitted to bar, 1991, Indiana and U.S. District Court, Northern and Southern Districts of Indiana. *Education:* Indiana University (B.A., B.S., 1972); Indiana University (J.D., 1990). *Member:* Indianapolis, Indiana State and American Bar Associations. ***PRACTICE AREAS:*** Bankruptcy; Real Estate; Foreclosure; Creditors Rights. ***Email:*** jsouthwick@feiwellhannoy.com

JEFFREY S. WILSON, born Lansing, Michigan, June 4, 1963; admitted to bar, 1990, Indiana. *Education:* Wabash College (A.B., 1986); Indiana University (J.D., cum laude, 1989). *Member:* Indianapolis and Indiana State Bar Associations. ***PRACTICE AREAS:*** Real Estate; Foreclosure; Creditors' Rights. ***Email:*** jwilson@feiwellhannoy.com

BRUCE G. ARNOLD, born Anderson, Indiana, September 27, 1959; admitted to bar, 1999, Indiana and U.S. District Court, Northern and Southern Districts of Indiana. *Education:* Florida Institute of Technology (B.A., 1982); Indiana University School of Law (J.D., 1999). *Member:* Indianapolis and Indiana State Bar Associations. ***PRACTICE AREAS:*** Creditors' Rights; Real Estate; Foreclosure. ***Email:*** barnold@feiwellhannoy.com

RANDY C. EYSTER, born Indianapolis, Indiana, December 5, 1960; admitted to bar, 1998, Indiana. *Education:* Purdue University (B.S., 1983); Indiana University School of Law (J.D., 1997). *Member:* Indianapolis and Indiana State Bar Associations. ***PRACTICE AREAS:*** Bankruptcy; Creditors' Rights; Commercial Law. ***Email:*** reyster@feiwellhannoy.com

BRYAN K. REDMOND, born Warren, Ohio, October 22, 1971; admitted to bar, 2000, Indiana. *Education:* Vanderbilt University (B.A., 1994); Washington University School of Law (J.D., 1999). *Member:* Indianapolis and Indiana State Bar Associations. ***PRACTICE AREAS:*** Foreclosures; Real Estate; Creditors Rights. ***Email:*** bredmond@feiwellhannoy.com

LEANNE S. TITUS, born New Castle, Pennsylvania, July 21, 1975; admitted to bar, 2000, Indiana. *Education:* Arizona State University (B.S., 1997); Indiana University School of Law (J.D., 2000). *Member:* Indianapolis and Indiana State Bar Associations. ***PRACTICE AREAS:*** Foreclosures; Real Estate; Creditors Rights. ***Email:*** ltitus@feiwellhannoy.com

TIMOTHY L. BLACK, born Hammond, Indiana, July 23, 1950; admitted to bar, 1976, Indiana and Illinois. *Education:* Valparaiso University (B.A., 1972); John Marshall Law School (J.D., 1976). Author: "Fundamentals of Bankruptcy Law," National Business Institute, 1995-2003; "How to Protect Secured Creditors," National Business Institute, 1996-2001. *Member:* Indianapolis and Indiana State Bar Associations. ***PRACTICE AREAS:*** Commercial Law; Bankruptcy; Creditors Rights; Commercial Litigation; Business Acquisitions; Business Transactions.

(This Listing Continued)

AMY S. THURMOND, born Indiana, March 22, 1971; admitted to bar, 1997, Indiana. *Education:* Indiana University (B.S., 1993; J.D., 1996). *Member:* Indianapolis and Indiana State Bar Associations.

JEFFREY D. WOLFE, born Winchester, Indiana, March 4, 1975; admitted to bar, 2002, Indiana. *Education:* Ball State University (B.A., 1997); Indiana University School of Law - Indianapolis (J.D., 2002). *Member:* Indianapolis and Indiana State Bar Associations.

MICHAEL GHOSH, born Elkhart, Indiana, January 26, 1973; admitted to bar, 1999, Indiana. *Education:* DePauw University (B.A., 1995); Indiana University School of Law - Indianapolis (J.D., 1999). *Member:* Indianapolis, Indiana State and American Bar Associations.

CARYN M. BEOUGHER, born Fort Wayne, Indiana, April 14, 1978; admitted to bar, 2003, Indiana. *Education:* Purdue University (B.S., 2000); Indiana University School of Law - Indianapolis (J.D., 2003). *Member:* Indianapolis and Indiana State Bar Associations.

ROSE K. FELTEN, born Corydon, Indiana, November 8, 1972; admitted to bar, 2002, Wisconsin; 2003, Indiana. *Education:* Purdue University (B.S., 1995; M.A., 1997); Indiana University School of Law - Indianapolis (J.D., 2002). *Member:* State Bar of Wisconsin; Indianapolis and Indiana State Bar Associations.

ALAN W. McEWAN, born Indianapolis, Indiana, July 1, 1976; admitted to bar, 2003, Indiana. *Education:* Wabash College (A.B., 1999); Indiana University School of Law - Indianapolis (J.D., 2003). *Member:* Indianapolis, Indiana State and American Bar Associations.

ANDREW P. SEIWERT, born Rochester, Indiana, December 26, 1959; admitted to bar, 1986, Indiana. *Education:* Purdue University (B.A., 1982); Indiana University (J.D., 1985). *Member:* Indianapolis Municipal Lawyers Association; Indianapolis and Indiana State Bar Associations. ***PRACTICE AREAS:*** Government Liability (100%).

CRAIG E. BEOUGHER, born Logansport, Indiana, March 21, 1977; admitted to bar, 2004, Indiana. *Education:* Purdue University (B.S., 2000); Indiana University School of Law (J.D., 2003). *Member:* Indianapolis and Indiana Bar Associations.

STEPHANIE REINHART, born Barberton, Ohio, December 14, 1977; admitted to bar, 2004, Indiana. *Education:* Walsh University (B.A., cum laude, 1999); University of Akron School of Law (J.D., magna cum laude, 2004). *Member:* Indianapolis and Indiana Bar Associations.

REPRESENTATIVE CLIENTS: Aames Home Loans; Aurora Home Loans; Bank of America; Bremner & Wiley, Inc.; Cenlar Mortgage; Chase Manhattan Mortgage Corp.; Citifinancial Mortgage; Citimortgage & Select Portfolio; Countrywide Home Loans; EMC Mortgage Corporation; Fidelity Foreclosure Solutions; Fifth Third Bank; First American National Default; Flaherty & Collins Properties; GMAC Mortgage Corp.; Green Tree Servicing; Homecomings Financial; Household Financial; Indy Mac; Interbay Funding; Key Home Equity; Leader Mortgage; Litton Loan Services; M & T Mortgage Corp.; National City Mortgage; Ocwen Federal Bank, FSB; Option One; Revel & Underwood; Saxon Mortgage; Security National Servicing Corp.; The Veterans Administration; Washington Mutual Bank; Wells Fargo Home Mortgage; Wendover Funding; Wilshire Credit Corp.
REFERENCES: Fifth Third Bank; Bank One Leasing; National Bank of Indianapolis.

FINDLING GARAU GERMANO & PENNINGTON, P.C.

151 N. DELAWARE STREET, SUITE 1515
INDIANAPOLIS, INDIANA 46204
Telephone: 317-822-9530
Telecopier: 317-822-9531
Email: fggplaw@iquest.net
URL: http://www.lawyers.com/fggplaw

General Civil Trial and Appellate Practice. Medical Malpractice, Personal Injury, Commercial Litigation, Employment Discrimination.

MARY ARLIEN FINDLING, born Muncie, Indiana, May 8, 1950; admitted to bar, 1986, Indiana and U.S. District Court, Southern and Northern Districts of Indiana. *Education:* Purdue University (B.A., with highest distinction, 1972); University of Michigan (M.A., 1974); Indiana University School of Law-Indianapolis (J.D., summa cum laude, 1986). Phi Beta Kappa; Phi Kappa Phi. Executive Articles and Production Editor, Indiana Law Review, 1985-1986. Co-author: "Underinsurance in Indiana: An Illusion of Coverage?" 21 Indiana Law Review 1, 1988. Lecturer: "Illusionary Underinsured Coverage-Reports of Its Demise are Exaggerated," Indiana Trial Lawyers Association Seminar, March 1990; "The Discovery Rule in Indiana," ICLEF Medical Malpractice Seminar, June 1991; "A to Z of Uninsured and Underinsured," ICLEF Seminar, 1992; "Multiple Victim Underinsured Motorist Cases," ICLEF UM/UIM Seminar, December 1992; "Medical Negligence Litigation," ICLEF Seminar, 1993; "Indiana Medical Malpractice Act-The Need for Reform," ICLEF Medical Malpractice Seminar, June 1993; "The Year in Review," ICLEF Seminar, 1995, 1996, 1998 and 2001; "The Discovery Rule in Medical Malpractice," ITLA Seminar, 1997. *Member:* Indianapolis, Indiana State and American Bar Associations; Indiana Trial Lawyers Association (Board of Directors, 1993—); Indiana Trial Lawyer of the Year, 1999; The Association of Trial Lawyers of America. ***LANGUAGES:*** German. ***REPORTED CASES:*** Cacdac v. West 705 N.E.2d 506 (Ind.App. 1999); Martin v. Richey, 711 N.E.2d 1273 (Ind. 1999); Cundiff by Cundiff v. Daviess County Hosp. 656 N.E.2d 298 (Ind.App. 1995); Mayhue v. Sparkman 653 N.E.2d 1834 (Ind. 1995); Reed v. Central Soya Co. Inc. 644 N.E.2d 84 (Ind. 1994); Terre Haute Regional Hosp., Inc. v. Trueblood 600 N.E.2d 1358 (Ind. 1992); McCarty v. Hospital Corp. of America 580 N.E.2d 228 (Ind. 1991); Landis v. American Interinsurance Exchange 542 N.E.2d 1351 (Ind.App. 1 Dist. 1989). ***PRACTICE AREAS:*** Medical Malpractice Law; Personal Injury Law. ***Email:*** mfind@iquest.net

JERRY A. GARAU, born Martinsville, Indiana, December 9, 1960; admitted to bar, 1986, Indiana; U.S. Court of Appeals, Seventh Circuit; U.S. District Court, Southern District of Indiana. *Education:* Franklin College (B.A., summa cum laude, 1983); Indiana University (J.D., cum laude, 1986). Order of Barristers. Articles Editor, Indiana Law Review, 1985-1986. Listed: "Best Lawyers Consumer Guide." Lecturer: "Breach of Trust," ITLA Seminar, March, 1996; "Appellate Practice," ICLEF Seminar, July, 1993. Author: "The Effect of NCAA v. Board of Regents on the NCAA's Power to Impose Television Sanctions,"

(This Listing Continued)

FINDLING GARAU GERMANO & PENNINGTON, P.C., Indianapolis—Continued

18 Indiana Law Review 937, 1987. Law Clerk to Hon. Patrick D. Sullivan, Indiana Court of Appeals, 1986-1987. *Member:* Indianapolis and Indiana State Bar Associations; The Association of Trial Lawyers of America; American Board of Trial Advocates. Fellow, Indiana Bar Foundation. ***REPORTED CASES:*** In re Estate of Wade, 768 N.E.2d 957 (Ind.App. 2002); Cacdac v. West, 705 N.E.2d 506 (Ind.App. 1999); Clemans v. Wishard Memorial Hospital, 727 N.E.2d 1084 (Ind.App. 2000); Terre Haute Regional Hosp., Inc. v. Trueblood 600 N.E.2d 1358 (Ind. 1992); Annon II, Inc. v. Rill 597 N.E.2d 320 (Ind.App. 1 Dist. 1992); Calvary Temple Church, Inc. v. Paino 555 N.E.2d 190 (Ind.App. 1 Dist. 1990). ***PRACTICE AREAS:*** Personal Injury Law; Commercial Litigation; Employment Law; Products Liability. ***Email:*** jgarau@fggplaw.com

BARBARA J. GERMANO, born South Bend, Indiana, May 2, 1956; admitted to bar, 1989, Indiana and U.S. District Court, Northern and Southern Districts of Indiana. *Education:* Indiana University-Bloomington (B.A., 1978); Indiana University School of Law at Indianapolis (J.D., 1988). Co-Author: "Underinsurance in Indiana: An Illusion of Coverage?" 21 Indiana Law Review 1, 1989. Lecturer: "Impaired Earning Capacity Proving the Full Measure of the Loss," ITLA Seminar, March 1996; IUPUI Division of Continuing Studies Mini Law School--Medical Malpractice, October 1996. Guest Instructor: Indiana University School of Law at Bloomington Trial Practice Program, 1996-1998. *Member:* Indianapolis and Indiana State American Bar Associations; Indiana Trial Lawyers Association; The Association of Trial Lawyers of America; Outstanding Lawyers of America. ***REPORTED CASES:*** Green v. Maginn 684 N.E.2d 553 (Ind.App. 1997); Indiana Patient's Compensation Fund v. Anderson 661 N.E.2d 907 (Ind.App. 1996); Jackson v. Indiana State Lottery Comm. 585 N.E.2d 276 (Ind.App. 3 Dist. 1992); Garnelis v. Indiana State Dept. of Health 806 N.E.2d 365 (Ind.App.2004). ***PRACTICE AREAS:*** Personal Injury Law; Medical Malpractice Law. ***Email:*** bgermano@fggplaw.com

DEBORAH K. PENNINGTON, born Oklahoma City, Oklahoma, June 20, 1952; admitted to bar, 1981, Michigan; 1982, Indiana; U.S. District Court, Northern and Southern Districts of Indiana; U.S. District Court, Eastern District of Michigan; U.S. Court of Claims. *Education:* Purdue University (B.A., 1973); Wayne State University (M.S., 1976; J.D., 1980). Author: "Survey Results and Integration of Trial Preparation and Discovery," ICLEF, 1982; "Medical Negligence" Practice Skills, ICLEF, 1990, 1991, 1992. Lecturer: "Preparing A Winning Submission to the Medical Review Panel," Indiana Trial Lawyers Association, 1990; "Early Detection in Breast and Cervical Cancer, an Evolving Standard of Care," ITLA, 1992; "Heart Attacks as a Preventable Event-- Assessing the Physicians' Liability," ITLA, 1996; "Taking the Defendant's Deposition," ICLEF, 1998. *Member:* Johnson County and Indiana State Bar Associations; Indiana Trial Lawyers Association; The Association of Trial Lawyers of America; Outstanding Lawyers of America. ***REPORTED CASES:*** Indiana Patient's Compensation Fund v. Anderson 661 N.E.2d 907, trans. den (Ind.App. 1996); Mayhue v. Sparkman 653 N.E.2d 1384 (Ind. 1995); Follett v. Davis 636 N.E.2d 1282, trans. den (Ind.App. 1 Dist. 1994). ***PRACTICE AREAS:*** Medical Malpractice Law. ***Email:*** dpenning@fggplaw.com

JENNIFER STEPHENS LOVE, born Indianapolis, Indiana, May 21, 1971; admitted to bar, 1996, Indiana; U.S. Court of Appeals, Seventh Circuit; U.S. District Court, Southern District of Indiana. *Education:* Indiana University (B.A., 1993; J.D., 1996). Order of Barristers. Articles Editor, Indiana International and Comparative Law Review. *Member:* Indianapolis and Indiana State Bar Associations; Indiana Trial Lawyers Association; The Association of Trial Lawyers of America. ***PRACTICE AREAS:*** Medical Malpractice Law; Personal Injury Law. ***Email:*** jlove@fggplaw.com

MARSHALL S. HANLEY, born Indianapolis, Indiana, 1952; admitted to bar, 1977, Indiana, U.S. District Court, Southern and Northern Districts of Indiana and U.S. Court of Appeals, 7th Circuit. *Education:* Northwestern University (B.S., 1974); Indiana University (J.D., cum laude, 1977). Contributing Author and Panelist: "Medical Negligence Litigation," Indiana Continuing Legal Education Forum, 1986; "Medical Malpractice in Indiana," National Business Institute, Inc., 1987; "Indiana Medical Malpractice," Indiana Continuing Legal Education Forum, 1989; Loyola University Conference on Law and Medicine, Medical Malpractice, November, 1993; "Medical Malpractice," Indiana Continuing Legal Education Forum, 2000. Listed, Indiana Trial Lawyer of the Year, 2004. Law Clerk to S. Hugh Dillin, Judge, U.S. District Court, Southern District of Indiana, 1977-1979. Member, Indiana Commission for Higher Education, 1990-1994. *Member:* Indianapolis, Indiana State and American Bar Associations; Indiana Trial Lawyers Association; The Association of Trial Lawyers of America; American Society of Law and Medicine, Inc. ***REPORTED CASES:*** McCarty v. Sanders 805 N.E.2d 894 (Ind.App.2004). ***PRACTICE AREAS:*** Medical Malpractice; Personal Injury Litigation. ***Email:*** mhanley@fggplaw.com

DAVID B. ALLEN, born Martinsville, Indiana, March 12, 1962; admitted to bar, 1995, Indiana; U.S. District Court, Southern District of Indiana. *Education:* Indiana University (B.S., Criminal Justice, 1991; J.D., 1995). Author: "Should the Peer Review Privilege be Eliminated?," The Indiana Lawyer, 1/2/02; "Medical Malpractice in Indiana," February 2004, published and presented by National Business Institute. *Member:* Indianapolis and Indiana State Bar Associations; Indiana Trial Lawyers Association; Association of Trial Lawyers of America. ***REPORTED CASES:*** Indiana Ins. Guar. Ass'n. v. Davis 768 N.E.2d 902 (Ind.App.2002), trans. den. 783 N.E.2d 701 (Ind.2002). ***PRACTICE AREAS:*** Medical Malpractice; Products Liability; Personal Injury; Litigation. ***Email:*** dallen@fggplaw.com

FRANK & KRAFT

A PROFESSIONAL CORPORATION

FIRST INDIANA PLAZA, SUITE 1100
135 NORTH PENNSYLVANIA STREET
INDIANAPOLIS, INDIANA 46204-2400
Telephone: 317-684-1100
Telefax: 317-684-6111
Email: info@frankkraft.com
URL: http://www.frankkraft.com

Estate Planning, Business, Corporate, Real Estate, Federal and State Taxation, Probate, Estate Administration, Employee Benefits, Mergers and Acquisitions, Medicaid Planning.

MARVIN J. FRANK, born South Bend, Indiana, November 19, 1939; admitted to bar, 1966, Indiana; 1968, U.S. Tax Court; U.S. District Court, Southern District of Indiana. *Education:* Indiana University (B.S., 1962; J.D., 1966). Beta Gamma Sigma; Beta Alpha Psi. Certified Public Accountant, Indiana, 1968. Tax Manager, Arthur Andersen & Co., 1962-1967. Contributing Author: "LEGACY, Plan, Protect and Preserve Your Estate," 1996; "Generations, Planning Your Legacy," 1999. Author and Lecturer, "The Bankruptcy Tax Act and Other Important Matters," Indiana Tax Institute, 1983; "The Best Tax Advantaged Investment—Qualified Retirement Plans," Dean Witter Reynolds, 1983, 1984, 1986; "Marriage, Death and Taxes; Reducing the Taxes," ICLEF, 1984; "Considerations in Buying or Selling a Business in Indiana," NBI, 1990, 1991. *Member:* Indianapolis, Indiana State (Member, Taxation Law Section) and American Bar Associations; Estate Planning Council of Indianapolis; National Network of Estate Planning Attorneys (Founding Member); American Academy of Estate Planning Attorneys (Charter Member). ***PRACTICE AREAS:*** Estate Planning Law; Mergers and Acquisitions Law; Real Estate Law; Corporate Law; Federal and State Taxation Law.

PAUL A. KRAFT, born Indianapolis, Indiana, August 1, 1961; admitted to bar, 1986, Indiana; U.S. District Court, Northern and Southern Districts of Indiana; 1986, U.S. Tax Court. *Education:* Indiana University (B.S., 1983; J.D., 1986). Phi Delta Phi. Contributing Author: "LEGACY, Plan, Protect and Preserve Your Estate," 1996; "Generations, Planning Your Legacy," 1999. Lecturer, "Cafeteria Plans After the Tax Reform Act of 1986" and "How to Avoid Probate and Save Taxes - Using a Revocable Living Trust," 1990-1999; "Avoiding the Nursing Home Traps-Medicaid Planning," 1992. *Member:* Indianapolis (Member, Taxation, Business Law and Estate Planning Sections), Indiana State (Member, Taxation Section) and American (Member, Taxation Section) Bar Associations; Indiana CPA Society; Estate Planning Council of Indianapolis; National Network of Estate Planning Attorneys (Founding Member); American Academy of Estate Planning Attorneys (Charter Member). ***PRACTICE AREAS:*** Estate Planning Law; Corporate Law; Estate Administration Law; Medicaid Planning; Real Estate Law; Federal and State Taxation Law.

RONALD D'AVIS, born Denver, Colorado, August 28, 1950; admitted to bar, 1987, Indiana; U.S. District Court, Southern District of Indiana; 1987, U.S. Tax Court. *Education:* Northern Arizona University (B.A., 1972); Indiana University (J.D., cum laude, 1987). Articles Editor, Indiana Law Review, 1986-1987. *Member:* Indianapolis (Member, Sections on Taxation, Estate Planning and Administration), Indiana State (Member, Sections on Taxation, Trust and Real Property) and American (Member, Sections on Taxation, Real Property and Probate) Bar Associations. ***PRACTICE AREAS:*** Federal and State Taxation Law; Estate Planning and Administration Law; Employee Benefits Law; Probate Law; Medicaid Planning.

ROBERT M. HAMLETT, born Wichita, Kansas, September 2, 1943; admitted to bar, 1970, Missouri; 1971, Illinois; U.S. District Court, Eastern District of Missouri and U.S. Court of Appeals, Eighth Circuit; 1998, Indiana and U.S. District Court, Northern and Southern Districts of Indiana. *Education:* Kansas State University (B.S. Ch.E., 1965); St. Louis University (J.D., cum laude, 1970). Phi Alpha Delta; Sigma Tau Engineering Honor Society. *Member:* Indianapolis, Indiana State, Illinois State and American Bar Associations. ***REPORTED CASES:*** Capitol Products Corp. v. Hernon, 457 F.2d 541 (8th Cir. 1972); Dillard v. Rowland, 520 S.W. 2d 81 (Mo.App. 1974); Barnes Hospital v. Leggett, 589 S.W. 2d 241 (Mo. 1979); Barnes Hospital v. Leggett, 646 S.W. 2d 889 (Mo.App. 1983); Jarrett v. Hill, 648 S.W. 2d 170 (Mo.App. 1983). ***PRACTICE AREAS:*** Business; Corporate; Real Estate; Mergers and Acquisitions.

REBECCA W. GEYER, born Indianapolis, Indiana, November 17, 1974; admitted to bar, 1999, Indiana; U.S. District Court, Northern and Southern Districts of Indiana. *Education:* Indiana University (B.A., 1996; J.D., 1998). Delta Theta Phi. Author: "Playing the Name Game: A Glimpse at the Future of the Internet Domain Name System," Federal Communications Law Journal, Vol. 51, March 1999. *Member:* Indianapolis (Member, Estate Planning, Administration and Taxation Sections), Indiana State and American Bar Associations. ***PRACTICE AREAS:*** Estate Planning Law; Federal and State Taxation.

REPRESENTATIVE CLIENTS: Bright Tower Communications, Inc.; Community Cancer Care, Inc.; Continental Products, Inc.; First National Bank of Odon; Heating-Cooling Distributors, Inc.; Indiana Food Brokerage Co., Inc.; Indiana Veneers Corp.; Innovative Computer Products, Inc.; International Pizza Supply Corp.; Midwest Institute for Clinical Research; Mobile Roof Systems, Inc.; Photographic Instant Memories, Inc.; Universal Reagents, Inc.; Wise Builders, Inc.

GILDAY & ASSOCIATES, P.C.

Established in 2004

BANK ONE CENTER TOWER
111 MONUMENT CIRCLE, SUITE 3300
INDIANAPOLIS, INDIANA 46204-5176
Telephone: 317-624-0033
Fax: 317-638-0300
Email: lawyer@gildaylegal.com
URL: http://www.lawyers.com/gildaylegal

Tax Law, Taxation, Tax Controversies, Real Estate Tax, Real Estate, Business Law, Business Planning, Contracts, Business Litigation, Business Enterprises, Corporate Law, Partnership Law, Limited Liability Company Law, Small Businesses, Business Formations, Starting a Business, Buying and Selling a Business, Wills, Probate, Trusts and Estates, Asset Protection, Estate Planning, Non-profit Charitable Organizations.

(This Listing Continued)

JAMES K. GILDAY, born Indianapolis, Indiana, June 26, 1956; admitted to bar, 1986, Indiana, U.S. District Court, Southern and Northern Districts of Indiana and U.S. Tax Court. *Education:* Xavier University (A.B., 1978); University of Indianapolis (M.B.A., 1983); Indiana University School of Law (J.D., 1986). Certified Public Accountant, Indiana, 1987. Lecturer, State and Local Tax, Indiana University School of Law at Indianapolis. *Member:* Indianapolis, Indiana State (Member, Sections on: Taxation; Business Law) and American (Member, Sections on: Real Property, Probate and Trust Law; Taxation) Bar Associations; Indiana Society of Certified Public Accountants. **Email:** jgilday@gildeylegal.com

GILLILAND & CAUDILL

3905 VINCENNES ROAD, SUITE 204
INDIANAPOLIS, INDIANA 46268
Telephone: 317-704-2400
Fax: 317-704-2410URL:
URL: http://www.gilliland.com
Email: thefirm@gilliland.com
URL: http://www.lawyers.com/gilliland

Health Law, Labor and Employment Law, Administrative Law, Civil Litigation, Corporate Law, Privacy Law.

JOHN C. GILLILAND, II, born Bellefonte, Pennsylvania, June 4, 1945; admitted to bar, 1971, Pennsylvania (inactive); 1979, Indiana; 1991, Kentucky; 1992, Ohio; U.S. District Court, Eastern District of Kentucky; U.S. District Court, Southern District of Indiana; U.S. District Court, Central District of Illinois; U.S. Court of Appeals, Seventh Circuit. *Education:* Pennsylvania State University (B.A., Pre-Law, 1967); Georgetown University (J.D., 1971). Fellow, Rotary Foundation, Queen's University of Belfast, Belfast, Northern Ireland, 1968-1969. *Member:* Kentucky, Ohio State, Indiana State and American Bar Associations; American Health Lawyers Association (Dispute Resolver, Alternative Dispute Resolution Service). [Capt., U.S. Army Military Intelligence; Reserves, 1967-1976, active duty, 1971-1972]. ***PRACTICE AREAS:*** Health Law; Labor and Employment. **Email:** jcg@gilliland.com

ASSOCIATES

ROBERT W. MARKETTE, JR., born Highland Park, Illinois, May 18 1972; admitted to bar, 1998, Indiana; U.S. District Court, Northern and Southern Districts of Indiana; U.S. Court of Appeals, Seventh Circuit. *Education:* Hanover College (B.A., 1994); Indiana University School of Law (J.D., 1998). ***REPORTED CASES:*** Advantage v. Indiana State Department of Health. ***PRACTICE AREAS:*** Civil Litigation; Administrative Law; Health Law; Privacy Law. **Email:** rwm@gilliland.com

JENNIFER S. MILLIGAN, born Brazil, Indiana, March 27, 1972; admitted to bar, 1999, Indiana and U.S. District Court, Southern and Northern Districts of Indiana. *Education:* Indiana State University (B.S., cum laude, 1996); Valparaiso University School of Law (J.D., magna cum laude, 1999). *Member:* Indianapolis and Indiana State Bar Associations. ***PRACTICE AREAS:*** Labor and Employment Law; Health Law. **Email:** jsm@gilliland.com

OF COUNSEL

VIRGINIA WRIGHT CAUDILL, born Pittsburgh, Pennsylvania, November 29, 1966; admitted to bar, 1992, Pennsylvania and U.S. District Court, Western District of Pennsylvania; 1995, Indiana, U.S. District Court, Northern and Southern Districts of Indiana and U.S. District Court, Central District of Illinois. *Education:* University of Pittsburgh (B.A., history/psychology, magna cum laude, 1989; J.D., 1992). Legal Counsel: Indiana State Department of Health, 1998-2000; Indiana Department of Natural Resources, 1995-1998. *Member:* Indianapolis, Indiana State and American Bar Associations; American Health Lawyers Association. ***PRACTICE AREAS:*** Administrative Law; Health Law. **Email:** vwc@gilliland.com

REPRESENTATIVE CLIENTS: Indiana Association for Home and Hospice Care; Kentucky Home Health Association; Housecall Medical Resources; Arrowhead Plastics Engineering; Home Services Unlimited; EKF Management, Inc.; Visiting Nurse Association of Southwest Indiana; National Private Duty Association; Sunrise At-Home Services; Visiting Nurse & Hospice Home; Sunshine Home Health Services; Maxim Healthcare Servuces; Midwest Residential Services, Inc.; Guardian Angel Hospice, Inc.

RICHARD B. GONON

9465 COUNSELORS ROW, SUITE 200
INDIANAPOLIS, INDIANA 46240
Telephone: 317-805-4816
Fax: 317-805-4817
Email: rgonon@aol.com
URL: http://www.rbgononlaw.com

Collection Agency Representation, Collections, Commercial Law, Creditor's Rights in Bankruptcy, Fair Debt Collection Practices Act Defense Litigation, Subrogation.

RICHARD B. GONON, born New York, New York, 1955; admitted to bar, 1984, Indiana and U.S. District Court, Northern and Southern Districts of Indiana. *Education:* University of Rhode Island (B.A., 1977); University of La Verne (J.D., 1980). Seminar Panelist: Fair Debt Collection Practices Act Lecturer, "Collections," ICLEF, February, 1991; Fair Debt Collection Practices Act Lecturer, "Current Trends," Midwest Regional Debt Collectors Conference, May, 2000. Lecturer, Advanced Collection Law in Indiana, Lorman Educational Services, December 2001. Fair Debt Collection Practices Act Lecturer, Indiana Collectors Association, May 2002. *Member:* Indianapolis and Indiana State Bar Associations; Indiana Creditors' Bar; American Collectors Association (Indiana State Chair; Member, Attorney Program). ***PRACTICE AREAS:*** Collection Agency; Consumer Collections; Commercial Collections; Creditors Rights in Bankruptcy; Fair Debt Collection Practices Act; Defense Litigation; Subrogation.

GONZALEZ, SAGGIO & HARLAN, L.L.P.

Established in 1989
201 NORTH ILLINOIS STREET, SUITE 1900
INDIANAPOLIS, INDIANA 46204
Telephone: 317-686-9800
Fax: 317-686-9821
Email: main@gshllp.com
URL: http://www.gshllp.com

West Des Moines, Iowa Office: 1501 42nd Street, Suite 465, 50266. Telephone: 515-453-8509. Fax: 515-267-1408.
Cincinnati, Ohio Office: Carew Tower, 441 Vine Street, Suite 3615, 45202. Telephone: 513-651-3456. Fax: 513-651-3446.
Milwaukee, Wisconsin Office: 225 East Michigan, 4th Floor, 53202. Telephone: 414-277-8500. Fax: 414-277-8521.
Chicago, Illinois Office: 208 LaSalle Street, Suite 1460, 60604. Telephone: 312-236-0475. Facsimile: 312-236-1750.

Business and Corporate Law, Civil Litigation, Insurance Defense Law, Equal Opportunities and Employment, School Law, Municipal Finance, Business and Commercial Litigation, Real Estate, Construction, Condemnation Law, Environmental, Taxation, Utilities Law, Trials and Appeals, Government Relations.

FIRM PROFILE: Gonzalez, Saggio & Harlan, L.L.P. is one of the fastest growing law firms in the Midwest. This growth is a reflection of the firm's devotion to quality, efficiency and frank communication in servicing client needs. Furthermore, as a minority-owned law firm, we believe that our diverse backgrounds add value to those clients wanting to better serve a changing and dynamic environment.

MIRIAM A. RICH, born Frankfort, Indiana, July 12, 1962; admitted to bar, 1993, Indiana, U.S. District Court, Northern and Southern Districts of Indiana and U.S. Court of Appeals, Seventh Circuit. *Education:* Indiana University (B.S., Business Management, 1985); Indiana University School of Law - Indianapolis (J.D., 1993). Member, Order of the Barristers. *Member:* Defense Trial Counsel of Indiana (Member, Sections on: Workers' Compensation; Trial Tactics; In-house Counsel). ***PRACTICE AREAS:*** Litigation; Workers Compensation. **Email:** miriam_rich@gshllp.com

REPRESENTATIVE CLIENTS: Accenture; Alliant Energy; Bear, Stears & Co.; Chubb Insurance Company; City of Milwaukee; CNH Global N.V.; Darden Restaurants, Inc.; Denny's; Eastman Kodak Company; E.I. du Pont de Nemours and Company; Family Dollar Stores, Inc.; Forest County Potawatomi Community; Harley-Davidson Motor Company; Kohl's Corporation; Luxottica Group; Menard, Inc.; Midwest Airlines; PepsiAmericas, Inc.; Starwood Hotels & Resorts Worldwide, Inc.; State of Wisconsin; Target Corporation; Time Warner Cable; We Energies; Wisconsin Housing and Economic Development Authority (WHEDA); Zale Corporation.

(For complete biographical data on all personnel, see Professional Biographies at Milwaukee, Wisconsin)

GOODIN ABERNATHY & MILLER, L.L.P.

Established in 1984
KEYSTONE AT THE CROSSING
8900 KEYSTONE CROSSING
SUITE 1100
INDIANAPOLIS, INDIANA 46240
Telephone: 317-843-2606
Fax: 317-574-3095
URL: http://www.gamlawyers.com

Civil Litigation, Corporate, Business, Real Estate, Insurance Defense, Employment and ERISA Litigation, Aviation and Transportation Law, Probate and Estate Planning, Estate Administration, Family/Domestic Relations, Mediation and Alternative Dispute Resolution.

JAMES A. GOODIN, born Indianapolis, Indiana, April 26, 1947; admitted to bar, 1973, Indiana and U.S. District Court, Southern District of Indiana; 1979, U.S. Court of Appeals, Seventh Circuit. *Education:* Marquette University (B.A., 1968); Indiana University (J.D., 1973). Member, Panel of Arbitrators, American Arbitration Association. *Member:* Indianapolis and Indiana State Bar Associations; The Defense Research Institute, Inc.; Defense Trial Counsel of Indiana. ***PRACTICE AREAS:*** Civil Practice; Litigation; Arbitration; Insurance Defense. **Email:** jgoodin@gamlawyers.com

JON C. ABERNATHY, born Elkhart, Indiana, December 6, 1957; admitted to bar, 1983, Indiana and U.S. District Court, Southern and Northern Districts of Indiana; U.S. Court of Appeals, Seventh Circuit. *Education:* Georgetown College (B.A., cum laude, 1980); Valparaiso University (J.D., 1983). Law Clerk to the Hon. Wesley W. Ratliff, Jr., Court of Appeals of Indiana, 1983-1984. *Member:* Indianapolis (Member, Litigation Section) and Indiana State Bar Associations; The Defense Research Institute, Inc. ***PRACTICE AREAS:*** Civil Practice; Aviation Litigation; Insurance; Appellate Practice; Commercial; Litigation; ERISA. **Email:** jabernathy@gamlawyers.com

PATRICK L. MILLER, born Birdseye, Indiana, February 23, 1965; admitted to bar, 1990, Indiana. *Education:* University of Evansville (B.S., magna cum laude, 1987); Indiana University (J.D., cum laude, 1989). *Member:* Indianapolis (Member, Litigation Section), Indiana State (Member, Young Lawyers Section) and American (Member, Tort and Insurance Practice and Litigation Section) Bar Associations; The Defense Research Institute, Inc.; Defense Trial Counsel of Indiana. ***PRACTICE AREAS:*** Civil Practice; Defense Litigation; Insurance Defense. **Email:** pmiller@gamlawyers.com

KARL G. POPOWICS, born Manchester, Connecticut, August 15, 1969; admitted to bar, 1996, Indiana and U.S. District Court, Northern and Southern Districts of Indiana. *Education:* DePauw University (B.A., 1991); Indiana University (J.D., 1996). *Member:* Indianapolis and Indiana State Bar Associations. ***PRACTICE AREAS:*** Civil Litigation; Workers Compensation. **Email:** kpopowics@gamlawyers.com

CHRISTOPHER E. CLARK, born Indianapolis, Indiana, September 26, 1968; admitted to bar, 1995, Indiana and U.S. District Court, Southern and Northern Districts of

(This Listing Continued)

GOODIN ABERNATHY & MILLER, L.L.P., Indianapolis—Continued

Indiana. *Education:* University of Arizona (B.A., 1990); Indiana University (J.D., 1995). *Member:* Indiana State Bar Association (Member, Young Lawyers Section); Defense Trial Counsel of Indiana; Defense Research Institute. ***PRACTICE AREAS:*** Insurance Defense; Civil Practice; Defense Litigation; Real Estate; Business Law. ***Email:*** cclark@gamlawyers.com

JAMES R. BROWNE, born Marion, Indiana, March 14, 1969; admitted to bar, 1994, Indiana and U.S. District Court, Northern and Southern Districts of Indiana. *Education:* DePauw University (B.A., 1991); Indiana University, School of Law, Indianapolis (J.D., 1994). Deputy Prosecutor, Marion County, Indiana, 1996-1999. Member, Defense Trial Counsel of Indiana. *Member:* Indianapolis and Indiana State Bar Associations. ***LANGUAGES:*** Spanish. ***Email:*** jbrowne@gamlawyers.com

ASSOCIATES

THOMAS B. BAYS, born Indianapolis, Indiana, July 29, 1964; admitted to bar, 1990, Indiana. *Education:* Indiana University (B.A., 1986; J.D., 1990). Judicial Law Clerk to both the Hon. Marc R. Kellams, Monroe Circuit Court, 1989-1990 and the Hon. V. Sue Shields, Indiana Court of Appeals, 1990-1992. *Member:* Boone County, Indiana State, Indianapolis and American Bar Associations; Defense Research Institute; Defense Trial Counsel of Indiana. ***Email:*** tbays@gamlawyers.com

CHRISTIE A. SEIFERT, born Omaha, Nebraska, April 14, 1968; admitted to bar, 1998, Indiana and U.S. District Court, Northern and Southern Districts of Indiana. *Education:* Indiana University (B.A., 1990); John Marshall Law School (J.D., 1998). Staff Editor, John Marshall Law School Law Review, 1997-1998. *Member:* Indianapolis and Indiana State Bar Associations; Defense Trial Counsel of Indiana; Defense Research Institute. ***PRACTICE AREAS:*** Insurance Defense; Insurance Coverage Defense; Civil Practice. ***Email:*** cseifert@gamlawyers.com

BRADLEY J. SCHULZ, born Neenah, Wisconsin, March 3, 1971; admitted to bar, 1999, Indiana; 2000, U.S. District Court, Northern and Southern Districts of Indiana. *Education:* Butler University (B.A., high honors, 1993); Indiana University School of Law (J.D., 1999). Member, Moot Court Order of Barristers. *Member:* Indianapolis and Indiana Bar Associations. ***PRACTICE AREAS:*** Civil Practice; Insurance Defense; Creditors Rights. ***Email:*** bschulz@gamlawyers.com

LIA R. LUKAART, born Hammond, Indiana, June 24, 1975; admitted to bar, 2000, Indiana and Illinois. *Education:* Purdue University (B.S., 1997); Valparaiso University (J.D., 2000). Moot Court, 1998-1999. Moot Court Executive Board, 1999-2000. ***PRACTICE AREAS:*** Civil Litigation; Commercial Litigation; Business Law. ***Email:*** llukaart@gamlawyers.com

OF COUNSEL

JOSEPH P. MURDOCK (1928-2003)

WILSON S. STOBER, born 1940; admitted to bar, 1965, Indiana, U.S. District Court, Southern District of Indiana and U.S. Court of Appeals, Seventh Circuit; 1981, Florida; 1984, U.S. Supreme Court. *Education:* St. Thomas College (B.A., 1962); Wayne University (J.D., 1965). Articles Editor, Wayne Law Review, 1964-1965. *Member:* Indianapolis (Member, Sections on: Land Use; Family Law) and Indiana State (Member, Family Law Section) Bar Associations; The Florida Bar. ***PRACTICE AREAS:*** Family Law; Civil Litigation; Land Use Regulation Law; Real Estate Law. ***Email:*** wstober@gamlawyers.com

R.D. ZINK, born Indianapolis, Indiana, August 28, 1948; admitted to bar, 1978, Indiana and U.S. District Court, Southern District of Indiana. *Education:* Rose-Hulman Institute of Technology (B.S.M.E., with honors, 1970); Indiana University (J.D., 1978). Blue Key; Pi Tau Sigma; Phi Delta Phi. *Member:* Indianapolis, Indiana State and American Bar Associations; Defense Trial Counsel of Indiana; Defense Research Institute; Arbitrator American Arbitration Association; Indiana State Certified Civil Mediator. [LTJG, U.S. Navy, 1970-1973]. ***PRACTICE AREAS:*** Insurance Defense; Civil Litigation; Construction Law; Alternative Dispute Resolution. ***Email:*** rzink@gamlawyers.com

AMY WHITE SEVIER, born Indianapolis, Indiana, September 15, 1963; admitted to bar, 1988, Indiana. *Education:* Indiana University (B.S., Finance, 1985; J.D., 1988). *Member:* Indianapolis (Member: Business Law, Estate Planning and Administration and Family Law Section; Young Lawyers Division Executive Council, 1991-1998; Chairman, 1995), Indiana State (Member: Family and Juvenile Law and Probate, Trust and Real Property Section) and American Bar Associations. ***PRACTICE AREAS:*** Probate; Real Estate; Business Law; Trusts and Estates; Family Law.

ROBERT C. LEE, born Indianapolis, Indiana, December 1969; admitted to bar, 1995, Indiana and U.S. District Court, Northern and Southern Districts of Indiana. *Education:* Indiana University (B.A., with distinction, 1992); Vanderbilt University (J.D., 1995). *Member:* Indianapolis (Member, Estate Planning and Administration and Business Law Sections) and Indiana State (Member, Probate, Trust and Real Property and Business Law Sections) Bar Associations; Estate Planning Council of Indianapolis. ***PRACTICE AREAS:*** Wills; Trusts and Estates; Estate Administration; Business Organization; Business Transactions. ***Email:*** robert@rleelaw.com

REPRESENTATIVE CLIENTS: Allstate Insurance Companies; American National Property and Casualty Co.; Continental Western Insurance Company; Federated Insurance; General Casualty Companies; Genuine Parts Company, Inc.; Greg Smith Associates, Inc.; Habitat for Humanity Hamilton County, Inc.; Hamilton County Humane Society; Hardee's Food Systems, Inc.; IFI, Inc.; IHDS of Michigan, Ltd.; McDaniel & Lloyd, Inc.; National Healthcare Technologies, Inc.; State Farm Insurance Companies; T&W Corp.; West Bend Insurance Co.; United Technologies; Universal Underwriters; Zotos International, Inc.; Dealers Eraine Sales; Bohren Logistics.

JENNIFER L. GRAHAM

1111 E. 54TH STREET, SUITE 138
INDIANAPOLIS, INDIANA 46220
Telephone: 317-257-7640
Fax: 317-257-7642

Commercial Litigation, Plaintiffs Personal Injury, Bankruptcy Litigation, Contract Litigation.

(This Listing Continued)

JENNIFER L. GRAHAM, born Indianapolis, Indiana, 1947; admitted to bar, 1983, Indiana; U.S. District Court, Southern District of Indiana; 1992, U.S. Supreme Court; U.S. Court of Appeals, Sixth and Seventh Circuits. *Education:* Walsh College (B.B.A., 1978); Indiana University (J.D., 1983). Walsh Management Scholar, 1978. *Member:* Indianapolis and Indiana State Bar Associations; Association of Trial Lawyers of American; Indiana Trial Lawyers Association. ***PRACTICE AREAS:*** Commercial Litigation; Plaintiffs Personal Injury; Bankruptcy Litigation; Contract Litigation.

HACKMAN HULETT & CRACRAFT, LLP

Established in 1929

ONE INDIANA SQUARE, SUITE 2400
INDIANAPOLIS, INDIANA 46204-2030
Telephone: 317-636-5401
Facsimile: 317-686-3288
URL: http://www.hhclaw.com

General Civil Practice. Corporate, Acquisitions and Mergers, Real Estate, Public Utility, Administrative, Municipal Finance, Environmental, Litigation in Federal and State Courts, Commercial, State and Local Taxation, Probate and Estate Planning.

FIRM PROFILE: The Firm was formed in 1929 by the late William H. Thompson, a prominent Indianapolis attorney, under the name of Thompson Rabb & Stevenson. Following a tradition of identifying itself with its most senior members, the Firm became Hackman Hulett & Cracraft, LLP in 1998. The Firm provides high quality legal services in business-oriented practice areas on a cost-efficient and timely basis.

The Firm represents corporations, partnerships, limited liability companies, governmental and other types of organizations engaged in a variety of business activities and handles trial and appellate litigation in state and federal courts, hearings before state and federal administrative agencies, as well as arbitrations, mediations and other forms of alternative dispute resolution. In addition, the Firm represents individuals in connection with estate planning and administration, charitable giving and guardianships.

Thompson Rabb & Stevenson	1929-1941
Thompson O'Neal & Smith	1941-1966
Smith Morgan & Ryan	1966-1986
Hackman McClarnon & McTurnan	1986-1988
Hackman McClarnon Hulett & Cracraft	1989-1998

MEMBERS OF FIRM

MARVIN L. HACKMAN, born Jasper, Indiana, January 29, 1934; admitted to bar, 1959, Indiana. *Education:* St. Joseph's College (A.B., summa cum laude, 1956); Indiana University (J.D., with high distinction, 1959). Phi Delta Phi; Delta Epsilon Sigma; Order of the Coif. Editor-in-Chief, Indiana Law Journal, 1958-1959. Law Clerk, Judge William E. Steckler, U.S. District Court, Southern District of Indiana, 1959-1961. *Member:* Indianapolis, Indiana State and American Bar Associations. ***PRACTICE AREAS:*** Corporate Law; Real Estate Law; Secured Lending Law. ***Email:*** mhackman@hhclaw.com

ROBERT S. HULETT, born Indianapolis, Indiana, August 18, 1944; admitted to bar, 1969, Indiana. *Education:* DePauw University (B.A., 1966); Indiana University (J.D., 1969). Phi Alpha Delta. *Member:* Indianapolis (Counsel to the Board of Managers, 1995; Vice President, 1986-1988), Indiana State and American Bar Associations. ***PRACTICE AREAS:*** Corporate Law; Real Estate Law; Civil Litigation. ***Email:*** rhulett@hhclaw.com

MICHAEL B. CRACRAFT, born Indianapolis, Indiana, November 7, 1945; admitted to bar, 1973, Indiana. *Education:* Miami University (B.A., 1968); Indiana University (J.D., magna cum laude, 1973). Phi Delta Phi. *Member:* Indianapolis, Indiana State and American Bar Associations; Indiana Municipal Lawyers Association. ***PRACTICE AREAS:*** Public and Municipal Utilities Law; State Taxation Law; Environmental Law; Civil Litigation. ***Email:*** mcracraft@hhclaw.com

TIMOTHY K. RYAN, born Indianapolis, Indiana, May 24, 1955; admitted to bar, 1980, Indiana. *Education:* Rollins College (B.A., 1977); Indiana University (J.D., cum laude, 1980). Phi Delta Phi; Omicron Delta Kappa. *Member:* Indianapolis, Indiana State and American Bar Associations. ***PRACTICE AREAS:*** Corporate Law; Real Estate Law; Probate Law; Estate Planning Law. ***Email:*** tryan@hhclaw.com

PHILIP B. McKIERNAN, born New York, New York., May 16, 1952; admitted to bar, 1983, Indiana. *Education:* University of Notre Dame (B.A., with honors, 1974; M.A., 1975; M.S.A., 1980); Indiana University (J.D., magna cum laude, 1983). Order of the Coif. Member, Indiana Law Journal, 1981-1983. *Member:* Indianapolis, Indiana State and American Bar Associations. ***PRACTICE AREAS:*** Administrative Law; Civil Litigation; Environmental Law; Public Utilities Law; Municipal Utilities Law. ***Email:*** pmckiernan@hhclaw.com

VICKI L. ANDERSON, born Indianapolis, Indiana, December 19, 1948; admitted to bar, 1985, Indiana. *Education:* Indiana University (B.A., 1973); Saint Francis College (M.S., summa cum laude, 1979); Indiana University (J.D., magna cum laude, 1985). Associate Editor, Indiana Law Review, 1984-1985. *Member:* Indianapolis, Indiana State and American Bar Associations; Estate Planning Council of Indianapolis, Inc. Fellow, The American College of Trust and Estate Counsel (ACTEC). ***PRACTICE AREAS:*** Probate and Estate Planning; Real Estate Law. ***Email:*** vanderson@hhclaw.com

JOHN D. COCHRAN, JR., born Washington, D.C., April 18, 1945; admitted to bar, 1971, Indiana. *Education:* Wabash College (B.A., 1968); University of Louisville (J.D., 1971). Delta Theta Phi. *Member:* Indianapolis, Indiana State and American Bar Associations; Indiana Defense Lawyers Association. ***PRACTICE AREAS:*** Civil Litigation; Business Litigation; Contract; Personal Injury; Products Liability; Fire; Appellate Practice; Insurance Law; Coverages; Bad Faith. ***Email:*** jcochran@hhclaw.com

MARK S. ALDERFER, born Marion, Indiana, February 22, 1958; admitted to bar, 1983, Indiana and Illinois. *Education:* Indiana University (A.B., 1980; J.D., 1983). Deputy Prosecuting Attorney, Monroe County, 1984-1986. *Member:* Indianapolis, Indiana State

(This Listing Continued)

and American Bar Associations. ***PRACTICE AREAS:*** Civil Litigation; Business Litigation; Contract; Personal Injury; Products Liability; Insurance Law. ***Email:*** malderfer@hhclaw.com

DAVID J. BODLE, born Lafayette, Indiana, December 15, 1952; admitted to bar, 1978, Indiana. *Education:* Marquette University (B.A., 1974); Wake Forest University (J.D., 1978). Speaker and Co-Author: "Building Indiana Companies from the Ground Up: Legal Issues," Indiana Continuing Legal Education Forum, December 2003; "Health Law in Indiana: The Legal Implications of Health Care Delivery Systems and Managed Care," National Business Institute, August, 2004; March, 2001; February, 2000; "Complying with the Health Insurance Portability and Accountability Act in Indiana," National Business Institute, September, 1997. *Member:* Indianapolis, Indiana State (Co-Chair, Written Publications Committee, 1992-1994; Chair, Editorial Board, 2000) and American Bar Associations; National Health Lawyers Association; Fellow, Indiana Bar Foundation. ***PRACTICE AREAS:*** Corporate Law; Health Care Law; Insurance Law; Administrative Law. ***Email:*** dbodle@hhclaw.com

STEVEN W. KROHNE, born Indianapolis, Indiana, February 20, 1971; admitted to bar, 1998, Indiana. *Education:* Indiana University (B.S., 1993); Indiana University School of Law (J.D., summa cum laude, 1998). Executive Articles Editor, Indiana International and Comparative Law Review, 1997-1998. *Member:* Indianapolis, Indiana State and American Bar Associations. ***PRACTICE AREAS:*** Public Utility Law; Municipal Utility Law; Environmental Law; Administrative Law. ***Email:*** skrohne@hhclaw.com

ELLEN MORRISON TOWNSEND, born Attica, Indiana, December 15, 1971; admitted to bar, 1997, Indiana. *Education:* DePauw University (B.A., cum laude, 1994); Indiana University School of Law (J.D., cum laude, 1997). Member, 1995-1997 and Articles Editor, 1996-1997, Indiana Law Journal. National Moot Court Traveling Team, 1996-1997. Author: "Insurance Discrimination Against Battered Women: Proposed Legislative Protections," 72 Indiana Law Journal 259 (1996). *Member:* Indianapolis (Member, Executive Committee, Women in the Law Division, 1997—), Indiana State and American Bar Associations; Defense Research Institute; Indiana Trial Lawyers Association; The Association of Trial Lawyers of America. ***PRACTICE AREAS:*** Civil Litigation; General Corporate Law. ***Email:*** etownsend@hhclaw.com

JOSEPH M. HENDEL, born Beech Grove, Indiana, April 9, 1972; admitted to bar, 1997, Indiana. *Education:* Indiana University (B.A., 1994); Indiana University School of Law (J.D., 1997). Executive Articles Editor, Indiana International & Comparative Law Review, 1996-1997. Law Clerk, Indiana Court of Appeals, 1997-2000. Author: Note "Equity in the American Courts and in the World Court: Does the End Justify the Means?" 6 Ind. Int'l & Comp. L. Rev. 637. *Member:* Indiana State Bar Association. ***PRACTICE AREAS:*** Civil Litigation. ***Email:*** jhendel@hhclaw.com

ANTHONY S. RIDOLFO, JR., born Ames, Iowa, July 31, 1970; admitted to bar, 1995, Oregon; 2001, Indiana. *Education:* Wabash College (A.B., 1992); Willamette University College of Law (J.D., 1995). Author, Contributor, "Occupational Safety and Health", 2000 Cumulative Supplement, Chapter 28, Oregon State Bar Workers' Compensation . Assistant Attorney General, Oregon Department of Justice, 1995-2001. ***PRACTICE AREAS:*** Insurance Defense; Litigation; Occupational Safety and Health; Civil Rights. ***Email:*** aridolfo@hhclaw.com

DAVINA L. CURRY, born Indianapolis, Indiana, March 19, 1968; admitted to bar, 2003, Indiana and U.S. District Court, Northern and Southern Districts of Indiana. *Education:* Purdue University (B.A., 1998); Indiana University School of Law - Indianapolis (J.D., 2002). *Member:* Indianapolis, Indiana State and American Bar Associations. ***PRACTICE AREAS:*** Civil Litigation. ***Email:*** dcurry@hhclaw.com

REPRESENTATIVE CLIENTS: Citizens Gas & Coke Utility; Citizens Thermal Energy; State Farm Mutual Automobile Insurance Company; Verizon Wireless; F.C. Tucker Company, Inc.; Title Services, L.P.; Tucker Mortgage, LLC; Tucker Associates, Inc.; Meridian Real Estate Services; Texas Eastern Products Pipeline Company; Indiana Municipal Power Agency; Indiana Municipal Electric Association, Inc.; AquaSource, Inc.; St. Paul Fire and Marine Insurance Company; Kemper Insurance Company; Allstate Insurance Company; Walker Information, Inc.; I.V.C. Industrial Coatings, Inc.; OfficeWorks, Inc.; Central Indiana Community Foundation (The Indianapolis Foundation); Indiana White River State Park Development Commission; Indiana Commission For Higher Education; National Printing Plate Company, Inc.; Merchants Property Insurance Company; Manufacturers Life Insurance Company; J.D. Gould Company, Inc.; Harry W. Moore Funeral Chapels.

HALL, RENDER, KILLIAN, HEATH & LYMAN, P.S.C.

Established in 1967

SUITE 2000, ONE AMERICAN SQUARE
BOX 82064
INDIANAPOLIS, INDIANA 46282
Telephone: 317-633-4884
Fax: 317-633-4878
Email: info@hallrender.com
URL: http://www.HallRender.com

Indianapolis North Office: Suite 820, 8402 Harcourt Road, 46260. Telephone: 317-871-6222. Fax: 317-338-3946.

Louisville, Kentucky Office: 614 West Main Street, Suite 4000, 40202. Telephone: 502-568-1890. Fax: 502-568-4878.

Troy, Michigan Office: Hall, Render, Killian, Heath & Lyman, PLLC, Columbia Center, Suite 315, 201 West Big Beaver Road, 48084. Telephone: 248-740-7505. Fax: 248-740-7501.

Milwaukee, Wisconsin Office: 411 East Wisconsin Avenue, Suite 900, 53202. Telephone: 414-721-0442. Fax: 414-721-0491.

Health Law, Managed Care Law, Medical Malpractice Defense, Antitrust, Corporations, Labor and Employment, Mediation, Environmental, Employee Benefits, Securities, Probate and Estate Planning, Real Estate and Taxation Law. Litigation and Appeals, Public Finance, Medicare and Medicaid Reimbursement, Computer Law, Construction and Engineering Law, Intellectual Property.

(This Listing Continued)

FIRM PROFILE: The firm's primary area of concentration is in providing a comprehensive range of legal services to the health care industry. Some of the firm's attorneys have gained experience in the health care field as either hospital administrators, managers, registered nurses, professors or in-house hospital counsel. Other firm members have gained experience in the health care regulatory field as administrators of state programs within the Board of Health and Health Professions Bureau. This experience, combined with the experience of other firm attorneys, has enabled Hall, Render, Killian, Heath & Lyman to engage in representation of health care clients on a regional and national level. The firm also has an extensive practice outside the health care industry including manufacturing, general business and individual clients.

JOHN C. RENDER, admitted to bar, 1971, Indiana; 1987, District of Columbia; 2003, Michigan. *Education:* Butler University (B.S., 1966); Indiana University - Indianapolis (J.D., 1971). ***PRACTICE AREAS:*** Health Law; Corporate Law; Business Law; Government Relations; Medicare and Medicaid Appeals. ***Email:*** jrender@hallrender.com

R. TERRY HEATH, admitted to bar, 1978, Indiana; 1979, U.S. Tax Court. *Education:* Purdue University (B.S., 1975); Indiana University - Indianapolis (J.D., cum laude, 1978); Georgetown University Law Center (LL.M., 1979). ***PRACTICE AREAS:*** Health Law; Tax Law; Corporate Law; Business Law. ***Email:*** heath@hallrender.com

STEPHEN W. LYMAN, admitted to bar, 1974, Indiana; 1981, U.S. Court of Appeals, Seventh Circuit. *Education:* Indiana University (B.S., Marketing, with distinction, 1971; J.D., 1974). Certified Mediator. ***PRACTICE AREAS:*** Labor and Employment; Mediation; Litigation. ***Email:*** slyman@hallrender.com

L. RICHARD GOHMAN, admitted to bar, 1971, Indiana; 1980, U.S. Supreme Court; 1985, U.S. Court of Appeals, Seventh Circuit; 1986, District of Columbia; 1991, U.S. District Court, District of Columbia; 1992, U.S. Court of Appeals for the Federal Circuit. *Education:* Indiana University (A.B., Economics, 1965; M.S., Education, 1967); Indiana University - Indianapolis (J.D., 1971). ***PRACTICE AREAS:*** Health Law; Health Economics; Medicare and Medicaid Appeals; Health Care; Fraud and Abuse; False Claims Defense; Corporate Law; Business Law. ***Email:*** rgohman@hallrender.com

JEFFREY PEEK, admitted to bar, 1983, Indiana, Indiana Tax Court and U.S. Tax Court. *Education:* Butler University (B.S., in Accounting, cum laude, 1979); Indiana University - Indianapolis (J.D., 1983). Certified Public Accountant. ***PRACTICE AREAS:*** Tax Law; Corporate Law; Business Law; Estate Planning; Tax Exempt. ***Email:*** catfish@hallrender.com

CLIFFORD A. BEYLER, admitted to bar, 1984, Indiana. *Education:* Indiana University (B.A., 1974); Indiana University - Indianapolis (J.D., 1983). ***PRACTICE AREAS:*** Health Law; Long Term Care Law; Government Relations. ***Email:*** cbeyler@hallrender.com

TIMOTHY C. LAWSON, admitted to bar, 1986, Indiana; 1991, Kentucky. *Education:* University of Notre Dame (B.B.A., 1972); Arizona State University (M.B.A., 1973; M.H.S.A., 1976); University of Louisville (J.D., 1986). ***PRACTICE AREAS:*** Health Law; Hospital Law; Managed Care Law; Corporate Law; Business Law. ***Email:*** tlawson@hallrender.com

DOUGLAS P. LONG, admitted to bar, 1979, Indiana; 1980, Illinois; 1981, U.S. Tax Court. *Education:* Indiana University (B.S., with highest distinction, 1976); Harvard University (J.D., 1979). ***PRACTICE AREAS:*** Tax Law; Corporate Law; Business Law; Estate Planning. ***Email:*** dlong@hallrender.com

WILLIAM H. THOMPSON, admitted to bar, 1987, Indiana; U.S. Court of Appeals, Seventh Circuit; 1993, U.S. Court of Federal Claims. *Education:* Indiana University - Indianapolis (B.S., 1980; M.H.A., 1983; J.D., 1987). ***PRACTICE AREAS:*** Health Law; Corporate Law; Business Transactions; Managed Care. ***Email:*** bthompson@hallrender.com

TIMOTHY W. KENNEDY, admitted to bar, 1983, Indiana; 1984, U.S. Tax Court, U.S. Claims Court and U.S. Court of Appeals, Seventh Circuit. *Education:* Wabash College (A.B., 1980); Indiana University - Indianapolis (J.D., 1983). ***PRACTICE AREAS:*** Health Law; Government Relations. ***Email:*** tkennedy@hallrender.com

STEVEN H. PRATT, admitted to bar, 1983, Indiana. *Education:* DePauw University (B.A., cum laude, 1980); Indiana University School of Law at Indianapolis (J.D., 1983). ***PRACTICE AREAS:*** Health Law; Managed Care Law; Corporate Law; Business Law. ***Email:*** spratt@hallrender.com

N. KENT SMITH, admitted to bar, 1981, Indiana. *Education:* Valparaiso University (B.S., with high distinction, 1978); Indiana University - Indianapolis (J.D., cum laude, 1981). ***PRACTICE AREAS:*** Litigation; Health Law. ***Email:*** ksmith@hallrender.com

MARY C. GAUGHAN, admitted to bar, 1987, Indiana; 1991, Florida. *Education:* Indiana University-Purdue University at Indianapolis (B.A., 1982); Indiana University - Indianapolis (J.D., 1987). ***PRACTICE AREAS:*** Health Law; Corporate Law; Business Law. ***Email:*** mgaughan@hallrender.com

FRED J. BACHMANN, admitted to bar, 1987, Indiana; 1991, U.S. Tax Court. *Education:* Ball State University (B.S., cum laude, 1980); Indiana University - Indianapolis (J.D., 1987). *Member:* Indiana CPA Society; American Institute of Certified Public Accountants. ***PRACTICE AREAS:*** Employee Benefits; Corporate Law; Business Law; Tax Law; Estate Planning. ***Email:*** bachmann@hallrender.com

MAUREEN O'BRIEN GRIFFIN, admitted to bar, 1983, Indiana. *Education:* Purdue University (A.D., Nursing, 1978; B.S., Nursing, 1980); Indiana University - Indianapolis (J.D., 1983). *Member:* American Health Lawyers Association. ***PRACTICE AREAS:*** Health Law; Medicare/Medicaid Reimbursement. ***Email:*** mgriffin@hallrender.com

ROBERT A. HICKS, admitted to bar, 1988, Indiana. *Education:* Hanover College (B.A., magna cum laude, 1985); Indiana University (J.D., 1988). ***PRACTICE AREAS:*** Real Estate Law; Eminent Domain Law; Property Tax Law. ***Email:*** rhicks@hallrender.com

(This Listing Continued)

HALL, RENDER, KILLIAN, HEATH & LYMAN, P.S.C., Indianapolis—Continued

KEVIN P. SPEER, admitted to bar, 1989, Indiana. *Education:* Purdue University (B.A., 1986); Valparaiso University (J.D., 1989); Gulf Coast Regional National Institute of Trial Advocacy, 1991. ***PRACTICE AREAS:*** Health Law. ***Email:*** kspeer@hallrender.com

GREGORY W. MOORE (Resident, Troy, Michigan Office)

DONALD R. RUSSELL, admitted to bar, 1983, Indiana and Georgia. *Education:* Indiana University (B.A., 1972); Butler University (M.B.A., 1979); Indiana University (J.D., magna cum laude, 1982). ***PRACTICE AREAS:*** Real Estate Law; Corporate Law; Business Law. ***Email:*** drussell@hallrender.com

JEFFREY W. SHORT, admitted to bar, 1991, Indiana. *Education:* Wabash College (B.A., 1988); Indiana University - Indianapolis (J.D., 1991). ***PRACTICE AREAS:*** Intellectual Property Law; Computer Law; Privacy Law; Business Law; Corporate Law; Securities Law; Public Finance Law. ***Email:*** jshort@hallrender.com

CLIFTON E. JOHNSON, admitted to bar, 1980, Ohio; 1992, Indiana. *Education:* Ohio Northern University (B.A., 1977); Syracuse University (M.B.A., 1980; J.D., 1980). ***PRACTICE AREAS:*** Health Law; Health Economics; Antitrust Law; Managed Care Law. ***Email:*** cjohnson@hallrender.com

GERALD L. STOVALL (Resident, Louisville, Kentucky Office)

JON F. SPADORCIA, admitted to bar, 1975, Indiana. *Education:* Tulane University of Louisiana and Butler University (B.S., 1969); Indiana University - Indianapolis (J.D., 1975). ***PRACTICE AREAS:*** Estate Planning; Probate; Trust; Real Property; Taxation; Business Law. ***Email:*** jspadorcia@hallrender.com

JOHN C. MEADE, admitted to bar, 1974, Michigan and Illinois; 1983, Indiana; 1984, District of Columbia. *Education:* Indiana University (A.B., 1967); University of Michigan (J.D., 1973). ***PRACTICE AREAS:*** Public Finance Law. ***Email:*** jmeade@hallrender.com

GREGG M. WALLANDER, admitted to bar, 1993, Indiana; 1994, U.S. Court of Appeals, Seventh Circuit. *Education:* Indiana University (B.S., 1988; J.D., magna cum laude, 1993). ***PRACTICE AREAS:*** Health Law; Managed Care Law; Corporate Law; Business Law. ***Email:*** gwally@hallrender.com

SAMUEL H. DeSHAZER (Resident, Louisville, Kentucky Office)

TODD J. SELBY, admitted to bar, 1990, Indiana. *Education:* Indiana University - Indianapolis (B.S., 1984; J.D., 1990). ***PRACTICE AREAS:*** Long Term Care Law; Health Law. ***Email:*** tselby@hallrender.com

JAMES B. HOGAN, admitted to bar, 1994, Indiana. *Education:* Hanover College (B.A., 1982); Indiana University - Indianapolis (M.B.A., 1986; J.D., 1994). ***PRACTICE AREAS:*** Health Law; Hospital and Health Systems; Medical Staff Credentialing; Peer Review; EMTALA. ***Email:*** jhogan@hallrender.com

CHRISTOPHER L. RIEGLER, admitted to bar, 1984, Michigan; 1993, Ohio; 1996, Indiana. *Education:* Cornerstone College (B.A., summa cum laude, 1980); Wayne State University School of Law (J.D., cum laude, 1984). ***PRACTICE AREAS:*** Litigation; Health Law. ***Email:*** criegler@hallrender.com

WILLIAM D. ROBERTS (Resident, Louisville, Kentucky Office)

A. COURTNEY GUILD, JR. (Resident, Louisville, Kentucky Office)

RENÉ REMEK SAVARISE (Resident, Louisville, Kentucky Office)

JAMES R. WILLEY, JR., admitted to bar, 1995, Indiana. *Education:* Hanover College (B.A., cum laude, 1987); Indiana University - Indianapolis (J.D., 1995). ***PRACTICE AREAS:*** Tax Law; Corporate Law; Business Law; Estate Planning. ***Email:*** jwilley@hallrender.com

KEITH D. BARBER, admitted to bar, 1995, Texas; 1996, Indiana. *Education:* Texas A & M University (B.S., 1981); Baylor University (M.H.A., 1990); University of Houston (J.D., cum laude, 1995). ***PRACTICE AREAS:*** Health Economics; Medicare/Medicaid Reimbursement; Health Care Fraud and Abuse; Health Law; Corporate Compliance. ***Email:*** kbarber@hallrender.com

SUSAN D. BIZZELL, admitted to bar, 1996, Indiana. *Education:* Indiana University Southeast (B.A., 1992); Indiana University (J.D.- M.H.A., 1996). ***PRACTICE AREAS:*** Health Law. ***Email:*** sbizzell@hallrender.com

DOUGLAS M. KINSER, admitted to bar, 1997, Indiana. *Education:* Indiana University (B.S., 1971; J.D., 1996); Ball State University (M.A., 1978). ***PRACTICE AREAS:*** Health Law; Government Relations. ***Email:*** dkinser@hallrender.com

KIMBERLY JO COMMINS (Resident, Troy, Michigan Office)

ARTHUR F. DEVAUX (Not admitted in Indiana; Resident, Troy, Michigan Office)

NORRIS CUNNINGHAM, admitted to bar, 1996, Indiana. *Education:* Aurora College (B.A., 1988); Central Michigan University (M.S., 1991); Indiana University - Indianapolis (J.D., 1996). ***PRACTICE AREAS:*** Medical Malpractice Defense; Health Law; Litigation. ***Email:*** ncunningham@hallrender.com

JULI K. SHIELDS, admitted to bar, 1987, Indiana. *Education:* Franklin College of Indiana (B.A., cum laude, 1984); Indiana University - Indianapolis (J.D., 1987). ***PRACTICE AREAS:*** Health Law; Corporate Law; Business Law; HIPAA Compliance. ***Email:*** jshields@hallrender.com

JOHN P. RYAN, admitted to bar, 1998, Indiana; 2003, Michigan. *Education:* Indiana University (B.A., Economics, 1995; J.D., 1998). ***PRACTICE AREAS:*** Employment; Labor; Immigration. ***Email:*** jpryan@hallrender.com

ANGELA M. SMITH, admitted to bar, 1994, Indiana; U.S. Court of Appeals, Seventh Circuit. *Education:* Indiana University (B.S. in Marketing, 1989; J.D., 1994). ***PRACTICE AREAS:*** Litigation; Medical Malpractice Defense. ***Email:*** asmith@hallrender.com

(This Listing Continued)

DAVID B. HONIG, admitted to bar, 1987, Florida; 1992, Illinois; 2000, Indiana. *Education:* Washington University (B.A., 1984); University of Florida (J.D., with honors, 1987). ***PRACTICE AREAS:*** Health Law; White Collar Crime; Fraud; Corporate Compliance. ***Email:*** dhonig@hallrender.com

STEPHAN C. MASONCUP, admitted to bar, 1994, Illinois; 2001, Indiana. *Education:* Southern Illinois University (B.S., Finance, 1991); John Marshall Law School (J.D., 1994). ***PRACTICE AREAS:*** Health Law; Managed Care; Corporate Law. ***Email:*** smasoncup@hallrender.com

LAWRENCE K. COON (Resident, Milwaukee, Wisconsin Office)

SCOTT J. GEBOY (Resident, Milwaukee, Wisconsin Office)

LINDA S. McPIKE (Resident, Milwaukee, Wisconsin Office)

PAUL W. SEIDENSTRICKER (Resident, Milwaukee, Wisconsin Office)

DAVID H. SNOW (Resident, Milwaukee, Wisconsin Office)

THOMAS R. STREIFENDER (Resident, Milwaukee, Wisconsin Office)

SCOTT W. TAEBEL (Resident, Milwaukee, Wisconsin Office)

LORI A. WINK (Resident, Milwaukee, Wisconsin Office)

KIRK R. JOCHAM, admitted to bar, 2001, Indiana. *Education:* University of Southern Indiana (B.A., 1998); Indiana University School of Law - Indianapolis (J.D., 2001). ***PRACTICE AREAS:*** Litigation; Medical Malpractice.

CRAIG M. WILLIAMS, admitted to bar, 1997, Kentucky; 1999, Indiana; 2004, U.S. Court of Appeals, Seventh Circuit and U.S. Supreme Court. *Education:* Wabash College (A.B., 1994); Indiana University School of Law - Indianapolis (J.D., 1997). ***PRACTICE AREAS:*** Labor and Employment.

ADAM J. RICHTER, admitted to bar, 2005, Indiana. *Education:* Indiana University (B.A., 2002; J.D., 2005). ***PRACTICE AREAS:*** Real Estate.

ERIN D. ABRAHAM, admitted to bar, 2005, Indiana. *Education:* Indiana University (B.S., 1999); Indiana University School of Law - Indianapolis (J.D., 2005). *Member:* American Health Lawyers Association. ***PRACTICE AREAS:*** Health Law.

MARY LIATTI HILL, admitted to bar, 1996, Indiana. *Education:* University of Cincinnati (B.S.N., summa cum laude, 1984); Indiana University - Indianapolis (J.D., summa cum laude, 1995). ***PRACTICE AREAS:*** Labor and Employment; Litigation; Health Law. ***Email:*** mhill@hallrender.com

MONICA C. HOCUM (Resident, Milwaukee, Wisconsin Office)

DAVID C. LIND, II, admitted to bar, 1997, Indiana; 1999, U.S. Tax Court. *Education:* Indiana University (B.S., Business in Accounting, with distinction, 1994); Northwestern University (J.D., Concentration in Business Associations, 1997). ***PRACTICE AREAS:*** Corporate Law; Business Law; Real Estate Law; Tax Law. ***Email:*** dlind@hallrender.com

TODD A. NOVA (Resident, Milwaukee, Wisconsin Office)

EDWARD L. SCHOENBAECHLER (Resident, Louisville, Kentucky Office)

TIMOTHY A. McGEATH, admitted to bar, 1999, Indiana. *Education:* Hanover College (B.A., with honors, 1984); Georgetown University (M.A., 1988); Indiana University - Indianapolis (J.D., cum laude, 1999). ***PRACTICE AREAS:*** Corporate Law; Business Law; Estate Planning; Intellectual Property; Computer Law; Securities. ***Email:*** tmcgeath@hallrender.com

BARBARA A. KILLIAN, admitted to bar, 1999, Indiana. *Education:* California State University (B.A., 1995); Indiana University - Indianapolis (J.D., 1999). ***PRACTICE AREAS:*** Health Law; Corporate Compliance; HIPAA; EMTALA; Computer Law; Information Technology Law. ***Email:*** bkillian@hallrender.com

THOMAS A. JENKINS, admitted to bar, 1968, Indiana. *Education:* Purdue University (B.A., 1965); Indiana University (J.D., 1968). ***PRACTICE AREAS:*** Trust and Estate Administration; Estate Planning; Business; Tax. ***Email:*** tjenkins@hallrender.com

JAY P. TURNER (Resident, Louisville, Kentucky Office)

CHARISE R. FRAZIER, admitted to bar, 2001, Indiana. *Education:* Valparaiso University (B.S., 1997); Indiana University - Indianapolis (J.D., 2001; M.H.A., 2001). ***PRACTICE AREAS:*** Health Law. ***Email:*** cfrazier@hallrender.com

MICHAEL J. PHILBRICK (Resident, Troy, Michigan Office)

LAURA M. NAPIEWOCKI (Resident, Troy, Michigan Office)

CHRISTOPHER J. ALLMAN (Resident, Troy, Michigan Office)

JAMES M. SHAFER, admitted to bar, 1998, Indiana. *Education:* Indiana University (B.A., Liberal Arts-History, 1994; J.D., cum laude, 1998). ***PRACTICE AREAS:*** Corporate Law; Business Law; Tax Law; Employee Benefits; Estate Planning; Estate Administration. ***Email:*** jshafer@hallrender.com

DOUGLAS J. KOCHELL, admitted to bar, 1989, Indiana. *Education:* Indiana University (B.S., Accounting, 1986); Indiana university School of Law (J.D., 1989). (Attorney). ***PRACTICE AREAS:*** Real Estate Law; Corporate and Business Law. ***Email:*** dkochell@hallrender.com

REGAN E. TANKERSLEY, admitted to bar, 2002, Indiana. *Education:* University of Illinois at Urbana-Champaign (B.S., 1997); Indiana University (J.D., 2002). Registered Mediator. *Member:* American Health Lawyers Association. ***PRACTICE AREAS:*** Health Law. ***Email:*** rtankersley@hallrender.com

JONATHAN C. BUMGARNER, admitted to bar, 2002, Indiana. *Education:* Wabash College (B.A., magna cum laude, 1995); Indiana University (J.D., summa cum laude, 2002). Certified Mediator. ***PRACTICE AREAS:*** Employment and Labor. ***Email:*** jbumgarner@hallrender.com

CHARLES P. SUKURS, admitted to bar, 2002, Indiana. *Education:* Indiana University School of Law (B.S., 1997; B.A., 1999); Vanderbilt University (J.D., 2002). ***PRACTICE AREAS:*** Corporate and Securities Law; Estate Planning and Administration; Tax Law. ***Email:*** csukurs@hallrender.com

(This Listing Continued)

KEVIN A. STELLA, admitted to bar, 2002, Indiana. *Education:* Indiana University School of Law (B.A., 1997); University of Notre Dame (J.D., 2002). *Member:* American Health Lawyers Association. ***PRACTICE AREAS:*** Health Law; Employment and Labor; Medical Staff Credentialing; Professional Licensure Defense. ***Email:*** kastella@hallrender.com

NEAL A. COOPER, admitted to bar, 1998, Illinois; 2003, Indiana. *Education:* Millikin University (B.S., 1988); John Marshall Law School (J.D., 1998). Certified Public Accountant. *Member:* American Health Lawyers Association. ***PRACTICE AREAS:*** Health Law; Health Economics; HIPAA; Stark/Antikickback/Fraud and Abuse. ***Email:*** ncooper@hallrender.com

MICHAEL L. KIM, admitted to bar, 1996, Missouri; 2003, Indiana. *Education:* Washington University (B.A., 1993); University of Tulsa College of Law (J.D., 1996). *Member:* American Immigration Lawyers Association. ***PRACTICE AREAS:*** Immigration. ***Email:*** mkim@hallrender.com

CHRISTOPHER C. EADES, admitted to bar, 1997, Indiana. *Education:* Indiana University, Bloomington (B.A., Political Science, 1994; J.D., 1997). *Member:* Defense Trial Counsel of Indiana. ***PRACTICE AREAS:*** Litigation; Medical Malpractice Defense. ***Email:*** ceades@hallrender.com

JENNIFER FOUTS SKEELS, admitted to bar, 1991, Illinois; 1997, Indiana. *Education:* Purdue University (A.A.S., 1983; B.S., Nursing, 1985); Loyola University of Chicago School of Law (J.D., 1991). *Member:* American Health Lawyers Association. ***PRACTICE AREAS:*** Health Law. ***Email:*** jskeels@hallrender.com

ELIZABETH CALLAHAN-MORRIS (Resident, Troy, Michigan Office)

JOHN F. WILLIAMS, III, admitted to bar, 2003, Indiana. *Education:* Embry-Riddle Aeronautical University (B.S., Aeronautical Science, 1992); George Mason University School of Law (J.D., 2002). *Member:* Indiana State Bar Association. ***PRACTICE AREAS:*** Litigation; Medical Malpractice Defense. ***Email:*** jwilliams@hallrender.com

KRISTINE S. PYZYNA, admitted to bar, 1985, Illinois; 2003, Indiana. *Education:* North Park College (B.S., in Nursing, 1979); DePaul University College of Law (J.D., 1985); John Marshall Law School (L.L.M., in Tax, 2003). Registered Nurse, Illinois, 1979. *Member:* American Health Lawyers Association. ***PRACTICE AREAS:*** Health Law; HIPAA; Tax Law; Corporate Organizations; Business Organizations; Mergers and Acquisitions. ***Email:*** kpyzyna@hallrender.com

LARA D. ENGELKING, RN, admitted to bar, 1997, Indiana. *Education:* Indiana University (B.S.N., with highest distinction, 1992; J.D., 1996). Sigma Theta Tau International Honor Society of Nursing. Licensed Registered Nurse, Indiana, 1992. *Member:* American Association of Nurse Attorneys; Defense Trial Counsel of Indiana. ***PRACTICE AREAS:*** Health Care Law; Litigation. ***Email:*** lengelking@hallrender.com

THOMAS D. SHRACK, admitted to bar, 2003, Indiana and U.S.District Court, Northern District of Indiana. *Education:* Miami University (B.A., English, 1987); Indiana Univeristy School of Law - Indianapolis (J.D., 2003). Member: American Registry of Diagnostic Medical Sonographers; Society of Vascular Ultrasound. *Member:* Indianapolis, Indiana State and American Bar Associations. ***PRACTICE AREAS:*** Health Law. ***Email:*** tshrack@hallrender.com

JOAN L. LOWES (Resident, Troy, Michigan Office)

MELISSA L. MARKEY, admitted to bar, 1991, Texas; 1992, Michigan (Not admitted in Indiana). *Education:* St. Louis University (B.A., Psychology, 1984; J.D., summa cum laude, 1991). *Member:* American Health Lawyers Association. ***PRACTICE AREAS:*** Health Law. ***Email:*** mmarkey@hallrender.com

ADELE MERENSTEIN, admitted to bar, 1993, Massachusetts; 1995, District of Columbia; 2004, Indiana. *Education:* State University of New York at Buffalo (B.S., Physical Therapy, 1980); Case Western Reserve University (J.D., 1992). ***PRACTICE AREAS:*** Health Law. ***Email:*** amerenstein@hallrender.com

KATHRYN A. ELIAS, admitted to bar, 1997, Indiana. *Education:* Indiana University (B.S., Biochemistry, 1989); University of Notre Dame (J.D., 1997). ***PRACTICE AREAS:*** Health Law; Litigation. ***Email:*** kelias@hallrender.com

KAREN D. BOLTON (Resident, Troy, Michigan Office)

ANJALI M. HERKE, admitted to bar, 1996, Indiana. *Education:* Indiana University (B.A., 1992); Indiana University School of Law at Indianapolis (J.D., 1995). ***PRACTICE AREAS:*** Estate Planning; Estate Administration. ***Email:*** aherke@hallrender.com

MICHAEL T. BATT, admitted to bar, 1999, Indiana. *Education:* University of Evansville (B.A., 1996); Indiana University School of Law at Indianapolis (J.D., 1999). ***PRACTICE AREAS:*** Computer; Information Technology. ***Email:*** mbatt@hallrender.com

DANA E. STUTZMAN, admitted to bar, 2002, Indiana. *Education:* Indiana University (B.A., 1999); Indiana University School of Law at Indianapolis (J.D., 2002). ***PRACTICE AREAS:*** Labor and Employment. ***Email:*** dstutzman@hallrender.com

HEATHER H. MACEK, admitted to bar, 2004, Indiana. *Education:* Indiana University (B.A., 1996); Indiana University School of Law at Indianapolis (J.D., 2004). ***PRACTICE AREAS:*** Health Law; Education. ***Email:*** hmacek@hallrender.com

BRIAN C. BETNER, admitted to bar, 2004, Indiana. *Education:* Indiana University (B.A., 1999); Indiana University School of Law at Indianapolis (J.D., 2004). ***PRACTICE AREAS:*** Health Law; Administrative Law.

KEVIN J. GFELL, admitted to bar, 2004, Indiana. *Education:* Indiana University (B.S., 2001); Indiana University School of Law at Indianapolis (J.D., 2004). ***PRACTICE AREAS:*** Health Law; Litigation. ***Email:*** kgfell@hallrender.com

ROBBIN S. CRADDOCK (Resident, Louisville, Kentucky Office)

COUNSEL

G. WELDON JOHNSON, admitted to bar, 1957, Indiana. *Education:* Indiana University (B.S., 1952; J.D., 1957). President: Indianapolis Bar Association, 1982; Estate Planning Council, 1981-1982. Fellow, American College of Trust and Estate Counsel. Accredited Estate Planner, National Association of Estate Planners. Best Lawyers in America, Who's Who in American Law (1996-1997). ***PRACTICE AREAS:*** Estate Planning; Administration. ***Email:*** wjohnson@hallrender.com

COLLEEN McKINLEY (Resident, Louisville, Kentucky Office)

OF COUNSEL

MARK R. ADAMS (Resident, Troy, Michigan Office)

REPRESENTATIVE CLIENTS: Ascension Health; St. Vincent Health (Indianapolis, IN); St. John Health (Detroit, MI); Porter Hospital (Valparaiso, IN); Indiana Hospital & Health Association; Michigan Health & Hospital Association; Beverly Enterprises, Inc.; Spectrum Health (MI); Texas Heart Hospital of the Southwest (Dallas, TX); St. Joseph Hospital (Kokomo, IN); City of Carmel (IN); Gaylor Group (IN); Carson Tahoe Hospital (Carson City, NV); Oldham County Sewer District (KY).

HARRISON & MOBERLY, LLP

Established in 1950

135 NORTH PENNSYLVANIA STREET, SUITE 2100
INDIANAPOLIS, INDIANA 46204
Telephone: 317-639-4511
Fax: 317-639-9565; 1-800-425-4511
Email: attorneys@h-mlaw.com
URL: http://www.harrisonmoberly.com

Marion Office: 315 South Adams Street, 3rd Floor, Marion, Indiana, 46952. Telephone: 765-673-6499.

Acquisitions and Mergers, Complex and Multi-District Litigation, Administrative Law, Antitrust and Trade Regulation. Appellate Practice (State and Federal), Arson and Fraud, Business Litigation, Collections, Construction Law, Contracts, Corporate Law, Business Transactions, Labor and Employment, Environmental Law, Environmental Compliance, Trusts and Estates, Financial Institutions, Health Care, Insurance Defense (First Party and Third Party) and Policyholder Law, Intellectual Property, Labor Law, Litigation, Medical Malpractice, Probate Litigation, Products Liability, Product Safety, Real Estate, Taxation (State, Federal, Estate and Gift), Toxic Torts, Trademarks, Copyrights, Warranty, Workers Compensation and Zoning, Planning and Land Use.

FIRM PROFILE: Harrison & Moberly is a comprehensive, full-service law firm located at the crossroads of America, with offices in Indianapolis, Carmel, and Marion, Indiana. The firm has a long history and tradition, going all the way back to its founding in 1950. Although the firm's headquarters are in the Midwest, Harrison & Moberly serves its clients' needs locally, nationally and internationally.

PARTNERS

STEPHEN E. ARTHUR, born Bluefield, West Virginia, February 16, 1955; admitted to bar, 1979, Indiana, U.S. District Court, Southern and Northern Districts of Indiana, U.S. Court of Military Appeals, U.S. Court of Appeals, Seventh Circuit and U.S. Supreme Court; 1995, U.S. Tax Court. *Education:* University of Indianapolis (B.A., magna cum laude with honors, 1976); Indiana University School of Law - Indianapolis (J.D., cum laude, 1979). Editor, Indiana Law Review, 1978-1979. Law Clerk to Chief Justice Richard M. Givan, Indiana Supreme Court, 1977-1979. Author: *Indiana Procedural Forms* and *Indiana Civil Trial Practice*,, West Publishing, 1996—. Contributing Author: chapter on Appellate Brief, *The Attorney's Guide to the Seventh Circuit Court of Appeals,* 1987 and Supplement, 1998—. Faculty, National Institute of Trial Advocacy and National Trial Advocacy College. Member, 1993-1998 and Secretary, 1995, Indiana Supreme Court Continuing Legal Education Commission. Member, Committee on Local Rules of United States District Court for the Southern District of Indiana, 1992-1998. *Member:* Seventh Circuit Bar Association; American Board of Trial Advocates (Associate Member, 1998—). Indiana Supreme Court Committee on Character and Fitness; American Society of Writers on Legal Subjects; Outstanding Lawyers of America. Fellow, Indiana Bar Foundation. [Capt., U.S. Marine Corps, 1979-1982]. (Certified as a Civil Trial Advocacy Specialist by the National Board of Trial Advocacy). ***PRACTICE AREAS:*** Complex Commercial Litigation; Products Liability; Antitrust; Commercial Litigation; Real Estate Litigation; Tax Litigation. ***Email:*** sarthur@h-mlaw.com

TIMOTHY J. HULETT, born East Chicago, Indiana, May 2, 1957; admitted to bar, 1982, Indiana, U.S. District Court, Northern and Southern Districts of Indiana, U.S. Court of Appeals, Seventh Circuit and U.S. Supreme Court. *Education:* Wabash College (A.B., cum laude, 1979); Indiana University (J.D., 1982). Phi Delta Phi. Member, Moot Court Society. Contributing Author and Panelist, "Subrogation-Spoilation of Evidence," Indiana Continuing Legal Education Forum, 1995; "Fire Litigation-Conducting the Fire Investigation," 1999; "ICLEF 2000 Year in Review: Insurance Law". *Member:* Indianapolis, Indiana State and American (Member, Tort and Insurance Practice Section) Bar Associations; Defense Research Institute; International Association of Defense Counsel; Defense Trial Counsel of Indiana. ***REPORTED CASES:*** State Farm Fire and Casualty Company v. Graham, 567 N.E.2d 1139; Burr v. United Farm Bureau Mutual Insurance Company, 560 N.E.2d, 1250; Northern Assurance Company v. William J. Summers, 17 F.3d 956 (7th Cir. 1994). ***PRACTICE AREAS:*** Complex Litigation; Arson and Fraud Defense; Complex Tort and Business Litigation. ***Email:*** timhulett@h-mlaw.com

PATRICIA POLIS McCRORY, born Indianapolis, Indiana, June 22, 1954; admitted to bar, 1980, Indiana and U.S. District Court, Northern and Southern Districts of Indiana; U.S. Court of Appeals, 7th Circuit. *Education:* University of Indianapolis (B.S., cum laude, 1976); Indiana University (J.D., 1979). Associate Editor, Indiana Law Review, 1978-1979. Law Clerk to Honorable Cale J. Holder, U.S. District Court, Southern District of Indiana, 1980-1983. Contributing Author and Panelist: "Litigation in the 1990's," Annual Meeting of the Seventh Circuit Bar Association, 1997; "Federal Court Practice," Environmental Issues and Toxic Tort Litigation Updates, 1998; "Superfund Recycling Act," 2000; "Environmental Cov. Issues," 2001; CERCLA Updates, 2002; "So You Have a Chemical Spill - Now What?" 2002; Mold, 2003; "Long Term Care and Nursing Home Litigation," 1999, 2000, 2002, 2003. Instructor, The Indiana Trial Advocacy College, 1998-2002. Presenter, Kiwanis International Convention, "The Kiwanis Foundation: Why Contributions Should

(This Listing Continued)

(This Listing Continued)

HARRISON & MOBERLY, LLP, Indianapolis—Continued

Go To A 501(c)(3) Entity," 1995/1996. Graduate of the National Institute for Trial Advocacy Advanced Litigation Series. Listed in: International Who's Who of Professionals; National Registry of Who's Who; Outstanding Lawyers of America, 2003. *Member:* Indianapolis (Chair, Environmental Section; Member, Sections on: Health Care; Litigation), Indiana State (Member, Sections on: Environmental; Health Care; Litigation), Seventh Circuit (First Vice President) and American Bar Associations; Defense Trial Counsel of Indiana; Defense Research Institute; International Association of Defense Counsel. Distinguished Fellow of the Indianapolis Bar Foundation. ***REPORTED CASES:*** State Farm Fire & Casualty Company v. Miles, 730 F.Supp. 1462 (S.D.Ind., 1990) aff'd 930 F.2d 25 (7th Cir. 1991); State Farm Fire & Casualty Company v. First Nat'l. Bank of Madison Co., as Guardian of the Est. of Stacy L. Murdock and James Murdock, 969 F.2d 521 (7th Cir. 1992); State Farm Fire & Casualty Company v. Sanders, 805 F.Supp. 1453 (S.D.Ind., 1992); Speedway International Trucks, Inc. v. Tony and Gladys Rosselle, et al. (1995), Ind., 648 N.E.2D 1168; First Community Bank and Trust, as successor in interest to Bargersville Federal Savings Bank, Walter M. Umbarger, Merrill M. Wesemann, and Eugene W. Morris v. Kelley, Hardesty, Smith and Company, Inc., Larry D. Smith and Garry Autry, 663 N.E.2d 218 (Ind.App. 1996); Noblesville Redevelopment Commission v. Noblesville Associates Limited Partnership, Mercantile Bank of St. Louis, et al., 674 N.E.2d 558 (Ind. 1996). ***PRACTICE AREAS:*** Enviromental Law; Toxic Torts; Health Care; Financial Institutions Law; Nonprofit Corporations. ***Email:*** pmccrory@h-mlaw.com

RICHARD L. McOMBER, born Gary, Indiana, September 18, 1946; admitted to bar, 1983, Indiana and U.S. District Court, Southern District of Indiana. *Education:* Butler University (B.A., 1969; M.S., 1974); Indiana University (J.D., 1983). Law Clerk to Chief Justice Richard M. Givan, Indiana Supreme Court, 1981-1983. Deputy Prosecuting Attorney, 19th Judicial Circuit, 1983-1987. *Member:* Indianapolis and Indiana State Bar Associations; American Board of Trial Advocates. ***PRACTICE AREAS:*** Personal Injury; Litigation; Municipal Liability; Insurance Coverage; Insurance Fraud. ***Email:*** rmcomber@h-mlaw.com

JANET A. McSHARAR, born Huntington, Indiana, July 22, 1956; admitted to bar, 1984, Indiana and U.S. District Court, Northern and Southern Districts of Indiana. *Education:* Indiana University (B.A., 1978); Indiana University School of Law - Indianapolis (J.D., 1983). Contributing Author and Speaker: Indiana Continuing Legal Education; National Business Institute; Lorman Business Center; Indiana Health Care Association; Indiana Association of Homes and Services for the Aging Annual Convention and for seminars about Nursing Homes. *Member:* Indianapolis, Indiana State and American Bar Associations; American Health Lawyers. ***PRACTICE AREAS:*** Health Care Regulation; Health Care Reimbursement; Health Care Licensing; Health Care Fraud; Administrative Law; Civil Litigation; Health Care Contracts; Health Care Mergers and Acquisitions; Employment Law. ***Email:*** jmcsharar@h-mlaw.com

RORY O'BRYAN, born 1947; admitted to bar, 1972, Indiana. *Education:* Indiana University (A.B., 1969; J.D., first in class, 1972). Order of the Coif. Note Editor, Indiana Law Journal, 1971-1972. Speaker, Author: "Indiana LLC Formations and Conversions: Law, Tax & Practice," PESI, 2002; "Drafting and Negotiating Commercial Leases in Indiana," National Business Institute, 2002; "Partnerships, LLCs and LLPs in Indiana," Lorman, 2002; "Agency Law for Indiana Real Estate Brokers and Salespersons;" Indiana Real Estate Conference, Indiana Board of Commercial Realtors. Author: "Real Estate Options and Rights May Be Invalidated by Rule Against Perpemities," The Indiana Lawyer, Nov. 26-Dec. 9, 1997; "Synthetic Lease Latest Rage in Real Estate World," The Indiana, July 23-Aug. 5, 1997; "Third-Generation Sublease Clauses Protect Landlords," Indianapolis Business Journal, April 24-30, 1995; "Like-Kind Real Estate Exchanges," Lorman, 1993. Listed in: Who's Who in American Law; The Best Lawyers in America; Outstanding Lawyers of America. Adjunct Professor, Indiana University School of Law, 1998—. Fellow, Indiana Bar Foundation. *Member:* Indiana State (Member, Probate, Trust and Real Property Section) and American (Member: Real Property, Probate and Trust Law Section; Committee on Commercial Leasing; Corporation, Banking and Business Law Section; Taxation Section) Bar Associations; American College of Real Estate Lawyers; International Association of Attorneys and Executives in Corporate Real Estate (Past Chairman, Board of Directors; Chairman, Publications Committee and Co-Editor, "Corporate Real Estate and the Law"). Indiana Bar Foundation. ***REPORTED CASES:*** Mid-west Fed. Sav. Bank v. Kerlin, 672 N.E.2d 82 (Ind.App. 1996). ***PRACTICE AREAS:*** Real Estate Law; Partnerships Law; Limited Liability Company Law. ***Email:*** rob@h-mlaw.com

JEFFREY W. SCRIPTURE, born Shelbyville, Indiana, February 7, 1962; admitted to bar, 1987, Indiana and U.S. District Court, Southern District of Indiana. *Education:* Wabash College (B.A., cum laude, 1984); Indiana University (J.D., 1987). Recipient, American Jurisprudence Award in Torts. Member, Board of Directors of Carmel City Chamber of Commerce. *Member:* Indianapolis, Indiana State and American Bar Associations; Builders Association of Greater Indianapolis (Board Member); Hancock County Builders Council (Board Member); Indiana State Builders Association (Board Member). ***PRACTICE AREAS:*** Construction Law; Real Estate; Zoning, Planning and Land Use. ***Email:*** jscript@h-mlaw.com

A. DONALD WILES, II, born Indianapolis, Indiana, December 8, 1938; admitted to bar, 1966, Indiana; U.S. District Court, Southern and Northern Districts of Indiana, U.S. Tax Court, and U.S. Supreme Court. *Education:* Princeton University (A.B., 1961); Columbia University (LL.B., cum laude, 1966). Contributing Author and Panelist for seminar on Advanced Real Estate Law with article "Securing Clear Title to Real Estate"; for seminar on Basic Corporate Law in Indiana with article "Partnerships, Limited Partnerships and Federal Taxation of Partnerships;" for seminar on Choice of Business Entity in Indiana with articles "The Fundamentals of Limited Liability Companies and Limited Liability Partnerships" and "Limited Partnerships;" for seminar on Family Limited Partnerships and Limited Liability Companies in Indiana with articles "Comparison of Limited Liability Companies to Family Limited Partnerships" and "Drafting of Family Limited Partnership and Limited Liability Documents;" for seminar on Exempt Organizations and Charitable Activities in Indiana with article "Introduction to Tax Exempt Organizations.". *Member:* Indianapolis, Indiana State and American (Member, Real Property, Probate and Trust Law Sections) Bar Associations. ***REPORTED CASES:*** Lowe as Trustee v. Johnson, 469 N.E.2d 768 (Ind. App. 2 Dist. 1984); Arsenal Savings Association v. Westfield Lighting Co. Inc., 471 N.E.2d 322 (Ind. App. 4 Dist. 1984); First Community Bank and Trust, as successor in interest to Bargersville Federal Savings Bank, Walter M. Umbarger, Merrill M. Wesemann, and Eugene W. Morris v. Kelley, Hardesty, Smith and Company, Inc., Larry D. Smith and Garry Autry, 663 N.E.2d 218 (Ind. App. 1996); First Community Bank and Trust, et al. v. Kelley, Hardesty, Smith and Company, Inc., et al., 663 N.E.2d 218 (Ind.App. 1996); Noblesville Redevelopment Commission v. Noblesville Associates Limited Partnership, Mercantile Bank of St. Louis, et al., 674 N.E.2d 558 (Ind. 1996); First Federal Savings Bank of Wabash v. United States, 118 F.3d 532 (7th Cir. Ct.App. 1997); Sheehan v. Mahoney Chevrolet-Olds, Inc., 23 F.Supp.2d 926 (N.D.Ind. 1998); PCL/Calumet v. Entercitement, L.L.C., et al., 760 N.E.2d 633 (Ind. App. 2001); The City of Jasper v. Collingnon, et al., 789 N.E.2d 80 (Ind. App. 2003); Lake Central School Corp. v. Hawk Development Corp., et al., 793 N.E.2d 1080 (Ind.App. 2003). ***PRACTICE AREAS:*** Real Estate; Construction; Business. ***Email:*** dwiles@h-mlaw.com

(This Listing Continued)

PAUL (RICK) RAUCH, III, born Cleveland, Ohio, March 6, 1964; admitted to bar, 1994, Indiana and U.S. District Court, Northern and Southern Districts of Indiana; 2001, U.S. Court of Appeals, Seventh Circuit. *Education:* Wabash College (A.B., 1986); Florida State University (M.S.M., 1990); Indiana University School of Law - Indianapolis (J.D., 1994). Seminar Speaker, Collection Law in the Health Care Industry. *Member:* Indianapolis, Indiana State and American Bar Associations. ***REPORTED CASES:*** Chicagoland Christian Village v. Sullivan, 671 NE2d 174 (Ind.Ct.App. 1996); Zeigler Coal Company v. William Hawker, 326 F.3d 894 (7th Circuit 2003). ***PRACTICE AREAS:*** Health Care Law; Corporate Law; Debtor and Creditor; Mergers and Acquisitions; Personal Injury; Civil Trial and Appellate Practice; Black Lung; Probate; Wills; Guardianship. ***Email:*** rrauch@h-mlaw.com

PAUL C. SWEENEY, born Burbank, California, March 7, 1972; admitted to bar, 1997, Indiana; U.S. District Courts, Northern and Southern Districts of Indiana; U.S. Court of Appeals, Seventh Circuit; U.S. Supreme Court. *Education:* Indiana University, Bloomington (B.A., 1994); Indiana University School of Law, Indianapolis (J.D., magna cum laude, 1997). Phi Delta Phi; Pi Kappa Alpha (Member, Housing Corporation, Delta Xi Chapter, 1996—). Research Fellow, Law and Education Research Fellowship, Indiana University, 1996-1997. Recipient, George O. Dix Writing Award, 1997. Student Note Editor, Indiana International & Comparative Law Review, 1996-1997. Judicial Intern to: Honorable Randall T. Shepard, Chief Justice, Indiana Supreme Court, 1996-1997; Honorable Kennard P. Foster, Magistrate Judge, U.S. District Court, Southern District of Indiana, 1995. Author: "Abuse, Misuse & Abrogation of the Use of Legislative History: Title IX & Peer Sexual Harassment," 66 University of Missouri-Kansas City L. Rev. 41 (1997). Co-Chair, 2000—, Hamilton County Youth as Resources Action Board. *Member:* Indianapolis, Seventh Circuit, Indiana State and American Bar Associations; Defense Trial Counsel of Indiana; Defense Research Institute. ***PRACTICE AREAS:*** Civil Litigation; Insurance Defense Litigation; Healthcare Litigation; Business Law. ***Email:*** psweeney@h-mlaw.com

DAVID WILLIAMS RUSSELL, born Lockport, New York, April 5, 1945; admitted to bar, 1976, Illinois and U.S. District Court, Northern and Federal Districts of Indiana; 1983, Indiana and U.S. District Court, Northern and Southern Districts of Indiana. *Education:* Dartmouth College (A.B., 1967); Amos Tuck School of Business Administration (M.B.A., Finance Major, 1969); Northwestern University (J.D., cum laude, 1976). *Member:* Indianapolis, Indiana State, Illinois State, American and International Bar Associations; Dartmouth Lawyers Association; International Lawyers Network; Board of Neutral Arbitrators; National Association of Securities Dealers. ***PRACTICE AREAS:*** Domestic and Global Business; Transactions; Debt; Securities; Financings; Intellectual Property; Technologies Law; Computer Law; Privacy Law; Marketing and Distribution Law; Antitrust; Real Estate; Litigation; Arbitration. ***Email:*** drussell@h-mlaw.com

COUNSEL

R. DAVY EAGLESFIELD, III, born Indianapolis, Indiana, September 21, 1941; admitted to bar, 1971, Indiana and U.S. District Court, Southern District of Indiana; 1974, U.S. Court of Appeals, Seventh Circuit; 1976, U.S. Supreme Court. *Education:* Indiana University (A.B., 1963; J.D., summa cum laude, 1971). Assistant Professor, Torts and Criminal Law, Indiana University Law School at Indianapolis, 1973-1974. *Member:* Indianapolis and American Bar Associations. ***PRACTICE AREAS:*** Environmental Law; Toxic Torts; Complex and Multi-District Litigation. ***Email:*** deaglesfield@h-mlaw.com

WILLIAM J. HANCOCK, born Indianapolis, Indiana, May 15, 1957; admitted to bar, 1982, Indiana and U.S. District Court, Northern and Southern Districts of Indiana; 1984, U.S. Court of Appeals, Seventh Circuit and U.S. Court of Federal Claims; 1990, U.S. District Court, Eastern District of Michigan; 2001, U.S. Supreme Court. *Education:* Indiana University, Indianapolis (B.S., 1979); Indiana University School of Law - Indianapolis (J.D., cum laude, 1982). Phi Delta Phi. Managing Editor, Indiana Law Review, 1981-1982. Recipient, Harold R. Woodard Fellowship, 1982. Speaker and Lecturer: Indiana Continuing Legal Education Forum; National Business Institute; Lorman Business Center, Inc.; Professional Education Systems, Inc.; Associated General Contractors of Indiana; Mechanical Contractors Association of Indiana, Inc.; Indiana Constructors, Inc.; Asphalt Pavement Association of Indiana, Inc.; Indiana Mineral Aggregates, Inc.; Indiana Women in Construction; Construction Specifications Institute (Indiana Chapter); AACE International (Indiana Section); Glazing Contractors Association (Detroit, MI); Purdue University Superintendents Conference; George S. Olive & Co. Construction Industry Conference. Member, Indianapolis Construction Advisory Committee and Panel Member, American Arbitration Association. Member, National Panel of Construction Arbitrators, Registered Civil Mediator, Indiana Commission for Continuing Legal Education Registry of Approved Court Mediators. *Member:* Indianapolis, Indiana State and American (Member: Public Contract Law; Forum Committee on the Construction Industry) Bar Associations. (Resident, Carmel Office). ***PRACTICE AREAS:*** Construction Law; Public Contract Law; Commercial Law. ***Email:*** whancock@h-mlaw.com

SENIOR COUNSEL

KEITH BEALL, born 1961; admitted to bar, 1987, Indiana and U.S. District Court, Southern and Northern Districts of Indiana. *Education:* Indiana University at Bloomington (B.S., 1984); University of Dayton School of Law (J.D., 1987). Panel Member on: The National Association of Water Companies Annual Issues Forum; Indiana Telephone Association Annual Conference; National Association of State Utility Consumer Advocates forum

(This Listing Continued)

on gas capacity release issues. Registered Civil Mediator, Indiana Commission for Continuing Legal Education Registry of Approved Court Mediators. Administrative Law Judge representative on Legislative Study Alternative Dispute Resolution for Administrative Agency Proceedings. *Member:* Indiana State Bar Association (Member, Utility Law Section). ***PRACTICE AREAS:*** Utility Law; Communications Law; Business Law; Litigation; Commercial Law; Real Estate; Property Taxes; Alternative Dispute Resolution. ***Email:*** kbeall@iquest.net

ROBERT J. HOFFMAN, born Indianapolis, Indiana, September 29, 1945; admitted to bar, 1974, Indiana and U.S. District Court, Southern District of Indiana. *Education:* Indiana University (A.B., 1968); Indiana University School of Law - Indianapolis (J.D., summa cum laude, 1974). Law Clerk, Indiana Court of Appeals, 1973-1974. Author: Handbook for Subcontractors and Material Suppliers, Indiana Subcontractors Association, 1979, 1980; "Indiana Chapter," State and Municipal Laws Sourcebook, American Bar Association, Public Contract Law Section, 1996; "Suing The Material Supplier," Construction Litigation: Representing the Contractor, John Wiley & Sons, 1986. Adjunct Professor, Contract Law, Indiana University School of Law - Indianapolis, 1975-1979. Member, Associated General Contractors of Indiana, 1982—. Member, Associated Builders and Contractors, Indiana Chapter, 1999—. Member, Indiana Association of Cities and Towns - Municipal Lawyers Association, 1996—. *Member:* Indianapolis, Indiana State and American (Member: Public Contract Law Section; Forum Committee on the Construction Industry) Bar Associations; American Arbitration Association (Member, National Panel of Construction Arbitrators, Indiana Advisory Committee, Large and Complex Case Program, 1985-2001). (Resident, Carmel Office). ***PRACTICE AREAS:*** Construction Law. ***Email:*** rhoffman@h-mlaw.com

SPECIAL COUNSEL

JAMES J. McGRATH, born Philadelphia, Pennsylvania, 1942; admitted to bar, 1967, Pennsylvania; 1968, U.S. Tax Court; 1974, Indiana. *Education:* LaSalle College (A.B., 1964); Villanova University (J.D., 1967). *Member:* Indianapolis (Treasurer, 1982-1984), Indiana State (Chairman, Taxation Section, 1978-1979) and American (Member, Sections on: Taxation; Corporation; Real Property, Probate and Trust; Business Law) Bar Associations. ***PRACTICE AREAS:*** Estate Planning; Trust Law; Taxation; Probate. ***Email:*** jmcgrath@h-mlaw.com

ASSOCIATES

THADDEUS R. AILES, born 1971; admitted to bar, 1997, Indiana. *Education:* Butler University (B.S., cum laude, 1994); Indiana University School of Law - Bloomington (J.D., magna cum laude, 1997). *Member:* Indianapolis and Indiana State Bar Associations. (Resident, Carmel Office). ***PRACTICE AREAS:*** Real Estate. ***Email:*** tailes@h-mlaw.com

RAYMOND A. BASILE, born Indianapolis, Indiana, January 10, 1974; admitted to bar, 1999, Indiana and U.S. District Court, Southern and Northern Districts of Indiana. *Education:* Indiana University (B.S., 1996); Indiana University School of Law - Indianapolis (J.D., 1999). Order of the Barristers. Recipient, Outstanding Young Lawyer Award, 2003. Member, Indianapolis Bar Association Bar Leadership Series. *Member:* Indianapolis and Indiana State (Member, Litigation Section) Bar Associations. ***PRACTICE AREAS:*** Corporate Litigation; Business Litigation. ***Email:*** basile@h-mlaw.com

STEPHEN D. LePAGE, born Flint, Michigan, November 30, 1963; admitted to bar, 1990, Illinois; 2000, Indiana; U.S. District Court, Northern and Southern Districts of Indiana. *Education:* Michigan State University (B.S., Political Science, 1985); DePaul University College of Law (J.D., 1988). Author: "Indiana's Uniform Athlete Agents Act Examined," Indiana Lawyer, August 2001; "Ergonomics Program Standard Moves Forward," Indiana Lawyer, January 2001. *Member:* Indianapolis, Indiana State and American Bar Associations; Defense Trial Counsel of Indiana (Publications Chairman). ***LANGUAGES:*** Spanish. ***PRACTICE AREAS:*** Labor and Employment; Construction Law. ***Email:*** slepage@h-mlaw.com

MARK WILLIAM PFEIFFER, born Indianapolis, Indiana, April 29, 1958; admitted to bar, 1995, Indiana and U.S. District Court, Northern and Southern Districts of Indiana. *Education:* Community College of the Air Force Maxwell AFB, AL (A.S., 1988); Indiana University (B.S.,with high distinction, 1991; J.D., cum laude, 1995). Contributing Author and Presenter, "Partnerships, LLCs and LLPs in Indiana" and "Indiana Tax Exempt Organizations," Seminars. *Member:* Indianapolis and Indiana State Bar Associations. [U.S. Air Force, 1983-1989]. ***PRACTICE AREAS:*** Estate Planning; Estate Administration; Estate and Gift Taxation; Business Transactions; Business Law. ***Email:*** mpfeiff@h-mlaw.com

ANDERSON R. WHITE, born Louisville, Kentucky, May 6, 1966; admitted to bar, 1999, Indiana, U.S. District Court, Southern and Northern Districts of Indiana and Seventh Circuit Court of Appeals. *Education:* Indiana University (B.A., with distinction, 1988; J.D., 1999). Member, Order of Barristers, Indiana University Moot Court Society. Semi-Finalist, National Products Liability Moot Court Competition. ***PRACTICE AREAS:*** Civil Litigation; Insurance Defense; Torts; Business Litigation; Arson; Fraud. ***Email:*** awhite@hmlaw.com

A. BARCLAY WONG, born September 25, 1975; admitted to bar, 2001, California; 2002, Indiana; U.S. Supreme Court; U.S. District Court, Southern and Northern Districts of Indiana. *Education:* Oberlin College (B.A. 1997); Loyola Law School (J.D. 2000). Deputy Attorney, General Medical Licensing, 2002-2004. *Member:* Indianapolis (Member, Health Care Section) and Indiana State (Member, Sections on: Elder Law; Healthcare; Medicine) Bar Associations. ***PRACTICE AREAS:*** Administrative Law; Health Care; Mediacare and Medicaid; Civil Practice. ***Email:*** awong@h-mlaw.com

OF COUNSEL

JAMES D. HARRISON, born Logansport, Indiana, September 16, 1914; admitted to bar, 1937, Indiana. *Education:* Indiana University (J.D., 1937). Sigma Delta Kappa. Author: "Chiropractic Practice Liability," International Chiropractors Association, 1990. Deputy Attorney General, 1943-1945. Traffic Safety Director, State of Indiana, 1947-1948. Member, Supreme Court Committee on Character and Fitness, 1974—. *Member:* Indianapolis,

(This Listing Continued)

Indiana State and American Bar Associations. ***PRACTICE AREAS:*** Wills; Trust Law; Nonprofit Corporations; Chiropractors Malpractice; Non Profit and Charitable Organizations. ***Email:*** jharris@h-mlaw.com

LEGAL SUPPORT PERSONNEL

THERESE M. MILLER, born Beech Grove, Indiana, March, 1953. *Education:* Indiana University (A.S., Respiratory Therapy, 1974; B.S., Nursing, 1980). Registered Nurse, 1980—. Member: American Association of Legal Nurse Consultants (Member, Greater Indianapolis and National). ***Email:*** terrim@h-mlaw.com

Ace Battery, Inc.; Advantage Medical Equipment & Supply, Inc.; AmeriCare Living Centers; American Express Company; B&B Farms, Inc.; Bonar Group, Inc.; CarDon & Associates, Inc.; Care Centers, Inc.; CGU Insurance Co.; Charming Shoppes, Inc.; Chicago Title Insurance Co.; Chisholm Lumber and Supply Co., Inc.; Cincinnati Insurance Co.; Citicorp USA, Inc.; City of Greencastle; City of Jasper; City of Lafayette Employee Alliance; Conestoga Title Insurance Company; Crown Equipment Corporation; CUNA Mutual Insurance Co.; Custom Facilities, Inc.; Dallman Industrial Corporation; Davis Ide Indiana Health Care Properties, L.L.C.; Edgeworth-Laskey Properties, LLC; Edwards Electrical and Mechanical, Inc.; Electrical Equipment, Inc.; Extendicare Health Services; Farm Bureau Insurance; Farmers Insurance Group; Fidelity National Title Insurance Company; Forum Credit Union; Freyn Brothers Heating and Air Conditioning; General Electric Capital Corporation; Goff Real Estate; Guide One Insurance Group; Greencroft, Inc; Harco; Hendricks County Bank and Trust Company; Hoosier Enterprises; Huston Electric, Inc.; Indiana Asbury Towers; Indiana Farmer's Mutual Insurance; Indiana Ready Mix Concrete Association; Inliner Technologies, LLC; International Chiropractors Association of Indiana; JFW Industries, Inc.; JTB Construction, Inc.; Kiwanis International Foundation; IVAX Corporation; Leach & Russell Mechanical, Inc.; L.D. Mechanical Contractors, Inc.; Lee Alan Bryant Health Care Facilities, Inc.; Management Resources, Inc.; Mid-West Peat, Inc.; Mid-West Reproductive Medicine; Milestone Contractors, L.P.; Miller's Health Systems, Inc.; Mitsubishi Heavy Industries Climate Control, Inc.; Naab Road Medical Group; National Bank of Indianapolis; National Medical Alliance; Oakwood Corp.; Options for Better Living, Inc.; Perfect Pullets, Inc.; Pleasant Run Farms, Inc.; Porter Development Corp.; Powers & Sons Construction, Inc.; Precision Truss Systems, Inc.; Providence Health Care, Inc.; R.E. Griesemer Mechanical Contractors, Inc.; R.W. Armstrong & Associates, Inc.; Renk Corporation; Resources for Healthcare, LLC; Reynolds, Inc.; Rieth-Riley Construction Co. Inc.; Robin Run Health Care;Royal Spa; Safeco Insurance Co.; Silver Springs Stock Farm, Inc.; STAR Financial Bank; State Farm Fire & Casualty Company; T.L.C. Management, Inc.; Ticor Title Insurance Company; Toyoshima Indiana, Inc.; United Steel Fabricators, Inc.; United Title Insurance Company; West Central Indiana Plumbing, Inc.; Wesley Manor; Westminster Village North; Zenith Goldline Pharmaceuticals.

HILL, FULWIDER, McDOWELL, FUNK & MATTHEWS

PROFESSIONAL CORPORATION

Established in 1981

SUITE 2000, ONE INDIANA SQUARE
INDIANAPOLIS, INDIANA 46204-2031

Telephone: 317-488-2000
FAX: 317-630-2768
URL: http://www.hillfulwider.com

General Practice. Litigation. Corporation, Hospital, Federal and State Taxation, Aviation Law. Suretyship. Trusts and Estate Planning Law. General Business Law and Business Enterprises, Wills, Probate, Medical Malpractice, Insurance Defense.

FIRM PROFILE: Established in 1981, Hill, Fulwider, McDowell, Funk & Matthews has experienced steady growth, attributable to their providing high quality service at a reasonable cost. With a concentration in commercial litigation, the firm has developed expertise in the areas of tort liability defense, including professional and products liability and related insurance coverage matters. Additionally, firm attorneys are frequently asked to serve as mediators, arbitrators, and medical review panel chairmen. Long standing service in the area of probate, tax, estate planning and general business matters rounds out the practice for this group of attorneys who share high professional standards and commitment to excel in the quality of service and results provided to clients.

DOUGLAS J. HILL, born Detroit, Michigan, January 8, 1933; admitted to bar, 1960, Indiana. *Education:* University of Michigan (B.B.A., 1955; LL.B., 1960). *Member:* Indianapolis, Indiana State and American Bar Associations; Defense Trial Counsel of Indiana. ***PRACTICE AREAS:*** Civil Litigation; Product Liability Law; Medical Malpractice Law; Mediation. ***Email:*** doug@hfmfm.com

RICHARD R. McDOWELL, born Topeka, Kansas, May 9, 1937; admitted to bar, 1965, Indiana. *Education:* Vanderbilt University (B.E., 1959; LL.B., 1965). Phi Delta Phi. Member, Board of Editors, Vanderbilt Law Review, 1963-1965. Member, Indianapolis Civilian Police Merit Board, 1981-1988. *Member:* Indianapolis, Indiana State and American Bar Associations; Lawyers-Pilots Bar Association; Defense Trial Counsel of Indiana. ***PRACTICE AREAS:*** Civil Litigation; Product Liability Law; Toxic Tort; Drug and Medical Device Law; Aviation Law; Mediation. ***Email:*** dick@hfmfm.com

NORMAN T. FUNK, born Fort Wayne, Indiana, April 18, 1945; admitted to bar, 1971, Indiana. *Education:* Indiana University (B.S., 1967; J.D., 1971). National Finalist, National Moot Court. Author: "1987-1988 Survey of Recent Developments in the Indiana Law of Evidence," Vol. 22 Indiana Law Review, Issue I (1988). Co-Author: "Discovery of Dishonesty Under the Financial Institution Bond and Other Fidelity Bonds," Defense Research Institute Issue No. 2 (1989). Author: "Survey of Recent Developments in the Indiana Rules of Trial Procedure and Their Interpretation," 23 Indiana Law Review 2, 1990. Adjunct Professor of Law, Trial Practice, Indiana University School of Law, 1999—. Executive Director, Indiana Civil Code Study Commission and Indiana Judicial Study Commission, 1971-1972. Member, Indiana Supreme Court Committee on Rules of Practice and Procedure, 1993-1998. *Member:* Defense Trial Counsel of Indiana (Board of Directors, 1990-1997; President, 1996). Fellow: American College of Trial Lawyers. ***PRACTICE AREAS:*** Civil Litigation.

JAMES F. MATTHEWS, born Indianapolis, Indiana, May 12, 1933; admitted to bar, 1963, Indiana. *Education:* Indiana University (B.S., 1955; J.D., 1963). Phi Delta Phi. *Mem-*

(This Listing Continued)

HILL, FULWIDER, McDOWELL, FUNK & MATTHEWS, PROFESSIONAL CORPORATION, Indianapolis—Continued

ber: Indianapolis and Indiana State (Chairman, Probate, Trust and Real Property Section, 1982) Bar Associations. ***PRACTICE AREAS:*** Estates Law; Trusts Law; Taxation Law. ***Email:*** jim@hfmfm.com

KEITH A. KINNEY, born Warsaw, Indiana, June 10, 1958; admitted to bar, 1983, Indiana. *Education:* DePauw University (B.A., cum laude, 1980); Indiana University (J.D., 1983). Phi Delta Phi. Associate Editor, Indiana Law Review, 1982-1983. Law Clerk, Justice Donald Hunter, Indiana Supreme Court, 1983-1984. Law Clerk, Judge James Noland, U.S. District Court, Southern District of Indiana, 1984-1986. Author: "Different Standards for Deciding Motions for Summary Judgment on Punitive Damage Claims: The State Court and Federal Court Approaches," The Indiana Lawyer, Vol. 5, No. 10. *Member:* Indianapolis, Indiana State and American Bar Associations; Defense Trial Counsel of Indiana; Defense Research Institute. ***PRACTICE AREAS:*** Civil Litigation. ***Email:*** keith@hfmfm.com

MICHAEL G. GETTY, born Chicago, Illinois, February 28, 1962; admitted to bar, 1987, Illinois, U.S. District Court, Central District of Illinois and U.S. Court of Appeals, Seventh Circuit; 1993, Indiana and U.S. District Court, Southern and Northern Districts of Indiana. *Education:* University of Michigan (B.A., 1984); Southern Illinois University (J.D., cum laude, 1987). Editor in Chief, Southern Illinois University Law Journal, 1986-1987; Assistant Editor, Journal of Legal Medicine, 1987—. Law Clerk to the Honorable Richard Mills, U.S. District Court, Central District of Illinois, 1987-1989. *Member:* Indianapolis and American (Member, Health Law Section) Bar Associations; Defense Research Institute; American College of Legal Medicine. ***PRACTICE AREAS:*** Professional Liability Litigation; Insurance Defense Law; Insurance Coverage. ***Email:*** mike@hfmfm.com

PETER H. DONAHOE, born Woonsockett, Rhode Island, July 14, 1955; admitted to bar, 1984, Indiana; 1989, U.S. Tax Court. *Education:* Indiana University (B.S., 1977; M.B.A., 1984; J.D., 1984). Certified Public Accountant, Indiana, 1981-1996. *Member:* Indianapolis (Chair, Estate Planning Section), Indiana State (Vice Chair, Tax Section Council) and American (Member Sections on: Estate Planning, Tax and Business Law) Bar Associations; Indiana CPA Society (Chairman, Federal Tax Committee, 1995; President, Indianapolis Chapter, 1995). Fellow, American College of Trust and Estate Counsel (ACTEC). ***PRACTICE AREAS:*** Estate Planning; Trust Planning; Estate Litigation; Trust Litigation; Business Tax; Real Estate; Federal and State Tax Controversies. ***Email:*** pete@hfmfm.com

KNIGHT S. ANDERSON, born Fall River, Massachusetts, January 22, 1968; admitted to bar, 1993, Indiana and U.S. District Court, Northern and Southern Districts of Indiana and U.S. Court of Appeals, Seventh and Third Circuits. *Education:* University of Notre Dame (B.A, 1990); Indiana University (J.D., cum laude, 1993). Omicron Delta Epsilon. Order of the Barristers. Member, National Moot Court Team, 1992-1993. Champion and Best Oralist, Sherman Minton Moot Court Competition, 1992. Moot Court Board, 1992-1993. Associate Editor, Adelphia Law Journal, 1991-1992. *Member:* Indianapolis, Indiana State and American Bar Associations; Indianapolis American Inn of Court; Defense Trial Counsel of Indiana; Defense Research Institute (Member, Young Lawyers Committee). ***REPORTED CASES:*** Harris v. AC&S et al., 915 F.Supp. 1420 (S.D. Ind. 1995), aff'd Harris v. OCF, 102 F.3d 1429 (7th Cir. 1996); Roberts v. ALCOA, Inc. et al., _N.E.2d_, 2004 WL 1505705 (Ind.App. Jul 07, 2004); Ritcher v. Asbestos Insulating & Roofing 790 N.E.2d 1000, (Ind.App. 2003); Allied Signal, Inc. v. Ott, 785 N.E.2d 1068 (Ind. 2003); Black v. A.C. & S., Inc. 785 N.E.2d 1084, (Ind. 2003); Black v. ACandS, Inc. 752 N.E.2d 148 (Ind.App. 2001); Fulk v. Allied Signal, Inc., 755 N.E.2d 1198, (Inc.App. 2001); Holmes v. ACandS, Inc., 711 N.E.2d 1289, (Ind.App. 1999) (decision on hearing); Holmes v. ACandS, Inc., 709 N.E.2d 26, (Ind.App. 1999); Harris v. A.C.&S. Inc. et al., 102 F.3d 1429 (7th Cir. 1996); Harris v. A.C.&S. Inc. et al., 915 F.Supp. 1420 (S.D.Ind. 1995). ***PRACTICE AREAS:*** Civil Litigation; Trademark Litigation; Products Liability; Toxic Tort; Commercial; Environmental; Insurance Coverage. ***Email:*** knight@hfmfm.com

ELIZABETH H. KNOTTS, born Indianapolis, Indiana, August 12, 1964; admitted to bar, 1991, Indiana. *Education:* Indiana University (B.A., 1986; J.D., cum laude, 1991). Phi Delta Phi, (Membership Chairman, 1990-1991). Recipient, American Jurisprudence Award in Property and Products Liability. Associate Editor, Indiana Law Review, 1990-1991. *Member:* Indianapolis (Vice President, 2001 and 2004), Indiana State and American Bar Associations. ***PRACTICE AREAS:*** Civil Litigation; Medical Malpractice Law; Products Liability. ***Email:*** beth@hfmfm.com

ALAN J. IRVIN, born Indianapolis, Indiana, October 31, 1966; admitted to bar, 1992, Indiana. *Education:* Indiana University (B.A., 1989; J.D., cum laude, 1992). Recipient, Team Championship and Best Brief Award, Chicago Bar Association Moot Court Competition, 1991. Law Clerk to the Honorable Edward W. Najam, Jr., Court of Appeals of Indiana, 1993-1995. Author: "A Comparison of Duties Owed Among Owners of Indiana Business Entities," ICLEF, 2003. *Member:* Indianapolis, Indiana State and American Bar Associations; Indiana Land Title Association. ***REPORTED CASES:*** Zurich American Ins. Group v. Wynkoop, 746 N.E.2d 985 (Ind. Ct. App. 2001); Azhar v. Town of Fishers, 744 N.E.2d 947 (Ind. Ct. App. 2001); Midwest Sec. Life Ins. Co. v. Stroup, 730 N.E.2d 163 (Ind. 2000); Long v. Methodist Hosp. of Indiana, Inc., 699 N.E.2d 1164 (Ind. Ct. App. 1998). ***PRACTICE AREAS:*** Business Litigation; Commercial Litigation; Real Estate Transactions; Business Transactions; Appellate Practice; Insurance Coverage. ***Email:*** alan@hfmfm.com

RORI LISA GOLDMAN, born Brooklyn, New York, February 27, 1970; admitted to bar, 1996, New York; 1997, Indiana and U.S. District Court, Northern and Southern Districts of Indiana. *Education:* Indiana University (B.A., 1992); Hofstra University (J.D., 1995). Member, Property Law Journal. Law Clerk to Hon. John T. Sharpnack, Court of Appeals of Indiana, 1995-1997. *Member:* Indianapolis, Indiana State and American Bar Associations; Defense Research Institute. ***PRACTICE AREAS:*** Civil Litigation; Premises Liability; Medical Malpractice; Workers Compensation. ***Email:*** rori@hfmfm.com

---

TY MICHAEL CRAVER, born Indianapolis, Indiana, May 18, 1972; admitted to bar, 1998, Indiana and U.S. District Court, Northern and Southern Districts of Indiana. *Education:* Indiana University (B.S., 1994; J.D., 1998). *Member:* Indianapolis (Member, Executive Board, Young Lawyers Division), Indiana State and American Bar Associations; Defense Trial Counsel of Indiana; Defense Research Institute. ***PRACTICE AREAS:*** Civil Litigation; Workers Compensation; Products Liability; Toxic Tort; Nursing Home Liability; Commercial; Insurance Coverage; Insurance Defense. ***Email:*** ty@hfmfm.com

EMILY D. SMITH, born Clarinda, Iowa, March 14, 1979; admitted to bar, 2003, Indiana. *Education:* University of Louisville (B.A., 2000); Indiana University, Bloomington (J.D., 2003). Recipient, Merit Scholarship. Member, Moot Court. Member, Indiana University Law Journal. *Member:* Indianapolis, Indiana State and American Bar Associations; Defense Research Institute; Defense Trial Counsel of Indiana. ***PRACTICE AREAS:*** Litigation; Workers Compensation; Personal Injury; Professional Malpractice. ***Email:*** emily@hfmfm.com

OF COUNSEL

CONSTANCE J. GUSTAFSON, born Lafayette, Indiana, September 28, 1951; admitted to bar, 1977, Indiana and U.S. District Court, Southern District of Indiana. *Education:* Indiana University (B.A., 1973); Indiana University School of Law - Indianapolis (J.D., 1977). Chairman, Indiana Corporate Law Survey Commission, 1984—. Reporter, Corporate Law Study Commission. Chairman, Drafting Committee, Nonprofit Corporation Act, 1991. Member, Limited Liability Company Act Task Force. *Member:* Indianapolis, Indiana State (Past Chairman, Corporate Banking and Business Law Section) and American Bar Associations.

REPRESENTATIVE CLIENTS: A.I.G.; Amerigas Propane, Inc.; Associated Electric & Gas Insurance Services, Ltd. (AEGIS); Atlanta Casualty Co.; Atlanta International Insurance Co.; Atlantic Mutual Insurance Co.; Casualty Indemnity Exchange; CBS Corporation; Celina Insurance Group; Chubb & Son, Inc.; Clarian Health Partners, Inc.; Country Mutual Insurance Co.; The Doctor's Company; Essex Insurance Co.; General Casualty Insurance Co.; Great American Insurance Group; The Hartford; Indiana Gas Company; Minnesota Mining & Manufacturing Co.; Monroe Guaranty Insurance Co.; SABER Management, LLC; Sears, Roebuck and Co.; Southern Indiana Gas & Electric Company; Stewart Title Guaranty Co.; St. Paul Travelers; The Midwestern Indemnity Co.; The Stanley Works; Trump Hotels & Casino Resorts; United States Steel; Utica Mutual Insurance Co.; USX Corporation; VECTREN Corporation; Viacom, Inc.; Wausau Insurance Cos.; Westinghouse Electric Corporation; Zurich-American Insurance, Co.
REFERENCE: Union Planters.

HINKLE & GIBBS

INDIANAPOLIS, INDIANA

(See Danville)

Civil and Criminal Trial Practice in all State and Federal Courts. Litigation, Bankruptcy, Personal Injury, Corporate, Probate and Estate Planning, Real Estate, Family, Domestic Relations and Banking Law.

HOCKER & ASSOCIATES

Established in 1993

7202 NORTH SHADELAND AVENUE, SUITE 207
INDIANAPOLIS, INDIANA 46250-2086
Telephone: 317-578-1630
Fax: 317-849-1892
URL: http://www.hockerlaw.com
Email: janethocker@aol.com
URL: http://www.hockerlawfirm.com

Business Litigation, Business Planning, Business Enterprises, Corporate, Small Business, Partnerships, Limited Liability Companies, Business Law, Real Estate, Estate Planning, Trusts and Estates, Wills and Probate, Bankruptcy and Corporate Formation (Sub S, C Corp. and LLC), Starting a Business, Buying and Selling a Business).

FIRM PROFILE: Small general practice firm located on the Northeast side of Indianapolis. Janet Davis Hocker is the sole attorney/owner of the firm which she founded in 1993 with Ronald J. Hocker. The firm serves individuals and business clients statewide.

Translation and interpretation services available for all languages.

JANET DAVIS HOCKER, born Logansport, Indiana, 1965; admitted to bar, 1993, Indiana. *Education:* Ball State University (B.S., 1988); Valparaiso University (J.D., 1993). Phi Alpha Delta. Member, Moot Court Society. Indiana Title Insurance Agent. *Member:* Indianapolis and Indiana State Bar Associations; Indiana Land Title Association. ***PRACTICE AREAS:*** Real Estate; Business Law; Wills; Probate; Bankruptcy. ***Email:*** janethocker@aol.com

LEGAL SUPPORT PERSONNEL

KELLY PABERZS, born Greenfield, Indiana, December 21, 1975. *Education:* Ivy Tech State College (A.A.S., 1991).

REPRESENTATIVE CLIENTS: First Indiana Bank; Valley Title Services of Indianapolis, LLC; National Attorneys Title Assurance Fund, Inc.; Hyatt Resorts; Indiana Land Title Association; Weber Concrete Construction Co.

HOLLAND & HOLLAND

Established in 1987

8888 KEYSTONE CROSSING, SUITE 848
INDIANAPOLIS, INDIANA 46240
Telephone: 317-581-4400
Fax: 317-705-3644
Email: hhlaw@sbcglobal.net

Civil Trial Practice. Negligence, Medical Malpractice, Products Liability, Railroad Crossing Accidents and Air Crash Litigation, Wrongful Death.

(This Listing Continued)

C. WARREN HOLLAND, born Indianapolis, Indiana, April 1, 1928; admitted to bar, 1952, Indiana, U.S. Supreme Court, U.S. Court of Appeals, Seventh Circuit and U.S. District Court, Southern District of Indiana. *Education:* University of Notre Dame (A.B., 1951; LL.B., 1952). Deputy Prosecutor, Marion County, 1959-1961. *Member:* Indianapolis, Indiana State and American Bar Associations; The Association of Trial Lawyers of America (Sustaining Member); American Board of Trial Advocates. ***PRACTICE AREAS:*** Personal Injury; Civil Litigation; Medical Malpractice; Product Liability; Railroad Litigation.

MICHAEL W. HOLLAND, born Indianapolis, Indiana, June 24, 1957; admitted to bar, 1982, Indiana; 1985, Florida, U.S. Court of Appeals, Seventh Circuit and U.S. District Court, Southern District of Indiana. *Education:* University of Notre Dame (B.A., summa cum laude, 1979); University of Michigan (J.D., 1982). Phi Beta Kappa. Associate Editor, Michigan Journal of Law Reform, 1981-1982. *Member:* Indianapolis, Indiana State and American Bar Associations; The Association of Trial Lawyers of America. ***PRACTICE AREAS:*** Personal Injury; Civil Litigation; Medical Malpractice; Product Liability; Railroad Litigation.

OF COUNSEL

GRETCHEN HOLLAND ETLING, born Indianapolis, Indiana, October 29, 1962; admitted to bar, 1988, Indiana, U.S. Court of Appeals, Seventh Circuit and U.S. District Court, Northern and Southern Districts of Indiana. *Education:* St. Mary's of the Lake (B.A., cum laude, 1985); Indiana University (J.D., 1988). Delta Theta Phi. *Member:* Indianapolis, Indiana State and American Bar Associations; The Association of Trial Lawyers of America. ***PRACTICE AREAS:*** Personal Injury; Civil Litigation; Medical Malpractice; Product Liability.

CHARLES G. REEDER, born Dayton, Ohio, July 3, 1939; admitted to bar, 1965, Indiana; 1967, U.S. Tax Court; 1970, U.S. Court of Appeals, 7th Circuit and U.S. District Court, Southern District of Indiana. *Education:* Miami University (B.S., 1961); Indiana University (J.D., with distinction, 1965). Phi Eta Sigma; Order of the Coif. Instructor of Law, Indiana University School of Law-Indianapolis, 1967. Adjunct Professor of Law, Indiana University School of Law-Indianapolis, 1973-1976; 1983. *Member:* Indianapolis and Indiana State Bar Associations; Indiana Trial Lawyers Association; The Association of Trial Lawyers of America. ***PRACTICE AREAS:*** Personal Injury; Civil Litigation; Medical Malpractice; Product Liability.

HOOVER HULL BAKER & HEATH LLP

111 MONUMENT CIRCLE, SUITE 4400
P.O. BOX 44989
INDIANAPOLIS, INDIANA 46244-0989
Telephone: 317-822-4400
Fax: 317-822-0234
URL: http://www.hooverhull.com

Civil Trial and Appellate Practice in all Federal and State Courts. Practice before Administrative Agencies and Alternative Dispute Resolution Proceedings. Art Law Litigation, Business & Commercial Litigation, Class Action Proceedings, Constitutional Law, Construction Disputes and Litigation, Education Law and School Litigation, Election Campaign and Political Law Litigation, Employee Benefits and Employment Litigation, Tort and Product Liability Litigation, Insurance Litigation, Professional Liability Litigation, Sports Law Litigation.

FIRM PROFILE: A firm devoted to the representation of clients in all forms of business, professional liability, employment and tort litigation. The firm provides litigation services in the areas of complex commercial disputes, class actions, fiduciary, director and officer liability, ERISA and employment disputes, reinsurance and insurance coverage, professional liability, construction disputes and torts. Attorneys will represent clients in state and federal trial and appellate courts, arbitration proceedings and other forms of dispute resolution.

JOHN DAVID HOOVER, born Minneapolis, Minnesota, September 7, 1951; admitted to bar, 1980, Indiana; U.S. District Court, Northern and Southern Districts of Indiana; U.S. Court of Appeals, Seventh Circuit; U.S. Supreme Court. *Education:* Vanderbilt University (B.A., 1973); Indiana University (J.D., cum laude, 1980). Associate Editor, Indiana Law Review, 1979-1980. Law Clerk to: Hon. Gene E. Brooks, U.S. District Court, Southern District of Indiana, 1980-1981; Hon. Robert Lybrook, Indiana Court of Appeals, 1977-1979. *Member:* Indianapolis, Indiana State, Seventh Circuit and American Bar Associations; Federation of Defense and Corporate Counsel; Defense Research Institute. ***PRACTICE AREAS:*** Commercial Litigation; Complex Litigation; Professional Liability Defense; Art Law. ***Email:*** jdhoover@hooverhull.com

ANDREW W. HULL, born Pontiac, Michigan, December 12, 1957; admitted to bar, 1986, Indiana; U.S. District Court, Northern and Southern Districts of Indiana; U.S. Court of Appeals, Seventh and Eleventh Circuits; U.S. Supreme Court. *Education:* University of Michigan (B.G.S., 1981); Indiana University (J.D., cum laude, 1986). Associate Editor, Indiana Law Journal, 1986. *Member:* Indianapolis, Indiana State, Seventh Circuit and American Bar Associations; Defense Trial Counsel of Indiana; Defense Research Institute. ***PRACTICE AREAS:*** ERISA Litigation; Commercial Litigation; Employment Litigation. ***Email:*** awhull@hooverhull.com

ROBERT M. BAKER III, born Oak Park, Illinois, August 21, 1950; admitted to bar, 1976, Indiana; U.S. District Court, Southern and Northern Districts of Indiana; U.S. Court of Appeals, Seventh Circuit; U.S. Supreme Court. *Education:* Miami University (B.S., Business, 1972); Indiana University (J .D., cum laude, 1976). Registered Civil Mediator, 1997. *Member:* Indianapolis, Indiana State and American Bar Associations; Defense Research Institute. ***PRACTICE AREAS:*** Civil Litigation; Products Liability; Personal Injury; Professional Liability; Toxic Torts; Insurance. ***Email:*** rbaker@hooverhull.com

G. RONALD HEATH, born Indianapolis, Indiana, December 30, 1938; admitted to bar, 1965, Indiana; U.S. District Court, Northern and Southern Districts of Indiana; U.S. Court of Appeals, Seventh Circuit. *Education:* Indiana University (B.A., Government/History, 1962; LL.B., 1965). Delta Theta Phi. *Member:* Indianapolis, Indiana State and American Bar Associations; Federation of Defense and Corporate Counsel; Defense Research Institute; Defense Trial Counsel of Indiana. ***PRACTICE AREAS:*** Civil Litigation; Products Liability; Professional Liability; Reinsurance Law; Insurance Coverage Law. ***Email:*** grheath@hooverhull.com

ALICE McKENZIE MORICAL, born West Lafayette, Indiana, May 13, 1969; admitted to bar, 1995, Indiana; U.S. District Court, Northern and Southern Districts of Indiana; U.S. Court of Appeals, Seventh Circuit. *Education:* Miami University (B.A., cum laude, 1991); Indiana University - Bloomington (J.D., magna cum laude, 1994). Order of the Coif. Member, Indiana Law Journal, 1993-1994. Law Clerk, Judge John D. Tinder, U.S. District Court, Southern District of Indiana, 1994-1995. *Member:* Indianapolis, Indiana State, Seventh Circuit and American Bar Associations. ***PRACTICE AREAS:*** Commercial Litigation; Employment Litigation; ERISA Litigation. ***Email:*** amorical@hooverhull.com

---

SEAN T. WHITE, born Indianapolis, Indiana, October 8, 1968; admitted to bar, 1997, Indiana; U.S. District Court, Northern and Southern Districts of Indiana; U.S. Court of Appeals, Seventh Circuit. *Education:* Indiana University, Bloomington (B.S., 1990); Indiana University, Indianapolis (J.D., summa cum laude, 1997). *Member:* Indianapolis, Indiana State, Seventh Circuit and American Bar Associations. ***PRACTICE AREAS:*** Complex Litigation; Commercial Litigation; Construction Law. ***Email:*** swhite@hooverhull.com

SARAH STITES FANZINI, born Mare Island, California, April 11, 1971; admitted to bar, 1999, Indiana; U.S. District Court, Northern and Southern Districts of Indiana. *Education:* Purdue University (B.A., Political Science/Communications, cum laude, with distinction, 1992); Indiana University (J.D., 1999). Phi Beta Kappa. *Member:* Indianapolis, Indiana State (Member, Written Publications Committee, 2001—) and American Bar Associations. ***PRACTICE AREAS:*** Professional Liability Defense. ***Email:*** sfanzini@hooverhull.com

MARK A. DRUMMOND, born Indianapolis, Indiana, February 13, 1963; admitted to bar, 1990, Indiana; U.S. District Court, Northern and Southern Districts of Indiana. *Education:* Indiana University (B.A., Telecommunications/Political Science, 1986; J.D., magna cum laude, 1990). Business Editor, Indiana Law Review, 1990. Winner, Thompson Memorial Writing Competition, 1990. *Member:* Indianapolis, Indiana State and American Bar Associations. ***PRACTICE AREAS:*** Commercial Litigation; Professional Liability Defense. ***Email:*** mdrummond@hooverhull.com

MICHAEL A. DORELLI, born Hammond, Indiana, August 2, 1971; admitted to bar, 1998, Indiana and U.S. District Court, Southern and Northern Districts of Indiana; 2001, U.S. Court of Appeals, Seventh Circuit. *Education:* Indiana University (B.S., 1994; J.D., magna cum laude, 1998). Executive Managing Editor, Indiana Law Review, 1997-1998. *Member:* Indianapolis, Indiana State and American Bar Associations. ***PRACTICE AREAS:*** Commercial Litigation. ***Email:*** mdorelli@hooverhull.com

GREGORY C. BRUBAKER, born Fort Wayne, Indiana, May 10, 1971; admitted to bar, 1998, Indiana and U.S. District Court, Southern and Northern Districts of Indiana. *Education:* DePauw University (B.A., 1994); Indiana University School of Law (J.D., cum laude, 1998). *Member:* Indianapolis, Indiana State and American Bar Associations. ***PRACTICE AREAS:*** Commercial Litigation; Employment Law and Litigation; ERISA Litigation. ***Email:*** gbrubaker@hooverhull.com

WILLIAM JOSEPH SPALDING, born Wichita, Kansas, March 16, 1976; admitted to bar, 2003, Indiana; U.S. District Court, Northern and Southern Districts of Indiana; U.S. Court of Appeals, Seventh Circuit. *Education:* Indiana University (B.A., 1998; J.D., 2003). Associate Editor, Indiana Law Journal. *Member:* Indianapolis, Indiana State and American Bar Associations. ***PRACTICE AREAS:*** ERISA Litigation; Commercial Litigation; Medical Malpractice Litigation. ***Email:*** wspalding@hooverhull.com

JASON L. FULK, born Bluffton, Indiana, January 5, 1976; admitted to bar, 2004, Indiana and U.S. District Court, Northern and Southern Districts of Indiana. *Education:* Indiana University Kelley School of Business - Bloomington (B.S., Marketing, B.S., Computer Information Systems); Indiana University School of Law - Bloomington (J.D., 2004). Managing Editor, Indiana Law Journal, 2004. *Member:* Indianapolis, Indiana State and American Bar Associations. ***PRACTICE AREAS:*** Commercial Litigation. ***Email:*** jfulk@hooverhull.com

REPRESENTATIVE CLIENTS: ACE USA; Ameritech Publishing, Inc.; Baltimore Life Insurance Company; Benicorp Insurance Company; Ceres Group, Inc.; Comcast Cablevision, Inc; CNA, EHOB, Inc.; Fortis Insurance Company; Goran Capital Company; Granite Reinsurance Company Limted; Great American Insurace Company; Indiana Heart Physicians, Inc.; Indiana High School Athletic Association, Inc.; Indiana Lumbermens Mutual Insurance Company; Individualized Care Management; Koch Air LLC, Nationwide Insurance Company; ProAssurance of Indiana; SanDor Development Corp.; SBC Ameritech; Spanierman Gallery, LLP.; Star Scientific, Inc.; Stone Capital Corporation; The Chubb Group of Insurance Companies; The Indiana Insurance Guaranty Association; The Prudential Insurance Company of America.

HOPPER BLACKWELL, P.C.

Established in 1987
BANK ONE CENTER/CIRCLE
111 MONUMENT CIRCLE, SUITE 452
INDIANAPOLIS, INDIANA 46204-5170
Telephone: 317-635-5005
Facsimile: 317-634-2501
URL: http://www.hopperblackwelllaw.com

Bankruptcy, Banks and Banking, Collections, Commercial Law, Corporate Law, Debtor and Creditor, Litigation, Commercial Litigation, Civil Litigation, Trial Practice, Mergers, Acquisitions and Divestitures.

FIRM PROFILE: Hopper Blackwell, P.C. concentrates in Commercial Litigation, Creditor's Rights, Transactions and Business Law. We have been committed to providing businesses and individuals the highest quality legal work at a reasonable price since 1987. Hopper Blackwell, P.C. offers legal representation at all levels of state and federal court.

(This Listing Continued)

HOPPER BLACKWELL, P.C., Indianapolis—Continued

GEORGE W. HOPPER, born Mineola, New York, February 11, 1957; admitted to bar, 1982, Indiana and U.S. District Court, Southern and Northern Districts of Indiana; 1984, U.S. Court of Appeals, Seventh Circuit; 1988, U.S. Court of Appeals, Sixth Circuit; 1994, U.S. Supreme Court. *Education:* Vanderbilt University (B.A., magna cum laude, 1979; J.D., 1982). Author and Lecturer, Indiana Continuing Legal Education Forum. *Member:* Indianapolis (Past Chairman, Commercial and Bankruptcy Law Section), Indiana State and American (Member, Business Law Section) Bar Associations; American Bankruptcy Institute; Indiana Association for Corporate Renewal. ***PRACTICE AREAS:*** Litigation; Commercial Litigation; Civil Litigation; Bankruptcy; Collections; Debtor and Creditor. ***Email:*** ghopper@hopperblackwell.com

THOMAS B. BLACKWELL, born Indianapolis, Indiana, June 18, 1960; admitted to bar, 1985, Indiana. *Education:* Vanderbilt University (B.A., 1982); Indiana University School of Law (J.D., 1985). Phi Delta Phi. *Member:* Indianapolis and Indiana State Bar Associations; Federation of Defense and Corporate Counsel; Indiana Association for Corporate Renewal. ***PRACTICE AREAS:*** Mergers, Acquisitions and Divestitures; Commercial Law; Corporate Law; Litigation; Loans. ***Email:*** tblackwell@hopperblackwell.com

JEFFREY E. RAMSEY, born Hammond, Indiana, July 18, 1958; admitted to bar, 1985, Indiana and U.S. District Court, Northern and Southern Districts of Indiana; U.S. Court of Appeals, Seventh Circuit. *Education:* Valparaiso University (B.A., 1980; J.D., 1985). Note Editor, Valparaiso University Law Review, 1984-1985. Judicial Clerk for Honorable Wesley W. Ratliff, Jr., Chief Judge, Court of Appeals of Indiana, 1985-1987. *Member:* Indianapolis and Indiana State Bar Associations. ***PRACTICE AREAS:*** Bankruptcy; Collections; Debtor and Creditor; Litigation. ***Email:*** jramsey@hopperblackwell.com

RONALD W. BUCHMEIER, born Garrett, Indiana, February 4, 1952; admitted to bar, 1979, Indiana and U.S. District Court Southern District of Indiana. *Education:* Manchester College (B.S., 1974); Indiana University (J.D., cum laude, 1979). Law Clerk to Hon. Nicholas W. Sufana, U.S. Bankruptcy Court, Southern District of Indiana, 1979-1982. *Member:* Indianapolis (Member, Commercial and Bankruptcy Section) and Indiana State (Member, Bankruptcy and Creditors Rights Section) Bar Associations; Conference on Consumer Finance. ***PRACTICE AREAS:*** Bankruptcy; Collections; Debtor and Creditor; Litigation. ***Email:*** rbuchmeier@hopperblackwell.com

JASON R. BURKE, born West Point, New York, November 5, 1968; admitted to bar, 1994, Florida; 1997, Indiana and U.S. District Court, Southern District of Indiana; 2000, U.S. District Court, Northern District of Indiana. *Education:* University of Georgia (A.B., cum laude, 1991); Washington & Lee University (J.D., cum laude, 1994). Phi Beta Kappa. Recipient, Law School Honor Scholarship, Washington & Lee University. Assistant State Attorney, Fourth Judicial Circuit, Florida, 1994-1996. *Member:* Indianapolis, Indiana State and American Bar Associations. ***PRACTICE AREAS:*** Bankruptcy; Collections; Debtor and Creditor; Litigation. ***Email:*** jburke@hopperblackwell.com

CHRISTOPHER C. HAGENOW, born Logansport, IN, April 4, 1967; admitted to bar, 1992, Indiana and U.S. District Court, Southern and Northern Districts of Indiana. *Education:* University of Notre Dame (B.A., 1989); Washington & Lee University (J.D., 1992). Phi Delta Phi. *Member:* Indianapolis (Member, Executive Committee, Young Lawyers Division, 1997-2001), Indiana State (Chair, Young Lawyers Section, 2004-2005) and American (Member, Business Law Section) Bar Associations; Defense Trial Counsel of Indiana (Member, Executive Committee, Products Liability Section, 1998-2000; Membership Chair, 2002). ***PRACTICE AREAS:*** Mergers, Acquisitions and Divestitures; Corporate Law; Litigation; Loans; Bankruptcy. ***Email:*** chagenow@hopperblackwell.com

NICCOLE R. SADOWSKI, born Milwaukee, Wisconsin, March 7, 1974; admitted to bar, 1999, Indiana and U.S. District Court, Southern and Northern Districts of Indiana. *Education:* Xavier University (B.A., magna cum laude, 1996); University of Dayton (J.D., cum laude, 1999). Phi Delta Phi. *Member:* Indianapolis and Indiana State Bar Associations. ***PRACTICE AREAS:*** Bankruptcy; Collections; Litigation. ***Email:*** nsadowski@hopperblackwell.com

REPRESENTATIVE CLIENTS: Bank One/J.P. Morgan Chase Bank; Fifth Third Bank; First Indiana Bank; First National Bank & Trust; Key Bank; Monroe Bank; National City Bank; Union Federal Bank; Anderson Family Medicine; Bond Safeguard Insurance; Collision Team of America; Dreambuilder Investments, Inc.; Health Care Economics, Inc.; InFlight Entertainment, LLC; Indiana Fiber Network; Indy Telcom Center, LLC; Lifeline Data Centers, LLC; M.D. Logistics; New Sesco, Inc.; Party Time Rentals; Patriot Software Solutions; RJE Business Interiors; Shares, Inc.; Star Environmental; Symons International Group, Inc.; West Coast Capital Group, Inc.

HOSTETLER & KOWALIK, P.C.

Established in 1987

101 WEST OHIO STREET

SUITE 2100

INDIANAPOLIS, INDIANA 46204

Telephone: 317-262-1001

Fax: 317-262-1010

URL: http://www.lawyers.com/hostetler&kowalik

Commercial, Bankruptcy, Debtors and Creditors Rights Law.

FIRM PROFILE: With each attorney having more than 20 years experience in the areas of bankruptcy, debtor/creditor rights and commercial litigation, Hostetler & Kowalik, P.C., offers individualized service to corporate, partnership and individual clients in these areas of practice. The varied experience of the attorneys in the firm has allowed them to work with a wide range of clients - from the individual consumer to state-wide banking institutions, to corporations with offices throughout the United States. Hostetler & Kowalik, P.C., represents both debtors and creditors in proceedings under the Bankruptcy Code and in out-of-court arrangements. The firm prides itself on being recognized in Indianapolis and Indiana as a specialized firm capable of resolving the most complex legal issues in their areas of practice.

GARY LYNN HOSTETLER, born Scottsburg, Indiana, September 3, 1953; admitted to bar, 1979, Indiana, U.S. District Court, Southern District of Indiana and U.S. Court of Appeals, Seventh Circuit. *Education:* Indiana University (B.S., high honors, 1975; J.D., 1979). Lecturer and Author: "Exemptions: Tenancy by the Entireties and Exemption Planning," Indiana Continuing Legal Education Forum, 1986, 1988 and 1991; "Advanced Practice Under Chapters 7 and 13: Current Developments," Indiana Continuing Legal Education Forum, 1994; "Advanced Chapter 7 and 13 Roundtable," Indianapolis Bar Association, Co-Chairman, 1997-2005; "Annual Bankruptcy Institute," Indiana Legal Education Forum, 1993-2005; "Bankruptcy Basics for the General Bar," Indiana Continuing Legal Education Forum, 1992; "Considerations in Preparation of Schedules, Statement of Affairs and The Chapter 13 Budget," Indiana Continuing Legal Education Forum, 1989; "Chapter 12 in Indiana," National Business Institute, 1987. *Member:* Indianapolis, Morgan County, Indiana State and American Bar Associations. ***PRACTICE AREAS:*** Commercial Law; Bankruptcy Law; Debtors and Creditors Rights Law. ***Email:*** glh@hostetler-kowalik.com

(This Listing Continued)

JAMES S. KOWALIK, born Lombard, Illinois, November 23, 1950; admitted to bar, 1978, Indiana, U.S. District Court, Southern District of Indiana and U.S. Court of Appeals, Seventh Circuit; 1987, U.S. Supreme Court. *Education:* Purdue University (B.A., with honors, 1972); Indiana University (J.D., cum laude, 1978). Law Clerk to Judge J. Robertson, Indiana Court of Appeals, 1978-1980. Lecturer and Author: "Recent Developments in Preference Law," Indianapolis Bar Association, 1985; "Consumer Bankruptcy Practice and Procedure," Indianapolis Bar Association, 1989; "Litigation of Common Bankruptcy Issues," Indianapolis Bar Association, 1991; "How to Guide Your Client Through a Chapter 7 Unscathed," Indiana Continuing Legal Education Forum, 1992; "Annual Bankruptcy Institute," Indiana Continuing Legal Education Forum, 1993, 1994, 2000; "Foreclosure and Related Bankruptcy and Title Issues," National Business Institute, 1998. *Member:* Indianapolis, Indiana State and American Bar Associations. ***PRACTICE AREAS:*** Commercial Law; Corporate Law; Bankruptcy Law; Debtors and Creditors Rights Law; Business Transactions; Probate. ***Email:*** jsk@hostetler-kowalik.com

DAVID R. KREBS, born Butler, Pennsylvania, October 18, 1956; admitted to bar, 1983, Indiana, U.S. District Court, Southern District of Indiana and U.S. Court of Appeals, Seventh Circuit. *Education:* DePauw University (B.A., 1978); Indiana University (J.D., 1983). Lecturer and Author: "Foreclosure and Repossession in Indiana," National Business Institute, 1989, 1991, 1992, 1995, 1996, 1999 and 2003; "Collecting Judgments in Indiana," National Business Institute, 1992, 1993, 1995, 1996 and 2000; "The Impact of Bankruptcy on Dissolution of Marriage in Indiana," National Business Institute, 1997, 1999, 2001, 2002; "Counseling the Business Entrepreneur in Indiana," National Business Institute, 1999, 2004; "Tax Consequences of Insolvency," Indiana Tax Institute, 1997; "Introduction to Collection Law," Lorman Education Services, 2000, 2001; "Advance Collection Law," Lorman Educational Services, 2000; "Loan Workout and Collateral Liquidation in Indiana," Lorman Educational Services, 2001, 2002; "Bankruptcy in Indiana," Lorman Educational Services, 2003; "Family Law Meets the World of Bankruptcy," Indiana Continuing Legal Education Forum, 2003, 2004. *Member:* Indianapolis (Chair, Commercial and Bankruptcy Law Section, 2000), Indiana State and American Bar Associations. ***PRACTICE AREAS:*** Commercial Law; Bankruptcy Law; Debtors and Creditors Rights Law. ***Email:*** drk@hostetler-kowalik.com

J. BRADLEY SCHOOLEY, born Kansas City, Missouri, April 30, 1945; admitted to bar, 1978, Indiana; U.S. District Court, Southern District of Indiana. *Education:* Denison University (B.A., 1967); Michigan State University (M.A.T., 1969); Indiana University (J.D., magna cum laude, 1978). Associate Editor, Indiana Law Review, 1978. Author: Note, "Ademption by Extinction in Indiana," Volume 11-4, Indiana Law Review, 1979. *Member:* Indianapolis, Shelby County (President, 1994) and Indiana State Bar Associations; Indiana Trial Lawyers Association. ***REPORTED CASES:*** Hash v. Catt, 368 F.3d 789 (2004); David A. Ryker Painting Co., Inc. v. Nunamaker, 818 N.E. 2d 898 (Ind. App. 2004). ***PRACTICE AREAS:*** Commercial Litigation; Creditors Rights; Real Estate; Probate. ***Email:*** jbs@hostetler-kowalik.com

JOHN W. GRAUB, II, born Indianapolis, Indiana, November 18, 1948; admitted to bar, 1975, Indiana, U.S. District Court, Southern and Northern Districts of Indiana and U.S. Court of Appeals, Seventh Circuit; 1984, U.S. Tax Court. *Education:* Indiana University (B.S., 1971; J.D., cum laude, 1974). Associate Editor, Indiana University Law Review, 1972-1973. *Member:* Indianapolis, Indiana State and American Bar Associations; Mortgage Bankers Association of America; Indiana Mortgage Bankers Association; American Bankruptcy Institute. ***PRACTICE AREAS:*** Bankruptcy; Commercial Law; Debtor and Creditor Rights; Foreclosures; Mechanics Liens; Real Estate; Secured Transactions. ***Email:*** jwg@hostetler-kowalik.com

CHRISTOPHER E. BAKER, born Cincinnati, Ohio, August 5, 1952; admitted to bar, 1981, Indiana and U.S. District Court, Southern and Northern Districts of Indiana and U.S. Court of Appeals, 7th Circuit. *Education:* Wabash College (B.A., 1974); Indiana University (M.P.A., 1976; J.D., magna cum laude, 1981). Author: "Mechanic's Lien and Bankruptcy," ICLEF, 1988; "Turning Judgments into Green," ICLEF, 1993; "Collecting/Post-Judgment Remedies," ICLEF, 1990; "Managing The Small & Medium Size Law Firm - Collection of Accounts Receivable," ICLEF, 1988. Law Clerk, Indiana Court of Appeals, 1979-1980. *Member:* Indianapolis (Vice President, 1998; Secretary, 1999-2000; Counsel, Board of Managers, 2001), Indiana State (Chair, Bankruptcy and Creditors Rights Section, 2004-2005) and American Bar Associations; The Association of Trial Lawyers of America; Indiana Trial Lawyers Association; Indianapolis Bar Foundation. ***PRACTICE AREAS:*** Bankruptcy; Commercial Litigation; Creditors Rights; Appellate Practice. ***Email:*** ceb@hostetler-kowalik.com

REPRESENTATIVE CLIENTS: ORIX Credit Alliance, Inc.; United Farm Bureau Mutual Insurance Co.; Airtron, Inc.; NBD Bank of Marion; Industrial Anodizing, Inc.; Farm Credit Services; Agra Bank; McBride Corp.; First National Bank & Trust; S.C. Nestel, Inc.; Shelby County Bank; Schrader Real Estate & Auction Co., Inc.; Autumn Glen Realty; CDC Appliances, Inc.; United Producers International; Service Crane Company; Fifth-Third Bank; Union Planters Bank, N.A.; Madison Community Bank; Bloomfield State Bank; First Community Bank & Trust.

HOVDE, DASSOW & DEETS LLC

Established in 1972

10585 NORTH MERIDIAN STREET, SUITE 205
P.O. BOX 40849
INDIANAPOLIS, INDIANA 46240-0849
Telephone: 317-818-3100
Fax: 317-818-3111
Email: firm@hovdelaw.com
URL: http://www.hovdelaw.com

Aviation, Personal Injury, Automobile Accidents, Head and Spinal Injuries, Nursing Home Abuse, Slip and Fall, Wrongful Death, Trucking Accidents, Drugs and Medical Devices, Medical Malpractice, Construction, Product Liability, Insurance, Securities Fraud and Consumer Fraud.

FIRM PROFILE: Hovde, Dassow & Deets LLC represents plaintiffs who are the victims of personal injury or death in the areas of automobile, truck and aviation accidents, premises, product and construction site accidents and medical malpractice. The members of the firm are dedicated trial lawyers who support the right to trial by jury and are actively involved in those organizations dedicated to its preservation.

F. BOYD HOVDE, born Minneapolis, Minnesota, August 7, 1934; admitted to bar, 1959, Indiana; 1977, U.S. Supreme Court. *Education:* Princeton University (B.A., 1956); University of Michigan (J.D., 1959). Member: Indiana Supreme Court, Committee on Rules of Practice and Procedure, 1980-1992; Committee on Character & Fitness, 1976-2000; Board of Visitors, Indiana University School of Law, 1984-1992. *Member:* Indianapolis Bar Association (President, 1979); Indiana Trial Lawyers Association (President, 1976-1977); The Association of Trial Lawyers of America. Fellow: Indiana College of Trial Lawyers; American College of Trial Lawyers; International Academy of Trial Lawyers; Indianapolis Bar Foundation.

FREDERICK R. HOVDE, born Lafayette, Indiana, October 1, 1955; admitted to bar, 1980, Indiana. *Education:* Southern Methodist University (B.B.A., 1977); Indiana University (J.D., 1980). Board of Visitors, Indiana University School of Law, 1993—. *Member:* Indianapolis Bar Association; Indiana Trial Lawyers Association (President, 2002); The Association of Trial Lawyers of America; American Board of Trial Advocates. Fellow: American College of Trial Lawyers; Indianapolis Bar Foundation; Indiana College of Trial Lawyers; Sagamore American Inn of Court, 1998-2000.

ROBERT T. DASSOW, born Sheboygan, Wisconsin, January 4, 1965; admitted to bar, 1990, Indiana. *Education:* Beloit College (B.A., 1987); Valparaiso University (J.D., 1990). Vollrath Scholar at Beloit College. Editor, Valparaiso University Law Review, 1989-1990. Associate Professor of Business Law, Valparaiso University, 1989-1990. *Member:* Indianapolis, Indiana State and American Bar Associations; Young Entrepreneur Organization; Indiana Trial Lawyers Association.

NICHOLAS C. DEETS, born Bloomington, Indiana, December 9, 1966; admitted to bar, 1993, Indiana. *Education:* Purdue University (B.S.I.M., with distinction, 1989); Indiana University (J.D., cum laude, 1993). Managing Editor, Indiana University, Journal of Global Legal Studies, 1992-1993. Summer Intern for the Honorable Michael S. Kanne, U.S. Court of Appeals for the Seventh Circuit. President, Tippecanoe County Criminal Defense Bar, 1997. *Member:* Tippecanoe County, Indiana State and American Bar Associations; Indiana Trial Lawyers Association.

STEPHEN LEE HUDDLESTON

INDIANAPOLIS, INDIANA

(See Franklin)

General Civil, Trial and Appellate Practice. Banking, Corporate, Zoning, Juvenile, Family/Domestic Relations, Real Estate and Probate and Estate Planning.

HUFFER & WEATHERS, P.C.

Established in 1997

1850 MARKET SQUARE CENTER
151 NORTH DELAWARE STREET
INDIANAPOLIS, INDIANA 46204-2522
Telephone: 317-822-8010
Toll Free: 888-822-8010
Fax: 317-822-8088
Email: info@hufferandweathers.com
URL: http://www.hufferandweathers.com

Alternative Dispute Resolution, Annuities, Arbitration, Appellate Practice, Bank Foreclosures, Business Litigation, Civil Practice, Class Actions, Commercial Law, Commercial Arbitration, Commercial Litigation, Contracts, Contract Litigation, Corporate Litigation, ERISA, Health Benefits, Fraud and Deceit, General Practice, Health Care, Home Health Care, Long Term Care, Nursing Home Litigation, Nursing Home Negligence, Insurance, Disability Insurance, Excess and Reinsurance, Extra Contractual Insurance Claims, Insurance Agents and Brokers Defense Insurance Agents and Brokers Errors and Omissions, Insurance Bad Faith, Insurance Coverage, Insurance Fraud, Life and Health Insurance, Reinsurance Arbitration, Insurance Coverage Defense, Legal Ethics and Professional Negligence, Federal Litigation, Premises Liability Defense, Professional Liability Insurance Coverage.

FIRM PROFILE: The lawyers of Huffer & Weathers, P.C. have over 40 years' combined litigation experience in the areas of life and health insurance, including bad faith and class actions. The firm, with Martindale-Hubbell's highest rating, serves the needs of its clients across the United States.

STEVEN K. HUFFER, born Fort Wayne, Indiana, November 1, 1958; admitted to bar, 1984, Indiana and U.S. District Court, Northern and Southern Districts of Indiana; 1985, U.S. Court of Appeals, 7th Circuit; 1987, Ohio; 2003, U.S. Court of Appeals, Sixth and Eighth Circuits and U.S. District Court, Northern and Southern Districts of Ohio. *Education:* Carleton College (B.A., magna cum laude, 1981); Indiana University (J.D., summa cum laude, 1984). Phi Beta Kappa. Author: "Amendments Curing Defendant Misnomers Under Trial Rule 15 (C)," 20 Indiana Law Review 139 (1987). Contributing Author: *Harvey, Indiana Practice* (Second Edition 1987); "Indiana Trial Systems Workbook," ICLEF, 1994. Seminars - Speaker: Insurance Coverage Law in Indiana, 2004; Adjusting Motor Vehicle Accident/Premises Liability Personal Injury Claims in Indiana, 2003; Speaker, Handling the Automobile Injury Claim in Indiana, A Strategy Seminar, 2002. *Member:* Indianapolis, Columbus, Indiana State and American Bar Associations. ***REPORTED CASES:*** Mark v. Moser, 746 NE2d 410 (Ind. App. 2001); Trustees of First Union, etc. v. Mandell, 987 F2d 1286 (7th. Cir. 1993); Hibler v. Conseco, 744 N.E. 2d 1012 (Ind.App. 2001); Walker v. Conseco Services, 252 F.Supp.2d 524 (N.D.Ohio 2003); Yoder v. American Travellers Life Ins. Co., 821 A.2d 588 (Penn. 2003). ***PRACTICE AREAS:*** Civil Practice; Reinsurance; Appellate Practice; Federal Litigation; Business Litigation; Class Actions; Commercial Law; Arbitration; Insurance; Extra Contractual Insurance Claims; Insurance Coverage Defense; Legal Ethics and Professional Responsibility; Insurance Agents and Brokers Errors and Omissions. ***Email:*** steve_huffer@hufferandweathers.com

SCOTT A. WEATHERS, born Castro Valley, California, March 13, 1960; admitted to bar, 1986, Indiana and U.S. District Court, Southern and Northern Districts of Indiana; 1994, U.S. Court of Appeals, Seventh Circuit; 1996, U.S. Supreme Court. *Education:* Gonzaga University (B.A., cum laude, 1982); Washington College of Law of American University (J.D., 1986). Dean's Fellow, 1984-1985. Author: "The Savings Clause of Trial Rule 60 (B): Muddy Waters?" 21 Indiana Law Review 73 (1988); "Misrepresentations on Application Can Void Policy," Vol. 15, Indianapolis Business Journal, No. 42 (1995); "Evidence of Emotional Distress," Lorman Education Services, (2004). Speaker: "Long Term Care, A Legal Perspective," 3rd Annual Intercompany LTCI Conference, Las Vegas (2003); "Daubert and Wrongful Death" Seminar, Indianapolis Bar Association, 2000; "Litigating Emotional Damages," Indiana Continuing Legal Education Forum, 2000; "Managing Objections at Trial," National Business Institute, 1999; "Winning Ways with Direct and Cross Examination," National Business Institute, 1998; "Trial of the Difficult Premises Liability Case," National Business Institute, 1997; Seminars: Author and Speaker, Indiana Nursing Home Law, 2004; Speaker, Health Insurance Basics in Indiana, 2003; Speaker, Reinsurance in Indiana, A Strategy Seminar, 2002. *Member:* Indianapolis (Past Chair, Litigation Section, 2001) and American (Member, Sections on: Litigation; Tort and Insurance Practice) Bar Associations; The Association of Trial Lawyers of America. ***REPORTED CASES:*** Terre Haute Regional Hospital v. Trueblood, 600 N.E.2d 1358 (Ind. 1992); State v. Huffman, 632 N.E.2d 899 (Ind. 1994); Tapia v. Heavner, 648 N.E.2d 1202 (Ind.App. 1995); In re McClain, 662 N.E.2d 935 (Ind. 1996); Mira v. Nuclear Measurement Corp., 107 F.3d 466 (7th Cir. 1997); Beverly Enterprises v. Spragg, 695 N.E.2d 1019 (Ind.App. 1998); Delta Tau Delta v. Johnson, 712 N.E.2d 968 (Ind. 1999); Hibler v. Conseco, 744 N.E.2d 1012 (Ind.App. 2001). ***PRACTICE AREAS:*** Reinsurance; Life and Health Insurance; Commercial Litigation; Professional Negligence; ERISA; Arbitration; Nursing Home Litigation; Nursing Home Negligence; Home Health Care; Insurance Agents and Brokers Errors and Omissions; Insurance Fraud; Insurance Bad Faith Defense; Legal Negligence; Legal Professional Liability; Accountants Liability; Accountants Malpractice; Agents and Brokers Liability; Professional Liability Defense; Professional Liability Insurance Coverage. ***Email:*** scott_weathers@hufferandweathers.com

---

CHRISTOPHER B. CARPENTIER, born Birmingham, Alabama, April 29, 1974; admitted to bar, 2000, Indiana and U.S. District Court, Southern and Northern Districts of Indiana; 2001, U.S. Court of Appeals, Seventh Circuit. *Education:* Indiana University (B.S., 1996); Indiana University (J.D., 2000). Co-Author: "Trial Tactics and Objection," ICCEF, 2001. Seminars - Speaker, Health Insurance Basics in Indiana, 2003; Speaker, Reinsurance in Indiana, A Strategy Seminar, 2002. *Member:* Indianapolis, Indiana and American Bar Associations. ***PRACTICE AREAS:*** Commercial Litigation; Reinsurance; Life and Health Insurance; Health Insurance Defense; Long Term Care; Excess and Reinsurance; Insurance Bad Faith; Insurance Coverage; Insurance Fraud. ***Email:*** chris_carpentier@hufferandweathers.com

SHANNON D. BOGARD, born Beech Grove, Indiana, April 29, 1975; admitted to bar, 2001, Indiana and U.S. District Court, Southern and Northern Districts of Indiana. *Education:* Butler University (B.A., cum laude, 1997); Indiana University School of Law - Indianapolis (J.D., magna cum laude, 2001). Member, Dean's Tutorial Society, 1999-2001. *Member:* Indiana State and American Bar Associations; Defense Research Institute. ***PRACTICE AREAS:*** Life Insurance; Health Insurance; Federal Litigation; Employment Law. ***Email:*** shannon_bogard@hufferandweathers.com

LEGAL SUPPORT PERSONNEL

EMILY T. MESECAR, born Indianapolis, Indiana, February 9, 1969. *Member:* Indianapolis Bar Association. (Office Manager/Paralegal). ***Email:*** emily_mesecar@hufferandweathers.com

REPRESENTATIVE CLIENTS: Bankers Life and Casualty Company; Conseco, Inc.; Conseco Life Insurance Company; Dr. Pepper/Seven Up Bottling Group and Subsidiaries; E&O Professionals; Freedom Life Insurance Company of America; Universal American Financial Companies; Pennsylvania Life Insurance Company; Site Technologies; State Auto Mutual Insurance Company; Legrand Morand and Partners; Beal Bank; Goieta National Bank; Noble Romans; Lanter Eye Care.
REFERENCES: Available Upon Request.

HUNT SUEDHOFF KALAMAROS LLP

6323 S. EAST STREET
INDIANAPOLIS, INDIANA 46227
Telephone: 317-784-4966
Fax: 317-784-5566
URL: http://www.hsk-law.com

South Bend, Indiana Office: 120 West LaSalle Avenue, Twelfth Floor, P.O. Box 4156, 46634-4156. Telephone: 574-232-4801. Fax: 574-232-9736.

(This Listing Continued)

HUNT SUEDHOFF KALAMAROS LLP, Indianapolis—Continued

Fort Wayne, Indiana Office: 803 South Calhoun Street, Ninth Floor, P.O. Box 11489, 46858-1489. Telephone: 260-423-1311. Fax: 260-424-5396.
St. Joseph, Michigan Office: 608 S. Pleasant Street, P.O. Box 46, 49085-0046. Telephone: 269-983-4405. Fax: 269-983-5645.

General Civil Trial and Appellate Practice. Insurance Defense Litigation. Commercial Real Estate Financing and Transactions. Corporate and Commercial Law. Probate and Estate Planning.

MEMBER OF FIRM

BRIAN L. ENGLAND, born Warsaw, Indiana, September 21, 1966; admitted to bar, 1992, Indiana and U.S. District Court, Northern and Southern Districts of Indiana; 1995, U.S. Court of Appeals, Seventh Circuit. *Education:* Indiana University (B.A., 1989; J.D., magna cum laude, 1992). Delta Theta Phi. Associate, Indiana Law Journal, 1990-1992. *Member:* Allen County, Indiana State and American Bar Associations; Defense Trial Counsel of Indiana; Defense Research Institute; Indiana Worker's Compensation Institute. ***PRACTICE AREAS:*** Workers Compensation; Labor Law; Insurance Litigation.

ASSOCIATES

KEVIN R. LESLIE, born Joliet, Illinois; admitted to bar, 2001, Indiana and U.S. District Court, Northern and Southern Districts of Indiana. *Education:* Purdue University (B.A., Elementary Education, 1994); Indiana University School of Law - Indianapolis (J.D., 2001). Formerly with Johnson County Prosecutor's Office. *Member:* Indianapolis Bar Association. [Member: Indiana Army National Guard, 1989-1994; Indiana Air National Guard, 2002—]. ***PRACTICE AREAS:*** Insurance Defense.

MARCUS HENDERSON, born Elwood, Indiana, February 3, 1978; admitted to bar, 2003, Indiana. *Education:* Indiana University, Bloomington (B.A., Journalism, 2000); Indiana University School of Law - Bloomington (J.D., 2003). *Member:* Indiana State and American Bar Associations. ***PRACTICE AREAS:*** Insurance Litigation.

ELIZABETH JOSEPH, born Fort Wayne, Indiana, September 6, 1978; admitted to bar, 2004, Indiana and U.S. District Court, Northern and Southern Districts of Indiana. *Education:* Indiana University (B.S., 2000; J.D., 2004). Phi Alpha Delta (Marshall, 2002-2003). Vice President, Health Law Society, 2003-2004. *Member:* Indianapolis, Indiana State and American Bar Associations. ***PRACTICE AREAS:*** Insurance Litigation. **Email:** ejoseph@hsk-law.com

ICE MILLER

Established in 1910

ONE AMERICAN SQUARE
BOX 82001
INDIANAPOLIS, INDIANA 46282-0002
Telephone: 317-236-2100
Fax: 317-236-2219
Email: info@icemiller.com
URL: http://www.icemiller.com

REVISER OF THE INDIANA LAW DIGEST FOR THIS DIRECTORY.

Chicago, Illinois Office: 200 West Madison, Suite 3500. Telephone: 312-726-1567. Fax: 312-726-7102. Internet Email: info@icemiller.com. Web Site Address: http://www.icemiller.com.
Washington, D.C. Office: 1090 Vermont Avenue, N.W., Suite 920. Telephone: 202-824-8600. Fax: 202-824-8601. Email: info@icemiller.com.Web Site Address: http://www.icemiller.com

Administrative Law, Antitrust, Appellate Practice, Architectural Malpractice Law, Banking, Bankruptcy, Broadcasting and Communications, Cable TV, Cable TV Franchising, Civil and Criminal Litigation, Civil Rights, Coal Law, College and University Law, Commercial and Business Litigation, Complex Litigation, Computer Law, Contracting and Litigation, Construction Law, Corporate Law, Corporate Finance, Creditors Rights Law, Drug and Medical Device Litigation, Economic Development and Incentives, Education Law, Employee Benefits Law, Entrepreneurial Services, Environmental Law, Estate Development and Finance, Franchise Law, Gaming Law, Gift and Estate Tax, Governmental Affairs, Governmental Relations, Governmental Services and Lobbying, Government Law, Government (Public) Contract Law, Government Procurement, Guardianship, Health Care Law, Immigration Law, Insurance Law, Intellectual Property and Licensing, International Law, Labor and Employment Law (including Equal Employment Litigation, ERISA Practice and Occupational Safety and Health Matters), Liability Risk Management, Licensing, Management Labor Relations Law, Mergers and Acquisitions, Minerals and Mining, Municipal Finance (Bond) Law, Municipal Finance (Bond), Dispute Resolution and Litigation, Municipal Litigation, Municipal Solid Waste Resource Recovery, Municipal Utility Regulation, Occupational Hazards Law (Black Lung, Asbestosis, etc.), Patent, Trademark and Copyright, Plaintiff's Trial Practice, Probate Law, Product Liability Law, Public Agency, Public Authority Financing Law, Public Contract Law, Public Employment Relations, Public Entity Law, Public Finance, Public Health Law, Public Housing Law, Public Schools, Public Sector Collective Bargaining, Public Utility Law, Public Works, Professional Malpractice Law, Real Estate Law (including Sales, Development and Financing, Mortgage Banking, Secured Transactions, Sale/Leasebacks, Condominiums and Zoning), Regulation, Risk and Claims Management, Securities Regulation Law, Sports Law, Taxation (Federal, State and Local), Tax Exempt Organizations, Tort Law, Toxic Torts, Transportation Law, Utility Law, Venture Capital, Venture Finance Services, Workers' Compensation.

FIRM PROFILE: A full-service law firm that also offers professional business advice, with offices in Indianapolis, South Bend and Chicago, Ice Miller has provided counsel on a local, state and national level since 1910.

The Firm was founded in Indianapolis on April 28, 1910, when three general practitioners formed a partnership under the name of Henley Matson Gates. The Firm experienced continuous growth and acquired a national reputation and a national practice. The Firm presently consists of 220 lawyers and 41 paraprofessionals, and an additional 250 staff employees, making it the largest law firm in Indianapolis.

Ice Miller's core departments are Corporate Law, Litigation, Labor and Employment, Real Estate Development, and Municipal Finance. From these core disciplines, Ice Miller lawyers have developed in-depth experience and knowledge in a variety of highly refined areas of concentration which allows the Firm to put together teams of attorneys to satisfy the increasingly sophisticated and multi-faceted needs of its clients. These areas of concentration are set forth below.

Most notable growth areas include: Advanced Technology Law Banking Law, Construction Law, Drug and Device Law, Employee Benefits Dispute Resolution, Environmental Law, Entrepreneurial Law, Governmental Services, Health Law, Intellectual Property (including Patent Law), International Law, Merger and Acquisition Law, Municipal Law, Occupational Hazards Law, Professional Liability Law, and Sports and Entertainment Law.

Ice Miller also has the largest litigation practice in the state, representing national, regional and locally domiciled clients for which it has obtained numerous "landmark" decisions in areas which include corporate, probate, professional, drug and device, and contractual liability.

LAW FIRM ALLIANCES/ASSOCIATIONS: **UNITED STATES LAW FIRM GROUP:** *United States Law Firm Group (USLFG) - www.uslfg.com.*
EMPLOYMENT LAW ALLIANCE: *Employment Law Alliance (ELA) - www.employmentlawalliance.com.*

Henley Matson & Gates	1910-1912
Matson Gates & Ross	1912-1914
Matson Kane & Ross	1914-1922
Matson Carter Ross & McCord	1922-1930
Matson Ross McCord & Clifford	1930-1939
Matson Ross McCord & Ice	1939-1942
Ross McCord Ice & Miller	1942-1963
Ice Miller Donadio & Ryan	1963-2000.

PARTNERS

WAYNE O. ADAMS, III, born Renton, Washington, April 7, 1949; admitted to bar, 1974, Indiana and U.S. District Court, Southern District of Indiana; 1975, U.S. District Court, Northern District of Indiana; 1977, U.S. Court of Appeals, Seventh Circuit; 1981, U.S. Supreme Court. *Education:* Wabash College (B.A., 1971); Indiana University School of Law - Indianapolis (J.D., cum laude, 1974). Author: "Sexual Harassment - Handling the Most Controversial Case in the Workplace," ABA Annual Meeting, 1992; "The Americans with Disabilities Act - An Overview," ABA Annual Meeting, 1991; "Illegal Discrimination Against Partners-When is a Partner Really an Employee?" ICLEF, 2002; "The Year in Review," (A Summary of the Year's Development in Employment Law), ICLEF, 1991-2001; "Hot Tips in Employment Law," ICLEF, 2001; "Updates on the Family and Medical Leave Act and Sexual Harassment," ICLEF, 1997; "Employment Discrimination Meets the Jury Box," ICLEF, 1997; "Harassment in the Workplace," ICLEF, 1993; "Employment Law Legislative Update," ICLEF, 1991; "Legal Update on Responding to Unions in the Workplace," ICLEF, 1990; "Sexual Harassment in the Workplace," Association of Indiana Counties, 2000; "Summary Judgement from the Defendant's Perspective," ICRC, 2000; Mediating Employment Disputes - The Final Agreement," The Indiana Lawyer, 1999; "Forms and Guidelines for Complying with the ADA," Indiana Chamber of Commerce, 1999; "Avoiding Liability in the Workplace," Federal Publications, 1998; "Shocking Developments in Personnel Law," NADFD, 1994. Contributing Editor: "The Developing Labor Law," BNA, 1982-1988; "Employment Discrimination Law," BNA, 1996. *Member:* Indianapolis (Chair, Labor Law Section, 1985), Indiana State (Chair, Labor Law Section, 1986) and American (Chair, Labor Law Committee, General Practice Section, 1987-1994) Bar Associations. ***REPORTED CASES:*** Wilkerson v. Service Corporation International, et al., 2003 WL 21052128 (S.D. Ind. 2003); Heims v. Subaru-Isuzu Automotive Inc., 2003 WL 1086362 (N.D. Ind. 2003); Ross v. Indiana State Teachers Association, et al., 159 F.3d 1001 (7th Cir. 1998), cert. denied 119 S.Ct. 1113 (1999); Richter v. Hook-SupeRX, Inc., 142 F.3d 1024 (7th Cir. 1998); Dalton v. Subaru-Isuzu Automotive, Inc., 141 F.3d 667 (7th Cir. 1998); Jasmantas v. Subaru-Isuzu Automotive, Inc., 139 F.3d 1155 (7th Cir. 1998); Bassett v. Subaru-Isuzu Automotive Inc., 948 F.Supp. 811 (N.D. Ind. 1996); Worthington v. Subaru-Isuzu Automotive Inc., 868 F. Supp. 1067 (N.D. Ind. 1994); Gorman v. Northeastern REMC, 594 N.E. 2d 843 (Ind. App. 1992), trasfer denied 597 N.E.2d 366 (Ind. 1992); Zapp v. United Transportation Union, 879 F.2d 1439)7th Cir. 1989), cert.denied 110 S.Ct. 722 (1990); Beard v. Whitley County REMC, 840 F.2d 405 (7th Cir. 1988); South Bend Federation of Teachers v. NEA - South Bend, 389 N.E. 2d 33 (Ind. App. 1979). *Labor Arbitrations:* Indiana State Teachers Association and Indiana Associate Staff Organization, 114 LA 686 (Brunner, 2000); Indiana State Teachers Association and ISTA Professional Staff Organization, 104 LA 137 (Paolucci, 1995); Indiana State Teachers Association and ISTA Professional Staff Organization, 94 LA 1239 (Feldman, 1990); Indiana State Teachers Association and ISTA Professional Staff Organization, 90 LA 579 (Heekin, 1988). ***PRACTICE AREAS:*** Employment Discrimination Litigation; Labor (Management) Law; Noncompete and Trade Secret Litigation; College and University Law. **Email:** adamsw@icemiller.com

ADAM ARCENEAUX, born Cambridge, Maryland, January 12, 1966; admitted to bar, 1993, Indiana; U.S. District Court, Southern and Northern Districts of Indiana; 1999, U.S. Court of Appeals, Seventh Circuit; 2002, U.S. District Court, Southern District of Illinois; 2005, U.S. District Court, Southern District of Texas. *Education:* Indiana University (B.S., highest honors, Marketing and Business Analysis, 1988); Indiana University School of Law, Indianapolis (J.D., summa cum laude, 1993). Phi Delta Phi. Member, Order of Barristers. Associate Editor, Indiana Law Review, 1992-1993. Former President and Current Member, Indiana University School of Law - Indianapolis Alumni Board of Directors. Graduate, Stanley K. Lacy Executive Leadership Series, Class XXVI. *Member:* Indianapolis, Seventh Circuit and Indiana State Bar Associations. ***REPORTED CASES:*** Utility Center, Inc. v. City of Fort Wayne, 2005 WL 2233576 (Ind. App. 2005); Conde v. SLS West,

(This Listing Continued)

LLC, 2005 WL 1661747 (S.D. Ind. 2005); City of North Vernon v. Jennings Northwest Regional Utilities, 829 N.E.2d 1 (Ind. 2005); Bloomington Country Club, Inc. v. City of Bloomington, 827 N.E.2d 1213 (Ind. App. 2005); U.S. Land Services v. U.S. Surveyor, 826 N.E.2d 49 (Ind. App. 2005); Marwil v. Farah, 2003 WL 23095657 (S.D. Ind. 2003); E & S Mems, LLC v. Eagen, 795 N.E. 2d 508 (Ind. App. 2003); CSL Community Ass'n, Inc. v. Jennings Northwest Regional Utilities, 794 N.E.2d 567 (Ind. App. 2003); Made2Manage Systems, Inc. v. ADS Information Systems, Inc., 2003 WL 21508235 (S.D. Ind. 2003); Quality Carriers, Inc. v. MJK Distribution, Inc., 2002 WL 506997 (S.D. Ill. 2002); Schwentker v. A.G. Edwards & Sons, Inc., 2000 U.S. Dist. LEXIS 10133 (S.D. Ind. 2000); Kenro, Inc. v. Fax Daily, Inc., 962 F.Supp. 1162 (S.D. Ind. 1997); Kenro, Inc. v. Fax Daily, Inc., 904 F.Supp. 912 (S.D. Ind. 1995). ***PRACTICE AREAS:*** Litigation; Business Litigation; Commercial Litigation; Insurance Litigation; Complex Litigation; Federal Litigation; Covenants Not To Compete; Noncompetition and Non-Solicitation Agreements; Restrictive Covenants; Unfair Competition; Breach of Contract; Contract Litigation; Real Estate Litigation; Product Liability Law; Appellate Practice (Appeals); Administrative Agency Practice; Administrative Litigation; Class Actions; Trade Secrets; Utility Law. ***Email:*** adam.arceneaux@icemiller.com

MARK B. BARNES, born Springfield, Ohio, February 7, 1953; admitted to bar, 1977, Indiana. *Education:* Wright State University (B.A., summa cum laude, 1974); Ohio State University College of Law (J.D., summa cum laude, 1977). ***PRACTICE AREAS:*** Banks and Banking; Securities; Insurance; Business Law; Mergers, Acquisitions and Divestitures; Corporate Law; Finance; Investments. ***Email:*** barnes@icemiller.com

PHILLIP L. BAYT, born Indianapolis, Indiana, March 8, 1952; admitted to bar, 1980, Indiana. *Education:* Macalester College (B.A., summa cum laude, 1974); Indiana University (M.B.A., 1980; J.D., cum laude, 1980). Phi Beta Kappa; Beta Gamma Sigma; Order of the Coif. *Member:* Indianapolis and Indiana State Bar Associations; American College of Real Estate Lawyers. ***PRACTICE AREAS:*** Construction Contract Law; Land Sales Registration and Compliance; Real Estate Development and/or Syndication Law; Condominium Law; Lending Law Compliance; Gaming Law. ***Email:*** bayt@icemiller.com

FRED R. BIESECKER, born Milwaukee, Wisconsin, December 28, 1953; admitted to bar, 1980, New York; 1984, Indiana; 1989, U.S. Court of Appeals, Seventh Circuit. *Education:* Indiana University (B.A., 1976); Yale Law School (J.D., 1979). Chief Counsel to Indiana Governor Frank O'Bannon, 1997-2001. Sagamore of the Wabash, 2001. Recipient, Distinguished Alumni Award, Indiana University, 1984. *Member:* Indiana State and American (Member: Forum Committee on the Construction Industry, 1990-1996) Bar Associations. ***REPORTED CASES:*** Federal Deposit Insurance Corporation v. Bierman, 2 F.3d 1424 (7th Cir. 1993); Wright-Moore Corp. v. Ricoh Corp., 908 F.2d 128 (7th Cir. 1990). ***PRACTICE AREAS:*** Appellate Practice; Litigation; Government Services; Business Litigation; Commercial Litigation; Construction Law; Professional Liability. ***Email:*** biesecke@icemiller.com

MICHAEL A. BLICKMAN, born Indianapolis, Indiana, October 24, 1953; admitted to bar, 1978, Indiana; 1979, New York. *Education:* Miami University (B.A., 1975); Boston College (J.D., cum laude, 1978). Phi Beta Kappa; Phi Kappa Phi; Omicron Delta Kappa. Editor-in-Chief, Boston College International and Comparative Law Journal, 1977-1978. *Member:* Indianapolis (Past Chairman, Labor and Employment Law Section), Indiana State and American (Member, Labor and Employment Law Section) Bar Associations. ***PRACTICE AREAS:*** Labor and Employment Law; Health Care and Hospital Law; Entrepreneurial Services; Civil Rights Law; Equal Employment Law; Education Law. ***Email:*** michael.blickman@icemiller.com

MICHAEL H. BOLDT, born Detroit, Michigan, October 11, 1950; admitted to bar, 1975, Indiana; 1979, U.S. Court of Appeals, 7th Circuit; 1980, U.S. Supreme Court; 1983, U.S. Court of Appeals for the District of Columbia Circuit. *Education:* University of Detroit and Wayne State University (B.A., 1972); University of Michigan (J.D., 1975). Phi Beta Kappa, 1972. Author: "The Jobsite: Problems and Solutions," published by Associated General Contractors of Indiana, 1983, revised 1987, 1991, 2004; "Collective Bargaining Guide and Legal Analysis," published by the Mechanical Contractors Association of America, 2002. Featured Speaker on videotape "Drawing the Line: How to Prevent Sexual and Other Harassment on the Construction Site," published by Associated General Contractors of America, 1994. *Member:* Indianapolis, Indiana State and American (Member, Section on Labor and Employment Law) Bar Associations. ***PRACTICE AREAS:*** Labor and Employment Law; Employee Benefits Law; Construction Law. ***Email:*** michael.boldt@icemiller.com

S. R. BORN, born Atwood, Illinois, April 19, 1945; admitted to bar, 1970, Indiana and U.S. District Court, Southern District of Indiana; 1975, U.S. Court of Appeals, Seventh Circuit; 1990, U.S. District Court, Northern District of Indiana; 2002, U.S. Supreme Court. *Education:* Northwestern University, American University and Simpson College (B.A., 1967); Indiana University (J.D., 1970). Phi Alpha Delta. Member, Staff, 1968-1969 and Editorial Board, 1969-1970, Indiana Law Journal. Co-Author: *Safety and Health Guide for Indiana Business,* Fifth Edition, 2004. Certified Civil Mediator, Indiana. *Member:* Indianapolis (Vice-President, 1985; President, 1988; Member, Board of Managers, 1989-1995; Member, Labor Law Section), Indiana State (Board of Managers, 1986-1991, 1993-1999; President, 1997-1998; Member, Labor and Employment Law Section), American (Member House of Delegates, 1988-1998; Member, Section of Labor and Employment Law) and Seventh Circuit Bar Associations. ***PRACTICE AREAS:*** Labor Law; OSHA Law; Collective Bargaining; Civil Rights Law; Arbitration Law; Public Employment Relations Law; Mediation. ***Email:*** born@icemiller.com

MARY BETH BRAITMAN, born Indianapolis, Indiana, September 23, 1950; admitted to bar, 1981, Indiana. *Education:* Indiana University (B.S., 1971; J.D., summa cum laude, 1981). Publications and Seminars: "Everything You Wanted to Know About EGTRRA Implementation" (National Association of Public Pension Plan Attorneys Annual Conference, June 2002); "Recent Pension Regulatory Developments for Public Pension Plans" (National Association of Public Pension Plan Attorneys Winter Meeting, February 2002); "A Retirement Odyssey" (National Association of State Retirement Administrators Annual Conference, August 2001); "Retirement Savings Legislation Included in Tax Relief Bill Applicable to Governmental Plans" and "Advanced Tax-Retiree Medical" (National Association of Public Pension Plan Attorneys Annual Conference, June 2001); "Tax Section Update" (National Association of Public Pension Plan Attorneys Winter Meeting, February 2001); "Defined Benefit Plans vs Defined Contribution Plans: Systems Respond with Creative Plan Designs" (National Council on Teacher Retirement Annual Conference, 2000); "Frequently Asked Questions on Federal Pension Law" and "Working from Here to Eternity: Post-Retirement Employment" (National Association of Public Pension Plan Attorneys Annual Conference, 2000); "Health and Pension Legislative Update" (International Foundation of Employee Benefit Plans, Benefits Conference for Public Employees, 2000); "Primer on Pension Qualification Rules Applicable to Governmental Plans" and "Advanced Session on Pension Qualification Issues Service Credit Purchases" (National Association of Public Pension Plan Attorneys Annual Conference, 1999); "School Corporation Update" and "Investment Choices and Education for Employees" (Circle City Seminar, IMDR, 1999); "New Plan Design Issues," (457 Plans and Qualified Excess Benefit Plans; National Association of Public Pension Plan Attorneys Annual Conference, 1997); "Recent Legislative Developments Affecting Governmental Plans," (Benefits Conference for Public Employees, International Foundation of Employee Benefit Plans, 1997); Public Safety Employees Pension and Benefits Conference (1997); "A Guidebook for Qualified Governmental Retirement Plans" (1997 & 1999); "A Guidebook for School System Retirement/Severance Programs" (1999); "Alternative Retirement Arrangements" (National Association of Public Pension Attorneys Annual Conference, 1995); "Public Fund Litigation Mock Court Presentation" (National Association of State Retirement Administrators Annual Conference, 1994); Tax Qualification Issues (National Association of Public Pension Attorneys Annual Conferences, 1998, 1995, 1994, 1993); "Governmental Plan Status" (National Association of Public Pension Attorneys Annual Conference, 1996); "Healthcare Responsibilities" (WEB, 1993); "Direct Rollover Distributions and Fiduciary Responsibilities" (WEB, 1993); "Americans with Disabilities Act" (Indiana Association of Cities & Towns and Association of Indiana Counties, 1992); Employee Benefit Issues (Indiana Tax Institute, 1991 and 1985); "Managing the Esoteric -- Practicalities of the Older Workers Benefit Protection Act and Nondiscrimination Rules of the Internal Revenue Service (School Board Association, 1991); "Individual Retirement Accounts -- Distribution Rules" (Notre Dame Institute, 1992); ERISA -- Employee Benefit Issues (Indiana Continuing Legal Education Forum Programs, 1995, 1992, 1990, 1989, 1985); "Taking Control of Your Benefit Program" (Indiana Chamber of Commerce, 1994); Briefings on Issues of Importance to College and University Officials, Employee Benefits," Seminar for Colleges and Universities, 1988. Member: Indiana Pension Conference; Indiana Municipal Attorneys Association; Network of Professionals Working in Employee Benefits (WEB); National Association of Public Pension Attorneys. Registered Lobbyist in Indiana. ***PRACTICE AREAS:*** Qualified Retirement Plans; Public Pension Plans; Public Employee Retirement; Municipal Pensions; ERISA; Employee Benefit Taxation; Pension Plans; Pension Taxation; Legislative Lobbying; Flexible Benefits; Deferred Compensation; Pension and Profit Sharing Plans. ***Email:*** braitman@icemiller.com

DAVID J. CARR, born Goshen, Indiana, December 31, 1958; admitted to bar, 1984, Indiana, U.S. Supreme Court and U.S. Court of Appeals, Seventh Circuit. *Education:* DePauw University (B.A., summa cum laude, 1981); Georgetown University Law Center (J.D., 1984). Phi Beta Kappa. 1988 Res Gestae Award (Outstanding Legal Article-Indiana State Bar Association). Contributing Author: "Covenants-Not-To-Compete: A State-by-State Analysis," BNA, 1991; "Employee Duty of Loyalty: A State by State Analysis," BNA, 1995; "Indiana Employment-At-Will at the Crossroads," 11 Res Gestae 506, May 1988; "Harvey on Indiana Practice—Rules of Procedure Annotated," West Publishing, 1987. Diplomate, Court Practice Institute. *Member:* Indianapolis (Chair, Labor and Employment Law Section, 1996), Indiana State and American Bar Associations; Bar Association of the Seventh Federal Circuit; Christian Legal Society. ***REPORTED CASES:*** JAK Productions, Inc. v. Wiza, 986 F.2d 1080 (7th Cir. 1993); Hudson v. Indiana Limestone Co., 143 F.Supp. 2d 1032 (S.D. Ind. 2001); Barnes Group Inc. v. Rinehart 2001 WL 301433 (S.D. Ind. 2001); Volunteers of America v. Premier Auto Acceptance Corp., 755 N.E.2d 656 (Ind. Ct. App. 2001); Beard v. Whitley Co. REMC, 840 F.2d 405 (7th Cir. 1988); Zapp v. UTU, 879 F.2d. 1439 (7th Cir. 1989). ***PRACTICE AREAS:*** Labor Law; Employment Discrimination Litigation; Litigation. ***Email:*** carr@icemiller.com

RALPH A. COHEN, born Indianapolis, Indiana, September 21, 1938; admitted to bar, 1964, Indiana. *Education:* Indiana University (B.S., 1960; J.D., 1964). Order of the Coif. Listed in Best Lawyers in America. Note Editor, Indiana Law Journal, 1963-1964. Chairman, National Invitational Conference on Unreliable Expert Witness Testimony, 1989. *Member:* Indianapolis and Indiana State Bar Associations; Defense Research Institute, Inc. (Chairman, Medical-Legal Committee, 1981-1983; Chairman, Drug and Device Liability Committee, 1985-1988); American College of Trial Lawyers. ***PRACTICE AREAS:*** Drug and Medical Device Litigation; Toxic Torts; Class Actions; Mass Torts; Complex Litigation. ***Email:*** cohen@icemiller.com

JAMES S. CUNNING, born Indianapolis, Indiana, June 20, 1952; admitted to bar, 1977, Indiana. *Education:* DePauw University (B.A., first in class, 1974); University of Michigan (J.D., cum laude, 1977). Phi Beta Kappa. *Member:* Indianapolis, (Member: Business Law Section; Labor and Employment Law Section, Chairman, 1989), Indiana State and American (Member, Business Law Section and Labor and Employment Law) Bar Associations; Indiana Chamber of Commerce (Executive Committee and General Counsel); Indiana Legal Foundation (Board of Directors and General Counsel). ***LANGUAGES:*** French. ***REPORTED CASES:*** Fields v. Cummins Employees Federal Credit Union, 540 NE 2d 631 NLRB v. Mosey Manufacturing Co., Inc., 701 F. 2d 610 Keller Manufacturing Co., Inc., 272 NLRB 763. ***PRACTICE AREAS:*** Arbitration Law; Business Acquisitions Law; Corporate Law; Employment Discrimination Law; Labor Law. ***Email:*** cunning@icemiller.com

TERRI ANN CZAJKA, born Heidelberg, Germany, October 28, 1958; admitted to bar, 1983, Minnesota; 1984, U.S. District Court, District of Minnesota; 1988, Indiana and U.S. District Court, Southern and Northern Districts of Indiana; 1990, U.S. Court of Appeals, Seventh Circuit; 1997, U.S. Court of International Trade, U.S. District Court, Western District of Michigan and Northern District of Alabama. *Education:* Creighton University (B.A., cum laude, 1980); University of Minnesota (J.D., cum laude, 1983). Member, Philip Jessup International Moot Court Program; Assistant to Professor Steven Nichols. Instructor, University of Cincinnati College of Law, 1984-1986. Attorney Advisor, Office of Administrative Law Judges, U.S. Department of Labor, Cincinnati, Ohio, 1986-1987. *Member:* Indiana State and Seventh Circuit Bar Associations. ***PRACTICE AREAS:*** Environmental Law; Gaming Law; Administrative Law; Toxic Torts. ***Email:*** czajka@icemiller.com

(This Listing Continued)

ICE MILLER, Indianapolis—Continued

GARY J. DANKERT, born Indianapolis, Indiana, August 14, 1952; admitted to bar, 1977, Indiana; 1978, Illinois. *Education:* Purdue University; Indiana University (B.A., 1974; J.D. cum laude, 1977). Law Clerk to Hon. Justice Donald H. Hunter, Indiana Supreme Court, 1977-1978. Publications and Seminars: Construction Law in the 90's (Indiana Continuing Legal Education Forum, 1992); Damages in Litigation (Indiana Continuing Legal Education Forum, 1990); Conference of Invited Attorney (Speaker, 1993); Indiana Construction Law (National Business Institute, 1987, 1990); Construction Claims and Job Profitability (National Business Institute, 1988); Architect-Engineer Liability (Cambridge Institute, 1988, 1989); Indiana Mechanics Liens and Bonds (Cambridge Institute, 1993, 1994). *Member:* Indianapolis, Indiana State and American Bar Associations. ***PRACTICE AREAS:*** Construction Law; Litigation Defense; Employee Benefit Law; ERISA; Multi-Employer Benefits. ***Email:*** dankert@icemiller.com

KRISTINE CAMRON DANZ, born Adrian, Michigan, July 27, 1971; admitted to bar, 1997, Indiana. *Education:* Michigan State University (B.A., in Political Theory, 1993); University of Michigan Law School (J.D., 1997). National Football League Players Association Certified Contract Advisor and National Basketball Players Association Certified Player Agent. *Member:* Indianapolis, Indiana State and American Bar Associations. ***PRACTICE AREAS:*** Mergers and Acquisitions; Corporate Law; Securities; Venture Capital; Title IX Discrimination; Entertainment Law; Professional Sports Law; Sports Contracts. ***Email:*** gerard@icemiller.com

JOSEPH E. DEGROFF, born Lafayette, Indiana, May 21, 1953; admitted to bar, 1979, Indiana. *Education:* Hanover College (B.A., 1975); Indiana University (M.B.A., 1979; J.D., magna cum laude, 1979). Author: "Corporate Reform: Best of Class Governance Issues Abound," BizVoice (Indiana Chamber of Commerce), November/December, 2002; "New Watchdog—Attorneys as Whistleblowers?" Indiana Lawyer, December, 2002. Member and Vice Chairman, Board of Directors and Member, Executive Committee, Indiana Sports Corporation. Member: Board of Advisors, Purdue University Discover Park and Burton D. Morgan Entrepreneurship Center; Marion County Economic Development Advisory Board. *Member:* American Bar Association. ***TRANSACTIONS:*** Representative transactions include: Joint Venture Between Great Lakes Chemical Corporation and Occidental Chemical Corporation, 2004; Sale of Brightpoint (Ireland) Limited, 2004; $175 million Note Offering for Magnequench, 2004; Sale of JWF Insurance Companies to Old National Bancorp, 2005; Recapitalization of Healthx, Inc., 2005. ***PRACTICE AREAS:*** Corporate Law; Securities; Mergers, Acquisitions and Divestitures; Business Law. ***Email:*** joseph.degroff@icemiller.com

JAMES V. DONADIO, born December 3, 1905; admitted to bar, 1927, Indiana; died August 7, 1998.

THOMAS K. DOWNS, born New Albany, Indiana, January 10, 1949; admitted to bar, 1980, Indiana. *Education:* Indiana University (B.A., 1977; J.D., magna cum laude, 1980). Municipal Finance Section Chairman. Order of the Coif. Executive Editor, Indiana Law Journal, 1979-1980. Founding Fellow, American College of Bond Counsel. Frequent Speaker and Author on subjects relating to Municipal Finance. Founding Fellow, Government Relations Committee, American College of Bond Counsel. National Association of Bond Lawyers (Bond Attorneys Workshop Steering Committee, 1985, 1986, 1990-1995, 2000; Committee on Opinions, 1993-1997; Committee on Professional Responsibility, 1994-1997; Chairman, 2001-2002; Education Committee, 1995, 1996; Chairman, Bond Banks Workshop, 1985, 1986; Tax Increment Workshop, 1989; Opinions and Roles and Responsibility of Bond Counsel Workshop, 1990, 1992, 1993, 1994; Panelist: Bond Banks Workshop, 1987; Tax Increment Workshop, 1988; Solid Waste Workshop, 1989; Government Obligations Workshop, 1989, 1990, 1991; Opinions and Professional Responsibility Workshop, 1990, 1991, 1995-1999. Faculty, Fundamentals of Municipal Bond Law, Opinions and Professional Responsibility, 1989, 1990, 1993, 1994, 1995, 1996, 1997; Vice Chairman, 1995, Chairman, 1996 Washington Seminar, 1995); Indiana Continuing Legal Education Forum (Chairman, Municipal Law Seminars, 1984-1992; Chairman, Practical Impact of Tax Reform Act of 1986, 1986; Panelist, Municipal Utility Finance, 1988, Public Law 10-1991); Indiana Municipal Lawyers Association, Inc. (Member, Board of Directors, 1983—); Indiana Association of Cities and Towns Foundation (Vice President, Board of Directors, 1994, 1995, President 1996—); Indiana Economic Development Association (Member, Board of Directors, 1994-1997); Co-Chair, Midwest Bond Buyer Conference, 1998. Southern Indiana Rural Development Project (Board of Directors, 1999). Included in Marquis' Who's Who in America in 1998 and 1999 and in the 1994-1995 Edition of Who's Who in American Law. Author of the Professional Responsibility quarterly feature in the Municipal Finance Journal 1999. Author of the General Law Section and Editor of the Professional Responsibility Section of "Fundamentals of Municipal Bond Law, " 1994-2002. ***PRACTICE AREAS:*** Municipal Law; Government; Government Contracts; Finance; Leases and Leasing; Public Finance. ***Email:*** Thomas.Downs@icemiller.com

HENRY A. EFROYMSON, born Indianapolis, Indiana, March 28, 1957; admitted to bar, 1982, Indiana and U.S. District Court, Southern and Northern Districts of Indiana; U.S. Court of Appeals, Seventh Circuit. *Education:* Indiana University (B.A., 1979; J.D., cum laude, 1982). Editor, The Order for Relief, Indiana State Bar Association, 1992-1994. Co-Author: "Mechanics Liens and the Bankruptcy Code: An Overview," Indiana Continuing Legal Education Forum, 1985. Author: "Environmental Issues in Chapter 11," Indiana Continuing Legal Education Forum, 1987; "Bankruptcy Reform Act of 1994, An Overview," Res Gestae, 1994; "Indiana Adopts Uniform Fraudulent Transfer Act," Res Gestae, 1995. Lecturer: Indiana Continuing Legal Education Bankruptcy Seminar, 1987-1989, 1995, 1999; 2000, 2001; ICLEF Advanced Bankruptcy Roundtable, 2002. Member, Advisory Board of the Central States Bankruptcy Workshop. National Bankruptcy Institute, Inc., Practicing Law Institute Seminar. Indiana Continuing Education Forum, "Representing the Business Creditor," Seminar, 1993. Listed in Best Lawyers in America, 1998, 2001. *Member:* Indianapolis (Member, Section on Commercial Law and Bankruptcy; Chairman, 1991) and Indiana State (Member, Section on Creditors' Rights and Bankruptcy, Chairman, 1996-1997; Chair, Task Force on Uniform Commercial Code Revised Article 9, 1999) Bar Associations; American Bankruptcy Institute (Regional Membership Committee Chairman, 1993-1997). ***REPORTED CASES:*** In re Potter Material Co., Inc., 781 F.2d 99; In re Environmental Waste Control, Inc., 122 BR 546. ***PRACTICE AREAS:*** U.C.C.; Creditors' Rights Law; Debtor-Creditor Law; Debtor's Remedies; Bankruptcy Law. ***Email:*** efroymso@icemiller.com

(This Listing Continued)

LUCY A. EMISON, born Rome, New York, September 13, 1950; admitted to bar, 1985, Indiana. *Education:* DePauw University (B.A., cum laude, 1972); Indiana University (M.B.A., 1979; J.D., summa cum laude, 1985). Member, 1984-1985 and Associate Editor, 1985, Indiana Law Review. Author: "Judicial Review of Shareholder Derivative Suits: Directors' Diminishing Control of Corporate Litigation," Indiana Law Review 18:2, 1985. Chairman, Indiana University Law School, Indianapolis, Alumnae Network, 2000-2002. Chairman, Firm Professional Services Evaluation Committee, 2002-2005. President, Tabernacle Presbyterian Church Endowment Fund Board of Trustees, 2001-2002. Bond Counsel: Indiana Bond Bank Taxable School Severance Funding Bonds, Series 1-10, 2002-2004; Indianapolis Local Public Improvement Bond Bank Notes Tax Warrant Program, 1988-2005; Indiana Municipal Power Agency Power Supply System Revenue Bonds, 2004 Series A; Indianapolis Local Public Improvement Bond Bank Bonds, Series 2004I (Indianapolis Airport Authority Project); Noblesville, Indiana Building Corporation First Mortgage Bonds, Series 2005. *Member:* Indiana State Bar Association; National Association of Bond Lawyers; Indiana Municipal Lawyers Association; Federalist Society; Indiana Economic Development Association. ***PRACTICE AREAS:*** Municipal Law; Public Finance; Tax-Exempt Securities; Municipal Leasing; Tax Increment Finance; Ad Valorem Tax. ***Email:*** Lucy.Emison@icemiller.com

SHERRY A. FABINA-ABNEY, born Johnstown, Pennsylvania, May 1, 1963; admitted to bar, 1988, Indiana, U.S. District Court, Northern and Southern Districts of Indiana; 1989, U.S. Court of Appeals, Seventh Circuit. *Education:* Purdue University (B.A., 1985); Indiana School of Law (J.D., magna cum laude, 1988). Managing Editor, Indiana Law Journal, 1987-1988. Co-Author: "Hospital and Physician Liability: A Legal Overview," National Health Lawyers Association, Focus Series, 1992. Law Clerk for the Honorable Michael S. Kanne, U.S. Court of Appeals for the Seventh Circuit, 1989. *Member:* Indianapolis, Indiana State and American (Member, Health Care Section) Bar Associations; American Health Lawyers Association; Defense Research Institute. ***PRACTICE AREAS:*** Health Care Liability; Health Care Litigation; Physicians Licensing; Medical Staff Credentialing; Hospital Peer Review; Medical Law. ***Email:*** sherry.fabina-abney@icemiller.com

JAMES R. FISHER, born South Bend, Indiana, April 15, 1947; admitted to bar, 1972, Indiana; U.S. District Court, Southern District of Indiana; U.S. Court of Appeals, Seventh Circuit. *Education:* Indiana University (A.B., 1969; J.D., summa cum laude, 1971). Voted to Indiana "Super Lawyer" list, 2004 and 2005. Co-Author: "Personal Injury Law and Practice," Vol. 23 of West's Indiana Practice Series. Chair, Ice Miller's "Senior Partner Mediation Group". Legal Examiner, "Corporate Physical" Risk Assessment Examination Program. *Member:* Indiana State Bar Association; Indiana Trial Lawyers Association. ***PRACTICE AREAS:*** Appellate Practice (Appeals); Mediation; Arbitration; Civil Litigation; Risk Management and Avoidance. ***Email:*** james.fisher@icemiller.com

MARY KAY FLEMING, born Evansville, Indiana, January 1, 1960; admitted to bar, 1990, Indiana. *Education:* Indiana State University (B.S., 1982); Indiana University (J.D., 1990). Phi Delta Phi. Order of Barristers. Author: "A Modest Proposal—The Prohibition of All Adult Communities By the Fair Housing Amendments Act of 1988," 22 Ind. L.Rev. 1021. Clerk to: Gene E. Brooks, Chief Judge, Southern District of Indiana, 1990-1992; Basil H. Lorch, III, U.S. Bankruptcy Judge, Southern District of Indiana, 1992-1993. Chief Counsel, Indiana Gaming Commission, 1993-1999. *Member:* Indiana State and American Bar Associations. ***PRACTICE AREAS:*** Administrative Law; Gaming Law; Gaming Licensing; Governmental Law; Minority Business Law; Business Law. ***Email:*** kay.fleming@icemiller.com

MARK W. FORD, born Indianapolis, Indiana, January 7, 1949; admitted to bar, 1974, Indiana and U.S. District Court, Southern and Northern Districts of Indiana; U.S. Court of Appeals, Seventh Circuit; U.S. Supreme Court. *Education:* DePauw University (B.A., 1971); Indiana University (J.D., cum laude, 1974). Former President, Student Bar Association. Co-Author, "Personnel and Employment Law in Indiana," Federal Publications, Inc., 1991-1995. Senate Majority Attorney, Indiana General Assembly, 1976, 1979, 1980. Chief Counsel, Indiana Senate Majority, 1976-1977, 1980. Senate Minority Counsel, Indiana General Assembly, 1977, 1978. *Member:* Indianapolis, Indiana State (Member, 1988-1989 and Chairman, 1989-1990, Labor and Employment Law Section) and American Bar Associations. ***REPORTED CASES:*** Rush v. McDonald's Corp., No. 91-2151, U.S. Court of Appeals for the Seventh Circuit, 966 F.2d 1104, 1992 U.S. App. LEXIS 14925, argued April 8, 1992, decided June 29, 1992; Mozee v. American Commercial Marine Serv. Co., No. 90-2660, U.S. Court of Appeals for the Seventh Circuit, 963 F.2d 929, 1992 U.S. App. LEXIS 9857, decided May 7, 1992, as amended May 18, 1992; Mozee v. American Commercial Marine Serv. Co., No. 90-2660 U.S. Court of Appeals for the Seventh Circuit, 940 F.2d 1036, 1991 U.S. App. LEXIS 18498, argued January 23, 1991, decided August 14, 1991; Mozee v. Jeffboat, Inc., Nos. 83-2243, 83-2244, U.S. Court of Appeals for the Seventh Circuit, 746 F.2d 365, 1984 U.S. App. LEXIS 17761, argued May 31, 1984, decided October 12, 1984; Borton v. United Parcel Service, Inc., No. 81-1536, U.S. Court of Appeals for the Seventh Circuit, 679 F.2d 893, 1982 U.S. App. LEXIS 21144, reversed March 9, 1982; Borton v. United Parcel Service, Inc., No. 82-211, U.S. Supreme Court of the United States, 459 U.S. 957, 103 S. Ct. 271, petition for writ of certiorari to the U.S. Court of Appeals for the Seventh Circuit denied, October 18, 1982; Swartz v. McDonald's Corp., U.S. District Court for the Northern District of Indiana, 87 F.Supp.2d 863, 2000 U.S. Dist. LEXIS 2786, decided January 28, 2000; Cornell v. Delco Elecs. Corp., U.S. District Court for the Southern District of Indiana, 103 F.Supp.2d 1116, 2000 U.S. Dist. LEXIS 6566, decided January 3, 2000; Satyshur v. General Motors Corporation, U.S. District Court for the Northern District of Indiana, 38 F.Supp.2d 744, 1999 U.S. Dist. LEXIS 2961, decided March 15, 1999, filed March 15, 1999; Erwin v. Northwestern Mut. Life Ins. Co., U.S. District Court for the Southern District of Indiana, 999 F.Supp.1227, 1998 U.S. Dist. LEXIS 4269, decided March 17, 1998, opinion filed, March 17, 1998; Rush v. McDonald's Corp., U.S. District Court for the Southern District of Indiana, 760 F.Supp.1349, 1991 U.S. Dist. LEXIS 5207, decided April 12, 1991; Steele v. McDonald's Corp., Court of Appeals of Indiana, 686 N.E.2d 137, 1997 Ind. App. LEXIS 990, filed July 28, 1997, appellant's rehearing denied October 7, 1997, appellant's transfer denied February 18, 1998; 114 Lab. Arb. (BNA) 1436, Pasminco Zinc, FMCS Case No. 99/09261, July 15, 2000; 104 Lab. Arb. (BNA) 964, Savage Zinc, Inc., FMCS Case No. 94-000837, July 24, 1995; 78 Lab. Arb. (BNA) 836, United Parcel Service, Inc., FMCS Case No. 81K/27874, February 22, 1982. ***PRACTICE AREAS:*** Labor and Employment (95%). ***Email:*** fordm@icemiller.com

SARAH K. FUNKE, born Tipton, Indiana, May 21, 1969; admitted to bar, 1994, Indiana. *Education:* Indiana University-Bloomington (B.A., with highest distinction, 1991); In-

(This Listing Continued)

diana University School of Law, Bloomington (J.D., magna cum laude, 1994). Order of the Coif. *Member:* Indiana State and American Bar Associations. ***PRACTICE AREAS:*** Real Property; Real Estate Sales; Real Estate Acquisitions; Real Property Development; Real Property Finance; Real Estate Leasing. ***Email:*** sarah.funke@icemiller.com

BONNIE L. GALLIVAN, born Bluffton, Indiana; admitted to bar, 1983, Indiana. *Education:* Indiana University (A.B., 1972; M.A.T., 1974); Indiana University School of Law-Indianapolis (J.D., summa cum laude, 1983). Articles Editor, Indiana University Law Review, 1982-1983. *Member:* International Association of Defense Counsel; Defense Research Institute; Product Liability Advisory Council. ***REPORTED CASES:*** Todd v. Merrell Dow Pharmaceuticals, Inc., 942 F.2d 1173; Porter v. American Home Products Corp., 9 F.2d 607 (7th Cir. 1993). ***PRACTICE AREAS:*** Medical Malpractice Defense; Drugs and Medical Device Law; Toxic Tort; Product Liability Law. ***Email:*** bonnie.gallivan@icemiller.com

ROBERT L. GAUSS, born Indianapolis, Indiana, July 3, 1968; admitted to bar, 1993, Indiana and U.S. District Court, Northern and Southern Districts of Indiana. *Education:* DePauw University (B.A., 1990); Indiana University - Indianapolis (J.D., 1993). *Member:* Indianapolis, Indiana State and American Bar Associations; Defense Research Institute. [Capt., USMCR, 1994-1997]. ***PRACTICE AREAS:*** Civil Litigation; Business Litigation; Products Liability; Toxic Torts; Asbestos Litigation; Construction Litigation; Family Law; Class Action Litigation. ***Email:*** gauss@icemiller.com

PHILIP C. GENETOS, born Gary, Indiana, August 2, 1952; admitted to bar, 1977, Indiana. *Education:* Cornell University (A.B., with distinction, 1974); Indiana University (M.B.A., 1977; J.D., magna cum laude, 1977). Order of the Coif. Member, 1975-1977 and Articles Editor, 1976-1977, Indiana Law Journal. Founding Member, American College of Bond Lawyers. Member, Indiana University Law Alumni Board of Directors. Board Chairman, Orchard Country Day School. Member, Board of Trustees, Indianapolis Childrens' Museum. President, Board of Directors: Park Tudor Foundation. Chairman, Board of Directors, AAA Hoosier Motor Club, Inc. Parish Council, Holy Trinity Greek Orthodox Church. *Member:* Indiana State and American Bar Associations; Indiana Municipal Lawyers Association; National Association of Bond Lawyers (Vice Chairman, Fundamentals of Bond Law Seminar, 1993, Chairman, 1994; Vice Chairman, Committee on Arbitrage, 1995). (Managing Partner). ***PRACTICE AREAS:*** Municipal Finance or Bond Law; Airport Law; Industrial Revenue Bond Law; Multi-Family Residential Real Estate; Health and Hospital Law; Housing and Community Development. ***Email:*** genetos@icemiller.com

GINA M. GIACONE, born Benton, Illinois, March 28, 1970; admitted to bar, 1995, Indiana. *Education:* Southern Illinois University (B.S., Accounting, magna cum laude, 1992); Vanderbilt University (J.D., 1995). *Member:* Indianapolis and Indiana State Bar Associations. ***PRACTICE AREAS:*** Estate Planning; Estate and Gift Taxation; Probate; Trust Law; Charitable Trusts; Tax Exempt Organizations. ***Email:*** gina.giacone@icemiller.com

ALAN H. GOLDSTEIN, born Chicago, Illinois, May 16, 1944; admitted to bar, 1969, Indiana. *Education:* Indiana University (B.A., 1965; J.D., cum laude, 1969). Editorial Board, Indiana Legal Forum, 1968-1969. Adjunct Professor, Conflicts of Law, 1974-1975 and Civil Procedure, 1975-1980, Indiana University School of Law- Indianapolis. Executive Secretary, Indiana Civil Code Study Commission, 1968-1969; Indiana Judicial Study Commission, 1969. Panelist and Author: Construction Management: Making the Right Choice, Definitional Approaches to the Different Project Delivery Methods-Contractor as CM; American Bar Forum on the Construction Industry, April, 1992; "Resolving Construction Failures," Indiana Continuing Legal Education Forum Seminar, 1987; "Understanding and Negotiating Construction Contracts from the General Contractors Perspective," Indiana Continuing Legal Education Forum 1988; "The A201 General Conditions and the Various Owner/Contractor Forms of Agreement from the Contractor's Point of View," ICLEF, 1988; "Collecting from the Construction Lender," ICLEF, 1990; "Performance and Payment Problems, Remedies and Claims," ICLEF, 1992; "Construction Management," ICLEF Forum Committee of Construction Industry, American Bar Association, 1995; "Five Top Issues Facing Construction," ICLEF Forum, 1995. President, Indianapolis Jewish Community Relations Council, 1980-1983. Fellow, Wexner Heritage Foundation. *Member:* Indianapolis, Indiana State and American (Member, Forum on the Construction Industry) Bar Associations. ***PRACTICE AREAS:*** Corporate and Construction Litigation; Construction Contracts; Construction Law; Construction Arbitration; Mold Claims. ***Email:*** alan.goldstein@icemiller.com

DOREEN J. GRIDLEY, born Ithaca, New York, May 17, 1955; admitted to bar, 1995, Indiana and U.S. District Court, Northern and Southern Districts of Indiana; registered to practice before U.S. Patent and Trademark Office, 1991. *Education:* Slippery Rock State College (B.S., summa cum laude, 1977); University of Virginia (M.S., 1979); Indiana Wesleyan University (M.S., 1987); Indiana University School of Law, Indianapolis (J.D., magna cum laude, 1995). *Member:* Indianapolis, Indiana State and American (Member, Intellectual Property Section) Bar Associations; American Intellectual Property Law Association. ***PRACTICE AREAS:*** Intellectual Property; Technology Law; Computer Law; Contracts; Sports Law. ***Email:*** Doreen.Gridley@icemiller.com

BRIAN D. GWITT, born Buffalo, New York, June 22, 1972; admitted to bar, 1999, New York and U.S. District Court, Western District of New York2002, Indiana and U.S. District Court, Northern and Southern Districts of Indiana. *Education:* State University of New York at Fredonia (B.A., 1994); State University of New York at Buffalo (J.D., 1998). Member, Buffalo Law Review, 1996-1998. National Trial Technique Team, 1998. *Member:* Indianapolis and American Bar Associations. ***PRACTICE AREAS:*** Commercial Litigation; Uniform Commercial Code; Debtor and Creditor Litigation; Tax Litigation. ***Email:*** gwitt@icemiller.com

STEPHEN J. HACKMAN, born Indianapolis, Indiana, July 11, 1959; admitted to bar, 1984, Indiana. *Education:* Indiana University (B.S., with high distinction, 1981; J.D., magna cum laude, 1984). Beta Gamma Sigma; Order of the Coif. Member, Editorial Staff, Indiana Law Journal, 1983-1984. *Member:* Indianapolis (Chair, Business Section, 1994) and American Bar Associations. ***PRACTICE AREAS:*** Securities; Mergers and Acquisitions; Corporate Finance. ***Email:*** hackman@icemiller.com

JOHN R. HAMMOND, III, born Indianapolis, Indiana, June 13, 1954; admitted to bar, 1991, Indiana and U.S. District Court, Southern and Northern Districts of Indiana. *Education:* DePauw University (B.A., 1976); Indiana University (J.D., 1991). Administrative Assistant, 1977-1979 and Senior Executive Assistant, Education Policy and Legislative Af-

(This Listing Continued)

fairs to Governor Robert D. Orr, 1981-1988. ***PRACTICE AREAS:*** Government Relations; Municipal Law; Regulatory Law; Administrative Law; Insurance; Health Care. ***Email:*** hammond@icemiller.com

JANE NEUHAUSER HERNDON, born Farmington, Michigan, October 16, 1964; admitted to bar, 1989, Indiana. *Education:* DePauw University (B.A., 1986); George Washington University (J.D., with high honors, 1989). Order of the Coif. Attorney for Speaker, Indiana House of Representatives, 1992 Legislative Session. *Member:* Indiana State and American Bar Associations; National Association of Bond Lawyers; Indiana Municipal Lawyers Association. ***PRACTICE AREAS:*** Municipal Bonds; Municipal Finance; Municipal Leasing; Equipment Leasing; Lease Law; School Law; Public Authority Financing Law. ***Email:*** herndon@icemiller.com

JEFFREY A. HOKANSON, born Valparaiso, Indiana; admitted to bar, 1989, Indiana and U.S. District Court, Northern and Southern Districts of Indiana. *Education:* Indiana University-Purdue University at Indianapolis (B.S., 1986); Indiana University School of Law-Indianapolis (J.D., 1989). *Member:* Indianapolis and Indiana State Bar Associations; Indiana Association for Corporate Turnaround; American Bankruptcy Institute. ***PRACTICE AREAS:*** Bankruptcy Litigation; Bankruptcy Reorganization; Commercial Bankruptcy; Commercial Insolvency; Commercial Workouts; Insolvency; Liquidations; Out of Court Debt Restructuring; Pre-Bankruptcy Workouts; Workouts. ***Email:*** jeff.hokanson@icemiller.com

BRENDA S. HORN, born Beech Grove, Indiana, April 22, 1949; admitted to bar, 1981, Indiana. *Education:* Indiana University (A.B., with distinction, 1971; J.D., summa cum laude, 1981); Purdue University (M.S., 1975). Phi Beta Kappa; Phi Delta Phi. Member, Indiana Law Review, 1980-1981. *Member:* Indianapolis (Member, Board of Managers, 1992; Chair, Women and the Law Division, 1992) and American Bar Associations; National Association of Bond Lawyers; Indiana Municipal Lawyers Association; American College of Bond Counsel (President,1998-2001, Vice President, 1995-1998, Member, Board of Directors,1995— and Founding Fellow). ***PRACTICE AREAS:*** Municipal Finance; Municipal Law; Health Care Finance; Public Finance. ***Email:*** horn@icemiller.com

BRENT W. HUBER, born Winamac, Indiana, February 19, 1965; admitted to bar, 1991, Indiana and U.S. District Court, Northern and Southern Districts of Indiana. *Education:* Purdue University (B.S., with distinction, 1987); Indiana University (J.D., cum laude, 1991). Articles Editor, Indiana Law Journal, 1990-1991. Author: Note, "Target Corporations, Hostile Horizontal Takeovers and 'Antitrust Injury' Under Section 16 of the Clayton Act after Cargill," 66 Ind. L.J. 625. ***REPORTED CASES:*** Hartford Fire Ins. v. Guide Corp., 206 F.R.D. 249 (S.D. 2001); Spolnik v. Guardian Life, 94 F. Supp. 2d 998 (S.D. 2000); McFarland Foods Corp. v. Chevron USA, Inc. et al., 2000 WL 684265 (S.D. Ind. 2000); K&S Co. v. Sexton Investment Co., 1999 WL 92284 (S.D.N.Y. 1999); Sans v. Monticello Ins., 718 N.E.2d 814 (Ind. Ct. App. 1999), trans. denied; United States Auto Club v. Smith, 717 N.E.2d 919 (Ind. Ct. App. 1999), trans. denied; McGlothlin v. M & U Trucking, 688 N.E.2d 1243 (Ind. 1997); Wolf v. Kajima Int'l, 629 N.E.2d 1237 (Ind. 1994). ***PRACTICE AREAS:*** Federal Civil Practice; Motor Sports Law; Business Litigation; Environmental Litigation; Environmental Insurance Coverage; Insurance Coverage; Complex Litigation; Toxic Tort Defense. ***Email:*** brent.huber@icemiller.com

STEVEN HUMKE, born Springfield, Illinois, June 7, 1960; admitted to bar, 1985, District of Columbia; 1993, Indiana. *Education:* Duke University (A.B., summa cum laude, 1981); University of Chicago (J.D., cum laude, 1985). Phi Beta Kappa. Certified Public Accountant, Illinois, 1982. *Member:* District of Columbia Bar; Indiana State Bar Association. ***PRACTICE AREAS:*** Business Transactions; Business Planning; Entrepreneurial Services; Emerging Growth Companies; Business Organization. ***Email:*** steven.humke@icemiller.com

HARRY T. ICE, born October 17, 1904; admitted to bar, 1929; died September 8, 1982.

LACY M. JOHNSON, born Frederick, Oklahoma, September 9, 1952; admitted to bar, 1981, Indiana. *Education:* Purdue University (B.A., 1976); Valparaiso University; Indiana University (J.D., 1981). Instructor, Law Enforcement Academy, Criminal Procedure, 1979-1989. Lt. Col./Deputy Superintendent, Indiana State Police, 1976-1989. *Member:* Marion County and Indiana State Bar Associations. [Lt. Cmdr., USNR, 1983—]. ***PRACTICE AREAS:*** Legislative Practice; Governmental Affairs; Procurement Practice; Gaming Law; Alcohol and Tobacco Litigation; Lobbying. ***Email:*** lacy.johnson@icemiller.com

G. DANIEL KELLEY, JR., born Chicago, Illinois, October 28, 1940; admitted to bar, 1968, Indiana. *Education:* American University, Hanover College (A.B., 1962); Indiana University Graduate School of Business and Economics; Indiana University (J.D., magna cum laude, 1967). Phi Delta Phi; Order of the Coif. Editor-in-Chief, Indiana Legal Forum, 1966-1967. Law Clerk for Judge Donald H. Hunter of the Indiana Appellate Court, 1965-1966 and of the Indiana Supreme Court, 1966-1967. Assistant Professor, Torts and Criminal Law, Indiana University Law School, 1969-1970. Member, 1976-1990 and Chairman, 1990-1993, Disciplinary Commission of the Supreme Court of Indiana. ***PRACTICE AREAS:*** Natural Resources Law; Mining or Mineral Law; Complex Litigation; Arbitration; Appellate and Administrative Practice. ***Email:*** kelley@icemiller.com

JAMES D. KEMPER, born Olney, Illinois, February 23, 1947; admitted to bar, 1971, Indiana. *Education:* Indiana University (B.S., 1969; J.D., summa cum laude, 1971). Phi Eta Sigma; Order of the Coif. Note Editor, Indiana Law Journal, 1970-1971. Law Clerk for Judge John S. Hastings, U.S. Court of Appeals, Seventh Circuit. Publications and Seminars: Ice Miller Donadio & Ryan Circle City Seminar, March 5, 1999, Indianapolis, Indiana, "Taking the Bad with the Good: Employer Protections and Fiduciary Responsibility under ERISA"; Merrill Lynch Presentation, January 27, 1999, Indianapolis, Indiana, "401(k) and Defined Contribution and Pension Plan Liability: When is an Employer Exposed as a Fiduciary?; 1997 Employee Benefits Conference, February 27, 1997, Indianapolis, Indiana, "What Every Employer Needs to Know to Comply with Recent Federal Legislation and Case Law Affecting Employee Benefit Plans"; Tax Exempt and Governmental Employers Seminar, November 1, 1995, Indianapolis, Indiana, "Deferred Compensation for Tax Exempt Organizations and Universities - The Basics and Beyond"; Ice Miller Donadio & Ryan, November, 1995, Indianapolis, Indiana, "Deferred Compensation for Tax Exempt Organizations and Universities - The Basics and Beyond"; Ice Miller Donadio & Ryan, June 29, 1994, Indianapolis, Indiana, "Taking Control of Your Benefit Program"; Katz, Sapper & Miller - Certified Public Accountants, September 28, 1993, Indianapolis, Indiana,

(This Listing Continued)

ICE MILLER, Indianapolis—Continued

"Understanding 401(k) Plans -- The Basics"; CUPA Midwest Regional Conference, 1992; "Strategies for Complying with New IRS Tests for Section 403(b) Annuities and Qualified Retirement Plans;" Indiana Continuing Legal Education Forum and The Indiana Municipal Lawyers Association, 1991; Municipal Law VIII; "Mandated Social Security Coverage;" Indiana Chamber of Commerce Health Care Conference, 1990; "Regulating Group Health Plans - Problems, Pitfalls and Proposals;" Fort Wayne Chapter Indiana CPA Society, 1989; "Hot Tax Topics - 1989 - Current Issues Relating to Qualified Plans;" National Business Institute, Inc.; Employee Benefits in Indiana, 1989; "Section 125 - Cafeteria Plans;" Legal Forum for Hospital Attorneys and Administrators, 1988; "Fraud and Abuse--Current Trends In Criminal Enforcement;" American Academy of Hospital Attorneys and National Health Lawyers Association Ninth Annual Institute on Medicare and Medicaid Payment Issues, 1988; "Financing and Refinancing Under Prospective Payment System;" Indiana Medical Group Management Association, 1988; "Tax Reform Act of 1986 and Leased Employees, Affiliated Service Groups and Management Companies--Consequences for Employee Benefit Plans of Physician Groups and Joint Ventures;" Eighth Annual Institute on Medicare and Medicaid Payment Issues, 1987; "Financing and Refinancing Under Prospective Payment System; Indiana Continuing Legal Education Forum and Indiana State Bar Association, 1987; *Employee Benefit Provisions of Tax Reform Act of 1986;* "Qualified Plans--Coverage, Participation, Leased Employees;" "Qualified Plans--Vesting/Integration/Asset Reversions/Loans/IRS Filing Requirements." Member, Stanley K. Lacy Leadership Alumni Association. *Member:* Indiana State and American (Member, Employee Benefits Committee, Section on Taxation) Bar Associations; Indiana Pension Conference. Member, Board of Directors, Eitlejorg Museum. ***PRACTICE AREAS:*** Employee Benefit Law; ERISA; Deferred/Executive Compensation; Retirement Law; Business Law. ***Email:*** james.kemper@icemiller.com

MARTIN J. KLAPER, born Chicago, Illinois, January 12, 1947; admitted to bar, 1971, Indiana; 1972, U.S. Court of Appeals, Seventh Circuit; 1979, U.S. Supreme Court. *Education:* Indiana University (B.S., summa cum laude, 1969; J.D., summa cum laude, 1971). Order of the Coif. *Best Lawyers in America.Member:* Indiana State and American Bar Associations; College of Labor and Employment Lawyers. ***PRACTICE AREAS:*** Arbitration Law; Collective Bargaining; Employment Discrimination Law; Civil Rights Defense; Personnel Law; Labor Law; Affirmative Action; Age Discrimination in Employment; Employer Rights; Employment Disability Discrimination; Equal Employment Opportunity Law; Executive Employment Law; Executive Severance Contracts; Executive Transfers; Fair Employment Practices; Fair Labor Standards; Family Medical Leave Act; Harassment; Labor Strikes; Management Employment Law; Management Labor Law; National Labor Relations Act; Personnel Policies; Personnel Training; Reductions in Work Force; Title VII Discrimination; Unfair Labor Practices; Union Elections; Union Organization; Wage and Hour Law; WARN Act; Wrongful Termination; Employment at Will. ***Email:*** klaper@icemiller.com

KEVIN R. KNIGHT, born Ft. Wayne, Indiana, October 9, 1960; admitted to bar, 1990, Indiana. *Education:* St. Francis College (B.A., with honors, 1983); Indiana University (J.D., magna cum laude, 1990). Order of the Coif. Articles Editor, Indiana Law Review, 1989-90. Author: "The Life of *Riley:* ...," 23 Ind. L. Rev. (1990). Law Clerk for the Hon. Robert H. Staton, Indiana Court of Appeals, 1990-1992. *Member:* Indianapolis and Indiana State Bar Associations; Defense Research Institute. ***REPORTED CASES:*** JKB, Sr. v. Armour Pharmaceutical Co., 660 N.E.2d 602 (Ind.App. 1996); Brown v. Medtronic, Inc., 852 F.Supp. 717 (S.D. Ind. 1993); Dominguez v. Syntex Laboratories, Inc., 149 F.R.D. 166 (S.D. Ind. 1993). ***PRACTICE AREAS:*** Defense Litigation; Drug and Medical Device Litigation; Toxic Torts; Construction Law. ***Email:*** kevin.knight@icemiller.com

GARETH W. KUHL, born Niles, Michigan, February 15, 1969; admitted to bar, 1994, Indiana. *Education:* University of Michigan (B.B.A., with high distinction, 1991; J.D., cum laude, 1994). Phi Beta Kappa; Beta Gamma Sigma; Order of the Coif. Executive Editor, University of Michigan Journal of Law Reform. *Member:* Indianapolis, Indiana State and American Bar Associations. ***PRACTICE AREAS:*** Tax Law; Low Income Housing Tax Credits; Partnership Taxation; Affordable Housing; Low Income Housing; Multi-Family Housing; Housing Finance; Nonprofit Tax Law; Tax Exempt Organizations; Real Estate Finance. ***Email:*** kuhl@icemiller.com

MARY NOLD LARIMORE, born Haddonfield, New Jersey, July 4, 1956; admitted to bar, 1980, Indiana. *Education:* Indiana University (A.B., with distinction, 1977; J.D., cum laude, 1980). Phi Alpha Delta (Treasurer, 1979-1980). Note Editor, Indiana Law Journal, 1979-1980. Author: "Indiana Workmen's Compensation Act: Accidents Arising out of and in the Course of Employment," 55 Indiana Law Journal 375, 1980; "Judicial Sanctions Under Federal Rule 11," For The Defense, March, 1987. Co-Author: "Discoverability of Document Management Systems: Pitfalls and How to Avoid Them," Defense Counsel Journal, Vol. 64, No. 3, pp. 369-380, July 1997; Faculty: 1997 IADC Trial Academy, Boulder, Colorado; Eleventh Annual Trial Advocacy Skills Workshop, National Institute for Trial Advocacy, Indiana Continuing Legal Education Foundation, 1990. Speaker: The Law Society's Commerce and Industry Group, London, England, in association with Cameron McKenna "A Message from America, Restatement 3d, Impact on American Product Liability Law and Long-Arm Jurisdiction," March 1998; Analyzing Epidemiologic Evidence, IADC Annual Meeting, Bermuda, 1997; Discoverability of Document Management Systems, IADC Mid-Winter Meeting, Pebble Beach, California, 1997; "Federal Preemption and Products Liability Cases," International Association of Defense Counsel, San Francisco, 1995; "Rule 11" Defense Research Institute Seminar, Drug and Device Seminar, Seattle, Washington, 1995; "Rule 11, Seminar of Discovery Tools, Indiana Continuing Legal Education Foundation, 1998; "Ethical and Practical Considerations of Dealings with Plaintiff's Experts," Seminar on Expert Witnesses, Defense Research Institute, Baltimore, Maryland, 1987; "Rule 11 Sanctions Against Lawyers and Their Impact on the Conduct of Litigation," Defense Research Institute Seminar, Drugs and Devices, San Francisco, California, April 1987; "Rule 11 Sanctions," Joint Presentation with United State District Court Judge, Oklahoma Association of Defense Counsel, Dallas, Texas, 1987; "Coping with the Explosion in Perinatal Litigation," Joint Presentation by Richard Baum, M.D., Patent Care, Third International Conference, September 12, 1986. Program Chair, Multi-National Committee, IADC, 1999—; "Overview of Indiana Product Liability Law," 2004 Indiana Litigation Institute, Indianapolis, Indiana, October, 2004. Member, Character and Fitness Committee, Board of Bar Examiners - Appointed by the Indiana Supreme Court, 1996—. Member, 1999— and Chair, 2004—, Rules Committee of the Indiana Supreme Court, Appointed by the Indiana Supreme Court. *Member:* Indianapolis and Indiana State Bar Associations; International Association of Defense Counsel; Defense Research Institute; American College of Trial Lawyers (Vice Chair, Indiana State Committee). ***PRACTICE AREAS:*** Drug and Medical Device Litigation; Toxic Tort; Product Liability Law. ***Email:*** larimore@icemiller.com

LISA A. LEE, born New Castle, Indiana, April 19, 1963; admitted to bar, 1997, Indiana. *Education:* Ball State University (B.S., 1985; M.P.A., 1987); Indiana University School of Law (J.D., 1997). Frequent speaker on the issues of tax increment finance, economic development and general municipal finance; has also been a panelist at seminars held by NABL, the Indiana Association of Cities and Towns, the Association of Indiana Counties, the Indiana League of Municipal Clerks and Treasurers and the Indiana Economic Development Academy on these and other topics such as legal opinions, professional ethics, municipal utility financing and stormwater financing. *Member:* Indiana State and American Bar Associations; National Association of Bond Lawyers. ***PRACTICE AREAS:*** Municipal Finance. ***Email:*** lisa.leel@icemiller.com

MICHAEL J. LEWINSKI, born South Bend, Indiana, May 17, 1960; admitted to bar, 1985, Indiana. *Education:* Wabash College (A.B., summa cum laude, 1982); Indiana University (J.D., cum laude, 1985). Phi Beta Kappa; Delta Theta Phi. Executive Editor, Indiana Law Journal, 1984-1985. Author: Note "Visitation Beyond the Traditional Limitations," Indiana Law Journal Volume 60:1, 1985. *Member:* Indianapolis and Indiana State Bar Associations. ***PRACTICE AREAS:*** Breach of Contract; Litigation; Real Estate; Commercial Law. ***Email:*** lewinski@icemiller.com

JEFFREY O. LEWIS, born Urbana, Illinois, November 8, 1952; admitted to bar, 1979, Indiana. *Education:* DePauw University (B.A., with high distinction, 1974); Louisville Presbyterian Theological Seminary (M.Div., 1979); University of Illinois (J.D., cum laude, 1979). Phi Beta Kappa. Member, Moot Court Board. *Member:* Indianapolis Bar Association; Indiana Municipal Lawyers Association; National Association of Bond Lawyers; National Association of College and University Attorneys. ***PRACTICE AREAS:*** Tax Exempt Finance; Tax Exempt Securities; University Finance; Private Education Law; First Amendment Law; College and University Law. ***Email:*** jeffrey.lewis@icemiller.com

DAVID J. MALLON, JR., born Newark, New Jersey, September 1, 1946; admitted to bar, 1975, Indiana and U.S. Court of Appeals, Seventh Circuit; U.S. District Court, Southern and Nothern Districts of Indiana. *Education:* Cornell University (B.A., 1968); Indiana University (J.D., 1975). Order of the Coif. *Member:* Indianapolis and Indiana State Bar Associations; National Health Lawyers Association; Indiana Defense Lawyers Association; American Health Lawyers Association; Defense Trial Counsel of Indiana; Defense Research Insititute. [Lieut., U.S. Navy, 1968-1972]. ***PRACTICE AREAS:*** Litigation; Medical Law; Health Care and Hospital Law; Tort Law; Medical Staff Credentialing; Contracts; Medicare and Medicaid. ***Email:*** david.mallon@icemiller.com

DAVID M. MATTINGLY, born Indianapolis, Indiana, June 3, 1946; admitted to bar, 1971, Indiana. *Education:* Indiana University (B.S., 1968); University of Michigan (J.D., 1970). Indiana Defense Lawyer Association's 1996 "Lawyer of the Year". *Member:* Indianapolis, Indiana State and Seventh Circuit Bar Associations; American College of Trial Lawyers. ***PRACTICE AREAS:*** Trial and Appellate Practice; Sports Law; Entertainment Law; Business Law; Complex Litigation. ***Email:*** mattingl@icemiller.com

CURTIS W. McCAULEY, born Wabash, Indiana, December 23, 1960; admitted to bar, 1992, Indiana. *Education:* Harvard University (A.B., cum laude, 1984); University of Michigan (J.D., cum laude, 1991). *Member:* Indiana State and American Bar Associations. ***PRACTICE AREAS:*** Business Litigation; Information and Privacy; Technology Law. ***Email:*** mccauley@icemiller.com

DEBRA HANLEY MILLER, born Terre Haute, Indiana, May 9, 1960; admitted to bar, 1984, Indiana, U.S. District Court, Southern and Northern Districts of Indiana. *Education:* Indiana State University (B.S., cum laude, 1980); Indiana University (J.D., cum laude, 1984). *Member:* Indianapolis and Indiana State Bar Associations; National Association of Women Business Owners; American Board of Trial Advocates. (Certified as a Civil Trial Advocacy Specialist by the National Board of Trial Advocates). ***PRACTICE AREAS:*** Personal Injury; Appellate Practice; Trial Practice; Business Litigation; Torts. ***Email:*** miller@icemiller.com

MERLE H. MILLER, born January 12, 1904; admitted to bar, 1930, Indiana; died January 8, 1997.

MICHAEL E. MILLIKAN, born Indianapolis, Indiana, December 2, 1971; admitted to bar, 1998, Indiana. *Education:* Villanova University (B.A., 1994); Indiana University School of Law - Indianapolis (J.D., 1998). *Member:* Indianapolis and Indiana State Bar Associations. ***PRACTICE AREAS:*** Entrepreneurial Business Law; Mergers and Acquisitions; Securities. ***Email:*** millikan@icemiller.com

THOMAS E. MIXDORF, born Waterloo, Iowa, September 8, 1962; admitted to bar, 1992, Indiana. *Education:* University of Northern Iowa (B.A., highest honors, 1984); Indiana University (J.D., summa cum laude, 1992). *Member:* Indianapolis, Indiana State and American Bar Associations. ***PRACTICE AREAS:*** General Business Litigation; Natural Resources; Litigation; Patent Damages Litigation; Attorney Defense. ***Email:*** mixdorf@icemiller.com

MICHELLE M. MOLIN, born Hutchinson, Minnesota, July 21, 1965; admitted to bar, 1999, Indiana. *Education:* Purdue University (B.A., 1989); Indiana University (J.D., 1998). Phi Beta Kappa; Golden Key National Honor Society. ***PRACTICE AREAS:*** Corporate Law; Debt and Equity Finance; Mergers and Acquisitions; Motor Sports Law. ***Email:*** michelle.molin@icemiller.com

BYRON L. MYERS, born Kansas City, Missouri, October 16, 1946; admitted to bar, 1977, Indiana. *Education:* Rose-Hulman Institute of Technology (B.S.M.E., 1968); Indiana University (J.D., summa cum laude, 1977). Order of the Coif. Phi Alpha Delta. Member, Indiana Law Journal, 1976-1977. *Member:* Indianapolis, Indiana State and American Bar Associations. ***PRACTICE AREAS:*** Labor and Employment Law; Employment Discrimination Law; Wrongful Termination-Employment At Will; Employment Litigation. ***Email:*** myers@icemiller.com

(This Listing Continued)

TIMOTHY E. OCHS, born Indianapolis, Indiana, March 30, 1967; admitted to bar, 1992, Indiana. *Education:* Purdue University (B.S.C.E., 1989); Indiana University (J.D., cum laude, 1992). Author: National Business Institute Seminar: Mastering Real Estate Title and Title Insurance in Indiana, 1995; Zoning, Subdivision and Annexation, 2003, 2004, 2005; Professional Education Systems Institute, LLC Seminar: Indiana Boundary Law and Adjoining Landowner Disputes, 2003, 2004, 2005; Indiana Continuing Legal Education Forum: Negotiating and Documenting The Transaction: Due Diligence, 2004; Exactions and Takings in Indiana, 2003; Contract Drafting, 1999; Adverse Possession, Acquiescence of Boundary Lines and Recent Amendments to Indiana Legal Survey Statute - Third Annual Real Estate Symposium, 1995; Archeological and Historical Preservation Issues: "What To Do When You Discover Skeletons In Your Closet," 1995. Contributing Author: "Survey of Recent Land Uses and Zoning Cases in Legislative Development," 1994. Chairman, Real Estate Section, Allan County Bar Association, 1995-1996. *Member:* Indianapolis, Indiana State and American (Member: Real Estate Section; Land Use and Zoning Section) Bar Associations. ***PRACTICE AREAS:*** Real Estate Development; Real Estate Joint Ventures; Real Estate Leasing; Real Estate Law; Zoning, Planning and Land Use; Lease Law; Real Estate Finance. ***Email:*** ochs@icemiller.com

JUDY STAROBIN OKENFUSS, born Washington, D.C., May 6, 1962; admitted to bar, 1991, Indiana and U.S. District Court, Southern and Northern Districts of Indiana. *Education:* Washington University (B.S.Ch.E., cum laude, 1984; B.A. in Spanish, 1984; J.D., 1991). Order of the Coif; Phi Delta Phi; Tau Beta Pi, National Engineering Honorary Society. Primary Articles Editor, Washington University Law Quarterly. Former Engineer, McDonnell Douglas Corporation and Dow Corning Corporation. Currently Chair, Board of Peace Learning Center, Indianapolis, Indiana. *Member:* Indianapolis, Indiana State and American Bar Associations; Defense Research Institute. ***LANGUAGES:*** Spanish. ***REPORTED CASES:*** R.L. McCoy, Inc. v. Jack, 752 N.E.2d 67 (Ind. Ct. App. 2001), vacated by, 772 N.E.2d 987 (Ind. 2002); Gagne v. Trustees of Indiana University, 692 N.E.2d 489 (Ind. Ct. App. 1998); Sears v. Blubaugh, 613 N.E.2d 468 (Ind. Ct. App. 1993). ***PRACTICE AREAS:*** Products Liability; Risk Management; Civil Litigation; Warranty Law; Catastrophic Injury; Litigation; Telephone Consumer Protection Act Litigation. ***Email:*** judy.okenfuss@icemiller.com

E. VAN OLSON, born Amityville, New York, August 30, 1950; admitted to bar, 1980, Indiana. *Education:* Indiana University (B.S., 1974; J.D., magna cum laude, 1980). Member, Board of Editors, Indiana Law Review, 1979-1980. Clerk to Honorable Robert H. Staton, Indiana Court of Appeals, 1979-1980. Publications and Seminars: "Chapter 7 of *The ESOP Association Administration Handbook,* ERISA Reporting and Disclosure Requirements for Defined Contribution Plans," (2001); "The New Minimum Required Distribution Rules under Code Section 401(a)(9)," Ice Miller Church Plan Workshop IV (2001); "Estate and Tax Planning for Qualified Retirement Plans and IRAs," National Business Institute (2000); "An Overview of the Basic Legal Requirements for Administration of an ESOP," The 2000 Two-Day ESOP Conference (2000); "ESOP Administration Issues," The Great Lakes Regional ESOP Conference, Itasca, Illinois, March 10, 2000; "ESOPs and the Closely-Held Corporation," National Association of Insurance and Financial Advisers—Indiana Chapter, March 2, 2000; "Deduction and Annual Addition Limitations, and Participant Tax Rules," The ESOP Association Two Day ESOP Conference, Las Vegas, Nevada, November 4-5, 1999; "IRA Distributions, Insurance and Certain Tax Considerations for Estate and Retirement Income Planning," The Central Indiana Financial Planning Conference, Carmel, Indiana, September 17, 1999; "Pitfalls of Prototypes" and "Buying and Selling Privately Held Businesses," Ice Miller Donadio & Ryan Circle City Seminar, March 5, 1999; "Deductions, contributions & Dividend Rules for Employee Stock Ownership Plans—A General Overview," The ESOP Association Two Day ESOP Conference, Las Vegas, Nevada, November 5-6, 1998; "IRS Audit Guidelines for ESOPs, and Some Suggestions on How to Approach an Audit," The ESOP Association 21st Annual Conference (1998); "Limiting Your Risks, Tax Qualified Retirement Plans, IRAs and Insurance," International Association of Financial Planners (1998); "Deductions, Contributions and Dividend Rules for ESOPs," The ESOP Associations Two Day ESOP Conference (1998); "The Issues Involved in the Termination of Tax Qualified Retirement Plans Sponsored by Companies in Bankruptcy," Annual Meeting of Chapter 7 Trustees, Indiana and Central and Southern Illinois (1997); "A Broad Overview of the Legal Requirements in the Administration of an ESOP," The ESOP Association's Two Day Deal (1997); "A Broad Overview of the Issues Involved in the Termination of Retirement Plans Sponsored by Companies in Bankruptcy," Chapter 7 Trustees Panel, U.S. Department of Justice, United States Trustees Region 10 (1997); "IRS Audit Guidelines for ESOPS," The ESOP Association's Two Day ESOP Deal (1996): "A Primer on ESOP Administration," The ESOP Association (1996); "Rulings and Regulations Governing ESOP Companies," National Center for Employee Ownership (1996); "ESOP Administration 101, "The 1995 TWO DAY ESOP DEAL sponsored by The ESOP Association (1995); "Advanced Issues Track -- Litigation and Administrative Rulings," Fourteenth Annual Conference on Employee Ownership and Participation (1995); "Estate and Retirement Income Planning for Tax Qualified Retirement Plans and Individual Retirement Account Monies," Louisville Employee Benefits Council (1995); "Employee Stock Ownership Plans, and Individual Retirement Accounts-General Planning Considerations," The Central Indiana Society of Certified Financial Planners (1995). *Member:* Indianapolis and Indiana State Bar Associations; Indiana Pension Conference (Past Chairman); The ESOP Association (Member, Administration Advisory Committee); National Center for Employee Ownership; International Association of Financial Planners. ***PRACTICE AREAS:*** Employee Benefits; Deferred Compensation; Employee Benefit Taxation; Employee Benefit Trusts; Employee Stock Ownership Plans; Employee Stock Ownership Trusts; Equity Compensation; ERISA; ERISA Compliance; Executive Compensation; Executive Compensation Taxation; Flexible Benefit Plans; Multi-Employer Benefits; Multi-Employer Pensions; Non-qualified Benefits; Pension and Profit Sharing Plans; Pension Plans; Pension Taxation; Profit Sharing; Qualified Retirement Plans; Taft-Hartley Plans; 401(k) Plans; Business Succession Planning; Business Succession; Closely Held Business Estate Planning; Family Business Successions; Retirement Planning. ***Email:*** olson@icemiller.com

RICHARD E. PARKER, born Lafayette, Indiana, February 7, 1947; admitted to bar, 1972, Indiana. *Education:* Purdue University (B.S., with highest distinction, 1969); Harvard University (J.D., cum laude, 1972). Omicron Delta Kappa. *Member:* American Immigration Lawyers Association. ***PRACTICE AREAS:*** Employer-Employee Relations Law; Collective Bargaining; Labor Law; Immigration and Naturalization Law; Wage and Hour Law; Wrongful Discharge Law. ***Email:*** parker@icemiller.com

GREGORY L. PEMBERTON, born Danville, Illinois, December 8, 1952; admitted to bar, 1981, Indiana. *Education:* Monmouth College (B.A., cum laude, 1975); University of Illinois (J.D., magna cum laude, 1981). Order of the Coif; Phi Alpha Delta. Member, Legal Committee, American Association of Homes and Services for the Aging. Treasurer, Board of Directors, Fund For Hoosier Excellence. Vice President, Board of Directors, Walther Cancer Institute. President, Board of Directors, New World Youth Symphony Orchestra. Vice Chair, Board of Directors, Indiana Association of United Ways. Member: Board of Directors, Indiana State Museum Foundation; Finance Committee, United Way of Central Indiana. *Member:* Indianapolis (Former Chair, Health Care Section), Indiana State and American (Chair, Health Law Section) Bar Associations; American Health Lawyers Association. Fellow, American Bar Foundation. ***PRACTICE AREAS:*** Health Care and Hospital Law; Tax Exempt Organizations Law; Alternative Health Care Delivery Systems; Nursing Home; Medicare. ***Email:*** gregory.pemberton@icemiller.com

JAMES L. PETERSEN, born Bloomington, Illinois, February 3, 1947; admitted to bar, 1976, Indiana; 1980, Florida. *Education:* Illinois State University (B.A., 1970); University of Illinois at Springfield (M.A., 1973); Indiana University (J.D., magna cum laude, 1976). Order of the Coif; Omicron Delta Kappa honorary; Phi Gamma Mu history honorary. Associate Editor, Indiana Law Journal, 1975-1976. Speaker: "Specialized Lines of Insurance Coverage," Lorman Education Services Insurance Law in Indiana Seminar, February, 2003; "Product Liability and Tort Reform," DTCI Seminar, Fall, 1998. Author: "A Survey of Indiana's Franchise Law for the General Practitioner," Res Gestae, 2002; "State Tying Claims: Do You Know What May Be Lurking?" American Bar Association Franchise Law Journal, 2002; "Defining the Scope of Commercial Insurance Contracts," Insurance Advocate, 2001; "Law Governing Liability of Component Part Manufacturers," The Indiana Lawyer, 1999); "Product Liability and Tort Reform," The Indiana Lawyer, 1998; "The Risk Utility Test in Indiana Product Liability Law," The Indiana Lawyer, 1996; "Tort Reform, Act No. 1741," Res Gestae and The Indiana Lawyer, 1995. Past President, Illinois State University Alumni Association. Past President, Indiana University School of Law Alumni Association. Listed in Who's Who in America. Board Member, The Business Counsel, Inc. *Member:* Indiana State and American (Member: Litigation Section: Products Liability Committee, Insurance Coverage Litigation Committee, Committee on Commercial and Business Litigation; Forum on Franchising, Business Section; Tort Trial and Insurance Practice Section) Bar Associations; The Florida Bar; International Franchise Association (Member, Symposium Organizing Committee); Indiana Association of Defense Counsel (Past Co-Chair, Products Liability Committee; Diplomat, 1997); International Association of Defense Counsel. Fellow, American College of Trial Lawyers. ***REPORTED CASES:*** Published Trial Court Opinions: Creative Foods of Indiana, Inc. v. My Favorite Muffin Too, Inc., 2002 WL 244577 (S.D. Ind. Jan. 14, 2002) (No. IP01-0228-C-T/G); Creative Foods of Indiana, Inc. v. My Favorite Muffin Too, Inc., 2002 WL 244584 (S.D. Ind. Jan. 14, 2002) (No. IP01-0228-C-T/K); Continental Western Ins. Co. v. Reliance Nat. Indem. Co., 141 F.Supp.2d 968 (N.D. Ind. 2001); The Daiei, Inc. v. Ball Corp., 198 F.D.R. 658 (S.D. Ind. 2001); Pryor v. Resort Condominiums Int'l., Inc., 2000 WL 1006742 (S.D. Ind. 2000); Peters v. Systems Specialized Carriers, Inc., 1996 WL 204486 (N.D. Ind. 1996); Hamilton v. Ontario Forge Corp., 794 F.Supp. 291 (S.D. Ind. 1992); Scalf v. SCM Corp., 1981 U.S. Dist. LEXIS 10442 (No. IP 80-285-C) (S.D. Ind. Jan. 28, 1981). Published Appellate Decisions: United States Fire Ins. Co. v. Barker Car Rental, 944 F. Supp. 739 (S.D. Ind. 1996); 132 F.3d 1153 (7th Cir. 1997); Bates v. Baltimore and Ohio Railroad Co., 9 F.3d 29 (7th Cir. 1993); Dillon v. Combs, 895 F.2d 1175 (7th Cir. 1990); Bunker v. National Gypsum Co., 406 N.E.2d 1239 (Ind. Ct. App. 1980); 426 N.E.2d 422 (Ind. Ct. App. 1981); 441 N.E.2d 8 (Ind. 1982); 460 U.S. 1076, 103 S. Ct. 1761 (April 18, 1983); Anderson v. P.A. Radocy & Sons, Inc. and Miller Electric Manufacturing Company, 67 F.3d 619 (7th Cir. 1995); Allen v. LTV Steel Co., 2003 U.S. App. LEXIS 12349, No. 02-4094 (7th Cir. June 17, 2003); Shannon v. Sign Pros, 753 N.E.2d 17 (Ind. 2001); J.R. Brooks Construction, Inc. v. Curran Roofing Co., Memorandum Decision issued April 30, 2001 (Ind. Ct. App.) (No. 18A02-0007-CV-456); Hague v. Curran Roofing Co., 714 N.E.2d 314 (Ind. Ct. App. 1999); Wine-Settergren V. Lamey, 716 N.E.2d 381 (Ind. 1999); 726 N.E.2d 305 (Ind. 1999); 654 N.E.2d 920 (Ind. App. 1995); O'Donnell v. American Employers Ins. Co., 622 N.E.2d 570 (Ind. Ct. App. 1993); Ramon v. Glenroy Construction Co., 609 N.E.2d 1123 (Ind. Ct. App. 1993); Allied Resin Corp. v. Waltz, 559 N.E.2d 390 (Ind. Ct. App. 1990); 574 N.E.2d 913 (Ind. 1991); Stropes v. Heritage House Children's Center of Shelbyville, Inc., 547 N.E.2d 244 (Ind. 1989); Rasp v. Hidden Valley Lake, Inc., 519 N.E.2d 153 (Ind. Ct. App. 1988); Jager v. Katz, 511 N.E.2d 1092 (Ind. Ct. App. 1987); Black v. Seaboard System Railroad, 487 N.E.2d 468 (Ind. Ct. App. 1986); RAM Broadcasting of Indiana, Inc. v. Digital Paging Systems of Indiana, Inc., 463 N.E.2d 1104 (Ind. Ct. App.1984); 464 N.E.2d 336 (Ind. Ct. App. 1984); Bunker v. National Gypsum Co., 406 N.E.2d 1239 (Ind. Ct. App. 1980); 426 N.E.2d 422 (Ind. Ct. App. 1981); 441 N.E.2d 8 (Supreme Ct. Ind. 1982); 460 U.S. 1076, 103 S. Ct. 1761 (U.S. Ind., April 18,1983); Bridges v. Kentucky Stone Co., Inc., 408 N.E.2d 575 (Ind. Ct. App. 1980); 425 N.E.2d 125 (Ind. 1981); Ang v. Hospital Corp. of America, 395 N.E.2d 441 (Ind. Ct. App. 1979); Constanzi v. Ryan, 368 N.E.2d 12 (Ind. Ct. App. 1977). ***PRACTICE AREAS:*** Business Litigation; Covenants Not To Compete; Class Action Defense; Commercial Litigation; Uniform Commercial Code; Franchise Litigation; Insurance Coverage; Litigation; Complex Litigation; Products Liability; Heavy Equipment Products Liability; Manufacturers Liability; Broker Dealer Arbitration; Securities Litigation; Creditors Rights; Insurance Defense. ***Email:*** james.petersen@icemiller.com

THOMAS W. PETERSON, born Union City, Indiana, July 15, 1960; admitted to bar, 1986, Indiana. *Education:* Duke University (A.B., magna cum laude, 1983; J.D., 1986); University of Kent, Canterbury, England (University Diploma, 1982). Senior Editor, Alaska Law Review, 1985-1986. *Member:* National Association of Bond Lawyers. ***PRACTICE AREAS:*** Municipal Finance; Tax-Exempt Financing Law; Housing Finance; Industrial Revenue Bond Law; Lease Law; School Law. ***Email:*** peterson@icemiller.com

TODD W. PONDER, born Indianapolis, Indiana, August 22, 1959; admitted to bar, 1984, Georgia and U.S. District Court, Northern, Middle and Southern Districts of Georgia; 1987, Indiana and U.S. District Court, Northern and Southern Districts of Indiana; 1990, U.S. District Court, Southern District of Illinois; 1991, U.S. Court of Appeals, Seventh Circuit. *Education:* DePauw University (B.A., magna cum laude, 1981); University of Chicago (J.D., 1984). Phi Beta Kappa; Omicron Delta Epsilon; Alpha Lambda Delta; Gold

(This Listing Continued)

ICE MILLER, Indianapolis—Continued

Key; Mortar Board; Sigma Chi (President). Listed in Who's Who in American Law and Who's Who Among Rising Young Lawyers. *Member:* Indianapolis, Indiana State and American Bar Associations; State Bar of Georgia; National Association of Bond Lawyers; Indiana Municipal Lawyers Association. ***PRACTICE AREAS:*** Municipal Finance (Bond) Law; Tax Exempt Financing Law; Public Authority Financing Law; University Law; Non-Profit Organizations. ***Email:*** ponder@icemiller.com

JOHN F. PRESCOTT, JR., born Highland Park, Michigan, March 30, 1950; admitted to bar, 1979, Indiana; U.S. Court of Appeals, Seventh, Ninth and Federal Circuits; registered to practice before U.S. Patent and Trademark Office. *Education:* General Motors Institute (B.S.M.E., 1973); University of Michigan (M.S.M.E., 1973); Indiana University (J.D., summa cum laude, 1979). *Member:* Indiana State and American Bar Associations; American Intellectual Property Law Association. ***PRACTICE AREAS:*** Intellectual Property Litigation; Copyrights; Computer Software Litigation; Patent Litigation; Trade Secrets; Trademarks. ***Email:*** prescott@icemiller.com

MELISSA PROFFITT REESE, born Kansas City, Missouri, May 17, 1960; admitted to bar, 1985, Indiana. *Education:* Indiana University (B.A., with distinction, 1982; J.D., cum laude, 1985). Phi Beta Kappa; Phi Eta Sigma; Alpha Lambda Delta; Dean's List; Merit Scholarship. Seminars: "HIPAA & COBRA: Coordinating the New Health Care Law & the Old," sponsored by the 1998 Mid-America Human Resources Symposium, Cincinnati, Ohio, June 15, 1998; "HIPAA, NMHPA, MHPA - The Remaining Unanswered Questions," sponsored by the Central Indiana Chapter Certified Employee Benefit Specialist (CEBS), April 30, 1998. Publications: Nondiscrimination Rules for Welfare Benefit Plans, 9 IBJ No. 4 (May 9-15, 1988); Strikes and the Obligation to Continue Group Health Coverage Under COBRA, 39 Labor L.J., No. 11 (November, 1988); Repeal of Code Section 89 - Good News, Bad News, 10 IBJ No. 36 (December 18-24, 1989); How to Coordinate Employee Benefits with the Americans with Disabilities Act, 17 ALI-ABA Course Mat. J., No. 4 (February, 1993); Coordinating Employee Benefits with the Americans with Disabilities Act, ALI-ABA Course Mat. J. (September, 1993); A Day as a Medical Intern, 85 IMSB No. 7 (March, 1996); Companies Prepare for Speedy 401(k) Rules, 17 IBJ No. 24 (September 2-8, 1996); In Some Courts, It's Still a Man's World, 17 IBJ No. 26 (September 16-22, 1996); Health Care 1997-1998 Legislative Update, Issues in Business (September, 1997). Featured in "Significant New Requirements for Group Health Plans," Indiana Constructor, October/November, 1997. Co-Managing Partner, 2004—. Selected for the 2006 edition of "Best Lawyers in America," Corporate Counsel Magazine. Chosen for 2000 "Forty Under 40," Indianapolis Business Journal; 2004 and 2005 Indiana's "Top 25 Female Super Lawyers," and "Super Lawyer/2004 and 2005" in Employee Benefits, Indianapolis Monthly; "2002 Notable American Women," American Biographical Institute. Member: Team 100—Women Leaders for Lugar 2000; 10th Anniversary Celebration Committee for the Richard G. Lugar Excellence in Public Service Series - 1999; Chairman of the Fund Raising Committee, 1997, 1998 and 1999. President, 2000— and Member of Board of Governors and participant in the Richard G. Lugar Excellence in Public Service Series; Former Member of WEB, Inc.; Published in Who's Who in American Law; Published in Strathmore's Who's Who; Former Member of Network of Women in Business; Board Member of Social Health Association of Central Indiana 1994-2000; President, 1999-2000, Program Committee Chairperson, 1995-1996, Board Development Committee Chairperson, 1996-1997; Staff Benefits Study Committee for Orchard School, 1996-1997. Participant in the Indianapolis Medical Society's 1996 Mini-Internship Program; Member, United Way of Central Indiana Leadership Alumni Triad; Board Member, Indiana Leadership Coalition, Inc., 1994-1996; Participant, Executive Women's Leadership Program, United Way of Central Indiana, 1994-1995. Delegate, Republican National Convention, 2004. Member, Presidential Electoral College, 2004. ***PRACTICE AREAS:*** COBRA; Deferred Compensation; Employee Compensation; ERISA; Executive Compensation; Flexible Benefit Plans; Health Benefits; Non-Qualified Benefits; Pension and Profit Sharing Plans; Pension Plans; Profit Sharing; Qualified Retirement Plans; Retirement Benefit Plans; 401(k) Plans. ***Email:*** melissa.reese@icemiller.com

MARK J. RICHARDS, born Columbus, Indiana, June 5, 1960; admitted to bar, 1985, Indiana and U.S. District Court, Northern and Southern Districts of Indiana; U.S. Tax Court; U.S. Court of Appeals, Seventh Circuit. *Education:* Indiana University (B.S., with honors, 1982; J.D., summa cum laude, 1985). Beta Gamma Sigma. Associate Editor, Indiana Law Review, 1984-1985. *Member:* Indianapolis (Past-President, Taxation Section) and Indiana State (Member, Taxation Section) Bar Associations; Indiana Manufacturers Association (Member, Tax Committee); Indiana State Chamber of Commerce (Member, Tax Committee). ***REPORTED CASES:*** RCA Corporation v. State Board of Tax Comm's, 528 NE 2d 125, (1988); Amax Inc. v. State Board of Tax Comm's, 552 NE 2d 850, (1990); SFN Shareholders Grantor Trust v. Indiana Dept. of State Revenue, 603 NE 2d 194, (1992); F.A. Wilhelm Construction Co., Inc. v. Indiana Dept. of State Revenue, 586 NE 2d 953, (1992); Indiana Dept. of State Revenue v. Caylor-Nickel Clinic P.C., 587 NE 2d 1311, (1992); Lubricant Consultants, Inc. v. Indiana Dept. of State Revenue 621 N.E. 2d 677, (1993); Hammond Construction, Inc. v. Indiana Dept. of State Revenue 620 N.E. 2d 761, (1993); USAir, Inc. v. Indiana Dept. of State Revenue, 623 N.E.2d 466 (Ind. Tax, 1993); Universal Group Ltd. v. Indiana Dept of State Revenue, 642 N.E.2d 553 (Ind. Tax, 1994) City Securities Corp. v. Indiana Dept. of State Revenue 704 N.E. 2d 1122, (1998); Hyatt Corp. v. Indiana Dept. of State Revenue, 695 N.E. 2d 1051, (1998); First Chicago NBD Corp. v. Indiana Dept. of State Revenue, 708 N.E. 2d 631, (1999); Edgcomb Metals Co. v. Dept. of Local Gov't Fin., 762 N.E. 2d 259, (2002) Christine M. Hackl v. Comm'r of Internal Revenue, Albert J. Hackl v. Comm'r of Internal Revenue, 118 T.C. 279 (Mar 27, 2002); Aztar Indiana Gaming Corporation v. Indiana Dept. of State Revenue, 806 N.E. 2d 381 (Ind. Tax 2004); pet. for rev. denied, 2004 Ind. Tax LEXIS 73; Grand Victoria Casino & Resort, L.P. v. Indiana Dept. of State Revenue, 789 N.E. 2d 1041 (Ind. Tax 2003). ***PRACTICE AREAS:*** Business Law; Sports Law; Motor Sports Law; Sports Contracts; Federal Taxation; State Taxation; Tax Litigation; Tax Controversies. ***Email:*** mark.richards@icemiller.com

SUSAN BARNHIZER RIVAS, born Noblesville, Indiana, August 13, 1952; admitted to bar, 1984, Indiana; 1990, District of Columbia. *Education:* Purdue University (B.A., with distinction, 1974; M.A., 1976); Indiana University School of Law (J.D., summa cum laude, 1984). Associate Editor, Indiana Law Review, 1983-1984. Speeches: "American Bar Association, Health Law Section - Antitrust Analysis of Physicians' Unions, Critical Legal Topics for the Physician Lawyer and Medical Practitioner" (CABA-AMA June 18, 1999); "NHLA/AAHA - Antitrust in Healthcare Field," *Strategic Alliances for Hospitals and Managed Care* (NHLA/AAHA, 1998); "Antitrust Aspects of Mergers, Acquisitions and Joint Ventures," *Buying and Selling Privately Held Businesses* (The Cambridge Institute, 1997); "Antitrust Aspects of Mergers, Acquisitions and Joint Ventures," *Buying and Selling Privately Held Businesses* (The Cambridge Institute, 1996); "Analysis of Health Care Provider Networks Under Federal Antitrust Law," *Market Dynamics: Antitrust Developments in Health Care Transactions and Network Development* (Health Care Section of Indianapolis Bar Association, 1996); "Getting Your Hospital Ready for an Antitrust Investigation," (Healthcare Financial Management Association, April Educational Institute, 1996); "Issues under Federal Antitrust Law in Hospital Acquisitions, Mergers, Consolidations, Joint Ventures and Affiliations," *Legal Forum For Hospital Attorneys and Administrators* (25th Annual Indiana Hospital Attorneys Meeting, 1995). Publications: Author, "Skyrocketing Penalties Imposed for Noncompliance with Premerger Notification," *Indiana Journal of Commerce & Industry,* (June 15-July 14, 1997); Co-Author, "Negotiating Mergers, Acquisitions, and Joint Ventures—Avoiding Antitrust Pitfalls," *MMI Companies, Inc., Advisory,* Vol. XIII, No. 2 (June, 1997); Co-Author, "Getting Your Hospital Ready for an Antitrust Investigation (It Could Happen To You)," *Hoosier Times,* (Healthcare Financial Management Association, May, 1996). *Member:* American Bar Association. ***PRACTICE AREAS:*** Antitrust; Joint Ventures; Mergers and Acquisitions; Business Law. ***Email:*** rivas@icemiller.com

GEORGE P. RYAN, born February 4, 1906; admitted to bar, 1940; died October 29, 1977.

PHILLIP R. SCALETTA, III, born Iowa City, Iowa, December 18, 1949; admitted to bar, 1975, Indiana. *Education:* Purdue University (B.S.I.M., with highest distinction, 1971; M.S.I.A., with highest distinction, 1972); Indiana University (J.D., cum laude, 1975). Phi Beta Kappa; Beta Gamma Sigma; Phi Eta Sigma. Approved Court Civil Mediator. *Member:* Indianapolis and Indiana State Bar Associations; Defense Research Institute and The International Association of Defense Counsel. ***PRACTICE AREAS:*** Environmental Law; Business Litigation; Contract Litigation; Complex Litigation. ***Email:*** scaletta@icemiller.com

THOMAS F. SCHNELLENBERGER, born Corpus Christi, Texas, August 17, 1954; admitted to bar, 1979, Indiana. *Education:* University of Notre Dame (B.B.A., 1976); Indiana University, Bloomington (J.D., cum laude, 1979). *Member:* Indianapolis (Chair, Tax Section, 1995), Indiana State and American Bar Associations. ***PRACTICE AREAS:*** Federal Income Tax; Estate Planning. ***Email:*** schnelle@icemiller.com

MARC W. SCISCOE, born Elkhart, Indiana, February 3, 1954; admitted to bar, 1980, Indiana. *Education:* Brown University (A.B., magna cum laude, 1977); Harvard University (J.D., 1980). Phi Beta Kappa. Publications and Seminars: "Nondiscrimination Requirements for Welfare Plans," 1988; "Introduction to ESOPs," 1988; "Due Diligence/Employee Benefits Issues," 1988; "Current Issues Relating to Employee Benefit Plans," 1989; "Deferred Compensation for Executives," 1990; "Description and Purposes of Employee Stock Ownership Plans," 1990; "Selected Topics Involving Litigation and Administrative Sanctions Under ERISA," 1990; "ERISA Liabilities Arising Out of Multiemployer Plans," 1991; "Trustee Fiduciary Obligations and Responsibilities," 1991; "Final Regulations Under Sections 401(k) and 401 (m)," 1991; "ERISA Litigation Issues," 1992; "New Regulations Regarding Plan Distributions," 1992; "Legal Developments Affecting Employee Stock Ownership Plans;" "Recent Developments In Employee Benefits Litigation," 1993; "How to Successfully Design and Implement a 401 (k) Plan," 1994; "Controlling Financial and Legal Exposure With Respect to Your Employee Benefit Plans," 1994; "Comparison of Defined Benefit Plans to Defined Contribution Plans," 1995; "Employee Stock Ownership Plans," 1995; "Fiduciary Obligations of Employee Stock Ownership Trustees," 1996; "Introduction to Medical Savings Accounts," 1997; "ERISA Litigation Update," 1998; "Evolution of ERISA," 1999; "Retirement Plan Distributions," 2000; "Recent Developments Affecting Estate Planning For Retirement Plan Distributions," 2000; "ERISA Title I Fiduciary Responsibility," 2001; "Fiduciary Liabilities Under ERISA," 2002; "Employee Benefit Plan Impact of Sarbanes-Oxley Act," 2003; "Legal Requirements for Cafeteria Plans," 2003; "Equity-Based Incentive Compensation," 2004. *Member:* Indianapolis, Indiana State and American (Section of Taxation; Employee Benefits Committee) Bar Associations; Indiana Pension Conference. ***LANGUAGES:*** French and Spanish. ***PRACTICE AREAS:*** Employee Benefits Law; Executive Compensation; Leveraged ESOPs; ERISA; Retirement Law; Litigation. ***Email:*** marc.sciscoe@icemiller.com

REBECCA J. SEAMANDS, born Bloomington, Illinois, May 27, 1965; admitted to bar, 1992, Indiana and U.S. District Court, Northern and Southern Districts of Indiana. *Education:* University of Illinois (B.S., 1987); Indiana University (J.D., 1992). Author: "Lawsuit for Sale: Assignability of Legal Malpractice Claims," 25 Indiana Law Rev 257 (1991). *Member:* Indiana State Bar Association. ***PRACTICE AREAS:*** Construction Law; Business Litigation; General Litigation. ***Email:*** seamands@icemiller.com

CHRISTOPHER S. SEARS, born Atlanta, Georgia, March 16, 1968; admitted to bar, 1994, Indiana. *Education:* Indiana University (B.A., 1990); Indiana University School of Law (J.D., cum laude, 1994). Author: "The Indiana Network for Patient Care: A Case Study" (with Victoria M. Prescott, Esq. and Clement J. McDonald, M.D.), September, 2005; "HIPAA is Here: Has Your County Started Yet?" (with Stephanie Alden Smithey), Indiana News 92 (March/April 2003); "USERRA - Protecting Employees' Rights" (with Mary Beth Braitman), The Wyoming Banker (January 2002); "Why Do Managed Care Organizations Do Credentialing?" (with Sherry A. Fabina-Abney), National Association Medical Staff Services Journal (Spring 1996). Speaker: "The Perfect Storm of Legal Issues from the Interoperable Electronic Health Record," American Health Lawyers Association National Teleconference (December 16, 2004); "HIPAA Privacy Update and Security Rule for Employers and Health Plans," Indiana Benefits Conference, Indianapolis, IN (September 14, 2004); "Defined Contribution Alphabet Soup - HSAs, HRAs, FSAs & MSAs" and "Welfare Plan Roundtable," Church Plan Workshop, Scottsdale, AZ (April 19-21, 2004); "HIPAA Privacy: The Final Days Before Compliance," American Bar Association Joint Committee on Employee Benefits National Teleconference/Live Audio Webcast (March 2, 2004); "Welfare Plan Hot Topics: HIPAA, Domestic Partners, Subrogation & COBRA Notices," Employee Benefits Seminar, Indiana Chamber of Commerce, Indianapolis, IN (January 29, 2004); "What's New With COBRA?," American Bar Association Joint Committee on Employee Benefits National Teleconference/Live Audio Webcast (October 16,

(This Listing Continued)

2003); "HIPAA - Where are We Now?," 48th Annual Employee Benefits Conference, International Foundation of Employee Benefit Plans, Toronto, Ontario (September 21-22, 2002). Member, Board of Directors, Indiana Perinatal Network, Inc. *Member:* American Health Lawyers Association; American Bar Association (Member of Health Law Section and Vice-Chair of Employee Benefits Interest Group). ***REPORTED CASES:*** Spangler, Jennings & Dougherty v. Indiana Insurance, 729 N.E.2d 117 (Ind. 2000); Wine-Settergren v. Lamey, 716 N.E.2d 381 (Ind. 1999). ***PRACTICE AREAS:*** Health Care; Hospital Law; Employee Benefits; Privacy Law; Health Benefits; ERISA; Pension and Profit Sharing Plans. ***Email:*** christopher.sears@icemiller.com

MYRA C. SELBY, born Saginaw, Michigan, July 1, 1955; admitted to bar, 1980, District of Columbia, U.S. Court of Appeals, District of Columbia Circuit; 1983, Indiana; 1985, U.S. Court of Appeals, Eighth Circuit; 1991, U.S. Court of Appeals, Seventh Circuit. *Education:* Kalamazoo College (B.A., with honors, 1977); University of Michigan (J.D., 1980). Author: "Terminating the Physician-Patient Relationship," Marion County Medical Society Bulletin, March 1985; "Reform Revisited, a Review of the Indiana Medical Malpractice Act 10 Years Later," Indiana Law Review, Volume XIX, Number 4, 1986; "Health Law Update (1988)," 18th Annual Meeting, National Health Lawyers Association; "Institutional Review Boards and Human Research Issues," Risk Management Handbook for Health Care Facilities, 1990; "Hospital and Physician Liability: A Legal and Risk Management Overview," Focus Series, National Health Lawyers Association, 1992; Stanley K. Lacy Leadership Series XIII. Columnist, Indianapolis Business Journal, 2000—. Director, Health Care Policy, State of Indiana, 1993. Associate Justice, Indiana Supreme Court, 1995. Member and Chair, Indiana Supreme Court Commission on Race and Gender Fairness. Member: Wishard Advantage Advisory Committee; Indiana Women in Law Conference, 1998-2002. *Member:* Indiana State and American (Member: Standing Committee on Judicial Independence; Committee on Legal Education and Admission to the Bar; Coalition for Justice and State Justice Initiatives; Satellite Seminar, Health Law Update 2001, American College of Health Care Executives) Bar Associations; American Law Institute (Member and Advisor to Restatement of Torts 3d General Principles); National Health Lawyers Association (Member, Women in the Profession, Commission, 1988—). ***PRACTICE AREAS:*** Health Law; Hospital Law; Medicare and Medicaid; Professional Malpractice; Nursing Home Litigation. ***Email:*** selby@icemiller.com

JAMES A. SHANAHAN, born Rushville, Indiana, October 27, 1951; admitted to bar, 1977, Indiana; 1997, Illinois. *Education:* University of Notre Dame (B.B.A., cum laude, 1973); Indiana University (J.D., magna cum laude, 1977). Order of the Coif. *Member:* National Association of Bond Lawyers; Indiana Municipal Lawyers Association. ***PRACTICE AREAS:*** Municipal Finance; Bond Law; Lease Law; Airport Law; School Law; Tax-Exempt Financing Law. ***Email:*** shanahan@icemiller.com

PAUL H. SINCLAIR, born Green Bay, Wisconsin, March 20, 1966; admitted to bar, 1993, Indiana. *Education:* University of Wisconsin, Eau Claire; Brigham Young University (B.A., 1990); Southern Illinois University (J.D., summa cum laude, 1993). Phi Eta Sigma. Recipient, Marriott Scholarship. *Member:* Indiana State Bar Association (Council Member, Labor and Employment Law Section). ***PRACTICE AREAS:*** Employment Law; Labor Law; Wrongful Discharge; Employment Discrimination Law; Employee Drug Testing. ***Email:*** sinclair@icemiller.com

RICHARD A. SMIKLE, born St. Joseph, Michigan, July 30, 1955; admitted to bar, 1980, Indiana; U.S. Supreme Court; U.S. Court of Appeals, Seventh Circuit; U.S. District Court, Northern and Southern Districts of Indiana; U.S. District Court, Eastern District of Wisconsin. *Education:* Kalamazoo College (B.A., 1977); Drake University (J.D., cum laude, 1980); University of Notre Dame (E.M.B.A., with focus in Finance, cum laude, 2005). Law Clerk to Chief Judge, U.S. District Court, Northern District of Indiana, 1980-1982. *Member:* Indianapolis, Indiana State and American Bar Associations; The Association of Trial Lawyers of America; National Association of College and University Attorneys. ***PRACTICE AREAS:*** Trial Practice; Complex Litigation; Products Liability Law (Defective Products); Construction Law; Colleges and Universities; Probate Litigation; Business Litigation; Commercial Litigation; Dispute Resolution/Litigation; Employment Litigation; Federal Litigation. ***Email:*** richard.smikle@icemiller.com

THOMAS C. SMITH, born Fort Wayne, Indiana, 1961; admitted to bar, 1988, Illinois; 1992, Indiana. *Education:* Indiana University (B.A., 1983; J.D., cum laude, 1988). Phi Beta Kappa. *Member:* National Association of Bond Lawyers; National Council of State Housing Agencies. ***PRACTICE AREAS:*** Public Finance; Securities. ***Email:*** tom.smith@icemiller.com

DONALD M. SNEMIS, born Gary, Indiana, June 29, 1963; admitted to bar, 1988, Indiana and U.S. District Court, Northern and Southern Districts of Indiana; 1990, U.S. Court of Appeals, Seventh Circuit; 1994, U.S. Supreme Court; 2001, U.S. District Court, Southern District of Illinois. *Education:* Ball State University (B.A., 1985); University of Notre Dame (J.D., cum laude, 1988). Publications: "Practitioners Guide To Indemnity," 7 Res Gestae 309-314 (Jan., 1994). Seminars: "Successful Handling of Wrongful Death Cases: The Experts Share Their Secrets" (1998-2000); "Taking and Defending Depositions Effectively" (2001-2002); "Evidence, Cross Examination & Closing Argument" (2003); "Business Torts in Indiana" (2005). *Member:* Indiana State Bar Association; Defense Research Institute. ***REPORTED CASES:*** Dillon v. Combs, 895 F.2d 1175 (7th Cir. 1990); Loos v. Farmer's Tractor and Implement Co., Inc., 738 F.Supp. 323 (S.D. Ind. 1990); Allied Resin Corporation v. Waltz, 574 N.E.2d 913 (Ind. 1991); CSL Utilities, Inc. v. Jennings Water, Inc., 16 F.3d 130 (7th Cir. 1993); In re Commercial Explosives Litigation, 1996 WL 795270 (D. Utah 1996); Holtz v. Hilliard, 1 F.Supp.2d 887 (S.D. Ind. 1998); Lenhardt Tool & Die Company, Inc. v. Lumpe, 722 N.E.2d 824 (Ind. 2000); Zurich American Ins. Group v. Wynkoop, 746 N.E.2d 985 (Ind. Ct. App. 2001); Energy Plus Consulting, LLC v. Illinois Fuel Company, LLC, 371 F.3d 907 (7th Cir. 2004); United Consulting Engineers v. Board of Commissioners of Hancock County, 810 N.E.2d 351 (Ind. Ct. App. 2004). ***PRACTICE AREAS:*** Business Litigation; Environmental Law; Trial Practice; Product Liability Law; Tort Law; Personal Injury Law. ***Email:*** Donald.Snemis@icemiller.com

JACK R. SNYDER, born Gary, Indiana, June 24, 1940; admitted to bar, 1965, Indiana. *Education:* Brown University (A.B., 1962); University of Michigan (LL.B., 1964). Phi Delta Phi. *Member:* Indianapolis, Indiana State and American Bar Associations. ***PRACTICE AREAS:*** Closely Held Businesses; Entrepreneurial Services; Sports Law; Intellectual Property Law; Estate Planning. ***Email:*** jack.snyder@icemiller.com

(This Listing Continued)

BARTON T. SPRUNGER, born Berne, Indiana, March 18, 1946; admitted to bar, 1975, Indiana. *Education:* Purdue University (B.S., with honors, 1968); Wayne Law School and University of Michigan (J.D., cum laude, 1975). Sigma Pi Sigma. *Member:* Indianapolis, Indiana State and American (Member, Committee on State and Local Taxes, 1990—) Bar Associations. ***LANGUAGES:*** Spanish. ***REPORTED CASES:*** U-Haul International, Inc. v. Indiana Dep't of State Revenue, 826 N.E.2d 713; Knox County Property Tax Assessment Bd. of Appeals v. Grandview Care, Inc., 826 N.E.2d 177; Aztar Indiana Gaming Corp. v. Indiana Dep't of State Revenue, 806 N.E.2d 381; Grand Victoria Casino & Resort, L.P. v. Indiana Dep't of State Revenue, 789 N.E.2d 1041; U-Haul Co. of Indiana, Inc. v. Indiana Dep't of State Revenue, 784 N.E.2d 1078; Enterprise Leasing Company of Chicago v. Indiana Dep't of State Revenue, 779 N.E.2d 1284; B.P. Products North America, Inc. v. Dep't of Local Government Finance, 774 N.E.2d 122; Edgcomb Metals Co. v. Dept. of Local Government Finance, 762 N.E.2d 259; First Chicago NBD Corp. v. Indiana Dept. of Revenue, 708 N.E.2d 631; PPG Industries, Inc. v. State Board of Tax Commissioners, 706 N.E.2d 611; City Securities Corp. v. Indiana Dept. of Revenue, 704 N.E.2d 1122; Hyatt Corp. v. Indiana Dept. of Revenue, 695 N.E.2d 1051; SFN Shareholders Grantor Trust v. Indiana Dept. of Revenue, 603 N.E.2d 194; Indiana Dept. of Revenue v. Caylor-Nickel Clinic, 587 N.E.2d 1311; AMAX Inc. v. State Board of Tax Commissioners, 522 N.E.2d 850; RCA Corporation v. State Bd. of Tax Comm'rs, 528 N.E.2d 125; Indiana Dep't of State Revenue v. AMAX, Inc. 404 N.E.2d 1173; Indiana Dep't of State Revenue v. General Foods Corp., 427 N.E.2d 665; State Bd. of Tax Comm'rs v. Aluminum Co. of America, 402 N.E.2d 1316; Indiana Dep't of State Revenue v. Hertz Corp., 457 N.E.2d 246; Indiana Dep't of State Revenue v. Endress & Hauser, Inc., 404 N.E.2d 1173. ***PRACTICE AREAS:*** Federal Taxation; State Taxation; Local Taxation. ***Email:*** sprunger@icemiller.com

DALE E. STACKHOUSE, born Cambridge, Massachusetts, June 5, 1962; admitted to bar, 1988, Indiana. *Education:* DePauw University (B.A., 1984); Harvard Law School (J.D., 1988); Fletcher School of Law and Diplomacy (M.A.L.D., 1988). Phi Beta Kappa. ***LANGUAGES:*** Japanese and French. ***PRACTICE AREAS:*** International Business Law; Import and Export Law; Business Law; Corporate Law; Customs Law; U.S. Foreign Trade Zones; Joint Ventures; Distribution Agreements; Dealer and Distributor Termination; International Commercial Law; Corporate Reorganization; Mergers and Acquisitions. ***Email:*** dale.stackhouse@icemiller.com

LISA A. STONE, born Indianapolis, Indiana, July 3, 1954; admitted to bar, 1980, Indiana. *Education:* Indiana University (B.A., with distinction, 1976; M.B.A., 1980; J.D., magna cum laude, 1980). Phi Delta Phi. Member, 1988— and Board Member, 1996-1999, Planned Giving Group of Indiana. Board Member and President, IUPUI Jaguars Athletic Club, 1996— and Member, IUPUI Chancellor's Advisory Board, 1999—, Board Member: Community Hospitals Foundation, 1999—; Family Service Association, 2000-2001. Listed in: Best Lawyers in America, 1990—; Best Lawyers in Indianapolis, Indianapolis Monthly Magazine, 1997—. *Member:* Indianapolis (Estate Planning and Administration Section, 1988—; Executive Council, 1990-1995; Section Chairman, 1994), Indiana State and American (Member, Probate and Real Property and Taxation Sections) Bar Associations; Estate Planning Council of Indianapolis. Fellow, American College of Trust and Estate Counsel. ***REPORTED CASES:*** MacLean v. Ford Motor Company, 831 F.2d 723 (7th Circuit). ***PRACTICE AREAS:*** Tax Planning; Business Succession Planning; Transfer Tax; Trusts and Estates; Estate and Gift Taxation; Nonprofit and Charitable Organizations. ***Email:*** stone@icemiller.com

MICHAEL A. SWIFT, born South Bend, Indiana, May 11, 1957; admitted to bar, 1994, Indiana; registered to practice before U.S. Patent and Trademark Office. *Education:* Tri-State University (B.S.Che., 1980); Indiana University School of Law (J.D., cum laude, 1993). ***PRACTICE AREAS:*** Intellectual Property; Litigation; Information and Privacy; Business Law. ***Email:*** swift@icemiller.com

JAY G. TAYLOR, born Paducah, Kentucky, November 18, 1940; admitted to bar, 1967, Illinois and Indiana; (U.S. Court of Customs and Patent Appeals, 1976-1982); 1970, U.S. District Court, Northern District of Illinois including Trial Bar, Northern and Southern District of Indiana and U.S. Court of Appeals, Seventh Circuit; 1979, U.S. Court of Appeals, Second Circuit; 1982, U.S. Court of Appeals for the Federal Circuit; registered to practice before the U.S. Patent and Trademark Office. *Education:* University of Cincinnati (B.S.M.E., 1964); Indiana University (J.D., magna cum laude, 1967). Order of the Coif; Phi Delta Phi; Pi Tau Sigma. Note Editor, Indiana Law Journal, 1966-1967. Author: "Intellectual Property, A General Practitioner's Guide," Illinois Bar Journal, 1990; Res Gestae, 1991. Contributing Author: "The Art & Science of Patent Law," Aspatore Books, 2004. Registered Mediator, Indiana. *Member:* Indiana State (Past Chairman, Intellectual Property Section), Federal Circuit and American Bar Associations; Intellectual Property Law Association of Chicago; American Intellectual Property Law Association. [Capt., U.S. Army, 1967-1969]. ***REPORTED CASES:*** Consolidated Aluminum v. Foesco, 910 F. 2d 804; Faulkner v. Baldwin Piano & Organ Co., 561 F. 2d 677. ***PRACTICE AREAS:*** Intellectual Property; Patent; Trademark; Copyright; Trade Secrets Law; Unfair Competition; Computers and Software; Mediation. ***Email:*** jay.taylor@icemiller.com

JOHN J. THAR, born Evanston, Illinois, January 30, 1948; admitted to bar, 1975, Indiana and U.S. District Court, Southern District of Indiana; 1978, U.S Court of Appeals, Seventh Circuit. *Education:* Western Michigan University (B.A., 1970); Indiana University School of Law (J.D., magna cum laude, 1975). Former Member, United States Attorney's Office for the Southern District of Indiana, 1978-1993. Assistant U.S. Attorney, Chief of the Organized Crime Drug Enforcement Task Force, 1986-1993. Interim U.S. Attorney, 1993. First Executive Director, Indiana Gaming Commission, 1993-2002. ***PRACTICE AREAS:*** Gaming; Public Affairs; Litigation. ***Email:*** john.thar@icemiller.com

JOHN R. THORNBURGH, born Indianapolis, Indiana, March 9, 1955; admitted to bar, 1980, Indiana. *Education:* DePauw University (B.A., 1977); University of Illinois (J.D., 1980). Phi Delta Phi. Member, University of Illinois Law Review, 1979-1980. Member, International Moot Court Team. Author: Casenote, "Nelson v. Araiza," Illinois Bar Journal, March 1979; "IRS Rationale on Trustee—Substitution Powers May Spread to Powers of Appointment," The Journal of Taxation, October, 1981. *Member:* Indiana State Bar Association. ***PRACTICE AREAS:*** Corporate Law; Venture Capital Law; Mergers and Acquisitions; Finance Law; Sports and Entertainment Law; Corporate Finance Law. ***Email:*** thornbur@icemiller.com

RICHARD J. THRAPP, born Auburn, Indiana, January 5, 1958; admitted to bar, 1983, Indiana. *Education:* DePauw University (B.A., magna cum laude, 1980); Indiana Univer-

(This Listing Continued)

ICE MILLER, Indianapolis—Continued

sity, Bloomington (J.D., magna cum laude, 1983). Phi Beta Kappa; Omicron Delta Upsilon; Order of the Coif. Member: Indiana Corporate Law Survey Commission; Indiana Limited Liability Company Act Task Force; Indiana Nonprofit Corporation Act Study Committee; Board of Governors of Child Advocates, Inc.; Board of Directors, Indianapolis Zoological Society. *Member:* Indianapolis, Indiana State and American Bar Associations; Indiana Bar Foundation (Member, Board of Directors). Fellow, Indiana Bar Foundation. ***SPECIAL AGENCIES:*** Indiana Corporate Law Survey Commission; Indiana Nonprofit Corporation Act Study Committee; Indiana Limited Liability Company Act Task Force. ***PRACTICE AREAS:*** Business Law; Corporate Law; Commercial Law; Mergers and Acquisitions; Limited Liability Company Law. ***Email:*** richard.thrapp@icemiller.com

MICHAEL L. TOOLEY, born Hartford, Kentucky, April 16, 1966; admitted to bar, 1991, Indiana. *Education:* Vanderbilt University (B.A., summa cum laude, 1988); Duke University (J.D., with high honors, 1991). Member, Moot Court Board. Senior Editor, Law and Contemporary Problems, 1991. *Member:* Indianapolis and Indiana State Bar Associations. ***PRACTICE AREAS:*** Labor Law; Employment Law; Employment Discrimination; Collective Bargaining; Defamation. ***Email:*** tooley@icemiller.com

THOMAS A. WALSH, born White Plains, New York, June 9, 1964; admitted to bar, 1995, Indiana; registered to practice before U.S. Patent and Trademark Office. *Education:* Purdue University (B.S.I.E., 1986); Indiana University Kelley School of Business (M.B.A., 1993); Indiana University (J.D., 1995). ***PRACTICE AREAS:*** Patent Law; Computers and Software; Internet Law; Information and Privacy; Trademarks. ***Email:*** thomas.walsh@icemiller.com

ZEFF A. WEISS, born South Bend, Indiana, February 13, 1957; admitted to bar, 1983, Indiana, U.S. District Court, Northern and Southern Districts of Indiana and Seventh Circuit Court of Appeals. *Education:* Indiana University (B.S., with honors, 1979; J.D., with honors, 1983). Beta Gamma Sigma. Certified Public Accountant, Florida, 1980—. *Member:* Indianapolis, Indiana State and American Bar Associations; American Institute of Certified Public Accountants; American College of Real Estate Lawyers. ***PRACTICE AREAS:*** Real Estate Development; Real Estate Finance; Multi-Unit Residential Real Estate; Zoning Law; Construction Law; Eminent Domain; Foreclosure Law. ***Email:*** zeff.weiss@icemiller.com

L. ALAN WHALEY, born Bloomington, Indiana, May 25, 1954; admitted to bar, 1981, Indiana. *Education:* Indiana University (B.S., magna cum laude, 1977; M.M., magna cum laude, 1979; J.D., cum laude, 1981). President, Moot Court Board. Semifinalist, National Moot Court Competition. Member, Order of Barristers. Associate, Indiana Law Journal, 1979-1981. Associate Instructor, Appellate Advocacy, Indiana University School of Law at Bloomington, 1980-1981. Law Clerk to Hon. S. Hugh Dillin, U.S. District Court, Southern District of Indiana, 1981-1983. Faculty Member, Indiana Trial Advocacy Skills College, Indiana Continuing Legal Education Foundation. Former Chair: Advisory Committee, St. Vincent Hospice; Advisory Board, St. Vincent Stress Centers. Board Member and Former President, International Violin Competition of Indianapolis. Former Board Member and Officer, Indiana Repertory Theatre. Chair, Board of Directors, Indiana Blood Center. *Member:* Indiana State Bar Association (Member, Sections on: Health Law; Appellate Practice); American Health Lawyers Association. ***REPORTED CASES:*** In re Commitment of M.Z. v. Clarian Health Partners, 829 N.E.2d 634 (Ind. Ct. App. 2005); Longa v. Vicory, 829 N.E.2d 546 (Ind. Ct. App. 2005); In re Commitment of M.M. v. Clarian Health Parnters, 826 N.E.2d 90 (Ind. Ct. App. 2005); Goodwine v. Goodwine, 819 N.E.2d 824 (Ind. Ct. App. 2004); Monroe Guaranty Ins. v. Langreck, 816 N.E.2d 485 (Ind. Ct. App. 2004); The Osler Institute v. Forde, 333 F.3d 832 (7th Cir. 2003), cert. denied, 540 U.S. 1177, 124 S.Ct. 1407, 158 L.Ed.2d 78 (2004); Ziliak v. AstraZeneca, 324 F.3d 518 (7th Cir. 2003); Hearn v. Hinshaw, 762 N.E.2d 791 (Ind. Ct. App. 2001), trans. denied, 783 N.E.2d 690 (Ind. 2002), cert. denied, 538 U.S. 922, 123 S.Ct. 1573, 155 L.Ed.2d 312 (2003); Hopster v. Burgeson, 750 N.E.2d 841 (Ind.Ct. App. 2001); Butler ex rel. Estate of Butler v. Kokomo Rehabilitation Hospital, 744 N.E.2d 1041 (Ind. Ct. App. 2001); Narducci v. Tedrow, 736 N.E.2d 1288 (Ind. Ct. App. 2000); Etienne v. Caputi, 679 N.E.2d 922 (Ind. Ct. App. 1997); Matter of Lawrance, 579 N.E.2d 32 (Ind. 1991); Rodenbeck v. Marathon Petroleum Co., 742 F. Supp. 1448 (N.D. Ind. 1990); Hockett v. Breunig, 526 N.E.2d 995 (Ind. Ct. App. 1988); Sloan v. Metropolitan Health Council of Indianapolis, 516 N.E.2d 1104 (Ind. Ct. App. 1987). ***PRACTICE AREAS:*** Appellate Practice (25%); Litigation (20%); Health Law (15%); Long Term Care (15%); Nursing Home Regulation (15%); Administrative Law (10%). ***Email:*** whaley@icemiller.com

PHILIP A. WHISTLER, born Indianapolis, Indiana, March 30, 1952; admitted to bar, 1978, Indiana. *Education:* Stanford University (B.A., 1974); Harvard University (J.D., cum laude, 1978). Member, Board of Student Advisors, 1976-1978. Listed in: Chambers' America's Leading Business Lawyers; The Best Lawyers in America. Member: Civil Justice Reform Act Advisory Committee, S. District of Indiana, 1991—; Marion County Judicial Nominating Commission, 1988-1991; Board of Directors of Indianapolis Legal Aid Society, 2005. *Member:* Indianapolis, Indiana State and American (Member, Litigation Section, Antitrust Section and Forum Committee on Franchising) Bar Associations. ***REPORTED CASES:*** Harold Wright Co. v. E.I. DuPont de Nemours & Co., 49 F. 3d 308 (7th Cir, 1995); Hammes v. AAMCO Transmissions, Inc., 33 F. 3d 774; FDIC v. Bierman, 2 F. 3d 1424; Wright-Moore Corp. v. Ricoh, 908 F. 2d 128; Farmers State Bank of Wyatt v. Clark Equipment Co., 582 N.E. 2d 452; First National Bank of Logansport v. Logan Mfg. Co., Inc., 577 N.E. 2d 949; Husted v. McCloud, 450 N.E. 2d 491; Federal Deposit Insurance Corporation v. Stanley, 770 F.Supp. 1281; Great Escape, Inc. v. Union City Body Company, 791 F. 2d 532; Morrison v. Murray Biscuit Company, 797 F.2d 1430. ***PRACTICE AREAS:*** Antitrust Law; Trade Regulation Law; General Civil Litigation. ***Email:*** philip.whistler@icemiller.com

JANICE C. WILKEN, born Fort Riley, Kansas, February 17, 1972; admitted to bar, 1998, Indiana. *Education:* Butler University (B.A., 1995); Indiana University, Indianapolis (J.D., 1998). Phi Delta Phi; Order of the Barristers. Executive Articles Editor, Indiana Law Review. Author: "Title VII and Reverse Discrimination: The Prima Facie Case," Indiana Law Review 31. ***PRACTICE AREAS:*** Business. ***Email:*** whitesid@icemiller.com

MICHAEL A. WILKINS, born Fort Wayne, Indiana, April 10, 1963; admitted to bar, 1988, Indiana. *Education:* University of Notre Dame (B.A., 1985; J.D., 1988). Phi Alpha Delta. Member, National Moot Court Team. *Member:* Indianapolis Bar Association. ***REPORTED CASES:*** Kmart Corp. v. Brzezinski, 540 N.E.2d 1276 (Ind.Ct.App. 1989); Southlake Limousine and Coach, Inc. v. Brock, 576 N.E.2d 677 (Ind.Ct.App. 1991); The Lutheran Hospital of Ft. Wayne, Inc. v. Doe, 639 N.E.2d 687 (Ind.Ct.App. 1994); Bell v. A.R.H., 654 N.E.2d 29 (Ind.Ct.App. 1995); WTHR-TV v. Milam, 690 N.E.2d 1174 (Ind. 1998); Graber v. State Board of Tax Commissioners, 727 N.E.2d 802 (Ind.Tax 2000); Bobrow v. Bobrow, 810 N.E.2d 726 (Ind.Ct.App. 2004); Juarez v. Menard, 366 F.3d 479 (7th Cir. 2004). ***PRACTICE AREAS:*** Appellate Practice; Bad Faith Law; Insurance Defense Law; Media Law; Products Liability Law; Adoption Law; Family Law; Litigation; Sports Law. ***Email:*** wilkins@icemiller.com

GORDON D. WISHARD, born Indianapolis, Indiana, January 7, 1945; admitted to bar, 1969, Indiana and U.S. District Court, Southern District of Indiana; 1974, U.S Court of Appeals, Seventh Circuit; 1980, U.S. Supreme Court; 1988, U.S. Tax Court. *Education:* Williams College (B.A., 1966); Indiana University (J.D., 1969). *Member:* Indianapolis and Indiana State (Chair, Probate, Trust and Real Property Section, 1994) Bar Associations. Fellow, American College of Trust and Estate Counsel. ***PRACTICE AREAS:*** Estate Planning; Estate Administration; Estate and Gift Taxation Law; Charitable Planning; Probate and Trust Law; Estate Litigation; Trust Litigation. ***Email:*** wishard@icemiller.com

KEVIN C. WOODHOUSE, born Highland Park Michigan, May 31, 1964; admitted to bar, 1989, Indiana. *Education:* Indiana University (B.A. with highest distinction, 1985); University of Michigan (J.D., 1989). Phi Beta Kappa; Golden Key. Senior Judge, Writing and Advocacy Program, 1988-1989. *Member:* Indiana State and American Bar Associations; American Health Lawyers Association. ***PRACTICE AREAS:*** Health (Health Care) and Hospital Law; Alternative Health Care Delivery Systems; Health Care Contracts; Health Care Corporate Law; Health Care Mergers and Acquisitions; Health Care Regulation; Managed Care; Managed Care Contracts; Managed Care Liability; Nursing Home Regulation; Physicians Contracts. ***Email:*** woodhous@icemiller.com

MICHAEL A. WUKMER, born Dayton, Ohio, May 8, 1957; admitted to bar, 1984, Indiana. *Education:* University of Cincinnati (B.A., 1981; J.D., 1984). Executive Editor and Student Contributor, University of Cincinnati Law Review, 1983-1984. Writes and speaks regularly on various issues for clients and for members of the bar. Most recent articles, which can be found at *www.icemiller.com,* include *Confidential Information, Covenants Not to Compete & Trade Secrets* (August 2000), *Five Mistakes Employers Make About Restrictive Agreements with Employees* (August 2000) and *Restrictive Covenant Case Alert: Burk v. Heritage United Food & Commercial Workers Union Service Equipment, Inc.* (November 2000). *Member:* Indianapolis, Indiana State and American Bar Associations. ***PRACTICE AREAS:*** Alternative Dispute Resolution; Arbitration; Mediation; Antitrust and Trade Regulation; Covenants Not To Compete; Deceptive Trade Practices; Noncompetition and Non-Solicitation Agreements; Restrictive Covenants; Business Litigation; Business Torts; Federal Civil Practice; Commercial Litigation; Commercial Torts; Corporate Fiduciary Law; Corporate Litigation; Federal Practice; Health Care Litigation; Managed Care Litigation; Employment Contracts; Employment Termination; Executive Severance Contracts; Conflicts of Interest; Legal Ethics; Legal Malpractice; Legal Professional Liability; Defamation; Libel and Slander; Litigation; Civil Litigation; Complex Litigation; Federal Civil Litigation; Federal Litigation; Trial Practice; Municipal Liability; Partnership Dissolution; Products Liability; Securities Litigation; Technical Litigation; Civil Liability; Tort Liability; Trade Secrets; Theft of Trade Secrets; Land Use Litigation. ***Email:*** wukmer@icemiller.com

PATRICIA A. ZELMER, born South Bend, Indiana, December 8, 1960; admitted to bar, 1986, Indiana. *Education:* Indiana University (B.S., 1982); American University; University of Notre Dame (J.D., cum laude, 1986). *Member:* St. Joseph County, Indiana State and American Bar Associations; National Association of Bond Lawyers; Indiana Municipal Lawyers Association. ***PRACTICE AREAS:*** Municipal Finance; Municipal Utility Regulation; Water and Sewer Law. ***Email:*** zelmer@icemiller.com

SENIOR COUNSEL

CRAIG C. BURKE, born New Albany, Indiana, January 11, 1966; admitted to bar, 1994, Indiana. *Education:* Indiana University, Bloomington (B.S., 1988; J.D., magna cum laude, 1994). Order of the Coif. Member, Indiana Law Journal. *Member:* Indianapolis, Indiana State and American Bar Associations; ESOP Association. ***PRACTICE AREAS:*** Employee Stock Ownership Plans; Pension and Profit Sharing; Executive Compensation; ERISA; Flexible Benefits; Health Plans; COBRA; Retirement Plans. ***Email:*** burkec@icemiller.com

WILLIAM P. DIENER, born Indianapolis, Indiana, December 13, 1941; admitted to bar, 1968, Indiana; 1978, Florida; 1990, District of Columbia. *Education:* Wabash College (B.A., 1964); Indiana University (J.D., 1968); George Washington University (LL.M., with highest honors, 1972); Butler University (M.A., 1992). Author: 46 Tulane Law Review, No. 4 pp. 695-723 (1972); 5 Natural Resources Lawyer, No. 3 pp. 378-388 (1972). Adjunct Associate Professor of Law, Indiana University, Fall, 1980 and Spring, 1982. *Member:* Bar Association of the District of Columbia; The Florida Bar; Indiana State, Federal Energy and American (Chairman, Section of Natural Resources, Energy and Environmental Law, 1984-1985) Bar Associations. ***PRACTICE AREAS:*** Utility (Public and Municipal); Energy Regulation Law; Pari-Mutuel Racing; General Business Regulation. ***Email:*** diener@icemiller.com

MARK D. GRANT, born Louisville, Kentucky, October 11, 1959; admitted to bar, 1984, Texas; 1990, Indiana; 2003, Illinois. *Education:* Purdue University (B.S., 1981); University of Houston (J.D., 1984). *Member:* Indianapolis (Member, Business Law Section), Indiana State (Member, Probate, Trust and Real Property Section) and American (Member, Real Property Section and Forum on Affordable Housing and Community Development Law) Bar Associations; State Bar of Texas. ***PRACTICE AREAS:*** Land Acquisitions; Land Sales; Real Estate Leasing; Affordable Housing; Real Estate Acquisitions; Real Estate Contracts; Real Estate Development; Real Estate Finance; Real Estate Sales; Commercial Conveyancing; Low Income Housing. ***Email:*** mark.grant@icemiller.com

KATHLEEN S. KIEFER, born Evansville, Indiana, October 30, 1965; admitted to bar, 1991, Indiana. *Education:* Vanderbilt University (B.A., magna cum laude, 1988); Cor-

(This Listing Continued)

nell Law School (J.D., cum laude, 1991). *Member:* Indiana State Bar Association. ***PRACTICE AREAS:*** Corporate Law; Mergers and Acquisitions; Financing Transactions; Securities. ***Email:*** kathy.kiefer@icemiller.com

PEGGY J. NAILE, born Indianapolis, Indiana, August 12, 1948; admitted to bar, 1989, Indiana. *Education:* Vassar College (A.B. with honors, 1970); Indiana University at Indianapolis (J.D., magna cum laude, 1989). *Member:* Indianapolis and Indiana State Bar Associations. ***PRACTICE AREAS:*** Agricultural Law; Asset Based Finance; Banks and Banking; Business Law; Commercial Bankruptcy; Commercial Foreclosure; Commercial Law; Contracts; Corporate Law; Debtor and Creditor; Equipment Finance and Leasing; Finance; Mergers and Acquisitions; Nonprofit Organizations; Public Finance; Secured Transactions; Workouts. ***Email:*** peggy.naile@icemiller.com

GREGORY D. NICHOLS, born Philadelphia, Pennsylvania, 1955; admitted to bar, 1981, Indiana; U.S. District Court, Northern and Southern Districts of Indiana. *Education:* American University (B.A., 1976); Indiana University School of Law - Indianapolis (J.D., 1981). ***PRACTICE AREAS:*** Employee Benefits; Health Benefits; ERISA; Taft-Hartley Plans. ***Email:*** gregory.nichols@icemiller.com

RANDLE B. POLLARD, born Milwaukee, Wisconsin, July 4, 1963; admitted to bar, 1989, Maryland; 1990, District of Columbia; 1999, Wisconsin; 2004, Indiana. *Education:* Hampton University (B.S., magna cum laude, 1985); Georgetown University (J.D., 1988; LL.M. in Taxation, 1996). Board Member, Indiana State Board of Education. Board Member and Treasurer, Indianapolis Private Industry Council. Commissioner, Board of Commissioners, Indianapolis Housing Agency. *Member:* American (Member, Taxation Section) and National (Co-Chair, Tax Law Section) Bar Associations; National Association of Bond Lawyers. ***PRACTICE AREAS:*** Municipal Finance; Public Policy; State Government Law; Government Affairs; Municipal Bonds; State Tax Controversies; Taxation. ***Email:*** randle.pollard@icemiller.com

CYNTHIA PEARSON PURVIS, born Indianapolis, Indiana, 1961; admitted to bar, 1989, Indiana; U.S. Court of Appeals, Sixth and Seventh Circuits; U.S. District Court, Northern and Southern Districts of Indiana. *Education:* Butler University (B.S., 1982); Indiana University School of Law - Indianapolis (J.D., 1988). *Member:* Indianapolis Bar Association. ***PRACTICE AREAS:*** Employee Benefits; Non-Qualified Benefits; Qualified Retirement Plans; Health Benefits; Flexible Benefit Plans. ***Email:*** cynthia.purvis@icemiller.com

LINDA R. ROWINGS, born Rochester, New York, 1953; admitted to bar, 1978, Indiana. *Education:* University of Virginia (B.A., 1975); Indiana University School of Law, Bloomington (J.D.,1978). ***PRACTICE AREAS:*** Employee Benefits; COBRA; ERISA; Health Benefits. ***Email:*** linda.rowings@icemiller.com

MARILEE J. SPRINGER, born Spartansburg, Pennsylvania; admitted to bar, 1996, Indiana. *Education:* Purdue University (B.A., with distinction, 1993); Indiana University School of Law - Indianapolis (J.D., magna cum laude, 1996). *Member:* Indianapolis Bar Association (Member, Tax Section). ***PRACTICE AREAS:*** Nonprofit And Charitable Organizations (80%); Corporate Law (10%); Federal Taxation (10%). ***Email:*** marilee.springer@icemiller.com

TARA SCHULSTAD SCISCOE, born Indianapolis, Indiana, January 18, 1969; admitted to bar, 1994, Indiana. *Education:* Duke University (A.B., cum laude, 1991); University of Michigan (J.D., cum laude, 1994), Order of the Coif. Contributing Editor, University of Michigan Law Review, 1992-1994. Author: "Rethinking Deferred Compensation Plans for Executives of Tax-Exempt Employers," Journal of Deferred Compensation, Spring, 2003. Speaker: "Controlling Fiduciary Exposure in a Post-Enron World," NACUBO Annual Conference, 2004; "Non-Qualified Deferred Compensation Plans of Colleges and Universities," Tax Institute for Colleges and Universities, 2005; "Employee Benefits Round-Up," NACUA Annual Conference, 2005. *Member:* Indianapolis, Indiana State and American (Member: Tax Section; Employee Benefits Committee) Bar Associations; National Association of College and University Attorneys; National Association of College and University Business Officers. ***REPORTED CASES:*** Eaton v. Onan Corporation, 117 F.Supp. 2d 812 (S.D. Ind. 2000); Marriott Mgmt. Services Corp. v. School Employees Retirement System, Nos. 96-4191, 96-4194 (6th Cir. 1998); Fairfield Mfg. Co. v. Hartman, 132 F. Supp. 2d 1142 (N.D. Ind. 2001); Reilly v. Daly, 666 N.E.2d 439 (Ind. App. Ct. 1996). ***PRACTICE AREAS:*** ERISA Compliance; Employee Benefits Litigation; Qualified Retirement Plans; Non-Qualified Benefits; Executive Compensation; Equity Compensation; Health Benefits; COBRA; Deferred Compensation; Employee Compensation; ERISA; Disability Benefits; Flexible Benefit Plans; Pension and Profit Sharing Plans; Public Employee Retirement; Retirement Benefit Plans; 401(k) Plans; Employee Benefit Taxation; Non-Qualified Plans; ERISA Litigation. ***Email:*** tara.sciscoe@icemiller.com

STEPHANIE ALDEN SMITHEY, born Oklahoma City, Oklahoma, February 3, 1966; admitted to bar, 1991, Indiana. *Education:* University of Notre Dame (B.A., cum laude, 1988); Loyola University of Chicago (J.D., 1991). Sigma Tau Delta; Alpha Kappa Delta. Member, Wagner Memorial Moot Court Team. *Member:* Indiana State and American Bar Associations. ***PRACTICE AREAS:*** ERISA; Health Benefits; COBRA; Multi-Employer Benefits; Disability Benefits; Employee Benefit Taxation; Employee Benefit Trusts; ERISA Compliance; Flexible Benefit Plans; Fringe Benefits; Multi-Employer Pensions; Pension and Profit Sharing Plans; Pension Plans; Qualified Retirement Plans; Retirement Benefit Plans; Taft-Hartley Plans; 401(k) Plans. ***Email:*** stephanie.smithey@icemiller.com

TIMOTHY W. SULLIVAN, born Akron, Ohio, October 21, 1948; admitted to bar, 1973, Indiana. *Education:* Wabash College (B.A., 1970); Indiana University School of Law-Indianapolis (J.D., 1973). Phi Delta Phi. *Member:* Indianapolis and Indiana State Bar Associations. ***PRACTICE AREAS:*** Real Estate; Landlord and Tenant Law; Real Estate Finance; Partnerships; Lender Rights. ***Email:*** sullivat@icemiller.com

BRADLEY L. WILLIAMS, born Dayton, Ohio, July 20, 1950; admitted to bar, 1975, Indiana; 1976, U.S. Court of Appeals, Seventh Circuit; 1978, Ohio; U.S. Supreme Court. *Education:* Indiana University (A.B., 1972; J.D., 1975). Acting U.S. Attorney, 1987-1988; First Assistant U.S. Attorney, 1984-1987, Southern District of Indiana. Member, District Court Local Rules Advisory Committee, Southern District of Indiana. *Member:* Indianapolis (Member, Attorney Grievance Committee), Seventh Circuit (Member, Board of Governors), Federal (Past President, Indianapolis Chapter) and American (Chair, Subcommittee on Attorney-Client and Constitutional Privileges, Section of Taxation, Committee on Civil and Criminal Tax Penalties) Bar Associations; National Health Lawyers Association. ***PRACTICE AREAS:*** Criminal Law; Health Care Litigation; Environmental Law; Federal Taxation; Qui Tam. ***Email:*** williamb@icemiller.com

OF COUNSEL

KAREN L. ARLAND, born Landstuhl, Germany, March 29, 1957; admitted to bar, 1982, Indiana. *Education:* Butler University (B.A., 1979); Indiana University (J.D., 1982). Assistant Corporation Counsel, City of Indianapolis, 1984-1989. *Member:* Indiana State Bar Association (Member, Governmental Practice Section); Indiana Municipal Lawyers Association; National Association of Bond Lawyers. ***PRACTICE AREAS:*** Public Construction Law; Public Works; Lobbying; Brownfields Redevelopment; County Government Law; Government Ethics; Local Government Law; Local Government Contracts; Public Bidding; Municipal Bonds; Municipal Finance; Municipal Corporation Law; Municipal Redevelopment; Municipal Solid Waste; Municipal Taxation; Tax Increment Finance; Land Annexation; Government; Government Relations; State Legislative Practice. ***Email:*** arland@icemiller.com

SANDRA K. BICKEL, born Elkhart, Indiana, August 25, 1947; admitted to bar, 1982, Indiana. *Education:* Indiana University at South Bend (B.S., 1970; M.S., 1975); Indiana University School of Law-Indianapolis (J.D., 1982). First Place, Client Counseling Competition. Member: State Tax and Financing Policy Commission; Property Tax Replacement Study Commission. Board Member, Butler-Tarkington Neighborhood Association. Member, Reach for Youth Finance Committee. Board Member, T.R.U.S.T. *Member:* Indianapolis and Indiana State Bar Associations; Indiana Municipal Lawyers Association; International Association of Assessing Officials (Indiana Chapter). ***REPORTED CASES:*** Meridian Towers v. Washington Township Assessor, 805 N.E.2d 475 (Ind. Tax 2004). ***PRACTICE AREAS:*** Government Affairs (10%); Property Tax (80%); Municipal Law (5%); State and Local Government Budgets (5%). ***Email:*** sandra.bickel@icemiller.com

SUSAN ROGERS BROOKE, born Lexington, Kentucky, August 29, 1951; admitted to bar, 1978, Indiana; U.S. District Court, Northern and Southern Districts of Indiana; U.S. Court of Appeals, Ninth and Seventh Circuits. *Education:* University of Delaware (B.A. in Political Science, with highest honors and distinction, 1973); Indiana University School of Law (J.D., summa cum laude, 1978). Author: "Indemnification and the Anti-Indemnification Statues," in *Construction Contractors Handbook of Business and Law* (Wiley Law Publications, 1992, Robert Cushman, Ed.); "Protecting Design Builder with Appropriate Contract Clauses," *Design/Build Contracting Handbook,* (Wiley Law Publications, 1992, Robert Cushman, Ed.); Indiana Casenote Editor, *Construct!,* a publication of the Litigation Section of the American Bar Association, 1999—. *Member:* Indianapolis, Indiana State and American (Member, Forum on Construction Industry; Chair, Section on Construction Management and Design Build, 1991-1993) Bar Associations; American Bankruptcy Institute. ***PRACTICE AREAS:*** Construction Law; Commercial Litigation. ***Email:*** susan.brooke@icemiller.com

JENIFER M. BROWN, born Franklin, Indiana, June 26, 1972; admitted to bar, 1999, Indiana. *Education:* Ball State University (B.A., 1994); Indiana University (J.D., 1998). *Member:* American Immigration Lawyers Association. ***PRACTICE AREAS:*** Immigration and Naturalization; Immigration Law. ***Email:*** brownj@icemiller.com

JULIE M. CONRAD, born Saginaw, Michigan, August 20, 1968; admitted to bar, 1993, Indiana. *Education:* University of Michigan (B.A., 1989); Indiana University (J.D., cum laude, 1993). *Member:* Indianapolis, Indiana State and American Bar Associations. ***PRACTICE AREAS:*** Labor and Employment; Litigation. ***Email:*** julie.conrad@icemiller.com

KAREN A. DUTCHER, born Hinsdale, Illinois, January 6, 1960; admitted to bar, 1985, Kansas and U.S. District Court, District of Kansas; 1999, Indiana and U.S. District Court, Northern and Southern Districts of Indiana. *Education:* University of Kansas (B.S., 1982; J.D., 1985). Phi Beta Kappa. Adjunct Professor, Law of Higher Education, University of Kansas, 1998-1999. *Member:* Indiana State Bar Association; Defense Research Institute. ***PRACTICE AREAS:*** Products Liability; Civil Rights Litigation; Education Law. ***Email:*** karen.dutcher@icemiller.com

NATALIE M. FIEREK, born Plymouth, Indiana, August 14, 1976; admitted to bar, 2004, Indiana. *Education:* Ball State University (B.S., with honors, 1999); Indiana University School of Law - Indianapolis (J.D., 2004). *Member:* Indianapolis, Indiana State and American Bar Associations. ***PRACTICE AREAS:*** Workers Compensation. ***Email:*** natalie.fierek@icemiller.com

KARI H. HALBROOK, born Fort Wayne, Indiana, 1973; admitted to bar, 2000, Indiana; U.S. District Court, Northern and Southern Districts of Indiana. *Education:* Purdue University (B.A., 1995); Indiana University School of Law - Indianapolis (J.D., 2000). *Member:* Indianapolis, Indiana State and American Bar Associations. ***PRACTICE AREAS:*** Litigation.

MELISSA A. HARKINS, born South Bend, Indiana, August 20, 1973; admitted to bar, 2003, Indiana; U.S. District Court, Northern and Southern Districts of Indiana. *Education:* St. Mary's College (B.S.); Indiana University (J.D., 2002). *Member:* Indianapolis and Indiana State Bar Associations; Defense Research Institute; Indiana Defense Trial Council. ***PRACTICE AREAS:*** Litigation. ***Email:*** melissa.harkins@icemiller.com

LISA ERB HARRISON, born Rensselaer, Indiana, January 29, 1967; admitted to bar, 1992, Indiana and U.S. District Court, Northern and Southern Districts of Indiana; U.S. Court of Appeals, Seventh Circuit. *Education:* Butler University (B.A., summa cum laude, 1989); Indiana University (J.D., cum laude, 1992). Managing Editor, Indiana Law Journal, 1991-1992. Law Clerk to the Hon. William I. Garrard, Indiana Court of Appeals, 1993-1996. Member, National Association of Government Defined Contribution Plan Administrators. *Member:* Indianapolis and Indiana State (Member, Women in the Law Executive Committee) Bar Associations; National Association of Public Pension Attorneys. ***PRACTICE AREAS:*** Employee Benefits; Public Pension Plans; Qualified Retirement Plans; Deferred Compensation Plans; Employment Law. ***Email:*** harrison@icemiller.com

BETH H. HENKEL, born Fargo, North Dakota, 1952; admitted to bar, 1982, Indiana; U.S. Court of Appeals, Seventh Circuit; U.S. District Court, Northern and Southern Districts of Indiana. *Education:* Indiana University (B.A., 1975); Indiana University School of

(This Listing Continued)

ICE MILLER, Indianapolis—Continued

Law - Indianapolis (J.D., magna cum laude, 1982). *Member:* Indianapolis Bar Association. ***LANGUAGES:*** Spanish. ***PRACTICE AREAS:*** Taxation; State Taxation; Tax Law. ***Email:*** beth.henkel@icemiller.com

STEVEN L. JONES, born Elkhart, Indiana, April 12, 1971; admitted to bar, 1998, Indiana. *Education:* Purdue University (B.S., 1995); Indiana University School of Law (J.D., 1998). ***PRACTICE AREAS:*** Litigation; Construction Law. ***Email:*** steven.jones@icemiller.com

JEFFREY M. LOZER, admitted to bar, 1994, Indiana. *Education:* Davidson College (B.A., 1989); Indiana University School of Law - Indianapolis (J.D., cum laude, 1994). *Member:* Indiana State Bar Association. ***PRACTICE AREAS:*** Nonprofit Organizations Law; Education Law; Corporate Law. ***Email:*** jeffrey.lozer@icemiller.com

JOHN T. MURPHY, born Indianapolis, Indiana, November 24, 1956; admitted to bar, 1983, Indiana. *Education:* University of Notre Dame (B.B.A., cum laude, 1978); University of Michigan (J.D., cum laude, 1982). Qualified Independent Assessor, Insurance Marketplace Standards Association. Past President and Chairman, Board of Directors, Writers' Center of Indianapolis, Inc. *Member:* Indiana State Bar Association. ***PRACTICE AREAS:*** Insurance Law; Insolvency Law; Insurance Regulation. ***Email:*** john.murphy@icemiller.com

HEATHER K. OLINGER, born Indianapolis, Indiana, 1967; admitted to bar, 1992, Indiana. *Education:* Butler University (B.S., summa cum laude, 1989); Indiana University School of Law - Indianapolis (J.D., summa cum laude, 1992). Executive Director, Shelby County United Fund, Inc., Shelbyville, Indiana, 2001-2004. ***PRACTICE AREAS:*** Real Estate; Real Estate Development; Real Estate Finance; Real Estate Leasing. ***Email:*** heather.olinger@icemiller.com

KELLY BAUMAN PITCHER, born Plymouth, Indiana, September 20, 1956; admitted to bar, 1988, Indiana. *Education:* Indiana University-Bloomington (B.S., cum laude, 1979); Indiana University-Indianapolis (J.D., cum laude, 1988). Order of the Barristers. Law Clerk to Hon. Randall T. Shepard, Chief Justice of Indiana, 1986-1988. *Member:* Indiana State and American Bar Associations; Defense Research Institute; Defense Trial Counsel of Indiana. ***PRACTICE AREAS:*** Medical Malpractice Defense; Drug and Medical Device Litigation; General Civil Litigation. ***Email:*** kelly.pitcher@icemiller.com

JILL TABOR POWLICK, admitted to bar, 1995, Indiana; 2000, U.S. Court of Appeals for the Federal Circuit; U.S. District Court, Northern and Southern Districts of Indiana; registered to practice before U.S. Patent and Trademark Office. *Education:* Carnegie Mellon University (B.S., 1983); University of Pittsburgh (Master of Education, 1988); Indiana University School of Law - Indianapolis (J.D., magna cum laude, 1995). Order of the Coif. Recipient, American Jurisprudence Award for Property, Wills and Trusts. Law Clerk to: Hon. Myra C. Selby, Indiana Supreme Court, 1995-1996; Hon. S. Hugh Dillin, U.S. District Court, Southern District of Indiana, 1996-1998. ***PRACTICE AREAS:*** Intellectual Property; Biotechnology Patent Prosecution. ***Email:*** jill.powlick@icemiller.com

SCOTT JAMES PRESTON, born Wichita, Kansas, August 18, 1966; admitted to bar, 1997, California; 2005, Indiana. *Education:* University of Nebraska (B.S., 1991); Creighton University (J.D., 1997). ***REPORTED CASES:*** Boeing North American, Inc. v. Roche, 298 F.3d 1274 (Fed. Cir. 2002); Abraham v. Rockwell Intern. Corp., 326 F.3d 1242 (Fed.Cir. 2003); T & E Pastorino Nursery v. Duke Energy Trading and Marketing, L.L.C., et al., 2003 WL 22110491 (S.D.Cal., Aug. 27, 2003). ***PRACTICE AREAS:*** Drug and Medical Device Litigation; Appellate Practice. ***Email:*** scott.preston@icemiller.com

SUSAN BENDER PRICE, born Indianapolis, Indiana, October 10, 1976; admitted to bar, 2002, Indiana. *Education:* DePauw University (B.A., 1999); University of Cincinnati (J.D., 2002). *Member:* National Association of Bond Lawyers. ***PRACTICE AREAS:*** Municipal Finance (100%). ***Email:*** susan.price@icemiller.com

WILLIAM C. REYNOLDS, born Lebanon, Indiana, September 10, 1942; admitted to bar, 1968, Indiana. *Education:* Indiana University (1965); Indiana University School of Law (J.D., 1968). *Member:* Indianapolis and Indiana State (Member, Sections on: Probate, Trust, Property and Death Tax; Taxation; Senior Lawyers) Bar Associations. ***PRACTICE AREAS:*** Personal Services. ***Email:*** william.reynolds@icemiller.com

NANCY MENARD RIDDLE, born Kankakee, Illinois, 1950; admitted to bar, 1976, Illinois; 1980, U.S. District Court, Eastern and Southern Districts of Illinois; 1988, U.S. Court of Appeals, Seventh Circuit; 1990, Indiana; 1993, U.S. District Court, Southern District of Indiana. *Education:* Northern Illinois University (B.S.Ed., summa cum laude, 1972); University of Illinois (J.D., with honors, 1976). Order of the Coif; Mortar Board. Member, University of Illinois Law Forum, 1975-1976. Law Clerk, Illinois Appellate Court, Fourth District, 1976-1980. *Member:* Indianapolis and Indiana State Bar Associations; Defense Research Institute; Defense Trial Counsel of Indiana. ***REPORTED CASES:*** Small v. Centocor, Inc., 731 N.E.2d 22 (Ind. App., June 26, 2000); O'Neal v. Throop, 596 N.E.2d 984 (Ind. App. 1 Dist., July 30, 1992); Community Hospitals of Indianapolis, Inc. v. Medtronic, Inc., Neuro Div., 594 N.E.2d 448 (Ind. App. 1 Dist., April 15, 1992); Bremer v. Community Hospitals of Indianapolis, Inc., 583 N.E.2d 780 (Ind. App. 2 Dist., Dec. 30, 1991); Matter of Hilligoss, 849 F.2d 280, 11 Fed. R. Serv. 3d 720 (7th Cir. (Ill.), June 13, 1988); Cole Hosp., Inc. v. Champaign County Bd. of Review, 113 Ill. App. 3d 96, 446 N.E.2d 562, 68 Ill. Dec. 656 (Ill. App. 4 Dist., Mar 03, 1983); Schlessman v. Henson, 83 Ill. 2d 82, 413 N.E.2d 1252, 46 Ill. Dec. 139 (Ill., Dec 01, 1980). ***PRACTICE AREAS:*** Drug and Medical Device Litigation; Toxic Torts; Medical Malpractice Defense. ***Email:*** riddle@icemiller.com

JANE H. RUEMMELE, born Louisville, Kentucky, February 22, 1959; admitted to bar, 1984, Indiana. *Education:* University of Louisville (B.S., cum laude, 1980); Indiana University (J.D., 1984). Author: "Aggressive Advocacy in the Juvenile Context," Indiana Defender, March, 1998; "Failure to Properly Instruct Juries Should Constitute Fundamental Error," The Acquitter, May, 1997. Co-Author, Juvenile Justice Manual published by the Public Defender Council, 1999. Public Defender: Marion County Municipal Court, 1985-1987; State of Indiana, 1987-1990; Marion County Superior Court, 1993-1994. Owner and Inventor: Chronology, Chronology-Junior, Chronology-Sports Edition, released in the United States and Canada, 1996, published by The Great American Puzzle Factory, Norwalk, Connecticut, released in the United Kingdom, 1997, Mattel/H. Spier. *Member:* Indianapolis and Indiana State Bar Associations; Marion County Criminal Defense Bar Association. ***REPORTED CASES:*** Lannan v. State, 600 N.E.2d 1334 (Ind. 1992); Lee v. State, 550 N.E.2d 304 (Ind. 1990); James v. State, 541 N.E.2d 264 (Ind. 1989); Clark v. State, 728 N.E.2d 800 (Ind. Ct. App. 2000); E.P. v. Marion County Office of Family and Children, 653 N.E.2d 1026 (Ind. Ct. App.. 1995); Borders v. Noel, 800 N.E.2d 586 (Ind.Ct.App.2003). ***PRACTICE AREAS:*** Real Estate. ***Email:*** jane.ruemmele@icemiller.com

KATHLEEN K. SHORTRIDGE, born Pasadena, California, September 26, 1944; admitted to bar, 1984, Indiana and U.S. District Court, Southern District of Indiana. *Education:* Stanford University (B.A., 1966); University of Michigan (M.A., Pol. Science, 1968; M.A., Journalism, 1971); University of Louisville (J.D., cum laude, 1984). Law Clerk, Hon. John Paul Godich, Magistrate, U.S. District Court, Southern District of Indiana, 1984-1986. *Member:* Indianapolis and Indiana State Bar Associations. ***PRACTICE AREAS:*** Labor and Employment; Workers Compensation Law. ***Email:*** shortrid@icemiller.com

GARY L. STAGE, born Ypsilanti, Michigan, September 23, 1949; admitted to bar, 1976, Kentucky; 1999, Indiana. *Education:* College of William & Mary (A.B., 1971); University of Kentucky (J.D., with high distinction, 1976). Order of the Coif. Editor-in-Chief, Kentucky Law Journal, 1975-1976. Author: "Raising Equity Capital," Kentucky Business Organizations (UK CLE) 1989. Instructor, Legal Writing, University of Kentucky, 1976-1978. Member, Board of Directors and President, Mapleton-Fall Creek Development Corporation. *Member:* Indianapolis (Member, Business Law Section, Executive Committee), Kentucky (Member, Business Law Section), Indiana State (Member, Business Law Section) and American (Member, Business Law Section) Bar Associations. ***PRACTICE AREAS:*** Business Law; Mergers, Acquisitions and Divestitures; Corporate Law; Limited Liability Company Law; Partnership Law; Corporate Finance; Securities. ***Email:*** gary.stage@icemiller.com

EDWARD P. STEEGMANN, born Indianapolis, Indiana, February 28, 1964; admitted to bar, 1988, Indiana. *Education:* Indiana University (B.A., with highest distinction, 1985; J.D., magna cum laude, 1988). Phi Beta Kappa; Order of the Coif. Executive Editor, Indiana Law Journal, 1987-1988. Author: Note, "Of History and Due Process," 63 Indiana Law Journal 369, 1988. ***PRACTICE AREAS:*** Commercial Litigation; Administrative Law; Coal Law. ***Email:*** steegman@icemiller.com

MARGARET D. WIELENBERG, born West Bloomfield, Michigan, May 2, 1970; admitted to bar, 1995, California; 1996, Michigan; 1999, Illinois; 2003, Indiana. *Education:* Michigan State University (B.A., cum laude, 1992); University of Detroit Mercy School of Law (J.D., 1995). ***PRACTICE AREAS:*** Labor and Employment. ***Email:*** margaret.wielenberg@icemiller.com

GERMAINE W. WILLETT, born Des Plaines, Illinois, April 1, 1972; admitted to bar, 1998, Indiana. *Education:* DePauw University (B.A., 1994); Phi Beta Kappa; Indiana University, Bloomington (J.D., cum laude, 1998). Author: Indiana Law Journal Vol. 73 Winter, 1997. *Member:* Indianapolis and Indiana State Bar Associations; Defense Trial Counsel of Indiana; Defense Research Institute. ***REPORTED CASES:*** *Hutchison v. Old Indiana Limited Liability Co.,* 714 N.E. 2d 789 (Ind. Ct. App. 2000); *Metcalf v. Estate of Hastings,* 726 N.E. 2d 372, (Ind. Ct. App. 2000); *Zurich American Insurance Group v. Wynkoop,* 2001 WL 406641 (Ind. Ct. App.). ***PRACTICE AREAS:*** Civil Litigation; Personal Injury Defense; Premises Liability Defense; Products Liability Defense. ***Email:*** germaine.willett@icemiller.com

SENIOR ASSOCIATE

KRISTINE J. BOUAICHI, born Indianapolis, Indiana, August 29, 1967; admitted to bar, 1998, Florida and Indiana. *Education:* Indiana University (B.A., Psychology, 1989); Stetson University College of Law (J.D., cum laude, 1998). Phi Delta Phi. Recipient, Victor O. Wehle Trial Advocacy Award, 1998. Member, Board of Directors, Family Service of Central Indiana, 2001—. *Member:* Indiana State Bar Association, The Florida Bar. ***PRACTICE AREAS:*** Estate Planning; Family Wealth Transfer; Tax Planning; Trusts and Estates. ***Email:*** kristine.bouaichi@icemiller.com

ASSOCIATES

ANTHONY AARON, born Philadelphia, Pennsylvania; admitted to bar, 2002, Indiana; U.S. District Court, Northern and Southern Districts of Indiana. *Education:* United States Military Academy (B.S., 1991); University of Northern Colorado (M.S., 1995); Indiana University School of Law - Indianapolis (J.D., summa cum laude, 2002). *Member:* Indianapolis, Indiana State and American (Member, Sections on: Antitrust; Business) Bar Associations. [Armor and Field Artillery Officer, U.S. Army and Indiana Army National Guard; Capt., U.S. Army and Indiana Army National Guard, 1991-1999]. ***PRACTICE AREAS:*** Antitrust; Corporate Law; Securities; Aviation. ***Email:*** anthony.aaron@icemiller.com

JAY B. ADAMS, born Evansville, Indiana; admitted to bar, 2002, Indiana and U.S. District Court, Northern and Southern Districts of Indiana. *Education:* Wabash College (B.A., History, cum laude, 1997); Indiana University School of Law - Indianapolis (J.D., cum laude, 2002). *Member:* Indianapolis, Indiana State and American Bar Associations. ***PRACTICE AREAS:*** Business Law; Business Transactions; Corporate Law. ***Email:*** jay.adams@icemiller.com

KEVIN M. ALERDING, born Baltimore, Maryland, November 22, 1969; admitted to bar, 1995, Indiana. *Education:* Ball State University (B.S., 1992); Indiana University (J.D., 1995). [Cpt. U.S. Army Reserve, 1995—]. ***PRACTICE AREAS:*** Estate Planning; Estate Administration; Estate and Gift Taxation. ***Email:*** alerding@icemiller.com

NIQUELLE ALLEN, born Hobart, Indiana, 1977; admitted to bar, 2002, Tennessee; 2003, Illinois; 2004, Indiana and U.S. District Court, Northern and Southern Districts of Indiana. *Education:* Tennessee State University (B.S., magna cum laude, 1999); Vanderbilt University (J.D., 2002). *Member:* Indianapolis, Marion County, Indiana State, American and National Bar Associations; Black Women Lawyers' Association of Greater Chicago, Inc. ***PRACTICE AREAS:*** Labor and Employment; Employment Discrimination; Employment Law; Employment Litigation; Labor Arbitration; Labor Relations. ***Email:*** niquelle.allen@icemiller.com

(This Listing Continued)

JENNIFER M. ALVEY, admitted to bar, 2004, Indiana. *Education:* Indiana University (B.S., 1995); Indiana University School of Law - Indianapolis (J.D., 2004). Certified Public Accountant. *Member:* Indianapolis, Indiana State and American Bar Associations. ***PRACTICE AREAS:*** Nonprofit Tax Law; College and University Law; Municipal Bonds. ***Email:*** jennifer.alvey@icemiller.com

JENNIFER A. ANDRES, admitted to bar, 2003, Indiana. *Education:* Indiana University (B.S., 1996); Indiana University School of Law - Indianapolis (J.D., 2003). *Member:* Indianapolis, Indiana State and American Bar Associations. ***PRACTICE AREAS:*** Corporate Law; Environmental Law. ***Email:*** jennifer.andres@icemiller.com

BRIAN BAILEY, admitted to bar, 2003, Indiana. *Education:* Wabash College (B.A., summa cum laude, 1997); Indiana University School of Law - Bloomington (J.D., cum laude, 2000). ***PRACTICE AREAS:*** Litigation; Appellate Practice. ***Email:*** brian.bailey@icemiller.com

DENISE Y. BARKDULL, born Bluffton, Indiana, June 16, 1971; admitted to bar, 1998, Indiana. *Education:* Boise State University (B.B.A., cum laude, 1994); Indiana University (J.D., 1997; M.B.A., 1997). Recipient, Scribe Award for Excellence in Legal Writing, 1994-1995. Business Editor, Journal of Global Legal Studies, 1996-1997. Member, Indiana Association of Cities and Towns. *Member:* Indianapolis (Participant in Leader Series, 2003) and Indiana State Bar Associations; National Association of Bond Lawyers; Indiana Municipal Lawyers Association. ***PRACTICE AREAS:*** Public Finance; Municipal Finance; Airport Finance and Development; Municipal Bonds Taxation; Municipal Derivative Products; Tax Exempt Securities; Public Law; Finance Taxation; Health Care Finance; Municipal Solid Waste. ***Email:*** barkdull@icemiller.com

ALYSSA BEATTIE, admitted to bar, 2004, Indiana. *Education:* Indiana University - Indianapolis (B.A., highest distinction, 1999); Indiana University School of Law (J.D., cum laude, 2004). ***PRACTICE AREAS:*** Corporate Law; International Law. ***Email:*** alyssa.beattie@icemiller.com

MARK A. BOGDANOWICZ, born Elmhurst, Illinois, March 28, 1973; admitted to bar, 2000, Tennessee (Not admitted in Indiana). *Education:* Harvard University (A.B., 1995); Vanderbilt School of Law (J.D., 2000). ***PRACTICE AREAS:*** Creditors Rights. ***Email:*** mark.bogdanowicz@icemiller.com

TONYA J. BOND, born Indianapolis, Indiana; admitted to bar, 2004, Indiana. *Education:* Indiana University-Purdue University - Indianapolis (B.A., 2000); Indiana University School of Law (J.D., 2004). ***PRACTICE AREAS:*** Litigation; Insurance; Environmental Law; Risk Management; Premises Liability; Products Liability. ***Email:*** tonya.boller@icemiller.com

MICHAEL BUKER, born Indianapolis, Indiana, March 5, 1956; admitted to bar, 1998, California and Indiana. *Education:* Indiana University (B.S., Accounting, 1978); University of the Pacific, McGeorge School of Law (J.D., with great distinction, 1997); New York University (LL.M., Taxation, 1999). Order of the Coif. Faculty Select Award for Most Significant Contribution toward Overall Scholarship, 1997 and 1998. Roger J. Traynor Honor Society, 1996 and 1997. Appellate Advocacy Honors Board, 1996 and 1997. Appellate Advocacy Scholarship. Academic Achievement Scholarship. Certified Public Accountant, Kentucky, 1981. *Member:* Indiana State and American Bar Associations; State Bar of California; American Institute of Certified Public Accountants; Kentucky Society of CPAs. ***PRACTICE AREAS:*** Corporate Taxation; Partnership Taxation; Municipal Bonds; Low Income Housing Tax Credits; State Taxation. ***Email:*** buker@icemiller.com

DANIEL K. BURKE, born February 23, 1972; admitted to bar, 1999, Texas and U.S. District Court, Northern District of Texas; 2000, U.S. District Court, Eastern District of Texas; 2003, U.S. District Court, Southern District of Indiana; 2004, Indiana and U.S. District Court, Northern District of Indiana; 2005, U.S. District Court, Southern District of Texas. *Education:* Indiana University (B.S., 1994); Southern Methodist University (J.D., cum laude, 1999). *Member:* Dallas, Indiana State and American Bar Associations; State Bar of Texas; Dallas Association of Young Lawyers. ***PRACTICE AREAS:*** Litigation. ***Email:*** daniel.burke@icemiller.com

HILARY BUTTRICK, admitted to bar, 2002, Indiana. *Education:* DePauw University (B.A., 1999); Indiana University School of Law - Indianapolis (J.D., 2002). *Member:* American Bar Association. ***PRACTICE AREAS:*** Litigation. ***Email:*** hilary.buttrick@icemiller.com

TIMOTHY J. CAPEN, born Greenfield, Indiana, May 2, 1979; admitted to bar, 2004, Indiana. *Education:* Indiana University (B.A., 2001); Indiana University School of Law - Indianapolis (J.D., magna cum laude, 2004). *Member:* Indiana State and American Bar Associations. ***PRACTICE AREAS:*** Private Equity; Venture Finance; Mergers and Acquisitions; General Corporate; Sport and Entertainment. ***Email:*** tim.capen@icemiller.com

BEN T. CAUGHEY, born Morgantown, West Virginia, March 25, 1975; admitted to bar, 2001, Indiana. *Education:* University of Illinois (B.S., 1997); Indiana University (J.D., 2001). Lecturer: Indiana Continuing Legal Education Bankruptcy Seminar, 2004, 2005; Indiana Continuing Legal Education Airline Seminar, 2005. *Member:* Indianapolis and Indiana State Bar Associations; American Bankruptcy Institute. ***PRACTICE AREAS:*** Creditors Rights; Commercial Bankruptcy; Commercial Litigation. ***Email:*** ben.caughey@icemiller.com

ABIGAIL CELLA, admitted to bar, 2004, Indiana. *Education:* Pennsylvania State University (B.S., with high distinction, 2001); Indiana University School of Law (J.D., cum laude, 2004). ***PRACTICE AREAS:*** Litigation. ***Email:*** abby.cella@icemiller.com

KATRINA M. CLINGERMAN, born Carbondale, Illinois, March 21, 1972; admitted to bar, 1999, Indiana. *Education:* DePauw University (B.A., summa cum laude, 1993); Indiana University School of Law - Indianapolis (J.D., cum laude, 1999). Phi Beta Kappa, 1993. Forrest E. Jump Scholar, 1995-1999. Note Development Editor, Indiana Law Review, 1998-1999. Speaker: "Practical Information You Should Know When Serving on a Nonprofit Board," Women in Law Conference, 2004; "The Mire of Litigation Taxation," IBA Bench-Bar Conference, 2004; "Incorporating Policy Advocacy Work into Your Organization," IACED Annual Conference, 2004. Participant, IBA Bar Leader Series, 2004-2005. Board Member, Youth as Resources of Marion County, 2004—. *Member:* Indianapolis (Member, Tax Executive Council), Indiana State and American Bar Associations. ***PRACTICE AREAS:*** Employee Benefits; Nonprofit and Charitable Organizations; Taxation. ***Email:*** katrina.clingerman@icemiller.com

(This Listing Continued)

RHONDA L. COOK, admitted to bar, 2004, Indiana. *Education:* Indiana University (B.A., 1992); Ball State University (M.P.A., 1994); Indiana University School of Law - Indianapolis (J.D., 2004). *Member:* Indianapolis, Indiana State and American Bar Associations; Indiana Governmental Affairs Society; National Association of Bond Lawyers; Indiana Municipal Lawyers Association. ***PRACTICE AREAS:*** Government Finance; Public Affairs. ***Email:*** rhonda.cook@icemiller.com

DAVID E. COREY, born Grand Rapids, Michigan, April 3, 1969; admitted to bar, 2000, Michigan (Not admitted in Indiana). *Education:* Hope College (B.A., magna cum laude, 1991); Indiana University School of Law - Indianapolis (J.D., magna cum laude, 2000). *Member:* State Bar of Michigan; American Bar Association. ***PRACTICE AREAS:*** Real Estate; Title Insurance. ***Email:*** david.corey@icemiller.com

SARAH DANSKER COTTERILL, born Indianapolis, Indiana, April 10, 1978; admitted to bar, 2003, Indiana. *Education:* University of Virginia (B.A., cum laude, 2000); Indiana University School of Law - Bloomington (J.D., cum laude, 2003). *Member:* Indianapolis, Indiana State and American Bar Associations; American Health Lawyers Association. ***PRACTICE AREAS:*** Health Care. ***Email:*** sarah.cotterill@icemiller.com

BRIAN C. CRIST, born 1971; admitted to bar, 1997, Indiana; U.S. Court of Appeals, Seventh Circuit; U.S. District Court, Northern and Southern Districts of Indiana. *Education:* University of Missouri, Columbia (B.A., magna cum laude, 1994); Vanderbilt University (J.D., 1997). Stanley K. Lacy Executive Leadership Program, 2000-2001. *Member:* Indiana State Bar Association. ***PRACTICE AREAS:*** Real Estate; Environmental Law; Insurance Law. ***Email:*** brian.crist@icemiller.com

MICHAEL DALRYMPLE, admitted to bar, 2002, Indiana. *Education:* Earlham College (B.A., 1995); Indiana University School of Law (J.D., 2002). ***PRACTICE AREAS:*** Labor and Employment. ***Email:*** michael.dalrymple@icemiller.com

STEVEN R. DAVIS, born Muncie, Indiana, February 12, 1979; admitted to bar, 2004, Indiana. *Education:* Anderson University (B.A., with honors, 2001); Indiana University School of Law (J.D., 2004). ***PRACTICE AREAS:*** Corporate Law. ***Email:*** steve.davis@icemiller.com

JODY DeFORD, born November 2, 1972; admitted to bar, 2002, Indiana and U.S. District Court, Northern and Southern Districts of Indiana. *Education:* Indiana University (B.A., with distinction, 1995); Indiana University School of Law - Indianapolis (J.D., cum laude, 1999). *Member:* Indianapolis, Indiana State and American Bar Associations; American Health Lawyers Association. ***PRACTICE AREAS:*** Litigation. ***Email:*** jody.deford@icemiller.com

MATTHEW G. DeLARUELLE, born Mishawaka, Indiana, May 16, 1974; admitted to bar, 2003, Missouri; 2004, Indiana. *Education:* Purdue University (B.A., 1999); Washington University School of Law (J.D., 2003). ***PRACTICE AREAS:*** Real Estate; Business Law; Intellectual Property. ***Email:*** matt.del@icemiller.com

JASON R. DELK, born Muncie, Indiana, March 13, 1979; admitted to bar, 2004, Indiana; U.S. District Court, Northern and Southern Districts of Indiana and U.S. District Court, Central District of Illinois. *Education:* Ball State University (B.S., 2001); Indiana University School of Law - Indianapolis (J.D., summa cum laude, 2004). *Member:* Indianapolis, Indiana State and American Bar Associations. ***PRACTICE AREAS:*** Business Litigation; Wrongful Death; Plaintiffs Personal Injury; Personal Injury Defense; Personal Injury; Litigation; Civil Litigation; Defense Litigation; Federal Civil Litigation; Federal Litigation; Trial Practice; Products Liability. ***Email:*** jason.delk@icemiller.com

AARON J. DIXON, born Fresno, California, June 14, 1974; admitted to bar, 1999, Indiana. *Education:* University of Iowa (B.A., 1996; J.D., 1999). ***PRACTICE AREAS:*** Business Law; Corporate Law; Real Estate. ***Email:*** dixon@icemiller.com

DUSTIN S. DuBOIS, born Rochester, Indiana, February 16, 1970; admitted to bar, 2000, Indiana; registered to practice before U.S. Patent and Trademark Office. *Education:* Rose-Hulman Institute of Technology (B.S., 1992); Indiana University School of Law (J.D., 2000). Order of the Barristers for achievements in oral advocacy in Moot Court. *Member:* American Intellectual Property Law Association. ***PRACTICE AREAS:*** Intellectual Property; Patents; Business Transactions; Strategic Alliances; Joint Ventures; Emerging Growth Companies; Commercial Contracts; Buy-Sell Agreements; Intellectual Property Licensing; Intellectual Property Portfolio Management. ***Email:*** dustin.dubois@icemiller.com

GREGORY A. DUFF, born Lebanon, Indiana; admitted to bar, 1999, Illinois; 2004, Indiana; U.S. District Court, Northern and Southern Districts of Indiana; U.S. District Court, Northern District of Illinois; registered to practice before U.S. Patent and Trademark Office. *Education:* Purdue University (B.S.Ph., with honors, 1996); University of Virginia (J.D., 1999). *Member:* Indianapolis and Indiana State Bar Associations. ***PRACTICE AREAS:*** Intellectual Property; Intellectual Property Litigation. ***Email:*** gregory.duff@icemiller.com

TAMI A. EARNHART, born Milwaukee, Wisconsin, December 1, 1969; admitted to bar, 1999, Indiana and U.S. District Court, Northern and Southern Districts of Indiana. *Education:* University of Evansville (B.S., magna cum laude, 1990); Indiana University School of Law - Bloomington (J.D., magna cum laude, 1999). Order of the Coif. Sherman Minton Moot Court Board, 1998-1999. Senior Managing Editor, Indiana Law Journal, 1998-1999. Author, "Medicated Mental Disabilities Under the Americans With Disabilities Act: Diagnosing the Problem, Prescribing the Solution," 74 Indiana Law Journal. *Member:* Indianapolis (Secretary/Treasurer, Labor and Employment Section, 2002-2003), Indiana State and American (Member, Labor and Employment Law Section) Bar Associations. ***PRACTICE AREAS:*** Employment Law; Labor Law; Employment Discrimination; Affirmative Action; Employment Litigation; Family and Medical Leave Act. ***Email:*** earnhart@icemiller.com

ALISON EMERY, admitted to bar, 2003, Indiana. *Education:* Anderson College (B.A., magna cum laude, 1998); Valparaiso University (J.D., cum laude, 2003). *Member:* Indianapolis, Indiana State and American Bar Associations. ***PRACTICE AREAS:*** Tax. ***Email:*** alison.emery@icemiller.com

MARGARET R. EMMERT, born Indianapolis, Indiana, September 25, 1958; (admission pending). *Education:* Indiana University (B.S.N., 1987; J.D., cum laude, 2001). ***PRACTICE AREAS:*** Health Care; Tax Law. ***Email:*** emmert@icemiller.com

(This Listing Continued)

ICE MILLER, Indianapolis—Continued

HOMER W. FAUCETT, III, admitted to bar, 2003, Indiana. *Education:* Indiana University (B.S., summa cum laude, 2000); Indiana University School of Law - Indianapolis (J.D., summa cum laude, 2003). *Member:* Indiana State Bar Association. ***PRACTICE AREAS:*** Intellectual Property. ***Email:*** homer.faucett@icemiller.com

MATTHEW FECHTMAN, admitted to bar, 2003, Indiana. *Education:* University of Virginia (B.A., 1997); University of Illinois (J.D., cum laude, 2003). ***PRACTICE AREAS:*** Strategic Advisors. ***Email:*** matthew.fechtman@icemiller.com

AMY KATHLEEN FISHER, born Indianapolis, Indiana, February 14, 1976; admitted to bar, 2001, Indiana. *Education:* University of Notre Dame (B.A., 1998); Indiana University School of Law - Indianapolis (J.D., 2001). *Member:* Indianapolis and Indiana State Bar Associations; Defense Research Institute; Defense Trial Counsel of Indiana. ***PRACTICE AREAS:*** General Litigation; Health Litigation; Drug and Medical Device Litigation. ***Email:*** amy.fisher@icemiller.com

ALEXANDER D. FORMAN, born Elkhart, Indiana, March 21, 1975; admitted to bar, 2001, Indiana; registered to practice before U.S. Patent and Trademark Office. *Education:* Indiana University, Bloomington (B.B.A., 1997); Indiana University School of Law - Indianapolis (J.D., magna cum laude, 2001). Note Development Editor, Indiana Law Review, 2000-2001. Author: "A Call To Restore Limitations on Unbridled Congressional Delegations," 34 Indiana Law Review, 1477. ***PRACTICE AREAS:*** Intellectual Property. ***Email:*** forman@icemiller.com

JENNIFER BARTELS FRAHM, born Bloomington, Illinois, 1973; admitted to bar, 2003, Indiana. *Education:* Purdue University (B.S., 1995); Indiana University School of Law, Indianapolis (J.D., cum laude, 2003). Order of the Barristers. Member, Evans Constitutional Law National Moot Court Team. ***PRACTICE AREAS:*** Employee Benefits. ***Email:*** jennifer.frahm@icemiller.com

CASSANDRA A. GILES, born Indianapolis, Indiana, July 9, 1978; admitted to bar, 2004, Indiana and U.S. District Court, Southern and Northern Districts of Indiana. *Education:* Indiana University - Indianapolis (B.S. in Business Marketing and Distribution, with high distinction, 2001); Indiana University School of Law - Indianapolis (J.D., cum laude, 2004). Delta Sigma Pi; Alpha Lambda Delta; Phi Eta Sigma; Beta Gamma Sigma. Member: Golden Key; Marketing Club. Recipient: J. Dwight Peterson Key Award for Most Outstanding Undergraduate Business Student; Most Outstanding Marketing and Distribution Student Awards. Author: Note, "Shaking Price Waterhouse: Suggestions for a More Workable Approach to Title VIII Mixed Motive Disparate Treatment Discrimination Claims," 37 Indiana Law Review 815. Member, Indiana Law Review. Member: Dean's Tutorial Society; Black Law Students Association; Women's Caucus. *Member:* Indianapolis, Marion County (Secretary, 2005) and American Bar Associations. ***PRACTICE AREAS:*** Corporate Law (50%); Antitrust (25%); Minority Business Law (25%). ***Email:*** cassandra.giles@icemiller.com

BENJAMIN M. HABEGGER, admitted to bar, 1999, Indiana. *Education:* Hanover College (B.A., cum laude, 1996); Indiana University School of Law, Indianapolis (J.D., 1999). ***PRACTICE AREAS:*** Corporate Law; Business Transactions. ***Email:*** benjamin.habegger@icemiller.com

MELANIE E. HARRIS, admitted to bar, 2001, Indiana. *Education:* DePauw University (B.A., English Composition, 1997); University of Pittsburgh School of Law (J.D., magna cum laude, 2000). Order of the Coif. *Member:* Indianapolis and Indiana State Bar Associations; Defense Trial Counsel of Indiana; Defense Research Institute. ***PRACTICE AREAS:*** Litigation; Business Litigation; Commercial Litigation. ***Email:*** melanie.harris@icemiller.com

BETH E. HATFIELD, admitted to bar, 2004, Indiana. *Education:* Indiana University (B.S., magna cum laude, 1997); Indiana University School of Law - Indianapolis (J.D., 2004). ***PRACTICE AREAS:*** Labor and Employment. ***Email:*** beth.hatfield@icemiller.com

DONALD HOSTETLER, admitted to bar, 2003, Indiana. *Education:* The Ohio State University (B.A., magna cum laude, 1997); University of Illinois College of Law (J.D., magna cum laude, 2003). ***PRACTICE AREAS:*** Litigation. ***Email:*** donald.hostetler@icemiller.com

DEWAYNE A. HUGHES, born Evansville, Indiana, 1966; admitted to bar, 2000, Indiana; U.S. District Court, Northern and Southern Districts of Indiana; registered to practice before U.S. Patent and Trademark Office. *Education:* University of Evansville (B.S., 1988); Indiana University School of Law - Indianapolis (J.D., summa cum laude, 2000). *Member:* Indianapolis and Indiana State Bar Associations. ***PRACTICE AREAS:*** Intellectual Property; Computers and Software; Contracts; Internet Law. ***Email:*** dewayne.hughes@icemiller.com

PAUL M. JONES, JR., born December 1, 1975; admitted to bar, 2002, Indiana. *Education:* Indiana University, Bloomington (B.S., with distinction, 1998); Indiana University School of Law, Indianapolis (J.D., magna cum laude, 2001). Order of Barristers. Fellow, Program on Law and State Government, 2000. Associate Editor, Indiana Law Review. Author: "Nonphysical Personal Injury Settlements and Judgments: Amending the Internal Revenue Code to Exclude Attorney Fees," 35 Ind. L. Rev. 245 (2001); "New Markets Tax Credits: Alternative Financing for Community and Economic Development," NewsQuarterly (Am. Bar Ass'n Tax Section, Fall 2003); "New Markets Tax Credits in Indiana." Tax Talk (Indiana Manufacturers Ass'n, June 2004). *Member:* Indianapolis, Indiana State and American Bar Associations; National Association of Bond Lawyers. ***PRACTICE AREAS:*** Taxation; Federal and State Tax Law. ***Email:*** paul.jones@icemiller.com

STACY S. KILLIAN, born Aurora, Illinois, March 31, 1974; admitted to bar, 2000, Indiana. *Education:* University of Kent, Canterbury, United Kingdom (B.A., 1996); University of Notre Dame (J.D., 2000). *Member:* American Bar Association. ***PRACTICE AREAS:*** Corporate Law (50%); Securities Regulation (50%). ***Email:*** kilian@icemiller.com

DOROTHY KOONTZ, admitted to bar, 2003, Indiana. *Education:* Valparaiso University (B.A., with honors, 1999); University of Illinois (J.D., cum laude, 2003). ***PRACTICE AREAS:*** Litigation. ***Email:*** dorothy.koontz@icemiller.com

(This Listing Continued)

ANGELA PEASE KRAHULIK, born Beech Grove, Indiana, August 30, 1974; admitted to bar, 2001, Indiana. *Education:* Indiana University (B.A., 1997; J.D., summa cum laude, 2001). Phi Alpha Delta. Dean's Tutorial Society Fellow. Member, Client Counseling Board. *Member:* Indiana State and American Bar Associations; Defense Trial Counsel of Indiana; Indianapolis American Inn of Court. ***PRACTICE AREAS:*** Litigation. ***Email:*** krahulik@icemiller.com

SCOTT D. MATTHEWS, born Richmond, Indiana, August 6, 1970; admitted to bar, 1998, Indiana and U.S. District Court, Northern and Southern Districts of Indiana. *Education:* Indiana University (B.A. Telecommunications, 1993); Indiana University School of Law-Indianapolis (J.D., summa cum laude, 1998). Member, Order of Barristers. Member, Indiana Law Review. ***PRACTICE AREAS:*** Commercial Litigation; Trade Secrets; Covenants Not To Compete; Restrictive Covenants; Unfair Competition; Environmental Litigation. ***Email:*** matthewd@icemiller.com

WILLIAM MAYNIE, IV, admitted to bar, 2004, Indiana. *Education:* University of Illinois (B.S., 2000); University of Illinois College of Law (J.D., 2004). *Member:* Marion County Bar Association. ***PRACTICE AREAS:*** Business Law. ***Email:*** william.maynie@icemiller.com

MICHAEL McNALLY, admitted to bar, 2002, Indiana and U.S. District Court, Northern and Southern Districts of Indiana. *Education:* Indiana University (B.A., 1997; J.D., 2002; M.B.A., 2004). ***PRACTICE AREAS:*** Litigation. ***Email:*** mike.mcnally@icemiller.com

KIMBERLY C. METZGER, born Iowa, February 20, 1966; admitted to bar, 1997, Indiana. *Education:* University of Notre Dame (B.A., 1988); University of Illinois, Urbana-Champaign (Master of Social Work, with highest honors, 1992); University of Toledo (J.D., magna cum laude, 1996). *Member:* Indianapolis and Indiana State Bar Associations. ***PRACTICE AREAS:*** Litigation. ***Email:*** kimberly.metzger@icemiller.com

DREW MIROFF, born Indianapolis, Indiana, August 13, 1973; admitted to bar, 1999, Indiana and U.S. District Court, Northern and Southern Districts of Indiana. *Education:* University of Michigan (B.A., Psychology, with high honors, 1996); Northwestern University School of Law (J.D., cum laude, 1999). *Member:* Indiana State and American Bar Associations. ***REPORTED CASES:*** Ledbetter v. Ball Memorial Hosp., 724 N.E.2d 1113 (Ind.App., 2000). ***PRACTICE AREAS:*** Litigation. ***Email:*** miroff@icemiller.com

THOMAS B. MULHERN, born Rochester, New York, 1973; admitted to bar, 2003, New York (Not admitted in Indiana). *Education:* Haverford College (B.A., 1995); Duke University (J.D., 2002). ***LANGUAGES:*** Spanish. ***PRACTICE AREAS:*** Finance.

BRIAN J. PAUL, born DeKalb, Illinois, November 8, 1972; admitted to bar, 2000, Indiana. *Education:* Purdue University, Lafayette (B.A., with highest distinction, 1995; M.A., 1997) Phi Beta Kappa; Vanderbilt Law School (J.D., 2000). *Member:* Seventh Circuit, Indiana State (Member, Appellate Practice Section) and American (Member, Appellate Practice Section) Bar Associations; Defense Research Institute (Member, Appellate Practice Section). ***REPORTED CASES:*** Ziliak v. AstraZeneca, LP, 324 F.3d 518 (7th Cir. 2003); Murray v. Conseco, Inc., 795 N.E.2d 454 (Ind. 2003); E & Mems, L.L.C. v. Eagen, 795 N.E.2d 508 (Ind. Ct. App. 2003); St. Mary's Med. Ctr. v. Loomis, 783 N.E.2d 274 (Ind. Ct. App. 2002); Huntington County Cmty. Sch. Corp. v. State Bd. of Tax Comm'rs, 757 N.E.2d 235 (Ind. Tax Ct. 2001). ***PRACTICE AREAS:*** Appellate Practice; Federal Courts; Torts; Commercial Litigation; Insurance. ***Email:*** brian.paul@icemiller.com

STEVEN F. POCKRASS, born New York, N.Y., November 23, 1965; admitted to bar, 1995, Indiana. *Education:* Washington & Lee University (B.A., 1987); University of Virginia (J.D., 1995). Phi Beta Kappa. *Member:* Indianapolis, Indiana State and American Bar Associations; Defense Trial Counsel of Indiana; Defense Research Institute. ***PRACTICE AREAS:*** Labor and Employment. ***Email:*** pockrass@icemiller.com

RYAN M. POOR, born Lafayette, Indiana, January 10, 1973; admitted to bar, 1998, Indiana, U.S. District Court, Northern and Southern Districts of Indiana and U.S. Court of Appeals, Seventh Circuit. *Education:* Wabash College (A.B., summa cum laude, 1995); Indiana University School of Law - Bloomington (J.D., magna cum laude, 1998). Phi Beta Kappa; Order of the Coif. ***PRACTICE AREAS:*** Labor and Employment; Employment Litigation; Labor Law. ***Email:*** Ryan.Poor@icemiller.com

APRIL SPARKS PYATT, born Muncie, Indiana, March 8, 1971; admitted to bar, 1998, Indiana. *Education:* Ball State University (B.S., 1994); Ohio Northern University (J.D., with high distinction, 1998). *Member:* Indianapolis, Indiana and American Bar Associations. ***PRACTICE AREAS:*** Real Estate. ***Email:*** sparks@icemiller.com

ELIZABETH TOWNSEND LAUGHLIN RAYMOND, admitted to bar, 2002, Illinois and U.S. District Court, Northern District of Illinois; 2003, U.S. District Court, Central District of Illinois; 2004, Indiana and U.S. District Court, Northern and Southern Districts of Indiana. *Education:* DePauw University (B.A., magna cum laude, 1999); University of Michigan (J.D., 2002). ***PRACTICE AREAS:*** Litigation; Labor and Employment. ***Email:*** elizabeth.raymond@icemiller.com

SUSAN B. REED, born Evansville, Indiana, July 28, 1972; admitted to bar, 2002, South Carolina; 2004, Indiana; 2005, U.S. District Court, Southern District of Indiana. *Education:* Purdue University (B.A., 1994); Indiana University School of Law - Indianapolis (J.D., 2002). ***PRACTICE AREAS:*** Municipal Finance. ***Email:*** susan.reed@icemiller.com

MARK C. REICHEL, born Philadelphia, Pennsylvania, May 28, 1974; admitted to bar, 2002, Indiana and U.S. District Court, Northern and Soutnern Districts of Indiana; 2003, New York, New Jersey and U.S. District Court, District of New Jersey; registered to practice before U.S. Patent and Trademark Office. *Education:* State University of New York at Stony Brook (B.S., Biochemistry, 1996); Indiana University School of Law - Indianapolis (J.D., 2002); Indiana University (M.B.A., 2002). Phi Delta Phi. Student Note Candidate, 2000-2001 and Executive Production Editor, 2001-2002, Indiana International & Comparative Law Review. *Member:* Indianapolis (Member, Intellectual Property Executive Committee, 2005—), Indiana State and New York State (Member, Intellectual Property Section) Bar Associations. ***PRACTICE AREAS:*** Intellectual Property; Intellectual Property Prosecution. ***Email:*** mark.reichel@icemiller.com

JENNIFER L. RHODES, born Kokomo, Indiana, August 29, 1974; admitted to bar, 1999, Indiana. *Education:* Indiana University (B.S., Accounting, summa cum laude, with departmental honors, 1996; J.D., magna cum laude, 1999). Delta Theta Phi; Order of the

(This Listing Continued)

Coif; Order of Barristers. Finalist and External Team Member, Sherman Minton Moot Court. *Member:* Indiana State and American Bar Associations; American Institute of Certified Public Accountants. ***PRACTICE AREAS:*** Venture Capital; Private Equity Financing; Mergers, Acquisitions and Divestitures; Securities; Corporate. ***Email:*** jennifer.rhodes@icemiller.com

MATTHEW R. ST. LOUIS, admitted to bar, 2004, Indiana. *Education:* University of Michigan (B.A., 2000); Indiana University Kelley School of Business (M.B.A., 2004); Indiana University School of Law (J.D., 2004). ***PRACTICE AREAS:*** Corporate Law. ***Email:*** matthew.st.louis@icemiller.com

RACHEL ST. PETER, born Fond Du Lac, Wisconsin, July 30, 1974; admitted to bar, 1999, Indiana; registered to practice before the U.S. Patent and Trademark Office. *Education:* Butler University (B.S., Biology, cum laude, with departmental honors, 1996); Indiana University School of Law (J.D., magna cum laude, 1999). Delta Theta Phi. Order of the Coif. Managing Editor, Indiana Journal of Global Legal Studies. ***PRACTICE AREAS:*** Intellectual Property. ***Email:*** stpeter@icemiller.com

SAMUEL SCHMUTTE, admitted to bar, 2004, Indiana. *Education:* Marian College (B.S., 1993); Indiana University School of Law - Bloomington (J.D., cum laude, 2004). ***PRACTICE AREAS:*** Business Law. ***Email:*** samuel.schmutte@icemiller.com

ERIC C. SCROGGINS, born Muncie, Indiana; admitted to bar, 2002, Indiana and U.S. District Court, Northern and Southern Districts of Indiana. *Education:* Ball State University (B.S., 1994); Indiana University School of Law - Indianapolis (J.D., 2001). Member, Order of the Barristers. Recipient, Christopher Maine Advocacy Award for Appellate Advocacy. Named "Top Advocate" of Indiana University - Indianapolis Moot Court Competition. Named a Graduate of the Last Decade by Ball State University Alumni Association. Regular Speaker, Indiana Chamber of Commerce, Indiana Association of Cities and Towns, Association of Indiana Counties, Indiana School Board Association, Indiana Payroll Association, Lorman, National Business Institute and various human resources associations on a variety of employment-related issues. Named Distinguished Hoosier by Governor O'Bannon for Public Service as Deputy Director of Personnel, State of Indiana. *Member:* Indianapolis (Labor and Employment Division), Indiana State (Labor and Employment Division) and American (Labor and Employment Division) Bar Associations; Human Resources Association of Central Indiana. ***PRACTICE AREAS:*** Labor and Employment; Employment Litigation; Civil Rights; Municipal Law; Administrative Law; Government; Age Discrimination in Employment; Civil Service; Collective Bargaining; Confidentiality Agreements; Covenants Not To Compete; Employee Discipline; Employee Drug Testing; Employee Leasing; Employee Privacy; Employer Liability; Employer Rights; Employment Arbitration; Employment at Will; Employment Breach of Contract; Employment Civil Rights; Employment Contracts; Employment Defense; Employment Disability Discrimination; Employment Discrimination; Employment Law; Employment Mediation; Employment Termination; Equal Employment Opportunity Law; Executive Employment Law; Executive Severance Contracts; Fair Labor Standards; Family and Medical Leave Act; Harassment; Fair Employment Practices; Labor Arbitration; Labor Law; Labor Legislation; Labor Relations; Labor Strikes; Management Employment Law; Management Labor Law; National Labor Relations Act; National Origin Discrimination; Negligent Hiring; Noncompete Litigation; Noncompetition and Non-Solicitation Agreements; Outsourcing; Personnel Policies; Personnel Training; Public Sector Collective Bargaining; Public Sector Employment Law; Public Sector Labor Relations; Reductions in Force; Restrictive Covenants; Retaliatory Discharge; Sexual Harassment; Title VII Discrimination; Unfair Labor Practices; Wage and Hour Law; WARN Act; Whistleblower Litigation; Workplace Violence; Wrongful Termination Defense; Municipal Defense; Municipal Labor Law; County Government Law; County Liability; Governmental Defense; Governmental Law; Governmental Liability; Local Government Defense; Local Government Law; Local Government Liability; Local Government Relations; Political Subdivision Liability; Public Officials Liability; State Government Law; Township Law; Civil Rights Defense; Civil Rights Section 1983; Discrimination; Sex Discrimination; Race Discrimination. ***Email:*** eric.scroggins@icemiller.com

TIFFANY A. SHARPLEY, born Charleston, South Carolina, December 25, 1973; admitted to bar, 2001, Indiana. *Education:* Indiana University (B.S., high distinction, 1997; M.B.A., 2001; J.D., magna cum laude, 2001). Associate Editor, Indiana Law Review, 1999-2000. *Member:* Indianapolis, Indiana State and American Bar Associations. ***PRACTICE AREAS:*** Employee Benefits. ***Email:*** sharpley@icemiller.com

MARK I. SHUBLAK, born Indianapolis, Indiana, June 9, 1970; admitted to bar, 2001, Indiana. *Education:* Ball State University (B.A., cum laude, 1992); Indiana University School of Law - Indianapolis (J.D., 2000). ***PRACTICE AREAS:*** Government Relations; Legislative Practice; Lobbying; Administrative Law; Regulatory Law; Gaming Law; Liquor Licensing; Government Contracts; Campaign Finance; Election Law. ***Email:*** shublak@icemiller.com

CHERYL L. SILVERTHORNE, born Crown Point, Indiana, May 12, 1971; admitted to bar, 2003, Indiana; U.S. District Court, Northern and Southern Districts of Indiana. *Education:* Purdue University (B.S., 1993); Indiana University School of Law - Indianapolis (J.D., cum laude, 2002). *Member:* Indianapolis, Indiana State and American Bar Associations. ***PRACTICE AREAS:*** Creditors Rights; Corporate Law; Business Law; Bankruptcy; Corporate Reorganization. ***Email:*** cheryl.silverthorne@icemiller.com

JACK SKINNER, admitted to bar, 2003, Indiana; U.S. Court of Appeals, Third Circuit. *Education:* Bradley University (B.S., 1993); University of Illinois (J.D., summa cum laude, 2002). Order of the Coif. Managing Editor, University of Illinois Law Reivew, 2001-2002. Law Clerk to Hon. Richard L. Nygaard, U.S. Court of Appeals, Third Circuit, 2002-2003. *Member:* American Bar Association. [Linguist, U.S. Navy, 1993-1999]. ***LANGUAGES:*** Chinese-Mandarin. ***PRACTICE AREAS:*** International; Corporate Law; Securities. ***Email:*** jack.skinner@icemiller.com

RABEH M. A. SOOFI, born Tehran, Iran; admitted to bar, 2004, Indiana and U.S. District Court, Northern and Southern Districts of Indiana. *Education:* University of Michigan (B.A. in History and Political Science); University of Notre Dame (J.D.). Sigma Ioto Rho; Phi Alpha Theta; Pi Sigma Alpha; Delta Epsilon Iota. Recipient, Corinne Lyman Award for Excellence in Political Science. Former Judge, Moot Court Competition, Indiana University - Indianapolis Law School. Board Member, Michigan Journal of Political Science. Managing Editor, Journal of Legislation. Instructed: Introductory English Classes, Tutored English-as-a-Second Language and Provided Services for Deaf and Hearing-Impaired Students; Undergraduate International Relations Classes, University of Notre Dame Government Department. Clerked for the City of Chicago Corporation Counsel. Member, Student Bar Association. Involved with Organizations including the Homeless Shelter Legal Project, which provides Legal Assistance to Transient and Low-Income Individuals and Families in the Indianapolis Area. Devoted significant time to Pro Bono Matters coordinated by the Heartland Pro Bono Council. Regular Participant in Habitat for Humanity Projects. *Member:* Indianapolis, Indiana State and American Bar Associations; Indiana Trial Lawyers Association. ***LANGUAGES:*** French and Persian. ***PRACTICE AREAS:*** Insurance; Insurance Recovery. ***Email:*** rabeh.soofi@icemiller.com

(This Listing Continued)

MICHAEL C. STEELE, born Kokomo, Indiana, June 22, 1978; admitted to bar, 2003, Florida; 2005, Indiana. *Education:* Ball State University (B.S., 2000); University of Miami School of Law (J.D., 2002). ***PRACTICE AREAS:*** Drug and Medical Device Litigation. ***Email:*** michael.steele@icemiller.com

ERIC SWANK, born Pennsylvania, 1973; admitted to bar, 1999, Indiana. *Education:* St. Olaf College (B.A., magna cum laude, 1995); University of Michigan (J.D., cum laude, 1999). Phi Beta Kappa. *Member:* American Bar Association. ***PRACTICE AREAS:*** Employee Benefits; Public Pension Plans; Qualified Retirement Plans. ***Email:*** swank@icemiller.com

JENNIFER A. THOMAS, born Hollywood, Florida, April 8, 1974; admitted to bar, 1999, Indiana and U.S. District Court, Northern and Southern Districts of Indiana. *Education:* Bob Jones University (B.A., cum laude, 1996); Indiana University School of Law (J.D., cum laude, 1999). *Member:* Indianapolis Bar Association; Indiana State Bar Association; American Bar Association; American Health Lawyers Association. ***PRACTICE AREAS:*** Litigation. ***Email:*** jennifer.thomas@icemiller.com

ANN L. THRASHER PAPA, born 1971; admitted to bar, 2002, Indiana; U.S. District Court, Northern and Southern Districts of Indiana. *Education:* Indiana University (B.A., 1993); Indiana University School of Law - Indianapolis (J.D., 2001). *Member:* Indianapolis, Boone County, Indiana State and American Bar Associations. ***PRACTICE AREAS:*** Litigation. ***Email:*** ann.papa@icemiller.com

KRISTINA M. TRIDICO, born Minneapolis, Minnesota, September 17, 1974; admitted to bar, 1999, Indiana. *Education:* Ohio University (B.S., summa cum laude, 1996); University of Oregon School of Law (J.D., 1999). Phi Beta Kappa. Author: "Sustainable America in the Twenty-First Century," Journal of Natural Resources and Environmental Law. *Member:* Indianapolis (Treasurer, Environmental Executive Committee) and Indiana State Bar Associations. ***PRACTICE AREAS:*** Corporate Law; Environmental Law; Environmental Administrative Law; Environmental Corporate Law. ***Email:*** tridico@icemiller.com

NATHANIEL M. UHL, admitted to bar, 2004, Indiana. *Education:* Hanover College (B.A., cum laude, 2001); Indiana University School of Law (J.D., cum laude, 2004). ***PRACTICE AREAS:*** Litigation (100%). ***Email:*** nate.uhl@icemiller.com

ANDREW N. VENTO, born Youngstown, Ohio, July 13, 1974; admitted to bar, 2000, Indiana. *Education:* Indiana University (B.A., summa cum laude, 1996; J.D., cum laude, 2000). ***PRACTICE AREAS:*** Estate Planning. ***Email:*** vento@icemiller.com

KATHERINE A. WINCHESTER, born Lincoln, Nebraska, April 28, 1968; admitted to bar, 1997, Indiana. *Education:* Butler University (B.A., 1990); Indiana University (J.D., magna cum laude, 1997). Order of the Coif. ***PRACTICE AREAS:*** Products Liability Defense; Complex and Multi-District Litigation; Toxic Tort Defense; Drug and Medical Device Defense; Environmental Products Liability. ***Email:*** katherine.winchester@icemiller.com

REPRESENTATIVE CLIENTS: Aisin U.S.A. Inc. (Aisin Seiki Co., Ltd. & Aisin American, Inc.); Allied Signal; Aluminum Company of America; Amateur Athletic Union of the United States, Inc.; AMAX, Inc.; American United Life Insurance Co.; American Excess Insurance; American Home Products Corp.; Arnett Clinic; Associated Insurance Co.; Associated General Contractors of Indiana, Inc.; Avesta Sheffield; Ball State University; BankOne, Indiana, NA; Baptist Homes of Indiana, Inc.; Baxter Healthcare Corp.; Biomet, Inc.; Bloomington, City of; Butler University; Carpenter Manufacturing, Inc.; Carrier Corporation; Chrysler Corp.; Churchill Downs; CIBA-Giegy Corp.; CID Equity Partners; CID Venture Partners, L.P.; Citizens Gas & Coke Utility; CNA Insurance; Commercial Union; Community Hospital of Indianapolis; Community Hospitals of Indiana, Inc.; Community Hospital of Anderson; Community Action of Greater Indianapolis, Inc.; Cosco, Inc,; Cummins Engine Co.; D.A. INC. (Daiwa Kasei Kogyo); Dana Corporation; Delco Remy America; Diamet Corporation (Mitsubishi Metal America Corporation); Digital Audio Disc Corporation (Sony Corporation); E.T.S., Inc.; ELSA Corporation (Sakamoto Industry Co., Ltd.); Employers Insurance of Warsaw; Evansville, City of; F.A. Wilhelm Construction Co.; Fairbanks Communications; Federal Deposit Insurance Corp.; Ford Motor Company; Fort Harrison Reuse Authority; Fort Wayne Airport Authority; Fuji Component Parts USA, Inc. (Fuji Buhin Kogyo K.K.); GECOM Corporation (Mitsui Mining & Smelting Co., Ltd.); General Seating of America, Inc. (NHK Spring Co., Ltd. & Lear Siegler Seating); General Housewares Corp.; Haynes International, Inc.; Howard, Needles, Tammen & Bergendoff; ICT Corporation (Isuzu Motors, Ltd.); Indiana Educational Facility Authority; Indiana Housing Finance Authority; Indiana Japanese Language School, Inc.; Indiana Health Facilities Financing Authority; Indiana Insurance Co.; Indiana Chamber of Commerce; Indiana Association of Cities and Towns; Association of Indiana Counties; Indiana Association of Cities and Towns Foundation; Indiana Bankers Association; Indiana University; Indiana, State of; Indiana Development Finance Authority; Indiana Port Commission; Indianapolis Foundation; Indianapolis Airport Authority; Indianapolis, City of ; Indianapolis Motor Speedway Corp.; INTAT Precision, Inc. (Aisin Takaoka Co., Ltd.); Irwin Financial Corporation; Isuzu Motors America, Inc. (Isuzu Motors, Ltd.); Ivy Tech State College; JAYTEC, INC. (F.C.C. CO.,LTD.); Johnson and Johnson; Key Bank; Kmart Corp.; Kobelco Compressors (America), Inc.; Lafayette, City of; Lake Michigan Charters; Liberty Mutual; Lilly Industries, Inc.; Magnequench International, Inc.; Marion General Hospital; McGill Manufacturing Corp.; MMI Co.; Motorola; Mutual Security Life; Navistar International Transportation Corp.; Nucor Steel; Onkyo Manufacturing, Inc. (Onkyo Corporation); Ontario Corporation; Pedcor Investments; Perry County; PHICO Insurance Co.; Procter & Gamble Co.; Public Employees Retirement Fund; Purdue University; Reid Hospital and Health Care Services; Reilly Industries, Inc.; Resort Condominiums International, Inc.; Rexnord, Inc.; Robinson-Nugent, Inc.; Saint Joseph's College; Sexton Companies; Showboar Marina; Sintering Technologies Inc. (Hitachi Powdered Metals Co., Ltd. & Cummins Engine Co.); Sofamor Danek Group, Inc.; Software Artistry; Sony Corporation of America (Sony Corporation); St. Paul Insurance Co.; Steak n Shake, Inc.; Sunshine Promotions, Inc.; Takasago America, Inc. (Takasago Thermal Engineering); Target Stores Division of Dayton-Hudson Corporation; Taylor University; The Buckingham Cos.; The Upjohn Company; The DeMars Corp.; The Coco-Cola Co.; Thomson Consumer Electronics, Inc. (RCA); Toyota Industrial Equipment Mfg., Inc. (Toyota Automatic Loom Works, Ltd.); United Dominion Industries; Wabash Valley Broadcasting Corporation; Warner-Lambert Company; Wavetek; Wyeth-Ayers & Labs.

REVISER OF THE INDIANA LAW DIGEST FOR THIS DIRECTORY.

JENSEN & ASSOCIATES

7440 NORTH SHADELAND
SUITE 202
INDIANAPOLIS, INDIANA 46250
Telephone: 317-849-5834
Fax: 317-849-5974
URL: http://www.jensenlaw.com
Email: jensen@iquest.net
URL: http://www.jensenlaw-firm.com

Family Law, Adoptions, Child Custody, Child Support, Divorce, Visitation Rights, Business Law, Business Planning, Contracts, Insurance Business, Business Enterprises, Corporate, Closely Held Business, Limited Liability Companies, Partnerships, Small Business, Business Litigation, Buying and Selling a Business, Starting a Business, Civil Litigation, Wills and Probate, Trusts and Estates, Asset Protection, Guardianships, Estate Planning, Family and Civil Mediation.

HERBERT A. JENSEN, admitted to bar, 1975, Indiana. *Education:* University of Evansville (B.A., 1967); Indiana University, Indianapolis (J.D., 1975). Advisory Board: Salvation Army; Neighborhood Christian Legal Clinic. Board Member, 1st Church of the Nazarene Church. *Member:* Indianapolis Bar Association; National Lawyers Association; Christian Legal Society (National Board Member). [U.S. Marine Corp., 1969-1972; National Guard, 1972-1974]. ***Email:*** hajensen@iquest.net

ASSOCIATES

ARTHUR E. JOHNSON, admitted to bar, 1995, Indiana. *Education:* Ball State University (B.S., Distinguished Military Graduate and Distinguished Alumni, 1964); Auburn University (M.S., 1974); Air Command and Staff College (Distinguished Graduate, 1974); National War College (1980); Indiana University Law School (J.D., cum laude, 1995). Director, Strategic and Space Forces, Office of the Secretary of Defense, Joint Chiefs of Staff Representative to the Defense and Space Talks with the Former Soviet Union. Commander, 44th Strategic Missile Wing. Officer and Member, Celebration of Hope Executive Board, Military Officers Association of America. *Member:* Indianapolis (Secretary, Professional Responsibility Committee) and Indiana State Bar Associations; Christian Legal Society. [Brigadier General, U.S. Air Force, retired, 1992]. ***PRACTICE AREAS:*** General Practice; Business Law; Consumer Law; Business Litigation; Consumer Litigation; Real Estate; Estate Planning; Business Succession Planning; Civil Litigation; Personal Injury; Mediation. ***Email:*** jensen@iquest.net

KIMBERLY JACKSON, admitted to bar, 1986, Indiana. *Education:* Indiana University, Bloomington (B.A., 1982); Indiana University, Indianapolis (J.D., 1986). Law Clerk, Indiana Supreme Court Chief Justice Randall T. Shepard, 1986-1987. Staff Attorney, Assistant Administrator, 1987-1995, and Administrator, 1998-2002, Indiana Supreme Court. Chief Deputy Clerk, U.S. District Court, Southern District of Indiana, 1995-1998. *Member:* Christian Legal Society (Local Board Member). ***PRACTICE AREAS:*** Civil Litigation; Family Law; Appellate Practice. ***Email:*** jensen@iquest.net

JENNIFER L. D'ORSO, admitted to bar, 1995, Indiana. *Education:* Purdue University (B.Ch.E., 1990); Indiana University (J.D., 1995). *Member:* Christian Legal Society. ***PRACTICE AREAS:*** Family Law; Adoption Law; Guardianship. ***Email:*** jldorso@iquest.net

KAREN H. YOUNG, admitted to bar, 2005, Indiana. *Education:* Cedarville University (1999); Indiana University, Indianapolis (J.D., 2004). Law Clerk: Reilly Industries, Inc.; Lewis & Kappes, P.C.; Jensen & Associates, 2005. Volunteer, Neighborhood Christian Legal Clinic. *Member:* Indianapolis, Indiana State and American Bar Associations; Christian Legal Society. ***PRACTICE AREAS:*** Family Law; Small Business Law; Estate Planning. ***Email:*** jensen@iquest.net

OF COUNSEL

JEANNE LEE McMAINS, admitted to bar, 1995, Indiana. *Education:* Purdue University (B.A., with highest distinction, 1992); Indiana University, Indianapolis (J.D., 1995). Staff Attorney, Focus on the Family, National Christian Foundation. *Member:* Christian Legal Society. ***PRACTICE AREAS:*** Charitable Giving; Estate Planning. ***Email:*** jmcmains@nationalchristian.com

JOHNSON LAWHEAD BUTH & POPE, P.C.

INDIANAPOLIS, INDIANA

(See Barnes & Thornburg)

KATZ & KORIN, PC

334 NORTH SENATE AVENUE
INDIANAPOLIS, INDIANA 46204-1708
Telephone: 317-464-1100
Fax: 317-464-1111
URL: http://www.katzkorin.com

Appellate Practice, Art Law, Business Law, Bankruptcy, Charitable Planning, Collections, Commercial Lending, Contracts, Entertainment Law, Environmental Law, Estate Planning and Administration, Health Care Law, Housing and Community Development Law, Intellectual Property Rights, High Technology Law, Labor and Employee Relations Law, Litigation, Mediation Services, Personal Injury, Product Defense, Real Estate Law and Tax Law.

RONALD M. KATZ, born Gary, Indiana, April 2, 1958; admitted to bar, 1983, Indiana and U.S. Tax Court; 1984, District of Columbia. *Education:* Indiana University (B.S., 1980; J.D., 1983); Georgetown University (LL.M. in Taxation, 1985). Recipient: Prentice Hall Tax Award, 1983; 2002 Indianapolis Bar Association (IBA) Dr. John Morton Finney Excellence in Legal Education Award. Author: "Housing Tax Credits in Indiana," Metro Publishing Co., 1994—. Co-Author, "Housing Development Forms and Commentary," West Group, 1996-2001. Certified Public Accountant, Maryland, 1984. Adjunct Professor, Indiana University School of Law-Indianapolis (Real Estate Transactions). Instructor, Indiana Bar Review Courses on Wills, Administration and Trusts, Real Property Law and Personal Property Law, 1993—. General Counsel, 2004 and Member, 2005—, IBA Board of Managers. Member, Board of Directors, Indiana Equity Fund, Inc., 1994—. Member, Board of Directors, Coalition on Homelessness Intervention and Prevention, 2003—. Frequent Faculty for American Bar Association, Indiana Continuing Legal Education Forum, IBA and Indiana Housing and Community Development Authority conferences on commercial real estate financing, estate planning, trust administration and probate, and use of low-income housing credits and other affordable housing and community development initiatives, 1994—. Member, National Advisory Board, Housing and Development Reporter, 1994—. Chair, 2005-2006 and Governing Committee Member, 2000—, ABA Forum on Affordable Housing & Community Development Law. President, Jewish Community Center of Indianapolis, 1995-1998. ***PRACTICE AREAS:*** Real Estate Development; Business Development; Housing and Community Development Law; Estate Planning and Administration. ***Email:*** rkatz@katzkorin.com

OFFER KORIN, born Jerusalem, Israel, November 24, 1964; admitted to bar, 1988, Indiana, U.S. District Court, Northern and Southern Districts of Indiana and U.S. Court of Appeals, Fourth and Seventh Circuits; 1996, U.S. Supreme Court and U.S. District Court, Northern District of Illinois. *Education:* Indiana University (B.A., 1985; J.D., 1988). Member, Local Rules Committee, United States District Court, Southern District of Indiana. Recognized in several Editions of Who's Who in American Law. Past President, Jewish Community Relations Council. *Member:* Federal Bar Association (Past President, Indianapolis Chapter); Indiana Trial Lawyers Association. ***LANGUAGES:*** Hebrew. ***PRACTICE AREAS:*** Federal and State Civil Litigation; Business Planning and Transactions; Labor Law; Employee Relations; Intellectual Property Rights. ***Email:*** okorin@katzkorin.com

SALLY FRANKLIN ZWEIG, born St. Louis, Missouri, March 24, 1950; admitted to bar, 1986, Indiana; U.S. Supreme Court; U.S. Court of Appeals, Seventh Circuit. *Education:* Washington University (B.A., 1971); Indiana University (J.D., 1986). *Member:* Bar Association of the Seventh Federal Circuit; Indianapolis Inn of Court (Charter Member, Master and Past President; Member, Disciplinary Commission). ***PRACTICE AREAS:*** Federal and State Civil Litigation; Business Law; Products Liability Defense; Health Care; Medical Products; Technology; Art Law. ***Email:*** szweig@katzkorin.com

MICHAEL W. HILE, born Goshen, Indiana, February 22, 1960; admitted to bar, 1985, Indiana and U.S. District Court, Northern and Southern Districts of Indiana; 1992, New York. *Education:* Andrews University (B.A., with honors, 1982); Indiana University (J.D., 1985). Phi Alpha Delta. Law Clerk to the Honorable Michael H. Kearns, U.S. Bankruptcy Court Judge, 1985-1986. *Member:* Indianapolis, Indiana State and American Bar Associations. ***PRACTICE AREAS:*** Bankruptcy Law; Corporate Restructuring Law. ***Email:*** mhile@katzkorin.com

MICHAEL J. GABOVITCH, born Indianapolis, Indiana, December 20, 1960; admitted to bar, 1986, Indiana. *Education:* Indiana University (B.A., with honors, 1983); Indiana University School of Law (J.D., 1986). Phi Beta Kappa. Judge Forrest E. Jump Scholar. Member, Indianapolis Law Review. ***PRACTICE AREAS:*** Real Estate; Corporate; Municipal. ***Email:*** mgabovitch@katzkorin.com

MICHAEL J. KERSCHNER, born Chicago, Illinois, September 2, 1966; admitted to bar, 1992, Illinois and U.S. District Court, Northern District of Illinois; 1996, Indiana and U.S. District Court, Northern and Southern Districts of Indiana. *Education:* University of Illinois (B.S., Acct., 1988); Illinois Institute of Technology, Chicago-Kent College of Law (J.D., with honors, 1992). Instructor, Title Law in Indiana, National Business Institute, September 1999. Panelist: "Choice of Entity," "The Basics of the Low Income Housing Tax Credit," and "Putting Together Mixed Finance Deals." Certified Public Accountant, Illinois, 1988. *Member:* Chicago, Illinois State, Indiana State and American Bar Associations. ***PRACTICE AREAS:*** Housing and Urban Development Law; Estate Planning; Estate Administration; Real Estate Law. ***Email:*** mkerschner@katzkorin.com

CATHLEEN L. NEVIN, born April 22, 1952; admitted to bar, 1984, California and U.S. District Court, Central District of California; 1999, Indiana and U.S. District Court, Southern and Northern Districts of Indiana. *Education:* University of California at Los Angeles (B.A., 1980); Santa Barbara College of Law (J.D., 1984). Lecturer, University of California, Santa Barbara Extension, 1996-1999; Golden Gate University, Santa Barbara, 1981-1991. *Member:* State Bar of California. ***PRACTICE AREAS:*** Employment Law. ***Email:*** cnevin@katzkorin.com

---

RONALD G. SENTMAN, born 1951; admitted to bar, 1984, Indiana and U.S. District Court, Southern and Northern Districts of Indiana. *Education:* Indiana University (A.B., Journalism, 1972); Indiana University School of Law-Bloomington (J.D., cum laude, 1984). ***PRACTICE AREAS:*** Commercial Litigation; Litigation. ***Email:*** rsentman@katzkorin.com

LINDA L. VITONE, born Nazareth, Pennsylvania, March 7, 1968; admitted to bar, 2002, Indiana; registered to practice before the U.S. Patent and Trademark Office. *Education:* Moravian College (B.S., 1990); Indiana University School of Law (J.D., 2002). ***Email:*** lvitone@katzkorin.com

BRIAN S. KENWORTHY, born Dayton, Ohio, April 12, 1972; admitted to bar, 2002, Indiana and U.S. District Court, Northern and Southern Districts of Indiana. *Education:* Indiana University (B.A., 1996; J.D., cum laude, 2002). Editor, Indiana International and Comparative Law Review. *Member:* Indianapolis, Indiana State, American and Federal Bar Associations. ***PRACTICE AREAS:*** Business Litigation; Commercial Debt Collections; Consumer Debt Collections; Employment Law. ***Email:*** bkenworthy@katzkorin.com

ROBERT B. KIRSH, born Indianapolis, Indiana, March 19, 1969; admitted to bar, 1995, Indiana and U.S. District Court, Northern and Southern Districts of Indiana. *Education:* Indiana University (B.A., 1991); The University of Tulsa (J.D., 1994); Purdue University (M.S., Management, 1997). Phi Alpha Delta (President/Justice, 1994). *Member:* Indianapolis, Indiana State and American Bar Associations. ***Email:*** rkirsh@katzkorin.com

KRISTOPHER N. KAZMIERCZAK, born Michigan City, Indiana; admitted to bar, 1996, Indiana and U.S. District Court, Northern and Southern Districts of Indiana; U.S.

(This Listing Continued)

District Court, Central District of Illinois; U.S. District Court, Northern District of Ohio; U.S. District Court, Eastern and Western Districts of Michigan; U.S. District Court, Eastern District of Wisconsin; U.S. Court of Appeals, Seventh Circuit. *Education:* Indiana University (B.A., 1992); Indiana University School of Law (J.D., 1996). Member, Indianapolis Inn of Court, 2001-2003. *Member:* Federal Bar Association. ***PRACTICE AREAS:*** Business Litigation; Employment Litigation; Employment Law; Federal Civil Litigation; Civil Litigation. ***Email:*** kkaz@katzkorin.com

OF COUNSEL

BERNARD PYLITT, born Chicago, Illinois, April 16, 1948; admitted to bar, 1975, Indiana; U.S. District Court, Northern and Southern Districts of Indiana, U.S. Court of Appeals, Seventh Circuit and U.S. Supreme Court. *Education:* Indiana University (B.A., 1970); Indiana University School of Law - Indianapolis (J.D., 1975). Co-Author, "ATM Crime and Bank Liability," The Banker Magazine, March/April 1987 and Res Gestae, November 1987. Adjunct Professor, Criminal Law, University of Indianapolis, 1982-1990. Instructor, Criminal Trial Advocacy, Department of Justice Advocacy Institute, Washington, D.C., 1978. Moderator and Lecturer, Indiana Continuing Legal Education Forum. Deputy Prosecuting Attorney, 19th Judicial Circuit, Marion County, Indiana, 1975-1977. First Assistant U.S. Attorney, Southern District of Indiana, 1977-1981. Chief, Criminal Justice Division, Indianapolis, 1977-1981. Administrative Law Judge: Indiana Gaming Commission, 1996-2003; Indiana Horse Racing Commission, 1997-2003; Indiana Alcoholic Beverage Commission. Judge, Hamilton County Superior Court No. 2, 2004. *Member:* Indianapolis, Indiana State and Federal (Past President, Indianapolis Chapter, 1985-1986) Bar Associations. [JAGC, U.S. Army, 1971-1973]. ***PRACTICE AREAS:*** Alternative Dispute Resolution; Mediation; Federal Litigation; White Collar Criminal Defense; State Government Law. ***Email:*** bpylitt@katzkorin.com

(All Attorneys are members of the Indianapolis, Indiana State and American Bar Associations).

KENDALL, WOOD, LOWRY & KESSINGER

INDIANAPOLIS, INDIANA

(See Danville)

General Trial Practice in all Courts. Probate and Estate Planning, Personal Injury, Real Estate, School, Family, Domestic Relations and Criminal Defense Law.

DIANE HUBBARD KENNEDY

4911 EAST 56TH STREET
INDIANAPOLIS, INDIANA 46220-5719
Telephone: 317-254-1443
Fax: 317-254-1449
Email: d_kennedy@iquest.net
URL: http://www.dhkennedylaw.com

Estate Planning, Wills and Probate, Trusts and Estates, Estate and Gift Taxation Law.

DIANE HUBBARD KENNEDY, born Muncie, Indiana, December 27, 1950; admitted to bar, 1979, Indiana. *Education:* Ball State University (B.S., with great distinction, 1972); Indiana University (J.D., summa cum laude, 1979). Editor-in-Chief, Indiana Law Review, 1978-1979. Editorial Board, Probate & Property, 1995—. *Member:* Indianapolis (Chair, Estate Planning and Administration Section, 2000-2001), Indiana State (Chair, Probate, Trust and Real Property Section, 2003-2004) and American Bar Associations. Fellow, the American College of Trust and Estate Counsel.

KIEFER AND McGOFF

Established in 1992
8900 KEYSTONE CROSSING, SUITE 400
INDIANAPOLIS, INDIANA 46240-2146
Telephone: 317-848-2300
Fax: 317-574-3000
URL: http://www.kmlawyers.com
URL: http://www.lawyers.com/kiefer&mcgoff

Criminal Trials and Appeals, State and Federal Courts, Health Care Law, Attorney Legal Ethics and Professional Responsibility, Family Law, Civil Litigation.

J. RICHARD KIEFER, born Lafayette, Indiana, January 15, 1948; admitted to bar, 1975, Indiana; U.S. Supreme Court; U.S. Court of Appeals, Seventh Circuit; U.S. District Court, Northern and Southern Districts of Indiana. *Education:* Purdue University (B.A., 1970); Indiana University School of Law (J.D., cum laude, 1975). Adjunct Professor, Indiana University-Purdue University, Indianapolis, 1980-1984. *Member:* Indianapolis (Chairman, Criminal Justice Section, 1984-1985), Indiana State (Chairman, Criminal Justice Section, 1986-1987), American and Federal Bar Associations; Indiana Association of Criminal Defense Lawyers (Board of Directors, 1986—; President, 1992—); National Association of Criminal Defense Lawyers; Indiana Health Care Association; Indiana Trial Lawyers Association; The Association of Trial Lawyers of America. ***PRACTICE AREAS:*** Criminal Defense Law; Civil Litigation; Health Care Law. ***Email:*** jrk@kmlawyers.com

KEVIN P. McGOFF, born Cleveland, Ohio, April 25, 1953; admitted to bar, 1980, Indiana; U.S. Supreme Court; U.S. Court of Appeals, Seventh Circuit; U.S. District Court, Southern District of Indiana. *Education:* Indiana University (B.A., 1977; J.D., 1980). Staff, Indiana Supreme Court Disciplinary Commission, 1978-1981. Adjunct Professor, Indiana University School of Law, Indianapolis, 1992-1993; Indiana Supreme Court Committee on Rules of Evidence, 1992-1993. Board of Directors, Indiana Public Defender Council, 1988-1994; Chairman, 1991-1993. Author: "Disciplining Attorneys," 25 Res Gestae 9, 1981. Professional Responsibility Survey, Vo. 29, Indiana Law Review, 1996. *Member:* Indianapolis (Board of Managers, 2004—), Indiana State (Legal Ethics Committee, 1990—) and American Bar Associations; Indiana Association of Criminal Defense Lawyers; National Association of Criminal Defense Lawyers; Indiana Trial Lawyers Association; Association of Professional Responsibility Lawyers. ***LANGUAGES:*** French. ***PRACTICE AREAS:*** Legal Ethics and Professional Responsibility; Criminal Law; Family Law. ***Email:*** kpm@kmlawyers.com

ASSOCIATES

WHITNEY D. MAUK, born Jeffersonville, Indiana, July 6, 1974; admitted to bar, 1999, Indiana and U.S. District Court, Northern and Southern Districts of Indiana. *Education:* Indiana University (B.A., 1996; J.D., 1999). Delta Theta Phi. *Member:* Indianapolis, Indiana State (Ethics Committee; Women in Law Committee, Young Lawyer Section) and American (Young Lawyer Section) Bar Associations. ***PRACTICE AREAS:*** Civil Litigation; Health Care; Family Law; Attorney Discipline; Personal Injury. ***Email:*** wdm@kmlawyers.com

JAMES J. BELL, born Saskatoon, Saskatchewan, Canada, December 22, 1973; admitted to bar, 1999, Indiana. *Education:* DePauw University (B.A., 1996); Indiana University School of Law (J.D., 1999). Formerly with Marion County Public Defender Agency. *Member:* Indiana State Bar Association (Chair, Criminal Justice Section, 2004). ***REPORTED CASES:*** Conwell v. State, 714 N.E2d 764 (Ind. Ct. App. 1999); Chambers v. State, 734 N.E2d 578 (Ind. 2000); Benson v. State, 762 N.E2d 748 (Ind. 2002); Booher v. State, 776 N.E.2d 814 (Ind. 2002). ***PRACTICE AREAS:*** Criminal Defense; Attorney Discipline; Criminal Appeals; Federal Criminal Law; Sex Crimes. ***Email:*** jjb@kmlawyers.com

DARLENE R. SEYMOUR, born Indianapolis, Indiana, July 16, 1975; admitted to bar, 2001, Indiana and U.S. District Court, Southern and Northern Districts of Indiana. *Education:* Indiana University, Bloomington (B.S., 1997; J.D., 2001). Phi Delta Phi; Order of the Barristers; Moot Court. Member, Criminal Defense Clinic, 2000-2001. *Member:* Indiana Trial Lawyers Association. ***PRACTICE AREAS:*** Criminal Law; Family Law; Civil Litigation. ***Email:*** drs@kmlawyers.com

KIGHTLINGER & GRAY, LLP

Established in 1946
MARKET SQUARE CENTER, SUITE 600
151 NORTH DELAWARE STREET
INDIANAPOLIS, INDIANA 46204
Telephone: 317-638-4521
Telecopier: 317-636-5917
Email: info@k-glaw.com
URL: http://www.k-glaw.com

Evansville, Indiana Office: 7311 Eagle Crest Blvd., 47715. Telephone: 812-474-4400. Telecopier: 812-474-4414.

New Albany, Indiana Office: One Commerce Square, 4106 Charlestown Road, 47150. Telephone: 812-949-2300. Telecopier: 812-949-8556.

Civil Litigation, Commercial and Business Litigation, Drug and Medical Device Litigation, Environmental and Toxic Tort Litigation, Casualty, Surety and Life Insurance Law, General Litigation, Malpractice Litigation (Pharmacy, Medical, Legal, Architects and Engineers, Accountants, Insurance Agents, Real Estate Agents and School Boards), Products Liability Law, Trucking Defense Litigation, Construction Law, ICC Regulatory Law, Appeals (State and Federal), Worker's Compensation, Maritime Law, Civil Rights and Wrongful Discharge Law, all areas of Government Liability, including Law Enforcement Liability Litigation, Class Actions, Labor Law, Securities Litigation.

FIRM PROFILE: Kightlinger & Gray, LLP started over 59 years ago when Erle A. Kightlinger and Mark W. Gray began to practice together. The practice was general in nature with a strong emphasis on litigation. Erle and Mark believed that a litigation background would better equip the lawyers in the firm to recognize how important it can be for a client to avoid, when appropriate, the costs and uncertainties of lawsuits. Our practice priorities are making sure the interests of our clients are vigorously promoted without sacrificing any professional ethical obligations. This successful formula has resulted in Kightlinger & Gray being able to expand its practice to accommodate a growing number of valued clients. With offices in Indianapolis, Evansville, and New Albany, Indiana, we are well-equipped to meet the growing needs of clients throughout the entire state in both the public and private sectors.

LAW FIRM ALLIANCES/ASSOCIATIONS: ***GREAT LAKES LAW***

PARTNERS

DONALD L. DAWSON, born Indianapolis, Indiana, May 25, 1944; admitted to bar, 1970, Indiana; U.S. District Court, Northern and Southern Districts of Indiana; U.S. Court of Appeals, Seventh Circuit; U.S. Supreme Court. *Education:* Indiana University (B.A., 1966; J.D., 1969). Phi Delta Phi. *Member:* International Association of Defense Counsel; Defense Research Institute (Former State Chairman); Defense Trial Counsel of Indiana; American Board of Trial Advocates; American College of Trial Lawyers; Trucking Industry Defense Association. ***PRACTICE AREAS:*** Insurance Defense Law; Trial Practice; Professional Liability Law; Civil Rights; School Law; Product Liability Litigation; Insurance Defense; Insurance Bad Faith Defense; Class Actions; Class Action Defense; Commercial Litigation; Construction Law; Construction Insurance Defense; Construction Litigation; Labor and Employment; Employer Liability; Employment Defense; Employment Law; Employment Litigation; Employment Practices Liability Insurance; Labor Law; Legal Malpractice; Libel Defense; Complex Litigation; Defense Litigation; Medical Malpractice; Medical Malpractice Defense; Mental Health Professionals Malpractice; Physicians Professional Liability; Psychiatric Malpractice; Psychology Malpractice; Personal Injury; Personal Injury Defense; Securities Litigation; Securities Fraud Arbitration; Toxic Torts; Toxic Tort Class Actions; Toxic Tort Defense; Trademark Infringement; Copyright Infringement; Transportation; Common Carrier Liability Law; Motor Carrier Defense; Motor Carrier Liability; Transportation Liability; Truck Accidents; Trucking Law; Trucking Liability. ***Email:*** ddawson@k-glaw.com

PETER G. TAMULONIS, born Nashua, New Hampshire, January 3, 1950; admitted to bar, 1975, Indiana; U.S. District Court, Northern and Southern Districts of Indiana; U.S.

(This Listing Continued)

KIGHTLINGER & GRAY, LLP, Indianapolis—Continued

Court of Appeals, Seventh and Eighth Circuits; U.S. Supreme Court. *Education:* Butler University (B.A., summa cum laude, 1972); Vanderbilt University (J.D., 1975). Selected by Law & Politics magazine as an "Indiana Super Lawyer, " 2004. Life Member, National Registry of Who's Who. Listed in: International Who's Who of Professionals; Outstanding Lawyers of America; Indiana Super Lawyers 2004; Marquis Who's Who in American Law, 2005-2006 edition. Author and Speaker: "Construction Contract Claims from the Contractor's Perspective," INDOT Road School; "Subcontract Law," "Unions," Contractor's Manual, INDOT/DBE Program, Ind. Dept. of Commerce, Minority and Women Business Development Division; "How to Make Effective Oral Argument," ICLEF Appellate Practice, 1991; "Construction Contracting: Assigning Reponsibility and Allocating Risk," Evansville Business Journal, July 1993; "Indiana Construction Law: What Do You Do When...?" National Business Institute. Co-Editor: "Wage and Hour Issues," Indiana Chamber of Commerce. Member, Board of Advisors, Indianapolis Convention & Visitors Association. *Member:* Indianapolis, Seventh Circuit and Indiana State Bar Associations; Associated General Contractors (AGC) Labor and Employment Law Council. ***PRACTICE AREAS:*** Appellate Practice; Construction Law; Labor and Employment Law; Class Actions; Complex Litigation; Administrative Law; Administrative Litigation; Civil Appeals; Business Law; Business Litigation; Business Organization; Closely Held Business Law; Complex Business Litigation; Small Business Law; Civil Rights; Civil Rights Defense; Class Action Defense; Collections; Commercial Collections; Commercial Law; Commercial Litigation; Computer Law; Construction Defects; Construction Insurance Defense; Construction Liability; Construction Litigation; Contractors Liability; Contracts; Contract Litigation; Limited Liability Company Law; Private Business Law; Disabilities; Labor and Employment; Employer Liability; Employment Civil Rights; Employment Class Actions; Employment Defense; Employment Disability Discrimination; Employment Discrimination; Employment Law; Employment Litigation; Labor Law; Leasing; Mergers and Acquisitions; Partnership Law; Limited Liability Partnerships; Limited Partnerships; Partnership Organization. ***Email:*** ptamulonis@k-glaw.com

RICHARD A. YOUNG, born Indianapolis, Indiana, December 8, 1950; admitted to bar, 1976, Indiana; U.S. District Court, Northern and Southern Districts of Indiana. *Education:* Ball State University (B.S., cum laude, 1973); Indiana University (J.D., cum laude, 1976). *Member:* Indianapolis and Indiana State Bar Associations; Defense Trial Counsel of Indiana; Federation of Defense and Corporate Counsel (Presenter at '97 FICC Mid-Winter Convention); Trucking Industry Defense Association; American Board of Trial Advocates; Defense Research Institute; Lawyer's Club of Indianapolis. ***PRACTICE AREAS:*** Trial Practice; Negligence Law; Insurance Defense Law; Litigation; Civil Litigation; Complex Litigation; Defense Litigation; Federal Civil Litigation; Federal Litigation; Products Liability; Products Liability Defense; Products Liability Subrogation; Professional Liability; Professional Liability Defense; Professional Malpractice; Transportation; Common Carrier Liability Law; Motor Carrier Defense; Motor Carrier Liability; Transportation Liability; Truck Accidents; Trucking Law; Trucking Liability. ***Email:*** ryoung@k-glaw.com

MICHAEL E. BROWN, born Fort Wayne, Indiana, January 14, 1952; admitted to bar, 1978, Indiana. *Education:* Indiana University (B.A., 1974; M.B.A., with highest honors, 1978; J.D., magna cum laude, 1978). Phi Beta Kappa; Order of the Coif. Law Clerk to Judge James E. Noland, U.S. District Court, Southern District of Indiana, 1978-1979. *Member:* American Bar Association (Member: Tort and Insurance Practice Section; Property Law and Insurance Coverage Litigation Committee; Chair Elect, TIPS Health and Disability Committee, 2005). ***PRACTICE AREAS:*** Insurance Defense Law; Professional Liability Law; Fidelity and Surety Law; Administrative Law; Insurance Bad Faith Defense; First and Third Party Insurance Defense; Insurance Defense; Arson and Insurance Fraud; Fire Insurance Defense; Insurance Coverage Defense; Insurance Defense Subrogation; Class Action Defense; Commercial Litigation; Constitutional Law; First Amendment Law; Disabilities; Environmental Law; Casualty Insurance Subrogation; Insurance Agents and Brokers Defense; Malpractice; Insurance Litigation; Fire Insurance Subrogation; Intellectual Property; Professional Liability; Professional Discipline; Professional Liability Defense; Professional Liability Insurance Coverage; Professional Malpractice; Media Law; Copyright Infringement; Patent Infringement; Trademark Infringement. ***Email:*** mbrown@k-glaw.com

MARK D. GERTH, born St. Louis, Missouri, July 19, 1952; admitted to bar, 1977, Indiana; U.S. District Court, Northern and Southern Districts of Indiana; U.S. Court of Appeals, Seventh Circuit. *Education:* Indiana University (A.B., 1974); Indiana University School of Law (J.D., magna cum laude, 1977). Order of the Coif. *Member:* Indianapolis and Indiana State Bar Associations; Defense Research Institute; Defense Trial Counsel of Indiana. ***PRACTICE AREAS:*** Workers Compensation Law; Insurance Coverage Litigation; Appellate Practice; Civil Appeals; Insurance Defense; Insurance Bad Faith Defense; Insurance Coverage Defense. ***Email:*** mgerth@k-glaw.com

STEVEN E. SPRINGER, born Indianapolis, Indiana, June 25, 1948; admitted to bar, 1979, Indiana; U.S. District Court, Northern and Southern Districts of Indiana; U.S. Court of Appeals, Seventh Circuit. *Education:* Purdue University (B.S., Engineering, 1971); Indiana University (J.D., magna cum laude, 1979). Chartered Property Casualty Underwriter, 1994—. Selected by Law & Politics magazine as an "Indiana Super Lawyer," 2004. Member, Federation of Insurance and Corporate Counsel. Frequent speaker on broad range of topics involving engineering, the law, and trial tactics including issues involving products liability and construction. Faculty Member and Instructor, Indiana Trial Advocacy College. 1996 Chairman of the Indiana CLE Seminar on Insurance Subrogation. Lead Counsel in numerous State and Federal trials, including such notable cases as the Greenwood (Indiana) midair collision, the explosion at Fort Benjamin Harrison, the Mt. Vernon warehouse fire, and the helicopter crash at Camp Atterbury. *Member:* Indianapolis and Indiana State Bar Associations; Federation of Defense and Corporate Counsel; Chartered Property Casualty Underwriters (CPCU designation received 1994); Aircraft Owners and Pilots Association (Legal Counsel, 1987 —); Lawyer-Pilots Bar Association; Defense Research Institute; National Transportation Safety Board (NTSB); The Lawyers Club of Indianapolis. [Cmdr., *U.S. Naval Reserve, Naval Flight Officer*]. ***PRACTICE AREAS:*** Subrogation Law; Products Liability Law; Aviation Law; Construction Law; Engineering Defense; Professional Liability; Architects and Engineers Errors and Omissions; Architects and Engineers Liability; Architects and Engineers Malpractice; Design Professionals Errors and Omissions; Design Professionals Liability; Design Professionals Malpractice; Professional Errors and Omissions; Professional Liability Defense; Professional Liability Insurance Coverage; Professional Malpractice; Professional Negligence; Surveyors Malpractice; Airplane Crash Litigation; Aviation Accidents; Aviation Defense; Aviation Insurance; Aviation Liability; Aviation Litigation; Aviation Products Liability; Helicopter Crash Litigation; Federal Aviation Licenses; Architectural Law; Construction Accidents; Construction and Design Law; Construction Claims; Construction Defects; Construction Insurance Defense; Construction Liability; Construction Litigation; Construction Products Liability; Contractors Liability; Arson and Insurance Fraud; Automobile Liability Defense; Casualty Insurance Defense; Commercial Insurance Defense; Fire Insurance Defense; First and Third Party Insurance Defense; General Liability Defense; Insurance Defense Subrogation; Property Insurance Defense; Complex Litigation; Defense Litigation; Federal Civil Litigation; Civil Litigation; Trial Practice; Personal Injury; Personal Injury Defense; Products Liability Subrogation; Products Liability Insurance Coverage; Products Liability Defense; Professional Indemnity; Transportation; Common Carrier Liability Law; Motor Carrier Defense; Motor Carrier Law; Motor Carrier Liability; Transportation Liability; Truck Accidents; Trucking Law; Trucking Liability. ***Email:*** sspringer@k-glaw.com

RICHARD T. MULLINEAUX (Resident, New Albany Office)

ROBERT M. KELSO, born Chicago, Illinois, April 2, 1955; admitted to bar, 1981, Indiana; U.S. District Court, Northern and Southern Districts of Indiana; U.S. Court of Appeals, Seventh Circuit. *Education:* Indiana University, Bloomington (B.S., 1977); Indiana University, Indianapolis (J.D., 1981). Assistant Corporation Counsel, Consolidated City of Indianapolis-Marion County, 1981-1984. Author and Speaker: "Litigation of Bad Faith in Claims Handling," CPCU I-Day, 2002. *Member:* Defense Trial Counsel of Indiana; Defense Research Institute; Chartered Property Casualty Underwriter (1996—; Board of Directors, Central IN Chapter, 1998—); National School Board Assoc.'s Council of School Attorneys. ***PRACTICE AREAS:*** Civil Rights; Governmental; School Law; Employment Claims; Insurance Defense; Tort; Negligence Trial Practice; Personal Injury; Administrative Law; Administrative Litigation; Alternative Dispute Resolution; Class Actions; Class Action Defense; Commercial Litigation; First Amendment Law; Constitutional Law; Contracts; Contract Litigation; Education Law; School Board Defense; School Board Liability; School District Liability; Employee Benefits; Employee Benefits Litigation; Labor and Employment; Employment Civil Rights; Employment Defense; Employment Law; Employment Litigation; Labor Law; Government; Government Affairs; Casualty Insurance Defense; First and Third Party Insurance Defense; Insurance Defense Subrogation; Civil Litigation; Complex Litigation; Defense Litigation; Federal Civil Litigation; Federal Litigation; Trial Practice; Municipal Liability; Municipal Defense; Municipal Law; Personal Injury Defense; Products Liability; Products Liability Defense; Products Liability Insurance Coverage; Professional Liability; Agents and Brokers Liability; Professional Liability Defense; Professional Liability Insurance Coverage; Professional Malpractice; RICO; Transportation; Common Carrier Liability Law; Motor Carrier Defense; Motor Carrier Liability; Transportation Liability; Truck Accidents; Trucking Law; Trucking Liability. ***Email:*** rkelso@k-glaw.com

BRENT R. WEIL (Resident, Evansville Office)

JOHN B. DRUMMY, born Terre Haute, Indiana, January 28, 1960; admitted to bar, 1985, Indiana; U.S. District Court, Northern and Southern Districts of Indiana; U.S. Court of Appeals, Sixth and Seventh Circuits; U.S. Supreme Court. *Education:* Creighton University (B.S.B.A., cum laude, 1982); Indiana University (J.D., cum laude, 1985). Author and Speaker: "Interlocutory Appeals Under Appellate Rule 4(B)," ICLEF, 1991, 1996. Co-author, "The Requirements of Trial Rule 56," ICLEF, 1992. Co-author, 1994 and 1995 Cumulative Supplements to T. Smith and A. DeBonis, Appellate Handbook for Indiana Lawyers Practice Areas. Author: "The Tort of Bad Faith," Lorman Education Services, January 2002; "The Tort of Bad Faith," Central Indiana Chapter CPCU, February 2002; "Bad Faith: Then and Now," Insurance Institute of Indiana, June 2002. *Member:* Indianapolis, Seventh Circuit and Indiana State Bar Associations; Defense Trial Counsel of Indiana; Defense Research Institute. ***PRACTICE AREAS:*** State and Federal Appellate Practice; Labor and Employment Law; Insurance Coverage Litigation; Bad Faith Litigation; Class Actions; Securities Law; Commercial Litigation; Contracts; Insurance Defense; Insurance Bad Faith Defense; Insurance Coverage Defense; Intellectual Property; Complex Litigation; Defense Litigation; U.S. Supreme Court Litigation; Personal Injury; Personal Injury Defense; Products Liability; Products Liability Defense; Products Liability Insurance Coverage; Securities; Securities Arbitration; Securities Litigation; Securities Fraud Arbitration; Copyright Infringement; Trademark Infringement. ***Email:*** jdrummy@k-glaw.com

JAMES W. ROEHRDANZ, born Toledo, Ohio, August 16, 1953; admitted to bar, 1978, Indiana; U.S. District Court, Northern and Southern Districts of Indiana; U.S. Court of Appeals, Seventh Circuit. *Education:* Indiana University (B.S., 1975); Valparaiso University (J.D., 1978). Registered Civil Mediator. *Member:* Indianapolis and Indiana State Bar Associations; Defense Trial Counsel of Indiana; Defense Research Institute. ***PRACTICE AREAS:*** Trial Practice; Products Liability Law; Negligence Law; Construction Law; Construction Defects; Construction Insurance Defense; Construction Liability; Construction Litigation; Environmental Law; Environmental Business Law; Environmental Corporate Law; Environmental Criminal Defense; Environmental Insurance Defense; Fidelity and Surety Bonds; First and Third Party Insurance Defense; Insurance Defense Subrogation; Complex Litigation; Defense Litigation; Personal Injury; Personal Injury Defense; Products Liability; Products Liability Defense; Products Liability Insurance Coverage; Products Liability Subrogation; Professional Liability; Professional Liability Defense; Professional Liability Insurance Coverage; Professional Malpractice; Toxic Torts; Toxic Tort Defense; Transportation; Common Carrier Liability Law; Motor Carrier Defense; Motor Carrier Law; Motor Carrier Liability; Transportation Liability; Truck Accidents; Trucking Law; Trucking Liability; Mediation. ***Email:*** jroehrdanz@k-glaw.com

PETER A. VELDE, born Des Moines, Iowa, June 16, 1949; admitted to bar, 1976, Indiana and Minnesota; 1983, New York; U.S. District Court, Southern District of Indiana; U.S. Court of Appeals, Seventh Circuit. *Education:* Purdue University (B.A., 1971); Albany Law School (J.D., 1975). Approved CNR letter reviewer. Author and Speaker: "Basic Bankruptcy in Indiana," 1990; "The Impact of Bankruptcy on Dissolution of Marriage in Indiana," 1997, 1999; "Advanced Consumer Bankruptcy Issues in Indiana," 1999; 2001 Fair Debt Collection Practices Act/Fair Credit Reporting Act, National Healthcare Collectors Association; "Current Issues Surrounding Fair Debt Collections Practices Act Spring 2001," National Legal Malpractice Conference; 2002, 2003 and 2004 Fair Debt Collection

(This Listing Continued)

Practices Act, National Healthcare Collectors Association; 2002, 2003 and 2004 HIPAA and Fair Debt Collection Practices Act Update, Indiana Collectors Association; 2002 and 2003 Fair Debt Collection Practices Act and HIPAA, Kentucky Collectors Association. Regional Panel Counsel, FDCPA-related issues, Gulf/Travelers Insurance. Deputy Prosecuting Attorney, Shelby County, 1976-1978. Member, Purdue University Alumni Association. *Member:* Indianapolis, Seventh Circuit and Indiana State (MAP Representative) Bar Associations; Association of Credit and Collection Professionals (ACA/ MAP Program). [Lt. Col., Retired, Indiana Army National Guard]. ***PRACTICE AREAS:*** Commercial Litigation; Banking; Corporate; Bankruptcy; Zoning; Creditors Rights; Collections; Lien Law; Banks and Banking; Banking Law; Banking Litigation; Commercial Banking; Commercial Credit; Credit Law; Lenders Rights; Commercial Finance; Finance; Bankruptcy Collections; Bankruptcy Litigation; Commercial Bankruptcy; Commercial Recovery; Debtor and Creditor; Debtor and Creditor Collections; Debtor and Creditor Rights; Debtors Rights; Fair Debt Collection Practices Act; Secured Creditors Rights; Unsecured Creditors Rights; Business Law; Business Litigation; Complex Business Litigation; Class Actions; Class Action Defense; Commercial Collections; Professional Collections; Retail Collections; Secured Collections; Unsecured Collections; Commercial Law; Construction Law; Construction Litigation; Contracts; Contract Litigation; Land Use; Land Use Litigation; Zoning Law; Leases and Leasing; Leasing; Military Law; Professional Liability; Professional Liability Defense; Professional Malpractice; Real Estate; Condominium Law. ***Email:*** pvelde@k-glaw.com

THOMAS J. JARZYNIECKI, JR., born Buffalo, New York, May 25, 1959; admitted to bar, 1985, Indiana and Illinois; U.S. District Court, Northern and Southern Districts of Indiana. *Education:* State University of NY at Buffalo (B.A., 1982); Valparaiso University (J.D., 1985). Delta Theta Phi. Associate Note Editor, Valparaiso University Law Review, 1984-1985. Law Clerk to the Honorable William J. Garrard, Indiana Court of Appeals, 1985-1986. *Member:* Indianapolis, Indiana State and Illinois State Bar Associations; National Association of Subrogation Professionals; Indiana Arson and Crime Association; Defense Trial Counsel of Indiana; Defense Research Institute. ***PRACTICE AREAS:*** Fire Subrogation; Products Liability Law; Trial Practice; Family Law; Adoption Law; Construction Law; Contracts; Guardianship; Insurance Defense; Arson and Insurance Fraud; Insurance Defense Subrogation; First and Third Party Insurance Defense; Fire Insurance Defense; Litigation; Complex Litigation; Defense Litigation; Personal Injury Defense; Personal Injury; Probate; Products Liability; Products Liability Defense; Products Liability Insurance Coverage; Products Liability Subrogation. ***Email:*** tjarzyniecki@k-glaw.com

VAN T. WILLIS (Resident, New Albany Office)

MARY JO WETZEL (Resident, New Albany Office)

STEVEN K. PALMQUIST (Resident, New Albany Office)

WILLIAM E. SMITH, III (Resident, New Albany Office)

ERIC D. JOHNSON, born Indianapolis, Indiana, April 22, 1968; admitted to bar, 1993, Indiana; U.S. District Court, Northern and Southern Districts of Indiana; U.S. Court of Appeals, Seventh Circuit. *Education:* Indiana University (B.S., with high distinction, 1990; J.D., magna cum laude, 1993). Order of the Coif. Beta Gamma Sigma. Golden Key. Member, Indiana Law Journal, 1991-1993. Author: Note, "Sounds of Silence for the Walkman Generation: Rock Concerts and Noise Induced Hearing Loss," Indiana Law Journal, Volume 68, Issue 3. Co-editor, *Wage & Hour Issues Handbook*, issued by Indiana Chamber of Commerce, 1998-2002. Frequent speaker on Indiana and federal wage and hour issues. Speaker: "Family Medical Leave Act," Phenix Investigations, 2000; "Fair Labor Standards Act," Lorman Seminars, 2000; "Fair Labor Standards Act," New Albany Chamber of Commerce, 2002. *Member:* Indiana State Bar Association (Member, Appellate Practice Section); Association of Credit and Collection Professionals (ACA/MAP). ***REPORTED CASES:*** Published Opinions, Seventh Circuit Court of Appeals: Deckard v. General Motors Corp., 307 F.3d 556 (2002); Patton v. Indianapolis Public School Bd., 276 F.3d 334 (2002); Dunn v. Fairfield Community H.S. Dist. 225, 158 F.3d 962 (1998); Indiana Supreme Court Baca v. New Prime, Inc., 810 N.E.2d 711 (2004); Orr v. Westminster Village North, Inc., 689 N.E.2d 712 (1997); Mikel v. American Ambassador Casualty Co., 652 N.E.2d 503 (1995); Knoy v. Cary, 813 N.E.2d 1170 (Ind. 2004); Indiana Court of Appeals Phoenix Natural Resources, Inc. v. Messmer, 804 N.E.2d 842 (2004); Estate of Spry v. Beatty, 804 N.E.2d 250 (2004); Alexander v. PSB Lending Corp., 800 N.E.2d 984 (2003); Knoy v. Cary, 794 N.E.2d 592 (2003); Lashbrooks v. Schultz, 793 N.E.2d 1211 (2003); Coutee v. Lafayette Neighborhood Housing Services, Inc., 792 N.E.2d 907 (2003); American Standard Ins. Co. v. Rogers, 788 N.E.2d 873 (2003); Utica Mut. Ins. Co. v. Precedent Companies, LLC, 782 N.E.2d 470 (2003); Jones v. Kingsbury, 779 N.E.2d 951 (2002); Munsell v. Hambright, 776 N.E.2d 1272 (2002); Bennett v. Crownlife Ins. Co., 776 N.E.2d 1264 (2002); Indiana Lumbermans Mut. Ins. Co. v. American Log Homes, Inc., 774 N.E.2d 603 (2002); Baca v. New Prime, Inc., 763 N.E.2d 1014 (2002); Ward v. First Indiana Plaza Joint Venture, 725 N.E.2d 134 (2000); Mattingly v. Warrick County Drainage Bd., 743 N.E.2d 1245 (2001); Wallem v. CLS Industries, Inc., 725 N.E.2d 880 (2000); Gilman v. Hohman, 725 N.E.2d 425 (2000); Fort Wayne Intern. Airport v. Wilburn, 723 N.E.2d 967 (2000); Interstate Cold Storage, Inc. v. General Motors Corp., 720 N.E.2d 727 (1999); Elma Buchta Trucking, Inc. v. Stanley, 713 N.E.2d 925 (1999) (amicus curiae); Homes by Pate, Inc. v. DeHaan, 713 N.E.2d 303 (1999); J.C. Spence & Associates, Inc. v. Geary, 712 N.E.2d 1099 (1999); Cole v. Lantis Corp., 714 N.E.2d 194 (1999); Ryobi Dye Casting v. Montgomery, 705 N.E.2d 227 (1999); Ross v. State, 704 N.E.2d 141 (1998); Lenhardt Tool & Dye Co., Inc. v. Lumpe, 703 N.E.2d 1079 (1998); Flock v. Snider, 700 N.E.2d 466 (1998); Straley v. Kimberly, 687 N.E.2d 360 (1997); Shand Mining, Inc. v. Clay County Bd. of Commissioners, 671 N.E.2d 477 (1996); Wright v. Pennamped (II), 664 N.E.2d 394 (1996); Utley v. Healy, 663 N.E.2d 229 (1996); Vukovits v. Board of School Trustees of Rockville Comm. School Corp., 659 N.E.2d 174 (1995); Wright v. Pennamped (I), 657 N.E.2d 1223 (1995); Ostrander v. Board of Directors of Porter County Educ. Interlocal, 650 N.E.2d 1192 (1995); Dawson v. Hummer, 649 N.E.2d 653 (1995); Roe v. North Adams Community School Corp., 647 N.E.2d 655 (1995); Mikel v. American Ambassador Casualty Co., 644 N.E.2d 168 (1994); Johnson v. Owens, 639 N.E.2d 1016 (1994); Wright Motors, Inc. v. Marathon Oil Co., 631 N.E.2d 923 (1994); Howard v. Dravett, 813 N.E.2d 1217 (Ind. Ct. App. 2004); Shepherd v. Carlin, 813 N.E2d 1200 (Ind. Ct. App. 2004). ***PRACTICE AREAS:*** Insurance Defense Litigation; Appellate Practice; Labor and Employment Law; Civil Appeals; Insurance Defense; Insurance Bad Faith Defense; Insurance Coverage Defense; Creditors Rights; Fair Debt Collection Practices Act; Class Actions; Class Action Defense; Collections; Commercial Litigation; Contracts; Labor and Employment; Employment Law; Labor Law; Legal Malpractice; Legal Professional Liability; Legal Malpractice Defense; Complex Litigation; Defense Litigation; Civil Litigation; Trial Practice; Professional Liability Defense; Professional Liability Insurance Coverage; Professional Malpractice. ***Email:*** ejohnson@k-glaw.com

D. BRYCE ZOELLER, born New Albany, Indiana, April 2, 1969; admitted to bar, 1995, Illinois; 1997, Indiana; U.S. District Courts Northern District of Illinois and Northern and Southern Districts of Indiana. *Education:* Indiana University (B.A., 1991; J.D., with honors, 1995). Selected by Law & Politics magazine as an "Indiana Super Lawyer," 2004. Author and Speaker: "Overview of Premises Liability in Illinois," 1996; "Current Case Law Development," Indiana Defense Lawyers Seminar, 1997; "Cross Examination of the Medical Expert," "Deposing the Plaintiff," and "Discovery, What to do and When to do it," Automobile Insurance Law and Accident Litigation Seminar, 1999-2002. *Member:* Chicago, Indianapolis, Illinois State, Indiana State and Federal Bar Associations; Defense Trial Counsel of Indiana; Defense Research Institute (ADR Liaison, Young Lawyers Committee; Alternative Dispute Resolution State Liaison for Indiana). ***PRACTICE AREAS:*** Trial Litigation; Premises Liability; Automobile Liability; Construction Liability; Professional Liability; Alternative Dispute Resolution; Construction Law; Construction Insurance Defense; Construction Litigation; Insurance Coverage Defense; General Liability Defense; First and Third Party Insurance Defense; Commercial Insurance Defense; Civil Litigation; Complex Litigation; Defense Litigation; Trial Practice; Occupational Safety and Health; OSHA; Personal Injury; Personal Injury Defense; Products Liability; Products Liability Defense; Products Liability Insurance Coverage; Products Liability Subrogation; Transportation; Common Carrier Liability Law; Motor Carrier Defense; Motor Carrier Liability; Transportation Liability; Truck Accidents; Trucking Law; Trucking Liability. ***Email:*** bzoeller@k-glaw.com

ERIN A. CLANCY, born Weymouth, Massachusetts, March 23, 1973; admitted to bar, 1998, Massachusetts; 2000, Indiana; U.S. District Court, Northern and Southern Districts of Indiana. *Education:* Purdue University (B.S., Biology, 1995); Indiana University (J.D., 1998). Delta Theta Phi. Managing Editor, Indiana Journal of Global Legal Studies. Author: "The Tragedy of the Global Commons," Indiana Journal of Global Legal Studies, Spring 1998. Member, Purdue University Alumni Association. *Member:* Indianapolis and Indiana State Bar Associations; Defense Research Institute. ***PRACTICE AREAS:*** Complex Tort Litigation; Real Estate; Commercial Litigation; Construction Law; Insurance Defense; First and Third Party Insurance Defense; Insurance Coverage Defense; Complex Litigation; Copyright Infringement; Trademark Infringement; Personal Injury Defense; Products Liability; Professional Liability; Professional Liability Defense; Professional Malpractice; RICO; Toxic Torts; Transportation; Trucking Law; Truck Accidents; Trucking Liability; Transportation Liability; Motor Carrier Liability; Motor Carrier Defense; Common Carrier Liability Law. ***Email:*** eclancy@k-glaw.com

RICHARD O. HAWLEY, JR. (Resident, Evansville Office)

R. JEFFREY LOWE (Resident, New Albany Office)

PFENNE P. CANTRELL, born Indianapolis, Indiana, September 3, 1970; admitted to bar, 1995, Indiana. *Education:* Wabash College (A.B., 1992); Indiana University, Indianapolis (J.D., cum laude, 1995). *Member:* Indianapolis and Indiana State Bar Associations; Defense Trial Counsel of Indiana; Professional Liability Underwriting Society. ***PRACTICE AREAS:*** Insurance Defense; Products Liability Law; Aviation Accidents; Aviation Defense; Aviation Law; Aviation Liability; Aviation Litigation; Legal Malpractice; Complex Litigation; Defense Litigation; Personal Injury; Professional Liability; Professional Conduct; Professional Discipline; Professional Liability Defense; Professional Malpractice; Subrogation; Fire Insurance Subrogation. ***Email:*** pcantrell@k-glaw.com

GINNY L. PETERSON, born Effingham, Illinois, March 4, 1956; admitted to bar, 1997, Indiana; U.S. District Court, Northern and Southern Districts of Indiana. *Education:* Purdue University (B.A., highest distinction, 1977); Indiana University School of Law (J.D., 1997). Phi Beta Kappa. Chartered Property Casualty Underwriter (CPCU), 1987. Author and Speaker: "Commercial General Liability Insurance Policies - Legal Issues of Coverage Determination," Central Indiana Chapter of the Chartered Property Casualty Underwriters (CPCU) Society Industry Day, 2005; "Employment-Related Liability-The Insurer's Response," Indiana Lawyer, March 17, 1999; "General Liability Insurance Coverage-What Business Know (and Should Know) About the Insurance They and Others Purchase," presented at the Defense Trial Counsel of Indiana (DTCI) workshop; "Legal Issues for the Business Owner," May 13, 2004. Member: Purdue University Alumni Association; Indiana University Alumni Association. *Member:* Indianapolis, Indiana State (Member, Sections on: Litigation; Environmental Lawyers) and American Bar Associations; Defense Research Institute; Defense Trial Counsel of Indiana; Chartered Property Casualty Underwriters (Member, Central Indiana Chapter; Chair, Indiana Chapter "Connections" Committee, 2004); National CPCU Organization. ***PRACTICE AREAS:*** Insurance Defense; Litigation; First and Third Party Insurance Defense; Insurance Bad Faith Defense; Insurance Coverage Defense; Insurance Defense Subrogation; Fire Insurance Defense; Commercial Insurance Defense; Arson and Insurance Fraud; Commercial Litigation; Construction Law; Construction Insurance Defense; Construction Liability; Construction Litigation; Disabilities; Americans with Disabilities Act; Disability Discrimination; Disabled Rights; Environmental Law; Environmental Business Law; Environmental Corporate Law; Environmental Criminal Defense; Environmental Criminal Law; Environmental Insurance; Environmental Insurance Claims; Environmental Insurance Coverage; Environmental Insurance Defense; Environmental Liability; Environmental Litigation; Legal Malpractice; Legal Malpractice Defense; Legal Professional Liability; Civil Litigation; Complex Litigation; Defense Litigation; Federal Civil Litigation; Trial Practice; Professional Liability Defense; Professional Liability Insurance Coverage; Professional Malpractice; Toxic Torts; Toxic Tort Defense. ***Email:*** gpeterson@k-glaw.com

JEFFREY D. HAWKINS, born Indianapolis, Indiana, January 31, 1971; admitted to bar, 1996, Indiana and U.S. District Court, Northern and Southern Districts of Indiana. *Education:* Indiana University (B.A., 1993); John Marshall Law School (J.D., 1996). *Member:* Indianapolis and Indiana State Bar Associations; Defense Trial Counsel of Indiana; Defense Research Institute. ***REPORTED CASES:*** Carter v. Jones, 757 N.E.2d 224 (Ind. App. 2001); Carter v. Jones, 751 N.E.2d 344 (Ind. App. 2001). ***PRACTICE AREAS:*** Estate Planning; Probate; Guardianship; Insurance Defense; Legal Malpractice; Legal Profes-

(This Listing Continued)

(This Listing Continued)

KIGHTLINGER & GRAY, LLP, Indianapolis—Continued

sional Liability; Litigation; Complex Litigation; Defense Litigation; Medical Malpractice; Medical Malpractice Defense; Personal Injury; Personal Injury Defense; Products Liability; Products Liability Defense; Professional Liability Defense.

MARCIA A. MAHONY, born Dallas, Oregon, January 16, 1959; admitted to bar, 1995, Indiana; U.S. District Court, Northern and Southern Districts of Indiana. *Education:* University of Oregon (B.S., 1984); Indiana University School of Law (J.D., cum laude, 1995). National Moot Court Team Member. Indiana Law Journal. Best Oralist, Finals, Sherman Minton Moot Court Competition. Co-Editor, "Wage & Hour Issues," issued by Indiana Chamber of Commerce. *Member:* Indianapolis, Seventh Circuit, Indiana State and Federal Bar Associations; Defense Research Institute; Defense Trial Counsel of Indiana; National School Board Association Council of School Attorneys. ***PRACTICE AREAS:*** Employment Law; School Law; Litigation; Education Law; School Board Defense; School Board Liability; School District Liability; Public School Law; Labor and Employment; Employment Discrimination; Equal Employment Opportunity Law; Family and Medical Leave Act; Harassment; Labor Law; Sexual Harassment; Title VII Discrimination; Age Discrimination in Employment; Affirmative Action; Employer Liability; Employer Rights; Employment Civil Rights; Employment Disability Discrimination; Employment Litigation; Employment Rights; Race Discrimination; Sex Discrimination; Womens Rights; Disabilities; Americans with Disabilities Act; Disabled Rights; Mental Disability Law; Professional Liability; Professional Liability Defense; Professional Malpractice; Medical Malpractice; Medical Malpractice Defense; Physicians Professional Liability; Workers Compensation; Federal Workers Compensation; Workers Compensation Defense. ***Email:*** mmahony@k-glaw.com

OF COUNSEL

MARK WILLIAM GRAY, born Indianapolis, Indiana, October 19, 1916; admitted to bar, 1940, Indiana; U.S. District Court, Northern and Southern Districts of Indiana; U.S. Court of Appeals, Seventh Circuit; U.S. Supreme Court. *Education:* Indiana University (B.S., 1938; LL.B., 1940). Phi Delta Phi. Chartered Property Casualty Underwriter, 1952. Marion County Election Commissioner, 1951-1963. Member, Indianapolis Board of School Commissioners, 1966-1970. *Member:* Lawyers Club of Indianapolis; Federation of Insurance and Corporate Counsel; International Association of Defense Counsel; Defense Trial Counsel of Indiana (Diplomat). Fellow: Indianapolis Bar Foundation; Sagamore of the Wabash, 1995. ***PRACTICE AREAS:*** Insurance Defense Law; Probate; Workers Compensation; Litigation; Complex Litigation; Defense Litigation; Insurance Defense; Insurance Coverage Defense. ***Email:*** mgray@k-glaw.com

ASSOCIATES

J. TODD SPURGEON (Resident, New Albany Office)

SUSAN G. GAINEY, born Tampa, Florida, February 23, 1973; admitted to bar, 1999, Indiana; U.S. District Court, Northern and Southern Districts of Indiana; U.S. Court of Appeals, Seventh Circuit. *Education:* Indiana University (B.S., 1995); Valparaiso University School of Law (J.D., with senior honors and course honors, 1999). Author: "Tax Changes Ease Settlement," Indiana Lawyer, March 9-22, 2005. Treasurer, Commission on Continuing Legal Education and the Conclave on Education, Indiana Supreme Court. *Member:* Indianapolis (Member, Women in Law Division) and Indiana State (State Representative, Women In Law and Public Relations Committee) Bar Associations; Defense Research Institute; Defense Trial Counsel of Indiana. ***PRACTICE AREAS:*** Commercial; Civil Rights; Insurance Defense; Collections; Commercial Collections; Education Law; School Law; Labor and Employment; Employer Liability; Employer Rights; Employment Defense; Litigation; Complex Litigation; Defense Litigation; Civil Litigation; Municipal Law; Municipal Defense; Municipal Liability; Personal Injury; Personal Injury Defense; Products Liability; Products Liability Defense; Products Liability Insurance Coverage; Insurance Defense Subrogation; Fire Insurance Defense. ***Email:*** sgainey@k-glaw.com

LIBBY S. VALOS MOSS, born Muncie, Indiana, August 9, 1973; admitted to bar, 1999, Indiana; U.S. District Court, Northern and Southern Districts of Indiana. *Education:* Ball State University (B.S., 1995); Indiana University (J.D., 1999). Phi Delta Phi; Order of Barristers. *Member:* Indianapolis, Indiana State and American Bar Associations; Defense Trial Counsel of Indiana; Defense Research Institute. ***PRACTICE AREAS:*** Products Liability; Premises Liability; Workers Compensation; Insurance Defense; Civil Rights; Civil Rights Defense; Construction Law; Construction Litigation; Construction Products Liability; Guardianship; Fire Insurance Defense; First and Third Party Insurance Defense; Insurance Defense Subrogation; General Liability Defense; Casualty Insurance Defense; Automobile Liability Defense; Automobile Insurance Defense; Arson and Insurance Fraud; Intellectual Property; Complex Litigation; Defense Litigation; Trial Practice; Copyright Infringement; Patent Infringement; Trademark Infringement; Personal Injury; Personal Injury Defense; Products Liability Defense; Products Liability Insurance Coverage; Professional Liability; Professional Liability Defense; Professional Liability Insurance Coverage; Professional Malpractice; Toxic Torts; Toxic Tort Defense; Transportation; Motor Carrier Defense; Motor Carrier Liability; Transportation Liability; Truck Accidents; Trucking Law; Trucking Liability; Workers Compensation Defense. ***Email:*** lmoss@k-glaw.com

D. KEITH PULLIAM (Resident, New Albany Office)

ELLIOTT PINKIE, born East Chicago, Indiana, September 14, 1973; admitted to bar, 2000, Indiana; U.S. District Court, Northern and Southern Districts of Indiana. *Education:* Ball State University (B.S., 1995); Ohio Northern University (J.D., 2000). Phi Alpha Delta. *Member:* Indianapolis and Indiana State Bar Associations; Defense Trial Counsel of Indiana; Defense Research Institute. ***PRACTICE AREAS:*** Negligence; Product Liability; Insurance Defense; Bankruptcy; Bankruptcy Litigation; Commercial Bankruptcy; Creditor Bankruptcy; Debtor Bankruptcy; Debtor and Creditor; Creditors Rights; Creditors Rights in Bankruptcy; Debtor and Creditor Collections; Debtor and Creditor Rights; Commercial Collections; Commercial Litigation; Criminal Law; Criminal Defense; First and Third Party Insurance Defense; Insurance Defense Subrogation; Civil Litigation; Complex Litigation; Defense Litigation; Trial Practice; Medical Malpractice; Medical Malpractice Defense; Personal Injury; Personal Injury Defense; Probate; Probate Litigation; Products Liability; Products Liability Defense; Products Liability Insurance Coverage; Products Liability Subrogation; Toxic Torts; Toxic Tort Defense; Transportation; Common Carrier Liability Law; Motor Carrier Defense; Motor Carrier Law; Motor Carrier Liability; Transportation Liability; Truck Accidents; Trucking Law; Trucking Liability. ***Email:*** epinkie@k-glaw.com

JAMES C. WADE (Resident, New Albany Office)

KRISTEN M. CARROLL, born Louisville, Kentucky, March 19, 1973; admitted to bar, 2001, Indiana and U.S. District Court, Northern and Southern Districts of Indiana. *Education:* Samford University (B.S., cum laude, 1995); Indiana University (J.D., 2001). Order of Barristers. Moot Court. Certified Civil Mediator. *Member:* Indianapolis and Indiana State Bar Associations; Defense Trial Counsel of Indiana. ***PRACTICE AREAS:*** Trial Litigation; Automobile Litigation; Insurance Defense; Alternative Dispute Resolution; Collections; Commercial Collections; Construction Law; Contracts; Contract Litigation; Creditors Rights; Guardianship; Complex Litigation; Defense Litigation; Personal Injury; Transportation; Trucking Liability; Trucking Law; Truck Accidents; Transportation Liability; Motor Carrier Liability; Motor Carrier Defense; Common Carrier Liability Law. ***Email:*** kcarroll@k-glaw.com

MICHELLE HAWK KAZMIERCZAK, born Fort Wayne, Indiana, March 16, 1976; admitted to bar, 2001, Indiana; U.S. District Court, Northern and Southern Districts of Indiana. *Education:* Indiana University (B.S., cum laude, 1998; J.D., 2001). *Member:* Indianapolis and Indiana State Bar Associations; Defense Research Institute. ***PRACTICE AREAS:*** Insurance Defense Litigation; Insurance Bad Faith Defense; Insurance Coverage Defense; Insurance Defense; Collections; Criminal Law; Legal Malpractice; Litigation; Complex Litigation; Professional Liability; Professional Liability Defense; Professional Malpractice. ***Email:*** mhawkkazmierczak@k-glaw.com

JASON J. HOY, born Waukegan, Illinois, November 14, 1971; admitted to bar, 1998, Indiana and U.S. District Court, Northern and Southern Districts of Indiana. *Education:* Indiana University (B.A., 1994; J.D., 1998). *Member:* Indianapolis and Indiana State Bar Associations; Defense Trial Counsel of Indiana; Defense Research Institute. ***PRACTICE AREAS:*** Business Litigation; Insurance Defense; Business Law; Commercial Litigation; Construction Law; Construction Insurance Defense; Intellectual Property; Complex Litigation; Defense Litigation; Copyright Infringement; Patent Infringement; Trademark Infringement; Personal Injury; Personal Injury Defense; Products Liability; Products Liability Insurance Coverage; Products Liability Defense; Transportation; Trucking Liability; Trucking Law; Truck Accidents; Transportation Liability; Motor Carrier Liability; Motor Carrier Defense; Motor Carrier Law; Common Carrier Liability Law; Common Carrier Law. ***Email:*** jhoy@k-glaw.com

ADAM F. PACKER, born Wheeling, West Virginia, October 16, 1978; admitted to bar, 2003, Indiana; U.S. District Court, Northern and Southern Districts of Indiana. *Education:* Wabash College (A.B., magna cum laude, 2000); Washington & Lee University (J.D., 2003). Phi Beta Kappa. Moot Court Executive Board. ATLA National Mock Trial. Member, Federalist Society. *Member:* Indianapolis and Indiana State Bar Associations; Defense Trial Counsel of Indiana; Defense Research Institute. ***PRACTICE AREAS:*** Insurance Defense; Collections; First and Third Party Insurance Defense; Medical Malpractice; Medical Malpractice Defense; Personal Injury; Personal Injury Defense; Products Liability; Products Liability Defense; Products Liability Insurance Coverage; Products Liability Subrogation; Professional Liability; Professional Malpractice; Transportation; Common Carrier Liability Law; Motor Carrier Defense; Motor Carrier Liability; Transportation Liability; Truck Accidents; Trucking Law; Trucking Liability. ***Email:*** apacker@k-glaw.com

JENNIFER M. HERRMANN, born Greencastle, Indiana, May 8, 1978; admitted to bar, 2003, Indiana; U.S. District Court, Northern and Southern Districts of Indiana; U.S. Court of Appeals, Seventh Circuit. *Education:* DePauw University (B.A., cum laude, 2000); Indiana University - Bloomington (J.D., cum laude, 2003). *Member:* Indianapolis and Indiana State Bar Associations; Defense Research Institute; Defense Trial Counsel of Indiana. ***PRACTICE AREAS:*** Insurance Defense; Appellate Practice; Civil Appeals; Contracts; Contract Litigation; Commercial Contracts; Government Contracts; First and Third Party Insurance Defense; General Liability Defense; Insurance Coverage Defense; Insurance Defense Subrogation; Fire Insurance Defense; Civil Litigation; Complex Litigation; Defense Litigation; Products Liability; Products Liability Defense; Products Liability Insurance Coverage; Products Liability Subrogation. ***Email:*** jherrmann@k-glaw.com

NICHOLAS W. LEVI, born Rushville, Indiana, May 24, 1978; admitted to bar, 2003, Indiana; U.S. District Court, Northern and Southern Districts of Indiana. *Education:* Indiana University (B.A., 2000); Indiana University - Bloomington (J.D., 2003). *Member:* Indianapolis (Member, Sections on: Litigation; Young Lawyers), Indiana State (Member, Sections on: Litigation; Young Lawyers) and American Bar Associations; Defense Research Institute (DRI). ***PRACTICE AREAS:*** Insurance Defense; Litigation; Construction Law; Construction Defects; Construction Insurance Defense; Construction Liability; Construction Litigation; Construction Products Liability; Contractors Liability; First and Third Party Insurance Defense; Complex Litigation; Defense Litigation; Products Liability Insurance Coverage; Products Liability Defense. ***Email:*** nlevi@k-glaw.com

AUBREY G. KUCHAR, born Crown Point, Indiana, August 15, 1979; admitted to bar, 2004, Indiana and U.S. District Court, Northern and Southern Districts of Indiana. *Education:* Centre College (B.A., Government and Economics, 2001); Valparaiso University School of Law (J.D., 2004). Law Clerk to Judge John Baker, Court of Appeals, Indiana, 2003. Federal Judicial Clerk to Judge Philip Simon, U.S. District Court, Northern District of Indiana, 2003-2004. Extern to: Steve Carver, Attorney General, Indiana, 2004; U.S. Attorneys Office, Northern District of Indiana, 2003. Congressional Intern to: Congressman Steve Buyer, Fifth District of Indiana, 2001; Congressman Ernie Fletcher, Sixth District of Kentucky, 2000. *Member:* Indianapolis (Member, Sections on: Litigation; Young Lawyers) and Indiana State Bar Associations; Defense Trial Counsel of Indiana (DTCI); Defense Research Institute (DRI). ***PRACTICE AREAS:*** Civil Rights; Litigation; Civil Litigation; Complex Litigation; Defense Litigation; Federal Civil Litigation; Federal Litigation; Labor and Employment; Employment Law; Labor Law; Civil Rights Defense. ***Email:*** akuchar@k-glaw.com

ERIC E. LAMB, born Indianapolis, Indiana, October 11, 1978; admitted to bar, 2004, Indiana; U.S. District Court, Northern and Southern Districts of Indiana. *Education:* Kelley School of Business, Indiana University (B.S., Business, 2001); Indiana University School of Law (J.D., 2004). *Member:* Indianapolis and Indiana State Bar Associations; Defense

(This Listing Continued)

Trial Counsel of Indiana (DTCI); Defense Research Institute (DRI). ***PRACTICE AREAS:*** Banks and Banking; Banking Litigation; Finance; Commercial Finance; Bankruptcy; Bankruptcy Litigation; Creditors Rights; Creditors Rights in Bankruptcy; Business Law; Business Litigation; Closely Held Business Law; Complex Business Litigation; Collections; Commercial Collections; Contracts; Contract Litigation; Debtor and Creditor; Debtor and Creditor Collections; Debtor and Creditor Rights; Intellectual Property; Intellectual Property Litigation; Copyright Infringement; Patent Infringement; Trademark Infringement; Securities Litigation; Securities Fraud Arbitration; Civil Litigation; Complex Litigation; Defense Litigation; Federal Civil Litigation; Federal Litigation; Trial Practice. ***Email:*** elamb@k-glaw.com

MARIE L. VAN DAM, born Grand Rapids, Michigan, July 5, 1978; admitted to bar, 2003, Illinois; 2005, Indiana. *Education:* Michigan State University (B.A., Political Theory and Constitutional Democracy, with honors, 2000); Loyola University Chicago School of Law (J.D., 2003). *Member:* Chicago, Indianapolis, Illinois State and Indiana State Bar Associations; Defense Trial Counsel of Indiana (DTCI); Defense Research Institute (DRI). ***PRACTICE AREAS:*** Insurance Defense; First and Third Party Insurance Defense; Litigation; Complex Litigation; Defense Litigation; Trial Practice; Products Liability; Products Liability Defense. ***Email:*** mvandam@k-glaw.com

MICHAEL WROBLEWSKI, born Detroit, Michigan, February 5, 1977; admitted to bar, 2002, Illinois; 2005, Indiana; U.S. District Court, Northern and Southern Districts of Indiana and Northern District of Illinois. *Education:* Indiana University of Pennsylvania (B.A., Criminology, 1999); Valparaiso University School of Law (J.D., with honors, 2002). Member, and Associate Editor, Volume 36, Valparaiso University Law Review. Co-Author: "Lawsuit Negotiation," June, 2003; "Lawsuit Avoidance: Understanding the Legal Issues in Managing Crane and Rigging Operations," presented at the 2003 Crane and Rigging Safety Seminar, University of Wisconsin at Madison, Jan., 2003. *Member:* Chicago and Illinois State Bar Associations. ***PRACTICE AREAS:*** Construction Law; Construction Litigation; Insurance Defense; First and Third Party Insurance Defense; Intellectual Property; Intellectual Property Litigation; Civil Litigation; Complex Litigation; Defense Litigation; Federal Civil Litigation; Federal Litigation; Trial Practice; Medical Malpractice; Medical Malpractice Defense; Products Liability; Products Liability Defense; Professional Liability; Professional Liability Defense; Professional Malpractice. ***Email:*** mwroblewski@k-glaw.com

DONNA J. JENKINS (Resident, New Albany Office)

SACHA L. ARMSTRONG (Resident, Evansville Office)

CURTIS D. CONDICT (Resident, Evansville Office)

CHAD M. SMITH (Resident, Evansville Office)

VALERIE D. KESSLER (Resident, New Albany Office)

(For complete biographical data on Evansville, Indiana and New Albany, Indiana personnel, see Professional Biographies at those locations)

MARK A. KING
ATTORNEY AT LAW

155 E. MARKET STREET, SUITE 450
INDIANAPOLIS, INDIANA 46204
Telephone: 317-634-5544
Fax: 317-630-4824
URL: http://www.makinglaw.com

Criminal Law, Driving Under Influence, Felonies, Homicide, Family Law, Child Custody, Child Support, Business Law, Social Security, Social Security Disability, Personal Injury.

MARK A. KING, born Fort Wayne, Indiana, June 18, 1970; admitted to bar, 1998, Indiana and U.S. District Court, Southern and Northern Districts of Indiana. *Education:* Indiana University (B.A., 1995); Indiana University School of Law (J.D., 1998). Phi Kappa Theta. *Member:* Marion County and Indiana State Bar Associations.

LAW OFFICE OF ROBERT D. KING

Established in 2000
152 EAST WASHINGTON STREET
INDIANAPOLIS, INDIANA 46204-3680
Telephone: 317-916-0000
Fax: 317-633-7680
Email: rking@robertkinglaw.com
URL: http://www.lawyers.com/robking

Personal Injury, Automobile Accidents, Dog Bites, Railroad Accidents, Slip and Fall, Wrongful Death, Toxic Mold, Police Brutality, Construction Accidents, Products Liability, Medical Malpractice, Criminal Law, Driving While Intoxicated, Drug Crimes, Felonies, Homicide, Juvenile Law, Misdemeanors, Parole and Probation, Traffic Violations, Sex Offenses, Domestic Battery.

ROBERT D. KING, born Chicago, Illinois, March 17, 1970; admitted to bar, 1998, Indiana. *Education:* Manchester College, Oxford, England; Colegio de España, Salamanca, Spain; Boston College (B.A., summa cum laude, 1992); Utah State University (M.A., 1995); Indiana University-Bloomington (J.D., 1998). Associate Editor, Federal Communications Law Journal, 1996-1997, 1997-1998. Lyndon Baines Johnson Congressional Fellow, 1992. Associate Member, Sagamore American Inn of Court, 2002-2003. *Member:* Indiana State and American Bar Association; Association of Trial Lawyers of America. ***LANGUAGES:*** Spanish. ***REPORTED CASES:*** Crabtree v. State of Indiana, 762 NE2d 217 (Ind. Ct. App. 2002); State of Indiana v. Reynolds, 774 NE2d 902 (Ind. Ct. App. 2002); Kirk v. State, 797 NE2d 837 (Ind. Ct. App. 2003), transfer denied.

KIRSH & KIRSH, P.C.

Established in 1981
2930 EAST 96TH STREET (HAMILTON COUNTY)
INDIANAPOLIS, INDIANA 46240-3716
Telephone: 317-575-5555
Fax: 317-575-5631
URL: http://www.IndianaAdoption.com
Email: skirsh@kirsh.com
URL: http://www.kirshlawfirm.com

Adoption Law and Agency Adoptions.

FIRM PROFILE: Kirsh & Kirsh, P.C. is the successor firm of Friedlander & Kirsh, P.C., which was established in 1981. Beginning in 1983, Steven Kirsh began practicing Adoption Law. In 1987, he limited his practice to this area. Joel Kirsh joined the firm in 1984 and began handling adoptions in 1988. As of January 1, 1991, brothers Steven & Joel Kirsh began practicing together as Kirsh & Kirsh, P.C. and limit their practice to Adoption Law. Kirsh & Kirsh, P.C., is the only firm in Indiana which practices exclusively Adoption Law.

STEVEN M. KIRSH, born Indianapolis, Indiana, January 16, 1954; admitted to bar, 1979, Indiana. *Education:* Dartmouth College (A.B., magna cum laude, 1976); Indiana University School of Law (J.D., cum laude, 1979). Phi Delta Phi (President, Wilkie Inn, 1977-1978). Member, Indiana University Moot Court. Recipient: Wall Street Journal Award for Excellence in Business and Tax Law, 1979; Graduate of the Year, 1979. Member, Indiana University Law Review. Marion County Deputy Prosecuting Attorney, 1981. *Member:* Indianapolis, Hamilton County, Indiana State and American (Member, Family Law Section, Adoption Committee) Bar Associations; American Academy of Adoption Attorneys (Member, 1990—; Member, Board of Trustees, 1990-1997; President, 1992; Treasurer, 1993—). ***PRACTICE AREAS:*** Adoption Law (100%); Agency Adoptions. ***Email:*** skirsh@kirsh.com

JOEL D. KIRSH, born Indianapolis, Indiana, August 30, 1959; admitted to bar, 1984, Indiana. *Education:* Indiana University at Bloomington (B.S., Business, 1981); Indiana University School of Law at Indianapolis (J.D., 1984). Phi Delta Phi. *Member:* Indianapolis, Hamilton County, Indiana State and American Bar Associations; American Academy of Adoption Attorneys (Member, 1990—). ***PRACTICE AREAS:*** Adoption Law (100%); Agency Adoptions. ***Email:*** jkirsh@kirsh.com

REFERENCE: National Bank of Indianapolis.

KNOWLES & ASSOCIATES, LLC

INDIANAPOLIS, INDIANA

(See Carmel)

Practice limited to Wills and Probate, Business Law, Business Planning, Starting a Business, Buying and Selling a Business, Elder Law, Estate Planning, Litigation, Trusts and Estates, Tax Planning, Medicaid Planning.

KORTEPETER McPHERSON HUX & MINTON

A LEGAL PROFESSIONAL ASSOCIATION
INDIANAPOLIS, INDIANA

(See Sommer Barnard Attorneys, PC)

KRIEG DEVAULT LLP

Established in 1870
ONE INDIANA SQUARE, SUITE 2800
INDIANAPOLIS, INDIANA 46204-2079
Telephone: 317-636-4341
Fax: 317-636-1507
Email: contact@kdlegal.com
URL: http://www.kriegdevault.com

Indianapolis Northside Office: 12800 North Meridian Street, Suite 300, Carmel, Indiana 46032. Telephone: 317-566-1110. Fax: 317-636-1507.
Fort Wayne, Indiana Office: Krieg DeVault Lundy LLP, 825 Anthony Wayne Building, 203 East Berry Street, 46802. Telephone: 260-422-1534. Fax: 260-423-1590.
Hammond, Indiana Office: Krieg DeVault Galvin LLP, 5231 Hohman Avenue, 46320. Telephone: 219-933-0380. Fax: 219-933-0471.

Acquisitions, Divestitures and Mergers, Antitrust, Appeals, Banking, Bankruptcy, Business and Commercial, Copyright, Corporations, Creditors' Rights, Employee Benefits, Energy, Environmental, ERISA, Estate Planning and Probate, Family/Domestic Relations, Federal and State Taxation, Government Relations, Health Care, Hospital Law, Intellectual Property, Insurance, International, Labor and Employment, Legislative, Litigation, Patent, Public Finance, Public Utilities, Products Liability, Real Estate, Securities Law, Tax-Exempt and Nonprofit Organizations, Technology and E-Commerce, Trademark.

LAW FIRM ALLIANCES/ASSOCIATIONS: ***MERITAS:*** *Members of Meritas, serving the needs of clients in more than 145 markets worldwide.*

WILLIAM H. KRIEG (1907-1998)

PAUL J. DEVAULT (1908-1993)

JOHN A. ALEXANDER (1911-1998)

H. EARL CAPEHART, JR. (1922-1996)

(This Listing Continued)

KRIEG DEVAULT LLP, Indianapolis—Continued

PARTNERS

ANTHONY W. MOMMER, born Fort Wayne, Indiana, January 7, 1944; admitted to bar, 1968, Indiana and U.S. District Court, Southern District of Indiana; 1975, U.S. Court of Appeals, Seventh Circuit. *Education:* Indiana University (A.B., with distinction, 1965); Indiana University School of Law - Bloomington (J.D., cum laude, 1968). *Member:* Indianapolis, Indiana State, American and Federal Seventh Circuit Bar Associations. [Lieutenant Commander, U.S. Navy JAGC, 1968 - 1973]. ***PRACTICE AREAS:*** General Corporate and Commercial Litigation; Appellate Practice; Securities Litigation; Trust and Estate Litigation; Civil Litigation; Eminent Domain. ***Email:*** amommer@kdlegal.com

MAX W. HITTLE, JR., born Indianapolis, Indiana, August 31, 1944; admitted to bar, 1969, Indiana; 1991, U.S. Court of Appeals, Seventh Circuit; U.S. District Court, Southern District of Indiana. *Education:* DePauw University (B.A., 1966); Indiana University School of Law (J.D., 1969). *Member:* Indianapolis, Indiana State, American and Federal Seventh Circuit Bar Associations. [LCDR, JAGC, USNR, 1969-1973]. ***PRACTICE AREAS:*** Business Litigation; Corporate Litigation; Banking Litigation. ***Email:*** mhittle@kdlegal.com

WILLIAM R. NEALE, born Indianapolis, Indiana, June 15, 1948; admitted to bar, 1973, Indiana and U.S. District Court, Southern District of Indiana. *Education:* Indiana University (B.S., 1970); Indiana University School of Law - Indianapolis (J.D., cum laude, 1973). *Member:* Indianapolis and Indiana State Bar Associations. ***PRACTICE AREAS:*** Business Transactions; Business and Corporate Law; General Corporate and Securities Matters; Nonprofit Organizations Law; Health Care. ***Email:*** wneale@kdlegal.com

PAUL F. LINDEMANN, born St. Paul, Minnesota, October 22, 1948; admitted to bar, 1976, Indiana, U.S. District Court, Southern District of Indiana and U.S. Tax Court. *Education:* Valparaiso University (B.A., 1970); Indiana University School of Law - Indianapolis (J.D., summa cum laude, 1976). *Member:* Indianapolis, Indiana State and American Bar Associations. ***PRACTICE AREAS:*** Federal and State Taxation; Acquisitions, Divestitures and Mergers; Real Estate Development and Syndications; Employee Stock Ownership Plans; Pension and Profit Sharing. ***Email:*** plindemann@kdlegal.com

TIMOTHY M. HARDEN, born Indianapolis, Indiana, May 19, 1946; admitted to bar, 1975, Indiana and U.S. District Court, Southern District of Indiana. *Education:* Purdue University (B.A., 1969); Indiana University School of Law - Indianapolis (J.D., 1974). *Member:* Indianapolis, Indiana State and American Bar Associations. [U.S. Army, 1969-1970]. ***PRACTICE AREAS:*** Federal Securities; Financial Institutions; Public Finance; Corporate Finance. ***Email:*** tharden@kdlegal.com

ROBERT A. GREISING, born Chicago, Illinois, April 19, 1953; admitted to bar, 1979, Indiana, U.S. District Court, Southern and Northern Districts of Indiana. *Education:* DePauw University (B.A., 1975); Washington University (M.B.A., 1979); Washington University School of Law (J.D., 1979). *Member:* Indianapolis, Indiana State and American Bar Associations. ***PRACTICE AREAS:*** Corporate Law; Corporate Finance; Secured Lending; Venture Capital Law; Financial Institutions; Acquisitions, Divestitures and Mergers; International Business Transactions; Technology Law. ***Email:*** rgreising@kdlegal.com

JOHN W. TANSELLE, born Lebanon, Indiana, May 16, 1956; admitted to bar, 1981, Indiana and U.S. District Court, Southern District of Indiana. *Education:* Indiana University (B.S., summa cum laude, 1978); Indiana University School of Law - Indianapolis (J.D., magna cum laude, 1981). *Member:* Indianapolis, Indiana State and American Bar Associations. ***PRACTICE AREAS:*** Financial Institutions; Regulatory and Enforcement Matters; Securities; Executive Compensation; Acquisitions, Divestitures and Mergers; Capital Raising Matters; Corporate Law. ***Email:*** jtanselle@kdlegal.com

MARC A. HETZNER, born Logansport, Indiana, April 24, 1953; admitted to bar, 1983, Indiana, U.S. District Court, Southern District of Indiana and U.S. Tax Court. *Education:* Indiana University (A.B., 1975; M.B.A., 1983); Indiana University School of Law - Indianapolis (J.D., cum laude, 1983). Fellow: American College of Trust and Estate Counsel; Indiana Bar Foundation. *Member:* Indianapolis, Indiana State and American Bar Associations. [U.S. Army, 1975-1979]. ***PRACTICE AREAS:*** Federal and State Taxation; Tax Litigation; Estate Planning; Probate. ***Email:*** mhetzner@kdlegal.com

STEPHEN D. SMITH, born Muncie, Indiana, October 15, 1949; admitted to bar, 1975, Indiana; 1978, U.S. Supreme Court; 1983, U.S. Tax Court. *Education:* Indiana University (A.B., 1972); Indiana University School of Law - Indianapolis (J.D., 1975); Georgetown University Law Center (LL.M., Taxation, 1983). *Member:* Indianapolis, Indiana State and American Bar Associations. [JAGD, USAF, 1975-1980; Colonel, JAGDR, USAFR, 1980-2001]. ***PRACTICE AREAS:*** Employee Stock Ownership Plans; Executive Compensation. ***Email:*** ssmith@kdlegal.com

MARK J. R. MERKLE, born Chicago, Illinois, August 5, 1958; admitted to bar, 1983, Indiana, U.S. District Court, Southern and Northern Districts of Indiana and U.S. Court of Appeals, Seventh Circuit. *Education:* Wabash College (A.B., cum laude, 1980); Indiana University School of Law - Indianapolis (J.D., 1983). *Member:* Indianapolis and Indiana State Bar Associations; Defense Trial Counsel of Indiana. ***PRACTICE AREAS:*** Litigation; Products Liability; Employment Law. ***Email:*** mmerkle@kdlegal.com

MICHAEL E. WILLIAMS, born Muncie, Indiana, October 30, 1956; admitted to bar, 1982, Indiana. *Education:* Ball State University (B.S., summa cum laude, 1979); Indiana University School of Law - Indianapolis (J.D., 1982). Deputy Prosecutor, Marion County, 1982. *Member:* Indianapolis, Indiana State and American Bar Associations. ***PRACTICE AREAS:*** Corporate Law; Corporate Finance; Acquisitions, Divestitures and Mergers; Financial Institutions; Antitrust Law. ***Email:*** mwilliams@kdlegal.com

THOMAS R. NEAL, born Brazil, Indiana, July 1, 1945; admitted to bar, 1972, Indiana. *Education:* Indiana University (A.B., 1967); Indiana University School of Law - Indianapolis (J.D., 1972). Deputy Attorney General, Indiana, 1972-1974. Deputy Corporation Counsel, City of Indianapolis, 1976-1978. General Counsel, The Health and Hospital Corporation of Marion County, 1978-1994. *Member:* Indianapolis, Indiana State and American Bar Associations; American Health Lawyers Association. ***PRACTICE AREAS:*** Health Care; Health and Hospital Law; Transactional, Regulatory and Management Issues; Managed Care Contracts. ***Email:*** tneal@kdlegal.com

(This Listing Continued)

LEAH S. MANNWEILER, born Indianapolis, Indiana, July 2, 1950; admitted to bar, 1976, Indiana. *Education:* DePauw University (B.A., cum laude, 1973); Indiana University School of Law - Indianapolis (J.D., 1976). Supervising Deputy Prosecuting Attorney, Child Support Division, Marion County Prosecutor's Office, 1979-1985. Executive Assistant to the Governor, Health and Human Services, 1985-1989. *Member:* Indianapolis, Indiana State and American Bar Associations. ***PRACTICE AREAS:*** Health and Hospital Law; Human Services; Medicaid Hearings and Medicare; Government Relations. ***Email:*** lmannweiler@kdlegal.com

NICHOLAS J. CHULOS, born Chicago, Illinois, October 29, 1959; admitted to bar, 1985, Indiana and U.S. District Court, Southern District of Indiana. *Education:* Elmhurst College (B.S., with honors, 1981); Washington University School of Law (J.D., 1985). *Member:* Indianapolis, Indiana State and American Bar Associations. ***PRACTICE AREAS:*** Business and Corporate Law; Financial Institutions; Acquisitions, Divestitures and Mergers; Securities. ***Email:*** nchulos@kdlegal.com

THOMAS J. COSTAKIS, born Gary, Indiana, August 4, 1960; admitted to bar, 1985, Indiana, U.S. District Court, Southern and Northern Districts of Indiana; 1988, U.S. Court of Appeals, Seventh Circuit; 1996, U.S. District Court, Central District of Illinois and U.S. Supreme Court. *Education:* Purdue University (B.S., 1982); Indiana University School of Law - Indianapolis (J.D., cum laude, 1985). *Member:* Indianapolis, Indiana State and Federal Seventh Circuit Bar Associations. ***PRACTICE AREAS:*** Litigation; Appellate Practice; Environmental Law; Products Liability. ***Email:*** tcostakis@kdlegal.com

SWADESH S. KALSI, born Nairobi, Kenya, April 10, 1943; admitted to bar, 1970, England and Wales; 1977, Indiana and U.S. District Court, Southern District of Indiana. *Education:* London School of Economics (B.S., cum laude, 1965); Lincoln's Inn, London, U.K. (Barrister-at-Law, 1970); National Law Center, George Washington University (LL.M., 1972); Academy of American and International Law, Texas (Certificate in International Law, 1972); Hague Academy of International Law, The Netherlands (Certificate in International Law, 1973). *Member:* Indianapolis, Indiana State, American and England and Wales Bar Associations; American Society of International Law. ***LANGUAGES:*** Hindi, Punjabi. ***PRACTICE AREAS:*** International Business Transactions; Business and Corporate Law. ***Email:*** skalsi@kdlegal.com

MARK P. CANADA, born Valparaiso, Indiana, July 30, 1958; admitted to bar, 1983, Illinois; 1988, Indiana. *Education:* Huntington College (B.S., summa cum laude, 1980); University of California School of Law, Los Angeles (J.D., 1983). *Member:* Indiana State and American Bar Associations. ***PRACTICE AREAS:*** Employee Benefits. ***Email:*** mcanada@kdlegal.com

ELIZABETH G. RUSSELL, born Indianapolis, Indiana, February 23, 1957; admitted to bar, 1983, Kentucky and U.S. District Court, Eastern and Western Districts of Kentucky; 1988, Indiana and U.S. District Court, Southern and Northern Districts of Indiana; U.S. Court of Appeals, Sixth and Seventh Circuits. *Education:* DePauw University (B.A., cum laude, 1979); Indiana University School of Law - Indianapolis (J.D., 1983). *Member:* Indianapolis, Indiana State, Kentucky and Seventh Circuit Bar Associations. ***PRACTICE AREAS:*** Employment Law; Health Care; Human Services; Litigation. ***Email:*** erussell@kdlegal.com

THOMAS P. EWBANK, born Indianapolis, Indiana, December 29, 1943; admitted to bar, 1969, Indiana, U.S. District Court, Southern District of Indiana, Indiana Supreme Court, U.S. Tax Court and U.S. Court of Military Appeals; 1970, U.S. Court of Appeals, Seventh Circuit; 1974, U.S. Supreme Court. *Education:* Indiana University (B.A., 1965); Indiana University School of Law - Indianapolis (J.D., 1969). *Member:* Indianapolis, Indiana State and American Bar Associations. Fellow: Indianapolis Bar Foundation; Indiana Bar Foundation. ***PRACTICE AREAS:*** Estate Planning; Estate Administration; Tax; Trust Law. ***Email:*** tewbank@kdlegal.com

C. DANIEL MOTSINGER, born Fort Wayne, Indiana, October 16, 1956; admitted to bar, 1982, Indiana; 1983, Florida; 1988, California. *Education:* Hillsdale College (A.B., summa cum laude, 1979); University of Michigan Law School (J.D., cum laude, 1982). *Member:* Indianapolis and Indiana State Bar Associations; American Bankruptcy Institute. (Certified in Business Bankruptcy Law by the American Board of Certification). ***PRACTICE AREAS:*** Creditors Rights; Bankruptcy; Workouts; Commercial Law; Litigation; Business Law. ***Email:*** cmotsinger@kdlegal.com

PAUL J. DUNNE, born Providence, Rhode Island, September 10, 1955; admitted to bar, 1980, Indiana. *Education:* University of Notre Dame (B.B.A., 1977); Indiana University (M.B.A., 1986); Indiana University School of Law - Indianapolis (J.D., 1980). *Member:* Indianapolis, Indiana State and American Bar Associations. ***PRACTICE AREAS:*** Commercial Finance; Secured Lending; Leveraged Acquisitions; Letters of Credit; Real Estate Finance; Asset Based Finance. ***Email:*** pdunne@kdlegal.com

SHARON B. HEARN, born Warsaw, Indiana, November 12, 1956; admitted to bar, 1984, Indiana. *Education:* Indiana State University (B.S., magna cum laude, 1978); Indiana University School of Law - Indianapolis (J.D., cum laude, 1984). *Member:* Indianapolis, Indiana State and American Bar Associations. ***PRACTICE AREAS:*** Employee Benefits; Executive Compensation; Employee Stock Ownership Plans. ***Email:*** shearn@kdlegal.com

LAWRENCE W. SCHMITS, born Princeton, Indiana, May 27, 1948; admitted to bar, 1976, Indiana and U.S. District Court, Southern District of Indiana. *Education:* Wabash College (B.S., 1970); Indiana University School of Law - Indianapolis (J.D., cum laude, 1976). *Member:* Indianapolis, Indiana State and American Bar Associations. ***PRACTICE AREAS:*** Employee Benefits. ***Email:*** lschmits@kdlegal.com

MARK R. WENZEL, born Sheboygan, Wisconsin, March 10, 1956; admitted to bar, 1981, Indiana, U.S. District Court, Southern and Northern Districts of Indiana; 1994, U.S. Court of Appeals, Seventh Circuit. *Education:* Purdue University (B.A., cum laude, 1978); Indiana University School of Law - Indianapolis (J.D., cum laude, 1981). *Member:* Indianapolis, Indiana State, Seventh Circuit and American Bar Associations. ***PRACTICE AREAS:*** Creditors Rights; Bankruptcy; Real Estate; Commercial Law; Litigation. ***Email:*** mwenzel@kdlegal.com

JULIA A. CARPENTER, born Chicago, Illinois, October 16, 1963; admitted to bar, 1988, Indiana and U.S. District Court, Southern District of Indiana. *Education:* Butler University (B.S., 1985); Indiana University School of Law - Indianapolis (J.D., magna cum

(This Listing Continued)

laude, 1988). *Member:* Indianapolis, Indiana State and American Bar Associations. ***PRACTICE AREAS:*** Commercial Lending; Banking Law; Real Estate; Corporate Finance; Corporate Law. ***Email:*** jcarpenter@kdlegal.com

DEBORAH J. DANIELS, born Atlanta, Georgia, February 16, 1951; admitted to bar, 1977, Indiana, U.S. District Court, Southern District of Indiana and U.S. Court of Appeals, Seventh Circuit; 1987, U.S. Supreme Court. *Education:* DePauw University (B.A., with honors, 1973); Indiana University School of Law - Indianapolis (J.D., cum laude, 1977). Assistant Attorney General for the Office of Justice Programs, U.S. Department of Justice, 2001-2005. United States Attorney for the Southern District of Indiana, 1988-1993. ***PRACTICE AREAS:*** State and Community Strategic Planning and Disaster Preparedness; Homeland Security; Federal and State Regulatory Compliance. ***Email:*** ddaniels@kdlegal.com

KIPPER V. TEW, born Fort Wayne, Indiana, November 30, 1961; admitted to bar, 1989, Indiana. *Education:* Indiana University (B.S., 1984); Indiana University School of Law - Indianapolis (J.D., 1989). Chairman, Marion County Democratic Party, 1995-1997. *Member:* Indianapolis and Indiana State Bar Associations; Government Affairs Society of Indiana. ***PRACTICE AREAS:*** Government Relations. ***Email:*** ktew@kdlegal.com

RANDALL R. FEARNOW, born Augusta, Georgia, July 11, 1955; admitted to bar, 1981, Indiana and U.S. District Court, Southern District of Indiana; 1989, U.S. District Court, Northern District of Indiana; 1990, U.S. Court of Appeals, Seventh Circuit. *Education:* University of Indianapolis (B.A., magna cum laude, 1977); Indiana University School of Law - Indianapolis (J.D., 1981). Chief Counsel, Indiana State Senate, 1993-1998. *Member:* Indianapolis and Indiana State Bar Associations; American Health Lawyers Association. ***PRACTICE AREAS:*** Health Care; Litigation; Government Relations. ***Email:*** rfearnow@kdlegal.com

MICHAEL J. MESSAGLIA, born South Bend, Indiana, July 19, 1967; admitted to bar, 1993, Indiana. *Education:* University of Notre Dame (B.A., 1990); University of Notre Dame Law School (J.D., 1993). *Member:* Indianapolis and Indiana State Bar Associations. ***PRACTICE AREAS:*** Corporate Law; Financial Institutions; Securities; Taxation; Estate Planning. ***Email:*** mmessaglia@kdlegal.com

JOHN R. KIRKWOOD, born Kankakee, Illinois, February 12, 1954; admitted to bar, 1979, Indiana. *Education:* Indiana University (B.S., cum laude, 1976); Indiana University School of Law - Bloomington (J.D., cum laude, 1979). *Member:* Indianapolis, Indiana State and American Bar Associations; National Association of Bond Lawyers. ***PRACTICE AREAS:*** Municipal Finance; Public Finance Law; Securities; Taxation. ***Email:*** jkirkwood@kdlegal.com

JAMES T. CRAWFORD, JR., born Baltimore, Maryland, August 14, 1947; admitted to bar, 1973, Indiana and U.S. District Court, Southern District of Indiana. *Education:* Purdue University (B.S., 1969); Indiana University School of Law - Indianapolis (J.D., 1973). *Member:* National Association of Bond Lawyers. ***PRACTICE AREAS:*** Public Finance; Governmental Law; Affordable Housing; Legislative Practice. ***Email:*** jcrawford@kdlegal.com

STEVEN M. SHERMAN, born Columbus, Ohio, December 8, 1949; admitted to bar, 1974, Ohio and U.S. District Court, Southern District of Ohio; 1985, Indiana, U.S. District Court, Southern District of Indiana and District of Columbia; U.S. Supreme Court; U.S. Court of Appeals, District of Columbia, Seventh and Eleventh Circuits. *Education:* University of Toledo (B.A., 1971); University of Memphis Law School (J.D., 1974). *Member:* Indiana State Bar Association. ***PRACTICE AREAS:*** Energy and Utilities Law. ***Email:*** ssherman@kdlegal.com

LINDA J. COOLEY, born Hackensack, New Jersey, May 16, 1952; admitted to bar, 1992, Indiana, U.S. District Court, Southern and Northern Districts of Indiana; 2000, U.S. Seventh Circuit Court of Appeals; 2001, U.S. Supreme Court. *Education:* Taylor University (B.S., 1974); Ball State University (M.A., 1980); Indiana University School of Law - Indianapolis (J.D., cum laude, 1992). *Member:* Indianapolis, Indiana State and American Bar Associations. ***PRACTICE AREAS:*** Administrative Law; Alternative Dispute Resolution; Education Law; Employment Law; Family Law; Health Care; Litigation; Personal Injury; Products Liability. ***Email:*** lcooley@kdlegal.com

DAVID ELLIOTT JOSE, born Richmond, Indiana, July 29, 1953; admitted to bar, 1981, Indiana. *Education:* Earlham College (A.B., 1975); University of Wisconsin (M.A., 1976); Boston College Law School (J.D., with honors, 1981). *Member:* Indianapolis, Indiana State and American Bar Associations. ***PRACTICE AREAS:*** Health Care and Hospital Law; Business and Corporate Law; Administrative Law; Regulatory Law. ***Email:*** djose@kdlegal.com

ALASTAIR J. WARR, born Salisbury, England, February 16, 1965; admitted to bar, 1991, Indiana, U.S. District Court, Southern and Northern Districts of Indiana; 1994, U.S. Court of Appeals, Seventh Circuit; registered to practice before U.S. Patent and Trademark Office, 2000. *Education:* Indiana University (B.S., 1987; B.A., 1988); Indiana University School of Law - Indianapolis (J.D., 1991). *Member:* Indianapolis, Indiana State and Seventh Circuit Bar Associations; American Intellectual Property Lawyers Association. ***PRACTICE AREAS:*** Intellectual Property; Patents; Trademarks; Trade Secrets; Commercial Litigation; Corporate Law. ***Email:*** awarr@kdlegal.com

THOMAS N. HUTCHINSON, born Indianapolis, Indiana, August 3, 1970; admitted to bar, 1996, Indiana. *Education:* DePauw University (B.A., 1993); Indiana University School of Law - Indianapolis (J.D., 1996). *Member:* Indianapolis, Indiana State and American Bar Associations. ***PRACTICE AREAS:*** Health and Hospital Law; Business and Corporate Law; Nonprofit Organizations Law; Tax Exempt Organizations; Real Estate; Environmental Law. ***Email:*** thutchinson@kdlegal.com

MARTHA R. LEHMAN, born Chester, Pennsylvania, October 23, 1962; admitted to bar, 1987, Ohio; 1988, Indiana, U.S. District Court, Southern and Northern Districts of Indiana; 2001, U.S. Supreme Court. *Education:* University of Dayton (B.A., summa cum laude, 1984); Vanderbilt University School of Law (J.D., 1987). *Member:* Indianapolis and Indiana State Bar Associations. ***PRACTICE AREAS:*** Creditors Rights; Bankruptcy. ***Email:*** mlehman@kdlegal.com

SCOTT S. MORRISSON, born Valparaiso, Indiana, June 5, 1962; admitted to bar, 1987, Indiana and U.S. District Court, Southern District of Indiana; 1990, U.S. Court of Appeals, Seventh Circuit; 1998, Colorado; 2003, U.S. District Court, Northern District of

(This Listing Continued)

Indiana. *Education:* Hanover College (B.A., with distinction, 1984); Indiana University School of Law - Indianapolis (J.D., cum laude, 1987). Certified Mediator, Indiana. *Member:* Indianapolis, Indiana State and American Bar Associations; Defense Trial Counsel of Indiana; Defense Research Institute. Fellow, Indianapolis Bar Foundation. ***PRACTICE AREAS:*** Arbitration; Civil Litigation; Commercial Litigation; Corporate Litigation; Employment Law; Insurance; Tort Litigation. ***Email:*** smorrisson@kdlegal.com

JOHN R. CROMER, born Dayton, Ohio, May 27, 1946; admitted to bar, 1971, Indiana and U.S. District Court, Southern and Northern Districts of Indiana; 1978, U.S. Supreme Court; U.S. Court of Appeals, Sixth and Seventh Circuits; U.S. District Court, Eastern District of Michigan. *Education:* Hanover College (B.A., 1968); Indiana University School of Law - Indianapolis (J.D, 1971). *Member:* Indianapolis, Indiana State and American Bar Associations; Indiana Trial Lawyers Association. ***PRACTICE AREAS:*** Complex Litigation; Toxic Torts; Environmental Law; Environmental Litigation; Products Liability. ***Email:*** jcromer@kdlegal.com

CHARLES S. COLEMAN, II, born Knoxville, Tennessee, August 22, 1971; admitted to bar, 1996, Alabama; 1999, Indiana. *Education:* University of Notre Dame (B.B.A., 1993); University of Alabama School of Law (J.D., 1996). *Member:* Indianapolis, Indiana State and American Bar Associations; Alabama State Bar. ***PRACTICE AREAS:*** Business and Corporate Law; Securities Regulation; Public Finance; Business Succession Planning. ***Email:*** ccoleman@kdlegal.com

CHRISTOPHER D. LONG, born Indianapolis, Indiana, July 21, 1958; admitted to bar, 1983, Indiana and U.S. District Court, Southern and Northern Districts of Indiana. *Education:* Miami University (B.S., 1980); Indiana University School of Law - Indianapolis (J.D., summa cum laude, 1983). *Member:* Indianapolis, Indiana State and American Bar Associations. ***PRACTICE AREAS:*** Real Estate Transactions; Commercial and Real Estate Finance; Business and Corporate Matters. ***Email:*** clong@kdlegal.com

L. SCOTT PAYNTER, born Lexington, Kentucky, November 13, 1962; admitted to bar, 1994, Indiana; registered to practice before U.S. Patent and Trademark Office, 1996. *Education:* University of Kentucky (B.S., with highest distinction, 1987); Indiana University School of Law - Indianapolis (J.D., summa cum laude, 1994). ***PRACTICE AREAS:*** Patent and Trademark Prosecution; Patent Reissues, Reexaminations and Interferences; Copyright; Trade Secrets; Software; Licensing; Technology Related Agreements. ***Email:*** lpaynter@kdlegal.com

GREGORY B. COY, born Tampa, Florida, February 23, 1970; admitted to bar, 1996, Indiana and U.S. District Court, Southern District of Indiana. *Education:* Wabash College (B.A., 1992); Indiana University School of Law - Bloomington (J.D., 1995). ***PRACTICE AREAS:*** Patent and Trademark Prosecution; Oppositions. ***Email:*** gcoy@kdlegal.com

DOUGLAS A. COLLIER, born Greencastle, Indiana, February 3, 1968; admitted to bar, 1998, Indiana; registered to practice before U.S. Patent and Trademark Office. *Education:* Rose-Hulman Institute of Technology (B.S., magna cum laude, 1990); Indiana University (M.B.A., 1994); Indiana University School of Law - Indianapolis (J.D., magna cum laude, 1997). *Member:* Indianapolis and Indiana State Bar Associations. ***PRACTICE AREAS:*** Patent and Trademark Prosecution; Copyright; Trade Secrets; Agreements; Licensing. ***Email:*** dcollier@kdlegal.com

BRAD A. SCHEPERS, born Jasper, Indiana, October 23, 1967; admitted to bar, 1998, Indiana; registered to practice before U.S. Patent and Trademark Office. *Education:* University of Southern Indiana (B.S., magna cum laude, 1990); Indiana University School of Law - Indianapolis (J.D., summa cum laude, 1998). *Member:* Indiana State and American Bar Associations. ***PRACTICE AREAS:*** Patent and Trademark Prosecution; Due Diligence and Right-to-Practice Opinions; Copyright; Trade Secrets; Licensing; Agreements. ***Email:*** bschepers@kdlegal.com

JOHN H. ALLIE, born Rochester, New York, September 3, 1960; admitted to bar, 1993, Indiana and U.S. District Court, Southern District of Indiana; registered to practice before U.S. Patent and Trademark Office, 1995. *Education:* Rochester Institute of Technology (B.S.M.E., 1983); Indiana University School of Business (M.B.A., 1986); Indiana University School of Law - Indianapolis (J.D., summa cum laude, 1993). ***PRACTICE AREAS:*** Intellectual Property; Patents; Trademarks; Copyrights; Trade Secrets; Technology Related Agreements. ***Email:*** jallie@kdlegal.com

OF COUNSEL

JAMES G. McINTIRE, born Indianapolis, Indiana, November 30, 1949; admitted to bar, 1974, Indiana. *Education:* Indiana University (A.B., 1971); Indiana University School of Law - Indianapolis (J.D., magna cum laude, 1974). ***PRACTICE AREAS:*** Litigation; Business Law; Commercial Law; Employment Law; Products Liability; Health Care. ***Email:*** jmcintire@kdlegal.com

JOHN R. FERNANDEZ, admitted to bar, 1993, Illinois and Indiana. *Education:* Indiana University (B.S., 1985; M.P.A., 1989); Indiana University School of Law - Bloomington (J.D., 1992). Former Mayor, City of Bloomington. ***PRACTICE AREAS:*** Government Affairs; Municipal Law; Public Finance; Business. ***Email:*** jfernandez@kdlegal.com

SENIOR ATTORNEYS

DEBRA S. EASTERDAY, born Chicago, Illinois, September 18, 1956; admitted to bar, 1981, Indiana. *Education:* Hillsdale College (B.A., magna cum laude, 1978); Indiana University School of Law - Indianapolis (J.D., magna cum laude, 1981). *Member:* Indianapolis and Indiana State Bar Associations. ***PRACTICE AREAS:*** Financial Institutions Law. ***Email:*** deasterday@kdlegal.com

DEBORAH C. McNEAR, born Terre Haute, Indiana, June 1, 1952; admitted to bar, 1990, Indiana. *Education:* Indiana University (B.A., 1974); Indiana University School of Law - Indianapolis (J.D., cum laude, 1990). *Member:* Indianapolis, Indiana State and American Bar Associations. ***PRACTICE AREAS:*** Employee Benefits; Executive Compensation. ***Email:*** dmcnear@kdlegal.com

VICKI J. WRIGHT, born Martinsville, Indiana, December 15, 1959; admitted to bar, 1999, Indiana and U.S. District Court, Southern and Northern Districts of Indiana. *Education:* Indiana University (B.A., 1982); University of Missouri at Kansas City (Paralegal Certification, 1992); Indiana University School of Law - Indianapolis (J.D., 1998). Regis-

(This Listing Continued)

KRIEG DEVAULT LLP, Indianapolis—Continued

tered Mediator, Indiana. *Member:* Indianapolis, Indiana State and American Bar Associations. Fellow, American Bar Foundation. ***PRACTICE AREAS:*** Environmental Law; Complex and Multi-District Litigation; Occupational Safety and Health; Products Liability; Toxic Torts; Alternative Dispute Resolution; Commercial Law; Contracts. ***Email:*** vwright@kdlegal.com

ASSOCIATES

MARC T. QUIGLEY, born Indianapolis, Indiana, March 25, 1971; admitted to bar, 1998, Indiana, U.S. District Court, Southern and Northern Districts of Indiana. *Education:* Indiana University (B.A., With Highest Distinction, 1993); Indiana University School of Law - Bloomington (J.D., cum laude, 1998). *Member:* Indianapolis, Indiana State and American Bar Associations. ***PRACTICE AREAS:*** Commercial Litigation. ***Email:*** mquigley@kdlegal.com

JULIE C. BOLLING, born Portland, Indiana, February 28, 1972; admitted to bar, 1997, Indiana, U.S. District Court, Southern and Northern Districts of Indiana. *Education:* University of Indianapolis (B.S., magna cum laude, 1994); Indiana University School of Law - Indianapolis (J.D., magna cum laude, 1997). ***PRACTICE AREAS:*** Public Finance. ***Email:*** jbolling@kdlegal.com

BRIAN C. FRITTS, born Indianapolis, Indiana, January 12, 1973; admitted to bar, 1999, Indiana. *Education:* Purdue University (B.S., 1995; B.A., 1995); Indiana University School of Law - Indianapolis (J.D., 1999). *Member:* Indianapolis and Indiana State Bar Associations. ***PRACTICE AREAS:*** Real Estate; Estate Planning; Business and Corporate Law. ***Email:*** bfritts@kdlegal.com

DAVID E. CORBITT, born Indianapolis, Indiana, October 15, 1971; admitted to bar, 1997, Illinois; 2001, Indiana. *Education:* Central Connecticut State University (B.S., 1994); Indiana University School of Law - Bloomington (J.D., 1997). *Member:* Indiana State and American Bar Associations. ***PRACTICE AREAS:*** Business and Corporate Law; Mergers and Acquisitions; Securities; Financial Institutions. ***Email:*** dcorbitt@kdlegal.com

BRIAN K. BEELER, born Kokomo, Indiana, February 18, 1973; admitted to bar, 1998, Indiana and U.S. District Court, Southern and Northern Districts of Indiana. *Education:* Purdue University (B.A., 1995); Indiana University School of Law - Indianapolis (J.D., cum laude, 1998). *Member:* Indianapolis and Indiana State Bar Associations. ***PRACTICE AREAS:*** Health Care. ***Email:*** bbeeler@kdlegal.com

MATTHEW S. CARR, born Indianapolis, Indiana, July 27, 1971; admitted to bar, 2000, Indiana, U.S. District Court, Southern and Northern Districts of Indiana, U.S. Tax Court and Indiana Supreme Court. *Education:* Indiana University (B.S., 1994; M.P.A., 2000); Indiana University School of Law - Indianapolis (J.D., 2000). *Member:* Indiana State and American Bar Associations. ***PRACTICE AREAS:*** Federal Taxation; State Taxation; Estate Planning; Creditors Rights. ***Email:*** mcarr@kdlegal.com

JOSHUA D. HAGUE, born Indianapolis, Indiana, June 5, 1972; admitted to bar, 1998, Indiana, U.S. District Court, Southern and Northern Districts of Indiana. *Education:* Indiana University (B.A., 1994); Indiana University School of Law - Indianapolis (J.D., 1998). *Member:* Indianapolis and Indiana State Bar Associations; Defense Research Institute. ***PRACTICE AREAS:*** Commercial Litigation; Products Liability; Energy Regulation. ***Email:*** jhague@kdlegal.com

LARRY C. TOMLIN, born Langley, Virginia, February 20, 1968; admitted to bar, 2001, Indiana. *Education:* Indiana University (B.S., 1989); Webster University (M.A., 1992); Indiana University School of Law - Bloomington (J.D., 2001). ***PRACTICE AREAS:*** Corporate Law; Securities; Financial Institutions Law; Mergers, Acquisitions and Divestitures. ***Email:*** ltomlin@kdlegal.com

GREG A. SMALL, born Indianapolis, Indiana, October 13, 1974; admitted to bar, 2001, Indiana. *Education:* University of Pennsylvania (B.A., 1997); Indiana University School of Law - Bloomington (J.D., 2001). *Member:* Indianapolis, Indiana State and American Bar Associations. ***PRACTICE AREAS:*** Corporate Litigation; Commercial Litigation; Products Liability Defense; Eminent Domain; Arbitration; Covenants Not To Compete. ***Email:*** gsmall@kdlegal.com

LISA M. GLENN, born Indianapolis, Indiana, November 25, 1963; admitted to bar, 2000, Indiana, U.S. District Court, Southern and Northern Districts of Indiana and Indiana Supreme Court; 2005, U.S. Tax Court. *Education:* University of Indianapolis (B.S., summa cum laude, 1997); Indiana University School of Law - Indianapolis (J.D., 2000). Certified Public Accountant. *Member:* Indianapolis, Indiana State and American Bar Associations. ***PRACTICE AREAS:*** Estate Planning; Family Business Successions; Probate Administration; Nonprofit and Charitable Organizations; State Taxation; Federal Taxation. ***Email:*** lglenn@kdlegal.com

ALICIA MITCHELL CHANDLER, born Cincinnati, Ohio, October 15, 1975; admitted to bar, 2002, Indiana and U.S. District Court, Southern and Northern Districts of Indiana. *Education:* University of Cincinnati (B.S., magna cum laude, 1998); University of Cincinnati College of Law (J.D., 2002). *Member:* Indianapolis and Indiana State Bar Associations. ***PRACTICE AREAS:*** Creditors Rights. ***Email:*** achandler@kdlegal.com

ANDREA D. BRASHEAR, born Sullivan, Indiana, June 17, 1977; admitted to bar, 2002, Indiana. *Education:* DePauw University (B.A., 1999); Indiana University School of Law - Indianapolis (J.D., 2002). *Member:* Indianapolis, Indiana State and American Bar Associations. ***PRACTICE AREAS:*** Health Care. ***Email:*** abrashear@kdlegal.com

KRISTEN L. GENTRY, born Indianapolis, Indiana, February 19, 1976; admitted to bar, 2002, Indiana and U.S. District Court, Southern and Northern Districts of Indiana. *Education:* Indiana University (B.S, with distinction, 1998); Indiana University School of Law - Indianapolis (J.D, 2002). *Member:* Indianapolis and American Bar Associations. ***PRACTICE AREAS:*** Employee Benefits; Health and Hospital Law. ***Email:*** kgentry@kdlegal.com

MICHAEL L. GRIFFIN, born Valparaiso, Indiana, September 15, 1973; admitted to bar, 1998, Indiana and U.S. District Court, Southern and Northern Districts of Indiana; 1999, U.S. Court of Appeals, Seventh Circuit. *Education:* Purdue University (B.S., with highest distinction, 1995); Indiana University School of Law - Bloomington (J.D., cum laude, 1998). *Member:* Indiana State and American Bar Associations. [Captain, U.S.A.R., 1999—]. ***PRACTICE AREAS:*** Employee Stock Ownership Plans; Employee Benefits; Executive Compensation. ***Email:*** mgriffin@kdlegal.com

AMY J. ADOLAY, born Wauseon, Ohio, March 16, 1976; admitted to bar, 2001, Indiana. *Education:* Miami University of Ohio (B.A., cum laude, 1998); Indiana University (J.D., cum laude, 2001). *Member:* Indiana State and American Bar Associations. ***PRACTICE AREAS:*** Litigation; Employment Law. ***Email:*** aadolay@kdlegal.com

MATTHEW E. CONRAD, born Berne, Indiana, September 10, 1978; admitted to bar, 2003, Indiana and U.S. District Court, Southern and Northern Districts of Indiana; 2004, Florida. *Education:* Taylor University (B.S., magna cum laude, 2000); Indiana University School of Law - Bloomington (J.D., cum laude, 2003). *Member:* Indianapolis, Indiana State and American Bar Associations; The Florida Bar; American Institute of Certified Public Accountants. ***PRACTICE AREAS:*** Mergers and Acquisitions; Corporate Taxation; Partnership Taxation; Corporate Finance; Real Estate. ***Email:*** mconrad@kdlegal.com

ALEXANDER C. O'NEILL, born Valparaiso, Indiana, July 10, 1975; admitted to bar, 2003, Indiana and U.S. District Court, Southern and Northern Districts of Indiana. *Education:* Purdue University (B.S., with distinction, 1998); Indiana University School of Public & Environmental Affairs (M.P.A., 2003); Indiana University School of Law - Bloomington (J.D., cum laude, 2003). ***PRACTICE AREAS:*** Real Estate Law; Environmental Law; Business Law; Public Finance. ***Email:*** aoneill@kdlegal.com

LESLEY A. NEARPASS, born Toledo, Ohio, May 2, 1977; admitted to bar, 2003, Indiana. *Education:* Butler University (B.A., cum laude, 1999); Indiana University School of Law - Indianapolis (J.D., 2003). *Member:* Indianapolis, Indiana State and American Bar Associations. ***PRACTICE AREAS:*** Governmental Affairs; Health Care. ***Email:*** lnearpass@kdlegal.com

BRETT J. HENRY, born Indianapolis, Indiana, June 25, 1971; admitted to bar, 2003, Indiana and U.S. District Court, Southern and Northern Districts of Indiana. *Education:* Vanderbilt University (B.A., 1993); Indiana University School of Law - Indianapolis (J.D., 2003). *Member:* Indianapolis, Indiana State and American Bar Associations. ***PRACTICE AREAS:*** Real Estate; Land Use; Business Law; Commercial Law; Securities. ***Email:*** bhenry@kdlegal.com

JOSEPH C. BOWMAN, born Fort Wayne, Indiana, October 4, 1969; admitted to bar, 1998, Indiana and U.S. District Court, Southern and Northern Districts of Indiana. *Education:* Indiana University (B.S., 1992); Indiana University School of Law - Indianapolis (J.D., magna cum laude, 1998). *Member:* Indianapolis, Indiana State and American Bar Associations. ***PRACTICE AREAS:*** Public Finance. ***Email:*** jbowman@kdlegal.com

AARON R. RAFF, born Bloomington, Indiana, January 10, 1977; admitted to bar, 2002, Indiana and U.S. District Court, Southern and Northern Districts of Indiana. *Education:* Indiana University (B.A., 1999); Indiana University School of Law - Bloomington (J.D., magna cum laude, 2002). *Member:* Indianapolis, Indiana State and American Bar Associations. ***PRACTICE AREAS:*** Civil Litigation; Employment Litigation; Insurance Defense; Family Law. ***Email:*** araff@kdlegal.com

STACY WALTON LONG, born Champaign, Illinois, March 7, 1979; admitted to bar, 2004, Indiana and U.S. District Court, Southern and Northern Districts of Indiana. *Education:* University of Illinois (B.A., 2001); University of Illinois College of Law (J.D., cum laude, 2004). *Member:* Indiana State and American Bar Associations. ***PRACTICE AREAS:*** Creditors Rights; Bankruptcy; Litigation. ***Email:*** swalton@kdlegal.com

KELLY J. GREEN, born Muncie, Indiana, June 20, 1969; admitted to bar, 2004, Indiana and U.S. District Court, Southern and Northern Districts of Indiana. *Education:* Ball State University (B.S., 1995); Indiana University School of Law - Indianapolis (J.D., magna cum laude, 2004). *Member:* Indianapolis, Indiana State and American Bar Associations. ***PRACTICE AREAS:*** Health Care. ***Email:*** kgreen@kdlegal.com

REBECCA BILLER ELMORE, born Maywood, Illinois, October 18, 1978; admitted to bar, 2004, Indiana and U.S. District Court, Southern and Northern Districts of Indiana. *Education:* University of Michigan (B.A.,with distinction, 2000); Indiana University School of Law - Bloomington (J.D., 2004). *Member:* Indiana State Bar Association. ***LANGUAGES:*** Spanish. ***PRACTICE AREAS:*** Litigation; Employment Law. ***Email:*** relmore@kdlegal.com

ALEXANDER L. MOUNTS, born Newburgh, Indiana, February 7, 1979; admitted to bar, 2004, Indiana and U.S. District Court, Southern and Northern Districts of Indiana. *Education:* Taylor University (B.A., cum laude, 2001); Indiana University School of Law - Indianapolis (J.D., 2004). *Member:* Indianapolis, Indiana State and American Bar Associations. ***PRACTICE AREAS:*** Employee Benefits; Employee Stock Ownership Plans. ***Email:*** amounts@kdlegal.com

ANGELA L. HAMM, born South Bend, Indiana, March 19, 1974; admitted to bar, 1999, Indiana and U.S. District Court, Southern and Northern Districts of Indiana; U.S. Court of Appeals, Seventh Circuit. *Education:* Indiana University (B.A., 1996); Indiana University School of Law - Indianapolis (J.D., 1999). *Member:* Indianapolis, Indiana State and American Bar Associations. ***PRACTICE AREAS:*** Complex and Multi-District Litigation; Environmental Law; Products Liability; Toxic Torts; Appellate Practice. ***Email:*** ahamm@kdlegal.com

LISA A. DURHAM, born Mendota, Illinois, July 27, 1958; admitted to bar, 2005, Indiana. *Education:* University of Illinois (B.A., 1981); Indiana University School of Law - Indianapolis (J.D., magna cum laude, 2005). *Member:* Indianapolis and American Bar Associations; ESOP Association. ***PRACTICE AREAS:*** Employee Benefits; Employee Stock Ownership Plans. ***Email:*** ldurham@kdlegal.com

HEATH E. UPPENCAMP, born October 27, 1979; admitted to bar, 2005, Indiana. *Education:* Purdue University (B.A., with highest distinction, 2002); University of Illinois College of Law (J.D., cum laude, 2005). ***PRACTICE AREAS:*** Litigation. ***Email:*** huppencamp@kdlegal.com

MATTHEW C. BRANIC, born Indianapolis, Indiana, February 20, 1979; admitted to bar, 2005, Indiana. *Education:* Miami University (B.S., 2001); University of Dayton School of Law (J.D., cum laude, 2005). ***Email:*** mbranic@kdlegal.com

(This Listing Continued)

JASON A. PENNINGER, born Niles, Michigan, August 13, 1980; admitted to bar, 2005, Indiana. *Education:* Western Michigan University (2002); Michigan State College of Law (J.D., cum laude, 2005). *Member:* American Bar Association. ***PRACTICE AREAS:*** Intellectual Property; Patents; Trademarks; Copyrights. ***Email:*** jpenninger@kdlegal.com

NIGEL J. RIGGINS, born Chicago, Illinois, April 7, 1978; admitted to bar, 2005, Indiana. *Education:* DePauw University (B.A., 2000); Indiana University School of Law - Indianapolis (J.D., 2005). ***PRACTICE AREAS:*** Creditors Rights; Business Law; Real Estate; Litigation. ***Email:*** nriggins@kdlegal.com

RETIRED PARTNERS

HOWARD KAHLENBECK, JR., born Fort Wayne, Indiana, December 7, 1929; admitted to bar, 1957, Indiana. *Education:* Indiana University (B.S., with distinction, 1952); University of Michigan Law School (LL.B., 1957). Years at the Firm: 1955 - 2003.

FRANCIS S. MICHAEL CONNELLY, born Chicago, Illinois, July 9, 1935; admitted to bar, 1963, Illinois; 1967, Indiana; 1976, U.S. Tax Court. *Education:* University of Notre Dame (B.S., 1957); DePaul University (J.D., 1962). Years at the Firm: 1976 - 2004.

MALCOLM CARROLL MALLETTE, born Evansville, Indiana, May 19, 1941; admitted to bar, 1967, Indiana. *Education:* Purdue University (B.S., 1963); Indiana University School of Law (J.D., magna cum laude, 1967). Years at the Firm: 1968 - 2004.

RICHARD D. WAGNER, born January 9, 1933; admitted to bar, 1960, Indiana; U.S. District Court, Southern and Northern Districts of Indiana; U.S. Court of Appeals, Seventh Circuit; U.S. Supreme Court. *Education:* Indiana University (B.S., with distinction, 1957); Indiana University School of Law (J.D., with distinction, 1960). Years at the Firm: 1963 - 1999.

REPRESENTATIVE CLIENTS: Acordia, Inc.; ADESA Corporation; Advanced Physical Therapy, P.C.; AgReliant Genetics, LLC; Allied Physicians of Michiana, LLC; Alverno Clinical Laboratories, Inc.; American Express; American Senior Communities; Anchor Glass Corporation; Anesthesia Consultants of Indianapolis, LLC; August Mack Environmental, Inc.; Basic American Industries, Inc.; BehaviorCorp, Inc.; Blue River Bancshares, Inc.; Bridgestone/Firestone Americas Holdings, Inc.; Catholic Archdiocese of Indianapolis; Chromcraft Revington, Inc. and its subsidiaries; City of Vincennes; Conseco, Inc.; Cooper Tire Company; Crown Central Petroleum Corporation; Cummins Mid-States Power, Inc.; CUNA Mutual Group; D-A Lubricant Company, Inc.; Duke Realty Investments, Inc.; Enhanced Telecommunications Corporation; The Estridge Companies; Fairbanks Hospital, Inc.; Federal Home Loan Bank of Indianapolis; Fidelity Federal Bancorp; Fifth Third Bank; First Bankers Trust Company; First Financial Corporation; First Indiana Bank, N.A.; Franciscan Sisters of Chicago Service Health Services, Inc.; Golden Rule Insurance Company; Grain Dealers Mutual Insurance Company; GreatBanc Trust Company; Gregg Appliances, Inc.; Hamblen Gage Corporation; Hang Up Shoppes, Inc.; HCA; Health and Hospital Corporation of Marion County (Wishard Memorial Hospital); Horizon Bancorp; Indianapolis Indians, Inc.; Indianapolis-Marion County Building Authority; Indianapolis Public Transportation Corporation; Irwin Union Bank & Trust Company; ITT Corporation; JPMorgan Chase Bank, N.A.; LaSalle Bank National Association; Liberty Enterprises, Inc.; MainGate, Inc.; Mainscape, Inc.; Methodist Hospitals, Inc. (Gary); Midwest Natural Gas Corporation; Miller Pipeline Corporation; Mitsubishi Motors Corporation; Moore Foundation; The National Bank of Indianapolis; National City Bank of Indiana; Old National Bancorp and its subsidiaries; PaineWebber Incorporated; Panhandle Eastern Corporation; ProLiance Energy, LLC; R.J. Reynolds Company; Regeneration Technologies, Inc.; Regions Bank; Reliant Services, LLC; Resort Condominiums International, Inc.; Rolls-Royce Corporation; SEEMAC, Incorporated; Sisters of St. Francis Health Services, Inc.; St. Anthony Medical Center; St. Anthony Memorial Health Centers; St. Francis Hospital & Health Centers; St. James Hospital & Health Centers; St. Margaret Mercy Healthcare Centers; Star Bank, Indiana, N.A.; Texas Eastern Corporation; Town of Zionsville; Trilithic, Inc.; Union Federal Savings and Loan Association; United States Trust Company, N.A.; Veolia Water Indianapolis, LLC; Winkler, Inc.

KROGER, GARDIS & REGAS

Established in 1937

111 MONUMENT CIRCLE, SUITE 900
INDIANAPOLIS, INDIANA 46204-5125
Telephone: 317-692-9000
Telecopier: 317-264-6832
URL: http://www.kgrlaw.com

General Civil Practice, Bankruptcy and Commercial Litigation, Business Transactions and Litigation, Civil Litigation and Appeals, Collections, Corporate Representation, Environmental Law and Litigation, Municipal Representation, Real Estate and Lending Transactions.

FIRM PROFILE: Since its founding in 1937, Kroger, Gardis & Regas has served the legal needs of Indiana's business and financial community with a reputation of integrity and honesty. While known throughout the state for its commercial and bankruptcy litigation practice, the firm has become a recognized leader in the areas of environmental law and litigation, real estate and lending matters, business transactions and litigation and governmental representation.

As one of Indianapolis' twenty-five largest law firms, Kroger, Gardis & Regas offers a full range of legal services to its business and institutional clients, but our attorneys have not forgotten our founding philosophy - personal service, integrity and honesty.

PARTNERS

JAMES A. KNAUER, admitted to bar, 1971, Indiana; U.S. District Court, Southern District of Indiana; U.S. Court of Appeals, 7th Circuit; 1979, U.S. Supreme Court. *Education:* Indiana University at Bloomington (B.S., 1968); Indiana University (J.D., 1971). Listed: "Who's Who in American Law" 1985-2005; "The Best Lawyers in America" (Bankruptcy) 1987- 2005. Member, Indiana Legal Forum, 1970-1971. Adjunct Professor of Law, Indiana University School of Law, 1986, 1990-1991. Member, Panel of Trustees for the United States Bankruptcy Court, Southern District of Indiana, 1979-1987; Member of the Editorial Board of the Bankruptcy Law and Litigation Report National News Letter, 2005—. Appointments as a Federal Receiver: United States Securities & Exchange Commission vs. Heartland Financial Services, Inc. et al. (see heartlandfinancialinfo.com); United States Securities & Exchange Commission vs. Wellington Bank and Trust, et. al. (see wellingtonbankinfo.com); United States Securities & Exchange Commission vs. Donald Barry Tamres, et al.; United States Securities & Exchange Commission vs. James R. Harrold, et al. (see harroldinfo.com); United States Securities & Exchange Commission vs. Gateway Association, et. al.(see gatewayinfo.net). Appointed as Federall Bankruptcy Examiner In re OneStar Telecommunications, Inc. *Member:* Indianapolis (Chairman, Commercial Law and Bankruptcy Section, 1983), Seventh Circuit (Chairman, Indiana Bankruptcy Section, 1989-1991), Indiana State and American (Member, Secured Transactions Committee, Litigation Section, 1978-1985) Bar Associations; Commercial Law League of America; The Association of Trial Lawyers of America; American Bankruptcy Institute. ***PRACTICE AREAS:*** Commercial Law; Business Litigation; Class Action Litigation; Bankruptcy Law. ***Email:*** jak@kgrlaw.com

JOHN J. PETR, born Chicago, Illinois, October 16, 1952; admitted to bar, 1977, Indiana; U.S. Supreme Court, U.S. Court of Appeals, Seventh Circuit and U.S. District Court, Northern and Southern Districts of Indiana. *Education:* University of Illinois (B.S., with honors, 1974); Indiana University (J.D., cum laude, 1977). Chapter 7 Trustee for the U.S. Bankruptcy Court, Southern District of Indiana, Indianapolis Division, since 1979. *Member:* Indianapolis and Indiana State Bar Associations; Commercial Law League of America; National Association of Bankruptcy Trustees. ***PRACTICE AREAS:*** Commercial Law; Secured Creditor Representation; Bankruptcy Law. ***Email:*** jjp@kgrlaw.com

JAMES G. LAUCK, born Indianapolis, Indiana, December 28, 1953; admitted to bar, 1979, Indiana, 1981, U.S. Court of Appeals, Seventh Circuit. *Education:* University of Notre Dame (B.B.A., cum laude, 1975); Indiana University (J.D., cum laude, 1979). Certified Mediator, 1996; Lecturer: Indiana Continuing Legal Education Forum, Bankruptcy Reorganization 1987, Chapter 13 Bankruptcy, 1989; Family, Business and Environmental Issues in Bankruptcy, 1990; Representing the Business Creditor, 1993; National Business Institute, Foreclosure & Repossession, 1987, 1990, 1992, 1994, 1995; Basic Bankruptcy 1989; Legal Issues of Problem Collections in Indiana, 1991; Collecting Judgements in Indiana, 1992, 1993, 1996; Collection Law in Indiana, Lorman Education Services, 1998. Author: "Bankruptcy Bibliography Update," 91 Com L.J. 370, 1986, 96 Com. L.J. 212, 1991, 97 Com. L.J. 429, 1992, 98 Com. L.J. 406, 1993. *Member:* Indianapolis (Member, Sections on: Commercial and Bankruptcy Law; Chairman, 1996), Indiana State and American Bar Associations; Commercial Law League of America. ***PRACTICE AREAS:*** Commercial Law; Bankruptcy Law; Real Estate Foreclosure Law. ***Email:*** jgl@kgrlaw.com

BRIAN C. BOSMA, born Indianapolis, Indiana, October 31, 1957; admitted to bar, 1984, Indiana and U.S. District Court, Northern and Southern Districts of Indiana. *Education:* Purdue University (B.S.E., 1981); Indiana University (J.D., 1984). Phi Delta Phi (Vice Chancellor, Wilkie Inn, 1983-1984). Associate Editor, Indiana Law Review, 1983-1984. Lecturer: "Indiana Law Update," Indiana Continuing Legal Education Forum, 1987; "Environmental Pitfalls for Commercial Lawyers," Indianapolis Bar Association, 1988; "Regulation of Underground Storage Tanks," Indiana Hazardous Materials Conference, 1989; "Environmental Liability for Trust Departments and Fiduciaries," Indiana Bankers Association Annual Conference, 1990; "The Indiana Responsible Property Transfer Law," Indianapolis Bar Association, 1990; "Environmental Law Update," Keynote Address, Nineteenth Annual Environmental Symposium, Central Indiana Technical and Environmental Societies, 1990. Chairman, Indiana Continuing Legal Education Forum, Environmental Law Symposium, 1990; "Environmental Compliance and Liability," Indiana Banker's Association 1991 Trust Conference; "Advanced Real Estate Law in Indiana," National Business Institute, 1991, 1992, 1993, 1994, 1996; "Environmental Law Update," Indianapolis Bar Association 1991; "Environmental Issues Common to Business Transactions," Indiana Continuing Legal Education Forum, 1991; "Municipal Liability for Underground Storage Tanks," Indiana Continuing Legal Education Forum, 1992; "What's New in the Environment," Indiana Continuing Legal Education Forum, 1992, 1993; "Hazardous Waste in Indiana," National Business Institute, 1993, Panel Chairman, "Purchasing and Selling Business Interests," Indiana Continuing Legal Education Forum, 1994; "Environmental Regulation in Indiana," Institute of Business Law, 1995; "Selecting and Contracting with Environmental Consultants," Indianapolis Bar Association, 1995; "Environmental Liability in Real Estate and Banking Transactions," Indiana Continuing Legal Education Forum, 1995; "Recent Developments in Indiana Law," Indiana Continuing Legal Education Forum, 1995; "Environmental Law Update," Indiana Continuing Legal Education Forum, 1997. Author: "A Lender's Guide to Environmental Site Assessments," Hoosier Banker, January 1991; "Ethical Guidelines for Environmental Lawyers," Indiana Continuing Legal Education Forum 1991; "Avoiding Environmental Liability: Indiana's Legislative Step in the Right Direction," Hoosier Banker, September 1991; "Death, Taxes and Environmental Liability: Trustees Beware!" Hoosier Banker, June 1992; "The EPA Lender Liability Rule: Help or Hindrance for Secured Lenders," Indiana Continuing Legal Education Forum, 1993; "A Brief Commentary on the IDEM Civil Penalty Policy," Indiana Continuing Legal Education Forum, 1994; "The Law of Corporations in Indiana," The Lawyer's Bar Review, 1995-1999; "The Law of Agency and Partnership in Indiana," The Lawyers Bar Review, 1996-1999. Executive Assistant for Governmental Affairs to the Superintendent of the Indiana Department of Education, 1985-1986. Member, 1986— and Republican Floor Leader, 1994—, Indiana House of Representatives. Member, Indiana Environmental Policy Commission, 1986-1994. State Law Advisory Committee, Environmental Due Diligence Guide, Bureau of National Affairs, 1993—, Member, Indiana Supreme Court Character and Fitness Committee, 1988-1994. *Member:* Indianapolis (Member and Chairman, 1997, Business Law Section; Member, Environmental Law Section); Indiana State (Member, Banking and Business Law; Environmental Law) and American (Member, Sections on: Corporation, Banking and Business Law; Natural Resources Law) Bar Associations. ***PRACTICE AREAS:*** Environmental Law; Real Estate; Corporate Law; Municipal Law. ***Email:*** bcb@kgrlaw.com

JAY P. KENNEDY, born Indianapolis, Indiana, December 13, 1956; admitted to bar, 1982, Indiana and U.S. Supreme Court; 1984, U.S. Court of Appeals, Seventh Circuit. *Education:* Emory University (B.A., 1979); Indiana University (J.D., cum laude, 1982). Associate Editor, Indiana Law Review, 1981-1982. Lecturer: Exemption Planning—Pitfalls and Opportunities," ICLEF, 1989. Panelist and Author: Collection Law in Indiana, Lorman, 1991, 1992; Panelist: Recent Developments in Commercial Law, Indianapolis Bar Association, 1991. Panelist and Author: Discharge Actions on Bankruptcy, Indianapolis Bar Association, 1991; Advanced Collection and the Impact on Bankruptcy in Indiana, 1993; "1994 Bankruptcy Amendment," Indianapolis Bar Association, 1994; "Bankruptcy Problems After Bankruptcy," Annual Bankruptcy Institute, ICLEF, 1994. *Member:* Indianapolis (Member: Commercial and Bankruptcy Law Section; Chairman, Education Committee,

(This Listing Continued)

KROGER, GARDIS & REGAS, Indianapolis—Continued

1994; Executive Committee, Young Lawyers Division, 1984-1986), Indiana State and American Bar Associations; American Bankruptcy Institute. ***PRACTICE AREAS:*** Bankruptcy Law; Creditors Rights Law; Commercial Litigation. ***Email:*** jpk@kgrlaw.com

WILLIAM BOCK, III, born Orange, Texas, September 10, 1962; admitted to bar, 1989, Indiana and U.S. District Court, Northern and Southern Districts of Indiana. *Education:* Oral Roberts University (B.A., summa cum laude, 1985); University of Michigan (J.D., cum laude, 1989). Staff Member, Michigan Journal of Law Reform, 1988-1989. Law Clerk to the Honorable John Daniel Tinder, U.S. District Judge, Southern District of Indiana, 1990-1992. Parliamentarian, Indiana House of Representatives, 2005-2006. *Member:* Indianapolis (Past Chairman, Sports and Entertainment Section), Indiana State and American (Member, Sections on Sports and Entertainment; State and Local Government; Employment Law) Bar Associations; Sports Lawyers Association; Christian Legal Society; Federalist Society. ***PRACTICE AREAS:*** Litigation; Employment; Civil Rights; Sports Law. ***Email:*** wb@kgrlaw.com

GREGORY P. CAFOUROS, born Indianapolis, Indiana, October 27, 1950; admitted to bar, 1978, Indiana and U.S. District Court, Southern District of Indiana. *Education:* University of Notre Dame (B.S., Civil Engineering, 1972); Indiana University (J.D., 1978). Certified Mediator, 1996. Registered Professional Engineer, Indiana, 1977. Enforcement Attorney, Indiana Environmental Management Board, 1977-1979. Member, Board of Directors, 1984-1988, 1996-1999, Consulting Engineers of Indiana. Author: "Living with Leaking Underground Storage Tanks, Liability in the 90's," Indiana Continuing Legal Education Forum, Environmental Law and Toxic Tort, 1995; "Capping the Costs of Corrective Action Plans," Indiana State Bar Association, Environmental Section, 1997. *Member:* Indianapolis, Indiana State and American (Member, Sections on Environmental Law, Land Use and Zoning Law, Chair, 1999) Bar Associations. ***PRACTICE AREAS:*** Environmental Law; Real Estate Law; Corporate Law; Business Law; Transportation Law. ***Email:*** gpc@kgrlaw.com

MADALYN S. KINSEY, born Indianapolis, Indiana, July 23, 1953; admitted to bar, 1979, Illinois; 1982, California; 1986, Indiana. *Education:* Indiana University (B.S., 1976); Indiana University School of Law (J.D., cum laude, 1979). *Member:* Indianapolis, Indiana State and American Bar Associations; State Bar of California. ***PRACTICE AREAS:*** Banking Law; Commercial Lending; Real Estate; Corporate Law. ***Email:*** msk@kgrlaw.com

MARK COLUCCI, born Utica, New York, January 5, 1965; admitted to bar, 1995, Indiana. *Education:* State University of New York at Albany (B.A., Economics, 1987); Indiana University School of Law (J.D., magna cum laude, 1995). Member, Dean's Tutorial Society. Note Editor, Indiana University Law Review. *Member:* Indianapolis, Indiana State and American Bar Associations; Christian Legal Society. ***PRACTICE AREAS:*** Commercial Transactions; Business Start-Ups; Real Estate; Intellectual Property. ***Email:*** mjc@kgrlaw.com

BRETT R. FLEITZ, born Lafayette, Indiana, January 15, 1965; admitted to bar, 1990, Indiana and U.S. District Court, Northern and Southern Districts of Indiana. *Education:* Indiana University (B.A., 1987; J.D., 1990). Law Clerk to Justice Brent E. Dickson, Supreme Court of Indiana, 1990-1992. Adjunct Professor, Indiana Institute of Technology, 1997—. Author: "Original Actions in the Indiana Supreme Court: Writs of Mandamus and Prohibition," 36 Res Gestae 522 (May, 1993). Co-Author: "The Journey's Account Statute: The Litigator's Little-Known Friend," 35 Res Gestae 60 (1991), republished in 13 The Verdict 193 (1991). *Member:* Indianapolis Bar Association. ***LANGUAGES:*** German. ***PRACTICE AREAS:*** Commercial Litigation; Appellate Practice; Bankruptcy Law. ***Email:*** brf@kgrlaw.com

ASSOCIATES

MARCIA E. ROAN, born Indianapolis, Indiana, November 9, 1958; admitted to bar, 1985, Indiana and U.S. District Court, Southern and Northern Districts of Indiana. *Education:* Purdue University (B.S., with highest distinction, 1980); Indiana University (J.D., cum laude, 1984). Articles Editor, Indiana Law Review, 1984. Law Clerk to the Honorable Jonathan J. Robertson and the Honorable George B. Hoffman, Jr., Indiana Court of Appeals. Co-Author: "Bankruptcy Bibliography Update," Commercial Law Journal, Summer, 1991; Fall, 1992; Fall, 1993; "Collecting Judgments in Indiana," National Business Institute, 1992; "Foreclosure and Repossession in Indiana," Lorman Education Services, 1991. *Member:* Hendricks County, Indianapolis, Indiana State and American Bar Associations. ***REPORTED CASES:*** Shell Oil Co. v. Meyer, 705 N.E. 2d 962 (Ind. 1998); National City Bank, Indiana v. Shortridge, 689 N.E. 2d 1248 Ind. 1998); Otte v. Otte. 655 N.E.2nd 76 (Ind.App. 1995); Winkler v. V.G. Reed & Sons, Inc., 619 N.E.2d 597 (Ind.App, 1993), aff'd 638 N.E.2d 1228 (Ind. 1994); Nikou v. INB National Bank, 638 N.E.2d 448 (Ind.App. 1994). ***PRACTICE AREAS:*** Commercial Law; Bankruptcy Law; Probate and Estate Planning. ***Email:*** mer@kgrlaw.com

TRICIA A. LEMINGER, born Terre Haute, Indiana, April 21, 1971; admitted to bar, 1996, Indiana and U.S. District Court, Northern and Southern Districts of Indiana. *Education:* Purdue University (B.A., 1993); Indiana University (J.D., 1996). *Member:* Indianapolis and Indiana State Bar Associations. ***PRACTICE AREAS:*** Business Law; Real Estate; Municipal Law; Land Use; Zoning Law. ***Email:*** tal@kgrlaw.com

REYNOLDS B. BRISSENDEN, born Indianapolis, Indiana, July 29, 1972; admitted to bar, 1997, Indiana and U.S. District Court, Northern and Southern Districts of Indiana; 2003, U.S. Court of Appeals, Seventh Circuit. *Education:* Hope College (B.A., cum laude, 1994); Valparaiso University (J.D., cum laude, 1997). Contributing Author, "Marion County Prosecutor's Office, Trial Manual," 1996. Deputy Prosecuting Attorney, 19th Judicial Circuit, Marion County, Indiana, 1997-1999. Article: In Pari Delicto Doctrine May Bar Receiver's Third Party Claims: Knauer v. Jonathon Roberts, Inc., et. al., 3 De Paul Bus. & Comm. L. J. 169 (Winter 2005). *Member:* Indianapolis, Indiana State and American Bar Associations. ***PRACTICE AREAS:*** Business Litigation; Commercial Litigation. ***Email:*** rbb@kgrlaw.com

KURTIS A. MARSHALL, born Indianapolis, Indiana, October 15, 1972; admitted to bar, 2002, Indiana, U.S. District Court, Northern and Southern Districts of Indiana. *Education:* Indiana University (B.A., 1995; J.D., cum laude, 2002). *Member:* Indianapolis, Indiana State and American Bar Associations. ***PRACTICE AREAS:*** General Practice; Commercial Litigation.

JEFFREY L. LOGSTON, born Columbus, Indiana, May 18, 1973; admitted to bar, 2004, Indiana, U.S. District Court, Northern and Southern Districts of Indiana. *Education:* Indiana University (B.S., Business, 1995; J.D., 2004). *Member:* Indianapolis, Indiana State and American Bar Associations. ***PRACTICE AREAS:*** General Practice; Commercial Litigation; Municipal Law.

ANDREW R. FALK, born Clarinda, Iowa, October 20, 1974; admitted to bar, 2003, Indiana, U.S. District Court, Northern and Southern Districts of Indiana. *Education:* Indiana University (B.S., with highest distinction, university honors, 1999; J.D., cum laude, 2002). Law Clerk to the Honorable Brent E. Dickson, Supreme Court of Indiana. Judicial Clerk to the Honorable Kenneth L. Ryskamp, U.S. District Court, Southern District of Florida. *Member:* Indianapolis and Indiana State Bar Associations. ***PRACTICE AREAS:*** General Practice; Commercial Litigation.

HARLEY K. MEANS, born Indianapolis, Indiana, June 18, 1975; admitted to bar, 2001, Indiana, U.S. District Court, Northern and Southern Districts of Indiana. *Education:* Purdue University (B.S., 1997); Indiana University (J.D., 2001). *Member:* Indianapolis and Indiana State Bar Associations. ***PRACTICE AREAS:*** Secured Creditors Rights; Bankruptcy.

SENIOR COUNSEL

SYDNEY L. STEELE, born Martinsville, Indiana, September 6, 1939; admitted to bar, 1964, Indiana. *Education:* Purdue University (B.S.M.E., 1961); Indiana University (J.D., 1964). Pi Tau Sigma; Delta Theta Phi. Member, Indiana University Law Journal, 1963-1964. *Member:* Indianapolis, Indiana State and American (Member: Section on: Litigation; Construction Law Forum) Bar Associations; Indianapolis Law Club (Co-Founder). [Capt., U.S. Army, 1964-1967]. (Also Member, Lowe Gray Steele & Darko, LLP). ***PRACTICE AREAS:*** Trial Practice; Business Law; Construction Law.

DAVID E. WRIGHT, born 1951; admitted to bar, 1977, Indiana, U.S. District Court, Southern and Northern Districts of Indiana and U.S. Court of Appeals, Seventh Circuit. *Education:* Indiana University at Bloomington (B.S., 1973); Indiana University at Indianapolis (J.D., 1977). Civil Mediator, Seminar Panelist and Author: "Indiana Foreclosure Procedures," Lorman Ed. Serv., October, 1990; December, 1991; "Prevention, Avoidance and Resolution of Destructive Shareholder Disputes," Lorman Ed. Serv., September, 1992; "Structuring and Enforcing Secured Loans - Avoiding Lender Liability," Lorman Ed. Serv., October, 1993; "Class Action: Establishment of A Class and the Class Certification Process: The Defendant's Perspective," IN State Bar Association, ICLEF, April, 1995. *Member:* Indianapolis, Indiana State and American Bar Associations; Indiana Trial Lawyers Association; The Association of Trial Lawyers of America. ***PRACTICE AREAS:*** Civil Litigation; Business Torts.

OF COUNSEL

WILLIAM J. REGAS, born Michigan City, Indiana, August 19, 1918; admitted to bar, 1942, Indiana; 1956, U.S. Supreme Court. *Education:* Indiana University (B.S., 1940; LL.B., 1942). Phi Delta Phi. *Member:* Indianapolis (Past Member: Grievance Committee; Legal Economics Committee; Member, Board of Managers, 1970), Indiana State and American Bar Associations; Commercial Law League of America. (Retired). ***Email:*** wjr@kgrlaw.com

GARY A. SCHIFFLI, born Newnan, Georgia, March 3, 1954; admitted to bar, 1980, Indiana; 1981, U.S. Court of Appeals, Seventh Circuit. *Education:* Indiana University (B.S., 1976; J.D., 1980). Phi Eta Sigma. Law Clerk to Hon. James E. Noland, U.S. District Court, Southern District of Indiana, 1980-1981. Lecturer, "Fair Debt Collection Practices Act, Beware and Prepare". *Member:* Indianapolis, Indiana State, Federal and American Bar Associations; Commercial Law League of America. ***PRACTICE AREAS:*** Commercial; Retail Collections. ***Email:*** gas@kgrlaw.com

FOUNDERS

R. McDONALD KROGER (1912-2002)

JOHN E. GARDIS (1909-2002)

LEGAL SUPPORT PERSONNEL

PARALEGALS

DEBRA K. NIX, born August 16, 1953. *Education:* University of Indianapolis (A.S., 1990); Indiana University (B.S.). *Member:* Indianapolis Bar Association (Associate Member); Indiana Paralegal Association; Federation of Paralegal Associations. ***PRACTICE AREAS:*** Commercial Law; Bankruptcy Law; Real Estate Foreclosure Law. ***Email:*** dkn@kgrlaw.com

KIMBERLY M. WHIGHAM, born Bloomington, Indiana, April 1, 1967. *Education:* Ball State University (B.S., 1989); National Institution for Paralegal Training, Atlanta, Georgia (1993). *Member:* Indiana Paralegal Association, Inc.; National Federation of Paralegal Associations. ***PRACTICE AREAS:*** Bankruptcy; Creditors Rights; Litigation; Corporate Law. ***Email:*** kmw@kgrlaw.com

REPRESENTATIVE CLIENTS: Bank One Indianapolis; Brownsburg Fire Protection Territory; CART, Inc.; Centex Home Equity Corporation; City of Beech Grove; City of Carmel; Ford Motor Credit Company; Irwin Union Bank; KeyBank; Marion County Election Board; National Board of Osteopathic M.E.; Old National Bank; Star Financial Bank; United States Anti-Doping (USADA); White River Fire Township Protection.
REFERENCES: Bank One, Indiana, NA; Star Financial Bank.

(This Listing Continued)

KULT LAW OFFICE, LLC

9465 COUNSELORS ROW, SUITE 200
INDIANAPOLIS, INDIANA 46240
Telephone: 317-805-4770
Fax: 800-852-3369
Email: gkult@kultlaw.com
URL: http://www.kultlaw.com

Employment Law Counsel and Advocacy for Employers.

MEMBER OF FIRM

GREGORY P. KULT, admitted to bar, 1994, Indiana and Wisconsin, U.S. District Court, Northern and Southern Districts of Indiana; 1997, U.S. District Court, Eastern and Western Districts of Wisconsin. *Education:* Indiana University (B.A., Economics, with high distinction, 1990); University of Wisconsin (J.D., 1994). Phi Beta Kappa. Member: Society for Human Resource Management; American Society for Healthcare Human Resources Administration. *Member:* Indiana (Member, Labor and Employment Section) and American (Member, Labor and Employment and Litigation Sections) Bar Associations; State Bar of Wisconsin. ***PRACTICE AREAS:*** Employment Law; Personnel Training; Employment Litigation. ***Email:*** gkult@kultlaw.com

LADENDORF & LADENDORF

Established in 1997
7310 NORTH SHADELAND AVENUE
INDIANAPOLIS, INDIANA 46250
Telephone: 317-842-5800
Toll Free: 1-888-925-3700
Facsimile: 317-842-5858
URL: http://www.ladendorf.com
Email: mark@ladendorf.com
URL: http://www.ladendorflaw.com

Personal Injury, Medical Malpractice, Products Liability, Wrongful Death, Trials and Appeals.

FIRM PROFILE: Indianapolis attorney Mark C. Ladendorf offers his clients an expertise honed through over twenty-four years of highly successful legal service. Chosen to appear in the Bar Register of Preeminent Lawyers, Mr. Ladendorf provides expert representation throughout the state of Indiana in matters of personal injury, medical malpractice, product liability and wrongful death. Among Mr. Ladendorf's many accomplishments include one of the highest settlements in the State of Indiana on a flammable fabrics case involving children's day wear, as well as his status as the Indiana representative for Bikers Against Manslaughter (BAM) and his induction as a Life Member in The National Registry of Who's Who and College of Fellows, Indiana Trial Lawyers Association.

MARK C. LADENDORF, born Hammond, Indiana, June 17, 1955; admitted to bar, 1980, Indiana, U.S. Court of Appeals, 7th Circuit and U.S. District Court, Northern and Southern Districts of Indiana. *Education:* Indiana University (B.A., with distinction, 1977; J.D., magna cum laude, 1980). Life Member, The National Registry of Who's Who. Indiana Super Lawyers, Indianapolis Monthly, 2004, 2005. *Member:* Indianapolis, Indiana State and American (Tort and Insurance Practice Sections) Bar Associations; Indiana Trial Lawyers Association (Executive Committee, 2005—; Board of Directors, Emeritus, 2005—; Board of Directors, 1990-2005); The Association of Trial Lawyers of America (Sustaining Member); Attorney Information Exchange Group. ***REPORTED CASES:*** International Vacuum, Inc. v. Owens, (1982) 439 N.E.2d 188; DiBortolo v. Metropolitan School District of Washington Township, (1982) 440 N.E.2d 506; Rachel Riggs, et al. v. Alan Burrell, (1992) 595 N.E.2d 268; Armstrong v. Lake, (1983) 447 N.E.2d 1153; Gonzalez v. U-Haul of Central Indiana and Volvo of America Corp., (1985) 752 F.2d 295; Wildman v. Nat'l Fire & Marine Ins. Co., 03N.E.2d 683 (Ind. App. 1998). ***PRACTICE AREAS:*** Personal Injury; Medical Malpractice; Products Liability; Wrongful Death; Trial Practice; Appellate Practice. ***Email:*** mark@ladendorf.com

DANIEL ALLEN LADENDORF, born Hammond, Indiana, March 26, 1961; admitted to bar, 1987, Indiana. *Education:* Indiana University (B.S., 1983; J.D., 1986). Chief Deputy Clerk of the Marion Circuit and Superior Courts. Deputy Prosecuting Attorney, Marion County Prosecutor's Office - Grand Jury Investigative Division, Municipal Trial Division and Felony Trial Division. Court Administrator, Municipal Court of Marion County. Legislative Assistant, Indiana House of Representatives. Member, Indianapolis-Marion County Board of Ethics. General Counsel, Marion County (Indiana) Election Board. *Member:* Indianapolis and Indiana State Bar Associations; Indiana Trial Lawyers Association; Indiana Continuing Legal Education Forum (Faculty, 1993-1996). ***PRACTICE AREAS:*** Personal Injury; Wrongful Death; Medical Malpractice. ***Email:*** dan@ladendorf.com

GLORIA J. DANIELSON, born Kansas City, Missouri, November 8, 1954; admitted to bar, 2001, Indiana. *Education:* University of Indianapolis (A.S., Nursing, 1976; B.S., Nursing, 1995; J.D., 2000). Medical Records Management for Indiana Paralegals, IPE, 2001. Life Skills for Women, basic legal rights, domestic consumer, Johnson County Jail, 2001. Medical Records for Indiana Attorneys, NBI, 2001; Medical School for Lawyers, ICLEF, 2002. *Member:* Indianapolis Bar Association; Indiana Trial Lawyers Association (Sustaining Member); Indiana Continuing Legal Education Forum (Member, 1989—). ***PRACTICE AREAS:*** Medical Malpractice; Personal Injury; Wrongful Death. ***Email:*** gloria@ladendorf.com

---

AMY VAN OSTRAND, born Techachapi, California, June 30, 1974; admitted to bar, 1999, Indiana, U.S. District Court, Northern and Southern Districts of Indiana. *Education:* Claremont McKenna College (B.A., magna cum laude, 1996); University of Illinois College of Law (J.D., magna cum laude, 1999). *Member:* Indianapolis, Indiana State and American Bar Associations. ***PRACTICE AREAS:*** Personal Injury; Medical Malpractice; Civil Litigation. ***Email:*** amy@ladendorf.com

LANDMAN & BEATTY

1150 MARKET SQUARE CENTER
151 NORTH DELAWARE STREET
INDIANAPOLIS, INDIANA 46204-2518
Telephone: 317-236-1040
Fax: 317-236-1049
Email: info@landlaw.ws
Mailing Address: P.O. Box 44953, Indianapolis, IN 46244-0953

Real Estate, Real Estate Tax, Financing and Corporate Business Transactions, Wills and Probate, Probate and Estates, Personal Injury, Automobile Accidents, Wrongful Death, Libel and Defamation, Media, Municipal and Zoning, Employment and Housing Discrimination, Governmental, Tort Law, Civil Litigation, Bankruptcy and Appellate Practice.

MEMBERS OF FIRM

BERNARD LANDMAN, JR. (1928-1991)

JAMES W. BEATTY, born 1931; admitted to bar, 1955, Indiana. *Education:* University of Michigan (B.A., 1953; J.D., 1955). Order of the Coif. Assistant Editor, Michigan Law Review, 1954-1955. Corporation Counsel, City of Indianapolis, 1964-1966. ***PRACTICE AREAS:*** Real Estate Tax Appeals; Real Estate Development; Multi-Family Housing; Property Tax; Zoning. ***Email:*** jwbeatty@landlaw.ws

VIRGINIA DILL McCARTY, born 1924; admitted to bar, 1950, Indiana. *Education:* Indiana University (B.A., 1946) Indiana University School of Law/Indianapolis, (LL.B., cum laude, 1950). Order of the Coif; Phi Beta Kappa. Indianapolis Editor, Indiana Law Journal, 1949-1950. Assistant Attorney General of Indiana, 1965-1969. Member, Indiana State Board of Law Examiners, 1971-1976. Chief Counsel to Marion County Prosecuting Attorney, 1975-1976. U.S. Attorney, Southern District of Indiana, 1977-1981. Chairman of the Board, Indiana Department of Corrections, 1989—. ***PRACTICE AREAS:*** Partnership Law; Fair Housing; Equal Employment Opportunity; Decedents' Estates; Municipal Law. ***Email:*** vmccarty@landlaw.ws

JAMES F. BEATTY, born 1959; admitted to bar, 1984, Indiana. *Education:* Indiana University (B.S., 1981; J.D., 1984). Beta Gamma Sigma. Commissioner, Marion County Courts, 1990-1995. ***PRACTICE AREAS:*** Civil Litigation; Contract Litigation; Landlord and Tenant Law; Real Estate Law; Multi-Family Housing. ***Email:*** jfbeatty@landlaw.ws

COUNSEL

STEPHEN M. TERRELL, born 1952; admitted to bar, 1980, Indiana. *Education:* Ball State University (B.A., 1974); Indiana University (J.D., summa cum laude, 1980). Member: Board of Editors, Indiana Law Review, 1979-1980. Instructor, Litigation, Butler University, 1984-1988. Clerk to Hon. Chief Judge Paul H. Buchanan, Indiana Court of Appeals, 1977-1980. *Member:* Indianapolis Bar Association; Indiana State Bar Association (Editor, GP Reporter); Indiana Trial Lawyers Association; The Association of Trial Lawyers of America. ***PRACTICE AREAS:*** Appellate Practice; Commercial Litigation; Libel Slander and Defamation; Probate; Estate Litigation; Trial Practice. ***Email:*** sterrell@landlaw.ws

NANCY G. ENDSLEY, born 1947; admitted to bar, 1988, Indiana and U.S. District Court, Northern and Southern Districts of Indiana. *Education:* Indiana University (B.A., 1969; M.L.S., 1972; J.D., 1988). Law Clerk to Hon. Robert H. Staton, Indiana Court of Appeals, 1988-1990. Co-author and Lecturer: "Bankruptcy Basics for the General Bar, 1992," ICLEF. *Member:* Indianapolis and Indiana State Bar Associations. ***LANGUAGES:*** Spanish. ***PRACTICE AREAS:*** Appellate Practice; Bankruptcy Law; Debtor and Creditor. ***Email:*** nendsley@landlaw.ws

ASSOCIATES

J. CHRIS REININGA, born 1966; admitted to bar, 1996, Indiana. *Education:* Purdue University (B.S., 1989); Indiana University (J.D., magna cum laude, 1996). Member, Indiana Law Review. Law Clerk to Hon. Robert H. Staton, Indiana Court of Appeals, 1996-1998. *Member:* Indianapolis and Indiana State Bar Associations; Indiana Trial Lawyers Association. ***PRACTICE AREAS:*** Civil Litigation; Personal Injury; Corporate Law; Real Estate; Appellate Practice. ***Email:*** jcreininga@landlaw.ws

CYNTHIA L. BALL, born 1968; admitted to bar, 1995, Indiana. *Education:* Butler University (B.A., magna cum laude, 1991); Indiana University (J.D., 1995). *Member:* Hendricks County Bar Association (Vice-President, 1999-2000; Treasurer, 1997-1999); Indianapolis Bar Association (Member, Executive Committee for Women and the Law); Indiana State Bar Association. ***PRACTICE AREAS:*** Family Law; Landlord and Tenant Law; Litigation. ***Email:*** clball@landlaw.ws

LANDWERLEN & ROTHKOPF L.L.P.

244 NORTH COLLEGE AVENUE
INDIANAPOLIS, INDIANA 46202
Telephone: 317-639-3315
Fax: 317-639-3318
URL: http://www.landrothlaw.com

Business Law, Business Planning, Contracts, Lawsuits, Insurance, Business Enterprises, Limited Liability Companies, Franchises, Partnerships, Small Business, Closely Held Business, Buying and Selling Business, Debt Credit, Corporate Law, Contracts, Real Estate, Commercial Litigation, Family Law, Adoptions, Divorce, Child Custody, Child Support, Domestic Violence, Visitation Rights, Criminal Law, Felonies, Misdemeanors, Homicide, Driving While Intoxicated, Traffic Violations, Personal Injury, Automobile Accidents, Medical Malpractice, Employment Law, Wills and Probate, Trusts and Estates, Estate Planning, Guardianships, Elder Law.

(This Listing Continued)

LANDWERLEN & ROTHKOPF L.L.P., Indianapolis—Continued

THOMAS L. LANDWERLEN, born Indianapolis, Indiana, June 14, 1955; admitted to bar, 1980, Indiana, Florida, U.S. District Court, Southern District of Indiana; U.S. Court of Appeals, Seventh Circuit. *Education:* Indiana University (A.B., 1977); Stetson University; Indiana University (J.D., 1980). Outstanding Orator, Stetson University, 1976-1977. *Member:* Indianapolis and Indiana State Bar Associations; The Florida Bar; Indiana Trial Lawyers Association; Association of Trial Lawyers of America; The Barristers. (Resident, Indianapolis Office). ***PRACTICE AREAS:*** Business Law. ***Email:*** pgv@iquest.net

ROBERT C. ROTHKOPF, born Indianapolis, Indiana, May 24, 1955; admitted to bar, 1980, Indiana and U.S. District Court, Southern District of Indiana; 1981, Florida; 1991, U.S. District Court, Northern District of Indiana. *Education:* Indiana University (B.S., 1977; J.D., cum laude, 1980). Phi Delta Phi. *Member:* Indianapolis, Indiana State and American Bar Associations; The Florida Bar; The Association of Trial Lawyers of America. (Resident, Indianapolis Office). ***Email:*** robert.rothkopf@landrothlaw.com

LEWIS & KAPPES

PROFESSIONAL CORPORATION

Established in 1985

ONE AMERICA TOWER

ONE AMERICAN SQUARE, SUITE 1700

INDIANAPOLIS, INDIANA 46282

Telephone: 317-639-1210

Telecopier: 317-639-4882

Email: Office@Lewis-Kappes.com

URL: http://www.Lewis-Kappes.com

General Civil Practice. Appellate, Corporate, Family/Domestic Relations, Real Estate, Municipal, Zoning, Mergers and Acquisitions, Labor and Employment, Copyright, Probate and Estate Planning, Administrative, Environmental, Litigation, State and Federal Taxation, Regulatory, Energy and Utility, Legislative, Immigration and Nationality, Medical Malpractice, Intellectual Properties, Securities, Bankruptcy, Creditor's Rights, Business and Transactional and Intellectual Properties.

FIRM PROFILE: Lewis & Kappes are attorneys dedicated to the proposition of representing your best interests at all times. Since February 15, 1985, the years of experience of our highly skilled lawyers equip us to handle your needs in a discreet, efficient and cost effective manner.

TED B. LEWIS (1919-1991)

PHILIP S. KAPPES, born Detroit, Michigan, December 24, 1925; admitted to bar, 1948, Indiana. *Education:* Butler University (B.A., cum laude, 1945); University of Michigan (J.D., 1948). Tau Kappa Alpha. First Chairman, Ovid Butler Society, 1985. Trustee, Butler University, 1987-1990. President, Butler University Alumni Association, Inc., 1955-1957. Instructor, Business Law, 1948-1949. Director, Indiana Citizens for Modern Court System, 1970. Secretary, Director: Indiana Machine Works, Inc., K & K Realty, Inc. Manager: LABECO Properties. General Partner, Creston Group. Member: Crossroads of Am. Council, BSA, Dir., 1965—, past Chairman. Board Chairman, 1984-1985, Director, 1960-1988, Distinguished Advisor, 1988—, Children's Museum (Member, Audit and Nominating Committees). Chairman, 1988-91, Director, 1986-1993, Director Emeritus, 1994—, Fairbanks Hospital. Chairman: Scottish Rite of Indianapolis Foundation, Inc.; Indianapolis Scottish Rite Cathederal Foundation Inc. Vice Chairman, 32° Learning Center for Children. *Member:* Indianapolis (Treasurer, Board of Managers, 1959-1961, 1976-1977; Chairman, Judiciary Committee, 1962-1964; First Vice President, 1965 and 1969; President, 1970; Vice Chairman and Faculty Member Law in, American Society Seminar, 1971-1973; Chairman, Community Education and Court Liaison Committees, 1992—; Co-Chairman, Family Law Study Commission, 1992—; Counsel to Board, 1994), Indiana State (Chairman: Committee on American Citizenship, 1953; 11th District Grievance Committee, 1960-1961; Midwinter Meeting, 1965; Public Relations Executive Committee, 1966-1969; Law Practice Management Committee; Member, House of Delegates, 1958—; Secretary, 1973-1974; Member, Executive Committee and Board of Managers, 1973-1974; 11th District Representative, Board of Managers, 1976-1977) and American (Member, House of Delegates, 1970-1971; Chairman, Lawyers Title Guaranty Fund Committee, 1971-1973) Bar Associations; American Judicature Society; Lawyers Club of Indianapolis; Lawyers Association of Indianapolis. Fellow: Indianapolis Bar Foundation; Indiana Bar Foundation; American Bar Foundation. ***PRACTICE AREAS:*** Corporate Law; Contracts Law; Intellectual Property Law; Estate Planning Law; Business Acquisitions Law. ***Email:*** PKappes@Lewis-Kappes.com

DAVID W. GRAY, born Anderson, Indiana, February 26, 1950; admitted to bar, 1975, Indiana and U.S. District Court, Southern District of Indiana; 1976, U.S. Court of Appeals, Seventh Circuit. *Education:* Indiana University (B.S., 1972; J.D., cum laude, 1975). Associate Editor, Indiana Law Review, 1974-1975. Author: "Survey of Recent Developments in Indiana Law," 10 Indiana Law Review 142, 1976; "Recent Development, Schneckloth v. Bustamonte," 7 Indiana Law Review 592, 1974. Adjunct Faculty: Indiana Central University, 1982-1984; Indiana University, 1984-1986. Law Clerk to the Honorable S. Hugh Dillin, Chief Judge, U.S. District Court, Southern District of Indiana, 1975-1977. *Member:* Indianapolis, Indiana State, Federal and American Bar Associations. ***PRACTICE AREAS:*** Litigation; Labor Law; Environmental Law. ***Email:*** DGray@Lewis-Kappes.com

JOHN F. WICKES, JR., born Miami, Florida, January 21, 1947; admitted to bar, 1975, Indiana; 1979, District of Columbia. *Education:* Indiana University (B.A., 1969; J.D., cum laude, 1975). Legal Staff, U.S. Senate Veterans' Affairs and Labor and Human Resources Committees, 1975-1979. *Member:* Indianapolis, Indiana State and American Bar Associations. [Sgt. U.S. Army, active duty, 1969-1971]. ***PRACTICE AREAS:*** Utility Regulation Law; Energy Law; General Practice. ***Email:*** JWickes@Lewis-Kappes.com

GARY P. PRICE, born Chicago, Illinois, September 11, 1950; admitted to bar, 1978, Indiana. *Education:* University of Wisconsin at Milwaukee (B.A., 1974; M.A., 1975); Indiana University (J.D., magna cum laude, 1978); Diplomate: Court Practice Institute, 1980; National Institute for Trial Advocacy, Advanced Seminar, 1983. Recipient: Appellate Advocacy Award, Spring, 1977; Woodard Fellowship, 1977-1978. Author: "Administrative Law," 12 Indiana Law Review 30-42; "Workmen's Compensation," 12 Indiana Law Review 334-339. Adjunct Faculty: Indiana Central University, 1980-1981; Butler University, 1981-1982; Indiana University School of Law, 1988-1992. Faculty Member, ICLEF/NITA Trial Advocacy Seminars, 1987-1989. Law Clerk, Supreme Court of Indiana, 1977-1978. Member, Law School Development Council, Indiana University-Indianapolis Law School, 1984—. *Member:* Indianapolis and Indiana State Bar Associations; Indiana Trial Lawyers Association; The Association of Trial Lawyers of America. [With U.S. Army, 1968-1970]. ***PRACTICE AREAS:*** Civil Litigation; Appellate and Trial Practice; Constitutional Law; Scientific and Intellectual Property Litigation Mediation. ***Email:*** GPrice@Lewis-Kappes.com

STEVEN L. TUCHMAN, born Indianapolis, Indiana, September 3, 1946; admitted to bar, 1971, Indiana. *Education:* Indiana University (B.A., 1968; J.D., 1971); City College, London, England. Phi Delta Phi. Advisor, Den Danske Bank, Copenhagen, Denmark, 1971-1973. Real Estate Counsel, Melvin Simon & Associates, 1973-1981. Adjunct Professor, Real Estate Law, Indiana University School of Business, 1983-1984. President, Planned Parenthood of Central Indiana, 1991-1992. Member, Indiana's International Task Force. Chairman: American Cabaret Theatre, 2001—; Indiana Arts; Indianapolis Historic Preservation Commission, 2003—. Member, Indianapolis Committee on Foreign Relations, 1999—. Honorary Consul to Denmark, 2003—. Director, 1990—, President, 2001-2002, Lewis & Kappes, P.C. *Member:* Indianapolis (Member: Supreme Court Disciplinary Commission Grievance Committee, 1986—; Mediator, Marion County Municipal and Superior Court Mediation Program, 1987-1993; Court Certified Mediator, 1993—; Committee, Long Range Plans, 1987-1988; International Section, 1994—; Indiana State (Member, House of Delegates, 1986—) and American (Member, Sections on: Business; Real Estate; International Law) Bar Associations; American Immigration Lawyers Association (National Board of Governors, 1992-2002, Chapter Chair Indiana, 1992-1994; Liaison to the Nebraska Service Center, 2000-2002); Indianapolis Bar Foundation (Member, Indianapolis Committee on Foreign Relations, 1994—). ***LANGUAGES:*** Danish. ***PRACTICE AREAS:*** Immigration Law; Nationality Law; General Business Law; Corporate Representation; Probate Law; Wills; Trusts; Estate Law. ***Email:*** STuchman@Lewis-Kappes.com

THOMAS R. RUGE, born Valparaiso, Indiana, March 30, 1949; admitted to bar, 1976, Indiana and U. S. District Court, Northern and Southern Districts of Indiana; 1980, U. S. Supreme Court, U. S. Court of Appeals, 7th Circuit and U. S. Claims Court. *Education:* Indiana University (B.A., 1971); Valparaiso University (J.D., 1976). Adjunct Professor, Immigration Law, Indiana University School of Law at Indianapolis, 1991. Author: "Screening and Evaluating the Medical Malpractice and Other Personal Injury Cases," "Evaluation of Structured Settlement Proposals," and "Proving Causation in Medical Malpractice and Other Personal Injury Cases," Personal Injury Litigation Practice in Indiana, National Business Institute, Inc., 1988; "Medical Malpractice," Indiana Law Review, Volume 22, Number 1, 1989; "Survey of Recent Developments in Medical Malpractice Law," Indiana Law Review, Volume 23, Number 2, 1990. Member, Board of Directors, 1989 and President, 1990-1991, Forum for International Professional Services. Member: Governor's Task Force on International Business, 1990; Mayor's Task Force on Families and Justice. Project Supervisor, Legal Service Organization of Indiana, 1977-1981. Adjunct Professor, Immigration Law, Indiana University School of Law, Indianapolis. *Member:* Indianapolis and Indiana State Bar Associations; Indiana Trial Lawyers Association; The Association of Trial Lawyers of America; Association of Immigration Attorneys; American Immigration Lawyers Association (Chairman, Indiana Chapter, 1988-1989); World Trade Club. ***LANGUAGES:*** Spanish. ***PRACTICE AREAS:*** Litigation; Immigration Law; General Business. ***Email:*** TRuge@Lewis-Kappes.com

C. DUANE O'NEAL, born Indianapolis, Indiana, March 10, 1950; admitted to bar, 1985, Indiana, U.S. District Court, Southern and Northern Districts of Indiana, U.S. Court of Appeals, Seventh Circuit and U.S. Tax Court; U.S. Supreme Court. *Education:* Indiana University (B.A., 1972; M.B.A., 1979; J.D., summa cum laude, 1984). Associate Editor, Indiana Law Review, 1984-1985. Counsel, Indiana House of Representatives, 1987-1991. Commissioner, Greenwood Board of Public Works, 1993-1995. Judge, Greenwood City Court, 1994-1995. Member, Panel of Arbitrators and Mediator, American Arbitration Association. Registered Lobbyist, State of Indiana. *Member:* Indianapolis, Johnson County and Indiana State Bar Associations. ***LANGUAGES:*** French. ***PRACTICE AREAS:*** Zoning Law; Civil Litigation; Family Law; Bankruptcy Law; General Corporate Law; Construction Law; Mediation; Arbitration. ***Email:*** ONeal@Lewis-Kappes.com

TODD A. RICHARDSON, born St. Paul, Minnesota, March 15, 1961; admitted to bar, 1986, Massachusetts; 1987, U.S. District Court, District of Massachusetts; 1991, U.S. Court of Appeals, Federal Circuit; 1992, Indiana and U.S. District Court, Southern District of Indiana; 1994, U.S. District Court, Northern District of Indiana. *Education:* Harvard University (B.A., cum laude, general studies, 1983); University of Michigan (J.D., cum laude, 1986). Staff Member, University of Michigan Journal of Law Reform, 1984-1986. ***REPORTED CASES:*** Airco Industrial Gases v. Indiana Michigan Power Co., 614 N.E. 2d 951 (Ind. App. 1993); Wang Laboratories, Inc. v. Applied Computer Sciences, Inc., 958 F. 2d 355 (Fed. Cir. 1992). ***PRACTICE AREAS:*** Commercial Litigation; Intellectual Property; Trade Regulation Law. ***Email:*** TRichardson@Lewis-Kappes.com

BETTE J. DODD, born Fort Wayne, Indiana, February 7, 1952; admitted to bar, 1983, Indiana and the U.S. District Court, Northern and Southern Districts of Indiana; 1984, U.S. Court of Appeals, 7th Circuit; 1986, U.S. Court of Appeals, 11th Circuit; 1990, U.S. Court of Appeals, Eighth Circuit; 1991, U.S. Supreme Court. *Education:* Indiana University (B.A., 1975; J.D., magna cum laude, 1983). Law Clerk To: Hon. Justice Donald H. Hunter, Indiana Supreme Court, 1983; Hon. William E. Steckler, U.S. District Court, Southern District of Indiana, 1983-1986. *Member:* Indianapolis, Indiana State and American Bar Associations; Indiana Municipal Lawyers Association; National Association of Bond Lawyers. ***PRACTICE AREAS:*** Municipal Utility Regulation Law; Water and Sewer Law; Municipal Finance; Municipal Law. ***Email:*** BDodd@Lewis-Kappes.com

PETER S. FRENCH, born Bloomington, Indiana, December 21, 1966; admitted to bar, 1992, Indiana and U.S. District Court, Southern District of Indiana and U.S. Supreme Court. *Education:* College of William and Mary (A.B., 1989); Tulane University Law School (J.D., Environmental Law, 1989). Author: Tulane Environmental Law Journal, May, 1992, vol. 5, Issue 2; "Parent Corporation Liability An Evaluation of The Corporate Veil Piercing Doctrine and its Application to the Toxic Torts Arena," Tulane Environmental Law

(This Listing Continued)

Journal (199), vol. 4, Issue & Note. *Member:* Indiana State (Member, Indiana Bar Grievance Committee, May, 2001—) and American Bar Associations. ***PRACTICE AREAS:*** Commercial Law; Intellectual Property; Business Litigation; Trial Practice. ***Email:*** PFrench@Lewis-Kappes.com

BRIAN ANDREW STATZ, born St. Joseph, Michigan, April 18, 1969; admitted to bar, 1994, Indiana. *Education:* Indiana University (B.A., 1991); University of Michigan (J.D., 1994). Phi Beta Kappa. Author, "The Effect of Austin Lakes Joint Venture v. Avon Utilities on Dispute Resolution with Regulated Entities," Ind. State Bar Jour. (Nov. 1995). *Member:* Indianapolis (Chair, Liaison with Law Schools Committee, 1999; Homeless Project, 1995-1998), Indiana State and American Bar Associations. ***PRACTICE AREAS:*** Commercial Litigation; Utility Regulation Law. ***Email:*** BStatz@Lewis-Kappes.com

TIMOTHY L. STEWART, born Muncie, Indiana, January 19, 1951; admitted to bar, 1984, Indiana. *Education:* Indiana University (B.A., 1973; M.P.A., 1975; J.D., summa cum laude, 1984). Author: "Jones v. Schweiker, Illegitimate Children and Social Security Benefits," Indiana Law Review, Vol. 16, 1983. Work experience: Associate, Baker & Daniels, 1984-1992; Indiana Utility Consumer Counselor's Office and Vernon J. Petri, 1992-2000. *Member:* Indianapolis, Indiana State and American Bar Associations. ***PRACTICE AREAS:*** Corporate Law; Securities Law; Banking Law; Family Law; Utility Law. ***Email:*** TStewart@Lewis-Kappes.com

JAMES J. AMMEEN, JR., born New York, N.Y., 1963; admitted to bar, 1995, Indiana, U.S. District Court, Southern and Northern Districts of Indiana; U.S. Court of Appeals, Seventh Circuit. *Education:* Middlebury College (A.B., 1985); Indiana University School of Law (J.D., 1995). Co-Winner, Faculty Award For Outstanding Law Student. Order of Barristers. Editor-in-Chief, Indiana International and Comparative Law Review, 1994-1995. Law Clerk to Supreme Court of Indiana, 1995-1997. Director, Federalist Society; President, St. Thomas More Society. *Member:* American Bar Association. ***PRACTICE AREAS:*** Litigation; Bankruptcy; Creditors Rights; Utility Law; International Law; Business Law. ***Email:*** jammeen@lewis-kappes.com

KATHRYN KUNZ, born Indianapolis, Indiana, January 30, 1951; admitted to bar, 1983, Indiana and Illinois. *Education:* Skidmore College (B.A., 1973); John Marshall Law School (J.D., 1983). Phi Delta Phi. Law Clerk to Illinois Court of Appeals, 1983-1985. *Member:* Indianapolis, Indiana State and Illinois State American Bar Associations. ***TRANSACTIONS:*** Georgia Pacific acquisition of CeCorr, Inc. ***Email:*** kkunz@lewis-kappes.com

CHRISTOPHER POLING, born Harrisburg, Pennsylvania, December 18, 1961; admitted to bar, 1987, Ohio; 1994, Washington; 1995, Indiana; U.S. District Court, Southern District of Indiana; U.S. Court of Appeals, Federal Circuit. *Education:* Purdue University, Krannert School of Management (B.S., 1983); Capital University (J.D., 1987). *Member:* Indianapolis, Indiana State, Ohio State and Washington State Bar Associations. ***Email:*** cpoling@lewis-kappes.com

CHARLEYNE L. GABRIEL, born Indianapolis, Indiana, August 6, 1947; admitted to bar, 1973, Indiana; U.S. District Court, Northern and Southern Districts of Indiana; U.S. Court of Appeals, Seventh Circuit. *Education:* University of Pittsburgh (B.A., 1970); Indiana University (J.D., summa cum laude, 1973). Member, Indianapolis and Indiana State (Member, Environmental Section) Bar Associations. ***PRACTICE AREAS:*** Commercial Litigation; Litigation. ***Email:*** cgabriel@lewis-kappes.com

JAMES E. ZOCCOLA, born Indianapolis, Indiana, August 17, 1966; admitted to bar, 1991, Indiana. *Education:* Indiana University School of Business (B.S., Marketing, 1988); Indiana University School of Law (J.D., 1991). *Member:* Indianapolis Bar Association; Defense Trial Counsel of Indiana. ***Email:*** jzoccola@lewis-kappes.com

JAMES A. KLIMEK, born South Bend, Indiana, April 19, 1967; admitted to bar, 1993, Indiana. *Education:* Colby College (B.A., Philosophy, 1989); Indiana University (J.D., 1992). Phi Beta Kappa. Associate Editor, Adelphia Law Journal, 1991-1992. Chief Counsel to the Indiana Securities Commissioner, 1995-1997. Deputy Indiana Securities Commissioner, 1992-1995. Associate Counsel, Standard Management Corporation, 1997-1999. Formerly with, Maddox Koeller Hargett & Caruso, 2000-2002. *Member:* Indiana State and American (Member, Federal and State Securities Regulation Committees) Bar Associations. ***PRACTICE AREAS:*** Securities. ***Email:*** JKlimek@Lewis-Kappes.com

DAVID S. KLINESTIVER, born Indianapolis, Indiana, August 2, 1959; admitted to bar, 1985, Kentucky; 1987, Indiana. *Education:* Indiana University (B.A., 1981; J.D., 1985). *Member:* Indianapolis, Indiana State, Kentucky and American Bar Associations. ***PRACTICE AREAS:*** Intellectual Property Law; Franchise Law; Corporate Law; Business Law; Mergers and Acquisitions. ***Email:*** DKlinestiver@Lewis-Kappes.com

JENNIFER WHEELER TERRY, born Bloomington, Indiana, June 30, 1969; admitted to bar, 1998, Indiana. *Education:* Purdue University (B.S., Materials Science and Engineering, 1992); Indiana University (J.D., magna cum laude, 1998). *Member:* Indianapolis and Indiana State Bar Associations. ***PRACTICE AREAS:*** Utility Law; Family Law; Estate Planning. ***Email:*** JTerry@Lewis-Kappes.com

THOMAS H. RISTINE, born Crawfordsville, Indiana, February 26, 1950; admitted to bar, 1975, Indiana. *Education:* Wabash College (A.B., magna cum laude, 1972); Duke University (J.D., 1975). Phi Beta Kappa. *Member:* Indiana State and American Bar Associations. ***PRACTICE AREAS:*** Administrative Law; Banking Law; Business Law; Estate Planning; Non-Profit Law. ***Email:*** tristine@lewis-kappes.com

---

CHRISTOPHER R. TAYLOR, born Bloomington, Illinois, June 28, 1974; admitted to bar, 2002, Indiana. *Education:* DePauw University (B.A., 1996); Valparaiso University (J.D., cum laude, 2001). *Member:* Indianapolis, Indiana State and American Bar Associations. ***PRACTICE AREAS:*** Employment Law; Utility Law; Litigation; Products Liability. ***Email:*** ctaylor@lewis-kappes.com

SUZANNE R. GAIDOO, born Bloomington, Indiana, June 1, 1977; admitted to bar, 2002, Indiana. *Education:* Indiana State University (B.S., 1999); University of Cincinnati (J.D., 2002). *Member:* Indianapolis, Indiana State and American Bar Associations. ***PRACTICE AREAS:*** Commercial Law; Employment Law; Family Law; Immigration; International Law; Litigation. ***Email:*** SRobinson@Lewis-Kappes.com

(This Listing Continued)

MARCO A. MORENO, born Matamoros, Tamualipas, Mexico, November 6, 1973; admitted to bar, 2003, Indiana and U.S. District Court, Northern and Southern Districts of Indiana. *Education:* Tri-State University (B.A., magna cum laude, 2000); Indiana University School of Law (J.D., 2003). Law Clerk to Honorable Judge George E. Brown, LaGrange Superior Court. Legal Assistant, Howard S. Grimm, Jr., Public Defender. Interpreter, LaGrange County Superior, Circuit and Traffic Courts. Registered Mediator. Secretary, Indianapolis Latino Affairs Committee. *Member:* Indianapolis and American Bar Associations; American Immigration Lawyers Association. ***LANGUAGES:*** Spanish. ***PRACTICE AREAS:*** Immigration Law; International Law; Securities; Corporate Law. ***Email:*** mmoreno@lewis-kappes.com

PAULA L. ZELMAN-FINCH, born Cleveland, Ohio, June 3, 1971; admitted to bar, 2003, Indiana; U.S. District Court, Northern and Southern Districts of Indiana. *Education:* Purdue University (B.A., 1993); Indiana University School of Law - Indianapolis (J.D., 2002). Member, U.S. Rowing Association. *Member:* Indianapolis, Indiana State and American Bar Associations. ***Email:*** pzelman@lewis-kappes.com

STEVEN W. GRIESEMER, born Indianapolis, Indiana, November 15, 1968; admitted to bar, 1996, California; 2004, Indiana. *Education:* Indiana University Kelly School of Business, Bloomington (B.S., 1992); Pepperdine University School of Law, Malibu (J.D., magna cum laude, 1995). *Member:* Indiana State and American Bar Associations; State Bar of California. ***PRACTICE AREAS:*** Intellectual Property; Technology Law; Entertainment Law; Commercial Law; Utility Law; Litigation. ***Email:*** sgriesemer@lewis-kappes.com

ANGELA D. IZA, born Indianapolis, Indiana, November 10, 1974; admitted to bar, 2004, Indiana. *Education:* Indiana University, Bloomington (B.S., 1997); Indiana University School of Law - Indianapolis (J.D., 2004). *Member, Board of Directors, Hispanic Education Center. Member:* Indianapolis (Member, Latino Affairs Committee), Indiana State and American Bar Associations; American Immigration Lawyers Association; La Plaza Education Center Board of Directors; Mayor's commission on Latino Affairs. ***PRACTICE AREAS:*** Immigration Law; International Law; Education Law; Family Law; Litigation. ***Email:*** aiza@lewis-kappes.com

SARA R. BRADBURY, born Whittier, California, November 15, 1976; admitted to bar, 2004, Indiana. *Education:* Earlham College (B.A., with honors, 1999); Indiana University School of Law - Bloomington (J.D., cum laude, 2004). *Member:* Indiana State and American Bar Associations. ***PRACTICE AREAS:*** Bankruptcy; Landlord and Tenant Law; Commercial Law; Litigation. ***Email:*** sbradbury@lewis-kappes.com

HANNAH KAUFMAN, born Indianapolis, Indiana, March 30, 1979; admitted to bar, 2004, Indiana. *Education:* Indiana University College of Arts and Sciences, Bloomington (B.A., 2001); Indiana University School of Law - Indianapolis (J.D., 2004). *Member:* Indiana State Bar Association. ***PRACTICE AREAS:*** Securities; Business Litigation; Civil Litigation. ***Email:*** hkaufman@lewis-kappes.com

OF COUNSEL

LESLIE DUVALL, born Indianapolis, Indiana, February 23, 1924; admitted to bar, 1949, Indiana. *Education:* Butler University (B.A., 1948); Indiana University (J.D., 1949). Sigma Delta Kappa (National President, 1958-1959). Instructor, Public Utility Regulation, Indiana University School of Law, 1990-1993. Indianapolis Commissioner, Indiana Utility Regulatory Commission, 1958-1961 (PSCI), 1985-1989 (IURC) . Member, Public Service Commission of Indiana, 1958-1961. Indiana State Senator, 1967-1985. *Member:* Indianapolis (Member: Board of Directors, 1959; Grievance Committee, 1962; Chaired Committees to establish Marion County Public Defender and Unify Superior and Municipal Courts) and Indiana State Bar Associations. [With U.S. Army, 1943-1946]. ***PRACTICE AREAS:*** Public Utilities. ***Email:*** JLD@Lewis-Kappes.com

SCOTT D. YONOVER, born Gary, Indiana, April 21, 1964; admitted to bar, 1989, Indiana, Illinois, District of Columbia and U.S. District Court, Northern and Southern Districts of Indiana. *Education:* Indiana University (B.A., 1986; J.D., 1989). Order of Barristers; Jessup National Moot Court Team. *Member:* Indianapolis, Indiana State and American Bar Associations. ***PRACTICE AREAS:*** Municipal Financial; Government-Municipal. ***Email:*** SYonover@aol.com

REPRESENTATIVE CLIENTS: ALCOA; Central Indiana Neighborhood Health Centers, Inc.; The Children's Museum of Indianapolis, Inc.; The Christian Church-Disciples of Christ; City of Indianapolis; The Coca-Cola Company; Cook Group, Inc.; General Motors, Inc.; Indiana Health Centers, Inc.; Indiana Industrial Energy Consumers, Inc.; Indiana Primary Health Care Association; Indianapolis Valley of Scottish Rite; KeyBank National Association; Mexican Consulate (Indianapolis); Mittal Steel; Northwest Mutual Life Insurance Company; Rolls Royce Corporation; Tuchman Cleaners; Union Federal Bank; United States Steel Corporation; University of Notre Dame; ZVL-ZKL Bearings Corporation.

LEWIS WAGNER, LLP

Established in 1958

500 PLACE

501 INDIANA AVENUE, SUITE 200

INDIANAPOLIS, INDIANA 46202-3199

Telephone: 317-237-0500

Fax: 317-630-2790

Email: lewiswagner@aol.com

URL: http://www.lewiswagner.com

General Civil Trial Practice. Administrative Law, Appellate Practice, Business Law, Commercial Law, Construction Law, Contracts, Corporate Law, Drug and Medical Device, Elder Law, Election, Campaign and Political, Environmental Law, Family Law, Finance, Guardianships, Government, Insurance, Labor and Employment, Legal Malpractice, Litigation, Medical Malpractice, Products Liability, Real Estate, Securities, Taxation, Toxic Torts, Trucking and Transportation Law, Trusts and Estates, Wills and Probate, Workers' Compensation.

FIRM PROFILE: Founded by Edward D. Lewis in 1950, Lewis Wagner has grown to be one of the most prestigious Indianapolis law firms, dedicated to best serving the needs of its diverse clientele. Lewis Wagner prides itself on its unique and refreshing approach to law, one utilizing something all too rare today—common sense and accountability.

(This Listing Continued)

LEWIS WAGNER, LLP, Indianapolis—Continued

JUDITH TREVOR KIRTLAND (1947-1990)

EDWARD D. LEWIS (1922-1996)

MARK E. WALKER. *Education:* Washington University (B.A., 1991); Indiana University (J.D., 1994). (1969-2000)

ROBERT F. WAGNER, born Guilford, Connecticut, February 27, 1935; admitted to bar, 1967, Indiana and U.S. District Court, Southern District of Indiana; 1979, U.S. Court of Appeals, Seventh Circuit; U.S. Court of Appeals, Eleventh Circuit. *Education:* Nichols College and University of Connecticut (B.S., 1958); University of Tulsa and Indiana University (J.D., 1967). Faculty Indiana, National Institute for Trial Advocates, 1986—. Member: Sagamore American Inn of Court; American Board of Trial Advocates (Past President, Indiana Chapter). Member, International Association of Insurance Receivers. *Member:* Indiana State, Federal and American Bar Associations; Indiana Trial Lawyers Association; American Judicature Society; Defense Trial Counsel of Indiana (Diplomat, 2000); Defense Research Institute; The Association of Trial Lawyers of America; Indianapolis Bar Foundation. Fellow, International Academy of Trial Lawyers. ***PRACTICE AREAS:*** Litigation; Products Liability Defense Litigation; Medical Malpractice; Drug and Medical Device Litigation; General Liability; Insurance Law; Commercial Law. ***Email:*** rwagner@lewiswagner.com

DAVID KONNERSMAN, born Cincinnati, Ohio, February 7, 1940; admitted to bar, 1973, Indiana. *Education:* Indiana University (B.A., 1965); University of Toledo (J.D., 1972). Member, University of Toledo Law Review, 1971-1972. Recipient, American Jurisprudence Award. ***PRACTICE AREAS:*** Commercial Law; Corporations Law; Real Estate Law.

THOMAS C. HAYS, born Franklin, Indiana, March 3, 1951; admitted to bar, 1977, Georgia and U.S. District Court, Northern District of Georgia; 1979, Indiana and U.S. District Court, Southern District of Indiana. *Education:* Indiana University (A.B., 1973); John Marshall Law School; Woodrow Wilson College of Law (J.D., 1977). Member, Atlanta Bar Association, 1977-1979. *Member:* Indianapolis (Member, Litigation Section), Johnson County, Indiana State and American Bar Associations; State Bar of Georgia; American Board of Trial Advocates (President Elect, Indiana Chapter, 2005); International Association of Defense Counsel; Defense Research Institute; Defense Trial Counsel of Indiana (Chair, Trial Tactics Section, 1999-2002; Board of Directors, 2005). ***PRACTICE AREAS:*** Insurance Defense Litigation; Commercial Litigation; Products Liability; Mediation. ***Email:*** thays@lewiswagner.com

JOHN C. TRIMBLE, born Portsmouth, Virginia, August 12, 1955; admitted to bar, 1981, Indiana, U.S. District Court, Northern and Southern Districts of Indiana and U.S. Court of Appeals, Seventh Circuit. *Education:* The Citadel and Hanover College (B.A., 1977); Indiana University - Indianapolis (J.D., magna cum laude, 1981). Executive Editor, Indiana Law Review, 1980-1981. Recipient: Phi Delta Phi Graduate of the Year, 1981; Ben F. Small Memorial Fellowship, 1981; I.U. Law School Faculty Award, 1981. Named Indiana Defense Lawyer of the Year, 1991-1992. Named Fred H. Sievert Outstanding Defense Bar Leader Award by DRI, 1999. Author of numerous Law Review articles in the area of Insurance Law. Member, Board of Visitors, Indiana University School of Law, Indianapolis, 1988—. Member, Board of Trustees, Hanover College, 2000—. *Member:* Indianapolis and Indiana State Bar Associations; Defense Trial Counsel of Indiana (President, 1998-1999); Defense Research Institute (Board of Directors, 2002—); International Association of Defense Counsel. ***LANGUAGES:*** Spanish. ***PRACTICE AREAS:*** Insurance Contract and Coverage Litigation; Insurance Defense; Commercial Litigation; Mediation; Arbitration; Professional Negligence; Catastrophic Injury; Wrongful Death. ***Email:*** jtrimble@lewiswagner.com

KENNETH P. REESE, born El Dorado, Arkansas, February 27, 1948; admitted to bar, 1977, Indiana. *Education:* Indiana University-Purdue University at Indianapolis (A.B., with distinction, 1974); Indiana University (J.D., magna cum laude, 1977). Lecturer, Uninsured and Underinsured Motorist Law, 1999-2005. *Member:* Indianapolis, Indiana State and American Bar Associations; Defense Trial Counsel of Indiana; Defense Research Institute; Trucking Industry Defense Association (TIDA). ***PRACTICE AREAS:*** Trial Practice; Personal Injury; Construction Law; Trucking Law; Commercial Law; Insurance Law; Mediation. ***Email:*** kreese@lewiswagner.com

SHARON FUNCHEON MURPHY, born Lafayette, Indiana, January 8, 1954; admitted to bar, 1982, Indiana, U.S. Court of Appeals, Seventh Circuit and U.S. District Courts, Northern and Southern Districts of Indiana. *Education:* University of Dallas (B.A., cum laude, 1976); Indiana University (J.D., summa cum laude, 1982). Board of Barristers; Moot Court Society. Associate Editor, Indiana Law Review, 1981-1982. First Place, ABA National Appellate Advocacy Competition, 1982. *Member:* Indianapolis and American (Council Member, 1991-1994, Secretary, 1989-1991, Chair, Appellate Advocacy Committee, 1986-1987, Chair, Emerging Issues Committee, 1994-1995, Chair, Handbook and By-Laws Committee, 2002-2003, Chair Worker's Compensation and Employers Liability Committee, 2003-2004, Tort and Insurance Practice Section) Bar Associations; Defense Trial Counsel of Indiana (Chair, 2001-2002, Worker's Compensation Section). ***PRACTICE AREAS:*** Workers Compensation; Insurance Coverage; Insurance Defense. ***Email:*** smurphy@lewiswagner.com

JARRELL B. HAMMOND, born Indianapolis, Indiana, September 25, 1955; admitted to bar, 1982, Indiana and U.S. District Court, Southern District of Indiana. *Education:* DePauw University (B.A., 1978); Indiana University School of Law (J.D., 1982). Author of several articles and seminars on estate planning and probate litigation. *Member:* Indianapolis (Estate Planning and Administration Section), Indiana State (Probate and Property Section) and American (Real Property and Probate Section) Bar Associations; Indiana Trial Lawyers Association; Association of Trial Lawyers of America. Fellow, Indianapolis Bar Foundation. ***PRACTICE AREAS:*** Estate Planning; Probate; Trusts and Estates; Wills; Probate Litigation; Corporate Law; Business Law; Litigation; Guardianship; Real Estate. ***Email:*** jhammond@lewiswagner.com

THEODORE L. NICHOLAS, born 1958; admitted to bar, 1986, Indiana. *Education:* Indiana University (B.A., 1981; J.D., 1986). ***PRACTICE AREAS:*** Civil Litigation; Elder Law; Business Law. ***Email:*** tnicholas@lewiswagner.com

(This Listing Continued)

MARY FOLEY PANSZI, born Feuchtwangen, Germany, March 30, 1947; admitted to bar, 1988, Indiana and U.S. District Court, Southern District of Indiana. *Education:* University of Pittsburgh (B.A., political science, 1970); Indiana University (J.D., 1988). Phi Alpha Delta. Certified in Civil Mediation. Indiana Corporate Registered Agent, American Conciliatory Court System. Member, Alumnae Board of Directors, Indiana University at Indianapolis Law School. *Member:* Indianapolis (Chair, Criminal Law Section; Member, Family Law Section; Chair, Criminal Section, 1994), Indiana State (Member, Family Law Section) and American (Member, Family Law Section) Bar Associations. ***LANGUAGES:*** Spanish. ***PRACTICE AREAS:*** Family Law; High Asset Divorce; Child Custody; Personal Injury; Estate Planning.

SUSAN E. MEHRINGER, born Fort Wayne, Indiana, October 14, 1959; admitted to bar, 1989, Indiana and U.S. District Court, Northern and Southern Districts of Indiana. *Education:* Indiana University (B.A., 1981; J.D., 1989). *Member:* Indianapolis and Indiana State Bar Associations; Defense Trial Counsel of Indiana; Defense Research Institute. ***PRACTICE AREAS:*** Insurance Defense Litigation; Product Liability. ***Email:*** smehringer@lewiswagner.com

TAMMY J. MEYER, born Springdale, Arkansas, 1964; admitted to bar, 1989, Indiana; U.S. District Court, Northern and Southern Districts of Indiana. *Education:* Indiana Wesleyan University (B.S., summa cum laude, 1986); Indiana University (J.D., summa cum laude, 1989). Named: Super Lawyer, 2004 and 2005; One of Top 25 Women Lawyers in Indiana, 2004 and 2005. Faculty, National Institute for Trial Advocates. Board Member, Indiana University School of Law Alumni Association (Former President) and Indianapolis Bar Foundation. *Member:* Defense Research Institute; Defense Trial Counsel of Indiana; American Bar Association (Member, Trial Tactics Committee; Steering Committee and Newsletter Editor; National Forum for Environmental and Toxic Torts); Indianapolis and Indiana State (Member, House of Delegates) Bar Associations; International Association of Defense Counsel; Indianapolis Bar Foundation (Fellow and Board Member). ***PRACTICE AREAS:*** Litigation; Drug and Medical Device Defense; Environmental Insurance Coverage; Insurance Law. ***Email:*** tmeyer@lewiswagner.com

DAUN A. WELIEVER, born Indianapolis, Indiana, May 14, 1964; admitted to bar, 1990, Indiana and U.S. District Court, Southern and Northern Districts of Indiana. *Education:* Indiana University (B.S., 1986; J.D., 1990). *Member:* Indianapolis and Indiana State Bar Associations; Defense Trial Counsel of Indiana; Indiana Trial Lawyers Association; American Inn of Court (Associate, 1998-2000). ***PRACTICE AREAS:*** Litigation; Personal Injury; Products Liability; Premises Liability. ***Email:*** dweliever@lewiswagner.com

RICHARD K. SHOULTZ, born Indianapolis, Indiana, July 19, 1965; admitted to bar, 1990, Indiana and U.S. District Court, Northern and Southern Districts of Indiana; 1991, U.S. Court of Appeals, 7th Circuit. *Education:* Hanover College (B.A., 1987); Indiana University School of Law (J.D., 1990). Author, numerous survey articles and seminars on insurance law. *Member:* Indianapolis, Indiana State and American Bar Associations; Defense Research Institute (Young Lawyers Liaison to Appellate Advocacy Committee, 1998-1999); Defense Trial Counsel of Indiana. ***PRACTICE AREAS:*** Insurance Defense; Litigation; Products Liability; Insurance Coverage; Appellate Practice; Personal Injury; Commercial Law; Construction Law. ***Email:*** rshoultz@lewiswagner.com

DINA M. COX, born Anderson, Indiana, September 5, 1969; admitted to bar, 1995, Indiana; U.S. District Court, Northern and Southern Districts of Indiana; U.S. Court of Appeals, Seventh Circuit. *Education:* Ball State University (B.G.S., cum laude, 1991); Indiana University (J.D., cum laude, 1995). *Member:* Indianapolis, Marion County, Indiana State and American Bar Associations; The Defense Research Institute, Inc.; Defense Trial Counsel of Indiana. ***PRACTICE AREAS:*** Drug and Medical Device Litigation; Professional Liability; Products Liability; Insurance Defense Litigation; Business Litigation. ***Email:*** dcox@lewiswagner.com

ANTHONY M. ELEFTHERI, born Gary, Indiana, July 17, 1971; admitted to bar, 1996, Indiana. *Education:* Indiana University at Bloomington (B.A., in Economics, 1993); Indiana University at Indianapolis (J.D., 1996). *Member:* Indianapolis and Indiana State Bar Associations; Defense Research Institute; Defense Trial Counsel of Indiana. ***LANGUAGES:*** Greek. ***PRACTICE AREAS:*** Defense Litigation; Food Products Liability; Trucking Litigation; Appellate Practice. ***Email:*** eleftheri@lewiswagner.com

A. RICHARD M. BLAIKLOCK, born Stafford, England, November 30, 1968; admitted to bar, 1997, Indiana. *Education:* Hanover College (B.S., 1990); Indiana University Indianapolis (J.D., summa cum laude, 1997). Executive Editor, Indiana Law Review. Dean's Tutorial Society. ***PRACTICE AREAS:*** Torts; Business Law; Business Litigation; Appellate Law; Products Liability; Commercial Litigation; Corporate Litigation; Uniform Commercial Code. ***Email:*** rblaiklock@lewiswagner.com

ROBERT R. FOOS, born Clinton, Indiana, July 31, 1970; admitted to bar, 1997, Illinois; 1998, Indiana. *Education:* Indiana University at Bloomington (B.A., 1994); John Marshall Law School (J.D., 1997). *Member:* Indianapolis and Indiana State Bar Associations; Defense Trial Counsel of Indiana; Defense Research Institute. ***PRACTICE AREAS:*** Litigation; Construction Law; Trucking Law; Insurance Coverage. ***Email:*** rfoos@lewiswagner.com

ASSOCIATES

JOHN C. KRAUSE, born Des Plaines, Illinois, July 26, 1968; admitted to bar, 1997, Indiana. *Education:* Indiana University (B.A., Psychology, 1990); Indiana University School of Law - Indianapolis (J.D., cum laude, 1997). ***PRACTICE AREAS:*** Business Law; Commercial Litigation; Gaming Law. ***Email:*** jkrause@lewiswagner.com

KYLE A. LANSBERRY, born Indianapolis, Indiana, August 28, 1972; admitted to bar, 1998, Indiana and U.S. District Court, Southern District of Indiana; 1999, U.S. District Court, Northern District of Indiana. *Education:* Ball State University (B.S., cum laude, 1995); Indiana University (J.D., 1998). Author: "Recent Developments in Indiana Tort Law," Indiana Law Review, 1999 and 2000; "Challenging the Admission of Medical Bills and Medical Records," Indiana Lawyer, 1999; Deposition Preparation and Defense for the Young Lawyer," For the Defense, 2000; "Preparing for Witness Deposition and Defense," Michigan Lawyers Weekly, 2000; "Challenging the Objection to Trial Rule 26," Indiana Lawyer, 2000; "Beyond Billable Hours," For the Defense, 2001. *Member:* Indianapolis (Vice President), Indiana State and American Bar Associations; Defense Trial Counsel of

(This Listing Continued)

Indiana; Defense Research Institute. ***PRACTICE AREAS:*** Insurance Defense Litigation; Drug and Medical Device Defense; Products Liability; Environmental Insurance Coverage. ***Email:*** klansberry@lewiswagner.com

STEFANIE R. CRAWFORD, born Indianapolis, Indiana, 1971; admitted to bar, 1999, Indiana and U.S. District Court, Northern and Southern District of Indiana. *Education:* Butler University (B.S., 1993); Indiana University (J.D., 1999). *Member:* Indianapolis, Marion County, Indiana State and American Bar Associations; Defense Trial Counsel of Indiana; Defense Research Institute. ***PRACTICE AREAS:*** Insurance Defense; Civil Litigation. ***Email:*** scrawford@lewiswagner.com

STEPHANIE L. CASSMAN, born Terre Haute, Indiana, September 6, 1974; admitted to bar, 2000, Indiana and U.S. District Court, Northern and Southern Districts of Indiana. *Education:* Indiana University (B.A., 1997); Indiana University School of Law (J.D., 2000). *Member:* Indianapolis and Indiana State Bar Associations; Defense Trial Counsel of Indiana; Defense Research Institute. ***PRACTICE AREAS:*** Commercial Litigation; Insurance Defense Litigation; Premises Liability; Employment Law. ***Email:*** scassman@lewiswagner.com

SONIA C. DAS, born Oak Park, Illinois, September 17, 1975; admitted to bar, 2000, Indiana and U.S. District Court, Northern and Southern Districts of Indiana. *Education:* Indiana University (B.A., 1996; J.D., 2000). Recipient, Indiana University Scribe Award for Excellence in Legal Writing, 1998. Board Member and Quarterfinalist, Sherman Minton Moot Court Competition, 1998-2000. Managing Editor, 1999-2000, Federal Communications Law Journal. *Member:* Indianapolis and Indiana State Bar Associations; Defense Trial Counsel of Indiana; Defense Research Institute. ***PRACTICE AREAS:*** Litigation; Workers Compensation; Insurance Defense Litigation. ***Email:*** sdas@lewiswagner.com

VALERIE L. HUGHS, born Philadelphia, Pennsylvania, December 10, 1973; admitted to bar, 2000, Indiana; U.S. District Court, Northern and Southern Districts of Indiana. *Education:* West Virginia University (B.S., Exercise Physiology, 1996); Indiana University School of Law - Indianapolis (J.D., 2000). Associate Editor, Indiana International and Comparative Law Review, 1999-2000. ***PRACTICE AREAS:*** Insurance Defense; Products Liability; Construction Law; Premises Liability; Automobile Accidents and Injuries. ***Email:*** vhughs@lewiswagner.com

CHRISTI R. ANDERSON, born Indianapolis, Indiana, August 25, 1960; admitted to bar, 2003, Indiana. *Education:* Indiana University (B.S., 1991; J.D., 2003). *Member:* Indianapolis, Indiana State and American Bar Associations. ***PRACTICE AREAS:*** Business Litigation; Business Transactions; Probate Litigation; Estate Planning; Estate Administration. ***Email:*** canderson@lewiswagner.com

RYAN K. GARDNER, born Gary, Indiana, August 6, 1978; admitted to bar, 2004, Indiana and U.S. District Court, Southern and Northern Districts of Indiana. *Education:* Indiana University, Bloomington (B.A., 2000); Indiana University School of Law - Indianapolis (J.D., 2004). Phi Alpha Delta. Dean's List. Member, American Inns of Court, 2003-2004. ***PRACTICE AREAS:*** Insurance Defense; Workers Compensation; Employment Law. ***Email:*** rgardner@lewiswagner.com

SHANNON L. LOGSDON, born Augsburg, Germany, November 26, 1971; admitted to bar, 2005, Indiana. *Education:* University of Maryland, College Park (B.A., summa cum laude, 1998); Franklin College (B.A., 1998); Indiana University School of Law - Indianapolis (J.D., cum laude, 2004). Order of Barristers. Executive Notes Editor, Indiana Health Law Review. Associate Justice, Moot Court Board, 2003-2004. Indiana State Teaching License, 1998—. *Member:* Indianapolis and Indiana State Bar Associations; Defense Trial Counsel of Indiana; Defense Research Institute. ***PRACTICE AREAS:*** Civil Litigation; Business Law. ***Email:*** slogsdon@lewiswagner.com

OF COUNSEL

LISA M. DILLMAN, born Indianapolis, Indiana, September 9, 1969; admitted to bar, 1995, Indiana and U.S. District Court, Northern and Southern Districts of Indiana. *Education:* University of Illinois (B.A., cum laude, 1992); Indiana University School of Law (J.D., 1995). Order of the Barristers. Executive Articles Editor, Indiana Law Review. Recipient, American Jurisprudence Award in Torts and Secured Transactions. ***PRACTICE AREAS:*** Asbestos Defense Litigation; Commercial Litigation; Family Law.

FELSON BOWMAN, born Laurel County, Kentucky, April 13, 1939; admitted to bar, 1968, Indiana; 1973, U.S. Supreme Court. *Education:* Northwestern University and Butler University (B.S., 1964); Indiana University (J.D., 1968). Phi Delta Phi. *Member:* Indianapolis, Indiana State and American (Member, Subcommittee on Litigation, Section on Corporation, Banking and Business Law, 1969-1980) Bar Associations.

REPRESENTATIVE CLIENTS: ACE USA/ESIS, Inc.; AIG Technical Services, Inc.; AIMCO, Inc.; Acuity Insurance Company; Affirmative Insurance Company; Allied Insurance Group; Asplundh Tree Expert Company; Baldwin & Lyons, Inc.; Bash & Associates; Beazer Homes USA, Inc.; Bituminous Insurance Company; Bob Kinder & Sons, Inc; Brotherhood Mutual Insuarnce Company; Campbell Ventilation, Inc; Citizens Insurance Company/Allmerica Financial; D.G. Perry Building Contractors, Inc.; Eagle Martin Claims Administration Services; Electrolux, Inc.; Erie Insurance Group; Fireman's Fund Insurance Company; Go America Insurance Company; Grange Insurance; Gulf Insurance; Hardee's Food Systems, Inc.; Hillenbrand Industries; Indiana Insurance Company; Kemper Insurance Company; Key Life Insurance Company; Liberty Mutual Insurance Group; M-J Insurance Group; Marsh Supermarkets; Medmarc, A Division of Hamilton Resources; Mendota Insurance Company; Mid-America Elevator Company; National City Bank; National Bond and Trust Company, Inc.; Natkin Contracting Company; Navigators California Insurance Services, Inc.; Northside Surgical Specialists, P.C.; Ohio Casualty Group; Omni Insurance Group; Pacers Sports & Entertainment; Red Top Rentals, Inc.; S-K General Contracting; St. Paul Insurance Company; Safeco/American States Insurance Companies; Scott Foods Store; Shelby/Vesta Insurance Group; Simon Property Group; Smith & Nephew Richards, Inc.; Sublette Brothers Construction; Supervalu Holdings; The Outdoorsman Sport Shop; Theta Chi Fraternity; Titan/Victoria Insurance Company; Travelers Property Casualty Company; Utica Insurance Company; Wausau Insurance Company; Wells-Marvel, P.C.; Zurich-American Insurance Group.

LINDER & HOLLOWELL, P.C.

728 SOUTH MERIDIAN STREET
P.O. BOX 845
INDIANAPOLIS, INDIANA 46206-0845
Telephone: 317-637-3170
Fax: Available Upon Request
Mailing Address: P.O. Box 845, Indianapolis, IN 46206-0845

(This Listing Continued)

Insurance Defense, General Practice.

ROBERT HOLLOWELL (1899-1980)

CHARLES W. LINDER, JR., born Indianapolis, Indiana, April 10, 1937; admitted to bar, 1962, Indiana. *Education:* Columbia University (A.B., 1958); Indiana University (J.D., 1962); Northwestern University. Delta Theta Phi. Teaching Fellow, Northwestern University, 1962-1963. Assistant Professor: University of Tulsa, 1963-1964; Loyola University, 1964-1965. Member, Board of Editors, Defense Counsel Journal, 1989-1998. *Member:* Indiana State and American Bar Associations; International Association of Defense Counsel.

SHARON L. WRIGHT, born Anderson, Indiana, October 24, 1942; admitted to bar, 1975, California; 1982, Indiana. *Education:* Purdue University (B.S., 1964); San Francisco State University (1969); Hastings College of Law, University of California (J.D., 1975). Member, Hastings Law Journal, 1973-1974. Instructor, Business Law, Ivy Tech State College, 1987-1990, 1995—.

REPRESENTATIVE CLIENTS: ACE-USA; Capitol Indemnity Company; INA Ins. Co.; Ohio Casualty Insurance Group; Ohio Westfield Cos.; Old Republic Insurance Co.; St. Paul Insurance Cos.; WESTCO Insurance.

LOCKE REYNOLDS LLP

Established in 1917

201 NORTH ILLINOIS, SUITE 1000
P.O. BOX 44961
INDIANAPOLIS, INDIANA 46244-0961
Telephone: 317-237-3800
Fax: 317-237-3900
URL: http://www.locke.com

Business Services, Construction and Real Estate Services, Financial Institutions, Government and Regulatory Services, Healthcare, Individual Services, Litigation, Products and Manufacturing, Tort Litigation and Insurance Services.

FIRM PROFILE: Locke Reynolds was founded in 1917 when two firms merged to create a litigation practice, which over the years, has become highly regarded. While litigation has remained an important part of the practice, we have expanded our services in anticipation of and in response to the needs of our clients. We are one of Indiana's largest law firms, providing legal counsel to clients throughout Indiana and around the country in virtually all areas of law.

LAW FIRM ALLIANCES/ASSOCIATIONS: **HARMONIE GROUP:** *State Law Resources, Inc.*

PARTNERS

NELSON D. ALEXANDER, born Terre Haute, Indiana, March 20, 1968; admitted to bar, 1993, Indiana. *Education:* Wabash College (B.A., 1990); University of Chicago (J.D., 1993). *Member:* Indianapolis and American Bar Associations. ***PRACTICE AREAS:*** Business Litigation; Products Liability; Appellate Practice. ***Email:*** nalexander@locke.com

THOMAS F. BEDSOLE, born Sacramento, California, September 10, 1964; admitted to bar, 1991, Indiana. *Education:* Indiana University (B.S., 1986); The Ohio State University (J.D., with honors, 1991). Certified Public Accountant, Virginia, 1988. *Member:* Indianapolis, Indiana State and American Bar Associations. ***PRACTICE AREAS:*** Commercial Litigation; Construction Law. ***Email:*** tbedsole@locke.com

REX E. BENNETT, born Indianapolis, Indiana, May 7, 1953; admitted to bar, 1981, Indiana; 1989, Illinois. *Education:* Greenville College (B.A., 1975); Southern Methodist University (J.D., 1981). *Member:* Indianapolis, Indiana State and American Bar Associations. ***PRACTICE AREAS:*** Banking; Creditors Rights; Real Estate. ***Email:*** rbennett@locke.com

MICHAEL A. BERGIN, born Detroit, Michigan, July 14, 1944; admitted to bar, 1969, Indiana. *Education:* University of Michigan (B.A., 1966; J.D., 1969). *Member:* Indianapolis, Indiana State and American Bar Associations; American Academy of Hospital Attorneys; Defense Research Institute. ***PRACTICE AREAS:*** Commercial; Products Liability; Toxic Torts. ***Email:*** mbergin@locke.com

MICHAEL T. BINDNER, born Indianapolis, Indiana, April 8, 1952; admitted to bar, 1979, Indiana and U.S. Tax Court. *Education:* University of Notre Dame (B.B.A., 1974); Indiana University (J.D., cum laude, 1979). Certified Public Accountant, Indiana, 1977. *Member:* Indianapolis and Indiana State Bar Associations; American Institute of Certified Public Accountants; Indiana CPA Society. ***PRACTICE AREAS:*** Business Planning; Employee Benefits; Health Care Taxation; Professional Corporations; State Taxation. ***Email:*** mbindner@locke.com

DEAN R. BRACKENRIDGE, born Kalamazoo, Michigan, May 20, 1968; admitted to bar, 1995, Indiana. *Education:* University of Notre Dame (B.A., 1990); The Ohio State University (J.D., 1995). *Member:* Indianapolis, Indiana State and American Bar Associations. ***PRACTICE AREAS:*** Construction Law; Business Litigation. ***Email:*** dbrackenridge@locke.com

TERRENCE L. BROOKIE, born Indianapolis, Indiana, October 31, 1955; admitted to bar, 1981, Indiana. *Education:* Denison University (B.A., 1978); Indiana University (J.D., 1981). *Member:* Indianapolis, Indiana State and American Bar Associations. ***PRACTICE AREAS:*** Commercial Litigation; Construction Law; Contracts; Fidelity and Surety; Insurance Defense. ***Email:*** tbrookie@locke.com

ALAN S. BROWN, born East Brunswick, New Jersey, December 18, 1952; admitted to bar, 1978, Indiana. *Education:* Indiana University (A.B., 1974; J.D., cum laude, 1978). *Member:* Indianapolis Bar Association. ***PRACTICE AREAS:*** Breach of Contract; Commercial; Contract; Complex Litigation and Litigation. ***Email:*** abrown@locke.com

THOMAS J. CAMPBELL, born Madison, Wisconsin, September 7, 1948; admitted to bar, 1975, Indiana. *Education:* Wittenberg University (B.A., 1970); Indiana University

(This Listing Continued)

LOCKE REYNOLDS LLP, Indianapolis—Continued

(J.D., cum laude, 1975). Chief Litigation Counsel, City of Indianapolis, 1984-1988. *Member:* Indianapolis, Indiana State and American Bar Associations. ***PRACTICE AREAS:*** Litigation; Products Liability; Professional Liability. ***Email:*** tcampbell@locke.com

SUSAN E. CLINE, born Greensburg, Indiana, July 7, 1961; admitted to bar, 1990, Indiana. *Education:* University of Indianapolis (B.S., magna cum laude, 1983); Indiana University (J.D., 1990). *Member:* Indianapolis, Johnson County, Indiana State and American Bar Associations. ***PRACTICE AREAS:*** Medical Malpractice; Healthcare. ***Email:*** scline@locke.com

HOWARD R. COHEN, born Indianapolis, Indiana, January 16, 1953; admitted to bar, 1978, Indiana. *Education:* Indiana University (A.B., 1974; J.D., cum laude, 1978). *Member:* Indianapolis, Indiana State and American Bar Associations. ***PRACTICE AREAS:*** Banking; Business; Commercial. ***Email:*** hcohen@locke.com

JOHN H. DAERR, born Lafayette, Indiana, June 21, 1964; admitted to bar, 1989, Indiana. *Education:* DePauw University (B.A., 1986); Valparaiso University (J.D., 1989). Graduate of Leadership Bloomington-Monroe County, 2004. Member, Firm's Management Committee. *Member:* Indianapolis, Monroe County, Indiana State and American Bar Associations; Lawyer-Pilots Bar Association; Defense Research Institute (DRI); Defense Trial Counsel of Indiana (DTCI), (Chair, Tort Litigation Group). ***PRACTICE AREAS:*** Torts; Insurance Litigation; Aviation Law; Business Litigation; Employment Law; Professional Malpractice Defense. ***Email:*** jdaerr@locke.com

THOMAS L. DAVIS, born Cleveland, Ohio, September 18, 1950; admitted to bar, 1975, Indiana. *Education:* Indiana University (A.B., 1972; J.D., magna cum laude, 1975). *Member:* Indianapolis (President, 1994), Indiana State and American (Past-Chair, Economics of Torts and Insurance Law Practice Committee, Tort and Insurance Practice Section) Bar Associations; Defense Research Institute. ***PRACTICE AREAS:*** Civil Litigation; Commercial Litigation. ***Email:*** tdavis@locke.com

THOMAS E. DEER, born Indianapolis, Indiana, May 23, 1969; admitted to bar, 1994, Indiana; 1997, U.S. Court of Appeals, Seventh Circuit; 1999, Illinois. *Education:* Yale University (B.A., cum laude, 1991); Indiana University (J.D., cum laude, 1994). ***PRACTICE AREAS:*** Labor and Employment. ***Email:*** tdeer@locke.com

JEFFREY S. DIBLE, born Pittsburgh, Pennsylvania, January 7, 1955; admitted to bar, 1979, Indiana; 1986, New York and U.S. Tax Court; 1988, U.S. District Court, Eastern and Southern Districts of New York. *Education:* Purdue University (B.S., with highest distinction, 1976); Indiana University (J.D., magna cum laude, 1979). Order of the Coif. *Member:* Indiana State Bar Association. ***PRACTICE AREAS:*** Estate Planning; Contested Trusts and Estates; Tax Law; Tax Controversies; Tax Exempt Organizations. ***Email:*** jdible@locke.com

JAMES DIMOS, born Evanston, Illinois, May 23, 1961; admitted to bar, 1986, Indiana. *Education:* Wabash College (A.B., 1983); Washington University (J.D., 1986). *Member:* Indianapolis, Indiana State and American Bar Associations. ***PRACTICE AREAS:*** Intellectual Property Litigation; Piracy; Unfair Competition; Trade Secrets; Complex Litigation; Business Litigation; Professional Liability. ***Email:*** jdimos@locke.com

THOMAS W. FARLOW, born Indianapolis, Indiana, July 30, 1954; admitted to bar, 1979, Indiana. *Education:* Indiana University (B.A., 1976; J.D., 1979). *Member:* Indianapolis, Indiana State and American Bar Associations. ***PRACTICE AREAS:*** Commercial Litigation; Criminal Defense; Federal Litigation; White Collar Fraud. ***Email:*** tfarlow@locke.com

MARY MARGARET RUTH FELDHAKE, born Indianapolis, Indiana, April 29, 1958; admitted to bar, 1989, Indiana and U.S. District Court, Northern and Southern Districts of Indiana. *Education:* Indiana University (A.S., 1980; B.S., 1984; J.D., cum laude, 1989). Member: American Registry of Radiologic Technologists, 1980; Indiana State Board of Health Radiologic Technologists, 1980. *Member:* Indianapolis, Indiana State and American Bar Associations. ***PRACTICE AREAS:*** Health Care Litigation; Medical Malpractice Defense. ***Email:*** mfeldhake@locke.com

JULIA BLACKWELL GELINAS, born Fort Wayne, Indiana, February 17, 1953; admitted to bar, 1978, Indiana. *Education:* St. Mary's College (B.A., cum laude, 1975); Indiana University (J.D., cum laude, 1978). Member, Editorial Board, Indiana Law Review, 1977. Law Clerk, Hon. Dixon W. Prentice, Justice, Indiana Supreme Court, 1977-1979. *Member:* Indianapolis, Indiana State and American Bar Associations. ***PRACTICE AREAS:*** Appellate Practice; Commercial Litigation; Construction Law; Fidelity and Surety; Insurance Rehabilitation and Liquidation. ***Email:*** jgelinas@locke.com

DAVID M. HASKETT, born Elwood, Indiana, February 23, 1944; admitted to bar, 1969, Indiana. *Education:* Indiana University (A.B., 1966; J.D., 1969). *Member:* Indianapolis, Indiana State and American Bar Associations. ***PRACTICE AREAS:*** Environmental Law; Litigation. ***Email:*** dhaskett@locke.com

DAVID T. KASPER, born Bristol, Connecticut, November 12, 1944; admitted to bar, 1969, Indiana. *Education:* Union College (A.B., 1966); Indiana University (J.D., 1969). Law Clerk, Hon. James E. Noland, U.S. District Court, Southern District of Indiana, 1969-1971. *Member:* Indianapolis, Indiana State and American Bar Associations. ***PRACTICE AREAS:*** Insurance; Litigation. ***Email:*** dkasper@locke.com

KARL M. KOONS, III, born Chicago, Illinois, February 13, 1960; admitted to bar, 1985, Indiana. *Education:* Northwestern University (B.A., 1982); Indiana University (J.D., 1985). *Member:* Indianapolis, Indiana State and American Bar Associations. ***PRACTICE AREAS:*** Asbestos Toxic Torts; Hospital Liability Defense; Hospital Risk Management; Litigation; Medical Malpractice Defense. ***Email:*** kkoons@locke.com

JAMES D. MASUR II, born Indiana, Pennsylvania, January 11, 1959; admitted to bar, 1984, Michigan; 1985, Ohio; 1996, Indiana. *Education:* Miami University (A.B., 1981); University of Virginia (J.D., magna cum laude, 1984). *Member:* Indianapolis and Ohio State Bar Associations; State Bar of Michigan. ***PRACTICE AREAS:*** Labor and Employment; Healthcare. ***Email:*** jmasur@locke.com

JOHN K. McDAVID, born Hattiesburg, Mississippi, May 5, 1963; admitted to bar, 1989, Indiana. *Education:* University of Notre Dame (B.A., 1985); Indiana University (J.D., cum laude, 1989). *Member:* Indianapolis, Indiana State and American Bar Associations. ***PRACTICE AREAS:*** Bankruptcy; Commercial Litigation; Asbestos Toxic Torts; Fidelity and Surety. ***Email:*** jmcdavid@locke.com

MICHAEL D. MORIARTY, born Indianapolis, Indiana, November 14, 1950; admitted to bar, 1978, Indiana. *Education:* Indiana University (B.S., 1972; J.D., 1978). *Member:* American Bar Association. ***PRACTICE AREAS:*** Business Law; Corporate Law; Leases and Leasing; Real Estate. ***Email:*** mmoriarty@locke.com

JEFFREY J. MORTIER, born Ottawa, Illinois, May 15, 1965; admitted to bar, 1991, Indiana. *Education:* Northwestern University (B.A., 1987); Valparaiso University (J.D., 1991). *Member:* Indianapolis, Indiana State and American Bar Associations. ***PRACTICE AREAS:*** Products Liability; Defense Litigation; Fire Loss. ***Email:*** jmortier@locke.com

KEVIN CHARLES MURRAY, born Indianapolis, Indiana, July 26, 1953; admitted to bar, 1979, Indiana. *Education:* Indiana State University (B.S., magna cum laude, 1975); Indiana University (J.D., cum laude, 1979). Minority Attorney's Office, Indiana Senate, 1975-1976; Majority Attorney's Office, Indiana Senate, 1977-1978; Assistant Minority Attorney, Indiana Senate, 1979-1980; Minority Attorney, Indiana House of Representatives, 1981-1986. Counsel, Democratic Caucus, State Senate, Indiana General Assembly, 1997-1999. *Member:* Indianapolis and Indiana State Bar Associations; American Academy of Hospital Attorneys. ***PRACTICE AREAS:*** Medical Malpractice Defense; Physicians Professional Liability; Physicians Risk Management. ***Email:*** kmurray@locke.com

NICHOLAS C. PAPPAS, born Gary, Indiana, May 21, 1966; admitted to bar, 1991, Indiana. *Education:* University of Notre Dame (B.A., 1988); Indiana University (J. D., cum laude, 1991). *Member:* Indianapolis Bar Association. ***LANGUAGES:*** Greek. ***PRACTICE AREAS:*** Aviation Products Liability; Automotive Products Liability; Heavy Equipment Products Liability; Products Liability Defense; Professional Malpractice. ***Email:*** npappas@locke.com

ERIC A. RIEGNER, born Indianapolis, Indiana, September 13, 1963; admitted to bar, 1988, Indiana. *Education:* Indiana University (B.A., 1985; J.D., 1988). *Member:* Indianapolis and American Bar Associations. ***PRACTICE AREAS:*** Civil Litigation; Products Liability; Automotive Restraints; Premises Liability Law. ***Email:*** eriegner@locke.com

RANDALL R. RIGGS, born Evansville, Indiana, November 3, 1952; admitted to bar, 1977, Indiana. *Education:* Indiana University (A.B., cum laude, 1974; J.D., cum laude, 1977). *Member:* Indianapolis, Indiana State and American Bar Associations; International Association of Defense Counsel (Member, Committees on: Products Liability; Advocacy Practice and Procedures (Chair); Defense Research Institute (Vice-Chair, Products Liability Committee; Member, Law Institute; Indiana Representative, 1993-1997); Forum for the Construction Industry; Defense Trial Counsel of Indiana. Fellow, American College of Trial Lawyers. ***PRACTICE AREAS:*** Products Liability. ***Email:*** rriggs@locke.com

MARK J. ROBERTS, born Indianapolis, Indiana, February 19, 1952; admitted to bar, 1977, Indiana and Ohio. *Education:* Indiana University (A.B., 1974; J.D., cum laude, 1977). *Member:* Indianapolis, Indiana State and American Bar Associations. ***PRACTICE AREAS:*** Domestic Relations; Dram Shop; Insurance Coverage; Legal Malpractice. ***Email:*** mroberts@locke.com

KEVIN C. SCHIFERL, born Chicago, Illinois, August 7, 1963; admitted to bar, 1988, Indiana. *Education:* Purdue University (B.A., 1985); Indiana University (J.D., 1988). *Member:* Indianapolis, Indiana State and American Bar Associations; Defense Research Institute; Defense Trial Counsel of Indiana. ***PRACTICE AREAS:*** Products Liability Defense; Negligence Defense; Tort Defense; Commercial Litigation. ***Email:*** kschiferl@locke.com

STEVEN J. STRAWBRIDGE, born Indianapolis, Indiana, March 27, 1948; admitted to bar, 1973, Indiana. *Education:* Indiana University (B.S., 1970; J.D., 1973). *Member:* Indianapolis, Indiana State and American Bar Associations; International Association of Defense Counsel; Defense Research Institute. ***PRACTICE AREAS:*** Construction Law; Federal Civil Practice; Fidelity and Surety; Products Liability. ***Email:*** sstrawbridge@locke.com

JOEL E. TRAGESSER, born Kokomo, Indiana, June 13, 1973; admitted to bar, 1997, Tennessee; 1999, Indiana; registered to practice before U.S. Patent and Trademark Office. *Education:* Wabash College (A.B., magna cum laude, 1994); Vanderbilt University (J.D., 1997). Member, TechPoint. *Member:* Indiana State and American Bar Associations; International Trademark Association; American Intellectual Property Law Association; Tennessee Intellectual Property Law Association. ***PRACTICE AREAS:*** Business Litigation; Intellectual Property. ***Email:*** jtragesser@locke.com

THOMAS E. WHEELER II, born Minneapolis, Minnesota, September 12, 1962; admitted to bar, 1987, Indiana, Kentucky, U.S. District Court, Northern and Southern Districts of Indiana, U.S. District Court, Eastern District of Kentucky, U.S. Court of Appeals, Seventh and Ninth Circuits and U.S. Supreme Court. *Education:* Indiana University (B.S., 1984; J.D., 1987). *Member:* Federal Bar Association (Secretary, Indianapolis Chapter); National School Board Association Council of School Attorneys; Defense Trial Counsel of Indiana (Board Member); Defense Research Institute. ***PRACTICE AREAS:*** Labor and Employment Law; Education Law. ***Email:*** twheeler@locke.com

ASSOCIATES

Sylvia A. Bier
Daniel D. Bobilya
Jeffrey M. Boldt
John M.T. Chavis, II
Darren A. Craig
Todd A. Croftchik
Lucy R. Dollens
Wade D. Fulford
J. Matt Harnish
Jared A. Harts
Deborah K. Hepler
Daniel P. King
Matthew R. King
Daniel M. Long
Andrew A. Manna
Melanie D. Margolin
Leslie B. Morse
Angie L. Ordway
April R. Schilling
Ian L. Stewart
Robert B. Thornburg
Jennifer L. VanLandingham
Matthew P. Voors
Dirk E. Wallsmith
Karen M. R. Weber
Amy S. Wilson
Heather L. Wilson

(This Listing Continued)

SENIOR COUNSEL

RODNEY E. CORSON, born Fort Wayne, Indiana, November 3, 1947; admitted to bar, 1980, Indiana. *Education:* Purdue University (B.S., 1969); Indiana University (M.D., 1972; J.D., 1980). Member, Joint Indianapolis Bar Association-Indianapolis Medical Society Medical-Legal Committee, 1986—. *Member:* Indianapolis, Indiana State and American Bar Associations; American Medical Association; Indianapolis and Indiana State Medical Societies. Fellow, American College of Emergency Physicians.

JULIA F. CROWE, born Indianapolis, Indiana, March 27, 1959; admitted to bar, 1984, Colorado; 1986, Indiana. *Education:* Indiana University (A.B., 1981); University of Denver (J.D., 1984). **Email:** jcrowe@locke.com

MELISSA J. DE GROFF, born Fergus Falls, Minnesota, May 12, 1965; admitted to bar, 1992, Wisconsin; 1994, Washington; 2001, Indiana. *Education:* University of Wisconsin (B.A., summa cum laude, 1988); University of Wisconsin School of Law (J.D., 1992). *Member:* Indianapolis, Indiana State, Washington State and American Bar Associations. ***PRACTICE AREAS:*** Bankruptcy; Commercial Law; Business Reorganization. **Email:** mdegroff@locke.com

CARRIE G. DOEHRMANN, born Jeannette, Pennsylvania, June 18, 1965; admitted to bar, 1992, Indiana. *Education:* DePauw University (B.A., 1988); Indiana University School of Law - Indianapolis (J.D., 1992). **Email:** cdoehrmann@locke.com

STEVEN R. EICHHOLTZ, born Norfolk, Virginia, February 6, 1955; admitted to bar, 1980, Indiana. *Education:* Purdue University (B.S., 1977); Indiana University (J.D., cum laude, 1980). Phi Delta Phi (President, 1979-1980). Commissioner, Superior Court of Marion County, 1982-1984. Judge: Marion Municipal Court, 1991-1996; Marion Superior Court, 1997-2000 (Presiding Judge, Marion Unified Courts, 1995-1997; Associate Presiding Judge, Marion Superior Courts, 1997-2000). **Email:** seichholtz@locke.com

RAYMOND GOOD, born Buffalo, New York, April 11, 1929; admitted to bar, 1961, Indiana. *Education:* State University of New York at Buffalo (B.S.M.E., 1951); Indiana University (J.D., 1960). *Member:* Indianapolis (President, 1980), Indiana State and American Bar Associations. ***PRACTICE AREAS:*** Real Estate Development; Zoning; Business Law. **Email:** rgood@locke.com

ROBERT L. HARTLEY, born Indianapolis, Indiana, March 1, 1948; admitted to bar, 1975, Indiana. *Education:* Indiana University (B.A., with honors in Political Science, 1970; J.D., magna cum laude, 1975). Named Insurance Defense Lawyer of the Year, Defense Trial Counsel of Indiana, 1990. Note and Development Editor, Indiana Law Review, 1974-1975. Author, "Speedy Trial," Vol. 8 Indiana Law Review 3, 1975. Lecturer, Indiana University at Indianapolis Law School, 1981-1990. *Member:* Indianapolis (Vice President, 1991) and Indiana State Bar Associations; Defense Research Institute; Defense Trial Counsel of Indiana (President, 1992-1993; Diplomat). [1st Lt., USAR, 1970-1972]. ***PRACTICE AREAS:*** Litigation; Appellate Practice; Administrative Law; Utility Law. **Email:** rhartley@locke.com

WILLIAM V. HUTCHENS, born Shelbyville, Indiana, February 1, 1933; admitted to bar, 1963, Indiana. *Education:* Indiana University (B.S., 1955; LL.B., 1963). *Member:* Indianapolis and Indiana State Bar Associations; Lawyer Pilots Bar Association. [Lt. Col., USAF-Res., Retired]. **Email:** whutchens@locke.com

LLOYD H. MILLIKEN, JR., born South Bend, Indiana, July 17, 1935; admitted to bar, 1960, Indiana. *Education:* Indiana University (B.S., 1957; J.D., 1960). Recipient, Indiana Defense Lawyer of the Year, 1993. Member, Board of Directors, Lawyers for Civil Justice, 1998—. *Member:* Indianapolis, Indiana State and American Bar Associations; International Association of Defense Counsel (Chairman, Casualty Insurance Committee, 1988-1990); Defense Trial Counsel of Indiana (President, 1994); Defense Research Institute (Regional Vice-President, 1990-1993; Member, Board of Directors, 1993—; Second Vice-President, 1996; First Vice-President, 1997; President-Elect, 1998; President, 1999). Fellow, American College of Trial Lawyers. ***PRACTICE AREAS:*** Litigation; Personal Injury; Products Liability; Insurance Coverage. **Email:** lmilliken@locke.com

ANTHONY W. OVERHOLT, born Lagrange, Indiana, July 13, 1965; admitted to bar, 1992, Indiana. *Education:* Indiana University (B.A., 1987; J.D., 1991). Law Clerk, Indiana Supreme Court Disciplinary Commission, 1991-1992. Author, "Retaining the Retaining Lien," *Res Gestae*, Volume 36, Number 3, September 1992. *Member:* Indianapolis, Indiana State, and American Bar Associations. **Email:** aoverholt@locke.com

HUGH E. REYNOLDS, JR., born Indianapolis, Indiana, September 17, 1929; admitted to bar, 1953, Indiana. *Education:* University of Notre Dame (B.S., 1950); University of Michigan (J.D., 1953). Member, 1982-1990 and Chairman, 1987-1988, Governing Committee, Forum for the Construction Industry. *Member:* Indianapolis, Indiana State and American (Chairman, Fidelity and Surety Committee, Torts and Insurance Practice Section, 1987-1988; Chairman, Torts and Insurance Practice Section, 1994-1995; 1994-1995 TIPS Representative to the House of Delegates, 1996—; Member of Council, 1988—) Bar Associations; International Association of Defense Counsel; Federation of Insurance and Corporate Counsel (President, 1985-1986); Defense Research Institute (Member, Board of Directors, 1985-1989). Fellow: American College of Trial Lawyers; American College of Construction Lawyers. [Lt. Col., Army J.A.G.C., Retired]. Certified as a Civil Trial Advocate by the National Board of Trial Advocacy. **Email:** hreynolds@locke.com

THOMAS E. SATROM, born Minneapolis, Minnesota, August 1, 1953; admitted to bar, 1983, Indiana. *Education:* Williams College (A.B., cum laude, 1975); Indiana University (J.D., magna cum laude, 1983). *Member:* Indiana State Bar Association. **Email:** tsatrom@locke.com

B. KEITH SHAKE, born Terre Haute, Indiana, April 6, 1958; admitted to bar, 1983, Indiana; 2000, U.S. Tax Court. *Education:* Indiana University (A.B., 1980; J.D., magna cum laude, 1983). *Member:* Indianapolis, Indiana State and American Bar Associations; The Association of Trial Lawyers of America; National Association of Securities Dealers, Inc. Fellow, Indiana Bar Foundation. **Email:** kshake@locke.com

MAGGIE L. SMITH, born 1968; admitted to bar, 1996, Indiana. *Education:* University of Arizona (B.A., cum laude, 1991; J.D., magna cum laude, 1996). *Member:* Indianapolis, Indiana State, Seventh Circuit and American Bar Associations. ***PRACTICE AREAS:*** Appellate Practice. **Email:** mlsmith@locke.com

(This Listing Continued)

GREGORY G. TAYLOR, born Lake Providence, Louisiana, August 24, 1970; admitted to bar, 1997, Indiana. *Education:* Indiana University (B.A., 1992); Indiana University School of Law (J.D., 1996). **Email:** gtaylor@locke.com

THOMAS A. WITHROW, born Indianapolis, Indiana, October 17, 1942; admitted to bar, 1969, Indiana; 1998, Colorado. *Education:* University of Michigan (B.A., 1964); Indiana University (J.D., 1969). Phi Delta Phi. Deputy Prosecutor, State of Indiana, 1969. Arbitrator, American Arbitration Association. *Member:* Indianapolis, Indiana State and American Bar Associations. **Email:** twithrow@locke.com

OF COUNSEL

ROBERT C. RIDDELL, born Indianapolis, Indiana, October 7, 1932; admitted to bar, 1957, Indiana. *Education:* Butler University (B.A., 1954); Indiana University (J.D., 1957). *Member:* Indianapolis, Indiana State and American Bar Associations.

WILLIAM H. VOBACH, born Chicago, Illinois, December 25, 1929; admitted to bar, 1954, Michigan and Indiana. *Education:* Oberlin College (A.B., magna cum laude, 1951); University of Michigan (J.D., 1954). Indiana State Senator, 1983-1990. Chairman, State Environmental Policy Commission, 1989-1990. *Member:* Indianapolis, Indiana State and American Bar Associations; International Association of Defense Counsel.

RETIRED

EMERSON BOYD (1914-1986)

THEODORE L. LOCKE (1891-1981)

HUGH E. REYNOLDS (1900-1968)

WILLIAM B. WEISELL, born Bluffton, Indiana, May 21, 1912; admitted to bar, 1940, Indiana. *Education:* Culver Military Academy, Culver, Ind.; Columbia University (A.B., 1936; LL.B., 1940). *Member:* Indianapolis, Indiana State and American Bar Associations; International Association of Insurance Counsel.

REPRESENTATIVE CLIENTS: AIG; American Express Financial Services; American Honda Motor Co.; American Suzuki Motor Corporation; Arbor Homes; Associated Aviation Underwriters; Bank One; Bank One, N.A.; Black & Decker (U.S.) Inc.; CNA Insurance Cos.; CNA Surety Companies; Case Corporation; Caylor-Nickel Clinic, P.C.; Cinergy/PSI Energy; Citizens Financial Services, Citizens Insurance Co. (The Hanover Group); Clarion Health Partners, Inc.; Columbus Regional Hospital; Crown Equipment; Delphi Automotive System; Dorel Juvenile Group; Emerson Electric Co.; Executive Homes; Fifth Third Bank, Indiana; First Indiana Bank; First National Bank and Trust; Ford Motor Company; General Motors Corp.; Geupel, DeMars, Hagerman LLC; Hagerman Construction Corp.; Home Federal Savings Bank; IPALCO, Inc.; Indiana Association of General Contractors; Indiana Motor Truck Assn.; International Business Machines Corp.; KeyBank National Assn.; LaSalle Bank National Assn.; Louisiana Pacific; Mercantile National Bank of Indiana; Nationwide Insurance Co.; OMS National; PHICO Insurance Co.; Riverview Hospital; Royal Insurance Cos.; Shook LLC; St. Paul Companies; St. Paul Fire and Marine; St. Vincent Hospital; The Doctors' Company; The Hartford Insurance Co.; The Huntington National Bank; The Medical Protective Co.; The St. Paul Companies; Tonn and Blank Construction; Toyota Motor Sales, U.S.A., Inc.; Trump Indiana, Inc.; Urology of Indiana, L.L.C.; U.S. Aircraft Insurance Group; U.S.F & G. Cos.; Wal-Mart Stores, Inc.; Washington Mutual Bank, FA; Wishard Health Services; Women's Hospital of Indianapolis; Zurich.

MADDOX HARGETT & CARUSO, P.C.

INDIANAPOLIS, INDIANA

(See Fishers)

Mediation, Securities Arbitration, Securities Litigation.

MAGINOT MOORE & BECK

BANK ONE CENTER/TOWER
111 MONUMENT CIRCLE
SUITE 3000
INDIANAPOLIS, INDIANA 46204-5115
Telephone: 317-638-2922
Facsimile: 317-638-2139
URL: http://www.maginot.com

Patent, Trademark, Copyright, Intellectual Property, Licensing, Counseling and Litigation.

PAUL J. MAGINOT, born Hammond, Indiana, July 29, 1961; admitted to bar, 1989, Indiana and U.S. District Court, Southern District of Indiana; 1995, U.S. Court of Appeals for the Federal and Seventh Circuits; registered to practice before the U.S. Patent and Trademark Office. *Education:* Purdue University (B.S., 1983; M.S.E.-E.E., 1987); Indiana University (J.D., 1989). *Member:* Indiana State Bar Association (Vice-Chair, Intellectual Property Section, 2004-2005). ***PRACTICE AREAS:*** Patent Law; Trademark Law; Copyright Law. **Email:** pjmaginot@maginot.com

HAROLD C. MOORE, born Pittsburgh, Pennsylvania, February 25, 1966; admitted to bar, 1993, New York and U.S. District Court, Southern and Eastern Districts of New York; 1995, Indiana; 1996, U.S. District Court, Southern District of Indiana; registered to practice before the U.S. Patent and Trademark Office. *Education:* Lehigh University (B.S.E.E., with highest honors, 1988); Rutgers University, Newark Law School (J.D., 1992). Phi Beta Kappa; Tau Beta Pi; Eta Kappa Nu. Managing Production Editor, Rutgers Computer and Technology Law Journal, 1990-1992. *Member:* Indiana State Bar Association (Chair, Intellectual Property Section, 2003-2004). ***PRACTICE AREAS:*** Patent Law; Trademark Law; Licensing; Litigation. **Email:** hcmoore@maginot.com

MICHAEL D. BECK, born Indianapolis, Indiana, September 23, 1956; admitted to bar, 1986, Indiana; 1990, U.S. Court of Appeals for the Federal Circuit; 2003, U.S. Court of Appeals, Seventh Circuit; registered to practice before U.S. Patent and Trademark Office. *Education:* General Motors Institute (B.S.M.E., 1979); Georgia Institute of Technology (M.S.E.S.M., 1980); Thomas Jefferson School of Law (J.D., 1986). Executive Editor, Western State Law Review, 1985-1986. ***PRACTICE AREAS:*** Intellectual Property. **Email:** mdbeck@maginot.com

(This Listing Continued)

MAGINOT MOORE & BECK, Indianapolis—Continued

DAVID M. LOCKMAN, born Chattanooga, Tennessee, October 16, 1955; admitted to bar, 1989, Ohio; 1990, U.S. District Court, Southern District of Ohio, U.S. District Court, Northern District of Georgia, U.S. District Court, Southern District of Indiana and U.S. Court of Appeals for the Federal and Seventh Circuits; 1995, Georgia; 2005, Indiana; registered to practice before U.S. Patent and Trademark Office. *Education:* Vanderbilt University (B.E.E.E., 1977); Cleveland-Marshall College of Law (J.D., Cum laude, 1989); Asbury Theological Seminary (M. Div., 2002). Member, Moot Court, 1987-1989. Alfred J. Lerner Scholarship (Cleveland-Marshall). Author: "Copyright Law Preemption of State Law Claims," Ohio State Bar Association Intellectual Property Law News Bulletin, Spring, 1994. Speaker: "Software Patents," Ohio State Bar Association Convention, 1994; Intellectual Property Law Committee Section. *Member:* State Bar of Georgia (Member, Intellectual Property Law Section). ***PRACTICE AREAS:*** Intellectual Property; Computer and Software Patents; Patent Litigation; Trademark Litigation. ***Email:*** dmlockman@maginot.com

ASSOCIATES

JAMES D. WOOD, born Janesville, Wisconsin, November 4, 1960; admitted to bar, 1998, Indiana; U.S. District Court, Northern and Southern Districts of Indiana and U.S. Court of Appeals, Ninth Circuit; registered to practice before U.S. Patent and Trademark Office. *Education:* U.S. Naval Academy (B.S., 1983); American University (M.A., 1984); George Washington Law School (J.D., 1998). ***PRACTICE AREAS:*** Patents; Trademarks; Litigation. ***Email:*** jdwood@maginot.com

RUSSELL E. FOWLER, II, born Indianapolis, Indiana, March 31, 1970; admitted to bar, 1996, Indiana and U.S. District Court, Southern District of Indiana; registered to practice before U.S. Patent and Trademark Office. *Education:* Purdue University, Indianapolis (B.S.E.E., 1993); Indiana University School of Law - Indianapolis (J.D., cum laude, 1996). *Member:* Indiana State Bar Association; American Intellectual Property Law Association. ***PRACTICE AREAS:*** Patent Law; Trademark Law; Copyright Law; Intellectual Property Licensing. ***Email:*** refowler@maginot.com

DAVID R. MOORMAN, born Indianapolis, Indiana, June 10, 1970; admitted to bar, 2005, Indiana. *Education:* Purdue University, Indianapolis, Indiana (B.S. Comp. E, 2002); Indiana University School of Law, Indianapolis, Indiana (J.D., 2005). *Member:* Indiana State Bar Association; American Intellectual Property Law Association. [Sargeant, U.S. Marine Corps, 1992-1997]. ***PRACTICE AREAS:*** Trademarks; Patents; Intellectual Property Licensing. ***Email:*** drmoorman@maginot.com

GERALD W. ROBERTS, born Indianapolis, Indiana, January 3, 1964; admitted to bar, 1996, Indiana; registered to practice before U.S. Patent and Trademark Office. *Education:* Rose-Hulman Institute of Technology (B.S.E.E., 1985); Indiana University School of Law, Indianapolis, Indiana (J.D., cum laude, 1996). Member, Moot Court; Order of Barristers. *Member:* Indianapolis, Marion County and Indiana State Bar Associations; American Intellectual Property Law Association. ***REPORTED CASES:*** Mid-Continent Paper Converters, Inc. v. Brady, Ware & Schoenfeld, Inc. 715NE2d906 (Ind. Ct. App. 1999). ***PRACTICE AREAS:*** Patents; Patents; Trademarks; Trademarks; Copyrights; Copyrights; Litigation; Litigation. ***Email:*** gwroberts@maginot.com

REPRESENTATIVE CLIENTS: Acterna Corporation; Aero Industries, Inc.; AT&T Corporation; Beckman Coulter, Inc.; Datascape, Inc.; DePuy Orthopaedics, Inc.; Doric Products; Emerson Appliance Controls; Equipment Technologies, Inc.; Fanimation, Inc.; Fundex Games, Ltd.; Gem City Engineering Co.; Gilmour, Inc.; IMMI, Inc.; Indiana University Research and Technology; Infineon Technologies; Johnson & Johnson; Landis + Gyr, Inc.; LSI Logic, Inc.; Lucent Technologies, Inc.; Motorola; NCR Corporation; PHS Indiana, Inc.; Purdue University; Robert Bosch Corp.; Siemens Corporation; Vandor Corporation; Vermont American Corporation; Xerox Corporation.

MANN LAW FIRM

INDIANAPOLIS, INDIANA

(See Terre Haute)

Personal Injury and Business Trial Practice in State and Federal Courts, Condemnation, Eminent Domain, Land Acquisition, Medical Malpractice and Products Liability.

THE MARCUS LAW FIRM

INDIANAPOLIS, INDIANA

(See Fishers)

Healthcare Law, Elder Law, Personal Injury, Automobile Accidents, Slip and Fall, Wrongful Death, Legal Malpractice, Consumer Law, Medical Malpractice, Unsafe Products, Civil Rights, Employment law, Wrongful Termination, Discrimination, Harassment, Trial Practice, Family Law, Adoptions, Child Custody, Child Support, Divorce, Visitation Rights, Real Estate, Wills and Probate, Trusts and Estates, Estate Planning, Guardianships, Asset Protection, Business Law, Business Planning, Contracts, Lawsuits, Business Enterprises, Corporate, Limited Liability Companies, Partnerships, Buying and Selling a Business.

SHEILA A. MARSHALL

INDIANAPOLIS, INDIANA

(See Carmel)

Family Law, Divorce, Child Custody, Visitation Issues, Child Support, Prenuptial Agreements, Mediation.

MAURER RIFKIN & HILL, P.C.

INDIANAPOLIS, INDIANA

(See Carmel)

Labor and Employment Law, Disability Accommodation, Discrimination, Employee Benefits, Wrongful Termination, Sexual Harassment, Civil Rights, Business Law, Business Planning, Contracts, Business Litigation, Business Enterprises, Small Business, Partnerships, Limited Liability Companies, Buying and Selling a Business, Starting a Business, Corporate Law, Family Law, Adoptions, Child Custody, Child Support, Divorce, Wills, Probate, Trusts and Estates, Estate Planning.

(This Listing Continued)

McCLURE McCLURE DAVIS & HENN

Established in 1975

235 NORTH DELAWARE
INDIANAPOLIS, INDIANA 46204
Telephone: 317-221-0800
Facsimile: 317-221-0900
URL: http://www.lawyers.com/mcclure-law

Greenwood Office: 225 South Emerson Avenue, Suite F, 46143-1959. Telephone: 317-885-0041. Facsimile: 317-885-0506.

General Civil, Insurance Defense, Employment Law, Family/Domestic Relations, Adoption Law, Child Custody, Child Support, Divorce, Visitation Rights, Personal Injury, Automobile Accidents and Injuries, Slip and Fall, Dog Bites, Wrongful Death, Estate Planning, Wills, Probate, Trusts and Estates, Guardianship, Asset Protection, Corporate Law, Business Litigation, Business Law, Business Planning, Business Enterprises, and Real Estate. Trials and Appellate Practice before all Courts.

FIRM PROFILE: The group of attorneys practicing under the name of McClure McClure Davis & Henn is the successor of McClure, McClure established in 1966, and McClure, McClure & Kammen formed in 1975 and McClure McClure & Davis founded in 1990. Within the association are attorneys offering varying areas of concentration both in the state of Indiana and nationwide.

MEMBERS OF FIRM

DAVID E. McCLURE, born Indianapolis, Indiana, December 13, 1938; admitted to bar, 1965, Indiana. *Education:* Indiana University (A.B., 1960); Indiana University School of Law (LL.B., 1965). Phi Delta Phi. Chief Probation Officer, Marion County, 1963-1965. Presenter, Domestic Law in Indiana, March 14, 2000. *Member:* Indianapolis (Chairman, Family Law Committee, 1982), Indiana State and American Bar Associations. ***PRACTICE AREAS:*** Family Law; Probate; Personal Injury; Asbestos Litigation. ***Email:*** mcclureatty@aol.com

GROVER B. DAVIS, born Seymour, Indiana, January 5, 1944; admitted to bar, 1974, Indiana and U.S. District Court, Northern and Southern Districts of Indiana. *Education:* Indiana University (B.S., 1968); Indiana University School of Law (J.D., magna cum laude, 1973). Deputy Prosecuting Attorney, Marion County, 1974. *Member:* Indianapolis, Indiana State and American Bar Associations; Defense Research Institute; Indiana Defense Lawyers Association; Indiana Trial Lawyers Association. ***PRACTICE AREAS:*** Insurance Defense; Business Litigation; Civil Practice. ***Email:*** gbdavis@mmdhlaw.com

DAVID M. HENN, born Indianapolis, Indiana, November 26, 1968; admitted to bar, 1994, Indiana and U.S. District Court, Northern and Southern Districts of Indiana; 1996, U.S. Court of Appeals, 7th Circuit. *Education:* Indiana University (B.S., 1991); University of Louisville (J.D., 1994). Law Clerk, Indiana Court of Appeals, 1994-1996. Author: "Survey of Recent Developments in Indiana Product Liability Law," 34 IND. L.REV. 857 (2001). *Member:* Indianapolis, Indiana State and American Bar Associations; Americna Inn of Court. (Resident, Greenwood Office). ***PRACTICE AREAS:*** Employment Law; Discrimination; Wrongful Discharge; Wage Claims; Insurance Defense; Business Litigation; Real Estate; Commercial Leasing; Appellate Practice. ***Email:*** dhenn@mmdhlaw.com

ASSOCIATES

CHRISTOPHER STEINMETZ, born Indianapolis, Indiana, March 4, 1960; admitted to bar, 2003, Indiana. *Education:* Indiana University (B.S., 1987; J.D., 2002).

BRETT M. HAWORTH, born Rensselaer, Indiana, June 17, 1978; admitted to bar, 2003, Indiana. *Education:* Franklin College of Indiana (B.A., 2000); Indiana University (J.D., 2003). ***Email:*** bhaworth@mmdhlaw.com

JAMES T. FLANIGAN, born Quantico, Virginia, May 21, 1958; admitted to bar, 1992, Indiana, U.S. District Court, Northern and Southern Districts of Indiana and U.S. Court of Appeals, Seventh Circuit. *Education:* Purdue University (B.S., 1980); Indiana University (J.D., magna cum laude, 1992). Order of the Coif. *Member:* Indianapolis Bar Association. (Resident, Greenwood Office). ***PRACTICE AREAS:*** Criminal Defense; Administrative Law; Alcoholic Beverage Control; Appellate Practice.

REFERENCE: NBD.

PATRICIA L. McKINNON

333 EAST OHIO STREET, SUITE 200
INDIANAPOLIS, INDIANA 46204
Telephone: 317-686-1900
Fax: 317-686-5760
URL: http://www.indianafamilylawyer.com
Email: pmckinnon@indianafamilylawyer.com
URL: http://www.divorceindianalaw.com

Family Law, Adoption, Child Custody, Child Support, Divorce, Visitation Rights, Paternity, CHINS, Guardianship.

PATRICIA L. McKINNON, born Oak Park, Illinois, February 2, 1961; admitted to bar, 1994, Indiana and U.S. District Court, Northern and Southern Districts of Indiana. *Education:* Augustana College (B.A., 1983); University of Notre Dame (J.D., 1994). Recipient, Indiana State Bar Association's Presidential Citation Award, 2004. *Member:* Indianapolis, Indiana State and American Bar Associations.

McNAMAR & ASSOCIATES

111 MONUMENT CIRCLE, SUITE 3350
P.O. BOX 1883
INDIANAPOLIS, INDIANA 46206-1883
Telephone: 317-632-3350
Fax: 317-632-3353
Email: dfmcnamar@mcnamarlaw.com
URL: http://www.mcnamarlaw.com

Health Care Regulatory, Administrative Law, Business Organization, Joint Ventures, Mergers, Acquisitions and Divestitures, Shareholder Rights, Business Successions, Estate Planning, Wills, Probate, Trusts and Estates, Insurance Law, Real Estate, State Government Law, Municipal Law.

FIRM PROFILE: Our firm has extensive experience in the large and complex body of health and healthcare law. We represent nursing facilities, home health care agencies, with health planning, and mental health law as they are impacted by Indiana statutes, regulations, and Medicare and Medicaid statutes and regulations. We represent individual Medicare and Medicaid provider clients including nursing facilities, transportation providers, and home health care agencies. We also defend health care providers in negligence and malpractice cases. Our Insurance Law Practice concerns defending Medicare and Medicaid providers in malpractice actions. We also have brought "bad faith" cases against insurance companies. Finally, our practice includes matters such as land use and zoning issues. We have also handled Mandate Actions for the Courts when needed. McNamar & Associates is listed in Martindale-Hubbell's Bar Register of Preeminent Lawyers.

DAVID F. McNAMAR, born Terre Haute, Indiana, March 26, 1940; admitted to bar, 1968, Indiana, U.S. District Court, Northern and Southern Districts of Indiana, U.S. Court of Appeals, Seventh Circuit and U.S. Supreme Court. *Education:* Purdue University (B.S., 1962); Indiana University (J.D., 1968). Master Commissioner, Marion Superior Court, Criminal Division 4, 1979-1993. Former Mediator, Supreme Courts of Indiana and American Health Lawyers Association. *Member:* Indianapolis, Indiana State, Federal and American Bar Associations; American Health Lawyers Association. Fellow: Indianapolis Bar Association. [Capt., JAGC, USNR-Ret.]. ***Email:*** dfmcnamar@mcnamarlaw.com

McTURNAN & TURNER

Established in 1989

2400 MARKET TOWER
10 WEST MARKET STREET
INDIANAPOLIS, INDIANA 46204
Telephone: 317-464-8181
Telecopier: 317-464-8131
URL: http://www.mtlitig.com

Business Litigation in all State and Federal Trial and Appellate Courts, including Antitrust, Contracts, Securities Fraud, Corporate Governance, Public Utility, Accountants' Liability, Legal Professional Liability Law, Class Action Defense, Discrimination, Employment, Noncompetition Agreements, Product Liability, Lender Liability, Uniform Commercial Code, Commercial Fraud, Business Torts, Unfair Competition, Administrative, Tax Litigation, Media and First Amendment.

FIRM PROFILE: McTurnan & Turner concentrates in relatively complex business or commercial litigation. The firm's goal is to provide the high quality of representation expected from the largest firms with the responsive and efficient services that distinguish the best small firms. The firm has assembled a group of unusually talented lawyers who work closely with the client or corporate counsel to plan and implement strategies throughout pre-trial and trial proceedings.

LEE B. McTURNAN, born New York, New York, September 13, 1937; admitted to bar, 1965, Illinois; 1978, Indiana. *Education:* Harvard University (A.B., magna cum laude, 1959); Oxford University (Lincoln College), England (Diploma in Law, 1961, on Rotary Foundation Fellowship); University of Chicago (J.D., cum laude, 1963). Phi Beta Kappa; Order of the Coif. Editor-in-Chief, University of Chicago Law Review, 1962-1963. Law Clerk to Justice Goldberg, U.S. Supreme Court, 1963-1964. Associate, 1964-1969, and Partner, 1970-1978, Sidley & Austin, Chicago, Illinois. Listed in Naifeh & Smith, Best Lawyers in America, 1989-2005 (Business Litigation, Indiana). *Member:* Indianapolis, Chicago (Member, Board of Managers, 1977-1978), Indiana State, Illinois State, Seventh Circuit and American Bar Associations; Indianapolis Law Club (President, 1988-1990); Local Rules Advisory Committee for Southern District of Indiana, 1995-2000; Indianapolis American Inn of Court (Master). ***PRACTICE AREAS:*** Trial Practice; Complex Litigation; Class Action Defense; Securities Litigation; Employment Discrimination; Contract Litigation; Media and First Amendment; Accountants Liability; Legal Professional Liability; Appellate Practice. ***Email:*** lmcturnan@mtlitig.com

WAYNE C. TURNER, born Rising Sun, Indiana, January 26, 1960; admitted to bar, 1985, Indiana. *Education:* Purdue University (B.S., with highest distinction, 1982, G.A. Ross Outstanding Graduate); Indiana University (J.D., magna cum laude, 1985). The Order of Barristers. Note and Development Editor, Indiana Law Review, 1984-1985. Listed in Naifeh & Smith, Best Lawyers in America, 2005 (Business Litigation, Indiana). *Member:* Indianapolis, Indiana State, Seventh Circuit and American Bar Associations; Indianapolis Law Club; Defense Research Institute, Inc. ***PRACTICE AREAS:*** Trial Practice; Business Torts; Professional Liability Law; Employment Litigation; Injunctions; Class Action Defense; Derivative Actions; Appellate Practice. ***Email:*** wturner@mtlitig.com

STEVEN M. BADGER, born Indianapolis, Indiana, November 11, 1964; admitted to bar, 1992, Indiana. *Education:* Wabash College (B.A., summa cum laude, 1987); Indiana University (J.D., summa cum laude, 1992). Phi Beta Kappa; Order of the Coif. Managing Editor, Indiana Law Journal, 1991-1992. Member, Marion County Board of Zoning Appeals, 2001—. *Member:* Indianapolis, Indiana State, Seventh Circuit and American Bar Associations. ***PRACTICE AREAS:*** Trial Practice; Media and First Amendment; Legal Professional Liability; Contract Litigation; Noncompete Litigation; Employment Litigation; Appellate Practice. ***Email:*** sbadger@mtlitig.com

(This Listing Continued)

JOHN F. McCAULEY, born Worcester, Massachusetts, December 15, 1963; admitted to bar, 1998, Indiana. *Education:* College of the Holy Cross (B.A., 1986); Catholic University of America (M.A., with distinction, 1992); United States Naval War College (1993); Indiana University School of Law (J.D., magna cum laude, 1998). Associate Editor, Indiana Law Review, 1996-1997. Political-Military Advisor to Gen. Colin L. Powell, Chairman of the Joint Chief of Staff, 1992-1993. Special Assistant to Chief of Naval Operations, 1993-1994. *Member:* Indianapolis, Indiana State, Seventh Circuit and American Bar Associations. [Lieut. (Naval Aviator), U.S. Navy, 1986-1994]. ***PRACTICE AREAS:*** Trial Practice; Appellate Practice. ***Email:*** jmccauley@mtlitig.com

ASSOCIATES

JACQUELINE BOWMAN PONDER, born Indianapolis, Indiana, November 11, 1964; admitted to bar, 1990, Indiana and Texas. *Education:* Southern Methodist University (B.A., cum laude, 1986); Indiana University School of Law (J.D., summa cum laude, 1989). Phi Beta Kappa; Nathan Mendenhall Award; Chancellor's Scholar. Associate Editor, Indiana Law Review, 1988-1989. Law Clerk to Judge Tom Stagg, U.S. District Court, Western District of Louisiana, 1990-1992. *Member:* Indianapolis, Indiana State, Seventh Circuit and American Bar Associations; State Bar of Texas. ***LANGUAGES:*** Russian. ***PRACTICE AREAS:*** Trial Practice; Employment Litigation; Noncompete Litigation; Contract Litigation; Class Action Defense; Appellate Practice. ***Email:*** jponder@mtlitig.com

ANNE L. COWGUR, born Mt. Pulaski, Illinois, July 6, 1970; admitted to bar, 1999, Indiana. *Education:* University of Illinois (B.A., summa cum laude, 1992); University of Illinois College of Law (J.D., magna cum laude, 1999). Order of the Coif. Recipient, Bronze Tablet, University of Illinois. Articles Editor, University of Illinois Law Review, 1998-1999. *Member:* Indianapolis, Indiana State, Seventh Circuit and American Bar Associations. ***PRACTICE AREAS:*** Trial Practice; Appellate Practice. ***Email:*** acowgur@mtlitig.com

GREGORY A. NEIBARGER, born Kokomo, Indiana, November 29, 1973; admitted to bar, 2000, Indiana. *Education:* University of Missouri (B.S., high honors, 1996); Indiana University School of Law (J.D., summa cum laude, 1999). Big Eight Academic All-American. Cale J. Holder Scholar, 1999. Associate Editor, Indiana Law Review, 1998-1999. *Member:* Indianapolis, Indiana State, Seventh Circuit and American Bar Associations. ***PRACTICE AREAS:*** Trial Practice; Appellate Practice. ***Email:*** gneibarger@mtlitig.com

KENNETH J. MUNSON, born Harvey, Illinois, March 4, 1970; admitted to bar, 2001, Indiana. *Education:* Indiana University (B.S., 1992; J.D., summa cum laude, 2001). Articles Editor, Indiana Law Review, 2000-2001. *Member:* Indianapolis, Indiana State, Seventh Circuit and American Bar Associations. ***PRACTICE AREAS:*** Trial Practice; Appellate Practice. ***Email:*** kmunson@mtlitig.com

CARL A. HAYES, born Hagerstown, Indiana, September 4, 1966; admitted to bar, 2002, Indiana. *Education:* Ball State University (B.S., cum laude, 1989); Butler University (M.A., 1998); Indiana University School of Law (J.D., summa cum laude, 2002). Order of Barristers. G. Kent Frandsen Scholar. Dean's Merit Scholar. Articles Editor, Indiana Law Review, 2001-2002. *Member:* Indianapolis, Indiana State and American Bar Associations. ***PRACTICE AREAS:*** Trial Practice; Appellate Practice. ***Email:*** chayes@mtlitig.com

MICHAEL R. LIMRICK, born Indiana, Pennsylvania, September, 23, 1976; admitted to bar, 2001, Indiana. *Education:* Marietta College (B.A., 1998); University of Toledo College of Law (J.D., magna cum laude, 2001). Burton-Maddock Full-Tuition Law Scholarship, 1998-2001. Order of the Coif. University of Toledo Law Review, 1999-2000. Outstanding College of Law Graduate Award, 2001. Law Clerk to Justice Theodore R. Boehm, Indiana Supreme Court, 2001-2003. *Member:* Indianapolis, Indiana State and American Bar Associations. ***PRACTICE AREAS:*** Trial Practice; Appellate Practice. ***Email:*** mlimrick@mtlitig.com

SHANNON D. LANDRETH, born Centralia, Illinois, November 14, 1977; admitted to bar, 2002, Indiana. *Education:* Southeast Missouri State University (B.S., summa cum laude, 1999); University of Illinois College of Law (J.D., summa cum laude, 2002). Order of the Coif. Harno Fellow. Executive Administrative Editor, University of Illinois Law Review, 2001-2002. Law Clerk, Justice Frank Sullivan, Jr., Indiana Supreme Court, 2002-2003. *Member:* Indianapolis, Indiana State, Seventh Circuit and American Bar Associations. ***PRACTICE AREAS:*** Trial Practice; Appellate Practice. ***Email:*** slandreth@mtlitig.com

JULIANNA M. PLAWECKI, born Hammond, Indiana, September 6, 1977; admitted to bar, 2003, Indiana. *Education:* Purdue University (B.A., with highest distinction, 2000); Indiana University School of Law (J.D., summa cum laude, 2003). Phi Beta Kappa. G. Kent Frandsen Scholar. The Order of Barristers. Articles Editor, Indiana Law Review, 2002-2003. Law Clerk to Chief Justice Randall T. Shepard, Indiana Supreme Court, 2003-2004. *Member:* Indianapolis, Indiana State, Seventh Circuit and American Bar Associations. ***PRACTICE AREAS:*** Trial Practice; Appellate Practice. ***Email:*** jplawecki@mtlitig.com

ERIK C. JOHNSON, born Normal, Illinois, September 19, 1979; admitted to bar, 2004, Indiana. *Education:* DePaul University (B.S., magna cum laude, 2001); University of Chicago Law School (J.D., cum laude, 2004). Recipient: Thomas R. Mulroy Award for Excellence In Appellate Advocacy And Oral Argument; Semi-Finalist, Hinton Moot Court Competition; John M. Olin Fellow of Law & Economics, 2002-2003. *Member:* Indianapolis, Indiana State, Seventh Circuit and American Bar Associations. ***PRACTICE AREAS:*** Trial Practice; Appellate Practice. ***Email:*** ejohnson@mtlitig.com

REPRESENTATIVE CLIENTS: SBC Communications, Inc.; PricewaterhouseCoopers, LLP; Wachovia Corporation; ProLiance Energy LLC; Salomon Smith Barney; CitiFinancial; General Motors Corporation; Onkyo Corporation; Western Newspaper Publishing Co.; Earlham College; Redcats USA, LP; McGraw-Hill Broadcasting Co., Inc. (WRTV-6).

MEILS, THOMPSON, DIETZ & BERISH

Established in 1978

TWO MARKET SQUARE CENTER, SUITE 830
251 EAST OHIO STREET
INDIANAPOLIS, INDIANA 46204
Telephone: 317-637-1383
Fax: 317-264-2573
Email: joedietz@worldnet.att.net
Email: rmeils@home.com

General Civil and Trial Practice. Insurance Litigation. Probate and Estate Planning, Real Estate.

MEMBERS OF FIRM

RICK D. MEILS, born Bloomington, Illinois, April 8, 1950; admitted to bar, 1975, Indiana and U.S. District Court, Southern District of Indiana. *Education:* Indiana University (A.B., 1972; J.D., 1975). *Member:* Indianapolis, Indiana State and American Bar Associations; Indiana Trial Lawyers Association; The Association of Trial Lawyers of America; Defense Research Institute; Indiana Defense Lawyers Association. ***PRACTICE AREAS:*** Civil Litigation; Insurance Defense; Insurance Litigation. ***Email:*** rmeils@comcast.com

ROBERT C. THOMPSON, JR., born St. Charles, Illinois, August 24, 1948; admitted to bar, 1974, Indiana and U.S. District Court, Southern District of Indiana. *Education:* Indiana University (B.S., 1970; J.D., 1973). Deputy Prosecutor, 1974-1989. Member, Governors Commission on Guardianship, 1993-1996. *Member:* Indianapolis and Indiana State Bar Associations. ***PRACTICE AREAS:*** Estate; Guardianship; Adoption.

JOSEPH M. DIETZ, born Camp Atterbury, Indiana, October 15, 1951; admitted to bar, 1976, Indiana and U.S. District Court, Northern and Southern Districts of Indiana; Northern District of Mississippi; 1985, U.S. Supreme Court. *Education:* Butler University (B.A., 1973); Indiana University (J.D., magna cum laude, 1976). Phi Kappa Phi; Phi Eta Sigma. Clerk Indiana Court of Appeals, 1975-1976. Member, Board of Directors, 1972-1977 and Chairman, 1974, Public Action in Correctional Efforts. *Member:* Indianapolis, Indiana State and American Bar Associations; Indiana Defense Lawyers Association. ***PRACTICE AREAS:*** Personal Injury; Wrongful Death; Product Liability. ***Email:*** joedietz@att.net

WILLIAM M. BERISH, born Poughkeepsie, New York, April 1, 1970; admitted to bar, 1996, Indiana and U.S. District, Southern and Northern District of Indiana. *Education:* Depauw University (B.A., 1993); Indiana University School of Law (J.D., 1996). *Member:* Indianapolis, Indiana State, and American Bar Associations. ***PRACTICE AREAS:*** Civil Litigation; Insurance Defense; Insurance Litigation. ***Email:*** wberish@meilsatty.com

NEIL A. DAVIS, born Lafayette, Indiana, April 30, 1971; admitted to bar, 1996, Indiana; U.S. District Court, Northern and Southern Districts of Indiana. *Education:* Purdue University (B.S., 1993); Indiana University (J.D., 1996). Formerly with: Smith & Wade; Haskin Lauter Cohen & Larue.*Member:* Indianapolis and Indiana State Bar Associations. ***REPORTED CASES:*** Medlock v. Blackwell 724 NE2d 113 5 (IndCtApp 2000). ***PRACTICE AREAS:*** Civil Litigation; Insurance Defense; Personal Injury; Wrongful Death. ***Email:*** ndavis@meilsatty.com

ASSOCIATE

JOHN W. MERVILDE, born Southfield, Michigan, June 16, 1974; admitted to bar, 1999, Indiana. *Education:* Indiana University (B.A., 1996); University of Notre Dame (J.D., 1999). *Member:* Indianapolis and Indiana State Bar Associations; Defense Trial Counsel of Indiana. ***PRACTICE AREAS:*** Insurance Defense; Civil Litigation; Personal Injury.

REPRESENTATIVE CLIENTS: Liberty Mutual; GRE-Indiana Insurance Co.; Amerisure; Michigan Mutual Insurance Co.; Linder Machinery; American Family Insurance Co.; Northland Insurance Co.; Capitol Indemnity; Acceptance Insurance Co.; CIE Service Corporation; Monroe Guaranty Insurance Co.
REFERENCES: National City Bank; NBO Bank.

MEYER LAW OFFICE

10811 LEXINGTON DRIVE
INDIANAPOLIS, INDIANA 46280
Telephone: 317-407-4571
URL: http://www.gjmeyerlaw.com

Wills, Trusts and Estates, Probate Law, Charitable Giving, Non-profit Organizations, Small Business, Business Law, Real Estate, Income Tax, Estate and Gift Taxation and Wealth Preservation Law.

GRACIA-JEAN "G-J" MEYER, born Indianapolis, Indiana; admitted to bar, 1998, Indiana. *Education:* Hanover College (B.A., magna cum laude, 1993); Indiana University School of Law - Bloomington (J.D., 1997). Director, Planned Giving Group of Indiana. *Member:* Indianapolis (Member Business, Estate Planning and Tax Sections) and Indiana State (Member, Probate, Tax and Business Sections) Bar Associations; Estate Planning Council. ***PRACTICE AREAS:*** Wills; Probate; Estate Planning; Tax Planning; Asset Protection; Trusts and Estates; Charitable Giving; Business Planning; Business Law; Small Business Law; Nonprofit Tax Law. ***Email:*** gjm@gjmeyer.com

MISHKIN & DUVALL

SUITE 525
200 SOUTH MERIDIAN
INDIANAPOLIS, INDIANA 46225
Telephone: 317-634-9100
Fax: 317-634-9103
Email: mishkin-duvall@sbcglobal.net

General Civil Practice in all State and Federal Courts. Litigation. Construction Law. Real Estate and Commercial Law, Documentation of Business Transactions, Employment Law.

(This Listing Continued)

SIDNEY MISHKIN, born Donora, Pennsylvania, August 29, 1937; admitted to bar, 1964, Indiana and U.S. District Court, Southern and Northern Districts of Indiana; 1966, U.S. Court of Appeals for the Seventh Circuit; 1971, U.S. Supreme Court; 1990, Pennsylvania. *Education:* Wilmington College (A.B., 1959); Indiana University (J.D., 1962). Phi Delta Phi. Member, Indiana Law Journal, 1960-1961. Teaching Fellow, Indiana University School of Law, 1962-1964. Certified Mediator, Indiana, 1992—. *Member:* Indianapolis, Indiana State and American Bar Associations; The Association of Trial Lawyers of America; Indiana Trial Lawyers Association. ***PRACTICE AREAS:*** Civil Litigation; Construction; Real Estate; Commercial Transactions; Transactions. ***Email:*** sidneymishkin@sbcglobal.net

LESA C. DUVALL, born Madison, Indiana, April 12, 1962; admitted to bar, 1992, Indiana and U.S. District Court, Northern and Southern Districts of Indiana. *Education:* Ball State University (B.S., cum laude, 1984); Butler University; Indiana University (J.D., magna cum laude, 1992). *Member:* Indianapolis, Indiana State and American Bar Associations; The Association of Trial Lawyers of America; Indiana Trial Lawyers Association. ***PRACTICE AREAS:*** Civil Litigation; Employment Law; Construction; Real Estate; Commercial Law; Transactions. ***Email:*** lesaduvall@sbcglobal.net

REPRESENTATIVE CLIENTS: Borns Construction Co.; Standard Life Insurance Company; Heritage Realty Management, Inc.; Lee Supply Corp.; Omni Restaurants, Inc.; World Wide Motors Inc.; Win Properties, Inc.; Allied Wholesale Electrical Supply, Inc.; Sandor Development, Co.; O'Neal Steel, Inc.; Automatic Irrigation Supply, Inc.; Word Systems, Inc.; JLF Construction Co., Inc.; Pickwick Farms Apartments.

MITCHELL & ASSOCIATES

Established in 2000

3925 RIVER CROSSING PARKWAY, SUITE 270
INDIANAPOLIS, INDIANA 46240-2279
Telephone: 317-815-5900
Fax: 317-472-0966
Email: info@mitchell-law.net
URL: http://www.gmitchelllawfirm.com

Mitchell & Associates is an association of attorneys who offer services in all areas of family law, including but not limited to divorce and post-divorce modification; domestic litigation; family mediation; qualified domestic relations orders (QDROS); antenuptial agreements; child custody and support; visitation rights; paternity; adoption; domestic violence; guardianships; grandparent's visitation rights; simple wills and trusts and other related matters.

GLORIA K. MITCHELL, born Cincinnati, Ohio, 1961; admitted to bar, 1988, Indiana and U.S. District Court, Southern and Northern Districts of Indiana; 1993, U.S. Court of Appeals, 7th Circuit. *Education:* Miami University (B.A., 1983); Indiana University (J.D., 1988). Delta Theta Phi; Order of Barristers. Speaker/Panelist, Family Law, Various Seminars, 1994—. Lecturer, Family Law, People's Law School, 1994-1997. Master Commissioner, Civil Division, 1993-1997. Certified Family Law Mediator, 1996—. *Member:* Indianapolis (Member, Board of Managers, 1993 and 1994; Member, 1994— and Chair, 2004, Executive Committee, Family Law Section), Indiana and American Bar Associations; National Association Counsel for Children. Fellow, Indianapolis Bar Foundation, 1996—. ***REPORTED CASES:*** Fuehrer v. Fuehrer (Ind.App. 1995) 651 N.E.2d 1171; Sizemore v. H&R Farms, Inc. (Ind.App 1 Dist 1994) 638 N.E.2d 455; Fiste v. Fiste (Ind.App 1 Dist 1994) 627 N.E.2d 1368; Curtis v. American Community Mut. Ins. Co (Ind.App 4 Dist 1993) 610 N.E.2d 871; Miller v. Terre Haute Regional Hosp. (Ind. 1992) 603 N.E.2d 861; Stump v. Indiana Equipment Co., Inc. (Ind.App. 2 Dist 1992)601 N.E.2d 398; Miller v. Terre Haute Regional Hosp. (Ind.App 5 Dist 1992) 596 N.E.2d 913; Cunningham v. Hastings (Ind.App 1 Dist 1990) 556 N.E.2d 12; Greensburg Local No. 761 Printing Specialities v. Robbins (Ind.App 4 Dist 1990) 549 N.E.2d 79; DeBerry v. State 659 N.E.2d 665 (Ind.App. 1995); Carmichael v. Siegel (Ind. 1996) WL 532384; Cornett v. Cornett (Ind. App. 5 Dist 2000) 733 N.E2d 542. ***PRACTICE AREAS:*** Family Law; Alternative Dispute Resolution. ***Email:*** gmitchell@mitchell-law.net

ASSOCIATES

ROBIN L. KELLY, born Travis Air Force Base, California, January, 1970; admitted to bar, 1995, Indiana; 1996, U.S. Court of Appeals for the Armed Forces. *Education:* College of William & Mary (B.A., History, 1992); Indiana University School of Law (J.D., 1995). International Moot Court Competition, 1994. Recipient: American Jurisprudence Award; Criminal Defense Clinic, Fall, 1994 - Spring, 1995; Air Force Commendation Medal; Air Force Organization Excellence Award; Air Armament Center Commander's Briefing Team; Excellence in Briefing Award; Squadron Officer School, Residence Course; Company Grade Officer of the Quarter, Air Armament Center, July-September 1997; Company Grade Officer of the Year, Air Armament Center, 1997. Adjunct Professor, Embry-Riddle Aeronautical University; St. Leo's College, 1996-1998. Special Assistant U.S. Attorney, Pensacola, Florida, May, 1997- January, 1998. *Member:* Indianapolis (Member, Family Law Section) and Indiana State Bar Associations. [Lt., 1995 and Capt., 1996, U.S. Air Force]. ***PRACTICE AREAS:*** Family Law. ***Email:*** rkelly@mitchell-law.net

ELISABETH M. EDWARDS, born Middletown, Ohio, 1976; admitted to bar, 2003, Indiana and U.S. District Court, Northern and Southern Districts of Indiana. *Education:* Hanover College (B.A., English, 1998); Indiana University School of Law (J.D., 2002). Phi Alpha Delta (Secretary, 2000-2002). Client Counseling Competition and Executive Board, 2000-2001. Dean's Student Advisory Board, 1999-2002. Member, Student Bar Association, 2001. Teen Court Volunteer, 2001. Volunteer, Volunteer Tax Assistance Program (VITA), 2001-2002. Certified Domestic Mediator, 2003—. Student Attorney, 2001-2002 and Secretary, Board of Directors, 2002—, Protective Order Pro Bono Project of Greater Indianapolis, Inc. Co-Author: "Children's Records Law in Indiana," Lorman Seminar, February 13, 2003. Faculty, "QDRO Creation in Indiana: Building a Future After a Split," July 14, 2004. *Member:* Indianapolis (Member, Law Student Division, Executive Board, 2002—), Indiana State and American Bar Associations; Indianapolis American Inn of Court, 2000-2001. ***PRACTICE AREAS:*** Family Law; Wills; Alternative Dispute Resolution. ***Email:*** eedwards@mitchell-law.net

REFERENCE: National City Bank.

MITCHELL HURST JACOBS & DICK

Established in 1981

152 EAST WASHINGTON STREET

INDIANAPOLIS, INDIANA 46204

Telephone: 317-636-0808

1-800-636-0808

Fax: 317-633-7680

URL: http://www.mhjdlaw.com

URL: http://www.mhjd.com

Civil Litigation, Corporate, Business Litigation, Business Planning, Contracts, Real Estate, Commercial Leasing, Commercial Real Estate, Personal Injury Law, Automobile Accidents, Dog Bites, Slip and Fall, Wrongful Death, Medical Malpractice, Foreclosure, Products Liability, Construction, Lien.

FIRM PROFILE: Mitchell Hurst Jacobs & Dick is unique in that it combines a sophisticated business law and commercial litigation practice with one of Indiana's largest personal injury practices. Its experience ranges from large real estate developments to shareholder and contract disputes to complex personal injury and commercial litigation. The firm is listed in Martindale-Hubbell's Bar Register of Preeminent Lawyers.

Several members of the firm are listed in Best Lawyers in America.

MEMBERS OF FIRM

MARVIN H. MITCHELL, born Indianapolis, Indiana, October 5, 1937; admitted to bar, 1963, Indiana and U.S. District Court, Southern District of Indiana; 1969, U.S. Court of Appeals, 7th Circuit. *Education:* Ohio State University (B.A., 1959); Indiana University (J.D., 1963). Listed: Best Lawyers In America. Author: "A Lease Check List for the Tenant's Attorney," February, 1973; "A Lease Check List for the Landlord's Attorney," June, 1973; "A Check List of Selected Estate Planning Ideas," May, 1978, Res Gestae; "A Method for Evolving a Trial Strategy," The Practical Lawyer, June, 1981; "Advancing Your Position on Valuation of a Business," Fall 1989, 9 Fairshare 14; "Cross Examining an Opponent's Business Valuation Expert," March, 1989, 9 Fairshare 3; "Title Insurance Checklist," April 1989, Res Gestae. Co-Author and Co-Chairman: "Indiana Trial Notebook," ICLEF, 1985; Contributing Author and Panelist: "Commercial Real Estate Leasing," ICLEF, 1985; "New Indiana Business Corporation Law," ICLEF, 1986; "Estate Planning for the General Practitioner," ICLEF, 1986; "Basic Real Estate Leasing," ICLEF, 1987; "Basics of Real Estate Development," ICLEF, 1987; "Residential and Small Commercial Real Estate Transactions," ICLEF, 1991. Contributing Author: "The Valuation Expert in Divorce Litigation," American Bar Association, 1992; Editor, "The Encyclopedia of Real Estate-Forms," Indianapolis Bar Association, 1993. Co-Author and Co-Chairman, Indiana Trial Systems Workbook, ICLEF, 1994. "Strategies and Techniques for Cross-Examining the Business Valuation Expert," September, 1997, Res Gestae. Research Assistant to Amos Jackson, Chief Justice, Indiana Supreme Court, 1963. Member, Panel of Arbitrators, American Arbitration Association. *Member:* Indianapolis, Indiana State and American Bar Associations. ***PRACTICE AREAS:*** Litigation; Real Estate Law; Business Law. ***Email:*** mmitchell@MHJD.Com

WILLIAM W. HURST, born Robinson, Illinois, February 27, 1938; admitted to bar, 1966, Indiana. *Education:* Indiana University (B.A., in Chemistry, 1962; J.D., with distinction, 1966). Listed in Naifeh and Smith, The Best Lawyers in America. ITLA Lawyer of the Year, 1999. Member, Indiana Law Review, 1965-1966. Author: "Subdivision Control," Indiana Law Review, 1965. Author: Article, "The Dram Shop: Closing Pandora's Box," I.U. Law Journal, 1989. Deputy Attorney General, 1966-1967. Regional PAC Fund Development, ATLA, 1988-1991. *Member:* Indiana State and American Bar Associations; Indiana Trial Lawyers Association (Director, 1985-1998; Member, Executive Committee, 1981—); The Association of Trial Lawyers of America. ***PRACTICE AREAS:*** Negligence Law; Personal Injury Law; Plaintiffs Trial Practice. ***Email:*** WHurst@MHJD.Com

SAMUEL L. JACOBS, born Granite City, Illinois, January 26, 1949; admitted to bar, 1976, Indiana and U.S. District Court, Southern District of Indiana. *Education:* Indiana University (B.A., 1971); John Marshall Law School and Indiana University (J.D., summa cum laude, 1976). Contributing Author: "Indiana Trial Notebook," ICLEF, 1985; "Indiana Trial Systems Workbook," ICLEF, 1994. Panelist, ICLEF, 1986, 1991 and 1993. *Member:* Indianapolis, Indiana State and American Bar Associations; Indiana Trial Lawyers Association (Director, 1987—); The Association of Trial Lawyers of America; The American Board of Trial Advocates. ***PRACTICE AREAS:*** Negligence Law; Personal Injury Law; Plaintiffs Trial Practice. ***Email:*** SJacobs@MHJD.Com

RICHARD J. DICK, born Evansville, Indiana, January 30, 1948; admitted to bar, 1976, Indiana. *Education:* University of Evansville (B.A., cum laude, 1970); Indiana University (J.D., magna cum laude, 1976). Note and Development Editor, Indiana Law Review, 1975-1976. Co-Author: "Indiana Mechanic's Lien Law," The Michie Company, 1981. Author and Panelist, "Indiana Mechanic's Lien Law," Indiana Continuing Legal Education Forum, 1985; "Hot Topics & Issues in Current Real Estate, Commercial and Residential Transactions," Indiana Continuing Legal Education Forum, 1991. Indiana Legal Education Forum, Mechanics Lien Law, February, 1994 and November, 1999. Certified Mediator. *Member:* Indianapolis, Indiana State and American Bar Associations; Indiana Trial Lawyers Association; The Association of Trial Lawyers of America. ***PRACTICE AREAS:*** Construction Law; Litigation. ***Email:*** RDick@MHJD.Com

KIMBERLY H. DANFORTH, born Portsmouth, New Hampshire, November 19, 1960; admitted to bar, 1986, Indiana. *Education:* Miami University; Indiana University (B.A., 1982; J.D., 1985). *Member:* Indianapolis, Indiana State and American Bar Associations; Indiana Trial Lawyers Association; American Trial Lawyers Association. ***PRACTICE AREAS:*** Personal Injury; Litigation. ***Email:*** KDanforth@MHJD.Com

MICHAEL T. McNELIS, born Indianapolis, Indiana, October 21, 1962; admitted to bar, 1988, Indiana and U.S. District Court, Northern and Southern Districts of Indiana; 1990, U.S. Court of Appeals, 7th Circuit. *Education:* Illinois State University (B.S., 1985); Indiana University (J.D., summa cum laude, 1988). Author: "Prepayment Penalties and Due-On-Sale Clauses in Commercial Mortgages: What Next?," 20 Indiana Law Review 735, 1987. Law Clerk to Justice Brent E. Dickson, Indiana Supreme Court, 1987-1988. *Member:* Indianapolis, Indiana State and American Bar Associations. ***PRACTICE AREAS:*** Real Estate Law; Litigation; Business Law; Corporate Law. ***Email:*** MMcNelis@MHJD.Com

(This Listing Continued)

ASSOCIATES

STEPHEN P. KENLEY, born Kansas City, Missouri, October 17, 1953; admitted to bar, 1995, Missouri and U.S. District Court, Western District of Missouri; 1996, Kansas and U.S. District Court, District of Kansas; 1999, Indiana and U.S. District Court, Northern and Southern Districts of Indiana. *Education:* University of Missouri (B.S., cum laude, 1976); University of Missouri, Kansas City (J.D., 1995). Associate Articles Editor, The Urban Lawyer, 1993-1994. Technical Editor, University of Missouri at Kansas City Law Review, 1994-1995. *Member:* Kansas City Metropolitan, Indianapolis, Johnson County and Indiana State Bar Associations; The Missouri Bar. ***PRACTICE AREAS:*** Litigation; Business Law. ***Email:*** skenley@MHJD.com

JOHN C. BABIONE, born Denver, Colorado, July 25, 1972; admitted to bar, 2001, Georgia; 2002, Indiana. *Education:* Indiana University (B.S., 1995); Indiana University School of Law - Indianapolis (J.D., 2001). Member, Indiana International and Comparative Law Review. Author: "Mission Accomplished? Fifty-four Years of Suffering For the People of the Marshall Islands and the Latest Round of Endless Reconciliation," published in Vol. II No. I Ind. International and Comparative Law Review. *Indiana State and American Bar Associations; Indiana Trial Lawyers Association.* ***PRACTICE AREAS:*** Personal Injury; Products Liability. ***Email:*** jbabione@mhjd.com

GENERAL COUNSEL FOR: Calderon Bros. Vending Machines, Inc.; Power Train Services, Inc.; Frank E. Irish, Inc.; Bedding Liquidators; Industrial Laundry; Dr. Tavel's Vision Centers; Harcourt Management Co., Inc.; Kosene & Kosene Mgt. & Dev. Co., Inc.; Hasten Entities; Aaron Y. Cohen Enterprises; Seven-Eleven Supermarkets; Stygall Companies; Weston Group (developers).

LOCAL COUNSEL FOR: Jim Walter Homes, Inc.; Mid-State Homes, Inc.; Consolidated Freightways Corporation of Delaware.

REFERENCE: National City Bank, Indianapolis, Ind.

MORGAN & POTTINGER, P.S.C.

Established in 1974

9801 FALL CREEK ROAD #333

INDIANAPOLIS, INDIANA 46256-4802

Telephone: 317-287-3961

Telecopier: 317-536-3687

URL: http://www.morganandpottinger.com

Louisville, Kentucky Office: 601 West Main Street. Telephone: 502-589-2780. Telecopier: 502-585-3498.

Lexington, Kentucky Office: 133 West Short Street. Telephone: 859-253-1900. Telecopier: 859-255-2038.

Nashville, Tennessee Office: 5543 Edmondson Pike #25. Telephone: 615-831-9554. Telecopier: 615-831-9557.

Banking, Bankruptcy, Business, Collections, Commercial, Corporate, Consumer Credit.

FIRM PROFILE: Morgan & Pottinger, P.S.C. is a full-service commercial law firm offering comprehensive services in a banking, business, creditor, and transaction law practice. We serve Kentucky and Tennessee from three offices located in Louisville and Lexington, Kentucky, Nashville, Tennessee, and Indianapolis, Indiana. The firm represents a wide spectrum of clients ranging from national corporations and banks to small businesses on matters including multi-million dollar commercial loans, acquisitions, and workouts, lender liability and other commercial and regulatory defense, general business representation including employment law, and collections.

EDWARD A.B. CASTALDO, born Newburgh, New York, June 9, 1972; admitted to bar, 1998, Indiana and U.S. District Court, Northern and Southern Districts of Indiana. *Education:* University of Central Arkansas (B.C., 1995); University of Arkansas (J.D., 1998). Phi Alpha Delta. Member, Board of Advocates. Author: "The Way Forward: Navigating Your Collection Case Through Bankruptcy," National Business Institute Seminar, January 21, 2004; "Advanced Collection Strategies," National Business Institute Seminar, October 18, 2004. Indiana Deputy Attorney General, 2000-2002. *Member:* Indianapolis and Indiana State Bar Associations; Indiana Creditor's Rights Bar Association. ***PRACTICE AREAS:*** Creditors Rights; Creditors Rights in Bankruptcy. ***Email:*** ecastaldo@bbanda.com

REPRESENTATIVE CLIENTS: *Banking:* American Founders Bank; Ascencia Bank; Branch Banking & Trust Company; Central Bank; Commonwealth Bank and Trust Company; Community First Bank; Community Trust Bank; Federal Deposit Insurance Corporation; Federal Reserve Bank of St. Louis; Fifth Third Bank; First Security Bank of Lexington; JP Morgan Chase Bank; Kentucky Bankers Association; Louisville Community Development Bank; National City Bank; PNC Bank; Republic Bank & Trust Co.; Stock Yards Bank & Trust Company; The Bank-Oldham County, Inc.; The Farmers State Bank; U.S. Bank. *Financial Services:* Advest Bank; American General Corporation; Associates Housing Corporation and its affiliates; Bank of America Mortgage; Chrysler Financial Company; CitiFinancial; GE Capital; GE Commercial Distribution Finance; General Motors Acceptance Corporation; GMAC Commercial Mortgage; New Equity Mortgage, LLC; Singer Asset Finance Company; Textron Financial Corporation. *Credit Unions:* Beacon Credit F.C.U.; Blue Cross/Blue Shield F.C.U.; Brown & Williamson F.C.U.; Census Bureau F.C.U.; Kentucky Telco Employees F.C.U.; Louisville Medical Center F.C.U.; Philip Morris F.C.U. *Automobile Dealers:* Byerly Ford-Nissan, Inc.; Bob Hook Chevrolet; Commonwealth Dodge, Inc.; Coyle Dodge; Jim Cooke Autoa Center; Oxmoor Toyota; Star Ford; Swope Auto Company, LLC; Town & Country Ford, Inc. *General:* Atria; AST Industrial & Environmental Services, Inc.; Eckart, LLC; Engelhard Corp.; General Motors Corporation; Keller Ladders; Rogers Group, Inc.; Sears-Roebuck & Co.; Tantus Tobacco, LLC.

APPROVED AGENTS FOR: Commonwealth Land Title Insurance Company; Stewart Title Guaranty; Chicago Title Insurance Company.

NEWTON BECKER BOUWKAMP

3755 EAST 82ND STREET, SUITE 220
INDIANAPOLIS, INDIANA 46240
Telephone: 317-598-4529
Fax: 317-598-4530
Email: nbblaw@nbblaw.com
URL: http://www.nbblaw.com

General Practice. Business Law, Estate Planning, Family Law, Insurance Coverage Law, Litigation, Manufactured Housing and Recreational Vehicles Law, Mediation and Arbitration, Not-for-Profit Law and Real Estate Law.

MEMBERS OF THE FIRM

M. KENT NEWTON, born Indianapolis, Indiana, December 21, 1946; admitted to bar, 1973, Indiana; 1987, U.S. Supreme Court; 1984, District of Columbia. *Education:* Indiana University (B.S., 1968); Indiana University, School of Law (J.D., magna cum laude, 1973); Christian Theological Seminary (Master of Theological Studies, 2001). Registered Mediator and Arbitrator. *Member:* Indianapolis and Indiana State Bar Associations; Christian Legal Society. [Lt., U.S. Navy, 1968-1970]. ***PRACTICE AREAS:*** Litigation; Family Law; Trade Association Law; Business Law; Corporate Law. ***Email:*** knewton@nbblaw.com

CARL J. BECKER, born Red Bud, Illinois, June 11, 1966; admitted to bar, 1991, Indiana; 1997, North Carolina. *Education:* University of Illinois (B.S., with high honors, 1988; J.D., cum laude, 1991). *Member:* Indianapolis and Indiana State Bar Associations. ***PRACTICE AREAS:*** Family Law; Litigation; Consumer Finance; Financial Institutions Law; Commercial Law; Wills. ***Email:*** cbecker@nbblaw.com

ALAN A. BOUWKAMP, born Lafayette, Indiana, May 4, 1962; admitted to bar, 1991, Indiana and U.S. District Court, Northern and Southern Districts of Indiana. *Education:* Indiana University (B.A., 1984; J.D., cum laude, 1990). *Member:* Indianapolis and Indiana State Bar Associations; International Association of Arson Investigators. ***REPORTED CASES:*** Birch v. Midwest, 790 N.E.2d 504 (Ind. Ct. App. 2003); Krueger v. Hogan, 780 N.E.2d 1119 (Ind. Ct. App. 2003); Summers v. AutoOwners, 719 N.E.2d 4112 (Ind. Ct. App. 1999). ***PRACTICE AREAS:*** Litigation; Family Law; Business Law; Insurance Coverage. ***Email:*** abouwkamp@nbblaw.com

JUDITH VALE NEWTON, born Indianapolis, Indiana, December 31, 1946; admitted to bar, 1979, Indiana and U.S. District Court, Southern District of Indiana. *Education:* Indiana University (BS., magna cum laude, 1968); Indiana University, School of Law (J.D., cum laude, 1979); Ball State University (M.A., summa cum laude, 1970). Law Clerk to The Honorable Robert H. Staton, Indiana Court of Appeals, 1979-1981. Author: "Skirting the Issue: Historical Women Artists of Indiana", Indiana Historical Society, 2004; "Beyond Realism: The Life and Art of Frederik Grue", 1995; "A Grand Tradition: The Art and Artists of the Hoosier Salon, 1925-1990", 1993; "The Hoosier Group: Five American Painters", 1985; "You Be the Judge", 1979. Co-Producer, Video: "England, The Treasured Isle", 1997. Attorney, Sparrenberger & Newton, 1981-1982. Member: Indianapolis-Marion County Metropolitan Board of Zoning Appeals, 1984-1989; The Authors Guild, New York, N.Y.; Women in Communications, Inc. *Member:* Indianapolis Bar Association; Heartland Pro Bono Council; Lawyers for the Creative Arts. ***PRACTICE AREAS:*** Estate Planning; Fine Arts Law. ***Email:*** jnewton@nbblaw.com

ASSOCIATE

LANA L. LENNINGTON, born Muncie, Indiana, September 4, 1971; admitted to bar, 1998, Tennessee; 2004, Indiana. *Education:* Ball State University (B.A., cum laude, 1992); Valparaiso University (J.D., 1997). *Member:* Indiana State Bar Association. ***PRACTICE AREAS:*** Family Law; Estate Planning; Litigation. ***Email:*** llennington@nbblaw.com

NORRIS CHOPLIN & SCHROEDER, LLP

Established in 1980

NINTH FLOOR
101 WEST OHIO STREET
INDIANAPOLIS, INDIANA 46204-4213
Telephone: 317-269-9330
Fax: 317-269-9338
Email: ncs@ncs-law.com

Civil Litigation and Dispute Resolution.

FIRM PROFILE: The law firm of Norris Choplin & Schroeder, LLP resolves civil disputes by negotiation, mediation, arbitration, trial and appeals in cases involving personal injury, wrongful death, property damage, subrogation claims, contract or other disputes in the following areas: accident insurance, agriculture, asbestos, automobile, aviation, church, civil rights, class action, commercial, construction, contracts, elder, employment, environmental, ERISA, excess/umbrella insurance, FAA certificate actions, fire, governmental liability, health care, health insurance, homeowner's insurance, inland marine insurance, insurance, life insurance, medical licensing board, medical malpractice, mold, motor vehicle, negligence, occupational disease, personal liability insurance, personal lines insurance, premises liability, probate, products liability, professional liability (accounting, architect, dental, engineering, insurance, legal, medical), property casualty, railroad, silica, special education, toxic torts, trucking, and workers' compensation law. The firm is also pleased to offer adoption law, co-counsel and local counsel services.

MEMBERS OF FIRM

RICHARD L. NORRIS, born Fort Wayne, Indiana, June 5, 1945; admitted to bar, 1971, Indiana and U.S. District Court, Southern District of Indiana; 1984, U.S. Court of Appeals, Seventh Circuit; 1991, U.S. District Court, Northern District of Indiana and U.S. District Court, Eastern District of Michigan; 1992, U.S. District Court, Western District of Michigan; 1996, U.S. Court of Appeals, Sixth Circuit; 1997, U.S. District Court, Central District of Illinois. *Education:* Butler University (B.S., 1967); Indiana University School of Law (J.D., 1971). Co-Author: "Aviation and The Law," Published by Wilson, Tabor & Holland, 1975; "Aviation Litigation," Indiana Continuing Legal Education Forum, 1986; "Passenger Rights and Airline Travel," Indiana Continuing Legal Education Forum, 2001; "Indiana Rules of Professional Conduct: In An Agency Setting," Indiana Continuing Legal Education Forum, 2002; "Nuances of Aircraft Litigation," Indiana Continuing Legal Education Forum, 2003. Registered Civil Mediator, 1993. *Member:* Indianapolis and Indiana State Bar Associations; Indianapolis Law Club; Lawyer-Pilots Bar Association; National Transportation Safety Board Bar Association; American Board of Trial Advocates (Advocate). ***PRACTICE AREAS:*** Aviation Law; Workers' Compensation; Arbitration; Mediation; Subrogation; Insurance; Negligence. ***Email:*** rnorris@ncs-law.com

JOHN M. CHOPLIN, II, born Cedar Rapids, Iowa, November 10, 1945; admitted to bar, 1974, Indiana and U.S. District Court, Southern District of Indiana; 1976, U.S. Court of Appeals, Seventh Circuit; 1977, U.S. Supreme Court; 1983, U.S. Court of Appeals, Sixth Circuit; 1991, U.S. District Court, Northern District of Indiana. *Education:* Drake University (B.A., with honors, 1967); University of Michigan (J.D., 1974). Phi Beta Kappa; Omicron Delta Kappa. Co-Author: "Aviation and The Law," Wilson, Tabor & Holland, 1975; "Preparing for the Decade, Law Firm Management Strategies for the 90's," 1990. *Member:* Indianapolis, Indiana State and American Bar Associations; Bar Association of the Seventh Federal Circuit; Indianapolis Law Club; Lawyer-Pilots Bar Association. [Capt., U.S.A.F., 1969-1973]. ***PRACTICE AREAS:*** Appellate Practice; Aviation Law; Commercial Law; Construction Law; Insurance; Motor Vehicle Accidents and Injuries; Negligence; Premises Liability; Products Liability; Subrogation; Toxic Torts. ***Email:*** jchoplin@ncs-law.com

PETER A. SCHROEDER, born Detroit, Michigan, March 21, 1954; admitted to bar, 1980, Indiana and U.S. District Court, Southern District of Indiana; 1983, U.S. Court of Appeals, Sixth Circuit; 1984, U.S. Court of Appeals, Seventh Circuit; 1991, U.S. District Court, Northern District of Indiana. *Education:* Indiana University (B.A., 1976; M.P.A., 1980); Indiana University School of Law (J.D., cum laude, 1980). Law Clerk to the Hon. Eugene N. Chipman, Indiana Court of Appeals, Fourth District, 1980-1981. Registered Civil Mediator, 1993. *Member:* Indianapolis and Indiana State Bar Associations; Indianapolis Law Club. ***PRACTICE AREAS:*** Subrogation; Fire Loss; Mediation; Arbitration; Professional Liability; Premises Liability; Products Liability; Appellate Practice. ***Email:*** pschroeder@ncs-law.com

BRUCE L. KAMPLAIN, born Indianapolis, Indiana, December 13, 1950; admitted to bar, 1977, Indiana; 1978, U.S. District Court, Southern District of Indiana; 1979, U.S. Court of Appeals, 7th Circuit; 1985, U.S. Supreme Court; 1993, U.S. District Court, Northern District of Indiana. *Education:* Hanover College (B.A., 1973); Indiana University School of Law (J.D., 1977). Indiana Deputy Attorney General, 1978-1985. *Member:* Indianapolis, Indiana State and American Bar Associations; Indianapolis Law Club. ***PRACTICE AREAS:*** Environmental Law; Insurance Coverage; Appellate Practice; Asbestos Defense; Toxic Torts; Product Liability; Employment Discrimination; Trial Practice. ***Email:*** bkamplain@ncs-law.com

RAYMOND L. FAUST, born Noblesville, Indiana, December 19, 1950; admitted to bar, 1976, Indiana and U.S. District Court, Southern District of Indiana; 1979, U.S. Supreme Court; 1991, U.S. District Court, Eastern District of Michigan; 1993, U.S. District Court, Western District of Michigan and U.S. District Court, Northern District of Indiana; 1995, U.S. Court of Appeals, Sixth Circuit. *Education:* Indiana University (B.A., 1973); Indiana University School of Law (J.D., cum laude, 1976). Attorney for Noblesville, Indiana Housing Authority, 1979—. Registered Civil Mediator, 1995. *Member:* Indianapolis, Hamilton County, Indiana State and American Bar Associations; Indianapolis Law Club. ***PRACTICE AREAS:*** Personal Injury; Premises Liability; Products Liability; Professional Liability; Mediation. ***Email:*** rfaust@ncs-law.com

KYLE A. JONES, born Indianapolis, April 11, 1963; admitted to bar, 1988, Indiana, U.S. District Court, Northern and Southern Districts of Indiana; 1989, U.S. Court of Appeals, Seventh Circuit. *Education:* Indiana University (B.A., 1985); Indiana University School of Law (J.D., 1988). Delta Theta Phi (President, 1987-1988). Co-Author, "Mandatory Random Drug Testing in the United States Department of Transportation: A Fourth Amendment Analysis," Volume 17, Denver University Transportation Law Journal, 1988. *Member:* Indianapolis, Hamilton County, Indiana State and Federal Bar Associations; Indianapolis Law Club; Council of Parent Attorneys and Advocates. ***PRACTICE AREAS:*** Civil Litigation; Negligence; Products Liability; Subrogation; Insurance Coverage. ***Email:*** kjones@ncs-law.com

NELSON A. NETTLES, born Franklin, Indiana, August 9, 1967; admitted to bar, 1992, Indiana and U.S. District Court, Northern and Southern Districts of Indiana; 1996, U.S. Court of Appeals, Sixth and Seventh Circuits; 1997, U.S. District Court, Central District of Illinois; 1998, U.S. Supreme Court. *Education:* Indiana University (B.A., 1989; J.D., 1992). Law Clerk to: the Hon. J. Patrick Endsley, Magistrate Judge, U.S. District Court for the Southern District of Indiana, 1992-1993; the Hon. Larry J. McKinney, District Judge, U.S. District Court for the Southern District of Indiana, 1994. *Member:* Indianapolis, Indiana State, Federal and American Bar Associations. ***PRACTICE AREAS:*** Litigation; Appellate Practice. ***Email:*** nnettles@ncs-law.com

ASSOCIATES

MATTHEW WALTON MELTON, born Indianapolis, Indiana, November 6, 1973; admitted to bar, 2000, Indiana and U.S. District Court, Southern and Northern Districts of Indiana. *Education:* Purdue University (B.A., 1996); Indiana University School of Law (J.D., 2000). *Member:* Indianapolis and Indiana State Bar Associations. ***Email:*** mmelton@ncs-law.com

RALPH E. DOWLING, born St. Louis, Missouri, February 1, 1957; admitted to bar, 1994, Indiana and U.S. District Court, Southern and Northern Districts of Indiana; 1996, U.S. Court of Appeals, Seventh Circuit. *Education:* University of Northern Colorado (B.A., 1979; M.A., 1980); University of Denver (Ph.D., 1984); Indiana University (J.D., summa cum laude, 1993). Associate Editor, Indiana Law Review, 1992-1994. Also editor/referee, several book publishers and academic journals. Author: "The Morals of the Story: Narrativity & Legal Ethics," 27 Indiana Law Review 191 (1993); "Wrongful Death in Indiana," The Indiana Lawyer, (1998); "Major Victory for Victims of Negligent Police," Trial Lawyers of Counsel (1994). Author/Co-Author: several book chapters and articles in: Political

(This Listing Continued)

Communication & Persuasion, 1989, 1990; Communication Studies, 1990; Conflict Quarterly, 1989; Western Journal of Speech Communication, 1986; Journal of Communication, 1986; Communication Education, 1983; and Journal of the American Forensic Association, 1981. Instructor: University of Northern Colorado; University of Denver; Ball State University; University of Indiana. *Member:* Muncie, Indianapolis, Indiana State and American Bar Associations. ***PRACTICE AREAS:*** Personal Injury; Insurance; Negligence; Appellate Practice. ***Email:*** rdowling@ncs-law.com

JOSEPH P. MAGUIRE, born Indianapolis, Indiana, October 6, 1955; admitted to bar, 1983, Indiana and U.S. District Court, Southern and Northern Districts of Indiana. *Education:* Indiana University (B.S., 1977; J.D., 1983). Associate Editor, Indiana Law Review, 1982-1983. *Member:* Indianapolis and Indiana State Bar Associations. ***PRACTICE AREAS:*** Personal Injury; Insurance; Subrogation. ***Email:*** jmaguire@ncs-law.com

SCOTT A. HARKNESS, born Indianapolis, Indiana, February 2, 1967; admitted to bar, 1992, Indiana and U.S. District Court, Northern and Southern Districts of Indiana. *Education:* DePauw University (B.A., 1989); Indiana University School of Law (J.D., 1992). *Member:* Indianapolis, Indiana State and American Bar Associations. ***Email:*** sharkness@ncs-law.com

J. KIRK LEBLANC, born Alton, Illinois, December 15, 1975; admitted to bar, 2001, Indiana and U.S. District Court, Northern and Southern Districts of Indiana. *Education:* Cedarville University (B.A., 1998); Indiana University (J.D., 2001). *Member:* Indianapolis and Indiana State Bar Associations. ***Email:*** kleblanc@ncslaw.com

EDWIN S. NORRIS, born Wabash, Indiana, May 29, 1975; admitted to bar, 2000, Indiana and U.S. District Court, Southern District of Indiana. *Education:* Indiana University, Bloomington (B.S., 1996); Indiana University School of Law - Bloomington (J.D., 1999). *Member:* Indianapolis and Indiana State Bar Associations. ***PRACTICE AREAS:*** Insurance Defense. ***Email:*** enorris@ncs-law.com

OF COUNSEL

MARY JO WEDDING, born Beech Grove, Indiana, December 15, 1962; admitted to bar, 1988, Indiana and U.S. District Court, Southern and Northern Districts of Indiana. *Education:* DePauw University (B.A., 1985); Indiana University School of Law (J.D., 1988). Phi Alpha Delta. Co-Author, "Recent Developments in Indiana State and Federal Evidence Law," 24 Indiana Law Review 865, 1991. Registered Civil Mediator, 2000. *Member:* Indianapolis, Indiana State and American Bar Associations. ***PRACTICE AREAS:*** Litigation; Negligence; Premises Liability; Professional Liability; Appellate Practice; Workers' Compensation; Products Liability. ***Email:*** mwedding@ncs-law.com

JAMES D. MATTHEWS, born Indianapolis, Indiana, February 7, 1919; admitted to bar, 1951, Indiana and U.S. District Court, Southern District of Indiana. *Education:* St. Ambrose University (B.S., 1948); University of Notre Dame (LL.B., 1951). *Member:* Indianapolis, Indiana State and American Bar Associations. ***PRACTICE AREAS:*** Insurance.

REFERENCE: National Bank of Indianapolis.

OGLETREE, DEAKINS, NASH, SMOAK & STEWART, P.C.

SUITE 4600, 111 MONUMENT CIRCLE
INDIANAPOLIS, INDIANA 46204
Telephone: 317-916-1300
Facsimile: 317-916-9076
Email: clientservices@ogletreedeakins.com
URL: http://www.ogletreedeakins.com

Atlanta, Georgia Office: 600 Peachtree Street, N.E., Suite 2100. Telephone: 404-881-1300.
Austin, Texas Office: 301 Congress Avenue, Suite 1250. Telephone: 512-344-4700.
Birmingham, Alabama Office: One Federal Place, Suite 1000, 1819 Fifth Avenue North. Telephone: 205-328-1900.
Charleston, South Carolina Office: 134 Meeting Street, Suite 160, P.O. Box 1808. Telephone: 843-853-1300.
Charlotte, North Carolina Office: 400 West Trade Street. Telephone: 704-342-2588.
Chicago, Illinois Office: Twenty-Fifth Floor, Two First National Plaza, 20 South Clark Street. Telephone: 312-558-1220.
Columbia, South Carolina Office: 1320 Main Street, Suite 600. Telephone: 803-252-1300.
Dallas, Texas Office: 700 Preston Commons, 8117 Preston Road. Telephone: 214-987-3800.
Greensboro, North Carolina Office: 2725 Horse Pen Creek Road, Suite 101. Telephone: 336-375-9737.
Greenville, South Carolina Office: The Ogletree Building, 300 North Main Street, P.O. Box 2757. Telephone: 864-271-1300.
Houston, Texas Office: One Allen Center, 500 Dallas Street, Suite 3000. Telephone: 713-655-0855.
Kansas City, Missouri Office: 4717 Grand Avenue, Suite 300. Telephone: 816-471-1301.
Los Angeles, California Office: 633 West Fifth Street, Suite 5300. Telephone: 213-239-9800.
Miami, Florida Office: 80 S.W. 8th Street, Suite 1830. Telephone: 305-374-0506.
Morristown, New Jersey Office: 10 Madison Avenue, Suite 402. Telephone: 973-656-1600.
Nashville, Tennessee Office: SunTrust Center, Suite 800, 424 Church Street. Telephone: 615-254-1900.
Phoenix, Arizona Office: 2415 East Camelback Road, Suite 800. Telephone: 602-778-3700.
Raleigh, North Carolina Office: 2301 Sugar Bush Road, Suite 600, P.O. Box 31608. Telephone: 919-787-9700.
San Antonio, Texas Office: 2600 Weston Centre, 112 East Pecan Street. Telephone: 210-354-1300.
St. Thomas, U.S. Virgin Islands Office: The Tunick Building, 1336 Beltjen Road, Suite 202. Telephone: 340-714-1235.
Tampa, Florida Office: 100 North Tampa Street, Suite 3600. Telephone: 813-289-1247.

(This Listing Continued)

Washington, D.C. Office: Fifth Floor, 2400 N Street, N.W. Telephone: 202-887-0855.

Labor Relations, Employment Litigation, Workers' Compensation. Civil Litigation in all State and Federal Courts and Administrative Agencies.

KIM F. EBERT, born Minneapolis, Minnesota, August 7, 1950; admitted to bar, 1976, Indiana. *Education:* Wabash College (B.A., cum laude, 1972); Indiana University (J.D., cum laude, 1976). Contributing Writer, Labor Law, Indianapolis Business Journal, 1982—. Listed in: Best Lawyers in America; Chambers USA America's Leading Lawyers for Business. *Member:* Indianapolis (Chairman, Labor Law Section, 1988), Indiana State and American (Member, Sections on: Litigation; Labor and Employment Law; Tort and Insurance Practice; Chair, National Programs, 1994-1996; Chair, CLE Board, 1997-1999; Chair, Employer-Employee Relations Committee, 2001-2002; Member, Standing Committee of Continuing Education of the Bar, 1997-2000) Bar Associations. Fellow, College of Labor and Employment Lawyers. ***PRACTICE AREAS:*** Labor and Employment; Litigation; Class Actions. ***Email:*** kim.ebert@ogletreedeakins.com

MICHIHARU HOMMA, born Nakano, Tokyo, Japan, 1950; admitted to bar, 1996, Indiana. ***EDUCATION:*** Hitotsubashi University (B.A., 1973); University of Cincinnati (J.D., 1994). ***LANGUAGES:*** Japanese. ***PRACTICE AREAS:*** Labor and Employment; Immigration Law. ***Email:*** michiharu.homma@ogletreedeakins.com

CHARLES B. BALDWIN, born Michigan City, Indiana, February 23, 1958; admitted to bar, 1983, Indiana and Ohio. *Education:* Valparaiso University (B.S., 1980); University of Dayton School of Law (J.D., 1983). Co-author: "Model Jury Instructions - Employment Litigation," published by the American Bar Association. Author: "Indiana Guide to Preventing Workplace Harassment," published by the Indiana Chamber. Seventh Circuit Editor: "Employment & Labor Relations Litigation Newsletter," published by the American Bar Association. Selected as a leading labor and employment lawyer in Chambers USA America's Leading Lawyers for Business (2004 and 2005 editions). Chosen as an Indiana Super Lawyer by Indianapolis Monthly (2005). Appointed to the Board of Directors for the Indiana Chamber (2003). Board of Trustees Member, University of Dayton School of Law Alumni. *Member:* Indianapolis, Indiana State, Federal, Seventh Circuit and American Bar Associations; American Employment Law Council; Defense Research Institute; Indiana Chamber of Commerce; United States Chamber of Commerce. ***LANGUAGES:*** Spanish. ***PRACTICE AREAS:*** Labor and Employment; Employee Benefits Litigation; ERISA Class Action; Employment Discrimination; Covenants Not To Compete; Age Discrimination in Employment; Employment Class Action; Employment Disability Discrimination; Labor Arbitration; Federal Civil Litigation; Labor Strikes. ***Email:*** charles.baldwin@ogletreedeakins.com

TODD J. KAISER, born Bremen, Indiana, May 2, 1961; admitted to bar, 1986, Indiana; U.S. District Court, Northern and Southern Districts of Indiana; U.S. Court of Appeals, Seventh Circuit; U.S. Supreme Court. *Education:* DePauw University (B.A., 1983); Indiana University (J.D., 1986). Law Clerk, Hon. William I. Garrard, Indiana Court of Appeals, 1986-1987. *Member:* Indianapolis, Indiana State and American Bar Associations. ***PRACTICE AREAS:*** Class Actions; Complex Litigation; Labor and Employment. ***Email:*** todd.kaiser@ogletreedeakins.com

BRIAN L. McDERMOTT, born Dubuque, Iowa, August 11, 1966; admitted to bar, 1992, Indiana and U.S. District Court, Northern and Southern Districts of Indiana; 1995, U.S. Court of Appeals, Seventh Circuit; 1999, Iowa; 2004, U.S. District Court, Northern District of Iowa and U.S. District Court, Northern District of Ohio. *Education:* Loras College (B.A., magna cum laude, 1988); University of Iowa (J.D., with distinction, 1991). Note and Comment Editor, Iowa Law Review, 1990-1991. Author: Indiana Employers' Guide to the ADA and FMLA, First Edition (2001) and Second Edition (2003); "The Constitutionality of Canon 7(B)(1)(c) of the Code of Judicial Conduct: Free Speech Rights of Judges," 25 Creighton Law Review 855 (1992); Note, "Defending the Defenseless: Murray v. Giarratano and the Right to Counsel in Capital Proceedings," 75 Iowa Law Review 1305 (1990); Chapter, How Arbitration Works, Alan Mills Ruben et al. eds., BNA Books (6th Edition 2001). Law Clerk, Honorable Donald J. Porter, U.S. District Court, District of South Dakota, 1991-1992. Member, Human Resources and Labor Committees, Indiana Chamber of Commerce. *Member:* Indianapolis (Chair, Labor and Employment Council, 2005), Indiana State (Chair, Labor and Employment Section, 2004) and American (Vice Chair, Civil Procedure and Evidence Committee, Tort and Insurance Practice Section, 2002—) Bar Associations; Human Resource Association of Central Indiana. ***PRACTICE AREAS:*** Employment Litigation; Management Labor Law; ERISA Litigation; Civil Rights Defense Law; Labor and Employment; Employee Benefits Litigation; Class Action Defense; Employment Discrimination; Covenants Not to Compete; Age Discrimination in Employment; Employment Arbitration; Employment Disability Discrimination; Labor Arbitration; Litigation of Restrictive Covenants; Labor Strikes; Wage and Hour Law. ***Email:*** brian.mcdermott@ogletreedeakins.com

KENNETH B. SIEPMAN, born Linton, Indiana, October 5, 1964; admitted to bar, 1990, Indiana; 1993, U.S. Court of Appeals, Seventh Circuit. *Education:* Wabash College (A.B., cum laude, 1987); Vanderbilt University (J.D., 1990). *Member:* Indianapolis, Indiana State and American (Member, Labor Law Section) Bar Associations. ***PRACTICE AREAS:*** Employment Law; Litigation; Management Labor Law; Wage and Hour Law; Public Sector Employment Law; Civil Rights Defense; OSHA. ***Email:*** kenneth.siepman@ogletreedeakins.com

MICHAEL A. MOFFATT, admitted to bar, 1989, Indiana; U.S. District Court, Northern and Southern Districts of Indiana; U.S. Court of Appeals, Seventh Circuit; U.S. Supreme Court. *Education:* DePauw University (B.A., 1986); Indiana University (J.D., 1989). Listed in: Who's Who in American Law; Who's Who in America; Who's Who in the World; National Registry of Who's Who. President, Fall Creek Little League. Past President, Indianapolis Exchange. *Member:* Indianapolis (Executive Council Member, Labor and Employment Section; Treasurer, 1999; Vice-Chair, 2000; Chairman, 2001), Indiana State (Executive Council Member) and American Bar Associations. ***PRACTICE AREAS:*** Labor and Employment; Employment Litigation; Class Actions; Litigation; Worker's Compensation. ***Email:*** michael.moffatt@ogletreedeakins.com

JAN MICHELSEN, born Chicago, Illinois; admitted to bar, 1994, Indiana. *Education:* Bradley University (B.S., summa cum laude, 1977); Kelley School of Business at Indiana University (M.B.A., 1987); Indiana University (J.D., summa cum laude, 1994). Editor in Chief, Indiana Law Review, Volume 27. Recipient, IU School of Law Faculty Award for

(This Listing Continued)

OGLETREE, DEAKINS, NASH, SMOAK & STEWART, P.C., Indianapolis—Continued

Scholarship, Leadership and Service, 1994. Pegasus Scholar (legal fellowship in United Kingdom, 1997). Contributing/Assistant Editor, "The Developing Labor Law," Section of Labor and Employment Law, American Bar Association, 1994-2001. *Member:* Indianapolis, Indiana State and American Bar Associations (Sections on: Labor and Employment Law; Litigation); Indianapolis Inn of Court, 1994-2000, Sagamore Inn of Court, 2001—; Trustee, American Inns of Court Foundation, 1997—. ***PRACTICE AREAS:*** Labor and Employment; Litigation; Employment Discrimination; Wage and Hour Law; Personnel Policies and Training; Workplace Violence; Employee Privacy. ***Email:*** jan.michelsen@ogletreedeakins.com

---

KRISTIN B. KELTNER, born St. Louis, Missouri, November 10, 1970; admitted to bar, 1998, Indiana. *Education:* Valparaiso University (B.A., summa cum laude, 1993); Indiana University (J.D., magna cum laude, 1998) Order of the Coif. Clerk, United States Court of Appeals for the Seventh Circuit, 2003-2004. *Member:* Indianapolis Bar Association. ***PRACTICE AREAS:*** Labor and Employment; Employment Discrimination; Harassment; Administrative Law; Litigation. ***Email:*** kristin.keltner@ogletreedeakins.com

BRANDON M. SHELTON, admitted to bar, 1998, Indiana; U.S. District Court, Southern and Northern Districts of Indiana and U.S. District Court, Western District of Arkansas. *Education:* Southern Illinois University (B.S., 1995); University of Illinois College of Law (J.D., 1998). *Member:* Indiana State, National and American Bar Associations. ***PRACTICE AREAS:*** Labor and Employment. ***Email:*** brandon.shelton@ogletreedeakins.com

MATTHEW S. EFFLAND, born Peoria, Illinois; admitted to bar, 1999, Indiana; 2000, Florida and U.S. Court of Appeals, Seventh and Eleventh Circuits; 2003, U.S. District Court, Eastern District of Michigan. *Education:* Cornell College (B.S.S., 1995); Texas Tech School of Law (J.D., cum laude, 1999). *Member:* The Florida Bar (Member, Sections on: Labor & Employment; Litigation); Indianapolis, Indiana State and American (Member, Sections on: Labor & Employment; Litigation) Bar Associations. ***PRACTICE AREAS:*** Labor and Employment Litigation; Commercial Litigation. ***Email:*** matthew.effland@ogletreedeakins.com

BONNIE L. MARTIN, born Silver Spring, Maryland; admitted to bar, 1997, Indiana and U.S. District Court, Southern and Northern Districts of Indiana. *Education:* Anderson University (B.A., summa cum laude, 1994); Wake Forest University (J.D., cum laude, 1997). Order of the Coif. Member: Moot Court Board; Association of Trial Lawyers of America Trial Team. Articles Editor, Wake Forest Law Review, 1996-1997. *Member:* Indiana State and American Bar Associations. ***PRACTICE AREAS:*** Employment Law; Litigation. ***Email:*** bonnie.martin@ogletreedeakins.com

CRAIG W. WILEY, born Beech Grove, Indiana; admitted to bar, 1998, Indiana, U.S. District Court, Northern and Southern Districts of Indiana; 2003, U.S. Court of Appeals, Sixth and Seventh Circuits. *Education:* Indiana University (B.S., 1995; J.D., 1998). Law clerk, United States Magistrate Judge Tim A. Baker, Southern District of Indiana, 2001-2003. Monthly columnist, Indiana Lawyer. Adjunct Instructor, Indiana University Purdue University - Indianapolis. *Member:* Indianapolis (Chair, Labor and Employment Law Section and Member, Board of Managers), Indiana (Treasurer, Employment and Labor Law Section) and Federal (Treasurer, Indianapolis Chapter) Bar Associations. ***PRACTICE AREAS:*** Employment Litigation; Commercial Litigation; Covenants Not To Compete. ***Email:*** craig.wiley@ogletreedeakins.com

DANE A. MIZE, born Indianapolis, Indiana; admitted to bar, 2001, Indiana; U.S. District Court, Southern and Northern Districts of Indiana. *Education:* Purdue University (B.A., 1998); Indiana University (J.D., cum laude, 2001). *Member:* Indiana State and American Bar Associations. ***PRACTICE AREAS:*** Labor and Employment; Litigation. ***Email:*** dane.mize@ogletreedeakins.com

ROBERT F. SEIDLER, admitted to bar, 2001, Ohio and U.S. District Court, Southern District of Ohio (Not admitted in Indiana). *Education:* Butler University (B.A., 1998); University of Notre Dame (J.D., 2001). Member and Coach, International Moot Court. *Member:* Ohio State and American Bar Associations. ***PRACTICE AREAS:*** Labor and Employment. ***Email:*** rob.seidler@ogletreedeakins.com

TANYA R. HATFIELD BELL, admitted to bar, 2000, Indiana and U.S. District Court, Southern and Northern Districts of Indiana. *Education:* Indiana State University (B.A., 1997); Indiana University School of Law - Indianapolis (J.D., cum laude, 2000). Article Development Editor, Indiana International & Comparative Law Review. *Member:* Indiana State Bar Association; Defense Trial Counsel of Indiana. ***PRACTICE AREAS:*** Employment Litigation; Business Litigation. ***Email:*** tanya.bell@ogletreedeakins.com

OF COUNSEL

STEVEN V. SHOUP, born Portland, Indiana, May 30, 1946; admitted to bar, 1974, Indiana and U.S. District Court, Southern District of Indiana; 1983, U.S. Court of Appeals, Seventh Circuit; 1995, U.S. District Court, Northern District of Indiana. *Education:* Indiana University (B.S., 1968; J.D., cum laude, 1974). *Member:* Indianapolis, Indiana State and American Bar Associations. ***PRACTICE AREAS:*** Labor and Employment Law; Collective Bargaining. ***Email:*** steven.shoup@ogletreedeakins.com

CANDACE S. WALKER, born New Castle, Indiana; admitted to bar, 1981, Indiana. *Education:* Ohio Wesleyan University (B.A., magna cum laude, 1974); Indiana University School of Law (J. D., magna cum laude, 1981). Phi Beta Kappa. *Member:* Indiana Bar Association; Indianapolis Bar Association; Chair-Labor Law Section, 1999. ***PRACTICE AREAS:*** Labor and Employment (95%); Municipal Law. ***Email:*** candace.walker@ogletreedeakins.com

JAN J. KINZIE, born Wabash, Indiana; admitted to bar, 1985, Indiana and U.S. District Court, Southern and Northern Districts of Indiana. *Education:* DePauw University (B.A., 1981); Indiana University (J.D., 1985). Assistant Corporation Counsel, Consolidated City of Indianapolis and Marion County, 1985-1988. *Member:* Indianapolis, Indiana State and American (Member, Sections on: Labor and Employment Law; Litigation) Bar Associations. ***Email:*** jan.kinzie@ogletreedeakins.com

(This Listing Continued)

KATY H.H. YANG-PAGE, born Taipei, Taiwan; admitted to bar, 1995, California; 1997, Hawaii; 2004, Indiana. *Education:* Northwestern University (B.A., 1990); New York University School of Law (J.D., 1994). Phi Beta Kappa (Northwestern). Adjunct Professor, Concord Law School, 2004—. Member, Asian Law Society, 1991-1994. ***LANGUAGES:*** Mandarin Chinese. ***PRACTICE AREAS:*** Employment Law; Employment Litigation; Immigration Law; Constitutional Law.

REPRESENTATIVE CLIENTS: BAA Indianapolis, LLC; BMG/Columbia House; CVS Pharmacy, Inc.; Cingular Wireless; Clarian Health Partners; ConAgra Foods, Inc.; Dalton Corporation; Home Depot; International Truck and Engine Corporation; Kraft Foods, Inc.; The Kroger Co.; Liquid Transport Corp.; Meijer, Inc.; Miller Pipeline Corporation; National Wine and Spirits, Inc.; SBC Communications; Sarkes Tarzian, Inc.; Subaru-Isuzu Automotive, Inc.; Sysco Corporation; Toyota Industrial Equipment Mfg., Inc.; Tractor Supply Company; Tyco; U.S. Foodservice.

O'KOON HINTERMEISTER, PLLC

101 WEST OHIO STREET, SUITE 1401
INDIANAPOLIS, INDIANA 46204
Telephone: 317-951-1401
Fax: 317-951-8470
URL: http://www.okoonlaw.com

Louisville, Kentucky Office: PNC Plaza, Suite 1100, 500 West Jefferson, 40202. Telephone: 502-581-1630. Fax: 502-581-1821.

General Civil Practice, Litigation, Personal Injury, Medical Malpractice, Automobile Negligence, Wrongful Death, Commercial Litigation, Employment Law, Bankruptcy, Corporations, Business, Limited Liability Companies, Family Law.

MARVIN R. O'KOON, born Louisville, Kentucky, June 15, 1945; admitted to bar, 1972, Kentucky and U.S. District Court, Western District of Kentucky; 1979, U.S. Supreme Court (Not admitted in Indiana). *Education:* University of Louisville (B.S.C., 1969; J.D., 1972). Member, Journal of Family Law, 1971-1972. *Member:* Louisville and Kentucky Bar Associations. (Resident, Louisville, Kentucky Office). ***PRACTICE AREAS:*** Litigation; Corporate Law; Limited Liability Company Law. ***Email:*** mokoon@okoonlaw.com

JEFFREY P. HINTERMEISTER, born Gary, Indiana, February 26, 1957; admitted to bar, 1985, Louisiana and Texas; 1987, Oklahoma; 1998, Kentucky; 1999, Indiana. *Education:* Louisiana State University (B.S., 1979; J.D., 1984); Emory University (LL.M., 1991). Teaching Seminars: Informal Means of Discovery in a Medical Device Case, Association of Trial Lawyers of America Annual Convention, July 1997; Winning Discovery Wars, Association of Trial Lawyers of America Seminar, January 1994. *Member:* Indiana State, Kentucky, Oklahoma, and Louisiana State Bar Associations; State Bar of Texas; The Association of Trial Lawyers of America. ***REPORTED CASES:*** Feldt v. Mentor Corp., 61 F.3d 431 (5th Cir 1995); Bingham v. Mentor Corp., 89 F.3d 203 (5th Cir. 1996). ***PRACTICE AREAS:*** Litigation. ***Email:*** jhintermeister@okoon.com

Benji J. Algase	***H. Andrew Sonneborn***
P. Lynn Bibbs	***Adina A. Teska***
Jane E. Griffin	***Julia R. Wilder***
Douglas E. Hiland	***Mark K. Zunk***
Lisa Maxwell-Frieden	***Katherine D. Zuran***
Dennis V. Panarisi	***Vicki J. Merriman***

(For information on additional personnel, see Professional Biographies at Louisville, Kentucky)

OSBORN HINER & LISHER, P.C.

Established in 1974

8500 KEYSTONE CROSSING, SUITE 480
INDIANAPOLIS, INDIANA 46240-2456
Telephone: 317-257-2400
Fax: 317-722-4840
URL: http://www.lawyers.com/ohllaw

General Civil Trial Litigation. Personal Injury, Insurance Defense Law, Probate and Estate, Wills and Trusts Planning, Workers Compensation, Products Liability. Appellate Law, Arson and Fraud.

FIRM PROFILE: Osborn, Hiner and Lisher was founded in 1974 by William M. Osborn and John R. Hiner, former partners in a large Indianapolis firm specializing in litigation. The firm has a general practice defending damage suits throughout the state. It specializes in the defense of personal injury suits, including products liability, automobile, premises liability, and insurance law. It defends several casualty insurance companies and several self-insured manufacturers.

JOHN R. HINER (1920-1986)

JOHN L. LISHER, born Indianapolis, Indiana, 1950; admitted to bar, 1975, Indiana. *Education:* Indiana University (A.B., with high honors, 1972; J.D., 1975). Phi Beta Kappa. *Member:* Indianapolis, Indiana State and American Bar Associations; Indiana Trial Lawyers Association; Indiana Defense Lawyers Association; Defense Research Institute. ***PRACTICE AREAS:*** Personal Injury Law; Insurance Defense; Products Liability. ***Email:*** jlisher@ohllaw.com

OF COUNSEL

WILLIAM M. OSBORN, born Indianapolis, Indiana, 1928; admitted to bar, 1952, Indiana; 1960, U.S. Supreme Court. *Education:* Butler University (B.S., cum laude, 1949); University of Michigan (J.D., 1952). Delta Theta Phi. Chairman, Indiana Continuing Legal Education Seminar on Products Liability Law, 1983. *Member:* Indianapolis, Indiana State (Chairman, Legal Ethics Committee, 1978-1981) and American Bar Associations. ***PRACTICE AREAS:*** Personal Injury Defense; Products Liability.

(This Listing Continued)

EDWARD A. STRAITH-MILLER, born Chicago, Illinois, 1910; admitted to bar, 1937, Indiana. *Education:* DePauw University (A.B., 1933); Indiana University (LL.B., 1937). Phi Delta Phi. *Member:* Indianapolis, Indiana State and American Bar Associations.

ROBERT S. O'DELL, born Indianapolis, Indiana, June 5, 1962; admitted to bar, 1987, Indiana and U.S. District Court, Northern and Southern Districts of Indiana; U.S. Court of Appeals, Third Circuit. *Education:* Wabash College (A.B., cum laude, 1984); Indiana University (J.D., cum laude, 1987). Delta Theta Phi. Member, Indiana University Trial Advocacy Team, 1987. Speaker, Indiana Bar Association, ICLER Seminar on Fire Litigation. *Member:* Indianapolis, Indiana State and American (Member, Tort and Insurance Practice Law Section) Bar Associations; The Association of Trial Lawyers of America; Indiana Defense Lawyers Association; Indiana Arson & Crime Association; International Association of Arson Investigators; Defense Research Institute. ***PRACTICE AREAS:*** Civil Litigation; Insurance Defense; Products Liability; Arson and Insurance Fraud; Tort Law. ***Email:*** rodell@ohllaw.com

JOHN K. ATKINSON, born Syracuse, New York, April 4, 1972; admitted to bar, 2002, Indiana. *Education:* Hanover College (B.A.B.A., 1995); Indiana University School of Law - Indianapolis (J.D., 2002). ***PRACTICE AREAS:*** Insurance; Subrogation. ***Email:*** jatkinson@ohllaw.com

RHONDA HANNA VEEN, admitted to bar, 1996, Indiana. *Education:* Oakland City University (B.S., Business Education, 1991); Indiana University School of Law - Bloomington (J.D., 1996). Prosecuting Attorney, Marion County, St. Joseph County and La Porte County, Indiana. ***PRACTICE AREAS:*** Insurance; Subrogation. ***Email:*** rveen@ohllaw.com

REPRESENTATIVE CLIENTS: Admiral-Merchants Motors Freight, Inc.; Alamo Rent-A-Car, Inc.; American Family Insurance Group; Amerisure; Buckeye Insurance Co.; Budget-Rent-A-Car; Centra Credit Union; CNA Insurance Cos.; The Continental Insurance Cos.; Continental Loss Adjusting Services; Countrywide Services Corp.; The Dow Chemical Co., Inc.; Federated Mutual Insurance Companies; Fireman's Fund Insurance Cos.; Frankenmuth Insurance Co.; Gulf Insurance Group; Hercules, Inc.; Hills Stores Co.; Indiana Residual Malpractice Insurance Authority; Insurancenter; Jack Cole-Dixie Highway Co.; Mattox & Moore, Inc.; The Mayflower Insurance Co.; The Medical Protective Co.; Medusa Corp.; Montana Sulphur & Chemical Co.; Motorist's Mutual Insurance Co.; Northrop Corp.; Porsche AG; Roper Corp.; The Royal Insurance Cos.; Rutland Fire Clay Inc.; Sequa; State Farm Fire & Casualty Co.; Stewart-Decatur Security Systems, Inc.; Transamerica Insurance Group; Traveler's Indemnity Co.; Vesta Insurance Group; Volkswagen of America, Inc.; Volvo North America Corporation; White Consolidated Industries, CNA; Zurich American Insurance Co.

JON R. PACTOR

Established in 1976

SUITE 2410, ONE INDIANA SQUARE
INDIANAPOLIS, INDIANA 46204
Telephone: 317-636-0686
Fax: 317-636-8094
Email: pactorlaw@iquest.net
URL: http://www.lawyers.com/pactorlaw

Legal Malpractice, Libel and Slander, General Practice.

JON R. PACTOR, born 1948; admitted to bar, 1976, Indiana, U.S. District Court, Southern District of Indiana and U.S. Court of Appeals, Seventh Circuit. *Education:* Wabash College (A.B., cum laude, 1971); Indiana University (J.D., 1976). Phi Beta Kappa. *Member:* Indianapolis, Indiana State (Member, Ethics Committee) and American Bar Associations; Indianapolis Law Club.

PADGETT LAW

Established in 2004

9000 KEYSTONE CROSSING, SUITE 230
INDIANAPOLIS, INDIANA 46240-2148
Telephone: 317-218-0316
Fax: 317-580-4960
Email: GP@IndianaEstateLaw.com
URL: http://www.IndianaEstateLaw.com

Will Contests, Trust Contests, Estate Litigation, Trust Litigation, Contested Wills, Contested Trusts, Probate Disputes, Probate Administration, Probate Litigation, Inheritance, Estate Claims, Estate Administration, Fiduciary Litigation, Contested Guardianships, Trial Practice, Complex Litigation.

FIRM PROFILE: Padgett Law is dedicated exclusively to providing the highest level of service and expertise in the field of estate and trust litigation.

GREGORY L. PADGETT, born Greenfield, Indiana, 1959; admitted to bar, 1984, Illinois; 1988, Indiana. *Education:* DePauw University (B.A., summa cum laude, 1981); Northwestern University (J.D., 1984). Phi Beta Kappa. Listed: Who's Who in American Law, 1994-2004; Outstanding Lawyers of America, 2003-2004. Co-Chair, Will Contests, ICLEF, 1996. *Member:* Indianapolis and Indiana State Bar Associations. ***REPORTED CASES:*** Hilligoss v. Associated Cos., 589 N.E.2d 1202; Allensworth v. GM, 945 F.2d 174; Rios v. Lane, 812 F.2d 1032. ***PRACTICE AREAS:*** Estate Litigation; Trust Litigation; Contested Wills; Contested Trusts and Estates; Estate Claims; Probate Disputes; Wills; Probate; Breach of Fiduciary Duty.

PARR RICHEY OBREMSKEY & MORTON

Established in 1899

201 N. ILLINOIS STREET, SUITE 300
INDIANAPOLIS, INDIANA 46204
Telephone: 317-269-2500
FAX: 317-269-2514
Email: indianapolis@parrlaw.com
URL: http://www.parrlaw.com

Lebanon, Indiana Office: Parr Building. 225 West Main Street. P.O. Box 668. Telephone: 765-482-0110; 317-269-2509. FAX: 765-483-3444.

Personal Injury, Products Liability, Insurance Defense, Business Litigation, Alternative Dispute Resolution, Appellate Practice, School, Business Transactions, Real Estate, Zoning, Utility Regulation and Finance, Estate Planning, Trusts and Estates, Wills and Probate.

PARTNERS OF FIRM

DAVID S. RICHEY, born 1932; admitted to bar, 1960, Indiana. *Education:* Butler University (B.S., 1954); Indiana University (J.D., 1960). Certified Mediator. Distinguished Alumni Service Award, Indiana University School of Law, Indianapolis, 1997. ***Email:*** drichey@parrlaw.com

PETER L. OBREMSKEY, born 1936; admitted to bar, 1961, Indiana. *Education:* Indiana University (B.S., 1958; J.D., 1961). Trustee, Indiana University (1998-2004). Fellow: American College of Trial Lawyers; International Society of Barristers. ***Email:*** pobremskey@parrlaw.com

DON F. MORTON, born 1939; admitted to bar, 1966, Indiana. *Education:* Kansas State University (B.S., 1962); Indiana University (J.D., 1966). General Counsel, Wabash Valley Power Association. ***Email:*** donm@wvpa.com

KENT M. FRANDSEN, born 1950; admitted to bar, 1975, Indiana. *Education:* Indiana University (B.S., 1972; J.D., 1975). Certified Mediator. Law Clerk to Hon. James E. Noland, U.S. District Court, Southern District of Indiana. ***Email:*** kfrandsen@parrlaw.com

CHARLES W. RITZ, III, born 1949; admitted to bar, 1974, Indiana. *Education:* Butler University (B.A., 1971); Indiana University (J.D., 1974). ***Email:*** critz@parrlaw.com

PAUL S. KRUSE, born 1955; admitted to bar, 1981, Indiana. *Education:* Indiana University (B.A., 1977; J.D., 1981). ***Email:*** pkruse@parrlaw.com

CAROL SPARKS DRAKE, born 1953; admitted to bar, 1978, Indiana. *Education:* Indiana University (B.A., 1975; J.D., 1978). Law Clerk, Indiana Court of Appeals. Administrative Law Judge, Indiana Utility Regulatory Commission. ***Email:*** cdrake@parrlaw.com

LARRY J. WALLACE, born 1937; admitted to bar, 1963, Indiana. *Education:* Indiana University (B.A., 1960; LL.B., 1962). Certified Mediator, Chairman, Indiana Utility Regulatory Commission. Founding Chairman, Utility Law Section, Indiana State Bar Association. ***Email:*** lwallace@parrlaw.com

JAMES A. L. BUDDENBAUM, born 1960; admitted to bar, 1989, Indiana. *Education:* Indiana University (B.A., 1983; J.D., 1989). ***Email:*** jbuddenbaum@parrlaw.com

ANTHONY W. PATTERSON, born 1967; admitted to bar, 1993, Indiana. *Education:* Southern Methodist University (B.A., 1990); Indiana University (J.D., 1993). ***Email:*** tpatterson@parrlaw.com

RANDOLPH G. HOLT, born 1957; admitted to bar, 1998, Indiana. *Education:* Ball State University (B.S., 1979); Indiana University (J.D., 1998). ***Email:*** rholt@parrlaw.com

ASSOCIATES

TAMIE JO MOROG, born 1958; admitted to bar, 1995, New York; 1999, Indiana. *Education:* Ball State University (B.S., 1980); State University of New York at Buffalo (J.D., 1994). Certified Mediator. Recipient, Judge William J. Regan Award. ***Email:*** tmorog@parrlaw.com

MONICA S. DOERR, born 1976; admitted to bar, 2003, Indiana. *Education:* Purdue University (B.S., Pharmacy, 1999); Indiana University (J.D., 2003). ***Email:*** mdoerr@parrlaw.com

RANDALL D. ROGERS, JR., born 1972; admitted to bar, 2000, Indiana. *Education:* Denison University (B.A., 1995); Indiana University (J.D., 1999). ***Email:*** rrogers@parrlaw.com

---

PASTORE & GOODEN P.C.

302 NORTH ALABAMA STREET
P.O. BOX 44947
INDIANAPOLIS, INDIANA 46244-0947
Telephone: 317-638-3333
Fax: 317-687-9707

Construction Law and Litigation, Business Law, Lawsuits, Contracts Law; Business Disputes, Business Enterprises, Partnerships, Limited Liability Companies, Corporate Law and General Civil Litigation.

FIRM PROFILE: The law firm of Pastore & Gooden, P.C. represents owners, design professionals, surveyors, construction managers, general contractors, subcontractors, material suppliers and manufacturers in all phases of the construction process, including contract negotiation, business advice and dispute resolution.

THOMAS A. PASTORE, born Bluffton, Indiana, December 7, 1964; admitted to bar, 1990, Indiana and U.S. District Court, Northern and Southern Districts of Indiana. *Education:* Purdue University (B.S., 1987); Indiana University School of Law (J.D., 1990). Co-Author: "Mechanic's Liens and Related Problems," ICLEF, 1990; "Mechanic's Lien Law and Strategy in Indiana," 1993; "Public Works Construction Contract Law," ABA, 1997; "Construction Contracting For Public Entities in Indiana," (Public Works Projects, Bidding

(This Listing Continued)

PASTORE & GOODEN P.C., Indianapolis—Continued

and Bid Protests in Indiana), Lorman Education Services, March 1999 and 2000. *Member:* Indianapolis, Indiana State and American (Member, Forum on Construction Industry) Bar Associations. ***LANGUAGES:*** English. ***REPORTED CASES:*** Merillville Conservancy Dist. v. Atlas Excavating, Inc., 712 N.E.2d 1114 (Ind. Ct. App. 1999), trans. denied, 726 N.E.2d 312 (Ind. 1999); Bigley v. MSD of Wayne Township Schools, 823 N.E.2d 278 (Ind. Ct. App. 2004), trans. denied; Amerisure, Inc. v. Wurster Const. Co., Inc., 818 N.E.2d 998 (Ind. Ct. App. 2004), decision clarified on reh'g, 822 N.E.2d 1115 (Ind. Ct. App. 2005); Brownsburg Community School Corp. v. Natare Corporation, 824 N.E.2d 336, 2005-1 Trade Cases P 74, 732 (Ind. 2005), reh'g denied. ***PRACTICE AREAS:*** Construction Litigation; Arbitration; Construction Contracts; Mechanics Liens Law. ***Email:*** tpastore@pastoregooden.com

WILLIAM W. GOODEN, born Muncie, Indiana, November 28, 1968; admitted to bar, 1996, Indiana and U.S. District Court, Northern and Southern Districts of Indiana. *Education:* Ball State University (B.S., 1992); Indiana University School of Law (J.D., 1996). Co-Author: "Tax Implications of Dissolution of Marriage," and "Marital Torts," ICLEF, December 1996; "Planning a Wrongful Death Case," National Business Institute, 1997; "Construction Payment Remedies," National Business Institute, 1999; "Construction Contracting for Public Entities in Indiana," Lorman Education Services, 1999 and 2000; "Indiana Residential Construction Law," ICLEF, May 2005; "Construction Defect and Mold," July 2003. Periodic Author, Articles on Legal Issues, Builder's Association of Greater Indianapolis Sites Magazine. Certified Civil Mediator. *Member:* Indianapolis, Indiana State and American (Member, Forum on the Construction Industry) Bar Associations; Builder's Association of Greater Indianapolis; Sagamore American Inn of Court. ***LANGUAGES:*** English. ***REPORTED CASES:*** Greg Allen Const. Co., Inc. v. Estelle 798 N. E. 22 171, Ind. LEXIS 923, 2003. ***PRACTICE AREAS:*** Construction Law; Litigation; Surety Law; Insurance Law; Insurance Litigation; Public Contract Law; Civil Litigation; Business Litigation; Personal Injury; Family Law; Divorce; Child Custody; Child Support; Adoption Law. ***Email:*** wgooden@pastoregooden.com

TROY MICHAEL MILLER, born Elkhart, Indiana, October 30, 1971; admitted to bar, 1999, Indiana and U.S. District Court, Northern and Southern Districts of Indiana. *Education:* Ball State University College of Architecture and Planning (B. Architecture, 1995; B.S. Environmental Design, 1995; M. Architecture, 1998); University of Dayton School of Law (J.D., 1999). Co-Author: "Indiana Public Works Statutes," Lorman, March 1999 and 2000; "Construction Contracting For Public Entities in Indiana," (Public Works Projects, Bidding and Bid Protests in Indiana), Lorman Education Services, March 1999 and 2000. *Member:* Indianapolis, Indiana State (Founding Member, Construction and Surety Law Section, Counsel Member,; Co-Chairman, Seminar and Education Committee) and American (Member, Forum on the Construction Industry) Bar Associations; American Institute of Architects; Builder's Association of Greater Indianapolis. ***LANGUAGES:*** English. ***REPORTED CASES:*** Amerisure Inc., v. Wurster Construction, Co., Inc. 818 N.E.2d 998 (Ind. Ct. App. 2004); Brownsburg Community School Corp. v. Nature Corporation, 824 ME. 2d 336 (Ind 2005); Bigley v. MSD of Wayne Township Schools 823 N.E 2d. 278 (Ind Ct. App 2005); Mark e. Savovee and Karen S. Savovee v. Industrial Contracting and Erecting, Inc. 789 ME2d 1013 (Ind Ct. App 2003). ***PRACTICE AREAS:*** Construction Contracts; Litigation; Public Contract Law; Mechanics Liens Law. ***Email:*** tmiller@pastoregooden.com

REPRESENTATIVE CLIENTS: Atlas Excavating, Inc.; Boles Custom Homes, Ltd.; Centimark Corporation; CFJ Properties, Inc.; Chance Bros. Marble & Tile, Inc.; Civil Designs, LLP.; Civil & Environmental Consultants, Inc.; Craftsman Builders, Inc.; Crider & Crider, Inc.; Design Organization, Inc.; Dry Wall Constructions, Inc.; E & B Paving, Inc.; Flying J. Inc.; Gradison Building Corp.; HES, Inc.; J.R. Lazaro Builders; Kyler Brothers Services, Inc.; Lebammon Concert Service; Mid-State Surety Corporation; PDG, Inc.; Paul H. Schwendener, Inc.; Paul I. Cripe, Inc.; Peterson Architure, P.C.; Recast Construction Company, Inc.; R.E. Geasome, Inc.; Suburban Glass Services, Inc.; US Automatic Sprinklers Corp.; Vester Associates, Inc.; Woolpert LLP; Wurster Construction Co., Inc.

GEORGE W. PENDYGRAFT, P.C.

BUILDING 1
6770 SPIRIT LAKE, SUITE 201
INDIANAPOLIS, INDIANA 46220
Telephone: 317-590-3398
Fax: 317-254-0448
Email: EcoLawyer@aol.com
URL: http://www.lawyers.com/ecolaw

National and International Environmental Matters, Toxic Tort Disputes, Environmental Insurance Coverage, Environmental Due Diligence, Utilities Regulations, and Patent, Trademark, and Copyright.

GEORGE W. PENDYGRAFT, born November 3, 1946; admitted to bar, 1976, Indiana and New York; registered to practice before U.S. Patent and Trademark Office. *Education:* Franklin College (A.B., first in class, 1968); University of Kentucky (Ph.D, Physical Organic Chemistry, 1972); Columbia University (J.D., 1975). *Member:* Indiana State Bar Association. (Of Counsel, Stewart & Irwin)

VERNON J. PETRI & ASSOCIATES

2124 EAST HANNA AVENUE
INDIANAPOLIS, INDIANA 46227
Telephone: 317-780-6610
Fax: 317-780-6620

Bodily Injury, Products Liability, Medical Malpractice, Pharmaceutical Litigation, Toxic Tort.

VERNON J. PETRI, born 1935; admitted to bar, 1966, Indiana, U.S. District Court, Southern District of Indiana and U.S. Supreme Court; 1973, U.S. Court of Appeals, 7th Circuit. *Education:* Indiana University (B.S., 1959; J.D., 1966). Phi Delta Phi. Prosecuting Attorney, Owen County, Indiana, 1967-1974. Member, Panel of Arbitration, American Arbitration Association. *Member:* Seventh Judicial Circuit, Hamilton County, Owen County, Indianapolis, Indiana State and American Bar Associations; Indiana Trial Lawyers Association (Member, Board of Directors, 1982); The Association of Trial Lawyers of America; Indiana Prosecuting Attorneys Association (President, 1974; Board Member, 1970-1975); American Judicature Society. Fellow, Indiana Bar Foundation. ***LANGUAGES:*** Spanish and Italian. ***PRACTICE AREAS:*** Bodily Injury; Products Liability; Medical Malpractice; Pharmaceutical Litigation; Toxic Tort.

PLEWS SHADLEY RACHER & BRAUN

Established in 1988
1346 NORTH DELAWARE STREET
INDIANAPOLIS, INDIANA 46202-2415
Telephone: 317-637-0700
Telecopier: 317-637-0710
Email: indy@psrb.com
URL: http://www.psrb.com

South Bend, Indiana Office: 53232 Generations Drive, 46635-1539. Telephone: 574-273-1010. Fax: 574-271-2050.

Environmental Litigation, Environmental Insurance Coverage, Environmental Cost Recovery, Complex Commercial Litigation, Environmental Corporate and Transaction Law, Environmental Administrative Law, Environmental Permitting, Superfund, Solid and Hazardous Waste, Underground Storage Tanks, Clean Air Act, Clean Water Act, Environmental Business Law, Intellectual Property, Commercial Real Estate and Land Use, Surface Coal Mining and Reclamation Act.

FIRM PROFILE: Since its founding in 1988, Plews Shadley Racher & Braun has concentrated its practice in environmental law and complex litigation. The firm serves clients from two offices in Indiana and has one of the largest environmental law practices in the Midwest. Its attorneys have substantial experience in a wide range of environmental matters including the prosecution and defense of claims involving CERCLA, RCRA, Clean Air and Water Acts, UST remediation and cost recovery, toxic torts, environmental property damage claims and governmental enforcement actions of all kinds. Its attorneys maintain a substantial practice representing policyholders in actions to recover insurance dollars, particularly for claims concerning environmental liabilities. The firm has actively participated in Superfund cases in a number of states and has organized committees to represent various interest groups in such efforts. It also advises clients on environmental issues in real estate and business transactions, such as wetlands and brownfields development, in conducting environmental due diligence and audit work, in undertaking voluntary cleanups, in developing programs for limiting liability exposure, and in drafting and monitoring legislation and rules. The firm also represents clients in a variety of other complicated legal matters such as products liability, class action and patent and trademark cases.

MEMBERS OF FIRM

GEORGE M. PLEWS, born 1952; admitted to bar, 1979, Indiana; 1981, U.S. Court of Appeals, Seventh Circuit; 1991, U.S. Supreme Court; 1994, U.S. District Court, Central District of Illinois. *Education:* Princeton University (A.B., magna cum laude, 1974); Worcester College, Oxford University, Oxford, England (B.A., Honours, 1976; M.A., 1981); Harvard University (J.D., cum laude, 1979). Phi Beta Kappa. Sachs Scholar. Senior Articles Editor, Harvard Civil Rights Civil Liberties Law Review, 1978-1979. Featured in "The Winners" Review of Outstanding Cases of 2001, Indiana Lawyer, December, 2001. Registered Civil Mediator. Listed in Best Lawyers in America, Environmental Law. ***PRACTICE AREAS:*** Litigation; Appellate Practice; Resource Conservation and Recovery Act; Insurance Coverage; Toxic Torts; Products Liability. ***Email:*** gplews@psrb.com

SUE A. SHADLEY, born 1952; admitted to bar, 1977, Indiana. *Education:* Purdue University (B.S., Environmental Science, 1974); Indiana University School of Law (J.D., 1977). Recipient, SBA Women in Law 2003 Achievement Award. Administrative Law Judge, Indiana Dept. of Natural Resources, 1984-1986. Recognized as Distinguished Alumnus, Purdue University, 2000. Inducted into the Hall of Fame, Indiana Chapter National Solid Waste Management Assn., 1992. Attorney: Air Pollution Control Div., State Board of Health, 1978 1982; Division of Reclamation, Indiana Dept. of Natural Resources, 1982-1984. General Counsel, Indiana Dept. of Envt'l. Mgt., 1986-1987. Director of Gov. Affairs, Waste Mgt. of North Am. and Chemical Waste Mgt. of Indiana, 1988. Listed in Best Lawyers in America, Environmental Law. ***PRACTICE AREAS:*** Resource Conservation and Recovery Act; Clean Air Act; Clean Water Act; SCMRA; Administrative Adjudication. ***Email:*** sshadley@psrb.com

PETER M. RACHER, born 1956; admitted to bar, 1986, Indiana. *Education:* Oberlin College (B.A., 1978); Indiana University (J.D., magna cum laude, 1986). Order of the Coif. Associate, Indiana Law Journal, 1985-1986. Recipient, Litigator of The Year Award, Hoosier Environmental Council, 1995. Listed in Best Lawyers in America, Environmental Law. *Member:* Indiana State Bar Association (Chair, Environmental Section, 1999). ***PRACTICE AREAS:*** Litigation; Environmental Cost Recovery; Resource Conservation and Recovery Act; Insurance Coverage; Underground Storage Tanks; Toxic Torts. ***Email:*** pracher@psrb.com

CHRISTOPHER J. BRAUN, born 1959; admitted to bar, 1984, District of Columbia; 1987, U.S. Supreme Court; 1988, Indiana and U.S. Court of Appeals, Seventh Circuit; U.S. District Court, Northern and Southern Districts of Indiana. *Education:* Wabash College (B.A., 1981); Centre for Medieval and Renaissance Studies, Oxford, England (1980-1981); Southern Methodist University (J.D., 1984). Phi Alpha Delta. Member, Southwestern Law Journal, 1982-1983. Adjunct Professor, Civil Mediation and Dispute Resolution, Indiana University Indianapolis Law School, 2001. General Counsel, Indiana Petroleum Marketers and Convenience Store Assn., 1993—. Associate: Baker & Botts, Washington, D.C., 1984 1986; Travis & Gooch, Washington, D.C., 1987. Associate, 1987-1991 and Partner, 1992-

(This Listing Continued)

1994, Baker & Daniels, Indianapolis, IN. Listed in Best Lawyers in America, Environmental Law. Registered Civil Mediator. ***PRACTICE AREAS:*** Complex Litigation; Real Estate; Environmental Law; Toxic Torts. ***Email:*** cbraun@psrb.com

JEFFREY D. CLAFLIN, born 1958; admitted to bar, 1990, Indiana. *Education:* Anderson College (B.A., 1981); Indiana University School of Law (J.D., 1990). Administrative Assistant/Acting Director, Office of Policy and Regulatory Analysis, Indiana Dept. of Envt'l Mgt., 1988. ***PRACTICE AREAS:*** Insurance Coverage; Environmental Law; Appellate Practice. ***Email:*** jclaflin@psrb.com

FREDERICK D. EMHARDT, born 1960; admitted to bar, 1985, Indiana; 1991, U.S. Court of Appeals, Seventh Circuit. *Education:* Wabash College (B.A., magna cum laude, 1982); University of Colorado at Boulder (J.D., 1985). Recipient, American Jurisprudence Award in Commercial Law. ***PRACTICE AREAS:*** Civil Litigation; Insurance Coverage; Products Liability; Solid Waste; Hazardous Waste; Toxic Torts; Zoning, Planning and Land Use. ***Email:*** emhardt@psrb.com

LEONARDO D. ROBINSON, born 1954; admitted to bar, 1986, Illinois; 1994, Indiana. *Education:* Carleton College (B.A., 1977); Antioch School of Law (J.D., 1981). RCRA/CERCLA Interface Expert, U.S. EPA Region V, 1989-1991. Section Chief, Solid Waste and Emergency Response Branch, Office of Regional Counsel, U.S. EPA Region V. Senior Envt'l. Counsel, Mid-West Region of Chemical Waste Management, 1991-1994. ***PRACTICE AREAS:*** Resource Conservation and Recovery Act; Administrative Adjudication. ***Email:*** ldrobinson@psrb.com

S. CURTIS DEVOE, born 1960; admitted to bar, 1988, Indiana; 1999, U.S. Court of Appeals, Seventh Circuit. *Education:* Princeton University (A.B., with distinction, 1982); Boalt Hall School of Law, University of California at Berkeley (J.D., 1988). Associate Editor and Executive Editor, Ecology Law Quarterly. ***PRACTICE AREAS:*** Environmental Permitting; Environmental Compliance; Environmental Cost Recovery; Resource Conservation and Recovery Act; Underground Storage Tanks; Clean Water Act; Clean Air Act; Wetlands Regulation; Voluntary Remediation Program; Brownfields Redevelopment; Administrative Adjudication; Solid Waste; Hazardous Waste; Real Estate Transactions; Environmental Business. ***Email:*** cdevoe@psrb.com

JOHN B. BRIDGE, born 1950; admitted to bar, 1976, New York; 1978, Indiana. *Education:* Wabash College (B.A., magna cum laude, 1972); Columbia University (J.D., 1975). Phi Beta Kappa. General Motors Scholar. Member, Columbia Journal of Law and Social Problems. Vice President, General Counsel and Secretary, VASA Insurance Group, Inc., 1984-1996. Executive Vice President, General Counsel and Secretary, VASA North America, Inc., 1990-1996. Vice President and Chief Legal Officer, Seaboard North American Holdings, Inc., 1995-1996. General Counsel and Secretary, Novia Holdings, Inc., 1997—. ***PRACTICE AREAS:*** Corporate Law; Real Estate; Business Transactions. ***Email:*** jbridge@psrb.com

STEPHEN A. STUDER, born 1951; admitted to bar, 1976, Illinois; 1979, U.S. Court of Appeals, Seventh Circuit; 1980, U.S. Supreme Court; 1992, Michigan and Indiana; 1993, U.S. Court of Appeals, Sixth Circuit. *Education:* University of Notre Dame (A.B., 1973); Loyola University (J.D., 1976). Notre Dame Scholar. Co-Author: "Environmental Site Assessments: An Integrated Approach," 1992 Environmental Site Assessment Conference, National Ground Water Association; "Advanced Real Estate Law in Indiana," National Business Institute, 1993. Speaker: CLE International Conference "Brownfields", Indianapolis and Chicago, 1998; Manufacturer's Education's Council, "Benefits", Cincinnati, 1999. Faculty Member, "Major Land Use Laws in Indiana", NBI, 1999. Panelist: Indiana Planning Association Conference, 1999; "Advanced Environmental Law," ICLEF, 2001. Deputy General Counsel, Heller Financial, Inc., 1985-1991. Mishawaka Assistant City Attorney for Land Use. Fellow, Indiana Bar Foundation. (Resident, South Bend Office). ***PRACTICE AREAS:*** Environmental Law; Real Estate; Real Estate Development; Zoning, Planning and Land Use.

JEFFREY A. TOWNSEND, born 1957; admitted to bar, 1988, Indiana; 1992, U.S. Court of Appeals, Seventh Circuit. *Education:* Indiana University (B.A., 1980); Indiana University School of Law (J.D., cum laude, 1988). ***PRACTICE AREAS:*** Commercial Litigation; Insurance Coverage; Environmental Litigation. ***Email:*** jtownsend@psrb.com

JEFFREY D. FEATHERSTUN, born 1967; admitted to bar, 1993, Indiana; 1997, U.S. Court of Appeals, Seventh Circuit. *Education:* Indiana University, Bloomington (B.A., with high distinction, 1989); University of Michigan (J.D., 1992). Phi Beta Kappa. ***PRACTICE AREAS:*** Litigation; Appellate Practice; Insurance Coverage; Underground Storage Tanks; Toxic Torts; Resource Conservation and Recovery Act; Products Liability. ***Email:*** jfeather@psrb.com

DONNA C. MARRON, born 1955; admitted to bar, 1994, Indiana. *Education:* Tufts University (B.S., summa cum laude, 1977); University of California at Berkeley (M.A., 1979; Ph.D., 1982); Indiana University (J.D., cum laude, 1993). Phi Beta Kappa; Sigma Xi. ***PRACTICE AREAS:*** Insurance Coverage; Environmental Law; Administrative Law; Water Law. ***Email:*** dmarron@psrb.com

JOHN H. LLOYD, IV, born 1967; admitted to bar, 1992, Indiana; 1996, Illinois. *Education:* Northwestern University (B.A., 1989); University of Notre Dame (J.D., 1992). Assistant City Atty., Hammond, Indiana, 1996-1999. Registered Civil Mediator, Indiana. (Resident, South Bend Office). ***PRACTICE AREAS:*** Litigation; Environmental Law; Complex Litigation; Zoning, Planning and Land Use. ***Email:*** jlloyd@psrb.com

JOHN M. KETCHAM, born 1955; admitted to bar, 1988, Michigan; 1998, Indiana; U.S. Court of Appeals, Sixth and Seventh Circuits. *Education:* Indiana University (B.A., 1980); Gordon Conwell Theological Seminary (M.Div., magna cum laude, 1983); University of Michigan (J.D., 1987). Law Clerk to Hon. John Feikens, U.S. District Judge, Eastern District of Michigan, 1988. ***PRACTICE AREAS:*** Civil Litigation; Commercial Litigation; Insurance Coverage; Environmental Litigation. ***Email:*** jketcham@psrb.com

ALEXANDRA S. SYLVIA, born 1971; admitted to bar, 1997, Indiana; 1999, Kentucky. *Education:* Indiana University (B.A., 1993; J.D., cum laude, 1996). Recipient, American Jurisprudence Award. ***PRACTICE AREAS:*** Environmental Law; Real Estate; Business Transactions; Litigation. ***Email:*** asylvia@psrb.com

BRETT E. NELSON, born 1973; admitted to bar, 2000, Indiana; registered to practice before U.S. Patent and Trademark Office. *Education:* Indiana University (B.S., Biology,

(This Listing Continued)

1992); Indiana University School of Law (J.D., cum laude, 1999). ***PRACTICE AREAS:*** Intellectual Property; Complex Litigation; Environmental Law. ***Email:*** bnelson@psrb.com

ASSOCIATES

DAVID L. PIPPEN, born 1969; admitted to bar, 1995, Indiana; U.S. District Court, Northern and Southern Districts of Indiana; 1996, U.S. Court of Appeals, Seventh Circuit. *Education:* Wabash College (A.B., 1991); Indiana University, Indianapolis (J.D., 1994). ***Email:*** dpippen@psrb.com

JOHN D. MORIARTY, born 1967; admitted to bar, 1996, Indiana. *Education:* Indiana University (B.S., 1989); University of Notre Dame (M.B.A., 1991); Indiana University School of Law (J.D., 1995). Recipient, Francis J. Feeney Tax Award, Indiana University School of Law, 1995. Deputy Prosecuting Atty., Miami County, Indiana, 1997-1999. ***PRACTICE AREAS:*** Environmental Law; Insurance Coverage; Civil Litigation; Underground Storage Tanks. ***Email:*** jmoriarty@psrb.com

TINA M. RICHARDS, born 1973; admitted to bar, 1998, Oregon; 2001, Indiana and U.S. District Court, Northern and Southern Districts of Indiana. *Education:* Purdue University (B.S., 1995); University of North Dakota (J.D., 1998); Lewis & Clark School of Law (Environmental Law Certificate, 1998); George Washington University (LL.M., Environmental Law, 2000). ***Email:*** trichards@psrb.com

KAREN B. SCHEIDLER, born 1949; admitted to bar, 1999, Indiana; 2000, U.S. Court of Appeals, Seventh Circuit. *Education:* Indiana University, Bloomington (B.A., 1972); Indiana University School of Law, Indianapolis (J.D., 1999). Associate Editor, Indiana International and Comparative Law Review, 1998-1999. Manager, Home Office Claims Administrator, American States Insurance Co., 1985-1998. ***PRACTICE AREAS:*** Environmental Litigation; Environmental Insurance Coverage. ***Email:*** kscheidler@psrb.com

AMY W. ROMIG, born 1973; admitted to bar, 2000, Indiana and Kentucky. *Education:* University of Louisville (B.S., Chemical Engineering, 1995); Indiana University (M.S., Environmental Sciences, 2000); Indiana University School of Law (J.D., magna cum laude, 2000). Tau Beta Pi; Pi Alpha Alpha. Notes Editor, Indiana Journal of Global Legal Studies, 1999-2000. ***PRACTICE AREAS:*** Clean Air Act; Clean Water Act; Wetlands Regulation; Indoor Air Quality; Litigation. ***Email:*** aromig@psrb.com

JONATHAN P. EMENHISER, born 1975; admitted to bar, 2000, Indiana. *Education:* Manchester College (B.S., summa cum laude, 1997); Indiana University School of Law - Bloomington (J.D., 2000). *Member:* Indianapolis, Indiana State and American Bar Associations.

TODD J. JANZEN, born 1973; admitted to bar, 2000, Indiana. *Education:* Philips University, Marburg, Germany (1993-1994); Bethel College of Kansas (B.A., summa cum laude, 1995); Indiana University School of Law (J.D., 2002). Note Editor, Indiana International and Comparative Law Review, 2001-2002. ***PRACTICE AREAS:*** Environmental Litigation; Environmental Insurance Coverage; Agricultural Law; Business Law; Real Estate. ***Email:*** tjanzen@psrb.com

JAMIE B. DAMERON, born 1969; admitted to bar, 2004, Indiana. *Education:* Indiana University (B.S., 1993); Indiana University School of Law - Bloomington (J.D., magna cum laude, 2004). Symposium Editor, Indiana Law Review, 2003-2004. Licensed Professional Geologist, Indiana. *Member:* Indianapolis, Indiana State and American Bar Associations.

GREGORY M. GOTWALD, born 1977; admitted to bar, 2004, Indiana. *Education:* Rose-Hulman Institute of Technology (B.S., 2001); Vermont Law School (J.D., 2004). ***Email:*** ggotwald@psrb.com

THAO T. NGUYEN, born 1979; admitted to bar, 2004, Indiana and U.S. District Court, Southern and Northern Districts of Indiana. *Education:* Oberlin College (B.A., 2001); Indiana University School of Law - Bloomington (J.D., 2004). (Resident, South Bend Office)

J. MICHAEL BOWMAN, born 1963; admitted to bar, 2004, Indiana. *Education:* University of Chicago (B.A., 1985); Purdue University (M.S., 1990, Don Bloodgood Outstanding Environmental Engineering Graduate); Indiana University School of Law (J.D., magna cum laude, 2004). Order of Barristers. Charles R. Oehrle Scholar. F. Emerson Boyd Scholar. Note Development Editor, Indiana Law Review, 2003-2004. *Member:* Indianapolis, Indiana State, Seventh Circuit and American Bar Associations. ***Email:*** jbowman@psrb.com

RUTH M. RIVERA, admitted to bar, 2005, Indiana. *Education:* University of Puerto Rico (B.S., 1984); Indiana Wesleyan University (M.B.A., 2000); Indiana University School of Law - Bloomington (J.D., 2004). *Member:* Indianapolis, Indiana State and American Bar Associations. ***LANGUAGES:*** Spanish.

OF COUNSEL

CHRISTINE C. H. PLEWS, born 1951; admitted to bar, 1979, Indiana. *Education:* Princeton University (A.B., magna cum laude, 1974); St. Hugh's College, Oxford University, Oxford, England (B.A., with honors, 1976; M.A., 1981); Harvard University (J.D., 1979). Phi Beta Kappa. Marshall Scholar. Senior Articles Editor, Harvard Civil Rights-Civil Liberties Law Review, 1978-1979. ***PRACTICE AREAS:*** Litigation; Appellate Practice. ***Email:*** cplews@psrb.com

MARY ANN FUCHS SAGGESE, born 1960; admitted to bar, 1989, Virginia; 1991, Indiana; U.S. Court of Appeals, Fourth Circuit. *Education:* Purdue University (B.S.C.E., 1982); George Washington University (J.D., 1989). Alpha Lambda Delta; Chi Epsilon; Tau Beta Pi. ***PRACTICE AREAS:*** Clean Air Act; Clean Water Act; OSHA; SARA; Wetlands Regulation; Administrative Adjudication. ***Email:*** psrb@psrb.com

F. RONALDS WALKER, born 1946; admitted to bar, 1976, Illinois; 1977, Indiana; 1989, U.S. Tax Court. *Education:* Yale University (B.A., 1968); University of Michigan (J.D., 1976). Sagamore of the Wabash. Associate General Counsel, Citizens Gas and Coke Utility, 1996-2000. Registered Civil Mediator. [U.S. Marine Corp. (Capt. 1968-1971).]. ***PRACTICE AREAS:*** Litigation; Oil and Gas Production; Utility Law; Insurance Coverage; Products Liability. ***Email:*** rwalker@psrb.com

DONALD P. BOGARD, born 1941; admitted to bar, 1971, Indiana, U.S. District Court, Northern and Southern Districts of Indiana, U.S. Court of Appeals, Second, Fifth,

(This Listing Continued)

PLEWS SHADLEY RACHER & BRAUN, Indianapolis—Continued

Seventh and District of Columbia Circuits and U.S. Supreme Court. *Education:* Ball State University (B.S., 1967; M.A., 1989); Indiana University School of Law - Bloomington (J.D., 1971); University of Indianapolis (M.B.A., 1999). *Member:* Indiana State Bar Association; American Corporate Counsel Association. ***PRACTICE AREAS:*** Litigation; Contracts; Intellectual Property.

P. KEVIN THOMPSON, born 1949; admitted to bar, 1983, Indiana. *Education:* Indiana University (A.B., Biological Science, 1975); Indiana University Graduate School of Business (M.B.A., 1977); Indiana University School of Law (J.D., 1983). Financial Analyst, Chrysler Corporation, 1977-1979. Vice President Risk Mgt., Mayflower Group, 1980-1994. Chief Financial Officer and Treasurer, Monroe Guaranty Insurance. Co., 1995-1999. Director of Risk Mgt., Eli Lilly & Co., 1999-2003. ***PRACTICE AREAS:*** Insurance Coverage; Commercial Insurance; Casualty Insurance; Property Insurance; Excess Coverage. ***Email:*** kthompson@psrb.com

REPRESENTATIVE CLIENTS: Dana Corp.; Eli Lilly & Co.; Cinergy Corp.; Lear Corp. Automotive Systems; Allied Waste Industries; Inland Paperboard & Packaging; Delphi Corp.; Norfolk Southern Corp.; American Commercial Barge Lines LLC; Recticel International; Heritage Environmental Services; World Kitchen, Inc.; TransMontaigne, Inc.; CGB Enterprises, Inc.; Railworks Corp.; Raytech Corp.; City of South Bend; City of Mishawaka; City of Elkhart; St. Joseph County; University of Notre Dame; Rumpke Consolidated Cos.; Kiel Brothers Oil Co.; Jeld Wen, Inc.; Novia Underwriters, Inc.; City of Gary; Petroleum Marketers & Convenience Store Assn.

PHILLIP V. PRICE

4249 LAFAYETTE ROAD
INDIANAPOLIS, INDIANA 46254
Telephone: 317-290-1800
Fax: 317-290-1863
Email: phillip@pvprice.net
URL: http://www.indianadisabilitylawyer.com

Social Security, Social Security, Disability, Wills, Probate, Trusts and Estates, Guardianship, Estate Planning.

PHILLIP V. PRICE, born Indianapolis, Indiana; admitted to bar, 1975, Indiana. *Education:* Purdue University and University of Wisconsin (B.A., 1971); Indianapolis Law School of Indiana University (J.D., 1975). Certified Elder Law Attorney, National Elder Law Foundation. *Member:* American Bar Association, Indianapolis and Indiana State Bar Associations; National Organization of Social Security Claimant's Representatives; National Academy of Elder Law. ***PRACTICE AREAS:*** Social Security Disability; Probate; Trust Law; Wills.

PRICE WAICUKAUSKI RILEY & DeBROTA, LLC

Established in 1985
THE HAMMOND BLOCK BUILDING
301 MASSACHUSETTS AVENUE
INDIANAPOLIS, INDIANA 46204
Telephone: 317-633-8787
Fax: 317-633-8797
Email: pricelaw@price-law.com
URL: http://www.price-law.com

Class Actions, Business Litigation, Personal Injury, Products Liability, Medical Malpractice, Legal Malpractice, Employment, Housing, Environmental Litigation, Actions Against Banks, Civil Trials, and Civil Appeals.

HENRY J. PRICE, born LaGrange, Indiana, March 26, 1937; admitted to bar, 1962, Indiana and District of Columbia; U.S. District Court, Northern and Southern Districts of Indiana; U.S. Court of Appeals, Seventh Circuit; U.S. Supreme Court. *Education:* Wittenberg University (A.B., cum laude, 1959); University of Michigan (J.D., 1962); Georgetown University (LL.M., 1963). ***Email:*** hprice@price-law.com

RONALD J. WAICUKAUSKI, born Carbondale, Illinois, June 13, 1948; admitted to bar, 1973, Indiana, U.S. District Court, Northern and Southern Districts of Indiana, U.S. Court of Appeals, Seventh Circuit and U.S. Supreme Court. *Education:* Northwestern University (B.S., cum laude, 1970); Harvard University (J.D., 1973); George Washington University (LL.M., summa cum laude, 1976). ***Email:*** rwaicukauski@price-law.com

WILLIAM N. RILEY, born Indianapolis, Indiana, October 9, 1963; admitted to bar, 1989, Indiana and U.S. District Court, Southern and Northern Districts of Indiana; 1992, U.S. Court of Appeals, 7th Circuit. *Education:* Indiana University (B.A., 1986; J.D., 1989). ***Email:*** riley@rileydebrota.com

AMY FICKLIN DeBROTA, born Indianapolis, Indiana, July 7, 1965; admitted to bar, 1993, Indiana and U.S. District Court, Northern and Southern Districts of Indiana; 1999, U.S. Court of Appeals, Seventh Circuit. *Education:* Indiana University at Bloomington (B.A., 1987); Indiana University at Indianapolis (J.D., cum laude, 1993). ***Email:*** debrota@rileydebrota.com

JANA K. STRAIN, born Seymour, Indiana, February 4, 1965; admitted to bar, 1998, Indiana. *Education:* Indiana State University (B.A., cum laude, 1986); Butler University (M.S., 1990); Indiana University School of Law (J.D., cum laude, 1997). ***Email:*** jstrain@price-law.com

CAROL A. NEMETH, born South Bend, Indiana, September 10, 1969; admitted to bar, 1994, Indiana; 1995, Ohio. *Education:* Indiana University (B.A., 1991; J.D., 1994). ***Email:*** cnemeth@price-law.com

SENIOR COUNSEL

ARLENE G. ANDERSON, born Elizabeth, New Jersey, November 2, 1944; admitted to bar, 1982, Indiana. *Education:* Hope College (A.B., cum laude, 1966); Indiana University School of Law (J.D., cum laude, 1982). ***Email:*** aanderson@price-law.com

GABRIEL A. HAWKINS, born Mt. Olive, Illinois; admitted to bar, 2002, Indiana. *Education:* Southern Illinois University (B.A., 1998); Indiana University School of Law, Indianapolis (J.D., cum laude, 2002). ***Email:*** ghawkins@price-law.com

CAROLYN A. CLAY, born Indianapolis, Indiana; admitted to bar, 2003, Indiana. *Education:* Ohio Weslyan University (B.A., cum laude, 2000); Indiana University School of Law, Indianapolis (J.D., cum laude, 2003). ***Email:*** jsweeney@price-law.com

JAMIE R. SWEENEY, born Vincennes, Indiana; admitted to bar, 2004, Indiana. *Education:* Ball State University (B.S.); Indiana University School of Law, Indianapolis (J.D.). ***Email:*** jsweeney@price-law.com

(This Listing Continued)

REIBER LAW OFFICE

6745 GRAY ROAD, SUITE G
INDIANAPOLIS, INDIANA 46237
Telephone: 317-888-5097
Fax: 317-783-7599
Email: indylaw2000@yahoo.com

Family Law, Adoptions, Child Custody, Child Support, Divorce, Domestic Violence, Visitation Rights, Criminal Law, Driving While Intoxicated, Drug Crimes, Juvenile Crimes, Parole and Probation, Traffic Violations, Discrimination, Sexual Harassment, Insurance Defense, Personal Injury, Automobile Accidents, Slip and Fall, Wrongful Death, Dog Bites, Real Estate, Business Law, Contracts, Business Litigation, Limited Liability Companies, Partnerships, Small Business Law, Collections, Debt and Credit.

ANTOLIN J. REIBER, born Clinton, Indiana, October 28, 1971; admitted to bar, 1998, Indiana and U.S. District Court, Southern District of Indiana. *Education:* Indiana University, Purdue University (B.S., Business, 1994; J.D., 1997). Phi Delta Phi. *Member:* Indiana State Bar Association.

RESOLUTION LAW GROUP, P.C.

1 NORTH PENNSYLVANIA STREET, SUITE 530
INDIANAPOLIS, INDIANA 46204
Telephone: 317-633-6780
Fax: 317-633-6725
Email: firm@resolutionlawgroup.com
URL: http://www.resolutionlawgroup.com

Lafayette, California Office: 3717 Mt. Diablo Boulevard, Suite 200, 94549. Telephone: 925-284-0840. Facsimile: 925-284-0870. Email: firm@resolutionlawgroup.com. URL: http://www.resolutionlawgroup.com

Washington, D.C., Office: 5335 Wisconsin Avenue, N.W., Suite 305, 20015. Telephone: 202-686-4844. Fax: 202-686-4843. Email: firm@resolutionlawgroup.com. URL: http://www.resolutionlawgroup.com

Woodland Hills, California Office: 21800 Oxnard Street, Suite 780, 91367. Telephone: 323-878-0969. Fax: 323-878-0913. Email: firm@resolutionlawgroup.com. URL: http://www.resolutionlawgroup.com

Civil Litigation, Insurance Coverage, Insurance Bad Faith Litigation, Environmental Law, Environmental Litigation, Toxic Torts Litigation, Securities Litigation and Arbitration.

MICHAEL O. NELSON, born Carmichael, California, February 12, 1968; admitted to bar, 1996, California and U.S. Court of Appeals, Ninth Circuit; 1998, U.S. District Court, Central, Eastern and Southern Districts of California; 2002, Indiana. *Education:* University of California, San Diego (B.A., 1990); Hastings College of Law (J.D., 1996). Editor in Chief, Hasting West-Northwest Journal of Environmental Law and Policy. *Member:* Indianapolis Bar Association; State Bar of California (Environmental Law Section). ***PRACTICE AREAS:*** Environmental Litigation; Insurance Coverage; Insurance Bad Faith; Toxic Tort Litigation. ***Email:*** michael.nelson@resolutionlawgroup.com

RILEY BENNETT & EGLOFF, LLP

Established in 1979
141 EAST WASHINGTON STREET, FOURTH FLOOR
INDIANAPOLIS, INDIANA 46204
Telephone: 317-636-8000
Fax: 317-636-8027
Email: info@rbelaw.com
URL: http://www.rbelaw.com

Litigation, Labor and Employment (Management), Employee Benefits, Insurance Defence, Corporation, Real Estate, Commercial, Governmental Relations, Workers Compensation Defense, Environmental, Trusts and Estates, Asset Protection, Guardianships, Estate Planning, Probate and Toxic Torts, Asbestos Litigation.

FIRM PROFILE: Riley Bennett & Egloff, LLP maintains a comprehensive business and litigation practice, providing legal services to local, regional, national and international firms. The Firm is committed to providing the highest quality services in a timely and cost effective manner.

MEMBERS OF FIRM

BRYCE H. BENNETT, JR., born Jackson, Michigan, August 6, 1953; admitted to bar, 1978, Indiana. *Education:* Indiana University (B.S. Finance, with high distinction, 1975; J.D., magna cum laude, 1978). Beta Gamma Sigma. Associate Editor, Indiana Law Review, 1977-1978. Certified Alternative Dispute Resolution Mediator. Chair, Indianapolis Equal Opportunity Advisory Board, 1995-1997. *Member:* Indianapolis (Chair, Litigation Section, 1994; Member, Board of Managers, 1995-1997; Chair, Judicial Evaluation Committee, 1996), Indiana State (Member, House of Delegates and Litigation Section) and American

(This Listing Continued)

(Member, Construction Forum, Litigation and Intellectual Property Sections) Bar Associations; International Association of Defense Trial Counsel; Defense Research Institute; Defense Trial Counsel of Indiana. **PRACTICE AREAS:** Business Litigation; Insurance; Construction; Products Liability; Professional Liability. **Email:** bbennett@rbelaw.com

JOHN L. EGLOFF, born Saginaw, Michigan, November 27, 1953; admitted to bar, 1978, Indiana; 1990, U.S. Court of Appeals, Seventh Circuit; 1991, U.S. Supreme Court. *Education:* Michigan State University (B.A. with honors, 1975); Indiana University, School of Law (J.D., magna cum laude, 1978). Order of the Coif. Chair, Indiana Chapter, Midwest Pension Conference, 1986. Member, Indiana Employees Appeals Commission, 1993-1995. *Member:* Indianapolis (Member, Labor Law Section), Indiana State (Member, Employment Law Section) and American (Member, Sections on: Business Law; Real Property, Probate and Trust Law) Bar Associations. **PRACTICE AREAS:** Corporation; Employee Benefit. **Email:** johnegloff@rbelaw.com

DONALD S. SMITH, born St. Paul, Minnesota, November 1, 1955; admitted to bar, 1981, Indiana. *Education:* DePauw University (B.A., cum laude, 1978); Indiana University, School of Law (J.D., cum laude, 1981). Associate Editor, Indiana Law Review, 1980-1981. Member, Board of Barristers, 1979-1981. Member, National Labor Relations Board, Region 25, Seminar Faculty. *Member:* Indianapolis (Chair, 1993 and Member, Labor Law Section), Indiana State (Member, Labor Law Section) and American (Member, Labor and Employment Law Section) Bar Associations; Defense Trial Counsel of Indiana; Indiana Workers' Compensation Institute. **PRACTICE AREAS:** Labor (Management); Worker's Compensation; Litigation. **Email:** Dsmith@rbelaw.com

MARY K. REEDER, born Indianapolis, Indiana, June 24, 1957; admitted to bar, 1983, Indiana; 1985, U.S. Court of Appeals, Seventh Circuit. *Education:* Indiana University (B.S., 1979; J.D., cum laude, 1983). Phi Alpha Delta (Justice, 1982-1983). Associate Editor, Indiana Law Review, 1982-1983. Member, Indianapolis Air Pollution Control Board, 1996-2000. *Member:* Indianapolis (Member, Litigation Section), Indiana State (Member, Environmental Law Section) and American (Member, Litigation Law Section) Bar Associations; Defense Research Institute; International Association of Defense Counsel; Defense Trial Counsel of Indiana. **PRACTICE AREAS:** Litigation; Environmental; Toxic Tort. **Email:** Mreeder@rbelaw.com

LAURA S. REED, born Enid, Oklahoma, March 13, 1962; admitted to bar, 1987, Indiana; 1990, U.S. Court of Appeals, Seventh Circuit. *Education:* Carleton College (B.A., magna cum laude, 1984); Indiana University, School of Law (J.D., magna cum laude, 1987). Note and Development Editor, Indiana Law Review, 1986-1987. *Member:* Indianapolis (Member, Litigation Section), Indiana State (Member, Young Lawyers Section) and American (Member, Sections on: Litigation; Tort and Insurance Practice) Bar Associations; Defense Research Institute; Defense Trial Counsel of Indiana. **PRACTICE AREAS:** Litigation; Insurance. **Email:** Lreed@rbelaw.com

RYAN L. LEITCH, born Fort Wayne, Indiana, July 18, 1962; admitted to bar, 1987, Indiana. *Education:* Indiana University (B.S., 1984; J.D., 1987). Delta Theta Phi. Certified Arbitrator for the Better Business Bureau. *Member:* Indianapolis (Member, Sections on: Estate Planning; Administration; Litigation), Indiana State (Member, Sections on: Probate, Trust and Real Property; Litigation) and American (Member, Sections on: Probate and Trust; Litigation; Tort and Insurance) Bar Associations; Defense Trial Counsel of Indiana. **PRACTICE AREAS:** Litigation; Insurance; Estate Planning; Probate; Construction Law. **Email:** Rleitch@rbelaw.com

RAYMOND T. SEACH, born Pittsburgh, Pennsylvania, September 18, 1964; admitted to bar, 1993, Indiana. *Education:* University of Notre Dame (B.B.A. with high honors, 1986); Indiana University, School of Law (J.D., cum laude, 1993). Recipient, American Jurisprudence Award in Negotiable Instruments. Certified Public Accountant, California. *Member:* Indianapolis, Indiana State and American Bar Associations. **PRACTICE AREAS:** Business Law; Litigation; Insurance; Banking Law; Mergers and Acquisitions; Real Estate. **Email:** Rseach@rbelaw.com

R. TROY MULDER, born Grand Rapids, Michigan, April 16, 1967; admitted to bar, 1992, Indiana and U.S. District Court, Northern and Southern Districts of Indiana; 1994, U.S. Court of Appeals, Seventh Circuit. *Education:* Calvin College (B.A., 1989); Indiana University, School of Law (J.D., cum laude, 1992). *Member:* Indianapolis, Indiana State and American Bar Associations; Defense Trial Counsel of Indiana; Defense Research Institute. **PRACTICE AREAS:** Toxic Substance Liability; Tort Liability; Business Litigation. **Email:** Tmulder@rbelaw.com

ANTHONY R. JOST, born Kokomo, Indiana, December 3, 1967; admitted to bar, 1993, Indiana and U.S. District Court, Northern and Southern Districts of Indiana; 1994, Illinois; 1996, U.S. District Court, Central District of Illinois; 1997, U.S. Court of Appeals, Seventh Circuit. *Education:* DePauw University (B.A., cum laude, 1990); Indiana University, School of Law (J.D., 1993). Delta Theta Phi. Member, Indiana University Moot Court Team, 1992-1993. Notes Editor, Adelphia Law Journal, 1992. *Member:* Indianapolis, Indiana State, Illinois State and American Bar Associations; Defense Trial Counsel of Indiana; Defense Research Institute. **PRACTICE AREAS:** Litigation; Employment Law; Business Law; Bankruptcy; Real Estate. **Email:** Tjost@rbelaw.com

J. MARK McKINZIE, born Urbana, Illinois, April 20, 1953; admitted to bar, 1979, Illinois; 1989, Indiana. *Education:* University of Illinois (B.S., Finance, with high honors, 1974; M.B.A., with high honors, 1976); Indiana University (J.D., cum laude, 1978). *Member:* Indianapolis, Indiana State, Illinois State and American (Member, Tort and Insurance Practice and Business Law Sections) Bar Associations; Defense Research Institute; Defense Trial Counsel of Indiana. **PRACTICE AREAS:** Insurance; Corporate Law; Litigation. **Email:** mmckinzie@rbelaw.com

CHARLES C. DOUGLAS, born Valparaiso, Indiana, April 4, 1971; admitted to bar, 1996, Indiana and U.S. District Court, Northern and Southern Districts of Indiana. *Education:* Indiana University (B.S., 1993); Valparaiso University (J.D., 1996). Delta Theta Phi. *Member:* Indianapolis, Indiana State and American (Member: Forum on the Construction Industry; Real Property, Probate and Trust Law Section) Bar Associations; Defense Trial Counsel of Indiana; Defense Research Institute (Member, Construction Law Committee). **PRACTICE AREAS:** Business Litigation; Construction Law; Toxic Torts; Corporate Law. **Email:** Cdouglas@rbelaw.com

(This Listing Continued)

STACY L. HANEFELD, born Indianapolis, Indiana, February 25, 1971; admitted to bar, 1996, Indiana and U.S. District Court, Northern and Southern Districts of Indiana. *Education:* Indiana University (B.A., 1992; J.D., 1996). Phi Beta Kappa. Associate Editor, Indiana Law Review, 1995-1996. *Member:* Indianapolis and Indiana State Bar Associations; Defense Trial Counsel of Indiana. **PRACTICE AREAS:** Civil Litigation; Health Care; Insurance. **Email:** Shanefeld@rbelaw.com

OF COUNSEL

JAMES W. RILEY, JR., born Muncie, Indiana, May 5, 1947; admitted to bar, 1972, Indiana; U.S. District Court, Southern and Northern Districts of Indiana; U.S. Court of Appeals, Seventh Circuit; U.S. Supreme Court. *Education:* Purdue University (B.S, 1969); University of Michigan (J.D., 1972). Member, Local Rules Advisory Committee, 2000—, U.S. District Court, Southern District of Indiana. *Member:* Indianapolis, Indiana State (President-Elect, 2005; Chair, House of Delegates, 2003; Board of Governors, 1997-1999, 2001-2003), Federal, Seventh Circuit and American Bar Associations; Federation of Defense and Corporate Counsel; Defense Research Institute; Defense Trial Counsel of Indiana (Board of Directors, 1996-1999); Indiana Continuing Legal Education Forum (President, 2005). Fellow, Indianapolis, Indiana (Board of Directors, 2004) and American Bar Foundations. **PRACTICE AREAS:** Business Litigation; Products Liability; Insurance Coverage; Arbitration. **Email:** jriley@rbelaw.com

BLAIR R. VANDIVIER, born Rapid City, South Dakota, December 24, 1955; admitted to bar, 1981, Indiana and U.S. District Court, Southern District of Indiana. *Education:* Butler University (B.S., magna cum laude, 1978); Indiana University, School of Law (J.D., cum laude, 1981). Phi Delta Phi. Listed in Who's Who of American Law, 1987, 1991 and 1993 Eds. *Member:* Indianapolis, Indiana State and American Bar Associations. **PRACTICE AREAS:** General Corporate; Real Estate.

ASSOCIATES

MELINDA J. SCHWER, born Rushville, Indiana, October 1, 1971; admitted to bar, 1996, Indiana. *Education:* Indiana University (B.A., 1992; J.D., 1996). *Member:* Indianapolis and Indiana State Bar Associations; Defense Trial Counsel of Indiana (Member, Young Lawyers' Steering Committee); Defense Research Institute. **Email:** mgentry@rbelaw.com

KEVIN N. THARP, born Richmond, Indiana, March 5, 1975; admitted to bar, 2000, Indiana and U.S. District Court, Northern and Southern Districts of Indiana. *Education:* Indiana University, Indianapolis (B.S. with high distinction, 1997; J.D., magna cum laude, 2000). Order of the Coif. Notes Editor, Federal Communications Law Journal, 1999-2000. *Member:* Indianapolis, Indiana State and American Bar Associations. **PRACTICE AREAS:** Employment Law; Intellectual Property; Business Law; Mergers and Acquisitions; Commercial Litigation. **Email:** ktharp@rbelaw.com

JAIME L. MEYER, born Mishawaka, Indiana, October 15, 1976; admitted to bar, 2002, Indiana. *Education:* Butler University (B.A., with high honors, 1999); Indiana University School of Law - Indianapolis (J.D., magna cum laude, 2002). *Member:* Indianapolis and Indiana State Bar Associations. **PRACTICE AREAS:** Toxic Torts; Civil Litigation; Business Law. **Email:** jmeyer@rbelaw.com

JEFFREY D. ROBERTS, born Highland, Indiana, July 10, 1976; admitted to bar, 2002, Indiana. *Education:* Indiana University - Bloomington (B.S., Business, 1998; J.D., cum laude, 2002). *Member:* American (Member, Litigation Section), Indianapolis and Indiana State Bar Associations; Defense Trial Counsel of Indiana. **PRACTICE AREAS:** Toxic Torts; Civil Litigation; Insurance Defense; Business Law. **Email:** jroberts@rbelaw.com

STEVEN L. ZAKROCKI, born South Bend, Indiana, November 17, 1971; admitted to bar, 2001, Indiana. *Education:* Indiana University (B.S., Public Affairs, 1994); Indiana University School of Law - Indianapolis (J.D., 2001). Member, Indiana International and Comparative Law Review, 2000-2001. *Member:* Indianapolis, Indiana State and American Bar Associations. **PRACTICE AREAS:** Employment Law; Civil Rights; Wrongful Termination; Insurance Defense; Commercial Litigation. **Email:** szakrocki@rbelaw.com

LAURA K. TAYLOR, born Crawfordsville, Indiana, March 21, 1964; admitted to bar, 1990, Indiana. *Education:* Butler University (B.S., 1986); Indiana University School of Law - Indianapolis(J.D., 1989). *Member:* Indianapolis and Indiana State Bar Associations. **PRACTICE AREAS:** Insurance Defense; Products Liability; Commercial Litigation. **Email:** ltaylor@rbelaw.com

WILLIAM P. MEANS, born Indianapolis, Indiana, June 24, 1971; admitted to bar, 2001, Indiana. *Education:* Purdue University (B.A., Psychology, B.A., General Communications, 1993); Indiana University School of Law - Indianapolis (J.D., cum laude, 2001). *Member:* Indiana State and American (Member, Litigation and Family Law Sections) Bar Associations. **PRACTICE AREAS:** Commercial Litigation; Medical Malpractice Defense. **Email:** wmeans@belaw.com

CHERYL D. FINCHUM, born Martinsville, Indiana, March 5, 1973; admitted to bar, 2001, Indiana. *Education:* Ball State University (B.S., Political Science, 1995); Indiana University School of Law - Indianapolis (J.D., 2001). *Member:* Indiana State and American (Member, Litigation and Family Law Sections) Bar Associations; Indiana Worker's Compensation Institute. **PRACTICE AREAS:** Workers Compensation. **Email:** cfinchum@belaw.com

JEFFREY B. FECHT, born Philadelphia, Pennsylvania, October 10, 1973; admitted to bar, 1998, Indiana and U.S. District Court, Northern and Southern Districts of Indiana. *Education:* Vanderbilt University (B.A., 1995; J.D., 1998). Phi Alpha Delta; International Law Society President, 1997-1998. *Member:* Indianapolis, Indiana State, and American Bar Associations. **LANGUAGES:** German. **PRACTICE AREAS:** Insurance Defense; Commercial Litigation. **Email:** jfecht@rbelaw.com

ROBERT C. BRANDT, born Brooklyn, New York, January 16, 1972; admitted to bar, 2002, Indiana and U.S. District Court, Southern District of Indiana. *Education:* Marist College (B.A., Communication Arts, 1994); Indiana University School of Law - Bloomington (J.D., 2002). Notes Editor, Federal Communications Law Journal, 2001-2002. Deputy Pros-

(This Listing Continued)

RILEY BENNETT & EGLOFF, LLP, Indianapolis—Continued

ecutor, Hamilton County, Indiana, 2003-2004. *Member:* Indianapolis (Member, Litigation Section) and Indiana State Bar Associations. ***PRACTICE AREAS:*** Commercial Litigation; Insurance Defense. ***Email:*** rbrandt@rbelaw.com

AUSTIN A. SHADLE, born Marion, Indiana, January 23, 1977; admitted to bar, 2004, Indiana and U.S. District Court, Northern and Southern Districts of Indiana. *Education:* Purdue University (B.S., 1999); Indiana University School of Law - Indianapolis (J.D., 2004). *Member:* Indianapolis, Indiana State and American Bar Associations. ***PRACTICE AREAS:*** Civil Litigation; Business Law; Real Estate; Appellate Practice; Insurance Defense. ***Email:*** ashadle@rbelaw.com

TIMOTHY H. BUTTON, born Summit, New Jersey, July 8, 1966; admitted to bar, 2004, Indiana and U.S. District Court, Northern and Southern Districts of Indiana. *Education:* Hamilton College (A.B., English, 1989); Indiana University School of Law - Indianapolis (J.D., 2004). Certified Civil Mediator. *Member:* Indianapolis and Indiana State Bar Associations. ***Email:*** tbutton@rbelaw.com

REPRESENTATIVE CLIENTS: *Financial and Real Estate:* City of Firsts Federal Credit Union; Drover Street Federal Credit Union; Duke Realty Investments, Inc.; Fair Finance; Fifth Third Bank; First Community Bank; Forum Credit Union; Hansen & Horn; Harrington Wealth Management Co.; Indiana Members Credit Union; Jones Mortgage Group, LLC; Meridian Investment Advisors; National City Bank of Indiana; NRC Corporation; Premiere Credit of North America, LLC; Solidarity Federal Credit Union; Stock Yards Bank & Trust Company; The National Bank of Indianapolis; Transmission Builders Federal Credit Union; Trinity Environmental Services; Union Equity Corporation; VanRooy Properties. *Manufacturing, Construction, Transportation and Technology:* Accent Technical Services, Inc.; Air Products and Chemicals, Inc.; American Trans Air; Apex Precision Technologies, Inc.; Benchmark Products, Inc.; Bennett's Contracting, LLC; Bloomfield Manufacturing Co., Inc.; Contract Lumber, Inc.; Copasetic Construction, LLC; Eagle Flooring Co., Inc.; Electric League of Indiana; Excel Graphics, Inc.; Federal Express; Forge Industrial Staffing, Inc.; Glasrite, a Division of PSC of Kentucky, Inc.; Hays & Sons Complete Restoration; Hiatt Metal Products; Hunt Construction Group, Inc.; Indiana Fiber Work; Integrity Engineering, Inc.; JetStar, Inc.; Knight Transportation; KONE, Inc.; Lakewood Engineering and Mfg. Company; Lear Corporation; Lehigh Cement Company; Liggett Group, Inc.; Lock Tight, LLC; Long Electric Company, Inc.; Malisipino Restoration, Inc.; McCord Corporation; Mims Construction Company; Morrell, Inc.; Neal Scrap Metals, LLC; Obsidian Enterprises, Inc.; Otis Elevator Company; PCL Construction Services, Inc.; Penske Truck Leasing Co.; PMC, Inc.; Relcon, Inc.; S.C. Johnson Wax; Site Technologies, LLC; Stone City Ironworks, Inc.; Tectonic Systems, Inc.; The Indiana Rail Road Company; Under Construction, LLC; USF Holland, Inc. *Insurance and Claims:* Argonaut Insurance Co.; Cambridge Integrated Services Group, Inc.; Carolina Casualty Insurance Co.; CGU Insurance Company; Chelsea-Rhone, LLC; Cincinnati Insurance Company; Citizens Insurance Company; Commercial Union Insurance Co.; Conseco; Constitution States Service Company; Corporate Claims Management, Inc.; Crum & Forster Unit; Diversified Insurance Brokerage Group; Employers Mutual Casualty; Farm Bureau Insurance Companies; Farmers Truck Insurance Exchange; Fireman's Fund Insurance Companies; First State Management Group; Foremost Insurance Company; Frank Gates Service Company; GAB Robins North America, Inc.; Gallagher Bassett Services, Inc.; Great American Insurance Companies; Illinois Farmers Insurance Company; Indiana Lumbermens Mutal Insurance Company; Indiana Public Employer's Plan, Inc.; Indianapolis Insurance Group, Inc.; Insurance Institute of Indiana; Klinger Associates, Inc.; Liberty Mutual Insurance Company; Medical Assurance of Indiana; MetLife Auto & Home; Mid Century Insurance Company; Mitsui Sumitomo Marine, USA; National Farmers Union; Neace Lukens Insurance Agency; ProClaim America, Inc.; RMA Brokerage, LLC; RSKCo; SAFECO; St. Paul Travelers; Sedgwick Claims Management; TIG Insurance Company; Transcontinental Insurance Company; Western Reserve Group; Zurich American. *Wholesale and Retail:* Acorn Distributors, Inc.; Charming Shoppes, Inc.; Cotto-Waxo Co.; Dollar General Corporation; Frito Lay, Inc.; Indianapolis City Market Corporation; J-Town Jewelry, Inc.; McDonald's Corporations; Meijer Corporation; Quaker Oats; Recognize U, Inc.; The Pillsbury Co.; Tom Lange Company, Inc.; University Loft Company; Verizon Wireless. *Health Care Products and Services:* Community Hospitals of Indiana, Inc.; Curative Health Services, Inc.; DaVita, Inc.; EyeQ Optometry, P.C.; Follas Labs; Fresenius North America; Health South Holdings; Jasneek Medical Staffing; Maddox Chiropractic Clinic; Maus & Elam Dental Lab; Novartis Pharmaceuticals; Oak Grove Christian Retirement Village; Oliver Family Healthcare; Reid Hospital; RepuCare, Inc.; Resista Temps, Inc.; Select Medical Supply; St. Vincent Hospitals; Staff America, Inc.
EDUCATION AND OTHER BUSINESSES: ADESA Corporation; Beacon Education Management, Inc.; Edison Schools; Frontline Communications; LaPetite Academy; Mentzer Printing, Inc.; Southern Yankee Routisserie Pit Smokers; The Duncan Group; Worksmart Systems, Inc. *Sports, Media & Entertainment:* Indiana Lawyer; Indianapolis Business Journal; Leading Edge Motorsports; Lighthouse Sportstech Racing; Media Indiana, Inc.; National Collegiate Athletic Association (NCAA); Perkins Nichols Media; Raccoon Lake Golf Course; Sollars Teleproducts, Inc.; United Skates of America, Inc.

JEFFERY B. RISINGER, P.C.

INDIANAPOLIS, INDIANA

(See Fishers)

Business Law, Finance, Securities and Investments, Business Enterprises, Closely Held Business Law, Corporate, Franchises, Limited Liability Companies, Partnership Law, Small Business Law, Buying and Selling of Businesses, Business Planning, Contracts, Real Estate, Commercial Leasing, Business Start-Ups, Strategic Alliances, Joint Ventures, Mergers, Taxation, Tax Planning, Water Law, Sewer Utilities.

ROCAP WITCHGER LLP

Established in 1904

6666 EAST 75TH STREET, SUITE 410
INDIANAPOLIS, INDIANA 46250
Telephone: 317-577-5380
Fax: 317-577-5385
Email: rocap@rocap-witchger.com
URL: http://www.lawyers.com/rocapwitchger

General Practice. Litigation and Insurance Defense, Motor Carrier Law, Wills and Probate, Trusts and Estates, Estate Planning, Estate Administration, Real Estate, Banking, Commercial, Tax and Corporate Law, Mediation Services, Business Law, Contracts, Business Planning, Business Enterprises, Family Law, Child Custody, Child Support, Divorce, Visitation Rights, Employment Law, Discrimination, Sexual Harassment, Wrongful Death.

FIRM PROFILE: Rocap Witchger LLP has been an integral part of the Indianapolis and Indiana legal community since its founding in 1904 by James E. Rocap, Sr., offering services in all areas of law. The firm concentrates its efforts in litigation of all types, including insurance defense, products liability, professional negligence and commercial. As a full service firm, our staff is able to provide the services to our clients to enable them to effectively and efficiently plan for the future.

JAMES E. ROCAP, SR. (1881-1969)
JOHN T. ROCAP (1909-1980)
KEITH C. REESE (1920-1993)
JAMES E. ROCAP, JR. (Retired)

MEMBERS OF FIRM

JAMES D. WITCHGER, born Detroit, Michigan, September 19, 1949; admitted to bar, 1974, Indiana. *Education:* University of Notre Dame (B.A., 1971); Indiana University (J.D., 1974). Certified Civil Mediator. *Member:* Indianapolis, Indiana State and American Bar Associations; Defense Trial Counsel of Indiana. ***PRACTICE AREAS:*** General Litigation; Products Liability Litigation; Defense Litigation; Civil Mediation. ***Email:*** jdw@rocap-witchger.com

RICHARD A. ROCAP, born Indianapolis, Indiana, April 8, 1955; admitted to bar, 1980, Indiana. *Education:* University of Notre Dame (B.B.A., 1977); Indiana University (J.D., 1980). Certified Domestic Relations Mediator. *Member:* Indianapolis and Indiana State Bar Associations; Defense Trial Counsel of Indiana; Commercial Law League of America. ***PRACTICE AREAS:*** Commercial and Defense Litigation; Banking Law; Corporate Law; Real Estate Law; Probate Law; Family Law. ***Email:*** rar@rocap-witchger.com

ASSOCIATE

JEFFREY A. MUSSER, born September 21, 1959; admitted to bar, 1996, Indiana. *Education:* University of Cincinnati (B.A., Urban Planning, 1989); Indiana University School of Law (J.D., 1996).

REPRESENTATIVE CLIENTS: Phillips Petroleum Co.; The Travelers Insurance Co.; Motorists Mutual; Union Federal Savings Bank; Wolf & Swickard Machine Co.; Denny's Restaurant; ABF Freight Systems; Indiana Materials & MFG., Inc.; Target Stores; Sedgwick Claims Management Services; Agora Syndicate; KinderCare Learning Centers; American Modern Home Insurance; Hardee's Food Services, Inc.; CKE Restaurants; Carrier Corporation; RLI Insurance; Boreal Insurance Company; Tyson Food, Inc.; Rieth-Riley Construction Co., Inc.; Bituminous Insurance Companies; Komatsu America International; KIA Motors of America; Mt. Hawley Insurance Company; Smurfit Stone Container Corporation; Marten Transport, Ltd.; Metromedia Restaurant Group; Alpha Insurance Corporation; American Hardware Insurance Co.; Willis Administrative Services; Gallagher-Bassett; Crawford & Company; Cybercom; Hertz Claim Management; Pfizer, Inc.; Terminix International; Nissan North America; CIGNA.
REFERENCE: Union Federal Bank of Indianapolis, Inc.

RUBIN & LEVIN, P.C.

Established in 1976

500 MAROTT CENTER
342 MASSACHUSETTS AVENUE
INDIANAPOLIS, INDIANA 46204-2161
Telephone: 317-634-0300
Toll Free: 800-860-0500
Telecopier: 317-263-9411
Email: law@rubin-levin.net
URL: http://www.rubin-levin.com

Creditors' Rights, Insolvency Reorganization, Commercial Collections, Bankruptcy, Banking, Corporate, Real Estate, Foreclosure, Federal and State, Civil Trial and Appellate Practice.

FIRM PROFILE: Rubin & Levin, P.C., is one of Indiana's largest firms concentrating in the commercial practice. For over 25 years we have dedicated ourselves to meeting our clients' business needs through aggressive litigation and good communication. Our dedicated staff and knowledge of commercial law allows us to handle cases throughout Indiana. We are also experienced in pre-litigation workouts, mediation, arbitration and the art of negotiation.

We believe a vital part of our mission requires participation in professional associations and education. Our attorneys are often published in their areas of practice, frequently lecture and chair educational seminars.

Our commercial practice has evolved from years of hard work and experience in the legal profession. We are dedicated to serving our clients' business needs.

GEORGE A. RUBIN, born Michigan City, Indiana, June 11, 1932; admitted to bar, 1959, Indiana; 1960, Illinois, U.S. District Court, Southern and Northern Districts of Indiana and U.S. Court of Appeals, Seventh Circuit. *Education:* Indiana University (B.S., 1954); Northwestern University (J.D., 1959). Phi Alpha Delta (Justice, 1959). Law Clerk, Supreme Court of Indiana, 1959-1960. Deputy Attorney General of Indiana, 1960-1961. Indiana State Senate, 1968-1972. Chairman, Senate Judiciary Committee, 1970-1972. Member, Judicial Nominating Commission of Marion County, Indiana 1977-1981. *Member:* Indianapolis, Indiana State (Council Member, Appellate Practice Section, 2002-2004) and American Bar Associations; Commercial Law League of America (Chairman, Young Member Section and Seventh District Members Association, 1973-1974; Member, Board of Governors, 1976-1979; Member, Board of Directors, Fund for Public Education, 1994-2000). [Officer, U.S.A.F., 1955-1957]. (Certified in Creditors' Rights Law by the American Board of Certification). ***Email:*** george@rubin-levin.net

ELLIOTT D. LEVIN, born Chicago, Illinois, September 9, 1941; admitted to bar, 1966, Indiana, U.S. District Court, Southern and Northern Districts of Indiana, U.S. Court of Appeals, Seventh Circuit and U.S. Supreme Court. *Education:* Indiana University (B.S., 1963; J.D., magna cum laude, 1966). Beta Gamma Sigma; Phi Delta Phi; Order of the Coif. Krannert Fellowship. Managing Editor, Indiana Law Journal, 1965-1966. Adjunct Professor of Law, Indiana University, 1983 to 2001, Bankruptcy and Corporate Reorganization Seminar. Author: "Bankruptcy," ICLEF, 1982; "Rights and Remedies of an Indiana Creditor," ICLEF, 1980; "Collecting From Business Debtors," ICLEF, 1982; "Basic Bankruptcy

(This Listing Continued)

and Reorganization Law," Seventh Circuit Bar Association, 1981; "Retention of Ownership Interest Over Creditor Objection-How Intangible and Unsubstantial May the Substantial Contribution Be?" Commercial Law Journal, 1987; "Statute of Limitations for Bankruptcy Avoidance Actions Brought by Debtors in Possession," Commercial Law Journal, Winter, 1992. Member: American College of Bankruptcy; Indiana Lawyer Roundtable, 1993; Private Panel of U.S. Trustees, Southern District of Indiana, Indianapolis Division, 1990—; Advisory Committee, Local Rules of the Bankruptcy Court, Southern District of Indiana; Annual Speaker, Sigmund J. Beck Bankruptcy Roundtable, 1990—. *Member:* Indianapolis (Member, Board of Managers, 1980-1982; Board Member and Chairman, Bankruptcy and Insolvency Section, 1982-1986); Indiana State and American Bar Associations; Commercial Law League of America (Chairman, National Bankruptcy Committee, 1981-1985; Chairman, Midwestern Regional Members Association, 1987; Council Member and Chairman, Bankruptcy and Insolvency Section, 1983-1988); Commercial Law League of America (Attorney Board Member, Board of Governors, 1990; President Elect, 1993-1994; President, 1994-1995; Chairman, Board of Associate Editors, CLLA); American Judicature Society; The Association of Trial Lawyers of America; Indiana Trial Lawyers Association; American Bankruptcy Institute; American College of Bankruptcy. [Captain, Armored Force, U.S. Army, 1967-1968]. ***Email:*** edl@rubin-levin.net

SUE FIGERT MEYER, born Rochester, Indiana, February 17, 1955; admitted to bar, 1981, Indiana and U.S. District Court, Southern and Northern Districts of Indiana; 1984, U.S. Court of Appeals, Seventh Circuit. *Education:* Butler University (B.A., 1977); Indiana University (J.D., summa cum laude, 1981). Author: "Judgment Liens and Execution - How to Collect in the New Millennia," ICLEF (2000); "Attorney's Fees and Collections," ICLEF (2000); "Creating and Writing Credit Documents," IACM (2000); "Advanced Collection Law in Indiana" (Lorman 2000); "Judgment Liens and Executions," ICLEF (2001); "Judgment Liens and Executions," IBA (2003). Seminar Chair: "Planning Your First Bankruptcy/ Collection," ICLEF, 2000; "Liens on Real Estate," ICLEF, 2001; "Lien and Bond Claims Against Federal, State, and Local Projects," ICLEF, 1998, 1999, 2003, 2005. *Member:* Indianapolis, Indiana State and American Bar Associations; Indianapolis Bar Foundation. ***Email:*** sue@rubin-levin.net

CHRISTINE HAYES HICKEY, born 1966; admitted to bar, 1993, Indiana. *Education:* Purdue University (B.A., 1988); Indiana University, Indianapolis (J.D., magna cum laude, 1993). Order of the Barristers. Recipient, American Jurisprudence Award, Corporate Reorganization and Bankruptcy, 1992. Recipient: Board of Managers Award, Indianapolis Bar Association, 2003; Best Article Award, 1995-1996. Author and Co-Author of many practice-related articles in Creditors' Rights since 1994, examples include: "Complying with the Fair Debt Collection Practices Act," Res Gestae, (1996); "Collecting From the Creative Debtor: Actions for Fraudulent Conveyances and Successor Liability Within a Proceedings Supplemental," ICLEF (1997); "Spousal Avoidance Powers: Regulation B As a Defense," CLLA, Creditors' Rights Section Free Press (1998); "The Best Defense is No Defense: Article 2A and the Finance Lease," CLLA, Creditors Rights Section Free Press (1999); "Introduction to Collection Law in Indiana," Lorman Education Services (2000; 2001); Indiana Collection Law Update, ICLEF (2005). *Member:* Indianapolis(CLE Commission, 1998-2003; Board of Managers, 1999-2001; 2002-2004; Chair, Judicial Excellence Political Action Committee; Justice Center Task Force Committee) Indiana State and American Bar Associations; Commercial Law League of America (Member, Board of Governors; Past-Chair, Creditors' Rights Section, 2003-2004; Midwest Region Secretary; Chair, National Professional Responsibility Committee); American Board of Certification (Board of Directors); Indianapolis Bar Foundation (President; Board of Directors; Distinguished Fellow). (Certified in Creditors' Rights Law by the American Board of Certification). ***Email:*** ch@rubin-levin.net

R. BROCK JORDAN, born Sioux City, Iowa, May 11, 1966; admitted to bar, 1993, Indiana, U.S. Court of Appeals, Seventh Circuit; U.S. District Court, Southern and Northern Districts of Indiana. *Education:* Iowa State University (B.S., 1988); University of Iowa (J.D., with distinction, 1992). Firm Director, Appellate Practice Section. *Member:* Indianapolis, Indiana State (Council Member, Appellate Section) and American Bar Associations. ***REPORTED CASES:*** Krose v. National Bank of Indianapolis, 815 N.E.2d 137 (Ind. Ct. App. 2004); National City Bank of Indiana v. All-Phase Electrical Supply Co., 790 N.E.2d 488 (Ind. Ct. App. 2003); Zollman v. Geneva Leasing Association, Inc., 780 N.E.2d 387 (Ind. Ct. App. 2002); Nwannunu v. Weichman and Associates, P.C., 770 N.E.2d 871 (Ind. Ct. App. 2002); Noble Roman's Inc., V. Ward, 760 N.E.2d 1132 (Ind. Ct. App. 2002); Bartle v. HCFP Funding, Inc., 756 N.E.2d 1034 (Ind. Ct. App. 2001); Eskew v. Cornett, 744 N.E.2d 954 (Inc. Ct. App. 2001); Peoples Bank & Trust Co. v. Price, 714 N.E.2d 712 (Ind. Ct. App. 1999); Bitner v. Hull, 695 N.E.2d 181 (Ind. Ct. App. 1998). ***Email:*** brock@rubin-levin.net

JOHN C. HOARD, born Fort Wayne, Indiana, April 7, 1955; admitted to bar, 1980, Indiana, U.S. District Court, Northern and Southern Districts of Indiana; U.S. Tax Court. *Education:* Northwestern University (B.S., 1977); Indiana University (J.D., 1980). Certified Public Accountant, Indiana, 1988. Associate Editor, Indiana Law Review. Co-author/ Author: "Revised Article Nine: Default and Enforcement Provisions," ICEF (2000); "Enforceability of Third Party Releases and Injunctions in Chapter 11 Plans," Annual Bankruptcy Institute, ICLEF (2000); Fraudulent Conveyances," ICLEF (2001); "Revised Article Nine of the Indiana UCC," Seminar Chair, Lorman (2002). Author: Article, "Ethical Issues in Bankruptcy," Panel Chair, Annual Bankruptcy Institute, ICLEF (2003); Article, Tax Implications of BAPCPA, ICLEF (2005). Panelist: Sigmund Beck Bankruptcy Roundtable, "UCC Update," ICLEF (2004); Aligning Your Practice with the BAPCPA of 2005, NBI (2005). *Member:* Indianapolis, Indiana State and American Bar Associations; American Bankruptcy Institute; Commercial Law League of America; Indiana CPA Society. Distinguished Fellow, Indianapolis Foundation. ***REPORTED CASES:*** Bohnke v. Estate of Bohnke, 454 N.E.2d 446 trans. denied (Ind. Ct. App. 1983); Isp.com, LLC v. Theising 805 N.E2d 767 (Ind. 2004). ***Email:*** johnh@rubin-levin.net

---

JAMES T. YOUNG, born Fort Wayne, Indiana, July 28, 1961; admitted to bar, 1987, Indiana; 1993, Tennessee; U.S. Court of Appeals, 7th Circuit; U.S. District Court, Northern and Southern Districts of Indiana. *Education:* Indiana University, Bloomington (B.S., 1983; M.B.A., 1987; J.D., 1987). Law Clerk to the Honorable John W. Montgomery, Circuit Court Judge, St. Joseph County, Indiana, 1986. *Member:* Indianapolis (Bankruptcy and Creditor Rights Section), Indiana State (Member, Sections on: Bankruptcy and Creditors Rights; Intellectual Property) and American Bar Associations; Bar Association of the Seventh Federal Circuit. ***Email:*** james@rubin-levin.net

GENE A. WHEELER, born Franklin, Indiana, November 14, 1964; admitted to bar, 1999, Indiana. *Education:* Ball State University (B.A., 1987); Indiana University (J.D., cum laude, 1999). Phi Alpha Delta. Member, 1997-1999 and Associate Editor, 1998-1999 Indiana Law Review. *Member:* Indianapolis, Indiana State and American Bar Associations. ***Email:*** gene@rubin-levin.net

JAMES E. ROSSOW, JR., born Saginaw, Michigan, March 2, 1972; admitted to bar, 1998, Indiana. *Education:* Indiana University (B.A., 1994); Indiana University School of Law (J.D., 1998). *Member:* Indianapolis, Indiana State and American Bar Associations; American Bankruptcy Institute. ***Email:*** jim@rubin-levin.net

JENNIFER E. RILEY, born Louisville, Kentucky, August 10, 1976; admitted to bar, 2001 Indiana and U.S. District Court, Northern and Southern Districts of Indiana. *Education:* University of Kentucky (B.A., summa cum laude, 1998); Indiana University - Indianapolis (J.D., magna cum laude, 2001). Associate Editor, Indiana Law Review. *Member:* Indianapolis and Indiana State Bar Associations. ***Email:*** jennifer@rubin-levin.net

S. BRENT POTTER, born Martinsville, Indiana, February 1, 1954; admitted to bar, 1986, Indiana. *Education:* Indiana University (B.S.P.A., 1979); Indiana University School of Law (J.D., 1985). *Member:* Indianapolis, Indiana State and American Bar Associations. ***PRACTICE AREAS:*** Banks and Banking; Real Estate; Corporate Law. ***Email:*** brent@rubin-levin.net

TAMARA L. WEISFELD, born Indianapolis, Indiana, April 9, 1961; admitted to bar, 1986, Indiana and U.S. District Court, Northern and Southern Districts of Indiana. *Education:* Indiana University (B.S., 1983; J.D., 1986). *Member:* Indianapolis, Indiana State and American Bar Associations; Indiana Creditors Bar Association. ***Email:*** tweisfeld@rubin-levin.net

EDWARD R. CARDOZA, born Bristol, Rhode Island, August 7, 1953; admitted to bar, 1997, Indiana. *Education:* Indiana University - Purdue University at Indianapolis (B.A., 1987); Indiana University School of Law (J.D., cum laude, 1997). *Member:* Indiana State Bar Association. [Staff Sergeant, U.S. Air Force, 1971-1978]. ***REPORTED CASES:*** Ransom v. State of Indiana, 741 N.E.2d 419 (Ind. App. 2000). ***Email:*** ecardoza@rubin-levin.net

OF COUNSEL

DIANE WITHEM ROE, born Beech Grove, Indiana, August 27, 1956; admitted to bar, 1981, Illinois; 1982 Missouri; 1989, Indiana and U.S. District Court, Northern and Southern Districts of Indiana. *Education:* Indiana University (B.S., 1978); University of Illinois (J.D., 1981). Beta Gamma Sigma. *Member:* Indianapolis and Indiana State Bar Associations. ***Email:*** diane@rubin-levin.net

DIXON B. DANN, born Indianapolis, Indiana, January 6, 1943; admitted to bar, 1967, Indiana. *Education:* Miami University (B.S., in Acc., 1964); University of Michigan (J.D., 1967). *Member:* Indianapolis (Member, Land Use Section), Indiana State and American (Member, Sections on Real Property, Probate and Trust Law, Land Use and Zoning Law) Bar Associations. ***Email:*** dixon@rubin-levin.net

JENNIFER LEVIN SINDER, born Louisville, Kentucky, October 29, 1968; admitted to bar, 1994, Indiana and U.S. District Court, Southern and Northern Districts of Indiana. *Education:* University of Arizona (B.S., 1991); Indiana University (J.D., 1994). *Member:* Indianapolis, Indiana State and American Bar Associations. ***LANGUAGES:*** French. ***Email:*** jsinder@rubin-levin.net

JOHN M. ROGERS, born St. Louis, Missouri, February 6, 1951; admitted to bar, 1980, Indiana. *Education:* Northwestern University (B.A., 1973); Indiana University (M.A., 1976; J.D., cum laude, 1979). Research Editor, Indiana University Law Journal, 1978-1979. Lecturer, Indiana University School of Law, Bloomington, 2000-2003. Law Clerk to Justice Stanley B. Miller, Indiana Court of Appeals, 1980-1982. *Member:* Indianapolis and Indiana State Bar Associations. ***Email:*** johnr@rubin-levin.net

ANDREA L. COHEN, born Indianapolis, Indiana, December 7, 1962; admitted to bar, 1990, Indiana. *Education:* Indiana University (B.A., with high honors, 1985; J.D., cum laude, 1990). Phi Beta Kappa. *Member:* Indianapolis and Indiana State Bar Associations. ***Email:*** acohen@rubin-levin.net

REPRESENTATIVE CLIENTS: Associates Housing Finance; General Electric Capital Corp.; Goodwill Industries of Central Indiana, Inc.; ITT Commercial Finance, Inc.; American Credit Association of Indiana; Graybar Electric; GMAC Mortgage Corp.; Kimball International; The National Bank of Indianapolis; Dun & Bradstreet; Monroe Bank; Bloomfield State Bank; Fidelity National Services, Inc.; Temple-Inland; Citicapital Commercial Corporation.

RUPPERT & SCHAEFER, P.C.

2910 E. 96TH STREET
SUITE D
INDIANAPOLIS, INDIANA 46240
Telephone: 317-580-9295
Facsimile: 317-580-9298
Email: law@netdirect.net
URL: http://www.ruppertandschaefer.com

Family Law, Divorce, Pre-marital Agreements, Child Custody, Child Support, Paternity, Visitation Rights, Step Parent Adoptions.

FIRM PROFILE: Ruppert & Schaefer, P.C. represents clients in Central Indiana in all aspects of the legal field known as "family law". Specifically, our practice is limited to divorce, pre-marital agreements, paternity and post-decree matters involving child support, custody and visitation. Our firm combines more than 50 years of experience to help you pursue your legal rights, protect your financial interests, and understand your options in your family law case. Michael G. Ruppert has received the designation, "Certified Family Law Specialist.".

(This Listing Continued)

RUPPERT & SCHAEFER, P.C., Indianapolis—Continued

MICHAEL G. RUPPERT, born Lafayette, Indiana, August 15, 1952; admitted to bar, 1978, Ohio and Indiana, U.S. District Court, Southern District of Indiana. *Education:* Indiana University (B.A., 1974); Cleveland Marshall College of Law (J.D., 1977). Named, as a SuperLawyer by Law & Politics Magazine in 2005. Staff Attorney, Children's Rights Project, Legal Services Organization of Indiana, Inc., 1978-1981. Co-author "Recent Development in Indiana Family Law," Indiana Law Review, 2005; "Survey of Developments in Indiana Family Law," Indiana Law Review, 2004; "Survey of Indiana Family Law in 1996," 30 Indiana Law Review 1073 (1997); "Survey of Indiana Family Law," 29 Indiana Law Review 913 (1996); "The Continuing Evolution of Indiana's Family Law," 25 Indiana Law Review 1243 (1992); "Survey of Recent Developments in Family Law," 23 Ind. Law Rev. 363 (1990); "The Impact of Child Relocation on Custody Litigation," ICLEF - Family Law: An Analysis of Current Issues of Interest to the Practitioner, 1989. Lecturer, Indianapolis Bar Association Bar Review Course, 1998—. *Member:* Indianapolis (Member, Executive Committee, Family Law Section), Indiana State (Member, Family Law Section) and American (Member, Family Law Section) Bar Associations. (Board Certified, Family Law Specialist, Indiana State Bar Association, Family Law Certification Board). ***REPORTED CASES:*** Hammes v. Brumley, 659 N.E.2d 1021 (1995). ***PRACTICE AREAS:*** Family Law; Divorce. ***Email:*** mruppert@randsfamilylaw.com

PAULA J. SCHAEFER, born Huntingburg, Indiana, 1969; admitted to bar, 1994, Indiana and U.S. District Court, Southern District of Indiana. *Education:* Ball State University (B.S., 1991); Indiana University (J.D., 1994). Co-Author: "Survey of Developments in Indiana Family Law," Indiana Family Law Review, 2004; "Survey of Indiana Family Law in 1996," 30 Indiana Law Review 1073 (1997); "Survey of Indiana Family Law," 29 Indiana Law Review 913 (1996). Lecturer, Indianapolis Bar Association Bar Review Course, 1998—. Mediator, Family Law. *Member:* Indianapolis (Young Lawyers Division, Executive Committee and Family Law Section), Indiana State (Family Law Section) and American (Member, Family Law Section) Bar Associations. ***REPORTED CASES:*** Hubbard v. Hubbard, 690 NE.2d 1219 Ind.Ct.App. (1998). ***PRACTICE AREAS:*** Family Law; Divorce; Mediation. ***Email:*** pschaefer@randsfamilylaw.com

LAINIE A. HURWITZ, born Indianapolis, Indiana, 1973; admitted to bar, 1998, Indiana; 1999, U.S. District Court, Northern and Southern Districts of Illinois. *Education:* Indiana University (B.S., 1995); University of Dayton (J.D., 1998). *Member:* Indianapolis (Member, Family Law Section) and Indiana State Bar Associations. ***PRACTICE AREAS:*** Family Law.

JOSEPH W. RUPPERT, born Lafayette, Indiana, July 7, 1951; admitted to bar, 1979, Indiana and U.S. District Court, Southern District of Indiana; 1980, U.S. District Court, Northern District of Indiana. *Education:* Purdue University (B.A., 1973); St. Mary's University of San Antonio (J.D., with distinction, 1979). Phi Delta Phi. Member, John H. Harlan Society. Instructor, Legal Research and Writing, St. Mary's University, Spring, 1979. Co-Author: "Recent Development in Indiana Family Law," Indiana Law Review, 2005. ***PRACTICE AREAS:*** Family Law. ***Email:*** jruppert@randsfamilylaw.com

STEVEN SAMS

8720 CASTLE CREEK PARKWAY, SUITE 323
INDIANAPOLIS, INDIANA 46250
Telephone: 317-577-1620
Fax: 317-577-1619
Email: steven.sams@stevensamslaw.com
URL: http://www.stevensamslaw.com

Employment Law, Wrongful Termination, Disability Accomodation, Employee Benefits, Sexual Harassment, Workers Compensation, Civil Rights, Discrimination, Sexual Harassment, Family Law, Adoptions, Divorce, Child Custody, Child Support, Visitation Rights, Wills, Probate, Trusts and Estates, Estate Planning, Guardianship, Personal Injury, Automobile Accidents, Medical Malpractice, Business Law, Contracts, Commercial Leasing, Business Enterprise, Business Formation, Buying and Selling of Businesses, Mold Litigation, State, Federal and Appellate Courts.

STEVEN SAMS, born Cairo, Illinois, September 28, 1954; admitted to bar, 1998, Indiana; U.S. District Court, Northern and Southern Districts of Indiana and U.S. Court of Appeals, 7th Circuit. *Education:* Washington University, St. Louis Missouri (B.S., 1979; M.H.A., 1984); Indiana University School of Law, Indianapolis (J.D., 1997). Author: "Involuntary Termination of Employment: Legal and Practical Considerations." *Member:* Indianapolis, Indiana State (Member: Labor and Employment Law, General Practice and Solo and Small Firm Sections) and American Bar Associations; The Association of Trial Lawyers of America.

SCHUCKIT & ASSOCIATES, P.C.

Established in 2005
30TH FLOOR MARKET TOWER
10 WEST MARKET STREET
SUITE 3000
INDIANAPOLIS, INDIANA 46204
Telephone: 317-363-2400
Fax: 317-363-2257
URL: http://www.schuckitlaw.com

Business Litigation in State and Federal Trial and Appellate Courts, Property Tax Appeals and Business Transactions.

ROBERT J. SCHUCKIT, born Milwaukee, Wisconsin, August 14, 1957; admitted to bar, 1982, Wisconsin and Illinois; 1990, Indiana; 1993, U.S. Court of Appeals, Seventh Circuit. *Education:* Brandeis University (B.A., cum laude, 1979); University of Wisconsin Law School-Madison (J.D., 1982). Former-Partner, Keck, Mahin & Cate, Chicago, Illinois. Member, Board of Directors and Executive Committee, Hasten Hebrew Academy of Indianapolis. *Member:* Indianapolis, Indiana, Illinois State and Seventh Circuit Bar Associations; State Bar of Wisconsin; Indiana Trial Lawyers Association. ***PRACTICE AREAS:*** Civil Litigation (90%); Property Tax (9%); Eminent Domain (1%). ***Email:*** rschuckit@schuckitlaw.com

ASSOCIATES

CHRISTOPHER T. LANE, born Saginaw, Michigan, September 4, 1971; admitted to bar, 1999, Indiana. *Education:* University of Notre Dame (B.A., 1994); Indiana University School of Law (J.D., 1998). *Member:* Indianapolis, Indiana State and Federal Bar Associations; Indianapolis Inn of Court (Barrister). ***PRACTICE AREAS:*** Civil Litigation. ***Email:*** clane@schuckitlaw.com

ROBERT E. DUFF, born Rockford, Illinois, August 14, 1967; admitted to bar, 1992, Indiana. *Education:* Purdue University (B.A., double major, with distinction, 1989); Indiana University School of Law (J.D., cum laude, 1992). *Member:* Indianapolis and Federal Bar Associations. ***PRACTICE AREAS:*** Civil Litigation. ***Email:*** reduff@schuckitlaw.com

MICKEY J. LEE, born Indianapolis, Indiana; admitted to bar, 2000, Indiana and U.S. District Court, Northern and Southern Districts of Indiana. *Education:* Indiana University (B.S.; J.D.). *Member:* Indianapolis, Indiana State and Federal Bar Associations. ***PRACTICE AREAS:*** Fair Credit Reporting Act; Labor and Employment; Civil Litigation. ***Email:*** mjlee@schuckitlaw.com

CAMILLE R. NICODEMUS, admitted to bar, 1997, New York; 2004, Indiana; U.S. District Court, Southern and Eastern Districts of New York; U.S. District Court, Southern District of Indiana. *Education:* Hunter College of the City University of New York (B.A., 1991); New York University (J.D., 1996). Phi Beta Kappa (Elected). *Member:* Indiana and American Bar Associations. ***PRACTICE AREAS:*** Employment Litigation; Employment Counseling; Commercial Litigation. ***Email:*** cnicodemus@schuckitlaw.com

SCHULTZ & POGUE, LLP

INDIANAPOLIS, INDIANA

(See Carmel)

Insurance Defense, Personal Injury, Medical Malpractice, Pharmacy Law, Drugs and Medical Devices, Health Care, Administrative Law, Appellate Practice, Government Liability, Products Liability, Construction Law, Labor and Employment.

SCOPELITIS, GARVIN, LIGHT & HANSON, P.C.

Established in 1978
10 WEST MARKET STREET, SUITE 1500
INDIANAPOLIS, INDIANA 46204-2968
Telephone: 317-637-1777
FAX: 317-687-2414
Email: indianapolis@scopelitis.com
URL: http://www.scopelitis.com

Chicago, Illinois Office: 30 West Monroe Street, Suite 600, 60603-2427. Telephone: 312-422-1200. Fax: 312-422-1224.
Washington, D.C. Office: 1850 M Street, N.W., Suite 280, 20036-5804. Telephone: 202-783-9222. Fax: 202-783-9230.
Kansas City, Missouri Office: Two Pershing Square, 2300 Main Street, Suite 900, 64108. Telephone: 816-279-9835. Fax: 816-279-1973.
Pasadena, California Office: 790 East Colorado Boulevard, 9th Floor, 91101. Telephone: 626-795-4700. Fax: 626-795-4790.

General Civil Practice. Litigation in all State and Federal Courts, including Appellate Practice, Transportation, Motor Carrier, Trucking Law, International Trade, Corporate, Mergers & Acquisitions, Administrative, Antitrust and Trade Regulation, Business, Insurance, Insurance Defense, Negligence, Labor and Employment, Employee Benefits, Immigration, Environmental, Workers Compensation, Probate and Estate Planning and Public Utility Law.

FIRM PROFILE: Scopelitis, Garvin, Light & Hanson, P.C. is a full-service law firm that offers a wide range of legal services to clients in many industries, including manufacturing, e-commerce, retail products, construction, and environmental concerns. Of particular note is the firm's knowledge of the transportation industry and its long-standing history of service to motor carriers, shippers, brokers and insurance companies nationwide. From its offices in Indianapolis, Chicago, Washington, D.C., Kansas City and Pasadena, the firm offers clients knowledge and experience in many business-related disciplines and also seeks to meet its clients' more individual needs in such areas as personal injury litigation, estate planning and probate administration.

NORMAN R. GARVIN, born Terre Haute, Indiana, February 1, 1948; admitted to bar, 1973, Indiana and Florida. *Education:* Indiana State University (B.A., 1970); Indiana University (J.D., magna cum laude, 1973). *Member:* The Florida Bar; American Trucking Associations; Association for Transportation Law, Logistics and Policy; Canadian Transport Lawyers Association; Truckload Carriers Conference; National Tank Truck Carriers, Inc.; Transportation Lawyers Association. ***SPECIAL AGENCIES:*** U.S. Department of Transportation, Federal Motor Carrier Safety Administration; Indiana Department of Revenue. ***PRACTICE AREAS:*** Transportation Law; Mergers and Acquisitions; Restructuring; Trucking Law; Transportation Regulation; International Transportation Law; Motor Carrier Law; Motor Carrier Regulation; Freights and Claims; Contract Law; Corporate Law. ***Email:*** ngarvin@scopelitis.com

ANDREW K. LIGHT, born Indianapolis, Indiana, November 10, 1954; admitted to bar, 1980, Indiana. *Education:* Indiana University (B.A., with distinction, 1977; J.D., 1980). Phi Beta Kappa. *Member:* Indianapolis and Indiana State Bar Associations; Association for Transportation Law, Logistics and Policy; Transportation Lawyers Association (Member,

(This Listing Continued)

Executive Committee); American Trucking Associations. ***SPECIAL AGENCIES:*** Indiana Department of Revenue; U.S. Department of Transportation, Federal Highway Administration. ***PRACTICE AREAS:*** Transportation; Administrative Law; Regulatory Law; Insurance; International Trade; Cargo Claims; Trucking Liability; State Taxation. ***Email:*** alight@scopelitis.com

JAMES H. HANSON, born Chicago, Illinois, January 5, 1956; admitted to bar, 1981, Indiana. *Education:* Anderson University (B.A., magna cum laude, 1978); Indiana University (J.D., magna cum laude, 1981). *Member:* Indianapolis, Indiana State and American Bar Associations; Christian Legal Society; North American Transportation Employee Relations Association (Vice-Chairman, 2001—). ***SPECIAL AGENCIES:*** National Labor Relations Board; Equal Employment Opportunity Commission; Indiana Civil Rights Commission; U.S. Department of Labor; Indiana Department of Labor. ***PRACTICE AREAS:*** Labor and Employment; Business and Commercial Transactions; Civil Litigation; Motor Carrier Transportation Law. ***Email:*** jhanson@scopelitis.com

LYNNE D. LIDKE, born Michigan City, Indiana, December 6, 1957; admitted to bar, 1982, Indiana. *Education:* Purdue University (B.A., 1979); Indiana University (J.D., cum laude, 1982). Note and Development Editor, Indiana Law Review, 1981-1982. Law Clerk to the Honorable Paul H. Buchanan, Jr., Indiana Court of Appeals, 1982-1984. *Member:* Indiana State and American Bar Associations. ***SPECIAL AGENCIES:*** Indiana Department of Revenue. ***PRACTICE AREAS:*** Appellate Practice; Insurance Coverage; Insurance Defense; State Taxation; Trucking Liability. ***Email:*** llidke@scopelitis.com

THOMAS E. FARRELL, born Indianapolis, Indiana, February 6, 1950; admitted to bar, 1986, Indiana. *Education:* Indiana University (B.A., 1979; J.D., 1986). Certified Civil Mediator. *Member:* Indianapolis, Indiana State and American (Member, Sections on: Tort and Insurance Practice; Litigation) Bar Associations; Defense Research Institute; Indiana Defense Lawyers Association; Trucking Industry Insurance Defense Association. ***PRACTICE AREAS:*** Litigation; Insurance Defense; Insurance. ***Email:*** tfarrell@scopelitis.com

GREGORY M. FEARY, born LaGrange, Illinois, November 18, 1957; admitted to bar, 1988, Indiana. *Education:* Eastern Illinois University (B.A., 1979); Indiana University (J.D., 1988). Author and Panelist, "Workers' Compensation in Indiana, Issues and Answers," National Business Institute, 1992, 1995; "Occupational Accident Insurance," American Trucking Associations, 1997; "1995 Development in Workers Compensation," 29 Ind. L. Rev. 1139 (1996); "Captives," National Accounting and Finance Council, 2000. Special Counsel for: American Trucking Associations, 1994-1999; The American Movers Conference, 1997. *Member:* Indiana Defense Lawyers Association (Vice Chairman, Workers' Compensation Section, 1994-1996; Chairman Elect, 1997). ***SPECIAL AGENCIES:*** Insurance Department of Indiana; Workers' Compensation Board of Indiana; Federal Highway Administration; Internal Revenue Service. ***PRACTICE AREAS:*** Contracts; Insurance Law; Motor Carrier Law. ***Email:*** gfeary@scopelitis.com

ROBERT L. BROWNING, born Bellefontaine, Ohio, March 19, 1962; admitted to bar, 1988, Arizona; 1990, Indiana. *Education:* Purdue University (B.S., 1985); Indiana University (J.D., 1988). Instructor, Indiana Bar Review. ***PRACTICE AREAS:*** Civil Litigation; Commercial and Business Transactions; Motor Carrier Transportation Law; Cargo Claims; Creditor's Rights Law. ***Email:*** rbrowning@scopelitis.com

STEVEN A. PLETCHER, born Goshen, Indiana, June 2, 1958; admitted to bar, 1991, Indiana. *Education:* Indiana University (B.S., 1986); Valparaiso University (J.D., magna cum laude, 1991). Member, National Moot Court Team. Author, "1995 Development in Workers Compensation," 29 Ind. L. Rev. 1139 (1996). Senior Editorial Staff, "The Alternative Workforce," American Bar Association. *Member:* Indianapolis, Indiana State and American Bar Associations; National Association of Professional Employer Organizations. ***SPECIAL AGENCIES:*** Internal Revenue Service; U.S. Department of Transportation, Federal Highway Administration; Indiana Department of Revenue. ***PRACTICE AREAS:*** Employee Benefits; Employment Taxes; State Taxation; Workers Compensation; Labor and Employment Law. ***Email:*** spletcher@scopelitis.com

TIMOTHY W. WISEMAN, born Indianapolis, Indiana, April 1, 1966; admitted to bar, 1993, Indiana. *Education:* Indiana University (LL.B., magna cum laude, 1993). *Member:* Indianapolis, Indiana State and American Bar Associations. ***PRACTICE AREAS:*** Transportation Law; Workers Compensation; Transportation Safety. ***Email:*** twiseman@scopelitis.com

JAY D. ROBINSON, JR., born Indianapolis, Indiana, July 2, 1959; admitted to bar, 1988, Indiana. *Education:* Southern Methodist University (B.A., 1982); Indiana University (J.D., 1988). *Member:* Indianapolis and Indiana State Bar Associations. ***PRACTICE AREAS:*** Business Law; Construction Law; Corporate and Partnership; Sales; Mergers and Acquisitions. ***Email:*** jrobinson@scopelitis.com

MICHAEL B. LANGFORD, born New Castle, Indiana, February 19, 1969; admitted to bar, 1994, Indiana. *Education:* Wabash College (B.A., cum laude, 1991); Indiana University (J.D., 1994). Order of the Barristers. National Moot Court Team. National Moot Court Honor Board. ***PRACTICE AREAS:*** Insurance Defense; Commercial Litigation; Employment and Labor Law; Insurance Law; Motor Carrier Liability Law. ***Email:*** mlangford@scopelitis.com

ANGELA S. CASH, born Louisville, Kentucky, December 10, 1966; admitted to bar, 1995, Indiana and U.S. District Court, Northern and Southern Districts of Indiana. *Education:* Butler University (B.S., cum laude, 1989); Indiana University (J.D., summa cum laude, Forrest Jump Scholar, 1995). Note Development Editor, Indiana Law Review, 1994-1995. *Member:* Indianapolis, Indiana State and American Bar Associations. ***PRACTICE AREAS:*** Litigation; Probate; Transportation Law; Truck Accidents. ***Email:*** acash@scopelitis.com

JEFFREY S. TOOLE, born Indianapolis, Indiana, January 9, 1967; admitted to bar, 1997, Indiana. *Education:* Indiana University (B.S., 1989; J.D., summa cum laude, 1996). Member. 1994-1996 and Editor-in-Chief, 1995-1996, Indiana Law Review. Intern for The Honorable Chief Justice Randall T. Sheperd, Indiana Supreme Court, 1996. *Member:* Indianapolis, Indiana and American Bar Associations. ***PRACTICE AREAS:*** Insurance; Employee Benefits; Taxation; Trusts and Estates; Business Law. ***Email:*** jtoole@scopelitis.com

DAVID D. ROBINSON, born Indianapolis, Indiana, May 11, 1965; admitted to bar, 1991, Indiana. *Education:* DePauw University (B.A., 1987); Indiana University School of Law (J.D., 1991). Indiana Law Review, 1991. *Member:* Indianapolis, Indiana State and American Bar Associations. ***PRACTICE AREAS:*** Labor and Employment Law. ***Email:*** drobinson@scopelitis.com

(This Listing Continued)

W. TODD METZGER, born Marietta, Georgia, February 7, 1971; admitted to bar, 1997, Indiana. *Education:* Purdue University (B.S. with Distinction, 1993); Indiana University School of Law (J.D., magna cum laude, 1997). Recipient, Krannert School of Management Outstanding Senior Award, Purdue. Scholarship, Forrest E. Jump, Indiana University. ***PRACTICE AREAS:*** Corporate Law; Business Transactions Law; Real Estate Law; Litigation. ***Email:*** tmetzger@scopelitis.com

CHRISTOPHER R. WHITTEN, born Fort Rucker, Alabama, January 28, 1971; admitted to bar, 1997, Indiana. *Education:* University of California, San Diego (B.A., 1993); Valparaiso University School of Law (J.D., magna cum laude, 1997). Editorial Board Member, Valparaiso University Law Review, 1996-1997. ***PRACTICE AREAS:*** Transportation; Commercial Litigation; Cargo Claims; Insurance Defense Litigation. ***Email:*** cwhitten@scopelitis.com

CRAIG J. HELMREICH, born Des Plaines, Illinois, October 10, 1975; admitted to bar, 2000, Indiana. *Education:* Butler University (B.A., 1997); Indiana University (J.D., cum laude, 2000). Law Alumni Scholar. ***PRACTICE AREAS:*** Litigation; Motor Carrier Law; Intellectual Property. ***Email:*** chelmreich@scopelitis.com

A. JACK FINKLEA, born Indianapolis, Indiana, August 29, 1967; admitted to bar, 2000, Indiana. *Education:* Indiana University (B.A., 1996; J.D., summa cum laude, 2000). *Member:* Indiana State Bar Association; Legal Aid Society. ***PRACTICE AREAS:*** Labor and Employment; Appellate Practice; Civil Litigation. ***Email:*** jfinklea@scopelitis.com

REBECCA S. SMITH, born Knox, Indiana, March 7, 1975; admitted to bar, 2002, Indiana and U.S. District Court, Northern and Southern Districts of Indiana. *Education:* Valparaiso University (B.S., 1997; J.D., 2002). *Member:* Indianapolis, Indiana State and American Bar Associations. ***PRACTICE AREAS:*** Transportation; Insurance. ***Email:*** rsmith@scopelitis.com

SHANNON M. COHEN, born Salem, Indiana, May 1, 1976; admitted to bar, 2002, Indiana and U.S. District Court, Southern and Northern Districts of Indiana. *Education:* Indiana University, Bloomington (B.S., 1998); Indiana University School of Law - Bloomington (J.D., cum laude, 2002). *Member:* Indianapolis, Indiana State, and American Bar Associations. ***PRACTICE AREAS:*** Transportation; Litigation. ***Email:*** scohen@scopelitis.com

ERIC K. HABIG, born Indianapolis, Indiana, July 29, 1971; admitted to bar, 1999, Indiana and U.S. District Court, Northern and Southern Districts of Indiana. *Education:* DePauw University (B.A., 1993); Indiana University School of Law (J.D., 1999). *Member:* Indianapolis and Indiana State Bar Associations; Defense Trial Counsel Institute; Defense Research Institute. ***PRACTICE AREAS:*** Litigation; Insurance Defense; Motor Carrier Liability. ***Email:*** ehabig@scopelitis.com

ALLISON OWEN SMITH, born Stamford, Connecticut, July 28, 1965; admitted to bar, 1996, Indiana and U.S. District Court, Northern and Southern Districts of Indiana. *Education:* University of Colorado at Boulder (B.A., 1987); Indiana University School of Law - Indianapolis (J.D., 1996). Member, Board of Directors, Indianapolis Bar Foundation. *Member:* Indianapolis and Indiana State Bar Associations. Fellow, Indianapolis Bar Foundation. ***PRACTICE AREAS:*** Business Development. ***Email:*** asmith@scopleitis.com

RONALD J. MORELOCK, born Tipton, Indiana, July 17, 1963; admitted to bar, 1993, Indiana. ***PRACTICE AREAS:*** Taxation. ***Email:*** rmorelock@scopelitis.com

R. JAY TAYLOR, JR., born Philadelphia, Pennsylvania, January 26, 1970; admitted to bar, 1996, Indiana and U.S. District Court, Northern and Southern Districts of Indiana. *Education:* University of Richmond (B.A., 1992); University of Richmond School of Law (J.D., cum laude, 1996). Member, McNeill Law Society. ***PRACTICE AREAS:*** Litigation; Appellate Practice; Transportation Liability Defense.

OF COUNSEL

ALKI E. SCOPELITIS, born South Bend, Indiana, April 12, 1937; admitted to bar, 1964, Indiana. *Education:* Yale University (B.A., 1959); Georgetown University (LL.B., 1964). Phi Delta Phi. *Member:* Indiana State Bar Association. [1st Lt., USMC, 1959-1961]. ***PRACTICE AREAS:*** Mediation; Transportation Law; Administrative/Regulatory Matters; Labor and Employment Law; Estate Planning; Probate; Business Transactions; Commercial Transactions. ***Email:*** ascopelitis@scopelitis.com

CARLA R. HOUNSHEL, born Seymour, Indiana, March 23, 1971; admitted to bar, 1996, Indiana and U.S. Court of Appeals, Seventh Circuit. *Education:* Vanderbilt University (B.A., History, magna cum laude, 1993); Indiana University (J.D., cum laude, 1996). Indiana Law Review, 1994-1996; Symposium Editor, 1995-1996. *Member:* Indianapolis, Indiana State and American Bar Association. ***PRACTICE AREAS:*** Labor and Employment Law; Civil Litigation; Workers Compensation Law. ***Email:*** chounshel@scopelitis.com

RICHARD A. CLARK, born Indianapolis, Indiana, February 16, 1958; admitted to bar, 1983, Indiana and U.S. District Court, Northern and Southern Districts of Indiana; 1987, U.S. Court of Appeals, Seventh Circuit. *Education:* Wabash College (B.A., 1980); Indiana University School of Law (J.D., cum laude, 1983). *Member:* American Bar Association; Transportation Lawyers Association. ***PRACTICE AREAS:*** Transportation; Litigation; Motor Carrier Law; Trucking Law; Transportation Regulation. ***Email:*** rclark@scopelitis.com

GREGORY A. OSTENDORF, born Vincennes, Indiana, March 3, 1955; admitted to bar, 1980, Texas; 1996, Illinois; 2005, Indiana. *Education:* Western Kentucky University (B.S., 1977); Indiana University School of Law - Indianapolis (J.D., 1980). *Member:* Houston Bar Association. ***PRACTICE AREAS:*** Commercial Transactions; Business Transactions; Bankruptcy; Mergers and Acquisitions. ***Email:*** gostendorf@scopelitis.com

REPRESENTATIVE CLIENTS: Carey International, Inc.; Celadon Trucking Services, Inc.; Comcar Industries, Inc.; Dana Corporation; Dean Foods; Diakon Logistics, Inc.; Exel; FedEx; Graebel Van Lines; Great West Casualty Company; Hanjin Shipping Company; J.B. Hunt

(This Listing Continued)

SCOPELITIS, GARVIN, LIGHT & HANSON, P.C., Indianapolis—Continued

Transport, Inc.; Lancer Insurance; Landstar System, Inc.; Liquid Transport Corp.; Maersk, Inc.; Mansur Real Estate Services, Inc.; McLane Foodservices, Inc.; Northland Insurance; Overnite Transportation Company; Penske System, Inc.; Pepsi Americas, Inc.; Roadlink USA: Schneider National Inc.; SIRVA/Allied Van Line, Inc./North American Van Lines, Inc.; Steak 'n Shake; Swift Transportation, Co.; Tyson Foods, Inc.; USA Truck, Inc.; Unigroup, Inc./Mayflower Transit, LLC/United Van Lines, LLC; Watkins Associated Industries, Inc.; Yellow Roadway Corporation.

SHIPLEY & ASSOCIATES

INDIANAPOLIS, INDIANA

(See Fort Wayne)

Bankruptcy other than consumer bankruptcy, Commercial Law, Commercial Litigation.

CURTIS E. SHIRLEY

Established in 1991

156 EAST MARKET STREET, SUITE 600
INDIANAPOLIS, INDIANA 46204
Telephone: 317-685-6512
Toll Free: 877-953-4900
Facsimile: 317-685-6505
URL: http://www.curtisshirleylaw.com
Email: curtis@shirleylaw.net
URL: http://www.shirleylaw.net

Wills and Probate, Guardianships, Contested Wills, Contested Trusts and Estates, Estate Litigation, Trust Litigation, Probate Litigation, Probate Taxation, Probate Administration, Estate Administration, Business Litigation, Complex Business Litigation, Fraud, Securities Fraud, Breach of Contract, Criminal Tax Defense.

FIRM PROFILE: Curtis E. Shirley is listed in Martindale-Hubbell's Bar Register of Preeminent Lawyers.

CURTIS E. SHIRLEY, born Portsmouth, Ohio, October 10, 1960; admitted to bar, 1991, Indiana; U.S. District Court, Northern and Southern Districts of Indiana; U.S. Court of Appeals, Seventh Circuit; U.S. Supreme Court. *Education:* University of Evansville (B.M.E., 1983); Indiana University (M.M.,1985; J.D., summa cum laude, 1991). Phi Delta Phi (President, 1990-1991). Alumni Scholar, Indiana University. Cale J. Holder Fellow. Lloyd Balfour Scholar. Harold R. Woodard Fellow. Associate Editor, Indiana Law Review, 1990-1991. Law Clerk to Honorable James E. Noland, U.S.D.C., Indianapolis, 1991-1992. Law Clerk to Honorable Daniel A. Manion, Seventh Circuit, 1992-1993. Partner, Cremer, Miller & Burroughs, 1993-2000. Author: "Taxation in Contested Estates," ICLEF 2000; "Tortious Interference With An Expectancy," Res Gestae, V.41, No. 4 1997. Author and Presenter, ICLEF Probate Litigation Seminars, 1997—; "The Legacy of Larry Inlow," ICLEF, 2004; "Taxation of Settlements," ICLEF, 2001; "Evidentiary Matters in Probate Litigation," ICLEF, 2002. Co-Author: "An Overview of Trust Litigation," ICLEF Seminar 1998. Author and Presenter, "Trust Litigation." Chairman, National Estate and Trust Litigation Institute, 2002. *Member:* Indianapolis, Seventh Circuit and Indiana State (Member, Sections on: Taxation Law; Probate Trust and Real Property) Bar Associations; Indiana Trial Lawyers Association; Estate Planning Council of Indianapolis, Inc.; Indianapolis Legal Aid Society (Chairman, Board of Directors, 1993—); National Institute for Trial Advocacy; Federal Law Clerk Society. ***REPORTED CASES:*** Hickman v. Irwin Union Bank, 811 N.E.2d 843 (Ind.App. 2004); Guardianship of Hickman, 805 N.E.2d 808 (Ind.App. 2004); Wagner v. Spurlock, 803 N.E.2d 1174 (Ind.App. 2004); Keith v. Dooley, 802 N.E.2d 54 (Ind.App. 2004) (cited Mr. Shirley); Saler v. Irick, 800 N.E.2d 960 (Ind.App. 2003); Miller v. NBD Bank, 701 N.E.2d 282 (Inc.App. 1998); Spears v. City of Indianapolis, 74 F.3d 153 (7th Cir. 1996); U.S. v. Caswell, 36 F.3d 29 (7th Cir. 1994); Harris v. AC & S, 915 F.Supp. 1420 (S.D.Ind. 1995).

ASSOCIATE

MOLLY C. JOHNSON, born Connersville, Indiana, December 19, 1974; admitted to bar, 2003, Indiana; U.S. District Court, Northern and Southern Districts of Indiana. *Education:* Purdue University (B.A., 1997); Loyola University, Chicago and Loyola University, Rome, Italy (J.D., 2001). Delta Gamma; Phi Alpha Delta. Golden Key. International Law Society. Public Interest Law Society. Dean's List (nine semesters). Director of Rush Personnel, Purdue University Panhellenic Association, 1994-1995; Vice-President of Administration, 1995-1996; Vice-President of Operations, 1995-1996. President, Mid-American Greek Council Association, 1995-1996. Greek Judicial Chair, Purdue University, 1995-1996. Law Clerk, Office of Attorney General Steve Carter, Indiana, 2001-2003.

SKEKLOFF, ADELSPERGER & KLEVEN, LLP

INDIANAPOLIS, INDIANA

(See Fort Wayne)

Bankruptcy, Creditors' Rights, Insolvency, and related Commercial Litigation and Transactions.

MARK SMALL

6434 NORTH COLLEGE AVENUE, SUITE B
INDIANAPOLIS, INDIANA 46220-2426
Telephone: 317-252-4800; 317-253-7476
Fax: 317-475-9578
Email: marksmall2001@yahoo.com
URL: http://www.smalllaw.com

Appeals, Criminal, Drug Crimes, Driving While Intoxicated, Death Penalty Cases, Personal Injury.

(This Listing Continued)

MARK SMALL, born Kokomo, Indiana, June 11, 1955; admitted to bar, 1989, Indiana and U.S. District Court, Southern and Northern Districts of Indiana; 1990, U.S. Court of Appeals, Seventh and Ninth Circuits; 1998, U.S. Supreme Court; U.S. Court of Appeals, Federal Circuit, District of Columbia. *Education:* DePauw University (B.A., 1978); Indiana University (J.D., 1989). Member: Order of Barristers; Indiana University School of Law Moot Court Society; American Bar Association National Appellate Advocacy Competition Team. *Member:* Indianapolis, Indiana State (Member, Appellate Section) and American Bar Associations. ***REPORTED CASES:*** Doe v. Methodist Hospital, 690 N.E.2d 681 (Ind. 1997).

JANICE E. SMITH
ATTORNEY AT LAW

617 E. MICHIGAN STREET, SUITE A
INDIANAPOLIS, INDIANA 46202
Telephone: 317-624-4220
Fax: 317-624-4224
URL: http://www.jansmithlaw.com
Email: jsmithlawofc@indy.rr.com
URL: http://www.jsmithlawofc.com

Criminal, Family and Education Law.

JANICE E. SMITH, born Bluffton, Indiana, October 28, 1941; admitted to bar, 1992, Indiana and U.S. District Court, Northern and Southern Districts of Indiana. *Education:* Purdue University (B.A., English and Spanish, 1962; M.S., Guidance and Counseling, 1967; Ed. Admin., Administration Certification, 1975); Indiana University - Bloomington (Ed.D., Educational Psychology, 1976); Indiana University - Indianapolis (J.D., 1992). Recipient: EPDA Fellowship for Doctorate Program, Indiana University; NDEA Fellowship for Masters Program, Purdue University; Valedictorian Merit Scholarship, Purdue University. Superintendent of Public Schools, Life License. School Psychologist License. Teacher, Secondary, Life License, Indiana. Basic Certificate, License, Indiana Board of Examiners in Psychology. Speaker: "After a Disturbance, How To Come Out a Winner with Innovation Programming," International Conference of the Correctional Education Association; "Delivery of Education to Inmates," Vocational Education Administrators Conference; "Effecting New Roles in School Psychology," Regional Correctional Education Association and Indiana Psychological Association; "Intervention on the Kindergarten Level," Indiana Council for Exceptional Children; "Working with Schools," Indiana Psychological Association; "Consultation and Change Models," State Department of Public Instruction Workshop; "Integration of Programmatic Services in a Correction Setting," TIE Conference. Former Member: Governor's Round Table, Charter Member; Governor's Task Force on Drunk Driving; Resource Committee, Governor's Panel on Vocational Education; State Library Advisory Council; State Advisory Council to Vocational Education; Indiana Office of Occupational Development Advisory Council. ***PRACTICE AREAS:*** Criminal Law; Family Law; Education Law.

THEODORE F. SMITH, JR.

INDIANAPOLIS, INDIANA

(See Anderson)

Social Security Disability, Personal Injury, Wrongful Death.

SOMMER BARNARD ATTORNEYS, PC

Established in 1969

ONE INDIANA SQUARE, SUITE 3500
INDIANAPOLIS, INDIANA 46204
Telephone: 317-713-3500
Fax: 317-713-3699
Email: mail@sommerbarnard.com
URL: http://www.sommerbarnard.com

North Office: 8888 Keystone Crossing, Suite 1400, Indianapolis, Indiana, 46240-4609. Telephone: 317-844-4744. Fax: 317-844-4780.

Antitrust and Trade Regulation, Banking, Bankruptcy and Debtors' and Creditors' Rights. Business and Corporate Transactions, Mergers and Acquisitions, Civil Trial and Appellate Litigation, Computer Law, Environmental Litigation and Regulatory Consultation, Debt and Equity Financing, Probate and Estate Planning, Administration, Federal and State Income Tax Planning, Consultation and Litigation, Federal and State Securities Regulation, Telecommunications; Utility Regulatory Law, Franchising and Licensing, Insurance Regulation and Insolvencies, International Law, Labor and Employment, ERISA Law and Litigation, Collective Bargaining and Arbitration, Employment Discrimination Law, Real Estate, Technology Based Transactions, Intellectual Property, Public Finance, Plaintiff Litigation, International, Agricultural Law.

FIRM PROFILE: Founded in 1969, Sommer Barnard engages in a general and diverse civil practice representing individuals, corporations and other business entities in local, regional, national and international matters. The Firm continues to develop and maintain its professional capabilities by hiring outstanding law school graduates and experienced, highly capable attorneys. Many of the firm's attorneys are active in a wide range of civic, charitable and professional organizations.

EDWARD W. HARRIS, III, admitted to bar, 1968, Indiana. *Education:* Amherst College (B.A., 1964); University of Michigan (J.D., cum laude, 1967). ***PRACTICE AREAS:*** Antitrust Law; Commercial Litigation. **Email:** eharris@sommerbarnard.com

FREDERICK M. KING, admitted to bar, 1964, Indiana. *Education:* Indiana University (B.S., 1959; J.D., 1964). ***PRACTICE AREAS:*** Labor Relations Law; Collective Bargaining and Arbitration; Employment Discrimination Law; Employment Litigation. **Email:** fking@sommerbarnard.com

(This Listing Continued)

JERALD I. ANCEL, admitted to bar, 1968, Indiana. *Education:* Indiana University (B.S., Accounting, 1965; J.D., 1968). Phi Delta Phi. ***PRACTICE AREAS:*** Bankruptcy and Debtors' and Creditors' Rights. ***Email:*** jancel@sommerbarnard.com

JAMES A. STRAIN, admitted to bar, 1969, Indiana and U.S. District Court, Southern District of Indiana; 1970, U.S. Court of Appeals, Seventh Circuit; 1976, Supreme Court. *Education:* Indiana University (A.B., 1966; J.D., cum laude, 1969). Law Clerk: to Hon. John S. Hastings, Senior Circuit Judge, U.S. Court of Appeals for the Seventh Circuit, 1970-1971; Hon. William H. Rehnquist, Justice, U.S. Supreme Court, 1972-1973. *Member:* Indianapolis, Seventh Circuit (Past President), Indiana State and American Bar Associations. ***REPORTED CASES:*** CTS Corporation v. Dynamics Corporation of America, 481 U.S. 69 (1987). ***PRACTICE AREAS:*** Mergers and Acquisitions; Corporate; Securities. ***Email:*** strain@sommerbarnard.com

LINDA L. PENCE, admitted to bar, 1974, Indiana, U.S. District Court, Southern and Northern Districts of Indiana, U.S. Temporary Emergency Court of Appeals and U.S. Court of Appeals, Fourth, Seventh, Ninth, Tenth and Federal Circuits; 1982, District of Columbia and U.S. Supreme Court. *Education:* Indiana University (B.A., 1971; J.D., 1974). Chief, Special Projects Branch, Deputy Chief, Government Fraud Section, Criminal Division, 1978-1983 and Trial Attorney, Civil Division, 1974-1978, U.S. Department of Justice, Washington, D.C. ***PRACTICE AREAS:*** White Collar Criminal Defense; Civil Litigation. ***Email:*** lpence@sommerbarnard.com

ERIC R. JOHNSON, admitted to bar, 1975, California (inactive) and Indiana. *Education:* Indiana University (B.A., with distinction, 1971); Stanford University (J.D., 1975). Phi Beta Kappa. ***PRACTICE AREAS:*** Mergers and Acquisitions; Business and Corporate Transactions; Insurance Regulation and Insolvencies. ***Email:*** ejohnson@sommerbarnard.com

ROBERT D. SWHIER, JR., admitted to bar, 1975, Indiana. *Education:* Purdue University (B.S., with highest distinction, 1971); London School of Economics, London, England (M.S., 1972); Harvard University (J.D., magna cum laude, 1975). Phi Beta Kappa. Rotary Foundation Fellowship, London School of Economics. ***PRACTICE AREAS:*** Municipal Finance; Municipal Law; Securities; Corporate Law. ***Email:*** rswhier@sommerbarnard.com

DONALD K. DENSBORN, admitted to bar, 1976, Indiana. *Education:* Indiana University (B.S., Business, magna cum laude, 1973; J.D., magna cum laude, 1976). Beta Gamma Sigma. Member, National Conference of Commissioners on Uniform State Laws. ***PRACTICE AREAS:*** Mergers and Acquisitions Law; Corporate Law; Finance Law; Real Estate Law. ***Email:*** ddensborn@sommerbarnard.com

GORDON L. PITTENGER, admitted to bar, 1977, Indiana. *Education:* DePauw University (A.B., with high distinction, 1973); Indiana University (J.D., magna cum laude, 1977). Phi Beta Kappa. ***PRACTICE AREAS:*** Computer Law; Civil Trial and Appellate Litigation; Legal Ethics and Professional Responsibility. ***Email:*** gpittenger@sommerbarnard.com

MARK A. PALMER, admitted to bar, 1977, Georgia; 1979, Indiana, U.S. Supreme Court, U.S. Court of Appeals, Seventh Circuit and U.S. District Court, Southern District of Indiana. *Education:* Kentucky Wesleyan College (B.A., 1974); Mercer University (J.D., 1977). ***PRACTICE AREAS:*** Legislative and Regulatory Affairs; Government Services. ***Email:*** mpalmer@sommerbarnard.com

FRANK J. DEVEAU, admitted to bar, 1980, Indiana. *Education:* Indiana University (A.B., 1976; J.D., summa cum laude, 1980). ***PRACTICE AREAS:*** Environmental Litigation; Regulation and Administrative Proceedings; Municipal Law; Local Government Practice; Insurance Litigation. ***Email:*** fdeveau@sommerbarnard.com

ROBERT R. CLARK, admitted to bar, 1979, Indiana; U.S. District Court, Northern and Southern Districts of Indiana; U.S. Supreme Court; U.S. Court of Federal Claims; U.S. Court of Appeals, 7th and Federal Circuits. *Education:* Valparaiso University (B.A., 1976; J.D., 1979). Judicial Clerk, Indiana Court of Appeals, 4th District, 1979-1980. ***PRACTICE AREAS:*** Environmental Law; Litigation. ***Email:*** rclark@sommerbarnard.com

MICHAEL C. TERRELL, admitted to bar, 1984, Indiana. *Education:* Indiana University (B.S., with high distinction, 1981; J.D., cum laude, 1984). ***PRACTICE AREAS:*** Labor and Employment Law; Employment Discrimination; Employment Law Litigation; Civil Trial and Appellate Litigation; Municipal Law; Municipal Utility Regulation. ***Email:*** mterrell@sommerbarnard.com

THOMAS A. BARNARD, admitted to bar, 1982, Indiana, U.S. District Court, Northern and Southern Districts of Indiana, U.S. Court of Federal Claims and U.S. Court of Appeals, Seventh Circuit. *Education:* Purdue University (B.S., with distinction, 1979); Indiana University (J.D., cum laude, 1982). Phi Kappa Phi; Phi Eta Sigma; Beta Gamma Sigma. ***PRACTICE AREAS:*** Environmental Law; Litigation. ***Email:*** tbarnard@sommerbarnard.com

MARLENE REICH, admitted to bar, 1983, Indiana; U.S. District Court, Northern and Southern Districts of Indiana and U.S. Court of Appeals, Seventh Circuit. *Education:* Indiana University (B.A., cum laude, 1976; J.D., cum laude, 1983). Phi Beta Kappa. *Member:* Indianapolis (Member, Commercial and Bankruptcy Law Section, Chair, 1993), Indiana State (Member, Bankruptcy and Creditors' Rights Section, Contributing Editor, The Order for Relief, 1992-1998) and American (Member, Corporation, Banking and Business Law Section) Bar Associations; American Bankruptcy Institute. ***PRACTICE AREAS:*** Bankruptcy and Debtors' and Creditors' Rights. ***Email:*** mreich@sommerbarnard.com

RICHARD C. RICHMOND, III, admitted to bar, 1983, Indiana; U.S. Court of Appeals, Seventh Circuit; U.S. District Court, Southern District of Indiana; U.S. District Court, Northern District of Indiana. *Education:* Franklin College of Indiana (B.A., cum laude, 1980); Indiana University (J.D., 1983). ***PRACTICE AREAS:*** Commercial Litigation; Debtors; Landlord and Tenant; Construction. ***Email:*** rrichmond@sommerbarnard.com

STEVEN C. SHOCKLEY, admitted to bar, 1984, Indiana; 1986, Florida (inactive). *Education:* Indiana University (B.A., 1978; J.D., magna cum laude, 1984). Phi Beta Kappa. ***PRACTICE AREAS:*** Civil Trial and Appellate Litigation. ***Email:*** sshockley@sommerbarnard.com

(This Listing Continued)

JOHN H. SHARPE, admitted to bar, 1981, Indiana, U.S. District Court, Southern District of Indiana and U.S. Court of Appeals, Seventh Circuit. *Education:* Indiana University (B.A., 1972; M.P.A., 1974; J.D., 1981). Phi Delta Phi. *Member:* Indiana State Bar Association; National Health Lawyers Association. ***PRACTICE AREAS:*** Business Transactions; Administrative Law; Health Care Regulation; Health Care Reimbursement; Civil and Appellate Practice. ***Email:*** jsharpe@sommerbarnard.com

ERICK D. PONADER, admitted to bar, 1985, Illinois and U.S. District Court, Northern District of Illinois; 1988, Indiana and U.S. District Court, Northern District of Indiana; U.S. District Court, Southern District of Indiana. *Education:* Indiana University (B.A., Chemistry, 1982; J.D., 1985). ***PRACTICE AREAS:*** Real Estate Law; Business; Corporate Transactions; Intellectual Property Law. ***Email:*** eponader@sommerbarnard.com

ROBERT J. HICKS, admitted to bar, 1987, Indiana. *Education:* Butler University (B.S., Business Accounting, cum laude, 1984; B.S., Accounting, with high honors, 1984); Marshall-Wythe School of Law, College of William and Mary (J.D., 1986). Order of the Coif. Member, William and Mary Law Review. Certified Public Accountant. ***PRACTICE AREAS:*** Complex Business and Commercial Transactions; Merger, Acquisition and Joint Venture Transactions; Business Advisory Services. ***Email:*** rhicks@sommerbarnard.com

LAWRENCE A. VANORE, admitted to bar, 1986, Indiana. *Education:* Hofstra University (B.A., 1981); Indiana University (M.P.A., 1986; J.D., magna cum laude, 1986). Order of the Coif. ***PRACTICE AREAS:*** Environmental Law; Insurance Law; Zoning, Planning and Land Use; Occupational Safety and Health. ***Email:*** lvanore@sommerbarnard.com

DONALD C. BIGGS, admitted to bar, 1979, Indiana. *Education:* Indiana University (B.S., with highest distinction, 1976); Indiana University School of Law-Bloomington (J.D., magna cum laude, 1979). Beta Gamma Sigma; Phi Eta Sigma. ***PRACTICE AREAS:*** Environmental Law; Commercial Litigation. ***Email:*** dbiggs@sommerbarnard.com

GAYLE A. REINDL, admitted to bar, 1987, Indiana; 1988, U.S. Court of Appeals, 7th Circuit; 1996, U.S. Court of Appeals, 10th Circuit; 1998, U.S. Court of Appeals, 3rd Circuit. *Education:* Cornell University (B.S.N., with distinction, 1970); University of Colorado (M.S., 1973); Indiana University (J.D., summa cum laude, 1987). Law Clerk to the Honorable S. Hugh Dillin, United States District Court, Southern District of Indiana, 1987-1989. ***PRACTICE AREAS:*** Business and Antitrust Litigation. ***Email:*** greindl@sommerbarnard.com

MICHAEL P. O'NEIL, admitted to bar, 1986, Illinois; 1987, Arizona; 1999, Indiana. *Education:* Marquette University (B.A., 1983); University of Michigan (J.D., 1986). ***PRACTICE AREAS:*** Bankruptcy; Creditors Rights; Commercial Litigation; Nonprofit and Charitable Organizations. ***Email:*** moneil@sommerbarnard.com

DAVID C. BROMUND, admitted to bar, 1988, Indiana and U.S. District Court, Northern and Southern Districts of Indiana. *Education:* Wabash College (A.B., 1985); Vanderbilt University School of Law (J.D., 1988). ***PRACTICE AREAS:*** Health Law; Managed Care; Securities; Mergers and Acquisitions; Business Transactions; Tax Exempt Organizations. ***Email:*** dbromund@sommerbarnard.com

GEOFFREY G. SLAUGHTER, admitted to bar, 1989, Illinois; 1995, Indiana; U.S. Supreme Court; U.S. Court of Appeals, Seventh and Federal Circuits; U.S. District Court, Northern District of Illinois; U.S. District Court, Northern and Southern Districts of Indiana; U.S. Court of Federal Claims. *Education:* Indiana University - Bloomington (B.A., Economics, with high distinction, 1985; M.B.A., Finance, 1989; J.D., cum laude, 1989). Phi Beta Kappa. Law Clerk, Chief Judge Allen Sharp, Northern District of Indiana, 1989-1991. Member, Local Rules Advisory Committee, Northern District of Indiana. President, Alumni Board, Indiana University School of Law-Bloomington, 2005-2006. Chairman, Indiana Public Employees Relations Board, 2001-2005. ***PRACTICE AREAS:*** Administrative Law; Antitrust; Appellate Practice; Business Law; Constitutional Litigation. ***Email:*** gslaughter@sommerbarnard.com

PHILIP L. McCOOL, admitted to bar, 1978, Indiana. *Education:* University of Michigan (B.A., 1975); Indiana University (J.D., 1978). ***PRACTICE AREAS:*** Federal and State Securities Regulation; Mergers and Acquisitions; Franchising. ***Email:*** pmccool@sommerbarnard.com

ANN CARR MACKEY, admitted to bar, 1974, Illinois; 1975, Missouri; 1980, U.S. Supreme Court; 1987, Indiana; U.S. Court of Appeals, Sixth and Seventh Circuits; U.S. District Court, Southern District of Indiana; U.S. District Court, Central District of Illinois. *Education:* Principia College (B.A., with honors, 1969); Washington University (J.D., 1974). ***PRACTICE AREAS:*** Employee Benefits. ***Email:*** amackey@sommerbarnard.com

EDWIN J. BROECKER, admitted to bar, 1991, Indiana. *Education:* Wabash College (B.A., cum laude, 1988); Indiana University (J.D., summa cum laude, 1991). Law Clerk to Hon. Sarah Evans Barker, U.S. District Court, Southern District of Indiana, 1990-1991. ***PRACTICE AREAS:*** Business Law; Real Estate. ***Email:*** ebroecker@sommerbarnard.com

THOMAS R. DeVOE, admitted to bar, 1992, Indiana and U.S. District Court, Northern and Southern Districts of Indiana. *Education:* Princeton University (A.B., 1988); Indiana University (J.D., magna cum laude, 1992). ***PRACTICE AREAS:*** Labor and Employment. ***Email:*** tdevoe@sommerbarnard.com

MARY T. DOHERTY, admitted to bar, 1992, Indiana and U.S. District Court, Northern and Southern Districts of Indiana; 1993, U.S. Courts of Appeals for the Federal Circuit; 1996, U.S. Court of Appeals, Tenth Circuit; 1998, U.S. Court of Appeals, Fourth Circuit; 2000, U.S. Court of Appeals, Seventh Circuit. *Education:* University of Dayton (B.A., 1983); Indiana University School of Law (J.D., summa cum laude, 1992). ***PRACTICE AREAS:*** Litigation. ***Email:*** mdoherty@sommerbarnard.com

SCOTT R. ALEXANDER, admitted to bar, 1992, Indiana, U.S. District Court, Northern and Southern Districts of Indiana, U.S. Court of Appeals, Seventh and Third Circuits and U.S. Supreme Court. *Education:* Wabash College (B.A., summa cum laude, 1989); Indiana University School of Law (J.D., summa cum laude, 1992). Phi Beta Kappa. *Member:* Indiana State and American Bar Associations. ***PRACTICE AREAS:*** Environmental; Litigation; General Practice. ***Email:*** salexander@sommerbarnard.com

(This Listing Continued)

SOMMER BARNARD ATTORNEYS, PC, Indianapolis—Continued

REGINA M. SHARROW, admitted to bar, 1991, California; 1996, Indiana. *Education:* University of Michigan (1987); Boalt Hall School of Law, University of California at Berkeley (J.D., 1991). *Member:* Indiana State Bar Association (Past Chair, Business Section). ***PRACTICE AREAS:*** Corporate; Business Transactions; Securities Law. ***Email:*** rsharrow@sommerbarnard.com

RALPH A. CARUSO II, admitted to bar, 1994, Indiana and U.S. District Court, Northern District of Indiana; 1996, U.S. Court of Appeals, Seventh Circuit; 1997, U.S. Tax Court. *Education:* Le Moyne College (B.S., magna cum laude, 1991); University of Notre Dame (J.D., 1994). ***PRACTICE AREAS:*** Mergers, Acquisitions and Divestitures; Joint Ventures; Business; Gaming Transactions. ***Email:*** rcaruso@sommerbarnard.com

PAUL T. DEIGNAN, admitted to bar, 1980, Indiana, U.S. District Court, Southern and Northern Districts of Indiana and U.S. Court of Appeals, Seventh Circuit. *Education:* Mount St. Paul College (B.A., 1968); Loyola University of Chicago (M. Ed., 1972); Indiana University (J.D., 1980). Law Clerk to Hon. Robert K. Rodibaugh, U.S. Bankruptcy Court, Northern District of Indiana, 1981-1983. ***PRACTICE AREAS:*** Business Workouts; Bankruptcy Matters; Commercial Law. ***Email:*** pdeignan@sommerbarnard.com

RICHARD A. KEMPF, admitted to bar, 1987, Indiana and U.S. District Court, Southern and Northern Districts of Indiana; 1988, U.S. Court of Appeals, Seventh Circuit. *Education:* Indiana University (B.S., 1976; J.D., cum laude, 1987); Ball State University (M.A., 1981). ***PRACTICE AREAS:*** Complex Civil and Commercial Litigation; White Collar Criminal Matters; Bankruptcy Litigation; Contract Disputes; Personal Injury. ***Email:*** rkempf@sommerbarnard.com

WILLIAM C. WAGNER, admitted to bar, 1992, Indiana, Illinois and U.S. District Court, Northern and Southern Districts of Indiana; U.S. Court of Federal Claims; U.S. Court of Appeals, Seventh Circuit; U.S. Supreme Court. *Education:* Valparaiso University (B.A., 1988; J.D., cum laude, with honors, 1992). ***PRACTICE AREAS:*** Complex Litigation; Business Disputes; Fraud Cases; Government Investigations; White Collar Criminal Defense; Securities Disputes; ERISA Litigation. ***Email:*** wwagner@sommerbarnard.com

F. ANTHONY PAGANELLI, admitted to bar, 1995, Indiana and U.S. District Court, Northern and Southern Districts of Indiana; 1996, U.S. Court of Appeals, Seventh Circuit; 1997, U.S. District Court, Northern District of Illinois; 2000, U.S. District Court, Eastern District of Michigan. *Education:* University of Notre Dame (B.A., 1992); Indiana University School of Law (J.D., cum laude, 1995). ***PRACTICE AREAS:*** Business Litigation; Criminal Defense; Real Estate/Construction Litigation; Bankruptcy Litigation. ***Email:*** paganelli@sommerbarnard.com

DAVID J. HENSEL, admitted to bar, 1986, Illinois; 1989, District of Columbia; 1990, Indiana. *Education:* Wabash College (B.A., 1979); Indiana University School of Law (J.D., cum laude, 1986). Judicial Law Clerk for the Honorable James T. Moody, Northern District of Indiana, 1986-1988. Marion County Superior Court Judge, 1999-2000. ***LANGUAGES:*** Bahasa Malaysia. ***PRACTICE AREAS:*** Criminal Law; Civil Litigation; Environmental Law. ***Email:*** dhensel@sommerbarnard.com

JACKIE M. BENNETT, JR., admitted to bar, 1983, Indiana. *Education:* Hanover College (B.A., 1980); Indiana University School of Law (J.D., 1983). Law Clerk to: Honorable Cale J. Holder, 1983-1984; Honorable Sarah Evans Barker, 1984-1985, U.S. District Court, Southern District of Indiana. ***PRACTICE AREAS:*** Business Litigation; White Collar Criminal Defense. ***Email:*** jbennett@sommerbarnard.com

JOHN D. PAPAGEORGE, admitted to bar, 1992, Indiana and U.S. District Court, Northern and Southern Districts of Indiana; 2001, U.S. Court of Appeals, Seventh Circuit. *Education:* Indiana University (B.A., 1989) Valparaiso University (J.D., cum laude, 1992). *Member:* Indiana State Bar Association (Member, Employment Law Section; Past Chair, Vice-Chair and Secretary/Treasurer, Litigation Section); American Bar Association (Member, Litigation and Employment Law Sections); Indianapolis Bar Association; Seventh Circuit Bar Association; Indianapolis American Inn of Court (Barrister). ***PRACTICE AREAS:*** Litigation; Labor and Employment Law. ***Email:*** jpapageorge@sommerbarnard.com

MICHELLE KAISER BRAY, admitted to bar, 1995, Illinois; 1997, California; 2003, Indiana; U.S. District Court, Northern District of Illinois; U.S. District Court, Northern and Southern Districts of Indiana; U.S. District Court, Central District of California; U.S. Court of Appeals, Seventh Circuit. *Education:* Xavier University (B.A., 1991); John Marshall Law School (J.D., 1994); McGeorge School of Law (LL.M., 1995). ***PRACTICE AREAS:*** Intellectual Property; Business; Technology; Internet Law. ***Email:*** mbray@sommerbarnard.com

BLAKE J. BURGAN, admitted to bar, 1995, Indiana. *Education:* Indiana University (B.S., 1989); University of Louisville School of Law (J.D., cum laude, 1994). Law Clerk for the Honorable Larry J. McKinney, Chief Judge of the United States District Court, Southern District of Indiana, 2000-2002. ***PRACTICE AREAS:*** Labor and Employment; Litigation. ***Email:*** bburgan@sommerbarnard.com

DAVID H. BENZ, admitted to bar, 1996, Indiana; 1997, Nevada; 2004, California. *Education:* Purdue University (B.S., 1992); Indiana University School of Law - Indianapolis (J.D., 1996). ***PRACTICE AREAS:*** Tax Law; Business Law. ***Email:*** dbenz@sommerbarnard.com

THOMAS F. O'GARA, admitted to bar, 1996, Indiana. *Education:* DePauw University (B.A., magna cum laude, 1992); Indiana University, Indianapolis (J.D., summa cum laude, 1996). Phi Beta Kappa. ***PRACTICE AREAS:*** Commercial Litigation; Civil Litigation. ***Email:*** togara@sommerbarnard.com

MICHAEL D. CHAMBERS, admitted to bar, 1997, Illinois and Indiana. *Education:* University of Notre Dame (B.S., with high honors, 1991); University of Illinois, Urbana-Champaign (M.S., with highest honors, 1994); University of Chicago (J.D., with honors, 1997). Phi Beta Kappa; Alpha Epsilon Delta. ***PRACTICE AREAS:*** Environmental; Administrative Law; Litigation. ***Email:*** mchambers@sommerbarnard.com

(This Listing Continued)

JAMES R.A. DAWSON, admitted to bar, 1997, Indiana and U.S. District Court, Northern and Southern Districts. *Education:* Indiana University (B.A., 1993); Indiana University School of Law-Indianapolis (J.D., 1997). ***PRACTICE AREAS:*** Debtor and Creditor Rights Litigation; Landlord and Tenant Law. ***Email:*** jdawson@sommerbarnard.com

STACEY A. HUSE, admitted to bar, 1998, Kentucky (Not admitted in Indiana). *Education:* DePauw University (B.A., 1985); Louis D. Brandeis School of Law, University of Louisville (J.D., cum laude, 1997). Managing Editor, 1996-1997 and Member, 1995-1996, Journal of Family Law. *Member:* Louisville, Kentucky and American Bar Associations. ***PRACTICE AREAS:*** Employee Benefits.

KAREN L. DE HAAN, admitted to bar, 1998, Kentucky; 2001, Indiana. *Education:* Northeast Missouri State University (B.S., 1990); University of Louisville (J.D., cum laude, 1998). Phi Kappa Phi; Delta Sigma Pi; Brandeis Honor Society. ***PRACTICE AREAS:*** Business Transactions; Taxation; Employee Benefits; Non-Profit Entities. ***Email:*** kdehaan@sommerbarnard.com

JEFFREY J. GRAHAM, admitted to bar, 1998, Indiana; U.S. District Court, Southern and Northern Districts of Indiana. *Education:* University of Notre Dame (B.A., cum laude, 1995); Valparaiso University School of Law (J.D., summa cum laude, 1998). Chief Justice, Valparaiso University School of Law Moot Court Society. Co-champion of Luther M. Swygert Moot Court Competition, Valparaiso University School of Law. Law Clerk to the Hon. S. Hugh Dillin, United States District Court for the Southern District of Indiana, 1998-2001. Speaker: "Commercial Lending In Indiana," National Business Insitute CLE 2004; "The Scope And Extent of Bankruptcy Jurisdiction Post Confirmation," ICLEF Annual Bankrutpcy Institute 2004 (co-speaker). Co-Author: American Bankruptcy Institute Journal "On The Edge" July/August 2001, 2002, 2003, 2004 & 2005. *Member:* Indianapolis and Indiana State Bar Associations; American Bankruptcy Institute. ***PRACTICE AREAS:*** Bankruptcy; Creditors Rights; Commercial Litigation. ***Email:*** jgraham@sommerbarnard.com

BRADLEY R. SUGARMAN, admitted to bar, 1998, Colorado (inactive); 2000, Indiana. *Education:* University of Virginia (B.A., 1994); Vermont Law School (J.D. 1998). ***PRACTICE AREAS:*** Environmental Law and Litigation; Zoning, Planning and Land Use; Government Practice. ***Email:*** bsugarman@sommerbarnard.com

ALEXA L. WOODS, admitted to bar, 1999, Indiana. *Education:* Purdue University at University of Indiana, Indianapolis (B.A., Political Science, 1995); Indiana University School of Law - Indianapolis (J.D., cum laude, 1999). Judicial Law Clerk to Honorable Patrick D. Sullivan, Indiana Court of Appeals, 1999-2000. ***PRACTICE AREAS:*** Commercial Real Estate. ***Email:*** awoods@sommerbarnard.com

ANDREW T. KIGHT, admitted to bar, 1998, Indiana. *Education:* Hamilton College (B.A., 1993); Indiana University School of Law-Bloomington (J.D., cum laude, 1997). ***PRACTICE AREAS:*** Business Workouts; Bankruptcy; Creditors Rights. ***Email:*** akight@sommerbarnard.com

STEPHANIE A. HALE, admitted to bar, 1999, Kentucky; 2002, Indiana. *Education:* Bellarmine College (B.A., 1996); University of Notre Dame (J.D., 1999). ***PRACTICE AREAS:*** Intellectual Property; Business Law; Mergers and Acquisitions. ***Email:*** shale@sommerbarnard.com

JOHN R. HUMPHREY, admitted to bar, 1999, Indiana. *Education:* Indiana University (B.S., 1989); Texas A&M University (M.B.A., 1992); Indiana University School of Law-Indianapolis, (J.D., 1999). Certified Public Accountant, Indiana. ***PRACTICE AREAS:*** Bankruptcy Matters; Commercial Law; Litigation. ***Email:*** jhumphrey@sommerbarnard.com

BRADLEY W. SCHWER, admitted to bar, 2000, Indiana. *Education:* Ball State University (B.S., 1996); E.W. Kelley School of Business, Indiana University (M.B.A., 1999); Indiana University School of Law-Indianapolis (J.D., 1999). Phi Delta Phi. ***PRACTICE AREAS:*** Business Transactions; Mergers and Acquisitions; Emerging Growth Companies. ***Email:*** bschwer@sommerbarnard.com

ANGELA M. HOPPER, admitted to bar, 2000, Indiana. *Education:* Indiana University, Fort Wayne (B.S., 1995); Indiana University School of Law - Indianapolis (J.D., cum laude, 2000). ***PRACTICE AREAS:*** Business Litigation; Employment Litigation; Civil Litigation. ***Email:*** ahopper@sommerbarnard.com

ANDREA K. MARSH, admitted to bar, 2000, Indiana. *Education:* Indiana University (B.A., in English and Biology, 1997); Washington University (J.D., 2000). *Member:* Indianapolis Bar Association. ***PRACTICE AREAS:*** Litigation. ***Email:*** amarsh@sommerbarnard.com

ROD L. MICHAEL, admitted to bar, 2002, Indiana and U.S. District Court, Northern and Southern Districts of Indiana. *Education:* Indiana University Purdue University - Indianapolis (B.S., 1996); Indiana University School of Law - Indianapolis (J.D., 2002). *Member:* Indiana State and American Bar Associations. ***PRACTICE AREAS:*** Business Law; Complex Litigation. ***Email:*** rmichael@sommerbarnard.com

DAVID J. BAYT, admitted to bar, 2001, Indiana. *Education:* Indiana University (B.A., 1997); Spanish American Institute for International Education, Seville, Spain; Indiana University School of Law - Bloomington (J.D., 2001). Law Clerk for Chief Judge Basil H. Lorch, III, U.S. Bankruptcy Court, New Albany, Indiana, 2002-2003. ***LANGUAGES:*** Spanish. ***PRACTICE AREAS:*** Bankruptcy; Business Workouts. ***Email:*** dbayt@sommerbarnard.com

IAN D. ARNOLD, admitted to bar, 2001, Indiana. *Education:* Hanover College (B.A., cum laude, 1998); Indiana University School of Law (J.D., cum laude, 2001). *Member:* Indianapolis, Indiana State and American Bar Associations. ***PRACTICE AREAS:*** Business; Mergers and Acquisitions. ***Email:*** iarnold@sommerbarnard.com

LONNIE JOHNSON, admitted to bar, 2003, Indiana. *Education:* Drake University (B.S. in Business Management, summa cum laude, 2000; M.B.A., 2002; J.D., with honors, 2002). Beta Gamma Sigma, Presidential Scholar. ***PRACTICE AREAS:*** Business Transactions; Mergers and Acquisitions; Emerging Growth Companies. ***Email:*** ljohnson@sommerbarnard.com

(This Listing Continued)

HANNAH L. MEILS, admitted to bar, 2003, Indiana and U.S. District Court, Northern and Southern Districts of Indiana. *Education:* Indiana University (B.A., with distinction, 1998); Indiana University School of Law (J.D., magna cum laude, 2003). Phi Beta Kappa; Order of the Coif. ***PRACTICE AREAS:*** Labor and Employment; Employment Immigration. ***Email:*** hmeils@sommerbarnard.com

MILDRED F. KRIZMANICH, admitted to bar, 2004, Indiana. *Education:* Texas A&M University (B.S., magna cum laude, 2000); University of Notre Dame (J.D., cum laude, 2003). Articles Editor, Notre Dame Law Review, 2002-2003. Judicial Clerk to Associate Justice Theodore R. Boehm, Supreme Court of Indiana, 2003-2005. ***PRACTICE AREAS:*** Litigation. ***Email:*** mkrizmanich@sommerbarnard.com

PETER J. PRETTYMAN, admitted to bar, 2004, Indiana. *Education:* Vanguard University of Southern California, (B.A., cum laude, 1996); Indiana University School of Law-Indianapolis, (J.D., cum laude, 2004). Recipient of the 2003 David R. Papke Prize for best student Law Review Note (published in 2004 by the Indiana Law Review); Recipient of the 2004 George O. Dix Writing Competition Prize for best scholarly paper by a graduating student; Note Development Editor for the Indiana Law Review; Law Clerk Externship, Governor Joseph Kernan's Office; Law Clerk Externship, Judge L. Mark Bailey, Indiana Court of Appeals; Author: "How to Discriminate Against Old Lawyers: The Status of Partners, Shareholders, and Members Under the Age Discrimination in Employment Act," 37 Ind. L. Rev. 545 (2004). *Member:* Indianapolis and Indiana State Bar Associations. ***PRACTICE AREAS:*** Civil Litigation; Environmental Litigation. ***Email:*** pprettyman@sommerbarnard.com

SHELLEY S. FRASER, admitted to bar, 2004, Indiana. *Education:* Indiana University (B.A., 1999); Indiana University School of Law-Indianapolis (J.D., 2004). ***PRACTICE AREAS:*** Business; Health Care. ***Email:*** sfraser@sommerbarnard.com

TRACY N. BETZ, admitted to bar, 2004, Indiana and U.S. District Court, Southern and Northern Districts of Indiana. *Education:* Indiana University (B.A., 2000; J.D., cum laude, 2004). *Member:* American (Member: Sections on Labor and Employment; Litigation; Young Lawyers) Indiana (Member, Sections on: Labor and Employment; Litigation; Young Lawyers) and Indianapolis (Member, Sections on: Labor and Employment; Litigation; Young Lawyers) Bar Associations. ***PRACTICE AREAS:*** Litigation; Labor and Employment. ***Email:*** tbetz@sommerbarnard.com

BRIAN V. POWERS, admitted to bar, 2005, Indiana. *Education:* Syracuse University (B.S., Environmental Engineering, cum laude, 1996); Indiana University School of Law-Indianapolis (J.D., 2005). ***PRACTICE AREAS:*** Business Law.

JAYNA M. CACIOPPO, admitted to bar, 2005, Indiana. *Education:* Georgetown University, Walsh School of Foreign Service (B.S., 1998); Indiana University School of Law-Indianapolis (J.D., magna cum laude, 2005). Articles Editor, 2004-2005 and Member, 2003-2004, Indiana Law Review. *Member:* Indiana State and American Bar Associations. ***LANGUAGES:*** Italian. ***PRACTICE AREAS:*** Litigation.

LINDY B. ARWOOD, admitted to bar, 2005, Indiana. *Education:* University of Tennessee at Chattanooga (B.S., magna cum laude, 2002); Valparaiso University School of Law (J.D., magna cum laude, 2005). Editor-in-Chief, Volume 39 Valparaiso University Law Review. *Member:* Indianapolis, Indiana State and American Bar Associations; Association for Supervision and Curriculum Development. ***PRACTICE AREAS:*** Litigation.

MICHAEL S. BYRON, admitted to bar, 2000, Indiana. *Education:* Indiana University (B.A., 1995); Valparaiso University (J.D., 1999). ***PRACTICE AREAS:*** Probate; Estate Planning; Environmental Law.

OF COUNSEL

JAMES K. SOMMER, admitted to bar, 1959, Indiana. *Education:* Yale University (B.A., 1954); Harvard University (LL.B., cum laude, 1959). ***PRACTICE AREAS:*** Business and Corporate Transactions; Mergers and Acquisitions; Securities. ***Email:*** jsommer@sommerbarnard.com

DAN G. STERNER, admitted to bar, 1962, Indiana. *Education:* Northwestern University (B.A., 1955); Indiana University (J.D., 1962). ***PRACTICE AREAS:*** Real Estate; Commercial Law; Business. ***Email:*** dsterner@sommerbarnard.com

STEVEN H. ANCEL, admitted to bar, 1960, Indiana. *Education:* Indiana University (A.B., 1958; J.D., 1960). Phi Delta Phi. Chairman, Bankruptcy and Insolvency Section, 1995 and Director, 1984-1988, Indianapolis Bar Association; Chairman, Bankruptcy and Creditors Rights Section, 1985 and Board of Directors, 1985-1986, Indiana State Bar Association; Board of Directors, 1987-1993, Treasurer, 1990-1993, Seminar Lecturer, 1976-1980 and Bankruptcy Seminar Chairman, 1980-2005, Indiana Continuing Education Forum; Indiana Bankruptcy Roundtable Chairman, 1990-2005; Listed in: Who's Who in American Law; Who's Who in America; Best Lawyers in America. *Member:* Indianapolis, Indiana State and American Bar Associations. Fellow: Indianapolis Bar Association; Indiana State Bar Association; American College of Bankruptcy. ***PRACTICE AREAS:*** Business Workouts; Bankruptcy Matters; Commercial Law and Litigation. ***Email:*** sancel@sommerbarnard.com

JERRY WILLIAMS, admitted to bar, 1968, Indiana; 1969, U.S. Tax Court. *Education:* Butler University (B.A., 1964); Indiana University (J.D., cum laude, 1968). ***PRACTICE AREAS:*** Business and Tax. ***Email:*** jwilliams@sommerbarnard.com

W. WILLIAM WEEKS, admitted to bar, 1979, Indiana; 2004, District of Columbia. *Education:* Indiana University (B.A., 1975); Indiana University School of Law (J.D., magna cum laude, 1979). ***PRACTICE AREAS:*** Environmental Law. ***Email:*** wweeks@sommerbarnard.com

JOHN K. SMELTZER, admitted to bar, 1980, Indiana. *Education:* Indiana University (B.A., 1975; J.D., 1980). *Member:* Indianapolis and Indiana State Bar Associations. Fellow, Indiana Bar Foundation. ***PRACTICE AREAS:*** Business Law; Real Estate. ***Email:*** jsmeltzer@sommerbarnard.com

MARCI A. REDDICK, admitted to bar, 1985, Indiana. *Education:* Indiana University at Indianapolis (B.A., 1978); Indiana University School of Law at Indianapolis (J.D., 1984). *Member:* American Bar Association (Member, Business Law Section, Partnership and Unincorporated Associations Section, and Subcommittee on Limited Liability Companies); Indiana State Bar Association (Past Chair and Member, Business Law Section); Indianapolis Bar Association (Member, Business Law, Land Use and Planning Sections). ***PRACTICE AREAS:*** Business Law; Real Estate Law. ***Email:*** mreddick@sommerbarnard.com

DEBRA McVICKER LYNCH, admitted to bar, 1986, Indiana. *Education:* University of Miami (B.A., magna cum laude, 1977); Indiana University (J.D., summa cum laude, 1986). Special Master, Bridgestone/ Firestone Tires Products Liability MDL, 2000—. Law Clerk to the Honorable Sarah Evans Barker, United States District Judge for the Southern District of Indiana, 1986-1988. ***PRACTICE AREAS:*** Business Litigation. ***Email:*** dlynch@sommerbarnard.com

CATHERINE R. REESE, admitted to bar, 1989, Indiana. *Education:* Purdue University (B.S., 1981); University of Michigan (J.D., cum laude, 1989). ***PRACTICE AREAS:*** Employee Benefits; Pension and Profit Sharing Plans; Qualified Retirement Plans; Flexible Benefit Plans; Health Benefits; Fringe Benefits; Executive Compensation; Non-Qualified Benefits; ERISA Compliance; COBRA. ***Email:*** creese@sommerbarnard.com

RICHARD L. ROWLEY, admitted to bar, 1990, Indiana and U.S. District Court, Southern and Northern Districts of Indiana; 1991, U.S. Tax Court. *Education:* Indiana University-Bloomington (B.S., 1986); Indiana University School of Law-Indianapolis (J.D., 1990). *Member:* Indianapolis and Marion County Bar Associations. ***PRACTICE AREAS:*** Business; Mergers and Acquisitions. ***Email:*** rrowley@sommerbarnard.com

THOMAS G. BURROUGHS, admitted to bar, 1990, Indiana; 1991, Illinois. *Education:* Indiana University (B.S., cum laude, 1987); Indiana University School of Law (J.D., summa cum laude, 1990). ***PRACTICE AREAS:*** Business; Litigation. ***Email:*** tburroughs@sommerbarnard.com

ANNE M. HAMILTON, admitted to bar, 1992, Indiana. *Education:* Wheaton College (B.A., 1988); Indiana University School of Law - Indianapolis (J.D., 1992). ***PRACTICE AREAS:*** Estate Planning; Administration. ***Email:*** ahamilton@sommerbarnard.com

JOSEPH W. CADE, admitted to bar, 1992, Alabama, U.S. District Court, Northern and Middle Districts of Alabama and U.S. Court of Appeals, Eleventh Circuit; 2004, Indiana. *Education:* University of Alabama at Tuscaloosa (B.S., 1985; J.D., 1992). *Member:* Indianapolis and Indiana State Bar Associations; Alabama State Bar. ***PRACTICE AREAS:*** Business Law; Real Estate Law; Mergers and Acquisitions. ***Email:*** jcade@sommerbarnard.com

SEAN J. FAHEY, admitted to bar, 1993, New York and U.S. Tax Court; 1995, Illinois; 2002, Indiana. *Education:* University of Rochester (B.A., 1989); Case Western Reserve University (J.D., 1992). ***PRACTICE AREAS:*** Estate Planning; Family Wealth Transfer; Business Succession Planning; Estate Administration; Trust Administration; Business Law. ***Email:*** sfahey@sommerbarnard.com

CHARLES R. O'KEEFE, JR., admitted to bar, 1994, Indiana and U.S. District Court, Northern and Southern Districts of Indiana; 2001, Wisconsin; U.S. District Court, Eastern and Western Districts of Wisconsin and U.S. Court of Appeals, Seventh Circuit. *Education:* Beloit College (B.A., 1985); Indiana University School of Law - Indianapolis (J.D., magna cum laude, 1994). *Member:* Indianapolis (Member, Sections on: Labor and Employment; Litigation), Indiana State (Member, Sections on: Labor and Employment, 1994—; Litigation, 1994—) and American (Member, Sections on: Labor and Employment, 1994—; Litigation, 1994—) Bar Associations; State Bar of Wisconsin. ***PRACTICE AREAS:*** Labor and Employment; Litigation; School Law. ***Email:*** cokeefe@sommerbarnard.com

DAVID J. TIPTON, admitted to bar, 1984, Indiana and Florida. *Education:* Manatee Junior College (A.A., 1977); Indiana University (B.A., 1979; J.D., cum laude, 1984). *Member:* The Florida Bar; Indiana State Bar Association. ***PRACTICE AREAS:*** Policyholder Insurance Coverage; Commercial Litigation. ***Email:*** dtipton@sommerbarnard.com

GRETCHEN K. GUTMAN, admitted to bar, 1997, Indiana. *Education:* Indiana University (A.B., 1986; M.P.A., 1987; J.D., 1997). *Member:* Indiana State and American Bar Associations; National Bond Lawyers Association. ***PRACTICE AREAS:*** Government Services; Public Finance; Bond Finance; Public Finance Taxation; Public Law. ***Email:*** ggutman@sommerbarnard.com

DEAN E. McCONNELL, admitted to bar, 1997, Indiana; registered to practice before U.S. Patent and Trademark Office. *Education:* Purdue University (B.S., 1994); Temple University (J.D., 1997). *Member:* Indianapolis and Indiana State Bar Associations; American Intellectual Property Law Association. ***PRACTICE AREAS:*** Intellectual Property; Patents. ***Email:*** dmcconnell@sommerbarnard.com

STANLEY TALESNICK, admitted to bar, 1950, Indiana; 1961, U. S. Court of Appeals, Seventh Circuit; 1980, U. S. Supreme Court; 1991, U. S. District Court, Eastern District of Wisconsin. *Education:* Indiana University (A.B., 1948); Indiana University School of Law (LL.B., 1950; Special J.D., 1967). Sigma Alpha Mu; Phi Delta Phi. ***PRACTICE AREAS:*** Business Bankruptcy; Commercial Transactions; Real Estate Matters. ***Email:*** stalesnick@sommerbarnard.com

HEATHER McPHERSON, admitted to bar, 1976, Indiana. *Education:* Wellesley College (B.A., 1970); Indiana University School of Law - Indianapolis (J.D., 1976). Associate Editor, Indiana Law Review, 1975-1976. Fellow, Indianapolis Bar Foundation. ***LANGUAGES:*** French. ***PRACTICE AREAS:*** Trusts and Estates; Estate Planning; Probate; Taxation.

ALAN M. HUX, admitted to bar, 1972, Illinois and U.S. District Court, Eastern District of Illinois; 1975, U.S. Court of Appeals, 7th Circuit; 1980, Indiana. *Education:* DePauw University (B.A., 1969); Washington University (J.D., 1972). ***PRACTICE AREAS:*** Real Estate; Business Law; Sewer Utilities; Water Utilities.

PAUL F. KORTEPETER, admitted to bar, 1956, District of Columbia and Indiana. *Education:* Wabash College; Harvard University (A.B., 1951); Duke University (LL.B., 1956). ***PRACTICE AREAS:*** Trusts and Estates; Estate Planning; Business Law; Taxation; Tax Exempt Organizations.

PHILLIP H. MINTON, admitted to bar, 1957, Indiana; U.S. District Court, Southern District of Indiana; U.S. Court of Appeals, Seventh Circuit. *Education:* DePauw University (A.B., 1951); Indiana University School of Law - Bloomington (J.D., 1956).

REPRESENTATIVE CLIENTS: Arvin Industries, Inc.; Bradford Group, Inc.; British Gas; Broadcast Music, Inc.; Burger King International; Chrysler Financial Corporation; Cincinnati Gas and Electric Co.; City of New Haven; Comerica Bank; Computer Systems Corp.; Consolidated Freightways; Control Devices, Inc.; Cook Group Inc.; Design Printing, Inc.; Dataflow

(This Listing Continued)

SOMMER BARNARD ATTORNEYS, PC, Indianapolis—Continued

Systems, Inc.; Equity Office Properties, L.L.C.; Exide Corp.; Family Auto Dealerships; Federal Express Corp.; Financialware, Inc.; First Internet Bank of Indiana; Globe Ticket & Label Co.; Grinnell Corp.; Grobet File Company of America; Hammond, Kennedy, Whitney & Co., Inc.; Heartland Capital Management, Inc.; Heartland Industries, Inc.; Howard W. Sams & Co.; HPS, Inc.; Huntington National Bank; Indiana Energy, Inc.; Indiana Life and Health Insurance Guaranty Assn.; Indiana Steel Fabricating, Inc.; Indiana Veneers Corp.; Indiana Veterinary Diagnostic Labs, Inc.; Inter-State Studio of Indiana, Inc.; City of Kokomo; Lamar Advertising Co.; Lincoln National Corp.; Maine Rubber International; MCS Consultants; Melvin Simon & Associates, Inc.; Merchants Property Insurance Company of Indiana; Metalworking Lubricants Co.; Monsanto Co.; Muncie Sanitary District; National Bank of Indianapolis; National Collegiate Athletic Association; National Wine & Spirits Corp.; Navistar International Transportation Corp.; New Holland North America Inc.; Newcourt Credit Group; PCL Packaging, Inc.; Peoples Loan & Trust Bank; Precision Rings, Inc.; Proffitt's, Inc.; re: Member Data Services, Inc.; RealMed Corp.; ReliaStar Life Insurance Co.; Relm Communications, Inc.; Roadway Express, Inc.; Roadway Package System, Inc.; Rose Acre Farms, Inc.; Ryan Fireprotection, Inc.; Saks Incorporated; Skinner & Broadbent Co.; Slater Steels; Star Financial Bank; Syncor International Corp.; Time Warner Communications; TRW, Inc.; Vincennes University; Virtual Financial Services, Inc.; Zollner Corp.

SPANGLER, JENNINGS & DOUGHERTY, P.C.

Established in 1952

9200 KEYSTONE CROSSING
SUITE 410
INDIANAPOLIS, INDIANA 46240
Telephone: 317-571-7690
Facsimile: 317-571-7686
Email: sjd.indy@gte.net
URL: http://www.sjdlaw.com

Merrillville, Indiana Office: 8396 Mississippi Street, 46410-6398. Telephone: 219-769-2323. Facsimile: 219-769-5007.
Valparaiso, Indiana Office: 150 Lincolnway, Suite 3001. Telephone: 219-462-6151. FAX: 219-477-4935.

General Trial and Appellate Practice. Administrative, Banking, Bankruptcy, Business Reorganizations, Business Transactions, Civil Rights, Commercial, Construction, Corporate, Creditors' Rights, Criminal Litigation, Family/Domestic Relations, Drug and Device, Eminent Domain, Environmental, ERISA and Employee Benefits, Probate and Estate Planning and Administration, Fire/Arson, Guardianships, Health Care, Insurance, Labor and Employment, Municipal and Zoning, Personal Injury, Product Liability, Professional Liability, Medical Malpractice Defense, Real Estate, School, Federal, State and Local Taxation, Toxic Torts, Transportation, Workers Compensation, Land Development.

FIRM PROFILE: In 1952, our founding partners created what is now the law firm of Spangler, Jennings & Dougherty to serve a broad range of clients' legal needs. Today, we continue to provide our clients with legal counsel based on extensive litigation experience, integrity, practicality and dedicated team effort.

Spangler, Jennings & Dougherty consists of 43 attorneys, fifteen paralegals, and a large and experienced support staff, making it Northwest Indiana's largest private law firm. In addition to years of legal experience and training, our firm has members with professional experience in public accounting and health care. We also have trial attorneys who belong to the prestigious American College of Trial Lawyers.

MICHAEL L. CARTER, born Indianapolis, Indiana, April 2, 1954; admitted to bar, 1985, Indiana. *Education:* Indiana University at Bloomington (B.A., 1977); Indiana University School of Law at Indianapolis (J.D., 1985). Author, "Using Daubert to Challenge Expert Testimony of Treating Doctorson Causation", Indiana Lawyer, Sept. 25, 2002. *Member:* Indianapolis, Indiana and American Bar Associations. ***REPORTED CASES:*** Jones v. Wasserman. (ind. App.1995); Sherman v. Four County Counseling Center (7th Cir. 1993); Ridlen v. Four County Counseling Center, (N.D. 1992); Bradley v. Stiller (Ind App. 1992); Edwards v. Vermillion County Hospital (Ind. App.1991); Kopec v. Memorial Hospital of South Bend. (Ind. App. 1990); Friedman v. Memorial Hospital of South Bend, (Ind. App. 1988). ***PRACTICE AREAS:*** Litigation; Insurance Defense; Medical Malpractice Defense. ***Email:*** mcarter@sjdlaw.com

GREGORY A. PURVIS, born Kokomo, Indiana, November 9, 1951; admitted to bar, 1977, Indiana; U.S. Court of Appeals, Seventh Circuit; U.S. Supreme Court. *Education:* Ball State University (B.S., 1974); Indiana University School of Law (J.D., 1977). *Member:* Indiana State Bar Association. ***PRACTICE AREAS:*** Real Estate Foreclosure; Creditor's Rights; Bankruptcy.

REPRESENTATIVE CLIENTS: Airborne Express; American National Property and Casualty Co.; Ancilla; Allstate Insurance Co.; American International Group; Associates Financial; Auto Owners; Bank One; Beneficial Finance; CNA Insurance; Community Hospital of Munster; Crown Point Community Schools; Farmers Insurance; Federal Employees Credit Union; 5th Third Bank; First Union Bank; Ford Motor Company; Horace Mann Insurance; Household Finance; IBEW Local 697; I.R.M.I.A.; Ispat/Inland Steel; Lake County; Leman Brothers; Liberty Mutual Co.; Medical Assurance of Indiana; Milwaukee Insurance; Munster Community Schools; Novogroder Development; PHICO; PICOM; PICI; Pro National Insurance Co.; Ryder Truck Lines; Safeco Insurance Co. of America; St. Anthony's Health Center; St. Mary Medical Center; St. Paul Insurance; State Farm Insurance; TIG Insurance; Town of Porter; United Farm Bureau; U.S.F.&G.; Wausau Insurance; Zurich Ins. Co.

STARK DONINGER & SMITH

Established in 1978

SUITE 700, 50 SOUTH MERIDIAN STREET
INDIANAPOLIS, INDIANA 46204
Telephone: 317-638-2400
Fax: 317-633-6618; 633-6619

General Civil and Business Litigation, Acquisitions and Mergers, Corporate and Business Transactions, Real Estate, Estate Planning and Administration, Commercial Lending, Family, Employment, Americans with Disabilities Act Compliance, Environmental, Health Care, Employee Benefits, Zoning and Land Use and Creditors' Rights and Bankruptcy Law.

(This Listing Continued)

MEMBERS OF FIRM

BRUCE E. SMITH, born South Bend, Indiana, September 2, 1947; admitted to bar, 1972, Indiana. *Education:* Indiana University (A.B., 1969); University of Michigan (J.D., 1972). Phi Beta Kappa. *Member:* Indianapolis, Indiana State and American Bar Associations. ***PRACTICE AREAS:*** Acquisitions and Mergers; Corporate and Business Transactions; Real Estate; Securities; Commercial Lending. ***Email:*** bsmith@sdsfirm.com

JOHN W. VAN BUSKIRK, born Indianapolis, Indiana, May 20, 1952; admitted to bar, 1978, Indiana. *Education:* Indiana University (B.A., 1974; J.D., 1978). Lecturer in Law, Indiana University School of Business, 1981-1989. Law Clerk, Indiana Court of Appeals, First District, 1977-1978. Author: "Environmental Site Assessments", Indianapolis Bar Association, 1990; "The Preparation and Presentation of a Zoning or Variance Case-A Look From The Inside", Indianapolis Bar Association, 1990; "Major Land Use Laws in Indiana," National Business Institute, 1998; "Indiana Real Estate Practice for Paralegals," HMS Continuing Legal Education, 1998. Mayor's Neighborhood Forum Environmental Subcommittee, 1992. Brownfields Legislation and RISC Policy Subcommittees. Civil Mediator. *Member:* Indianapolis, Indiana State (Member, Environmental Law Section) and American Bar Associations. ***PRACTICE AREAS:*** Real Estate; Construction Law; Environmental Law; Zoning and Land Use Law; Commercial Transactions; Civil Mediation. ***Email:*** jvanbuskirk@sdsfirm.com

RICHARD W. DYAR, born Indianapolis, Indiana, March 18, 1955; admitted to bar, 1981, Indiana and Florida. *Education:* Indiana University (A.B., 1977; M.B.A., 1981; J.D., 1981). *Member:* Indianapolis, Indiana State and American Bar Associations; The Florida Bar. ***PRACTICE AREAS:*** Corporate and Business Transactions; Securities; Employment Law; Real Estate. ***Email:*** rdyar@sdsfirm.com

PATRICIA SEASOR BAILEY, born Indianapolis, Indiana, March 22, 1956; admitted to bar, 1981, Indiana. *Education:* Anderson College (B.S.W., B.A., 1978); Indiana University (J.D., 1981). Phi Alpha Delta. Note and Development Editor, Indiana Law Review, 1980-1981. Lecturer in Legal Writing, Indiana University School of Law, 1981-1982. *Member:* Indianapolis, Indiana State and American Bar Associations. ***PRACTICE AREAS:*** Acquisitions and Mergers; Corporate and Business Transactions; Estate Planning and Administration; Business Succession Planning. ***Email:*** pbailey@sdsfirm.com

BRIAN J. TUOHY, born Indianapolis, Indiana, September 7, 1955; admitted to bar, 1984, Indiana. *Education:* Indiana University (B.S., 1977; J.D., 1983). Indiana Licensed Real Estate Broker, 1977. *Member:* Indianapolis (Chairman, Land Use Section), Indiana State and American Bar Associations; Indiana Trial Lawyers Association. ***PRACTICE AREAS:*** Zoning and Land Use Law; General Civil Litigation; Business Litigation; Corporate and Business Transactions; Real Estate; Development Litigation. ***Email:*** btuohy@sdsfirm.com

MARK A. BAILEY, born Anderson, Indiana, May 29, 1955; admitted to bar, 1986, Indiana. *Education:* Anderson University (B.A., 1977); Indiana University (M.B.A., 1985; J.D., 1985); Ball State University (M.A., 1986). Associate Editor, Indiana Law Review, 1984-1985. *Member:* Indianapolis, Indiana State and American Bar Associations. ***PRACTICE AREAS:*** Acquisitions and Mergers; Corporate and Business Transactions. ***Email:*** mbailey@sdsfirm.com

LEWIS E. WILLIS, JR., born Bridgeton, New Jersey, June 7, 1962; admitted to bar, 1987, Indiana. *Education:* Indiana University (B.A., 1984); Valparaiso University (J.D., 1987). *Member:* Indianapolis, Indiana State and American Bar Associations. ***PRACTICE AREAS:*** Corporate and Business Transactions; Real Estate; Acquisitions and Mergers; General Civil and Business Litigation; Employee Benefits Law. ***Email:*** lwillis@sdsfirm.com

THOMAS A. BRODNIK, born Indianapolis, Indiana, July 23, 1959; admitted to bar, 1989, Indiana, California and U.S. District Court, Southern District of Indiana and Central and Southern Districts of California. *Education:* Marian College (B.S., Acct., 1982); Indiana University (J.D., summa cum laude, 1989). *Member:* Indianapolis, Indiana State and American Bar Associations; State Bar of California. ***PRACTICE AREAS:*** Civil Litigation; Criminal Defense; Tax; Business Litigation. ***Email:*** tbrodnik@sdsfirm.com

ASSOCIATES

RICHARD B. KAUFMAN, born Evanston, Illinois, August 20, 1958; admitted to bar, 1983, Indiana; 2001, U.S. Court of Appeals, Seventh Circuit. *Education:* DePauw University (B.A., 1980); Indiana University School of Law, (J.D., 1983). Member, Board of Editors, Indiana Law Journal, Vol. 58, 1982-1983. Law Clerk to Hon. Robert L. Bayt, U.S. Bankruptcy Judge, Southern District of Indiana, 1985-1987. *Member:* Indianapolis, Indiana State and American Bar Associations. ***PRACTICE AREAS:*** General Civil and Business Litigation; Creditors Rights; Bankruptcy Law. ***Email:*** rkaufman@sdsfirm.com

ANTHONY B. RATLIFF, born Pikeville, Kentucky, November 13, 1969; admitted to bar, 1994, Indiana and U.S. District Court, Northern and Southern Districts of Indiana. *Education:* Morehead State University (B.A., magna cum laude, 1991); Indiana University School of Law (J.D., cum laude, 1994). *Member:* Indianapolis, Indiana State and American Bar Associations. ***PRACTICE AREAS:*** Civil Litigation; Insurance Coverage; Insurance Litigation. ***Email:*** aratliff@sdsfirm.com

JOHN J. MOORE, born Houston, Texas, March 21, 1972; admitted to bar, 1998, Indiana. *Education:* Indiana University (B.S., 1993); University of Minnesota (J.D., 1997). Member, Intellectual Property Moot Court. *Member:* Indianapolis, Indiana State and American Bar Associations. ***PRACTICE AREAS:*** Business Transactions; Commercial Litigation; Real Estate; Zoning, Planning and Land Use. ***Email:*** jjmoore@sdsfirm.com

DENNIS R. TYLER, born Lebanon, Indiana, January 9, 1964; admitted to bar, 1998, Indiana. *Education:* Ball State University (B.S., 1986); Indiana University School of Law (J.D., 1998). Articles Editor, Indiana International and Comparative Law Review, 1997-1998. *Member:* Indianapolis, Indiana State and American Bar Associations. ***PRACTICE AREAS:*** Corporate Law; Business Transactions; Commercial Loans; Civil Litigation; Real Estate; Business Litigation. ***Email:*** dtyler@sdsfirm.com

DONALD J. SMITH, born San Diego, California, July 15, 1973; admitted to bar, 2003, Indiana, U.S. District Court, Northern, Southern Districts of Indiana. *Education:* Indiana University (B.A., 1995); Cleveland State University (J.D., cum laude, 2003). Associate,

(This Listing Continued)

2001-2002 and Executive Editor, Executive Committee, 2002-2003, Cleveland State Law Review. *Member:* Indianapolis, Indiana State and American Bar Associations. ***PRACTICE AREAS:*** Real Estate; Business Transactions; Zoning, Planning and Land Use; Civil Litigation. ***Email:*** dsmith@sdsfirm.com

DANICA L. EYLER, born Vincennes, Indiana, February 7, 1979; admitted to bar, 2004, Indiana. *Education:* Indiana University (B.S., 2001); Indiana University School of Law (J.D., 2004). *Member:* Indianapolis, Indiana State and American Bar Associations. ***LANGUAGES:*** German. ***PRACTICE AREAS:*** Civil Litigation; Real Estate; Zoning, Planning and Land Use. ***Email:*** deyler@sdsfirm.com

SENIOR COUNSEL

JOHN C. STARK, born Indianapolis, Indiana, January 2, 1935; admitted to bar, 1964, Indiana. *Education:* DePauw University (B.A., 1955); Indiana University (J.D., 1964). Phi Delta Phi; Order of the Coif. Associate Editor, Indiana Law Journal, 1963-1964. *Member:* Indianapolis, Indiana State and American Bar Associations. ***PRACTICE AREAS:*** Business Litigation; Acquisitions and Mergers; Corporate and Business Transactions; Commercial Lending. ***Email:*** jstark@sdsfirm.com

COUNSEL

WILLIAM K. BYRUM, born Indianapolis, Indiana, August 1, 1933; admitted to bar, 1959, Indiana and U.S. District Court, Southern District of Indiana. *Education:* Butler University (A.B., 1955); Indiana University (J.D., 1958). Phi Delta Phi. Deputy Trial Prosecutor, Marion County, 1962-1965. Member, Marion County Council, Mass Transportation Authority, 1966-1970. *Member:* Indianapolis, Indiana State and American Bar Associations. [Captain, U.S. Air Force, Judge Advocate General's Department, active duty, 1959-1961]. ***PRACTICE AREAS:*** Corporation; Insurance; Construction; Probate; Transportation Litigation.

CLARENCE H. DONINGER, born Evansville, Indiana, October 8, 1935; admitted to bar, 1960, Indiana. *Education:* Indiana University (B.S., 1957; J.D., 1960). Phi Delta Phi; Order of the Coif; Beta Gamma Sigma. Member, Board of Editors, Indiana Law Journal, 1959-1960. President, Legal Services Organization of Indiana, Inc., 1975-1977. Director, Athletics-Indiana University, 1991-2001. *Member:* Indianapolis, Indiana State and American Bar Associations. ***PRACTICE AREAS:*** Corporate; Business Transactions; Mergers and Acquisitions; Real Estate. ***Email:*** cdoninger@sdsfirm.com

GREGORY S. FEHRIBACH, born Lafayette, Indiana, August 21, 1958; admitted to bar, 1986, Indiana. *Education:* Ball State University (B.S., 1981; M.A., 1983); Ohio Northern University (J.D., 1985). Attended International Program, Notre Dame, London, England, 1984. Trustee: Ball State University; Health and Hospital Corporation of Marion County. *Member:* Indianapolis and American Bar Associations. ***PRACTICE AREAS:*** American with Disabilities Act Consulting; Guardianship Administration; Estate Administration. ***Email:*** gregoryfehribach@ameritech.net

ROBERT D. MAAS, born Indianapolis, Indiana, April 12, 1952; admitted to bar, 1982, Indiana; U.S. District Court, Southern and Northern Districts of Indiana and U.S. Court of Appeals, Seventh Circuit. *Education:* Indiana University (A.B., 1974; J.D., 1982). Associate Editor, Indiana Law Review, Vol. 14, 1981. *Member:* Indianapolis, Indiana State and American Bar Associations; Defense Research Institute. ***PRACTICE AREAS:*** General Civil and Business Litigation; Alternative Dispute Resolution; Real Estate; Family Law; Environmental Law. ***Email:*** rdmaas@sdsfirm.com

REPRESENTATIVE CLIENTS: Acorn Group; American Consulting Engineers, Inc.; Basic American Industries, Inc.; Bunzl Corp.; Cornerstone Companies; C.P. Morgan Communities, L.P.; Deer Creek Music Center; Gasamerica Services, Inc.; Integrity Development Partners; National Bank of Indianapolis; Sun Life Insurance Co.; Ost Enterprises; Premier Ventures; Royal Pin Leisure Centers, Inc.; Rugby USA, Inc.; Wm. E. Schmidt & Associates; Speedco, Inc.; Storms-McMullen Electric, Inc.; Sullivan Corp.; Summit Construction Co., Inc.; Thomas & Associates, Inc.; Wurster Enterprises.
REFERENCE: National Bank of Indianapolis.

STARKEY LAW GROUP, PC

30 SOUTH MERIDIAN STREET
SUITE 850
INDIANAPOLIS, INDIANA 46204
Telephone: 317-705-8888
Facsimile: 317-705-8884
Email: mts@starkey-law.com
URL: http://www.starkey-law.com

Estate Planning, Wills and Probate, Trusts and Estates, Estate and Trust Administration, Probate and Fiduciary Litigation, Business and International Law, Real Estate.

FIRM PROFILE: Martha T. Starkey's twenty three-year probate law practice was officially incorporated under the name Starkey Law Group, PC in 2000. Located in Indianapolis, Indiana, and with offices located in Troy, Michigan, the law firm concentrates in the areas of wills, trusts, estates and related complex litigation, business and international law and real estate. While the growth of the firm under Ms. Starkey's leadership reflects a commitment to offering the best services possible, the attorneys and staff remain dedicated to providing personal assistance for each client.

MARTHA T. STARKEY, born Evansville, Indiana; admitted to bar, 1981, Indiana and U.S. District Court, Northern and Southern Districts of Indiana. *Education:* University of Evansville (B.S., cum laude, 1976); Indiana University School of Law - Indianapolis (J.D., 1981). Selected as an Indiana Super Lawyer, 2004 and 2005. Law Clerk to the Honorable Richard W. Vandivier, U.S. Bankruptcy Court, 1981-1982. Faculty: Indiana Practical Estate Planning and Will Drafting, 1989; Administration of the Estate in Indiana, 1990-1991; How to Build and Run a Probate Practice, 1992; ICLEF Estate Planning 101, 1993; Winning Financial Strategies for Women, 1993-1994; Business Succession Planning, 1993; Basic Tax Issues in Estate Administration, 1994; ICLEF Forms and Procedures for Transfers of Assets to Living Trusts, 1995; ICLEF Avoiding Malpractice, 1995; ICLEF National Estate and Trust Litigation, 2003. Member, National Conference of Commissioners on Uniform

(This Listing Continued)

State Laws (Indiana Chair, 1992—; Division Chair, 1997-1999 and 2003-2005; Drafting Committee, Uniform Trust Code, 1994-1999). Member, Board of Directors: Alumni Association of University of Evansville, 1994-1999; Wheeler Mission, 1989—; Ballet Internationale, 2003—; Neighborhood Christian Legal Clinic, 2003—. *Member:* Indianapolis (Chair, Estate Planning and Administration Section, 1996-1997; Judicial Evaluation Committee, 1999—; (Co-Chair, 2002; Judicial Selection Committee, 2001; Vice-President, Board of Managers, 2001; Judicial Excellence Political Action Committee, 2005), Indiana State and American Bar Associations; Christian Legal Society. ***LANGUAGES:*** German. ***PRACTICE AREAS:*** Probate; Probate Litigation; Trusts and Estates; Estate Planning. ***Email:*** mts@starkey-law.com

HONG-SIK CHUNG, born Chun-Ju, Korea; admitted to bar, 2001, Indiana and U.S. District Court, Northern and Southern Districts of Indiana. *Education:* Chung-Ang University, Korea (B.A., 1993; M.A., 1996); University of California at Los Angeles (Certificate, Professional Designation of International Trade and Commerce, 1998); Indiana University School of Law - Bloomington (J.D., 2001). *Member:* Indianapolis, Indiana State and American Bar Associations. ***LANGUAGES:*** Korean. ***PRACTICE AREAS:*** Corporate Law; Mergers and Acquisitions; International Business Transactions; Real Estate; Business Immigration; Trusts and Estates. ***Email:*** hsc@starkey-law.com

LISA M. ADLER, born Lafayette, Indiana; admitted to bar, 2004, Indiana, U.S. District Court, Northern and Southern Districts of Indiana; 2005, Illinois. *Education:* Indiana University - Bloomington (B.S., summa cum laude, 1998; J.D., cum laude, 2004). *Member:* Indiana State and American Bar Associations; American Immigration Lawyers Association. ***PRACTICE AREAS:*** Estate Planning; Estate Administration; Trust Administration; International Law; Business Law; Litigation; Immigration Law. ***Email:*** lma@starkey-law.com

JUSSARA SILVA, born Managua, Nicaragua, November 23, 1978; admitted to bar, 2004, Indiana. *Education:* University of Miami (B.A., cum laude, Psychology, 2001); Indiana University School of Law (J.D., 2004). Phi Alpha Delta; Florida Academic Scholar; Golden Key. *Member:* Indiana State and American Bar Associations. ***LANGUAGES:*** Portuguese and Spanish. ***PRACTICE AREAS:*** Estate Planning; Estate Administration; Trust Administration; Litigation. ***Email:*** jss@starkey-law.com

MARK T. BERNHARDT, born Indianapolis, Indiana, June 13, 1977; admitted to bar, 2005, Indiana. *Education:* Indiana State University (B.S., 1999); Thomas M. Cooley Law School (J.D., 2004). ***PRACTICE AREAS:*** Estate Planning; Probate; Business Law. ***Email:*** mtb@starkey-law.com

STECKLER & RYAN

An Association, Not A Partnership
CHAMBER OF COMMERCE BUILDING
320 NORTH MERIDIAN STREET, SUITE 901
INDIANAPOLIS, INDIANA 46204
Telephone: 317-264-1000
Fax: 317-264-1004
URL: http://www.stecklerryan.com

General Practice. Civil and Criminal Trials and Appeals, Tax, Business, Real Estate, Probate and Estate Planning.

W. RUDOLPH STECKLER (1941-2000)

DAVID J. RYAN, born Schenectady, New York, May 6, 1947; admitted to bar, 1977, Indiana. *Education:* University of Notre Dame (B.A., 1969); Boston College (J.D., 1975); New York University (LL.M., Taxation, 1977). Assistant United States Attorney, Chief Tax and Fraud Section, Southern District of Indiana, 1983-1988. Tax Counsel, Peter Kiewit Sons', Inc., 1982-1983. Assistant United States Attorney, District of Nebraska, 1980-1982. Attorney, Office of the Chief Counsel, Internal Revenue Service, 1978-1980. ***PRACTICE AREAS:*** Federal and State Civil Litigation; Federal and State Criminal Litigation; Tax Litigation; Business Litigation; Corporate and Business Law.

A. DOUGLAS STEPHENS

9211 CRAWFORDSVILLE ROAD
INDIANAPOLIS, INDIANA 46234
Telephone: 317-299-5297
Fax: 317-299-5005
Email: indylaws@aol.com
URL: http://www.indylawfirms.com

Criminal Law, Driving While Intoxicated, Drug Crimes, Traffic Violations, Felonies Misdemeanors, Real Estate, Collections, Debtor and Creditor, Bankruptcy, Family Law, Child Support, Adoptions, Wills and Probate, Trusts and Estates, Business Law.

A. DOUGLAS STEPHENS, born Shelbyville, Indiana, March 1, 1959; admitted to bar, 1988, Indiana and U.S. District Court, Northern and Southern Districts of Indiana. *Education:* Indiana University (B.A., 1981; J.D., 1987). Recipient, Englehart Scholarship. Small Claims Judge, Pike Township (2003—) *Member:* Indianapolis Bar Association. ***PRACTICE AREAS:*** Criminal Law; Land Use; Litigation.

STEPHENSON MOROW & SEMLER, P.C.

Established in 1986
8710 NORTH MERIDIAN STREET
SUITE 200
INDIANAPOLIS, INDIANA 46260-5307
Telephone: 317-844-3830
Fax: 317-573-4194
URL: http://www.stephlaw.com

Governmental and Insurance Defense Law.

(This Listing Continued)

STEPHENSON MOROW & SEMLER, P.C., Indianapolis—Continued

FIRM PROFILE: Since its incorporation as a firm in 1986, the law practice of Stephenson, Morow and Semler has served the state of Indiana with special expertise in the areas of defense of governmental entities in civil rights, employment and tort litigation, and general insurance defense.

JAMES S. STEPHENSON, born Oak Park, Illinois, January 16, 1953; admitted to bar, 1979, Illinois and U.S. District Court, Northern District of Illinois; U.S. Court of Appeals, Seventh Circuit; 1986, Indiana; U.S. District Court, Northern and Southern Districts of Indiana. *Education:* Northwestern University (B.A., 1975); Case Western Reserve University (J.D., 1979). Associate Editor, Case Western Reserve Law Review, 1978-1979. *Member:* Indiana State Bar Association; Defense Research Institute; Defense Trial Counsel of Indiana. ***PRACTICE AREAS:*** Municipal; Civil Rights; Insurance Defense. ***Email:*** jstephenson@stephlaw.com

MICHAEL R. MOROW, born Hammond, Indiana, November 24, 1951; admitted to bar, 1977, Indiana; 1980, Illinois; 1982, New Mexico; U.S. District Court, Northern and Southern Districts of Indiana; U.S. Court of Appeals, Seventh Circuit. *Education:* Ball State University (B.A., magna cum laude, 1974); Valparaiso University (J.D., 1977). Associate Note Editor, Valparaiso University Law Review, 1977. *Member:* Indiana State Bar Association; Defense Research Institute, Inc. ***PRACTICE AREAS:*** Municipal; Insurance Defense. ***Email:*** mmorow@stephlaw.com

RONALD J. SEMLER, born New Castle, Indiana, April 25, 1952; admitted to bar, 1978, Indiana and U.S. District Court, Southern District of Indiana; 1979, U.S. Court of Appeals, Seventh Circuit; 1993, U.S. District Court, Northern District of Indiana. *Education:* Ball State University (B.S. magna cum laude,); Indiana University School of Law (J.D. cum laude, 1978). Deputy Attorney General, 1978-1980, 1982-1993; Deputy Prosecuting Attorney, 1980-1982. ***PRACTICE AREAS:*** Civil Rights; State Torts. ***Email:*** rsemler@stephlaw.com

---

TONYA M. ARETZ (1959-1999)

G. RICHARD POTTER (1946-2001)

MARK A. HOLLOWAY, born South Bend, Indiana, October 16, 1958; admitted to bar, 1992, Indiana and U.S. District Court, Northern and Southern Districts of Indiana; U.S. Court of Appeals, Seventh Circuit. *Education:* Indiana University (B.S., Finance, 1982; J.D., cum laude, 1992). *Member:* Indiana State Bar Association; Defense Research Institute; Indiana Defense Trial Counsel. ***PRACTICE AREAS:*** Municipal Law; Civil Rights; Insurance Defense; Mediation. ***Email:*** mholloway@stephlaw.com

ROSEMARY L. BOREK, born New York, N.Y., December 21, 1971; admitted to bar, 1997, Indiana. *Education:* University of Miami (B.A., 1993); Indiana University (J.D., 1997). Phi Beta Kappa; Indiana Law Journal. Deputy Attorney General, Indiana, 1997-2001. ***PRACTICE AREAS:*** Municipal Law; Insurance. ***Email:*** rborek@stephlaw.com

WAYNE E. UHL, born Pittsburgh, Pennsylvania, July 28, 1956; admitted to bar, 1981, Tennessee (Not Active); 1989, Indiana. *Education:* Allegheny College (B.A., 1978); Vanderbilt University (J.D., 1981). Deputy Attorney General, Indiana, 1989-2002. Assistant Attorney General, Tennessee, 1981-1989. ***REPORTED CASES:*** Barnes v. Glen Theatre, 501 U.S. 560 (1991). ***PRACTICE AREAS:*** Civil Rights Defense; Employment Defense; Personal Injury Defense. ***Email:*** wuhl@stephlaw.com

GARY J. MARKSBERRY, born Henderson, Kentucky, October 27, 1973; admitted to bar, 2003, Indiana and U.S. District Court, Northern and Southern Districts of Indiana. *Education:* University of Southern Indiana (B.S., 1997); Michigan State University College of Law (J.D., 2002). *Member:* Indiana State Bar Association. ***PRACTICE AREAS:*** Insurance Defense. ***Email:*** jmarksberry@stephlaw.com

OF COUNSEL

WILLIAM W. KURNIK, born Chicago, Illinois, November 25, 1946; admitted to bar, 1975, Illinois and U.S. District Court, Northern District of Illinois; U.S. Court of Appeals, Seventh Circuit; U.S. Supreme Court; 1986, Indiana; U.S. District Court, Northern and Southern Districts of Indiana. *Education:* Illinois Institute of Technology-Chicago Kent College of Law (B.S., 1968); University of Chicago; John Marshall Law School (J.D., with distinction, 1975). Order of John Marshall. Gavel Society Award. Editor, John Marshall Law Review, 1974-1975. *Member:* Chicago, Illinois State, Indiana State and American Bar Associations; Illinois Defense Council; Defense Research Institute, Inc. ***PRACTICE AREAS:*** Municipal; Insurance Defense. ***Email:*** wkurnik@stephlaw.com

REPRESENTATIVE CLIENTS: Governmental Interinsurance Exchange; Liberty Mutual Insurance; Crum & Forster Commercial Insurance; National Fire and Casualty Co.; Indiana Insurance; St. Paul Fire & Marine Ins. Co.; Municipal Insurance Alliance; HAS Claims Service; Gallagher Bassett Services; Hamilton Mutual Insurance; Network Adjusters; Trident Insurance Services.

STEWART & IRWIN

PROFESSIONAL CORPORATION

Established in 1921

TWO MARKET SQUARE CENTER, SUITE 1100
251 EAST OHIO STREET
INDIANAPOLIS, INDIANA 46204-2147
Telephone: 317-639-5454
Fax: 317-632-1319
Email: hr@stewart-irwin.com
URL: http://www.silegal.com

General Civil Practice. Insurance, Administrative, Business, Taxation, Corporate, Probate, Estate Planning. Environmental, Trial and Appellate Practice, Bankruptcy and Creditor's Rights. International Law and Gaming Law, Transactions, Mergers and Acquisitions, Employment, Labor Law, Real Estate, Medical Malpractice Defense, Automotive Retail, Municipal Finance, Bond and Securities, Banking and Lending, Telecommunications and Utility, Transportation, Insurance Coverage.

FIRM PROFILE: Stewart & Irwin is a full-service law firm with 45 attorneys on staff. Languages spoken: Spanish, Chinese, French and German.

RICHARD E. AIKMAN, JR., admitted to bar, 1973, Indiana. *Education:* DePauw University (B.A., 1969); Indiana University (J.D., 1973). ***PRACTICE AREAS:*** Litigation; Environmental Law; Utility Law; Communications Law; Transportation.

STEPHEN W. SUTHERLIN, admitted to bar, 1965, Indiana. *Education:* DePauw University (B.A., 1961); Indiana University (J.D., 1966). ***PRACTICE AREAS:*** Securities Law; Corporate Law; Real Estate Law.

RONALD C. SMITH, admitted to bar, 1968, Indiana. *Education:* Indiana University (B.S. 1965); Indiana University School of Law-Indianapolis (J.D., 1968). ***PRACTICE AREAS:*** Employment Law; Business Entity Law; Commercial Litigation; Transactions; Estate Planning; Probate; Tax. ***Email:*** rsmith@stewart-irwin.com

DONN H. WRAY, admitted to bar, 1980, Indiana and Illinois. *Education:* Indiana University; Valparaiso University (B.A., with distinction, 1977; J.D., 1980). ***PRACTICE AREAS:*** Litigation and Appeals; UST; RCRA; OSHA Compliance; CERCLA; Personal Injury Law; Automotive Retail Law.

JAMES W. BRAUER, admitted to bar, 1976, Indiana. *Education:* Indiana University (B.S., 1971; J.D., 1975). ***PRACTICE AREAS:*** Insurance Defense Law; Medical Malpractice.

DOUGLAS R. BROWN, admitted to bar, 1985, Indiana. *Education:* Vanderbilt University (B.A., 1981); Indiana University-Indianapolis (J.D., 1984). ***PRACTICE AREAS:*** Gaming Law; Real Estate Law; Finance Law; Commercial Litigation; Domestic and International Business Transactions; Litigation.

KEITH A. GASTON, born Shelbyville, Illinois, June 19, 1953; admitted to bar, 1979, Indiana. *Education:* Millikin University (B.A., summa cum laude, 1975); Indiana University (J.D., cum laude, 1979). ***PRACTICE AREAS:*** Motor Carrier Law; Premises Liability Law; Products Liability Law; Defense Litigation. ***Email:*** kgaston@silegal.com

ANNE E. BECKER, born Columbus, Indiana, July 31, 1961; admitted to bar, 1988, Indiana. *Education:* St. Mary's College (B.A., 1983); University of Notre Dame (J.D., 1988).

EDWARD G. BIELSKI

THOMAS W. BLESSING, admitted to bar, 1991, Indiana. *Education:* DePauw University (B.A., Political Science, cum laude, 1987); Indiana University (J.D., 1991). ***PRACTICE AREAS:*** Civil Litigation.

GLENN D. BOWMAN, born Amarillo, Texas, March 3, 1958; admitted to bar, 1983, Indiana. *Education:* Indiana University (B.A., 1980); Indiana University School of Law-Indianapolis (J.D., 1983). ***SPECIAL AGENCIES:*** Volunteer, Indianapolis Legal Aid Society. ***PRACTICE AREAS:*** Commercial Law; Corporate Law; Commercial Litigation.

CHAD J. BRADFORD

WILLIAM R. BROWN, born Indianapolis, Indiana, October 11, 1939; admitted to bar, 1970, Indiana. *Education:* Franklin College of Indiana (A.B.); Indiana University, Indianapolis (J.D.).

LARRY R. CHAMPION

SONIA S. CHEN

ROBERT D. EMMERSON

RICHARD L. FAIRCHILD, admitted to bar, 1965, Indiana. *Education:* DePauw University (A.B., 1962); University of Michigan Law School (J.D., 1965). ***PRACTICE AREAS:*** Insurance Defense Law; Medical Malpractice.

WILLIAM R. FATOUT, admitted to bar, 1976, Indiana. *Education:* Indiana University (A.B., 1973); Indiana University School of Law - Bloomington (J.D., 1975; M.B.A., 1982). ***PRACTICE AREAS:*** Estate Planning; Probate.

FRED W. GARVER

ANDREA L. HERMER, admitted to bar, 1990, Indiana. *Education:* Indiana University (B.A., 1987; J.D., cum laude, 1990). ***PRACTICE AREAS:*** Telecommunications Law; Real Estate; Litigation.

EDWARD B. HOPPER, II, admitted to bar, 1964, Tennessee; 1967, Indiana; 1997 Illinois;. *Education:* Vanderbilt University (B.A., with honors, dean's list, 1961; LL.B., 1964). ***PRACTICE AREAS:*** Bankruptcy; Creditors Rights; Commercial Litigation.

MICHAEL K. IRWIN, admitted to bar, 1972, Indiana. *Education:* DePauw University (B.A., 1969); Indiana University (J.D., 1972). ***PRACTICE AREAS:*** Insurance Defense Law; School Law; Products Liability Law.

WILLIAM N. IVERS, admitted to bar, 1987, Indiana. *Education:* Purdue University (B.A., 1984); Valparaiso University (J.D., 1987). ***PRACTICE AREAS:*** Appellate Law; Insurance Defense Law; Environmental Law; Employment Law; Business Litigation; Automotive Retail Law.

PETER S. KOVACS, admitted to bar, 1992, Indiana. *Education:* University of Connecticut (B.A., 1984); Indiana University (J.D., 1992). ***PRACTICE AREAS:*** Business Litigation; Administrative; Regulatory; Telecommunications Law.

GEOFFREY C. LAMBERT

JUSTIN W. LEVERTON, born Indianapolis, Indiana, 1979; admitted to bar, 2005, Indiana. *Education:* Illinois Wesleyan University (B.A., Public Accounting and Economics, 2002); Indiana University School of Law (J.D., 2005). ***PRACTICE AREAS:*** Commercial Litigation; Corporate Finance; Securities; Tax Litigation.

CYNTHIA M. LOCKE, born Indianapolis, Indiana, May 11, 1949; admitted to bar, 1985, Indiana. *Education:* Butler University (B.A., 1981); Indiana University (J.D., 1985). ***PRACTICE AREAS:*** Toxic Tort Defense; Insurance Defense; ERISA; Employment Discrimination; Life and Health Insurance. ***Email:*** clocke@silegal.com

(This Listing Continued)

JOHN T. LOFTUS, born Chicago, Illinois, 1955; admitted to bar, 1991, Illinois (Not admitted in Indiana). *Education:* Elmhurst College (B.S., 1984; B.A., 1984); Chicago-Kent College of Law (J.D., 1990).

JILL L. McCRORY, admitted to bar, 1988, Indiana. *Education:* Indiana State University (A.D., Nursing, 1981; B.S., Nursing, magna cum laude, 1984); Indiana University (J.D., cum laude, 1988). ***PRACTICE AREAS:*** Insurance Defense; Medical Malpractice; Health Care Risk Management.

CHARLES R. MERCER, JR., born Kentucky, March 8, 1942; admitted to bar, 1968, Indiana. *Education:* Indiana University (B.S., Business, 1965; J.D., 1968).

RODERICK H. MORGAN, admitted to bar, 1979, District of Columbia; 1992, Indiana. *Education:* United States Military Academy (B.S., 1970); Georgetown University Law Center (J.D., 1978). ***LANGUAGES:*** Spanish, French, German. ***PRACTICE AREAS:*** Municipal Finance.

MARK R. NELSON, admitted to bar, 1993, Indiana and Illinois. *Education:* Indiana University (B.S., 1989; J.D., 1993). ***PRACTICE AREAS:*** Corporate Law; Commercial Law; Commercial Lending; Commercial Leasing; Mergers and Acquisitions; Estate Planning.

PAMELA A. PAIGE, born Teaneck, New Jersey, April 16, 1961; admitted to bar, 1989, New Jersey and U.S. District Court, District of New Jersey; 1990, New York; 1991, Indiana; 1992, District of Columbia. *Education:* Marquette University; California State University at Fullerton (B.A., 1984); Pace University (J.D., 1989). ***PRACTICE AREAS:*** Insurance Defense Litigation; Products Liability Defense; Workers Compensation. ***Email:*** ppaige@silegal.com

STEPHEN J. PETERS, admitted to bar, 1981, Indiana. *Education:* Amherst College (B.A., cum laude, 1977); Indiana University (J.D., 1980). ***PRACTICE AREAS:*** Appellate Law; Insurance Coverage Litigation; Employment Law; Business Litigation; Personal Injury.

LISA CROSS PRICE

RICHARD H. RIEGNER, born Indianapolis, Indiana, February 13, 1936; admitted to bar, 1965, Indiana. *Education:* Butler University and Indiana University (B.S., 1958); Indiana University (J.D., cum laude, 1965). ***PRACTICE AREAS:*** Administrative Law; Litigation; Commercial Law; Insurance Law; Probate Law; Estate Planning; Wills and Trusts; Insurance Coverage Counsel. ***Email:*** rriegner@silegal.com

DAVID I. RUBIN

MICHAEL J. RUSNAK

MARY F. SCHMID, admitted to bar, 1993, Indiana. *Education:* Indiana University (B.A., 1987); Indiana University, School of Law (J.D., 1993). ***PRACTICE AREAS:*** Business Litigation.

BRADLEY W. SKOLNIK, born Benton Harbor, Michigan, November 27, 1955; admitted to bar, 1981, Indiana, U.S. District Court, Southern District of Indiana and U.S. Court of Appeals, Seventh Circuit. *Education:* Michigan State University (B.A., 1978); Indiana University, Bloomington (J.D., 1981). ***PRACTICE AREAS:*** Securities Regulation; Financial Services Law.

PETER B. STEWART, admitted to bar, 1966, Indiana. *Education:* Butler University (A.B., 1963); Indiana University (LL.B., 1966). ***PRACTICE AREAS:*** Insurance Defense Law; Product Liability Law; Domestic Relations Law; Probate.

PHILIP R. THOMPSON

WILLIAM A. WICK

MARK E. WIREY, admitted to bar, 1990, Indiana. *Education:* Indiana University (B.S., 1975; J.D., cum laude, 1990); Butler University (M.B.A., 1984). ***PRACTICE AREAS:*** Estate Planning; Probate Law; Tax Law; Business Law.

STUART & BRANIGIN LLP

Established in 1878

SUITE 640
8888 KEYSTONE CROSSING
INDIANAPOLIS, INDIANA 46240
Telephone: 317-574-7245
Fax: 317-574-7050
Email: sb@stuartlaw.com
URL: http://www.stuartlaw.com

Lafayette, Indiana Office: 300 Main Street, Suite 900, P.O. Box 1010. Telephone: 765-423-1561. Fax: 765-742-8175.

General Practice. Trials and Appeals. Administrative, Banking, Commercial, Computer, Construction, Copyright and Trademark, Corporation, Creditors' Rights, Environmental, Estate Planning, Hospital and Health Care, Insurance, Labor and Employment, Pension, Probate, Railroad, Real Estate, Securities, Taxation, Utility and Zoning Law.

FIRM PROFILE: Stuart & Branigin LLP, one of the oldest law firms in Indiana, had its origin in Lafayette, Indiana, in 1878, and today consists of over 30 lawyers. Our firm members over the years have included two former justices of the Indiana Supreme Court, one governor of the state of Indiana, and four presidents of the Indiana State Bar Association. Stuart & Branigin LLP serves the entire state and represents national clients throughout the United States. The firm encourages its members to participate actively in legal education seminars, professional association activities and civic affairs.

MEMBERS OF FIRM

JOHN M. STUCKEY, born Lafayette, Indiana, August 9, 1964; admitted to bar, 1989, Indiana, U.S. Court of Appeals, Seventh Circuit, and U.S. District Court, Northern and Southern Districts of Indiana. *Education:* Purdue University (B.A., 1986); College of William and Mary (J.D., 1989). Member, William and Mary Law Review, 1988-1989. *Member:* Tippecanoe County, Indiana State and American Bar Associations; Defense Research Institute; Defense Trial Counsel of Indiana; National Association of Railroad Trial Counsel. Fellow: Indiana Bar Foundation. (Also at Lafayette Office). ***PRACTICE AREAS:*** Construction Law; Commercial Litigation; Civil Litigation. ***Email:*** jms@stuartlaw.com

(This Listing Continued)

BRUCE A. HUGON, born Fort Worth, Texas, July 3, 1954; admitted to bar, 1979, Indiana and U.S. District Court, Southern District of Indiana; 1984, U.S. Court of Appeals, Seventh Circuit; 1999, U.S. District Court, Northern District of Indiana; 2002, U.S. District Court, Central District of Illinois. *Education:* Purdue University (B.A., 1975); Indiana University School of Law (J.D., cum laude, 1979). *Member:* Indianapolis, Indiana State and American Bar Associations; National Association of Railroad Trial Counsel; Defense Research Institute; Defense Trial Counsel of Indiana. ***REPORTED CASES:*** Herriman v. Consolidated Rail Corporation, 887 F.Supp. 1148 (N.D. Ind. 1995); Shots v. CSX Transportation, Inc., 887 F.Supp. 206 (S.D. Ind. 1995); Herriman v. Consolidated Rail Corporation, 883 F. Supp. 303 (N.D. Ind. 1995); Shots v. CSX Transportation, Inc., 38 F.3d 304 (7th Cir. 1994); Fisher v. National R.R. Passenger Corp., 152 F.R.D. 145 (S.D. Ind. 1993); Reno v. Consolidated Rail Corporation, 797 F.Supp. 700 (S.D. Ind. 1992); Taylor v. National R.R. Passenger Corp., 920 F.2d 1372 (7th Cir. 1990); Cannon v. Northside Transfer Co., Inc., 427 N.E.2d 712 (Ind. Ct. App. 1981). ***PRACTICE AREAS:*** Civil Litigation; Railroad Law. ***Email:*** bah@stuartlaw.com

GEOFFREY L. BLAZI, born South Bend, Indiana, November 6, 1965; admitted to bar, 1993, Indiana. *Education:* University of Notre Dame (B.A., 1988; J.D., 1992). Phi Delta Phi. Member, National Moot Court Team. Recipient: A. Harold Weber Moot Court Award for Outstanding Achievement in the Art of Oral Argument; William T. Kirby Award for Excellence in Legal Writing. *Member:* Tippecanoe County, Indiana State and American Bar Associations; Indiana Defense Lawyers Association; National Association of Railroad Trial Counsel. ***PRACTICE AREAS:*** Civil Litigation; Water Resources Law; Construction Law; Commercial Litigation; Railroad Law. ***Email:*** glb@stuartlaw.com

OF COUNSEL

NICHOLAS C. NIZAMOFF, born Indianapolis, Indiana, July 29, 1942; admitted to bar, 1969, Indiana and U.S. District Court, Southern District of Indiana; 1974, U.S. Court of Appeals, Seventh Circuit; 1997, U.S. Supreme Court. *Education:* Wabash College (A.B., 1964); Indiana University (J.D., cum laude, 1969). *Member:* Indianapolis, Indiana State and American Bar Associations; International Association of Defense Counsel; Defense Research Institute; National Association of Railroad Trial Counsel; American Institute of Architects (Allied Member); Defense Trial Counsel of Indiana. ***PRACTICE AREAS:*** Design Professional Liability; Legal Malpractice; Railroad Law. ***Email:*** ncn@stuartlaw.com

ASSOCIATE

TRENTEN D. KLINGERMAN, born Plymouth, Indiana, May 22, 1971; admitted to bar, 2001, Indiana and U.S. District Court, Northern and Southern Districts of Indiana. *Education:* Purdue University (B.S., 1994); Indiana University School of Law (J.D., 2001). Recipient: Glenn D. Peters Scholarship; Lila B. Louden Scholarship; Class of 1998 Scholarship. Managing Editor, Indiana Law Journal, 2000-2001. *Member:* Tippecanoe County (Secretary 2005-2006), Indiana State and American Bar Associations; Defense Trial Counsel of Indiana; National Association of College and University Attorneys. ***Email:*** tdk@stuartlaw.com

GENERAL COUNSEL FOR: Lafayette Savings Bank; North Central Health Services, Inc.; Purdue Research Foundation; Purdue University; Tippecanoe School Corp.
STATE COUNSEL FOR: Norfolk Southern Railway Co.; CSX Transportation, Inc.; Canadian Pacific Railway.
REPRESENTATIVE CLIENTS: Advanced Process Cominatorics, Inc.; Aluminum Company of America; Amoco Oil Co.; BioLab, Inc.; Camico Mutual Insurance Company; Caterpillar Tractor Co.; Cinergy; DPIC Companies; DiscoverRe; The Egyptian Lacquer Manufacturing Co.; Eli Lilly & Co.; Fairfield Manufacturing Co., Inc.; Fifth Third Bank; GAB Business Services, Inc.; Gerling America Insurance Company; Great Lakes Chemical Corp.; Greater Lafayette Health Services, Inc.; Indiana Lumbermens Mutual Insurance Co.; The Indiana Railroad Co.; Kettelhut Construction, Inc.; Kirby Risk Corporation; Lafayette Instrument Company, Inc.; Lafayette Life Insurance Company; Lafayette Savings Bank; Lafayette Venetian Blind, Inc.; Leffler Industries, Inc.; National Railroad Passenger Corp.; Nissan Chemical America Corp.; Perry Chemical & Manufacturing Company, Inc.; Regions Bank; Roman Catholic Diocese of Lafayette-in-Indiana; Sisters of St. Francis Hospital Service; Tippecanoe Community Health Clinic; Wabash Valley Hospital, Inc.; West Bend Mutual Insurance Co.

(For complete biographical data on all personnel, see professional biographies at Lafayette, Indiana)

JOHN J. SULLIVAN

Established in 1976

8900 KEYSTONE CROSSING
SUITE 1250
INDIANAPOLIS, INDIANA 46240
Telephone: 317-574-4500
Fax: 317-574-4501
Email: jsullivan@millermuller.com
URL: http://www.johnsullivanlaw.com

General Civil Litigation in all State and Federal Courts. Bankruptcy, Government Relations, Health Care, Medical Malpractice, Personal Injury, Automobile Accidents, Wrongful Death, Products Liability, Wills and Probate, Estate Planning, Trusts and Estates, Guardianship, Asset Protection, Insurance, General Negligence and Trials and Appeals.

JOHN J. SULLIVAN, born Indianapolis, Indiana, May 2, 1951; admitted to bar, 1976, Indiana; 1982, U.S. Court of Appeals, Seventh Circuit; 1986, U.S. Supreme Court. *Education:* College of the Holy Cross (A.B., cum laude, 1973); Indiana University (J.D., 1976). Member, Marion County Convention Center and Recreational Facilities Commission, 1985-1995. Chairman, Indiana Recount Commission, 1988. *Member:* Indianapolis and Indiana State Bar Association.

REPRESENTATIVE CLIENTS: Brebeuf Jesuit Preparatory School; Indiana State Democratic Party; Golden Rule Insurance Co.; Indiana Restaurant and Hospitality Association; Medical Savings Insurance Co.
REFERENCES: National City Bank; Bank One, Indiana.

TABBERT HAHN EARNEST & WEDDLE LLP

Established in 1988

SUITE 1900, ONE INDIANA SQUARE
INDIANAPOLIS, INDIANA 46204-2032
Telephone: 317-639-5444
Fax: 317-639-5232
Email: thew@tabberthahn.com
URL: http://www.tabberthahn.com

Civil and Criminal Litigation (Complex), Medical Malpractice Defense, Drug Liability, Product Liability, Legal Malpractice, Healthcare Law, Estate Planning, Estate Administration, Gaming Industry Law, Environmental Law, Family Law, Business Law, Housing Law, Real Estate Law, Corporate Law, Commercial Litigation, International Business, Eminent Domain, Outdoor Advertising.

FIRM PROFILE: Tabbert Hahn Earnest & Weddle LLP counsels individuals and businesses on local, regional and national levels. We cover all practice areas with particular concentrations in complex civil and criminal litigation, medical malpractice defense, drug and product liability, estate planning and administration, business organizations, housing, real estate and a special emphasis in the gaming industry.

GREGORY F. HAHN, born Winchester, Indiana, October 14, 1949; admitted to bar, 1974, Indiana and U.S. District Court, Southern District of Indiana. *Education:* University of Evansville (B.S., 1971); Indiana University School of Law (J.D., 1974). Chief Deputy Prosecutor, Indianapolis, 1974-1978. *Member:* Indianapolis (Vice Chairman, Grievance Committee, 1978-1979), Seventh Circuit (Member, Domestic Law Committee, 1975-1978), Indiana State and American Bar Associations; National District Attorney's Association; Indiana Trial Lawyers Association; The Association of Trial Lawyers of America; International Gaming Attorneys Association (International Masters of Gaming Law); Indiana Bar Foundation (Board of Director; Chair, Building Committee); Fellow, Indiana Bar Foundation. ***SPECIAL AGENCIES:*** Member, Board of Directors: Indianapolis Opera Company, 1981-1983; Pleasant Run Children's Home, 1981-1983; University of Evansville, Board of Trustees, 1981-1984; Area Youth Ministries Board; Indiana Sports Corporation; Washington Township Foundation Board; Pathways Inc.; Indiana Private Industry Counsel Board Member, 2003—, Treasurer, 1974-1980, Counsel, 2000—, Marion County Democratic Party, ; Treasurer, State Democratic Party, 1980-1984. ***PRACTICE AREAS:*** Civil Litigation; Business Law; Family Law; Corporate Law; Administrative Law; Real Estate; Gaming Licensing; Government Affairs. ***Email:*** greghahn@tabberthahn.com

LANTE K. EARNEST, born Rushville, Indiana, September 21, 1946; admitted to bar, 1973, Indiana, U.S District Court, Southern District of Indiana, U.S. Court of Appeals, Seventh Circuit. *Education:* Indiana University (B.S., 1969); Indiana University School of Law (J.D., 1972). Recipient, 1994, Distinguished Alumni Award. Member of Board of Directors of Heritage Trust and Indiana Natural Resources Foundation, 1998—. Named Indiana Super Lawyer, 2004, 2005. *Member:* Indianapolis, Indiana State and American (Member, Sections on: Business law; Commercial Law; Corporate Law) Bar Associations; Indianapolis Bar Foundation (Board of Directors, 2000—; President, 2003 and 2004). ***PRACTICE AREAS:*** Business Law; Estate Planning; Housing; Real Estate; Corporate Law; Contracts. ***Email:*** lke@tabberthahn.com

ROBERT G. WEDDLE, born Houston, Texas, October 21, 1943; admitted to bar, 1972, Indiana, U.S. District Court, Northern and Southern Districts of Indiana and U.S. Court of Appeals, Seventh Circuit. *Education:* Purdue University (B.S., Chemical Engineering, 1967); Indiana University School of Law (J.D., cum laude, 1972). Author: "Legal Implications of AIDS - an Overview," Indiana Medico-Legal Bar Association, 1987; "Legal Implications of Aids in Indiana," Indiana Continuing Legal Education Forum, 1988; "Controlling Litigation Costs," Handbook for Indiana Defense Lawyers Association, 1989; "Protection of Owners' Security Interest on a Construction Project," Handbook for ABA Forum on the Construction Industry, 1990; "The Admissibility of Expert Witness Testimony," 1996. *Member:* Indianapolis, Indiana State and American Bar Associations; National Institute for Trial Advocacy; American Board of Trial Advocates. ***PRACTICE AREAS:*** Medical Malpractice Defense; Drug and Medical Device Defense; Legal Malpractice; Toxic Torts; Products Liability; Insurance Defense. ***Email:*** rgw@tabberthahn.com

JUDY M. TYRRELL, born Indianapolis, Indiana, September 19, 1949; admitted to bar, 1991, Virginia; 1992, District of Columbia; 1993, Maryland; 1995, Indiana and U.S. District Court, Southern District of Indiana; 1997, U.S. Court of Appeals, Seventh Circuit. *Education:* Indiana University (A.B., 1971; M.A., 1974); George Mason University (J.D., with distinction, 1991). Recipient, American Jurisprudence Awards: Criminal Law; Torts. Member, George Mason University Law Review. Former Clerk to the Honorable Thomas J. Middleton (retired), Circuit Court of Fairfax County, Virginia. Certified Family Law Specialist. Family Law Mediator. Author: Interpretation of Virginia's Medical Malpractice Act, George Mason University Law Review. Author and Speaker, for Following Continuing Education Courses: Family Law in Indiana; Family Law Litigation in Indiana; Successful Divorce Mediation in Indiana. Indianapolis Monthly Super Lawyer, 2004, 2005. *Member:* Indianapolis, Indiana State, Virginia, Maryland State and American Bar Associations; The District of Columbia Bar; Virginia State Bar. ***LANGUAGES:*** French. ***PRACTICE AREAS:*** Family Law; Family Mediation. ***Email:*** jtyrrell@tabberthahn.com

E. SCOTT TREADWAY, born Hamilton, Ohio, February 22, 1962; admitted to bar, 1989, Indiana, U.S. District Court, Northern and Southern Districts of Indiana and U.S Court of Appeals, Seventh Circuit. *Education:* Ball State University (B.S., 1984); Indiana University (J.D., with honors, 1988). Pi Gamma Mu; Alpha Lamda Delta. Who's Who in American College Students. Dillon Scholar. Associate Editor, Indiana Law Review, 1987-1988. Teaching Faculty and Associate Member, Metropolitan Indianapolis Board of Realtors, 1993-1996. Recipient, 2000 Hoosier Environmental Counsel Litigator of the year. Approved Real Estate Continuing Education Instructor by Indiana State Professional Licensing. Continuing Education Instructor and Speaker on the following topics: Construction Damage Calculations, Mechanics Liens, Construction Contracts, License Law, Agency Law, Ethics Law, Defects Disclosure Law and Real Estate Litigation. Instructor for National Business Institute, Indiana Continuing Legal Education Foundation, Lorimar and Real Estate Career Institute. Named Indiana Super Lawyer, 2004. *Member:* Indianapolis and American Bar Associations; Associated General Contractors; Associated Builders and Contractors. ***PRACTICE AREAS:*** Commercial Litigation; Construction; Real Estate; Municipal Law. ***Email:*** streadway@tabberthahn.com

DAVID A. SHELTON, born Indianapolis, Indiana, March 24, 1964; admitted to bar, 1989, Indiana and U.S. District Court, Northern and Southern District of Indiana. *Education:* Butler University (B.S., cum laude, 1986); Indiana University School of Law (J.D., summa cum laude, 1989). Recipient, American Jurisprudence Award. Member, Indianapolis Historic Preservation Commission. *Member:* Indianapolis, Indiana State and American Bar Associations. ***SPECIAL AGENCIES:*** Indianapolis-Marion County Metropolitan Division of Planning and Zoning. ***PRACTICE AREAS:*** Real Estate; Commercial Transactions; Corporate Law; Business Law; Finance; Credit Transactions; Construction Law; Commercial Litigation. ***Email:*** dshelton@tabberthahn.com

MATTHEW W. CONNER, born Elwood, Indiana, July 31, 1967; admitted to bar, 1993, Indiana and U.S. District Court, Northern and Southern Districts of Indiana. *Education:* Ball State University (B.S., cum laude, 1990); Indiana University, School of Law (J.D., 1993). *Member:* Indianapolis and Indiana State Bar Associations; Defense Trial Counsel of Indiana. ***PRACTICE AREAS:*** Medical Malpractice Defense; Litigation. ***Email:*** mattc@tabberthahn.com

ROBERT S. DANIELS, born Greenwood, Indiana, September 11, 1970; admitted to bar, 1996, Indiana. *Education:* DePauw University (B.A., Political Science, 1993); Indiana University School of Law-Bloomington (J.D., 1996). Phi Eta Sigma; Alpha Lambda Delta; Delta Tau Delta. Recipient: Municipal Law Scholarship; Academic Scholarship. *Member:* Indianapolis, Indiana State and American Bar Associations. ***PRACTICE AREAS:*** Business Law; Real Estate Transactions and Litigation; Commercial Transactions and Litigation; Construction Law; Mergers and Acquisitions; Municipal Law; Banking Law. ***Email:*** rdaniels@tabberthahn.com

---

MARK J. PIZUR, born Chicago, Illinois, June 16, 1973; admitted to bar, 1999, Indiana. *Education:* St. Joseph's College (B.S., 1995); Chicago-Kent College of Law (J.D., 1998). ***PRACTICE AREAS:*** Employment Law; Civil Rights; Civil Litigation; Business Law; Construction Law. ***Email:*** mpizur@tabberthahn.com

JOAN ISAACS, born Fort Wayne, Indiana, November 15, 1957; admitted to bar, 1994, Indiana. *Education:* Purdue University (B.S., Psychology, 1989); Indiana University (J.D., 1994). *Member:* Indianapolis, Indiana State and American Bar Associations. ***PRACTICE AREAS:*** Medical Malpractice Defense; Civil Practice; Trial Practice; Administrative Law; Health Care; Insurance Defense. ***Email:*** joan@tabberthahn.com

LINDA H. HAVEL, born Chattanooga, Tennessee, January 22, 1966; admitted to bar, 1994, Kentucky; 1999, Indiana; U.S. District Court, Northern and Southern Districts of Indiana; U.S. District Court, Eastern and Western Districts of Kentucky and U.S. District Court, District of Hawaii. *Education:* Vanderbilt University (B.A., 1988); University of Louisville (J.D., 1994). *Member:* Tippecanoe County, Indiana State, Kentucky and American Bar Associations; Indiana Trial Lawyers Association. ***PRACTICE AREAS:*** Business Law; Complex Commercial Litigation; Real Estate Litigation; Construction Litigation; Personal Injury; Wrongful Death. ***Email:*** lhavel@tabberthahn.com

CHARLES R. WHYBREW, born Wabash, Indiana, January 16, 1972; admitted to bar, 1998, Indiana. *Education:* Wabash College (B.A., cum laude, 1994); Indiana University, School of Law (J.D., 1998). *Member:* Indianapolis (Member: Sports and Entertainment Executive Committee, 1999-2003; Treasurer, 2001), Indiana State and American Bar Associations. ***PRACTICE AREAS:*** Bankruptcy; Creditors Rights; Products Liability Defense; Civil Litigation; Construction Law; Insurance Defense; Administrative Law. ***Email:*** chuckw@tabberthahn.com

CHAD T. WALKER, born Loogootee, Indiana; admitted to bar, 2001, Indiana and U.S. District Court, Northern and Southern Districts of Indiana. *Education:* University of Evansville (B.S., Business Administration, 1996); Indiana University School of Law (J.D., 2001). ***PRACTICE AREAS:*** Commercial Real Estate; Business Transactions; Business Law; Corporate Law; Estate Planning; Housing Law. ***Email:*** cwalker@tabberthahn.com

KEVIN M. QUINN, born Indianapolis, Indiana, November 21, 1977; admitted to bar, 2003, Indiana and U.S. District Court, Northern and Southern Districts of Indiana. *Education:* Indiana University, Bloomington (B.S. with high distinction, 2000); Indiana University, Indianapolis (J.D., 2003). ***PRACTICE AREAS:*** Civil Litigation; Construction Law; Business Law. ***Email:*** kevinq@tabberthahn.com

DAVID J. DUNCAN, born Lafayette, Indiana, June 6, 1978; admitted to bar, 2004, Indiana, U.S. District Court, Northern and Southern Districts of Indiana. *Education:* Indiana University (B.S., 2001); Indiana University School of Law (J.D., 2004). ***PRACTICE AREAS:*** Business Transactions; Real Estate; Mergers and Acquisitions; Corporate Law; Business Law. ***Email:*** davidd@tabberthahn.com

OF COUNSEL

DON A. TABBERT, born Hamilton, Ohio, August 21, 1928; admitted to bar, 1953, Indiana and U.S. District Court, Northern and Southern Districts of Indiana; 1956, U.S. Court of Appeals, 7th Circuit; 1959, U.S. Supreme Court and U.S. Tax Court. *Education:* Indiana University (A.B., 1950); Indiana University School of Law (LL.B., 1953). Phi Delta Phi. Assistant U.S. Attorney, 1954-1957. U.S. Attorney, Southern District of Indiana, 1957-1961. *Member:* Indianapolis, Indiana State, Federal (President, Indianapolis Chapter, 1961-1962) and American Bar Associations. ***PRACTICE AREAS:*** Civil Litigation; Criminal Law; Antitrust; International Law; Business Planning; Estate Planning; Federal Taxation; State Taxation; Administrative Law. ***Email:*** dat@tabberthahn.com

JOSEPH W. HAMMES, born Minneapolis, Minnesota, June 3, 1946; admitted to bar, 1972, Indiana and U.S. District Court, Southern District of Indiana. *Education:* University of Notre Dame (A.B., 1968); Indiana University School of Law (J.D., 1972). Author: "Taking Property by Eminent Domain, and Advising Clients Prior to Condemnation," National Business Institute, 1997; "Eminent Domain, Relocation Assistance: More Than Just Compensation," Indiana Continuing Legal Education Forum, 1997; "Land Use Planning and Eminent Domain in Indiana," National Business Institute, 2002; "Eminent Domain and Land Valuation Litigation," Indiana Continuing Legal Education Forum, 2003. Trial Attor-

(This Listing Continued)

ney, Office of the Attorney General, State of Indiana, 1972-1973. Chief Trial Deputy, Eminent Domain Section, 1973-1975. Member, Panel of Trustees for the U.S. Bankruptcy Court, Southern District of Indiana, Indianapolis Division, 1979—. *Member:* Indianapolis, Indiana State and American Bar Associations; National Association of Bankruptcy Trustees. ***PRACTICE AREAS:*** Civil Practice; Outdoor Advertising; Business Law; Eminent Domain; Real Estate. ***Email:*** hammes@tabberthahn.com

MARK K. SULLIVAN, born Indianapolis, Indiana, November 2, 1952; admitted to bar, 1979, Indiana and U.S. District Court, Southern District of Indiana; 1984, U.S. Court of Appeals, Seventh Circuit. *Education:* St. Joseph's College (B.S., 1974); University of Louisville (J.D., 1979). Deputy Prosecuting Attorney, 1979-1982 and Prosecuting Attorney, 1983-1990, 83rd Judicial District. Deputy Prosecutor, 1991-1992 and Chief Deputy Prosecutor, 1993-1994, Marion County (Indianapolis). *Member:* Indianapolis, Seventh Circuit and Indiana State Bar Associations; Indiana Trial Lawyers Association; The Association of Trial Lawyers of America; National Association of Criminal Defense Lawyers. ***PRACTICE AREAS:*** Civil Litigation; Criminal Law; Gaming Law; Healthcare Law; Family Law; Administrative Law; Entertainment Law. ***Email:*** msullivan@tabberthahn.com

DALE E. SPORLEDER, born Lake City, Iowa, November 7, 1940; admitted to bar, 1967, Missouri; 1979, Iowa; 1983, North Carolina; 1989, Indiana. *Education:* Northwest Missouri State University (B.A., 1963); University of Missouri (J.D., 1967). Author: Appeal of Orders and Decisions of the Missouri Public Service Commission, 28 Journal of the Missouri Bar 376 (August 1972); Missouri Practical Skills Course, The Missouri Bar (1978), Chapter 8, Administrative Law; Missouri Administrative Law, The Missouri Bar (1979), Chapter 6, Public Service Commission (co-authored). ***PRACTICE AREAS:*** Public Utility Law. ***Email:*** sporleder@tabberthahn.com

DARLA Y. WILLIAMS, born Indianapolis, Indiana, December 16, 1963; admitted to bar, 2001, Indiana. *Education:* Purdue University (B.S., 1996); University of Tulsa College of Law (J.D., 1999). ***PRACTICE AREAS:*** Personal Injury (35%); Criminal Law (35%); Governmental Law (10%); Gaming Law (10%); Environmental Law (10%). ***Email:*** darla@tabberthahn.com

REPRESENTATIVE CLIENTS: Bayer Corporation; Trump Indiana, Inc.; State of Indiana, Department of Insurance; Clarion Health Partners, Inc.; Bally Gaming; Phico Insurance Group; Alliance Gaming; Medical Inter-Insurance Exchange; Ohio Hospital Insurance Co.; Lab Plus, Inc.; Robinson Supply; Clear Channel Outdoor Advertising, City of Indianapolis; Clifton-Gunderson, LLC; Indiana Insurance Guaranty Assoc.; St. Paul Insurance Companies.

THRELKELD REYNOLDS, LLP

Established in 2000

CENTURY BUILDING, SUITE 720
36 SOUTH PENNSYLVANIA STREET
INDIANAPOLIS, INDIANA 46204
Telephone: 317-655-5200
Telefax: 317-655-3150
Email: tr@threlkeld-reynolds.com
URL: http://www.lawyers.com/threlkeld-reynolds

General Practice, Litigation and Insurance Defense, Motor Carrier Law, Probate and Estate Planning, Estate Administration, Real Estate, Banking, Commercial, Tax and Corporate Law, Mediation Services.

PARTNERS

W. BRENT THRELKELD, born Indianapolis, Indiana, March 23, 1946; admitted to bar, 1972, Indiana, U.S. District Court, Southern District of Indiana, U.S. Court of Appeals, Seventh Circuit, U.S. Court of Military Appeals and U.S. Supreme Court. *Education:* Indiana State University (B.S., 1968); Indiana University, School of Law (J.D., 1971). Phi Alpha Delta. Lecturer: "Litigation and Understanding the Medical Injury," ICLEF, 1995; "Trying the Automobile Injury Case in Indiana," NBI, 1999; "Masters in Trial," ABOTA, 1999. Deputy Prosecuting Attorney, 1979-1982. Judge Advocate, Military Judge, 1974 and 1975. *Member:* Indianapolis (Member, Litigation Section) and Indiana State Bar Associations; Defense Trial Counsel of Indiana; Defense Research Institute, Inc.; American Board of Trial Advocates (Associate, 1996). [Capt., USMC, 1972-1975, Judge Advocate, Military Judge, 1974 and 1975]. ***PRACTICE AREAS:*** Insurance Defense; Trial Practice. ***Email:*** brent@threlkeld-reynolds.com

THOMAS TODD REYNOLDS, born Indianapolis, Indiana, May 1, 1954; admitted to bar, 1981, Indiana, U.S. District Court, Northern and Southern Districts of Indiana and U.S. Court of Appeals, Seventh Circuit. *Education:* Indiana University, Bloomington (B.S., 1976; M.P.A., J.D., 1981). Pi Alpha Alpha; Phi Alpha Delta. Assistant Corporation Counsel, Indianapolis, 1981-1982. *Member:* Indianapolis (Chair, Litigation Section, 1989) and Indiana State Bar Associations; Defense Trial Counsel of Indiana. (Managing Partner). ***PRACTICE AREAS:*** Insurance Defense; Trial Practice. ***Email:*** tom@threlkeld-reynolds.com

ASSOCIATES

RICHARD W. McMINN, born Indianapolis, Indiana, April 13, 1961; admitted to bar, 1987, Indiana, U.S. Court of Appeals, Seventh Circuit, U.S. District Court, Northern and Southern Districts of Indiana, U.S. District Court, Eastern District of Illinois, U.S. Court of Courts Martial, U.S. Court of Military Appeals and U.S. Court of Federal Claims. *Education:* University of Indianapolis (B.S., Education, 1983); University of Toledo (J.D., 1987); University of Virginia Government Contracts School (1990). *Member:* Indianapolis, Indiana State and American Bar Associations; Veterans of Foreign Wars; American Legion; Association of General Contractors; Association of Building Contractors and Builders Association of Greater Indianapolis. [Capt., U.S.A.F. JAG Corps., 1988-1992]. ***PRACTICE AREAS:*** Construction Litigation; State Commercial Litigation; Federal Commercial Litigation; Public Contract Law; Contract Appeals. ***Email:*** richard@threlkeld-reynolds.com

THOMAS W. KRAMER, born Fort Wayne, Indiana, December 18, 1971; admitted to bar, 1998, Indiana and U.S. District Court, Southern District of Indiana. *Education:* University of Dayton (B.A., History, 1994); Indiana University, Indianapolis (J.D., 1997). Deputy Prosecuting Attorney, 1998-2004. *Member:* Indianapolis and Indiana State Bar Associations. ***PRACTICE AREAS:*** Insurance Defense. ***Email:*** tkramer@threlkeld-reynolds.com

LISA MARIE LEWIS, born Indianapolis, Indiana, May 19, 1976; admitted to bar, 2001, Indiana and U.S. District Court, Northern and Southern Districts of Indiana. *Education:* Purdue University (B.A., Law and Society and Psychology, 1998); Indiana University School of Law - Indianapolis (J.D., 2001). Phi Beta Kappa; Phi Delta Phi; Golden Key National Honors Society. *Member:* Indianapolis and Indiana State Bar Associations. ***PRACTICE AREAS:*** Insurance Defense. ***Email:*** lisa@threlkeld-reynolds.com

AMY M. JONES, born Fort Wayne, Indiana, March 13, 1974; admitted to bar, 2001, Indiana and U.S. District Court, Southern District of Indiana. *Education:* Purdue University (B.A., Public Relations and Political Science, 1996); Thomas M. Cooley Law School (J.D., cum laude, 2000). Phi Alpha Delta. Deputy Prosecuting Attorney, Marion County, 2002-2005. *Member:* Indianapolis and Indiana State Bar Associations. ***Email:*** amy@threlkeld-reynolds.com

CHRISTINE M. RIESNER, admitted to bar, 2002, Indiana. *Education:* Indiana University (B.A., 1998); John Marshall Law School (J.D., 2002). *Member:* Indianapolis and Indiana State Bar Associations. ***PRACTICE AREAS:*** Insurance Defense. ***Email:*** criesner@threlkeld-reynolds.com

REPRESENTATIVE CLIENTS: American Family Insurance Co.; Budget Rent-A-Car Corp.; Gateway Insurance Co.; Guide One; Harleysville Insurance Co.; Highlands Insurance Group; Lake States Insurance Co.; Met Life Insurance Co.; Penn America Group; RSKCo; Reliance National Insurance; St. Paul Insurance Co.; State Farm Mutual Insurance Co.; State Auto Insurance Co.; TIG; Travelers Insurance Cos.

TOWNSEND & MONTROSS

Established in 1941

230 EAST OHIO STREET
INDIANAPOLIS, INDIANA 46244-0902
Telephone: 317-264-4444
Fax: 317-264-2080
Email: townsendmontross@aol.com
URL: http://www.townsendmontross.com

General Civil Trial Practice in all State and Federal Courts. Personal Injury, Products Liability, Malpractice and Aviation Law. Trials and Appeals.

FIRM PROFILE: The firm was founded in 1941. It has always limited its practice to the representation of individuals with claims for personal injury or death. A significant portion of the practice is devoted to medical malpractice and product liability claims.

JOHN F. TOWNSEND (1916-2001)

JOHN F. TOWNSEND, JR., born Indianapolis, Indiana, June 19, 1942; admitted to bar, 1967, Indiana. *Education:* University of Michigan (B.A., 1964); Harvard University (J.D., 1967). Phi Beta Kappa; Phi Kappa Phi. *Member:* Indianapolis, Indiana State and American Bar Associations; The Association of Trial Lawyers of America (State Committeeman, 1974-1978; Member, Board of Governors, 1988-1991); Indiana Trial Lawyers Association (Member, Board of Directors, 1979—; Legislative Chairman, 1978-1981; Director, 1980; Vice-President 1981; President, 1982-1983; Lifetime Director, 1983). Fellow: Indiana College of Trial Lawyers; American College of Trial Lawyers; Indianapolis Bar Foundation. ***LANGUAGES:*** Italian. ***REPORTED CASES:*** Scott v. Krueger, 151 Ind. App. 479, 280 NE2d 336 (1972); Motorists Mutual Ins. Co. v. Simpson, 494 F2d 850 (7th Cir., 1975); Carrow v. Streeter, 410 NE2d 1369 (Ind. App., 1980); Napa General Auto Parts v. Whitcomb, 481 NE2d 1335 (Ind. App., 1985); Miller v. Todd (Suzuki), 551 NE2d 1139 (Ind., 1990); Baltimore & Ohio R.R. Co. v. Taylor 589 NE2d 267 (Ind. App., 1992); 600 NE2d 543 (Sup. Ct. 1992). ***PRACTICE AREAS:*** Personal Injury; Wrongful Death; Product Liability; Aviation Accidents; F.E.L.A.; Insurance; Medical Malpractice. ***Email:*** townsendmontross@aol.com

W. SCOTT MONTROSS, born Milwaukee, Wisconsin, April 16, 1947; admitted to bar, 1971, Indiana. *Education:* University of Michigan (B.B.A., 1969); Indiana University (J.D., 1971). President, Indianapolis Law Club, 1986. *Member:* Indianapolis (Chairman: Legal Aid to Homeless, 1991—; Juvenile Court Legal Aid Project; Chairman, 1993—), Indiana State and American Bar Associations; Indiana Trial Lawyers Association (Member, Board of Directors, 1982—; Treasurer, 1984; Secretary, 1985; lst Vice-President, 1986; President-Elect, 1987; President, 1988; Lifetime Director, 1989); The Association of Trial Lawyers of America (State Public Relations Chairman, 1986); American Board of Trial Advocates; American Judicature Society; Indianapolis Legal Aid Society (Member, Board of Directors); Heartland Pro Bono Council (Member, Board of Directors, 2003—; Secretary, 2003—). Fellow: Indianapolis Bar Foundation; Indiana State Bar Foundation; Indiana College of Trial Lawyers; American College of Trial Lawyers. ***REPORTED CASES:*** Ford Motor Co. v. Ammerman, 705 N.E.2d 539 (Ind.App. 1999) (transfer denied); Sears Roebuck & Co. v. Manuilov, 742 N.E.2d 453 (Ind. Supreme Court, 2001); Groves v. Taylor, 729 N.E.2d 569 (Ind. Supreme Court, 2000). ***PRACTICE AREAS:*** General Personal Injury; Insurance Claims; Medical Malpractice; Product Liability Law; Aviation Law; F.E.L.A. Law; Wrongful Death. ***Email:*** townsendmontross@aol.com

JOHN F. TOWNSEND, III, born Indianapolis, Indiana, May 11, 1971; admitted to bar, 1996, Indiana, U.S. District Court, Northern and Southern Districts of Indiana and U.S. Court of Appeals, Seventh Circuit. *Education:* University of Salamanca, Spain; University of Michigan (B.A., 1993); Indiana University (J.D., 1996). Order of the Coif. *Member:* Indianapolis, Indiana State and American Bar Associations. Indiana Trial Lawyers Association (Sustaining Member; Board of Directors, 2004—); The Association of Trial Lawyers of America (Member, Board of Governors, New Lawyers Division, 2002—); Seventh Circuit Bar Association. Fellow: Indiana Bar Foundation. ***LANGUAGES:*** Spanish. ***REPORTED CASES:*** Crossno v. State, 726 N.E. 2d 375 (Ind. App. 2000); Sears Roebuck & Co. v. Manuilov, 742 N.E.2d 453 (Ind. Supreme Court, 2001); Fort v. C.W. Keller Trucking 330 F. 3d 1006 (7th Cir. 2002); Carolina Casualty Insurance Company v. E.C. Trucking —F.3d—

(This Listing Continued)

TOWNSEND & MONTROSS, Indianapolis—Continued

(7th Cir. 2005). ***PRACTICE AREAS:*** Automobile Negligence; Insurance Claims; Product Liability; Medical Malpractice; Personal Injury; Aviation Law; Wrongful Death; Federal Employers Liability Act (FELA). ***Email:*** ejtownsendiii@cs.com

REFERENCE: Bank One of Indianapolis.

WILLIAM J. TUCKER & ASSOCIATES, LLC

Established in 1999

429 NORTH PENNSYLVANIA STREET, SUITE 400
INDIANAPOLIS, INDIANA 46204-1816
Telephone: 317-833-3030
Facsimile: 317-833-3031
Email: wtucker@wjtucker.com
URL: http://www.wjtucker.com

Business Law, Bankruptcy, Commercial Law, Debtor and Creditor Rights, Corporate Law, Collections, Taxes.

FIRM PROFILE: William J. Tucker & Associates, LLC is one of the leading Commercial Law and Bankruptcy Firms in central Indiana. Located in downtown Indianapolis, our Firm of four attorneys and four legal assistants provides a service equal to much larger firms, yet on a far more cost effective basis. Known widely as one of the top Individual Business and Corporate Reorganization firms in Indianapolis, we also regularly represent Creditors in state and Bankruptcy Court, businesses and individuals in commercial Transactions and Litigation and individuals and businesses with taxation and insolvency issues.

MEMBERS

WILLIAM J. TUCKER, born Batesville, Indiana, May 14, 1949; admitted to bar, 1975, Indiana and Ohio; 1977, Florida. *Education:* Indiana State University (B.S., 1971); Salmon P. Chase College of Law, Northern Kentucky University (J.D., 1975). *Member:* Indianapolis and Indiana Bar Associations; National Association of Bankruptcy Trustees; Commercial Law League of America; American Bankruptcy Institute. ***Email:*** wtucker@wjtucker.com

STEVEN K. DICK, born Springfield, Ohio, February 8, 1953; admitted to bar, 1981, Ohio; 2000, Indiana. *Education:* Ohio State University (B.S.C.E., 1975); University of Cincinnati (J.D., 1981). *Member:* American Bar Association; American Bankruptcy Institute. ***Email:*** sdick@wjtucker.com

JEFFREY MICHAEL HESTER, born Silver Springs, Maryland, September 12, 1973; admitted to bar, 1999, Hawaii; 2000, Indiana. *Education:* Indiana University at Bloomington (B.A., 1995); Indiana University School of Law, Indianapolis (J.D., 1998). ***LANGUAGES:*** Mandarin Chinese. ***Email:*** hester@wjtucker.com

ASSOCIATE

C. ABRAHAM MURPHY, born Indianapolis, Indiana, March 25, 1972; admitted to bar, 2002, Indiana. *Education:* Indiana University (B.S., Criminal Justice, 1999; J.D., 2002). ***PRACTICE AREAS:*** Commercial Law; Collections; Bankruptcy. ***Email:*** amurphy@wjtucker.com

LEGAL SUPPORT PERSONNEL

KATHY SHAMBLIN (Paralegal)

REPRESENTATIVE CLIENTS: Annex Railroad; KRB Music Companies, Inc.; Indianapolis Water Company; Indianapolis Power & Light Co.; Vinylcraft, Inc.; Alliant Foodserice, Inc.; Northwest Internal Medicine Associates; KMS Computer Services, Inc.; Standt's Fine Jewelry; First Horizon Home Loans; Old Republic National Title.

TYRA & COLLESANO, P.C.

8470 ALLISON POINTE BOULEVARD, SUITE 420 (CASTLETON)
INDIANAPOLIS, INDIANA 46250-4364
Telephone: 317-567-2222
Fax: 317-567-2220
Email: kevin.tyra@tycolaw.com
URL: http://www.tycolaw.com

Trial and Appellate Practice. Insurance Defense, including Medical Malpractice, Nursing Home Cases, Workers Compensation, Insurance Coverage, Insurance Fraud Investigation. Wills and Probate, Trusts and Estates, Estate Planning, Business, Corporate, Construction Law, Contracts and Employment Law. General Civil Litigation. Arbitration and Mediation.

JAMES F. BLEEKE, born Bluffton, Indiana, August 25, 1960; admitted to bar, 1985, Indiana, U.S. District Court, Northern and Southern Districts of Indiana and U.S. Court of Appeals, Seventh Circuit. *Education:* Indiana University (B.A., with highest distinction, 1982; J.D., cum laude, 1985). Phi Beta Kappa. Note Editor, Indiana Law Journal, 1984-1985. Author: "Intentional Infliction of Emotional Distress in the At-Will Employment Setting," 59:2 Indiana Law Journal, 1984. Co-Author: "Insurance Coverage in Automobile Accident Cases," Indiana Continuing Legal Education Forum, 1986. Panel Member, Indiana Medical Malpractice Seminar, Indiana Continuing Legal Education Forum, 2000. *Member:* Indiana State (Member, Litigation Section) and American Bar Associations; Defense Research Institute; Defense Trial Counsel of Indiana. ***PRACTICE AREAS:*** Medical Malpractice; Nursing Homes; Insurance Defense; General Civil Litigation; Natural Resources Law; Warranty Law; Black Lung Law; Health Care; Litigation. ***Email:*** jim.bleeke@tycolaw.com

STANLEY F. COLLESANO, born Buffalo, New York, August 4,1968; admitted to bar, 1995, New York and U.S. District Court, Western District of New York; 1999, Indiana and U.S. District Court, Northern and Southern Districts of Indiana. *Education:* Canisius College (B.S., 1990); Thomas M. Cooley Law School (J.D., 1994). *Member:* Indiana State Bar Association; Defense Trial Counsel of Indiana; Builders Association of Greater Indianapolis. ***PRACTICE AREAS:*** Business Law; Corporate Law; Estate Planning; Estate Administration; Trust Administration; Construction Law; Real Estate; Liability; Insurance Defense; Tax Law. ***Email:*** stan.collesano@tycolaw.com

DORIS L. SWEETIN, born Nürnberg, Germany, February 15, 1963; admitted to bar, 1995, Ohio; 1998, U.S. District Court, Southern District of Ohio; 2000, Indiana and U.S. District Court, Southern District of Indiana; 2002, U.S. District Court, Northern District of Indiana; U.S. Court of Appeals, Seventh Circuit. *Education:* Wichita State University (B.A., cum laude, 1988); University of Cincinnati (J.D., 1995). Arbitrator, Mediator and Advocate, Collaborative Law Institute, Cincinnati, Ohio. *Member:* Indiana State and Ohio State Bar Associations; Defense Trial Counsel of Indiana; Indiana Workers' Compensation Institute. ***PRACTICE AREAS:*** Insurance Defense; Workers Compensation; Construction Law. ***Email:*** doris.sweetin@tycolaw.com

KEVIN C. TYRA, born Saginaw, Michigan, November 22, 1956; admitted to bar, 1981, Tennessee; 1986, U.S. Court of Military Appeals; 1987, Indiana and U.S. District Court, Southern District of Indiana; 1996, U.S. District Court, Northern District of Indiana and U.S. Court of Appeals, Seventh Circuit. *Education:* Purdue University (B.A., cum laude, 1978); Vanderbilt University (J.D., 1981). Phi Beta Kappa. Certified Civil and Family Mediator. *Member:* Indiana State Bar Association; Defense Trial Counsel of Indiana. [LT., JAGC, USNR, active duty, 1981-1987]. ***PRACTICE AREAS:*** Insurance Defense; Insurance Coverage; Insurance Fraud; Employment Law; Medical Malpractice; Workers Compensation; Arbitration; Mediation. ***Email:*** kevin.tyra@tycolaw.com

---

KORI L. McOMBER, born Indianapolis, Indiana, August 10, 1976; admitted to bar, 2001, Indiana; U.S. District Court, Northern and Southern Districts of Indiana. *Education:* Miami University (B.A., International Studies, 1998); Indiana University, School of Law-Indianapolis (J.D., 2001). *Member:* Indianapolis (Executive Board, Young Lawyers Division, 2004—) and Indiana State Bar Associations; Defense Trial Counsel of Indiana. ***LANGUAGES:*** French. ***PRACTICE AREAS:*** Insurance Defense; Insurance Coverage; Insurance Fraud. ***Email:*** kori.mcomber@tycolaw.com

PEGGY K. LITTLE, born Rushville, Indiana, January 18, 1956; admitted to bar, 2002, Indiana; U.S. District Court, Northern and Southern Districts of Indiana. *Education:* University of Indianapolis (B.S., summa cum laude, 1999); Indiana University, School of Law (J.D., 2002). Order of Barristers. *Member:* Indianapolis and Indiana State Bar Association; Defense Trial Counsel of Indiana. ***PRACTICE AREAS:*** Insurance Defense; Nursing Homes; Workers Compensation. ***Email:*** peggy.little@tycolaw.com

REPRESENTATIVE CLIENTS: Autumn Glen Communities; EmCare; First State Management Group; GMAC Insurance; HCR Manor Care; HVAC Design, Inc.; IFG Companies; Illinois State Medical Insurance Services; Indiana Department of Insurance (Patient Compensation Fund); Infinity Document Solutions; Innovative Exercise Research, Inc.; Integrity Document Solutions, Inc.; Meadowbrook Insurance Group; Menard, Inc.; Met Life Auto and Home; Ohio Casualty Group; Point Construction, Inc.; R.F. Mattei & Associates; Rockford Mutual; Selective Insurance; State Farm; Western Litigation Specialists; GECI; QMedtrix; Ward North America; Zurich North America.

THE WADDICK LAW FIRM, P.C.

Established in 1993

9000 KEYSTONE CROSSING, SUITE 1000
INDIANAPOLIS, INDIANA 46240
Telephone: 317-843-3980
FAX: 317-573-5280
Email: wwaddick@inct.net
URL: http://www.lawyers.com/williamwaddick

Personal Injury, Commercial, Corporate.

WILLIAM A. WADDICK, born Chicago, Illinois, December 7, 1931; admitted to bar, 1961, Indiana. *Education:* Xavier University and University of Notre Dame (B.S. in Com., 1957); Indiana University (J.D., 1961). Phi Delta Phi. Law Clerk, Supreme Court of Indiana, 1961. Listed in: Who's Who in the U.S., 1975—; Noteable Americans, 1976—; Who's Who in American Law, 1985—; Strathmore's Who's Who, 1997—. *Member:* Indianapolis and The Indiana State Bar Associations; The Indiana Trial Lawyers Association; The Association of Trial Lawyers of America. ***LANGUAGES:*** Spanish. ***REPORTED CASES:*** Allstate Indemnity Company v. Lee O. Brown, Jr., Indiana Court of Appeals, Appeal No. 49A04-9710-CV-452, decided June 30, 1998, transfer denied. ***PRACTICE AREAS:*** Personal Injury; Corporations Law. ***Email:*** wwaddick@inct.net

WALLACK SOMERS & HAAS, P.C.

Established in 1999

ONE INDIANA SQUARE, SUITE 1500
INDIANAPOLIS, INDIANA 46204
Telephone: 317-231-9000
FAX: 317-231-9900
URL: http://www.wshlaw.com

Real Estate, Finance, Investment, Development, Construction, Leasing, Corporate, Business, Mediation.

FIRM PROFILE: Wallack Somers & Haas, P.C. is a boutique firm concentrating its practice on serving the commercial real estate and business community. Our commitment is to provide the highest degree of legal expertise and experience, while our entrepreneurial "small firm" setting promotes prompt and cost effective legal services, satisfying both the client's "bottom line" and its business objectives. The firm is listed in Chambers USA America's Leading Business Lawyers, as a Leading Firm in Real Estate, 2003-2005.

BARRY Z. WALLACK, born New York, New York, April 13, 1941; admitted to bar, 1965, Indiana. *Education:* University of Wisconsin (B.S., 1962; J.D., 1965). Order of the Coif. Editorial Board, University of Wisconsin Law Review, 1964-1965. Listed in: Best

(This Listing Continued)

Lawyers in America, 2000-2005; Indianapolis Monthly as Real Estate Super Lawyer, 2004; Chambers USA America's Leading Business Lawyers, as a Leading Individual, 2003-2005. ***PRACTICE AREAS:*** Real Estate; Finance; Investment; Construction; Leasing; Corporate; Business; Mediation. ***Email:*** bzw@wshlaw.com

MICHAEL S. WALLACK, born Indianapolis, Indiana, December 2, 1965; admitted to bar, 1992, Indiana. *Education:* Northwestern University (B.A., 1988); Indiana University (J.D., cum laude, 1991). ***PRACTICE AREAS:*** Real Estate; Finance; Investment; Construction; Leasing; Corporate; Business. ***Email:*** msw@wshlaw.com

GEORGE W. SOMERS, born 1947; admitted to bar, 1979, Indiana. *Education:* St. Olaf College (B.A., magna cum laude, 1969); Harvard University (M.T.S., cum laude, 1971); Duke University (M.A., 1974); University of Chicago (J.D., 1979). Phi Beta Kappa. James B. Duke Scholar. Listed in: Best Lawyers in America, 1997-2005; Indianapolis Monthly as Real Estate Super Lawyer, 2004; Chambers USA America's Leading Business Lawyers, as a Leading Individual, 2003-2005. ***PRACTICE AREAS:*** Real Estate; Finance; Investment; Construction; Leasing. ***Email:*** gws@wshlaw.com

KARL P. HAAS, born 1960; admitted to bar, 1985, Indiana. *Education:* Indiana University (B.S., with highest distinction, 1982; J.D., summa cum laude, 1985). Beta Gamma Sigma. Edwards Fellow. Jump Scholar. Listed in: Best Lawyers in America, 2005; Chambers USA America's Leading Business Lawyers, as a Leading Individual, 2003-2005. ***PRACTICE AREAS:*** Real Estate; Finance; Investment; Construction; Leasing. ***Email:*** kph@wshlaw.com

JENNIFER R. SHOUP, born 1967; admitted to bar, 1996, Indiana. *Education:* Butler University (B.S., with high honors, 1989); Indiana University (J.D., summa cum laude, 1996). ***PRACTICE AREAS:*** Real Estate; Finance; Investment; Construction; Leasing. ***Email:*** jrs@wshlaw.com

JODIE L. EDMINSTER, born 1970; admitted to bar, 1999, Indiana. *Education:* Fairleigh Dickinson University (B.A., summa cum laude, 1992); Indiana University School of Law (J.D., cum laude, 1999). Phi Beta Kappa. Presidential Scholar, Psi Chi. ***PRACTICE AREAS:*** Real Estate; Finance; Leasing; Business Law. ***Email:*** jle@wshlaw.com

SAMUEL J. ARENA, born Bedford, Indiana, May 14, 1976; admitted to bar, 2001, Wisconsin; 2005, Indiana. *Education:* Indiana University (B.A., with distinction, 1997; J.D., cum laude, 2001). Phi Alpha Theta; Phi Delta Phi (Vice President, 2001). *Member:* Milwaukee and American Bar Associations; State Bar of Wisconsin. ***PRACTICE AREAS:*** Real Estate; Finance; Leasing; Business Law. ***Email:*** sja@wshlaw.com

REPRESENTATIVE CLIENTS: Kite Realty Group Trust; Old National Bank; The City of Carmel, Indiana; Fifth Third Bank; Browning Investments, Inc.; REI Investments, Inc.; Republic Services, Inc.; ING; Earlham College; BMG.
REFERENCE: National Bank of Indianapolis.

WARD & WARD

Established in 1963
1014 CIRCLE TOWER BUILDING
55 MONUMENT CIRCLE
INDIANAPOLIS, INDIANA 46204
Telephone: 317-639-9501
Email: cpw@wardlawfirm.com

Personal Injury, Products Liability, Wrongful Death, Aviation, Automobile Accidents, Medical Malpractice, Federal Employers Liability Act, Civil Trial, Wills, Probate, Trusts and Estates, Guardianships, Asset Protection, Estate Planning.

FIRM PROFILE: The firm of Ward & Ward expanded in 1991 when Charles P. Ward joined his father in practice. Ward & Ward offers expert legal services throughout Indiana. This Bar Register listed firm concentrates particularly on the areas of plaintiff auto and trucking accidents and products liability.

MEMBERS OF FIRM

DONALD W. WARD, born Peoria, Illinois, October 5, 1928; admitted to bar, 1954, Indiana, U.S. District Court, Southern District of Indiana and U.S. Court of Appeals, Seventh Circuit. *Education:* Hanover College (A.B., 1951); University of Notre Dame (J.D., 1954). Deputy Trial Prosecutor, Marion County, 1962-1965. Deputy Corporation Counsel, City of Indianapolis, 1975-1980. Member, Indiana Judicial Nominating Commission and Indiana Judicial Qualification Commission, 1978-1984, 1993-1995 and 2001—. *Member:* Indianapolis (Vice-President, 1975) and Indiana State Bar Associations; Indiana Trial Lawyers Association (President, 1978-1979; Lifetime Director and Recipient of 1996, Lifetime Achievement Award); The Association of Trial Lawyers of America (Governor, 1979-1982 and 1997—). Fellow, Indiana College of Trial Lawyers. ***PRACTICE AREAS:*** Personal Injury; Products Liability; Wrongful Death; Aviation; Medical Malpractice; Federal Employers Liability Act; Civil Practice; Probate; Trusts and Estates.

CHARLES P. WARD, born Indianapolis, Indiana, April 17, 1963; admitted to bar, 1989, Indiana and U.S. District Court, Northern and Southern Districts of Indiana. *Education:* Butler University (B.A., cum laude, 1985); Indiana University (J.D., 1989). Law Clerk to Justice Richard M. Givan, Indiana Supreme Court, 1990-1991. *Member:* Indianapolis and Indiana State Bar Associations; Indiana Trial Lawyers Association; The Association of Trial Lawyers of America (State Delegate, 1996—; Governor, Young Lawyers Divisions, 1995-1999); Indianapolis Inn of Court. ***PRACTICE AREAS:*** Personal Injury; Products Liability; Wrongful Death; Aviation; Medical Malpractice; Federal Employers Liability Act; Civil Practice; Probate; Trusts and Estates. ***Email:*** cpw@wardlawfirm.com

REFERENCE: Bank One.

GARY R. WELSH, ATTORNEY AT LAW, P.C.

Established in 2002
320 N. MERIDIAN, SUITE 615
INDIANAPOLIS, INDIANA 46204
Telephone: 317-684-0099
Fax: 317-634-1754
Email: gwelsh@ameritech.net
URL: http://www.welshatlaw.com

Business, Real Estate, Immigration, Family Law.

GARY R. WELSH, born Terre Haute, Indiana, November 30, 1962; admitted to bar, 1993, Indiana. *Education:* Eastern Illinois University (B.A., cum laude, 1984); Indiana University School of Law (J.D., magna cum laude, 1993). Phi Delta Phi. *Member:* Indiana State Bar Association; American Immigration Lawyers Association. ***PRACTICE AREAS:*** Business Law; Real Estate; Immigration and Naturalization; Family Law; Business Litigation.

WESSELS & PAUTSCH, P.C.

MARKET TOWER
10 WEST MARKET STREET, SUITE 1770
INDIANAPOLIS, INDIANA 46204
Telephone: 317-656-8800
Fax: 317-656-8855
Email: wessels@stch.w-p.com
URL: http://www.w-p.com

Milwaukee, Wisconsin Office: Two Plaza East, 330 East Kilbourn Avenue, Suite 1475. Telephone: 414-291-0600. Fax: 414-291-0200.
Chicago, Illinois Office: Chicago Bar Association Building, 321 South Plymouth Court, Suite 900. Telephone: 312-461-0500. Fax: 312-461-0595.
Davenport, Iowa Office: Northwest Bank Building, 101 W. Second Street, Suite 307. Telephone: 563-333-9102. Fax: 563-333-9105.
Minneapolis, Minnesota Office: MoneyGram Tower, 1550 Utica Avenue South, Suite 450. Telephone: 952-746-1700. Fax: 952-746-1704.

Representing Employers in Labor and Employment Law Matters. NLRA, RLA, all Federal and State Employment Discrimination Laws, Federal and State Disability Laws, Wrongful Discharge, Employment Contracts, Collective Bargaining Negotiations and Arbitrations, Employee Substance Abuse, Safety and Health, Unemployment Insurance, Benefits Law, Wage and Hour, and Employment-Based Immigration Matters. Litigation before all Federal and State Courts and Agencies, Trial and Appellate Practice.

FREDERICK D. PAYNE, born December 3, 1971; admitted to bar, 1999, Indiana, U.S. District Court, Northern and Southern Districts of Indiana, U.S. District Court, Northern and Central Districts of Illinois and U.S. Court of Appeals, Eleventh Circuit. *Education:* Grambling State University (B.A., 1994); University of Northern Iowa (M.A., 1998); Indiana University School of Law, Bloomington, (J.D., 1998). Phi Alpha Delta. Board Member, Indiana State Pro bono Commission. Member, Indianapolis & Marian County Justice Center Joint Task Force. *Member:* Indianapolis, Marion County, Indiana State (Member, House of Delegates) and American (Member, Employment Law Section) Bar Associations. ***Email:*** frpayne@indy.w-p.com

BRUCE F. MILLS, born Chicago, Illinois, October 27, 1946; admitted to bar, 1998, Wisconsin and U.S. District Court, Eastern and Western Districts of Wisconsin; 2004, Indiana, U.S. District Court, Northern District of Illinois and U.S. District Court, Northern and Southern Districts of Indiana. *Education:* Indiana State University (B.S., 1968; M.S., 1971; PH.D., 1973); University of Wisconsin (J.D., 1998). Author: "Will the 1991 Amendments to Title VII Prohibit Section 1983 Actions for Public Employees?" Labor Law Journal, 1999. *Member:* Milwaukee, Indiana State and American Bar Associations; State Bar of Wisconsin; National Trial Lawyers Association. ***Email:*** brmills@indy.w-p.com

(For complete biographical data on other personnel, see Professional Biographies at Chicago, Illinois; Milwaukee, Wisconsin; Davenport, Iowa; and Minneapolis, Minnesota)

STEVEN E. WILLSEY

Established in 1983
4040 SOUTH MERIDIAN STREET
INDIANAPOLIS, INDIANA 46217
Telephone: 317-783-2500
1-888-783-2500
Fax: 317-782-2994
Email: swillsey01@sbcglobal.net
URL: http://www.lawyers.com/stevenwillseylaw

Personal Injury, Automobile Accidents and Injuries, Wrongful Death, Construction Site Accidents, Medical Malpractice, Motorcycle Accidents.

STEVEN E. WILLSEY, born Indianapolis, Indiana, November 18, 1957; admitted to bar, 1983, Indiana. *Education:* Indiana University (B.A., 1980; J.D., 1983). *Member:* Indianapolis Bar Association. ***PRACTICE AREAS:*** Plaintiff's Personal Injury.

WILSON, KEHOE & WININGHAM

Established in 1970

2859 NORTH MERIDIAN
INDIANAPOLIS, INDIANA 46208
Telephone: 317-920-6400
Fax: 317-920-6405
Email: mailbox@wkw.com
URL: http://www.wkw.com

Richmond, Indiana Office: 2901 East Main Street, 47374. Telephone: 765-962-9113.
Muncie, Indiana Office: 3620 N. Everbrook Lane, Suite A, 47304. Telephone: 765-284-2474. Fax: 765-288-8655.

Civil Trial Practice in State and Federal Courts. Aviation, Medical Legal, Personal Injury, Product Liability, Medical Malpractice, Wrongful Death, Insurance.

FIRM PROFILE: The Law Firm of Wilson, Kehoe & Winingham represents plaintiffs who are personal injury or wrongful death victims of automobile and aviation accidents, product liability, fires and explosions, and medical malpractice.

Wilson, Kehoe & Winingham have frequently been called upon to assist lawyers in preparing cases for trial dates on short notice and actively litigate in courts throughout the United States.

MEMBERS OF FIRM

HARRY A. WILSON, JR. (1930-2004)

D. BRUCE KEHOE, born Evansville, Indiana, November 27, 1950; admitted to bar, 1980, Indiana, U.S. District Court, Northern and Southern Districts of Indiana and U.S. Court of Appeals, Seventh Circuit. *Education:* Indiana University (B.S., 1973; J.D., 1980). Recipient, ITLA's Trial Lawyer of the Year Award, 2001. Author: "Expanding Hahn v. Moore in the Loss of a Teenage Child," Indiana Continuing Legal Education Forum, 1985; Indiana Practitioner Series, "Personal Injury and Torts-Pleading and Practice and Aviation Accidents," 1996. Inducted: American College of Trial Lawyers. *Member:* Indianapolis, Indiana State and American Bar Associations; Indiana Trial Lawyers Association (Member, Board of Directors, 1987—); The Association of Trial Lawyers of America (Sustaining Member). ***PRACTICE AREAS:*** Medical Malpractice Law; Medical Products Law; General Tort. ***Email:*** kehoe@wkw.com

WILLIAM E. WININGHAM, JR., born Indianapolis, Indiana, March 13, 1952; admitted to bar, 1979, Indiana; U.S. District Court, Northern and Southern Districts of Indiana; U.S. Court of Appeals, Seventh Circuit. *Education:* Indiana University (B.A., 1975); Indiana University School of Law-Indianapolis (J.D., 1979). Recipient, ITLA's Trial Lawyer of the Year Award, 2002. Author: "Working with the Grieving Client," Indiana Continuing Legal Education Forum, 1989; "Nursing Services Provided to the Plaintiff by Family Members - The Neglected Damage Element," Indiana Trial Lawyers Association Seminar, 1989; Indiana Practitioner Series, "Personal Injury and Torts-Pleading and Practice," 1996; "Depositions: Strategies, Tactics & Mechanics," Professional Education Systems, Inc. Seminar, 1990; "Plaintiff's Perspective in Premises Liability Cases," Indianapolis Bar Association, 1992; "Plaintiff's Perspective in Personal Injury Litigation Practice in Indiana," National Business Institute Seminar, 1993; "Dealing with Expert Witnesses," Indiana Continuing Legal Education Forum, 1993; "Bad Faith Litigation," National Business Institute Seminar, 1995; "Expert Evidence Under Rule 702 and Daubert," Indiana Continuing Legal Education Forum, 1996; "Surviving Daubert Issues in Federal Court," Indiana Trial Lawyers Association, 2000; "64 Tips for Punitive Damages," Indiana Continuing Legal Education Forum, 2002; "Indiana Bad Faith Litigation," National Business Institute, 2003. Marion County Deputy Prosecutor, 1979-1982. Assistant U.S. Attorney, 1982-1985. *Member:* Indianapolis, Indiana State and American Bar Associations; The Association of Trial Lawyers of America; Indiana Trial Lawyers Association. ***PRACTICE AREAS:*** General Tort; Products Liability Law; Fire and Explosion Law. ***Email:*** winingham@wkw.com

ASSOCIATES

GERALD A. GRIFFIN, M.D., born Hammond, Indiana, November 14, 1952; admitted to bar, 1996, Indiana; U.S. District Court, Northern and Southern Districts of Indiana. *Education:* Indiana University (M.D.,1981); Indiana University School of Law (J.D., cum laude, 1995). Legal Authorships: "(THI) Traumatic Head Injury Defined," May, 1993; "Skin Physiology & The Treatment of Burns," Autumn, 1993; "Whiplash Injuries Of The Head and Neck," Summer 1994,"; Low Back Pain - Part II: Diagnostic," Winter, 1995; Trial Lawyers of Counsel. Trial Lawyers of Counsel. Authored and copyrighted as part of a series of education seminars, Continuing Legal Education Credit for attendees: "Lawyers Medical Resource Guide," Lawyers Consulting Service, Inc., 1993; "Lawyers Medical Resource Guild-Second Edition," Lawyers Consulting Service, Inc., 1994. Professional License: Physician License, 1981. *Member:* Indianapolis, Indiana State Bar Associations; American Trial Lawyers Association; Indiana Trial Lawyers Association. Member, American College of Forensic Examiners, 1996. Fellow American College of Legal Medicine (Membership, 1993, Fellowship awarded, 1996). ***PRACTICE AREAS:*** Medical Malpractice; Personal Injury. ***Email:*** griffin@wkw.com

CHRISTOPHER G. STEVENSON, born Lafayette, Indiana, February 13, 1974; admitted to bar, 2004, Indiana and U.S. District Court, Northern and Southern Districts of Indiana. *Education:* Purdue University (B.S., 1996); Indiana University School of Law (J.D., 2003). ***PRACTICE AREAS:*** Aviation Law; Products Liability Law; General Tort. ***Email:*** cstevenson@wkw.com

OF COUNSEL

GERALD L. LAWLIS, born Indianapolis, Indiana, March 22, 1938; admitted to bar, 1966, Indiana; U.S. District Court, Northern and Southern Districts of Indiana; U.S. Supreme Court. *Education:* Purdue University (B.S., 1960); University of Michigan (J.D., 1966). *Member:* Indianapolis (Chair, Lawyers Assistance Committee, 1991, 1992), Indiana State and American Bar Associations; Indiana Trial Lawyers Association; The Association of Trial Lawyers of America. ***Email:*** jlawlis@wkw.com

REFERENCE: Fifth Third Bank.

JUDITH J. WODDELL

SUITE 1420, 151 NORTH DELAWARE STREET
INDIANAPOLIS, INDIANA 46204
Telephone: 317-269-6262
Fax: 317-269-0016

Probate and Estate Planning, Estate Administration, Taxation Law, Corporate Law.

JUDITH J. WODDELL, born Indianapolis, Indiana, November 25, 1940; admitted to bar, 1969, Indiana; 1970, U.S. Tax Court. *Education:* Butler University (B.S., 1962); Indiana University (J.D., 1969). *Member:* Indianapolis and Indiana State Bar Associations.

WOODARD, EMHARDT, MORIARTY, McNETT & HENRY LLP

Established in 1879

BANK ONE CENTER/TOWER
111 MONUMENT CIRCLE, SUITE 3700
INDIANAPOLIS, INDIANA 46204-5137
Telephone: 317-634-3456
Telecopier: 317-637-7561
URL: http://www.uspatent.com

Patent, Trademark, Copyright, Unfair Competition, Computer, Franchise and related Antitrust Law. Trials and Appeals.

FIRM PROFILE: Located in Indianapolis, Indiana, Woodard, Emhardt, Moriarty, McNett and Henry LLP is among the nation's oldest intellectual property law firms. Founded in 1879 - the same year Thomas Edison perfected the light bulb -the firm's practice is thoughtfully focused on patent, trademark, copyright and unfair competition law, including litigation of intellectual property issues. Forty of the firm's attorneys are members of the patent bar.

The Firm's critical mass of technical expertise provides a breadth and depth of experience to serve clients in diverse industries and with specialized needs. The firm carefully selects attorneys for their degrees in engineering, biology, chemistry and other technical specialties that complement their knowledge of intellectual property law.

Members of the firm work either directly with the client, or with a client's business lawyer to provide comprehensive legal representation in all areas of intellectual property law. The firm services domestic and foreign clients in every corner of the globe. Clients include Fortune 500 corporations, small business owners, individual inventors, general practice attorneys and corporate counsel. Industries served include biomedical, advanced manufacturing, and telecommunications among many, many others. The firm's depth of its talent, breadth of technical expertise and exclusive focus allow it to quickly position the right attorney with every client's unique intellectual property need.

MEMBERS OF FIRM

C. DAVID EMHARDT, born 1931; admitted to bar, 1955, District of Columbia; 1958, Indiana; registered to practice before U.S. Patent and Trademark Office. *Education:* Culver Military Academy; Purdue University (B.S.E.M.E., 1952; A.S.E.E.T., 1966); Harvard University (LL.B., 1955). *Member:* District of Columbia Bar; Indiana State (Chairman, Patent Section, 1967-1968) Bar Association; American Intellectual Property Law Association. [Capt., Indiana Nat'l Guard, Asst. Staff Judge Advocate, 38th Division, 1964-1966]. ***PRACTICE AREAS:*** Patents; Trademarks; Copyrights. ***Email:*** demhardt@uspatent.com

JOHN V. MORIARTY, born 1940; admitted to bar, 1969, Indiana; registered to practice before U.S. Patent and Trademark Office. *Education:* University of Notre Dame (B.S.A.E., 1963); Indiana University (M.B.A., 1967; J.D., 1969). Registered Professional Engineer, Indiana, 1968. Trial Deputy, Marion County Prosecutor's Office, 1975-1976. *Member:* Indiana State (Secretary-Treasurer, Patent Section, 1971-1972) Bar Association. ***PRACTICE AREAS:*** Patents; Trademarks; Copyrights. ***Email:*** jmoriarty@uspatent.com

JOHN C. McNETT, born 1944; admitted to bar, 1970, Indiana; registered to practice before U.S. Patent and Trademark Office. *Education:* Purdue University (B.S., 1967); George Washington University (J.D., 1970). *Member:* Seventh Circuit, Federal Circuit and Indiana State (Chairman, Patent Section, 1978-1979) Bar Associations; Institute of Electrical and Electronics Engineers; American Intellectual Property Law Association; American Chemical Society. ***PRACTICE AREAS:*** Patents; Trademarks; Copyrights. ***Email:*** jmcnett@uspatent.com

THOMAS Q. HENRY, born 1952; admitted to bar, 1975, Indiana; registered to practice before U.S. Patent and Trademark Office. *Education:* Purdue University (B.S., Chem. Eng., cum laude, 1972); Indiana University (J.D., magna cum laude, 1975). Author: "What The General Practitioner Should Know About Patent Laws," Res Gestae, August, 1979; "Intellectual Property in the Business Environment," Basic Corporate Practice, 1987. Judicial Law Clerk, Indiana Court of Appeals, 1974-1975. *Member:* Indianapolis (President, 1991; Chairman, Young Lawyers, 1986), Seventh Circuit and Indiana State (Chairman, Patent Section, 1985-1986) Bar Associations; American Chemical Society. ***PRACTICE AREAS:*** Patents; Trademarks; Copyrights. ***Email:*** thenry@uspatent.com

JAMES M. DURLACHER, born 1946; admitted to bar, 1976, Indiana; registered to practice before U.S. Patent and Trademark Office. *Education:* Purdue University (B.S.M.E., 1968; M.S., 1972); Indiana University (J.D., 1976). *Member:* Seventh Circuit Bar Association. ***PRACTICE AREAS:*** Patents; Trademarks; Copyrights. ***Email:*** jdurlacher@uspatent.com

CHARLES R. REEVES, born 1951; admitted to bar, 1977, Indiana; registered to practice before U.S. Patent and Trademark Office. *Education:* Purdue University (B.S., Met. Engr., cum laude, 1973); Indiana University (J.D., summa cum laude, 1977). Judicial Law Clerk, Indiana Court of Appeals, 1975-1976. Author: Indiana Chapter, "State Trademark

(This Listing Continued)

and Unfair Competition Law," 64. *Member:* Seventh Circuit and Federal Circuit Bar Associations; American Society for Metals; American Institute for Mining, Metallurgical and Petroleum Engineers. ***PRACTICE AREAS:*** Patents; Trademarks; Copyrights. ***Email:*** creeves@uspatent.com

VINCENT O. WAGNER, born 1951; admitted to bar, 1976, Indiana; registered to practice before U.S. Patent and Trademark Office. *Education:* University of Notre Dame (B.S., cum laude, 1973); Indiana University (J.D., cum laude, 1976). Phi Delta Phi. *Member:* Seventh Circuit and Federal Circuit Bar Associations. ***PRACTICE AREAS:*** Patents; Trademarks; Copyrights. ***Email:*** vwagner@uspatent.com

STEPHEN E. ZLATOS, born 1951; admitted to bar, 1977, Indiana; registered to practice before U.S. Patent and Trademark Office. *Education:* Purdue University (B.S.E., 1973); Indiana University (J.D., 1977). Associate Editor, Indiana Law Review, 1976-1977. Deputy Attorney General and Chief Attorney, Environmental Section, State of Indiana, 1977-1981. *Member:* Seventh Circuit and Indiana State (Chairman, Patent Section, 1991-1992) Bar Associations. ***PRACTICE AREAS:*** Patents; Trademarks; Copyrights. ***Email:*** stevezlatos@uspatent.com

SPIRO BEREVESKOS, born 1956; admitted to bar, 1981, Indiana; 1983, U.S. Court of Appeals, Federal Circuit; 1985, U.S. Supreme Court; registered to practice before U.S. Patent and Trademark Office. *Education:* Purdue University (B.S., Indus. Engr., with honors, 1977); Indiana University, Bloomington (J.D., cum laude, 1981). ***LANGUAGES:*** Greek. ***PRACTICE AREAS:*** Patents; Trademarks; Copyrights.

CLIFFORD W. BROWNING, born 1950; admitted to bar, 1978, Indiana; registered to practice before U.S. Patent and Trademark Office. *Education:* Purdue University (B.S. in Chem. Eng., 1972); Indiana University (J.D., 1978). Editor-in-Chief, Indiana Law Review, 1977-1978. Law Clerk to Judge James E. Noland, U. S. District Court, Southern District of Indiana, 1978-1980. Senior Editor, Editorial Board, The Trademark Reporter. Adjunct Professor of Trademark and Unfair Competition Law at the Indiana University School of Law, Indianapolis. ***PRACTICE AREAS:*** Patents; Trademarks; Copyrights. ***Email:*** browning@worldip.com

R. RANDALL FRISK, born 1959; admitted to bar, 1985, Indiana; registered to practice before U.S. Patent and Trademark Office. *Education:* Purdue University (B.S.M.E., 1981); Indiana University (J.D., 1985). Phi Delta Phi. Member, ABA National Moot Court Competition, 1981. ***PRACTICE AREAS:*** Patents; Trademarks; Copyrights. ***Email:*** rfrisk@uspatent.com

DANIEL J. LUEDERS, born 1960; admitted to bar, 1986, Indiana; registered to practice before U.S. Patent and Trademark Office. *Education:* Northwestern University (B.S.C.E., 1983); Indiana University, Bloomington (J.D., cum laude, 1986). Member: Moot Court Board; National Moot Court Team. Adjunct Professor, Patent Law and Trademark Law, Indiana University School of Law. Co-Author, Indiana Chapter: "INTA's State Trademark and Unfair Competition Law" treatise. Part-time Deputy Prosecutor, 1991-1992. ***PRACTICE AREAS:*** Patents; Trademarks; Copyrights; Trade Secrets. ***Email:*** lueders@uspatent.com

KENNETH A. GANDY, born 1962; admitted to bar, 1988, Indiana; registered to practice before U.S. Patent and Trademark Office. *Education:* Indiana University (B.S., Biochemistry, 1985; J.D., cum laude, 1988). *Member:* American Intellectual Property Law Association. ***PRACTICE AREAS:*** Patents; Trademarks; Copyrights. ***Email:*** kgandy@uspatent.com

TIMOTHY N. THOMAS, born 1954; admitted to bar, 1990, Indiana; registered to practice before U.S. Patent and Trademark Office. *Education:* Purdue University (B.S., 1980; M.S., 1984); Indiana University (J.D., magna cum laude, 1990). Executive Editor, Indiana Law Review, 1989-1990. Author: "Institutional Arrangements Governing the Construction of Electric Generating Units," 22 Ind. Law Review 1174, 1990. ***PRACTICE AREAS:*** Patents; Trademarks; Copyrights. ***Email:*** tnt@uspatent.com

KURT N. JONES, born 1961; admitted to bar, 1992, Indiana; registered to practice before U.S. Patent and Trademark Office. *Education:* Rose-Hulman Institute of Technology (B.S., 1984); University of Colorado (M.B.A., 1989); Indiana University (J.D., 1992). Chauncey Rose Scholar. *Member:* American Intellectual Property Law Association. ***PRACTICE AREAS:*** Patents; Trademarks; Copyrights. ***Email:*** kjones@uspatent.com

HOLIDAY W. BANTA, born 1970; admitted to bar, 1994, Indiana; U.S. District Court, Northern and Southern Districts of Indiana; U.S. District Court, Western District of Texas; U.S. Court of Appeals, Seventh Circuit; U.S. Court of Appeals, Ninth Circuit; U.S. Court of Appeals for Federal Circuit; U.S. Supreme Court; registered to practice before U.S. Patent and Trademark Office. *Education:* Indiana University (B.A., summa cum laude, 1990); Vanderbilt School of Law (J.D., 1994). Phi Beta Kappa. Area Certificate in Environmental Studies, 1990. Presenter, Sycamore School Girls Conference, March 2004, "Settle or Sue: An Overview of Patents and Patent Litigation," Guest Lecturer, July 2003, ITT Technical Institute: "Enforcement of Intellectual Property Rights," CLE Presentation, March 2003: "Patent Infringement Basics: An Overview of Infringement Case Analysis," CLE Presentation, January 2001: "Insurance Considerations for Trademark Infringement; Drafting Licenses That Concern Information: The New Article 2B," The Indiana Lawyer, October 1997. *Member:* Indianapolis, Indiana State and American Bar Associations. ***PRACTICE AREAS:*** Patents; Trademarks; Copyrights; Intellectual Property Arbitration; Intellectual Property Infringement; Intellectual Property Licensing; Intellectual Property Litigation; Intellectual Property Portfolio Management; Intellectual Property Procurement; Intellectual Property Rights; International Intellectual Property; International Licensing; Internet Intellectual Property; Literary Property; Mechanical Intellectual Property; Medical Intellectual Property; Piracy; Proprietary Rights; Biotechnology Patents; Business Methods Patents; Design Patents; International Patents; Mechanical Patents; Medical Patents; Patent Infringement; Patent Licensing; Patent Litigation; Patent Protection; Counterfeiting; International Trademarks; Internet Trademarks; Lanham Act; Trade Dress; Trade Names; Trademark Arbitration; Trademark Infringement; Trademark Licensing; Trademark Litigation; Trademark Prosecution; Trademark Protection; Trademark Registration; Copyright Infringement; Copyright Licensing; Copyright Litigation; Copyright Prosecution; Copyright Protection; Copyright Registration. ***Email:*** hbanta@world-ip.com

TROY J. COLE, born 1963; admitted to bar, 1994, Indiana; registered to practice before U.S. Patent and Trademark Office. *Education:* Bradley University (B.S.E.E., 1985); Southern Methodist University (J.D., 1994). Leading Articles Editor, SMU Law Review. Licensed Professional Engineer, Texas, 1993. Author: "Zoning Control of Airport Expansion By Host Cities," J. of Air Law & Comm., Vol. 59, No. 1 (1993). *Member:* American Intellectual Property Law Association. ***PRACTICE AREAS:*** Patents; Trademarks; Copyrights. ***Email:*** tjcole@uspatent.com

CHARLES J. MEYER, born 1970; admitted to bar, 1995, Indiana; registered to practice before U.S. Patent and Trademark Office. *Education:* DePauw University (B.A., cum laude, 1992); Indiana University (J.D., cum laude, 1995). Author: "National and International Copyright Liability for Electronic Systems Operators," 2 J. Global Legal Studies 497, 1995. ***PRACTICE AREAS:*** Patents; Trademarks; Copyrights. ***Email:*** cmeyer@uspatent.com

LISA A. HIDAY, born 1964; admitted to bar, 1995, Indiana; registered to practice before U.S. Patent and Trademark Office. *Education:* Purdue University (B.S.A.A.E., summa cum laude, 1986; Ph.D., 1992); Stanford University (M.S.A.A.E., 1987); Indiana University (J.D., 1995). Sigma Gamma Tau. Phi Delta Phi. Order of the Engineer. Recipient: American Intellectual Property Law Association, Robert C. Watson Award; Indiana University Scribe Award. Purdue Forever Fellowship for Ph.D. Candidates; David Ross Fellowship; Purdue University Graduate Fellowship; Indiana University Law Fellowship; Glenn D. Peters Law Fellowship; Stanford University Graduate Fellowship; Amelia Earhart Fellowship, Zonta International. Author: "Drifting Toward Trademark Rights in Gross," 85 Trademark Reporter 19 (1995). *Member:* American Intellectual Property Law Association; American Institute of Aeronautics & Astronautics. ***PRACTICE AREAS:*** Patents; Trademarks; Copyrights. ***Email:*** lhiday@uspatent.com

JOHN V. DANILUCK, born Indianapolis, Indiana, September 28, 1952; admitted to bar, 1995, Indiana and U.S. District Court, Northern and Southern Districts of Indiana; registered to practice before the Patent and Trademark Office. *Education:* Purdue University (B.S.M.E., 1976, M.S.M.E., 1978); Indiana University (J.D., 1995). Licensed Professional Engineer, Indiana. Chief Project Engineer, Advanced Military Engines, General Motors. Engineering Supervisor, Missile Systems Group, Hughes Aircraft Company. Staff Engineer, Rolls-Royce Corporation. Research Assistant and Teaching Assistant, Purdue University. ***PRACTICE AREAS:*** Patents; Trademarks; Copyrights. ***Email:*** jdaniluck@uspatent.com

CHRISTOPHER A. BROWN, born Indianapolis, Indiana, March 14, 1967; admitted to bar, 1996, Indiana and U.S. District Court, Northern and Southern Districts of Indiana; registered to practice before the U.S. Patent and Trademark Office. *Education:* Wabash College (A.B., summa cum laude, 1989); Indiana University School of Law (J.D., 1996). Articles Editor, Indiana Law Review, 1995-1996. Author: "The Worsening Problem of Trial Publicity: Is 'New' Model Rule 3.6 Solution or Surrender?", Indiana Law Review, Vol. 29, No. 2, 1995. *Member:* Indiana State Bar Association. ***PRACTICE AREAS:*** Patents; Trademarks; Copyrights. ***Email:*** cbrown@uspatent.com

SCOTT J. STEVENS, born Saginaw, Michigan, July 30, 1952; admitted to bar, 1977, New Jersey; 1978 Connecticut; 1999, Indiana; registered to practice before U.S. Patent and Trademark Office. *Education:* Michigan State University (B.S.E.E., 1974); Rutgers University Law School, Newark (J.D., 1977). ***PRACTICE AREAS:*** Patents; Trademarks; Copyrights. ***Email:*** sstevens@uspatent.com

CHARLES P. SCHMAL, born Huntingdon Valley, Pennsylvania, May 14, 1969; admitted to bar, 2000, Virginia and Indiana; registered to practice before U.S. Patent and Trademark Office. *Education:* Purdue University (B.S.I.E., 1992); George Mason University (J.D., 1999). *Member:* Indiana State Bar Association. ***PRACTICE AREAS:*** Patent; Trademark. ***Email:*** cschmal@uspatent.com

ASSOCIATES

JOHN M. BRADSHAW, born Indianapolis, Indiana, March 1, 1972; admitted to bar, 1999, Indiana; registered to practice before U.S. Patent and Trademark Office. *Education:* University of Notre Dame (B.S., Chemical Engineering, summa cum laude, 1994); University of Florida (M.S., Chemical Engineering, 1996); Indiana University School of Law (J.D., summa cum laude, 1999). ***PRACTICE AREAS:*** Copyrights; Patents; Trademarks. ***Email:*** jmbradshaw@uspatent.com

QUENTIN G. CANTRELL, admitted to bar, 2000, Indiana; registered to practice before U.S. Patent and Trademark Office. *Education:* Purdue University (B.S., 1995); Indiana University School of Law (J.D., 2000). Federalist Society Treasurer, 1997-1998. ***PRACTICE AREAS:*** Copyrights; Patents; Trademarks. ***Email:*** qcantrell@uspatent.com

JOHN J. EMANUELE, JR., born Milwaukee, Wisconsin, August 9, 1956; admitted to bar, 2002, Wisconsin, Indiana and U.S. District Court, Northern District of Indiana; registered to practice before U.S. Patent and Trademark Office. *Education:* University of Wisconsin-Milwaukee (B.S., Chemistry, 1985); University of Wisconsin-Madison (J.D., 2002). ***PRACTICE AREAS:*** Patents; Trademarks; Copyrights. ***Email:*** jemanuele@uspatent.com

MICHAEL S. WHERRY, born Valparaiso, Indiana, January 8, 1968; admitted to bar, 2003, California and Indiana; registered to practice before U.S. Patent and Trademark Office. *Education:* Rose-Hulman Institute of Technology (B.S., 1990); Indiana University School of Law (J.D., 2002). ***PRACTICE AREAS:*** Copyrights; Patents; Trademarks. ***Email:*** mwherry@uspatent.com

DOUGLAS G. GALLAGHER, admitted to bar, 2003, Indiana. *Education:* University of Colorado, Boulder (B.A., 1986); University of Alabama (M.S., 2003); Indiana University School of Law (J.D., 2003). ***PRACTICE AREAS:*** Copyrights; Patents; Trademarks. ***Email:*** dgallagher@uspatent.com

MARTA L. PUCKETT, born Anderson, Indiana, September 24, 1977; admitted to bar, 2003, Indiana. *Education:* Purdue University (B.S.C.E., 2000); Indiana University School of Law - Indianapolis (J.D., 2003). Dean's List. Member: Women's Caucus, 2000-2002; Society of Women Engineers, 1997-2000; American Society of Civil Engineers, 1998-2000. ***PRACTICE AREAS:*** Copyrights; Patents; Trademarks. ***Email:*** mpuckett@uspatent.com

ELIZABETH A. SHUSTER, born Peoria, Illinois, May 28, 1970; admitted to bar, 2003, Indiana; registered to practice before U.S. Patent and Trademark Office. *Education:*

(This Listing Continued)

WOODARD, EMHARDT, MORIARTY, McNETT & HENRY LLP, Indianapolis—Continued

University of Illinois (B.S., 1993; M.S., 1994); Indiana University School of Law - Bloomington (J.D., 2003). Professional Engineer, Illinois. *Member:* American Bar Association. ***PRACTICE AREAS:*** Copyrights; Patents; Trademarks. ***Email:*** eshuster@uspatent.com

MICHAEL A. BENEFIELD, born 1973; admitted to bar, 2004, Indiana; U.S. District Court, Southern and Northern Districts of Indiana; registered to practice before U.S. Patent and Trademark Office. *Education:* Rose-Hulman Institute of Technology (B.S., Chem. Eng., cum laude, 1995); Indiana University (J.D., magna cum laude, 2004). *Member:* Indianapolis and Indiana State Bar Associations. ***PRACTICE AREAS:*** Patents; Trademarks; Copyrights. ***Email:*** mbenefield@uspatent.com

TIMOTHY B. PAUL, born 1976; admitted to bar, 2004, Indiana; registered to practice before U.S. Patent and Trademark Office. *Education:* University of Louisville (B.S., Chemical Engineering, with high honors, 1999); Indiana University School of Law - Bloomington (J.D., 2004). ***PRACTICE AREAS:*** Patents; Copyrights; Trademarks. ***Email:*** tpaul@uspatent.com

TERESA E. KNIGHT, born 1972; admitted to bar, 2004, Indiana; registered to practice before U.S. Patent and Trademark Office. *Education:* Whittier College (B.A., Biochemistry and Philosophy, 1995); Indiana University School of Law, Indianapolis (J.D., cum laude, 2004). *Member:* Indianapolis and Indiana State Bar Associations. ***PRACTICE AREAS:*** Patents; Trademarks; Copyrights. ***Email:*** tknight@uspatent.com

ADAM W. BORGMAN, admitted to bar, 2005, Indiana; U.S. District Court, Northern and Southern Districts of Indiana; registered to practice before U.S. Patent and Trademark Office. *Education:* Rose-Hulman Institute of Technology (B.S., Chemical Engineering, summa cum laude, 2001); Indiana University School of Law, Indianapolis (J.D., 2005). *Member:* Indianapolis and American Bar Associations. ***PRACTICE AREAS:*** Patents; Trademarks; Copyrights. ***Email:*** aborgman@uspatent.com

WILLIAM A. McKENNA, born 1980; admitted to bar, 2005, Indiana. *Education:* Rose-Hulman Institute of Technology (B.S., Computer Science and Mathematics, cum laude, 2002); Indiana University School of Law, Bloomington (J.D., 2005). ***PRACTICE AREAS:*** Patents; Copyrights; Trademarks. ***Email:*** wmckenna@uspatent.com

MARK T. STEPHENSON, admitted to bar, 2005, Indiana. *Education:* Purdue University (B.S. Aeronautical and Astronautical Engineering, 1995); Franklin Pierce Law Center (J.D., cum laude, 2005). *Member:* American Bar Association; American Intellectual Property Law Association. ***PRACTICE AREAS:*** Trademarks; Copyrights; Patents. ***Email:*** mstephenson@uspatent.com

JAMES R. BLAUFUSS, born 1969; admitted to bar, 2005, Indiana. *Education:* University of Utah (B.S., Mechanical Engineering, 1992; M.E., Mechanical Engineering, 1999); Indiana University School of Law, Indianapolis (J.D., 2005). ***PRACTICE AREAS:*** Patents; Trademarks; Copyrights. ***Email:*** jblaufuss@uspatent.com

OF COUNSEL

JOSEPH A. NAUGHTON, JR., born 1930; admitted to bar, 1960, Indiana; registered to practice before U.S. Patent and Trademark Office. *Education:* University of Notre Dame (B.S. in Mech. Engr., 1951); Chrysler Institute of Engineering (M.S. in Automotive Engr., 1953); Indiana University (LL.B., 196 0). *Member:* Indiana State (Chairman, Patent Section, 1974-1975) Bar Association. ***PRACTICE AREAS:*** Patents; Trademarks; Copyrights. ***Email:*** jnaughton@uspatent.com

EDWARD E. SOWERS, born Crawfordsville, Indiana, November 26, 1942; admitted to bar, 1991, Indiana and U.S. District Court, Northern and Southern Districts of Indiana; registered to practice before U.S. Patent and Trademark Office. *Education:* Wabash College (A.B., 1964); Tufts University (Ph.D., 1970); Indiana University School of Law (J.D., 1990). Cale Holder Scholar. *Member:* Indiana State and American Bar Associations; American Chemical Society. ***PRACTICE AREAS:*** Patents; Trademarks; Copyrights. ***Email:*** esowers@uspatent.com

GARY M. GRON, born East Cleveland, Ohio, October 20, 1938; admitted to bar, 1966, Ohio; 1972, U.S. District Court, Southern District of Ohio; 2004, Indiana; registered to practice before U.S. Patent and Trademark Office. *Education:* Case Western Reserve University (B.S.M.E., 1960); Cleveland Marshall Law School (J.D., 1965). Registered Professional Engineer, Ohio, 1965. ***PRACTICE AREAS:*** Patent Law; Trademark Law. ***Email:*** ggron@uspatent.com

JOHN R. TROLL, born 1947; admitted to bar, 1981, New York; 1984, Ohio; 1985, U.S. District Court, Northern District of Ohio; 1997, Michigan; 2002, Indiana. *Education:* Antioch College (B.A., 1970); State University of New York at Buffalo (J.D., 1980). *Member:* Ohio State Bar Association; State Bar of Michigan; Indianapolis Bar Association; American Intellectual Property Law Association; International Trademark Association (Member Designee). ***PRACTICE AREAS:*** Intellectual Property. ***Email:*** dtroll@uspatent.com

The Firm is an Associate Member of the International Trademark Association. All Attorneys are Members of the Indianapolis, Indiana State and American Bar Associations.

WOODEN & McLAUGHLIN LLP

Established in 1970

ONE INDIANA SQUARE, SUITE 1800
INDIANAPOLIS, INDIANA 46204-4208
Telephone: 317-639-6151
Fax: 317-639-6444
URL: http://www.woodmaclaw.com

General Civil Practice. Litigation, Banking, Corporate and Business, Real Estate, Commercial, Tax, Probate and Estate Planning, Labor and Employment Law, Environmental Law, Medical Malpractice, Wrongful Death, Airplane and Helicopter Crash Litigation, Railroad Accidents, Drug and Medical Device Litigation, Eminent Domain and Administrative Law.

(This Listing Continued)

FIRM PROFILE: Wooden & McLaughlin is a general practice law firm founded in 1970, which renders legal services in most areas of civil law.

The firm has an extensive and varied trial and appellate practice in state and federal courts, with an emphasis on the handling of products liability, commercial, municipal liability, premises liability, condemnation or eminent domain, contract, construction, employment, environmental, insurance coverage, design professional liability, personal injury, property damage and fidelity claims and cases. The firm's trial practice is frequently national in scope, as several of the firm's trial lawyers are routinely involved in handling cases in jurisdictions in various parts of the country outside Indiana. The firm's employment law practice includes the defense of employment discrimination cases and general consultation regarding federal, state and local laws and regulations.

Wooden & McLaughlin's transactional practice covers real estate, finance, banking, commercial and general business services as well as a variety of specialized services. The firm's transactional practice has been involved in many of the most significant real estate developments in central Indiana.

LAW FIRM ALLIANCES/ASSOCIATIONS: ***MACINTYRE STRÄTER INTERNATIONAL LIMITED:*** *A Worldwide Association of Independent Professional Firms.*

MEMBERS OF FIRM

MICHAEL C. COOK, born Chicago, Illinois, May 7, 1944; admitted to bar, 1970, Indiana. *Education:* Butler University (B.S., 1966); Indiana University (J.D., 1970). Phi Delta Phi. Certified Mediator. *Member:* Indianapolis and Indiana State Bar Associations; Defense Trial Counsel of Indiana. ***Email:*** mcook@woodmaclaw.com

RONALD G. SALATICH, born Indianapolis, Indiana, June 27, 1945; admitted to bar, 1971, Indiana. *Education:* Butler University (B.A., 1967); University of Michigan and Indiana University (J.D., 1971). *Member:* Indianapolis and Indiana State Bar Associations. ***PRACTICE AREAS:*** Business Law; Corporate Law; Partnership Law; Trusts and Estates. ***Email:*** rsalatich@woodmaclaw.com

THOMAS W. DINWIDDIE, born Toledo, Ohio, May 29, 1947; admitted to bar, 1973, Indiana. *Education:* DePauw University (A.B., 1969); Indiana University (J.D., 1973). Phi Delta Phi. *Member:* Indianapolis and Indiana State (Chairman, Corporation, Banking and Business Law Section, 1982-1983) Bar Associations. ***Email:*** tdinwiddie@woodmaclaw.com

JOHN D. NELL, born Indianapolis, Indiana, January 28, 1946; admitted to bar, 1974, Indiana. *Education:* Butler University (B.S., 1968); Indiana University (J.D., cum laude, 1974). *Member:* Indianapolis and Indiana State Bar Associations; Bar Association of Seventh Federal Circuit; American Health Lawyers Association; Defense Trial Counsel of Indiana (Member, Board of Directors). Fellow: International Association of Defense Counsel; American College of Trial Lawyers. ***Email:*** jnell@woodmaclaw.com

DOUGLAS B. KING, born Valparaiso, Indiana, June 15, 1951; admitted to bar, 1976, Indiana and U.S. District Court, Southern District of Indiana; 1982, U.S. Court of Appeals, 7th Circuit; 1983, U.S. Supreme Court; 1990, U.S. Court of Appeals, 3rd Circuit. *Education:* Butler University (B.S., 1973); Indiana University (J.D., summa cum laude, 1976). Associate Editor, Indiana Law Review, 1975-1976. Member, National Moot Court Team, 1975-1976. Law Clerk, Hon. Patrick D. Sullivan, Indiana Court of Appeals, 1975-1976. Approved Counsel, MEDMARC Mutual Insurance Co. *Member:* Indianapolis and Indiana State Bar Associations; Bar Association of the Seventh Federal Circuit; Defense Research Institute. Fellow, International Association of Defense Counsel. ***Email:*** dking@woodmaclaw.com

DALE W. EIKENBERRY, born Delphi, Indiana, June 12, 1953; admitted to bar, 1978, Indiana. *Education:* Purdue University (B.A., 1975); Northwestern University (J.D., 1978). *Member:* Indianapolis, Indiana State and American (Member, Sections on Antitrust and Tort and Insurance Practice) Bar Associations; Defense Research Institute (Business Litigation Section); Defense Trial Counsel of Indiana. ***PRACTICE AREAS:*** Litigation; Environmental Litigation; Insurance Litigation; Insurance Coverage. ***Email:*** deikenberry@woodmaclaw.com

ANDREW C. CHARNSTROM, born Indianapolis, Indiana, July 8, 1954; admitted to bar, 1979, Indiana. *Education:* University of Evansville; Indiana University (B.A., with honors, 1976; J.D., with honors, 1979). Certified Civil, Family Mediator. *Member:* Indianapolis, Indiana State and American (Member, Sections on: Litigation; Labor and Employment Law) Bar Associations; Bar Association of the Seventh Federal Circuit. ***PRACTICE AREAS:*** Appellate Practice; Construction Law; Litigation; Professional Liability. ***Email:*** acharnstrom@woodmaclaw.com

DANIEL D. TRACHTMAN, born Frederick, Maryland, May 21, 1953; admitted to bar, 1978, Indiana. *Education:* Hamilton College (B.A., 1975); Indiana University (J.D., 1978). Order of the Barristers. *Member:* Indianapolis, Indiana State and American (Member, Section on Tort and Insurance Practice) Bar Associations; Defense Trial Counsel of Indiana. ***PRACTICE AREAS:*** Products Liability; Premises Liability; Toxic Torts. ***Email:*** dtrachtman@woodmaclaw.com

THOMAS M. HANAHAN, born Franklin, Indiana, April 10, 1961; admitted to bar, 1986, Indiana; U.S. District Court, Northern and Southern Districts of Indiana. *Education:* University of Notre Dame (B.A., 1983); Indiana University (J.D., 1986). *Member:* Indianapolis and Indiana State (Member, Sections on Business Law) Bar Associations. ***PRACTICE AREAS:*** Banks and Banking; Finance; Commercial Real Estate. ***Email:*** thanahan@woodmaclaw.com

KENT M. BROACH, born Lafayette, Indiana, July 20, 1960; admitted to bar, 1985, Indiana. *Education:* Purdue University (B.A., 1982); Indiana University (J.D., 1985). Associate Editor, Indiana Law Review, 1984-1985. *Member:* Indianapolis and Indiana State (Member, Sections on Taxation) Bar Associations. ***PRACTICE AREAS:*** Business Law; Corporate Law; Probate; Trusts and Estates. ***Email:*** kbroach@woodmaclaw.com

JEFFREY L. McKEAN, born Indianapolis, Indiana, May 5, 1963; admitted to bar, 1990, Indiana and U.S. District Court, Northern District of Indiana; U.S. District Court, Southern District of Indiana. *Education:* Purdue University (B.S.I.M., 1986); Indiana Uni-

(This Listing Continued)

versity (J.D., cum laude, 1990). Order of the Barristers. *Member:* Indianapolis and Indiana State Bar Associations; Defense Trial Counsel of Indiana. ***PRACTICE AREAS:*** Alcoholic Beverages; Litigation; Products Liability. ***Email:*** jmckean@woodmaclaw.com

HOLLY HAPAK BETZ, born Indianapolis, Indiana, June 22, 1965; admitted to bar, 1990, Indiana. *Education:* Indiana University (B.S., 1987); Boston University (J.D., 1990). *Member:* Indianapolis and Indiana State (Member, Sections on Business Law) Bar Associations. ***Email:*** hbetz@woodmaclaw.com

MICHAEL RABINOWITCH, born Bloomington, Indiana, May 28, 1968; admitted to bar, 1994, Indiana. *Education:* DePauw University (B.A., 1990); Indiana University (J.D., 1994). *Member:* Indianapolis and Indiana State Bar Associations; Defense Trial Counsel of Indiana; Defense Research Institute. ***PRACTICE AREAS:*** Trade Secrets; Litigation; Torts; Labor and Employment. ***Email:*** mrabinowitch@woodmaclaw.com

JOHN W. HAMILTON, born Fort Wayne, Indiana, May 7, 1963; admitted to bar, 1993, Virginia; 1996, Indiana. *Education:* Davidson College (B.A., 1986); Washington & Lee University (J.D., cum laude, 1993). Editor, Washington & Lee Law Review. *Member:* Indianapolis and Indiana State (Member, Sections on Business Law) Bar Associations. ***PRACTICE AREAS:*** Real Estate; Commercial Real Estate; Leases and Leasing; Finance; Business Law. ***Email:*** jhamilton@woodmaclaw.com

JANE ANN HIMSEL, born Evansville, Indiana, August 2, 1964; admitted to bar, 1990, Indiana and U.S. District Court, Southern and Northern Districts of Indiana; 1992, U.S. Court of Appeals, Seventh Circuit; 2000, U.S. Supreme Court; 2001, U.S. Court of Appeals, Sixth Circuit. *Education:* Vanderbilt University (B.A., cum laude, 1986); Northwestern University (J.D., 1989). Associate Articles Editor, Journal of Criminal Law and Criminology, 1988-1989. Judicial Clerk, Randall T. Shepard, Chief Justice of Indiana, 1989-1991. *Member:* Indianapolis (Member, Labor and Employment Law Section), Seventh Circuit, Indiana State (Member, Sections on: Labor and Employment Law; Appellate Practice) and American (Member: Labor and Employment Law Section; EEO and State Labor and Employment Law Developments Committees) Bar Associations. ***PRACTICE AREAS:*** Labor and Employment. ***Email:*** jhimsel@woodmaclaw.com

JOHN D. WALLER, born Washington, Indiana, March 18, 1968; admitted to bar, 1993, Indiana and U.S. District Court, Northern and Southern Districts of Indiana. *Education:* DePauw University (B.A., 1990); Indiana University (J.D., 1993). *Member:* Indianapolis and Indiana State Bar Associations; Defense Trial Counsel of Indiana. ***PRACTICE AREAS:*** Medical Malpractice Defense; Business Litigation; Torts. ***Email:*** jwaller@woodmaclaw.com

E. JOSEPH KREMP, born Washington, Indiana, September 18, 1965; admitted to bar, 1994, Indiana. *Education:* Duke University (A.B., 1988); Indiana University (M.B.A., 1991); Indiana University School of Law, Bloomington (J.D., 1994). Formerly In-House: Midwest Bankers Group; Newcourt Credit Group. *Member:* Indiana State Bar Association; American Corporate Counsel Association. ***LANGUAGES:*** French. ***PRACTICE AREAS:*** Real Estate; Finance; Leases and Leasing; Business Law. ***Email:*** jkremp@woodmaclaw.com

ASSOCIATES

JAMES M. BOYERS, born Indianapolis, Indiana, June 2, 1972; admitted to bar, 1998, Indiana and U.S. District Court, Northern and Southern Districts of Indiana. *Education:* Hanover College (B.A., 1994); Indiana University (J.D., 1998). Managing Editor, Indiana Journal of Global Legal Studies, 1997-1998. *Member:* Indiana State and American Bar Associations; Defense Trial Counsel of Indiana. ***Email:*** jboyers@woodmaclaw.com

CHRISTINE K. JACOBSON, born Bremen, Indiana, January 9, 1960; admitted to bar, 1992, Indiana and U.S. District Court, Northern and Southern Districts of Indiana. *Education:* Indiana University (B.S., high distinction, 1982); Georgetown University (J.D., cum laude, 1992). Certified Public Accountant, Indiana, 1983. *Member:* Indianapolis and Indiana State Bar Associations. ***Email:*** cjacobson@woodmaclaw.com

MAUREEN E. WARD, born Sullivan, Indiana, October 25, 1953; admitted to bar, 1993, Indiana, Kentucky and U.S. District Court, Southern District of Indiana; 1995, U.S. Court of Appeals, Seventh Circuit. *Education:* Indiana University (B.A., Journalism and English, 1975); Murray State University (M.S., Communications, summa cum laude, 1992); University of Louisville (J.D., cum laude, 1992). Executive Editor, Journal of Family Law, 1991-1992. Law Clerk, Hon. S. Hugh Dillin, U.S. District Court for the Southern District of Indiana, 1992-2002. *Member:* Indianapolis and Indiana Bar Associations; Defense Trial Counsel of Indiana. ***Email:*** mward@woodmaclaw.com

JEREMY B. JOHNSON, born Indianapolis, Indiana, May 5, 1977; admitted to bar, 2002, Indiana and U.S. District Court, Northern and Southern Districts of Indiana. *Education:* Franklin College of Indiana (B.A., 1999); Indiana University School of Law - Indianapolis (J.D., 2002). Order of Barristers. *Member:* Indianapolis and Indiana State Bar Associations. ***Email:*** jjohnson@woodmaclaw.com

DAYNA L. SWITZER, born Alton, Illinois; admitted to bar, 2001, Illinois; 2002, Missouri; 2003, Indiana. *Education:* Eastern Illinois University (B.S., summa cum laude, 1997); St. Louis University School of Law (J.D., magna cum laude, 2001). ***Email:*** dswitzer@woodmaclaw.com

JEFFREY A. HAMMOND, born Yuma, Arizona, October 10, 1973; admitted to bar, 1999, Illinois and U.S. District Court, Northern District of Illinois; 2004, Indiana and U.S. District Court, Northern and Southern Districts of Indiana. *Education:* Purdue University (B.A., 1995); Indiana University School of Law (J.D., 1999). *Member:* Indiana State and Illinois State Bar Associations. ***PRACTICE AREAS:*** Commercial Litigation; Construction Litigation; Trademark And Copyright. ***Email:*** jhammond@woodmaclaw.com

MARK T. MONROE, born Indianapolis, Indiana, June 23, 1971; admitted to bar, 2003, Indiana and U.S. District Court, Northern and Southern Districts of Indiana. *Education:* Ball State University (B.S., Environmental Design, with honors; B.U.P.D., Urban Planning & Development, with honors, 1994); Indiana University (J.D., 2003). Presidential Scholar. Registered Civil Mediator, Indiana. Member: American Institute of Certified Planners; American Planning Association. *Member:* Indianapolis, Indiana State and American Bar Associations. ***PRACTICE AREAS:*** Real Estate Law; Land Use Law; Alternative Dispute Resolution. ***Email:*** mmonroe@woodmaclaw.com

(This Listing Continued)

ROBERT F. INSELBERG, born Cleveland, Ohio, April 6, 1979; admitted to bar, 2004, Indiana. *Education:* Indiana University (B.S., 2001); Indiana University School of Law (J.D., 2004). *Member:* Indianapolis, Indiana State and American Bar Associations. ***PRACTICE AREAS:*** Real Estate; Finance; Corporate; Commercial. ***Email:*** rinselberg@woodmaclaw.com

TIMOTHY J. HIGHTOWER, born Louisville, Kentucky, October 9, 1966; admitted to bar, 2001, Indiana and U.S. District Court, Southern and Northern Districts of Indiana. *Education:* Indiana University (B.A., 1997); University of Indiana School of Law (J.D., 2001). Recipient: Cali Award in Banking and Finance Law, Indiana University School of Law. *Member:* Indiana State and American Bar Associations. ***PRACTICE AREAS:*** Real Estate; Finance; Banking. ***Email:*** thightower@woodmaclaw.com

OF COUNSEL

WILLIAM P. WOODEN, born Holland, Michigan, July 7, 1933; admitted to bar, 1958, Indiana. *Education:* DePauw University (A.B., 1955); University of Michigan (J.D., 1958). Order of the Coif; Phi Alpha Delta. Assistant Editor, Michigan Law Review, 1957-1958. Member, Large Complex Case Panel of Arbitrators, American Arbitration Association. *Member:* Indianapolis and Indiana State (Chairman, House of Delegates, 1972-1973) Bar Associations; Bar Association of the Seventh Federal Circuit; National Association of Railroad Trial Counsel; Defense Trial Counsel of Indiana. Fellow: American College of Trial Lawyers; International Association of Defense Counsel; International Society of Barristers; American Bar Foundation. ***Email:*** wwooden@woodmaclaw.com

ROBERT L. McLAUGHLIN, born Indianapolis, Indiana, June 25, 1936; admitted to bar, 1961, Indiana. *Education:* Indiana University (A.B., 1958); University of Michigan (J.D., 1961). Order of the Coif. Assistant Editor, Michigan Law Review, 1960-1961. *Member:* Indianapolis and Indiana State Bar Associations. ***Email:*** rmclaughlin@woodmaclaw.com

DONALD W. BUTTREY, born Terre Haute, Indiana, 1935; admitted to bar, 1961, Indiana. *Education:* Indiana State University (B.S., 1956); Indiana University, Bloomington (J.D., 1961). Note Editor, Indiana Law Journal, 1960-1961. Law Clerk, U.S. District Court, Southern District of Indiana, 1961-1963. Trustee, Indiana State University, 1992-2000 (Vice-President of Board, 1997-2000). *Member:* Indianapolis (President, 1990), Indiana State (Member, Board of Governors, 1994-1996) and American Bar Associations. Fellow: Indiana Bar Foundation; Indianapolis Bar Foundation (President, 1993-1996); American Bar Foundation; American College of Tax Counsel. ***Email:*** dbuttrey@woodmaclaw.com

REPRESENTATIVE CLIENTS: AIG Aviation, Inc.; AT&T; Apartment Association of Indiana, Inc.; Barrett & Stokely, Inc.; Bechtel Corporation; BP Products North America, Inc.; CB Richard Ellis; Central Hockey League; Clark Refining and Marketing; Columbia/HCA; CVS Corporation; Dresser Industries; Fifth Third Bank; Flintkote Company; Gallagher Bassett Services, Inc.; H.P. Products Corp.; Health Care Indemnity, Inc.; Hughes Group, Inc.; Huntington National Bank; Indiana Mortgage Bankers, Inc.; Indiana University; International Insurance Company; Irwin Mortgage Corp.; J. M. Foster, Inc.; Lauth Properties; Lexington Insurance Co.; Metropolitan Life Insurance Co.; Northrop Corporation; Peabody Coal Co.; P/R Mortgage & Investment Corp.; Rapid-American Corporation; Skinner-Broadbent Co.; Terre Haute Regional Hospital; U.S. Aviation Insurance Group; U.S. Bank.

PETER L. WORMSER

156 EAST MARKET STREET, SUITE 1300
INDIANAPOLIS, INDIANA 46204
Telephone: 317-624-6700
Fax: 317-624-6701
Email: schleppers@aol.com
URL: http://www.lawyers.com/peterwormser

Family Law, Divorce, Child Custody, Child Support, Guardianship, Adoption Law, Visitation Rights, Social Security Disability, Consumer Law, Bankruptcy.

FIRM PROFILE: I am a sole practitioner, admitted to practice in Indiana in 1968, with emphasis on Family Law and Social Security disability cases.

PETER L. WORMSER, born Terre Haute, Indiana, May 1, 1943; admitted to bar, 1968, Indiana and U.S. District Court, Southern District of Indiana. *Education:* Indiana University (B.S., 1965); Indiana University School of Law (J.D., 1968).

YARLING & ROBINSON

Established in 1963
151 NORTH DELAWARE, SUITE 1535
P.O. BOX 44128
INDIANAPOLIS, INDIANA 46204
Telephone: 317-262-8800
Fax: 317-262-3046
Email: yrhl@yarling.com
URL: http://www.yarling.com

General and Appellate Practice. Negligence, Insurance, Commercial, Bankruptcy, Corporation, Products Liability and Probate and Estate Planning. Trials and Appeals.

MEMBERS OF FIRM

CHARLES F. ROBINSON, JR., born Indianapolis, Indiana, January 2, 1940; admitted to bar, 1966, Indiana. *Education:* Marian College (A.B., 1962); Indiana University (J.D., 1966). Phi Delta Phi. Law Clerk, Indiana Appellate Court, 1965-1966. Marion County Deputy Prosecutor, 1972-1974. *Member:* Indianapolis (Secretary, 1977) and Indiana State Bar Associations; Lawyers Association of Indianapolis (Secretary-Treasurer, 1967-1970). ***PRACTICE AREAS:*** Tort Litigation. ***Email:*** crobinson@yarling.com

LINDA Y. HAMMEL, born Shelbyville, Indiana, October 5, 1945; admitted to bar, 1975, Indiana and U.S. Court of Appeals for the Seventh Circuit. *Education:* Indiana University (B.M.E., cum laude, 1967; J.D., summa cum laude, 1975). Phi Delta Phi. Author: "Appellate Review of Circumstantial Evidence in Indiana Criminal Cases," Indiana Law

(This Listing Continued)

YARLING & ROBINSON, Indianapolis—Continued

Review, Vol. 7, No. 5, 1974. Law Clerk to Judge Robert H. Staton, Indiana Court of Appeals, 1972-1976. *Member:* Indianapolis and Indiana State Bar Associations. ***PRACTICE AREAS:*** Appellate Practice; Probate Law; Products Liability Law; Insurance Defense Law; Negligence; Insurance Coverage Law. ***Email:*** lhammel@yarling.com

MATTHEW C. ROBINSON, born Indianapolis, Indiana, September 18, 1966; admitted to bar, 1991, Indiana. *Education:* Wabash College (B.A., 1988); Valparaiso University (J.D., 1991). Deputy Prosecuting Attorney, Marion County (1991-1993); Deputy Indiana Attorney General (1994). Member, Marion County Election Board, 1995-1996. *Member:* Indianapolis, Indiana State and American Bar Association. ***PRACTICE AREAS:*** Civil Litigation. ***Email:*** mrobinson@yarling.com

BRIAN L. NEHRIG, born Williamsport, Indiana, May 28, 1966; admitted to bar, 1991, Indiana and U.S. District Court, Northern and Southern Districts of Indiana. *Education:* Wabash College (B.A., 1988); Valparaiso University (J.D., 1991). Delta Theta Phi. *Member:* Marion County, Indiana State and American Bar Associations. ***PRACTICE AREAS:*** Consumer and Commercial Collections Law; Creditors' Rights. ***Email:*** bnehrig@yarling.com

ASSOCIATES

SARAH DILLINGER, born Indianapolis, Indiana, May 10, 1972; admitted to bar, 2003, Indiana. *Education:* Indiana University, Bloomington (B.S.W., 1994); Indiana University, Indianapolis (J.D., 2003). *Member:* Indiana State Bar Association. ***PRACTICE AREAS:*** Commercial Law; Foreclosures; Bankruptcy; Insurance Defense. ***Email:*** sdillinger@yarling.com

CHRISTOPHER P. HAMILTON, born Fort Wayne, Indiana, June 7, 1962; admitted to bar, 1989, Indiana and U.S. District Court, Northern and Southern Districts of Indiana. *Education:* DePauw University (B.A., 1984); Washington University (J.D., 1989). Phi Delta Phi. Registered Civil Mediator. *Member:* Allen County, Indiana State and American Bar Associations. ***LANGUAGES:*** Spanish. ***PRACTICE AREAS:*** Insurance Defense; Negligence; Workers Compensation Defense; Insurance Coverage. ***Email:*** chamilton@yarling.com

OF COUNSEL

SETH M. LAHN, born August 17, 1957; admitted to bar, 1984, New York; 1990, Indiana. *Education:* Yale University (B.A, summa cum laude, 1979); Yale University Law School (J.D., 1982). Phi Beta Kappa. Law Clerk, U.S. District Judge Edward N. Cahn, Philadelphia, Pennsylvania, 1982-1983. Lecturer, Indiana University School of Law, Bloomington, 1995—. *Member:* Indiana State Bar Association. ***PRACTICE AREAS:*** Commercial Litigation; Insurance Defense. ***Email:*** slahn@yarling.com

RICHARD W. YARLING, born Shelbyville, Indiana, October 18, 1921; admitted to bar, 1949, Indiana. *Education:* Indiana University (A.B., 1943; J.D., with distinction, 1949). Sigma Delta Kappa; Order of the Coif. Associate Editor-in-Chief, Indiana Law Journal, 1948-1949. Deputy Attorney General, State of Indiana, 1950-1953, 1965-1969. Chairman, Editorial Board, Indiana Products Liability Handbook, 1968. *Member:* Indianapolis, Indiana State (Chairman, Trial Lawyers Section, 1972) and American (Member, Trial Techniques Committee, 1971—) Bar Associations; Federation of Insurance Counsel. ***PRACTICE AREAS:*** Products Liability Law; Insurance Defense Law; General Negligence Law.

REPRESENTATIVE CLIENTS: INSURANCE DEFENSE: Allstate Insurance Co.; American Family Insurance Group; DaimlerChrysler Services of North America; Hartford/Omni Insurance Company; Monroe Guaranty Insurance Company; Progressive Insurance Company; Superior/Pafco General Insurance Company; Symons International Group; United National Insurance Company. COMMERCIAL: Banc One Leasing; CIT Group; CitiFinancial Mortgage; Equicredit Service; Fairbanks Capital; Fairbanks n/k/a Select Portfolio; Fidelity National Foreclosure Services Corporation; Franklin Credit Management Corporation; GMAC Mortgage Corporation; Greenwich Investors XI, LLC; Indy Mac Bank; ITC Acceptance; Litton Loan Servicing Corporation; M & I Bank; New South Federal Savings Bank; Paccar Financial; Provident Bank; Security National Servicing Corporation; Wells Fargo; Wilshire Credit. BANKRUPTCY: American Investment Bank; Chrysler Financial Services Corporation; CitiFinancial Services; Forum Credit; General Motors Acceptance Corporation; ITC Acceptance Norwest Financial Services.
REFERENCE: Union Planters, Indiana

ROBERT W. YORK & ASSOCIATES

7212 NORTH SHADELAND AVENUE
SUITE 150
INDIANAPOLIS, INDIANA 46250-2030
Telephone: 317-842-8000
Fax: 317-577-7321
Email: rwyork@york-law.com
URL: http://www.yorklaw-firm.com

Personal Injury, Automobile Accidents, Wrongful Death, Insurance Disputes, Insurance Bad Faith, Unsafe Products, Family Law, Divorce, Child Support, Child Custody, Trial Practice, Insurance Law, Business Law, Business Planning, Contracts, Lawsuits, Business Enterprises, Corporate, Partnerships, Limited Liability Companies, Small Business, Starting a Business, Buying and Selling a Business, Strategic Alliances, Products Liability, Wills and Probate, Trusts and Estates, Estate Planning, Guardianships, Asset Protection, Estate Disputes.

MEMBER OF FIRM

ROBERT W. YORK, born Fort Wayne, Indiana, September 19, 1944; admitted to bar, 1973, Indiana and U.S. District Court, Northern and Southern Districts of Indiana; 1984, U.S. Tax Court; 1991, U.S. Supreme Court. *Education:* Indiana University (B.S., 1969; J.D., cum laude, 1973). Phi Alpha Delta. Listed in Martindale Hubbell Bar Register of Preeminent Lawyers, 2000—. Life Member, National Registry of Who's Who, 2001. Author, Indiana Product Liability Guide, 1995. Member, Head Injury Foundation. Senior Counsel Member, American College of Barristers, 2001. *Member:* Hamilton County, Indianapolis Indiana State and American Bar Associations; Indiana Trial Lawyers Association (Member: Board of Directors, 1983—; President, 1998-1999; College of Fellows, 1993—); The Association of Trial Lawyers of America (Sustaining Member). ***PRACTICE AREAS:*** Insurance; Medical Malpractice; Family Law; Business Law; Products Liability; Automobile Accidents and Injuries; Wills; Probate; Personal Injury; Divorce; Negligence; Trial Practice. ***Email:*** rwyork@york-law.com

LAWRENCE T. NEWMAN, born Cleveland, Ohio, December 17, 1954; admitted to bar, 1981, Ohio; 1982, U.S. District Court, Northern District of Ohio; 1987, Indiana and U.S. District Court, Southern District of Indiana. *Education:* Ohio State University (B.S., 1977); Case Western Reserve University (J.D., 1981). Phi Alpha Delta; Order of The Coif. ***REPORTED CASES:*** Park Hoover v. Ardsley/Park Hoover 766 NE2d 13 (Ind. Ct. App. 2002). ***Email:*** lnewman@york-law.com

OF COUNSEL

JAMES A. MELLOWITZ, born South Bend, Indiana, October 19, 1956; admitted to bar, 1988, Indiana. *Education:* Indiana University-Bloomington (B.A., 1979); Indiana University-Indianapolis (J.D., cum laude, 1987). Author, "Bad Faith in Third Party Med Pay Claims," 1998 ITLA; "Spoliation of Evidence," 1997 ITLA. Adjunct Professor, Journalism, 1990-1991 and Political Science, 1995. *Member:* Indiana State Bar; Indiana Trial Lawyers Association; The Association of Trial Lawyers of America. ***REPORTED CASES:*** Van Winkle v. Nash, 761 N.E.2d 856 (Ind. Ct. App. 2002); Midwestern Indemnity Company v. Laikin, 119 F. Supp. 2d 831 (S.D. Ind. 2000); Scaggs v. Consolidated Rail Corp. 6 F.3d 1290 (7th Cir. 1993); and Wilhoite v. Mel Simon & Associates, et. al., 640 N.E. 2d 382 (Ind. Ap. 1994). ***PRACTICE AREAS:*** Litigation; Personal Injury; Traffic Violations; Slip and Fall; Products Liability; Medical Malpractice; Insurance Bad Faith; Dental Malpractice; Nursing Malpractice. ***Email:*** jmellowitz@york-law.com

LAW OFFICES OF J. DAVID YOUNG

Established in 1988
3850 PRIORITY WAY S. DRIVE
SUITE 100
INDIANAPOLIS, INDIANA 46240
Telephone: 317-580-2582
Facsimile: 317-571-0177
Email: jdyjd@aol.com
URL: http://www.jdyounglawfirm.com

Creditor Rights, Product Liability Defense, Insurance Defense, Business Law, Contracts, Business Litigation, Business Enterprises, Corporate, Partnerships, Limited Liability Companies, Small Business, Buying and Selling a Business, Starting a Business, Debt and Credit, Collections, Business Planning, Entertainment & Sports Law, Real Estate, Commercial Litigation, Wills and Probate, Contested Wills Litigation, Art Law, Intellectual Property, Insurance Law, Environmental Law, Construction Law, Family Law, Divorce, Child Custody, Adoption Law, Employment Law, Personal Injury, Automobile Accidents, Wrongful Death.

FIRM PROFILE: Having previously practiced law with a large San Francisco, California law firm, Attorney Young continues to provide a wide variety of services to his clients.

J. DAVID YOUNG, born Pittsburgh, Pennsylvania, June 10, 1950; admitted to bar, 1977, California; U.S. District Court, Northern District of California; 1988, Indiana and U.S. District Court, Northern and Southern Districts of Indiana. *Education:* Indiana University (B.A., 1972); New College of California (J.D., 1977). *Member:* Indianapolis and American Bar Associations; Indiana Trial Lawyers Association.

REPRESENTATIVE CLIENTS: Environomental Assurance Company; Recovery Management Associates.; Lowes; Home Depot; Meridian Psychological Associates; Baldoni Entertainment; Sabre Demolition Company; Global Environmental Outfitters; Nordstrom; J.C. Penney.

ZEIGLER COHEN & KOCH

9465 COUNSELORS ROW, SUITE 104
INDIANAPOLIS, INDIANA 46240
Telephone: 317-844-5200
Facsimile: 317-844-7200

Health Care and Hospital Law, Medical Malpractice Defense. Civil Trial and Appellate Practice. Insurance Defense, Products Liability Law.

ROBERT G. ZEIGLER, born Washington, D.C., January 14, 1950; admitted to bar, 1980, Indiana. *Education:* Illinois College (B.A., 1970); University of Illinois (M.A., 1971; J.D., 1980).

STEVEN J. COHEN, born Peoria, Illinois, November 24, 1952; admitted to bar, 1980, Indiana. *Education:* Northwestern University (B.S., 1974); Indiana University (J.D., 1980).

EDNA M. KOCH, born Terre Haute, Indiana, October 12, 1951; admitted to bar, 1980, Indiana. *Education:* Indiana State University (B.S., cum laude, 1977); St. Anthony Hospital School of Nursing, 1972; Indiana University (J.D., cum laude, 1980). Registered Nurse, Indiana, 1972.

DAVID BECSEY, born Grand Rapids, Michigan, February 27, 1953; admitted to bar, 1991, Indiana. *Education:* Duke University (B.H.S., magna cum laude, 1984); Indiana University, Indianapolis (J.D., 1991). Registered Nurse, Indiana, 1981.

ROGER K. KANNE, born Oak Park, Illinois, April 11, 1957; admitted to bar, 1983, California; 1993, Indiana. *Education:* Indiana University (B.A., 1979); University of San Diego (J.D., 1982); Indiana Law Enforcement Training Board, Law Enforcement Officer (1978).

(This Listing Continued)

ASSOCIATES

MARILYN A. YOUNG, born Indianapolis, Indiana, January 22, 1960; admitted to bar, 1989, Indiana. *Education:* Purdue University (B.S., 1983); Indiana University (J.D., cum laude, 1989). Licensed Pharmacist, Indiana, 1983.

JOSEPH D. McPIKE, II, born Bedford, Indiana, October 30, 1966; admitted to bar, 1993, Indiana. *Education:* Auburn University (B.S., cum laude, 1990); Indiana University (J.D., 1993).

JENNIFER A. STRICKLAND-PADGETT, born Indianapolis, Indiana, March 27, 1976; admitted to bar, 2001, Indiana. *Education:* Northwestern University (B.A., 1998); Indiana University School of Law (J.D., cum laude, 2001).

ANDREW R. BLOCH, born Indianapolis, Indiana, January 11, 1978; admitted to bar, 2003, Indiana. *Education:* Xavier University (B.S.B.A., 2000); Indiana University (J.D., 2003).

BOBBY J. AVERY-SEAGRAVE, born Tennyson, Indiana, September 2, 1976; admitted to bar, 2002, Indiana. *Education:* Indiana State University (B.S., magna cum laude, 1998); Indiana University School of Law - Indianapolis (M.H.A.; J.D., 2001).

REPRESENTATIVE CLIENTS: A List of Representative Clients will be Furnished Upon Request.

BINGHAM McHALE LLP

212 WEST SIXTH STREET
JASPER, INDIANA 47546
Telephone: 812-482-5500
Fax: 812-482-2017
Email: firm@binghammchale.com
URL: http://www.binghammchale.com

Indianapolis, Indiana Office: Bingham McHale LLP, 2700 Market Tower, 10 West Market Street. Telephone: 317-635-8900. Fax: 317-236-9907.
Noblesville, Indiana Office: Bingham McHale LLP, 970 Logan Street, Telephone: 317-776-8668. Fax: 317-776-8651.
Vincennes, Indiana Office: Bingham Mchale LLP, 112 North 7th Street. Telephone: 812-886-9970. Fax: 812-886-0776.

General Civil Practice, Business Law, Business Litigation, Environmental Law, Estate Planning and Administration, Governmental Services, Intellectual Property, Labor and Employment, Patent, Public Finance, Public Utility Law, Real Estate, Zoning, Planning and Land Use.

FIRM PROFILE: Bingham McHale LLP was formed by the merger of Bingham Summers Welsh & Spilman and McHale Cook & Welch on January 1, 2002. Evident in the nearly 130 year combined history of both firms is the longstanding commitment to one ideal: providing high quality legal services at an affordable cost. Both firms individually earned a reputation founded upon client service, and will continue and improve upon that tradition collectively as it continues to provide the highest level of service to business, government, utility and land use clients and their individual owners.

JOHN S. CHAPPELL, born Evansville, Indiana, 1947; admitted to bar, 1972, Indiana; 1974, U.S. Court of Appeals, Seventh Circuit and U.S. District Court, Southern District of Indiana. *Education:* Indiana University (B.S., 1969; J.D., 1972). Law Clerk to Hon. S. Hugh Dillin, U.S. District Court, Southern District of Indiana, 1972-1974. (Also Of Counsel, Indianapolis Office). ***PRACTICE AREAS:*** Corporate Law; Probate; Estate Planning; Real Estate. ***Email:*** jchappell@binghammchale.com

WILLIAM J. KAISER, JR., born Jasper, Indiana, 1965; admitted to bar, 1990, Indiana. *Education:* Wabash College (B.A., 1987); Indiana University, Indianapolis (J.D., cum laude, 1990). (Also Member, Indianapolis Office). ***LANGUAGES:*** German. ***PRACTICE AREAS:*** Corporate Law; Real Estate; Environmental Law; Zoning, Planning and Land Use. ***Email:*** bkaiser@binghammchale.com

REPRESENTATIVE CLIENTS: A.M. Bohnert Rice Plantation, Inc.; Best Chairs, Inc.; Buehler Foods, Inc.; Ditto Sales, Inc.; Dubois County Block & Brick; Indiana Furniture Industries; Jasper Seating Company, Inc.; MasterBrand Cabinets, Inc.; Patoka Valley Regional Health Care Co-op, Inc.

(For complete biographical data on all personnel, see Professional Biographies at Indianapolis, Indiana)

BIRK & BIRK

ATTORNEYS AT LAW, P.C.
Established in 1995
520 MAIN STREET, SUITE 1
P.O. BOX 1024
JASPER, INDIANA 47547-1024
Telephone: 812-482-2093
Fax: 812-482-7218
URL: http://www.lawyers.com/birklaw
URL: http://www.birklawfirm.com

Banking, Civil Litigation, Commercial Collections, Construction Law, Creditors Rights and Bankruptcy, Environmental, General Business and Commercial Practice, Government, Municipal, and Administrative, Insurance Defense, Health Care Law, Real Estate, Probate and Estate Planning, Healthcare Planning, Insurance Subrogation, Employment Law & Labor Relations, Intellectual Property Law.

JOHN E. BIRK, born Jasper, Indiana, March 10, 1959; admitted to bar, 1989, Indiana and U.S. District Court, Southern and Northern Districts of Indiana. *Education:* United States Military Academy (B.S., 1981); Indiana University School of Law (J.D., 1989). Phi Kappa Phi. *Member:* Indianapolis, Dubois County, Indiana State and American Bar Associations. [Captain, U.S. Army, 1984-1986]. ***PRACTICE AREAS:*** Insurance Defense; Insurance Defense Subrogation; Workers Compensation; Defense Litigation; Commercial Collections; Estate Planning; Health Care; Probate. ***Email:*** jebirk@birklawfirm.com

(This Listing Continued)

THOMAS H. BIRK, born Jasper, Indiana, April 8, 1956; admitted to bar, 1981, Indiana, U.S. District Court, Southern District of Indiana and U.S. Court of Appeals, Seventh Circuit. *Education:* Purdue University (B.S.M.E., 1978); Vanderbilt University (J.D., 1981). Phi Kappa Phi; Pi Tau Sigma; Tau Beta Pi. *Member:* Dubois County (President, 1984) and Indiana State Bar Associations; Commercial Law League of America Who's Who. ***SPECIAL AGENCIES:*** Assistant City Attorney, City of Jasper, Indiana (concentration in municipal utilities), 1994-2000. General Counsel, State Lottery Commission of Indiana, 1991. Staff Attorney, Indiana Department of Administration, 1992-1993. ***PRACTICE AREAS:*** Business Law; Bankruptcy; Creditors Rights; Real Estate; Environmental Law; Municipal Law; Administrative Law; Commercial Collections; Banking Law. ***Email:*** thbirk@birklawfirm.com

LOCAL COUNSEL FOR: The Ohio Casualty Group of Insurance Companies; The American Family Insurance Group; Safeco; Auto Owners Insurance Group; The Cincinnati Insurance Companies; Indiana Farmers Mutual Insurance Group; Procol, Inc.; Western Reserve Mutual Insurance Group.
REPRESENTATIVE CLIENTS: The German American Bank; German American Bank Trust Department; Old National Trust Company; Memorial Hospital & Health Care Center; Donan Engineering, Inc.; Disinger Jewelers; The Claims Group; North American Products Corporation; Springs Valley Bank & Trust Co.; Styline Industries, Inc.; Betz Bros. Construction & Supply, Inc.; Classic Bulk Trucking, Inc.; Dubois County Physician Services, Inc.; Eckert Industrial Supplies, Inc.; Graber Agri-Builders Co., Inc.; Jasper Pediatric Associates, P.C.; Siebert's, Inc.; Procol, Inc.; Birk Title Corporation.
REFERENCES: The German American Bank, Jasper, Indiana; Styline Industries, Inc.; Memorial Hospital & Health Care Center, Jasper, Indiana; The Ohio Casualty Group of Insurance Companies, Lombard, Illinois; Donan Engineering, Inc., Jasper, Indiana; Old National Bank.

KAHN, DEES, DONOVAN & KAHN, LLP

JASPER, INDIANA
(See Evansville)

General Civil Practice including Litigation, Environmental, Labor Management, Corporate, Pension, Banking, Hospital, Insurance Defense, Real Estate, Workers' Compensation, Tax, Construction, Immigration and General Civil Law.

LAW OFFICE OF BART COLOMB

JEFFERSONVILLE, INDIANA
(See New Albany)

Social Security, Workers Compensation and Family Law.

FIFER, VOGT & LANUM

JEFFERSONVILLE, INDIANA
(See Stites & Harbison, PLLC)

LYNCH, COX, GILMAN & MAHAN, P.S.C.

JEFFERSONVILLE, INDIANA
(See Louisville, Kentucky)

General Civil Practice. Estate Planning and Probate. Corporation, Taxation, Insurance, Labor Relations, Patent, Trademark, Negligence and Commercial Law. Trials. Real Estate, Civil Rights, Class Action and Personal Injury Law. Consumer Litigation. Workers Compensation, Insurance. Employee Benefits. Telecommunications. Asbestos and Toxic Torts.

MATTOX MATTOX & WILSON

JEFFERSONVILLE, INDIANA
(See New Albany)

Civil Trial Litigation. Personal Injury and Wrongful Death, Products Liability, Medical Malpractice, Insurance Law, Corporate Law, Business Torts, Family Law, Aviation Law, Labor and Employment Law, Health Care Regulations.

MERKLEY LAW OFFICE

538 E. COURT AVENUE
JEFFERSONVILLE, INDIANA 47130
Telephone: 812-285-9787
Fax: 812-288-0811
Email: lmerkley@sbcglobal.net
URL: http://www.merkleylaw.net

Family Law, Criminal Law, Estates and Wills, Personal Injury, Municipal Law.

LESLIE D. MERKLEY, born Salem, Indiana, February 24, 1969; admitted to bar, 1997, Indiana and U.S. District Court, Northern and Southern Districts of Indiana. *Education:* Indiana University at New Albany (B.A., 1991); Thomas M. Cooley Law School (J.D., 1997). *Member:* Indiana State and American Bar Associations. ***PRACTICE AREAS:*** Family Law; Criminal Law; Estate; Wills; Personal Injury; Government. ***Email:*** lmerkley@merkleylaw.net

CHARLES R. MURPHY

JEFFERSONVILLE, INDIANA

(See New Albany)

Real Estate, Elder Law, Business Law, Buying or Selling a Home, Eminent Domain, Landlord and Tenant Law, Zoning and Land Use, Tax Deferred Exchanges, Business Start-Ups, Buying or Selling a Business, Business Enterprises, Limited Liability Company Law, Corporations, Partnerships, Small Business Law.

LAW OFFICE OF EDWIN S. SEDWICK

417 EAST COURT AVENUE
JEFFERSONVILLE, INDIANA 47130
Telephone: 812-282-7200
Facsimile: 812-282-7393
Email: edwinsedwick@sbcglobal.net
URL: http://www.edwinsedwick.com

General Personal Injury, Wrongful Death, Insurance Claims, Trials and Appeals, Family Law.

EDWIN S. SEDWICK, born Indianapolis, Indiana, October 3, 1946; admitted to bar, 1972, Indiana, U.S. Court of Appeals, Seventh Circuit and U.S. District Court, Southern District of Indiana. *Education:* Indiana University (B.S., 1968); University of Louisville (J.D., magna cum laude, 1972). Phi Kappa Phi. Lecturer, University of Louisville, 1973-1974. Public Defender, Harrison-Crawford Counties, 1977. Certified Civil Mediator. *Member:* Clark County (President, 1982) and Indiana State Bar Associations; Indiana Trial Lawyers Association (Member, Board of Directors, 1991-1994); The Association of Trial Lawyers of America. ***REPORTED CASES:*** Cornell Harbison Excavating, Inc. vs. May (1989) Ind., 546 N.E.2d1186; Rubin vs. Johnson (1990) Ind. App., 550 N.E.2d324; Rauck vs Hawn (1990) Ind. App., 564 N.E.2d334.

SEWELL AND ASSOCIATES

JEFFERSONVILLE, INDIANA

(See Louisville, Kentucky)

Personal Injury and Insurance Defense, Commercial Litigation, Employment Defense and Disability Discrimination Litigation.

STITES & HARBISON, PLLC

Formerly Fifer, Vogt & Lanum

323 EAST COURT AVENUE
JEFFERSONVILLE, INDIANA 47130
Telephone: 812-282-7566
Fax: 812-284-5519
Email: general@stites.com
URL: http://www.stites.com

REVISER OF THE KENTUCKY LAW DIGEST FOR THIS DIRECTORY.

Atlanta, Georgia Office: 303 Peachtree Street, N.E., 2800 SunTrust Plaza, 30308. Telephone: 404-739-8800. Fax: 404-739-8870.
Frankfort, Kentucky Office: 421 West Main Street, 40601-0634. Telephone: 502-223-3477. Fax: 502-223-4124.
Lexington, Kentucky Office: 250 West Main Street, Suite 2300, 40507-1758. Telephone: 859-226-2300. Fax: 859-253-9144.
Louisville, Kentucky Office: 400 West Market Street, Suite 1800, 40202-3352. Telephone: 502-587-3400. Fax: 502-587-6391.
Nashville, Tennessee Office: 424 Church Street, Suite 1800, 37219-2376. Telephone: 615-244-5200. Fax: 615-782-2371.
Washington, D.C. Office: 1200 G Street, N.W., Suite 800, 20005. Telephone: 202-682-4700. Fax: 703-938-0143.
Alexandria, Virginia Office: 1199 North Fairfax Street, Suite 900, 22314. Telephone: 703-739-4900. Fax: 703-739-9577.

General Civil Practice in all State and Federal Courts. Acquisitions, Divestitures and Mergers, Administrative Hearings and Appeals, Admiralty, Antitrust, Appellate Practice, Aviation, Banking, Bankruptcy, Charitable Trusts and Foundations, Commercial, Complex Litigation, Construction, Corporation, Defense of Legal and Medical Malpractice and Personal Injury, Dissolution of Marriage, Employment, Environmental, Equine, Estate Planning and Probate Administration, Health Care, Insurance Defense, Labor Legislative Practice, Litigation, Mineral, Planning and Zoning, Public Finance, Products Liability Litigation, Real Estate, Securities, Social Security Disability, Taxation (Local, State, Federal Income, Estate and Gift), Toxic Torts Litigation, Trust(s) and Utilities. Intellectual Property, including Patents (Mechanical, Biochemical, Chemical, Computer, Medical, Metallurgical, Pharmaceutical, Electromechanical), Trademarks, Copyrights, and Trade Secrets, Franchising and Licensing Law, and Litigation Related to Intellectual Property Matters, including Infringement, Unfair Competition, and Deceptive Trade Practices.

FIRM PROFILE: Stites & Harbison, PLLC, strives to be a preeminent law firm based in strategic Southeastern locations and sought by business and institutional clients nationwide for sophisticated transactions, difficult litigation and complex regulatory matters. Stites & Harbison is a full service firm practicing through departmental groupings with specialty and industry teams whose seven locations function as a single law office. The firm, which traces its origins to 1832, has been the Kentucky editor of the Martindale-Hubbell Law Digest since 1917.

LAW FIRM ALLIANCES/ASSOCIATIONS: **BUSINESS COUNCIL, INC.**

HARMONIE GROUP

SOUTHERN LAW NETWORK

TOLEDO CONFERENCE GROUP

MEMBERS

ALLEN L. MORRIS, born New Albany, Indiana, October 5, 1948; admitted to bar, 1978, Kentucky; 1980, Indiana, U.S. District Court, Southern and Northern Districts of Indiana and U.S. District Court, Western and Eastern Districts of Kentucky; U.S. Court of Appeals, Seventh Circuit. *Education:* University of Louisville (A.B., 1971; J.D., 1978). Pi Sigma Alpha. City Attorney, City of Jeffersonville, Indiana, 1984-1987. Author: Post Judgement Remedies Overview; Debtor/Creditor Relations in Kentucky, 1991. *Member:* Louisville, Clark County, Kentucky, Indiana State and American Bar Associations; American Bankruptcy Institute. [U.S. Naval Reserve, 1971-1991, LCDR]. ***PRACTICE AREAS:*** Asset Based Lending; Banking Law; Bankruptcy Chapter 11 and 12; Bankruptcy Law; Collection Law; Creditor Bankruptcy; Creditors Rights Law; Debtor Creditor Law; Firearms Law; Lender Liability; Lending Law Compliance; Bankruptcy Stay; Litigation; Municipal Law; Prejudgment and Post Judgment Collection; Zoning and Subdivision Law; Zoning Law. ***Email:*** amorris@stites.com

DOUGLAS B. BATES, born Memphis, Indiana, June 17, 1965; admitted to bar, 1992, Indiana, Kentucky, U.S. District Court, Southern and Northern Districts of Indiana and U.S. District Court, Western District of Kentucky. *Education:* Indiana University (B.A., 1989; J.D., cum laude, 1992). Alpha Chi. *Member:* Clark County, Indiana State and American Bar Associations; Defense Research Institute. ***PRACTICE AREAS:*** Litigation. ***Email:*** dbates@stites.com

COUNSEL

J. SPENCER HARMON, born November 3, 1942; admitted to bar, 1973, Indiana; U.S. Court of Appeals, Seventh Circuit; U.S. District Court, Southern District of Indiana. *Education:* University of Kansas (B.S., Business, 1964); Indiana University School of Law, Indianapolis (J.D., cum laude, 1973). Certified Mediator, Indiana Continuing Legal Education Forum, 1992. Leadership Southern Indiana, Class of 1990. Member, Board of Trustees and Chairman, Southern Indiana Economic Development Council, 2002. Chairman, Southern Indiana Chamber of Commerce, 1999. Member, Board of Directors and President, Floyd Memorial Foundation, 1995. *Member:* Floyd County, Clark County, Indiana State and American Bar Associations. [Captain, U.S. Army, 1964-1970]. ***PRACTICE AREAS:*** Real Estate; Corporate Law; Commercial Litigation; Environmental Law. ***Email:*** sharmon@stites.com

OF COUNSEL

ROBERT W. LANUM, born Jeffersonville, Indiana, October 19, 1936; admitted to bar, 1968, Indiana and U.S. District Court, Southern District of Indiana; 1969, U.S. Tax Court. *Education:* Indiana University (B.S., 1959); University of Louisville (J.D., 1968). Delta Theta Phi (Secretary, 1966-1967). President, Clark-Floyd Estate Planning Council, 1972-1973. Member, 1984-1991 and Vice Chairman, 1986-1987, Indiana Probate Study Commission. Fellow, American College of Trust and Estate Counsel. *Member:* Clark County (Vice-President, 1979; President, 1980-1981), Indiana State (Member, Sections of: Taxation; Probate, Trust and Real Property) and American (Member, Sections of: Corporation; Trust and Probate; Taxation) Bar Associations. ***PRACTICE AREAS:*** Corporate Law; Taxation Law; Probate Law; Business Planning Law; Closely Held Business Law; Closely Held Corporation Law; Living Trust Law; Tax Exempt Organizations; Income, Estate and Gift Tax; Taxation of Individuals and Business Entities; Trust Administration; Trust Law; Trustee Rights; Will Contests; Will. ***Email:*** rlanum@stites.com

REPRESENTATIVE CLIENTS: Adams USA, Inc.; Aegon USA Investment Management, Inc.; A.H. Belo Corporation; Alcoa Fujikura Ltd.; Alstom Power; Ambrake Corporation; American Electric Power Service Corporation (Kentucky Power Co.); American General Corporation; American Institute of Steel Construction, Inc.; Anthem Inc.; Bank One, Kentucky, N.A.; Baptist Healthcare System; The Beck Group; BellSouth Telecommunications, Inc.; Beverly Enterprises, Inc.; Brainstorm USA LLC; Bridgestone/Firestone, Inc.; Brown-Forman Corporation; Brown & Williamson Tobacco Corporation; Caldwell Tanks, Inc.; Catskill Development, LLC; CHA HMO, Inc.; Dynergy Power Corp.; Electrolux LLC; Fidelity National Bank; Fleet Financial Corp.; Fortune Brands; Frontier Insurance Corporation; GE Capital Corporation; GlaxoSmithKline; The Goodyear Tire & Rubber Company; International Port of Kentucky; James N. Gray Company; Holder Construction Company; ITT Financial; J.P. Morgan Mortgage Capital; Kajima Construction Services, Inc.; Kentucky Economic Development Finance Authority (KEDFA); KFC Corporation; Lexington-Fayette Urban County Airport Board; Life Insurance Company of Georgia; Louisville Regional Airport Authority; Metropolitan Nashville Airport Authority; Microsoft; Modis Professional Services, Inc.; National City Bank of Kentucky; National Health Investors, Inc.; National Renal Alliance, LLC; New Life Corporation of America; New York Department of Insurance; Northern Life Insurance Company; Pizza Magia International, LLC; Presco Steel, Inc.; Purdue Pharma LP; Regions Bank; Lin R.Rogers Electrical Contractors; Russell Athletic Corporation; Southern Land Company; Steel Technologies, Inc.; Stock Yards Bank & Trust Co.; SunTrust Bank; Synaxis Group, Inc.; ThermoView Industries, Inc.; Tricon Global Restaurants; Tyson Foods, Inc.; Union Planters Bank, N.A.; University Medical Center, Inc.; University of Kentucky; University of Louisville; Vanderbilt University; Whayne Supply Company; Zurich American Insurance Companies.

REVISER OF THE KENTUCKY LAW DIGEST FOR THIS DIRECTORY.

(This Listing Continued)

WEBER & ROSE

PROFESSIONAL SERVICE CORPORATION

JEFFERSONVILLE, INDIANA

(See Louisville, Kentucky)

General Civil Practice, Medical Malpractice, Healthcare Law, Insurance Defense, Media Law, Commercial Litigation, Bankruptcy, Taxation, Estate Planning, Corporate Law, Labor and Employment and Railroad Defense.

BLACKBURN & GREEN

KENDALLVILLE, INDIANA

(See Fort Wayne)

Litigation, Personal Injury Law.

ROEBUCK & ASSOCIATES, P.C.

KENDALLVILLE, INDIANA

(See Ft. Wayne)

Personal Injury, Automobile Accidents, Boat Accidents, Motorcycle Accidents, Truck Accidents, Slip and Fall, Dog Bites, Medical Malpractice, Head Injuries, Nursing Home Abuse and Neglect, Products Liability, Insurance, Social Security, Social Security Disability, and Wrongful Death.

STOUT, WHEELER & ZABONA

KENDALLVILLE, INDIANA

(See Angola)

General Practice, DUI, Driving While Intoxicated, Drug Crimes, Juvenile Crimes, Parole and Probation, Traffic Violations, White Collar Crime, Criminal Law, Domestic Violence, Adoptions, Child Custody, Child Support, Divorce, Domestic Violence, Visitation Rights, Prenuptial Agreements, Unmarried Couples, Guardianships, Automobile Accidents, Dog Bites, Head and Spinal Injuries, Nursing Home Abuse, Sexual Abuse, Slip and Fall, Trucking Accidents, Wrongful Death, Class Actions, Construction Accidents, Personal Injury, Railroad Accidents, Natural Disasters, Business Enterprises, General Business, Starting a Business, Buying or Selling a Home, Construction, Eminent Domain, Environmental, Landlord and Tenant, Zoning and Land Use, Neighbors and Pets, Natural Disasters, Asset Protection, Estate Planning, Wills and Probate.

YODER & MOWERY, PC

Established in 1991

515 PROFESSIONAL WAY
P.O. BOX 633
KENDALLVILLE, INDIANA 46755
Telephone: 260-347-9400
Fax: 260-347-0692
Email: mike.ym@mchsi.com
Email: jim.ym@mchsi.com
Email: myoder@yoderlawoffice.com

General Trial Practice. Probate and Estate Planning, Elder Law, Medicaid Planning, Personal Injury, Corporate, Real Estate and Family/Domestic Relations and Criminal Law.

FIRM PROFILE: Yoder & Mowery, PC is an integral part of the Kendallville law community concentrating in Civil and Criminal Trial Practice and Elder Law. Mr. Yoder is a law graduate of Notre Dame University and has over 30 years of legal experience. Mr. Yoder served as LaGrange County Prosecuting Attorney from 1975 through 1982. Mr. Yoder served as Kendallville City Attorney from 1996 through 2003 and is a member of the East Noble School Board. Mr. Mowery currently serves as Noble County Attorney.

MICHAEL M. YODER, born Kendallville, Indiana, October 14, 1947; admitted to bar, 1971, Indiana, U.S. District Court, Northern District of Indiana and Michigan; U.S. Court of Appeals, Seventh Circuit. *Education:* Ball State University (B.S., 1968); Notre Dame University (J.D., 1971). Kendallville, City Attorney (1996-2003). Deputy Prosecuting Attorney, 1973-1974 and Prosecuting Attorney, 1975-1982, LaGrange County, Indiana. *Member:* Noble County, Indiana State and American Bar Associations; State Bar of Michigan; Indiana Trial Lawyers Association; National Academy of Elder Law Attorneys. ***PRACTICE AREAS:*** Personal Injury; Probate; Estate Planning; Corporate; Real Estate; Family; Domestic Relations; Criminal Law. ***Email:*** mike.ym@mchsi.com

JAMES B. MOWERY, born Olathe, Kansas, August 3, 1972; admitted to bar, 1997, Indiana and U.S. District Court, Northern and Southern Districts of Indiana. *Education:* Purdue University (B.A., 1994); Valparaiso University (J.D., 1997). Deputy Public Defender, Noble County, 1998-1999 and 2001-2002. County Attorney, Noble County, 2000—. *Member:* Noble County (Secretary, 1999—); Indiana State and American Bar Associations. ***PRACTICE AREAS:*** Municipal Law; Criminal Defense; Family Law; Corporate Law; Real Estate. ***Email:*** jim.ym@mchsi.com

LEGAL SUPPORT PERSONNEL

DIXIE L. VANCE, (Paralegal)

CAROL FORKER, (Paralegal)

REPRESENTATIVE CLIENTS: B&J Specialty, Inc.; Wick-Fab, Inc.; Frisco, Inc.; Begley Track, LLC; Campbell & Fetter Bank.
REFERENCES: Lake City Bank; Campbell & Fetter Bank.

RICHARD BALLARD
ATTORNEY AT LAW

KENTLAND, INDIANA

(See Knox)

Criminal Law, DUI, Drug Crimes, Juvenile Crimes, Traffic Violations, White Collar Crimes, Family Law, Adoptions, Child Custody, Child Support, Divorce, Visitation Rights, Personal Injury, Medical Malpractice, Auto Accidents, Wrongful Death, Slip and Fall, Real Estate.

NED TONNER
ATTORNEY AT LAW

KENTLAND, INDIANA

(See Rensselaer)

Personal Injury, Criminal Law, Estates, Trusts, Real Estate, Divorce, Family Law.

RICHARD BALLARD
ATTORNEY AT LAW

52 E. WASHINGTON STREET
KNOX, INDIANA 46534
Telephone: 571-772-0455
Fax: 571-772-0455
URL: http://www.richardballardlaw.com

Criminal Law, DUI, Drug Crimes, Juvenile Crimes, Traffic Violations, White Collar Crimes, Family Law, Adoptions, Child Custody, Child Support, Divorce, Visitation Rights, Personal Injury, Medical Malpractice, Auto Accidents, Wrongful Death, Slip and Fall, Real Estate.

RICHARD BALLARD, born Tipton, Indiana, October 16, 1946; admitted to bar, 1985, Indiana. *Education:* Indiana University (1968-1972); Valparaiso University (J.D., 1985). Chief Deputy Prosecuting Attorney, Starke County 44th Judicial Circuit. *Member:* American, Starke-Pulaski County and Indiana State Bar Associations.

MATTHEW D. LATULIP
ATTORNEY AT LAW

KNOX, INDIANA

(See Schererville)

Personal Injury, Medical Malpractice, Auto Accidents, Slip and Fall, Wrongful Death, Criminal, DUI, Traffic Violations, Juvenile Crimes, Employment Discrimination, Sexual Harassment, Nursing Home Abuse, Insurance.

MORRIS & RUIZ, P.C.

KNOX, INDIANA

(See Plymouth)

Business Transactions, Corporate Law, Bankruptcy, Litigation, Personal Injury, Domestic Relations, Criminal Law, Juvenile Law, Automobile Accidents, Driving While Intoxicated, Juvenile Criminal Law, Parole and Probation, Traffic Violations, White Collar Crimes.

NED TONNER
ATTORNEY AT LAW

KNOX, INDIANA

(See Rensselaer)

Personal Injury, Criminal Law, Estates, Trusts, Real Estate, Divorce, Family Law.

BAYLIFF, HARRIGAN, CORD & MAUGANS, P.C.

Established in 1966

THE SECURITY BUILDING
123 NORTH BUCKEYE
P.O. BOX 2249
KOKOMO, INDIANA 46904-2249
Telephone: 765-459-3941
Fax: 765-459-3974
URL: http://www.bhcmlaw.com

Personal Injury Litigation, Real Estate, Probate and Estate Planning, Estate Administration, Corporations and Family/Domestic Relations, Product Liability, Medical Malpractice, Wrongful Death Law.

FIRM PROFILE: This firm was established by the present members in 1966. The firm maintains a general practice with a strong emphasis on personal injury litigation, including some defense work, in all state and federal courts. It employs thirteen additional personnel including an investigator and five paralegals. The firm encourages continuing education for lawyers, paralegals, and secretaries as well as participation in professional and civic organizations.

EDGAR W. BAYLIFF

DANIEL J. HARRIGAN, born Indianapolis, Indiana, October 30, 1937; admitted to bar, 1963, Indiana. *Education:* Indiana University (B.S., 1959; J.D., 1962). Phi Alpha Delta. Note Editor, Indiana Law Journal, 1962. Law Clerk to Judge Dewey Kelley, Indiana Appellate Court, 1963. Listed in The Best Lawyers in America. *Member:* Howard County (President, 1987) and Indiana State Bar Associations; Indiana Trial Lawyers Association (Director, 1977—; Treasurer, 1978-1982; Second Vice President, 1982-1984; President, 1984; Member, College of Fellows, 1985—); President, College of Fellow, 1995-1996. The Association of Trial Lawyers of America (State Committeeman, 1980-1983; Member, Board of Governors 1991-1997; Vice-Chair, 1993-1994 and Chair, 1994-1995, Railroad Law Section); College of Master Advocates and Barristers. Fellow, Indiana Bar Foundation. (Certified as a Civil Trial Advocate by the National Board of Trial Advocacy). ***PRACTICE AREAS:*** Personal Injury Law; Railroad Law. ***Email:*** dan.harrigan@bhcmlaw.com

C. MICHAEL CORD, born Connersville, Indiana, June 2, 1935; admitted to bar, 1962, Indiana. *Education:* Indiana University (B.S., 1959; J.D., 1962). Phi Delta Phi. Law Clerk to Honorable S. Hugh Dillin, U.S. District Court, Southern District of Indiana, 1962-1964. Civil Mediation, 1994. Member, Board of Directors, Indiana Continuing Legal Education Forum, 1989-1996. *Member:* Howard County (President, 1971) and Indiana State (Member, Board of Governors, 2003-2005) Bar Associations; Indiana Trial Lawyers Association. Fellow, Indiana Bar Foundation. ***PRACTICE AREAS:*** Mediation (750); Personal Injury Litigation; Estate Planning; Probate Law; Civil Mediation. ***Email:*** mike.cord@bhcmlaw.com

(This Listing Continued)

BAYLIFF, HARRIGAN, CORD & MAUGANS, P.C., Kokomo—Continued

J. CONRAD MAUGANS, born Miami County, Indiana, May 10, 1938; admitted to bar, 1962, Indiana; 1963, U.S. Court of Military Appeals. *Education:* Manchester College (A.B., 1960); Indiana University (J.D., 1962). Order of the Coif; Phi Delta Phi. *Member:* Howard County (President, 1989) and Indiana State Bar Associations; Indiana Trial Lawyers Association; The Association of Trial Lawyers of America. Fellow, Indiana Bar Foundation. Lifetime Fellow, Roscoe Pound-American Trial Lawyers Foundation. ***REPORTED CASES:*** Green v. Estate of Green, 724 N.E.2d 260 (Ind.Ct.App. 2000); Bagko Development Co. v. Damitz, 640 N.E.2d 67 (Ind. Ct.App.1994); Campbell v. State, 284 N.E.2d 733 (Ind. 1972). ***PRACTICE AREAS:*** Civil Trial Practice; Real Estate Law; Estate Planning; Probate Law. ***Email:*** connie.maugans@bhcmlaw.com

DAVID A. COX, born Rantoul, Illinois, September 28, 1955; admitted to bar, 1982, Indiana and U.S. District Court, Northern and Southern Districts of Indiana. *Education:* Manchester College (B.S., 1977); Indiana University School of Law (J.D., 1982). Instructor, Indiana University-Kokomo, paralegal program, 1991-1995. Judge, Howard County Superior Court III, 2001-2002. *Member:* Howard County and Indiana State Bar Associations; Indiana Trial Lawyers Association. ***PRACTICE AREAS:*** Family Law; Real Estate; Personal Injury; Zoning, Planning and Land Use. ***Email:*** dave.cox@bhcmlaw.com

A List of Representative Clients will be Furnished Upon Request.
REFERENCE: National City Bank, Kokomo.

WILLIAM E. BECK II

Established in 1976

401 WEST WALNUT
P.O. BOX 868
KOKOMO, INDIANA 46903-0868
Telephone: 765-456-1318
FAX: 765-456-1323
Email: bbecklaw@aol.com

Civil Trial, Personal Injury, Wrongful Death, Workman's Compensation.

FIRM PROFILE: William Beck II, solo practitioner and lifelong resident of Kokomo primarily practices trial law.

WILLIAM E. BECK, II, born Indianapolis, Indiana, July 30, 1950; admitted to bar, 1976, Indiana and U.S. District Court, Southern District of Indiana; 1993, U.S. Supreme Court. *Education:* Northwestern College of Law; Indiana University (B.S., 1972; J.D., 1975). Recipient, Indiana State Bar Association Award for outstanding leadership in improving the availability of legal assistance in the community, 1986. Chairperson, Howard County Public Defender Board, 2005. *Member:* Howard County (President, 1988) and Indiana State Bar Associations; Indiana Trial Lawyers Association; The Association of Trial Lawyers of America. ***REPORTED CASES:*** Gyer vs. City of Logansport 370 NE 2d 333 (1977). ***PRACTICE AREAS:*** Plaintiff; Accidents; Automobile Accidents and Injuries; Automobile Negligence; Bodily Injury; Brain Injury; Head Injury; Motor Vehicle Accidents and Injuries; Motorcycle Accidents; Plaintiffs Personal Injury; Severe Burns; Wrongful Death; Dram Shop Liability; Liquor Liability; Health Care Litigation; Hospital Negligence; Automobile Insurance; Accident Insurance; Excess Coverage; Insurance Bad Faith; Insurance Litigation; Uninsured and Underinsured Motorists; Medical Liability; Nursing Malpractice; Nursing Negligence; Tort Liability; Motor Carrier Liability; Truck Accidents.

LEGAL SUPPORT PERSONNEL

SUE GIBSON, born Kokomo, Indiana, June 26, 1960. *Education:* Ball State (Associate Degree, 1980); Indiana University at Kokomo.

SARA THATCHER, born Warsaw, Indiana, November 12, 1958. *Education:* Indiana State University (B.S., 1980).

DARRIAN STORY, born May 2, 1981. *Education:* Earlham College (B.A., 2003).

BUTTON, McGARVEY, TRAURING, WILSON & OAKS

ASSOCIATION OF INDEPENDENT ATTORNEYS

515 WEST SYCAMORE STREET
P.O. BOX 958
KOKOMO, INDIANA 46903-0958
Telephone: 765-457-9321
Telecopier: 765-452-0882
Email: lawkokomo@aol.com

General Civil Practice. Litigation, Real Estate, Corporate Law, Business Organizations, Insurance, Estate Planning and Estate Administration.

FIRM PROFILE: Button, McGarvey, Trauring, Wilson & Oaks have been serving clients in business and personal matters throughout North Central Indiana since 1964, offering personalized legal services with a clear view towards meeting each client's particular needs. Button, McGarvey, Trauring, Wilson & Oaks are committed to the highest standards of professionalism and quality in the delivery of legal services.

ATTORNEYS

THOMAS J. TRAURING, born Muncie, Indiana, June 6, 1945; admitted to bar, 1972, Indiana. *Education:* Miami University and Indiana University (B.S., 1967; J.D., 1972). *Member:* Howard County and Indiana State Bar Associations; Defense Research Institute,

(This Listing Continued)

Inc.; Defense Trial Counsel of Indiana; Association of Defense Trial Attorneys. Fellow, American College of Trial Lawyers. ***PRACTICE AREAS:*** Estate Planning; Probate Law; Business Law; Corporate Law; Litigation. ***Email:*** tomtrauring@yahoo.com

ALAN D. WILSON, born Marion, Indiana, May 17, 1961; admitted to bar, 1986, Indiana. *Education:* Purdue University (B.A., 1983); Indiana University (J.D., 1986). *Member:* Howard County and Indiana State Bar Associations; Defense Research Institute; Defense Trial Counsel of Indiana; Association of Defense Trial Attorneys. ***PRACTICE AREAS:*** Litigation; Insurance Defense; Business Law; Commercial Law; Government Tort Liability. ***Email:*** lawkokomo@sbcglobal.net

BRIAN L. OAKS, born Lafayette, Indiana, March 20, 1964; admitted to bar, 1990, Indiana. *Education:* Wabash College (B.A., 1986); Indiana University (J.D., 1989). Assistant Attorney, Howard County, 1995—. *Member:* Howard County (President, 1995) Indiana State and American Bar Associations; Commercial Law League of America. ***PRACTICE AREAS:*** Civil Litigation; Debtor and Creditor; Automobile Insurance. ***Email:*** boaks.attorney@sbcglobal.net

REPRESENTATIVE CLIENTS: Syndicate Sales, Inc.; Haynes International, Inc.; Hospital Authority of the City of Kokomo; Mervis Industries, Inc.; Hewitt Tool & Die, Inc.; Wildcat Creek Golf Course, L.L.C.; Gerber Plumbing Fixtures Corp.; Kokomo Lumber Co., Inc.; Functional Devices, Inc.; Kokomo Municipal Airport; Mid America Beverage, Inc.; Select Equipment Co., Inc.
INSURANCE COS.: American Family Mutual Insurance Group; Century Insurance Co.; Cincinnati Insurance Co.; General Casualty Cos.; Grange Mutual Casualty Co.; Hartford Insurance Group; Indiana Farmers Mutual Insurance Co.; Meridian Insurance Co.; National General Insurance Co.
REFERENCES: First National Bank & Trust; KeyBank.

RUSSELL, McINTYRE, HILLIGOSS & WELKE

Established in 1987

116 NORTH MAIN STREET
P.O. BOX 1047
KOKOMO, INDIANA 46903-1047
Telephone: 765-456-3827
Telecopier: 765-456-3839
Email: rrussell@kokomolaw.com
URL: http://www.kokomolawfirm.com

General Trial and Appellate Practice in State and Federal Courts. Banking, Bankruptcy, Business and Corporate, Collections and Creditor's Rights, Criminal Defense, Employment, Family/Domestic Relations, Health, Mediation, Medical Malpractice, Personal Injury, Probate and Estate Planning, Real Estate and School Law and Product Liability, Intellectual Property Law.

FIRM PROFILE: Russell, McIntyre, Hilligoss & Welke is a full service firm. This preeminent law firm is represented in Martindale-Hubbell's Bar Register, serves North Central Indiana providing its clients with the highest caliber legal services available. Their focus remains on personal service, cost effectiveness and quality representation. The people-oriented philosophy extends further as they are actively involved in community affairs.

MEMBERS OF FIRM

RICHARD L. RUSSELL, born Kokomo, Indiana, December 13, 1946; admitted to bar, 1975, Indiana; U.S. District Court, Northern and Southern Districts of Indiana. *Education:* Purdue University (B.A., 1970); Indiana University School of Law-Indianapolis (J.D., 1975). Deputy Prosecutor, 1978 and Chief Deputy, 1983-1986, Howard County, Indiana. City Attorney, City of Kokomo, Indiana, 1978-1979. Attorney, City of Kokomo Economic Development Commission, 1978-1979. Chairman, Board Kokomo Economic Development Commission, 1996-1997. Certified Civil and Family Law Mediator. Chairman, Board Kokomo-Howard County Chamber of Commerce, 1997-1998. *Member:* Howard County (President, 1982), Indiana State and American Bar Associations; Indiana Trial Lawyers Association; The Association of Trial Lawyers of America. ***PRACTICE AREAS:*** Medical Malpractice Law; Personal Injury Law; Personal Injury; Mediation; Family Law. ***Email:*** rrussell@kokomolaw.com

JAMES B. McINTYRE, born Jersey City, New Jersey, February 5, 1944; admitted to bar, 1970, Indiana; U.S. District Court, Northern and Southern Districts of Indiana. *Education:* DePauw University (A.B., 1966); Indiana University School of Law-Indianapolis (J.D., 1970). Phi Delta Phi. Certified Civil and Family Law Mediator. Chairman, Community Foundation of Howard County. *Member:* Indianapolis, Howard County (President, 1990-1991) and Indiana State Bar Associations. ***PRACTICE AREAS:*** Estate and Financial Planning Law; Probate Law; Corporate and Business Law; Real Estate Law. ***Email:*** jmcintyre@kokomolaw.com

THOMAS J. HILLIGOSS, JR., born Kokomo, Indiana, May 3, 1947; admitted to bar, 1979, Indiana; U.S. District Court, Northern and Southern Districts of Indiana. *Education:* Indiana University (A.B., 1974; J.D., 1979). Certified Civil and Family Law Mediator. Assistant County Attorney, 1989-1992. Member, Board of Trustees, Howard Community Hospital, 1999—. Member, Board of Trustees, 1985-1991, President, 1989-1990, General Counsel, 2000—. Kokomo Center Township Consolidated School Corporation. *Member:* Howard County and Indiana State Bar Associations. ***PRACTICE AREAS:*** Banking and Bankruptcy Law; Creditor's Rights Law; School Law; Family Law; Personal Injury Law; Real Estate Law; Collections. ***Email:*** thilligoss@kokomolaw.com

CURTIS C. WELKE, born Peru, Indiana, December 23, 1946; admitted to bar, 1973, California; 1977, Indiana; U.S. District Court, Northern and Southern Districts of Indiana. *Education:* Purdue University (B.S.I.M., 1969); Pepperdine University (J.D., 1973). Member, Board of Directors: Community First Bank; Kokomo Rescue Mission. Member, Board of Deacons, Our Redeemer Lutheran Church. *Member:* Howard County and Indiana State Bar Associations; State Bar of California. ***PRACTICE AREAS:*** Personal Injury Law; Medical Malpractice Law; Family Law; Bankruptcy. ***Email:*** cwelke@kokomolaw.com

REBECCA R. VENT, born Indianapolis, Indiana, July 11, 1966; admitted to bar, 1996, Indiana, U.S. District Court, Northern and Southern Districts of Indiana. *Education:* Uni-

(This Listing Continued)

versity of Florida (B.A., 1989); Ohio Northern University (J.D., 1996). *Member:* Howard County and Indiana State and American Bar Associations. ***PRACTICE AREAS:*** Personal Injury; Family Law; Adoption Law; Collections. ***Email:*** rvent@kokomolaw.com

OF COUNSEL

JOHN E. FELL, JR., born Kokomo, Indiana, December 5, 1933; admitted to bar, 1957, Indiana. *Education:* University of Arizona and Indiana University (B.S., 1955; J.D., 1957). Phi Delta Phi. *Member:* Howard County, Indiana State and American Bar Associations. ***PRACTICE AREAS:*** Banking Law; Probate Law; Real Estate Law. ***Email:*** jfell@kokomolaw.com

REPRESENTATIVE CLIENTS: Furnished Upon Request.
REFERENCE: First National Bank, Kokomo, Ind.

THEODORE F. SMITH, JR.

KOKOMO, INDIANA

(See Anderson)

Social Security Disability, Personal Injury, Wrongful Death.

BALL EGGLESTON, PC

Established in 1954

810 BANK ONE BUILDING
P.O. BOX 1535
LAFAYETTE, INDIANA 47902-1535
Telephone: 765-742-9046
Fax: 765-742-1966
Email: info@ball-law.com
URL: http://www.ball-law.com

Personal Injury and Wrongful Death, Product Liability, Medical Malpractice, Professional Malpractice, Probate and Estate Planning, Trusts and Estates, Wills, Guardianships, Asset Protection, Corporation and Business Organizations, Business Enterprises, Corporate, Partnerships, Limited Liability Companies, Contracts, Business Law, Business Planning, Family Law, Real Estate, Zoning and Land Use, Municipal Law, Administrative Law, Mediation, Commercial Collections, Insurance, Workers Compensation, General Practice.

FIRM PROFILE: The Firm was founded in 1950 as a general practice firm serving in Indiana and Federal Courts. The firm continues to practice in diverse areas of the law with emphasis in trials and appeals, estate planning and probate and real estate development. The firm is a member of the International Society of Primerus Law Firms and committed to six key principles in the practice of law: integrity; excellence of work product; reasonableness in fees; continuing legal education; civility to court's officers, judges and lawyers and community service.

LAW FIRM ALLIANCES/ASSOCIATIONS: ***PRIMERUS***

CABLE G. BALL (1904-1981)
OWEN CROOK (1908-1977)
WARREN N. EGGLESTON (1923-1991)

JOSEPH T. BUMBLEBURG, born Lafayette, Indiana, January 5, 1937; admitted to bar, 1961, Indiana. *Education:* University of Notre Dame (A.B., 1958); Indiana University (J.D., 1961). Phi Delta Phi. Trustee, Ivy Tech Community College of Indiana (Chairman, 2000-2001). *Member:* Tippecanoe County (Secretary, 1965-1966; President, 1982-1983), Indiana State and American Bar Associations; American Judicature Society; Judge Advocates Association. Master Fellow, Indiana Bar Foundation. Fellow, Indiana University School of Law, Academy of Law Alumni Fellows. [Capt., U.S. Army, J.A.G.C., 1961-1964]. ***PRACTICE AREAS:*** Alternative Dispute Resolution; Municipal Law; Zoning Law; Subdivision Law. ***Email:*** jbumbleburg@ball-law.com

JOHN K. McBRIDE, born Cincinnati, Ohio, January 15, 1943; admitted to bar, 1968, Indiana and Ohio. *Education:* Denison University (A.B., 1965); University of Cincinnati (J.D., 1968). Order of the Coif; Phi Delta Phi. Officer and Member, Board of Editors, University of Cincinnati Law Review, 1967-1968. President, Estate Planning Council of Lafayette, Indiana, 1978. Member, Board of Directors of Banc One, Lafayette, N.A. 1991-1999. *Member:* Tippecanoe County (Treasurer, 1971-1972; Past President), Indiana State (Member: Probate, Trust and Real Property Section; Corporate Counsel) and American (Member: Real Property, Probate and Trust Section) Bar Associations. Master, Fellow, Indiana Bar Foundation. ***PRACTICE AREAS:*** General Business Law; Corporate and Partnership Law; Municipal Corporations Law; Estate Planning; Trust Law; Probate; Elder Law. ***Email:*** jmcbride@ball-law.com

JACK L. WALKEY, born Lafayette, Indiana, April 21, 1946; admitted to bar, 1971, Indiana. *Education:* Ohio State University (B.S., 1968); Indiana University (J.D., 1971). Phi Alpha Delta. *Member:* Tippecanoe County (President, 2000), Indiana State (Member, Real Property, Probate and Trust Law Section) and American (Member, Real Property, Probate and Trust Law Section; Taxation Section) Bar Associations; Estate Planning Council of Lafayette (President, 1986). ***PRACTICE AREAS:*** Residential Real Estate; Commercial Real Estate; Farm Real Estate; Estate Planning Law; Tax Planning; Trusts Law; Tax Deferred Exchanges; Probate. ***Email:*** jwalkey@ball-law.com

MICHAEL J. STAPLETON, born Chicago, Illinois, October 8, 1947; admitted to bar, 1972, Indiana. *Education:* University of Kentucky (A.B., 1970; J.D., 1972). Phi Delta Phi. *Member:* Tippecanoe County and Indiana State Bar Associations; Indiana Trial Lawyers Association (Board of Directors, 2004—); The Association of Trial Lawyers of America; Seventh Circuit Bar Association; Trial Lawyers for Public Justice. Master Fellow: Indiana Bar Foundation; American College of Trial Lawyers; American Board of Trial Associations (Associate); Roscoe Pound Foundation. ***PRACTICE AREAS:*** Personal Injury Law; Professional Malpractice; Commercial Litigation; Insurance; Products Liability. ***Email:*** mstapleton@ball-law.com

(This Listing Continued)

JEFFREY J. NEWELL, born Lafayette, Indiana, May 30, 1955; admitted to bar, 1980, Indiana. *Education:* Purdue University (B.S. and B.A., with honors, 1977); Indiana University (J.D., magna cum laude, 1980). Order of the Coif. *Member:* Tippecanoe County and Indiana State Bar Associations. ***PRACTICE AREAS:*** Creditors Rights Law; Landlord and Tenant Rights Law; Collections. ***Email:*** jnewell@ball-law.com

BRIAN WADE WALKER, born Frankfort, Indiana, September 17, 1957; admitted to bar, 1984, Indiana. *Education:* Purdue University (B.A., 1981); Indiana University School of Law-Indianapolis (J.D., 1984). *Member:* Tippecanoe County, Indiana State and American Bar Associations; American Trial Lawyers Association. ***PRACTICE AREAS:*** Personal Injury Litigation; Trial Practice; Appellate Practice; Worker's Compensation Law; Family Law; Insurance Law. ***Email:*** bwalker@ball-law.com

CHERYL M. KNODLE, born Beloit, Wisconsin, September 9, 1946; admitted to bar, 1987, Indiana. *Education:* University of Illinois (B.A., 1968); Indiana University-Bloomington (M.L.S., 1975); Indiana University-Indianapolis (J.D., magna cum laude, 1987). Phi Beta Kappa; Phi Alpha Delta. *Member:* Indiana State Bar Association. ***PRACTICE AREAS:*** Elder Law; Contracts Law; Appellate Practice. ***Email:*** cknodle@ball-law.com

RANDY J. WILLIAMS, born Rome, New York, September 24, 1956; admitted to bar, 1982, New York; 1989, Indiana. *Education:* Hamilton College (B.A., 1978); Albany Law School of Union University (J.D., 1981). *Member:* Tippecanoe County and Indiana State Bar Associations; Indiana Trial Lawyers Association. ***PRACTICE AREAS:*** Civil Litigation; Criminal Law; Real Estate; Zoning Law; Insurance; Municipal Law. ***Email:*** rwilliams@ball-law.com

STEVEN P. MEYER, born Lafayette, Indiana, July 9, 1959; admitted to bar, 1984, Indiana; U.S. District Court, Northern and Southern Districts of Indiana; 2001, U.S. Supreme Court. *Education:* St. Joseph's College (B.S., suma cum laude, 1981); Indiana University (J.D., 1984). Phi Delta Phi (President, 1984). Instructor, Business Law, Ivy Tech State College, 1988 and Indiana University, 1989. Member, Lafayette City Council, 1992—. Member, Public Defender Council, Indiana. Public Defender, Tippecanoe County, 1984-2000. *Member:* Tippecanoe County (Secretary, 1995) and Indiana State Bar Associations; Indiana Trial Lawyers Association. ***PRACTICE AREAS:*** General Practice; Personal Injury; Criminal Law; Family Law; Civil Practice; Estate Litigation. ***Email:*** smeyer@ball-law.com

BRENDA MITHOEFER CLAPPER, born Lafayette, Indiana, May 30, 1972; admitted to bar, 1997, Indiana and U.S. District Court, Northern and Southern Districts of Indiana; U.S. Supreme Court. *Education:* Purdue University (B.A., 1994); Indiana University (J.D., 1997). *Member:* Tippecanoe County, Indiana State and American Bar Associations. ***PRACTICE AREAS:*** Estate Planning; Probate Law; Elder Law; Adoption Law; Employment Law. ***Email:*** bclapper@ball-law.com

MATTHEW G. McQUEEN, born Lafayette, Indiana, June 6, 1972; admitted to bar, 1997, Illinois; 2002, Indiana, U.S. District Court, Northern and Southern Districts of Indiana, U.S. Supreme Court. *Education:* Indiana University (B.A., with high distinction, 1994); University of Michigan (J.D., magna cum laude, 1997). Phi Beta Kappa; Order of the Coif. Note Editor, University of Michigan Journal of International Law, 1996-1997. *Member:* Tippecanoe County, Indiana State and American Bar Associations. ***PRACTICE AREAS:*** Business Law; Corporate Law; Partnership Law; Contracts; Real Estate; Zoning Law; Secured Transactions. ***Email:*** mmcqueen@ball-law.com

GENERAL COUNSEL FOR: The Lafayette Union Railway Co.
REPRESENTATIVE CLIENTS: City of Lafayette Board of Park and Recreation Commissioners; Equitable Life Assurance Society; West Lafayette Community Library (Trustees); Lafayette Regional Association of Realtors; Greater Lafayette Public Transportation Company; American Family Insurance Company; Town of Dayton, Indiana; Lend-Lease Agri-Business; Town of Battle Ground, Indiana.
REFERENCES: Bank One, Indiana, N.A.; Lafayette Bank & Trust Co.

JOHN MICHAEL BURGETT

Established in 1963

510 MAIN STREET
LAFAYETTE, INDIANA 47901-1447
Telephone: 765-742-6006
FAX: 765-429-7368

Practice limited to Real Estate, Estates, Estate Planning, Trusts, Wills, Guardianships, Adoptions, Agricultural and Business Law and Litigation.

JOHN MICHAEL BURGETT, born Indianapolis, Indiana, December 26, 1936; admitted to bar, 1963, Indiana, U.S. District Court, Northern and Southern Districts of Indiana, U.S. Court of Appeals, Seventh Circuit and U.S. Supreme Court. *Education:* DePauw University and Indiana University at Bloomington (A.B., 1959); Indiana University at Indianapolis (J.D., 1962). Publications: "Residential Leasing," *Indiana Real Estate Transactions,* Lawyers Cooperative Publishing, 1996. *Member:* Tippecanoe County (President, 1985-1986) and Indiana State (Member, Sections on: Probate, Trust and Real Property; Trial Lawyers) Bar Associations; Indiana Trial Lawyers Association; The Association of Trial Lawyers of America. ***PRACTICE AREAS:*** Wills; Powers of Attorney; Trusts Law; Estates Law; Tax Planning; Estate Administration; Residential Real Estate; Farm and Ranch Law.

Representative Clients will be furnished upon request.
REFERENCES: Lafayette Bank and Trust Company; Bank One Trust Company, N.A.;Union Planters Bank; Salin Bank.

DOWELL BAKER

Established in 2003

1001 MAIN STREET
LAFAYETTE, INDIANA 47901
Telephone: 765-429-4004
Fax: 765-429-4114
URL: http://www.dowellbaker.com

Oak Park, Illinois Office: 229 Randolph Street, 60302. Telephone: 708-660-1413. Fax: 312-873-4466.

(This Listing Continued)

DOWELL BAKER, Lafayette—Continued

General Practice.

MEMBER OF FIRM

ANTHONY E. DOWELL, born Frankfort, Indiana, April 26, 1966; admitted to bar, 1994, Illinois and U.S. District Court, Northern District of Illinois including Trial Bar; 2003, Indiana; registered to practice before U.S. Patent and Trademark Office. *Education:* Purdue University (I.D.E., 1989); Notre Dame University (J.D., magna cum laude, 1994). Senior Editor, Notre Dame Law Review. Recipient, American Jurisprudence Awards in Trial Advocacy and Civil Procedure. Author: "Trade Dress Protection of Product Designs: Stifling the Progress of Science and the Useful Arts for an Unlimited Time," 70 Notre Dame L. Rev. 137 (1994). *Member:* Indiana State, Illinois State and American Bar Associations. ***PRACTICE AREAS:*** Intellectual Property; Litigation. ***Email:*** aedowell@dowellbaker.com

THOMAS J. HERR

324 MAIN STREET, SUITE D
P.O. BOX 710
LAFAYETTE, INDIANA 47902-0710
Telephone: 765-420-0230
Email: therr@tjherrlaw.com

Civil Litigation, Personal Injury, Collections, Family Law, Divorce, General Civil Practice, Wills and Probate, Trusts and Estates.

THOMAS J. HERR, born Gary, Indiana, October 14, 1955; admitted to bar, 1983, Indiana; 1983, U.S. District Court, Northern District Indiana; 1986, U.S. Court of Appeals, 7th Circuit; 1987, U.S. Claims Court; 1997, U.S. Supreme Court. *Education:* Indiana University (B.A., 1978; J.D., cum laude, 1983). Forrest E. Jump Scholar. *Member:* Tippecanoe County and Indiana State Bar Associations. ***REPORTED CASES:*** Green v. Hendrickson Publishers, 751 N.E.2d 815 (Ind. App. 2001); Hoovler v. State, 668 N.E. 2d 1229 (Ind. 1996); Ward v. Ward, 611 N.E.2d 167 (Ind. App., 1993).

HOFFMAN, LUHMAN & MASSON, P.C.

Established in 1957
201 MAIN STREET
P.O. BOX 99
LAFAYETTE, INDIANA 47902-0099
Telephone: 765-423-5404
Fax: 765-742-6448
Email: hlb@hlblaw.com
URL: http://www.hlblaw.com

Commercial Law, General Civil Practice, Personal Injury, Insurance, Probate, Estate Planning, Banking, Appellate Practice, Bankruptcy, Federal Civil Practice, Collections, County Government Law, Insurance Defense, Negligence Defense, Trusts and Estates.

DAVID W. LUHMAN, born Fort Wayne, Indiana, December 22, 1950; admitted to bar, 1977, Indiana. *Education:* Purdue University (B.S., 1973); Indiana University (J.D., 1977). Phi Alpha Delta. Tippecanoe County Attorney, 1998—. *Member:* Tippecanoe County, The Indiana State and American Bar Associations; Bar Association of the Seventh Federal Circuit; Defense Research Institute; Commercial Law League of America; National Association of Retail Collection Attorneys; American Judicature Society. ***Email:*** dwl@hlblaw.com

DOUGLAS J. MASSON, born Richmond, Indiana, August 8, 1971; admitted to bar, 1996, Indiana; 2003, U.S. Court of Appeals, 7th Circuit. *Education:* Miami University (B.A., 1993); Indiana University (J.D., cum laude, 1996). Author: "Fixation on Fixation: Why Imposing Old Copyright Law on New Technology Will Not Work," 71 Ind. L.J. 1049 (1996); "The Genie Let Loose: Ineffectual Encryption Export Restriction Business," 2 J.Tech.L.&Pol'y 4 (Fall 1996). *Member:* Tippecanoe County, Indiana State and American Bar Associations; Commercial Law League of America. ***Email:*** djm@hlhlaw.com

REPRESENTATIVE CLIENTS: Tippecanoe County; Hastings Mutual Insurance Company; Lafayette Accounts Service, Inc.; National Swine Registry; State Farm Insurance Companies; Argent Healthcare Financial Services; Industrial Federal Credit Union; Allied Collection Service, Inc.; Tippecanoe Emergency Ambulance Service; Life Employment Service.
REFERENCES: Lafayette Bank & Trust Co., Lafayette, Indiana; Lafayette Savings Bank, Lafayette, Indiana; Bank One, Lafayette, Indiana; Sand Ridge Bank, Lafayette, Indiana.

HOLDER LAW OFFICE

Established in 1975
12 NORTH THIRD STREET
P.O. BOX 757
LAFAYETTE, INDIANA 47902-0757
Telephone: 765-742-1124
Fax: 765-742-5140
Email: all@hdslaw.com

Family Law, General Civil and Trial Practice, Probate and Estate Planning, Real Estate, Corporate, Guardianships and Adoption.

FIRM PROFILE: Holder Law Office traces its roots to Carolyn S. Holder, who established the firm in 1975. Over the last 26 years, the firm has maintained a high level of service to Tippecanoe and surrounding counties. Holder Law Office is proud to offer legal representation.

(This Listing Continued)

MEMBER OF FIRM

CAROLYN S. HOLDER, born Lafayette, Indiana, December 15, 1947; admitted to bar, 1973, Indiana; U.S. Supreme Court; U.S. Court of Appeals, Seventh Circuit and U.S. District Court, Northern and Southern Districts of Indiana. *Education:* Purdue University (B.A., 1970); Indiana University (J.D., 1973). Deputy Prosecuting Attorney, 1973-1974. *Member:* Tippecanoe County (Secretary, 1977), Indiana State and American (Member, Sections on: Economics of Law Practice; Family Law) Bar Associations; Indiana Trial Lawyers Association. ***PRACTICE AREAS:*** Civil Practice; Trial Practice; Family Law; Estate Planning; Probate; Real Estate; Corporate; Guardianship; Adoption Law. ***Email:*** cholder@hdslaw.com

KIRK G. EICHER-MILLER, born Ephrata, Pennsylvania, June 20, 1974; admitted to bar, 2003, Indiana. *Education:* Goshen College (B.A., 1996); Temple University (J.D., 1999). *Member:* Tippecanoe County and American Bar Associations. ***PRACTICE AREAS:*** General Practice. ***Email:*** kmiller@hdslaw.com

OF COUNSEL

WILLIAM C. BURNS, born Hartford City, Indiana, April 13, 1933; admitted to bar, 1957, Indiana; 1958, U.S. District Court, Northern District of Indiana. *Education:* Indiana University (B.S., 1955; J.D., 1957). Phi Delta Phi. *Member:* Tippecanoe County, Indiana State and American Bar Associations. ***PRACTICE AREAS:*** General Practice Law (100%).

REFERENCES: Salin Bank; Bank One, Lafayette.

LAW OFFICE OF DIANE RAE HURTT

136 NORTH 3RD STREET
LAFAYETTE, INDIANA 47901
Telephone: 765-429-5333
Fax: 765-428-8660
Email: dhurtt@drhlawoffice.com
URL: http://www.drhurttlaw.com

Immigration Law, Family Law, Business Transactions, Corporate Law, Collections.

DIANE RAE HURTT, born Cleveland, Ohio, April 5, 1953; admitted to bar, 1996, Indiana and U.S. District Court, Northern District of Indiana. *Education:* Purdue University (B.A., 1990); Indiana University of School Law, Indianapolis (J.D., 1996). Phi Beta Kappa. Member, 1994-1995 and Articles Editor, 1995-1996, Indiana Law Review. Member, Board of Directors, Lafayette Chamber of Commerce, 2002 to present. Vice President, Legal Aid Corporation, Tippecanoe County. *Member:* Tippecanoe County and Indiana State Bar Associations; American Immigration Lawyers Association. ***PRACTICE AREAS:*** Immigration Law; Family Law; Business Transactions; Corporate Law; Collections.

LASZYNSKI & MOORE

P.O. BOX 848
LAFAYETTE, INDIANA 47902-0848
Telephone: 765-423-5626
Fax: 765-429-5776
URL: http://www.laszynskimoorelaw.com

Civil and Criminal Trial Litigation in all Courts, Business Law, Real Estate, Probate and Estate Planning, Family Law, Domestic Relations and School Law.

ROBERT S. LASZYNSKI, born Dowagiac, Michigan, August 27, 1953; admitted to bar, 1978, Indiana and U.S. District Court, Northern District of Indiana. *Education:* University of Notre Dame (B.S., 1975); Indiana University at Indianapolis (J.D., magna cum laude, 1978). Phi Delta Phi. *Member:* Tippecanoe County (Secretary, 1980-1981), Indiana State and American Bar Associations; National Academy of Elder Law Attorneys. ***PRACTICE AREAS:*** Wills; Real Estate; General Practice. ***Email:*** blaszynski@laszynskimoore.com

E. KENT MOORE, born Wilmington, North Carolina, July 31, 1943; admitted to bar, 1968, Indiana and U.S. District Court, Northern and Southern Districts of Indiana. *Education:* Wabash College (A.B., 1965); Indiana University (J.D., 1968). Attorney: Lafayette School Corporation, 1974—; Lafayette Redevelopment Commission, 1974-1995. *Member:* Tippecanoe County (President, 1990-1991) and Indiana State Bar Associations; National Association of Criminal Defense Lawyers; National School Board Attorneys Association. ***PRACTICE AREAS:*** Family Law; Criminal Law; School Law. ***Email:*** ekmoore@laszynskimoore.com

ASSOCIATE

DANIEL J. MOORE, born Lafayette, Indiana, May 3, 1977; admitted to bar, 2002, Indiana and U.S. District Court, Northern and Southern Districts of Indiana. *Education:* Indiana University (B.A., 1999; J.D., cum laude, 2002). Member: Indiana Law Journal, 2000-2002; Sherman Minton Moot Court Board, 2001-2002. Law Clerk: Indiana Attorney General's Office; Barnes & Thornburg. *Member:* Indiana State and Tippecanoe County Bar Associations. ***LANGUAGES:*** Japanese. ***PRACTICE AREAS:*** Criminal Law; Civil Litigation. ***Email:*** dmoore@laszynskimoore.com

LAYDEN & LAYDEN

Established in 1986

SUITE 712, BANK ONE BUILDING
201 MAIN STREET
P.O. BOX 909
LAFAYETTE, INDIANA 47902-0909
Telephone: 765-742-7646
Fax: 765-742-0983
Email: cmlayden@iquest.net
URL: http://www.laydenlawfirm.com

General Civil Practice. Wills and Probate, Trusts and Estates, Guardianships, Asset Protection, Estate Planning, Real Estate, Business, Business Enterprises, Personal Injury, Automobile Accidents, Wrongful Death, Insurance and Products Liability, Civil Trials.

MEMBERS OF FIRM

CHARLES MAX LAYDEN, born Lafayette, Indiana, November 10, 1941; admitted to bar, 1967, Indiana and U.S. District Court, Northern and Southern Districts of Indiana; 1970, U.S. Court of Appeals, 7th Circuit; 1986, U.S. Tax Court. *Education:* Purdue University (B.A., 1964); Indiana University (J.D., 1967). Phi Delta Phi. *Member:* Tippecanoe County (President, 1995-1996) Indiana State and American Bar Associations; Indiana Trial Lawyers Association (Director, 1982—); The Association of Trial Lawyers of America; Association of Hospital Attorneys; American Board of Trial Advocates. ***PRACTICE AREAS:*** Personal Injury; Civil Litigation; Probate and Estate Planning.

LYNN M. LAYDEN, born Minneapolis, Minnesota, June 15, 1941; admitted to bar, 1967, Indiana; U.S. District Court, Northern and Southern Districts of Indiana. *Education:* Carleton College (B.A., 1963); Indiana University (J.D., 1967). Phi Beta Kappa; Order of the Coif. Indiana Certified Mediator. *Member:* Tippecanoe County, Indiana State and American Bar Associations.

REPRESENTATIVE CLIENTS: Available Upon Request.
REFERENCE: Bank One Lafayette.

MAYFIELD & BROOKS LLC

8 NORTH THIRD STREET, SUITE 405
P.O. BOX 650
LAFAYETTE, INDIANA 47902
Telephone: 765-423-5454
Fax: 765-420-8114
Email: info@mayfieldbrooks.com
URL: http://www.mayfieldbrooks.com

Wills, Revocable Living Trusts, Irrevocable Trusts, Heath Care Documents, Living Wills, Life Insurance Trusts, Durable Powers of Attorney, Estate Planning, Probate, Estate and Trust Settlement, Real Estate, Small Business and Corporate Formation, Bankruptcy, Personal Injury, Collections.

THOMAS L. BROOKS, born Lafayette, Indiana, February 16, 1932; admitted to bar, 1959, Indiana. *Education:* Indiana University (B.S., 1954); University of Louisville (J.D., magna cum laude, 1959). Assistant Professor, Business Law, Purdue University, 1962-1999. ***PRACTICE AREAS:*** Probate; Estates; Estate Planning; Real Estate. ***Email:*** tbrooks@mayfieldbrooks.com

THOMAS L. BROOKS, JR., born Nurnberg, Germany, November 1, 1955; admitted to bar, 1992, Indiana. *Education:* Xavier University (B.S., Business Administration, 1978); Valparaiso University (J.D., 1992). Lecturer, Business Law, Purdue University, 1996—. Attorney: City of Lafayette Police Civil Service Commission; West Lafayette Police Merit Commission; Tippecanoe County CASA Program. ***PRACTICE AREAS:*** General Practice; Bankruptcy; Children. ***Email:*** tbrooksjr@mayfieldbrooks.com

OF COUNSEL

PHILLIP J. SCALETTA, JR., born Sioux City, Iowa, August 20, 1925; admitted to bar, 1950, Iowa; 1966, Indiana and U.S. Supreme Court. *Education:* Morningside College (B.S., 1948); University of Iowa College of Law (J.D., with distinction, 1950). Professor and Head, Business Law Department, Purdue University. ***PRACTICE AREAS:*** Business Law (45%); Probate (55%). ***Email:*** pscaletta@mayfieldbrooks.com

REPRESENTATIVE CLIENTS: DeFouw Chevrolet, Inc.; National Attorneys' Title Insurance Fund, Inc.
REFERENCES: Lafayette Bank & Trust Co.; NBD Bank, N.A.

LAW OFFICE OF EARL McCOY

424 COLUMBIA STREET
LAFAYETTE, INDIANA 47901
Telephone: 765-742-4394
Fax: 765-420-0407
Email: earl.mccoy@verizon.net
URL: http://earlmccoylawfirm.com

Family Law, Criminal Defense, Personal Injury.

EARL McCOY, born Torrance, California, June 13, 1969; admitted to bar, 1996, Indiana and U.S. District Court, Northern and Southern Districts of Indiana. *Education:* Purdue University (B.S., 1992); Indiana University School of Law (J.D., 1996). *Member:* Tippecanoe County and Indiana State Bar Associations. ***PRACTICE AREAS:*** Family Law; Criminal Defense; Personal Injury.

(This Listing Continued)

ASSOCIATES

LADONA E. KNIGHT, born 1973; admitted to bar, 1997, Indiana. *Education:* Boston University (B.A., 1994); Indiana University School of Law (J.D., 1997). *Member:* Indiana State and American Bar Associations. ***PRACTICE AREAS:*** Family Law; Civil Litigation; Estate Planning.

TRICIA L. THOMPSON, born Lebanon, Indiana, June 28, 1969; admitted to bar, 1994, Vermont; 1999, Indiana. *Education:* Purdue University (B.A., 1991); University of Vermont, School of Law (J.D., 1994). *Member:* Indianapolis and Indiana State Bar Associations.

REILING, TEDER & SCHRIER, LLC

Established in 1972

415 COLUMBIA STREET SUITE 3000
P.O. BOX 280
LAFAYETTE, INDIANA 47902-0280
Telephone: 765-423-5333
Fax: 765-423-4564
Email: info@reilingtederschrier.com
URL: http://www.reilingtederschrier.com

General Business, Contracts, Business Planning, Business Enterprises, Buying and Selling Businesses, Commercial and Business Litigation, Corporations, Banking Law, Business Transactions and Acquisitions, Creditor Representation, Commercial Law, Real Estate, Agriculture Law, Zoning, Wills, Trusts & Estates, Probate and Employment Law.

FIRM PROFILE: Reiling, Teder & Schrier, LLC, a preeminent law firm represented in the Martindale-Hubbell Bar Register, has provided legal services throughout Indiana since 1972. The firm serves individuals, partnerships, corporations and various other entities.

MEMBERS OF FIRM

ROBERT C. REILING, JR., born Hamilton, Ohio, March 16, 1947; admitted to bar, 1972, Indiana. *Education:* Purdue University (B.S., 1969); George Washington University (J.D., cum laude, 1972). Author: "Representing the Franchisee in Negotiating A Franchise Agreement," Franchises and Other Methods of Distribution, I.C.L.E.F., May 1982. Continuing Lecturer, Business Law, Purdue University, 1976-1987; 1999—. President, Tippecanoe County Election Board, 1988—. Chairman, Lafayette Urban Enterprise Assoc., Inc., 1997—. Chairman, Greater Lafayette Community Development Corporation, 2001—. Member, Lafayette Redevelopment Commission, 2000-2003. Attorney, West Lafayette School Corp., 2000—. *Member:* Tippecanoe County and Indiana State Bar Associations. Fellow, Indiana Bar Foundation. ***PRACTICE AREAS:*** Commercial Law; Corporate Law; School Law; Business Transactions and Acquisitions; Estate Planning. ***Email:*** rcr@rtslawfirm.com

DANIEL A. TEDER, born Vallejo, California, August 22, 1946; admitted to bar, 1972, Indiana; 1973, U.S. District Court, Northern and Southern Districts of Indiana. *Education:* Purdue University (B.S., 1968); Indiana University (J.D., 1972). Phi Delta Phi. Visiting Lecturer, Business Law, Purdue University, 1977-1981. Deputy Prosecuting Attorney, 1973-1975. Attorney, City of West Lafayette, 1980-1987. Attorney, West Lafayette Economic Development Commission, 1980-1986. Member, Lafayette Redevelopment Commission, 1994—. *Member:* Tippecanoe County and Indiana State (Member: Probate, Trust, and Real Estate Sections) Bar Associations; Fellow, Indiana Bar Foundation. ***PRACTICE AREAS:*** Real Estate Law; Probate Law; Zoning; Corporate Law; Estate Planning. ***Email:*** dat@rtslawfirm.com

JAMES R. SCHRIER, born Crawfordsville, Indiana, 1952; admitted to bar, 1988, Indiana; U.S. District Court, Northern and Southern Districts of Indiana; U.S. Court of Appeals, Seventh Circuit. *Education:* Purdue University (B.S., 1974); Indiana University School of Law, Indianapolis (J.D., cum laude, 1988). Associate Editor, Indiana Law Review, 1987-1988. Lecturer, Business Law, Purdue University, 1998-1999. Registered Civil Mediator. *Member:* Tippecanoe County, Indiana State and American Bar Associations; Commercial Law League of America. ***PRACTICE AREAS:*** Business Litigation; Bankruptcy; Commercial Law; Agricultural Law; Corporate Law; Estate Planning. ***Email:*** jrs@rtslawfirm.com

ASSOCIATES

WAYNE T. SZULKOWSKI, born Chicago, Illinois, 1969; admitted to bar, 1997, Illinois; 2003, Indiana, U.S. District Court Northern District of Illinois; 2004, U.S. District Court Northern District of Indiana. *Education:* Purdue University (B.S., 1991); John Marshall Law School (J.D., 1997). *Member:* Tippecanoe County, Indiana State and American Bar Associations. ***PRACTICE AREAS:*** Business Litigation; Corporate Law; Commercial Law; Real Estate. ***Email:*** wts@rtslawfirm.com

KEVIN J. RILEY, born Lafayette, Indiana, September 17, 1974; admitted to bar, 2002, Tennessee; 2004, Indiana, U.S. District Court, Northern District of Indiana. *Education:* Purdue University (B.A., 1997); University of Tennessee (J.D., 2002). Law Clerk, Honorable W. Frank Crawford, Presiding Judge, Western Section, Tennessee Court of Appeals, 2002-2004. ***PRACTICE AREAS:*** Business Law; Commercial Law; Corporate Law; Education Law. ***Email:*** kjr@rtslawfirm.com

OF COUNSEL

WILLIAM BONSIGNORE, born Elmira, New York, November 24, 1958; admitted to bar, 1983, Indiana; 1993, North Carolina. *Education:* State University of New York at Fredonia (B.S., magna cum laude 1980); Union University Albany Law School (J.D., 1983). ***PRACTICE AREAS:*** Taxation; Business Transactions; Business Acquisitions; Corporate Law. ***Email:*** wb@rtslawfirm.com

REPRESENTATIVE CLIENTS: Salin Bank; Oscar Winski Inc.; Ace Industries; Irvin's Concrete Products, Inc.; Irvin's Interstate Brick and Block Co., Inc. of Indianapolis; Stetler's Chevrolet and Cadillac; Physicians Homecare, Inc.; Advantage Title Company; Coyote Crossing Golf Course; Dilling Mechanical Contractors, Inc.; Lafayette Eye Center; Industrial

(This Listing Continued)

REILING, TEDER & SCHRIER, LLC, Lafayette—Continued

Federal Credit Union; Lafayette Ambulatory Surgery Center; Dome Systems, Inc.; Smith Office Supply; West Lafayette School Corp.; State Bank of Oxford; Lafayette Bank and Trust; Leming Supply, Inc.; Purdy Materials, Inc.; Huth Thompson, LLP; Hydro Conduit Corp. APPROVED ATTORNEYS FOR: National Attorneys Title Assurance Fund, Inc. References: Bank One of Lafayette; Salin Bank; Huntington Bank; Regions Bank; Lafayette Bank and Trust.

SEEGER, HODSON & FORBES

106 NORTH 9TH STREET
P.O. BOX 878
LAFAYETTE, INDIANA 47902
Telephone: 765-742-4529
Fax: 765-742-6445
URL: http://www.shf-law.net
URL: http://www.lawyers.com/seeger-forbes

Estates, Estate Planning, Trusts, Trust Planning, Trust Administration, Living Trusts, Wills, Living Wills, Guardianship, Medicaid Planning, Probate Administration, Business Law, Limited Liability Partnerships, Corporations, Business Transactions, Collections, Creditors Rights, Real Estate, Contracts, Civil Litigation, Trial Practice, Tort Liability, Personal Injury, Automobile Accidents, Medical Malpractice, Elder Law, Health Care Law, Wrongful Death, Federal Litigation, Corporate Litigation, Commercial Litigation.

JAY T. SEEGER, born Lafayette, Indiana, June 11, 1952; admitted to bar, 1978, Indiana and U.S. District Court, Southern and Northern Districts of Indiana; 1980, U.S. Court of Appeals, Seventh Circuit; 1983, U.S. Supreme Court; 1999, Florida. *Education:* Purdue University (B.S., 1974); Indiana University (J.D., cum laude, 1978). Author: "The Liability of Purveyors of Alcoholic Beverages in Indiana," Auto Accidents - Non-Driver Liability, Indiana Continuing Legal Education Forum. *Member:* Tippecanoe County, Indiana State and American Bar Associations; The Florida Bar; The Association of Trial Lawyers of America; Indiana Trial Lawyers Association. ***PRACTICE AREAS:*** Trusts and Estates; Business Law; Litigation; Real Estate. ***Email:*** jay@shf-law.net

JAMES T. HODSON, born Muncie, Indiana, February 21, 1954; admitted to bar, 1982, Indiana. *Education:* Purdue University (B.S., with distinction, 1976); Valparaiso University (J.D., 1982). Beta Gamma Sigma. *Member:* Tippecanoe County, Indiana State and American Bar Associations. ***PRACTICE AREAS:*** Creditors Rights Law; Bankruptcy Law; Commercial Law.

RODNEY E. FORBES, born Huntington, Indiana, March 27, 1964; admitted to bar, 1990, Indiana and U.S. District Court, Southern and Northern Districts of Indiana; 1995, Illinois and U.S. District Court, Northern, Central and Southern Districts of Illinois. *Education:* Indiana University (B.A., 1986; J.D., 1989). *Member:* Tippecanoe County, Illinois State and Indiana State Bar Associations; The Association of Trial Lawyers of America; Indiana Trial Lawyers Association; Illinois Trial Lawyers Association. ***PRACTICE AREAS:*** Civil Litigation; Personal Injury; Medical Malpractice; Products Liability. ***Email:*** rod@shf-law.net

STUART & BRANIGIN LLP

Established in 1878

THE LIFE BUILDING
300 MAIN STREET, SUITE 900
P.O. BOX 1010
LAFAYETTE, INDIANA 47902-1010
Telephone: 765-423-1561
Telecopier: 765-742-8175
Email: sb@stuartlaw.com
URL: http://www.stuartlaw.com

Indianapolis, Indiana Office: Suite 640, 8888 Keystone Crossing, 46240. Telephone: 317-574-7245. Fax: 317-574-7050.

General Practice. Trials and Appeals. Administrative, Banking, Commercial, Computer, Construction, Copyright and Trademark, Corporation, Creditors' Rights, Education, Environmental, Hospital and Health Care, Insurance, Labor and Employment, Pension, Mergers, Acquisitions and Divestitures, Wills and Probate, Trusts and Estates, Estate Planning, Products Liability, Railroad, Real Estate, Securities, Taxation, Utility and Zoning Law.

FIRM PROFILE: Stuart & Branigin LLP, one of the oldest law firms in Indiana, had its origin in Lafayette, Indiana, in 1878, and today consists of over 30 lawyers who graduated from nine different law schools. Our firm members over the years have included two former justices of the Indiana Supreme Court, one governor of the state of Indiana, and four presidents of the Indiana State Bar Association. Stuart & Branigin LLP serves the entire state and represents national clients throughout the United States. The firm encourages its members to participate actively in legal education seminars, professional association activities and civic affairs.

MEMBERS OF FIRM

ALLISON ELLSWORTH STUART (1886-1950)

ROGER D. BRANIGIN (1902-1975)

THOMAS R. McCULLY, born Rushville, Indiana, March 10, 1941; admitted to bar, 1966, Indiana. *Education:* Wabash College (A.B., 1963); Indiana University (J.D., with distinction, 1966). Phi Delta Phi; Blue Key. Recipient, Pro Bono Publico Award, Indiana Bar Foundation, 1995. Member, Board of Visitors, Indiana University Law School, Bloomington, 1994—. President, Alumni Association, 1996. Member of Staff, Indiana Law Journal, 1964-1965. Listed, The Best Lawyers in America, 1989—. *Member:* Tippecanoe County (President, 1991), Indiana State (Chair, Land Use and Zoning Section, 1992-1994) and American Bar Associations; American Health Lawyers Association. Master Fellow, Indiana Bar Foundation. ***PRACTICE AREAS:*** Real Estate Law; Zoning Law; Health Care Law; Labor and Employment Law. ***Email:*** trm@stuartlaw.com

LARRY R. FISHER, born Marion, Indiana, September 29, 1939; admitted to bar, 1968, Indiana. *Education:* Indiana University (B.S., 1965; J.D., 1968). Beta Gamma Sigma; Phi Alpha Delta. Member, Indiana Law Journal, 1966-1968. *Member:* Tippecanoe County, The Indiana State and American Bar Associations; Indiana Defense Lawyers Association (President, 1985; Member of Board, 1979-1991; Diplomat); Bar Association of the Seventh Federal Circuit; Association of Defense Trial Attorneys (Executive Council, 1998-2001). Fellow: American College of Trial Lawyers; Indiana Bar Foundation. ***PRACTICE AREAS:*** Professional Malpractice Litigation; Products Liability; Toxic Torts; Civil Litigation; Health Care Law. ***Email:*** lrf@stuartlaw.com

NINA B. KIRKPATRICK, born Lafayette, Indiana, October 29, 1942; admitted to bar, 1975, Wisconsin and Indiana. *Education:* Purdue University (B.S., 1964); Miami University (M.S., 1966); University of Wisconsin-Madison (J.D., with honors, 1975). *Member:* Tippecanoe County, Indiana State and American Bar Associations; State Bar of Wisconsin. Fellow, Indiana Bar Foundation. ***PRACTICE AREAS:*** Health Care Law; Real Estate Law; Estate Planning and Administration Law. ***Email:*** nbk@stuartlaw.com

MARK LILLIANFELD, born Brooklyn, New York, February 22, 1949; admitted to bar, 1974, Indiana. *Education:* State University of New York at Stony Brook (B.A., cum laude, 1970); Indiana University (J.D., cum laude, 1974); New York University (LL.M., Taxation, 1975). *Member:* Tippecanoe County, Indiana State and American Bar Associations. ***PRACTICE AREAS:*** Federal and State Taxation Law; Employee Benefit Plans Law; Estate Planning Law. ***Email:*** mil@stuartlaw.com

STEPHEN R. PENNELL, born Cheyenne, Wyoming, April 7, 1952; admitted to bar, 1976, Indiana. *Education:* Indiana University (A.B., summa cum laude, 1973; J.D., magna cum laude, 1976). Phi Beta Kappa; Order of the Coif. Recipient, American Jurisprudence Prize Award, 1976. Note Editor, Indiana Law Journal, 1975-1976. *Member:* Tippecanoe County, Indiana State (Chairman, Litigation Section, 2004) and American Bar Associations; Bar Association of the Seventh Federal Circuit; Defense Trial Counsel of Indiana (President 2004; Member, Board of Directors); Defense Research Institute; Indiana State Representative (Member, 1998-2000); Association of Defense Trial Attorneys. ***PRACTICE AREAS:*** Civil Litigation; Insurance Law; Products Liability; Appellate Practice. ***Email:*** srp@stuartlaw.com

ANTHONY S. BENTON, born Decatur, Illinois, January 28, 1949; admitted to bar, 1976, Indiana and Illinois. *Education:* University of Illinois (B.A., with honors, 1971); Indiana University (J.D., summa cum laude, 1976). Phi Alpha Delta. Legal Counsel to The Trustees of Purdue University. *Member:* Tippecanoe County, Indiana State, Illinois State and American Bar Associations; American Judicature Society; National Association of Railroad Trial Counsel; National Association of College and University Attorneys. Fellow, Indiana Bar Foundation; American Bar Foundation. ***PRACTICE AREAS:*** Education Law; Environmental Law; Employment Law. ***Email:*** asb@stuartlaw.com

ERIK D. SPYKMAN, born Amsterdam, Netherlands, November 4, 1954; admitted to bar, 1980, Indiana; 1981, Michigan. *Education:* Calvin College (B.A., 1977); University of Notre Dame (J.D., 1980). Director, Indiana Continuing Legal Education Forum, 1987-1993. *Member:* Tippecanoe County, Indiana State and American Bar Associations; State Bar of Michigan. Fellow: Indiana Bar Foundation. ***LANGUAGES:*** German. ***PRACTICE AREAS:*** Corporate Law; Business Law; Mergers and Acquisitions; Estate Planning; Trusts and Estates; Business Succession Planning. ***Email:*** eds@stuartlaw.com

WILLIAM E. EMERICK, born Peoria, Illinois, August 4, 1950; admitted to bar, 1977, California; 1978, Indiana and Illinois. *Education:* University of Illinois (A.B., 1972); University of San Fernando Valley (J.D., 1977). Delta Theta Phi. Deputy Prosecuting Attorney, Tippecanoe County, Indiana, 1978-1981. Chief Deputy Prosecuting Attorney, 1980-1981. Adjunct Instructor, Purdue University. *Member:* Tippecanoe County, Illinois State, Indiana State and American Bar Associations; State Bar of California; The Association of Trial Lawyers of America; National Association of College and University Attorneys. Master Fellow, Indiana Bar Foundation. ***PRACTICE AREAS:*** Civil and Criminal Litigation. ***Email:*** wee@stuartlaw.com

JOHN C. DUFFEY, born Burnettsville, Indiana, September 8, 1956; admitted to bar, 1982, Indiana; 1995, Illinois, U.S. District Court, Northern and Southern Districts of Indiana, U.S. District Court, Central and Northern Districts of Illinois including Trial Bar and U.S. Court of Appeals, Southern Seventh Circuit; 2004, Ohio. *Education:* Franklin College (B.A., 1979); Georgetown University (J.D., 1982). Fellow, American College of Trial Lawyers. ***PRACTICE AREAS:*** Litigation; Railroad Litigation. ***Email:*** jcd@stuartlaw.com

BRUCE McSPADDEN, born Wabash, Indiana, July 5, 1951; admitted to bar, 1982, Indiana. *Education:* University of Idaho (B.S., summa cum laude, 1974); Indiana University (J.D., summa cum laude, 1982). Order of the Coif. Assistant General Counsel, Great Lakes Chemical Corporation, 1990-1997. *Member:* Tippecanoe County, Indiana State (Council Member, Business Law Section, 1998—) and American Bar Associations; American Society of International Law. ***PRACTICE AREAS:*** Corporate Law; Business; Mergers, Acquisitions and Divestitures; Insurance Coverage. ***Email:*** blm@stuartlaw.com

MARK E. DeYOUNG, born Lafayette, Indiana, December 13, 1956; admitted to bar, 1983, Indiana. *Education:* Calvin College; Purdue University; Indiana University (B.A., 1980; J.D., summa cum laude, 1983). Phi Alpha Delta. Member, Indiana Law Review, 1982-1983. *Member:* Tippecanoe County and Indiana State Bar Associations. ***PRACTICE AREAS:*** Real Estate Law; Business Organizations; Commercial Litigation; Estate Planning; Education Law. ***Email:*** med@stuartlaw.com

THOMAS B. PARENT, born Manchester, New Hampshire, January 16, 1960; admitted to bar, 1986, Indiana. *Education:* Purdue University (B.S., with highest distinction, 1982); Indiana University School of Law (J.D., magna cum laude, 1986). Beta Gamma Sigma; Order of the Coif. Administrative Editor, Indiana Law Journal, 1985-1986. Assistant Legal Counsel to the Trustees of Purdue University. *Member:* Tippecanoe County, Indiana State and American Bar Associations; National Association of College and University Attorneys American Health Lawyers Association. ***PRACTICE AREAS:*** Corporate Law; Mergers and Acquisitions; Estate Planning Law; Intellectual Property Law; Education Law. ***Email:*** tbp@stuartlaw.com

(This Listing Continued)

KEVIN D. NICOSON, born Brazil, Indiana, January 27, 1963; admitted to bar, 1988, Indiana. *Education:* Indiana University (B.A., 1985; J.D., magna cum laude, 1988). Recipient: American Jurisprudence Awards, Remedies; Land Use Control. Associate, Indiana Law Journal, 1987-1988. *Member:* Tippecanoe County, Indiana State (Former Chairman, Bankruptcy and Creditors' Rights Section, 2003-2004) and American Bar Associations; American Bankruptcy Institute; Commercial Law League of America. ***PRACTICE AREAS:*** Banking Law; Creditors Rights Law; Commercial Litigation. **Email:** kdn@stuartlaw.com

SUSAN K. ROBERTS, born Gary, Indiana, February 28, 1959; admitted to bar, 1986, Indiana, U.S. Court of Appeals, Seventh Circuit and U.S. District Court, Northern and Southern Districts of Indiana. *Education:* Indiana University (B.S., with distinction, 1981; J.D., 1986). Beta Alpha Psi; Beta Gamma Sigma. Law Clerk to the Honorable Paul H. Buchanan, Jr., Chief Judge, Court of Appeals of Indiana, 1986-1988. Indiana High School Mock Trial Association (President, 1993—). *Member:* Tippecanoe County, Indiana State, Seventh Circuit and American Bar Associations; Defense Trial Counsel of Indiana; American Bankruptcy Institute; National Association of College and University Attorneys. Fellow, Indiana Bar Foundation. ***PRACTICE AREAS:*** Commercial Litigation; Creditors Rights Law; Insurance Defense Law; Accountants Malpractice. **Email:** skr@stuartlaw.com

JOHN M. STUCKEY, born Lafayette, Indiana, August 9, 1964; admitted to bar, 1989, Indiana, U.S. Court of Appeals, Seventh Circuit, and U.S. District Court, Northern and Southern Districts of Indiana. *Education:* Purdue University (B.A., 1986); College of William and Mary (J.D., 1989). Member, William and Mary Law Review, 1988-1989. *Member:* Tippecanoe County, Indiana State and American Bar Associations; Defense Research Institute; Defense Trial Counsel of Indiana; National Association of Railroad Trial Counsel. Fellow: Indiana Bar Foundation. (Also at Indianapolis Office). ***PRACTICE AREAS:*** Construction Law; Commercial Litigation; Civil Litigation. **Email:** jms@stuartlaw.com

DEBORAH B. TRICE, born Lafayette, Indiana, April 20, 1963; admitted to bar, 1990, Indiana, U.S. District Court, Northern and Southern Districts of Indiana, U.S. District Court, Central District of Illinois and U.S. Court of Appeals, Seventh Circuit. *Education:* Purdue University (B.A., with distinction, 1985); Indiana University School of Law - Indianapolis (J.D., 1989). Associate Editor, Indiana Law Review, 1988-1989. *Member:* Tippecanoe County, Indiana State, Seventh Circuit and American Bar Associations; National Association of College and University Attorneys; Defense Research Institute; Defense Trial Counsel of Indiana. Fellow: Indiana Bar Foundation. ***PRACTICE AREAS:*** Employment Law; College and University Law; Administrative Law. **Email:** dbt@stuartlaw.com

WILLIAM P. KEALEY, born Elkhorn, Wisconsin, 1963; admitted to bar, 1989, California; 1991, District of Columbia; 1996, Indiana. *Education:* Harvard University (B.A., magna cum laude, 1985); Cambridge University (M.Phil., 1987); Stanford University (J.D., 1989). Truman Scholar. Henry Fellow. ***PRACTICE AREAS:*** Commercial Litigation; Intellectual Property; Technology Law; Environmental Law. **Email:** wpk@stuartlaw.com

DAVID A. STARKWEATHER, born Grand Rapids, Michigan, August 17, 1967; admitted to bar, 1992, Indiana, U.S. District Court, Northern and Southern Districts of Indiana, U.S. District Court, Western District of Michigan, U.S. Court of Appeals, Seventh Circuit. *Education:* Wheaton College (B.A., 1989); Indiana University School of Law - Bloomington (J.D., magna cum laude, 1992). Order of the Coif. Managing Editor, Indiana Law Journal. *Member:* Tippecanoe County, Indiana State and American Bar Associations; Defense Trial Counsel of Indiana; Defense Research Institute; National Association of Railroad Trial Counsel. ***PRACTICE AREAS:*** Products Liability; Commercial Litigation; General Civil Litigation; Corporate; Insurance Defense; Railroad Litigation. **Email:** das@stuartlaw.com

MARIANNE MITTEN OWEN, born Indianapolis, Indiana, January 3, 1964; admitted to bar, 1991, Indiana, U.S. District Court, Northern and Southern Districts of Indiana. *Education:* Wellesley College (B.A., 1986); Indiana University School of Law - Bloomington (J.D., 1991). Delta Theta Phi. Real Estate Broker, Indiana, 1985-1997. *Member:* Tippecanoe County (Treasurer, 1993-1994), Indiana State (Chair, Young Lawyers Section, 2001-2002) and American Bar Associations. Fellow, Indiana Bar Foundation. ***PRACTICE AREAS:*** Real Estate; Land Use; Zoning; Business Law; Commercial Finance. **Email:** mmo@stuartlaw.com

KAREN R. ORR, born Danville, Illinois, July 31, 1963; admitted to bar, 1989, Indiana, U.S. District Court, Northern and Southern Districts of Indiana; 1997, U.S. Court of Appeals, Seventh Circuit and U.S. Supreme Court. *Education:* Indiana University (B.A., 1985); Indiana University School of Law - Indianapolis (J.D., cum laude, 1989). Phi Beta Kappa. Associate Editor, Indiana Law Review, 1988-1989. Law Clerk, Honorable Patrick D. Sullivan, Indiana Court of Appeals. *Member:* Tippecanoe County, Indiana State and American Bar Associations; American Health Lawyers' Association. Fellow: Indiana Bar Foundation. ***PRACTICE AREAS:*** Business Transactions; Health Care Law; Education Law. **Email:** kro@stuartlaw.com

DAVID A. LOCKE, born Anderson, Indiana, March 8, 1957; admitted to bar, 1995, Indiana, U.S. District Court, Northern and Southern Districts of Indiana; 1996, U.S. Court of Appeals, Seventh Circuit; 2005, U.S. Supreme Court. *Education:* Butler University (B.A., 1992); Indiana University School of Law - Bloomington (J.D., 1995). Editor-in-Chief, Indiana Law Journal, 1994-1995. Law Clerk, Honorable Allen Sharp, Chief Judge, U.S. District Court, Northern District of Indiana, 1995-1997. Author: "Counterspeech as an Alternative to Prohibition: Proposed Federal Regulation of Tobacco Promotion in American Motorsport," 70 Ind. L.J. 217 (1994). *Member:* Tippecanoe County, Indiana State (Council Member, Appellate Practice Section, 2004—) and American Bar Associations; Bar Association of the Seventh Federal Circuit; Defense Trial Counsel of Indiana; Defense Research Institute; National Association of Railroad Trial Counsel. ***PRACTICE AREAS:*** Railroad Litigation; Appellate Practice. **Email:** dal@stuartlaw.com

BARRY L. LOFTUS, born Euclid, Ohio, February 16, 1963; admitted to bar, 1998, Indiana and U.S. District Court, Northern and Southern Districts of Indiana. *Education:* University of Maryland; Marquette University (B.A., 1985); Indiana University School of Law - Indianapolis (J.D., cum laude, 1998). Author: "Seminole Tribe and Superfund: A Federalism Gamble," 31 Ind. L. Rev. 183 (1998). *Member:* Tippecanoe County, Indiana State and American Bar Associations; Defense Research Institute; Defense Trial Counsel of Indiana; National Association of Railroad Trial Counsel; National Association of College and University Attorneys. ***PRACTICE AREAS:*** Litigation; Business Transactions; Estate Planning. **Email:** bll@stuartlaw.com

SENIOR COUNSEL

RUSSELL H. HART, born Chicago, Illinois, May 1, 1928; admitted to bar, 1956, Indiana. *Education:* DePauw University (A.B., 1950); Indiana University School of Law - Bloomington (J.D., 1956). Phi Delta Phi; Order of the Coif. Senior Associate Editor, Indiana Law Journal, 1955-1956. *Member:* Tippecanoe County, Indiana State (President, 1987-1988) and American Bar Associations; Defense Trial Counsel of Indiana; National Association of Railroad Trial Counsel (President, 1995-1996). Fellow: American College of Trial Lawyers; International Academy of Trial Lawyers; International Society of Barristers; Indiana Bar Foundation; American Bar Foundation; Indiana University School of Law, Academy of Law Alumni, 1997. ***PRACTICE AREAS:*** Railroad Litigation; Toxic Tort Litigation; Commercial Litigation; Insurance Litigation. **Email:** rhh@stuartlaw.com

COUNSEL

JAMES V. McGLONE, born Terre Haute, Indiana, December 31, 1932; admitted to bar, 1964, Indiana. *Education:* Purdue University (B.S., 1955); Indiana University School of Law - Bloomington (J.D., with high distinction, 1964). Order of the Coif. Member, Board of Editors, Indiana Law Journal, 1962-1964. *Member:* Tippecanoe County, Indiana State and American Bar Associations; Bar Association of the Seventh Federal Circuit; Indiana Defense Lawyers Association (Member of Board, 1978; Diplomat). Fellow, American College of Trial Lawyers. ***PRACTICE AREAS:*** Insurance Defense Litigation; Products Liability Litigation; Commercial Litigation. **Email:** jvm@stuartlaw.com

THOMAS L. RYAN, born Cincinnati, Ohio, January 29, 1929; admitted to bar, 1958, Indiana. *Education:* Indiana University (B.S., 1951; J.D., with high distinction, 1958). Order of the Coif. Articles and Book Review Editor, Indiana Law Journal, 1957-1958. Former Counsel to The Trustees of Purdue University. *Member:* Tippecanoe County, Indiana State and American Bar Associations; National Association of College and University Attorneys. Fellow, Indiana Bar Foundation. ***PRACTICE AREAS:*** Education Law; Corporate Law; Banking Law; Creditors Rights Law. **Email:** tlr@stuartlaw.com

ASSOCIATES

TRENTEN D. KLINGERMAN, born Plymouth, Indiana, May 22, 1971; admitted to bar, 2001, Indiana and U.S. District Court, Northern and Southern Districts of Indiana. *Education:* Purdue University (B.S., 1994); Indiana University School of Law (J.D., 2001). Recipient: Glenn D. Peters Scholarship; Lila B. Louden Scholarship; Class of 1998 Scholarship. Managing Editor, Indiana Law Journal, 2000-2001. *Member:* Tippecanoe County (Secretary 2005-2006), Indiana State and American Bar Associations; Defense Trial Counsel of Indiana; National Association of College and University Attorneys. **Email:** tdk@stuartlaw.com

SHANNON A. MIDDLETON, born Danville, Illinois, September 20, 1975; admitted to bar, 2002, Indiana. *Education:* Purdue University (B.S., 1998); Indiana University (J.D., 2002). Notes Editor, Indiana International and Comparative Law Review, 2001-2002. Author: "Women's Rights Unveiled: Taliban's Treatment of Women in Afghanistan," Indiana International & Comparative Law Review, Vol. 11, No. 2. *Member:* Tippecanoe County, Indiana State and American Bar Associations. ***PRACTICE AREAS:*** Business Transactions. **Email:** sam@stuartlaw.com

K. CAMPBELL WHITE, born Danville, Illinois, March 12, 1977; admitted to bar, 2003, Indiana, U.S. District Court, Northern and Southern Districts of Indiana. *Education:* Purdue University (B.S.B.A., 2000); Indiana University (J.D., 2003). Order of the Coif. Managing Editor, Indiana Law Journal, 2002-2003. *Member:* Tippecanoe County, Indiana State and American Bar Associations; Defense Trial Counsel of Indiana. ***LANGUAGES:*** French. ***PRACTICE AREAS:*** Business Transactions; Civil Litigation.

SARAH N. SNOEBERGER, born Lafayette, Indiana, April 21, 1977; admitted to bar, 2002, Indiana; 2004, U.S. District Court, Northern and Southern Districts of Indiana. *Education:* Purdue University (B.S., with highest distinction, 1999); Indiana University School of Law (J.D., cum laude, 2002). Executive Articles Editor, Indiana Law Review, Vol. 35, 2001-2002. ***LANGUAGES:*** Spanish. ***PRACTICE AREAS:*** Civil Litigation.

MARGARETT A. WYATT, born Elkhart, Indiana, April 3, 1974; admitted to bar, 2005, Indiana, U.S. District Court Northern and Southern Districts of Indiana and U.S. Tax Court. *Education:* San Jose State University (B.A., 1998); Tulane Law School (J.D., 2003); New York University, School of Law (LL.M., Taxation, 2004). *Member:* Tippecanoe County, Indiana State and American Bar Associations. ***PRACTICE AREAS:*** Taxation; Business Transactions; Trusts and Estates. **Email:** maw@stuartlaw.com

GENERAL COUNSEL FOR: Lafayette Savings Bank; North Central Health Services, Inc.; Purdue Research Foundation; Purdue University; Tippecanoe School Corp.
STATE COUNSEL FOR: Norfolk Southern Railway Co.; CSX Transportation, Inc.; Canadian Pacific Railway.
REPRESENTATIVE CLIENTS: Advanced Process Cominatorics, Inc.; Aluminum Company of America; Amoco Oil Co.; BioLab, Inc.; Camico Mutual Insurance Company; Caterpillar Tractor Co.; Cinergy; DPIC Companies; DiscoverRe; The Egyptian Lacquer Manufacturing Co.; Eli Lilly & Co.; Fairfield Manufacturing Co., Inc.; Fifth Third Bank; GAB Business Services, Inc.; Gerling America Insurance Company; Great Lakes Chemical Corp.; Greater Lafayette Health Services, Inc.; Indiana Lumbermens Mutual Insurance Co.; The Indiana Railroad Co.; Kettelhut Construction, Inc.; Kirby Risk Corporation; Lafayette Instrument Company, Inc.; Lafayette Life Insurance Company; Lafayette Savings Bank; Lafayette Venetian Blind, Inc.; Leffler Industries, Inc.; National Railroad Passenger Corp.; Nissan Chemical America Corp.; Perry Chemical & Manufacturing Company, Inc.; Regions Bank; Roman Catholic Diocese of Lafayette-in-Indiana; Sisters of St. Francis Hospital Service; Tippecanoe Community Health Clinic; Wabash Valley Hospital, Inc.; West Bend Mutual Insurance Co.

ANTHONY F. TAVITAS ATTORNEYS AT LAW

A PROFESSIONAL CORPORATION

LAFAYETTE, INDIANA

(See Munster)

Insurance Defense, Trial Practice, Personal Injury, Insurance Coverage, Workers Compensation.

TRUITT & RAY LLP

Established in 1991

324 MAIN STREET, SUITE C

P.O. BOX 711

LAFAYETTE, INDIANA 47902

Telephone: 765-742-7040

Facsimile: 765-429-5591

URL: http://www.truittraylaw.com

URL: http://www.truittraylawfirm.com

Civil Litigation in all State and Federal Courts, Trials and Appeals, Wills, Trusts and Estates, Probate and Estate Planning, Corporation and Business Law, Personal Injury, Automobile Accidents, Wrongful Death, Collections, Family Law, Adoptions, Divorce, Child Custody, Child Support, Real Estate.

FIRM PROFILE: A Tippecanoe County law firm located in Lafayette, Indiana providing general legal services in the areas of estate planning and administration, business and corporate law, real estate, family law, collections, personal injury and general litigation.

PARTNERS OF FIRM

PATRICIA PEYTON TRUITT, born Lafayette, Indiana, April 26, 1939; admitted to bar, 1979, Indiana; 1983, U.S. Supreme Court; 1984, U.S. Court of Appeals, Seventh Circuit; U.S. District Court, Northern and Southern Districts of Indiana. *Education:* Duke University (B.A., 1961); Purdue University (M.A., 1963); Indiana University (J.D., cum laude, 1979). Phi Delta Phi. Note and Development Editor, Indiana Law Review, 1978-1979. National Finalist, American Bar Association National Appellate Advocacy Competition, 1977. Indiana Super Lawyers, 2004, 2005. *Member:* Tippecanoe County (Treasurer), Indiana State (Board of Governors, House of Delegates, Chair, Honors and Necrology; Chair, General Practice, Solo and Small Firm Section; Member: Probate, Trust and Real Property, Family, GP Solo and Small Firms, Elderlaw Sections) and American Bar Associations. Indiana Bar Foundation (President; Fellow). ***PRACTICE AREAS:*** Estate Planning & Probate; Business & Corporate Law; Real Estate Law.

ROD A. RAY, born Greencastle, Indiana, August 14, 1953; admitted to bar, 1980, Indiana and U.S. District Court, Southern District of Indiana; 1981, U.S. District Court, Northern District of Indiana. *Education:* Purdue University (B.S., 1975); Pepperdine University (J.D., 1980). Phi Alpha Delta. Member, Moot Court Board. *Member:* Tippecanoe County and Indiana State Bar Associations; Indiana Trial Lawyers Association. ***PRACTICE AREAS:*** Probate and Estate Planning; Business and Corporate Law; Family Law; Personal Injury; Collections.

THOMAS D. SARVER, born Crawfordsville, Indiana, 1977; admitted to bar, 2004, Indiana, U.S. District Court, Northern and Southern Districts of Indiana. *Education:* Wabash College (B.A., summa cum laude, with honors, 1999); Drake University (M.A., 2003; J.D., 2003). *Member:* Montgomery County, Indiana State and American Bar Associations; Indiana Trial Lawyers Association. ***PRACTICE AREAS:*** Administrative Law; Agricultural Law; Food and Agriculture; Broadcast Applications; Broadcast Licensing; Broadcast Regulation; Broadcast Television; Cable TV; FCC Regulation; Mass Media Law; Media and First Amendment; Education Law; Entertainment Law; General Practice; County Government Law; Government; Federal Legislative Practice; Government Affairs; Government Relations; Governmental Law; Legislative Practice; Local Government Relations; Public Policy; State Government Law; State Legislative Practice; Real Property; Landlord and Tenant Law.

REPRESENTATIVE CLIENTS: Radian Research, Inc.; HemoCleanse, Inc.; Greater Lafayette Health Services, Inc.; Grace United Methodist Church of Lafayette, Inc.; Covenant Presbyterian Church, Inc.; St. Elizabeth Healthcare Center; State Auto Insurance Companies; Ash Access Technology Inc.
References Available Upon Request.

WITHERED, CORRIGAN & BURNS, LLP

8 NORTH THIRD STREET, SUITE 401

P.O. BOX 499

LAFAYETTE, INDIANA 47902-0499

Telephone: 765-742-1988

Fax: 765-742-8774

Email: info@witheredlaw.com

URL: http://www.witheredlaw.com

Civil Litigation and Appellate Practice, Personal Injury, Medical Malpractice, Workers Compensation, Family Law, Adoptions, Wills, Trusts and Estates.

FIRM PROFILE: The firm primarily engages in trial and appellate practice, representing individuals, small businesses and others throughout central Indiana. The firm is listed in the Bar Register of Preeminent Lawyers.

JEROME L. WITHERED, born Batesville, Indiana, August 5, 1951; admitted to bar, 1980, Indiana and U.S. District Court, Southern and Northern Districts of Indiana; U.S. Supreme Court; U.S. Court of Appeals, Seventh Circuit. *Education:* Purdue University

(This Listing Continued)

(B.S., 1973); University of Virginia (M.A., 1976); Indiana University (J.D., summa cum laude, 1980). Co-Author: "Civil Trial Practice," West's Indiana Practice, Vols. 21 and 22, 1996. Visiting Lecturer, Business Law, Purdue University, 1981-1983. Law Clerk to Chief Justice Richard M. Givan, Indiana Supreme Court, 1977-1979. Deputy Public Defender, Tippecanoe County, 1980-1981. Member, 1982-1997, Secretary, 1985-1986, President, 1986-1988 and Treasurer, 1988-1992, Indiana State Board of Law Examiners. Chairman, Tippecanoe County Republican Party, 1989-1991. Board of Trustees, Tippecanoe County Public Library, 1997—. *Member:* Tippecanoe County, Indiana State (Board of Governors, 1994-1996) and American Bar Associations; Indiana Trial Lawyers Association; The Association of Trial Lawyers of America. Master Fellow, Indiana Bar Foundation (Director, 1990-1994). (Certified as a Civil Trial Advocate by the National Board of Trial Advocacy). ***REPORTED CASES:*** Drake Ins. Co. v. Carroll Co. Sheriff's Dept, 427 N.E.2d 1153 (Ind.App. 1981); Fuston v. Nat'l Mutual Ins. Co., 440 N.E.2d 751 (Ind.App. 1982); Williams v. Lafayette Production Credit Ass'n, 508 N.E.2d 579 (Ind.App. 1987); Village Furniture, Inc. v. Associated Ins. Managers, Inc., 541 N.E.2d 306 (Ind.App. 1989); Ingersoll-Rand Corp. v. Scott, 557 N.E.2d 679 (Ind.App. 1990); Foster v. Purdue Univ. Chapter, Beta Theta Pi, 567 N.E.2d 865 (Ind.App. 1991); Dible v. City of Lafayette, 713 N.E.2d 269 (Ind. 1999); Doe v. City of Lafayette, 377 F.3d 757 (7th Cir. 2004). ***PRACTICE AREAS:*** Litigation; Personal Injury; Business Law; Corporate Law. ***Email:*** jwithered@witheredlaw.com

CHRISTOPHER D. CORRIGAN, born Osage, Iowa, February 3, 1963; admitted to bar, 1988, Indiana and U.S. District Court, Northern and Southern Districts of Indiana. *Education:* Purdue University (B.S., 1985); Indiana University (J.D., 1988). Deputy Prosecuting Attorney, Tippecanoe County, 1991. Deputy Public Defender, Tippecanoe County, 1992-1994. I.C.L.E.F. Seminar, Workers' Compensation, November, 1997. Instructor, Purdue University, 2000—. *Member:* Tippecanoe County and Indiana State Bar Associations; Indiana Trial Lawyers Association; The Association of Trial Lawyers of America. ***PRACTICE AREAS:*** Personal Injury; Product Liability; Worker's Compensation; Criminal Law; Medical Malpractice. ***Email:*** ccorrigan@witheredlaw.com

ERIC H. BURNS, born Lafayette, Indiana, February 18, 1957; admitted to bar, 1982, Indiana; 1988, U.S. Court of Appeals, Seventh Circuit. *Education:* Wabash College (B.A., 1979); Washington & Lee University (J.D., 1982). City Attorney, Lafayette Corporation Counsel, 1996-2003. *Member:* Tippecanoe County (Treasurer, 1987-1988) and Indiana State (Probate, Trust and Real Property Section) Bar Associations; Estate Planning Council of Greater Lafayette. ***PRACTICE AREAS:*** Corporate Law; Guardianship; Real Estate; Wills; Trusts and Estates; Litigation; Business Law; Government Law. ***Email:*** eburns@witheredlaw.com

---

SEAN M. PERSIN, born Bedford, Ohio, January 9, 1973; admitted to bar, 2001, Indiana and U.S. District Court, Southern District of Indiana; 2003, U.S. District Court, Northern District of Indiana. *Education:* Purdue University (B.S., 1996); University of Wyoming (J.D., 2001). National Order of Barristers. Deputy Prosecuting Attorney, Tippecanoe County Indiana, 2001-2003. *Member:* Tippecanoe County and Indiana State Bar Associations; Indiana Trial Lawyers Association. ***PRACTICE AREAS:*** Personal Injury; Workers Compensation; Family Law; Collections; Litigation. ***Email:*** spersin@witheredlaw.com

REPRESENTATIVE CLIENTS: Countrywide Home Loans; Wee Engineer, Inc.; Blue Print Specialties, Inc.; Family Inns of America; St. Anthony Healthcare, Inc.; Haan Foundation, Inc.; Lehe Farm Corp.; Henry Poor Lumber Co.; Warren Industries; Lafayette Housing Authority; Millennium Supply, Inc.; American Suburban Utilities, Inc.; ORC Plastics; Arnett Clinic.
REFERENCES: Salin Bank; Huntington Bank.

BEERS MALLERS BACKS & SALIN, LLP

108 WEST MICHIGAN STREET

LAGRANGE, INDIANA 46761

Telephone: 260-463-4949

FAX: 260-463-4905

URL: http://www.beersmallers.com

Fort Wayne, Indiana Office: 110 West Berry Street, Suite 1100. Telephone: 260-426-9706.

General Trial and Appellate Practice in all State and Federal Courts. Administrative Law, Bankruptcy, Banks and Banking, Business Law, Civil Rights, Collections, Commercial Law, Computers and Software, Construction Law, Contracts, Copyrights, Corporate Law, Debtor and Creditor, Elder Law, Environmental Law, Estate Planning and Administration, Franchising and Licensing, Government, Health Care, Insurance, Litigation, Mergers, Acquisitions and Divestitures, Municipal Law, Personal Injury, Probate, Products Liability, Public and Private Sector Labor and Employment (Management), Public Finance, Real Estate, Securities, Trademarks, Trusts and Estates, Zoning, Planning and Land Use.

MEMBERS OF FIRM

KURT RUSSELL BACHMAN, born LaGrange, Indiana, May 31, 1964; admitted to bar, 1989, Indiana and U.S. District Court, Northern and Southern Districts of Indiana. *Education:* Manchester College (B.S., 1986); Indiana University, School of Law (J.D., 1989). Publication: "Waiting for the Hammer to Fall: A General Overview of Auction Law" 2002. *Member:* Fort Wayne Estate Planning Council, LaGrange County (Secretary/Treasurer, 1993; Vice President, 1994; President, 1995-1996), Indiana State and American Bar Associations; National Association of Bond Lawyers. ***PRACTICE AREAS:*** Corporate Law; Real Estate; Estate Planning; Municipal Law; Taxation; Auction Law. ***Email:*** krbachman@beersmallers.com

KEVIN P. BRUNS, born Ft. Wayne, Indiana, April 16, 1966; admitted to bar, 1993, Indiana and U.S. District Court, Northern District of Indiana. *Education:* Indiana University (B.A., 1989); Cleveland-Marshall College of Law (J.D., 1992). *Member:* LaGrange County and Indiana State Bar Associations. ***PRACTICE AREAS:*** Estate Administration; Business Law; Real Estate. ***Email:*** kpbruns@beersmallers.com

ASSOCIATE

LISA M. BOWEN-SLAVEN, born Seattle, Washington, July 20, 1967; admitted to bar, 1993, Indiana and U.S. District Court, Northern District of Indiana. *Education:* Purdue

(This Listing Continued)

University (B.S., 1990); Valparaiso University (J.D., 1993). *Member:* La Grange County and Indiana State Bar Associations; American Academy of Adoption Attorneys. ***PRACTICE AREAS:*** Adoption Law; Medicaid Planning; Guardianships; Elder Law. ***Email:*** lbslaven@beersmallers.com

REPRESENTATIVE CLIENTS: Allen County, Indiana; Allen County Public Library; Angola Public Library; Cole Hardwood Co., Inc.; Construction Control, Inc.; D.O. McComb & Sons, Inc.; Economy Co.; Electrolux; Estate Securities General Insurance Agency, Inc.; First Union Corp.; Fort Wayne Patrolman's Benevolent Association, Inc.; Fraternal Order of Police Lodge #14; F.W. Toenges Orthotics, Inc.; Town of Fremont; Fremont Public Library; Granite Broadcasting Corp. (WPTA-TV); Herdrich Petroleum; Howe Military School; Humphries Developments of Northern Indiana, Inc.; Indiana Custom Tracks, LLC; Indiana Dimension, Inc.; LaGrange County, Indiana; LaGrange County Public Library; LaGrange County REMC; LIN Television Corp. (WANE-TV); Millennium Development, Inc.; Mid-America Management; National Serv-All, Inc.; Oberlin-Jackson Marketing Co.; Pac-Tec, Inc.; Parkview Health System, Inc.; PHD, Inc.; Preferred Automotive Group, Inc.; Republic Services, Inc.; Salin Bancshares, Inc.; Salin Bank & Trust Co.; The Town of Shipshewana, Indiana; Shorewood Packaging Corp.; STAR Financial Bank; Steuben County EMS, Indiana; SUPERVALU, INC.; Time Services, Inc.; Tri-State Sports Corp.; Wabash Valley Refuse Removal Co.; Wheat First Union: Winn-Dixie; Wright-Moore Corp.

(For Complete Personnel and Biographical Data, See Professional Biographies at Fort Wayne, Indiana)

BLACKBURN & GREEN

LAGRANGE, INDIANA

(See Fort Wayne)

Litigation, Personal Injury Law.

DRESSER, DRESSER, HAAS & CAYWOOD, P.C.

LAGRANGE, INDIANA

(See Sturgis, Michigan)

General Civil Practice. Business, Banking, Probate and Estate Planning. Environmental, Real Property, Labor and Employment (Management), Employee Benefits and Pensions, Taxation Law. Litigation and Mediation Services, Product Liability, Insurance Defense, Family, Negligence and Personal Injury, Intellectual Property, Technology, Creditors Rights and Commercial Law.

STOUT, WHEELER & ZABONA

LAGRANGE, INDIANA

(See Angola)

General Practice, DUI, Driving While Intoxicated, Drug Crimes, Juvenile Crimes, Parole and Probation, Traffic Violations, White Collar Crime, Criminal Law, Domestic Violence, Adoptions, Child Custody, Child Support, Divorce, Domestic Violence, Visitation Rights, Prenuptial Agreements, Unmarried Couples, Guardianships, Automobile Accidents, Dog Bites, Head and Spinal Injuries, Nursing Home Abuse, Sexual Abuse, Slip and Fall, Trucking Accidents, Wrongful Death, Class Actions, Construction Accidents, Personal Injury, Railroad Accidents, Natural Disasters, Business Enterprises, General Business, Starting a Business, Buying or Selling a Home, Construction, Eminent Domain, Environmental, Landlord and Tenant, Zoning and Land Use, Neighbors and Pets, Natural Disasters, Asset Protection, Estate Planning, Wills and Probate.

RICHARD BALLARD
ATTORNEY AT LAW

LA PORTE, INDIANA

(See Knox)

Criminal Law, DUI, Drug Crimes, Juvenile Crimes, Traffic Violations, White Collar Crimes, Family Law, Adoptions, Child Custody, Child Support, Divorce, Visitation Rights, Personal Injury, Medical Malpractice, Auto Accidents, Wrongful Death, Slip and Fall, Real Estate.

R. TRACY CRUMP

LA PORTE, INDIANA

(See New Carlisle)

Intellectual Property, Copyrights, Licensing Agreements, Patents, Trade Secrets, Trademarks.

MATTHEW D. LATULIP
ATTORNEY AT LAW

LA PORTE, INDIANA

(See Schererville)

Personal Injury, Medical Malpractice, Auto Accidents, Slip and Fall, Wrongful Death, Criminal, DUI, Traffic Violations, Juvenile Crimes, Employment Discrimination, Sexual Harassment, Nursing Home Abuse, Insurance.

NEWBY, LEWIS, KAMINSKI & JONES, LLP

Established in 1904

916 LINCOLNWAY

LA PORTE, INDIANA 46350

Telephone: 219-362-1577

Direct Line Michigan City: 219-879-6300

Fax: 219-362-2106

Email: nlkj@nlkj.com

URL: http://www.nlkj.com

Mailing Address: P.O. Box 1816, La Porte, IN 46352-1816

(This Listing Continued)

Civil Practice, Corporate Law, Real Estate, Appellate Practice, Personal Injury, Automobile Accidents, Wrongful Death, Wills and Probate, Trusts and Estates, Estate Planning, Civil Rights, Insurance Defense, Labor and Employment Law, Environmental Law, Education Law, Criminal Law, Driving While Intoxicated, Drug Crimes, Bankruptcy Law, Family Law, Adoptions, Divorce, Child Custody, Child Support, Visitation Rights, Medical Malpractice Defense, Mediation Services, Zoning Law.

FIRM PROFILE: Newby, Lewis, Kaminski & Jones, LLP and its predecessors have provided general legal services in Northern Indiana for over ninety years. In addition to meeting the legal needs of individuals, families, businesses, banks, and insurance companies, the firm actively pursues continuing education, participates in leadership positions in the Bar, and serves the community on government boards and non-profit agencies.

MEMBERS OF FIRM

DANIEL E. LEWIS (1910-1997)

DANIEL E. LEWIS, JR., born LaPorte, Indiana, June 13, 1935; admitted to bar, 1961, Indiana, U.S. Tax Court and U.S. District Court, Northern and Southern Districts of Indiana. *Education:* DePauw University (A.B., 1958); University of Michigan (J.D., 1961). Order of the Coif; Phi Beta Kappa; Phi Alpha Delta. Associate Editor, Michigan Law Review, 1960-1961. Reviewing Editor, Indiana Estate Planning and Probate Practice. Deputy Prosecuting Attorney, La Porte County, 1961-1966. *Member:* LaPorte County, Indiana State (Chairman, Probate, Trust and Real Property Section, 1992-1993) and American Bar Associations. Fellow: Indiana Bar Foundation; American College of Trust and Estate Counsel. ***PRACTICE AREAS:*** Business Law; Probate; Health Care; Estate Planning. ***Email:*** delewis@nlkj.com

GENE M. JONES, born Loogootee, Indiana, January 25, 1939; admitted to bar, 1963, Indiana and U.S. District Court, Northern and Southern Districts of Indiana. *Education:* Indiana University (A.B., 1961; LL.B., 1963). *Member:* Indiana State Bar Association (Member, Board of Managers, 1985-1986); Defense Trial Counsel of Indiana (President, 1989-1990; Diplomate Award, 1991). Fellow: Indiana Bar Foundation; American College of Trial Lawyers; International Association of Defense Counsel. [Captain, Judge Advocate Office, U.S.A.F., 1963-1966]. ***PRACTICE AREAS:*** Civil Litigation; Personal Injury; Products Liability; Toxic Torts. ***Email:*** gmjones@nlkj.com

EDWARD L. VOLK, born LaPorte, Indiana, December 29, 1944; admitted to bar, 1971, Illinois; 1972, Indiana; 1978, U.S. Supreme Court. *Education:* Loyola University (B.S., 1967); Indiana University (J.D., magna cum laude, 1970). Phi Sigma Tau; Order of the Coif. Board of Editors, Indiana Law Journal, 1969-1970. Law Clerk to the Honorable Jesse E. Eschbach, U.S. District Court, Northern District of Indiana, 1970-1971. Certified Alternative Dispute Resolution Mediator by the Indiana Commission for Continuing Legal Education. Member, LaPorte Municipal Airport Authority, 1973—. *Member:* LaPorte County (President, 1988-1989), Indiana State (Chairman, Aviation Law Committee, 1983-1991) and Illinois State Bar Associations; Lawyer-Pilots Bar Association. Fellow, Indiana Bar Foundation. ***PRACTICE AREAS:*** Business Law; Probate; Estate Planning. ***Email:*** elvolk@nlkj.com

MARK L. PHILLIPS, born Evansville, Indiana, September 9, 1950; admitted to bar, 1976, Indiana and U.S. District Court, Northern and Southern Districts of Indiana; U.S. Court of Appeals, Seventh Circuit. *Education:* Purdue University (B.S.I.M., 1972); Indiana University (J.D., cum laude, 1976). Delta Theta Phi. Law Clerk to Honorable Robert B. Lybrook, Court of Appeals of Indiana, 1974-1976. Member, Indiana Supreme Court Northwest Regional Committee on Rules of Evidence, 1992-1993. Certified Alternative Dispute Resolution Mediator by the Indiana Commission for Continuing Legal Education. *Member:* LaPorte County, Indiana State (Member, House of Delegates, 1984-1997) and American Bar Associations; Defense Trial Counsel of Indiana. Fellow, Indiana Bar Foundation. ***PRACTICE AREAS:*** Labor and Employment; Workers Compensation; Personal Injury; Mediation. ***Email:*** mlphillips@nlkj.com

MARTIN W. KUS, born Hammond, Indiana, March 16, 1951; admitted to bar, 1978, Indiana and U.S. District Court, Northern and Southern Districts of Indiana; U.S. Court of Appeals, Seventh Circuit; U.S. Supreme Court. *Education:* Indiana University (B.S., 1973); Drake University (J.D., 1978). Law Clerk to the Hon. Allen Sharp, Chief Judge, U.S. District Court, Northern District of Indiana, 1978-1980. *Member:* Indiana State Bar Association (Council Member, District 3, Litigation Section). ***PRACTICE AREAS:*** Civil Litigation; Employment Law; Civil Rights; Criminal Defense. ***Email:*** mwkus@nlkj.com

MARK A. LIENHOOP, born 1956; admitted to bar, 1981, Indiana. *Education:* Valparaiso University (B.A., 1978; J.D., 1981). Voted by peers as Indiana "Super Lawyer," 2004. Accepted into American Board of Trial Advocates, 2002. Board of Directors, Defense Trial Counsel of Indiana, 1995-2001. Editor-in-Chief, Indiana Civil Litigation Review. Member, 2d District Council, Litigation Section, Indiana State Bar Association. Mr. Lienhoop has attained Martindale-Hubbell's highest rating for legal ability and ethical standards. ***PRACTICE AREAS:*** Civil Trials; Civil Appeals. ***Email:*** MALienhoop@nlkj.com

JAMES W. KAMINSKI, born LaPorte, Indiana, February 9, 1961; admitted to bar, 1986, Nebraska, Indiana and U.S. District Court, Northern and Southern Districts of Indiana. *Education:* Marquette University (B.S., 1983); Creighton University (J.D., 1986). *Member:* LaPorte County, Indiana State and Nebraska State Bar Associations. ***PRACTICE AREAS:*** Probate; Healthcare; Transactions. ***Email:*** jwkaminski@nlkj.com

WILLIAM S. KAMINSKI, born LaPorte, Indiana, December 9, 1965; admitted to bar, 1992, Indiana and U.S. District Court, Northern and Southern Districts of Indiana; U.S. Court of Appeals, Seventh Circuit. *Education:* Creighton University (B.S.Soc., 1988; J.D., 1991). Phi Alpha Delta. Deputy Public Defender, LaPorte County, Indiana, 1994—. *Member:* LaPorte County, Indiana State and American Bar Associations. ***PRACTICE AREAS:*** Litigation; Criminal Law; Zoning Law; Domestic Relations. ***Email:*** wskaminski@nlkj.com

DAVID P. JONES, born Ogden, Utah, August 10, 1964; admitted to bar, 1993, Indiana and U.S. District Court, Northern and Southern Districts of Indiana; U.S. Court of Appeals, Seventh Circuit. *Education:* Indiana University (B.S., 1987; M.S., 1990); Valparaiso University (J.D., 1993). Deputy Public Defender, LaPorte County, 1995—. *Member:* LaPorte County, Seventh Circuit, Indiana State and American Bar Associations; National Associa-

(This Listing Continued)

NEWBY, LEWIS, KAMINSKI & JONES, LLP, La Porte—Continued

tion of Criminal Defense Lawyers; Indiana Trial Lawyers Association; Association of Trial Lawyers of America. ***PRACTICE AREAS:*** Plaintiffs Personal Injury; Criminal Defense. ***Email:*** dpjones@nlkj.com

ASSOCIATES

MATTHEW J. HAGENOW, admitted to bar, 2000, Indiana and U.S. District Court, Northern and Southern Districts of Indiana. *Education:* University of Notre Dame (B.S., 1994; J.D., cum laude, 2000). *Member:* LaPorte County and Indiana State Bar Associations. ***PRACTICE AREAS:*** Civil Litigation; Appellate Practice. ***Email:*** mjhagenow@nlkj.com

MICHAEL A. BIANCO, born Merrillville, Indiana, December 10, 1963; admitted to bar, 1996, Oregon and U.S. District Court, District of Oregon; 2000, Indiana. *Education:* U.S. Merchant Marine Academy (B.S., 1986); Loyola University (J.D., 1996). *Member:* Multnomah County and American Bar Associations; Oregon State Bar. [Capt., U.S. Army, Infantry, 1986-1989]. ***LANGUAGES:*** Spanish. ***Email:*** mabianco@nlkj.com

BRADLEY J. ADAMSKY, born Troy, Ohio, May 19, 1977; admitted to bar, 2003, Indiana. *Education:* University of Notre Dame (B.A., 1999; J.D., 2003). ***Email:*** bjadamsky@nlkj.com

KRISTINA J. JACOBUCCI, born Indianapolis, September 30, 1979; admitted to bar, 2004, Indiana. *Education:* St. Mary's College (B.A., 2001); Valparaiso University School of Law (J.D., 2004). Member, Moot Court Honor Society. ***Email:*** kjjacobucci@nlkj.com

JASON M. MASSARO, born Chicago, Illinois, December 23, 1971; admitted to bar, 1996, Indiana; U.S. District Court, Northern and Southern Districts of Indiana. *Education:* Purdue University (B.S., 1993); Valparaiso University (J.D., magna cum laude, 1996). ***PRACTICE AREAS:*** General Civil Practice.

SENIOR COUNSEL

LEON R. KAMINSKI, born LaPorte, Indiana, November 21, 1924; admitted to bar, 1950, Indiana; U.S. District Court, Northern and Southern Districts of Indiana; U.S. Court of Appeals, 7th Circuit; U.S. Supreme Court. *Education:* Indiana University (A.B., 1946; J.D., 1950). Phi Delta Phi. Recipient: Distinguished Alumni Service Award, Indiana University, Indianapolis School of Law, 1988; Indiana Bar Foundation, The Fifty Year Award, 2000. Deputy Prosecuting Attorney, La Porte County, Indiana, 1953-1958. Certified Alternative Dispute Resolution Mediator by the Indiana Commission for Continuing Legal Education. Member, 1971-1976 and Vice President, 1972, Indiana State Board of Bar Examiners. Member: Indiana Supreme Court Committee on Character and Fitness, 1991—; United States District Court for the Northern District of Indiana Advisory Committee on Local Rules and Civil Justice Reform Act, 1991-1992. *Member:* LaPorte County (President, 1972-1973), Indiana State (Member, Board of Managers, 1977-1978; Vice President, 1980-1981; President Elect, 1981-1982; President, 1982-1983) and American Bar Associations; American Academy of Hospital Lawyers; Defense Trial Counsel of Indiana (Diplomate). Fellow: American College of Trial Lawyers (State Chairman, 1981-1982); Indiana Bar Foundation (Chairman of Fellows, 1991-1992); American Bar Foundation; International Society of Barristers (State Chairman, 1985-1995). ***PRACTICE AREAS:*** Mediation; Litigation; Professional Liability Defense. ***Email:*** nlkj@nlkj.com

COUNSEL FOR: La Porte Transit Co.; Bridgestone/Firestone; Kingsbury Industrial & Development Corp.; American International Group; State Farm Insurance Co.; Howmet Corp.; United Farm Bureau Mutual Insurance Co.; Medical Protective Co.; The Doctor's Co.; T-P Orthodontics, Inc.; Atlanta Cos.; Dwyer Products Corp.; New York Blower Company; Cincinnati Insurance Co.; Caster Maintenance Co., Inc.; LaPorte Regional Health System; Aero Metals, Inc.; St. Paul Insurance Co.; West Bend Mutual Insurance Co.

SWEENEY, DABAGIA, THORNE, JANES & PAGOS, L.L.P.

LA PORTE, INDIANA

(See Michigan City)

General Civil and Trial Practice in State and Federal Courts, Municipal, Personal Injury, Mediation, Probate and Estate Planning, Corporate, Banking and Creditors Rights, Real Estate, Family Law, Appeals and Criminal Law, Bankruptcy.

ANTHONY F. TAVITAS ATTORNEYS AT LAW

A PROFESSIONAL CORPORATION

LA PORTE, INDIANA

(See Munster)

Insurance Defense, Trial Practice, Personal Injury, Insurance Coverage, Workers Compensation.

O. JERROLD WINSKI

LA PORTE, INDIANA

(See Michigan City)

Business Law, Commercial Real Estate, Residential Real Estate, Labor and Employment, Leases and Leasing, Civil Litigation, Business Acquisitions, Business Divestitures, Personal Injury, Mediation, Trusts and Estates, Wills and Probate, Estate Planning, Zoning, Planning and Land Use.

RENDIGS, FRY, KIELY & DENNIS, L.L.P.

LAWRENCEBURG, INDIANA

(See Cincinnati, Ohio)

Trial and General Practice, Appellate Practice, Products Liability, Insurance Litigation, Personal Injury, Medical Liability, Medical Malpractice, Nursing Home Litigation, Health Law, Hospital Law, Professional Liability, Construction Law, Mold Claims, Corporate Law, Business Law, Maritime Law, Aviation Law, Commercial Law, Taxation, Real Estate, Probate, Trusts and Estates, Wills, Bankruptcy, Family Law, Environmental Law, Transportation, Medical Devices, Civil Rights, Premises Liability, Premises Security, Labor Law, Employment Law, Employee Benefits, Criminal Law, Class Actions, Complex and Multi-District Litigation, Alternative Dispute Resolution, Legal Professional Liability, Workers' Compensation Defense, Zoning, Planning and Land Use.

WAITE, SCHNEIDER, BAYLESS & CHESLEY CO., L.P.A.

LAWRENCEBURG, INDIANA

(See Cincinnati, Ohio)

General Civil Practice. Aviation, Antitrust Litigation, Class Action, Commercial Litigation, Complex Litigation, Corporate Law, Federal Employees Liability, General Civil Trials and Appeals in all Courts, Insurance, Labor, Consolidated and Multi-district Litigation, Products Litigation, Securities Litigation and Wrongful Death.

WOOD & LAMPING, L.L.P.

208 WALNUT STREET
LAWRENCEBURG, INDIANA 47025
Telephone: 812-537-2375
Fax: 812-537-2368

Cincinnati, Ohio Office: Wood & Lamping, L.L.P., 600 Vine Street, Suite 2500, 45202-2491. Telephone: 513-852-6000. Fax: 513-852-6087.

Civil and Commercial Litigation, Corporate and Business, including Mergers and Acquisitions, Tax, Labor and Employment, Workers Compensation, Real Estate, Municipal and Administrative, Admiralty, Products Liability Defense, Insurance Defense, Securities, Bankruptcy, Estate Planning, Probate, Family Law, Land Use and Zoning, Employee Benefits, Health and Hospital Law.

MEMBER OF FIRM

LISA DEHART LEHNER, born Lawrenceburg, Indiana, March 31, 1966; admitted to bar, 1993, Arizona; 1996, Indiana; 2001, Ohio. *Education:* Miami University (B.A., 1988); American University (J.D., 1992). Member, American University Journal of International Law and Policy. *Member:* Cincinnati, Dearborn County, Ohio State and Indiana State Bar Associations; State Bar of Arizona. (Also at Cincinnati, Ohio Office). ***LANGUAGES:*** German. ***PRACTICE AREAS:*** Business Law; Estate Administration; Estate Planning; Real Estate; Governmental Law. ***Email:*** ldlehner@woodlamping.com

ASSOCIATE

THOMAS R. BLONDELL, born Evanston, Illinois, October 1, 1960; admitted to bar, 1988, Illinois; 2002, Indiana; U.S. District Court, Northern and Central Districts of Illinois; U.S. District Court, Southern District of Indiana; U.S. Court of Appeals, Seventh Circuit. *Education:* Millikin University (B.A., 1982); John Marshall Law School (J.D., 1988). *Member:* Dearborn County and Indiana State Bar Association; First Amendment Lawyers Association. ***PRACTICE AREAS:*** Civil Litigation; Criminal Law. ***Email:*** trblondell@woodlamping.com

(For complete biographical data on all personnel, see Professional Biographies at Cincinnati, Ohio)

PARR RICHEY OBREMSKEY & MORTON

Established in 1899

PARR BUILDING
225 WEST MAIN STREET
P.O. BOX 668
LEBANON, INDIANA 46052
Telephone: 765-482-0110; 317-269-2509
FAX: 765-483-3444
Email: lebanon@parrlaw.com
URL: http://www.parrlaw.com

Indianapolis, Indiana Office: 201 N. Illinois Street, Suite 300, 46204. Telephone: 317-269-2500. FAX: 317-269-2514.

Personal Injury, Products Liability, Insurance Defense, Business Litigation, Alternative Dispute Resolution, Appellate Practice, School, Business Transactions, Real Estate, Zoning, Utility Regulation and Finance, Estate Planning, Trusts and Estates, Wills and Probate.

(For Complete Biographical Data on all Personnel, see Professional Biographies at Indianapolis, Indiana).

THOMPSON LAW OFFICE

LIBERTY, INDIANA

(See Connersville)

Personal Injury, Debt Collection, Estate Planning, Criminal Law, Appellate Practice, Bankruptcy, Environmental Law, Family Law.

BLACKBURN & GREEN

LOGANSPORT, INDIANA

(See Fort Wayne)

Litigation, Personal Injury Law.

STARR AUSTEN TRIBBETT MYERS & MILLER

Established in 1982

201 SOUTH THIRD STREET

LOGANSPORT, INDIANA 46947

Telephone: 574-722-6676

Telefax: 574-753-3299

URL: http://www.satmlaw.com

General Civil Practice in State and Federal Courts. Personal Injury Litigation, Securities Fraud Arbitration and Litigation, Insurance, Class Action Litigation, Banking, Corporation, Wills and Probate, Trusts and Estates; Estate Planning, Environmental and Toxic Tort Law, Real Estate Law, Family/Domestic Relations, Appellate Practice.

MEMBERS OF FIRM

SCOTT L. STARR, born Indianapolis, Indiana, May 15, 1955; admitted to bar, 1980, Indiana, U.S. District Court, Northern and Southern Districts of Indiana and U.S. Court of Appeals, Seventh Circuit. *Education:* Ball State University (B.S., summa cum laude, 1977); Indiana University (J.D., magna cum laude, 1980). Phi Delta Phi. Recipient: Defense Research Institute Exceptional Performance Citation, 1998; Diplomat Award of Defense Trial Counsel of Indiana, 2003. Voted Super Lawyer, Indianapolis Magazine Poll, 2003-2004. *Member:* American College of Trial Lawyers; Cass County (President), Indiana State (Member, Litigation Section) and American (Member, Litigation Section) Bar Associations; Indiana Trial Lawyers Association; The Association of Trial Lawyers of America; Indiana Defense Lawyers Association (Past President); Defense Research Institute. **PRACTICE AREAS:** Securities Fraud; Personal Injury; Insurance Defense; Toxic Torts; Commercial Litigation; Class Actions. **Email:** starr@satmlaw.com

JAMES H. AUSTEN, born Indianapolis, Indiana, April 21, 1953; admitted to bar, 1981, Indiana, U.S. District Court, Northern and Southern Districts of Indiana. *Education:* Ball State University (B.S., 1975); Indiana University (J.D., magna cum laude, 1981). Phi Alpha Delta. Associate Editor, Indiana Law Review, 1981. Cass County Deputy Prosecutor, 1986. *Member:* Cass County (Secretary/Treasurer, 1986-1987; Vice President, 1987-1990; President, 1991-1993), Indiana State and American Bar Associations; Indiana Defense Lawyers Association. **PRACTICE AREAS:** Insurance Defense; Securities Fraud. **Email:** austen@satmlaw.com

DONALD J. TRIBBETT, born Logansport, Indiana, January 23, 1950; admitted to bar, 1975, Indiana; 1977, Illinois; 1981, U.S. Supreme Court and U.S. Court of Appeals, 7th Circuit. *Education:* Butler University (B.A., 1972); Indiana University (J.D., magna cum laude, 1975). Associate Editor, Indiana Law Review, 1974-1975. Law Clerk, Indiana Supreme Court, 1974-1977. Attorney: Logansport/Cass County Airport Authority; Twin Lakes Regional Sewer District. City Attorney, City of Logansport, Indiana, 2000-2004. *Member:* Indiana State (Member, Sections on: Appellate Practice; Probate) and American Bar Associations. **PRACTICE AREAS:** Commercial Litigation; Appellate; Probate; Estate Planning; Personal Injury; Municipal Law. **Email:** tribbett@satmlaw.com

JON M. MYERS, born Logansport, Indiana, April 11, 1959; admitted to bar, 1989, Indiana, U.S. District Court, Northern and Southern Districts of Indiana; U.S. Supreme Court and U.S. Court of Appeals, Seventh Circuit. *Education:* Wabash College (A.B., 1981); Indiana University (J.D., 1989). Phi Alpha Delta. Eli Lilly Scholar. Town Attorney, Galveston, Indiana. *Member:* Cass County, Indiana State and American (Tort and Insurance Practice and Litigation Sections) Bar Associations; Indiana Trial Lawyers Association. Fellow, Indiana Bar Foundation. **PRACTICE AREAS:** Insurance Coverage; Insurance Defense; Securities Fraud; Family Law; Toxic Torts. **Email:** myers@satmlaw.com

ANDREW B. MILLER, born Munster, Indiana, April 28, 1968; admitted to bar, 1995, Indiana; U.S. District Court, Northern and Southern Districts of Indiana. *Education:* Wabash College (A.B., 1990); Saint Louis University (J.D., cum laude, 1995). Deputy City Attorney, City of Logansport, Indiana, 2000-2002. *Member:* Cass County, Indiana State and American Bar Associations; Defense Trial Counsel of Indiana. **PRACTICE AREAS:** Insurance Defense; Securities Fraud; Personal Injury. **Email:** miller@satmlaw.com

REPRESENTATIVE CLIENTS: National City Bank of Indiana; Community State Bank; Royal Center, Indiana; Community BanCorp.; Cincinnati Insurance Co.; Indiana Farmers Insurance Group; Logansport Clinic for Women, Inc.; Maiben's, Inc.; Pekin Insurance Co.; Prudential Property & Casualty Insurance Co.; United Farm Bureau Mutual Insurance Co.; Mike Anderson Pontiac GMC, Inc.; Overway Petroleum, Inc.; Select Seed Hybrids, Inc.; Statesman Insurance Group, Insurance Cos.; Kemper Insurance Cos.; Shelter Insurance Cos.; Baker Specialty and Supply Co., Inc.; Brown Constuction Co., Inc.; Fireman's Fund Co.; Grange Insurance Co.; The Travelers Companies; Sequa Corp.; General Casualty Companies; Globe American Casualty Company; Logansport Lumber Co., Inc.; Game Time, Inc.; LaSalle Consulting Group, Inc.; Markley Abstract Co., Inc.; Pasquale Trucking Co., Inc.; Dennis Foods, Inc.; Transport Insurance Co.; Meridian Mutual Insurance Co.; John Hancock Mutual Life Insurance Co.; State Farm Fire and Casualty Co.; Edlo Sales & Engineering; Shidcler Electric Co.; Town of Galveston; Twin Lakes Regional Sewer District; Zenith Corporation.

BARLOW LAW OFFICE

Established in 1897

201 EAST MAIN STREET

MADISON, INDIANA 47250-3493

Telephone: 812-273-4440

FAX: 812-273-2329

General Civil and Criminal Practice, Probate, Personal Injury and Domestic Relations Law, Real Estate, Banking, Corporation, Municipal, Probate and Estate Planning, Collections.

(This Listing Continued)

FIRM PROFILE: Since its establishment in 1897 by Emerson Lemen, the firm has grown over the years. The names have changed but it has maintained a small town general practice focusing on Personal Injury and Municipal Law. The firm represents a variety of clients throughout Southeastern Indiana but is not limited to that area. The firm has experienced, knowledgeable and result orientated members.

MEMBER OF FIRM

ROBERT L. BARLOW, II, born Indianapolis, Indiana, January 20, 1949; admitted to bar, 1980, Georgia and Indiana; U.S. District Court, Southern District of Indiana. *Education:* Ball State University (B.S., 1972); Mercer University (J.D., 1980). Phi Delta Phi; Phi Alpha Theta. Member, 1978-1979 and Associate Editor, 1979-1980, Mercer Law Review. Author: "Treatment of Guest Passengers: Georgia Maintains Its Minority Rule," 31 Mercer Law Review 1061, 1980. Teaching Assistant, Legal Bibliography, Walter F. George School of Law, Mercer University, 1979. Madison City Attorney, 1995—. *Member:* Jefferson County (President, 1992-2000) and Indiana State Bar Associations; State Bar of Georgia; Indiana Trial Lawyers Association; Association of Trial Lawyers of America. **PRACTICE AREAS:** Civil Litigation; Probate and Estate Planning; Municipal and Zoning; Auto Negligence; Personal Injury Defense. **Email:** rbarlow@blueriver.net

---

MARY B. McCUSKEY, born Chicago, Illinois, January 6, 1951; admitted to bar, 1975, Kansas and U.S. District Court, District of Kansas; 1977, Iowa and U.S. District Court, Northern District of Iowa; 1989, Tennessee; 1991, U.S. District Court, Middle District of Tennessee; 1999, Indiana; 2004, U.S. District Court, Southern District of Indiana. *Education:* University of Kansas (B.A., 1972); Washburn University School of Law (J.D., 1975). *Member:* Jefferson County and Indiana, Bar Associations. **LANGUAGES:** English. **PRACTICE AREAS:** Family Law; Construction Law; Alternative Dispute Resolution. **Email:** mccuskey@blueriver.net

KRISTEN D. VANDEWATER, born Carrollton, Kentucky, October 24, 1976; admitted to bar, 2002, Indiana. *Education:* Indiana University, New Albany (D.Psych., 1999); University of Louisville (J.D., 2002). Member, Indiana Pro Bono Council, 2002—. *Member:* Jefferson County and Indiana State Bar Associations; Indiana Trial Lawyers Association; The Association of Trial Lawyers of America. (Also of Counsel, Mason, Schilling & Mason Co., L.P.A., Cincinnati, Ohio). **PRACTICE AREAS:** Banking Law; Commercial Law; Collections; Real Estate; Family Law; Criminal Law; Personal Injury.

REPRESENTATIVE CLIENTS: City of Madison, Indiana; Madison Bank & Trust Company; Hanover College; Farmers Bank of Milton; Fifth Third Bank; Indiana Gas Company; Aetna Casualty and Insurance Company; Hartford Accident and Indemnity Company; Dupont Water Company, Inc.; Canaan Utilities Corporation; Town of Brooksburg, Indiana; United Farm Bureau Mutual Insurance Company; Viking Insurance Company.
APPROVED ATTORNEYS FOR: National Attorneys Title Assurance Fund.

COLUSSI LAW OFFICE

Established in 1990

427 EAST MAIN

MADISON, INDIANA 47250

Telephone: 812-265-4455

Fax: 812-265-4461

Email: colussilaw@msn.com

Civil and Criminal Trials, Appellate and Federal Practice, Insurance, Corporate, Personal Injury, Real Estate, Commercial, Probate, Estate Planning, Trusts, Domestic Relations, and Bankruptcy.

MEMBER OF FIRM

JOSEPH A. COLUSSI, born Cincinnati, Ohio, February 18, 1956; admitted to bar, 1981, Missouri; 1986, Indiana; U.S. Supreme Court. *Education:* Hanover College (B.A., cum laude, 1978); Indiana University (J.D., 1981). Note Editor, Indiana Law Journal, 1979-1981. Law Clerk to Hon. Scott O. Wright, U.S. District Court, Western District of Missouri, 1981-1983. Deputy Prosecuting Attorney, 1986-1990. **PRACTICE AREAS:** Insurance Defense; Family Law; Personal Injury; Trusts and Estates; Real Estate; Bankruptcy. **Email:** colussilaw@msn.com

REPRESENTATIVE CLIENTS: Wal-Mart Stores, Inc.; Target Stores; Wolohan Lumber Cos.; Northern Star Minerals, Inc.; Irving Materials, Inc.; Western Reserve Ins. Co.; The Travelers Insurance Co.; The Grange Insurance Co.; Century Surety Co.; Allied Insurance Group; M.S.I. Insurance Co.; Westfield Insurance Co.; Ohio Casualty Insurance Co.; Fifth Third Bank; Heritage Community Bank; Friendship State Bank; Clifty Creek Credit Union.

MASON, SCHILLING & MASON CO., L.P.A.

Established in 1973

201 EAST MAIN STREET

MADISON, INDIANA 47250

Telephone: 513-489-0829

800-840-3514

Fax: 513-489-0834

Email: msm@mason-law.com

URL: http://www.mason-law.com

Cincinnati, Ohio Office: 11340 Montgomery Road, Suite 210. Telephone: 513-489-0829; 800-840-3514. Fax: 513-489-0834.
Covington, Kentucky Office: Heritage International, Suite 203, P.O. Box 2158. Telephone: 513-489-0829. Fax: 513-489-0834.
Columbus Office: 460 E. Main Street. Telephone: 513-489-0829. Fax: 513-489-0834.
Dayton, Ohio Office: 319 Liberty Tower. Telephone: 513-489-0829. Fax: 513-489-0834.
Lima, Ohio Office: P.O. Box 937. Telephone: 513-489-0829. Fax: 513-489-0834.

(This Listing Continued)

MASON, SCHILLING & MASON CO., L.P.A., Madison—Continued

Commercial, Creditors Rights, Bankruptcy, Collection, Banking and Financial Institution Law, Civil Litigation, Federal Consumer Law Litigation, Foreclosures, Automobile Deficiencies, Credit Cards, Medical Debts, Bad Checks, Business Loans/Commercial Debt, Vehicle and Property Repossessions, Landlord Representation/Evictions/Lease Litigation, Equipment Leasing.

FIRM PROFILE: Mason, Schilling & Mason Co., L.P.A., since its founding over 30 years ago, exclusively concentrates in the areas of creditor representation, in all aspects of commercial litigation, banking law, leasing law, bankruptcy law, and creditors' rights law.

We have developed a full service staff of attorneys in all aspects of representation to the credit granting community. Our legal services concentrate exclusively on representing creditors in all facets of legal representation concerning credit management and credit granting, commercial law, and bankruptcy law on behalf of the credit management community.

Further, of particular attention, is the providing of legal services to the banking and credit management community throughout the entire States of Ohio and Kentucky. Our attorneys appear in all State and federal courts in both states.

The value of our law firm rests with the dependable level of service that we provide to all creditor-clients. We pride ourselves in the personalized service and the conscientious follow through that has been a trade mark throughout over three decades of providing legal services to our creditor and banking clients.

REPRESENTATIVE CLIENTS: First Interstate Bank; Global Leasing Corp.; Barnett Banks; Share Fax Credit Union; Republic Bank; Mohawk Industries; The Fifth Third Bancorp; The Fifth Third Bank; Citicorp and Citibank, N.A.; Contel Credit Corp.; Borg-Warner Acceptance Corporation; Caterpillar Financial Corp.; Commercial Union Insurance Co.; First Financial Savings Bank; General Ionics, Inc., Subsidiary of Ionics, Inc.; Health and Education Credit Union; Superior Savings Bank; Hobart Corporation; Central Transport, Inc.; Dunlop Tire Co.; General Electric Credit Corporation; GTE Leasing Corp.; Hallmark Cards Inc.; Globe Furniture Rentals, Inc.; 84 Lumber Company; Transamerica Commercial Finance, Inc.; Transit Credit Union; Toyota Motor Credit Corp.; Mercedes-Benz Credit Corp.; Mason-Dixon Lines, Inc.; Novus Financial Services (formerly Sears); GCM Group of Pittsburgh and Cleveland, Inc.; Connecticut Mutual Life Insurance Co.; Jewish Hospital Credit Union; Union Federal Savings Bank; ITT Hartford Insurance Co.; ORIX Leasing Services; Parisian Credit Services; Xerox Credit Services; Key Corp Bank; Autofinance Group; Nationsbank; Cincinnati Bell, Inc.; Nike, Inc.; Arcadia Health Services; Volvo Financial Services; Mellon Bank; Colonial Pacific Corp.; U.S. Bank; Provident Bank Information Leasing Corp.; Park National Bank; Morgan Stanley Dean Witter.
SPECIAL COUNSEL FOR: State of Wisconsin; State of Minnesota; State of Arizona; State of New York; Allstate Insurance Co.; Nationwide Insurance Co.; Liberty Mutual Insurance Co.; Midwest Payment Systems; Bank of Louisiana; Associates Financial; ITT Credit Corp.; Fifth-Third Leasing Co.
REFERENCES: Fifth-Third Bank of Cincinnati; Fifth-Third Bank of Northern Kentucky.

(For Complete Biographical Data on all Personnel, see Professional Biographies at Cincinnati, Ohio)

MATTOX MATTOX & WILSON

MADISON, INDIANA

(See New Albany)

Civil Trial Litigation. Personal Injury and Wrongful Death, Products Liability, Medical Malpractice, Insurance Law, Corporate Law, Business Torts, Family Law, Aviation Law, Labor and Employment Law, Health Care Regulations.

KILEY, KILEY, HARKER, MICHAEL & CERTAIN

300 WEST THIRD STREET
P.O. BOX 899
MARION, INDIANA 46952-0899
Telephone: 765-664-9041
Fax: 765-664-8119

General Civil Practice. Corporation, Insurance, Trusts and Estates, Personal Injury, Family Law, Guardianships, Zoning and Real Estate Law. Trials. Appeals.

FIRM PROFILE: Since its establishment in 1930 by Robert Ralph Batton and Albert L. Harker, the firm has maintained a General Practice with an emphasis on defense trial. The firm represents a variety of clients statewide with its practice centered in Grant County and the surrounding counties.

MEMBERS OF FIRM

ROBERT RALPH BATTON (1890-1963)

ALBERT L. HARKER (1904-1965)

ALBERT BONNER BROWN (1911-1981)

THOMAS W. MICHAEL (1944-2002)

MICHAEL J. KILEY, born Marion, Indiana, July 15, 1934; admitted to bar, 1959, Indiana. *Education:* University of Notre Dame (A.B., 1956); Georgetown University (J.D., 1959). Member of Staff, Georgetown Law Journal, 1957-1958. City Judge, Marion, 1964-1971. Chairman, Indiana Natural Resources Commission, 1990—. Certified Mediator. *Member:* Grant County, Indiana State (Member, Board of Managers, 1976-1978) and American Bar Associations. ***PRACTICE AREAS:*** Business; Commercial; Real Estate; Probate; Environmental Law. ***Email:*** mkiley@kileylaw.net

ALBERT C. HARKER, born Marion, Indiana, January 16, 1936; admitted to bar, 1962, Indiana. *Education:* Indiana University (B.A., 1958); University of Virginia (LL.B., 1962). *Member:* Grant County, Indiana State and American Bar Associations; Defense Research Institute. ***PRACTICE AREAS:*** Litigation; Insurance Defense; Appellate Practice; Corporate Law; Probate; Mental Health Law. ***Email:*** aharker@kileylaw.net

HARRY J. CERTAIN, born Marion, Indiana, May 13, 1944; admitted to bar, 1969, Indiana; 1973, Florida. *Education:* Loras College (B.A., 1966); Indiana University (J.D., 1969). *Member:* Grant County and Indiana State Bar Associations; The Florida Bar. ***REPORTED CASES:*** Bowman Agri-Corp. v. First Farmers Nat., 561 N.E.2d 841; Fullenkamp v. Newcomer, 508 N.E.2d 37; Chesnut v. Chesnut, 499 N.E.2d 783. ***PRACTICE AREAS:*** Litigation; Insurance; Labor and Employee; Commercial Law. ***Email:*** jcertain@kileylaw.net

ASSOCIATES

JOSHUA M. HOWELL, born Minneapolis, Minnesota, November 30, 1967; admitted to bar, 1997, Indiana. *Education:* Michigan State University (B.A., 1991); Indiana University School of Law (J.D., cum laude, 1997). *Member:* Grant County and Indiana State Bar Associations. ***PRACTICE AREAS:*** Civil Litigation; Insurance Defense; Real Estate. ***Email:*** howell@kileylaw.net

TERI A. POLLETT, born Neenah, Wisconsin, April 12, 1960; admitted to bar, 2000, Indiana and Illinois. *Education:* University of Wisconsin-Stout (B.S., 1993); Indiana University School of Law (J.D., 1999). *Member:* Grant County and Indiana State Bar Associations.

MARTIN A. HARKER, born Marion, Indiana, April 17, 1975; admitted to bar, 2000, Indiana. *Education:* University of Cincinnati (B.A., 1997); University of Akron Law School (J.D., 2000). *Member:* Grant County and Indiana State Bar Associations.

OF COUNSEL

DAVID L. KILEY, SR., born January 24, 1928; admitted to bar, 1953, Indiana. *Education:* Georgetown University (B.S., cum laude, 1950; J.D., 1953). Member of Staff, Georgetown Law Journal, 1950-1953. City Judge, 1956-1959. City Attorney: Marion, 1960-1963; Gas City, 1968—. *Member:* Grant County and Indiana State Bar Associations. ***PRACTICE AREAS:*** Litigation; Insurance Defense; Personal Injury; Family Law; Divorce; Child Custody. ***Email:*** dkiley@kileylaw.net

JULES SCOTT WALKER, born October 26, 1931; admitted to bar, 1969, Indiana. *Education:* Wabash College (B.A., 1954); Indiana University (M.S., 1956); Indiana University School of Law (J.D., 1969). Assistant City Attorney, 1975-1978. Bankruptcy Trustee, 1979-1993. *Member:* Grant County and Indiana State Bar Associations. ***PRACTICE AREAS:*** General Practice; Bankruptcy; Probate; Estates. ***Email:*** jmwalker@busprod.net

GENERAL COUNSEL FOR: First Federal Savings Bank; Greene Line Manufacturing Co.; Mississinewa Community Schools; Atlas Foundry Co.; Grant Blackford Mental Health, Inc.; Marion Community Schools; Marion General Hospital; Garcor Supply Co.; City of Gas City; DeVoe Chevrolet Cadillac; Miami Nation of Indians of the State of Indiana, Inc.; Marion Public Library Building Corp.
LOCAL ATTORNEYS FOR: Bank One, Indiana, N.A.; Travelers Insurance Co.; America Family Group; Cincinnati Ins. Co.; Pekin Ins. Co.; Indiana Insurance Co.; Ohio Casualty Co.; Prudential Insurance Co.; Marion Mfg. Division of Dana Corp.; Brotherhood Mutual; Motorists Mutual Insurance Co.; General Motors Corp.; GenCorp; Governmental Interinsurance Exchange; Hartford Insurance Co.; Indiana Lumbermen's Mutual Insurance Co.; First National Bank & Trust of Kokomo; Gallaher-Bassett Insurance Service; American Electric Power Co.; Ford Motor Company; Salin Bank & Trust Co.

ROGERS & ROGERS, P.C.

525 SOUTH WASHINGTON STREET
P.O. BOX 925
MARION, INDIANA 46952
Telephone: 765-664-0003
Fax: 765-664-0373
Email: Rogers1law@aol.com

General Civil Practice. Banking, Probate, Business and Commercial Litigation.

KIM A. ROGERS, born Indianapolis, Indiana, March 5, 1939; admitted to bar, 1964, Indiana. *Education:* Indiana University (B.S., 1961; LL.B., 1964). Author: "Why Avoid Probate or the Virtues of Probate," How To Avoid Probate--but Should You?, ICLEF, 1993. Deputy Prosecuting Attorney, 1967-1968, 1998—. Attorney for Town of Sweetser, 1984—. *Member:* Grant County, Indiana State and American Bar Associations. [1st Lt., U.S. Army, 1964-1966]. ***PRACTICE AREAS:*** Banking; Creditors Rights; Business Law; Probate.

OF COUNSEL

GEORGE ROBB ROGERS, born Marion, Indiana, July 28, 1968; admitted to bar, 1994, Indiana. *Education:* Miami University (B.A., 1990); Indiana University at Bloomington (J.D., 1994). Intern, United States Federal District Court for the Southern District of Indiana, 1992. Author, "Legislative Intent vs. Executive Non-Enforcement," 69 Ind. L.J. 1257, 1994. Part-Time Deputy Prosecutor, Felonies and Domestic Violence, 1997. Assistant Majority Counsel, Indiana Senate, sessions of 1998-1999. Legislative Assistant for Technology, Antitrust, Crime, Elections Law and the Judiciary, Senator Richard G. Lugar, 1999-2001. Counsel, Subcommittee on Technology and Procurement Policy, Committee on Government Reform, U.S. House of Representatives, 2001-2003. General Counsel, Committee on Rules, U.S. House Representatives, 2003—. *Member:* Grant County, Indiana State and American Bar Associations. ***PRACTICE AREAS:*** Litigation; Business and Commercial; General Practice.

SPITZER HERRIMAN STEPHENSON HOLDEREAD MUSSER & CONNER, LLP

Established in 1931

ONE TWENTY TWO EAST FOURTH STREET
P.O. BOX 927
MARION, INDIANA 46952-0927
Telephone: 765-664-7307
Fax: 765-662-0574
Email: bsh@nxco.com

General Practice in State and Federal Courts. Corporate, Insurance, Probate and Estate Planning, Real Estate and Trial Practice. Municipal and Zoning, Personal Injury, Medical, Appeals.

(This Listing Continued)

MEMBERS OF FIRM

HERBERT A. SPITZER, JR., born Indianapolis, Indiana, June 1, 1940; admitted to bar, 1966, Indiana; 1971, U.S. Supreme Court. *Education:* Marian College (A.B., 1962); Indiana University School of Law (J.D., 1966). Phi Delta Phi. Law Clerk, Appellate Court of Indiana, 1964-1965. *Member:* Grant County and Indiana State Bar Associations; Defense Trial Counsel of Indiana. ***PRACTICE AREAS:*** Litigation; Zoning; Probate and Estate Planning; Real Estate; Personal Injury; Corporate. ***Email:*** hspitzer@nxco.com

CHARLES E. HERRIMAN, born Gary, Indiana, September 15, 1941; admitted to bar, 1966, Indiana. *Education:* Franklin College of Indiana (A.B., 1963); Indiana University School of Law (LL.B., 1966). Deputy Prosecuting Attorney, 1968-1969. Assistant City Attorney, 1969-1971. Member, Panel of Arbitrators, American Arbitration Association. *Member:* Grant County, Indiana State and American Bar Associations; Defense Trial Counsel of Indiana. Fellow, American College of Trial Lawyers. ***PRACTICE AREAS:*** Civil Trial; Litigation; Real Estate; Corporate; Probate and Estate Planning. ***Email:*** cherriman@nxco.com

PHILLIP E. STEPHENSON, born Muncie, Indiana, October 8, 1947; admitted to bar, 1973, Indiana; 2000, U.S. Supreme Court. *Education:* Ball State University (B.S., 1969); Indiana University School of Law (J.D., cum laude, 1973). Deputy Prosecuting Attorney, 1974-1977. Author: "Bad Faith in Indiana," ICLEF Seminar, 1991; "Insurance Law Update For 1996," ICLEF Seminar. *Member:* Grant County, Indiana State Bar Associations; Defense Trial Counsel of Indiana; Indiana Trial Lawyers Association. ***PRACTICE AREAS:*** Commercial Litigation; Personal Injury; Real Estate; Corporate Law. ***Email:*** psteph@nxco.com

JEROME T. HOLDEREAD, born Plymouth, Indiana, March 2, 1948; admitted to bar, 1977, Indiana. *Education:* Manchester College (B.S., with distinction, 1970); Ball State University (M.P.A., 1972); Indiana University (J.D., magna cum laude, 1976). Adjunct Professor, Business Law, Taylor University, 1987—. *Member:* Grant County, Indiana State and American Bar Associations. ***PRACTICE AREAS:*** Banking; Creditor's Rights; Real Estate; Probate and Estate Planning. ***Email:*** jth@nxco.com

JOSEF D. MUSSER, born Marion, Indiana, June 17, 1951; admitted to bar, 1980, Indiana. *Education:* Indiana University (A.B., 1974; J.D., 1980). Deputy Prosecuting Attorney, 1980-1982. Corporate Counsel, City of Marion, 2002-2003. *Member:* Grant County and Indiana State Bar Associations; Defense Trial Counsel of Indiana. ***PRACTICE AREAS:*** Civil Litigation (10%); Insurance Defense (50%); Probate (10%); Estate Planning (10%); School Law (20%). ***Email:*** jmusser@nxco.com

MICHAEL D. CONNER, born Marion, Indiana, September 14, 1960; admitted to bar, 1988, Indiana and U.S. District Court, Northern and Southern Districts of Indiana; 2000, U.S. Supreme Court. *Education:* Ohio University (A.B., summa cum laude, 1983); Indiana University School of Law (J.D., 1988). Deputy Attorney General, 1988-1989. Public Defender, 1990 and Deputy Prosecutor, 1991, Grant County. *Member:* Grant County, Indiana State and American Bar Associations; Defense Trial Counsel of Indiana. ***PRACTICE AREAS:*** Insurance Defense; Medical Malpractice Defense; Commercial Litigation; Civil Litigation; Personal Injury; Employment Law; School Law; Corporate Law; Probate. ***Email:*** conner@nxco.com

MARK E. SPITZER, born Indianapolis, Indiana, August 22, 1965; admitted to bar, 1990, Indiana and U.S. District Court, Northern and Southern Districts of Indiana; 1997, U.S. Court of Appeals, Seventh Circuit. *Education:* University of Notre Dame (B.A., 1987); Indiana University (J.D., magna cum laude, 1990). Phi Delta Phi. Senior Clerk to the Honorable Robert H. Staton, Court of Appeals of Indiana, 1990-1992. Deputy Prosecutor, Grant County, 1992-1995. Corporate Counsel, City of Marion, 2004—. *Member:* Grant County and Indiana State Bar Associations. ***PRACTICE AREAS:*** Appellate Law (5%); Litigation (20%); Municipal Law (30%); Corporate (30%). ***Email:*** mspitzer@nxco.com

KYLE C. PERSINGER, born Marion, Indiana, October 20, 1968; admitted to bar, 1999, Indiana and U.S. District Court, Northern and Southern Districts of Indiana. *Education:* University of Indianapolis (B.S., 1991); Indiana University (J.D., 1999). Member, Board of Trustees, Marion Community Schools, 1997—. *Member:* Grant County and Indiana State Bar Associations. ***PRACTICE AREAS:*** Litigation; School Law; Municipal Law; Insurance Defense. ***Email:*** persinger@nxco.com

---

LeANN HOPPER, born Noblesville, Indiana, February 24, 1974; admitted to bar, 2004, Indiana. *Education:* Indiana University, Bloomington (B.A., 1996); Indiana University School of Law - Indianapolis (J.D., 2004). *Member:* Grant County and Indiana State Bar Associations. ***PRACTICE AREAS:*** Civil Litigation; Family Law. ***Email:*** lhopper@nxco.com

GENERAL COUNSEL FOR: Marion Community Schools; Madison-Grant United School Corp.; Indiana Wesleyan University; City of Marion, IN; Marion School Employees FCU; Bradner Village Health Care Center; Wesleyan Health Care Center; Marion Steel Fabrication, Inc.; Moorehead Electric Co., Inc.; Fairmount State Bank; Farmers State Bank; Tulox Plastics Corp.; Marion Service Utility Board; Grant Co., IN; Marion Municipal Airport; CVS Systems, Inc.; NX Communications, Inc.; Grant County Abstract; Grant County State Bank; Town of Matthews; Grant County Economic Growth Council; J.G. Bowers, Inc.
LOCAL COUNSEL FOR: Medical Protective Co.; State Farm Mutual Ins. Co.; United Farm Bureau Ins. Co.; American Family Ins. Co.; Auto Owners Ins. Co.; State Auto Ins. Co.; Salin Bank; Hartson-Kennedy Cabinet Top, Inc.; Cafaro Inc.; Gannett; American Electric Power.

MALLOR CLENDENING GRODNER & BOHRER LLP

MARTINSVILLE, INDIANA

(See Bloomington)

Civil Litigation, Insurance Defense, Business Law, Wills, Trusts and Estates, Family Law, Personal Injury, Taxation, Corporate Law, Real Estate, Probate, Labor and Employment.

RUPPERT & SCHAEFER, P.C.

MARTINSVILLE, INDIANA

(See Indianapolis)

Family Law, Divorce, Pre-marital Agreements, Child Custody, Child Support, Paternity, Visitation Rights, Step Parent Adoptions.

P.R. SMITH AND ASSOCIATES, P.C.

Established in 1979

1589 BURTON LANE
P.O. BOX 1452
MARTINSVILLE, INDIANA 46151-1548
Telephone: 765-342-7148
Fax: 765-342-0739

General Practice. Real Estate, Wills and Probate, Trusts and Estates, Estate Planning, Family, Domestic, Civil Litigation, Personal Injury, Trials.

FIRM PROFILE: Since the firm's establishment by William H. Wehrle and Phillip R. Smith, the firm has maintained a general practice with an emphasis on civil trial work, commercial and collections. The firm primarily represents corporations, small businesses and individuals throughout Central Indiana. The firm is listed in the Bar Register of Preeminent Lawyers.

PHILLIP R. SMITH, born Washington, D.C., July 26, 1942; admitted to bar, 1969, Indiana. *Education:* Indiana University (B.S., 1966; J.D., 1969). Judge, Morgan Superior Court, 1976-1979. Morgan County Attorney. *Member:* Morgan County (President, 1982-1983), Indianapolis, Indiana State and American Bar Associations. ***PRACTICE AREAS:*** Family; Domestic; Real Estate; Probate; Estate Planning; Civil Litigation.

REPRESENTATIVE CLIENTS: Home Bank, S.B.; Citizens Bank in Mooresville; Town of Morgantown; Morgantown Plan Commission and Board of Zoning Appeals.
REFERENCES: Citizens Bank, Mooresville, Indiana; Home Bank, S.B., Martinsville, Indiana.

ANDERSON & WARD, P.C.

BARRISTER COURT
9211 BROADWAY
MERRILLVILLE, INDIANA 46410
Telephone: 219-769-1892
Facsimile: 219-769-1107
URL: http://www.andersonward.com
Email: law@andersonward.com
URL: http://www.andersonwardlaw.com

Real Estate, Zoning and Land Use Law, Business Law, Corporate Law, Contracts, Law Suits, Business Enterprises, Partnerships, Limited Liability Companies, Wills and Probate, Trusts and Estates, Estate Planning, Guardianships, Banking Law, Family Law, Adoptions, Divorce, Child Custody, Child Support, Visitation Rights, Bankruptcy, Debtor and Creditor Law, Collections, Taxation.

RICHARD E. ANDERSON, born Gary, Indiana, March 30, 1948; admitted to bar, 1973, Indiana, U.S. District Court, Northern District of Indiana, U.S. Court of Appeals, Seventh Circuit and U.S. Tax Court. *Education:* Indiana University (B.S., 1970); Indiana University School of Law (J.D., cum laude, 1973). Phi Alpha Delta. *Member:* Lake County, Indiana State and American Bar Associations. ***PRACTICE AREAS:*** Real Estate; Zoning Law; Corporate Law; Estate Planning; Probate Law; Banking; Civil Practice. ***Email:*** randerson@andersonward.com

MEGAN L. WARD, born Valparaiso, Indiana, May 19, 1976; admitted to bar, 2001, Indiana; U.S. District Court, Northern and Southern Districts of Indiana; U.S. Court of Appeals, Seventh Circuit. *Education:* Indiana University (B.S., 1998); Indiana University School of Law (J.D., 2001). *Member:* Lake County, Indiana State and American Bar Associations. ***PRACTICE AREAS:*** Bankruptcy; Family Law; Collections; Estate Planning; Guardianship; Divorce. ***Email:*** mward@andersonward.com

---

ARSHAD, PANGERE & WARRING, LLP

7899 TAFT STREET
MERRILLVILLE, INDIANA 46410
Telephone: 219-736-6500
Fax: 219-736-6591
URL: http://www.apwlaw.net

Estate Planning, Trusts and Estates, Wills and Probate, Guardianship, Asset Protection, Elder Law, Business Law, Business Planning, Contracts, Business Litigation, Business Enterprises, Corporate, Starting a Business, Buying and Selling a Business, Personal Injury, Automobile Accidents, Slip and Fall, Wrongful Death, Medical Malpractice, Family Law, Adoptions, Child Custody, Child Support, Divorce, Domestic Violence, Immigration, Municipal, Criminal Law, Driving While Intoxicated, Drug Crimes, Parole and Probation, Juvenile Law.

FIRM PROFILE: A full service law firm concentrating in the areas of Family Law, Criminal Law, Personal Injury and Business.

SOPHIA J. ARSHAD, born Eloise, Michigan, June 24, 1975; admitted to bar, 2003, Indiana and U.S. District Court, Northern and Southern Districts of Indiana; 2004, Illinois. *Education:* University of Chicago (B.A., Psychology, 1996); Valparaiso University (J.D., cum laude, 2003; M.A., Psychology, 2003). Psi Chi, National Honor Society in Psychology. *Member:* Chicago, Lake County, Illinois State, Indiana State and American Bar Associations. ***PRACTICE AREAS:*** Estate Planning; Elder Law; Business Planning; Personal Injury; Family Law; Immigration. ***Email:*** sjarshad@apwlaw.net

VASILIA M. PANGERE, born Merrillville, Indiana, July 28, 1978; admitted to bar, 2003, Indiana and U.S. District Court, Northern and Southern Districts of Indiana. *Educa-*

(This Listing Continued)

ARSHAD, PANGERE & WARRING, LLP, Merrillville—Continued

tion: Valparaiso University (B.A., Economics, 2000; J.D., 2003). *Member:* Lake County, Indiana State and American Bar Associations. ***PRACTICE AREAS:*** Family Law; Personal Injury; Elder Law; Municipal; Business. ***Email:*** vmpangere@apwlaw.net

MATTHEW J. WARRING, born Waterbury, Connecticut; admitted to bar, 2003, Indiana and U.S. District Court, Northern and Southern Districts of Indiana. *Education:* Indiana University (B.S., Business Management, 2000); Valparaiso University (J.D., 2003). *Member:* Lake County, Indiana State and American Bar Associations. ***PRACTICE AREAS:*** Criminal Law; Employment Law; Personal Injury; Civil Rights; Medical Malpractice. ***Email:*** mjwarring@apwlaw.net

BROWN & BROWN

ATTORNEYS AT LAW, P.C.

Established in 1928

7448 BROADWAY

MERRILLVILLE, INDIANA 46410

Telephone: 219-769-4230

Fax: 219-769-4237

Email: gwblaw@aol.com

URL: http://www.lawyers.com/gwblaw

Lowell, Indiana Office: 771 West Commercial, 46356. Telephone: 219-696-8009.

Civil Litigation, Personal Injury, Criminal Law, Trusts and Estates, Probate, Real Estate.

FIRM PROFILE: Edwin T. Brown, Sr. began practicing law in the small town of Spencer, Indiana in 1928. Edwin T. Brown, Jr. joined the firm in 1951 at which time the firm practiced in Gary, Indiana. The firm was moved to Merrillville, Indiana in the 1970's. Gregory W. Brown joined the firm in 1989 after having practiced law with a Hammond law firm for two years. The firm now has offices in Lowell and Merrillville, Indiana.

GREGORY W. BROWN, born Gary, Indiana, May 9, 1962; admitted to bar, 1987, Indiana; 1988, Illinois. *Education:* Valparaiso University (B.S., 1984; J.D., 1987). Former President, Merrillville Optimist Club. *Member:* Lake County, Illinois State, Indiana State and American Bar Associations; The Association of Trial Lawyers of America. ***REPORTED CASES:*** Lovings v. Cleary, NE2d (Ind. App. 2003); In Re: Dzurovcak, 650 NE2d 337 (Ind. App. 1995); Timm v. State, 644 NE2d 1235 (Ind. App. 1994); Thomas v. State, 515 NE2d 880 (Ind. App. 1987). ***PRACTICE AREAS:*** Real Estate; Personal Injury; Civil Litigation; Criminal Defense. ***Email:*** gwblaw@aol.com

BURKE COSTANZA & CUPPY LLP

Established in 1928

9191 BROADWAY

MERRILLVILLE, INDIANA 46410-7064

Telephone: 219-769-1313

Fax: 219-769-6806

URL: http://www.bcclegal.com

Munster, Indiana Office: 900 Ridge Road, Suite L. Telephone: 219-513-1000. Fax: 219-513-1001.

Valparaiso, Indiana Office: 57 Franklin Street, Suite 203. Telephone: 219-531-0134. Fax: 219-531-0507.

General Civil Practice in State and Federal Courts, Trials, Appeals, Civil Mediation, Administrative, Business Law, Business Planning, Contracts, Business Litigation, Business Enterprises, LLC's, Partnerships, Small Business, Corporate, Real Estate, Employee Benefits/ ERISA, Banking, Commercial, Insurance Defense, Personal Injury, Automobile Accidents, Wrongful Death, Wills and Probate, Trusts and Estates, Estate Planning, Medical Malpractice, Legal Malpractice, Family Law, Adoptions, Child Custody, Child Support, Divorce, Visitation Rights, Municipal and Zoning, Environmental.

PARTNERS

JOSEPH E. COSTANZA, born Chicago, Illinois, March 2, 1936; admitted to bar, 1961, Indiana and Illinois. *Education:* Wabash College (B.A., 1958); Northwestern University (J.D., 1961). Phi Alpha Delta. ***PRACTICE AREAS:*** Probate; Trusts and Estates; Taxation; Taxation Appeals; Municipal Law. ***Email:*** costanza@bcclegal.com

GEORGE W. CARBERRY, born Chicago, Illinois, August 22, 1952; admitted to bar, 1977, Indiana. *Education:* University of Notre Dame (A.B., 1974); Valparaiso University (J.D., 1977). ***PRACTICE AREAS:*** Business Law; Health Care; Real Estate; Trusts and Estates. ***Email:*** carberry@bcclegal.com

DAVID K. RANICH, born Chicago, Illinois, June 20, 1951; admitted to bar, 1977, Indiana. *Education:* DePauw University and Indiana University (B.S., with honors, 1973); Rutgers University (J.D., 1977). Beta Gamma Sigma. ***PRACTICE AREAS:*** Business Law; Commercial Law; Corporate Law; Real Estate; Trusts and Estates; Litigation. ***Email:*** ranich@bcclegal.com

ROBERT F. PARKER, born Springfield, Ohio, November 4, 1951; admitted to bar, 1977, Indiana. *Education:* University of Notre Dame (B.A., with honors, 1974); Indiana University at Bloomington (J.D., cum laude, 1977). ***PRACTICE AREAS:*** Professional Liability; Product Liability; Commercial Litigation. ***Email:*** parker@bcclegal.com

KATHRYN D. SCHMIDT, born Gary, Indiana, May 4, 1947; admitted to bar, 1980, Indiana. *Education:* Indiana University (B.S., 1969); Indiana State University (M.S., 1974); Valparaiso University (J.D., with high distinction, 1980). ***PRACTICE AREAS:*** Litigation; Appeals; Civil Mediation; Commercial Law; Civil Rights; Employment Law. ***Email:*** schmidt@bcclegal.com

PAUL A. LEONARD, JR., born Dayton, Ohio, June 20, 1953; admitted to bar, 1982, Indiana. *Education:* College of the Holy Cross (B.A., 1975); University of Dayton (M.A., 1978); Valparaiso University (J.D., 1982). (Board Certified, Family Law Specialist, Indiana State Bar Association, Family Law Certification Board). ***PRACTICE AREAS:*** Family Law. ***Email:*** leonard@bcclegal.com

PAULA E. NEFF, born Gary, Indiana, November, 11, 1953; admitted to bar, 1982, Illinois; 1983, Indiana. *Education:* Indiana University (A.S., 1974; B.S., 1976; M.S., 1978); The John Marshall Law School (J.D., 1982). ***PRACTICE AREAS:*** Health Care; Environmental; Civil Litigation; Commercial Law; Corporate; Administrative Proceedings; Employment Law. ***Email:*** neff@bcclegal.com

TODD A. ETZLER, born Hammond, Indiana, January 20, 1966; admitted to bar, 1991, Indiana. *Education:* Purdue University (B.S., 1988); Indiana University (J.D., 1991). ***PRACTICE AREAS:*** Real Estate; Business Law; Construction Law; Zoning, Planning and Land Use; Trusts and Estates. ***Email:*** etzler@bcclegal.com

KEVIN E. STEELE, born Gary, Indiana, November 24, 1967; admitted to bar, 1993, Indiana. *Education:* University of Notre Dame (B.A., 1990); Indiana University (J.D., 1993). Notre Dame Scholar. ***PRACTICE AREAS:*** Litigation; Construction Law; Commercial Law; Insurance Defense; Mortgages. ***Email:*** steele@bcclegal.com

VICTOR H. PRASCO, born Gary, Indiana, September 27, 1965; admitted to bar, 1993, Indiana and Illinois. *Education:* Indiana University (B.S., 1988); Valparaiso University (J.D., magna cum laude, 1993). ***PRACTICE AREAS:*** Estate Planning; Probate; Taxation; Business Law; Real Estate. ***Email:*** prasco@bcclegal.com

NATALIE V. SHRADER, born Gary, Indiana, October 27, 1967; admitted to bar, 1994, Indiana. *Education:* Purdue University (B.S., 1990); Valparaiso University (J.D., 1994). ***PRACTICE AREAS:*** Litigation; Insurance Defense; Leases and Leasing; Housing Law. ***Email:*** shrader@bcclegal.com

ASSOCIATES

ANDREW L. KRAEMER, born Waterloo, Iowa, July 14, 1964; admitted to bar, 1989, Indiana. *Education:* Augustana College (A.B., 1986); Valparaiso University (J.D., 1989). Delta Theta Phi. ***PRACTICE AREAS:*** Bankruptcy; Debtor and Creditor; Mortgages; Commercial Law. ***Email:*** kraemer@bcclegal.com

JON A. SCHMALTZ, born LaPorte, Indiana, October 20, 1973; admitted to bar, 1999, Indiana. *Education:* Purdue University (B.S., 1996); Indiana University School of Law - Indianapolis (J.D., 1999). ***PRACTICE AREAS:*** Real Estate; Business Law; Zoning, Planning and Land Use; Trusts and Estates. ***Email:*** schmaltz@bcclegal.com

CHAD J. MELCHI, born Angola, Indiana, July 21, 1972; admitted to bar, 2001, Indiana. *Education:* Indiana University (B.S., 1995); Indiana University School of Law (J.D., 2001). Associate Editor, Indiana Law Review, 1998-2000. ***PRACTICE AREAS:*** Medical Malpractice; Insurance Defense; Business Litigation; Commercial Litigation. ***Email:*** melchi@bcclegal.com

JOSEPH A. SAMRETA, born June 19, 1973; admitted to bar, 1999, Indiana. *Education:* Wabash College (A.B., 1995); Indiana University (J.D., 1999). ***PRACTICE AREAS:*** Civil Litigation; Civil Appeals; Insurance Defense; Business Litigation; Commercial Litigation. ***Email:*** samreta@bcclegal.com

BARRY W. PRUETT, born Harvey, Illinois, January 23, 1970; admitted to bar, 2005, Indiana. *Education:* Miami University (B.S., 1993); Valparaiso University (J.D., 2005). ***PRACTICE AREAS:*** Business Law; Real Estate Law; Contracts; Probate. ***Email:*** pruett@bcclegal.com

OF COUNSEL

EDWARD L. BURKE, born Gary, Indiana, October 17, 1930; admitted to bar, 1954, Indiana. *Education:* University of Notre Dame (LL.B., magna cum laude, 1954). ***PRACTICE AREAS:*** Probate; Estate Planning; Real Estate; Taxation. ***Email:*** burke@bcclegal.com

FREDERICK M. CUPPY, born Indianapolis, Indiana, June 2, 1941; admitted to bar, 1966, Indiana. *Education:* Indiana University (B.S., 1962; J.D., 1966). ***PRACTICE AREAS:*** International Estate Planning; Asset Protection. ***Email:*** fcuppy@bcclegal.com

GREGORY R. LYMAN, born Flint, Michigan, September 27, 1952; admitted to bar, 1977, Michigan; 1978, Indiana. *Education:* Michigan State University (B.S., magna cum laude, 1974); Valparaiso University (J.D., with high honors, 1977). ***PRACTICE AREAS:*** Employee Benefits; ERISA; Labor Law; Employment Law; Civil Mediation. ***Email:*** lyman@bcclegal.com

JOHN G. DONNER, born South Bend, Indiana, July 3, 1951; admitted to bar, 1977, Indiana. *Education:* Indiana University (A.B., 1974; J.D., 1977). ***PRACTICE AREAS:*** Business Law; Real Estate Law. ***Email:*** donner@bcclegal.com

REPRESENTATIVE CLIENTS: Lehigh Portland Cement Company; Continental Machine & Engineering Co., Inc.; Gary Steel Products Corp.; Superior Construction Co., Inc.; Federal National Mortgage Association; St. Catherine Hospital of East Chicago, Indiana; Simon DeBartolo Property Group; The Travelers Insurance Companies (Panel Counsel); Guide One Insurance Companies; The City of East Chicago (Contract Counsel).

JOHN P. BUSHEMI & ASSOCIATES

Established in 1974

8959 BROADWAY

MERRILLVILLE, INDIANA 46410

Telephone: 219-769-8100

Facsimile: 219-769-8170

URL: http://www.bushemilawfirm.com

Email: jbushatt@netnitco.net

URL: http://www.bushemilaw.com

Civil Trial Practice in State and Federal Courts, Collections, Corporate, Domestic Relations, Adoption, Divorce, Child Custody, Child Support, Employment, Wills and Probate, Trusts and Estates, Guardianship, Estate Planning, Medical Malpractice, Municipal, Personal Injury, Product Liability, Public Utilities, Real Estate, State Agencies, Workers Compensation and Zoning.

(This Listing Continued)

JOHN P. BUSHEMI, born Chicago, Illinois, April 13, 1948; admitted to bar, 1974, Indiana; U.S. Court of Appeals, Seventh Circuit. *Education:* Indiana University (A.B., 1970; J.D., 1973). Indiana State Senator, 1976-1990. Indiana Department of Revenue Attorney, 1992—. Lake County Sheriff's Attorney, 1995-2002. Hobart City Attorney, 1996—; Schererville Fire Commission Attorney, 2001-2003; Schererville Park Board Attorney, 2001—. Schererville Plan Commission Attorney, 2004—. Schererville Board of Zoning Appeals Attorney, 2004—. Schererville Police Commission Attorney, 2004—. Hammond Public Safety Attorney, 2004—.

ASSOCIATE

KEVIN E. WERNER, born Laporte, Indiana, July 9, 1972; admitted to bar, 2001, Indiana and U.S. District Court, Northern and Southern Districts of Indiana. *Education:* Purdue University (B.A., 1996); Southern Illinois University (J.D., 2000). Member, Purdue University Alumni Association, 1996—. *Member:* Lake County and Indiana State Bar Associations. ***Email:*** kwerner@bushemilaw.com

CHARLES E. ENSLEN

500 EAST 86TH AVENUE
MERRILLVILLE, INDIANA 46410
Telephone: 219-791-4000
Fax: 219-769-1302
Email: charlesenslen@aol.com
URL: http://www.enslenlaw.com

Commercial Law, Personal Injury, Automobile Accidents, Slip and Fall, Wrongful Death, Negligence, Bankruptcy, Business Law, Contracts, Litigation, Business Planning, Business Enterprises, Corporate, Small Business, Partnerships, Limited Liability Company Law, Real Estate, Family Law, Divorce, Child Custody, Child Support, Adoption Law, Visitation Rights, Mediation.

CHARLES E. ENSLEN, born Gary, Indiana, March 15, 1952; admitted to bar, 1977, Indiana; 1981, U.S. Court of Appeals, Seventh Circuit; 1995, U.S. Supreme Court. *Education:* Indiana University (A.B., 1974); Valparaiso University (J.D., 1977). Phi Alpha Delta. *Member:* Lake County (Member, Board of Directors, 1990-1993, 1996-2003; President, 1995), Indiana State (Member, House of Delegates, 1993—) and American Bar Associations; Indiana Trial Lawyers Association; Commercial Law League of America; Fellow, Indiana Bar Foundation.

REPRESENTATIVE CLIENTS: U.S. Steel Corp.; Combined Transport Systems, Inc.; Smith Motors, Inc. of Hammond; Smith Ford of Lowell, Inc.; Volvo Commercial Finance, LLC; The Americas, First Source Bank; Amerititle, Inc.

MARCE GONZALEZ, JR.

TWIN TOWERS BUILDING
1000 E. 80TH PLACE, 502 NORTH
MERRILLVILLE, INDIANA 46410
Telephone: 219-769-3030
FAX: 219-769-3031
Email: marceglaw@netnitco.net

Criminal Defense, Drug Crimes, Driving While Intoxicated, Juvenile Law, Felonies and Misdemeanors, Appellate, Traffic Violations, Personal Injury, Automobile Accidents, Slip and Fall, Dog Bites, Wrongful Death, Attorney Discipline Defense.

MARCE GONZALEZ, JR., born Gary, Indiana, March 8, 1954; admitted to bar, 1983, Indiana and U.S. District Court, Northern District of Indiana; 1992, U.S. Supreme Court; 1993, U.S. Court of Appeals, Seventh Circuit. *Education:* Indiana University at Bloomington (B.S., 1976; J.D., 1982). Author: "Representing Traffic Offenders in Indiana," Practice Skills Seminar, ICLEF, 1992. Author and Panelist: "Hot Topics 1999" ("Recent Trends in Professional Responsibility"), Indiana Lawyer Seminar; Defending Death Cases ("An Overview of the Lawyer Discipline Process"), IPDC, 1999; Criminal Law, 2000 ("2001: An Appellate Odyssey," Lake County Bar Association Seminar; "Hot Topics 2001," (Ethics), Lake County Bar Association; "Indiana Legal Ethics and Malpractice," Lorman, 2002. Panelist, "Developing Appellate Skills, 2001," ICLEF; "Managing Attorney-Client Privilege and the Work Product Doctrine in Indiana," NBI, 2002. Co-Author: "Criminal Appeals and Post-Conviction Relief," Criminal Law Seminar, ICLEF, 1992. Co-Author and Chair: DWI ("Developing a Medical Defense To Insufficient Breath Test Refusal Cases") ICLEF, 1998. Contributing Author and Panelist: "We The Jury" ("Post-Trial Juror Contact: Ethical Considerations"), Indiana Lawyer Seminar, 1998; "Everything You'd Better Know About Civil Law" (Professionalism in The Civil Practice), ICLEF, 1996; "Juristic Park" (Ethical Considerations) ICLEF, 1995. Panelist: "Defending Death Cases," Seminar, IPDC, 1998. Appellate Public Defender, Lake County Criminal Courts, 1986—. Public Defender, Lake Station City Court, 1991-1994. Member: Public Defenders Council, 1986—; Supreme Court Committee on Character & Fitness, 1992—. Commissioner, Indiana Supreme Court Disciplinary Commission, 1994-1999. *Member:* Lake County, Seventh Circuit and Indiana State Bar Associations; Indiana Trial Lawyers Association. ***REPORTED CASES:*** Roark v. State (1994) Ind., 644 N.E. 2d 565; Cobbs v. State, 528 NE 2d 62; Kelly v. State, 561 NE 2d 771; Ward v. State, 567 NE 2d 85; Wolfe v. State, 549 NE 2d 1024; Niksich v. State, 596 N.E. 2d 268 (Ind. 1992); McCarthy v. State, 726 N.E. 2d 789 (Ind. App. 2000); Gallant Insurance Co. v. Amaizo Federal Credit Union, 726 N.E. 2d 860 (Ind. App. 2000); Udarbe v. State, 749 N.E. 2d 562 (Ind.App. 2001). ***PRACTICE AREAS:*** Criminal Defense; Criminal Appeals; Civil Appeals; Personal Injury; Traffic Violations; Nursing and Health Care Professionals Defense; Attorney Discipline Defense.

THOMAS M. GREENBERG, P.C.

99 EAST 86TH AVENUE, SUITE E-2
MERRILLVILLE, INDIANA 46410-6267
Telephone: 219-769-2600
Fax: 219-769-2688
Email: tmg@jorsm.com

General Practice, Trusts and Estates, Estate Planning, Probate, Real Estate, Real Estate Transactions, Employment Law, Employee Benefits, Business Law, Business Formation, Business Enterprises, Limited Liability Company Law, Commercial Law, Professional Practices, Tax Exempt Organizations, Health Law, Mental Health Law, Local Government Law, General Civil Litigation.

THOMAS M. GREENBERG, born Hammond, Indiana, December 15, 1948; admitted to bar, 1973, Indiana, Illinois and U.S. District Court, Northern and Southern Districts of Indiana; 1990, U.S. U.S. Court of Appeals, Seventh Circuit and U.S. Tax Court. *Education:* Indiana University (B.A., 1970); Northwestern University (J.D., 1973). Editor, Clearinghouse Review, 1971-1973. City Attorney, City of Hobart, 1974-1975. District Attorney, Independence Hill Conservancy, 1978-1995. *Member:* Lake County, Indiana State, Illinois State and American Bar Associations. Fellow, Indiana Bar Foundation. ***Email:*** tmg@jorsm.com

REPRESENTATIVE CLIENTS: Southlake Community Mental Health Center, Inc.; Geminus Corp.; Radiologic Associates of Northwest Indiana, Inc.; Haire Group; Calumet Orthopedic & Prosthetics Co.
REFERENCE: Fifth Third Bank, Merrillville, Indiana.

HODGES & DAVIS, P.C.

Established in 1906
8700 BROADWAY
MERRILLVILLE, INDIANA 46410
Telephone: 219-641-8700
Fax: 219-641-8710
URL: http://www.hodgesdavis.com

Portage, Indiana Office: 6082 Lute Road. P.O. Box 1037. Telephone: 219-762-9129. Fax: 219-762-2826.

General Civil Practice in all State and Federal Courts, Trials and Appeals, Insurance Defense, Corporation, Health and Hospital, Municipal and Zoning Law, Criminal, Driving While Intoxicated, Financing, Tax and Administrative Law. EEOC, Negligence, Products Liability, Environmental, Wills and Probate, Trusts and Estates, Estate Planning, Real Estate and Foreclosure Law. Consumer and Commercial Collections, Business Law, Business Planning, Business Litigation, Business Enterprises, Corporate, Partnerships, Small Business, Buying and Selling a Business, Business Start-Ups.

FIRM PROFILE: Established in 1906, Hodges & Davis is a progressive law firm providing a wide range of legal services to the residents of Northwest Indiana. The firm's attorneys work closely with one another, combining their knowledge, skills and experience to provide innovative and cost-effective solutions to the legal problems they are called upon to address.

WILLIAM F. HODGES (1877-1954)
CLAUDE V. RIDGELY (1881-1963)
THOMAS M. HODGES (1906-1969)
HERSCHEL B. DAVIS (1901-1990)
GILBERT GRUENBERG (1902-1989)
BRUCE E. SAYERS (1939-1990)
WILLIAM B. DAVIS (Retired)

CLYDE D. COMPTON, born Grand Forks, North Dakota, March 23, 1940; admitted to bar, 1965, Indiana; 1978, U.S. Supreme Court. *Education:* Columbia University and DePauw University (B.A., 1962); Indiana University (LL.B., 1965). City Council Attorney, Portage, Indiana, 1973-1987. Water Reclamation Board Attorney, Portage, Indiana, 1976—. Member, Board of Visitors, Indiana University Law School, 1986-1988, 2002—. President: Indiana University Law School Alumni Association, 1988-1989; Visiting Nurse Association of Northwest Indiana, 1994-1996. *Member:* Lake County (Treasurer, 1986-1987), Indiana State (Treasurer, 1989-1992, Secretary, 1992-1994; Member: Mandatory Legal Education Task Force, 1985-1986; Board of Managers, 1977-1979; House of Delegates, 1970-1992; Chairman: Committees on: Legal Economics, 1983-1985; Competency, 1979-1982; Budget and Finance, 1986-1992; Draft Committee of the House of Delegates, 1986; Staff Compensation Committee, 1990-1996; Chairman, House of Delegates, 2001; Vice President, 2002-2003; President-Elect, 2003-2004; President, 2004-2005) and American Bar Associations; Indiana Bar Foundation (Treasurer, 1990-1992; Secretary, 1992-1994; President-Elect, 1994-1996; President, 1996-1998). Master, Calumet American Inn of Court. ***PRACTICE AREAS:*** Trial Practice; Real Estate; Corporate and Business Law. ***Email:*** ccompton@hodgesdavis.com

EARLE F. HITES, born Indianapolis, Indiana, October 18, 1947; admitted to bar, 1972, Indiana. *Education:* Indiana University (B.S., 1969); Valparaiso University (J.D., 1972). Member, Editorial Board, Valparaiso University Law Review, 1971-1972. Author: Student Note, "Student Voting Rights," 6 Valparaiso University Law Review. *Member:* Lake County, Indiana State and American Bar Associations; American Health Lawyers Association. ***PRACTICE AREAS:*** Health Care Law; Corporate and Business; Real Estate; Creditors Rights Law. ***Email:*** ehites@hodgesdavis.com

R. LAWRENCE STEELE, born Valparaiso, Indiana, March 28, 1947; admitted to bar, 1974, Indiana and Wisconsin. *Education:* Indiana University (B.S., 1969); Indiana University at Indianapolis (J.D., 1974). Phi Delta Phi. Lake County Deputy Prosecutor, Felony Division, 1976-1978. Porter County Deputy Prosecutor, 1980-1981. U.S. Attorney for Northern District of Indiana, 1981-1985. Attorney: Porter County Plan Commission, 1993-2002; Porter County Board of Zoning Appeals, 1993-2002; Certified Civil Mediator. *Member:* Lake County, Porter County, Indiana State (Member, Environmental Law Section),

(This Listing Continued)

HODGES & DAVIS, P.C., Merrillville—Continued

Federal and American (Member, Sections on: Litigation; Labor and Employment Law) Bar Associations; State Bar of Wisconsin; National Association of Former U.S. Attorneys. ***PRACTICE AREAS:*** Civil and Criminal Litigation; Employment Law; Business Law; Health Care Law; Real Estate. ***Email:*** rsteele@hodgesdavis.com

GREGORY A. SOBKOWSKI, born Gary, Indiana, January 10, 1957; admitted to bar, 1982, Indiana. *Education:* University of Notre Dame (B.A., cum laude, 1979; J.D., 1982). City Attorney, Portage, Indiana, 1988—. Attorney, Portage Township Schools, 1995—. *Member:* Lake County, Indiana State (Chairman, Young Lawyers Section, 1989-1990; Member, ICLEF Board of Directors, 1990-1991; Treasurer, 1999-2000) and American (Delegate, House of Delegates 1991-1994, 1999—) Bar Associations. ***PRACTICE AREAS:*** Municipal Law; Corporate and Business; Health Care Law; Real Estate; Estate Planning; Probate. ***Email:*** gsobkowski@hodgesdavis.com

BONNIE C. COLEMAN, born Neenah, Wisconsin, September 3, 1960; admitted to bar, 1984, Indiana. *Education:* Ripon College (A.B., magna cum laude, 1981); Valparaiso University (J.D., 1984). Phi Beta Kappa. Adjunct Professor, Valparaiso University. Director, Boys & Girls Club of NW Indiana (President, 1998; Vice-President, 1995-1997; Treasurer, 1994). *Member:* Lake County, Indiana State and American Bar Associations. ***PRACTICE AREAS:*** Health Care Law; Corporate and Business; Municipal Law; Estate Planning; Probate; Real Estate; Finance. ***Email:*** bcoleman@hodgesdavis.com

LAURA B. FROST, born Evanston, Illinois, July 20, 1965; admitted to bar, 1991, Indiana and Illinois. *Education:* Illinois Wesleyan University (B.A., magna cum laude, 1987); Valparaiso University (J.D., summa cum laude, 1991). Phi Kappa Phi; Phi Delta Phi. Note Editor, Valparaiso University Law Review, 1990-1991. Author: Student Note, "He Who Controls the Mind Controls the Body: False Imprisonment, Religious Cults, and the Destruction of Volitional Capacity," 25 Valparaiso University Law Review 407. Attorney, Town of Dune Acres, 1994-1998; Portage Plan Commission, 1994-1995; Portage Board of Zoning Appeals, 1994-1995. Director, 2000-2005, President, 2003-2005 and Vice President, 2002, Lake County Foundation for the Retarded. *Member:* Lake County, Indiana State and American Bar Associations. ***PRACTICE AREAS:*** Health Care Law; Corporate; Business. ***Email:*** lfrost@hodgesdavis.com

BENJAMIN T. BALLOU, born Hammond, Indiana, October 23, 1973; admitted to bar, 1999, Indiana. *Education:* University of Chicago (B.A., 1996); Valparaiso University School of Law (J.D., 1999). *Member:* Lake County and Indiana State Bar Associations. ***PRACTICE AREAS:*** Probate; Estate Planning; Corporate; Health Law; General Practice. ***Email:*** bballou@hodgesdavis.com

DAVID H. KREIDER, born Akron, Ohio, October 17, 1941; admitted to bar, 1970, Indiana. *Education:* Indiana University (A.B., 1964; J.D., 1970). Deputy Attorney General, Indiana, 1971-1977. District Counsel, U.S. Small Business Administration, Indianapolis District Office, 1977-1983. Assistant United States Attorney, Northern District of Indiana, 1983-1985. Senior Attorney, FDIC, Indianapolis Consolidated Office, 1985-1986. *Member:* Lake County and Indiana State Bar Associations. ***PRACTICE AREAS:*** Commercial Law; Bankruptcy Law; Litigation; Health Care Law. ***Email:*** dkreider@hodgesdavis.com

R. TIMOTHY FLETCHER, born La Porte, Indiana, September 16, 1971; admitted to bar, 2003, Indiana. *Education:* Indiana State University (B.S., magna cum laude, 1995); Valparaiso University School of Law (J.D., 2003). Author: 37 Val. U. L. Rev. 983 Summer 2003. *Member:* Lake County, Indiana State and American Bar Associations. ***Email:*** rfletcher@hodgesdavis.com

REBECCA C. HOPKINS, born Gary, Indiana, November 7, 1959; admitted to bar, 2003, Indiana. *Education:* Purdue University (B.S., 1982); Valparaiso University (J.D., 2003). Pharmacist, 1982. *Member:* Lake County, Indiana State and American Bar Associations. ***Email:*** rhopkins@hodgesdavis.com

OF COUNSEL

EDWARD J. HUSSEY, born Detroit, Michigan, April 6, 1947; admitted to bar, 1975, Indiana. *Education:* University of Notre Dame (B.B.A., 1969); Indiana University (J.D., 1975). Author: "Indemnifying Corporate Officials for Williams Act Violations," 50 Indiana Law Journal 826, 1975. *Member:* Lake County, Indiana State and American Bar Associations.

REPRESENTATIVE CLIENTS: *Banks:* Centier Bank. *Mortgage Broker:* Lake Mortgage Co., Inc. *Municipal:* Gary Fire Civil Service Commission; Gary Police Pension Fund; Hobart Fire Civil Service Commission; Merrillville Community School Corporation; City of Portage, Indiana; Portage Township Schools; Portage Redevelopment Commission; Portage Water Reclamation Board. *Insurance Companies:* Hartford Insurance Co.; Liberty Mutual Insurance Co. *Health Care Providers:* The Methodist Hospitals, Inc.; Amputee Care Center, Inc.; Edgewater Systems for Balanced Living, Inc.; Geminus Corp.; Home Health Service of Porter County, Indiana, Inc.; Visiting Nurse Association of Porter County, Indiana, Inc.; Whispering Pines Nursing Home. *Auto Dealerships:* Lake Shore Ford, Inc.; Michigan City Motors, Inc.; Nielsen Buick Subaru, Inc.; Nielsen Automotive Group, Inc.; Nielsen Ford Lincoln Mercury; Nielsen Nissan; Pine Chevrolet, Inc.; Pine-Mitsubishi-Kia; Shaver Motors, Inc. *Real Estate:* Aberdeen Limited Partnership; Accent Homes, Inc.; Andover Management; Century 21 Heritage, Inc.; DeNovo Development; Inland Real Estate Group; Purdue Research Foundation. *Other:* Hawk Enterprises; Indiana-American Water Co.; Lakehead Pipe Line Co., Inc.; Vector Pipe Line Co.; Liberty Homes, Inc.; R.A.S. Construction Co., Inc.; WilTel Communications, LLC.

HOEPPNER WAGNER & EVANS LLP

Established in 1976

TWIN TOWERS, SUITE 606 SOUTH
1000 EAST 80TH PLACE
P.O. BOX 10627
MERRILLVILLE, INDIANA 46410-0627
Telephone: 219-769-6552; 800-263-1466 (IN, IL)
Fax: 219-738-2349
Email: hwe@hwelaw.com
URL: http://www.hwelaw.com

Valparaiso, Indiana Office: 103 East Lincolnway, P.O. Box 2357, 46384-2357. Telephone: 219-464-4961; 800-879-2246 (IN, IL). Fax: 219-465-0603. Email: hwe@hwelaw.com

(This Listing Continued)

General Practice. Trials and Appeals in State, Federal and Tax Courts. Bankruptcy, Commercial and Banking, Corporate, Creditors' Rights, Probate, Estate Planning, Estate Administration, Financial Resources Planning, Insurance Defense, Municipal Bonds, Municipal Law, Personal Injury, Product Liability, Professional Malpractice, Real Estate, Taxation, Workers Compensation, Zoning Law, Labor and Employment Law. Mediation, OSHA, Employee Benefits Law.

RESIDENT MEMBERS

LARRY G. EVANS, admitted to bar, 1962, Indiana; 1978, U.S. Supreme Court. *Education:* Valparaiso University (A.B., 1960; J.D., 1962). Delta Theta Phi. Author: "Article Eight of the Federal Rules of Evidence: The Hearsay Rule," 8 Val. U.L. Rev. 261, 1974. Adjunct Professor of Trial Advocacy, Valparaiso University School of Law, 1972-1980. Deputy Prosecuting Attorney, 67th Indiana Judicial Circuit, 1963. President, Porter County Chapter, American Inns of Court. Local Civil Rules Advisory Committee, U.S. District Court, Northern District of Indiana. *Member:* Porter County, Indiana State, Federal (President, N.W. Indiana Chapter, 1985) and American Bar Associations; Defense Research Institute, Inc.; Indiana Defense Lawyers Association; International Association of Defense Counsel; Indiana Defense Trial Counsel (Diplomate). Director and Fellow, Indiana Bar Foundation. ***PRACTICE AREAS:*** Employment Law; Civil Litigation. ***Email:*** levans@hwelaw.com

JOHN E. HUGHES, admitted to bar, 1971, Indiana; 1978, U.S. Supreme Court; U.S. Court of Appeals, Seventh Circuit; U.S. District Court, Northern and Southern Districts of Indiana. *Education:* Capital University (B.A., 1968); Valparaiso University (J.D., 1971). Phi Alpha Delta. Associate Editor, Valparaiso University Law Review, 1970-1971. Adjunct Professor, Valparaiso University School of Law, 1991-1995. *Member:* Porter County, Lake County, Indiana State, Federal and American Bar Associations; Indiana Defense Lawyers Association. ***PRACTICE AREAS:*** Civil Litigation; Commercial Litigation; Insurance Defense; Labor and Employment Law; Personal Injury; Municipal Law; Mediation. ***Email:*** jhughes@hwelaw.com

F. JOSEPH JASKOWIAK, admitted to bar, 1979, Indiana and Illinois. *Education:* Illinois Wesleyan University (B.A., 1976); Valparaiso University (J.D., 1979). Associate Editor, Valparaiso University Law Review, 1978-1979. Author: "The Meaning of the Term 'Accident' in the Indiana Workmen's Compensation Act," 13 Val. U.L. Rev. 533, 1979; "Covenants Not to Compete in Employment Agreements Under Indiana Law," Res Gestae, April, 1983; "Advantages of Designating the Physician in Workmen's Compensation Cases," Indiana Business, December, 1983. *Member:* Porter County, Lake County, Indiana State, Federal and American Bar Associations; Indiana Defense Lawyers Association. ***PRACTICE AREAS:*** Civil Litigation; Products Liability; Insurance Defense; Employment Law. ***Email:*** fjaskowiak@hwelaw.com

J. BRIAN HITTINGER, admitted to bar, 1990, Illinois, U.S. District Court, Northern District of Illinois and Supreme Court; 1992, Indiana, U.S. District Court, Northern and Southern Districts of Indiana and Supreme Court. *Education:* Indiana University at Bloomington (B.S., 1982); Valparaiso University (J.D., with high distinction, 1990). Certified Public Accountant, 1986—. *Member:* Porter County, and Lake County, Indiana State and American Bar Associations; American Institute of Certified Public Accountants; Illinois and Indiana State Certified Public Accountant Societies. ***PRACTICE AREAS:*** Tax Law; General Business Law; Trusts and Estates. ***Email:*** bhittinger@hwelaw.com

JACK A. KRAMER, admitted to bar, 1995, Indiana and U.S. District Court, Southern and Northern Districts of Indiana; 1997, U.S. Court of Appeals, Seventh Circuit; 1998, U.S. Supreme Court. *Education:* Ball State University (B.S., 1992); Valparaiso University (J.D., 1995). Valparaiso University Law Review, 1994-1995. Moot Court Society. Author: Note, "Vouching For Federal Educational Choice: If You Pay Them, They Will Come," 29 Val. U.L. Rev. 1005, 1995. *Member:* Porter County, Lake County, Indiana State and American Bar Associations. ***PRACTICE AREAS:*** Asbestos Litigation; Products Liability; Insurance Bad Faith; Litigation. ***Email:*** jkramer@hwelaw.com

JAY S. PATHEJA, admitted to bar, 1994, Illinois; 1997, Indiana; 2000, Michigan. *Education:* Indiana University (B.A., 1991); Loyola University (J.D., 1994). Vice President, Loyola Environmental Law Society, 1992-1994. *Member:* Chicago, Porter County, Lake County, Illinois State, Indiana State and American Bar Associations. ***PRACTICE AREAS:*** Estate Planning; Probate; Wills; Corporate; Real Estate. ***Email:*** jpatheja@hwelaw.com

TINA M. BENGS, admitted to bar, 1997, Indiana and U.S. District Court, Northern and Southern Districts of Indiana; 1998, U.S. Court of Appeals, Seventh Circuit. *Education:* Indiana University (B.S., 1989); Thomas M. Cooley Law School (J.D., cum laude, 1996). Member: Indiana Workers Compensation Institute; Society for Human Resource Management. *Member:* Porter County, Lake County, Indiana State and American Bar Associations; Indiana Defense Lawyers Association. ***PRACTICE AREAS:*** Employment Law; Workers Compensation. ***Email:*** tbengs@hwelaw.com

RESIDENT ASSOCIATES

MICHAEL EUGENE TOLBERT, admitted to bar, 2000, Indiana and and U.S. District Court, Northern and Southern Districts of Indiana. *Education:* Valparaiso University (B.A., 1997; J.D., cum laude, 2000). *Member:* Lake County, Porter County, Indiana State and American Bar Associations; American Inns of Court. ***Email:*** mtolbert@hwelaw.com

ERIC P. MATHISEN, admitted to bar, 1996, Indiana. *Education:* Carthage College (B.A., 1992); Valparaiso University (J.D., 1996). Moot Court Society, 1995-1996. Listed in Who's Who Among American Law Students, 1994-1996. Certified Mediator, 1998—. Real Estate License, St. Joseph County, In., 1996. Formerly with Konopa, Reagan & Kenyon, P.C. Member, Indiana HIPAA Workgroup. *Member:* Lake County, Porter County, St. Joseph County, Indiana State and American Bar Associations; Defense Research Institute, Inc.; Defense Trial Counsel of Indiana; Porter County Chapter, American Inn of Court. ***PRACTICE AREAS:*** Civil Litigation; Mediation; Products Liability; Wrongful Death; Brain Injury; Insurance Litigation; Nursing Home Abuse and Neglect. ***Email:*** emathisen@hwelaw.com

GEROLD L. STOUT, admitted to bar, 2002, Indiana. *Education:* Purdue University (B.A., 1996); Valparaiso University (J.D., 2001). Pi Sigma Alpha. Listed, *Who's Who:*

(This Listing Continued)

American Law Students, 1999-2001. Member: Lake County, Indiana State and American Bar Associations. ***PRACTICE AREAS:*** Estate Planning; Corporate Law; Taxation. ***Email:*** gstout@hwelaw.com

CINTRA D.B. GEAIRN, admitted to bar, 1998, Illinois (Not admitted in Indiana). *Education:* University of Rochester (B.A., cum laude, 1992); Chicago-Kent College of Law, Illinois Institute of Technology (J.D., summa cum laude, 1998). Order of the Coif. Member, Moot Court. Executive Board, Law Review. author, "A Pregnant Pause: Are Women Who Undergo Fertility Treatment to Achieve Pregnancy Within the Scope of Title VII's Pregnancy Discrimination Act?", 73 Chicago-Kent L. Rev. 391 (1998). *Member:* American Bar Association (Member, Labor and Employment Section); National Association of Women Lawyers (Member, Amicus Committee). ***PRACTICE AREAS:*** Labor and Employment. ***Email:*** cgeairn@hwelaw.com

SEAN E. KENYON, admitted to bar, 1991, Indiana and U.S. District Court, Northern and Southern Districts of Indiana; 1995, U.S. District Court, Northern District of Illinois and U.S. Court of Appeals, Seventh Circuit. *Education:* St. Bonaventure University (B.B.A., 1982); Indiana University (B.A., 1985; J.D., cum laude, 1991). Clerk to the Honorable Allen Sharp, U.S. District Court, Northern District of Indiana, 1991-1993. Visiting/Adjunct Lecturer, Indiana University, South Bend, 1992-1995. *Member:* St. Joseph County, Indiana State and American Bar Associations; Defense Trial Counsel of Indiana; Robert A. Grant Inn of Court. ***REPORTED CASES:*** Xantech Corp. v. Ramco Industries, Inc., 159 F.3d 1089 (7th Cir. 1998); Grand Trunk Western Rail Road Co. v. Kapitan, 698, N. E. 2d 363 (Ind. Ct App. 1998); Levee v. Beeching, 729 N. E. 2d 215 (Ind. Ct. App. 2000); Beeching v. Levee, 764 N. E. 2d 669 (Ind. Ct App 2002). ***PRACTICE AREAS:*** Civil Litigation; Appellate Practice; Insurance Coverage.

LUCRETIA A. THORNTON, admitted to bar, 1982, Indiana. *Education:* Purdue University (B.S., 1967; R.N., 1975); Valparaiso University (J.D., 1982). *Member:* Indiana State and American Bar Associations. ***PRACTICE AREAS:*** Risk Management; Hospital Law.

LEE I. LANE, admitted to bar, 2005, Indiana. *Education:* University of Denver (B.A., 1985); Valparaiso University (J.D., cum laude, 2004). Associate Editor, Valparaiso University Law Review, 2002-2003. Regional Champion, Negotiation Team, 2003; Client Counseling Team, 2002. Member, Northeast Indiana World Trade Council. *Member:* Porter County, Indiana State and American Bar Associations. [Army Reserves, 1991-1995; CW2, Illinois Army National Guard, 1995-2005]. ***PRACTICE AREAS:*** Real Estate; Corporate. ***Email:*** llane@hwelaw.com

(For complete biographical information on all Personnel, see Professional Biographies at Valparaiso, Indiana)

LAW OFFICES OF DAVID W. HOLUB

A PROFESSIONAL CORPORATION

8913 BROADWAY

MERRILLVILLE, INDIANA 46410

Telephone: 219-736-9700

Fax: 219-736-9704

Email: d.holub@verizon.net

URL: http://www.davidholublaw.com

Personal Injury, Medical Malpractice and Wrongful Death Litigation.

DAVID W. HOLUB, admitted to bar, 1982, Indiana and U.S. District Court, Northern and Southern Districts of Indiana; 1995, U.S. Supreme Court. *Education:* Olivet College (B.A., magna cum laude, 1979); Valparaiso University (J.D., 1982). Delta Theta Phi; Omicron Delta Kappa. Associate Editor, Valparaiso University Law Review, 1981-1982. Author: "The Contributory Negligence Defense as Applied Against Children in Indiana," 16 Valparaiso University L. Rev. 319-359, 1982. Co-Author: "Indiana Not-For-Profit Corporations' Standing to Maintain A Derivative Suit on Behalf of the Corporation, A Member's Suit to Enforce Membership Rights or a Citizen's Suit to Enforce Performance of Charitable Obligations," 25 Valparaiso University L. Rev. 249, 1991; Latent Heart Injury Following Vehicular Impact or Other Blunt Chest Trauma," 35 Trial Lawyer's Guide 3, Callahan, 1991. Certified Member, "The Million Dollar Advocates Forum - The Top Trial Lawyer's in America." *Member:* Lake County and Indiana State Bar Associations; The Association of Trial Lawyer's of America; Indiana Trial Lawyers Association. (Board Certified Civil Trial Attorney, National Board of Trial Advocacy). ***PRACTICE AREAS:*** Personal Injury; Products Liability; Trial; Class Actions. ***Email:*** d.holub@verizon.net

JOHNSON & RAPPA, LLC

(Formerly Spangler, Johnson & Associates)

250 EAST 90TH DRIVE

MERRILLVILLE, INDIANA 46410-8102

Telephone: 219-769-0087

Fax: 219-769-0092

URL: http://www.JohnsonRappa.com

URL: http://www.johnsonrappalaw.com

Trial, Appellate, Personal Injury, Automobile Accidents, Slip and Fall, Wrongful Death, and Defense Practice in State and Federal Courts. Insurance, Civil Rights, Labor and Employment, Wrongful Termination, Employment Contracts, Mediation and Arbitration, Class Actions, Construction, Administrative, Products Liability and Transportation Law.

FIRM PROFILE: Johnson & Rappa, LLC are litigators providing to its clients in Merrillville and the Lake Region in Northwest Indiana with a full service civil trial practice in State and Federal Courts. The highly rated firm's attorneys are experienced in personal injury, products liability, as well as questions of construction and transportation law and insurance defense. They are active members of state and national attorneys organizations and trial lawyers organizations.

STEVEN A. JOHNSON, born Providence, Rhode Island, March 27, 1949; admitted to bar, 1975, Indiana and U.S. District Court, Northern and Southern Districts of Indiana; 1976, Florida; 1977, U.S. Court of Appeals, Seventh Circuit; 1979, U.S. Supreme Court; 1990, U.S. District Court, Northern District of Illinois. *Education:* University of Florida; Loyola University (B.B.A., 1971); University of Miami (J.D., 1975). *Member:* Seventh Circuit, Lake County, Indiana State and American Bar Associations; The Florida Bar; Inn of Court. ***PRACTICE AREAS:*** Civil Litigation; Labor and Employment; Class Actions; Insurance; Product Liability; Construction. ***Email:*** saj@JohnsonRappa.com

MICHAEL J. RAPPA, born Milwaukee, Wisconsin, October 17, 1963; admitted to bar, 1993, Indiana and U.S. District Court, Northern and Southern Districts of Indiana; 1994, Florida. *Education:* University of Wisconsin-Madison (B.A., 1986); Valparaiso University (J.D., 1993). *Member:* The Florida Bar; Inn of Court. ***PRACTICE AREAS:*** Civil Litigation; Labor and Employment; Class Actions; Insurance; Product Liability; Construction. ***Email:*** mjr@JohnsonRappa.com

GEORGE S. IVANCEVICH, born Chicago, Illinois, February 6, 1955; admitted to bar, 1984, Indiana and Illinois. *Education:* Indiana University (B.A., 1977); John Marshall Law School (J.D., 1983). Magistrate, Lake Circuit Court (1999-2005). Probate Commissioner (1997-1999). Member, Lake County Bar Association (2003-2004). Certified Family Law Mediator. Master, Calumet Chapter, American Inn of Court (1997—). ***PRACTICE AREAS:*** Civil Litigation; Plaintiffs Personal Injury; Insurance Defense; Family Law; Labor and Employment. ***Email:*** gsi@JohnsonRappa.com

REPRESENTATIVE CLIENTS: Insurance: Citizens Insurance Company of America; Claims America, Inc.; Crawford & Company; Design Professionals Insurance Company; Liberty International Insurance Company; Gallagher Barnett Services, Inc.; Hanover Insurance Company; Standard Mutual Insurance Co.; The United Fire Group; Inventors Insurance Group; North American Specialty; Northland Insurance Companies; Westfield Insurance Company; Zurich-American Insurance Group. Non-Insurance: Americall Telemarketing Corporation; Buffington Harbor Riverboats, LLC; Calumet Builders' Association; City of Crown Point Library Board; City of Gary, Indiana; East Chicago FOP; Gough Construction Co., Inc.; Home Depot, U.S.A., Inc.; Indiana Landscapers Association; Mental Health Associates; Metromedia Steakhouse Company, LP; McDonalds, Inc.; National Steel Corporation; Plumbing & Piping Contractors Association of Northern Indiana; Purdue University; Rieth-Riley Construction Co., Inc.; Sequa Corporation; Superior Construction Company, Inc.; Whiteco Industries, Inc.; City of Crown Point; Town of Merrillville; Town of Winfield.

KOPKO GENETOS & RETSON LLP

Established in 1999

8585 BROADWAY

SUITE 480

MERRILLVILLE, INDIANA 46410

Telephone: 219-755-0400

Fax: 219-755-0410

URL: http://www.kgr-law.com

Bankruptcy, Debtor and Creditor, Landlord and Tenant Law, Foreclosure, Affordable Housing, Multi-Family Housing, Real Estate, Banks and Banking, Commercial Law, Consumer Law, Taxation, Estate Planning, Business Law and Litigation.

MEMBERS OF FIRM

ANDREW J. KOPKO, born Gary, Indiana, December 20, 1939; admitted to bar, 1964, Indiana and Illinois. *Education:* University of Notre Dame (B.B.A., 1961, J.D., 1964). Member, Notre Dame Lawyer, 1963-1964, *Member:* Lake County and Indiana State Bar Associations; American Bankruptcy Institute. ***PRACTICE AREAS:*** Bankruptcy; Debtor and Creditor; Landlord and Tenant; Foreclosures; Real Estate. ***Email:*** kgrbky@kgr-law.com

LAMBERT C. GENETOS, born Gary, Indiana, December 9, 1945; admitted to bar, 1970, Indiana. *Education:* Indiana University (A.B., 1967; J.D., 1970). *Member:* Lake County, Indiana State and American Bar Associations; Commercial Law League; American Bankruptcy Institute. ***PRACTICE AREAS:*** Banks and Banking; Commercial Law; Consumer Law; Bankruptcy; Debtor and Creditor. ***Email:*** genetos@kgr-law.com

DEMETRI J. RETSON, born Chicago, Illinois, January 23, 1952; admitted to bar, 1977, Illinois; 1986, Indiana. *Education:* Northwestern University (B.A., 1974; M.A., 1974); Harvard University (J.D., 1977). ***PRACTICE AREAS:*** Real Estate Finance; Commercial Banking; Taxation; Estate Planning; Affordable Housing; Multi-Family Housing. ***Email:*** retson@kgr-law.com

STACIA L. YOON, born Sioux City, Iowa, November 26, 1963; admitted to bar, 1992, Indiana. *Education:* Butler University (B.A., 1986); Indiana University at Bloomington (M.A., 1989; J.D., 1992). Chapter 7 Trustee, Northern District of Indiana, Gary Division. *Member:* Lake County, Indiana State and American Bar Associations; National Association of Bankruptcy Trustees. ***PRACTICE AREAS:*** Bankruptcy; Litigation; Commercial Law; Consumer Law. ***Email:*** syoon@kgr-law.com

MARCO A. MOLINA, born East Chicago, Indiana, August 22, 1973; admitted to bar, 1999, Texas; 2001, Indiana. *Education:* Indiana University (B.S., 1995; J.D., 1999). *Member:* Lake County, Indiana State and American Bar Associations; State Bar of Texas; Hispanic National Bar Association. ***LANGUAGES:*** Spanish. ***PRACTICE AREAS:*** Business Law; Real Estate; Commercial Banking. ***Email:*** molina@kgr-law.com

ASSOCIATE

SETH R. BUITENDORP, born Grand Haven, Michigan, July 1, 1974; admitted to bar, 2001, Wisconsin; 2002, Indiana. *Education:* University of Michigan, Ann Arbor (B.A., 1998); Valparaiso University School of Law (J.D., 2001). Phi Beta Kappa. Former Associate, Britton & Reiher, P.C. ***PRACTICE AREAS:*** Bankruptcy; Banking Law; Commercial Law; Debtor and Creditor; Consumer Law. ***Email:*** buitendorp@kgr-law.com

OF COUNSEL

RICHARD L. MOSTAK, born Gary, Indiana, June 23, 1949; admitted to bar, 1975, Indiana. *Education:* Indiana University at Bloomington (B.S., 1972); Indiana University at Indianapolis (J.D., 1975). *Member:* Lake County, Indiana State and American Bar Associations. ***PRACTICE AREAS:*** Outdoor Advertising; Real Estate; Debtor and Creditor; Contracts; Sports Law.

(This Listing Continued)

KOPKO GENETOS & RETSON LLP, Merrillville—Continued

LILY M. SCHAEFER, born Valparaiso, Indiana, August 29, 1953; admitted to bar, 1979, Indiana; 1980, U.S. District Court, Northern District of Indiana. *Education:* Valparaiso University (B.A., with honors in History, cum laude, 1976; J.D., 1979). Board Member, Catholic Family Services, 2000-2003. *Member:* Lake County (Member, Board of Managers, 1991-1995), Porter County, and Indiana State Bar Associations. ***LANGUAGES:*** German. ***REPORTED CASES:*** Maxey v. Board of Zoning Appeals, 180 NE2d 589; Beta Tau Housing Corp. v. Board of Zoning Appeals, 499 NE2d 780. ***PRACTICE AREAS:*** Commercial Litigation; Creditors Rights; Municipal Zoning; Probate; Trust Litigation; Family Law. ***Email:*** schaefer@kgr-law.com

REPRESENTATIVE CLIENTS: Bank One, N.A.; Centier Bank; Fifth Third Bank; Mercantile National Bank; Sterling Bank & Trust, FSB; Tech Credit Union; Tri-Electronics, Inc.; Personal Finance Company; Sand Ridge Bank; Thomas Dodge of Highland, Inc.; MB Bank; Citizens Financial Services FSB; Advance Financial Federal Credit Union; Allegius Federal Credit Union; G.W Berkheim Co., Inc.; Educational Credit Management Corp.; Gary Metal Mfg. LLC; City of Portage Board of Parks and Recreation.

MICHAEL LAMBERT

500 WEST LINCOLN HIGHWAY, SUITE Q
MERRILLVILLE, INDIANA 46410
Telephone: 219-769-6171
Fax: 219-769-6172
URL: http://www.lambertlawfirm.com

Criminal Law, Drug Crimes, Driving While Intoxicated, Parole and Probation, Juvenile Crimes, Traffic Violations, Family Law, Adoption, Divorce, Child Custody, Child Support, Domestic Violence, Visitation Rights, Employment Law, Wrongful Termination, Sexual Harassment, Civil Rights, Discrimination, Personal Injury, Automobile Accidents, Slip and Fall, Wrongful Death, Bankruptcy, Wills and Probate, Guardianships, Business Law, Contracts, Lawsuits, Business Enterprises.

MICHAEL LAMBERT, born Chicago, Illinois, August 15, 1969; admitted to bar, 2000, Indiana and U.S. District Court, Northern District of Indiana; 2001, Illinois. *Education:* Indiana University (B.A., 1995); John Marshall Law School (J.D., 2000). [U.S. Army, 1987-1991]. ***LANGUAGES:*** German. ***PRACTICE AREAS:*** Criminal Law; Civil Practice; Trust Law; Real Estate.

HERBERT S. LASSER & ASSOCIATES, P.C.

3700 EAST U.S. 30
MERRILLVILLE, INDIANA 46410
Telephone: 219-942-3710
Fax: 219-942-0064
URL: http://www.lawyers.com/lasserlaw

Personal Injury, Wrongful Death, Automobile and All Accidents, Construction Law, Family Law, Divorce, Child Custody, Child Support, Domestic Violence, Visitation Rights, Work Accidents, Trials and Appeals, Business Law, Business Planning, Contracts, Law Suits, Insurance, Business Enterprises, Closely Held Business, Corporate, Limited Liability Companies, Partnerships, Small Business, Franchises, Buying and Selling A Business, Debt and Credit, Collections, Creditors Rights, Banking and Finance, Venture Capital, Employee Benefits, Employment Contracts, Human Resources, Discrimination, Sexual Harassment, Workers Compensation, Wrongful Termination, Real Estate, Buying or Selling, Commercial Leasing, Environmental, Landlord and Tenant, Zoning and Land Use, Starting a Business, Strategic Alliances, Joint Ventures, Mergers, Civil Rights, Consumer Law, Consumer Fraud, Unsafe Products, Criminal Law, Drunk Driving, Misdemeanors, Drug Crimes, Juvenile Crimes, Parole and Probation, Traffic Violations, Medical Malpractice, Legal Malpractice, Products Liability, Slip and Fall, Wills and Probate, Trusts and Estates, Asset Protection, Estate Planning, General Civil and Criminal Practice, General Practice, Trademark Patent Litigation.

HERBERT S. LASSER, born Gary, Indiana, August 17, 1928; admitted to bar, 1953, Indiana and Illinois, U.S. District Court, Northern District of Indiana and Northern District of Illinois, and U.S. Court of Appeals, Seventh Circuit. *Education:* Indiana University (B.A., 1950); Valparaiso University (J.D., 1953). Phi Alpha Delta. *Member:* Lake County, Indiana State and Illinois State Bar Associations; Association of Trial Lawyers of America. ***PRACTICE AREAS:*** Real Estate and Construction Law (60%); Personal Injury Law (20%); General Practice (20%). ***Email:*** hslasser@yahoo.com

ROBERT A. PLANTZ, born Lafayette, Indiana, April 4, 1973; admitted to bar, 2000, Indiana, U.S. District Court, Northern and Southern Districts of Indiana, and U.S. Court of Appeals, Seventh Circuit. *Education:* Purdue University (B.A., 1996); Valparaiso University (J.D., 1999). Alpha Kappa Delta. *Member:* Lake County and Indiana State Bar Associations; Association of Trial Lawyers of America. ***Email:*** robertplantz@yahoo.com

LUCAS, HOLCOMB & MEDREA LLP

Established in 1949
300 EAST 90TH DRIVE
MERRILLVILLE, INDIANA 46410
Telephone: 219-769-3561
Fax: 219-756-7409
Email: lhm@lhmlaw.com

General Practice, State and Federal Courts. Trials and Appeals. Corporate, Business, Business Litigation, Contracts, Business Planning, Business Enterprises, Commercial, Employment, Wrongful Termination, Banking, Tax, Wills and Probate, Trusts and Estates and Estate Planning, Insurance, Bankruptcy, Personal Injury, Automobile Accidents, Wrongful Death, Products Liability, Family/Domestic Relations, Adoptions, Child Custody, Child Support, Divorce, Visitation Rights, Hospital, Real Estate, Municipal and Zoning Law, Consumer and Commercial Collection Law, Construction Litigation.

FIRM PROFILE: Since 1949, the preeminent firm of Lucas, Holcomb & Medrea has offered clients in Merrillville and Northwest Indiana a full-service Civil Trial Practice, with appeals in State and Federal Courts, concentrating on Business and Commercial Litigation, Personal Injury, Product Liability, Probate, Hospital Law and Employment Law. In addition, the firm has extensive experience in Business Law matters, including Corporate Law, Bankruptcy, Commercial Leases and Litigation, as well as Estate Planning, Family/Domestic Relations, Real Estate and Zoning. Members of the firm are active in state and national lawyer associations, and in local governance.

MEMBERS OF FIRM

ROBERT A. LUCAS (1922-1999)

JAMES A. HOLCOMB, born Saginaw, Michigan, March 9, 1934; admitted to bar, 1961, Indiana. *Education:* Flint Community College (A.A., 1954); University of Michigan (B.A., 1958; J.D., 1961). Park Board Attorney, City of Gary, 1962-1968. President, Legal Aid Society of Gary, 1968-1970. Secretary-Treasurer, 1971-1972; Vice President, 1972-1973 and President, 1973-1974, Gary Bar Association. Corporation Counsel, City of Gary, 1972-1973. Attorney, Gary Public Transportation Corporation, 1974-1994. Member, Board of Directors, Indiana Lawyers Commission, 1977-1989. Member, 1984— and President, 1984-1988, Community Corrections Advisory Board. Member, Board of Directors, Indiana Natural Resources Foundation, 1990—. Trustee, Indiana Heritage Trust, 1990—. *Member:* Indiana State Bar Association (Secretary, Young Lawyers Section, 1965-1966; Vice Chairman, 1966-1967; Chairman, 1967-1968; Member of Board of Managers, 1967-1968); American Health Lawyers Association; Indiana Bar Foundation (President, Board of Directors, 1982-1984). Fellow: Indiana State Bar Foundation; American Bar Foundation (Life Fellow). ***PRACTICE AREAS:*** Banking Law; Hospital Law; Health Care Law; Business Law.

JOHN O. STILES, born Gary, Indiana, 1932; admitted to bar, 1958, Illinois; 1959, Indiana. *Education:* Indiana University (A.B., 1953); Harvard University (LL.B., cum laude, 1958). Phi Beta Kappa. Author: "Antenuptial Agreements and The Subsequent Marriage," Will & Trust Drafting-A Case Study Approach, Indiana Continuing Legal Education Forum, 1988. *Member:* Lake County Bar Association. ***PRACTICE AREAS:*** Real Estate Law; Probate Law; Corporate Law; Commercial Leases.

DANIEL A. MEDREA, born East Chicago, Indiana, April 10, 1944; admitted to bar, 1969, Indiana; 1970, Illinois; 1971, Florida; 1984, U.S. Court of Appeals, Seventh Circuit; 1993, U.S. Supreme Court. *Education:* University of Notre Dame (A.B., magna cum laude, 1966); Indiana University (J.D., 1969). Member, Board of Directors, Legal Aid Society of Gary, 1972-1977. Member, Panel of Arbitrators, American Arbitration Association. Member, Board of Directors, 1991-2001 and Chairman of Board, 1995-1998, South Suburban Hospital, Hazelcrest, Illinois. Certified Civil Mediator. *Member:* Lake County, Indiana State (Member, Executive Council, 1971-1974, Secretary-Treasurer, 1974-1975, Chairman-Elect, 1975-1976 and Chairman, 1976-1977, Young Lawyers Section; Board of Managers, 1981-1983), Illinois State and American (Executive Council, Young Lawyers Division, 1977-1979) Bar Associations; The Florida Bar; Seventh Circuit Bar Association; Calumet Inns of Court. ***PRACTICE AREAS:*** Civil Litigation; Employment Law; Business Law; Civil Mediation.

ROBERT F. PETERS, born Wausau, Wisconsin, June 23, 1946; admitted to bar, 1971, Indiana; 1972, U.S. District Court, Southern District of Indiana; 1976, U.S. District Court, Northern District of Indiana and U.S. Court of Appeals, 7th Circuit; 1977, U.S. Supreme Court. *Education:* Valparaiso University (B.A., 1968; J.D., 1971). Attorney, Gary Model Cities Agency, 1971-1972. Deputy Prosecuting Attorney, Lake County, 1973-1980. *Member:* Lake County, Indiana State and American Bar Associations; The Association of Trial Lawyers of America; The American Health Lawyers Association. ***PRACTICE AREAS:*** Personal Injury; Products Liability; Civil Litigation; Insurance Defense Law; Employment Law; Construction Litigation. ***Email:*** rpeters@lhmlaw.com

STEPHEN R. PLACE, born Evanston, Illinois, May 28, 1946; admitted to bar, 1972, Indiana and U.S. District Court, Southern and Northern Districts of Indiana. *Education:* Duke University (A.B., 1968); Indiana University (J.D., 1972). Phi Delta Phi. Deputy Prosecuting Attorney, Lake County, 1974-1980. Certified Family and Civil Law Mediator. Treasurer, Indiana Federal Community Defender Corp Calumet Inns of Court. Board of Directors, Legacy Foundation, Inc., 2004—. *Member:* Lake County (Member, Board of Directors, 1989-1990; 1995-1998; Vice President, 2001; President Elect, 2002; President, 2003), Indiana State (Member: Family Law Section; House of Delegates, 2001—) and American Bar Associations. ***PRACTICE AREAS:*** Family Law; Real Estate Law; Bankruptcy Law; Corporate Law. ***Email:*** splace@lhmlaw.com

MARY LINDA CASEY, born Milan, Indiana, March 7, 1945; admitted to bar, 1970, Indiana. *Education:* Indiana University (B.A., 1967; J.D., 1970). Appointee, Indianapolis District Director, Federal Women's Program Coordinator for Indianapolis District, 1973-1975. Attorney, Internal Revenue Service, Estate Tax Division, 1970-1978. Member: Internal Revenue Service District Equal Opportunity Advisory Committee, 1973-1974; Internal Revenue Service District Training Committee, 1976-1977. Awarded Certificate of Appreciation by Indianapolis District Director, 1975. Director, Indianapolis Council of Federal Agencies, 1975-1976. President, Indiana University Women's Club of Indianapolis, 1976-1977. Member, Indiana University Alumni Executive Council, 1979-1983. Member, Board of Directors, Legacy Foundation, Inc., 1992-2001. Seminar Chairman, Tax Issues in Estate Administration, Indiana Continuing Legal Education Forum, 1993. Jasper County Library Board, 1982-1998. Member, Indiana University (Bloomington) Law School Alumni Board, 1998—. *Member:* Lake County, Indiana State (Unauthorized Practice of Law Committee, 1998—) and American Bar Associations. Fellow, American College of Trust and Estate Council (ACTEC). ***PRACTICE AREAS:*** Estate Planning; Probate; Real Estate Tax; Business Law. ***Email:*** casey3745@yahoo.com

GLENN R. PATTERSON, born Jeffersonville, Indiana, October 3, 1951; admitted to bar, 1976, Indiana and U.S. District Court, Northern District of Indiana; 1985, U.S. Supreme Court. *Education:* Indiana University (B.A., with distinction, 1973); Indiana Uni-

(This Listing Continued)

versity School of Law, Bloomington (J.D., cum laude, 1976). Phi Beta Kappa; Phi Alpha Delta. Licensed Private Pilot, USA, 1989. *Member:* Lake County, Indiana State and American Bar Associations. [1st Lt. USAR, Army, 1969-1984]. ***PRACTICE AREAS:*** Corporate Law; Finance Law; Real Estate Law; Land Use Regulation; Business Organization; Commercial Law; Commercial Transactions; Mortgage Finance; Commercial Loans. ***Email:*** gpatterson@lhmlaw.com

MARK S. LUCAS, born Grosse Pointe, Michigan, January 28, 1955; admitted to bar, 1980, Indiana. *Education:* University of Notre Dame (B.A., 1977); Indiana University (J.D., 1980). Member, Board of Trustees, 1993—, Vice President, 1993-1994, 1996-1997,1997-1998, 1998-1999, 2000-2001, 2003-2005 and President, 1994-1995, 1995-1996, 1999-2000, 2001-2002, 2005-2006, Merrillville Community School Corporation. Member, Board of Directors, Bank One, Merrillville, N.A., 1993-1998. *Member:* Lake County (Member, Board of Managers, 1987-1992; Vice-President, 1991 and 1992), Indiana State (District 1 Board Member; Business Law Section) and American Bar Associations. ***PRACTICE AREAS:*** Elder Law; Corporate Law; Real Estate Law. ***Email:*** mlucas@lhmlaw.com

C. DONALD EMERY, III, born Augusta, Maine, April 3, 1958; admitted to bar, 1985, Pennsylvania; 1987, Indiana. *Education:* Taylor University; Pennsylvania State University (B.B.A., 1981); Valparaiso University (J.D., 1985). Author: "Funding of Revocable Trust Agreements," ICLEF, 1998; "Death Taxes," ICLEF, 2001. Member, Crown Point Indiana Redevelopment Commission, 2004—. *Member:* Lake County and Indiana State Bar Associations. ***PRACTICE AREAS:*** Trusts and Estates; Probate; Wills; Real Estate; Elder Law; Business Law. ***Email:*** demery@lhmlaw.com

JAMES L. CLEMENT, JR., born Gary, Indiana, April 23, 1962; admitted to bar, 1991, Indiana. *Education:* Bob Jones University (B.A., 1985); Valparaiso University (J.D., cum laude, 1991). *Member:* Lake County and Indiana State Bar Associations; Lake County Community Corrections Advisory Board; Christian Legal Society; Calumet Inns of Court. ***PRACTICE AREAS:*** Personal Injury; Civil Litigation; Criminal Defense; Appellate Practice. ***Email:*** jclement@lhmlaw.com

ASSOCIATE

BROOKE SHREVE, born East Chicago, Indiana, March 8, 1975; admitted to bar, 2001, Indiana and U.S. District Court, Northern and Southern Districts of Indiana. *Education:* Purdue University (B.S., 1997); Valparaiso University (J.D., 2001). Phi Beta Kappa; Phi Kappa Phi. *Member:* Lake County, Indiana State and American Bar Associations. ***PRACTICE AREAS:*** Civil Litigation. ***Email:*** bshreve@lhmlaw.com

REPRESENTATIVE CLIENTS: Bank One, Merrillville, N.A.; Fifth Third Bank; WPM Construction LLC (Formerly Whiteco Construction Services LLC); Community Foundation of Northwest Indiana (Community Healthcare System); St. Catherine Hospital, Inc.; Munster Medical Research Foundation, Inc. (Operating "The Community Hospital"); Regency Hospital; St. Mary Medical Center Continental Electric Co.; Western Union; Gary Public Transportation Corp.; Gas City Limited; The Trustees of Indiana University; Walsh and Kelly (Paving Contractors); Ellas Construction Co., Inc. (Paving Contractors); Knox Mall Shopping Center, Knox, Indiana; Five Star Food Centers; Legacy Foundation, Inc. (charitable foundation); Van's Industrial; 2-Alloy, Inc.; Fitzsimmons Furniture; Illiana Disposal, Inc.; Temple Corp.; Munster Med-Inn (Extended Care Facility); Greenwald Surgical Instrument Co.; Calumet Surgi-Center; Tri-State Telecommunications of Northeast Indiana, Inc.; Midwest Construction Services, Inc.; Pruzin Funeral Home, Inc.; Classic Steel Co.; Doug Flanagin Excavating, Inc.; Marblehead Lime Co.; ATM Corp.; Coldwell Banker Residential Brokerage; City of Whiting, Indiana; Rieter Automotive Company; New State Mortgage, LLC; First American Real Estate; Superior Construction; Guy and Allen Funeral Home; Moke Realty; Re-Max Commercial; Property Solutions; Bank Calumet Trust Department; Mercantile National Bank of Hammond Trust Department.
REFERENCES: Bank One, Merrillville, N.A.; Fifth Third Bank; Bank Calumet Trust Department; Mercantile National Bank of Hammond Trust Department.

PINKERTON AND FRIEDMAN

PROFESSIONAL CORPORATION

MERRILLVILLE, INDIANA

(See Munster)

Federal Income and State Taxation, Probate and Estate Planning, Estate Administration, Trusts, Wills, Real Estate, Partnership, Business and Corporate Law. Municipal and Zoning Law, Employee Benefits, Business Litigation, Real Estate, Health Care Law.

QUERREY & HARROW, LTD.

Established in 1939

8585 BROADWAY, SUITE 510

MERRILLVILLE, INDIANA 46410

Telephone: 219-738-1820
Fax: 219-738-1821
Email: jclymer@querrey.com
URL: http://www.querrey.com

Chicago, Illinois Office: 175 West Jackson Boulevard, Suite 1600. Telephone: 312-540-7000. Fax: 312-540-0578.
Crystal Lake, Illinois Office: 651 West Terra Cotta Avenue, Suite 221. Telephone: 815-479-1929. Fax: 815-479-1978.
Wheaton, Illinois Office: 310 South County Farm Road, Third Floor. Telephone: 630-653-2600. Fax: 630-653-0178.
Waukegan, Illinois Office: 415 West Washington Street, Suite 205. Telephone: 847-249-4440. Fax: 847-249-4932.
Joliet, Illinois Office: 2 Rialto Square, Suite 401, 116 North Chicago Street. Telephone: 815-726-1600. Fax: 815-726-1674.
New York, N.Y. Office: 120 Broadway, Suite 2800. Telephone: 212-233-0130. Fax: 212-233-0172.
London, England Office: 141-142 Fenchurch Street, Fifth Floor. Telephone: 207-929-6670. Fax: 207-929-6671.

General Practice and Trial Practice.

(This Listing Continued)

MEMBERS OF FIRM

GALEN A. BRADLEY, admitted to bar, 1995, Indiana; 1995, Illinois. *Education:* Eastern Illinois University (B.S., 1988); Valparaiso University School of Law (J.D., 1995). *Member:* Lake County, Porter County and Indiana State Bar Associations; Illinois Trial Lawyers Association. (Also at Chicago, Illinois Office). ***PRACTICE AREAS:*** Insurance Defense; Workers Compensation.

JEFFREY W. CLYMER, admitted to bar, 1992, Indiana and Michigan. *Education:* Kalamazoo College (B.A., 1983); Valparaiso University (J.D., magna cum laude, 1992). (Resident). ***PRACTICE AREAS:*** Litigation. ***Email:*** jclymer@querrey.com

JOHN H. HALSTEAD, admitted to bar, 2002, Indiana. *Education:* Brigham Young University (B.A., cum laude, 1999); Indiana University School of Law - Bloomington (J.D., magna cum laude, 2002). (Resident). ***PRACTICE AREAS:*** Litigation. ***Email:*** jhalstead@querrey.com

(For complete biographical data on all personnel, see Professional Biographies at Chicago, Illinois)

SPANGLER, JENNINGS & DOUGHERTY, P.C.

Established in 1952

8396 MISSISSIPPI STREET

MERRILLVILLE, INDIANA 46410-6398

Telephone: 219-769-2323
Facsimile: 219-769-5007
Email: spangler@sjdlaw.com
URL: http://www.sjdlaw.com

Valparaiso, Indiana Office: 150 Lincolnway, Suite 3001. Telephone: 219-462-6151. FAX: 219-477-4935.
Indianapolis, Indiana Office: 9200 Keystone Crossing, Suite 410. Telephone: 317-571-7690. Facsimile: 317-571-7686.

General Trial and Appellate Practice. Administrative, Banking, Bankruptcy, Business Reorganizations, Business Transactions, Civil Rights, Commercial, Construction, Corporate, Creditors' Rights, Criminal Litigation, Family/Domestic Relations, Drug and Device, Eminent Domain, Environmental, ERISA and Employee Benefits, Probate and Estate Planning and Administration, Fire/Arson, Guardianships, Health Care, Insurance, Labor and Employment, Municipal and Zoning, Personal Injury, Product Liability, Professional Liability, Medical Malpractice Defense, Real Estate, School, Federal, State and Local Taxation, Toxic Torts, Transportation, Workers Compensation, Land Development.

FIRM PROFILE: In 1952, our founding partners created what is now the law firm of Spangler, Jennings & Dougherty to serve a broad range of clients' legal needs. Today, we continue to provide our clients with legal counsel based on extensive litigation experience, integrity, practicality and dedicated team effort.

Spangler, Jennings & Dougherty consists of 39 attorneys, ten paralegals, and a large and experienced support staff, making it Northwest Indiana's largest private law firm serving all of Indiana. In addition to years of legal experience and training, our firm has members with professional experience in public accounting and health care. We also have trial attorneys who belong to the prestigious American College of Trial Lawyers.

RICHARD A. MAYER, born Gary, Indiana, July 27, 1934; admitted to bar, 1961, Indiana. *Education:* Indiana University (B.S., 1956; J.D., 1961). Founder of Calumet American Inn of Court. Fellow, American College of Trial Lawyers. ***PRACTICE AREAS:*** Construction; Environmental Law; Personal Injury; Product Liability; Professional Liability. ***Email:*** rmayer@sjdlaw.com

JOHN P. McQUILLAN, born Pittsburgh, Pennsylvania, November 21, 1940; admitted to bar, 1965, Indiana; 1981, U.S. Supreme Court. *Education:* University of Notre Dame (B.B.A., 1962; LL.B., 1965). Note Editor, Notre Dame Lawyer, 1964-1965. *Member:* Indiana State Bar Association; Indiana Defense Lawyers Association; Defense Research Institute; Federation of Insurance and Corporate Counsel. ***PRACTICE AREAS:*** Civil Trial Practice; Environmental; Insurance Law; Personal Injury; Product Liability. ***Email:*** jpmcquillan@sjdlaw.com

SAMUEL J. BERNARDI, JR., born Highland Park, Illinois, January 30, 1941; admitted to bar, 1966, Indiana and Illinois. *Education:* Miami University (B.B.S., 1963); University of Notre Dame (J.D., 1966). Greys Inn. *Member:* Porter County, Indiana State and American Bar Associations; Indiana Defense Lawyers Association; Defense Research Institute (President, 1983). (Resident, Valparaiso Office). ***PRACTICE AREAS:*** Civil Trial Practice; Insurance Defense; Personal Injury; Products Liability. ***Email:*** spangler@sjdlaw.com

JON F. SCHMOLL, born Fort Wayne, Indiana, December 20, 1941; admitted to bar, 1967, Indiana. *Education:* Indiana University (A.B., 1964; J.D., 1967). Law Clerk, Indiana Court of Appeals, 1965-1967. *Member:* Indiana State (Chairman, Trial Lawyers Section, 1989) and American Bar Associations; American Academy of Health Care Attorneys; International Association of Defense Counsel; American Board of Trial Advocates (President, Indiana Chapter, 1997; National Board of Directors, 2000—); American College of Trial Lawyers. ***PRACTICE AREAS:*** Medical Malpractice; Personal Injury; Litigation; Hospital Law; Products Liability; Insurance Law. ***Email:*** spangler@sjdlaw.com

ROBERT D. HAWK, born Calumet City, Illinois, February 25, 1938; admitted to bar, 1967, Indiana. *Education:* Indiana University (B.S., 1963; J.D., 1967). ***PRACTICE AREAS:*** Construction; Insurance; Personal Injury; Transportation Law; Medical Malpractice. ***Email:*** spangler@sjdlaw.com

DANIEL A. GIOIA, born Bellerose, New York, December 23, 1950; admitted to bar, 1975, Indiana. *Education:* Georgetown University (A.B., 1972); American University (J.D., 1975). Certified Mediator, Civil and Domestic Relations. Indiana Supreme Court Commission for Continuing Legal Education, 1991-1997. *Member:* Lake County (President, 1990)

(This Listing Continued)

SPANGLER, JENNINGS & DOUGHERTY, P.C., Merrillville—Continued

and Indiana State Bar Associations. ***PRACTICE AREAS:*** Civil Trial Practice; Domestic Relations; Health Care; Personal Injury; Professional Liability; Medical Malpractice Defense. ***Email:*** dgioia@sjdlaw.com

JAMES D. McQUILLAN, born Hammond, Indiana, January 19, 1950; admitted to bar, 1975, Iowa and Indiana. *Education:* Wabash College (B.A., 1972); University of Iowa (J.D., 1975). *Member:* Indiana State Bar Association. ***PRACTICE AREAS:*** Civil Trial Practice; Health Care; Insurance; Personal Injury. ***Email:*** jdmcquillan@sjdlaw.com

DAVID L. ABEL, II, born Indianapolis, Indiana, March 28, 1950; admitted to bar, 1976, Indiana. *Education:* DePauw University (B.A., 1972); Indiana University (J.D., magna cum laude, 1976). Law Clerk, Indiana Court of Appeals, 1973-1976. *Member:* Lake County (Past Member Board of Managers), Seventh Circuit and Indiana State Bar Associations; Defense Research Institute; Indiana Defense Lawyers Association. ***PRACTICE AREAS:*** Fire/Arson; Insurance; Personal Injury; Professional Liability. ***Email:*** dabel@sjdlaw.com

LAWRENCE A. KALINA, born Hammond, Indiana, May 11, 1951; admitted to bar, 1977, Indiana, U.S. District Court, Northern District of Indiana, U.S. Court of Appeals, Seventh Circuit and U.S. Tax Court. *Education:* Villanova University (B.A., 1973); University of Miami (J.D., 1977); DePaul College of Law (LL.M. in Taxation, 1981). Phi Delta Phi. Associate Editor, University of Miami Inter-American Law Review, 1976-1977. *Member:* Lake County, Indiana State, Federal, American and Seventh Circuit Bar Associations. ***PRACTICE AREAS:*** Bankruptcy; Commercial; Corporate; Federal, State and Local Taxation. ***Email:*** lkalina@sjdlaw.com

ROBERT P. STONER, born Valparaiso, Indiana, July 25, 1953; admitted to bar, 1978, Indiana and U.S. District Court, Southern District of Indiana; 1979, U.S. District Court, Northern District of Indiana. *Education:* University of Tennessee (B.A., 1975); Indiana University at Indianapolis (J.D., 1978); John Marshall Law School (LL.M., 1988). Law Clerk, Indiana Court of Appeals, 1976-1977. *Member:* Porter County (President, 1997; Member, Board of Directors, 1991—) and Indiana State Bar Associations; Indiana Defense Lawyers Association; Defense Research Institute. ***PRACTICE AREAS:*** Civil Trial Practice; Insurance; Products Liability. ***Email:*** rstoner@sjdlaw.com

GREGORY J. TONNER, born Rensselaer, Indiana, July 28, 1957; admitted to bar, 1982, Indiana, Oklahoma and U.S. District Court, Northern and Southern Districts of Indiana; 1983, U.S. Court of Appeals, Seventh Circuit; 1990, U.S. Supreme Court. *Education:* Indiana University at Bloomington (B.S., 1979); University of Tulsa (J.D., 1982). Law Clerk to Hon. Michael S. Kanne, U.S. District Court, Northern District of Indiana, 1982-1984. *Member:* Lake County, Indiana State, Oklahoma and Federal Bar Associations; Defense Research Institute. ***PRACTICE AREAS:*** Civil Trial Practice; Personal Injury; Insurance; Products Liability; Medical Devices; Construction. ***Email:*** gtonner@sjdlaw.com

KATHLEEN M. MAICHER, born East Chicago, Indiana, October 22, 1949; admitted to bar, 1983, Indiana and U.S. District Court, Northern and Southern Districts of Indiana; 1984, Illinois and U.S. District Court, Northern District of Illinois; 1985, U.S. Court of Appeals, Seventh Circuit. *Education:* Indiana State University at Terre Haute (B.A., cum laude, 1971); Purdue University (M.A., 1974); Loyola University of Chicago School of Law (J.D., 1983). Member, Loyola University Law Journal, 1982-1983. Law Clerk to the Honorable Allen Sharp, Chief Judge, U.S. District Court, Northern District of Indiana, 1983-1985. *Member:* Indiana State, Illinois State and American Bar Associations. ***PRACTICE AREAS:*** Civil Trial Practice; Medical Malpractice Defense; School Law. ***Email:*** kmaicher@sjdlaw.com

PAUL B. PORACKY, born Chicago, Illinois, July 27, 1953; admitted to bar, 1984, Illinois; 1986, Indiana, Texas, U.S. District Court, Northern and Southern Districts of Indiana, U.S. District Court, Eastern District of Illinois and U.S. Court of Appeals, Seventh Circuit. *Education:* Purdue University (B.S., 1975); Indiana University (M.B.A., 1978); The John Marshall Law School (J.D., 1984). *Member:* Illinois State and Indiana State Bar Associations; State Bar of Texas. ***PRACTICE AREAS:*** Business Transactions; Corporate; Insurance; Products Liability. ***Email:*** pporacky@sjdlaw.com

ROBERT D. BROWN, born Spring Valley, Illinois, April 27, 1958; admitted to bar, 1986, Indiana and U.S. District Court, Northern and Southern Districts of Indiana; 1987, U.S. Supreme Court and U.S. Court of Appeals, Seventh Circuit. *Education:* Illinois State University (B.S., magna cum laude, 1983); Valparaiso University (J.D., 1986). Phi Delta Phi. *Member:* Indiana State Bar Association; Calumet American Inn of Court. ***PRACTICE AREAS:*** Civil Trial Practice; Insurance; Personal Injury; Products Liability. ***Email:*** rbrown@sjdlaw.com

ROBERT J. DIGNAM, born Evergreen Park, Illinois, June 26, 1960; admitted to bar, 1986, Indiana and U.S. District Court, Northern and Southern Districts of Indiana; 1993, U.S. Court of Appeals, Seventh Circuit and U.S. Supreme Court. *Education:* St. Xavier University (B.A., 1983); Valparaiso University (J.D., 1986). *Member:* Lake County, Indiana State and American Bar Associations; Defense Research Institute and Trial Lawyers Association; Defense Trial Counsel of Indiana; Calumet American Inn of Court. ***PRACTICE AREAS:*** Civil Trial Practice; Civil Rights; Hospital Law; Medical Malpractice. ***Email:*** rdignam@sjdlaw.com

JAMES M. PORTELLI, born Detroit, Michigan, March 9, 1968; admitted to bar, 1993, Indiana, U.S. District Court, Northern and Southern Districts of Indiana and U.S. Court of Appeals, Seventh Circuit. *Education:* University of Michigan (B.A., in Philosophy, with distinction, 1990); Indiana University (J.D., 1993). Delta Theta Phi. Associate Editor, Adelphia Law Journal, 1991-1992. Member, Federalist Society, 1992-1993. *Member:* Lake County, Indiana State and American Bar Associations. ***PRACTICE AREAS:*** Insurance Defense; Civil Litigation; Medical Malpractice; Insurance; Personal Injury; Products Liability. ***Email:*** jportelli@sjdlaw.com

ROBERT D. HAWK, JR., born Hammond, Indiana, June 20, 1968; admitted to bar, 1995, Indiana. *Education:* Knox College (B.A., 1990); Drake University (J.D., with honors, 1995). Member, Drake University Law Review. ***LANGUAGES:*** Hungarian. ***PRACTICE AREAS:*** Insurance Defense; Employment Law; Construction Law; Medical Malpractice; Products Liability; Special Education Law; Workman's Comp. ***Email:*** rhawkjr@sjdlaw.com

RICARDO A. HALL, born Barbados, West Indies, April 1, 1964; admitted to bar, 1996, Indiana. *Education:* Virginia Union University (B.A., 1986); Howard University (M.M.E., 1988); Indiana University (J.D., 1995). Listed in Who's Who in American Colleges. ***PRACTICE AREAS:*** Medical Malpractice; Insurance; Contracts. ***Email:*** rhall@sjdlaw.com

SHARON L. STANZIONE, born Gary, Indiana, April 24, 1971; admitted to bar, 1997, Indiana and Illinois. *Education:* Purdue University (B.A., with distinction, 1993); Indiana University (J.D., 1996). Phi Beta Kappa; Golden Gavel; Golden Key; Alpha Lambda Delta; Skull and Crescent; Delta Theta Phi. Best Oralist, Evan A. Evans Constitutional Law Moot Court Competition, Moot Court Honors Board. Articles Editor, Federal Communications Law Journal. *Member:* Chicago, Lake County, Indiana State, Illinois State and Federal Communications Bar Associations. ***LANGUAGES:*** French. ***PRACTICE AREAS:*** Insurance Defense; Medical Malpractice; Civil Litigation; Employment Law. ***Email:*** sstanzione@sjdlaw.com

CHRISTOPHER GRABAREK, born South Bend, Indiana, March 12, 1967; admitted to bar, 1993, Indiana; U.S. District Court, Northern and Southern Districts of Indiana. *Education:* University of Notre Dame (B.A., English Literature, 1989); Holy Cross College (A.A., 1987); Valparaiso University School of Law (J.D., 1992). Co-Author: Article, "Towards the Destruction of Legal Relativism," St. Thomas University Law Review. Deputy Prosecuting Attorney, Porter County, Indiana, 1993-1997. (Resident, Valparaiso Office). ***PRACTICE AREAS:*** Insurance Defense Litigation; General Liability. ***Email:*** cgrabarek@sjdlaw.com

ASSOCIATES

JAMES L. HOUGH, born South Bend, Indiana, February 18, 1971; admitted to bar, 1998, Indiana. *Education:* Grand Rapids Baptist College (B.A., magna cum laude, 1994); Valparaiso University (J.D., summa cum laude, 1998). Valparaiso University School of Law Moot Court Society, 1996-1998. *Member:* Indiana State Bar Association. ***PRACTICE AREAS:*** Litigation; Insurance Defense. ***Email:*** jhough@sjdlaw.com

KETAKI SIRCAR, born Dover, New Jersey, February 16, 1971; admitted to bar, 1996, Indiana. *Education:* University of Michigan (B.A., 1993); Indiana University School of Law (J.D., 1996). Moot Court Coach, 1995. Instructor, International Business College Pre-Law Substitute, 1997. *Member:* Indiana State and American Bar Associations; Asian-Pacific American Law Student Association. ***LANGUAGES:*** Indian dialect of Bengali and French. ***PRACTICE AREAS:*** Civil Litigation; Insurance Defense. ***Email:*** ksircar@sjdlaw.com

GREGORY A. PURVIS, born Kokomo, Indiana, November 9, 1951; admitted to bar, 1977, Indiana, U.S. Court of Appeals, Seventh Circuit and U.S. Supreme Court. *Education:* Ball State University (B.S., 1974); Indiana University School of Law (J.D., 1977). Former Staff Attorney, Fidelity Financial Services, Inc. *Member:* Indiana State Bar Association (Member, Creditors Rights and Bankruptcy Section). (Resident, Indianapolis Office). ***PRACTICE AREAS:*** Real Estate Foreclosure; Creditor's Rights; Bankruptcy. ***Email:*** gpurvis@sjdlaw.com

JON S. DISTON, born Bryn Mawr, Pennsylvania, January 28, 1967; admitted to bar, 2000, Indiana. *Education:* Delaware County Community College (A.A., 1988); Eastern College (B.A., cum laude, 1990); Valparaiso University (J.D., 1999). Phi Alpha Delta. (Resident, Valparaiso Office). ***PRACTICE AREAS:*** Insurance Defense; Civil Litigation. ***Email:*** jdiston@sjdlaw.com

MARIAN C. DRENTH, born Chicago, Illinois; admitted to bar, 1995, Indiana. *Education:* Loyola University (B.A., cum laude, 1992); Valparaiso University (J.D., 1995). *Member:* Indiana State Bar Association; Defense Research Institute; Defense Trial Counsel of Indiana. ***PRACTICE AREAS:*** Civil Trial Practice; Insurance Defense; General Civil Litigation; Commercial Litigation; Medical Malpractice; Health Care Law. ***Email:*** mdrenth@sjdlaw.com

MICHELLE P. BURCHETT, born Jeffersonville, Indiana, November 3, 1961; admitted to bar, 1987, New York; 1988, Virginia and U.S. Tax Court; 1989, U.S. District Court, Eastern District of Virginia and U.S. Court of Appeals, Fourth Circuit; 1994, Indiana. *Education:* College of William & Mary (B.A., 1983); University of Virginia (J.D., 1986). Omicron Delta Epsilon. Managing Editor, Virginia Tax Review, 1984-1985. ***PRACTICE AREAS:*** Medical Malpractice. ***Email:*** mburchett@sjdlaw.com

MELISSA J. WRAY, born Terre Haute, Indiana, March 16, 1967; admitted to bar, 2002, Indiana and U.S. District Court, Northern and Southern Districts of Indiana. *Education:* Boise State University (B.S., Nursing, cum laude, 1995); Valparaiso University School of Law (J.D., 2002). Sigma Theta Tau. ***PRACTICE AREAS:*** Medical Malpractice.

CALEB S. JOHNSON, born Chicago, Illinois, June 10, 1977; admitted to bar, 2003, Indiana and U.S. District Court, Northern and Southern Districts of Indiana. *Education:* Purdue University Calumet (B.S., 1999); Valparaiso University (J.D., 2002). *Member:* Indiana State and American Bar Associations. ***PRACTICE AREAS:*** Insurance Defense. ***Email:*** cjohnson@sjdlaw.com

MICHAEL L. CARTER, born Indianapolis, Indiana, April 2, 1954; admitted to bar, 1985, Indiana. *Education:* Indiana University at Bloomington (B.A., 1977); Indiana University School of Law at Indianapolis (J.D., 1985). Author, "Using Daubert to Challenge Expert Testimony of Treating Doctorson Causation", Indiana Lawyer, Sept. 25, 2002. *Member:* Indianapolis, Indiana and American Bar Associations. ***REPORTED CASES:*** Jones v. Wasserman. (ind. App.1995); Sherman v. Four County Counseling Center (7th Cir. 1993); Ridlen v. Four County Counseling Center, (N.D. 1992); Bradley v. Stiller (Ind App. 1992); Edwards v. Vermillion County Hospital (Ind. App.1991); Kopec v. Memorial Hospital of South Bend. (Ind. App. 1990); Friedman v. Memorial Hospital of South Bend, (Ind. App. 1988). ***PRACTICE AREAS:*** Litigation; Insurance Defense; Medical Malpractice Defense. ***Email:*** mcarter@sjdlaw.com

(This Listing Continued)

WILLIAM M. KOCH, born New Brunswick, New Jersey, March 31, 1960; admitted to bar, 1988, New Jersey; 1997, Indiana. *Education:* Montclair State University (B.A., 1982); Valparaiso University (J.D., 1988). *Member:* Lake County and Indiana State Bar Associations.

JANIS G. SIMS, born Florence, Alabama, September 7, 1948; admitted to bar, 2004, Indiana and U.S. District Court, Northern and Southern Districts of Indiana. *Education:* Indiana University, South Bend (B.A., Behavioral Sciences, highest distinction, 2002); Indiana University School of Law - Indianapolis (J.D., 2003). *Member:* Lake County and Indiana State Bar Associations. ***Email:*** jsims@sjdlaw.com

DERRICK A. MASON, born Marion, Indiana, 1980; admitted to bar, 2005, Indiana and U.S. District Court, Northern and Southern Districts of Indiana. *Education:* Indiana University (B.S., 2002; J.D., 2005).

FREDERICK L. CARPENTER, born Peru, Indiana, 1970; admitted to bar, 2005, Indiana and U.S. District Court, Northern and Southern Districts of Indiana. *Education:* Purdue University (B.A., 1998); Valparaiso University (J.D., 2005).

ANN MARIE WOLWINE, born Hobart, Indiana, 1979; admitted to bar, 2005, Indiana and U.S. District Court, Northern and Southern Districts of Indiana. *Education:* Indiana University (B.A., 2002); Valparaiso University (J.D., 2005).

OF COUNSEL

HARRY J. JENNINGS, born Shumway, Illinois, May 15, 1923; admitted to bar, 1949, Illinois; 1952, Indiana. *Education:* State University of Iowa; Chicago-Kent College of Law (LL.B., 1949). Phi Delta Phi. *Member:* Lake County and Indiana State Bar Associations. Fellow, American College of Trial Lawyers. ***PRACTICE AREAS:*** Personal Injury; Professional Liability. ***Email:*** spangler@sjdlaw.com

PATRICK J. DOUGHERTY, born Gary, Indiana, February 26, 1928; admitted to bar, 1953, Ohio; 1954, Indiana. *Education:* St. Joseph College; University of Cincinnati (LL.B., 1953). Phi Delta Phi. *Member:* Porter County and Indiana State Bar Associations; Indiana Defense Lawyers Association. (Resident, Valparaiso Office). ***PRACTICE AREAS:*** Civil Trial Practice; Insurance Defense; Real Estate Law. ***Email:*** spangler@sjdlaw.com

REPRESENTATIVE CLIENTS: Airborne Express; American National General Insurance; American National Property and Casualty Co.; Allstate Insurance Co.; American International Group; Ancilla; Ansal, Inc.; Associates Financial; Auto Owners; Community Hospital of Munster; Crown Point Community Schools; CUNA Mutual; Farmers Insurance; Federal Employees Credit Union; 5th Third Bank; First Union Bank; Ford Motor Company; Hanover Community School Corporation; Hanover School Corporation; Horace Mann Insurance; Household Finance; IBEW Local 697; I.R.M.I.A.; Ispat/Inland Steel; Lake County; Leader-Infinity Group; Leman Brothers; Liberty Mutual Co.; Medical Assurance of Indiana; Met-Life/St. Paul; Milwaukee Insurance; Munster Community Schools; PICOM; PICI; Pro National Insurance Co.; Ryder Truck Lines; Safeco Insurance Co. of America; Safeway Insurance Co.; St. Anthony's Health Center; St. Mary Medical Center; St. Paul Insurance; State Farm Insurance; TIG Insurance; Town of Porter; United Farm Bureau; Unitran Insurance; Unitrin Multi-Lines Insurance including: Trinity Universal Insurance Co; Milwaukee Insurance Co.; Valley Insurance Co; U.S.F.&G.; Wausau Insurance; Zurich Ins. Co.

TAUBER, WESTLAND & JASAITIS, P.C.

MERRILLVILLE, INDIANA

(See Schererville)

General Civil and Trial Practice in all State and Federal Courts. Real Estate, Municipal and Zoning, Corporate, Business, Business Planning, Contracts, Lawsuits, Strategic Planning, Banking, Wills and Probate, Trusts and Estates, Asset Protection, Estate Planning, Guardianships, Personal Injury, Automobile Accidents, Negligence Litigation, Wrongful Death, Slip and Fall, Family Law, Adoptions, Child Custody, Child Support, Divorce, Domestic Violence, Visitation Rights, Creditors' Rights and Creditor Bankruptcy, Real Estate, Criminal Law, Driving While Intoxicated, Traffic Violations.

UNTERBERG & ASSOCIATES P.C.

8050 CLEVELAND PLACE
MERRILLVILLE, INDIANA 46410
Telephone: 219-736-5579
Fax: 219-756-1810

Mortgage Banking Foreclosures/Bankruptcies and Related Litigation, Real Estate and Title Insurance Law.

KENNETH W. UNTERBERG, born Chicago, Illinois, 1955; admitted to bar, 1980, Illinois and U.S. District Court, Northern District of Illinois; 1987, Indiana; 1988, Wisconsin; U.S. District Court, Northern and Southern Districts of Indiana. *Education:* Loyola University of Chicago (B.A., 1977); DePaul University (J.D., 1980). *Member:* DuPage, Indiana State Bar Association; State Bar Wisconsin; Mortgage Bankers Association of America.

REPRESENTATIVE CLIENTS: Available upon request.

LAW OFFICES OF MINH C. WAI

1000 E. 80TH PLACE, SUITE 502N
MERRILLVILLE, INDIANA 46410
Telephone: 219-793-9000
Fax: 219-793-9211
Email: minh_wai@sbcglobal.net
URL: http://www.wailaw.com

General Practice, Personal Injury, Auto and Railroad Accidents, Construction Accidents, Property Damage, Slip and Fall, Unsafe Products, Wrongful Death, Bankruptcy, Insurance Defense and Coverage, Corporate Law, Contracts, Landlord-Tenant, Business Defense, Personal Injury Defense, Subrogation, Immigration Law.

(This Listing Continued)

MINH C. WAI, born Saigon, Vietnam, February 23, 1974; admitted to bar, 1999, Wisconsin and U.S. District Court, Eastern and Western Districts of Wisconsin; 2001, Indiana and U.S. District Court, Northern and Southern Districts of Indiana; 2005, Illinois and U.S. District Court, Northern District of Illinois. *Education:* Grinnell College (B.A., 1996); Marquette University (J.D., 1999). *Member:* Lake County, Illinois State and Indiana State Bar Associations; State Bar of Wisconsin; Defense Research Institute. ***PRACTICE AREAS:*** General Practice; Personal Injury; Auto Accidents; Railroad Accidents; Construction Accidents; Property Damage; Slip and Fall; Unsafe Products; Wrongful Death; Bankruptcy; Insurance Defense; Insurance Coverage; Corporate Law; Contracts; Landlord and Tenant; Business Defense; Personal Injury Defense; Subrogation; Immigration Law.

BECKMAN, KELLY & SMITH

MICHIGAN CITY, INDIANA

(See Hammond)

General Practice, Commercial, Corporation, Transportation and Trucking, Products and Professional Liability Defense, Elder Law, Estate and Trust Planning and Administration, Franchising, Real Estate, Employment, Taxation and Environmental Law, Trials and Appeals in all Courts, Medical Malpractice Defense and Workers Compensation Defense.

BRAJE & NELSON, LLP

Established in 1976
126 WEST FOURTH STREET
P.O. BOX 1006
MICHIGAN CITY, INDIANA 46361-8206
Telephone: 219-872-2100
Fax: 219-873-9163
URL: http://www.braje-nelson.com

General Civil and Criminal Trial Practice. Commercial, Real Estate, Family, Domestic Relations, Personal Injury Law, Estate Planning, Probate and Bankruptcy.

MEMBERS OF FIRM

CRAIG V. BRAJE, born Melrose Park, Illinois, October 21, 1949; admitted to bar, 1974, Indiana and Illinois. *Education:* Western Illinois University (B.A., 1971); Valparaiso University (J.D., 1974). Recipient, American Jurisprudence Award, 1972. Corporation Counsel, City of Michigan City, Indiana, 1976-1979. LaPorte County Deputy Prosecutor, 1979-1987. LaPorte County Public Defender, 1994—. *Member:* La Porte County, Porter County, Indiana State, Illinois State and American Bar Associations; Indiana Trial Lawyers Association; American Trial Lawyers Association; National Association of Criminal Defense Lawyers. ***LANGUAGES:*** English. ***PRACTICE AREAS:*** Civil and Criminal Litigation; Personal Injury; Commercial Law; Real Estate Law; Family Law; Domestic Relations Law; Medical Malpractice. ***Email:*** cvb@adsnet.com

WILLIAM J. NELSON, JR., born La Porte, Indiana, January 8, 1965; admitted to bar, 1992, Indiana. *Education:* Taylor University (B.A., 1987); Valparaiso University (J.D., 1992). LaPorte County Deputy Public Defender, 1994—. Counsel, Michigan City Sanitary District. *Member:* La Porte County, Porter County, Indiana State and American Bar Associations; National Association of Criminal Defense Lawyers; American Trial Lawyers Association. ***LANGUAGES:*** English. ***PRACTICE AREAS:*** Civil and Criminal Trial Practice; Domestic Law; Personal Injury Law; Real Estate Law; Products Liability. ***Email:*** wjn@adsnet.com

KURT R. EARNST, born Knoxville, Illinois, October 6, 1970; admitted to bar, 1996, Indiana, Illinois and U.S. District Court, Northern and Southern Districts of Indiana. *Education:* Purdue University (B.A., 1992); Valparaiso University (J.D., 1996). *Member:* La Porte County, Porter County, Indiana State, Illinois State and American Bar Associations; The Association of Trial Lawyers of America; National Association of Criminal Defense Lawyers. ***LANGUAGES:*** English. ***PRACTICE AREAS:*** Civil Litigation; Criminal Litigation; Family Law; Domestic Relations; Adoption Law; Bankruptcy; Real Estate; Personal Injury; Traffic Law. ***Email:*** kre@adsnet.com

ELIZABETH ANN FLYNN, born Valparaiso, Indiana, March 22, 1970; admitted to bar, 1995, Illinois; 1998, Indiana. *Education:* University of Evansville (B.A., cum laude, 1992); Valparaiso University (J. D., cum laude, 1995). States Attorney's Office, Chicago, Illinois, 1995-1999. *Member:* LaPorte County, Porter County, Indiana State, Illinois State and American Bar Associations. ***LANGUAGES:*** English. ***PRACTICE AREAS:*** Civil Litigation; Criminal Litigation; Traffic Law; Domestic Relations; Personal Injury; Medical Malpractice. ***Email:*** eaf@adsnet.com

---

CHRISTOPHER L. WILLOUGHBY, born Michigan City, Indiana, July 17, 1970; admitted to bar, 2002, Indiana and U.S. District Court, Northern and Southern Districts of Indiana. *Education:* North Central College (B.A., 1994); Valparaiso University (J.D., 2001). Phi Delta Phi. *Member:* LaPorte County, Porter County, Indiana State and American Bar Associations. ***PRACTICE AREAS:*** Estate Planning; Probate; Business Law; Real Estate; Bankruptcy; Debtor and Creditor Rights. ***Email:*** clw@adsnet.com

CARRI N. CRIDER, born Greenfield, Indiana, April 4, 1974; admitted to bar, 1999, Indiana. *Education:* Indiana University (B.A., 1996); Valparaiso University (J.D., 1999). Member, Moot Court Society, 1997-1999. Formerly with Austgon, Decker & Phillips, P.C. *Member:* Lake County, LaPorte County, Porter County and Indiana State Bar Associations. ***LANGUAGES:*** German. ***REPORTED CASES:*** Bursuk v. Town of St. John, 820 N.E.2d 118 (Ind. 2005); Gary Bd. of Zoning Appeals v. Eldridge, 774 N.E.2d 579 (End Gr. App. 2002). ***PRACTICE AREAS:*** Civil Litigation; Criminal Law; Municipal Law; Real Estate; Land Use; Land Development; Employment Law; Labor Law; Appellate Practice. ***Email:*** cnc@adsnet.com

(This Listing Continued)

BRAJE & NELSON, LLP, Michigan City—Continued

RETIRED

C. T. KITOWSKI, born Michigan City, Indiana, 1925; admitted to bar, 1952, Indiana. *Education:* Valparaiso University (J.D., 1952). Former LaPorte County Chief Deputy Prosecuting Attorney. *Member:* Porter County, Indiana State and American Bar Associations.

LEGAL SUPPORT PERSONNEL

PATTI L. PISHKUR

LYNN A. OWENS

Language: English.

REPRESENTATIVE CLIENTS: B & E Marine, Inc.; Delco, Inc.; LaPorte County Hospital Authority; Commercial Investment Transactions, Inc.; Northern Indiana Education Foundation; Frech USA; Automated Data Systems, Inc.; Concrete Specialists, Inc.; R.L. Roofing, Inc.; Dominiack Mechanical, Inc.; Sanitary District of Michigan City; Members Advantage Credit Union; Moore Surgical Associates, P.C.; Library Board of Michigan City; Michigan City Housing Authority; Boys and Girls Club of Michigan City; Wiesemann Plumbing and HVAC, Inc.
REFERENCE: Bank One, N.A.

HUELAT & MACK

Established in 2005

MARQUETTE MALL OFFICE BUILDING
450 ST. JOHN ROAD, SUITE 204
MICHIGAN CITY, INDIANA 46360
Telephone: 219-879-3253
Fax: 219-879-3090
URL: http://www.huelatandmack.com

Civil Trials and Appeals in State and Federal Courts, Insurance Defense, Insurance Coverage, Personal Injury, Automobile Accidents, Slip and Fall, Sexual Abuse, Wrongful Death, Products Liability, Libel and Slander, Fraud, Insurance, Legal Malpractice, Civil Rights, Discrimination, Consumer Law, Consumer Fraud, Unsafe Products, Warranties, Employment Law, Sexual Harassment, Wrongful Termination, Construction.

FIRM PROFILE: Huelat & Mack concentrates its practice in civil insurance defense litigation, including trial and appellate practice, motor vehicle and trucking litigation, products liability, libel and slander, construction, fraud, premises liability, insurance coverage issues and disputes, arsons, etc. The firm's goal is to provide its clients with the highest quality legal representation in a timely and efficient manner.

JERRY E. HUELAT, born Chicago, Illinois, March 7, 1953; admitted to bar, 1981, Indiana and U.S. District Court, Northern and Southern Districts of Indiana; U.S. Court of Appeals, Seventh Circuit. *Education:* Pennsylvania State University (B.A., 1977); Northern Illinois University (J.D., 1981). *Member:* Michigan City, LaPorte County, St. Joseph County and Indiana State (Board Member, Ethics Committee) Bar Associations; Defense Trial Counsel of Indiana; Defense Research Institute. [United States Marine Corps, 1972-1974]. ***REPORTED CASES:*** Daisy v. Roach, 811 N.E. 2d 862 (Ind.App. 2004); Westfield Co. v. Knapp, 804 N.E. 2d 1270 (Ind. App. 2004); Meridian Ins. Co. v. Zepeda, 734 N.E. 2d 1126 (Ind. App. 2000). ***PRACTICE AREAS:*** Civil Litigation; Insurance Defense; Arson Claims; Fire Losses; Coverage Issues; Personal Injury; Product Liability.

BEVERLY J. MACK, born Olney, Illinois, July 25, 1961; admitted to bar, 1989, Illinois; 1990, U.S. District Court, Central District of Illinois; 1991, U.S. District Court, Southern District of Illinois; 1995, U.S. Court of Appeals, Seventh Circuit; 1996, Indiana; 1998, U.S. District Court, Northern District of Indiana. *Education:* Olney Central College (A.S., 1981); Eastern Illinois University (B.A., 1983); University of Illinois (J.D., 1989). *Member:* Illinois State and Indiana State Bar Associations; Defense Trial Counsel of Indiana; and Defense Research Institute. ***REPORTED CASES:*** Stiff v. E. Ill. Area of Special Educ., 279 Ill. App.3d 1076 (4th Dist. 1996); GoodKnight v. Piraino, 255 Ill. App.3d 738 (4th Dist. 1993). ***PRACTICE AREAS:*** Civil Litigation; Insurance Defense; Products Liability; Personal Injury; Insurance Coverage. ***Email:*** bmack@huelatandmack.com

ASSOCIATES

MICHAEL KREPPEIN, born Staten Island, New York, December 2, 1971; admitted to bar, 2000, Indiana and U.S. District Court, Northern and Southern Districts of Indiana; 2004, U.S. Court of Appeals, Seventh Circuit. *Education:* University of Illinois at Chicago (B.A., 1994); Valparaiso University (J.D., 2000). Member/President, Student Association, Trial Lawyers Mock Trial Team, 1998-2000. *Member:* Indiana State Bar Association (District Representative, Young Lawyers Section); Defense Trial Counsel of Indiana. ***PRACTICE AREAS:*** Insurance Defense; Products Liability; Personal Injury; Civil Litigation; Insurance Coverage. ***Email:*** mkreppein@huelatandmack.com

JAIME M. OSS, born La Porte, Indiana, August 31, 1978; admitted to bar, 2003, Indiana and U.S. District Court, Southern and Northern Districts of Indiana. *Education:* Indiana University; Purdue University, Indianapolis (B.A., 2000); Valparaiso University (J.D., 2003). Phi Alpha Delta. *Member:* Indiana State Bar Association. ***PRACTICE AREAS:*** Insurance Defense; Civil Litigation; Personal Injury; Insurance Coverage; Products Liability. ***Email:*** joss@huelatandmack.com

DAVID BACHMAN, born Chicago, Illinois, November 28, 1975; admitted to bar, 2003, Indiana and U.S. District Court, Northern and Southern Districts of Indiana. *Education:* Valparaiso University (B.A., 1997; J.D., 2002). *Member:* Indiana State Bar Association. ***PRACTICE AREAS:*** Civil Litigation; Insurance Defense; Insurance Coverage; Personal Injury; Products Liability. ***Email:*** dbachman@huelatandmack.com

REPRESENTATIVE CLIENTS: Acuity; American National Property and Casualty; Auto Owners Insurance; Bituminours Insurance Company; Brotherhood Mutual Insurance Company; Cincinnati Insurance Company; Employers Mutual Insurance Company; Erie Insurance Company; Farm Bureau Insurance; Farmers Group Insurance; Foremost Insurance Group; GAB Robins; Indiana Farmers Mutual Insurance Company; Meridian Mutual Insurance; National Indemity Company; OneBeacon Insurance; Safeco Insurance Company; Scott Fetzer Company; St. Paul Travelers; State Auto Insurance Companies; Victoria Fire & Casualty Company; Westfield Companies; Wolverine Mutual Insurance Company.

(This Listing Continued)

NEWBY, LEWIS, KAMINSKI & JONES, LLP

MICHIGAN CITY, INDIANA

(See La Porte)

Civil Practice, Corporate Law, Real Estate, Appellate Practice, Personal Injury, Automobile Accidents, Wrongful Death, Wills and Probate, Trusts and Estates, Estate Planning, Civil Rights, Insurance Defense, Labor and Employment Law, Environmental Law, Education Law, Criminal Law, Driving While Intoxicated, Drug Crimes, Bankruptcy Law, Family Law, Adoptions, Divorce, Child Custody, Child Support, Visitation Rights, Medical Malpractice Defense, Mediation Services, Zoning Law.

SWEENEY, DABAGIA, THORNE, JANES & PAGOS, L.L.P.

An Indiana Registered Limited Liability Partnership

Established in 1971

709 FRANKLIN SQUARE
P.O. BOX 769
MICHIGAN CITY, INDIANA 46361-0769
Telephone: 219-879-5321
Fax: 219-879-2942
Email: dwp@sdtjp.com

General Civil and Trial Practice in State and Federal Courts. Municipal, Personal Injury, Mediation, Probate and Estate Planning, Corporate, Banking and Creditors Rights, Real Estate, Family Law, Appeals and Criminal Law, Bankruptcy.

MEMBERS OF FIRM

CLARENCE T. SWEENEY (1899-1980)

JOHN H. SWEENEY (Retired)

LEE W. DABAGIA (Retired)

JEFFREY L. THORNE, born Gary, Indiana, September 14, 1952; admitted to bar, 1978, Indiana, U.S. District Court, Northern and Southern Districts of Indiana, U.S. Court of Appeals, Seventh Circuit and U.S. Supreme Court. *Education:* Indiana University (A.B., 1974); Valparaiso University (J.D., 1978). Law Clerk to Honorable Andrew V. Giorgi, Senior Judge of the Criminal Division of Lake County Superior Court, 1976-1978. Attorney: Town of Long Beach, 1981—; Town of Pottawattomie Park, 1999—. Board of Aviation Commissioners, City of Michigan City, 2002—. *Member:* Michigan City (President, 1988-1989), La Porte County, Indiana State and American Bar Associations. ***PRACTICE AREAS:*** Probate; Estate Planning; Municipal Law; Corporate Law; Social Security Disability Benefits; Bankruptcy; Real Estate. ***Email:*** jthorne@sdtjp.com

WILLIAM JANES, born Chicago, Illinois, December 20, 1953; admitted to bar, 1978, Indiana and Illinois. *Education:* Ball State University (B.S., 1975); Northern Illinois University (J.D., 1978). *Member:* Michigan City (Vice President, 1990; President, 1991), LaPorte County (Secretary/Treasurer, 1990; President, 1993), Indiana State, Illinois State and American Bar Associations. ***PRACTICE AREAS:*** Matrimonial Law; Family; Domestic Relations; Creditors Rights Law; Collection Law; Bankruptcy; Criminal Defense. ***Email:*** wjanes@sdtjp.com

DONALD W. PAGOS, born Oakland, California, July 4, 1956; admitted to bar, 1981, Indiana and U.S. District Court, Northern and Southern Districts of Indiana; U.S. Court of Appeals, Seventh Circuit, and U.S. Supreme Court. *Education:* Ball State University (B.S., 1978); Valparaiso University (J.D., 1981). Law Clerk to Honorable Donald D. Martin, Judge, LaPorte County Superior Court No. 1, 1980-1981. Adjunct Professor of Law, Valparaiso University, 1995-1997. Deputy City Attorney, Michigan City, Indiana, 1981-1986. Member, 1983-1986 and President, 1984-1986, Michigan City Board of Public Works and Safety. Community Correction Advisory Board, Member, 1992-2002. Author: "Understanding and Challenging DNA Statistics," Indiana Defender, March 1990. "Probation Officer Advocacy," July 1995. Member, Board of Directors, Indiana Public Defender Council, 1994-2001. National Association of Criminal Defense Lawyers, 1992-2002.*Member:* Michigan City (President, 1993), La Porte County (President, 1995-1997), Indiana State and American Bar Associations; Bar Association of the Seventh Federal Circuit; The Association of Trial Lawyers of America; Indiana Trial Lawyers Association. (Board Certified as a Trial Specialist by the National Board of Trial Advocacy). ***PRACTICE AREAS:*** Civil Litigation; Criminal Law; Civil Appeals; Criminal Appeals; Personal Injury; Corporate Law. ***Email:*** dwp@sdtjp.com

ASSOCIATE

AIMEE M. TALIAN, born Hobart, Indiana, January 23, 1975; admitted to bar, 2001, Indiana and U.S. District Court, Northern and Southern Districts of Indiana. *Education:* Ball State University (B.S., 1998); Valparaiso University (J.D., 2001). Phi Alpha Delta, 1999-2001. Attorney, La Porte County Public Defender's Office, 2004—. *Member:* Michigan City, La Porte County, Indiana State and American Bar Associations. ***PRACTICE AREAS:*** Civil Litigation; Criminal Law; Bankruptcy; Social Security Disability; Family Law; Personal Injury. ***Email:*** talian@sdtjp.com

REPRESENTATIVE CLIENTS: Town of Long Beach; Geberit Manufacturing, Inc.; Michigan City Aviation Commission; Town of Pottawattomie Park; Yacht Brite Products, Inc.; Horizon Bank, N.A.; Global Sourcing Solutions; Opti Gloss Products; Bratchat Music.
REFERENCE: Horizon Bank, N.A.

O. JERROLD WINSKI

601 FRANKLIN STREET, SUITE 200
DRAWER K
MICHIGAN CITY, INDIANA 46361
Telephone: 219-874-4276
Fax: 219-874-9699
Email: oscarwins@comcast.net
URL: http://www.lawyers.com/winskilaw

Business Law, Commercial Real Estate, Residential Real Estate, Labor and Employment, Leases and Leasing, Civil Litigation, Business Acquisitions, Business Divestitures, Personal Injury, Mediation, Trusts and Estates, Wills and Probate, Estate Planning, Zoning, Planning and Land Use.

O. JERROLD WINSKI, born Michigan City, Indiana, September 3, 1937; admitted to bar, 1962, Illinois; 1963, Indiana; 1984, Texas. *Education:* University of Michigan (B.B.S., 1959; LL.B., 1962). *Member:* Michigan City (President, 1976), La Porte County (President, 1978), Indiana State and American Bar Associations; State Bar of Texas.

REPRESENTATIVE CLIENTS: Ticor Title Insurance Co.; Tri-State Electrical Supply, Inc.; Radio Communications, Inc.; Michigan City Radiologists, Inc.; Indiana Paging Network, Inc.; Woodruff & Sons Contractors; Michigan City Department of Water Works; Sanlo Manufacturing Co. Inc.; Sager Metal Strip Co., Inc.; Serviscape, LLC Circle R; Mechanical, Inc.; Communication Properties, LLC; Central States Manufacturing, Inc.

JAY LAUER

MISHAWAKA, INDIANA

(See South Bend)

General Civil Practice in All State and Federal Courts. Criminal Law, Driving While Intoxicated, Drug Crimes, Juvenile Law, Parole and Probation, Traffic Violations, White Collar Crime, Labor, Employment Discrimination, Sexual Harassment, Wrongful Termination, Medical Malpractice, Personal Injury, Automobile Accidents and Injuries, Slip and Fall, Wrongful Death, Product Liability, Social Security Disability, Workers Compensation, Bankruptcies, Investment Fraud, Municipal Law, Real Estate, Wills, Probate, Trusts and Estates, Estate Planning, Asset Protection, Guardianships, Domestic Relations, Family Law, Adoptions, Child Custody, Child Support, Divorce, Domestic Violence, Visitation Rights.

MAY OBERFELL LORBER

Established in 1856

4100 EDISON LAKES PARKWAY
MISHAWAKA, INDIANA 46545-3422
Telephone: 574-243-4100
Facsimile: 574-232-9789
URL: http://www.maylorber.com

South Bend, Indiana Office: 300 North Michigan Street, Suite 414, 46601. Telephone: 574-232-2031. Fax: 574-232-9789.

Corporate and Commercial Transactions, Litigation, Environmental Law, Real Estate, Labor and Employment, Banking and Bank Related Matters, Estate Planning, Municipal and Administration Law, Products Liability, Alternative Dispute Resolution, Health Care, Medical Malpractice Defense, Insurance Litigation, Trademark and Copyright, Tax, Plaintiff's Litigation, General Civil and Appellate Practice in State and Federal Courts.

FIRM PROFILE: For over 145 years, the law firm of May, Oberfell & Lorber has expanded and reorganized its professional and support staff to meet a broad spectrum of its client's needs throughout north central Indiana. Beginning with Andrew Anderson in 1856, May, Oberfell & Lorber now consists of over 20 attorneys and paralegals, making it one of the largest law firms in north central Indiana. During the firm's distinguished history, its members have served as Indiana Attorney General, Indiana Public Service Commissioner, as state and federal court judges and in the United States Congress.

LAW FIRM ALLIANCES/ASSOCIATIONS: **NETWORK OF LEADING LAW FIRMS**

MEMBERS OF FIRM

JOHN H. PEDDYCORD, born LaPorte, Indiana, October 15, 1944; admitted to bar, 1971, Indiana, U.S. District Court, Northern District of Indiana and U.S. Court of Appeals, Seventh Circuit. *Education:* Ball State University (A.B., 1967); University of Notre Dame (J.D., 1971). Law Clerk to the Hon. Robert A. Grant, U.S. District Court, Northern District of Indiana, 1971-1973. *Member:* St. Joseph County (Past Member, Board of Governors), Indiana State (Member, Probate, Trust and Real Property Section) and American Bar Associations; Michiana Estate Planning Council. ***PRACTICE AREAS:*** Estate Planning; Probate; Real Estate; Municipal Law. ***Email:*** jpeddycord@maylorber.com

E. SPENCER WALTON, JR., born Mishawaka, Indiana, February 22, 1952; admitted to bar, 1979, Indiana and U.S. District Court, Northern and Southern Districts of Indiana; U.S.Tax Court; U.S.Court of Federal Claims and U.S. District Court of Eastern District of Michigan. *Education:* Indiana University (B.S., with distinction, 1974); Indiana University School of Law (J.D., 1979). Beta Gamma Sigma; Phi Eta Sigma. Recipient, Sagamore of the Wabash Award, Indiana's Governor, 2002. *Member:* St. Joseph County, Indiana State (President, 2000-2001) and American Bar Associations. ***PRACTICE AREAS:*** Litigation; Trial Practice; Products Liability; Commercial Law; Mediation; Arbitration; Personal Injury. ***Email:*** ewalton@maylorber.com

JEFFERY A. JOHNSON, born South Bend, Indiana, September 30, 1955; admitted to bar, 1980, Indiana, U.S. District Court, Northern and Southern Districts of Indiana and U.S. Court of Appeals, Seventh Circuit. *Education:* Indiana University, South Bend (B.S., Public Affairs, with distinction, 1977); University of Notre Dame (J.D., 1980). Pi Alpha Alpha. *Member:* St. Joseph County and Indiana State Bar Associations. ***PRACTICE AREAS:*** Banking Law; Commercial Transactions; Commercial Litigation; Corporate Law; Bankruptcy. ***Email:*** jjohnson@maylorber.com

(This Listing Continued)

ROBERT J. PALMER, born Fort Wayne, Indiana, October 23, 1954; admitted to bar, 1980, Indiana, U.S. District Court, Northern and Southern Districts of Indiana, U.S. Court of Appeals, Sixth and Seventh Circuits and U.S. Supreme Court. *Education:* University of Notre Dame (B.A., Psychology, 1977); Valparaiso University (J.D., 1980). Note Editor, Valparaiso University Law Review, 1979-1980. Author: "The Case for a Speech or Debate Privilege for State Legislators in Federal Courts," 13 Valparaiso University Law Review 501. Law Clerk to the Honorable George B. Hoffman, Jr., Indiana Court of Appeals, 1980-1982. Adjunct Assistant Professor of Law, University of Notre Dame Law School. *Member:* St. Joseph County, Seventh Circuit, Indiana State and American Bar Associations; Robert A. Grant Inn of Court. ***PRACTICE AREAS:*** Appellate Practice; Litigation; Products Liability; Alternative Dispute Resolution. ***Email:*** rpalmer@maylorber.com

WENDELL W. WALSH, born Indianapolis, Indiana, September 13, 1955; admitted to bar, 1980, Indiana and U.S. District Courts, Northern and Southern Districts of Indiana. *Education:* University of Notre Dame (B.A., 1977; J.D., 1980). Coach, Notre Dame Law School Trial Competition Team, 1992-2000. Faculty Member: Indiana Trial Advocacy Skills Workshop, 1993-1995; NITA Mid-Central Regional Program, 1999-2000. *Member:* St. Joseph County and Indiana State Bar Associations; Defense Trial Counsel of Indiana; Robert A. Grant American Inn of Court (Past President). Fellow, American College of Trial Lawyers. ***PRACTICE AREAS:*** Litigation; Medical Malpractice; Insurance. ***Email:*** wwalsh@maylorber.com

PATRICIA E. PRIMMER, born South Bend, Indiana, January 4, 1950; admitted to bar, 1984, Indiana and U.S. District Court, Northern and Southern Districts of Indiana. *Education:* Indiana University (B.A., 1971; M.S., 1981); University of Notre Dame (M.A., 1979); Valparaiso University (J.D., 1984). Executive Editor of Student Writing, Valparaiso University Law Review, 1983-1984. Law Clerk to the Honorable Robert K. Rodibaugh, U.S. Bankruptcy Court, Northern District of Indiana, 1985-1986. *Member:* St. Joseph County and Indiana State Bar Associations; Indiana Continuing Legal Education Forum (Member, Board of Directors, 1994-1999). ***PRACTICE AREAS:*** Banking Law; Commercial Transactions; Creditors Rights; Bankruptcy; Commercial Litigation; Business Law; Corporate. ***Email:*** pprimmer@maylorber.com

W. TODD WOELFER, born Waukegan, Illinois, August 17, 1967; admitted to bar, 1993, Michigan, Indiana and U.S. District Court, Northern and Southern Districts of Indiana; 1995, U.S. District Court, Western and Eastern Districts of Michigan. *Education:* Valparaiso University (B.S., 1990; J.D., cum laude, 1993). Notes Editor, Valparaiso Law Review, 1992-1993. Law Extern for the Honorable Robert K. Rodibaugh, U.S. Bankruptcy Court, Northern District of Indiana. *Member:* St. Joseph County, Indiana State and American Bar Associations; State Bar of Michigan; Robert A. Grant Inn of Court. ***PRACTICE AREAS:*** Environmental Law; Commercial Transactions; Commercial Litigation; Creditors Rights; Bankruptcy; Business Law; Corporate Law. ***Email:*** wwoelfer@maylorber.com

BRADLEY L. VARNER, born Tell City, Indiana, December 20, 1960; admitted to bar, 1986, Indiana and U.S. District Court, Northern and Southern Districts of Indiana; 1987, U.S. Court of Appeals, Seventh Circuit; 1995, U.S. Supreme Court. *Education:* Purdue University (B.A., 1983); Valparaiso University (J.D., 1986). Law Clerk to the Honorable Allen Sharp, Chief Judge, U.S. District Court, Northern District of Indiana, 1986-1988. Deputy Prosecuting Attorney, Elkhart County, Indiana, 1989-1993. *Member:* Elkhart City, St. Joseph County and Indiana State Bar Associations. ***PRACTICE AREAS:*** Commercial Litigation; Insurance; Products Liability; Trial Practice; Personal Injury; Family Law; Medical Malpractice Defense; Workers Compensation Defense. ***Email:*** bvarner@maylorber.com

D. ANDREW SPALDING, born Indianapolis, Indiana, July 4, 1961; admitted to bar, 1986, Indiana and U.S. District Court, Northern and Southern Districts of Indiana and U.S. Court of Federal Claims. *Education:* Miami University (A.B., 1983); Valparaiso University (J.D., 1986). Instructor, Business Law, College of Business Administration, Valparaiso University, 1985-1986. Adjunct Professor: Law of Medical Malpractice, Valparaiso University School of Law, 1996-1997; Law of Medical Malpractice, University of Notre Dame School of Law, 2001—. *Member:* St. Joseph County and Indiana State Bar Associations. ***PRACTICE AREAS:*** Litigation; Medical Malpractice; Health Care; Products Liability. ***Email:*** dspalding@maylorber.com

JANE F. BENNETT, born Peru, Indiana, June 20, 1952; admitted to bar, 1977, Indiana and U.S. District Court, Northern and Southern Districts of Indiana. *Education:* Indiana University (B.A., 1974); University of Notre Dame (J.D., 1977). Phi Beta Kappa. *Member:* St. Joseph County (President, 1995-1996) and Indiana State Bar Associations. ***PRACTICE AREAS:*** Medical Malpractice Defense; Insurance; Personal Injury. ***Email:*** jbennett@maylorber.com

RICHARD F. NUGENT, JR., born Newark, New Jersey, January 10, 1955; admitted to bar, 1980, Indiana; 1981, Pennsylvania and U.S. District Court, Western District of Pennsylvania; 2001, U.S. District Court, Northern District of Indiana. *Education:* University of Notre Dame (B.A., 1977); Valparaiso University, School of Law (J.D., 1980). Assistant Professor, Dept. of Economics, University of Notre Dame, 2000-2001.*Member:* St. Joseph County and Indiana State Bar Associations. ***PRACTICE AREAS:*** Labor and Employment Law; Corporate Law. ***Email:*** rnugent@maylorber.com

CHRISTOPHER R. PUTT, born South Bend, Indiana, February 11, 1972; admitted to bar, 1998, Indiana. *Education:* University of Notre Dame (B.A., 1994; J.D., 1998). *Member; St. Joseph County, Indiana State and American (Member:* Tort and Insurance Law, Intellectual Property and Law Practice Management Sections) Bar Associations. ***PRACTICE AREAS:*** Commercial Litigation; Insurance Defense; Labor and Employment; Intellectual Property; Corporate Law. ***Email:*** cputt@maylorber.com

OF COUNSEL

JOHN J. LORBER, born Springfield, Illinois, April 8, 1937; admitted to bar, 1962, Indiana; 1963, U.S. District Court, Northern and Southern Districts of Indiana, U.S. Court of Appeals, Seventh Circuit and U.S. Court of Military Appeals of the Armed Forces. *Education:* Indiana University (A.B., 1959); Indiana University School of Law (J.D., 1962). Order of the Coif; Phi Delta Phi. Member, Board of Editors, Indiana Law Journal, 1961-1962. *Member:* St. Joseph County, Indiana State and American Bar Associations. [Capt.,

(This Listing Continued)

MAY OBERFELL LORBER, Mishawaka—Continued

U.S. Army, Post Judge Advocate, Fort Douglas, Utah, 1963-1965]. ***PRACTICE AREAS:*** Litigation; Insurance; Products Liability; Medical Malpractice Defense. ***Email:*** jlorber@maylorber.com

ASSOCIATES

GEORGIANNE M. WALKER, born South Bend, Indiana, May 17, 1975; admitted to bar, 2001, Indiana and U.S. District Court, Northern and Southern Districts of Indiana; 2002, Michigan. *Education:* Indiana University, South Bend (B.S., 1998); Valparaiso University School of Law (J.D., 2001). *Member:* St. Joseph County, Indiana State Bar Associations; State Bar of Michigan; American Inns of Court. ***PRACTICE AREAS:*** Insurance Defense; Corporate Litigation; Civil Litigation. ***Email:*** gwalker@maylorber.com

MICHAEL W. ARNOLD, born South Bend, Indiana, January 27, 1978; admitted to bar, 2003, Indiana. *Education:* Wabash College (A.B., 2000); Valparaiso University (J.D., 2003). *Member:* St. Joseph County and Indiana State Bar Associations. ***PRACTICE AREAS:*** Litigation; Commercial Litigation; Commercial Transactions; Bankruptcy. ***Email:*** marnold@maylorber.com

REPRESENTATIVE CLIENTS: All American Homes, Inc.; ASA Corp.; Bayer Corporation; Cambridge Integrated Services; Cast Products Corp.; CNA Insurance Company; Coachman Industries, Inc.; Communitywide Federal Credit Union; Daimler Chrysler Corp.; Dearborn & Crane Engineering, Inc.; Ditmer Trucking Co.; Eagle Products, Inc.; Health Care Indemnity, Inc.; JB Products, Inc.; Keybank; Keystone RV Company; Madison Center & Hospital; Memorial Hospital of South Bend, Inc.; Memorial Health System, Inc.; Memorial Home Care, Inc.; The Medical Protective Co.; Metro Beverages, Inc.; Miles Distributors, Inc.; National Guardian Risk Retention Group, Inc.; NMB Technologies Corp.; Pro Assurance Group; Pro Assurance Insurance Company; Rustoleum, Inc.; South Bend Chocolate Co.; St. Paul Fire & Marine Insurance Co.; St. Joseph Capital Bank; State Farm Fire & Casualty Co.; State Farm Mutual Automobile Insurance Co.; Thor Industries, Inc.; Town of North Liberty; Trinity Health; TriStar Distributing, LP; Trustmark Insurance Co.; Unitrin Specialty Lines Insurance Co.; Wise International Trucks, Inc.; Worksport Rehabilitation Services; Zurich North American Insurance Group.

STUTSMAN, MULVANEY & DeBOER

MISHAWAKA, INDIANA

(See Elkhart)

General Civil and Appellate Practice in all State and Federal Courts. Personal Injury, Automobile Accidents, Slip and Fall, Wrongful Death, Workers Compensation, Medical Malpractice, Corporate, Wills and Probate, Trusts and Estates, Asset Protection, Guardianships, Estate Planning, Real Estate, Internet Law.

THORNE • GRODNIK, LLP

420 LINCOLN WAY WEST
P.O. BOX 1210
MISHAWAKA, INDIANA 46544
Telephone: 574-256-5660
FAX: 574-674-6835
Email: firm@tglaw.us
URL: http://www.tglaw.us

Elkhart, Indiana Office: 228 West High Street. Telephone: 574-294-7473. FAX: 574-294-5390.

Commercial and Civil Litigation, Creditors Rights, Bankruptcy, Banking and Bank Related Matters, Corporate and Commercial Transactions, Insurance Defense, Personal Injury, Automobile Accidents, Slip and Fall, Wrongful Death, Real Estate and Zoning, Wills and Probate, Trusts and Estates, Estate Planning, School Law and Family Law, Adoptions, Divorce, Child Custody, Child Support, Visitation Rights, Mediation.

FIRM PROFILE: The firm of Thorne • Grodnik, LLP traces its roots to 1963. The core of the firm's practice remains Litigation, Business Matters and Civil Mediation.

MEMBERS OF FIRM

STEVEN L. HOSTETLER, born Kokomo, Indiana, July 12, 1958; admitted to bar, 1983, Indiana. *Education:* Olivet Nazarene University (B.S., magna cum laude, 1980); Indiana University (J.D., cum laude, 1983). Author: "Farm Reorganizations Under Chapter 12 of the Bankruptcy Code," Res Gestae, Indiana State Bar Association Journal, November, 1987; "Doing Business with Bankrupt Companies," Indiana Business Magazine, April, 1992. *Member:* St. Joseph County and Indiana State Bar Associations. ***PRACTICE AREAS:*** Bankruptcy; Creditors Rights; Commercial Litigation; Real Estate; Corporations. ***Email:*** slhostetler@tglaw.us

MICHAEL A. TRIPPEL, born Mishawaka, Indiana, June 17, 1963; admitted to bar, 1992, Indiana. *Education:* Indiana University (B.S., 1985); Valparaiso University (J.D., cum laude, 1992). Mishawaka Common Council Attorney, 2004—. *Member:* St. Joseph County and Indiana State Bar Associations; Robert A. Grant Inn of Court. (Resident). ***PRACTICE AREAS:*** Civil Litigation; Corporate; Real Estate; Banking Law; Probate Administration. ***Email:*** mtrippel@tglaw.us

ASSOCIATE

JAMIE C. WOODS, born Mishawaka, Indiana, March 4, 1974; admitted to bar, 1999, Indiana and U.S. District Court, Northern and Southern Districts of Indiana. *Education:* Manchester College (B.S., 1996); Indiana University (J.D., 1999). Attorney, Town of Osceola, Indiana. Member, Penn-Harris-Madison School Board of Trustees. Author and Presenter: "Mastering the Trial Notebook in Indiana," Institute for Paralegal Education Seminar, June 2004; "Arbitration of Construction Disputes," St. Joseph Valley Association of Plumbing-Heating-Cooling Contractors, Inc., March, 2004; "Construction Payment Remedies," St. Joseph Valley Association of Plumbing-Heating-Cooling Contractors, Inc., October, 2002; "An Overview of Preferential Transfers and Debtor in Possession Accounts," The Michigan Credit Management Association, November, 2002. *Member:* St. Joseph

(This Listing Continued)

County and Indiana State Bar Associations. ***PRACTICE AREAS:*** Creditors Rights; Construction Law; Civil Litigation. ***Email:*** jwoods@tglaw.us

WEISMAN ASSOCIATES

PROFESSIONAL CORPORATION
400 LINCOLNWAY EAST
P.O. BOX 683
MISHAWAKA, INDIANA 46544
Telephone: 574-254-1151
Fax: 574-254-9388
Email: DBW294@MSN.COM

General Civil and Criminal Trial Practice. Drug Crimes, Driving While Intoxicated, Parole and Probation, Traffic Violations, Negligence, Real Estate, Business Law, Contracts, Partnership Law, Corporate, Wills and Probate, Trusts and Estates, Estate Planning, Commercial Law, Real Estate, Commercial Leasing, Family Law, Adoption Law, Child Custody, Child Support, Divorce, Visitation Rights.

DAVID B. WEISMAN, born Columbus, Ohio, April 6, 1935; admitted to bar, 1960, Indiana and Michigan; U.S. Supreme Court; U.S. Court of Appeals, 7th Circuit; U.S. District Court, Northern and Southern Districts of Indiana. *Education:* Ohio Wesleyan University (B.A., 1957); University of Michigan (J.D., 1960). Delta Theta Phi. Deputy Prosecuting Attorney, 60th Judicial Circuit, Indiana, 1963-1966. Attorney for Area Plan Commission of St. Joseph County, Indiana, 1967-1997. Code Enforcement Hearing Officer, Mishawaka, Indiana, 1985-1987. ***Email:*** DBW294@MSN.COM

WILLIAM H. MULLIS, P.C.

Established in 1998
112 SOUTH SEVENTH STREET
P.O. BOX 35
MITCHELL, INDIANA 47446
Telephone: 812-849-9087
Facsimile: 812-849-6938
Email: WHM@mullislaw.com
URL: http://www.mullislaw.com

General Civil Trial and Appellate Practice in State and Federal Courts. Insurance Defense, Insurance Coverage, Products Liability, Probate and Estate Planning, Business Law and Estates.

FIRM PROFILE: Litigation-oriented law practice concentrated in defending third- and first-party liability claims for insurance companies throughout southern Indiana.

WILLIAM H. MULLIS, born Bedford, Indiana, January 28, 1957; admitted to bar, 1985, Texas and U.S. Army Court of Military Review; 1989, U.S. Supreme Court; 1991, Indiana and U.S. District Court, Southern District of Indiana; 1994, Kentucky and U.S. District Court, Western District of Kentucky; 1996, U.S. Court of Appeals, Sixth Circuit. *Education:* Indiana University (B.A., 1979); Baylor University (J.D., 1985); The Judge Advocate General's School-Army (LL.M., 1989). *Member:* Evansville, Indiana State and Kentucky Bar Associations; State Bar of Texas. [Captain, U.S. Army, 1979-1991]. ***PRACTICE AREAS:*** Insurance Defense Law; Insurance Coverage; Products Liability Defense Law; Civil Litigation; Business Law; Estate Planning. ***Email:*** WHM@mullislaw.com

REPRESENTATIVE CLIENTS: GuideOne Insurance Company; Pekin Insurance Company; National Indemnity Group; Secura Insurance Company; Bituminous Insurance Companies; Clean Burn, Inc.; Western Reserve Group; Hastings Mutual Insurance Company; Argonaut Great Central Insurance Company.

NED TONNER
ATTORNEY AT LAW

MONTICELLO, INDIANA

(See Rensselaer)

Personal Injury, Criminal Law, Estates, Trusts, Real Estate, Divorce, Family Law.

ALLYN & GIVENS

Established in 1972
204 MAIN STREET
MT. VERNON, INDIANA 47620
Telephone: 812-838-4476
Fax: 812-838-4491
Email: agblaw@aol.com

General Civil and Criminal Practice in all State and Federal Courts. Probate, Trusts, Real Estate and Natural Resources Law.

OTIS B. ALLYN (1912-1985)

DAVID O. GIVENS, born Mt. Vernon, Indiana, January 8, 1943; admitted to bar, 1971, Indiana. *Education:* University of Evansville; Indiana University (B.S., 1968); Indiana University School of Law (J.D., 1971). Phi Delta Phi. Attorney, Mt. Vernon Planning Commission, 1974-1976. *Member:* Evansville (Member, Board of Directors, 1985), Posey County (President, 1981-1986), Indiana State (Member, Professional Services Committee, 1976-1987) and American Bar Associations. ***PRACTICE AREAS:*** Probate Law; Civil Practice; Real Estate; Corporate Law.

BAMBERGER, FOREMAN, OSWALD AND HAHN, LLP

Established in 1959

309 MAIN STREET

MT. VERNON, INDIANA 47620

Telephone: 812-838-4495

Evansville, Indiana Office: 20 NW Fourth Street, Suite 708, P.O. Box 657, 47708. Telephone: 812-425-1591. Fax: 812-421-4936.

Indianapolis, Indiana Office: Market Tower, Suite 2950, 10 West Market Street, 46204. Telephone: 317-464-1591. Fax: 317-464-1592. Toll Free: 888-994-7976.

Poseyville, Indiana Office: 178 South Lockwood, 47633. Telephone: 812-874-3365. Fax: 812-874-3366.

Princeton, Indiana Office: 302 N. Prince Street, 47670. Telephone: 812-386-6482. Fax: 812-386-6480.

Administrative Law, Antitrust Law, Appellate Practice, Arbitration, Banking Law, Bankruptcy Law, Business Law, Civil Rights, Civil Trial Practice, Commercial Law, Commercial Litigation, Communications Law, Construction Law, Corporate Law, Creditors' Rights, Elder Law, Energy Law, Environmental Law, Health Care Law, Insurance Defense, Intellectual Property Law, Labor and Employment Law, Land Use Law, Medical Malpractice, Mergers and Acquisitions, Product Liability Law, Public Utilities Law, Real Estate Law, Trademark, Copyright and Unfair Competition, Trusts and Estates, Wills and Probate.

REPRESENTATIVE CLIENTS: Available Upon Request.

(For complete biographical data on all personnel, see Professional Biographies at Evansville, Indiana)

JOHN ANDREW GOODRIDGE LAW OFFICE

MT. VERNON, INDIANA

(See Evansville)

Bankruptcy and Federal Criminal Law.

KAHN, DEES, DONOVAN & KAHN, LLP

MT. VERNON, INDIANA

(See Evansville)

General Civil Practice including Litigation, Environmental, Labor Management, Corporate, Pension, Banking, Hospital, Insurance Defense, Real Estate, Workers' Compensation, Tax, Construction, Immigration and General Civil Law.

OLSEN, WHITE & HAMBIDGE, LLP

MT. VERNON, INDIANA

(See Evansville)

Probate, Business Law, Family Law, Wills, Personal Injury, Criminal Law, Real Estate.

RUDOLPH, FINE, PORTER & JOHNSON LLP

MT. VERNON, INDIANA

(See Evansville)

General Corporate Practice. Health Care Law, Commercial Litigation, Insurance Defense, Real Estate, Zoning and Land Use Law, Mediation and Arbitration, Bankruptcy Law, Mergers and Acquisitions. Probate and Estate Planning, Tax, Employment Law, Appeals, Banking. Trials in all State and Federal Courts.

TERRELL, BAUGH, SALMON & BORN, LLP

MT. VERNON, INDIANA

(See Evansville)

General Civil Trial and Appellate Practice in State and Federal Courts. Insurance Defense, Commercial Transactions, Business Organizations, Employment, Construction, Bankruptcy, Probate and Estate Planning and Administration, Real Estate, Personal Injury, Environmental, Mediation, Zoning, Shopping Center Development and Leasing.

ZIEMER, STAYMAN, WEITZEL & SHOULDERS, LLP

MT. VERNON, INDIANA

(See Evansville)

General Civil Practice. Litigation in Federal and State Courts. Banking, Bankruptcy and Business Reorganization, Business and Commercial Transactions, Construction, Corporation, Creditors Rights, Environmental Law, Hospital and Medical, Insurance, Negligence and Products Liability, Labor and Employment Discrimination, Oil and Gas and Mining, Probate, Estate Planning and Administration, Mergers and Acquisitions, Real Estate, and Workers Compensation. Environmental Law.

BALES AND ALEXANDER

Established in 1923

116 NORTH WALNUT STREET

MUNCIE, INDIANA 47305

Telephone: 765-289-2268

FAX: 765-289-2270

Email: calexander@balesandalexander.com

Collection Law, Probate and Estate Planning and Administration and Real Estate.

FIRM PROFILE: Bales and Alexander began as the sole practice of William H. Bales, Sr., in 1923, who was joined by his son, William H. Bales, Jr., in 1954, and by Chip A. Alexander in 1980. Drawing on over 60 years of legal expertise, the firm specializes in Collection Law, Probate and Estate Planning and Administration, Real Estate and Banking.

MEMBERS OF FIRM

WILLIAM H. BALES (1895-1975)

WILLIAM H. BALES, JR., born Winchester, Indiana, March 25, 1927; admitted to bar, 1952, Colorado; 1954, Indiana. *Education:* DePauw University (A.B., 1949); University of Michigan (LL.B., 1952). *Member:* Muncie and Indiana State Bar Associations. ***PRACTICE AREAS:*** Probate; Real Estate; Estate Planning; Banking.

CHIP ALEXANDER, born Muncie, Indiana, October 29, 1955; admitted to bar, 1980, Indiana. *Education:* Brown University (A.B., 1977); Indiana University (J.D., 1980). *Member:* Muncie and Indiana State Bar Associations. ***PRACTICE AREAS:*** Probate; Estate Planning; Real Estate; Collection Law; Wills; Trusts. ***Email:*** calexander@balesandalexander.com

REFERENCES: Star Financial Bank; Old National Trust; First Merchants Bank, N.A.

BEASLEY & GILKISON LLP

MUTUAL FEDERAL BUILDING

110 EAST CHARLES STREET

P.O. BOX 1648

MUNCIE, INDIANA 47308

Telephone: 765-289-0661

Facsimile: 765-282-4966

Email: email@beasleylaw.com

URL: http://www.beasleylaw.com

General Practice. Civil Litigation and Personal Injury Law, Commercial Law, Corporate Law, Business Law, Probate, Wills, Banking Law, Real Estate, Labor and Employment, Creditors Rights, Bankruptcy, Municipal Law, Zoning Law, School Law, Elder Law, Environmental Law, Family Law, Adoptions Law.

FIRM PROFILE: Beasley & Gilkison LLP and its predecessors have been in practice in Muncie for more than 100 years. We represent clients throughout East Central Indiana and our practice includes a full range of civil matters in federal and state trial and appellate courts. The size and structure of our law practice allows us to respond promptly to the needs of our clients. We value our reputation for skillful advocacy and quality legal service.

MEMBERS OF FIRM

WILLIAM F. WHITE (1871-1946)

WILLIAM T. HAYMOND (1880-1964)

WALTER D. WHITE (1900-1981)

GEORGE W. PIERCE (1908-1975)

JOHN B. BEASLEY (1917-2003)

CHARLES R. CLARK, born Muncie, Indiana, June 9, 1934; admitted to bar, 1962, Indiana. *Education:* Indiana University and DePauw University (A.B., 1959); Indiana University (LL.B., 1962). Phi Delta Phi. *Member:* Muncie (President, 1964-1965), Indiana State and American Bar Associations; Indiana Trial Lawyers Association; The Association of Trial Lawyers of America. ***REPORTED CASES:*** Burger Man, Inc., and Vesco Corporation v. Jordan Paper Products, Inc., 352 N.E.2d 821 (1976). ***PRACTICE AREAS:*** Civil Litigation; Personal Injury; Corporate Law. ***Email:*** clark@beasleylaw.com

WILLIAM V. HUGHES, born Muncie, Indiana, October 31, 1947; admitted to bar, 1972, Indiana. *Education:* Johns Hopkins University (A.B., 1969); Duke University (J.D., 1972). Phi Delta Phi. *Member:* Muncie (President, 1989-1990) and Indiana State Bar Associations. ***REPORTED CASES:*** Lakeview Country Club, Inc. v. State Board of Tax Commissioners, Ind. Tax, 565 N.E.2d 392; Board of School Trustees v. Barnell, Ind.Ct.App., 678 N.E.2d 799. ***PRACTICE AREAS:*** Real Estate Law; Zoning Law; School Law; Banking Law; Environmental Law. ***Email:*** hughes@beasleylaw.com

J. PHILIP UPDIKE, born Elwood, Indiana, March 22, 1950; admitted to bar, 1975, Indiana. *Education:* Indiana University and DePauw University (B.A., 1972); Indiana University (J.D., 1975). Member, Legal Services Organization of Indiana, Inc., 1999—. *Member:* Muncie, Indiana State and American Bar Associations. ***PRACTICE AREAS:*** Banking Law; Commercial Law; Creditors Rights; Bankruptcy Law; Contracts; Wills. ***Email:*** updike@beasleylaw.com

MARK A. ERVIN, born Muncie, Indiana, April 23, 1959; admitted to bar, 1993, Indiana. *Education:* Ball State University (B.S., magna cum laude, 1981; M.A., 1985); Indiana University (J.D., cum laude, 1992). Recipient: G. Kent Frandsen Memorial Scholarship; Ball State University Outstanding Young Alumnus Award, 1994. *Member:* Muncie, Indiana State and American Bar Associations. ***PRACTICE AREAS:*** Civil Litigation; Wills; Probate; Adoption Law; Business Law; Corporate Law; Copyright Infringement; Trademark Infringement. ***Email:*** ervin@beasleylaw.com

SARA E. SHADE, born Anderson, Indiana, September 5, 1976; admitted to bar, 2001, Indiana and U.S. District Court, Southern and Northern Districts of Indiana. *Education:*

(This Listing Continued)

BEASLEY & GILKISON LLP, Muncie—Continued

DePauw University (B.A., 1998); Indiana University School of Law, Bloomington (J.D., 2001). Managing Editor, Federal Communications Law Journal, 2000-2001. *Member:* Muncie, Indiana State and American Bar Associations. ***PRACTICE AREAS:*** Elder Law; Wills; Probate. ***Email:*** shade@beasleylaw.com

ASSOCIATES

M. EDWARD KRAUSE, born Baltimore, Maryland, August 23, 1976; admitted to bar, 2004, Indiana. *Education:* Indiana University (B.A., 1998); Indiana University School of Law (J.D., 2004). ***PRACTICE AREAS:*** Civil Litigation; Municipal Law. ***Email:*** krause@beasleylaw.com

TIMOTHY R. HOLLEMS, born Fort Wayne, Indiana, March 28, 1965; admitted to bar, 1997, Wisconsin; 2001, Illinois; 2004, Indiana. *Education:* Beloit College (B.A., 1987); University of Wisconsin-Madison (J.D., 1997). ***PRACTICE AREAS:*** Family Law; Labor and Employment; Creditors Rights. ***Email:*** hollems@beasleylaw.com

OF COUNSEL

FRANK E. GILKISON, born Washington, Indiana, October 19, 1926; admitted to bar, 1950, Indiana. *Education:* Indiana University (A.B., 1948; J.D., 1950). Delta Theta Phi. *Member:* Muncie (President, 1961-1962), Indiana State and American Bar Associations; Indiana Trial Lawyers Association. Fellow: American College of Trial Lawyers; Indiana Bar Foundation. ***REPORTED CASES:*** State of Indiana et al. v. King et al. 413 N.E.2d 1016 (1980); Reed v. Central Soya Company, Inc. et al. 621 N.E.2d 1069 (1993); modified on rehearing, 644 N.E.2d 84; Ball Memorial Hospital v. Freeman 196 N.E.2d 274 (1964), 9 ALR3d 567. ***PRACTICE AREAS:*** Civil Litigation; Personal Injury Law; Wills. ***Email:*** gilkison@beasleylaw.com

CHARLES V. RETHERFORD, born Indianapolis, Indiana, April 6, 1927; admitted to bar, 1952, Indiana. *Education:* Harvard University (A.B., 1949; J.D., 1952). *Member:* Muncie (President, 1963-1964), Indiana State and American Bar Associations. Fellow: American College of Trust and Estate Counsel. ***PRACTICE AREAS:*** Wills; Probate; Real Estate Law. ***Email:*** retherford@beasleylaw.com

JACK E. BUCKLES, born Fort Wayne, Indiana, June 8, 1927; admitted to bar, 1953, Indiana. *Education:* Indiana University (B.S., 1950; J.D., 1953). Phi Delta Phi. *Member:* Muncie (President, 1960-1961), Indiana State and American Bar Associations. ***PRACTICE AREAS:*** Business Law; Wills; Probate. ***Email:*** buckles@beasleylaw.com

LEGAL SUPPORT PERSONNEL

DEANNA L. MYERS, born Elwood, Indiana, May 25, 1938. Paralegal Experience: 24 years. *Member:* East Central Indiana Human Resources Association. (Paralegal). ***PRACTICE AREAS:*** Mortgage Foreclosures; Human Resources; Corporations; Collections. ***Email:*** myers@beasleylaw.com

MALIA K. BRAUN, born Honolulu, Hawaii, October 9, 1968. Paralegal Experience: 7 Years. (Paralegal). ***PRACTICE AREAS:*** Litigation Support. ***Email:*** braun@beasleylaw.com

KIMBERLY N. MILLER, born Muncie, Indiana, June 8, 1980. *Education:* Ivy Tech State College (A.S., 2004). ***PRACTICE AREAS:*** Probate Administration and Support; Estate Planning; Elder Law Support. ***Email:*** miller@beasleylaw.com

COUNSEL FOR: MFS Financial, Inc.; Mutual Federal Savings Bank; Farm Credit Services of Mid-America; American Electric Power; Adoption Support Center, Inc.; CDS Leopold Corp.; Clancy's Car Washes, Inc.; DMI Distribution, Inc.; Daleville Construction Partnership; Dobrow Services, Inc.; Duffy Tool & Stamping, Inc.; Emar, Inc.; Fred Stewart Trucking, Inc.; Harrison-Washington Community Schools; Hartford Concrete Products, Inc.; Hartford Glass Co., Inc; Indiana-American Water Co., Inc.; Indiana Public Employer's Plan, Inc.; Littler Diecast, Inc.; Liberty-Perry Community School Corp.; Ludwig's of Dunkirk, Inc.; City of Muncie; Odle Inc.; Muncie Community Schools; Norrick Petroleum; Ontario Corp.; Pathologists Associated; Reber Machine & Tool Co., Inc.; Reliable Technical Services, Inc.; Reliance Machine Co., Inc.; Sherry Laboratories, Inc.; Society Enterprises, Inc.; Standt's, Inc.; Storer Scholarship Foundation; Taurus Tool & Engineering, Inc.; Robert G. Taylor, Inc; Terhunes, Inc.

BLACKBURN & GREEN

MUNCIE, INDIANA

(See Fort Wayne)

Litigation, Personal Injury Law.

BOSTON, BEVER, KLINGE, CROSS & CHIDESTER

MUNCIE, INDIANA

(See Richmond)

General Civil, Trial and Appellate Practice, Banking, Business, Commercial, Corporations, Creditors' Rights, Criminal, Family and Domestic Relations, Insurance, Personal Injury, Probate and Estate Planning, Real Estate and Zoning Law.

BROOKE & MAWHORR

112 EAST GILBERT STREET
MUNCIE, INDIANA 47305
Telephone: 765-741-1375; 1-800-481-0900
Fax: 765-288-7763

Civil Trial and Appeals, Insurance Defense, Family, Custody and Business Law.

MEMBERS OF FIRM

JOHN H. BROOKE, born Terre Haute, Indiana, May 17, 1959; admitted to bar, 1984, Indiana; U.S. District Court, Northern and Southern Districts of Indiana and U.S. Court of Appeals, Seventh Circuit. *Education:* Ball State University (B.S., cum laude, 1981); Indiana University (J.D., 1984). Deputy Prosecutor, 1986-1989. *Member:* Indianapolis, Muncie, Indiana State and American (Natural Resources and Construction Law Forum) Bar Associations. ***PRACTICE AREAS:*** Insurance Defense; Contracts; Firearms Products Liability; Business Litigation.

(This Listing Continued)

DOUGLAS K. MAWHORR, born Columbus, Georgia, October 6, 1965; admitted to bar, 1998, Indiana, U.S. District Court, Northern and Southern Districts of Indiana. *Education:* Wabash College (A.B., 1988); Indiana University (J.D., 1997). *Member:* Delaware County, Indianapolis, Indiana and American Bar Associations. ***PRACTICE AREAS:*** Business Litigation; Insurance Defense; Family Law; Misdemeanors; Criminal Law; Wills; Probate.

REPRESENTATIVE CLIENTS: Fast Cash, USA; American Cash Advance; United Farm Family Insurance; Sagamore Insurance; Scott Trout, DDS; Terry W. Davis, DDS; Daniel Wheeler, DDS.

P. GREGORY CROSS

315 EAST CHARLES STREET
MUNCIE, INDIANA 47305
Telephone: 765-747-1953
Fax: 765-747-1991
Email: pgcross@thecrosslawfirm.com

Civil Litigation, Products Liability, Personal Injury Law, Wrongful Death, Commercial Litigation.

P. GREGORY CROSS, born Shelbyville, Indiana, October 26, 1952; admitted to bar, 1977, Indiana; registered to practice before U.S. Patent and Trademark Office. *Education:* Purdue University (B.S., Engineering, with highest distinction, 1974); University of Michigan (J.D., cum laude, 1977). Phi Beta Kappa; Tau Beta Pi. Participant as speaker and author at numerous continuing education programs; Named Indiana Trial Lawyer of the Year, 1992. Listed, The Best Lawyers in America. *Member:* Muncie and Indiana State Bar Associations; Indiana Trial Lawyers Association (Director, 1982-1998; Director Emeritus, 1998—; Chairman, Amicus Curiae Committee, 1984-1997, Treasurer, 1992; Secretary, 1993; Vice-President, 1994-1995; President Elect, 1996-1997; President, 1997-1998); The Association of Trial Lawyers of America (Indiana State Delegate, 1995; Board of Governors, 2003—); Trial Lawyers for Public Justice. Fellow, Indiana College of Trial Lawyers. (Certified Civil Trial Advocate by the National Board of Trial Advocacy). ***PRACTICE AREAS:*** Civil Litigation; Wrongful Death; Products Liability; Personal Injury Law; Commercial Law.

CROSS, MARSHALL, SCHUCK & DeWEESE

PROFESSIONAL CORPORATION
Established in 1954
200 EAST WASHINGTON STREET
P.O. BOX 3229
MUNCIE, INDIANA 47307-3229
Telephone: 765-289-6151
Fax: 765-289-6158
URL: http://www.crossmarshall.com

General Practice, Negligence, Probate and Estate Planning, Corporations, Family/Domestic Relations, Elder Law, Social Security Law, Bankruptcy.

J. RICHARD MARSHALL, born Muncie, Indiana, June 5, 1937; admitted to bar, 1962, Indiana. *Education:* Purdue University (B.S., 1959); University of Michigan (J.D., 1962). Delta Theta Phi. Member, Board of Trustees, Muncie Community Schools, 1969-1977. Member, Board of Directors, Ball State University Foundation (Director, 1977—; Vice Chairman, 1982-1997; Chairman, 1997-2000). *Member:* Muncie and Indiana State (Probate, Trust and Real Property Section) Bar Associations; East Central Indiana Estate Planning Council. [Lt., U.S. Navy, Staff of the Judge Advocate General, 1963-1966]. ***PRACTICE AREAS:*** Probate and Estate Planning; Corporate Law; Personal Injury Law. ***Email:*** jrmarshall1@crossmarshall.com

KENNETH P. SCHUCK, born Muncie, Indiana, November 6, 1944; admitted to bar, 1969, Indiana. *Education:* Ball State University (A.B., 1966); University of Illinois (J.D., 1969). Phi Delta Phi. Deputy Prosecuting Attorney, 1975-1976. Member, Muncie Growth Commission (1994); Member, Muncie Historic Preservation & Restoration Commission (1999—). *Member:* Muncie, Indiana State Bar Association; National Organization of Social Security and Representatives (Sustaining Member). ***PRACTICE AREAS:*** Real Estate Law; Personal Injury Law; Social Security Law. ***Email:*** kpschuck@crossmarshall.com

THOMAS L. DeWEESE, born Evansville, Indiana, June 6, 1943; admitted to bar, 1975, Indiana. *Education:* Ball State University (B.S., 1968; M.B.A., 1969); Indiana University (J.D., 1975). Phi Delta Phi. City Attorney, 1980-1983. Attorney: Delaware-Muncie Metropolitan Plan Commission, 2003—; Delaware-Muncie Metropolitan Board of Zoning Appeals, 2003—. Member, Board of Trustees, Ball State University, 1987—; President 1996—; Member, Board of Directors, Ball State University Foundation (1995—). *Member:* Muncie (President, 1984-1985), Indiana State and American Bar Associations. ***PRACTICE AREAS:*** Corporate Law; Personal Injury; Bankruptcy. ***Email:*** tldeweese@crossmarshall.com

DEFUR VORAN LLP

Established in 1906

SUITE 400, 201 EAST JACKSON STREET
MUNCIE, INDIANA 47305-2847
Telephone: 765-288-3651
Telecopier: 765-288-7068
Email: atty's first initial, last name"@defur.com
URL: http://www.defur.com

Fishers, Indiana Office: 8409 Fishers Centre Drive, 46038. Telephone: 317-585-8085. Telecopier: 317-585-8858.

General Civil Practice. Business Organizations, Personal Planning, Education, Health, Personnel and Employment, Banking, Real Estate, Taxation, Employee Benefit/Retirement Plans, Creditor's Rights, Civil Litigation, Mediation, Intellectual Property, Family.

FIRM PROFILE: East Central Indiana's leading law firm, DeFur Voran LLP has been in existence for nearly a century, providing a broad range of legal services for individual, corporate and institutional clients.

MEMBERS OF FIRM

EARL G. DEFUR (1903-1986)

MARSHALL E. HANLEY (1920-1981)

REED D. VORAN (1913-1994)

WILLIAM F. RADCLIFF (1922-2002)

JON H. MOLL, born Wauseon, Ohio, September 5, 1942; admitted to bar, 1967, Indiana; 1968, U.S. Court of Military Appeals; 1979, U.S. Court of Appeals, Seventh Circuit. *Education:* Indiana University (A.B., 1964; J.D., cum laude, 1967). Order of the Coif; Phi Alpha Delta. Senior Writer, Indiana Law Journal, 1966-1967. *Member:* Muncie (President, 1979-1980), Indiana State and American Bar Associations; National Association of College and University Attorneys. [Lieut., JAGC, USNR, 1967-1971]. ***REPORTED CASES:*** Riggin v. Board of Trustees of Ball State University, 499 N.E. 2d 243 (Ind. 1986); Korf v. Ball State University, 726 F.2d 1222 (7th Cir. 1984); Swartz v. Scruton, 964 F.2d 607 (7th Cir. 1992); Bright v. Ball Memorial Hospital Association, 616 F.2d 328 (7th Cir. 1980). ***PRACTICE AREAS:*** Higher Education Law; Employee Benefits Law; Banking Law. ***Email:*** jmoll@defur.com

GREGORY A. HUFFMAN, born Fort Wayne, Indiana, September 29, 1947; admitted to bar, 1972, Indiana. *Education:* Indiana University (A.B., 1969); University of Michigan (J.D., 1972). Phi Alpha Delta. *Member:* Muncie, Indiana State and American Bar Associations. ***PRACTICE AREAS:*** Banking Law; Commercial Law; Bankruptcy Law; Real Estate Law. ***Email:*** ghuffman@defur.com

STEVEN D. MURPHY, born Hartford City, Indiana, May 25, 1951; admitted to bar, 1976, Indiana. *Education:* Wabash College (B.A., cum laude, 1973); Duke University (J.D., 1976). Past Board Member, Indiana Continuing Legal Education Forum. Master Commissioner, Delaware County Superior Court No. 2, 1998-2000. *Member:* Muncie (President, 1986-1987), Indiana State and American Bar Associations. ***PRACTICE AREAS:*** Civil Litigation; Education Law; Mediation. ***Email:*** smurphy@defur.com

SCOTT E. SHOCKLEY, born Muncie, Indiana, May 8, 1951; admitted to bar, 1978, Colorado; 1984, Indiana and U.S. Supreme Court. *Education:* Yale University (B.A., 1973); University of Denver (J.D., 1977). Member, Board of Editors, Denver Law Journal, 1976-1977. Deputy, Chief Deputy District Attorney, Denver, Colorado, 1978-1983. Assistant U.S. Attorney, Southern District of Indiana, 1983-1985. Corporate Counsel, City of Muncie, 1992-1995. Lecturer and Contributing Author: "Fraud and Abuse," ICLEF, 1986; "Home Health Care," ICLEF, 1988; "Rico Legislation," ICLEF, 1989. *Member:* Muncie, Indiana State, Federal and American Bar Associations; American Health Lawyers Association; Indiana Trial Lawyers Association; National Association of College and University Attorneys. ***REPORTED CASES:*** Dugan v. Ball State University 815 F.2d 1132 (7th Cir. 1986); Smart v. Ball State University, 89 F.3d 437 (7th Cir. 1996); Kuhn v. Ball State University, 78 F.3d 330 (7th Cir. 1996); Webb v. Ball State University, 167 F. 3d 1146; Ray v. Saint Johns Health Care Corp. 582 NE 2d 464 (Ind. App. 1991); Family and Social Services Administration v. Community Care Centers, Inc. 641 N.E.2d, 1012 (Ind. App. 1994); Rollins Burdick Hunter v. Ball State University 665 NE 2d 914 (Ind. App. 1996); Indiana Health Centers v. Cardinal Health System, 774 N.E. 2d, 992 (Ind. App. 2002). ***PRACTICE AREAS:*** Litigation. ***Email:*** sshockley@defur.com

JAMES P. BORGMANN, born Cincinnati, Ohio, August 22, 1962; admitted to bar, 1987, Indiana. *Education:* Purdue University (B.S., 1984); Indiana University (J.D., 1987). *Member:* Muncie (President, 2001-2002), Indiana State and American Bar Associations; Indiana Certified Public Accountant Society. ***PRACTICE AREAS:*** Taxation Law; Estate Planning and Estate Administration; Business/Corporate Law. ***Email:*** jborgmann@defur.com

JAMES R. WILLIAMS, born Oxford, Ohio, January 7, 1966; admitted to bar, 1991, Indiana and U.S. District Courts, Northern and Southern Districts of Indiana. *Education:* Wabash College (A.B., summa cum laude, 1988); Indiana University (J.D., cum laude, 1991). Judge, Union County Circuit Court, 1998-2004. Lecturer and Contributing Author: "Conflicts of Interest and a Brief Survey of Other Ethical Considerations for Indiana Lawyers," ICLEF, 2002; "Indiana's Landlord-Tenant Law--A Survey," ICLEF Seminar, 2003; "Judges in the Historical Arena," Indiana Judicial Center, 2004. *Member:* Muncie, Indiana State and American Bar Associations. ***PRACTICE AREAS:*** Litigation; Mediation; Banking Law; Education Law. ***Email:*** jwilliams@defur.com

WILLIAM H. LUTZ, born Ann Arbor, Michigan, September 7, 1959; admitted to bar, 1991, Missouri; 1992, Indiana. *Education:* Valparaiso University (B.S.W., 1981); Indiana University (M.S.B.A., 1986); St. Louis University (J.D., cum laude, 1991). Recipient: Academic Achievement Award in Administrative Law, St. Louis University. Articles Editor, St. Louis University Public Law Review, 1990-1991. Law Clerk to Hon. William Crandall, Missouri Court of Appeals, 1991-1992. Author: "The House Rich But Cash Poor Elderly: A Solution For First Time Home Buyers," St. Louis University Public Law Review, Vol. X, No. 2, p. 531, 1990. *Member:* Muncie, Indiana State and American Bar Associations; The Missouri Bar; National Academy of Elder Law Attorneys. ***PRACTICE AREAS:*** Elder Law; Estate Planning; Estate Administration. ***Email:*** wlutz@defur.com

ASSOCIATES

MICHELLE L. COOPER, born Muncie, Indiana, May 5, 1973; admitted to bar, 1999, Indiana, U.S. District Court, Northern and Southern Districts of Indiana. *Education:* Ball State University (B.S., 1995); Indiana University (J.D., cum laude, 1999). Executive Note Development Editor, Indiana International and Comparative Law Review. Law Clerk to the Honorable Patricia Riley, Indiana Court of Appeals, 1998. *Member:* Hamilton County, Indianapolis, Indiana State and American Bar Associations. ***PRACTICE AREAS:*** Labor and Employment; Litigation; Intellectual Property. ***Email:*** mcooper@defur.com

DAVID R. BROCK, born Hanford, California, November 11, 1946; admitted to bar, 2002, Indiana. *Education:* California State University at Fresno (B.A., 1968); University of Dayton School of Law (J.D., 2002). *Member:* Muncie, Indiana State and American Bar Associations; East Central Indiana Estate Planning Council. ***PRACTICE AREAS:*** Estate Planning; Estate Administration; Business Law; Real Estate. ***Email:*** dbrock@defur.com

SHAWNANNE NEAL, born Muncie, Indiana, August 26, 1971; admitted to bar, 2000, Indiana and U.S. District Court, Northern and Southern Districts of Indiana. *Education:* Ball Sate University (B.S., 1994); Indiana University School of Law (J.D., cum laude, 2000). Articles Editor, Indiana Law Review, 1999-2000. *Member:* Muncie, Indiana State and American Bar Associations. ***PRACTICE AREAS:*** Civil Practice; Appellate Practice; Employment Law; Education Law. ***Email:*** sneal@defur.com

BRIAN M. PIERCE, born Muncie, Indiana, October 18, 1976; admitted to bar, 2003, Indiana, U.S. District Court, Northern and Southern Districts of Indiana. *Education:* Ball State University (B.A., 1999); Indiana University School of Law (J.D., 2003). *Member:* Muncie, Indiana State and American Bar Associations. ***PRACTICE AREAS:*** Litigation; Labor and Employment Law; Appellate Practice. ***Email:*** bpierce@defur.com

SARAH L. PIERCE, born Denver, Colorado, November 25, 1977; admitted to bar, 2004, Indiana. *Education:* Ball State University (B.S., 2000); Indiana University School of Law (J.D., 2004). *Member:* Muncie, Indiana State and American Bar Associations. ***PRACTICE AREAS:*** Estate Planning; Health Law. ***Email:*** spierce@defur.com

OF COUNSEL

RICHARD D. HUGHES, born Valparaiso, Indiana, October 30, 1942; admitted to bar, 1969, Indiana; 1979, U.S. Tax Court. *Education:* Wabash College (B.A., 1965); Indiana University (J.D., 1969). Phi Delta Phi. Muncie Community School Board of Trustees, 1984-1988. Approved Court Civil Mediator, Indiana. *Member:* Muncie (President, 1973-1974), Indiana State and American Bar Associations; American Health Lawyers Association. ***PRACTICE AREAS:*** Health Care; Taxation; Estate Planning and Estate Administration; Corporate Law; Civil Mediation. ***Email:*** rhughes@defur.com

GENERAL COUNSEL FOR: Ball State University; Cardinal Health System, Inc.; Ball Memorial Hospital, Inc.; First Merchants Bank, N.A.; Mount Pleasant Township Community Schools; Muncie Housing Authority; AGBEST, LLC; Westminster Village Muncie, Inc.; Muncie Power Products, Inc.; Ball Brothers Foundation; Complete Masonry Services, Inc.; Delaware Community School Corp.; Blackford County Schools; The Community Foundation of Muncie and Delaware County, Inc.; Muncie Aviation Co.; Gale Tschuor Company, Inc.; Mid-West Metal Products Co., Inc.; Gate City Steel, Inc.; Youth Opportunity Center, Inc.; City Machine Tool & Die Co., Inc.
REPRESENTATIVE CLIENTS: Delaware Advancement Corporation; Cardinal Greenway, Inc.; LifeStream Services, Inc.; Muncie Family YMCA; Performance Dynamics, Inc.; Park One/332; Sanyo-Verbatim CD Company, LLC; Old National Bank; Old National Trust; Integra Health Services, LLC.

JILL A. GONZALEZ, ATTORNEY AT LAW

114 E. WASHINGTON STREET
MUNCIE, INDIANA 47305
Telephone: 765-282-2246
Fax: 765-282-2256
URL: http://www.jillgonzalez.com

Family Law, Personal Injury, Criminal Law, Divorce.

JILL A. GONZALEZ, born Gary, Indiana, March 1, 1960; admitted to bar, 2000, Indiana. *Education:* Ball State University (B.S., 1997); Thomas M. Cooley Law School (J.D., 2000).

THEODORE F. SMITH, JR.

MUNCIE, INDIANA

(See Anderson)

Social Security Disability, Personal Injury, Wrongful Death.

WILSON, KEHOE & WININGHAM

Established in 1970

3620 N. EVERBROOK LANE, SUITE A
MUNCIE, INDIANA 47304
Telephone: 765-284-2474
Fax: 765-288-8655
Email: mailbox@wkw.com
URL: http://www.wkw.com

Richmond, Indiana Office: 2901 East Main Street, 47374. Telephone: 765-962-9113.
Indianapolis, Indiana Office: 2859 North Meridian, 46208. Telephone: 317-920-6400.

Civil Trial Practice in State and Federal Courts. Aviation, Medical Legal, Personal Injury, Product Liability, Medical Malpractice, Wrongful Death.

(This Listing Continued)

WILSON, KEHOE & WININGHAM, Muncie—Continued

FIRM PROFILE: The Law Firm of Wilson, Kehoe & Winingham represents plaintiffs who are personal injury or wrongful death victims of automobile and aviation accidents, product liability, fires and explosions, and medical malpractice.

Wilson, Kehoe & Winingham have frequently been called upon to assist lawyers in preparing cases for trial dates on short notice and actively litigate in courts throughout the United States.

(For complete biographical data on all personnel, see Professional Biographies at Indianapolis, Indiana)

BURKE COSTANZA & CUPPY LLP

Established in 1928

900 RIDGE ROAD, SUITE L
MUNSTER, INDIANA 46321
Telephone: 219-513-1000
Fax: 219-513-1001
URL: http://www.bcclegal.com

Merrillville, Indiana Office: 9191 Broadway. Telephone: 219-769-1313. Fax: 219-769-6806.

Valparaiso, Indiana Office: 57 Franklin Street, Suite 203. Telephone: 219-531-0134. Fax: 219-531-0507.

General Civil Practice in State and Federal Courts, Trials, Appeals, Civil Mediation, Administrative, Business Law, Business Planning, Contracts, Business Litigation, Business Enterprises, LLC's, Partnerships, Small Business, Corporate, Real Estate, Employee Benefits/ERISA, Banking, Commercial, Insurance Defense, Personal Injury, Automobile Accidents, Wrongful Death, Wills and Probate, Trusts and Estates, Estate Planning, Medical Malpractice, Legal Malpractice, Family Law, Adoptions, Child Custody, Child Support, Divorce, Visitation Rights, Municipal and Zoning, Environmental.

PARTNERS

JOSEPH E. COSTANZA, born Chicago, Illinois, March 2, 1936; admitted to bar, 1961, Indiana and Illinois. *Education:* Wabash College (B.A., 1958); Northwestern University (J.D., 1961). Phi Alpha Delta. ***PRACTICE AREAS:*** Probate; Trusts and Estates; Taxation; Taxation Appeals; Municipal Law. ***Email:*** costanza@bcclegal.com

DAVID K. RANICH, born Chicago, Illinois, June 20, 1951; admitted to bar, 1977, Indiana. *Education:* DePauw University and Indiana University (B.S., with honors, 1973); Rutgers University (J.D., 1977). Beta Gamma Sigma. ***PRACTICE AREAS:*** Business Law; Commercial Law; Corporate Law; Real Estate; Trusts and Estates; Litigation. ***Email:*** ranich@bcclegal.com

NATALIE V. SHRADER, born Gary, Indiana, October 27, 1967; admitted to bar, 1994, Indiana. *Education:* Purdue University (B.S., 1990); Valparaiso University (J.D., 1994). ***PRACTICE AREAS:*** Litigation; Insurance Defense; Leases and Leasing; Housing Law. ***Email:*** shrader@bcclegal.com

REPRESENTATIVE CLIENTS: NBD Bank, N.A.; The Post Tribune (Knight Ridder Publications); Continental Machine & Engineering Co., Inc.; Portland Lehigh Cement Company; Gary Steel Products Corp.; Superior Construction Co., Inc.; Federal National Mortgage Association; Morrison Construction Co.; St. Catherine Hospital of East Chicago, Indiana; Travelers/Aetna Casualty Corporation (Regional Consultants for Commercial and Personal Lines).

(For Biographical data on all Personnel, see Professional Biographies at Merrillville, Indiana)

COHEN, KELLY, OLSON, DeHAAN & RICHTER, L.L.C.

Established in 1872

9337 CALUMET AVENUE, SUITE A-1
MUNSTER, INDIANA 46321
Telephone: 219-836-1171
Facsimile: 312-836-2003

Chicago, Illinois Office: Kelly, Olson, Michod, DeHaan & Richter, L.L.C., 30 South Wacker Drive, Suite, 2300, 60606. Telephone: 312-236-6700. Facsimile: 312-236-6706.

Estate Planning, Probate, Banking Litigation, Transactions, Finance, Construction Law, Creditors Rights, General Civil Practice, Personal Injury Law, Mechanics Lien Litigation, Corporate Law, Mediation and Arbitration, Family Law, Divorce.

MEMBER OF FIRM

STEPHEN B. COHEN, born East Chicago, Indiana, March 14, 1939; admitted to bar, 1965, Indiana and Illinois. *Education:* Harvard University (A.B., 1961); Vanderbilt University (J.D., 1964); University of Cambridge, Downing College, England (LL.M., International Law, with honors, 1966); Diploma in International Law, 1972. ISBA ADR Section Council (Secretary). Certified for Court Ordered mediation, Indiana. ***PRACTICE AREAS:*** Real Estate; Litigation; Civil Practice; Estate Planning; Business Transactions; OWI; Traffic Citations; Civil Mediation; Arbitration. ***Email:*** scohen@komdr.com

(For complete biographical listings, see Kelly, Olson, Michod, DeHaan & Richter, L.L.C., Chicago, Illinois)

LAW OFFICES OF EUGENE M. FEINGOLD

625 RIDGE ROAD, SUITE A
MUNSTER, INDIANA 46321-1611
Telephone: 219-836-8800
Fax: 219-836-8944
Email: emfeingoldlaw@aol.com
URL: http://www.feingoldlawfirm.com

General Civil Trial Practice in all State and Federal Courts. Real Estate, Insurance, Corporation, Municipal and Zoning Law, Wills and Probate, Trusts and Estates, Estate Planning Law.

EUGENE M. FEINGOLD, born Hazleton, Pennsylvania, May 12, 1929; admitted to bar, 1953, Pennsylvania; 1954, Indiana. *Education:* University of Pittsburgh (B.S., 1950); Harvard University Law School (J.D., 1953). Author: "Legal Inventory of Applicable Indiana and Federal Law Affecting Indiana Coastal Zone," Indiana State Planning Services Agency, October, 1976. Attorney, Town of Munster, 1962—. Legal Consultant, State of Indiana Coastal Zone Management Program, 1976-1978. *Member:* Lake County, Indiana State and American Bar Associations. ***PRACTICE AREAS:*** Civil Litigation; Municipal Law; Corporate Law; Probate; Estate Planning.

ASSOCIATE

STEVEN P. KENNEDY, born Louisville, Kentucky, August 27, 1949; admitted to bar, 1974, Indiana. *Education:* Wabash College (A.B., magna cum laude, 1971); Vanderbilt University (J.D., 1974). *Member:* Lake County and Indiana State Bar Associations. ***PRACTICE AREAS:*** Civil Litigation; Municipal; General Practice. ***Email:*** emfeingoldlaw@aol.com

REPRESENTATIVE CLIENTS: Furnished Upon Request.

BURTON A. PADOVE

533 RIDGE ROAD, SUITE C
MUNSTER, INDIANA 46321
Telephone: 219-836-2200
Fax: Available Upon Request
Email: BurtonAP@aol.com
URL: http://www.lawyers.com/burtonpadove

Personal Injury, Products Liability, Medical Malpractice, Family Law, Divorce, Adoptions, Criminal Law, Wills and Probate, Trusts and Estates, Real Estate, Business Law.

BURTON A. PADOVE, born June 21, 1956; admitted to bar, 1981, Illinois; 1987, Indiana. *Education:* Loyola University (B.A., 1977); Chicago Kent College of Law (J.D., 1981). ***PRACTICE AREAS:*** Personal Injury; Medical Malpractice; Real Estate.

PINKERTON AND FRIEDMAN

PROFESSIONAL CORPORATION

Established in 1975

THE FAIRMONT
9245 CALUMET AVENUE
SUITE 201
MUNSTER, INDIANA 46321
Telephone: 219-836-3050
Fax: 219-836-2955
URL: http://www.pflawoffice.com

Federal Income and State Taxation, Probate and Estate Planning, Estate Administration, Trusts, Wills, Real Estate, Partnership, Business and Corporate Law. Municipal and Zoning Law, Employee Benefits, Business Litigation, Real Estate, Health Care Law.

FIRM PROFILE: Since 1975, Pinkerton and Friedman has counseled individual and corporate clients in Northwest Indiana and in Chicago, Illinois on Federal and State Taxation and Business Law, while adhering to the highest standards of integrity and diligence. In addition, the Firm concentrates on Estate Planning and Administration, Municipal Law, Litigation and Health Care Law.

MILTON ROTH (1925-1996)

KIRK A. PINKERTON, born Hammond, Indiana, December 29, 1949; admitted to bar, 1975, Indiana and U.S. District Court, Northern District of Indiana; 1979, U.S. Tax Court; 1996, U.S. Court of Appeals, Seventh Circuit. *Education:* Indiana University (B.A., with honors, 1972; J.D., 1975). Phi Beta Kappa. ***PRACTICE AREAS:*** Employee Benefits Law; Corporate Law; Tax Law; Business Law; Probate and Estate Planning Law; Business Litigation; Health Care. ***Email:*** kpinkerton@paflaw.com

STUART J. FRIEDMAN, born New York, N.Y., November 1, 1952; admitted to bar, 1978, Florida and Illinois; 1978, U.S. Tax Court; 1979, Indiana and U.S. District Court, Northern District of Indiana; 1980, District of Columbia. *Education:* Queens College of the City University of New York (B.A., cum laude, 1974); University of Miami (J.D., 1977; LL.M., 1978). Phi Alpha Delta. Recipient, American Jurisprudence Award in Business Association, 1977. *Member:* Illinois State, Indiana State and American Bar Associations; District of Columbia Bar; The Florida Bar. ***PRACTICE AREAS:*** Probate and Estate Planning Law; Federal Taxation Law; Estate Administration; Business Law. ***Email:*** sfriedman@paflaw.com

JEFFREY F. GUNNING, born Pittsburgh, Pennsylvania, April 26, 1955; admitted to bar, 1988, Indiana and U.S. District Courts, Northern and Southern Districts of Indiana; 1990, Illinois; 1997, U.S. Court of Appeals, Seventh Circuit. *Education:* Wabash College (B.A., 1977); Valparaiso Law School (J.D., 1988). Town Councilman, Merrillville, 1984-

(This Listing Continued)

1991. Member, Northwestern Indiana Regional Planning Commission, 1988-1989. Town Attorney, Ogden Dunes, Indiana, 1990—. City Attorney, Hobart, Indiana, 1992-1995. Town Attorney, Beverly Shores, Indiana, 1996-2004. *Member:* Chicago, Lake County, Indiana State, Illinois State and American Bar Associations; Indiana Municipal Lawyers Association (Member, Board of Directors). ***PRACTICE AREAS:*** Litigation; Business Law; Municipal Law; Zoning and Land Use. ***Email:*** jgunning@paflaw.com

RICHARD N. SHAPIRO, born Des Moines, Iowa, July 6, 1955; admitted to bar, 1994, Indiana; U.S. District Court, Northern and Southern Districts of Indiana and U.S. Tax Court. *Education:* Wabash College (B.A., cum laude, 1977); Valparaiso University School of Law (J.D., 1994). *Member:* Lake County and Indiana State Bar Associations. ***PRACTICE AREAS:*** Corporate Law; Probate Law; Business Law; Litigation. ***Email:*** rshapiro@paflaw.com

KEITH WOLAK, born Hammond, Indiana, December 30, 1969; admitted to bar, 1998, Indiana, U.S. District Court, Northern and Southern Districts of Indiana and U.S. Tax Court; U.S. Court of Appeals, Seventh Circuit. *Education:* Indiana University (B.S., with honors of high distinction, 1992; J.D., 1998). Certified Public Accountant, 1996 *Member:* Lake County Bar Association. ***PRACTICE AREAS:*** Corporate Law; Tax Law. ***Email:*** kwolak@paflaw.com

Reference Clients Available on Request.

ANTHONY F. TAVITAS ATTORNEYS AT LAW

A PROFESSIONAL CORPORATION

900 RIDGE ROAD, SUITE T
MUNSTER, INDIANA 46321
Telephone: 219-836-0900
Fax: 219-836-1931
Email: AnthonyFTavitas@aftlawoffice.com
URL: http://www.aftlawfirm.com

Insurance Defense, Trial Practice, Personal Injury, Insurance Coverage, Workers Compensation.

FIRM PROFILE: The firm concentrates its practice in civil defense litigation, including trial practice in premises liability, motor vehicle and trucking litigation, workers compensation, SIU and coverage issues. The firm's trial verdicts are regularly reported in the Indiana Jury Verdict Reporter. The firm practices in all Northern and Central courts of Indiana, and in Cook County and surrounding counties in the State of Illinois. The firm's goal is to move its cases quickly and efficiently without compromising the highest quality of legal representation.

ANTHONY F. TAVITAS, born Chicago, Illinois, February 27, 1963; admitted to bar, 1989, Indiana; U.S. District Court, Northern and Southern Districts of Indiana. *Education:* Indiana University (B.S. Finance/Economics, 1985); University of Notre Dame (J.D., 1988). Certified Civil Mediator and Arbitrator. *Member:* Lake County (Member, Board of Managers), Indiana State and American Bar Associations; Defense Trial Counsel of Indiana. ***PRACTICE AREAS:*** Insurance Defense; Trial Practice; Personal Injury.

ASSOCIATE

JULIE A. DUGAN, born Hammond, Indiana; admitted to bar, 2001, Indiana and U.S. District Court, Northern and Southern Districts of Indiana. *Education:* Hanover College, Hanover, Indiana (B.A., with honors, 1996); University of Cincinnati (J.D., with honors, 1999). *Member:* Lake County and Indiana State Bar Associations; Lake County Pro Bono Commission. ***REPORTED CASES:*** Smith v. Jones, 99 N.J. Super. 999 (App. Div. 2001); Smith v. Doe, 999 F.Supp. 9999 (S.D.N.Y. 2000). ***PRACTICE AREAS:*** Insurance Defense; Insurance Coverage; Workers Compensation; Trial Practice; Appellate Practice; Personal Injury; Products Liability; Federal Civil Rights; Estate Planning. ***Email:*** jadugan@aftlawoffice.com

REPRESENTATIVE CLIENTS: AAA Insurance Company; Allstate Insurance Company; American Family Insurance Company; American National Property & Casualty Company; Capitol Indemnity Corporation; Carl Warren & Company; Case's General Store; Comcast Cable Communications; Costco Wholesale; Eric Insurance Group; Gordon food Services; Hobby Lobby, Inc.; Indiana Farmers Mutual Insurance Company; Majestic Star Casino; Moose International, Inc.; State Auto/Meridian Insurance; State Farm Mutual Automobile Insurance Company; Starbucks Coffee Company; Trump Casino; United Fire Group; USF Insurance Company; Western Reserve Group; Zurich Insurance Company.

BUNGER & ROBERTSON

NASHVILLE, INDIANA

(See Bloomington)

General Practice, Civil Practice, Trial Practice, Corporate Law, Business Law, Banking Law, Wills and Probate, Trusts and Estates, Guardianships, Elder Law, Estate Planning, Insurance, Hospital Law, Health Care, Education Law, School Law, Real Estate, Land Use, Contracts, Lawsuits, Business Planning, Business Enterprises, Limited Liability Companies, Partnerships, Small Business.

BOEHL STOPHER & GRAVES, LLP

ELSBY EAST, SUITE 204
400 PEARL STREET
NEW ALBANY, INDIANA 47150
Telephone: 812-948-5053
Fax: 812-948-9233
URL: http://www.bsg-law.com

Louisville, Kentucky Office: Suite 2300, AEGON Center, 400 West Market Street. Telephone: 502-589-5980. Fax: 502-561-9400.

(This Listing Continued)

Lexington, Kentucky Office: 444 West Second Street. Telephone: 859-252-6721. Fax: 859-253-1445.
Paducah, Kentucky Office: 410 Broadway. Telephone: 270-442-4369. Fax: 270-442-4689.
Pikeville, Kentucky Office: 137 Main Street, Suite 200. Telephone: 606-432-9670. Fax: 606-432-9680.

General Civil Practice.

RESIDENT PARTNERS

JAMES L. FISCHER, JR., born Lexington, Kentucky, November 11, 1963; admitted to bar, 1989, Indiana, Kentucky, U.S. District Court, Southern and Northern Districts of Indiana and U.S. District Court, Western and Eastern Districts of Kentucky. *Education:* Indiana University (B.A., 1986); University of Louisville (J.D., 1989). University of Louisiana Law Scholarship Recipient. Outstanding Student in Social and Political Science. Member, Student Trial Lawyers Association. Deputy Prosecuting Attorney, Prosecutor's Office, Clark County, 1990-1998. *Member:* Indiana State and Kentucky Bar Associations; Defense Research Institute; Defense Trial Counsel Indiana; Kentucky Defense Counsel; Sherman Minton American Inn of Court (Barrister). ***PRACTICE AREAS:*** Civil Litigation; Insurance Defense. ***Email:*** jfischer@bsg-in.com

JEFFREY L. HANSFORD, born New Albany, Indiana, July 27, 1953; admitted to bar, 1987, Indiana and U.S. District Court, Southern and Northern Districts of Indiana. *Education:* Indiana University (B.G.S., 1984); University of Louisville (J.D., 1987). ***PRACTICE AREAS:*** Workers Compensation Defense; Tort Defense; Mediation; Insurance Defense; Federal Civil Practice. ***Email:*** jhansford@bsg-law.com

MATTHEW HUNTER JONES, born Louisville, Kentucky, December 20, 1961; admitted to bar, 1987, Indiana, U.S. Court of Appeals, Seventh Circuit and U.S. District Court, Northern and Southern Districts of Indiana. *Education:* Indiana University (B.A., with distinction, 1984); University of Louisville (J.D., 1987). Member, Brandeis Society. Recent Cases Editor, Journal of Family Law, 1986-1987. *Member:* Floyd County (President, 1992-1993), Indiana State and American Bar Associations. ***PRACTICE AREAS:*** Litigation; Insurance Defense Law; Medical Malpractice Defense; Personal Injury Defense; Premises Liability Defense; Automobile Liability Defense; Defense Litigation. ***Email:*** mjones@bsg-in.com

RESIDENT ASSOCIATES

ELIZABETH A. SCHOTT, born Louisville, Kentucky, April 19, 1969; admitted to bar, 1996, Kentucky; 1999, Indiana. *Education:* University of Louisville (B.A., 1992; J.D., 1996). Phi Alpha Delta. *Member:* Louisville, Floyd County, Kentucky, Indiana State and American Bar Associations. ***PRACTICE AREAS:*** Insurance Defense; Workers Compensation. ***Email:*** eschott@bsg-in.com

FREDERICK M. REINECKE, born Louisville, Kentucky, December 19, 1968; admitted to bar, 1999, Kentucky and Indiana. *Education:* University of Kentucky (B.A., 1991); University of Louisville (J.D., 1996). *Member:* Louisville, Floyd County, Indiana State, Kentucky and American Bar Associations. ***PRACTICE AREAS:*** Civil Litigation. ***Email:*** freinecke@bsg-in.com

CURTIS P. MOUTARDIER, born Bedford, Indiana, June 29, 1974; admitted to bar, 2002, Indiana and U.S. District Court, Northern and Southern Districts of Indiana. *Education:* Indiana University (B.A., Political Science and Psychology, with distinction, 1996; J.D., magna cum laude, 2002). *Member:* Floyd County, Indiana State and American Bar Associations. ***PRACTICE AREAS:*** Insurance Defense Litigation. ***Email:*** cmoutardier@bsg-in.com

BROWN, TODD & HEYBURN PLLC

NEW ALBANY, INDIANA

(See Frost Brown Todd LLC)

LAW OFFICE OF BART COLOMB

400 PEARL STREET, SUITE 100
NEW ALBANY, INDIANA 47150
Telephone: 812-945-0282
Fax: 812-945-1051
URL: http://www.lawyers.com/colomb

Social Security, Workers Compensation and Family Law.

BART COLOMB, born Louisville, Kentucky, November 16, 1960; admitted to bar, 1986, Kentucky; 1987, U.S. District Court, Eastern District of Kentucky; 1993, Indiana. *Education:* Centre College of Kentucky (B.A., 1982); University of Louisville (J.D., 1986). Delta Theta Phi. *Member:* Kentucky, Indiana State and American Bar Associations; Kentucky Academy of Trial Attorneys; The Association of Trial Lawyers of America. ***PRACTICE AREAS:*** Workers Compensation; Social Security; Family Law.

STANLEY O. FAITH

412 E. MAIN STREET
NEW ALBANY, INDIANA 47150
Telephone: 812-542-0048
Fax: 812-941-4026
Email: staff@stanfaith.com
URL: http://www.lawyers.com/stanleydfaith

Corporate Law, Family Law, Criminal Law, Labor Law, Civil Rights.

FIRM PROFILE: Stanley O. Faith has served as Prosecutor of Floyd County, Indiana for sixteen years. He has extensive litigation experience.

(This Listing Continued)

STANLEY O. FAITH, New Albany—Continued

STANLEY O. FAITH, born New Albany, Indiana; admitted to bar, 1982, Indiana and U.S. District Court, Northern and Southern Districts of Indiana. *Education:* Indiana University (B.S., 1966; M.S., 1979); Indiana School of Law - Bloomington (J.D., 1982). Prosecutor of Floyd County, Indiana for sixteen years. Member, Sherman Minton Section, Inns of Court. *Member:* Indiana State and American (Criminal Section) Bar Associations. ***PRACTICE AREAS:*** Corporate Law; Family Law; Criminal Law; Labor Law; Civil Rights.

FROST BROWN TODD LLC

120 WEST SPRING STREET, SUITE 400
NEW ALBANY, INDIANA 47150-3655
Telephone: 812-948-2800
Telecopier: 812-948-7994
Email: info@fbtlaw.com
URL: http://www.frostbrowntodd.com

Cincinnati, Ohio Office: 2200 PNC Center, 201 East Fifth Street, 45202-4182. Telephone: 513-651-6800. Telecopier: 513-651-6981.
Columbus, Ohio Office: One Columbus, 10 West Broad Street, 43215-3467. Telephone: 614-464-1211. Telecopier: 614-464-1737.
Middletown, Ohio Office: 300 North Main Street, Suite 200, 45042-1919. Telephone: 513-422-2001. Telecopier: 513-422-3010.
Lexington, Kentucky Office: 250 West Main Street, Suite 2700, 40507-1742. Telephone: 859-231-0000. Telecopier: 859-231-0011.
Louisville, Kentucky Office: 400 West Market Street, 32nd Floor, 40202-3363. Telephone: 502-589-5400. Telecopier: 502-581-1087.
Nashville, Tennessee Office: 424 Church Street, Suite 1600, 37219-2308. Telephone: 615-251-5550. Telecopier: 615-251-5551.

Alternative Dispute Resolution, Bankruptcy and Reorganization, Business Acquisitions, Business and Corporate, Commercial Finance, Commercial Litigation, Commercial/Real Estate, Construction, Copyright, Corporate Responsibility and Defense, Employee Benefits, Energy and Natural Resources, Entrepreneurial, Environmental, Equine, Estate Planning and Administration, Financial Institutions, Fire and Explosion, Health Care, Immigration, International, Intellectual Property, International Business, Internet and Electronic Commerce, Labor and Employment Law, Litigation, Media, Mold and Water Intrusion, Multi-District Litigation, Patent Litigation, Personal Planning and Family Business, Privacy and Information Security, Product Liability, Public Finance, Securities, Tax, Tort & Insurance Law, Trademark, Venture Capital, General Trial Practice in all State and Federal Courts.

FIRM PROFILE: Frost Brown Todd LLC is the result of the November 1, 2000 merger of Brown, Todd & Heyburn PLLC and Frost & Jacobs LLP. This super-regional law firm of approximately 370 attorneys has seven offices in New Albany, Indiana; Louisville and Lexington, Kentucky; Cincinnati, Columbus and Middletown, Ohio; and Nashville, Tennessee. The increased breadth of practice experience, combined with the depth of service and expanded geographic scope, allows the combined firm to effectively serve the growing and changing needs of its institutional, commercial and individual clients at the local, regional, national and international level.

MEMBER

GENE F. PRICE, born Princeton, Kentucky, December 25, 1956; admitted to bar, 1989, Kentucky; 1991, Indiana. *Education:* University of Louisville (B.A., 1980; J.D., 1988). ***PRACTICE AREAS:*** Civil Litigation; ERISA; Insurance Matters; Employment Litigation. ***Email:*** gprice@fbtlaw.com

SENIOR ASSOCIATE

STEVEN P. LANGDON, born Bedford, Indiana, 1972; admitted to bar, 1997, Indiana. *Education:* Indiana University, SouthEast (B.A., 1989); Indiana University School of Law - Indianapolis (J.D., 1997). ***PRACTICE AREAS:*** Litigation. ***Email:*** slangdon@fbtlaw.com

ASSOCIATES

KEITH R. CONRAD, born Louisville, Kentucky, March 9, 1972; admitted to bar, 1997, Indiana and U.S. District Court, Nothern and Southern Districts of Indiana. *Education:* Indiana University (B.A., 1994; J.D., 1997). Author: "Media Mergers: First Step In A New Shift of Antitrust Analysis?" 49 Fed. Comm. L.J. 675. *Member:* Floyd County, Indiana State and American Bar Associations. ***PRACTICE AREAS:*** Sports Law; Entertainment Law; Products Liability; Insurance Defense; Litigation. ***Email:*** kconrad@fbtlaw.com

KRISTEN L. REESE, born Jeffersonville, Indiana, November 6, 1975; admitted to bar, 2001, Kentucky; 2003, Indiana. *Education:* Indiana University, Bloomington (B.A., cum laude, 1998); University of Kentucky College of Law (J.D., 2001). Phi Beta Kappa. *Member:* Louisville, Kentucky, Indiana State and American Bar Associatons; National Bar Association; Women's Lawyer's Association of Jefferson County. ***PRACTICE AREAS:*** Litigation; Personal Injury; Tort Defense. ***Email:*** kreese@fbtlaw.com

JOSHUA T. ROSE, born Louisville, Kentucky, January 31, 1977; admitted to bar, 2003, Indiana; 2004, Kentucky. *Education:* University of Kentucky (B.A., cum laude, 1999); Louis D. Brandeis School of Law, University of Louisville (J.D., 2003). Graduated First in Class, Louis D. Brandeis School of Law, University of Louisville, 2003. *Member:* Louisville and American Bar Associations. ***LANGUAGES:*** Spanish. ***PRACTICE AREAS:*** Litigation; Commercial Litigation; Insurance Coverage Litigation and Bad Faith. ***Email:*** jtrose@fbtlaw.com

REPRESENTATIVE CLIENTS: AAF-McQuay Inc.; AEGON USA Realty Advisors, Inc.; AIG Insurance Group; AK Steel Corporation; Anthem Health Plans; Broadwing Inc.; Brown & Williamson Tobacco Corporation; Catholic Healthcare Partners; Central Bank & Trust Company; Chapelthorp plc; Chiquita Brands International; ClubLink Corporation; Convergys Corporation; Coolmore Castlehyde and Associated Stud Farms; Federated Department Stores, Inc.; FieldTurf, Inc.; Firstar/U.S. Bank; Taco Bell Franchise Management Advisory Council (FRANMAC); General Electric Company; ICI Paints World Group; Jewish Hospital HealthCare Services, Inc.; LensCrafters, Inc.; Lexis-Nexis; LG&E Energy Corp.; Liberty Mutual Insurance Group; Lightyear Communications, Inc.; MidAmerica Bancorp; New Horizon Resources, Inc.; NTS Development Company; OneBeacon Insurance Group; Progressive Insurance Company; PNC Bank Corp. and PNC Bank; Res-Care, Inc.; The Rouse Companies, LLC; Services Net Incorporated; Smithkline Beecham Clinical Lab; Terex Corporation; Turner Construction Company; Unified Foodservice Purchasing Co-op, LLC; United Parcel Service; Vincor International Inc.; Waste Management of North America; Western Southern Life Insurance Company.

KIGHTLINGER & GRAY, LLP

ONE COMMERCE SQUARE
4106 CHARLESTOWN ROAD
NEW ALBANY, INDIANA 47150
Telephone: 812-949-2300
Telecopier: 812-949-8556
Email: info@k-glaw.com
URL: http://www.k-glaw.com

Indianapolis, Indiana Office: Market Square Center, Suite 600, 151 North Delaware Street, 46204. Telephone: 317-638-4521. Telecopier: 317-636-5917.
Evansville, Indiana Office: 7311 Eagle Crest Blvd., 47715. Telephone: 812-474-4400. Telecopier: 812-474-4414.

Civil Litigation, Commercial and Business Litigation, Drug and Medical Device Litigation, Environmental and Toxic Tort Litigation, Casualty, Surety and Life Insurance Law, General Litigation, Malpractice Litigation (Pharmacy, Medical, Legal, Architects and Engineers, Accountants, Insurance Agents, Real Estate Agents and School Boards), Products Liability Law, Trucking Defense Litigation, Construction Law, ICC Regulatory Law, Appeals (State and Federal), Worker's Compensation, Maritime Law, Civil Rights and Wrongful Discharge Law, All areas of Government Liability, including Law Enforcement Liability Litigation, Class Actions, Labor Law, Securities Litigation.

SENIOR PARTNER

SAMUEL A. DAY (1952-2003)

RESIDENT PARTNERS

RICHARD T. MULLINEAUX, born Corpus Christi, Texas, July 30, 1952; admitted to bar, 1978, Virginia; 1980, Indiana; U.S. District Court, Southern District of Indiana and Eastern District of Virginia; U.S. Court of Appeals, Seventh Circuit. *Education:* Indiana University (B.S., 1974); George Mason University (J.D., 1978). *Member:* Floyd County, Seventh Circuit and Indiana State Bar Associations; Defense Research Institute; Defense Trial Counsel of Indiana; Trucking Industry Defense Association; American Board of Trial Advocates; Southern Indiana Chamber of Commerce; Sherman Minton American Inns of Court. ***PRACTICE AREAS:*** Insurance Defense; Products Liability Law; Trial Practice; Professional Malpractice Liability; Civil Rights; Business; Transportation; Insurance Bad Faith Defense; Fire Insurance Defense; First and Third Party Insurance Defense; Insurance Coverage Defense; Insurance Defense Subrogation; General Liability Defense; Property Damage Defense; Property Insurance Defense; Automobile Insurance Coverage; Casualty Insurance Subrogation; Fire Insurance Subrogation; Fire Loss; Malpractice; Insurance Litigation; Property Subrogation; Class Actions; Class Action Defense; Commercial Litigation; Constitutional Law; First Amendment Law; Construction Law; Construction Insurance Defense; Construction Litigation; Education Law; Public School Law; School Board Defense; School Board Liability; School District Liability; School Law; Legal Malpractice; Legal Malpractice Defense; Legal Professional Liability; Libel Defense; Civil Litigation; Complex Litigation; Defense Litigation; Medical Malpractice; Medical Malpractice Defense; Personal Injury; Personal Injury Defense; Products Liability; Products Liability Defense; Products Liability Insurance Coverage; Products Liability Subrogation; Toxic Torts; Toxic Tort Defense; Common Carrier Liability Law; Motor Carrier Defense; Motor Carrier Liability; Truck Accidents; Trucking Liability; Trucking Law.

VAN T. WILLIS, born Franklin, Kentucky, December 18, 1959; admitted to bar, 1988, Kentucky; 1990, Indiana; U.S. District Court, Southern District of Indiana; U.S. District Court, Eastern and Western Districts of Kentucky; U.S. Court of Appeals, Sixth and Seventh Circuits. *Education:* University of Kentucky (B.A., 1983; J.D., 1988). Law Clerk to Judge Gene E. Brooks, U.S. District Court, Southern District of Indiana, 1989-1991. *Member:* Louisville, Floyd County, Kentucky and Indiana State Bar Associations; Defense Trial Counsel of Indiana; Defense Research Institute; Sherman Minton American Inns of Court; Southern Indiana Chamber of Commerce. ***PRACTICE AREAS:*** Insurance Defense Law; Civil Rights; Corporate and Business Law; Workers Compensation; Products Liability; Business Law; Business Litigation; Business Start-Ups; Business Organization; Closely Held Business Law; Complex Business Litigation; Limited Liability Company Law; Private Business Law; Professional Practices; Small Business Law; Sole Proprietorships; Civil Rights Defense; Contracts; Contract Litigation; Employment Defense; Employment Law; Employment Litigation; Insurance Defense; First and Third Party Insurance Defense; Leasing; Complex Litigation; Defense Litigation; Federal Civil Litigation; Federal Litigation; Trial Practice; Civil Litigation; Nonprofit Organizations Law; Partnership Law; Limited Liability Partnerships; Limited Partnerships; Partnership Organization; Transportation; Common Carrier Liability Law; Motor Carrier Defense; Motor Carrier Liability; Truck Accidents; Trucking Law; Trucking Liability; Workers Compensation Defense. ***Email:*** vwillis@k-glaw.com

MARY JO WETZEL, admitted to bar, 1975, Kentucky; 1976, Indiana; U.S. District Court, Southern District of Indiana; U.S. District Court, Eastern and Western Districts of Kentucky; U.S. Court of Appeals, Sixth Circuit. *Education:* Indiana University (B.A., 1971); University of Louisville (J.D., 1975). *Member:* Louisville, Floyd County, Kentucky and Indiana State Bar Associations; Kentucky Defense Counsel; Defense Research Institute, Inc.; Defense Trial Counsel of Indiana; Sherman Minton American Inns of Court. ***PRACTICE AREAS:*** Trials; Insurance Defense; Product Liability Litigation; Insurance Bade Faith Defense; First and Third Party Insurance Defense; Litigation; Civil Litigation; Complex Litigation; Defense Litigation; Federal Litigation; Trial Practice; Products Liabil-

(This Listing Continued)

ity; Products Liability Defense; Products Liability Insurance Coverage; Products Liability Subrogation; Professional Liability; Professional Liability Defense; Professional Liability Insurance Coverage; Professional Malpractice. ***Email:*** mwetzel@k-glaw.com

STEVEN K. PALMQUIST, born Moline, Illinois, September 9, 1954; admitted to bar, 1979, Indiana; 1980, Kentucky; U.S. District Court, Southern District of Indiana and Eastern and Western Districts of Kentucky. *Education:* Cornell College (B.A., cum laude, 1976); University of Cincinnati (J.D., 1979). Active in Southern Indiana Chamber of Commerce; Wall Street United Methodist Church; Council on Finance and Administration; South Indiana Conference, United Methodist Church; Habitat for Humanity; Vice President, Board of Directors, Regional Youth Services, Inc.; Co-President Elect, Board of Directors, Hanover College Parents Association. *Member:* Floyd County, Kentucky and Indiana State (Member, Probate, Trust and Real Property Section) Bar Associations; Southern Indiana Realtors Association (Affiliate Member); Indiana Land Title Association; Southern Indiana Chamber of Commerce. ***PRACTICE AREAS:*** Real Estate; Estate Planning; Estate Administration; Corporate Law; Banks and Banking; Banking Law; Banking Litigation; Commercial Banking; Consumer Banking; Fair Lending; Lender Liability; Lender Law; Lenders Rights; Loans; Commercial Litigation; Commercial Law; Complex Commercial Litigation; Business Law; Business Estate Planning; Business Formation; Business Litigation; Business Organization; Business Planning; Business Start-Ups; Business Succession Planning; Business Successions; Business Trusts; Closely Held Business Estate Planning; Closely Held Business Law; Closely Held Business Taxation; Complex Business Litigation; Entrepreneurial Business Law; Limited Liability Company Law; Professional Practices; Small Business Law; Condominium Association Law; Community Association Law; Condominium Law; Land Acquisitions; Land Sales; Land Trusts; Real Estate Acquisitions; Real Estate Banking Law; Real Estate Development; Real Estate Finance; Real Estate Litigation; Real Estate Partnerships; Real Estate Restructuring; Real Estate Title; Real Estate Title Examination; Real Estate Title Insurance; Residential Real Estate; Residential Real Estate Acquisitions; Right of Way Easements; Contracts; Commercial Contracts; Contract Litigation; Trusts and Estates; Estate Planning for Parents of Handicapped Children; Estate Planning for the Disabled; Estate Planning for the Elderly; Estate Planning for Unmarried Couples; Estate Settlements; Family Trusts; Fiduciary Liability; Fiduciary Litigation; Financial Planning; Living Trusts; Personal Planning; Special Needs Trusts; Trust Administration; Trust Law; Trust Litigation; Trust Planning; Wills; Living Wills; Guardianships and Conservatorship; Adult Guardianship; Elder Guardianship; Guardianship; Guardianship Administration; Leases and Leasing; Commercial Leasing; Landlord and Tenant Law; Leasing; Office Leasing; Retail Leasing; Partnership Law; Limited Liability Partnerships; Limited Partnerships; Partnership Formation; Partnership Dissolution; Partnership Organization; Probate; Probate Administration; Probate Litigation; Zoning, Planning and Land Use; Land Development; Land Use; Land Use Litigation; Rezoning; Zoning Law. ***Email:*** spalmquist@k-glaw.com

WILLIAM E. SMITH, III, born Neptune, New Jersey, December 18, 1953; admitted to bar, 1979, Indiana; 1980, Kentucky; U.S. District Court, Southern District of Indiana and Eastern and Western Districts of Kentucky; U.S. Court of Appeals, Sixth Circuit. *Education:* Franklin College of Indiana (B.A., magna cum laude, 1976); University of Dayton (J.D., 1979). Phi Alpha Delta; Blue Key. Member: Southern Indiana Chamber of Commerce; Rotary Club; Clark County Chapter, American Red Cross; Morton Memorial United Methodist Church. Attorney: Town of Borden, Indiana, 1982—. *Member:* Louisville, Clark County, Floyd County, Indiana State and Kentucky Bar Associations; Association of Credit and Collection Professionals (ACA/MAP); Sherman Minton American Inns of Court. ***PRACTICE AREAS:*** Real Estate; Bankruptcy; Creditors Rights; Corporate Law; Estate Planning; Estate Administration; Adoption Law; Banks and Banking; Banking Law; Banking Litigation; Commercial Banking; Commercial Loans; Credit Law; Financial Law; Lender Law; Lender Liability; Lender Rights; Savings and Loan Law; Commercial Litigation; Commercial Law; Complex Commercial Litigation; Bankruptcy Collections; Bankruptcy Litigation; Fair Debt Collection Practices Act; Business Law; Business Estate Planning; Business Litigation; Complex Business Litigation; Professional Practices; Small Business Law; Sole Proprietorships; Environmental Law; Environmental Business Law; Environmental Corporate Law; Environmental Criminal Defense; Environmental Litigation; Trusts and Estates; Estate Litigation; Fiduciary Litigation; Trust Administration; Trusts and Estate Collections; Trust Law; Trust Litigation; Trust Planning; Guardianship; Municipal Law; Municipal Defense; Zoning Law; Land Use; Land Use Litigation; Real Estate Litigation. ***Email:*** wsmith@k-glaw.com

R. JEFFREY LOWE, born Blowing Rock, North Carolina, January 26, 1972; admitted to bar, 1998, Kentucky; 1999, Indiana; U.S. District Court, Southern District of Indiana and Western District of Kentucky. *Education:* University of North Carolina (B.A., History, 1994); Louis D. Brandeis School of Law at the University of Louisville (J.D., 1998). *Member:* Louisville, Floyd County, Kentucky and Indiana State Bar Associations; Defense Research Institute; Defense Trial Counsel of Indiana; Southern Indiana Chamber of Commerce; Sherman Minton American Inns of Court. ***PRACTICE AREAS:*** Litigation; Insurance Defense; Insurance Bad Faith Defense; First and Third Party Insurance Defense; Insurance Coverage Defense; Insurance Defense Subrogation; Life Insurance Defense; Civil Rights; Civil Rights Defense; Constitutional Law; Legal Malpractice; Legal Malpractice Defense; Legal Professional Liability; Libel Defense; Civil Litigation; Complex Litigation; Defense Litigation; Municipal Law; Municipal Defense; Municipal Liability; Personal Injury; Personal Injury Defense; Products Liability; Products Liability Defense; Products Liability Insurance Coverage; Professional Malpractice; Professional Liability Insurance Coverage; Professional Liability Defense; Fire Insurance Defense. ***Email:*** jlowe@k-glaw.com

RESIDENT ASSOCIATES

J. TODD SPURGEON, born Brownstown, Indiana, February 19, 1974; admitted to bar, 1999, Indiana; U.S. District Court, Southern District of Indiana. *Education:* Wabash College (B.A., 1996); Indiana University (J.D., cum laude, 1999). Delta Theta Phi. Member, Philip Jessup International Law Moot Court. Articles Editor, Indiana Journal of Global Legal Studies. Author and Speaker: Article, "Ethical Considerations Raised in Insurance Defense Practice"; ICLEF Seminar: "42 Things You Need To Know About Insurance Law," March 24, 2000; "Issues Regarding the Use of Interpreters in Depositions in Indiana," Indiana Lawyer article, Vol. 13, No. 18, November 20, 2002. Program Co-Chair: Young Lawyers Summit, 2003 and 2004. Panelist: "Dealing with the SOB Litigator". Member: Board of Directors, Junior Achievement of Southern Indiana; Lions Club of New Albany. *Member:* Floyd County, Indiana State (Young Lawyer Representative, 2005-2007; Ninth District Representative, Young Lawyer's Section; Member, Professionalism Committee) and American (Member, House of Delegates) Bar Associations; Defense Trial Counsel of Indiana; Defense Research Institute; Southern Indiana Chamber of Commerce; Sherman Minton American Inns of Court; Young Professionals Association of Louisville. ***PRACTICE AREAS:*** Insurance Defense; Municipal Law; Zoning and Land Use; Insurance Bad Faith Defense; First and Third Party Insurance Defense; Insurance Coverage Defense; Insurance Defense Subrogation; Arson and Insurance Fraud; Fire Insurance Defense; General Liability Defense; Insurance Fraud Defense; Property Damage Defense; Property Insurance Defense; Civil Rights; Civil Rights Defense; Commercial Litigation; Eminent Domain; Government; Government Affairs; Land Use; Land Use Litigation; Zoning Law; Rezoning; Zoning, Planning and Land Use; Complex Litigation; Defense Litigation; Trial Practice; Municipal Defense; Personal Injury; Personal Injury Defense; Products Liability; Products Liability Defense; Products Liability Insurance Coverage; Products Liability Subrogation; Professional Liability; Professional Liability Defense; Professional Liability Insurance Coverage; Professional Malpractice; Legal Malpractice Defense; Real Estate; Real Estate Litigation; Transportation; Common Carrier Liability Law; Motor Carrier Defense; Motor Carrier Liability; Transportation Liability; Truck Accidents; Trucking Law; Trucking Liability. ***Email:*** tspurgeon@k-glaw.com

D. KEITH PULLIAM, born Louisville, Kentucky, August 22, 1975; admitted to bar, 2000, Indiana and Kentucky. *Education:* Indiana University (B.A., 1997; J.D., cum laude, 2000). Author and Speaker: Southern Indiana Small Business Development Center (SBDC) Pre-Business Workshop; SBDC Managing Your Accounts Receivable and Collections Workshop. Chairman, Southern Indiana SBDC Youth Entrepreneurial Success (YES) Program, 2002- 2004. *Member:* Louisville, Indiana State and Kentucky Bar Associations; Sherman Minton American Inns of Court; Hispanic Connection of Southern Indiana, Inc.; Southern Indiana Chamber of Commerce (Director and Treasurer). ***LANGUAGES:*** Spanish. ***PRACTICE AREAS:*** Litigation; Estate Planning; Business Law; School Law; Business Litigation; Small Business Law; Partnership Law; Limited Liability Partnerships; Limited Partnerships; Partnership Organization; Commercial Litigation; Contracts; Contract Litigation; Leases and Leasing; Commercial Landlord and Tenant Law; Commercial Leasing; Landlord and Tenant Law; Labor and Employment; Labor Law; Employment Litigation; Employment Defense; Trusts and Estates; Estate Administration; Estate Litigation; Trust Law; Trust Litigation; Trust Planning; Intellectual Property; Intellectual Property Litigation; Immigration and Naturalization; Business Immigration; Employment Authorizations; Employment Immigration; Employment Visas; Immigration Discrimination; Immigration Law. ***Email:*** kpulliam@k-glaw.com

JAMES C. WADE, born Reno, Nevada, January 8, 1971; admitted to bar, 1998, Kentucky; 2002, Indiana; U.S. District Court, Eastern and Western Districts of Kentucky; U.S. District Court, Southern District of Indiana. *Education:* Bellarmine College (B.A., cum laude, 1993); University of Louisville (J.D., cum laude, 1998). *Member:* Louisville, Floyd County, Kentucky and Indiana State (Member, Young Lawyers Section) Bar Associations; Sherman Minton American Inns of Court; Defense Research Institute; Southern Indiana Chamber of Commerce. ***PRACTICE AREAS:*** Civil Litigation Defense; Construction Law; Insurance Law; Surety Law; Insurance Defense; Insurance Bad Faith Defense; Collections; Commercial Collections; Construction Litigation; Contracts; Contract Litigation; Fidelity and Surety Bonds; Complex Litigation; Defense Litigation; Trial Practice. ***Email:*** jwade@k-glaw.com

DONNA J. JENKINS, born New Albany, Indiana, June 4, 1961; admitted to bar, 1987, Kentucky; 1997, Indiana; U.S. District Court, Western District of Kentucky. *Education:* Indiana University Southeast (B.A., Political Science, 1983); University of Louisville School of Law (J.D., 1987). *Member:* Floyd County, Kentucky and Indiana State Bar Associations; Sherman Minton American Inns of Court; Hispanic Connection of Southern Indiana, Inc. (Secretary); American Immigration Lawyers Association. ***PRACTICE AREAS:*** Business Law; Contracts Law; Immigration; Insurance Defense. ***Email:*** djenkins@k-glaw.com

VALERIE D. KESSLER, born Louisville, Kentucky, August 15, 1971; admitted to bar, 2003, Kentucky; 2005, Indiana. *Education:* Georgetown College of Kentucky (B.A., 1993); University of Kentucky (M.A., English, 1996); University of Kentucky College of Law (J.D., 2003). *Member:* Kentucky and American Bar Associations; Defense Research Institute (DRI); Defense Trial Counsel of Indiana (DTCI). ***PRACTICE AREAS:*** Commercial Litigation; Insurance Defense; First and Third Party Insurance Defense; Complex Litigation; Defense Litigation; Trial Practice. ***Email:*** vkessler@k-glaw.com

(For complete biographical data on Indianapolis, Indiana and Evansville, Indiana personnel, see Professional Biographies at those locations)

MATTOX MATTOX & WILSON

SUITE 420 ELSBY BUILDING
P.O. BOX 1203
NEW ALBANY, INDIANA 47151-1203
Telephone: 812-944-8005
Facsimile: 812-944-2255
Email: mmlaw@win.net

Civil Trial Litigation. Personal Injury and Wrongful Death, Products Liability, Medical Malpractice, Insurance Law, Corporate Law, Business Torts, Family Law, Aviation Law, Labor and Employment Law, Health Care Regulations.

MEMBERS OF FIRM

RICHARD L. MATTOX, born Columbus, Indiana, January 19, 1934; admitted to bar, 1962, Indiana, U.S. Court of Appeals, Seventh Circuit and U.S. District Court, Southern District of Indiana. *Education:* Indiana University (B.S., 1956; J.D. 1962). Author: " Punitive Damages in Wrongful Death Cases," Indiana Continuing Legal Education Forum, 1985; "Powers, Duties and Responsibilities of Airport Board Members," Indiana Continuing Legal Education Forum, 1987; "Examination and Cross-Examination of Medical Experts," Indiana Continuing Legal Education Forum, 1989; "The Medical Malpractice Ac-

(This Listing Continued)

MATTOX MATTOX & WILSON, New Albany—Continued

tion in Indiana," Louisville Bar Association, 1991; General Counsel, Robinson Nugent, Inc. *Member:* Floyd County (President, 1964), Indiana State and American Bar Associations; Lawyer-Pilots Bar Association; Indiana Trial Lawyers Association; Indiana Defense Lawyers Association (Director, 1992; Diplomat). Fellow, American College of Trial Lawyers. [Capt., U.S. Air Force, 1956-1964]. (Board Certified, Family Law Specialist, Indiana State Bar Association, Family Law Certification Board). ***PRACTICE AREAS:*** Litigation; Personal Injury; Domestic Relations; Insurance Bad Faith. ***Email:*** rmottox@win.net

S. FRANK MATTOX, born Rushville, Indiana, February 4,1956; admitted to bar, 1981, Indiana, U.S. District Court, Southern District of Indiana and U.S. Court of Appeals, Seventh Circuit. *Education:* Wabash College (B.A., 1978); Indiana University (J.D., 1981). Certified Family Law Mediator. Faculty ICLEF Family Law Institute, 2003. Public Defender, Harrison Circuit Court, 1982-1986. Attorney, Harrison County Department of Public Works, 1986-2002. *Member:* American (Executive Council, Young Lawyers Division, 1987-1991), Indiana State (Executive Council, Young Lawyers Section, 1987-1991, Chairman, Indiana Teen Law Committee, 1989-1991, Director, Indiana Bar Foundation, 1996-2000, Executive Council, Professional Legal Education and Development Section, 2002), Clark County, Floyd County (Delegate to ISBA House of Delegates, 1988—) Harrison-Crawford County, Louisville, Kentucky Bar Associations; Indiana Trial Lawyers Association; The Association of Trial Lawyers of America; Indiana Association of Criminal Defense Lawyers; National Association of Council for Children. Fellow, Indiana Bar Foundation. (Board Certified, Family Law Specialist, Indiana State Bar Association, Family Law Certification Board). ***REPORTED CASES:*** Straub v. B.M.T., 645 N.E. 2d 597, 1994 Ind. LEXIS 219, (Ind. 1994); Cooper v. Cooper, 730 N.E. 2d 212, 2000 Ind. App. LEXIS 892 (Ind. 2000); Obremski v. Henderson, 497 N.E. 2d 909, 1986 Ind. LEXIS 1276 (Ind. 1986); In the Matter of : Y.D.R. and J.C.R. Children Alleged to be Children in Need of Services; M.L.R. v. Harrison County Welfare Dept., 567 N.E.2d 872, 1991 Ind. App. LEXIS 529 (Ind. 1991). ***PRACTICE AREAS:*** Litigation; Personal Injury; Domestic Relations; Insurance Bad Faith. ***Email:*** matlaw@win.net

DERRICK H. WILSON, born Louisville, Kentucky, July 6, 1966; admitted to bar, 1991, Kentucky, Indiana, U.S. District Court, Southern District of Indiana, U.S. District Court, Western District of Kentucky and U.S. Court of Appeals, Seventh Circuit. *Education:* University of Louisville (B.A., summa cum laude, 1988; J.D., cum laude, 1991). Author: "Winning Techniques for Taking and Defending Depositions," (Program Chair, 1998); *Member:* Indiana State (Council, Young Lawyers Section, 1997-1999), Kentucky and American Bar Associations. (Certified as a Civil Trial Specialist by the National Board of Trial Advocacy). ***REPORTED CASES:*** Law v. Law, 676 N.E.2d 771 (briefs only) (Ind. App. 1997); Sword v. NKC, 661 N.E.2d 10 (briefs and argument) (Ind. App. 1996); Straub v. B.M.T., 645 N.E.2d 597 (briefs only) (Ind. 1994). ***PRACTICE AREAS:*** Litigation; Commercial Transactions; Medical Malpractice. ***Email:*** mmlaw@win.net

ASSOCIATES

KAREN R. GOODWELL, born New Albany, Indiana, February 9, 1959; admitted to bar, 1985, Indiana and U.S. District Court, Southern District of Indiana. *Education:* DePauw University (B.A., cum laude, 1981); Indiana University School of Law (J.D., 1984). Corporate Counsel, Statesman Insurance Co., 1987-1992. *Member:* Indiana State and American (Member, Labor and Employment Sections) Bar Associations. ***PRACTICE AREAS:*** Insurance; Labor and Employment Law. ***Email:*** mmlaw@win.net

DEBRA S. AUDRY, born Anderson, Indiana, September 7, 1961; admitted to bar, 2004, Indiana. *Education:* Indiana University (B.S.N., 1983; J.D., 2004). Registered Nurse, 1983. *Member:* Indiana State and American Bar Associations; The American Association of Nurse Attorneys. ***PRACTICE AREAS:*** Civil; Family Law; Medical Malpractice. ***Email:*** dandry@mmwlaw.net

REPRESENTATIVE CLIENTS: AAOMS National Insurance; Cablelink, Inc.; Clark Memorial Hospital; Coyle Chevrolet, Inc.; Fashion Shops of Columbus, Inc.; Floyd County Plan Commission; Floyd Memorial Hospital; Harrison County Hospital; General Casualty Co.; Hap's Aerial Enterprises, Inc.; John Jones GM City, Inc.; Kimball International, Inc.; The Medical Protective Co.; New Albany Housing Authority; Papa Johns Intl., Inc.; PHICO Insurance Co.; Physicians Group, Inc.; Robinson Nugent, Inc.

MERKLEY LAW OFFICE

NEW ALBANY, INDIANA

(See Jeffersonville)

Family Law, Criminal Law, Estates and Wills, Personal Injury, Municipal Law.

MORGAN & POTTINGER, P.S.C.

NEW ALBANY, INDIANA

(See Louisville, KY)

Banking, Bankruptcy, Business, Collections, Commercial, Corporate, Consumer Credit, Employment Law, Estate Planning, Litigation, Probate, Real Estate, Secured Transactions, State and Federal Trial Practice, Tax, Trusts.

CHARLES R. MURPHY

3707 CHARLESTOWN ROAD, SUITE D
NEW ALBANY, INDIANA 47150-0254
Telephone: 812-944-0515
Fax: 812-944-2996
Email: terrax@win.net
URL: http://www.lawyers.com/charlesrmurphy

Real Estate, Elder Law, Business Law, Buying or Selling a Home, Eminent Domain, Landlord and Tenant Law, Zoning and Land Use, Tax Deferred Exchanges, Business Start-Ups, Buying or Selling a Business, Business Enterprises, Limited Liability Company Law, Corporations, Partnerships, Small Business Law.

(This Listing Continued)

CHARLES R. MURPHY, born Bedford, Indiana, March 5, 1955; admitted to bar, 1981, Indiana and U.S. District Court, Southern District of Indiana. *Education:* Indiana University, Bloomington (B.S., 1977); Indiana University, Indianapolis (J.D., cum laude, 1981). Secretary Treasurer, Clark County Bar Association, 1983-1984. *Member:* Floyd County and Indiana State Bar Associations.

JOHN M. NADER & ASSOCIATES

NEW ALBANY, INDIANA

(See Louisville, Kentucky)

Bankruptcy, Transportation, Corporate Law, Civil Litigation.

O'BRYAN, BROWN & TONER, PLLC

NEW ALBANY, INDIANA

(See Louisville, Kentucky)

SCOTT, FORREST & BOURNE

821 MOUNT TABOR ROAD, SUITE 302
NEW ALBANY, INDIANA 47150
Telephone: 812-945-9151
Fax: 812-945-6131
Email: sfb@sfb-law.com
URL: http://www.sfb-law.com

Wrongful Death, Products Liability and Medical Malpractice Law.

FIRM PROFILE: We limit our practice to cases involving wrongful death and serious personal injury arising from product failure, medical malpractice and, on occasion, other types of catastrophic occurrences. Each of the partners has over 30 years experience trying such cases in State and Federal Courts. Our partners are active in their professional associations and regularly teach continuing legal education seminars in their fields of practice.

Our clients are individuals and families who have experienced serious injury or wrongful death as result of the fault of another person or company, healthcare provider or product manufacturer or seller.

DAVID V. SCOTT, born Greenville, Mississippi, October 25, 1942; admitted to bar, 1970, Indiana and U.S. District Court, Southern District of Indiana; 1977, U.S. Court of Appeals, Seventh Circuit; 1979, Kentucky and Michigan (inactive); 1982, U.S. District Court, Western District of Kentucky; 1987, U.S. Court of Appeals, Sixth Circuit; 1997, U.S. District Court, Eastern District of Kentucky. *Education:* Baker University (B.A., 1966); University of Louisville (J.D., 1969). *Member:* Indiana State and American Bar Associations; The Association of Trial Lawyers of America; Indiana Trial Lawyers Association (Emeritus Director, 1989—); American Board of Trial Advocates. ***PRACTICE AREAS:*** Products Liability; Motor Vehicle Accidents and Injuries. ***Email:*** dave@sfb-law.com

DONALD R. FORREST, born Washington, D.C., November 9, 1940; admitted to bar, 1966, Indiana and U.S. District Court, Southern District of Indiana; 1985, U.S. Court of Appeals, Seventh Circuit; 1986, Kentucky and U.S. District Court, Western District of Kentucky; 1990, U.S. Court of Appeals, Sixth Circuit. *Education:* Indiana University (A.B., 1962; LL.B., 1966). Trial Lawyers for Public Justice. *Member:* Indiana State, Louisville, Kentucky and American Bar Associations; Indiana Trial Lawyers Association; Kentucky Academy of Trial Attorneys; Association of Trial Lawyers of America; American Board of Trial Advocates. ***PRACTICE AREAS:*** Medical Negligence; Products Liability; Highway Design Liability. ***Email:*** dforrest@sfb-law.com

JAMES E. BOURNE, born Charleston, West Virginia, January 13, 1940; admitted to bar, 1965, Indiana and U.S. District Court, Southern District of Indiana; 1969, U.S. Court of Appeals, 7th Circuit; 2003, U.S. Supreme Court. *Education:* Indiana University (B.A., 1962; J.D., 1965). Chair, Commission on Continuing Legal Education, 1991-1992 and Member, Character and Fitness Committee, 1993—, Indiana Supreme Court. *Member:* Indiana State (President, 2002-2003; Chair, House of Delegates, 1997-1998) and American Bar Associations; The Association of Trial Lawyers of America; Indiana Trial Lawyers Association; American College of Trial Lawyers. ***PRACTICE AREAS:*** Wrongful Death; Personal Injury; Product Liability. ***Email:*** jbourne@sfb-law.com

WYATT, TARRANT & COMBS, LLP

(Formerly Orbison, O'Connor, MacGregor & Mattox)

THE COMMUNITY BANK BUILDING
101 WEST SPRING STREET, SUITE 500
NEW ALBANY, INDIANA 47150-3440
Telephone: 812-945-3561
Telecopier: 812-949-2524
URL: http://www.wyattfirm.com

Louisville, Kentucky Office: 500 West Jefferson Street. Telephone: 502-589-5235. Telecopier: 502-589-0309.

Lexington, Kentucky Office: 250 West Main Street, Suite 1600. Telephone: 859-233-2012. Telecopier: 859-259-0649.

Bowling Green, Kentucky Office: 918 State Street. Telephone: 270-842-1050. Telecopier: 270-842-4720.

Nashville, Tennessee Office: 2525 West End Avenue, Suite 1500. Telephone: 615-244-0020. Telecopier: 615-256-1726.

Memphis, Tennessee Office: The Renaissance Center, 1715 Aaron Brenner Drive, Suite 800. Telephone: 901-537-1000. Telecopier: 901-537-1010.

(This Listing Continued)

Administrative Law, Alternative Dispute Resolution, Antitrust and Trade Regulation, Appellate Practice, Bankruptcy, Banks and Banking, Commercial Law, Commercial Real Estate, Communications and Media, Construction Law, Copyrights, Corporate Law, Debtor and Creditor, Education Law, Employee Benefits, Energy Law, Equine, Environmental Law, Franchises and Franchising, Government, Health Care, Hospital Law, Immigration and Naturalization, Insurance, Insurance Defense, Intellectual Property, International Law, International Trade, Labor and Employment, Leases and Leasing, Legal Ethics and Professional Responsibility, Litigation, Medicare and Medicaid, Merger Acquisitions and Divestitures, Mortgages, Municipal Law, Natural Resources, Nonprofit and Charitable Organizations, Occupational Safety and Health, Partnership Law, Probate, Public Finance, Securities, Taxation, Technology and Science, Trade Secrets, Trademarks, Trusts and Estates, Utility Law, Wills, Workers Compensation, Zoning Planning and Land Use.

FIRM PROFILE: Wyatt, Tarrant & Combs, LLP is a regional law firm with 210 attorneys in six offices throughout Tennessee, Kentucky and Southern Indiana.

PARTNERS

TELFORD B. ORBISON (1901-1990)

CHARLES E. MACGREGOR, born Clarksville, Indiana, November 11, 1930; admitted to bar, 1954, Indiana. *Education:* Indiana University (B.A., 1952); University of Louisville (J.D., 1954). *Member:* Floyd County (Past President), Indiana State (State Delegate Member) and American Bar Associations; Indiana Defense Lawyers Association. ***PRACTICE AREAS:*** Business Law; Real Estate Lending; Commercial Lending Law; Tort and Insurance Defense. ***Email:*** cmacgregor@wyattfirm.com

THOMAS W. SINEX, born New Albany, Indiana, November 5, 1940; admitted to bar, 1965, Indiana. *Education:* Wabash College (A.B., summa cum laude, 1962); Harvard Law School (J.D., 1965). Phi Beta Kappa; Delta Phi Alpha. Member and Past President, Southern Indiana Estate Planning Council. *Member:* American Bar Association. Fellow, American College of Trust and Estate Counsel. ***PRACTICE AREAS:*** Business Law; Estate Planning; Public Finance. ***Email:*** tsinex@wyattfirm.com

RICHARD A. BIERLY, born Elizabeth, Indiana, May 7, 1946; admitted to bar, 1976, Indiana. *Education:* Indiana University (B.A., 1972; J.D., magna cum laude, 1976). Order of the Coif. Law Clerk to Hon. Phil McNagny, U.S. District Judge Northern District of Indiana, 1976-1978. *Member:* American Bar Association; Defense Trial Counsel of Indiana Past President (2000-2001). ***PRACTICE AREAS:*** Employment Law; Tort and Insurance Defense. ***Email:*** rbierly@wyattfirm.com

GEORGE L. SEAY, JR., born Tullahoma, Tennessee, June 19, 1948; admitted to bar, 1973, Kentucky; 1975, Indiana; U.S District Court, Eastern and Western Districts of Kentucky; U.S. Court of Appeals, Sixth Circuit; U.S. District Court, Northern District of Alabama; U.S. Court of Appeals, Eleventh Circuit; U.S. Supreme Court; U.S. Court of Appeals for the District of Columbia Circuit. *Education:* Hanover College (B.A., 1970); University of Louisville (J.D., 1973). Chief Law Clerk, Kentucky Court of Appeals (now Supreme Court), 1973-1974. Departmental Attorney, Kentucky Department for Natural Resources of Environmental Protection, 1945-1978. Best Lawyers in America, 1997-2002. *Member:* Louisville, Franklin County (Secretary-Treasurer, 1979-1980; President, 1998), Indiana State, Kentucky and American (SONREL Litigation) Bar Associations; Eastern Mineral Law Foundation; The Association of Trial Lawyers of America; Kentucky Association of Trial Attorneys. ***PRACTICE AREAS:*** Environmental Law; Mineral Law; Administrative Law; Natural Resources; Energy; Litigation. ***Email:*** gseay@wyattfirm.com

CYNTHIA W. YOUNG, born Louisville, Kentucky, August 26, 1955; admitted to bar, 1982, Indiana and Kentucky. *Education:* Indiana University Southeast (B.A., 1978); University of Louisville (J.D., 1982). Brandeis Society. Recipient, Edwin O. Davis Award to Valedictorian, 1982. *Member:* Indiana State Bar Association. ***PRACTICE AREAS:*** Banking Law; Bank Mergers and Acquisitions; Buying and Selling of Businesses; Mergers and Acquisitions; Mergers and Acquisitions Finance; Securities. ***Email:*** cyoung@wyattfirm.com

WILLIAM H. HOLLANDER, born Evansville, Indiana, April 5, 1953; admitted to bar, 1984, Indiana and Kentucky. *Education:* Harvard University (A.B., cum laude, 1975); Indiana University School of Law (J.D., summa cum laude, 1984). Order of the Coif. *Member:* Kentucky, Indiana State and American Bar Associations; International Trademark Association. ***PRACTICE AREAS:*** Labor and Employment; Intellectual Property; Media and First Amendment; Trademark; Computers and Software. ***Email:*** whollander@wyattfirm.com

JEFFREY E. WALLACE, born Valparaiso, Indiana, October 16, 1962; admitted to bar, 1987, Indiana and Kentucky. *Education:* Purdue University (B.A., 1984); Valparaiso University (J.D., 1987). Member, Board of Editors, Valparaiso University Law Review. *Member:* Indiana State and American Bar Associations. ***LANGUAGES:*** Japanese and Spanish. ***PRACTICE AREAS:*** Aircraft Finance and Leasing; International Business Law; Commercial Real Estate Acquisitions; Commercial Real Estate Finance; International Real Estate. ***Email:*** jwallace@wyattfirm.com

JOHN W. WOODARD, JR., born Indianapolis, Indiana, July 15, 1961; admitted to bar, 1991, Indiana; 2003, Kentucky. *Education:* Indiana University (B.A., 1987; J.D., 1991). Associate Editor, Indiana Law Review, 1990-1991. *Member:* American Bar Association. ***PRACTICE AREAS:*** Commercial Litigation. ***Email:*** jwoodard@wyattfirm.com

COUNSEL

LARRY R. CHURCH, born Portsmouth, Ohio, August 3, 1966; admitted to bar, 1991, Ohio; 1993, Kentucky; 1996, Indiana. *Education:* Kent State University (B.A., 1988); University of Cincinnati (J.D., 1991). Phi Beta Kappa. Member, Moot Court Executive Board. Attorney, Kentucky Department of Public Advocacy. *Member:* Louisville and Ohio State Bar Associations. ***PRACTICE AREAS:*** Insurance Defense. ***Email:*** lchurch@wyattfirm.com

ALLEN C. PLATT III, born Louisville, Kentucky, October 12, 1968; admitted to bar, 1995, Indiana and Kentucky. *Education:* Indiana University (B.A., 1991); Valparaiso University (J.D., magna cum laude, 1995). *Member:* Louisville, Floyd County, Indiana State and Kentucky Bar Associations. (Resident, New Albany, Indiana Office). ***PRACTICE AREAS:*** Business Law; Litigation. ***Email:*** aplatt@wyattfirm.com

All Lawyers are Members of The Floyd County Bar Association and The Indiana State Bar Association.

REPRESENTATIVE CLIENTS: Allstate Insurance Co.; American Society of Composers, Authors and Publishers; Appleton Papers; Arch Coal, Inc.; Ashland Inc.; Bank One, Kentucky, NA; Baptist Healthcare System, Inc.; Churchill Downs, Incorporated; CIGNA Companies; Destec Energy, Inc.; E.I. du Pont de Nemours and Company; Ford Motor Co.; Franklin Industries Inc.; GAMBRO Healthcare Patient Services, Inc.; General Electric Company; Heaven Hill Distilleries, Inc.; Jefferson County, Ky. Board of Education; JRN, Inc.; Kentucky Hospital Assn; Merrill Lynch; Metropolitan Life Insurance Co.; Thomas Nelson, Inc.; Norton Healthcare, Inc.; Perdue Farms, Inc.; PNC Bank, National Association; Quantum Chemical Corporation; Reynolds Metals Co.; Joseph E. Seagram & Sons, Inc.; Sumitomo Rubber Industries, LTD.; Henry Vogt Machine Co.; Thorntons Inc.; Westvaco Corporation; WMX Technologies, Inc.

(For Complete Biographical Data on other Personnel, See Professional Biographies at Louisville, Lexington and Bowling Green, Kentucky and Memphis and Nashville, Tennessee)

BRINKERHOFF RILEY LLC

NEWBURGH, INDIANA

(See Evansville)

Family Law, Child Custody, Divorce, Juvenile Matters, Criminal Defense, Felonies, Misdemeanors, Probation Violations, Small Claims, Contract Disputes, Medical Malpractice and Employment Law.

R. TRACY CRUMP

P.O. BOX 604
NEW CARLISLE, INDIANA 46552
Telephone: 574-654-8222
Fax: 574-654-8577
Email: rtc@rtclaw.com
URL: http://www.rtclaw.com

Intellectual Property, Copyrights, Licensing Agreements, Patents, Trade Secrets, Trademarks.

R. TRACY CRUMP, born San Antonio, Texas, February 9, 1965; admitted to bar, 1992, Indiana; registered to practice before U.S. Patent and Trademark Office. *Education:* Butler University (B.S., with honors in Physics, 1987); Valparaiso University (J.D., 1992); Indiana University (M.B.A, 1999). *Member:* St. Joseph County and Indiana State Bar Associations. ***PRACTICE AREAS:*** Patent; Trademark; Copyright; Intellectual Property.

JAMES E. DAVIS ATTORNEY AT LAW

NEW CASTLE, INDIANA

(See Greenfield)

Personal Injury, Social Security Disability, Wrongful Death, Medical Malpractice, Wills and Probate Law, Automobile Accidents and Injuries, Head Injury, Spinal Injury, Slip and Fall, Trucking Accidents, Construction Accidents, Railroad Accidents, Nursing Home and Abuse and Neglect.

HAYES COPENHAVER CRIDER

Established in 1911

214 SOUTH MAIN STREET
NEW CASTLE, INDIANA 47362-4286
Telephone: 765-529-2100
Fax: 765-529-3532
Email: attorneys@hcclaw.com
URL: http://www.hcclaw.com

Civil Litigation, Trial Practice, Probate Administration, Estate Planning, Medicaid Planning, Bodily Injury, Zoning Law, Banking Law, Divorce, Municipal Law, Real Property.

MEMBERS OF FIRM

E. G. SCOTTEN (1877-1957)

J. R. HINSHAW (1883-1970)

JAMES R. STANLEY (1910-1980)

GEORGE W. HAND (1919-1995)

R. SCOTT HAYES, born Lafayette, Indiana, July 9, 1946; admitted to bar, 1972, Indiana. *Education:* Purdue University (B.S., with honors, 1968); Indianapolis Law School of Indiana University (J.D., cum laude, 1971). *Member:* Henry County, Indiana State (Member, Board of Managers, 1977-1979; Chairman, House of Delegates, 1987-1988) and American Bar Associations; Commercial Law League of America; The Association of Trial Lawyers of America; Indiana Trial Lawyers Association; 7th Circuit Bar Association. (Board Certified Civil Trial Advocate, National Board of Trial Advocacy). ***PRACTICE AREAS:*** Litigation; Personal Injury; Defense Litigation; Family Law; Banking. ***Email:*** shayes@hcclaw.com

DAVID L. COPENHAVER, born Muncie, Indiana, September 24, 1950; admitted to bar, 1976, Indiana and U.S. District Court, Southern District of Indiana. *Education:* Valparaiso University (B.A., 1972); Indiana University (J.D., cum laude, 1976). Pi Sigma Alpha. Former Member, Indiana House of Representatives. Certified Indiana Mediator. *Member:* Henry County, Indiana State and American Bar Associations; Indiana Trial Lawyers

(This Listing Continued)

HAYES COPENHAVER CRIDER, New Castle—Continued

Association; The Association of Trial Lawyers of America. ***PRACTICE AREAS:*** Civil Practice; Domestic Relations; Local Government Law. ***Email:*** dcopenhaver@hcclaw.com

GREGORY L. CRIDER, born Shelbyville, Indiana, May 27, 1950; admitted to bar, 1981, Indiana. *Education:* Indiana University (A.B., 1971; Ph.D., 1975; J.D., magna cum laude, 1981). Phi Beta Kappa; Order of the Coif. Author: "Indiana's Implied Warranty of Fitness for Habitation: Limited Protection for Used Home Buyers," Indiana Law Journal 57:3, Fall, 1982. *Member:* Henry County, Indiana State and American Bar Associations. ***PRACTICE AREAS:*** Estate Planning; Probate Administration; Family Wealth Transfer; Living Trusts; Medicaid Planning. ***Email:*** gcrider@hcclaw.com

ASSOCIATE

JOEL E. HARVEY, born Muncie, Indiana, August 26, 1976; admitted to bar, 2002, Indiana; U.S. District Court, Northern and Southern Districts of Indiana. *Education:* Wabash College (B.A., 1999); University of Dayton School of Law (J.D., magna cum laude, 2002). Associate Editor and Executive Editor, University of Dayton Law Review, 2001-2002. Assistant City Attorney, Richmond, 2003—. *Member:* Henry County, Indiana State and American Bar Associations.

GENERAL COUNSEL: Ameriana Bank & Trust.
REPRESENTATIVE CLIENTS: Town of Knightstown; Blue River Valley School Corp.; Henry County Memorial Hospital; Riverside Mfg.; Eastern Indiana Federal Credit Union; Perfect Circle Credit Union; City of New Castle; Town of Middletown.

AYRES CARR & SULLIVAN, P.C.

136 SOUTH NINTH STREET
NOBLESVILLE, INDIANA 46060-2619
Telephone: 317-773-0882
Fax: 317-773-0943

Indianapolis, Indiana Office: 251 East Ohio Street, Suite 500. Telephone: 317-636-3471. Fax: 317-636-6575.

General Civil and Criminal Practice in all State and Federal Courts. Administrative, Corporation, Insurance and Probate and Estate Planning, Real Estate, Taxation, Transportation, Trial and Appellate Practice.

(For Complete Biographical Data on Personnel, See Professional Biographies at Indianapolis, Indiana.)

BINGHAM McHALE LLP

Established in 1912
970 LOGAN STREET
NOBLESVILLE, INDIANA 46060
Telephone: 317-776-8668
Telecopier: 317-776-8651
URL: http://www.binghammchale.com

Indianapolis, Indiana Office: Bingham McHale LLP, 2700 Market Tower, 10 West Market Street. Telephone: 317-635-8900. Fax: 317-236-9907.
Jasper, Indiana Office: Bingham McHale LLP, 212 West Sixth Street. Telephone: 812-482-5500. Fax: 812-482-2017.
Vincennes, Indiana Office: Bingham Mchale LLP, 112 North 7th Street. Telephone: 812-886-9970. Fax: 812-886-0776.

General Civil Practice, Architects and Engineers, Business Law, Business Litigation, Commercial Transactions, Construction Law, Corporate Finance, Estate Planning and Administration, Governmental Services, Matrimonial and Family Law, Public Finance, Public Utility Law, Real Estate, Zoning, Planning and Land Use.

FIRM PROFILE: Bingham McHale LLP was formed by the merger of Bingham Summers Welsh & Spilman and McHale Cook & Welch on January 1, 2002. Evident in the nearly 130 year combined history of both firms is the longstanding commitment to one ideal: providing high quality legal services at an affordable cost. Both firms individually earned a reputation founded upon client service, and will continue and improve upon that tradition collectively as it provides the highest level of service to business, government, utility and land use clients and their individual owners.

MEMBER OF FIRM

STEVEN D. HARDIN, born Indianapolis, Indiana, 1963; admitted to bar, 1992, Indiana. *Education:* Indiana University (B.S., 1989; J.D., summa cum laude, 1992). Order of the Coif; Order of Barristers. *Indiana State Bar Association (Chair, Young Lawyers Section, 1999-2000).* (Also Member, Indianapolis Office). ***PRACTICE AREAS:*** Real Estate; Zoning; Planning and Land Use. ***Email:*** sdhardin@binghammchale.com

Bingham McHale LLP attorneys are members of the American, Indiana State, Indianapolis, Hamilton County, Federal and Seventh Circuit Bar Associations.

REPRESENTATIVE CLIENTS: Adams & Marshall; Allisonville Nursery, Inc.; Asset Midwest, LLC; Beazer Homes, Inc.; The Bradford Group, Inc.; Bremner & Wiley, Inc.; Bressler Outdoor, LLC; CP Morgan, Inc.; Centex Homes; Chicago Title Insurance Co.; City of Carmel; City of Noblesville; CR White Development, LLC; Crossmann Communities, Inc.; Davis Homes, Inc.; Duke Realty Corp.; Equicor Development Corporation; Gradison Building Corporation; Hamilton Southeastern Utilities, Inc.; Heritage Environmental Services, LLC; Intracoastal, Inc.; JC Partners, LLC; LandAmerica Title Insurance Co.; Lawyers Title Insurance Co.; Mid-States Engineering; Meyer Najem Corporation; Old Republic Title Insurance; Paul I. Cripe, Inc.; Portrait Homes; Republic Development Corporation; Sandcreek Partners, LLC; SCM Development, Inc.; Shamrock Builders, Inc.; Trinity Homes, LLC; Tri-North Development, LLC.

(For complete biographical data on all personnel, see Professional Biographies at Indianapolis, Indiana)

CAMPBELL KYLE PROFFITT LLP

Established in 1915
198 SOUTH NINTH STREET
P.O. BOX 2020
NOBLESVILLE, INDIANA 46061-2020
Telephone: 317-773-2090
Fax: 317-776-5051
Email: ckplaw@ckplaw.com
URL: http://www.ckplaw.com

Carmel Office: 11595 N. Meridian, Suite 701. Telephone: 317-846-6514. Fax: 317-843-8097.

Civil Practice. State and Federal Courts and Administrative Agencies, Domestic Relations, Family Law, Divorce, Adoptions, Personal Injury, Corporation, Business Law, Utility Law, Insurance, Wills and Probate, Trusts and Estates, Estate Planning and Elder Law, Real Estate, Zoning, Employment Law, Criminal Law. Contracts, Taxation, Real Estate, Commercial Litigation.

FIRM PROFILE: Campbell Kyle Proffitt LLP has provided legal services to clients in central Indiana since 1915. The firm serves individuals, partnerships, corporations and various municipal and other public entities. While we are a general practice firm, the members of the firm concentrate their respective work within a few areas of the law. For complex matters it is not unusual for two or more members of the firm to become involved. Our touchstone is prompt personal attention to our clients' needs.

MEMBERS OF FIRM

FRANK S. CAMPBELL (1880-1964)
FRANK W. CAMPBELL (1916-1991)
ROBERT F. CAMPBELL (1946-2004)

JOHN M. KYLE, born Gary, Indiana, 1927; admitted to bar, 1954, Indiana. *Education:* Indiana University (B.S., 1951; J.D., 1954). Phi Delta Phi. City Attorney, Noblesville, 1972-1976. Member, Board of Directors, Indiana Bar Foundation. *Member:* Hamilton County and Indiana State (Member, Board of Managers, 1986-1988) Bar Associations. ***PRACTICE AREAS:*** Corporate Law; Probate; Estate Planning; Real Estate; Taxation. ***Email:*** jkyle@ckplaw.com

JOHN D. PROFFITT, born Lebanon, Indiana, 1932; admitted to bar, 1959, Missouri; 1963, Indiana. *Education:* Wabash College (A.B., 1954); University of Chicago (J.D., 1959). *Member:* Hamilton County, Indiana State (Treasurer, 1991-1992; Vice President, 1993-1994; President, 1995-1996) and American Bar Associations; Fellow: American College of Trial Lawyers; American Academy of Matrimonial Lawyers; American Bar Foundation; Indiana State Bar Foundation. (Resident, Carmel Office). ***PRACTICE AREAS:*** Civil Practice; Personal Injury; Business Litigation; Family Law; Domestic Relations. ***Email:*** jproffitt@ckplaw.com

JEFFREY S. NICKLOY, born Toledo, Ohio, 1948; admitted to bar, 1973, Indiana. *Education:* Wabash College (B.A., 1970); Duke University (J.D., 1973). Phi Beta Kappa. Author: "Non-Competition Clauses in Employment Contracts," Res Gestae, August 1983; "Handling Employee Records - A Brief Guide," Res Gestae, February 1996. *Member:* Hamilton County and Indiana State (Member: Legal Ethics Committee, Chair, 1999-2001; Labor and Employment Law Section, Chair, 2001-2002, Business Law Section) Bar Associations. ***PRACTICE AREAS:*** Corporate Law; Contracts; Employment Law; Commercial Litigation. ***Email:*** jnickloy@ckplaw.com

DEBORAH L. FARMER, born Indianapolis, Indiana, 1954; admitted to bar, 1983, Indiana. *Education:* Butler University (B.S., cum laude, 1976); Indiana University School of Law (J.D., magna cum laude, 1983). Certified Family Law Specialist. Author, "Survey of Recent Developments in Family Law," Indiana Law Review, Vol. 29, Nov. 3, 1991. *Member:* Hamilton County and Indiana State (Member, Board of Managers, 1990-1992; Counsel to the President, 1993; Chair, Family and Juvenile Law Section, 1995-1997) Bar Associations. Fellow, Indiana Bar Foundation (President, 1998-2000). American Academy of Matrimonial Lawyers. (Resident, Carmel Office). ***PRACTICE AREAS:*** Domestic Relations; Mediation. ***Email:*** dfarmer@ckplaw.com

WILLIAM E. WENDLING, JR., born Kendallville, Indiana, 1950; admitted to bar, 1983, Indiana. *Education:* Texas A. & I. University (B.A., 1973); Indiana University School of Law (J.D., 1983). Law Clerk to the Hon. James E. Noland, Chief Judge, U.S. District Court, Southern District of Indiana, 1983-1984. Member, Indiana Education Employment Relations Board, 1989—. Treasurer, Indiana Bar Foundation. *Member:* Hamilton County and Indiana State Bar Associations. (Resident, Carmel Office). ***PRACTICE AREAS:*** Civil Practice; Real Estate; Zoning Law; Family Law; Domestic Relations; Personal Injury; Criminal Law; Business Litigation. ***Email:*** wwendling@ckplaw.com

ANNE HENSLEY POINDEXTER, born Salina, Kansas, 1962; admitted to bar, 1988, Indiana. *Education:* Ball State University (B.S., 1984); Indiana University School of Law (J.D., cum laude, 1988). Registered Mediator. Tax Analyst, Supervisor, 1985-1987 and Administrator, 1987-1988, Inheritance Tax Division, Indiana Department of Revenue. *Member:* Hamilton County (President, 1996-1998), Indiana State and American Bar Associations. (Resident, Carmel Office). ***PRACTICE AREAS:*** Civil Practice; Probate; Estate Planning; Domestic Relations; Mediation; Public Utility Law. ***Email:*** apoindexter@ckplaw.com

ANDREW M. BARKER, born Indianapolis, Indiana, 1960; admitted to bar, 1989, Indiana. *Education:* Indiana University (B.S., 1983); Indiana University School of Law (J.D., 1989). Phi Delta Phi. *Member:* Hamilton County and Indiana State Bar Associations;. ***PRACTICE AREAS:*** Civil Practice; Family Law; Personal Injury; Criminal Law. ***Email:*** abarker@ckplaw.com

MICHAEL A. CASATI, born Milwaukee, Wisconsin, 1959; admitted to bar, 1992, Indiana. *Education:* Indiana University (B.A., with distinction, 1982; J.D., cum laude, 1992). Indiana University Police Academy, 1981. Indiana State Police Academy, 1983. Certified

(This Listing Continued)

Family Law Specialist. *Member:* Hamilton County and Indiana State Bar Associations. Fellow, Indiana Bar Foundation. (Resident, Carmel Office). ***PRACTICE AREAS:*** Family Law; Civil Litigation; Criminal Litigation. ***Email:*** mcasati@ckplaw.com

RODNEY T. SARKOVICS, born Buffalo, New York, 1970; admitted to bar, 1996, Indiana. *Education:* Canisius College (B.S., 1992); Ohio Northern University (J.D. with distinction, 1996). Phi Kappa Phi; American Inns of Court. Editor, Ohio Northern Law Review. Author: "How Loud Is Too Loud," Indiana State Bar Association Young Lawyer's Section Network, Fall, 1999; Case Summaries: Family Matters, 1999—. *Member:* Hamilton County, Indiana State and American Bar Associations. (Resident, Carmel Office). ***PRACTICE AREAS:*** Family Law; Criminal Law; Civil Litigation. ***Email:*** rsarkovics@ckplaw.com

JOHN S. TERRY, born Indianapolis, Indiana, 1972; admitted to bar, 1998, Indiana. *Education:* Wabash College (A.B., 1995); Indiana University (J.D., 1998). *Member:* Hamilton County (Treasurer, 2004-2005) and Indiana State Bar Associations. ***PRACTICE AREAS:*** Wills; Probate; Trusts and Estates; Corporate Law; Business Law; Real Estate; Personal Injury. ***Email:*** jterry@ckplaw.com

ASSOCIATES

SCOTT P. WYATT, born Dubuque, Iowa, 1970; admitted to bar, 1998, Indiana. *Education:* Northeast Missouri State University (B.A., 1993); Indiana University (J.D., 1998). Phi Delta Phi. Past Deputy Prosecutor, Marion County Prosecutors Office, 1998-2001. *Member:* Indiana State and American Bar Associations. (Resident, Carmel Office). ***PRACTICE AREAS:*** Criminal Law; Family Law; Civil Litigation; Utilities. ***Email:*** swyatt@ckplaw.com

AMY E. HIGDON, born Marion, Indiana, 1975; admitted to bar, 1999, Indiana. *Education:* Ball State University (B.S., summa cum laude, 1996); Indiana University School of Law-Indianapolis (J.D., cum laude, 1999). Phi Delta Phi. Law Clerk to the Hon. Margret G. Robb, Indiana Court of Appeals, 1999-2001. *Member:* Hamilton County, Indiana State (Member, Family Law Section) and American Bar Associations. (Resident, Carmel Office). ***PRACTICE AREAS:*** Family Law. ***Email:*** ahigdon@ckplaw.com

STEPHENIE K. GOOKINS, born Greensburg, Indiana, 1972; admitted to bar, 1998, Indiana and U.S. District Court, Southern District of Indiana. *Education:* Indiana University (B.A., Public Affairs, 1994; J.D., 1998). Member, Hamilton Community Corrections Advisory Board, 2002—. *Member:* Hamilton County Bar Association. ***PRACTICE AREAS:*** Criminal Defense; Civil Litigation; Contracts; Family Law; Disability Benefits. ***Email:*** sgookins@ckplaw.com

N. SCOTT SMITH, born Benton Harbor, Michigan, 1976; admitted to bar, 2005, Indiana. *Education:* Purdue University (B.A., 1999); Indiana University School of Law (J.D, 2004). Runner Up, Moot Court Barrister Championship. Recipient, John J. Dillon Scholarship. Realtor, 2001. (Resident, Carmel Office). ***LANGUAGES:*** Spanish. ***Email:*** ssmith@ckplaw.com

ANNE E. BRANT, born Indianapolis, Indiana, 1978; admitted to bar, 2004, Indiana. *Education:* Indiana University (B.S., 2001; J.D., 2004). ***Email:*** abrant@ckplaw.com

GENERAL COUNSEL FOR: Clay Township Regional Waste District; Lake Santee Regional Waste District; Industrial Dielectrics, Inc.; Beck's Superior Hybrids, Inc.; Underwriters Surety, Inc.; Carmel Clay Public Library; Advanced Marketing Technologies, Inc.; Lake Santee Property Owners Association.
REPRESENTATIVE CLIENTS: PSI Energy, Inc.; Mobil Oil Corp.; Minnesota Mining & Manufacturing Co.; Conseco Insurance Companies; Inland Paperboard and Packaging, Inc.; Mohawk Industries, Inc.; Metro Plastics Technology, Inc.

CHURCH, CHURCH, HITTLE & ANTRIM

Established in 1880
938 CONNER STREET
P.O. BOX 10
NOBLESVILLE, INDIANA 46061-0010
Telephone: 317-773-2190
Telecopier: 317-773-5320
Email: dchurch@cchalaw.com
URL: http://www.cchalaw.com

General Civil Trial Practice in all State and Federal Courts. Appellate and Federal Practice, Personal Injury, Automobile Accidents, Wrongful Death, Family Law, Adoption Law, Child Custody, Child Support, Divorce, Visitation Rights, Municipal and Governmental Regulations, Real Estate, Zoning Law, Land Use, Commercial Leasing, Wills, Probate, Trusts and Estates, Estate Planning, Asset Protection, Guardianship Law, Estate Administration and Litigation, Tax Planning, Tax Controversies, Business Law, Contracts, Litigation, Business Enterprises, Business Transactions, Corporate Formation, Corporate Litigation, School Law, Commercial Litigation, Professional License Defense, Medical Malpractice, Bankruptcy, Criminal Law, Driving While Intoxicated, Drug Crimes, Felonies, Misdemeanors, Mediation.

FIRM PROFILE: Church, Church, Hittle & Antrim was founded in 1880 by Joseph A. Roberts. The office of the law firm has been in the same location for the past 120 years. The firm has a statewide practice and provides general and specialized legal services. Members participate as faculty and students of professional development and bar related programs.

MEMBERS OF FIRM

DOUGLAS D. CHURCH, born Indianapolis, Indiana, January 22, 1944; admitted to bar, 1970, Indiana. *Education:* Indiana University (A.B., 1966; J.D., 1970). Phi Delta Phi (Magister, 1968-1969). Law Clerk, Appellate Court of Indiana, 1968-1970. *Member:* Hamilton County (President, 1980-1981), Indiana State (Chairman: Young Lawyers Section, 1980-1981; Local Government Law Section, 1981-1982) and American Bar Associations; Indiana Trial Lawyers Association; American Board of Trial Advocates (Advocate); Indiana Municipal Lawyers Association (President, 1999-2000). ***PRACTICE AREAS:*** General Negligence Law; Administrative Law; Domestic Relations Law; General Civil Trial Practice in all State and Federal Courts; Commercial Litigation; Personal Injury. ***Email:*** dchurch@cchalaw.com

(This Listing Continued)

JACK G. HITTLE, born Indianapolis, Indiana, August 27, 1948; admitted to bar, 1973, Indiana. *Education:* Butler University (B.A., 1970); Indiana University (J.D., 1973). Associate Editor, Indiana Law Review, 1972-1973. *Member:* Hamilton County (President, 1993), Indianapolis and Indiana State (Chairman, Probate, Trust and Real Property Section, 1988-1989; Member, Board of Governors, 1995-1996) Bar Associations; Indiana Bar Foundation (Board Member, 2001—). Fellow, American College of Trust and Estate Counsel. ***PRACTICE AREAS:*** Probate Law; Real Estate Law; Commercial Transactions; School Law; General Civil Trial Practice in all State and Federal Courts.

J. MICHAEL ANTRIM, born Ann Arbor, Michigan, August 28, 1950; admitted to bar, 1975, Indiana. *Education:* Indiana University (B.S., cum laude, 1972; J.D., cum laude, 1975). Associate Editor, Indiana Law Review, 1974-1975. *Member:* Hamilton County (President, 1987-1988) and Indiana State Bar Associations; Indiana Trial Lawyers Association (Member, Board of Directors); The Association of Trial Lawyers of America. ***PRACTICE AREAS:*** Civil Practice; Personal Injury Law; General Civil Trial Practice in all State and Federal Courts. ***Email:*** antrim@cchalaw.com

MARTIN E. RISACHER, born Washington, Indiana, April 23, 1947; admitted to bar, 1975, Indiana. *Education:* Indiana State University (B.A., magna cum laude, 1972); Indiana University (J.D., 1975). Phi Delta Phi. Author: "Professional Responsibility and Liability," 22 Indiana Law Review 1. Faculty Member, National Judicial College, Reno Nevada, 1980-1986. Judge of Dubois-Martin County Court, 1976-1980. Judge of Dubois Superior Court, 1980-1986. Staff Counsel, Indiana Supreme Court Disciplinary Committee, 1987-1988. Registered Civil Mediator. *Member:* Hamilton County and Indiana State Bar Associations; Indiana Trial Lawyers Association; The Association of Trial Lawyers of America. [With U.S. Army, 1966-1969, 1st Lt.]. ***PRACTICE AREAS:*** Civil Practice; Trials; Personal Injury Law; Products Liability Law; Professional License Defense; General Civil Trial Practice in all State and Federal Courts; Commercial Litigation. ***Email:*** risacher@cchalaw.com

DAVID R. DAY, born Mount Summit, Indiana, September 14, 1952; admitted to bar, 1977, Indiana. *Education:* Ball State University (B.S., summa cum laude, 1973); Harvard University (J.D., cum laude, 1977). Director, National School Board Association, Council of School Attorneys, 1990-1994. *Member:* Indianapolis and Indiana State Bar Associations. ***PRACTICE AREAS:*** Education Law; Estate Planning; Probate; Business Transactions; Real Estate Transactions. ***Email:*** day@cchalaw.com

BRUCE M. BITTNER, born Champaign, Illinois, December 18, 1954; admitted to bar, 1981, Illinois and Arizona; 1984, Texas; 1989, Indiana. *Education:* Indiana University-Bloomington (B.S., Accounting, 1976); Arizona State University (J.D., 1981). Certified Public Accountant. *Member:* Indiana Society of Certified Public Accountants. *Member:* Hamilton County and Indiana Bar Associations. Fellow, Indiana Bar Foundation. ***PRACTICE AREAS:*** Estate Planning; Probate; Tax Planning and Tax Controversies; Elder Law; Zoning Law; Business, Commercial and Real Estate Transactions. ***Email:*** bittner@cchalaw.com

LESLIE CRAIG HENDERZAHS, born Louisville, Kentucky, November 15, 1964; admitted to bar, 1990, Indiana and U.S. District Court, Northern and Southern Districts of Indiana; 1992, U.S. Court of Appeals, Seventh Circuit. *Education:* Indiana University (B.A., 1986; J.D., 1990). Phi Delta Phi (Exchequer). Law Clerk, U.S. District Court for Southern District of Indiana, 1990-1992. Registered Civil Mediator. *Member:* Indianapolis, Hamilton County, Indiana State (Member, House of Delegates, 1998—) and American Bar Associations. Fellow, Indiana Bar Foundation; Indiana Trial Lawyers Association; Association of Trial Lawyers of America. ***PRACTICE AREAS:*** Personal Injury; Zoning Law; Domestic Relations Law; General Civil Trial Practice in all State and Federal Courts. ***Email:*** henderzahs@cchalaw.com

JORDAN D. CHURCH, born Indianapolis, Indiana, July 25, 1970; admitted to bar, 1997, Indiana and U.S. District Court, Northern and Southern Districts of Indiana. *Education:* Wabash College (A.B., 1992); Indiana University (J.D., 1997). *Member:* Hamilton County, Indiana State and American Bar Associations. ***Email:*** jchurch@cchalaw.com

AMBER D. SULLIVAN, born Greencastle, Indiana, January 11, 1974; admitted to bar, 2000, Indiana and U.S. District Court, Northern and Southern Districts of Indiana. *Education:* DePauw University (B.A., cum laude, 1996); Indiana University School of Law (J.D., 2000). Phi Delta Phi, Exchequer, 1999-2000. *Member:* Hamilton County, Indiana State (Member: Probate Trust and Real Property Sections; Legal Ethics Committee, 2003—) and American Bar Associations; National Academy of Elder Law Attorneys. ***PRACTICE AREAS:*** Estate Planning; Probate; Estate Litigation; Elder Law; Commercial Transactions; Real Estate Transactions; School Law. ***Email:*** sullivan@cchalaw.com

ERIC M. DOUTHIT, born Indianapolis, Indiana, July 11, 1972; admitted to bar, 1997, Indiana. *Education:* Vanderbilt University (B.S., 1994); Indiana University School of Law (J.D., 1997). ***PRACTICE AREAS:*** Business Law; Trusts and Estates; Real Estate; General Practice. ***Email:*** edouthit@cchalaw.com

ASSOCIATES

SAMUEL R. ROBINSON, born Muncie, Indiana, September 1, 1973; admitted to bar, 2000, Indiana. *Education:* Asbury College (B.A., 1996); Indiana University-Indianapolis (J.D., 2000). *Member:* Hamilton County and Indiana State Bar Associations. ***PRACTICE AREAS:*** Criminal Law (30%); Family Law (30%); Personal Injury (30%). ***Email:*** srobinson@cchalaw.com

ANN M. O'HARA, born Indianapolis, Indiana, August 21, 1963; admitted to bar, 1990, Indiana. *Education:* St. Joseph's College (B.S., summa cum laude, 1985); Trinity College, Dublin University (1986-1987) Attended on Ambassadorial Scholarship granted by International Rotary Foundation; Indiana University (J.D., 1990). Lecturer for the Federal Estate and Gift Tax Section for the Indianapolis Bar Association Bar Review Course, 2000—. Member, Board of Trustees St. Joseph's College, 1992—. Director/Counsel, Corporations Division of the Indiana Secretary of State, 1990. *Member:* Indianapolis and Indiana State Bar Associations. ***PRACTICE AREAS:*** Probate and Estate Planning (60%); Business Transactions (20%); Municipal Law (10%); Zoning Law (10%). ***Email:*** aohara@cchalaw.com

(This Listing Continued)

CHURCH, CHURCH, HITTLE & ANTRIM, Noblesville—Continued

OF COUNSEL

Manson E. Church

COUNSEL FOR: Noblesville Schools; MSD Lawrence Township Schools; MSD Warren Towhship Schools; Carmel Clay Schools; Westfield-Washington Schools; Community Bank; Metrobank; Towns of Westfield, Fishers and Pendleton; Reynolds Farm Equipment; Weihe Engineering; Historic Railroad Multijurisdictional Port Authority; Metropolitan School Districts of Lawrence and Warren Townships; Anderson Community School Corp.; Carmel Clay Schools.

HOLT, FLECK & ROMINE

Established in 1975

83 SOUTH 9TH STREET

NOBLESVILLE, INDIANA 46060

Telephone: 317-773-5997
Facsimile: 317-773-5960
Email: hfr@hfrlaw.com
URL: http://www.hfrlaw.com

Civil and Criminal Trials in all Courts, Criminal Law, Drug Crimes, Driving While Intoxicated, Parole and Probation, Traffic Violations, Wills and Probate, Trusts and Estate, Guardianships, Asset Protection, Estate Planning, Business, Contracts, Business Planning, Lawsuits, Business Enterprises, Closely Held Business, Corporate, Partnerships, Limited Liability Companies, Small Business, Real Estate, Buying and Selling Real Estate, Commercial Leasing, Family Law, Adoptions, Child Custody, Child Support, Divorce, Visitations Rights, Domestic Violence, Domestic Relation, Personal Injury, Automobile Accidents, Slip and Fall, Wrongful Death, Medical Malpractice, Unsafe Products, Bankruptcy, Elder Law.

STEVEN A. HOLT, born Indianapolis, Indiana, July 10, 1948; admitted to bar, 1973, Indiana and U.S. District Court, Southern District of Indiana. *Education:* DePauw University (B.A., Political Science, 1970); Indiana University (J.D., 1973). Certified Civil Mediator, 1996. President, Crossroads of America Council, Boys Scouts of America, 1996-1998. Member: Hamilton County Commissioners, 1989—; Drainage Board, 1989—; Plan Commission, 1991—; Hamilton County Alliance Executive Board, 1994—, Legacy Fund Board of Governors, Hamilton County. *Member:* Hamilton County (President, 1984-1986) and Indiana State Bar Associations; Indiana Trial Lawyers Association; The Association of Trial Lawyers of America; National Association of Criminal Defense Lawyers. ***PRACTICE AREAS:*** Criminal; Divorce; Personal Injury; Civil Litigation; Mediation. ***Email:*** sholt@hfrlaw.com

K. SEAN FLECK, born Noblesville, Indiana, July 13, 1956; admitted to bar, 1981, Indiana and U.S. District Court, Southern District of Indiana. *Education:* Purdue University (B.S., 1977); Indiana University (J.D., 1980). Chairman, Hamilton County Alcoholic Beverage Commission, 1993—. Board of Directors, 2001— and President, 2005—, Noblesville Main Street, Inc. *Member:* Hamilton County (President, 1998-2000) and Indiana State Bar Associations. ***PRACTICE AREAS:*** Probate Administration; Estate Planning; Wills; Trust Law; Business Formation; Bankruptcy; Real Estate; Zoning Law. ***Email:*** ksfleck@hfrlaw.com

OF COUNSEL

CAROL JEAN ROMINE, born Chicago, Illinois, January 10, 1942; admitted to bar, 1996, Indiana and U.S. District Court, Southern District of Indiana. *Education:* Indiana University (B.A., Science, with distinction, 1977); Indiana University, Indianapolis (J.D., 1996). Registered Family Law Mediator. *Member:* Hamilton County, Indianapolis and Indiana State Bar Associations. ***PRACTICE AREAS:*** Divorce; Post Divorce Modification; Child Custody; Visitation Rights; Child Support. ***Email:*** cjromine@hfrlaw.com

ASSOCIATE

CHRISTL P. GLIER, born South Korea, January 9, 1979; admitted to bar, 2004, Indiana. *Education:* Indiana University, Bloomington (B.A., 2001); Indiana University School of Law - Indianapolis (J.D., 2004). *Member:* Indiana State and American Bar Associations. ***PRACTICE AREAS:*** Personal Injury; Civil Litigation; Workers Compensation; Contract Law; Social Security Disability. ***Email:*** cglier@hfrlaw.com

THE MARCUS LAW FIRM

NOBLESVILLE, INDIANA

(See Fishers)

Healthcare Law, Elder Law, Personal Injury, Automobile Accidents, Slip and Fall, Wrongful Death, Legal Malpractice, Consumer Law, Medical Malpractice, Unsafe Products, Civil Rights, Employment law, Wrongful Termination, Discrimination, Harassment, Trial Practice, Family Law, Adoptions, Child Custody, Child Support, Divorce, Visitation Rights, Real Estate, Wills and Probate, Trusts and Estates, Estate Planning, Guardianships, Asset Protection, Business Law, Business Planning, Contracts, Lawsuits, Business Enterprises, Corporate, Limited Liability Companies, Partnerships, Buying and Selling a Business.

JANICE E. SMITH
ATTORNEY AT LAW

NOBLESVILLE, INDIANA

(See Indianapolis)

Criminal, Family and Education Law.

McCONNELL AND FINNERTY

Established in 1952

38 NORTH 5TH STREET
P.O. BOX 90

NORTH VERNON, INDIANA 47265

Telephone: 812-346-5201
FAX: 812-346-8470
Email: lawyers@mcconnelllaw.net

Probate and Estate Planning, Personal Injury and Commercial Law, Family/Domestic Relations. Civil Litigation. Trials, Appeals and Banking.

MEMBERS OF FIRM

IRA B. HAMILTON (1899-1982)

HAROLD H. McCONNELL, born Seymour, Indiana, 1918; admitted to bar, 1948, Indiana. *Education:* Bard College; Indiana University (LL.B., 1948). Phi Delta Phi. Recipient, Indiana Bar Foundation 50 Year Award, 1999. *Member:* Jennings County, Indiana State (Member, Board of Managers, 1960-1962) and American Bar Associations; Indiana Trial Lawyers Association; The Association of Trial Lawyers of America. ***LANGUAGES:*** French. ***PRACTICE AREAS:*** Real Estate Law; Probate Law; Banking Law.

CORINNE R. FINNERTY, born Seymour, Indiana, 1956; admitted to bar, 1981, Indiana, U.S. District Court, Northern and Southern Districts of Indiana, U.S. Court of Appeals, Seventh Circuit and U.S. Supreme Court. *Education:* Indiana University (A.B., magna cum laude, 1978; J.D., magna cum laude, 1981). Phi Beta Kappa. Phi Alpha Delta. Member, Order of the Coif. President, Mortar Board, 1977-1978. Recipient: Elvis J. Starr Outstanding Senior Award at Indiana University, 1978; Amjur Award for Outstanding Achievement in Criminal Law, 1979. North Vernon City Attorney. Chief Deputy Prosecuting Attorney, 1987, 1991-1992; Deputy Prosecuting Attorney, 1993-1995. Member, Indiana Supreme Court Disciplinary Commission, 2003—. *Member:* Jennings County, Indiana State and American Bar Associations; Indiana Trial Lawyers Association; Association of Trial Lawyers of America. ***PRACTICE AREAS:*** Real Estate Law; Probate Law; Civil Litigation; Corporate Litigation; Banking Law; Employment Law.

ASSOCIATE

CHARLES R. WAGGONER, born Franklin, Indiana, 1950; admitted to bar, 1989, Indiana and U.S. District Court, Northern and Southern Districts of Indiana; 1990, U.S. Court of Appeals, Seventh Circuit; 2004, U.S. Supreme Court. *Education:* Purdue University (B.S., 1984); Indiana University (J.D., 1989). Phi Alpha Delta. Recipient, Am Jur Award for Outstanding Achievement in Trial Practice, 1988. Lt. (Ret.), Indiana State Police, 1970-1991. Proscecuting Attorney, 54th Indiana Judicial Circuit, 1999-2002. *Member:* Jennings County and Indiana State Bar Associations; Association of Indiana Prosecuting Attorneys (Board Member, 2000-2002; Treasurer, 2002). [337th General Hospital, U.S. Army Reserve, 1969-1975]. ***PRACTICE AREAS:*** Asset Protection; Criminal Law; Family Law; Guardianship and Conservatorship; Law Enforcement; Real Estate; Trusts and Estates; White Collar Crime; Wills. ***Email:*** crw@mcconnelllaw.net

REPRESENTATIVE CLIENTS: Heritage Community Bank; First Financial Bank; Decatur Mold, Tool, and Engineering, Inc.; Home Federal Savings Bank; Rose Acre Farms, Inc.; CPX, Inc.; North Vernon Industry Corp.; NAC, Inc.; Decatur Plastics, Inc.; National Loan Investors, L.P.

BLACKBURN & GREEN

PERU, INDIANA

(See Fort Wayne)

Litigation, Personal Injury Law.

JOHN ANDREW GOODRIDGE LAW OFFICE

PETERSBURG, INDIANA

(See Evansville)

Bankruptcy and Federal Criminal Law.

RICHARD BALLARD
ATTORNEY AT LAW

PLYMOUTH, INDIANA

(See Knox)

Criminal Law, DUI, Drug Crimes, Juvenile Crimes, Traffic Violations, White Collar Crimes, Family Law, Adoptions, Child Custody, Child Support, Divorce, Visitation Rights, Personal Injury, Medical Malpractice, Auto Accidents, Wrongful Death, Slip and Fall, Real Estate.

BLACKBURN & GREEN

PLYMOUTH, INDIANA

(See Fort Wayne)

Litigation, Personal Injury Law.

DORAN • BLACKMOND LLP

PLYMOUTH, INDIANA

(See South Bend)

Civil Trial and Appellate Practice in Federal and State Courts, Insurance Defense and Coverage Questions, Special Investigation, Personal Injury, Product Liability, Architect and Engineer Liability, Legal Malpractice, Worker's Compensation, Construction Law, Commercial, Creditor's Rights, Bankruptcy and Reorganization, Mediation and Arbitration.

KIZER & NEU, LLP

Established in 1951

319 WEST JEFFERSON STREET
P.O. BOX 158
PLYMOUTH, INDIANA 46563
Telephone: 574-936-2169
FAX: 574-936-2642
URL: http://www.kizerneu.com

Bremen, Indiana Office: 1406 West Plymouth Street, P.O. Box 158. Telephone: 574-546-2626. FAX: 574-546-2608.

General Practice. Litigation and Trials in all Courts. Corporate, Labor and Employment, Wills and Probate, Trusts and Estates, Estate Planning, Administrative Law, Bankruptcy Law, Creditor's Rights.

MEMBERS OF FIRM

MARSHALL F. KIZER (1907-1988)

JAMES H. NEU (1917-1991)

RICHARD F. JOYCE (Retired)

HAROLD L. WYLAND, born LaPorte, Indiana, April 16, 1946; admitted to bar, 1973, Indiana. *Education:* Indiana University (B.S., Accounting, 1968; J.D., 1972). Attorney, Plymouth Community School Corporation, 1976-1994, Culver Community Schools Corporation, 1987—. *Member:* Marshall County, Indiana State and American Bar Associations. ***PRACTICE AREAS:*** Business Transactions; Corporation Law; Real Estate Law; Probate Law; Estate Planning; School Law. ***Email:*** wyland@kizerneu.com

JERE L. HUMPHREY, born Louisville, Kentucky, September 10, 1944; admitted to bar, 1972, Indiana. *Education:* Ball State University (B.S., 1966); Indiana University (J.D., 1972). *Member:* Marshall County, Indiana State and American Bar Associations. [Capt., USAF, 1966-1970]. ***REPORTED CASES:*** Wilson Fertilizer & Grain, Inc. v. ADM Mill Co., 654 N.E.2d 848 (Ind.App. 1995); Carpenter v. Farm Credit Services of Mid-America, ACA, 654 N.E.2d 1125 (Ind. 1995); Estate of Decker v. Farm Credit Services of Mid-America, ACA, 653 N.E.2d 534 (Ind.App. 1995);Farm Credit Services of Mid-America, ACA v. Estate of Decker, 624 N.E.2d 491 (Ind.App. 5 Dist. 1993); Fager v. Hundt, 610 N.E.2d 246 (Ind. 1993); Farmers State Bank of Wyatt v. Clark Equipment Co., 582 N.E.2d 452 (Ind.App. 3 Dist. 1991); Stevens v. State, 580 N.E.2d 274 (Ind.App. 3 Dist. 1991); LaPorte Production Credit Ass'n. v. Kalwitz, 567 N.E.2d 1202 (Ind.App. 3 Dist. 1991); Faulkner v. State, 556 N.E.2d 1 (Ind.App. 3 Dist. 1989); Deluxe Sheet Metal, Inc. v. Plymouth Plastics, Inc., 555 N.E.2d 1296 (Ind.App. 3 Dist. 1990); Crider v. State, 531 N.E.2d 1151 (Ind. 1988); Reed v. State, 491 N.E.2d 182 (Ind. 1986); Martin v. State, 488 N.E.2d 1160 (Ind.App. 3 Dist. 1986); Davis v. State, 477 N.E.2d 889 (Ind. 1985); Visitation of Menzie, In re, 469 N.E.2d 1225 (Ind.App. 3 Dist. 1984); Teague v. Boone, 442 N.E.2d 1119 (Ind.App. 3 Dist. 1982); Howard v. State, 431 N.E.2d 868 (Ind.App. 3 Dist. 1982);Williams v. State, 430 N.E.2d 759 (Ind. 1982); Williams v. State, 426 N.E.2d 662 (Ind. 1981); Dolph v. Mangus, 440 N.E.2d 189 (Ind.App. 3 Dist. 1980); Knaub v. State, 394 N.E.2d 201 (Ind.App 3 Dist. 1979); Carter v. State, 392 N.E.2d 448 (Ind. 1979); Swan v. State, 375 N.E.2d 198 (Ind. 1978); Patten v. Smith, 360 N.E2d 233 (Ind.App. 3 Dist. 1977); Western State Bank of South Bend v. First Union Bank & Trust Co. of Winamac, 360 N.E.2d 254 (Ind.App. 3 Dist. 1977); Metz v. Transit Mix, 828 F.2d 1202 (7th Cir 1987); Knight v. United Farm Bureau Mutual Insurance Company, 950 F.2d 377 (7th Cir. 1991); Berger Farms, Inc. v. Estes, et al., N.E.2d (Ind.App. 1996). ***PRACTICE AREAS:*** Litigation; Appeals; Personal Injury; Domestic Relations; Criminal Law. ***Email:*** jere@kizerneu.com

MARK E. WAGNER, born Bremen, Indiana, February 20, 1950; admitted to bar, 1975, Indiana. *Education:* University of St. Francis (B.A., 1972); Indiana University (J.D., 1975). Attorney, Bremen Public Schools, 1979—. Town Attorney, Bourbon, Indiana, 1984—. Chapter 12 Trustee, U.S. Bankruptcy Court, South Bend, Indiana. *Member:* Marshall County and Indiana State Bar Associations. (Resident at Bremen). ***PRACTICE AREAS:*** Bankruptcy; Creditor's Rights; Estates & Estate Planning; Real Estate; Collections; Agricultural Law. ***Email:*** mark_wagner@earthlink.net

RONALD D. GIFFORD, born Battle Creek, Michigan, January 6, 1951; admitted to bar, 1976, Georgia and Indiana. *Education:* Albion College (B.A., 1973); Emory University (J.D., 1976). Phi Delta Phi. City Attorney, Plymouth, Indiana, 1980-1987. Town Attorney: Argos, Indiana, 1977-1991, 2000—; Walkerton, Indiana, 1980-1983; Culver, Indiana, 1996—; Lake of The Woods Regional Sewer District, 1988—. *Member:* Marshall County, Indiana State and American Bar Associations; State Bar of Georgia. ***PRACTICE AREAS:*** Business Transactions; Corporation Law; Probate Law; Estate Planning; Real Estate Law; Municipal Law. ***Email:*** rgifford@kizerneu.com

JAMES N. CLEVENGER, born South Bend, Indiana, June 3, 1952; admitted to bar, 1978, Indiana. *Education:* Hanover College (B.A., 1974); Valparaiso University and Indiana University (J.D., 1978). Marshall County Attorney, 1997—. Town Attorney, Culver, Indiana, 1984-1991 and Walkerton, Indiana, 1984-1987. Attorney, Argos Community School Corporation, 1999—. *Member:* Marshall County, Indiana State and American Bar Associations. ***PRACTICE AREAS:*** Litigation; Personal Injury; Domestic Relations; Criminal Law; Juvenile Law; Municipal Law. ***Email:*** jclevenger@kizerneu.com

ANTHONY J. WAGNER, born Bremen, Indiana, February 9, 1979; admitted to bar, 2004, Indiana. *Education:* University of Notre Dame (B.A., 2001; J.D., 2004). ***Email:*** awagner@kizerneu.com

COUNSEL FOR: 1st Source Bank; Farm Credit Services; Pi-Rod, Inc., Plymouth, Indiana; Hoosier Racing Tire Corp., Lakeville, Indiana; American Containers, Inc.; Bomarko, Inc.; U.S. Granules Corp., all of Plymouth, Indiana; Bremen Castings, Inc.; Bornemann Products, Inc., all of Bremen, Indiana; Niff-Corr, Inc., Tippecanoe, Indiana; Town Attorney, Bourbon, Indiana; Bremen Community Hospital; Bremen Development, Inc.; Bremen Public Schools; Culver Community Schools Corp.; Argos Community School Corporation; Town Attorney, Culver, Indiana; Town Attorney, Argos, Indiana; County Attorney, Marshall County, Indiana.
REFERENCE: 1st Source Bank

MATTHEW D. LATULIP
ATTORNEY AT LAW

PLYMOUTH, INDIANA

(See Schererville)

Personal Injury, Medical Malpractice, Auto Accidents, Slip and Fall, Wrongful Death, Criminal, DUI, Traffic Violations, Juvenile Crimes, Employment Discrimination, Sexual Harassment, Nursing Home Abuse, Insurance.

MORRIS & RUIZ, P.C.

401 N. CENTER STREET
PLYMOUTH, INDIANA 46563
Telephone: 574-935-9500
Fax: 574-935-9537
URL: http://www.lawyers.com/morrisandruiz

Business Transactions, Corporate Law, Bankruptcy, Litigation, Personal Injury, Domestic Relations, Criminal Law, Juvenile Law, Automobile Accidents, Driving While Intoxicated, Juvenile Criminal Law, Parole and Probation, Traffic Violations, White Collar Crimes.

JOSEPH R. MORRIS, born Plymouth, Indiana, August 28, 1965; admitted to bar, 1996, Indiana and U.S. District Court, Northern and Southern Districts of Indiana. *Education:* Ball State University (B.S., with distinction, departmental honors, 1991); Valparaiso University (J.D., summa cum laude, 1996). *Member:* Marshall County, Indiana State and American Bar Associations; The Association of Trial Lawyers of America. ***PRACTICE AREAS:*** Business Transactions; Corporate Law; Bankruptcy; Litigation; Personal Injury; Domestic Relations; Criminal Law; Juvenile Law; Automobile Accidents and Injuries; Driving While Intoxicated; Juvenile Criminal Law; Parole and Probation; Traffic Violations; White Collar Crime.

EDWARD R. RUIZ, born Plymouth, Indiana, December 30, 1969; admitted to bar, 1995, Indiana and U.S. District Court, Northern and Southern Districts of Indiana. *Education:* Butler University (B.A., with honors, 1992); Indiana University (J.D., 1995). *Member:* Indianapolis and Indiana State Bar Associations. ***PRACTICE AREAS:*** Civil Practice; Defense Litigation; Insurance Defense.

STEVENS, TRAVIS, FORTIN & LUKENBILL

Established in 1885

119 WEST GARRO STREET
P.O. BOX 517
PLYMOUTH, INDIANA 46563
Telephone: 574-936-4041
Fax: 574-936-3060
Email: stfl@kconline.com

General Civil Practice. Real Estate, Wills and Probate, Trusts and Estates, Guardianships, Asset Protection. Estate Planning, Corporation and Insurance Litigation. Law.

MEMBERS OF FIRM

WILLIAM L. FORTIN, born Hammond, Indiana, December 20, 1938; admitted to bar, 1965, Indiana and Illinois. *Education:* Indiana University; St. Joseph's College (A.B., 1961); Loyola University, Chicago (J.D., 1964). Instructor, Business Law, Ancilla College, 1982—2004; Deputy Attorney General, Indiana, 1965-1969. City Attorney, Plymouth, 1972-1980 (Member, Supreme Court Committee on Character and Fitness of State Board of Law Examiners). *Member:* Marshall County and Indiana State Bar Associations.

KENNETH H. LUKENBILL, born Indianapolis, Indiana, December 11, 1942; admitted to bar, 1969, Indiana. *Education:* Indiana University (A.B., 1965; J.D., 1969). Phi Delta Phi. Deputy Attorney General, Indiana, 1970-1972. Attorney: Marshall County Plan Commission, 1984—; Union-North United School Corporation, 1972—. Instructor, Business Law, Ancilla College 2005-. *Member:* Marshall County, Indiana State and American Bar Associations.

OF COUNSEL

MICHAEL A. DERUCKI, born Chicago, Illinois, August 7, 1963; admitted to bar, 1988, Illinois; 1990, Indiana. *Education:* Bradley University (B.S., 1985) Illinois Institute of Technology/Chicago-Kent College of Law (J.D., 1988). *Member:* Indiana State, Illinois State and American Bar Associations. ***PRACTICE AREAS:*** Family Law; Traffic Violations; Contracts; Litigation; Estate Planning.

LEGAL SUPPORT PERSONNEL

DAVID W. FORTIN, born Indianapolis, Indiana, January 21, 1967. *Education:* Purdue University (B.S., 1990); Indiana University (M.B.A., 1994); Valparaiso University (J.D., 2004). (Intern)

HODGES & DAVIS, P.C.

Established in 1906

6082 LUTE ROAD
P.O. BOX 1037
PORTAGE, INDIANA 46368
Telephone: 219-762-9129
Fax: 219-762-2826
URL: http://www.hodgesdavis.com

Merrillville, Indiana Office: 8700 Broadway. Telephone: 219-641-8700. Fax: 219-641-8710.

(This Listing Continued)

HODGES & DAVIS, P.C., Portage—Continued

General Civil Practice in all State and Federal Courts, Trials and Appeals, Insurance Defense, Corporation, Health and Hospital, Municipal and Zoning Law, Criminal, Driving While Intoxicated, Financing, Tax and Administrative Law. EEOC, Negligence, Products Liability, Environmental, Wills and Probate, Trusts and Estates, Estate Planning, Real Estate and Foreclosure Law. Consumer and Commercial Collections, Business Law, Business Planning, Business Litigation, Business Enterprises, Corporate, Partnerships, Small Business, Buying and Selling a Business, Business Start-Ups.

CLYDE D. COMPTON, born Grand Forks, North Dakota, March 23, 1940; admitted to bar, 1965, Indiana; 1978, U.S. Supreme Court. *Education:* Columbia University and DePauw University (B.A., 1962); Indiana University (LL.B., 1965). City Council Attorney, Portage, Indiana, 1973-1987. Water Reclamation Board Attorney, Portage, Indiana, 1976—. Member, Board of Visitors, Indiana University Law School, 1986-1988, 2002—. President: Indiana University Law School Alumni Association, 1988-1989; Visiting Nurse Association of Northwest Indiana, 1994-1996. *Member:* Lake County (Treasurer, 1986-1987), Indiana State (Treasurer, 1989-1992, Secretary, 1992-1994; Member: Mandatory Legal Education Task Force, 1985-1986; Board of Managers, 1977-1979; House of Delegates, 1970-1992; Chairman: Committees on: Legal Economics, 1983-1985; Competency, 1979-1982; Budget and Finance, 1986-1992; Draft Committee of the House of Delegates, 1986; Staff Compensation Committee, 1990-1996; Chairman, House of Delegates, 2001; Vice President, 2002-2003; President-Elect, 2003-2004; President, 2004-2005) and American Bar Associations; Indiana Bar Foundation (Treasurer, 1990-1992; Secretary, 1992-1994; President-Elect, 1994-1996; President, 1996-1998). Master, Calumet American Inn of Court. ***PRACTICE AREAS:*** Trial Practice; Real Estate; Corporate and Business Law. ***Email:*** ccompton@hodgesdavis.com

EARLE F. HITES, born Indianapolis, Indiana, October 18, 1947; admitted to bar, 1972, Indiana. *Education:* Indiana University (B.S., 1969); Valparaiso University (J.D., 1972). Member, Editorial Board, Valparaiso University Law Review, 1971-1972. Author: Student Note, "Student Voting Rights," 6 Valparaiso University Law Review. *Member:* Lake County, Indiana State and American Bar Associations; American Health Lawyers Association. ***PRACTICE AREAS:*** Health Care Law; Corporate and Business; Real Estate; Creditors Right Law. ***Email:*** ehites@hodgesdavis.com

R. LAWRENCE STEELE, born Valparaiso, Indiana, March 28, 1947; admitted to bar, 1974, Indiana and Wisconsin. *Education:* Indiana University (B.S., 1969); Indiana University at Indianapolis (J.D., 1974). Phi Delta Phi. Lake County Deputy Prosecutor, Felony Division, 1976-1978. Porter County Deputy Prosecutor, 1980-1981. U.S. Attorney for Northern District of Indiana, 1981-1985. Attorney: Porter County Plan Commission, 1993-2002; Porter County Board of Zoning Appeals, 1993-2002. Certified Civil Mediator. *Member:* Lake County, Porter County, Indiana State, Federal and American (Member, Sections on: Litigation; Labor and Employment Law) Bar Associations; State Bar of Wisconsin; Seventh Circuit Bar Association; National Association of Former U.S. Attorneys. ***PRACTICE AREAS:*** Civil and Criminal Litigation; Employment Law; Business Law; Health Care Law; Real Estate. ***Email:*** rsteele@hodgesdavis.com

GREGORY A. SOBKOWSKI, born Gary, Indiana, January 10, 1957; admitted to bar, 1982, Indiana. *Education:* University of Notre Dame (B.A., cum laude, 1979; J.D., 1982). City Attorney, Portage, Indiana, 1988—. Attorney, Portage Township Schools, 1995—. *Member:* Lake County, Indiana State (Chairman, Young Lawyers Section, 1989-1990; Member, ICLEF Board of Directors, 1990-1991; Treasurer, 1999-2000) and American (Delegate, House of Delegates 1991-1994; 1999—) Bar Associations. ***PRACTICE AREAS:*** Municipal Law; Corporate and Business; Health Care Law; Real Estate; Estate Planning; Probate. ***Email:*** gsobkowski@hodgesdavis.com

BONNIE C. COLEMAN, born Neenah, Wisconsin, September 3, 1960; admitted to bar, 1984, Indiana. *Education:* Ripon College (A.B., magna cum laude, 1981); Valparaiso University (J.D., 1984). Phi Beta Kappa. Adjunct Professor, Valparaiso University. Director, Boys & Girls Club of NW Indiana (President, 1998; Vice-President, 1995-1997; Treasurer, 1994). *Member:* Lake County, Indiana State and American Bar Associations. ***PRACTICE AREAS:*** Health Care Law; Corporate Law; Business Law; Municipal Law; Estate Planning; Probate; Real Estate; Finance. ***Email:*** bcoleman@hodgesdavis.com

LAURA B. FROST, born Evanston, Illinois, July 20, 1965; admitted to bar, 1991, Indiana and Illinois. *Education:* Illinois Wesleyan University (B.A., magna cum laude, 1987); Valparaiso University (J.D., summa cum laude, 1991). Phi Kappa Phi; Phi Delta Phi. Note Editor, Valparaiso University Law Review, 1990-1991. Author: Student Note, "He Who Controls the Mind Controls the Body: False Imprisonment, Religious Cults, and the Destruction of Volitional Capacity," 25 Valparaiso University Law Review 407. Attorney, Town of Dune Acres, 1994-1998; Portage Plan Commission, 1994-1995; Portage Board of Zoning Appeals, 1994-1995. Director, 2000-2005, President, 2005 and Vice President, 2002, Lake County Foundation for the Retarded. *Member:* Lake County, Indiana State and American Bar Associations. ***PRACTICE AREAS:*** Health Care Law; Corporate; Business. ***Email:*** lfrost@hodgesdavis.com

BENJAMIN T. BALLOU, born Hammond, Indiana, October 23, 1973; admitted to bar, 1999, Indiana. *Education:* University of Chicago (B.A., 1996); Valparaiso University School of Law (J.D., 1999). *Member:* Lake County and Indiana State Bar Associations. ***PRACTICE AREAS:*** Probate; Estate Planning; Corporate; Health Law; General Practice. ***Email:*** bballou@hodgesdavis.com

DAVID H. KREIDER, born Akron, Ohio, October 17, 1941; admitted to bar, 1970, Indiana. *Education:* Indiana University (A.B., 1964; J.D., 1970). Deputy Attorney General, Indiana, 1971-1977. District Counsel, U.S. Small Business Administration, Indianapolis District Office, 1977-1983. Assistant United States Attorney, Northern District of Indiana, 1983-1985. Senior Attorney, FDIC, Indianapolis Consolidated Office, 1985-1986. *Member:* Lake County and Indiana State Bar Associations. ***PRACTICE AREAS:*** Commercial Law; Bankruptcy Law; Litigation; Health Care Law. ***Email:*** dkreider@hodgesdavis.com

R. TIMOTHY FLETCHER, born LaPorte, Indiana, September 16, 1971; admitted to bar, 2003, Indiana. *Education:* Indiana State University (B.S., magna cum laude, 1995); Valparaiso University School of Law (J.D., 2003). Author: 37 Val. U. L. Rev. 983 Summer 2003. *Member:* Lake County, Indiana State and American Bar Associations. ***Email:*** rfletcher@hodgesdavis.com

REBECCA C. HOPKINS, born Gary, Indiana, November 7, 1959; admitted to bar, 2003, Indiana. *Education:* Purdue University (B.S., 1982); Valparaiso University (J.D., 2003). Pharmacist, 1982. *Member:* Lake County, Indiana State and American Bar Associations. ***Email:*** rhopkins@hodgesdavis.com

REPRESENTATIVE CLIENTS: *Banks:* Centier Bank. *Mortgage Broker:* Lake Mortgage Co., Inc. *Municipal:* Gary Fire Civil Service Commission; Gary Police Pension Fund; Hobart Fire Civil Service Commission; Merrillville Community School Corporation; City of Portage, Indiana; Portage Township Schools; Portage Redevelopment Commission; Portage Water Reclamation Board. *Insurance Companies:* Hartford Insurance Co.; Liberty Mutual Insurance Co. *Health Care Providers:* The Methodist Hospitals, Inc.; Amputee Care Center, Inc.; Edgewater Systems for Balanced Living, Inc.; Geminus Corp.; Home Health Service of Porter County, Indiana, Inc.; Visiting Nurse Association of Porter County, Indiana, Inc.; Whispering Pines Nursing Home. *Auto Dealerships:* Lake Shore Ford, Inc.; Michigan City Motors, Inc.; Nielsen Buick Subaru, Inc.; Nielsen Automotive Group, Inc.; Nielsen Ford Lincoln Mercury; Nielsen Nissan; Pine Chevrolet, Inc.; Pine-Mitsubishi-Kia; Shaver Motors, Inc. *Real Estate:* Aberdeen Limited Partnership; Accent Homes, Inc.; Andover Management; Century 21 Heritage, Inc.; DeNovo Development; Inland Real Estate Group; Purdue Research Foundation. *Other:* Hawk Enterprises; Indiana-American Water Co.; Lakehead Pipe Line Co., Inc.; Vector Pipe Line Co.; Liberty Homes, Inc.; R.A.S. Construction Co., Inc.; WilTel Communications, LLC.

(For Complete Biographical Data on all Personnel see Professional Biographies at Merrillville, Indiana)

AIMEE C. ZEMAITIS

3437 AIRPORT ROAD
PORTAGE, INDIANA 46368
Telephone: 219-764-7172
Fax: 219-763-0519
Email: aczlaw@hotmail.com

Personal Injury, Family Law, Wills, Trusts and Estates, Business Law, Traffic Violations.

AIMEE C. ZEMAITIS, born Hammond, Indiana, December 15, 1976; admitted to bar, 2002, Indiana and U.S. District Court, Northern and Southern Districts of Indiana; 2003, Illinois. *Education:* Purdue University, Lafayette (B.A., 1999); Valparaiso University School of Law (J.D., 2002). *Member:* Lake County, Illinois State and Indiana State Bar Associations. ***PRACTICE AREAS:*** Personal Injury; Family Law; Wills; Trusts and Estates; Business Law; Traffic Violations.

BLACKBURN & GREEN

PORTLAND, INDIANA

(See Fort Wayne)

Litigation, Personal Injury Law.

JILL A. GONZALEZ, ATTORNEY AT LAW

PORTLAND, INDIANA

(See Muncie)

Family Law, Personal Injury, Criminal Law, Divorce.

HINKLE, RACSTER, LOPEZ & CLAMME

PROFESSIONAL CORPORATION
Established in 1937
121 WEST HIGH STREET
PORTLAND, INDIANA 47371
Telephone: 260-726-8104
Fax: 260-726-9113
Email: hrl@jayco.net

General Civil Practice. Corporation, Probate and Estate Planning, Personal Injury and Real Estate Law. Trial and Appellate Practice, Family/Domestic Relations, Collections. Mediation.

WAYNE W. HINKLE (1906-2000)

LON R. RACSTER, born Evansville, Indiana, July 14, 1942; admitted to bar, 1967, Indiana; 1972, U.S. Supreme Court; 1987, U.S. Tax Court. *Education:* Indiana University (A.B., 1964; J.D., 1967). Portland City Attorney, 1980-1991; Jay County Attorney, 1969-1972; Jay School Corporation Attorney, 1969-1978; Jay County Hospital Attorney, 1978-1992. Certified Indiana Mediator. *Member:* Jay County, Indiana State and American Bar Associations. ***PRACTICE AREAS:*** Corporate; Probate; Personal Injury. ***Email:*** lrr@jayco.net

WILLIAM W. HINKLE, born Portland, Indiana, September 24, 1946; admitted to bar, 1971, Indiana. *Education:* Indiana University (B.S., 1968; J.D., 1971). Dunkirk City Attorney, 1976—. Jay County Attorney, 1981-1984, 1991-1992. Portland City Attorney, 2001— *Member:* Jay County, Indiana State and American Bar Associations. ***PRACTICE AREAS:*** Real Estate; Probate; Trusts and Estates; Personal Injury; Family. ***Email:*** wwh@jayco.net

GEORGE O. LOPEZ, born Mexico City, Mexico, April 11, 1954; admitted to bar, 1979, Indiana and U.S. District Court, Southern District of Indiana. *Education:* Xavier University (B.S., 1976); Salmon P. Chase College (J.D., 1979). Phi Alpha Delta. Prosecutor, Jay County, 1995—. *Member:* Jay County, Indiana State and American Bar Associations; The Association of Trial Lawyers of America. ***LANGUAGES:*** Spanish. ***PRACTICE AREAS:*** Family Law; Personal Injury; Collections; Mediation; Insurance Defense. ***Email:*** golopez@jayco.net

ROBERT A. CLAMME, born Hartford City, Indiana, May 25, 1945; admitted to bar, 1973, Indiana. *Education:* Ball State University (B.S., 1970); Indiana University School of Law (J.D., 1973). Prosecuting Attorney, Jay County, 1975-1994; Chief Deputy Prosecuting

(This Listing Continued)

Attorney, Jay County, 1995— Member: Jay County Planning Commission, 1991-1998; Jay County Board of Health, 1990— *Member:* Jay County and Indiana State Bar Associations. ***PRACTICE AREAS:*** Probate Law; Personal Injury; Family Law; Collections; Real Estate Law. ***Email:*** rclammeatty@jayco.net

COUNSEL FOR: The First National Bank of Portland; Community First Bank & Trust; Second National Bank; Mercer Savings Bank; Indiana Glass Co.; Teledyne-Portland Forge; Createc Corp.; City of Portland; City of Dunkirk; Moser Engineering; Jay Products, Inc.; Jay Petroleum, Inc.; Jay Co. Council; Jay County Abstract Co., Inc.
APPROVED ATTORNEYS FOR: Commonwealth Title Insurance Co.; Lawyers Title Insurance Co.
REFERENCES: The First National Bank of Portland; MainSource Bank.

BAMBERGER, FOREMAN, OSWALD AND HAHN, LLP

Established in 1959

302 N. PRINCE STREET
PRINCETON, INDIANA 47670
Telephone: 812-386-6482
Fax: 812-386-6480
Email: info@bamberger.com
URL: http://www.bamberger.com

Evansville, Indiana Office: 20 NW Fourth Street, Suite 708, 47708. Telephone: 812-425-1591. Fax: 812-421-4936.
Indianapolis, Indiana Office: Market Tower, Suite 2950, 10 West Market Street, 46204. Telephone: 317-464-1591. Fax: 317-464-1592. Toll Free: 888-994-7976.
Mt. Vernon, Indiana Office: 309 Main Street, 47620. Telephone: 812-838-4495. Fax: 812-838-9445.
Poseyville, Indiana Office: 178 South Lockwood, 47633. Telephone: 812-874-3365. Fax: 812-874-3366.

Administrative Law, Antitrust Law, Appellate Practice, Arbitration, Banking Law, Bankruptcy Law, Business Law, Civil Rights, Civil Trial Practice, Commercial Law, Commercial Litigation, Communications Law, Construction Law, Corporate Law, Creditors' Rights, Elder Law, Energy Law, Environmental Law, Health Care Law, Insurance Defense, Intellectual Property Law, Labor and Employment Law, Land Use Law, Medical Malpractice, Mergers and Acquisitions, Product Liability Law, Public Utilities Law, Real Estate Law, Trademark, Copyright and Unfair Competition, Trusts and Estates, Wills and Probate.

For a list of Representative Clients, see Professional Biographies at Evansville.

(For other personnel, see Professional Biographies at Evansville, Indiana)

HALL, PARTENHEIMER & KINKLE

Established in 1960

219 NORTH HART STREET
P.O. BOX 13
PRINCETON, INDIANA 47670
Telephone: 812-386-0050
FAX: 812-385-2575
Email: hpk@insightbb.com
URL: http://www.hpklawyers.com

General Civil Practice. Personal Injury, Probate and Estate Planning, Real Estate, Mining, Oil and Gas and Corporate Law, Municipal Law, Trials.

MEMBERS OF FIRM

VERNER P. PARTENHEIMER, born Princeton, Indiana, May 5, 1936; admitted to bar, 1960, Indiana. *Education:* Indiana University (A.B., 1958; LL.B., 1960). Delta Theta Phi; Order of the Coif; Phi Beta Kappa. Editor-in-Chief, Indiana Law Journal, 1959-1960. *Member:* Gibson County, Indiana State and American Bar Associations; Eastern Mineral Law Foundation. ***PRACTICE AREAS:*** Probate and Estate Planning; Oil and Gas; Mineral Law; Environmental Litigation; Real Estate; Business Organization. ***Email:*** vernp@insightbb.com

J. ROBERT KINKLE, born Evansville, Indiana, September 29, 1944; admitted to bar, 1969, Indiana and U.S. District Court, Southern District of Indiana. *Education:* Indiana University (A.B., 1966; J.D., 1969). Phi Alpha Delta. Deputy Prosecuting Attorney, Vanderburgh County, 1975-1980. *Member:* Evansville, Gibson County, Indiana State and American Bar Associations. [With U.S. Marine Corps, active duty, 1970-1973; Major, USMCR]. ***PRACTICE AREAS:*** Real Estate Law; Personal Injury Law; Oil and Gas; Domestic Relations; Probate and Estate Planning; Business Organization; Municipal Law. ***Email:*** hpk@insightbb.com

REPRESENTATIVE CLIENTS: Toyota Motor Manufacturing, Indiana, Inc.; Marathon Oil Co.; Interlake Inc.; Fifth Third Bank; United States Fidelity & Guaranty Co.; South Gibson School Corp.; East Gibson School Corporation; Union Planters Bank; Cyprus Amax Minerals; Triad Mining, Inc.; Allionce Coal, LLC; Kindill Mining, Inc.; City of Oakland; Gibson County Solid Waste Management District; Lower Patoke River Conservancy District; Fifth Third Bank; Old National Bank.
APPROVED ATTORNEYS FOR: Lawyers Title Insurance; National Attorneys Title Assurance Fund and Stewart Title.
REFERENCES: Fifth Third Bank; Old National Bank; Union Planters Bank.

HART BELL LLC

PRINCETON, INDIANA

(See Vincennes)

General Practice. Litigation, Insurance, Banking, Corporate, Employment, Probate and Estate Planning, State and Federal Tax Law, Real Estate, Construction, Commercial, Business, Elder, Creditors Rights, Personal Injury, Family Law and Criminal Defense.

HIGGINBOTHAM LAW OFFICE

Established in 1989

208 EAST STATE STREET
PRINCETON, INDIANA 47670
Telephone: 812-386-3040; 812-386-3041
Fax: 812-386-7306
Email: higglaw@gibsoncounty.net
URL: http://www.higglaw.com

Civil and Criminal Litigation, Real Estate, Commercial Law, Probate, Family, Divorce, Custody, Separation Agreements, Personal Injury, Oil and Gas, Collections.

C. DEAN HIGGINBOTHAM, born New Haven, Connecticut, October 24, 1947; admitted to bar, 1983, Indiana and U.S. District Court, Southern District of Indiana; U.S. Court of Appeals, Seventh Circuit. *Education:* Purdue University (B.A., 1970; M.S., 1971; Ph.D., 1983); Indiana University (J.D., 1982). Phi Kappa Phi; Phi Delta Phi. David Ross Fellow, Purdue University, 1973-1974. *Member:* Gibson County, Indiana State and American Bar Associations; The Association of Trial Lawyers of America. ***LANGUAGES:*** Russian. ***REPORTED CASES:*** Kirby v. Ashland Oil, Inc. (Ind.App. 1984) 463 N.E.2d 1127; Gibson County Farm Bureau Co-op v. Greer (Ind., 1994) 643 N.E.2d 313; U.S. v. Arthur Gerber (7th Cir., 1993) 999 F.2d 1112.

COUNSEL FOR: Town of Mackey; Town of Somerville; Midwest Archaeological Conference, Inc.; Council for Conservation of Indiana Archaeology.
REPRESENTATIVE CLIENTS: Citizens Bank; Credit Bureau of Evansville; T.E.C. Consulting Engineers; Perdue Farms; Federal Assembly, Inc.; Owensville Lumber & Supply, Inc.; Miles Farm Supply, Inc.; DeKalb Genetics Corporation; Lin-Gas, Inc.; Powers Motor Parts, Inc.; Bradford Supply Co.; Woebkenberg Farms; Fireman's Fund Insurance Co.; Interstate Trucker; Archaeological Conservancy.
APPROVED ATTORNEY FOR: Lawyers Title Insurance.
REFERENCE: Fifth Third Bank.

KAHN, DEES, DONOVAN & KAHN, LLP

PRINCETON, INDIANA

(See Evansville)

General Civil Practice including Litigation, Environmental, Labor Management, Corporate, Pension, Banking, Hospital, Insurance Defense, Real Estate, Workers' Compensation, Tax, Construction, Immigration and General Civil Law.

RUDOLPH, FINE, PORTER & JOHNSON LLP

PRINCETON, INDIANA

(See Evansville)

General Corporate Practice. Health Care Law, Commercial Litigation, Insurance Defense, Real Estate, Zoning and Land Use Law, Mediation and Arbitration, Bankruptcy Law, Mergers and Acquisitions. Probate and Estate Planning, Tax, Employment Law, Appeals, Banking. Trials in all State and Federal Courts.

JOHN T. CASEY

REMINGTON, INDIANA

(See Rensselaer)

Civil Litigation, Administrative Law, Probate, Estate Planning, Real Estate.

RICHARD BALLARD ATTORNEY AT LAW

RENSSELAER, INDIANA

(See Knox)

Criminal Law, DUI, Drug Crimes, Juvenile Crimes, Traffic Violations, White Collar Crimes, Family Law, Adoptions, Child Custody, Child Support, Divorce, Visitation Rights, Personal Injury, Medical Malpractice, Auto Accidents, Wrongful Death, Slip and Fall, Real Estate.

BLACKBURN & GREEN

RENSSELAER, INDIANA

(See Fort Wayne)

Litigation, Personal Injury Law.

JOHN T. CASEY

217 EAST WASHINGTON STREET
RENSSELAER, INDIANA 47978
Telephone: 219-866-4656
Fax: 219-866-4219

Civil Litigation, Administrative Law, Probate, Estate Planning, Real Estate.

JOHN T. CASEY, born San Antonio, Texas, January 5, 1946; admitted to bar, 1972, Indiana; 1977, U.S. Tax Court. *Education:* DePauw University (B.A., 1967); Indiana University (J.D., 1972); George Washington University (LL.M., with highest honors, 1977). Deputy Prosecuting Attorney, 1982-1984. *Member:* Newton County (President, 1986-1987), Jasper County and Indiana State Bar Associations. [With USMC, 1968-1970]. ***PRACTICE AREAS:*** Civil Litigation; Administrative Law; Probate; Estate Planning.

DUMAS, WEIST & MAHNESMITH

Established in 1946

119 WEST HARRISON STREET
RENSSELAER, INDIANA 47978
Telephone: 219-866-4158
FAX: 219-866-2274
Email: edd@nwiis.com
URL: http://www.dumas-moriarty.com

Fowler, Indiana Office: Weist Building, P.O. Box 101, 47944-0101. Telephone: 765-884-1840. Fax: 765-884-8450.

General Civil and Criminal Trial Practice. Personal Injury, Wills and Probate, Trusts and Estates, Estate Planning, Corporate, Municipal and Zoning Law, Elder Law, Medicaid Planning.

THOMAS B. DUMAS (1918-1998)

WILLIAM J. MORIARTY, JR. (1939-1993)

MEMBERS OF FIRM

EDWARD P. DUMAS, born Rensselaer, Indiana, April 16, 1951; admitted to bar, 1976, Indiana. *Education:* Regis College (B.A., 1973); Valparaiso University (J.D., 1976). *Member:* Indiana State and American Bar Associations; Indiana Trial Lawyers Association. ***PRACTICE AREAS:*** Personal Injury; Civil Litigation; Probate and Estate Planning. ***Email:*** edd@nwiis.com

WILLIAM B. WEIST (Resident, Fowler, Indiana Office)

KENT E. MAHNESMITH, born Garrett, Indiana, November 10, 1966; admitted to bar, 1993, Indiana. *Education:* University of Indianapolis (B.S., 1989); Valparaiso University (J.D., 1993). *Member:* Indiana State and American Bar Associations. ***PRACTICE AREAS:*** Medicaid Planning; Elder Law; Estate Planning; Probate; Real Estate; Personal Injury; Civil Litigation. ***Email:*** kentm@nwiis.com

REPRESENTATIVE CLIENTS: DeMotte State Bank; St. Joseph's College; Rensselaer Central Schools Corp.; Kankakee Valley School Corp.; West Central School Corp.; Jasper County Abstract Co.; Rensselaer Auto Parts; Jasper County Hospital; Jasper County Public Library; Jasper County Economic Development Commission; Jasper County Drainage Board; Fowler State Bank; Farmers & Merchant State Bank of Boswell; Commissioners of Benton County.

MICHAEL LAMBERT

RENSSELAER, INDIANA

(See Crown Point)

Criminal Law, Drug Crimes, Driving While Intoxicated, Parole and Probation, Juvenile Crimes, Traffic Violations, Family Law, Adoption, Divorce, Child Custody, Child Support, Domestic Violence, Visitation Rights, Employment Law, Wrongful Termination, Sexual Harassment, Civil Rights, Discrimination, Personal Injury, Automobile Accidents, Slip and Fall, Wrongful Death, Bankruptcy, Wills and Probate, Guardianships, Business Law, Contracts, Lawsuits, Business Enterprises.

MATTHEW D. LaTULIP
ATTORNEY AT LAW

RENSSELAER, INDIANA

(See Schererville)

Personal Injury, Medical Malpractice, Auto Accidents, Slip and Fall, Wrongful Death, Criminal, DUI, Traffic Violations, Juvenile Crimes, Employment Discrimination, Sexual Harassment, Nursing Home Abuse, Insurance.

NED TONNER
ATTORNEY AT LAW

203 N. CULLEN STREET
RENSSELAER, INDIANA 47978
Telephone: 219-866-8888
Fax: 219-866-0474
Email: ned@tonnerlaw.com
URL: http://www.lawyers.com/tonnerlaw

Personal Injury, Criminal Law, Estates, Trusts, Real Estate, Divorce, Family Law.

NED J. TONNER, born Rensselaer, Indiana, August 7, 1960; admitted to bar, 1986, Indiana and U.S. District Court, Northern and Southern Districts; 1988, Illinois; 1989, California. *Education:* Indiana University (B.S., 1982); University of Tulsa (J.D., 1985). City Attorney, Rensselaer, 1996—. *Member:* Jasper County and Indiana State Bar Associations; Indiana Trial Lawyers Association; Association of Trial Lawyers of America. ***PRACTICE AREAS:*** Personal Injury; Criminal Law; Trusts and Estates; Real Estate; Divorce; Family Law.

ALLEN • WELLMAN • McNEW

RICHMOND, INDIANA

(See Greenfield)

General Civil and Criminal Practice in all Courts. Trials, Personal Injury, Medical Malpractice, Family/Domestic Relations, Real Estate, Business Association, Trusts, Probate and Estate Planning, Commercial, Litigation, Business Law, Personal and Corporate Bankruptcy, Appeals, Zoning, Mediation.

BOSTON, BEVER, KLINGE, CROSS & CHIDESTER

Established in 1911

27 NORTH EIGHTH STREET
RICHMOND, INDIANA 47374-3028
Telephone: 765-962-7527
Fax: 765-966-4597
Email: bbkcc@infocom.com

General Civil, Trial and Appellate Practice, Banking, Business, Commercial, Corporations, Creditors' Rights, Criminal, Family and Domestic Relations, Insurance, Personal Injury, Probate and Estate Planning, Real Estate and Zoning Law.

MEMBERS OF FIRM

JOHN M. HARLAN (Retired)

RICHARD E. BOSTON, born Sullivan, Indiana, October 18, 1946; admitted to bar, 1971, Indiana and U.S. District Court, Southern District of Indiana. *Education:* Indiana University (B.S., 1968; J.D., 1971). Standing Trustee, U.S. Bankruptcy Court, Southern District of Indiana, Indianapolis Division, 1979—. *Member:* Wayne County, Indianapolis, Indiana State and American Bar Associations; Commercial Law League of America; National Association of Bankruptcy Trustees; American Bankruptcy Institute; National Association of Retail Collection Attorneys. ***PRACTICE AREAS:*** Bankruptcy; Creditors Rights; Real Estate Law; Commercial Law; Retail Collections; Commercial Collections; Trusts and Estates. ***Email:*** reboston@bbkcc.com

ROBERT L. BEVER, born Richmond, Indiana, April 30, 1953; admitted to bar, 1978, Indiana. *Education:* DePauw University (B.A., with distinction, 1975); Indiana University (J.D., magna cum laude, 1978). Pi Sigma Alpha; Phi Delta Phi. Richmond City Attorney, 1996—. Listed in Who's Who in American Law. *Member:* Wayne County, Indiana State and American Bar Associations. ***REPORTED CASES:*** Great Atlantic & Pacific Tea Co. v. Wilson, (Ind App) 408 NE2d 144-11 ALR4th 569. ***PRACTICE AREAS:*** Banking Law; Commercial Real Estate; Commercial Law; Corporation; Municipal Law; Physician Practices; Health Law. ***Email:*** bbever@bbkcc.com

KENT G. KLINGE, born Indianapolis, Indiana, August 5, 1939; admitted to bar, 1968, Indiana. *Education:* Hanover College (A.B., 1963); Indiana University School of Law (J.D., 1967). Phi Delta Phi. Assistant City Attorney, Richmond, 1968-1972. *Member:* Wayne County, Indiana State (Member, House of Delegates) and American Bar Associations; Indiana Trial Lawyers Association; The Association of Trial Lawyers of America. ***PRACTICE AREAS:*** Insurance Defense; Civil Litigation; Commercial Law. ***Email:*** kgklinge@bbkcc.com

RONALD L. CROSS, born Monticello, Kentucky, February 10, 1947; admitted to bar, 1976, Indiana. *Education:* Indiana University (B.A., 1970; J.D., magna cum laude, 1976). Phi Beta Kappa; Omicron Delta Epsilon. Wayne County Attorney, 2001—. *Member:* Wayne County, Indiana State and American Bar Associations. ***PRACTICE AREAS:*** Banking Law; Commercial Law; School Law; Municipal Law; Civil Litigation; Creditors Rights. ***Email:*** ronc@bbkcc.com

WALTER S. CHIDESTER, born Coshocton, Ohio, August 31, 1946; admitted to bar, 1978, Indiana. *Education:* Heidelberg College (A.B., 1968); Drake University (J.D., 1977). *Member:* Wayne County, Indiana State and American Bar Associations. ***PRACTICE AREAS:*** Domestic Relations; Guardianship; Probate. ***Email:*** walt@bbkcc.com

DOUGLAS B. OLER, born Richmond, Indiana, March 19, 1940; admitted to bar, 1965, Indiana, U.S. District Court, Southern District of Indiana and U.S. Tax Court. *Education:* DePauw University (B.A., cum laude, 1962); University of Michigan (J.D., 1965). *Member:* Wayne County and Indiana State Bar Associations; National Academy of Elder Law Attorneys. ***PRACTICE AREAS:*** Business; Corporate; Estate Planning; Elder Law; Probate. ***Email:*** dboler@bbkcc.com

ASSOCIATE

J. CLAYTON MILLER, born Muncie, Indiana, September 17, 1971; admitted to bar, 2000, Indiana and U.S. District Court, Northern and Southern Districts of Indiana. *Education:* Indiana University (B.S., 1994); Drake University (J.D., with honors; M.P.A., 2000). Pi Alpha Alpha; Delta Theta Phi. Member, Editorial Board, Drake Journal of Agriculture Law. Public Administration Honor Society. Assistant Wayne County Attorney, 2001—. *Member:* Wayne County, Indiana State and American Bar Associations. ***Email:*** cmiller@bbkcc.com

OF COUNSEL

TERRY O'MALEY, born Richmond, Indiana, November 10, 1954; admitted to bar, 1980, Indiana and U.S. District Court, Southern District of Indiana. *Education:* Indiana University (B.S., 1977; J.D., with honors, 1980). Wayne County Prosecutor, 1991-1998. *Member:* Wayne County and Indiana State Bar Associations. ***PRACTICE AREAS:*** Domestic Relations; Family Law; Personal Injury; Criminal Law; Probate; Litigation. ***Email:*** tomaley@bbkcc.com

REPRESENTATIVE CLIENTS: City of Richmond; Wayne County Government; Richmond Community Schools; Northeastern Wayne Schools; Union School Corporation; Eaton National Bank & Trust Co.; First Bank, Richmond N.A.; Crown Chrysler, Inc.; Fred First Ford, Inc.; Victory Chevrolet, Inc.; Cinergy (local counsel); Wayne County Health Dept.; Carpenter's Excavating, Inc.; J.M. Hutton and Co., Inc.; Smarelli General Contractors; Mac-Del, Inc. (trucking); Brady, Ware & Schoenfeld, Inc. (CPA's); General Home Maintenance, Inc.; Kent's Harbor, Inc.; Tom Raper, Inc.; Nixon Tool Co.; Eastgate Electric; Wharton Home Improvement; Pediatric and Internal Medicine Center, Inc.; OB-GYN, Inc.; Eastern Indiana Center for Ambulatory Surgery; Anesthesia Associates, LLC; Richmond Cardiologists, Inc.; Emergency Medicine of Eastern Indiana; Richmond Radiologists, Inc.; Motorists Insurance Co.; Ohio Casualty Co.; Prudential Insurance Co.; Travelers Insurance Group; Friends Fellowship Community, Inc.; State Farm Insurance; Ahaus Tool & Engineering, Inc.; Richmond Casting, Inc.; Urban Enterprise Association of Richmond, Inc.; Green Acres, Inc.; Cope Environmental Center; Richmond-Wayne County Chamber of Commerce; Brewer Broadcasting; Brower's Gaar Nurseries; Rose City Nursery; Midwest Orthopedics, Inc.; Rodefeld Company, Inc.; Cabinet Supply, Inc.; Forest Hills Country Club, Inc.; Richmond Power & Light; Georgia Direct Carpet, Inc.; Mancino's Industries, Inc.; Richmond Roosters Baseball.

BURTON AND SIMKIN

Established in 1966

25 NORTH 7TH STREET

RICHMOND, INDIANA 47374-3088

Telephone: 765-966-5518

Fax: 765-966-5510

Email: dburton@infocom.com

URL: http://www.lawyers.com/burton&simkin

Personal Injury, Medical Malpractice, Wrongful Death, Civil Trial Practice, Criminal Trial Practice, Real Estate, Family and Domestic Relations, Driving While Intoxicated, Business, Corporate, Employment, Probate and Estate Planning, Bankruptcy, Traffic Violations, Real Estate.

FIRM PROFILE: Serving the needs of Richmond/Wayne County and East-Central Indiana, Burton and Simkin was founded by Robert G. Burton in 1966. Donald L. Simkin joined the firm in 1974 and David J. Burton in 1995.

MEMBERS OF FIRM

ROBERT G. BURTON, born South Bend, Indiana, September 6, 1937; admitted to bar, 1963, Indiana and U.S. District Court, Southern District of Indiana; 1964, Arizona; 1965, California; 1985, U.S. Court of Appeals, 7th Circuit; 1986, U.S. Supreme Court. *Education:* Indiana University (A.B., 1959); University of Michigan (J.D., 1962). Judge, Richmond City, 1967-1971. City Attorney, Richmond City, 1973-1975. *Member:* Wayne County (President, 1984), Indiana State and American Bar Associations; State Bar of Arizona; State Bar of California; The Association of Trial Lawyers of America; Indiana Trial Lawyers Association; National Institute of Trial Advocacy. ***PRACTICE AREAS:*** Personal Injury; Civil Trial Practice; Real Estate; Corporate; Probate; Estate Planning; Wills; Trusts.

DONALD L. SIMKIN, born Elkhart, Indiana, January 11, 1949; admitted to bar, 1974, Indiana and U.S. District Court, Southern District of Indiana; 1985, U.S. Court of Appeals, 7th Circuit; 1986, U.S. Supreme Court. *Education:* Indiana University (B.S., 1971; J.D., cum laude, 1974). Assistant City Attorney, Richmond City, 1974-1975. Member, Board of Directors, Indiana University School of Law, Indianapolis Alumni Association (1999—). *Member:* Wayne County (President, 1999-2000), Indiana State and American Bar Associations; The Association of Trial Lawyers of America; Indiana Trial Lawyers Association. ***PRACTICE AREAS:*** Personal Injury; Civil Trial Practice; Criminal Trial Practice; Real Estate; Family/Domestic Relations; Corporate; Probate; Estate Planning; Divorce; Child Custody; Driving While Intoxicated; Traffic Violations; Bankruptcy.

DAVID J. BURTON, born Richmond, Indiana, July 4, 1966; admitted to bar, 1992, Indiana; U.S. District Court, Southern and Northern Districts of Indiana. *Education:* University of Michigan (A.B., 1988); Indiana University (J.D., cum laude, 1992). *Member:* Wayne County, Indiana State and American Bar Associations; The Association of Trial Lawyers of America (Member, Motor Vehicle, Collision, Highway, and Premises Liability Section); Indiana Trial Lawyers Association (Sustaining Member). ***REPORTED CASES:*** Wimmer Temporaries Inc. v. Massoff, 740 N.E.2d 886 (Ind. App.2001). ***PRACTICE AREAS:*** Personal Injury; Medical Malpractice; Civil Trial Practice; Real Estate; Corporate; Probate; Estate Planning; Wills; Trusts; Employment. ***Email:*** dburton@infocom.com

REPRESENTATIVE CLIENTS: Furnished Upon Request.
REFERENCES: Firstar Bank, Richmond; West End Savings Bank, Richmond.

JAMES E. DAVIS
ATTORNEY AT LAW

RICHMOND, INDIANA

(See Greenfield)

Personal Injury, Social Security Disability, Wrongful Death, Medical Malpractice, Wills and Probate Law, Automobile Accidents and Injuries, Head Injury, Spinal Injury, Slip and Fall, Trucking Accidents, Construction Accidents, Railroad Accidents, Nursing Home and Abuse and Neglect.

GARDNER, SAYRE & WEIKART

Established in 1910

TWO NORTH EIGHTH, THIRD FLOOR

RICHMOND, INDIANA 47374-3090

Telephone: 765-966-6688

FAX: 765-966-6618

Email: gswinlaw@aol.com

General Civil and Trial Practice. Corporation, Probate and Estate Planning, Real Estate, Personal Injury and Commercial Transactions.

FIRM PROFILE: The firm was established in 1910. The firm has a General Civil and Trial Practice with a Concentration on Corporation, Probate and Estate Planning, Real Estate, Personal Injury Commercial Transactions. The firm offers its services to East Central Indiana representing primarily National and Regional Corporations and Banking Institutions.

MEMBERS OF FIRM

ALONZO M. GARDNER (1886-1941)
WILFRED JESSUP (1900-1944)
FRANK K. CHAMBERS (1938-1955)
FLOYD W. GARDNER (1933-1965)
JOHN R. HARRINGTON (1907-1999)
CLIFFORD M. HAWORTH (1923-1967)
GAYLE W. GARDNER (Retired)

(This Listing Continued)

JOHN M. SAYRE, III, born Rensselaer, Indiana, December 23, 1940; admitted to bar, 1965, Indiana. *Education:* DePauw University (B.A., 1962); Indiana University (LL.B., 1965). Delta Theta Phi. President, Eastern Indiana Estate Planning Council, 1991. *Member:* Wayne County (President, 1991), Indiana State and American Bar Associations. [U.S. Air Force, JAG, 1965-1968]. ***PRACTICE AREAS:*** Banking Law; Probate and Trusts; Estate Planning; Business Transactions; Civil Litigation.

KIRK A. WEIKART, born Springfield, Missouri, October 16, 1962; admitted to bar, 1987, Indiana. *Education:* Lewis and Clark College (B.S., 1984); Indiana University (J.D., 1987). *Member:* Wayne County, Indiana State and American Bar Associations. ***PRACTICE AREAS:*** Personal Injury; Real Estate; Commercial Transactions; Business Law; Litigation. ***Email:*** kaw2gswinlaw@aol.com

---

APRIL BLAIR, born Marion, Indiana, April 6, 1977; admitted to bar, 2003, Indiana. *Education:* Georgetown College (B.A., 1999); Indiana University School of Law (J.D., 2003). *Member:* Wayne County, Indiana State and American Bar Associations.

GENERAL COUNSEL FOR: Dunn Mental Health Center, Inc.; Richmond Housing Authority; The Recycling Center, Inc.; US Bank, NA; Paul Casket Company, Inc.; Cambridge City Casket Co., Inc.; Hawkins Auto Stores, Inc.; Richmond Anesthesiologists, Inc.; R Hoppe, Inc.; Robbins Matherly Dils Insurance; Harrington-Hoch, Inc. (insurance); Freedom Title Company, Inc.; Milso Industries; Stanley W. Hayes Research Foundation, Inc.; Wayne Family Health Care P.C.; Enviro Finishing of Indiana; Hospital Bed Remanufacturing; Precision Wire Assemblies, Inc.; First National Bank and Trust; Spartech Plastics; The Safety Zone.
LOCAL COUNSEL FOR: CIGNA; Equitable Life Assurance Society of the United States, Employers Group; Franklin Iron & Metal Corp.; South Brooklyn Casket Co; Gannet News Service; The Palladium Item Newspaper.

THOMPSON LAW OFFICE

RICHMOND, INDIANA

(See Connersville)

Personal Injury, Debt Collection, Estate Planning, Criminal Law, Appellate Practice, Bankruptcy, Environmental Law, Family Law.

WILSON, KEHOE & WININGHAM

Established in 1970

2901 EAST MAIN STREET

RICHMOND, INDIANA 47374

Telephone: 765-962-9113

Email: mailbox@wkw.com

URL: http://www.wkw.com

Indianapolis, Indiana Office: 2859 North Meridian, 46208. Telephone: 317-920-6400. Fax: 317-920-6405.

Muncie, Indiana Office: 3620 N. Everbrook Lane, Suite A, 47304. Telephone: 765-284-2474.

Civil Trial Practice in State and Federal Courts. Aviation, Medical Legal, Personal Injury, Product Liability, Medical Malpractice, Wrongful Death.

FIRM PROFILE: The Law Firm of Wilson, Kehoe & Winingham represents plaintiffs who are personal injury or wrongful death victims of automobile and aviation accidents, product liability, fires and explosions, and medical malpractice.

Wilson, Kehoe & Winingham have frequently been called upon to assist lawyers in preparing cases for trial dates on short notice and actively litigate in courts throughout the United States.

(For complete biographical data on all personnel, see Professional Biographies at Indianapolis, Indiana)

BLACKBURN & GREEN

ROCHESTER, INDIANA

(See Fort Wayne)

Litigation, Personal Injury Law.

MORRIS & RUIZ, P.C.

ROCHESTER, INDIANA

(See Plymouth)

Business Transactions, Corporate Law, Bankruptcy, Litigation, Personal Injury, Domestic Relations, Criminal Law, Juvenile Law, Automobile Accidents, Driving While Intoxicated, Juvenile Criminal Law, Parole and Probation, Traffic Violations, White Collar Crimes.

KAHN, DEES, DONOVAN & KAHN, LLP

ROCKPORT, INDIANA

(See Evansville)

General Civil Practice including Litigation, Environmental, Labor Management, Corporate, Pension, Banking, Hospital, Insurance Defense, Real Estate, Workers' Compensation, Tax, Construction, Immigration and General Civil Law.

CLARKSON & GULDE, P.C.

Established in 1927
127 WEST 2ND STREET
P.O. BOX 279
RUSHVILLE, INDIANA 46173
Telephone: 765-932-2227
Fax: 765-932-2197
Email: clarkson@cnz.com

Accidents and Personal Injury, Family Law, Criminal Law, Probate, General Trial Practice.

C. JACK CLARKSON, born Rushville, Indiana, December 18, 1930; admitted to bar, 1959, Indiana; U.S. District Court, Southern and Northern Districts of Indiana, U.S. Supreme Court. *Education:* Butler University (B.A., 1957); Indiana University (J.D., with distinction, 1958). Phi Delta Phi; Order of the Coif. Recipient, Indiana Trial Lawyer of the Year, 1986. Prosecuting Attorney, Rush County, 1959-1966. *Member:* Rush County (President, 1961-1962), Indiana State Bar Association; Indiana Trial Lawyers Association (Director, 1985—); The Association of Trial Lawyers of America; American Board of Trial Advocates. Fellow, ITLA. ***Email:*** clarkson@cnz.com

ROBERT G. GULDE, born Rushville, Indiana, September 26, 1965; admitted to bar, 1991, Indiana and U.S. District Court, Southern and Northern District of Indiana. *Education:* Indiana University (B.A., 1988; J.D., 1991). Public Defender, Rush County Court, 1992-1994. Chief Deputy Prosecuting Attorney, Rush County, 1994-2001. *Member:* Rush County, Indiana State Bar Association; Indiana Trial Lawyers Association; The Association of Trial Lawyers of America. ***Email:*** clarkson@cnz.com

A List of Representative Clients will be Furnished upon request.

EARNEST, FOSTER, EDER & LEVI

Established in 1959
114 WEST THIRD STREET
P.O. BOX 430
RUSHVILLE, INDIANA 46173
Telephone: 765-932-4118
Fax: 765-932-4486
Email: efel@verizon.net

General Practice. Trials. Personal Injury, Probate and Estate Planning, Real Estate, Commercial and Corporation Law.

KENNETH L. EARNEST (1916-1995)

OF COUNSEL

JAMES S. FOSTER, born Pittsburgh, Pennsylvania, March 12, 1927; admitted to bar, 1952, Indiana; 1954, U.S. Court of Appeals, Seventh Circuit; 1958, U.S. Supreme Court. *Education:* Indiana University (B.S., 1949; J.D., 1952). *Member:* Rush County, Indiana State and American Bar Associations.

MEMBERS OF FIRM

ROBERT J. EDER, born North Vernon, Indiana, December 4, 1927; admitted to bar, 1955, Indiana. *Education:* St. Joseph's College and Indiana University (B.S., 1953); Indiana University (J.D., 1955). Note Editor, Indiana Law Journal, 1954-1955. *Member:* Rush County and Indiana State Bar Associations. ***PRACTICE AREAS:*** Probate and Estate Planning; Real Estate; Tax; Corporate.

RICHARD K. LEVI, born Rushville, Indiana, March 31, 1945; admitted to bar, 1971, Indiana. *Education:* Indiana University (B.S., 1967); Indiana University at Indianapolis (J.D., 1971). Blue Key. County Attorney, 1973-1981. *Member:* Rush County, Indiana State and American Bar Associations; Indiana Trial Lawyers Association. ***PRACTICE AREAS:*** Civil Litigation; Probate and Estate Planning; Real Estate; Tax.

ASSOCIATE

LEIGH S. MORNING, born Indianapolis, Indiana, August 10, 1971; admitted to bar, 1996, Indiana and U.S. District Court, Northern and Southern Districts of Indiana. *Education:* Indiana University (B.A., 1992; J.D., 1996). Phi Alpha Delta. County Attorney, Rush County, 1997—. *Member:* Indianapolis, Rush County, Indiana State and American Bar Associations. ***PRACTICE AREAS:*** Civil Litigation; Domestic Relations; Collections.

REPRESENTATIVE CLIENTS: Rush Memorial Hospital; The Sampler, Inc.; Ticor Title Insurance Co.; Farm Bureau Insurance Co.; Dawson Oil Company, Inc.; Harcourt Outlines, Inc.; Harcourt Pencil Co., Inc.
REFERENCE: Wells Fargo Bank of Rushville.

KEATON AND KEATON, P.C.

Established in 1937
126 WEST SECOND STREET
RUSHVILLE, INDIANA 46173-1874
Telephone: 765-932-3947
Fax: 765-938-2803
Email: keatonlaw@nraonline.com

General Practice concentrated in Family Law, Probate and Personal Injury.

WALTER B. KEATON (1912-1980)

WILLIAM B. KEATON, born Rushville, Indiana, November 30, 1945; admitted to bar, 1971, Indiana and U.S. District Court, Southern District of Indiana. *Education:* Missouri Military Academy; Indiana University (B.A., 1968; J.D., 1971). Court Crier, U.S. District Court, Southern District of Indiana for Honorable Cale J. Holder, 1968-1971. Prosecuting Attorney, 1971-1986 (President, Indiana Prosecuting Attorney Association, 1982; Director, 1976-1981, 1983-1986). *Member:* Rush County, Indiana State and American Bar Associations. ***LANGUAGES:*** Spanish. ***REPORTED CASES:*** Reno v. Haler, 734 NE 2d 1095 (Ind. Ct. App. 2000); Reno v. Haler, 743 NE 2d 1139 (Ind. Ct. App. 2001); Reddick v. Carfield, 656 NE 2d 518 (Ind. Ct. App. 1995); Motorists Mutual Ins. Co. v. Morris, 654 NE 2d 861(Ind. Ct. App. 1995). ***PRACTICE AREAS:*** Probate (15%); Personal Injury (35%); Family Law (50%). ***Email:*** keatonlaw@nraonline.com

THOMPSON LAW OFFICE

RUSHVILLE, INDIANA

(See Connersville)

Personal Injury, Debt Collection, Estate Planning, Criminal Law, Appellate Practice, Bankruptcy, Environmental Law, Family Law.

LAW OFFICE OF BART COLOMB

SALEM, INDIANA

(See New Albany)

Social Security, Workers Compensation and Family Law.

MATTOX MATTOX & WILSON

SALEM, INDIANA

(See New Albany)

Civil Trial Litigation. Personal Injury and Wrongful Death, Products Liability, Medical Malpractice, Insurance Law, Corporate Law, Business Torts, Family Law, Aviation Law, Labor and Employment Law, Health Care Regulations.

MERKLEY LAW OFFICE

SALEM, INDIANA

(See Jeffersonville)

Family Law, Criminal Law, Estates and Wills, Personal Injury, Municipal Law.

HINSHAW & CULBERTSON LLP

Hinshaw & Culbertson LLP is an Illinois registered limited liability partnership that has elected to be governed by the Illinois Uniform Partnership Act (1997)

Established in 1934
222 INDIANAPOLIS BOULEVARD
SUITE 202
SCHERERVILLE, INDIANA 46375
Telephone: 219-864-5051
Facsimile: 219-864-5052
Telex: 880248
Email: kfox@hinshawlaw.com
URL: http://www.hinshawlaw.com

Other Office Locations: Chicago, Illinois; Appleton, Wisconsin; Belleville, Illinois; Boston, Massachusetts; Champaign, Illinois; Crystal Lake, Illinois; Edwardsville, Illinois; Fort Lauderdale, Florida; Jacksonville, Florida; Joliet, Illinois; Lisle, Illinois; Los Angeles, California; Miami, Florida; Milwaukee, Wisconsin; Minneapolis, Minnesota; New York, New York; Peoria, Illinois; Phoenix, Arizona; Portland, Oregon; Providence, Rhode Island; Rockford, Illinois; St. Louis, Missouri; San Francisco, California; Springfield, Illinois; Tampa, Florida; Waukegan, Illinois.

Appellate, Banking & Financing, Bankruptcy & Creditors' Rights, Class Action Litigation, Civil Rights Defense, Commercial Litigation, Corporate, Construction Law, Director & Officer Liability, Employee Benefits, Environmental, Fidelity & Surety, General Liability Litigation, Government, Health Care, Insurance Coverage, Insurance and Reinsurance, Labor & Employment, Legal Malpractice, Medical Malpractice, Mergers & Acquisitions, Municipal Liability, Personal Injury Defense, Public Law, Products Liability Litigation, Professional Liability, Regulatory, Real Estate, School Law, Securities, Taxation, Transportation, White Collar Crime and Workers' Compensation Defense.

FIRM PROFILE: Hinshaw & Culbertson LLP is a national AMLaw 200 firm with 425 lawyers in 27 offices coast-to-coast. The firm offers a full-service practice, with an emphasis in commercial and defense litigation, corporate, environmental, employment and construction law, as well as the representation of professionals in their liability and risk management matters.

Hinshaw provides services to a range of clients in financial services, construction, health care, not-for-profit, insurance, legal, manufacturing, real estate, transportation and other industries. Firm clients also include government agencies, municipalities and schools.

Hinshaw was founded in 1934. The firm is headquartered in Chicago, and maintains offices in 12 states: Arizona, California, Florida, Illinois, Indiana, Massachusetts, Minnesota, Missouri, New York, Oregon, Rhode Island and Wisconsin.

PARTNERS

JENNIFER KALAS, born Valparaiso, Indiana, November 22, 1966; admitted to bar, 1993, Indiana, Illinois, U.S. District Court, Northern District of Indiana and U.S. District Court, Northern District of Illinois; 2001, U.S. District Court, Southern District of Indiana. *Education:* University of Evansville (B.S., summa cum laude, 1989); Valparaiso University (J.D., summa cum laude, 1993). Author: "Indiana's Peer Review Privilege Statute and its Effect on a Claim of Negligent Credentialing: Analysis and Proposed Statutory Reform,"

(This Listing Continued)

27 Valparaiso University Law Review 411 (1993). *Member:* Lake County Bar Association. ***PRACTICE AREAS:*** General Liability Litigation; Workers; Products Liability Litigation; Employment. ***Email:*** jkalas@hinshawlaw.com

RENEE J. MORTIMER, born Chicago, Illinois, February 1, 1967; admitted to bar, 1991, Illinois; 1992, U.S. District Court, Northern and Central Districts of Illinois; 1998, Indiana and U.S. District Court, Northern District of Indiana; 2000, U.S. District Court, Southern District of Indiana. *Education:* Indiana University (B.A., English, 1988); Loyola University of Chicago School of Law (J.D., 1991). *Member:* Lake County Bar Association; Illinois State Bar Association; Calumet American Inn of Court; Women's Bar Association of Illinois; Defense Research Institute. (Also at Chicago, Illinois Office). ***PRACTICE AREAS:*** Medical Malpractice Defense; Transportation; Defense Litigation; Products Liability Defense; Municipal Defense; Municipal Liability; ERISA Litigation; National and Regional Litigation Programs; Risk Management. ***Email:*** rmortimer@hinshawlaw.com

MICHAEL E. O'NEILL, born Chicago, Illinois, February 11, 1960; admitted to bar, 1991, Indiana, U.S. District Court, Southern and Northern Districts of Indiana and U.S. Court of Appeals, Seventh Circuit; 1992, Illinois; 2001, U.S. Supreme Court. *Education:* Loyola University (B.A., 1984); University of Notre Dame Law School (J.D., 1991). Member, Jessup International Moot Court Team. *Member:* Indianapolis, Lake County, Indiana State and American Bar Associations; Defense Trial Counsel of Indiana. ***PRACTICE AREAS:*** Professional Liability Litigation; Medical Malpractice; Legal Malpractice; General Liability Litigation; Insurance Coverage; Appellate. ***Email:*** moneill@hinshawlaw.com

ASSOCIATES

SCOTT B. COCKRUM, born Wiesbaden, West Germany, December 24, 1969; admitted to bar, 1998, Indiana and U.S. District Court, Northern and Southern Districts of Indiana; 2002, U.S. Court of Appeals, Seventh Circuit. *Education:* University of Southern Indiana (B.S., 1993); Indiana State University (M.A., 1995); Notre Dame Law School (J.D., 1998). Member, Moot Court Board, 1997-1998. Instructor, Paralegal Studies, Calumet College of St. Joseph, Whiting, Indiana, 2000—. *Member:* Indiana State Bar Association. ***REPORTED CASES:*** In re Estate of Harold G. Meyer, 747 N.E.2d 1159 (Ind. Ct. App. 2001); Palmer & Sons Paving, Inc. v. Northern Indiana Public Service Company, 758 N.E.2d 550 (Ind. Ct. App. 2001); Gallant Insurance Company v. Oswalt, 762 N.E.2d 1254 (Ind. Ct. App. 2002); Loomis v. Ameritech Corp., 764 N.E.2d 658 (Ind. Ct. App. 2002); McGarrity v. Berlin Metals, Inc., 774 N.E.2d 71 (Ind. Ct. App. 2002). ***PRACTICE AREAS:*** Medical Malpractice Litigation; Legal Malpractice Defense; Insurance Coverage; Appellate Advocacy; Personal Injury Defense; Insurance Defense; Products Liability Defense. ***Email:*** scockrum@hinshawlaw.com

PATRICK P. DEVINE, born Hammond, Indiana, March 14, 1971; admitted to bar, 1996, Indiana, Illinois, U.S. District Court, Southern and Northern Districts of Indiana and U.S. District Court, Northern District of Illinois. *Education:* Indiana University School of Business (B.S., Accounting, 1992); DePaul University College of Law (J.D., with honors, 1996). Member, Order of the Coif; Recipient, CALI Award for Excellence in Advanced Trial Advocacy. 2001, Recipient, Citizens/Allmerica Exceptional Performance Award. *Member:* St. Joseph County, Lake County (Indiana) and Indiana State Bar Associations. ***PRACTICE AREAS:*** Personal Injury Litigation; Medical Malpractice Defense; General Liability Litigation; Legal Malpractice Defense; Products Liability Litigation; Construction Litigation; Bad Faith Litigation; Commercial Litigation. ***Email:*** pdevine@hinshawlaw.com

MARCUS E. ELLISON, born South Bend, Indiana, April 14, 1976; admitted to bar, 2001, Indiana and U.S. District Court, Northern and Southern Districts of Indiana; 2003, U.S. Court of Appeals, Seventh Circuit. *Education:* Georgetown University (B.A., 1998); Notre Dame Law School (J.D., 2001); University of Phoenix (M.B.A., 2004). Assistant Coach, South Bend John Adams Mock Trial Team, 1999. Instructor, Ivy Tech State College, 2003-2004. Instructor, Michiana College, 2003. Instructor Grand Canyon University, 2005. Instructor, Devry University, 2005. Speaker, "Incarceration Nation: The Warehousing of America's Poor," Ivy Tech State College, South Bend, Indiana, 2003. Member, Fraternal Order of Police, 2002-2005. Member, Notre Dame Black Alumni Association, 2001-2005. Saint Joseph County Deputy Prosecutor, 2001-2004. *Member:* Lake County, Saint Joseph County and Indiana State Bar Associations. ***PRACTICE AREAS:*** Insurance Litigation; Insurance Coverage; General Liability Litigation; Transportation Litigation. ***Email:*** mellison@hinshawlaw.com

---

MATTHEW D. LaTULIP
ATTORNEY AT LAW

7654 HARVEST DRIVE
SCHERERVILLE, INDIANA 46375
Telephone: 219-864-9055
Fax: 219-864-9062
Email: mlatulip@hmllaw.net
URL: http://www.lawyers.com/latuliplaw

Personal Injury, Medical Malpractice, Auto Accidents, Slip and Fall, Wrongful Death, Criminal, DUI, Traffic Violations, Juvenile Crimes, Employment Discrimination, Sexual Harassment, Nursing Home Abuse, Insurance.

MATTHEW D. LaTULIP, born East Chicago, Indiana, January 16, 1974; admitted to bar, 2000, Indiana; U.S. District Court Northern and Southern Districts of Indiana; 2005, U.S. Court of Appeals, Seventh Circuit. *Education:* Indiana University (B.S., 1996) Indiana University School of Law (J.D., 2000). Alpha Phi Sigma; Phi Alpha Alpha. Member, Moot Court Society, Executive Production Editor Indiana International and Comparative Law Review, 1999-2000; President, Criminal Law Association, 1999-2000. *Member:* Lake County Bar Association. ***PRACTICE AREAS:*** Personal Injury; Medical Malpractice; Auto Accidents; Slip and Fall; Wrongful Death; Criminal; DUI; Traffic Violations; Juvenile Crimes; Employment Discrimination; Sexual Harassment; Nursing Home Abuse; Insurance.

TAUBER, WESTLAND & JASAITIS, P.C.

1415 EAGLE RIDGE DRIVE
SCHERERVILLE, INDIANA 46375
Telephone: 219-865-8400
Fax: 219-865-8484
URL: http://www.tauberwestland.com
Email: dww@twjlaw.com
URL: http://www.twjlawfirm.com

General Civil and Trial Practice in all State and Federal Courts. Real Estate, Municipal and Zoning, Corporate, Business, Business Planning, Contracts, Lawsuits, Strategic Planning, Banking, Wills and Probate, Trusts and Estates, Asset Protection, Estate Planning, Guardianships, Personal Injury, Automobile Accidents, Negligence Litigation, Wrongful Death, Slip and Fall, Family Law, Adoptions, Child Custody, Child Support, Divorce, Domestic Violence, Visitation Rights, Creditors' Rights and Creditor Bankruptcy, Real Estate, Criminal Law, Driving While Intoxicated, Traffic Violations.

RHETT L. TAUBER, born Hammond, Indiana, January 8, 1949; admitted to bar, 1974, Indiana, U.S. District Court, Northern District of Indiana, U.S. Court of Appeals, Seventh Circuit and U.S. Supreme Court. *Education:* Valparaiso University (B.A., 1971; J.D., 1974). Attorney, Town of Highland, 1981—. *Member:* Lake County, Indiana State and American Bar Associations; Indiana Trial Lawyers Association; The Association of Trial Lawyers of America. ***PRACTICE AREAS:*** Civil Litigation; Personal Injury; Municipal Law; Real Estate; Banking. ***Email:*** rtauber@twjlaw.com

DAVID W. WESTLAND, born Chicago, Illinois, July 15, 1970; admitted to bar, 1995, Indiana; U.S. District Court, Northern of Indiana; U.S. District Court, Southern District of Indiana. *Education:* Augustana College (B.A., magna cum laude, 1992); Valparaiso University (J.D., cum laude, 1995). Delta Theta Phi. Note Writer, 1993-1994, and Executive Editor of Publications, 1994-1995, Valparaiso University Law Review. Public Defender, 2000—. *Member:* Lake County, Indiana State and American Bar Associations. ***PRACTICE AREAS:*** Civil Litigation; Personal Injury; Banking Law; Municipal Law; Criminal Law. ***Email:*** dwestland@twjlaw.com

MICHAEL J. JASAITIS, born East Chicago, Indiana, October 5, 1974; admitted to bar, 2000, Indiana, Illinois, U.S. District Court, Northern and Southern Districts of Indiana and U.S. District Court, Northern District of Illinois. *Education:* Valparaiso University (B.A., with Honors, 1997); Valparaiso University School of Law (J.D., magna cum laude, 2000). Phi Delta Phi. Note Writer and Associate Editor, Valparaiso University Law Review. *Member:* Lake County, Indiana State, Illinois State and American Bar Associations. ***PRACTICE AREAS:*** Civil Practice; Civil Litigation; Criminal Law. ***Email:*** mjasaitis@twjlaw.com

---

NICOLE BENNETT SPICER, born Lansing, Michigan, June 3, 1973; admitted to bar, 1998, Indiana and U.S. District Court, Northern District of Indiana. *Education:* Alma College (B.A., cum laude, 1994); Valparaiso University School of Law (J.D., 1997). National Historical Honor Society; Women's Honor Society. President, Student Division, The Association of Trial Lawyers of America, 1996-1997. Formerly with: Office of the Lake County Prosecuting Attorney, 1998-2004. ***PRACTICE AREAS:*** Civil Practice; Civil Litigation; Criminal Law. ***Email:*** nspicer@twjlaw.com

REPRESENTATIVE CLIENTS: Sand Ridge Bank; Town of Highland; Greater Northwest Indiana Association of Realtors, Inc.; Willie and Steiner, Inc.; Schererville Go Center, Inc.; Bell Parts Supply, Inc.; The Calumet Press; Bank Calumet; South Central Bank; Hammond Development Corporation; City of Hammond; Lake County Transfer, Inc.; Best Disposal, Inc.; Bert's Towing and Recovery, Inc.; Double T Towing & Recovery, Inc; Buffalo Wild Wings Grill & Bar; Red Robin Gourmet Burgers & Spirits; A.P.A. Development, LLC; Krygier Properties, LLC; NIES Engineering; Orthopaedic Speialists of Northwest Indiana, Inc.

LAW OFFICE OF BART COLOMB

SCOTTSBURG, INDIANA

(See New Albany)

Social Security, Workers Compensation and Family Law.

MATTOX MATTOX & WILSON

SCOTTSBURG, INDIANA

(See New Albany)

Civil Trial Litigation. Personal Injury and Wrongful Death, Products Liability, Medical Malpractice, Insurance Law, Corporate Law, Business Torts, Family Law, Aviation Law, Labor and Employment Law, Health Care Regulations.

MERKLEY LAW OFFICE

SCOTTSBURG, INDIANA

(See Jeffersonville)

Family Law, Criminal Law, Estates and Wills, Personal Injury, Municipal Law.

LAW OFFICE OF BART COLOMB

SELLERSBURG, INDIANA

(See New Albany)

Social Security, Workers Compensation and Family Law.

JEWELL, CRUMP, ANGERMEIER & PRALL

SEYMOUR, INDIANA

(See Columbus)

General Civil and Criminal Trial Practice. Driving While Intoxicated, Drug Crimes, Juvenile Law, Parole and Probation, Traffic Violations, Personal Injury, Automobile Accidents, Slip and Fall, Wrongful Death, Wills and Probate, Trusts and Estates, Estate Planning, Taxation, Business Organizations, Commercial Law, Business Law, Business Litigation, Business Planning, Contracts, Buying and Selling a Business, Business Start-Ups, Debtor and Creditor, Collections, Business Enterprises, Corporate, Limited Liability Companies, Small Business, Partnerships, Family/Domestic Relations, Child Custody, Child Support, Divorce, Visitation Rights, Adoptions, Insurance Defense, Real Estate and Title Insurance Law.

THE PARDIECK LAW FIRM

Established in 1985

100 NORTH CHESTNUT STREET
P.O. BOX 608
SEYMOUR, INDIANA 47274
Telephone: 812-523-8686
Fax: 812-522-4199
Email: lawyers@pardiecklaw.com

Personal Injury and Wrongful Death Claims. Products and Professional Liability Law, Commercial Litigation.

FIRM PROFILE: Founded in 1985. Committed to providing clients the highest caliber of legal services available. Roger Pardieck is the first and only Indiana lawyer to be invited into The Inner Circle of Advocates. Membership is limited to one hundred lawyers across the U.S. who have been lead counsel in more than fifty jury trials and obtained one or more million dollar verdicts.

ROGER L. PARDIECK, born Seymour, Indiana, March 1, 1937; admitted to bar, 1963, Indiana. *Education:* Indiana University (A.B., 1959; LL.B., 1963); International Graduate School, University of Stockholm, Sweden. Member, The Inner Circle of Advocates, 1995—. *Member:* Indiana State (Member, Board of Governors, 1980-1982) and American Bar Associations; The Association of Trial Lawyers of America (Member, Board of Governors, 1985-1988); American Board of Trial Advocates (Advocate); Trial Lawyers for Public Justice (State Coordinator, 1992—). Fellow: American College of Trial Lawyers; Indiana Trial Lawyers Association (Member, Board of Directors, 1971—; President, 1975-1976); Indiana College of Trial Lawyers;. (Certified Civil Trial Advocate, National Board of Trial Advocacy). ***Email:*** rlp@pardiecklaw.com

---

ANDREW M. PARDIECK, born Columbus, Indiana, January 18, 1968; admitted to bar, 1996, Indiana. *Education:* Harvard College (A.B., magna cum laude, 1990); Indiana University (J.D., magna cum laude, 1996); Hokkaido University (Ph.D., 2000). Order of the Coif. Articles Editor in Journal of Global Legal Studies. Books: Shoken Torihiki Kanyu Kisei: Kaiji Gimu, Setsumei Gimu o Koete (Regulating the Solicitation of Securities Transactions: Beyond Disclosure and the Duty to Explain) (Shoji Homu Kenkyukai, March, 2002). Articles: The Formation and Transformation of Securities Law in Japan: From the Bubble to the Big Bang, UCLA Pacific Basin Law Journal, Fall 2001; Hengakuhoken Ni Kansuru Saikosai No Nihanketsu (A Study of Two Supreme Court Opinions Concerning Variable Life Insurance), Hanrei Times, No. 990 (1999); Amerika No Sosho Shakai: Zofuku Sarete Iru Gokai (American Litigiousness: Amplified Misunderstandings), Kokusai Shoji Ho Ronshu, Vol 26, No. 5, 1998; Virtuous Ways and Beautiful Customs: The Role of Alternative Dispute Resolution In Japan, Temple International and Comparative Law Journal, Spring 1997; Foreign Legal Consultants: The Changing Role of the Lawyer in a Global Economy, Indiana Journal of Global Legal Studies, Spring 1996. Translations: Kou v. Japan, Japanese Annual of International Law, No. 41, 1999. *Member:* Indiana State Bar Association; Trial Lawyers for Public Justice. ***LANGUAGES:*** Japanese. ***Email:*** amp@pardiecklaw.com

KAREN J. MELLENCAMP DAVIS, born Seymour, Indiana, July 24, 1965; admitted to bar, 1994, Indiana. *Education:* Indiana University, Bloomington (B.A., 1987; J.D., cum laude, 1994). Phi Beta Kappa. Articles Editor, Indiana Law Journal. Author: "Reading, Writing, and Sexual Harassment: Finding a Constitutional Remedy when Schools Fail to Address Peer Abuse," Indiana Law Journal, Vol. 69, Fall 1994. *Member:* Jackson County and Indiana State Bar Associations; Indiana Trial Lawyers Association; The Association of Trial Lawyers of America. ***Email:*** kmd@pardiecklaw.com

REFERENCE: Home Federal Savings Bank, Seymour, Indiana.

ADAMS & CRAMER

Established in 1947

33 WEST WASHINGTON STREET
P.O. BOX 746
SHELBYVILLE, INDIANA 46176
Telephone: 317-398-6626
Fax: 317-392-1962

Trials. General Practice. Real Estate, Insurance, Administrative Law. Wills, Probate, Trusts and Estates, Estate Planning. Banking, Tax and Corporation Law, Elder Law.

FIRM PROFILE: The firm was established in 1947 by Ralph Adams and Fred V. Cramer. The firm has a General Practice and represents clients throughout the state of Indiana. The firm's clients are primarily trusts, partnerships, limited liability, companies, estates, corporations and individuals.

RALPH ADAMS (1901-1986)

(This Listing Continued)

FRED V. CRAMER (1907-1998)

MEMBERS OF FIRM

ROBERT W. ADAMS, born Shelbyville, Indiana, 1942; admitted to bar, 1967, Indiana and U.S. District Court, Southern District of Indiana; 1971, U.S. Tax Court. *Education:* Wabash College (A.B., 1964); London School of Economics, London, England; Northwestern University (J.D., 1967). Phi Alpha Delta. *Member:* Indianapolis, Shelby County, Indiana State and American (Member, Tax Section; Member, Committees on: Partnership; Fiduciary Tax) Bar Associations. ***PRACTICE AREAS:*** Estate Planning; Probate; Real Estate; Administrative. ***Email:*** radams@lighthound.com

N. GREGG GRAHAM, born 1946; admitted to bar, 1972, Indiana. *Education:* Butler University (B.S., bus. adm., 1968); Indiana Universitiy School of Law (J.D., 1972). *Member:* Shelby County and Indiana State Bar Associations. ***PRACTICE AREAS:*** Estate Planning; Probate; Real Estate; Agricultural Law; Zoning Law.

ROBERT E. MARSHALL

Established in 1958

ONE COURTSIDE BUILDING
18 WEST POLK STREET
SHELBYVILLE, INDIANA 46176
Telephone: 317-398-9745
Fax: 317-398-1013
Email: remarshall@lightbound.com
URL: http://www.remarshalllaw.com

General and Trial Practice, Personal Injury, Wrongful Death, Automobile Accidents, Slip and Fall, Dog Bites, Products Liability, Medical Negligence, Wills, Trusts and Estates, Estate Planning, Asset Protection, Guardianships, Family Law, Domestic Relations, Adoptions, Child Custody, Child Support, Divorce, Visitation Rights, Business Law, Business Contracts, Business Litigation, Business Planning, Business Enterprises, Partnerships, Small Business, Corporate, Limited Liability Company Law, Buying and Selling a Business, Business Start-Ups, Criminal Law, Drug Crimes, DWI, DUI, Traffic Violations.

ROBERT E. MARSHALL, born Shelbyville, Indiana, August 29, 1931; admitted to bar, 1956, Indiana; 1961, U.S. District Court, Southern District of Indiana; 1964, U.S. Supreme Court. *Education:* Indiana University (B.S., 1953; J.D., 1956). Member, Board of Trustees, Carnegie Public Library, Shelbyville, 1965-1970. *Member:* Shelby County (Secretary, Treasurer, 1960-1961; Vice President, 1969-1970; President, 1970-1971) and Indiana State (Chairman, Sub-Committee on Publicity, Public Relations Executive Committee, 1964-1970; Member, Legal Economics Committee, 1980-1982) Bar Associations; Indiana Trial Lawyers Association; The Association of Trial Lawyers of America; American Board of Trial Advocates. [Staff Judge Advocate, USAF, 1956-1958]

REFERENCE: Bank One, Indianapolis, N.A., Shelbyville, Indiana.

HART BELL LLC

SHOALS, INDIANA

(See Vincennes)

General Practice. Litigation, Insurance, Banking, Corporate, Employment, Probate and Estate Planning, State and Federal Tax Law, Real Estate, Construction, Commercial, Business, Elder, Creditors Rights, Personal Injury, Family Law and Criminal Defense.

BAKER & DANIELS LLP

Established in 1863

FIRST BANK BUILDING
205 WEST JEFFERSON BOULEVARD, SUITE 250
SOUTH BEND, INDIANA 46601
Telephone: 574-234-4149
Fax: 574-239-1900
URL: http://www.bakerdaniels.com

Indianapolis, Indiana Office: 300 North Meridian Street, Suite 2700, 46204. Telephone: 317-237-0300. Fax: 317-237-1000.

Fort Wayne, Indiana Office: 111 East Wayne Street, Suite 800, 46802. Telephone: 260-424-8000. Fax: 260-460-1700.

Elkhart, Indiana Office: 317 West Franklin Street, P.O. Box 507, 46515-0507. Telephone: 574-296-6000. Fax: 574-296-6001.

Indianapolis-96th Street, Indiana Office: Parkwood Six, 600 East 96th Street, Suite 600, 46240. Telephone: 317-569-9600. Fax: 317-569-4800.

Washington, D.C. Office: 805 15th Street, N.W., Suite 700, 20005. Telephone: 202-312-7440. Fax: 202-312-7460.

Qingdao, China Office: 4/F, Office Tower, Crowne Plaza Qingdao, No. 76 Hong Kong Middle Road, 266071. Telephone: +011-86-532-575-1051. Fax: +011-86-532-575-1055.

Beijing, China Office: Room 1919, Tower 2, China World Trade Center, No. 1 JianGuoMenWai Avenue, 100004. Telephone: +86-10-6505-7733. Fax: +86-10-6505-8730.

Antitrust, Bankruptcy, Business Planning, Commercial, Corporate Finance, Creditors Rights, Employee Benefits, Employment, Environment, Estate and Probate, Family, Financial, Food and Drug, Government Affairs, Health Care, Insurance, Intellectual Property, International, Legislative, Litigation, Medical Technology Regulation, Municipal, Nonprofit, Product Liability, Real Estate, Securities, Sports, Tax, Transportation, Utilities, Year 2000, Zoning and Land Use Law.

(This Listing Continued)

FIRM PROFILE: Since 1863 we have been helping clients do business throughout Indiana, across the country and around the world. From Fortune 500 corporations to regional businesses, local governments and individuals, clients look to Baker & Daniels LLP for excellence in all areas of legal practice, for a creative and individualized approach to solving client problems, and for a deep understanding of business, law and government. More than 350 Baker and Daniels' professionals serve clients from the firm's seven offices in Indiana, Washington, D.C. and China (we are one of only 31 U.S. law firms licensed to practice in China). Our service to clients is enhanced by our Washington, D.C. government affairs consulting subsidiary, Sagamore Associates, and our exclusive Indiana membership in Lex Mundi, an association of more than 158 independent law firms around the world.

LAW FIRM ALLIANCES/ASSOCIATIONS: **TAGLAW (The Appleton Group Legal Network):** *The Firm is a member of TAGLaw, an international association of prominent law firms and an exclusive Indiana Member of Lex Mundi.*

MEMBERS OF FIRM

THOMAS J. BRUNNER, JR., admitted to bar, 1966, Indiana. *Education:* University of Notre Dame (A.B., 1963; J.D., 1966). Staff Attorney, National Labor Relations Board, Washington, D.C., 1968. Legislative Assistant to U.S. Senator R. Vance Hartke, 1969-1971. Adjunct Professor, Labor and Equal Employment Opportunity Law, Indiana University at South Bend, 1976-1985. City Attorney, South Bend, Indiana, 1976-1979. Member, Indiana Supreme Court Disciplinary Commission, 1996-2001. *Member:* St. Joseph County, Indiana State and Seventh Circuit Bar Associations. ***PRACTICE AREAS:*** Employment Law; Commercial and Employment Litigation. ***Email:*** thomas.brunner@bakerd.com

GERARD T. GALLAGHER, born 1966; admitted to bar, 1992, Indiana and U.S. District Court, Northern and Southern Districts of Indiana; 1996, U.S. Court of Appeals for the Federal Circuit; registered to practice before U.S. Patent and Trademark Office. *Education:* University of Notre Dame (B.S., 1989; J.D., cum laude, 1992). Member, 1991, Lead Articles Editor, 1992, Notre Dame Law Review. Author: "State Action and the Peremptory Challenges: Evolution of the Court's Treatment and Impressions for Georgia v. McCollum," 67 Notre Dame Law Rev. 1049, 1992. *Member:* American Intellectual Property Law Association. ***PRACTICE AREAS:*** Intellectual Property. ***Email:*** gerard.gallagher@bakerd.com

CARL A. GRECI, born 1962; admitted to bar, 1993, Indiana and U.S. District Court, Northern and Southern Districts of Indiana; 1994, U.S. Court of Appeals, Seventh Circuit. *Education:* Indiana University (B.A., 1983); Indiana University School of Law (J.D., cum laude, 1993); Miami University (M.G.S., 1985). Managing Editor, Indiana Law Journal. Author: Note, "Use It and Lose It: The Employer's Absolute Right Under ERISA Section 510 to Engage in Post-Claim Modifications of Employee Welfare Benefit Plans," Vol. 68, Indiana Law Journal, pg. 177, 1992. *Member:* St. Joseph County, Seventh Circuit and Indiana State Bar Associations. ***PRACTICE AREAS:*** Commercial Litigation. ***Email:*** carl.greci@bakerd.com

M. PATRICIA HACKETT, admitted to bar, 1991, Indiana and Michigan. *Education:* University of Notre Dame (B.A., cum laude, 1981; M.A., 1983; J.D., cum laude, 1991). ***PRACTICE AREAS:*** Health Care. ***Email:*** patricia.hackett@bakerd.com

RICHARD L. HILL, born 1947; admitted to bar, 1972, Indiana; 1985, U.S. Supreme Court. *Education:* LaSalle University (B.A., 1969); University of Notre Dame (J.D., 1972). Adjunct Professor, University of Notre Dame Graduate School of Business, 1988-1989. Staff Attorney, 1972, Deputy Director, 1973, Executive Director, 1974-1980, Legal Services Program of Northern Indiana. City Attorney, South Bend, Indiana, 1980-1985. State Chairperson, 1985-1986 and Member, Committee on Local Government, Finance, Bonds and Taxation, 1986, National Institute of Municipal Law Officers. Corporation Counsel, South Bend, Indiana, 1985-1986. *Member:* St. Joseph County and Indiana State Bar Associations; National Association of Bond Lawyers. ***PRACTICE AREAS:*** Corporation Law; Municipal Finance; Municipal Law; Sports Law. ***Email:*** richard.hill@bakerd.com

JAMES M. MATTHEWS, born 1960; admitted to bar, 1985, Indiana; U.S. District Court, Northern and Southern Districts of Indiana; U.S. Court of Appeals, Seventh Circuit. *Education:* Wabash College (A.B., summa cum laude, 1982); Ohio State University (J.D., with honors, 1985). Phi Beta Kappa; Delta Theta Phi. *Member:* St. Joseph County and Indiana State Bar Associations. ***PRACTICE AREAS:*** Bankruptcy; Litigation. ***Email:*** james.matthews@bakerd.com

RANDOLPH R. ROMPOLA, born 1962; admitted to bar, 1991, Indiana. *Education:* Luzerne County Community College (A.S., 1982); King's College (B.A., magna cum laude, 1984); Notre Dame Law School (J.D., magna cum laude, 1991). Symposium and Note Editor, Notre Dame Law Review, 1990-1991. *Member:* St. Joseph County, Indiana State and American Bar Associations; National Association of Bond Lawyers. [Captain, U.S. Air Force, 1984-1988]. ***PRACTICE AREAS:*** Municipal Law; Public Finance; Government. ***Email:*** randolph.rompola@bakerd.com

EDWARD A. SULLIVAN, III, born 1961; admitted to bar, 1993, Indiana; U.S. District Court, Southern and Northern Districts of Indiana. *Education:* Villanova University (B.A., 1983); University of Notre Dame (J.D., 1993). Recipient: The A. Harold Weber Award for Achievement in Oral Argument; The Jon E. Krupnick Award for Excellence in Trial Advocacy; The Kraft W. Eidman Award, National Trial Competition National Championship Team, 1993. ***PRACTICE AREAS:*** Litigation. ***Email:*** edward.sullivan@bakerd.com

PETER G. TRYBULA, born 1955; admitted to bar, 1983, Illinois and U.S. District Court, Northern District of Illinois; 1991, Indiana. *Education:* Wabash College (B.A., magna cum laude, 1977); Harvard Law School (J.D., magna cum laude, 1983). Phi Beta Kappa. ***PRACTICE AREAS:*** Mergers and Acquisitions; Commercial Finance; Securities; Real Estate. ***Email:*** peter.trybula@bakerd.com

COUNSEL

D. LUCETTA POPE, born 1962; admitted to bar, 1988, Illinois; 1994, Minnesota; 1996, Indiana. *Education:* Princeton University (B.A., summa cum laude, 1984); Stanford University (J.D., 1987). Member, Stamford Law Review. ***PRACTICE AREAS:*** Litigation. ***Email:*** lucetta.pope@bakerd.com

(This Listing Continued)

ROBERT A. WADE, born 1963; admitted to bar, 1989, Ohio; 1993, Indiana. *Education:* Bowling Green State University (B.A., summa cum laude, 1986); The Ohio State University College of Law (J.D., summa cum laude, 1989). Order of the Coif. Managing Editor, Ohio State Law Journal. General Counsel and Organizational Integrity Officer for St. Joseph Regional Medical Center, Inc. *Member:* American Bar Association (Member, Health Law Section); American Health Lawyers Association. ***PRACTICE AREAS:*** Health Care; Corporate Law; Sports Law. ***Email:*** robert.wade@bakerd.com

ASSOCIATES

CARA R. BROOK, admitted to bar, 2004, Indiana. *Education:* Indiana University (B.A., 2000); University of Miami (J.D., 2004). Recipient: John T. Evans Scholarship; Dean's Certificate of Achievement for Outstanding Academic Performance in Lawyering Skills and Ethics, University of Miami School of Law. *Member:* St. Joseph County and Indiana State Bar Associations. ***PRACTICE AREAS:*** Civil Litigation. ***Email:*** cara.brook@bakerd.com

ALISON G. FOX, born 1970; admitted to bar, 1995, Illinois; 1999, Indiana. *Education:* University of Illinois (B.S., 1992); Northwestern University (J.D., 1995). Law Clerk to Honorable Robert L. Miller, Jr., U.S. District Court, Northern District of Indiana. ***PRACTICE AREAS:*** Litigation; Employment Law; Product Liability. ***Email:*** alison.fox@bakerd.com

PETER J. GILLIN, born 1969; admitted to bar, 1998, Rhode Island; 2000, Massachusetts (Not admitted in Indiana). *Education:* University of Notre Dame (B.A., 1992); Boston College Law School (J.D., cum laude, 1998). Formerly with: Hale and Dorr, Boston, Massachusetts, 2000-2003; Edwards and Angell, Providence, Rhode Island, 1998-1999. ***Email:*** peter.gillin@bakerd.com

JEFF R. HECK, born 1956; admitted to bar, 1998, Indiana. *Education:* University of Notre Dame (B.B.A., 1991; J.D., magna cum laude, 1998). *Member:* St. Joseph County and Indiana State Bar Associations; Seventh Circuit Bar Association; Transportation Lawyers Association; Association for Transportation Law, Logistics and Policy. ***PRACTICE AREAS:*** Litigation; Transportation; Products Liability. ***Email:*** jeff.heck@bakerd.com

RAELEE C. HUDSON, born 1972; admitted to bar, 1999, Indiana. *Education:* University of California, Los Angeles (B.A., summa cum laude, 1994); Valparaiso University School of Law (J.D., summa cum laude, 1999). Phi Beta Kappa. Executive Editor, Student Writing, Valparaiso University Law Review. Author: Note, Striking a Balance in Indiana: Employee Access to Employment Records Maintained by Employers, 33 Val. U.L. Rev. (1999). ***PRACTICE AREAS:*** Estate Planning; Business Planning. ***Email:*** raelee.hudson@bakerd.com

JENNIFER BICKLEY HULL, admitted to bar, 1997, Michigan; 1998, Indiana. *Education:* Michigan State University (B.A., 1993); University of Detroit Mercy School of Law (J.D., 1997). ***PRACTICE AREAS:*** Labor and Employment. ***Email:*** jennifer.hull@bakerd.com

THOMAS J. MAUCH, admitted to bar, 2001, Indiana. *Education:* Wayne State University (B.S., 1996); University of Notre Dame School of Law (J.D., 2001). *Member:* Indiana State Bar Association. ***PRACTICE AREAS:*** Intellectual Property. ***Email:*** tom.mauch@bakerd.com

SHAWN E. PETERSON, admitted to bar, 2003, Indiana. *Education:* Indiana University, Kelley School of Business, Bloomington (B.S., with high distinction, 2000); University of Notre Dame Law School (J.D., 2003). White Scholar, Journal of Law Ethics and Public Policy. Invitee, Notre Dame Law Review. ***Email:*** shawn.peterson@bakerd.com

DAVID R. PRUITT, born 1970; admitted to bar, 1999, Virginia and U.S. Court of Appeals, Fourth Circuit; 2000, District of Columbia; 2002, U.S. District Court, Eastern District of Virginia and U.S. District Court, Northern District of Oklahoma; 2003, U.S. District Court, Northern District of Indiana (Not admitted in Indiana). *Education:* University of Notre Dame (B.B.A., cum laude, 1992; J.D., cum laude, 1999). Member, Notre Dame University Law Review. *Member:* American Bar Association; Defense Research Institute; Intellectual Property Law Association. ***PRACTICE AREAS:*** Products Liability; Intellectual Property. ***Email:*** david.pruitt@bakerd.com

AMY M. STEKETEE, admitted to bar, 2004, Indiana. *Education:* Indiana University (B.A., 1992; M.S. Ed., 1995); Indiana University School of Law - Bloomington (J.D., cum laude, 2004). Managing Editor, Indiana Journal of Global Legal Studies, 2002-2004. *Member:* Indiana State Bar Association. ***PRACTICE AREAS:*** Business Litigation. ***Email:*** amy.steketee@bakerd.com

DANIEL TYCHONIEVICH, admitted to bar, 1996, Indiana and U.S. District Court, Northern and Southern Districts of Indiana; registered to practice before U.S. Patent and Trademark Office. *Education:* Ohio State University (B.S.W.E., 1981); Notre Dame Law school (J.D., cum laude, 1996). Registered Professional Engineer, Ohio, 1986—. ***PRACTICE AREAS:*** Intellectual Property. ***Email:*** daniel.tychonievich@bakerd.com

(For complete biographical data on other Members of Firm, Of Counsel and Associates, See Professional Biographies at Indianapolis, Fort Wayne, Elkhart, Indiana, Washington, D.C., Qingdao and Beijing, China)

BARNES & THORNBURG LLP

600 1ST SOURCE BANK CENTER
100 NORTH MICHIGAN
SOUTH BEND, INDIANA 46601-1632
Telephone: 574-233-1171
FAX: 574-237-1125
URL: http://www.btlaw.com

Indianapolis, Indiana Office: 11 South Meridian Street, 46204. Telephone: 317-236-1313. FAX: 317-231-7433.

Fort Wayne, Indiana Office: 600 One Summit Square, 46802. Telephone: 260-423-9440. FAX: 260-424-8316.

Elkhart, Indiana Office: 121 West Franklin Street, Suite 200, 46516. Telephone: 574-293-0681. FAX: 574-296-2535.

(This Listing Continued)

BARNES & THORNBURG LLP, South Bend—Continued

Chicago, Illinois Office: One North Wacker Drive, Suite 4400, 60606-2833. Telephone: 312-357-1313. FAX: 312-759-5646.
Washington, D.C. Office: 750 17th Street, N.W., Suite 900, 20006. Telephone: 202-289-1313. FAX: 202-289-1330.
Grand Rapids, Michigan Office: 300 Ottawa Avenue, N.W., Suite 500, 49503. Telephone: 616-742-3930. FAX: 616-742-3999.

Acquisitions and Divestitures, Ad Valorem Tax, Administrative Law, Affirmative Action, Agriculture Law, Americans with Disabilities Act, Antidumping, Antitrust, Antitrust and Trade Regulation, Appellate Practice, Attorney Grievances, Automotive Warranty Law, Aviation and Aerospace, Aviation Law, Banking Law, Banking Regulations, Bankruptcy, Bankruptcy Reorganization, Banks and Banking, Biochemical Patents, Biomedical Products Liability, Biomedical Technology, Biotechnology Patent Prosecution, Bond Law, Brain Injury, Breach of Warranty, Brown Fields Redevelopment, Business Immigration, Business Law, Business Litigation, Business Planning, Business Regulatory and Administrative, Business Start-ups, Business Succession Planning, Business Taxation, Business Torts, Business Transactions, Business Transfers, Buying and Selling of Businesses, Cable TV, Cargo Claims, Charitable Trusts and Foundations, Chemical Intellectual Property, Chemical Patent Prosecution, Chemical Patents, Chemical Products Liability, Civil Appeals, Civil Litigation, Civil Practice, Civil RICO, Class Action Defense, Clean Air Act, Clean Water Act, Closely Held Business Estate Planning, Closely Held Businesses, Closely Held Business Law, Closely Held Corporations, Collective Bargaining, Commercial Bankruptcy, Commercial Finance Law, Commercial Law, Commercial Leasing and Financing, Commercial Litigation, Commercial Conveyancing, Commercial Real Estate, Commercial Real Estate Acquisition, Commercial Real Estate Development, Commercial Real Estate Finance, Commercial Transactions, Commodities Fraud, Communications and Media, Complex Commercial Litigation, Complex Litigation, Computer and Software Patents, Computer Law, Computers and Software, Conflicts of Interest, Construction Labor Law, Construction Law, Consumer Credit, Contract Litigation, Cooperatives, Copyrights, Corporate Finance, Corporate Formation, Corporate Law, Corporate Taxation, Corporate Tax Planning, Countervailing Duties, Covenants Not To Compete, Creditors Rights, Creditors Rights in Bankruptcy, Criminal Defense, Criminal Law, Criminal Tax Audits, Customs Law, Dealer and Distributor Termination, Debt and Equity Finance, Decedents Estates, Defense Litigation, Design Patents, Disability Insurance Defense, Discrimination, Distribution, Drug and Medical Device Defense, Economic Development, Education Law, Elder Law, Election, Campaign and Political Law, Electric Power, Electric Utilities, Electrical Intellectual Property, Electrical Patents, Electro-mechanical Patents, Electronic Commerce, Electronic Patents, Eminent Domain, Employee Benefits, Employee Stock Ownership Plans, Employment Defense, Employment Discrimination, Employment Law, Employment Litigation, Energy, Energy Contracts, Energy Regulation, Environmental Administrative Law, Environmental Cleanup, Environmental Compliance, Environmental Criminal Defense, Environmental Law, Environmental Litigation, Environmental Permitting, Environmental Real Estate, Environmental Regulation, Environmental Risk Management, Equal Employment Opportunity Law, ERISA Litigation, Estate Administration, Estate and Gift Taxation, Estate Planning, Estate Planning and Taxation, Estate Planning and Administration, Estate Planning and Probate, Estate Planning for Parents of Handicapped Children, Estate Planning for Unmarried Individuals, Executive Compensation, Executive Severance Contracts, Export Regulation, Fair Employment Practices, Family and Medical Leave Act, Family Business Successions, Family Wealth Transfer, Federal and State Administrative Regulatory Practice, Federal and State Legislative Practice, Federal Civil Litigation, Federal Civil Practice, Federal Criminal Law, Federal Estate and Gift Taxation, Federal Litigation, Federal Tax Controversies, Federal Taxation, Fiduciary Income Tax, Finance, Financial Transactions, First Party Insurance, Foreign Investment in the United States, Freight Claims, Freight Loss and Damage, Gaming Law, Gaming Licensing, Gas Utilities, General Litigation, Government, Government Affairs, Government Agency Practice, Government Contracts, Government Investigations, Government Relations, Groundwater Contamination, Hazardous Materials and Substances, Hazardous Waste, Hazardous Waste Liability, Head Injury, Health Care, Health Care Corporate Law, Health Care Contracts, Health Care Fraud, Health Care Licensing, Health Care Litigation, Health Care Mergers and Acquisitions, Health Care Regulation, Health Care Reimbursement, Health Law, Heavy Equipment Products Liability, Immigration Law, Industrial Revenue Bond Law, Inheritance Tax, Initial Public Offerings, Insurance, Insurance Bad Faith, Insurance Coverage, Insurance Litigation, Insurance Regulation, Integrated Health Care Delivery Systems, Intellectual Property, Intellectual Property General Prosecution, Intellectual Property Infringement, Intellectual Property Licensing, Intellectual Property Litigation, Intellectual Property Procurement, Intellectual Property Protection, Intellectual Property Rights, International Business Law, International Intellectual Property, International Law, International Patents, International Trade, International Transportation Law, Internet Law, Internet Trademark Law, Joint Ventures, Labor and Employment, Labor Arbitration, Labor Law, Labor Relations, Land Use, Lease Law, Leasing, Legal Ethics and Professional Responsibility, Legal Malpractice Defense, Legislative Practice, Licensing, Life Insurance Defense, Limited Liability Company Law, Limited Partnerships, Liquor Licensing, Litigation, Loans, Lobbying, Local Government Law, Logistics, Long Term Care, Managed Care, Managed Care Contracts, Management Employment Law, Management Labor Law, Manufacturers Liability, Maritime Regulations, Mechanical Intellectual Property, Mechanical Patents, Media Law, Mediation, Medical Antitrust, Medical Intellectual Property, Medical Patents, Mental Health Law, Mergers, Acquisitions and Divestitures, Mergers and Acquisitions, Mineral Taxation, Molecular Biology Patents, Motor Carrier Law, Motor Carrier Regulation, Multi-Employer Pensions, Municipal Bonds, Municipal Bonds Taxation, Municipal Finance, Municipal Law, Municipal Leasing, Municipal Redevelopment, Municipal Securities, Municipal Taxation, National Labor Relations Act, Neurolaw, Nonprofit and Charitable Organizations, Nonprofit Organizations Law, North American Free Trade Agreement, Occupational Safety and Health, OSHA, Partnership Law, Partnership Taxation, Patent Infringement, Patent Interference Practice, Patent Litigation, Patent Prosecution, Patents, PCT Legal Export, Personal Injury, Personal Injury Defense, Pesticide Litigation, Pharmaceutical Intellectual Property, Pharmaceutical Patents, Physician Contracts, Physician Practices, Planning and Land Use, Power Line Contact Injury, Probate, Probate Litigation, Products Liability, Products Liability Defense, Professional Liability, Property Law, Property Tax, Property Tax Abatement, Property Tax Appeals, Psychological Injury, Public Finance, Public Sector Labor Relations, Public Utility Law, Railroad Law, Real Estate, Real Estate Acquisitions, Real Estate Contracts, Real Estate Development, Real Estate Finance, Real Estate Licensing, Real Estate Secured Lending, Real Estate Title Insurance, Real Property, Real Property Acquisitions, Real Property Finance, Reorganizations, Resource Conservation and Recovery Act (RCRA), Retirement Benefit Plans, School Law, Securities, Securities Litigation, Securitization, Semiconductor Technology, Sexual Harassment, Small Business Corporations, State Government Law, State Tax Controversies, State Taxation, Structured Finance, Succession Planning, Superfund, Tax Controversies, Tax Exempt Finance, Tax Exempt Organizations, Tax Increment Finance, Tax Law, Tax Litigation, Taxation, Technology and Science, Technology Law, Technology Licensing, Technology Transfers, Telecommunications Competition, Telecommunications Law, Theft of Trade Secrets, Title VII Discrimination, Title IX Discrimination, Tort Defense, Toxic Exposure, Toxic Tort Class Actions, Toxic Torts, Toxic Tort Defense, Trade Dress, Trade Secrets, Trademark Litigation, Trademarks, Trademark Prosecution, Trademark Protection, Trademark Registration, Transportation, Transportation Safety, Trial Practice, Trusts and Estates, Unfair Competition, Unfair Trade, Uniform Commercial Codes, Union Contract Negotiations, Union Elections, Utilities, Utility Law, Wage and Hour Law, WARN Act, Water Pollution, Water Quality, Water Utilities, Wetland Regulation, White Collar Crime, White Collar Criminal Defense, Wills, Workers Compensation, Workouts, World Trade Organization, Wrongful Death, Wrongful Termination, Wrongful Termination Defense, Zoning, Planning and Land Use.

FIRM PROFILE: Quality. Service. Efficiency. Communication. These are the cornerstones of the firm's culture and the keys to its success.

Established on January 1, 1982, Barnes & Thornburg LLP is relatively young; however, its founding date belies the firm's rich history. The firm's roots can be traced to two cities, South Bend and Indianapolis. Our northern Indiana presence began in 1926 with the establishment of Seebirt Oare & Omacht, and later grew when they merged with an Elkhart firm, Cawley and Harman. In Indianapolis, four partners opened Barnes Hickam Pantzer & Boyd on September 13, 1940. They began the firm with 13 people in an office of 13 rooms on the 13th floor of the Merchants Bank Building, the tallest in Indiana at that time. The number 13 has proven to be a lucky number for Barnes & Thornburg LLP.

Since 1982, the firm has opened offices in Chicago, Fort Wayne, Washington, D.C., Grand Rapids and merged with Jenkins, Coffey, Hyland, Badger & Conard, an intellectual property firm; Roberts, Ryder, Rogers & Scism, a labor and employment law firm; Church, Nilsson & Paulen of Elkhart; Roemer & Mintz, LLP, of South Bend and, most recently, Lee, Mann, Smith, McWilliams, Sweeney & Ohlson of Chicago. The firm has also been joined by Gallucci, Hopkins & Theisen, P.C., a Fort Wayne firm with an extensive labor and employment practice, and Johnson Lawhead Buth & Pope, P.C., an Indianapolis firm with a concentration in estate planning. Today Barnes & Thornburg LLP is the largest law firm in Indiana and one of the largest in the Midwest. More than 390 attorneys provide legal services to more than 11,000 international, national, regional and local clients.

With offices in Indianapolis, Fort Wayne, South Bend, Elkhart, Chicago, Washington, D.C., and Grand Rapids, we are a business-minded law firm serving clients ranging from Fortune 100 companies and governmental entities to individuals and nonprofit organizations. We represent the interests of businesses in our primary practices: business, tax and real estate, creditors' rights, energy, telecommunications and utilities, environmental law, governmental services and finance, healthcare, intellectual property, labor and employment law, litigation, appellate, business and technology, construction law, e-commerce, economic development, entrepreneurial services, financial institutions, international, media, pension and benefits litigation, property tax, transportation and white collar crime. Each of our offices offers a unique blend of services which collectively make Barnes & Thornburg LLP a diverse and dynamic legal resource for our clients and communities.

We have lawyers involved at city, state and national levels of the legal profession as officers, chairpersons and committee members in legal organizations. Others are authors, presenters and drafters of legislation. Most of our lawyers are active in their communities and provide civic leadership. Each office sponsors, contributes to, and often leads, an array of community activities.

LAW FIRM ALLIANCES/ASSOCIATIONS: **TECHLAW GROUP**

TERRALEX, THE WORLDWIDE NETWORK OF INDEPENDENT LAW FIRMS

PARTNERS

STEPHEN A. SEALL, admitted to bar, 1966, Indiana. *Education:* Purdue University (B.A., with distinction, 1963); Cornell University Graduate School of Business and Public Administration; University of Notre Dame (LL.B., 1966). Book Review and Survey Note Editor, Notre Dame Law Review, 1965-1966. *Member:* Indiana State (Chair, Taxation Section, 1977-1978) and American (Section of Taxation, Civil and Criminal Tax Penalties Committee) Bar Associations. Fellow: American College of Tax Counsel; American Bar Foundation; Indiana Bar Foundation. ***PRACTICE AREAS:*** Taxation; Mergers, Acquisitions and Divestitures; Federal Tax Controversies; Criminal Tax Audits; Corporate Law; Real Estate. ***Email:*** stephen.seall@btlaw.com

NELSON J. VOGEL, JR., admitted to bar, 1971, Indiana and Michigan. *Education:* Miami University (B.S., with honors, 1968); University of Notre Dame (J.D., cum laude, 1971). Executive Editor, Notre Dame Lawyer, 1970-1971. Certified Public Accountant, Indiana, 1974. *Member:* Indiana State Bar Association (Chair, Taxation Section, 1981-1982); State Bar of Michigan. ***PRACTICE AREAS:*** Business Law; Taxation; Buying and Selling of Businesses; Business Succession Planning; Family Business Successions; Closely Held Business Law. ***Email:*** nelson.vogel@btlaw.com

ROGER W. BENKO, admitted to bar, 1972, Indiana and Michigan. *Education:* Northwestern University (B.S., 1968); Valparaiso University (J.D., 1972). Phi Alpha Delta. ***PRACTICE AREAS:*** Corporate Law; Real Estate; Labor and Employment. ***Email:*** roger.benko@btlaw.com

BRIAN J. LAKE, admitted to bar, 1971, Michigan; 1972, Indiana and Florida. *Education:* University of Notre Dame (B.A., 1968); University of Michigan (J.D., cum laude, 1971). *Member:* St. Joseph County, Indiana State and American Bar Associations; State Bar

(This Listing Continued)

of Michigan; The Florida Bar. ***PRACTICE AREAS:*** Business Law; Business Succession Planning; Buying and Selling of Businesses; Employee Benefits; Employee Stock Ownership Plans; Executive Compensation. ***Email:*** brian.lake@btlaw.com

RICHARD L. MINTZ, admitted to bar, 1972, Michigan; 1976, Indiana. *Education:* University of Oxford, England and Antioch College (B.A., 1969); University of Michigan (J.D., 1971). *Member:* St. Joseph County, Indiana State and American Bar Associations. ***PRACTICE AREAS:*** Business; Real Estate. ***Email:*** dick.mintz@btlaw.com

LAURENCE A. McHUGH, admitted to bar, 1973, Illinois; 1988, Arizona; 1989, Indiana. *Education:* Indiana University (A.B., magna cum laude, 1970; J.D., cum laude, 1973). Phi Beta Kappa. Environmental Rulemaking Study Committee, Indiana General Assembly, 1994. *Member:* Indiana State (Member, Environmental Law Section), Illinois State (Chair, Council, Environmental Control Law Section, 1982-1983) and American (Chair, Administrative and Governmental Law Committee, 1986-1987; Chair, Natural Resources Committee, General Practice Section, 1990; Chair, Environmental Law Committee, 1990-1991; Member, Air Quality Committee and Water Quality Committee, Environment, Energy & Resources Section, 1990—) Bar Associations; Air and Waste Management Association; Northern Indiana Environmental Management Association; St. Joseph County Solid Waste Management Advisory Committee (Chair, 1991—); Environmental Task Force, Chamber of Commerce of St. Joseph County (Chair, 1997—). ***PRACTICE AREAS:*** Environmental Law; Clean Air Act; Clean Water Act; Resource Conservation and Recovery Act (RCRA); Superfund; Environmental Real Estate. ***Email:*** larry.mchugh@btlaw.com

DOUGLAS K. DIETERLY, admitted to bar, 1980, Indiana. *Education:* Ball State University (B.A., summa cum laude, 1977); Indiana University (J.D., magna cum laude, 1980). National Product Liability Defense Counsel: Whirlpool Corporation; UHaul International, Inc.; Dometic Corporation. *Member:* St. Joseph County, Indiana State and American Bar Associations; Defense Research Institute; Indiana Bar Foundation. ***REPORTED CASES:*** Estate of Shebel v. Yaskaw Elec. Am., Inc., 713 N.E.2d 275 (ind. 1999); Mlott v. Whirlpool Corporation, 252 A.D.2d 990; 676 N.Y.S.2d 383 (N.Y. App. Div. 1998); York v. Union Carbide Corporation, 586 N.E.2d 861 (In.App. 1992). ***PRACTICE AREAS:*** Litigation; Products Liability; Neurolaw; Brain Injury; Head Injury; Personal Injury Defense; Power Line Contact Injury; Psychological Injury; Canadian Product Litigation Defense; Product Safety; Product Warning Labels; Product Documentation. ***Email:*** douglas.dieterly@btlaw.com

ALAN B. FELDBAUM, admitted to bar, 1981, Kentucky; 1989, Indiana; 1994, Illinois. *Education:* Indiana University (B.A., 1977); University of Kentucky (J.D., 1981). Phi Beta Kappa; Phi Delta Phi. *Member:* National Association of Bond Lawyers. ***PRACTICE AREAS:*** Municipal Law; Municipal Bonds; Business Law; Mergers, Acquisitions and Divestitures; Health Care Mergers and Acquisitions; Loans. ***Email:*** alan.feldbaum@btlaw.com

TIMOTHY J. ABESKA, admitted to bar, 1982, Indiana; 1986, Michigan. *Education:* University of Michigan (B.A., with distinction, 1979); University of Notre Dame (J.D., 1982). Member, Panel of Arbitrators, American Arbitration Association. *Member:* St. Joseph County, Indiana State and American Bar Associations; State Bar of Michigan; Association of Transportation Law Professionals; Robert A. Grant Inn of Court; Defense Research Institute. Fellow, Indiana Bar Foundation. ***PRACTICE AREAS:*** Litigation; Construction Claims; Business Torts; Creditors Rights. ***Email:*** tim.abeska@btlaw.com

GERALD F. LUTKUS, admitted to bar, 1982, Illinois; 1987, Indiana. *Education:* University of Notre Dame (B.A., 1974; J.D., 1982). Executive Editor, Notre Dame Lawyer, 1981-1982. Law Clerk to Hon. Charles Clark, Chief Judge, U.S. Court of Appeals, Fifth Circuit, 1982-1983. ***PRACTICE AREAS:*** Labor and Employment Law; Collective Bargaining; Employment Litigation; Management Labor Law; Litigation; Media Law. ***Email:*** gerald.lutkus@btlaw.com

NANCY L. ICKLER, admitted to bar, 1984, Indiana. *Education:* Michigan State University (B.A., summa cum laude, 1972); University of California at Berkeley (Ph.D., 1981); University of Notre Dame (J.D., summa cum laude, 1984). Phi Beta Kappa. ***PRACTICE AREAS:*** Trusts and Estates; Estate Planning; Estate Administration; Estate and Gift Taxation; Tax Exempt Organizations; Charitable Trusts and Foundations. ***Email:*** nancy.ickler@btlaw.com

KATHLEEN K. BRICKLEY, admitted to bar, 1982, Indiana; U.S. District Court, Northern and Southern Districts of Indiana; U.S. Court of Appeals, Seventh Circuit. *Education:* Miami University (B.S., 1977); University of Notre Dame (J.D., 1982). ***PRACTICE AREAS:*** Labor and Employment; Employment Litigation; Employment Discrimination; Fair Employment Practices; Sexual Harassment; Age Discrimination in Employment; Title VII Discrimination; Employment Disability Discrimination; Title IX Discrimination; Employee Privacy; Employee Drug Testing; Employee Discipline; Employer Liability; Workplace Violence; Personnel Policies; Union Elections; Unfair Labor Practices; National Labor Relations Act; Family and Medical Leave Act; Retaliatory Discharge; Wrongful Termination Defense; Employment at Will; Employment Breach of Contract; Whistleblower Litigation. ***Email:*** kathy.brickley@btlaw.com

MICHAEL B. WATKINS, admitted to bar, 1986, Indiana; U.S. District Court, Northern and Southern Districts of Indiana and U.S. Court of Appeals, Seventh Circuit. *Education:* Indiana University (B.A., 1979; J.D., summa cum laude, 1986). Phi Delta Phi. Articles Editor, Indiana Law Review, 1985-1986. American Bankruptcy Institute. (Certified in Business Bankruptcy Law by the American Board of Certification). ***PRACTICE AREAS:*** Bankruptcy Reorganization; Commercial Bankruptcy; Commercial Transactions; Commercial Real Estate; Real Estate Leasing; Workouts. ***Email:*** Michael.Watkins@btlaw.com

SETH D. LINFIELD, admitted to bar, 1984, New York; 1985, Pennsylvania; 1988, Indiana. *Education:* New York University (B.A., 1980); Stanford University (J.D., 1983). Phi Beta Kappa. Law Clerk to Hon. Lawrence T. Lydick, U.S. District Court to the Central District of California, 1983-1985; to Hon. Daniel A. Manion, U.S. Court of Appeals for the Seventh Circuit, 1986-1988. Adjunct Assistant Professor, Mendoza College of Business, University of Notre Dame, 1999—. (Co-chair, Business Technology Practice Group; Chair, Technology Transactions Group). ***PRACTICE AREAS:*** Computers and Software; Technology and Science; Intellectual Property; Communications and Media; Corporate Finance. ***Email:*** seth.linfield@btlaw.com

(This Listing Continued)

TIMOTHY D. HERNLY, admitted to bar, 1986, Indiana and Florida; 1992, U.S. Tax Court; Indiana Tax Court; U.S. Court of Appeals, Seventh Circuit. *Education:* Indiana University - Bloomington (B.S., Accounting, 1982; M.B.A., Finance and Taxation, 1985; J.D., cum laude, 1985). Listed in *Best Lawyers in America (Tax Law). Indiana Registered Legislative Lobbyist.* Certified Public Accountant, Indiana and Florida, 1986. *Member:* Indiana State (Chair, Section of Taxation, 1997-1998) and American (State and Local Taxation Committee) Bar Associations; Indiana Property Tax Institute (Chair, 1998—); Indiana Chamber of Commerce (Tax Committee); Indiana Manufacturers Association (Tax Committee); Chamber of Commerce of St. Joseph County (Chair, Taxation Task Force, 2000—); Institute for Professionals in Taxation; Appraisal Institute; International Association of Assessing Officers; American Institute of Certified Public Accountants; Indiana Assessors Association; Iron and Steel Society. (Tax Partner)(Chairman, Property Tax Practice Group). ***PRACTICE AREAS:*** Property Tax Appeals; Tax Law; Buying and Selling of Businesses; Tax Litigation; State Tax Controversies; Property Tax Abatement. ***Email:*** tim.hernly@btlaw.com

JOSEPH R. FULLENKAMP, admitted to bar, 1988, Indiana and U.S. District Court, Northern and Southern Districts of Indiana; 2003, U.S. Court of Appeals, Seventh Circuit. *Education:* University of Iowa (B.A., 1985; J.D., with distinction, 1988). *Member:* St. Joseph County and Indiana State Bar Associations; Robert A. Grant Inn of Court. ***REPORTED CASES:*** I/N Tek v. Hitachi, Ltd., 734 N.E.2d 584 (Ind.App. 2000); Drake v. Maid-Rite Co., 681 N.E.2d 734 (Ind. App. 1997); Hefty v. Certified Settlement Class, 638 N.E.2d 1284 (Ind. App. 1994), rev. by 680 N.E.2d 843 (Ind. 1997); Terra-Products v. Kraft General Foods, 653 N.E.2d 89 (Ind. App. 1995); State ex rel Firestone v. Parke Circuit Court, 621 N.E.2d 1113 (Ind. 1993); Hardy v. South Bend Sash & Door Co., 603 N.E.2d 895 (Ind. App. 1992); In re Train Collision at Gary, Indiana, 670 N.E.2d 902 (Ind. App. 1996); Massachusetts Mutual v. Associated Dry Goods, 786 F. Supp. 1403 (N.D. Ind. 1992). ***PRACTICE AREAS:*** Civil Litigation; Commercial Litigation; Appellate Practice; Class Action Defense; Insurance Coverage; Products Liability. ***Email:*** joseph.fullenkamp@btlaw.com

GRETA ROEMER LEWIS, admitted to bar, 1989, Indiana. *Education:* University of Notre Dame (B.A., 1986); DePaul University (J.D., 1989). *Member:* St. Joseph County and Indiana State Bar Associations. ***PRACTICE AREAS:*** Estate Planning and Probate; Elder Law. ***Email:*** greta.lewis@btlaw.com

MICHAEL D. HARDY, admitted to bar, 1990, Indiana. *Education:* University of South Florida (B.A., with high honors, 1986); Indiana University (J.D., magna cum laude, 1990). Order of the Coif. ***PRACTICE AREAS:*** Banking Law; Commercial Real Estate; Zoning, Planning and Land Use; Commercial Law; Creditors Rights. ***Email:*** michael.hardy@btlaw.com

JANILYN BROUWER DAUB, admitted to bar, 1991, Michigan, Indiana, U.S. District Court, Northern and Southern Districts of Indiana and Western District of Michigan; 1993, U.S. Court of Appeals, Seventh Circuit. *Education:* Hope College (B.A., magna cum laude, 1988); Ohio State University (J.D., 1991). Phi Beta Kappa. Managing Editor, The Ohio State Law Journal, 1990-1991. *Member:* St. Joseph County and Indiana State (Member, Labor and Employment Law Section) Bar Associations; State Bar of Michigan (Member, Labor and Employment Law Section). ***PRACTICE AREAS:*** Labor and Employment; Management Employment Law; Employment Litigation; Employment Discrimination; Harassment; Wrongful Termination Defense; Family and Medical Leave Act; Labor Arbitration; Wage and Hour Law; Employee Discipline; Employee Drug Testing; Personnel Policies; Personnel Training; Workplace Violence; Reductions in Force; WARN Act; Employment Contracts; Noncompetition and Non-solicitation Agreements. ***Email:*** janilyn.daub@btlaw.com

TRACY D. KNOX, admitted to bar, 1991, Indiana; 1994, Michigan. *Education:* U.S. Military Academy (B.S., 1984); University of Notre Dame (J.D., summa cum laude, 1991). ***PRACTICE AREAS:*** Litigation; Products Liability; Commercial Litigation. ***Email:*** tracy.knox@btlaw.com

MARK J. ADEY, admitted to bar, 1988, Indiana. *Education:* Indiana University (B.A., 1985); University of Notre Dame (J.D., 1988). *Member:* American Bankruptcy Institute. Certified in Business Bankruptcy Law by the American Board of Certification. ***PRACTICE AREAS:*** Creditors Rights; Bankruptcy; Commercial Law. ***Email:*** mark.adey@btlaw.com

JEANINE M. GOZDECKI, admitted to bar, 1992, Indiana. *Education:* University of Notre Dame (B.A., with honors, 1985; J.D., 1992). Recipient: American Jurisprudence Award in Trial Advocacy; Barrett Award for Excellence in Trial Advocacy. Past Chair, Indiana Supreme Court Commission for Continuing Legal Education. Adjunct Faculty, Notre Dame Law School. Guest Faculty Member, National Institute for Trial Advocacy. *Member:* St. Joseph County (Past President; Chair, Law-Media Committee) and Indiana State Bar Associations; Robert A. Grant Inn of Court. ***PRACTICE AREAS:*** Employment Litigation; Labor and Employment. ***Email:*** jeanine.gozdecki@btlaw.com

DOUGLAS D. ANDERSON, admitted to bar, 1992, Illinois; 1993, California; 1994, Indiana. *Education:* University of Notre Dame (B.A., 1989; J.D., 1992). *Member:* St. Joseph County, Indiana State and American Bar Associations. ***PRACTICE AREAS:*** Estate Planning; Business Law; Real Estate. ***Email:*** doug.anderson@btlaw.com

GEORGE E. HORN, JR., admitted to bar, 1987, Indiana, Michigan and U.S. District Court, Northern District of Indiana; 1996, U.S. District Court, Western District of Michigan; 1998, U.S. District Court, Southern District of Indiana and U.S. District Court, Northern District of Texas; 1999, U.S. Court of Appeals, Seventh Circuit; 2001, U.S. District Court, Western District of Pennsylvania; 2002, U.S. District Court, Eastern District of Texas. *Education:* University of Notre Dame (B.A., with honors, 1984; J.D., 1987). Law Clerk, U.S. Department of Justice, 1985-1987; Chief Assistant Prosecutor, Cass County, Michigan, 1987-1991; Deputy Prosecutor, Marion County, Indiana, 1991-1995; Special Assistant U.S. Attorney, Southern District of Indiana, 1994-1995. Past Lecturer, National College of District Attorneys; Prosecuting Attorneys Association of Michigan; Indiana Continuing Legal Education Fund. Television and radio commentary on various high profile criminal cases. *Member:* Indiana State, Seventh Circuit and American Bar Associations; State Bar of Michigan; National Association of Criminal Defense Attorneys. (Co-Chair, White Collar Crime Practice Group). ***PRACTICE AREAS:*** White Collar Crime; Criminal Law; Products Liability; Litigation. ***Email:*** geroge.horn@btlaw.com

(This Listing Continued)

BARNES & THORNBURG LLP, South Bend—Continued

JODY H. ODELL, admitted to bar, 1995, Indiana, U.S. District Court, Northern and Southern Districts of Indiana and U.S. Court of Appeals, Seventh Circuit; 2002, U.S. Supreme Court. *Education:* Wheaton College (B.A., magna cum laude, 1992); University of Notre Dame (J.D., magna cum laude, 1995). Law Clerk to Judge Kenneth F. Ripple. *Member:* Seventh Circuit and American Bar Associations (Member, ABA AIDS Coordinating Committee); Robert A. Grant Inn of Court. ***REPORTED CASES:*** Diann Grube v. Lau Industries, Inc., 257 F.3d 723 (7th Cir. 2001); Jackson v. Miller, 260 F.3d 769 (7th Cir. 2000); Hiner v. Penn-Harris-Madison School Corp., 256 F. Supp. 2d 854 (N.D. Ind. 2003). ***PRACTICE AREAS:*** Litigation; Labor and Employment Law; Employment Defense. ***Email:*** jody.odell@btlaw.com

JOHN C. SMARRELLA, admitted to bar, 1996, Indiana. *Education:* Greenville College (B.A., magna cum laude, 1991); University of Notre Dame (J.D., magna cum laude, 1996). Law Clerk to the Hon. John G. Baker, 1996-1997. Lead Research & Project Editor, Notre Dame Law Review, 1995-1996. *Member:* St. Joseph County and Indiana State Bar Associations. ***PRACTICE AREAS:*** Corporate Law; Taxation; Employee Benefits. ***Email:*** john.smarrella@btlaw.com

OF COUNSEL

BRIAN E. CASEY, admitted to bar, 1992, Maryland; 1994, Colorado; 1995, District of Columbia; 2002, Indiana. *Education:* Rice University (B.A., cum laude, 1989); Yale University Law School (J.D., 1992). ***PRACTICE AREAS:*** ERISA Litigation; Securities Litigation; Appellate Practice; Federal Civil Litigation. ***Email:*** brian.casey@btlaw.com

PHILIP J. FACCENDA, JR., admitted to bar, 1992, Indiana. *Education:* University of Notre Dame (B.A., 1989; J.D., 1992). *Member:* St. Joseph County and Indiana State Bar Associations. ***PRACTICE AREAS:*** Corporate Law; Municipal Finance. ***Email:*** philip.faccenda@btlaw.com

MICHAEL P. PALMER, admitted to bar, 1997, Illinois and U.S. District Court, Northern District of Illinois; U.S. Court of Appeals, Seventh Circuit (Not admitted in Indiana). *Education:* University of Notre Dame (B.A., 1994); Loyola University - Chicago (J.D., cum laude, 1997). *Member:* Chicago, Illinois State and American Bar Associations. ***PRACTICE AREAS:*** Labor and Employment. ***Email:*** michael.palmer@btlaw.com

TIMOTHY J. MAHER, admitted to bar, 1990, Missouri; 1991, Illinois; 1992, Indiana, U.S. District Court, Northern and Southern Districts of Indiana, U.S. District Court, Eastern District of Missouri and U.S. Court of Appeals, Fifth and Seventh Circuits. *Education:* Cornell College (B.S.S., 1987); University of Notre Dame (J.D., 1990). Concannon Programme of International Law, London, England, 1988-1989. Instructor, Trial Advocacy, Notre Dame Law School. *Member:* Bar Association of Metropolitan St. Louis; St. Joseph County, Indiana State and Illinois State Bar Associations; The Missouri Bar; Defense Research Institute; Notre Dame Law Association; Robert A. Grant Inn of Court. ***PRACTICE AREAS:*** Civil Litigation; Commercial Litigation; School Law. ***Email:*** tim.maher@btlaw.com

ASSOCIATES

RICHARD J. DEAHL, admitted to bar, 1998, Indiana. *Education:* Indiana University (B.S., 1994); Indiana University School of Law Indianapolis (J.D., 1998); Indiana University Kellogg School of Business (M.B.A., 1998). ***PRACTICE AREAS:*** Business Law; Real Estate Acquisitions; Buying and Selling of Businesses; Property Tax. ***Email:*** richard.deahl@btlaw.com

D. MICHAEL ANDERSON, admitted to bar, 1998, Indiana; U.S. Court of Appeals, Seventh Circuit; U.S. District Court, Northern District of Indiana; U.S. District Court, Southern District of Indiana. *Education:* Indiana State University (B.S., 1989); Indiana University (J.D., magna cum laude, 1998). ***PRACTICE AREAS:*** Trademarks; Trademark Litigation; Trade Secrets; Civil Litigation. ***Email:*** mike.anderson@btlaw.com

JAMES W. TUESLEY, admitted to bar, 1999, Indiana. *Education:* Indiana University - Kelley School of Business (B.S., 1996; M.B.A., 1999); Indiana University - Bloomington (J.D., 1999). ***PRACTICE AREAS:*** Business Law; Taxation; Health Care. ***Email:*** jim.tuesley@btlaw.com

BRIEN P. CROTTY, admitted to bar, 1998, Indiana. *Education:* Valparaiso University (B.A., 1995); University of Notre Dame (J.D., 1998). Editor-in-Chief, Journal of College and University Law, 1998. *Member:* St. Joseph County, Indiana State and American Bar Associations; Robert A. Grant Inn of Court. ***PRACTICE AREAS:*** Litigation; Products Liability; Business Torts; Computer Law; Creditors Rights. ***Email:*** brien.crotty@btlaw.com

DAMON R. LEICHTY, admitted to bar, 1999, Indiana and U.S. District Court, Northern and Southern Districts of Indiana; 2004, U.S. Court of Appeals, Seventh Circuit. *Education:* Wabash College (B.A., summa cum laude, 1994); Indiana University School of Law - Bloomington (J.D., cum laude, 1999); University of Aberdeen, King's College, Aberdeen, Scotland (M.Litt., 1999). Order of the Barristers. Law Clerk to Hon. Robert L. Miller, Jr., Chief Judge of U.S. District Court for Northern District of Indiana. Member, Robert A. Grant Inn of Court. *Member:* St. Joseph County and Indiana State Bar Associations. ***PRACTICE AREAS:*** Appellate Practice; Litigation. ***Email:*** damon.leichty@btlaw.com

MICHAEL V. KNIGHT, admitted to bar, 2000, Illinois and Indiana. *Education:* Brown University (A.B., 1979); Valparaiso University (J.D., magna cum laude, 1999). *Member:* St. Joseph County and Lake County Bar Associations. ***PRACTICE AREAS:*** Civil Litigation; Uniform Commercial Code; Contract Litigation; Construction Law; Real Estate; Zoning. ***Email:*** michael.knight@btlaw.com

ANDREW P. HECK, admitted to bar, 2000, Indiana and U.S. District Court, Northern and Southern Districts of Indiana. *Education:* Wabash College (B.A., cum laude, 1997); Valparaiso University (J.D., summa cum laude, 2000). Associate Editor, Valparaiso University Law Review, 1999-2000. ***PRACTICE AREAS:*** Trusts and Estates; Wills; Corporate Law; Taxation. ***Email:*** andrew.heck@btlaw.com

MICHAEL J. HAYS, admitted to bar, 2002, Indiana; U.S. District Court, Northern and Southern Districts of Indiana; 2003, U.S. Court of Appeals, Seventh Circuit. *Education:* DePauw University (B.A., summa cum laude, 1999); University of Notre Dame (J.D., summa cum laude, 2002). Phi Beta Kappa. Note Editor, Notre Dame Law Review. Author, "The E-SIGN Act of 2000: The Triumph of Function Over Form in American Contract Law," 76 Notre Dame L. Rev. 1183, 2001. *Member:* St. Joseph County, Indiana State, and American Bar Associations; Robert A. Grant Inn of Courts. ***REPORTED CASES:*** Rust-Oleum Corp. v. Fitz, 801 N.E.2d 754 (Ind. Ct. App. 2004); Pizel v. Monaco Coach Corp., 364 F. Supp. 2d 790 (N.D. Ind. 2005). ***PRACTICE AREAS:*** Federal Civil Practice; Labor and Employment; Litigation. ***Email:*** michael.hays@btlaw.com

GREGORY P. RIPPLE, admitted to bar, 2003, Indiana and U.S. District Court, Southern and Northern Districts of Indiana; 2004, U.S. Court of Appeals, Seventh Circuit. *Education:* University of Notre Dame (B.A., magna cum laude, 1994; J.D., magna cum laude, 2003); Fordham University (M.A., 1996; M. Phil., 2000). ***Email:*** greg.ripple@btlaw.com

LAURA D. SENG, admitted to bar, 2003 Indiana and U.S. District Court, Northern and Southern Districts of Indiana. *Education:* University of Evansville (B.S. Nursing, summa cum laude, 1985); Valparaiso University School of Law (J.D., summa cum laude, 2003). Adjunct Faculty, Valparaiso University School of Law; ABA Commission on Law & Aging: 2003 Student Essay Contest, First Place. Author: "Legal and Regulatory Barriers to Adequate Pain Control for Elders in Long-Term Care Facilities," New York City Law Review, Fall 2003. *Member:* Indiana State and American Bar Associations; American Health Lawyers Association. ***PRACTICE AREAS:*** Health Care; Business Law. ***Email:*** laura.seng@btlaw.com

KATE E. MUELLER, admitted to bar, 2004, Indiana and U.S. District Court, Northern District of Indiana. *Education:* University of Notre Dame (B.A., summa cum laude, 2001; J.D., 2004). Phi Beta Kappa. Note Editor, Journal of College and University Law. *Member:* St. Joseph County, Indiana State and American (Member, Litigation Section) Bar Associations; Robert A. Grant Inn of Court. ***LANGUAGES:*** Spanish. ***PRACTICE AREAS:*** Litigation. ***Email:*** kate.mueller@btlaw.com

REPRESENTATIVE CLIENTS: lst Source Bank; AM General Corporation; Beta Steel Corporation; Bethlehem Steel Corporation; Bowne & Co., Inc.; Burkhart Advertising, Inc.; Cadence Environmental Energy; Crowe, Chizek and Company LLP; Fairmont Homes, Inc.; Gast Manufacturing Corporation; Gates Automobile Dealerships; Hamilton Grove; LeMaster Steel Erectors, LLC; Madison Center, Inc.; Massachusetts Mutual Life Insurance Company; Medical Group of Michigan City, P.C.; Memorial Hospital of South Bend; Midwest Medical, LLC; Mittler Steel Supply, Inc.; Nishikawa Standard Company; Morgan Drive Away, Inc.; National Steel Corporation; NIBCO, Inc.; Press Ganey Co., Inc.; Reinke Construction Corporation; Rieth-Riley Construction Co., Inc.; Saint Mary's College; Schurz Communications, Inc.; Skyline Corporation; South Bend Clinic, L.L.P.; South Bend Tribune; Steel Warehouse Co. Inc.; Teachers Credit Union; Tire Rack, Inc.; Universal Bearings, Inc.; University of Notre Dame; Utilimaster; Whirlpool Corporation; Whiteford, Inc.; WSBT, Inc.

MARY ANN BOULAC

535 PARKOVASH AVENUE
P.O. BOX 11654
SOUTH BEND, INDIANA 46617
Telephone: 574-236-7230
Fax: 574-236-8907
Email: boulac@sbcglobal.net

General Business, Real Estate, Estate Planning, Trusts and Estates, Asset Protection, Guardianships, Elder Law, Medicaid, Wills and Probate.

MARY ANN BOULAC, born 1943; admitted to bar, 1983, Indiana. *Education:* St. Mary's College, Notre Dame, Indiana (B.A., 1965); University of Notre Dame (J.D., 1983). *Member:* St. Joseph County and Indiana State Bar Associations.

BOVERI MURPHY RICE & LaDUE, LLP

400 PLAZA BUILDING
210 SOUTH MICHIGAN STREET
SOUTH BEND, INDIANA 46601
Telephone: 574-232-0300
Fax: 574-232-0400
URL: http://www.bmrl-law.com

Litigation, State and Federal Trial Practice.

MARK D. BOVERI, born March 31, 1960; admitted to bar, 1986, Indiana and Michigan. *Education:* Indiana University (B.S., 1982); University of Notre Dame (J.D., 1985). Associate Editor, Notre Dame Law Review, 1983-1985.*Member:* St. Joseph County and Indiana State Bar Associations; State Bar of Michigan; Robert A. Grant Inn of Court. ***REPORTED CASES:*** Beanstalk Group, Inc. v. A.M. General Corp., 283 F.3d 856 (7th Cir. 2002); Koval v. Simon-Telelect, Inc., 979 F.Supp. 1222 (N.D. Ind. 1997); St. Joseph County v. State Board of Tax Comm'rs, 683 N.E.2d 1379 (Ind. Tax Ct. 1997); Transamerica Ins. Co. v. Henry, 563 N.E.2d 1265 (Indiana 1990). ***PRACTICE AREAS:*** Litigation; State and Federal Trial Practice; Labor and Employment. ***Email:*** mboveri@bmrl-law.com

PATRICK D. MURPHY, born South Bend, Indiana, December 24, 1962; admitted to bar, 1988, Indiana. *Education:* University of Notre Dame (B.B.A., 1985); Indiana University (J.D., 1988); University of Illinois (LL.M., 1995). Associate Editor, Indiana Law Review, 1987-1988. Law Clerk to: Hon. James E. Noland, U.S. District Court, S.D. of Indiana, 1988-1990. Member, Local Rules Advisory Committee, U.S. District Court for the Northern District of Indiana, 1999—. Publication: A Federal Practitioner's Guide to Supplemental Jurisdiction under 28 U.S.C. § 1367, 78 Marq. L. Rev. 973 (1995). *Member:* St. Joseph County and Indiana State Bar Associations. Robert A. Grant Inn of Court (Secretary/Treasurer, 2003—). [1 Lt., JAG Corps, USAR, 1985-1994]. ***REPORTED CASES:*** Rhodes v. Wright 805 N.E. 2d 382 (Ind. 2004); Title Search Co., Inc. v. 1st Source Bank, 765 N.E. 2d 167 (Ind. App. 2002); Beanstalk Group, Inc. v. A.M. General Corp., 283 F.3d 856 (7th Cir. 2002); Feltner v. Title Search Co., 283 F.2d 838 (7th Cir. 2002); Hochstedler v. St. Joseph Coun. Solid Waste Management District, 770 N.E. 2d 910 (Ind. App. 2002). ***PRACTICE AREAS:*** Litigation (100%). ***Email:*** pmurphy@bmrl-law.com

CHARLES P. RICE, born Manhasset, New York, May 16, 1963; admitted to bar, 1989, Indiana; 1990, Illinois. *Education:* University of Notre Dame (B.A., 1985; J.D., 1988).

(This Listing Continued)

Member: St. Joseph County and Indiana State Bar Associations. ***REPORTED CASES:*** Pence v. General Assembly (Ind., 1995) 652 NE 2nd 486; Adoption of AMK 698 NE 2d 845 (Ind. App. 1998); Adoption of JP 713 NE 2d 873 (Ind. App. 1999); Estate of Penzenik 749 NE 2d 61 (2001) Ind. App.; Wallar v. Osterloo 758 NE 2d 59 (Ind. App. 2001). ***PRACTICE AREAS:*** Litigation. ***Email:*** crice@bmrl-law.com

JOHN D. LaDUE, born Dearborn, Michigan, March 1, 1962; admitted to bar, 1990, Michigan; 1996, Indiana. *Education:* Michigan State University (B.A., 1984); University of Notre Dame (J.D., 1990). Editor-in-Chief, Notre Dame Law Review, 1989-1990. Adjunct Professor of Law, Trial Advocacy and Deposition Skills, University of Notre Dame Law School, 2003—. *Member:* St. Joseph County and Indiana State Bar Associations; State Bar of Michigan; Robert A. Grant Inn of Court. [Judge Advocate, U.S. Marine Corps, 1990-1996]. ***REPORTED CASES:*** AM General Corporation and General Motors Corporation v. Daimler Chrysler Corporation, 311 F.3d 796 (7th Cir., 2002); Zimmerman v. Tribble, 226 F.3d 568 (7th Cir. 2000); Markley Enterprises v. Grover, 716 N.E.2d 559 (Ind.App.1999); Moore v. University of Notre Dame, 968 F.Supp. 1330 (N.D.Ind. 1997). ***PRACTICE AREAS:*** Commercial Litigation; Trademark Litigation; Labor and Employment; Trade Secrets; Noncompete Litigation; Federal Litigation; White Collar Crime. ***Email:*** jladue@bmrl-law.com

---

JOHN D. FALVEY, born Springfield, Massachusetts, March 28, 1962; admitted to bar, 1997, Indiana; 1999, Missouri; 2000 Kansas. *Education:* Indiana University (B.A., 1985); Seton Hall University (M.A.); Valparaiso University (J.D., 1996). Former Special Agent, F.B.I. *Member:* St. Joseph County and Indiana State Bar Associations; State Bar of Missouri; Robert A. Grant Inn of Court. ***PRACTICE AREAS:*** Litigation. ***Email:*** jfalvey@bmrl-law.com

R. JOHN KUEHN, III, born Grand Forks, North Dakota, March 4, 1975; admitted to bar, 2000, Indiana. *Education:* University of Notre Dame (B.A., 1997; J.D., 2000). Adjunct Assistant Professor of Law, Deposition Skills, University of Notre Dame Law School, 2004—. *Member:* St. Joseph County, Seventh Circuit and Indiana State Bar Associations; Robert A. Grant Inn of Court; The Association of Trial Lawyers of America. ***PRACTICE AREAS:*** Civil Litigation; Labor and Employment; Commercial Litigation; Trade Secrets; Noncompete Litigation. ***Email:*** jkuehn@bmrl-law.com

TIMOTHY M. CURRAN, admitted to bar, 2000, Wisconsin, U.S. Court of Appeals, Seventh Circuit and U.S. District Court, Western and Eastern Districts of Wisconsin; 2003, Indiana and U.S. District Court, Northern and Southern Districts of Indiana. *Education:* University College, Galway, Ireland, 1995; Marquette University (B.A., 1997); University of Notre Dame (J.D., 2000). Phi Beta Kappa. Notre Dame Moot Court. *Member:* State Bar of Wisconsin; Indiana State and American (Member, Business Torts; Membership Coordinator) Bar Associations; The Association of Trial Lawyers of America; American Inns of Court. ***PRACTICE AREAS:*** Litigation. ***Email:*** tcurran@bmrl-law.com

R. TRACY CRUMP

SOUTH BEND, INDIANA

(See New Carlisle)

Intellectual Property, Copyrights, Licensing Agreements, Patents, Trade Secrets, Trademarks.

ALADEAN M. DeROSE

105 EAST JEFFERSON BOULEVARD, SUITE 512
SOUTH BEND, INDIANA 46601
Telephone: 574-234-5091
Fax: 574-289-4618
Email: aderose@ci.south-bend.in.us
URL: http://www.deroselaw.com

Bankruptcy, Collections, Wills and Probate, Trusts and Estates, Estate Planning, Family/Domestic Relations, Adoptions, Divorce, Child Custody, Child Support, Visitation Rights, Personal Injury, Automobile Accidents, Slip and Fall, Wrongful Death, Social Security Disability, Employment Discrimination, Workers Compensation, Civil Trial Litigation in all State and Federal Courts.

FIRM PROFILE: Ms. DeRose began her own practice in 1982 and has been practicing law in South Bend for over 20 years. Her mission is to provide personalized attention, attentiveness to detail and reasonable rates to her clients in Northern Indiana. With strong litigation and appellate experience, Ms. DeRose concentrates on many aspects of general practice including banking, family law and employment discrimination law.

ALADEAN M. DeROSE, born Chicago, Illinois, September 20, 1951; admitted to bar, 1978, Indiana, U.S. District Court, Northern District of Indiana and U.S. Court of Appeals, 7th Circuit. *Education:* Georgetown University (B.S., 1973); Indiana University (J.D., 1978). Certified Mediator, Mediation and Civil/Family. Deputy City Attorney, South Bend, *1990-1999. Chief Assistant City Attorney, South Bend, 1999—.* Adjunct Faculty, Bankruptcy, Indiana University, 1991. Lecturer: Custody Law. Board of Governors, St. Joseph County Bar Association. *Member:* Indiana State Bar Association (Member, Board of Law Examiners Character and Fitness Committee); Indiana Trial Lawyers Association; Michiana Association of Mediators (Co-Chair, 1999—. ***LANGUAGES:*** French. ***REPORTED CASES:*** Luson International Distributors, Inc. v. Mitchell, 939 F.2d 493, 1991; Garza v. Sullivan, 753 F.Supp. 737, 1991; In re: Stookey Holsteins, Inc., 112 B.R. 942, Bankr. N.D. Ind., 1990; In re: Merrill, 587 N.E.2d 188, Ind. App., 1992; Ind. Dept. of Public Welfare v. Carmen Delvalle, 596 N.E.2d 301, Ind. App., 1992; Molnar v. Otis Elevator, 37 F.3d 335, 1994; Kimsey v. City of South Bend.

DIAMOND AND DIAMOND

405 WEST WAYNE STREET
P.O. BOX 1875
SOUTH BEND, INDIANA 46634-1875
Telephone: 574-232-6918
Fax: 574-233-2267
Email: attydiamond@prodigy.net

General Civil Practice in all Courts. Corporation, Probate and Estate Planning, Real Estate, Business, Family/Domestic Relations, Labor and Employment, Bankruptcy and Collections Law.

ARTHUR M. DIAMOND (1925-2000)

ERIC L. DIAMOND, born South Bend, Indiana, August 15, 1958; admitted to bar, 1983, Indiana. *Education:* University of Notre Dame (B.B.A., with honors, 1980; J.D., cum laude, 1983). Co-Author: "New Federalism is Not Enough: The Privatization of Nonpublic Goods," Harvard Journal of Law and Public Policy, Vol. 7 p. 321, Fall, 1984. Member of Faculty, Paralegal Studies Program, Probate Law, Indiana University at South Bend, 1989-1992. *Member:* St. Joseph County, Indiana State and American (Member: Section on Real Property, Probate and Trust Law; Probate and Trust Division Committee on Creditors Rights in Estates and Trusts, 1987-1993) Bar Associations. ***PRACTICE AREAS:*** Collection Law (45%); Probate and Estate Planning (45%); Real Estate (10%).

JEFFREY M. JANKOWSKI, born South Bend, Indiana, January 6, 1962; admitted to bar, 1988, Indiana. *Education:* Holy Cross College; University of Notre Dame (B.A., 1984; J.D., 1987). Delta Theta Phi. Assistant City Attorney, 1990—. Attorney, St. Joseph County Prosecutor's Office, 1989-1990. *Member:* St. Joseph County, Indiana State (Member, Family Law Section) and American Bar Associations; Young Lawyers Association. ***REPORTED CASES:*** Civil City of South Bend, IN v. Conrail Cite as 880 F. Supp. 595 (N.D. Ind. 1995). ***PRACTICE AREAS:*** Labor and Employment Law (10%); Domestic Relations (34%); Bankruptcy (5%); Litigation (15%); Corporate Law (5%); Business Law (10%); Retail Collections (3%); Post Judgment Collections (3%); Garnishments (3%); Commercial Collections (3%); Collections (3%); Unsecured Collections (3%); Secured Collections (3%).

RAE D. BEEHLER, born Mishawaka, Indiana, August 18, 1962; admitted to bar, 2001, Indiana. *Education:* Indiana University (B.A., 1984); Valparaiso University (J.D., 2001). *Member:* St. Joseph County, Indiana State and American Bar Associations. ***PRACTICE AREAS:*** Creditors Rights (75%); Probate (20%); Estate Planning (5%).

REPRESENTATIVE CLIENTS: Creed Excavating Co., Inc.; Ideal Consolidated, Inc.; International Bakers Service, Inc.; The Centre, P.C.; Radiology, Inc.; Absolute Communications, Inc.
REFERENCES: South Bend; Wells Fargo Bank, Indiana N.A., South Bend.

DORAN • BLACKMOND LLP

Established in 1989
CITY CENTER
211 W. WASHINGTON STREET
SUITE 1700
SOUTH BEND, INDIANA 46601
Telephone: 574-288-1800
Fax: 574-236-4265
Email: firm@doranblackmond.com
URL: http://www.doranblackmond.com

Civil Trial and Appellate Practice in Federal and State Courts, Insurance Defense and Coverage Questions, Special Investigation, Personal Injury, Product Liability, Architect and Engineer Liability, Legal Malpractice, Worker's Compensation, Construction Law, Commercial, Creditor's Rights, Bankruptcy and Reorganization, Mediation and Arbitration.

FIRM PROFILE: Doran • Blackmond evolved from a firm started in 1927 by M. Edward Doran and Clarence Manion, former dean of Notre Dame Law School. Members of the firm are experienced trial lawyers, having tried a substantial number of cases to juries in federal and state courts. The firm is committed to providing its clients with the highest quality of legal services available anywhere in the State of Indiana. From its offices located in South Bend, the firm can cost-effectively represent clients in federal courts located in Fort Wayne, Hammond, and South Bend, and state courts in Allen, Cass, De Kalb, Elkhart, Fulton, Huntington, Jasper, Kosciusko, La Grange, Lake, La Porte, Marshall, Miami, Newtown, Noble, Pulaski, Porter, St. Joseph, Starke, Steuben, Wabash, and Whitley counties.

MEMBERS OF FIRM

M. EDWARD DORAN (1895-1982)
JOHN E. DORAN (Retired)

DON G. BLACKMOND, born Dowagiac, Michigan, February 4, 1940; admitted to bar, 1966, Indiana. *Education:* DePauw University (B.A., 1962); Valparaiso University (J.D., 1965). Phi Alpha Delta. Certified Mediator, Indiana ADR Rules. Faculty Member, National Institute for Trial Advocacy, 1984. *Member:* St. Joseph County, Indiana State and American Bar Associations; Indiana Defense Lawyers Association; Defense Research Institute; Robert A. Grant Inns of Court. ***PRACTICE AREAS:*** Federal and State Trials; Civil Litigation; Personal Injury; Insurance Defense; Commercial Litigation; Product Liability; Legal Malpractice; Annexation; Mediation and Arbitration. ***Email:*** dblackmondsr@doranblackmond.com

DON GREGORY BLACKMOND, born South Bend, Indiana, February 20, 1968; admitted to bar, 1994, Indiana and U.S. District Court, Northern and Southern Districts of Indiana; 1996, U.S. Court of Appeals, Seventh Circuit. *Education:* Michigan State University (B.S., 1991); Valparaiso Law School (J.D., cum laude, 1994). Former Law Extern for the Honorable Robert K. Rodibaugh, United States Bankruptcy Court, Northern District of Indiana. *Member:* St. Joseph County and Indiana State Bar Associations; Defense Research

(This Listing Continued)

DORAN • BLACKMOND LLP, South Bend—Continued

Institute. ***REPORTED CASES:*** Breneman v. Slusher, 768 N.E. 2d 451 (Ind. App. 2002); Paper Mfrs. Co. v. Rescuers, Inc., 60 F. Supp. 2d 869 (N.D. Ind. 1999); Stanford v. Woltman, WL 792181 (N.D. Ind. 1998); Beiger Heritage Corp. v. Carnegie Properties, Inc., 667 N.E.2d 184 (Ind. App. 1996); Agnew v. St. Joseph County Jail, WL 534928 (N.D. Ind. 1996). ***PRACTICE AREAS:*** State and Federal Civil Trials; Insurance Defense; Insurance Coverage; Product Liability; Construction; Commercial Litigation; Legal Malpractice; Personal Injury; Workers Compensation. ***Email:*** dblackmond@doranblackmond.com

SALLY P. NORTON, born Elkhart, Indiana, January 28, 1964; admitted to bar, 1991, Indiana and U.S. District Court, Northern and Southern Districts of Indiana. *Education:* Indiana University (B.A., 1986; J.D., 1989). Author: "Investigating and Documenting Worker's Compensation Claims," Lorman Education Services, 1998; Worker's Compensation: The Employer's Perspective, Lorman Education Service 2000. *Member:* St. Joseph County and Indiana State Bar Associations; Defense Trial Counsel of Indiana; Robert A Grant, Inn of Court. ***PRACTICE AREAS:*** Workers Compensation; Civil Litigation; Personal Injury; Insurance Defense. ***Email:*** snorton@doranblackmond.com

OF COUNSEL

A. HOWARD WILLIAMS, born Fort Wayne, Indiana, January 13, 1950; admitted to bar, 1976, Indiana. *Education:* Indiana University (B.S., 1971); University of Notre Dame (J.D., 1976). Certified Mediator, Indiana ADR Rules. Associate Editor, Notre Dame Journal of Legislation, 1975-1976. St. Joseph County Police Attorney, 1976-1982, 1995-1998. *Member:* St. Joseph County, Indiana State and American Bar Associations; The Association of Trial Lawyers of America. ***REPORTED CASES:*** Burks v. Bolerjack, 427 N.E.2d 887 (Ind. 1981); Osborne v. Wenger, 572 N.E.2d 1343 (Ind.App. 1991); American Economy Ins. Co. v. Liggett, 426 N.E.2d 136 (Ind.App. 1981). ***PRACTICE AREAS:*** Federal and State Trials; Personal Injury; Commercial Litigation; Bankruptcy; Worker's Compensation. ***Email:*** ahw@gte.net

LEGAL SUPPORT PERSONNEL

KATRINA L. CURFISS, born Cincinnati, Ohio, October 4, 1980. *Education:* University of Cincinnati (A.A.B., cum laude, 2001). *Member:* Cincinnati and Michiana Paralegal Associations. (Paralegal). ***Email:*** kcurfiss@doranblackmond.com

REPRESENTATIVE CLIENTS: Allstate Insurance Company; CNA Insurance Cos.; Crum and Forster Commercial Insurance; CIGNA Insurance Cos.; FCCI/Monroe Guaranty; Fireman's Fund Insurance Co.; General Casualty Cos.; Hoosier Inc. Co.; Horace Mann Insurance Co.; Integon Insurance Company; Liberty Mutual Insurance Co.; Maryland Casualty Co.; National Rifle Assn.; Reliance Insurance; First Reinsurance of Hartford; Royal Sun Alliance; RSKCo. Claim Services; Sentry Insurance Co.; State Auto Mutual Insurance Co.; Universal Underwriters Insurance Group; Zurich Insurance Co.
REFERENCES: National City Bank, South Bend, Indiana; LaSalle National Bank, Chicago, Illinois.

FOLEY & SMALL

Established in 1995

1002 EAST JEFFERSON BOULEVARD
SOUTH BEND, INDIANA 46617
Telephone: 574-288-7676; 800-276-2525
Fax: 574-288-4939
Email: info@foleyandsmall.com
URL: http://www.foleyandsmall.com

Regional Offices at: Knox, LaPorte, Plymouth and Rochester, Indiana.

Personal Injury, Premises Liability, Products Liability, Wrongful Death, Automobile Accidents, Insurance Litigation, and General Litigation.

MEMBERS OF FIRM

EDMOND W. FOLEY, born Lebanon, Missouri, November 19, 1951; admitted to bar, 1979, Illinois; 1982, Indiana, U.S. District Court, Northern District of Indiana and U.S. Court of Appeals, Seventh Circuit. *Education:* University of Notre Dame (B.B.A. in Accounting, 1974; J.D., cum laude, 1979). Certified Public Accountant, Illinois, 1977. Law Clerk to the Honorable Robert A. Grant, U.S. District Court, Northern District of Indiana, 1980-1981. *Member:* St. Joseph County and Indiana State Bar Associations. ***PRACTICE AREAS:*** Personal Injury; Premises Liability; Products Liability; Wrongful Death; Automobile Accidents and Injuries; Insurance Litigation; Litigation. ***Email:*** efoley@foleyandsmall.com

DOUGLAS D. SMALL, born Knox, Indiana, November 8, 1957; admitted to bar, 1983, Indiana, U.S. District Court, Northern District of Indiana, U.S. Court of Appeals, Seventh Circuit and U.S. Supreme Court; U.S. Court of Claims. *Education:* Indiana University (B.A. high honors in History, 1980; J.D., cum laude, 1983). Phi Beta Kappa. Member National Moot Court Board. Partner, Barnes & Thornburg, 1983-1994. *Member:* St. Joseph County, Indiana State and American Bar Associations; American Trial Lawyers Association. ***PRACTICE AREAS:*** Personal Injury; Premises Liability; Products Liability; Wrongful Death; Automobile Accidents and Injuries; Insurance Litigation; Litigation. ***Email:*** dsmall@foleyandsmall.com

HAHN, WALZ AND KNEPP

A PROFESSIONAL ASSOCIATION

Established in 1986

509 WEST WASHINGTON AVENUE
SOUTH BEND, INDIANA 46601-1527
Telephone: 574-234-2118; 574-232-5988
Fax: 574-234-2119
Email: Lawyers@hahnwalz.com
URL: http://www.hahnwalz.com/

Business and Corporate Law, Elder Law, Estate Planning and Probate, Real Estate, General Civil Litigation (Federal and State Courts), Bankruptcy, Collections, commercial Law, Personal Injury, Labor Law, Wills and Trusts Law, Family Law, Adoptions.

FIRM PROFILE: The Association was established in 1986 with the merger of the practices of Hahn and Knepp with the practices of Wilford V. Walz and Thomas M Walz.

CHARLES W. HAHN (1909-1985)

WILFORD V. WALZ (1902-1993)

JAMES P. KNEPP, born Chicago, Illinois, June 21, 1947; admitted to bar, 1975, Indiana and U.S. District Court, Northern and Southern Districts of Indiana; 1995, U.S. District Court, Northern District of Illinois including Trial Bar. *Education:* Indiana University (B.S., summa cum laude, 1973; J.D., cum laude, 1975). Beta Gamma Sigma. Instructor, Indiana University at South Bend Paralegal Studies Program. *Member:* St. Joseph County, Indiana State (Member, Probate and Real Property, Business and General Practice Sections) and American (Member, General Practice Section) Bar Associations. ***PRACTICE AREAS:*** Elder Law; Estate Planning and Probate; Wills and Trusts; Real Estate; Business and Corporate; Adoption. ***Email:*** jknepp@hahnwalz.com

THOMAS M. WALZ, born South Bend, Indiana, January 20, 1953; admitted to bar, 1978, Indiana and U.S. District Court, Northern and Southern Districts of Indiana; 1994, U.S. Court of Appeals, Seventh Circuit. *Education:* Indiana University (B.S., 1975); Pepperdine University (J.D., 1978). *Member:* St. Joseph County, Indiana State and American Bar Associations. ***PRACTICE AREAS:*** Estate Planning and Probate; Wills and Trusts; Commercial Law; Collections and Bankruptcy; Business and Corporate; Personal Injury; Real Estate; Adoption; Elder Law. ***Email:*** twalz@hahnwalz.com

ANDREA KUREK SLAGH, born South Bend, Indiana, April 7, 1972; admitted to bar, 1998, Indiana and U.S. District Court, Northern and Southern Districts of Indiana. *Education:* University of Notre Dame (B.A., 1994); Valparaiso University School of Law (J.D., cum laude, 1998). *Member:* St. Joseph County; Indiana State and American Bar Associations. ***PRACTICE AREAS:*** Civil Litigation; Trusts and Estates; Estate Planning; Probate; Wills and Trusts; Collections; Bankruptcy; Labor and Employment; Personal Injury; Business Law; Corporate Law; Real Estate; Adoption Law; Elder Law. ***Email:*** aslagh@hahnwalz.com

REPRESENTATIVE CLIENTS: Meridian Title Corp.; Associates Commercial Corp.; Associates Leasing, Inc.; A.I. Credit Corp.; Amsted Industries, Inc.; Chrysler Credit Corp.; Tandy Corp.; Indiana Carton Company; X-Cel Controls, Inc.; Patrick Industries; ILC Metal Products Co.; Polycast Technology Corp.; Uniroyal Plastics Acquisition Corp; Pre-Melt Systems, Inc.; Emergent Mortgage Corp.; Datasearch, Inc.; Red Hen Turf Farm, Inc.; Century Surety Company; Chapel Hill Funeral Home and Memorial Gardens, Inc.; Citicapital; Jamil Packaging Corp.; Prudential; One Realty, L.L.C.; Mortgage One, L.L.C.; Palmer Funeral Homes, Inc. References provided upon request.

HAINS LAW FIRM, LLP

Established in 1991

125 NORTH ST. PETER STREET
SOUTH BEND, INDIANA 46617
Telephone: 574-234-7606
Fax: 574-282-1360
URL: http://www.hainslawfirm.com

General Civil and Criminal Trial Practice in all State and Federal Courts, Appellate Practice, Business Litigation, Domestic Relations, Family Law, Bankruptcy, Real Estate, Intellectual Property, Adoption, Child Custody, Child Support, Divorce, Visitation Rights, Wills and Probate.

MEMBERS OF FIRM

FRED R. HAINS, born South Bend, Indiana, March 15, 1948; admitted to bar, 1974, Indiana; 1982, U.S. District Court, Northern District of Indiana. *Education:* Wittenberg University (B.A., 1970); Valparaiso University (J.D., 1974). *Member:* St. Joseph County, Indiana State and American Bar Associations. ***REPORTED CASES:*** Freidline v. Shelby Ins. Co., 774 N.E. 2d 37 (Ind. 2002); Paternity of V.A.M.C., 768 N.E. 2d 990 (Ind. Ct. App. 2002), instructions on remand modified by 773 N.E.2d 359 (Ind. Ct. App. 2002); In Re Adoption of I.K.E.W., 724 N.E.2d 245 (Ind. Ct. App. 2000); U.S. v. Johnson, 185 F.3d 765 (7th Cir. 1999); John Wendt & Sons v. Edward C. Levy Co., 685 N.E.2d 183 (Ind. Ct. App. 1997); Kiskowski v. O'Hara 622 N.E.2d 991 (Ind. Ct. App. 1993). ***Email:*** fhains@hainslawfirm.com

PETER M. YARBRO, born Madison, Wisconsin, August 31, 1974; admitted to bar, 1999, Indiana and U.S. District Court, Northern and Southern Districts of Indiana; 2001, U.S. Court of Appeals, Seventh Circuit. *Education:* Johns Hopkins University (B.A., 1996); University of Notre Dame (J.D., 1999). Phi Alpha Delta Law Fraternity (Member, 1996—; Hoynes Chapter Justice, 1997-1998). Recipient: Dean's Award, Pleadings Discovery and Pre Trial, Fall 1998; Dean's Award, Roman Law, Spring 1999. *Member:* St. Joseph County, Indiana State and American (Member, Litigation Section) Bar Associations. ***PRACTICE AREAS:*** Business Law; Civil Litigation; Real Estate; Appellate Practice; Bankruptcy. ***Email:*** pyarbro@hainslawfirm.com

HAMILTON LAW FIRM

A PROFESSIONAL CORPORATION

300 NORTH MICHIGAN STREET
SUITE 454
SOUTH BEND, INDIANA 46601
Telephone: 574-289-9987
Fax: 574-289-8138
Email: jch@HamiltonFirm.com

Civil Trial and Appellate Practice in Federal and State Courts. Commercial, Employment and Environmental Law.

JOHN C. HAMILTON, born New York, New York, November 26, 1940; admitted to bar, 1968, California; 1977, Indiana; 1984, U.S. Supreme Court. *Education:* University of Notre Dame (B.A., 1964); Harvard University (J.D., 1967). Author: "Environmental Law: The Roles of Commerce, Citizens and the Land In an Era of Intensifying Competition," 26 Ind.L.Rev. 921 (1993). Faculty Member, National Institute for Trial Advocacy, 1987-1990; Indiana Continuing Legal Education Forum, 1983, 1987, 1989, 1990, 1993, 1995-2002. Member, 1995-2000, and Chairman, 1998-2000, Indiana Clean Manufacturing Technology and Safe Materials Board. Deputy Attorney General, California Department of Justice, 1968-1970. Deputy City Attorney, Los Angeles, California, 1974-1977. *Member:* St. Joseph County, Indiana State (Member: Appellate Section, 1996—) and The Seventh Circuit (Northern District Indiana Liaison) Bar Associations; State Bar of California; National Employment Lawyers Association; The Association of Trial Lawyers of America; Indiana Trial Lawyers Association. ***REPORTED CASES:*** Olinger v. U.S. Golf Assn., 205 F.3d 1001 (7th Cir. 2000), cert. granted and remanded, 121 S.Ct. 2212 (2001); Williams v. Pharmacia, Inc., 137 F.3d 944 (7th Cir. 1998); Wolvos v. Meyer, 668 N.E.2d 671 (Ind. 1996); Millenium Club, Inc. v. Avila, 809 N.E.2d 906 (Ind.Ct.App. 2004); The Waste Inc. Cost Recovery Group v. Allis-Chalmers Corp., 51 F. Supp. 2d 936 (ND. Ind. 1999). **Email:** jch@HamiltonFirm.com

REFERENCE: Wells Fargo, South Bend, Indiana.

HUNT SUEDHOFF KALAMAROS LLP

120 WEST LASALLE AVENUE, TWELFTH FLOOR
P.O. BOX 4156
SOUTH BEND, INDIANA 46634-4156
Telephone: 574-232-4801
Fax: 574-232-9736
URL: http://www.hsk-law.com

Fort Wayne, Indiana Office: 803 South Calhoun Street, Ninth Floor, P.O. Box 11489, 46858-1489. Telephone: 260-423-1311. Fax: 260-424-5396.

Indianapolis, Indiana Office: 6323 S. East Street, 46227. Telephone: 317-784-4966. Fax: 317-784-5566.

St. Joseph, Michigan Office: 608 S. Pleasant Street, P.O. Box 46, 49085-0046. Telephone: 269-983-4405. Fax: 269-983-5645.

General Civil Trial and Appellate Practice, Insurance Defense Litigation, Commercial Real Estate Financing and Transactions, Corporate and Commercial Law, Probate and Estate Planning.

FIRM PROFILE: Hunt Suedhoff, LLP was founded in 1950 by the late Leigh L. Hunt, a noted trial lawyer. Kalamaros and Associates was founded in 1960 by the late Edward N. Kalamaros, a noted worker's compensation lawyer. Recently, the two firms with so much in common joined forces. This solidified Hunt Suedhoff Kalamaros LLP as the premier law firm with the largest litigation practice in Northern Indiana. The firm presently serves the casualty insurance industry, as well as many regional and national corporations.

The lawyers of the firm are recognized by their peers as specialists in their fields, and frequently are called upon to participate in the training of other lawyers in various workshops and seminars sponsored by the National Institute for Trial Advocacy, the National Business Institute and the Indiana Continuing Legal Education Forum.

MEMBERS OF FIRM

THOMAS F. COHEN, born South Bend, Indiana, September 3, 1953; admitted to bar, 1978, Indiana and U.S. District Court, Northern District of Indiana; 1980, U.S. Court of Appeals, Seventh Circuit. *Education:* University of Notre Dame (A.B. cum laude, 1975); Indiana University School of Law (J.D., cum laude, 1978). Author: "Indiana Worker's Compensation Benefits," Professional Education Systems, Inc., 1989; "Time Limitations in Worker's Compensation Cases," ICLEF, 1990; "Changing Benefit Levels," Professional Education Systems, Inc., 1991; "Indiana Workers' Compensation Law," Professional Education Systems, Inc., 1992; "Practical Aspects of Indiana Workers' Compensation Law," ICLEF, 1993; "Independent Contractor and Special Employee Situations," ICLEF, 1994; "Cross Examination of Vocational Experts," ICLEF, 1996; "Ethical Considerations in Worker's Compensation Cases", ICLEF, 1998. Inclusion in The Best Lawyers in America Woodward/White 1995. *Member:* St. Joseph County, Indiana State and American Bar Associations; Defense Trial Counsel of Indiana. ***PRACTICE AREAS:*** Workers Compensation; Litigation; Insurance Defense; Civil Appeals.

ROBERT DEANE WOODS, born Marley, Idaho, September 30, 1936; admitted to bar, 1984, Indiana. *Education:* University of Kansas (B.S., 1965; J.D., 1983); Naval Post Graduate School (M.S., with distinction, 1976). Author, "Worker's Compensation -- The Challenges and Opportunities," National Business Institute, 1991 Edition. *Member:* St. Joseph County and Indiana State Bar Associations; Defense Trial Counsel of Indiana. [CMR, USN, Ret., 1957-1980]. ***PRACTICE AREAS:*** Defense Litigation; Workers Compensation Defense; Appellate Practice.

KEVIN W. KEARNEY, born Morristown, New Jersey, February 20, 1961; admitted to bar, 1986, New Jersey; 1993, Indiana. *Education:* University of Notre Dame (B.A., 1983); Seton Hall University (J.D., 1986). Law Clerk to the Hon. Charles J. Harrington, Jr., Superior Court of New Jersey, 1986-1987. Assistant Prosecutor, Essex County, New Jersey, 1987-1990. *Member:* St. Joseph County and Indiana State Bar Associations; Defense Trial Counsel of Indiana. ***PRACTICE AREAS:*** Civil Litigation; Workers Compensation.

PHILIP E. KALAMAROS, born South Bend, Indiana, April 21, 1962; admitted to bar, 1987, Indiana, U.S. District Court, Northern and Southern Districts of Indiana and U.S. Court of Appeals, Seventh Circuit; 1995, U.S. Supreme Court; 2002, Michigan. *Education:* University of Notre Dame (B.B.A., 1984; J.D., 1987). Author and/or Speaker: "Temporary Partial Disability, Getting the Numbers Right," Res Gestae, October 1989; "Preparing Yourself for Mediation," ITLA Summertime Torts, August 1992; "Bad Faith and Collateral Actions in Workers' Compensation," LBC Insurance Law Update, May 1993; "Overview of the Workers Compensation Act," Workers Compensation Deskbook ICLEF, 1994; "Constitutional Challenge to Tort Reform, IDLA, June 1996; "Fraudulent Concealment and the Statute of 1997, Limitations in Medical Malpractice," IDLA, Winter 1996; "1997 Indiana Workers Compensation Legislation Summary"; The Indiana Lawyer, June 11, 1997; "Making it Work" and "Defense Bar and Industry Relations," Defense Seminar, Insurance Institute of Indiana, 1998; "Defense Approach: Getting A Clue," Planning Your First Tort Case, ICLEF Seminar Summer 2000; "Depositions for Fun and Profit," IDLA Rookie Seminar, April 1995, 1997, 1999, 2001, 2003; "Times They Have Changed: The Business of Being a Defense Lawyer Affecting the Art of Being a Defense Lawyer," ICLEF Masters Series, Summer 2001; "Defending the Bad Faith Action," Bad Faith Claims in Litigation, ICLEF, Fall 2003. Other: Mediator/Arbitrator. Inclusion in: The Best Lawyers in America, Woodward/White 1995/1998/2001; Marquis Who's Who; Strathmore's Who's Who; Indiana Superlawyers, 2003-2004. Member: American Bar Association, 1987-2003; The Association of Trial Lawyers of America, 1987-2003; Indiana Trial Lawyers Association, 1987-2003. *Member:* St. Joseph County (Member, Board of Governors, 1989-1990; Secretary, 1990-2003), Berrien County, Seventh Circuit and Indiana State Bar Associations; Defense Trial Counsel of Indiana (Amicus Chairman, 1992-1997, Director, 1997—); Defense Trial Counsel of Michigan; Defense Research Institute; National Council of Self Insureds; Indiana Self Insurers Association; National Health Lawyers Association; Notre Dame Law Association. Fellow, Indiana Bar Foundation. ***REPORTED CASES:*** Court View Centre, L.L.C. v. Witt, 753 N.E.2d 75 (Ind.App., Aug 7, 2001); Beaver v. Grand Prix Karting Ass'n, Inc., 246 F.3d 905 (7th Cir. (Ind.), Mar 30, 2001); Coble v. Joseph Motors, Inc., 695 N.E.2d 129 (Ind.App.., Apr. 29, 1998); Cincinnati Ins. Co. v. Moen, 940 F.2d 1069 (7th Cir. (Ind.), Aug. 19, 1991); Chang v. Michiana Telecasting Corp., 900 F.2d 1085, 17 Media L. Rep. 1768 (7th Cir. (Ind.), Apr. 24, 1990). ***PRACTICE AREAS:*** Insurance Coverage; Errors and Omissions; Employment Practices Liability Insurance; Civil Appeals; Insurance Defense; Workers Compensation; Medical Malpractice Defense; Professional Malpractice; Civil Rights Defense; Torts; Civil Litigation; First Party Insurance Defense; Business Planning.

LYNN E. KALAMAROS, born St. Charles, Illinois, June 13, 1968; admitted to bar, 1993, Indiana and Illinois. *Education:* University of Notre Dame (B.A., cum laude, 1990; J.D., cum laude, 1993). *Member:* St. Joseph County and Indiana State Bar Associations; Defense Counsel of Indiana; Council Oak Inn of Court. ***PRACTICE AREAS:*** Civil Litigation; Employment Discrimination; Civil Rights; Insurance Defense.

CAROL A. VOGEL, born South Bend, Indiana, January 11, 1950; admitted to bar, 1994, Colorado, Wyoming, U.S. District Court, Districts of Wyoming and Colorado and U.S. Court of Appeals, Tenth Circuit; 1995, Nebraska; 1997, Indiana; U.S. District Court, Southern and Northern Districts of Indiana. *Education:* Indiana University, South Bend (B.S., Business, 1982); Indiana University School of Law, Bloomington (J.D., 1994). Beta Gamma Sigma; Omicron Delta Epsilon; Sigma Iota Epsilon. Recipient, American Jurisprudence Award, Trial Team, 1993. Listed in: Who's Who Among American Law Students, 1994. Hearing Officer for the South Bend Human Rights Commission, 2000—. *Member:* St. Joseph County, Laramie County, Colorado, Indiana State, Nebraska State and American Bar Associations; Wyoming State Bar; The Association of Trial Lawyers of Americ; Robert A. Grant Inn of Court. ***PRACTICE AREAS:*** Insurance Defense; Litigation.

LYLE R. HARDMAN, born Milwaukee, Wisconsin, January 14, 1966; admitted to bar, 1991, Indiana and U.S. District Court, Southern and Northern Districts of Indiana; 1993, U.S. Court of Appeals, Seventh Circuit. *Education:* DePauw University (B.A., cum laude, 1988); Indiana University (J.D., 1991). *Member:* Lake County, Seventh Circuit, Indiana State and American Bar Associations; Defense Research Institute. ***PRACTICE AREAS:*** Medical Malpractice; Litigation; Appellate Practice.

ASSOCIATES

THOMAS R. HAMILTON, born New Castle, Indiana, December 17, 1955; admitted to bar, 1983, Indiana and U.S. District Court, Northern and Southern Districts of Indiana; 1984, U.S. Court of Appeals, Seventh Circuit. *Education:* Wabash College (A.B., 1978); Valparaiso University (J.D., 1983). *Member:* Elkhart City, St. Joseph County and Indiana State Bar Associations; Defense Trial Counsel of Indiana. ***PRACTICE AREAS:*** Personal Injury Defense; Civil Litigation; Commercial Litigation; Family Law; General Practice.

CHARLES H. BASSFORD, IV, born Green Bay, Wisconsin, September 12, 1955; admitted to bar, 1984, Tennessee; 1994, Indiana. *Education:* Bryan College (B.S.B.A., 1978); Tennessee Technological University (M.B.A., 1979); University of Memphis (J.D., 1983). ***PRACTICE AREAS:*** Commercial; Creditor Rights; Business; Workers' Compensation; Insurance.

KEITH C. DOI, born South Bend, Indiana, January 18, 1963; admitted to bar, 1990, Indiana and U.S. District Court, Southern and Northern Districts of Indiana. *Education:* Indiana University at Bloomington (B.A., 1985; J.D., 1988). St. Joseph County Deputy Prosecuting Attorney, 1990-1993. Elkhart County Deputy Prosecuting Attorney, 1994-1997. Director, Title IV-D Program for Elkhart County, 1994-1997. *Member:* Elkhart City (Secretary, 1996) and St. Joseph County Bar Associations; Defense Trial Counsel of Indiana. ***PRACTICE AREAS:*** Litigation; Insurance Defense; Personal Injury; Family Law; General Practice.

PETER J. BAGIACKAS, born Rhinebeck, New York, May 19, 1961; admitted to bar, 1994, Indiana. *Education:* University of Notre Dame (B.A., 1983); Indiana University (J.D., 1994). *Member:* Indiana State Bar Association; Defense Trial Counsel of Indiana. ***PRACTICE AREAS:*** Workers Compensation; Medical Malpractice Defense; Insurance Defense; Civil Litigation.

(This Listing Continued)

HUNT SUEDHOFF KALAMAROS LLP, South Bend—Continued

DEANNE M. VOLHEIM, born Hobart, Indiana, July 3, 1974; admitted to bar, 2001, Indiana. *Education:* Valparaiso University (B.A., 1996; J.D., 2001). ***PRACTICE AREAS:*** Insurance Defense; Civil Rights Defense.

(For complete biographical data on all personnel, see Professional Biographies at Fort Wayne, Indiana)

JOHNSON LAW GROUP

SOUTH BEND, INDIANA 46601
Telephone: 877-333-2889
Fax: 309-827-3991
Email: johnson.law@verizon.net

Okemos, Michigan Office: 3474 Alaiedon Parkway, 47764. Telephone: 877-333-2889.
Canton, Ohio Office: 4571 Stephen Circle N.W., 44718. Telephone: 877-333-2889.
Bloomington, Illinois Office: 115 W. Front Street, 61701. Telephone: 309-827-3670.

Felonies, Murder, White Collar Crime, Drugs, Domestic Violence, DWI.

FIRM PROFILE: Johnson Law Group provides aggressive criminal defense representation throughout the entire States of Illinois, Indiana, Michigan and Ohio. Our Criminal Defense Attorneys are recognized in Illinois, Indiana, Michigan and Ohio for providing premier criminal defense services. The attorneys at Johnson Law Group place cutting edge aggressive defensive strategies at the top of their priority list. Johnson Law Group has developed a process that allows a client 24 hours a day, 7 days a week access to a client service representative who will work closely with the client and our experienced criminal defense lawyers to make sure that every possible angle in a case is covered. To learn more about our process, visit our website at johnsoncriminaldefenselawgroup.com.

Languages: Japanese and Greek.

(For complete biographical data on all personnel, see Professional Biographies at Bloomington, Illinois)

TIMOTHY E. KALAMAROS LAW OFFICE, P.C.

328 NORTH MICHIGAN STREET, SUITE S-2
SOUTH BEND, INDIANA 46601
Telephone: 574-232-4802
Fax: 574-232-3839
Email: teklaw@sbcglobal.net

Wills and Probate, Trusts and Estates, Estate Planning, Elder Law, Business Law, Business Planning, Business Enterprises, Starting a Business, Buying and Selling a Business, Real Estate.

TIMOTHY E. KALAMAROS, born South Bend, Indiana, 1971; admitted to bar, 1996, Indiana, Illinois and U.S. District Court, Northern and Southern Districts of Indiana. *Education:* University of Notre Dame (B.B.A., 1993); Loyola University of Chicago (J.D., 1996). Author: "Defining Estate Administration," and "How and When to Close the Estate," Estate Planning and Probate for the Paralegal/Legal Assistant in Indiana, April 2000; "Indiana Spousal Electives," and "Indiana Law of Interstate Succession," The Probate Process From Start to Finish in Indiana, August 2004. *Member:* Chicago and Indiana State Bar Associations. ***PRACTICE AREAS:*** Business Law; Wills; Probate; Trusts and Estates; Estate Planning; Real Estate Law. ***Email:*** teklaw@sbcglobal.net

THOMAS P. KELLER

THE TOWER BUILDING, SUITE 720
218 W. WASHINGTON
SOUTH BEND, INDIANA 46601
Telephone: 574-234-2990
Fax: 574-234-9960
Email: thomas.keller@tkellerlaw.com
URL: http://www.tkellerlaw.com

Criminal Law, Felonies, Misdemeanors, Drug Crimes, Traffic Violations, Driving While Intoxicated, White Collar Crime, Personal Injury, Automobile Accidents, Slip and Fall, Wrongful Death, Debt Collection, Debtor and Creditor Law.

THOMAS P. KELLER, born Clarendon Hills, Illinois, March 17, 1966; admitted to bar, 1993, Michigan; 1994, Indiana. *Education:* Fairfield University (B.A., cum laude, 1988); University of Notre Dame (J.D., cum laude, 1992). *Member:* St. Joseph County and Indiana State Bar Associations; State Bar of Michigan. ***PRACTICE AREAS:*** Criminal Law; Debt Collection; Personal Injury; Civil Litigation.

REPRESENTATIVE CLIENTS: CBM Accounts Service, Inc.; American Safety and First Aid.

KONOPA, REAGAN & AIGOTTI, P.C.

Established in 1993
212 EAST LASALLE AVENUE, SUITE 200
SOUTH BEND, INDIANA 46617
Telephone: 574-239-1000
Fax: 574-239-1001
URL: http://www.konopa.com

General Civil Practice. Personal Injury, Automobile Accidents, Products Liability, Brain Injury, Truck Accidents, Nursing Home Negligence, Wrongful Death, Insurance (Personal and Commercial Lines), and Commercial Law. Business Law, Contracts, Litigation, Trial and Appellate Practice in all State and Federal Courts. Mediations and Arbitrations.

(This Listing Continued)

FIRM PROFILE: Since the firm was founded, March 1, 1993, it is dedicated to serve the people of Northern Indiana. Based in South Bend, the firm extends service to Elkhart, La Porte, La Grange, Kosciusko, Fulton, Porter, Noble, Whitley, Starke, Marshall, Lake and Steuben counties. The practice specializes in the areas of Civil Litigation, Personal Injury, Products Liability and Business Law. The firm is committed to provide quality, cost-effective representation reflecting the highest diligence and integrity.

DIRECTORS OF FIRM

ROBERT J. KONOPA, born Manistee, Michigan, August 1, 1941; admitted to bar, 1967, Indiana, U.S. District Court, Northern and Southern Districts of Indiana and U.S. Court of Appeals, Seventh Circuit. *Education:* University of Notre Dame (A.B., 1963; M.A., 1964; LL.B., 1967). Associate Lecturer, Indiana University of South Bend, 1965-1977, 1983. Certified Mediator. Listed in *Best Lawyers in America,* 1987—. *Member:* St. Joseph County (Member, Board of Governors, 1976-1979), Indiana State (Member: Board of Managers, 1988-1990; Trial Section) and Seventh Circuit Bar Association; National Lawyers Association; Defense Research Institute, Inc.; Diplomat, Defense Trial Counsel of Indiana (Member, Board of Directors, 1996-1998); The Association of Trial Lawyers of America; Indiana Trial Lawyers Association. Robert A. Grant Inn of Court (Emeritus; President, 1997-1999). Fellow, American College of Trial Lawyers. ***PRACTICE AREAS:*** Civil Litigation; Mediation; Personal Injury; Wrongful Death; Brain Injury; Truck Accidents; Products Liability; Insurance Litigation; Commercial Disputes; Railroad Accidents. ***Email:*** rkonopa@konopa.com

MARGOT FISHER REAGAN, born Springfield, Illinois, February 10, 1955; admitted to bar, 1987, Indiana; U.S. District Court, Northern and Southern Districts of Indiana; U.S. Court of Appeals, Seventh Circuit; U.S. Supreme Court. *Education:* St. Mary's College (B.B.A., 1977); University of Akron; University of Notre Dame (J.D., cum laude, 1987). Author: Note, "Judicial Review of an Administrative Agency Rescission," 18 Akron Law Review 153, 1984. Clerk for Judge Allen Sharp, U.S. District Court, Northern District of Indiana, 1987-1989. *Member:* St. Joseph County (Member, Board of Governors, 2001-2003), Indiana State and American Bar Associations; Indiana Trial Lawyers Association; Robert A. Grant Inn of Court. ***PRACTICE AREAS:*** Civil Litigation; Personal Injury; Brain Injury; Nursing Home Abuse and Neglect; Wrongful Death; Products Liability; Insurance Litigation; Commercial Disputes. ***Email:*** mreagan@konopa.com

CLAIRE KONOPA AIGOTTI, born South Bend, Indiana, September 15, 1971; admitted to bar, 1996, Indiana. *Education:* University of Notre Dame (B.A., 1993); St. Thomas University (J.D., 1996). Phi Delta Phi. Certified Mediator. *Member:* St. Joseph County and Indiana State Bar Associations; Defense Research Institute, Inc.; Defense Trial Counsel of Indiana; Robert A. Grant Inn of Court. ***PRACTICE AREAS:*** Civil Litigation; Mediation; Products Liability; Wrongful Death; Brain Injury; Truck Accidents; Nursing Home Abuse and Neglect; Insurance Litigation; Medical Malpractice; Family Law; Divorce; Child Custody. ***Email:*** caigotti@konopa.com

REPRESENTATIVE CLIENTS: Allstate Insurance Co.; Auto Owners Insurance Co.; Rockford Mutual Insurance Co.; Grand Trunk Western Railroad Co.; Employers Mutual Insurance Co.; Minnesota Mutual Insurance Co.; Liberty Bell Agency; Hamilton Mutual Insurance Co.; American Family Mutual Insurance Co.; AM Reliable; Guide One; American Bankers Ins. Co.
REFERENCE: St. Joseph Capital Bank.

JAY LAUER

400 TRIGON BUILDING
224 WEST JEFFERSON BOULEVARD
SOUTH BEND, INDIANA 46601-1824
Telephone: 574-288-5562
Fax: 574-233-9342
URL: http://www.jaylauer.com

General Civil Practice in All State and Federal Courts. Criminal Law, Driving While Intoxicated, Drug Crimes, Juvenile Law, Parole and Probation, Traffic Violations, White Collar Crime, Labor, Employment Discrimination, Sexual Harassment, Wrongful Termination, Medical Malpractice, Personal Injury, Automobile Accidents and Injuries, Slip and Fall, Wrongful Death, Product Liability, Social Security Disability, Workers Compensation, Bankruptcies, Investment Fraud, Municipal Law, Real Estate, Wills, Probate, Trusts and Estates, Estate Planning, Asset Protection, Guardianships, Domestic Relations, Family Law, Adoptions, Child Custody, Child Support, Divorce, Domestic Violence, Visitation Rights.

FIRM PROFILE: Mr. Lauer began practicing law in South Bend in 1978 and has served Northern Indiana in his present practice since 1988. As a solo general practitioner, Mr. Lauer's mission is to treat his clients with respect and to provide reasonable and fair fees. He has significant experience in labor law, employment discrimination, medical malpractice, personal injury, and other general practice areas.

JAY LAUER, born Hammond, Indiana, June 16, 1952; admitted to bar, 1978, Indiana and U.S. District Court, Northern District of Indiana. *Education:* Wabash College; Valparaiso University (B.A., 1975; J.D., 1978). Arbitrator, NASDAQ, 1990-1991. *Member:* St. Joseph County, Indiana State and American Bar Association. ***REPORTED CASES:*** ServiceMaster Diversified Health Services, L.P. v. Wiley, 790 N.E.2d 1056 (Ind.App. Jul 02, 2003); Northern Indiana Public Service Co. v. Dabagia, 721 N.E.2d 294, 15 IER Cases 1785 (Ind.App. Dec 27, 1999); Pedraza ex rel. Pedraza v. Grande, 712 N.E.2d 1007 (Ind.App. May 24, 1999); Choung v. Iemma, 708 N.E.2d 7 (Ind.App. Mar 16, 1999); Citizens Action Coalition of Indiana, Inc. v. Public Service Co. of Indiana, 450 N.E.2d 98, 29 A.L.R.4th 606 (Ind.App. 4 Dist. Jun 20, 1983); Marozsan v. Review Bd. of Indiana Employment Sec. Division, 429 N.E.2d 986 (Ind.App. 4 Dist. Jan 12, 1982); Citizens Action Coalition of Indiana, Inc. v. Public Service Commission of Indiana, 425 N.E.2d 178 (Ind.App. 3 Dist. Aug 31, 1981); Martin v. Review Board of Indiana Employment Sec. Division, 421 N.E.2d 653 (Ind.App. 4 Dist. Jun 08, 1981); Molina v. Review Bd. of Indiana Employment Sec. Division, 418 N.E.2d 1198 (Ind.App. 4 Dist. Apr 08, 1981); Matter of Fries, 416 N.E.2d 908 (Ind.App. 3 Dist. Mar 02, 1981); Jones v. Review Bd. of Indiana Employment Sec. Division, 399 N.E.2d 844 (Ind.App. 3 Dist. Feb 04, 1980); Washington v. LaPorte County Sheriff's Dept., 306F.3d 515 (7th Cir.(Ind.) Oct 07, 2002); U.S. v. Nelson,

(This Listing Continued)

143 F.3d 373 (7th Cir.(Ind.) May 06, 1998); Addis v. Holy Cross Health System Corp., 88 F.3d 482, 65 USLW 2122, 1997-1 Trade Cases P 71,728 (7th Cir.(Ind.) Jul 08, 1996); U.S. v. Phillips, 205 F.Supp.2d 995 (N.D.Ind. May 15, 2002); Addis v. Holy Cross Health System Corp., Not Reported in F.Supp., 1995 WL 429270 (N.D.Ind. Feb 07, 1995).

LEE AND GROVES

PROFESSIONAL ASSOCIATION

Established in 1972

SUITE 502
205 WEST JEFFERSON BOULEVARD
SOUTH BEND, INDIANA 46601-1812
Telephone: 574-232-5923
Fax: 574-232-5942
URL: http://www.leesandgroves.com

General Civil and Trial Practice in all State and Federal Courts. Personal Injury, Products Liability, Family/Domestic Relations, Insurance, Administrative, Negligence, Corporation and Real Estate Law.

ROBERT D. LEE, born Los Angeles, California, May 29, 1939; admitted to bar, 1966, Indiana and U.S. District Court, Northern and Southern Districts of Indiana. *Education:* University of Notre Dame (B.B.S., 1961); Valparaiso University (J.D., 1966). Delta Theta Phi. Co-founder and Business Director of Valparaiso University Law Review, 1966. *Member:* St. Joseph County (Chairman, Bench and Bar Committee, 1983-1984), Indiana State and American Bar Associations; Indiana Trial Lawyers Association; The Association of Trial Lawyers of America (Member, Litigation Section); Indiana Defense Lawyers Association. Fellow, Indiana Bar Foundation. ***PRACTICE AREAS:*** Personal Injury Litigation; Family Law; Domestic Relations; Insurance Defense. ***Email:*** robertdlee@aol.com

JAMES F. GROVES, born South Bend, Indiana, January 6, 1947; admitted to bar, 1972, Indiana. *Education:* Notre Dame University (A.B., 1969; J.D., 1972). Roseland Town Attorney, 1974-1987. Faculty: National Institute for Trial Advocacy; American Inns of Court, Council Oaks Chapter. *Member:* South Bend, St. Joseph County (Chairman, Bench and Bar Committee, 1975-1979; Board of Directors, 1992-1998, and Member, Judicial Selection Commission, 1982-1987, President, St. Joseph County Bar Association, 1996), Indiana State (Member, Committee on Professional Services Corporation Act, 1975-1977) and American Bar Associations; American College of Trial Lawyers; American Judicature Society; Indiana Defense Lawyers Association; Fellow, American College of Trial Lawyers. [Captain, U.S. Army Infantry, 1972-1973]. ***LANGUAGES:*** Spanish. ***PRACTICE AREAS:*** Malpractice Law; Personal Injury Litigation; Product Liability; Insurance Defense; Commercial Litigation. ***Email:*** jimfgroves@aol.com

---

CLINT A. ZALAS, born South Bend, Indiana, March 24, 1974; admitted to bar, 2001, Indiana. *Education:* Purdue University (B.A., 1996); Valparaiso University (J.D., 2001). *Member:* American Inn of Court, Council Oak Chapter. ***PRACTICE AREAS:*** Medical Malpractice; Personal Injury; Insurance Defense; Commercial Litigation. ***Email:*** clintanthonyzalas@yahoo.com

DAVID E. BALLARD, born Middletown, Ohio, October 7, 1961; admitted to bar, 1987, Ohio; 1995, North Carolina; 1997, Indiana. *Education:* Miami University (B.A., 1984); Ohio State University (J.D., 1987). *Member:* St. Joseph County, Indiana State and American Bar Associations. ***PRACTICE AREAS:*** Insurance Defense (60%); Medical Malpractice (20%); Commercial Litigation (20%); Appellate Practice. ***Email:*** ballard7@peoplepc.com

Languages: Spanish.

REPRESENTATIVE CLIENTS: Farm Bureau Insurance Co.; Secura Insurance Co.; Wolverine Mutual Insurance Co.; Canal Insurance Co.; Goodville Mutual Insurance Co.; Westfield Companies; South Bend Mishawaka New Car Dealers Association; Jordan Motors, Inc.; B & R Oil Co., Inc.; Indiana Waste Systems; St. Joseph Valley, Inc.; County Commissioners of St. Joseph County, Indiana.
REFERENCES: 1st Source Bank; KeyBank; National City Bank; MFB Financial.

ERIC MARSHALL

1318 MISHAWAKA AVENUE
SOUTH BEND, INDIANA 46615
Telephone: 574-234-9334
Fax: 574-288-1066
URL: http://www.ericmarshall.com
Email: sericmarshall@aol.com
URL: http://www.southbendelderlaw.com

Elder Law, Elder Care, Health Care Law, Estate Planning, Trusts and Estates, Wills and Probate, Estate Litigation, Asset Protection, Guardianship and Conservatorship, Charitable Giving, Taxation, Estate and Gift Taxation, Income Tax, Property Tax, Long Term Care, Medicare and Medicaid, Nursing Home Litigation, Real Estate.

ERIC MARSHALL, born South Bend, Indiana, August 28, 1957; admitted to bar, 1992, Indiana. *Education:* Indiana University (B.S., 1980); University of Notre Dame (J.D., 1992). Treasurer, Phi Delta Phi, 1991-1992. Certified Public Accountant, Indiana, 1983. Previous employment: Coopers & Lybrand, CPAs, 1980-1988; Crowe Chizek, CPAs, 1988-1989. Member: American Institute of Certified Public Accountants, 1983—; Indiana C.P.A. Society, 1983-1990. *Member:* Indiana State and American Bar Associations; National Academy of Elder Law Attorneys. ***PRACTICE AREAS:*** Tax; Estate Planning; Corporate; Health Care.

MAY OBERFELL LORBER

Established in 1856

300 NORTH MICHIGAN STREET, SUITE 414
SOUTH BEND, INDIANA 46601
Telephone: 574-232-2031
Facsimile: 574-232-9789
URL: http://www.maylorber.com

Mishawaka, Indiana Office: 4100 Edison Lakes Parkway, 46545-3422. Telephone: 574-243-4100. Fax: 574-232-9789.

Corporate and Commercial Transactions, Litigation, Environmental Law, Real Estate, Labor and Employment, Banking and Bank Related Matters, Estate Planning, Municipal and Administration Law, Products Liability, Alternative Dispute Resolution, Health Care, Medical Malpractice Defense, Insurance Litigation, Trademark and Copyright, Tax, Plaintiff's Litigation, General Civil and Appellate Practice in State and Federal Courts.

FIRM PROFILE: For over 145 years, the law firm of May, Oberfell & Lorber has expanded and reorganized its professional and support staff to meet a broad spectrum of its client's needs throughout north central Indiana. Beginning with Andrew Anderson in 1856, May, Oberfell & Lorber now consists of over 20 attorneys and paralegals, making it one of the largest law firms in north central Indiana. During the firm's distinguished history, its members have served as Indiana Attorney General, Indiana Public Service Commissioner, as state and federal court judges and in the United States Congress.

LAW FIRM ALLIANCES/ASSOCIATIONS: **NETWORK OF LEADING LAW FIRMS**

JOHN H. PEDDYCORD, born LaPorte, Indiana, October 15, 1944; admitted to bar, 1971, Indiana, U.S. District Court, Northern District of Indiana and U.S. Court of Appeals, Seventh Circuit. *Education:* Ball State University (A.B., 1967); University of Notre Dame (J.D., 1971). Law Clerk to the Hon. Robert A. Grant, U.S. District Court, Northern District of Indiana, 1971-1973. *Member:* St. Joseph County (Past Member, Board of Governors), Indiana State (Member, Probate, Trust and Real Property Section) and American Bar Associations; Michiana Estate Planning Council. ***PRACTICE AREAS:*** Estate Planning; Probate; Real Estate; Municipal Law. ***Email:*** jpeddycord@maylorber.com

REPRESENTATIVE CLIENTS: All American Homes, Inc.; ASA Corp.; Bayer Corporation; Cambridge Integrated Services; Cast Products Corp.; CNA Insurance Company; Coachman Industries, Inc.; Communitywide Federal Credit Union; Daimler Chrysler Corp.; Dearborn & Crane Engineering, Inc.; Ditmer Trucking Co.; Eagle Products, Inc.; Health Care Indemnity, Inc.; JB Products, Inc.; Keybank; Keystone RV Company; Madison Center & Hospital; Memorial Hospital of South Bend, Inc.; Memorial Health System, Inc.; Memorial Home Care, Inc.; The Medical Protective Co.; Metro Beverages, Inc.; Miles Distributors, Inc.; National Guardian Risk Retention Group, Inc.; NMB Technologies Corp.; Pro Assurance Group; Pro Assurance Insurance Company; Rustoleum, Inc.; South Bend Chocolate Co.; St. Paul Fire & Marine Insurance Co.; St. Joseph Capital Bank; State Farm Fire & Casualty Co.; State Farm Mutual Automobile Insurance Co.; Thor Industries, Inc.; Town of North Liberty; Trinity Health; TriStar Distributing, LP; Trustmark Insurance Co.; Unitrin Specialty Lines Insurance Co.; Wise International Trucks, Inc.; Worksport Rehabilitation Services; Zurich North American Insurance Group.

(For biographical data on all personnel, see Professional Biographies at Mishawaka)

MICHAEL C. MURPHY ELDER LAW P.C.

CAMDON PARK ON HICKORY
1001 HICKORY ROAD, SUITE 7B
SOUTH BEND, INDIANA 46615
Telephone: 574-235-7950
Fax: 574-235-7954
Email: mike@murphyelderlaw.com
URL: http://www.michianaelderlaw.com

Elder Law, Estate Planning, Trust and Estates, Wills and Probate, Medicare, Medicaid, Guardianships and Conservatorship, Asset Protection, Health Care.

MICHAEL C. MURPHY, born Oakland, California, August 4, 1953; admitted to bar, 1979, Indiana and U.S. District Court, Southern and Northern Districts of Indiana. *Education:* University of Notre Dame (B.B.A., 1975; J.D., 1979); International Christian University, Tokyo, Japan. Lecturer: "Indiana Elder Law: The Basics & Beyond," 1991; "Planning Opportunities With Living Trusts in Indiana," 1992; "Estate Planning for the Professional," 1998; "Divorce and Remarriage for the Older Client," 1998. *Member:* St. Joseph County and Indiana State Bar Associations; National Academy of Elder Law Attorneys; St. Joseph County Estate Planning Council. ***PRACTICE AREAS:*** Elder Law; Aged and Aging; Medicare and Medicaid; Trusts and Estates; Wills; Guardianship and Conservatorship. ***Email:*** mike@murphyelderlaw.com

NEWBY, LEWIS, KAMINSKI & JONES, LLP

SOUTH BEND, INDIANA

(See La Porte)

Civil Practice, Corporate Law, Real Estate, Appellate Practice, Personal Injury, Automobile Accidents, Wrongful Death, Wills and Probate, Trusts and Estates, Estate Planning, Civil Rights, Insurance Defense, Labor and Employment Law, Environmental Law, Education Law, Criminal Law, Driving While Intoxicated, Drug Crimes, Bankruptcy Law, Family Law, Adoptions, Divorce, Child Custody, Child Support, Visitation Rights, Medical Malpractice Defense, Mediation Services, Zoning Law.

NICKLE & PIASECKI

Established in 1979

205 WEST JEFFERSON BOULEVARD, SUITE 600
SOUTH BEND, INDIANA 46601
Telephone: 574-232-4747
Fax: 574-232-4904

Commercial Transactions, Corporate and Business Law, Real Estate, Commercial Collections, Creditors' Rights, Personal Injury Litigation. Practice in all State and Federal Courts.

FIRM PROFILE: Nickle & Piasecki was founded in 1979 by Andrew Nickle and Carmen Piasecki. Thomas Singer, with a recognized specialty of litigation, became Of Counsel to the firm in 1988.

ANDREW W. NICKLE, born Jamestown, New York, April 2, 1949; admitted to bar, 1974, Indiana and U.S. District Court, Northern District of Indiana. *Education:* Hillsdale College (A.B., 1971); University of Notre Dame (J.D., 1974). Omicron Delta Kappa. Instructor, St. Mary's College, Business Law, 1978. Intern, White House, 1970. *Member:* St. Joseph County (Chairman, Probate, Trust and Real Estate Section, 1982-1983), Indiana State (Member, Sections on: Probate, Trust and Real Property and Business Law; Member, House of Delegates, 1981) and American (Member, Consumer Finance Committee, 1981-1993) Bar Associations. **Email:** nickleaw@aol.com

CARMEN M. PIASECKI, born South Bend, Indiana, December 10, 1948; admitted to bar, 1973, Indiana and U.S. District Court, Northern District of Indiana. *Education:* St. Mary of the Woods College (B.A., 1970); University of Notre Dame (J.D., 1973). Assistant U.S. Attorney, 1975-1979. Law Clerk to Hon. George N. Beamer, Sr., and Hon. Robert A. Grant, U.S. District Court, Northern District of Indiana, 1973-1975. *Member:* St. Joseph County (President, 1986-1987) and Indiana State (Secretary, 1984-1985; Member: Board of Managers, 1982-1984) Bar Associations; National Institute for Trial Advocacy. **Email:** CMPiasec@aol.com

OF COUNSEL

THOMAS H. SINGER, admitted to bar, 1960, Indiana; 1971, U.S. Supreme Court. *Education:* University of Michigan (A.B., 1956; LL.B., 1959). Hon. Jim R. Carrigan Fellow, 1997. Recipient, NITA Faculty Award, 1992. Faculty: University of Notre Dame Law School Adjunct Professor of Law, 1979-1986; 1988—; National Institute for Trial Advocacy, 1975—. Listed: in *The Best Lawyers in America* (Business Litigation and Personal Injury, 1987—); Top 50 Indiana Super Lawyers by Law and Politics, Indianapolis Monthly 2004, 2005. Member: Indiana Judicial Nominating Commission and Indiana Commission on Judicial Qualifications, 1984-1989; 1994-1996; Indiana Supreme Court Committee on Rules of Evidence, 1992-1993. Fellow: International Society of Barristers; American College of Trial Lawyers. **Email:** singert@infionline.net

REPRESENTATIVE CLIENTS: 1st Source Bank; American Electric Power Company; Agdia, Inc.; ABRO Industries, Inc.; Real Estate Management Company, LLC; Underwriters Laboratories Inc.; Coldwell Banker-Anchor Real Estate; Interlogic Outsourcing, Inc.; Carleton, Inc.; Chematics, Inc.; Chem-Elec, Inc.; National Institute for Trial Advocacy; Robert Bradley Associates; CB Richard Ellis/South Bend; Office Interiors, Inc.; Master Metal Machinery, Inc.; H.G. Christman Construction Co.
REFERENCE: 1st Source Bank.

PLEWS SHADLEY RACHER & BRAUN

Established in 1988

53732 GENERATIONS DRIVE
SOUTH BEND, INDIANA 46635-1539
Telephone: 574-273-1010
Fax: 574-271-2050
Email: sbend@psrb.com
URL: http://www.psrb.com

Indianapolis, Indiana Office: 1346 North Delaware Street, 46202-2415. Telephone: 317-637-0700. Telecopier: 317-637-0710.

Environmental Litigation, Environmental Insurance Coverage, Environmental Cost Recovery, Complex Commercial Litigation, Environmental Corporate and Transaction Law, Environmental Administrative Law, Environmental Permitting, Superfund, Solid and Hazardous Waste, Underground Storage Tanks, Clean Air Act, Clean Water Act, Environmental Business Law, Intellectual Property, Commercial Real Estate and Land Use, Surface Coal Mining and Reclamation Act.

FIRM PROFILE: Since its founding in 1988, Plews Shadley Racher & Braun has concentrated its practice in environmental law and complex litigation. The firm serves clients from two offices in Indiana and has one of the largest environmental law practices in the Midwest. Its attorneys have substantial experience in a wide range of environmental matters including the prosecution and defense of claims involving CERCLA, RCRA, Clean Air and Water Acts, UST remediation and cost recovery, toxic torts, environmental property damage claims and governmental enforcement actions of all kinds. Its attorneys maintain a substantial practice representing policyholders in actions to recover insurance dollars, particularly for claims concerning environmental liabilities. The firm has actively participated in Superfund cases in a number of states and has organized committees to represent various interest groups in such efforts. It also advises clients on environmental issues in real estate and business transactions, such as wetlands and brownfields development, in conducting environmental due diligence and audit work, in undertaking voluntary cleanups, in developing programs for limiting liability exposure, and in drafting and monitoring legislation and rules. The firm also represents clients in a variety of other complicated legal matters such as products liability, class action and patent and trademark cases.

JOHN H. LLOYD, IV, born 1967; admitted to bar, 1992, Indiana; 1996, Illinois. *Education:* Northwestern University (B.A., 1989); University of Notre Dame (J.D., 1992). Assistant City Atty., Hammond, Indiana, 1996-1999. Registered Civil Mediator, Indiana. (Resident). **PRACTICE AREAS:** Litigation; Environmental Law; Complex Litigation; Zoning, Planning and Land Use. **Email:** jlloyd@psrb.com

STEPHEN A. STUDER, born 1951; admitted to bar, 1976, Illinois; 1979, U.S. Court of Appeals, Seventh Circuit; 1980, U.S. Supreme Court; 1992, Michigan and Indiana; 1993, U.S. Court of Appeals, Sixth Circuit. *Education:* University of Notre Dame (A.B., 1973); Loyola University (J.D., 1976). Notre Dame Scholar. Co-Author: "Environmental Site Assessments: An Integrated Approach," 1992 Environmental Site Assessment Conference, National Ground Water Association; "Advanced Real Estate Law in Indiana," National Business Institute, 1993. Speaker: CLE International Conference "Brownfields", Indianapolis and Chicago, 1998; Manufacturer's Education's Council, "Benefits", Cincinnati, 1999. Faculty Member, "Major Land Use Laws in Indiana", NBI, 1999. Panelist: Indiana Planning Association Conference, 1999; "Advanced Environmental Law," ICLEF, 2001. Deputy General Counsel, Heller Financial, Inc., 1985-1991. Mishawaka Assistant City Attorney for Land Use. Fellow, Indiana Bar Foundation. **PRACTICE AREAS:** Environmental Law; Real Estate; Real Estate Development; Zoning, Planning and Land Use.

ASSOCIATE

THAO T. NGUYEN, born 1979; admitted to bar, 2004, Indiana and U.S. District Court, Southern and Northern Districts of Indiana. *Education:* Oberlin College (B.A., 2001); Indiana University School of Law - Bloomington (J.D., 2004).

(For Complete Biographical Data on all Personnel, see Professional Biographies at Indianapolis, Indiana)

ROEMER & MINTZ, LLP

SOUTH BEND, INDIANA

(See Barnes & Thornburg)

LAW OFFICES
ROWE & ROWE

Established in 1995

1003 NORTH HICKORY
SOUTH BEND, INDIANA 46615
Telephone: 574-233-8200
Fax: 574-234-5987
Email: Rowe.Rowe@attbi.com
URL: http://www.roweandrowe.com

Insurance Defense. Trials and Appeals in State and Federal Courts. Personal Injury, Automobile Accidents, Truck Accidents, Slip and Fall, Traumatic Brain Injury, Wrongful Death, Unsafe Products, Medical Malpractice, Legal Malpractice.

R. KENT ROWE, born South Bend, Indiana, June 21, 1930; admitted to bar, 1955, Indiana and U.S. Court of Military Appeals; 1959, U.S. District Court, Northern District of Indiana; 1960, U.S. Court of Appeals, Seventh Circuit. *Education:* St. Edward's University (A.B., cum laude, 1952); University of Notre Dame (J.D., 1955). Listed in Naifeh and Smith's "The Best Lawyers in America," 1995—. County Attorney, St. Joseph County, 1965-1969. Lecturer in Advanced Trial Law, University of Notre Dame, 1968—. *Member:* St. Joseph County, Indiana State and American Bar Associations; Notre Dame Law Association; Defense Trial Counsel of Indiana; American Judicature Society; International Association of Insurance Counsel; Defense Research Institute; American Board of Trial Advocates. **PRACTICE AREAS:** Civil Litigation; Insurance Defense; Medical Malpractice; Corporate Law; Products Liability; Mediation. **Email:** Rowe.Rowe@Comcast.net

R. KENT ROWE, III, born San Antonio, Texas, January 1, 1956; admitted to bar, 1981, Indiana; 1982, U.S. District Court, Northern District of Indiana; 1984, U.S. Court of Appeals, Seventh Circuit. *Education:* Indiana University (A.B., 1978); Tulane University of Louisiana (J.D., 1981). Listed in Naifeh and Smith's "The Best Lawyers in America," 1997—. *Member:* St. Joseph County and Indiana State Bar Associations; Defense Research Institute; Defense Trial Counsel of Indiana; The Association of Trial Lawyers of America (ATLA). **PRACTICE AREAS:** Civil Litigation; Insurance Defense; Medical Malpractice; Product Liability; Personal Injury. **Email:** Rowe.Rowe@Comcast.net

ASSOCIATE

GREGORY J. HAINES, born Goshen, Indiana, March 20, 1965; admitted to bar, 1991, Indiana. *Education:* University of Notre Dame at South Bend (B.A., 1987); Indiana University (J.D., 1991). *Member:* St. Joseph County and Indiana State Bar Associations.

SANDERS • PIANOWSKI, LLP

SOUTH BEND, INDIANA

(See Elkhart)

General Practice, Corporate, Business Law, Civil Litigation, Insurance, Bank Collection and Foreclosure, Commercial Litigation, Labor and Employment, Mergers and Acquisitions, Real Estate, Estate Planning, Trusts and Estates, Probate, Wills and Estate Administration, Environmental, Family Law, Adoption, Child Custody, Child Support, Divorce, Visitation Rights.

THE SHEDLAK LAW FIRM

402 W. WASHINGTON STREET, SUITE 200
SOUTH BEND, INDIANA 46601
Telephone: 574-233-7701
Fax: 574-233-7721
URL: http://www.shedlaklaw.com

Business Litigation, Real Estate, Land Use, Construction Litigation, Business Torts, Civil Litigation, Commercial Litigation, Condominium Law, Employment Law, Business Transactions, Contracts, Personal Injury, Insurance Law, Business Law, Municipal Law.

(This Listing Continued)

MEMBER OF FIRM

CHARLES R. SHEDLAK, born Marion, Indiana, May 28, 1964; admitted to bar, 1991, Wisconsin and U.S. District Court, Eastern and Western Districts of Wisconsin; 1992, U.S. Court of Appeals, Seventh Circuit; 1996, U.S. District Court, Northern and Southern Districts of Indiana; 1998, Indiana. *Education:* University of Notre Dame (B.A., 1985); University of Delaware (M.A., 1987); Cornell University (J.D., cum laude, 1991). Recipient: American Jurisprudence Award, Professional Ethics. *Member:* St. Joseph County, Indiana State (Member, Legal Ethics Committee; Improvements in the Judicial System Committee), Wisconsin (Member, Board of Bar Examiners Review Committee), Seventh Circuit and American Bar Associations; Notre Dame Law Association; American Planning Association. [U.S. Army Reserve, 1984-1992]. ***PRACTICE AREAS:*** Business Litigation; Business Torts; Real Estate; Land Use; Construction Litigation; Condominium Law; Employment Law. ***Email:*** crs@shedlaklaw.com

OF COUNSEL

CATHERINE F. PIERONEK, born Detroit, Michigan, August 14, 1962; admitted to bar, 1995, Indiana. *Education:* University of Notre Dame (B.S.A.E., cum laude, 1984; J.D., magna cum laude, 1995); University of California at Los Angeles (M.S.A.E., 1987). ***PRACTICE AREAS:*** Business Transactions; Title IX Discrimination; Civil Litigation; College and University Law. ***Email:*** cfp@shedlaklaw.com

SOPKO, NUSSBAUM & INABNIT

PLAZA BUILDING, 5TH FLOOR
210 SOUTH MICHIGAN STREET
P.O. BOX 300
SOUTH BEND, INDIANA 46624
Telephone: 574-234-3000
Telecopier: 574-234-4220
Email: SNI@SNI-Law.com
URL: http://www.sni-law.com

General Civil and Trial Practice in State and Federal Courts. Corporate Banking Law, Probate Litigation, Estate Planning, Real Estate, Family/Domestic Relations, Commercial Law, Personal Injury, Franchise Law and Computer Law.

MEMBERS OF FIRM

THOMAS C. SOPKO, born Warren, Ohio, March 21, 1945; admitted to bar, 1970, Indiana. *Education:* Xavier University (B.S., 1967); University of Notre Dame (J.D., 1970). Deputy Prosecuting Attorney, St. Joseph County, 1975-1978. Attorney, Town of Osceola, Indiana, 1975-1982. *Member:* St. Joseph County (Member, Judicial Nominating Committee; Chairman: Public Defenders' Committee, 1983-1986; Grievance Committee, 1984-1986; President, 1994), Indiana State (District Chairman, Trial Lawyers Section, 1979-1980; Member, Board of Governors, 1990-1995) and American Bar Associations; Indiana Trial Lawyers; The Association of Trial Lawyers of America; Master of the Bench Council Oak Inn of Court. Fellow, Indiana Bar Foundation. [Capt., USAR, 1970-1978]. ***PRACTICE AREAS:*** Civil Litigation; Corporate Law; Probate and Estate Planning; Real Estate; Banking. ***Email:*** toms@sni-law.com

RICHARD A. NUSSBAUM, II, born Pittsburgh, Pennsylvania, September 4, 1952; admitted to bar, 1977, Indiana and U.S. District Court, Northern District of Indiana; 1978, Michigan; U.S. Court of Appeals, Seventh Circuit, U.S. Supreme Court. *Education:* University of Notre Dame (B.A., cum laude, 1974; J.D., 1977). Corporation Counsel, City of South Bend, 1988-1998. General Counsel: Lt. Governor of State of Indiana, 1998-2003. Special Counsel, Governor of State of Indiana, 2003-2005. Secretary and Legal Counsel, Midwest League of Professional Baseball Clubs, Inc., 1993. *Member:* St. Joseph County (President, 1993-1994), Indiana State and American Bar Associations; State Bar of Michigan. ***PRACTICE AREAS:*** Real Estate; Corporate Law; Municipal Law; Sports Law; Estate Planning. ***Email:*** dickn@sni-law.com

BRENT E. INABNIT, born Indianapolis, Indiana, April 22, 1965; admitted to bar, 1990, Illinois; U.S. District Court, Northern District of Illinois; 1993, Indiana; U.S. District Court, Northern District of Indiana. *Education:* Ball State University (B.S., 1987); Valparaiso University School of Law (J.D., with distinction, 1990). *Member:* St. Joseph County Bar Association. ***PRACTICE AREAS:*** Civil Practice; Commercial Litigation; Personal Injury. ***Email:*** brenti@sni-law.com

MATTHEW R. KACZMAREK, born Milwaukee, Wisconsin, January 3, 1968; admitted to bar, 1996, Indiana and U.S. District Court, Northern and Southern Districts of Indiana; 1999, U.S. Court of Appeals, Seventh Circuit. *Education:* Marquette University (B.A., 1990); Valparaiso University School of Law (J.D., with distinction, 1996). Court Appointed Special Advocate, 1992—. Attorney, Town of Dune Acres, Indiana, 1998-1999; Associate Attorney, Town of Chesterton, Indiana and Town of Burns Harbor, Indiana 1996-1999. *Member:* St. Joseph County (Member, Board of Governors, 2003—), Indiana State and American Bar Associations; The Association of Trial Lawyers of America; Robert A. Grant Inn of Court. ***PRACTICE AREAS:*** Appellate Practice; Business Law; Civil Practice; Commercial Law; Corporate Law; Litigation; Municipal Law; Personal Injury; Torts; Trade Secrets. ***Email:*** mattk@sni-law.com

ASSOCIATES

CHRISTOPHER M. KEEFER, born Fort Wayne, Indiana, July 2, 1974; admitted to bar, 1999, Indiana and U.S. District Court, Northern and Southern Districts of Indiana. *Education:* University of Notre Dame (B.B.A., 1996); Indiana University at Bloomington (J.D., 1999). Delta Theta Phi. Author: Comment, Indiana Law Journal Volume 74, Issue 4, Page 1375. *Member:* St. Joseph County and Indiana State Bar Associations. ***PRACTICE AREAS:*** Civil Practice; Personal Injury; Commercial Litigation; Corporate Law; Appellate Practice. ***Email:*** chrisk@sni-law.com

JOSHUA A. VISSER, born Grand Rapids, Michigan, July 26, 1979; admitted to bar, 2004, Indiana and U.S. District Court, Northern District of Indiana. *Education:* University of Michigan (B.A.); Valparaiso University (J.D., 2004). *Member:* Indiana State Bar Association. ***PRACTICE AREAS:*** Civil Practice; Commercial Litigation; Corporate Law. ***Email:*** joshv@sni-law.com

OF COUNSEL

RONALD J. JAICOMO, born South Bend, Indiana, October 23, 1932; admitted to bar, 1959, Illinois; 1960, U.S. District Court, Northern District of Illinois; 1975, Indiana and U.S. District Court, Northern District of Indiana; 1979, U.S. Tax Court. *Education:* Bradley University (B.S., 1954); University of Illinois (J.D., 1959). Associate Editor, Illinois Law Forum, 1957-1959. Certified Public Accountant, Illinois, 1963. Listed in Who's Who in American Law. Instructor, Paralegal Studies Program, Indiana University at South Bend, 1987-1996. Past President, Estate Planning Council of St. Joseph County, 1994-1995. *Member:* St. Joseph County (President, Board of Governors, 2004-2005) and Indiana State Bar Associations. Fellow, Indiana Bar Foundation. ***PRACTICE AREAS:*** Trusts and Estates; Corporate Law; Taxation. ***Email:*** ronj@sni-law.com

REPRESENTATIVE CLIENTS: Notre Dame Federal Credit Union; Priests of Holy Cross; Gurley-Leep Mercedes, Buick; Rock Oldsmobile Cadillac; University Park Chrysler/Plymouth; Peterson Pontiac-GMC Truck; Saturn of Michiana, Inc.; Gurley-Leep Audi, Honda and Volkswagen, Team Toyota Inc.; Gurley-Leep Dodge, Inc. d/b/a Dodge City; Holy Cross College; Gurley-Leep Ford, Inc.; Cressy & Everett Realtors, Inc.; Edison Lakes Corporate Park; Linebacker Lounge; Quality Dining, Inc., d/b/a Chili's; Burger King; Grady's American Grill; Ironwood Health & Rehabilitation Center; Underground Pipe and Valve Inc.; Michiana Plastics, Inc.; Jack Post Corporation; Elkhart General Hospital; Midwest League of Professional Baseball Clubs, Inc.; Hobby Lobby Stores, Inc.; Kaser Spraker Construction, Inc.; Cargo Systems, Inc.; Bamar Plastics, Inc.; Hoosier Molded Products, Inc.; Brothers of Holy Cross Midwest Province; Brothers of Holy Cross Southwest Province; Fifth Third Bank; Merrill Lynch; Extendicare Health Facilities, Inc.
REFERENCES: 1st Source Bank; Notre Dame Federal Credit Union; Key Bank.

STUTSMAN, MULVANEY & DeBOER

SOUTH BEND, INDIANA
(See Elkhart)

General Civil and Appellate Practice in all State and Federal Courts. Personal Injury, Automobile Accidents, Slip and Fall, Wrongful Death, Workers Compensation, Medical Malpractice, Corporate, Wills and Probate, Trusts and Estates, Asset Protection, Guardianships, Estate Planning, Real Estate, Internet Law.

THORNE • GRODNIK, LLP

SOUTH BEND, INDIANA
(See Elkhart)

Commercial and Civil Litigation, Creditors Rights, Bankruptcy, Banking and Bank Related Matters, Corporate and Commercial Transactions, Insurance Defense, Personal Injury, Automobile Accidents, Slip and Fall, Wrongful Death, Real Estate and Zoning, Wills and Probate, Trusts and Estates, Estate Planning, School Law and Family Law, Adoptions, Divorce, Child Custody, Child Support, Visitation Rights, Mediation.

TUESLEY & HALL, LLP

RIVERPLACE PROFESSIONAL CENTER
212 EAST LASALLE AVENUE, SUITE 100
SOUTH BEND, INDIANA 46617
Telephone: 574-232-3538
Facsimile: 574-232-3790
Email: attorneys@tuesley-hall.com
URL: http://www.tuesley-hall.com

Corporate and Business Law, Business Litigation, Business Formation, Mergers, Buying and Selling a Business, Commercial Transactions, Taxation and Estate Planning, Probate, Commercial Litigation, Real Estate, Land Use, and Construction Law, Personal Injury and Defense Litigation, Automobile Accidents, Wrongful Death, Health Care Law, General Civil and Trial Practice in State and Federal Courts.

FIRM PROFILE: Firm is a Member of LawPact.

MEMBERS OF FIRM

MALCOLM J. TUESLEY, born South Bend, Indiana, February 16, 1948; admitted to bar, 1973, Indiana and Michigan; 1983, U.S. Tax Court. *Education:* Indiana University (A.B., 1970); Indiana University School of Law, Indianapolis (J.D., 1973). Administrative Law Judge, Indiana Department of Workforce Development, 1974-1995. *Member:* St. Joseph County, Indiana State and American Bar Associations; State Bar of Michigan. [Captain, U.S. Army Reserves, Retired]. ***PRACTICE AREAS:*** Probate; Taxation; Estate Planning; Corporate Law; Business Law; Real Estate. ***Email:*** mtuesley@tuesley-hall.com

THOMAS J. HALL, born South Bend, Indiana, April 30, 1948; admitted to bar, 1974, Indiana and U.S. District Court, Northern District of Indiana; U.S. Court of Appeals, Seventh Circuit and U.S. Tax Court. *Education:* Indiana University (A.B., 1971); Indiana University School of Law, Indianapolis (J.D., magna cum laude, 1974). Law Clerk, Indiana Court of Appeals, 1973-1974. Former Chairman, The Chamber of Commerce of St. Joseph County. Financial Services Advocate of the Year, Indiana/SBA, 1988. Member, Statewide Advisory Council for Indiana Small Business Development Centers.*Member:* St. Joseph County, Indiana State and American Bar Associations; Attorneys for Family-Held Enterprises. ***PRACTICE AREAS:*** Corporate Law; Business Law; Commercial Transactions; Health Care Law; Taxation. ***Email:*** thall@tuesley-hall.com

JOHN K. HANSON, born Knox, Indiana, July 23, 1959; admitted to bar, 1984, Indiana; 1988, Michigan; 1998, Arizona. *Education:* Indiana University, Bloomington (B.S., with distinction, 1981); Indiana University School of Law, Bloomington (J.D., 1984). Beta Gamma Sigma; Beta Alpha Psi. Certified Public Accountant, Indiana, 1991. *Member:* St. Joseph County and Indiana State Bar Associations; State Bar of Michigan; State Bar of Arizona; Indiana Certified Public Accountants Society; American Association of Attorney-

(This Listing Continued)

TUESLEY & HALL, LLP, South Bend—Continued

Certified Public Accountants; American Institute of Certified Public Accountants; Indiana Land Title Association. ***PRACTICE AREAS:*** Estate Planning; Probate; Taxation; Real Estate Law; Corporate Law. ***Email:*** jhanson@tuesley-hall.com

OF COUNSEL

SUSAN R. HANSON, born Franklin, Indiana, August 26, 1960; admitted to bar, 1985, Indiana and U.S. District Court, Northern and Southern Districts of Indiana; 1987, Michigan. *Education:* Miami University (B.A., 1982); Indiana University School of Law, Bloomington (J.D., 1984). Mortar Board; Omicron Delta Kappa; Phi Alpha Delta. Member, Editorial Board, Indiana Law Journal, 1983-1984. Law Clerk, Indiana Court of Appeals, 1985. *Member:* St. Joseph County and Indiana State (Member, Sections on: Employment Law; Appellate Practice) Bar Associations; State Bar of Michigan (Member, Section on Employment Law). ***REPORTED CASES:*** SMDFund, Inc. v. Fort Wayne-Allen County Airport Authority, 831 N.E. 2d 725 (Ind. 2005); VanVactor Farms, Inc. v. Marshall Co. Plan Commission, 793 N.E. 2d 1136 (Ind. Ct. App. 2004); Pioneer Hi-Bred International v. Key Bank, 742 N.E. 2d 967 (Ind. Ct. App. 2001); Smith v. Miller Builders, 741 N.E. 2d 731 (Ind. Ct. App. 2001); Ackles v. Hartford 699 N.E. 2d 740 (Ind. Ct. App. 1998). ***PRACTICE AREAS:*** Employment Law; Commercial Litigation; Appellate Practice. ***Email:*** shanson@tuesley-hall.com

EDWARD P. BENCHIK, born Wurzburg, Germany, June 4, 1966; admitted to bar, 1991, Ohio; 1992, U.S. District Court, Northern District of Indiana, U.S. District Court, Northern District of Ohio and U.S. Court of Appeals, Seventh Circuit; 1993, Indiana and U.S. District Court, Southern District of Indiana; 2003, U.S. Tax Court. *Education:* University of Notre Dame (B.A., with honors, 1988); Indiana University School of Law, Bloomington (J.D., 1991). Instructor, Business Organizations, Indiana University, South Bend, 1998-1999. ***LANGUAGES:*** French. ***REPORTED CASES:*** RSR Corp. v. Avanti Dev., Inc., 68 F. Supp. 2d 1037 (S.D. Ind., 1999); Sheehan v. Mahoney Chevrolet-Olds, 23 F. Supp. 2d 926, (N.D. Ind. 1998); In re Terry Ltd. Partnership, 169 B.R. 182 (Bankr. N.D. Ind. 1993); Frankenmuth Mut. Ins. Co. v. Williams, 690 N.E.2d 675 (Ind. 1997); Colley v. Indiana Farmers Mut. Ins. Group, 691 N.E.2d 1259 (Ind. Ct. App. 1998); Plumrose USA v. Review Bd. of the Indiana Dep't of Workforce Dev., 654 N.E.2d 827 (Ind. Ct. App. 1995). ***PRACTICE AREAS:*** Business Law; Business Planning; Contracts; Business Enterprises; Business Formation; Corporate Structuring; Limited Liability Companies; Partnerships; Small Business; Banking Law; Finance; Strategic Alliances; Commercial Litigation; Taxation; Tax Planning; IRS Audits; Wills; Probate; Trust and Estates; Asset Protection; Estate Planning; Bankruptcy; Creditors Rights. ***Email:*** tbenchik@tuesley-hall.com

SENIOR ASSOCIATE

ERIC W. SEIGEL, born Mankato, Minnesota, October 3, 1970; admitted to bar, 1999, Indiana and U.S. District Court, Northern and Southern Districts of Indiana; 2001, Michigan. *Education:* Michigan State University (B.A., General Business Admn., 1993); University of Notre Dame (J.D., 1999). *Member:* St. Joseph County, Indiana State and American Bar Associations. ***PRACTICE AREAS:*** Corporate Law; Business Law; Commercial Transactions. ***Email:*** eseigel@tuesley-hall.com

REPRESENTATIVE CLIENTS: *Agri Business:* Big D's Little Farm Corp.; R & P Grapevine Acres Inc.; Sycamore Farms, Inc.; Waggoners' Dairy Farm, Inc.; *Commercial and Defense Litigation*; McDonald's Corp.; Onan Corp.; Western World Insurance Co.; *Construction*: Big C Lumber Co., Inc.; Miller Builders, Inc.; Moser Homes; Smessaert Custom Homes, Inc.; *Distributors and Dealers:* Cutting Tools, Inc.; Discount Muffler and Tire Cos.; North End Cycle Shop, Inc.; Postle Distributors, Inc.; The Ridge Company; Vanson, LLC; Vanderboegh Cos.; VanAndle Propane Cos.; Waggoner Fuel; JHK, Inc. d/b/a American Safety and First Aid; St. Joseph Paper and Packaging Inc.; Correlated Products, Inc.; Road Solutions, Inc.; *Environmental Law:* Heartland Environmental Resources, Inc.; *Finance and Insurance:* Dunbar Mortgage Co., LLC; Mellinger Financial Services, Inc.; Strategic Employee Benefit Services of N.I., Inc. (Northwestern Mutual Life Insurance Company, General Agent); St. Joseph Capital Bank; Korhorn Financial Group, Inc.; *Health Care Law:* Northern Indiana Oncology Associates, LLC; Houser, Norborg, McGregor, P.C.; *Manufacturing:* A.K. Industries, Inc.; Penz Products, Inc.; Burnham Glove Factory; Daman Products Co., Inc.; Imagineering Enterprises, Inc.; South Bend Modern Molding, Inc.; Plastic Solutions, Inc.; Owens-Illinois, Inc.; *Food Service:* The LaSalle Grill; *Technology:* Anjon Systems, Inc.; Nextt Priority, Ltd.; Bidspotter, Inc.; *Condominium Communities:* Oakhill Condominiums Association, Inc.; Sandpiper Cove Condominium Association, Inc.; Brendon Hills Park Home Owners Association.

URDA PROFESSIONAL CORPORATION

Established in 1980

112 WEST JEFFERSON BOULEVARD, SUITE 503
SOUTH BEND, INDIANA 46601
Telephone: 574-234-2161
Fax: 574-233-6533
Email: rurda@gte.net

Pension and Profit Sharing, ERISA, Employee Benefits, Professional Corporations, Wills and Probate, Trusts and Estates, Estate Planning and Taxation Law.

RICHARD B. URDA, JR., born Pittsburgh, Pennsylvania, April 24, 1950; admitted to bar, 1975, Indiana and Michigan; 1976, U.S. Court of Appeals, 7th Circuit and U.S. Tax Court. *Education:* University of Notre Dame (B.A., summa cum laude, 1972); University of Michigan (J.D., cum laude, 1975). Phi Beta Kappa. *Member:* St. Joseph County, Indiana State and American Bar Associations; State Bar of Michigan. Fellow, The American College of Trust and Estate Counsel. ***Email:*** rurda@gte.net

REFERENCES: Bank One; 1st Source Bank; KeyBank National Association; Wells Fargo Bank.

WEISMAN ASSOCIATES

PROFESSIONAL CORPORATION

SOUTH BEND, INDIANA

(See Mishawaka)

General Civil and Criminal Trial Practice. Drug Crimes, Driving While Intoxicated, Parole and Probation, Traffic Violations, Negligence, Real Estate, Business Law, Contracts, Partnership Law, Corporate, Wills and Probate, Trusts and Estates, Estate Planning, Commercial Law, Real Estate, Commercial Leasing, Family Law, Adoption Law, Child Custody, Child Support, Divorce, Visitation Rights.

ZAPPIA ZAPPIA & STIPP

Established in 1976

52582 STATE ROAD 933 NORTH
SOUTH BEND, INDIANA 46637
Telephone: 574-277-8720
Fax: 574-272-8167
Email: zappialaw.com
URL: http://www.zappialaw.com

Zoning, Planning and Land Use, Business Law, Business Planning, Contracts, Law Suits, Business Enterprises, Corporate Law, Partnerships, Limited Liability Companies, Civil Practice, Criminal Law, Driving While Intoxicated, Drug Crimes, Juvenile Law, Parole and Probation, Traffic Violations, Civil Litigation, Defense Litigation, Trial Practice, Personal Injury, Automobile Accidents, Slip and Fall, Wrongful Death, Bankruptcy, Family Law, Adoptions, Child Custody, Child Support, Divorce, Visitation Rights, Wills, Trusts and Estates, Estate Planning, Real Estate, Worker's Compensation, Family Mediation, Leases, Collections, Grandparents Visitation Rights.

MEMBERS OF FIRM

ANTHONY M. ZAPPIA, born South Bend, Indiana, October 2, 1949; admitted to bar, 1976, Indiana and U.S. District Court, Northern and Southern Districts of Indiana. *Education:* University of Notre Dame (B.S., cum laude, 1972); Valparaiso University (J.D., 1976). Deputy Prosecuting Attorney, St. Joseph County, 1976-1986. Mishawaka City Council Attorney, 1981-1986. St. Joseph County Attorney, 1986—. Member: St. Joseph County Judicial Nominating Committee; St. Joseph County Public Defender's Advisory Committee. Supreme Court, State of Indiana, Committee for Fitness & Character; Indiana Supreme Court Disciplinary Commission, 2001—. *Member:* St. Joseph County (President-Elect, 1989-1990; President, 1990-1991), Indiana State and American Bar Associations; Indiana Trial Lawyers Association; Association of Trial Lawyers of America. ***PRACTICE AREAS:*** Personal Injury; Criminal Defense; Domestic Relations; Zoning; Civil Practice; Civil Litigation; Trial Practice. ***Email:*** azappia@zappialaw.com

MARIO J. ZAPPIA, born South Bend, Indiana, March 5, 1964; admitted to bar, 1990, Indiana. *Education:* Northwestern University (B.A., 1986); Valparaiso University (J.D., 1990). Assistant St. Joseph County Attorney, 1990—. Board Attorney, Solid Waste Management District, 1991—. Member, Board of Directors, Legal Services Program of Northern Indiana, Inc., 1997-1999. Certified Family Law Specialist, 2002—. *Member:* St. Joseph County (Immediate Past President, 2003-2004; President, 2001-2003; Board of Governors, 1995-2001; Member, 1991— and Co-Chairman, 1998-2000, Family Law Committee), Indiana State (Third District Representative of the Young Lawyers Section, 1993-1997) and American (Member, Sections on: Real Property; Probate; Trust Law; Family Law, Law Practice Management) Bar Associations. ***PRACTICE AREAS:*** Family Law; Adoption Law; Matrimonial Law; Separation Agreements; Spousal Support; Child Custody; Alimony; Divorce. ***Email:*** marioz@zappialaw.com

THOMAS SEAN STIPP, born Terre Haute, Indiana, November 19, 1970; admitted to bar, 1996, Indiana and U.S. District Court, Northern and Southern Districts of Indiana. *Education:* Indiana University at Bloomington (B.A., 1993); Notre Dame Law School (J.D., 1996). Certified Family Law Specialist. *Member:* St. Joseph County, Indiana State and American Bar Associations. ***PRACTICE AREAS:*** Domestic relations; Personal Injury; Civil Practice; Civil Litigation; Trial Practice; Family Law; Paternity; Adoption Law; Visitation Rights; Child Support; Grandparents Visitation Rights; Leases, Leasing; Business Law. ***Email:*** tsstipp@zappialaw.com

ASSOCIATE

ARIC J. RUTKOWSKI, born Indianapolis, Indiana, December 2, 1971; admitted to bar, 1997, Indiana. *Education:* Indiana University (B.A., 1993); Indiana University School of Law (J.D., 1996). *Member:* Indiana State and St. Joseph County Bar Associations. ***REPORTED CASES:*** Brooks v. McGee, 776 NE2d 952 (Ind. Ct. App. 2002); Smith v. Smith, 793 NE2d 282 (Ind. Ct. App. 2003); Pedraza v. Gasperson, 813 NE2d 1173 (Ind. 2004). ***PRACTICE AREAS:*** Domestic Law; General Litigation; Corporate Law; Real Estate; Appellate Practice. ***Email:*** arutkowski@zappialaw.com

REPRESENTATIVE CLIENTS: Budget Rent A Car; St. Joseph County Economic Development Commission; St. Joseph County; Solid Waste Management District of St. Joseph County; St. Joseph County Redevelopment Commission; Underground Pipe & Valve, Inc.; Sergio's Pools & Spas; 1st Response Construction; Michiana Industrial Supply, Inc.; Jo-To-Go.
REFERENCE: 1st Source Bank and Trust Company of South Bend, Indiana.

MICHAEL K. BONNELL

63 EAST MARKET STREET
P.O. BOX 533
SPENCER, INDIANA 47460
Telephone: 812-829-2209
URL: http://www.bonnelllawoffice.com
Email: mkbonnell@hotmail.com
URL: http://www.bonnelllaw.com

Bankruptcy, Criminal Law, Driving While Intoxicated, Drug Crimes, Juvenile Law, Parole and Probation, Traffic Violations, Employment Law, Wrongful Termination, Discrimination, Family Law, Adoptions, Child Custody, Child Support, Divorce, Visitation Rights, Personal Injury, Wrongful Death, Automobile Accidents, Real Estate, Buying and Selling Real Estate, Commercial Leasing, Construction, Zoning and Land Use, Trusts and Estates, Estate Planning, Wills and Probate, Business Law, Business Planning, Contracts, Litigation, Business Enterprises, Corporate, Small Business, Starting a Business, Buying and Selling a Business.

MICHAEL K. BONNELL, born Alton, Illinois, December 16, 1954; admitted to bar, 1986, Indiana; U.S. District Court, Northern and Southern Districts of Indiana; U.S. Court of Appeals, Seventh Circuit; U.S. Court of International Trade. *Education:* Indiana University (B.A., 1983); Indiana University School of Law, Bloomington (J.D., 1986). Deputy Prosecutor, 1986-1987, Public Defender, 1998—, and Attorney, 1999—, Monroe County. Administrative Law Judge, and Chairman, Unemployment Insurance Review Board, Indiana, 1992. Deputy Commissioner, Indiana Department of Workforce Development, 1993-1996. City Councilman, Bloomington, Indiana, 1995-1996. *Member:* Owen County, Monroe County and Indiana State Bar Associations; Association of Trial Lawyers of America. ***PRACTICE AREAS:*** Employment Law; Family Law; Civil Practice; Criminal Law; Probate.

REPRESENTATIVE CLIENTS: L & C Enterprise, Inc.; Lane, Inc.; P & L, Inc.; Minnick Drywall & Insulation; Stop & Go Muffler Center, Inc.; J & K Newsom, Inc.; Abstract & Real Estate; Owen County State Bank; Owen Community Bank; First National Bank; Tri Professional Realty, Inc.
APPROVED ATTORNEY FOR: Conestoga Title Insurance Co.

CHAPMAN & NELSON, P.C.

SPENCER, INDIANA

(See Bloomington)

Criminal Law, Driving While Intoxicated, Traffic Violations, Personal Injury, Litigation, Family Law, Dissolutions of Marriage, Adoption Law, Guardianship, Modification of Support and Visitation, Name Changes.

MALLOR CLENDENING GRODNER & BOHRER LLP

SPENCER, INDIANA

(See Bloomington)

Civil Litigation, Insurance Defense, Business Law, Wills, Trusts and Estates, Family Law, Personal Injury, Taxation, Corporate Law, Real Estate, Probate, Labor and Employment.

HART BELL LLC

SULLIVAN, INDIANA

(See Vincennes)

General Practice. Litigation, Insurance, Banking, Corporate, Employment, Probate and Estate Planning, State and Federal Tax Law, Real Estate, Construction, Commercial, Business, Elder, Creditors Rights, Personal Injury, Family Law and Criminal Defense.

HAWKINS LAW PC

Established in 2001

999 NORTH SECTION STREET
P.O. BOX 382
SULLIVAN, INDIANA 47882-0382
Telephone: 812-268-8777; 812-847-7000
Fax: 812-268-8838
Email: info@hawkinslaw.com
URL: http://www.HawkinsLaw.com

Estate Planning, Trusts and Estates, Wills and Probate, Estate Planning, Elder Law, Wills and Probate, Business Law, Business Planning, Contracts, Lawsuits, Business Enterprises, Small Business, Corporate, Limited Liability Companies, Adoption Law, Real Estate, Municipal Law.

FIRM PROFILE: Estate, trust and business attorneys serving southwestern and south central Indiana.

JEFF R. HAWKINS, born Sullivan, Indiana, January 16, 1966; admitted to bar, 1992, Indiana, U.S. District Court, Northern and Southern Districts of Indiana. *Education:* Indiana University, Bloomington (B.S., 1988); University of Louisville (J.D., 1992). Faculty, Advanced Elder Law 2003, Indiana Continuing Legal Education Forum, Inc.; Faculty, Annual Elder Law 2003, Indiana Continuing Legal Education Forum, Inc.; Estate Planning and Administration in Review 2003, Indiana Continuing Legal Education Forum, Inc.; Faculty, Annual Elder Law 2004, Indiana Continuing Legal Education Forum, Inc. Member, Board of Directors, Indiana Continuing Legal Education Forum, 1998-1999. *Member:* Sullivan County, Indiana State (Member: Probate, Trust and Real Property Section; Business Law Section; Bankruptcy and Creditor's Rights Section; Professional Legal Education, Admission and Development Section (Chair, 2000-2001); Elder Law Section; Agricultural Section; Clients Assistance Fund Committee; Board of Governors, 1996-1998; House of Delegates) and American (Member: Real Property, Probate and Trust Law Section; Business Law Section) Bar Associations; National Academy of Elder Law Attorneys. Fellow, Indiana Bar Foundation. ***PRACTICE AREAS:*** Estate Planning; Trusts and Estates; Wills; Probate; Elder Law; Business Law; Real Estate. ***Email:*** jeff@hawkinslaw.com

JENNIFER J. HAWKINS, born Sullivan, Indiana, November 2, 1965; admitted to bar, 1992, Indiana and U.S. District Court, Northern and Southern Districts of Indiana. *Education:* Indiana University, Bloomington (B.M.E., 1988); University of Louisville (J.D., 1992). Member, Journal of Law and Education, University of Louisville, 1991. Greene County Deputy Prosecutor, 1993-1994, 1998. Board Member, Sullivan County, Community Foundation. *Member:* Sullivan County and Indiana State (Member, Probate, Trust and Real Property Section) Bar Associations. ***PRACTICE AREAS:*** Trusts and Estates; Elder Law; Adoption Law; Real Estate. ***Email:*** jennifer@hawkinslaw.com

APPROVED ATTORNEYS FOR: Lawyers Title Insurance Corporation.

HUNT, HASSLER & LORENZ LLP

SULLIVAN, INDIANA

(See Terre Haute)

Insurance Defense, Family/Domestic Relations, Adoptions, Child Custody, Child Support, Divorce, Visitation Rights, Business Law, Business Planning, Contracts, Business Litigation, Business Enterprises, Corporate, Limited Liability Companies, Partnerships, Small Business, Starting a Business, Buying and Selling a Business, Employment Law, Employment Litigation, Wrongful Termination, Commercial, Real Estate, Wills and Probate, Trusts and Estates, Asset Protection, Guardianships, Estate Planning, Insurance Law. Trials and Appeals.

EDWARD McGLONE LAW OFFICE

SULLIVAN, INDIANA

(See Terre Haute)

Personal Injury, Automobile Accidents, Slip and Fall, Dog Bites, Wrongful Death, Criminal Law, Traffic Violations, Driving While Intoxicated, Juvenile Law, Drug Crimes, Felonies, Misdemeanors.

WILKINSON, GOELLER, MODESITT, WILKINSON & DRUMMY

SULLIVAN, INDIANA

(See Terre Haute)

General Civil Practice in all Courts. Taxation, Corporation, Trust, Probate, Estate Planning, Insurance Law, Health Law, Municipal Law, Bankruptcy, and Creditors Rights. Insurance Defense, Business Litigation, Mediation and Arbitration.

SNYDER BIRCH CORNWELL & MORGAN LLP

200 WEST MAIN STREET
SYRACUSE, INDIANA 46567
Telephone: 574-457-5727
Fax: 574-457-2056
URL: http://www.sbcmlaw.com

Fort Wayne, Indiana Office: 904 South Calhoun Street, 46802. Telephone: 260-407-0915. Fax: 260-407-7005.

Business Litigation, Business Law, Zoning, Planning and Land Use, Real Estate, Civil Litigation, Estate Planning, Trust, Probate, Guardianship, Elder Law, Tax, Banking Law, Employee Benefits, ERISA.

STEPHEN R. SNYDER, born 1947; admitted to bar, 1971, Indiana and U.S. District Court, Northern and Southern Districts of Indiana; U.S. Court of Appeals, Seventh Circuit. *Education:* Valparaiso University (B.A., 1969; J.D., 1971). Phi Alpha Delta. Warsaw, Indiana, City Attorney, 1990-1997. *Member:* Kosciusko County, Indiana State and American Bar Associations; Indiana Trial Lawyers Association; The Association of Trial Lawyers of America. ***SPECIAL AGENCIES:*** Indiana Department of Natural Resources; United States Army Corps of Engineers. ***PRACTICE AREAS:*** Business Litigation; Zoning, Planning and Land Use; Real Estate; Civil Litigation; Business Law. ***Email:*** srs@sbcmlaw.com

JACK C. BIRCH, born June 15, 1966; admitted to bar, 1991, Indiana and U.S. District Court, Northern and Southern Districts of Indiana. *Education:* Indiana University (B.A., 1988; J.D., 1991). Phi Alpha Delta. Mortar Board. Recipient, American Jurisprudence Award in Real Estate. Town Attorney, North Webster, Indiana. *Member:* Kosciusko County, Indiana State (House of Delegates, 1998—) and American Bar Associations. ***PRACTICE AREAS:*** Business Law; Real Estate; Civil Litigation; Zoning, Planning and Land Use. ***Email:*** jcb@sbcmlaw.com

DAVID D. CORNWELL, born 1950; admitted to bar, 1976, Indiana and U.S. District Court, Northern and Southern Districts of Indiana. *Education:* Indiana University (A.B., 1972; M.B.A. in Finance, J.D., 1976). Beta Gamma Sigma. Contributing Author: "Lending Considerations & Documenting Residential Mortgages," ICLEF, 1994; "Real Estate Skills Series," 1994; "Closing Estates," ICLEF; "Planning your First Probate Administration," 1997 and 1998. President, Fort Wayne Estate Planning Council, 2002-2003. Law and Banking Instructor, American Institute of Banking, 1978-1986. former Vice President, and General Counsel, Summcorp and Summit Bank, Fort Wayne, Indiana, 1983-1992. *Member:* Allen County, Kosciusko County, Indiana State and American Bar Associations. (Also at Fort Wayne Office). ***PRACTICE AREAS:*** Estate Planning; Trust; Probate; Guardianship; Elder Law; Tax; Business Law; Banking Law; Employee Benefits; ERISA. ***Email:*** ddc@sbcmlaw.com

(This Listing Continued)

SNYDER BIRCH CORNWELL & MORGAN LLP, Syracuse—Continued

RANDALL L. MORGAN, born November 11, 1968; admitted to bar, 1994, Indiana and U.S. District Court, Northern and Southern Districts of Indiana; 2000, U.S. Court of Appeals, Seventh Circuit. *Education:* Indiana University (B.S., 1991; J.D., 1994). *Member:* Kosciusko County, Indiana State and American Bar Associations. ***PRACTICE AREAS:*** Business Law; Real Estate Law; Land Use and Zoning; Civil Litigation; Appellate Practice. ***Email:*** rlm@sbcmlaw.com

BRAD BOUGH

321 OHIO STREET
TERRE HAUTE, INDIANA 47807
Telephone: 812-234-8458
Fax: 812-232-3232
Email: brad@boughlaw.com
URL: http://www.bradboughlaw.com

General Civil Litigation, Personal Injury, Automobile Accidents, Slip and Fall, Wrongful Death, Wills and Probate, Trusts and Estates, Insurance Defense, Mediation.

BRAD BOUGH, born South Bend, Indiana, March 25, 1958; admitted to bar, 1983, Indiana, U.S. District Court, Southern District of Indiana and U.S. Court of Appeals, Seventh Circuit. *Education:* Indiana State University (B.S., cum laude, 1980); Indiana University School of Law-Indianapolis (J.D., magna cum laude, 1983). Deputy Prosecuting Attorney, Vigo County, 1983-1989 and 1990—. Certified Civil Mediator, 1992—. *Member:* Terre Haute (Treasurer, 1989-1992), Indiana State and American Bar Associations; Indiana Association of Mediators. ***REPORTED CASES:*** Estate of Cullop v. State of Indiana, et al., 821 N.B. 2d 403 2005, Ind.App. Lexis 536 (2005) cert. denied, 2005 Ind. App. Lexis 536 (2005); Rice v. Meridian Ins. Co., 751 N.E.2d 685 (Ind.App. 2001); Haltom v. Bruner and Meis, Inc., 680 N.E.2d 6 (Ind.App. 1997); Ashcraft v. Northeast Sullivan County School Corp., 706 N.E.2d 1101, 132 Ed. Law Rep. 897 (Ind.App. 1999); Smith v. Beaty, 639 N.E.2d 1029 (Ind.App. 1994). ***PRACTICE AREAS:*** Personal Injury; Torts; Probate; Wills; Mediation; Insurance Defense.

REFERENCES: State Auto Insurance; Meridian Insurance; West Bend Insurance; Terre Haute Medical Laboratory, Inc.; Pathology Associates, P.C.; Lehman Communication Service, Inc.; Premier Manufactured Homes, Inc.

COX, ZWERNER, GAMBILL & SULLIVAN, LLP

511 WABASH AVENUE
P.O. BOX 1625
TERRE HAUTE, INDIANA 47808-1625
Telephone: 812-232-6003
Fax: 812-232-6567

General Civil Practice. Trials. Federal and State, Tax, Probate and Estate Planning, Corporate, Real Estate, Banking and Insurance Law, Education/School Law, Mediation, Employment Law.

FIRM PROFILE: Cox, Zwerner, Gambill & Sullivan was established prior to 1900 and is one of the oldest law firms in West Central Indiana. The firm provides a broad range of legal services to individuals as well as business and industry.

The firm's clients include banks, newspapers, colleges and universities, real estate developers, contractors, insurance companies, manufacturers, auto dealers, medical professionals, small business owners, retailers and service providers.

The firm strives to serve its clients by providing quality legal services in an efficient manner.

MEMBERS OF FIRM

ERNEST J. ZWERNER (1918-1980)

BENJAMIN G. COX (1915-1988)

GILBERT W. GAMBILL, JR. (1921-2001)

JAMES E. SULLIVAN, born Franklin, Pennsylvania, November 6, 1919; admitted to bar, 1957, Indiana, Florida and U.S. District Court, Southern District of Indiana; U.S. Court of Appeals, 7th Circuit; U.S. Supreme Court; U.S. Claims Court and U.S. Tax Court. *Education:* Duquesne University; University of Notre Dame (B.S.C., 1955; J.D., 1957). Registered Civil Mediator. *Member:* Terre Haute, Indiana State and American Bar Associations; The Florida Bar. ***PRACTICE AREAS:*** Education/School Law; Litigation; Corporate and Business Law; Taxation; Labor; Probate and Estate Planning.

B. GUILLE COX, JR., born Terre Haute, Indiana, April 13, 1946; admitted to bar, 1971, Indiana, U.S. Court of Appeals, Seventh Circuit and U.S. Tax Court. *Education:* Massachusetts Institute of Technology (B.S., 1968); Harvard Law School (J.D., 1971). Sigma Xi. Vice President, Harvard Voluntary Defenders, 1969-1971. Rose-Hulman Institute of Technology (Honorary Doctorate, Engineering, 2002). *Member:* Terre Haute, Indiana State and American Bar Associations. ***PRACTICE AREAS:*** Trusts and Estate Planning; Corporate and Business Law; Banking Law; Real Estate; Taxation.

DAVID W. SULLIVAN, born Sewickley, Pennsylvania, July 29, 1948; admitted to bar, 1973, Indiana and U.S. District Court for the Southern District of Indiana; 1975, U.S. Court of Appeals, Seventh Circuit. *Education:* University of Notre Dame (B.B.A., 1970); Indiana University (J.D., cum laude, 1973). Law Clerk, Honorable Cale J. Holder, Judge, U.S. District Court for Southern District of Indiana, 1973-1975. *Publications:* "Initial Preparation of Defense Cases," Indiana Continuing Legal Education Forum, 1989; "Underinsured Motorist Coverage from the Defendant's Perspective," Indiana Defense Lawyers Association Seminar, 1995; "Summary Judgment from the Defense Perspective-Drafting and Defending Them," Indiana Continuing Legal Education Forum, 1995; "Hot Topics in Employment Law," Indiana Continuing Legal Education Forum, 1998; "Labor and Employment Law

(This Listing Continued)

Update," ICLEF 2003, 2004, 2005; "Variety is the Spice of Employment Law," ICLEF, 2005. Speaker: Project Peace (Peaceful Endings Through Attorneys, Children and Educators) Training Seminars, Indiana State Bar Association. Registered Civil Mediator. *Member:* Terre Haute, Indiana State (Project Peace Volunteer Attorney, Council Member, Labor and Employment Section, Facilities Review Committee, 2001-2003, Membership Benefits Committee 1996—, Vice-Chairman, Honors Committee 2003—, Nominating Committee, 1998-1999, 2004-2005; Long Range Planning Committee, 2004—), American and Federal Bar Associations; Defense Trial Counsel of Indiana (Recipient: Diplomat Award, 1993); Defense Research Institute; Indiana Continuing Legal Education Forum Board of Directors, 1997-2003, Secretary 1998-1999. Master Fellow, Indiana Bar Foundation (Member, Board of Directors, 2002—). ***PRACTICE AREAS:*** Employment Law; Mediation; Arbitration; Corporate and Business Litigation; Personal Injury Litigation. ***Email:*** DSullivan@coxlaw.net

LOUIS F. BRITTON, born Terre Haute, Indiana, March 5, 1953; admitted to bar, 1977, Indiana. *Education:* Indiana University (B.S., with distinction and departmental honors, 1974; J.D., magna cum laude, 1977). Phi Beta Kappa; Order of the Coif. Member, National Moot Court Team. Publications: "State and Federal Income Tax Credits for Historic Preservation," Indiana Continuing Legal Education Forum, 1994; "Gathering Information and Preparing Simple Wills," Indiana Continuing Legal Education Forum, 1993. *Member:* Terre Haute, Indiana State and American Bar Associations. ***PRACTICE AREAS:*** Commercial Transactions; Real Estate; Business Organizations; Banking; Zoning, Planning and Land Use. ***Email:*** LBritton@coxlaw.net

RONALD E. JUMPS, born Danville, Illinois, September 16, 1943; admitted to bar, 1989, Indiana, U.S. District Court, Northern and Southern Districts of Indiana. *Education:* Purdue University (B.S., 1966); Eastern New Mexico University (M.B.A., 1976); Indiana University (J.D., cum laude, 1989). Phi Delta Phi (Vice Magister, 1987-1988; Magister, 1988-1989). *Member:* Terre Haute, Indiana State and American Bar Associations. [U.S. Air Force, 1966-1986, Lt. Col.]. ***PRACTICE AREAS:*** General Civil Practice; Real Estate; Probate; Business. ***Email:*** RJumps@coxlaw.net

SCOTT CRAIG, born Clinton, Indiana, August 15, 1971; admitted to bar, 1997, Indiana and U.S. District Court, Northern and Southern Districts of Indiana. *Education:* Wabash College (B.A., magna cum laude, 1994); Indiana University (J.D., magna cum laude, 1997). Order of The Coif. Author: An Employer's Responsibilities and Liabilities Following the End of the Employment Relationship," Indiana Continuing Legal Education Forum, 2004. Co-Author: "Employment Law Update," Indiana Continuing Legal Education Forum, 2003 and 2004. *Member:* Terre Haute, Indiana State and American Bar Associations. Fellow, Indiana Bar Foundation; Indiana Continuing Legal Education Forum (Member, Board of Directors, 2003—). ***PRACTICE AREAS:*** Employment Law; Municipal Law; Appellate Practice; Insurance Defense. ***Email:*** scraig@coxlaw.net

DONALD J. BONOMO, born Terre Haute, Indiana, May 7, 1975; admitted to bar, 2000, Indiana and U.S. District Court, Northern and Southern Districts of Indiana. *Education:* Indiana State University (B.S., cum laude, 1997); Indiana University at Indianapolis (J.D., 2000). Beta Gamma Sigma. *Member:* Terre Haute, Indiana State and American Bar Associations. ***PRACTICE AREAS:*** Real Estate; Civil Practice; Bankruptcy. ***Email:*** dbonomo@coxlaw.net

LAKSHMI REDDY, born Hyderabad, India, May 29, 1970; admitted to bar, 1997, Indiana; U.S. District Court, Northern and Southern Districts of Indiana; U.S. Court of Appeals, Seventh Circuit. *Education:* Vanderbilt University (B.S., 1992); Indiana University (J.D., cum laude, 1997). Indiana Law Review, 1996-1997. Law Clerk to the Honorable Frank Sullivan, Jr., Supreme Court of Indiana, 1996-1997. *Member:* Terre Haute, Indiana State and American Bar Associations. ***PRACTICE AREAS:*** Health Care; Trust Planning; Estate Planning; Appellate Practice; Corporate Law; Business Law; Insurance Defense; Employment Law. ***Email:*** lreddy@coxlaw.net

COUNSEL FOR: Applied Extrusion Technologies, Inc.; Amoco Pipeline Co.; Bob Bowen Ford; City of Clinton; Clay County Redevelopment Commission; EBC, Inc.; Equitable Life Assurance Society of U.S.; Farmers Insurance Group; Federated Mutual Insurance Co.; Fireman's Fund; First Financial Bank, NA; Futurex Automotive Products, Inc.; General Accident Group; Great Dane Trailers; Guaranty National Ins.; Heitman Properties; Hercules Incorporated; Indiana-American Water Co.; Indiana Business Equipment; Indiana State University; Jiffy Mini-Marts, Inc.; Marathon Oil Co., Inc.; Milwaukee Mutual Ins. Co.; Ohio Casualty Insurance Co.; Old National Bank (Terre Haute); Pekin Insurance Co.; Pfizer Inc.; Rose-Hulman Ventures; Rose-Hulman Institute of Technology; Sears Roebuck Co. (local area); Sisters of Providence; Sullivan County Redevelopment Commission; Terre Haute Board of Santary Commissioners; The Hartford Insurance Co.; Travelers/Aetna; Tribune-Star Publishing Co., Inc.; Tri-Remanufacturing; Town of Montezuma, Indiana; United Services Auto Assn.; Vernon Insurance Companies; Vigo County Public Library; Viking Insurance Co.; Wal Mart; Clinton Public Library; Clinton Redevelopment Commission; Hoosier Insurance Co.
APPROVED TITLE ATTORNEYS FOR: Lawyers Title Insurance Corp.; Stewart Title Guaranty Co. and Ticor.
TITLE INSURANCE AGENTS FOR: Old Republic National Title Insurance Company.

HUNT, HASSLER & LORENZ LLP

Established in 1932
100 CHERRY STREET
P.O. BOX 1527
TERRE HAUTE, INDIANA 47808
Telephone: 812-232-9691
Telecopier: 812-234-2881
URL: http://www.huntlawfirm.net

Insurance Defense, Family/Domestic Relations, Adoptions, Child Custody, Child Support, Divorce, Visitation Rights, Business Law, Business Planning, Contracts, Business Litigation, Business Enterprises, Corporate, Limited Liability Companies, Partnerships, Small Business, Starting a Business, Buying and Selling a Business, Employment Law, Employment Litigation, Wrongful Termination, Commercial, Real Estate, Wills and Probate, Trusts and Estates, Asset Protection, Guardianships, Estate Planning, Insurance Law. Trials and Appeals.

DAVID E. ROSENFELD (1906-1979)

ROBERT G. WOLFE (1916-1997)

(This Listing Continued)

MEMBERS OF FIRM

ROBERT F. HUNT, born Anderson, Indiana, April 19, 1948; admitted to bar, 1973, Indiana and U.S. District Court, Southern District of Indiana; 1978, U.S. Court of Appeals, Seventh Circuit; 1983, U.S. Supreme Court; 1989, U.S. Court of Appeals, Tenth Circuit; 1997, U.S. District Court, Western District of Michigan and U.S. Court of Appeals, Sixth Circuit; 1998, U.S. Court of Federal Claims; 2004, U.S. District Court, Central District of Illinois. *Education:* Indiana University (B.S., 1970; J.D., 1973). *Member:* Terre Haute (Secretary, 1976-1984; President, 1986-1987), Indiana State and American Bar Associations; Defense Research Institute. ***PRACTICE AREAS:*** Trials; Insurance Law. **Email:** hunt@huntlawfirm.net

MARK D. HASSLER, born Greencastle, Indiana, July 8, 1956; admitted to bar, 1981, Indiana and U.S. District Court, Southern District of Indiana; 1982, U.S. Court of Appeals, Seventh Circuit. *Education:* Indiana State University (B.S., cum laude, 1978); Indiana University (J.D., with honors, 1981). Registered Mediator, Civil Litigation, Indiana, 1992. *Member:* Terre Haute (Secretary, 1986-1992; President, 1996-1997), Indiana State Bar Associations. ***PRACTICE AREAS:*** Business Litigation; Real Estate Law; Insurance Law. **Email:** hassler@huntlawfirm.net

TERI M. LORENZ, born Iowa City, Iowa, June 4, 1948; admitted to bar, 1979, Indiana and U.S. District Court, Southern District of Indiana. *Education:* Indiana University (B.S., cum laude, 1970; M.S., 1973; J.D., cum laude, 1979). Certified Family Law Specialist and Mediator. *Member:* Terre Haute and Indiana State Bar Associations. ***PRACTICE AREAS:*** Divorce; Family Law; Trust Law; Probate Law; Real Estate Law; Corporate Law. **Email:** lorenz@huntlawfirm.net

ROBERT P. KONDRAS, JR., born Camden, New Jersey, August 6, 1967; admitted to bar, 1994, Indiana and U.S. District Court, Southern and Northern Districts of Indiana; 1997, U.S. Court of Appeals, Seventh Circuit; 2001, U.S. District Court, Central and Southern Districts of Illinois; 2003, U.S. District Court, District of North Dakota. *Education:* University of Richmond (B.A., magna cum laude, 1989); University of Indiana, Bloomington (M.A. in English, 1992; J.D., 1994). Phi Beta Kappa. *Member:* Terre Haute and Indiana State Bar Associations; Association of Trial Lawyers of America. ***PRACTICE AREAS:*** Employment Law; Family Law. **Email:** kondras@huntlawfirm.net

ATTORNEYS FOR: Auto Owners Insurance Co.; Indiana Insurance Co.; Wausau Insurance Co.; Go America Auto Insurance; Empire Fire and Marine Insurance Co.; American Motorists Insurance Co.; Liberty Mutual Insurance Co.; The Kemper Group; Horace Mann Insurance Co.; Indiana Farmers Mutual Insurance Group; Pinkerton's Inc.; Morris Trucking Co., Inc.; TRW, Inc.; Acceptance Insurance Company; Britt Tools, Inc.; Computer Solutions, Inc.; Futerex Industries; Hane Industrial Training; Northstar Computer Consultants; Terre Haute Police Department Merit Commission; Terre Haute Fire Department Merit Commission; Kirkham Hardwoods, Inc.; Advance Waste Management; Dump Trucks, Inc.; Andrews Heating & Air Conditioning, Inc.; Bennett and Hair General Contractors, Inc.; Fleetwood Enterprises, Inc.
REFERENCE: Terre Haute First National Bank.

DANIEL W. KELLY

321 OHIO STREET
TERRE HAUTE, INDIANA 47808
Telephone: 812-234-1292
Fax: 812-232-3232
Email: danmbk@aol.com
URL: http://www.dankellylawfirm.com

Personal Injury, Family Law, Wills, Estate Administration, Bankruptcy.

DANIEL W. KELLY, born Terre Haute, Indiana, July 25, 1961; admitted to bar, 1988, Indiana, U.S. District Court, Southern and Northern Districts of Indiana. *Education:* Purdue University (B.A., 1984); Valparaiso University (J.D., 1988). Author: "Using The Indiana Child Support Guidelines", ICLEF, November 1993 and 1994. Co-Author: "The Indiana Responsible Property Transfer Act: Environmental Disclosure Statements Between Buyers, Sellers and Lenders," ICLEF, March 1991. Deputy Prosecutor, Vigo County, 1995—. Registered Mediator, June 1998—. *Member:* Terre Haute (President, 1997-1998) and Indiana State (Director, Young Lawyers Section, 1992-1995) Bar Associations; Indiana Trial Lawyers Association. ***PRACTICE AREAS:*** Personal Injury; Family Law; Wills; Estate Administration; Bankruptcy.

WILLIAM J. MAHER

140 CHERRY STREET
TERRE HAUTE, INDIANA 47807
Telephone: 812-232-6617
Fax: 812-235-2041
URL: http://www.lawyers.com/wjmaherlaw

General Civil Trial Practice in State and Federal Courts. Personal Injury, Automobile Accidents, Slip and Fall, Dog Bites, Wrongful Death, Product Liability, Wills, Probate, Trusts and Estates, Guardianships, Asset Protection, Estate Planning, Business Law, Contracts, Business Litigation, Business Enterprises, Corporate, Real Estate, Workers Compensation, Social Security Disability, Bankruptcy.

WILLIAM J. MAHER, born Terre Haute, Indiana, October 28, 1945; admitted to bar, 1970, Indiana. *Education:* Indiana State University (B.S., 1967); Indiana University at Bloomington (J.D., 1970). Deputy Prosecutor, Vigo County, 1970-1972. Second County Attorney, Vigo County, 1970-1972. *Member:* Terre Haute, Indiana State and American Bar Associations; Indiana Trial Lawyers Association; The Association of Trial Lawyers of America.

REFERENCES: First Financial Bank; Old National Bank; 5/3 Bank.

MANN LAW FIRM

646 WALNUT STREET
P.O. BOX 1643
TERRE HAUTE, INDIANA 47808-1643
Telephone: 812-232-0107
FAX: 812-232-3414
Email: mannlawfirm.com
URL: http://www.mannlawfirm.com

Personal Injury and Business Trial Practice in State and Federal Courts, Condemnation, Eminent Domain, Land Acquisition, Medical Malpractice and Products Liability.

FIRM PROFILE: Since its establishment in 1937 by Hansford C. Mann, the trial firm has specialized in litigation for injury victims and damaged businesses. The firm handles a wide variety of litigation, ranging from the most serious injury cases to the most complex business and contractual disputes. The firm represents clients throughout Western Indiana and Eastern Illinois but is not limited to those areas.

MEMBERS OF FIRM

HANSFORD C. MANN (1911-1998)

MAX E. GOODWIN [Lt. Comdr., USNR, JAGC, 1967-1971]. (1941-2001)

STEPHEN L. WILLIAMS, born Terre Haute, Indiana, January 10, 1949; admitted to bar, 1973, U.S. Court of Appeals, 7th Circuit; 1974, Illinois, Indiana and U.S. District Court, Northern and Southern Districts of Indiana. *Education:* Indiana State University (B.S., 1971); Indiana University (J.D., magna cum laude, 1974); National Institute for Trial Advocacy, Chapel Hill, N.C. (1984) National Institute for Trial Advocacy, Advanced Trial Advocacy Skills, Houston, Texas (1985). Sigma Pi Alpha. Recipient, Indiana State University Distinguished Alumni Award, 1999. Member, Board of Editors, Indiana Law Review, 1973-1974. Alumni Counsel, Indiana State University, 1986-1991. Member, Board of Directors, Indiana University Law School Alumni Association, 1987—. Author: "Recent Developments," 6 Indiana Law Review 314, 1972 and 6 Indiana Law Review 812, 1972; Note, "Risk of Loss Under the U.C.C.," 7 Indiana Law Review 711, 1974; Article, "Indiana's Medical Malpractice Act—The Developing Law," Vol. XXVII No. 10, Res Gestae 494, 1984; Article, "Maximizing the Benefits and Avoiding the Pitfalls of Comparative Fault," ICLEF Seminar on Impact of Comparative Fault, September, 1984. Article and Seminar Lecturer: "Insurance Carrier's Duty of Good Faith & Fair Dealing To Its Insureds," ICLEF Seminar, September, 1986; "The Mechanics-Procedural Devises For Keeping Evidence Out," ICLEF Seminar, March, 1988; Article and Seminar Lecturer, "The Current Status of Premises Liability," ICLEF and ISBA Seminar, October, 1989; Article and Seminar Lecturer, "The Preparation and Trial of Dog Bite Cases," ITLA Seminar, March 1990. Article and Seminar Lecturer, "New Developments in Comparative Fault," ITLA Seminar, March, 1991; Author: Chapter 57, "Cranes," Product Liability Practice Guide, (Matthew Bender & Co., Inc., October, 1991); "Is it Whiplash Or Is It Myofacial Pain Syndrome," ITLA Seminar, March, 1992. Article and Seminar Lecturer: Article, "Pain Syndromes with Positive Test Results and Objective Symptoms," Spring, 1992, Verdict; ITLA Seminar, March 1993, Article and Seminar Lecturer, "Consistent and Inconsistent Statements-Correct Use and Evidentiary Impact," October, 1993. Seminar Lecturer, "Processing A Civil Lawsuit," St. Mary of the Woods College, December, 1993—. Seminar Chairman, Indiana Trial Lawyers 1993 Annual Institute. Article and Seminar Lecturer, "Using Experts Under Indiana's New Rules of Evidence," ITLA Seminar, March, 1994. ITLA Seminar, March 1994; Article and Seminar Lecturer, "Practical Tips For Handling Complex Business Litigation," ICLEF; Seminar on Current Issues In Business Litigation, November 10, 1994; Article and Seminar Lecturer, "Pain Syndromes With Positive Test Results And Objective Symptoms," ITLA Seminar, March, 1995; Article and Seminar Lecturer, "Product Liability Defenses After Tort Reform," August, 1996; Article and Seminar Lecturer, "Admissibility Of Computer Generated Graphics," ITLA Seminar, March, 1997. Article and Seminar Lecturer, "The Limitations on Admissibility of Medical Records Under the Indiana Rules of Evidence," ITLA Seminar, April, 1998. Article and Seminar Lecturer, "Medical Records - Admissible April, 1999, ITLA Seminar; Article and Seminar Lecturer, "Civility In The Law," ICLEF Seminar, October, 1999; Article and Seminar Lecturer, "Discovery - Medical Records," June, 2000, ITLA Seminar. Instructor, Labor Law, Indiana University, 1978-1981. Faculty, National Institute of Trial Advocacy, May 1989. 1990, 1991, 1992, 1993, 1994. Recipient: Outstanding Young Man of America, U.S. Jaycees, 1983; Trial Lawyer of the Year, Indiana Trial Lawyer's Association, 1989; Sagamore of the Wabash Award, Indiana Governor Evan Bayh, 1990. Listed in Best Lawyers in America, 1975—. *Member:* Terre Haute and Indiana State (Counsel, Trial Lawyers Section, 1985-1989) Bar Associations; Bar Association of the 7th Federal Circuit; Indiana Trial Lawyers Association (Member, Board of Directors, 1988—; Member, Executive Committee, 1998—); The Association of Trial Lawyers of America. Fellow, American College of Trial Lawyers. Indiana Trial Lawyer's Association. Fellow, Indiana Bar Association. Certified as a Civil Trial Advocate by the National Board of Trial Advocacy. ***PRACTICE AREAS:*** Personal Injury; Medical Malpractice; Torts. **Email:** steve@mannlawfirm.com

BRUCE D. AUKERMAN, born Newport, Indiana, December 16, 1961; admitted to bar, 1988, Indiana and U.S. District Court, Northern and Southern Districts of Indiana. *Education:* Indiana University (B.S., Accounting, 1985); Southern Illinois University (J.D., 1988). Phi Delta Phi. National Moot Court Team. Recipient: Order of the Barristers Award; Indiana Trial Lawyers Association Trial Lawyer of the Year 2003. *Member:* Terre Haute and Indiana State Bar Associations; Indiana Trial Lawyers Association (Chairman, Securities Litigation Committee 1991-1992). ***PRACTICE AREAS:*** Plaintiff's Business and Securities Litigation; Personal Injury; Products Liability. **Email:** bruce@mannlawfirm.com

JOHN T. ROACH III, born Alton, Illinois, October 6, 1961; admitted to bar, 1988, Missouri; 1989, Illinois; 1994, Indiana and U.S. District Court, Northern and Southern District of Indiana; U.S. Court of Appeals, 7th Circuit; Eastern District of Missouri and Southern District of Illinois. *Education:* Southern Illinois University-Carbondale (B.A., Political Science, 1985); Southern Illinois University School of Law (J.D., magna cum laude, 1988). President, Moot Court Board; Recipient, Order of the Barristers Award; National Moot Court Team. National Institute for Trial Advocacy (1992 and 1995). *Member:* Terre Haute, Indiana State, Illinois State and American Bar Associations; The Missouri Bar; Indiana

(This Listing Continued)

MANN LAW FIRM, Terre Haute—Continued

Trial Lawyers Association; The Association of Trial Lawyers of America. ***PRACTICE AREAS:*** Personal Injury; Medical Malpractice; Products Liability. ***Email:*** john@mannlawfirm.com

CHRIS A. WREDE, admitted to bar, 2000, Indiana and Illinois; 2001, U.S. District Court, Northern and Southern District of Indiana, U.S. District Court, Central and Southern District of Illinois and U.S. Court of Appeals, Seventh Circuit. *Education:* Indiana State University (B.S., 1996); Indiana University School of Law (J.D., cum laude, 2000). Member: Dean's Tutorial Society. Articles Editor, Indiana Law Review. *Member:* Indiana State Bar Association; Indiana Trial Lawyers Association. ***Email:*** chris@mannlaw.com

REFERENCES: Terre Haute First National Bank; Indiana State Bank.

EDWARD McGLONE LAW OFFICE

2022 WABASH AVENUE, SUITE B
TERRE HAUTE, INDIANA 47807
Telephone: 812-478-3442
Fax: 812-478-3462
Email: edmcglonelaw@aol.com

Personal Injury, Automobile Accidents, Slip and Fall, Dog Bites, Wrongful Death, Criminal Law, Traffic Violations, Driving While Intoxicated, Juvenile Law, Drug Crimes, Felonies, Misdemeanors.

EDWARD McGLONE, born Terre Haute, Indiana, September 19, 1964; admitted to bar, 1989, Indiana and U.S. District Court, Northern and Southern Districts of Indiana. *Education:* Indiana State University (B.S., cum laude, 1986); Indiana University School of Law (J.D., 1989). Phi Delta Phi; Beta Gamma Sigma. Member, National District Attorneys Association, 1991-1995. Chief Deputy Prosecuting Attorney, Greene County, Indiana, 1991-1995. *Member:* Terre Haute, Vigo, Green County, Indiana State and American Bar Associations; The Association of Trial Lawyers of America; Indiana Trial Lawyers Association; National Association of Criminal Defense Lawyers. ***PRACTICE AREAS:*** Personal Injury; Criminal Law; Traffic Violations; Driving While Intoxicated; Juvenile Law.

McGLONE LAW

Established in 1967
1717 S. THIRD STREET
TERRE HAUTE, INDIANA 47802
Telephone: 812-234-4000
Fax: 812-234-4900
Toll free: 812-234-8400
Email: jerry@2344000.com

Trial Practice in State and Federal Courts. Personal Injury, Workers Compensation, Products Liability, Construction and Probate.

FIRM PROFILE: Since the firm's establishment in 1967 by Gerald H. McGlone, the firm has maintained a trial practice with an emphasis on personal injury, products liability, workers compensation and construction site accidents. The firm has a support staff that includes an investigator and case management. The firm primarily represents individuals and small business throughout West Central Indiana. The firm has achieved the highest rating given by Martindale-Hubbell. The firm is listed in the Bar Register of Preeminent Lawyers in the field of personal injury.

MEMBERS OF FIRM

GERALD H. McGLONE, born Terre Haute, Indiana, December 31, 1932; admitted to bar, 1964, Indiana and U.S. District Court, Southern District of Indiana; 1972, U.S. Court of Appeals, Seventh Circuit. *Education:* Rose Polytechnic Institute (B.S., with honors, 1955); Indiana University (J.D., with high distinction, 1964). Member, Panel of Arbitrators, American Arbitration Association. *Member:* Terre Haute, Indiana State and American Bar Associations; The Association of Trial Lawyers of America; Indiana Trial Lawyers Association. ***PRACTICE AREAS:*** Personal Injury; Wrongful Death; Product Liability; Probate and Estate. ***Email:*** jerry@2344000.com

DANIEL J. McGLONE, born Bloomington, Indiana, January 28, 1963; admitted to bar, 1988, Indiana and U.S. District Court, Northern and Southern Districts of Indiana. *Education:* Indiana State University (B.S., cum laude, University Honors Program, 1985); Indiana University (J.D., 1988). Vigo County Deputy Prosecutor, 1989—. *Member:* Terre Haute, Indiana State and America Bar Associations; The Association of Trial Lawyers of America; Indiana Trial Lawyers Association. ***PRACTICE AREAS:*** Personal Injury; Wrongful Death; Product Liability; Workers Compensation. ***Email:*** dan@2344000.com

REFERENCE: Regions Bank.

SACOPULOS, JOHNSON & SACOPULOS

676 OHIO STREET
TERRE HAUTE, INDIANA 47807
Telephone: 812-238-2565
FAX: 812-238-1945
Email: office@sacopulos.com

Civil Litigation, Corporate, Insurance, and Probate and Estate Planning. General Practice, Employment, Medical Malpractice.

(This Listing Continued)

MEMBERS OF FIRM

GUS SACOPULOS, born Gary, Indiana, August 3, 1935; admitted to bar, 1960, Indiana and U.S. District Court, Southern and Northern Districts of Indiana; U.S. Court of Appeals, Seventh Circuit. *Education:* Indiana University (A.B., 1957; J.D., 1960). Phi Delta Phi; Delta Sigma Rho; Pi Sigma Alpha; Delta Tau Delta. Listed in Best Lawyers in America. Designated Indiana Super Lawyer, 2004 and 2005. *Member:* Terre Haute (President, 1972-1973), Seventh Circuit, Indiana State, Federal and American Bar Associations; Indiana Defense Lawyers Association (Diplomat; Member, Board of Directors); Association of Insurance Attorneys; Defense Research and Trial Lawyers Association; American Board of Trial Advocates (Vice President, Indiana Chapter, 1982-1985; President, 1986-1988); American Society of Hospital Attorneys; International Society of Barristers (Fellow); American Society of Legal Medicine. Fellow: Indiana Bar Foundation; American College of Trial Lawyers; International Association of Defense Counsel. ***PRACTICE AREAS:*** Civil Litigation; Insurance Law; Mediation; Medical Malpractice; Toxic Torts; Asbestos Defense. ***Email:*** gus.sacopulos@sacopulos.com

R. STEVEN JOHNSON, born Terre Haute, Indiana, November 8, 1945; admitted to bar, 1972, Indiana and U.S. District Court, Southern District of Indiana. *Education:* Indiana State University (B.S., 1967); Indiana University (J.D., 1972). Phi Alpha Delta. Deputy Prosecuting Attorney, 1972-1973; Assistant City Attorney, 1973, Terre Haute, Indiana. *Member:* Terre Haute, Indiana State and American Bar Associations; Defense Research and Trial Lawyers Association; Indiana Defense Lawyers Association. ***PRACTICE AREAS:*** Civil Litigation; Corporate Law; Insurance Law; Mediation; Medical Malpractice Defense. ***Email:*** steve.johnson@sacopulos.com

PETER J. SACOPULOS, born Evansville, Indiana, February 11, 1963; admitted to bar, 1988, Indiana, U.S. District Court, Southern District of Indiana. *Education:* Tulane University (B.A., cum laude, 1985); Indiana University (J.D., 1988). Author: "Establishing Jurisdiction over International Terrorists," The TVI Report, Vol. IX No. I 1989. *Member:* Terre Haute (President), Indiana State and American Bar Associations; Indiana Defense Trial Lawyers Association; American Judicature Society; International Association of Defense Counsel. ***PRACTICE AREAS:*** Insurance Defense Litigation; Mediation; Business Law; Toxic Torts; Latex Allergy Litigation; Trusts and Estates; Estate Planning. ***Email:*** pete.sacopulos@sacopulos.com

MICHAEL J. SACOPULOS, born Terre Haute, Indiana, May 19, 1969; admitted to bar, 1995, Indiana and U.S. District Court, Southern and Northern Districts of Indiana. *Education:* Harvard College (A.B., magna cum laude, 1991); Indiana University (J.D., cum laude, 1994). *Member:* Terre Haute, Indiana State and American Bar Associations; Indiana Defense Trial Lawyers Association; National Association of Retail Collection Attorneys. ***PRACTICE AREAS:*** Insurance Defense Litigation; Civil Litigation; Medical Malpractice Defense; Commercial Litigation; Trusts and Estates; Estate Planning. ***Email:*** mike.sacopulos@sacopulos.com

ASSOCIATE

JOHN J. KLOTZ, born West Terre Haute, Indiana, September 28, 1978; admitted to bar, 2004, Indiana and U.S. District Court, Southern District of Indiana. *Education:* Indiana State University (B.S., 2001); Valparaiso University (J.D., 2004). ***PRACTICE AREAS:*** General Practice; Civil Practice; Trial Practice; Corporate; Insurance; Probate. ***Email:*** john_klotz@sacopulos.com

REPRESENTATIVE CLIENTS: Auto-Owners Insurance Co.; Champion Home Builders Co.; Credit Life Insurance Co.; Professional Mutual Insurance Co.; The Medical Protective Co.; Bituminous Insurance Cos.; Employers Mutual Insurance Cos.; Universal Fire & Casualty Insurance Co.; Indiana Insurance Co.; Centennial Insurance Co.; Security Insurance Co.; Crown Life Insurance Co.; United Insurance Company of America; American Economy Insurance Co.; Meridian Mutual Insurance Co.; CNA Insurance Co.; Canadian Universal Insurance Co.; Employers of Wausau Insurance Co.; American Professionals Ins. Co.; Minnesota Mutual Ins. Co.; Peerless Ins. Co.; Amerisure Cos.; Great America Ins. Co.; Progressive Insurance Co.; Risk Management Claims Service; American Family Insurance Co., Inc.; Indiana Residual Medical Malpractice Authority; Amerisure Cos.; WalMart Stores, Inc.; Physicians & Surgeons Insurance Co.; Citizens Ins. Co.; USF&G; Victoria Ins. Co.; Motorists Mutual; Safeco; Beazer East Inc.

SMOCK AND ETLING

77 CHERRY STREET
TERRE HAUTE, INDIANA 47807
Telephone: 812-238-1751
FAX: 812-238-1752
Email: smock.etling@verizon.net
URL: http://www.smock-etling.com

Criminal, Personal Injury Law, Family Law.

MEMBERS OF FIRM

WILLIAM G. SMOCK, born Terre Haute, Indiana, December 22, 1946; admitted to bar, 1972, Indiana, U.S. District Court, Southern District of Indiana, U.S. Court of Appeals, Seventh Circuit and U.S. Supreme Court. *Education:* Indiana State University (B.S., 1968); Indiana University (J.D., 1971). Phi Delta Phi. Deputy Attorney General, 1972. Assistant Public Defender, 1973. *Member:* Terre Haute (President, 1991-1992), Indiana State and American Bar Associations; Seventh Circuit Bar Association (Chairman, 1988—, Indiana Section of the Committee on Criminal Law and Procedure); Indiana Trial Lawyers Association; The Association of Trial Lawyers of America; American Board of Trial Advocates; National Association of Criminal Defense Lawyers; Indiana Association of Criminal Defense Lawyers (Member, Board of Directors, 1986-1987). ***PRACTICE AREAS:*** Personal Injury; Criminal.

JOSEPH K. ETLING, born Terre Haute, Vigo County, Indiana, June 7, 1963; admitted to bar, 1988, Indiana, U.S. District Court, Southern District of Indiana, U.S. Court of Appeals, Seventh Circuit and U.S. Supreme Court. *Education:* Wabash College (B.A., 1985); Indiana University (J.D., 1988). Omicron Delta Epsilon; Delta Theta Phi. *Member:* Terre Haute, Indiana State and American Bar Associations; Seventh Circuit Bar Association; In-

(This Listing Continued)

diana Trial Lawyers Association; The Association of Trial Lawyers of America; National Association of Criminal Defense Lawyers; Indiana Association of Criminal Defense Lawyers. ***PRACTICE AREAS:*** Personal Injury; Criminal.

ASSOCIATE

MICHAEL A. SLAGLE, born Hamilton, Ohio, January 23, 1969; admitted to bar, 1998, Indiana and U.S. District Court, Southern and Northern Districts of Indiana. *Education:* Ball State University (B.S., 1995); Indiana University (J.D., 1998). *Member:* Terre Haute, Indiana State and American Bar Associations; Indiana Trial Lawyers Association. [Army 1987-1991, Specialist/E-4]. ***PRACTICE AREAS:*** Criminal Defense; Personal Injury; Family Law. ***Email:*** smock.etling@verizon.net

---

WILKINSON, GOELLER, MODESITT, WILKINSON & DRUMMY

Established in 1898

333 OHIO STREET
P.O. BOX 800
TERRE HAUTE, INDIANA 47808-0800
Telephone: 812-232-4311
Fax: 812-235-5107
Email: BCWilkinson@wilkinsonlaw.com
URL: http://www.wilkinsonlaw.com

General Civil Practice in all Courts. Taxation, Corporation, Trust, Probate, Estate Planning, Insurance Law, Health Law, Municipal Law, Bankruptcy, and Creditors Rights. Insurance Defense, Business Litigation, Mediation and Arbitration.

FIRM PROFILE: The Wilkinson, Goeller, Modesitt, Wilkinson & Drummy law firm evolved from the 70-year legal practice of George O. Dix, who founded the firm in 1898. The firm's practice has long focused on litigation, corporate, real estate, and tax matters. As the largest firm in west central Indiana, the firm continues its general practice with specialty work in mass tort/environmental and insurance defense litigation, real estate and title insurance, health and hospital law, creditor's rights, small business, commercial and probate law and extensive work in civil litigation in both state and federal courts.

MEMBERS OF FIRM

DAVID H. GOELLER, born Columbus, Indiana, July 1, 1935; admitted to bar, 1963, Indiana. *Education:* Indiana University (B.S., 1959; J.D., with distinction, 1963). Beta Gamma Sigma; Phi Delta Phi; Order of the Coif. Member, Board of Editors, Indiana Law Journal, 1961-1963. *Member:* Terre Haute, Indiana State and American Bar Associations. ***PRACTICE AREAS:*** Real Estate Law; Banking Law; Corporate and General Business Law; Estate Planning and Probate Law. ***Email:*** DHGoeller@wilkinsonlaw.com

RAYMOND H. MODESITT, born Terre Haute, Indiana, June 30, 1943; admitted to bar, 1968, Indiana. *Education:* Indiana University (A.B., 1965; J.D., 1968). Phi Alpha Delta. *Member:* Terre Haute, Indiana State and American Bar Associations; Indiana Defense Lawyers Association; Defense Research Institute; Indiana Defense Lawyers Association (Diplomat). Fellow, American College of Trial Lawyers. ***PRACTICE AREAS:*** Toxic Tort Litigation; Environmental Litigation; Product Liability Litigation; Medical Malpractice Litigation; Commercial and Business Litigation; Corporate Commercial Law. ***Email:*** RHModesitt@wilkinsonlaw.com

B. CURTIS WILKINSON, born Pomona, California, July 29, 1947; admitted to bar, 1972, Indiana. *Education:* Indiana State University (A.B., 1969) Indiana University (J.D., with distinction, 1972). Pi Gamma Mu; Phi Alpha Delta. *Member:* Terre Haute, Seventh Circuit, Indiana State and American Bar Associations; Indiana Defense Lawyers Association; Defense Research Institute; American Academy of Hospital Attorneys; National Health Lawyers Association. ***PRACTICE AREAS:*** Health and Hospital Law; Insurance Defense Litigation; Corporate and General Business Law. ***Email:*** BCWilkinson@wilkinsonlaw.com

WILLIAM W. DRUMMY, born Omaha, Nebraska, November 12, 1948; admitted to bar, 1975, Nebraska; 1977, Indiana. *Education:* Indiana University (B.S., 1970); Creighton University (J.D., cum laude, 1975). Member and Associate Editor, Creighton Law Review, 1974-1975. Author: "The Hospital and the Staff Physician—An Expanding Duty of Care," 7 Creighton Law Review 249, 1973; "Constitutional Law—Due Process—Iowa Harmless Error Rule Denies Remedy for Deprivation of Property Contrary to Fuentes v. Shevin," 6 Creighton Law Review 410, 1973. Indiana Super Lawyer, 2004 and 2005. *Member:* Terre Haute, Indiana State and American Bar Associations; American Board of Trial Advocates (Advocate); Defense Research Institute; Indiana Trial Lawyers Association; The Association of Trial Lawyers of America. Fellow, American College of Trial Lawyers. ***REPORTED CASES:*** E.E.O.C v. North Knox School Corp. 154 F.3d744, 77 Fair Empl.Prac.Case. (BNA) 1306, 74 Empl.Prac.Dec. P45, 524, 129 Ed. Law Rep. 59 (7th Cir. (Ind.), Sep 8, 1998) (NO. 97-3704; Doherty v. Crow, 2000 WL 1006620 (S.D.Ind., Jul 19, 2000) (NO. TH 99-216-C-T/H); Harris v. Cacdac, 512 N.E.2d 1138 (Ind.App. 4 Dist., Sep 23, 1987) (NO. 83A04-8603-CV-85); Carie v. PSI Energy, Inc., 715 N.E.2d 853 (Ind., Sep 3, 1999) (NO. 83S01-9811-CV-695); Goldhart v. Board of Com'rs of County of Parke, 533 N.E.2d 605 (Ind.App. 1 Dist., Feb 2, 1989) (NO. 61A01-8802-CV-54); First Bank & Trust Co. of Clay County v. Bunch, 460 N.E.2d 517 (Ind.App. 1 Dist., Feb 29, 1984) (NO. 1-1182 A 327); Power v. Brodie, 460 N.E.2d 1241 (Ind.App. 1 Dist., Mar 29, 1984) (NO. 1-1282 A 364); Terre Haute First Nat. Bank v. Stewart, 455 N.E.2d 362 (Ind.App. 1 Dist., Oct. 19, 1983) (NO. 1-1282 A 351); ConAgra, Inc. v. Farrington, 635 N.E.2d 1137 (Ind.App. 1 Dist., Jun 23, 1994) (NO. 84A01-9312-CV-386); Hunter v. Byrd, 602 N.E.2d 1052 (Ind.App. 1 Dist., Nov 19, 1992) (NO. 77A01-9205-CV-151); Hershberger v. Brooker, 421 N.E.2d 672 (Ind.App. 1 Dist., Jun 9, 1981) (NO. 1-1180 A 330); Carie v. PSI Energy, Inc., 694 N.E.2d 729 (Ind.App., Apr 23, 1998) (NO. 83A01-9707-CV-229); Young v. Butts, 685 N.E.2d 147 (Ind.App., Sep 16, 1997) (NO. 32A05-9607-CV-151). ***PRACTICE AREAS:*** Personal Injury Trials; Medical Malpractice Defense; Products Liability Defense; Direct Action Defense; Age Discrimination; Commercial and Business Litigation; Municipal Law; Employment Law; Defense. ***Email:*** WWDrummy@wilkinsonlaw.com

KELVIN L. ROOTS, born Indianapolis, Indiana, July 22, 1954; admitted to bar, 1981, Indiana. *Education:* DePauw University (B.A., cum laude, 1976); Indiana University (J.D., cum laude, 1981). *Member:* Terre Haute, Indiana State (Member, Section on Bankruptcy and Creditors Rights) and American Bar Associations; Commercial Law League of America. ***PRACTICE AREAS:*** Bankruptcy Law; Commercial and Business Litigation; General Practice. ***Email:*** KLRoots@wilkinsonlaw.com

JOHN C. WALL, born Rochester, New York, September 19, 1948; admitted to bar, 1982, Indiana. *Education:* Principia College (B.A., 1971); Colgate University (M.A., cum laude, 1975); Indiana University (J.D., summa cum laude, 1982). Associate Editor, Indiana Law Review, 1980-1982. *Member:* Terre Haute, Indiana State and American Bar Associations; Defense Trial Counsel of Indiana. ***PRACTICE AREAS:*** Insurance Defense Litigation; Medical Malpractice Defense; Appeals; General Practice. ***Email:*** JCWall@wilkinsonlaw.com

WILLIAM M. OLAH, born Terre Haute, Indiana, August 9, 1952; admitted to bar, 1978, Indiana and U.S. District Court, Southern District of Indiana; 1979, Arkansas and U.S. Court of Appeals, Seventh Circuit; 2000, U.S. Supreme Court. *Education:* Rose-Hulman Institute of Technology (B.S., cum laude, 1974); University of Arkansas (J.D., with honors, 1978). Phi Delta Phi. Citations Editor, Arkansas Law Review, 1977. *Member:* Terre Haute, Indiana State (Member, Probate, Trust and Real Property Section) and American (Member, Taxation Section) Bar Associations; Seventh Circuit Bar Association. ***PRACTICE AREAS:*** Corporate and Commercial Law; Taxation Law; Real Estate Law; Estate and Trust Planning and Probate Law. ***Email:*** WMOlah@wilkinsonlaw.com

CRAIG M. McKEE, born Frankfort, Indiana, April 17, 1958; admitted to bar, 1983, Indiana, U.S. Court of Appeals, Seventh Circuit and U.S. Tax Court. *Education:* Indiana State University (B.S., 1979); Indiana University (J.D., 1983). Law Clerk to U.S. District Judge, Gene E. Brooks, Southern District of Indiana, 1983-1985. Certified Mediator. *Member:* Terre Haute (President, 1995-1996), Indiana State and American Bar Associations; Seventh Circuit Bar Association; American Health Lawyers Association; Indiana Defense Lawyers Association. ***PRACTICE AREAS:*** Insurance Defense Litigation; Health Care; General Corporate and Probate Practice; Mediation. ***Email:*** CMMcKee@wilkinsonlaw.com

SCOTT M. KYROUAC, born Kankakee, Illinois, June 13, 1960; admitted to bar, 1985, Indiana. *Education:* University of Illinois (B.S., high honors, 1982); Indiana University (J.D., 1985). Delta Theta Phi. Author: "Bad Faith Litigation," 2003 ICLE; "Crashworthiness Revisited," Indiana Lawyer, 1996; "The Art of Being Local Counsel," Indiana Lawyer, 1999. *Member:* Terre Haute, Indiana State and American (Member, Sections on: Litigation; Environmental Law; Sports and Entertainment Law) Bar Associations; Indiana Defense Lawyers Association; Defense Research Institute; American Board of Trial Advocates (Advocate). ***REPORTED CASES:*** McCullough v. Archbold, 605 N.E. 2d 175 (Ind. 1993); Harbour v. Arelco, Inc., 678 N.E. 2d 381 (Ind. 1999); Shelton v. Wick, 715 N.E. 2d 890 (1999); trans. denial 736 N.E. 2d 219 (2000). ***PRACTICE AREAS:*** Personal Injury; Insurance Defense; Medical Malpractice Defense; Products Liability; Environmental Law; Employment Law; Municipal Law. ***Email:*** SMKyrouac@wilkinsonlaw.com

JEFFREY A. BOYLL, born Sullivan, Indiana, August 17, 1956; admitted to bar, 1983, Indiana. *Education:* DePauw University (B.A., summa cum laude, 1978); Indiana University (J.D., magna cum laude, 1983). Phi Beta Kappa. Editor, Indiana Law Journal, 1982-1983. Author: Note, 58 Indiana Law Journal, 1983. *Member:* Clay County, Terre Haute, Indiana State and American Bar Associations. ***PRACTICE AREAS:*** Insurance Defense Litigation; Education/School Law. ***Email:*** JABoyll@wilkinsonlaw.com

DAVID P. FRIEDRICH, born South Bend, Indiana, February 3, 1965; admitted to bar, 1990, Indiana. *Education:* Butler University (B.S., cum laude, 1987); Indiana University (J.D., 1990). *Member:* Terre Haute, Indiana State and American Bar Associations; Indiana Defense Lawyers Association. ***PRACTICE AREAS:*** Insurance Defense Litigation; Business Litigation; General Practice. ***Email:*** DPFriedrich@wilkinsonlaw.com

JEFFREY A. LEWELLYN, born Indianapolis, Indiana, March 7, 1963; admitted to bar, 1990, Indiana. *Education:* Murray State University (B.S., 1985); Indiana University (J.D., 1990). Phi Delta Phi. City Attorney, City of Seymour, Indiana, 1994-1996. Deputy City Attorney, City of Seymour, Indiana, 1993. *Member:* Jackson County (President, 1994), Terre Haute, Indiana State and American Bar Associations; Indiana Trial Lawyers Association; The Association of Trial Lawyers of America. ***PRACTICE AREAS:*** Real Estate; Banking Law; Corporate Law; Business Law; Estate Planning; Probate. ***Email:*** JALewellyn@wilkinsonlaw.com

TRACY M. WEBER, born Pinckneyville, Illinois, August 25, 1969; admitted to bar, 1998, Indiana and Illinois. *Education:* University of Illinois (B.S., 1991); Southern Illinois University (J.D., magna cum laude, 1998). Phi Delta Phi. Member: Graduate and Professional Student Council; Lincoln's Inn; Southern Illinois American Inns of Court. Casenote/Comment Editor, Southern Illinois University Law Journal, 1997-1998. Author: "Name-Clearing Hearings, Gratuitous Remedies, and Common Law Writs of Certiorari - Are They Worth Their Weight in Gold?" Southern Illinois University Law Journal, Volume 22, Page 201 (Fall 1997). President, Student Bar Association, 1997-1998. *Member:* Terre Haute, Indiana State, Illinois State and American Bar Associations; Indiana Defense Lawyers Association. ***PRACTICE AREAS:*** Estate Planning; Real Estate; Business Law; Family Law; Probate. ***Email:*** TMWeber@wilkinsonlaw.com

---

WILLIAM S. FRANKEL, IV, born Terre Haute, Indiana, August 6, 1978; admitted to bar, 2004, Indiana; 2005, Illinois. *Education:* Indiana State University (B.S., 2001); Indiana University School of Law - Indianapolis (J.D., cum laude, 2004). Beta Gamma Sigma; Phi Kappa Phi; Order of the Barristers; Golden Key National Honor Society; Dean's Tutorial Society. Member, Indiana Volunteer Firefighters Association. *Member:* Indiana, Terra Haute, Indianapolis and American Bar Associations. ***Email:*** wsfrankel@wilkinsonlaw.com

(This Listing Continued)

WILKINSON, GOELLER, MODESITT, WILKINSON & DRUMMY, Terre Haute—Continued

REPRESENTATIVE CORPORATE CLIENTS: Old National Bank; Old National Trust Company; CSX, Inc.; Chicago Title Insurance Co.; Terre Haute Board of Realtors; Union Hospital; Associated Physicians and Surgeons Clinic, LLC.; Health Care Excel; City of Terre Haute; Templeton Coal Co.; Farm Credit Services of Mid-America, ACA; Bethesda Elderly Housing Corp.; CDI, Inc.; Hannig Construction, Inc.; Gartland Foundry; Cinergy PSI; AET; Gibault, Inc.; Westminster Village of Terre Haute, Inc.; Turbines, Inc.; White Construction, Inc.; Terre Haute Housing Authority; Honey Creek-Vigo Conservancy District; Apple House, Inc.; Shenango Industries, Inc.; Ragle & Company; TRI Aerospace, LLC; Richard Jenkins Construction; Owens Corning Fiberglas.
REPRESENTATIVE INSURANCE CLIENTS: State Farm Mutual Insurance; Medical Protective Co.; Prudential Insurance Co.; Motorists Mutual Insurance Co.; Country Companies; Crum & Forster Group; GEICO; Chubb & Sons, Inc.; Nationwide Insurance Co.; Celina Mutual Insurance Co.; Indiana Insurance Cos.; State Farm Fire & Casualty Co.; American Family Insurance; Western Indemnity; Midwest Claims Service; Scottsdale Insurance Co.; Rockford Mutual Insurance Co.; John Hancock Insurance; Farmland Insurance Co.; Monroe Guaranty Insurance Co.; Old American Insurance Co.; Pro Assurance.

BINGHAM, FARRER & WILSON, A PROFESSIONAL CORPORATION

TIPTON, INDIANA

(See Elwood)

General Practice, Banking and Finance, Bankruptcy, Business Planning, Sales and Acquisitions, Consumer and Commercial Law, Consumer and Commercial Collections, Transactions and Litigation, Contracts, Corporate Law, Creditors Rights, Debtor-Creditor Law, Elder Law, Family Law, Domestic Relations, Adoption Law, Child Support, Custody, Dissolution/Divorce, Separation and Visitation, Government Relations, Zoning, Planning and Land Use, Municipal Law, Probate, Guardianship, Estate Planning, Wills and Trusts, Real Estate, Foreclosures, Mechanics Liens.

BLACKBURN & GREEN

TIPTON, INDIANA

(See Fort Wayne)

Litigation, Personal Injury Law.

BEN B. HOBBS

Established in 1972

118 SOUTH INDEPENDENCE STREET
P.O. BOX 219
TIPTON, INDIANA 46072
Telephone: 765-675-9000
Fax: 765-675-9020
Email: bbhatty@tiptontel.com
URL: http://www.lawyers.com/benbhobbslawfirm

Wills, Trusts and Estates, Probate and Estate Planning, Real Estate Transactions, Contracts, Commercial Litigation, Wills, Trust and Estates, Trust and Estate Administration, Business Law, Corporate, Business Entrepreneurs, Small Business, Buying and Selling an Business, Starting a Business, Municipal Law.

BEN B. HOBBS, born Elwood, Indiana, October 30, 1944; admitted to bar, 1972, Indiana. *Education:* Indiana University (B.S., 1966; J.D., cum laude, 1972). Member, Moot Court Board. Attorney, Tipton County, 1973-1991. Attorney for: Tipton County Office of Family and Children, 1972-1995; Tipton County Drainage Board, 1973—. Tipton County Public Library, 1978—. Member, Supreme Court Committee on Character and Fitness. *Member:* Tipton County (President, 1981-1982; 1985-1986), Indiana State (Delegate, 1979-1982) and American Bar Associations. Fellow, Indiana Bar Foundation.

QUIGLEY & QUIGLEY

117 NORTH MAIN STREET
TIPTON, INDIANA 46072
Telephone: 765-675-6949 • 765-675-4675
Fax: 765-675-8835

General Civil Practice. Real Estate, Business and Probate Law, Estate Planning, Municipal Law, Utility Law.

DAVID B. QUIGLEY, born Lafayette, Indiana, February 10, 1947; admitted to bar, 1974, Indiana. *Education:* Indiana University (B.S., 1969; J.D., 1974). Tipton City Attorney, 1980-1983, 1988-1992, 1992—and Utilities Attorney, 1980-1987, 1992—. *Member:* Tipton County, Indiana State and American Bar Associations. ***Email:*** dbq@tiptonteh.com

MATTHEW B. QUIGLEY, born Kokomo, Indiana, September 27, 1975; admitted to bar, 2001, Indiana. *Education:* Indiana University (B.S., 1998; J.D., 2001). City of Tipton Board of Zoning Appeals and Plan Commission Attorney, 2002—. Chief Deputy Prosecuting Attorney for Tipton County, 2003—. *Member:* Tipton County and Indiana State Bar Associations.

BECKMAN, KELLY & SMITH

VALPARAISO, INDIANA

(See Hammond)

General Practice, Commercial, Corporation, Transportation and Trucking, Products and Professional Liability Defense, Elder Law, Estate and Trust Planning and Administration, Franchising, Real Estate, Employment, Taxation and Environmental Law, Trials and Appeals in all Courts, Medical Malpractice Defense and Workers Compensation Defense.

BURKE COSTANZA & CUPPY LLP

Established in 1928

57 FRANKLIN STREET, SUITE 203
VALPARAISO, INDIANA 46383
Telephone: 219-531-0134
Fax: 219-531-0507
URL: http://www.bcclegal.com

Merrillville, Indiana Office: 9191 Broadway. Telephone: 219-769-1313. Fax: 219-769-6806.
Munster, Indiana Office: 900 Ridge Road, Suite L. Telephone: 219-513-1000. Fax: 219-513-1001.

General Civil Practice in State and Federal Courts, Trials, Appeals, Civil Mediation, Administrative, Business Law, Business Planning, Contracts, Business Litigation, Business Enterprises, LLC's, Partnerships, Small Business, Corporate, Real Estate, Employee Benefits/ ERISA, Banking, Commercial, Insurance Defense, Personal Injury, Automobile Accidents, Wrongful Death, Wills and Probate, Trusts and Estates, Estate Planning, Medical Malpractice, Legal Malpractice, Family Law, Adoptions, Child Custody, Child Support, Divorce, Visitation Rights, Municipal and Zoning, Environmental.

PARTNERS

GEORGE W. CARBERRY, born Chicago, Illinois, August 22, 1952; admitted to bar, 1977, Indiana. *Education:* University of Notre Dame (A.B., 1974); Valparaiso University (J.D., 1977). ***PRACTICE AREAS:*** Business Law; Health Care; Real Estate; Trusts and Estates. ***Email:*** carberry@bcclegal.com

TODD A. ETZLER, born Hammond, Indiana, January 20, 1966; admitted to bar, 1991, Indiana. *Education:* Purdue University (B.S., 1988); Indiana University (J.D., 1991). ***PRACTICE AREAS:*** Real Estate; Business Law; Construction Law; Zoning, Planning and Land Use; Trusts and Estates. ***Email:*** etzler@bcclegal.com

ASSOCIATE

Jon A. Schmaltz

(For complete biographical data on all personnel, see Professional Biographies at Merrillville)

DOUGLAS, KOEPPEN & HURLEY

14 INDIANA AVENUE
P.O. BOX 209
VALPARAISO, INDIANA 46384-0209
Telephone: 219-462-2126
Fax: 219-477-4408
URL: http://www.dkhlawfirm.com

General Civil Practice. Corporation, Banking, Personal Injury, Insurance, Probate and Estate Planning, Trial Practice, Municipal and Zoning, Family/Domestic Relations.

MEMBERS OF FIRM

HERBERT K. DOUGLAS, born Valparaiso, Indiana, October 3, 1934; admitted to bar, 1958, Indiana; 1959, U.S. District Court, Northern District of Indiana. *Education:* DePauw University (A.B., 1956); Indiana University (J.D., 1958). Delta Theta Phi. *Member:* Porter County, Indiana State and American Bar Associations. ***PRACTICE AREAS:*** Probate; Estate Planning; Civil Litigation.

R. BRADLEY KOEPPEN, born Gary, Indiana, July 9, 1954; admitted to bar, 1984, Florida and Indiana. *Education:* Ball State University (B.S., 1976); Kent State University (M.A., 1978); Valparaiso University (J.D., 1983). Fulbright Scholar, United States Educational Foundation, 1976. City Attorney, Valparaiso, Indiana, 1985-1988. *Member:* Porter County, Indiana State and American Bar Associations; The Florida Bar; American Trial Lawyers Association. ***LANGUAGES:*** Greek. ***PRACTICE AREAS:*** Personal Injury; Real Estate; Business Law; Probate; Estate Planning; Family; Domestic Relations.

BRIAN J. HURLEY, born Appleton, Wisconsin, March 30, 1958; admitted to bar, 1984, Indiana and U.S. District Court, Northern and Southern Districts of Indiana; 1997, U.S. Court of Appeals, Seventh Circuit. *Education:* St. Norbert College (B.A., magna cum laude, 1980); Valparaiso University (J.D., 1984). Member, Moot Court Team, 1982-1983. Member, Valparaiso University Law Review, 1983-1984. Law Clerk for Hon. Wesley W. Ratliff Jr., Court of Appeals, State of Indiana, 1984-1985. Author: "Confrontation and the Unavailable Witness: Searching for a Standard," 18 Valparaiso University Law Review 193, 1983. Adjunct Professor, Valparaiso University School of Law, 1995—. Deputy Prosecuting Attorney, 1987-1991. Attorney, County Planning Commission and Board of Zoning Appeals, 1986-1993. *Member:* Indiana State and American Bar Associations. ***PRACTICE AREAS:*** Municipal and Zoning; Civil; Criminal Litigation; Real Estate; Personal Injury; Employment Law.

MARK A. HARDWICK, born Valparaiso, Indiana, May 1, 1968; admitted to bar, 1993, Indiana. *Education:* Indiana University (B.A., 1990); Valparaiso University (J.D., 1993). *Member:* Porter County, Indiana State and American Bar Associations. ***PRACTICE AREAS:*** Family Law; Mediation; Adoption Law; Divorce; Child Custody; Child Support; Wills; Probate; Trusts and Estates; Business Law; Corporate Law; Bankruptcy.

ATTORNEYS FOR: Northern Indiana Public Service Co.; Urschel Laboratories, Inc.; Park District, City of Valparaiso; Porter County Drainage Board, Emerson Electric; First National Bank, Valparaiso; Kankakee Valley Rural Electric Membership Cooperative; Smith Ready Mix, Inc.; Spesco, Inc.; Century Pipe & Supply, Inc.; Von Tobel Lumber & Supply, Inc.; Builders Plumbing & Supply, Inc.

HARRIS, WELSH & LUKMANN

VALPARAISO, INDIANA

(See Chesterton)

General Civil Practice in all State and Federal Courts. Corporation, Wills and Probate, Trusts and Estates, Estate Planning, Personal Injury, Automobile Accidents, Wrongful Death, Insurance, Real Property, Eminent Domain, Banking and Municipal Law. Trials.

HODGES & DAVIS, P.C.

VALPARAISO, INDIANA

(See Merrillville)

General Civil Practice in all State and Federal Courts, Trials and Appeals, Insurance Defense, Corporation, Health and Hospital, Municipal and Zoning Law, Criminal, Driving While Intoxicated, Financing, Tax and Administrative Law. EEOC, Negligence, Products Liability, Environmental, Wills and Probate, Trusts and Estates, Estate Planning, Real Estate and Foreclosure Law. Consumer and Commercial Collections, Business Law, Business Planning, Business Litigation, Business Enterprises, Corporate, Partnerships, Small Business, Buying and Selling a Business, Business Start-Ups.

HOEPPNER WAGNER & EVANS LLP

Established in 1976

103 EAST LINCOLNWAY
P.O. BOX 2357
VALPARAISO, INDIANA 46384-2357
Telephone: 219-464-4961; 800-879-2246 (IN, IL)
Fax: 219-465-0603
Email: hwe@hwelaw.com
URL: http://www.hwelaw.com

Merrillville, Indiana Office: Twin Towers, Suite 606 South, 1000 East 80th Place, P.O. Box 10627, 46419-0627. Telephone: 219-769-6552; 800-263-1466 (IN, IL). Fax: 219-738-2349. Email: hwe@hwelaw.com

General Practice. Trials and Appeals in State, Federal and Tax Courts. Bankruptcy, Commercial and Banking, Corporate, Creditors' Rights, Probate and Estate Planning, Estate Administration, Financial Resources Planning, Insurance Defense, Municipal Bonds, Municipal and Zoning, Personal Injury, Product Liability, Professional Malpractice, Real Estate, Taxation, Workers Compensation, Labor and Employment. Mediation, OSHA, Employee Benefits Law.

RETIRED

DELMAR R. HOEPPNER, admitted to bar, 1954, Indiana; 1978, U.S. Supreme Court. *Education:* Valparaiso University (A.B., 1952; J.D., 1954). Phi Alpha Delta. *Member:* Porter County, Indiana State and American Bar Associations. (Retired). ***PRACTICE AREAS:*** Corporations Law; Probate Law; Tax Law; Mediation.

OF COUNSEL

WILLIAM H. WAGNER, admitted to bar, 1958, Indiana; 1959, Michigan. *Education:* Valparaiso University (B.A., 1956; J.D., 1958). Phi Alpha Delta. *Member:* Porter County, Indiana State and American Bar Associations; Association of College and University Attorneys. ***PRACTICE AREAS:*** Educational Law; Municipal Corporations Law; Probate; Real Estate Law; Zoning Law; Mediation. ***Email:*** wwagner@hwelaw.com

MEMBERS OF FIRM

LARRY G. EVANS, admitted to bar, 1962, Indiana; 1978, U.S. Supreme Court. *Education:* Valparaiso University (A.B., 1960; J.D., 1962). Delta Theta Phi. Author: "Article Eight of the Federal Rules of Evidence: The Hearsay Rule," 8 Val. U.L. Rev. 261, 1974. Adjunct Professor of Trial Advocacy, Valparaiso University School of Law, 1972-1980. Deputy Prosecuting Attorney, 67th Indiana Judicial Circuit, 1963. President, Porter County Chapter, American Inns of Court. Local Civil Rules Advisory Committee, U.S. District Court, Northern District of Indiana. *Member:* Porter County, Indiana State, Federal (President, N.W. Indiana Chapter, 1985) and American Bar Associations; Defense Research Institute, Inc.; Indiana Defense Lawyers Association; International Association of Defense Counsel; Indiana Defense Trial Counsel (Diplomate). Director and Fellow, Indiana Bar Foundation. (Resident, Merrillville Office). ***PRACTICE AREAS:*** Employment Law; Civil Litigation. ***Email:*** levans@hwelaw.com

WILLIAM F. SATTERLEE, III, admitted to bar, 1966, Indiana; 1978, U.S. Supreme Court. *Education:* Marietta College (B.A., 1960); Valparaiso University (J.D., 1966). *Member:* Porter County, Lake County, Indiana State, Federal and American Bar Associations; The Association of Trial Lawyers of America; Indiana Trial Lawyers Association; Indiana Defense Lawyers Association; Indiana Association of Mediators. ***PRACTICE AREAS:*** Civil Litigation; Education Law; Labor and Employment Law; Mediation. ***Email:*** wsatterlee@hwelaw.com

JOHN E. HUGHES, admitted to bar, 1971, Indiana; 1978, U.S. Supreme Court; U.S. Court of Appeals, Seventh Circuit; U.S. District Court, Northern and Southern Districts of Indiana. *Education:* Capital University (B.A., 1968); Valparaiso University (J.D., 1971). Phi Alpha Delta. Associate Editor, Valparaiso University Law Review, 1970-1971. Adjunct Professor, Valparaiso University School of Law, 1991-1995. *Member:* Porter County, Lake County, Indiana State, Federal and American Bar Associations; Indiana Defense Lawyers Association. (Resident, Merrillville Office). ***PRACTICE AREAS:*** Civil Litigation; Commercial Litigation; Insurance Defense; Labor and Employment Law; Personal Injury; Municipal Law; Mediation. ***Email:*** jhughes@hwelaw.com

MORRIS A. SUNKEL, admitted to bar, 1974, Indiana; 1978, U.S. Tax Court and U.S. Supreme Court. *Education:* University of Illinois (B.S., 1970); Valparaiso University (J.D., 1974); John Marshall (LL.M., Taxation, 1996). *Member:* Porter County and Indiana State Bar Associations; Indiana Society of Certified Public Accountants. ***PRACTICE AREAS:*** Tax Law; Probate and Estate Planning Law. ***Email:*** msunkel@hwelaw.com

JAMES L. JORGENSEN, admitted to bar, 1974, Indiana; 1976, Florida; 1978, U.S. Supreme Court. *Education:* St. Olaf College (B.A., summa cum laude, 1969); University of Washington (M.A., 1970); Valparaiso University (J.D., 1974). Phi Beta Kappa. Associate Editor, Valparaiso University Law Review, 1973-1974. Adjunct Professor, Valparaiso University School of Law, 1975—. *Member:* Porter County, Lake County, Indiana State and American Bar Associations; The Florida Bar. ***PRACTICE AREAS:*** Commercial Law; Banking Law; Labor and Employment Law. ***Email:*** jjorgensen@hwelaw.com

RONALD P. KUKER, admitted to bar, 1976, Indiana. *Education:* University of Missouri (B.S., 1973); Valparaiso University (J.D., 1976). *Member:* Porter County, Lake County, Indiana State, and American Bar Associations; Indiana Defense Lawyers Association; Indiana Trial Lawyers Association; Indiana Association of Mediators (1998-2003); Indiana Supreme Court Commission on Continuing Legal Education; Indiana Trial Lawyers Association; Indiana Defense Lawyers Association. ***PRACTICE AREAS:*** Alternative Dispute Resolution; Mediation; Arbitration; Civil Litigation; Workers Compensation. ***Email:*** rkuker@hwelaw.com

F. JOSEPH JASKOWIAK, admitted to bar, 1979, Indiana and Illinois. *Education:* Illinois Wesleyan University (B.A., 1976); Valparaiso University (J.D., 1979). Associate Editor, Valparaiso University Law Review, 1978-1979. Author: "The Meaning of the Term 'Accident' in the Indiana Workmen's Compensation Act," 13 Val. U.L. Rev. 533, 1979; "Covenants Not to Compete in Employment Agreements Under Indiana Law," Res Gestae, April, 1983; "Advantages of Designating the Physician in Workmen's Compensation Cases," Indiana Business, December, 1983. *Member:* Porter County, Lake County, Indiana State, Federal and American Bar Associations; Indiana Defense Lawyers Association. (Resident, Merrillville Office). ***PRACTICE AREAS:*** Civil Litigation; Employment Law. ***Email:*** jjaskowiak@hwelaw.com

RICHARD M. DAVIS, admitted to bar, 1980, Indiana. *Education:* Valparaiso University (B.A., 1975); Indiana University School of Law-Bloomington (J.D., 1980). Deputy Prosecutor, Lake County, Indiana, 1982-1985. *Member:* Porter County, Lake County, Indiana State and American Bar Associations. ***PRACTICE AREAS:*** Litigation; Criminal Defense; Personal Injury; First Party Insurance Law; Insurance Defense. ***Email:*** rdavis@hwelaw.com

MARK E. SCHMIDTKE, admitted to bar, 1981, Indiana, Indiana Supreme Court and U.S. District Court, Southern District of Indiana; 1982, U.S. District Court, Northern District of Indiana; 1983, U.S. Court of Appeals, Seventh Circuit; 1991, U.S. Court of Appeals, Eighth Circuit and U.S. Supreme Court; 1993, U.S. District Court, Central District of Illinois and U.S. District Court, Southern District of Illinois; 1995, U.S. Court of Appeals, Tenth Circuit; 1996, U.S. Court of Appeals, Second and Eleventh Circuits; 1997, U.S. Court of Appeals, Fourth, Fifth and Sixth Circuits; 1998, U.S. District Court, Eastern District of Michigan and U.S. District Court, District of Colorado; 1999, U.S. District Court, Eastern District of Wisconsin; 2000, U.S. Court of Appeals, Ninth Circuit; 2001, U.S. Court of Appeals, Third Circuit; 2003, U.S. District Court, Northern District of Illinois. *Education:* Valparaiso University (B.A., 1978; J.D., 1981). Phi Alpha Theta; Omicron Delta Epsilon. Associate Editor, Valparaiso University Law Review, 1980-1981. Law Clerk to: Hon. George B. Hoffman, Jr., Indiana Court of Appeals, 1981; Hon. James T. Moody, U.S. District Court, Northern District of Indiana, 1982-1983. Author: "Carving Out a Special Warrant Requirement: Arkansas v. Sanders," 14 Valparaiso University Law Review 157, 1979. Co-Author: *ERISA Case Digest* (John Wiley & Sons, 1992); *ERISA Litigation Form Book* (John Wiley & Sons, 1992); *ERISA Litigation Primer* (Defense Research Institute, 1992-2003). Contributing Author, *Employee Benefits Law* (BNA, 1992-1998). *Member:* Porter County, Indiana State, Federal and American (Member, Employee Benefits Committee, Section on Labor and Employment Law) Bar Associations. ***PRACTICE AREAS:*** ERISA; Employment Litigation. ***Email:*** mschmidtke@hwelaw.com

TODD A. LEETH, admitted to bar, 1988, Indiana. *Education:* Indiana University (B.A., 1982); Valparaiso University (J.D., 1988). *Member:* Porter County, Lake County, Indiana State and American Bar Associations; Indiana Municipal Lawyers Association. ***PRACTICE AREAS:*** Municipal; Zoning; Real Estate Law. ***Email:*** tleeth@hwelaw.com

J. BRIAN HITTINGER, admitted to bar, 1990, Illinois, U.S. District Court, Northern District of Illinois and Supreme Court; 1992, Indiana, U.S. District Court, Northern and Southern Districts of Indiana and Supreme Court. *Education:* Indiana University at Bloomington (B.S., 1982); Valparaiso University (J.D., with high distinction, 1990). Certified Public Accountant, 1986—. *Member:* Porter County, Lake County, Indiana State and American Bar Associations; American Institute of Certified Public Accountants; Illinois and Indiana State Certified Public Accountant Societies. (Resident, Merrillville Office). ***PRACTICE AREAS:*** Tax Law; General Business Law; Trust and Estates. ***Email:*** bhittinger@hwelaw.com

LAUREN K. KROEGER, admitted to bar, 1989, Pennsylvania; 1993, Indiana. *Education:* Miami University (B.S.B.A., 1986); Dickinson School of Law (J.D., magna cum laude, 1989). Comment Editor, Dickinson Law Review. *Member:* Porter County, Lake County, Indiana State and American Bar Associations. ***PRACTICE AREAS:*** Labor and Employment Law; Civil Litigation. ***Email:*** lkroeger@hwelaw.com

ROBERT L. CLARK, admitted to bar, 1990, Illinois and U.S. District Court, Northern District of Illinois; 1992, Indiana and U.S. District Court, Northern and Southern Districts of Indiana. *Education:* Loyola University of Chicago (B.A., 1987); University of South Carolina (J.D., 1990). *Member:* Porter County, Indiana State and American Bar Associations; Illinois Trial Lawyers Association; Indiana Trial Lawyers Association; Association of Trial Lawyers of America. ***PRACTICE AREAS:*** Civil Litigation; Commercial Litigation; Employment Litigation; ERISA; Labor Law; Products Liability. ***Email:*** rclark@hwelaw.com

JACK A. KRAMER, admitted to bar, 1995, Indiana and U.S. District Court, Southern and Northern Districts of Indiana; 1997, U.S. Court of Appeals, Seventh Circuit; 1998, U.S. Supreme Court. *Education:* Ball State University (B.S., 1992); Valparaiso University (J.D., 1995). Valparaiso University Law Review, 1994-1995. Moot Court Society. Author: Note, "Vouching For Federal Educational Choice: If You Pay Them, They Will Come," 29 Val. U.L. Rev. 1005, 1995. *Member:* Porter County, Lake County, Indiana State and American

(This Listing Continued)

HOEPPNER WAGNER & EVANS LLP, Valparaiso—Continued

Bar Associations. (Resident, Merrillville Office). ***PRACTICE AREAS:*** Products Liability; Insurance Bad Faith; Asbestos Litigation; Litigation. ***Email:*** jkramer@hwelaw.com

JAY S. PATHEJA, admitted to bar, 1994, Illinois; 1997, Indiana; 2000, Michigan. *Education:* Indiana University (B.A., 1991); Loyola University (J.D., 1994). Vice President, Loyola Environmental Law Society, 1992-1994. *Member:* Chicago, Porter County, Lake County, Illinois State, Indiana State and American Bar Associations. (Resident, Merrillville Office). ***PRACTICE AREAS:*** Estate Planning; Probate; Wills; Corporate; Real Estate. ***Email:*** jpatheja@hwelaw.com

TINA M. BENGS, admitted to bar, 1997, Indiana and U.S. District Court, Northern and Southern Districts of Indiana; 1998, U.S. Court of Appeals, Seventh Circuit. *Education:* Indiana University (B.S., 1989); Thomas M. Cooley Law School (J.D., cum laude, 1996). Member: Indiana Workers Compensation Institute; Society for Human Resource Management. *Member:* Porter County, Lake County, Indiana State and American Bar Associations; Indiana Defense Lawyers Association. (Resident, Merrillville Office). ***PRACTICE AREAS:*** Employment Law; Workers Compensation. ***Email:*** tbengs@hwelaw.com

KEVIN G. KERR, admitted to bar, 1997, Indiana; 1998, U.S. District Court, Northern and Southern Districts of Indiana; 1998, U.S. Court of Appeals, Seventh Circuit. *Education:* Blackburn College (B.S., summa cum laude, 1978); Western Illinois University (M.A., 1981); Valparaiso University (J.D., magna cum laude, 1997). *Member:* Porter County, Lake County, Indiana State (Member, Sections on: Litigation; Appellate) and American Bar Associations. ***PRACTICE AREAS:*** Insurance Defense; Appellate Practice; Legal Writing. ***Email:*** kkerr@hwelaw.com

ASSOCIATES

WILLIAM A. FERNGREN, admitted to bar, 1999, Indiana and U.S. District Court, Northern and Southern Districts of Indiana. *Education:* Purdue University (B.S., Construction Management, 1991); Valparaiso University (J.D., 1999). Dean's List, 1995. Course Honors, American Legal History Seminar. *Member:* Porter County, Lake County and Indiana State (Member, Real Estate Section) Bar Associations. ***PRACTICE AREAS:*** Municipal Law; Zoning Law; Real Estate. ***Email:*** wferngren@hwelaw.com

MICHAEL EUGENE TOLBERT, admitted to bar, 2000, Indiana and and U.S. District Court, Northern and Southern Districts of Indiana. *Education:* Valparaiso University (B.A., 1997; J.D., cum laude, 2000). *Member:* Porter County, Indiana State and American Bar Associations; American Inns of Court. (Resident, Merrillville Office). ***PRACTICE AREAS:*** Civil Litigation; Commercial Litigation; Insurance Defense. ***Email:*** mtolbert@hwelaw.com

ERIC P. MATHISEN, admitted to bar, 1996, Indiana. *Education:* Carthage College (B.A., 1992); Valparaiso University (J.D., 1996). Moot Court Society, 1995-1996. Listed in Who's Who Among American Law Students, 1994-1996. Certified Mediator, 1998—. Real Estate License, St. Joseph County, In., 1996. Formerly with Konopa, Reagan & Kenyon, P.C. Member, Indiana HIPAA Workgroup. *Member:* Lake County, Porter County, St. Joseph County, Indiana State and American Bar Associations; Defense Research Institute, Inc.; Defense Trial Counsel of Indiana; Porter County Chapter, American Inn of Court. (Resident, Merrillville Office). ***PRACTICE AREAS:*** Civil Litigation; Mediation; Products Liability; Wrongful Death; Brain Injury; Insurance Litigation; Nursing Home Abuse and Neglect. ***Email:*** emathisen@hwelaw.com

GEROLD L. STOUT, admitted to bar, 2002, Indiana. *Education:* Purdue University (B.A., 1996); Valparaiso University (J.D., 2001). Pi Sigma Alpha. Listed, *Who's Who:* American Law Students, 1999-2001. Member: Lake County, Indiana State and American Bar Associations. (Resident, Merrillville Office). ***PRACTICE AREAS:*** Estate Planning; Corporate Law; Taxation. ***Email:*** gstout@hwelaw.com

THOMAS L. CHRZANOWSKI, admitted to bar, 1995, Indiana. *Education:* Indiana University (B.S., 1989); California Western School of Law (J.D., 1994). Phi Alpha Delta. *Member:* Indianapolis and Indiana State Bar Associations. ***PRACTICE AREAS:*** Corporate Law; Business Law; Litigation; Tax Law; Real Estate. ***Email:*** tchrzanowski@hwelaw.com

CINTRA D.B. GEAIRN, admitted to bar, 1998, Illinois (Not admitted in Indiana). *Education:* University of Rochester (B.A., cum laude, 1992); Chicago-Kent College of Law, Illinois Institute of Technology (J.D., summa cum laude, 1998). Order of the Coif. Member, Moot Court. Executive Board, Law Review. author, "A Pregnant Pause: Are Women Who Undergo Fertility Treatment to Achieve Pregnancy Within the Scope of Title VII's Pregnancy Discrimination Act?", 73 Chicago-Kent L. Rev. 391 (1998). *Member:* American Bar Association (Member, Labor and Employment Section); National Association of Women Lawyers (Member, Amicus Committee). ***PRACTICE AREAS:*** Labor and Employment. ***Email:*** cgeairn@hwelaw.com

SEAN E. KENYON, admitted to bar, 1991, Indiana and U.S. District Court, Northern and Southern Districts of Indiana; 1995, U.S. District Court, Northern District of Illinois and U.S. Court of Appeals, Seventh Circuit. *Education:* St. Bonaventure University (B.B.A., 1982); Indiana University (B.A., 1985; J.D., cum laude, 1991). Clerk to the Honorable Allen Sharp, U.S. District Court, Northern District of Indiana, 1991-1993. Visiting/Adjunct Lecturer, Indiana University, South Bend, 1992-1995. *Member:* St. Joseph County, Indiana State and American Bar Associations; Defense Trial Counsel of Indiana; Robert A. Grant Inn of Court. (Resident, Merrillville Office). ***REPORTED CASES:*** Xantech Corp. v. Ramco Industries, Inc., 159 F.3d 1089 (7th Cir. 1998); Grand Trunk Western Rail Road Co. v. Kapitan, 698, N. E. 2d 363 (Ind. Ct App. 1998); Levee v. Beeching, 729 N. E. 2d 215 (Ind. Ct. App. 2000); Beeching v. Levee, 764 N. E. 2d 669 (Ind. Ct App 2002). ***PRACTICE AREAS:*** Civil Litigation; Appellate Practice; Insurance Coverage.

LUCRETIA A. THORNTON, admitted to bar, 1982, Indiana. *Education:* Purdue University (B.S., 1967; R.N., 1975); Valparaiso University (J.D., 1982). *Member:* Indiana State and American Bar Associations. ***PRACTICE AREAS:*** Risk Management; Hospital Law.

LEE I. LANE, admitted to bar, 2005, Indiana. *Education:* University of Denver (B.A., 1985); Valparaiso University (J.D., cum laude, 2004). Associate Editor, Valparaiso University Law Review, 2002-2003. Regional Champion, Negotiation Team, 2003; Client Counseling Team, 2002. Member, Northeast Indiana World Trade Council. *Member:* Porter County, Indiana State and American Bar Associations. [Army Reserves, 1991-1995; CW2, Illinois Army National Guard, 1995-2005]. ***PRACTICE AREAS:*** Real Estate; Corporate. ***Email:*** llane@hwelaw.com

(This Listing Continued)

REPRESENTATIVE CLIENTS: Aldi Inc.; American Family Insurance Group; American National Property & Casualty; American States Insurance Co.; Anthem Insurance Company; Aon Insurance Company; Babcock & Wilcox; Bank One; CGU Insurance Co.; Chester, Inc.; Citizens Financial Services, FSB; Coldwell First American, Inc.; Combined Insurance Company; East Porter County Schools; Fifth-Third Bank; First National Bank; GAB Robins; Illinois StateMedical Insurance Services; Indiana Insurance Co.; ISG, Inc.; JWP Hyre Electric; Lear Corp.; Meridian Mutual Ins. Co.; Noridian Insurance Company; Okaya Electric America, Inc.; Porter-Starke Services, Inc.; Security Life of Denver; State Farm Insurance Cos.; Sun Life Assurance Company of Canada; Task Force Tips, Inc.; The Travelers; Toys R Us Corp.; Tri-State Coach Lines, Inc.; Unitrin Insurance Co.; Unum Provident Corporation; Valparaiso University; Whiteco Industries, Inc.; White Lodging Services Corp.; Worldwide Services Co.

JOHNSON & RAPPA, LLC

VALPARAISO, INDIANA

(See Merrillville)

Trial, Appellate, Personal Injury, Automobile Accidents, Slip and Fall, Wrongful Death, and Defense Practice in State and Federal Courts. Insurance, Civil Rights, Labor and Employment, Wrongful Termination, Employment Contracts, Mediation and Arbitration, Class Actions, Construction, Administrative, Products Liability and Transportation Law.

TIMOTHY F. KELLY AND ASSOCIATES

VALPARAISO, INDIANA

(See Dyer)

General Practice, Commercial, Business Law, Business Planning, Contracts, Business Litigation, Business Enterprises, Wills and Probate, Trusts and Estates, Asset Protection, Guardianships, Estate Planning, Corporation, Real Estate, Labor and Employment, Trials and Appeals in all Courts, Insurance Defense, Automobile Accidents, Slip and Fall, Wrongful Death, Products Liability, Professional Liability and Medical Malpractice.

MICHAEL LAMBERT

VALPARAISO, INDIANA

(See Crown Point)

Criminal Law, Drug Crimes, Driving While Intoxicated, Parole and Probation, Juvenile Crimes, Traffic Violations, Family Law, Adoption, Divorce, Child Custody, Child Support, Domestic Violence, Visitation Rights, Employment Law, Wrongful Termination, Sexual Harassment, Civil Rights, Discrimination, Personal Injury, Automobile Accidents, Slip and Fall, Wrongful Death, Bankruptcy, Wills and Probate, Guardianships, Business Law, Contracts, Lawsuits, Business Enterprises.

HERBERT S. LASSER & ASSOCIATES, P.C.

VALPARAISO, INDIANA

(See Merrillville)

Personal Injury, Wrongful Death, Automobile and All Accidents, Construction Law, Family Law, Divorce, Child Custody, Child Support, Domestic Violence, Visitation Rights, Work Accidents, Trials and Appeals, Business Law, Business Planning, Contracts, Law Suits, Insurance, Business Enterprises, Closely Held Business, Corporate, Limited Liability Companies, Partnerships, Small Business, Franchises, Buying and Selling A Business, Debt and Credit, Collections, Creditors Rights, Banking and Finance, Venture Capital, Employee Benefits, Employment Contracts, Human Resources, Discrimination, Sexual Harassment, Workers Compensation, Wrongful Termination, Real Estate, Buying or Selling, Commercial Leasing, Environmental, Landlord and Tenant, Zoning and Land Use, Starting a Business, Strategic Alliances, Joint Ventures, Mergers, Civil Rights, Consumer Law, Consumer Fraud, Unsafe Products, Criminal Law, Drunk Driving, Misdemeanors, Drug Crimes, Juvenile Crimes, Parole and Probation, Traffic Violations, Medical Malpractice, Legal Malpractice, Products Liability, Slip and Fall, Wills and Probate, Trusts and Estates, Asset Protection, Estate Planning, General Civil and Criminal Practice, General Practice, Trademark Patent Litigation.

LUCAS, HOLCOMB & MEDREA LLP

VALPARAISO, INDIANA

(See Merrillville)

General Practice, State and Federal Courts. Trials and Appeals. Corporate, Business, Business Litigation, Contracts, Business Planning, Business Enterprises, Commercial, Employment, Wrongful Termination, Banking, Tax, Wills and Probate, Trusts and Estates and Estate Planning, Insurance, Bankruptcy, Personal Injury, Automobile Accidents, Wrongful Death, Products Liability, Family/Domestic Relations, Adoptions, Child Custody, Child Support, Divorce, Visitation Rights, Hospital, Real Estate, Municipal and Zoning Law, Consumer and Commercial Collection Law, Construction Litigation.

MICHAEL B. MILLER, P.C.

701 EAST LINCOLNWAY
VALPARAISO, INDIANA 46383
Telephone: 219-465-1197
Fax: 219-531-0683
Email: miller.law@gte.net
URL: http://www.mmillerlawfirm.com

Estate Planning, Trusts and Estates, Asset Protection, Living Trusts, Wills and Probate, Retirement Planning, Guardianship, Elder Law, Medicaid, Corporations, Business Law, Contracts, Premarital Agreements, Leases and Leasing, Real Estate, Condemnation, Taxation, Personal Injury, Accidents, Automobile Accidents and Injuries, Slip and Fall, Wrongful Death.

MICHAEL B. MILLER, born Valparaiso, Indiana, November 27, 1957; admitted to bar, 1994, Indiana and U.S. District Court, Northern and Southern Districts of Indiana. *Education:* Indiana University (B.S., 1979); Valparaiso University (J.D., 1994).

PHILLIP A. NORMAN, P.C.

2110 CALUMET AVENUE
VALPARAISO, INDIANA 46383
Telephone: 219-462-5104
Fax: 219-462-9344
Email: phil@normanattorney.com

Civil Litigation, Commercial Law, Banking Law, Municipal Law, Zoning Law, Creditor's Rights, Family Law, Mediation.

PHILLIP A. NORMAN, born Dayton, Ohio, May 26, 1962; admitted to bar, 1987, Indiana. *Education:* Georgetown College (B.A., cum laude, 1984); Valparaiso University (J.D., 1987). Phi Alpha Delta. Attorney, Town of Merrillville Board of Zoning Appeals, 1988-1992. *Member:* Porter County and Indiana State Bar Associations. ***PRACTICE AREAS:*** Civil Litigation; Commercial Law; Banking Law; Municipal Law; Zoning Law; Creditor's Rights; Family Law; Mediation. ***Email:*** phil@normanattorney.com

REPRESENTATIVE CLIENTS: Countrywide Home Loans; Litton Loan Servicing; Ticor Title Insurance Company.

JILL SISSON

15 NORTH FRANKLIN STREET
SUITE 220
VALPARAISO, INDIANA 46383
Telephone: 219-465-3717
Fax: 219-531-0728
Email: mjsisson@verizon.net
URL: http://www.lawyers.com/jillsisson

Interstate Adoptions, Private Placement Adoptions, Step Parent Adoptions, Family/Domestic Relations, Divorce, Child Custody, Child Support, Visitation Rights.

FIRM PROFILE: Ms. Sisson spent six years Hoeppner Wagner and Evans in Valparaiso before starting her own practice in 1995. She handles all aspects of family and domestic relations law, primarily in Northwest Indiana. As a family law attorney, Ms. Sisson concentrates on all facets of adoption, including interstate, private placement, and step parent adoptions.

JILL SISSON, born Grand Rapids, Michigan, December 11, 1951; admitted to bar, 1980, Indiana; 1984, Michigan. *Education:* Aquinas College (B.A., cum laude, 1974; B.S., 1976); Valparaiso University (J.D., 1980). *Member:* Porter County, Indiana State (Member, Family Law Section) and American (Member, Family Law Section) Bar Associations; State Bar of Michigan (Member, Family Law Section). ***PRACTICE AREAS:*** Domestic Law; Family Law; Adoptions.

REFERENCE: Centier Bank.
REPRESENTATIVE CLIENTS: Available Upon Request.

SPANGLER, JENNINGS & DOUGHERTY, P.C.

Established in 1952
150 LINCOLNWAY, SUITE 3001
VALPARAISO, INDIANA 46383
Telephone: 219-462-6151
Fax: 219-477-4935
Email: spangler@sjdlaw.com
URL: http://www.sjdlaw.com

Merrillville, Indiana Office: 8396 Mississippi Street. Telephone: 219-769-2323.
Indianapolis, Indiana Office: 9200 Keystone Crossing, Suite 410. Telephone: 317-571-7690. Facsimile: 317-571-7686.

General Trial and Appellate Practice. Administrative, Banking, Bankruptcy, Business Reorganizations, Business Transactions, Civil Rights, Commercial, Construction, Corporate, Creditors' Rights, Criminal Litigation, Family/Domestic Relations, Drug and Device, Eminent Domain, Environmental, ERISA and Employee Benefits, Probate and Estate Planning and Administration, Fire/Arson, Guardianships, Health Care, Insurance, Labor and Employment, Municipal and Zoning, Personal Injury, Product Liability, Professional Liability, Medical Malpractice Defense, Real Estate, School, Federal, State and Local Taxation, Toxic Torts, Transportation, Workers Compensation, Land Development.

FIRM PROFILE: In 1952, our founding partners created what is now the law firm of Spangler, Jennings & Dougherty to serve a broad range of clients' legal needs. Today, we continue to provide our clients with legal counsel based on extensive litigation experience, integrity, practicality and dedicated team effort.

(This Listing Continued)

Spangler, Jennings & Dougherty consists of 43 attorneys, fifteen paralegals, and a large and experienced support staff, making it Northwest Indiana's largest private law firm. In addition to years of legal experience and training, our firm has members with professional experience in public accounting and health care. We also have trial attorneys who belong to the prestigious American College of Trial Lawyers.

PARTNERS

SAMUEL J. BERNARDI, JR., born Highland Park, Illinois, January 30, 1941; admitted to bar, 1966, Indiana and Illinois. *Education:* Miami University (B.B.S., 1963); University of Notre Dame (J.D., 1966). Greys Inn. *Member:* Porter County, Indiana State and American Bar Associations; Indiana Defense Lawyers Association; Defense Research Institute (President, 1983). ***PRACTICE AREAS:*** Civil Trial Practice; Insurance Defense; Personal Injury; Products Liability. ***Email:*** spangler@sjdlaw.com

CHRISTOPHER GRABAREK, born South Bend, Indiana, March 12, 1967; admitted to bar, 1993, Indiana; U.S. District Court, Northern and Southern Districts of Indiana. *Education:* University of Notre Dame (B.A., English Literature, 1989); Holy Cross College (A.A., 1987); Valparaiso University School of Law (J.D., 1992). Co-Author: Article, "Towards the Destruction of Legal Relativism," St. Thomas University Law Review. Deputy Prosecuting Attorney, Porter County, Indiana, 1993-1976. ***PRACTICE AREAS:*** Insurance Defense Litigation; General Liability. ***Email:*** cgrabarek@sjdlaw.com

JON S. DISTON, born Bryn Mawr, Pennsylvania, January 28, 1967; admitted to bar, 2000, Indiana. *Education:* Delaware County Community College (A.A., 1988); Eastern College (B.A., cum laude, 1990); Valparaiso University (J.D., 1999). Phi Alpha Delta. ***PRACTICE AREAS:*** Insurance Defense; Civil Litigation. ***Email:*** jdiston@sjdlaw.com

OF COUNSEL

PATRICK J. DOUGHERTY, born Gary, Indiana, February 26, 1928; admitted to bar, 1953, Ohio; 1954, Indiana. *Education:* St. Joseph College; University of Cincinnati (LL.B., 1953). Phi Delta Phi. *Member:* Porter County, Indiana State and American Bar Associations; Indiana Defense Lawyers Association. ***PRACTICE AREAS:*** Civil Trial Practice; Insurance Defense; Real Estate Law. ***Email:*** spangler@sjdlaw.com

REPRESENTATIVE CLIENTS: Airborne Express; American National Property and Casualty Co.; Ancilla; Allstate Insurance Co.; American International Group; Associates Financial; Auto Owners; Bank One; Beneficial Finance; CNA Insurance; Community Hospital of Munster; Crown Point Community Schools; Farmers Insurance; Federal Employees Credit Union; 5th Third Bank; First Union Bank; Ford Motor Company; Hanover School Corporation; Horace Mann Insurance; Ispat/Inland Steel; Lake County; Leman Brothers; Liberty Mutual Co.; Medical Assurance of Indiana; Milwaukee Insurance; Munster Community Schools; PICI; Pro National Insurance Co.; Ryder Truck Lines; Safeco Insurance Co. of America; St. Anthony's Health Center; St. Mary Medical Center; St. Paul Insurance; State Farm Insurance; TIG Insurance; Town of Porter; United Farm Bureau; U.S.F.&G.; Wausau Insurance; Zurich Ins. Co.

(For Complete Biographical Data on all Personnel, See Professional Biographies at Merrillville)

JOSEPH STALMACK & ASSOCIATES, P.C.

VALPARAISO, INDIANA

(See Hammond)

General Practice. Trials and Appeals. Insurance, Products Liability, Probate and Estate Planning, Transportation, Asbestos Litigation, Automobile, Common Carrier, Complex and Multi-District Litigation, Computer, Construction, Environmental and Industrial Disease, Environmental, Fire Insurance, Hazardous Materials, Legal Malpractice, Medical Malpractice, Mediation Services, Professional Malpractice, Subrogation, Toxic Substances and Toxic Torts Law, Personal Injury.

STUTSMAN, MULVANEY & DEBOER

VALPARAISO, INDIANA

(See Elkhart)

General Civil and Appellate Practice in all State and Federal Courts. Personal Injury, Automobile Accidents, Slip and Fall, Wrongful Death, Workers Compensation, Medical Malpractice, Corporate, Wills and Probate, Trusts and Estates, Asset Protection, Guardianships, Estate Planning, Real Estate, Internet Law.

ANTHONY F. TAVITAS
ATTORNEYS AT LAW

A PROFESSIONAL CORPORATION

VALPARAISO, INDIANA

(See Munster)

Insurance Defense, Trial Practice, Personal Injury, Insurance Coverage, Workers Compensation.

AIMEE C. ZEMAITIS

VALPARAISO, INDIANA

(See Portage)

Personal Injury, Family Law, Wills, Trusts and Estates, Business Law, Traffic Violations.

MCCONNELL AND FINNERTY

VERNON, INDIANA

(See North Vernon)

Probate and Estate Planning, Personal Injury and Commercial Law, Family/Domestic Relations. Civil Litigation. Trials, Appeals and Banking.

EATON & DAY

123 SOUTH MAIN STREET
P.O. BOX 275
VERSAILLES, INDIANA 47042-9442
Telephone: 812-689-5111
Fax: 812-689-5165
Email: leaton@seidata.com
URL: http://www.lawyers.com/leatonlaw

General Trial and Appellate Practice. Negligence, Corporation, Probate and Estate Planning and Real Estate Law. School Law.

FIRM PROFILE: The firm was established in 1968 by Larry L. Eaton. The firm represents clients throughout the state of Indiana with a primary focus on Ripley, Dearborn, Ohio, Switzerland, Jefferson, Jennings, Decatur and Franklin counties. The firm has represented most businesses, municipalities and schools over the past 30 years. It is a well established and stable law firm.

MEMBERS OF FIRM

LARRY L. EATON, born Osgood, Indiana, February 9, 1940; admitted to bar, 1966, Indiana. *Education:* Indiana University (A.B., 1962; J.D., 1966). Phi Delta Phi. *Member:* Ripley County, Indiana State and American Bar Associations. ***REPORTED CASES:*** Fraley v. Minger. ***PRACTICE AREAS:*** Corporate Law; Real Estate; Banking Law; School Law; Civil Litigation; Probate. ***Email:*** eaton1aw@suscom.net

TIMOTHY B. DAY, born Greensburg, Indiana, June 14, 1964; admitted to bar, 1989, Indiana and U.S. District Court, Southern District of Indiana. *Education:* Ball State University (B.S., 1986); Indiana University (J.D., 1989). Deputy Prosecuting Attorney, Decatur County, 1989-1991. *Member:* Decatur County (Vice-President, 1990; President, 1991), Indiana State and American Bar Associations. ***PRACTICE AREAS:*** General Practice. ***Email:*** thdlaw@etczone.com

REPRESENTATIVE CLIENTS: Milan Community School Corp.; CDA, Inc.; Tom Tepe Autocenter; C.S. Gibbs Corporation; Wal-Mart Stores, Inc.; Tuscany Bay LLC.

BINGHAM McHALE LLP

Established in 1914
112 N. 7TH STREET
P.O. BOX 139
VINCENNES, INDIANA 47591
Telephone: 812-886-9970
Telecopier: 812-886-0776
Email: jgregg@binghammchale.com

Indianapolis, Indiana Office: Bingham McHale LLP, 2700 Market Tower, 10 West Market Street. Telephone: 317-635-8900. Fax: 317-236-9907.
Jasper, Indiana Office: Bingham McHale LLP, 212 West Sixth Street. Telephone: 812-482- 5500. Fax: 812-482-2017.
Noblesville, Indiana Office: Bingham McHale LLP, 970 Logan Street. Telephone: 317-776-8668. Fax: 317-776-8651.

General Civil Practice including: Administrative Law; Agricultural Law; Alternative Dispute Resolution; Antitrust and Trade Regulation; Appeals; Appellate; Architects and Engineers Liability Defense; Banks and Banking; Bankruptcy and Reorganization; Business Law; Business Litigation; Cable Telecommunications Law; Collective Bargaining; Commercial Transactions; Construction Law; Contract Negotiation; Copyright; Corporate Finance; Complex Litigation; Class Actions; Corporate Law; Creditors' Rights; Drug and Medical Device Law; Election, Campaign Finance and Political Law; Employee Benefits; Environmental Law; Estate Planning and Administration; Family Law; Finance; Franchising and Licensing; Gaming Law; Governmental Services; Health Care; Hospital Law; Insurance; Intellectual Property; Labor and Employment; Leases and Leasing; Legal Malpractice, Discipline and Licensing; Libel, Slander and Defamation; Litigation; Lobbying; Matrimonial and Family Law; Media Law; Medicare and Medicaid Reimbursement, Medical and Dental Liability Defense and Disciplines and Licensing; Mergers and Acquisitions; Natural Resources Law; Occupational Safety and Health; Patent; Probate; Product Liability; Professional Liability Defense; Public Finance; Public Utility Law; Real Estate; Securities Law; Tax-Exempt Finance, Taxation (Controversies, Corporate Planning, Income, Gift and Estate, Individual, Partnership, Property, Nonprofit Organizations), Toxic Torts Law; Trademark; White Collar Criminal Defense; Zoning, Planning and Land Use.

FIRM PROFILE: Bingham McHale LLP was formed by the merger of Bingham Summers Welsh & Spilman and McHale Cook & Welch on January 1, 2002. Evident in the nearly 130 year combined history of both firms is the longstanding commitment to one ideal: providing high quality legal services at an affordable cost. Both firms individually earned a reputation founded upon client service, and will continue and improve upon that tradition collectively as it provides the highest level of service to business, government, utility and land use clients and their individual owners.

JOHN R. GREGG, born Sanborn, Indiana, 1954; admitted to bar, 1984, Indiana. *Education:* Vincennes University (A.S., 1974); Indiana University (B.A., 1976; J.D., 1984); Indiana State University (M.P.A., 1978). Recipient: Governing Magazine's "Public Officials of the Year" Award, 2002; Governor's Heroism Award, 1997; Hoosier Hero Award, 1996; 4 Sagamore of the Wabash Awards, 1989, 1996, 2002 and 2003; Honorary Doctorate Degree, Vincennes University, 2002. Outstanding Freshman Legislator, 1986. Faculty, New Speakers Conference, Harvard, February 2003. Speaker of the House, Indiana House of Representatives, 1996-2002. Interim President, Vincennes University, August 2003-July 2004. Democratic Leader, Indiana House of Representatives, 1994-1996. Majority Leader, Indiana House of Representatives, 1990-1994. State Representative, 1986-2002. Member: Good Samaritan Hospital Foundation; Knox County Community Foundation; Vincennes University Foundation. *Member:* Knox County Bar Association. ***PRACTICE AREAS:*** Business Law; Commercial Law; Government Affairs.

Bingham McHale LLP attorneys are members of the American, Indiana State, Indianapolis, Federal and Seventh Circuit Bar Associations.

REPRESENTATIVE CLIENTS: ADESA Corporation; Aearo Company; Albertsons, Inc.; Altrista Corporation; American Society of Composers, Authors and Publishers (ASCAP); American United Life Insurance Co.; Asphalt Materials, Inc.; Averitt Express, Inc.; Bangs Laboratories, Inc.; Bank One, Indiana, NA; Barth Electric Co., Inc.; Baxter Healthcare Corp.; Best Chairs, Inc.; BKD, LLP; Boone County; BP Products; Bremner & Wiley, Inc.; Bressler Outdoor, LLC; Buehler Foods, Inc.; Capital Improvement Board of Managers (RCA Dome, Conseco Fieldhouse & Victory Field, Indiana Convention Center); Chase Manhattan Bank; Cinergy Inc.; City of Carmel; City of Ft. Wayne; City of Greenwood; City of Indianapolis; Comcast Cablevision; Community Bankers Association of Indiana; CTI Billing Solutions; Davis Homes, Inc.; Deere Credit Services, Inc.; DePauw University; Duke Energy; Duke Realty Corp.; EDS, Inc.; Ericsson Mobile Communications; Fanimation, Inc.; Farbest Foods, Inc.; FEPCO; Fifth Third Bank of Central Indiana; First Merchants Corporation; Frontier Financial; Gatorade Trust; Hamilton Southeastern Utilities, Inc.; Heritage Environmental Services, LLC; Hoosier State Press Association; Indiana Bond Bank; Indiana Development Finance Authority; Indiana Heart Physicians; Indiana Horse Racing Commission; Indiana Manufacturers Association; Indiana State Poultry Association, Inc.; Indiana University; Indianapolis Housing Agency; Indianapolis Opthalomology; Insight Communications; Interstate Brands Corporation; Jasper Seating Company, Inc.; Jostens Inc.; Key Bank; Klipsch LLC; Knowledge Resource Group; Kocolene Marketing LLC; Lehigh Cement Company; LIN Television; Litho Press, Inc.; Marathon Oil Company; Market Square Partners; MasterBrand Cabinets, Inc.; Meridian Plastic Surgery Center; Midland Life Insurance Co.; Midwest Bankers Group, Inc.; Morgan Guaranty Trust Company of New York; National Association of Broadcasters; National City Bank, Indiana; National Collegiate Athletic Association (NCAA); Old National Bank; Pedigo Chevrolet; Pfizer Inc; Philip Morris, Inc.; Pizza King, Inc.; Provident Bank; Purdue University; Reeves Buick Pontiac; Resort Condominiums International (RCI); SAFECO; Sagamore Health Network, Inc.; Saint-Gobain Containers, Inc.; SBC Communications, Inc.; Schering Plough Corp.; Shell Oil Co.; Simon Property Group; Simon & Schuster, Inc.; State Farm Mutual Automobile Insurance Company; Subaru-Isuzu Automotive Inc.; SYM Financial Corporation; Tera Pharmaceuticals; The Medical Protective Co.; Thomson Multimedia, Inc.; Time Warner Cable; Wabash Valley Produce, Inc.; Xerox Corporation.

(For complete biographical data on all personnel, see Professional Biographies at Indianapolis, Indiana)

EMISON DOOLITTLE KOLB & ROELLGEN

Established in 1819
EIGHTH & BUSSERON STREETS
P.O. BOX 215
VINCENNES, INDIANA 47591
Telephone: 812-882-2280
FAX: 812-885-2308
Email: general@emisonlaw.com

General Practice. Trials, Estate Planning and Administration, Family Law, Bankruptcy, Corporation, Commercial and Insurance Law.

FIRM PROFILE: Samuel Judah, the firm's founder, arrived from New Jersey in 1819, making this firm the oldest in the State of Indiana and among the oldest in the nation. Contrasted with this antiquity is the firm's adaptation to new skills and knowledge of the law and technology. Active members of the firm display this interest by service upon the governing board of the Indiana Continuing Legal Education Forum, repeated service as lecturers at training seminars and offices in the Indiana State Bar Association. An active member served as President of the State Bar and the Continuing Legal Education Forum and received the American Bar Association Spirit of Excellence Award. An active partner is presently serving upon the board of the Continuing Legal Education Forum and is past president of the Indiana Bar Foundation. Three partners sat on the ISBA Board of Governors. Three served as Vincennes City Attorneys.

MEMBERS OF FIRM

ROBERT P. DOOLITTLE, born Mishawaka, Indiana, August 30, 1940; admitted to bar, 1965, Indiana. *Education:* Indiana University (B.S., 1962; LL.B., 1965). *Member:* Knox County (President, 1968), Indiana State and American (Member, Business Law Section) Bar Associations. ***PRACTICE AREAS:*** Alternative Dispute Resolution; Business Law; Bankruptcy Law; Commercial Law; Creditors' Rights Law; Real Estate; Non-Profit Organizations. ***Email:*** doolittle@emisonlaw.com

JEFFREY B. KOLB, born Ft. George Meade, Maryland, May 28, 1951; admitted to bar, 1976, Indiana and U.S. District Court, District of Indiana; 1977, Illinois; 1987, Seventh Circuit Court of Appeals; 1991, U.S. Tax Court. *Education:* Indiana University (B.A., 1973; J.D., 1976). Author: "Henry's Probate Law and Practice," Volume 8, Indiana Estate Planning System, ICLEF (Hot docs software) and numerous books and articles on estate planning and administration. *Member:* Knox County, Indiana State (Lifetime Service Award, Probate, Trust and Real Property Section; Co-Editor, Indiana Probate, Trust, Property and Death Tax Newsletter, 1981—; Chairman, Probate, Trust and Real Property Section, 1986-1987; Board of Managers, 1990-1992); Chair, UPL Committee, 2004—; Indiana Continuing Legal Education Forum (Board of Directors, 1996-2004); Illinois State and American Bar Associations; Indiana Bar Foundation (Board of Directors, 1991—; President, 2000-2002); National Academy of Elder Law Attorneys; The American College of Trust and Estate Counsel. ***PRACTICE AREAS:*** Estate Planning and Administration; Trusts and Estates; Wills; Probate; Personal Injury; Oil and Gas Law; Real Estate; Business Planning; Buying and Selling of Businesses; Elder Law; Drainage and Levee; Guardianship; Medicaid. ***Email:*** kolb@emisonlaw.com

J. DAVID ROELLGEN, born Vincennes, Knox County, Indiana, November 6, 1953; admitted to bar, 1979, Indiana and U.S. District Court, Southern District of Indiana; 1981, U.S. Court of Appeals, Seventh Circuit; 1988, U.S. Court of Military Appeals; 1990, Illinois. *Education:* Vincennes University (A.S., 1974); Indiana State University (B.S., 1976); Indiana University-Indianapolis (J.D., cum laude, 1979). Phi Delta Phi. Attorney, 1992-1996. Associate City Attorney, 2000-2002 and City Attorney, 2003—, City of Vincennes. Contributing Author: Numerous articles on family and military law. *Member:* Knox County (President, 1996), Indiana State (Past-Chairman, Family and Juvenile Law Section, 1993-1995; Board of Governors, 2000-2002), Illinois State and American Bar Associations; In-

(This Listing Continued)

diana Bar Foundation; Indiana Equal Justice Fund (Board Member); Defense Trial Counsel of Indiana (Board Member). [LTC, Indiana Army National Guard, 1985—; Staff Judge Advocate, 38th ID (MECH)]. ***PRACTICE AREAS:*** Family Law; Personal Injury; Custody Law; Litigation; Insurance Defense; Municipal Law; Mediation; Family Mediation. ***Email:*** roellgen@emisonlaw.com

YVETTE CHARMAINE KIRCHOFF, born Vincennes, Indiana, July 22, 1962; admitted to bar, 1998, New Jersey and U.S. District Court, District of New Jersey; 1999, Indiana, Illinois, U.S. District Court, Northern and Southern Districts of Indiana and U.S. District Court, Northern District of Illinois; 2000, District of Columbia and U.S. District Court, District of Columbia; 2004, U.S. District Courts, Central and Southern Districts of Illinois. *Education:* Vincennes University (A.A., 1982); Purdue University (A.A.S., 1986; B.S., 1988); Seton Hall University (J.D., cum laude, 1998). Associate City Attorney, 2003—. *Member:* The District of Columbia Bar; Knox County (Treasurer, 2004-2005), Indiana State, New Jersey State, Illinois and American Bar Associations; Defense Trial Counsel of Indiana. ***PRACTICE AREAS:*** Family Law; Real Estate; Litigation; Insurance Defense. ***Email:*** kirchoff@emisonlaw.com

OF COUNSEL

RABB EMISON, born Vincennes, Indiana, February 3, 1925; admitted to bar, 1950, Indiana; 1989, U.S. Court of Appeals, Seventh Circuit. *Education:* DePauw University (A.B., 1947); Indiana University School of Law (LL.B., 1950). Phi Delta Phi. Recipient, 2003 American Bar Association Spirit of Excellence Award. *Member:* Knox County, Indiana State (Member, Board of Managers, 1975-1977; Chairman, House of Delegates, 1979; President, 1986-1987) and American (Member, Sections on: Litigation; Economics of Law Practice) Bar Associations; American Bar Foundation. (Retired). ***Email:*** emison@emisonlaw.com

ASSOCIATE

TONYA R. SHAW, born Washington, Indiana, December 27, 1979; admitted to bar, 2005, Indiana. *Education:* Vincennes University (A.A., summa cum laude, 2000); Indiana State University (B.A., magna cum laude, 2002); Valparaiso University (J.D., with honors, 2005). Honor's Program Graduate from Valparaiso University School of Law. Member: Christian Legal Society 2002-2004; Golden Key National Honor Society 2000-2002; Alpha Lambda Delta Honor Society 2000-2002; Recipient: Outstanding Pre-Law Student, Vincennes University 2000; Awarded Highest - Most Promising in Social Science Department, Vincennes University, 2000. ***Email:*** shaw_tonya@yahoo.com

REPRESENTATIVE CLIENTS: Sun-Commercial Newspaper (a Gannett paper); Old National Bank; Old National Trust; Gemtron Corporation (Mfrs); Vincennes Housing Authority; Miller Construction Company; Knox County Association For Retarded Citizens, Inc.; Cinergy; Amoco Pipeline; El Paso Energy; Tennessee Gas Pipeline; Brevoort Levee Conservancy District; McGinnis Levee Committee; American Family Insurance; Cincinnati Insurance; Sentry Insurance; GRE Insurance; Prudential Insurance; WAOV; WZDM; WBBL; WUZR; The Original Company, Inc.; Old Northwest Broadcasting, Inc.; Fox Ridge Development Co.; Sievers Construction; Children & Family Services, Inc.; R & H Trucking, Inc.; Second Street Development, LLC; First Street Development, LLC; City of Vincennes; Duke Energy.

GOSNELL, BORDEN, ENLOE & SLOSS, LTD.

VINCENNES, INDIANA

(See Lawrenceville)

General Practice. Insurance Defense. Trials. Probate Law. Oil and Gas Law. Personal Injury, Family Law.

HALL, PARTENHEIMER & KINKLE

VINCENNES, INDIANA

(See Princeton)

General Civil Practice. Personal Injury, Probate and Estate Planning, Real Estate, Mining, Oil and Gas and Corporate Law, Municipal Law, Trials.

HART BELL LLC

Established in 1884

513 MAIN STREET
P.O. BOX 979
VINCENNES, INDIANA 47591
Telephone: 812-882-8935
Fax: 812-882-5186; 812-882-9272

General Practice. Litigation, Insurance, Banking, Corporate, Employment, Probate and Estate Planning, State and Federal Tax Law, Real Estate, Construction, Commercial, Business, Elder, Creditors Rights, Personal Injury, Family Law and Criminal Defense.

FIRM PROFILE: Hart Bell LLC has maintained a continuous practice in Knox County for well over 100 years. Our former partners include two Justices on the Indiana Supreme Court, a President of the Indiana State Bar Association, a President of the State Board of Law Examiners, and a Mayor of Vincennes. We are proud of our firm's continuing contributions to the legal profession and our extended community.

A full service law firm, we provide the broad spectrum of legal services required for our business, banking, insurance, and public employer clients. We also maintain an active civil litigation practice in the state and federal courts throughout Southwestern Indiana and Southeastern Illinois.

We are committed to providing quality cost effective legal services to meet the simple and complex legal needs of our diverse client base. We view our role as problem solvers. We continuously invest in our library, technology, staff, continuing education, and facilities to be ready to meet our clients' needs. We take pride in our clients' successes, and the confidence and trust they place in us.

(This Listing Continued)

MEMBERS OF FIRM

L. EDWARD CUMMINGS, born Indianapolis, Indiana, November 25, 1946; admitted to bar, 1973, Indiana. *Education:* Indiana University (A.B., 1968; J.D., 1973). ***PRACTICE AREAS:*** Civil Trials; Real Estate Law; Construction Law. ***Email:*** ecummings@hartbell.com

MARK EWING, born Vincennes, Indiana, May 1, 1951; admitted to bar, 1977, Indiana; 1978, Illinois. *Education:* Syracuse University (B.A., 1973); Williamette University (J.D., 1976); New York University (LL.M. in Taxation, 1977). ***PRACTICE AREAS:*** Estate Planning; Tax Law; Business Transactions; Real Estate; Tax Controversies. ***Email:*** mewing@hartbell.com

BRENT STUCKEY, born Vincennes, Indiana, June 27, 1953; admitted to bar, 1978, Indiana; 1980, Illinois. *Education:* Drury College (B.A., summa cum laude, 1975); Indiana University (J.D., magna cum laude, 1978). ***PRACTICE AREAS:*** Employment Law; Civil Litigation; Insurance Litigation; Personal Injury. ***Email:*** bstuckey@hartbell.com

JEFFERY S. NEAL, born Crawfordsville, Indiana, December 28, 1971; admitted to bar, 1997, Indiana and Illinois. *Education:* Indiana University (B.A., 1994); Indiana University School of Law (J.D., 1997). Phi Beta Kappa. ***PRACTICE AREAS:*** Family Law; Civil Litigation; Criminal Defense; Civil Forfeiture; Divorce; Child Custody; Child Support; Adoption Law; Guardianship. ***Email:*** jneal@hartbell.com

DANIEL L. SIEWERS, born Vincennes, Indiana, September 23, 1974; admitted to bar, 1999, Indiana and Illinois. *Education:* Franklin College (B.A., summa cum laude, 1996); Indiana University School of Law (J.D., magna cum laude, 1999). ***PRACTICE AREAS:*** Civil Litigation; Elder Law; Medicaid Planning; Estate Planning; Real Estate; Business Transactions. ***Email:*** dsiewers@hartbell.com

RUDOLPH, FINE, PORTER & JOHNSON LLP

VINCENNES, INDIANA

(See Evansville)

General Corporate Practice. Health Care Law, Commercial Litigation, Insurance Defense, Real Estate, Zoning and Land Use Law, Mediation and Arbitration, Bankruptcy Law, Mergers and Acquisitions. Probate and Estate Planning, Tax, Employment Law, Appeals, Banking. Trials in all State and Federal Courts.

STURM, SMITH & PARMENTER

312 MAIN STREET
P.O. BOX 393
VINCENNES, INDIANA 47591
Telephone: 812-882-1303
Fax: 812-886-0786
URL: http://www.ssplawfirm.com
URL: http://www.lawyerspages.com/firms/ssp/

Litigation, Commercial, Bankruptcy, Business, Collections, Workers Compensation, Social Security, Probate, Estate Planning, Personal Injury, Real Estate, Family.

MEMBERS OF FIRM

GREGORY W. STURM, born Evansville, Indiana, August 23, 1945; admitted to bar, 1970, Indiana. *Education:* University of Notre Dame (B.B.A., 1967); Indiana University School of Law (J.D., 1970). Member, Advisory Council, University of Notre Dame Law School, 1987—. *Member:* Indiana Trial Lawyers Association; The Association of Trial Lawyers of America. Fellow, Indiana Bar Foundation. ***PRACTICE AREAS:*** Probate; Estate Planning; Real Estate; Corporate; Personal Injury; Banking. ***Email:*** gsturm@cbnstl.com

BRUCE A. SMITH, born Terre Haute, Indiana, January 4, 1952; admitted to bar, 1976, Indiana; 1984, Illinois; 2002, Kentucky. *Education:* Indiana State University (B.S., 1973); Indiana University School of Law (J.D., cum laude, 1976). *Member:* Indiana State (Chair, Bankruptcy and Creditors' Rights Section, 1994-1995) Bar Association. Fellow, Indiana Bar Foundation. (Certified Specialist Business Bankruptcy and Consumer Bankruptcy Law American Bankruptcy Board of Certification). ***PRACTICE AREAS:*** Creditors Rights; Bankruptcy. ***Email:*** bsmith@cbnstl.com

MATTHEW PARMENTER, born Vincennes, Indiana, February 8, 1955; admitted to bar, 1985, Indiana; 1988, Illinois. *Education:* University of Evansville (B.S., 1978); Indiana University (J.D., cum laude, 1985). *Member:* The Association of Trial Lawyers of America (Sustaining Member); Indiana Trial Lawyers Association (Sustaining Member); Illinois Trial Lawyers Association. ***PRACTICE AREAS:*** Personal Injury; Wrongful Death. ***Email:*** parmenter@cbnstl.com

JASON C. FIELD, born October 8, 1970; admitted to bar, 2000, Indiana. *Education:* Indiana University (B.S., 2000); Valparaiso University (J.D., 2000). ***PRACTICE AREAS:*** Bankruptcy; Creditors Rights; Family Law. ***Email:*** jfield@cbnstl.com

REPRESENTATIVE CLIENTS: Regions Bank; Integra Bank; JOFCO, Inc.; Wabash Coffee, Inc.; Inwood Office Furniture, Inc.; Farm Credit Services; Vincennes Community School Corp.; Vincennes Utilities Service Board, Knox County, Indiana.

KILEY, KILEY, HARKER, MICHAEL & CERTAIN

WABASH, INDIANA

(See Marion)

JAMES S. BUTTS

119 E. CENTER STREET, SUITE B-5
WARSAW, INDIANA 46580-2852
Telephone: 574-269-9500
Fax: 574-269-2888
Email: jsblawfirm@abanet.org

Civil Litigation, Family Law, Adoptions, Child Custody, Child Support, Divorce, Visitation Rights, Wills, Probate, Trust and Estates, Estate Planning, Personal Injury, Automobile Accidents, Truck Accidents, Wrongful Death.

JAMES S. BUTTS, born Fort Wayne, Indiana, May 23, 1951; admitted to bar, 1979, Indiana, U.S. District Court, Northern and Southern Districts of Indiana and U.S. Supreme Court; 1984, U.S. Court of Appeals, Seventh Circuit. *Education:* Indiana University (B.A., 1973); Southern Methodist University (J.D., 1979). *Member:* Kosciusko County, Indiana State and American (Member, Sections on: Litigation; General Practice; Solo and Small Firm; Family Law) Bar Associations; American Trial Lawyers Association. ***PRACTICE AREAS:*** General Family Practice; Family Law; Dissolution of Marriage; Child Custody; Visitation Rights; Parenting Time; Child Support; Adoption Law; Guardianship; Real Estate Transactions; Business Law; Sole Proprietorships; Partnership Law; Corporate Law; Civil Litigation; Trial Practice; Appellate Practice; Products Liability; Personal Injury; Estate Planning; Health Care; Wills; Last Wills and Testaments; Trusts and Estates; Probate.

DAVID C. KOLBE, P.C.

Established in 1992
221 NORTH WASHINGTON STREET
WARSAW, INDIANA 46580
Telephone: 574-267-5353
Fax: 574-267-0151
URL: http://www.dkolbelawfirm.com
Email: dkolbelaw@kconline.com
URL: http://www.dkolbelaw.com

Personal Injury, Automobile Accidents, Dig Bites, Head and Spinal Injuries, Nursing Home Abuse, Sexual Abuse, Slip and Fall, Truck Accidents, Products Liability, Drug and Medical Devices, Medical Malpractice, Criminal Law, Drug Crimes, Driving While Intoxicated (DWI), DUI, Juvenile Criminal Law, Parole and Probation, Traffic Violations, White Collar Crime, Family Law, Adoption Law, Child Custody, Child Support, Divorce, Domestic Violence, Visitation Rights, Business Law, Business Planning, Business Litigation, Contract, Commercial Law, Business Enterprises, Small Business Law, Partnership Law, Corporate Law, Limited Liability Company Law (LLC), Buying and Selling a Business, Business Start-Ups, Real Estate, Wills and Probate, Trusts and Estates, Elder Law, Guardianship, Asset Protection, Estate Planning.

FIRM PROFILE: The firm is dedicated to assisting the legal matters of injured workers, those charged with crimes, persons injured in a variety of accidents, and those with family law matters.

DAVID C. KOLBE, born Clearfield, Pennsylvania, January 21, 1955; admitted to bar, 1981, Indiana; 1982, U.S. District Court, Northern District of Indiana and Western District of Michigan. *Education:* DePauw University; Indiana University at South Bend (B.A., 1977); Valparaiso University (J.D., 1981). Author: "Double Jeopardy and the Habitual Offender Enhancement," Res Gestae, Indiana State Bar Journal, 1988—; "Bad Faith Statute Trumps Indiana Constitution," Res Gestae, Indiana State Bar Journal, Res Gestae, 2003. Instructor, "Elements of Law," "Business Law" and "Introduction to American Politics," Indiana University/Purdue University, Fort Wayne and Indiana University at South Bend. Public Defender, 1983-1993. Kosciusko County Prosecutor, 54th Judicial Circuit, 1995-1998. Delegate, People to People, Cuban Republic, 2002. *Member:* Kosciusko County and Indiana State Bar Associations; Christian Legal Society; National Institute for Trial Advocacy; Indiana Public Defender Council. ***LANGUAGES:*** Spanish. ***PRACTICE AREAS:*** Product Liability; Personal Injury; Workers Compensation; Criminal Law. ***Email:*** dkolbelaw@kconline.com

---

JOHN D. BARRETT, born Terre Haute, Indiana, March 31, 1966; admitted to bar, 2004, Indiana and U.S. District Court, Northern and Southern Districts of Indiana. *Education:* University of New Mexico (B.A., 2000); Indiana University School of Law, Indianapolis (J.D., 2003). *Member:* Kosciusko County (Vice President, 2005) and Indiana State Bar Associations; Indiana Public Defense Counsel. ***PRACTICE AREAS:*** Family Law; Domestic Relations; Criminal Defense; Contracts; Estates. ***Email:*** dkolbelaw@kconline.com

Languages: Spanish.

LAVENDER & BAUER, P.C.

Established in 1985
116 NORTH BUFFALO STREET
WARSAW, INDIANA 46580
Telephone: 574-267-4151
Toll Free: 800-567-4151
Fax: 574-267-6263
Email: lavenderlaw@kconline.com

Torts, Criminal Law, Drug Crimes, DWI, DUI, Traffic Violations, Will and Probate, Trusts and Estates, Family Law, Adoptions, Child Custody, Child Support, Divorce, Visitation Rights, Domestic Relations, Probate, Corporate Law, Business Law, Business Planning, Business Contracts, Business Litigation, Business Enterprises, Buying and Selling a Business, Starting a Business.

(This Listing Continued)

J. L. LAVENDER, born Wellston, Ohio, January 21, 1949; admitted to bar, 1982, Indiana and U.S. District Court, Northern and Southern Districts of Indiana. *Education:* Otterbein College (B.A., 1971); Capital University (J.D., 1982). Delta Theta Phi. Chief Trial Deputy Attorney, Kosciusko County Prosecutor's Office, 1983-1988. *Member:* Kosciusko County, Indiana State and American Bar Associations; The Association of Trial Lawyers of America. ***PRACTICE AREAS:*** Torts; Criminal Law; Domestic Relations; Probate; Corporate Law; Business Law. ***Email:*** lavenderlaw@kconline.com

TORREY J. BAUER, born Grand Rapids, Michigan, October 4, 1964; admitted to bar, 1991, Indiana and U.S. District Court, Northern and Southern Districts of Indiana. *Education:* Grace College (B.S., 1986); Indiana University (J.D., cum laude, 1991). *Member:* Kosciusko County, Indiana State and American Bar Associations; The Association of Trial Lawyers of America. ***PRACTICE AREAS:*** Torts; Criminal Law; Domestic Relations. ***Email:*** lavenderlaw@kconline.com

Language: Spanish.

MORRIS & RUIZ, P.C.

WARSAW, INDIANA

(See Plymouth)

Business Transactions, Corporate Law, Bankruptcy, Litigation, Personal Injury, Domestic Relations, Criminal Law, Juvenile Law, Automobile Accidents, Driving While Intoxicated, Juvenile Criminal Law, Parole and Probation, Traffic Violations, White Collar Crimes.

ROCKHILL PINNICK LLP

105 EAST MAIN STREET
WARSAW, INDIANA 46580-2742
Telephone: 574-267-6116
Telecopier: 574-269-9264
Email: rockhill@rexnet.net
URL: http://www.rockhillattorneys.com

General Civil Trial Practice in all State and Federal Courts. Business Law, Business Planning, Contracts, Business Litigation, Business Enterprises, Partnerships, Corporate, Limited Liability Companies, Small Business, Family Law, Construction Law, Mediation, Wills and Probate, Trusts and Estates, Estate Planning, Asset Protection, Banking, Real Estate, Land Use, Municipal and Zoning, Insurance Law.

MEMBERS OF FIRM

STANLEY E. PEQUIGNOT, born Warsaw, Indiana, December 31, 1942; admitted to bar, 1968, Indiana. *Education:* Indiana University (B.S., 1965; J.D., 1968). Phi Alpha Delta. *Member:* Kosciusko County, Indiana State and American Bar Associations. ***PRACTICE AREAS:*** Trusts and Estates; Wills; Business Law.

RICHARD K. HELM, born Indianapolis, Indiana, January 1, 1945; admitted to bar, 1973, Indiana. *Education:* Wabash College (A.B., 1967); Indiana University (M.S., 1970; J.D., 1973). Certified Civil Mediator. *Member:* Kosciusko County (President, 1979-1984), Indiana State and American Bar Associations. ***PRACTICE AREAS:*** Litigation; Zoning, Planning and Land Use; Real Estate.

VERN K. LANDIS, born Dallas, Texas, April 20, 1951; admitted to bar, 1976, Indiana. *Education:* Indiana University (B.S., 1973; J.D., 1976). Certified Family/Civil Mediator. Beta Gamma Sigma. *Member:* Kosciusko County, Indiana State and American Bar Associations. ***PRACTICE AREAS:*** Trusts and Estates; Business Law; Debtor/Creditor.

JAY A. RIGDON, born Syracuse, Indiana, April 7, 1960; admitted to bar, 1984, Indiana. *Education:* George Washington University (B.A., 1981); Indiana University (J.D., 1984). *Member:* Kosciusko County, Indiana State and American Bar Associations. ***PRACTICE AREAS:*** Litigation; Criminal Law; Debtor/Creditor.

CHRISTOPHER D. KEHLER, born Warsaw, Indiana, December 12, 1961; admitted to bar, 1987, Indiana. *Education:* Franklin College of Indiana (B.A., 1984); Valparaiso University (J.D., 1987). ***PRACTICE AREAS:*** Family Law; Criminal Defense; Civil Trial Practice; Wills; Trusts and Estates.

DANA LEON, born Mt. Clair, New Jersey, June 3, 1973; admitted to bar, 1998, Indiana. *Education:* Indiana University (B.A., 1995); Indiana University School of Law (J.D., 1998). Order of Barristers. *Member:* Kosciusko County, Indiana State and American Bar Associations. ***LANGUAGES:*** Spanish. ***PRACTICE AREAS:*** General Practice; Family Law; Criminal Law.

REPRESENTATIVE CLIENTS: FarmersState Bank, Mentone, Indiana; Warsaw Times-Union Newspaper; State Farm Insurance Cos.; Milford, Indiana; Motorists Mutual Ins. Co.; Otis R. Bowen Center for Human Services, Inc.; Phend & Brown, Inc.; Warsaw Production Welding Inc.; Symmetry Medical, Inc.; Legacy Homes, Inc.; Koscusko Community Foundation, Inc.; Petro Bros Chrysler; Petro-Buick-GMC-Cadillac; Bambi's Roofing, Inc.; R.L. Gilbert Utility Contractors, Inc.

ROTHBERG LOGAN & WARSCO LLP

Established in 1952
(Successor by merger to, Rothberg & Logan and Warsco Brogan)
212 NORTH BUFFALO STREET
WARSAW, INDIANA 46580
Telephone: 574-267-8802
Telefax: 574-267-0605
Email: law@rlwlawfirm.com
URL: http://www.rlwlawfirm.com

Fort Wayne, Indiana Office: 2100 National City Center, 110 West Berry Street, P.O. Box 11647, 46859-1647. Telephone: 260-422-9454. Telefax: 260-422-1622.

(This Listing Continued)

General Civil Litigation in all Courts. Corporate, Banking, Bankruptcy, Commercial, Insurance, Labor and Employment Law, Municipal Law, Municipal Finance, Securities, Real Estate, Construction, Probate and Estate Planning, Transportation, Tax, Creditors' Rights, Agricultural Law, Family/Domestic Relations, Health Care Law.

FIRM PROFILE: Rothberg Logan & Warsco LLP was founded in 1952 by Sol Rothberg, Thomas A. Gallmeyer, and Richard T. Doermer. In 2000, the firm merged with Warsco Brogan and in 2002, the firm opened a Warsaw, Indiana office. The firm has developed a wide-ranging practice serving many of the region's leading banks and businesses as well as its international airport and community transit system.

MICHAEL E. ARMEY, born Fort Wayne, Indiana, December 6, 1942; admitted to bar, 1974, Indiana; U.S. Tax Court. *Education:* Purdue University (B.S., with distinction, 1971); Indiana University (J.D., cum laude, 1974). Beta Gamma Sigma. Supervising Editor, Indiana Law Journal, 1973-1974. *Member:* Kosciusko County, Indiana State (Member, Board of Governors, 1998-2000; Business Law Section, Chairman, 1993-1994) and American Bar Associations. Fellow, Indiana Bar Foundation. ***PRACTICE AREAS:*** Business; Banking; Environmental; Real Estate; Labor. ***Email:*** marmey@rlwlawfirm.com

R. STEVEN HEARN, born Wabash, Indiana, July 30, 1937; admitted to bar, 1966, Indiana. *Education:* Purdue University and Southern Methodist University (B.B.A., 1961); Indiana University (J.D., 1966). Sheriff to Indiana Supreme Court, 1963-1965. Law Clerk, Indiana Supreme Court, 1965-1966. Prosecuting Attorney, Kosciusko County, Indiana, 1969-1977. Member: Judicial Study Commission, State of Indiana, Juvenile Justice Division, 1976-1977; Kosciusko County Election Board, 1982—. Chief Counsel, 1983-2002 and President, 2003—, American Power Boat Association. *Member:* Kosciusko County (President, 1975-1976) and Indiana State (Member of Counsel, Litigation Section, 1993) Bar Associations; Indiana Prosecuting Attorneys Association (Director, 1974-1976). ***PRACTICE AREAS:*** Products Liability Litigation; Entertainment and Sports Law; Civil Litigation; Family Law; Personal Injury; Real Estate and Estates. ***Email:*** rshearn@rlwlawfirm.com

APPROVED ATTORNEYS FOR: Ameriquest Mortgage Company; Aon Corporation; Avis Industrial Corp.; Bank One, N.A.; Busak + Shamban, Inc.; Cameron Memorial Community Hospital; Construction Management Engineering, Inc.; City of Fort Wayne; Dell Computer Corp.; Farm Credit Services of Mid-America, ASA; Fifth Third Bank; Fort Wayne-Allen County Airport Authority; Fort Wayne Public Transportation Corporation, d/b/a Citilink; ; K & K Insurance Group, Inc.; Lake City Bank; National City Bank of Indiana; Parkview Health System; R.E. Crosby & Sons, Inc.; Slater Fort Wayne Federal Credit Union; Tower Bank; Weigand Construction Co., Inc.; Wells Fargo Bank Indiana, N.A.; Wells Fargo Home Mortgage Company; Wolf Corporation.

(For complete biographical data on all personnel, see Professional Biographies at Fort Wayne, Indiana)

STUTSMAN, MULVANEY & DEBOER

WARSAW, INDIANA

(See Elkhart)

General Civil and Appellate Practice in all State and Federal Courts. Personal Injury, Automobile Accidents, Slip and Fall, Wrongful Death, Workers Compensation, Medical Malpractice, Corporate, Wills and Probate, Trusts and Estates, Asset Protection, Guardianships, Estate Planning, Real Estate, Internet Law.

EMISON DOOLITTLE KOLB & ROELLGEN

WASHINGTON, INDIANA

(See Vincennes)

General Practice. Trials, Estate Planning and Administration, Family Law, Bankruptcy, Corporation, Commercial and Insurance Law.

HART BELL LLC

WASHINGTON, INDIANA

(See Vincennes)

General Practice. Litigation, Insurance, Banking, Corporate, Employment, Probate and Estate Planning, State and Federal Tax Law, Real Estate, Construction, Commercial, Business, Elder, Creditors Rights, Personal Injury, Family Law and Criminal Defense.

BOSE MCKINNEY & EVANS LLP

Established in 1955

SUITE B2-204
3000 KENT AVENUE
WEST LAFAYETTE, INDIANA 47906
Telephone: 765-464-3200
Facsimile: 765-464-3225
URL: http://www.boselaw.com

Indianapolis, Indiana Office: 2700 First Indiana Plaza, 135 North Pennsylvania Street, 46204. Telephone: 317-684-5000. Facsimile: 317-684-5173.
Indianapolis, Indiana North Office: 600 East 96th Street, Suite 500 46240. Telephone: 317-684-5300. Facsimile: 317-684-5316.
Washington, D.C. Office: 700 North One Lafayette Centre, 1120 20th Street, N.W., 20036. Telephone: 202-973-1229. Fax: 202-973-1212.
Crown Point, Indiana Office: 3577 West Lakeshore Drive, 46307. Telephone: 219-663-2968. Fax: 219-663-2969.
Chesterton, Indiana Office: P.O. Box 957, 46304. Telephone: 219-983-1552. Fax: 219-983-1741.

(This Listing Continued)

General Civil Practice in all Courts including Agricultural Law, Antitrust, Appellate Practice, Capital Strategies, Civil Rights, Commercial Law, Communications and Media, Constitutional Law, Corporate Law, Creditors Rights, Creditors Rights in Bankruptcy, Debtor Bankruptcy, Education Law, Employee Benefits, Entertainment and the Arts, Entrepreneurial Services, Environmental Law, Finance, Financial Institutions Law, Government Contracts, Government Relations, High Technology, Insurance, Intellectual Property, International Law, Labor and Employment, Legislative Practice, Litigation, Mergers and Acquisitions, Municipal Finance, Municipal Law, Planning and Land Use, Probate, Real Estate, Regulated Industries, Regulatory Agency Practice, Securities, Taxation, Trusts and Estates, Utility Law, Wills and Zoning.

OF COUNSEL

EYAL H. BARASH, born Lafayette, Indiana, June 5, 1969; admitted to bar, 1997, Illinois; 1998, District of Columbia; 2005, Indiana; registered to practice before U.S. Patent and Trademark Office. *Education:* Indiana University (B.S., Chemistry, 1991; B.A., History, 1991); University of California at Berkeley (M.S., Chemistry, 1994); Northwestern University (J.D., 1997). *Member:* Illinois State and Indiana State Bar Associations; The District of Columbia Bar. ***PRACTICE AREAS:*** Intellectual Property; Patents.

RICHARD BALLARD
ATTORNEY AT LAW

WINAMAC, INDIANA

(See Knox)

Criminal Law, DUI, Drug Crimes, Juvenile Crimes, Traffic Violations, White Collar Crimes, Family Law, Adoptions, Child Custody, Child Support, Divorce, Visitation Rights, Personal Injury, Medical Malpractice, Auto Accidents, Wrongful Death, Slip and Fall, Real Estate.

MATTHEW D. LATULIP
ATTORNEY AT LAW

WINAMAC, INDIANA

(See Schererville)

Personal Injury, Medical Malpractice, Auto Accidents, Slip and Fall, Wrongful Death, Criminal, DUI, Traffic Violations, Juvenile Crimes, Employment Discrimination, Sexual Harassment, Nursing Home Abuse, Insurance.

NED TONNER
ATTORNEY AT LAW

WINAMAC, INDIANA

(See Rensselaer)

Personal Injury, Criminal Law, Estates, Trusts, Real Estate, Divorce, Family Law.

BLACKBURN & GREEN

WINCHESTER, INDIANA

(See Fort Wayne)

Litigation, Personal Injury Law.

DONNA J. BAYS

ZIONSVILLE, INDIANA

(See Indianapolis)

Family Law, Divorce, Child Custody, Paternity, Premarital Agreements.

KNOWLES & ASSOCIATES, LLC

ZIONSVILLE, INDIANA

(See Carmel)

Practice limited to Wills and Probate, Business Law, Business Planning, Starting a Business, Buying and Selling a Business, Elder Law, Estate Planning, Litigation, Trusts and Estates, Tax Planning, Medicaid Planning.

McDONALD, BROWN & FAGEN

ADEL, IOWA

(See Dallas Center)

General Practice, including: Real Estate, Wills, Trusts, Estate Planning, and Probate, Business and Commercial, Taxation Law and Tax Returns, Family Law, Litigation and Appeals, Debtor and Creditor, Municipal and School Law.

JOSEPH F. STARCEVIC

13 S. CLINTON STREET
P.O. BOX 576
ALBIA, IOWA 52531
Telephone: 641-932-7802
Fax: 641-932-5768
Email: JStarcevic@AlbiaLaw.com
URL: http://www.AlbiaLaw.com

General Practice, including but not limited to: Wills, Trusts, Estate Planning and Probate Law; Real Estate Law; Business Law and Corporate Law.

JOSEPH F. STARCEVIC, born Ottumwa, Iowa, April 19, 1956; admitted to bar, 1981, Iowa. *Education:* Ottumwa Heights College (A.A., with Highest Distinction, 1975); University of Iowa (B.A., with Highest Distinction, 1977); Iowa College of Law (J.D., with High Distinction, 1981). Phi Theta Kappa; Phi Beta Kappa. Member: Board of Directors, Linn County Bar, 1990. Trust Officer, Peoples Bank & Trust Company, Cedar Rapids, Iowa, 1981-1987. Assistant General Counsel, Teleconnect Company, Cedar Rapids, Iowa, 1987-1990. Senior Corporate Counsel, MCI Telecommunications Corporation, Atlanta, Georgia, 1990-1997. Albia Chamber of Commerce, President 2006. Albia Library Board. *Member:* Iowa State (Vice Chair, Corporate Counsel Section, 2003-2004) and American Bar Associations. ***PRACTICE AREAS:*** General Practice; Wills; Trusts and Estates; Estate Planning; Probate; Real Estate; Business Law; Corporate Law.

PETERSON & LIPPS

6 EAST STATE STREET
P.O. BOX 575
ALGONA, IOWA 50511
Telephone: 515-295-9494
Fax: 515-295-9493
Email: info@petelipp.com
URL: http://www.petersonlipps.com

General Practice and Trial Practice. Personal Injury, Workers Compensation, Real Estate, Insurance, Corporation, Tax, Probate, Trusts, Collections, Domestic Relations, Commercial, Estate Planning.

MARTIN W. PETERSON, born Scranton, Iowa, March 25, 1943; admitted to bar, 1968, Iowa. *Education:* Drake University (B.S., 1965); University of Iowa (J.D., 1968). Phi Delta Phi. *Member:* Kossuth County, Iowa State and American Bar Associations. ***Email:*** mpete@petelipp.com

THOMAS W. LIPPS, born Nebraska, July 30, 1954; admitted to bar, 1979, Nebraska; 1981, Iowa; U.S. Supreme Court; U.S. Court of Appeals, Eighth Circuit; U.S. District Court, District of Nebraska and U.S. District Court, Northern and Southern Districts of Iowa; U.S. Tax Court. *Education:* University of Nebraska-Lincoln College of Agriculture (B.S. with high distinction, 1976); University of Nebraska-Lincoln (J.D., 1979). Gamma Sigma Delta; Phi Eta Sigma. Judicial Magistrate, 1985-1989. Recipient, Iowa Trial Lawyers Association 2000 Public Justice Award. Member, Iowa Democratic Party (Fifth Congressional District; State Central Committee, 1998-2002; Chair, 2000-2002. *Member:* Kossuth County, Iowa State, Nebraska State and American Bar Associations; Iowa Trial Lawyers Association (Member, Board of Governors, 1998-2004); The Association of Trial Lawyers of America. Fellow, Iowa Academy of Trial Lawyers. (Board Certified, Civil Trial Specialist, National Board of Trial Advocacy). ***Email:*** tlipps@petelipp.com

DAVID L. SHUMWAY (Retired)

REFERENCE: Iowa State Bank, Algona, Iowa.

BEATTIE LAW FIRM, P.C.

AMES, IOWA

(See Des Moines)

Civil Litigation, Personal Injury, Product Liability, Workers Compensation, Wrongful Death, Dog Bites, Legal Malpractice, Business Litigation, Automobile Accidents.

BECKMAN AND HIRSCH

AMES, IOWA

(See Burlington)

Personal Injury, Appeals, Corporation, Taxation, Probate, Insurance, Real Estate, Criminal Defense, Commercial Litigation, Computer Law, Family Law, General Trial Practice in State and Federal Courts.

HUBER, BOOK, CORTESE, HAPPE & LANZ, P.L.C.

AMES, IOWA

(See Des Moines)

Civil Trial and Appellate Practice. Insurance Defense, Workers' Compensation, Insurance, Products Liability, Professional Malpractice Defense and Administrative Law. Commercial, Business and Insurance Litigation.

NEWBROUGH, JOHNSTON, BREWER, MADDUX AND HOWELL, L.L.P.

Established in 1935
612 KELLOGG AVENUE
P.O. BOX 847
AMES, IOWA 50010
Telephone: 515-232-1761
Fax: 515-232-8962
Email: atty@newbroughlaw.com
URL: http://www.lawyers.com/newbroughlaw

General Practice. Trials and Appeals. Estate Planning, Probate, Corporation, Real Estate Law, Personal Injury, Employee Benefits and ERISA.

MEMBERS OF FIRM

D. R. NEWBROUGH, born Eagle Grove, Iowa, November 29, 1928; admitted to bar, 1953, Iowa; U.S. District Court, Northern and Southern Districts of Iowa and Central District of Illinois and U.S Court of Appeals, Eighth Circuit. *Education:* Iowa State University; University of Iowa (B.A., 1951; LL.B., 1953). Delta Theta Phi (Dean, 1951-1952). Mayor, Ames, Iowa, 1967-1968. *Member:* Story County (Past President, 1968-1969), Iowa State (Member, Probate Section) and American Bar Associations. ***PRACTICE AREAS:*** Probate. ***Email:*** atty@newbroughlaw.com

JAMES A. BREWER, born Des Moines, Iowa, December 17, 1936; admitted to bar, 1961, Iowa; U.S. District Court, Northern and Southern Districts of Iowa; U.S. Court of Appeals, Eighth Circuit and U.S. Supreme Court. *Education:* Drake University (B.S., 1959; LL.B., 1961). *Member:* Story County (President, 1973), Iowa State and American Bar Associations; Iowa Academy of Trial Lawyers (Member, Board of Governors, 2000—)' Association of Trial Lawyers of Iowa (Member, Board of Governors, 1976-1979); Iowa Association of Workers Compensation Attorneys; American Board of Trial Advocates; Association of Defense Trial Attorneys. Fellow, American College of Trial Lawyers. ***PRACTICE AREAS:*** Civil Litigation; Personal Injury; Business Litigation; Products Liability; Professional Malpractice.

JERE C. MADDUX, born Detroit, Michigan, January 20, 1940; admitted to bar, 1971, Iowa; U.S. District Court, Northern and Southern Districts of Iowa and U.S. Court of Appeals, 8th Circuit. *Education:* Ottawa University (B.A., 1963); Drake University (J.D., 1971). Phi Alpha Delta. *Member:* Story County (President, 1981-1982), Iowa State and American Bar Associations; The Association of Trial Lawyers of America. [First Lieut., U.S. Army, active duty, 1963-1966 (one Vietnam tour)]. ***PRACTICE AREAS:*** Domestic Relations; Family Law; Wills; Estates; Probate Law. ***Email:*** atty@newbroughlaw.com

STEPHEN J. HOWELL, born Omaha, Nebraska, January 3, 1956; admitted to bar, 1997, Iowa. *Education:* University of Nebraska at Omaha (B.S., 1984); Drake University (J.D., 1997). Phi Alpha Delta. *Member:* Story County, Iowa State and American Bar Associations. ***PRACTICE AREAS:*** Corporate Law; Business Law; Real Estate; Wills; Estates. ***Email:*** showell@newbroughlaw.com

WILLIAM T. TALBOT, born Carroll, Iowa, November 27, 1951; admitted to bar, 1990, Iowa. *Education:* University of Northern Iowa (B.A., 1974); Drake University (J.D., with honors, 1989). Delta Theta Phi. *Member:* Story County Bar Association (President, 2004-2006). ***PRACTICE AREAS:*** Family Law; Criminal Law; Civil Practice; Trial Practice; Real Estate; Commercial Law.

ASSOCIATES

ANGELINA M. THOMAS, born Oceanside, California, June 24, 1969; admitted to bar, 1994, Iowa. *Education:* Iowa State University (B.S., 1990); University of Iowa (J.D., with distinction, 1994). Phi Alpha Delta. Member, University of Iowa Law Review, 1993-1994. Assistant Iowa Attorney General, Criminal Appeals Division, 1994-1996. Assistant County Attorney, 1996-2002 and Chief Criminal Assistant Attorney, 2002, Story County Attorney's Office. *Member:* Story County (President 2002-2003; Vice President, 2001-2002; Secretary-Treasurer, 2000-2001), Iowa State and American Bar Associations. ***PRACTICE AREAS:*** Civil Litigation; Personal Injury; Family Law; Criminal Defense. ***Email:*** athomaslaw@yahoo.com

EMIL PETERSON, born Worthington, Minnesota, October 8, 1946; admitted to bar, 1978, Illinois; 1989, Massachusetts; 1997, Iowa. *Education:* Augustana College (B.A., 1968); Chicago-Kent College of Law, Illinois Institute of Technology (J.D., with honors, 1978). *Member:* Story County and Iowa State Bar Associations. ***PRACTICE AREAS:*** Employee Benefits; ERISA; Real Estate; Probate; Business Law. ***Email:*** epeterson@newbroughlaw.com

OF COUNSEL

FRANK B. JOHNSTON, born Fort Dodge, Iowa, October 22, 1934; admitted to bar, 1961, Iowa. *Education:* University of Iowa (B.A., 1958; J.D., 1961). Phi Delta Phi. Assistant County Attorney, Story County, 1963-1964. *Member:* Story County (Secretary-Treasurer, 1961-1970; President, 1976-1977), Iowa State and American Bar Associations.

LOCAL COUNSEL: Todd & Sargent, Inc.; Northcrest, Inc. (Retirement home); American Home Assurance Co.; New Hampshire Insurance Group; Gary Thompson Oil Co.; First National Bank, Ames, Iowa; Greater Iowa Credit Union; Iowa State University Research Park;

(This Listing Continued)

NEWBROUGH, JOHNSTON, BREWER, MADDUX AND HOWELL, L.L.P., Ames—Continued

ALMACO; Swine Genetics International, Ltd.; United Fire and Casualty; Hawkeye Security Co.; First American Bank; Agora Group; Harold Pike Construction Co.; Nikkel & Associates, Inc.; Engineering Plus, Inc.
REFERENCES: First National Bank; Greater Iowa Credit Union.

NYEMASTER, GOODE, WEST, HANSELL & O'BRIEN

A PROFESSIONAL CORPORATION
1416 BUCKEYE AVENUE
AMES, IOWA 50010
Telephone: 515-233-3000
Telecopier: 515-232-3846
URL: http://www.nyemaster.com

Des Moines, Iowa Office: 700 Walnut, Suite 1600, Des Moines, Iowa 50309. Telephone: 515-283-3100. Telecopier: 515-283-3108.

General Civil Practice including Corporate, Securities, Antitrust, Insurance, Banking, Commercial Law, Cooperative Law, Probate, Real Estate, Taxation, Workers Compensation, Municipal, Legislative, Labor, Administrative Law and Trials in all Courts.

DAVID W. BENSON, born Marshalltown, Iowa, January 20, 1952; admitted to bar, 1978, Iowa, U.S. District Court, Southern and Northern Districts of Iowa and U.S. Tax Court. *Education:* Iowa State University (B.S., 1974); Creighton University (J.D., 1978). President, Story County Bar Association, 1991. (Resident). ***PRACTICE AREAS:*** Estate Planning; Estate Administration; Real Estate; Corporate Law; Taxation. ***Email:*** dwb@nyemaster.com

BRIAN J. HUMKE, born Iowa Falls, Iowa, April 6, 1956; admitted to bar, 1982, Iowa; 1985, U.S. District Court, Southern District of Iowa; 1989, U.S. District Court, Northern District of Iowa. *Education:* University of Northern Iowa (B.A., 1978); Drake University (J.D., 1981). Author: "The Evolution of Joint Custody in Iowa," 34 Drake Law Review 769; Case Note, "Settlement of Insurance Litigation Without Full Disclosure to the Insured: Rogers v. Robson, et al. (Illinois 1980)," 30 Drake Law Review. Instructor, Domestic Relations, Des Moines Area Community College, 1985; Teaching Assistant, Drake University Law School, 1980-1981. Member, 1988—, President, 1994-1995, 1998-1999, 2003-2004, Ankeny School Board. Director, Iowa Bar Review School, Inc, 1988-1994. *Member:* National Association of Criminal Defense Attorneys. ***PRACTICE AREAS:*** Civil Trial Practice; Criminal Trial Practice. ***Email:*** bjh@nyemaster.com

DEBORAH S. KRAUTH, born Atlantic, Iowa, July 23, 1952; admitted to bar, 1983, Iowa. *Education:* University of Northern Iowa (B.A., 1974); University of Iowa (J.D., with high honor, 1983). Recipient, Trial Lawyers Award. Law Clerk, Hon. George G. Fagg, Eighth Circuit Court of Appeals, 1990. *Member:* Iowa State Bar Association (Chair, General Practice Section Council, 1994-1995; Member, Council Probate Section, 2002-2005; Chair, 1997-1998; Member, Taxation Section Council, 1998-2001); Story County Bar Association. ***Email:*** dsk@nyemaster.com

BARRY NADLER, born Mason City, Iowa, May 15, 1956; admitted to bar, 1981, Iowa; 1982, U.S. District Court, Northern and Southern Districts of Iowa; 1992, U.S. Court of Appeals, Eighth Circuit; 1993, United States Supreme Court. *Education:* University of Iowa (B.A., with honors, 1978; J.D., with high distinction, 1981). Phi Beta Kappa; Phi Eta Sigma. Member, Iowa Law Review, 1981. Author: Note, "Avoiding the Iowa Hearsay Rule With Evidence of the Whole Story of the Crime," 66 Iowa Law Review 961 (1981). *Member:* Association of Trial Lawyers of Iowa; American Board of Trial Advocates. ***Email:*** bjn@nyemaster.com

All members, associates and of counsel are members of the Story County, Iowa State and American Bar Associations.

REPRESENTATIVE CLIENTS: The Burlington Northern and Santa Fe Railway Company; BP Amoco Co.; General Electric Co.; Deere & Co.; Chevron Chemical Co.; Eli Lilly and Co.; Monsanto Agricultural Co.; The Hertz Corp.; Aventis; 3M Corp.; HON Industries; The Waldinger Corp.; Equitable of Iowa Cos., Inc.; Wells Fargo Bank Iowa, N.A.; American International Group.; Wellmark Blue Cross and Blue Shield; Land O'Lakes; Iowa Automobile Dealers Assn.; Iowa Life and Health Insurance Assn.; Iowa Medical Society; Iowa Newspaper Assn.; Iowa Chapter, American Institute of Architects; Iowa Society of Certified Public Accountants; Iowa Grocery Industry Assn.; Hubbell Realty Co.; U-Haul International; Locust Street Securities; Iowa Health System; Grinnell College; American Insurance Assn.; CHUBB Group of Insurance Cos.; ING Groep N.V.; Novartis; Safeco Insurance Co.; GuideOne Insurance Group; The Iowa Clinic, P.C.; McFarland Clinic, P.C.; Amerus Life Insurance Co.; Story Construction Co.; Jacobson Warehouse Co., Inc.; Pepsi-Cola General Bottlers, Inc.; Mary Greeley Medical Center; Bank of America, N.A.; American Gas Assn.; Iowa Association of Electric Cooperatives; Qwest Communications Corp.; Lighthouse Communications, Inc.; Helena Chemical Co.; John Deere Health Care, Inc.; Alliant Energy; FPL Energy LLC; Midwest Renewable Energy Corporation; Meredith Corporation; The Cincinnati Insurance Cos.; American Family Mutual Insurance Co.; UNUMProvident Companies; LaSalle Bank National Association; AEGON N.V.

(For complete biographical data on all personnel, see Professional Biographies at Des Moines, Iowa)

PASLEY AND SINGER LAW FIRM, L.L.P.

323 SIXTH STREET
P.O. BOX 664
AMES, IOWA 50010
Telephone: 515-232-4732
Fax: 515-232-4756
Email: email@singerlaw.com

General Practice. Trials and Appeals in all Courts. Personal Injury and Tort Law, Commercial Litigation, Tax, Corporation, Insurance, Municipal, Adoption Law, Family Law, Probate, Trusts and Estates and Real Estate.

(This Listing Continued)

C.H. PASLEY (1876-1952)
ROBERT G. PASLEY (Retired)
WILLIAM A. SINGER (Retired)

MEMBERS OF FIRM

CLARKE A. PASLEY, born Ames, Iowa, March 4, 1941; admitted to bar, 1965, Iowa. *Education:* Iowa State University (B.S., 1963); University of Iowa (J.D., with distinction, 1965). Phi Delta Phi. Author, Case Comment, 49 Iowa Law Review 945. Assistant County Attorney, 1968-1972. Instructor, Real Estate, Iowa State University, 1984-1985. *Member:* Story County (President, 1977-1978), Iowa State and American Bar Associations. ***PRACTICE AREAS:*** Wills; Estate Planning; Probate; Business Organization; Corporate Law; Real Estate. ***Email:*** cap@singerlaw.com

STEVAN A. HOLM, born Cedar Rapids, Iowa, November 18, 1941; admitted to bar, 1966, Iowa. *Education:* University of Iowa (B.A., 1963; J.D., with distinction, 1966). Phi Delta Phi. Assistant County Attorney, Story County, Iowa, 1973-1975. Instructor, Business Law and Real Estate, Iowa State University, 1983-1990. *Member:* Story County (President, 1979-1980), Iowa State (Member, Title Standards Committee, 1991-1993) and American Bar Associations. [Capt., U.S. Army, J.A.G.C., 1966-1970]. ***PRACTICE AREAS:*** Real Estate; Probate; Wills; Trusts and Estates. ***Email:*** sholm@singerlaw.com

JOHN L. TIMMONS, born Washington, D.C., November 2, 1946; admitted to bar, 1975, Iowa and Minnesota; 1976, U.S. District Court, Southern and Northern Districts of Iowa; 1979, U.S. Supreme Court and U.S. Court of Appeals, Eighth Circuit; 1988, U.S. District Court, District of Minnesota; 1994 U.S. Court of Federal Claims. *Education:* Loras College; Iowa State University (B.S., honors, 1968); University of Iowa (J.D., with distinction, 1975). Law Clerk, Minnesota District Court, 1975-1976. Mediator, Alternative Dispute Resolution. *Member:* Story County (President, 1984-1985), Iowa State and American Bar Associations; Association of Trial Lawyers of Iowa; The Association of Trial Lawyers of America. ***PRACTICE AREAS:*** Litigation; Personal Injury; Torts; Professional Liability; Family Law. ***Email:*** jtimmons@singerlaw.com

JANE MELSON MATHISON, born Des Moines, Iowa, September 30, 1952; admitted to bar, 1977, Iowa and U.S. District Court, Southern and Northern Districts of Iowa; 1980, U.S. Supreme Court, U.S. Court of Appeals, 8th Circuit. *Education:* University of Strasbourg, France; Iowa State University (B.S., with distinction, 1974); University of Iowa (J.D., with distinction, 1977). Phi Beta Kappa; Order of the Coif; Phi Kappa Phi. *Member:* Story County (President, 1990-1991), Iowa State (Member, Committee on Professional Ethics and Conduct, 1990-1993; Adoption Committee, 1997—) and American Bar Associations. ***PRACTICE AREAS:*** Adoption Law; Family Law; Probate; Trusts and Estates; Real Estate. ***Email:*** jmathison@singerlaw.com

LARRY R. CURTIS, born Norman, Oklahoma, September 23, 1945; admitted to bar, 1973, Iowa; 1974, U.S. District Court, Northern and Southern Districts of Iowa; 1980, Minnesota. *Education:* Iowa State University (B.S., 1968); University of Iowa (M.B.A., 1973; J.D., 1973). Pi Tau Sigma. Adjunct Assistant Professor, Business Law, Iowa State University, 1973—. Councilman at Large, Ames City Council, 1979-1989. Mayor, 1989-1997. [Specialist 5th Class, U.S. Army, 1969-1970]. ***PRACTICE AREAS:*** Business Organization; Probate; Residential Real Estate. ***Email:*** lcurtis@singerlaw.com

SCOTT L. HIPPEN, born Fort Dodge, Iowa, November 21, 1960; admitted to bar, 1994, Iowa and U.S. District Court, Southern and Northern Districts of Iowa; 1998, U.S. Supreme Court. *Education:* Central University of Iowa (B.A., Economics, magna cum laude, 1983); Drake University (J.D., with honors, 1994); Iowa State University (M.S., Economics, 1995). Arbitrator, National Futures Association. *Member:* Story County and Iowa State Bar Associations. ***PRACTICE AREAS:*** Personal Injury; Torts; Family Law; Civil Litigation; Criminal Law; Probate; Estate Planning. ***Email:*** shippen@singerlaw.com

ALEXANDER P. GALYON, born Bloomington, Indiana, April 14, 1959; admitted to bar, 1994, Iowa, U.S. District Court, Southern and Northern Districts of Iowa and U.S. Court of Appeals, Eighth Circuit. *Education:* Iowa State University (B.S., 1987); Drake University (J.D., with honors, 1994). *Member:* Story County and Iowa State Bar Associations. ***PRACTICE AREAS:*** Real Estate; Bankruptcy; Family Law; Juvenile Law; Criminal Law; Probate. ***Email:*** apgalyon@singerlaw.com

References available upon request.

EELLS & TRONVOLD LAW OFFICES, P.L.C.

ANAMOSA, IOWA

(See Cedar Rapids)

General Practice with emphasis on Personal Injury, Litigation, Probate and Estate Planning, Trusts and Wills, Business Law and Mediation.

WHITE & JOHNSON, P.C.

ANAMOSA, IOWA

(See Cedar Rapids)

General Practice. Trials, Personal Injury, Insurance, Workers' Compensation, Tax, Corporate, Real Estate, Probate, Domestic Relations.

WILLIAM J. BRIBRIESCO & ASSOCIATES

2407 18TH STREET, SUITE 200
BETTENDORF, IOWA 52722
Telephone: 563-359-8266
Fax: 563-359-5010
URL: http://www.wjbribriescolaw.com

Personal Injury, Workers Compensation, Products Liability, Business Law.

(This Listing Continued)

WILLIAM J. BRIBRIESCO, born Davenport, Iowa, May 28, 1955; admitted to bar, 1981, Iowa. *Education:* University of Iowa (B.B.A., 1978; J.D. 1980). *Member:* Scott County and Iowa State Bar Associations; Iowa Trial Lawyers Association; The Association of Trial Lawyers of America. ***PRACTICE AREAS:*** Personal Injury; Workers Compensation.

ASSOCIATE

DANIEL BERNSTEIN, born Chicago, Illinois, September 10, 1951; admitted to bar, 1995, Minnesota; 1996, Iowa. *Education:* University of Iowa (B.S., 1976; J.D., 1995). *Member:* Iowa State Bar Association (Member, Young Lawyers Division); Iowa Trial Lawyers Association; The Association of Trial Lawyers of America. ***PRACTICE AREAS:*** Personal Injury; Workers Compensation; Products Liability; Business Law.

GALLAGHER, MILLAGE & GALLAGHER

BETTENDORF, IOWA

(See Davenport)

General Civil Practice, including Business, Banking, Real Estate and Corporate Law, Business Transactions, Trusts and Estates, Wills and Probate, and General Litigation.

GOSMA, TARBOX & ASSOCIATES, P.L.C.

BETTENDORF, IOWA

(See Davenport)

General Civil Practice, including Business and Corporate Organization and Transactions, Banking, Real Estate, Estate Planning, Elder Law, Trust and Estate Administration, and Personal Injury, Business and Probate Litigation, Medical Malpractice, Business Enterprises, Slip and Fall, Personal Injury, Automobile Accidents, Wrongful Death, Buying and Selling, Zoning and Land Use, Construction, Asset Protection, Guardianships, Banking and Finance, Closely Held Business, Corporate, Franchise, Limited Liability, Small Business, Partnerships, Buying and Selling of Businesses, Creditors Rights, Contracts, Business Planning, Law Suites, Insurance, Commercial Leasing, Business Start-Ups.

KERSTEN BROWNLEE HENDRICKS, LLP

BOONE, IOWA

(See Fort Dodge)

General Practice. Personal Injury Law, Corporation, Insurance Defense, Workers Compensation, Bankruptcy, Banking, Probate and Estate Planning and Taxation Law. Trials.

ASPELMEIER, FISCH, POWER, ENGBERG & HELLING, P.L.C.

Established in 1877

FIRST FEDERAL SAVINGS BANK
321 NORTH THIRD STREET
P.O. BOX 1046
BURLINGTON, IOWA 52601
Telephone: 319-754-6587
Fax: 319-754-7514

Mediapolis, Iowa Office: 621 Main Street. Telephone: 319-394-3136. Fax: 319-394-3493. *West Point, Iowa Office:* 420 Avenue "E". Telephone: 319-837-6614. Fax: 319-837-8813.

Insurance Defense, Estate Planning, Real Estate, Municipal Law, Negligence, Corporate Law, Probate, Taxation, Banking Law, Personal Injury, Workers Compensation, Civil Trial Practice in all State and Federal Courts.

John J. Seerley	1877-1884
Seerley & Clark	1884-1928
Seerley, Clark & Hale	1928-1935
Clark, Hale & Plock	1935-1938
Clark, Pryor, Hale & Plock	1938-1948
Clark, Pryor, Hale, Plock & Riley	1948-1952
Pryor, Hale, Plock, Riley & Jones	1952-1959
Pryor, Riley, Jones & Walsh	1959-1976
Pryor, Riley, Jones & Aspelmeier	1976-1985
Aspelmeier, Fisch, Power, Warner & Engberg	1985-2001

JAMES F. FISCH, born Le Mars, Iowa, February 11, 1940; admitted to bar, 1965, Iowa. *Education:* St. John's University (B.A., 1962); University of Iowa (J.D., 1965). *Member:* Des Moines County (President, 1978-1979) and Iowa State Bar Associations.

WILLIAM SCOTT POWER, born Lambs Grove, Iowa, March 16, 1945; admitted to bar, 1971, Iowa, U.S. District Court, Southern District of Iowa and U.S. Court of Appeals, Eighth Circuit. *Education:* University of Iowa (B.A., with high distinction, 1967; J.D., with distinction, 1971). Phi Beta Kappa. Part-time U.S. Magistrate Judge, 1972-1997. *Member:* Des Moines County (President, 1984-1985) and Iowa State Bar Associations.

ROBERT A. ENGBERG, born Burlington, Iowa, August 13, 1946; admitted to bar, 1973, Iowa; 1978, U.S. Supreme Court. *Education:* University of Iowa (B.B.A., 1968; J.D., with distinction, 1973). Des Moines County Magistrate, 1973-1974. Member, State Judicial Nominating Commission, 1987-1993. *Member:* Des Moines County (President, 1987-1988), Iowa State (Member, Litigation Section) and American Bar Associations; Defense Research Institute; Iowa Defense Counsel Association (Member, Board of Directors, 1987—; Secretary, 1994-1995; President-Elect, 1995-1996; President, 1996-1997).

BRIAN J. HELLING, born Fort Madison, Iowa, August 27, 1964; admitted to bar, 1989, Iowa and Illinois. *Education:* Southeastern Community College (A.A., 1984); University of Iowa (B.B.A., 1986; J.D., with distinction, 1989). Certified Public Accountant, Iowa, 1993. *Member:* Des Moines County, Iowa State, Illinois State and American Bar Associations.

WILLIAM R. JAHN, JR., born Iowa City, Iowa, February 5, 1969; admitted to bar, 1994, Iowa; 1997, U.S. District Court, Southern District of Iowa. *Education:* Grinnell College (B.A., with honors, 1991); University of Iowa (J.D., with distinction, 1994). *Member:* Des Moines County and Iowa State Bar Association.

BRENT RUTHER, born Burlington, Iowa, January 10, 1968; admitted to bar, 1993, Colorado; 1995, U.S. District Court, District of Colorado; 1997, U.S. Court of Appeals, Tenth Circuit; 1999, Iowa and U.S. District Court, Southern District of Iowa; 2000, U.S. Court of Appeals, Eighth Circuit. *Education:* University of Iowa (B.A., Psychology, 1990); University of Denver (J.D., 1993). *Member:* Colorado, Des Moines County and Iowa State Bar Associations; Iowa Defense Counsel Association (Member, Board of Directors, 2001—); Defense Research Institute.

WYATT P. PETERSON, born Mount Pleasant, Iowa, April 12, 1978; admitted to bar, 2003, Iowa and U.S. District Court, Southern District of Iowa. *Education:* Iowa State University (B.S., Agricultural Business, 2000); Drake University (J.D., with honors, 2003). Editor-in-Chief, Drake Journal of Agricultural Law, 2002-2003. *Member:* Des Moines County, Iowa State (District Representative, Young Lawyers Division, 2004—) and American Bar Associations; Iowa State Bar Review School (Board of Directors, 2003—).

OF COUNSEL

KENNETH A. ASPELMEIER, born Burlington, Iowa, March 21, 1935; admitted to bar, 1960, Iowa. *Education:* Parsons College (B.A., 1957); New York University (LL.B., 1960). *Member:* Des Moines County (President, 1972-1973) and Iowa State (Member, Committee on Probate, Property and Trust Law, 1982-1987) Bar Associations.

GENERAL COUNSEL FOR: Mediapolis Savings Bank; Pilot Grove Savings Bank; City of Mediapolis, Iowa; City of West Point, Iowa; Winegard Realty Co.; City of Burlington, Iowa; Burlington Municipal Waterworks; West Point Municipal Utility; Des Moines County Drainage Districts Nos. 7 and 8; Louisa-Des Moines Drainage District No. 4; Iowa River-Flint Creek Levee District No. 16; Green Bay Levee and Drainage District; First Federal Savings Bank of Iowa (Burlington Branch); City of St. Paul, Iowa..
INSURANCE COMPANY CLIENTS: EMC Insurance Companies; Iowa Mutual Insurance Co.; Metropolitan life Insurance Co.; Mutual Fire and Automobile Insurance Co.; Hawkeye Security Insurance Co.; United Fire & Casualty Co.; United Security Insurance Co.; Farm Bureau Mutual Insurance Co.; Heritage Cos.; Auto-Owners Insurance Co.; Tri-State Insurance Company of Minnesota; Farm & City Insurance Co.; West Bend Mutual Insurance Co.; Country Mutual Insurance Company.

BECKMAN AND HIRSCH

Established in 1901

314 NORTH FOURTH STREET
BURLINGTON, IOWA 52601
Telephone: 319-754-8404
Fax: 319-754-6302
URL: http://www.iowalaw.com

Personal Injury, Appeals, Corporation, Taxation, Probate, Insurance, Real Estate, Criminal Defense, Commercial Litigation, Computer Law, Family Law, General Trial Practice in State and Federal Courts.

STEPHEN J. BECKMAN (1873-1950)

RICHARD R. BECKMAN (1915-1993)

DAVID D. BECKMAN, born Burlington, Iowa, 1950; admitted to bar, 1976, Iowa. *Education:* Iowa State University (B.S.I.E., 1973); University of Iowa (M.B.A., J.D., 1976). Gamma Epsilon Sigma. Certified Public Accountant, Iowa, 1977. Member, Iowa Supreme Court Commission on Courts in the 21st Century (Team Co-Chair, Steering Committee). *Member:* Des Moines County (President, 1994-1995), Iowa State (Member, Board of Governors, 1990-1996; President, 1998-1999; Chair, Technology Committee, 1999—) and American (Chair, Lotus Notes Interest Group, 1994-1998; Member, Commission on Responsibility in Client Development, 1999—, Chair, 2000—) Bar Associations; American Institute of Certified Public Accountants; Iowa Society of Certified Public Accountants (Member, Board of Directors; Secretary, Executive Committee, 1985-1988; Member, Ethics Committee, 1988—; Chair, By Laws Committee, 1987-1989; Member, Continuing Professional Education Committee, 1983-1986). Fellow, Iowa State Bar Foundation. ***PRACTICE AREAS:*** Tax Law; Probate Law; Real Estate; General Practice; Corporate Law; Computer Law. ***Email:*** ddb@iowalaw.com

DAVID A. HIRSCH, born Chicago Heights, Illinois, 1947; admitted to bar, 1973, Iowa. *Education:* Michigan State University (B.S., 1970); University of Iowa (J.D., with distinction, 1973). Law Clerk to Justice Clay LeGrand, Iowa Supreme Court, 1973-1974. *Member:* Des Moines County (President, 1990-1991), Iowa State (Member, Judicial Administration Committee, 1994— and Multi Jurisdictional Practice Committee, 2001—) and American Bar Associations; The Association of Trial Lawyers of America; The Iowa Trial Lawyers Association. ***PRACTICE AREAS:*** Litigation; Personal Injury; Appeals; Corporate Law; Insurance; Real Estate; Criminal Law; General Practice; Insurance Defense; Computer Law; Commercial Litigation. ***Email:*** david@iowalaw.com

ASSOCIATE

JENNIFER E. KLEVER-KIRKMAN, born Independence, Iowa, 1980; admitted to bar, 2005, Iowa, U.S. District Court, Northern and Southern Districts of Iowa, U.S. Court of Appeals and U.S. Tax Court. *Education:* University of Iowa (B.A. with Honors in Communication Studies, 2001; International Business Certificate, 2001); University of Iowa (J.D, 2004). Moot Court Board Member., 2003-2004. Recipient, Glovka Trial Advocacy Law Foundation Scholarship, 2004. Quarterfinalist VanOosterhout Moot Court Competition, 2003. Finalist, Roy L. Stephenson Trial Advocacy Competition, 2003. Director Roy L. Stephenson Trial Advocacy Competition, 2004. Trial Advocacy Board Member, 2004.

(This Listing Continued)

(This Listing Continued)

BECKMAN AND HIRSCH, Burlington—Continued

Member: Des Moines County, Iowa State and American Bar Associations; Iowa Trial Lawyers Association; Iowa Organization of Women Attorneys. ***PRACTICE AREAS:*** General Practice; Litigation; Family Law; Criminal Law; Commercial Law; Personal Injury.

WILLIAM J. BRIBRIESCO & ASSOCIATES

BURLINGTON, IOWA

(See Bettendorf)

Personal Injury, Workers Compensation, Products Liability, Business Law.

ROBBERTS LAW OFFICE

205 WASHINGTON STREET, SUITE 201
P.O. BOX 427
BURLINGTON, IOWA 52601
Telephone: 319-758-9800
Fax: 319-758-9801
Email: rloffice1001@qwest.net
URL: http://www.robbertslawoffice.com

Family Law, Divorce, Personal Injury, Appellate Practice, Corporate Law, Litigation, Probate, Insurance, Real Estate, Criminal Law, General Practice.

MARLIS J. ROBBERTS, born Council Bluffs, Iowa, March 14, 1971; admitted to bar, 1997, Iowa; 2000, Illinois. *Education:* University of Northern Iowa (B.A., 1993); University of Iowa (J.D., with distinction, 1997). Member, Grievance Commission, Supreme Court of Iowa, 1999-2005. *Member:* Des Moines County, Iowa State, Illinois State and American Bar Associations; The Association of Trial Lawyers of America; Iowa Trial Lawyers Association. ***PRACTICE AREAS:*** Family Law; Divorce; Personal Injury; Appellate Practice; Corporate Law; Litigation; Probate; Insurance; Real Estate; Criminal Law; General Practice.

BEECHER, FIELD, WALKER, MORRIS, HOFFMAN & JOHNSON, P.C.

CEDAR FALLS, IOWA

(See Waterloo)

General Practice. Taxation, Real Estate, Probate, Estate Planning, Trust and Corporation Law, Bankruptcy, Personal Injury, Family Law, Banking, Environmental, Workers Compensation, Health Care, Employment Law, Social Security, Business Litigation, Consumer and Commercial Collections.

EELLS & TRONVOLD LAW OFFICES, P.L.C.

CEDAR FALLS, IOWA

(See Cedar Rapids)

General Practice with emphasis on Personal Injury, Litigation, Probate and Estate Planning, Trusts and Wills, Business Law and Mediation.

LAW OFFICES OF C. KEVIN McCRINDLE

CEDAR FALLS, IOWA

(See Waterloo)

Agricultural Law, Business Planning, Real Estate, Probate, Estate Planning, Trusts and Estates, Taxation and Health Care.

McGUIRE LAW FIRM, P.C.

CEDAR FALLS, IOWA

(See Mason City)

Personal Injury Law, Medical Malpractice, Severe Burns, Water Heater Flammable Vapor Litigation, Products Liability, Railroad Litigation, Trial Practice.

REDFERN, MASON, DIETER, LARSEN & MOORE, P.L.C.

Established in 1898
415 CLAY STREET
P.O. BOX 627
CEDAR FALLS, IOWA 50613
Telephone: 319-277-6830
Facsimile: 319-277-3531
Email: RMDLM@cflaw.com
URL: http://www.cflaw.com

Insurance, Litigation, Medical Malpractice and Product Liability, Wills, Trusts, Estate Planning and Probate Law, Taxation and Tax Returns, Labor Law, Employment Law, Commercial Law, Contracts, Elder Law, Mergers and Acquisitions, Trial Law, Workers' Compensation, Franchise Law, Municipal Law, Real Estate, Business Law, Corporate Law, Family Law, Public Utility Law, Civil Trial Practice in all Courts.

(This Listing Continued)

JAMES B. NEWMAN (1870-1958)

GEORGE F. NEWMAN (1908-1988)

WILLIAM W. McKINLEY (1926-1981)

LeROY H. REDFERN, born Peru, Nebraska, April 16, 1919; admitted to bar, 1948, Iowa; 1975, U.S. Tax Court. *Education:* Nebraska State College, Peru (A.B., 1941); University of Michigan (J.D., 1948). Recipient: Community Service Award, 2001; Peru State College Distinguished Service Award, 2002. Assistant Editor, Michigan Law Review, 1947-1948. City Attorney, Cedar Falls, 1951-1955. Member, Title Guaranty Division Board, Iowa Finance Authority, 1985-1989. *Member:* Black Hawk County (President, 1963-1964), Iowa State (Chairman, Committee on Title Standards, 1967-1989; Member, Probate, Property and Trust Law Committee, 1965-1975; Recipient, Award of Merit, 1979) and American Bar Associations; American Bar Foundation. ***PRACTICE AREAS:*** Probate; Real Estate.

DAVID R. MASON, born Elma, Iowa, July 20, 1944; admitted to bar, 1969, Iowa; 1972, U.S. District Court, Northern District of Iowa; 1975, U.S. Tax Court. *Education:* University of Iowa (B.A., 1966; J.D., 1969). Phi Eta Sigma; Phi Beta Kappa; Phi Alpha Delta. Assistant City Attorney, Cedar Falls, 1973-1977. Iowa Board of Law Examiners, 1996-2005. *Member:* Black Hawk County, Iowa State (Member, Board of Governors, 1989-1995; Chair, Lawyers Professional Liability Insurance Committee, 1994—, Chair, 1997-2000; Strategic Planning Committee, 2002-2003) and American Bar Associations; American Bar Foundation; Iowa Academy of Trial Lawyers; Iowa Defense Counsel Association; Iowa Bar Foundation. [First Lieut., U.S. Army, 1969-1971]. ***Email:*** mason@cflaw.com

ROBERT J. DIETER, born Carroll, Iowa, September 30, 1946; admitted to bar, 1974, Iowa; 1976, U.S. District Court, Northern District of Iowa; 1979, U.S. District Court, Southern District of Iowa. *Education:* University of Northern Iowa (B.A., 1972); University of Iowa (J.D., with distinction, 1974). American Association of Alternative Dispute Resolution Attorneys. *Member:* Black Hawk County and Iowa State (Member, Sections on: Real Estate, Mediation) Bar Associations. ***PRACTICE AREAS:*** Mediation; Real Estate; Civil Litigation; Business Litigation. ***Email:*** rjdieter@cflaw.com

JOHN C. LARSEN, born Waterloo, Iowa, March 28, 1953; admitted to bar, 1978, Iowa; 1980, U.S. District Court, Northern District of Iowa. *Education:* Wartburg College (B.A., summa cum laude, 1975); University of Iowa (J.D., with high distinction, 1978). Alpha Chi. *Member:* Black Hawk County (President, 1989-1990; Member, Estate Planning Council), Iowa State (Member, Probate and Trust Law, Real Estate and Title Law, and Business Law Sections) and American Bar Associations. ***Email:*** jclarsen@cflaw.com

STEVEN D. MOORE, born Omaha, Nebraska, May 19, 1950; admitted to bar, 1975, Iowa; 1980, U.S. District Court, Northern District of Iowa. *Education:* University of Iowa (B.A., with highest distinction, 1972; J.D., with high distinction, 1975); George Washington Law Center (LL.M. in Taxation, 1978). Phi Beta Kappa; Order of the Coif; Phi Eta Sigma. Co-editor, Journal of Corporation Law, 1974-1975. Author, Case Comment, "From Brophy to Diamond to Schein: Muddled Thinking, Excellent Result," 1 Journal of Corporation Law 83 (1975). Assistant County Attorney, Black Hawk County, 1978-1985. Assistant City Attorney, 1986-1999; City Attorney, 1999—, City of Cedar Falls. *Member:* Black Hawk County (Member, Estate Planning Council, Title Standards Committee) and Iowa State (Member, Sections on: Taxation Law, Probate and Trust Law, Real Estate, Title Law and Government Practice) Bar Associations; Iowa Municipal Attorneys Association. [Lt., J.A.G.C., U.S. Navy, 1975-1978]. ***Email:*** moore@cflaw.com

DONALD B. REDFERN, born Nebraska City, Nebraska, June 9, 1945; admitted to bar, 1973, Ohio; 1976, California; 1982, Iowa and Minnesota; U.S. District Court, Northern and Southern Districts of Iowa; U.S. District Court, Northern and Central Districts of California; U.S. Court of Appeals, Eighth Circuit. *Education:* Carleton College (B.A., 1967); Columbia University (J.D., 1973). State Senator, 1993—. *Member:* Black Hawk County, Iowa State and American Bar Associations; Iowa Bar Foundation. ***Email:*** dbredfern@cflaw.com

MARK W. FRANSDAL, born Willmar, Minnesota, February 20, 1960; admitted to bar, 1985, Iowa; 1988, U.S. District Court, Northern District of Iowa; 1992, U.S. District Court, Southern District of Iowa. *Education:* University of Iowa (B.B.A., with high distinction, 1982; J.D., with honors, 1985). Beta Gamma Sigma. Assistant County Attorney, Black Hawk County, 1985-1990. *Member:* Black Hawk County, Iowa State (Member, Litigation and Workers Compensation Law Sections) and American Bar Associations; The Association of Trial Lawyers of America; Iowa Trial Lawyers Association. ***PRACTICE AREAS:*** Personal Injury Litigation; Insurance Litigation; Employment Litigation. ***Email:*** mwfransdal@cflaw.com

MARK S. ROLINGER, born Waterloo, Iowa, October 16, 1965; admitted to bar, 1991, Iowa and U.S. District Court, Northern District of Iowa. *Education:* Wartburg College (B.A., cum laude, 1988); University of Iowa (J.D., with distinction, 1991). Phi Delta Phi. *Member:* Black Hawk County, Iowa State (Member, Business Law, Probate and Trust Law, Real Estate and Title Law Sections) and American Bar Associations. ***Email:*** mrolinger@cflaw.com

BRUCE L. GETTMAN, JR., born Mason City, Iowa, January 29, 1959; admitted to bar, 1985, Iowa and U.S. District Court, Northern District of Iowa. *Education:* North Iowa Area Community College (A.A., 1979); University of Iowa (B.A., 1982); University of Arkansas (J.D., 1985). *Member:* Black Hawk County and Iowa State (Advisory Rules Committee for Association Workers Compensation Section; Litigation Section) Bar Associations; Iowa Association Workers Compensation Lawyers; Iowa Defense Council Association (Member Jury Instructions Committee); Iowa Trial Lawyers Association;. ***PRACTICE AREAS:*** Workers Compensation Law; Insurance Defense Litigation; Personal Injury Litigation. ***Email:*** bgettman@cflaw.com

ASSOCIATES

MICHAEL J. MILLER, born Strawberry Point, Iowa, April 25, 1976; admitted to bar, 2002, Iowa. *Education:* University of Iowa (B.A., with honors and highest distinction, 1998; J.D., with high distinction, 2002). *Member:* Black Hawk County and Iowa State Bar Associations. ***Email:*** miller@cflaw.com

(This Listing Continued)

CHET A. MELLEMA, born Mason City, Iowa, December 9, 1977; admitted to bar, 2003, Iowa. *Education:* Drake University (B.S., 2000); University of Iowa (J.D., 2003). **Email:** mellema@cflaw.com

DAVID H. MASON, JR., born Cedar Falls, Iowa, November 6, 1972; admitted to bar, 1998, Minnesota; 2005, Iowa. *Education:* Miami University (B.S., magna cum laude, 1995); University of Iowa (J.D., with distinction, 1998). ***PRACTICE AREAS:*** Business Law. **Email:** masonjr@cflaw.com

REPRESENTATIVE CLIENTS: Wells Fargo Bank Iowa N.A.; Community National Bank; Cedar Falls Utilities; City of Cedar Falls; University of Northern Iowa Foundation; Cedar Falls Community School District; Fireman's Fund Insurance Cos.; Cincinnati Insurance Co.; Secura Companies; Northwestern National Insurance Group; Newcor, Inc.; Standard Golf Co.; Lockard Development, Inc.; Martin Brothers Distributing Co., Inc.; Cedar Falls Construction Co., Inc.; University of Northern Iowa Credit Union; Hawkeye Corrugated Box Co.; Blue Line Moving & Storage, Inc.; Holdiman Motor, Inc.; Waterloo Wood Bearing Company; Heating & Cooling Supply Co.; Iowa Laser Technology, Inc.; Iowa Metal Spinners, Inc.; Pekin Ins. Co.; Safeco Ins. Co.; Bituminous Ins. Co.; Symons-Pafco/Superior Ins. Co.; GRE/Globe Ins. Co.; Old Republic Ins. Co.; Continental Western Ins. Co.; The St. Paul Companies; EBI-The Net Worth Advisors; State Farm Ins. Co.; ANPAC Ins. Co.; United Jackson Companies; Black Hawk Economic Development, Inc.; Omega Cabinets, Ltd.; Jerry Roling Motors, Inc.; Trapp & Associates Realtors, Inc.; HealthCare Solutions, Inc.; Power Engineering and Manufacturing, Ltd.; Atlantic Mutual Ins. Co.

BRADLEY & RILEY PC

Attorneys and Counselors

Established in 1981

2007 FIRST AVENUE SE

P.O. BOX 2804

CEDAR RAPIDS, IOWA 52406-2804

Telephone: 319-363-0101

Fax: 319-363-9824

URL: http://www.bradleyriley.com

Iowa City, Iowa Office: One South Gilbert Street, 52240-3914. Telephone: 319-466-1511. Fax: 319-358-5560.

General Practice, Administrative, Antitrust, Arbitration, Banking, Bankruptcy, Civil Trial and Appellate Practice in all State and Federal Courts, Condominiums, Construction, Copyright, Corporate, E-Commerce, Employee Benefits, Environmental, Estate Planning, General Business, Government, Immigration, Insurance, Intellectual Property Labor and Employment Relations, Land Use, Mergers and Acquisitions, Municipal Bonds, Non-Profit, Pension and Profit Sharing, Personal Injury, Probate, Product Liability, Professional Liability, Real Estate, Securities, Taxation, Trademark and Trust Law.

F. JAMES BRADLEY, born Bancroft, Iowa, May 7, 1927; admitted to bar, 1950, Iowa. *Education:* Loras College and University of Iowa (B.A., 1948); University of Iowa (J.D., 1950). Delta Theta Phi. Member, Board of Editors, Iowa Law Review, 1950. Recipient, Iowa Bar Association Award of Merit, 1983. Member: Iowa Supreme Court Judicial Nominating Commission, 1965-1971; District Court Judicial Nominating Commission, 1964-1971; Iowa Supreme Court Advisory Council, 1975-1976. Member, Iowa Client Security and Attorney Disciplinary Commission, 1986-1995; Chairman, 1995. *Member:* Linn County (President, 1967-1968; Member, Board of Governors, 1968-1970, 1984-1985), Iowa State (Member: Special Committee on Corporation and Business Law, 1963-1974; Board of Governors, 1972-1974; Vice President, 1974-1975; President-Elect, 1975-1976; President, 1976-1977; Chairman, Scope and Correlation Committee, 1977-1984; Member, 1995-1997 and American (Member, House of Delegates, 1982-1988) Bar Associations. Fellow: Iowa State Bar Foundation; American College of Trust and Estate Counsel; American Bar Foundation. ***PRACTICE AREAS:*** Estate Planning; Probate; Corporate Law; Business Law. **Email:** jbradley@bradleyriley.com

BYRON G. RILEY, born Burlington, Iowa, December 7, 1930; admitted to bar, 1957, Iowa. *Education:* University of Iowa (B.S.C., 1952; J.D., with distinction, 1957). Phi Delta Phi. Member, Board of Editors, Iowa Law Review, 1956-1957. *Member:* Linn County (President, 1990-1991), Iowa State (President, Junior Bar Section, 1964-1965; Chairman, Special Committee on Prepaid Legal Services, 1974-1976; Member, Committee on Corporation and Business Law, 1979-1983; Member, Board of Governors, 1983-1988; Member: Probate, Property and Trust Law Section, 1990—; Corporate Counsel Section, 1990-1997) and American Bar Associations. Fellow, American College of Trust and Estate Lawyers and the American Bar Foundation. ***PRACTICE AREAS:*** Wills, Trusts, Estates and Probate; Corporation and Business Law; Family Business Successions; Taxation. **Email:** briley@bradleyriley.com

MICHAEL K. DENNEY, born Leavenworth, Kansas, October 8, 1948; admitted to bar, 1973, Iowa, Kansas and U.S. District Court, Northern and Southern Districts of Iowa. *Education:* University of Kansas (B.S., 1970; J.D. with honors, 1973). Order of the Coif. Member: Moot Court Board, 1971-1972; Board of Governors, Kansas Law Review, 1972-1973. *Member:* Linn County (Secretary, 1987-1989), Iowa State (Member, Bar Economics and Law Operations Committee, 1981-1989; Chairman, 1986-1989; Member, Corporations and Business Law Committee, 1989-1990; Member, Council of Corporation, Banking and Business Law Section, 1990-1993), Kansas and American Bar Associations. ***PRACTICE AREAS:*** Business Law; Securities Law; Mergers and Acquisitions; Corporate Law. **Email:** mdenney@bradleyriley.com

PATRICK M. COURTNEY, born Fort Dodge, Iowa, August 30, 1949; admitted to bar, 1974, Iowa, Nebraska and U.S. District Court, Northern and Southern Districts of Iowa; 1982, U.S. Tax Court and U.S. Court of Appeals, Eighth Circuit. *Education:* University of Iowa (B.B.A., 1971); Creighton University (J.D., 1974); Georgetown University (LL.M. in Taxation, 1980). Certified Public Accountant, District of Columbia, 1981. Staff Attorney, Office of Associate Chief Counsel, Technical, Internal Revenue Service, Washington, D.C., 1976-1982. State of Iowa Reporter, American Bar Association Real Property, Probate and Trust Committee on Significant Developments in Iowa. *Member:* Linn County, Iowa State (Council Member, Section on Taxation, 1982-1992) and American Bar Associations; American Association of Attorney-Certified Public Accountants; Iowa Society of Certified

(This Listing Continued)

Public Accountants. Fellow, American College of Trust and Estate Counsel. ***PRACTICE AREAS:*** Taxation; Corporation and Business Law; Wills, Estate and Probate; Estate Planning. **Email:** pcourtney@bradleyriley.com

DONALD G. THOMPSON, born Grand Island, Nebraska, July 1, 1949; admitted to bar, 1976, Nebraska, U.S. District Court, District of Nebraska and U.S. Court of Appeals, Eighth Circuit; 1983, Iowa and U.S. District Court, Northern and Southern Districts of Iowa; 1990, U.S. Supreme Court; 1992, U.S. District Court, Central District of Illinois; 1993, U.S. Court of Appeals, Seventh Circuit and U.S. Tax Court. *Education:* University of Nebraska at Lincoln (B.A., 1971; J.D., with distinction, 1976). Order of the Coif. Member, 1974-1975 and Competition Supervisor, 1975-1976, Allen Moot Court Board. Faculty Member: National Institute for Trial Advocacy, Mid-America Regional, 1984-1985, 1988-1991, 1994; Pacific Regional, 1990-1991; Southern California Regional, 1991; Deposition Program, Denver, 1990, 1992; Drake Legal Services Program, 2003. Past President, Dean Mason L. Ladd Inn of Court, 1991-1992. *Member:* Linn County, Iowa State (Chair, Federal Practice Committee, 1991-1995; Litigation Section Council, 1996-1999; Law Practice Management Section Council, 2000-2003), Nebraska State and American (Construction Industry Forum-Iowa Casenotes Editor of Construct, 2001—; Dispute Resolution, Law Practice Management, and Litigation Sections) Bar Associations; Iowa Trial Lawyers Association; The Association of Trial Lawyers of America; Defense Research Institute. ***PRACTICE AREAS:*** Civil Trials; Commercial Litigation; Construction Law; Appeals; Mediation; Arbitration. **Email:** dthompson@bradleyriley.com

KELLY R. BAIER, born Creston, Iowa, February 20, 1953; admitted to bar, 1979, Iowa and District of Columbia; 1982, U.S. District Court, District of Columbia; 1983, U.S. District Court, Northern and Southern Districts of Iowa and U.S. Court of Appeals for the District of Columbia Circuit; 1993, Central District of Illinois Court of Appeals, Eighth Circuit. *Education:* Iowa State University (B.A., with distinction, 1975); University of Iowa (J.D., with high distinction, 1978; M.A., 1979). Phi Beta Kappa; Phi Kappa Phi; Order of the Coif. Adjunct Assistant Professor, University of Iowa College of Law and College of Business, 1994-1995, 2002. Contributing Author: "Issues in the Evolving Use of Arbitration Agreements by Employers," 2005; "Settlement and Mediation of Employment Law Claims," 2003; "Dealing with FMLA, ADA and Workers Compensation Benefits," 2002; "The FMLA, ADA and Workers Compensation: Confusion to the Third Degree," 1999; "Wrongful Termination in Retaliation for Seeking Worker's Compensation Benefits," 1999; "Terminating Employees in Light of the FMLA and the ADA: Protecting Your Business From Lawsuits and Substandard Work Performance," 1998; "Employment and Labor Law in Iowa," 1998; "Employment Trade Secret Litigation," 1998; "Employment and Labor Law in Iowa," 1997; "Employment and Labor Law in Iowa," 1996; "Preventing and Defending Sexual Harassment Claims in Iowa," 1996; "Defending Wrongful Discharge Claims," 1995; "Employment and Labor Law in Iowa," 1995; Practical Evolution of the American With Disabilities Act in Iowa," 1995; "Discharge and Documentation in Iowa," 1995; "A Hands on Approach to Labor and Employment Law in Iowa," 1995. *Member:* Linn County (Member, Board of Governors, 1992-1993, 2001-2004; President, 2002-2003), Iowa State (Member, Labor Law Committee, 1984-1990; Labor and Employment Law Section, 1990—; Labor and Employment Law Council, 1990-1993, 1996-1999) and American Bar Associations; Industrial Relations Research Association. ***PRACTICE AREAS:*** Discrimination and Civil Rights Law; Labor and Employment Law; Civil Trials. **Email:** kbaier@bradleyriley.com

GREGORY J. SEYFER, born Cedar Rapids, Iowa, September 26, 1954; admitted to bar, 1979, Iowa and U.S. District Court, Northern and Southern Districts of Iowa. *Education:* Drake University (B.A., cum laude, 1976; J.D., with honors, 1979). Phi Alpha Delta. *Member:* Linn County (Member, Title Standards Committee, 1984—), Iowa State (Member: Title Standards Committee, 1988; Young Lawyers Section, Real Estate Practice Manual, 1989 and 1990; Real Property Committee, 1991-1996 and 2000—) and American Bar Associations. ***PRACTICE AREAS:*** Real Estate Law; Banking and Credit Union Law. **Email:** gseyfer@bradleyriley.com

DEAN A. SPINA, born Cedar Rapids, Iowa, September 9, 1952; admitted to bar, 1981, Iowa and U.S. District Court, Southern District of Iowa; 1983, U.S. District Court, Northern District of Iowa and U.S. Court of Appeals, Eighth Circuit. *Education:* University of Iowa (B.A., honors with High Distinction, 1975; J.D., High Distinction, 1981). Order of the Coif. Author: "State and Local Incentives: A Well-Stocked Candy Store," 5 Journal of Corporation Law 517 (1980). Law Clerk, U.S. Judge Harold D. Vietor, Southern District of Iowa, 1981-1983. *Member:* Linn County, Iowa State (Member: Business Law and Governmental Practice Sections) and American (Member: State and Local Government Law Section; Forum on Affordable Housing); National Association of Bond Lawyers. ***PRACTICE AREAS:*** Real Estate Development; Real Estate Transactions; Affordable Housing; Zoning; Property Tax; Local Government Law; Private Activity Bonds; Charitable Organizations Law. **Email:** dspina@bradleyriley.com

JOSEPH E. SCHMALL, born Dubuque, Iowa, September 16, 1958; admitted to bar, 1984, Iowa and U.S. District Court, Northern and Southern Districts of Iowa; 1992, U.S. District Court, Central District of Illinois. *Education:* Loras College (B.A., maxima cum laude, 1981); University of Iowa (J.D., with High Distinction, 1984). Phi Delta Phi (Historian, 1983-1984). Member, Moot Court Board. *Member:* Linn County, Iowa State (Member: Commercial and Bankruptcy Law Section Council, 1999-2001 and 2004-2006; Professionalism Committee, 1998-2002; Commission on Unauthorized Practice of Law, 1999-2008) and American Bar Associations. ***PRACTICE AREAS:*** Real Estate; Pension Plans; Employee Benefits; Commercial Law; Bankruptcy. **Email:** jschmall@bradleyriley.com

BRADLEY G. HART, born Burlington, Iowa, November 23, 1955; admitted to bar, 1982, Texas; 1990, Iowa. *Education:* Iowa State University (B.A., 1978); South Texas College of Law (J.D., 1982). Order of Lytae. *Member:* Linn County, Iowa State (Member, Corporate Counsel Section) and American (Member, Business Law Section) Bar Associations; State Bar of Texas. ***PRACTICE AREAS:*** Corporation and Business Law; Mergers and Acquisitions of Business. **Email:** bhart@bradleyriley.com

WILLIAM J. NEPPL, born Carroll, Iowa, November 27, 1950; admitted to bar, 1978, Iowa. *Education:* University of South Dakota (B.S., 1973); University of Iowa (M.A., 1974; J.D., 1978). Phi Eta Sigma; Phi Delta Phi. Administrative Assistant to City Manager, Iowa City, Iowa, 1974-1975. Author: "Comparisons of Partnerships, S and C Corporations, and Limited Liability Companies" as published in LLCs: Advising Small Business Start-Ups and Larger Companies in Iowa, by Lorman Education Services (2005); "Letters of Intent"

(This Listing Continued)

BRADLEY & RILEY PC, Cedar Rapids—Continued

as published in Current Land Development Issues in Iowa, by Lorman Education Services (2005); "Limited Liability Companies in Iowa - Practical Operating Procedures" as published in Limited Liability Companies in Iowa, by National Business Institute, Inc. (2002); "Entity Choice & Estate Planning" as published in the Iowa State Bar Association Probate and Trust Law Section Seminar (October 1999). *Member:* Linn County (Member, Linn County Title Standards Committee, 1981—), Iowa State (Member, Iowa State Title Standards Committee, 1987-1990, 1998-2001; Member, Sections on: Business Law; Probate and Trust Law; Real Estate and Title Law) and American (Member, Sections on: Business Law; Real Property; Probate; Trust; Taxation) Bar Associations; Cedar Rapids Estate Planning Council (Officer and Board of Directors, 1990-1994). ***PRACTICE AREAS:*** Corporate and Business Law; Real Estate Law; Municipal Law; Wills, Trusts, Estates and Probate Law. ***Email:*** wneppl@bradleyriley.com

WILLIAM T. McCARTAN, born Omaha, Nebraska, June 30, 1965; admitted to bar, 1991, Illinois and U.S. District Court, Northern District of Illinois; 1994, U.S. District Court, Central District of Illinois; 1994 Iowa; 1995, U.S. District Court, Northern and Southern Districts of Iowa; 2000, U.S Court of Appeals, Seventh and Eighth Circuit. *Education:* Creighton University (B.A., 1987); University of Notre Dame (J.D., magna cum laude, 1991). Member, National Moot Court Team, 1991. *Member:* Linn County (Member, Board of Governors, 1999-2001), Iowa State (Member, Securities Regulation Subcommittee of Business Law Section; Young Lawyers Division Executive Council, 1995-1997; Subcommittee on Securities Regulation), Illinois State and American (Member, Sections on: Litigation, Subcommittee on Securities Litigation) Bar Associations. ***PRACTICE AREAS:*** Securities Law; Corporate Law; Business Law; Securities Litigation. ***Email:*** bmccartan@bradleyriley.com

MAUREEN G. KENNEY, born Council Bluffs, Iowa, May 18, 1962; admitted to bar, 1994, Iowa. *Education:* St. Mary's College (B.S., 1984); University of Iowa (J.D., with distinction, 1994). *Member:* Linn County, Iowa State (Member, Sections on: Tax, Business Law and Probate) and American (Member, Sections on: Tax, Real Property; Probate and Trust; Business Law) Bar Associations; Iowa Society of Certified Public Accountants; American Institute of Certified Public Accountants. ***PRACTICE AREAS:*** Estate Planning; Probate; Corporate Law; Business Law. ***Email:*** mkenney@bradleyriley.com

VERNON P. SQUIRES, born Evanston, Illinois, March 22, 1964; admitted to bar, 1993, Illinois and U.S. District Court, Northern District of Illinois; 1995, Iowa and U.S. District Court, Northern and Southern Districts of Iowa; 1998, U.S. Court of Appeals, Eighth Circuit. *Education:* Institute for European Studies, Vienna, Austria (1984); Williams College (B.A., 1986); University of Minnesota at Minneapolis (J.D., cum laude, 1993). Member, Moot Court Board; Dean Mason Ladd Inn of Court, 1995-1997. Contributing Author: "Preventing Lawsuits for Wrongful Termination," 2005; "Safeguarding Against Sexual Harassment," 2005; "The Ultimate Right to Fire," 2005; "Iowa FMLA Update," 2005. Employee Privacy in the Workplace," 2005; "Negligence in the Workplace," 2004-2005; "Sexual Harassment: Employer and Employee Rights and Responsibilities," 2003; "Everything You Need to Know About Employee Departure Issues, Including RIF's, Severance Agreements, Non-Competes and Non-Disclosures," 2003; "Current Exemptions under the FLSA," 2003; "Sex, Race and Other Harassment in the Workplace," 2003; "Recent ADA Developments in Reasonable Accommodation," 2003; "Trade Secrets and Intellectual Property Protection," 2002; "Employee Leave Issues," 2002; "Trade Secrets and Unfair Competition," 2002; "Hiring Issues in Iowa," 2002; "Employee Leave Rights Under State and Federal Law," 2001; "Corporate Trade Secret Protection in Iowa," 2001; "Family and Medical Leave Act in Iowa," 2001; "Circuit City adds Power to Employment Arbitration Agreements," 2001. *Member:* Linn County, Iowa State and American (Member, Sections on: Litigation; Labor and Employment; Intellectual Property) Bar Associations. ***PRACTICE AREAS:*** Labor and Employment; Commercial Litigation; Intellectual Property. ***Email:*** vsquires@bradleyriley.com

TIMOTHY J. HILL, born Cedar Rapids, Iowa, February 28, 1966; admitted to bar, 1991, Illinois and U.S. District Court, Northern District of Illinois; 1997, U.S. District Court, Eastern District of Michigan; 1998, Iowa, U.S. District Court, Northern and Southern Districts of Iowa and U.S. District Court, Central District of Illinois. *Education:* University of Iowa (B.A., summa cum laude, 1988); University of Virginia (J.D., 1991). Phi Beta Kappa. Author: "Evaluating and Litigating Iowa Insurance Coverage Disputes," National Business Institute (2005); "Succeeding in Federal Court," National Business Institute (2005); "Mastering the Trial Notebook in Iowa," National Business Institute (2004). Attendee, National Trial Advocacy Skills Program presented by the National Institute of Trial Advocacy. *Member:* American (Litigation Section), Iowa State (Litigation Section Council and Annual Meeting Committee), Linn County and Chicago Bar Associations. ***PRACTICE AREAS:*** Commercial Litigation; Insurance. ***Email:*** thill@bradleyriley.com

PAUL D. BURNS, born Waterloo, Iowa, March 2, 1967; admitted to bar, 1993, Iowa; 1995, U.S. District Court, Southern and Northern Districts of Iowa. *Education:* University of Northern Iowa (B.A., 1989); University of Iowa (J.D., with high distinction, 1993). Order of the Coif (1993). Articles Editor, Iowa Law Review, Vol. 78, 1992-1993. Law Clerk to the Hon. Harold D. Vietor, U.S. District Judge, Southern District of Iowa, 1993-1995. Contributor to: the Iowa section in the 50 State Survey of Payment Provisions in Construction Contacts, ABA Construction Lawyer Journal, Vol. 24 No. 4 (2004). Author: "Construction Contracting and Change Orders," Lorman Education Services (2004); "Overview of Mechanic's Lien Law in Iowa," Lorman Education Services (2003); "Licensing Issues in Design-Build," Lorman Education Services (2002); "Iowa Public Bidding Law," Lorman Education Services (2002); "Iowa Code Chapter 573" (Public Contracting), Lorman Education Services (2002); "State and Federal MBE/DBE Requirements," Lorman Education Services (2001). Co-author: "Computer Law" chapter in the Iowa Legal Research Guide (2003). Speaker, "Spoilation of Evidence: What Every Defense Lawyer Needs to Know," Iowa Defense Counsel Association Seminar (2005). *Member:* Linn County, Iowa State (Vice-Chair, Federal Practice Committee, 2005-2006; Chair, e-Commerce Section Council) and American Bar Associations (Litigation Section); Dean Mason Ladd Inn of Court. (Resident, Iowa City Office). ***PRACTICE AREAS:*** Commercial Litigation. ***Email:*** pburns@bradleyriley.com

MICHAEL J. PUGH, born Pomona, California, July 16, 1965; admitted to bar, 1991, Illinois; 1992, U.S. District Court, Northern District of Illinois; 1994, Iowa. *Education:* University of Iowa (B.A., 1987); Indiana University (J.D., 1991). Co-Author: "Limited Liability Partnerships and Limited Liability Companies in Iowa,: 2001; "Limited Liability Companies in Iowa," 2002; "Iowa Land Use," 2003; "Zoning and Land Use in Iowa," 2004. President, Greater Iowa City Area Homebuilder's Association, 2005. Adjunct Lecturer, University of Iowa College of Business. Assistant State's Attorney, Cook County, Illinois, 1991-1994. Formerly with, Phelan, Tucker, Mullen, Walker, Tucker & Gelman, L.L.P., Iowa City, Iowa, 1994-2003. *Member:* Johnson County (Co-Chair, Title Standards/Real Estate Committee, 1999—), Iowa State (Member: Business Law Section Council, 2002—; Limited Liability Companies Subcommittee; Real Estate and Title Law Section; Probate and Trust Law Section) and American (Member: Forum on the Construction Industry; Business Law Section; Partnerships and Unincorporated Business Organizations Committee; Real Property, Probate and Trust Section) Bar Associations; Urban Land Institute. (Resident, Iowa City Office). ***PRACTICE AREAS:*** Real Estate; Zoning, Planning and Land Use; Construction Law; Business Law; Banking Law; Wills; Trust Law. ***Email:*** mpugh@bradleyriley.com

(This Listing Continued)

JANICE J. KERKOVE, born Sigourney, Iowa, January 23, 1968; admitted to bar, 1999, Iowa. *Education:* Indiana Wesleyan University (B.S., summa cum laude, 1995); Drake University (J.D., with highest honors, 1999). Order of the Coif. Author: "Probate and Trust Law," chapter of the Iowa Legal Research Guide, 2003. Co-Chair, Iowa's 48th Annual Spring Tax Institute, 2003. Iowa State Bar Association Probate & Trust Law Section Council (2004-2007). *Member:* Iowa State Bar Association (Member, Sections on: Probate and Trust Law; Tax); American Bar Association (Member, Real Property, Probate and Trust Law Section); Cedar Rapids Estate Planning Council (Board Member, 2002-2004). ***PRACTICE AREAS:*** Wills; Trust Law; Estate Planning; Probate; Tax Law. ***Email:*** jkerkove@bradleyriley.com

SHANNON P. THOMPSON, born Dallas, Texas, February 6, 1974; admitted to bar, 2000, Iowa. *Education:* University of Iowa (B.A., 1996; J.D., with distinction, 1999). Author: "The 1998 Russian Federation Family Code Provisions on Intercountry Adoption Break the Hague Convention Ratification Gridlock," Transnational Law and Contemporary Problems, Vol. 9, No. 2 (Fall 1999). *Member:* Linn County Bar Association; Iowa State Bar Association. ***PRACTICE AREAS:*** Real Estate; Corporate Law; Business Law; Securities Law. ***Email:*** sthompson@bradleyriley.com

KEVIN C. PAPP, born Columbus, Ohio, March 2, 1973; admitted to bar, 1998, Iowa; 2002, U.S. District Court, Northern and Southern Districts of Iowa. *Education:* University of San Diego (B.S., magna cum laude, 1995); University of Iowa (J.D., with distinction, 1998). Law Clerk: Hon. Van D. Zimmer, Iowa Court of Appeals, Jan-Aug 1999; Hon. Louis A. Lavorato, Chief Justice of the Iowa Supreme Court, 1999-2001; Jeffrey Axelrad, United States Department of Justice. Author: "Environmental Constitutional Protection, Human Rights, and the Eighth Draft of the Temporary Constitution for the Palestinian National Authority in the Transitional Period," Transnat'l L. and Contemp. Probs. 529, 1997. *Member:* American Bar Association (Young Lawyers Division and Litigation Section- Appellate Practice, Bankruptcy and Insolvency, and Commercial & Business Litigation Committees); Iowa State Bar Association (Litigation and Commercial Bankruptcy Committees); Linn County Bar Association (Bench Bar Relations Committee). ***PRACTICE AREAS:*** Commercial Litigation; Construction Litigation; Creditors Rights; Appellate Practice. ***Email:*** kpapp@bradleyriley.com

LAURA C. MUELLER, born Cedar Rapids, Iowa, June 27, 1972; admitted to bar, 1998, Missouri; 1999, Kansas; U.S. District Court, Western District of Missouri; 2001, U.S. District Court, Central District of Illinois; 2002, Iowa and U.S. District Court, Northern and Southern Districts of Iowa. *Education:* Northwestern University (B.A., with honors, 1994); The University of Iowa (M.A., 1995; J.D., with distinction, 1998). *Member:* Lynn County, Iowa State and American Bar Associations. ***PRACTICE AREAS:*** Labor and Employment; Civil Rights Law; Civil Litigation. ***Email:*** lmueller@bradleyriley.com

DAVID J. ZYLSTRA, born Cedar Rapids, Iowa, June 12, 1972; admitted to bar, 1998, Missouri; 1999, Kansas; 2002, Iowa. *Education:* Duke University (A.B., Economics, 1994); University of Iowa (J.D., with high distinction, 1998). Order of the Coif. Member, Iowa Law Review. ***PRACTICE AREAS:*** Corporate Law; Business Law; Mergers and Acquisitions; Taxation. ***Email:*** dzylstra@bradleyriley.com

KIMBERLY H. BLANKENSHIP, born Wyoming, Iowa, October 24, 1975; admitted to bar, 2001, Iowa. *Education:* University of Iowa (B.A., 1998; J.D., 2001). Attendee, National Trial Advocacy Skills Program presented by the National Institute of Trial Advocacy. *Member:* Iowa State Bar Association (Committee Chair, Emergency Services Task Force). ***PRACTICE AREAS:*** General Practice; Litigation; Business Law; Immigration Law. ***Email:*** kblankenship@bradleyriley.com

SARAH E. SWARTZENDRUBER, born Iowa City, Iowa, April 30, 1976; admitted to bar, 2001, Iowa. *Education:* University of Iowa (B.A., 1997; J.D., with high distinction, 2001). Order of the Coif. Adjunct Lecturer, University of Iowa College of Business. Formerly with, Phelan, Tucker, Mullen, Walker, Tucker & Gelman, L.L.P., 2001-2003. Author: "Use of LLCs in Real Estate Transactions" as published in LLCs: Advising Small Business Start-Ups and Larger Companies by Lorman Business Center, Inc. (2005); "Restrictive Covenants and Common Interest Community Issues" as published in Current Land Development Issues in Iowa by Lorman Business Center, Inc. (2005). *Member:* Johnson County, Iowa State and American (Member: Business Law Section; Real Property, Probate and Trust Section) Bar Associations; Urban Land Institute. (Resident, Iowa City Office). ***PRACTICE AREAS:*** Business Law; Real Estate; Contracts; Commercial Transactions; Construction Law; Zoning, Planning and Land Use. ***Email:*** sswartzendruber@bradleyriley.com

TYLER G. OLSON, born Cedar Rapids, Iowa, June 21, 1976; admitted to bar, 2003, Iowa. *Education:* Claremont McKenna College (B.A., 1998); University of Iowa (J.D., 2003). *Member:* American; Iowa State (Young Lawyers Division, Justice for All Committee), Linn County and Johnson County Bar Associations; Linn Law Club (Treasurer). ***PRACTICE AREAS:*** Business Law; Corporate Law; Real Estate. ***Email:*** tolson@bradleyriley.com

(This Listing Continued)

JOSEPH W. YOUNKER, born Decatur, Indiana; admitted to bar, 2005, Iowa. *Education:* Creighton University (B.A., 2001); University of Iowa College of Law (J.D., 2005). (Resident, Iowa City Office)

OF COUNSEL

MELISSA WEETS ANDERSON, born Lost Nation, Iowa, April 23, 1962; admitted to bar, 1987, Iowa and U.S. District Court, Southern District of Iowa; 1988, U.S. District Court, Northern District of Iowa; 1989, U.S. Tax Court; 1990, U.S. Court of Appeals, Eighth Circuit; 1997, Massachusetts. *Education:* Cornell College (B.A., with honors, magna cum laude, 1984); University of Iowa (J.D., with distinction, 1987). Phi Beta Kappa; Phi Delta Phi. National Merit Scholar. Member, Moot Court Board, 1986-1987. Barrister, Dean Mason L. Ladd Inn of Court (Executive Committee, 1990-1992, 1993-1995). Law Clerk to Hon. James H. Carter, Iowa Supreme Court, 1988-1989. *Member:* Iowa State (Chair, Managed Health Care Committee, 1994-1996; Young Lawyers Division Executive Council, 1993-1995), Massachusetts (Member, Health Law Division) and American Bar Associations (Member, Health Law Forum); American Health Lawyers Association. ***PRACTICE AREAS:*** Health Care Regulation; Physician Practice and Professional Rights; Organized Care Delivery Systems; Labor and Employment Law; Litigation. ***Email:*** manderson@bradleyriley.com

REPRESENTATIVE CLIENTS: Ahrens Concrete Company; Alliant Energy; APAC Customer Services, Inc.; Arlington Development, Inc.; Berthel Fisher & Company Financial Services, Inc.; Berthel Growth & Income Trust I; Bjornsen Investment Company; Blackford Farms, Inc.; Cardiologists, P.C.; Cedar Rapids Bank and Trust Company; Cellular Engineering Technologies, Inc.; Chubb Group of Insurance Companies; Collins Community Credit Union; Commercial Federal Bank; The Dexter Company; ESCO Electric Company; Fastek International, Ltd.; FOX 28 KFXA; Guaranty Bank and Trust Co.; Heartland Hotel Corp.; High Development Corp.; Highway Equipment Company; Hills Bank and Trust Company; Intuit, Inc.; Iowa Eye Center, P.C.; Iowa First Capital Fund, LP; Iowa Glass Depot, Inc.; Iowa Land and Building Co.; Investamerica Investment Advisors, Inc.; King's Material, Inc.; Kirkwood Community College; Knutson Construction Services Midwest, Inc.; K's Merchandise; Lil' Drug Store Products, Inc.; Linn Area Credit Union; Linn County OB-GYN, P.C.; Manpower Inc. of Cedar Rapids; Master Builders of Iowa (AGC Building Chapter of Iowa); Maxwell Construction, Inc.; McLeodUSA Incorporated; Merit Construction Company; MidAmerica Housing Partnership; Millhiser-Smith Insurance Agency, Inc.; MorAmerica Capital Corporation; Mount Mercy College; National Computer Systems, Inc.; Physicians Clinics of Iowa; Prime Ventures Development Inc.; Regency Homes of Eastern Iowa, L.C.; Roy J. Carver Charitable Trust; Telecommunications Income Fund IX, X & XI L.P.; United Fire & Casualty Co.; United Life Insurance Co.; University of Iowa Foundation; U.S. Bank, N.A.; Wells Fargo Bank, N.A.; Wholesale Feeds, Inc.; Worley Warehousing, Inc.; Woodward Communications, Inc.; Yellow Book.
REFERENCES: US Bank; Collins Community Credit Union.

BRADY & O'SHEA, P.C.

2735 FIRST AVENUE SOUTHEAST
CEDAR RAPIDS, IOWA 52402
Telephone: 319-866-9277
Fax: 319-866-9280
URL: http://www.lawyers.com/bradyoshea
Email: bbrady@bradyoshea.com
URL: http://www.bradyoshea.com

Personal Injury, Wrongful Death, Business Litigation, Class Actions, Products Liability, Premises Liability, Professional Negligence, Employment Law, Real Estate, Corporate Law, Estate Planning, Probate, Taxation, Appellate Practice, Civil Trial Practice, Worker's Compensation, Accidents, Automobile Accidents and Injuries, Trademark Litigation, Franchise Litigation, Trusts and Estates, Estate Planning, Probate, Wills.

BRAD J. BRADY, born Anamosa, Iowa, September 18, 1952; admitted to bar, 1978, Iowa, U.S. District Court, Northern and Southern Districts of Iowa; U.S. District Court, Western District of Michigan and U.S. Court of Appeals, Eighth Circuit. *Education:* Cornell College (B.A., summa cum laude, 1974); University of Iowa (J.D., with distinction, 1978). *Member:* Linn County, Iowa State and American Bar Associations; The Association of Trial Lawyers of America; Iowa Trial Lawyers Association. Fellow, Iowa Academy of Trial Lawyers. ***REPORTED CASES:*** Rieff v. Evans, 672 N.W.2d 728, (Iowa, Dec 17, 2003); Rieff v. Evans, 630 N.W.2d278 (Iowa, May 31, 2001)(NO.99-0313); Luker v. Wal-Mart Stores, Inc., 1999 WL 33655475 (N.D.Iowa, Nov 15, 1999); GreatAmerica Leasing Corp. v. Telular Corp., 1999 WL 33656867 (N.D.Iowa, Apr 20, 1999); Great Rivers Co-op of Southeastern Iowa v. Farmland Industries, Inc., 120 F.3d 893, 148 A.L.R. Fed. Sec L. Rep. P99,490 (8th Cir. (Iowa), Jul 29, 1997) (NO. 96-2751); Gutierrez v. Givens, 989 F. Supp. 1033 (S.D. Cal. 1997); Great Rivers Co-op of Southeastern Iowa v. Farmland Industries, Inc. 934 F.Supp. 302; Jolly v. Pittore, 1995 WL 566002 (S.D.N.Y., Sep 22, 1995) (NO. 92 CIV.3593 (JSM), 92 CIV. 5244 (JSM); Great Rivers Co-op. of Southeastern Iowa v. Farmland Industries, Inc. 59 F.3d 764, Fed. Sec. L. Rep. P98,807,31 Fed. R. Serv. 3d 1205 (8th Cir. (Iowa), July 12, 1995) NO. 95-1249); Kalell v. Petersen, 498 N.W. 2d 413 (Iowa App., Feb 02, 1993) (NO.2-614, 92-475); Nichols v. Schweitzer, 472 N.W. 2d 266 (Iowa, Jun 19, 1991) (NO. 89-1507); In re Marriage of Hasley, 433 N.W. 2d 40, 50 Ed. Law Rep. 1186 (Iowa App., Sep 28, 1988) (NO. 87-1114); U.S. v. Cooper, 709 F.Supp. 905 (N.D.Iowa, Sep 14, 1988) (NO. C86-0160);Taylor v. Wiebold, 390 N.W.2d 128 (Iowa, Jul 23, 1986) (NO. 85-1661); Smalley v. Dewberry, 379 N.W.2d 922, 54 USLW 2420 (Iowa, Jan 15, 1986) (NO. 85-367); Munz v. State, 382 N.W.2d 693 (Iowa App., Dec 18, 1985) (NO. 84-1109); In re Voss, 20 B.R. 598 (Bankr.N.D.Iowa, Jun 04, 1982) (NO. 81-00070, 81-0309). ***PRACTICE AREAS:*** Personal Injury; Wrongful Death; Commercial Litigation; Class Actions; Products Liability; Mediation. ***Email:*** bbrady@bradyoshea.com

ROBERT J. O'SHEA, born Cresco, Iowa, June 2, 1969; admitted to bar, 1995, Iowa, U.S. District Court, Northern and Southern Districts of Iowa and U.S. Tax Court; U.S. District Court, Western District of Michigan. *Education:* Coe College (B.A., cum laude, 1991); Drake University (J.D., with honors, 1995). Order of the Coif. *Member:* Linn County (Member, Title Standards Committee), Iowa State and American Bar Associations. ***PRACTICE AREAS:*** Real Estate; Corporate Law; Business; Estate Planning; Probate; Taxation; Trusts and Estates; Wills. ***Email:*** roshea@bradyoshea.com

MATTHEW L. PRESTON, born Cedar Rapids, Iowa, September 10, 1971; admitted to bar, 1996, Iowa, U.S. District Court, Northern and Southern Districts of Iowa and Western District of Michigan. *Education:* University of Iowa (B.B.A., with honors, 1992; J.D., with distinction, 1996). National Moot Court Advocate, 1995. Member, Iowa Law Review, 1994-1995. *Member:* Linn County (Vice President, 1998-2000), Iowa State (President, Young Lawyers Division) and American (Member Sections on: Tort and Insurance Practice, Intellectual Property; Franchise Forum) Bar Associations. ***PRACTICE AREAS:*** Commercial Litigation; Trademark Litigation; Franchise Litigation; Personal Injury. ***Email:*** mpreston@bradyoshea.com

ANN E. BROWN-GRAFF, born DeWitt, Iowa, April 18, 1980; admitted to bar, 2004, Iowa, U.S. District Court, Northern and Southern Districts of Iowa. *Education:* Cornell College (B.A., cum laude, Political Science, 2001); University of Iowa (J.D., with distinction, 2004). Phi Sigma Alpha. Recipient, Mark E. Hutchinson Scholarship for Excellence in Political Science. Selected to participate in the Van Oosterhout Memorial Moot Court Competition. *Member:* Iowa State Bar Association; Iowa Trial Lawyers Association; Iowa Organization of Women Attorneys; American Trial Lawyers Association. ***PRACTICE AREAS:*** Personal Injury; Lead Poisoning. ***Email:*** abrown-graff@bradyoshea.com

CRAWFORD, SULLIVAN, READ & ROEMERMAN, P.C.

1800 1ST AVENUE NE
SECOND FLOOR
CEDAR RAPIDS, IOWA 52402-5435
Telephone: 319-364-0171
Fax: 319-364-1370
Email: csrr@crawfordsullivan.com
URL: http://www.crawfordsullivan.com

Insurance Defense, Personal Injury, Products Liability, Workers Compensation, Commercial Litigation and Transactions, Corporate Law, Employment Law, Real Estate, Probate, Family Law, Appellate Practice, Civil Trial Practice in all State and Federal Courts.

JAMES W. CRAWFORD (1911-1988)

GERALD T. SULLIVAN, born Washington, D.C., September 24, 1937; admitted to bar, 1963, Iowa; 1964, District of Columbia and United States Court of Military Appeals. *Education:* Iowa State College and University of Iowa (B.A., 1960); Georgetown University (J.D., 1963). *Member:* Linn County, Iowa State and American Bar Associations; Iowa Defense Counsel Association; Defense Research Institute. Fellow, Iowa Academy of Trial Lawyers (President, 1997-1998); American Academy of Alternative Dispute Resolution Attorneys. [Major, U.S. Army, active duty, 1963-1968]. ***PRACTICE AREAS:*** Mediation; General Practice; Personal Injury; Products Liability; Insurance Law; Civil Appeals; Litigation; Discrimination; Civil Rights; Professional Negligence. ***Email:*** sullivan@crawfordsullivan.com

THOMAS B. READ, born Des Moines, Iowa, April 7, 1949; admitted to bar, 1975, Iowa; 1976, U.S. Tax Court. *Education:* Cornell College (B.A., 1971); University of Iowa; Drake University (J.D., 1975). Author: Casenote, "Physical Contact Requirement in a Hit-and-Run Claim," 8 Defense Update 1, 1995, 24 Drake Law Review 709; "Occupying the Vehicle--An Analysis for Defending UIM Cases," 9 Defense Update 3, 1996. Law Clerk to Hon. Robert C. Landess, Iowa Industrial Commissioner, 1974, *Member:* Linn County and Iowa State Bar Associations; Iowa Association of Workers Compensation Lawyers; Iowa Defense Counsel Association; Defense Research Institute. Fellow, Iowa Academy of Trial Lawyers. ***PRACTICE AREAS:*** General Practice; Workers Compensation; Personal Injury Defense; Insurance Law; Litigation; Civil Appeals. ***Email:*** read@crawfordsullivan.com

WILLIAM H. ROEMERMAN, born Blakburg, Iowa, January 31, 1953; admitted to bar, 1977, Iowa. *Education:* University of Iowa (B.A., with honors, 1975; J.D. with distinction, 1977). Phi Beta Kappa. Author: "Damages in First Party Bad Faith Actions...Peering Through the Fog," 3 Defense Update 3, 1990; "Tenants and Subrogation," Vol. V Defense Update 4; "Defending the Tortfeasor: A Proposal for UIM Insurers," Vol. IX Defense Update 4. *Member:* Linn County (Member, Insurance Committee, 1982-1988), Iowa State (Member: Committee on Legal Ethics Education, 1980-1981; Litigation Section; Labor and Employment Section) and American Bar Associations; Linn County Criminal Law Association (Board of Governors, 1979-1980); Iowa Defense Counsel Association; Defense Research Institute. Fellow, Iowa Academy of Trial Lawyers. ***PRACTICE AREAS:*** General Practice; Real Estate; Personal Injury; Litigation; Civil Appeals; Insurance Law; Labor and Employment; Administrative Law; Civil Rights; Municipal Law. ***Email:*** wroemerman@crawfordsullivan.com

ROBERT S. HATALA, born Fort Madison, Iowa, April 21, 1952; admitted to bar, 1983, Iowa. *Education:* Iowa State University (B.A., 1974); University of Iowa (M.A., 1983; J.D., 1983). Pi Sigma Alpha. Mayor, Fort Madison, Iowa, 1977-1979. Member, Board of Directors, League of Iowa Municipalities, 1978. *Member:* Linn County, Iowa State and American Bar Associations; Iowa Defense counsel Association; Defense Research Institute. ***PRACTICE AREAS:*** General Practice; Personal Injury; Products Liability; Business Law; Construction Law; Insurance Law; Municipal Law; Probate. ***Email:*** rhatala@crawfordsullivan.com

JAMES L. SINES, born St. Cloud, Minnesota, April 15, 1957; admitted to bar, 1983, Iowa. *Education:* University of Iowa (B.A., 1979; J.D., 1983). Assistant County Attorney, Linn County, 1983-1985. *Member:* Linn County, Iowa State and American Bar Associations; Iowa Trial Lawyers Association; The Association of Trial Lawyers of America. ***PRACTICE AREAS:*** General Practice; Domestic Relations; Family Law; Personal Injury; Real Estate; Criminal Law. ***Email:*** jsines@crawfordsullivan.com

THOMAS J. WILKINSON, JR., born Iowa City, Iowa, July 20, 1934; admitted to bar, 1962, Iowa; 1972, U.S. Supreme Court. *Education:* Coe College (B.A., 1956); University of Iowa (J.D., 1962). PSI CHI; Phi Alpha Delta. Author and Lecturer: Continuing Legal Education Presentation, e.g.; "Emerging Substantive Legal Issues In The Computer Area," Association of Trial Lawyers of Iowa Seminar, Cedar Rapids, Iowa, April 22, 1988; "Electronic Legal Research," Annual meeting, Iowa State Bar Association, Des Moines, Iowa,

(This Listing Continued)

CRAWFORD, SULLIVAN, READ & ROEMERMAN, P.C., Cedar Rapids—Continued

June, 1988. Contributing Author and Lecturer: "Basic Corporation Law in Iowa," National Business Institute's Law Review Series, Cedar Rapids, Iowa, July 25, 1991; "Limited Liability Companies in Iowa," National Business Institute, Cedar Rapids, Iowa, July 25, 2000. Assistant Linn County Attorney, 1963-1967. *Member:* Linn County (Secretary, 1968-1971) and Iowa State (Chairman, Special Committee on Law and Behavioral Sciences, 1975-1980; Chairman, Electronic Research Committee, 1984-1991) Bar Associations; Cedar Rapids Area Estate Planning Council. ***PRACTICE AREAS:*** General Practice; Corporate Law; Real Estate Law; Wills; Probate Law; Energy Law; Business Law; Estate Planning. ***Email:*** tjwlaw@crawfordsullivan.com

---

PETER B. WELCH, born Cedar Rapids, Iowa, November 1, 1950; admitted to bar, 1981, California; 1982, Iowa. *Education:* San Diego State University (B.S., 1972); Pepperdine University (M.B.A., 1977); University of San Francisco (J.D., 1981). Phi ETA Sigma; Beta Gamma Sigma. Chair, Cedar Rapids Veteran Commission. *Member:* Iowa State and American Bar Associations; The State Bar of California. [Capt., SC (ret), U.S. Navy, 1971-2002]. ***PRACTICE AREAS:*** General Practice; Family Law; Wills; Probate; Domestic Relations; Military Law. ***Email:*** pwelch@crawfordsullivan.com

SHERRY L. SCHULTE, born Chicago, Illinois, October 7, 1965; admitted to bar, 1990, Iowa; U.S. District Court, Northern and Southern Districts of Iowa. *Education:* Luther College (B.A., 1987); University of Iowa College of Law (J.D., 1990). Contributing Author and Lecturer: "Financial Problems in Divorce in Iowa," National Business Institute, Cedar Rapids, Iowa, March 6, 1996. *Member:* Linn County and Iowa State (Member, Family Law Section) Bar Associations. ***PRACTICE AREAS:*** Family Law. ***Email:*** sschulte@crawfordsullivan.com

REPRESENTATIVE CLIENTS: Fireman's Fund Insurance Cos.; Farm Bureau Mutual Insurance Co.; Iowa Mutual Insurance Co.; Mutual Fire and Automobile Insurance Co.; Le Mars Mutual Insurance Co.; Chubb Insurance Group; Utica of New York; AFIA (American Foreign Insurance) World Wide Insurance; Insurance Company of North America; Appalachian Insurance Co.; Minnesota Mutual Fire and Casualty; Reliance Insurance Co.; Fremont Indemnity; Gallagher Bassett Services, Inc.; Farmland Industries, Inc.; North American Van Lines, Inc.; O.F. Paulson Construction Co.; City of Ely, Iowa; City of Quasqueton, Iowa; City of Walker, Iowa; Walker Ag Center; United States Fire Insurance Co.; Omaha Property and Casualty; Meadowbrook Insurance; First Mercury Insurance.
Names of References on request.

EELLS & TRONVOLD LAW OFFICES, P.L.C.

Established in 1994

1921 51ST STREET, N.E.
CEDAR RAPIDS, IOWA 52402
Telephone: 319-393-1020
Fax: 319-393-4000
Email: Jeff@eells-tronvold.com
URL: http://www.eells-tronvoldlaw.com

General Practice with emphasis on Personal Injury, Litigation, Probate and Estate Planning, Trusts and Wills, Business Law and Mediation.

MR. LEW EELLS, born Belle Plaine, Iowa, November 29, 1943; admitted to bar, 1968, Iowa and U.S. District Court, Northern District of Iowa; 1969, U.S. District Court, Southern District of Iowa; 1970, U.S. Court of Appeals 8th Circuit; 1987, U.S. Tax Court. *Education:* State College of Iowa (B.A., 1966); University of Iowa (J.D., 1968). Phi Alpha Delta; Phi Delta Phi. Editor, Iowa Young Lawyers Newspaper, 1973-1974. Recipient: Bureau of National Affairs, Inc. Award; Most Satisfactory Progress in Field of Law, University of Iowa, 1968; American Jurisprudence Award in Law and Psychiatry. Assistant County Attorney, Felony Trial Division, Linn County, Iowa, 1975-1982. Trustee, Cedar Rapids Public Library, 1988-1998. *Member:* Linn County and Iowa State Bar Associations. ***PRACTICE AREAS:*** General Practice; Personal Injury; Litigation; Wills; Trusts; Estate Planning; Probate; Family Law; Divorce; Adoption Law; Criminal Law; Contracts; Collections; Real Estate; Business Law.

MR. JEFFREY R. TRONVOLD, born Newton, Iowa, May 3, 1966; admitted to bar, 1998, Iowa; 1999, U.S. Court of Appeals, Eighth Circuit and U.S. District Court, Northern and Southern Districts of Iowa. *Education:* United States Military Academy (B.S., 1988); Boston University (M.A., 1993); University of Iowa (J.D., with distinction, 1997; M.B.A., 1998). *Member:* Linn County and Iowa State Bar Associations; Association of Trial Lawyers of Iowa; The Association of Trial Lawyers of America. [Captain, United States Army, 1988-1994]. ***PRACTICE AREAS:*** Personal Injury; Civil Rights; Discrimination; Medical Malpractice; Legal Malpractice; Professional Malpractice; Wrongful Death; Products Liability; Toxic Torts; Premises Liability; Eminent Domain; Civil Litigation; Trial Practice; Libel, Slander and Defamation; Birth Trauma; Brain Injury; Automobile Accidents and Injuries; Mold Litigation; Agricultural Law; Pesticide Litigation. ***Email:*** jeff@eells-tronvold.com

REFERENCES: Bankers Trust, Cedar Rapids.

ELDERKIN & PIRNIE, P.L.C.

Established in 1900

Successor to Barnes and Chamberlain

115 FIRST AVENUE, S.E.
P.O. BOX 1968
CEDAR RAPIDS, IOWA 52406
Telephone: 319-362-2137
Fax: 319-362-1640

Civil Trial and Appellate Practice in all State and Federal Courts. Construction, Insurance Defense, Professional Liability, Personal Injury, Toxic Torts, Corporation and Business Associations, Health Care and Hospital Law, Estate Planning, Family, Probate, Real Estate, Taxation, Workers Compensation, Bankruptcy.

(This Listing Continued)

FIRM PROFILE: Elderkin & Pirnie, P.L.C. evolved from the Barnes and Chamberlain firm which was established in Cedar Rapids, Iowa, in 1918. Mr. David M. Elderkin became a partner in the firm in 1950 while Mr. Thomas H. Pirnie became a partner in 1957. The firm offers a wide range of legal services.

THOMAS H. PIRNIE (Deceased)

DAVID M. ELDERKIN, born Cedar Rapids, Iowa, November 5, 1913; admitted to bar, 1937, Iowa. *Education:* State University of Iowa (B.A., 1935; J.D., with distinction, 1937). Phi Delta Phi; Pi Gamma Mu; Omicron Delta Kappa. Assistant County Attorney, Linn County, 1946-1950. Member, 1959-1968 and Chairman, 1968, Iowa State Board of Bar Examiners. Supreme Court Appointee, Legislative Ethics Committee, 1969-1973. Member, Iowa Supreme Court Advisory Committee on Rules of Civil Procedure, 1971-1980. Recipient, Iowa Bar Association Award of Merit, 1972. *Member:* Linn County (President, 1973), Iowa State (Member, Board of Governors, 1962-1966; Vice President, 1965-1966; President, 1966-1967; Chairman, Committee on Rules of Civil Procedure, 1967-1970; Lecturer, Trial Tactics Seminars, 1960-1984; Contributor, Iowa Trial Handbook, 1969; Co-Author, "Defense of Cancer Cases,"; Member: Scope and Correlation Committee, 1967-1980; Special Select Legislative Study Committee, 1976-1980) and American Bar Associations; American Judicature Society; Judge Advocate General Association; American Society of Hospital Attorneys. Fellow: Iowa Academy of Trial Lawyers (Member, Board of Governors, 1965—; President, 1982, Dean of the Academy, 1989); American Bar Foundation; Iowa Bar Foundation; American Board of Trial Advocates; American College of Trial Lawyers (State Chairman, 1976-1978). [Captain, United States Marine Corps, World War II]. ***PRACTICE AREAS:*** Civil Litigation; Health Care Law.

JOHN K. VON LACKUM, born Cedar Rapids, Iowa, February 13, 1929; admitted to bar, 1954, Iowa. *Education:* Grinnell College and Northwestern University (B.S., 1951); University of Michigan (J.D., 1954). Delta Theta Phi. Assistant County Attorney, Linn County, 1961-1963. *Member:* Linn County (President, 1987-1988), Iowa State and American Bar Associations. ***PRACTICE AREAS:*** General Practice.

DAVID A. ELDERKIN, born Cedar Rapids, Iowa, June 4, 1941; admitted to bar, 1966, Iowa; 1970, U.S. Supreme Court. *Education:* University of Iowa (B.B.A., 1963; J.D., 1966). Assistant Attorney General of Iowa, 1966. Assistant Attorney General in Charge of Criminal Appeals Division, 1967-1969. Special Assistant Attorney General in Charge of Tort Claims Division, 1970-1972. Advisory Member, Iowa Crime Commission, 1967. Member, Iowa Law Enforcement Academy Council, 1967-1972. Member, Client Security and Attorney Disciplinary Commission, 1973-1985. Member, Judicial Qualifications Commission, 1988-1999. *Member:* Linn County (Member, Ethics and Grievance Committee) and Iowa State (Member, Litigation Section) Bar Associations; Dean Mason Ladd Inns of Court; American Board of Trial Advocates; Iowa Society of Hospital Attorneys. Fellow: American College of Trial Lawyers; Iowa Academy of Trial Lawyers (President, 1992-1993). ***PRACTICE AREAS:*** Civil Litigation; Appellate Practice; Insurance Law; Hospital Law. ***Email:*** DAElderkin@elderkinpirnie.com

PATRICK M. ROBY, born Bremerhaven, Germany, April 7, 1947; admitted to bar, 1972, Iowa. *Education:* Upper Iowa College (B.A., 1969); University of Iowa (J.D., with distinction, 1972). Phi Delta Phi. Member: Iowa Supreme Court Advisory Committee on Rules of Civil Procedure, 1981-1987; Iowa Supreme Court Special Committee on Discovery, 1986-1988. Independent Counsel, Iowa Senate Ethics Committee, 1992. *Member:* Linn County, Iowa State and American Bar Associations; Iowa Defense Counsel Association (President, 1988-1989); Iowa Academy of Trial Lawyers; Defense Research Institute; American Board of Trial Advocates (President, Iowa Chapter, 1989-1993). Fellow, American College of Trial Lawyers. ***LANGUAGES:*** French. ***PRACTICE AREAS:*** Civil Litigation. ***Email:*** proby@elderlinpirnie.com

MARK L. COPPOCK, born Cedar Rapids, Iowa, December 30, 1947; admitted to bar, 1975, Iowa. *Education:* University of Iowa (B.B.A., 1970); Creighton University and Drake University (J.D., 1975). *Member:* Linn County, Iowa State (Member: Title Guaranty Committee, 1983-1986; Health Law Committee, 1988-1989; Member, Council of Health Law Section 1990-1992) and American Bar Associations; Iowa Society of Hospital Attorneys; American Health Lawyers Association. ***PRACTICE AREAS:*** Health (Health Care) & Hospital Law; Business Law; Estate Planning; Probate Law; Real Estate. ***Email:*** mcoppock@elderkinpirnie.com

EDWARD M. BLANDO, born Aberdeen, South Dakota, September 29, 1938; admitted to bar, 1968, South Dakota; 1976, Iowa. *Education:* Northern State University (B.S., 1962); University of South Dakota (J.D., 1968). Phi Delta Phi. Assistant Attorney General, South Dakota, 1968-1969. States Attorney, Hughes County, South Dakota, 1971-1975. Assistant Attorney General, Area Prosecutor's Section, Iowa, 1978-1980. *Member:* Linn County (Chair, Continuing Legal Education Committee, 1988-1997), Iowa State (Member, Litigation Section; Chairman, Membership Services and Long Range Planning Committee; Member, Section Council Chair, 1999-2002; Chair, Professionalism Committee, 1994-1998; Member, Supreme Court Advisory Committee on Rules, 2002—Member, Iowa Jury Instruction Committee, 2002—) and American Bar Associations; Iowa Trial Lawyers Association; Association of Trial Lawyers of America. Fellow: Iowa Academy of Trial Lawyers; American Board of Trial Advocates. ***PRACTICE AREAS:*** Civil Trial Practice; Personal Injury; Medical Malpractice; Environmental Injury; Insurance Law. ***Email:*** eblando@elderkinpirnie.com

JAMES W. AFFELDT, born Cedar Rapids, Iowa, October 22, 1943; admitted to bar, 1968, Iowa. *Education:* University of Notre Dame (B.A., 1965); University of Iowa (J.D., 1968). Phi Delta Phi. Assistant County Attorney, Linn County, 1970-1976. President, Cedar Rapids Law Club, 1973-1974. *Member:* Linn County (Vice President, 1974-1975) and Iowa State Bar Associations. ***PRACTICE AREAS:*** Real Estate; Family Law; Civil Trial Practice; Estate Planning; Business Law. ***Email:*** jaffeldt@elderkinpirnie.com

JACK C. PAIGE, born Cedar Falls, Iowa, October 21, 1950; admitted to bar, 1980, Iowa. *Education:* University of Northern Iowa (B.A., with highest distinction, 1977); University of Iowa (J.D., 1980). Phi Delta Phi. *Member:* Iowa State Bar Association (Member, Workers Compensation Section); Iowa Defense Counsel Association; Iowa Association of Workers Compensation Attorneys. Fellow, Iowa Academy of Trial Lawyers. ***PRACTICE AREAS:*** Workers Compensation; Personal Injury; Civil Trial. ***Email:*** jpaige@elderkinpirnie.com

(This Listing Continued)

DAN CHILDERS, born Bowling Green, Kentucky, March 25, 1954; admitted to bar, 1982, Iowa; U.S. District Court, Northern and Southern Districts of Iowa and U.S. Court of Appeals, Eighth Circuit. *Education:* Western Kentucky University (B.A., cum laude, 1976); University of Iowa (J.D., 1982). Research Editor, Journal of Corporation Law, 1981-1982. Law Clerk to the Hon. Wm. W. Thinnes, U.S. Bankruptcy Judge, Northern District of Iowa, 1982-1984. Certified, Business Bankruptcy, American Board of Certification. *Member:* Linn County and Iowa State Bar Associations; Commercial Law League of America; American Bankruptcy Institute. ***PRACTICE AREAS:*** Bankruptcy Reorganizations; Commercial Transactions. ***Email:*** dchilders@elderkinpirnie.com

TODD W. ANDERSON, born China Lake, California, July 13, 1963; admitted to bar, 1988, Iowa and U.S. District Court, Northern and Southern Districts of Iowa. *Education:* Wartburg College (B.A., magna cum laude, 1985); University of Iowa (J.D., with distinction, 1988). Phi Delta Phi. *Member:* Linn County (Member, Board of Governors, 2003—) and Iowa State (Member, Sections on: Probate and Trust Law; Real Estate) Bar Associations; Cedar Rapids Area Estate Planning Council (Board of Directors, 1994-1995). ***PRACTICE AREAS:*** Wills; Trust Law; Real Estate Law; Corporate Law; Business Law; Probate Law. ***Email:*** tanderson@elderkinpirnie.com

CHRISTOPHER LEE BRUNS, born Clarinda, Iowa, September 17, 1965; admitted to bar, 1991, Iowa. *Education:* Drake University (B.A., summa cum laude, 1988; J.D., 1991). Phi Beta Kappa; Phi Kappa Phi; Order of the Coif. Editor in Chief, Drake Law Review, 1990-1991. *Member:* Linn County and Iowa State Bar Associations; Iowa Defense Counsel Association; Defense Research Institute. [Lieutenant J.A., U.S. Army, 1991-1996]. ***PRACTICE AREAS:*** Insurance Defense; Employment Law; Civil Rights. ***Email:*** cbruns@elderkinpirnie.com

---

CYNTHIA HANNA, born Albert Lea, Minnesota, July 15, 1956; admitted to bar, 1981, Illinois; 1982, Iowa. *Education:* Augustana College (B.A., magna cum laude, 1978); DePaul University (J.D., 1981). *Member:* Linn County and Iowa State (Member, Sections on: Probate and Trust Law; Real Estate and Title) Bar Associations. ***PRACTICE AREAS:*** Probate; Real Estate; Wills; Adoption Law. ***Email:*** channa@elderkinpirnie.com

TAMRA L. MITCHELL, born Cedar Rapids, Iowa, April 29, 1960; admitted to bar, 1989, Iowa. *Education:* Loras College; Mount Mercy College (B.S.N., cum laude, 1984); University of Iowa (J.D., with distinction, 1989). Sigma Theta Tau. Member, Journal of Corporation Law, 1987-1989. Registered Nurse, Iowa, 1984—. *Member:* Linn County (Member, Board of Governors, 1999-2001), Iowa State (Member, Health Law Section) and American Bar Associations; Iowa Society of Hospital Attorneys. ***PRACTICE AREAS:*** Health Care and Hospital Law. ***Email:*** tmitchell@elderkinpirnie.com

DANIEL DENBESTE, born St. Paul, Minnesota, December 11, 1949; admitted to bar, 1978, Iowa; 1986, U.S. Tax Court. *Education:* Coe College (B.A., cum laude, 1972); Brigham Young University (J.D., 1978); Chicago-Kent College of Law, Illinois Institute of Technology (LL.M., 1988). Co-Author: "Labor and Employment Law: Compliance and Litigation," Callaghan & Co., 1986-1990. *Member:* Linn County, Iowa State and American Bar Associations. [1st Lieut., USAF, 1972-1975]. ***PRACTICE AREAS:*** Taxation; Employee Benefits. ***Email:*** ddenbeste@elderkinpirnie.com

ROBERT M. HOGG, born Iowa City, Iowa, January 24, 1967; admitted to bar, 1995, Minnesota; 1998, Iowa. *Education:* University of Iowa (B.A., 1988); University of Minnesota (J.D., 1995). Order of the Coif. Managing Editor, Minnesota Law Review, 1994-1995. Law Clerk: to Hon. Donald P. Lay, Circuit Judge, U.S. Court of Appeals, Eighth Circuit, 1995-1996; to Hon. Michael J. Melloy, Chief Judge U.S. District Court, Northern District of Iowa, 1998-1999. *Member:* Linn County and Iowa State Bar Associations. ***PRACTICE AREAS:*** Civil Litigation. ***Email:*** rhogg@elderkinpirnie.com

PAULA L. ROBY, born Cedar Rapids, Iowa, September 1, 1973; admitted to bar, 2000, Iowa. *Education:* University of Northern Iowa (B.A., 1996); University of Iowa (J.D., with distinction, 1999). *Member:* Linn County and Iowa State (Member, Young Lawyers Division) Bar Associations; Iowa Trial Lawyers Association. Dean Mason Ladd Inn of Court. ***PRACTICE AREAS:*** Trial Practice. ***Email:*** plroby@elderkinpirnie.com

ANN M. KLOSTERMANN MCCREA, born Dubuque, Iowa, October 29, 1968; admitted to bar, 1999, Iowa, U.S. Court of Appeals, Eighth Circuit and U.S. District Court, Northern and Southern Districts of Iowa. *Education:* University of Iowa (B.G.S., 1991); Mount Mercy College (B.S., 1996); William Mitchell College of Law (J.D., 1999). Member, Cedar Rapids Estate Planning Council, 1999—. *Member:* Linn County and Iowa State (Member: Probate and Trust Section, 1999—; Young Lawyers Division, 1999—; YLD Executive Council, 2002; Trust Code Committee, 2000—; YLD Services to Elderly Committee, 1999—; YLD Membership Committee, 2000-2003) Bar Associations. ***PRACTICE AREAS:*** Wills; Trusts; Estate Planning; Corporate; Business; Real Estate; Taxation; Health Law; Hospital Law. ***Email:*** amccrea@elderkinpirnie.com

REPRESENTATIVE CLIENTS: Allied Insurance Co.; AMCO Insurance Company; Bank Iowa; Metco Credit Union; Heritage Insurance Co.; Mayo Foundation; Mercy Medical Center; Virginia Gay Hospital.
GENERAL COUNSEL FOR: Mercy Foundation; Centro Inc.; Bruce McGrath Pontiac, Inc.; Midwest Metal Products Co.; Community Plus Credit Union; Securian Advisors Midwest, Inc.; The Lutheran Home for the Aged Association; Ouel Finance, Inc.; Shelton Technologies, Inc.

GARTELOS, WAGNER & AMENT

CEDAR RAPIDS, IOWA

(See Waterloo)

General Trial Practice and Appeals. Corporation, Family, Insurance, Personal Injury, Real Estate, Probate, Estate Planning, Workers Compensation and Bankruptcy Law.

GRAY, STEFANI & MITVALSKY, P.L.C.

Established in 1938

200 AMERICAN BUILDING
CEDAR RAPIDS, IOWA 52401
Telephone: 319-364-1535
FAX: 319-364-1562
URL: http://www.gsmlawyers.com
Mailing Address: P.O. Box 456, Cedar Rapids, IA 52406-0456

General Practice. Family Law, Juvenile, Real Estate, Professional Liability, Products Liability, Wills, Trusts and Estates, Estate Planning, Probate, Insurance, Environmental Law, Commercial Law, Corporate Law. Trials and Appeals.

RAYMOND R. STEFANI, born Des Moines, Iowa, April 25, 1929; admitted to bar, 1955, Iowa, U.S. District Court, Northern and Southern Districts of Iowa, U.S. District Court, Southern District of Illinois and U.S. Court of Appeals, Eighth Circuit. *Education:* University of Iowa; Drake University (B.A., 1953; J.D., 1955). Delta Theta Phi. Member, Federal Advisory Committee, U.S. Court of Appeals, Eighth Circuit, 1988-1992 . *Member:* Linn County (President, 1986-1987), Iowa State and American Bar Associations; Iowa Defense Counsel Association (Member, Board of Directors, 1980—; President, 1984-1985); Defense Research Institute. Fellow, American College of Trial Lawyers; Fellow, Iowa Academy of Trial Lawyers. ***LANGUAGES:*** Italian. ***PRACTICE AREAS:*** Civil Litigation Defense; Medical Malpractice; Dental Malpractice; Products Liability; Employment Law; Environmental Law. ***Email:*** rstefani@gsmlawyers.com

FRANK S. MITVALSKY, born Cedar Rapids, Iowa, May 31, 1943; admitted to bar, 1968, Iowa, U.S. District Court, Northern and Southern Districts of Iowa and U.S. Court of Appeals, Eighth Circuit. *Education:* Northwestern University (B.A., 1965); University of Iowa (J.D., 1968). Phi Delta Phi. *Member:* Linn County (President, 1994-1995), Iowa State and American Bar Associations. ***PRACTICE AREAS:*** Business Law; Family Law; Probate; Real Estate; Civil Litigation. ***Email:*** fsmitvalsky@gsmlawyers.com

RAYMOND R. STEFANI, II, born Des Moines, Iowa, January 10, 1953; admitted to bar, 1979, Iowa, U.S. District Court, Northern and Southern Districts of Iowa and U.S. Court of Appeals, Eighth Circuit. *Education:* Drake University (B.F.A., 1975; J.D., 1979). Phi Alpha Delta. *Member:* Linn County; Iowa State and American Bar Associations; Iowa Defense Counsel Association; American Board of Trial Advocates. ***PRACTICE AREAS:*** Civil Litigation Defense; Medical Malpractice; Dental Malpractice; Products Liability; Workers' Compensation; Construction Claims; Personal Injury; Real Estate. ***Email:*** rstefaniii@gsmlawyers.com

RICHARD A. STEFANI, born Des Moines, Iowa, July 27, 1954; admitted to bar, 1980, Iowa, U.S. District Court, Northern and Southern Districts of Iowa and U.S. Court of Appeals, Eighth Circuit. *Education:* University of Iowa (B.B.A., 1976); Creighton University (J.D., 1980). Alpha Sigma Nu. Author: "Assumption of Risk and the Automobile Guest: Time to Reevaluate Their Relationship," 13 Creighton Law Review 251, 1979. *Member:* Linn County, Iowa State and American Bar Associations; Iowa Defense Counsel Association (Member, Board of Directors, 1988-1991); Defense Research Institute. Fellow, Iowa Academy of Trial Lawyers. ***PRACTICE AREAS:*** AIDS Litigation; Products Liability; Drug and Medical Device Litigation; Medical Malpractice; Employment Law. ***Email:*** rickstefani@gsmlawyers.com

THOMAS F. OCHS, born Frankfurt, West Germany, September 27, 1962; admitted to bar, 1988, Iowa, U.S. District Court, Northern and Southern Districts of Iowa and U.S. Court of Appeals, Eighth Circuit. *Education:* Northwestern University (B.A., 1985); Drake University (J.D., 1988). *Member:* Linn County and Iowa State Bar Associations; Iowa Defense Counsel Association. ***LANGUAGES:*** German. ***PRACTICE AREAS:*** Civil Litigation; Products Liability; Medical Malpractice; Family Law; Appellate Practice. ***Email:*** thomaso@gsmlawyers.com

RICHARD F. MITVALSKY, born Cedar Rapids, Iowa, April 3, 1971; admitted to bar, 1996, Iowa; 2000, U.S. District Court, Northern District of Iowa. *Education:* University of Michigan (A.B., 1993); Drake University (M.A., J.D., with honors, 1996). Delta Theta Phi. Member, Drake Journal of World Agricultural Law. *Member:* Linn County, Iowa State (Chair, Young Lawyers Division Juvenile Law Committee, 2000-2002; Member, Family Law Section) and American Bar Associations; Iowa Supreme Court (Member, Juvenile Court Services Advisory Committee (2002-2003). ***PRACTICE AREAS:*** Civil Litigation; Family Law; Wills; Trust Law; Probate; Juvenile Law; Business Law; Guardian Ad Litem. ***Email:*** rmitvalsky@gsmlawyers.com

REPRESENTATIVE CLIENTS: Altorfer Inc.; American Hospitality Concepts, Inc.; Bayer Corporation; Casey's General Stores; Radiology Consultants of Iowa; Consolidated Freightways; DaimlerChrysler Corp.; Darrahs, Inc.; Deere & Company; First Property Management Corp.; GreatAmerica Leasing Corporation; The Ground Round, Inc.; J. B. Hunt Transport, Inc.; Lumbermans Investment Corp.; Massey-Ferguson, Inc.; McGrath Automotive Group, Inc.; Wal-Mart, Inc.; Kwik-Way Products, Inc.; Lake Delhi Recreation Association.
INSURANCE: Blue Cross and Blue Shield of Iowa; DaimlerChrysler Insurance Company; Commercial Union Insurance Cos.; Medical Claims Management Group; The Atlantic Cos.; The Hartford Insurance Group; GE Medical Protective Co.; CIGNA; Gallagher-Bassett Insurance Services; Scottsdale Insurance Co.; U.S. Insurance Group; Zurich-American Insurance Group; Chubb Insurance Group; National General Insurance Co.; Rice Insurance Services Company, LLC; Medmarc Casualty Insurance Company; Preferred Physician Medical Risk Retention Group, Inc.; RLI Insurance Company; GMAC Insurance; Sentry Insurance.

JACKSON & JACKSON P.L.C.

SUITE 250 ARMSTRONG CENTRE
222 THIRD AVENUE, SOUTHEAST
CEDAR RAPIDS, IOWA 52401
Telephone: 319-363-2683
Fax: 319-363-3028

Family Law, Adoptions, Child Custody, Child Support, Divorce, Domestic Violence, Visitation Rights, Real Estate, Probate, and Civil Trial Practice, Wills, Trusts, Estates.

(This Listing Continued)

JACKSON & JACKSON P.L.C., Cedar Rapids—Continued

MEMBERS

STEPHEN B. JACKSON, born Cedar Rapids, Iowa, July 9, 1936; admitted to bar, 1964, Iowa; 1970, U.S. Supreme Court and U.S. District Court, Northern and Southern Districts of Iowa. *Education:* Coe College (B.A., 1959); George Washington University; University of Iowa (J.D., 1964). Recipient, Volunteer Lawyer Project Award, 2000. Assistant County Attorney, 1964-1970. City Attorney: City of Center Point, Iowa, 1974-1980; City of Lisbon, Iowa, 1984-1989. Member, City Planning Commission of Cedar Rapids, 1988-1993. *Member:* Linn County (Treasurer, 1965-1967; Member, Board of Governors, 1977-1978; Family Law Committee, 1998—; Chair, 1998—) and Iowa State (Member, Family Law Section) Bar Associations; The Criminal Law Association of Linn County (Member, Board of Governors, 1975-1979; Chair, 1978); The Association of Trial Lawyers of Iowa (Member, Board of Governors, 1976-1979; Treasurer, 1979; Secretary, 1979-1981; Recipient, Outstanding Key Person Award, 1978); The Association of Trial Lawyers of America (Member, Family Law Section). ***Email:*** stevesr@jackson-law

STEPHEN B. JACKSON, JR., born May 12, 1966; admitted to bar, 1991, Illinois (Inactive) and U.S. District Court, Northern District of Illinois (Inactive); 1994, Iowa and U.S. District Court, Northern and Southern Districts of Iowa. *Education:* University of Notre Dame (B.A., 1988); University of Iowa (J.D., with distinction, 1991). *Member:* Linn County and Iowa State (Member, Family Law Section) Bar Associations; The Association of Trial Lawyers of America; The Association of Trial Lawyers of Iowa. Recipient, Volunteer Lawyer Project Award, 2000. ***Email:*** stevejr@jackson-law.com

REFERENCE: Hills Bank and Trust.

KLINGER, ROBINSON & FORD, L.L.P.

Established in 1979

401 OLD MARION ROAD, N.E.
P.O. BOX 10020
CEDAR RAPIDS, IOWA 52410-0020
Telephone: 319-395-7400
FAX: 319-395-9041
Cable: TESHUB
Email: Krflaw@mcleodusa.net
URL: http://www.krflawoffice.com

General Civil Practice. Federal Criminal Defense, Including White Collar Crimes and Drug Crimes, Real Estate, Probate, Environmental, Equal Employment Opportunity, Bankruptcy, Insolvency, Corporate and Commercial Law. Litigation, Family Law, Estate Planning, Drug, Insurance, Municipal Law, Appellate Practice, Mediation, Wills and Probate, Trusts and Estates, DWI, Traffic Violations, Divorce, Juvenile Crimes, Probation.

ROBERT E. FORD, born Cedar Rapids, Iowa, October 22, 1925; admitted to bar, 1952, Iowa; 1954, U.S. District Court, Northern District of Iowa. *Education:* Coe College; University of Iowa (B.A., 1949; J.D., with distinction, 1952). Phi Delta Phi. Chairman, Cedar Rapids Riverfront Improvement Commission, 1960-1976. District Court Judge, Iowa District Court, 1977-1985. *Member:* Linn County and Iowa State Bar Associations. [U.S. Navy, 1943-1946]

PHILLIP D. KLINGER, born Cedar Rapids, Iowa, December 8, 1942; admitted to bar, 1968, Iowa and U.S. District Court, Northern District of Iowa; 1971, U.S. Supreme Court. *Education:* University of Iowa (B.B.A., 1964; J.D., 1968). Assistant Linn County Attorney, 1968-1974. *Member:* Linn County and Iowa State (Member: Environmental Law Section; Real Estate Law Section) Bar Associations. ***PRACTICE AREAS:*** Real Estate; Estate Planning; Corporations; Environmental Law. ***Email:*** Pklinger.krflaw@mcleodusa.net

GARY L. ROBINSON (1947-1998)

JEFFREY P. TAYLOR, born Waterloo, Iowa, December 29, 1962; admitted to bar, 1989, Iowa and U.S. District Court, Northern and Southern Districts of Iowa and U.S. Court of Appeals, Eighth Circuit. *Education:* University of Iowa (B.B.A., with distinction, 1985; J.D., with high distinction, 1988). *Member:* Linn County, Iowa State and American Bar Associations. ***PRACTICE AREAS:*** Commercial Law; Bankruptcy; Civil Litigation; Family Law; Estate Planning. ***Email:*** Jtaylor.krflaw@mcleodusa.net

JONATHAN B. HAMMOND, born New York City, N.Y., November 29, 1954; admitted to bar, 1984, Iowa; 1987, U.S. District Court, Northern District of Iowa; 1991, U.S. Court of Appeals, Eighth Circuit. *Education:* University of Iowa (B.A., 1978; J.D., with distinction, 1984). Master of the Bench, Dean Mason Ladd Inn of Court. Assistant Linn County Attorney, 1984-1987. Special Prosecutor: Linn County, 1992; Jones County, 1995, 1996; Benton County, 1993, 1996, 1997. *Member:* Linn County and Iowa State (Member, Criminal Law Section) Bar Associations; National Association of Criminal Defense Lawyers. ***PRACTICE AREAS:*** Criminal Law; Municipal Law. ***Email:*** Jhammond.krflaw@mcleodusa.net

STEPHEN A. SWIFT, born Grand Rapids, Michigan, August 26, 1949; admitted to bar, 1975, Iowa and U.S. District Court, Northern District of Iowa; 1981, U.S. District Court, Southern District of Iowa; 1990, U.S. Court of Appeals, Eighth Circuit and U.S. Supreme Court. *Education:* Michigan State University (B.A., 1971); University of Iowa College of Law (J.D., 1974). *Member:* Linn County and Iowa State Bar Associations; National Association of Criminal Defense Lawyers. ***PRACTICE AREAS:*** Criminal Law; Family Law; Collections; Estate Planning; Wills; Mediation. ***Email:*** sswift.krflaw@mcleodusa.net

DANIEL L. SEUFFERLEIN, born Cedar Falls, Iowa, November 12, 1973; admitted to bar, 2001, Iowa and U.S. District Court, Northern District of Iowa; 2002, U.S. Court of Appeals, Eighth Circuit. *Education:* Arkansas State University (B.A., 1997); University of Iowa (J.D., 2001). *Member:* Linn County and Iowa State (District Representative, Young Lawyers Division) Bar Associations; Iowa Trial Lawyers Association. ***PRACTICE AREAS:*** Civil Litigation; Trial Practice.

(This Listing Continued)

REPRESENTATIVE CLIENTS: General Mills, Inc.; Guaranty Bank & Trust Co.; First State Bank of Manchester, Iowa; Duffy Schamberger Motor Company; United Security Savings Bank; Lone Star Restaurant and Saloon Co.; Bettenbender Manufacturing Co.; Village Winery, Inc.; Community State Bank; Patriot Bank; City of Springville; Aurora National Life Insurance, Co.; Advantage Chevrolet; Advantage Chrysler, Plymouth Dodge; Iowa Motor Co.-Lincoln Ford Mercury; Cendant Mortgage; PHH Mortgage; Instamortgage.com.; Iowa Golf Association; Iowa Section PGA.
REFERENCES: Provided on Request.

KRUG LAW FIRM, P.L.C.

Established in 1996

THE HACH BUILDING, SUITE 330
401 FIRST STREET S.E.
P.O. BOX 186
CEDAR RAPIDS, IOWA 52406-0186
Telephone: 319-297-7515
Fax: 319-297-7518
Email: ekrug@kruglawfirm.com
URL: http://www.kruglawfirm.com

General Civil Trial Practice emphasizing Insurance Defense, Labor and Employment Law (Management), Railroad/Transportation, Workers' Compensation, Mediation and Family Law.

FIRM PROFILE: See Website.

EDWARD J. KRUG, born Newark, New Jersey, December 28, 1956; admitted to bar, 1982, Massachusetts; 1988, Iowa. *Education:* Coe College (B.A., 1979); Boston College (J.D., 1982). Staff Member, Boston College Environmental Affairs Law Review, 1980-1981. *Member:* Linn County, Iowa State and American Bar Associations; Iowa Defense Counsel Association; Defense Research Institute; National Association of Railroad Trial Counsel; Association for Transportation Law, Logistics and Policy; Trucking Industry Defense Association. ***PRACTICE AREAS:*** Railroad/Transportation Litigation; Civil Litigation; Employment Law; Mediation. ***Email:*** ekrug@kruglawfirm.com

BOBBI J. LAMMER, born Dubuque, Iowa, September 21, 1977; admitted to bar, 2004, Iowa. *Education:* University of Iowa (B.A., J.D., 2004). *Member:* Iowa State Bar Association. ***PRACTICE AREAS:*** General Practice. ***Email:*** blammer@kruglawfirm.com

REPRESENTATIVE CLIENTS: General Electric Company; Werner Enterprises, Electric Insurance Company; Chicago Central & Pacific Railroad Company; Gordon Sevig Trucking Company; American Freightways; Iowa Interstate Railroad, Ltd.; Lancer Insurance Company; AIG (Trucking Group); Swiss Reinsurance America; Affordable Plumbing and Construction; Dakota & Iowa Railroad; Cherokee Insurance Company.

JOHN L. LANE

Established in 1981

THE LAW BUILDING, SUITE 310
225 SECOND STREET S.E.
CEDAR RAPIDS, IOWA 52406-5245
Telephone: 319-363-3839
Fax: 319-363-4851
Email: attyjohnlane@msn.com

Federal Criminal Defense, including White Collar Crimes and Drug Cases.

JOHN L. LANE, born Davenport, Iowa, July 21, 1952; admitted to bar, 1981, Iowa, U.S. District Court, Northern and Southern Districts of Iowa and U.S. Court of Appeals, Eighth Circuit. *Education:* University of Iowa (B.A., 1978; J.D., 1981). *Member:* Linn County, Iowa State (Member, Criminal Law Section) and American (Member, Criminal Law Section) Bar Associations; National Association of Criminal Defense Lawyers. [U.S. Marine Corps, 1971-1974]. ***PRACTICE AREAS:*** Federal Criminal Law (100%).

PETE LEEHEY LAW FIRM, P.C.

6105 ROCKWELL DRIVE N.E.
P.O. BOX 10316
CEDAR RAPIDS, IOWA 52410-7490
Telephone: 319-294-4424
Fax: 319-294-4993
Email: pleehey@leeheylaw.com
URL: http://www.lawyers.com/leeheylaw

Personal Injury, Workers' Compensation, Automobile Accidents, Dog Bites, Sexual Abuse, Slip and Fall, Wrongful Death, Wrongful Termination, Medical Malpractice, Nursing Home Abuse.

PETE LEEHEY, born Iowa City, Iowa, March 9, 1959; admitted to bar, 1984, Iowa; U.S. Supreme Court; U.S. Court of Appeals, Eighth Circuit; U.S. District Court, Northern and Southern Districts of Iowa. *Education:* University of Iowa (B.A., 1981; J.D., 1984). Formerly with Trevino & Leehey, 1989-1994; Leehey & Valentine, 1994-1998; Wertz & Leehey, 1998-2001. *Member:* Linn County and Iowa State (Chair, Workers' Compensation Section, 1997-1999) Bar Associations; The Association of Trial Lawyers of America; Iowa Trial Lawyers Association (Member: Board of Governors, 1991-1998; Executive Committee, 1998-2005); Iowa Association of Workers' Compensation Lawyers (Member, Board of Governors, 1998—). ***PRACTICE AREAS:*** Personal Injury; Workers' Compensation; Automobile Accidents and Injuries; Dog Bites; Sexual Abuse; Slip and Fall; Wrongful Death; Wrongful Termination; Medical Malpractice; Nursing Home Abuse and Neglect. ***Email:*** pleehey@leeheylaw.com

(This Listing Continued)

ASSOCIATE

KENT SMITH, born Ames, Iowa, April 4, 1978; admitted to bar, 2005, Iowa. *Education:* Central College (B.A., 2001); Drake University (J.D., 2005; Legislative Practice Certificate, 2005). *Member:* Iowa State (Member, Young Lawyers Division) and American Bar Associations; Iowa Trial Lawyers Association.

LYNCH DALLAS, P.C.

Established in 1926

526 SECOND AVENUE SE
P.O. BOX 2457
CEDAR RAPIDS, IOWA 52406-2457
Telephone: 319-365-9101
Facsimile: 319-365-9512
Email: attorneys@lynchdallas.com
URL: http://www.lynchdallas.com

General Civil Practice.

CHARLES J. LYNCH (1905-1983)

WILLIAM M. DALLAS (1905-1981)

DONALD G. RIBBLE, born Cedar Rapids, Iowa, July 16, 1930; admitted to bar, 1955, Iowa. *Education:* Coe College (B.A., 1952); University of Iowa (J.D., 1955). Comments Editor, Iowa Law Review, 1954-1955. *Member:* Linn County (President, 1985-1986) and Iowa State Bar Associations; Dean Mason Ladd American Inn of Court (President, 1993-1994). Fellow: Iowa Academy of Trial Lawyers; American College of Trial Lawyers; Iowa and American Bar Foundations. ***PRACTICE AREAS:*** Civil Litigation. ***Email:*** dribble@lynchdallas.com

H. EDWARD BEATTY, born Shellsburg, Iowa, December 9, 1934; admitted to bar, 1961, Iowa. *Education:* Colorado College (B.A., 1956); University of Iowa (J.D., 1961). *Member:* Linn County, Iowa State and American Bar Associations. ***PRACTICE AREAS:*** Real Estate; Trust Law; Estate Planning; Probate. ***Email:*** hbeatty@lynchdallas.com

SCOTT E. McLEOD, born Marshalltown, Iowa, March 9, 1942; admitted to bar, 1967, Iowa. *Education:* University of Iowa (B.A., 1964; J.D., 1967). Member, Board of Editors, Iowa Law Review, 1967. *Member:* Linn County, Iowa State and American Bar Associations; Iowa Defense Counsel Association; Iowa Association of Worker's Compensation Lawyers; Defense Research Institute. Fellow, Iowa Academy of Trial Lawyers. ***PRACTICE AREAS:*** Civil Litigation; Workers Compensation. ***Email:*** smcleod@lynchdallas.com

WILFORD H. STONE, born Lake County, Illinois, April 18, 1956; admitted to bar, 1984, Iowa. *Education:* College of Wooster (B.A., 1978); Cornell University (M.I.L.R., 1980); University of Iowa (J.D., 1984); Georgetown University (LL.M., 1987). Attorney, National Labor Relations Board, 1984-1987. Arbitrator, Iowa Public Employment Relations Board. *Member:* Linn County, Iowa State and American Bar Associations. ***PRACTICE AREAS:*** Civil Litigation; Labor and Employment. ***Email:*** wstone@lynchdallas.com

SEAN W. McPARTLAND, born Cedar Rapids, Iowa, October 28, 1958; admitted to bar, 1984, Missouri; 1989, Iowa. *Education:* University of Iowa (B.A., 1981; J.D., 1984). Phi Beta Kappa. *Member:* Linn County, Iowa State and American Bar Associations; The Missouri Bar; Iowa Defense Counsel Association; Defense Research Institute; National Association of Railroad Trial Counsel. ***PRACTICE AREAS:*** Civil Litigation; Railroad Law; Transportation Litigation; Labor and Employment; Insurance Litigation. ***Email:*** smcpartland@lynchdallas.com

MATTHEW J. NAGLE, born Davenport, Iowa, November 28, 1961; admitted to bar, 1987, Iowa. *Education:* Loras College (B.A., 1984); University of Iowa (J.D., 1987). Adjunct Professor, Trial Advocacy, University of Iowa. *Member:* Linn County, Iowa State and American Bar Associations; Iowa Association of Workers' Compensation Lawyers; Fellow: Iowa Academy of Trial Lawyers; Iowa Defense Counsel Association. ***PRACTICE AREAS:*** Civil Litigation; Workers' Compensation. ***Email:*** mnagle@lynchdallas.com

JANET HONG, born Fairfield, Iowa, April 26, 1949; admitted to bar, 1990, California; 1993, Iowa. *Education:* University of Iowa (B.A., 1971; J.D., 1990). Phi Beta Kappa. *Member:* Linn County, Iowa State and American Bar Associations; State Bar of California; Dean Mason Ladd American Inn of Court. ***PRACTICE AREAS:*** Debt and Bankruptcy; Commercial Law; Criminal Law. ***Email:*** jhong@lynchdallas.com

SUSAN L. HENSE, born Milwaukee, Wisconsin, September 20, 1960; admitted to bar, 1996, Iowa. *Education:* Coe College (B.A., 1993); University of Iowa (J.D., 1996). Board Chair, Moot Court, 1996. *Member:* Linn County, Iowa State and American Bar Associations. ***PRACTICE AREAS:*** Real Estate; Probate; Tax Law. ***Email:*** shense@lynchdallas.com

PATRICK J. O'CONNELL, born Clinton, Iowa, January 6, 1970; admitted to bar, 1995, Iowa; 1999, U.S. District Court, Northern and Southern Districts of Iowa. *Education:* Luther College (B.A., 1992); University of Iowa College of Law (J.D., 1995). Dean Mason Ladd Inn of Court, 1999. Judge Advocate, U.S. Marine Corps, Camp Lejeune, North Carolina, 1996-1999. *Member:* Linn County and Iowa State Bar Association. [Major, U.S. Marine Corps; Judge Advocate, U.S. Marine Corps, 1996-1999.]. ***PRACTICE AREAS:*** Railroad Litigation; Insurance Defense; Workers Compensation; Employment Law. ***Email:*** poconnell@lynchdallas.com

CORINNE R. BUTKOWSKI, born Saint Cloud, Minnesota, December 21, 1962; admitted to bar, 1997, Iowa. *Education:* Mankato State University (B.S.N., 1985); University of Iowa (J.D., 1997). Moot Court Board, 1996. Senior Note and Comment Editor, Journal of Corporation Law, 1996-1997. Registered Nurse, Iowa, 1985. *Member:* Linn County, Iowa State and American Bar Associations. ***Email:*** cbutkowski@lynchdallas.com

TODD A. SLAGTER, born Fargo, North Dakota, June 6, 1975; admitted to bar, 2001, Iowa and U.S District Court, Northern and Southern Districts of Iowa. *Education:* University of Minnesota, Duluth (B.A., summa cum laude, 1997); University of Denver (J.D., 2000; LL.M., Taxation, 2000). Business Editor, Preventive Law Reporter, University of Denver, 1999. Member, Cedar Rapids Estate Planning Council. *Member:* Linn County, Iowa State (Member, Probate Trust Law Section and Taxation Section) and American (Member, Tax Section) Bar Associations. ***PRACTICE AREAS:*** Taxation; Estate Planning; Business Planning; Probate.

AMY L. REASNER, born Phoenix, Arizona, August 13, 1971; admitted to bar, 2001, Iowa. *Education:* University of Iowa (B.A., 1993; J.D., 2001). Editor, Moot Court Board. Recipient, Iowa Bar Association Award. ***Email:*** areasner@lynchdallas.com

GREGORY L. CLEVENGER, born East Lansing, Michigan, September 27, 1970; admitted to bar, 2003, Iowa. *Education:* University of Iowa (B.A., 1999; J.D., 2003). ***Email:*** gclevenger@lynchdallas.com

JASON M. CRAIG, born Omaha, Nebraska, October 21, 1978; admitted to bar, 2004, Iowa and U.S. District Court, Northern and Southern Districts of Iowa. *Education:* University of Iowa (B.A., 2000; J.D., with high distinction, 2004). Order of the Coif. *Member:* Linn County, Iowa State and American Bar Associations. ***Email:*** jcraig@lynchdallas.com

REPRESENTATIVE CLIENTS: Alliant Transportation; American States Insurance Co.; CRANDIC Railway; CIGNA Cos.; General Casualty Insurance Companies; Progressive Insurance Companies; Rockwell Collins, Inc.; State Farm Insurance Cos.; The Travelers Insurance Cos.

(This Listing Continued)

MOYER & BERGMAN, P.L.C.

Established in 1961

2720 FIRST AVENUE, N.E.
P.O. BOX 1943
CEDAR RAPIDS, IOWA 52406-1943
Telephone: 319-366-7331
Telecopier: 319-366-3668
Email: mb@moyerbergman.com
URL: http://www.moyerbergman.com

General Practice in all Courts State and Federal. Business and Corporate, Employment and Labor, Real Estate, Insurance Defense, Collection and Bankruptcy, Appellate Practice, Banking and Financial Institutions, Commercial Transactions, Computer Law, Construction Claims, Family Law, Fidelity and Surety Law, Government Contracts, Civil Rights and Discrimination Law, Immigration, Intellectual Property, Interstate Commerce, Motor Carrier Transportation Litigation, Municipal Law, Personal Injury, Professional Malpractice Defense, Wills, Trusts, Probate, Estate Planning, Worker's Compensation and Trademark, Copyright Law, Franchise Law.

FIRM PROFILE: Moyer & Bergman, P.L.C. was founded in 1961 and is a full service law firm. The Firm provides advice and counsel to clients throughout Iowa, as well as across the country. Moyer & Bergman has Attorneys who are licensed to practice in Illinois, Minnesota, Nebraska, Washington and Wisconsin.

The Firm operates within four-practice group: Business and Tax, Employment and Labor Law, Litigation and Risk Management and Commercial Litigation. These groups provide a framework of specialists to meet your needs. The Practice group work together to provide the expertise that is needed for each client.

RETIRED

WILLIAM A. BERGMAN, born Fort Madison, Iowa, March 15, 1924; admitted to bar, 1949, Iowa; 1951, U.S. Tax Court. (Retired)

MEMBERS OF FIRM

ROBERT E. KONCHAR, born Madrid, Iowa, June 5, 1939; admitted to bar, 1965, Iowa, U.S. District Court, Northern and Southern Districts of Iowa, U.S. Court of Appeals, Third, Eighth, Eleventh and District of Columbia Circuits and U.S. Supreme Court. *Education:* Iowa State University; University of Iowa (B.B.A., 1962; J.D., 1965). Phi Delta Phi. *Member:* Linn County, Iowa State and American (Member, Sections on: Labor and Employment Law; Torts and Insurance Practice) Bar Associations; Defense Research Institute; Iowa Defense Counsel Association; American Trucking Association; National Trucking Industrial Relations Association; Iowa Academy of Trial Lawyers. ***PRACTICE AREAS:*** Civil Litigation; Commercial Litigation; Discrimination; Employment Contracts; Employment Law; Labor Law; Litigation; Appellate Practice; Motor Carrier Law; Sexual Harassment; Transportation. ***Email:*** bkonchar@moyerbergman.com

STEPHEN C. NELSON, born Ogden, Iowa, March 15, 1942; admitted to bar, 1967, Iowa. *Education:* Iowa State University (B.S., 1964); University of Iowa (J.D., 1967). Tau Beta Pi. President, Cedar Rapids Area Estate Planning Council, 1979-1980. *Member:* Linn County (Member, Board of Governors, 1981-1983, 1989-1993; Title Standards Committee, 1982—), Iowa State (Chairman, Legal Forms Committee, 1980-1984; Real Estate Committee, 1991—) and American (Member, Real Property Section, Probate and Trust Law Section, 1988—, State Chair of Affordable Housing, 1999—) Bar Associations. ***PRACTICE AREAS:*** Estate Planning; Housing Law; Zoning, Planning and Land Use; Landlord and Tenant Law; Probate; Estate Administration; Real Estate; Taxation; Trusts and Estates; Wills. ***Email:*** SNelson@moyerbergman.com

J. SCOTT BOGGUSS, born Moline, Illinois, September 19, 1946; admitted to bar, 1971, Iowa; 1972, U.S. District Court, Northern and Southern Districts of Iowa and U.S. Tax Court. *Education:* University of Iowa (B.B.A., 1968; J.D., 1971). Beta Gamma Sigma; Phi Delta Phi. Fellow, American College of Trust & Estate Counsel. *Member:* Linn County, Iowa State (Vice Chairman, Tax Section, 1993-1994) and American (Member, 1975-1983 and Adjunct Member, 1983-2000, Committee on Employee Benefits, Taxation Section; Member, Sections on: Business Law; Law Practice Management) Bar Associations.

(This Listing Continued)

MOYER & BERGMAN, P.L.C., Cedar Rapids—Continued

PRACTICE AREAS: Business Law; Business Organization; Commercial Law; Estate Planning; Franchise Law; Pension and Profit Sharing Plans; Probate Administration; Estate Administration; Real Estate; Securities Law; Taxation. ***Email:*** SBogguss@moyerbergman.com

LARRY G. GUTZ, born Storm Lake, Iowa, July 4, 1939; admitted to bar, 1964, Iowa; 1968, U.S. District Court, Northern and Southern Districts of Iowa; 1970, District of Columbia, U.S. Court of Appeals, Eighth Circuit and U.S. Supreme Court; 1990, Wisconsin; 1993, U.S. District Court, Eastern District of Wisconsin. *Education:* Iowa State University; University of Iowa (B.A., 1962; J.D., cum laude, 1964). Phi Delta Phi. *Member:* Linn County (Chairman: Medical-Legal Malpractice Panel, 1982-1984; Fee Arbitration Committee, 1982-1986; Ethics and Grievance Committee, 1989-1992; Member, Board of Governors, 1977, 1978, 1990-1994; President, 1992-1993), Sixth Judicial District (Member, Board of Governors, 1980-1981; President, 1981), Iowa State (Member, Board of Governors, 1982-1986) and American (Member, Law Office Management Section) Bar Associations; Defense Research Institute; American Bankruptcy Institute; Iowa Defense Counsel Association; American Trucking Association Litigation Center. ***PRACTICE AREAS:*** Bankruptcy; Commercial Litigation; Debtor and Creditor; Family Law; Transportation. ***Email:*** LGutz@moyerbergman.com

PHILIP D. BROOKS, born Webster City, Iowa, August 14, 1950; admitted to bar, 1977, Iowa and U.S. District Court, Northern and Southern Districts of Iowa. *Education:* University of Iowa (B.B.A., 1972; M.B.A., 1974); Creighton University (J.D., 1977). Chartered Property Casualty Underwriter (CPCU), 1976—. Chartered Life Underwriter (CLU), 1980—. *Member:* Linn County (Member: Ethics and Grievance Committee, 1988-1989; Fee Arbitration Committee, 1989—) Iowa State (Member: Committee on Insurance, 1984-1987; Lawyer's Professional Liability Committee, 1989—) and American Bar Associations. ***PRACTICE AREAS:*** Agricultural Law; Antitrust and Trade Regulation; Business Law; Business Organization; Estate Planning; Health Care Law; Insurance; Mergers and Acquisitions; Taxation. ***Email:*** PBrooks@moyerbergman.com

J. MICHAEL WESTON, born Anderson, Indiana, February 15, 1955; admitted to bar, 1980, Iowa; U.S. Supreme Court; U.S. Court of Appeals, Eighth Circuit; U.S. District Court, Northern and Southern Districts of Iowa. *Education:* University of Iowa (B.A., 1977; J.D., 1980). Omicron Delta Kappa. Editor, Moot Court Board, 1980. Adjunct Professor, Mount Mercy College, 1981-1987. *Member:* Linn County (Chairman: Fee Arbitration Committee, 1988-1992; Chairman, Ethics and Grievance Committee, 1992-1998; Member, Board of Governors, 1996-2001; President, 1999-2000), Iowa State (Member: Litigation Section; Board of Governors, 2000—) and American (Member, Sections on: Litigation; Tort and Insurance Practice) Bar Associations; Iowa Defense Counsel Association (Member, Board of Directors, 1995—; Chairman: Jury Instruction Committee, 1996-1997; Chairman, Legislative Committee, 1997-2002; Secretary, 2000-2001; President Elect, 2001-2002; President, 2002-2003); International Association of Defense Counsel (Member, Advocacy, Practice and Procedure and Casualty Insurance Committees; Faculty, IADC Trial Academy, 2003); Defense Research Institute (Member, Product Liability and Casualty Insurance Committees). Fellow: Iowa State Bar Association; Iowa Academy of Trial Lawyers. ***PRACTICE AREAS:*** Casualty Insurance Defense; Civil Litigation; Commercial Litigation; Insurance; Litigation; Appellate Practice; Medical Malpractice; Personal Injury; Products Liability; Professional Liability; Torts. ***Email:*** MWeston@moyerbergman.com

KEVIN J. VISSER, born Warrensburg, Missouri, November 10, 1956; admitted to bar, 1980, Iowa; 1981, U.S. District Court, Northern and Southern Districts of Iowa; 1986, U.S. Court of Appeals, Eighth Circuit and U.S. Supreme Court. *Education:* Central Missouri State University (B.S., Econ., 1978); University of Iowa (J.D., 1980). *Member:* Linn County (Member, Ethics and Grievance Committee) Iowa State (Member, Sections on: Litigation; Labor and Employment; Trade Regulation) and American (Member, Sections on: Labor and Employment Law; Litigation) Bar Associations; Iowa Trial Lawyers Association; Association of General Contractors' Labor Lawyers Council; National Employment Lawyers' Association; American Board of Trial Advocates. Fellow, Iowa Academy of Trial Lawyers. Listed in Best Lawyers in America, Blair's ADR List. ***PRACTICE AREAS:*** Civil Rights; Commercial Litigation; Employment Law; Labor Law; Appellate Practice; Trial Law; Business Law. ***Email:*** KVisser@moyerbergman.com

RANDAL J. SCHOLER, born Burlington, Iowa, October 20, 1956; admitted to bar, 1981, Iowa and U.S. District Court, Northern and Southern Districts of Iowa. *Education:* Southeastern Community College (A.S., 1976); University of Iowa (B.B.A., 1978; J.D., with distinction, 1981). Member, Beta Gamma Sigma Scholastic Honorary Society. Editor, Moot Court Board, 1980-1981. *Member:* Linn County, Iowa State (Member, Sections on: Taxation and Corporate Counsel; Business Law; Agricultural Law; Probate and Trust Law) and American (Member, Sections on: Business Law; Taxation; Real Property, Probate and Trust Law; State and Local Government Law) Bar Associations; International Foundation of Employee Benefit Plans; Iowa Municipal Attorneys Association. ***PRACTICE AREAS:*** Administrative Law; Business Law; Business Organization; Commercial Law; Employee Benefits; Estate Planning; Mergers and Acquisitions; Municipal Law; Probate Administration; Estate Administration; Real Estate. ***Email:*** RScholer@moyerbergman.com

WILLIAM S. VERNON, born Cedar Rapids, Iowa, October 21, 1952; admitted to bar, 1977, Iowa; 1981, U.S. District Court, Northern and Southern Districts of Iowa and U.S. Tax Court. *Education:* Regis College (B.S., cum laude, 1974); Drake University (J.D., 1977); University of Missouri-Kansas City (LL.M., Taxation, 1981). Alpha Sigma Nu. Member, Moot Court Board, 1976-1977. Certified Public Accountant, Iowa, 1979. *Member:* Linn County, Iowa State (Member: Title Guaranty Committee, 1985-1987; Taxation Committee, 1985-1988; Iowa Title Standards Committee, 1990—) and American (Member, Sections on: Taxation; Urban, State and Local Government Law) Bar Associations. ***PRACTICE AREAS:*** Collections Law; Commercial Law; Commercial Litigation; Construction Law; Contracts; Corporate Law; Debtor and Creditor; Real Estate; Tax Controversies. ***Email:*** BVernon@moyerbergman.com

JAMES P. CRAIG, born Normal, Illinois, September 28, 1956; admitted to bar, 1983, Iowa, U.S. District Court, Northern and Southern Districts of Iowa and U.S. Court of Appeals, 8th Circuit. *Education:* University of Iowa (B.A., 1979; M.A., 1981; J.D., with distinction, 1983). *Member:* Linn County (Member, Board of Governors, 2001-2003; President, 2003-2004), Iowa State and American (Member, Sections on: Litigation; Tort and Insurance Practice) Bar Associations; Defense Research Institute; Iowa Defense Counsel Association. Fellow: Iowa Academy of Trial Lawyers; Iowa Municipal Attorneys Association. ***PRACTICE AREAS:*** Adoption Law; Casualty Insurance Defense; Civil Litigation; Medical Malpractice; Motor Vehicle Accidents and Injuries; Municipal Law; Personal Injury; Premises Liability; Products Liability; Professional Liability; Torts. ***Email:*** JCraig@moyerbergman.com

ERIC W. LAM, born Hong Kong B.C.C., October 21, 1956; admitted to bar, 1982, Iowa; U.S. Supreme Court; U.S. Court of Appeals, Eighth circuit; U.S. District Court, Northern and Southern Districts of Iowa. *Education:* Macalester College (B.A., cum laude, 1979); University of Iowa (J.D., with distinction, 1982). Recipient: Certificate of Merit, Writing Competition, International Association of Insolvency Practitioners (INSOL), Vancouver, British Columbia, Canada, June 22, 1989; First Prize, Writing Competition, American Bankruptcy Institute, Washington D.C., May 8, 1989. Managing Editor, Iowa Law Review, Vol. 67, 1981-1982. Law Clerk to: Hon. W. Ward Reynoldson, Chief Justice, Iowa Supreme Court, 1982-1983; Hon. William W. Thinnes, U.S. Bankruptcy Judge, Northern District of Iowa, 1983-1984. Author: Comment, "Toward a Valid Defense Contingent Fee Contract," Vol. 67 Iowa Law Review 373 (1982); "Recent Developments," 1984 Annual Survey of Bankruptcy Law, 327; "Cancellation of Insurance Bankruptcy Automatic Stay Implications," 59 American Bankruptcy Law Journal 267 (Summer 1985); "Of Exclusivity and For Cause: 11 U.S.C. Sec. 1121 (d) Re-examined," 36 Drake Law Review, 533 (Spring 1988); "Bankruptcy Code Section 304(b)(3): Other Appropriate Relief for Multinational Bankruptcy, "16 Brooklyn Journal of International Law, 4-79, 1990; "Municipal Bankruptcy: The Problem with Chapter 9 Eligibility--A Proposal to Amend 11 U.S.C. §109 (c)(2), 1988," 22 Arizona State Law Journal 625, 1990; "On The River of Artificial and Arbitrary Impairment: An Erroneous Analysis," 70. So. Dakota L. Rev. 993 (1994); "The Limit and Inconsistency of Application of the Plain Meaning Rule to Selected Provisions of the Bankruptcy Reform Act of 1994," 20 Hamline L Rev. 111 (Fall 1996); Book, *Bankruptcy in Iowa,* 1992. Lecturer (Bankruptcy), Iowa State Bar Review School, Inc. (January 1989, 1990-1996). Adjunct Professor, (Bankruptcy), University of Iowa College of Law, 1993. Bankruptcy Trustee, Chapter 7, 1990—. Member, Iowa Supreme Court Committee to Monitor and Implement "Equality in the Courts" Task Force Report, 1995-1997. *Member:* Linn County (Co-Chair, Membership Committee, 1993), Iowa State (Chair, Commercial and Bankruptcy Law Council, 1995-1996; Board of Governors, 1996-2000), Federal (Chair, Bankruptcy Section, 1993-1994) and American (Member, Litigation Section) Bar Associations; American Bankruptcy Institute. Fellow: Iowa State Bar Foundation; American College of Bankruptcy. ***PRACTICE AREAS:*** Bankruptcy Law; Creditors Rights. ***Email:*** ELam@moyerbergman.com

MICHAEL McDONOUGH, born Ottumwa, Iowa, February 28, 1954; admitted to bar, 1981, Nebraska; 1985, Iowa, U.S. District Court, Northern and Southern Districts of Iowa, U.S. District Court, District of Nebraska, U.S. Court of Appeals, Eighth Circuit and U.S. Claims Court. *Education:* University of Iowa (B.A., 1977); Creighton University (J.D., magna cum laude, 1981). Member, Creighton University Law Review, 1979-1981. Law Clerk to Chief Justice Norman Krivosha, Nebraska Supreme Court, 1981-1982. *Member:* Linn County, Iowa State, Nebraska State and American Bar Associations; Trucking Industry Defense Association. ***PRACTICE AREAS:*** Bankruptcy; Commercial Litigation; Construction Law; Construction Litigation; Insurance Coverage Defense; Motor Carrier; Personal Injury; Products Liability; Uniform Commercial Code. ***Email:*** MMcdonough@moyerbergman.com

BRENDA K. WALLRICHS, born Waterloo, Iowa, May 7, 1970; admitted to bar, 1995, Iowa and U.S. District Court, Northern and Southern Districts of Iowa; 2000, U.S. Court of Appeals, Eighth Circuit. *Education:* Drake University (B.A., cum laude, 1992); University of Iowa (J.D., with distinction, 1995). Articles Editor, Iowa Law Review, Vol. 80, 1994-1995. *Member:* Linn County, Iowa State and American (Member, Sections on: Tort and Insurance Practice) Bar Associations; Iowa Defense Counsel; Defense Research Institute. ***PRACTICE AREAS:*** Appellate Practice; Automobile Liability; Casualty Insurance Defense; Civil Litigation; Insurance; Litigation; Municipal Law; Personal Injury; Products Liability. ***Email:*** BWallrichs@moyerbergman.com

THOMAS D. WOLLE, born Sioux City, Iowa, March 5, 1966; admitted to bar, 1992, Iowa, Minnesota, U.S. District Court, Northern and Southern Districts of Iowa and U.S. Court of Appeals, Eighth Circuit. *Education:* Luther College (B.A., 1988); University of Iowa (J.D., with distinction, 1992). Associate Editor, Iowa Law Review, 1991-1992. *Member:* Linn County, Iowa State and American Bar Associations. ***PRACTICE AREAS:*** Civil Litigation; Commercial Litigation; Employment Law; Family Law; Labor Law; Workers Compensation. ***Email:*** TWolle@moyerbergman.com

MATTHEW J. KRIGBAUM, admitted to bar, 1997, Washington; 1998, Illinois and U.S. District Court, Northern District of Illinois; 1999, Iowa and U.S. District Court, Northern District of Iowa; 2001, U.S. District Court, Southern District of Iowa. *Education:* University of Oregon (B.A., 1994); Gonzaga University (J.D., 1997); John Marshall Law School (LL.M., Intellectual Property, 1998). *Member:* American (Member, Sections on: Intellectual Property, Business Law, Franchise Law, Science and Technology), Iowa State (Member, Sections on: Intellectual Property; Information Technology and Business Law), Illinois State and Washington State Bar Associations; American Intellectual Property Law Association; Computer Law Association; International Trademark Association; Licensing Executives Society). ***PRACTICE AREAS:*** Intellectual Property; Information Technology; Business Law; Computer Law; Corporate Law; Copyrights; Trademarks; Trade Secrets; Internet Law; Unfair Competition; Franchise Law. ***Email:*** MKrigbaum@moyerbergman.com

THOMAS N. DeBOOM, born Cedar Rapids, Iowa, December 25, 1973; admitted to bar, 1999, Iowa. *Education:* University of Iowa (B.S., with honors and distinction, 1996; J.D., with distinction, 1999). *Member:* Linn County, Iowa State and American (Member, Sections on: Business Law, Corporate Counsel, Probate and Trust Law and Taxation) Bar Associations; American Immigration Lawyers Association. ***PRACTICE AREAS:*** Business Immigration; Business Law; Business Organization; Contracts; Employee Benefits; Estate Planning; Mergers and Acquisitions; Pension and Profit Sharing Plans; Securities Law; Taxation. ***Email:*** TDeboom@moyerbergman.com

(This Listing Continued)

ASSOCIATES

MARK J. HERZBERGER, born Anamosa, Iowa, May 17, 1951; admitted to bar, 1987, Iowa; 1988, U.S. Tax Court and U.S. District Court, Nort hern District of Iowa; 1989, U.S. District Court, Southern District of Iowa; 1990, U.S. Court of Appeals, Eighth Circuit. *Education:* Kirkwood Community College (A.A., 1977); University of Iowa (B.B.A., 1979; J.D., with distinction, 1987). *Member:* Linn County, Iowa State and American Bar Associations; Defense Research Institute (Member, Trucking Law Committee); Trucking Industry Defense Association; Iowa Motor Truck Association (Member, Sections on: Construction Law; Insurance Law Practice). [USMC, 1969-1973]. ***PRACTICE AREAS:*** Civil Litigation; Commercial Litigation; Construction Law; Construction Litigation; Contracts; Motor Carrier Law; OSHA; Torts; Trade Secrets; Transportation. ***Email:*** MHerzberger@moyerbergman.com

CYNTHIA SCHERRMAN SUEPPEL, born Denver, Colorado, July 3, 1958; admitted to bar, 1984, Iowa and U.S. District Court, Northern and Southern Districts of Iowa. *Education:* University of Iowa (B.A., with highest honors, 1980; J.D., with distinction, 1984). *Member:* Linn County, Iowa State (Member, Sections on: Litigation Law; Workers Compensation Law) and American Bar Associations; Iowa Trial Lawyers Association (Member, Workers Compensation Section); Iowa Association of Workers Compensation Lawyers; Iowa Academy of Trial Lawyers.; Dean Mason Inn of Court. ***PRACTICE AREAS:*** Appellate Practice; Discrimination; Employment Law; Medical Malpractice; Personal Injury; Products Liability; Sexual Harassment; Torts; Workers Compensation. ***Email:*** CSueppel@moyerbergman.com

MARCIA V. HARRIS, born Salem, Oregon, October 8, 1962; admitted to bar, 1994, Minnesota; 1995, Wisconsin (Not admitted in Iowa). *Education:* North Dakota State University (B.S., 1986); William Mitchell College of Law (J.D., magna cum laude, 1994). ***PRACTICE AREAS:*** Civil Rights; Discrimination; Employment Law; Insurance; Torts; Litigation; Appellate Practice; Municipal Law; Personal Injury; Sexual Harassment; Toxic Torts. ***Email:*** MHarris@moyerbergman.com

BRIAN J. FAGAN, born Cedar Rapids, Iowa, December 1, 1971; admitted to bar, 2001, Iowa, U.S. District Court, Northern and Southern Districts of Iowa and U.S. Court of Appeals, Seventh and Eight Circuits; U.S. Court of Appeals for the District of Columbia. *Education:* University of Iowa (B.B.A., 1994); Drake University Law School (J.D., 2001). Law Clerk to Judge Michael J. Melloy, U.S. District Court, Northern District of Iowa and U.S. Court of Appeals for the Eighth Circuit. Member: Linn County, Iowa State and American (Member, Law Related Education Committee, Young Lawyers Division) Bar Associations. ***PRACTICE AREAS:*** Employment Law; Commercial Litigation. ***Email:*** BFagan@moyerbergman.com

MARK J. PARMENTER, born Grinnell, Iowa, January 31, 1963; admitted to bar, 2003, Iowa and U.S. District Court, Northern and Southern Districts of Iowa. *Education:* University of Missouri at Kansas City (B.A., 1993); Drake University Law School (J.D., 2003). *Member:* Linn County, Iowa State and American Bar Associations. ***PRACTICE AREAS:*** Corporate Law; Estate Administration; Estate Planning; Probate Administration; Real Estate. ***Email:*** MParmenter@moyerbergman.com

AMANDA D'AMICO, born Honolulu, Hawaii, December 15, 1979; admitted to bar, 2004, Iowa. *Education:* University of Iowa (B.B.A., 2001; J.D., 2004). Phi Delta Phi. Certified Public Accountant, 2001. *Member:* Linn County, Iowa State (Member, Bridge the Gap Committee) and American Bar Associations. ***PRACTICE AREAS:*** Business Law; Taxation. ***Email:*** adamico@moyerbergman.com

SASHA L. MONTHEI, born Iowa City, Iowa, June 20, 1980; admitted to bar, 2004, Iowa and U.S. District Court, Northern and Southern Districts of Iowa. *Education:* University of Iowa (B.A., 2001; J.D., 2004). Order of the Coif. ***PRACTICE AREAS:*** Litigation; Contracts; Insurance; Personal Injury; Transportation. ***Email:*** smonthei@moyerbergman.com

KIMBERLY K. HARDEMAN, born April 18, 1970; admitted to bar, 1996, Iowa. *Education:* St. Cloud State University (B.S., summa cum laude, 1992); Drake University (J.D., 1995). Associate Adjunct Professor, Civil Litigation, Kirkwood Community College. Formerly with John C. Wagner Law Offices, P.C. *Member:* Iowa County (President, 1996-1997), Linn County, Iowa State and American Bar Associations; Iowa Trial Lawyers Association; Dean Mason Inn of Court. ***PRACTICE AREAS:*** Litigation; Personal Injury; Insurance; Medical Malpractice; Workers Compensation. ***Email:*** khardeman@moyerbergman.com

MATTHEW J. ADAM, born Fairfield, Iowa, February 8, 1976; admitted to bar, 2002, Iowa. *Education:* Truman State University (B.S., 1998); University of Iowa (J.D., 2002); Henry B. Tipple School of Management (M.B.A., 2002). Phi Delta Phi, 1998-2002. Associate Editor, Journal of Corporation Law, 2001-2002. *Member:* Johnson County, Linn County, Iowa State and American Bar Associations. ***PRACTICE AREAS:*** Real Estate; Estate Planning; Business Law; Commercial Transactions; Probate. ***Email:*** madam@moyerbergman.com

OF COUNSEL

LARRY D. HELVEY, born Portland, Oregon, March 5, 1945; admitted to bar, 1985, Iowa; U.S. District Court, Northern and Southern Districts of Iowa. *Education:* University of Oregon (B.S., 1967; M.D., 1971); University of Iowa (J.D., 1985). Member, Alpha Omega Alpha Medical Honor Society. Board Certified in Emergency Medicine. Director of Emergency Medicine, St. Luke's Hospital, Cedar Rapids, Iowa, 1972—. *Member:* Linn County, Iowa State and American Bar Associations; Defense Counsel Association. ***PRACTICE AREAS:*** Medical Malpractice. ***Email:*** LHelvey@moyerbergman.com

NICOLE L. CLAUSSEN, born Grand Mound, Iowa, July 3, 1973; admitted to bar, 1999, Iowa and U.S. District Court, Northern District of Iowa. *Education:* Coe College (B.A. magna cum laude, with distinction, 1995); University of Iowa (J.D., 1998). *Member:* Linn County, Iowa State and American Bar Associations. ***PRACTICE AREAS:*** Child Support; Family Law; Insurance; Litigation; Appellate Practice; Motor Vehicle Accidents and Injuries; Municipal Law; Torts. ***Email:*** NClaussen@moyerbergman.com

REPRESENTATIVE CLIENTS: AEGON USA, Inc.; Ag Services of America, Inc.; American Family Insurance Group; Bankers Trust Co.; Bruening Rock Products; Capital Indemnity Ins. Co.; Carl A. Nelson & Co.; Cedar Graphics, Inc.; Cedar Valley Asphalt; CitiCaptial Commercial Corp.; City of Fairfax; City of Hiawatha; City of Lisbon; Communications Engr. Co.; CRST, Inc.; CRST Logistics, Inc.; Dan's Overhead Doors and More, Inc.; Deere & Co.; Employers Reinsurance Corp.; Farm Credit System Capital Corp.; Fauser Oil Co.; First Financial Center; Fred Carlson Co., Inc.; Gee Grading and Excavating; GEICO Casualty Company; GE Capital Corp.; GreatAmerica Leasing Corp.; Great West Casualty Co.; Gulf Insurance Co.; Hames Mobile Home, Inc.; Henderson Mfg.; Independent Ins. Agents of Iowa; Intermec Technologies Corp.; ITT Commercial Finance; KGAN-TV; Kuhlman Construction Co.; Lynch Ford, Inc.; Malone Freight Lines, Inc.; Maquoketa State Bank; Maytag Corporation; McLeod USA Incorporated; Mendota Insurance Co.; Metal Fabricators Co., Inc.; Modern Piping, Inc.; Monticello State Bank; Natl Farmer's Union Property & Cas.; North American Nutrition; Omega Cabinets; Omega Communications; Palo Coop. Telephone Assoc.; Permeate Refining, Inc.; Petroleum Equipment and Sercs., Inc.; Rexco Equipment, Inc.; Quintrex Data Systems; Safeco; Safeco Insurance Company; Springville Tel. Assn.; State Farm Insurance Companies; Three "I" Truck Lines, Inc.; Tipton State Bank; TrueNorth Companies; U.S. Bank, N.A.; United States Liability Insurance Group; Vector Group; Victor Plastics; Wausau Insurance Co.; Wendling Quarries, Inc.; West Bend Mutual Ins. Co.; Westfield Group; Wilbur-Ellis, Co.

(This Listing Continued)

NYEMASTER, GOODE, WEST, HANSELL & O'BRIEN

A PROFESSIONAL CORPORATION

CEDAR RAPIDS, IOWA

(See Des Moines)

General Civil Practice including Corporate, Securities, Antitrust, Insurance, Banking, Commercial Law, Cooperative Law, Probate, Real Estate, Taxation, Workers Compensation, Municipal, Legislative, Labor, Administrative Law and Trials in all Courts.

PICKENS, BARNES & ABERNATHY

Established in 1974

TENTH FLOOR AMERICAN BUILDING
101 2ND STREET SE
P.O. BOX 74170
CEDAR RAPIDS, IOWA 52407-4170
Telephone: 319-366-7621
Fax: 319-366-3158
Email: law@pbalawfirm.com
URL: http://www.pbalawfirm.com

Trials and Appeals in all Courts, Civil Litigation, Insurance Defense, Personal Injury, Workers Compensation, Commercial and Construction Litigation, Employment Law, Insurance Coverage, Products Liability, Creditors Remedies and Bankruptcy.

JAMES F. PICKENS (1929-2004)

MEMBERS OF FIRM

TERRY J. ABERNATHY, born Kansas City, Missouri, August 19, 1947; admitted to bar, 1973, Iowa and U.S. District Court, Northern and Southern Districts of Iowa. *Education:* Coe College (B.A., 1970); University of Iowa (J.D., with distinction, 1973). Finalist, National Moot Court Competition. Member, Sixth Judicial District Nominating Commission, 1991-1994. *Member:* Linn County (President, 1996-1997), Iowa State (Member, Litigation Section) and American Bar Associations; American Board of Trial Advocates; International Association of Defense Counsel; Iowa Academy of Trial Lawyers (Fellow); Defense Research Institute; Iowa Defense Counsel Association (Director, 1998-2003); Dean Mason Ladd Inn of Court. ***PRACTICE AREAS:*** Insurance Defense; Civil Litigation. ***Email:*** tabernathy@pbalawfirm.com

MATTHEW G. NOVAK, born Cedar Rapids, Iowa, December 3, 1956; admitted to bar, 1982, Iowa and U.S. District Court, Northern and Southern Districts of Iowa; 1987, U.S. Supreme Court. *Education:* Coe College (B.A., 1979); St. Louis University (J.D., 1982). Staff Member and Assistant Managing Editor, St. Louis University Law Journal, 1981-1982. *Member:* Linn County, Iowa State (Member, Executive Council, Young Lawyers Division, 1984-1992; Member, Workers Compensation Section; Co-Chair, Bench-Bar Committee, 1995-1998) and American Bar Associations; The Association of Trial Lawyers of America; Iowa Trial Lawyers Association; Iowa Academy of Trial Lawyers; Dean Mason Ladd Inn of Court (President, 1999-2000); Iowa Association of School Boards. ***PRACTICE AREAS:*** Civil Litigation; Personal Injury; Insurance Defense; Workers Compensation. ***Email:*** mnovak@pbalawfirm.com

THAD J. COLLINS, born Iowa City, Iowa, June 4, 1964; admitted to bar, 1990, Minnesota; 1994, U.S. Court of Appeals, Eighth Circuit; 1998, Iowa and U.S. District Court, Northern and Southern Districts of Iowa. *Education:* Macalester College (B.A., 1986); University of Iowa (J.D., with distinction, 1990). Associate Editor, Iowa Law Review, 1989-1990. Author: Note, "Forging Middle Ground: Revision of Student Loan Debts in Bankruptcy," 75 Iowa L. Rev 733, 1990. Law Clerk to: Judge David R. Hansen, U.S. Court of Appeals, Eighth Circuit, 1993-1995; Chief Judge Michael J. Melloy, U.S. District Court, Northern District of Iowa, 1992-1993; Chief Judge Michael J. Melloy, U.S. Bankruptcy Court, Northern District of Iowa, 1990-1992. *Member:* Linn County, Iowa State and American Bar Associations; Dean Mason Ladd Inn of Court. ***PRACTICE AREAS:*** Civil Litigation; Mediation; Personal Injury; Employment Law; Construction Law; Insurance Defense. ***Email:*** tcollins@pbalawfirm.com

STEPHANIE L. HINZ, born Des Moines, Iowa, August 2, 1969; admitted to bar, 1994, Iowa; 1997, U.S. District Court, Northern and Southern Districts of Iowa. *Education:* Iowa State University (B.A., 1991); Drake University (M.A., 1994; J.D., with distinction, 1994). *Member:* Linn County (Member, Board of Governors, 2000—), Iowa State and American Bar Associations; Linn County Women Attorneys Association; Linn Law Club (President, 2000-2001); Defense Research Institute. ***PRACTICE AREAS:*** Insurance Defense; Civil Litigation; Creditors Rights. ***Email:*** shinz@pbalawfirm.com

(This Listing Continued)

PICKENS, BARNES & ABERNATHY, Cedar Rapids—Continued

RETIRED

MINOR BARNES, born Mason City, Iowa, April 22, 1930; admitted to bar, 1961, Iowa and U.S. District Court, Southern District of Iowa; 1964, U.S. Supreme Court; 1968, U.S. District Court, Northern District of Iowa. *Education:* Carleton College; University of Iowa (B.A., 1952; J.D., with distinction, 1961). Phi Delta Phi. Member, Board of Editors, Iowa Law Review, 1960-1961. Legislative Assistant and Counsel to U.S. Senator Jack R. Miller, 88th Congress, 1963-1964. Member, Sixth Judicial District Nominating Commission, 1978-1984. Member, Iowa Supreme Court Nominating Commission, 1987-1993. *Member:* Linn County (President, 1982-1983), Iowa State and American (Member, Torts and Insurance Practice Section) Bar Associations; Iowa Defense Counsel Association; Defense Research Institute. Fellow, Iowa State Bar Foundation. [Lt., US Navy, 1952-1956]. ***PRACTICE AREAS:*** Insurance Defense.

REPRESENTATIVE CLIENTS: EMC Insurance Companies; Hy-Vee, Inc.; Allied Insurance; GuideOne Insurance; Iowa Mutual Insurance Company; Society Insurance; Acuity; Integrity Insurance; American Nat'l Prop. and Cas. Companies (ANPAC); Ford Motor Credit; General Motors Acceptance Corp.; SDG Macerich Properties; Linn-Mar Community School District; Merit Construction.
REFERENCES: Guaranty Bank and Trust Co., Cedar Rapids, Iowa.

RICCOLO & SEMELROTH, P.C.

SUITE 1140, APAC BUILDING
425 SECOND STREET, S.E.
CEDAR RAPIDS, IOWA 52401
Telephone: 319-365-9200; Toll Free: 1-888-546-6529
Fax: 319-365-1114
Email: rb@riccololaw.com
URL: http://www.riccololaw.com

Trials and Appeals in all State and Federal Courts. Personal Injury, Medical Malpractice, Professional Malpractice, Products Liability, Workers Compensation Law.

JOHN L. RICCOLO, born Pontiac, Illinois, November 16, 1950; admitted to bar, 1977, Illinois and Iowa, U.S. District Court, Northern and Southern Districts of Iowa and U.S. Court of Appeals, Eighth Circuit. *Education:* University of Notre Dame (B.A., 1972); John Marshall Law School (J.D., with honors, 1977). Member, John Marshall Journal of Practice & Procedure, 1976-1977. Member, National Labor Law Moot Court. Member, Supreme Court Study Committee on Lawyer Specialization, 1985-1986. Founding Sponsor, Civil Justice Foundation. Member, Trial Lawyers For Public Justice, 1989—. *Member:* Linn County, Iowa State (President, Young Lawyers Section, 1984-1985) and American (Member: Executive Council, Young Lawyers Division, 1983-1984; Litigation Section) Bar Associations; Iowa Trial Lawyers Association (Member, Board of Governors, 1980-1990; President, 1990-1991); Iowa Academy of Trial Lawyers (Member, Board of Governors, 1999—; President, 2003-2004); The Association of Trial Lawyers of America (Sustaining Member, Board of Governors, 1992—; Member, Birth Trauma Litigation Group; Member, Professional Negligence Section); Iowa Association of Workers Compensation Lawyers. ***PRACTICE AREAS:*** Personal Injury; Medical Malpractice; Professional Negligence. ***Email:*** jriccolo@riccololaw.com

TIMOTHY S. SEMELROTH, born Cedar Rapids, Iowa, September 8, 1971; admitted to bar, 1997, Iowa; 1998, U.S. District Court, Northern District of Iowa. *Education:* Drake University (B.A., summa cum laude, 1994); University of Iowa (J.D., with high distinction, 1997). Iowa Law Review, 1995-1996. Director, Trial Advocacy Board, 1996-1997. Law Clerk to Hon. John A. Jarvey, Chief Magistrate Judge, U.S. District Court, Northern District of Iowa, 1997-1998. *Member:* Linn County, Iowa State (President, Young Lawyers Division, 2002-2003) and American (Executive Council, Young Lawyers Division, 1998-2000, Litigation Section) Bar Associations; Iowa Trial Lawyers Association (Board of Governors, 2003—); The Association of Trial Lawyers of America (Member: Birth Trauma Litigation Group; Professional Negligence Section). ***PRACTICE AREAS:*** Personal Injury; Professional Negligence; Workers Compensation. ***Email:*** tsemelroth@riccololaw.com

DELL A. RICHARD

CEDAR RAPIDS, IOWA

(See Coralville)

Business Law, Commercial Real Estate, Corporate Law, Guardianships and Conservatorships, Leases and Leasing, Partnership Law, Probate, Real Estate Law, Trusts and Estates, Wills.

TOM RILEY LAW FIRM, P.L.C.

Established in 1980
4040 FIRST AVENUE N.E.
P.O. BOX 998
CEDAR RAPIDS, IOWA 52406-0998
Telephone: 319-363-4040
Fax: 319-363-9789; 319-298-2917
URL: http://www.trlf.com
URL: http://www.tomrileylaw.com

Iowa City Office: 1210 Highway 6 West. Telephone: 319-351-4996. Fax: 319-351-7063.

Personal Injury, Medical Malpractice, Products Liability, Civil Litigation, Workers' Compensation and Corporate Litigation.

TOM RILEY, admitted to bar, 1952, Iowa. *Education:* University of Iowa (B.B.A., 1950; J.D., 1952). Author: "Punitive Damages: When and When Not to Claim," Trial Diplomacy Journal, Vol. 1, No. 1, Spring 1978, reprinted in The Trial Masters: A Handbook of Strategies and Tactics That Win Cases, Prentice-Hall, 1984; "Punitive Damages: The Doctrine of Just Enrichment," 27 Drake Law Review 194, Summer 1978; "Opening Statement—Winning at the Outset," American Journal of Trial Advocacy, Vol. 3, No. 2, Fall 1979; "Proving Punitive Damages: The Complete Handbook," Prentice-Hall, 1981; "Toxic Shock Syndrome: Proving Causation Before Science Has," American Journal of Trial Advocacy, Vol. 6, No. 1, Summer 1982; "Cross Examination: The Art of Gentle Persuasion," Trial Diplomacy Journal, Vol. 6, No. I, Spring 1983; Article, "Protective Orders: Machiavelli Would Be Pleased," Trial, Vol. 20, No. 12, November 1984; "The Price of a Life: One Woman's Death from Toxic Shock," Adler & Adler, 1986; "The ABC's of Cross Examination," 41 Drake Law Review 35, 1992; "Trial Handbook for Iowa Lawyers," Lawyers Cooperative Pub. Co., 1997; Iowa Civil Litigation Handbook, 2000-2001 (West Group). Adjunct Professor, Trial Advocacy, University of Iowa College of Law, 1979. *Member:* Iowa Academy of Trial Lawyers (Member, Board of Governors, 1981-1990); Iowa Trial Lawyers Association (Member, Board of Governors, 1999-2002); The Association of Trial Lawyers of America. ***Email:*** EllenA@TRLF.COM

PETER C. RILEY, admitted to bar, 1980, Iowa. *Education:* University of Iowa (B.B.A., 1976; J.D., 1980). Certified Public Accountant, Iowa, 1980. *Member:* Iowa State Bar Association; Iowa Trial Lawyers Association; Iowa Academy of Trial Lawyers; The Association of Trial Lawyers of America. ***Email:*** PETERR@TRLF.COM

T. TODD BECKER, admitted to bar, 1980, Iowa. *Education:* University of Iowa (B.A., with high distinction, 1976; J.D., with distinction, 1980). Phi Beta Kappa; Phi Delta Phi. Recipient, American Jurisprudence Awards: Civil Procedure; Contracts. *Member:* Association of Trial Lawyers of America. Fellow, Iowa Academy of Trial Lawyers (1987—). ***Email:*** TODDB@TRLF.COM

MARK E. LIABO, admitted to bar, 1979, Iowa. *Education:* University of Iowa (B.A., 1975; M.A., 1976); Drake University (J.D., with honors, 1979). *Member:* Iowa State Bar Association; Iowa Academy of Trial Lawyers; Association of Trial Lawyers of America; Iowa Trial Lawyers Association. ***Email:*** MARKL@TRLF.COM

HUGH G. ALBRECHT, admitted to bar, 1980, Iowa. *Education:* Iowa State University (B.S., 1977); University of Iowa (J.D., with honors, 1980). *Member:* Iowa Academy of Trial Lawyers; Association of Trial Lawyers of America. ***Email:*** HUGHA@TRLF.COM

SARA RILEY, admitted to bar, 1986, Iowa. *Education:* University of Iowa (B.B.A., 1982); Drake University (J.D., 1985). Recipient, American Jurisprudence Award. Instructor, Mass Media Law, Drake Law School, Spring 1985. *Member:* The Association of Trial Lawyers of America; Iowa Trial Lawyers Association (Board of Governors). ***Email:*** SARAR@TRLF.COM

THOMAS J. CURRIE, admitted to bar, 1985, Iowa. *Education:* University of Iowa (B.A., 1982; J.D., with distinction, 1985). Phi Eta Sigma; Phi Beta Kappa. Author, Note-"Risk Contribution: An Undesirable New Method for Apportioning Damages in the DES Cases," 10 Journal of Corporation Law 743, 1985. *Member:* Iowa State Bar Association; The Association of Trial Lawyers of America; The Iowa Association of Worker's Compensation Lawyers, Inc.; Iowa Trial Lawyers Association. ***Email:*** TOMC@TRLF.COM

JAMES E. BENNETT, admitted to bar, 1968, Iowa. *Education:* Coe College; State University of Iowa (LL.B., 1968). *Member:* Iowa State Bar Association. ***Email:*** JIMB@TRLF.COM

GERALD J. KUCERA, admitted to bar, 1975, Iowa. *Education:* University of Iowa (B.A., 1973; J.D., with distinction, 1975). *Member:* Iowa State Bar Association; Iowa Trial Lawyers Association. ***Email:*** GARYK@TRLF.COM

NESTOR LOBODIAK, admitted to bar, 1989, Iowa. *Education:* University of Iowa (B.S., Pharmacy, 1980; J.D., with distinction, 1989). Associate Editor, Iowa Law Review, 1988-1989. Registered Pharmacist, Iowa, 1981. *Member:* Iowa Trial Lawyers Association. ***Email:*** nestorl@trlf.com

---

JAMES K. WESTON, II, admitted to bar, 1996, Iowa. *Education:* University of Iowa (B.A., 1992); Drake University (J.D., with honors, 1996). Production Editor, Drake Law Review, 1995-1996. Law Clerk to the Hon. Michael J. Streit, Iowa Court of Appeals, 1996. ***Email:*** JIMW@TRLF.com

RUSH & NICHOLSON, PLC

100 FIRST STREET S.W.
CEDAR RAPIDS, IOWA 52404
Telephone: 319-363-5209
Fax: 319-363-6664
URL: http://www.rushnicholson.com
Email: info@rushnicholson.com
URL: http://www.lawyers.com/rushlawfirm

Mailing Address: P.O. Box 637. Cedar Rapids, Iowa. 52406-0637

Personal Injury, Product Liability, Professional Liability, Labor and Employment, Workers Compensation.

ROBERT R. RUSH, born Lake Forest, Illinois, October 30, 1944; admitted to bar, 1970, Iowa. *Education:* Northwestern University (B.A., 1966); University of Iowa (J.D., 1970). Attorney, U.S. Department of Justice, (Civil Rights Division) 1971-1973. Special Assistant U.S. Attorney for the District of Columbia, 1973. Member, Iowa Senate, 1976-1982. *Member:* Linn County, Iowa State and American Bar Associations; Association of Trial Lawyers of America; Iowa Trial Lawyers Association; Iowa Association of Workers Compensation Lawyers; . Fellow, Iowa Academy of Trial Lawyers. ***PRACTICE AREAS:*** Personal Injury; Products Liability; Professional Liability; Labor and Employment; Workers Compensation. ***Email:*** bob@rushnicholson.com

WILLIAM G. NICHOLSON, born Cedar Rapids, Iowa, November 7, 1952; admitted to bar, 1980, Iowa; U.S. District Court, Northern and Southern Districts of Iowa; U.S. Court of Appeals, Eighth Circuit. *Education:* University of Iowa (B.A., with honors, 1977; J.D., with honors, 1980). Phi Beta Kappa. Member, University of Iowa College of Law Moot Court Board, 1979-1980. *Member:* Linn County and Iowa State Bar Associations; Iowa

(This Listing Continued)

Trial Lawyers Association; Fellow, Iowa Academy of Trial Lawyers. ***PRACTICE AREAS:*** Insurance Law; Products Liability Law; Negligence; Personal Injury Law; Trial Practice. ***Email:*** wnich@rushnicholson.com

---

JEANNE M. STEINER, born Bismarck, North Dakota, January 13, 1965; admitted to bar, 1992, Arizona; 2001, Minnesota and Iowa; 2005, U.S. District Court, Northern and Southern Districts of Iowa. *Education:* Moorhead State University (B.S., 1987); William Mitchell College of Law (J.D., 1992). *Member:* Iowa State and Minnesota State Bar Associations; State Bar of Arizona; Iowa Trial Lawyers Association. ***LANGUAGES:*** Spanish. ***PRACTICE AREAS:*** Trial Practice; Workers Compensation. ***Email:*** jsteiner@rushnicholson.com

SCHELDRUP LAW FIRM, P.C.

Established in 2002

LAW BUILDING

225 SECOND STREET S.E., SUITE 200

P.O. BOX 36

CEDAR RAPIDS, IOWA 52406-0036

Telephone: 319-286-1743

Fax: 319-286-1748

URL: http://www.scheldruplaw.com

General practice in state and federal courts and before administrative agencies, workers' compensation, labor and employment, professional malpractice defense, insurance defense, motor carrier transportation defense, family law.

FIRM PROFILE: The firm consists of attorneys with large firm litigation experience who now focus their practice in specific areas of law thereby providing clients the benefits of large firm specialization in the confines of a small firm environment.

CHRIS J. SCHELDRUP, born Evanston, Illinois, March 10, 1958; admitted to bar, 1986, Arizona and U.S. Court of Appeals, Ninth Circuit; 1989, Iowa. *Education:* University of Northern Iowa (B.A., with high distinction, 1980); University of Iowa (J.D., 1984). Member, Moot Court Board. Recipient, Sigma Alpha Epsilon Academic Excellence Award. Graduate, Arizona College of Trial Advocacy; Selected and Certified as Member of Million Dollar Advocates Forum. Former Adjunct Professor of Administrative Law, University of Northern Iowa. Instructor, Workers' Compensation, Kirkwood Community College. *Member:* Linn County, Iowa State and American (Member, Sections on: Tort and Insurance Practice) Bar Associations; State Bar of Arizona; Iowa Workers' Compensation Association; Iowa Defense Counsel. ***PRACTICE AREAS:*** Workers Compensation; Labor and Employment; Professional Malpractice Defense; Insurance Defense; Motor Carrier Transportation Defense. ***Email:*** cscheldrup@scheldruplaw.com

CHARLES A. BLADES, born Ann Arbor, Michigan, December 22, 1957; admitted to bar, 1985, Illinois; 1989, Iowa. *Education:* Dartmouth College (A.B., 1980); University of Iowa (J.D., 1985). Order of the Coif. Author: Iowa Tort Guide, 1993, 2000; "The Motorcycle Helmet Defense," 40 Federation of Insurance and Corporate Counsel Quarterly 243, Spring, 1990. *Member:* Linn County and Iowa State Bar Associations. ***PRACTICE AREAS:*** Professional Liability; Products Liability; Employment Discrimination; Commercial Litigation; Workers Compensation; Personal Injury; Insurance; Family Law. ***Email:*** cblades@scheldruplaw.com

DAVID E. SCHROCK, born Burlington, Iowa, September 2, 1967; admitted to bar, 1992, Iowa. *Education:* University of Iowa (B.A., 1989; J.D., 1992). Author: "Superholder" in Due Course Protection of FDIC Extended: Kilpatrick v. Riddle Bars Investors' Federal Securities Fraud Claims Under the D'Oench, Duhme Doctrine, Vol. 17:2 J.Corp.L., Winter 1992. *Member:* Linn County, Iowa State (Executive Council, Young Lawyers Division, 1992-2000) and American Bar Associations. ***PRACTICE AREAS:*** Civil Litigation; Insurance Litigation; Family Law; Personal Injury; General Practice; Insurance Defense; Workers Compensation. ***Email:*** dschrock@scheldruplaw.com

REPRESENTATIVE CLIENTS: Zurich American Insurance; United Fire & Casualty Group; West Side Transport; Barr-Nunn Transportation, Inc.; Florilli Transportation; TrueNorth Companies; TMC Trucking; Annett Holdings, Inc.; Risk Administrative Services; EMC Insurance Companies; ABCM Corporation; SISCO; Cambridge Integrated; Combined Specialty Insurance Company; Pickwick Manufacturing; Menard, Inc.; AUSCO; Great American Insurance Company.

SHUTTLEWORTH & INGERSOLL, P.L.C.

Established in 1853

115 THIRD STREET S.E., SUITE 500

CEDAR RAPIDS, IOWA 52401

Telephone: 319-365-9461

Fax: 319-365-8443

URL: http://www.shuttleworthlaw.com

Mailing Address: P.O. Box 2107, Cedar Rapids, IA 52406-2107

Administrative Law, Agricultural Law, Alternative Dispute Resolution, Arbitration, Mediation, Antitrust, Unfair Trade, Bankruptcy, Banks and Banking, Biotechnology, Civil Litigation and Appellate Practice in all State and Federal Courts, Civil Rights, Commercial Law, Commercial Real Estate, Communications and Media, Computers and Software, Constitutional Law, Construction Law, Contracts, Copyrights, Corporate Law, Debtor and Creditor, Disabilities, Education Law, Elder Law, Eminent Domain, Employee Benefits, Employment Law, Energy, Environmental Law, Estate Planning, General Practice, Health Care, Hospital Law, Insurance, Insurance Defense, Intellectual Property, Labor, Land Use, Medical Malpractice, Mergers, Acquisitions, and Divestitures, Municipal Law, Natural Resources, Nonprofit and Charitable Organizations, OSHA, Partnership Law, Patents, Personal Injury, Probate, Products Liability, Professional Liability, Real Estate, Securities, Tax Law, Technology and Science, Trademarks, Trusts and Estates, Utility Law, Wills, Workers Compensation, Zoning Law.

(This Listing Continued)

FIRM PROFILE: Shuttleworth & Ingersoll, P.L.C., traces its origin to 1853. The firm presently includes 40 lawyers (four of whom are registered patent lawyers), legal assistants and support staff. Shuttleworth & Ingersoll is committed to economically providing high quality legal services on a timely basis. As a full service law firm, Shuttleworth & Ingersoll emphasizes the development of areas of expertise to more efficiently handle client matters, utilizing specialized training and advanced technology. Members of Shuttleworth & Ingersoll participate in a variety of professional and community endeavors.

V.C. SHUTTLEWORTH (1900-1965)

T.M. INGERSOLL (1902-1972)

MICHAEL O. McDERMOTT, born Des Moines, Iowa, April 20, 1938; admitted to bar, 1963, Iowa. *Education:* State University of Iowa (B.B.A., 1960; J.D., 1963). Listed in The Best Lawyers in America, Tax Law. *Member:* Linn County, Iowa State (Member, Committee on Taxation, 1972-1990) and American Bar Associations. ***PRACTICE AREAS:*** Estate Planning; Tax Law; Real Estate; Probate; Partnership Law. ***Email:*** mom@shuttleworthlaw.com

JOHN M. BICKEL, born Tyler, Texas, September 21, 1943; admitted to bar, 1969, Iowa and Florida. *Education:* University of Colorado; Cornell College (B.A., 1966); Florida State University (J.D., with honors, 1969). Listed in The Best Lawyers in America. *Member:* Linn County, Iowa State (President, Young Lawyers Section, 1978-1979) and American Bar Associations; The Florida Bar; American College of Trial Lawyers (Iowa Chair, 1998-2000); Federation of Insurance and Corporate Counsel; American Board of Trial Advocates (Iowa President, 1997-1998; National Board, 2000—;) International Association of Defense Counsel; Iowa Academy of Trial Lawyers; Iowa Defense Counsel Association; Iowa Association of Workers Compensation Lawyers (Member, Board of Governors, 1980—); Iowa Industrial Commission Advisory Committee (Member, 1988—; President, 1992-1993); Defense Research Institute; National Association of College and University Attorneys; American Inns of Court (Emeritus Master). Fellow, Iowa State Bar Foundation. ***PRACTICE AREAS:*** Civil Litigation; Construction Law; Communications and Media; Professional Liability; Workers' Compensation. ***Email:*** jmb@shuttleworthlaw.com

ROBERT D. HOUGHTON, born Red Oak, Iowa, October 6, 1946; admitted to bar, 1971, Iowa. *Education:* University of Iowa (B.B.A., 1968; J.D., with distinction, 1971). *Member:* Linn County, Iowa State and American Bar Associations; Iowa Defense Council Association (President, 2000); Federation of Insurance and Corporate Counsel; American Board of Trial Advocates; Defense Research Institute; Fellow, Iowa Academy of Trial Lawyers; Fellow, American College of Trial Lawyers. ***PRACTICE AREAS:*** Civil Litigation; Personal Injury; Products Liability; Professional Liability; Drug and Medical Device Litigation. ***Email:*** rdh@shuttleworthlaw.com

RICHARD S. FRY, born Iowa City, Iowa, August 16, 1946; admitted to bar, 1974, Iowa. *Education:* University of Northern Iowa (B.A., 1968); University of Iowa (J.D., 1973). Order of the Coif. Listed in The Best Lawyers in America. *Member:* Linn County (President, 2001-2002), Iowa State and American Bar Associations; Iowa Defense Counsel Association; Iowa Academy of Trial Lawyers; American College of Trial Lawyers; International Association of Defense Counsel; Defense Research Institute; Iowa Bar Foundation. ***PRACTICE AREAS:*** Civil Litigation; Utility Law; Insurance law; Products Liability; Professional Liability. ***Email:*** rsf@shuttleworthlaw.com

RICHARD C. GARBERSON, born Cedar Rapids, Iowa, March 9, 1949; admitted to bar, 1974, Iowa. *Education:* University of Iowa (B.B.A., 1971); Drake University (J.D., 1974). Order of the Coif. *Member:* Linn County, Iowa State and American Bar Associations; Iowa Academy of Trial Lawyers; American Board of Trial Advocates; Iowa Defense Counsel Association; Iowa Association of Worker's Compensation Lawyers; American Inns of Court. ***PRACTICE AREAS:*** Civil Litigation; Personal Injury; Products Liability; Insurance Defense; Workers' Compensation. ***Email:*** rcg@shuttleworthlaw.com

GARY J. STREIT, born Sibley, Iowa, June 18, 1950; admitted to bar, 1975, Iowa. *Education:* Iowa State University (B.S., 1972); University of Iowa (J.D., 1975). Listed in The Best Lawyers in America, Tax Law and Employee Benefits Law. Certified Public Accountant, Iowa, 1975. *Member:* Linn County, Iowa State (Member, Sections on: Corporation, Banking and Business Law; Probate; Taxation) and American Bar Associations. Fellow, American College of Trust and Estate Counsel. ***PRACTICE AREAS:*** Estate Planning; Tax Law; ERISA; Mergers, Acquisitions and Divestitures; Non-Profit and Charitable Organizations. ***Email:*** gjs@shuttleworthlaw.com

CARROLL J. REASONER, born Washington, D.C., April 27, 1951; admitted to bar, 1976, Iowa; 1977, District of Columbia. *Education:* University of Pennsylvania; University of Iowa (B.A., 1973; J.D., 1976). Order of the Coif. Listed in The Best Lawyers in America, Corporate, Mergers and Acquisitions and Securities, Financial Institutions and Transactions, and Health Care Law; State Judicial Nominating Commission, 1998-2004. *Member:* Linn County, Sixth Judicial District (President, 1984-1988), Iowa State (Member: Board of Governors, 1985-1987, 1988-1990; President, Young Lawyers Section, 1986-1987; President, 1991-1992; Member, Sections on: Commercial and Bankruptcy Law; Business Law; Health Law;) and American (Member, Sections on: Antitrust; Business Law; Health Law; Law Practice Management) Bar Associations; Iowa Society of Hospital Attorneys; American Health Lawyers Association. American Bar Foundation; Iowa Bar Foundation. ***PRACTICE AREAS:*** Corporate Law; Banks and Banking; Mergers, Acquisitions and Divestitures; Antitrust and Trade Regulation; Hospital Law. ***Email:*** cjr@shuttleworthlaw.com

STEVEN J. PACE, born Clarinda, Iowa, August 20, 1952; admitted to bar, 1977, Iowa. *Education:* Iowa State University (B.A., 1974); University of Iowa (J.D., 1977). *Member:* Linn County, Iowa State (Sections on: Commercial and Bankruptcy Law, Council, 1998-2001; Environmental and Natural Resources Law, Section Chair, 2002-2004; Litigation) and American (Member, Sections on: Litigation; Environment, Energy and Resources) Bar Associations; Iowa Defense Council Association; American Board of Trial Advocates. Fellow: Iowa Academy of Trial Lawyers; Iowa Bar Foundation. ***PRACTICE AREAS:*** Civil Litigation; Environmental Law; Bankruptcy; Construction Law. ***Email:*** sjp@shuttleworthlaw.com

GLENN L. JOHNSON, born Akron, Ohio, May 24, 1950; admitted to bar, 1975, Iowa; U.S. Court of Appeals, Federal Circuit; registered to practice before U.S. Patent and Trade-

(This Listing Continued)

SHUTTLEWORTH & INGERSOLL, P.L.C., Cedar Rapids— Continued

mark Office. *Education:* Cornell College; University of Northern Colorado (B.A., 1973); University of Iowa (J.D., with distinction, 1975). Member, Linn County Attorney's Office, 1975-1979. *Member:* Linn County (Member, Ethics and Grievance Committee, 1985—), Iowa State (Member: Bridge-The-Gap-Seminar Committee, 1982-1985; Executive Council, Young Lawyers Section, 1984-1985; Annual Meeting Seminar Committee, 1988-1989; Labor Law Committee, 1988-1989; Labor Law Section, 1990—; Co-Chair: Federal/State EEO Developments Subcommittee, 1990-1991; Federal Practice Committee, 1996—; Litigation Section, 1990—; Intellectual Property Section, 1998—), Federal Circuit and American (Member, Sections on: Litigation, 1988—; Labor and Employment Law, 1988—; Intellectual Property Law, 1995—) Bar Associations; Defense Research Institute (Member, Employment Law Section); Iowa Intellectual Property Law Association; American Intellectual Property Law Association; Iowa Academy of Trial Lawyers. ***PRACTICE AREAS:*** Patents; Trademarks; Civil Litigation; Technology and Science; Employment Law. ***Email:*** glj@shuttleworthlaw.com

ROBERT W. HOKE, II, born Pittsburgh, Pennsylvania, September 13, 1951; admitted to bar, 1977, Iowa; 1983, Minnesota; registered to practice before U.S. Patent and Trademark Office. *Education:* Iowa State University (B.S., Chemical Engineering, 1973); University of Iowa (M.B.A.; J.D., 1977). Licensed Patent Attorney, 1978. *Member:* Linn County, Minnesota State, Iowa State and American Bar Associations; International Trademark Association (Director, 1997-2000); American Intellectual Property Law Association; Iowa Intellectual Property Law Association; Minnesota Intellectual Property Law Association. ***PRACTICE AREAS:*** Trademarks; Patents; Copyrights; Intellectual Property Licensing; Intellectual Property. ***Email:*** rwh@shuttleworthlaw.com

THOMAS P. PEFFER, born Iowa City, Iowa, June 24, 1953; admitted to bar, 1978, Iowa. *Education:* Bemidji State University (B.A., 1975); University of Iowa (J.D., with distinction, 1978). *Member:* Linn County, Iowa State (Chair: Unauthorized Practice Committee, 1989-1990; Litigation Section Council, 1993-1995) and American (Member: Commercial Torts Committee; Products, General Liability and Consumer Law Committee) Bar Associations; American Board of Trial Advocates; Iowa Defense Counsel Association; Defense Research Institute. ***PRACTICE AREAS:*** Medical Malpractice; Civil Litigation; Insurance Defense. ***Email:*** tpp@shuttleworthlaw.com

DENNIS J. McMENIMEN, born Mason City, Iowa, August 15, 1953; admitted to bar, 1978, Iowa; 2005, Wyoming. *Education:* St. John's University (B.A., 1975); University of Iowa (J.D., with distinction, 1978). Listed in The Best Lawyers in America, Commercial Real Estate. *Member:* Linn County, Iowa State (Member, Real Estate and Title Law Section, 1990—, Section Council, 1995-1999, Chairman, Real Property Committee, 1999-2000, Chairman, CLE Sub-committee 1990-1991; Commercial and Bankruptcy Law Section, 1990—, Chairman, Membership Committee, 1990-1991; Corporation, Banking and Business Law Section, 1990—, Section Council, 2000-2003; Chairman, Limited Liability Company Subcommittee, 2000-2001; UCC Subcommittee, 1990-1994, Partnership Committee, 1997-1998; Environmental Law Section, 1990—; Title Standards Committee, 1981-1986; Corporation and Business Law Committee, 1987-1989) and American Bar Associations; American College of Mortgage Attorneys. ***PRACTICE AREAS:*** Commercial Real Estate; Commercial Law; Corporate Law; Energy; Natural Resources. ***Email:*** djm@shuttleworthlaw.com

KEVIN H. COLLINS, born Cedar Rapids, Iowa, May 7, 1955; admitted to bar, 1981, Iowa; 1982, Hawaii. *Education:* Creighton University (B.A., 1978); University of Iowa (J.D., 1980). Member, Panel of Arbitrators, American Arbitration Association. Listed in The Best Lawyers in America. *Member:* Linn County, Iowa State (President, 2003-2004; Member, Board of Governors, 1998-2001; Co-Chair: Committee on the Delivery of Legal Services to the Elderly, 1989-1990; Member, Law Practice Management Committee, 1991-1998), Hawaii State and American Bar Associations; Iowa Academy of Trial Lawyers; American Board of Trial Advocates; Iowa Bar Foundation; Federation of Insurance and Corporate Counsel; The College of Master Advocates & Barristers. ***PRACTICE AREAS:*** Civil Litigation; Alternative Dispute Resolution; Construction Law. ***Email:*** khc@shuttleworthlaw.com

WILLIAM P. PROWELL, born New York, N.Y., May 28, 1954; admitted to bar, 1981, Iowa. *Education:* Trinity College (B.A., 1976); Drake University (J.D., 1981). *Member:* Linn County (Member, Title Standards Committee), Iowa State and American Bar Associations. ***PRACTICE AREAS:*** Corporate Law; Real Estate; Zoning Law; Eminent Domain; Municipal Law. ***Email:*** wpp@shuttleworthlaw.com

DIANE KUTZKO, born Bronx, New York, October 24, 1946; admitted to bar, 1981, Iowa. *Education:* Universite de Nancy, France (Certificat de Propedeutique, 1966); Brooklyn College of the City University of New York (B.A., 1967); University of Wisconsin-Madison (M.A., 1969); University of Iowa (J.D., 1981). Listed in The Best Lawyers in America, Health Care Law. Member, 1995-2003 and Chair, 2000-2003, Iowa Board of Law Examiners. *Member:* Linn County, Iowa State (Bar Liaison, Iowa Medical Society, 1989-1995; Member: Board of Governors, 1992-1996) and American (Member, House of Delegates, 1996-2001; Standing Committee on Legal Aid and Indigent Defendants, 2002—) Bar Associations; American Health Lawyers Association; Iowa Society of Hospital Attorneys (President, 2001); Legal Services Corporation of Iowa (President, 1998-2002); Iowa Bar Foundation (President, 1998-1999; Member, Board of Directors, 2002—). ***LANGUAGES:*** French. ***PRACTICE AREAS:*** Health Law; Hospital Law; Appellate Practice; Administrative Law; Constitutional Law. ***Email:*** dhk@shuttleworthlaw.com

MARK L. ZAIGER, born Audubon, Iowa, February 5, 1953; admitted to bar, 1980, Wisconsin; 1983, Iowa. *Education:* Harvard University (A.B., 1975); University of Iowa (J.D., with distinction, 1979). Listed in The Best Lawyers in America. Law Clerk to Judge Frank M. Johnson, Jr., U.S. Court of Appeals, Fifth Circuit, 1979-1980. *Member:* Linn County, Iowa State (Member, Litigation Section; Employment Section, Council Chair, 2001-2003) and American (Member, Labor & Employment Section; Chair, Federal Practice Committee, Northern District of Iowa, 1997-2002) Bar Associations; American Board of Trial Advocates; Iowa Defense Counsel Association. Iowa Academy of Trial Lawyers. ***PRACTICE AREAS:*** Civil Litigation; Labor Law; Employment Law; Disabilities; Personal Injury. ***Email:*** mlz@shuttleworthlaw.com

(This Listing Continued)

DOUGLAS R. OELSCHLAEGER, born Cedar Rapids, Iowa, April 22, 1957; admitted to bar, 1981, Iowa. *Education:* University of Iowa (B.A., 1978; J.D., with distinction, 1981). Law Clerk to Justice Arthur A. McGiverin, Supreme Court of Iowa, 1981-1982. *Member:* Linn County, Iowa State and American (Member: Workers' Compensation and Employers Liability Law Committee, Employer-Employee Relations Committee and Employee Benefits Law Committee, Tort and Insurance Practice Section; Insurance Coverage Litigation Committee, Litigation Section) Bar Associations; Iowa Association of Workers Compensation Lawyers, Inc.; Federation of Defense and Corporate Counsel; American Board of Trial Advocates; Iowa Defense Counsel Association; Defense Research Institute. ***PRACTICE AREAS:*** Civil Litigation; Administrative Law; Constitutional Law; Municipal Law; Insurance; Real Estate Tax Appeals. ***Email:*** dro@shuttleworthlaw.com

WESLEY B. HUISINGA, born Waterloo, Iowa, April 7, 1956; admitted to bar, 1981, Iowa; 1986, Nebraska. *Education:* University of Northern Iowa (B.A., 1977); University of Iowa (J.D., with distinction, 1981). Assistant United States Trustee, 1987. United States Trustee, Region 12, 1987-1994. Acting United States Trustee, Region 7, 1991. Member, Panel of Bankruptcy Trustees, Northern and Southern Districts of Iowa. *Member:* Linn County, Iowa State (Member, Sections on: Commercial and Bankruptcy; Agriculture Law), Nebraska State and American (Member, Business Law Section) Bar Associations; Commercial Law League of America (Member, Sections on: Bankruptcy; Creditors Rights); American Bankruptcy Institute; National Association of Chapter 13 Trustees; National Association of Bankruptcy Trustees; American League of Lobbyists. ***PRACTICE AREAS:*** Bankruptcy; Commercial Litigation; Agricultural Law; Debtor and Creditor; Workouts. ***Email:*** wbh@shuttleworthlaw.com

DEAN R. EINCK, born Ossian, Iowa, September 7, 1957; admitted to bar, 1982, Iowa. *Education:* University of Northern Iowa (B.A., 1979); University of Iowa (J.D., with distinction, 1982). Certified Public Accountant, Iowa, 1979. Listed in The Best Lawyers In America: Tax Law, 1997-2006; Trusts and Estates, 1993-2006. *Member:* Linn County, Iowa State and American (Member, Sections on: Taxation; Real Property, Probate and Trust Law; Communication Law Forum) Bar Associations; Iowa Society of Certified Public Accountants; American Institute of Certified Public Accountants; Cedar Rapids Area Estate Planning Council, Inc. (President, 1996-1997). ***PRACTICE AREAS:*** Mergers, Acquisitions and Divestitures; Tax Law; Estate Planning; Communications and Media; Employee Benefits. ***Email:*** dre@shuttleworthlaw.com

LINDA M. KIRSCH, born Dubuque, Iowa, May 1, 1959; admitted to bar, 1984, Iowa. *Education:* Loras College (B.A., 1981); University of Iowa (J.D., 1984). Order of the Coif. *Member:* Linn County, Iowa State (Member, Sections on: Commercial and Bankruptcy Law; Real Estate and Title Law; International Law) and American (Member, Sections on: Real Property; Probate and Trust Law; Business Law; International Law) Bar Associations. ***PRACTICE AREAS:*** Commercial Real Estate; Commercial Law; Securities; Real Estate; Debtor and Creditor. ***Email:*** lmk@shuttleworthlaw.com

CONNIE ALT, born Dubuque, Iowa, January 14, 1961; admitted to bar, 1985, Iowa. *Education:* University of Iowa (B.B.A., 1982; J.D., 1985). Order of the Coif. Law Clerk to Justice Harvey Uhlenhopp, Iowa Supreme Court, 1985-1986. *Member:* Linn County, Iowa State (Member, Sections on: Health Law; Employment; Litigation) and American (Member, Sections on: Health Law; Labor & Employment Law) Bar Associations; Iowa Defense Counsel Association; American Board of Trial Advocates (Secretary, 2005); Defense Research Institute; Iowa Academy of Trial Lawyers (Board Member; Vice President 2005); American College of Trial Lawyers. ***PRACTICE AREAS:*** Medical Malpractice; Products Liability; Employment Law; Civil Litigation; Insurance Defense. ***Email:*** cma@shuttleworthlaw.com

WILLIAM S. HOCHSTETLER, born Iowa City, Iowa, January 15, 1955; admitted to bar, 1986, Iowa. *Education:* Eastern Mennonite College (B.A., 1977); University of Iowa (J.D., 1986). Order of the Coif. Certified Public Accountant. *Member:* Linn County, Iowa State (Member, Sections on: Business Law; Probate and Trust Law; Taxation) and American (Member, Sections on: Real Property, Probate and Trust Law) Bar Associations; Cedar Rapids Area Estate Planning Council (President, 2004-2005). ***PRACTICE AREAS:*** Estate Planning; Tax Law; Business Planning; Trusts and Estates; Computers and Software. ***Email:*** wsh@shuttleworthlaw.com

BRIAN D. BERGSTROM, born Mount Pleasant, Iowa, December 11, 1962; admitted to bar, 1989, Illinois; 1996, Iowa. *Education:* Harvard University (A.B., 1985; J.D., 1989). *Member:* Linn County, Iowa State (Member, Sections on: Business Law; Corporate Counsel) and American (Member: Business Law Section; Venture Capital and Private Equity Committee; Angel Venture Capital Subcommittee; Committee on Negotiated Acquisitions) Bar Associations. ***PRACTICE AREAS:*** Securities; Corporate Law; Mergers, Acquisitions and Divestitures; Equity Finance. ***Email:*** bdb@shuttleworthlaw.com

GILDA L. BOYER, born Philadelphia, Pennsylvania, January 6, 1962; admitted to bar, 1991, Iowa. *Education:* Cornell College (B.S.S., magna cum laude, 1984); University of Iowa (J.D., high distinction, 1991). *Member:* Linn County, Iowa State and American Bar Associations. ***PRACTICE AREAS:*** Employment Law; Employee Benefits; Business Law; Estate Planning; Non-Profit and Charitable Organizations; Health Law. ***Email:*** glb@shuttleworthlaw.com

NANCY J. PENNER, born Ottumwa, Iowa, December 28, 1958; admitted to bar, 1994, Iowa. *Education:* Mount Mercy College (B.S., 1981); University of Iowa (M.A., 1985; J.D., 1994). Order of the Coif. Registered Nurse, Iowa, 1981. *Member:* Linn County, Iowa State (Member, Employment Law Section; Health Law Section, Council, 1998-2001, 2003—, Chair, 2003-2004) and American (Member, Sections on Health Law; Employment Law) Bar Associations; Iowa Society of Hospital Attorneys; Iowa Defense Counsel Association; American Health Lawyers Association; American Association of Nurse Attorneys. ***PRACTICE AREAS:*** Health Care; Hospital Law; Appellate Practice; Employment Law. ***Email:*** njp@shuttleworthlaw.com

KEVIN J. CASTER, born Ottumwa, Iowa, May 14, 1960; admitted to bar, 1995, Iowa. *Education:* University of Northern Iowa (B.A., 1982); University of Iowa (J.D., with distinction, 1995). Author: "The Future of Self Funded Health Plans," Iowa Law Review 79:2 (1994); "ERISA Preemption Overview and Updates," Defense Update: The Iowa Defense Counsel Association Newsletter XIII: 4 (Oct. 2000). *Member:* Linn County, Iowa State and American (Member, Construction Industry Forum; Litigation Section; Tort and Insurance

(This Listing Continued)

Practice Section) Bar Associations; Iowa Defense Counsel Association. ***PRACTICE AREAS:*** Insurance Defense; Construction Law; Commercial Litigation; ERISA Litigation. ***Email:*** kjc@shuttleworthlaw.com

THERESA C. DAVIS, born Kewanee, Illinois, July 1, 1967; admitted to bar, 1995, Iowa. *Education:* Western Illinois University (B.A., 1989); University of Iowa (J.D., with high distinction, 1995). *Member:* Linn County, Iowa State (Past Co-Chair: Professional Development Committee, Young Lawyers Division); and American Bar Associations; American Inns of Court, Dean Mason Ladd Chapter; Iowa Defense Counsel Association; Defense Research Institute; Iowa Association of Workers Compensation Attorneys. ***PRACTICE AREAS:*** Civil Litigation; Appellate Practice; Insurance Defense; Personal Injury; Workers' Compensation. ***Email:*** tcd@shuttleworthlaw.com

SARAH J. GAYER, born Sioux City, Iowa, April 6, 1971; admitted to bar, 1997, Iowa. *Education:* Duke University (B.A., 1993); University of Iowa (J.D., 1997). Order of the Coif. *Member:* Linn County, Iowa State (Member, Federal Practice Committee) and American Bar Associations. ***PRACTICE AREAS:*** Appellate Practice; Civil Litigation; Commercial Litigation; Insurance Defense. ***Email:*** sjg@shuttleworthlaw.com

LAURIE L. DAWLEY, born Charles City, Iowa, June 10, 1973; admitted to bar, 1998, Iowa. *Education:* Wartburg College (B.A., summa cum laude, 1995); University of Iowa (J.D., with high distinction, 1998). Articles Editor, Journal of Corporation Law, 1997-1998. Author: "The Continuing Debate Regarding the Lease Versus Disguised Security Interest Issue: Did the Edison Court Correctly Find a True Lease?" 24 Journal of Corporation Law 169, 1998. *Member:* Linn County, Iowa State (Chair, Membership Committee, Young Lawyers Division; Member, Sections on: Business Law; Commercial and Bankruptcy Law; Real Estate and Title Law) and American Bar Associations. ***PRACTICE AREAS:*** Creditors Rights; Commercial Law; Real Estate; Corporate Law. ***Email:*** lld@shuttleworthlaw.com

JENNIFER E. RINDEN, born Rock Island, Illinois, December 21, 1967; admitted to bar, 1997, Iowa; 1998, Illinois. *Education:* University of Texas (B.A., 1993); Drake University (J.D., 1997). Order of the Barristers. Law Clerk to Hon. Mark W. Bennett, U.S. District Court, Northern District of Iowa, 1997-1999. *Member:* Chicago, Linn County, Illinois State, Iowa State and American Bar Associations. ***PRACTICE AREAS:*** Civil Litigation; Insurance Defense; Personal Injury; Products Liability; Employment Law. ***Email:*** jer@shuttleworthlaw.com

---

PATRICIA L. HOFFMAN-SIMANEK, born Vinton, Iowa, May 12, 1976; admitted to bar, 2001, Iowa. *Education:* Mount Mercy College (B.A., summa cum laude, 1998); University of Notre Dame (J.D., cum laude, 2001). Recipient, Dean's Award in Legal Research. Production Editor, Journal of College & University Law, 2000-2001. *Member:* Linn County, Iowa State (Member: Sections on: Employment; Health; Litigation; Young Lawyers Division, Mock Trial Committee, 2002—) and American (Member, Sections on: Litigation; Tort and Insurance Practice; Young Lawyers Division) Bar Associations; American Inns of Court (Dean Mason Ladd Chapter); Iowa Defense Counsel Association. ***PRACTICE AREAS:*** Insurance Defense; Employment Law; Civil Litigation; Medical Malpractice. ***Email:*** phs@shuttleworthlaw.com

MARTY L. SUTCLIFFE, born Burlington, Iowa, March 10, 1978; admitted to bar, 2001, Iowa. *Education:* University of Iowa (B.A., with honors and high distinction, 1998; J.D., with distinction, 2001). *Member:* Linn County, Iowa State (Member, Commercial and Bankruptcy Law Section; Real Estate and Title Law Section; Young Lawyers Division, Services to the Elderly Committee, 2002; Membership Committee, 2003) and American Bar Associations; American Bankruptcy Institute. ***PRACTICE AREAS:*** Bankruptcy; Debtor and Creditor; Real Estate; Real Estate Title; Commercial Law. ***Email:*** mls@shuttleworthlaw.com

JACE T. BISGARD, born Emmetsburg, Iowa, November 25, 1976; admitted to bar, 2002, Iowa. *Education:* University of Iowa (B.A., 1999; J.D., 2002). *Member:* Linn County, Iowa State (Member, Young Lawyers Division) and American Bar Associations. ***PRACTICE AREAS:*** General Practice; Civil Litigation; Insurance Defense. ***Email:*** jtb@shuttleworthlaw.com

RYAN N. CARTER, born Midland, Michigan, September 18, 1975; admitted to bar, 2002, Iowa; registered to practice before U.S. Patent and Trademark Office. *Education:* University of Iowa (B.S., Chemistry, 1998); Southern Illinois University (J.D., cum laude, 2002). *Member:* Linn County, Iowa State (Member, Young Lawyers Division) and American Bar Associations; American Intellectual Property Law Association; Iowa Intellectual Property Law Association. ***PRACTICE AREAS:*** Patent; Trademark; Intellectual Property; General Practice; Copyrights. ***Email:*** rnc@shuttleworthlaw.com

HEATHER L. FLEMING, born Geneva, Illinois, January 4, 1977; admitted to bar, 2002, Iowa. *Education:* University of Northern Iowa (B.A., magna cum laude, Political Science, 1999); Drake University (J.D., with honors, 2002). *Member:* Linn County, Iowa State (Member, Young Lawyers Division) and American Bar Associations. ***PRACTICE AREAS:*** Civil Litigation; Insurance Defense; Personal Injury; General Practice. ***Email:*** hlf@shuttleworthlaw.com

OF COUNSEL

THOMAS M. COLLINS, born Rock Island, Illinois, November 10, 1927; admitted to bar, 1952, Iowa. *Education:* University of Iowa (B.A., 1950; J.D., 1952). Listed in The Best Lawyers in America, Corporate Law. Co-Chair, Federal Practice Committee, Northern District of Iowa, 1981-1988. Member, State of Iowa Board of Regents, 1993-1996. Member, Iowa Law School Foundation Board. *Member:* Linn County, Iowa State and American Bar Associations; Iowa Academy of Trial Lawyers. Fellow: American Bar Foundation; Iowa Bar Foundation. ***PRACTICE AREAS:*** Corporate Law. ***Email:*** tmc@shuttleworthlaw.com

WILLIAM R. SHUTTLEWORTH, born Cedar Rapids, Iowa, December 3, 1926; admitted to bar, 1953, Iowa. *Education:* University of Iowa (B.A., 1949; M.A., 1951); Yale University (LL.B., 1953). Listed in The Best Lawyers in America, Real Estate Law. *Member:* Linn County, Iowa State and American Bar Associations. Fellow, American College of Trust and Estate Counsel. ***PRACTICE AREAS:*** College and University Law; Condominium Law; Real Estate; Probate. ***Email:*** wrs@shuttleworthlaw.com

(This Listing Continued)

JAMES C. NEMMERS, born Des Moines, Iowa, December 29, 1931; admitted to bar, 1957, Iowa; registered to practice before U.S. Patent and Trademark Office. *Education:* Iowa State University (B.S., 1952); University of Iowa (J.D., 1957). Listed in The Best Lawyers in America, Intellectual Property Law. Lecturer, Patent and Intellectual Property Law, College of Law, University of Iowa, 1964-1990. *Member:* Linn County (President, 1993-1994), Iowa State (Chairman, Intellectual Property Law Section, 1995-1996) and American Bar Associations; Iowa Intellectual Property Law Association (President, 1984-1985). ***PRACTICE AREAS:*** Patents; Trademarks; Copyrights; Intellectual Property. ***Email:*** jcn@shuttleworthlaw.com

COUNSEL

JENNA M. WISCHMEYER, born Davenport, Iowa, August 3, 1973; admitted to bar, 1999, Kansas; 2003, Iowa. *Education:* Iowa State University (B.S., 1996); University of Kansas (J.D., 1999). *Member:* Linn County, Iowa State (Member, Environmental and Natural Resources Section) and American (Member, Environment, Energy and Resources Section) Bar Associations. ***PRACTICE AREAS:*** Environmental Law. ***Email:*** jmw@shuttleworthlaw.com

REPRESENTATIVE CLIENTS: Abbe Center for Community Mental Health; Aegon USA, Inc.; Amana Society; Archer-Daniels-Midland Co.; Barilla America, Inc.; Cargill, Inc.; Cedar Rapids Television Company (KCRG TV 9); Coe College; Commercial Federal Bank; Cornell College; Cryovac Co., a Division of W.R. Grace Co.; Employee Group Services, Ltd.; Gazette Communications, Inc.; General Growth Management, Inc.; General Mills, Inc.; Hunter's Specialties, Inc.; Kirkwood Community College; Life Investors Insurance Company of America; MCI Telecommunications; McLeod Telecommunication Group, Inc.; Met-Coil Systems Corp.; National Systems Contractors Assn.; Penford Products; Pfizer, Inc.; PMX Industries, Inc.; Quaker Oats Co.; SCI Financial Group; Sears Roebuck and Co.; Square D Company; St. Luke's Hospital; St. Martin Land Company; U. S. Bank, N. A.; Vanguard Appraisals.
REPRESENTATIVE PATENT CLIENTS: Aegon USA, Inc.; Met-Coil Systems Corp.; Diamond V. Mills, Inc.; PMX Industries, Inc.; Swiss Valley Farms; American Trencher, Inc.; Iowa Precision Industries, Inc.; Stamats Communications, Inc.
REPRESENTATIVE INSURANCE CLIENTS: Auto Owners Ins.; CNA Insurance Co.; The Doctors' Company; Farmers Insurance Group of Cos.; Farmland Mutual Insurance Co.; Federated Mutual Insurance Co.; Fireman's Fund Insurance Cos.; General Casualty Company of Wisconsin; Grinnell Mutual Insurance Co.; Meridian Mutual Ins. Co.; Pekin Insurance; Scottsdale Insurance Company; United Fire & Casualty Company; Universal Underwriters Group; Wasau Insurance Cos.

SIMMONS, PERRINE, ALBRIGHT & ELLWOOD, P.L.C.

Established in 1916

115 THIRD STREET S.E.
SUITE 1200
CEDAR RAPIDS, IOWA 52401
Telephone: 319-366-7641
Telecopier: 319-366-1917
URL: http://www.simmonsperrine.com

Iowa City Office: Third Floor Tower Place, 22 South Linn Street, 52240. Telephone: 319-887-1368. Fax: 319-887-1372.

General Practice. Trial and Appellate Practice, Commercial, Insurance, Personal Injury, Professional Malpractice, Workers' Compensation, Environmental, Labor, Employment, Banking, Bankruptcy, Antitrust and Unfair Competition, Construction and Products Liability, Corporation Practice, Tax, Probate, Estate Planning, Real Estate, Pension, Profit-Sharing and Employee Benefits, ERISA, Mergers and Acquisitions, International and Domestic Patent and Trademark Law, Domestic Copyright Law, Family Law.

FIRM PROFILE: Simmons, Perrine, Albright & Ellwood, P.L.C. is a full service, eastern Iowa-based law firm providing high quality legal services and holding the performance of its lawyers to the highest ethical standards. We have a long history as a litigation firm in Iowa with extensive experience in federal and state courts, arbitration and mediation in Iowa and across the nation. Simmons, Perrine, Albright & Ellwood, P.L.C. has developed a comprehensive business practice consulting services. With skilled and experienced attorneys in nearly all fields of law, we serve individual and corporate clients from eastern Iowa and throughout the United States.

Our main office is in Cedar Rapids, Iowa. Our Iowa City office provides all of the services of our firm and a complete listing of all of the members of the firm as well as their biography information can be found in the Cedar Rapids Martindale-Hubbell listing.

MEMBERS

DARREL A. MORF, born Fredericksburg, Iowa, December 24, 1943; admitted to bar, 1969, Iowa. *Education:* University of Iowa (B.A., 1966; J.D., with high distinction, 1969). Phi Alpha Delta; Omicron Delta Kappa; Phi Beta Kappa; Order of the Coif. Special Projects Editor, Iowa Law Review, 1968-1969. Listed in The Best Lawyers in America. Law Clerk, Hon. Donald P. Lay, U.S. Circuit Court of Appeals, 8th Circuit, 1969-1970. Lecturer, Estate Planning, University of Iowa College of Law, 1973-1991. *Member:* Linn County (President, 1998-1999), Iowa State (Board of Governors, 1999-2002; Member, Special Committee on Probate, Property and Trust Law, 1977-1988; Council Member, Probate and Trust Law Section, 1990-1991 and 1995-1998) and American (Member: Sections on Real Property, Probate and Trust Law; Committee on D-8 Federal Death Tax Problems of Estates and Trusts, 1985-1987) Bar Associations. Fellow, The American College of Trust and Estate Counsel. ***PRACTICE AREAS:*** Estate Planning; Probate; Corporate Law. ***Email:*** dmorf@simmonsperrine.com

JAMES E. SHIPMAN, born Shell Rock, Iowa, October 10, 1943; admitted to bar, 1970, Iowa; 1973, U.S. District Court, Southern and Northern Districts of Iowa and U.S. Court of Appeals, Eighth Circuit. *Education:* United States Merchant Marine Academy (B.S., 1967); Loyola University (J.D., 1970). Alpha Sigma Nu Jesuit Honor Society. Executive Editor, Loyola University Law Journal, 1969-1970. Captain, National Moot Court Team, 1968-1970. *Member:* Linn County, Iowa State and American Bar Associations. Fellow: Iowa Academy of Trial Lawyers; American Board of Trial Advocates (Advocate Mem-

(This Listing Continued)

SIMMONS, PERRINE, ALBRIGHT & ELLWOOD, P.L.C., Cedar Rapids—Continued

ber); Iowa Defense Counsel Association; Association of Defense Trial Attorneys; Defense Research Institute. ***PRACTICE AREAS:*** Civil Litigation; Medical Malpractice Defense. ***Email:*** jshipman@simmonsperrine.com

STEPHEN J. HOLTMAN, born Burlington, Iowa, January 21, 1945; admitted to bar, 1972, Iowa; 1973, U.S. Court of Appeals, Eighth Circuit; 1977, U.S. Court of Appeals, Fifth Circuit; 1979, U.S. Supreme Court; 1981, Wisconsin; 1982, U.S. Court of Appeals, Sixth and Ninth Circuits; 1983, U.S. Court of Appeals, Eleventh Circuit; 1984, U.S. Court of Appeals, Fourth Circuit; 1987, U.S. Court of Appeals, Tenth Circuit; 1992, U.S. Court of Appeals, Third Circuit and Federal Circuit. *Education:* University of Iowa (B.S., 1967; J.D., with distinction, 1972). Listed in The Best Lawyers in America. Law Clerk to Hon. Donald P. Lay, Judge, U.S. Court of Appeals, 8th Circuit, 1972-1973. Member, Panel of Arbitrators, American Arbitration Association. *Member:* Linn County, Iowa State (Member: Federal Practice Committee, 1979, 1991-1994; Litigation Section, 1990; Trade Regulation Section, 1981—(Chairman, 1987-1990); Patent, Trademark & Copyright Section, 1991—; Iowa Supreme Court Advisory Committee on Rules, 2001—) and American Bar Associations; State Bar of Wisconsin; Iowa Defense Counsel Association; American Law Institute (Adviser, Restatement (Third) of Torts, Apportionment of Liability). Fellow: Iowa State Bar Foundation; American College of Trial Lawyers; American Board of Trial Advocates. ***PRACTICE AREAS:*** Commercial Litigation; Antitrust; Intellectual Property Litigation. ***Email:*** sholtman@simmonsperrine.com

IRIS E. MUCHMORE, born Parkston, South Dakota, April 25, 1949; admitted to bar, 1975, Iowa; 1981, Wisconsin. *Education:* University of South Dakota and Grinnell College (B.A., 1971); Drake University (J.D., 1975). Member: Order of the Coif; Order of the Barristers. Staff Member, Drake Law Review, 1973-1975. Law Clerk to Justice W. W. Reynoldson, Iowa Supreme Court, 1975-1976. Member, 1987-1991 and Chair, 1991-1993, Supreme Court Advisory Committee on Rules. Member, Iowa Supreme Court's Rules of Professional Conduct Drafting Committee, 2000-2002. *Member:* Linn County (President, 1989-1990), Iowa State (Member: Labor and Employment Law Section Council, 1990-1992; Appellate Practice Committee, 1999-2004; Strategic Planning Committee, 2000-2002) and American Bar Associations; Iowa Academy of Trial Lawyers. ***PRACTICE AREAS:*** Labor; Employment. ***Email:*** imuchmore@simmonsperrine.com

GREGORY M. LEDERER, born Sioux City, Iowa, November 25, 1951; admitted to bar, 1977, Iowa. *Education:* University of Nebraska (B.A., 1973); Drake University (J.D., 1977). Law Clerk: Justice M. E. Rawlings, 1977-1978; Chief Justice W. W. Reynoldson, 1978-1979, Iowa Supreme Court. Contributor: Evidence in America, The Federal Rules in the States, 1987. Contributing Author: USGF Gymnastics Safety Manual, 1990; U.S. Diving Safety Manual, 1990, 1999. Commissioner, Iowa State Judicial Nominating Commission, 1993-1999. Chair, U.S. District Court Magistrate Judge Merit Selection Panel, Northern District of Iowa, 1995-1996. Member, Federal Practice committee, Northern District of Iowa, 2002—. *Member:* Linn County, Iowa State (Member: Litigation Section, 1990—; Litigation Section Council, 1994-1997; Committee on Administrative Law, 1980-1986) and American Bar Associations; Iowa Academy of Trial Lawyers; American Board of Trial Advocates; Iowa Defense Counsel Association (Board of Directors, 1991—; Secretary, 1992-1993; President-Elect, 1993-1994; President, 1994-1995; Member, Civil Jury Instructions Task Force); International Association of Defense Counsel (Member, Executive Committee, 2001-2004; Chair, General Convention, 2001; President-Elect, 2004—; Past Chair, Legal Malpractice Committee; Member, Product Liability Committee; Faculty Member, 1995 Trial Academy); Defense Research Institute (Member, Board of Directors, 2001—; State Representative, 1997-2001). ***PRACTICE AREAS:*** Civil Litigation. ***Email:*** glederer@simmonsperrine.com

JAMES A. GERK, born Mason City, Iowa, September 1, 1955; admitted to bar, 1980, Iowa. *Education:* University of Iowa (B.B.S., 1977; J.D., with distinction, 1980). Executive Editor, Journal of Corporation Law, 1979-1980. *Member:* Linn County, Iowa State and American Bar Associations; American College of Trial Lawyers (Fellow); Iowa Academy of Trial Lawyers; American Board of Trial Advocates; Iowa Defense Counsel Association; Iowa Association for Hospital Attorneys; Defense Research Institute. ***PRACTICE AREAS:*** Civil Litigation. ***Email:*** jgerk@simmonsperrine.com

ROGER W. STONE, born Dakota City, Iowa, June 7, 1954; admitted to bar, 1980, Iowa. *Education:* University of Iowa (B.A., 1975; J.D., with highest distinction, 1980); Columbia University (M.A., 1977). Phi Beta Kappa; Order of the Coif. International Fellow; Recipient: Hancher-Finkbine Medallion; Iowa State Bar Academic Excellence Award. Editor-in-chief, Journal of Corporation Law, 1979-1980. Author: "Construction Damages in Iowa," 52 Drake Law Rev. 449, 2004; "Architect's and Engineer's Liability Under Iowa Construction Law," 50 Drake Law Rev. 33, 2001; "Mechanic's Liens in Iowa," 30 Drake Law Review 39, 1980; "Mechanic's Lien Law in Iowa - Revisited," 49 Drake Law Review 1, 2000. Co-Author: "Iowa Construction Law," National Business Institute, 1987 and 1998. Law Clerk to Hon. Donald P. Lay, Chief Judge, U.S. Court of Appeals, 8th Circuit, 1980-1981. Chairperson, Cedar Rapids Area Chamber of Commerce, 2000-2001; State of Iowa Democratic Central Committee, 1983-1990; Linn County Democratic Chairperson, 1987-1988; President, Cedar Rapids Art Museum, 1998. *Member:* Linn County, Iowa State (Member, Environmental Law Council) and American (Member: Construction Industry Forum; Section on Environmental Law) Bar Associations; Iowa Academy of Trial Lawyers; American Arbitration Association National Registry of Arbitrators. ***PRACTICE AREAS:*** Construction; Environmental Law; Banking; Litigation. ***Email:*** rstone@simmonsperrine.com

DAVID A. HACKER, born Waterloo, Iowa, February 12, 1944; admitted to bar, 1982, Iowa and U.S. District Court, Northern District of Iowa; 1983, U.S. Court of Appeals, Eighth Circuit; 1984, U.S. Court of Appeals, Federal Circuit; 1987, U.S. Court of Appeals, Tenth Circuit; 1990, U.S. Court of Appeals, Ninth Circuit; 1992, U.S. Court of Appeals, Third Circuit and U.S. Supreme Court; 1992, U.S. District Court, Southern District of Iowa. *Education:* University of Notre Dame (B.A., 1966); University of Iowa (Ph.D., 1972; J.D., with high distinction, 1982). Author: "The Admission Exception to the Iowa Statute of Frauds: An Inefficient Approach to the Enforcement of Oral Contracts," 67 Iowa Law Review 3, 1982. Member, Order of the Coif. *Member:* Linn County, Johnson County, Iowa State (Member, Sections on: Trade Regulations; Litigation; Patent, Trademark and Copyright) and American Bar Associations; Iowa Defense Counsel Association; American Intellectual Property Law Association; Iowa Intellectual Property Law Association. ***PRACTICE AREAS:*** Commercial Litigation; Intellectual Property Litigation. ***Email:*** dhacker@simmonsperrine.com

DAVID W. KUBICEK, born Birmingham, Alabama, August 21, 1946; admitted to bar, 1973, Iowa. *Education:* Iowa State University (B.S., 1968); University of Iowa (J.D., with distinction, 1972). Phi Delta Phi. Listed in the Best Lawyers in America: Real Estate Law, 1993-2004. Co-Author: "Selected Topics in Examination of Abstracts of Title," 26 Drake L. Review, 1977. *Member:* Linn County (Chair, 1982-1997, Member, 1975—, Title Standards Committee), Iowa State (Chair, 1982-1983 and Member, 1976-1983, Real Estate Practice Manual Committee, Young Lawyers Section; Member, 1982—; Chair, 1991—, Title Standards Committee) and American (Member, Section on Real Property, Probate and Trust Law) Bar Associations; American College of Real Estate Lawyers. ***PRACTICE AREAS:*** Real Estate; Probate and Estate Planning. ***Email:*** dkubicek@simmonsperrine.com

MATTHEW J. BRANDES, born Waverly, Iowa, October 6, 1953; admitted to bar, 1981, Minnesota; 1985, Iowa. *Education:* University of Notre Dame (B.A., 1975); William Mitchell College of Law (J.D., cum laude, 1981). Law Clerk, Honorable Edward J. McManus, Chief Judge, Northern District of Iowa, 1983-1985. *Member:* Linn County (Member, Family Law Procedures Committee, 2001-2003), Iowa State (Section Council, Family and Juvenile Law; Co-Chair, ADR Sub-Committee) and American (Member, Sections on: Family Law; Litigation) Bar Associations; Association of Family and Conciliation Courts; Iowa Association of Workers' Compensation Lawyers, Inc. ***PRACTICE AREAS:*** Family Law; Mediation; Workers' Compensation; Insurance Defense; Personal Injury. ***Email:*** mbrandes@simmonsperrine.com

JAMES M. PETERS, born Ft. Dodge, Iowa, April 23, 1955; admitted to bar, 1980, Iowa. *Education:* University of Iowa (B.A., with high distinction, 1977; J.D., with distinction, 1980). Phi Beta Kappa. Law Clerk to Hon. Arthur A. McGiverin, Supreme Court of Iowa, 1980-1981. Private Practice, Dickinson Law Firm, Des Moines, Iowa 1981-1983. Assistant Iowa Attorney General, 1983-1986. *Member:* Linn County, Iowa State and American Bar Associations. ***PRACTICE AREAS:*** Workers' Compensation; Employment; Civil Litigation; Insurance Defense. ***Email:*** jpeters@simmonsperrine.com

LEONARD T. STRAND, born Sioux City, Iowa, July 14, 1965; admitted to bar, 1990, Iowa and U.S. District Court, Northern and Southern Districts of Iowa; 1992, U.S. Court of Appeals, Third and Eighth Circuits. *Education:* University of Iowa (B.A., with high distinction, 1987; J.D., with highest distinction, 1990). Phi Beta Kappa; Order of the Coif. Recipient, John F. Murray Prize. Member, Journal of Corporation Law, 1989. Author: Comment, "*Noerr* Immunity in the Private Standard-Setting Context: *Allied Tube & Conduit Corp. v. Indian Head, Inc.*," 14 Journal of Corporation Law 1033 (1989). *Member:* Linn County, Iowa State and American Bar Associations; Iowa Defense Counsel Association. ***PRACTICE AREAS:*** Commercial and Employment Litigation; Contract Law. ***Email:*** lstrand@simmonsperrine.com

MARK H. OGDEN, born Oskaloosa, Iowa, December 25, 1947; admitted to bar, 1977, Iowa and U.S. District Court, Northern District of Iowa. *Education:* Grinnell College (B.A., 1970); Drake University (J.D., with honors, 1976). Order of Coif. Staff Member, Drake University, Law Review, 1975-1976. *Member:* Linn County (Chairman, Title Standards Committee), Iowa State (Member, Taxation, Probate and Trust Law and Real Estate and Title Law Sections) and American Bar Associations. ***PRACTICE AREAS:*** Probate; Real Estate; Estate Planning; Taxation. ***Email:*** mogden@simmonsperrine.com

WEBB L. WASSMER, born Cedar Rapids, Iowa, April 11, 1964; admitted to bar, 1989, Iowa; 1992, U.S. District Court, Northern and Southern Districts of Iowa; 1993, U.S. Court of Appeals, Eighth Circuit and for the Federal Circuit. *Education:* Washington University (B.A., cum laude, 1986); University of Pennsylvania (J.D., 1989). Law Clerk: Honorable David R. Hansen, U.S. District Court, Northern District of Iowa, 1989-1991; Honorable David R Hansen, U.S. Court of Appeals, Eighth Circuit, 1991-1992. *Member:* Linn County, Iowa State (Member, 1999-2002 and Chair, 2001-2002, Environmental Law Section Council; Iowa Jury Instruction Committee, 2000—) and American Bar Associations; Iowa Defense Counsel Association; Defense Research Institute. ***PRACTICE AREAS:*** Civil Litigation; Environmental Law; Construction Law. ***Email:*** wwassmer@simmonsperrine.com

MARK A. ROBERTS, born Ames, Iowa, December 1, 1966; admitted to bar, 1993, Iowa. *Education:* Iowa State University (B.A., 1989); University of Nebraska at Lincoln (J.D., with high distinction, 1993). Order of the Coif. Executive Editor, Nebraska Law Review. *Member:* Linn County, Iowa State and American Bar Associations. ***PRACTICE AREAS:*** Civil Litigation. ***Email:*** mroberts@simmonsperrine.com

CHAD M. VON KAMPEN, born Ogallala, Nebraska, June 12, 1967; admitted to bar, 1992, Nevada; 1993, Iowa. *Education:* Concordia College (B.A., highest distinction, 1989); University of Nebraska at Lincoln (J.D., with highest distinction, 1992). Sigma Tau Delta; Order of the Coif. Author, "Solid Waste Regulation," Chapter in "Nevada Environmental Law Handbook." *Member:* Linn County, Iowa State and American Bar Associations; Iowa Defense Counsel Association. ***PRACTICE AREAS:*** Civil Litigation. ***Email:*** cvonkampen@simmonsperrine.com

GREGORY G. WILLIAMS, born San Diego, California, March 23, 1959; admitted to bar, 1985, Iowa and U.S. District Court, Northern and Southern Districts of Iowa; 1986, U.S. Court of Appeals for the Federal and Eighth Circuits; 2001, U.S. Supreme Court; registered to practice before U.S. Patent and Trademark Office. *Education:* University of Iowa (B.A. in Physics, 1982; J.D., 1985; M.B.A., 1997). Adjunct Instructor of Business Law, University of Iowa and Mount Mercy College. *Member:* Linn County, Johnson County and Iowa State Bar Associations; Iowa Intellectual Property Law Association (Member, Board of Governors, 1988-1991; President, 1999). ***PRACTICE AREAS:*** Patents; Trademark and Unfair Competition; Copyrights. ***Email:*** gwilliams@simmonsperrine.com

ALLISON M. HEFFERN, born Des Moines, Iowa, January 4, 1960; admitted to bar, 1987, Iowa; 1990, U.S. District Court, Northern and Southern Districts of Iowa. *Education:* Clarke College (B.A., 1982); University of Iowa (J.D., 1987). *Member:* Linn County (Member, Board of Governors, 2002—), Iowa State (Litigation and Health Law Sections) and American Bar Associations; Iowa Defense Counsel Association; Defense Research Insti-

(This Listing Continued)

tute; American Health Lawyers Association; Dean Mason Ladd American Inn of Court (Past Treasurer). ***PRACTICE AREAS:*** Civil Litigation; Insurance Defense. ***Email:*** aheffern@simmonsperrine.com

LYNN WICKHAM HARTMAN, born Dubuque, Iowa, January 4, 1962; admitted to bar, 1987, Iowa, U.S. Court of Appeals, Eighth Circuit and U.S. District Court, Northern and Southern Districts of Iowa. *Education:* University of Iowa (B.A., with distinction, 1984; J.D., with distinction, 1987). Recipient, American Jurisprudence Award in Education Law. Associate Editor, Iowa Law Review, 1986-1987. Author: "Standards Governing the News: Their Use, Their Character, and Their Legal Implications," 72 Iowa Law Review 637 (1987). *Member:* Linn County and Iowa State (Member, Business Law Section, Uniform Commercial Code Committee Member; Corporate Counsel Section; Member, Commercial and Bankruptcy Law Section) Bar Associations; Linn County Women Attorneys (Past President); Dean Mason Ladd American Inn of Court (Past Treasurer). ***PRACTICE AREAS:*** Banking Law; Commercial Law; Mortgages; Creditor's Rights; Real Estate Finance. ***Email:*** lhartman@simmonsperrine.com

KATHLEEN A. KLEIMAN, born Cedar Rapids, Iowa, December 16, 1963; admitted to bar, 1988, Illinois; 1989, U.S. Court of Appeals, Seventh Circuit; 1997, Iowa. *Education:* University of Iowa (B.B.A., with highest distinction, 1985); Yale Law School (J.D., 1988). Law Clerk to Judge Walter J. Cummings, U.S. Court of Appeals, Seventh Circuit. *Member:* Illinois State and Iowa State Bar Associations. ***PRACTICE AREAS:*** Corporate Law; Business Sales and Acquisitions; Employee Benefits. ***Email:*** kkleiman@simmonsperrine.com

NICOLAS ABOU-ASSALY, born Beirut, Lebanon, September 2, 1966; admitted to bar, 1992, Texas; 1995, Iowa. *Education:* University of Iowa (B.B.A., with honors, 1989; J.D., with distinction, 1992). *Member:* Linn County, Iowa State and American Bar Associations; State Bar of Texas. ***LANGUAGES:*** Arabic. ***PRACTICE AREAS:*** Real Estate; Corporate; Real Estate Taxation; Immigration Law. ***Email:*** nick@simmonsperrine.com

PAUL P. MORF, born Cedar Rapids, Iowa, February 12, 1972; admitted to bar, 1998, Iowa, U.S. District Court, Northern and Southern Districts of Iowa and U.S. Court of Appeals, Eighth Circuit. *Education:* Dartmouth College (A.B., summa cum laude, 1994); Yale University (J.D., 1997). Phi Beta Kappa. Editor-in-Chief, Yale Journal on Regulation, 1996-1997. Law Clerk to David R. Hansen, U.S. Court of Appeals, Eighth Circuit, 1997-1998. Adjunct Professor, Estate Planning, University of Iowa College of Law, 2003—. *Member:* Linn County, Iowa State (Member, Sections on: Probate and Trust Law, Litigation, Health Law, Business and Taxation; Chair, Probate and Trust Code Reconciliation Committee, 2003-2004) and American (Member, Sections on: Taxation, Business Law, State and Local Government, Litigation, Real Property, Probate and Trust Law) Bar Associations. ***PRACTICE AREAS:*** Litigation; Trusts and Estates; Wills; Estate Planning; Probate; Business Law. ***Email:*** pmorf@simmonsperrine.com

PHILIP A. BURIAN, born Iowa City, Iowa, March 11, 1968; admitted to bar, 1996, Iowa, Illinois and U.S. District Court, Northern and Southern Districts of Iowa. *Education:* Kirkwood Community College (A.A., Liberal Arts, with honors, 1989); Coe College (B.A., cum laude, 1993); University of Iowa (J.D., high distinction, 1996). Phi Beta Kappa; Phi Kappa Phi; Order of the Coif. Ruth A. Outland Scholar. Member: Van Oosterhout Moot Court Competition, 1995; National Moot Court Team, 1995. *Member:* Linn County, Iowa State and American Bar Associations; Iowa Association of Defense Counsel. ***PRACTICE AREAS:*** Civil Litigation. ***Email:*** pburian@simmonsperrine.com

CHRISTINE L. CONOVER, born North Platte, Nebraska, July 3, 1973; admitted to bar, 1998, Iowa; 2000, U.S. District Court, Northern and Southern Districts of Iowa. *Education:* Iowa State University (B.A., 1995) Phi Beta Kappa; University of Iowa (J.D., with high distinction, 1998). Member, National Moot Court Team. Law Clerk to Justice J.L. Larson, Iowa Supreme Court, 1998-1999. Author: "The Violence Against Women," Act 1 Journal of Gender, Race & Justice 269 (1997). *Member:* Linn County, Iowa State and American Bar Associations; Iowa Association of Defense Counsel (Board Member, 2003—); Iowa Organization of Women Attorneys (Board Member, 1999-2002; President, 2002-2003). ***PRACTICE AREAS:*** Civil Litigation; Medical Malpractice. ***Email:*** cconover@simmonsperrine.com

DAVID C. KUTCHER, born Iowa City, Iowa, November 13, 1974; admitted to bar, 2001, Illinois; 2003, Iowa. *Education:* Western Illinois University (B.S., cum laude, 1997); University of Iowa (J.D., with distinction, 2000). *Member:* Linn County, Iowa State and Illinois State Bar Associations. ***PRACTICE AREAS:*** Corporate Law; Business Law; Contracts; Public Finance. ***Email:*** dkutcher@simmonsperrine.com

ASSOCIATES

MICHAEL F. WILLIAMS, born Norman, Oklahoma, December 17, 1960; admitted to bar, 1991, Iowa; registered to practice before U.S. Patent and Trademark Office. *Education:* Wartburg College (B.A., Mathematics, B.A., Computer Science, with honors, 1983); University of Illinois (M.S., with honors, 1985); University of Iowa (J.D., with honors, 1989). *Member:* Linn County, Iowa State and American Bar Associations; American Intellectual Property Law Association. ***PRACTICE AREAS:*** Intellectual Property; Patents; Trademarks. ***Email:*** mwillia@simmonsperrine.com

ELIZABETH V. CROCO, born Paris, France, November 9, 1974; admitted to bar, 2000, Iowa and U.S. District Court, Northern and Southern Districts of Iowa. *Education:* Grinnell College (B.A., 1996); University of Iowa (J.D., with high distinction, 2000). *Member:* Linn County, Iowa State and American Bar Associations; Iowa Association of Defense Counsel; Iowa Organization of Women Attorney (Board Member, 2003—). ***LANGUAGES:*** French, Spanish and German. ***PRACTICE AREAS:*** Civil Litigation; Family Law. ***Email:*** ecroco@simmonsperrine.com

PATSY A. THIMMIG, born Sheboygan, Wisconsin, July 12, 1966; admitted to bar, 1999, Missouri; 2000, Illinois; 2001, Iowa; 2002, U.S. District Court, Northern District of Iowa. *Education:* Colorado College (B.A., 1988); University of Denver (M.A., 1991); St. Louis University (J.D., magna cum laude, 1999). Law Clerk, Hon. David R. Hansen, U.S. Court of Appeals, Eighth Circuit, 1999-2001. Author: "Not Your Average School Day: Reading, Writing and Stripsearching," 43 St. Louis University Law Journal 1389 (1998). *Member:* Linn County and Iowa State Bar Associations. ***PRACTICE AREAS:*** Civil Litigation. ***Email:*** pthimmig@simmonsperrine.com

(This Listing Continued)

JASON M. STEFFENS, born Cedar Rapids, Iowa, December 29, 1977; admitted to bar, 2003, Iowa and U.S. District Court, Northern and Southern Districts of Iowa. *Education:* Wartburg College (B.A., 2000); University of Iowa (J.D., with distinction, 2003). Note and Comment Editor, Iowa Law Review, Vol. 88. Author: "The 'Peculiar' Being: The Rights of an Unborn Child in Iowa," 88 Iowa Law Review 217 (2002). *Member:* Linn County and Iowa State Bar Associations. ***PRACTICE AREAS:*** Civil Litigation. ***Email:*** jsteffens@simmonsperrine.com

LORIE E. REINS-SCHWEER, born Waterloo, Iowa, July 2, 1962; admitted to bar, 2003, Iowa. *Education:* University of Northern Iowa (B.A., 1984); University of Iowa (J.D., 2003). Order of the Coif. Member, Journal of Corporation Law, 2002-2003. Recipient: Justice Randy Holland Award for Corporate Scholarship; ABA Medal for Excellence in Bankruptcy Studies. Author: "The Power of 'Except as Otherwise Provided': Carry Forward of Passive Activity Losses From a Closely Held C Corporation to an S Corporation," Journal of Corp. Law 28-2. Certified Public Accountant, 1984. Member, American Institute of Certified Public Accountants, 1984—. *Member:* Iowa State Bar Association. ***PRACTICE AREAS:*** Taxation; Business Law; Estate Planning; Wills; Probate; Debtor and Creditor; Bankruptcy. ***Email:*** lreins-schweer@simmonsperrine.com

LANCE R. STAKER, born Fredericksburg, Iowa, April 30, 1971; admitted to bar, 1997, Iowa; 1999, Illinois. *Education:* Coe College (B.A., 1993); University of Iowa (J.D., with high distinction, 1997); University of Iowa (M.B.A., 1997). *Member:* Iowa State Bar Association. ***Email:*** lstaker@simmonsperrine.com

OF COUNSEL

James R. Snyder
Robert M. Jilek

REPRESENTATIVE CLIENTS: D.C. Taylor Roofing Co.; Kleiman Construction Co.; Garling Construction Co.; Wells Fargo Bank, N.A.; City of Iowa City; Hills Bank & Trust; Commercial Federal Bank, N.A.; Alliant Energy Resources; Gazette Co.; Grain Processing Corp., a division of Varied Investments, Inc.; Kinze Manufacturing Co.; Crystal Group, Inc.; Diversified Software, Inc.; Amana Company, a Division of Goodman, Inc.; Cedar Memorial Funeral Home Co.; Croell Redi Mix Co.; Pickwick Manufacturing Co.; Grant Wood Area Education Agency; Herbert Hoover Presidential Library; Halls-Perrine Foundation; Greater Cedar Rapids Community Foundation; Raytheon Co.; Cryovac, Inc., a subsidiary of Sealed Air Corporation; Kent Feeds; Penford Products Co.; Weyerhaeuser Paper Co.; Longview Fibre Co.; Howard R. Green Co.; Varied Investments, Inc.; Norand Corp.; Firstar Bank, N.A.; Iowa Comprehensive Petroleum Underground Storage Tank Fund; Crawford and Company; Intermec Technologies Corp.; IES Utilities, Inc.; Mutual Service Insurance Companies.
REPRESENTATIVE PATENT CLIENTS: Norand Mobile Data Systems; Rockwell International Corporation.
INSURANCE COMPANY CLIENTS: XL America Insurance Co.; American States Insurance Co.; American International Group, Inc.; American International Underwriters; National Union Insurance Cos.; New Hampshire Insurance Group; Allstate Insurance Co.; Grinnell Mutual Reinsurance Co.; Hawkeye-Security Insurance Co.; Milwaukee Mutual Insurance Co.; The St. Paul Cos.; State Farm Fire & Casualty Company; Farmers Casualty Company Mutual; IMT Insurance Company; GAB Business Services; National Chiropractic Mutual Ins. Co.; Prudential Property & Casualty Insurance Company; Pharmacists Mutual Insurance Co.; Reliance Insurance Company; Pacific Employers Insurance Company.

TERPSTRA, EPPING & WILLETT

An Association of Sole Practitioners

118 THIRD AVENUE, S.E.
SUITE 500, HIGLEY BUILDING
CEDAR RAPIDS, IOWA 52401-1424
Telephone: 319-364-2467
Fax: 319-364-2460
Email: info@tewlaw.net

Creditors Rights, Real Estate, Civil Litigation, Bankruptcy Litigation, Commercial Transactions, Probate.

HARRY R. TERPSTRA (1929-1998)

H. RAYMOND TERPSTRA, II, born Cedar Rapids, Iowa, August 4, 1956; admitted to bar, 1981, Iowa and U.S. District Court, Northern and Southern Districts of Iowa; U.S. Supreme Court; U.S. Court of Appeals, Eighth Circuit. *Education:* Allegheny College (B.S., with distinction, 1978); Drake University (J.D., with distinction, 1981). *Member:* Linn County, Iowa State and Federal Bar Associations; American Bankruptcy Institute. ***PRACTICE AREAS:*** Creditors Rights; Foreclosures; Workouts; Lender Liability; Commercial Law; Commercial Collections; Litigation. ***Email:*** rterpstra@tewlaw.net

GREGORY J. EPPING, born Davenport, Iowa, January 4, 1955; admitted to bar, 1980, Iowa and U.S. District Court, Northern and Southern Districts of Iowa. *Education:* Iowa State University (B.S., with distinction, 1977); University of Iowa (J.D., with distinction, 1980). *Member:* Linn County and Iowa State Bar Associations. ***PRACTICE AREAS:*** Bankruptcy; Creditors Rights; Probate; Real Estate; Conservatorship; Buying and Selling of Businesses; Commercial Law; Business Litigation. ***Email:*** gepping@tewlaw.net

ALFRED E. WILLETT

FORREST W. ROSSER

REPRESENTATIVE CLIENTS: Cat Financial Services Corp; Central State Bank, Muscatine, IA; Chelsea Savings Bank; Farmers Savings Bank, Walford; Hills Bank and Trust Co., Hills, IA; Kerndt Bros. Savings Bank; Regions Bank, N.A.; Textron Financial Corp.; TSB Bank, Marshalltown, IA; Wells Fargo Bank Iowa, N.A.; Wells Fargo Equipment Finance Corp.; West Bank, Iowa City, IA.
REFERENCES: Farmers and Merchants Savings Bank, Cedar Rapids, IA; Hills Bank & Trust Co., Hills, IA.

JOHN M. TITLER

320 8TH AVENUE, SOUTH EAST
P.O. BOX 1168
CEDAR RAPIDS, IOWA 52401-2018
Telephone: 319-363-5563
Fax: 319-363-5678
Email: jmt@t-mlawcr.com
URL: http://www.lawyers.com/johnmtitler

Bankruptcy, Real Estate, Business Law, Probate, Wills, Trusts, Estates.

JOHN M. TITLER, born Cedar Rapids, Iowa, July 19, 1947; admitted to bar, 1974, Colorado; 1978, Iowa. *Education:* Loras College; University of Iowa (B.A., 1969); University of Notre Dame (J.D., 1974). *Member:* Linn County, Iowa State and American Bar Associations.

WERTZ LAW FIRM, P.C.

1500 CENTER STREET, N.E.
P.O. BOX 849
CEDAR RAPIDS, IOWA 52406-0849
Telephone: 319-861-3001
Fax: 319-861-3007
Email: twertz@wertzlaw.com
URL: http://www.wertzlaw.com

Mailing Address: P.O. Box 849, Cedar Rapids, IA 52406-0849

Workers Compensation, Personal Injury.

THOMAS M. WERTZ, born Cedar Rapids, Iowa, January 10, 1953; admitted to bar, 1978, Iowa. *Education:* University of Iowa (B.A., 1975); University of Tulsa (J.D., 1978). Member: Arthritis Foundation; State of Iowa Board. Chair, Eastern Iowa Board, 1994—. Member, Board of Directors, USA Rugby, 1997-2002. President, Midwest Rugby Union, 1996-2002. Outstanding Member of the Year, Iowa Trial Lawyers Association, 2002. *Member:* Iowa State Bar Association; Iowa Trial Lawyers Association (Chair, Workers Compensation Section, 1998—; Board of Governors, 1998—); Association of Trial Lawyers of America; Work Injury Litigation Group (WILG). ***PRACTICE AREAS:*** Workers Compensation. ***Email:*** twertz@wertzlaw.com

---

MATTHEW D. DAKE, born Cedar Rapids, Iowa, June 6, 1971; admitted to bar, 1997, Iowa. *Education:* University of Northern Iowa (B.A., Business, with honors, 1994); Creighton University (J.D., cum laude, 1997). *Member:* Linn County and Iowa State Bar Associations; Iowa Trial Lawyers Association. ***PRACTICE AREAS:*** Personal Injury; Workers Compensation. ***Email:*** mdake@wertzlaw.com

---

WHITE & JOHNSON, P.C.

FIRST FLOOR
AMERICAN BUILDING
101 2ND STREET, S.E.
P.O. BOX 5878
CEDAR RAPIDS, IOWA 52406-5878
Telephone: 319-364-0900
Facsimile: 319-364-7212
Email: w&j@wjpc.com
URL: http://www.wjpc.com

General Practice. Trials, Personal Injury, Insurance, Workers' Compensation, Tax, Corporate, Real Estate, Probate, Domestic Relations.

TIMOTHY S. WHITE, born Carroll, Iowa, November 14, 1941; admitted to bar, 1967, Iowa; U.S. Supreme Court; U.S. Court of Appeals, Eighth Circuit; U.S. District Court, Northern and Southern Districts of Iowa; 2001, Wisconsin. *Education:* University of Iowa (B.A., 1964; J.D., 1967); Northwestern University School of Law (Certification for Prosecuting Attorneys, 1969). Assistant Linn County Attorney, 1968-1972. *Member:* Linn County (Member, Board of Governors, 1987-1988), Iowa State (Member, Litigation Legislation Committee, 1979—) and American Bar Associations; Iowa Academy of Trial Lawyers; Association of Trial Lawyers of Iowa (Member, Board of Governors, 1973-1981; President, 1978-1979); The Association of Trial Lawyers of America (State Committeeman, 1979-1980). ***PRACTICE AREAS:*** Personal Injury Law; Products Liability Law; Trial Practice. ***Email:*** w&j@wjpc.com

J. RICHARD JOHNSON, born Milton, Massachusetts, June 4, 1952; admitted to bar, 1978, Iowa; U.S. Court of Appeals, Eighth Circuit; U.S. District Court, Northern and Southern Districts of Iowa. *Education:* Marietta College (B.A., 1974); University of Iowa (J.D., 1978). Phi Delta Phi. Articles Editor, The Journal of Corporation Law, 1977-1978. Author: "Piper v. Chris-Craft Industries, Inc. - The Uncertain Evolution of Private Actions Under The Williams Act," 3 Journal of Corporation Law 364 (1978). *Member:* Linn County and Iowa State Bar Associations; Iowa Defense Counsel Association; The Iowa Association of Workers' Compensation Lawyers, Inc. ***PRACTICE AREAS:*** Insurance Law; Workers' Compensation Law; Trial Practice. ***Email:*** rjohnson@wjpc.com

JAMES W. RADIG, born Minneapolis, Minnesota, March 13, 1959; admitted to bar, 1985, Iowa; 1986, U.S. District Court, Northern District of Iowa; 1987, U.S. District Court, Southern District of Iowa; 1988, South Dakota. *Education:* University of North Dakota (B.A., summa cum laude, 1981); University of Iowa (J.D., with high distinction, 1984). Law Clerk to: Honorable Richard F. Stageman, U.S. Bankruptcy Judge, Southern District of Iowa, 1985-1986; Honorable Dick R. Schlegel, Iowa Court of Appeals, 1984-1985. *Member:* Linn County, Iowa State and American Bar Associations. ***PRACTICE AREAS:*** Probate; Estate Planning; Commercial Litigation; Bankruptcy; Real Estate; Corporate Law. ***Email:*** jradig@wjpc.com

---

DEBORAH M. SKELTON, born Sioux Falls, South Dakota, June 27, 1953; admitted to bar, 1996, Iowa; 1997, U.S. District Court, Northern District of Iowa. *Education:* Mount Mercy College (B.A., magna cum laude, 1993); University of Iowa (J.D., 1996). *Member:* Linn County, Benton County (Vice President, 1998—), Iowa State and American Bar Associations; Association of Women Lawyers of Linn County (Vice President, 1998—). ***PRACTICE AREAS:*** Family Law; Criminal Law; Juvenile Law. ***Email:*** dskelton@wjpc.com

MATT J. REILLY, born Des Moines, Iowa, January 17, 1972; admitted to bar, 1988, Iowa; 2001, U.S. District Court, Northern and Southern Districts of Iowa. *Education:* University of Iowa (B.A., 1994); Drake University (J.D., with high honors, 1998). Order of the Coif. Law Clerk, for the Honorable Donald E. O'Brien, Senior District Court Judge for the U.S. District, Northern District of Iowa. Staff Attorney, U.S. Court of Appeals, 8th Circuit, 1998-1999. ***PRACTICE AREAS:*** Employment Law; Personal Injury. ***Email:*** mreilly@wjpc.com

ROBERT J. LEGISLADOR, born Cleveland, Ohio, January 18, 1972; admitted to bar, 2000, Iowa and U.S. District Court, Northern District of Iowa; U.S. District Court, Southern District of Iowa and U.S. Court of Appeals, Eighth Circuit. *Education:* University of Iowa (B.S., 1996); Drake University (J.D., 2000). *Member:* Linn County, Iowa State and American Bar Associations. ***PRACTICE AREAS:*** General Practice. ***Email:*** rlegisla@wjpc.com

LANDON R. DUFOE, born Cedar Rapids, Iowa, January 15, 1971; admitted to bar, 2004, Iowa and U.S. District Court, Southern and Northern Districts of Iowa. *Education:* Coe College (B.A., cum laude, 2001); University of Iowa College of Law (J.D., 2003). Phi Kappa Phi; Phi Beta Kappa. *Member:* Iowa State Bar Association. ***PRACTICE AREAS:*** Insurance Defense; General Practice. ***Email:*** ldufoe@wjpc.com

DOMINIC F. PECHOTA, born Martin, South Dakota, February 24, 1978; admitted to bar, 2004, Iowa. *Education:* University of Nebraska at Lincoln (B.A., 2000); University of Iowa (J.D., 2004). *Member:* Iowa State Bar Association. ***PRACTICE AREAS:*** Civil Litigation. ***Email:*** dpechota@wjpc.com

RENEE V. SNEITZER, born Brooklyn, New York; admitted to bar, 1993, Iowa; U.S. Court of Appeals, Eighth Circuit; U.S. District Court, Northern District of Iowa. *Education:* Iowa State University (B.A., 1987); University of Iowa (J.D., 1990). Assistant County Attorney: Johnson County, Iowa, 1993-94; Black Hawk County, Iowa, 1994-96; Commissioned, National Appeals Committee for ELCA, 1993-99; Appointed, Panel Attorney, Federal Criminal Justice Act, 2001—; Governor Appointee, Iowa State Board of Corrections, 2003. *Member:* Johnson County, Black Hawk County, Linn County and Iowa State Bar Associations; Iowa Trial Lawyers Association; American Inns of Court (Dean Mason Ladd Inn of Court). ***PRACTICE AREAS:*** Family Law; Criminal Law; Personal Injury.

INDEPENDENT COUNSEL

RONALD L. LUEHRSMANN, born Dubuque, Iowa, June 11, 1942; admitted to bar, 1969, Iowa and U.S. District Court, Northern and Southern Districts of Iowa; 1970, U.S. Court of Appeals, Eighth Circuit; 1975, U.S. Supreme Court. *Education:* Loras College (B.A., 1964); University of Iowa (J.D., 1969). Assistant Linn County Attorney, Cedar Rapids, Iowa, 1970-1975. Linn County Judicial Magistrate Appointment Commission, 1970-1975. *Member:* Linn County and Iowa State Bar Associations; Association of Trial Lawyers of Iowa (Member, Board of Governors, 1970-1975). ***PRACTICE AREAS:*** Litigation; Sports Law. ***Email:*** ronl@wjpc.com

CAROLYN J. BEYER, born Omaha, Nebraska, March 8, 1952; admitted to bar, 1977, Wisconsin; 1985, Illinois; 1991, Iowa and U.S. District Court, Northern and Southern Districts of Iowa. *Education:* University of Nebraska (B.A., 1974); Creighton University (J.D., 1977). *Member:* Linn County, Iowa State and American Bar Associations; Iowa Association of Trial Lawyers; The Association of Trial Lawyers of America. ***PRACTICE AREAS:*** Trial Practice; Family Law. ***Email:*** cbeyer@wjpc.com

REPRESENTATIVE INSURANCE CLIENTS: Cincinnati Insurance Co.; The Farmers Alliance Insurance; Bituminous Casualty Corp.; Agora Syndicate; Freemont Compensation Insurance Group; T.I.G. Insurance; Ohio Casualty Insurance; Selective Insurance Co.; United Fire & Casualty.
REPRESENTATIVE CLIENTS: The Procter & Gamble Co.; Novartis, Inc.; Family Health Center, P.C.; Wholesale Feeds, Inc.; Great Plains Supply Co.; Cedar Rapids Lumber Co.; Austin Construction Co.; Employee Group Services, Ltd.; Cedar Rapids Dermatology; Access Direct Telemarketing, Inc.; F & W Mack Truck Sales, Inc.; Financial Life Resources Group, Inc.; Squaw Creek Village Home Sales, Inc.; Caldwell Banker Hedges Realty; Winmor Construction Co; Shelton Technologies, Inc.; Duball Electric, Inc.; McDonald's Corporation.

KARLA M. WOLFF

866 FIRST AVENUE NE
CEDAR RAPIDS, IOWA 52402
Telephone: 319-366-7516
Fax: 319-366-7880
Email: kmwolff2@aol.com
URL: http://www.lawyers.com/kmwolff

Family Law, Divorce, Custody, Juvenile Law, Adoption Law.

KARLA M. WOLFF, born Valley City, North Dakota, June 14, 1961; admitted to bar, 1990, Iowa; 1991, U.S. District Court, Northern and Southern Districts of Iowa. *Education:* Moorhead State University (B.A., cum laude, 1984); University of Iowa (J.D., with distinction, 1990). *Member:* Linn County, Iowa State and American Bar Associations. ***PRACTICE AREAS:*** Family Law; Divorce; Custody; Juvenile Law; Adoption Law.

VERLE W. NORRIS

CENTERVILLE, IOWA

(See Corydon)

ORSBORN, BAUERLE, MILANI & GROTHE, L.L.P.

105 WEST VAN BUREN STREET
P.O. BOX 518
CENTERVILLE, IOWA 52544
Telephone: 641-856-3251
Fax: 641-856-5548
Email: obmgc@sirisonline.com
URL: http://www.obmglaw.com

Ottumwa, Iowa Office: 110 East Third, P. O. Box 878. Telephone: 641-682-5447. Fax: 641-682-6940.

General Practice in all Courts. Litigation, Probate and Real Estate.

FIRM PROFILE: In the early 1900's, Merrill Gilmore began practice in Ottumwa. Wilbur Dull joined the firm in 1946. George A Milani joined Tom Fee in the practice of law in Centerville, Iowa, in 1928. The two firms merged in 1989 with offices in Ottumwa and Centerville. The firm has continuously engaged in the practice of law for more than a century. The firm offers a wide range of legal services throughout Southeastern Iowa.

JAMES G. MILANI, born Centerville, Iowa, May 7, 1933; admitted to bar, 1958, Iowa. *Education:* State University of Iowa (B.A., 1958; J.D., 1958). Phi Delta Phi. Law School Class Agent, 78-90 and 98—. County Attorney, Appanoose County, 1959-1967. Trustee, First Methodist Church, 1965-1969. Area Chairman, Iowa Law School Foundation, 1967—. Member, National Panel of Arbitrators, American Arbitration Association, 1967—. President, Centerville National, Inc., 1968-1976. Secretary to the Lay Advisory Board, St. Joseph Mercy Hospital, 1969-1997. Government Appeal Agent, Selective Service Board, 1970-1972. President, Indian Hills Community College Foundation, 1974-1976. Member, Iowa Board of Law Examiners, 1980-1984. *Member:* Judicial District 8-A (Secretary-Treasurer, 1959-1961), Iowa State Junior (Member, Executive Council, 1967-1968), Iowa State (Member, Law School Panel Committee, 1960-1964; Member, 1963-1968 and Chairman, 1967-1968, Committee on Unauthorized Practice of Law; Commissioner, Grievance Commission, Professional Ethics Committee, 1984-1988) and American (Member, Sections on: General Practice; Real Property, Probate and Trust Law) Bar Associations; Iowa Trial Lawyers Association; Iowa Cattleman's Association (State Board of Directors). Fellow, Iowa Academy of Trial Lawyers; The Association of Trial Lawyers of America. [Comm, R.O.T.C. 2nd Lt. Inf., 1958.]. (Resident). ***PRACTICE AREAS:*** Real Estate; Estate Planning; Probate Law; Personal Injury; General Civil and Trial Practice.

BRADLEY M. GROTHE, born Burlington, Iowa, July 29, 1967; admitted to bar, 1994, Iowa. *Education:* Iowa State University (B.S., 1990); Drake University (J.D., 1994). Board Member, Appanoose County Foundation. *Member:* Appanoose, Iowa and American Bar Associations. ***PRACTICE AREAS:*** Estate Planning; Wills; Trusts; Probate; Real Estate; Creditors Rights; Civil Litigation; Trial Practice. ***Email:*** bradg@sirisonline.com

GEORGE A. MILANI (1900-1992)

REPRESENTATIVE CLIENTS: Iowa Trust and Savings Bank, Centerville; Farmers Bank of Northern Missouri, N.A.; Centerville, Iowa; Firstar Bank N.A., Centerville; Indian Hills Community College, Centerville; The Continental Holdings Corporation, Centerville; Wells Fargo Bank, Iowa, N.A. .

(For Additional Biographical Data on Other Personnel, see Professional Biographies at Ottumwa, Iowa).

KENNEDY AND KENNEDY

CHARLES CITY, IOWA

(See New Hampton)

Probate, Real Estate, Criminal Law, Trial Practice.

LAW OFFICE OF DAVID J. BLAIR, P.C.

425 SUMNER STREET
P.O. BOX 458
CHEROKEE, IOWA 51012
Telephone: 712-225-2323
Fax: 712-225-2727
Email: davidblair@blairadr.com
URL: http://www.blairadr.com

ADR, Mediation, Arbitration.

FIRM PROFILE: Founded 1991 by David J. Blair, a former Iowa District Court Judge and U.S. Magistrate. The Firm offers Neutral ADR Services including Mediation and Arbitration. Statewide, Regional, National Practice.

DAVID J. BLAIR, born Omaha, Nebraska, December 22, 1942; admitted to bar, 1968, Iowa; 1970, U.S. District Court, Northern and Southern Districts of Iowa and U.S. Court of Appeals, Eighth Circuit. *Education:* Harvard University (B.A., 1965); University of Iowa (J.D., 1968). Order of the Coif. Law Clerk to Hon. William C. Hanson, U.S. District Court, Northern and Southern Districts of Iowa, 1968-1970. Judge, Third Judicial District of Iowa, 1976-1981. U.S. Magistrate, Northern District of Iowa, 1973-1976. Panel Memberships: American Arbitration Association; Duke University Private Adjudication Center; CPR Institute for Dispute Resolution. Chairman, Civil Justice Reform Act Advisory Group, U.S.

(This Listing Continued)

District Court, Northern District of Iowa, 1991-1993. Member: Iowa Supreme Court's Advisory Committee on Media Coverage of the Courts, 1979-1980; Iowa Supreme Court's Commission on Planning For the 21st Century, 1995-1996; Iowa Attorney General's Task Force on Mediation, 1996-2000. *Member:* Iowa State and American Bar Associations; American Bar Foundation; Iowa Academy of Trial Lawyers (President, 1993-1994). ***SPECIAL AGENCIES:*** Commissioner, Iowa Racing and Gaming Commission, 1992-1994. ***PRACTICE AREAS:*** Mediation; Arbitration. ***Email:*** davidblair@blairadr.com

A List of Representative Clients Will Be Furnished Upon Request.

HERRICK, ARY, COOK, COOK, COOK & COOK

Established in 1869

209 WEST WILLOW STREET
P.O. BOX 209
CHEROKEE, IOWA 51012
Telephone: 712-225-5175
FAX: 712-225-5178

General Practice. Estate Planning, Probate, Corporation, Personal Injury, Commercial Litigation and Taxation Law. Trials.

MEMBERS OF FIRM

WILLIAM K. HERRICK (1878-1944)

LESTER C. ARY (1893-1962)

JOHN HOWARD COOK (1917-1996)

JOHN H. COOK, JR., born Chicago, Illinois, August 10, 1949; admitted to bar, 1974, Iowa. *Education:* Iowa State University (B.S., 1971); Drake University (J.D., 1974). Order of the Coif; Phi Alpha Delta; Delta Sigma Rho-Tau Kappa Alpha. Member, Order of Barristers. Member, Drake Law Review, 1972-1974. *Member:* Cherokee County, Iowa State and American Bar Associations; Association of Trial Lawyers of Iowa. ***Email:*** jcook@iowabar.org

RICHARD ARY COOK, born Cherokee, Iowa, August 1, 1958; admitted to bar, 1983, Iowa. *Education:* Iowa State University (B.S., 1980); Drake University (J.D., 1983). *Member:* Cherokee County, Iowa State and American Bar Associations; Association of Trial Lawyers of Iowa. ***Email:*** rcook@iowabar.org

WILLIAM D. COOK, born Cherokee, Iowa, June 6, 1960; admitted to bar, 1987, Iowa; 1999, Minnesota. *Education:* Iowa State University (B.S., 1982); Washburn University (J.D., 1987). *Member:* Cherokee County, Iowa State and American Bar Associations; Association of Trial Lawyers of Iowa. ***Email:*** wcook@iowabar.org

ATTORNEYS FOR: Cherokee State Bank; Cherokee Community School District; Lundell Construction Co., Inc.; Tiel Sanford Memorial Fund; Simonsen Mill Inc.; Obeco Inc.; Christensen Brothers Concrete; First Trust and Savings Bank of Aurelia; Farm Bureau Mutual Insurance Company; Cherokee County Rural Water; North Star Community Credit Union.

SAYRE, WITTGRAF & MELOY

Established in 1912

223 PINE STREET
P.O. BOX 535
CHEROKEE, IOWA 51012
Telephone: 712-225-6481
Fax: 712-225-5300
Email: swmlaw@mchsi.com

General, Trial and Appellate Practice, Probate, Estate Planning, Corporation, Personal Injury, Taxation and Real Estate Law.

LEW McDONALD (1884-1963)

DAVID L. SAYRE (Retired)

MEMBERS OF FIRM

GEORGE W. WITTGRAF, born Washington, D.C., September 25, 1945; admitted to bar, 1975, Iowa; 1977, U.S. District Court, Northern District of Iowa. *Education:* Grinnell College (B.A., 1967); Rutgers University (M.A., 1968); Drake University (J.D., 1974). Administrative Assistant, Lt. Governor, Iowa, 1973-1976. Assistant Cherokee County Attorney, 1976-1983. Chairman, Board of Directors, Legal Services Corporation, 1990-1993. *Member:* Cherokee County, Iowa State (Director, Iowa Law PAC, 1987-1994) and American Bar Associations. [Capt., Iowa Army National Guard, 1968-1974]. ***PRACTICE AREAS:*** Probate; Estate Planning; Corporate Law; Personal Injury; Taxation; Real Estate. ***Email:*** swmlaw@mchsi.com

DANIEL A. MELOY, born Cherokee, Iowa, July 27, 1958; admitted to bar, 1995, Iowa. *Education:* Iowa State University (B.S., 1980); Creighton University (J.D., 1995). Member: Cherokee Community School Board, 1995-2001; Sioux Valley Memorial Hospital Board, 1997—. *Member:* Cherokee County, Iowa State and American Bar Associations. ***PRACTICE AREAS:*** Probate; Estate Planning; Corporate Law; Personal Injury; Taxation; Real Estate. ***Email:*** swmlaw@netins.net

REPRESENTATIVE CLIENTS: Central Bank, Cherokee, Iowa; C-M-L Telephone Cooperative Association of Meriden, Iowa; Beck Ranch, Inc.; Valley Pharmacy Corp.; Schoon Construction Inc.; Sioux Valley Memorial Hospital; Cherokee Area Economic Development Corp.

TURNER, JONES & BITTING

301 EAST MAIN STREET
P.O. BOX 231
CLARINDA, IOWA 51632
Telephone: 712-542-2151
Fax: 712-542-2031
Email: tjblaw@clarinda.heartland.net

General Practice. Probate, Real Estate and Banking Law. Trials.

MEMBERS OF FIRM

CLINTON H. TURNER (1909-1969)

SANFORD A. TURNER, born Bedford, Iowa, March 1, 1935; admitted to bar, 1963, Iowa. *Education:* Iowa State University; Northwest Missouri State College (B.S., 1959); State University of Iowa (J.D., 1963). With Federal Bureau of Investigation, 1963-1966. City Attorney, 1968—. Member, Client Security and Attorney Disciplinary Commission, 1973-1984; Grievance Commission, 1985-1988. *Member:* Page County, Southwest Iowa (President, 1975) and Iowa State (Member, Board of Governors, 1988-1995) Bar Associations. [U.S. Armed Forces, active duty, 1955-1958]

PAUL W. JONES, born Bedford, Iowa, February 20, 1937; admitted to bar, 1962, Iowa; 1963, Oregon. *Education:* Grinnell College (B.A., 1959); University of Michigan (J.D., 1962). *Member:* Page County and Iowa State Bar Associations; Oregon State Bar.

RONNY M. BITTING, born Hanford, Washington, January 29, 1945; admitted to bar, 1973, Iowa. *Education:* University of Northern Iowa (B.A., 1967); Drake University (J.D., 1973). *Member:* Page County and Iowa State Bar Associations.

REPRESENTATIVE CLIENTS: Citizens State Bank, Clarinda, Iowa; Cities of Clarinda, Coin, Braddyville, Shambaugh, Blanchard and Northboro, Iowa; Lisle Corp., Clarinda, Iowa; City of Clarinda; NSK Bearing Co.; Clarinda Printing Graphics; Welhausen Farms, Inc.; Oxley Farms, Inc.; Page County Federal Savings.
REFERENCES: Citizens State Bank; Page County State Bank of Clarinda, Iowa; State Savings Bank of Bedford, Iowa.

MALLOY LAW FIRM

CLARION, IOWA

(See Goldfield)

General Trial and Appellate Practice Before State and Federal Courts and Administrative Agencies, Agricultural, Corporate, Insurance, Personal Injury, Real Estate, Probate, Estate Planning Law.

FREY, HAUFE & CURRENT, P.L.C.

408 SOUTH 2ND STREET
P.O. BOX 668
CLINTON, IOWA 52733-0668
Telephone: 563-242-1832
Fax: 563-242-1845
Email: jhc@cis.net

General Practice. Corporation, Business, Real Estate, Probate, Domestic, Criminal, Administrative Law, Trials and Appeals, Insurance Defense Law, Estate Planning, Personal Injury.

L. L. JURGEMEYER (1918-1980)

A. JOHN FREY, JR., born Little Falls, Minnesota, December 2, 1944; admitted to bar, 1969, Iowa; 1973, U.S. District Court, Northern and Southern Districts of Iowa; U.S Supreme Court. *Education:* Loras College; University of Iowa (B.A., 1967; J.D., with distinction, 1969). Phi Alpha Delta. Special Agent, Federal Bureau of Investigation, 1969-1973. Member, Clinton City Council, 1984-1987. *Member:* Clinton County (President, 1976) and Iowa State Bar Associations; Iowa Trial Lawyers Association. ***PRACTICE AREAS:*** Litigation; Personal Injury; Insurance Defense; Probate; Real Estate.

STEPHEN D. HAUFE, born St. Louis, Missouri, October 19, 1948; admitted to bar, 1974, Iowa and U.S. District Court, Northern and Southern Districts of Iowa. *Education:* Carleton College (B.A., 1971); Duke University (J.D., with distinction, 1974). *Member:* Clinton County and Iowa State Bar Associations. ***PRACTICE AREAS:*** Real Estate; Commercial Law; Corporate Law; Banking; Probate; Estate Planning.

T. RANDY CURRENT, born Maquoketa, Iowa, November 28, 1956; admitted to bar, 1982, Iowa and U.S. District Court, Northern and Southern Districts of Iowa. *Education:* University of Iowa (B.A., 1979; J.D., with honors, 1982). Phi Delta Phi. *Member:* Clinton County (President, 1988), Iowa State and American Bar Associations. ***PRACTICE AREAS:*** Adoption; Insurance Defense; Personal Injury; Real Estate.

COUNSEL FOR: Clinton Printing Co.; Bull Livestock, Inc.; PFC Center; Metal Tech Mfg., Inc.; Custom-Pak; Clinton Area Dev. Corp.
LOCAL COUNSEL FOR: Equistar Chemicals, L.P; Chevron Texaco Corporation.; Alliance Pipeline Company.
OTHER REPRESENTATIVE CLIENTS: Ohio Casualty Co.; The Western Insurance Co.; City of Clinton; The Hartford Insurance Co.; American Inter Insurance Exchange; Gateway State Bank; Chicago Title Insurance Co.; Super 8 Motel; Northwestern National Insurance Co.; GRE Insurance Group; Clinton National Bank; CNA Health Pro; Clinton Area Chamber of Commerce; Quality Concrete Co.; Lutheran Services in Iowa.
REFERENCES: Chicago Title Insurance Company; Clinton National Bank; U.S. Bank; Gateway State Bank; Sterling Federal Bank.

McCARTHY, LAMMERS & HINES

CLINTON, IOWA

(See Davenport)

General Civil Practice. Trials, Personal Injury, Workers Compensation, Wills, Trusts, Probate, Criminal Law, Real Estate, Family Law, Divorce, Child Custody, Estate Planning, Bankruptcy, Juvenile.

VAN SCOY & KROSS, P.C.

Established in 1950
410 SOUTH SECOND STREET
CLINTON, IOWA 52732
Telephone: 563-242-2827
Fax: 563-242-0540

General Practice. Probate, Wills, Corporate Law, Real Estate, Personal Injury, Bankruptcy, Trials and Appeals, Family Law, Estate Planning, School Law, Business Law.

JERRY D. VAN SCOY, born Ames, Iowa, February 3, 1947; admitted to bar, 1972, Iowa; 1974, U.S. District Court, Northern and Southern Districts of Iowa; 1990, U.S. Tax Court. *Education:* Iowa State University (B.S., 1969); University of Iowa (J.D., with distinction, 1972). Phi Alpha Delta. Student Editor for Mason Ladd, Dean Emeritus, Iowa Law School, 1971-1972. Member, Board of Directors and President, Iowa Council of School Board Attorneys, 1990—. *Member:* Clinton County, Iowa State (Member: Title Standards Committee, 1979-1985; Board of Governors, 1998—) and American Bar Associations.

EDWARD J. KROSS, born Clinton, Iowa, January 7, 1949; admitted to bar, 1974, Iowa and U.S. District Court, Northern and Southern Districts of Iowa. *Education:* St. Ambrose College (B.A., 1971); University of Iowa (J.D., with distinction, 1974). *Member:* Clinton County, Iowa State and American Bar Associations.

REPRESENTATIVE CLIENTS: Firststar Bank; Clinton Community School District; Camanche Community School District; Mercy Health Center; Iowa American Water Co.
REFERENCES: Clinton Community School District; Camananche Community School District; Samaritan Health System; Clinton National Bank.

PETOSA, PETOSA & BOECKER, L.L.P.

1350 NORTHWEST 138TH STREET, SUITE 100
CLIVE, IOWA 50325-8308
Telephone: 515-222-9400
Fax: 515-222-9121
Email: spetosa@petosalaw.com

General Civil and Trial Practice. Corporation, Real Estate, Foreclosure, Zoning, Municipal, Taxation, Probate, Estate Planning and Bankruptcy Law.

MEMBERS OF FIRM

STEPHEN J. PETOSA, born April 24, 1943; admitted to bar, 1968, Iowa and U.S. District Court, Southern and Northern Districts of Iowa; 1972, U.S. Supreme Court and U.S. Court of Appeals, Eighth Circuit. *Education:* University of Iowa (J.D., 1968). Assistant Attorney General, Iowa, 1968-1970. *Member:* Iowa State (Member: Special Committee on Iowa Property Law, 1979—; Probate, Property and Trust Law Committee, 1989—; Council, Real Estate and Title Law Section, 1990-1992 and Chair, 1991-1992; Contributing Author, Iowa Real Estate Practice Manual) Bar Association. ***PRACTICE AREAS:*** Real Estate; Probate and Trusts.

THEODORE R. BOECKER, born Des Moines, Iowa, November 20, 1947; admitted to bar, 1973, Iowa and U.S. District Courts, Southern and Northern Districts of Iowa and U.S. Court of Appeals, Eighth Circuit; 1977, U.S. Supreme Court. *Education:* Drake University (J.D., 1973). Assistant Attorney General, Iowa, 1973-1979. ***PRACTICE AREAS:*** Real Estate.

BENJAMIN W. HOPKINS, born Des Moines, Iowa, June 7, 1964; admitted to bar, 1997, Iowa and U.S. District Court, Southern and Northern Districts of Iowa. *Education:* University of Iowa (B.S., 1987); Drake Law School (J.D., with high honors, 1996). Order of the Coif. ***PRACTICE AREAS:*** Real Estate.

REPRESENTATIVE CLIENTS: Aames Home Loan; Bank of America; Charter Bank; Chase Manhattan Mortgage Corp.; CitiFinancial Mortgage; Countrywide Funding Corp.; Earlham Savings Bank; Fairbanks Capital Corp.; InterBay Funding; Midland Mortgage Co.; Neighborhood Finance Corp.; Washington Mutual Bank; West Bank.

EELLS & TRONVOLD LAW OFFICES, P.L.C.

CORALVILLE, IOWA

(See Cedar Rapids)

General Practice with emphasis on Personal Injury, Litigation, Probate and Estate Planning, Trusts and Wills, Business Law and Mediation.

PAUL McANDREW LAW FIRM

Established in 1999
2590 HOLIDAY ROAD, SUITE 100
CORALVILLE, IOWA 52241
Telephone: 319-887-1690
Fax: 319-887-1693
Email: paulm@paulmcandrew.com
URL: http://www.mcandrewlaw.com

Workers' Compensation, Social Security.

FIRM PROFILE: A firm practicing primarily in Iowa workers' compensation law.

PAUL J. McANDREW, JR., born Kalona, Iowa, March 8, 1957; admitted to bar, 1983, Iowa and U.S. District Court, Southern and Northern Districts of Iowa; 1987, U.S. Claims Court; 1999, U.S. Court of Appeals, Eighth Circuit; 2000, U.S. Supreme Court. *Education:* University of Iowa (B.A., 1979; J.D., with high distinction, 1983). Omicron Delta Kappa; Phi Alpha Delta; Phi Beta Kappa. Editor, Contemporary Studies Project, Iowa Law Review, 1982-1983. Law Clerk to Honorable William C. Stuart, U.S. District Court, Southern District of Iowa, 1983-1985. Author: "Harmless Error in Criminal Appeals," 67 Iowa Law Review 607, 1982. Iowa Representative, National Board of Governors, Work-

(This Listing Continued)

place Injury Litigation Group, 1997—. *Member:* Johnson County, Iowa State (Chair, Workers' Compensation Section, 1993-1995) and American Bar Associations; Iowa Trial Lawyers Association (Representative, Board of Governors, 1993—; Secretary, Workers' Compensation Section, 1997-1999); The Association of Trial Lawyers of America (Chair, Workers' Compensation Section, 2002-2003); Iowa Workers' Compensation Advisory Committee (Claimant's Counsel Representative, 2000—); Iowa Association of Workers' Compensation Attorneys (Representative, Board of Governors, 1993—). ***REPORTED CASES:*** University of Iowa Hospitals v. Waters, 674 N.W.2d 92 (Iowa 2004); Wal-Mart Stores v. Caselman, 657 N.W.2d 493 (Iowa 2003); Sioson v. Manpower Temporary Services, 529 N.W. 259 (Iowa 1995); Mortimer v. Fruefauf Corp., 502 N.W.2d 12 (Iowa 1993); Heartland Express, Inc. v. Terry, 631 N.W.2d 260 (Iowa 2001). ***PRACTICE AREAS:*** Workers Compensation. ***Email:*** paulm@paulmcandrew.com

Language: Spanish.

MEARDON, SUEPPEL & DOWNER P.L.C.

CORALVILLE, IOWA

(See Iowa City)

General Practice.

DELL A. RICHARD

Established in 1981

1150 5TH STREET, SUITE 280
CORALVILLE, IOWA 52241
Telephone: 319-354-9592
Facsimile: 319-354-7957
Email: dell@darichardlaw.com
URL: http://www.dellarichard.com

Business Law, Commercial Real Estate, Corporate Law, Guardianships and Conservatorships, Leases and Leasing, Partnership Law, Probate, Real Estate Law, Trusts and Estates, Wills.

FIRM PROFILE: The firm has been providing legal services to the Iowa City area since the 1970's. The areas of concentration in the firm have historically included all areas of corporation and business law, real estate and probate and estate planning.

DELL A. RICHARD, born Leon, Iowa, December 30, 1949; admitted to bar, 1975, Iowa; U.S. Court of Appeals, Eighth Circuit; U.S. District Court, Northern and Southern Districts of Iowa. *Education:* Central College (B.A., with honors, 1972); University of Iowa (J.D., with distinction, 1975). Phi Alpha Delta. Law Clerk to Chief Justice Moore, Iowa Supreme Court, 1975-1976. Member, 1977-1984, and Chairman, 1978-1984, Johnson County Board of Social Welfare. Member, Board of Temporary Bar Examiners, 1985—. *Member:* Johnson County (Member, Title Standards Committee, 1999—), Iowa State (Member: ISBA Tax School Committee, 1996-1999; Spring Tax Institute Committee, 1999—; Chairman, 2000-2001, 2003-2004) and American (Member, Sections on: Corporation, Banking and Business Law; Economics of Law Practice; Real Estate, Estate Planning, Real Property, Probate, Trust Law and Taxation) Bar Associations. ***PRACTICE AREAS:*** Real Estate; Corporate; Probate; Estate Planning; Trusts and Wills.

ASSOCIATE

COREY W. SCHATZ, born Monticello, Iowa; admitted to bar, 2005, Iowa. *Education:* University of Iowa (B.B.A., with honors, 1999); University of Iowa (J.D., 2004).

REFERENCES: Hills Bank & Trust, Hills, Iowa; Iowa State Bank & Trust Company, Iowa City, Iowa.
REPRESENTATIVE CLIENTS: Furnished upon request.

STANLEY, LANDE & HUNTER

A PROFESSIONAL CORPORATION

2201 EAST GRANTVIEW DRIVE, SUITE 200
CORALVILLE, IOWA 52241
Telephone: 319-248-9000
Facsimile: 319-248-9001
Email: Contact.us@slhlaw.com
URL: http://www.slhlaw.com

Davenport, Iowa Office: 900 U.S. Bank Center, 201 West Second Street. Telephone: 563-324-1000. Facsimile: 563-326-6266.
Wilton, Iowa Office: 115 West Fourth, P.O. Box 481. Telephone: 563-732-4000. Facsimile: 563-732-2318.

General Civil and Trial Practice. Corporation, Business, Banking, Taxation, Securities, Tax-Exempt Financing, Labor, Employment Discrimination, Administrative, Creditor Bankruptcy and Agricultural Law, Insurance Defense, Personal Injury and Property Damage Law, Pension and Profit-Sharing, Real Estate, Probate, Estate Planning and Charitable Trusts and Foundations Law.

REPRESENTATIVE CLIENTS: Bandag Incorporated; Carver Enterprise Group; Central Can Company; Central State Bank; Connoisseur Communications; Dovetail Development Group; Farm Bureau Mutual Insurance Co.; Farmers and Merchants Savings Bank (Lone Tree); First National Bank of Muscatine; General Motors Acceptance Corp.; Great American Insurance Co.; H.J. Heinz Company; HON INDUSTRIES, Inc. and its subsidiaries; IPSCO Steel Inc.; Liberty Trust & Savings Bank (Durant); Milwaukee Mutual Insurance Company; Monsanto Company; Tech Systems, Inc.; The Family Credit Union; The Stanley Foundation; The Travelers Group, Inc.; Stanley Consultants, Inc. and subsidiaries; Texaco, Inc.; Union Federal Savings and Loan Association of Kewanee, Illinois; Varied Investments, Inc. (Grain Processing Corporation, Kent Feeds, Inc.); West Liberty State Bank.
GENERAL COUNSEL FOR: HWH Corporation; John Keady's General Motors Superstore; Lujack's Northpark Auto Plaza; M.A. Ford Mfg. Co.; Royale International Beverage Co.; The State Bank of Annawan; BT Prime-Mover, Inc.; Tri State Companies, Inc.; Unity Health System; Wilton Industrial Development Corp.; Wilton Precision Steel; WTC Communications, Inc.

(For Complete Biographical Data on all Personnel, see Professional Biographies at Davenport, Iowa)

VERLE W. NORRIS

300 WEST MARION
P.O. BOX 256
CORYDON, IOWA 50060
Telephone: 641-872-1363
Facsimile: 641-872-2468
URL: http://www.vnorris.com

Humeston, Iowa Office: 125 Broad Street, P.O. Box 117, 50123. Telephone: 641-877-9700. Fax: 641-877-2204.

VERLE W. NORRIS, born Cedar Rapids, Iowa, March 1, 1963; admitted to bar, 1990, Iowa and U.S. District Court, Southern District of Iowa. *Education:* Calvin College (B.A., 1985); Drake University (J.D., 1990). Magistrate, Wayne County, 1997—. *Member:* Wayne County and Iowa State Bar Associations. ***SPECIAL AGENCIES:*** Iowa Utilities Board. ***PRACTICE AREAS:*** Administrative Law; Real Estate Law; Bankruptcy.

ASSOCIATE

JAMES G. ROWE, born Des Moines, Iowa, August 28, 1975; admitted to bar, 2005, Iowa. *Education:* Grand View College (B.A., 1998); Regent University School of Law (J.D., with distinction, 2005). Senior Editor, Regent University Journal of International Law, 2004. Chair, Regent University Alternative Dispute Resolution and Client Counseling Board, 2005. ***PRACTICE AREAS:*** Litigation; Bankruptcy; Employment Law; Debtor and Creditor; Estate Planning; Wills; Trusts; Probate. ***Email:*** jgr@norrislw.com

BRUMBAUGH & QUANDAHL, P.C., L.L.O.

COUNCIL BLUFFS, IOWA

(See Omaha)

Commercial Law and Creditor Bankruptcy, Consumer Collections, Corporate Reorganization and General Business Litigation, Consumer and Retail Collections.

ENGLES, KETCHAM, OLSON & KEITH, P.C.

COUNCIL BLUFFS, IOWA

(See Omaha, Nebraska)

General Civil Practice, Insurance Defense, Litigation, Trials. Insurance, Negligence, Workers Compensation, Personal Injury, Admiralty and Marine Law. Banking, Insurance and Commercial Fraud Law. Labor and Employment, Corporate, Business and Corporation, Product Liability, Automobile Accidents and Injuries, Discrimination, Legal Malpractice, Personal Injury, Real Estate, Appeals, Construction Law, Contracts, Guardianship & Conservatorship, Highways, Premises Liability, Professional Liability, Torts, Agricultural Law, Alternative Dispute Resolution, Animal Law, Civil Litigation, Civil Rights, Commercial and Environmental Litigation.

DONALD G. FURLOW

COUNCIL BLUFFS, IOWA

(See Omaha, Nebraska)

Real Estate, Commercial, Bankruptcy, Creditors' Rights, Employment, Banking, Foreclosures and Collections, Estate Planning, Acquisitions and Liquidations, Business Formation.

LAMSON, DUGAN AND MURRAY, LLP

COUNCIL BLUFFS, IOWA

(See Omaha, Nebraska)

General Practice. Litigation, Business Law, Insurance, Government Relations, Banking, Reinsurance, Railroad Law, Bankruptcy, Insolvency Law, Trial Practice Litigation, Trusts and Estates, Commercial Law, Insurance Regulation, Commercial Litigation, Complex Litigation, Torts, Product Liability Defense, Professional Liability Defense, Labor Relations, Insurance Insolvency, Corporate Law, Taxation, Labor Employment, Mergers and Acquisitions, Public Utility.

LOCHER, CELLILLI, PAVELKA & DOSTAL, L.L.C.

500 WEST BROADWAY, SUITE 307
COUNCIL BLUFFS, IOWA 51503
Telephone: 402-898-7000
Fax: 402-898-7130
URL: http://www.lcpdlaw.com

Omaha, Nebraska Office: 200 The Omaha Club, 2002 Douglas Street, 68102. Telephone: 402-898-7000. Fax: 402-898-7130.

General Civil Practice, Trials, General Negligence, Personal Injury, Admiralty and Maritime Law, Banking and Creditor Bankruptcy, Insurance and Commercial Fraud.

(For Complete Biographical Data on all Personnel, see Professional Biographies at Omaha, Nebraska)

SUELLEN OVERTON

Established in 1994

404 PARK BUILDING
500 WILLOW AVENUE
COUNCIL BLUFFS, IOWA 51503
Telephone: 712-322-6585
Fax: 712-325-6112
Email: soverton@cblaw.omhcoxmail.com
URL: http://www.lawyers.com/suellenoverton

General Practice, Family Law, Personal Injury, Child Custody, Child Support, Divorce, Collections, Bankruptcy, Social Security, Wills and Probate Law.

FIRM PROFILE: Suellen Overton has served and continues to serve in various local and state leadership positions. She serves on the judicial nominating commission, served 12 years on the State Board of Corrections and more than 22 years with the Iowa Air National Guard.

SUELLEN OVERTON, born Des Moines, Iowa, February 12, 1962; admitted to bar, 1990, Iowa; 1992, Nebraska. *Education:* Drake University (B.A., magna cum laude, 1987; J.D., 1990). Phi Alpha Delta. Named, ABWA Woman of the Year, 1999. Member, State Board of Corrections, Representing Fourth Congressional District, Appointed by Governor Vilsack. *Member:* Omaha, Pottawattamie County, Iowa State, Nebraska State and Southwest Iowa Bar Associations. [Lt. Col., Iowa Air National Guard JAG, 1982—]

PETERS LAW FIRM, P.C.

Established in 1895

233 PEARL STREET
P.O. BOX 1078
COUNCIL BLUFFS, IOWA 51502-1078
Telephone: 712-328-3157
FAX: 712-328-9092
Email: peterslawfirm@hotmail.com
URL: http://www.peterslawfirm.com

Glenwood, Iowa Office: 10 North Walnut. Telephone: 712-527-4877. FAX: 712-527-3418.
Neola, Iowa Office: 401 Front Street, P.O. Box 282. Telephone: 712-485-2265.
South Omaha, Nebraska Office: 4828 South 24th Street, Suite 200, 68107. Telephone: 402-731-1711. Fax: 402-731-3363.

Personal Injury Litigation and Commercial Litigation. Insurance, Tax, Real Estate, Corporation, Probate and Bankruptcy Law.

JAMES A. CAMPBELL, born Carroll, Iowa, October 4, 1940; admitted to bar, 1965, Iowa; 1975, U.S. Supreme Court; 2003, Nebraska. *Education:* University of Iowa (B.A., 1962; LL.B., 1965; J.D., 1993). Phi Delta Phi. Iowa Supreme Court Board of Professional Ethics and Conduct, 1996-2004. *Member:* Pottawattamie County (President, 1992-1993), Iowa State (Chair, Committee on Lawyer Advertising, 1992-1994) and American (Member, Sections on: Business Law; Real Property) Bar Associations. ***PRACTICE AREAS:*** Business; Estate Planning; Probate; Real Estate. ***Email:*** jimc@peterslawfirm.com

DENNIS M. GRAY, born Sioux City, Iowa, July 15, 1943; admitted to bar, 1968, Iowa. *Education:* University of Iowa (B.A., 1965; J.D., 1968). *Member:* Iowa State Bar Association; American College of Trial Lawyers; Iowa Academy of Trial Lawyers (Past President and Member, Board of Governors); The Association of Trial Lawyers of America; Iowa Trial Lawyers Association; Iowa Defense Counsel Association; Iowa Association of Workers' Compensation Lawyers (Past President and Member, Board of Governors, 1982—). [Major General, USAFR, Ret.]

JAMES A. THOMAS, born Council Bluffs, Iowa, April 14, 1942; admitted to bar, 1967, Iowa. *Education:* Morningside College (B.S., 1964); University of Iowa (J.D., 1967). Phi Delta Phi. Mills County Attorney, 1968-1972. *Member:* Mills County, Iowa State, Southwest Iowa (President, 1987-1988) and American Bar Associations.

LYLE W. DITMARS, born Council Bluffs, Iowa, January 15, 1951; admitted to bar, 1977, Iowa. *Education:* University of Nebraska at Omaha (B.S., magna cum laude, 1973); Creighton University (J.D., 1977). Adjunct Professor, Creighton University Law School, 1991-2002. *Member:* Iowa State and American Bar Associations; Iowa Defense Counsel Association (Member, Board of Directors, 2000—); Defense Research Institute; Iowa Academy of Trial Lawyers.

SCOTT H. PETERS, born Council Bluffs, Iowa, April 1, 1950; admitted to bar, 1975, Iowa; 1976, U.S. Court of Military Appeals; 1998, U.S. Court of Federal Claims; 1999, Nebraska. *Education:* Drake University (B.A., 1972; J.D., 1975). *Member:* Iowa State Bar Association; Iowa Trial Lawyers Association (President, 1991-1992; Member, Board of Governors, 1986-1993); The Association of Trial Lawyers of America (Member, Board of Governors, 1989-1993); American Board of Trial Advocates (President, 2002); Iowa Academy of Trial Lawyers; Trial Lawyers for Public Justice; The Civil Justice Foundation. Certified as a Civil Trial Specialist by the National Board of Trial Advocacy (Diplomate). ***PRACTICE AREAS:*** Trials and Appeals.

JOHN M. McHALE, born Minneapolis, Minnesota, July 16, 1957; admitted to bar, 1982, Iowa and Nebraska. *Education:* St. John's University (B.A., 1979); University of Nebraska at Lincoln (J.D., 1982). *Member:* Iowa State, Nebraska State and American Bar Associations. Fellow, Iowa Academy of Trial Lawyers; Iowa Trial Lawyers Association; The Association of Trial Lawyers of America; Legal Services Corporation of Iowa (Member, Board of Directors, 1987-2003; President, 1994-1998). ***PRACTICE AREAS:*** Civil Trial. ***Email:*** JMMPLF@hotmail.com

JACOB J. PETERS, born Council Bluffs, Iowa, March 14, 1960; admitted to bar, 1985, Iowa. *Education:* Iowa State University (B.S., 1982); Creighton University (J.D., 1985). *Member:* Iowa State Bar Association (Member, Workers' Compensation Advisory Committee); Iowa Academy of Trial Lawyers; Iowa Trial Lawyers Association (Member, Workers' Compensation Committee). ***PRACTICE AREAS:*** Civil Trial; Workers' Compensation. ***Email:*** jakep@peterslawfirm.com

(This Listing Continued)

LEO P. MARTIN, born Red Oak, Iowa, May 30, 1953; admitted to bar, 1982, Minnesota; 1985, Iowa; 1989, Nebraska. *Education:* Iowa State University (B.S., 1975; M.S., 1979); University of Minnesota (J.D., 1982). Author: "Estate Planning: Playing the Odds," Rural Practice Journal, Mason Publishing, St. Paul, Minnesota, November, December, 1984. *Member:* Iowa State (Chair, Agricultural Law Section, 1994-1996), Nebraska State and American Bar Associations; American Agricultural Law Association.

SCOTT J. ROGERS, born Council Bluffs, Iowa, September 7, 1961; admitted to bar, 1987, Iowa and U.S. District Court, District of Iowa. *Education:* Dana College (B.S., magna cum laude, 1984); Creighton University (J.D., 1987). Board Member, American Red Cross. Board of Directors, Western Iowa Grape Growers Association. *Member:* Pottawattamie County, Southwest Iowa, Iowa State (Member, Real Estate, Probate, Property and Trust Law Sections) and Nebraska State Bar Associations; Iowa Trial Lawyers Association; Iowa Municipal Attorneys Association; Council Bluffs Estate Planning Council (Board Member and Vice President). ***PRACTICE AREAS:*** Estate Planning; Probate; Real Estate; Family Law.

JON E. HEISTERKAMP, born Lake City, Iowa, September 14, 1964; admitted to bar, 1990, Iowa and U.S. District Court, Northern and Southern Districts of Iowa; 1995, Nebraska; 2001, Texas. *Education:* Drake University (B.S.B.A., 1987; J.D., 1990). Board Member, Co Bluffs Chamber of Commerce Commission. Member, (IOLTA) Supreme Court Commission. Board Member, Iowa Trial Lawyers Association. *Member:* Iowa State (Member, Young Lawyers Division, 1992-1999), Pottawattamie County, Southwest Iowa and Nebraska State Bar Associations; State Bar of Texas. ***PRACTICE AREAS:*** Personal Injury; Family Law; Criminal Law. ***Email:*** jeheisterkamp@yahoo.com

JOHN M. FRENCH, born Harlan, Iowa, July 6, 1948; admitted to bar, 1974, Iowa; 1976, U.S. District Court, Northern and Southern Districts of Iowa; 1978, U.S. Court of Appeals, Eighth Circuit; 1980, Washington; 1989, Nebraska; 1991, U.S. District Court, District of Nebraska; 1996, U.S. Supreme Court. *Education:* Drake University; University of Northern Iowa (B.S., 1971); Drake University (J.D., 1974). Staff Attorney, Iowa Supreme Court, 1976-1978. *Member:* Pottawattamie County, Southwest Iowa, Iowa State, Washington State, Nebraska State and American Bar Associations; American College of Trial Lawyers; Iowa Academy of Trial Lawyers; Iowa Trial Lawyers Association; Association of Trial Lawyers of America. ***PRACTICE AREAS:*** Litigation. ***Email:*** john.french@peterslawfirm.com

MATTHEW G. WOODS, born Cedar Rapids, Iowa, November 11, 1966; admitted to bar, 1993, Iowa. *Education:* University of Iowa (B.B.A., 1989); Creighton University (J.D., 1993). *Member:* Mills County Bar Association (President, 1999—); Iowa State and Southwest Iowa Bar Associations; Iowa Municipal Attorneys Association. ***Email:*** matthew.woods@peterslawfirm.com

---

JOHN C. RASMUSSEN, born December 1, 1960; admitted to bar, 1985, Nebraska; 1991, Iowa; 1994, U.S. Tax Court; 1995, U.S. Supreme Court. *Education:* Creighton University (B.S.B.A., 1983; J.D., 1985). Board Member and Past Trustee, SID Zole, Douglas County, Nebraska. Past Director, Montessori Parents Co-op for Children, Omaha, Nebraska. Past President and Director, Council Bluffs Estate Council. Director and Past President, Bluffs Arts Council. ***PRACTICE AREAS:*** Taxation Law.

JOHN D. KWAPNIOSKI, born Omaha, Nebraska, December 8, 1972; admitted to bar, 1998, Nebraska and U.S. District Court, District of Nebraska; 2001, Iowa and U.S. District Court, Southern District of Iowa. *Education:* University of Nebraska at Omaha (B.S., magna cum laude, 1995); University of Nebraska at Lincoln (J.D., 1998). Authorized to electronically file in U.S. District Courts, including Bankruptcy Courts, Nebraska and Southern District of Iowa. Board Member, Metropolitan Community College Legal Assistant Advisory Board. *Member:* Pottawattamie County, Nebraska State (Member, Real Estate, Probate, and Trust Law Section) and Iowa State (Member, Sections on: Commercial and Bankruptcy Law; Probate, Property and Trust Law) Bar Associations; Council Bluffs Estate Planning Council.

JENNIFER K. SEWELL, born Watertown, South Dakota, February 22, 1975; admitted to bar, 2001, Iowa and U.S. District Court, Southern District of Iowa; 2002, Nebraska. *Education:* South Dakota State University (B.A., with honors, 1997); Creighton University (J.D., cum laude, 2001). *Member:* Pottawattamie County, Iowa State and Nebraska State Bar Associations; Iowa Trial Lawyers Association.

JUSTIN R. WYATT, born Loma Linda, California, July 5, 1975; admitted to bar, 2003, Iowa; 2004, Nebraska. *Education:* Creighton University (B.S., 1998; J.D., 2003). *Member:* Iowa State and Nebraska State Bar Associations. ***Email:*** justin@peterslawfirm.com

REPRESENTATIVE CLIENTS: Grinnell Mutual Re-Insurance Co.; Horace Mann Ins. Cos.; Kemper Group: Shelter Ins. Co.; State Farm Mutual Auto Ins.; United Fire & Casualty; The Cities McClelland, Glenwood, Underwood, Neola and Minden, IA; Iowa West Racing Assn.; Mills County State Bank; Glenwood State Bank; 1st Community National Bank; Citizens Savings Bank; Peoples National Bank; Randolph State Bank; MidStates Bank; Ameristar Casino; North Pointe Insurance Co.; Edwards Archer Auto Plaza.
REFERENCE: Mid States Bank.

RASMUSSEN & MITCHELL

COUNCIL BLUFFS, IOWA

(See Omaha, Nebraska)

Corporate, Securities, Real Estate, Bankruptcy Reorganization, Trial Practice in all State and Federal Courts with Emphasis on Bankruptcy Litigation, Professional Liability Litigation, Personal Injury Litigation, Commercial Litigation, Estate Planning and Probate.

REILLY, HANNAN & DREISMEIER, P.L.C.

215 SOUTH MAIN STREET
P.O. BOX 1016
COUNCIL BLUFFS, IOWA 51502-1016
Telephone: 712-328-1575
Fax: 712-328-1562

Personal Injury Litigation. General Practice in all Courts. Probate, Real Estate, Corporation, Domestic Relations, Workers Compensation, Bankruptcy, Construction and Insurance Law. Discrimination and Civil Rights Law. Trials and Appeals. Criminal Law.

FIRM PROFILE: Reilly, Petersen & Hannan was originally founded in the 1920's by Proctor R. Perkins and the present lawyers have a combined experience of over 70 years. Serving clients throughout the state of Iowa with an emphasis in the southwestern area and the 4th Judicial District. The firm engages in a General Practice.

C. R. HANNAN, born Council Bluffs, Iowa, August 20, 1943; admitted to bar, 1968, Iowa and South Dakota; 1969, Nebraska and U.S. District Court, Northern and Southern Districts of Iowa. *Education:* University of Notre Dame; Creighton University (A.B., 1965; J.D., 1968). Phi Alpha Delta. Part Time Judicial Magistrate, 1973-1979. *Member:* Pottawattamie County (Secretary, 1976-1979), Southwest Iowa, Iowa State, Federal (Member, Iowa Chapter) and American Bar Associations; Iowa Trial Lawyers Association; American Bankruptcy Institute. [With U.S. Army, 1968-1970]. ***PRACTICE AREAS:*** Bankruptcy Law; Family Law; Probate; Workers Compensation. ***Email:*** crhannan@rphlaw.com

MICHAEL G. REILLY, born Fonda, Iowa, July 17, 1957; admitted to bar, 1981, Iowa, Nebraska and U.S. District Court, Northern and Southern Districts of Iowa and District of Nebraska. *Education:* Creighton University (B.S. in Bus. Adm., 1979; J.D., 1981). *Member:* Pottawattamie County, Southwest Iowa, Iowa State, Nebraska State and American Bar Associations; Iowa Trial Lawyers Association (President, 1998-1999); Iowa Academy of Trial Lawyers; Nebraska Association of Trial Attorneys; The Association of Trial Lawyers of America; American Board of Trial Advocates. Certified as a Civil Trial Advocate by the National Board of Trial Advocacy. ***PRACTICE AREAS:*** Personal Injury Litigation. ***Email:*** mreilly@rphlaw.com

CRAIG M. DREISMEIER, born Omaha, Nebraska, June 7, 1967; admitted to bar, 1992, Iowa; 1993, Nebraska and U.S. District Court, Northern and Southern Districts of Iowa and District of Nebraska. *Education:* University of Nebraska at Omaha (B.S., Criminal Justice, 1989); Creighton University (J.D., 1992). *Member:* Pottawattamie County, Iowa State, Nebraska State and Federal Bar Associations; Southwest Iowa; Iowa Trial Lawyers Association. ***PRACTICE AREAS:*** Criminal Law; Bankruptcy; Family Law. ***Email:*** dreismeier@rphlaw.com

REFERENCE: Peoples National Bank of Council Bluffs.

RYAN M. SEWELL

215 SOUTH MAIN STREET
COUNCIL BLUFFS, IOWA 51503
Telephone: 712-328-1575
Fax: 712-328-1562
Email: rsewell@cox.net
URL: http://www.lawyers.com/sewelllaw

General Practice including, but not limited to, Criminal Law, Personal Injury, Insurance Law, Litigation and Trials.

FIRM PROFILE: Sole Practitioner engaged in general practice including, but not limited to, Criminal Law, Personal Injury, Insurance Law, Litigation, and Trials.

RYAN M. SEWELL, born Omaha, Nebraska, April 14, 1975; admitted to bar, 2002, Nebraska and U.S. District Court, District of Nebraska; 2003, Iowa; 2004, U.S. District Court, Southern District of Iowa;. *Education:* University of Nebraska at Lincoln (B.A., 2004); Creighton University School of Law (J.D., cum laude, 2002). Assistant Editor, Creighton Law Review; Member, Moot Court Board. *Member:* Pottawattamie County Bar Association; Iowa State Bar Association; Nebraska State Bar Association; Association of Trial Lawyers of America; Iowa Trial Lawyers Association; Nebraska Association of Trial Attorneys.

SMITH PETERSON LAW FIRM, LLP

Established in 1908
35 MAIN PLACE, SUITE 300
P.O. BOX 249
COUNCIL BLUFFS, IOWA 51502
Telephone: 712-328-1833
Fax: 712-328-8320
URL: http://www.smithpeterson.com
Email: email@smithpeterson.com
URL: http://www.lawyers.com/smithpeterson

Litigation, Discrimination and Civil Rights, Workers Compensation, Appeals, Insurance Law, Administrative Law, Corporation and Business Law, Debt and Bankruptcy, Environmental, Municipal, Real Estate, Estates and Probate Law and Banking Law, Commercial Law, Collection, Labor and Employment Law, Mediation, Taxation and Insurance Defense.

MEMBERS OF FIRM

RAYMOND A. SMITH (1892-1977)
JOHN LeROY PETERSON (1895-1969)

OF COUNSEL

HAROLD T. BECKMAN

(This Listing Continued)

PARTNERS

ROBERT J. LAUBENTHAL, born April 14, 1939; admitted to bar, 1965, Iowa; 1989, Nebraska. *Education:* State College of Iowa (B.A., 1961); University of Iowa (J.D., 1965). Phi Alpha Delta. President, Pottawattamie County Bar Association, 1982-1983. *Member:* Nebraska State Bar Association; Iowa Academy of Trial Lawyers; Federation of Insurance Corporate Counsel; Iowa Defense Counsel Association; Iowa Association of Workers Compensation Lawyers. ***PRACTICE AREAS:*** Civil Litigation; Municipal Law; Construction Law; Mediation and Arbitration; Complex and Multi-District Litigation; Environmental Law; Government; Insurance; Products Liability; Professional Liability; Insurance Defense; Agricultural Law; Workers' Compensation; Wrongful Termination. ***Email:*** rjlaubenthal@smithpeterson.com

RICHARD A. HEININGER, born September 21, 1945; admitted to bar, 1970, Iowa and U.S. District Court, Northern and Southern Districts of Iowa; 1985, Nebraska. *Education:* Blackburn College (B.A., 1967); Drake University (J.D., 1970). Delta Theta Phi. Student Contributor, Drake Law Review, 1969-1970. Participant, Title Guaranty Division of the Iowa Finance Authority. ***PRACTICE AREAS:*** Real Estate; Probate; Estate Planning; Corporate Law; Municipal Law. ***Email:*** raheininger@smithpeterson.com

LAWRENCE J. BECKMAN, born September 13, 1948; admitted to bar, 1973, Iowa; 1988, Nebraska. *Education:* Knox College (B.A., 1970); University of Iowa (J.D., 1973). Phi Delta Phi. Member, Committee on Taxation, Iowa State Bar Association, 1977-1990. Member, 1992-1999 and Section Chair, 1997-1999, Tax Section Council, Iowa State Bar Association. ***PRACTICE AREAS:*** Taxation; Corporate Law; Contracts; Employment Law; Mergers and Acquisitions; Trusts and Estates; Real Estate; Probate. ***Email:*** ljbeckman@smithpeterson.com

GREGORY G. BARNTSEN, born February 2, 1946; admitted to bar, 1975, Iowa; 1983, Nebraska. *Education:* University of Iowa (B.B.A., 1968; J.D., with distinction, 1974). *Member:* Nebraska State Bar Association; Iowa Defense Counsel Association (Member, Board of Governors, 1989—); Iowa Association of Workers Compensation Lawyers; Defense Research Institute; Iowa Academy of Trial Lawyers. ***PRACTICE AREAS:*** Insurance Law; Insurance Defense; Products Liability; Workers' Compensation; Wrongful Termination; Civil Litigation; Agricultural Law; Crop Damage; Tort Claims; Personal Injury. ***Email:*** ggbarntsen@smithpeterson.com

STEVEN H. KROHN, born May 12, 1953; admitted to bar, 1978, Iowa; 1983, Nebraska. *Education:* University of Nebraska at Lincoln (B.S., 1975; J.D., with distinction, 1978). Member, Order of the Coif. *Member:* Nebraska State Bar Association; American Bankruptcy Institute; Commercial and Bankruptcy Law Section Council. ***PRACTICE AREAS:*** Agricultural Law; Banking; Bankruptcy; Business Law; Collections; Commercial Law; Contracts; Corporate Law; Debtor and Creditor Law; Real Estate; Trusts and Estates. ***Email:*** shkrohn@smithpeterson.com

JOSEPH D. THORNTON, born August 26, 1959; admitted to bar, 1984, Iowa; 1991, Nebraska. *Education:* University of Iowa (B.B.A., 1982; J.D., with distinction, 1984). Certified Public Accountant of Iowa, 1982. President, Young Lawyers Division, Iowa State Bar Association, 1992-1993. ***PRACTICE AREAS:*** Business Law; Workers Compensation; Insurance Defense; Labor and Employment; Personal Injury; Corporate Law; Taxation. ***Email:*** jdthornton@smithpeterson.com

T. J. PATTERMANN, born Winfield, Illinois, July 23, 1968; admitted to bar, 1994, Iowa; 1995, Nebraska. *Education:* Drake University (B.A., cum laude, 1990); University of Iowa (J.D., with distinction, 1994). Phi Delta Phi. International Council Member, 1997-2001. Member, Journal of Corporation Law. *Member:* Iowa State (Member, Young Lawyer Division Executive Council, 1998-2002) and Nebraska Bar Associations. ***PRACTICE AREAS:*** Insurance Defense; Personal Injury; Appellate Practice; Workers Compensation. ***Email:*** tjpattermann@smithpeterson.com

DANIEL L. FRETHEIM, born March 29, 1968; admitted to bar, 1995, Iowa. *Education:* University of Northern Iowa (B.A., 1990); Drake University (J.D., with honors, 1994). *Member:* Pottawattamie County, Southwest Iowa, Iowa State (Member, Young Lawyers' Division) and American Bar Associations. ***PRACTICE AREAS:*** Taxation; Corporate Law; Contracts. ***Email:*** dlfretheim@smithpeterson.com

ASSOCIATES

MARVIN O. KIECKHAFER, born Plainview, Nebraska, January 25, 1949; admitted to bar, 1981, Nebraska, U.S. District Court, District of Nebraska and U.S. Court of Appeals, Eighth Circuit; 2001, Iowa. *Education:* Hastings College (B.A., 1971); University of Nebraska (J.D., 1981). ***PRACTICE AREAS:*** Litigation; Insurance Defense; Workers Compensation. ***Email:*** mok@smithpeterson.com

NATHAN R. WATSON, born Council Bluffs, Iowa, June 7, 1978; admitted to bar, 2004, Iowa; 2005, Nebraska. *Education:* Boston University (B.A., magna cum laude, 2001); Drake University (J.D., with high honors, 2004). ***PRACTICE AREAS:*** Litigation; Transactional Law. ***Email:*** nrwatson@smithpeterson.com

Most Attorneys are Members of the Pottawattamie County, Southwest Iowa, Iowa State and Nebraska State Bar Associations.

REPRESENTATIVE CLIENTS: Allied Group Insurance; Allstate Insurance Co.; Amber Enterprises; American States Insurance Co.; Bituminous Insurance Co.; Bluffs Run Casino; Bunge Corporation; Catholic Mutual Group; Children's Square U.S.A.; Continental Western Insurance Co.; Council Bluffs Nonpareil Newspaper Group; Employers Mutual Insurance Co.; Farm Bureau Mutual Insurance; Bank Iowa; Fresco Systems, USA; General Casualty Insurance Co.; Great American Insurance Co.; GAB Robinson Co.; Grinnell Mutual Insurance Co.; Hawkeye Security Insurance Co.; Iowa Pipeline Association, Inc.; Iowa West Foundation; Iowa Western Community College; John Deere Co.; Metropolitan Life Insurance; Midwest Resources; Mutual Fire and Auto Insurance; Nonthe Pointe; Paxton Vierling Steel Co.; Peoples National Bank; Redland Insurance Co.; Silverstone Group, Incorporated; Travelers Co.; United Group; Wausau Insurance Co.; St. Paul Fire and Marine Insurance Co.; Council Bluffs Water Works.

SODORO, DALY & SODORO, P.C.

COUNCIL BLUFFS, IOWA

(See Omaha, Nebraska)

Trial and Appellate Practice in Local State and Federal Courts and the U.S. Supreme Court. General Practice, Trials and Appeals, Insurance Defense, Medical Malpractice, Professional Malpractice, Professional Liability, Personal Injury, Workers' Compensation Law, General Negligence, Product Liability, Discrimination and Civil Rights, Insurance Coverage, Insurance Law, Environmental Law, Real Estate Law, Business Law, Commercial Law, Estate and Probate Law, Banking Law, Health Care Law, Business Law, Employment Law, Employee Benefits Law, Officers and Directors Liability, Fidelity and Surety Law, Legal Ethics, Professional Responsibility and Toxic Torts.

STUART, TINLEY, PETERS, THORN, HUGHES, FAUST & MADSEN

U.S. WEST BUILDING
310 WEST KANESVILLE BOULEVARD, SECOND FLOOR
P.O. BOX 398
COUNCIL BLUFFS, IOWA 51502-0398
Telephone: 712-322-4033
Fax: 712-322-6243
Email: lawoffice@stuarttinley.com
URL: http://www.stuarttinley.com

Litigation, Trial Law, Products Liability, Discrimination and Civil Rights, Workers' Compensation, Personal Injury, Malpractice, Professional Negligence, Insurance Law, Bankruptcy, Environmental, Real Estate, Wills, Estates and Probate Law, Insurance Defense Litigation, Commercial Litigation, Mediation, Business Law, Family Law, Municipalities, School Law, Divorce, Child Custody.

FIRM PROFILE: Our law firm has been practicing continuously for nearly a century. Our partners have served and continue to serve in various leadership positions with the Iowa State Bar Association and various other legal organizations, including the IADC and DRI. Firm members have served on judicial selection commissions for both state and federal courts. Stuart, Tinley is a full service law practice. We serve Western Iowa and Eastern Nebraska with attorneys licensed in both states.

MEMBERS OF FIRM

JAMES E. THORN, born LuVerne, Iowa, May 28, 1935; admitted to bar, 1963, Iowa. *Education:* Wartburg College (B.A., 1962); University of Iowa (J.D., 1963). Phi Alpha Delta. *Member:* Pottawattamie County, Southwest Iowa, Iowa State and American Bar Associations; Iowa Association of Workers' Compensation Lawyers. ***Email:*** thorn.james@stuarttinley.com

WILLIAM R. HUGHES, JR., born Council Bluffs, Iowa, September 23, 1948; admitted to bar, 1980, Iowa and Nebraska. *Education:* University of Iowa (B.S., 1970); Drake University (M.A., 1973); University of Nebraska at Lincoln (J.D., 1979; Ph.D., 1985). Order of the Coif. Member, Nebraska Law Review, 1978-1979. *Member:* Pottawattamie County, Southwest Iowa and Iowa State Bar Associations; International Association of Defense Counsel. ***Email:*** hughes.william@stuarttinley.com

GARY R. FAUST, born Alta, Iowa, June 9, 1944; admitted to bar, 1974, Iowa. *Education:* University of Northern Iowa (B.A., 1970); Drake University (J.D., 1973). *Member:* Pottawattamie County, Southwest Iowa, Iowa State and American Bar Associations; Iowa Supreme Court Commission on Continuing Legal Education. ***Email:*** faust.gary@stuarttinley.com

KRISTOPHER K. MADSEN, born Council Bluffs, Iowa, October 18, 1963; admitted to bar, 1989, Iowa; 1990, U.S. District Court, Southern and Northern Districts of Iowa; 1996, Nebraska; U.S. Court of Appeals, Eighth Circuit. *Education:* St. Olaf College (B.A., 1986); Drake University (J.D., 1989). Delta Theta Phi. *Member:* Pottawattamie County, Southwest Iowa, Iowa State, Nebraska State and American Bar Associations; Iowa Trial Lawyers Association; Iowa Defense Counsel; Iowa Academy of Trial Lawyers. ***Email:*** madsen.kristopher@stuarttinley.com

RICHARD D. CROWL, JR., born Council Bluffs, Iowa, September 24, 1959; admitted to bar, 1985, Iowa and U.S. Tax Court; U.S. District Court, Southern District of Iowa; 2003, Nebraska and U.S. Court of Appeals, Eighth Circuit. *Education:* Iowa State University (B.A., 1982); University of Iowa (J.D., with distinction, 1985). Pottawattamie County Attorney, 1991-2002. *Member:* Pottawattamie County, Southwest Iowa, Iowa State and American Bar Associations; Iowa Trial Lawyers Association (Member, Criminal Law Board of Directors and Worker's Compensation Section). ***Email:*** crowl.rick@stuarttinley.com

ROBERT M. STUART (1914-1986)

JACK W. PETERS (1931-1993)

EMMET TINLEY (1916-2002)

ASSOCIATE

ROBERT LIVINGSTON, admitted to bar, 2000, Iowa and Nebraska. *Education:* Colorado State University (B.S., 1993); Iowa State University (M.S., 2000); Drake University (J.D., with honors, 2000). *Member:* Pottawattamie, Southwest Iowa, Iowa State (President, Bar Review Committee, Young Lawyers Division), Nebraska State and American Bar Associations. ***Email:*** livingston.robert@stuarttinley.com

REPRESENTATIVE CLIENTS: U.S. Bank Iowa, N.A.; Burlington-Northern; National Cooperative Refinery Association. *Insurance Companies:* Travelers; Hartford; St. Paul; Liberty Mutual; Fireman's Fund-American; Continental; Ohio Casualty Group; Great American Insurance Cos.; Union Insurance Co.; The Maryland; Northwestern National Insurance Co.; Tri-State Insurance Co.; CIGNA; Iowa Mutual; Horace Mann; American States; Economy Fire & Casualty Co.; Prudential; State Farm Insurance Companies; General Casualty Company; Pafco Insurance Company; Florists' Mutual Insurance Co.; Orion Insurance Company; Public Entity Risk Services; Progressive Insurance Company; Municipal Housing Agency of Council Bluffs.

SWANSON LAW FIRM

COUNCIL BLUFFS, IOWA

(See Red Oak)

General Civil and Trial Practice in all Courts, Personal Injury and Negligence Litigation, Probate, Domestic Relations, Taxation, Real Estate.

TELPNER, PETERSON, SMITH, RUESCH, THOMAS & SIMPSON

25 MAIN PLACE, SUITE 200
P.O. BOX 248
COUNCIL BLUFFS, IOWA 51502-0248
Telephone: 712-325-9000
Fax: 712-328-1946
Email: email@telpnerlaw.com

Commercial/Banking Law, Corporate Bankruptcy, Real Estate Law, Personal Injury/Workers Compensation, Probate, Estate Planning, Domestic Relations, Environmental, Civil Trial Practice, Unfair Trade Practices, Eminent Domain, Business, Zoning, Debtor and Creditor, Professional Liability and General Practice in State and Federal Courts.

MEMBERS OF FIRM

RICHARD W. PETERSON, born Council Bluffs, Iowa, September 29, 1925; admitted to bar, 1951, Iowa and U.S. District Court, Southern District of Iowa; 1991, U.S. Supreme Court; 1997, U.S. Court of Appeals, Eighth Circuit. *Education:* State University of Iowa (B.A., 1949; J.D., with distinction, 1951). Phi Delta Phi; Delta Sigma Rho; Omicron Delta Kappa. Author: "Federal Magistrates Act," Article 56 Iowa Law Review 62 October, 1970; "The Court Moves West," Southside Press of the Midlands, Copyright 1988; "West of the Nishnabotna," Southside Press of the Midlands, 1998. Co-Author: "No One is Above the Law: the Story of Southern Iowa's Federal Court," Copyright, 1994. Member, Board of Directors Council Bluffs Community School District, 1958-1964; President, 1963. U.S. Magistrate Judge, Southern District of Iowa (part-time), 1970—. Member, 1964—, and President, 1978-1979, National Council U.S. Magistrates. Verifying Official, Prisoner Transfer Commission, Mexico City, 1977; Bolivia, 1980-1981; Peru, 1981. President, Historical Society of U.S. Courts in the Eighth Circuit, 1989—. *Member:* Pottawattamie County (President, 1979-1980), Iowa State (Member, 1975-1981, and Chairman, 1978-1980, Federal Practice Committee; Member, Legal Education and Admission to the Bar Committee, 1983-1987; Member: Probate & Trust Law Council, 1996—; Probate & Trust Law Section, 1996—); Iowa Conference of Bar Association Presidents (President, 1985-1987), Federal, American (Member, Real Estate, Probate and Trust Law Section) and Inter-American Bar Associations; American Judicature Society. Life Fellow, American Bar Foundation. ***PRACTICE AREAS:*** Probate. ***Email:*** rpeterson@telpnerlaw.com

CHARLES L. SMITH, born Mason City, Iowa, September 22, 1948; admitted to bar, 1974, Iowa and U.S. District Court, Southern District of Iowa; 1978, U.S. District Court, Northern District of Iowa; U.S. Court of Appeals, Eighth Circuit; 1988, Nebraska and U.S. District Court, District of Nebraska. *Education:* University of Notre Dame (B.A., 1971); Creighton University (J.D., 1974). Member, City Council, 1982-1985 and Mayor, 1984, Council Bluffs, Iowa. *Member:* Pottawattamie County (President, 2001-2002), Southwest Iowa, Iowa State (Board of Governors, 2001—), Nebraska State, Federal and American Bar Associations; National Association of Bankruptcy Trustees; Association of Trial Lawyers of Iowa; The Association of Trial Lawyers of America; American Bankruptcy Institute. ***PRACTICE AREAS:*** Bankruptcy; Environmental; Commercial Banking; Debtor and Creditor. ***Email:*** csmith@telpnerlaw.com

JACK E. RUESCH, born Monroe, Wisconsin, June 1, 1951; admitted to bar, 1976, Iowa; 1977, U.S. District Court, Southern and Northern Districts of Iowa, U.S. Court of Appeals, Eighth Circuit; 1988, Nebraska and U.S. District Court, District of Nebraska. *Education:* Iowa State University (B.S., 1973); Creighton University (J.D., 1976). Assistant City Attorney, City of Council Bluffs, 1980-1983. Member: Council Bluffs City Council, 1990-1994; Supreme Court Grievance Commission, 1996—. *Member:* Pottawattamie County, Southwest Iowa, Iowa State, Nebraska State, Federal and American Bar Associations; Association of Trial Lawyers of Iowa; The Association of Trial Lawyers of America; American Bankruptcy Institute; American Agricultural Law Association. ***PRACTICE AREAS:*** Commercial Banking; Real Estate; Probate; Estate Planning; Eminent Domain; Business Law; Zoning, Planning and Land Use. ***Email:*** jruesch@telpnerlaw.com

WALTER P. THOMAS, born Spencer, Iowa, August 4, 1953; admitted to bar, 1981, Iowa; 1984, Nebraska; 1994, U.S. District Court, Southern District of Iowa. *Education:* University of Iowa (B.B.A., with distinction, 1976; J.D., 1980). Member, Attorney General's Crime Victims Assistance Board of Directors, 1992-1994; Iowa Supreme Court Commissioner on CLE, 1994—. Public Defender, 1981-1994 and Chief Public Defender, 1983-1994, Pottawattamie County, Iowa. *Member:* Pottawattamie County, Iowa State, Nebraska State and Southwest Iowa Bar Associations; Iowa Trial Lawyers Association. ***PRACTICE AREAS:*** Personal Injury; Workers' Compensation; Trial Law; Professional Liability. ***Email:*** wthomas@telpnerlaw.com

SHANNON DELL'ORFANO SIMPSON, born Los Angeles, California, February 6, 1969; admitted to bar, 1997, Iowa, U.S. District Court, Southern District of Iowa and U.S. Court of Appeals, Eighth Circuit. *Education:* Northern Arizona University (B.S., 1994); Creighton University (J.D., 1997). Member, Historical Society, U.S. Court of Appeals, 8th Circuit, 1998. *Member:* Pottawattamie County, Southwest Iowa, Nebraska State, Iowa State and American Bar Associations; Iowa Trial Lawyers Association. ***PRACTICE AREAS:*** Trial Practice; Domestic Relations; Employment Law. ***Email:*** ssimpson@telpnerlaw.com

---

NICOLE B. ENGELHARDT, born Waverly, Iowa, March 2, 1978; admitted to bar, 2003, Iowa, Nebraska and U.S. District Court, District of Nebraska and Northern and

(This Listing Continued)

Southern Districts of Iowa. *Education:* Creighton University (B.S.B.A., summa cum laude, 2000); Creighton University Law School (J.D., magna cum laude, 2003). Phi Alpha Delta. *Member:* Pottawattamie County, Iowa State, Nebraska State, Federal and American Bar Associations; Iowa Trial Lawyers Association. ***PRACTICE AREAS:*** Bankruptcy; Commercial Law; Evictions. ***Email:*** nengelhardt@telpnerlaw.com

RETIRED

MAYNARD S. TELPNER

REPRESENTATIVE CLIENTS: Kellogg Company Employees Credit Union; Sapp Bros. Petroleum Co.; ERC Properties Inc.; De Bruce Grain, Inc.; US Bank; Citizens State Bank of Clarinda; State Savings Bank, Bedford, Iowa; Security State Bank of Red Oak; Oakland State Bank; First Nebraska Credit Union; Omaha Employee Credit Union; Heartland Area Credit Union; Southwest 8 Senior Services Incorporation; Bethany Foundation; Pottawattamie County Development Corporation; P.J. Morgan Realty; Marathon Realty; Signa Development Locs. Inc.; Historic General Dodge House; City of Council Bluffs.
REFERENCE: US Bank, Council Bluffs, Iowa.

WELSH & WELSH, P.C., L.L.O.

COUNCIL BLUFFS, IOWA

(See Omaha, Nebraska)

Automobile Accidents, Motorcycle Accidents, Medical Malpractice, Farm Accidents, Railroad Accidents, Dangerous Products, Wrongful Death, Animal Attacks, Gas Explosions, Birth Injury, Workers Compensation, Pharmaceutical Injuries, Burn Injuries, Automobile Negligence, Personal Injury, Products Liability, Aviation, Pharmaceutical Litigation, Class Actions, Nursing Home Abuse, Car Accidents, Semi-Truck Accidents, ATU Accidents, Professional Malpractice, Gastric Bypass/Banding Malpractice, Vioxx.

WILLSON & PECHACEK, P.L.C.

421 WEST BROADWAY, SUITE 200
P.O. BOX 2029
COUNCIL BLUFFS, IOWA 51502
Telephone: 712-322-6000
Fax: 712-322-6200
Email: info@willsonpechacek.com
URL: http://www.willsonpechacek.com

Oakland, Iowa Office: 109 North Main. Telephone: 712-482-6999.
Red Oak, Iowa Office: 608 Second Street, Suite 100. Telephone: 712-623-9623.
Treynor, Iowa Office: 15 East Main Street. Telephone: 712-487-3444.
Harlan Iowa Office: 1121 7th Street. Telephone: 712-755-1111.
Carroll, Iowa Office: 110 West 8th Street. Telephone: 712-792-0001.

Civil and Business Litigation, Insurance, Trial Practice, Product Liability, Malpractice or Professional Negligence, Personal Injury, Workers' Compensation, Employment, Governmental Regulations and Administrative Law, Agriculture, Environmental, Corporations and Limited Liability Companies, Business Transactions, Taxation, Real Estate, Commercial and Retail Collections, Will, Estate, and Probate.

MEMBERS OF FIRM

PHILIP J. WILLSON, born September 30, 1923; admitted to bar, 1949, Iowa and U.S. District Court, Northern and Southern Districts of Iowa; 1951, U.S. Court of Appeals, Eighth Circuit; 1953, U.S. District Court, District of Nebraska and U.S. Supreme Court; 1994, Nebraska. *Education:* Parsons College (B.A., 1946); Yale University (LL.B., 1949). Recipient: Iowa State Bar Association Award of Merit, 1985; President's Award, 2000; Community Service Award, 2000, Co-author: "Iowa Practice," Vestal and Willson, 1974. Member, Iowa Supreme Court: Model Rules of Professional Conduct; Advisory Committee on Iowa Rules Evidence. *Member:* Omaha, Pottawattamie County (President, 1963-1964), Iowa State (President, 1977-1978; Member, Sections on: Litigation; Workers' Compensation), Southwest Iowa, Nebraska State and American (Member, Sections on: Litigation ;Tort and Insurance Practice) Bar Associations; Iowa Defense Counsel Association (President, 1969-1970); Iowa Association of Workers' Compensation Lawyers; Defense Research Institute. Fellow: American College of Trial Lawyers; Iowa Academy of Trial Lawyers; Iowa State Bar Foundation. ***PRACTICE AREAS:*** Trial Practice; Arbitration; Alternative Dispute Resolution. ***Email:*** pwillson@willsonpechacek.com

FRANK W. PECHACEK, JR., born May 1, 1944; admitted to bar, 1969, Iowa and U.S. District Court, Southern District of Iowa; 1970, U.S. Court of Appeals, Eighth Circuit and U.S. District Court, Northern District of Iowa; 1980, U.S. Court of Federal Claims; 1982, U.S. Tax Court; 1983, Nebraska and U.S. District Court, District of Nebraska; 1992, U.S. Supreme Court; 1999, U.S. Court of Appeals for the Federal Circuit; U.S. District Court, District of North Dakota. *Education:* University of Northern Iowa (B.A., with distinction, 1966); University of Iowa (J.D., with distinction, 1969). Phi Delta Phi. Student Contributor, Iowa Law Review, 1968-1969. Commissioner, Iowa Supreme Court Commission on Continuing Legal Education, 1976-1982. Member, Iowa Judicial Nominating Commission, 1991-1997. *Member:* Pottawattamie County, Iowa State (Member, Sections on: Law Practice Management; Probate and Trust; Chair, Business Law Section; Member, Sections Council: Business and Corporate Law, 1992-1994, 1999-2001; Law Practice Management, 1995-1999), Southwest Iowa, Nebraska State and American (Member, Business Law and Law Practice Management) Bar Associations. Fellow: Iowa State Bar Foundation (1999); Federal Circuit Bar Association. ***PRACTICE AREAS:*** Corporate Law; Business Law; Banking Law; Wills; Estates; Probate. ***Email:*** fpechacek@willsonpechacek.com

BRUCE B. GREEN, born Manchester, Iowa, June 29, 1968; admitted to bar, 1993, Iowa and Nebraska; U.S. District Court, Northern and Southern Districts of Iowa; U.S. District Court, District of Nebraska; U.S Court of Appeals, Eighth Circuit; 1999, U.S. District Court, District of North Dakota; U.S. Court of Federal Claims; U.S. Court of Appeals for the Federal Circuit. *Education:* University of Iowa (B.A., with highest distinction, 1990; J.D., with high distinction, 1993). Phi Eta Sigma; Phi Beta Kappa. Member, Moot Court Board. Recipient, American Jurisprudence Award, Contract and Sales Transactions.. *Member:* Omaha, Pottawattamie County, Nebraska State (Member, Sections on: Employment Law; Insurance Law; General Practice), Southwest Iowa, Iowa State (Member, Sections on: Labor and Employment Law; General Practice) and American (Member, Sections on: Labor and Employment Law; Environment Energy and Resources; Young Lawyers) Bar Associations; Nebraska Association of Trial Attorneys; National Employment Lawyers Association; Defense Research Institute. ***PRACTICE AREAS:*** Personal Injury; Employment Law; Administrative Law; Agricultural Law; Insurance. ***Email:*** bgreen@willsonpechacek.com

M. BRETT RYAN, born Redondo Beach, California, September 18, 1970; admitted to bar, 1999, Iowa; 2000, Nebraska, U.S. District Court, Northern and Southern Districts of Iowa. *Education:* University of Northern Iowa (NB.A., 1993); University of Iowa (J.D., with high distinction, 1999). Member, Iowa Law Review, 1997-1998. *Member:* Omaha, Pottawattamie County, Nebraska State, Iowa State, Southwest Iowa and American (Member, Sections on Litigation and Young Lawyers) Bar Associations; The Association of Trial Lawyers of America; Iowa Trial Lawyers Association. ***PRACTICE AREAS:*** Litigation; General Practice; Government; Administrative Law. ***Email:*** bryan@willsonpechacek.com

ASSOCIATES

JAMIE L. COX, born Rock Island, Illinois, January 2, 1976; admitted to bar, 2002, Iowa and Nebraska; 2003, U.S. District Court, Southern and Northern Districts of Iowa, U.S. District Court, District of Nebraska. *Education:* University of Iowa (B.A., with honors and distinction, 1998; J.D., 2001). *Member:* Pottawattamie County, Southwest Iowa Bar Associations. ***PRACTICE AREAS:*** Alternative Dispute Resolution Litigation; E-Commerce. ***Email:*** jcox@willsonpechacek.com

LONNY L. KOLLN II, born Denison, Iowa, March 22, 1977; admitted to bar, 2002, Iowa; 2003, Nebraska. *Education:* University of Northern Iowa (B.A., summa cum laude, 1999); University of Iowa (J.D., with distinction, 2002). Member, Council Bluffs Estate Planning Council. *Member:* Pottawattamie County, Southwest Iowa, Iowa State (Member Sections on: Real Estate and Title Law, Taxation) Nebraska State and American (Member, Sections on: Real Property, Probate, Trust Law and Young Lawyers) Bar Associations. ***PRACTICE AREAS:*** Taxation; Corporate Law; Real Estate; Wills; Probate; Agricultural Law; Trust Law. ***Email:*** lkolln@willsonpechacek.com

REPRESENTATIVE CLIENTS: Agri General Insurance Company; Agro National, L.L.C.; American Equine Insurance Group, Ltd.; Amoco Corporation; Auto-Owners Insurance; Baltzell Agri-Products; Centering Corporation; Century Indemnity Company; CIGNA; Citizens Security Group; Citizens State Bank; EMC Insurance Companies; Farm Bureau Mutual; Farmers Crop Insurance Alliance; Fireman's Fund; First Bank Iowa, F.S.B.; Firstar Bank Iowa N.A.; Fremont County Savings Bank; Historical Society of Pottawattamie County; The Home Agency, Inc.; Lozier Corp.; Mobil Corp.; North Pointe Insurance Company; Rain and Hail Insurance Service, Inc.; Rain and Hail, L.L.C.; Scottsdale Insurance Companies; Treynor State Bank; United National Group; Western Ventures, Inc.

McDONALD, BROWN & FAGEN

Established in 1933
502-15TH STREET
P.O. BOX 250
DALLAS CENTER, IOWA 50063-0250
Telephone: 515-992-3728
Fax: 515-992-3971
Email: dalctlaw@mindspring.com
URL: http://www.dallascenterlawyers.com

Grimes, Iowa Office: 306 South First Street. Telephone: 515-986-9888. Fax: 515-986-9876.

General Practice, including: Real Estate, Wills, Trusts, Estate Planning, and Probate, Business and Commercial, Taxation Law and Tax Returns, Family Law, Litigation and Appeals, Debtor and Creditor, Municipal and School Law.

FIRM PROFILE: The firm is listed in the Martindale-Hubbell Bar Register of Preeminent Lawyers.

OF COUNSEL

JOHN C. McDONALD, born Lorimor, Iowa, February 19, 1924; admitted to bar, 1948, Iowa, U.S. District Court, Southern District of Iowa, U.S. Court of the Armed Forces and U.S. Supreme Court. *Education:* Simpson College (1941-1943); Drake University (J.D., 1948). Dallas County Attorney, 1958-1962. Member, 1975-1978 and Chairman, 1978, Board of Visitors U.S. Air Force Academy. Member, 1981-1987 and President, 1985-1987, Iowa State Board of Regents. Member, American Battle Monuments Commission, 1982-1992. *Member:* Dallas County and Iowa State Bar Associations. [USAF, 1943-1946, 1951-1953; Colonel, USAF Reserve, 1953-1975]

MEMBERS OF FIRM

RALPH R. BROWN, born Mt. Pleasant, Iowa, December 13, 1944; admitted to bar, 1969, Iowa, U.S. District Court, Southern and Northern Districts of Iowa, U.S. Court of Appeals, Eighth Circuit and U.S. Supreme Court; 2002, District of Columbia. *Education:* Drake University (B.A., with honors, 1967; J.D., 1969). Secretary of the Iowa State Senate, 1973-1975. Dallas Center City Attorney, 1984—. Granger City Attorney, 1990—. Member, President's Commission on Model State Drug Laws, 1992-1993. Director, 1994— and Vice Chairman, 1996—, National Alliance for Model State Drug Laws. *Member:* Dallas County, Iowa State and American Bar Associations. ***PRACTICE AREAS:*** Business Law; Commercial Law; Business Organization; Wills; Trust Law; Estate Planning; Probate; Taxation; Real Estate; Municipal Law; School Law; Election, Campaign and Political Law. ***Email:*** ralphbrown@mindspring.com

CHARLES H. FAGEN, born Spencer, Iowa, December 2, 1960; admitted to bar, 1986, Iowa; 1989, Minnesota and U.S. District Court, Southern District of Iowa; 1998, U.S. Tax Court. *Education:* Drake University (BS., 1983; J.D., 1986). Certified Public Accountant, Iowa, 1985. *Member:* Dallas County, Iowa State and American Bar Associations. ***PRACTICE AREAS:*** Real Estate; Taxation; Wills; Trust Law; Estate Planning; Probate; Agricultural Law; Business Organization; Commercial Law; Debtor and Creditor; Family Law; Personal Injury. ***Email:*** chuckfagen@mindspring.com

(This Listing Continued)

McDONALD, BROWN & FAGEN, Dallas Center—Continued

ASSOCIATE

BENJAMIN L. ROUSE, born Emmetsburg, Iowa, March 23, 1980; admitted to bar, 2005, Iowa. *Education:* Iowa State University (B.S. in Agronomy, 2002); University of Utah (J.D., 2005). *Member:* Dallas County and Iowa State Bar Associations. (Also at Grimes Office). ***PRACTICE AREAS:*** Agricultural Law; Real Estate; Wills; Probate; Taxation; Family Law; Business Organization.

REPRESENTATIVE CLIENTS: City of Dallas Center; City of Granger; DCI Group, L.L.C.; Dallas Center-Grimes Community School District; Dallas County Care Facility, Inc.; Dallas Mutual Insurance Co.; GPS Ventures, L.L.C.; McK Construction, Inc.; National Alliance for Model State Drug Laws; Spurgeon Manor, Inc.; TSE Enterprises, L.L.C.

BETTY, NEUMAN & McMAHON

Established in 1907

111 EAST THIRD STREET, SUITE 600
DAVENPORT, IOWA 52801
Telephone: 563-326-4491
Fax: 563-326-4498
Email: bnmcm@bettylawfirm.com
URL: http://www.bettylawfirm.com

General Civil Practice in State and Federal Courts, Trials and Appeals, Insurance Defense, Estate Planning, Trusts and Probate, Real Estate, Family, Taxation, Business and Corporation Law.

FIRM PROFILE: Betty, Neuman & McMahon was founded in 1907 by brothers Harry and Frank Betty, graduates of Chicago University and Michigan University Law Schools, respectively. The Firm has a general practice serving clients throughout Iowa and Illinois.

MEMBERS OF FIRM

H. B. BETTY (1874-1953)

FRANK F. BETTY (1880-1974)

THOMAS F. DALEY, JR. (1930-1979)

HENRY N. NEUMAN (1905-1986)

RICHARD M. McMAHON (1920-1994)

HENRY G. NEUMAN, born Davenport, Iowa, August 17, 1948; admitted to bar, 1974, Iowa; U.S. District Court, Northern and Southern Districts of Iowa; 1989, Illinois; 1991, Colorado. *Education:* Augustana College (B.A., 1970); University of Colorado (J.D., 1973). Trustee, Iowa Cultural Trust Board. Trustee and Past President: Community Foundation of the Great River Bend, 1993-2000; Davenport Museum of Art, 1995-2003. President, Museum of Art Foundation, 1999-2004. *Member:* Scott County (President, 1992-1993), Iowa State, Illinois State and American Bar Associations; Quad City Estate Planning Council (President, 1998-1999); American Academy of ADR Attorneys. ***PRACTICE AREAS:*** Business Law; Corporate Law; Civil Litigation; Real Estate; Estate Planning; Trusts and Probate. ***Email:*** hgn@bettylawfirm.com

STEVEN H. JACOBS, born Davenport, Iowa, October 8, 1944; admitted to bar, 1969, Iowa; U.S. District Court, Northern and Southern Districts of Iowa. *Education:* State University of Iowa (B.B.A., 1966; J.D., 1969); New York University, School of Law (LL.M. in Taxation, 1974). Phi Delta Phi. Chair, Iowa State Board of Tax Review, 1979-1985. *Member:* Scott County (Treasurer, 1986—), Iowa State and American Bar Associations. [Capt., JAGC, U.S. Army, 1969-1973]. ***PRACTICE AREAS:*** Business Law; Corporate Law; Family Law; Real Estate; Estate Planning; Trusts and Probate. ***Email:*** shj@bettylawfirm.com

ROGER A. LATHROP, born Fairfield, Iowa, August 24, 1951; admitted to bar, 1976, Iowa; U.S. District Court, Northern and Southern Districts of Iowa and U.S. District Court, Central District of Illinois. *Education:* Drake University; University of Northern Iowa (B.A. with honors, 1973); University of Iowa (J.D. with distinction, 1976). *Member:* Scott County (Vice President, 1986-1987 and President, 1987-1988), Iowa State (Member, Federal Practice Committee) and American Bar Associations; Iowa Academy of Trial Lawyers; Iowa Defense Counsel Association; Defense Research Institute (Member, Products Liability Committee); International Association of Defense Counsel (Member, Committees on: Products Liability; Toxic Torts; Professional Liability); American Board of Trial Advocates. ***PRACTICE AREAS:*** Civil Trials and Appeals; Product Liability; Negligence; Personal Injury Law. ***Email:*** ral@bettylawfirm.com

CRAIG A. LEVIEN, born Davenport, Iowa, June 14, 1953; admitted to bar, 1979, Iowa; U.S. District Court, Northern and Southern Districts of Iowa; 1980, Illinois; U.S. District Court Northern and Central Districts of Illinois. *Education:* Boston College (B.A., 1975); University of Iowa (J.D. with distinction, 1979). *Member:* Scott County, Rock Island County, Iowa State and Illinois State Bar Associations; Iowa Defense Counsel; Iowa Association of Workers' Compensation Lawyers; Iowa Academy of Trial Lawyers; Illinois Association of Defense Trial Counsel; American Board of Trial Advocates. Fellow, American College of Trial Lawyers. ***PRACTICE AREAS:*** Civil Litigation; Workers Compensation. ***Email:*** cal@bettylawfirm.com

GREG A. EGBERS, born Berwyn, Illinois, March 15, 1954; admitted to bar, 1979, Iowa; U.S. District Court, Northern and Southern Districts of Iowa. *Education:* Purdue University (B.S. with honors, 1975); Drake University (J.D., 1979). Phi Alpha Delta. Recipient, International Academy of Trial Lawyers Award. Co-Chair, Iowa Workers' Compensation Symposium, 1989-1990. *Member:* Scott County, Iowa State and American Bar Associations; Iowa Defense Counsel Association; Iowa Association of Workers' Compensation Lawyers; Iowa Academy of Trial Lawyers (Member, Board of Governors, 2001—); Defense Research Institute; International Association of Industrial Accident Boards and Commissions; American Board of Trial Advocates. Fellow, American College of Trial Lawyers. ***PRACTICE AREAS:*** Civil Litigation; Medical Malpractice; Workers Compensation. ***Email:*** gae@bettylawfirm.com

(This Listing Continued)

MARK A. WOOLLUMS, born Ottumwa, Iowa, March 9, 1961; admitted to bar, 1986, Iowa; U.S. District Court, Northern and Southern Districts of Iowa; 1987, Illinois; U.S. District Court, Northern, Southern and Central Districts of Illinois; U.S. Court of Appeals, Seventh and Eighth Circuits. *Education:* Iowa State University (B.A., 1982); Drake University (J.D., 1986). *Member:* Scott County, Iowa State, Illinois State and American Bar Associations; Iowa Defense Counsel; Iowa Association of Workers' Compensation Lawyers; Illinois Association of Defense Trial Counsel; Defense Research Institute; Association of Trial Lawyers of America. ***PRACTICE AREAS:*** Civil Litigation and Appeals in State and Federal Courts; Appeals; Workers Compensation; Negligence; Employment Law; Products Liability. ***Email:*** maw@bettylawfirm.com

DEBORAH A. DUBIK, born Erie, Pennsylvania, April 12, 1955; admitted to bar, 1980, Iowa. *Education:* Gannon University (B.A., 1976); Drake University (J.D., 1980). Phi Alpha Delta. Administrative Law Judge, State of Iowa, 1981-1987; Deputy Iowa Industrial Commissioner, 1987-1992. Member, Iowa Supreme Court Commission on Continuing Legal Education, 1992-1999. Co-Chair, Iowa Workers' Compensation Symposium, 1995-1996. *Member:* Scott County, Iowa State and American Bar Associations; Iowa Association of Workers' Compensation Lawyers (Member, Board of Governors, 1994-2002); Iowa Defense Counsel Association; Defense Research Institute. ***PRACTICE AREAS:*** Workers Compensation; Employment Law. ***Email:*** dad@bettylawfirm.com

MARTHA L. SHAFF, born Clinton, Iowa, August 11, 1964; admitted to bar, 1989, Iowa; 1993, Illinois; U.S. District Court, Northern and Southern Districts of Iowa and Northern and Central Districts of Illinois; U.S. Court of Appeals, Seventh and Eighth Circuits; U.S. Supreme Court. *Education:* St. Olaf College (B.A., 1986); Drake University (J.D. with honors, 1989). Delta Theta Phi (Treasurer, 1987-1988). Member, Drake Law Review. Board Member, Moot Court Board, 1988-1989. *Member:* Scott County, Iowa State, Illinois State and American Bar Associations; Iowa Defense Counsel Association (Member: Board of Directors, 2001—; Seventh Judicial District Nomination Committee, 2000—); Illinois Association of Defense Trial Counsel; Iowa Academy of Trial Lawyers. ***PRACTICE AREAS:*** Civil Litigation; Products Liability; Employment Law; Appeals in State and Federal Court. ***Email:*** mls@bettylawfirm.com

JEAN DICKSON FEENEY, born Northfield, Minnesota, November 21, 1967; admitted to bar, 1992, Iowa; U.S. District Court, Northern and Southern Districts of Iowa; 1993, Illinois; U.S. District Court, Central District of Illinois; U.S. Court of Appeals, Eighth Circuit. *Education:* Luther College (B.A., cum laude, 1989); University of Iowa (J.D. with high distinction, 1992). Phi Delta Phi. Recipient, American Jurisprudence Book Award, Professional Responsibility, 1992. Law Clerk to Hon. Allen L. Donielson, Iowa Court of Appeals, 1992-1993. Co-Chair, Iowa Workers' Compensation Symposium, 2005. Member, State Judicial Nominating Commission, 2005—. *Member:* Scott County (President, 2000-2001), Iowa State, Illinois State and American Bar Associations; Iowa Association of Workers' Compensation Lawyers (Member, Board of Governors, 2002—); Iowa Defense Counsel Association. ***PRACTICE AREAS:*** Workers' Compensation; Civil Litigation; Appeals. ***Email:*** jdf@bettylawfirm.com

PETER J. THILL, born Aurora, Illinois, August 4, 1969; admitted to bar, 1995, Iowa, U.S. District Court, Northern and Southern Districts of Iowa, Illinois and U.S. District Court, Central District of Illinois. *Education:* Illinois Wesleyan University (B.A., 1991); Drake University (J.D., 1995). Member: Order of Barristers; National Moot Court Team, 1994-1995; Insurance Law Moot Court Team, 1993-1994. Law Clerk to Chief Justice Arthur McGiverin, Iowa Supreme Court, 1995-1996. Author: "Insurers' and Courts' Response to High Dose Chemotherapy with Autologous Bone Marrow Transplant in the Treatment of Breast Cancer: A Tragedy or Necessity?" 43 Drake L. Rev. 863, 1995. *Member:* Scott County, Iowa State and American Bar Associations; Iowa Defense Counsel Association; Iowa Association of Workers' Compensation Lawyers; Quad City Claims Association. ***PRACTICE AREAS:*** Workers' Compensation; Civil Litigation; Appeals. ***Email:*** pjt@bettylawfirm.com

ASSOCIATES

RONI N. HALABI, born Monrovia, Liberia, July 26, 1972; admitted to bar, 1999, Iowa; 2002, Illinois; 2003, U.S. District Court, Southern District of Iowa. *Education:* Bradley University (B.A., summa cum laude, 1994); Drake University (J.D., 1998). Editor-in-Chief, Drake Journal of Agricultural Law, 1997-1998. Law Clerk to: Justice Linda K. Neuman, Iowa Supreme Court, 1998-1999; Justice James H. Carter, Iowa Supreme Court, 1999-2000. Author: "Stability in the Middle East Through Economic Development: An Analysis of the Peace Process, Increased Agricultural Trade, Joint Ventures and Free Trade Agreements," 2 Drake J. Agric. L. 275, 1997. *Member:* Scott County (Chair, CLE Committee, 2002—), Iowa State, Illinois State and American Bar Associations. ***PRACTICE AREAS:*** Business Law; Corporate Law; Real Estate; Employment Law; Commercial Litigation; Estate Planning; Trust Law; Probate. ***Email:*** rnh@bettylawfirm.com

CARRIE N. ROSEBERRY, born Cedar Rapids, Iowa, June 3, 1977; admitted to bar, 2003, Iowa; 2004, Illinois. *Education:* Iowa State University (B.A., 1999); Drake University (J.D., with honors, 2002). *Member:* Scott County, Iowa State, Illinois State and American Bar Associations; Iowa Defense Counsel Association. ***PRACTICE AREAS:*** Workers Compensation; Civil Defense. ***Email:*** cnr@bettylawfirm.com

EDWARD J. ROSE, born Atlantic, Iowa, July 7, 1976; admitted to bar, 2002, Iowa; 2004, Illinois; 2005, U.S. District Court, Southern District of Iowa. *Education:* University of Iowa (B.A., 1999); University of Wyoming (J.D., with honors, 2002). Phi Delta Phi. Law Clerk for the Fifth Judicial District of Iowa, 2002-2004. *Member:* Scott County, Iowa and Illinois State Bar Associations. ***PRACTICE AREAS:*** Workers Compensation; Civil Practice. ***Email:*** ejr@bettylawfirm.com

TIMOTHY J. REICHWALD, born Green Bay, Wisconsin, April 19, 1978; admitted to bar, 2004, Iowa. *Education:* Ripon College (B.A., cum laude, 2000); Drake University (J.D., with honors, 2004). *Member:* Scott County and Iowa State Bar Associations. ***PRACTICE AREAS:*** Workers Compensation; Civil Litigation. ***Email:*** tjr@bettylawfirm.com

COUNSEL FOR: Kraft Foods, Inc.; Oscar Mayer Foods; Hartford Insurance Co.; Greater Davenport Board of Realtors; The St. Paul Cos.; The Travelers Insurance Co.; The Fireman's Fund American; Kemper Insurance Group; Federated Mutual Insurance Co.; The Bituminous Casualty Corp.; The Ohio Casualty Group; CNA Insurance Co.; Auto-Owners Mutual; Liberty Mutual; Employers Insurance of Wausau; Aetna Life Insurance Co.; Davenport Association of Insurance Agents; Junior League of the Quad-Cities; Mississippi Valley Girl Scout Council;

(This Listing Continued)

Economy Fire & Casualty; West Bend Mutual Insurance Co.; The Granite State Insurance Group; American International Adjustment Co.; U. S. Automobile Association; American States Insurance Co.; First American Title Insurance Co.; CIGNA Insurance Cos.; General Motors; American Home Insurance Co.; U. S. Fidelity & Guaranty; Grinnell Mutual Insurance Co.; Continental Western Insurance Co.; United Fire & Casualty Insurance Co.; Westfield Insurance Co.; May Department Stores; Louis Rich Co.; Northwest Bank & Trust Co.; Scott Schools Credit Union; PepsiCo; Boy Scouts of America; Chubb Insurance Group; Ralston Purina; American Home Products; Archer Daniels Midland Co.; Crawford Co.; BWI/Kartridg Pak Co.; Virginia Surety Co.; Cargill, Inc.; Quaker Oats Co.; Sears Roebuck & Co.; Lowes; City of Rock Island; Deans Foods; Zenith Insurance Co.; Cafe New Holland.

BITTNER, LAMBERT & WERNER

A Partnership including Professional Corporations

Established in 1986

1000 U.S. BANK CENTER
201 WEST 2ND STREET
DAVENPORT, IOWA 52801
Telephone: 563-328-3333
Fax: 563-328-3352

All members are admitted and engage in Civil and Trial Practice in Iowa District Courts and in U.S. District Court, Northern and Southern Districts of Iowa, Central District of Illinois and U.S. Court of Appeals. General Practice including but not limited to Wills, Trusts, Estate Planning and Probate Law, Real Estate, Banking Law, Employment Law, Business Law.

JOHN A. HELLSTROM (1921-1992)

JOHN J. CARLIN (Retired, 1993)

MEMBERS OF FIRM

R. RICHARD BITTNER, (P.C.), born Lincoln, Nebraska, October 18, 1928; admitted to bar, 1957, Iowa. *Education:* Iowa State University (B.S., 1950); State University of Iowa (J.D., 1957). ***PRACTICE AREAS:*** Business Law; Taxation; Wills; Trusts; Estate Planning; Probate Law. ***Email:*** loseband@blwlaw.com

ROBERT D. LAMBERT, (P.C.), born Davenport, Iowa, October 3, 1951; admitted to bar, 1977, Iowa. *Education:* University of Illinois (B.A., with highest distinction, 1974); Drake University (J.D., 1977). Order of Barristers. *Member:* National Association of College and University Attorneys. ***PRACTICE AREAS:*** Employment Law; Banking Law; Real Estate. ***Email:*** rlambert@blwlaw.com

CLEMENS A. WERNER, JR., born Davenport, Iowa, April 25, 1947; admitted to bar, 1974, Iowa. *Education:* Middlebury College (B.A., 1969); University of Iowa (J.D. with distinction, 1972). ***PRACTICE AREAS:*** Wills; Trusts; Estate Planning; Probate Law; Real Estate; Business Law; Banking Law. ***Email:*** cwerner@blwlaw.com

COUNSEL FOR: Bechtel Trusts & Foundation; Iowa Mutual Insurance Co.; Lawyers Title Insurance; Palmer Chiropractic University; Ragan Mechanical, Inc.; H.R. Schaefer Construction Co.; Walcott Trust and Savings Bank; The Salvation Army; CUNA Mutual Group; Iowa-Illinois Taylor Insulation Co.; Nestle Purina PetCare Company; U.S. Bank.

BOZEMAN, NEIGHBOUR, PATTON & NOE, LLP

4300 E. 53RD STREET, SUITE 103
DAVENPORT, IOWA 52807
Telephone: 563-449-1037
Fax: 309-764-1371
URL: http://www.bnpn.com

Moline, Illinois Office: 1630 5th Avenue, P.O. Box 659, 61266-0659. Telephone: 309-797-0850. Fax: 309-764-1371.

General Practice in State and Federal Courts. Trials. Corporation, Taxation, Commercial, Insurance Defense, Insurance Coverage, Product Liability, Medical and Professional Liability, Labor and Employment, Bankruptcy, Probate, Trusts and Estates, Real Estate and Workers Compensation.

JOHN P. HARRIS, born Normal, Illinois, March 2, 1955; admitted to bar, 1980, Iowa and Illinois. *Education:* Hope College; University of Iowa (B.A., 1977; J.D., 1980). *Member:* Rock Island County, Scott County, Illinois State and Iowa State Bar Associations. (Also at Moline, Illinois Office)

GARY L. SISSEL, born Davenport, Iowa, April 23, 1948; admitted to bar, 1973, Iowa; 1986, California; 1988, Illinois. *Education:* University of Iowa (B.A., 1970; J.D., with honors, 1973). *Member:* Rock Island County, Scott County (Member, Executive Council, 1982-1987), Illinois State, Iowa State and American Bar Associations; State Bar of California. (Also at Moline, Illinois Office)

RICHARD M. BATCHER, born Waterloo, Iowa, August 9, 1941; admitted to bar, 1967, Iowa; 1968, Illinois. *Education:* Iowa State University (B.S.M.E., 1963); University of Iowa (J.D., 1967). *Member:* Rock Island County, Scott County, Illinois State, Iowa State and American Bar Associations. (Also at Moline, Illinois Office)

WILLIAM P. RECTOR, born Davenport, Iowa, January 6, 1962; admitted to bar, 1987, Illinois; 1999, Iowa. *Education:* Wake Forest University (B.A., cum laude, 1984); University of Iowa (J.D., with distinction, 1987). *Member:* Rock Island County, Iowa State and American Bar Associations; Professional Liability Underwriting Society. (Also at Moline, Illinois)

(For Complete Biographical Data on Firm Personnel, see Professional Biographies at Moline, Illinois)

WILLIAM J. BRIBRIESCO & ASSOCIATES

DAVENPORT, IOWA

(See Bettendorf)

Personal Injury, Workers Compensation, Products Liability, Business Law.

BROOKS & TRINRUD

A PROFESSIONAL CORPORATION

Established in 1990

220 EMERSON PLACE
DAVENPORT, IOWA 52801
Telephone: 563-326-4900
Fax: 563-326-4944
Email: info@btlawpc.com
URL: http://www.BTLawPC.com

Rock Island, Illinois Office: 3725 Blackhawk Road, P.O. Box 3487, 61204-3487. Telephone: 309-786-4900. Fax: 309-786-4940.

General Practice, Civil Litigation, Workers Compensation, Bankruptcy, Estate Planning, Trusts and Probate, Business Law (including Corporations, Partnerships), Family Law, Commercial Collections, Real Estate Foreclosure, Real Estate, Commercial Real Estate.

(For Complete Biographical Data on all Personnel, see Professional Biographies at Rock Island, Illinois)

CALIFF & HARPER, P.C.

DAVENPORT, IOWA

(See Moline, Illinois)

Corporate, Commercial, Civil Litigation in all State and Federal Courts, Labor, Employment, Banking, Governmental, School, Administrative (including N.L.R.B.), Products Liability, Insurance, Taxation, Estate Planning and Probate Law, Real Estate, Land Development and Zoning, Business Enterprises, Closely Held Business, Limited Liability Companies, Partnerships, Small Business, Buying or Selling a Business, Collections, Employee Benefits, Employment Contracts, Human Resources, Contracts, Business Lawsuits, Internet Law, E-Commerce, Commercial Leasing, Landlord and Tenant; Buying or Selling a Home; Tax Planning and Asset Protection.

EELLS & TRONVOLD LAW OFFICES, P.L.C.

DAVENPORT, IOWA

(See Cedar Rapids)

General Practice with emphasis on Personal Injury, Litigation, Probate and Estate Planning, Trusts and Wills, Business Law and Mediation.

GALLAGHER, MILLAGE & GALLAGHER

Established in 1945

AMERICAN BANK BUILDING
4301 EAST 53RD STREET, SUITE 300
DAVENPORT, IOWA 52807
Telephone: 563-388-8417
Fax: 563-388-9240
Email: gmg@gmglawfirm.com
URL: http://www.gmglawfirm.com

General Civil Practice, including Business, Banking, Real Estate and Corporate Law, Business Transactions, Trusts and Estates, Wills and Probate, and General Litigation.

FIRM PROFILE: Gallagher, Millage & Gallagher is a preeminent full service law firm located on the border of Davenport and Bettendorf, Iowa. We represent businesses and individuals throughout the state of Iowa, Wisconsin and Eastern Illinois. The firm engages in a general practice with an emphasis in trusts and estates, banking, real estate, business law, business transactions, wills and probate, and general litigation. The firm has available effective, trained support personnel.

ROBERT H. GALLAGHER, born Annapolis, Maryland, December 27, 1944; admitted to bar, 1969, Iowa. *Education:* University of Iowa (B.S., 1966; J.D., 1969). Phi Delta Phi. Assistant County Attorney, 1970-1978. *Member:* Scott County (President, 1986-1987), Iowa State (Former Member, Board of Governors) and American Bar Associations. ***PRACTICE AREAS:*** Banks and Banking; Business Transactions; Commercial Law; Corporate Law; Family Law; Litigation; Probate; Real Estate; Trusts and Estates; Wills; Zoning, Planning and Land Use. ***Email:*** rgallaghersr@gmglawfirm.com

DAVID A. MILLAGE, born Portland, Oregon, February 26, 1953; admitted to bar, 1978, Iowa. *Education:* University of Iowa (B.B.A., with distinction, 1974; J.D., with distinction, 1978). Member, Iowa House of Representatives, 1991-2002. *Member:* Scott County and Iowa State Bar Associations. ***PRACTICE AREAS:*** Bankruptcy; Civil Practice; Contracts; Debtor and Creditor; Litigation; Medical Malpractice; Personal Injury; Products Liability; Social Security; Workers Compensation; Family Law; General Practice; Real Estate; Trusts and Estates; Wills. ***Email:*** dmillage@gmglawfirm.com

ROBERT S. GALLAGHER, born Iowa City, Iowa, July 20, 1969; admitted to bar, 1994, Wisconsin and U.S. District Court, Eastern District of Wisconsin; 1995, Iowa and U.S. District Court, Western District of Iowa; 1997, U.S. District Court, Northern District of Iowa; U.S. District Court, Central District of Illinois. *Education:* University of Iowa (B.A., 1991); Marquette University (J.D., 1994). *Member:* Scott County, Iowa State Bar Associa-

(This Listing Continued)

GALLAGHER, MILLAGE & GALLAGHER, Davenport—Continued

tion; State Bar of Wisconsin; The Association of Trial Lawyers of America; Iowa Trial Lawyers Association. ***PRACTICE AREAS:*** Civil Practice; Civil Rights; Criminal Defense; Family Law; Labor and Employment; Litigation; Personal Injury; Real Estate; Trusts and Estates; Wills. ***Email:*** rgallagherjr@gmglawfirm.com

ASSOCIATES

MATTHEW A. LEDDEN, born Hinsdale, Illinois, April 19, 1975; admitted to bar, 2001, Iowa. *Education:* University of Iowa (B.A., History and Political Science, 1997); Drake University Law School (J.D., 2001). *Member:* Scott County and Iowa State Bar Associations. Dillion Inn of Court. ***PRACTICE AREAS:*** Criminal Defense; Family Law; Personal Injury. ***Email:*** mledden@gmglawfirm.com

BRIAN KENNEDY, born Boston, Massachusetts, February 14, 1964; admitted to bar, 1991, Iowa. *Education:* Iowa State University (B.A., 1987); Drake University (J.D., 1991). *Member:* Iowa State Bar Association. ***PRACTICE AREAS:*** Government Relations. ***Email:*** bkennedy@gmglawfirm.com

ALICIA D. GIECK, born Denver, Colorado, November 15, 1973; admitted to bar, 2000, Georgia; 2001, Illinois and Iowa. *Education:* Drake University (B.A., 1996); University of Iowa (J.D., 2000). *Member:* Scott County, Island County, Iowa State and Illinois Bar Associations. ***PRACTICE AREAS:*** Personal Injury; Family Law; Civil Litigation; Workers Compensation. ***Email:*** aliciagieck@gmglawfirm.com

REPRESENTATIVE CLIENTS: Blue Grass Savings Bank; Eldridge Lumber Co., Inc.; Great River Bank & Trust; Parochetti Enterprises (Taco Bell franchisee); Saddlebrook Homes Development, Inc.; Scott County Regional Authority; Douglas Industries, Inc.; Riverboat Development Authority; Harmony Enterprises, Inc.

GOSMA, TARBOX & ASSOCIATES, P.L.C.

Established in 1998

AMERICAN BANK BUILDING
4301 EAST 53RD STREET, SUITE 300
DAVENPORT, IOWA 52807
Telephone: 563-388-8417
Fax: 563-388-9240
URL: http://www.gt-lawfirm.com
Email: jgosma@gt-lawfirm.com
URL: http://www.gosma-gallagherplc.com

General Civil Practice, including Business and Corporate Organization and Transactions, Banking, Real Estate, Estate Planning, Elder Law, Trust and Estate Administration, and Personal Injury, Business and Probate Litigation, Medical Malpractice, Business Enterprises, Slip and Fall, Personal Injury, Automobile Accidents, Wrongful Death, Buying and Selling, Zoning and Land Use, Construction, Asset Protection, Guardianships, Banking and Finance, Closely Held Business, Corporate, Franchise, Limited Liability, Small Business, Partnerships, Buying and Selling of Businesses, Creditors Rights, Contracts, Business Planning, Law Suites, Insurance, Commercial Leasing, Business Start-Ups.

FIRM PROFILE: Gosma, Tarbox & Associates possesses expertise and capabilities greater then its size might indicate. Its lawyers are experienced and sophisticated in the areas in which they practice. John Gosma has practiced law since 1969, when he completed an appointment as a law clerk for the Iowa Supreme Court. He then practiced in business, transactional, banking and real estate law until 1987 with the firm of Rehling, Lindburg & Gosma, which subsequently merged with a larger firm. Marie Tarbox had several years of banking, probate and trust experience before entering private practice with a twenty member firm in 1990. John and Marie decided in 1992 that they could better serve their clients in a small firm atmosphere. In 1998, they were joined by Jim Noth. Jim had been a sole practitioner practicing in probate, trusts, estates and real estate law for many years before joining Gosma, Tarbox & Associates. David Mahl has practiced primarily in personal injury law for approximately ten years. He is engaged in general practice, with an emphasis on litigation.

Gosma, Tarbox & Associates practices primarily in those areas in which its attorneys have substantial experience and expertise, including business and banking law and transactions, elder law, trusts, estates and estate planning, residential and commercial real estate, and litigation in business, probate, trust, personal injury, and real estate cases. We have chosen not to attempt to provide services in all areas of the law. This approach allows us to serve our clients efficiently, and to provide the highest quality services at a reasonable cost.

JOHN S. GOSMA, born Davenport, Iowa, July 26, 1942; admitted to bar, 1968, Iowa; 1969, U.S. District Court, Southern District of Iowa and U.S. District Court, Central District of Illinois; 1970, U.S. Court of Appeals, Eighth Circuit. *Education:* University of Iowa (B.A., 1965; J.D., 1968). Phi Delta Phi. Law Clerk to Justice Clay LeGrand, Supreme Court of Iowa, 1968-1969. *Member:* Scott County (President, 1984-1985), Iowa State and American Bar Associations. ***PRACTICE AREAS:*** Business Law; Banks and Banking; Real Estate; Trusts and Estates; Business Transactions; Probate Litigation; Business Litigation. ***Email:*** jgosma@gt-lawfirm.com

MARIE R. ROLLING-TARBOX, born Estherville, Iowa, March 13, 1958; admitted to bar, 1987, Iowa; 1991, Illinois. *Education:* University of Iowa (B.A., 1983; J.D., with distinction, 1987). Author, "Powers of Appointment Under the Bankruptcy Code: A Focus on General Testamentary Powers," 72 Iowa Law Review 1041, 1987. *Member:* Scott County, Rock Island County, Iowa State, Illinois State and American Bar Associations. ***PRACTICE AREAS:*** Trusts and Estates; Wills; Probate; Guardianship and Conservatorship; Elder Law; Real Estate; Banks and Banking; Business Law; Corporate Law. ***Email:*** mtarbox@gt-lawfirm.com

DAVID A. MAHL, born Davenport, Iowa, September 7, 1965; admitted to bar, 1991, Minnesota; 1992, Iowa. *Education:* University of Iowa (B.B.A., 1988); St. Louis University (J.D., 1991). Pi Alpha Delta. *Member:* Minnesota State and Iowa State Bar Associations. ***PRACTICE AREAS:*** Personal Injury; Business Law; Estates. ***Email:*** dmahl@gt-lawfirm.com

JAMES G. NOTH, born Davenport, Iowa, September 3, 1920; admitted to bar, 1948, Iowa and District of Columbia. *Education:* St. Ambrose College (B.A., 1942); Georgetown University (J.D., 1948). Member, Phi Delta Phi, 1946-1948. *Member:* Scott County, Iowa State and American Bar Associations; The District of Columbia Bar. [U.S. Army Engr., Sgt., 1942-1945]. ***PRACTICE AREAS:*** Trusts and Estates; Real Estate.

REPRESENTATIVE CLIENTS: Ambank Holdings, Inc. and its subsidiaries including American Bank and Trust Company; Davenport Homes, Inc.; First Trust and Savings Bank; Miller Container Corp.; The National Republic Bank of Chicago; Salzman International, Inc.; Purina Mills, Inc.; St. Paul Insurance Companies; Wells Fargo Bank; Wheatland Bancorp.

LAW OFFICE OF JAY R. HAMILTON, PLC

Established in 2003

NEW VENTURES CENTER, SUITE 100
331 W. 3RD STREET
DAVENPORT, IOWA 52801
Telephone: 563-441-0207
Fax: 563-823-4637
Email: jay@qcpatents.com
URL: http://www.qcpatents.com

Member: Patent Prosecution and Licensing, Intellectual Property, Trademarks, Copyrights, Trade Secrets, Consumer Fraud.

FIRM PROFILE: The Law Office of Jay R. Hamilton, PLC was founded in 2003 by Jay R. Hamilton and serves a wide spectrum of clients including individuals and start-ups as well as companies ranging in size from small to large located across the United States in intellectual property matters, including prosecution, transactional and litigation support.

JAY R. HAMILTON, born Davenport, Iowa, January 4, 1969; admitted to bar, 2000, Illinois; 2001, Iowa; registered to practice before U.S. Patent and Trademark Office. *Education:* University of Iowa (B.S.Ch.E., 1991; M.B.A., Finance & Entrepreneurship, 1999; J.D., with distinction, 2000). Member, Iowa Law Review, 1997. *Member:* Iowa State and Illinois State Bar Associations. ***LANGUAGES:*** English. ***PRACTICE AREAS:*** Patent Prosecution; Intellectual Property; Trademarks; Copyrights; Trade Secrets. ***Email:*** jay@qcpatents.com

Language: English.

REPRESENTATIVE CLIENTS: Calmer Corn Heads, LLC; Sentry Pools; Genesis III; In Pro Seals and Douglas Industries.

HENINGER AND HENINGER

PROFESSIONAL CORPORATION

Established in 1966

SUITE 501, 101 WEST SECOND STREET
DAVENPORT, IOWA 52801
Telephone: 563-324-0418
Fax: 563-324-5808
URL: http://www.heningerlaw.com
URL: http://www.lawyers.com/heningerlaw

General Practice. Business Law, Probate, Real Estate, Health Care, Labor and Employment, Personal Injury, Estate Planning, Medical Malpractice, Professional Liability, Trial Practice.

FIRM PROFILE: Heninger and Heninger is a family law firm spanning four generations of lawyers beginning with Charles C. Heninger who commenced the practice of law in 1900. In 1932, his son, Ralph U. Heninger, joined the practice in Sigourney, Iowa. In 1966, Ralph U. Heninger and Ralph H. Heninger re-established the firm in Davenport, Iowa. Today, Ralph H. Heninger and Ralph W. Heninger continue the family's tradition in the general practice of law in Iowa and Illinois from their office overlooking the Mississippi River.

RALPH U. HENINGER (1908-1993)

RALPH H. HENINGER, born Iowa City, Iowa, March 7, 1933; admitted to bar, 1961, Iowa; 1991, Illinois; U.S. Court of Appeals for the Federal, Seventh and Eighth Circuits; U.S. Supreme Court. *Education:* University of Iowa (B.A., 1955; J.D., 1961). Phi Delta Phi. *Member:* Scott County, Rock Island County, Iowa State (Member, 1979-1984 and Chairman, 1981-1984, Committee on Lawyers Professional Insurance; Member: Business Law Section Council, 1996—; Environmental Law Committee, 1976), Federal and American Bar Associations; Iowa Society of Healthcare Attorneys (President, 1985-1988; Chair, NonProfit Corporation Law Subcommittee, 1991-1994); American Health Lawyers Association. ***REPORTED CASES:*** Ryerson v. First Trust & Sav. Bk., 430 N.W.2d 442 (Iowa 1988). ***PRACTICE AREAS:*** Corporate Law; Probate; Real Estate; Estate Planning; Admiralty Law; Health Care; Family Law. ***Email:*** rhh@heningerlaw.com

RALPH W. HENINGER, born Iowa City, Iowa, March 14, 1959; admitted to bar, 1984, Iowa; 1985, Illinois; U.S. Court of Appeals, Seventh and Eighth Circuits; U.S. Supreme Court. *Education:* Colorado College (B.A., cum laude, 1981); University of Iowa (J.D., with distinction, 1984). *Member:* Scott County (Chair, CLE Committee, 1991-1992; Member, Executive Committee, 1998-2000), Rock Island County, Iowa State, Illinois State and American Bar Associations; Iowa Trial Lawyers Association. ***REPORTED CASES:*** Tredrea v. Anesthesia & Analgesia, P.C., 584 N.W.2d 276 (Iowa 1998); Welte v. Bello, 482 N.W.2d 437 (Iowa 1992); Johnston v. Tri-City Blacktop, 577 N.E.2d 529 (Illinois 1991); Davies v Dooley, 2001 WL 539609. ***PRACTICE AREAS:*** Litigation; Health Care; Labor and Employment; Personal Injury; Medical Malpractice; Trial Practice; Professional Liability. ***Email:*** rwh@heningerlaw.com

(This Listing Continued)

REPRESENTATIVE CLIENTS: Anesthesia & Pain Consultants; Braaten Health; Caronia Corporation; Catlin Underwriting Agency; CNA PRO Insurance; Davenport Emergency Physicians, P.C.; ENT Professional Services; Gastrointestinal Clinic of Quad City; Grampp Realty; HCR ManorCare; Hematology Medical Oncology Assoc.; Illinois-Iowa Blacktop; Midwest Therapy Center; New Choices Incorporated; Quad City Occupational Health; Quad City Safety, Inc.; The Rem Centers; Russell Construction Co.; Sitrick & Assoc., L.L.C.; Tri City Blacktop; Wyffels Hybrids, Inc.

JAMES M. HOOD

Established in 1970

220 EMERSON PLACE, SUITE 100

DAVENPORT, IOWA 52801

Telephone: 563-323-5255

Fax: 563-323-7015

URL: http://www.lawyers.com/jhood

Email: james@jameshood.com

URL: http://www.jameshood.com

Plaintiffs Trial Practice in all Courts. Personal Injury including Automobile Accidents and Injuries, Workers Compensation.

FIRM PROFILE: James M. Hood established his office in 1970. He limits his practice exclusively to personal injury (automobile accidents primarily) and workers' compensation in eastern Iowa. He has over 30 years of experience.

JAMES M. HOOD, born Des Moines, Iowa, March 27, 1945; admitted to bar, 1970, Iowa and U.S. District Court, Southern District of Iowa; 1972, U.S. District Court, Northern District of Iowa; 1973, U.S. District Court, Southern District of Illinois; 1978, U.S. Supreme Court. *Education:* Drake University (B.A., 1967; J.D., 1970). Delta Theta Phi. *Member:* Scott County, Iowa State and American (Member, Sections on: Insurance, Negligence and Compensation Law; Litigation) Bar Associations; Association of Trial Lawyers of Iowa; The Association of Trial Lawyers of America; Iowa Association of Workers Compensation Lawyers. ***PRACTICE AREAS:*** Personal Injury; Automobile Accidents and Injuries; Workers Compensation.

HOPKINS & HUEBNER, P.C.

100 EAST KIMBERLY ROAD., SUITE 704

DAVENPORT, IOWA 52806-5944

Telephone: 319-445-2264

Fax: 319-445-2267

Des Moines, Iowa Office: Suite 111, Terrace Center, 2700 Grand Avenue, 50312-5213. Telephone: 515-244-0111. Fax: 515-244-8935.

General Practice. Insurance, Casualty, Workers Compensation, Corporation, Employment, Municipal, Civil Rights, Products Liability, Contracts. Trials in all Courts, Business and Corporation Law, and Real Estate.

M. ANNE McATEE, born 1961; admitted to bar, 1989, Iowa; 1998, Illinois. *Education:* University of Iowa (B.B.A., 1982); St. Ambrose University (M.B.A., 1986); Creighton University (J.D., 1989). *Member:* Iowa Association of Workers' Compensation Lawyers.

MICHAEL C. WALKER, born 1965; admitted to bar, 1992, Iowa and Illinois. *Education:* Iowa State University (B.A., with distinction, 1988); University of Iowa (J.D., 1992). *Member:* American, Iowa State, Illinois State, Scott County and Rock Island County Bar Associations; Iowa Trial Lawyers Association. ***Email:*** mwalker@hopkinsandhuebner.com

---

PAUL SALABERT, JR., born 1970; admitted to bar, 1996, Illinois; 2003, Iowa. *Education:* Augustana College (B.A., 1992); Northwestern University School of Law (J.D., 1995). *Member:* Illinois Trial Lawyers Association (Member, Workers Compensation Committee, 1996—); The Association of Trial Lawyers of America (Member, Workers' Compensation and Workplace Injury Section, 1996—); Rock Island County (Board Member, 2001—) and Illinois State Bar Associations. ***Email:*** psalaber@hopkinsandhuebner.com

NATHAN M. SONDGEROTH, born 1979; admitted to bar, 2004, Iowa. *Education:* Augustana College (B.A., cum laude, 2001); University of Iowa College of Law (J.D., 2004). *Member:* Scott County and Iowa State Bar Associations. ***Email:*** nsondger@hopkinsandhuebner.com

(For complete biographical data on all personnel, see Professional Biographies at Des Moines, Iowa)

KATZ, HUNTOON & FIEWEGER, P.C.

DAVENPORT, IOWA

(See Moline)

Civil Trial and Appellate Practice. Personal Injury, Insurance, Commercial, Banking, Bank and Savings and Loan Failures, Bankruptcy, Corporation, Probate, Real Estate, Labor Relations, Taxation, Professional Malpractice, Products Liability, Workers Compensation, Employment, Administrative, Public, School and Municipal Law and Business Crimes.

LANE & WATERMAN LLP

Established in 1854

220 NORTH MAIN STREET, SUITE 600

DAVENPORT, IOWA 52801

Telephone: 563-324-3246

Fax: 563-324-1616

URL: http://www.l-wlaw.com

Rock Island, Illinois Office: 224 18th Street, Suite 500. Telephone: 309-786-1600. Fax: 309-786-1794.

(This Listing Continued)

General Civil Practice, Corporation, Business, Banking, Taxation, Securities, Labor, Employment Discrimination, Environmental, Health Care, Insurance Defense, Pension and Profit-Sharing, Real Estate, Estate and Probate, Wills and Trusts.

Davison & True .... (1854-1873)
Davison & Lane .... (1873-1902)

MEMBERS OF FIRM

JOE R. LANE (1902-1931)

CHARLES M. WATERMAN (1902-1924)

WILLIAM C. DAVIDSON, born June 24, 1941; admitted to bar, 1968, Illinois and Iowa. *Education:* Bradley University (B.A., 1965); University of Illinois (J.D., 1968). Phi Delta Phi. Fellow: Iowa Academy of Trial Lawyers; Iowa Council of School Board Attorneys. ***PRACTICE AREAS:*** Labor and Employment Law; Education Law; Litigation. ***Email:*** wdavidson@l-wlaw.com

C. DANA WATERMAN, III, born November 28, 1946; admitted to bar, 1971, Iowa. *Education:* Phillips Academy and Dartmouth College (A.B., 1968); University of Iowa (J.D., 1971). Phi Delta Phi. *Member:* American Society of Corporate Secretaries; Iowa Council of School Board Attorneys (Chairman, 1989). ***PRACTICE AREAS:*** Securities Law; Corporate Law; Communications Law. ***Email:*** dwaterman@l-wlaw.com

CHARLES E. MILLER, born June 13, 1945; admitted to bar, 1973, Iowa; 1989, Illinois. *Education:* Phillips Exeter Academy and Northwestern University (A.B., 1966); University of Iowa (J.D., with distinction, 1973). Phi Delta Phi. Member, Dillon Inn of Court (Treasurer, 1993-1995). Member: Iowa Supreme Court Advisory Committee on the Rules of Civil Procedure, 1993-1998; Iowa Uniform Court Instruction Committee, 1983-1986. *Member:* Iowa Academy of Trial Lawyers; Iowa Defense Counsel Association (President, 1995-1996); International Association of Defense Counsel. [CDR, U.S. Navy, 1966-1969]. ***PRACTICE AREAS:*** Labor and Employment Law; Defense Litigation; Malpractice Defense. ***Email:*** cmiller@l-wlaw.com

JAMES A. MEZVINSKY, born September 30, 1948; admitted to bar, 1973, Texas; 1987, Iowa. *Education:* Northwestern University; University of Iowa (B.B.A., 1970); Southern Methodist University (J.D., 1973). Certified Public Accountant: Iowa, 1975; Illinois, 1982. ***PRACTICE AREAS:*** Banking Law; Corporate Law; Taxation; Estate Planning. ***Email:*** jmezvinsky@l-wlaw.com

DAVID A. DETTMANN, born March 30, 1949; admitted to bar, 1974, Iowa; 1993, Illinois. *Education:* Luther College (B.A., 1971); Drake University (M.B.A., 1974; J.D., 1974). Certified Public Accountant, Iowa, 1976. *Member:* National Association of Estate Planners - Accredited Estate Planner; American College of Real Estate Lawyers (1994—). Fellow, The American College of Trust and Estate Counsel. ***PRACTICE AREAS:*** ERISA; Estate Planning; Real Estate (Property) Law. ***Email:*** ddettmann@l-wlaw.com

DANA M. CRAIG, born June 12, 1950; admitted to bar, 1975, Iowa; 1989, Illinois. *Education:* Iowa State University (B.S., with distinction, 1972); University of Michigan (J.D., 1975). *Member:* Iowa Defense Counsel Association; Propane Gas Defense Association; American Intellectual Property Association. ***PRACTICE AREAS:*** Litigation; Product Liability Law; Construction Law; Computer Law; Trademark, Copyright and Unfair Competition. ***Email:*** dcraig@l-wlaw.com

TERRY M. GIEBELSTEIN, born April 8, 1953; admitted to bar, 1976, Iowa; 1977, Illinois. *Education:* University of Iowa (B.A., 1974; J.D., with highest distinction, 1976). Phi Beta Kappa; Order of the Coif. ***PRACTICE AREAS:*** Commercial Law; Litigation. ***Email:*** tgiebelstein@l-wlaw.com

RAND S. WONIO, born July 17, 1950; admitted to bar, 1977, Iowa. *Education:* St. Ambrose College (B.A., 1973); St. Louis University (J.D., cum laude, 1977). Fellow, Iowa Academy of Trial Lawyers. ***PRACTICE AREAS:*** Accident and Personal Injury; Products Liability Law; Business Litigation. ***Email:*** rwonio@l-wlaw.com

CURTIS E. BEASON, born January 14, 1952; admitted to bar, 1980, Iowa. *Education:* DePauw University (B.A., 1974); Southern Methodist University (M. Th., 1980; J.D., 1980). Phi Beta Kappa. ***PRACTICE AREAS:*** Zoning Law; Gaming Law; Environmental Law. ***Email:*** cbeason@l-wlaw.com

ROBERT V. P. WATERMAN, JR., born November 20, 1955; admitted to bar, 1981, Iowa; 1983, Illinois. *Education:* Northwestern University (B.A., 1978); University of Iowa (J.D., 1981). Fellow: American College of Trial Lawyers; Iowa Academy of Trial Lawyers; Iowa Defense Counsel Association; Illinois Association of Defense Trial Counsel; Quad City Claims Association (President, 1987-1988). ***PRACTICE AREAS:*** Litigation; Insurance Law; Environmental Coverage Litigation. ***Email:*** bwaterman@l-wlaw.com

PETER J. BENSON, born March 7, 1957; admitted to bar, 1982, Iowa; 1983, Illinois. *Education:* Northwestern University (B.A., 1979); University of Iowa (J.D., with high distinction, 1982). Order of the Coif. *Member:* Iowa Society of Hospital Attorneys (President, 1997-1998); American Health Lawyers Association. ***PRACTICE AREAS:*** Health (Health Care) and Hospital Law; Corporate Law. ***Email:*** pbenson@l-wlaw.com

MICHAEL L. NOYES, born October 13, 1946; admitted to bar, 1971, Iowa. *Education:* University of Iowa (B.A., 1968; J.D., 1971). Phi Delta Phi. Faculty, National Institute for Trial Advocacy, Mid-America Regional, 1994. Trustee, Davenport Public Library, 1984— (President, 1995-2000). *Member:* Iowa Academy of Trial Lawyers; Iowa Defense Counsel Association; Defense Research Institute; American Judicature Society. ***PRACTICE AREAS:*** Business Litigation; Business Law. ***Email:*** mnoyes@l-wlaw.com

R. SCOTT VAN VOOREN, born March 10, 1957; admitted to bar, 1983, Iowa; 1990, Illinois. *Education:* Creighton University (B.S.B.A., cum laude, 1979); University of Iowa (J.D., with distinction, 1983). Beta Alpha Psi. Certified Public Accountant, Nebraska, 1980; Iowa, 1983. *Member:* Iowa State (Member: Committee on Taxation, 1988-1990; Council of Taxation Section, 1990-1991 and 1994-1997; Council of Probate and Trust Law Section, 1991-1994) and American (Member, Sections on: Taxation; Business Law; Member, Forum Committee on Franchising) Bar Associations. ***PRACTICE AREAS:*** Business Law; Estate Planning. ***Email:*** svanvooren@l-wlaw.com

THOMAS D. WATERMAN, born June 25, 1959; admitted to bar, 1984, Iowa; 1985, Illinois; 1986, U.S. District Court, Northern and Southern Districts of Iowa; 1988, U.S. Dis-

(This Listing Continued)

LANE & WATERMAN LLP, Davenport—Continued

trict Court, Central District of Illinois; U.S. Court of Appeals, Eighth Circuit; 1997, U.S. Court of Appeals, Seventh Circuit; 2003, U.S. Supreme Court. *Education:* Dartmouth College (B.A., cum laude, 1981); University of Iowa (J.D., 1984). Order of the Coif. *Member:* Iowa Academy of Trial Lawyers; Iowa Defense Counsel Association; Defense Research Institute; Federation of Defense & Corporate Counsel. ***PRACTICE AREAS:*** Litigation; Product Liability. ***Email:*** twaterman@l-wlaw.com

JOHN D. TELLEEN, born April 26, 1958; admitted to bar, 1984, Iowa; 1985, Illinois. *Education:* Augustana College (B.A., cum laude, 1980); University of Iowa (J.D., with distinction, 1984). *Member:* Iowa Defense Counsel Association; Illinois Association of Defense Trial Counsel. ***PRACTICE AREAS:*** Civil Litigation; Insurance Law; Environmental Coverage Litigation. ***Email:*** jtelleen@l-wlaw.com

RICHARD A. DAVIDSON, born September 12, 1959; admitted to bar, 1984, Iowa; 1986, Illinois. *Education:* Drake University (B.S.B.A., magna cum laude, 1981; J.D., with honors, 1984). Beta Alpha Psi; Order of the Coif. Law Clerk, Fifth Judicial District of Iowa, 1984-1985. ***PRACTICE AREAS:*** Real Estate; Commercial Law; Bankruptcy Law; Probate Law. ***Email:*** rdavidson@l-wlaw.com

MICHAEL P. BYRNE, born May 12, 1960; admitted to bar, 1986, Iowa; 1987, Illinois. *Education:* University of Iowa (B.B.A., 1982); University of Kansas (J.D., 1986). Order of the Coif. Member: Iowa Board of Professional Ethics and Conduct, 1994—; Iowa Board of Medical Examiners, 2000—. *Member:* Iowa Defense Counsel Association; American Health Lawyers Association; Iowa Society of Hospital Attorneys; Iowa State Board of Medical Examiners; Iowa Supreme Court Board of Ethics and Conduct. ***PRACTICE AREAS:*** Health (Healthcare) and Hospital Law; Insurance Coverage. ***Email:*** mbyrne@l-wlaw.com

EDMUND H. CARROLL, JR., born February 21, 1958; admitted to bar, 1985, Wisconsin; 1986, Iowa; 1987, Illinois. *Education:* Georgetown University (B.A., with distinction, 1980); University of Wisconsin Law School; Marquette University (J.D., 1985). ***PRACTICE AREAS:*** Business Acquisitions Law; Securities; Closely Held Business; Zoning Law. ***Email:*** ecarroll@l-wlaw.com

JEFFREY W. PAUL, born November 29, 1951; admitted to bar, 1989, Iowa and Illinois. *Education:* Iowa State University (B.S., 1974); University of Iowa (J.D., with distinction, 1989). ***PRACTICE AREAS:*** Estate Planning; Real Estate; Agricultural Law. ***Email:*** jpaul@l-wlaw.com

THEODORE F. OLT III, born February 23, 1962; admitted to bar, 1995, Iowa and Illinois. *Education:* United States Naval Academy (B.S., 1985); University of Iowa (J.D., 1994). Order of the Coif. [LT., U.S. Navy, 1985-1992]. ***Email:*** tolt3@l-wlaw.com

CAMERON A. DAVIDSON, born February 24, 1968; admitted to bar, 1995, Iowa; 1997, Illinois. *Education:* St. Norbert College (B.A., cum laude, 1990); Hamline University (J.D., with honors, 1995). ***Email:*** cdavidson@l-wlaw.com

JUDITH L. HERRMANN, born April 15, 1969; admitted to bar, 1994, Illinois; 1996, Iowa. *Education:* Augustana College (B.A., 1991); Valparaiso University (J.D., summa cum laude, 1994). Sigma Tau Delta; Phi Delta Phi. ***Email:*** jherrmann@l-wlaw.com

ROBERT BLAKE McMONAGLE, born June 5, 1963; admitted to bar, 1995, Illinois; 1996, California; 1997, Iowa. *Education:* University of Notre Dame (B.A., 1985; J.D., 1994). Law Clerk, Hon. John J. Hargrove, U.S. Bankruptcy Court, Southern District of California, 1994-1995. Assistant State's Attorney, Cook County, Illinois, 1995-1996. [Lt. Col., U.S. Marine Corps Reserve, 1985—]. ***Email:*** rmcmonagle@l-wlaw.com

CHRISTOPHER J. CURRAN, born August 6, 1971; admitted to bar, 1997, Iowa; 1998, Illinois. *Education:* St. Ambrose University (B.A., summa cum laude, 1994); University of Iowa (J.D., with distinction, 1997). ***Email:*** ccurran@l-wlaw.com

JOSEPH C. JUDGE, born January 6, 1970; admitted to bar, 1998, Iowa and Illinois. *Education:* University of Northern Iowa (B.A., 1993); University of Iowa College of Law (J.D., with high distinction, 1997). Order of the Coif. Certified Public Accountant, Iowa, 1993. ***Email:*** jjudge@l-wlaw.com

JASON J. O'ROURKE, born March 24, 1973; admitted to bar, 1998, Iowa; 1999, Illinois. *Education:* Creighton University (B.A., cum laude, 1995; J.D., magna cum laude, 1998). ***PRACTICE AREAS:*** Products Liability; Construction Law; Insurance Defense. ***Email:*** jo'rourke@l-wlaw.com

TROY D. VENNER, born December 26, 1971; admitted to bar, 1998, Iowa; 1999, Illinois. *Education:* University of Wisconsin - La Crosse (B.A., 1995); Drake University (J.D., 1998). ***Email:*** tlv@l-wlaw.com

COURTNEY M. KAY-DECKER, born May 7, 1973; admitted to bar, 1997, Iowa; 1998, Illinois. *Education:* Northwestern University (B.A., 1994); University of Iowa (J.D., with distinction, 1997). *Member:* Iowa State Board of Tax Review. ***PRACTICE AREAS:*** Corporate; Estate Planning. ***Email:*** ckay-decker@l-wlaw.com

TROY A. HOWELL, born March 9, 1974; admitted to bar, 1999, Iowa; 2000, Illinois. *Education:* University of Illinois (B.A., 1996); University of Iowa (J.D., 1999). ***PRACTICE AREAS:*** Civil Defense Litigation. ***Email:*** thowell@l-wlaw.com

DIANE M. REINSCH, born September 14, 1958; admitted to bar, 1996, Iowa and Illinois. *Education:* Iowa State University (B.A., with high distinction, 1984); University of Iowa (M.A., 1989; J.D., with high distinction, 1995). ***PRACTICE AREAS:*** Civil Litigation; Insurance Defense. ***Email:*** dreinsch@l-wlaw.com

ASSOCIATES

CATHERINE E.E. HULT, born March 8, 1974; admitted to bar, 1999, Iowa; 2000, Illinois. *Education:* University of South Dakota (B.S., summa cum laude, 1996); Creighton University School of Law (J.D., summa cum laude, 1999). ***PRACTICE AREAS:*** Real Estate; Estate Planning. ***Email:*** chult@l-wlaw.com

MIKKIE R. SCHILTZ, born February 28, 1973; admitted to bar, 1997, Illinois; 2000, Georgia; 2002, Iowa. *Education:* University of West Florida (B.A., magna cum laude, 1994); University of Illinois (J.D., summa cum laude, 1997). Phi Delta Phi. ***Email:*** mschiltz@l-wlaw.com

(This Listing Continued)

DIANE E. PUTHOFF, born December 29, 1975; admitted to bar, 2001, Iowa; 2002, Illinois. *Education:* Marquette University (B.A., 1998); Creighton University School of Law (M.B.A., 2001; J.D., cum laude, 2001). Law Clerk, Hon. Linda K. Neuman, Iowa Supreme Court, 2001-2002. ***Email:*** dputhoff@l-wlaw.com

STACEY L. HAWKE, born Mesa, Arizona, July 28, 1976; admitted to bar, 2003, Iowa. *Education:* University of Missouri (B.A., B.J., magna cum laude, 1998); University of Iowa (J.D., with high distinction, 2003). ***Email:*** shawke@l-wlaw.com

WENDY S. MEYER, born Garner, Iowa, June 16, 1972; admitted to bar, 2003, Iowa. *Education:* University of Iowa (B.A., 1995; J.D., with distinction, 2003). ***Email:*** wmeyer@l-wlaw.com

ERIKA L. GILMORE, born September 21, 1977; admitted to bar, 2005, Illinois (Not admitted in Iowa). *Education:* Purdue University (B.S., 2000); University of Iowa (J.D., with distinction, 2004). ***Email:*** egilmore@l-wlaw.com

OF COUNSEL

ROBERT A. VAN VOOREN, born May 28, 1933; admitted to bar, 1960, Iowa and Illinois. *Education:* Marquette University (B.S., 1955); Northwestern University (J.D., 1960). Davenport City Attorney, 1974. Member, American Bar Association House of Delegates, 1994-1996. *Member:* Iowa State Bar Association (Member, Board of Governors, 1978-1982; Vice President, 1982-1983; President-Elect, 1983-1984; President, 1984-1985; President & Board Member, Volunteer Lawyers Project, 1988-1991). Fellow: Iowa Academy of Trial Lawyers (Member, Board of Governors, 1981-1982; Vice President, 1982-1983; President, 1983-1984); Advocate, American Board of Trial Advocates. Fellow, American Bar Foundation. Fellow, American College of Trial Lawyers. ***PRACTICE AREAS:*** Litigation; Commercial Law; Environmental Law. ***Email:*** rvanvooren@l-wlaw.com

THOMAS N. KAMP, born April 13, 1938; admitted to bar, 1965, Iowa. *Education:* University of Notre Dame (B.B.A., 1960); University of Iowa (J.D., with high distinction, 1965). Order of the Coif; Phi Delta Phi. *Member:* Scott County (Member, Executive Board, 1985-1995) and Iowa State (President, 1994; President-Elect, 1993; Vice President, 1992; Board of Governors, 1986-1992) Bar Associations; Iowa Defense Counsel Association; Iowa Association of Workers Compensation Lawyers, Inc. (Board of Governors, 1990-1992; Treasurer, 1993; Secretary, 1994; Vice-President, 1995; President, 1996); Iowa Worker's Compensation Advisory Committee, Inc. (President, 1987; Vice President, 1986; Treasurer, 1985). Fellow: American College of Trial Lawyers (State Chair, 1997-1998); Iowa Academy of Trial Lawyers; Iowa State Bar Foundation. [LCDR, U.S. Navy, 1960-1962]. ***PRACTICE AREAS:*** Workers Compensation Law; Defense Litigation. ***Email:*** tkamp@l-wlaw.com

All attorneys are members of the Iowa State and Scott County Bar Associations.

COUNSEL FOR: Bettendorf Community School District; Davenport Community School District;Eastern Iowa Community College District; North Scott Community School District; Pleasant Valley Community School District; St. Ambrose University; Alter Companies; Diocese of Davenport;Estes Company; Genesis Health System; Happy Joe's Pizza & Ice Cream Parlor, Inc.; Iowa-American Water Co.; Isle of Capri Casinos; Lee Enterprises, Incorporated; McCarthy Improvement Co.; McGladrey & Pullen, L.L.P.; Mel Foster Co., Inc.; MidAmerican Energy Co.;THE National Bank, N.A.; Ruhl & Ruhl, Realtors; Russell Construction, Inc.; The Schebler Co.;Sears Manufacturing Co.; Swiss Valley Farms Co.; Von Maur, Inc.; Whitey's Ice Cream Manufacturers, Inc. LOCAL COUNSEL FOR: Aluminum Company of America; Commercial Union Insurance Co.;Deere & Co.; Employers Mutual Companies; Farm Bureau Mutual Insurance Co.; VerizonWireless; The Hartford Insurance Group; Insurance Company of North America; Maryland Insurance Co.; Medical Protective Co.; Midwest Medical Insurance Company; Ryan Companies;Winegard Company; Quad City Bank & Trust.

McCARTHY, CALLAS, FUHR & ELLISON, P.C.

DAVENPORT, IOWA

(See Rock Island, Illinois)

Divorce, Commercial and Residential Real Estate, Labor Law, Labor Relations, Labor Arbitration, Commercial Litigation, Criminal Defense, Probate and Probate Administration, Inheritance, Dram Shop Law, Liquor Liability, Casualty Insurance, Medical Negligence, Debtor/Creditor Bankruptcy, ERISA, Personal Injury, Wrongful Death, Maritime Accidents, Products Liability, Traffic Violations.

McCARTHY, LAMMERS & HINES

701 KAHL BUILDING
DAVENPORT, IOWA 52801
Telephone: 563-324-9117
Fax: 563-324-8367
Email: mjmccarthylwr@aol.com
URL: http://www.mccarthylammershines.com

General Civil Practice. Trials, Personal Injury, Workers Compensation, Wills, Trusts, Probate, Criminal Law, Real Estate, Family Law, Divorce, Child Custody, Estate Planning, Bankruptcy, Juvenile.

MEMBERS OF FIRM

MARTIN F. McCARTHY (1904-1987)

MICHAEL J. McCARTHY, born Davenport, Iowa, January 6, 1949; admitted to bar, 1976, Iowa; U.S. District Court, Southern District of Iowa and Central District of Illinois; U.S. Court of Appeals, Seventh and Eighth Circuits. *Education:* University of Iowa (B.A., 1971); Creighton University (J.D., 1976). Member, Editorial Staff, Creighton Law Review, 1975-1976. Member, National Moot Court Team, 1975. *Member:* Iowa State and American Bar Associations; Association of Trial Lawyers of Iowa; The Association of Trial Lawyers of America. ***Email:*** mjmccarthylwr@aol.com

LAWRENCE J. LAMMERS, born Davenport, Iowa, May 20, 1953; admitted to bar, 1978, Iowa. *Education:* University of Notre Dame (B.A., 1975); Creighton University (J.D., 1978). *Member:* Scott County, Iowa State and American Bar Associations.

(This Listing Continued)

MICHAEL T. HINES, born Davenport, Iowa, November 9, 1956; admitted to bar, 1984, Iowa; U.S. District Court, Southern District of Iowa. *Education:* College of St. Thomas (B.A. in English, 1979); St. Louis University (J.D., 1983). *Member:* Scott County, Iowa State and American Bar Associations; Association of Iowa Trial Lawyers.

REFERENCE: Wells Fargo, Davenport, Iowa.

McDONALD, WOODWARD & IVERS, P.C.

Established in 1942

JERSEY RIDGE OFFICE CENTER
3432 JERSEY RIDGE ROAD
P.O. BOX 2746
DAVENPORT, IOWA 52809-2746
Telephone: 563-355-6478
Fax: 563-355-1354
URL: http://www.mwilawyers.com

Civil Trial Practice and Appeals in State and Federal Courts. Insurance Defense, Workers Compensation, Personal Injury, Real Estate, Professional Negligence, Business Law, Litigation, Probate, Wills, Trusts, Employment Discrimination, Contracts, Corporate Law, Wrongful Death, Medical Malpractice, Commercial Litigation, Construction Litigation.

ELLIOTT R. McDONALD, III, born Davenport, Iowa, March 6, 1956; admitted to bar, 1981, Iowa; U.S. District Court, Southern and Northern Districts of Iowa; U.S. District Court, Central District of Illinois; U.S. Court of Appeals, Eighth Circuit; 1993, Illinois. *Education:* University of Iowa (B.A., 1978; J.D., with distinction, 1981). Phi Beta Kappa. *Member:* Scott County, Rock Island County, Illinois State and Iowa State Bar Associations; Defense Research Institute; Illinois Association of Defense Trial Counsel. ***PRACTICE AREAS:*** Civil Litigation; Personal Injury; Products Liability; Professional Liability; Construction Litigation; Workers Compensation. ***Email:*** emcdonald3@mwilawyers.com

PATRICIA RHODES CEPICAN (1950-2004)

PATRICK L. WOODWARD, born Davenport, Iowa, February 17, 1957; admitted to bar, 1983, Iowa; 1986, Washington; U.S. District Court, Southern and Northern Districts of Iowa, U.S. District Court, Central District of Illinois and U.S. Court of Appeals, Seventh and Eighth Circuits. *Education:* St. Ambrose College (B.A., with honors, 1979); University of Iowa (J.D., with distinction, 1983). *Member:* Scott County, Washington State, Iowa State and American (Member, Sections on: Tort and Insurance Practice) Bar Associations; Iowa Defense Counsel Association; Iowa Association of Trial Lawyers; Defense Research Institute; The Association of Trial Lawyers of America.nl. [Lt., U.S. Navy, JAGC, 1983-1986]. ***PRACTICE AREAS:*** Insurance Litigation; Workers Compensation; Personal Injury; Trial Practice. ***Email:*** pwoodward@mwilawyers.com

BRIAN C. IVERS, born Ft. Benning, Georgia, September 24, 1962; admitted to bar, 1990, Iowa and Illinois; U.S. District Court, Southern and Northern Districts of Iowa. *Education:* University of Iowa (B.G.S., 1987; J.D., with distinction, 1990). Recipient: Stephenson Competition Best Advocate Award; Iowa Academy of Trial Lawyers Best Advocate Award. *Member:* Scott County, Iowa State, Illinois State and American Bar Associations; Iowa Defense Counsel Association; Illinois Defense Counsel Association. [Sgt., U.S. Army, 1st 75th Ranger Batt., 1982-1985]. ***PRACTICE AREAS:*** Trial Practice; Insurance Defense; Plaintiff Personal Injury; Workers Compensation. ***Email:*** bivers@mwilawyers.com

ELLIOTT R. (JACK) McDONALD, JR., born Peoria, Illinois, February 10, 1929; admitted to bar, 1952, Iowa; 1954, Illinois. *Education:* State University of Iowa (B.A., 1950; J.D., 1952). Phi Alpha Delta. Member, 1990-1999 and Chairman, 1996-1999, Iowa Board of Law Examiners. *Member:* Scott County (President, 1975-1976), Iowa State and American Bar Associations. ***PRACTICE AREAS:*** Real Estate; Workers Compensation; Probate. ***Email:*** mcdonaldjr@mwilawyers.com

---

HEATHER L. CARLSON, born Sterling, Illinois; admitted to bar, 1999, Kansas; 2000, Missouri and Illinois; 2005, U.S. District Court, Central District of Illinois (Not admitted in Iowa). *Education:* Augustana College (B.A., cum laude, 1996); St. Louis University (J.D., cum laude, 1999). Executive Editor, St. Louis University Public Law Review, 1998-1999. Author: "Freedom at Risk: The Implications of the City of Boerne v. Flores on the Merger of Catholic and Non-Catholic Hospitals," 17 St. Louis U. Pub.L. Rev. 157 (1997).*Member:* Illinois State Bar Association; The Missouri Bar. ***PRACTICE AREAS:*** Personal Injury; Workers Compensation; Insurance Litigation. ***Email:*** hcarlson@mwilawyers.com

HOWARD ZIMMERLE II, born Fort Dodge, Iowa, July 3, 1981; admitted to bar, 2005, Iowa. *Education:* University of Northern Iowa (B.A., cum laude, 2002); University of Iowa College of Law (J.D., 2005). Author: Note: "Common Sense v. The EEOC: Co-Worker Ostracism and Shunning as Retaliation Under Title VII," 30 J. Corp. L 627 (2005). *Member:* Iowa State and Scott County Bar Associations. ***PRACTICE AREAS:*** Insurance Litigation; Personal Injury; Workers Compensation. ***Email:*** hzimmerle@mwilawyers.com

REPRESENTATIVE CLIENTS: Altorfer Machinery Co.; American Family Insurance; CNA Insurance; Nationwide Insurance Co.; Scottsdale Insurance Co.; Sentry Insurance Co.; Shelter Insurance Co.; State Farm Fire & Casualty Co.; Ohio Casualty Ins.; PAFCO/SYMONS Int'l; Prudential Property & Casualty Co.; Chubb Insurance; Empire Fire & Casualty; Farm Bureau; Encompass Insurance; Merchants Bonding Co.; Unitrin Specialty Lines.
REFERENCE: Northwest Bank and Trust Co.

JOHN O. MOELLER

601 BRADY STREET, SUITE 303
DAVENPORT, IOWA 52803
Telephone: 563-323-3014
Fax: 563-323-9403
Email: moellerj@muscanet.com
URL: http://www.johnmoeller.com

General Practice including but not limited to trial and appellate practice concerning criminal law, personal injury, product liability, real estate, business law, admirality law and maritime law in all State and Federal Courts.

(This Listing Continued)

JOHN O. MOELLER, born 1953; admitted to bar, 1979, Iowa. *Education:* University of Iowa (B.G.S., 1976; J.D., 1978). *Member:* Scott County and Iowa State Bar Associations; The Association of Trial Lawyers of America; National Association of Criminal Defense Lawyers.

NYEMASTER, GOODE, WEST, HANSELL & O'BRIEN

A PROFESSIONAL CORPORATION

DAVENPORT, IOWA

(See Des Moines)

General Civil Practice including Corporate, Securities, Antitrust, Insurance, Banking, Commercial Law, Cooperative Law, Probate, Real Estate, Taxation, Workers Compensation, Municipal, Legislative, Labor, Administrative Law and Trials in all Courts.

PAPPAS & SCHNELL, P.C.

DAVENPORT, IOWA

(See Rock Island, Illinois)

Labor and Employment, Litigation, Trusts and Estates, Probate, Taxation, Corporate, Business Law, Real Estate, Education.

PASTRNAK LAW FIRM, P.C.

313 WEST THIRD STREET
DAVENPORT, IOWA 52801
Telephone: 563-323-7737
Fax: 563-323-7739
Email: tpastrnak@pastrnak.com

Moline, Illinois Office: 1535-47th Avenue, Suite 3, 61265. Telephone: 309-757-7737. Fax: 309-763-3858.

General Civil and Trial Practice. Corporation, Business, Banking, Tax-Exempt Financing, Labor, Employment Discrimination, Administrative, Creditor Bankruptcy, Personal Injury and Property Damage Law, Real Estate, Probate, Estate Planning and Family Law.

THOMAS J. PASTRNAK, born Inglewood, California, January 7, 1959; admitted to bar, 1984, Iowa, Illinois, U.S. Supreme Court and U.S. Court of Appeals, Eighth Circuit. *Education:* University of Chicago (B.A., 1981); Drake University (J.D., 1984). Staff Member, Drake Law Review, 1982-1984. *Member:* Scott County, Rock Island County, Iowa State (Member, Sections on: Business Law, Bankruptcy, and Health Law), Illinois State and American Bar Associations. ***PRACTICE AREAS:*** Business; Creditor-Debtor; Health Law. ***Email:*** tpastrnak@pastrnak.com

CANDY K. PASTRNAK, born Guthrie Center, Iowa, March 2, 1958; admitted to bar, 1983, Iowa; 1985, Illinois and U.S. District Court, Central District of Illinois; 1987, U.S. Court of Appeals, Seventh Circuit; 1990, U.S. District Court, Southern District of Iowa; 1992, U.S. Supreme Court. *Education:* Drake University (B.A., magna cum laude, 1980; J.D., 1983). Editor, Drake Legal Research Service, 1982-1983. Judicial Clerk, District 2B, Iowa State Judiciary, 1984-1985. Member, Board of Directors, 1992-1998, Vice-President, 1993-1995, President, 1995-1996 and Board Member, 2004—, YWCA of the Quad Cities. *Member:* Rock Island County (Illinois), Scott County (Iowa), Illinois State and Iowa State (Member, Sections on: Civil Practice; Family Law; Workers Compensation) Bar Associations; Iowa Trial Lawyers Association. ***Email:*** ckpastrnak@pastrnak.com

OF COUNSEL

THOMAS R. SCHULZ

ASSOCIATE

WILLIAM P. LAIRD, born Moline, Illinois, July 14, 1949; admitted to bar, 1975, Iowa, Illinois and U.S. District Court, Central District of Illinois. *Education:* Drake University (B.S., 1971; J.D., 1975). Previous Term as: Assistant State's Attorney; Assistant Public Defender; Special Illinois Assistant Public Defender; Special Illinois Assistant Attorney General. Village Attorney for Hillside, Illinois. Member, Rock Island Public Building Commission. *Member:* Winnebago County, Scott County, Rock Island County (Board Member, Continuing Legal Education Committee), Illinois State and Iowa State Bar Associations. ***PRACTICE AREAS:*** Workmen's Compensation; Personal Injury; Criminal Law; Bankruptcy; Real Estate. ***Email:*** wplaird@pastrnak.com

REPRESENTATIVE CLIENTS: *Financial Institutions:* Wells Fargo Bank Iowa, N.A.; Wells Fargo Bank & Trust Company; Mercantile Bank, FSB; First Midwest Bank, N.A.; I.H. Mississippi Valley Credit Union; Pinnacle Bank. *Corporations:* Crowe Thomas Group, Inc.; Gierke-Robinson Co., Inc.; Kelly Construction of Davenport, Inc.; Quad City Freight Services, Inc.; Quad City Consolidation & Distribution, Inc.; Russell Construction Co., Inc.; Star Cres International Resources & Development, Inc.; Whitehall Funding Inc. *Health Care Providers:* Quad Cities Health Providers Group. *Charitable Corporations:* Partnership For Affordable Housing, Inc.

SCHEBLER, WINE & COLLINS

1414 WEST LOCUST STREET
DAVENPORT, IOWA 52804
Telephone: 563-324-1387
Fax: 563-324-1389
Email: swclaw@netexpress.net
URL: http://www.lawyers.com/scheblerwine

Trusts, Wills, Estate Planning, Probate, Buying/Selling, Real Estate, Elder Law, Mortgage Foreclosure, Landlord/Tenant Law.

(This Listing Continued)

SCHEBLER, WINE & COLLINS, Davenport—Continued

MEMBERS OF FIRM

THOMAS G. SCHEBLER, born Davenport, Iowa; admitted to bar, 1961, Iowa and U.S. District Court, Southern District of Iowa. *Education:* St. Ambrose College (B.A., 1957); University of Iowa (J.D., 1961). *Member:* Scott County and Iowa State Bar Associations. ***PRACTICE AREAS:*** Trusts; Wills; Estate Planning; Real Estate; Business Law; Elder Law. ***Email:*** swclaw@netexpress.net

THOMAS L. WINE, born Oelwein, Iowa; admitted to bar, 1961, Iowa. *Education:* University of Iowa (B.S.C., 1959; J.D., 1961). *Member:* Scott County (President, 1982) and Iowa State Bar Associations. ***PRACTICE AREAS:*** Buying and Selling a Home; Wills; Probate; Elder Law; Landlord/Tenant Law; Mortgage Foreclosure. ***Email:*** swclaw@netexpress.net

JOHN J. COLLINS (1923-2005)

KENT A. SIMMONS

Established in 1981

601 BRADY STREET, SUITE 211

DAVENPORT, IOWA 52803

Telephone: 563-322-7784

Fax: 563-323-9309

Email: ttswlaw@bigplanet.com

URL: http://www.kentasimmons.com

Criminal Law, Post Conviction and Habeas Corpus, Trial and Appellate Practice, DWI, Drug Crimes, Felonies, Homicide and Sexual Assault.

KENT A. SIMMONS, born 1955; admitted to bar, 1981, Iowa, U.S. District Court, Northern and Southern Districts of Iowa, U.S. District Court, Central District of Illinois, U.S. Court of Appeals, Eighth Circuit and U.S. Supreme Court. *Education:* University of Iowa (B.A., 1977; J.D., 1980). Commissioner, State of Iowa District Judicial Nominating Commission, 1998-2004.*Member:* Scott County (President, 1996-1997, Vice-President, 1995-1996) and Iowa State (Member, Uniform Jury Instruction Committee, 2001-2007) Bar Associations; National Association of Criminal Defense Lawyers; Iowa Association of Criminal Defense Lawyers; American Inns of Court (Local President, 2002-2003). ***REPORTED CASES:*** State v. Liggins, 524 NW2d 181 (Iowa 1994); State v. Nance, 533 NW2d 557 (Iowa 1995); State v. Sutton, 636 NW2d 107 (Iowa 2001); U.S. v. Hernandez, 301 F.3d 886 (8th Cir. 2002); Fullenwider v. State, 674 NW 2d 73 (Iowa 2004); State v. Tague, 676 N.W.2d 197 (Iowa 2004; State v. McCoy 692 N.W. 2d 6 (Iowa 2005). ***PRACTICE AREAS:*** Criminal Defense.

SNYDER, PARK & NELSON, P.C.

DAVENPORT, IOWA

(See Rock Island, Illinois)

Banking, Bankruptcy, Commercial, Corporation, General Civil Litigation in all State and Federal Courts, Insurance, Labor Law, Probate, Real Estate, Taxation, Estate Planning, Trials, Employment Law, Workers Compensation, Construction and Commercial Litigation and Administrative Law.

STANLEY, LANDE & HUNTER

A PROFESSIONAL CORPORATION

900 U.S. BANK CENTER

201 WEST SECOND STREET

DAVENPORT, IOWA 52801

Telephone: 563-324-1000

Facsimile: 563-326-6266

Email: Contact.us@slhlaw.com

URL: http://www.slhlaw.com

Muscatine, Iowa Office: 301 Iowa Avenue, Suite 400. Telephone: 563-264-5000. Facsimile: 563-263-8775.

Wilton, Iowa Office: 115 West Fourth, P.O. Box 481. Telephone: 563-732-4000. Facsimile: 563-732-2318.

Coralville, Iowa Office: 2201 East Grantview Drive, Suite 200. Telephone: 319-248-9000. Facsimile: 319-248-9001.

General Civil and Trial Practice. Corporation, Business, Banking, Taxation, Securities, Tax-Exempt Financing, Labor, Employment Discrimination, Administrative, Creditor Bankruptcy and Agricultural Law, Insurance Defense, Personal Injury and Property Damage Law, Pension and Profit-Sharing, Real Estate, Probate, Estate Planning and Charitable Trusts and Foundations Law.

ROGER L. LANDE, born Lake Mills, Iowa, November 7, 1936; admitted to bar, 1961, Iowa. *Education:* Iowa State University; University of Iowa (B.A., 1961); University of Iowa (J.D., with distinction, 1961). Member, Editorial Advisory Board, The Journal of Corporation Law, 1976-1999. Director, American Judicature Society, 1982-1986. Director, Iowa Law School Foundation, 1988-2000. Member, Iowa Board of Regents, 1996-2001. *Member:* Muscatine County (President, 1971-1972), Iowa State (Member: Executive Council, Young Lawyers Section, 1968-1973; Committee on Corporation and Business Law, 1970-1977; Board of Governors, 1977-1979; President, 1981-1982) and American Bar Associations. Fellow, American Bar Foundation; Member: Iowa Association of Business and Industry (Director, 1983-1993, Treasurer, 1989-1990, Vice Chairman, 1990-1991 and Chairman, 1991-1992). ***PRACTICE AREAS:*** Corporate Law; Business Acquisitions; Employment Law. ***Email:*** rlande@slhlaw.com

CHARLES R. COULTER, born Webster City, Iowa, June 10, 1940; admitted to bar, 1965, Iowa. *Education:* University of Iowa (B.A., 1962; J.D., with high distinction, 1965). Order of the Coif. *Member:* Muscatine County (President, 1975-1976), Iowa State (Member: Committee on Membership, 1973-1979; Committee on Bar Economics and Law Office Operations, 1979-1987, Chairman, 1981-1986) and American (Member, Section of Law Practice Management; Council Member, 1985-1988; Secretary, 1988-1989; Chair, 1991-1992; Coordinating Commission on Legal Technology, 1991-1997, Chair, 1994-1997; Standing Committee on Technology and Information Systems, 1997-1998) Bar Associations. Fellow: American Bar Foundation; The American College of Trust and Estate Counsel; Iowa State Bar Foundation. ***PRACTICE AREAS:*** Corporate Law; Law Practice Management; Real Estate; Probate. ***Email:*** chuckcoulter@slhlaw.com

ROBERT L. LANDE, born Mason City, Iowa, April 17, 1947; admitted to bar, 1972, Washington; 1973, Iowa; 1977, Illinois; 1979, U.S. Supreme Court. *Education:* University of Iowa (B.S., 1969; J.D., with distinction, 1972). *Member:* Muscatine County (President, 1984-1985), Iowa State (Member, Trade Regulation, Corporate Counsel & Business Law Sections) and American Bar Associations. ***PRACTICE AREAS:*** Business Law; Banking Law; Commercial Law; Construction Law. ***Email:*** blande@slhlaw.com

STEVEN T. HUNTER, born Maquoketa, Iowa, September 29, 1950; admitted to bar, 1974, Iowa; 1978, U.S. District Court, Southern District of Iowa. *Education:* St. Ambrose University (B.A., 1972); University of Iowa (J.D., with distinction, 1974). City Attorney, Riverdale, Iowa. Director, Davenport Commission School District. *Member:* Scott County, Iowa State (Member, Commercial Law and Bankruptcy Law Section) and American Bar Associations. ***PRACTICE AREAS:*** Corporate Law; Commercial Law; Bankruptcy Law; Banking Law; Real Estate. ***Email:*** shunter@slhlaw.com

DAVID J. MELOY, born Dubuque, Iowa, July 27, 1950; admitted to bar, 1975, Iowa; 1976, U.S. District Court, Southern District of Iowa; 1977, Illinois. *Education:* Iowa State University; University of Iowa (B.A., 1972; J.D., with high distinction, 1975). Order of the Coif; Phi Delta Phi. Law Clerk to Justice Harvey Uhlenhopp, Iowa Supreme Court, 1975-1976. *Member:* Muscatine County (President, 1990-1991), Iowa State and American Bar Associations. ***PRACTICE AREAS:*** Business Law; Environmental Law. ***Email:*** dmeloy@slhlaw.com

PATRICK W. DRISCOLL, born Bernard, Iowa, March 17, 1945; admitted to bar, 1978, Iowa and U.S. District Court, Northern and Southern Districts of Iowa. *Education:* Loras College (B.A., 1967); Loyola University, Chicago (J.D., 1978). *Member:* Scott County, Iowa State (Member, American Citizenship Committee, 1994—) and American Bar Associations; American Trial Lawyers Association; Association of Trial Lawyers of Iowa (Current President and Chairman of Technology). ***PRACTICE AREAS:*** Civil Trial; General Practice; Litigation; Landlord and Tenant Law. ***Email:*** patdriscoll@slhlaw.com

JOAN U. AXEL, born Fargo, North Dakota, January 21, 1943; admitted to bar, 1982, Iowa. *Education:* Iowa State University (B.S., 1964); University of Iowa (J.D., 1982). Member: 1974-1978 and Chair, 1977-1978, Iowa State Lottery Commission 1986-1991. Member: Iowa Telecommunication and Technology Commission, 1994-2000; Muscatine County Board of Supervisors . Director, Iowa Law School Foundation, 2000—. *Member:* Muscatine County, Iowa State (Member, Supreme Court Commission on Unauthorized Practice of Law, 1996—; Former Member: Supreme Court Grievance Commission; Supreme Court Commission on Rules of Civil Procedure) and American Bar Associations; Iowa Bar Foundation. ***PRACTICE AREAS:*** Health Law; Real Estate; Estate Planning; Probate. ***Email:*** juaxel@slhlaw.com

ERIC J. THOMSEN, born Mason City, Iowa, March 19, 1953; admitted to bar, 1978, Iowa, Wisconsin and U.S. Tax Court. *Education:* Iowa State University (B.S., 1975); University of Iowa (J.D., with distinction, 1978). Certified Public Accountant, Iowa, 1982. Board Member: Lutheran Homes Society; Muscatine Humane Society; Muscatine Community Y Endowment Foundation. *Member:* Muscatine County and Iowa State Bar Associations; American Institute of Certified Public Accountants; Iowa Society of Certified Public Accountants. (Probate, Estate Planning and Tax Department Chair). ***PRACTICE AREAS:*** Estate Planning; Individual Income Tax Planning; Business Tax Planning. ***Email:*** ethomsen@slhlaw.com

CURT A. OPPEL, born Colorado Springs, Colorado, May 16, 1963; admitted to bar, 1988, Nebraska; 1992, Iowa, U.S. District Court, Northern and Southern Districts of Iowa and U.S. Tax Court. *Education:* University of Iowa (B.B.A., 1985); Drake University (J.D., with honors, 1988). Certified Public Accountant, Nebraska, 1990. Author: "An Overview of Section 89," Nebraska Certified Public Accountant Newsletter, April, 1989. *Member:* Scott County, Nebraska State and Iowa State Bar Associations; U.S. Tax Court Bar; American Institute of Certified Public Accountants; Quad City Estate Planning Council; Iowa Society of Certified Public Accountants. ***PRACTICE AREAS:*** Employee Benefits; ERISA; Taxation Law; Estate Planning; Probate Law; Trust Administration; Health Law. ***Email:*** caoppel@slhlaw.com

JOHN A. KUHL, born Ithaca, New York, June 19, 1969; admitted to bar, 1994, Iowa; 1995, Illinois; U.S. District Court, Southern District of Iowa. *Education:* Marquette University (B.S., magna cum laude, 1991); University of Iowa College of Law (J.D., with high distinction, 1994); University of Iowa (M.A., Industrial Relations and Human Resources, 1995). Member, National Moot Court Team, 1993-1994. Recipient, American Jurisprudence Award in Corporations II. City Attorney, Nichols, Iowa. Author: Municipal Policy Leaders' Handbook and 1995 Index of Iowa Laws Relating to Cities. *Member:* Scott County, Iowa State, Illinois State and American Bar Associations; Society for Human Resource Managers; Great River Human Resource Association. ***PRACTICE AREAS:*** Employment Law; Corporate Law; Municipal Law. ***Email:*** jkuhl@slhlaw.com

JOEL K. HERIFORD, born Rock Island, Illinois, March 28, 1957; admitted to bar, 1985, Arizona; 1991, Illinois and Iowa. *Education:* Illinois State University (B.S., 1979); De Paul University College of Law (J.D., 1985). Certified Public Accountant, Illinois, 1979. *Member:* State Bar of Arizona; Illinois State and Iowa State Bar Associations. ***PRACTICE AREAS:*** Estate Planning; Business Transactions; Commercial Real Estate; Residential Real Estate; Probate; Trust Administration. ***Email:*** jheriford@slhlaw.com

H. J. PRIES, born Klagenfurt, Austria, August 4, 1948; admitted to bar, 1977, Iowa; 1997, Illinois; U.S. District Court, Northern and Southern Districts of Iowa; U.S. District Court, Central District of Illinois. *Education:* Ohio State University (B.S., Education, 1971; J.D., 1973). Board, Center for Alcohol and Drug Services, Inc., 1980-1982. Member, Quad

(This Listing Continued)

Cities Old Boy Rugby Football Club. Board Member President, Illinois-Iowa Center for Independent Living. *Member:* Scott County, Rock Island County, Iowa State, Illinois State and American Bar Associations; U.S. Army Special Forces Association (Life Member); U.S. Army Pathfinder Association. [Lt. Col U.S. Army Reserves (Ret.), 1st Special Forces Regiment]. ***PRACTICE AREAS:*** Family Law; Criminal Law; Real Estate; Contracts; Civil Litigation. ***Email:*** hpries@slhlaw.com

STEVEN J. HAVERCAMP, born Bettendorf, Iowa, June 10, 1965; admitted to bar, 1998, Iowa; 1999, Illinois, U.S. District Court, Northern and Southern Districts of Iowa and U.S. District Court, Central District of Illinois; U.S. Bankruptcy Court, Northern and Southern District of Iowa; U.S. Bankruptcy Court, Central District of Illinois. *Education:* University of Northern Iowa (B.A., cum laude, 1992); Drake University (J.D., with honors, 1998). Research Editor, Drake Law Review, 1997-1998. Recipient, Jeff Gilbert Memorial Award, 1996-1997. Co-Author: "China's Environmental Puzzle: Theory and Practice," Journal of Developing Societies, 1994. Board Member, Friends of Davenport Museum of Art, Museum of Art Foundation, 1999-2003; Habitat for Humanity, Habitat Re Store, Quad Cities. *Member:* Scott County, Iowa State and American Bar Associations. ***PRACTICE AREAS:*** Commercial Law; Collections Law; Construction Law; Personal Injury Law; Products Liability. ***Email:*** shavercamp@slhlaw.com

---

BRANDY DULCEAK, born Winfield, Illinois, October 1, 1972; admitted to bar, 2001, Iowa; 2002, Illinois. *Education:* University of Iowa (B.A., Communications, with honors, 1998; J.D., 2001). Recipient, National Association of Women Lawyers Award, 2001. Representative, Seventh District, I.O.W.A., 2001—. Chairperson, Membership Committee, I.O.W.A., 2002—. *Member:* Muscatine County (President, 2004—), Scott County, Iowa State (Member, 2001— and Member, Publicity Committee, 2001—, Young Lawyers Division) and American Bar Associations; Iowa Organization of Women Attorneys. ***PRACTICE AREAS:*** General Practice. ***Email:*** brandyd@slhlaw.com

JEAN E. DRAGON, born Chicago, Illinois, December 19, 1961; admitted to bar, 1995, Illinois; 2003, Iowa. *Education:* University of Dubuque (B.A., 1989); University of Iowa (J.D., with distinction, 1994). ***PRACTICE AREAS:*** General Practice. ***Email:*** jdragon@slhlaw.com

WES A. FOWLER, born Macomb, Illinois, January 10, 1976; admitted to bar, 2001, Iowa. *Education:* University of Iowa (B.A., Political Science, with distinction, 1998; J.D., 2001). *Member:* Iowa State and American Bar Associations. ***PRACTICE AREAS:*** General Practice. ***Email:*** wfowler@slhlaw.com

ANGELA N. REIER, born Winfield, Illinois, June 16, 1980; admitted to bar, 2005, Iowa. *Education:* Northwestern University (B.S., Human Development and Psychological Services, 2002); University of Iowa (J.D., with distinction, 2005). *Member:* Scott County, Iowa and American Bar Associations. ***PRACTICE AREAS:*** General Practice. ***Email:*** areier@slhlaw.com

ANDREW M. TELSCHOW, born Dover, New Jersey, October 20, 1978; admitted to bar, 2004, Iowa. *Education:* Rutgers University (B.A., Political Science, with honors, 2001); University of Iowa (J.D., 2004). Recipient: Michelle Benn Client Representation Award, 2004; Henry Rutgers Scholar. *Member:* Scot County, Iowa State and American Bar Associations. ***PRACTICE AREAS:*** General Practice. ***Email:*** atelschow@slhlaw.com

OF COUNSEL

THOMAS O. LINDBURG

REPRESENTATIVE CLIENTS: Bandag, Incorporated; Carver Enterprise Group; Central Can Company; Central State Bank; Connoisseur Communications; Dovetail Development Group; Farm Bureau Mutual Insurance Co.; Farmers and Merchants Savings Bank (Lone Tree); First National Bank of Muscatine; General Motors Acceptance Corp.; Great American Insurance Co.; H.J. Heinz Company; Hon Industries, Inc. and its subsidiaries; IPSCO Steel Inc.; Liberty Trust & Savings Bank (Durant); Milwaukee Mutual Insurance Company; Monsanto Company; Tech Systems, Inc.; The Family Credit Union; The Stanley Foundation; The Travelers Group, Inc.; Stanley Consultants, Inc, and subsidiaries; Texaco, Inc.; Union Federal Savings and Loan Association of Kewanee, Illinois; Varied Investments, Inc. (Grain Processing Corporation, Kent Feeds, Inc.); West Liberty State Bank.
GENERAL COUNSEL FOR: HWH Corporation; John Keady's General Motors Superstore; Lujack's Northpark Auto Plaza; M.A. Ford Mfg. Co.; Royale International Beverage Co.; The State Bank of Annawan; BT Prime-Mover, Inc.; Tri State Companies, Inc.; Unity Health System; Wilton Industrial Development Corp.; Wilton Precision Steel; WTC Communications, Inc.

STURM & FIX LLP

304 NORTHWEST BANK BUILDING-DOWNTOWN
101 WEST SECOND STREET
DAVENPORT, IOWA 52801-1813
Telephone: 563-323-9731
Fax: 563-323-9709
URL: http://www.hsllp.com

Des Moines, Iowa Office: 206 Sixth Avenue, Suite 1213, 50309-4076. Telephone: 515-288-9589. Fax: 515-288-4860.

Patent, Trademark, Copyright and Unfair Competition Law, Federal Trial Practice, Intellectual Property.

FIRM PROFILE: Sturm & Fix LLP was founded in 1962 and serves a wide spectrum of U.S. and International clients in intellectual property matters, including prosecution and litigation.

MEMBER OF FIRM

JOHN E. CEPICAN, born 1948; admitted to bar, 1974, Iowa; registered to practice before U.S. Patent and Trademark Office. *Education:* Iowa State University (B.S., physics, 1971); Drake University (J.D., 1974). ***Email:*** Cepican@hsllp.com

(For complete biographical data on all personnel, see Professional Biographies at Des Moines, Iowa)

DAVID R. TREIMER

Established in 1992

601 BRADY STREET, SUITE 211
DAVENPORT, IOWA 52803
Telephone: 563-323-7889
Fax: 563-323-9309
Email: ttswlaw@bigplanet.com
URL: http://www.dtreimer.com

State and Federal Criminal Defense, Felonies, Driving While Intoxicated, White Collar Crime, Drug Crimes, Parole and Probation, Traffic Violations, Juvenile Law.

FIRM PROFILE: Primarily engaged in criminal defense in both State and Federal courts in the Midwest.

DAVID R. TREIMER, born Davenport, Iowa, November 16, 1954; admitted to bar, 1992, Iowa; 1993, U.S. District Court, Southern District of Iowa and U.S. District Court, Central District of Illinois; 2003, U.S. District Court, Northern District of Iowa. *Education:* Iowa State University (B.S., 1990); University of Iowa (J.D., 1992). *Member:* Iowa State Bar Association. ***REPORTED CASES:*** U.S. v. Hernandez, 301 F.3d 886 (8th Cir. 2002); U.S. v. Banks, 257 F.3d 908 (8th Cir. 2001); U.S. v. Collins, 350 F3d 773 (8th Cir. 2003). ***PRACTICE AREAS:*** Criminal Defense; Felonies; Driving While Intoxicated; White Collar Crime.

WESSELS & PAUTSCH, P.C.

NORTHWEST BANK BUILDING
101 WEST SECOND STREET, SUITE 307
DAVENPORT, IOWA 52801
Telephone: 563-333-9102
Fax: 563-333-9105
Email: wessels@stch.w-p.com
URL: http://www.w-p.com

St. Charles, Illinois Office: Dunham Center, 2035 Foxfield Drive. Telephone: 630-377-1554. Fax: 630-377-1653.
Milwaukee, Wisconsin Office: Two Plaza East, 330 East Kilbourn Avenue, Suite 1475. Telephone: 414-291-0600. FAX: 414-291-0200.
Chicago, Illinois Office: Chicago Bar Association Building, 321 South Plymouth Court, Suite 900. Telephone: 312-461-0500. Fax: 312-461-0595.
Minneapolis, Minnesota Office: MoneyGram Tower, 1550 Utica Avenue South, Suite 450. Telephone: 952-746-1700. Fax: 952-746-1704.
Indianapolis, Indiana Office: Market Tower, 10 West Market Street, Suite 1770. Telephone: 317-656-8800. Fax: 317-656-8855.

Representing Employers in Labor and Employment Law Matters. NLRA, RLA, all Federal and State Employment Discrimination Laws, Federal and State Disability Laws, Wrongful Discharge, Employment Contracts, Collective Bargaining Negotiations and Arbitrations, Employee Substance Abuse, Safety and Health, Unemployment Insurance, Benefits Law, Wage and Hour, and Employment-Based Immigration Matters. Litigation before all Federal and State Courts and Agencies, Trial and Appellate Practice.

RICHARD H. WESSELS, born Geneva, Illinois, June 29, 1939; admitted to bar, 1967, Illinois; 1972, U.S. District Court, Northern District of Illinois; 1989, Wisconsin; 1994, Iowa; U.S. Court of Appeals, Seventh Circuit. *Education:* Knox College (B.A., 1961); DePaul University (J.D., 1967). *Member:* Chicago, DuPage County, Kane County, Illinois State, Iowa State and American Bar Associations; State Bar of Wisconsin. ***Email:*** riwessels@stch.w-p.com

JOSEPH H. LAVERTY, born Evergreen Park, Illinois, August 19, 1968; admitted to bar, 1994, Illinois, Iowa and U.S. District Court, Northern District of Illinois; 1995, U.S. District Court, Central District of Illinois and U.S. District Court, Southern District of Iowa; 1999, U.S. Supreme Court; 2000, U.S. Court of Appeals, Eighth Circuit; 2002, U.S. District Court, Northern District of Iowa. *Education:* St. Ambrose University (B.A., 1990); Thomas M. Cooley Law School (J.D., cum laude, 1994). *Member:* Scott County, Rock Island County, Iowa State, Illinois State and American Bar Associations. ***Email:*** jolaverty@dav.w-p.com

(For complete biographical data on other personnel, see Professional Biographies at Chicago, Illinois; Milwaukee, Wisconsin; Davenport, Iowa; Minneapolis, Minnesota and Indianapolis, Indiana)

WINSTEIN, KAVENSKY & WALLACE

DAVENPORT, IOWA

(See Rock Island, Illinois)

General Civil Practice in all State and Federal Courts. Trial and Appellate Practice. Personal Injury, Products Liability, Labor, Workers Compensation, Matrimonial, Criminal, Bankruptcy, Probate, Real Estate and Commercial Litigation Law.

MILLER, PEARSON, GLOE, BURNS, BEATTY & COWIE, P.L.C.

301 WEST BROADWAY
DECORAH, IOWA 52101
Telephone: 563-382-4226
Fax: 563-382-3783
Email: millerlaw@dybb.com

General Practice, all Courts. Insurance Law, Estate Planning, Personal Injury, Family Law, Taxation and Probate.

(This Listing Continued)

MILLER, PEARSON, GLOE, BURNS, BEATTY & COWIE, P.L.C., Decorah—Continued

FRANK R. MILLER (1915-1977)

JAMES BURNS, born Burlington, Iowa, February 19, 1948; admitted to bar, 1974, Iowa; 1990, Minnesota. *Education:* Cornell College (B.A., 1970); University of Iowa (J.D., 1973). Phi Delta Phi. *Member:* Winneshiek County (President, 1977), Iowa State and American Bar Associations; Iowa State Trial Lawyers Association; The Association of Trial Lawyers of America; National Association of College and University Attorneys. ***PRACTICE AREAS:*** Trials and Appeals; Workman's Compensation; Personal Injury; Banking; Creditors Rights.

MARION L. BEATTY, born Vinton, Iowa, April 24, 1953; admitted to bar, 1977, Iowa; 1986, Minnesota. *Education:* Luther College (B.A., magna cum laude, 1975); University of Iowa (J.D., 1977). Phi Delta Phi. *Member:* Winneshiek County (President, 1979), Iowa State (Member, Board of Governors, 1998-2004; Vice President, 2004-2005; President Elect, 2005-2006), Minnesota State and American Bar Associations; Iowa Academy of Trial Lawyers (Member, Board of Directors, 2003—); The Association of Trial Lawyers of America; Iowa Defense Counsel Association (President, 2000-2001; President-elect, 1999-2000; Board of Directors, 1993-2000; Recipient, Edward F. Seitzinger Award, Outstanding Director, 1994); Iowa Association of Hospital Attorneys; National Association of College and University Attorneys; Defense Research Institute. Fellow: American College of Trial Lawyers; International Association of Defense Counsel. (Certified as a Civil Trial Advocate by the National Board of Trial Advocacy). ***PRACTICE AREAS:*** Trial Litigation; Personal Injury; Insurance Defense; Domestic Relations. ***Email:*** beatty@dybb.com

ROBERT J. COWIE, JR., born Peoria, Illinois, October 21, 1955; admitted to bar, 1980, Iowa; 1982, U.S. Tax Court. *Education:* Northern Illinois University (B.A., 1977); University of Iowa (J.D., with distinction, 1980); Washington School of Law (LL.M., Taxation, 1995). *Member:* Winneshiek County (President, 1983), Iowa State (Chair, Probate Section; Member, Title Standards Committee) and American Bar Associations. Fellow, American College of Estate and Trust Counsel. ***PRACTICE AREAS:*** Taxation; Probate; Corporations; Real Estate. ***Email:*** cowie@dybb.com

---

LAURA J. PARRISH MAKI, born Kendall, Wisconsin, December 19, 1978; admitted to bar, 2004, Iowa. *Education:* Cornell College (B.A., 2001); University of Iowa (J.D., 2004). *Member:* Winneshiek County and Iowa State (Member, Young Lawyer's Division) Bar Associations; Iowa Organization of Women Attorneys. ***PRACTICE AREAS:*** Family Law; Criminal Defense; General Practice. ***Email:*** imaik@dybb.com

OF COUNSEL

FLOYD S. PEARSON, born McGregor, Iowa, October 27, 1918; admitted to bar, 1948, Iowa. *Education:* State University of Iowa (B.A., 1940; J.D., 1948). Gamma Eta Gamma. Member, Iowa Conservation Commission, 1952-1957. Chairman, Winneshiek County Conservation Board, 1960-1974. *Member:* Winneshiek County (President, 1957-1958), Iowa State and American Bar Associations.

DONALD H. GLOE, born Gladbrook, Iowa, June 6, 1935; admitted to bar, 1961, Iowa. *Education:* State University of Iowa (B.A., 1958; J.D., with distinction, 1961). Phi Delta Phi. State Counsel, Iowa State Highway Commission, 1961-1964. *Member:* Winneshiek County, Iowa State and American Bar Associations; Iowa Academy of Trial Lawyers; Iowa Defense Counsel Association; Defense Research Institute. ***PRACTICE AREAS:*** Trial Litigation; Insurance Defense.

COUNSEL FOR: Luther College; Decorah Community School District; Winneshiek County Memorial Hospital; Community First National State Bank; Viking State Bank; Waukon State Bank.
LOCAL COUNSEL FOR: Farmland Insurance Co.; Allied Mutual Insurance Co.; Royal Insurance Co.; Ohio Casualty Insurance Co.; Iowa Farm Mutual Insurance Co.; Employers Mutual Liability Insurance Co. of Wisconsin; Continental Casualty Co.; Employers Mutual Casualty Co.; Employers Mutuals of Wausau, Wisconsin; Firemans Fund Group; Hawkeye Security Insurance Co.; The Atlantic Co.; Continental Insurance Co.; Iowa Mutual Insurance Co.; Motor Club of America; Auto Owners Insurance Co.; General Casualty; Grinnell Mutual Reinsurance Co.; Milbank Mutual Insurance Co.; Northwestern National Insurance Group.

RICHARD D. ZAHASKY

309 WEST WATER STREET
P.O. BOX 257
DECORAH, IOWA 52101
Telephone: 563-382-8409
Fax: 563-382-8400

General, Civil and Trial Practice. Personal Injury, Probate, Real Estate, Insurance, Corporate and Municipal Law. Collective Bargaining Negotiations.

RICHARD D. ZAHASKY, born Marshalltown, Iowa, May 29, 1947; admitted to bar, 1973, Iowa and Nebraska. *Education:* Loras College (B.S., 1970); Creighton University (J.D., 1972). City Attorney, Cities of Decorah, Lawler, Fort Atkinson and Lansing, Iowa, 1982—. *Member:* Winneshiek County (President, 1976) and Iowa State Bar Associations; Iowa Municipal Attorneys Association; The Association of Trial Lawyers of America.

REPRESENTATIVE CLIENTS: City of Decorah, Iowa; City of Lawler, Iowa; City of Fort Atkinson, Iowa; City of Lansing; City of Calmar, Iowa; Citizens Savings Bank, Spillville and Fort Atkinson, Iowa; Jirak Farms, Ltd.; Decorah Mobile Glass, Inc.; Benefits, Inc.; City of New Albin.

AHLERS & COONEY, P.C.

Established in 1888
100 COURT AVENUE, SUITE 600
DES MOINES, IOWA 50309-2231
Telephone: 515-243-7611
Fax: 515-243-2149
URL: http://www.ahlerslaw.com

General Practice. Litigation, Municipal Bonds, Public Finance, Government, Administrative, Business Law, Corporate, Banking, Environmental, Taxation, Securities, Antitrust, Education, Municipal, Workers Compensation, Pension, Profit Sharing, Employee Benefits, Real Estate, Labor and Employment, Insurance, Utility, Estate Planning and Probate Law. Practice before State and Federal Courts, Administrative and Regulatory Agencies.

FIRM PROFILE: The Firm and its predecessor partnerships have been practicing Law in Des Moines, Iowa since at least 1888. The Firm's practice groups include: Litigation, Public Finance, Business, Local Government and Employment Law. Some lawyers practice in more than one group.

Lawyers in the Firm have law degrees from the Cornell, Drake, Georgetown, Iowa, Michigan, North Dakota, Washburn, and Valparaiso Law Schools.

PAUL F. AHLERS (1913-2002)

JAMES EVANS COONEY (1917-1998)

PHILIP J. DORWEILER (Retired)

JOHN F. McKINNEY, JR., born Hannibal, Missouri; admitted to bar, 1965, Iowa; 1970, U.S. Supreme Court. *Education:* Drake University (B.A., 1962; J.D., 1965). City Prosecutor, 1965; Assistant City Attorney, 1965-1968; City Solicitor, City of Des Moines, 1968-1971. *Member:* Polk County, Iowa State and American (Member, Section of Local Government) Bar Associations; Iowa Municipal Attorneys Association; National Association of Bond Lawyers. ***PRACTICE AREAS:*** Securities; Government; Taxation; Municipal Law; Public Finance. ***Email:*** jmckinney@ahlerslaw.com

RICHARD G. SANTI, born Ames, Iowa; admitted to bar, 1969, Iowa. *Education:* Iowa State University (B.S., with distinction, 1966); University of Iowa (J.D., with high distinction, 1969). Murray Scholar; Order of the Coif; Phi Alpha Delta. Note and Comments Editor, Iowa Law Review, 1968-1969. Law Clerk to Hon. William C. Hanson, U.S. District Judge, 1969-1971. Listed in: The Best Lawyers in America, 1993—; Chambers USA America's Leading Business Lawyers. *Member:* Polk County, Iowa State and American Bar Associations; American College of Trial Lawyers (Iowa Chair, 2000-2002); Iowa Defense Counsel Association (Director, 1998-2001; President, 2003-2004); Defense Research Institute; Iowa Academy of Trial Lawyers; Blackstone Inn of Court (Emeritus). ***PRACTICE AREAS:*** Litigation; Insurance; Products Liability; Torts; Business Litigation. ***Email:*** rsanti@ahlerslaw.com

EDGAR H. BITTLE, born Des Moines, Iowa; admitted to bar, 1967, Iowa. *Education:* Cornell University (B.A., 1964); University of Michigan (J.D., 1967). Author: "The Fact-Finding Process in Iowa-Last Chance for Voluntary Settlement on the Road to Final Offer Binding Arbitration," Broader Perspectives in Dispute Resolution, Society of Professionals in Dispute Resolution, 1978; "Due Process for School Officials: A Guide for the Conduct of Administrative Proceedings," NOLPE, 1986; "The School Attorney: A Practical Guide to Employing School Legal Counsel," NSBA, 1986; "Drug Testing," West Publishing Co., Education Law Reporter, April 3, 1987; "Contracting for Asbestos Abatement," West Publishing Co., Education Law Reporter, March 1, 1990; "School Building Programs, Equipment Acquisitions and Cash Flow: The Anatomy of School Debt Financing," 73 Ed. Law 593, 1992; "Planning and Financing School Improvement and Construction Projects," ABA-NOLPE 1996. Iowa State Representative, 65th and 66th General Assemblies, 1973-1976. Member, Board of Directors, National Organization on Legal Problems of Education, 1980-1984. Chairman, National Council of School Attorneys, 1980-1981. Co-Chair, Higher Education Task Force of the Iowa General Assembly, 1988-1990. *Member:* Polk County, Iowa State (Chairman: Special Committee on Labor Law, 1978-1980; Political Action Committee, 1981-1985; Committee on Administrative Law, 1985-1986; Member, Foundation Board of Trustees, 2000-2004) and American (Committee on Public Education, Section of Urban, State and Local Government Law, Vice Chairman, 1979-1985; Chairman, 1985-1989; 1994-1995; Member of Council, 1989-1994) Bar Associations; National Association of Bond Lawyers. ***PRACTICE AREAS:*** Education Law; Securities; Government. ***Email:*** ebittle@ahlerslaw.com

LANCE A. COPPOCK, born Indianola, Iowa; admitted to bar, 1972, Iowa. *Education:* Drake University (B.S., 1970; J.D., 1972). Law Clerk to Hon. Roy L. Stephenson, U.S. Circuit Judge, 8th Circuit Court of Appeals, 1973-1975. *Member:* Polk County, Iowa State and American Bar Associations; Iowa Municipal Attorneys Association; National Association of Bond Lawyers. Fellow: American College of Bond Counsel; Iowa State Bar Foundation. ***PRACTICE AREAS:*** Government; Securities; Taxation; Public Finance; Municipal Bonds. ***Email:*** lcoppock@ahlerslaw.com

DAVID H. LUGINBILL, born South Bend, Indiana; admitted to bar, 1976, Iowa. *Education:* University of Iowa (B.A., 1973); Drake University (J.D., with honors, 1976). Member: Order of the Coif; National Order of the Barristers; National Moot Court Team. Case Notes Editor, Drake University Law Review, 1975-1976. *Member:* Polk County, Iowa State and American Bar Associations; International Association of Defense Counsel; Iowa Defense Counsel Association (Board of Directors); Defense Research Institute; American Academy of ADR Attorneys. ***PRACTICE AREAS:*** Products Liability; Toxic Torts; Professional Liability; Employment Litigation. ***Email:*** dluginbill@ahlerslaw.com

MARK W. BEERMAN, born Mason City, Iowa; admitted to bar, 1973, Iowa. *Education:* Valparaiso University (B.A., 1969; J.D., 1972); Georgetown University (LL.M. in Taxation, 1976). Member, Board of Editors, Valparaiso Law Review, 1971-1972. Law Clerk to Hon. M.L. Mason, Justice of Iowa Supreme Court, 1972-1973. Attorney, National Office, Internal Revenue Service, 1973-1977. *Member:* Iowa State and American Bar Associations. Fellow, American College of Trust and Estate Counsel. ***PRACTICE AREAS:*** Probate, Trusts and Estate Law; Taxation; Employee Benefits; Business. ***Email:*** mbeerman@ahlerslaw.com

(This Listing Continued)

EDWARD W. REMSBURG, born Lake City, Iowa; admitted to bar, 1973, Iowa. *Education:* University of Iowa (B.B.A., with highest distinction, 1970; J.D., with high distinction, 1973). Beta Gamma Sigma; Phi Eta Sigma; Order of the Coif; Phi Delta Phi. Member, Board of Editors, Iowa Law Review, 1972. Author: "Contemporary Studies Project: Perspectives on the Administration of Criminal Justice in Iowa," Vol. 57, Iowa Law Review, 1972. Law Clerk to Judge Roy L. Stephenson, U.S. Court of Appeals, 8th Circuit, 1976-1978. *Member:* Polk County (Member, Fee Arbitration Committee, 1984-1989), Iowa State (Member: Federal Practice Committee, 1995-2003, 2005—; Professionalism Committee, 1996-2003, Chairman 2003; Alternatives to Resolving Disputes Committee, Young Lawyers, 1982-1984; Environmental Law Committee, 1986-1987; Trade Regulation Committee, 1987-1993, 2003; Council Member, 1999—) and American Bar Associations; American College of Trial Lawyers; C. Edwin Moore American Inns of Court (Emeritus); Civil Justice Reform Act Advisory Group. [Lt., JAGC, U.S. Navy, 1973-1976]. ***PRACTICE AREAS:*** Litigation; Labor and Employment Law; Business Litigation; Construction Law; Environmental Law; Antitrust and Trade Regulation. ***Email:*** eremsburg@ahlerslaw.com

RANDALL H. STEFANI, born Des Moines, Iowa; admitted to bar, 1981, Iowa. *Education:* University of Iowa (B.B.A., 1978; J.D., with distinction, 1981). Certified Public Accountant, Iowa, 1980. Member, Judicial Nominating Commission, District 5C, 2002—. *Member:* Polk County, Iowa State and American Bar Associations; Iowa Trial Lawyers Association (Member, Board of Governors, 1998-2000). ***PRACTICE AREAS:*** Personal Injury Law; Professional Liability; Litigation; Workers Compensation. ***Email:*** rstefani@ahlerslaw.com

ELIZABETH GREGG KENNEDY, born Chicago, Illinois; admitted to bar, 1981, Iowa. *Education:* Macalester College and Drake University (B.A., cum laude, 1976); Drake University (J.D., 1981). Member, Moot Court Board. Member: Greater Des Moines Partnership (Board of Directors); The Blood Center of Iowa (Board of Directors); Past member Polk County Legal Aid Board of Directors; Iowa Supreme Court Commission on Unauthorized Practice of Law; Fifth Judicial District Nominating Commission; Greater Des Moines Partnership Community Development Board. *Member:* Polk County (Board of Directors, 2004—), Iowa State (Board of Directors, 2004—, Labor and Employment Section; Chair, 1998-1999) and American Bar Associations; National Association of College and University Attorneys; Blackstone Inn of Court (Member, Bencher Emeritus); Lincoln Inn of Court. ***PRACTICE AREAS:*** Civil Rights; Employment Law; Education Law. ***Email:*** ekennedy@ahlerslaw.com

WADE R. HAUSER III, born Washington, Iowa; admitted to bar, 1981, Iowa. *Education:* Iowa State University (B.S., 1973; M.S., 1976); University of Iowa (J.D., with high distinction, 1981). Editor-in-Chief, Iowa Law Review, 1980-1981. Recipient, Iowa State Bar Certificate of Merit, 1981. Law Clerk to Hon. W.W. Reynoldson, Chief Justice of Iowa Supreme Court, 1981-1982. *Member:* Polk County (Board of Directors, 1995-1997), Iowa State and American Bar Associations. Fellow: Iowa Academy of Trial Lawyers; C. Edwin Moore American Inns of Court (Master). ***PRACTICE AREAS:*** Litigation; Banking Law; Commercial Law; Contracts; Business Law; Appellate Practice. ***Email:*** whauser@ahlerslaw.com

WILLIAM J. NOTH, born Davenport, Iowa; admitted to bar, 1982, Iowa. *Education:* St. John's University (B.A., 1975); University of Iowa (J.D., with distinction, 1982). Note and Comment Editor, Iowa Law Review, 1981-1982. Author: Comment, "A Functional Expansion of the Attorney Corporate-Client Privilege: Upjohn Company v. United States," 67 Iowa Law Review 161, 1981. Law Clerk to Hon. K. David Harris, Justice of Iowa Supreme Court, 1982-1983. *Member:* Polk County, Iowa State and American Bar Associations; National Association of Bond Lawyers (Member, Board of Directors, 1999-2003; President, 2001-2002); American College of Bond Counsel; Iowa Municipal Attorneys Association. ***PRACTICE AREAS:*** Government; Securities; Taxation; Public Finance; Municipal Bonds; Corporate. ***Email:*** wnoth@ahlerslaw.com

LINDA L. KNIEP, born Brookfield, Missouri; admitted to bar, 1981, Iowa. *Education:* Drake University (B.A., summa cum laude, 1965; D.A. in English, 1977); University of Iowa (J.D., with highest distinction, 1981). Phi Beta Kappa; Order of the Coif. Recipient of John F. Murray Award. Member, Moot Court Board. *Member:* Polk County, Iowa State and American Bar Associations; National Association of Bond Lawyers. ***PRACTICE AREAS:*** Government; Securities; Taxation; Public Finance; Municipal Bonds. ***Email:*** lkniep@ahlerslaw.com

JOHN D. HINTZE, born Davenport, Iowa; admitted to bar, 1973, Iowa. *Education:* University of Iowa (B.B.A., 1970; J.D., 1973). Beta Alpha Psi; Beta Gamma Sigma; Order of the Coif. Certified Public Accountant, Iowa, 1973. Instructor: Drake University, Wills and Trusts, 1980; Employee Benefits, 1983-1988. ***PRACTICE AREAS:*** Business Law; Employee Benefits; Corporate; Taxation. ***Email:*** jhintze@ahlerslaw.com

PETER L. J. PASHLER, born Toronto, Canada; admitted to bar, 1986, Iowa. *Education:* DePauw University (B.A., 1969); University of Illinois (M.A., 1974); Drake University (J.D., with honors, 1986). Instructor, Adjunct Faculty, Drake Law School, Labor Law, 1995. Author: Comment, 35, Drake Law Review, May 1986. Director, 1974-1980 and Member, 1980-1986, Iowa Public Employment Relations Board. Director, Mid-West Consortium of Neutral Agencies, 1979-1986. Arbitrator, American Arbitration Association. *Member:* Polk County, Iowa State and American Bar Associations; Society of Professionals in Dispute Resolution; Association of Labor Relations Agencies; Federal Mediation Conciliation Service. ***PRACTICE AREAS:*** Employee Benefits; Employment Law; Education Law. ***Email:*** ppashler@ahlerslaw.com

IVAN T. WEBBER, born Hayward, California; admitted to bar, 1973, Iowa; 1974, U.S. District Court, Northern and Southern Districts of Iowa; 1977, U.S. Supreme Court; 1980, U.S. Court of Appeals, Eighth Circuit; 1985, U.S. Court of Appeals, District of Columbia Circuit. *Education:* University of Iowa (B.A., with honors in Political Science, 1969; J.D., with distinction, 1973). Corporation Counsel, City of Des Moines, 1986-1989. Author: *Making Objections and Laying Foundations in Iowa,* Association of Trial Lawyers of Iowa (1983); Second Edition (2005). *Member:* Iowa State (Member, Committee on Specialization, 1980-1990; Chair, Government Practice Section, 1997-1999) and American Bar Associations; Association of Trial Lawyers of Iowa (Outstanding Member, 1981-1982; Member, Board of Directors, 1981-1986); Iowa Municipal Attorneys Association. ***LANGUAGES:*** Spanish. ***PRACTICE AREAS:*** Municipal Law; Government Law; Environmental Law; Communications; Zoning, Planning and Land Use. ***Email:*** iwebber@ahlerslaw.com

(This Listing Continued)

JANE B. McALLISTER, born Kansas City, Kansas; admitted to bar, 1974, Kansas; 1988, Iowa. *Education:* University of Kansas (B.S., 1971); Washburn University (J.D., 1974); University of Missouri (LL.M., 1982). Attorney, U.S. Environmental Protection Agency, Region VII, 1978-1987. *Member:* Polk County, Iowa State and American Bar Associations. ***PRACTICE AREAS:*** Environmental Law; Real Estate. ***Email:*** jmcallister@ahlerslaw.com

JAMES C. HANKS, born Chicago, Illinois; admitted to bar, 1975, Iowa; 1976, Nebraska. *Education:* University of Iowa (B.A., 1972; J.D., with high distinction, 1975). Phi Beta Kappa. Director, 1978— and Chairman, 1984-1985, Iowa Council of School Board Attorneys. Director, National School Boards Association, Council of School Attorneys, 1984-1995; Chairman, 1990-1991. *Member:* Iowa State (Member, 1981— and Chairman, 1977-1990, Committee on Labor Law), Nebraska State and American (Member, Section Council, Section of State and Local Government, 1999-2003; Chairman, Public Education Committee of the Section of State and Local Government, 1995-1999) Bar Associations. ***PRACTICE AREAS:*** Education Law; Employment Law; Employee Benefits; Local Government Law. ***Email:*** jhanks@ahlerslaw.com

R. MARK CORY, born Nevada, Iowa; admitted to bar, 1986, Iowa; U.S. District Court, Northern and Southern Districts of Iowa, U.S. Court of Appeals, Eighth Circuit and U.S. Supreme Court. *Education:* University of Northern Iowa (B.A., with honors, 1982); Drake University (J.D., with honors, 1986). Member: Order of the Coif; Order of the Barristers. Guest Lecturer: Drake Law School, Iowa State University, Iowa Municipal Clerks Institute. Member, Drake Law School Board of Counsellors. *Member:* Polk County, Iowa State and American Bar Associations; National Association of Bond Lawyers; Iowa Municipal Attorneys Association. ***PRACTICE AREAS:*** Municipal Bonds; Public Finance; Government; Securities; Taxation. ***Email:*** rcory@ahlerslaw.com

RONALD L. PEELER, born Nebraska City, Nebraska; admitted to bar, 1987, Iowa. *Education:* Iowa State University (B.S., 1983); Drake University (J.D., with honors, 1987). Order of the Coif. Case Notes Editor, Drake University Law Review, 1986-1987. *Member:* Polk County, Iowa State and American Bar Associations; Iowa Council of School Board Attorneys. ***PRACTICE AREAS:*** Education Law; Employment Law; Employee Benefits. ***Email:*** rpeeler@ahlerslaw.com

ANDREW J. BRACKEN, born Chicago, Illinois; admitted to bar, 1988, Iowa, U.S. District Court, Northern and Southern Districts of Iowa, U.S. Court of Appeals, Eighth Circuit and U.S. Supreme Court. *Education:* University of Iowa (B.S., 1984); Drake University (J.D., with honors, 1988). Order of the Barristers. Articles Editor, Drake Law Review, 1987-1988. Author: The Legal Handbook For Iowa School Administrators (Omni Publishing Co., 1998); Casenote, 36 Drake Law Review 813 (1986-1987). Adjunct Professor, College of Education, Iowa State University, 1998—. Law Clerk to Hon. Arthur A. McGivern, Chief Justice Iowa Supreme Court, 1988-1989. *Member:* Polk County, Iowa State and American Bar Associations; National School Boards Association (Director, Council of School Attorneys, 2002—); Iowa Council of School Attorneys (Chair, 2001-2002); National Association of College and University Attorneys. ***PRACTICE AREAS:*** Education Law; Employment Law. ***Email:*** abracken@ahlerslaw.com

STEVEN L. SERCK, born Rock Valley, Iowa; admitted to bar, 1989, Iowa; U.S. District Court, Northern and Southern Districts of Iowa. *Education:* University of Northern Iowa (B.A., with highest distinction, 1986); University of Iowa (J.D., with high distinction, 1989). Order of the Coif. Author: Comment, "Taylor v. Wiebold and Rules of Civil Procedure 48 & 55: Do Statutes of Limitations Still Matter in Iowa?" 73 Iowa Law Review 975 (1988). *Member:* Polk County, Iowa State and American Bar Associations; National Association of College and University Attorneys; Iowa Defense Counsel; Defense Research Institute. ***PRACTICE AREAS:*** College and University Law; Commercial Litigation; Insurance; Personal Injury Litigation; Products Liability; Torts. ***Email:*** sserck@ahlerslaw.com

STEVEN MICHAEL NADEL, born Des Moines, Iowa; admitted to bar, 1992, Iowa. *Education:* University of Iowa (B.B.A., in Accounting, with highest distinction, 1989); Cornell University (J.D., 1992). Law Clerk to Hon. David Harris, Justice, Iowa Supreme Court, 1992-1993. *Member:* Polk County, Iowa State and American Bar Associations. ***PRACTICE AREAS:*** Employment Law; Employee Benefits; Workers Compensation Law. ***Email:*** snadel@ahlerslaw.com

ELIZABETH A. GROB, born St. Louis, Missouri; admitted to bar, 1996, Iowa. *Education:* University of Mississippi (B.A., 1988); University of Missouri (M.A., 1990); Drake University (J.D., with honors, 1996). Order of the Coif. Author: "Fundamentals in Competitive Bidding, Planning and Financing School Improvement and Construction Projects," 68 (Edgar H. Bittle, ed. 1996); "Recent Developments in Public Education Law," 28 The Urban Lawyer, 895 (1996); "Recent Developments in Public Education Law," 29 The Urban Lawyer 837 (1997); "Recent Developments in Public Education Law," 31 The Urban Lawyer 955 (1999). *Member:* Dallas County, Polk County, Iowa State and American Bar Associations; National Council of School Board Attorneys; Iowa Council of School Board Attorneys; National Association of Bond Lawyers. ***PRACTICE AREAS:*** Education; Government; Local Government Law; Public Finance; Municipal Bonds. ***Email:*** egrob@ahlerslaw.com

JENNIFER A. CLENDENIN, born Cedar Rapids, Iowa; admitted to bar, 1997, Iowa. *Education:* University of Notre Dame (B.A., 1994); Drake University (J.D., with high honors, 1997). Order of the Coif. Order of the Barristers. Author: "A Guide for Lower Courts in Factoring Religion Into Child Custody Disputes," 45 Drake Law Review 733. *Member:* Polk County, Iowa State and American Bar Associations. ***PRACTICE AREAS:*** Litigation; Employment Law; Workers Compensation. ***Email:*** jclendenin@ahlerslaw.com

NATHAN J. OVERBERG, born Mt. Pleasant, Iowa; admitted to bar, 1997, Iowa. *Education:* Central College (B.A., summa cum laude, 1994); University of Iowa (J.D., with highest distinction, 1997). Order of the Coif. Member, National Moot Court Team, 1996-1997. Member, 1995-1996 and Associate Editor, 1996-1997, Iowa Law Review. Law Clerk: Hon. Harold D. Vietor, Senior U.S. District Court Judge, Southern District of Iowa, 1997-1999. *Member:* Polk County, Iowa State (Member: Federal Practice Committee; Labor and Employment Law Section Council) and American Bar Associations; Iowa Municipal At-

(This Listing Continued)

AHLERS & COONEY, P.C., Des Moines—Continued

torneys Association; National Association of College and University Attorneys; C. Edwin Moore Inns of Court. ***PRACTICE AREAS:*** General Civil Litigation; Employment Law; Education Law. ***Email:*** noverberg@ahlerslaw.com

JOHN H. BUNZ, born Manning, Iowa; admitted to bar, 1990, Iowa; 1991, Kansas; 1992, Missouri. *Education:* Luther College (B.A., 1987); Drake University (J.D., with honors, 1990). Phi Delta Theta. Vice President, Student Bar Association, 1988-1989. Member, Moot Court Team. Staff Member, Drake University Law Review, 1988-1990. Law Clerk, Hon. K. David Harris, Justice of the Iowa Supreme Court, 1990-1991. *Member:* Polk County, Iowa State and American Bar Associations. ***PRACTICE AREAS:*** Public Finance; Municipal Bonds; Securities; Real Estate Finance. ***Email:*** jbunz@ahlerslaw.com

DANIELLE JESS HAINDFIELD, born Belmond, Iowa; admitted to bar, 1999, Iowa. *Education:* Drake University (B.A., magna cum laude, 1996; J.D., with high honors, 1999). Order of the Coif. Article Editor, Drake Law Review, 1998-1999. Author: "Wall of Separation or Path to Interaction: The Uncertain Constitutional Future of School Vouchers in Light of Inconsistent Developments in Judicial Neutrality Between Church and State," 48 Drake Law Review, 403; Contributing Author: "America's Children at Risk," American Bar Association (2000) and "School Violence: From Discipline to Due Process," American Bar Association (2004). *Member:* Polk County, Iowa State and American Bar Associations; Iowa and National School Board Association Council of School Attorneys. ***PRACTICE AREAS:*** Education Law; Employment Law; Local Government Law. ***Email:*** dhaindfield@ahlerslaw.com

OF COUNSEL

KENNETH H. HAYNIE, born Omaha, Nebraska; admitted to bar, 1957, Iowa. *Education:* DePauw University (B.A., 1954); University of Michigan (J.D., 1957). Delta Theta Phi; Order of the Coif. Member, Board of Editors, Michigan Law Review, 1956. *Member:* Polk County, Iowa State (Chairman, Joint Committee with Iowa Investment Bankers Association, 1976) and American (Member, Committees on General Obligation Bonds, 1970-1973, Liaison with the Securities Industry Association, 1973-1977 and Liaison with the Municipal Finance Officers Association, 1978, Section of Urban, State and Local Government Law) Bar Associations; National Association of Bond Lawyers; American College of Bond Counsel (Director, 1995-2004). ***PRACTICE AREAS:*** Securities; Government; Taxation; Corporate; Public Finance; Municipal Bonds. ***Email:*** khaynie@ahlerslaw.com

ROBERT G. ALLBEE, born Muscatine, Iowa; admitted to bar, 1955, Iowa. *Education:* Grinnell College; Colorado College (A.B., 1952); Drake University (J.D., 1955). Order of the Coif; Order of the Barristers; Omicron Delta Kappa; Phi Alpha Delta. Co-Author: "Error Preservation in Civil Litigation: A Primer for the Iowa Practitioner," 35 Drake Law Review 1. Justice, Iowa Supreme Court, 1978-1982. Chief Judge, Iowa Court of Appeals, 1976-1978. Judge, Iowa District Court, 1975-1976. *Member:* Iowa Defense Counsel Association (President, 1972-1973). Fellow: American College of Trial Lawyers; American Academy of Appellate Lawyers; American Bar Foundation; Moore Inn of Court (Co-Founder).

H. RICHARD SMITH, born Moravia, Iowa; admitted to bar, 1958, Iowa. *Education:* Simpson College (B.S., 1953); Drake University (J.D., 1958). Order of the Coif: Delta Theta Phi. Assistant Editor, Drake University Law Review, 1957-1958. Member, Board of Trustees, Simpson College, 1974—. Chairman, Supreme Court Advisory Committee on Rules of Civil Procedure, 1981-1985. *Member:* Polk County (President, 1980-1981), Iowa State (Member, Board of Governors, 1981-1985; Vice-President, 1985-1986; President, 1987-1988; Chair, Litigation Section, 1990-1992) and American Bar Associations; Iowa Defense Counsel Association; Iowa Academy of Trial Lawyers. Fellow: American College of Trial Lawyers; American Bar Foundation. ***PRACTICE AREAS:*** Litigation.

RONALD L. SUTPHIN, born Des Moines, Iowa; admitted to bar, 1964, Iowa. *Education:* Drake University (B.A., 1962; J.D., 1964). Delta Theta Phi. Assistant Editor, Drake Law Review, 1963-1964. Author, "Federal Standard of Search and Seizure," 13 Drake Law Review, 1965. Lecturer in Law, Securities Regulation, Drake University, 1970. Police Judge Pro Tem, Windsor Heights, Iowa, 1971-1973. *Member:* Polk County (Member: Admissions Committee, 1974-1984; Grievance Committee, 1984-1987), The Iowa State and American (Member, Sections of Corporation, Banking and Business Law; Taxation; Labor and Employment Law; Real Property, Probate and Trust Law; Chair, Business Corporations Committee of the Business Law Section, 1995-1996) Bar Associations. [Capt., Judge Advocate, U.S. Air Force, active duty, 1966-1969]. ***PRACTICE AREAS:*** Business Law; Labor and Employment Law; Probate, Trusts and Estates Law; Securities; Corporate Law. ***Email:*** rsutphin@ahlerslaw.com

DOUGLAS R. SMITH, born Syracuse, New York; admitted to bar, 1970, Iowa; 1989, Colorado. *Education:* Iowa State University (B.S., with distinction, 1968); University of Iowa (J.D., with high distinction, 1970). *Member:* Iowa State Bar Association. ***PRACTICE AREAS:*** Business Law; Corporate; Employee Benefits. ***Email:*** dsmith@ahlerslaw.com

JANE A.B. EPPINK, born Sac City, Iowa; admitted to bar, 1989, Indiana; 1991, Iowa. *Education:* Indiana University (B.A., with highest distinction, 1984); Massachusetts Institute of Technology (S.M. 1987); Indiana University (J.D., summa cum laude, 1989). *Member:* Iowa State Bar Association. ***PRACTICE AREAS:*** Real Estate Finance. ***Email:*** jeppink@ahlerslaw.com

---

PATRICIA A. WESTEMEYER, born New Hampton, Iowa; admitted to bar, 1998, Iowa. *Education:* Iowa State University (B.A., 1995); University of Iowa College of Law (J.D., with distinction, 1997). Member, Journal of Corporation Law, 1996-1997. *Member:* Polk County, Iowa State and American Bar Associations; National Association of Bond Lawyers. ***PRACTICE AREAS:*** Public Finance; Municipal Bonds; Taxation; Securities; Government; Commercial Real Estate Finance. ***Email:*** pwestemeyer@ahlerslaw.com

JAMES R. WAINWRIGHT, born Providence, Rhode Island; admitted to bar, 1999, Iowa. *Education:* Boston College (B.A., 1992); Drake University (J.D., with honors, 1999). *Member:* Polk County, Iowa State and American Bar Associations; Iowa Defense Counsel Association; Defense Research Institute; Iowa Municipal Attorneys Association; Blackstone Inn of Court. ***PRACTICE AREAS:*** Civil Litigation; Local Government Law. ***Email:*** jwainwright@ahlerslaw.com

J. ERIC BOEHLERT, born Syracuse, New York; admitted to bar, 1999, Iowa. *Education:* Drake University (B.A., cum laude, 1996; J.D., with honors, 1999). Delta Theta Phi. Law Clerk to Hon. Mark S. Cady, Justice of Iowa Supreme Court. *Member:* Polk County, Iowa State and American Bar Associations; National Association of Bond Lawyers. ***PRACTICE AREAS:*** Local Government Law; Public Finance. ***Email:*** eboehlert@ahlerslaw.com

ANDREW T. TICE, born Des Moines, Iowa; admitted to bar, 2001, Iowa. *Education:* Iowa State University (B.A., 1998); University of Illinois (J.D., cum laude, 2001). Associate Editor, Elder Law Journal. *Member:* Polk County, Iowa State and American Bar Associations; Iowa Defense Counsel Association; Blackstone Inn of Court. ***PRACTICE AREAS:*** Workers Compensation; Employment Law; Litigation. ***Email:*** atice@ahlerslaw.com

COLIN J. WITT, born Colorado Springs, Colorado; admitted to bar, 1999, Iowa; U.S. District Court, Northern and Southern Districts of Iowa. *Education:* University of Iowa (B.A., with honors, 1996; J.D., with distinction, 1999). Editor-in-Chief, Journal of Corporation Law, Volume 24, 1998-1999. Law Clerk to Ronald E. Longstaff, Chief Judge, U.S. District Court, Southern District of Iowa, 1999-2002. Magistrate, Polk County (part-time), 2005—. Member, Criminal Justice Act Panel. *Member:* Polk County, Iowa State and American Bar Associations; Iowa Association of Magistrate Judges; Eighth Circuit Bar Association. ***PRACTICE AREAS:*** Litigation; Business Law. ***Email:*** cwitt@ahlerslaw.com

MICHAEL M. GALLOWAY, born Coon Rapids, Iowa; admitted to bar, 1997, Iowa. *Education:* Iowa State University (B.B.A., with distinction, 1993); Drake University (J.D., with honors, 1996). *Member:* Polk County, Iowa State and American Bar Associations. ***PRACTICE AREAS:*** Education Law; Employment Law; Employee Benefits; Local Government Law. ***Email:*** mgalloway@ahlerslaw.com

GORDON D. GRETA, born St. Paul, Minnesota; admitted to bar, 1974, Iowa. *Education:* University of Iowa (B.A., with honors in Political Science, 1968; J.D., 1974). Board of Editors, Iowa Law Review, 1973. Contemporary Projects Editor, Iowa Law Review, 1974. Author: "Home-State Preference in Public Contracting: A Study in Economic Balkanization," 58 Iowa Law Review, 576-595, and "National and State Bank Interest Rates Under the National Bank Act: Preference or Party?" 58 Iowa Law Review, 1250-1267. Editor: "Contemporary Studies Project: Large Farm Estate Planning and Probate in Iowa," 58 Iowa Law Review, 794-999. *Member:* Iowa State and American Bar Associations. ***PRACTICE AREAS:*** Local Government Law; Public Finance; Utility Law. ***Email:*** ggreta@ahlerslaw.com

---

AHLERS, COONEY, DORWEILER, HAYNIE, SMITH & ALLBEE, P.C.

DES MOINES, IOWA

(See Ahlers & Cooney, P.C.)

ANDERSON & TULLY

A PROFESSIONAL CORPORATION

DES MOINES, IOWA

(See West Des Moines)

General Civil and Trial Practice in State and Federal Courts. Corporation, Securities, Estate Planning, Trusts, Probate, Real Estate, Insurance, Personal Injury, Workers Compensation and Administrative Law.

BABICH, GOLDMAN, CASHATT & RENZO, P.C.

100 COURT AVENUE, SUITE 403
DES MOINES, IOWA 50309-2200
Telephone: 515-244-4300
Fax: 515-244-2650

Family Law, Domestic Relations, Personal Injury, Employment Law, Discrimination, Civil Rights, Constitutional Law, Criminal Law, Juvenile Law, Trials and Appeals and Mediation Services.

FIRM PROFILE: Babich, Goldman, Cashatt & Renzo, P.C. has been serving clients for over 20 years regionally with an emphasis in Iowa. The firm was established in 1977 and is primarily known for its work in the areas of personal injury, civil rights, employment discrimination, family and domestic relations law and mediation services.

LESLIE BABICH, born Detroit, Michigan, February 21, 1949; admitted to bar, 1974, Iowa. *Education:* Simpson College (B.A., 1971); Drake University (J.D., 1974). Instructor, Domestic Relations, Des Moines Area Community College Legal Assistant Program, 1978-1990. *Member:* Polk County and Iowa State Bar Associations. ***PRACTICE AREAS:*** Family Law; Domestic Relations. ***Email:*** lbabich@babichlaw.com

TODD E. BABICH, born Detroit, Michigan, January 5, 1963; admitted to bar, 1989, Iowa, U.S. Tax Court and U.S. District Court, Southern District of Iowa. *Education:* University of Michigan; Drake University (B.A., 1985; J.D., 1988). *Member:* Polk County (Member: Family Law Committee; Juvenile Law Committee) and Iowa State (Member: Family Law Committee; Juvenile. Law Committee) Bar Associations. ***PRACTICE AREAS:*** Family Law; Juvenile Law; Domestic Relations; Mediation Services. ***Email:*** tbabich@babichlaw.com

MICHAEL J. CARROLL, born Los Angeles, California, July 15, 1964; admitted to bar, 1989, New Mexico (inactive); U.S. District Court, District of New Mexico; 1991, Iowa and U.S. District Court, Northern and Southern Districts of Iowa; U.S. Court of Appeals, Eighth Circuit and Federal Circuit. *Education:* University of Iowa (B.A., Political Science, 1987); Drake University (J.D., 1989). Delta Theta Phi. Member, Drake National Mock Trial

(This Listing Continued)

Team. *Member:* Iowa State and American (Member, Committees on: Bridge the Gap, 1992—; Law Related Education, 1993—) Bar Associations; The Association of Trial Lawyers of America; National Employment Lawyers Association (Iowa Affiliate Leader). ***PRACTICE AREAS:*** Employment Law; Civil Rights; Discrimination. ***Email:*** mcarroll@babichlaw.com

BRENT A. CASHATT, born Des Moines, Iowa, March 7, 1962; admitted to bar, 1989, Iowa and U.S. District Court, Northern and Southern District of Iowa; U.S. Court of Appeals, Eighth Circuit. *Education:* Grand View College (B.A., with distinction, 1986); Drake University (J.D., 1989). *Member:* Polk County, Iowa State (Member, Sections on: Family Law and Alternative Dispute Resolution, Chairperson, 2000—) and American (Member, Sections on: Family Law and Alternative Dispute Resolution) Bar Associations; Association for Conflict Resolution; Sports Lawyers Association. ***PRACTICE AREAS:*** Family Law; Domestic Relations; Litigation; Conflict Resolution; Mediation Services. ***Email:*** bcashatt@babichlaw.com

DAVID H. GOLDMAN, born Des Moines, Iowa, April 3, 1942; admitted to bar, 1977, Iowa; U.S. Supreme Court; U.S. Court of Appeals, Eighth Circuit; U.S. Court of Federal Claims; U.S. District Court, Northern and Southern Districts of Iowa. *Education:* Brandeis University (B.A., with honors, 1964); St. John's College, Oxford University (1964-1967); University of Iowa (J.D., with honors, 1977). Panel Member, Iowa District Court Mediation Program. *Member:* Polk County (Member, Alternative Dispute Resolution Committee), Iowa State (Member, Sections on: Alternative Dispute Resolution; Labor and Employment Law; Litigation) and American (Member, Sections on: Labor and Employment Law; Dispute Resolution) Bar Associations; Iowa Trial Lawyers Association; National Employment Lawyers Association; American Academy of ADR Attorneys (Board Certified Mediator); Association for Conflict Resolution. ***PRACTICE AREAS:*** Employment Law; Civil Rights; Mediation. ***Email:*** dgoldman@babichlaw.com

KODI A. PETERSON, born Storm Lake, Iowa, July 31, 1979; admitted to bar, 2005, Iowa, U.S. Court of Appeals, Eighth Circuit and U.S. District Court, Northern and Southern Districts of Iowa. *Education:* Simpson College (B.A., summa cum laude, 2001); Drake University (J.D., with highest honors, 2004). *Member:* Polk County, Iowa State and American Bar Associations; National Employment Lawyers Association. ***PRACTICE AREAS:*** Employment Law; Civil Rights; Discrimination; Appellate Practice. ***Email:*** kpetersen@babichlaw.com

JOSEPH A. RENZO, born Des Moines, Iowa, April 15, 1949; admitted to bar, 1992, Iowa and U.S. District Court, Southern District of Iowa. *Education:* University of New Mexico (B.A., 1971); Drake University (J.D., with honors, 1991). *Member:* Polk County and Iowa State Bar Associations. ***PRACTICE AREAS:*** Criminal Law; Personal Injury; Juvenile Law. ***Email:*** jrenzo@babichlaw.com

ALEXANDER R. RHOADS, born Dixon, Illinois, June 29, 1965; admitted to bar, 1996, Iowa and U.S. District Court, Northern and Southern Districts of Iowa. *Education:* Grinnell College (B.A., 1987); Drake University (J.D., 1996). *Member:* Dallas County, Iowa State and American Bar Associations; Iowa Trial Lawyers Association; The Association of Trial Lawyers of America (Member, Litigation Section). ***PRACTICE AREAS:*** Civil Litigation; Domestic Relations; Family Law. ***Email:*** arhoads@babichlaw.com

STACEY N. WARREN, born La Grange, Illinois, March 18, 1969; admitted to bar, 1994, Iowa; 1995, U.S. District Court, Northern and Southern Districts of Iowa. *Education:* University of Kansas (B.A., with honors, 1991; J.D., 1993). Member, 1992-1993 and Associate Editor, 1993, Kansas Journal of Law and Public Policy Staff. Law Clerk to Honorable Terry L. Huitink, Judge, Iowa Court of Appeals, 1994-1995. *Member:* Polk County, Iowa State (Member, Sections on: Family Law; Litigation) and American (Member, Sections on: Family Law; Litigation; Young Lawyers Division, Member, Family Law Executive Subcommittee) Bar Associations. ***PRACTICE AREAS:*** Family Law; Domestic Relations; Appellate Practice. ***Email:*** swarren@babichlaw.com

REFERENCE: Wells Fargo Bank Iowa, N.A.

BARNHILL & ASSOCIATES, P.C.

DES MOINES, IOWA

(See West Des Moines)

Construction Law, Government Contracts, Public Construction, Business Law, Contracts, Real Estate, Architectural Copyrights, Corporate Law and Litigation, Eminent Domain, Intellectual Property, Labor and Employment Law, Civil Practice, Class Actions, Construction Litigation, Highways, Commercial Law, Litigation, Trusts and Estates Litigation, Zoning, Planning and Land Use, Unfair Competition, Trade Secrets, Collections, Public Bids and Bidding, Tax Litigation, Business Litigation, Shareholder and Business Valuation Litigation, Trademark and Copyright Litigation.

BEATTIE LAW FIRM, P.C.

4300 GRAND AVENUE
DES MOINES, IOWA 50312
Telephone: 515-263-1000
Fax: 515-263-1411
Email: beattielaw@beattielawfirm.com
URL: http://www.donbeattielaw.com

Civil Litigation, Personal Injury, Product Liability, Workers Compensation, Wrongful Death, Dog Bites, Legal Malpractice, Business Litigation, Automobile Accidents.

DONALD G. BEATTIE, born Des Moines, Iowa, November 30, 1947; admitted to bar, 1977, Iowa; 1978, Court of Appeals, Northern and Southern Districts of Iowa. *Education:* Simpson College (B.A., with honors, 1970); Drake University (J.D., with honors, 1977). Delta Theta Phi. Order of the Coif. Recipient, Double SS Award for Outstanding Achievement after College, 1993. Author: Casenote, 24 Drake Law Review, Vol. 4, 1975; Note, "First Party Torts: Extra-Contractual Liability of Insurers Who Violate The Standard of Good Faith and Fair Dealing," 25 Drake Law Review, Vol. 4, 1976. Lecturer: Settlement Techniques, Iowa Trial Lawyers Association Seminar, Des Moines, Iowa, 1992; Full Disclosure and Discovery, Iowa's Trial Lawyers Association Seminar, Des Moines, Iowa, July 1996; Legal Hurdles and Obstacles in Propane Gas Explosion Litigation, 50th Anniversary American Trial Lawyers Association Seminar, Boston, Massachusetts, July 1996; Rapid Fire, Warnings, Iowa Trial Lawyers Association Seminar, Des Moines, Iowa, May 1997. Pro Hoc Vice: Michigan, New Mexico, Arizona, Colorado, Nebraska, Illinois, Minnesota, North Dakota, South Dakota. Listed: Who's Who Among American Universities and Colleges, 1977. *Member:* Polk County (Board of Directors, 1993; Board of Governors, 1989-1994; Ethics Committee, 1989-1993) and Iowa State Bar Associations; The Association of Trial Lawyers of America; Iowa Trial Lawyers Association; Million Dollar Advocates Forum; Blackstone Inn of Court. [Capt., USMCR, 1970-1974; Flight Officer, U.S. Navy, 1971-1974]. (Certified as a Civil Trial Advocacy Specialist by the National Board of Trial Advocacy). ***REPORTED CASES:*** Scherle v. McClellan, 1.8 Million (1989); DeJong v. Phillips Petroleum, et al, 3.2 Million (1990); Timmens v. Kaneb Pipeline, 1.6 Million (1991); Walter v. Phillips Petroleum et al, 6.2 Million (1993). ***PRACTICE AREAS:*** Civil Litigation; Propane Products Liability; Products Liability; Workers Compensation; Legal Malpractice; Personal Injury; Business Litigation.

(This Listing Continued)

BECKMAN AND HIRSCH

DES MOINES, IOWA

(See Burlington)

Personal Injury, Appeals, Corporation, Taxation, Probate, Insurance, Real Estate, Criminal Defense, Commercial Litigation, Computer Law, Family Law, General Trial Practice in State and Federal Courts.

BELIN LAMSON McCORMICK ZUMBACH FLYNN

A PROFESSIONAL CORPORATION
THE FINANCIAL CENTER
666 WALNUT STREET, SUITE 2000
DES MOINES, IOWA 50309-3989
Telephone: 515-243-7100
Fax: 515-558-0715
URL: http://www.belinlaw.com

General Practice. Civil and Criminal Trials and Appeals, Taxation, Labor and Employment, Probate, Trusts and Estates, Banks and Banking, Bankruptcy, Corporate Law, Real Estate, Antitrust, Environmental Law, Legislative, Education Law.

FIRM PROFILE: Belin Lamson McCormick Zumbach Flynn is listed in the Martindale-Hubbell Bar Register of Preeminent Lawyers.

DAVID W. BELIN (1928-1999)

ROGER T. STETSON (1953-2004)

JEFFREY E. LAMSON, born Oak Park, Illinois, May 29, 1941; admitted to bar, 1966, Iowa. *Education:* University of Iowa (B.A., with high distinction, 1963); Harvard Law School (J.D., 1966). Phi Beta Kappa; Omicron Delta Kappa. *Member:* Polk County, Iowa State and American Bar Associations. ***Email:*** jelamson@belinlaw.com

MARK McCORMICK, born Fort Dodge, Iowa, April 13, 1933; admitted to bar, 1960, Iowa; 1961, U.S. District Court, Northern and Southern Districts of Iowa, U.S. Court of Appeals, Eighth Circuit and U.S. Supreme Court. *Education:* Villanova University (A.B., 1955); Georgetown University (LL.B., 1960); University of Virginia (LL.M., 1982). Delta Epsilon Sigma; Alpha Sigma Nu. Author: "Opinion Evidence in Iowa," 19 Drake Law Review 245, 1970; "Appellate Congestion in Iowa: Dimensions and Remedies," 25 Drake Law Review 133, 1975; "Scientific Evidence: Defining a New Approach to Admissibility," 67 Iowa Law Review 879, 1982. Co-Author with V. Hale Starr, *Jury Selection,* Little Brown and Company, 1985, Second Edition, 1993. Faculty Member, Evidence Subjects, National Judicial College, 1976-1979. Law Clerk for Harvey A. Johnson, Chief Judge, U.S. Court of Appeals, 8th Circuit, 1960-1961. Assistant County Attorney, Webster Co., 1963-1967; District Judge, 1968-1972; Associate Justice, Supreme Court of Iowa, 1972-1986. Chair, Governor's Public Investment Task Force, 1992. Co-Chair, Iowa Legislative Reform Committee on Government Ethics and Procedures, 1992. Chair, U.S. Magistrate Merit Selection Panel, Southern District, Iowa, 1990-1991, 1994. Chair, Joint State Government Ethics Committee, 1992-1993. Chair, Governor's State Institutional Task Force, 1995-1996. Member: Iowa State Ethics and Campaign Finance Disclosure Board, 1999-2003; Iowa State Judicial Nominating Commission, 1996-2001. *Member:* Polk County, Iowa State (Member, Jury Instruction Committee, 1969-1972, 1986-1994; Chair, 1991-1994; Chair, Appellate Practice Committee, 1999-2002) and American Bar Associations; American Academy of Appellate Lawyers; Iowa Academy of Trial Lawyers (Hon.). [U.S., Navy, 1955-1958, Lt.]. ***PRACTICE AREAS:*** Civil Litigation; Administrative Agency Practice; Civil Appeals. ***Email:*** mmccormick@belinlaw.com

STEVEN E. ZUMBACH, born Manchester, Iowa, January 12, 1950; admitted to bar, 1975, Iowa. *Education:* Iowa State University (B.S., 1973; Ph.D., in Economics, 1980); University of Iowa (J.D., 1975). Phi Kappa Phi; Gamma Sigma Delta; Omicron Delta Kappa; Order of the Coif. Member, Cardinal Key. Certified Public Accountant, Iowa, 1977. Author: BNA Portfolio 833, Special Use Valuation; 1984, "Divorce Corporate Style," The Practical Accountant, 1984. Member: National Planning Board for the White House Conference on Aging, 1970-1972; Iowa State Board of Regents, 1973-1977. President, Iowa State University Alumni Association, 1986-1987. President, Des Moines Estate Planning Council, 1990—. Chair, Greater Des Moines Partnership, 2003. Deputy National Chair, Iowa State University Partnership For Prominence Capital Campaign, 1993. *Member:* Iowa State Bar Association; Iowa Society of Certified Public Accountants; American Agricultural Economics Association. Fellow, The American College of Trust and Estate Counsel. ***PRACTICE AREAS:*** Mergers and Acquisitions; Trusts & Estates; Taxation. ***Email:*** sezumbach@belinlaw.com

(This Listing Continued)

BELIN LAMSON McCORMICK ZUMBACH FLYNN, A PROFESSIONAL CORPORATION, Des Moines—Continued

THOMAS L. FLYNN, born Mitchell, South Dakota, February 24, 1946; admitted to bar, 1972, Iowa, U.S. District Court, Northern and Southern Districts of Iowa and U.S. Court of Appeals, Eighth Circuit. *Education:* Morningside College (B.A., with honors, 1968); Drake University (J.D., with honors, 1972). Delta Theta Phi. Member, Drake Law Review, 1971-1972. *Member:* Polk County, Iowa State (Chairman: Bankruptcy and Commercial Committee, 1983-1989) and American Bar Associations. Fellow: American College of Bankruptcy. ***PRACTICE AREAS:*** Banks & Banking; Business Law; Bankruptcy; Real Estate; Estate Planning. ***Email:*** tlflynn@belinlaw.com

JON L. STAUDT, born Marble Rock, Iowa, August 13, 1949; admitted to bar, 1976, Iowa. *Education:* University of Iowa (B.A., with highest distinction, 1972; J.D., with high distinction, 1976). Order of the Coif; Phi Beta Kappa. *Member:* Polk County, Iowa State (Member, Taxation & Corporate Sections) and American Bar Associations. ***PRACTICE AREAS:*** Taxation; Trusts & Estates; Business Law. ***Email:*** jlstaudt@belinlaw.com

JAMES L. KRAMBECK, born Clinton, Iowa, July 19, 1939; admitted to bar, 1964, Iowa; 1965, U.S. Court of Military Appeals; 1968, U.S. District Court, Southern District of Iowa; 1970, U.S. District Court, Northern District of Iowa and U.S. Court of Appeals, 8th Circuit; 1972, U.S. Supreme Court. *Education:* University of Iowa (B.A., 1961); University of Michigan (J.D., 1964). Partner, Ahlers, Cooney, Dorweiler, Haynie, Smith & Allbee, Des Moines, Iowa, 1968-1991. Senior Vice-President and General Counsel, Kirke-Van Orsdel, Inc., 1991-1999. Author: "Conducting Corporate Business and Meetings Under the New Iowa Business Corporation Act," 40 Drake Law Review, 1991. *Member:* Polk County (Board of Directors, 1992-1996; Grievance Committee, 1983-1986), Iowa State (Board of Governors, 1992-1996; Vice Chairman, 1989-1990, Chair, 1990-1991, Corporation and Banking, Business Law Section and Council Member, 2001—, Business Law Section; Board of Editors, Business Law Practice Manual, 2002-2005; Member, Corporate Counsel Section, 1990—; Member, 1983-1985, and Vice Chairman 1989-1990; Lawyers' Professional Insurance Committee) and American (Member, Sections on: Business Law; Tort and Insurance Practice; Health Law; Dispute Resolution) Bar Associations; American Corporate Counsel Association (President, Iowa Chapter, 1995-1998). [Judge Advocate, U.S.A.F., 1964-1967]. ***Email:*** jlkrambeck@belinlaw.com

RICHARD W. LOZIER, JR., born Minneapolis, Minnesota, January 2, 1944; admitted to bar, 1969, Iowa. *Education:* University of Iowa (B.A., 1966; J.D., 1969); Exeter University, Exeter, England. Phi Delta Phi. Special Agent, Federal Bureau of Investigation, 1969-1971. *Member:* Polk County (President, 1986-1987), Iowa State (Member: Board of Governors, 1987-1991) and American Bar Associations. ***Email:*** rwlozier@belinlaw.com

JAMES V. SARCONE, JR., born Newport, Rhode Island, August 11, 1944; admitted to bar, 1969, Iowa; 1972, District of Columbia. *Education:* Rockhurst College (B.A., 1966); Georgetown University (J.D., 1969). Assistant City Attorney, City of Des Moines, 1971-1973. *Member:* The District of Columbia Bar; Polk County and Iowa State Bar Associations. [U.S. Army, active duty, 1969-1971]. ***Email:*** jvsarcone@belinlaw.com

JAMES R. SWANGER, born Muncie, Indiana, August 15, 1946; admitted to bar, 1971, Iowa, U.S. Court of Appeals, Eighth Circuit and U.S. District Court, Southern and Northern Districts of Iowa. *Education:* Drake University (B.A., 1968; J.D., 1971). Phi Alpha Delta. Associate Editor, Drake Law Review, 1970-1971. Chairman, Drake Moot Court Board, 1970-1971. President, Board of Trustees, Legal Aid Society of Polk County, 1983. *Member:* Polk County, Iowa State (Member, Special Committee on Labor Law, 1982-1990; Chairman, Section on Labor and Employment Law, 1990-1991) and American (Member: Section on Labor and Employment Law; Federal Labor Standards Legislation Committee, 1974—) Bar Associations. ***PRACTICE AREAS:*** Labor Law; Employment Law (Management). ***Email:*** jrswanger@belinlaw.com

JEREMY C. SHARPE, born Spokane, Washington, 1950; admitted to bar, 1975, Iowa. *Education:* Columbia University (B.A., magna cum laude, 1972; J.D., 1975). Phi Beta Kappa. Harlan Fiske Stone Scholar. Articles Editor, Columbia Journal of Law and Social Problems, 1974-1975. Author: "State Taxation of Interstate Businesses and the Multistate Tax Compact: The Search for a Delicate Uniformity," 11 Columbia Journal of Law and Social Problems 231, 1975. *Member:* Polk County, Iowa State and American (Member, Real Property, Probate and Trust Law Section) Bar Associations. ***PRACTICE AREAS:*** Commercial Real Estate. ***Email:*** jcsharpe@belinlaw.com

SUE LUETTJOHANN SEITZ, born Cedar Rapids, Iowa, October 18, 1952; admitted to bar, 1976, Iowa, U.S. District Court, Northern and Southern Districts of Iowa, U.S. Court of Appeals, Eighth Circuit and U.S. Supreme Court. *Education:* University of Iowa (B.A., with highest distinction, 1973; J.D., with highest distinction, 1976). Phi Beta Kappa; Phi Delta Phi; Order of the Coif; Moot Court Board. *Member:* Polk County (Member, Arbitration Committee, 1987-1997) and Iowa State (Chair, 1989-1992, Administrative Law Section; Fellow, 1995—) Bar Associations; National Council of School Board Attorneys; Iowa Council of School Board Attorneys (Member, Executive Committee, 1983-1993, 1999—; President, 1985 and 2003). ***PRACTICE AREAS:*** Education Law; Labor Law; Employment Law. ***Email:*** slseitz@belinlaw.com

JOHN T. SEITZ, born Des Moines, Iowa, July 16, 1949; admitted to bar, 1976, Iowa. *Education:* Stanford University (B.A., 1971); University of Iowa (J.D., with highest distinction, 1976). Order of the Coif. *Member:* Polk County and Iowa State Bar Associations. ***PRACTICE AREAS:*** Secured Lending; Uniform Commercial Code; Consumer Banking. ***Email:*** jtseitz@belinlaw.com

ROBERT A. MULLEN, born Clarinda, Iowa, March 31, 1949; admitted to bar, 1978, Iowa. *Education:* Iowa State University (B.S., with distinction, 1971); Drake University (J.D., with honors, 1977). Order of the Coif. Member, Drake Law Review, 1976-1977. Certified Public Accountant, Iowa, 1972; *Member:* Iowa State Bar Association; Iowa Society of CPAs. ***PRACTICE AREAS:*** Banks & Banking; Corporate Law; Mergers; Business Acquisitions; Business Divestitures. ***Email:*** ramullen@belinlaw.com

PATRICIA A. SHOFF, born Colby, Kansas, 1948; admitted to bar, 1973, Iowa. *Education:* University of Iowa (B.A., with honors, 1970; J.D., with distinction, 1973). Listed in The Best Lawyers in America, Family Law, Labor and Employment Law, 2005. Member, 1987-1999 and Vice Chair, State of Iowa Board of Law Examiners. Member, Iowa Law School Foundation, 1992-2004. *Member:* Polk County (Member, Board of Directors, 1987-1999; Vice President, 1992; President-Elect, 1993; President, 1994), Iowa State (Member, Board of Governors, 1995-1999; Member, 1987— and Chairperson, 1991, Labor and Employment Law Section) and American (Member: Labor and Employment Law Committee, 1982—; Family Law Committee) Bar Associations. ***PRACTICE AREAS:*** Civil Rights; Labor and Employment; Family Law; Health Law.

WILLIAM D. BARTINE, born Marshalltown, Iowa, April 15, 1952; admitted to bar, 1977, Iowa. *Education:* Iowa State University (B.A., with distinction, 1974); University of Iowa (J.D., with high distinction, 1977). Order of the Coif. *Member:* Polk County, Iowa State (Member, Title Standards Committee, 1984-2000 and 2001—; Member, Real Estate and Title Law Section Council, 1990-1993, 1997-2000. Chair, Real Estate and Title Law Section, 1992-1993; Chair, Real Estate Practice Manual Committee, 1986-1988) and American Bar Associations. ***PRACTICE AREAS:*** Real Estate; Land Use Regulations. ***Email:*** wdbartine@belinlaw.com

QUENTIN R. BOYKEN, born Titonka, Iowa, September 13, 1954; admitted to bar, 1982, Iowa, U.S. District Court, Northern and Southern Districts of Iowa, U.S. Court of Appeals, Eighth Circuit and U.S. Tax Court. *Education:* Iowa State University (B.S., with distinction, 1976); University of Michigan (J.D., cum laude, 1982). Phi Beta Kappa; Phi Kappa Phi. Certified Public Accountant, Iowa, 1977 and Minnesota, 1979. Norwegian Consul for State of Iowa. *Member:* Polk County, Iowa State (Member, Section on Corporation, Banking and Business Law; Section on, E-Commerce) and American (Member, Section on Corporation, Banking and Business Law) Bar Associations; Iowa Society of Certified Public Accountants; IOWAccess Advisory Council. ***PRACTICE AREAS:*** Business Acquisitions; Corporate Law; Nonprofit and Charitable Organizations. ***Email:*** qrboyken@belinlaw.com

CHARLES F. BECKER, born Dubuque, Iowa, April 8, 1954; admitted to bar, 1979, Iowa. *Education:* University of Iowa (B.B.A., 1976; J.D., 1979). Managing Editor, Iowa Law Review, 1978-1979. Author: "Willful Blindness as a Substitute for Criminal Knowledge," 63 Iowa Law Review 466, 1978; "Guide to Iowa Environmental Laws and Regulations," Iowa Association of Business and Industry, 1990; "Lender Liability for the Environment: What Can A Lender Do?" The Disclosure Magazine, 1991: "Environmental Liability and the CGL Policy: Why is There Coverage?" CPCU Journal, 1992; "Environmental Liability Under Iowa Law," Iowa Commerce Magazine, 1996; "Minimizing Environmental Problems for Iowa Businesses," The Cambridge Institute, 1996; "The Iowa Environmental Audit Priviledge and Immunity Act," Iowa State Bar Association, 1998. Contributing Author: "Brown Fields: A Comprehensive Guide to Redeveloping Contaminated Property," Second Edition, 2002. Contributing Editor, Iowa Environmental Newsletter, 1990-2000. Law Clerk to: Justice Clay LeGrand, Iowa Supreme Court, 1979-1980; Judge Donald E. O'Brien, U.S. District Court, Northern and Southern Districts of Iowa, 1980-1982. Member, Environmental Committee, Iowa Association of Business and Industry, 1989—. *Member:* Polk County, Iowa State (Council Member, Governing Council, Environmental and National Resources Section, 1991-2000) and American (Section of Natural Resources Law) Bar Associations. ***PRACTICE AREAS:*** Environmental Law; Civil Litigation. ***Email:*** cfbecker@belinlaw.com

SHEILA K. TIPTON, born Martins Ferry, Ohio, August 4, 1951; admitted to bar, 1980, Iowa, U.S. District Court, Northern and Southern Districts of Iowa and U.S. Court of Appeals, Eighth Circuit. *Education:* Ohio University (B.S., 1973); Drake University (J.D., with honors, 1980). Phi Alpha Delta. *Member:* Polk County, Iowa State (Member, Administrative Law Section, Section Council, 1989-1991; Member, Business Law Section, Section Council, 1993-1995, Chair, International Trade and Investment Committee, 1992-1994; Member, Trade Regulation Section; Co-Chair, Task Force on the Quality of Life, 1993-1996), American (Member, Business Law, Labor and Employment Law and Public Utilities Law Sections) and Federal Energy (Co-Chair, Power Generation Committee, 2005-2006) Bar Associations. ***PRACTICE AREAS:*** Business Law; Public Utility; Employment; Corporate Governance and Compliance; Corporate; Securities; Administrative Law; Employment Law. ***Email:*** tktipton@belinlaw.com

MARK E. WEINHARDT, born Cedar Rapids, Iowa, September 17, 1960; admitted to bar, 1985, Illinois and U.S. District Court, Northern District of Illinois; 1989, Iowa; 1991, U.S. District Court, Southern and Northern Districts of Iowa, U.S. Court of Appeals, Eighth Circuit. *Education:* Dartmouth College (A.B., magna cum laude, 1982); University of Michigan (J.D, cum laude, 1985). Assistant State's Attorney, Winnebago County (Rockford), Illinois 1988-1991. Special Assistant State's Attorney, 1995-1996, 1999. Member, Local Rules Committee, U.S. District Court, Northern and Southern Districts of Iowa, 2000-2002; Federal Defender Panel, 1992—. *Member:* Polk County and Iowa State Bar Associations; State Bar of Illinois; National Association of Criminal Defense Lawyers; Iowa Association of Criminal Defense Lawyers. Fellow, Iowa Academy of Trial Lawyers. ***PRACTICE AREAS:*** Trial Practice; Commercial Litigation; White Collar Criminal Defense. ***Email:*** meweinhardt@belinlaw.com

DENNIS P. OGDEN, born Cedar Rapids, Iowa, June 14, 1957; admitted to bar, 1982, Iowa; 1983, U.S. District Court, Northern and Southern Districts of Iowa; 1984, U.S. Court of Appeals, Eighth Circuit. *Education:* Iowa State University (B.A., 1979); University of Iowa (J.D., with distinction, 1982). *Member:* Polk County, Iowa State (Member, Executive Council, Young Lawyers Division, 1989-1991; Labor and Employment Law and Litigation Sections, 1992—) and American Bar Associations; Trucking Industry Defense Association. ***PRACTICE AREAS:*** Civil Litigation; Motor Vehicle Accidents and Injuries; Employment Litigation; Commercial Litigation. ***Email:*** dpogden@belinlaw.com

EDWARD M. MANSFIELD, born Cambridge, Massachusetts, January 12, 1957; admitted to bar, 1983, Arizona; 1993, Kansas; 1996 Iowa. *Education:* Harvard University (A.B., magna cum laude, 1978); Yale University (J.D., 1982). Phi Beta Kappa. Law Clerk to Honorable Patrick E. Higginbotham, U.S. Court of Appeals, Fifth Circuit, 1982-1983. Author: "Reflections on Current Limits on Component and Raw Material Supplier Liability and the Proposed Third Restatement," 84 Kentucky Law Journal 221, 1996. ***PRACTICE AREAS:*** Commercial Litigation; Appellate Practice. ***Email:*** emmansfield@belinlaw.com

STEPHEN R. ECKLEY, born Euclid, Ohio, March 18, 1957; admitted to bar, 1981, Missouri; 1984, Iowa; U.S. Supreme Court of Appeals, Eighth Circuit; U.S. District Court, Northern and Southern Districts of Iowa; 2003, Colorado. *Education:* Drake University

(This Listing Continued)

(B.A., summa cum laude, 1977); Harvard University (J.D., 1981). Phi Beta Kappa. *Member:* Polk County, Iowa State and American Bar Associations; American Board of Trial Advocates. ***PRACTICE AREAS:*** Civil Litigation.

DAVID SWINTON, born Des Moines, Iowa, July 4, 1956; admitted to bar, 1981, Colorado; 1984, Iowa. *Education:* University of Iowa (B.A., with high distinction, 1977); Duke University (J.D., with distinction, 1981). Phi Beta Kappa. *Member:* Polk County, Colorado, Iowa State and American Bar Associations. ***PRACTICE AREAS:*** Litigation; Business Law; Contracts; ERISA Litigation.

MARGARET C. CALLAHAN, born Kansas City, Missouri, October 15, 1957; admitted to bar, 1984, Missouri; 1987, Iowa; U.S. Court of Appeals, Eighth Circuit; U.S. District Court, Northern and Southern Districts of Iowa. *Education:* Drake University (B.A., summa cum laude, 1979); Duke University (J.D., high honors, 1984). Law Clerk to Judges John R. Gibson, 1984-1985, Roger L. Wollman, 1985-1986 and George G. Fagg, 1986-1987, U.S. Court of Appeals, 8th Circuit. *Member:* Polk County and Iowa State Bar Associations; The Missouri Bar; Eighth Circuit Bar Association (Director, 2003-2004; Secretary, 2005). ***PRACTICE AREAS:*** Civil Appeals. ***Email:*** mccallahan@belinlaw.com

ROBERT D. SHARP, born Charles City, Iowa, May 4, 1954; admitted to bar, 1987, Iowa; U.S. Court of Appeals, Eighth Circuit; U.S. District Court, Northern and Southern Districts of Iowa. *Education:* University of Northern Iowa (B.A., with honors, 1984); Drake University Law School (J.D., with honors, 1987). Order of the Coif; Order of Barristers. Articles Editor, Drake Law Review, 1986-1987. Author: Note, 36 Drake Law Review 389. *Member:* Polk County, Iowa State and American Bar Associations. ***PRACTICE AREAS:*** Civil Litigation. ***Email:*** rdsharp@belinlaw.com

GARTH D. ADAMS, born Lansing, Michigan, June 5, 1963; admitted to bar, 1990, New York; 1992, Iowa. *Education:* Drake University (B.A., 1985; M.P.A., 1986); Columbia University (J.D., 1989). Harlan Fiske Stone Scholar. Certified Public Accountant, Iowa, 1989. *Member:* American Bar Association (Member, Business Law Section, Committees on: Negotiated Acquisitions; Federal Securities Regulation, 1933 Act and 1934 Act; Uniform Commercial Code, Article 9). ***PRACTICE AREAS:*** Mergers and Acquisitions; Finance; Securities; Commercial Real Estate; Corporate Law. ***Email:*** gdadams@belinlaw.com

MICHAEL R. RECK, born Ottumwa, Iowa, February 11, 1965; admitted to bar, 1991, Illinois; 1994, Iowa. *Education:* The University of Iowa (B.A., with distinction, 1988); Harvard University (J.D., cum laude, 1991). Phi Beta Kappa; Omicron Delta Kappa; Mortar Board. *Member:* Illinois State, Iowa State and American Bar Associations. ***PRACTICE AREAS:*** Civil Litigation; Employment Litigation; Anti-Trust. ***Email:*** mrreck@belinlaw.com

WAYNE E. REAMES, born Cedar Rapids, Iowa, October 8, 1975; admitted to bar, 2000, Iowa, U.S. District Court, Northern and Southern Districts of Iowa, U.S. Court of Appeals, Eighth Circuit and U.S. Tax Court. *Education:* Luther College (B.A., summa cum laude 1997); University of Michigan (J.D., cum laude, 2000); New York University (LL.M, Taxation, 2001). Phi Beta Kappa. Clarence Darrow Scholar. Certified Public Accountant. Iowa, 1997. Member, Iowa Society of Certified Public Accountants. Member, American Institute of Certified Public Accountants. *Member:* Polk County, Iowa State and American Bar Associations. ***PRACTICE AREAS:*** Taxation; Nonprofit Organizations Law; Business Law; Trusts and Estates. ***Email:*** wereames@belinlaw.com

---

S. CHRISTIAN NELSON, born Des Moines, Iowa, February 19, 1975; admitted to bar, 2001, Iowa. *Education:* University of Iowa (B.B.A., with highest distinction and with honors, 1998); University of Michigan, Ann Arbor (J.D., cum laude, 2001). Certified Public Accountant, Iowa, 2000. *Member:* Polk County and Iowa State Bar Association. ***PRACTICE AREAS:*** Business Acquisitions; Corporate Law; Mergers and Acquisitions; Family Business Law; Corporate Organization. ***Email:*** scnelson@belinlaw.com

HOLLY M. LOGAN, born Bloomfield, Iowa, July 31, 1976; admitted to bar, 2001, Iowa and U.S. District Court, Southern and Northern Districts of Iowa; U.S. Court of Appeals, Eighth Circuit; U.S. Supreme Court. *Education:* University of Dayton (B.S., Business Administration, magna cum laude, 1998); University of Iowa (J.D., with high distinction, 2001). Phi Delta Phi. Member, 1999-2000, and Note and Comment Editor, 2000-2001, Journal of Corporation Law. *Member:* Polk County (Member, Board of Directors, Volunteer Lawyer Project), Iowa State and American (Member, Litigation and Criminal Law Sections) Bar Associations; Iowa Association of Criminal Defense Lawyers. ***PRACTICE AREAS:*** Civil Litigation; Criminal Defense; Employment Defense. ***Email:*** hmlogan@belinlaw.com

LAURA E. HAMADY, born Madison, Wisconsin, January 5, 1975; admitted to bar, 2002, Iowa. *Education:* Yale University (B.A., 1997); University of California, Berkeley (J.D., 2002). ***PRACTICE AREAS:*** Promotion Law; Marketing Law; Intellectual Property; Corporate Law. ***Email:*** lehamady@belinlaw.com

LANCE W. LANGE, born Davenport, Iowa, September 21, 1972; admitted to bar, 2001, Illinois; 2005, Iowa. *Education:* Stanford University (A.B., with honors, 1996); University of Iowa (M.A., 1998); Columbia University (J.D., 2001). *Member:* Polk County, Iowa State and American Bar Associations. ***LANGUAGES:*** German. ***PRACTICE AREAS:*** Civil Litigation; Defamation; Intellectual Property Litigation; Corporate Investigations; Antitrust Litigation. ***Email:*** lwlange@belinlaw.com

SILVIA J. HANSELL, born Georgetown, South Carolina, October 23, 1970; admitted to bar, 2004, Iowa. *Education:* Duke University (A.B., cum laude, 1993); University of Michigan (J.D., 1997). Member, 1995-1997 and Executive Editor, 1996-1997, Michigan Law Review. *Member:* Polk County and American Bar Associations. ***LANGUAGES:*** German. ***PRACTICE AREAS:*** Family Law; Commercial Litigation. ***Email:*** sjhansell@belinlaw.com

TRICIA A. JOHNSTON, born Iowa City, Iowa, August 21, 1964; admitted to bar, 1993, Iowa. *Education:* University of Colorado; University of Iowa (B.A., 1988; J.D., 1992). ***LANGUAGES:*** Spanish. ***PRACTICE AREAS:*** Criminal Law; Employment Law.

MATTHEW C. McDERMOTT, born Carroll, Iowa, November 22, 1977; admitted to bar, 2003, Iowa. *Education:* University of Iowa (B.A., with distinction and honors, 2000); University of California, Berkeley (J.D., 2003). Executive Editor, California Law Review, 2002-2003. *Member:* Polk County, Iowa State and American Bar Associations. ***Email:*** mmcdermott@belinlaw.com

OF COUNSEL

DANIELLE M. SHELTON, born Fort Wayne, Indiana, July 21, 1970; admitted to bar, 1995, Iowa, Illinois and U.S. District Court, Northern and Southern Districts of Iowa. *Education:* Augustana College (B.A., summa cum laude, 1992); Harvard Law School (J.D., magna cum laude, 1995). Phi Beta Kappa. Law Clerk to Judge Ed Carnes, U.S. Court of Appeals, Eleventh Circuit, 1995-1996. *Member:* Polk County, Illinois State, Iowa State and American Bar Associations. ***PRACTICE AREAS:*** Trial Practice; Civil Litigation. ***Email:*** dmshelton@belinlaw.com

---

BRADSHAW, FOWLER, PROCTOR & FAIRGRAVE, P.C.

Established in 1917
801 GRAND AVENUE, SUITE 3700
DES MOINES, IOWA 50309-2727
Telephone: 515-243-4191
Fax: 515-246-5808
URL: http://www.bradshawlaw.com

General Civil Practice, including Litigation, Insurance, Corporation, Commercial, Probate, Taxation, Real Estate, Antitrust, Bankruptcy and Reorganization, Public Utility, Workers' Compensation, Motor Carrier and Administrative Law.

FIRM PROFILE: History and Management: The firm has been providing legal services for nearly a century and is recognized in the State for its stability and steady growth. The firm is administered by a four person Management Committee working with a professional office administrator.

Delivery of Services: Practice groups in the Firm include Commercial Litigation, Transaction Law, and Insurance Defense Litigation including all aspects of liability and property insurance as well as workers' compensation. Each practice group is responsible for the assignment of work and the timely and efficient delivery of services.

Client Base: Clients of the Firm include corporate leaders in the fields of insurance, mortgage lending, banking, health care and utilities. While a substantial portion of the Firm's client base is made up of larger corporations, the Firm represents a significant number of small businesses and individuals.

CHARLES S. BRADSHAW (1871-1953)
REX H. FOWLER (1893-1972)
W. Z. PROCTOR (1902-1995)
D. J. FAIRGRAVE (1906-1990)
HOWARD A. STEELE (1909-1973)
HARRIS M. COGGESHALL (1907-1993)
ROBERT E. DREY (1931-1997)
DAN STAMATELOS (1934-2001)
HOMER E. BRADSHAW (1914-2005)
JOHN V. SYNHORST (Retired)

KENT M. FORNEY, born Hull, Iowa, September 17, 1932; admitted to bar, 1958, Iowa. *Education:* University of Iowa (B.A., 1956; J.D., with distinction, 1958). *Member:* Polk County (President, 1975-1976), Iowa State (Board of Governors, 1976-1978) and American Bar Associations; American Board of Trial Advocates; International Association of Defense Counsel; Association of Insurance Attorneys; Iowa Academy of Trial Lawyers (President, 1977-1978); Iowa Defense Counsel Association; International Society of Barristers; Defense Research Institute. Fellow: American College of Trial Lawyers; American Bar Foundation. ***PRACTICE AREAS:*** Insurance Defense; Insurance Regulation; Corporate Insurance. ***Email:*** forney.kent@bradshawlaw.com

MICHAEL H. FIGENSHAW, born Jefferson, Iowa, July 18, 1940; admitted to bar, 1964, Iowa. *Education:* Creighton University and University of Iowa (B.A., 1962); University of Iowa (J.D., with honors, 1964). Member, Board of Editors, Iowa Law Review, 1963-1964. *Member:* Polk County, Iowa State (Chairman, Professional Ethics and Conduct Committee, 1987-1991) and American Bar Associations; Iowa Academy of Trial Lawyers; Iowa Defense Counsel Association; American Board of Trial Advocates. Fellow: American College of Trial Lawyers. ***PRACTICE AREAS:*** Civil Practice; Trial Practice; Insurance Defense Law; Personal Injury Law. ***Email:*** figenshaw.mike@bradshawlaw.com

JOHN C. CORTESIO, JR., born Centerville, Iowa, February 1, 1938; admitted to bar, 1962, Iowa; 1963, U.S. Court of Military Appeals; 1987, U.S. Supreme Court. *Education:* University of Notre Dame (B.A., cum laude, 1959); University of Iowa (J.D., with high distinction, 1962). Order of the Coif. Note Editor, Iowa Law Review, 1961-1962. Member, Board of Editors, Federal Bar Journal, 1964. *Member:* Polk County (Member, Board of Directors, 1991-1995), Iowa State (Chairman, Trade Regulation Section, 1997-1999; Member, Board of Governors, 1991-1995; Member, Trade Regulation Section Council, 1990-1992 and 1997-1999; Chairman, Trade Regulation Committee, 1981-1987; Member, Grievance Commission, 1980-1981) and American (Member, Sections on: Antitrust Law; Litigation) Bar Associations; American Health Lawyers Association. Fellow, Iowa State Bar Foundation. [Capt., J.A.G.C., U.S. Army, 1962-1965]. ***PRACTICE AREAS:*** Corporate and Business Law; Antitrust and Trade Regulations; Appellate Practice. ***Email:*** cortesio.john@bradshawlaw.com

EDWARD E. JOHNSON, born Greenfield, Iowa, January 30, 1943; admitted to bar, 1968, Iowa. *Education:* Grinnell College (B.A., 1965); University of Iowa (J.D., 1968). Phi Delta Phi; Phi Beta Kappa; Order of the Coif. Member, Board of Editors, Iowa Law Review,

(This Listing Continued)

BRADSHAW, FOWLER, PROCTOR & FAIRGRAVE, P.C., Des Moines—Continued

1967-1968. *Member:* Polk County, Iowa State and American Bar Associations. ***PRACTICE AREAS:*** Corporate; Business; Probate, Trust and Estate. ***Email:*** johnson.edward@bradshawlaw.com

LARRY D. SPAULDING, born Muscatine, Iowa, June 22, 1941; admitted to bar, 1970, Iowa. *Education:* University of Northern Iowa (B.A., 1967); Drake University (J.D., 1970). Delta Theta Phi. *Member:* Polk County, Iowa State and American Bar Associations; Iowa Defense Counsel Association; Iowa Academy of Trial Lawyers (Member, Tort and Insurance Law Practice, 1990); American Board of Trial Advocates. ***PRACTICE AREAS:*** Civil Practice; Trial Practice; Insurance Defense; Personal Injury Law. ***Email:*** spaulding.larry@bradshawlaw.com

WILLIAM F. FANTER, born Elgin, Illinois, September 28, 1944; admitted to bar, 1969, Iowa. *Education:* University of Iowa (B.B.A., 1966; J.D., 1969). Phi Delta Phi. *Member:* Polk County, Iowa State and American (Member, Property Insurance Law Committee, Section on Tort and Insurance Practice, 1981—) Bar Associations; Iowa Defense Counsel Association; Federation of Defense and Corporate Counsel (President, 2000-2001); Defense Research Institute; American Board of Trial Advocates. ***PRACTICE AREAS:*** Civil Litigation; Trial Practice; Civil Defense; Personal Injury; Arson Law; Fraud. ***Email:*** fanter.william@bradshawlaw.com

DAVID J. W. PROCTOR, born Des Moines, Iowa, April 1, 1946; admitted to bar, 1971, Iowa. *Education:* University of Iowa (B.A., 1968; J.D., with distinction, 1971). Phi Delta Phi. Member, Iowa Defense Council. Contract Instructor: Bureau of Alcohol, Tobacco and Firearms, ATF National Academy; Arson Course of Instruction, Federal Law Enforcement Training Center, Glynco, Georgia, 2000—. Lecturer, Fire and Arson Investigation Course, sponsored by the State Fire Marshal's Office, 1985—. Member, International Association of Arson Investigators (Member, Attorney Advisory Committee). Member, Board of Directors, Iowa Chapter, International Association of Arson Investigators, 1985—. *Member:* Polk County, Iowa State and American Bar Associations. ***PRACTICE AREAS:*** Insurance Fraud; Property Insurance. ***Email:*** proctor.david@bradshawlaw.com

JAMES M. HOLCOMB, born Sioux City, Iowa, June 21, 1943; admitted to bar, 1971, Iowa. *Education:* Iowa State University (B.S., 1965); University of Iowa (J.D., with distinction, 1971). Phi Delta Phi. Adjunct Professor, Modern Real Estate Transactions, Drake University College of Law, 2001-2002.*Member:* Polk County (Chair, Title Standards Committee, 2002—; Board of Directors, 1995-1999), Iowa State (Member: Board of Governors, 1995-1999; Real Estate and Title Law Section) and American (Member, Sections on: Real Property, Probate and Trust Law; Corporation, Banking and Business Law) Bar Associations; American College of Real Estate Lawyers. ***PRACTICE AREAS:*** Real Estate; Business; Bankruptcy; Probate Law. ***Email:*** holcomb.james@bradshawlaw.com

DENNY M. DENNIS, born Des Moines, Iowa, March 30, 1946; admitted to bar, 1970, Iowa; 1976, U.S. Supreme Court. *Education:* Drake University (B.A., 1967; J.D., with honors, 1970). Order of the Coif; Delta Theta Phi. Member, Drake University Law Review, 1969-1970. *Member:* Polk County, Iowa State and American (Member, Sections on: Litigation; Tort and Insurance Practice) Bar Associations; Iowa Defense Counsel Association; Defense Research Institute; Iowa Academy of Trial Lawyers. [Lt., JAGC, U.S. Navy, 1970-1974]. ***PRACTICE AREAS:*** Commercial Litigation; Business Litigation; Insurance Litigation. ***Email:*** dennis.denny@bradshawlaw.com

DONALD F. NEIMAN, born Hammond, Indiana, October 17, 1944; admitted to bar, 1969, Iowa; 1972, U.S. Court of Appeals, 8th Circuit and U.S. District Court, Northern and Southern Districts of Iowa. *Education:* University of Iowa (B.B.A., 1966); Drake University (J.D., 1969). Phi Alpha Delta. Trustee, U.S. Bankruptcy Court, Southern District of Iowa, 1974-2002. *Member:* Polk County, Iowa State (Member, 1983-2002, and Chairman, 1983-1984, Commercial Law and Bankruptcy Committee, 1992-2002), Federal and American Bar Associations; Commercial Law League of America; National Association of Bankruptcy Trustees. [Captain, Judge Advocate, USAF, 1969-1972]. ***PRACTICE AREAS:*** Bankruptcy Law; Business; Commercial Law. ***Email:*** neiman.donald@bradshawlaw.com

MARK L. TRIPP, born Kansas City, Missouri, August 18, 1952; admitted to bar, 1981, Iowa. *Education:* Iowa State University (B.S., with distinction, 1978); Drake University (J.D., with honors, 1980). Pi Sigma Alpha. Member, Drake University Law Review, 1979-1980. *Member:* Polk County, Iowa State and American Bar Associations; Iowa Defense Counsel Association (Past President, 1999); Defense Research Institute. ***PRACTICE AREAS:*** Products Liability; Civil Defense; Personal Injury; Insurance Litigation. ***Email:*** tripp.mark@bradshawlaw.com

DAVID L. JENKINS, born Aurora, Illinois, May 30, 1951; admitted to bar, 1976, Iowa and U.S. Court of Military Appeals. *Education:* Vanderbilt University; Drake University (B.S., 1973; J.D., with honors, 1976). Beta Gamma Sigma. Member, Midwest Judicature Society. *Member:* Polk County, Iowa State and American (Member, Sections on: Tort and Insurance Practice; Labor and Employment) Bar Associations; Defense Research Institute; Iowa Association of Workers' Compensation Lawyers, Inc. (Member, Board of Governors, 1997—). [Capt., JAGD, U.S. Air Force, 1976-1982]. ***PRACTICE AREAS:*** Workers' Compensation; Civil Practice; Trial Practice; Insurance Defense; Personal Injury. ***Email:*** jenkins.david@bradshawlaw.com

STEVEN M. AUGSPURGER, born Bloomfield, Iowa, October 10, 1961; admitted to bar, 1987, Iowa. *Education:* University of Iowa (B.B.A., 1984); University of Iowa (J.D., with distinction, 1987). Managing Editor, Journal of Corporation Law, Volume 12. Author: "Empirical Research Project, Defensive Tactics to Hostile Tender Offers—An Examination of Their Legitimacy and Effectiveness," 11 J. Corp. L. 651, 1986. *Member:* Polk County, Iowa State and American Bar Associations; Iowa Association of Workers' Compensation Lawyers; Iowa Defense Counsel Association; Defense Research Institute, Inc. ***PRACTICE AREAS:*** Civil Practice; Trial Practice; Insurance Defense; Workers' Compensation. ***Email:*** augspurger.steven@bradshawlaw.com

GREGORY A. WITKE, born Des Moines, Iowa, November 15, 1961; admitted to bar, 1987, Iowa. *Education:* Iowa State University (B.S., with distinction, 1984); University of Iowa (J.D., with distinction, 1987). Phi Kappa Phi; Phi Eta Sigma; Alpha Lambda Delta; Phi Delta Phi. Member, Moot Court Board. *Member:* Polk County, Iowa State and American Bar Associations; Iowa Defense Counsel Association; Defense Research Institute; Federation of Defense and Corporate Counsel. ***PRACTICE AREAS:*** Civil Litigation; Commercial Litigation; Personal Injury; Medical Malpractice; Products Liability. ***Email:*** witke.greg@bradshawlaw.com

KENNETH R. MUNRO, born Chicago, Illinois, August 29, 1963; admitted to bar, 1988, Iowa. *Education:* University of Notre Dame (B.A., 1985); University of Iowa (J.D., with distinction, 1988). Member, Iowa Law Review, 1986-1988. *Member:* Polk County, Iowa State and American Bar Associations; Iowa Defense Counsel Association; Defense Research Institute. ***PRACTICE AREAS:*** Personal Injury; Insurance Defense. ***Email:*** munro.kenneth@bradshawlaw.com

D. BRIAN SCIESZINSKI, born Iowa City, Iowa, March 16, 1962; admitted to bar, 1987, Iowa. *Education:* University of Iowa (B.S., 1984; J.D., with high distinction, 1987). *Member:* Polk County, Iowa State and American (Member, Workers Compensation Law Committee) Bar Associations; Iowa Association of Workers' Compensation Lawyers; Iowa Trial Lawyers Association. ***PRACTICE AREAS:*** Workers' Compensation; Insurance Defense; Personal Injury. ***Email:*** scieszinski.brian@bradshawlaw.com

GREGORY L. KENYON, born Creston, Iowa, January 27,1954; admitted to bar, 1978, Iowa; 1980, U.S. District Court, Southern and Northern Districts of Iowa. *Education:* Buena Vista College (B.A., 1975); Drake University (J.D., 1978). Former Member, United States Arbitration and Mediation of Iowa. Regular Speaker and Presenter, Continuing Legal Education, Estates, Trusts, Elder Law, Medicaid and Long Term Care Planning. Lecturer, Des Moines Area Community College, Legal Assistant Program, 1982-1984. *Member:* Polk County (Board Member, 1997-2002), Iowa State (Member: Probate Section, 1987—; Probate Section Council, 1993-1997 and 1999— and Chair 1996-1997 and 2000-2002) and American Bar Associations; American College of Trust and Estate Counsel. ***PRACTICE AREAS:*** Estate Planning; Elder Law; Probate; Trust Law; Real Estate; Corporate Law. ***Email:*** kenyon.gregory@bradshawlaw.com

KELLY L. McCARTY, born Des Moines, Iowa, July 11, 1957; admitted to bar, 1982, Iowa. *Education:* University of Iowa (B.B.A., 1979; J.D., 1982). Member, Association of Business and Industry Commerce and Tax Committees, 2000-2002. Certified Public Accountant, Iowa, 1980. Member, Editorial Board, The Journal of Multistate Taxation, 1991-1996. Author: "Magazine and Newspaper Distinction Unclear," The Journal of Multistate Taxation, March/April 1991; "New Seed Capital Credit Encourages Investment," The Journal of Multistate Taxation, May/June 1991; "Technological Innovations Compel Economic Presence," The Journal of Multistate Taxation, September/October 1991; "Limitations Statute Runs From Due Date With Extensions," The Journal of Multistate Taxation, May/June 1992; "Consultant Services Increase Scope of Sales Tax," The Journal of Multistate Taxation, July/August 1992; "Field Condensate was Subject to Tax as Oil," The Journal of Multistate Taxation, Jan./Feb. 1993; "Voluntary Settlement Not Affected by Later Court Holding," The Journal of Multistate Taxation, March/April 1993; "U.S. Supreme Court Hits Back at State Tax Authorities," International Financial Law Review, October 1992; "Tax Bill Impact on Banks," The Northwestern Banker, October, 1987; "Iowa Sales & Use Taxes," American Bar Association, Section of Taxation, Sales & Use Tax Desk Book, 1988-1996. Presenter, Professional and Nonprofessional Groups on Various Business and Taxation Issues. *Member:* Polk County, Iowa State (Taxation, Business Law and Corporate Counsel Sections, 2000-2002) and American (Member, Sections on: Taxation; Corporation; Banking and Business Law) Bar Associations. ***PRACTICE AREAS:*** Business Transactions; Finance; Taxation; Securities. ***Email:*** mccarty.kelly@bradshawlaw.com

KARL TAGE OLSON, born South Weymouth, Massachusetts, October 9, 1958; admitted to bar, 1992, New Mexico; 1993, Iowa. *Education:* College of William and Mary (B.A., 1980); Drake University (J.D., with honors, 1992). Delta Theta Phi. Order of the Coif. Editor-in-Chief, Drake Law Review. Member, Drake Trial Competition Team. Author: Case Note: Missouri v. Jenkins, 41 Drake Law Review 223, 1992; Note "The Constitutionality of Department of Defense Press Restrictions on Wartime Correspondents Covering the Persian Gulf War," 41 Drake Law Review 511, 1992. *Member:* Polk County, Iowa State and American Bar Associations; Defense Research Institute; Iowa Defense Counsel Association. [U.S. Army, 1980-1989, Capt.; U.S.A.R., Maj., 1989-1993]. ***PRACTICE AREAS:*** Insurance Coverage; Personal Injury; Commercial Litigation; Construction Law. ***Email:*** olson.karl@bradshawlaw.com

ELIZABETH A. NIGUT, born Des Moines, Iowa, July 19, 1969; admitted to bar, 1994, Iowa. *Education:* Simpson College (B.A., cum laude, 1991); Drake University (J.D., 1994). Delta Theta Phi. *Member:* Polk County, Iowa State (Member, Employment Law and Litigation Sections) and American (Member, Employment and Labor Law, Tort and Insurance Practice Sections) Bar Associations; Defense Research Institute; Iowa Defense Counsel Association. ***PRACTICE AREAS:*** Personal Injury; Commercial Litigation; Employment Law. ***Email:*** nigut.beth@bradshawlaw.com

CYNTHIA A. HURLEY, born Elmhurst, Illinois, December 5, 1968; admitted to bar, 1994, Iowa. *Education:* University of Iowa (B.A., with honors, 1991); Drake University (J.D., with honors, 1994). Delta Theta Phi. Member, Order of the Coif. *Member:* Polk County, Iowa State and American Bar Associations. ***PRACTICE AREAS:*** Estate Planning; Real Estate; Corporate; Taxation. ***Email:*** hurley.cynthia@bradshawlaw.com

MICHAEL L. MOCK, born Holbrook, Nebraska, December 2, 1969; admitted to bar, 1995, Iowa. *Education:* Drake University (B.A., magna cum laude, 1992; J.D., with honors, 1995). Delta Theta Phi; Phi Beta Kappa; Order of the Coif. Editor in Chief, Drake Law Review, 1994-1995. *Member:* Polk County, Iowa State and American Bar Associations; Iowa Defense Counsel; Defense Research Institute. ***PRACTICE AREAS:*** Worker's Compensation; Insurance Defense Law. ***Email:*** mock.michael@bradshawlaw.com

JEFFREY D. GOETZ, born Brooklyn, New York, May 21, 1956; admitted to bar, 1992, California and U.S. District Court, Southern, Central and Eastern Districts of California; 2001, Iowa and U.S. District Court, Southern District of Iowa; 2002, U.S. District Court, Northern District of Iowa. *Education:* University of California at Santa Barbara (B.A., History, 1978); California Western School of Law (J.D., 1987). Recipient, State Bar of California Wiley W. Manual Award for Pro Bono Legal Services, 2000. Guest Lecturer, San Diego City College, Downtown Campus, Paralegal Program, 1995. Seminar Lecturer, San Diego Volunteer Lawyers Program, AID/HIV Law Panel, Bankruptcy Law, 1993. Member, U.S. Bankruptcy Court, Southern District of California, Committee on Electronic Bankruptcy Filings, 1996-1999. Member, Case Management/Electronic Case Filing Users

(This Listing Continued)

Group, U.S. Bankruptcy Court, Southern District of California, 1999-2001. Seminar Faculty: Iowa State Bar Association, Young Lawyers Division. Summer Seminars: "The Revised UCC Article Nine," 2002; Bankruptcy Seminars, Inc., 32nd Annual Bankruptcy Seminar,"The Revised UCC Article Nine," 2002; Sterling Educational Services, LLC, Creditor's Rights and Protection of Security Interests in Bankruptcy, "Problems for Secured Creditors in Bankruptcy" and "Insuring That a Security Agreement and Financing Statement are Valid," 2002. *Member:* Polk County, Iowa State and American (Business Law Section) Bar Associations; American Bankruptcy Institute. ***PRACTICE AREAS:*** Bankruptcy; Corporate Transactions. ***Email:*** goetz.jeffrey@bradshawlaw.com

DOUGLAS A. FULTON, born Waterloo, Iowa, December 18, 1957; admitted to bar, 1986, Iowa, U.S. District Court, Southern District of Iowa; 1988, U.S. Court of Appeals, Eighth Circuit; 1989, U.S. District Court, Southern District of Iowa; 1992, U.S. Supreme Court. *Education:* University of Northern Iowa (B.A., 1980); Drake University (J.D., with honors, 1985). *Member:* Iowa State and American Bar Associations; American Trial Lawyers Association. ***PRACTICE AREAS:*** Real Estate; Corporations; Health Law; Employment Law. ***Email:*** fulton.douglas@bradshawlaw.com

IRIS J. POST, born Hartley, Iowa, October 9, 1956; admitted to bar, 1981, Iowa, Illinois and U.S. District Court, Southern and Northern Districts of Iowa and U.S. Court of Appeals, Eighth Circuit. *Education:* University of Iowa (B.A., 1977; J.D., 1980). Assistant Attorney General, State of Iowa, 1981-1984. Iowa Workers' Compensation Commissioner, 1996-2002. Appt. by Secretary of Energy Richardson, Jan. 2001 for 2 yr. term on Advisor Comm. to Federal Worker Advocacy Office of the Dept. of Energy. *Member:* Iowa State (Member: Workers Compensation Committee, 1988-1992; Professionalism Committee, 1993-1995; Women and Minorities Committee, 1990-1997; Environmental Section Council, 1993-1996; IAIABC Board Member, 1996-2000) and American Bar Associations. ***PRACTICE AREAS:*** Workers Compensation; Personal Injury; Bad Faith Litigation; Environmental Litigation. ***Email:*** post.iris@bradshawlaw.com

GORDON R. FISCHER, born Oak Park, Illinois, November 24, 1964; admitted to bar, 1994, Iowa. *Education:* University of Iowa (B.A., 1991); Southern Illinois University (J.D., summa cum laude, 1994). Captain, Southern Illinois University Environmental Law Moot Court Team, 1993-1994. Editor, Southern Illinois University Law Journal, 1993-1994. Law Clerk, Honorable Maynard J.V. Hayden, Iowa Court of Appeals, 1994-1995. Monthly Columnist, The Iowa Lawyer Magazine, 1996-1999; Quarterly Columnist, In Brief Magazine, 1997-1999. Chosen "40 Most Influential Leaders Under 40," Des Moines Business Record, 2002. Graduated, Greater Des Moines Leadership Institute, 1996. Member: Society for Human Resource Management, 1998—; Central Iowa Society for Human Resource Management, 1998—. Chair, Iowa Democratic Party, 2002—. *Member:* Polk County (Ethics Committee), Iowa State and American Bar Associations; Iowa Defense Counsel Association; Iowa Trial Lawyers Association (Amicus Curiae Committee); Defense Research Institute, Inc. ***LANGUAGES:*** German. ***PRACTICE AREAS:*** Employment Law. ***Email:*** fischer.gordon@bradshawlaw.com

ANN C. SPELLMAN, born Iowa City, Iowa, April 10, 1969; admitted to bar, 1994, Iowa; 1995, U.S. District Court, Northern and Southern Districts of Iowa. *Education:* University of Iowa (B.A., 1991); Drake University (J.D., 1994). Delta Theta Phi. *Member:* Polk County, Iowa State and American Bar Associations; Iowa Defense Counsel Association; Defense Research Institute. ***PRACTICE AREAS:*** Workers Compensation; Insurance Defense; Civil Litigation. ***Email:*** spellman.ann@bradshawlaw.com

SEAN M. O'BRIEN, born St. Louis Park, Minnesota, November 24, 1969; admitted to bar, 1995, Iowa. *Education:* Grinnell College (B.A., in Economics, with honors, 1992); University of Iowa College of Law (J.D., with distinction, 1995). Phi Beta Kappa. Senior Note and Comment Editor, Journal of Corporation Law, 1994-1995. Author: Note, "Caveat Venditor: A Case for Granting Subsequent Purchasers a Cause of Action Against Builder-Vendors for Latent Defects in the Home," 20 J.Corp.L. 525 (1995). Law Clerk to Justice David Harris, Iowa Supreme Court, 1995-1996. Adjunct Professor, Business Law, Drake University, 1996—. *Member:* Polk County, Iowa State and American Bar Associations; Defense Research Institute; Iowa Defense Council Association; International Association of Arson Investigators (Iowa Chapter). ***PRACTICE AREAS:*** Insurance Fraud; Arson; Property Insurance; Fire and Explosion Litigation; Construction; Zoning Law. ***Email:*** obrien.sean@bradshawlaw.com

TODD A. STROTHER, born Des Moines, Iowa, September 15, 1968; admitted to bar, 1995, Illinois and U.S. District Court, Northern District of Illinois; 1997, U.S. Court of Appeals, Seventh Circuit; 2000, Iowa; 2001, U.S. District Court, Southern District of Iowa; 2002, U.S. District Court, Northern District of Iowa. *Education:* University of Iowa (B.B.A., Finance, 1991; J.D., with high distinction, 1995). Member, Iowa Law Review, Moot Court Board. Co-Author: "Private Rights of Action Under the CEA Defined Further," *Futures & Derivative Law Report,* Vol. 18, No. 9 (Dec. 1998). Assistant Author: "Discovery & Mandatory Disclosures," *Lawyers Cooperative Federal Practice Guide: Federal Civil Procedure Before Trial,* Vol. 3, Ch. 14 (1998). *Member:* American Bar Association; Defense Research Institute; Iowa Defense Counsel Association. ***PRACTICE AREAS:*** Securities; General Trial Practice; Commercial Litigation; Insurance Litigation. ***Email:*** strother.todd@bradshawlaw.com

PATRICK D. SMITH, born Canoga Park, California, April 19, 1967; admitted to bar, 1993, Iowa and U.S. District Court, Northern and Southern Districts of Iowa. *Education:* Drake University (B.A., magna cum laude, 1989); University of Iowa (J.D., with high distinction, 1993). Note and Comment Editor, Journal of Corporation Law, 1992-1993. Author: Comment, "The Court Opens the Door to Arbitration of Employment Disputes," 17 Journal of Corporation Law 865. *Member:* Polk County, Iowa State (Member, Sections on: Employment Law; Litigation; Workers' Compensation) and American Bar Associations; Iowa Defense Counsel Association; Defense Research Institute, Inc. ***PRACTICE AREAS:*** Civil Litigation; Insurance; Construction Law; Employment Litigation; Personal Injury; Worker's Compensation. ***Email:*** smith.patrick@bradshawlaw.com

JASON T. MADDEN, born Mason City, Iowa, January 28, 1972; admitted to bar, 1997, Iowa, U.S. District Court, Northern and Southern Districts of Iowa and U.S. Court of Appeals, 8th Circuit. *Education:* Wartburg College (B.A., with honors, 1994); Drake University (J.D., with honors, 1997). Member, 1995-1996 and Vice-President, 1996-1997, Moot Court Board. Member, 1995-1996 and Articles Editor, 1996-1997, Drake Journal of Agricultural Law. *Member:* Iowa State and American Bar Associations; Defense Research Institute; Blackstone Inn of Court. ***PRACTICE AREAS:*** Product Liability and Insurance Defense Litigation. ***Email:*** madden.jason@bradshawlaw.com

LORI A. BRANDAU, born Waverly, Iowa, February 2, 1971; admitted to bar, 1997, Iowa. *Education:* Wartburg College (B.A., 1993); University of Iowa (J.D., 1997). Member, National Moot Court Team, 1996-1997. *Member:* Polk County, Iowa State and American Bar Associations; Defense Research Institute, Inc.; Association of Business and Industry. ***PRACTICE AREAS:*** Workers Compensation Law. ***Email:*** brandau.lori@bradshawlaw.com

DAVID N. MAY, born Kirksville, Missouri, May 23, 1971; admitted to bar, 1998, Iowa; U.S. Court of Appeals, Eighth Circuit; U.S. District Court, Northern and Southern Districts of Iowa; 2000, Minnesota. *Education:* University of Missouri (B.A., 1993); University of Oklahoma Health Sciences Center (M.P.H., 1995); Drake University (J.D., high honors, 1998). Order of the Coif. Associate Editor, Drake Law Review, 1997-1998. Author: Note, "Inhouse Defenders of Insureds: Some Ethical Considerations," 46 Drake L. Rev. 881, 1998; "Pioneer's Paradox: Appellate Rule 4(a)(5) and the Rule Against Excusing Ignorance of Law," 48 Drake L. Rev. 677, 2000. Co-author: "Hedge to Arrive Contracts and the Commodity Exchange Act: A Textual Alternative," 47 Drake L. Rev. 319, 1999. ***PRACTICE AREAS:*** Insurance Fraud; Insurance Litigation; Insurance Coverage; Commercial Litigation; Appellate Litigation. ***Email:*** may.david@bradshawlaw.com

JASON C. PALMER, born Gainesville, Georgia, August 19, 1970; admitted to bar, 1997, Wisconsin; 1998, Iowa, U.S. District Court, Northern and Southern Districts of Iowa. *Education:* University of Iowa (B.S., 1994); Drake University (J.D., with honors, 1997). Member, 1995-1997, and Managing Editor, 1995-1997, Drake Law Review. Clerk, Iowa Supreme Court, Justice K. David Harris, 1997-1998. *Member:* Iowa State Bar Association. ***PRACTICE AREAS:*** Commercial Litigation; Insurance Defense. ***Email:*** palmer.jason@bradshawlaw.com

PATRICK T. BURK, born Waterloo, Iowa, July 19, 1965; admitted to bar, 1992, Iowa. *Education:* University of Northern Iowa (B.A., 1989); Drake University (J.D., with honors, 1991). *Member:* Polk County and Iowa State (Member, Sections on: Real Estate; Title) Bar Associations. ***PRACTICE AREAS:*** Real Estate; Zoning; Development; Financing; Leasing; Business Law; Corporate Law. ***Email:*** burk.patrick@bradshawlaw.com

MATTHEW J. HAINDFIELD, born Onawa, Iowa, September 26, 1971; admitted to bar, 1999, Iowa, U.S. District Court, Northern and Southern Districts of Iowa and U.S. Court of Appeals, Eighth Circuit. *Education:* Iowa State University (B.S., 1994); Drake University Law School (J.D., with honors, 1999). Order of the Barristers. *Member:* Polk County (Member, Bench and Bar Committee), Iowa State (Member, YLD Bar Review Committee) and American (Member, Litigation and Tort and Insurance Sections) Bar Associations; Iowa Defense Counsel Association; Defense Research Institute; American Inns of Court. ***PRACTICE AREAS:*** Commercial and Insurance Defense Litigation. ***Email:*** haindfield.matt@bradshawlaw.com

---

LORI E. COLE, born Cresco, Iowa, October 10, 1970; admitted to bar, 1999, Iowa and U.S. District Court, Northern and Southern Districts of Iowa. *Education:* University of Northern Iowa (B.A., 1993); Drake University (J.D., with honors, 1998). Delta Theta Phi. William F. Starr Insurance Law Moot Court Team, 1997-1998 (finalist and best brief); National Mock Trial Team, 1998. *Member:* Polk County and Iowa State Bar Associations; The Association of Trial Lawyers of America; Iowa Organization of Women Attorneys. [U.S. Army National Guard, 1994-1997]. ***PRACTICE AREAS:*** Litigation. ***Email:*** cole.lori@bradshawlaw.com

MATTHEW M. CARVER, born Des Moines, Iowa, January 25, 1972; admitted to bar, 2001, Iowa; 2002, Minnesota. *Education:* University of Notre Dame (B.A., 1994); University of Iowa (J.D., 2001). *Member:* Polk County, Iowa State, Minnesota State and American Bar Associations. [Captain, Iowa Army National Guard, 1998—]. ***PRACTICE AREAS:*** Real Estate; Corporate. ***Email:*** carver.matthew@bradshawlaw.com

MEGAN ALTHOFF WOLFE, born Cascade, Iowa, August 13, 1975; admitted to bar, 2000, Iowa and U.S. District Court, Northern and Southern Districts of Iowa. *Education:* University of Iowa (B.B.A., 1997; J.D., with distinction, 2000). Articles Editor, Journal of Corporation Law, 1999-2000. Law Clerk to Justice Mark S. Cady, Iowa Supreme Court, 2000-2002. Author: Note, "The National Bank Act's Federal Preemption of State Electronic Funds Transfer Acts," 25J.Corp.L.843, 2000. *Member:* Polk County, Iowa State and American Bar Associations; Iowa Defense Counsel Association; Defense Research Institute, Inc. ***LANGUAGES:*** Spanish. ***PRACTICE AREAS:*** Insurance Defense and Commercial Litigation. ***Email:*** althoffwolfe.megan@bradshawlaw.com

THOMAS D. LEAHY, born Des Moines, Iowa, October 17, 1967; admitted to bar, 2002, Iowa. *Education:* Drake University (B.S.B.A., cum laude, 1990; J.D., with honors, 2002). *Member:* Polk County, Iowa State and American Bar Associations. ***PRACTICE AREAS:*** Estate Planning; Probate; Real Estate and Business Law. ***Email:*** leahy.thomas@bradshawlaw.com

STACIE M. CODR, born Norfolk, Nebraska, December 30, 1976; admitted to bar, 2002, Iowa. *Education:* University of Iowa (B.A., 1998; J.D., with honors, 2002). Articles Editor, Journal of Gender, Race & Justice. *Member:* Polk County, Iowa State and American Bar Associations. ***PRACTICE AREAS:*** Insurance Defense Litigation. ***Email:*** codr.stacie@bradshawlaw.com

BRIAN R. KOHLWES, born Collins, Iowa, January 17, 1978; admitted to bar, 2003, Iowa. *Education:* Iowa State University (B.S., 2000); Drake University (J.D., with honors, 2002). *Member:* Iowa State Bar Association. ***PRACTICE AREAS:*** Worker's Compensation and Insurance Defense Litigation.

ANDREW C. JOHNSON, born Ames, Iowa, July 16, 1978; admitted to bar, 2003, Iowa. *Education:* Iowa State University (B.A., Political Science, 2000); University of Iowa (J.D., 2003). *Member:* Iowa State Bar Association; Iowa Defense Council. ***PRACTICE AREAS:*** Commercial Litigation; Insurance Defense Litigation. ***Email:*** johnson.andrew@bradshawlaw.com

WILLIAM J. MILLER, born Joliet, Illinois, March 30, 1977; admitted to bar, 2002, Iowa. *Education:* Augustana College (B.A., cum laude, 1999); Drake University (J.D.,

(This Listing Continued)

BRADSHAW, FOWLER, PROCTOR & FAIRGRAVE, P.C., Des Moines—Continued

highest honors, 2002). Member and President, Beaverdale Neighborhood Associations. *Member:* Polk Count Bar and Iowa State Bar Associations; Iowa Supreme Court Commission on Continuing Legal Education; American Judicature Society. ***PRACTICE AREAS:*** Commercial Litigation; Insurance Defense Litigation. ***Email:*** miller.william@bradshawlaw.com

KARIN A. STRAMEL, born LeCrosse, Wisconsin, May 5, 1979; admitted to bar, 2004, Iowa. *Education:* Luther College (B.A. magna cum laude, 2001); Drake University University (J.D., high honors, 2004). ***PRACTICE AREAS:*** Insurance Defense Litigation; Commercial Litigation. ***Email:*** stramel.karin@bradshawlaw.com

CATHERINE M. DREXLER, born Iowa City, Iowa, April 21, 1976; admitted to bar, 2004, Iowa. *Education:* Iowa State University (B.S., 1999); Drake University Law School (J.D., 2004). *Member:* Polk County Women Attorneys Association. ***PRACTICE AREAS:*** Workers Compensation. ***Email:*** drexler.catherine@bradshawlaw.com

ANNE R. CHU, born Taipei, Taiwan, September 7, 1979; admitted to bar, 2004, Kansas; 2005, Iowa. *Education:* University of Iowa (B.B.A., Management, 2001); University of Kansas (J.D., 2004). *Member:* Polk County, Iowa State, Kansas and American Bar Associations. ***LANGUAGES:*** Mandarin Chinese. ***PRACTICE AREAS:*** Estate Planning; Corporate Law; Taxation; Real Estate; Health Law.

OF COUNSEL

J. EDWARD POWER, born Peoria, Illinois, December 2, 1938; admitted to bar, 1964, Iowa. *Education:* Knox College and University of Iowa (B.A., 1960); University of Iowa (J.D., 1964). Phi Delta Phi. Member, Board of Editors, Iowa Law Review, 1963-1964. Law Clerk to Chief Judge, Roy L. Stephenson, U.S. District Court for the Southern District of Iowa, 1964-1965. *Member:* Polk County, Iowa State (Chairman, Committee on Probate, Property and Trust Law, 1983-1987) and American Bar Associations. Fellow: American College of Trust and Estate Counsel (State Chair, 1995-2000); American College of Real Estate Lawyers. ***PRACTICE AREAS:*** Real Estate; Probate; Estate Planning Law. ***Email:*** power.edward@bradshawlaw.com

GENERAL COUNSEL: Employers Mutual Companies; IMT Insurance Company (Mutual); Iowa Association of Realtors; Iowa Insurance Guaranty Association; NCMIC Insurance Company; Appliance Manufacturers Assurance Company RRG.
REPRESENTATIVE CLIENTS: Allied Group; American Feed Industry Risk Retention Insurance Co.; Atlanta Casualty Company; Auto-Owners Insurance Company; C.I.T. Corporation; Calexico Special Financing Authority; Cargill, Inc.; Caterpillar; Central Soya Co., Inc.; Chubb/Pacific Indemnity Group; The Cincinnati Cos.; CNA Insurance; Continental Western Group; CUNA Mutual Insurance Group; Earlham Savings Bank; First American Bank; First State Bank of Stuart; Frontier Communications; General Casualty Insurance Company; Grove Worldwide; The Hartford; Hawkeye Security Insurance; Hy-Vee, Inc.; The Integrity Group; Iowa Long Term Care Risk Management Assoc.; JLG Industries; John Hancock Mutual Life Insurance Co.; Leader National Insurance Co.; Lincoln Financial Advisors; Lincoln National Life Insurance Co.; The Medical Protective Co.; Metropolitan Life Insurance Co.; MidAmerican Energy Company; National Council on Compensation Insurance; Osteopathic Mutual Insurance Co.; Pacific Coast Investment/Wisconsin North, LLC; Pella Corporation; PIC-Wisconsin; Preferred Physicians Insurance Co.; Principal Capital Management, LLC; Principle Life Insurance Co.; Principal Residential Mortgage, Inc.; The Prudential Insurance Company of America; The Rouse Company; Smufit-Stone Corp.; St. Paul Insurance Company; State Farm Mutual Automobile Insurance Co.; TMC Transportation, Inc.; United of Omaha Life Insurance Co.; United States Fidelity & Guaranty Co.; Universal Premium Acceptance Corp.; Wausau Insurance; Wells Fargo Bank; Wells Fargo Home Mortgage; Zurich-American Insurance Co.

BRICK, GENTRY, BOWERS, SWARTZ, STOLTZE, SCHULING & LEVIS, P.C.

SUITE 200, 550 THIRTY-NINTH STREET
39TH AND INGERSOLL
DES MOINES, IOWA 50312
Telephone: 515-274-1450
Telecopier: 515-274-1488
URL: http://www.brickgentrylaw.com

General and Civil Practice and Trials in all Courts. Administrative Law, Public Utility, Telecommunications, Energy, Banking, Corporate, Labor, Municipal, Real Estate, Personal Injury, Federal and State Taxation, Legislative, School, Estate Planning, Health Care, Agricultural Cooperatives and Workers' Compensation Law.

JOSEPH S. BRICK, born Des Moines, Iowa, May 24, 1937; admitted to bar, 1962, Iowa, U.S. Court of Appeals, Eighth Circuit and U.S. District Court, Southern and Northern Districts of Iowa. *Education:* St. Ambrose College (B.A., 1959); University of Iowa; Drake University (J.D., 1962). Special Assistant Attorney General, Tort Claims Division, 1965-1967. Mayor, City of Urbandale, 1970-1974. Member, Board of Directors, Bank of America, 1983—. Civilian Aid, State of Iowa to Secretary of the U.S. Army. Board of Trustees, Des Moines Civic Center; Board Member, National Policy Council, New England Financial Company. *Member:* Polk County, Iowa State and American Bar Associations; National Health Lawyers Association. ***PRACTICE AREAS:*** Health Care; Agricultural Cooperatives; Business. ***Email:*** joseph.brick@brickgentrylaw.com

JAMES E. BRICK, born Des Moines, Iowa, June 15, 1939; admitted to bar, 1970, Iowa and U.S. Court of Appeals, Eighth Circuit; 1975, U.S. District Court, Northern District of Iowa; 1982, U.S. District Court, Southern District of Iowa; 1984, U.S. Supreme Court; 1989, Nebraska. *Education:* University of Maryland (B.A., 1967); Drake University (J.D., 1970). *Member:* Polk County and Iowa State Bar Associations. ***PRACTICE AREAS:*** Litigation; Labor Law; Environmental Law; Municipal Law; Zoning Law. ***Email:*** jim.brick@brickgentrylaw.com

NOLDEN GENTRY, born Rockford, Illinois, August 30, 1937; admitted to bar, 1964, Iowa. *Education:* University of Iowa (B.S., 1960; J.D., 1964). Special Agent, Federal Bureau of Investigation, 1964-1965. Assistant Attorney General, 1965-1966. Member, Board of Directors: Delta Dental Plan of Iowa, 1971—; Firstar Bank Iowa, N.A., 1978-1996; MidAmerican Energy, 1989-1999; Mid-Iowa Health Foundation, 1995—; Bankers Trust Co., 1996—; Prairie Meadows Race Track & Casino, 2003—; Greater Des Moines Community Foundation, 1970-2003; Iowa Public Television Foundation, 1987-1993. Member, State Board of Public Instruction, 1968-1970, Des Moines Independent School District Board of Directors, 1970-1983, President 1974-1975 and 1982-1983. *Member:* Polk County and Iowa State Bar Associations. ***Email:*** nolden.gentry@brickgentrylaw.com

JAMES R. BOWERS, born Fairfield, Iowa, March 30, 1949; admitted to bar, 1974, Iowa, U.S. Court of Appeals, 8th Circuit and U.S. District Courts, Southern and Northern District of Iowa. *Education:* University of Iowa (B.A., 1971; J.D., 1974). Omicron Delta Epsilon; Phi Delta Phi. Assistant City Attorney, City of Grinnell, 1975-1979. *Member:* The Association of Trial Lawyers of Iowa. ***PRACTICE AREAS:*** Civil Litigation; Personal Injury. ***Email:*** jim.bowers@brickgentrylaw.com

CLIFFORD S. SWARTZ, born Des Moines, Iowa, July 31, 1942; admitted to bar, 1979, Iowa; 1980, U.S. District Court, Northern and Southern Districts of Iowa; 1984, U.S. Tax Court. *Education:* Conception College (B.A., 1960); University of Northern Iowa (M.A., 1972); Drake University (J.D., with honors, 1978). Member, Drake Law Review, 1977-1978. Order of the Coif. *Member:* Polk County, Iowa State and American Bar Associations. ***PRACTICE AREAS:*** Business; Health Care; Probate; Estate Planning; Real Estate. ***Email:*** cliff.swartz@brickgentrylaw.com

BRUCE H. STOLTZE, born Ute, Iowa, October 30, 1953; admitted to bar, 1977, Iowa; 1978, U.S. District Court, Southern District of Iowa; 1983, U.S. Court of Appeals, Eighth Circuit; 1985, U.S. District Court, Northern District of Iowa; 1989, U.S. Supreme Court; 1992, U.S. Court of Appeals, Tenth Circuit; 2002, U.S. Court of Appeals, Fifth Circuit. *Education:* University of Iowa (B.S., 1975; J.D., with high distinction, 1977). Phi Delta Phi. *Member:* Polk County, Iowa State and American Bar Associations; Association of Trial Lawyers of America; Association of Trial Lawyers of Iowa. ***PRACTICE AREAS:*** Personal Injury; Workers Compensation; Civil Litigation; Employment Litigation. ***Email:*** bruce.stoltze@brickgentrylaw.com

MARK R. SCHULING, born Germany, June 6, 1955; admitted to bar, 1980, Iowa; 1981, U.S. District Court, Northern and Southern Districts of Iowa; 1983, U.S. Court of Appeals, Eighth Circuit; 1984, U.S. Tax Court. *Education:* Drake University (B.A., 1976; J.D., 1980). Phi Alpha Delta (Chapter Justice, 1978-1979). Order of Barristers. Moot Court Board, 1979-1980. Certified Public Accountant, Iowa, 1984. Assistant Attorney General, Iowa Department of Revenue, 1980-1984. Family Law Mediator, Polk County District Court. Member: Board of Directors, Youth Law Center, 2002—. Board of Directors, Des Moines Independent School District, 1996-2002; President, 2000-2001; Vice President, 1999-2000. Board of Directors, Greater Des Moines Chambers of Commerce, 1996-2000. *Member:* Polk County and Iowa State (Member: Tax Committee, 2001-2004; District Associate Nomination Commission; 5c; Iowa Legislature Property Tax Implementation Committee, 2003-2004) Bar Associations; Iowa Society of Certified Public Accountants. ***PRACTICE AREAS:*** Property Tax Assessments; Property Tax Appeals; Cable Communications; State Taxation. ***Email:*** mark.schuling@brickgentrylaw.com

THOMAS J. LEVIS, born Chariton, Iowa, January 20, 1953; admitted to bar, 1977, Iowa and U.S. District Court, Northern and Southern Districts of Iowa; U.S. Court of Appeals, Eighth Circuit; U.S. Supreme Court. *Education:* Drake University (B.A., 1974; J.D., 1977). Member, Board of Directors, First Bank, 1999—. *Member:* Polk County (Member, Bench Bar Committee; Former Member, Iowa Fee Arbitration Committee), Iowa State (Former Member, Alternative Dispute Resolution Council; Member, General Practice Section) and American Bar Associations; Association of Trial Lawyers of Iowa; The Association of Trial Lawyers of America; C. Edwin Moors Inns of Court (Master of the Bench). ***PRACTICE AREAS:*** Civil Litigation; Personal Injury; Corporate Law; Real Estate; Family Law. ***Email:*** tom.levis@brickgentrylaw.com

AMY S. BEATTIE, born Des Moines, Iowa, June 3, 1958; admitted to bar, 1983, Iowa; 1988, Louisiana. *Education:* Los Angeles Baptist College (B.A., 1980); Drake University (J.D., 1983); Tulane University (M.B.A., 1989). *Member:* Polk County, Iowa State and Louisiana State Bar Associations. ***PRACTICE AREAS:*** Corporate; Municipal; Real Estate; Probate. ***Email:*** amy.beattie@brickgentrylaw.com

KENNETH L. BUTTERS, born Oelwein, Iowa, June 25, 1945; admitted to bar, 1971, Iowa. *Education:* University of Northern Iowa and University of Iowa (B.B.A., 1968); University of Iowa (J.D., with distinction, 1971). Phi Delta Phi. *Member:* Iowa State Bar Association; The Association of Trial Lawyers of Iowa. ***Email:*** ken.butters@brickgentrylaw.com

STEVEN P. BRICK, born Des Moines, Iowa, June 23, 1967; admitted to bar, 1993, Iowa and U.S. District Court, Southern and Northern Districts of Iowa; U.S. Court of Appeals, Eighth Circuit. *Education:* University of Iowa; Creighton University (B.A., 1990); Drake University (J.D., 1992). Delta Theta Phi. *Member:* Polk County, Iowa State and American Bar Associations; Iowa Trial Lawyers Association; Edwin Moore Inn of Court (Barrister). ***PRACTICE AREAS:*** Civil Litigation; Personal Injury; Corporate Law; Real Estate; Municipal Law. ***Email:*** steve.brick@brickgentrylaw.com

THOMAS P. SCHLAPKOHL, born Davenport, Iowa, March 17, 1951; admitted to bar, 1981, Iowa and U.S. District Court, Southern and Northern Districts of Iowa. *Education:* Cornell College (B.A., 1973); Drake University (J.D., 1981). *Member:* Polk County, Iowa State and American Bar Associations; Iowa Trial Lawyers Association; The Association of Trial Lawyers of America; Blackstone Inns of Court (Bencher). ***Email:*** tom.schlapkohl@brickgentrylaw.com

JAMES E. NERVIG, born Grinnell, Iowa, October 22, 1950; admitted to bar, 1976, Iowa; 1982, U.S. District Court, Southern District of Iowa; 1983, U.S. District Court, Northern District of Iowa; 1985 U.S. Court of Appeals, Eighth Circuit. *Education:* University of Iowa (M.B.A., 1976; J.D., 1976). Past Employment, Petosa, Petosa, Boecker & Nervig, LLP. Member, Board of Editors, Journal of Corporation Law, 1975-1976. City Solicitor, Des Moines, 1979-1988. Iowa Municipal Attorneys Association, 1981—. *Member:* Polk County and Iowa State (Member, Section: Legal Forms) Bar Associations. ***PRACTICE AREAS:*** Real Estate; Municipal Law; Litigation; Estate Planning; Corporate Law. ***Email:*** jim.nervig@brickgentrylaw.com

PAUL A. DREY, born Storm Lake, Iowa, September 18, 1966; admitted to bar, 1992, Iowa and U.S. District Court, Southern and Northern Districts of Iowa; 1994, U.S. Court of Appeals, Eighth Circuit. *Education:* University of Notre Dame (B.A., 1989; J.D., 1992). Phi

(This Listing Continued)

Beta Kappa. Notre Dame Scholar; McCafferty Law Scholar. Former President, Student Bar Association. *Member:* Polk County, Iowa State (Member: Real Estate Section; Health Law Section; Bankruptcy and Commercial Law Section), American and Federal (Co-Chair, Iowa Federal Bar Association Bankruptcy Seminar, 2002-2005; Treasurer, 2004-2005) Bar Associations. ***PRACTICE AREAS:*** Health Law; Bankruptcy; Corporate Law. ***Email:*** paul.drey@brickgentrylaw.com

STEPHANIE L. BRICK DREY, born Des Moines, Iowa, December 9, 1966; admitted to bar, 1992, Iowa and U.S. District Court, Southern and Northern Districts of Iowa. *Education:* University of Notre Dame (B.A., with honors, 1989); University of Iowa (J.D., with distinction, 1992). Pi Sigma Alpha; Phi Delta Phi. Member, Iowa Law Review, 1990-1991. *Member:* Polk County, Iowa State and American Bar Associations. ***PRACTICE AREAS:*** Probate; Estate Planning; Real Estate. ***Email:*** stephanie.drey@brickgentrylaw.com

DAVID E. BRICK, born Des Moines, Iowa, December 23, 1971; admitted to bar, 1998, Iowa and U.S. District Court, Southern and Northern Districts of Iowa. *Education:* Boston College (B.A., 1994); University of Iowa College of Law (J.D., 1998). *Member:* Polk County, Iowa State and American Bar Associations. ***PRACTICE AREAS:*** Family Law; Litigation; Commercial Transactions; Personal Injury. ***Email:*** dave.brick@brickgentrylaw.com

NOLDEN BRIAN GENTRY, born Des Moines, Iowa, April 15, 1970; admitted to bar, 1996, Iowa. *Education:* Lake Forest College (B.S., Political Science, 1992); University of Iowa (J.D., 1996). Author: "Defining the Appropriateness of Class Certification in Anti-Trust Cases," Journal of Corporation of Law, Volume 22, No. 1, Fall 1996. ***PRACTICE AREAS:*** Municipal Law; Business Law; Civil Litigation. ***Email:*** brian.gentry@brickgentrylaw.com

MATTHEW T. CRONIN, born Galesburg, Illinois, August 23, 1975; admitted to bar, 2000, Iowa. *Education:* University of Missouri (B.A., magna cum laude, 1997); University of Iowa (J.D., with highest distinction, 2000). Order of the Coif. Member, American Bankruptcy Institute. Author: "Uncitral Model Law on Cross-Border Insolvency A Procedural Approach To A Substantive Problem", 24 J.Corp.L. 709 (1999); "Self Settled Spendthrift Trusts, Move Close to Home," American Bankruptcy Journal, Sept. 2000 at 10. *Member:* Iowa State Bar Association; American Bankruptcy Institute. ***PRACTICE AREAS:*** Bankruptcy; Corporate Law; Litigation.

MATTHEW S. BRICK, born Des Moines, Iowa, October 2, 1972; admitted to bar, 2001, Iowa, District of Columbia, Minnesota, Nebraska, U.S. District Court, Northern and Southern Districts of Iowa and U.S. Court of Appeals, Eighth Circuit; 2004, U.S. Supreme Court, U.S. Court of Appeals, Fifth Circuit and U.S. District Court, Northern District of Texas. *Education:* University of Iowa (B.S., Psychology with honors, 1995; J.D., with high distinction, 2000). Member, Windsor Heights City Council, 2000-2004. *Member:* Iowa State, Nebraska State and American (Member, Sections: Employment and Litigation) Bar Associations; The District of Columbia Bar. ***PRACTICE AREAS:*** Employment Law; Municipal Law; Litigation. ***Email:*** matt.brick@brickgentrylaw.com

BILLY J. MALLORY, born Natchez, Mississippi, March 5, 1973; admitted to bar, 2001, Iowa; U.S. District Court, Northern and Southern Districts of Iowa. *Education:* University of Iowa (B.S., 1995); Drake University (J.D., 1998). *Member:* Polk County and Iowa State Bar Associations; Iowa Trial Lawyers Association. ***PRACTICE AREAS:*** Environmental Law; Municipal Law; Real Estate; Litigation. ***Email:*** bill.mallory@brickgentrylaw.com

REFERENCES: Bankers Trust; First Bank; US Bank Des Moines, N.A.

W. KENDALL BROWN

558 28TH STREET
DES MOINES, IOWA 50312
Telephone: 515-282-7702
Fax: 515-282-7706
Email: Kendall@DPS8.com

General Civil Practice. Taxation, Corporate, Probate and Estate Planning, Employee Benefits, Banking and Administrative Law.

W. KENDALL BROWN, born Cedar Rapids, Iowa, October 13, 1943; admitted to bar, 1968, Arizona; 1969, Iowa; 1971, U.S. Claims Court; 1976, U.S. Tax Court. *Education:* California Institute of Technology (B.S., 1965); University of Colorado (J.D., 1968). Order of the Coif. *Member:* Iowa State and American Bar Associations; State Bar of Arizona.

BROWN, WINICK, GRAVES, GROSS, BASKERVILLE AND SCHOENEBAUM, P.L.C.

666 GRAND AVENUE, SUITE 2000
DES MOINES, IOWA 50309-2510
Telephone: 515-242-2400
Fax: 515-283-0231
Email: bwg@ialawyers.com
URL: http://www.ialawyers.com

Pella, Iowa Office: 616 Franklin Place, 50219. Telephone: 641-628-4513. Fax: 641-628-8494.
West Des Moines, Iowa Office: Regency West 5, 4500 Westown Parkway, Suite 277, 50266-6717. Telephone: 515-242-2400. Fax: 515-242-2448.

General Civil Practice, including but not limited to, Administrative Law, Adoption Law, Agricultural Law, Alternate Dispute Resolution, Antitrust and Trade Regulation, Appellate Practice, Banking Law, Bankruptcy, Business Law, Civil Rights and Discrimination, Commercial Law, Construction Law, Contracts, Corporate Law, Debtor and Creditor, Election, Campaign and Political, Eminent Domain, Employee Benefits, Employment Law, Energy, Entertainment and Sports, Environmental Law, Estate Planning, Family Law, Finance, Franchise Law, Government, Health Care, Insurance, Intellectual Property, International Law, International Trade, Labor Law, Litigation, Medical Malpractice, Mergers and Acquisitions, Occupational Safety and Health, Pension and Profit Sharing Law, Personal Injury, Product Liability, Professional Liability, Public Utility Law, Real Estate, Securities, Taxation, Toxic Torts, Trademarks and Copyright Law, Transportation, Trial Law, Trusts and Estates, Wills and Probate, Workers' Compensation, Zoning, Planning and Land Use. Litigation in all Courts.

FIRM PROFILE: Brown, Winick, Graves, Gross, Baskerville and Schoenebaum, P.L.C. is a major law firm with offices in Des Moines, West Des Moines, and Pella, Iowa. The firm originated as a tax law specialty firm in downtown Des Moines in 1951. Today the firm offers a broad range of legal services to clients throughout Iowa, regionally and nationally. The firm serves as counsel to a wide variety of service, manufacturing and commercial businesses and professionals. The firm's mission is to attract, retain and develop clients by providing effective and innovative solutions. We will provide a comprehensive range of legal services primarily to businesses, as well as to individuals in need of high quality legal services, inside and outside the State of Iowa.

WALTER R. BROWN (1921-2000)

RICHARD W. BASKERVILLE, born Monona, Iowa, July 28, 1935; admitted to bar, 1959, Iowa. *Education:* University of Dubuque; Miami University; University of Iowa (LL.B., 1959). Member, Board of Editors, Iowa Law Review, 1958-1959. Member, Supreme Court Day Arguments, 1959. *Member:* Polk County and Iowa State Bar Associations. ***PRACTICE AREAS:*** Wills; Trusts; Estate Planning; Probate Law. ***Email:*** baskerville@ialawyers.com

BRUCE GRAVES, born October 5, 1939; admitted to bar, 1964, Iowa and Nebraska. *Education:* University of Omaha (B.S., 1961); University of Nebraska (J.D., cum laude, 1964). Order of the Coif. *Member:* Polk County, Iowa State (Member, Board of Governors, 1994-1998; President, 2000-2001), Nebraska State, Federal and American (Member, Sections on: Taxation; Business Law; Litigation) Bar Associations. ***Email:*** graves@ialawyers.com

STEVEN C. SCHOENEBAUM, born Quincy, Illinois, August 5, 1946; admitted to bar, 1970, Iowa. *Education:* University of Iowa (B.A., 1968); Drake University (J.D., with honors, 1970). Order of the Coif. Staff Member, Drake Law Review, 1969-1970. Instructor, Legal Research and Writing, Drake University Law School, 1970. Executive Secretary, Iowa Reciprocity Board, State of Iowa, 1971-1972. *Member:* Iowa State and American Bar Associations; Iowa Institute for Cooperatives. ***Email:*** schoenebaum@ialawyers.com

HAROLD N. SCHNEEBECK, born Colorado Springs, Colorado, November 20, 1942; admitted to bar, 1976, Iowa; U.S. District Court, Southern and Northern Districts of Iowa; U.S. Court of Appeals, Eighth Circuit; U.S. Court of Federal Claims; U.S. Court of Appeals for the Federal Circuit; U.S. Tax Court. *Education:* University of Iowa (Ph.D., 1973; J.D., with high distinction, 1976). Order of the Coif. *Member:* Polk County, Iowa State and American Bar Associations. ***Email:*** schneebeck@ialawyers.com

PAUL D. HIETBRINK, born Lincoln, Nebraska, May 22, 1952; admitted to bar, 1977, Iowa and Nebraska. *Education:* University of Nebraska (B.A., 1973; J.D., with distinction, 1976). Order of the Coif. *Member:* Polk County, Iowa State, Nebraska State and American Bar Associations. (Also at Pella, Iowa Office). ***Email:*** hietbrink@ialawyers.com

WILLIAM C. BROWN, born November 2, 1953; admitted to bar, 1977, Iowa. *Education:* University of Iowa (B.A., with honors in Psychology, 1974; J.D., with high distinction, 1977). Order of the Coif. *Member:* Iowa State (Member, Taxation Section; Corporate Law; Banking and Business Law; Taxation Council, 1996-1999, 2000-2002, 2003—) and American (Member: Taxation Section; Committee on S Corporations) Bar Associations. ***LANGUAGES:*** Italian. ***PRACTICE AREAS:*** Taxation. ***Email:*** brown@ialawyers.com

RICHARD K. UPDEGRAFF, born Iowa City, Iowa, September 17, 1951; admitted to bar, 1976, Iowa and Arizona. *Education:* University of Iowa (B.A., 1973; J.D., with high distinction, 1976). Member, Board of Editors, Iowa Law Review, 1975-1976. *Member:* Polk County and Iowa State (Member: Litigation Legislation Committee, 1989-1990; Commercial and Bankruptcy Law Committee, 1994—; Appellate Practice Committee, 2001—) and American (Litigation Section) Bar Associations; State Bar of Arizona. ***Email:*** updegraff@ialawyers.com

PAUL E. CAREY, born Des Moines, Iowa, December 16, 1954; admitted to bar, 1982, Iowa; 1984, U.S. Tax Court. *Education:* Drake University (B.S.B.A., 1977; J.D., with honors, 1981). Phi Eta Sigma; Beta Alpha Psi; Order of the Coif. *Member:* Polk County, Iowa State and American (Member, Taxation Section) Bar Associations; Iowa Taxpayer Association. ***PRACTICE AREAS:*** Taxation. ***Email:*** carey@ialawyers.com

DOUGLAS E. GROSS, born Earling, Iowa, December 28, 1954; admitted to bar, 1986, Iowa; 1989, U.S. District Court, Southern District of Iowa. *Education:* Iowa Wesleyan College (B.A., summa cum laude, 1977); Drake University (J.D., with honors, 1985). Recipient, American Jurisprudence Award. Legislative Liaison for Governor Robert D. Ray, 1981-1983. Chief of Staff to Governor Terry E. Branstad, 1984-1989. Republican Candidate for Governor of Iowa, 2002. *Member:* Polk County, Iowa State and American Bar Associations.

JOHN D. HUNTER, born Omaha, Nebraska, November 27, 1960; admitted to bar, 1986, Iowa; 1987, Colorado; 1989, Nebraska. *Education:* University of Nebraska at Lincoln (B.S., with distinction, 1983; J.D., with distinction, 1986). Order of the Coif. Member, 1984-1986 and Executive Editor, 1985, Nebraska Law Review. *Member:* Polk County, Iowa State, Colorado, Nebraska State and American Bar Associations; National Association of Bond Lawyers. (Also at West Des Moines, Iowa Office). ***Email:*** hunter@ialawyers.com

JAMES H. GILLIAM, born Weed, California, October 5, 1955; admitted to bar, 1980, Iowa; 1988, U.S. District Court, Northern and Southern Districts of Iowa. *Education:* University of Iowa (B.A., 1977; J.D., with distinction, 1980). General Counsel, Iowa Public Employment Relations Board, 1984-1988. *Member:* American Bar Association. [Capt., U.S. Army, JAGC, 1980-1984]. ***Email:*** gilliam@ialawyers.com

ROBERT D. ANDEWEG, born Pella, Iowa, August 26, 1962; admitted to bar, 1987, Iowa. *Education:* Central College (B.A., 1984); Drake University (J.D., with honors, 1987). Member, Urbandale City Council. Candidate, Certified Commercial Investment Member

(This Listing Continued)

BROWN, WINICK, GRAVES, GROSS, BASKERVILLE AND SCHOENEBAUM, P.L.C., Des Moines—Continued

(CCIM). *Member:* Iowa State (Member, Real Estate and Title Law Section) and American Bar Associations. (Also at West Des Moines, Iowa Office). ***Email:*** andeweg@ialawyers.com

ALICE EASTMAN HELLE, born Fort Dodge, Iowa, May 29, 1951; admitted to bar, 1988, Iowa. *Education:* Iowa State University (B.S., with distinction, 1973); Drake University (J.D., with honors, 1988). Order of the Coif. Member, 1986-1987 and Executive Editor, 1987-1988, Drake Law Review. *Member:* Polk County, Iowa State (Chair, Employee Benefits Taxation Committee, 1994-1995) and American Bar Associations; Polk County Women Attorneys, Inc. ***PRACTICE AREAS:*** Pension and Profit Sharing Law. ***Email:*** helle@ialawyers.com

MICHAEL R. BLASER, born Cedar Rapids, Iowa, July 25, 1960; admitted to bar, 1985, Iowa. *Education:* University of Iowa (B.B.A., 1982; J.D., with distinction, 1985). Certified Public Accountant, Iowa, 1983. *Member:* Polk County, Iowa State (Member: Agricultural Law Section Council; Environmental and Natural Resources Law Section) and American Bar Associations; Iowa Society of Certified Public Accountants (Board of Directors, 1995-1998); American Agricultural Law Association. (Also at West Des Moines, Iowa Office). ***PRACTICE AREAS:*** Environmental Law. ***Email:*** blaser@ialawyers.com

THOMAS D. JOHNSON, born February 6, 1962; admitted to bar, 1990, Illinois; 1992, Iowa. *Education:* University of Iowa (B.B.A., 1984; J.D., with high distinction, 1990). Member, Journal of Corporation Law, 1988-1990. Certified Public Accountant, Illinois, 1985. *Member:* Polk County, Illinois State, Iowa State (Business Law Section) and American Bar Associations; Iowa Society of Certified Public Accountants. ***PRACTICE AREAS:*** Securities; Corporate Law. ***Email:*** johnson@ialawyers.com

CHRISTOPHER R. SACKETT, born Creston, Iowa, August 9, 1967; admitted to bar, 1993, Wisconsin; 1994, Iowa. *Education:* Central College (B.A., magna cum laude, 1989); University of Iowa (J.D., with distinction, 1993). Member, National Moot Court Team. *Member:* Polk County, Iowa State and American (Member; Business Law Section; Forum on Franchising) Bar Associations; State Bar of Wisconsin. ***Email:*** sackett@ialawyers.com

SEAN P. MOORE, born Milwaukee, Wisconsin, January 11, 1962; admitted to bar, 1991, California and Iowa;1995, U.S. District Court, Northern and Southern Districts of Iowa; 1998, U.S. Court of Appeals, Eighth Circuit. *Education:* University of Iowa (B.B.A., 1984; J.D., with high distinction, 1991). Note and Comment Editor, Journal of Corporation Law, 1990-1991. *Member:* Iowa State Bar Association; State Bar of California. ***Email:*** moore@ialawyers.com

NANCY SHIMANEK BOYD, born December 1, 1947; admitted to bar, 1973, Iowa and U.S. District Court, Northern and Southern Districts of Iowa. *Education:* Clarke College (B.A., cum laude, 1970); University of Iowa (J.D., 1973). Assistant to Governor Robert D. Ray, 1981-1983. Executive Assistant to Chief Justice W.W. Reynoldson, Supreme Court of Iowa, 1984-1987. Member: Iowa House of Representatives, 1977-1981; Iowa Utilities Board, 1987-1997. ***PRACTICE AREAS:*** Government; Energy. ***Email:*** boyd@ialawyers.com

JAMES L. PRAY, born Monterey, California, October 17, 1959; admitted to bar, 1985, Iowa, U.S. District Court, Southern and Northern Districts of Iowa. *Education:* University of Nebraska at Omaha (B.S., magna cum laude, 1980); University of Iowa (J.D., with distinction, 1984). *Member:* Polk County, Iowa State (Chair, Environmental and Natural Resources Law Council, 1998-1999; 2004-2006) and American Bar Associations. ***PRACTICE AREAS:*** Environmental Law. ***Email:*** pray@ialawyers.com

BRENTON D. SODERSTRUM, born Story City, Iowa, November 17, 1963; admitted to bar, 1989, Iowa and U.S. District Court, Northern and Southern Districts of Iowa. *Education:* Luther College (B.A., 1986); University of Iowa (J.D., with high distinction, 1989). Associate Editor, Iowa Law Review, 1988-1989. *Member:* Iowa Defense Counsel Association; Mechanical Contractors Association; Sheet Metal Contractors Association; Construction Specifications Institute (President, 1996-1997). ***PRACTICE AREAS:*** Construction Law. ***Email:*** soderstrum@ialawyers.com

MICHAEL D. TREINEN, born LeMars, Iowa, August 11, 1941; admitted to bar, 1972, Iowa. *Education:* Creighton University (B.A., 1964); University of Iowa (J.D., 1972). Phi Alpha Delta. The Principal Financial Group, 1977-1999. *Member:* Iowa State and American Bar Associations; Iowa Taxpayers Association. [U.S. Army, 1964-1969; Col., USAR, 1969-1994]. ***PRACTICE AREAS:*** Government. ***Email:*** treinen@ialawyers.com

SCOTT L. LONG, born Belmond, Iowa, July 5, 1962; admitted to bar, 1987, Arizona and U.S. District Court, District of Arizona; 1994, U.S. Court of Appeals, Ninth Circuit; 1997, Iowa and U.S. District Court, Northern and Southern Districts of Iowa. *Education:* University of Iowa (B.B.A., with distinction, 1984); University of Michigan (J.D., 1987). Beta Gamma Sigma. *Member:* Polk County, Iowa State and American Bar Associations; State Bar of Arizona; Defense Research Institute, Inc. ***Email:*** scottlong@ialawyers.com

RONNI F. BEGLEITER, born Tupper Lake, New York, July 7, 1948; admitted to bar, 1983, Iowa; 1985, U.S. Tax Court. *Education:* Cornell University (B.A., with distinction, 1969); Columbia University (M.L.S., with honors, 1971); Drake University (J.D., with honors, 1982). Phi Beta Kappa; Beta Phi Mu; Order of the Coif. Member, Clive City Council, 2002-2003, 2004—. ***PRACTICE AREAS:*** Wills; Trusts; Estate Planning; Probate Law; Employee Benefits. ***Email:*** begleiter@ialawyers.com

MIRANDA L. HUGHES, born Grinnell, Iowa, March 25, 1967; admitted to bar, 1992, Iowa; 1996, U.S. District Court, Southern and Northern Districts of Iowa. *Education:* University of Iowa (B.A., 1989; J.D., with distinction, 1992). Law Clerk to Hon. Russell J. Hill, U.S. Bankruptcy Court, Southern District of Iowa, 1993-1996. *Member:* Iowa State, Federal (Treasurer, 2002-2003; Vice President, 2004-2005) and American Bar Associations. ***Email:*** hughes@ialawyers.com

KELLY D. HAMBORG, born Des Moines, Iowa, August 31, 1955; admitted to bar, 1985, Iowa. *Education:* University of Iowa (B.B.A., 1977); Drake University (J.D., 1985). *Member:* Polk County and Iowa State Bar Associations; American Health Lawyers Association; Iowa Hospital Association; Iowa Society of Healthcare Attorneys. (Also at West Des Moines, Iowa Office). ***PRACTICE AREAS:*** Health Care; Real Estate. ***Email:*** hamborg@ialawyers.com

WILLIAM E. HANIGAN, born Dunlap, Iowa, November 12, 1967; admitted to bar, 1993, Iowa; 1997, Nebraska; 1998, U.S. District Court, Northern and Southern Districts of Iowa; 2005, Minnesota. *Education:* Creighton University (B.S.B.A., magna cum laude, 1990; J.D., 1993). Certified Public Accountant, Iowa, 1991. Legislative Tax Counsel to United States Senator Charles E. Grassley, 1995-1997. *Member:* Iowa State and Nebraska State Bar Associations; Iowa Renewable Fuels Association; Renewable Fuels Association. ***Email:*** hanigan@ialawyers.com

MARY A. ERICSON, born Madison, Wisconsin, October 18, 1942; admitted to bar, 1979, Iowa. *Education:* University of Wisconsin (B.A., 1964); Drake University (M.A., 1970; J.D., 1978). *Member:* Polk County and Iowa State Bar Associations; Polk County Women Attorneys, Inc. ***LANGUAGES:*** Russian and French. ***PRACTICE AREAS:*** Taxation. ***Email:*** ericson@ialawyers.com

BARBARA BROOKER BURNETT, born Fond du Lac, Wisconsin, September 19, 1956; admitted to bar, 1984, Iowa; 1986, U.S. District Court, Southern District of Iowa. *Education:* Drake University (B.A., 1978; J.D., 1983). Administrative Counsel, Governor Branstad, 1985-1990. Past Vice President: Science Center of Iowa, 1995-2003; Community School Board, West Des Moines, 2003—. *Member:* Iowa State (Member, Administrative Law Section, 1986-1987) and American Bar Associations; Polk County Women Attorneys, Inc. ***PRACTICE AREAS:*** Government. ***Email:*** burnett@ialawyers.com

G. BRIAN PINGEL, born Fort Dodge, Iowa, August 30, 1940; admitted to bar, 1970, Wisconsin; 1973, Minnesota; 1977, Iowa; registered to practice before U.S. Patent and Trademark Office. *Education:* Iowa Central (A.A., 1963); University of Iowa (B.S.E.E., 1966); University of Nebraska (J.D., with distinction, 1970). *Member:* Polk County, Iowa State and American Bar Associations; Iowa Intellectual Property Law Association. (Also at West Des Moines, Iowa Office). ***PRACTICE AREAS:*** Patents; Trademarks; Copyrights. ***Email:*** bpingel@ialawyers.com

MICHAEL J. GREEN, born Cascade, Iowa, March 14, 1948; admitted to bar, 1976, Iowa. *Education:* Loras College (B.A., 1970); Drake University (J.D., 1975). *Member:* Polk County (Member, Sections on: Real Estate Title Standards; Business), Iowa State (Member, Sections on: Real Estate; Business) and American (Member, Sections on: Business Law; Real Estate) Bar Associations. (Also at West Des Moines, Iowa Office). ***PRACTICE AREAS:*** Business Law; Real Estate. ***Email:*** mgreen@ialawyers.com

MICHAEL A. DEE, born Des Moines, Iowa, April 13, 1962; admitted to bar, 1988, Pennsylvania; 1990, District of Columbia; 1995, Iowa. *Education:* Iowa State University (B.S., with distinction and honors, 1984); University of Iowa (J.D., 1987). *Member:* Polk County (Member, Board of Directors, 2002—) and American Bar Associations; District of Columbia Bar; Iowa Trial Lawyers Association. ***Email:*** mdee@ialawyers.com

CAMILLE L. URBAN, born Humboldt, Iowa, February 12, 1964; admitted to bar, 1998, Iowa; registered to practice before U.S. Patent and Trademark Office. *Education:* Iowa State University (B.S., Chemistry, 1985); University of Iowa (M.A.T., with high distinction, 1987; J.D., with high honors, 1998). *Member:* Polk County, Iowa State and American Bar Associations; Intellectual Property Law Association (Member, Board of Directors, 2000—; President, 2005—). (Also at West Des Moines, Iowa Office). ***PRACTICE AREAS:*** Patents; Trademarks; Copyrights. ***Email:*** curban@ialawyers.com

DANIELLE DIXON SMID, born Pella, Iowa, March 2, 1973; admitted to bar, 1998, Iowa; U.S. Court of Appeals, Eighth Circuit, and U.S. District Court, Northern and Southern Districts of Iowa. *Education:* Iowa State University (B.S., 1995); Drake University (J.D., with honors, 1998). *Member:* Polk County, Iowa State and American Bar Associations; Polk County Women Attorneys, Inc. ***PRACTICE AREAS:*** Employment Law. ***Email:*** dixon@ialawyers.com

BRIAN P. RICKERT, born Mankato, Minnesota, December 10, 1972; admitted to bar, 1998, Missouri and U.S. District Court, Western District of Missouri; 1999, Kansas, Iowa and U.S. District Court, District of Kansas; 2000, U.S. District Court, Northern and Southern Districts of Iowa. *Education:* University of Iowa (B.B.A., 1995); Drake University (J.D., with honors, 1998). *Member:* Polk County, Iowa State, Kansas and American (Forum on the Construction Industry) Bar Associations; The Missouri Bar; American Agricultural Law Association. ***PRACTICE AREAS:*** Construction Law. ***Email:*** rickert@ialawyers.com

VALERIE D. BANDSTRA, born Oskaloosa, Iowa, July 14, 1975; admitted to bar, 2000, Iowa. *Education:* Iowa State University (B.S., with distinction, Economics, 1998); University of Iowa (J.D., with high distinction, 2000). *Member:* Polk County, Iowa State and American Bar Associations. ***Email:*** bandstra@ialawyers.com

ANN HOLDEN KENDELL, born Jefferson, Iowa, June 19, 1973; admitted to bar, 1998, Iowa, U.S. District Court, Northern and Southern Districts of Iowa and U.S. Court of Appeals, Eighth Circuit. *Education:* Iowa State University (B.S., 1995); Drake University (J.D., 1998). Law Clerk to the Hon. K. David Harris, Iowa Supreme Court, 1998-1999. *Member:* Polk County, Iowa State and American Bar Associations; Polk County Women Attorneys, Inc. (Board, 2000—; President-Elect, 2005). ***PRACTICE AREAS:*** Employment Law. ***Email:*** kendell@ialawyers.com

---

ALEXANDER M. JOHNSON, born Ames, Iowa, December 31, 1973; admitted to bar, 1999, Iowa, U.S. District Court, Northern and Southern Districts of Iowa and U. S. Bankruptcy Court. *Education:* Iowa State University (B.A., English, 1996); Drake University (J.D., with honors, 1999). *Member:* Polk County and Iowa State Bar Associations; Iowa Trial Lawyers Association. ***Email:*** ajohnson@ialawyers.com

JAMES S. NIBLOCK, born Des Moines, Iowa, April 27, 1959; admitted to bar, 1996, Iowa. *Education:* University of Iowa (B.A., 1982; B.B.A., 1984; J.D., with distinction, 1996). Certified Public Accountant, Iowa, 1987. *Member:* Story County, Iowa State and American Bar Associations; Iowa's Society of Certified Public Accountants; American Institute of Certified Public Accountants. ***PRACTICE AREAS:*** Taxation. ***Email:*** niblock@ialawyers.com

(This Listing Continued)

REBECCA A. BROMMEL, born Des Moines, Iowa, January 13, 1976; admitted to bar, 2001, Iowa, U.S. District Court, Southern and Northern Districts of Iowa and U.S. Court of Appeals, Eighth Circuit. *Education:* Drake University (B.A., magna cum laude, 1998; J.D., with highest honors, 2001). Order of the Coif. *Member:* Polk County, Iowa State and American (Member, Litigation Section) Bar Associations; Iowa Trial Lawyers Association. ***Email:*** brommel@ialawyers.com

MARK E. ROTH, born Portland, Oregon, March 21, 1954; admitted to bar, 2002, Iowa. *Education:* University of Notre Dame (B.S., Chemical Engineering, 1976); University of Chicago (M.B.A., 1979); Drake University (J.D., 2002). *Member:* Polk County, Iowa State and American Bar Associations. ***Email:*** roth@ialawyers.com

TINA R. THOMPSON, born St. Paul, Minnesota, October 16, 1974; admitted to bar, 2003, Iowa. *Education:* Wartburg College (B.A., magna cum laude, 1997); University of Iowa (J.D., 2003). *Member:* Polk County, Iowa State (Member, Young Lawyers Division) and American Bar Associations; Polk County Women Attorneys, Inc. ***Email:*** thompson@ialawyers.com

BRIAN M. GREEN, born Dubuque, Iowa, August 3, 1969; admitted to bar, 1996, Iowa. *Education:* University of Kansas (B.S., Journalism, 1994); Drake University (J.D., 1996). *Member:* Polk County, Iowa State (Member, For Profit Corporation Committee, Business Section) and American (Business Law Section) Bar Associations. ***PRACTICE AREAS:*** Business Law; Securities. ***Email:*** bgreen@ialawyers.com

DUSTIN D. SMITH, born Kirksville, Missouri, December 10, 1970; admitted to bar, 1997, Iowa. *Education:* University of Iowa (B.A., 1993); Drake University (J.D., 1997). *Member:* Polk County, Iowa State (Member, Real Estate Section) and American (Member, Real Estate Section) Bar Associations. (Also at West Des Moines, Iowa Office). ***Email:*** dsmith@ialawyers.com

ADAM W. JONES, born Carlisle, Iowa, February 18, 1974; admitted to bar, 2003, Iowa; registered to practice before U.S. Patent and Trademark Office. *Education:* University of Rochester (B.A., Biology, 1996); Michigan State University (M.A., Botany and Plant Pathology, 2000); Drake University (J.D., with high honors, 2003). *Member:* Polk County, Iowa State and American Bar Associations; Iowa Intellectual Property Law Association. (Also at West Des Moines, Iowa Office). ***Email:*** ajones@ialawyers.com

CATHERINE E. COWNIE, born Des Moines, Iowa, April 16, 1975; admitted to bar, 1999, Iowa; U.S. Court of Federal Claims. *Education:* Chaminade University (B.A., Psychology, summa cum laude, 1996); University of Iowa (J.D., 1999). *Member:* Polk County, Iowa State (Co-Chair, Young Lawyers Division, Justice for all Committee) and American Bar Associations; Polk County Women Attorneys, Inc.; American Health Lawyers Association; Society of Healthcare Attorneys; Iowa Hospital Association. ***Email:*** cownie@ialawyers.com

ERICK D. PROHS, born Hugo, Colorado, April 24, 1973; admitted to bar, 2002, Iowa and U.S. District Court, Northern and Southern Districts of Iowa. *Education:* Colorado State University (B.S.B.A., 1995); University of Colorado (M.B.A., 1998); University of Iowa (J.D., 2001). Member, Journal of Corporation Law, 2000-2001. Author: "Periodic Financial Reporting - A Relic of the Past?" 27 J. Corp. L. 333, 481 (2002). *Member:* Polk County, Iowa State, American and Federal Bar Associations. ***Email:*** prohs@ialawyers.com

LAURA N. MARTINO, born Jefferson, Iowa, March 16, 1978; admitted to bar, 2003, Iowa; 2004, Missouri. *Education:* Loras College (B.A., maxima cum laude, 2000); University of Iowa (J.D., with distinction, 2003). Law Clerk, Seventh Judicial District, State of Iowa, 2003-2004. *Member:* Polk County, Iowa State and American Bar Associations; The Missouri Bar. ***Email:*** martino@ialawyers.com

AMY R. PIEPMEIER, born St. Joseph, Missouri, April 4, 1979; admitted to bar, 2004, Iowa; U.S. Bankruptcy Court. *Education:* University of Missouri, Columbia (B.S., Ag. Econ.; Minor, International Agriculture, 2001); University of Iowa (J.D., 2004). *Member:* Polk County, Iowa State and American Bar Associations. ***Email:*** piepmeier@ialawyers.com

ELIZABETH A. COONAN, born Berwyn, Illinois, July 30, 1977; admitted to bar, 2002, Iowa; 2003, U.S. District Court, Northern and Southern District of Iowa; U.S. Court of Appeals, Eighth Circuit. *Education:* Miami University (B.A., Political Science; B.A., International Studies, 1999); Drake University (J.D., with honors, 2002). *Member:* Polk County, Iowa State and American Bar Associations; Polk County Women Attorneys, Inc.

BRITNEY L. SCHNATHORST, born Ames, Iowa; admitted to bar, 2005, Iowa. *Education:* Drake University (B.A., History, Law, Politics and Society, summa cum laude, 2002); Drake University Law School (J.D., with highest honors, 2005). Order of the Coif. Drake Law Review, 2004-2005. *Member:* Polk County, Iowa State and American Bar Associations. ***Email:*** bls@ialawyers.com

SARA L. KEENAN, born Kearny, Arizona, 1973; admitted to bar, 2005, Iowa. *Education:* University of New Mexico (B.A., 1995); Creighton University School of Law (J.D., cum laude, 2005). Phi Delta Phi. Member, Creighton Law Review, 2003-2005. International Moot Court Board, Problem Director, 2004-2005. Author: Case Note, "Interactive Products Corp. v. A2Z Mobile Office Solutions, Inc.: The Sixth Circuit Failed to Conduct a Thorough Analysis in Determining Whether Using a Trademark in the Post-Domain Path of a URL is Trademark Infringement," 37 Creighton L.Rev. 967 (2004). *Member:* Polk County, Iowa State and American Bar Associations. ***Email:*** keenan@ialawyers.com

REBECCA A. REISINGER, born Manhattan, Kansas, 1974; admitted to bar, 2005, Iowa. *Education:* University of Northern Iowa (B.A., Political Science, magna cum laude, 1996); George Mason University (J.D., 2005). Office of U.S. Senator Charles Grassley, 1997-2000. U.S. Senate Aging Committee, Professional Staff, 2000-2001. U.S. Senate Finance Committee, Health Policy Advisor, 2001-2002. ***Email:*** reisinger@ialawyers.com

WARREN BURGE

2428 S.W. 9TH STREET, SUITE 3
DES MOINES, IOWA 50315
Telephone: 515-285-2600
Email: WrnBrg@aol.com
URL: http://www.warrenburge.com
Bankruptcy, Divorce and Criminal Defense.

WARREN BURGE, born Warrensburg, Missouri, February 28, 1944; admitted to bar, 1984, Iowa and U.S. District Court, Northern District of Iowa. *Education:* Drake University (B.A., 1981; J.D., with honors, 1984). *Member:* Iowa State Bar Association. [With USAF, 1963-1967]. ***PRACTICE AREAS:*** Bankruptcy; Divorce; Criminal Defense.

CARNEY, APPLEBY, NIELSEN & SKINNER, P.L.C.

Established in 1976
400 HOMESTEAD BUILDING
303 LOCUST STREET
DES MOINES, IOWA 50309
Telephone: 515-282-6803
Fax: 515-282-4700
URL: http://www.carneylawfirmiowa.net
Email: recept@carneylawfirmiowa.com
URL: http://www.lawyers.com/carneylaw

General Practice. Legislative Law, Business Law, Torts, Real Estate, Family Law, Administrative Law, Insurance Law, Criminal Law, Family Law, Wills and Trusts, Probate, Bankruptcy, Malpractice. Trials and Appeals in Federal and State Courts.

FIRM PROFILE: Carney, Appleby, Nielsen & Skinner, P.L.C., was founded by James W. Carney in 1976 and serves clients throughout the State of Iowa. The firm engages in a General Practice with a heavy emphasis on civil litigation and legislation. The Firm has trained support personnel available.

JAMES W. CARNEY, born Centerville, Iowa, August 24, 1948; admitted to bar, 1975, Iowa, U.S. District Court, Southern and Northern Districts of Iowa, U.S. Claims Court, U.S. Tax Court, U.S. Court of Appeals, Eighth Circuit and U.S. Supreme Court. *Education:* University of Iowa (B.A., 1970); Drake University (J.D., 1975). Delta Theta Phi. Fellow, Iowa State Bar Association. *Member:* Polk County, Iowa State and American (Member, Sections on: Administrative Law; Family Law; Litigation) Bar Associations; Association of Trial Lawyers of Iowa; Iowa Academy of Trial Lawyers; Blackstone Inns of Court; American Board of Trial Advocates; National Association of Bar Executives (Past Chair, Government Relations Section); The Advocacy Group (TAG). [With U.S. Army, 1970-1972]. ***PRACTICE AREAS:*** Plaintiffs and Defendants Personal Injury; Medical Negligence; State Legislative Practice. ***Email:*** carney@carneylawfirmiowa.com

GEORGE W. APPLEBY, born Cedar Rapids, Iowa, August 10, 1947; admitted to bar, 1979, Iowa, U.S. District Court, Southern District of Iowa and U.S. Court of Appeals, Eighth Circuit; 1980, U.S. District Court, Northern District of Iowa and U.S. Court of Appeals, Court of Federal Claims. *Education:* Iowa State University (B.S., 1969); University of Iowa (J.D., 1979). Member: Polk County Charter Commission 1989-1990; Greater Des Moines Area Commission, 1990-1991; Polk County Compensation Commission. Member, 1991-2003 and Chair, 2000-2001, Iowa Medical Assistance Advisory Council. *Member:* Polk County, Iowa State and American Bar Associations; Blackstone Inns of Court (Emeritus). ***PRACTICE AREAS:*** Administrative Agency Practice; Criminal Defense; Divorce; State Legislative Practice; Civil Litigation; Plaintiffs Personal Injury; Civil Liability; General Liability Defense. ***Email:*** appleby@carneylawfirmiowa.com

STEPHEN V. NIELSEN, born Des Moines, Iowa, October 15, 1963; admitted to bar, 1991, Iowa and U.S. District Court, Southern District of Iowa. *Education:* University of Iowa (B.A., 1988); Thomas M. Cooley Law School (J.D., cum laude, 1991). Member, Thomas M. Cooley Law Review. Author: 7 Cooley Law Review 491 (1990). *Member:* Iowa State and American Bar Associations; The Association of Trial Lawyers of America; Iowa Trial Lawyers Association; Blackstone Inn of Court. [LCPL, United States Marine Corps, 1983-1985]. ***PRACTICE AREAS:*** Personal Injury; Wills; Trusts and Estates; Real Estate; Civil Litigation; Divorce Mediation; Medical Negligence; Real Estate Contracts; Real Estate Title Examination; Corporate Organization; Probate Administration; Mediation; Automobile Accidents and Injuries. ***Email:*** nielsen@carneylawfirmiowa.com

TROY A. SKINNER, born Des Moines, Iowa, October 31, 1969; admitted to bar, 1996, Iowa and U.S. District Court, Southern and Northern Districts of Iowa. *Education:* University of Iowa (B.B.A., 1992); Creighton University (J.D., 1996). *Member:* Iowa State Bar Association; Iowa Trial Lawyers Association. (Also practicing individually at same address). ***PRACTICE AREAS:*** Personal Injury; Family Law; Probate; Estate Planning; Employment Law. ***Email:*** skinner@carneylawfirmiowa.com

---

DIANE L. DORNBURG, born Wheaton, Minnesota, April 28, 1951; admitted to bar, 1976, Michigan; 1977, Iowa and U.S. District Court, Southern District of Iowa. *Education:* Gustavus Adolphus College (B.A., Sociology, magna cum laude, 1973); University of Michigan Law School (J.D., 1976). Co-Author: *Family Law and Custody Issues: Family Violence and Substance Abuse*, published by Lorman Educational Services, August, 1994. Author: *Family Law for Social Work*, University of Iowa text, re-edited for each class. *Member:* Polk County (Member, Family Law Committee) and Iowa State (Member, Family Law Section) Bar Associations. ***PRACTICE AREAS:*** Family Law; Child Custody; Child Support; Divorce; Domestic Violence; Visitation Rights; Guardianships. ***Email:*** dornburg@carneylawfirmiowa.com

JENNIFER ANN TYLER, born Stillwater, Oklahoma, November 14, 1959; admitted to bar, 1988, Iowa. *Education:* University of Iowa (B.A., with highest distinction, 1981; J.D., with distinction, 1985). Phi Beta Kappa; Phi Eta Sigma. Commissioner: Des Moines Historic District Commission, 1992-1994; Des Moines Plan and Zoning Commission,

(This Listing Continued)

CARNEY, APPLEBY, NIELSEN & SKINNER, P.L.C., Des Moines—Continued

1994-1996. *Member:* Iowa State Bar Association. ***PRACTICE AREAS:*** Legislative Lobbying; Government Affairs; Administrative Law. ***Email:*** tyler@carneylawfirmiowa.com

REPRESENTATIVE CLIENTS: Meredith Corp.; Anheuser Busch, Inc.; Iowa Veterinary Medical Assn.; Iowa State Bar Assn.; Accountants Association of Iowa; Printing Industries of Iowa; Iowa Manufactured Housing Assn.; AT&T; Iowa Assn. of Nurse Anesthetists; Magellan Behavioral Care of Iowa, Inc.; Iowa Consumer Credit Coalition; CitiGroup; HSBC North America; Wells Fargo Financial; Iowa Council of Health Care Centers; Iowa Association of Community Providers; Iowa Competitive Bidding Alliance, Inc.; Mediacom Communications Corporation; Appriss; Anderson Financial; Explore Information Services.
REFERENCE: Wells Fargo.

ROXANNE B. CONLIN AND ASSOCIATES, P.C.

Established in 1991

319 7TH STREET, SUITE 600
DES MOINES, IOWA 50309-3826
Telephone: 515-283-1111
Fax: 515-282-0477
Email: rconlin@roxanneconlinlaw.com
URL: http://www.roxanneconlinlaw.com

Trial and Appellate Practice. Personal Injury, Medical Malpractice, Products Liability, Employment Discrimination Law.

FIRM PROFILE: Roxanne B. Conlin has been practicing law in the community since 1966. Serving clients for over 35 years throughout the midwest with an emphasis on Iowa. The firm engages in the practice of consumer law.

ROXANNE B. CONLIN, born Huron, South Dakota, June 30, 1944; admitted to bar, 1966, Iowa. *Education:* Drake University (B.A., 1964; J.D., 1966; M.P.A., 1979). Phi Beta Kappa; Alpha Lambda Delta; Kappa Beta Phi; Pi Alpha Alpha. Chi Omega Service Award, 1964. Member, Drake University Law Review, 1965-1966. Student Representative, American Law Student Association, 1963-1964. Fischer Foundation Scholar. Co-Editor, "ATLA's Litigating Tort Cases," 6 Vol West, 2002. Deputy Industrial Commissioner, 1967-1968. Assistant Attorney General, Iowa, 1969-1976. Director, Iowa Civil Rights Section, Department of Justice, 1969-1976. Iowa Commission on the Status of Women, 1972-1978. Founder and State Chairperson, Iowa Women's Political Caucus, 1973-1975. Consultant, United States Commission on the Observance of International Women's Year, 1976-1977. Adjunct Professor of Law, University of Iowa, 1977-1979. U.S. Attorney, Southern District of Iowa, 1977-1981. Attorney General's Advisory Committee of United States Attorneys, 1977-1981. Consultant, Attorney General's Advocacy Institute, 1977-1981. Member, Law Board of Counselors, Drake University Law School, 1977-1986. Board of Directors, IOWA SHARES, 1979-1981. Vice-President and President, Federal Executive Council, 1979-1981. President, Drake Law School Endowment Trust, 1985-1986. Named one of the 50 Most Influential Women Lawyers in the U.S., National Law Journal. Named in 100 Most Influential Lawyers in United States in 1991, National Law Journal; Top 10 Litigators in the U.S. *Member:* Iowa State and American Bar Associations; The Association of Trial Lawyers of America (Secretary, Vice President, President-Elect, President); Association of Trial Lawyers of Iowa (Member, Board of Governors); Inner Circle of Advocates; International Academy of Trial Lawyers; Trial Lawyers Care (Board of Directors). ***REPORTED CASES:*** Madison v. IBP 257 F.3d 780 (8th Cir. 2001); Channon v. UPS 625 NW2d 835 (2001); Krauel v. Iowa Methodist Medical Center, 95 F.3d 674, 65 USLW 2186, 71 Fair Empl. Prac. Cas. (BNA) 1326, 69 Empl. Prac. Dec. P 44, 315, 20 Employee Benefits Cas. 1809, 5 A.D. Cases 1503, 18 A.D.D. 112, 8 NDLR P 317 (8th Cir. (Iowa), Sep 11, 1996) (NO. 95-3768); Frideres v. Schiltz, 540 N.W.2d 261 (Iowa, Nov 22, 1995) (NO. 94-400); Courtney v. American Nat. Can Co., 537 N.W.2d 681, 4 A.D. Cases 1583, 7 NDLR P 99 (Iowa, Sep 20, 1995) (NO. 94-183); Brodersen v. Sioux Valley Memorial Hosp., 902 F.Supp. 931, 43 Fed. R. Evid. Serv. 567 (N.D.Iowa, Sep 19, 1995) (NO. C 93-4011); Doe v. Cherwitz, 894 F.Supp. 344 (S.D.Iowa, Aug 28, 1995) (NO. CIV. 3-92-70138); Falczynski v. Amoco Oil Co., 533 N.W.2d 226, 71 Fair Empl. Prac. Cas. (BNA) 1029, 4 A.D. Cases 777, 6 NDLR P 359 (Iowa, May 24, 1995) (NO. 93-1575, 81); Langner v. Simpson, 533 N.W.2d 511 (Iowa, May 24, 1995) (NO. 93-1364); Doe v. Cherwitz, 518 N.W.2d 362 (Iowa, Jun 22, 1994) (NO. 93-1269); Beeman v. Manville Corp. Asbestos Disease Compensation Fund, 496 N.W.2d 247, Prod. Liab. Rep. (CCH) P 13,424 (Iowa, Feb 17, 1993) (NO. 90-1514); Lynch v. City of Des Moines, 464 N.W.2d 236 (Iowa, Dec 19, 1990) (NO. 89-1589); Lynch v. City of Des Moines, 454 N.W.2d 827, 57 Fair Empl. Cas. (BNA) 1331, 54 Empl. Prac. Dec. P 40,097 (Iowa, Apr 18, 1990) (NO. 89-222); Gail v. Clark, 410 N.W.2d 662 (Iowa, Jul 22, 1987) (NO. 86-493); Moore v. City of Des Moines, Iowa, 766 F.2d 343, 38 Fair Empl. Prac. Cas. (BNA) 189, 37 Empl. Prac. Dec. P 35, 366, 38 Empl. Prac. Dec. P 35, 666 (8th Cir. (Iowa), Jun 25, 1985) (NO. 84-2514); U.S. v. May, 625 F.2d 186 (8th Cir. (Iowa), May 30, 1980) (NO. 79-1790) Copr. (C) West 1997 No claim to orig. U.S. govt. works; State ex rel. Turner v. Beuchele, 236 N.W.2d 322 (Iowa, Dec 17, 1975) (NO. 2-58022); Cedar Rapids Community School Dist. v. Parr, 227 N.W.2d 486, 12 Fair Empl. Prac. Cas. (BNA) 54, 9 Empl. Prac. Dec. P 10,016 (Iowa, Mar 19, 1975) (NO. 2-56518) Copr. (C) West 1997 No claims to orig. U.S. govt. works; State v. Bartz, 224 N.W.2d 632 (Iowa, Dec 18, 1974) (NO. 55707); Wilson-Sinclair Co. v. Griggs, 211 N.W.2d 133, 6 Fair Empl. Prac. Cas. (BNA) 1057, 6 Empl. Prac. Dec. P 8839 (Iowa, Sep 19, 1973) (NO. 55918); Iron Workers Local NO. 67 v. Hart, 191 N.W.2d 758, 4 Fair. Empl. Prac. Cas. (BNA) 137, 4 Empl. Prac. Dec. P 7565 (Iowa, Nov 11, 1971) (NO. 54741). ***PRACTICE AREAS:*** Trial and Appellate Practice; Personal Injury Law; Medical Malpractice; Products Liability Law; Employment Discrimination Law. ***Email:*** rconlin@roxanneconlinlaw.com

CONNOLLY, O'MALLEY, LILLIS, HANSEN & OLSON, L.L.P.

Established in 1917

BANK OF AMERICA BUILDING
317 6TH AVENUE, SUITE 300
DES MOINES, IOWA 50309-4127
Telephone: 515-243-8157
Fax: 515-243-3919
Email: colho@connollylawfirm.com
URL: http://www.connollylawfirm.com

General Trial Practice, State and Federal Courts. Probate, Real Estate, Zoning, Municipal, Corporation, Workers Compensation, Personal Injury, Administrative, Family, Bankruptcy, Environmental Law and Hospital Law.

FIRM PROFILE: Connolly, O'Malley, Lillis, Hansen & Olson, L.L.P. was founded in 1917 by John Connolly, Jr. Serving clients throughout Polk, Dallas, Jasper, Warren, Madison, Story, Marion and surrounding counties. All attys in B/R General Practice, Real Estate, Trusts and Estates, Wills and Probate.

MEMBERS OF FIRM

WILLIAM J. LILLIS, born Williamsburg, Iowa, January 31, 1943; admitted to bar, 1968, Iowa and U.S. District Court, Northern and Southern Districts of Iowa; 1975, U.S. Supreme Court. *Education:* Drake University (B.A., 1965); University of Iowa; Creighton University (J.D., 1968). Phi Alpha Delta. Assistant Polk County Attorney, 1968-1970. *Member:* Polk County (President, 1981), Iowa State (Member, Board of Governors, 1982) and American Bar Associations. ***PRACTICE AREAS:*** Real Estate; Zoning; Banking; Condemnation; Business Law. ***Email:*** wlillis@connollylawfirm.com

RUSSELL J. HANSEN, born Watkins, Iowa, July 7, 1945; admitted to bar, 1970, Iowa and U.S. District Court, Southern District of Iowa; 1971, U.S. District Court, Northern District of Iowa. *Education:* Iowa State University (B.S., 1967); Drake University (J.D., 1970). Phi Alpha Delta. Diplomate, Court Practice Institute, 1974. *Member:* Polk County, Iowa State and American Bar Associations; The Association of Trial Lawyers of Iowa. ***PRACTICE AREAS:*** Real Estate; Litigation; Corporate Law; Business Law; Probate; Trusts and Estates. ***Email:*** rhansen@connollylawfirm.com

MICHAEL W. O'MALLEY, born Des Moines, Iowa, October 27, 1949; admitted to bar, 1974, Iowa and U.S. District Court, Northern and Southern District of Iowa. *Education:* Loras College and Creighton University (A.B., 1971); Creighton University (J.D., 1974). *Member:* Polk County, Iowa State and American Bar Associations. ***PRACTICE AREAS:*** Probate; Personal Injury; Real Estate; Family Law; Estate Planning. ***Email:*** momalley@connollylawfirm.com

EUGENE E. OLSON, born Ames, Iowa, May 4, 1943; admitted to bar, 1968, Iowa and U.S. District Court, Northern and Southern Districts of Iowa. *Education:* University of Iowa (B.A., with honors, 1965; J.D., 1968). Omicron Delta Kappa. Assistant City Attorney, Des Moines, 1968-1975. City Solicitor, Des Moines, 1975-1978. *Member:* Polk County, Iowa State (Member, Board of Governors, 1987-1991) and American Bar Associations; American Academy of Hospital Attorneys; American Hospital Association. ***PRACTICE AREAS:*** Real Estate; Zoning; Health Care Law; Hospital Law. ***Email:*** eolson@connollylawfirm.com

STREETAR CAMERON, born Bloomfield, Iowa, January 29, 1957; admitted to bar, 1983, Iowa. *Education:* University of Iowa (B.A., 1979); Drake University (J.D., with honors, 1983). *Member:* Polk County and Iowa State (Member, Sections on: Probate and Trust; Real Estate) Bar Associations. ***PRACTICE AREAS:*** Real Estate; Probate; Corporate Law. ***Email:*** scameron@connollylawfirm.com

DANIEL L. MANNING, born Des Moines, Iowa, July 17, 1958; admitted to bar, 1983, Iowa and U.S. District Court, Southern and Northern Districts of Iowa; U.S. Army Court of Military Review. *Education:* Creighton University (B.A., 1980; J.D., 1983). *Member:* Polk County and Iowa State Bar Associations; Iowa Trial Lawyers Association. [CAPT., JAGC, 1983-1987]. ***PRACTICE AREAS:*** Personal Injury; Litigation; Condemnation; Zoning Law. ***Email:*** dmanning@connollylawfirm.com

CHRISTOPHER R. POSE, born Waterloo, Iowa, May 15, 1963; admitted to bar, 1989, Iowa; U.S. District Court, Southern and Northern Districts of Iowa; U.S. Supreme Court. *Education:* University of Iowa (B.A., 1986); Drake University (J.D., 1989). Delta Theta Phi. Order of the Barristers. Member: Moot Court Board, 1988-1989; National Appellate Advocacy Team; Midwest Regional Appellate Advocacy Team, 1988. Recipient, Rodney L. Hudson Senior Advocacy Award, 1989. Contributing Author: "Environmental Law and Practice Manual," 1996. *Member:* Polk County, Iowa State (Council Member, Natural Resources and Environmental Law Section, 1995-1997) and American Bar Associations. ***PRACTICE AREAS:*** Zoning; Environmental Law; Litigation. ***Email:*** cpose@connollylawfirm.com

ADAM C. VAN DIKE, born Sioux City, Iowa, January 11, 1975; admitted to bar, 2001, Iowa and U.S. District Court, Southern District of Iowa. *Education:* University of Iowa (B.A., 1998); Creighton University of Law (J.D., 2001). Board Member, International Moot Court Board, 2000-2001. Member, Board of Adjustment, City of Clive, Iowa. *Member:* Polk County and Iowa State Bar Associations. ***PRACTICE AREAS:*** Real Estate; Corporate Law; Foreclosures; Zoning Law; Litigation. ***Email:*** avandike@connollylawfirm.com

A list of Representative Clients will be furnished upon request.
References will be furnished upon request.

CRAWFORD LAW FIRM

1701 RUAN CENTER
666 GRAND AVENUE
DES MOINES, IOWA 50309
Telephone: 515-245-5420
Fax: 515-245-5421
Email: crawford@crawfordlawfirm.com

Civil Litigation, National and International Government Relations Strategies, Plaintiff's Personal Injury, Administrative Law, Racing and Gaming / Sports Law.

FIRM PROFILE: The Crawford Law Firm prides itself on providing the highest quality legal services to a variety of clients including individuals, local businesses and multinational corporations. The firm is committed to excellence in personal and professional service as measured by the results we achieve for our clients.

GERALD W. (JERRY) CRAWFORD, born Indianola, Iowa, October 26, 1949; admitted to bar, 1975, Iowa. *Education:* Macalester College (B.A., 1971); University of Iowa (J.D., 1975). Board of Directors, Democratic Governor's Association. Commissioner, Iowa Judicial Compensation Commission. *Member:* Polk County, Iowa State and American Bar Associations; Association of Trial Lawyers of Iowa; The Association of Trial Lawyers of America. ***PRACTICE AREAS:*** Civil Litigation; Government Relations; Plaintiffs Personal Injury; Gaming Law; Sports Law. ***Email:*** crawford@crawfordlawfirm.com

JAMES R. QUILTY, born 1968; admitted to bar, 1993, Illinois; 1994, Missouri; 1999, Iowa, U.S. District Court, Northern and Southern Districts of Iowa, U.S. District Court, Southern District of Illinois and U.S. District Court, Eastern District of Missouri. *Education:* St. Ambrose University (B.A., 1990); University of Illinois (J.D., magna cum laude, 1993). Former Assistant Attorney General to The State of Missouri Stemming from representation of the State in the tobacco litigation. *Member:* Polk County and Iowa State Bar Associations; American Trial Lawyers Association; Iowa Trial Lawyers Association; Greater Des Moines Leadership Institute. ***PRACTICE AREAS:*** Plaintiffs Personal Injury; Medical Malpractice; Product Liability; Commercial Litigation. ***Email:*** quilty@crawfordlawfirm.com

LAW CHAMBERS OF NICHOLAS CRITELLI, P.C.

Established in 1967
SUITE 950, 317 SIXTH AVENUE
DES MOINES, IOWA 50309-4128
Telephone: 515-243-3122
Toll Free: 1-877-243-3122
Telecopier: (Fax) 515-243-2932
Email: critelli@critellilaw.com
URL: http://www.CritelliLaw.com

London, England Office: 9 Stone Buildings, Lincoln's Inn. Telephone: 011-44-171-404-5055. Fax: 011-44-171-405-1551.

Practice limited to acting as local Counsel and trial counsel to members of the Bar in matters concerning Commercial Litigation, International, Insurance, Intellectual Property, Trademark, Copyright, Unfair Competition, Business Crime, Mediation and Arbitration.

FIRM PROFILE: Nicholas Critelli, P.C. established the firm in 1967 as a specialty trial law firm. In the United States, the firm limits its practice to acting for members of the Bar as local or trial counsel in matters involving litigation and advocacy in the state and federal courts in matters concerning commercial litigation, intellectual property, fraud, antitrust, negligence, malpractice and business and commercial related crime. In England and Wales, Mr. Critelli practices in the areas of international civil litigation and commercial matters and business crime.

NICK CRITELLI, JR., born Des Moines, Iowa, February 15, 1944; admitted to bar, 1967, Iowa; 1971, U.S. Supreme Court; 1990, New York; 1991, England and Wales (Barrister Middle Temple). *Education:* Drake University (B.A., 1966; J.D., 1967). Adjunct Professor of Trial Law and Practice, Drake University Law School, 1980-1989. Member, Iowa Supreme Court Advisory Committee on Rules of Evidence, 1982—, Chairman, 1983-1989. Member, Civil Justice Reform Act Committee, U.S. District Court, 1990-1997. Chairman, Iowa State Bar Association Professionalism Committee, 1989-1996. Chairman, Iowa State Bar Association Special Committee on Foreign Practice, 1989-1995. Chairman, Iowa State Bar Association Litigation Legislation Committee, 1988-1990. Governor, 1981—, Iowa Academy of Trial Lawyers, President, 1986-1987. Barrister, Honourable Society of Middle Temple Inn of Court (London, England). President and Master of the Bench, Honorable Society of Blackstone Inn of Court, Des Moines, Iowa. *Member:* Iowa State (President, 2004; Member, Litigation Section), New York State (Member, Litigation and International Law Sections), American (Member, Litigation, Torts and Insurance and International Law Sections) and International Bar Associations; American Board of Trial Advocates (Diplomat); American Arbitration Association. Fellow: American College of Trial Lawyers; International Society of Barristers; Iowa Criminal Defense Association (Board of Governors, 1997—); Society of Advanced Legal Studies, London. (Certified as Civil Trial Advocate by National Board of Trial Advocacy). ***LANGUAGES:*** Italian. ***PRACTICE AREAS:*** Litigation; International Practice; Securities Litigation; Trademark Law; Copyright Law; Unfair Competition; Mediation; Arbitration. ***Email:*** nick@critellilaw.com

LYLEA DODSON CRITELLI, born Ottawa, Illinois, May 12, 1956; admitted to bar, 1981, Iowa, U.S. District Court, Southern District of Iowa and U.S. Court of Appeals, Eighth Circuit; 1982, U.S. District Court, Northern District of Iowa; 1985, U.S. Supreme Court. *Education:* Illinois Wesleyan University (B.A., cum laude, 1978); Drake University (J.D., 1981). Phi Alpha Delta (Vice Justice, 1980). Member, Board of Directors, 1985 and Treasurer, 1986, Legal Services Corporation of Iowa. Member, Drake University Law School Board of Counselors, 1991-1994. *Member:* Polk County (Chair, Special Projects, 1990-1992, Member, Board of Directors, 1992-1993; Member, Juvenile Justice Committee, 1985-1986), Iowa State (Member: Chair, Public Relations Committee, 1998-1999; Conference 2000, Chair, 1993; Board of Governors, 1987-1990; Living Farms Committee, 1981-1982; Chairman, 1982-1983; Member, Bridge-the-Gap Committee, 1982-1984; Co-Chairman, 1984-1986; Member, Executive Council, Young Lawyers Section, 1983-1987; Secretary, 1987-1988; President-Elect, 1988-1989; President, 1989-1990), Federal (Secretary, Iowa Chapter, 1989-1990) and American (District 19 Representative, 1986-1988; Member, Sections on: Litigation; Young Lawyers; Assistant Executive Council Coordinator, 1987-1988; Member, Long Range Planning Committee, 1989-1990) Bar Associations; Blackstone Inn of Court (Barrister, 1989-1993; Bencher, 1997-1999). ***LANGUAGES:*** Spanish. ***Email:*** Lylea@critellilaw.com

N. TRÉ CRITELLI, born Des Moines, Iowa, April 2, 1966; admitted to bar, 1996, Iowa and U.S. District Court, Northern and Southern Districts of Iowa; U.S. Court of Appeals, 8th Circuit; 1999, U.S. Supreme Court; 2002, England and Wales; Barrister, Middle Temple. *Education:* Loras College (B.A., 1988); Drake University (J.D., 1995). Phi Alpha Delta. Participant: National Institute of Trial Advocacy Trial School, 1996, 1999; American Academy of ADR Attorneys Mediation Training, 1999. Adjunct Professor, Drake University Law School, 2000. Co-Moderator, CaseMap Users Yahoo! Group, 2000—. *Member:* Iowa State Bar Association (Member, Young Lawyers' Division: Chair, Publicity Committee, 2000-2002; District Representative, 1998-2000, 2002—; Member, State Fair Committee, 1996-2000; Member, Professional Development Committee, 1996-2000); Iowa Association of Criminal Defense Lawyers (Member, Board of Directors, 1997-1999); Iowa Trial Lawyers Association (Member, Continuing Legal Education Committee, 2000—); American Intellectual Property Lawyers Association; C. Edwin Moore American Inn of Court (Lawyer Pupil, 1997-1999; Barrister, 2000—); Honourable Society of the Middle Temple (Pupil, 2001-2002). ***LANGUAGES:*** Japanese. ***Email:*** Tre@critellilaw.com

REFERENCE: Iowa State Bar Association.

CUTLER LAW FIRM, P.C.

DES MOINES, IOWA

(See West Des Moines)

HARRY W. DAHL, P.C.

Established in 1972
974 73RD STREET #16
DES MOINES, IOWA 50312
Telephone: 515-224-1070
Fax: 515-224-4620
Email: harrywdahl@msn.com

Workers Compensation Law.

FIRM PROFILE: Harry W. Dahl, P.C. was founded by Harry W. Dahl in 1972, serving clients throughout the region with an emphasis in the state of Iowa. The firm focuses its practice in the area of workers compensation.

HARRY W. DAHL (1927-1996)

HARRY W. DAHL, born Des Moines, Iowa, November 6, 1958; admitted to bar, 1984, Iowa; 1985, Nebraska. *Education:* Drake University (B.A., summa cum laude, 1981; J.D., 1984). Phi Beta Kappa. *Member:* Polk County, Iowa State, Nebraska State and American Bar Associations; Iowa Trial Lawyers Association; Iowa Association of Workers' Compensation Lawyers (Member, Board of Governors). ***PRACTICE AREAS:*** Workers Compensation Defense; Workers Compensation Appeals; Workers Compensation Subrogation; Workers Compensation Mediation.

PAMELA GREENMAN DAHL, born Des Moines, Iowa, February 8, 1959; admitted to bar, 1984, Iowa. *Education:* Graceland College; Drake University (B.A., magna cum laude, 1981; J.D., with honors, 1984). Order of the Coif. Iowa Assistant Attorney General, 1984-1988. *Member:* Polk County, Iowa State and American Bar Associations. ***PRACTICE AREAS:*** Workers Compensation Appeals.

REPRESENTATIVE CLIENTS: Broadspire; Crum & Forster Commercial Insurance; ESIS; Iowa Municipalities Workers' Compensation Association; Metzeler Automotive Profile Systems; OneBeacon Insurance Group; Silverstone Group; The Zenith Insurance Company; Zurich Services Corporation.

DAVIS, BROWN, KOEHN, SHORS & ROBERTS, P.C.

THE FINANCIAL CENTER
666 WALNUT STREET, SUITE 2500
DES MOINES, IOWA 50309-3993
Telephone: 515-288-2500
Cable: Davis Law
Facsimile: 515-243-0654
Email: info@lawiowa.com
URL: http://www.lawiowa.com

West Des Moines, Iowa Office: 4201 Westown Parkway, Suite 300, 50266. Telephone: 515-288-2500. Fax: 515-246-7997.

Administrative, Agricultural, Alternative Dispute Resolution, Antitrust and Trade Regulation, Appellate Practice, Bankruptcy, Banks and Banking, Biotechnology, Business Law, Civil, Class Actions, Commercial, Commercial Real Estate, Communications and Media, Complex and Multi-District Litigation, Computers and Software, Constitutional, Construction, Consumer, Contracts, Copyrights, Corporate, Debtor and Creditor, Education, Employee Benefits, Energy, Environmental, Equipment Finance and Leasing, Family, Finance, Franchises and Franchising, Government, Government Contracts, Guardianship and Conservatorship, Health

(This Listing Continued)

DAVIS, BROWN, KOEHN, SHORS & ROBERTS, P.C., Des Moines—Continued

Care, Hospital Law, Human and Civil Rights, Immigration and Naturalization, Insurance, Insurance Defense, Intellectual Property, International Law, International Trade, Labor and Employment, Leases and Leasing, Legal Ethics and Professional Responsibility, Libel, Slander and Defamation, Litigation, Media Law, Medical Malpractice, Mergers, Acquisitions and Divestitures, Municipal Law, Natural Resources, Nonprofit and Charitable Organizations, Partnership, Patents, Personal Injury, Probate. Products Liability, Professional Liability, Property, Public Finance, Real Estate, Regulatory, Securities, Taxation, Technology and Science, Torts, Trade and Professional Associations, Trade Secrets, Trademarks, Transportation, Trusts and Estates, Utilities, Wills, Workers Compensation, Zoning, Planning and Land Use.

FIRM PROFILE: Davis, Brown, Koehn, Shors & Roberts, P.C., and its predecessors, have been practicing law in Des Moines since 1929. The Firm is the Iowa representative in Lex Mundi, the world's leading association of independent law firms, as well as the Iowa member of World Services Group, a worldwide professional services organization.

For a full description visit the firm's web site at www.lawiowa.com.

JOHN D. SHORS, born Fort Dodge, Iowa, 1937; admitted to bar, 1964, Iowa. *Education:* Iowa State University (B.S., Elec. Eng., 1959); University of Iowa (J.D., with high distinction, 1964). Order of the Coif. Listed in The Best Lawyers in America, Health Care. Co-Author: "Closely Held Corporations in Business and Estate Planning," Little Brown and Company, 1983. Member, Board of Governors, 1984—and Chairman of Board, 1988-1991, Iowa State University Foundation. *Member:* Polk County (President, 1985-1986), Iowa State (President, 1992-1993) and American (Fellow; Member, House of Delegates, 1992-1993) Bar Associations. ***PRACTICE AREAS:*** Corporate Law; Health Care; Hospital Law; Mergers and Acquisitions; Technology and Science. ***Email:*** John.Shors@lawiowa.com

STEPHEN W. ROBERTS, born Des Moines, Iowa, 1939; admitted to bar, 1964, Iowa. *Education:* Princeton University (B.A., 1961); University of Michigan (J.D., 1964). Chairman, Iowa Republican Party, 1977-1981. Member, Republican National Committee, 1977-1981, 1988—. ***PRACTICE AREAS:*** Administrative Law; Antitrust and Trade Regulation; Business Law; Casino and Gambling; Corporate Law; Government; State Legislative Practice; State Taxation. ***Email:*** Steve.Roberts@lawiowa.com

WILLIAM R. KING, born Des Moines, Iowa, 1939; admitted to bar, 1966, Iowa; 1967, U.S. District Court, Southern and Northern Districts of Iowa; 1977, U.S. Supreme Court; 1980, U.S. Court of Appeals, Seventh Circuit; 1982, U.S. Court of Appeals, Eighth Circuit and U.S. District Court, Central District of Illinois. *Education:* Iowa State University and University of Iowa (B.A., 1961); University of Iowa (J.D., 1966). *Member:* American Bar Association (Member, Forum Committee on the Construction Industry, 1977—). ***PRACTICE AREAS:*** Alternative Dispute Resolution; Construction Law; Medical Malpractice; Negligence. ***Email:*** Bill.King@lawiowa.com

ROBERT F. HOLZ, JR., born Dubuque, Iowa, 1942; admitted to bar, 1967, Iowa. *Education:* Loras College (B.A., 1964); University of Iowa (J.D., with distinction, 1967). Listed in The Best Lawyers in America, Public Utility Law. *Member:* Polk County, Iowa State and American Bar Associations; American Health Lawyers Association; Iowa Society of Healthcare Attorneys. ***PRACTICE AREAS:*** Administrative Law; Health Care; Utility Law; Telecommunications Law. ***Email:*** Bob.Holz@lawiowa.com

ROBERT A. GAMBLE, born Des Moines, Iowa, 1938; admitted to bar, 1962, Iowa. *Education:* State University of Iowa (B.A., 1960; LL.B., 1962). Phi Delta Phi. Member, Iowa Supreme Court Grievance Commission, 1990-1995. *Member:* Polk County, Iowa State (Member, Sections on: Business Law; Commercial and Bankruptcy Law) and American (Member, Section on Business Law) Bar Associations. ***PRACTICE AREAS:*** Banks and Banking. ***Email:*** Beau.Gamble@lawiowa.com

MICHAEL G. KULIK, born Miami Beach, Florida, 1945; admitted to bar, 1970, Iowa. *Education:* University of Iowa (B.B.A., 1967; J.D., with distinction, 1970). Notes and Comments Editor, Iowa Law Review, 1969-1970. *Member:* Polk County, Iowa State and American (Member, Sections on: Communications, Real Property, Probate and Trust Law; Corporation, Banking and Business Law) Bar Associations. ***PRACTICE AREAS:*** Business Law; Telecommunications Law; Contracts; Corporate Law; Mergers and Acquisitions; Probate; Trust, Estates and Wills. ***Email:*** Mike.Kulik@lawiowa.com

THOMAS E. SALSBERY, born Milwaukee, Wisconsin, 1946; admitted to bar, 1972, Iowa. *Education:* University of Iowa (B.A., 1968; J.D., with distinction, 1972). Lecturer: Commercial Paper, 1974; Commercial Transactions, 1992, Drake University College of Law. *Member:* Polk County, Iowa State and American Bar Associations; American Agricultural Law Association. ***PRACTICE AREAS:*** Commercial Law; Consumer Law; Professional Liability. ***Email:*** Tom.Salsbery@lawiowa.com

FRANK J. CARROLL, born Albuquerque, New Mexico, 1947; admitted to bar, 1973, Iowa. *Education:* St. Louis University (B.S., cum laude, 1969); University of Illinois (J.D., 1973). Listed in The Best Lawyers in America, Tax Law, Corporate, Mergers and Acqusitions, 1995-2003. Certified Public Accountant, Illinois, 1970. Adjunct Professor: Planning of Corporate Transactions, Drake University College of Law, 1976-1986; Corporate Taxation, Drake University, College of Business, Masters of Tax Program, 1987-1993. Member, IRS Commissioners Advisory Group, 1989. *Member:* Polk County, Iowa State and American Bar Associations. ***PRACTICE AREAS:*** Business Law; Corporate Law; Mergers, Acquisitions and Divestitures; Taxation. ***Email:*** Frank.Carroll@lawiowa.com

BRUCE I. CAMPBELL, born Mason City, Iowa, 1947; admitted to bar, 1973, Iowa. *Education:* Upper Iowa University (B.A., summa cum laude, 1969); Harvard University (J.D., cum laude, 1973). Listed in The Best Lawyers in America, Tax Law, Trusts and Estates, 1995-2003. *Member:* Polk County, Iowa State and American (Member, Sections on: Taxation; Real Property, Probate and Trust Law) Bar Associations. Fellow, American College of Trust and Estate Counsel. ***PRACTICE AREAS:*** Estate Gift Taxation; Estate Planning; Trust Law; Decedents Estates. ***Email:*** Bruce.Campbell@lawiowa.com

JONATHAN C. WILSON, born Montezuma, Iowa, 1945; admitted to bar, 1971, Iowa. *Education:* Morningside College (B.A., cum laude, 1967); University of Iowa (J.D., with distinction, 1971). Order of the Coif. Member, Iowa Law Review, 1970-1971. Law Clerk, U.S. Court of Appeals, Eighth Circuit, 1971-1972. Lecturer: Australian National University, Canberra, Australia, 1972-1974; Modern Real Estate Transactions, Drake University College of Law, 1975. ***PRACTICE AREAS:*** Civil Practice; Contracts; Government; Litigation; Real Estate; Transportation; Zoning, Planning and Land Use. ***Email:*** Jonathan.Wilson@lawiowa.com

STEVEN L. NELSON, born Baraboo, Wisconsin, 1952; admitted to bar, 1976, Iowa; 1978, U.S. District Court, Northern and Southern Districts of Iowa; 1979, U.S. Court of Appeals, Eighth Circuit; 1987, U.S. Tax Court; 1981, U.S. Supreme Court. *Education:* University of Iowa (B.B.A., 1973; J.D., 1976). Order of the Coif. Law Clerk to Hon. W.W. Reynoldson, Supreme Court of Iowa, 1976-1977. ***PRACTICE AREAS:*** Product Liability; Class Actions; Torts; Trade Secrets; Business Litigation. ***Email:*** Steve.Nelson@lawiowa.com

DAVID B. VANSICKEL, born Mason City, Iowa, 1953; admitted to bar, 1977, Iowa. *Education:* University of Northern Iowa (B.A., magna cum laude, 1974); University of Iowa (J.D., with honors, 1977). *Member:* Polk County, Iowa State and American Bar Associations; National Association of Bond Lawyers. ***PRACTICE AREAS:*** Public Finance and Securities. ***Email:*** David.VanSickel@lawiowa.com

GENE R. LA SUER, born Newton, Iowa, 1953; admitted to bar, 1979, Iowa. *Education:* Iowa State University (B.S., 1976); University of Iowa (J.D., with honors, 1979). *Member:* Polk County, Iowa State (Member, Litigation and Labor and Employment Law Sections) and American (Member, Sections on; Litigation; Labor and Employment Law) Bar Associations. ***PRACTICE AREAS:*** Civil Rights; Labor and Employment; Personal Injury; Insurance Defense; Professional Liability. ***Email:*** Gene.LaSuer@lawiowa.com

DEBORAH M. THARNISH, born Des Moines, Iowa, 1955; admitted to bar, 1980, Iowa. *Education:* Iowa State University (B.A., 1977); University of Iowa (J.D., with high distinction, 1980). Phi Beta Kappa. Member, Order of the Coif. Articles Editor, Iowa Law Review, 1979-1980. *Member:* Polk County, Iowa State and American Bar Associations; Iowa Defense Counsel (Member, Board of Directors). ***PRACTICE AREAS:*** Antitrust and Trade Regulation; Labor and Employment; Litigation; Adoption. ***Email:*** Deb.Tharnish@lawiowa.com

KENT A. HERINK, born Marshalltown, Iowa, 1955; admitted to bar, 1982, Iowa; registered to practice before the U.S. Patent and Trademark Office. *Education:* Coe College (B.A., magna cum laude, 1976); University of Iowa (M.S., 1979; J.D., with distinction, 1982). Phi Eta Sigma. Listed in The Best Lawyers in America, Intellectual Property, 1995-2004. *Member:* Polk County, Iowa State (Member, Patent, Trademark and Copyright Section, 1990—) and American (Member: Section of Patent, Trademark and Copyright Law; Biosciences Committee, 1984-2002) Bar Associations; Iowa Intellectual Property Law Association (President, 1992-1993). ***PRACTICE AREAS:*** Intellectual Property; Trademarks. ***Email:*** Kent.Herink@lawiowa.com

ROBERT J. DOUGLAS, JR., born Mason City, Iowa, 1957; admitted to bar, 1982, Iowa. *Education:* St. John's University (B.S., cum laude, 1979); University of Iowa (J.D., with distinction, 1982). *Member:* Polk County, Iowa State (Member, Banking/Financial Institutions Committee, 1993-1995) and American (Member: Banking Committee, 1990—; Subcommittee on Community Bank Corporate Activities, 1990—) Bar Associations. ***PRACTICE AREAS:*** Financial Institutions Law; Real Estate. ***Email:*** Bob.Douglas@lawiowa.com

MARK D. WALZ, born St. Louis, Missouri, 1958; admitted to bar, 1983, Missouri; 1986, Iowa, U.S. District Court, Northern and Southern Districts of Iowa and U.S. Court of Appeals, Eighth Circuit. *Education:* University of Iowa (B.A., 1980; J.D., with distinction, 1983). *Member:* Polk County and Iowa State (Member, Section on Commercial and Bankruptcy Law) Bar Associations; The Missouri Bar; American Bankruptcy Institute. ***PRACTICE AREAS:*** Bankruptcy; Commercial Law. ***Email:*** Mark.Walz@lawiowa.com

GARY M. MYERS, born Storm Lake, Iowa, 1961; admitted to bar, 1986, Iowa. *Education:* Iowa State University (B.A., 1983); University of Iowa (J.D., with high distinction, 1986). Order of the Coif. *Member:* Polk County, Iowa State and American Bar Associations. ***PRACTICE AREAS:*** Real Estate; Environmental Law. ***Email:*** Gary.Myers@lawiowa.com

STANLEY J. THOMPSON, born Red Oak, Iowa, 1960; admitted to bar, 1985, Iowa. *Education:* Iowa State University (B.A., with distinction, 1982); George Washington University (J.D., with honors, 1985). Law Clerk to Allen L. Danielson, Iowa Court of Appeals, 1985-1986. Member, Board of Directors, 1999-2005 and Chair, 2003-2004, Iowa State University Alumni Association. Republican Nominee for Congress, Iowa District 3, 2002 and 2004. ***PRACTICE AREAS:*** Litigation; Antitrust and Trade Regulation. ***Email:*** Stan.Thompson@lawiowa.com

DAVID A. TANK, born Marshalltown, Iowa, 1959; admitted to bar, 1984, Iowa. *Education:* Colgate University (B.A., 1981); University of Iowa (J.D., with high distinction, 1984). *Member:* Polk County, Iowa State and American Bar Associations. ***PRACTICE AREAS:*** Litigation; Intellectual Property Litigation; Products Liability; Complex and Multi-District Litigation; Class Actions; Toxic Torts; Torts. ***Email:*** Dave.Tank@lawiowa.com

DAVID M. ERICKSON, born Ames, Iowa, 1953; admitted to bar, 1979, Iowa. *Education:* Drake University (B.A., 1974; J.D., with honors, 1979). Order of the Coif. Member, Editorial Board and Honorary Board Member, Drake Law Review, 1978-1979. ***PRACTICE AREAS:*** Real Estate; Mortgages; Commercial Real Estate; Zoning Planning and Land Use; Property Law. ***Email:*** Dave.Erickson@lawiowa.com

LORI TORGERSON CHESSER, born Flagstaff, Arizona, 1962; admitted to bar, 1987, Iowa. *Education:* Western Illinois University (B.B.A., Finance, with high honors, 1984); University of Georgia (J.D., magna cum laude, 1987). Order of the Coif. *Member:* Polk County, Iowa State and American Bar Associations; Polk County Women Attorneys (President, 1992); American Immigration Lawyers Association (Co-founder and Chair, Iowa/Nebraska Chapter, 1998-1999). ***PRACTICE AREAS:*** Immigration and Naturalization Law. ***Email:*** Lori.Chesser@lawiowa.com

JO ELLEN WHITNEY, born Des Moines, Iowa, 1963; admitted to bar, 1988, Iowa. *Education:* Duke University (B.A., magna cum laude, 1984; J.D., 1988). *Member:* Polk County, Iowa State and American Bar Associations; Polk County Women Attorneys Inc.

(This Listing Continued)

PRACTICE AREAS: Alternative Dispute Resolution; Health Care; Hospital Law; Housing Law; Labor and Employment; Litigation; Privacy Law. ***Email:*** JoEllen.Whitney@lawiowa.com

BECKY S. KNUTSON, born Decorah, Iowa, 1957; admitted to bar, 1981, Iowa. *Education:* University of Iowa (B.A., with honors, 1978; J.D., with distinction, 1981). Student Director, Trial Advocacy Board, University of Iowa College of Law. Adjunct Professor, Drake University Law School, 1996-2000. Counsel, Republican Party of Iowa, 1999-2000. Member, Iowa Senate Ethics Committee, 1991-1992. *Member:* Polk County, Iowa State and American Bar Associations; Iowa Defense Council. ***PRACTICE AREAS:*** Alternative Dispute Resolution; Family Law; Labor and Employment; Workers Compensation; OSHA. ***Email:*** Becky.Knutson@lawiowa.com

JULIE JOHNSON McLEAN, born Cedar Rapids, Iowa, 1956; admitted to bar, 1981, Iowa. *Education:* Coe College (B.A., with honors, 1978); University of Iowa (J.D., with distinction, 1981). Phi Beta Kappa. *Member:* Polk County, Iowa State, Federal (President, 1997-1999; National Delegate, Iowa Chapter) and American Bar Associations. ***PRACTICE AREAS:*** Corporate Law; Commercial Law; Debtor and Creditor; Mergers, Acquisitions and Divestitures; Banks and Banking; Equipment Finance and Leasing; Business Law; Bankruptcy. ***Email:*** Julie.McLean@lawiowa.com

BEVERLY EVANS, born Rushville, Nebraska, 1949; admitted to bar, 1979, Nebraska, U.S. District Court, District of Nebraska and U.S. Court of Appeals, 8th Circuit; 1996, Iowa. *Education:* Creighton University (B.A., 1971); University of Nebraska College of Law (J.D., 1979). *Member:* Polk County, Iowa State (Member, Business Law Section Council), Nebraska State and American Bar Associations. ***PRACTICE AREAS:*** Securities; Business Law; Contracts; Corporate Law; Mergers, Acquisitions and Divestitures; Partnership Law. ***Email:*** Bev.Evans@lawiowa.com

M. DANIEL WATERS, born Des Moines, Iowa, 1964; admitted to bar, 1989, Iowa. *Education:* University of Iowa (B.B.A., with highest distinction, 1986; J.D., with high distinction, 1989). Order of the Coif. Member, Iowa Law Review, 1988-1989. Member: Iowa Institute for Cooperatives; National Council of Farmer Cooperatives; Lex Mundi Agribusiness Practice Group (Chair). ***PRACTICE AREAS:*** Agricultural Law; Business Law; Contracts; Corporate Law; Finance; Leases and Leasing; Mergers, Acquisitions and Divestitures. ***Email:*** Dan.Waters@lawiowa.com

CHRISTOPHER P. JANNES, born Moline, Illinois, 1963; admitted to bar, 1989, Iowa and Illinois; 1990, U.S. Court of Appeals, Eighth Circuit and U.S. District Court, Northern and Southern Districts of Iowa; 1993, U.S. Supreme Court. *Education:* Augustana College (B.A., cum laude, 1985); University of Iowa (J.D., with distinction, 1989). *Member:* Polk County, Iowa State and American Bar Associations; Iowa Defense Counsel Association; Defense Research Institute. ***PRACTICE AREAS:*** Litigation. ***Email:*** Chris.Jannes@lawiowa.com

SHARON K. MALHEIRO, born Chicago, Illinois, 1956; admitted to bar, 1989, Iowa. *Education:* Drake University (B.A., 1978; J.D., with honors, 1989). Articles Editor, Drake Law Review, 1988-1989. Adjunct Professor, Iowa State University, College of Journalism. Law Clerk to the Honorable Louis A. Lavorato, Iowa Supreme Court, 1989-1990. *Member:* Polk County, Iowa State and American Bar Associations; Polk County Women Attorneys. ***PRACTICE AREAS:*** Labor and Employment; Litigation; Communications and Media. ***Email:*** Sharon.Malheiro@lawiowa.com

KRIS HOLUB TILLEY, born Grand Forks, North Dakota, 1965; admitted to bar, 1990, Iowa; 1991, U.S. District Court, Southern District of Iowa; 1993, U.S. District Court, Northern District of Iowa and U.S. Court of Appeals, 8th Circuit; 1996, U.S. Court of Appeals, Federal Circuit. *Education:* Mount Mercy College (B.A., cum laude, 1987); University of Iowa (J.D., with high distinction, 1990). ***PRACTICE AREAS:*** Litigation; Product Liability; Insurance Defense; Torts. ***Email:*** Kris.Tilley@lawiowa.com

WILLIAM A. BOATWRIGHT, born Des Moines, Iowa, 1963; admitted to bar, 1989, Illinois; 1994, Iowa. *Education:* Drake University (B.A., 1985); University of Iowa (J.D., with distinction, 1989). Phi Beta Kappa. *Member:* Polk County, Illinois State, Iowa State and American Bar Associations. ***LANGUAGES:*** Japanese. ***PRACTICE AREAS:*** Nonprofit and Charitable Organizations; Estate Planning; Probate; Corporate Tax Law; Individual Taxation; International Law. ***Email:*** Bill.Boatwright@lawiowa.com

THOMAS J. HOUSER, born Belmond, Iowa, 1964; admitted to bar, 1989, Iowa. *Education:* College of St. Thomas (B.A., 1986); University of Iowa (J.D., 1989). *Member:* Polk County, Iowa State and American Bar Associations. ***PRACTICE AREAS:*** Business Law; Contracts; Corporate Law; Guardianship and Conservatorship; Probate; Real Estate; Trusts, Wills and Estates. ***Email:*** Tom.Houser@lawiowa.com

KENDALL R. WATKINS, born Cedar Rapids, Iowa, 1960; admitted to bar, 1985, Iowa and U.S. District Court, Southern District of Iowa. *Education:* Knox College (B.A., 1982); Drake University (J.D., 1985). Senior Staff Member, Drake Law Review, 1984-1985. *Member:* Polk County, Iowa State and American Bar Associations; American Health Lawyers Association. ***PRACTICE AREAS:*** Health Law; Administrative Law; Aged and Aging; Medicare and Medicaid. ***Email:*** Ken.Watkins@lawiowa.com

SCOTT M. BRENNAN, born Des Moines, Iowa, 1962; admitted to bar, 1994, Iowa. *Education:* Grinnell College (B.A., 1985); University of Iowa (J.D., 1993). Author: "Due Process Comes Due: An Argument for the Clear and Convincing Evidentiary Standard in Sentencing Hearings," 77 Iowa Law Review 1803, 1992. Aide to U.S. Senator Tom Harkin, 1982-1990. *Member:* Polk County, Iowa State and American Bar Associations. ***PRACTICE AREAS:*** Insurance Defense; Civil Litigation; Commercial LItigation; Construction Litigation; Administrative Litigation. ***Email:*** Scott.Brennan@lawiowa.com

DEBRA RECTENBAUGH PETTIT, born Creston, Iowa, 1969; admitted to bar, 1994, Iowa; 1995, U.S. District Court, Northern and Southern Districts of Iowa; 1997, U.S. Court of Appeals, Eighth Circuit. *Education:* Drake University (B.A., summa cum laude, 1991); Northwestern University School of Law (J.D., cum laude, 1994). Clerk for Chief Justice McGiverin, Iowa Supreme Court, 1994-1995. ***PRACTICE AREAS:*** Construction Law; Insurance Defense; Libel, Slander and Defamation; Litigation; Negligence; Personal Injury; Product Liability; Torts; Commercial Litigation. ***Email:*** DebraRPettit@lawiowa.com

MATTHEW E. LAUGHLIN, born Omaha, Nebraska, 1969; admitted to bar, 1996, Iowa and Nebraska. *Education:* Simpson College (B.A., 1992); University of Nebraska at Lincoln (J.D., with distinction, 1996). *Member:* Polk County, Iowa State, Nebraska State and American Bar Associations. ***PRACTICE AREAS:*** Business Law; Real Estate; Commercial Law; Commercial Litigation. ***Email:*** Matt.Laughlin@lawiowa.com

JUDITH R. "LYNN" BOES, born Columbus, Ohio, 1956; admitted to bar, 1996, Iowa. *Education:* University of Iowa (B.S.N., 1979); Drake University (J.D., 1996). *Member:* Polk County, Iowa State and American Bar Associations; American Health Lawyers Association; Polk County Women Attorneys; Iowa Nurses' Association; Iowa Public Health Association. ***PRACTICE AREAS:*** Health Law; Administrative Law; Aged and Aging. ***Email:*** Lynn.Boes@lawiowa.com

DANIEL A. ROSENBERG, born Des Moines, Iowa, 1956; admitted to bar, 1997, Iowa; registered to practice before U.S. Patent and Trademark Office. *Education:* Iowa State University (B.S., 1981); Drake University (J.D., 1997). Order of the Coif. *Member:* Polk County, Iowa State and American Bar Associations; Iowa Intellectual Property Law Association. ***PRACTICE AREAS:*** Intellectual Property; Trademarks; Copyrights; Patents. ***Email:*** Dan.Rosenberg@lawiowa.com

WILLIAM P. KELLY, born Peoria, Illinois, 1967; admitted to bar, 1999, Iowa. *Education:* Brown University (B.A., 1990); Drake University (J.D., with honors, 1999). Managing Editor, Drake Law Review, 1999. Author, "Scope of Advertising Injury Under Iowa Law in Commercial General Liability Policies," Drake Law Review, 48:4, 2000.*Member:* Polk County and Iowa State and American Bar Associations. [JAG Officer Army National Guard; Trained Mediator]. ***PRACTICE AREAS:*** Litigation; Alternative Dispute Resolution; Family Law; Insurance Defense. ***Email:*** Bill.Kelly@lawiowa.com

SUSAN J. FREED, born Cherokee, Iowa, 1973; admitted to bar, 1999, Iowa; 2000, Illinois. *Education:* University of Iowa (B.S., 1996); DePaul University (J.D., 1999). *Member:* Polk County, Iowa State and American Bar Associations; American Health Lawyers Association. ***PRACTICE AREAS:*** Employee Benefits; Health Care. ***Email:*** Susan.Freed@lawiowa.com

WILLIAM J. KOEHN, born Winterset, Iowa, 1936; admitted to bar, 1963, Iowa; 1971, U.S. Supreme Court and U.S. Court of Appeals, Eighth Circuit. *Education:* Drake University; University of Iowa (B.A., 1958; J.D., 1963). Order of the Coif. Member, Board of Editors, Iowa Law Review, 1962-1963. *Member:* Polk County, Iowa State (Member: Council on Environmental Law; Professionalism Committee) and American Bar Associations; The Iowa Trial Lawyers Association. ***PRACTICE AREAS:*** Class Actions; Complex and Multi-District Litigation; Construction Law; Litigation; Products Liability; Personal Liability; Toxic Torts. ***Email:*** Bill.Koehn@lawiowa.com

ASSOCIATES

DENISE R. CLATON, born Des Moines, Iowa, 1970; admitted to bar, 1996, Iowa. *Education:* Drake University (B.A., summa cum laude, 1992); University of Iowa (J.D., with distinction, 1996). Phi Beta Kappa. *Member:* Iowa State Bar Association; American Immigration Lawyers Association. ***PRACTICE AREAS:*** Immigration and Naturalization. ***Email:*** Denise.Claton@lawiowa.com

BEHNAZ SOULATI, born Iran, 1969; admitted to bar, 1999, Iowa, U.S. District Court, Northern and Southern Districts of Iowa and U.S. Court of Appeals, Eighth Circuit. *Education:* University of Iowa (B.A., with highest distinction, 1993; M.A., 1995; J.D., with distinction, 1999). Phi Beta Kappa. Judicial Clerk, Seventh Judicial District of Iowa, 1999-2000. *Member:* Polk County, Iowa State and American Bar Associations; Polk County Women Association; American Blind Lawyers Association. ***LANGUAGES:*** Azerbaijani, Farsi, French, Turkish. ***PRACTICE AREAS:*** Litigation. ***Email:*** Behnaz.Soulati@lawiowa.com

HEATHER L. PALMER, born Minneapolis, Minnesota, 1970; admitted to bar, 1999, Iowa, U.S. District Court, Northern and Southern Districts of Iowa and U.S. Court of Appeals, Eighth Circuit. *Education:* University of Iowa (B.A., 1993; M.A., 1994); Drake University College of Law (J.D., with honors, 1999). *Member:* Polk County Women Attorneys (Board Member); Iowa Organization of Women Attorneys (Board Member); National Conference of Women's Bar Associations (Secretary). ***PRACTICE AREAS:*** Environmental Law; Insurance Defense; Labor and Employment; Business Litigation. ***Email:*** Heather.Palmer@lawiowa.com

JASON M. STONE, born Des Moines, Iowa, 1973; admitted to bar, 2000, Iowa and U.S. Tax Court. *Education:* University of Iowa (B.S., 1996); Washburn University of Topeka (J.D., magna cum laude, 2000); New York University (LL.M., 2001). Editor, Washburn Law Journal, 1999-2000. *Member:* Polk County, Iowa State and American Bar Associations. ***PRACTICE AREAS:*** Taxation; Business Law; Mergers, Acquisitions and Divestitures. ***Email:*** Jason.Stone@lawiowa.com

AMY M. LANDWEHR, born Des Moines, Iowa, 1974; admitted to bar, 2001, Iowa. *Education:* University of Central Florida (B.A., cum laude, 1996); Louis Brandeis School of Law, University of Louisville (J.D., cum laude, 2001). Member: Brandeis Law Journal, 1990-2000; Journal of Law and Education, 1999-2000. *Member:* Polk County, Iowa State and American Bar Associations; Polk County Women Attorneys Association; American Immigration Lawyers Association. ***PRACTICE AREAS:*** Immigration and Naturalization. ***Email:*** Amy.Landwehr@lawiowa.com

JOSEPH M. PAWLOSKY, born Waynesburg, Pennsylvania, 1959; admitted to bar, 1996, Illinois; 2002, Iowa. *Education:* West Virginia University (B.S., cum laude, 1985; M.B.A., 1986); DePaul University (J.D., with honors, 1996). Order of the Coif. Member, DePaul Law Review, 1994-1996. *Member:* Polk County, Iowa State and Illinois State Bar Associations. ***PRACTICE AREAS:*** Employee Benefits.

JOHN C. PIETILA, born Watertown, South Dakota, 1974; admitted to bar, 2002, Iowa. *Education:* South Dakota State University (B.A., 1997); University of Iowa (J.D., with distinction, 2002). Phi Delta Phi. Member, Journal of Corporation Law. *Member:* Polk County and Iowa State Bar Associations. ***PRACTICE AREAS:*** Business Law; Corporate Law; Telecommunications Law. ***Email:*** John.Pietila@lawiowa.com

JASON M. ROSS, born Freeport, Illinois, 1973; admitted to bar, 1999, Wisconsin; 2000, Illinois; 2003, Iowa. *Education:* University of Illinois-Urbana (B.A., magna cum laude, 1995); University of Iowa (J.D., with distinction, 1999). Phi Beta Kappa; Phi Delta Phi. Member, University of Iowa Law Review. *Member:* Illinois State Bar Associaton; State

(This Listing Continued)

DAVIS, BROWN, KOEHN, SHORS & ROBERTS, P.C., Des Moines—Continued

Bar of Wisconsin. ***LANGUAGES:*** German. ***PRACTICE AREAS:*** Commercial Transactions; Commercial Finance; Franchises and Franchising; Business Acquisitions; Consumer Credit. ***Email:*** Jason.Ross@lawiowa.com

EMILY E. HARRIS, born Des Moines, Iowa, 1976; admitted to bar, 2003, Iowa. *Education:* Grinnell College (B.A., 1998); University of Iowa (J.D., 2003). *Member:* Polk County and Iowa State Bar Associations; Polk County Women Attorneys; Iowa Organization of Women Attorneys (Treasurer); Iowa Intellectual Property Association. ***PRACTICE AREAS:*** Intellectual Property; Intellectual Property Litigation; Patents; Trademarks; Copyrights. ***Email:*** Emily.Harris@lawiowa.com

JODIE L. CLARK, born Des Moines, Iowa, 1979; admitted to bar, 2004, Iowa. *Education:* Iowa State University (B.A., 2001); University of Arizona, James E. Rogers College of Law (J.D., cum laude, 2004). *Member:* Polk County and Iowa State Bar Associations. ***PRACTICE AREAS:*** Litigation; Labor and Employment; Commercial Litigation; Torts. ***Email:*** Jodie.Clark@lawiowa.com

DENISE M. HILL, born Davenport, Iowa, 1969; admitted to bar, 1996, Iowa. *Education:* Wartburg College (B.A., magna cum laude, 1992); Drake University of Business and Public Administration (M.P.A., 1995); Drake University Law School (J.D., magna cum laude, 1996). Registered Mediator, American Health Lawyers Association. *Member:* Polk County and Iowa State Bar Associations; American Health Lawyers Association; Iowa Society of Healthcare Attorneys (Member, Executive Committee). ***PRACTICE AREAS:*** Health Care; Alternative Dispute Resolution; Administrative Law; Government Relations; Estate Planning; Estate Planning for Parents of Handicapped Children; Guardianship and Conservatorship; Labor and Employment.

TARA L. ZAGER, born Des Moines, Iowa, 1980; admitted to bar, 2005, Iowa. *Education:* University of Iowa (B.A., 2002); Drake University Law School (J.D., 2005). *Member:* Polk County and Iowa State Bar Associations. ***PRACTICE AREAS:*** Litigation; Civil Litigation.

OF COUNSEL

DONALD J. BROWN, admitted to bar, 1958, Iowa. *Education:* Creighton University and University of Iowa (B.A., 1956); University of Iowa (J.D., 1958); Georgetown University (LL.M., 1961). ***Email:*** Don.Brown@lawiowa.com

DAVID W. DUNN, admitted to bar, 1980, Iowa and U.S. District Court, Southern District of Iowa; 1983, U.S. Supreme Court; 1984, U.S. Court of Appeals, Eighth Circuit; 1986, U.S. District Court, Northern District of Iowa; 1987, U.S. Tax Court. *Education:* Drake University (B.A., cum laude, 1976); American University (J.D., 1980). (Also Member, David W Dunn Law Firm PLC, Eldora). ***PRACTICE AREAS:*** Litigation. ***Email:*** Dave.Dunn@lawiowa.com

C. CARLETON FREDERICI, admitted to bar, 1965, Iowa; 1966, New York. *Education:* University of Iowa (B.A., 1960; J.D., with high distinction, 1965). ***PRACTICE AREAS:*** Litigation. ***Email:*** Carl.Frederici@lawiowa.com

A. J. GREFFENIUS, admitted to bar, 1950, Minnesota; 1959, North Dakota; 1967, Iowa. *Education:* Valley City State University (B.A.,Ed., 1947); University of Michigan (LL.B., 1950). ***Email:*** Al.Greffenius@lawiowa.com

DENNIS D. JERDE, born Clarion, Iowa, 1942; admitted to bar, 1967, Iowa. *Education:* University of Iowa (B.A., 1964; J.D., with distinction, 1967). Member, Board of Editors, Iowa Law Review, 1966-1967. *Member:* Polk County, Iowa State (Member: Iowa Jury Instructions Committee, 1993-2002; Lawyers Professional Liability Insurance Committee, 1992-1993) and American Bar Associations. ***PRACTICE AREAS:*** Litigation. ***Email:*** Dennis.Jerde@lawiowa.com

RICHARD E. RAMSAY, admitted to bar, 1961, Iowa. *Education:* Drake University (B.A., 1959; J.D., 1961). ***Email:*** Dick.Ramsay@lawiowa.com

NEAL E. SMITH, admitted to bar, 1950, Iowa. *Education:* Syracuse University; University of Missouri; Drake University (J.D., 1950). [Maj., U.S. Army Air Corps, 1942-1945]. ***Email:*** Neal.Smith@lawiowa.com

WILLIAM D. THOMAS, admitted to bar, 1973, Ohio; 1975, Iowa. *Education:* University of Iowa (B.S., 1967; J.D., with high distinction, 1973). (Also practicing individually at Pocahontas)

DICKINSON, MACKAMAN, TYLER & HAGEN, P.C.

Established in 1936

1600 HUB TOWER
699 WALNUT STREET
DES MOINES, IOWA 50309-3986
Telephone: 515-244-2600
Fax: 515-246-4550
Email: info@dickinsonlaw.com
URL: http://www.dickinsonlaw.com

Washington, D.C. Office: 1660 L Street, NW, Suite 506, 20036-5603. Telephone: 202-463-6330. Fax: 202-463-6328.

Administrative, Antitrust, Banking, Casualty Insurance and Workers Compensation, Commercial Litigation, Corporate, Energy, Environmental, Family Law, Fidelity and Surety Law, General Practice, Immigration, Intellectual Property, Labor and Employment Law, Probate, Public Utility, Real Estate, School Law, Telecommunications, Trials and Appeals.

FIRM PROFILE: Dickinson, Mackaman, Tyler & Hagen, P.C. can be traced to the year 1936 when L. Call Dickinson founded a law firm devoted primarily to tax law. He was joined in 1940 by his father, former United States Senator L.J. Dickinson and the firm quickly grew in its representation of clients in many areas of law. The firm's attorneys are a diverse group with solid academic backgrounds and significant experience in their areas of concentration. Our firm represents diverse business enterprises of all sizes, many of which operate on a national basis. We serve as Iowa counsel for numerous out-of-state corporations and routinely act as co-counsel to a variety of national law firms. Our firm also has experience representing trade industry associations and in working with governmental entities at all levels. In addition to our work for businesses and organizations, we have traditionally provided a full array of personal legal services for individual clients.

L. J. DICKINSON (1873-1968)

L. CALL DICKINSON (1905-1974)

HELEN C. ADAMS, born Fort Rucker, Alabama, June 20, 1959; admitted to bar, 1988, Missouri; 1990, Iowa, U.S. District Court, Northern and Southern Districts of Iowa and U.S. Court of Appeals, Eighth Circuit; 1997, U.S. Supreme Court. *Education:* University of Iowa (B.S., 1985; J.D., with high distinction, 1988). Order of the Coif. Winner: Faculty Recognition Award, 1988. 1st Vice-Chairperson, University of Iowa Moot Court Board, 1987-1988. Editor, Revised Federal Practice Manual, Iowa Bar Association, 1994. Law Clerk to the Honorable Harold D. Vietor, Federal District Court, Southern District of Iowa, 1988-1990. Chairperson: Federal Practice Committee of the Southern District of Iowa, 1996-2001; Federal Practice Committee, Iowa State Bar Association, 1999—. *Member:* Polk County, Iowa State (Member: Federal Practice Committee; Litigation and Employment Law Sections) and American (Member, Litigation, Employment & Alternative Dispute Resolution Sections) Bar Associations; Lincoln Inn, American Inns of Court (Pupil, Blackstone Inn of Court, 1989-1990), Defense Research Institute, Inc. (Employment and Litigation). ***PRACTICE AREAS:*** Employment Law; Discrimination; Civil Rights; Trial Practice. ***Email:*** hadams@dickinsonlaw.com

JOSEPH A. CACCIATORE, born Des Moines, Iowa, August 22, 1965; admitted to bar, 1993, Iowa; 1996, U.S. District Court, Northern and Southern Districts of Iowa. *Education:* University of Northern Iowa (B.A., magna cum laude, 1987); Drake University (J.D., with honors, 1992). Order of the Coif. Articles Editor, Drake Law Review, 1991-1992. Author: Casenote: "State v. Mabry," 41 Drake Law Review 351. Author: Annual Supplement to LaMarca, "Iowa Pleading and Causes of Action," 1993-1994. *Member:* Polk County, Iowa State (Member: Litigation Section; Workers' Compensation Section) and American Bar Associations; The Association of Trial Lawyers of America; Iowa Trial Lawyers Association; Iowa Association of Workers' Compensation Lawyers. ***PRACTICE AREAS:*** Litigation; Personal Injury; Workers Compensation. ***Email:*** jcacciat@dickinsonlaw.com

BRET A. DUBLINSKE, born Waterloo, Iowa, July 29, 1965; admitted to bar, 1994, Iowa; 1996, U.S. Court of Appeals, Eighth Circuit and U. S. District Court, Northern and Southern Districts of Iowa. *Education:* Iowa State University (B.S., B.A., 1988); University of Iowa (J.D., with high distinction, 1994). Recipient, Iowa State Bar Association Graduating Senior Award. University of Iowa Moot Court Board, 1993-1994, Moot Court National Team, 1993-1994. Law Clerk to the Honorable Harold D. Vietor, U.S. District Ct., S.D. Iowa, 1994-1996. Author: "Free Speech, the Internet, and the CDA: Is a "Decent" Opinion Just a Dream?," 30 Creighton L. R. 1229 (1997); "Sec. 1983 Redux: The Case for Section 1983 Liability in Wireless Tower Siting Cases," 1 Telecom Land Management Law Report, Vol. 1, No. 9 (July 1999). *Member:* Polk County, Iowa State (Member, Litigation Section) and American (Member, Communications and Litigation Sections) Bar Associations; Federal Communications Bar Association. ***PRACTICE AREAS:*** Communications and Media; Regulatory Law; Utility Law. ***Email:*** bdublins@dickinsonlaw.com

REBECCA BOYD DUBLINSKE, born Iowa City, Iowa, December 10, 1959; admitted to bar, 1986, Iowa; 1987, U.S. District Court, Northern and Southern Districts of Iowa; 1988, U.S. Court of Appeals, Eighth Circuit. *Education:* University of Iowa (B.A., with distinction, 1983; J.D., with honors, 1986). Phi Beta Kappa. *Member:* Iowa State (Member, sections on: Labor and Employment; Litigation) and American (Member, sections on: Labor and Employment; Litigation) Bar Associations; Defense Research Institute (Member, Commercial Litigation, Employment Law, Product Liability and Trial Tactics Committees). ***PRACTICE AREAS:*** Employment Law; Employment Litigation; Litigation. ***Email:*** rdublinske@dickinsonlaw.com

GREGORY G.T. ERVANIAN, born Bloomfield Hills, Michigan, May 12, 1962; admitted to bar, 1990, Nebraska and U.S. District Court, District of Nebraska; 1991, Iowa and U.S. District Court, Southern District of Iowa. *Education:* University of Iowa (B.G.S., 1987); Creighton University (J.D., 1990). *Member:* Polk County (Member, Corporate Counsel, Real Property, Trusts and Business Law Sections), Iowa State, Nebraska State and American (Member, Real Property Corporate Counsel and Business Law Sections) Bar Associations. ***Email:*** gervanian@dickinsonlaw.com

JOAN M. FLETCHER, born Fort Dodge, Iowa, December 28, 1952; admitted to bar, 1989, Iowa, U.S. District Court, Northern and Southern Districts of Iowa and U.S. Court of Appeals, Eighth Circuit. *Education:* University of Iowa (B.S., 1975); Kansas State University (M.A., 1977); Drake University (J.D., 1989). Order of the Coif. Case Notes Editor, Drake Law Review, 1987-1988. *Member:* Polk County, Iowa State and American (Member, Litigation and Tort, Trial and Insurance Sections) Bar Associations; Defense Research Institute (Member, Commercial Litigation, Trial Tactics and Techniques and Product Liability Committees); Iowa Defense Counsel Association. ***PRACTICE AREAS:*** Trial Practice; Commercial Litigation; Products Liability; OSHA. ***Email:*** jfletcher@dickinsonlaw.com

HOWARD O. HAGEN, born Homestead, Iowa, November 10, 1948; admitted to bar, 1973, Iowa; 1978, U.S. Claims Court, U.S. Court of Appeals, Eighth Circuit and U.S. District Court, Northern and Southern Districts of Iowa. *Education:* Grinnell College (B.A., with honors, 1970); Washington Semester Program (Phi Beta Kappa); University of Chicago (J.D., 1973). National Law Honor Scholarship. Iowa Assistant Attorney General, Director of the Division of Administrative Law, 1979-1985. General Counsel, Iowa Superintendent of Banking and Iowa Dept of Banking, 1979-1985. Lecturer, Bank Acquisitions, Iowa School of Banking, 1996-1997. Instructor-Lecturer, School of Central Banking for Central and Eastern Europeans, Iowa State University, 1993. Co-Author: "Banking Law," Chapter 13.3, Iowa Legal Research Guide, 2002 Edition. Instructor-Lecturer, Summer Institute in Agricultural Law, Drake Law School, 1986. Member, Governor's Task Force on Privacy, 2001. *Member:* Polk County, Iowa (Member, Corporation, Banking and Business Law Section, Electronic Commerce Working Groups; Chairman and Member, Banking, Financial Institutions Committee, 1990-2000; 2002—) and American (Member: Banking,

(This Listing Continued)

Currency and Treasury Committee, Administrative Law Section, 1989-1996; Corporation, Banking and Business Law Section; Participant, Electronic Commerce Working Groups; Committee on the Law of Commerce in Cyberspace; Information Security and Electronic Funds Transfer Committees, Science and Technology Section; Franchising Law Section) Bar Associations. ***PRACTICE AREAS:*** Banking Law; Business Law; Corporate Law. ***Email:*** hhagen@dickinsonlaw.com

PAUL E. HORVATH, born Martins Ferry, Ohio, February 23, 1947; admitted to bar, 1976, Iowa and U.S. District Court, Northern and Southern Districts of Iowa. *Education:* Ohio University (B.A., with honors, 1969); University of Iowa; Washington University (J.D., 1975). Member, Board of Editors, Washington University Law Quarterly, 1974-1975. *Member:* Polk County, Iowa State (Member, Sections: Litigation; Environmental Law) and American (Member, Sections: Litigation; Energy, Communications and Transportation Law) Bar Associations. ***Email:*** phorvath@dickinsonlaw.com

JEFFREY A. KRAUSMAN, born Evanston, Illinois, January 31, 1949; admitted to bar, 1975, Iowa. *Education:* Michigan State University; Drake University (B.A., 1971; J.D., 1975). Administrative Law Judge, Iowa Public Employment Relations Board, 1975-1977. *Member:* Polk County, Iowa State (Member: Labor and Employment Law Section, 1979—Chair, 1987-1988; Litigation Section) and American (Member, Section on Labor and Employment Law) Bar Associations; National Council of School Board Attorneys; Iowa Council of School Board Attorneys (Member, Executive Committee, 1994-2003; President, 1997-1998). ***PRACTICE AREAS:*** Labor Relations; Employment Litigation; School Law. ***Email:*** jkrausman@dickinsonlaw.com

F. RICHARD LYFORD, born New York, New York, July 24, 1944; admitted to bar, 1972, Iowa. *Education:* University of Chicago (B.A., 1966); University of Iowa (J.D., 1972). Co-Author: "Balancing the Rights of the Government and Taxpayers in Adopting and Enforcing Statute of Limitations in the Area of Taxation," 9 Journal of State Taxation 65, October 1990. Co-Editor, Iowa Chapter, ABA Sales & Use Tax Deskbook. *Member:* Polk County, Iowa State and American (Member, Litigation, Torts and Insurance Practice Sections) Bar Associations; The Association of Trial Lawyers of America; Association of Trial Lawyers of Iowa. ***PRACTICE AREAS:*** Litigation; Appellate Practice; Administrative Law; State Government Law; Local Government Law; Municipal Law. ***Email:*** rlyford@dickinsonlaw.com

RICHARD A. MALM, born Pensacola, Florida, August 6, 1949; admitted to bar, 1974, Iowa. *Education:* Iowa State University (B.S.E.E., 1971); Drake University (J.D., with honors, 1974). Tau Beta Pi; Order of the Coif. Associate Editor, Drake Law Review, 1973-1974. Author: Note, "Securities Depositories and Revision of the Uniform Commercial Code," 22 Drake Law Review 657; "Contracts for Future Delivery of Grain, An Overview of Common Legal Problems," 2 Agricultural Law Journal, 4:3, 1981. Editor, Iowa Chapter, ABA Sales & Use Tax Deskbook. *Member:* Polk County, Iowa State (Member, Agricultural Law Section) and American (Member, State and Local Tax Committee of Section of Taxation) Bar Associations. ***Email:*** rmalm@dickinsonlaw.com

ARTHUR F. OWENS, born Des Moines, Iowa, April 20, 1948; admitted to bar, 1973, Iowa. *Education:* Simpson College (B.A., summa cum laude, 1970); Drake University (J.D., with honors, 1973). Associate Editor, Drake Law Review, 1972-1973. Order of the Coif. *Member:* Polk County, Iowa State (Chairman, Committee on Lawyer Advertising, 1986-1989; Member, Business Law Section Council, 1997-1999; Chairman, Business Law Section, Newsletter/Publications Committee, 1990-1997) and American (Member, Business Law Section) Bar Associations. ***Email:*** aowens@dickinsonlaw.com

MOLLIE M. PAWLOSKY, born Des Moines, Iowa, June 29, 1970; admitted to bar, 1996, Illinois and U.S. District Court, Northern District of Illinois; 2000, U.S. District Court, Central District of Illinois; 2002, Iowa; 2003, U.S. District Court, Northern and Southern Districts of Iowa and U.S. Court of Appeals, Eighth Circuit; 2005, U.S. Court of Appeals, Seventh Circuit. *Education:* Grinnell College (B.A., with honors, 1992), IES Madrid Semester Program, Phi Beta Kappa; DePaul University College of Law (J.D., with honors, 1996), Order of the Coif. Member: DePaul Law Review. Author: "When Justice is Lost in the 'Translation'...Gonzalez v. United States, and 'Interpretation' of the Court Interpreters Act of 1978," 45 DePaul Law Rev. 435 (1995). *Member:* Polk County (Co-Chair, Membership Committee, 2003—), Iowa State and American (Member, Litigation Section) Bar Associations. ***PRACTICE AREAS:*** Commercial Litigation. ***Email:*** mpawlosky@dickinsonlaw.com

DAVID M. REPP, born Perry, Iowa, January 14, 1961; admitted to bar, 1990, Iowa and Missouri. *Education:* University of Iowa (B.B.A., with high distinction, 1987; M.A., Accounting, 1990; J.D., with distinction, 1990). Phi Delta Phi. Managing Editor, Journal of Corporation Law, 1989-1990. Author: "Limited Liability Company May Not Be the Best Entity for Family Estate Planning-But Don't Give Up the Ship," 1 LLC Advisor No. 5, Jan. 29, 1996; "Antidumping and Countervailing Duties: Protection at a Cost," 15:1 Journal of Corporation Law, 1989; "Limited Liability Companies in an IRA?," Parts I & II, LLC Advisor, Commerce Clearing House Issue Nos. 42 & 43, February 22, 1999 and March 23, 1999. Co-Author: "Planning Opportunities Under the Nexus Approach to Consolidated Reporting," Journal of Multistate Taxation 52, May/June 1993; "State Taxation of Nonresident Pension Income: Whose Golden Years?," 11 Journal of State Taxation 25, Fall 1992 and 11 Journal of State Taxation 34, Winter 1992; "Supreme Court Rules on Constitutionality of State Value Added Tax, 10 Journal of State Taxation 1, Fall, 1991. *Member:* Polk County, Iowa State (Member, Agricultural Law; Corporate, Banking and Business Law; Corporate Counsel; Taxation Sections) and American (Member, Real Property, Probate and Trust; and Taxation Sections) Bar Associations. ***PRACTICE AREAS:*** Taxation. ***Email:*** drepp@dickinsonlaw.com

RUSSELL L. SAMSON, born West Point, Nebraska, August 6, 1948; admitted to bar, 1975, Iowa. *Education:* Iowa State University (B.S., 1970; M.S., 1972); Georgetown University (J.D., 1975). *Member:* Polk County, Iowa State and American (Member, Labor and Employment Law Section) Bar Associations. ***Email:*** rsamson@dickinsonlaw.com

PHILIP E. STOFFREGEN, born Greeley, Colorado, December 10, 1947; admitted to bar, 1977, Iowa, U.S. District Court, Northern and Southern Districts of Iowa and U.S. Court of Appeals, Eighth Circuit; 1980, District of Columbia; 1981, U.S. Supreme Court. *Education:* University of Iowa (B.A., 1969; M.S., 1970; M.A., 1972; J.D., with high distinction, 1977). Order of the Coif. Author: "Telecommunications Deregulation: A State-by-State Analysis of Legislation," Telecom Publishing Group, 1st ed., 1988, 2nd ed. 1989,

(This Listing Continued)

3rd ed. 1990; "Trends in State Telecommunications Deregulation," Public Utility Regulation in an Environment of Change," Michigan St. University, 1987. Assistant Iowa Attorney General, 1982-1983. Assistant Professor, Engineering Law, Department of Industrial Engineering, Iowa State University, 1983. General Counsel, Iowa State Commerce Commission, 1983-1985. *Member:* American, Iowa State (Member: Public Utility Law, Energy Law, Telecommunications Law Sections) and Polk County Bar Associations; Computer Law Association. ***PRACTICE AREAS:*** Public Utility Law; Energy Law; Telecommunications Law. ***Email:*** pstoffre@dickinsonlaw.com

JON P. SULLIVAN, born Newton, Iowa, January 22, 1954; admitted to bar, 1979, Iowa. *Education:* University of Northern Iowa (B.A., with highest honors, 1976); University of Iowa (J.D., with distinction, 1979). Author: Comment, 63 Iowa Law Review 708, 1978; Note, 64 Iowa Law Review 65, 1978; "Iowa Real Estate Mortgage Foreclosure," West Publishing Company, Third edition, 2003. Note and Comment Editor, Iowa Law Review, 1978-1979. Law Clerk to Hon. Harvey Uhlenhopp, Supreme Court of Iowa, 1979-1980. *Member:* Polk County, Iowa State (Member, Commercial and Bankruptcy Law Section) and American (Member, Section on Business Law; UCC Task Force on State Certificate of Title Laws) Bar Associations. ***PRACTICE AREAS:*** Debtor and Creditor Law; Real Estate. ***Email:*** jsulliva@dickinsonlaw.com

PAUL R. TYLER, born Lenox, Iowa, December 22, 1942; admitted to bar, 1967, Iowa and Wisconsin. *Education:* University of Iowa (B.A., with honors and distinction, 1964; J.D., with distinction, 1967). Phi Beta Kappa; Phi Delta Phi. Member, Supreme Court Grievance Commission, 1995—. *Member:* Polk County (Chairman, Grievance Committee, 1985-1987; Member, Board of Directors, 1989-1993; 1995—; President, 2002-2003), Iowa State (Member, Board of Governors, 1995-1999, 2003—; Chairman, Real Estate and Title Law Section, 1993-1994, Chairman, Legal Forms Committee, 1984-1988; Chairman, Multi-Jurisdictional Practice Committee, 1999-2003; Member, Land Title Standards Committee, 1989-1995; Member, Board of Directors, Volunteer Lawyers Project, 2004—; President's Award, 2001) and American Bar Associations; State Bar of Wisconsin; Iowa Land Title Association; American Land Title Association; American College of Real Estate Lawyers; Polk County Legal Aid Society (Member, Board of Directors, 2000-2002). ***PRACTICE AREAS:*** Banks and Banking; Business Law; Real Estate; Wills. ***Email:*** ptyler@dickinsonlaw.com

JOHN K. VERNON, born Cedar Rapids, Iowa, August 22, 1946; admitted to bar, 1975, Iowa and U.S. District Court, Northern and Southern Districts of Iowa; 1989, U.S. Supreme Court. *Education:* St. Benedict's College (B.A., 1968); Drake University; University of Puget Sound (J.D., 1975). Member, Board of Directors, Youth Law Center, 2003—. *Member:* Polk County, Iowa State (Member: Board of Governors, 1999-2003, Family Law Section) and American (Member: Family Law Section) Bar Associations. [Capt., USMC, 1968-1971]. ***PRACTICE AREAS:*** Family Law; Employment Law; Insurance; Litigation; Appellate Practice. ***Email:*** jvernon@dickinsonlaw.com

J. MARC WARD, born Springfield, Missouri, February 24, 1958; admitted to bar, 1984, Iowa. *Education:* Iowa State University (B.S., 1980); Drake University (J.D., with honors, 1984). Order of the Coif. Projects Editor, Drake Law Review, 1983-1984. Author: "Limited Liability Companies Guide" (CCH), 1995; "A Guide to the Iowa Limited Liability Company Act," 42 Drake Law Review 385, 1993. Adjunct Professor of Law, Drake Law School, Business Planning, 1996. Member: Board of Education, 1997-2003; President of the Board, 2002-2003, Des Moines Public Schools; Board of Directors, Greater Des Moines Partnership, 2002—; Board of Directors, Downtown Community Alliance; Board of Trustees, Civic Center of Greater Des Moines, 2000—; Board of Directors, Park and Recreation Board, City of Des Moines, 2002-2003; United Way Campaign Cabinet, 2001-2002; Greater Des Moines Leadership Institute, Class of 2000. *Member:* Polk County, Iowa State (Member: Corporation, Banking and Business Law Section; Business Law Council; Committees: Chair, Limited Liability Companies, 1992-1994, 1996-1999, 2002—; Chair, Banking Law, 2000-2001; For Profit Corporation, 2000—) and American (Member, Banking Law Committee; Partnerships and Unincorporated Business Organizations Committee, Business Law Section) Bar Associations. ***PRACTICE AREAS:*** Corporate Law; Business Law. ***Email:*** mward@dickinsonlaw.com

ASSOCIATES

JENNIFER L. HODGE, born Rock Island, Illinois, August 18, 1977; admitted to bar, 2002, Iowa. *Education:* University of Iowa (B.B.A., Finance, 1999; J.D., 2002). *Member:* Polk County, Iowa State (Member: Young Lawyers Division, Probate Property & Trust Law, Real Estate and Title Law) and American (Young Lawyers Division, Real Property, Probate & Trust Law, Business Law Section) Bar Associations; Polk County Women Attorneys Association. ***Email:*** jhodge@dickinsonlaw.com

JILL R. JENSEN-WELCH, born Harlan, Iowa, June 1, 1961; admitted to bar, 2003, Iowa and U.S. District Court, Southern District of Iowa; 2004, U.S. District Court, Northern District of Iowa and U.S. Court of Appeals, Eighth Circuit. *Education:* Drake University (B.A., Psychology and Sociology, magna cum laude, 1982; M.S., Mental Health Counseling, 1994); Drake University Law School (J.D., with high honors, 2003). Order of the Coif. Certification in Senior Professional in Human Resources, Human Resource Certification Institute, Washington, D.C., 1989. *Member:* Iowa State (Member: Labor & Employment, Young Lawyer Division) and American (Member: Labor and Employment, Litigation, ADR, Young Lawyers Division, Appellate Practice Sections) Bar Associations; Polk County Women Attorneys Association; Society for Human Resource Management. ***PRACTICE AREAS:*** Employment Law; Litigation. ***Email:*** jjenson@dickinsonlaw.com

BRIDGET R. PENICK, born Council Bluffs, Iowa, August 10, 1973; admitted to bar, 1998, Illinois and U.S. District Court, Northern District of Illinois; 2002, Iowa and U.S. District Court, Northern and Southern Districts of Iowa; U.S. Court of Appeals, Eighth Circuit. *Education:* Central College (B.A., magna cum laude, 1995); University of Iowa College of Law (J.D., with high distinction, 1998). Phi Delta Phi (Vice President, 1996-1997). Author: "Give the Child a Legal Father," Iowa Law Review, 1998. *Member:* Iowa (Member: Young Lawyers Division Executive Council), American (Labor & Employment Law Section) and Polk County Bar Associations; American Immigration Lawyers Association. ***PRACTICE AREAS:*** Labor and Employment Law; Litigation; Immigration Law. ***Email:*** bpenick@dickinsonlaw.com

(This Listing Continued)

DICKINSON, MACKAMAN, TYLER & HAGEN, P.C., Des Moines—Continued

CHARLES M. SCHNEIDER, born Davenport, Iowa, June 24, 1973; admitted to bar, 2002, Iowa and U.S. Tax Court. *Education:* Creighton University (B.A., Political Science, 1995); University of Iowa (J.D., M.B.A., 2002). Phi Delta Phi. Moot Court participant. Student Judge, Jessup International Moot Court. Recipient, Jim H. Houtz Fellowship in Business Graduate Scholarship. Board Member and Student Writer, Law Review. Member, Board of Directors, Chruches United (Homeless Shelter), Des Moines, Iowa. *Member:* Polk County, Iowa State (Member: Banking and Business Law Section, International Law Section and Young Lawyers Division) and American (Member: Young Lawyers Division; Banking & Business Law Section, Dispute Resolution Section, International Law and Practice Section, Real Property Section, Probate and Trust Law Section, and State and Local Government Law Section) Bar Associations. ***Email:*** cschneider@dickinsonlaw.com

KRISTA K. TANNER, born Des Moines, Iowa, March 16, 1974; admitted to bar, 2000, Iowa; 2004, U.S. District Court, Northern and Southern Districts of Iowa. *Education:* University of Northern Iowa (B.A., 1996); Drake University (J.D., with honors, 2000); Drake University Law School (Legislative Practice Certificate, 2000). *Member:* Polk County, Iowa State (Member: Administrative Law and Litigation Sections) and American Bar Associations; Polk County Women Attorneys. ***Email:*** ktanner@dickinsonlaw.com

KRISTI A. TRAYNOR, born Maquoketa, Iowa, August 28, 1972; admitted to bar, 1998, Iowa; 1999, U.S. District Court, Southern District of Iowa; 2003, U.S. Court of Appeals, Eighth Circuit; 2004, U.S. District Court, Northern District of Iowa. *Education:* Central College (B.A., 1994); University of Iowa (J.D., with distinction, 1998). *Member:* Polk County, Iowa State and American Bar Associations. ***LANGUAGES:*** Spanish. ***PRACTICE AREAS:*** Workers Compensation.

OF COUNSEL

JANET G. HUSTON, born Seattle, Washington, August 4, 1950; admitted to bar, 1983, Iowa. *Education:* Augsburg College (B.A., 1972); Drake University (J.D., 1983). National Order of Barristers, 1986. Board Member, 1981-1983; Vice Chairperson, Moot Court Board, 1982-1983. Recipient, Alumni Service Award, Moot Court Board, Drake University Law School, 1986. Listed in Who's Who Among Students in American Universities and Colleges, 1983. Member, Board of Counselors, Drake Law School, 1986-1990, 2001—. President, Iowa Lawyers Assistance Program, 1999—. *Member:* Polk County, Iowa State (Founding Member, Council, E-Commerce Section, 2000-2002; Section Chair, E-Commerce, 2002—; Member, Lawyers Helping Lawyers Committee) and American (Member, Business Law Section, Cyberspace Committee) Bar Associations; Polk County Women Attorneys Association; American Intellectual Property Law Association. Iowa State Bar Foundation, 2002. ***Email:*** jhuston@dickinsonlaw.com

JOHN R. MACKAMAN, born Des Moines, Iowa, July 27, 1929; admitted to bar, 1956, Iowa. *Education:* Drake University (B.A., with honors, 1951; J.D., with honors, 1956). Phi Alpha Delta; Phi Beta Kappa; Order of the Coif. Editor, Drake Law Review, 1955. *Member:* Polk County (President, 1988-1989), Iowa State (Chairman, Legal Forms Committee, 1976-1980; Chairman, Title Guaranty Committee, 1981-1988; Member, Board of Governors, 1980-1984, 1989-1993) and American Bar Associations; American Judicature Society. Fellow, Iowa State Bar Foundation (Chair, 1994-1995). ***Email:*** jmackama@dickinsonlaw.com

WASHINGTON, D.C. OF COUNSEL

GENE C. LANGE, born Sac City, Iowa, July 31, 1947; admitted to bar, 1973, District of Columbia; U.S. Supreme Court; U.S. Court of Appeals for the District of Columbia; U.S. Claims Court. *Education:* Iowa State University (B.S., 1969); Georgetown University (J.D., 1972). Member, Charles Fahy Inn of Court. *Member:* The District of Columbia Bar. (Also Member, Luman, Lange, Thomas & McMullen, LLP, Washington, DC). ***PRACTICE AREAS:*** Corporate; Immigration Law. ***Email:*** glange@dickinsonlaw.com

JOHN W. THOMAS, born Carroll, Iowa, October 9, 1949; admitted to bar, 1974, Virginia; 1975, District of Columbia; 1996, U.S. District Court, Eastern District of Virginia. *Education:* Iowa State University (B.S., with honors, 1971); George Washington University National Law Center (J.D., with honors, 1974). Co-Author: Thomas, J. and Terry, M. "Professional Labeling and Animal Drugs," 56 Journal of Association Food & Drug Officials. *Member:* Fairfax Bar Association; U.S. Animal Health Association; American Veterinary Medical Law Association; American Society of Association Executives. (Also Member, Luman, Lange, Thomas & McMullen, LLP, Washington, D.C.). ***PRACTICE AREAS:*** Business Law; Nonprofit Organizations; Food and Drug Law; Government Relations. ***Email:*** jthomas@dickinsonlaw.com

REPRESENTATIVE CLIENTS: Adventure Lands of America; America Online; Ankeny Community Schools; Associated Builders and Contractors of Iowa; Bankers Trust Company; Budget Marketing; Calpine Corporation; Central Iowa KFC; Des Moines Area Association of Realtors; Des Moines Board of Water Works; Farm and City Insurance Co.; FCStone Group, Inc.; Foods, Inc.; Git-N-Go Convenience Stores, Inc.; Guide One Mutual Insurance Co.; Hills Bank and Trust Co.; IKON Office Solutions; Iowa Association of Business and Industry; Life Care Retirement Communities, Inc.; MCI; Monfort Inc.; Meredith Corp.; Merit Resources; Mid-States Ford Truck Sales, Inc.; QuikTrip Corporation; Telecorp PCS; U.S. Cellular; Urbandale Community School District; Utilicorp; Verizon Wireless; Waukee State Bank; Wells Fargo Bank, Iowa; Wells Fargo Mortgage; Wesley Retirement Services, Inc.; Williams Cos.
REFERENCE: Wells Fargo Bank, Iowa, N.A.

DORSEY & WHITNEY LLP

801 GRAND, SUITE 3900
DES MOINES, IOWA 50309
Telephone: 515-283-1000
Fax: 515-283-1060
URL: http://www.dorsey.com

Minneapolis, Minnesota Office: Suite 1500, 50 South Sixth Street, 55402-1498. Telephone: 612-340-2600.
Seattle, Washington Office: U.S. Bank Centre, 1420 Fifth Avenue, Suite 3400, 98101. Telephone: 206-903-8800.

(This Listing Continued)

New York, New York Office: 250 Park Avenue, 10177. Telephone: 212-415-9200.
Washington, D.C. Office: 1001 Pennsylvania Avenue, N.W., Suite 400 South, 20004. Telephone: 202-442-3000.
Denver, Colorado Office: 370 Seventeenth Street, Republic Plaza Building, Suite 4700, 80202-5647. Telephone: 303-629-3400.
London, England Office: 21 Wilson Street, EC2M 2TD. Telephone: 011-44-207-588-0800.
Hong Kong Office: Suite 3008, One Pacific Place, 88 Queensway, Hong Kong. Telephone: 011-852-252-65000. Fax: 011-852-252-43000.
Shanghai, China Office: Suite 6211-12, Plaza 66, No. 1266 Nanjing Xi Lu, Shanghai, 200040. Telephone: 86-21-6288-2323. Fax: 86-21-6288-3222.
Toronto, Ontario Office: BCE Place, 161 Bay Street, Suite 4310, P.O. Box 512, M5J 2S1. Telephone: 416-367-7370. Fax: 416-367-7371.
Vancouver, British Columbia Office: 666 Burrard Street, Suite 500, V6C 3P6. Telephone: 604-687-5151.
Anchorage, Alaska Office: 1031 West 4th Avenue, Suite 600, 99501-5907. Telephone: 907-276-4557.
Salt Lake City, Utah Office: Wells Fargo Plaza, 170 South Main Street, Suite 900, 84101. Telephone: 801-933-7360.
Southern California Office: 38 Technology Drive, Irvine, 92618-5310. Telephone: 949-932-3600.
Fargo, North Dakota Office: 51 North Broadway, Suite 402, P.O. Box 1344, 58107-1344. Telephone: 701-235-6000.
Great Falls, Montana Office: 507 Davidson Building, 8 Third Street North, P.O. Box 1566, 59401. Telephone: 406-727-3632.
Missoula, Montana Office: 125 Bank Street, Suite 600, 59802-4407. Telephone: 406-721-6025. Fax: 406-543-0863.
Paramus, New Jersey Office: 95 Route 17 South, Suite 203, 07652. Telephone: 201-291-8904. Fax: 201-712-9444.
Palo Alto, California Office: 1717 Embarcadero Road, 94303. Telephone: 650-857-1717.
San Francisco, California Office: 555 California Street, Suite 1000, 94104-1513. Telephone: 415-781-1989.

Banking and Commercial, Corporate Finance, Employee Benefits, Environmental, Estate Planning and Administration, Foreign Trade, Health Law, Government and Regulatory Affairs, Intellectual Property, International, Labor and Employment Law, Litigation, Real Estate, Tax, and Municipal and Public Authority Financing. Indian and Gaming Law and Venture Capital.

FIRM PROFILE: Clients have relied on Dorsey since 1912 as a valued, cutting-edge business partner. With over 700 lawyers in 20 locations in the USA, Canada, Europe and Asia, we provide an integrated, proactive approach to our clients' legal and business needs. Dorsey represents a number of the world's most successful Fortune 500 companies from a variety of industries including leaders in the financial services, investment banking, life sciences, securities, technology and energy sectors as well as nonprofit and government entities.

MEMBERS OF FIRM

DAVID L. CLAYPOOL, born 1946; admitted to bar, 1975, Iowa. *Education:* Illinois College (B.A., 1968); University of Iowa (J.D., with high distinction, 1975). Order of the Coif. Notes and Comments Editor, Iowa Law Review, 1974-1975. Author: Comment, 59 Iowa Law Review 655, 1973; Note 59, Iowa Law Review 1161, 1974. *Member:* Polk County and Iowa State Bar Associations; National Association of Bond Lawyers; Iowa Municipal Attorneys Association. ***Email:*** claypool.david@dorsey.com

DAVID D. GROSSKLAUS, born 1968; admitted to bar, 1994, Iowa. *Education:* University of Northern Iowa (B.A., with high honors, 1990); Drake University (J.D., 1993). *Member:* Polk County and Iowa State Bar Associations; Iowa Municipal Attorneys Association; National Association of Bond Lawyers. ***Email:*** grossklaus.david@dorsey.com

DENNIS W. JOHNSON, born 1949; admitted to bar, 1975, Arizona; 1978, Iowa and U.S. Supreme Court; U.S. Court of Appeals, Eighth and Ninth Circuits; U.S. District Court, Northern and Southern Districts of Iowa. *Education:* University of Iowa (B.A., with honors, 1972; J.D., with high distinction, 1975). Editor-in-Chief, Iowa Law Review, 1974-1975. Phillip C. Jessup International Law Moot Court Team, 1975. Author: Comment, "To Deduct or Capitalize, a Conflict Between Sections 167 and 263," 59 Iowa Law Review 420, 1974. Iowa Solicitor General, 2000-2002. *Member:* Polk County and Iowa State (Member, Litigation and Administrative Law Sections) Bar Associations; Blackstone Inn of Court (Barrister). (Board Certified Civil Trial Specialist, National Board of Trial Advocacy). ***Email:*** johnson.dennis@dorsey.com

ROBERT E. JOSTEN, born 1942; admitted to bar, 1972, District of Columbia; 1977, Iowa. *Education:* Morningside College (B.A., magna cum laude, 1964); George Washington University (J.D., 1969). Executive Director, League of Iowa Municipalities, 1974-1977. Board of Directors, National League of Cities, 1975-1977. Des Moines Planning and Zoning Commission, 1978-1980. Secretary, Iowa Municipal Attorneys Association, 1982-1994. *Member:* Polk County and Iowa State Bar Associations; The District of Columbia Bar; National Association of Bond Lawyers. ***Email:*** josten.robert@dorsey.com

BRIAN J. LAURENZO, born 1961; admitted to bar, 1988, Illinois and U.S. District Court, Northern District of Illinois; 1991, Iowa and U.S. District Court, Northern and Southern Districts of Iowa; 1992, U.S. District Court, Central District of Illinois; 1993, U.S. Court of Appeals, Seventh, Eighth and Federal Circuits and U.S. Supreme Court; registered to practice before U.S. Patent and Trademark Office. *Education:* Iowa State University (B.S., Construction Engineering, 1984); DePaul University (J.D., 1988). *Member:* Polk County and Iowa State (Chair, Intellectual Property Law Section, 2000-2001) Bar Associations; Iowa Intellectual Property Law Association (President, 1996). ***Email:*** laurenzo.brian@dorsey.com

EDWIN N. McINTOSH, born 1950; admitted to bar, 1976, Iowa. *Education:* University of Iowa (B.A., 1972; J.D., with high distinction, 1976). Order of the Coif. Moot Court Case Editor. *Member:* Polk County (Magistrate Appointing Commission, 1984-1996) and Iowa State (Member: Litigation Section; Health Law Section) Bar Associations; American Health Lawyers Association. ***Email:*** mcintosh.edwin@dorsey.com

(This Listing Continued)

ASSOCIATES

Amy Bjork	*Angela Dralle*
Heather Campbell	*Darla M. Giese*
John Danos	*Jason M. Hunt*

Cristina Kuhn

ATTORNEY

MICHAEL C. GILCHRIST, born 1968; admitted to bar, 1995, Iowa; 1998, U.S. District Court, Northern and Southern Districts of Iowa; 1999, U.S. Court of Appeals for the Federal Circuit; registered to practice before U.S. Patent and Trademark Office. *Education:* University of Iowa (B.S.E., 1991; J.D., with high distinction, 1995). Managing Editor, Iowa Law Review, Vol. 80, 1994-1995. *Member:* Polk County, Iowa State Bar Associations; Iowa Intellectual Property Law Association. ***Email:*** gilchrist.michael@dorsey.com

(For personnel and biographical data on Dorsey & Whitney's other offices, see that specific city and state listing)

DREHER, SIMPSON & JENSEN, P.C.

THE EQUITABLE BUILDING
604 LOCUST STREET, SUITE 222
DES MOINES, IOWA 50309-3723
Telephone: 515-288-5000
Telecopier: 515-288-7718
Email: LSimpson@dreherlaw.com
URL: http://www.dreherlaw.com

General Civil Practice, Corporation, Insurance, Probate, Administrative, Labor, Employment, Personal Injury, Workers Compensation, Real Estate and Business Law, Trials and Appeals, Estate Planning, Tax and Tax Litigation.

FIRM PROFILE: Firm established in 1927 as Brunk & Janss and engaged in general practice and insurance regulatory law. A full service firm with emphasis on civil litigation, business, real estate, and estate planning. The firm has experience in class action and antitrust litigation, construction, corporate and employment matters.

GREGORY BRUNK (1894-1965)

PETER W. JANSS (1904-1969)

MARVIN R. ADAMS (1930-1982)

ROBERT E. DREHER

WALTER T. HART

ALBERT L. HARVEY

LYLE L. SIMPSON, born Des Moines, Iowa, October 15, 1937; admitted to bar, 1963, Iowa, U.S. District Court, Southern and Northern Districts of Iowa, U.S. Court of Appeals, 8th Circuit, U.S. Tax Court; U.S. Court of Military Appeals, and U.S. Supreme Court. *Education:* Drake University (B.A., 1960; J.D., 1963). Delta Theta Phi. *Member:* Polk County, Iowa State and American Bar Associations. [Capt., Signal Corps. USNG, 1955-1968; CDR, Judge Advocate, U.S. Navy Reserve, 1968-1986]. ***PRACTICE AREAS:*** Corporation; Business Development; Estate Planning; Real Estate. ***Email:*** lsimpson@dreherlaw.com

DICK L. JENSEN, born Audubon, Iowa, October 25, 1930; admitted to bar, 1954, Iowa, U.S. Supreme Court, U.S. Courts of Appeals, Eighth Circuit and Federal Circuit and U.S. District Court, Northern and Southern Districts of Iowa and U.S. Tax Court. *Education:* University of Iowa (LL.B., 1954). Phi Delta Phi. *Member:* Polk County, Iowa State and American Bar Associations. ***Email:*** djensen@dreherlaw.com

MARCUS F. ABELS, born Des Moines, Iowa, June 6, 1958; admitted to bar, 1983, Iowa and U.S. Tax Court. *Education:* University of Iowa (B.B.A., 1980); Drake University (J.D., with honors, 1982). *Member:* Polk County, Iowa State and American Bar Associations. ***PRACTICE AREAS:*** Real Estate. ***Email:*** mabels@dreherlaw.com

GARY R. FISCHER, born Cedar Rapids, Iowa, October 24, 1964; admitted to bar, 1990, Iowa, U.S. Court of Appeals, Eighth Circuit and U.S. District Court, Northern and Southern Districts of Iowa. *Education:* Central College (B.A., 1987); Drake University (J.D., with honors, 1990). *Member:* Polk County, Iowa State, Federal and American (Member, Labor and Employment, Litigation Sections) Bar Associations. ***PRACTICE AREAS:*** Employment and Labor Law; Litigation. ***Email:*** gfischer@dreherlaw.com

MICHAEL F. BURGER, born Iowa City, Iowa, September 7, 1948; admitted to bar, 1974, Iowa and U.S. District Court, Northern and Southern Districts of Iowa and U.S. Tax Court. *Education:* University of Chicago (B.A., 1970); University of Kansas (J.D., 1973). *Member:* Polk County, Iowa State and American (Member, Construction Law Forum) Bar Associations. ***PRACTICE AREAS:*** Construction; Litigation. ***Email:*** mburger@dreherlaw.com

D. SCOTT SIMPSON, born Des Moines, Iowa, July 26, 1966; admitted to bar, 1993, Iowa. *Education:* Drake University (B.S., 1989; J.D., 1993). Delta Theta Phi. Co Author, Chapter 15, Estate Planning, *Leveraging with Legal Assistants,* American Bar Section of Law Practice Management (1993); Chapter I, Special Problems of Closely Held Corporations, Business Practice Manual, Iowa State Bar Association. *Member:* Iowa State Bar Association. ***PRACTICE AREAS:*** Business Law; Estate Planning; Probate. ***Email:*** dscott@dreherlaw.com

JOHN M. BOUSLOG, born Macomb, Illinois, January 2, 1958; admitted to bar, 1985, Iowa; 1986, U.S. District Court, Northern and Southern Districts of Iowa and U.S. Court of Appeals, Eighth Circuit; U.S. Tax Court. *Education:* Western Illinois University (B.B., with honors, 1980); Drake University (M.B.A.; J.D., 1985). Dean's List. Blue Key. Beta Gamma Sigma; Phi Eta Sigma; Delta Theta Phi. *Member:* Polk County, Iowa State and American Bar Associations; Student Bar Association. ***PRACTICE AREAS:*** Corporate Law; Business Law; Real Estate Law; Estate Planning. ***Email:*** jbouslog@dreherlaw.com

(This Listing Continued)

JOEL D. HUSTON, born Joliet, Illinois, August 9, 1975; admitted to bar, 2004, Iowa. *Education:* Drake University (B.A., 1997; J.D., 2004). *Member:* Iowa State, Polk County and American Bar Associations. ***PRACTICE AREAS:*** Estate Planning; Business Planning; Real Estate; Litigation. ***Email:*** joelh@dreherlaw.com

COUNSEL FOR: Iowa State Bank; M. Peterson Construction Co.; A-1 Ready Mix Co.; Gene Miller Co.; Iowa Roofing Co.; GNA Concrete, Inc.
REPRESENTATIVE CLIENTS: Ago Systems, Inc.; Batten, Batten, Hudson and Swab, Inc.; Cemen Tech, Inc.; Keck, Inc.; Ambico, Inc.; Shivvers Incorporated; Dieomatic Inc.; Cosma International, Inc.; Investment Consulting Service, Inc.; Century Software, Limited; Ameristar Casino's, Inc.; S. Joseph and Sons, Incorporated.

DUNCAN, GREEN, BROWN & LANGENESS

A PROFESSIONAL CORPORATION
Established in 1993
400 LOCUST STREET, SUITE 380
DES MOINES, IOWA 50309-2363
Telephone: 515-288-6440
Fax: 515-288-6448
URL: http://www.duncangreenlaw.com

General Civil Practice, Trials and Appeals State and U.S. Courts, Corporate and Business, Taxation, Real Estate, Estate Planning and Probate, Banking, Trade Regulation, Employment, Products Liability, Legal and Medical Malpractice, Antitrust, Personal Injury, Commercial Litigation, Education, Health, Administrative, Insurance Defense, Coverage and Regulation.

HEARST R. (RANDY) DUNCAN, JR., born Osage, Iowa, March 15, 1937; admitted to bar, 1963, Iowa. *Education:* State University of Iowa (B.A., 1959); Southern Methodist University and Drake University (J.D., 1963). Delta Theta Phi. *Member:* Polk County, Iowa State and American Bar Associations; National Association of Railroad Trial Counsel. Fellow: American College of Trial Lawyers; International Society of Barristers; American Inns of Court (Emeritus Edwin Moore Inn). Fellow, Iowa Academy of Trial Lawyers; Iowa Defense Counsel Association. ***PRACTICE AREAS:*** Aviation Law; Legal Malpractice; Personal Injury; Products Liability. ***Email:*** rduncan@duncangreenlaw.com

BRENT B. (CHRIS) GREEN, born Spencer, Iowa, March 7, 1941; admitted to bar, 1965, Iowa; 1966, New York. *Education:* University of Iowa (B.A., 1963; J.D., with distinction, 1965). Phi Delta Phi. Member, Board of Editors, Iowa Law Review, 1964-1965. Co-Author: "Iowa Tort Law," published in *Tort Handbook: A Fifty State Compendium. Member:* The Association of the Bar of the City of New York; Polk County, Iowa State and American (Member, Sections on: Antitrust Law; Litigation; Tort and Insurance Practice) Bar Associations; Association of Trial Lawyers of Iowa; Iowa Defense Counsel Association. Fellow: Iowa Academy of Trial Lawyers; American College of Trial Lawyers; International Society of Barristers; American Academy of Appellate Lawyers; American Inns of Court (Master, C. Edwin Moore Inn); American Board of Trial Advocates. ***PRACTICE AREAS:*** Antitrust; Commercial Litigation; Insurance Defense; Insurance; Professional Liability. ***Email:*** bgreen@duncangreenlaw.com

GREGORY R. BROWN, born Emmetsburg, Iowa, July 11, 1953; admitted to bar, 1978, Iowa. *Education:* University of Iowa (B.A., with high distinction, 1975; J.D., with distinction, 1978). Phi Beta Kappa; Omicron Delta Kappa; Phi Delta Phi. *Member:* Polk County and Iowa State Bar Associations; Defense Research Institute; American Inns of Court (Master, C. Edwin Moore Inn). ***PRACTICE AREAS:*** Civil Practice; Insurance Defense; Litigation. ***Email:*** gbrown@duncangreenlaw.com

JAMES B. LANGENESS, born Des Moines, Iowa, November 11, 1954; admitted to bar, 1980, Iowa. *Education:* Syracuse University and Wharton School of Business, University of Pennsylvania (B.S., Economics, 1977); Drake University (J.D., 1979). Certified Public Accountant, Iowa, 1977. Iowa Society of Certified Public Accountants (State Taxation Committee, 1994-2005). Listed, Best Lawyers in USA - Estates and Trusts Category. *Member:* Polk County, Iowa State (Member: Taxation Council, 1995-1998; Probate/Trust Law Council, 2001-2004; Probate/Trust Law and Taxation Sections) and American (Member: Real Property, Probate & Trust Law Section; Taxation Section) Bar Associations. Fellow, American College of Trust and Estate Counsel. ***PRACTICE AREAS:*** Wills; Trusts; Estate Planning; Probate Law; Taxation; Business Law. ***Email:*** jlangeness@duncangreenlaw.com

RANDOLPH MATHIESON (MATT) DUNCAN, born Des Moines, Iowa, September 30, 1962; admitted to bar, 1988, Iowa and Missouri; 1989, District of Columbia; U.S. Court of Appeals, Eighth and Tenth Circuits; U.S. District Court, Northern and Southern Districts of Iowa. *Education:* University of Iowa (B.A., 1985); Drake University (J.D., with honors, 1988). Order of the Coif; Delta Theta Phi. Managing Editor, Drake University Law Review, 1987-1988. *Member:* Polk County, Iowa State and American (Member, Litigation, Business Law and Real Estate Sections) Bar Associations; District of Columbia Bar; The Missouri Bar. ***PRACTICE AREAS:*** Corporate Law; Business Law; Insurance; Real Estate. ***Email:*** rmduncan@duncangreenlaw.com

MARICLARE THINNES CULVER, born Dubuque, Iowa, December 23, 1964; admitted to bar, 1990, Iowa; U.S. Court of Appeals, Eighth Circuit; U.S. District Court, Northern and Southern Districts of Iowa. *Education:* Loras College; University of Iowa (B.A., 1987; J.D., with distinction, 1990). Vice-Chairperson, Moot Court Executive Board, 1989-1990. *Member:* Polk County, Iowa State and American Bar Associations; Iowa Trial Lawyers Association. ***PRACTICE AREAS:*** Labor and Employment; Civil Rights; Civil Practice; Insurance Defense; Legal Malpractice. ***Email:*** mculver@duncangreenlaw.com

BRADLEY C. OBERMEIER, born Des Moines, Iowa, March 25, 1970; admitted to bar, 1997, Iowa; U.S. District Court, Southern District of Iowa. *Education:* University of Iowa (B.B.A., 1992; J.D., with high distinction, 1997). Chairperson, Moot Court Board, 1996-1997. Member, Iowa Law Review, 1996-1997. Co-Author: "Iowa Tort Law," published in *Tort Handbook: A Fifty State Compendium. Member:* Polk County (Member, Membership Committee, 1999—), Iowa State (Member, Executive Council, Young Lawyers Division, 1999-2003) and American (Member, Young Lawyers Division; Chairman,

(This Listing Continued)

DUNCAN, GREEN, BROWN & LANGENESS, A PROFESSIONAL CORPORATION, Des Moines—Continued

Law Practice Committee, 2002-2003) Bar Associations; American Inns of Court (Pupil, C. Edwin Moore Inn). ***PRACTICE AREAS:*** Civil Practice; Commercial Litigation; Legal Malpractice. ***Email:*** bobermeier@duncangreenlaw.com

MARTIN J. KENWORTHY, born Des Moines, Iowa, June 28, 1958; admitted to bar, 1989, Ohio, U.S. District Court, Southern District of Ohio, U.S. District Court, Eastern District of Kentucky and U.S. Court of Appeals, Sixth Circuit; 1990, Kentucky; 1992, Florida; 1998, Iowa and U.S. District Court, Southern District of Iowa; 2003, U.S. Supreme Court. *Education:* Bradley University (B.S., magna cum laude, 1980); Salmon P. Chase College of Law (J.D., cum laude, 1989). Editor, Salmon P. Chase College of Law Review, 1988-1989; Tax Moot Court, 1989. Author: "The Feres Doctrine: Should It Bar Claims by Military Personnel Against Civilian Federal Employees?" 15 N.Ky.L.R. 559 (1988). Chairman, Union Township Board of Zoning Appeals, 1990-1997. *Member:* Cincinnati (Chairman, Construction Law Committee, 1995-1997), Polk County, Iowa State and American (Member, Forum on the Construction Industry, 1989—) Bar Associations; The Florida Bar. ***PRACTICE AREAS:*** Commercial Litigation; Construction Law; Business Law. ***Email:*** mkenworthy@duncangreenlaw.com

---

CHRISTINE B. LONG, born South Bend, Indiana, September 16, 1965; admitted to bar, 1991, Arizona and U.S. District Court, District of Arizona; 1992, U.S. Court of Appeals, Sixth Circuit; 1997, Iowa. *Education:* College of the Holy Cross (B.A., 1988); University of Iowa (J.D., with distinction, 1991). *Member:* Polk County and Iowa State Bar Associations; State Bar of Arizona. ***PRACTICE AREAS:*** Estate Planning; Trust Administration; Probate. ***Email:*** clong@duncangreenlaw.com

MICHELE M. RAMSEY, born Des Moines, Iowa, November 11, 1971; admitted to bar, 1997, Iowa and U.S. District Court, Southern and Northern Districts of Iowa; 1998, Illinois. *Education:* Central College (B.A., magna cum laude, 1994); University of Iowa (J.D., with high distinction, 1997). Phi Delta Phi. *Member:* Polk County, Illinois State and Iowa State Bar Associations (Member, Executive Committee, Young Lawyers Division, 2000-2003; Vice-Chair, Mock Trial Committee, Young Lawyers Division, 2001-2003). ***PRACTICE AREAS:*** Litigation; Employment Law. ***Email:*** mramsey@duncangreenlaw.com

KIRK W. BAINBRIDGE, born Iowa City, Iowa, September 23, 1975; admitted to bar, 2002, Iowa; 2003, Illinois. *Education:* University of Iowa (B.A., 1998; J.D., 2002). *Member:* Iowa State Bar Association; C. Edward Moore American Inn of Court. ***PRACTICE AREAS:*** Business Litigation (25%); Professional Malpractice (50%); Civil Litigation (25%). ***Email:*** kbainbridge@duncangreenlaw.com

LYNN M. GAUMER, born Park Ridge, Illinois, May 21, 1968; admitted to bar, 1993, South Dakota; 1994, Illinois; 2002, Iowa. *Education:* University of Iowa (B.A., 1990); University of South Dakota (J.D., 1993). ***PRACTICE AREAS:*** Wills; Trusts; Estate Planning; Probate Law. ***Email:*** lgaumer@duncangreenlaw.com

OF COUNSEL

TIMOTHY S. ECKLEY, born New Haven, Connecticut, February 1, 1962; admitted to bar, 1987, Iowa; 1989, U.S. District Court, Southern and Northern Districts of Iowa. *Education:* University of Iowa (B.A., 1983; J.D., 1987). Phi Beta Kappa; Phi Delta Phi. Managing Editor, Iowa Law Review, 1986-1987. Law Clerk to Justice Charles R. Wolle, Iowa State Supreme Court, 1987 and U.S. District Court, Southern District of Iowa, 1987-1989. Author: "Invoking the Presence of God at Public High School Graduation Ceremonies", 71 Iowa Law Review 1247. *Member:* Polk County, Iowa State and American Bar Associations. ***Email:*** tseckley@duncangreenlaw.com

REPRESENTATIVE CLIENTS: American Republic Insurance Co.; Asplundh Tree Expert Co.; Bauer Built Inc.; Bridgestone/Firestone, Inc.; City of Des Moines; Coca Cola Corp.; Charles Gabus Ford, Inc.; The Coleman Co.; Continental Insurance Company; Cotter and Company; Des Moines Chrysler Plymouth; Earl May Seed & Nursery, L.P.; Federated Rural Electric Insurance Corporation; Firstar Bank, N.A.; The Goodyear Co.; Heller Financial, Inc.; Inter-City Products Corporation (USA); Iowa One Call; Krause Gentle Corp., A.A.U.; Liberty Savings Bank; Meredith Corporation; Merrill Lynch and Co.; MidAmerican Energy Company; Mississippi Chemical Company; Mobil Oil Corp.; Morton Buildings, Inc.; Nellis Corporation; New York Life Insurance Co.; R.R. Donnelley & Sons Co.; Reader's Digest Assn.; Reliance Insurance Co.; Risk Enterprise Management, Ltd.; Sears Roebuck & Co.; Sisters of Mercy Health Corporation; Software and Informtion Technology of Iowa; United Insurance Company of America; Vasa North Atlantic Ins. Co.; Wausau Underwriters Insurance Company; Wells Fargo Bank Iowa N.A.; West Des Moines State Bank; Whink Products Company; White Consolidated Industries.

ELVERSON, VASEY & PETERSON, L.L.P.

100 COURT AVENUE, SUITE 405
DES MOINES, IOWA 50309
Telephone: 515-243-1914
Fax: 515-243-2235
URL: http://www.evpllp.com

General Practice, Insurance Defense, Business Law, Corporation Law, Bankruptcy, Divorce, Family Law, Child Custody, Personal Injury, Automobile Accidents, Social Security, Real Estate, Wills, Probate, Trusts and Estates, Criminal Law, Medical Malpractice.

MEMBERS OF FIRM

TODD A. ELVERSON, born Bloomington, Minnesota, March 16, 1956; admitted to bar, 1981, Iowa and U.S. District Court, Southern District of Iowa. *Education:* Drake University (B.F.A., with honors, 1978; J.D., 1981). Author: "Procuring and Insuring Free and Clear Title," Advanced Real Estate Law in Iowa NBI, 1992, 1994. Member, Des Moines Estate and Financial Planners, Vice President, 1992; President, 1993. *Member:* Polk County (Member, Title Standards Committee, 1989-1991) and Iowa State (Member, Sections on: Probate and Trust Law; Corporation and Business Law; Real Estate and Title Law) Bar Associations. ***PRACTICE AREAS:*** Corporate Law; Business Law; Real Estate; Family Law; Wills; Probate. ***Email:*** todd.elverson@elversonlaw.com

JON A. VASEY, born Sioux Falls, South Dakota, December 4, 1957; admitted to bar, 1983, Iowa; 1984, U.S District Court, Southern District of Iowa. *Education:* Iowa State University; University of Iowa (B.B.A., 1980); Drake University (J.D., 1983). Delta Theta Phi (Vice Dean, 1981-1982; Dean, 1982-1983). *Member:* Polk County (Member, Unauthorized Practice Committee) and Iowa State (Member: Insurance Committee, 1989-1993; Young Lawyers Section, 1989-1991) Bar Associations. Member, Iowa Defense Counsel Association; Defense Research and Trial Lawyers Association. ***PRACTICE AREAS:*** Insurance Defense. ***Email:*** jon.vasey@elversonlaw.com

GREGORY W. PETERSON, born Charles City, Iowa, June 8, 1953; admitted to bar, 1979, Iowa; 1985, U.S. District Court, Southern and Northern Districts of Iowa; 1990, Nebraska, Wisconsin, Michigan, U.S. Court of Appeals, Fifth, Eighth, Ninth and Eleventh Circuits. *Education:* Cornell College (B.A., 1975); Drake University (J.D., 1978). *Member:* Polk County and Iowa State Bar Associations; Iowa Trial Lawyers Association. ***PRACTICE AREAS:*** Personal Injury; Bankruptcy; Social Security; Medical Malpractice. ***Email:*** greg.peterson@elversonlaw.com

ASSOCIATES

ALLISON R. ABBOTT, born Greensboro, North Carolina, July 20, 1973; admitted to bar, 1999, Iowa. *Education:* Arizona State University (B.A., 1994); Drake University (J.D., with honors, 1999). Delta Theta Phi. *Member:* Polk County and Iowa State Bar Associations. ***PRACTICE AREAS:*** Insurance Defense; General Practice. ***Email:*** allison.martin@elversonlaw.com

JENNIFER L. OETKER, born Dubuque, Iowa, March 21, 1973; admitted to bar, 1999, Iowa. *Education:* Iowa State University (B.A., 1996); Drake University (J.D., with honors, 1999). Delta Theta Phi. *Member:* Polk County and Iowa State Bar Associations. ***PRACTICE AREAS:*** Family Law; Criminal Law; General Practice. ***Email:*** jennifer.oetker@elversonlaw.com

REPRESENTATIVE CLIENTS: State Farm Mutual Automobile Insurance Co.; Allstate Insurance Co.; Farmers Casualty Co. Mutual; CIGNA Cos.; Pella Co.; Iowa Automobile Dealers Assn.; Peerless Supply, Inc.; State Farm Credit Union; Mid-Plains Ins. Co.; State Farm Fire and Casualty Co.; Amoco Oil Corporation; State Auto Insurance Co.; West Bend Mutual Insurance Company; Wells Fargo Home Mortgage, Inc.; Universal Casualty Co.
REFERENCE: West Bank.

FAEGRE & BENSON LLP

801 GRAND AVENUE, SUITE 3100
DES MOINES, IOWA 50309-8002
Telephone: 515-248-9000
Facsimile: 515-248-9010
Email: info@faegre.com
URL: http://www.faegre.com

REVISER OF THE MINNESOTA LAW DIGEST FOR THIS DIRECTORY.

Minneapolis, Minnesota: 2200 Wells Fargo Center, 90 South Seventh Street. Telephone: 612-766-7000. Facsimile: 612-766-1600.

Denver, Colorado: 3200 Wells Fargo Center, 1700 Lincoln Street. Telephone: 303-607-3500. Facsimile: 303-607-3600.

London, England: 7 Pilgrim Street, EC4V 6LB. Telephone: 44-20-7450-4500. Facsimile: 44-20-7450-4545.

Frankfurt, Germany: Theodor-Heuss-Allee 108, 60486 Frankfurt am Main. Telephone: 011-49-69-631-561-0. Facsimile: 011-49-69-631-561-11.

Shanghai, China: Shanghai Centre, Suite 425, 1376 Nanjiing Road West, Shanghai, 200040 China. Telephone: 011-86-21-6279-8988. Facsimile: 011-86-21-6279-8968.

General Practice including Agribusiness, Corporate, Banking, E-Commerce, Employment, Insurance, Media and Communications, Products Liability, Real Estate, Antitrust and Commercial Litigation.

RESIDENT MEMBERS

MICHAEL A. GIUDICESSI, born Des Moines, Iowa, 1953; admitted to bar, 1979, Iowa. *Education:* University of Missouri (B.J., 1976); University of Iowa (J.D., with distinction, 1979). Law Clerk to Honorable Leo E. Oxberger, Chief Judge, Iowa Court of Appeals, 1979-1980. ***Email:*** mgiudicessi@faegre.com

KIMBERLY J. WALKER, born Washington, Iowa, 1954; admitted to bar, 1979, Iowa and California. *Education:* University of Iowa (B.S., with honors, 1976; J.D., with high distinction, 1979). Law Clerk to Honorable William C. Stuart, Chief Judge, U.S. District Court, Iowa, 1979-1981. ***Email:*** kwalker@faegre.com

TERRI L. COMBS, born Joplin, Missouri, 1957; admitted to bar, 1983, District of Columbia; 1984, New York; 1994, Iowa. *Education:* Southwest Missouri State University (B.S., summa cum laude, 1979); Georgetown University (J.D., 1982). Case and Notes Editor, The Tax Lawyer, 1981-1982. Law Clerk to Honorable Myron H. Bright, Judge U.S. Court of Appeals, Eighth Circuit, 1982-1983. ***Email:*** tcombs@faegre.com

SUSAN M. BOE, born Sioux City, Iowa, 1949; admitted to bar, 1986, Minnesota; 1988, Iowa. *Education:* Iowa State University (B.S., 1971); University of Iowa College of Law (J.D., with highest distinction, 1985). Order of the Coif. ***Email:*** sboe@faegre.com

ROSS W. JOHNSON, born Racine, Wisconsin, 1970; admitted to bar, 1997, Arizona; 2001, Iowa. *Education:* Arizona State University (B.A., summa cum laude, 1993); University of Iowa (J.D., with high distinction, 1997). Phi Beta Kappa; Order of the Coif. Member, Iowa Law Review, 1995-1997. ***Email:*** rwjohnson@faegre.com

SPECIAL COUNSEL

BRIAN L. CAMPBELL, born Hampton, Iowa, 1949; admitted to bar, 1977, Nebraska; 1982, Iowa; 2002, Minnesota. *Education:* University of Northern Iowa (B.A., 1971); Creighton University (J.D., 1977). Member, Creighton University Law Review, 1974-1976.

(This Listing Continued)

REPORTED CASES: Edmund v. Mid American Energy, Co., F.3d., 2002 WL 178436 (8th Cir. 2002); Grove v. Principal Mutual Life Insurance Co., 200 F.R.D. 434 (S.D. Iowa 2001); Howard v. Coventry Health Care of Iowa, Inc., 158 F. Supp. 2d 937 S.D. Iowa (2001); J.A.H. Ex.rel. R.M.H. v. Wadle and Associates, P.C., 589 N.W. 2d. 256 (Iowa 1999); Johnson v. Knoxville Community School district, 570 N.W. 2d. 633, 122 Ed. Law. Rep. 778 (Iowa 1997); Pierce v. Iowa-MO. Conference of Seventh Day Adventists, 534 N.W. 2d. 425, 130 Lab. Cas. P. 57, 983 (Iowa 1995); 205 Corp. v. Brndow, 517 N.W. 2d 548 (Iowa 1994); Borschel v. City of Perry, 512 N.W. 2d. 565 (Iowa 1994); Porter v. Pioneer Hi-Bred International, Inc., 497 N.W. 2d. 870, 126 Lab. Cas. P. 57465 (Iowa 1993); Croblin Xpress v. Iowa Insurance Guaranty Association, 461 N.W. 2d 175 (Iowa 1990); Mortved v. Bethany Manor, 458 N.W., 2d 2 (Iowa 1990); Speck v. Unit Handling Div., a Div. of Litton Systems, Inc., 366 N.W. 2d. 543 (Iowa 1985); American States Insurance Co., v. Estate of Tollari, 362 N.W. 2d. 519 (Iowa 1985); Millard v. State Department of Education, 277 N.W. 2d. 71 (Neb. 1979). ***PRACTICE AREAS:*** Business Litigation; Employment Litigation; Construction Litigation. ***Email:*** bcampbell@faegre.com

THOMAS L. SLAUGHTER, born Des Moines, Iowa, 1954; admitted to bar, 1979, Iowa; 1987, New York. *Education:* McPherson College (B.A., summa cum laude, 1976); University of Iowa (J.D., with distinction, 1979). Vice President-General Counsel and Secretary, Meredith Corporation, 1994-1999. ***Email:*** tslaughter@faegre.com

ANDREW R. ANDERSON, born Cedar Falls, Iowa, October 19, 1964; admitted to bar, 1993, Iowa and Minnesota; 1997, Arizona. *Education:* Luther College (B.A., 1987); Australian National University (M.A., with distinction, 1991); University of Iowa College of Law (J.D., with distinction, 1992). Law Clerk, Fifth Judicial District of Iowa, 1993-1994. ***PRACTICE AREAS:*** Public Project Financing; Corporate Finance; Banking Law; Gaming Law. ***Email:*** aanderson@faegre.com

RESIDENT ASSOCIATES

WILLIAM J. HUNNICUTT, born Edina, Minnesota, 1971; admitted to bar, 1996, Iowa. *Education:* University of Notre Dame (B.A., cum laude, 1993); Drake University (J.D., with honors, 1996). Order of the Coif. Articles Editor, Drake Law Review, 1995-1996. Law Clerk to the Honorable Bruce Snell, Jr., Iowa Supreme Court, 1996-1997. ***Email:*** bhunnicu@faegre.com

CHAD R. ANDERSON, born Muscatine, Iowa, 1971; admitted to bar, 1999, Wisconsin; 2003, Iowa. *Education:* University of Iowa (B.A., with highest distinction, 1993; J.D., with high distinction, 1999). Order of the Coif. ***PRACTICE AREAS:*** Business Litigation; Antitrust; Intellectual Property. ***Email:*** canderson@faegre.com

ANGELA J. MORALES, born Des Moines, Iowa, 1976; admitted to bar, 2001, Iowa. *Education:* Drake University (B.A., summa cum laude, 1998; J.D., with highest honors, 2001). Associate Editor, Drake Law Review, 2000-2001. ***Email:*** amorales@faegre.com

CHRISTOPHER L. McDONALD, born Bangkok, Thailand, 1974; admitted to bar, 2001, Iowa. *Education:* Grand View College (B.A., 1997); University of Iowa (J.D., with highest distinction, 2001). Order of the Coif. Associate Editor, Iowa Law Review, 2000-2001. Law Clerk, Honorable David R. Hansen, Chief Judge, U.S. Court of Appeals, Eighth Circuit, 2001-2003. ***PRACTICE AREAS:*** Business Litigation. ***Email:*** cmcdonald@faegre.com

BRIAN S. McCORMAC, born Iowa City, Iowa, 1974; admitted to bar, 2000, Wisconsin and U.S. District Court, Eastern and Western Districts of Wisconsin; 2003, U.S. Supreme Court; 2004, Iowa, U.S. District Court, Southern District of Iowa and U.S. Court of Appeals, 8th Circuit. *Education:* Coe College (B.A., 1997); University of Iowa (J.D., with distinction, 2000). Member, Iowa Law Review, 1998-1999. *Member:* Iowa State Bar Association; State Bar of Wisconsin. ***PRACTICE AREAS:*** Commercial Litigation; Antitrust; Products Liability. ***Email:*** bmccormac@faegre.com

JESSE LINEBAUGH, born Ottumwa, Iowa, 1976; admitted to bar, 2002, Texas; 2004, Iowa. *Education:* University of Iowa (B.B.A., with honors and high distinction, 1999); Duke University (J.D., 2002). Member, Park and Recreation Advisory Board, City of Duncanville. *Member:* State Bar of Texas. ***Email:*** jlinebaugh@faegre.com

JACOB D. BYLUND, born Criston, Iowa, 1978; admitted to bar, 2003, Iowa. *Education:* Iowa State University (B.A., 2000); University of Iowa (J.D., with high distinction, 2003). ***PRACTICE AREAS:*** Litigation. ***Email:*** jbylund@faegre.com

JENNIFER PETERSON, born Des Moines, Iowa, 1974; admitted to bar, 2003, Iowa. *Education:* University of Iowa (B.A., 1996; J.D., 2003). Member, Junior League of Des Moines. *Member:* Polk County Women Attorneys (Publicity Chair). ***Email:*** jpeterson@faegre.com

REVISER OF THE MINNESOTA LAW DIGEST FOR THIS DIRECTORY.

(For complete Biographical Data on all personnel, see Professional Biographies at Minneapolis, Minnesota)

FERNANDEZ LAW FIRM

DES MOINES, IOWA

(See Urbandale)

Family Law, Bankruptcy, Personal Injury, Divorce, General Practice.

FINLEY, ALT, SMITH, SCHARNBERG, CRAIG, HILMES & GAFFNEY, P.C.

699 WALNUT STREET, SUITE 1900
DES MOINES, IOWA 50309
Telephone: 515-288-0145
Telecopier: 515-288-2724

REVISER OF THE IOWA LAW DIGEST FOR THIS DIRECTORY.

(This Listing Continued)

General Civil Practice, Litigation and Appeals in all Courts. Banking, Civil Trial, Commercial, Communication, Corporate, Education, ERISA, Employment Law, Estate Planning, Health Care, Insurance, Personal Injury, Product Liability, Professional Malpractice, Probate, Real Estate, Taxation, Transportation, Trust and Workers Compensation.

FIRM PROFILE: History: The firm was founded in 1924 under the name of Carr, Cox, Evans & Riley. In the firm's 80 year history the firm name has changed a number of times. In 1998, the firm name was changed to FINLEY, ALT, SMITH, SCHARNBERG, CRAIG, HILMES & GAFFNEY, P.C.

Areas of Emphasis: FINLEY, ALT, SMITH, SCHARNBERG, CRAIG, HILMES & GAFFNEY, P.C., is a full service law firm with particular emphasis on Personal Injury, Insurance Defense, Corporation, Business, Finance, Banking, Employment Law, Health Law, Estate Planning and Probate, Professional Malpractice and Real Estate Law. The firm has 15 lawyers and 4 paraprofessionals.

Firm Activities: The firm encourages participation in community activities and mandates CLE hours for each lawyer each year. A practice management committee supervises the assignment of work and monitors the work of younger lawyers. Monthly meetings of all lawyers and paraprofessionals are held to discuss new and revised laws and regulations. All lawyers are members of the American Bar Association, the Iowa State Bar Association and the Polk County Bar Association. In addition, firm members are encouraged to belong to specialized groups such as the Association of Trial Lawyers of America, National Association of Railroad Trial Counsel, Defense Research Institute, American Academy of Hospital Attorneys and National Health Lawyers Association.

Client Base: Clients represent leaders in their industries such as insurance, mortgage lending, railroads, banking, health care and retirement living. Although a significant amount of work comes from corporations, the firm continues to represent individuals and small businesses.

THOMAS A. FINLEY, born Mason City, Iowa, December 22, 1940; admitted to bar, 1966, Iowa; U.S. District Court, Northern and Southern Districts of Iowa. *Education:* University of Iowa (B.A., 1965; LL.B., 1966). Chair, Iowa State Bar Association Committees on: Professional Ethics; Professionalism; Appointed Special Master, Iowa Supreme Court to study attorney advertising. Co-Author: "Tort Reform and Medical Malpractice—Iowa Past, Present and Future," 36 Drake Law Review 669, 1987. Co-Author Iowa Section of: "Fifty States Construction Lien and Bond Law." Frequent author and lecturer on Medical Malpractice issues. *Member:* Polk County, Iowa State and American Bar Associations. Fellow: The Iowa Academy of Trial Lawyers; Iowa Trial Lawyers Association; American College of Trial Lawyers; American Board of Trial Advocates; Iowa Defense Counsel; C. Edwin Moore American Inn of Court; Defense Research Institute. ***PRACTICE AREAS:*** Professional Malpractice; Product Liability; Insurance; Corporate Litigation.

JERRY P. ALT, born Kalona, Iowa, September 25, 1940; admitted to bar, 1968, Iowa; U.S. District Court, Northern and Southern Districts of Iowa. *Education:* University of Iowa (B.A., 1963); Drake University (J.D., with honors, 1968). Order of the Coif. Notes Editor, Drake Law Review, 1967. Phi Alpha Delta. *Member:* Polk County, Iowa State and American Bar Associations. ***PRACTICE AREAS:*** Real Estate; Corporate; Construction Law; General Practice.

GLENN L. SMITH, born Des Moines, Iowa, February 27, 1944; admitted to bar, 1968, Iowa; U.S. District Court, Northern and Southern Districts of Iowa; U.S. Court of Appeals, Eighth Circuit; U.S. Supreme Court. *Education:* Drake University (B.A., 1965; J.D., 1968). Associate and Case Notes Editor, Drake Law Review, 1967-1968. Phi Alpha Delta. Member, Iowa Supreme Court Board of Professional Ethics and Conduct, 1992-2001. *Member:* Polk County, Iowa State and American Bar Associations. ***PRACTICE AREAS:*** Copyright; Professional Liability; Insurance Coverage; Corporate Litigation; Business Litigation; General Practice.

STEVEN K. SCHARNBERG, born Muscatine, Iowa, May 13, 1949; admitted to bar, 1974, Iowa; U.S. District Court, Northern and Southern Districts of Iowa. *Education:* University of Iowa (B.A., with high distinction, 1971; J.D., 1974). Moot Court Board. Phi Beta Kappa; Phi Eta Sigma; Phi Kappa Psi. *Member:* Polk County, Iowa State and American Bar Associations; American Board of Trial Advocates; Iowa Defense Counsel. Fellow, Iowa Academy of Trial Lawyers. ***PRACTICE AREAS:*** Personal Injury; Professional Liability; Product Liability; Fire and Property Damage; Health Law.

DAVID C. CRAIG, born Des Moines, Iowa, April 11, 1947; admitted to bar, 1975, Iowa; U.S. Tax Court; U.S. District Court, Southern District of Iowa. *Education:* Regis University (B.S., magna cum laude, 1969); University of Iowa (J.D., with high distinction, 1975). Order of the Coif; Alpha Sigma Nu. *Member:* Polk County (President, 1999-2000), Iowa State (Member, Board of Governors, 2000—; Member, Sections on: Tax, Probate) and American (Member, Sections on: Taxation; Business) Bar Associations. [Lt. USNR, 1969-1972]. ***PRACTICE AREAS:*** Business Law; Estate Planning; Probate; Employee Benefits.

JOHN D. (JACK) HILMES, born Des Moines, Iowa, September 8, 1954; admitted to bar, 1979, Iowa; U.S. District Court, Northern and Southern Districts of Iowa; U.S. Court of Appeals, Eighth Circuit. *Education:* University of Northern Colorado (B.A., 1976); Drake University (J.D., 1979). Author: "The Continued Availability of The Open and Obvious Defense," Products Liability, Commentary and Cases, November, 1986. *Member:* Polk County, Iowa State and American Bar Associations; American Board of Trial Advocates; Defense Research Institute; Iowa Defense Counsel Association. Fellow: Iowa Academy of Trial Lawyers; American College of Trial Lawyers; C. Edwin Moore American Inn of Court (Master of the Bench). ***PRACTICE AREAS:*** Professional Malpractice; Product Liability; Insurance; Personal Injury.

R. TODD GAFFNEY, born Storm Lake, Iowa, November 11, 1953; admitted to bar, 1979, Iowa; 1994, Missouri; Iowa Supreme Court; Missouri Supreme Court; U.S. District Court, Northern and Southern Districts of Iowa; U.S. Court of Appeals, Eighth Circuit. *Education:* Drake University (B.S.B.A., 1976); John Marshall Law School and Drake University (J.D., 1979). Omicron Delta Kappa. Staff Member, Drake Law Review, 1978-1979. Law Clerk for Honorable Donald E. O'Brien, United States District Court, Northern and Southern Districts of Iowa, 1979-1981. Member, Drake University Board of Trustees, 1989-1995. *Member:* Polk County, Iowa State (Chair, Litigation Section, 1998-2000) and

(This Listing Continued)

FINLEY, ALT, SMITH, SCHARNBERG, CRAIG, HILMES & GAFFNEY, P.C., Des Moines—Continued

American Bar Associations; The Missouri Bar; Iowa Trial Lawyers; Defense Research Institute; Iowa Defense Counsel; National Association of Railroad Trial Counsel; The Association of Trial Lawyers of America; American Board of Trial Advocates. ***PRACTICE AREAS:*** Insurance Defense; Litigation; Railroad Law.

KERMIT B. ANDERSON, born Des Moines, Iowa, June 6, 1950; admitted to bar, 1975, Iowa; U.S. District Court, Northern and Southern Districts of Iowa; U.S. Court of Appeals, Eighth Circuit. *Education:* University of Iowa (B.B.A., with high distinction, 1972; J.D., 1975). Phi Delta Phi; Phi Eta Sigma; Beta Gamma Sigma. Law Clerk to Honorable William C. Stuart, U.S. District Court, Southern District of Iowa, 1975-1977. Assistant U.S. Attorney, 1977-1981 and U.S. Attorney, 1981-1982, Southern District of Iowa. *Member:* Polk County, Iowa State and American Bar Associations; Iowa Defense Counsel Association (Board of Editors, Defense Update, 1990—). ***PRACTICE AREAS:*** Civil Litigation; Insurance Defense; Insurance Law; Employment Law; Commercial Law.

KEVIN J. DRISCOLL, born Dubuque, Iowa, February 11, 1960; admitted to bar, 1988, Missouri; 1998, Iowa; 1999, Minnesota. *Education:* Loras College (B.A., cum laude, 1982); Drake University (J.D., with honors, 1987). Order of the Coif; Order of Barristers. Staff Member, Drake Law Review, 1987. *Member:* Polk County, Iowa State, Minnesota State and American Bar Associations; The Missouri Bar; The Association of Trial Lawyers of America. ***PRACTICE AREAS:*** Employment Law; Commercial Litigation; Construction Law; Products Liability; Professional Malpractice; Insurance Defense.

CONNIE L. DIEKEMA, born Pella, Iowa, May 27, 1961; admitted to bar, 1988, Iowa; 1990, U.S. District Court, Northern and Southern Districts of Iowa, U.S. Court of Appeals, Eighth Circuit and U.S. Tax Court. *Education:* Morningside College (B.S., 1983); Drake University (J.D., 1987); University of Osteopathic Medicine and Health Sciences (M.H.A., 1999). Member, Iowa Board of Governors (2005). *Member:* Polk County (Secretary, 1999, 2000; Treasurer, 2001; Vice-President, 2002; President Elect, 2003; President, 2004), Iowa State and American Bar Associations; Iowa Defense Counsel; Iowa Society of Healthcare Attorneys; Iowa Trial Lawyers Association. ***PRACTICE AREAS:*** Professional Malpractice; Personal Injury; Health Law. ***Email:*** mail@finleylaw.com

FREDERICK T. HARRIS, born Jefferson, Iowa, May 11, 1964; admitted to bar, 1994, Iowa, Nebraska and U.S. District Court, District of Nebraska; U.S. District Court, Northern and Southern Districts of Iowa; U.S. Court of Appeals, Eighth Circuit. *Education:* Loras College (B.A., magna cum laude, 1987); Drake University (M.B.A., 1989); Creighton University (J.D., 1993). *Member:* Iowa State, Nebraska State and American Bar Associations; Iowa Defense Counsel; Defense Research Institute.

BRIAN L. STOWE, born La Crosse, Wisconsin, February 11, 1972; admitted to bar, 2000, Iowa; 2001, Minnesota. *Education:* Wartburg College (B.A., 1994); Drake University (J.D., with honors, 2000). *Member:* Polk County, Iowa State, Minnesota State and American Bar Associations; Iowa Defense Counsel.

THOMAS J. JOENSEN, born Ames, Iowa, February 23, 1972; admitted to bar, 2003, Iowa. *Education:* Iowa State University (B.A., 1994); University of Iowa (M.A., 1997; J.D., 2003). Co-Author: "Model Act for Genetic Privacy and Conntrol (MAGPAC)," 88 Iowa Law Review 121 (2002). *Member:* Polk County, Iowa State and American Bar Associations.

KAMI M. LANG, born Baraboo, Wisconsin, October 9, 1976; admitted to bar, 2002, Iowa. *Education:* Loras College (B.A., magna cum laude, 1999); Drake University (J.D., with highest honors, 2002). Order of the Coif. Law Clerk to Hon. Robert Mahan, Iowa Court of Appeals. *Member:* Polk County, Iowa State and American Bar Associations.

ERIC G. HOCH, born Appleton, Wisconsin, June 17, 1974; admitted to bar, 2004, Iowa. *Education:* University of Iowa (B.A., 1997; J.D., with distinction, 2004). *Member:* Polk County, Iowa State and American Bar Associations. [Captain, U.S. Air Force, 1997-2001]

OF COUNSEL

KERRY A. FINLEY, born Iowa City, Iowa, June 15, 1965; admitted to bar, 1993, Iowa. *Education:* Dartmouth College (B.A., 1987); University of Iowa (J.D., with distinction, 1990). Phi Delta Phi. *Member:* Iowa State and American Bar Associations.

IOWA ATTORNEYS FOR: Midwest Medical Insurance Co.
DISTRICT ATTORNEYS FOR: Norfolk and Southern Railroad; Soo Line Railroad Company.
REPRESENTATIVE CLIENTS: Allied Insurance Group; American Society of Composers, Authors and Publishers; Catholic Health Initiatives Corporation; Chubb Insurance Companies; CIGNA; CNA; Farmers Mutual Hail Insurance Co.; Ford Motor Co.; Hy-Vee, Inc.; Iowa Methodist Medical Center; Mercy Hospital Medical Center; Midwest Medical Insurance Co.; Minnesota Lawyers Mutual Insurance Co.; Mutual Fire and Automobile Insurance Co.; PIC Wisconsin; Stephen R. Grubb Construction, Inc.; St. Paul Companies; Stivers Lincoln-Mercury; Travelers Property Casualty; The Wittern Group.
TRANSPORTATION CLIENTS: CP Rail System; Norfolk and Southern Railroad; Soo Line Railroad Co.; Chicago Central and Pacific Railroad.

REVISER OF THE IOWA LAW DIGEST FOR THIS DIRECTORY.

GALLIGAN, DOYLE & REID, P.C.

SUITE 5 THE PLAZA
300 WALNUT
DES MOINES, IOWA 50309-2292
Telephone: 515-282-3333; 1-800-217-9312
Fax: 515-282-0318
Email: lawyers@galliganlaw.com
URL: http://www.galliganlaw.com

Litigation, Medical Malpractice, Products Liability and Personal Injury.

MICHAEL J. GALLIGAN, born Syracuse, New York, July 14, 1942; admitted to bar, 1967, California; 1971, Iowa. *Education:* Drake University (B.A., 1964); Boalt Hall, University of California (J.D., 1967). Listed in: "Best Lawyers In America," Eighth Ed. (Personal Injury); Bar Register of Preeminent Lawyers (Medical Malpractice), 2000. Member: Advisory Committee, Rules of Civil Procedure, Iowa Supreme Court, 1983-1986; Supreme Court Committee on Costs of Litigation. Diplomate: National Board of Trial Advocacy; Board of Governors; National College of Advocacy, 1992-1997. Trustee, Civil Justice Foundation, 1993-1999; Faculty, N.C.A. Ultimate Trial Advocacy, June, 1994; Birth Trauma Litigation Group. *Member:* Polk County, Iowa State and American (Member Sections on: Litigation; Labor Law) Bar Associations; State Bar of California; Association of Trial Lawyers of Iowa (Chairman, Legal Education Committee, 1975-1978; Board of Governors, 1977-1992; President, 1983-1984); The Association of Trial Lawyers of America (State Delegate, 1983-1985; Board of Governors, 1986-1992). Fellow: Iowa Academy of Trial Lawyers; AIEG. [JAGC, U.S. Air Force, 1968-1971]. Certified as a Civil Trial Advocate by the National Board of Trial Advocacy. ***PRACTICE AREAS:*** Litigation; Medical Malpractice Law; Products Liability; Personal Injury Law. ***Email:*** mgalligan@galliganlaw.com

RICHARD H. DOYLE, born Elgin, Illinois, August 8, 1949; admitted to bar, 1976, Iowa, U.S. Court of Appeals, 8th Circuit and U.S. District Courts for the Northern and Southern Districts of Iowa; U.S. Supreme Court. *Education:* Drake University (B.A., 1971; J.D., 1976). Member, Drake Law Review. Assistant Attorney General, State of Iowa, 1976-1977. *Member:* Polk County; Iowa State and American Bar Associations; Iowa Trial Lawyers Association; The Association of Trial Lawyers of America; Lincoln Inn of Court. Fellow, Iowa Academy of Trial Lawyers. [U.S. Army, 1971-1973]. ***PRACTICE AREAS:*** Personal Injury Law. ***Email:*** rdoyle@galliganlaw.com

TIMM W. REID, born Des Moines, Iowa, September 7, 1963; admitted to bar, 1989, Iowa; U.S. District Court, Northern and Southern Districts of Iowa and U.S. Court of Appeals, Eighth Circuit. *Education:* Bob Jones University (B.A., 1986); Drake University (J.D., 1989). Recipient, Defense Fund, National Litigation Academy graduate and Honor Guard, 2001, 2004—. Chief Counsel, Iowa Liberty and Justice Center, 2001—. *Member:* Polk County, Iowa State and American Bar Associations; Iowa Trial Lawyers Association (Member, Board of Governors, 1994-1998; Legislative Committee, 1992-1998); The Association of Trial Lawyers of America (Member, Key Person Committee, 1995-1998). ***PRACTICE AREAS:*** Personal Injury; Products Liability; Medical Negligence. ***Email:*** treid@galliganlaw.com

---

BRIAN P. GALLIGAN, born Des Moines, Iowa, October 10, 1974; admitted to bar, 2000, Iowa; U.S. District Court, Northern and Southern Districts of Iowa. *Education:* Colorado College (B.A., 1997); University of Iowa (J.D., 2000). Order of the Coif. *Member:* Polk County, Iowa State and American Bar Associations; Iowa Trial Lawyers Association (Member, CLE Committee, 2004—); The Association of Trial Lawyers of America (National College of Advocacy, Advocate). ***PRACTICE AREAS:*** Personal Injury; Products Liability; Medical Malpractice. ***Email:*** bgalligan@galliganlaw.com

JOSEPH MICHAEL GALLIGAN, born West Point, New York, December 11, 1969; admitted to bar, 2002, Iowa. *Education:* Cornell College (B.S.S., 1997); Drake University School of Law (J.D., 2001). [US Navy, 1991-1993, SN]. ***Email:*** jgalligan@galliganlaw.com

OF COUNSEL

JAMES A. ALBERT, born Cedar Rapids, Iowa, July 2, 1947; admitted to bar, 1976, Iowa; 1978, U.S. Court of Military Appeals; 1979, U.S. Tax Court. *Education:* Drake University (B.F.A., 1971); University of Notre Dame Law School (J.D., 1976). Order of the Coif; Delta Theta Phi; Alpha Epsilon Rho. Attorney Advisor, Federal Communications Commission, Washington, D.C., 1976-1978. Professor, University of South Dakota, 1978-1981. Professor of the Year: University of South Dakota, 1979. Professor of Law, Drake University, 1981—. Leland Stanford Forest Outstanding Law Professor of the Year, Drake University Law School, 1983; 1988; 1999; 2000; 2003; 2004. Outstanding Law Professor in the Nation, Delta Theta Phi, 1989; 1999; 2001. Iowa Supreme Court Sesquicentennial Committee, 1988-1989. Chairman, Iowa Ethics and Campaign Disclosure Board, 2001—. Author: *The Broadcaster's Legal Guide*, Pluribus Books, 1985; *Pay Dirt*, Branden Press, 1989; *Jim Bakker:* Miscarriage of Justice? Carus Publishing Co., 1997; *Potomac Meltdown*, 2004. *Member:* Iowa State and American Bar Associations; Iowa Trial Lawyers Association; The Association of Trial Lawyers of America; Notre Dame Law Association. ***PRACTICE AREAS:*** Personal Injury; Products Liability.

REFERENCE: US Bank.

GAUDINEER, COMITO & GEORGE, L.L.P.

P.O. BOX 4628
DES MOINES, IOWA 50306
Telephone: 515-327-1750
Fax: 515-327-1250
Email: gaudineercomito@qwest.net
URL: http://www.gaudineercomitogeorge.com

General Civil, Trial and Appellate Practice in State and Federal Courts. Corporation, Insurance, Labor, Municipal, Administrative, Workers' Compensation, Employment, Civil Rights, Probate, Real Estate, Taxation, Personal Injury, Product Liability and Criminal.

MEMBERS OF FIRM

LEE H. GAUDINEER, JR., born Des Moines, Iowa, March 10, 1932; admitted to bar, 1958, Iowa; U.S. District Court, Northern and Southern Districts of Iowa, U.S. Court of Appeals, Eighth Circuit, U.S. Supreme Court and U.S. Tax Court. *Education:* Grinnell College (B.A., 1957); Drake University (J.D., 1958); University of Missouri (LL.M., 1967). Delta Theta Phi. Author: "Ethics: The Grievance Commission," Drake Law Review, 1972; "Ethics: The Zealous Advocate," 24 Drake Law Review 79, 1974; "Ethics and Malpractice," 26 Drake Law Review 99, 1976-1977. Member: Iowa House of Representatives,

(This Listing Continued)

1965-1967; Iowa Senate, 1967-1972. Minority Leader, Iowa Senate, 1970-1972. Member, Supreme Court Budget Committee, 1988-1999. Lecturer, Drake University College of Law, 1974—. *Member:* Polk County, Iowa State (Member, Committees on: Workmen's Compensation, 1966-1970; Public Relations, 1966-1970) and American Bar Associations.

FRANK A. COMITO, born Des Moines, Iowa, July 8, 1939; admitted to bar, 1963, Iowa; U.S. District Court, Northern and Southern Districts of Iowa; U.S. Court of Appeals, Eighth Circuit; U.S. Supreme Court; U.S. Court of Military Appeals. *Education:* Drake University (B.A., 1961; LL.B., 1963). Adjunct Professor: Post-Graduate Trial Advocacy, Drake University Law School, 1983. Assistant Polk County Attorney, 1965-1967. *Member:* Iowa State Bar Association (Member, Ethics Counsel, 1982-1984); Iowa Academy of Trial Lawyers; Association of Trial Lawyers of Iowa; Iowa Defense Counsel Association; Defense Research and Trial Lawyers Association; Blackstone Inn of Court, Fellow, Charter Institute of Arbitrators. [U.S. Army (Iowa National Guard), 1963-1965; Grade Specialist Forth Class; U.S. Navy Reserve, 1965—, Lieut. Cmdr.]

TOM W. GEORGE, born Oskaloosa, Iowa, May 20, 1940; admitted to bar, 1965, Iowa and U.S. District Court, Southern and Northern Districts of Iowa. *Education:* University of Iowa (B.B.A., 1962); Drake University (J.D., 1965). *Member:* Iowa State Bar Association (Member; Sections on: Probate; Real Estate; Litigation). [JAGC, USNR]. ***PRACTICE AREAS:*** Real Estate; Probate; Litigation.

CARLTON G. SALMONS, born Beloit, Wisconsin, October 13, 1947; admitted to bar, 1976, Iowa; U.S. District Court, Northern and Southern Districts of Iowa; U.S. Court of Appeals, Seventh and Eighth Circuits; U.S. Supreme Court. *Education:* Illinois State University (B.S., summa cum laude, 1973); Drake University (J.D., 1975). Assistant Attorney General of Iowa, 1977-1978. *Member:* Polk County, Iowa State and American Bar Associations.

JON K. SWANSON, born Des Moines, Iowa, September 3, 1954; admitted to bar, 1979, Iowa; U.S. District Court, Northern and Southern Districts of Iowa; U.S. Court of Appeals, Eighth Circuit; U.S. Supreme Court. *Education:* University of South Dakota (B.S., cum laude, 1976); University of Iowa (J.D., with distinction, 1979). Phi Delta Phi. Assistant Attorney General, Iowa, 1979-1982. *Member:* Polk County, Iowa State and American Bar Associations; Iowa Defense Counsel Association; Defense Research Institute; Iowa Association of Workers' Compensation Lawyers.

PATRICK J. HOPKINS, born Storm Lake, Iowa, September 14, 1950; admitted to bar, 1975, Iowa and Nebraska; 1982, District of Columbia; U.S. District Court, Northern and Southern Districts of Iowa; U.S. Court of Appeals, Eighth Circuit. *Education:* University of Iowa (B.A., 1972); Creighton University (J.D., 1975). Assistant Attorney General of Iowa, 1982-1985. Litigation Department Solicitor, City of Des Moines Legal Department, 1986-1989. Member: League of Municipalities; Blackstone Inn of Court, 1989-1992. *Member:* Polk County, Iowa State, Nebraska State and American Bar Associations; The District of Columbia Bar.

WILLIAM W. SCHWARZ, born Des Moines, Iowa, 1948; admitted to bar, 1979, Iowa, U.S. District Court, Northern and Southern Districts of Iowa and U.S. Court of Appeals, Eighth Circuit; 1982, U.S. Supreme Court. *Education:* University of North Dakota, University of Iowa and Drake University (B.S., 1971); Drake University (J.D., 1979). *Member:* Polk County, Iowa State (Member, Workers Compensation Section) and American Bar Associations; Iowa Defense Counsel Association; Defense Research Institute; Iowa Association of Workers Compensation Lawyers. ***Email:*** williamwschwarz@qwest.net

KENT A. GUMMERT, born Radcliffe, Iowa, August 15, 1966; admitted to bar, 1993, Iowa, U.S. District Court, Northern and Southern Districts of Iowa; U.S. Court of Appeals, Eighth Circuit. *Education:* Iowa State University (B.S., 1990); Drake University (J.D., 1992). Delta Theta Phi. *Member:* Polk County, Iowa State and American Bar Associations.

REPRESENTATIVE CLIENTS: Casey's General Stores, Inc.; Correctional Medical Services; First Mercury Insurance Syndicate, Southfield, Michigan; Fremont Indemnity Co., Los Angeles, California; Great American Insurance Company, Cincinnati, Ohio; The Hartford Insurance Group; Heartland Insurance Risk Pool; Iowa Communities' Assurance Pool; Iowa Jaycees; The Maytag Co., Newton, Iowa; National Casualty Company, Scottsdale, Arizona; Ohio Casualty Group; Reliance Insurance Company; Schwan's Sales Enterprises; Scottsdale Insurance Company, Scottsdale, Arizona.

GISLASON & HUNTER LLP

Established in 1937

LIBERTY BUILDING
418 SIXTH AVENUE, SUITE 1210
DES MOINES, IOWA 50309
Telephone: 515-244-6199
Facsimile: 515-244-6493.
URL: http://www.gislason.com

New Ulm, Minnesota Office: 2700 South Broadway, P.O. Box 458. Telephone: 507-354-3111. Facsimile: 507-354-8447.
Minneapolis, Minnesota Office: Suite 215E, 9900 Bren Road East, P.O. Box 5297. Telephone: 952-933-9900. Facsimile: 952-933-0242.
Mankato, Minnesota Office: Landkamer Building, Suite 200, 124 East Walnut Street, P.O. Box 4157. Telephone: 507-387-1115. Facsimile: 507-387-4413.

General Practice including Agricultural Law, Alternate Dispute Resolution, Banking Law, Bankruptcy, Commercial Law, Corporate Law, Environmental Law, Estate Planning, Family Law, Health Law, Insurance, Labor Law, Medical Malpractice, Personal Injury, Wills and Probate, Product Liability, Real Estate, Trial Law, Workers' Compensation.

FIRM PROFILE: Gislason & Hunter LLP, has been serving clients across the Midwest for more than sixty years. With offices in Des Moines, the Twin Cities, New Ulm, Mankato and Mapleton, the firm and its lawyers are active members of those communities. With its diverse experience in litigation, corporate, ADR, commercial, agricultural, and probate and estate matters, Gislason & Hunter is uniquely positioned to respond to the needs of its clients in the Midwest. Gislason & Hunter is committed to working in a cooperative manner in order to achieve excellent client results in the most efficient and cost effective manner possible.

(This Listing Continued)

MEMBERS OF FIRM

BARRY G. VERMEER, born 1955; admitted to bar, 1980, Minnesota; 1998, Iowa; U.S. District Court, District of Minnesota and Northern District of Illinois; U.S. District Court, Northern and Southern Districts of Iowa; U.S. Court of Appeals, Eighth Circuit. *Education:* University of Iowa (B.A., with high distinction, 1977); University of Minnesota (J.D., cum laude, 1980). *Member:* American Board of Trial Advocates. ***LANGUAGES:*** Spanish. ***Email:*** bvermeer@gislason.com

GARY W. KOCH, born 1954; admitted to bar, 1979, Iowa; 1981, Minnesota; 1991, Wisconsin; U.S. District Court, District of Minnesota and Northern District of Iowa; U.S. Court of Appeals, Eighth Circuit; U.S. Supreme Court. *Education:* University of Iowa (B.A., 1976; J.D., 1979). ***Email:*** gkoch@gislason.com

ROGER H. GROSS, born 1950; admitted to bar, 1984, Minnesota; U.S. District Court, District of Minnesota; U.S. Court of Appeals, Eighth Circuit; 2005, Iowa. *Education:* University of Minnesota (B.S., with distinction, 1978); William Mitchell College of Law (J.D., 1984). ***Email:*** rgross@gislason.com

REED H. GLAWE, born 1961; admitted to bar, 1986, Iowa, Minnesota and U.S. District Court, District of Minnesota; U.S. Court of Appeals, Eighth Circuit. *Education:* Iowa State University (B.S., with distinction, 1983); University of Iowa (J.D., with high distinction, 1986). Order of the Coif. ***Email:*** rglawe@gislason.com

WADE R. WACHOLZ, born 1960; admitted to bar, 1987, Minnesota and U.S. District Court, District of Minnesota; 2002, Iowa. *Education:* Concordia College (B.A., magna cum laude, 1982); Valparaiso University School of Law; University of Minnesota (J.D., cum laude, 1986). ***Email:*** wwacholz@gislason.com

LAURA L. MYSLIS, born 1956; admitted to bar, 1985, Minnesota; U.S. District Court, District of Minnesota; U.S. Court of Appeals, Eighth Circuit; 2002, Iowa. *Education:* Northwestern University (B.A., 1978); William Mitchell College of Law (J.D., 1985). ***Email:*** lmyslis@gislason.com

ANDREW A. WILLAERT, born 1958; admitted to bar, 1983, Minnesota; U.S. District Court, District of Minnesota; 2004, Iowa. *Education:* St. John's University (B.S., 1980); William Mitchell College of Law (J.D., 1983). ***Email:*** awillaert@gislason.com

DUSTAN J. CROSS, born 1969; admitted to bar, 1994, Iowa and Minnesota; 1995, U.S. District Court, District of Minnesota; 1998, U.S. Court of Appeals, Eighth Circuit. *Education:* University of Notre Dame (B.A., 1991); University of Iowa (J.D., with high honors, 1994) Order of the Coif. ***Email:*** dcross@gislason.com

LOREE A. NELSON, born 1957; admitted to bar, 1994, Iowa; U.S. District Court, Northern and Southern Districts of Iowa. *Education:* Weber State College (B.S., in Health Care Administration, magna cum laude, 1986); Drake University (J.D., with honors, 1994). Order of the Coif. Adjunct Professor, Drake Law School. ***Email:*** lnelson@gislason.com

---

JAMES R. GOWLING, born 1942; admitted to bar, 1969, Minnesota; U.S. District Court, District of Minnesota; 1970, U.S. Court of Appeals, Eighth Circuit; 1978, U.S. Supreme Court; 2003, Iowa; U.S. District Court, Northern and Southern Districts of Iowa. *Education:* Macalester College (B.A., 1964); William Mitchell College of Law (J.D., 1969). ***Email:*** jgowling@gislason.com

PETER M. SAND, born 1966; admitted to bar, 1993, Iowa and Illinois; 1994, U.S. District Court, Northern and Southern Districts of Iowa. *Education:* St. Ambrose College (B.A., History, 1987); Creighton University Law School (J.D., cum laude, 1993). ***Email:*** psand@gislason.com

REPRESENTATIVE CLIENTS: Affiliated Community Medical Centers; AgriBank, FCB; AgQuest Financial Services, Inc.; AgStar Financial Services; Alliance Bank; All American Foods, Inc.; Alpha Wireless Communications, Inc.; Alternative Insurance Management; American Artstone Company; American Mart Corporation; Americana Community Bank; Associated Milk Producers, Inc.; Auto-Owners Insurance Co.; Bank Midwest; Camden Physicians; Chicago Blackhawk Hockey Team; Christensen Family Farms; Citizens Bank Minnesota; Cysteel Manufacturing, Inc.; Davis Family Dairies; Deluca/Monarch Beverages of Las Vegas; Employers Mutual Casualty Co.; Fairview-University Hospitals; Farm Credit Leasing; Farm Credit Services; Farmers Home Group; Farmers Insurance Group; Farmland Mutual Insurance Co.; First Miami Bancorp, Inc.; First National Bank & Trust; First Security Trust & Savings Bank; Forman Realty Corporation; Frandsen Bank & Trust; Grinnell Mutual Reinsurance Co.; Harvest States Cooperatives; Heymann Construction Co.; Hickory Tech Internet; A.J. Hoffman & Sons, Inc.; Honeymead Products Co.; Hubbard Feeds Inc.; McLeod Bancshares, Inc.; Metropolitan Life Insurance Co.; Midwest Medical Insurance Co.; Mutual Service Insurance Co.; North Memorial Health Care; Northland Capital Financial Services; Palmer Bus Services; Pioneer Bank; Rabo AgServices, Inc.; St. Paul Companies; South Miami Corporation; United Center; University of Minnesota; Upper Midwest Management Company; U.S. Bank, N.A.; Valley Bank & Trust; Vetter Stone Co.; Wal-Mart Stores, Inc.; Wells Fargo; Wirtz Corporation; Zurich Insurance.
REFERENCES: Citizens Bank Minnesota; Alliance Bank, New Ulm; Frandsen Bank & Trust.

(For Biographical Data on other Personnel, see Professional Biographies at Minneapolis and Mankato, Minnesota)

GOODMAN & ASSOCIATES, P.C.

Established in 2001

P.O. BOX 12091
DES MOINES, IOWA 50312
Telephone: 515-267-8600
Facsimile: 515-224-2075
Email: jeff@gdmnlaw.com
URL: http://www.goodmanandassoc.com

West Des Moines Office: 1501 42nd Street, Suite 300, 50266. Telephone: 515-267-8600. Fax: 515-224-2075.

Civil Trial Practice, Products Liability, Design Defect Litigation, Construction Law, Employment Law, Commercial Law, State, County and Municipal Law, Professional Liability, Insurance Defense, Wrongful Death, Personal Injury.

JEFFREY L. GOODMAN, born Marshalltown, Iowa, January 12, 1959; admitted to bar, 1985, Iowa; 2002, Nebraska; U.S. District Court, Northern and Southern Districts of

(This Listing Continued)

GOODMAN & ASSOCIATES, P.C., Des Moines—Continued

Iowa; U.S. District Court, Northern and Southern Districts of Nebraska; U.S. Court of Appeals, Eighth Circuit; U.S. Supreme Court. *Education:* St. Olaf College; University of Iowa (B.A., 1981); Drake University (J.D., 1985). Co-Author: "The Attorney-Client Privilege and the Municipal Lawyer," 48 Drake L. Rev. 655 (2000). Speaker: International Municipal Lawyer Association, 65th Annual Meeting; American Bar Association, State and Local Government Section Meeting. Guest Lecturer: Drake Law School; Lorman, Cambridge and National Business Institute seminars. Assistant Black Hawk County Attorney, 1985-1987. Assistant U.S. Attorney, Northern District of Iowa, 1987-1988. Assistant City Attorney, City of West Des Moines, 1995. City Attorney, City of West Des Moines, 1996-1998. Commissioner, 5-C Judicial Nominating Commission, 1996-2002. *Member:* Polk County and Iowa State Bar Associations; Iowa Defense Counsel; Defense Research Institute; American Trial Lawyers Association; Iowa Trial Lawyers Association; Former Barrister, C. Edwin Moore Inn of Court, 2000-2002; Blackstone Inn of Court, 1991-1993. **Email:** jeff@gdmnlaw.com

---

MARCY A. O'BRIEN, born Sioux City, Iowa, March 1, 1970; admitted to bar, 1995, Iowa; 1996, U.S. Court of Appeals, Eighth Circuit and U.S. District Court, Northern and Southern Districts of Iowa. *Education:* Iowa State University (B.A., with distinction, 1992); University of Iowa (J.D., with distinction, 1995). Phi Beta Kappa, Phi Kappa Phi. Author, "Jenson v. Eveleth Co.: A Legal Standard for Class Action Sexual Harassment," Journal of Corporation Law, 1994. *Member:* Polk County, Iowa State and American Bar Associations. **Email:** marcy@gdmnlaw.com

GRETCHEN R. JENSEN, born Des Moines, Iowa, February 1, 1973; admitted to bar, 1998, Iowa and U.S. District Court, Northern and Southern Districts of Iowa. *Education:* University of Iowa (B.A., 1995); Drake University (J.D., with honors, 1998). Member, Drake Law Review, 1996-1998 (Associate Editor, 1997-1998). Co-Author, "What me? Prejudiced? Absolutely Not!," TRIAL, December, 2000. *Member:* Polk County, Iowa State (Labor and Employment Sections) and American Bar Associations; Iowa Trial Lawyers Association; Association of Trial Lawyers of America. **Email:** gretchen@gdmnlaw.com

---

THE GRAHAM LAW FIRM

A PROFESSIONAL CORPORATION
630 EQUITABLE BUILDING
604 LOCUST STREET
DES MOINES, IOWA 50309
Telephone: 515-282-0230
Fax: 515-282-4235
Email: wwg@grahamlawiowa.com
URL: http://www.wgrahamlaw.com

General Civil Practice. Trials and Appeals in all Courts. Business and Commercial Litigation. Corporate, Business, Employment, Products Liability and Construction Law.

WILLIAM W. GRAHAM, born Des Moines, Iowa, August 9, 1952; admitted to bar, 1977, Iowa; U.S. District Court, Northern and Southern Districts of Iowa; U.S. Court of Appeals, Eighth Circuit; U.S. Supreme Court. *Education:* University of Pennsylvania (B.A., cum laude, 1974); Boston College (J.D., 1977). *Member:* Polk County, Iowa State and American (Member, Sections on: Litigation; Business Law) Bar Associations. American Inns of Court (Master, C. Edwin Moore Inn of Court). ***PRACTICE AREAS:*** Civil Litigation; Business Law.

GREFE & SIDNEY, P.L.C.

Established in 1971
2222 GRAND AVENUE
P.O. BOX 10434
DES MOINES, IOWA 50306
Telephone: 515-245-4300
Fax: 515-245-4452
Email: grandfirm@grefesidney.com
URL: http://www.grefesidney.com

Pella, Iowa Office: 810 Washington Street, 50219. Telephone: 641-628-4300.

General Civil and Trial Practice in all State and Federal Courts. Appellate Practice, Product Liability, Insurance, Negligence, Environmental, Toxic Torts, Professional Liability, Employment, Discrimination, Personal Injury, Workers Compensation, Real Estate, Probate and Estate Planning, Corporate Practice, Family Law, Commercial Litigation and Elder Law.

FIRM PROFILE: Grefe & Sidney, P.L.C. has established itself as a litigation firm in both defense and plaintiff's matters, as well as offering a business, corporate and tax division having a broad range of experience. The firm is listed in the Martindale-Hubbell Bar Register of Preeminent Lawyers.

THOMAS W. CARPENTER, born Harlan, Iowa, June 17, 1932; admitted to bar, 1960, Iowa. *Education:* Grinnell College (B.A., 1954); University of Iowa (J.D., 1960). Phi Delta Phi; Phi Beta Kappa. *Member:* Polk County, Iowa State (Chairman, Committee on Taxation, 1981-1984) and American Bar Associations. Fellow: American Bar Foundation; American College of Trust and Estate Counsel. ***PRACTICE AREAS:*** Tax Law; Trusts and Estates; Wills; Probate. **Email:** tcarpenter@grefesidney.com

HENRY A. HARMON, born Fulton, Missouri, February 10, 1940; admitted to bar, 1965, Iowa. *Education:* Northwestern University and Drake University (B.A., 1962); University of Minnesota (J.D., 1965). *Member:* Polk County, Iowa State (Member, Supreme Court Advisory Committee on Rules, 1979-1982; Member, Board of Governors, 1988-1992; Chairman, Litigation Section, 1998) and American Bar Associations; Iowa Defense Counsel Association; Iowa Academy of Trial Lawyers; American Bar Foundation; Iowa State Bar Foundation; American Board of Trial Advocates. [CDR, JAGC, USNR]. **Email:** hharmon@grefesidney.com

STEPHEN D. HARDY, born Washington, Iowa, November 17, 1949; admitted to bar, 1974, Iowa. *Education:* University of Iowa (B.A., 1971; J.D., with distinction, 1974). Phi Delta Phi. Editor, Iowa Advocate, 1972-1974. Member, DMACC Legal Assistant Advisory Board, 1988-1995, 2000—. *Member:* Polk County, Iowa State (Chairman, Committee on Legal Assistants, 1993-2000) and American Bar Associations; Iowa Defense Counsel Association; Defense Research Institute. **Email:** shardy@grefesidney.com

ROBERT C. THOMSON, born Highland Park, Illinois, January 23, 1948; admitted to bar, 1973, Iowa. *Education:* University of Iowa (B.B.A., 1970); Drake University (J.D., 1973). *Member:* Polk County, Iowa State (Chair, Corporate Counsel Section, 1998-2000; Member, Sections on: Business Law; Labor and Employment; Commercial and Bankruptcy Law; Real Estate and Title Law; Probate and Trust) and American (Member, Sections on: Business Law; Real Property, Probate and Trust) Bar Associations. **Email:** rthomson@grefesidney.com

CRAIG S. SHANNON, born Burbank, California, November 6, 1953; admitted to bar, 1978, Iowa. *Education:* Dordt College (A.B., summa cum laude, 1975); Drake University (J.D., 1978). Member: Christian Legal Society; Noon Estate and Financial Planners. *Member:* Polk County and Iowa State (Member, Sections on: Business Law; Real Estate and Title; Taxation; Probate and Trust) Bar Associations; Iowa Trust Association; Lincoln Inne. ***PRACTICE AREAS:*** Estate Planning; Trusts and Estates; Corporate Law; Real Estate; Taxation. **Email:** cshannon@grefesidney.com

PATRICK J. McNULTY, born Jefferson, Iowa, August 29, 1951; admitted to bar, 1977, Iowa. *Education:* University of Iowa (B.A., 1974; J.D., 1977). Co-Author: "Liability for Aiding and Abetting by Silence of Inaction: An Unfounded Doctrine," 29 Tort and Ins. L.J. 14 (1993); "The Privacy Disclosure Tort and the First Amendment: Should the Community Decide Newsworthiness?" 64 Iowa Law Review 185, 1979. Author: "Dalia v. United States: The Validity of Covert Entry," 65 Iowa Law Review 931, 1980; "The Gertz Fault Standard and the Common Law of Defamation: An Argument for Predictability of Result and Certainty of Expectations," 35 Drake Law Review 51, 1986; "Central Bank of Denver v. First Interstate Bank of Denver: The End of Aiding and Abetting Liability Under Section 10 (b)," 29 Tort and Ins, L.J. 847 (1994); "The Law of Defamation: A Primer for the Iowa Practitioner," 44 Drake Law Review 639 (1996); "The Public Disclosure of Private Facts: There is Life After Florida Star," 50 Drake Law Review 93 (2001). *Member:* Polk County, Iowa State and American Bar Associations; Iowa Academy of Trial Lawyers. ***PRACTICE AREAS:*** Civil Practice; Trial Practice; Workers Compensation. **Email:** pmcnulty@grefesidney.com

MARK W. THOMAS, born Omaha, Nebraska, May 7, 1955; admitted to bar, 1981, Nebraska; 1986, Iowa. *Education:* Drake University (B.A., magna cum laude, 1977); Creighton University (J.D., cum laude, 1981). Phi Beta Kappa. Student Articles Editor, Creighton Law Review, 1980-1981. Author: Note, Vol. 13 Creighton Law Review, 1980. *Member:* Polk County, Nebraska State, Iowa and American Bar Associations. [JAG, USAF, 1982-1986; Lt.Col., Iowa Air National Guard, 1987—]. ***PRACTICE AREAS:*** Personal Injury; Employment Law. **Email:** mthomas@grefesidney.com

GUY R. COOK, born Des Moines, Iowa, August 23, 1956; admitted to bar, 1982, Iowa; U.S. District Court, Northern and Southern Districts of Iowa; U.S. Court of Appeals, Eighth Circuit; U.S. Court of Federal Claims; U.S. Tax Court. *Education:* University of Iowa (B.A., 1979); Drake University (J.D., 1981). Law Clerk to Hon. J.L. Larson, Justice, Supreme Court of Iowa, 1983-1987. Assistant U.S. Attorney, Southern District of Iowa, 1983-1987. Member, Merit Selection Panel, U.S. Magistrate Judge, Southern District of Iowa, 1994-1995. *Member:* Polk County (Chair, Continuing Legal Education Committee, 1995—; Board of Directors, 2000-2001; Treasurer, 2001-2003; President-Elect, 2004), Iowa State (Member, Federal Practice Committee, 1988-1998; Litigation Resources, 1997-1998; Iowa Civil Jury Instruction Committee, 1997— Editor, Federal Practice Manual, 1994), Federal and American (Member, Litigation Section) Bar Associations; American Judicature Society; Iowa Trial Lawyers Association; The Association of Trial Lawyers of America; Million Dollar Advocates Forum. Fellow, Iowa Academy of Trial Lawyers; American Board of Trial Advocates; Senior Counsel, American College of Barristers. (Board Certified Civil Trial Advocacy Specialist by the National Board of Trial Advocacy). ***PRACTICE AREAS:*** Personal Injury; Insurance; Trial Practice. **Email:** gcook@grefesidney.com

ANDREW D. HALL, born Aurora, Illinois, November 11, 1964; admitted to bar, 1990, Iowa. *Education:* Stanford University (B.A., 1987); University of Iowa (J.D., with distinction, 1990). Phi Delta Phi. Recipient, American Jurisprudence Award for Excellence in Criminal Procedure. Member, 1989-1990, Iowa Law Review. *Member:* Polk County, Iowa State and American Bar Associations. **Email:** ahall@grefesidney.com

DONNA R. MILLER, born Aberdeen Proving Grounds, Maryland, January 13, 1971; admitted to bar, 1995, Iowa. *Education:* Northeast Missouri State University (B.S., 1992); University of Iowa (J.D., 1995). Member, Order of the Coif. Law Clerk, 5th Judicial District of Iowa, 1995-1996. Law Clerk, U.S. District Court, Northern District of Iowa Chief Judge, Michael J. Melloy, 1996-1997. Author: "Unconstitutional Democracy: Ends and Means in Boris Yeltsin's Russia" 4. Transnational Law & Contemporary Problems 873. *Member:* Polk County, Iowa State and American Bar Associations; Iowa Defense Council Association. ***PRACTICE AREAS:*** Civil Litigation. **Email:** dmiller@grefesidney.com

---

MICHAEL A. CARMONEY, born Ashland, Ohio, March 9, 1966; admitted to bar, 1999, Iowa. *Education:* Wittenberg University (B.A., cum laude, 1987); Drake University (J.D., with high honors, 1999). Author: "When are Heart Attacks Compensable Injuries Under Iowa Workers' Compensation Law?," 49 Drake L.Rev 621, 2001. *Member:* Polk County and Iowa State Bar Associations; Blackstone Inn of Court. **Email:** mcarmoney@grefesidney.com

CLARK I. MITCHELL, born Davenport, Iowa, October 2, 1968; admitted to bar, 2000, Iowa; 2002, U.S. District Court, Southern and Northern Districts of Iowa. *Education:* Drake University (B.A., 1991; J.D., with honors, 2000). *Member:* Polk County, Iowa State and American Bar Associations; Iowa Defense Counsel Association. **Email:** cmitchell@grefesidney.com

(This Listing Continued)

LISA RENEE LEMONS PERDUE, born Des Moines, Iowa, August 15, 1975; admitted to bar, 2000, California and Iowa. *Education:* University of Northern Iowa (B.A., History, 1997); Drake University (J.D., 2000). Order of the Barristers, Spring 2000. Recipient: Rodney L. Hudson Senior Advocacy Award, Spring 2000; Davis Award for Excellence, Spring 2000. *Member:* Polk County, Iowa State and American Bar Associations. **Email:** lperdue@grefesidney.com

NICHOLAS J. MAURO, born Des Moines, Iowa, August 27, 1976; admitted to bar, 2002, Iowa. *Education:* University of Iowa (B.A., 1999; J.D., 2002). *Member:* Polk County, Iowa State and American Bar Associations. ***PRACTICE AREAS:*** Litigation. **Email:** nmauro@grefesidney.com

ANITA L. DHAR, born Iowa Falls, Iowa, August 8, 1977; admitted to bar, 2002, Iowa. *Education:* University of Iowa (B.S., Psychology, 1999); University of Iowa College of Law (J.D., 2002). Law Clerk, to Judge Robert W. Pratt, U.S. District Court for the Southern District of Iowa. *Member:* Polk County, Iowa State and American Bar Associations; Polk County Women Attorneys. ***PRACTICE AREAS:*** Litigation. **Email:** adhar@grefesidney.com

JEFFREY P. FISHER, born Decatur, Illinois, October 28, 1977; admitted to bar, 2003, Iowa. *Education:* Iowa State University (B.A., 2000); Hamline University School of Law (J.D., cum laude, 2003). *Member:* Polk County, Iowa State and American Bar Associations. **Email:** jfisher@grefesidney.com

SAMANTHA S. WILLETS, born Fort Dodge, Iowa, June 24, 1978; admitted to bar, 2003, Iowa. *Education:* University of Iowa (B.B.A., Accounting, 1999); Drake University Law School (J.D., 2003). Certified Public Accountant, 2001. Member: American Association of Attorney Certified Public Accountants, 2002; Iowa Society of CPA's. *Member:* Polk County, Iowa State and American Bar Associations; Polk County Women Attorneys. ***PRACTICE AREAS:*** Business Law. **Email:** swillets@grefesidney.com

AMY E. H. MILLER, born Burlington, Iowa, November 26, 1976; admitted to bar, 2004, Iowa. *Education:* Central College (B.A., 1999); Drake University (J.D., 2003). *Member:* Polk County and Iowa State Bar Associations. **Email:** amiller@grefesidney.com

E JACOB CUMMINGS, born Iowa City, Iowa, November 18, 1976; admitted to bar, 2004, Iowa. *Education:* University of Northern Iowa (B.A., 1999); Drake University (J.D., 2003). Delta Theta Phi. Member, Blackstone Inn of Court; Moot Court Board. Member, Drake University Law Review, 2002-2003. Law Clerk, to the Honorable Robert E. Mahan, Iowa Court of Appeals. *Member:* Polk County, Iowa State and American Bar Associations. **Email:** ecummings@grefesidney.com

ARTHUR KRIMSKY, born Tashkent, Uzbekistan, July 15, 1978; admitted to bar, 2004, Iowa. *Education:* Wartburg College (B.A., 1999); Drake Law School (J.D., 2004). *Member:* American, Iowa State and Polk County Bar Associations; The Association of Trial Lawyers of America. **Email:** akrimsky@grefesidney.com

JULIA L. ROOSE, born Pella, Iowa, January 22, 1976; admitted to bar, 2001, Iowa. *Education:* University of Northern Iowa (B.A., 1998); Drake University Law School (J.D., 2001). Order of the Coif. *Member:* Polk County, Iowa State and American Bar Associations. ***PRACTICE AREAS:*** Family Law. **Email:** jroose@grefesidney.com

---

JOHN WERNER, born Iowa City, Iowa, September 27, 1948; admitted to bar, 1973, Iowa. *Education:* Drake University (B.A., 1970); Drew University and London School of Economics and Political Science, London, England; University of Iowa (J.D., with high distinction, 1973). Order of the Coif. Editor-in-Chief, Iowa Law Review, Vol. 58. Author: "Perspectives on the Administration of Criminal Justice in Iowa," 57 Iowa Law Review 590, 1972. Special Assistant to the Attorney General of Iowa, Tort Claims Division, 1979-1980. *Member:* Polk County, Iowa State and American Bar Associations; Iowa Academy of Trial Lawyers; Iowa Defense Counsel Association; Defense Research Institute. **Email:** jwerner@grefesidney.com

ROLLAND E. GREFE (1920-2004)

REPRESENTATIVE CLIENTS: Adventurelands of America; Allied Mutual Group; Caseys General Stores, Inc.; Federal Express; Montgomery Elevator; Otis Elevator; Terminix; Neumann Brothers, Inc.
CASUALTY INSURANCE CLIENTS: Cincinnati Insurance Companies; Crum & Forster; Employers Mutual Insurance Companies; Liberty Mutual Insurance Co.; Reliance Insurance Co.; The State Farm Companies of Bloomington, IL; Zurich-American Group; The St. Paul Insurance Companies.

HANSEN, McCLINTOCK & RILEY

Established in 1939

FLEMING BUILDING, 8TH FLOOR
218 SIXTH AVENUE
DES MOINES, IOWA 50309-4092
Telephone: 515-244-2141
Fax: 515-244-2931
Email: info@hmrlawfirm.com
URL: http://www.hmrlawfirm.com

General Civil Trial Practice in all Courts. Professional Negligence, Workers' Compensation, Corporation and Real Estate Law, Credit Union, Insurance, Administrative Law, Appellate Practice and Products Liability.

FIRM PROFILE: Hansen, McClintock & Riley was founded by Haemer Wheatcraft and J. Rudolph Hansen in 1939. Serving clients throughout the State of Iowa with an emphasis on Polk and surrounding counties. The Firm engages in a General Trial Practice, with practice areas including but not limited to professional negligence, products liability, workers compensation law, insurance law, administrative law, personal injury, appellate practice, corporate and real estate law, probate and estates and credit unions. The Firm is also listed in the Martindale-Hubbell Bar Register of Preeminent Lawyers.

(This Listing Continued)

MEMBERS OF FIRM

HAEMER WHEATCRAFT (1904-1983)

J. RUDOLPH HANSEN (1904-1995)

RONALD A. RILEY (Retired)

JOHN A. McCLINTOCK, born Des Moines, Iowa, July 5, 1931; admitted to bar, 1958, Iowa. *Education:* Grinnell College (A.B., 1953); University of Iowa (J.D., 1958). Recipient, 1986 Award of Merit, Iowa State Bar. *Member:* Polk County (President, 1974-1975), Iowa State (Member: Special Committee on Uniform Court Instructions, 1967-1979; Board of Governors, 1975-1983; President 1982-1983; Administrative Committee, 1993-1994; Chair, Scope & Correlation Committee, 1993-1994) and American Bar Associations; Iowa Academy of Trial Lawyers (President, 1984-1985; Secretary-Treasurer, 1993—); American Inns of Court; C. Edwin Moore Inn of Court. Fellow: Iowa State and American Bar Foundations; American College of Trial Lawyers. **Email:** jmcclintock@hmrlawfirm.com

CHESTER C. WOODBURN, III, born Iowa City, Iowa, April 6, 1948; admitted to bar, 1975, Iowa. *Education:* University of Iowa (B.A., 1971); Drake University (J.D., 1975). Assistant Attorney, Polk County, 1975-1977. Major Offense Bureau, 1976. *Member:* Polk County, Iowa State and American Bar Associations; Iowa Academy of Trial Lawyers; American Board of Trial Advocates (Advocate). **Email:** cwoodburn@hmrlawfirm.com

WILLIAM D. SCHERLE, born Council Bluffs, Iowa, June 25, 1950; admitted to bar, 1975, Iowa and Nebraska; 1995, U.S. Supreme Court; 1977, U.S. Tax Court; U.S. Claims Court; U.S. Court of Appeals, Eighth and Federal Circuit; U.S. District Court, Southern District of Iowa. *Education:* Texas A & M University (B.A., 1972); Creighton University (J.D., 1975). Assistant Attorney General, Iowa, 1975-1976. Assistant U.S. Attorney, 1976-1977. Member, Eighth Circuit Court Annual Conference Planning Committee, 1993. Member, Board of Directors, Youth Law Center. *Member:* Polk County (President, 1991-1992), Iowa State (Vice President, 1995-1996; President, 1997-1998; President, Young Lawyers Section, 1985-1986; Chair, Federal Practice Commission, 1980-1982; Member and Chair, Ways & Means Committee, 1991-1992; Chair, Scope and Correlations; Membership Chair; Board of Governors, 1992-1994), Iowa State Bar Foundation (Strategic Planning Committee, 2002—); Nebraska State and American Bar Associations; Iowa Association of Workers Compensation Attorneys (Member, Board of Directors, Advisory Committee and Youth Law Center Board of Directors). **Email:** bscherle@hmrlawfirm.com

DAVID L. BROWN, born Decatur, Illinois, April 25, 1947; admitted to bar, 1976, Iowa. *Education:* Lawrence University (B.A., 1969); Michigan State University (M.A., 1972); Drake University (J.D., 1975). Recipient, 1999 Award of Merit, Iowa State Bar. Member: Drake Board of Counselors, 1980-1990; Drake Foundation Trust Board, 1990—. Assistant Attorney General, Iowa, 1976. Law Clerk to Iowa Supreme Court Chief Justice C. Edwin Moore, 1976-1978. *Member:* Polk County (President, Junior Bar, 1984-1985; Member, Lawyers Grievance Committee, 1984-1985, 1988-1990; Judicial Nomination Commission, 1992-1998), Iowa State (Member, Committees on: Uniform Court Instructions, 1988-2000; Chair, Litigation Section, 1993-1996; Co-Chair Task Force on Administrative Law, 1994-1998; Chair, Scope and Correlation Committee, 2001—; Chair, Judicial Administration Committee, 2002—), Federal, American (Member, House of Delegates, 1997—) and International Bar Associations; Iowa Defense Counsel Association (Member, Board of Directors, 1993-1998); Federation of Insurance and Corporate Counsel; International Association of Defense Counsel; American Arbitration Association; American Academy of Hospital Attorneys; Iowa Society of Hospital Attorneys; American Board of Trial Advocates (Advocate; President Iowa Chapter, 1999-2000); American Bar Foundation; Iowa State Bar Foundation; C. Edwin Moore Inn of Court (Master). Iowa Board of Bar Examiners (Supreme Court Commission, Proposed Iowa Rules of Professional Conduct, 2000-2002); Diplomate, National Board of Trial Advocacy; American Board of Professional Liability Attorneys. Fellow: Iowa Academy of Trial Lawyers (Member, Board of Governors, 1993— Vice President, 1999-2000; President, 2000-2001); American College of Trial Lawyers; International Society of Barristers; American Academy of Appellate Lawyers; International Academy of Trial Lawyers. **Email:** dlbrown@hmrlawfirm.com

JOHN E. SWANSON, born Monona, Iowa, August 30, 1956; admitted to bar, 1982, Iowa, U.S. District Court, Northern and Southern Districts of Iowa and U.S. Court of Appeals, Eighth Circuit. *Education:* Wartburg College (B.A., magna cum laude, 1979); Drake University (J.D., 1982). Member, Drake University Law Review. Author: Case Note, 30 Drake L. Rev. 650, 1980. *Member:* Polk County, Iowa State (Member, Workers' Compensation, 1998-2001) and American Bar Associations; Iowa Trial Lawyers Association. **Email:** jswanson@hmrlawfirm.com

AARON T. OLIVER, born Winfield, Kansas, May 25, 1971; admitted to bar, 1996, Iowa. *Education:* Kansas State University (B.S., 1993); Drake University (J.D., with honors, 1996). Chief Executive Editor, Drake Journal of Agricultural Law, 1995-1996. Law Clerk to Justice James H. Andreasen, Iowa Supreme Court, 1996-1997. Author: "Jury Nullification: Should the Type of Case Matter?," 6 Kansas Journal of Law and Public Policy, Volume VI, Number II, Winter 1997. *Member:* Polk County, Iowa State (YLD President, 2003—; YLD President-Elect, 2002-2003; YLD Secretary, 2001-2002; Annual Meeting, 1998—; YLD Membership, 1998-1999; Chair, YLD Know Your Constitution, 1999-2001; YLD District 5C representative, 1999-2001; Appellate Practice, 2002—) and American (YLD Assistant Editor, The Affiliate, 2002—)Bar Associations; Iowa Trial Lawyers Association. Fellow: Iowa State Bar Foundation. **Email:** aoliver@hmrlawfirm.com

ASSOCIATE

ALEXANDER WONIO, born Iowa City, Iowa, May 10, 1979; admitted to bar, 2004, Iowa. *Education:* Loras College (B.A., 2001); Drake University (J.D., 2004). *Member:* Iowa State and American Bar Associations. **Email:** awonio@hmrlawfirm.com

REPRESENTATIVE CLIENTS: American Fidelity; American Home Assurance Co.; American International Group; American International Recovery; Bituminous; British American Tobacco Company, Ltd.; CGU Hawkeye Security; Crawford & Company; Crum & Forster; EMC Risk; Farm Bureau; Farmland Insurance; GAB Insurance Services; Granite State; Great American Ins. Co.; Great West Casualty; Health Care Indemnity, Inc.; Highlands Group; ITT Hartford; Illinois National; Ins. Co. of Pennsylvania; Minnesota Lawyers Mutual; National Union Fire; New Hampshire Group; Pharmacists Mutual Ins. Co.; Podiatry Insurance (PICA); Sedgwick CMS; St. Paul Fire & Marine; Travelers Property Casualty; Broadlawns Medical Center; St.

(This Listing Continued)

HANSEN, McCLINTOCK & RILEY, Des Moines—Continued

Anthony Regional Hospital and Nursing Home; Deere Community Credit Union; Des Moines Asphalt & Paving Co.; Financial Plus Credit Union; Hoster Refrigeration Supply, Inc.; Iles Funeral Homes, Inc.; Iowa Credit Union League; Iowa Girls High School Athletic Union; Iowa National Guard Credit Union; Iowa Postal Credit Union; Vermeer Mfg.; Lear Corp.; Polk County Water District No. 1; PreNeed Systems; White Consolidated Industries; White Water University.

HANSON, BJORK & RUSSELL, L.L.P.

405 6TH AVENUE, SUITE 1300
DES MOINES, IOWA 50309
Telephone: 515-244-0177
Fax: 515-244-8258
URL: http://www.hbr-law.com

General Practice, Probate and Estate Planning, Trials and Appellate Practice, Insurance Law, Employment Law, Personal Injury Law, Health Care Law, Workers Compensation, Products Liability, Commercial Litigation, Business Planning, Business Formation, Real Estate Law, White Collar Crime, Tax.

FIRM PROFILE: The firm dates back to the 1920's and has been named Hanson, Bjork & Russell, L.L.P. since 1986. The firm provides a full range of legal services as shown above and serves clients throughout the state of Iowa as well as nationally.

MEMBERS OF FIRM

THOMAS D. HANSON, born Jefferson, Iowa, November 10, 1944; admitted to bar, 1970, Illinois; 1975, Iowa; 1984, U.S. Supreme Court. *Education:* University of Iowa (B.A., 1967); University of Chicago (J.D., 1970). *Member:* Polk County and Iowa State Bar Associations; Iowa Defense Counsel Association (President, 1987-1988). Fellow, American College of Trial Lawyers. ***PRACTICE AREAS:*** General Practice; Trial Practice; Appellate Practice; Products Liability; Commercial Litigation; White Collar Criminal Defense. ***Email:*** thanson@hbr-law.com

ALAN H. BJORK, born Des Moines, Iowa, March 22, 1949; admitted to bar, 1976, Iowa and U.S. District Court, Northern and Southern Districts of Iowa. *Education:* Cornell College (B.A., 1971); University of Iowa; Drake University (J.D., 1976). *Member:* Polk County, Iowa State and American Bar Associations. ***PRACTICE AREAS:*** General Practice; Probate; Trusts and Estates; Employment Law; Health Care Law; Workers Compensation Law; Products Liability. ***Email:*** abjork@hbr-law.com

BARRY A. RUSSELL, born Winnipeg, Manitoba, May 25, 1949; admitted to bar, 1976, Iowa; 1978, Wisconsin. *Education:* Cornell College (B.A., 1971); University of North Carolina (M.A., 1973); University of Iowa (J.D., 1976). Law Clerk, Judge William C. Hanson, U.S. District Court, Southern District of Iowa, 1976-1978. *Member:* Polk County, Iowa State and American Bar Associations; State Bar of Wisconsin; The Association of Trial Lawyers of America. ***PRACTICE AREAS:*** General Practice; Trial Practice; Appellate Practice; Insurance; Personal Injury; Products Liability; Commercial Litigation. ***Email:*** brussell@hbr-law.com

LU ANN WHITE, born Waterloo, Iowa, August 31, 1956; admitted to bar, 1981, Iowa and U.S. District Court, Northern and Southern Districts of Iowa; U.S. Court of Appeals, Eighth Circuit; U.S. Supreme Court. *Education:* Cornell College (B.A., 1978); University of Iowa (J.D., 1981). Note and Comment Editor, Iowa Law Review, 1980-1981. Law Clerk, U.S. Magistrate R.E. Longstaff, Southern District of Iowa, 1981-1982, 1984-1985. *Member:* Polk County, Iowa State and American Bar Associations; Polk County Women Attorneys; Iowa Organization of Women Attorneys; The Association of Trial Lawyers of America; Iowa Trial Lawyers Association. ***PRACTICE AREAS:*** General Practice; Trial Practice; Appellate Practice; Insurance; Personal Injury; Products Liability; Commercial Litigation. ***Email:*** lawhite@hbr-law.com

DALE A. KNOSHAUG, born Des Moines, Iowa, November 27, 1961; admitted to bar, 1987, Iowa, U.S. Court of Appeals, Eighth Circuit and U.S. District Court, Northern and Southern Districts of Iowa. *Education:* Iowa State University (B.S., 1984); Drake Law School (J.D., 1987). *Member:* Polk County, Iowa State and American Bar Associations; Iowa Defense Counsel Association. ***PRACTICE AREAS:*** General Practice; Trial Practice; Appellate Practice; Insurance Law; Personal Injury Law; Products Liability; Commercial Litigation. ***Email:*** dknoshaug@hbr-law.com

FRED E. BEAVER, born Des Moines, Iowa, November 20, 1949; admitted to bar, 1975, Iowa. *Education:* University of Iowa (B.B.A., with honors, 1972; J.D., with distinction, 1975). Founding Editor, Journal of Corporation Law, 1974-1976. Member, Board of Editors, Iowa Law Review, 1974-1975. Certified Public Accountant, Iowa, 1972. Author: Comment, 59 Iowa Law Review 726, 1973; Note, 60 Iowa Law Review 54, 1974. Co-Author: Beaver and Fleck "Revenue Act of 1978 Creates New Tax Planning Environment for Farm Co-ops," 50 Journal of Tax 138, 1978. *Member:* Polk County and Iowa State Bar Associations. ***PRACTICE AREAS:*** General Practice; Business Planning; Business Formation; Commercial Litigation; Accounting Law; White Collar Crime; Y2K; Litigation. ***Email:*** fbeaver@hbr-law.com

CLARK G. McDERMOTT, born Sibley, Iowa, May 6, 1965; admitted to bar, 1991, Iowa and U.S. District Court, Northern and Southern Districts of Iowa. *Education:* Drake University (B.A., magna cum laude, 1988); University of Minnesota (J.D., 1991). Phi Beta Kappa. *Member:* Polk County, Iowa State and American Bar Associations. ***PRACTICE AREAS:*** General Practice; Probate; Trusts and Estates; Insurance; Appellate Practice; Business Planning; Business Formation; Commercial Litigation. ***Email:*** cmcdermott@hbr-law.com

MICHAEL D. ENSLEY, born Jefferson City, Missouri, December 16, 1972; admitted to bar, 1998, Iowa, U.S. District Court, Northern and Southern Districts of Iowa. *Education:* Iowa State University (B.A., 1995); University of Iowa (J.D., 1998). Author: "Dealing with the Mentally Incapacitated Client: Ethical Issues Facing the Attorney," Family Law Quarterly, 1999. *Member:* Polk County, Iowa State and American Bar Associations; The Association of Trial Lawyers of America. ***PRACTICE AREAS:*** General Practice; Insurance Law; Products Liability; Personal Injury; Family Law. ***Email:*** mensley@hbr-law.com

(This Listing Continued)

ASSOCIATES

JONATHAN D. BERGMAN, born Des Moines, Iowa, June 12, 1977; admitted to bar, 2004, Iowa and U.S. District Court, Northern and Southern Districts of Iowa. *Education:* University of Iowa (B.A., 2000; J.D., 2004). *Member:* Polk County, Iowa State and American Bar Associations. ***Email:*** jbergman@hbr-law.com

KARA L. PETERSON, born Cresco, Iowa, May 5, 1980; admitted to bar, 2005, Iowa. *Education:* Iowa State University (B.A., 2002); University of Iowa (J.D., 2005). *Member:* American Bar Association.

REPRESENTATIVE CLIENTS: Aetna Life and Casualty; Alltel Corp.; Bankers Trust Company, N.A.; Casey's General Stores; Columbia Insurance Group; Conseco; Credit Suisse First Boston, Inc.; Employers Mutual Casualty Co.; Excel Corp.; Farm Bureau Mutual Insurance Co.; Intel Corp.; Iowa State Bank; Luther Care Services; National States Insurance Co.; St. Paul Insurance Co.; Travelers Insurance Co.; U.S. Bank; West Bend Mutual Insurance Co.

HAWKINS & NORRIS, PC

2501 GRAND AVENUE, SUITE C
DES MOINES, IOWA 50312-5399
Telephone: 515-288-6532
Fax: 515-288-9733

General Civil Trial, Trials and Appeals, Contract and Tort Litigation, Personal Injury, Antitrust and Business Litigation.

FIRM PROFILE: Hawkins & Norris, PC was founded by J. Riley McManus in the early 1920's. Serving clients regionally with a focus in the State of Iowa, the firm engages in a general civil trial practice. The firm is also listed in Martindale-Hubbell Bar Register of Preeminent Lawyers.

MEMBERS OF FIRM

LEX HAWKINS, born Red Oak, Iowa, December 17, 1925; admitted to bar, 1951, Iowa and U.S. District Court, Southern District of Iowa; 1960, U.S. District Court, Northern District of Iowa; 1965, U.S. Supreme Court; 1986, Texas; 1991, Colorado. *Education:* Drake University (B.A., 1948; J.D., 1951). Phi Alpha Delta. Member, Scribes. President, Iowa Workmen's Compensation Advisory Committee, 1964. *Member:* Polk County and Iowa State (Member: Special Committee on Workmen's Compensation Law, 1964-1966; Special Committee on Iowa Rules of Civil Procedure, 1965-1966; 1968-1969; Special Committee on Uniform Instruction, 1967-1969; Member, Special Select Legislative Study Committee 1976—) Bar Associations; The Association of Trial Lawyers of America (Associate Editor, American Trial Lawyers NACCA Law Journal, 1958; Lecturer, National Convention, 1965-1967; Member, Board of Governors, 1966-1967, 1967-1968; Member, Committee on Judicial Selection of Judicial Administration Section, 1970); Iowa Academy of Trial Lawyers (President, 1967-1968; Editor, Iowa Academy of Trial Lawyers, *Trial Handbook*, 1970, Second Edition, 1986); International Academy of Trial Lawyers (Member, Board of Directors, 1968-1972, 1976-1979, 1985—); International Society of Barristers. Fellow: American College of Trial Lawyers; American Bar Foundation. [With U.S. Navy, 1944-1946]. ***PRACTICE AREAS:*** Civil Practice; Personal Injury; Products Liability; Medical Malpractice; Business Tort. ***Email:*** lhawkins@2501grand.com

GLENN L. NORRIS, born Clarinda, Iowa, September 25, 1946; admitted to bar, 1971, Iowa and U.S. District Court, Northern District of Iowa; 1972, U.S. District Court, Southern District of Iowa; 1976, U.S. Supreme Court. *Education:* Simpson College (B.A., 1968); University of Iowa (J.D., with distinction, 1971). Member of Staff, Iowa Law Review, 1969-1970. Law Clerk to Hon. William C. Hanson, Chief U.S. District Judge, Southern and Northern Districts of Iowa, 1971-1973. *Member:* Polk County and Iowa State Bar Associations; Iowa Trial Lawyers Association (Governor, 1988—; Editor, The Iowa Trial Lawyer, 1976-1978); The Association of Trial Lawyers of America; American Judicature Society; American Board of Trial Advocates. Fellow, Iowa Academy of Trial Lawyers. ***PRACTICE AREAS:*** Civil Practice; Personal Injury; Products Liability; Medical Malpractice; Business Tort. ***Email:*** gnorris@2501grand.com

REFERENCE: West Des Moines State Bank.

HERRICK, LANGDON & LANGDON

1550 FINANCIAL CENTER
SEVENTH AND WALNUT
DES MOINES, IOWA 50309-3972
Telephone: 515-282-8150
Telecopier: 515-282-8226

General Civil Practice. Litigation and Appeals in Federal and State Courts. Insurance, Corporate and Business, Employment, Products Liability, Dram Shop, Personal Injury, Malpractice, Class Actions, Antitrust, Trade Regulation, Taxation, Real Estate, Estate Planning and Probate and Administrative Law.

FIRM PROFILE: Herrick, Langdon & Langdon was founded by Allan A. Herrick and Herschel G. Langdon in 1935, serving clients for over 69 years throughout the state of Iowa with an emphasis in Polk and its contiguous counties. The firm engages in a general civil practice focusing in all types of litigation, trusts, estates and business law.

MEMBERS OF FIRM

ALLAN A. HERRICK (1896-1989)

HERSCHEL G. LANGDON (1905-2002)

RICHARD G. LANGDON, born Des Moines, Iowa, July 9, 1936; admitted to bar, 1961, Iowa. *Education:* Harvard University (A.B., cum laude, 1958); Harvard Law School (J.D., 1961). *Member:* Polk County, Iowa State and American Bar Associations; International Association of Defense Counsel; Federation of Insurance and Corporate Counsel;

(This Listing Continued)

Iowa Academy of Trial Lawyers; Iowa Defense Counsel Association. Fellow, American College of Trial Lawyers. ***PRACTICE AREAS:*** Civil Litigation; Insurance Defense; Insurance Law; Corporate and Business Law; Estate Planning.

WILLIAM R. CLARK, JR., born Des Moines, Iowa, August 1, 1951; admitted to bar, 1976, Iowa and Illinois. *Education:* Drake University (B.A., 1973; J.D., with honors, 1975). Order of the Coif; Delta Theta Phi. Associate Editor, Drake Law Review, 1975. Law Clerk to Honorable Bruce M. Snell, Jr., Judge, Iowa Court of Appeals, 1976-1978. *Member:* Polk County, Iowa State and American Bar Associations. ***PRACTICE AREAS:*** Estate and Trust Administration; Estate Planning; Corporate and Business Law; Taxation; Real Estate.

RICHARD N. WINDERS, born Milwaukee, Wisconsin, April 13, 1945; admitted to bar, 1970, Iowa; 1975, U.S. Supreme Court. *Education:* Drake University (B.A., 1967; J.D., 1970). Assistant Attorney General, State of Iowa, 1970-1977. *Member:* Polk County, Iowa State and American Bar Associations; International Association of Defense Counsel; Iowa Academy of Trial Lawyers; The Association of Trial Lawyers of America; Iowa Defense Counsel Association; C. Edwin Moore American Inns of Court (President, 2003-2004). ***PRACTICE AREAS:*** Civil Litigation; Insurance Defense; Insurance Law; Environmental Law.

REPRESENTATIVE CLIENTS: Wells Fargo Bank Iowa, N.A.; Citicorp Services; MAPCO, Inc.; Mercedes Benz of North America, Inc.; Terra Affinity Claims International; J.B. Hunt Transport, Inc.; C.R. England and Sons, Inc.; Coregis Group; American Home Assurance Co.; Amex Insurance Co.; Canal Insurance Co.; Carolina Casualty; CIGNA; Cincinnati Insurance Co.; Connecticut General Insurance Co.; Connecticut Mutual Life Insurance Co.; CNA Health Pro; Empire Fire and Marine Insurance Cos.; Federal Kemper Life Insurance Co.; Fireman's Fund Insurance Co.; Globe American Casualty Co.; The Hanover Insurance Co.; ITT Hartford; Jefferson Insurance Group; Kemper National Property and Casualty Cos.; Lloyds of London; J.C. Penney Life Ins. Co.; Mutual Fire and Auto Insurance Co.; New York Life Insurance Co.; Ohio Casualty Insurance Group; Pafco Insurance Co.; Progressive Insurance Cos.; Royal Insurance Co.; Union Insurance Group; Home Insurance Cos.; National Home Life Assurance Co.; Werner Enterprises; Con-Agra; Northbrook Property and Casualty Co.; Provident Life and Accident Insurance Co.; Northwestern National Life Insurance Co.

HOFFMANN LAW FIRM, P.C.

Established in 1972

3708 75TH STREET
DES MOINES, IOWA 50322
Telephone: 515-270-8899
Fax: 515-270-0115
Email: hlf@hoffmannlawfirm.com
URL: http://www.iowaworkcomp.com

Workers' Compensation Law.

FIRM PROFILE: The firm is listed in the Martindale-Hubbell Bar Register of Preeminent Lawyers.

MICHAEL R. HOFFMANN, born Des Moines, Iowa, April 26, 1947; admitted to bar, 1972, Iowa and U.S. Court of Customs and Patent Appeals; 1974, U.S. District Courts, Southern and Northern Districts of Iowa; 1976, U.S. Court of Appeals, 8th Circuit; 1977, U.S. Supreme Court; registered to practice before U.S. Patent and Trademark Office. *Education:* University of Iowa (B.S., 1969); Drake University (J.D., 1972); George Washington University (LL.M., in Patent and Trade Regulation Law, 1973). Phi Alpha Delta (District Marshal, 1970). Recipient, American Jurisprudence Award, 1970 and 1972. Speaker, 25th and 33rd Annual Workers' Compensation Symposium, Iowa Workers' Compensation Advisory Committee, Inc., 1987 and 1995. Clerk, Jones, Hoffmann & Davison, Des Moines, 1970-1973. Associate: Bacon & Thomas, Arlington, Va., 1973-1974; Jones, Hoffmann & Davison, 1974-1979 and Partner, 1979-1983. President, Michael R. Hoffmann, P.C., 1983-1995. President, Michael R. Hoffmann PLC, 1994-1999; Partner, Jones, Hoffmann & Davison then Jones, Hoffmann & Huber, 1990. Member, Hoffmann & McConkey, P.L.C., 1999-2002; President, Hoffmann Law Firm, P.C., 2002—. *Member:* Polk County, Iowa State (Co-Chair, Workers' Compensation Technology Committee, 2000) and American Bar Associations: Iowa Patent Law Association (Charter Member); American Intellectual Property Law Association; Iowa Defense Counsel Association; Defense Research Institute; American Judicature Society; The Iowa Association of Workers' Compensation Lawyers, Inc,; International Association of Industrial Accident Boards and Commissions. ***PRACTICE AREAS:*** Workers Compensation. ***Email:*** mrh@hoffmannlawfirm.com

AMY M. HOFFMANN, born Des Moines, Iowa, December 16, 1970; admitted to bar, 2001, Iowa. *Education:* University of Iowa (B.S., 1994); Drake University (J.D., 2000). Associate: Hoffmann & McConkey, P.L.C., 2001-2002; Hoffmann Law Firm, P.C., 2002—. *Member:* Polk, Iowa State and American Bar Associations; Iowa Defense Counsel Association. ***PRACTICE AREAS:*** Workers Compensation. ***Email:*** amh@hoffmannlawfirm.com

REPRESENTATIVE CLIENTS: Accident Fund Company; Arby's; Argonout Insurance Company; BFI Waste Systems of North America; Burlington Coat Factory; Cargill; CNA Insurance Company; Constitution State Service Company; Conway Central Express; Crawford and Company; ETV, Inc; Emery Worldwide; Federated Rural Electric Insurance Corp.; Foodland Supermarkets; Frontier Insurance; Great Central Insurance; Grundy County REC; Harmon Glass; Jet Company, Inc.; Lumberman's Underwriting Alliance; Motel 6; RSKCo; National Gypsum; Northwest Iowa Power Cooperative; NPI Security; Old Republic; Prestige Products, Inc.; Risk Services, Inc.; Roberts Dairy; Royal Sun Insurance; RSK Co.; Ryder Services Corporation; Sedgwick Claims Management Services; Smurfit, Inc.; Travelers Insurance; Viskase; Weitz; Woodbury County REC; Des Moines YMCA.

HOPKINS & HUEBNER, P.C.

SUITE 111, TERRACE CENTER
2700 GRAND AVENUE
DES MOINES, IOWA 50312-5213
Telephone: 515-244-0111
Fax: 515-244-8935
URL: http://www.hopkinsandhuebner.com

Davenport, Iowa Office: 100 East Kimberly Road, Suite 704, 52806-5944. Telephone: 319-445-2264. Fax: 319-445-2267.

(This Listing Continued)

Adel, Iowa Office: 1009 Main Street, P.O. Box 99, 50003-1454. Telephone: 515-993-4545. Fax: 515-993-5214.

General Practice, Insurance, Casualty, Workers Compensation, Corporation, Employment, Municipal, Civil Rights, Products Liability, Contracts, Trials in all Courts, Business and Corporation Law, and Real Estate.

FRED D. HUEBNER (1919-1996)

MARVIN E. DUCKWORTH (1942-2003)

TERRENCE A. HOPKINS, born 1929; admitted to bar, 1954, Iowa. *Education:* Drake University (LL.B., 1954). *Member:* American, Polk County (President, 1982) and Iowa State Bar Associations; State Judicial Nominating Commission; Iowa Academy of Trial Lawyers; American College of Trial Lawyers.

FRANK T. HARRISON, born 1941; admitted to bar, 1967, Iowa and Nebraska. *Education:* Drake University (A.B., 1963); Creighton University (J.D., 1967). Deputy Workers Compensation Commissioner, 1967-1970. *Member:* American, Iowa State (Member Workers' Compensation Committee) and Nebraska State Bar Associations; Iowa Association of Workers' Compensation Lawyers (Chairman, Workers Compensation Advisory Committee; Trustee, Broadlawns Medical Center). ***Email:*** fharriso@hopkinsandhuebner.com

E. J. GIOVANNETTI, born 1941; admitted to bar, 1966, Iowa. *Education:* Creighton University (B.A., 1963; J.D., 1966). *Member:* American, Polk County and Iowa State Bar Associations; Iowa Association of Workers' Compensation Lawyers; Defense Research Institute. ***Email:*** ejgiovan@hopkinsandhuebner.com

JEFF H. JEFFRIES, born 1945; admitted to bar, 1970, Iowa. *Education:* Morningside College (B.A., 1967); Drake University (J.D., 1970). *Member:* American and Iowa State Bar Associations; Defense Research Institute; American College of Trial Lawyers. ***Email:*** jjeffrie@hopkinsandhuebner.com

R. RONALD POGGE, born 1951; admitted to bar, 1976, Iowa. *Education:* University of Notre Dame (B.A., 1973); Drake University (J.D., with honors, 1976). *Member:* Iowa State Bar Association; Iowa Trial Lawyers Association. ***Email:*** rpogge@hopkinsandhuebner.com

THOMAS J. LOGAN, born 1951; admitted to bar, 1976, Iowa. *Education:* Drake University (B.A., 1973; J.D., 1976). *Member:* American and Iowa State Bar Associations; Defense Research Institute. ***Email:*** tlogan@hopkinsandhuebner.com

DENNIS L. HANSSEN, born 1943; admitted to bar, 1968, Iowa. *Education:* Grinnell College (B.A., 1965); Drake University (J.D., 1968). Deputy Industrial Commissioner, 1972-1979.*Member:* Iowa State Bar Association; Iowa Association of Workers' Compensation Lawyers; The Association of Trial Lawyers of America; Iowa Trial Lawyers Association. [Staff Judge Advocate, U.S. Marine Corps, 1968-1972]. ***Email:*** dhanssen@hopkinsandhuebner.com

LORRAINE J. MAY, born 1952; admitted to bar, 1975, Iowa. *Education:* Drake University (B.A., 1973; J.D., with honors, 1975). *Member:* American, Polk County and Iowa State Bar Associations. ***Email:*** lmay@hopkinsandhuebner.com

JAMES E. VAN WERDEN, born 1939; admitted to bar, 1964, Iowa. *Education:* University of Iowa (J.D., 1964). *Member:* American, Iowa State and Dallas County Bar Associations; Association of Trial Lawyers of Iowa; The Association of Trial Lawyers of America. ***Email:*** jvanwerd@hopkinsandhuebner.com

WILLIAM L. DAWE, born 1945; admitted to bar, 1976, Iowa. *Education:* University of Maryland (B.S., 1973); Drake University (J.D., with honors, 1975). *Member:* American, Iowa State and Polk County Bar Associations; Iowa Academy of Trial Lawyers; Iowa Defense Counsel Association; Defense Research Institute. ***Email:*** wdawe@hopkinsandhuebner.com

PHILIP H. DORFF, JR., born 1949; admitted to bar, 1982, Iowa. *Education:* Colorado College (B.A., 1971); Drake University (J.D., 1982). *Member:* American and Iowa State Bar Associations; Defense Research Institute; Iowa Defense Counsel Association. ***Email:*** phdorff@hopkinsandhuebner.com

E. J. KELLY, born 1947; admitted to bar, 1973, Iowa. *Education:* College of St. Thomas (B.A., 1969); Creighton University Law School (J.D., 1973). Deputy Industrial Commissioner, 1979-1983. *Member:* American, Iowa State and Nebraska State Bar Associations; International Association of Defense Counsel; Defense Research Institute; Iowa Association of Workers' Compensation Lawyers. ***Email:*** ejkelly@hopkinsandhuebner.com

JOHN E. ORRELL, JR., born 1957; admitted to bar, 1982, Iowa. *Education:* University of North Dakota (B.S., 1979); Drake University (J.D., 1982). *Member:* Iowa State Bar Association; Defense Research Institute. ***Email:*** jorrell@hopkinsandhuebner.com

ROBERT C. LANDESS, born 1935; admitted to bar, 1962, Iowa. *Education:* University of Iowa (B.A., 1957); Drake University (J.D., 1962). *Member:* American, Polk County and Iowa State (Member, Workers' Compensation Advisory Committee) Bar Associations; International Association of Industrial Accident Boards and Commissions; Iowa Association of Workers' Compensation Lawyers. ***Email:*** rlandess@hopkinsandhuebner.com

GREGORY T. RACETTE, born 1950; admitted to bar, 1979, Iowa and Michigan. *Education:* University of Michigan (B.A., 1972); Thomas M. Cooley Law School (J.D., cum laude, 1979). *Member:* American, Iowa State and Polk County Bar Associations; The Association of Trial Lawyers of America; Iowa Trial Lawyers Association; Iowa Association of Workers' Compensation Lawyers. ***Email:*** gracette@hopkinsandhuebner.com

VALERIE A. LANDIS, born 1960; admitted to bar, 1987, Iowa. *Education:* University of Missouri-Columbia (B.E.S., 1984); Drake University (J.D., with honors, 1987). *Member:* American, Iowa State and Polk County Bar Associations; Iowa Association of Workers' Compensation Lawyers. ***Email:*** vlandis@hopkinsandhuebner.com

JEFF M. MARGOLIN, born 1955; admitted to bar, 1981, Iowa and Illinois. *Education:* University of Iowa (B.A., 1977); John Marshall Law School (J.D., 1981). *Member:* Iowa State and Polk County Bar Associations. ***Email:*** jmargoli@hopkinsandhuebner.com

ANNE L. CLARK, born 1960; admitted to bar, 1986, Iowa. *Education:* Drake University (B.A., 1982; J.D., 1985). *Member:* Iowa State Bar Association; Iowa Municipal Attorneys Association; Iowa Association of Workers' Compensation Lawyers. ***Email:*** aclark@hopkinsandhuebner.com

(This Listing Continued)

HOPKINS & HUEBNER, P.C., Des Moines—Continued

MATTHEW A. GROTNES, born 1963; admitted to bar, 1989, Iowa. *Education:* Luther College (B.A., 1986); Drake University (J.D., 1989). *Member:* American, Iowa State and Polk County Bar Associations; Iowa Association of Workers' Compensation Lawyers. ***Email:*** mgrotnes@hopkinsandhuebner.com

M. ANNE McATEE (Resident, Davenport Office)

JANE V. LORENTZEN, born 1963; admitted to bar, 1991, Iowa. *Education:* University of Iowa (B.S.N., 1986); Drake University Law School (J.D., 1991). Member, Drake Law School Board of Counselors, 1999—*Member:* American, Iowa State (Counsel, Workers' Compensation Section; Member, Advisory Committee) and Polk County (Member, Board of Directors, 2000—) Bar Associations; Iowa Association of Workers' Compensation Attorneys. ***Email:*** jlorentz@hopkinsandhuebner.com

HUGH J. CAIN, born 1955; admitted to bar, 1983, Iowa. *Education:* Creighton University (B.A., summa cum laude, 1978); University of Washington (J.D., 1982). *Member:* American (Member, Sections on: Labor and Employment) and Iowa State (Member, Sections on: Labor and Employment) Bar Associations; Defense Research Institute. ***Email:*** hcain@hopkinsandhuebner.com

TINA M. EICK, born 1967; admitted to bar, 1993, Iowa. *Education:* Iowa State University (B.A., with honors, 1989); Drake University (M.A., 1993; J.D., with honors, 1993). *Member:* American, Iowa State and Polk County Bar Associations. ***Email:*** teick@hopkinsandhuebner.com

MARK D. LOWE, born 1966; admitted to bar, 1993, Iowa. *Education:* Iowa State University (B.S., 1988); Drake University (J.D., with honors, 1993). *Member:* Iowa State, Polk County and Dallas County (President, 2003) Bar Associations. ***Email:*** mlowe@hopkinsandhuebner.com

BARBARA A. HERING, born 1956; admitted to bar, 1986, Iowa; 1987, U.S. Court of Appeals, Eighth Circuit. *Education:* Central College (B.A., 1978); Drake University (J.D., with honors, 1986). *Member:* American, Iowa State and Polk County Bar Associations; Iowa Defense Counsel Association; Defense Research Institute. ***Email:*** bhering@hopkinsandhuebner.com

DAVID S. GORHAM, born 1967; admitted to bar, 1993, Iowa. *Education:* Iowa State University (B.S., 1990); Drake University (J.D., with honors, 1993). *Member:* Iowa State Bar Association; Iowa Trial Lawyers Association. ***Email:*** dgorham@hopkinsandhuebner.com

MICHAEL C. WALKER (Resident, Davenport Office)

ERIN Q. PALS, born 1975; admitted to bar, 2000, Iowa. *Education:* Central College (B.A., 1997); Drake University (J.D., 2000). *Member:* American and Polk County Bar Associations. ***Email:*** epals@hopkinsandhuebner.com

APRYL M. DE LANGE, born 1974; admitted to bar, 2000, Iowa. *Education:* University of Northern Iowa (B.A., magna cum laude, 1997); Drake University (J.D., with honors, 2000). *Member:* American, Iowa State and Polk County Bar Associations. ***Email:*** adelange@hopkinsandhuebner.com

THOMAS P. MURPHY, born 1963; admitted to bar, 1992, Iowa. *Education:* Marquette University (B.A., 1985); Drake University (J.D., with honors, 1992). *Member:* American, Iowa State and Polk County Bar Associations; Iowa Trial Lawyers Association; The Association of Trial Lawyers of America. ***Email:*** tmurphy@hopkinsandhuebner.com

B. J. MILLER, born 1975; admitted to bar, 2002, Iowa. *Education:* University Northern Iowa (B.A., 1998); Drake Law School (J.D., with high honors, 2002). *Member:* American and Iowa Bar Associations. ***Email:*** bjmiller@hopkinsandhuebner.com

PAUL SALABERT, JR. (Resident, Davenport Office)

RANDALL P. SCHUELLER, born 1975; admitted to bar, 2003, Iowa. *Education:* University of Northern Iowa (B.A., 1997); Drake University School of Law (J.D., with high honors, 2003). ***Email:*** rschuell@hopkinsandhuebner.com

SARAH M. KOURI, born 1978; admitted to bar, 2003, Iowa. *Education:* University of Iowa (B.B.A., 2000); Drake University School of Law (J.D., with high honors, 2003). ***Email:*** skouri@hopkinsandhuebner.com

B.J. TERRONES, born 1977; admitted to bar, 2004, Iowa. *Education:* University of Iowa (B.A., 1999); Drake University (J.D., with honors, 2004). *Member:* Polk County, Iowa State and American Bar Associations; Iowa Trial Lawyers Association. ***Email:*** bterrone@hopkinsandhuebner.com

NATHAN M. SONDGEROTH (Resident, Davenport Office)

WENDY D BOKA, born 1980; admitted to bar, 2005, Iowa. *Education:* Simpson College (B.A., summa cum laude, 2002); Drake University Law School (J.D., with honors, 2005).

REFERENCES: Upon request.

HOWE, CUNNINGHAM & LOWE, P.L.C.

DES MOINES, IOWA

(See Urbandale)

General Practice including Trial and Appellate Practice in State and Federal Courts. Corporate, Transportation, Administrative, Insurance, Family, Divorce, Personal Injury, Estate Planning, Wills, Probate, Real Estate, and Creditor Law.

HUBER, BOOK, CORTESE, HAPPE & LANZ, P.L.C.

Established in 1920

2700 WESTOWN PARKWAY, SUITE 170
DES MOINES, IOWA 50266-1411
Telephone: 515-243-4148
Fax: 515-243-5481
Email: huber@desmoineslaw.com
URL: http://www.desmoineslaw.com

Civil Trial and Appellate Practice. Insurance Defense, Workers' Compensation, Insurance, Products Liability, Professional Malpractice Defense and Administrative Law. Commercial, Business and Insurance Litigation.

FIRM PROFILE: Huber, Book, Cortese, Happe & Lanz, P.L.C. was founded by William Carl Hoffmann in 1920. Serving clients throughout the state of Iowa with a focus in Polk and contiguous counties, the firm engages in an emphasis in trial work. The firm is also listed in the Martindale-Hubbell Bar Register of Preeminent Lawyers.

MEMBERS OF FIRM

JAMES C. HUBER, born New Prague, Minnesota, October 9, 1945; admitted to bar, 1970, Missouri and Iowa; 1971, U.S. District Courts, Northern and Southern Districts of Iowa; 1972, U.S. Court of Appeals, 8th Circuit; 1978, U.S. Supreme Court. *Education:* Carleton College (B.A., 1967); Washington University (J.D., 1970). *Member:* Polk County, Iowa State and American Bar Associations; Iowa Defense Counsel Association. ***PRACTICE AREAS:*** Civil Trial Practice; Workers Compensation Law. ***Email:*** jhuber@desmoineslaw.com

RICHARD G. BOOK, born Des Moines, Iowa, March 22, 1954; admitted to bar, 1979, Iowa and U.S. District Courts, Northern and Southern Districts of Iowa. *Education:* Northwestern University (B.A., in Biochemistry, 1976); University of Iowa (J.D., with distinction, 1979). *Member:* Polk County, Iowa State (Member, Litigation and Workers Compensation Sections) and American Bar Associations; Defense Research and Trial Lawyers Association; Iowa Association of Workers Compensation Lawyers; Iowa Defense Counsel Association. ***PRACTICE AREAS:*** Workers Compensation Law. ***Email:*** rbook@desmoineslaw.com

JOSEPH S. CORTESE II, born Des Moines, Iowa, August 17, 1955; admitted to bar, 1981, Iowa and U.S. District Courts, Northern and Southern Districts of Iowa; 1984, U.S. Court of Appeals, Eighth Circuit. *Education:* Indiana University (A.B., 1977); Creighton University and Drake University (J.D., with honors, 1981). Phi Alpha Delta. *Member:* Polk County, Iowa State and American Bar Associations; Iowa Defense Counsel Association; Defense Research and Trial Lawyers Association; Iowa Association of Workers' Compensation Lawyers; Iowa Defense Counsel Association. ***PRACTICE AREAS:*** Workers Compensation Law. ***Email:*** jcortese@desmoineslaw.com

JOSEPH A. HAPPE, born Carroll, Iowa, June 5, 1960; admitted to bar, 1985, Iowa; 1986, Missouri and U.S. District Court, Northern District of Iowa; 1988, U.S. District Court, Western District of Missouri; 1989, U.S. District Court, Southern District of Iowa. *Education:* Creighton University (B.A., 1982; J.D., 1985). Pi Sigma Alpha. *Member:* Polk County, Iowa State (Member, Workers Compensation Section) and American (Law Student Division Liaison, Section of General Practice Counsel, 1982-1983) Bar Associations; The Missouri Bar; Iowa Defense Counsel Association; Iowa Trial Lawyers Association; Iowa Association of Workers Compensation Lawyers; Defense Research Institute. ***PRACTICE AREAS:*** Trial Practice; Workers Compensation Law. ***Email:*** jhappe@desmoineslaw.com

JEFFREY W. LANZ, born Grand Forks, North Dakota, December 29, 1968; admitted to bar, 1995, Iowa and U.S. District Court, Northern and Southern Districts of Iowa and U.S. Court of Appeals, Eighth Circuit. *Education:* Iowa State University (B.B.A., 1990); Drake University Law School (M.B.A., 1995; J.D., with honors, 1995). Delta Theta Phi. *Member:* Polk County, Iowa State (Member, Workers' Compensation Section) and American Bar Associations; Iowa Trial Lawyers Association; Defense Research Institute. ***PRACTICE AREAS:*** Workers Compensation Law. ***Email:*** jlanz@desmoineslaw.com

WILLIAM H. GRELL, born Council Bluffs, Iowa, August 16, 1972; admitted to bar, 1997, Iowa and U.S. District Court, Northern and Southern Districts of Iowa. *Education:* Augustana College (B.A., cum laude, 1994); University of Iowa (J.D., with distinction, 1997). *Member:* Polk County and Iowa State Bar Associations. ***PRACTICE AREAS:*** Workers Compensation. ***Email:*** wgrell@desmoineslaw.com

NATHAN R. McCONKEY, born Des Moines, Iowa, March 20, 1968; admitted to bar, 1995, Iowa and U.S. District Court, Southern District of Iowa. *Education:* University of Iowa (B.B.A., 1990); Drake University Law School (J.D., 1995). Delta Theta Phi. Member, Hoffmann & McConkey, P.L.C. *Member:* Polk County, Iowa State (Member, Workers Compensation Section) and American Bar Associations; Iowa Defense Counsel Association; The Defense Research Institute, Inc. ***Email:*** nmcconkey@desmoineslaw.com

ASSOCIATES

KERRY A. GAINES, born Aurora, Colorado, September 19, 1977; admitted to bar, 2003, Iowa. *Education:* University of Wyoming (B.S., Political Science, 2000; J.D., 2003). Order of Barristers. Vice President, Board of Advocates. *Member:* Association of Trial Lawyers of America; American, Iowa State and Polk County Bar Associations. ***REPORTED CASES:*** Beldon v. State, 73 P.3d 1041 (Wyo. 2003); Huff v. State, 69 P.3d 400 (Wyo. 2003); Penner v. State, 78 P.3d 1045 (Wyo. 2003). ***PRACTICE AREAS:*** Litigation; Insurance Law; Workers Compensation. ***Email:*** kgaines@desmoineslaw.com

KATHERINE J. PRONK, born Mason City, Iowa, November 16, 1979; admitted to bar, 2004, Iowa. *Education:* Drake University (B.A., magna cum laude, 2001; J.D., with high honors, 2004). Legal Research and Writing Teacher's Assistant, 2002-2004. *Member:* Polk County, Iowa State and American Bar Associations. ***PRACTICE AREAS:*** Litigation; Insurance Defense; Workers Compensation. ***Email:*** kpronk@desmoineslaw.com

(This Listing Continued)

REPRESENTATIVE CLIENTS: Argonaut Insurance Co.; Atlantic Mutual Cos.; CNA Insurance Cos.; Chesterfield Services, Inc.; Crawford & Co.; Design Professional Insurance Co.; ESIS; Fidelity and Deposit Company of Maryland; Firemans Fund-American Insurance Cos.; GAB Business Services, Inc.; Gallagher Bassett; Gates McDonald; General Motors Acceptance Corp.; Indiana Lumbermen's Mutual Insurance Co.; Interstate Insurance Group; Laidlaw, Inc.; Liberty Mutual Insurance Co.; Lobo Claims Management; Markel Insurance Co.; Merastar Insurance Co.; Meridian Insurance; Nationwide Agribusiness; Prudential Property & Casualty Insurance Co.; RLI Insurance Companies; Sedgwick James; Union Insurance Co.; Ward North America, Inc.; Zurich Insurance.
REFERENCES: Wells Fargo, DesMoines; The Bankers Trust Co.; Bank of America.

THE JAMES LAW FIRM, P.C.

Established in 1988

630 EQUITABLE BUILDING
604 LOCUST STREET
DES MOINES, IOWA 50309
Telephone: 515-246-8484
Fax: 515-246-8767
URL: http://www.jameslawfirm.com

Personal Injury, Wrongful Death, Medical Malpractice, Product Liability, Business and Tort Litigation.

DWIGHT W. JAMES, born Des Moines, Iowa, June 30, 1934; admitted to bar, 1961, Iowa, U.S. District Court, Northern and Southern Districts of Iowa and U.S. Court of Appeals, Eighth Circuit. *Education:* Texas College of Arts & Industries (B.B.A., 1958); Drake University (LL.B., 1961). Iowa/American Board of Trial Advocates, Outstanding Advocate Award, 1998. Past President and Master, C. Edwin Moore Inn of Court, 1990—. President, Board of Counsellors, Drake Law School, 1967-1968. Author: "Wrongful Death Actions in Iowa," The Iowa Trial Lawyer, Winter 1982. Co-Author: "Tort Reform: An Elimination of Rights," Vol. 36, No. 4, Drake Law Review, 1986-1987. Listed, Best Lawyers in America. Board Certified as a Mediator by the American Association of ADR Attorneys. *Member:* Polk County and Iowa State (President, Junior Bar Section, 1968-1969; Chair, Committee on Independence Judiciary; (Chair, Litigation Section, 2003—); Iowa Trial Lawyers Association (President, 1977-1978); Trial Lawyers for Public Justice (Board Member, 1989-1998); The Association of Trial Lawyers of America (Governor, 1980-1986); American Board of Trial Advocates (Advocate; President, Iowa Chapter, 1993; National Board Representative, 1995-1998). Fellow: Iowa Academy of Trial Lawyers; American College of Trial Lawyers; Roscoe Pound Foundation. ***PRACTICE AREAS:*** Personal Injury Law; Wrongful Death Law; Medical Malpractice; Product Liability Law; Business Law; Tort Litigation. ***Email:*** dwjames@raccoon.com

FREDERICK W. JAMES, born Des Moines, Iowa, July 28, 1959; admitted to bar, 1988, Iowa and U.S. District Court, Northern and Southern Districts of Iowa; U.S. Court of Appeals, Eighth Circuit. *Education:* Coe College; University of Iowa (B.A., 1983); Drake University (J.D., 1987). Master of the Bench, C. Edwin Moore Inn of Court, 1999—. *Member:* Polk County Bar Association (Member, Admissions Committee, 1990-1995), Iowa State (Member, Committee on American Citizenship, 1990—); American Board of Trial Advocates; The Association of Trial Lawyers of America (Member: Public Relation Committee, 1989-1991; Young Lawyers Advisory Committee, 1991-1993); Iowa Trial Lawyers Association (Member, Continuing Legal Education Committee, 1989-1995; Chairperson, 1992-1995; Board of Governors, 1990-1995; Officer at Large, 1995-1996; Parliamentarian, 1996-1997; Secretary, 1997-1998; Vice President, Administration, 1998-2001; President Elect, 2001-2002; President, 2002-2003; Secretary Justice for all P.A.C., 1995-1998; Chair, 1998-1999). Fellow: Iowa Academy of Trial Lawyers; Roscoe Pound Foundation. (Certified as a Civil Trial Specialist by the National Board of Trial Advocacy). ***PRACTICE AREAS:*** Personal Injury; Wrongful Death; Medical Malpractice; Products Liability; Business; Tort Litigation. ***Email:*** fwjames@raccoon.com

JENNIFER GERRISH-LAMPE, born Seoul, Korea, May 15, 1972; admitted to bar, 1997, Iowa and U.S. District Court, Northern and Southern Districts of Iowa. *Education:* Drake University (B.A., 1994; J.D., with honors, 1996). *Member:* Polk County (Member, Board of Governors; Co-Chair, Bench Bar Committee), Iowa State (Member, YLD Committee) and American Bar Associations; Iowa Trial Lawyers Association (Chair, Tech Committee; Vice Chair, CLE Committee; Member, Board of Governors) The Association of Trial Lawyers of America; Iowa Delegate Minority Caucus. ***Email:*** jennifer@jameslawfirm.com

REFERENCE: Liberty Bank.

STEVEN C. JAYNE

5835 GRAND AVENUE
SUITE 201
DES MOINES, IOWA 50312
Telephone: 515-255-2945
Fax: 515-255-5997

Social Security, Workers Compensation, Personal Injury, Trials.

FIRM PROFILE: Steven C. Jayne has been serving clients for over 25 years throughout Polk and its contiguous counties. The firm was established in 1979 and practices in the area of litigation.

STEVEN C. JAYNE, born Carroll, Iowa, February 23, 1950; admitted to bar, 1979, Iowa and U.S. District Court, Northern and Southern Districts of Iowa; U.S. Court of Appeals, Eighth Circuit. *Education:* University of New Mexico (B.A., 1976); Drake University (J.D., 1978). *Member:* Iowa State and American Bar Associations; The Association of Trial Lawyers of America; Iowa Association of Workers Compensation Lawyers; Iowa Trial Lawyers Association.

KALINOSKI & CHAPLINSKY
ATTORNEYS AT LAW

100 COURT AVENUE, SUITE 205
DES MOINES, IOWA 50309
Telephone: 515-246-8800
Fax: 515-246-1920
URL: http://www.kclawoffice.net

General Practice.

MEMBERS OF FIRM

CHARLES J. KALINOSKI (1948-2003)

MARGARET M. CHAPLINSKY, born Lehighton, Pennsylvania, 1958; admitted to bar, 1983, Pennsylvania; 1985, U.S. Court of Appeals, Third Circuit; 1989, U.S. Court of Appeals, Tenth Circuit; 1992, Iowa and U.S. District Court, Southern District of Iowa; 1993, U.S. Court of Appeals, Eighth Circuit. *Education:* Villanova University (B.A., 1980); Delaware Law School of Widener University (J.D., 1983). Recipient, American Jurisprudence Award in Real Property. *Member:* Philadelphia, Polk County, Iowa State, Pennsylvania and American Bar Associations. ***LANGUAGES:*** Russian. ***Email:*** mmchaplinsky@kc-legal.com

DOROTHY L. KELLEY

808 INSURANCE EXCHANGE BUILDING
505 FIFTH AVENUE
DES MOINES, IOWA 50309-2317
Telephone: 515-243-5207
Fax: 515-243-5212

Litigation, Workers Compensation Law.

DOROTHY L. KELLEY, born Pittsburgh, Pennsylvania, February 23, 1944; admitted to bar, 1974, Iowa; 1976, U.S. Supreme Court, U.S. Claims Court, U.S. District Court, Northern and Southern Districts of Iowa and U.S. Court of Appeals, Eighth Circuit. *Education:* Drake University (B.A., 1971; J.D., 1974). Phi Kappa Phi; Phi Alpha Delta (Marshal, 1973-1974). Recipient: American Jurisprudence Award, 1973; Student Service Award, 1974. Registered Technologist, American Registry Radiologic Technology Iowa, 1965. Assistant Attorney General, Department of Justice, State of Iowa, 1974-1977. *Member:* Polk County, Iowa State and American Bar Associations; Iowa Defense Counsel Association; Defense Research Institute; Iowa Association of Workers Compensation Lawyers; American Society of Law and Medicine. ***PRACTICE AREAS:*** Litigation; Workers Compensation Law.

KUTAK ROCK LLP

Established in 1965

SUITE 124, HIGHLAND BUILDING
4201 WESTOWN PARKWAY
DES MOINES, IOWA 50266-6720
Telephone: 515-224-1266
Fax: 515-457-7669
URL: http://www.kutakrock.com

Atlanta, Georgia Office: Suite 2100, 225 Peachtree Street, NE, 30303-1731. Telephone: 404-222-4600. Facsimile: 404-222-4654.
Denver, Colorado Office: Suite 3100, 1801 California Street, 80202-2658. Telephone: 303-297-2400. Facsimile: 303-292-7799.
Kansas City, Missouri Office: Valencia Place, Suite 200, 444 West 47th Street, 64112-1914. Telephone: 816-960-0090. Telefax: 816-960-0041.
Fayetteville, Arkansas Office: The Three Sisters Building, 214 West Dickson Street, 72701-5221. Telephone: 501-973-4200. Facsimile: 501-973-0007.
Little Rock, Arkansas Office: Suite 1100, 425 West Capitol Avenue, 72201-3409. Telephone: 501-975-3000. Facsimile: 501-975-3001.
Los Angeles, California Office: Suite 3000, 555 West Fifth Street, 90013-1010. Telephone: 213-996-8478. Facsimile: 213-996-8479.
Oklahoma City, Oklahoma Office: Suite 475, 6305 Waterford Boulevard, 73118-1116. Telephone: 405-848-2475. Facsimile: 405-842-5748.
Omaha, Nebraska Office: The Omaha Building, 1650 Farnam Street, 68102-2186. Telephone: 402-346-6000. Facsimile: 402-346-1148.
Scottsdale, Arizona Office: Suite 300, 8601 N. Scottsdale Road, 85253-2742. Telephone: 480-429-5000. Facsimile: 480-429-5001.
Washington, D.C. Office: Suite 1000, 1101 Connecticut Avenue, NW, 20036-4374. Telephone: 202-828-2400. Facsimile: 202-828-2488.
Irvine, California Office: Suite 1100, 18201 Von Karman Avenue, 92612-1077. Telephone: 949-417-0999. Facsimile: 949-417-5394.
Pasadena, California Office: Suite 308, 201 South Lake Avenue, 91101-3004. Telephone: 626-432-1630. Facsimile: 626-432-1614.
Richmond, Virginia Office: Bank of America Center, Suite 800, 1111 East Main Street, 23219-3103. Telephone: 804-644-0313. Facsimile: 804-783-6192.
Chicago, Illinois Office: One South Wacker Drive, 60606-4614. Telephone: 312-602-4100. Facsimile: 312-602-4101.
Wichita, Kansas Office: Suite 370, 8301 East 21st Street North, 67206-2935. Telephone: 316-609-7900. Facsimile: 316-630-8021.

Civil Litigation and Bankruptcy, Public Finance, Corporate and Structured Finance, Banking and Commercial Lending, Real Estate Law, Taxation Law, Health Care and Hospital Law.

FIRM PROFILE: Founded in Omaha in 1965, Kutak Rock conducts a full-service, multidisciplinary practice. While the firm has long had a nationally recognized public and corporate finance practice, we have also developed a sophisticated business and litigation practice rep-

(This Listing Continued)

KUTAK ROCK LLP, Des Moines—Continued

resenting clients across the country in complex transactions and major litigation. Kutak Rock has represented every major investment banking firm in the United States; major European, Asian and domestic money-center banks; savings and loan associations; insurance companies; national real estate syndicators and developers; major national franchising enterprises; and numerous other financial institutions, businesses and state and local governmental units. The firm's litigation practice group represents corporate and individual clients in federal and state courts nationwide in complex civil litigation matters and represents clients in arbitration and mediation proceedings. The firm's Healthcare/hospital law group represents hospitals and physician organizations in numerous states.

PARTNER

NORENE D. JACOBS, born Hays, Kansas, July 24, 1942; admitted to bar, 1978, Iowa. *Education:* Fort Hays State University (A.B., summa cum laude, 1974); University of Kansas School of Law (J.D., 1977). Phi Kappa Phi. Moot Court Council, 1976-1977. ***PRACTICE AREAS:*** Health Care; Labor and Employment. ***Email:*** norene.jacobs@kutakrock.com

(For biographical data of Atlanta Lawyers, see Professional Biographies at Atlanta, Georgia).
(For biographical data of Chicago Lawyers, see Professional Biographies at Chicago, Illinois).
(For biographical data of Denver Lawyers, see Professional Biographies at Denver, Colorado).
(For biographical data of Fayetteville Lawyers, see Professional Biographies at Fayetteville, Arkansas).
(For biographical data of Kansas City Lawyers, see Professional Biographies at Kansas City, Missouri)
(For biographical data of Little Rock Lawyers, see Professional Biographies at Little Rock, Arkansas).
(For biographical data of Irvine Lawyers, see Professional Biographies at Irvine, California).
(For biographical data of New York Lawyers, see Professional Biographies at New York, N.Y.).
(For biographical data of Oklahoma City Lawyers, see Professional Biographies at Oklahoma City, Oklahoma).
(For biographical data of Omaha Lawyers, see Professional Biographies at Omaha, Nebraska).
(For biographical data of Pasadena Lawyers, see Professional Biographies at Pasadena, California).
(For biographical data of Pittsburgh Lawyers, see Professional Biographies at Pittsburgh, Pennsylvania).
(For biographical data of Richmond Lawyers, see Professional Biographies at Richmond, Virginia).
(For biographical data of Scottsdale Lawyers, see Professional Biographies at Scottsdale, Arizona).
(For biographical data of Washington Lawyers, see Professional Biographies at Washington D.C.).

LAMARCA & LANDRY, P.C.

1820 NW 118TH STREET, SUITE 200
DES MOINES, IOWA 50325
Telephone: 515-225-2600
Fax: 515-225-8581
URL: http://www.lamarcaandlandry.com

Trial Practice in State and Federal Courts. Aviation Law, Commercial Litigation, Personal Injury, Wrongful Death, Medical Malpractice, Legal Malpractice, Workers Compensation, Products Liability.

FIRM PROFILE: LaMarca & Landry was founded by George A. LaMarca and Gregory W. Landry in 1989. Serving clients for over 27 years throughout the State of Iowa as well as nationally. The firm engages in the practice of Personal Injury, Wrongful Death, Commercial Litigation and Medical Malpractice and Workers Compensation.

GEORGE A. LAMARCA, born Rockford, Illinois, June 21, 1945; admitted to bar, 1970, Iowa; 1971, U.S. District Court, Southern District of Iowa; 1976, U.S. District Court, Northern District of Iowa and U.S. Court of Appeals, Eighth Circuit; 1978, U.S. Supreme Court; 1982, U.S. Claims Court; 1986, Florida, U.S. District Court, Southern and Middle Districts of Florida and U.S. Court of Appeals, Eleventh Circuit. *Education:* Southern Illinois University, Carbondale (B.A., Political Science and English, 1967); Oxford University, England; Drake University Law School (J.D., 1970). Author: "Market Share Liability, Industry-Wide Liability, Alternative Liability and Concert of Action: Modern Legal Concepts Preserving Liability for Defective but Unidentifiable Products," 31 Drake Law Review 61, 1981-1982; "Overintrusive Surveillance of the Plaintiff in Personal Injury Cases," *The American Journal of Trial Advocacy,* Cumberland School of Law, Samford University, Volume 8:3, August, 1985; *Iowa Pleading and Causes of Action,* Vols. I and II, 1989, Butterworths. Contributing Editor, American Bar Association Journal of Litigation, 1976-1980. Member, Board of Editors, Trial Diplomacy Journal, 1989—. Associate Professor, Trial Advocacy, Drake University School of Law, 1983. *Member:* Iowa State and American (Member, Litigation and Insurance Sections) Bar Associations; The Florida Bar; Association of Trial Lawyers of Iowa (Member, Board of Governors, 1979-1983, 1987-1991; Parliamentarian, 1990-1991; Secretary, 1991-1992; Vice President, 1992-1994; President-Elect, 1994-1995; President, 1995-1996); American Board of Trial Advocates; American Board of Professional Liability Attorneys; Iowa Academy of Trial Lawyers; The Association of Trial Lawyers of America; Illinois Trial Lawyers Association; The Academy of Florida Trial Lawyers; Lawyer Pilots Bar Association. Certified as a Civil Trial Attorney by the National Board of Trial Advocacy; Board Certified as a Diplomate by the American Board of Professional Liability Attorneys (Also Of Counsel to Duffey & Davis, Sarasota, Florida). ***PRACTICE AREAS:*** Personal Injury; Commercial Litigation. ***Email:*** george@lamarcalandry.com

(This Listing Continued)

GREGORY W. LANDRY, born South Haven, Michigan, May 9, 1957; admitted to bar, 1983, Iowa; 1991, Missouri; 1993, Florida; 1988, U.S. Supreme Court; 1983, U.S. Court of Appeals, Eighth Circuit; U.S. Claims Court; U.S. District Court, Northern and Southern Districts of Iowa; U.S. Court of Appeals for the Federal Circuit. *Education:* University of Colorado at Boulder (B.A., 1980); Drake University Law School (J.D., 1983). *Member:* Polk County, Iowa State and American Bar Associations; The Association of Trial Lawyers of America; Association of Trial Lawyers of Iowa; Iowa Academy of Trial Lawyers; Iowa Association of Workers' Compensation Lawyers, Inc.; American Board of Trial Advocates; American Board of Professional Liability Attorneys; Lawyer Pilots Bar Association. Board Certified as a Diplomate by the American Board of Professional Liability Attorneys. ***PRACTICE AREAS:*** Personal Injury; Medical Malpractice. ***Email:*** greg@lamarcalandry.com

---

GARY G. MATTSON, born Osceola, Iowa, July 30, 1962; admitted to bar, 1988, Iowa; U.S. District Court, Northern and Southern Districts of Iowa; U.S. Court of Appeals, Eighth Circuit; U.S. Supreme Court;. *Education:* Luther College (B.A., 1985); Drake University Law School (J.D., 1988). Delta Theta Phi. *Member:* Polk County and Iowa State Bar Associations; Iowa Trial Lawyers Association; The Association of Trial Lawyers of America (Member, Sections on: Motor Vehicle Collision; Highway and Premises Liability); Iowa Association of Workers' Compensation Lawyers. ***PRACTICE AREAS:*** Workers Compensation; Personal Injury. ***Email:*** gary@lamarcalandry.com

JUSTIN E. LAVAN, born Spencer, Iowa, October 10, 1972; admitted to bar, 1998, Iowa, U.S. District Court, Northern and Southern Districts of Iowa and U.S. Court of Appeals, Eighth Circuit; 1999, Florida; 2002, U.S. Supreme Court; 2003, U.S. District Court, District of Nebraska; 2004, U.S. District Court, Northern District of Florida; U.S. District Court, Middle District of Florida. *Education:* Mankato State University (B.S., Political Science, magna cum laude, 1994); Drake University (J.D., with honors, 1998). Delta Theta Phi. Author: "Strategies to Avoid Enforcement of Arbitration Clauses", The Trial Lawyer Journal of Strategy, Technique and Case Management, Vol. 24, No. 2, March/April, 2001. *Member:* Iowa Bar Association; The Florida Bar; Iowa Trial Lawyers Association; Christian Legal Society. [JAG Officer, U.S. Army Reserves, 1990-2003]. ***PRACTICE AREAS:*** Business Litigation; Insurance Litigation; Personal Injury. ***Email:*** justin@lamarcalandry.com

ROMAN VALD, born Riga, Latvia, January 1, 1970; admitted to bar, 1995, Iowa. *Education:* University of Iowa (B.A., high distinction, 1992; J.D., 1995). Member, Phillips, McCollom, Kozlowski & Vald, P.L.C. *Member:* Polk County and Iowa State Bar Associations; Iowa Association Criminal Defense Lawyers. ***LANGUAGES:*** Russian. ***PRACTICE AREAS:*** Family Law (40%); Criminal Defense (40%); Personal Injury (20%). ***Email:*** valdlaw@yahoo.com

CHAD KNAPP, admitted to bar, 2002, Iowa. *Education:* Iowa State University (B.A., Political Science, 1999); Drake University Law School (J.D., 2002). *Member:* Iowa State Bar Association; Iowa Trial Lawyers Association. ***PRACTICE AREAS:*** Civil Litigation. ***Email:*** chad@lamarcalandry.com

SARA A. LAMME, born Winner, South Dakota, August 24, 1977; admitted to bar, 2003, Iowa; 2004, Nebraska. *Education:* Mount Marty College (B.A., magna cum laude, 2000); Creighton University School of Law (J.D., 2003). *Member:* Iowa State Bar Association; Nebraska State Bar Association. ***PRACTICE AREAS:*** Personal Injury; Workers Compensation. ***Email:*** sara@lamarcalandry.com

JAMES BISCOGLIA, born Atlanta, Georgia, February 6, 1969; admitted to bar, 1995, Florida and U.S. District Court, Middle District of Florida; 2004, Iowa. *Education:* Drake University (B.S., with honors, 1992; J.D., with honors, 1995). ***PRACTICE AREAS:*** Personal Injury; Medical Malpractice; Nursing Home Abuse and Neglect; General Litigation. ***Email:*** james@lamarcalandry.com

OF COUNSEL

MARTIN R. ANDERSON, born Vicksburg, Michigan, November 8, 1946; admitted to bar, 1976, Iowa; 1983, Alaska; 1986, U.S. District Court, District of Alaska. *Education:* Western Michigan University (B.A., 1972); Drake University Law School (J.D., 1975). Of Counsel, Perkins Cole, 1984-1990. Executive Vice-President and Manager, Alaska Pacific Trust Co., 1981. *Member:* Alaska and Iowa State and American Bar Associations. [Sgt., U.S. Air Force, 1967-1971]. ***PRACTICE AREAS:*** Estate Planning; Probate; Estate Administration.

NICK JAMES AVGERINOS, admitted to bar, 1981, Iowa and Illinois. *Education:* University of Kansas (B.A., 1978); Drake University Law School (J.D., 1981). Mediator, United States Arbitration and Mediation, 1992—. *Member:* Chicago and Iowa State Bar Associations; Illinois Trial Lawyers Association; Iowa and Illinois Workers' Compensation Lawyers Association. (Also member, Capron & Avgerinos, P.C., Chicago, Illinois). ***PRACTICE AREAS:*** Workers Compensation.

REPRESENTATIVE CLIENTS: American Administrators, Inc.; Burger Boat Company; Burger Yacht Sales, Inc.; Collective Investment Management, Ltd.; Construction Support Group, Inc.; Crown Ready-Mix, Inc.; Eco-Tech Contractors, Inc.; Heartland Plastic & Reconstructive Surgery, P.C.; Midwest Ready-Mix, Inc.; Schabel Trucking, Inc.; Ted Lare Design Build LLC; Ludwig Roofing; Bardwell Enterprises, LLC; Bardwell Construction, Inc.; Professional Drywall.

LAW FIRM OF STEVEN V. LAWYER & ASSOCIATES, P.L.C.

Established in 1997
FOURTH FLOOR FLEMING BUILDING
218 SIXTH AVENUE
DES MOINES, IOWA 50309-4011
Telephone: 515-282-2080
Fax: 515-282-1980; Toll Free: 1-877-282-2080
Email: Info@LawyerLawFirm.com
URL: http://www.lawyerlawfirm.com

Traumatic Brain Injury, Wrongful Death, Automobile Accidents and Injuries, Products Liability, Roadway Design Liability, Aircraft Accidents, Employment Law.

(This Listing Continued)

STEVEN VERNE LAWYER, born Des Moines, Iowa, July 9, 1965; admitted to bar, 1991, Iowa and U.S. District Court, Southern and Northern Districts of Iowa; U.S. Court of Appeals, Eighth Circuit; U.S. Supreme Court. *Education:* Iowa State University (B.S., in Physics, 1988); Drake University (J.D., with honors, 1991); University of Southern California, Institute of Safety and Systems Management (Aircraft Accident Investigation, 1991). Co-Editor, Supplement to Roehrick, Iowa Evidence, 1991. Author: "Owner Liability for Negligent Driving by a Co-Worker," 1996; "Maximizing Client Recovery in the Face of Hospital Liens and Insurance Subrogation," 2000; "Dealing with Medicare in a P.I. Case," 2001. *Member:* Iowa Trial Lawyers Association; The Association of Trial Lawyers of America; Aircraft Owners and Pilots Association (Panel Attorney); Iowa State Bar Association; Blackstone Inn of Court; American College of Barristers. ***LANGUAGES:*** French. ***PRACTICE AREAS:*** Personal Injury; Wrongful Death; Brain Injury; Automobile Accidents and Injuries; Unsafe Products; Aviation Law; Airplane Crash Litigation; Roadway Design; Medical Malpractice; Nursing Home Abuse and Neglect; Discrimination; Sexual Harassment.

LEWIS, WEBSTER, VAN WINKLE & KNOSHAUG, L.L.P.

620 LIBERTY BUILDING
418 SIXTH AVENUE
DES MOINES, IOWA 50309
Telephone: 515-243-1000
Fax: 515-288-7000
Email: attorneys@lewislaw-ia.com

Litigation in all Courts. Insurance, Negligence, Personal Injury, Workers' Compensation, Products Liability, Transportation Litigation, Commercial, Agency Law and Appeals.

FIRM PROFILE: Lewis, Webster, Van Winkle & Knoshaug, L.L.P. was established in 1994 with a combined experience of over 100 years practicing law in the community, serving clients throughout the state of Iowa. The firm engages in a trial practice as well as being involved in Dispute Resolution.

R. JEFFREY LEWIS, born Ames, Iowa, May 28, 1947; admitted to bar, 1972, Iowa. *Education:* University of Kansas (B.A., with honors, 1969); University of Minnesota (J.D., 1972). Recipient, Stone Scholarship Tutorial Program. *Member:* Polk County and Iowa State Bar Associations; Association of Trial Lawyers of Iowa; Iowa Defense Counsel Association; Defense Research Institute; Trucking Industry Defense Association. Fellow, Iowa Academy of Trial Lawyers. ***PRACTICE AREAS:*** Trial Practice; Appeals. **Email:** rjl@lewislaw-ia.com

KIMBERLY P. KNOSHAUG, born Waterloo, Iowa, November 23, 1963; admitted to bar, 1990, Illinois and U.S. District Court, Northern District of Illinois; 1993, Iowa; 1994, U.S. District Court, Northern District of Iowa; 1995, U.S. District Court, Southern District of Iowa; 1996, U.S. Court of Appeals, Eighth Circuit. *Education:* University of Iowa (B.A., 1985); Chicago-Kent College of Law, Illinois Institute of Technology (J.D., 1989). *Member:* Polk County and Iowa State Bar Associations. ***PRACTICE AREAS:*** Trial Practice. **Email:** kpk@lewislaw-ia.com

JASON B. WITTGRAF, born Des Moines, Iowa, November 30, 1975; admitted to bar, 2001, Iowa and U.S. District Court, Northern and Southern Districts of Iowa. *Education:* Ripon College (B.A., with honors, 1998); University of Iowa (J.D., 2001). *Member:* Polk County and Iowa State Bar Associations. ***PRACTICE AREAS:*** Trial Practice. **Email:** jbw@lewislaw-ia.com

ANGELA BROUGHTON-ROMAIN, born Shelbyville, Indiana, May 29, 1967; admitted to bar, 1994, Minnesota and U.S. District Court, District of Minnesota; 2002, U.S. District Court, Southern District of Indiana; 2003, Iowa. *Education:* Indiana University (B.A., with highest distinction, 1988) Phi Beta Kappa; New York University (M.A., 1991); Indiana University (J.D. magna cum laude, 1994);. Order of the Coif. Co-Author with Reid Carron: "When is 'No' Really 'No'?—The NLRB's Current Position on the Freedom of Contract, Management Rights and Waiver," 13 Lab. Law. 299 (Fall 1997). Co-Author: "International Legal Developments in Review," ABA International Employment Law Committee Reports, 1997, 32 Int'l. Law. 303 (Summer 1998) and 1998, 33 Int'l Law. 291 (Summer 1999). Adjunct Professor, Legal Writing: University of Minnesota, 1998-1999; William Mitchell College of Law, 1999-2000. *Member:* Polk County and Iowa State Bar Associations. ***LANGUAGES:*** French. ***PRACTICE AREAS:*** Trial Practice. **Email:** abr@lewislaw-ia.com

BENNETT A. WEBSTER (1923-2002)

COUNSEL

JOSEPH G. VAN WINKLE, born Detroit, Michigan, October 15, 1953; admitted to bar, 1978, Iowa and U.S. Court of the Armed Forces; 1980, U.S. Court of Appeals, District of Columbia Circuit; 1981, U.S. Supreme Court; 1986, U.S. District Court, Southern and Northern Districts of Iowa; 1987, U.S. Court of Appeals, Eighth Circuit; 1996, U.S. District Court, District of Nebraska; 2003, U.S. Court of Appeals, Fifth Circuit. *Education:* Iowa State University (B.S., with honors, 1975); University of Iowa (J.D., 1978). *Member:* Polk County (Treasurer, 2000-2001; Secretary, 2001-2003) and Iowa State (Member, Board of Governors, 2003-2004) Bar Associations; The Association of Trial Lawyers of America. [Lt. Commander, U.S. Navy, 1978-1986]. Certified in Trial Advocacy, National Board of Trial Advocacy. ***PRACTICE AREAS:*** Trial Practice; Appeals. **Email:** jvw@lewislaw-ia.com

REPRESENTATIVE CLIENTS: Great West Casualty Company; Farmland Industries, Inc.; Ferrellgas, Inc.; Iowa-Illinois Safety Council; Lincoln General Casualty Company; National By-Products, Inc.; Old Republic Insurance Company; Sentry Insurance Company; Tyson Fresh Meats, Inc.; Union Pacific Railroad Company, Universal Underwriters Insurance Company.

MARCUCCI & CONGER, P.L.C.

DES MOINES, IOWA

(See West Des Moines)

General Civil Trial Practice, Commercial Litigation, Negligence, Personal Injury.

McCARTHY & HAMROCK, P.C.

DES MOINES, IOWA

(See West Des Moines)

Criminal Law, Personal Injury, Driving While Intoxicated, Drug Crimes, Juvenile Criminal Law, Parole and Probation, Traffic Violations, Automobile Accidents, Slip and Fall, Wrongful Death.

McENROE, GOTSDINER, BREWER, BURDETTE & STEINBACH, P.C.

DES MOINES, IOWA

(See West Des Moines)

General Practice. Corporate, Real Estate, Bankruptcy, Commercial Collection, Personal Injury, Criminal, Probate, Domestic Relations, Transportation and Products Liability Law. Litigation in all Courts.

McGUIRE LAW FIRM, P.C.

DES MOINES, IOWA

(See Mason City)

Personal Injury Law, Medical Malpractice, Severe Burns, Water Heater Flammable Vapor Litigation, Products Liability, Railroad Litigation, Trial Practice.

McKEE, VOORHEES & SEASE, P.L.C.

Established in 1924
801 GRAND, SUITE 3200
DES MOINES, IOWA 50309-2721
Telephone: 515-288-3667
Facsimile: 515-288-1338
Email: patatty@ipmvs.com
URL: http://www.ipmvs.com

Intellectual Property and Technology Law, including Patent, Trademark, Copyright, Trade Secret, Licensing, Antitrust. State and Federal Trial Practice.

FIRM PROFILE: The Firm and it's predecessor partnerships have been practicing law in Des Moines since 1924. The Firm deals with all aspects of such technical and scientific areas as mechanical, electrical, chemical, biotechnical, medical, microbial and computer arts. Extensive litigation is conducted in all of these areas, as well as in the fields of copyrights and trademarks and related causes of action.

McKee, Voorhees & Sease is listed in the Martindale Hubbell Bar Register of Preeminent Lawyers.

MEMBERS OF FIRM

BRUCE W. McKEE, born Montezuma, Iowa, May 3, 1934; admitted to bar, 1959, Iowa; 1959-1982, U.S. Court of Customs and Patent Appeals; 1962, U.S. Supreme Court, U.S. Claims Court and U.S. Court of Military Appeals; 1963, U.S. District Courts of Iowa and U.S. Court of Appeals Eighth Circuit; 1982, U.S. Court of Appeals for the Federal Circuit; registered to practice before U.S. Patent and Trademark Office. *Education:* Iowa State University (B.S.E., 1956); American University (J.D., 1959). Delta Theta Phi. Patent Examiner, U.S. Patent Office, 1956-1959. Assistant Staff Judge Advocate, U.S.A.F., 1959-1962. *Member:* Polk County, Iowa State (Chairman: Law and Behavioral Science Committee, 1983-1986; Patent, Trademark, Copyright Law Section Council, 1991-1993; Intellectual Property Council, 1998-2000) and American Bar Associations; American Intellectual Property Law Association; Iowa Intellectual Property Law Association (President, 1977-1978); International Trademark Association. ***PRACTICE AREAS:*** Patents; Trademarks; Copyrights. **Email:** mckee@ipmvs.com

MICHAEL G. VOORHEES, born Des Moines, Iowa, April 17, 1941; admitted to bar, 1968, Iowa; 1969, Missouri; U.S. Circuit Court of Appeals, Eighth Circuit; 1970, U.S. District Courts of Iowa; 1975-1982, U. S. Court of Customs and Patent Appeals; 1982, U.S. Court of Appeals for the Federal Circuit; registered to practice before U.S. Patent and Trademark Office. *Education:* Iowa State University (B.S., 1964); Drake University (J.D., 1968). Member, Drake Law Review, 1968. Lecturer, Trademark, Patent and Copyright Law, Drake University Law School, 1977-1986. Adjunct Professor of Law, Drake University Law School, 1986-1990. *Member:* Polk County, Iowa State and American Bar Associations; The Missouri Bar; American Intellectual Property Law Association; Iowa Intellectual Property Law Association (President, 1981-1982); American Inns of Court. ***PRACTICE AREAS:*** Patents; Trademarks; Copyrights; Litigation. **Email:** voorhees@ipmvs.com

EDMUND J. SEASE, born Cherokee, Iowa, August 25, 1942; admitted to bar, 1967, Iowa; 1969, Ohio; 1972, U.S. Supreme Court; 1973, U.S. District Court, Northern and Southern Districts of Iowa; 1976, U.S. Court of Appeals, Eighth and Fifth Circuits; 1982, U.S. Court of Appeals for the Federal Circuit; 1990, U.S. Court of Appeals, Sixth Circuit; registered to practice before U.S. Patent and Trademark Office. *Education:* Iowa Central Community College (A.A., 1962); Drake University (B.A., in Chem., 1964; J.D., 1967). Phi Theta Kappa; Phi Beta Kappa; Order of the Coif; Phi Alpha Delta. Member, Editorial Board, Drake Law Review, 1966-1967. Lecturer, Patent, Trademark and Copyright Law,

(This Listing Continued)

McKEE, VOORHEES & SEASE, P.L.C., Des Moines—Continued

Drake University Law School, 1977-1986. Adjunct Professor of Law, Drake University Law School, 1986—. Lecturer, Patent Law, University of Iowa Law School, 1995. *Member:* Polk County, Iowa State, Ohio State and American Bar Associations; American Chemical Society; Iowa Intellectual Property Law Association; American Intellectual Property Law Association. ***REPORTED CASES:*** United States Supreme Court: J.E.M. Ag Supply Inc. v. Pioneer HI-BRED Int'l 534 U.S. 124 (2001). ***PRACTICE AREAS:*** Patents; Trademarks; Copyrights; Litigation. ***Email:*** sease@ipmvs.com

MARK D. HANSING, born Harlowton, Montana, September 23, 1956; admitted to bar, 1981, Iowa and U.S. District Court, Southern and Northern Districts of Iowa; 1983, U.S. Court of Appeals for the Federal Circuit; 1985, U.S. Court of Appeals, Eighth Circuit; registered to practice before U.S. Patent and Trademark Office. *Education:* Luther College (B.A., 1978); University of Iowa (J.D., 1981). *Member:* Polk County, Iowa State and American Bar Associations; Iowa Intellectual Property Law Association; American Intellectual Property Association. ***PRACTICE AREAS:*** Patents; Trademarks; Copyrights. ***Email:*** hansing@ipmvs.com

KIRK M. HARTUNG, born Des Moines, Iowa, September 10, 1955; admitted to bar, 1982, Iowa; 1983, U.S. District Court, Northern and Southern Districts of Iowa, U.S. Court of Appeals for the Federal Circuit and U.S. Supreme Court; registered to practice before U.S. Patent and Trademark Office. *Education:* Iowa State University (B.S., 1979); University of Iowa (J.D., 1982). Phi Delta Phi; Tau Beta Pi. *Member:* Polk County, Iowa State (President, Young Lawyers Division, 1991-1992) and American Bar Associations; Iowa Intellectual Property Law Association; American Intellectual Property Law Association. ***PRACTICE AREAS:*** Patents; Trademarks; Copyright Litigation. ***Email:*** hartung@ipmvs.com

HEIDI SEASE NEBEL, born Des Moines, Iowa, April 11, 1967; admitted to bar, 1992, Iowa; 1993, U.S. Court of Appeals for the Federal and Eighth Circuits; U.S. District Court, Northern and Southern Districts of Iowa; U.S. Supreme Court; registered to practice before U.S. Patent and Trademark Office. *Education:* University of Iowa (B.S., Molecular Biology, 1989); Drake University (J.D., with honors, 1992). Delta Theta Phi. *Member:* Polk County, Iowa State and American Bar Associations; American Intellectual Property Association; Iowa Patent Law Association; Iowa Biotechnology Association; Association of University Technology Managers (President, 2002-2003). ***PRACTICE AREAS:*** Intellectual Property; Biotechnology Patents. ***Email:*** nebel@ipmvs.com

WENDY K. MARSH, born Chicago, Illinois, December 13, 1967; admitted to bar, 1994, Iowa; U.S. Court of Appeals, Federal and Eighth Circuits and U.S. District Court, Northern and Southern Districts of Iowa; registered to practice before U.S. Patent and Trademark Office. *Education:* Drake University (B.S., Pharmacy, 1990; J.D., 1994). Delta Theta Phi. Licensed Pharmacist, Iowa, 1990. *Member:* Polk County, Iowa State (Chair, Intellectual Property Section, 2001-2002) and American (Chair, Inventors Committee, 1998-1999) Bar Associations; American Intellectual Property Law Association; American Pharmaceutical Association; Iowa Intellectual Property Law Association. ***PRACTICE AREAS:*** Intellectual Property; Chemical Patents; Pharmaceutical Patents; Trademarks; Copyrights. ***Email:*** marsh@ipmvs.com

JEFFREY D. HARTY, born Fort Dodge, Iowa, December 7, 1968; admitted to bar, 1995, Iowa, U.S. District Court, Northern and Southern Districts of Iowa, U.S. Court of Appeals, Sixth, Eighth and Federal Circuits, and U.S. Court of Federal Claims. *Education:* Iowa State University (B.S., in Industrial Engineering, 1991); University of Iowa (J.D., with high distinction, 1995). Lecturer, Copyright Law, University of Iowa Law School, 2001; Lecturer, Trademark and Copyright Law, Drake Law School, 2002; Lecturer, Intellectual Property Litigation, Drake Law School, 2004. Member, Polk County Bar Association, 2004. *Member:* Iowa State and American Bar Associations; Iowa Intellectual Property Law Association. ***PRACTICE AREAS:*** Patents; Trademarks; Copyrights; Litigation. ***Email:*** harty@ipmvs.com

CHRISTINE LEBRÓN-DYKEMAN, born Nashua, New Hampshire, December 23, 1969; admitted to bar, 1996, Massachusetts; 1998, Iowa; 2000, California and U.S. District Court, Northern and Southern Districts of Iowa and U.S. Court of Appeals, Federal and Ninth Circuit. *Education:* Smith College (A.B., 1991); University of Iowa (J.D., with distinction, 1996). Judicial Law Clerk, 1997-1999. *Member:* Iowa State, Massachusetts, California and American Bar Associations; State Bar of California. ***PRACTICE AREAS:*** Trademarks; Patent Litigation; Copyrights. ***Email:*** lebron-dykeman@ipmvs.com

R. SCOTT JOHNSON, born Des Moines, Iowa, August 8, 1973; admitted to bar, 2000, Iowa; U.S. District Court, Northern and Southern Districts of Iowa; registered to practice before U.S. Patent and Trademark Office. *Education:* Iowa State University (B.S., Aerospace Engineering, 1996); Drake University (J.D., with honors, 1999). *Member:* Polk County, Iowa State and American Bar Associations; American Institute of Aeronautics; American Intellectual Property Law Association; Iowa Intellectual Property Law Association; Iowa Trial Lawyers Association. ***PRACTICE AREAS:*** Intellectual Property; Patents; Trademarks; Copyrights; Litigation. ***Email:*** johnson@ipmvs.com

ASSOCIATES

JOHN D. GOODHUE, born Des Moines, Iowa, April 9, 1974; admitted to bar, 2000, Iowa; registered to practice before U.S. Patent and Trademark Office. *Education:* Rose-Hulman Institute of Technology (B.S., 1996); Drake University (J.D., 2000). Author: "Persuasive Presentations: The Essential Guide for Lawyers," ABA LPM, 2001. ***PRACTICE AREAS:*** Intellectual Property; Business Method Patents; Software Protection; Domain Names. ***Email:*** goodhue@ipmvs.com

LILA A.T. AKRAD, born Göes, The Netherlands, March 27, 1971; admitted to bar, 2003, Iowa; registered to practice before U.S. Patent and Trademark Office. *Education:* University of Kansas (B.S., Biology, 1994); Vermont Law School (J.D., 2001). *Member:* Polk County, Iowa State and American Bar Associations; American Intellectual Property Law Association; Iowa Intellectual Property Law Association; Iowa Biotechnology Association; American Seed Trade Association (Associate Member). ***PRACTICE AREAS:*** Intellectual Property; Patents; Biotechnology Patents; Trademarks; Copyrights. ***Email:*** akrad@ipmvs.com

(This Listing Continued)

STEVEN P. SMITH, born Des Moines, Iowa, July 26, 1974; admitted to bar, 2001, California; U.S. District Court, Northern and Central Districts of California; 2003, Nebraska; 2004, Iowa, U.S. District Court, Northern and Southern Districts of Iowa. *Education:* University of Northern Iowa (B.A., Management Information Systems, summa cum laude, 1997); Indiana University School of Law - Bloomington (J.D., magna cum laude, 2000). Order of the Coif. *Member:* State Bar of California. ***Email:*** steven.smith@ipmvs.com

ROBERT A. HODGSON, born Sioux Falls, South Dakota, August 26, 1977; admitted to bar, 2003, Iowa; registered to practice before U.S. Patent and Trademark Office. *Education:* University of Iowa (B.A., Biochemistry, 2000; J.D., 2003). Associate Articles Editor, Iowa Law Review. *Member:* Iowa State Bar Association. ***PRACTICE AREAS:*** Intellectual Property; Patents; Trademarks; Copyrights; Litigation. ***Email:*** hodgson@ipmvs.com

BART A. FISHER, born Wichita, Kansas, July 29, 1970; admitted to bar, 2004, Iowa; registered to practice before U.S. Patent and Trademark Office. *Education:* Kansas State University (B.S., Electrical Engineering, 1994); Friends University (M.S., Management, 2000); Washburn University School of Law (J.D., with honors, 2004). Phi Delta Phi. *Member:* Polk County and Iowa State Bar Associations; Institute of Electrical and Electronic Engineers. ***PRACTICE AREAS:*** Intellectual Property; Patents; Trademarks; Copyrights.

JANÁE LEHMAN BELL, born Austin, Texas, October 15, 1971; admitted to bar, 2004, Iowa; registered to practice before U.S. Patent and Trademark Office. *Education:* University of Nebraska at Omaha (B.S., Biotechnology, 1995); University of Nebraska Medical Center (Ph.D., Department of Pathology and Microbiology, 2001); University of Iowa (J.D., 2004). Associate Editor, Journal of Corporation Law. *Member:* Iowa State Bar Association. ***PRACTICE AREAS:*** Intellectual Property; Patents; Trademarks; Copyrights; Litigation.

JASON F. LINDH, born Aberdeen Washington, October 28, 1973; admitted to bar, 2005, Iowa. *Education:* Central Washington University (B.S., 1998); Gonzaga University (J.D., 2005). Member, IEEE, 2005—. ***Email:*** jason.lindh@ipmus.com

KURT VAN THOMME, born Des Moines, Iowa, February 21, 1976; admitted to bar, 2005, Iowa. *Education:* Drake University (B.A., 1996; J.D., 2005). Delta Theta Phi. Order of the Coif. Author: "Prosecution History Estoppel After *Festo:* Can An Equivalent Ever Break Through the File Wrapper?" volume 53:4 Drake Law Review, 1099 (2005). ***Email:*** kurt.vanthomme@ipmus.com

JANET E. PHIPPS-BURKHEAD, born Ft. Dodge, Iowa, December 11, 1954; admitted to bar, 2005, Iowa. *Education:* Iowa State University (B.S., 1978; M.P.A., 1988); Drake University (J.D., 2005). *Member:* Iowa State and American Bar Associations; Polk County Women Attorneys. [USAR, 1985-1996; Michigan Army National Guard, 1998-2001; Iowa Army National Guard, 1996-1998; Colonel, 2001—.]. ***PRACTICE AREAS:*** Intellectual Property Litigation. ***Email:*** janet.phippsburkhead@ipmus.com

REFERENCE: Bank of America (Des Moines, Iowa).

McLEISH LAW OFFICE

Established in 2004

6165 NW 86TH STREET

DES MOINES, IOWA 50131

Telephone: 515-252-2528

Cell: 515-224-1651

Fax: 515-252-2529

Email: mcleishlaw@iowabar.org

URL: http://www.mcleishlaw.com

Bankruptcy, Commercial Litigation, Wills and Trusts, and Divorce.

MEMBER

DARIA McLEISH, born Springfield, Missouri, 1974; admitted to bar, 2002, Iowa and U.S. District Court, Southern District of Iowa. *Education:* University of Northern Iowa (B.M., cum laude, 1999); Drake University (J.D., 2002). *Member:* Iowa State and American Bar Associations. ***PRACTICE AREAS:*** Living Wills; Wills; Divorce; Name Changes; Bankruptcy Chapter 7; Consumer Bankruptcy; Workouts; Personal Bankruptcy; Trusts and Estates; Living Trusts. ***Email:*** mcleishlaw@iowabar.org

MORAIN & PUGH, P.L.C.

DES MOINES, IOWA

(See West Des Moines)

General Practice, Corporation, Insurance, Administrative, Probate, Real Estate, Litigation and Appeals in Federal and State Courts.

NYEMASTER, GOODE, WEST, HANSELL & O'BRIEN

A PROFESSIONAL CORPORATION

Established in 1917

700 WALNUT, SUITE 1600

DES MOINES, IOWA 50309

Telephone: 515-283-3100

Telecopier: 515-283-3108

Email: info@nyemaster.com

URL: http://www.nyemaster.com

Ames, Iowa Office: 1416 Buckeye Avenue, Ames, Iowa 50010. Telephone: 515-233-3000. Telecopier: 515-232-3846.

(This Listing Continued)

General Civil Practice including Corporate, Securities, Antitrust, Insurance, Banking, Commercial Law, Cooperative Law, Probate, Real Estate, Taxation, Workers Compensation, Municipal, Legislative, Labor, Administrative Law and Trials in all Courts.

JAMES B. WEST, born Des Moines, Iowa, August 2, 1933; admitted to bar, 1960, Iowa. *Education:* Drake University (B.A., 1958; J.D., 1960). Order of the Coif. ***PRACTICE AREAS:*** Legislation and Regulation; Trade Associations; Corporate Insurance.

EDGAR F. HANSELL, born Leon, Iowa, October 12, 1937; admitted to bar, 1961, Iowa. *Education:* State University of Iowa (B.B.A., 1959; J.D., with distinction, 1961). Phi Delta Phi. Author: "Financing Under Article 9 of the Iowa Uniform Commercial Code," 17 Drake Law Review 143, 1968; "Bulk Transfers Under Article 6 of the Iowa Uniform Commercial Code," 19 Drake Law Review 275, 1970. Co-Author: "The Fundamentals of UCC Article 9, as Amended, for the Iowa Banker," The Iowa Bankers Association, 1974; "The Iowa Uniform Securities Act Exemptions Part I: The Securities Exemptions," 2 Journal of Corporation Law 437, 1977; "The Iowa Uniform Securities Act Exemptions Part II: The Transaction Exemptions," 3 Journal of Corporation Law 437, 1978; "Bulk Transfers Under Article 6 of the Iowa UCC Revisited," 31 Drake Law Review 303, 1982; "The Choice of Law Rules of the Iowa Uniform Commercial Code," 33 Drake Law Review 561, 1984; "Director Liability Under Iowa Law - Duties and Protections," 13 Journal of Corporation Law 369, 1988; "Duties of the Board of Directors Under the Iowa Business Corporation Act," 40 Drake Law Review 687, 1991. Member, Editorial Advisory Board, The Journal of Corporation Law, 1977—. Listed in: The Best Lawyers in America, Corporate, Mergers & Acquisitions, and Securities Law; Chambers USA America's Leading Lawyers for Business, Corporate/Mergers & Acquisitions. President, Young Lawyers Section, 1971-1972; Member: Board of Governors, 1971-1972, 1985-1987; Grievance Commission, 1973-1978; Special Committee on Corporation and Business Law, 1973-1985, Chairman, 1979-1985; President, 1989-1990, Iowa State Bar Association. ***PRACTICE AREAS:*** Corporation Law; Business Law; Health Law; Commercial Lending. ***Email:*** efh@nyemaster.com

R. CRAIG SHIVES, born Newton, Iowa, August 5, 1945; admitted to bar, 1970, Iowa. *Education:* Cornell College (B.A., 1967); Vanderbilt University and University of Iowa (J.D., 1970). Order of the Coif; Phi Delta Phi. Listed in, Best Lawyers in America, 1989—. ***PRACTICE AREAS:*** Pension; Profit Sharing; Employee Benefit Plans. ***Email:*** rcs@nyemaster.com

LAWRENCE E. MYERS, born Des Moines, Iowa, November 5, 1930; admitted to bar, 1956, Iowa. *Education:* University of Iowa (B.A., 1952); University of Iowa and Drake University (J.D., 1956). Phi Delta Phi. President, Polk County Bar Association, 1983-1984. Member, Board of Governors, Iowa State Bar Association, 1984-1988. ***Email:*** lem@nyemaster.com

KEITH E. LUCHTEL, born Milford, Iowa, September 7, 1941; admitted to bar, 1973, Iowa. *Education:* United States Air Force Academy (B.S., 1964); Drake University (J.D., 1973). Order of the Coif. Surveys Editor, Drake Law Review, 1972. [Capt., USAF, 1964-1970]. ***PRACTICE AREAS:*** Legislation and Regulation. ***Email:*** kel@nyemaster.com

GERALD J. NEWBROUGH, born Des Moines, Iowa, February 24, 1947; admitted to bar, 1973, Iowa. *Education:* Drake University (B.A., 1969; J.D., 1973). Phi Beta Kappa; Order of the Coif. Associate Editor, Drake Law Review, 1972-1973. ***PRACTICE AREAS:*** Commercial Litigation; Class Actions. ***Email:*** gjn@nyemaster.com

ROBERT A. VanORSDEL, born Omaha, Nebraska, September 6, 1944; admitted to bar, 1975, Iowa. *Education:* University of Iowa (B.B.A., 1967); Drake University (J.D., 1974). Order of the Coif. Associate Editor, Drake Law Review, 1974-1975. Certified Public Accountant, Iowa, 1972. Member, Committee on Taxation, Iowa State Bar Association, 1979-1990. Listed in, The Best Lawyers in America. *Member:* American College of Trust and Estate Counsel. ***Email:*** rav@nyemaster.com

RICHARD J. SAPP, born Monticello, Iowa, January 12, 1950; admitted to bar, 1976, Iowa. *Education:* Drake University (B.A., with honors, 1972; J.D., 1976). Order of the Coif; Omicron Delta Kappa. Staff Member, Drake Law Review, 1975-1976. Author: "Pre-Trial Challenges to Expert Testimony in Toxic Tort Cases," For The Defense (Defense Research Institute, 1989). Co-Author: *Products Liability 50 State Handbook* (West 1994); "Statutes of Limitation and Repose Applicable to Pharmaceutical and Medical Device Litigation" (Products Liability Litigation Committee, Section of Litigation, American Bar Association, 1997); "Products Liability," Report on Civil Jury Instructions (Iowa Defense Counsel Association, 1990). Listed in: Chambers USA America's Leading Lawyers for Business (2004, 2005); The Best Lawyers in America. Member, 1984-1990, Vice Chairman, 1988-1990, Litigation Legislation Committee; Litigation Section Council, 1993-1995, Iowa State Bar Association. Chair, Liability Reform Committee, Iowa Association of Business & Industry, 1996-1998. *Member:* Product Liability Advisory Council; International Association of Defense Counsel; American Board of Trial Advocates; Defense Research Institute; Iowa Defense Counsel Association (Member, Board of Directors, 1987-1994; President, 1993-1994). ***PRACTICE AREAS:*** Trial Practice; Products Liability. ***Email:*** rjs@nyemaster.com

G. R. NEUMANN, born Des Moines, Iowa, September 30, 1950; admitted to bar, 1976, Iowa. *Education:* University of Colorado at Boulder (B.A., 1972); Drake University (J.D., 1976). Co-Author: "The Iowa Uniform Securities Act Exemptions Part I: The Securities Exemptions," 2 Journal of Corporation Law 437, 1977; "The Iowa Uniform Securities Act Exemptions Part II: The Transaction Exemptions," 3 Journal of Corporation Law 437, 1978. Lecturer, Securities Law, Drake University Law School, 1981. Chair, City-County Consolidation Commission, 2002-2004. Member of Board, 2002— and Chair, 2005—, Iowa Capital Investment Board. Listed in: The Best lawyers in America, Corporate Law; Chambers USA America's Leading Lawyers for Business, Corporate/Mergers & Acquisitions. ***PRACTICE AREAS:*** Business Law. ***Email:*** grneumann@nyemaster.com

CARLTON T. KING, born Washington, D.C., March 4, 1944; admitted to bar, 1969, Iowa and Oklahoma. *Education:* Westminster College (B.A., 1966); University of Oklahoma (J.D., 1969). Phi Delta Phi. Listed in, The Best Lawyers in America. Member, Committee on Probate, Property and Trust Law, Iowa State Bar Association, 1984-1990. ***Email:*** ctk@nyemaster.com

GREGORY P. PAGE, born Des Moines, Iowa, April 4, 1952; admitted to bar, 1977, Iowa. *Education:* University of Iowa (B.A., 1974; J.D., with distinction, 1977). Phi Beta Kappa. Member, Moot Court Board, 1976-1977. Listed in, The Best Lawyers in America, 1995-2006. ***PRACTICE AREAS:*** Commercial Practice with emphasis on Financial Institutions; Commercial Lending; Corporate Transactions. ***Email:*** gpp@nyemaster.com

RANDALL G. HORSTMANN, born Iowa City, Iowa, December 16, 1948; admitted to bar, 1976, Iowa. *Education:* University of Iowa (B.A., 1971; M.A., 1973); Drake University (J.D., 1976). Order of the Coif. Editor-in-Chief, Drake Law Review, 1975-1976. Law Clerk, Chief Judge William C. Stuart, U.S. District Court, Southern District of Iowa, 1976-1978. Member, Tort and Insurance Practice and Litigation Section, American Bar Association. *Member:* Iowa Defense Counsel Association. ***PRACTICE AREAS:*** Trial Practice. ***Email:*** rgh@nyemaster.com

JAY EATON, born Waterloo, Iowa, February 24, 1946; admitted to bar, 1971, Iowa; 1972, Ohio (inactive); 1977, Wisconsin (inactive). *Education:* University of Iowa (B.B.A., 1968; J.D., with distinction, 1971). Member: Trade Regulation Committee, 1982-1987; Council, Trade Regulation Section, 1990-1992; Council, Environmental and Natural Resources Law Section, 1994-1998; Jury Instructions Committee, 1993-1998; Board of Governors, 1993-2001; President, 1999-2000, Iowa State Bar Association; Member: Board of Directors, 1989-1997; President, 1992-1993, Polk County Bar Association. ***PRACTICE AREAS:*** Trial Practice; Commercial and Tort Litigation; Environmental Law. ***Email:*** je@nyemaster.com

BURNS MOSSMAN, born Augusta, Georgia, March 12, 1943; admitted to bar, 1968, Iowa and Nebraska; 1970, U.S. Tax Court; U.S. District Court, Northern and Southern Districts of Iowa; U.S. Court of Appeals, Eighth Circuit; U.S. Court of Claims. *Education:* Cornell College, University of Iowa (B.S., 1965; J.D., with distinction, 1968). Phi Delta Phi. Trial Attorney, St. Paul, Minnesota, 1970-1978 and District Counsel, Des Moines, Iowa, 1978-1982, Office of Chief Counsel, Internal Revenue Service. Lecturer, Federal Tax Procedure, Drake University Law School, 1983-1985, 1987. Listed in, The Best Lawyers in America, 1987—. Member, Taxation Committee, 1981-1982, Taxation Council, 1995-1998, and Co-Chair, Iowa Tax Legislation Committee, 1994-1996, Iowa State Bar Association. Member, Court Procedure Committee, American Bar Association Taxation Committee, 1983-1991. Member, American College of Tax Counsel. ***PRACTICE AREAS:*** Taxation Law; Litigation of Disputed State and Federal Taxes. ***Email:*** bmossman@nyemaster.com

BRADFORD L. AUSTIN, born Minneapolis, Minnesota, 1948; admitted to bar, 1976, Iowa. *Education:* University of Minnesota (B.S.B., 1970); Drake University (J.D., 1976). Order of the Coif. Articles Editor, Drake Law Review, 1975-1976. Co-author: "Bulk Transfers Under Article 6 of the Iowa UCC Revisited," 31 Drake Law Review 383, 1982; "Director Liability Under Iowa Law - Duties and Protections," 13 Journal of Corporation Law 369, 1988; "Duties of the Board of Directors Under the Iowa Revised Model Business Corporation Act," 40 Drake Law Review, 1991. Instructor, Business Law, Upper Iowa University, 1978-1979. Judicial Magistrate, Floyd County, Iowa, 1979-1980. Listed in: The Best Lawyers in America; Chambers USA America's Leading Lawyers for Business. Member, Corporation and Business Law Committee 1985-1990, Corporation, Banking and Business Law Section, For Profit Corporations Committee, Chairman, 1990-1992, Iowa State Bar Association; State Chair, American College of Mortgage Attorneys, 1997—. ***PRACTICE AREAS:*** Real Estate; Business Law. ***Email:*** baustin@nyemaster.com

SARA J. SERSLAND, born Menasha, Wisconsin, July 1, 1948; admitted to bar, 1979, Iowa. *Education:* Luther College (B.A., magna cum laude, 1970); Northwestern University (M.A.T., 1971); University of Miami; Drake University (J.D., 1979). Order of the Coif. Executive Editor, Drake Law Review, 1978-1979. Law Clerk, Justice Robert G. Allbee, Supreme Court of Iowa, 1979-1980. Author: "Mental Disability Caused by Mental Stress: Standards of Proof in Workers' Compensation Cases," 33 Drake Law Review 751, 1984. Chair, 1991-1992, Workers' Compensation Section; Member, Board of Governors, 2004—, Iowa State Bar Association. Member, Board of Directors, 2004—, Polk County Bar Association. Member, Board of Governors, 1990—; Rules Committee Chair, 1992-1995; President, 2000-2001, Iowa Association of Workers' Compensation Lawyers, Inc. ***PRACTICE AREAS:*** Workers' Compensation. ***Email:*** sjs@nyemaster.com

HAYWARD L. DRAPER, born Stamford, Connecticut, August 28, 1949; admitted to bar, 1977, Massachusetts; 1979, Michigan; 1982, Iowa. *Education:* Yale University (B.A., magna cum laude, 1971); Harvard University (J.D., cum laude, 1976). Articles Editor, Harvard Journal on Legislation, 1974-1975. Law Clerk, Justice Christopher Armstrong, Massachusetts Appeals Court, 1976-1977. Assistant U.S. Attorney, 1979-1982, Assistant Chief, Civil Division, 1981-1982, Office of United States Attorney, Detroit, Michigan. Listed in, Chambers USA America's Leading Business Lawyers, Litigation. ***PRACTICE AREAS:*** Trial Practice; Professional Malpractice; Health Care; Insurance; Product Liability; Fraud; Banking Litigation. ***Email:*** hdraper@nyemaster.com

MICHAEL W. THRALL, born Manhattan, Kansas, May 26, 1955; admitted to bar, 1980, Iowa. *Education:* Iowa State University (B.S., 1977); University of Iowa (J.D., with high distinction, 1980). Chairperson, Moot Court Board, 1979-1980. Law Clerk, Judge Harold D. Vietor, U.S. District Court, Southern District of Iowa, 1980-1982. Listed in, The Best Lawyers in America. Member, Federal Practice Committee, 1988, Iowa Jury Instructions Committee, 1989-2000, E-Commerce Section Council, 2000-2003, Iowa State Bar Association. Member, United States District Court Federal Practice Committee, 1996. *Member:* Iowa Academy of Trial Lawyers; Iowa Defense Counsel Association (Director, 1997-2003; President-Elect, 2004); National Association of Railroad Trial Counsel; American Board of Trial Advocates; Defense Research Institute (Member, Committee on Health, Disability and Life Insurance); International Association of Defense Counsel; Master, C. Edwin Moore Inn of Court. Iowa State Bar Foundation. ***PRACTICE AREAS:*** Trial Practice. ***Email:*** mwt@nyemaster.com

MARK C. DICKINSON, born Colorado Springs, Colorado, April 23, 1955; admitted to bar, 1981, Iowa. *Education:* Grinnell College (B.A., 1977); University of Iowa (J.D., with distinction, 1981). Executive Editor, Journal of Corporation Law, 1980-1981. Law Clerk, Justice Harvey Uhlenhopp, Iowa Supreme Court, 1981-1982. Author: "Overview of Securities Laws" and "Third Party Legal Opinions," Business Law Practice Manual, Iowa State Bar Association. Lecturer, Securities Regulation, Drake University Law School, 1989. Listed in: The Best Lawyers in America, Corporate, Mergers & Acquisitions, and Securities Law; Chambers USA America's Leading Business Lawyers, Corporate and M&A. Council Member, Business Law Section, 1997-2000, 2003—; Chair, Business Law Section Securities Regulation Committee, 1993-1995; Chair, 1996-1997 and Council Member, 1994-

(This Listing Continued)

NYEMASTER, GOODE, WEST, HANSELL & O'BRIEN, A PROFESSIONAL CORPORATION, Des Moines—Continued

1997, Trade Regulation Section; Member, Electronic Research Committee, 1983-1989; Commercial Law Committee, 1989-1991, Iowa State Bar Association. ***PRACTICE AREAS:*** Corporation; Business; Securities; Franchising. ***Email:*** mcd@nyemaster.com

GREGORY B. WILCOX, born Des Moines, Iowa, September 22, 1954; admitted to bar, 1982, Iowa. *Education:* University of Iowa (B.B.A., 1976); Drake University (J.D., 1982). Order of the Coif. Associate Articles Editor, Drake Law Review, 1981-1982. Co-Author: "The Relative Priority of A Landlord's Lien and Article Nine Security Interest," 35 Drake Law Review 27, 1986; "Director Liability Under Iowa Law - Duties and Protections," 13 Journal of Corporation Law 369, 1988; "Duties of the Board of Directors Under the Iowa Business Corporation Act," 40 Drake Law Review 687, 1991. Co-Author: "Business Acquisitions" and "Third Party Legal Opinions" and Author: "Duties, Liabilities and Indemnification of Directors," Iowa State Bar Association Business Law Practice Manual, 2004; Commercial Law chapter, Iowa Legal Research Guide, 2003. Listed in, The Best Lawyers in America. Member, Committee on Legal Forms, 1985-1991, Chair, 1988-1991; Chair, Business Law Section Professional Corporation Committee, 1993-1994; Member, Business Law Section Council, 2003-2004, Iowa State Bar Association. ***PRACTICE AREAS:*** Corporate Law; Business Law; Mergers and Acquisitions; Cooperatives. ***Email:*** gbw@nyemaster.com

JOHN F. LORENTZEN, born Des Moines, Iowa, August 15, 1957; admitted to bar, 1982, Iowa. *Education:* St. Olaf College (B.A., cum laude, 1978); Drake University (J.D., with honors, 1982). Order of the Coif. Order of Barristers. Instructor, Insurance Law, Drake University Law School, 1990. Lecturer on Insurance Law, Iowa State Bar Review School, 1991-1996. ***PRACTICE AREAS:*** Commercial Litigation; ERISA Litigation; Insurance Law. ***Email:*** jfl@nyemaster.com

ROD KUBAT, born Arkansas City, Kansas, September 18, 1951; admitted to bar, 1976, Iowa, Kansas, U.S. District Court, Southern and Northern Districts of Iowa and U.S. Court of Appeals, 8th Circuit. *Education:* University of Iowa (B.B.A., with high distinction, 1973); University of Kansas (J.D., 1976). Member: Commercial and Bankruptcy Section; Council, 1990-1992, 2004-2005; Chair, 1991-1992; Member, Business Law Section; Council, 1996-1999, 2004—; For Profit Corporation Committee, 2000-2002, 2004—; UCC Committee, 2004—; Limited Liability Company Committee, 2005—, Iowa State Bar Association. ***PRACTICE AREAS:*** Business Law; Debtor and Creditor. ***Email:*** rpkubat@nyemaster.com

STEVEN J. ROY, born Des Moines, Iowa, March 1, 1959; admitted to bar, 1983, Iowa. *Education:* Drake University (B.S.B.A., summa cum laude, 1980; M.B.A., 1983; J.D., with honors, 1983). Beta Gamma Sigma. Order of the Coif. Articles Editor, Drake Law Review, 1982-1983. Certified Public Accountant, Iowa, 1980. Adjunct Professor, Drake University Law School, 1987-1998. Member, Council, Law Practice Management Section, Iowa State Bar Association, 1990-1993. Member, Ways and Means Committee, Iowa State Bar Association, 2000-2003. ***PRACTICE AREAS:*** Taxation Law. ***Email:*** sjr@nyemaster.com

FRANK B. HARTY, born Des Moines, Iowa, September 3, 1959; admitted to bar, 1984, Iowa. *Education:* University of Iowa (B.B.A., with honors, 1981); Drake University (J.D., 1984). Order of the Coif. Editor-in-Chief, Drake Law Review, 1983-1984. Professor, "Employment Law," Drake University Law School, 1998-1999. Lecturer, "Trial Advocacy," Drake University Law School, 1991-1992. Lecturer, "Business Law and Personnel Management," Simpson College, 1987. Lecturer, "Employment Law," Drake University Law School. Author: "Sex Discrimination in Iowa, An Analysis and Critique," 44 Drake Law Review 261 (1996); "Competition Between Employer and Employee: Drafting and Enforcing Restrictive Covenants in Employment Agreements," 35 Drake Law Review 251, 1986; "Expert Testimony Under the Iowa Rules of Evidence, Proffering and Resisting Expert Opinion," 36 Drake Law Review, 343 1987. Co-Author: "The Relative Priority of a Landlord's Lien and Article Nine Security Interest," 35 Drake Law Review 27, 1986; "Employment Torts: Emerging Areas of Employer Liability," 39 Drake Law Review 1, 1990. Associate Editor, American Bar Association Tort and Insurance Law Journal, 1993-1995. Listed in, The Best Lawyers in America; Chambers USA America's Leading Business Lawyers, Employment. Chair, Labor and Employment Law Section, 1995-1998; President, 1994-1995, Young Lawyers Division, Iowa State Bar Association. *Member:* American Bar Association; Iowa Defense Counsel Association; National Institute of Trial Advocacy; National Association of Diocesan Attorneys; Iowa Hospital Attorneys Association; Association of Trial Lawyers of America. ***PRACTICE AREAS:*** Labor and Employment; Collective Bargaining; Litigation; Tort and Insurance. ***Email:*** fharty@nyemaster.com

JAMES C. WINE, born Davenport, Iowa, February 7, 1957; admitted to bar, 1982, Iowa; 1984, Minnesota. *Education:* Princeton University (A.B., 1979); University of Iowa (J.D., with high distinction, 1982). Executive Editor, Journal of Corporation Law, 1981-1982. Law Clerk: Senior Judge Roy L. Stephenson, U.S. Court of Appeals, Eighth Circuit, 1982; Judge George G. Fagg, U.S. Court of Appeals, Eighth Circuit, 1982-1984. Author: "Lender Liability Under Iowa Law," 39 Drake Law Review 645 (1989-1990); "Organizing a Corporation Under Iowa's Business Corporation Act," 40 Drake Law Review 837, 1991; Co-Author: "A Survey of the Legality of Confessed Judgment Clauses in Commercial Transactions," 47 The Business Lawyer 792, 1992. Listed in: The Best Lawyers in America; Chambers USA America's Leading Business Lawyers, Real Estate. Recipient: Iowa State Bar Association Mason Ladd Legal Writing Award, First Place, 1990. Chair, Mortgage Lending Committee, American Bar Association Section of Real Property, Probate and Trust Law, 2005—; Member, American College of Real Estate Lawyers; Fellow, American College of Mortgage Attorneys. ***PRACTICE AREAS:*** Real Estate Finance; Real Estate; Land Use and Zoning Law. ***Email:*** jwine@nyemaster.com

BRUCE W. BAKER, born Burlington, Iowa, October 5, 1957; admitted to bar, 1982, Illinois; 1987, Iowa; U.S. Tax Court. *Education:* University of Iowa (B.B.A., with distinction, 1978); University of San Diego (J.D., cum laude, 1982). Trial Attorney, Office of Chief Counsel, Internal Revenue Service, 1982-1986. Certified Public Accountant, Iowa, 1982. Author: "Iowa Chapter, ABA Property Tax Deskbook." Listed in, The Best Lawyers in America. Member, Administrative Practice Committee, Section of Taxation, American Bar Association. Member, Taxation Council, Iowa State Bar Association, 1998-2000. Co-Chair, Iowa Tax Legislation Committee, 1994-1996; National Diocesan Attorneys Association. ***PRACTICE AREAS:*** Tax Controversies; Tax Deferred Exchanges; State Taxation; Trusts and Estates Taxation; Property Tax Appeals; Sales and Use Tax. ***Email:*** bwbaker@nyemaster.com

THOMAS W. FOLEY, born Chicago, Illinois, October 5, 1959; admitted to bar, 1985, Missouri; 1986, Iowa; U.S. District Court, Northern and Southern Districts of Iowa; U.S. Court of Appeals, Eighth Circuit. *Education:* University of Iowa (B.B.A., with honors, 1982; J.D., with high distinction, 1985). Lecturer, "Employment Law," Drake University Law School, 1999. Co-Author: "Employment Torts: Emerging Areas of Employer Liability," 39 Drake Law Review 1, 1990. Listed in, Chambers USA America's Leading Business Lawyers. Member, Labor and Employment Law Section, Iowa State Bar Association. ***Email:*** tfoley@nyemaster.com

STEVEN H. LYTLE, born Oskaloosa, Iowa, May 26, 1945; admitted to bar, 1976, Iowa. *Education:* Drake University (B.S.B.A., 1967; J.D., 1976). Phi Eta Sigma; Beta Gamma Sigma; Order of the Coif. Member, Drake Law Review, 1974-1976. Instructor in Law, Drake University Law School, 1976-1977, 1990. Listed in, The Best Lawyers in America, 1993—. Member, Family Law Committee, 1979-1993, Chairman, 1985-1990; Ethics Committee, 1996-2002, Chair, 1999-2002, Polk County Bar Association. Member, Family Law Section Council, 1990-1993, 1995-1998; Section Chair, 1997-1998; Supreme Court Budget Committee, 2001-2003; Board of Governors, 2002-2004, Iowa State Bar Association. Fellow, American Academy of Matrimonial Lawyers. [Capt., USAF, 1967-1972; Capt., ANG, 1972-1976]. ***PRACTICE AREAS:*** Family and Matrimonial Law. ***Email:*** shl@nyemaster.com

TERRY C. HANCOCK, born Hempstead, New York, September 16, 1946; admitted to bar, 1974, Iowa. *Education:* University of Nebraska (B.A., with distinction, 1968); Georgetown University and Drake University (J.D., with honors, 1973). Phi Beta Kappa; Order of the Coif. ***PRACTICE AREAS:*** Employee Benefits. ***Email:*** tch@nyemaster.com

ANTHONY A. LONGNECKER, born Storm Lake, Iowa, December 26, 1955; admitted to bar, 1980, Iowa. *Education:* Iowa State University (B.S., with honors, 1978); University of Iowa (J.D., with distinction, 1980). Phi Eta Sigma; Alpha Kappa Psi. *Member, American College of Mortgage Attorneys.* ***PRACTICE AREAS:*** Business Law; Banking Law; Real Estate Law. ***Email:*** aal@nyemaster.com

JOSEPH A. QUINN, born Des Moines, Iowa, October 22, 1961; admitted to bar, 1987, Iowa. *Education:* Drake University (B.S., 1984; J.D., with honors, 1987). Contributing Author: Iowa Legal Research Guide (2003). Member: Iowa Defense Counsel Association; Iowa Association of Workers' Compensation Lawyers. Member, 2000-2003, and Chair, 2001-2002, Iowa State Bar Association, Workers Compensation Council; Public Relations Committee, 1996-2002; Chair, Young Lawyers' Division, State Fair Committee, 1992-1997. Co-Chair, Polk County Bar Association Public Relations Committee, 1996-2000. ***PRACTICE AREAS:*** Trial Practice; Workers' Compensation. ***Email:*** jaq@nyemaster.com

WADE H. SCHUT, born Sioux Center, Iowa, June 16, 1962; admitted to bar, 1987, Iowa. *Education:* Northwestern College (B.A., 1984); University of Iowa (J.D., 1987). Order of the Coif. ***Email:*** whs@nyemaster.com

MARK D. ALJETS, born Ft. Dodge, Iowa, September 3, 1956; admitted to bar, 1983, Iowa. *Education:* Iowa State University (B.S., 1979); Drake University (J.D., 1983). Contributing Author: "Employment Discrimination" 3rd Ed., Schlei and Grossman. *Member:* C. Edwin Moore American Inns of Court (Barrister); Iowa Defense Counsel Association; The Defense Research Institute. ***PRACTICE AREAS:*** Products Liability; Labor Law; Trial Practice. ***Email:*** mda@nyemaster.com

G. THOMAS SULLIVAN, born Des Moines, Iowa, July 3, 1958; admitted to bar, 1985, Iowa. *Education:* Iowa State University (B.S., 1980); Drake University (M.B.A., 1982; J.D., 1985). *Member:* Association of Life Insurance Counsel. ***PRACTICE AREAS:*** Insurance; Real Estate; Securities; Corporation and Business Law. ***Email:*** gtsullivan@nyemaster.com

THOMAS H. WALTON, born Cedar Falls, Iowa, April 10, 1963; admitted to bar, 1989, Iowa. *Education:* University of Northern Iowa (B.A., with highest honors, 1986); University of Iowa (J.D., with high distinction, 1989). Order of the Coif. *Member:* Iowa Defense Counsel Association. ***PRACTICE AREAS:*** Trial Practice. ***Email:*** twalton@nyemaster.com

WILLARD L. BOYD III, born Iowa City, Iowa, October 22, 1959; admitted to bar, 1984, Iowa; 1986, Missouri; 1987, District of Columbia; 1988, Minnesota. *Education:* University of Michigan (B.A., with high honors and distinction, 1982); University of Iowa (J.D., with distinction, 1984). Associate Editor, Iowa Law Review, 1983-1984. Law Clerk, U.S. District Court, Northern and Southern Districts of Iowa, 1984-1986. Author: "Implied-In-Fact Contract: Contractual Recovery Against the Government Without An Express Agreement," 21 Public Contract Law Journal 84 (Fall 1991). Co-Author: "The Program Fraud Civil Remedies Act: The Administrative Adjudication of Fraud Against the Government," 50 Federal Contracts Report 691 (1988). Listed in, The Best Lawyers in America, Corporate Law. Member, Business Law Section Council, Health Law Section Council and Trade Regulation Section Council, Iowa State Bar Association. *Member:* American Health Lawyers Association. ***Email:*** wlb@nyemaster.com

JEFFREY WILLIAM COURTER, born Boone, Iowa, November 26, 1961; admitted to bar, 1987, Iowa. *Education:* Iowa State University (B.S., with honors and distinction, 1984); University of Iowa (J.D., 1987). Phi Kappa Phi. Law Clerk to Hon. W. Ward Reynoldson, Chief Justice, Iowa Supreme Court, 1987 and to Hon. Russell J. Hill, U.S. Bankruptcy Judge for the Southern District of Iowa, 1987-1989. Member, Sections on Commercial and Bankruptcy Law, Business and Litigation, Iowa State Bar Association. *Member:* Federal Bar Associations; American Bankruptcy Institute. ***Email:*** jwc@nyemaster.com

HALLIE E. STILL-CARIS, born Jefferson, Iowa, March 27, 1961; admitted to bar, 1986, Iowa; 1987, Illinois. *Education:* Iowa State University (B.S., 1983); University of Iowa (J.D., with distinction, 1986). Senior Note & Comment Editor, Iowa Law Review, 1985-1986. Author: "Legislative Reform: Redefining the Parent-Child Relationship in Cases of Adoption," 71 Iowa Law Review 265, 1985; "Informed Consent: What Doctors Should Understand About Their Duty to Disclose," 36 Federation of Insurance & Corporate

(This Listing Continued)

Counsel Quarterly 49, 1985. Member, 1998— and Chair, 1999-2001, Environmental and Natural Resources Law Council, Iowa State Bar Association. ***PRACTICE AREAS:*** Corporate Law; Real Estate Law; Environmental Law. ***Email:*** hsc@nyemaster.com

JOSEPH K. HAGGERTY, born Scranton, Pennsylvania, December 1, 1946; admitted to bar, 1973, Pennsylvania; 1994, Kentucky (inactive); 1997, Iowa. *Education:* Loyola University of Chicago, Rome, Italy Campus (1966-1967); Wheeling Jesuit University (B.A., History, 1968); University of Pittsburgh (J.D., 1973). Member, Bethel Park School Board, Bethel Park, Pennsylvania. Member: American Society of Corporate Secretaries, 1976-1984; Association of Life Insurance Counsel, 1997—. (With AMERUS Group). ***PRACTICE AREAS:*** Corporate Law; Securities; Insurance. ***Email:*** jhaggerty@nyemaster.com

TERRY L. MONSON, born Fargo, North Dakota, January 5, 1947; admitted to bar, 1972, Iowa. *Education:* North Dakota State University (B.A., with honors, 1969); Northwestern University (J.D., 1972). Phi Kappa Phi; Phi Eta Sigma. Listed in, Chambers USA America's Leading Business Lawyers. *Member:* Polk County (Member, Real Estate Committee), Iowa State (Member, Real Estate and Title Law Section) and American (Member: Public Utility, Communications and Transportation Law, Law Practice Management Sections) Bar Associations. ***PRACTICE AREAS:*** Real Estate Law; Wind Energy Development Law. ***Email:*** tmonson@nyemaster.com

BARRY NADLER, born Mason City, Iowa, May 15, 1956; admitted to bar, 1981, Iowa; 1982, U.S. District Court, Northern and Southern Districts of Iowa; 1992, U.S. Court of Appeals, Eighth Circuit; 1993, United States Supreme Court. *Education:* University of Iowa (B.A., with honors, 1978; J.D., with high distinction, 1981). Phi Beta Kappa; Phi Eta Sigma. Member, Iowa Law Review, 1981. Author: Note, "Avoiding the Iowa Hearsay Rule With Evidence of the Whole Story of the Crime," 66 Iowa Law Review 961 (1981). *Member:* Association of Trial Lawyers of Iowa; American Board of Trial Advocates. ***Email:*** bjn@nyemaster.com

DAVID W. BENSON, born Marshalltown, Iowa, January 20, 1952; admitted to bar, 1978, Iowa, U.S. District Court, Southern and Northern Districts of Iowa and U.S. Tax Court. *Education:* Iowa State University (B.S., 1974); Creighton University (J.D., 1978). *Member:* Story County Bar Association (President, 1991). (Resident, Ames Office). ***PRACTICE AREAS:*** Estate Planning; Estate Administration; Real Estate; Corporate Law; Taxation. ***Email:*** dwb@nyemaster.com

BRIAN J. HUMKE, born Iowa Falls, Iowa, April 6, 1956; admitted to bar, 1982, Iowa; 1985, U.S. District Court, Southern District of Iowa; 1989, U.S. District Court, Northern District of Iowa. *Education:* University of Northern Iowa (B.A., 1978); Drake University (J.D., 1981). Author: "The Evolution of Joint Custody in Iowa," 34 Drake Law Review 769; Case Note, "Settlement of Insurance Litigation Without Full Disclosure to the Insured: Rogers v. Robson, et al. (Illinois 1980)," 30 Drake Law Review. Instructor, Domestic Relations, Des Moines Area Community College, 1985; Teaching Assistant, Drake University Law School, 1980-1981. Member, 1988—, President, 1994-1995, 1998-1999, 2003-2004, Ankeny School Board. Director, Iowa Bar Review School, Inc, 1988-1994. *Member:* National Association of Criminal Defense Attorneys. ***PRACTICE AREAS:*** Civil Trial Practice; Criminal Trial Practice. ***Email:*** bjh@nyemaster.com

DEBORAH S. KRAUTH, born Atlantic, Iowa, July 23, 1952; admitted to bar, 1983, Iowa. *Education:* University of Northern Iowa (B.A., 1974); University of Iowa (J.D., with high honor, 1983). Recipient, Trial Lawyers Award. Law Clerk, Hon. George G. Fagg, Eighth Circuit Court of Appeals, 1990. Member, Board of Directors, Iowa Finance Authority, 1989-1999. *Member:* Iowa State Bar Association (Chair, General Practice Section Council, 1994-1995; Member, Council Probate Section, 2002-2005; Chair, 1997-1998. Member, Taxation Section Council, 1998-2001); Story County Bar Association. ***PRACTICE AREAS:*** Wills; Probate Law; Real Estate; Business Law. ***Email:*** dsk@nyemaster.com

PAULA S. DIERENFELD, born Sac City, Iowa, September 7, 1954; admitted to bar, 1985, Iowa. *Education:* University of Northern Iowa (B.A., 1981); Drake University (J.D., 1984). Commissioner, Iowa Utilities Board, 1997-1999. Legal Counsel, Governor Terry E. Branstad, 1991-1997. Senior Policy Staff, 1989-1991. Director, Senate Research Staff, Iowa General Assembly, 1986-1989. Staff Assistant, U.S. Senator Charles E. Grassley, 1984-1986. *Member:* Federal Energy Bar Association. ***Email:*** psd@nyemaster.com

COREEN K. SWEENEY, born Charles City, Iowa, March 3, 1965; admitted to bar, 1991, Iowa. *Education:* University of Iowa (B.B.A., 1987); Drake University (J.D., 1990). Delta Theta Phi. Author: AIDS in the Workplace: A Handicap Under the Rehabilitation Act?", Drake Law Review, 39:1 (1989-1990); "Establishment Clause - Adolescent Family Life Act Upheld as Facially Valid After First Amendment Constitutional Attack on the Right of Religious Organizations to Receive Federal Funding to Counsel and Teach Adolescents - Bowen v. Kendrick," Drake Law Review, 38:3 (1989-1990). Contributing Author, Iowa Legal Research Guide (2003). Iowa Association of Workers Compensation Lawyers (Treasurer, Board of Governors); Member, 1996—; Seminar Co-Chair, 1999-2000; Iowa Workers' Compensation Advisory Committee Symposium Co-Chair, 2003-2004. ***PRACTICE AREAS:*** Workers Compensation. ***Email:*** cksweeney@nyemaster.com

ANTONIO COLACINO, born Des Moines, Iowa, November 8, 1949; admitted to bar, 1974, Iowa. *Education:* University of Notre Dame (B.A., summa cum laude, 1971; J.D., cum laude, 1974). Phi Beta Kappa. Adjunct Professor, Modern Real Estate Transactions, Drake University Law School. Listed in: The Best Lawyers in America; Chambers USA America's Leading Business Lawyers, Real Estate. *Member:* Polk County, Iowa State and American Bar Associations. ***PRACTICE AREAS:*** Real Estate; Eminent Domain; Municipal; Zoning Law. ***Email:*** acolacino@nyemaster.com

JILL M. STEVENSON, born Clarion, Iowa, December 31, 1957; admitted to bar, 1995, Iowa. *Education:* Iowa State University (B.S., 1980); Drake University (M.B.A.; J.D., with honors, 1995). Order of the Coif. Law Clerk, Hon. Charles R. Wolle, U.S. District Court, Southern District of Iowa, 1995-1996. ***PRACTICE AREAS:*** Business Law. ***Email:*** jms@nyemaster.com

ANGEL A. WEST, born Jefferson, Iowa, December 17, 1971; admitted to bar, 1997, Iowa, U.S. District Court, Northern and Southern Districts of Iowa, and U.S. Court of Appeals, Eighth Circuit. *Education:* University of Iowa (B.A., with highest honors, 1994); Drake University (J.D., with high honors, 1997). Phi Beta Kappa; Pi Sigma Alpha. University of Iowa Collegiate Scholar. Associate Editor, Drake Law Review, 1996-1997; Staff Member, 1995-1996. ***PRACTICE AREAS:*** Litigation. ***Email:*** aaw@nyemaster.com

ANGELA L. WATSON COOK, born Des Moines, Iowa, October 1, 1970; admitted to bar, 1996, Iowa; 1998, U.S. Tax Court. *Education:* Drake University (B.S.B.A., 1993); University of Iowa (J.D., 1996). Senior Associate Editor, Journal of Corporation Law, 1995-1996. Certified Public Accountant, Iowa, 1996. Member, Iowa Society of CPAs, 1996—. ***PRACTICE AREAS:*** Tax. ***Email:*** alwcook@nyemaster.com

MARY E. FUNK, born Mt. Pleasant, Iowa, October 14, 1969; admitted to bar, 1995, Illinois and U.S. District Court, Northern and Central Districts of Illinois; 1996, Iowa; 1999, U.S. Court of Appeals, Seventh Circuit; 2000, U.S. Court of Appeals, Eighth Circuit; 2001, U.S. District Court, Northern and Southern Districts of Iowa. *Education:* Drake University (B.A., magna cum laude, 1992); University of Iowa (J.D., with distinction, 1995). Note and Comment Editor, Iowa Law Review, 1994-1995. *Member:* Illinois State and Iowa State Bar Associations; Iowa Defense Counsel Association. ***PRACTICE AREAS:*** Litigation; Labor and Employment. ***Email:*** mef@nyemaster.com

RANDALL D. ARMENTROUT, born Cedar Rapids, Iowa, June 23, 1965; admitted to bar, 1991, Iowa; 1994, U.S. District Court, Northern and Southern Districts of Iowa and U.S. Court of Appeals, Eighth Circuit; 1997, U.S. Court of Appeals, Tenth Circuit; 1998, U.S. Supreme Court. *Education:* University of Iowa (B.S., 1988); Drake University (J.D., with honors, 1991). Law Clerk to: Honorable James H. Carter, Iowa Supreme Court, 1991-1992; Honorable George G. Fagg, U.S. Court of Appeals, Eighth Circuit, 1992-1994. Listed in, Chambers USA America's Leading Business Lawyers, Employment. ***PRACTICE AREAS:*** Appellate Practice; Civil Litigation; Commercial Litigation; Discrimination; Employment Contracts; Employment Law; Equipment Leasing; Litigation; Sexual Harassment; Trade Secrets. ***Email:*** rdarmentrout@nyemaster.com

THOMAS M. CUNNINGHAM, born Des Moines, Iowa, June 23, 1959; admitted to bar, 1984, Missouri and U.S. District Court, Western District of Missouri; 1986, U.S. Court of Appeals, Eight Circuit; 1989, Iowa and U.S. District Court Northern and Southern Districts of Iowa; 1992, U.S. Supreme Court; 1994, U.S. Court of Appeals, Seventh Circuit; 1995, U.S. District Court, District of Nebraska; 1996, U.S. District Court, Central District of Illinois; 2003, U.S. District Court, District of Colorado; 2004, U.S. District Court, Western District of Michigan. *Education:* University of Iowa (B.A., with distinction, 1981; J.D., with distinction, 1984). Phi Beta Kappa; Omicron Delta Kappa; Phi Alpha Delta. Note and Comment Editor, Iowa Law Review, 1983-1984. Author: Comment, "Nixon v. Fitzgerald: A Justifiable Separation of Powers Argument for Absolute Presidential Civil Damages Immunity?" 68 Iowa L. Rev. 557 (1983). President, 1996, West Des Moines Chamber of Commerce. Listed in, Chambers USA America's Leading Lawyers for Business, Employment Law, 2004—. *Member:* Iowa State Bar Association (Chair, Federal Practice Committee, 2004—); The Missouri Bar; Defense Research Institute; Iowa Trial Lawyers Association; Iowa Defense Counsel Association; National Association of Railroad Trial Counsel; C. Edwin Moore American Inn of Court (Master, 2003—). ***PRACTICE AREAS:*** Labor and Employment Law; Trial Practice. ***Email:*** tmcunningham@nyemaster.com

DENISE M. MENDT, born Cherokee, Iowa, August 5, 1960; admitted to bar, 1986, Illinois; 1991, Iowa. *Education:* University of Northern Iowa (B.A., with honors, 1983); University of Iowa (J.D., with high distinction, 1986). Order of the Coif. Certified Public Accountant, Iowa, 1983. ***PRACTICE AREAS:*** Taxation Law. ***Email:*** dmmendt@nyemaster.com

DEBRA L. HULETT, born Cedar Rapids, Iowa, June 3, 1967; admitted to bar, 1997, Iowa; U.S. District Court, Northern and Southern Districts of Iowa; U.S. Court of Appeals, Eighth Circuit. *Education:* University of Iowa (B.A., with high distinction, 1989; J.D., with high distinction, 1997). Order of the Coif. Note and Comment Editor, Journal of Corporation Law, 1996-1997. Author: "COBRA Continuation Insurance: Is Pre-Existing Coverage Under a Spouse's Group Health Plan a Terminating Event?" 22 Journal of Corporation Law 747 (Summer, 1997). Law Clerk, Hon. Ronald E. Longstaff, U.S. District Court, Southern District of Iowa, 1997-1999. Member, Iowa Supreme Court Commission on Continuing Legal Education, 2005—. *Member:* Iowa Defense Counsel Association; Defense Research Institute. ***PRACTICE AREAS:*** Litigation. ***Email:*** dlhulett@nyemaster.com

MARK A. SCHULTHEIS, born Peru, Indiana, December 27, 1965; admitted to bar, 1993, Iowa and U.S. District Court, Northern and Southern Districts of Iowa; U.S. Court of Appeals, Eighth Circuit; 2003, U.S. Court of Appeals, Federal Circuit. *Education:* University of Iowa (B.A., 1990; J.D., with distinction, 1993). *Member:* Iowa Defense Counsel Association; Blackstone Inn of Court. ***PRACTICE AREAS:*** Civil Litigation. ***Email:*** maschultheis@nyemaster.com

JOHN T. CLENDENIN, born Iowa City, Iowa, January 13, 1972; admitted to bar, 1998, Iowa; U.S. District Court, Southern District of Iowa; 1999, U.S. District Court, Northern District of Iowa and U.S. Court of Appeals, Eighth Circuit. *Education:* University of Illinois at Urbana-Champaign (B.A., 1995); Drake University (J.D., with honors, 1998). Order of the Barristers. Member, C. Edwin Moore American Inn of Court. National Moot Court Team, 1996-1998; Moot Court Board, 1996-1998. Recipient, Rodney L. Hudson Senior Advocacy Award, 1998. Law Clerk to Hon. Terry L. Huitink, Iowa Court of Appeals, 1998-1999. Member, Board of Counselors, Drake University Law School, 2000—. Member, Iowa State Bar Association Appellate Practice Committee. *Member:* Iowa Defense Counsel Association; Defense Research Institute. ***PRACTICE AREAS:*** Litigation. ***Email:*** jtc@nyemaster.com

NEAL K. WESTIN, born Waterloo, Iowa, April 27, 1974; admitted to bar, 1999, Iowa. *Education:* University of Iowa (B.A., with high distinction, 1995); University of Texas (J.D., with honors, 1999). Phi Beta Kappa. Managing Editor, Texas Forum on Civil Liberties and Civil Rights, 1998-1999. ***PRACTICE AREAS:*** Real Estate; Business Law; Immigration. ***Email:*** nkwestin@nyemaster.com

STEPHANIE L. MARETT, born Des Moines, Iowa, February 28, 1973; admitted to bar, 1999, Iowa; U.S. District Court, Northern and Southern Districts of Iowa; U.S. Court of Appeals, Eighth Circuit. *Education:* Luther College (B.A., magna cum laude, 1995); Drake University (J.D., with high honors, 1999). Phi Beta Kappa; Phi Alpha Delta (Marshall, 1997-1999). Articles Editor, Drake Law Review, 1998-1999. *Member:* Polk County Bar Association (Co-Chair, Public Relations Committee, 2004—); Iowa Defense Counsel Association. ***PRACTICE AREAS:*** Litigation. ***Email:*** slm@nyemaster.com

(This Listing Continued)

NYEMASTER, GOODE, WEST, HANSELL & O'BRIEN,
A PROFESSIONAL CORPORATION, Des Moines—Continued

JORDAN B. HANSELL, born Des Moines, Iowa, October 20, 1970; admitted to bar, 2001, Iowa. *Education:* Duke University (A.B., summa cum laude, 1993); University of Michigan (M.A., 1998; J.D., magna cum laude,1998). Order of the Coif. Member, 1995-1997 and Note Editor, 1996-1997, Michigan Law Review. Law Clerk to the Honorable Antonin Scalia, Associate Justice, U.S. Supreme Court, 1999-2000. Law Clerk to the Honorable J. Harvie Wilkinson, III, Chief Judge, U.S. Court of Appeals, Fourth Circuit, 1998-1999. Intern: The Office of the Solicitor General, U.S. Department of Justice, 1998; Honorable Charles R. Wolle, Chief Judge, U.S. District Court, Southern District of Iowa, 1995. Author: "The Appearance of Impropriety: How the Ethics Wars Have Undermined American Government, Business, and Society," Michigan Law Review, May 1998; "Is HIV Extraordinary?" 96 Michigan Law Review 1095 (1998); Co-Author: "Issues Affecting All Business Organizations-Electronic Commerce," Iowa State Bar Association Business Law Section, Practice Manual (2004). ***LANGUAGES:*** Spanish. ***PRACTICE AREAS:*** Corporate; Business Law; Electronic Commerce. ***Email:*** jbhansell@nyemaster.com

---

L. W. "BILL" ROSEBROOK, born Milwaukee, Wisconsin, February 16, 1944; admitted to bar, 1969, Iowa. *Education:* University of Iowa (B.A., with honors, 1966; J.D., with distinction, 1969). Omicron Delta Kappa; Phi Delta Phi. Murray Scholar. Chairman, Committee on Litigation Legislation, Iowa State Bar Association, 1984-1989. *Member:* Iowa Defense Counsel Association; Defense Research Institute. ***PRACTICE AREAS:*** Litigation. ***Email:*** lwr@nyemaster.com

CORY R. HARRIS, born Des Moines, Iowa, August 16, 1971; admitted to bar, 2000, Iowa. *Education:* University of Iowa (B.B.A., 1994); Drake University (M.B.A.; J.D., with high honors, 2000). Order of the Coif; Delta Theta Phi. Co-Author: "Issues Affecting All Business Organizations-Electronic Commerce," Iowa State Bar Association Business Law Section, Practice Manual (2004). Member, Business Law and E-Commerce Sections, Iowa State Bar Association. ***PRACTICE AREAS:*** Corporate Law; Business Law. ***Email:*** crharris@nyemaster.com

PATRICK B. WHITE, born Des Moines, Iowa, March 30, 1973; admitted to bar, 2002, Iowa; 2003, U.S. District Court, Southern and Northern Districts of Iowa; U.S. Court of Appeals, Eighth Circuit. *Education:* Drake University (B.S.B.A., 1995; J.D., with highest honors, 2002). Order of the Coif. Member, Drake Law Review, 2001-2002. *Member:* Iowa State and American Bar Associations; Iowa Defense Council Association. ***PRACTICE AREAS:*** Litigation. ***Email:*** pwhite@nyemaster.com

STEPHANIE G. TECHAU, born Cedar Falls, Iowa, October 7, 1966; admitted to bar, 1992, Iowa. *Education:* University of Iowa (B.A., 1989; J.D., with distinction, 1992). Phi Delta Phi. Member, Iowa Law Review, 1990-1991. State Judicial Nominating Commission, Elected Representative District 5C, 2000-2007. Member, Supreme Court Board of Professional Ethics and Conduct (1996-2005; Vice Chairman, 2004-2005). Co-Author: "Negligent Misrepresentation," Defense Update, Vol. VIII, No. 1, January 1995. *Member:* Polk County (Membership Committee, 1999-2002) and Iowa State (Specialization Committee, 1995-1997; Iowa Workers' Compensation Advisory Committee, 1998-2001; Co-Chair, Young Lawyers Division Newsletter and Public Information Committee, 1995-1998; Member, Young Lawyers Division Justice for All Committee, 1993-1995) Bar Associations; Polk County Women Attorneys (Board of Directors, 1996; Chair, Social Committee, 1995; Recording Secretary, 1994); Iowa Association of Workers' Compensation Lawyers, Inc. (Co-Chair, Annual Seminar, 2001-2002; Board of Governors, 2002—); Iowa Defense Counsel Association. ***PRACTICE AREAS:*** Workers Compensation; Civil Litigation. ***Email:*** sgtechau@nyemaster.com

BRAD C. EPPERLY, born Oskaloosa, Iowa, April 30, 1968; admitted to bar, 1993, Iowa and Nebraska; 1996, U.S. District Court, District of Nebraska and U.S. District Court, Northern and Southern Districts of Iowa. *Education:* University of Iowa (B.B.A., with honors, 1990; J.D., with distinction, 1993). *Member:* Nebraska State, Iowa State and American Bar Associations. ***PRACTICE AREAS:*** Commercial Litigation; Bankruptcy; Commercial Transactions; Real Estate Financing. ***Email:*** bcepperly@nyemaster.com

SCOTT A. SUNDSTROM, born St. Andrews, Scotland, November 16, 1972; admitted to bar, 2000, California; 2001, U.S. Court of Appeals, Tenth Circuit and U.S. District Court, District of Colorado; 2002, Colorado; 2003, U.S. Court of Appeals, Eighth and Ninth Circuits; 2004, Iowa. *Education:* Carleton College (B.A., cum laude, 1995); New York University School of Law (J.D., cum laude, 1999). Articles Editor, New York University Law Review. Law Clerk to the Honorable Carlos F. Lucero, U.S. Court of Appeals, Tenth Circuit, 2000-2001. Author: "You've Got Mail! (And the Government Knows It): Applying the Fourth Amendment to Workplace E-Mail Monitoring," 73 NYU L. Rev., 2064, 1998. *Member:* Polk County, The Colorado, Iowa State and American Bar Associations; State Bar of California. ***REPORTED CASES:*** Colorado ex rel. Salazar v. Davidson, 79 P.3d 1221 (Colo. 2003). ***PRACTICE AREAS:*** Commercial Litigation. ***Email:*** sasundstrom@nyemaster.com

BENJAMIN P. ROACH, born Minneapolis, Minnesota, December 16, 1976; admitted to bar, 2003, Iowa. *Education:* University of Northern Iowa (B.A., 1999); University of Iowa (J.D., with high distinction, 2003). Order of the Coif. *Member:* Polk County, Iowa State and American Bar Associations. ***Email:*** bproach@nyemaster.com

ALLISON M. STEUTERMAN, born Des Moines, Iowa, November 18, 1978; admitted to bar, 2004, Iowa. *Education:* Truman State University (B.A., cum laude, 2001); Drake University Law School (J.D., with high honors, 2004). Order of the Coif. ***PRACTICE AREAS:*** Litigation. ***Email:*** amsteuterman@nyemaster.com

HANNAH M. ROGERS, born Hastings, Nebraska, January 23, 1975; admitted to bar, 2004, Iowa. *Education:* Drake University (B.A., 1997; J.D., with high honors, 2004). Order of the Coif. Author: Note, "School Vouchers: A Solution to an Educational Crisis or Impermissible Government Involvement in Religion?" 52 Drake Law Review 824 (2004). ***PRACTICE AREAS:*** Litigation. ***Email:*** hmrogers@nyemaster.com

KATHLEEN K. LAW, born Lake City, Iowa, November 15, 1961; admitted to bar, 2005, Iowa. *Education:* William Penn College (B.A., magna cum laude, 2002); Drake University (J.D., with highest honors, 2005). Order of the Coif. Member, Drake Moot Court Board, 2003-2005. Recipient, Iowa State Bar Association Graduating Senior Award, 2005. Research Assistant to Professor Andrea Charlow, 2003-2005. Associate Editor, Drake Law Review, 2004-2005. Member, American Inns of Court, 2004—. ***Email:*** kklaw@nyemaster.com

JASON L. GILES, born Salt Lake City, Utah, February 23, 1976; admitted to bar, 2003, Iowa. *Education:* Utah State University (B.A., cum laude, 2000); Drake University (J.D., 2003; M.B.A., with highest honors, 2003). Presidential Scholar. Opperman Scholar. Member, National Honor Society, Utah State University. Order of the Coif. Member, Drake Law Review. Law Clerk to the Honorable James E. Gritzner, U.S. District Court for the Southern District of Iowa, 2003-2005. ***LANGUAGES:*** Spanish. ***PRACTICE AREAS:*** Corporate Law. ***Email:*** jlgiles@nyemaster.com

MITCHELL R. KUNERT, born Hampton, Iowa, May 30, 1979; admitted to bar, 2005, Iowa. *Education:* Arizona State University (B.S., 2001); Drake University (J.D., with high honors, 2005). Order of the Coif. Associate Editor, Drake Law Review. President, Student Bar Association. Commencement Speaker. ***PRACTICE AREAS:*** Litigation. ***Email:*** mrkunert@nyemaster.com

OF COUNSEL

SAMUEL G. O'BRIEN, born Oskaloosa, Iowa, July 11, 1920; admitted to bar, 1947, Iowa. *Education:* State University of Iowa (B.A., 1943; J.D., 1947). Phi Delta Phi.

LEROY R. VOIGTS, born Greene, Iowa, October 2, 1927; admitted to bar, 1955, Iowa. *Education:* Wartburg College (B.A., 1948); Drake University (J.D., 1955). Omicron Delta Kappa; Order of the Coif. Editor, Drake University Law Review, 1954. Law Clerk, U.S. District Judge Henry N. Graven, 1955. President, Polk County Bar Association, 1978-1979. President, Young Lawyers Section, 1962-1963 and Member, Board of Governors, 1979-1983, Iowa State Bar Association. Member, House of Delegates, American Bar Association, 1989-1996. *Member:* Polk County, Iowa State and American Bar Associations; American College of Trial Lawyers; Iowa Defense Counsel Association; International Association of Defense Counsel; Iowa Academy of Trial Lawyers. ***PRACTICE AREAS:*** Trial Practice.

DREW R. TILLOTSON, born Des Moines, Iowa, July 2, 1930; admitted to bar, 1955, Iowa. *Education:* Drake University (B.S., 1955); University of Nebraska and Drake University (J.D., 1955). Order of the Coif; Beta Gamma Sigma; Omicron Delta Kappa; Delta Theta Phi. Author: "Better Homes and Gardens Income Tax Guide." Trial Attorney, Office of the Chief Counsel, Internal Revenue Service, 1955-1959. ***PRACTICE AREAS:*** Taxation Law.

FRANK B. COMFORT, born Des Moines, Iowa, May 11, 1924; admitted to bar, 1951, Iowa. *Education:* State University of Iowa (B.A., 1949; J.D., 1951). Phi Delta Phi.

RUSSELL E. SCHRAGE, born Waterloo, Iowa, March 13, 1938; admitted to bar, 1963, Iowa. *Education:* University of Iowa (B.B.A., 1960; LL.B., 1963); Drake University (M.A. in Economics, 1970). Phi Delta Phi. Member, Committee on Insurance, Iowa State Bar Association, 1978-1986. *Member:* American College of Real Estate Lawyers; American College of Investment Counsel; Association of Life Insurance Counsel. ***Email:*** res@nyemaster.com

ROGER L. FERRIS, born Dubuque, Iowa, December 17, 1943; admitted to bar, 1969, Iowa. *Education:* Grinnell College (B.A., 1965); Rutgers University (M.A., 1966); University of Iowa (J.D., 1969). Phi Sigma Alpha; Phi Delta Phi. Author: "Notice or Knowledge of Injury and Limitations of Actions Under the Iowa Workers' Compensation Act," 29 Drake Law Review 775, 1980. Deputy Iowa Industrial Commissioner, 1970-1971. Member, Committee on Workers' Compensation Law, 1974-1991; Member, Worker's Compensation Section Council, 1997-2000 and Chair, 1999-2000, Iowa State Bar Association. Chair, Legislative Committee, 1978-1980, Chair, Administrative Rules Committee, 1980-1990, Iowa Workers' Compensation Advisory Committee. *Member:* Iowa Association of Workers' Compensation Lawyers; Iowa Defense Counsel Association. ***PRACTICE AREAS:*** Workers Compensation.

LUTHER L. HILL, JR., born Des Moines, Iowa, August 21, 1922; admitted to bar, 1951, Iowa;. *Education:* Williams College (B.A., 1947); Harvard Law School (LL.B., magna cum laude, 1950). *Member:* Association of Life Insurance Counsel. ***LANGUAGES:*** German.

All Members and Associates of the Firm are Members of the County, Iowa State and American Bar Associations.
Firm is a Member of the State Capital Law Firm Group. (Member firms of the State Capital Law Firm Group practice independently and not in a relationship for the joint practice of law).

REPRESENTATIVE CLIENTS: The Burlington Northern and Santa Fe Railway Company; BP Amoco Co.; General Electric Co.; Deere & Co.; Eli Lilly and Co.; Monsanto Agricultural Co.; The Hertz Corp.; Aventis; 3M Corp.; HON Industries; The Waldinger Corp.; Equitable of Iowa Cos., Inc.; Wells Fargo Bank Iowa, N.A.; American International Group; Wellmark Blue Cross and Blue Shield; Land O'Lakes; Iowa Automobile Dealers Assn.; Federation of Iowa Insurers; Iowa Medical Society; Iowa Newspaper Assn.; Iowa Chapter, American Institute of Architects; Iowa Society of Certified Public Accountants; Iowa Grocery Industry Assn.; Hubbell Realty Co.; U-Haul International; Locust Street Securities; Iowa Health System; Grinnell College; American Insurance Assn; CHUBB Group of Insurance Cos.; ING Groep N.V.; Novartis; Safeco Insurance Co.; GuideOne Insurance Group; The Iowa Clinic, P.C.; McFarland Clinic, P.C.; AmerUs Life Insurance Co.; Story Construction Co.; Jacobson Warehouse Co., Inc.; Pepsi-Cola General Bottlers, Inc.; Mary Greeley Medical Center; Bank of America, N.A.; American Gas Assn.; Iowa Association of Electric Cooperatives; Qwest Communications Corp.; Lighthouse Communications, Inc.; Helena Chemical Co.; John Deere Health Care, Inc.; Alliant Energy; FPL Energy LLC; Midwest Renewable Energy Corporation; Meredith Corporation; The Cincinnati Insurance Cos.; American Family Mutual Insurance Co.; UNUMProvident Companies; LaSalle Bank National Association; AEGON N.V.; Lennox Industries, Inc.; American General Life Companies; Zurich American Insurance; MidAmerican Energy Company; FMC Corp.

(This Listing Continued)

OLSON LAW OFFICE, P.C.

3116 INGERSOLL AVENUE
DES MOINES, IOWA 50312-3910
Telephone: 515-271-9100
Fax: 515-271-8100
Email: lem@olson-law.net

ALAN O. OLSON, born Mankato, Minnesota, May 18, 1967; admitted to bar, 1993, Iowa; 1994, U.S. District Court, Southern District of Iowa; 1995, U.S. Court of Appeals, Eighth Circuit and U.S. District Court, Northern District of Iowa; 2000, U.S. Supreme Court. *Education:* Drake University (B.A., 1989; J.D., 1992). Law Clerk, Hon. Dick R. Schlegel, Iowa Court of Appeals, Des Moines, Iowa 1992-1993. Assistant Editor: Cumulative Supplement, Trial Handbook, Iowa Academy of Trial Lawyers, 1993. *Member:* Polk County, Iowa State (Member, Board of Governors, 1996-1999; Administrative Committee, 1998-1999) and American (Presidential Appointments Committee, 2002-2003; House of Delegates, 2003-2006; Standing Committee on Membership, 2002-2005; Chair, Young Lawyers Division, 2002-2003; Chair, General Practice, Solo and Small Firm Section, Corporate Sponsorship Committee, 2003-2004) Bar Associations; Iowa Trial Lawyers Association; Association of Trial Lawyers of America; American Mock Trial Association (Recipient, Chief Justice W.W. Reynoldson Award, 1993; Inductee, Judges Hall of Fame, 1999); National Order of Barristers. ***PRACTICE AREAS:*** Trial Practice; Personal Injury; Automobile Accidents and Injuries; Slip and Fall; Dog Bites; Wrongful Death. ***Email:*** aoo@olson-law.net

---

PATTERSON, LORENTZEN, DUFFIELD, TIMMONS, IRISH, BECKER & ORDWAY, L.L.P.

Established in 1965

505 FIFTH AVENUE, SUITE 729
DES MOINES, IOWA 50309-2390
Telephone: 515-283-2147
Fax: 515-283-1002
URL: http://www.pattersonfirm.com

General Civil Practice. Litigation and Appeals in State and Federal Courts. Insurance, Casualty and Workers Compensation Law. Corporation, Probate and Estate Planning Law.

FIRM PROFILE: The Patterson Law Firm was founded in 1965. Although it offers a wide range of services to its clients, the firm is best known as one of the most respected litigation firms in Iowa. The firm's history has been characterized by stability and steady growth while emphasizing professionalism in its dealings with clients, bench, and bar. The firm is listed in the Martindale-Hubbell Bar Register of Preeminent Lawyers.

MEMBERS OF FIRM

ROY M. IRISH, born Chicago, Illinois, January 23, 1939; admitted to bar, 1964, Iowa. *Education:* Drake University (B.S., 1962; J.D., 1964). *Member:* Polk County, Iowa State and American Bar Associations; Association of Trial Lawyers of Iowa. ***PRACTICE AREAS:*** Trial Practice; Insurance Law. ***Email:*** rirish@pattersonfirm.com

GARY D. ORDWAY, born Mason City, Iowa, February 10, 1942; admitted to bar, 1966, Iowa. *Education:* Drake University (B.S., 1964; J.D., 1966). Delta Theta Phi. *Member:* Polk County, Iowa State and American Bar Associations; Association of Trial Lawyers of Iowa; The Association of Trial Lawyers of America; American Academy of ADR Attorneys. ***PRACTICE AREAS:*** Trial Practice; Insurance Law. ***Email:*** gordway@pattersonfirm.com

ROBIN L. HERMANN, born Ames, Iowa, May 23, 1943; admitted to bar, 1968, Iowa. *Education:* United States Military Academy; University of Iowa (LL.B., 1968). Phi Delta Phi. *Member:* Polk County, Iowa State and American Bar Associations. ***PRACTICE AREAS:*** Malpractice; Trial Practice; Personal Injury Law. ***Email:*** rhermann@pattersonfirm.com

HARRY PERKINS, III, born Des Moines, Iowa, October 29, 1947; admitted to bar, 1973, Iowa. *Education:* Creighton University (B.S.B.A., 1970); Drake University (J.D., 1973). *Member:* Polk County, Iowa State and American Bar Associations; Federation of Defense and Corporate Counsel; Iowa Academy of Trial Lawyers; Iowa Defense Counsel Association; Defense Research Institute. ***PRACTICE AREAS:*** Trial Practice; Insurance Law. ***Email:*** hperkins@pattersonfirm.com

MICHAEL F. LACEY, JR., born Boone, Iowa, June 4, 1943; admitted to bar, 1976, Iowa. *Education:* Iowa State University (B.S., 1966); Golden Gate University (M.B.A., 1971); Drake University (J.D., 1976). Delta Theta Phi. *Member:* Polk County, Iowa State and American Bar Associations; Association of Trial Lawyers of Iowa; Association of Trial Lawyers of America; American Board of Trial Advocates; American Academy of ADR Attorneys. ***PRACTICE AREAS:*** Personal Injury; Insurance Law. ***Email:*** mlacey@pattersonfirm.com

GREGORY J. WILSON, born Joliet, Illinois, July 28, 1950; admitted to bar, 1977, Iowa; 1981, U.S. Tax Court. *Education:* University of Iowa (B.A., 1972); Marycrest College (M.A., 1973); Drake University (J.D., 1977). *Member:* Polk County, Iowa State and American (Member, Sections on: Real Property, Probate and Trust Law; International Law and Practice) Bar Associations. ***PRACTICE AREAS:*** International Trade and Investment; Real Estate; Wills; Estate and Probate Law. ***Email:*** gwilson@pattersonfirm.com

JEFFREY A. BOEHLERT, born Clinton, New York, November 16, 1953; admitted to bar, 1978, Iowa; 1987, Nebraska. *Education:* Syracuse University (B.S., magna cum laude, 1975); Drake University (J.D., 1978). *Member:* Polk County, Iowa State and American Bar Associations; Iowa Defense Counsel Association. ***PRACTICE AREAS:*** Professional Negligence; Personal Injury; Employment; Discrimination; Product Liability Law. ***Email:*** jboehlert@pattersonfirm.com

DOUGLAS A. HAAG, born Cokato, Minnesota, October 11, 1952; admitted to bar, 1979, Iowa. *Education:* Mankato State College (B.S., summa cum laude, 1975); Drake University (J.D., 1979). Phi Kappa Phi; Order of the Coif. *Member:* Polk County, Iowa State and American Bar Associations; Defense Research Institute. ***PRACTICE AREAS:*** Appeals; Insurance; Trial Law. ***Email:*** dhaag@pattersonfirm.com

JEFFREY A. BAKER, born Davenport, Iowa, October 19, 1960; admitted to bar, 1989, Iowa. *Education:* Winona State University (B.S., 1983); Drake University (J.D., 1989). President, Drake University Student Bar Association, 1988-1989. *Member:* Polk County, Iowa State and American Bar Associations; Iowa Association of Workers Compensation Attorneys. ***PRACTICE AREAS:*** Workers Compensation. ***Email:*** jbaker@pattersonfirm.com

JANICE M. THOMAS, born Pampa, Texas, June 11, 1964; admitted to bar, 1989, Iowa. *Education:* University of Iowa (B.B.A., 1986); Drake University (J.D., 1989). *Member:* Polk County, Iowa State and American Bar Associations; Defense Research Institute; Iowa Defense Counsel Association. ***PRACTICE AREAS:*** Trial Practice; Insurance Law; Workers Compensation. ***Email:*** jthomas@pattersonfirm.com

PATRICK V. WALDRON, born Keokuk, Iowa, December 23, 1969; admitted to bar, 1995, Iowa. *Education:* Marycrest College (B.A., magna cum laude, 1992); Drake University (J.D., with honors, 1995). Delta Theta Phi. Articles Editor, Drake University Agricultural and Food Law Journal. *Member:* Polk County, Iowa State and American Bar Associations. ***PRACTICE AREAS:*** Personal Injury; Workers Compensation. ***Email:*** pwaldron@pattersonfirm.com

MARTIN C. SPROCK, born Carroll, Iowa, January 1, 1952; admitted to bar, 1977, Iowa. *Education:* Drake University (B.A., 1974; J.D., 1977). Phi Beta Kappa; Omicron Delta Kappa; Beta Alpha Psi. *Member:* Polk County, Iowa State and American (Member, Taxation Section) Bar Associations; Iowa Society of Certified Public Accountants. ***PRACTICE AREAS:*** Taxation; Wills and Estate Law; Probate. ***Email:*** msprock@pattersonfirm.com

WILLIAM A. WICKETT, born Decorah, Iowa, January 19, 1945; admitted to bar, 1981, Iowa. *Education:* St. Olaf College (B.A., 1967); Drake University (J.D., with honors, 1980). *Member:* Polk County, Iowa State and American Bar Associations. ***PRACTICE AREAS:*** Personal Injury; Trial Law; Construction. ***Email:*** wwickett@pattersonfirm.com

FREDERICK M. HASKINS, born Des Moines, Iowa, October 18, 1947; admitted to bar, 1972, Iowa. *Education:* University of Iowa (B.B.A., 1969; J.D., 1972). Assistant Attorney General, State of Iowa, 1972-1991. Chief Counsel, Iowa Insurance Division, 1980-1991. Acting Insurance Commissioner of Iowa, 1986. *Member:* Polk County and Iowa State Bar Associations; Federation of Regulatory Counsel. ***Email:*** fhaskins@pattersonfirm.com

MICHAEL S. JONES, born Cedar Rapids, Iowa, November 26, 1962; admitted to bar, 1995, Iowa. *Education:* University of Iowa (B.B.A., 1985); Denver University; Drake University (J.D., with honors, 1995). Chartered Property and Casualty Underwriter (CPCU), Colorado, 1989. *Member:* Polk County, Iowa State and American Bar Associations; Iowa Defense Counsel Association; Defense Research Institute. ***PRACTICE AREAS:*** Insurance Law; Personal Injury. ***Email:*** mjones@pattersonfirm.com

RYAN M. CLARK, born Milwaukee, Wisconsin, April 22, 1973; admitted to bar, 1999, Iowa. *Education:* Arizona State University (B.A., 1995); Drake University (J.D., with honors, 1999). *Member:* Polk County, Iowa State and American Bar Associations; Iowa Association of Workers Compensation Attorneys. ***Email:*** rclark@pattersonfirm.com

---

MARK A. KING, born Ottumwa, Iowa, October 30, 1973; admitted to bar, 2001, Iowa. *Education:* Creighton University (B.S., 1997); Drake University (J.D., with honors, 2001). *Member:* Polk County, Iowa State and American Bar Associations. ***Email:*** mking@pattersonfirm.com

CORY D. ABBAS, born Des Moines, Iowa, April 3, 1973; admitted to bar, 2004, Iowa. *Education:* Drake University (B.S.B.A., magna cum laude, 1994; J.D., with high honors, 2004). *Member:* Polk County, Iowa State and American Bar Associations. ***Email:*** cabbas@pattersonfirm.com

GENERAL COUNSEL FOR: Iowa Insurance Institute.
REPRESENTATIVE CLIENTS: Allied Mutual Insurance Co./Nationwide; American Family Insurance Group; Bar-B Management, Inc.; Chubb Insurance Group; CGU/Hawkeye-Security Insurance Co.; CIGNA Insurance Co./ACE USA; CNA Excess & Select; CNA Health Pro; CNA Insurance Co.; General Casualty; Continental Western Insurance Co.; Columbia Insurance Group; Farmers Insurance Group; Farmland Insurance; Gentry Ltd.; Grinnell Mutual Reinsurance Co.; Iowa Mutual Insurance Co.; Iowa Realty Co., Inc.; Iowa Realty Commercial; MetLife Auto & Home Insurance Co.; Northland Insurance Co.; Qwest; St. Paul Travelers Insurance Company; Secura Insurance Co.; Sedgwick James Insurance Co.; Sentry Insurance Co.; Shelter Insurance Co.

PEARSON VAN HOUTEN PLC

DES MOINES, IOWA

(See West Des Moines)

Business Law, Banking Law, Probate, Estate Planning, Taxation, Trusts and Estates, Wills, Employee Benefits, Real Estate, Elder Law.

PEDDICORD, WHARTON, SPENCER AND HOOK, LLP

Established in 1965

700 DES MOINES BUILDING
405 SIXTH AVENUE
P.O. BOX 9130
DES MOINES, IOWA 50306
Telephone: 515-243-2100
Fax: 515-243-2132
1-800-383-2100
URL: http://www.peddicordwharton.com

Litigation—all Courts. Aviation, Insurance, Negligence, Personal Injury, Workers Compensation, Product Liability, Medical Malpractice, Professional Liability, Bankruptcy, Real Estate, Corporation and Employment Law, Medical Malpractice.

(This Listing Continued)

PEDDICORD, WHARTON, SPENCER AND HOOK, LLP, Des Moines—Continued

FIRM PROFILE: We are an aggressive, well-respected defense law firm that works throughout the entire state of Iowa serving clients since 1965. This firm was founded as a civil, litigation and insurance defense law firm that has an exceptional win-loss ratio regardless of the type of case being prosecuted or defended.

ROLAND D. PEDDICORD, born Van Meter, Iowa, March 29, 1936; admitted to bar, 1962, Iowa. *Education:* Drake University (B.S., 1961; J.D., 1962). Phi Eta Sigma; Delta Theta Phi; Order of the Coif, Beta Gamma Sigma; Omicron Delta Kappa. Editor-in-Chief, Drake Law Review, 1961-1962. Author: "Damages," Drake Law Review, Vol. 10-74; "Intersection Accidents in Iowa," Drake Law Review, Vol. 10-111; "Survey of Iowa Tort Law," Drake Law Review Vol. 20, Page 288, 1971. Lecturer in Law: College of Osteopathic Medicine and Surgery, 1965-1972; Drake University, 1970-1980. Assistant Attorney General, State of Iowa, 1962-1963. Edwin Moore, American Inns of Court (Past President). *Member:* Polk County, The Iowa State and American (Member: Aviation and Space Law Committee; Insurance, Negligence and Compensation Law Section) Bar Associations; Iowa Academy of Trial Lawyers; The Association of Trial Lawyers of America; Defense Research Institute; Lawyer-Pilots Bar Association; Iowa Defense Counsel Association; The Iowa Association of Workers Compensation Lawyers; American Board of Trial Advocates (Advocate). (Certified as a Civil Trial Advocacy Specialist by the National Board of Trial Advocacy). ***PRACTICE AREAS:*** Products Liability; Insurance; Medical Malpractice. ***Email:*** dale.peddicord@peddicord-law.com

JOHN M. WHARTON, born Ames, Iowa, June 16, 1944; admitted to bar, 1970, Iowa; 1972, Florida. *Education:* Iowa State University (B.S., 1967); Drake University (J.D., 1970). Phi Alpha Delta (Vice President, 1969-1970). Case Notes Editor, Drake Law Review, 1969-1970. Author: Casenote, 18 Drake Law Review 119, 1968; Note, 19 Drake Law Review 187, 1969. Member, Iowa Board of Law Examiners, 1983—. *Member:* Polk County, The Iowa State and American Bar Associations; The Florida Bar; Defense Research Institute; Iowa Academy of Trial Lawyers; Iowa Defense Counsel Association; Association of Trial Lawyers of Iowa; The Association of Trial Lawyers of America; Lawyer-Pilots Bar Association. [Capt., JAGD, USAF, 1970-1974]. ***PRACTICE AREAS:*** Insurance. ***Email:*** jack.wharton@peddicord-law.com

STEPHEN W. SPENCER, born Ravenna, Ohio, March 7, 1955; admitted to bar, 1980, Iowa. *Education:* Clinton Community College (A.A., magna cum laude, 1975); Drake University (B.A., summa cum laude, 1977); University of Iowa (J.D., with distinction, 1980). *Member:* Polk County, Iowa State (Member, Section on Workers Compensation) and American (Member, Sections on: Litigation; Administrative Law) Bar Associations; The Iowa Association of Workers Compensation Lawyers; Iowa Defense Counsel Association. ***PRACTICE AREAS:*** Workers Compensation. ***Email:*** stephen.spencer@peddicord-law.com

LEE P. HOOK, born Webster City, Iowa, February 19, 1956; admitted to bar, 1981, Iowa. *Education:* University of Iowa; Drake University (J.D., 1981). *Member:* Polk County, Iowa State and American Bar Associations; Iowa Trial Lawyers Association; Iowa Defense Counsel Association. ***PRACTICE AREAS:*** Workers Compensation; Insurance. ***Email:*** lee.hook@peddicord-law.com

JOSEPH M. BARRON, born Coon Rapids, Iowa, March 28, 1963; admitted to bar, 1988, Iowa. *Education:* University of Iowa, Iowa City, Iowa (B.A., 1985; J.D., with distinction, 1988). Member, Iowa Law Review. *Member:* Polk County, Iowa State and American Bar Associations. ***PRACTICE AREAS:*** Insurance. ***Email:*** joe.barron@peddicord-law.com

TIMOTHY W. WEGMAN, born Iowa City, July 15, 1964; admitted to bar, 1989, Missouri; 1990, Iowa; U.S. District Court, Southern and Northern Districts of Iowa. *Education:* University of Iowa, Iowa City (B.A., 1986); Drake University (J.D., with honors, 1989). Phi Alpha Delta. Member, 1987-1989 and Projects Editor, 1988-1989 Drake Law Review. *Member:* Polk County, Iowa State and American Bar Associations; The Missouri Bar; Iowa Trial Lawyers Association. ***PRACTICE AREAS:*** Insurance; Workers Compensation. ***Email:*** tim.wegman@peddicord-law.com

MICHAEL S. ROLING, born Spencer, Iowa, May 21, 1966; admitted to bar, 1994, Iowa. *Education:* Briar Cliff College (B.A., 1988); Drake University (J.D., with honors, 1993). Delta Theta Phi. *Member:* Polk County, Iowa State Bar Associations; Iowa Defense Counsel; Association of Trial Lawyers of Iowa; The Association of Trial Lawyers of America. ***PRACTICE AREAS:*** Workers Compensation; Insurance. ***Email:*** mike.roling@peddicord-law.com

STEVEN T. DURICK, born Lansing, Michigan, January 30, 1970; admitted to bar, 1995, Iowa; U.S. District Court, Southern and Northern Districts of Iowa. *Education:* Illinois State University (B.S., 1992); Drake University (J.D., with honors, 1995). American Jurisprudence Award in Administrative Law, 1993; Drake Achievement Award, Trial Advocacy, 1994. President, Drake Moot Court Board, 1994-1995. Member, Drake National Mock Trial Team, 1995. Member: C. Edwin Moore Inns of Court, 1994-1995; National Order of Barristers, 1995. *Member:* Polk County, Iowa State and American Bar Associations; Iowa Trial Lawyers Association. ***PRACTICE AREAS:*** Workers Compensation; Insurance. ***Email:*** steven.durick@peddicord-law.com

---

SCOTT J. BEATTIE, born Des Moines, Iowa, October 19, 1966; admitted to bar, 1992, Iowa. *Education:* Cedarville College (B.A., 1989); Drake University Law School (J.D., with honors, 1992). Member: Drake Law Review, 1991-1992; National Mock Trial Team, 1992. Assistant City Attorney, City of Des Mines, 1998-2002. *Member:* Polk County and Iowa State Bar Associations; Defense Research Institute. [Lt. Commander JAG Corps U.S. Navy, 1992-1998]. ***PRACTICE AREAS:*** Workers Compensation; Insurance Defense. ***Email:*** scott.beattie@peddicord-law.com

ANNE UPDEGRAFF, born Landstuhl, Germany, 1971; admitted to bar, 1996, Iowa; U.S. District Court, Southern and Northern Districts of Louisiana and U.S. Court of Appeals, Eighth Circuit. *Education:* University of Iowa (B.A., 1993); Drake University (J.D., with honors, 1996). Phi Beta Kappa; Order of the Coif. Recipient, American Jurisprudence Award in Constitutional Law. Law Clerk, Second District of Iowa, 1996-1997. *Member:* Iowa State Bar Association; Defense Research Institute. ***Email:*** Anne.Updegraff@peddicord-law.com

MARK A. BOSSCHER, born Cadillac, Michigan, November 11, 1975; admitted to bar, 2001, Iowa. *Education:* Central College (B.A., 1998); Drake University Law School (J.D., with honors, 2001). *Member:* Polk County, Iowa State and American Bar Associations; Iowa Trial Lawyers Association (Member, Sections on: Workers Compensation Committee); National Workers Compensation Defense Network. ***PRACTICE AREAS:*** Workers Compensation; Insurance Defense. ***Email:*** mark.Bosscher@peddicord-law.com

REPRESENTATIVE CLIENTS: AAO Services Inc.; Ace Group; Ace USA; Ace Westchester Spec. Group; Accident Fund of America; Administrative Claims Services; AIG Aviation; Aldi, Inc.; Amana Appliances/Maytag Corp; American Arbitration Assn; American Safety Insurance; Amex Assurance Company; AP Capital; Aramark Corporation; Arthur J. Gallagher & Co.; Auto Recon USA; Berkley Risk Administrators; Berkshire Hathaway; Broadspire; Budget Rent-A-Car Corporation; Cambridge Integrated Srvcs. Inc.; Carl Konz Agency; Catholic Health Initiatives; CCMSI; Cendant Car Rental; Claims Management Inc.; Clarke Companies; CNA Claims; Conagra Foods; Conagra Risk; Constitution State SVC; Continental Western; Comhuster Casualty; Country Companies; Crawford Insurance Adjusters; Crum & Forster Insurance; Dalmler Chrysler Motors; Dial Corporation; District Court Mediation Program; Donaldson Company; Dr. Pepper/7-Up; E & O Professionals; Employers Mutual; Employers Reinsurance/Westport; Enterprise Rent-A-Car; ESIS, Inc.; Essex Insurance; Farmer Bocken; Federal Express; Fireman's Fund Insurance Group; Fortress Insurance Company; Gab, Robins North America Inc.; Gallagher Bassett Services, Inc.; Gates, McDonald; Gelco Insurance; Great American Insur. Co.; Great West Casualty Company; Heartland Express; Heenan Agency; Heyl Truck Lines; Han Industries; In Service, Inc.; Integrated Asset Services; Integrity Mutual Insurance; Interstate Insurance Group; K & K Insurance; Lindsey Cunningham Claim Serv; Lumberman's Underwriting; Alliance; Meadowbrook Insurance Group; Mercury Ins. Co. of Florida; Metso Minerals; Midwest Industries; MMIC Insurance; MSI Insurance; National Employee Care Systems; National Indemnity Company; NECS; NPC Management; Nestle Beverage; Nestle Petcare; Octagon Risk Mngmt Services; OMS National Insurance Co.; Pamida Stores; Pekin Insurance Company; Piggott Office Pavillion; Progressive Insurance Companies; Reinhart Food Service, Inc.; Risk Admin SVCS Inc.; Rollins, Inc.; Royal Insurance; Ruan Dedicated Unit; Sagamore Insurance Company; Seaton Corp; Sedgwick James Group; Self Insured Services Company; Sedgwick Claims Management Services; Sentry Insurance Group; Society Insurance; Stealth Enterprises; SYSCO Food Services of Iowa; Specialty Risk Services; Swift & Company; Swiss Valley Farms; Travelers Property Casualty; Trinity Industries; Tristar Claim Administration; Tri-State Insurance of Minnesota; United Companies Lending Corp.; United Fire & Casualty; United Heartland Inc.; United National Insurance; Ward North America; Weltz Construction Company; Western National Insurance; Wheaton Franciscan Services; Winnebago Industries, Inc.; Workmens Auto Insurance; Zurich American Ins.

PETOSA, PETOSA & BOECKER, L.L.P.

DES MOINES, IOWA

(See Clive)

General Civil and Trial Practice. Corporation, Real Estate, Foreclosure, Zoning, Municipal, Taxation, Probate, Estate Planning and Bankruptcy Law.

THE POWELL LAW FIRM, P.C.

DES MOINES, IOWA

(See Norwalk)

Business Law, Construction Law, Family Law, Personal Injury, Real Estate, Administrative Law, Appellate Practice, Commercial Law, Consumer Law, Contracts, Federal Practice, Government Contracts, Guardianship and Conservatorship, Litigation, Probate, Trusts and Estates, Wills, Elder Law, Child Custody, Child Support, Divorce, Criminal Defense, Automobile Accidents and Injuries, Commercial Real Estate, Residential Real Estate Sales, Zoning Planning and Land Use, Corporate Law, Franchise Law, Small Business Law, Business Organization.

J. KEITH RIGG

SUITE 409
100 COURT AVENUE
DES MOINES, IOWA 50309
Telephone: 515-284-7930
Facsimile: 515-284-7928
URL: http://www.keithrigg.com
Email: jkrigg@dwx.com
URL: http://www.lawyers.com/jkeithrigg

Criminal Trial Practice in Federal and State Courts. Civil Litigation.

FIRM PROFILE: Mr. Rigg engages in a trial practice with an emphasis in criminal litigation in the state and federal courts.

J. KEITH RIGG, born Springfield, Illinois, June 24, 1958; admitted to bar, 1982, Iowa, U.S. District Court, Northern and Southern Districts of Iowa, U.S. Court of Appeals, Eight Circuit and U.S. Supreme Court. *Education:* Illinois State University (B.S., with honors, 1979); Drake University (J.D., with honors, 1982). First Assistant Public Defender, Woodbury County, Iowa, 1985-1986. First Assistant County Attorney, Woodbury County, Iowa, 1987-1988. *Member:* Polk County, Iowa State, Federal and American Bar Associations; National Association of Criminal Defense Lawyers; Iowa Association of Criminal Defense Lawyers. ***PRACTICE AREAS:*** Criminal Law; Federal Criminal Law; Criminal Conspiracy; Felonies.

ROSENBERG, STOWERS & MORSE

1010 INSURANCE EXCHANGE BUILDING
505 FIFTH AVENUE
DES MOINES, IOWA 50309
Telephone: 515-243-7600; 515-243-0583
URL: http://www.rosenbergstowersmorse.com
URL: http://www.lawyers.com/rosenbergstowersmorse

General Practice, Civil, Criminal Trial and Appellate practice in Federal and State Courts. Criminal Law, Personal Injury, Family Law, Business Litigation, Bankruptcy, White Collar Crimes, Criminal Appeals, Securities Litigation and Arbitration.

FIRM PROFILE: The partners of the Rosenberg, Stowers & Morse Law Firm are Dean Stowers, Brent Rosenberg and David A. Morse. The firm practices in the Federal and State Trial Courts throughout Iowa, as well as in the Federal and State Appeal Courts. The firm encourages continuing professional development and legal education. The firm has available effective, trained support personnel.

MEMBERS OF FIRM

DEAN A. STOWERS, born Madison, Wisconsin, March 5, 1964; admitted to bar, 1989, Iowa, Pennsylvania and U.S. Court of Appeals, Eighth Circuit and U.S. Supreme Court. *Education:* University of Wisconsin-Madison (B.S., 1986); Drake University (J.D., 1989). Member, Drake Law Review, 1988-1989. Author: Note, "Juror Bias Undiscovered During Voir Dire," 29 Drake L. Rev. 201, 1990; Casenote, 38 Drake L. Rev. 961 1989. Attorney, U.S. Sentencing Commission, 1989-1990. Listed, "The Best Lawyers in America." *Member:* Iowa State, Pennsylvania and American Bar Associations; National Association Criminal Defense Lawyers; Iowa Association Criminal Defense Lawyers (Board Member, 1995-1996). ***REPORTED CASES:*** U.S. v. Cornelius, 968 F.2d 703 (8th Cir. 1992); Huyser v. Iowa District Court, 499 N.W.2d (Iowa 1993); U.S. v. Cornelius, 999 F.2d 1293 (8th Cir. 1993); Ginsberg v. D.O.T., 508 N.W.2d 633 (Iowa 1993); U.S. v. O'Conner, 64 F.3d 355 (8th Cir. 1995); U.S. v. Halter, 217 F.3d 551 (8th Cir. 2000); U.S. v. Moyer, 244 F.3d 666 (8th Cir. 2001); State v. Hager, 630 N.W.2d 828 (Iowa 2001); U.S. v. Cruz. 285 F.3d 692 (8th Cir. 2002). ***PRACTICE AREAS:*** Criminal Defense; Criminal Appeals; Federal Criminal Law.

BRENT D. ROSENBERG, born Des Moines, Iowa, December 17, 1949; admitted to bar, 1980, Missouri; 1982, Texas; 1992, Iowa. *Education:* University of Iowa (B.G.S., 1975); Drake University (J.D., with honors, 1979). Order of the Coif. Member, Drake Law Review, 1978-1979. Author: Casenote, "Owen Equipment & Erection Co. v. Kroger," 28 Drake Law Review 198, 1979; Critique, "Ancillary and Pendent Party Jurisdiction in the Aftermath of Owen Equipment and Erection Co. v. Kroger," 28 Drake Law Review 758, 1979. *Member:* Iowa State Bar Association; State Bar of Texas. ***REPORTED CASES:*** United States v. Grimaldo, 214 F.3d 967 (8th Cir. 2000), cert.denied, 531 U.S. 1081, 121 S.Ct., 148 L.Ed.2d 680, 69 USLW 3456 (U.S. 2001); U.S. v. Licona-Lopez, 163 F.3d 1040 (8th Cir. 1998); Stanton v. Iowa Dist. Ct. for Polk County, 2001 WL 98951 (Iowa App. 2001); State v. Ross, 573 N.W.2d 906 (Iowa 1998); State v. Vogel, 548 N.W.2d 584 (Iowa 1996). ***PRACTICE AREAS:*** Business Litigation; Contract Litigation; Criminal Defense.

DAVID A. MORSE, born Mason City, Iowa, March 28, 1964; admitted to bar, 1989, Iowa. *Education:* Coe College (B.A., 1986); Drake University (J.D., with honors, 1989). Drake Moot Court Board, 1987-1989. *Member:* Polk County, Iowa State and American Bar Associations; Iowa Association of Criminal Defense Lawyers. ***LANGUAGES:*** German. ***REPORTED CASES:*** Leydens v. Des Moines, 484 N.W. 2d 594 (Iowa 1992); All Tech v. Power Products, Company, 581 N.W. 2d 202 (Iowa 1998); University of Iowa v. Dunbar, 590 N.W. 2d 510 (Iowa 1999); Cepelak v. Sears, 246 B.R. 341 (8th Cir. 2000); Dial National Bank v. Van Houweling, 258 B.R. 173 (BAP 8th Cir. 2001). ***PRACTICE AREAS:*** General Practice; Civil Litigation; Criminal Law; Appellate Practice; Personal Injury; Business Litigation; Securities Litigation; Bankruptcy; Family Law; Arbitration. ***Email:*** morse@rosenbergstowersmorse.com

REFERENCE: Firstar Bank, Des Moines, Iowa.

SMITH, SCHNEIDER, STILES & SERANGELI, P.C.

THE EQUITABLE BUILDING
604 LOCUST, SUITE 1000
DES MOINES, IOWA 50309
Telephone: 515-245-6789
Fax: 515-244-1328
Email: stelford@smithlawiowa.com

General Civil Trial, Civil, Criminal, Commercial and Tax Litigation and Appellate Practice in all Courts. Commercial, Corporation, Workers Compensation, Real Estate, Taxation, Personal Injury, Probate and Administrative Law, Business Transactions.

JAN MOHRFELD KRAMER, born West Point, Iowa, August 2, 1966; admitted to bar, 1991, Iowa, U.S. Court of Appeals, Eighth Circuit and U.S. District Court, Northern and Southern Districts of Iowa, U.S. Tax Court. *Education:* Drake University (B.S., 1987; J.D., with honors, 1990). Order of the Coif. *Member:* Polk County, Iowa State and American Bar Associations; Iowa Trial Lawyers Association. The Association of Trial Lawyers of America. ***PRACTICE AREAS:*** Employment Law; Commercial Litigation. ***Email:*** JMK@smithlawiowa.com

RONALD L. MOUNTSIER, born Geneva, Illinois, May 21, 1957; admitted to bar, 1982, Iowa, U.S. Court of Federal Claims, U.S. Tax Court; U.S. District Court, Southern and Northern Districts of Iowa and U.S. Court of Appeals, Eighth and Ninth Circuits. *Education:* Drake University (B.S.B.A., 1979; J.D., 1982). Certified Public Accountant, Iowa, 1979. Co-Author: "When Should The Election To Be Excluded From The Partnership Tax Provisions Be Made?" Taxation For Accountants, August, 1987. *Member:* Polk County, Iowa State and American (Member, Taxation Section) Bar Associations; Iowa Society of Certified Public Accountants. ***PRACTICE AREAS:*** Tax Law; Corporate Law; Business Law. ***Email:*** RMountsier@smithlawiowa.com

(This Listing Continued)

FRED R. SCHNEIDER, born Velasco, Texas, March 25, 1943; admitted to bar, 1967, Iowa; 1969, U.S. District Court, Northern and Southern Districts of Iowa, U.S. Court of Appeals, Eighth Circuit, U.S. Tax Court. *Education:* Drake University (B.A., 1965; J.D., with honors, 1967). Phi Beta Kappa; Order of the Coif; Phi Eta Sigma. Editor-in-Chief, Drake University Law Review, 1966-1967. Law Clerk to Hon. Roy L. Stephenson, Chief Judge, U.S. District Court, Southern District of Iowa, 1967-1969. Board of Counselors, Drake University Law School, 1981-1990. *Member:* Polk County, Iowa State and American (Member, Sections on: Corporation, Banking and Business Law) Bar Associations. ***PRACTICE AREAS:*** Corporate Law; Business Law; Business Transactions. ***Email:*** FSchneider@smithlawiowa.com

WILLIAM B. SERANGELI, born Fort Madison, Iowa, October 14, 1949; admitted to bar, 1975, Iowa; 1976, U.S. Tax Court, U.S. District Court, Southern and Northern Districts of Iowa, U.S. Court of Appeals, Eighth Circuit and U.S. Supreme Court. *Education:* Illinois State University (B.S.Ed., 1972); Drake University (J.D., with honors, 1975). Order of the Coif. The Order of Barristers. Staff Member, Drake University Law Review, 1974-1975. *Member:* Polk County, Iowa State (Member, Litigation Section) and American (Member, Litigation Section) Bar Associations; Fellow, The Iowa Academy of Trial Lawyers; The Association of Trial Lawyers of America; The Association of Trial Lawyers of Iowa; C. Edwin Moore American Inns of Court (Master); Iowa Defense Counsel Association. ***PRACTICE AREAS:*** Employment Law; Real Estate; Commercial Litigation. ***Email:*** WBS@smithlawiowa.com

WILLIAM S. SMITH, born Clearwater, Florida, February 25, 1944; admitted to bar, 1968, Iowa; 1972, U.S. Tax Court; U.S. District Court, Northern and Southern Districts of Iowa; U.S. District Court, Northern District California; U.S. Claims Court; U.S. Court of Appeals, Eighth and Ninth Circuits; U.S. Supreme Court. *Education:* University of Iowa (B.B.A., 1967; J.D., with high distinction, 1968). Phi Alpha Delta; Order of the Coif; Blackstone Inn of Court (Past President). Certified Public Accountant, Illinois and Iowa, 1970. Contributing Editor: Life Insurance Trusts in the Estate Plan, Drake Law Review (1995); Iowa Legal Research Guide in Criminal Law & Prosecution, Drake Law School, 2002. Lecturer, Taxation Law, Drake University Law School, 1982-2000. Former Member, Board of Directors, Lawyers Trust Account Commission of the Supreme Court of Iowa. *Member:* Polk County, Iowa State and American (Member, Committee on Civil and Criminal Tax Penalties, 1989-2002; Tax Council, 2001-2004; Criminal Justice Section, 1997-2004) Bar Associations; The Association of Trial Lawyers of America; Association of Federal Defense Attorneys. Fellow, Iowa State Bar Association. ***PRACTICE AREAS:*** White Collar Crime; Taxation; Business Law; Agricultural Law; Litigation. ***Email:*** WSSmith@smithlawiowa.com

WILLIAM R. STILES, born Stewartville, Minnesota, January 18, 1946; admitted to bar, 1973, Iowa. *Education:* Drake University (B.A., 1969; J.D., with honors, 1973). Order of the Coif; National Order of Barristers; Delta Theta Phi. Member, National Moot Court Team. Editor-in-Chief, Drake University Law Review, 1972-1973. Author: Case Note, 21 Drake Law Review 375, 1972; "Habeas Corpus Relief for the Military Prisoner; The Double Standard," 21 Drake Law Review 576, 1972; "Blackacre As a Shelf of Securities: Real Estate Syndications," 23 Drake Law Review 483, 1974. Lecturer, Securities Regulation Law, Drake University Law School, 1979. *Member:* Polk County, Iowa State (Member, Section on Real Estate and Title Law) and American (Member, Sections on: Real Estate, Probate and Trust Law; Taxation; Corporation, Banking and Business Law) Bar Associations. ***PRACTICE AREAS:*** Real Estate; Probate. ***Email:*** WStiles@smithlawiowa.com

CECELIA IBSON WAGNER, born Des Moines, Iowa, September 12, 1963; admitted to bar, 1989, Iowa, U.S. District Court, Northern and Southern District of Iowa and U.S. Court of Appeals Eighth, Ninth and Tenth Circuits. *Education:* Iowa State University (B.A., 1985); George Washington University (J.D., 1988). President, Phi Alpha Delta, 1987-1988. Member, George Washington Journal of International Law and Economics. Assistant Attorney General, Iowa, 1995-1999. Member, Des Moines 40 under 40 Business and Community Leaders, 2002. *Member:* Iowa State, Federal and American Bar Associations; Polk County Women Attorneys (President, 1994); Master C. Edwin Moore Inn of Court; Iowa Defense Council Association. ***PRACTICE AREAS:*** Insurance Defense; Real Estate; Commercial Litigation; Complex Litigation. ***Email:*** ciwagner@smithlawiowa.com

---

JOSEPH M. BORG, born Pella, Iowa, November 25, 1977; admitted to bar, 2003, Iowa. *Education:* Central College (B.A., summa cum laude, 2000); Drake University (J.D., with honors, 2003). Order of the Coif. Law Clerk to Judge Terry L. Huitink, Iowa Court of Appeals, 2003-2005. Articles Editor, Drake University Law Review. *Member:* Polk County, Iowa State (Member, Young Lawyers Division, 2003) and American Bar Associations. ***PRACTICE AREAS:*** Civil Litigation; Commercial Litigation; Real Estate.

AMY D. PLUMMER, born Eau Claire, Wisconsin, September 25, 1976; admitted to bar, 2002, Iowa and U.S. District Court, Southern District of Iowa. *Education:* University of Minnesota, Minneapolis (B.S., 1999); Pepperdine University School of Law (J.D., 2002). Fellow and Founding Student Board Member, Pepperdine School of Law Center for Entrepreneurship and Technology Law. Co-Author, "Internet Laws Affecting Iowa Companies," 2003. *Member:* Polk County, Iowa State (Member, Young Lawyers Division, 2002) and American Bar Associations; Polk County Women Attorneys. ***PRACTICE AREAS:*** Corporate Law; Business Law. ***Email:*** adplummer@smithlawiowa.com

Representative Clients provided on request.

STURM & FIX LLP

Established in 1962
206 SIXTH AVENUE, SUITE 1213
DES MOINES, IOWA 50309-4076
Telephone: 515-288-9589
Fax: 515-288-4860
Email: sturm@hsllp.com
URL: http://www.hsllp.com

Davenport, Iowa Office: 304 Northwest Bank Building-Downtown, 101 West Second Street, 52801-1813. Telephone: 563-323-9731. Fax: 563-323-9709.

(This Listing Continued)

STURM & FIX LLP, Des Moines—Continued

Patent, Trademark, Copyright and Unfair Competition Law, Federal Trial Practice, Intellectual Property.

FIRM PROFILE: Sturm & Fix LLP was founded in 1962 and serves a wide spectrum of U.S. and International clients in intellectual property matters, including prosecution and litigation.

MEMBERS OF FIRM

MICHAEL O. STURM, born 1943; admitted to bar, 1973, Virginia; 1974, Iowa; 1982, Nebraska; 1974, registered to practice before U.S. Patent and Trademark Office. *Education:* Iowa State University (B.S., Engr., 1966); Catholic University of America (J.D., 1973). Examiner, U.S. Patent and Trademark Office, 1966-1971. ***Email:*** Sturm@hsllp.com

JOHN E. CEPICAN, born 1948; admitted to bar, 1974, Iowa; 1974, registered to practice before U.S. Patent and Trademark Office. *Education:* Iowa State University (B.S., physics, 1971); Drake University (J.D., 1974). ***Email:*** Cepican@hsllp.com

RICHARD L. FIX, born 1943; admitted to bar, 1976, Iowa; 1985, Nebraska; registered to practice before U.S. Patent and Trademark Office. *Education:* University of Iowa (B.S., Ch.E., 1966; M.B.A., 1967); Drake University (J.D., 1975). ***Email:*** Fix@hsllp.com

REFERENCE: Wells Fargo Bank Iowa, N.A.

THE NAN TIERNAN LAW FIRM, P.L.C.

P.O. BOX 12034
DES MOINES, IOWA 50312
Telephone: 515-277-7136; 1-866-977-7136
Cell: 515-988-3540
Email: nantiernan@yahoo.com
URL: http://www.lawyers.com/nantiernan

Family Law, Adoptions, Interstate Adoptions, Step Parent Adoption, Child Custody, Child Support, Divorce, Parental Rights, Domestic Violence, Visitation Rights, Alimony, Grandparent Rights, General Practice, Wills and Probate, Bankruptcy, Guardianships, Appellate Practice, Post Divorce Modification, Surrogacy Law, Assisted Reproduction Technology, Termination of Parental Rights, Grandparent Adoption, Premarital Agreements, Mental Health and Developmental Disabilities, Incompetence Proceedings, Paternity, Spousal Support, Modification of Custody.

NAN TIERNAN, born Des Moines, Iowa, 1942; admitted to bar, 1995, Iowa and U.S. District Court, Southern District of Iowa. *Education:* Drake University (B.S., magna cum laude, 1965); University of Iowa (M.S., Education, Learning Disabilities, 1982; J.D., 1994). *Member:* Iowa State Bar Association (Member, Family Law Section). ***PRACTICE AREAS:*** Family Law; Adoption Law; Interstate Adoptions; Step Parent Adoptions; Child Support; Divorce; Parental Rights; Domestic Violence; Visitation Rights; Alimony; Grandparents Visitation Rights; General Practice; Wills; Probate; Bankruptcy; Guardianship; Appellate Practice; Post Divorce Modification; Surrogacy Law; Assisted Reproductive Technology; Termination of Parental Rights; Grandparents Custody; Premarital Agreements; Mental Health Law; Disabilities; Incompetency Proceedings; Paternity; Spousal Support.

TRIPP, P.C.

DES MOINES, IOWA
(See Pella)
Social Security Law, General Practice.

THE LAW OFFICES OF BRETT J. TROUT, P.C.

516 WALNUT STREET
DES MOINES, IOWA 50309
Telephone: 515-280-1939
Fax: 515-280-7114
URL: http://www.bretttrout.com
Email: trout@bretttrout.com
URL: http://www.brettjtrout.com

Patent, Trademark and Copyright Law, E-Commerce, Software Licensing, Intellectual Property, Information Technology, Trade Secrets.

BRETT J. TROUT, born Des Moines, Iowa, July 28, 1966; admitted to bar, 1992, Iowa and U.S. District Court, Northern and Southern Districts of Iowa and U.S. Supreme Court; U.S. Court of Appeals for the Federal Circuit; 2002, District of Columbia; registered to practice before U.S. Patent and Trademark Office. *Education:* Grinnell College (B.A., Chemistry, 1988); University of Iowa College of Law (J.D., with distinction, 1992). Articles Editor, Journal of Corporation Law, 1991-1992. Author: "Internet Laws Affecting Iowa Companies" 2002. The Law of Information Technology in Iowa; "A Patient Seeks a Portion of the Biotechnological Patent Profits in: Moore v. Regents of the University California," 17 J. Corp. L. 513 (1992). *Member:* Polk County and American Bar Associations; District of Columbia Bar; Iowa State Bar Association; Iowa Intellectual Property Law Association (President, 2001-2002). (Resident). ***PRACTICE AREAS:*** Intellectual Property; Information Technology; Patents; Trademarks; Copyrights; Software Licensing; Trade Secrets. ***Email:*** trout@bretttrout.com

TURNER LAW OFFICES

DES MOINES, IOWA
(See West Des Moines)

General Civil and Trial Practice in all State and Federal Courts. Litigation, Corporate and Business, Insurance, Labor and Employment, Construction, Personal Injury, Real Estate, Wills and Probate, Trusts and Estates.

WANDRO, BAER, APPEL AND CASPER, P.C.

Established in 1996
2501 GRAND AVENUE, SUITE B
DES MOINES, IOWA 50312
Telephone: 515-281-1475
Fax: 515-281-1474
Email: scarter@2501grand.com
URL: http://www.wandrolaw.com

General Civil and Trial Practice in all Courts, Commercial Litigation, Administrative Law, Personal Injury, Bankruptcy, Products Liability, Medical Malpractice and Business Law.

FIRM PROFILE: The Firm carries the highest legal ability rating in Martindale Hubble.

STEVEN P. WANDRO, born Charles City, Iowa, 1957; admitted to bar, 1984, Iowa and U.S. District Court, Northern District of Iowa; 1987, U.S. District Court, Southern District of Iowa. *Education:* University of Iowa (B.A., with high distinction, 1981; J.D., 1984). Phi Beta Kappa. Law Clerk to Hon. Lee M. Jackwig, U.S. Bankruptcy Court for Southern District of Iowa, 1987-1988. Chairman of the Board, Iowa Mediation Service. *Member:* Polk County, Iowa State and Federal (President, Iowa Chapter) Bar Associations; Agricultural Law Association; American Inns of Court. ***PRACTICE AREAS:*** Commercial Litigation; Agricultural Law; Bankruptcy; Personal Injury; Products Liability. ***Email:*** swandro@2501grand.com

KIMBERLEY K. BAER, born Des Moines, Iowa, August 31, 1963; admitted to bar, 1989, Illinois and U.S. District Court, Northern District of Illinois; 1995, Iowa; 1995, U.S. District Court, Southern District of Iowa. *Education:* University of Iowa (B.A., 1985); Washington College of Law, American University (J.D., summa cum laude, 1989). Member, American University Law Review, 1987-1989. Named, Woman of the Year 1999 by the Leukemia and Lymphoma Society. Associated with Skadden, Arps, Meagher & Flom, Chicago Office, 1989-1995. Appointed, Special Assistant Attorney General, 1990-1995 by Illinois Attorney General's Office. Graduate, Greater Des Moines Leadership Institute, 1996-1997. Board Member: Variety Club; Greater Des Moines Leadership Institute; Leukemia & Lymphoma Society; VIP Group, Habitat for Humanity, 1995-1998; Leadership Network, 1996-1999. *Member:* Polk County Bar Association; Iowa State Bar Association (Elected District Representative Young Lawyer Division); American Bar Association (Editor, Publications Board of ABA Tort and Insurance Practice Section; Vice-Chair, Young Lawyers Division Employment Law Section; Member, Sections on: Tort and Insurance Practice; Litigation; Young Lawyers Division); The Association of Trial Lawyers of America; Iowa Trial Lawyers Association. ***PRACTICE AREAS:*** Medical Malpractice; Personal Injury; Commercial Litigation; Products Liability; Insurance Defense. ***Email:*** kbaer@2501grand.com

BRENT R. APPEL, born Dubuque, Iowa, July 13, 1950; admitted to bar, 1978, California; 1979, Iowa; 1981, U.S. Supreme Court; U.S. Court of Appeals, Eighth Circuit and U.S. District Court, Northern and Southern Districts of Iowa. *Education:* Stanford University (B.A., with distinction and honors in History, 1973; M.A., 1973); University of California at Berkeley (J.D., 1977). Phi Beta Kappa. Winner: McBaine Moot Court Competition, 1977; Jamieson Award, Outstanding Scholar and Advocacy, 1977. Member, Board of Editors, 1975-1977 and Research Editor, 1976-1977, California Law Review. Law Clerk, U.S. Court of Appeals, District of Columbia Circuit, 1977-1978. Comment: "Emergency Mayor Power: An Exercise in Charter Interpretation," 65 Cal. L. Rev. 636, 1977; Author: "The Inevitable Discovery Exception to the Exclusionary Rule," 21 Crim. L. Bull. 101, 1985. Co-Author: with T. McGrane, "Client Perjury and the Criminal Justice System," 23 Am. Crim. L. Rev. 19, 1985; "Employment at Will in Iowa: A Journey Forward," Drake L. Rev. 67 (1989-1990). Author: Nix v. Whiteside, "The Role of Apples, Oranges and the Great Houdini in Constitutional Adjudication," 23 Crim. L. Bull. 5, 1987; "The Limited Impact of Nix v. Whiteside on Attorney-Client Relations," 136 U. Penn. L. Rev. 1913, 1988. Co-Author: "Employment at Will in Iowa: A Journey Forward," 39 Drake Law Review 67 (1989-1990); "Item Veto Litigation in Iowa: Marking the Boundaries Between Legislative and Executive Power," 41 Drake L. Rev. 1 (1992). First Assistant Attorney General of Iowa, 1979-1980. Deputy Attorney General of Iowa, 1983-1986. Member: Polk County Chamber Commission, 1990; Temporary State Reapportionment Advisory Committee, 1991; Greater Des Moines Government Reform Commission, 1991. *Member:* Polk County, Iowa State and American (Member, Litigation Section) Bar Associations; Iowa Trial Lawyers Association; Iowa Association of Trial Lawyers. American Inns of Court (Master C. Edwin Moore Inn of Court, 1999—). Fellow, Iowa State Bar Association Foundation. ***PRACTICE AREAS:*** Litigation; Employment Law. ***Email:*** bappel@2501grand.com

MICHELLE M. CASPER, born Des Moines, Iowa, October 17, 1970; admitted to bar, 1997, Iowa and U.S. District Court, Northern and Southern Districts of Iowa; 1998, U.S. Court of Appeals, Eighth Circuit. *Education:* University of Iowa (B.A., 1993; J.D., with distinction, 1997). Member, Iowa Law Review. Named, Woman of the Year 2001 by the Leukemia and Lymphoma Society. Member: Greater Des Moines Leadership Institute, 2001-2002; Leukemia & Lymphoma Society; Young Women's Resource Center, 1998-2005; Community Health Charities of Iowa Contract Negotiating Team, 2002. *Member:* Polk County, Iowa State and Iowa Federal Bar Associations; American Agricultural Law Association. ***PRACTICE AREAS:*** Commercial Litigation; Agricultural Law; Personal Injury; Products Liability. ***Email:*** mcasper@2501grand.com

JASON E. McCOLLOUGH, born Midwest City, Oklahoma, May 13, 1979; admitted to bar, 2004, Iowa, U.S. District Court, Southern and Northern Districts of Iowa. *Education:*

(This Listing Continued)

Oklahoma State University (B.S., 2001); Drake University (J.D., with honors, 2003). ***PRACTICE AREAS:*** Criminal Law; General Practice; Products Liability; Commercial Litigation; Trademarks; Copyrights. ***Email:*** jmccoll@2501grand.com

PHIL WATSON, P.C.

Established in 1975

535 EAST ARMY POST ROAD
DES MOINES, IOWA 50315
Telephone: 515-287-7000
Fax: 515-287-0875;
URL: http://philwatson.com
Email: firm@watsonpc.com
URL: http://www.watsonpc.com

Commercial and Retail Collections, Corporate and Commercial Law, Bankruptcy Law, Estate Planning, Probate, Real Estate and Business Litigation.

PHIL WATSON, born Des Moines, Iowa, June 19, 1941; admitted to bar, 1967, Iowa; 1969, U.S. District Court, Southern District of Iowa; 1974, U.S. Court of Appeals, Eighth Circuit. *Education:* Simpson College (B.A., 1964); Drake University (J.D., 1967). Phi Alpha Delta. Iowa Credit Association, President, 1989. Lincoln Inn, President, 1990. *Member:* Polk County and Iowa State Bar Associations. ***PRACTICE AREAS:*** Corporate Law; Business Litigation; Wills; Trust Law; Probate; Real Estate; Debtor and Creditor; Business Law. ***Email:*** phil@watsonpc.com

DRENNAN L. FISCHER, born Chicago, Illinois, October 16, 1973; admitted to bar, 2001, Iowa. *Education:* University of Iowa (B.A., English, 1996); California Western School of Law (J.D., 2001). *Member:* Polk County and Iowa State Bar Associations. ***PRACTICE AREAS:*** Probate; Wills; Trust Law; Real Estate; Estate Planning. ***Email:*** dfischer@watsonpc.com

BECKY J. PETERSEN, born Yankton, South Dakota, October 24, 1978; admitted to bar, 2003, Iowa; 2004, U.S. Tax Court. *Education:* University of Northern Iowa (B.A., Finance, with honors, 2000); Creighton University School of Law (J.D., cum laude, 2003). *Member:* Polk County and Iowa State Bar Associations. ***PRACTICE AREAS:*** Estate Planning; Real Estate; Probate; Business Law; Taxation. ***Email:*** bpetersen@watsonpc.com

ROCKY J. ROBBINS, born Hampton, Iowa, August 28, 1977; admitted to bar, 2004, Iowa. *Education:* University of Northern Iowa (B.A., magna cum laude, 2000); Drake University Law School (J.D., with high honors, 2004). Production Editor, Drake Law Review. ***PRACTICE AREAS:*** Criminal Law; Family Law; Litigation. ***Email:*** rrobbins@watsonpc.com

REPRESENTATIVE CLIENTS: Wells Fargo Card Services; Greyhound Lines, Inc.; John Deere Credit; Daiimler Chrysler Financial Corp.
REFERENCE: Community State Bank, Indianola, Iowa.

WHITFIELD & EDDY, P.L.C.

Established in 1928

317 6TH AVENUE, SUITE 1200
DES MOINES, IOWA 50309-4195
Telephone: 515-288-6041
Fax: 515-246-1474
Email: info@whitfieldlaw.com
URL: http://www.whitfieldlaw.com

Mt. Pleasant, Iowa Office: 110 North Jefferson, Suite 101, 52641-2016 Telephone: 319-385-9522. Fax: 319-385-3633. Email: info@whitfieldlaw.com. URL: http://www.whitfieldlaw.com.

Ankeny, Iowa Office: 213 North Ankeny Boulevard, Suite 100, 50023-1749. Telephone: 515-964-3633. Fax: 515-964-3692. Email: info@whitfieldlaw.com. URL: http://www.whitfieldlaw.com.

West Des Moines, Iowa Office: 3737 Woodland Avenue, Suite 400, 50266. Telephone: 515-558-0111. Fax: 515-222-0318. Email: info@whitfieldlaw.com. URL: http://www.whitfieldlaw.com.

General Practice including Trial and Appellate Practice and Business and Banking. Alternative Dispute Resolution, Antitrust and Trade Regulation, Arbitration, Bankruptcy, Banks and Banking, Business, Civil Rights, Commercial, Construction, Corporate, Criminal, Environmental, Family, Fidelity and Surety, Foreclosures, Health Care, Immigration and Naturalization, Insurance, Insurance Defense, Intellectual Property, Labor and Employment, Mediation, Municipal, Personal Injury, Probate, Products Liability, Professional Liability, Real Estate, Securities, Taxation, Transportation, Trust and Estates, Utility, Wills, Workers Compensation.

FIRM PROFILE: Whitfield & Eddy, P.L.C. has always maintained a strong emphasis on litigation focusing on insurance defense and products liability. The firm has diversified its practice to be responsive to the times, both in terms of developments in the economy and developments in the law. The firm endeavors to provide a wide variety of legal services to its clients at the highest level of quality and efficiency. Whitfield & Eddy has four locations in the state of Iowa. Please visit our web site for more detailed information on our practice areas, attorneys, locations and tradition of leadership in the legal community.

LAW FIRM ALLIANCES/ASSOCIATIONS: ***ALFA INTERNATIONAL***

EMPLOYERS COUNSEL NETWORK (ECN)

MEGAN M. ANTENUCCI, admitted to bar, 1985, Iowa. *Education:* Iowa State University (B.A., 1979); Drake University Law School (J.D., with honors, 1985). Order of the Coif; Order of the Barristers. Executive Editor, Drake Law Review, 1984-1985. Certified Mediator. *Member:* Polk County, Iowa State (Member, Litigation Section) and American (Member, Sections on: Law Practice Management; Litigation; Tort, Trial and Insurance Practice) Bar Associations. ***PRACTICE AREAS:*** Insurance; Litigation; Trial Law; Product Liability. ***Email:*** antenucci@whitfieldlaw.com

ROBERT G. BRIDGES, admitted to bar, 1961, Iowa. *Education:* University of Wisconsin-Madison (B.A., 1957); University of Iowa (J.D., 1961). *Member:* Polk County, Iowa State (Member, Sections on: Corporate Counsel; Real Estate and Title Law; Probate and Trust Law) and American (Member, Sections on: Litigation; Real Property, Probate and Trust Law; Tort, Trial and Insurance Practice) Bar Associations. ***Email:*** bridges@whitfieldlaw.com

THOMAS H. BURKE, admitted to bar, 1980, Iowa. *Education:* University of Iowa (B.A., with honors, 1977; J.D., with distinction, 1980). *Member:* Polk County, Iowa State (Member, Sections on: Agricultural Law; Business Law; Commercial and Bankruptcy Law), Federal and American (Member, Business Law Section) Bar Associations. ***PRACTICE AREAS:*** Banking Law; Business Law. ***Email:*** burke@whitfieldlaw.com

JASON M. CASINI, admitted to bar, 1993, Iowa. *Education:* University of Iowa (B.A., with distinction, 1990; J.D., with distinction, 1993). *Member:* Polk County, Iowa State (Member, Sections on: Intellectual Property Law; Labor and Employment Law; Litigation) and American (Member, Sections on: Labor and Employment Law; Law Practice Management; Litigation; Tort, Trial and Insurance Practice) Bar Associations. ***PRACTICE AREAS:*** Litigation; Product Liability; Labor and Employment; Insurance. ***Email:*** casini@whitfieldlaw.com

DANNY L. CORNELL, admitted to bar, 1995, Iowa; 2005, Illinois. *Education:* Evangel College (B.A., cum laude, 1989); University of Iowa (J.D., with high distinction, 1994). Member, Iowa Law Review. *Member:* Henry County, Iowa State (Member, Litigation Section) and American (Member, Sections on: Litigation; Tort, Trial and Insurance Practice) Bar Associations. (Resident, Mt. Pleasant Office). ***Email:*** cornell@whitfieldlaw.com

STEPHEN E. DOOHEN, admitted to bar, 1996, Iowa and South Dakota; 1997, Nebraska. *Education:* Morningside College (B.S., cum laude, 1993); University of Nebraska-Lincoln (J.D., 1996). *Member:* Polk County, Iowa State (Member, Litigation Section), Nebraska State and American (Member, Sections on: Litigation; Tort, Trial and Insurance Practice) Bar Associations; State Bar of South Dakota. ***PRACTICE AREAS:*** Litigation; Insurance Defense; Negligence; Premises Liability. ***Email:*** doohen@whitfieldlaw.com

WILLIAM L. FAIRBANK, admitted to bar, 1966, Iowa. *Education:* Drake University (B.A., 1964; J.D., 1966). *Member:* Polk County, Iowa State (Member, Sections on: Business Law; Probate and Trust Law; Real Estate and Title Law) and American (Member, Sections on: Business Law; Public Utility, Communications and Transportation Law; Real Property, Probate and Trust Law) Bar Associations. ***PRACTICE AREAS:*** Business Law; Transportation; Real Estate; Mortgages. ***Email:*** fairbank@whitfieldlaw.com

ROBERT L. FANTER, admitted to bar, 1969, Iowa. *Education:* University of Iowa (B.B.A., 1966; J.D., 1969). Authorized Mediator, American Academy of ADR Attorneys. *Member:* Polk County, Iowa State (Member, Sections on: Intellectual Property Law; Litigation) and American (Member, Litigation Section) Bar Associations; Defense Research Institute, Inc. (Past-President, 1997); American Board of Trial Advocates. ***PRACTICE AREAS:*** Product Liability; Litigation; Alternative Dispute Resolution; Intellectual Property. ***Email:*** fanter@whitfieldlaw.com

JOHN F. FATINO, admitted to bar, 1991, Iowa and Minnesota. *Education:* Concordia College (B.A., cum laude, 1987); Drake University (J.D., 1991). Order of Barristers. *Member:* Polk County, Iowa State (Member, Labor and Employment Law Section), Minnesota State and American (Member: Forum on the Construction Industry; Labor and Employment Law Section) Bar Associations. ***PRACTICE AREAS:*** Appellate Practice. ***Email:*** fatino@whitfieldlaw.com

GARY GATELY, admitted to bar, 1961, Iowa. *Education:* University of Iowa (B.S.C., 1957; J.D., 1961). *Member:* Polk County, Iowa State (Member, Sections on: Taxation; Probate and Trust Law) and American (Member, Sections on: Business Law; Taxation) Bar Associations. ***PRACTICE AREAS:*** Business Law; Corporate Law; Taxation; Wills; Trust Law; Estate Planning; Probate. ***Email:*** gately@whitfieldlaw.com

MARK R. GRAY, admitted to bar, 1986, Illinois; 1989, Iowa. *Education:* Truman State University (B.S., 1983); John Marshall Law School (J.D., 1986). *Member:* Polk County, Iowa State (Member, Sections on: General Practice; Probate and Trust Law; Real Estate and Title Law) and American Bar Associations. (Resident, Ankeny Office). ***PRACTICE AREAS:*** Business Law; Real Estate; Probate; Wills. ***Email:*** gray@whitfieldlaw.com

FRANK M. GRENARD, admitted to bar, 1977, Illinois; 1979, District of Columbia; 1989, Indiana; 1990, Michigan; 1999, Iowa; 2004, Nebraska. *Education:* California State University at Northridge (B.A., 1971); Northwestern University (J.D., 1977). *Member:* Polk County, Illinois State, Iowa State (Member, Sections on: Corporate Counsel; Environmental and Natural Resources), Nebraska State and American (Member, Sections on: Business Law; Environment, Energy and Resources) Bar Associations; State Bar of Michigan (Member, Environmental Law Section). ***PRACTICE AREAS:*** Banking Law; Real Estate; Environmental Law. ***Email:*** grenard@whitfieldlaw.com

MARK V. HANSON, admitted to bar, 1986, Iowa. *Education:* Iowa State University (B.S., 1970); Drake University (M.B.A., 1972); University of Iowa (J.D., with distinction, 1986). Associate Editor, Iowa Law Review, 1985-1986. *Member:* Polk County, Iowa State (Member, Sections on: Alternative Dispute Resolution; Business Law; Real Estate and Title Law; Probate and Trust Law) and American (Member, Sections on: Business Law; Real Property, Probate and Trust Law) Bar Associations. ***PRACTICE AREAS:*** Real Estate; Banking Law; Wills; Trust Law; Estate Planning; Probate. ***Email:*** hanson@whitfieldlaw.com

J. CAMPBELL HELTON, admitted to bar, 1995, Iowa. *Education:* University of Utah (B.S., 1992); Drake University (J.D., with honors, 1995). *Member:* Polk County, Iowa State (Member, Sections on: e-Commerce; Litigation; Workers' Compensation) and American (Member, Intellectual Property Law Section) Bar Associations. ***PRACTICE AREAS:*** Litigation; Intellectual Property; Labor and Employment; Commercial Law. ***Email:*** helton@whitfieldlaw.com

THOMAS HENDERSON, admitted to bar, 1980, Iowa. *Education:* Drake University (B.A., cum laude, 1977; J.D., 1980). Order of the Barristers. *Member:* Polk County, Iowa

(This Listing Continued)

WHITFIELD & EDDY, P.L.C., Des Moines—Continued

State (Member, Sections on: Litigation; Workers' Compensation) and American Bar Associations. ***PRACTICE AREAS:*** Litigation; Municipal Law; Personal Injury; Construction Law. ***Email:*** henderson@whitfieldlaw.com

RICHARD J. KIRSCHMAN, admitted to bar, 1991, Iowa. *Education:* Truman State University (B.S., cum laude, 1988); University of Iowa (J.D., with high distinction, 1991). Editor, Journal of Corporation Law, 1990-1991. *Member:* Polk County, Iowa State (Member, Sections on: Health Law; Litigation) and American (Member, Sections on: Health Law; Litigation; Tort, Trial and Insurance Practice) Bar Associations. ***PRACTICE AREAS:*** Insurance; Litigation; Product Liability; Appellate Practice. ***Email:*** kirschman@whitfieldlaw.com

PHILIP D. McCORMICK, admitted to bar, 1984, Iowa and Nebraska. *Education:* University of Iowa (B.B.A., 1981); Drake University (J.D., with honors, 1983). Order of the Coif. *Member:* Henry County, Iowa State (Member, Sections on: Real Estate and Title Law; Probate and Trust Law; Taxation), Nebraska State and American Bar Associations. (Resident, Mt. Pleasant Office). ***PRACTICE AREAS:*** Wills; Probate; Real Estate; Taxation; Banks and Banking; Trusts and Estates. ***Email:*** mccormick@whitfieldlaw.com

GREG A. NAYLOR, admitted to bar, 1978, Iowa; 1980, Michigan. *Education:* University of Iowa (B.A., with distinction, 1975); Drake University (J.D., 1978). Certified Mediator in Labor and Employment Law. *Member:* Polk County, Iowa State (Member: Labor and Employment Law Section) and American (Member, Labor and Employment Law Section) Bar Associations; State Bar of Michigan. (Resident, West Des Moines Office). ***PRACTICE AREAS:*** Labor and Employment; Civil Rights; Litigation. ***Email:*** naylor@whitfieldlaw.com

DAVID D. NELSON, admitted to bar, 1979, Iowa; 1995, Missouri. *Education:* Cornell College (B.A., 1970); Drake University (M.S.T., 1971; J.D., 1978). *Member:* Polk County, Iowa State (Member, Sections on: Environmental and Natural Resources; Real Estate and Title Law) and American (Member, Real Property, Probate and Trust Law Section) Bar Associations; The Missouri Bar. (Resident, Ankeny Office). ***PRACTICE AREAS:*** Real Estate; Business Law; Corporate Law; Zoning, Planning and Land Use. ***Email:*** nelson@whitfieldlaw.com

GARY A. NORTON, admitted to bar, 1984, Iowa. *Education:* Iowa State University (B.S., 1975); Washburn School of Law (J.D., with honors, 1984). Washburn Law Journal, 1982-1984. *Member:* Polk County, Iowa State (Member, Sections on: Commercial and Bankruptcy Law; e-Commerce; Environmental and Natural Resources), Federal and American (Member, Sections on: Business Law; Environment, Energy and Resources Law) Bar Associations. ***PRACTICE AREAS:*** Commercial Law; Bankruptcy; Debtor and Creditor; Environmental Law. ***Email:*** norton@whitfieldlaw.com

DAVID L. PHIPPS, admitted to bar, 1969, Iowa. *Education:* Drake University (B.A., 1967; J.D., with high honors, 1969). Order of the Coif. Member, Drake Law Review, 1968-1969. *Member:* Polk County, Iowa State (Member, Litigation Section) and American (Member, Litigation Section) Bar Associations; Iowa Defense Counsel Association (President, 1986-1987); Defense Research Institute, Inc. (State Chairman, 1988-1996). Fellow, American College of Trial Lawyers. Diplomate, American Board of Trial Advocates. ***PRACTICE AREAS:*** Litigation; Insurance Defense; Professional Liability; Personal Injury. ***Email:*** phipps@whitfieldlaw.com

SALLY A. REAVELY, admitted to bar, 1988, Iowa. *Education:* University of Iowa (B.S.N., with highest distinction, 1967; M.A., in Nursing, 1971); Drake University (J.D., with honors, 1988). Order of the Coif. *Member:* Polk County, Iowa State (Member, Sections on: General Practice; Health Law) and American (Member, Sections on: Health Law; General Practice, Solo and Small Firm) Bar Associations. ***PRACTICE AREAS:*** Health Care; Administrative Law; Aged and Aging. ***Email:*** s.reavely@whitfieldlaw.com

THOMAS S. REAVELY, admitted to bar, 1971, Iowa and Virginia. *Education:* College of William and Mary (B.A., 1968; J.D., 1971). *Member:* Polk County, Iowa State (Member, Sections on: Litigation; Workers' Compensation), Federal and American (Member, Sections on: Law Practice Management; Litigation; Tort, Trial and Insurance Practice) Bar Associations; Virginia State Bar. ***PRACTICE AREAS:*** Litigation; Personal Injury; Military Law; Securities. ***Email:*** reavely@whitfieldlaw.com

KEVIN M. REYNOLDS, admitted to bar, 1981, Iowa. *Education:* Iowa State University (B.A., 1978); University of Iowa (J.D., with distinction, 1981). *Member:* Polk County, Iowa State (Member, Litigation Section) and American (Member, Sections on: Litigation; Tort, Trial and Insurance Practice) Bar Associations. ***PRACTICE AREAS:*** Product Liability; Insurance Defense; Aviation and Aerospace. ***Email:*** reynolds@whitfieldlaw.com

G. MARK RICE, admitted to bar, 1983, Iowa and Nebraska. *Education:* University of South Dakota (B.A., 1978); Creighton University (J.D., 1982). Certified Mediator and Arbitrator. *Member:* Polk County, Iowa State (Member, Sections on: Business Law; Commercial and Bankruptcy Law; Real Estate and Title Law), Nebraska State, Federal and American (Member, Sections on: Business Law; Real Property, Probate and Trust Law) Bar Associations. ***Email:*** rice@whitfieldlaw.com

ROSCOE A. RIES, JR., admitted to bar, 1994, Iowa. *Education:* Drake University (B.S.B.A., magna cum laude, 1991; J.D., with honors, 1994). *Member:* Polk County, Iowa State (Member, Sections on: Business Law; Litigation) and American (Member, Sections on: Business Law; Litigation) Bar Associations. ***PRACTICE AREAS:*** Litigation; Insurance Defense; Appellate Practice; Criminal Law. ***Email:*** ries@whitfieldlaw.com

JAKI K. SAMUELSON, admitted to bar, 1980, Iowa. *Education:* Bradley University (B.A., summa cum laude, 1975); University of Iowa (J.D., with highest distinction, 1979). Order of the Coif. Editor, Iowa Law Review, 1978-1979. *Member:* Polk County, Iowa State (Member, Sections on: Labor and Employment Law; Trade Regulations) and American (Member, Labor and Employment Law Section) Bar Associations; Iowa Defense Counsel Association (President, 1997-1998). ***PRACTICE AREAS:*** Labor and Employment; Litigation; Trade Secrets; Unfair Competition. ***Email:*** samuelson@whitfieldlaw.com

ANJELA A. SHUTTS, admitted to bar, 1996, Iowa. *Education:* Luther College (B.A., 1993); Drake University (J.D., 1996). Order of the Barristers. Trained and Certified by Iowa Supreme Court as Family Law Mediator. *Member:* Polk County, Iowa State (Member, Sections on: Family and Juvenile Law; Litigation) and American (Member, Family Law Section) Bar Associations. ***PRACTICE AREAS:*** Alternative Dispute Resolution; Family Law. ***Email:*** shutts@whitfieldlaw.com

BERNARD L. "JERRY" SPAETH JR., admitted to bar, 1974, Iowa. *Education:* St. Thomas University (B.A., cum laude, 1971); University of Iowa (J.D., with high distinction, 1974). Order of the Coif. *Member:* Polk County, Iowa State (Member, Sections on: Family and Juvenile Law; Litigation) and American (Member, Sections on: Family Law; Litigation; Tort, Trial and Insurance Practice) Bar Associations. ***PRACTICE AREAS:*** Litigation; Family Law; Commercial Law; Business Law. ***Email:*** spaeth@whitfieldlaw.com

JEFFREY D. STONE, admitted to bar, 1993, Iowa. *Education:* Iowa State University (B.S., Construction Engineering, 1976); Drake University (J.D., with honors, 1992). Order of the Coif. *Member:* Polk County, Iowa State (Member, Alternative Dispute Resolution Section) and American (Member: Forum on the Construction Industry; Public Contract Law Section) Bar Associations. (Resident, West Des Moines Office). ***PRACTICE AREAS:*** Construction Law. ***Email:*** stone@whitfieldlaw.com

JOHN A. TEMPLER, JR., admitted to bar, 1975, Iowa. *Education:* University of Iowa (B.A., 1972; J.D., with high distinction, 1974). Certified Mediator in Construction Litigation. *Member:* Polk County, Iowa State (Member, Litigation Section) and American (Member: Forum on the Construction Industry; Litigation Sections) Bar Associations. (Resident, West Des Moines Office). ***PRACTICE AREAS:*** Construction Law; Litigation. ***Email:*** templer@whitfieldlaw.com

MAUREEN ROACH TOBIN, admitted to bar, 1987, Iowa. *Education:* University of Iowa (B.A., Economics, 1979); Drake University (J.D., with honors, 1987). *Member:* Polk County, Iowa State (Member, Sections on: Litigation; Workers' Compensation) and American (Member, Litigation Section) Bar Associations. ***PRACTICE AREAS:*** Workers Compensation; Litigation; Insurance Defense; Personal Injury. ***Email:*** tobin@whitfieldlaw.com

BENJAMIN B. ULLEM, admitted to bar, 1969, Iowa; 1982, Minnesota. *Education:* Drake University (B.A., 1966; J.D., 1969). Certified Mediator. *Member:* Polk County, Iowa State (Member, Sections on: Business Law; Real Estate and Title Law) and American (Member: Forum on the Construction Industry; Sections on: Business Law; Tort, Trial and Insurance Practice) Bar Associations. ***PRACTICE AREAS:*** Business Law; Fidelity and Surety; Real Estate; Corporate Law. ***Email:*** ullem@whitfieldlaw.com

---

RYAN M. ALBAUGH, admitted to bar, 1999, California; 2005, Florida and Iowa. *Education:* University of Iowa (B.B.A., Finance, with honors, 1996); Golden Gate University (J.D., with distinction, 1999). Associate Editor, Golden Gate University Law Review, 1998-1999. *Member:* Polk County, Iowa State and American Bar Associations; The Florida Bar; State Bar of California. (Resident, Ankeny Office). ***PRACTICE AREAS:*** Criminal Law; Family Law; Personal Injury; Trusts and Estates; Real Estate. ***Email:*** albaugh@whitfieldlaw.com

AARON D. BERNARD, admitted to bar, 2003, Arizona; 2004, Iowa. *Education:* Brigham Young University (B.A., International Law and Diplomacy, 2000); University of Notre Dame (J.D., 2003). *Member:* Polk County, Iowa State (Member, Sections on: Business Law; Labor and Employment Law) and American (Member, General Practice, Solo and Small Firm Section) Bar Associations. ***PRACTICE AREAS:*** Immigration and Naturalization; Business Law; Labor and Employment; Litigation. ***Email:*** bernard@whitfieldlaw.com

NICHOLAS O. COOPER, admitted to bar, 2004, Iowa. *Education:* University of Iowa (B.B.A., 2001); Drake University (J.D., with honors, 2004). Senior Staff Member, Drake Journal of Agricultural Law, 2003-2004. President, Drake Law School, 2003-2004. *Member:* Polk County, Iowa State (Member, Sections on: Business Law; Family and Juvenile Law; Litigation) and American (Member, Sections on: Business Law; Litigation) Bar Associations. ***Email:*** cooper@whitfieldlaw.com

JEFFREY D. EWOLDT, admitted to bar, 2000, Iowa; 2001, U.S. District Court, Northern and Southern Districts of Iowa; 2002, U.S. Court of Appeals, Eighth Circuit. *Education:* Iowa State University (B.S., with distinction, 1993); Drake University (J.D., with honors, 2000). Phi Kappa Phi; Phi Beta Kappa. Articles Editor, Drake Law Review, 1999-2000. Staff Writer: The Des Moines Register, 1992-1993; Quad City Times, 1994-1997; Sioux Falls Argus Leader, 1997. Co-Editor, Iowa Employment Law Newsletter (M. Lee Smith Publishers). *Member:* Polk County, Iowa State (Member, Labor and Employment Law Section) and American (Member, Labor and Employment Law Section) Bar Associations. ***Email:*** ewoldt@whitfieldlaw.com

ERIK S. FISK, admitted to bar, 2005, Iowa. *Education:* Drake University (B.A., summa cum laude, 1999; J.D., with highest honors, 2005); Indiana University (M.A., 2000). Order of the Coif. Projects Editor, Drake Law Review, 2004-2005. *Member:* Polk County, Iowa State and American Bar Associations. (Resident, West Des Moines Office). ***Email:*** fisk@whitfieldlaw.com

DREW J. GENTSCH, admitted to bar, 2000, Iowa. *Education:* Drake University (B.A., 1994; J.D., with honors, 2000). Member, Drake Journal of Agricultural Law. *Member:* Polk County, Iowa State (Member, Sections on: Agricultural Law; International Law; Labor and Employment Law) and American (Member: Forum on the Construction Industry; Sections on: International Law; Labor and Employment Law) Bar Associations. ***PRACTICE AREAS:*** Agricultural Law; Construction Law; Fidelity and Surety; Personal Injury. ***Email:*** gentsch@whitfieldlaw.com

GARY D. GOUDELOCK, admitted to bar, 2005, Iowa. *Education:* Oklahoma State University (B.A., German, 2002; B.A., Music, 2002); Drake University (J.D., with high honors, 2005). *Member:* Polk County, Iowa State and American (Member, Sections on: Litigation; Real Property, Probate & Trust Law; Tort, Trial & Insurance Practice) Bar Associations. ***PRACTICE AREAS:*** Wills; Trusts and Estates; Taxation; Commercial Law. ***Email:*** goudelock@whitfieldlaw.com

R. WILLIAM HANCOCK, JR., admitted to bar, 2004, Iowa. *Education:* University of North Carolina at Wilmington (B.A., cum laude, 1997); Drake University (J.D., with high honors, 2004). Order of the Coif; Order of the Barristers. Articles Editor, Drake Law Re-

(This Listing Continued)

view, 2003-2004. *Member:* Polk County, Iowa State and American (Member, Sections on: Administrative Law and Regulatory Practice; Litigation) Bar Associations. ***PRACTICE AREAS:*** Litigation; Torts; Consumer Law. ***Email:*** hancock@whitfieldlaw.com

JON K. HOFFMANN, admitted to bar, 1988, Iowa. *Education:* Drake University (B.S.B.A., Accounting, 1984; J.D., with honors, 1988). *Member:* Polk County, Iowa State (Member, Sections on: Litigation; Workers' Compensation) and American (Member, Tort, Trial and Insurance Practice Section) Bar Associations. ***PRACTICE AREAS:*** Civil Practice; Insurance Defense; Litigation; Real Estate. ***Email:*** hoffmann@whitfieldlaw.com

GRETCHEN WITTE KRAEMER, admitted to bar, 1999, Maryland; 2001, Iowa. *Education:* University of Richmond (B.A., summa cum laude, 1993); MCP-Hahnemann University (M.A., 1997; Ph.D., 2000); Villanova University (J.D., cum laude, 1999). Order of the Coif. Member, Villanova Law Review, 1998-1999. *Member:* Polk County, Iowa State (Member, Labor and Employment Law Section) and American (Member, Sections on: Litigation; Science and Technology Law) Bar Associations. ***Email:*** kraemer@whitfieldlaw.com

JONATHAN E. KRAMER, admitted to bar, 2002, Iowa. *Education:* Iowa State University (B.S., 1997); Drake University (J.D., with honors, 2002). Dwight D. Opperman Scholar, 1999-2002. *Member:* Polk County, Iowa State (Member, Sections on: Business Law; Commercial and Bankruptcy Law; Family and Juvenile Law; Probate and Trust Law) and American (Member, Sections on: Business Law; Family Law; Taxation) Bar Associations. ***PRACTICE AREAS:*** Debtor and Creditor; Family Law; Bankruptcy; Trusts and Estates. ***Email:*** kramer@whitfieldlaw.com

ADAM C. MANATT, admitted to bar, 2004, Iowa. *Education:* Iowa State University (B.A., with distinction, 2000); University of Iowa (J.D., 2004). Articles Editor, Journal of Corporation Law, 2002-2004. *Member:* Polk County, Iowa State (Member, Sections on: Labor and Employment Law; Litigation) and American (Member, Forum on the Construction Industry) Bar Associations. ***PRACTICE AREAS:*** Construction Law; Labor and Employment; Contracts; Litigation. ***Email:*** manatt@whitfieldlaw.com

STEPHEN D. MARSO, admitted to bar, 1999, Iowa. *Education:* Hope College (B.A., Spanish, magna cum laude, 1996); University of Iowa (J.D., with high distinction, 1999). Senior Managing Editor, Iowa Law Review, 1998-1999. *Member:* Polk County, Iowa State and American Bar Associations. ***PRACTICE AREAS:*** Construction Law; Criminal Law; Insurance; Litigation. ***Email:*** marso@whitfieldlaw.com

MARIA L. RUHTENBERG, admitted to bar, 1995, Iowa and U.S. District Court, Northern and Southern Districts of Iowa. *Education:* Indiana University (B.A., 1991); Drake University (J.D., with honors, 1995). Order of the Coif. Staff Member, 1993-1994 and Articles Editor, 1994-1995, Drake University Law Review. *Member:* Iowa State Bar Association. ***PRACTICE AREAS:*** Criminal Law; Federal Criminal Law; Search and Seizure; Criminal Appeals. ***Email:*** ruhtenberg@whitfieldlaw.com

THEODORE C. SIMMS, II, admitted to bar, 2001, Iowa. *Education:* University of Maryland (B.A., 1998); Drake University (J.D., 2001). Order of Barristers. Captain, National Championship Moot Court Team, 2001. Staff Member, Drake Journal of Agricultural Law, 1999-2000. *Member:* Polk County, Iowa State and American (Member, Labor and Employment Law Section) Bar Associations. ***PRACTICE AREAS:*** Appellate Practice; Litigation; Employment Law; Insurance. ***Email:*** simms@whitfieldlaw.com

KARA M. SINNARD, admitted to bar, 2002, Iowa. *Education:* University of Iowa (B.A., with honors, 1995); Drake University (J.D., with highest honors, 2002). Order of the Coif. Articles Editor, Drake Law Review, 2001-2002. *Member:* Polk County, Iowa State (Member, Sections on: Business Law; Commercial and Bankruptcy Law; Probate and Trust Law; Real Estate and Title Law) and American (Member, Sections on: Business Law; Real Property, Probate and Trust Law; Taxation) Bar Associations. ***PRACTICE AREAS:*** Business Law; Banking Law; Taxation; Real Estate. ***Email:*** sinnard@whitfieldlaw.com

B. MACPAUL "MAC" STANFIELD, admitted to bar, 2002, Massachusetts; 2003, Iowa. *Education:* University of Massachusetts, Boston (B.A., summa cum laude, 1995); University of Washington (M.A., 1998); Drake University (J.D., with highest honors, 2001). Dwight D. Opperman Scholar, 1998-2001. Research Editor, Drake Law Review, 2000-2001. *Member:* Polk County, Iowa State (Member, Sections on: Business Law; Commercial and Bankruptcy Law; e-Commerce; Intellectual Property Law; Real Estate and Title Law), Massachusetts (Member, Business Law Section) and American (Member: Entertainment and Sports Industries Forum; Sections on: Business Law; Intellectual Property Law) Bar Associations. ***PRACTICE AREAS:*** Intellectual Property; Commercial Law; Banking Law; Corporate Law. ***Email:*** stanfield@whitfieldlaw.com

OF COUNSEL

RONALD R. ADAMS, admitted to bar, 1977, Iowa; 1988, Nebraska. *Education:* Metropolitan State College (B.A., 1974); Washington & Lee University (J.D., 1977). *Member:* Polk County, Iowa State (Member, Sections on: Business Law; Commercial and Bankruptcy Law), Nebraska State, Federal and American Bar Associations. ***Email:*** adams@whitfieldlaw.com

WENDY L. CARLSON, admitted to bar, 1985, Iowa. *Education:* Drake University (B.S.B.A., magna cum laude, 1982); University of Notre Dame (J.D., 1985). Certified Public Accountant, Iowa, 1984. ***Email:*** carlson@whitfieldlaw.com

ALANSON K. ELGAR, admitted to bar, 1951, Iowa. *Education:* Iowa Wesleyan College (B.A., 1949); Drake University (J.D., 1951). *Member:* Henry County, Iowa State and American Bar Associations; Defense Research Institute, Inc. (State Chair, 1985-1986); Iowa Defense Counsel Association (President, 1983). (Resident, Mt. Pleasant Office). ***Email:*** elgar@whitfieldlaw.com

GEORGE H. FRAMPTON, admitted to bar, 1976, Iowa. *Education:* Drake University (B.S.B.A., Corporate Finance, 1973; J.D., 1976). Certified Public Accountant, Iowa, 1976. *Member:* Polk County, Iowa State (Member, Sections on: Probate and Trust Law; Real Estate and Title Law) and American Bar Associations. ***Email:*** frampton@whitfieldlaw.com

HARLEY A. WHITFIELD, admitted to bar, 1956, Iowa; 1983, District of Columbia. *Education:* Iowa State University (B.S., 1951); Drake University (J.D., 1956). Order of the Coif. *Member:* The District of Columbia Bar. ***Email:*** whitfield@whitfieldlaw.com

(This Listing Continued)

RETIRED

JOHN C. EDDY, admitted to bar, 1949, Iowa. *Education:* Dartmouth College (B.A., 1946); University of Virginia (LL.B., 1949). ***Email:*** eddy@whitfieldlaw.com

TIMOTHY J. WALKER, admitted to bar, 1965, Iowa. *Education:* Marquette University; Drake University (B.A., 1964; J.D., 1965). ***Email:*** walker@whitfieldlaw.com

A. ROGER WITKE, admitted to bar, 1959, Iowa. *Education:* Simpson College (B.A., 1954); University of Michigan (J.D., 1959). ***Email:*** witke@whitfieldlaw.com

REPRESENTATIVE CLIENTS: Acuity Insurance; AgStar Financial Services; Allied Group Insurance Co.; American Equity Investment Life Co.; Animal Rescue League of Iowa; Architectural Wall Systems; Associated General Contractors of Iowa; Bank of America; Bankers Trust Co.; Bituminous Insurance Co.; Brown Manufacturing Co.; City of Grimes, Iowa; City of Van Meter, Iowa; Clarke County State Bank; Commercial Federal Bank; Community State Bank; Conoco Phillips; Decker Truck Line, Inc.; Denis Della Vedova, Inc.; Essex Insurance Co.; Farm Credit Services; First National Bank in Fairfield; Fisher-Price, Inc.; Founders Insurance Co.; Gateway Savings Bank; Gillotti Companies; Graco Children's Products, Inc.; Graham Construction; Great Western Bank; Hamilton Beach/Proctor Silex, Inc.; Hawkeye-Security Insurance Co.; Henning Construction Co.; Home Services Lending; Hy-Vee/Weitz Construction; Iowa Landlord Association; J.S. Alberici Construction Co., Inc.; L&L Insulation & Supply Co.; Leachman Lumber Co.; Location Finders, International; Manatt's, Inc.; Marriott International, Inc.; Martin Marietta Materials, Inc.; Master Builders of Iowa; Mazda North American Operations; McAninch Corp.; Mechanical Contractors Association of Iowa; Mendota Insurance Co.; Merchants Bonding Co.; Metropolitan Life Insurance Co.; Midwest Heritage Bank, FSB; Midwest Livestock Services; Miller the Driller; National Apartment Association; Nationwide Insurance Co.; Nissan North America, Inc.; Neumann Brothers, Inc.; Old Republic Surety Co.; Pekin Insurance Co.; Penn-Co Construction, Inc.; Point Builders; Proctor Mechanical; Rasmussen Group, Inc.; Ritchie Industries; Royal and SunAlliance Insurance Co.; Scottsdale Insurance Co.; SISCO; Stearns Bank, NA; Story Construction; Stroh Corp.; Subaru of America, Inc.; Sunbeam Products, Inc.; Taylor Construction Group; Terrible's Lakeside Casino; The Hanson Co.; The Weitz Co.; Townsend Engineering Co.; Union Planters Bank, NA; United Fire & Casualty Co.; US Bank, NA; Walgreen Co.; Wells Fargo Bank Iowa, NA; West Bank; Westchester Savings Bank; Western World Insurance Co., Inc.; Zurich American Healthcare; Zurich North American.

WILLIAMS, BLACKBURN, HUDSON & MAHARRY, P.L.C.

740 BANK OF AMERICA BUILDING
317 6TH AVENUE
DES MOINES, IOWA 50309
Telephone: 515-280-3300
Fax: 515-280-3322
URL: http://www.desmoineslawfirm.com

General Civil and Legislative Practice. Securities Litigation and Arbitration, Real Estate Law, Insurance Regulation, Personal Injury.

TIMOTHY R. WILLIAMS, born Des Moines, Iowa, April 15, 1947; admitted to bar, 1973, Iowa; 1976, U.S. District Court, Southern and Northern Districts of Iowa; 1977, U.S. Court of Appeals, Eighth Circuit, U.S. Claims Court and U.S. Tax Court; 1980, U.S. Supreme Court. *Education:* University of Iowa (B.A., 1969); Drake University (J.D., with honors, 1973). Order of the Coif. Member, Lincoln Inn. *Member:* Polk County, Iowa State (Member, Corporation and Business Law Committee, 1982-1985) and American Bar Associations. ***PRACTICE AREAS:*** Real Estate; Probate; Business Law; Family Law. ***Email:*** timwilliams@desmoineslaw.xroads.net

JAMES S. BLACKBURN, born Des Moines, Iowa, April 6, 1954; admitted to bar, 1980, Iowa; 1981, U.S. District Court, Southern and Northern Districts of Iowa and U.S. Court of Appeals, Eighth Circuit. *Education:* University of Colorado (B.S., 1976); University of Northern Colorado; Drake University (J.D., 1979). *Member:* Polk County, Iowa State and American Bar Associations; Association of Trial Lawyers of Iowa; The Association of Trial Lawyers of America. ***PRACTICE AREAS:*** Trial Practice; Family Law; Personal Injury; Criminal Defense; Workers Compensation. ***Email:*** jamieblackburn@desmoineslaw.xroads.net

JOHN D. HUDSON, born Des Moines, Iowa, February 1, 1948; admitted to bar, 1973, Iowa, Southern and Northern Districts of Iowa, U.S. Court of Appeals, Eighth Circuit and U.S. Supreme Court. *Education:* University of Iowa (B.A., 1970; J.D., with distinction, 1973). Phi Delta Phi. Assistant Attorney General, State of Iowa, 1973-1976. *Member:* Polk County, Iowa State and American Bar Associations; Public Investors Arbitration Bar Association. ***PRACTICE AREAS:*** Securities; Litigation; Personal Injury. ***Email:*** jackhudson@desmoineslaw.xroads.net

RODNEY K. MAHARRY, born Iowa City, Iowa, July 18, 1968; admitted to bar, 1994, Iowa and U.S. District Court, Northern and Southern Districts of Iowa. *Education:* Iowa State University (B.B.A., 1989); Drake University Law School (J.D., 1994). *Member:* Polk County, American and Iowa State Bar Associations; Iowa Trial Lawyers Association; Blackstone Inns of Court. ***PRACTICE AREAS:*** Personal Injury; Criminal Defense; Family Law; Workers Compensation. ***Email:*** rodmaharry@desmoineslaw.xroads.net

JAMI J. HAGEMEIER, born Ida Grove, Iowa, August 27, 1977; admitted to bar, 2003, Iowa. *Education:* Iowa State University (B.S., 2000); Drake University (J.D., 2003; M.P.A., 2003). ***PRACTICE AREAS:*** Personal Injury; Family Law; Criminal Defense; Juvenile Law. ***Email:*** jjhagemeier@desmoineslaw.xroads.net

OF COUNSEL

JOHN C. SCHACHTERLE, born Des Moines, Iowa, October 29, 1958; admitted to bar, 1984, Iowa. *Education:* Iowa State University (B.S., 1981); Drake University (J.D., 1984). Phi Alpha Delta (Vice Justice, Cole Chapter, 1983-1984). Member, Polk County Foster Care Review Board, 1985-1987. *Member:* Polk County, Iowa State and American (Member, Sections on: Business Law; Tort and Insurance Practice; Health Law) Bar Associations; American Judicature Society. ***PRACTICE AREAS:*** Legislative; Regulatory; Insurance; Health; Corporate. ***Email:*** john@lobbyiowa.com

(This Listing Continued)

WILLIAMS, BLACKBURN, HUDSON & MAHARRY, P.L.C., Des Moines—Continued

COUNSEL FOR: Executive Relocation Corp.; Principal Residential Mortgage Inc.; Lawyers Title Insurance Corp.; Federation of Iowa Insurers; Iowa Managed Care Association; Iowa Financial Services Association; Midwest Ambulance Service of Iowa, Inc.

ZARLEY LAW FIRM, P.L.C.

CAPITAL SQUARE
400 LOCUST STREET, SUITE 200
DES MOINES, IOWA 50309-2350
Telephone: 515-558-0200
Fax: 515-558-7790
Email: tzarley@zarleylaw.com
URL: http://www.zarleylaw.com

Patents, Trademarks, Copyrights, Intellectual Property Litigation, Trade Secrets and Unfair Competition.

FIRM PROFILE: The Zarley Law Firm provides intellectual property services to clients both nationally and internationally.

TIMOTHY J. ZARLEY, born Des Moines, Iowa, December 1, 1960; admitted to bar, 1998, Iowa and U.S. District Court, Northern and Southern Districts of Iowa; U.S. District Court, Central District of Illinois, U.S. District Court, District of Colorado and U.S. Court of Appeals, Federal Circuit; registered to practice before U.S. Patent and Trademark Office. *Education:* Drake University (B.S., Business, 1984; M.B.A., 1988; J.D., with high honors, 1997). Member, Drake Law Review, 1996-1997. National Moot Court Team, 1997. Moot Court Board, 1996-1997. Order of the Barristers. *Member:* Polk County and Iowa State (Chair, Intellectual Property Section) Bar Associations; Iowa Intellectual Property Law Association (President Elect); American Intellectual Property Law Association. ***PRACTICE AREAS:*** Patent; Trademark; Copyright. **Email:** tzarley@zarleylaw.com

JOSEF LOUIS HOFFMANN, born Highland, Illinois, February 15, 1978; admitted to bar, 2003, Iowa and U.S. District Court, Southern District of Iowa; registered to practice before U.S. Patent and Trademark Office. *Education:* Bradley University (B.S.E.P. 2000); Drake University (J.D. with honors, 2003). Delta Theta Phi; Sigma Pi Sigma Physics Honor Society. *Member:* Polk County, Iowa State and American Bar Associations; Iowa Intellectual Property Law Association. ***PRACTICE AREAS:*** Patents; Trademarks; Copyrights. **Email:** jhoffmann@zarleylaw.com

VAN SCOY & KROSS, P.C.

DE WITT, IOWA
(See Clinton)

General Practice. Probate, Wills, Corporate Law, Real Estate, Personal Injury, Bankruptcy, Trials and Appeals, Family Law, Estate Planning, School Law, Business Law.

WILLIAM J. BRIBRIESCO & ASSOCIATES

DUBUQUE, IOWA
(See Bettendorf)

Personal Injury, Workers Compensation, Products Liability, Business Law.

EELLS & TRONVOLD LAW OFFICES, P.L.C.

DUBUQUE, IOWA
(See Cedar Rapids)

General Practice with emphasis on Personal Injury, Litigation, Probate and Estate Planning, Trusts and Wills, Business Law and Mediation.

FUERSTE, CAREW, COYLE, JUERGENS & SUDMEIER, P.C.

Established in 1965
200 SECURITY BUILDING
151 WEST 8TH STREET
DUBUQUE, IOWA 52001
Telephone: 563-556-4011
Telecopier: 563-556-7134
Email: mail@fccjs.com
URL: http://www.fccjs.com

General Practice, including Construction Law, Corporate and Commercial, Discrimination, Education Law, Employment and Labor, Estate Planning, Trusts and Wills, Probate, Family Law, Insurance, Litigation, Personal Injury, Products Liability, Workers Compensation and Wrongful Death.

FIRM PROFILE: The law firm of Fuerste, Carew, Coyle, Juergens & Sudmeier, P.C., is a general practice firm, located in Dubuque, Iowa, and serving clients throughout the tri-state area of northeast Iowa, southwest Wisconsin, and northeast Illinois. The historical roots of this law firm date to 1854 and the law firm of Cooley & Adams. The recent history of this firm starts with the formation of Fuerste & Carew by William C. Fuerste and Allan J. Carew in 1965. The firm and its predecessors have focused upon the needs of the people with and for whom it works, and to serve those needs, the firm has developed a broad range of practice areas.

WILLIAM C. FUERSTE, born Proctor, Minnesota, January 25, 1923; admitted to bar, 1947, Iowa. *Education:* University of Iowa (B.A., 1946; J.D., 1947). Law Clerk to Hon. Henry N. Graven, U.S. District Judge, 1947-1948. Member, Iowa Supreme Court Advisory Committee on Rules, 1968-1981. *Member:* Dubuque County, Iowa State and American Bar Associations. Fellow, American College of Trial Lawyers (Chairman, 1979-1981); Iowa Defense Counsel. Fellow, Iowa Academy of Trial Lawyers. **Email:** wfuerste@fccjs.com

ALLAN J. CAREW, born Dubuque, Iowa, March 15, 1933; admitted to bar, 1960, Iowa. *Education:* University of Northern Iowa and University of Iowa (B.S., 1957); University of Iowa (J.D., 1960). Phi Delta Phi. Member, Board of Editors, Iowa Law Review, 1959-1960. Member, Board of Governors, Iowa State Bar Association, 1989-1993. *Member:* Dubuque County (President, 1984-1985), Iowa State and American Bar Associations. **Email:** acarew@fccjs.com

MICHAEL J. COYLE, born Mason City, Iowa, March 18, 1945; admitted to bar, 1970, Iowa. *Education:* University of Iowa (B.B.A., 1967; J.D., 1970). Phi Delta Phi. *Fellow, American College of Trial Lawyers; American Board of Trial Advocates; Fellow, Iowa Academy of Trial Lawyers; International Association of Defense Counsel; Iowa Association of Worker's Compensation Lawyers; Dubuque County, Iowa State and American Bar Associations.* **Email:** mcoyle@fccjs.com

STEPHEN J. JUERGENS, born Dubuque, Iowa, March 6, 1947; admitted to bar, 1973, Iowa. *Education:* Loras College (B.A., 1969); University of Iowa (J.D., with high distinction, 1973). Phi Alpha Theta; Phi Alpha Delta. Member, Board of Governors, Iowa State Bar Association, 1998-2005. *Member:* Dubuque County (President, 1997-1998), Iowa State and American Bar Associations; Iowa Municipal Attorneys Association; Iowa Council of School Board Attorneys; National Association of Ski Defense Attorneys. **Email:** sjuergens@fccjs.com

ROBERT L. SUDMEIER, born Dubuque, Iowa, February 24, 1948; admitted to bar, 1973, Iowa; 1984, Wisconsin. *Education:* University of Iowa (B.B.A., with high distinction, 1970; J.D., with distinction, 1973). Beta Gamma Sigma; Phi Alpha Delta. *Member:* Dubuque County (President 2002-2003), Iowa State and American Bar Associations; State Bar of Wisconsin; Iowa Defense Counsel. Fellow, Iowa Academy of Trial Lawyers. **Email:** rsudmeier@fccjs.com

DOUGLAS M. HENRY, born Dubuque, Iowa, February 13, 1952; admitted to bar, 1977, Iowa. *Education:* University of Iowa (B.A., 1973; J.D., with honors, 1977). *Member:* Dubuque County, Iowa State and American Bar Associations; Iowa Defense Counsel; The Association of Trial Lawyers of America (Associate Member). **Email:** dhenry@fccjs.com

MARK J. WILLGING, born Dubuque, Iowa, January 13, 1953; admitted to bar, 1978, Iowa; U.S. District Court, Northern District of Iowa and U.S. Tax Court. *Education:* Loras College (B.A., magna cum laude, 1975); University of Iowa (J.D., with honors, 1978). *Member:* Dubuque County, Iowa State and American Bar Associations. **Email:** mwillging@fccjs.com

MICHAEL J. SHUBATT, born Iowa City, Iowa, February 27, 1965; admitted to bar, 1990, Iowa; 1991, Illinois; U.S. District Court, Northern and Central Districts of Illinois and U.S. Court of Appeals, Eighth Circuit. *Education:* University of Iowa (B.A., 1987; J.D., with distinction, 1990). Phi Delta Phi. *Member:* Dubuque County, Iowa State, Illinois State and American Bar Associations; Iowa Trial Lawyers Association; Iowa Council of School Board Attorneys. **Email:** mshubatt@fccjs.com

A. THEODORE HUINKER, born Dubuque, Iowa, July 18, 1973; admitted to bar, 1998, Iowa. *Education:* Loras College (B.A., magna cum laude, 1995); University of Iowa College of Law (J.D., 1998). Phi Delta Phi. *Member:* Dubuque County, Iowa State and American Bar Associations. **Email:** thuinker@fccjs.com

NORMAN J. WANGBERG, born Minneapolis, Minnesota, September 24, 1948; admitted to bar, 1976, Iowa. *Education:* Wartburg College (B.A., 1970); University of Iowa (J.D., with distinction, 1976). *Member:* Dubuque County, Iowa State and American Bar Associations. **Email:** dgrant@fccjs.com

DANITA L. GRANT, born Milwaukee, Wisconsin, November 14, 1975; admitted to bar, 2000, Iowa. *Education:* University of Wisconsin (B.A., magna cum laude, 1997); Drake University (J.D., with honors, 2000). Delta Theta Phi. District Representative, ISBA - YLD. *Member:* Dubuque County, Iowa and American Bar Associations. **Email:** nwangberg@fccjs.com

JOHN F. HODGES, born Hudson, New York, May 16, 1980; admitted to bar, 2005, Iowa. *Education:* Central College (B.A., 2002); Drake University (J.D., with honors, 2005). Delta Theta Phi. *Member:* Dubuque County, Iowa State and American Bar Associations. **Email:** jhodges@fccjs.com

REPRESENTATIVE CLIENTS:
BUSINESS: The Adams Company; Anderson-Weber Inc.; Aquila Networks; Art Pape Transfer, Inc.; Bethany Home; Conlon Construction Company; Cottingham & Butler Insurance Services, Inc.; Dubuque Bank & Trust Company; Dubuque Data Services; Dubuque Stamping & Manufacturing, Inc.; Dupaco Community Credit Union; The Durrant Group, Inc.; Eagle Window & Door, Inc.; Edwards Cast Stone Company; Edwards Pre-Cast Concrete Co.; Family Beer East, Inc.; First Community Trust; First Gear, Inc.; Flynn Company, Inc.; Geisler Brothers Co.; Jim Giese Commercial Roofing, Inc.; Heartland Financial USA, Inc.; Kaiser's Contract Cleaning Specialists, Inc.; Kehl River Boats, Inc.; Kennedy Mall, L.T.D., L.L.C.; Kirchhoff Distributing Company; A.Y. McDonald Mfg. Co.; Martin Luther Home; Mississippi Belle II Employees Ownership Co.; Mi-T-M Corporation; Molo Oil Company; Myers-Cox Co.; Norby Farm Fleet Supply Stores; Nordstrom; Packers' Chemical, Inc.; Peosta Warehousing, Inc.; Portzen Construction Company; Project Concern, Inc.; Rafoth Sheet Metal, Inc.; Royal Oaks Development Corporation; Sands Mortgage; Self Insured Services Company; Trausch Distributing Company; TFM Co.; Union-Hoermann Press; Unique Balance; U.S. Bank; Woodward Communications, Inc.; Zephyr Aluminum Products, Inc.
INSURANCE: Acuity Insurance; CNA Commercial Insurance; Chubb Group of Insurance Companies; EMC Insurance Companies; Farm Bureau Mutual Insurance Company; Gallagher Bassett Services; General Casualty; The Harleysville Insurance Companies; Highlands Insurance Group; K & K Insurance Group, Inc.; The Medical Protective Company; Minnesota Fire & Casualty Company; The Ohio Casualty Group; Partners Mutual Insurance; Pekin Insurance Company; Rice Insurance Company; St. Paul Travelers Insurance; Scottsdale Insurance Company; State Farm Mutual Automobile Insurance Company; State Farm Fire & Casualty Company; Ulico Casualty Company; Zurich-America Insurance Group.

(This Listing Continued)

PUBLIC: City of Asbury; Asbury Area Development Corporation; City of Cascade, Iowa; Dubuque Community School District; Keystone Area Education Agency 1; City of New Vienna; Northeast Iowa Community College; City of Sherrill; Western Dubuque County Community School District.

HAMMER, SIMON & JENSEN

770 MAIN STREET
DUBUQUE, IOWA 52001-6820
Telephone: 563-583-4010
Fax: 563-583-3402
Email: hsjlaw@hammerlawoffices.com

Galena, Illinois Office: 303 North Bench. Telephone: 815-777-1101. Fax: 815-777-9241.

General Trial and Appellate Practice. Litigation, Wills, Estate and Trusts, Corporate and Business, Real Estate, Domestic Relations and Workers Compensation.

DAVID L. HAMMER, born Newton, Iowa, June 6, 1929; admitted to bar, 1956, Iowa; 1989, Illinois. *Education:* Grinnell College (B.A., 1951); University of Iowa (J.D., with distinction, 1956). Member, Board of Editors, Iowa Law Review, 1955-1956. *Member:* Dubuque County (President, 1979-1980), Iowa State (President, Junior Bar Section, 1963-1964; Chairman, Continuing Legal Education Committee, 1964-1967; Member, Grievance Committee, 1973-1985; Member, Supreme Court Advisory Rules Committee, 1986-1990), Illinois State and American Bar Associations; Fellow, Iowa Academy of Trial Lawyers; The Association of Defense Trial Attorneys (Member, Executive Council, 1984-1987). Fellow, American College of Trial Lawyers; Iowa Defense Counsel Association (former President). ***PRACTICE AREAS:*** Litigation; Business. ***Email:*** dhammer@dhammerlawoffices.com

ANGELA C. SIMON, born Fort Sill, Oklahoma, October 29, 1949; admitted to bar, 1985, Iowa and Illinois. *Education:* Loras College (B.A., Maxima cum laude, 1981); University of Iowa (J.D., with distinction, 1985). Recipient: International Association of Trial Lawyers Award; Stephenson Trial Advocacy Competition "Best Litigator" Award. Past Member of Iowa Supreme Court Commission on Continuing Legal Education. Iowa Supreme Court Grievance Commission (1999—). ALJ, Dubuque Human Rights Commission. Past Member of Judicial Nominating Commission, Iowa. Board Member, Dubuque Racing Association, Past President. *Member:* Dubuque County (Past Member, Board of Governors), Jo Daviess County, Iowa State (Certified Mediator), Illinois State and American Bar Associations; State Bar of Wisconsin; Defense Trial Attorneys Association; Fellow, Iowa Academy of Trial Lawyers. ***REPORTED CASES:*** Waddell v. Forney, et. al., 108F.3d 889 (1997). ***PRACTICE AREAS:*** Litigation; General Practice. ***Email:*** asimon@hammerlawoffices.com

PHILIP F. JENSEN, born Chicago, Illinois, March 18, 1959; admitted to bar, 1984, Illinois; 1988, Iowa. *Education:* Illinois State University (B.S., 1981); University of Nebraska (J.D., 1984). Adjunct Faculty Member, Loras College, 1989. *Member:* Illinois State, Iowa State and American Bar Associations. ***PRACTICE AREAS:*** General Office Practice.

PAUL T. JENSEN, born Stambaugh, Michigan, August 3, 1950; admitted to bar, 1997, Illinois, 1998, Iowa. *Education:* North Park College (B.A., 1972); University of Iowa (J.D., with distinction, 1996). *Member:* Illinois and Iowa Bar Associations. ***PRACTICE AREAS:*** Personal Injury; Criminal Defense; Family Law; Business Law.

REPRESENTATIVE CLIENTS: Alliant Utilities; Boyes Auto & Truck Parts; YWCA; Allstate Insurance; American Home Assurance Co.; Federated Insurance; Hartford Insurance; Royal Insurance; St. Paul Fire & Marine Insurance; Travelers; City of Galena, Illinois; Apple Canyon Lake Property Owners Assn.; Country Companies Inc.; West Bend Insurance Company; Micoa Insurance Company; University of Dubuque; Liberty Mutual Insurance Co.; United Fire & Casualty Insurance Co.; Zurich Insurance Co.; Mike Finnin Ford; Cottingham & Butler Insurance Services.
APPROVED ATTORNEYS FOR: Alternative Dispute Resolution (ADR); General Motors; Navistar.

KANE, NORBY & REDDICK, P.C.

Established in 1993
2100 ASBURY ROAD, SUITE 2
DUBUQUE, IOWA 52001
Telephone: 563-582-7980
Fax: 563-582-5312

General Practice. Corporate/Commercial (including Litigation), Probate, Estate Planning, Trusts and Wills, Real Estate, Taxation and Contested Wills, Employee Benefits, Litigation, Workers' Compensation.

BRIAN J. KANE, born Dubuque, Iowa, March 28, 1957; admitted to bar, 1982, Iowa. *Education:* Loras College (B.A., magna cum laude, 1979); University of Iowa (J.D., 1982). Delta Epsilon Sigma. Certified Public Accountant, Iowa, 1987. *Member:* Dubuque County, Iowa State (Member, Taxation Section) and American (Member, Taxation Section) Bar Associations; Iowa Society of Certified Public Accountants; American Institute of Certified Public Accountants. Fellow, American College of Trust and Estate Counsel. ***PRACTICE AREAS:*** Corporate/Commercial Law; Taxation Law; Probate and Estate Planning; Real Estate. ***Email:*** bkane@kanenorbylaw.com

GARY K. NORBY, born Sibley, Iowa, December 18, 1941; admitted to bar, 1967, Iowa. *Education:* University of Iowa (B.A., 1964; J.D., 1967). Order of the Coif; Phi Beta Kappa; Phi Delta Phi. Member, Board of Editors, Iowa Law Review, 1966-1967. *Member:* Dubuque County, Iowa State (Member, Sections on: Corporation, Banking and Business Law; Real Estate and Title Law; Member, Professional Corporation Committee, 1991-1992) and American (Member, Section on Business Law) Bar Associations. ***PRACTICE AREAS:*** Banking; Real Estate; Employee Benefits; Corporate; Probate and Estate Planning. ***Email:*** gnorby@kanenorbylaw.com

LES V. REDDICK, born Harrisburg, Pennsylvania, January 9, 1948; admitted to bar, 1977, Iowa; 1989, Illinois. *Education:* University of Iowa (B.A., 1973; J.D., with honors, 1977). Author: "Comment on the Law," Iowa Defense Counsel Quarterly, Fall 1990; "Insurance Bad Faith Investigation," 1998. Co-author: "Twelve Years Under Iowa's Comparative Fault Act," 1996; "Iowa Motor Vehicle Law Handbook," 1999. Member, Judicial Nominating Commission, First Judicial District, 1984-1990. *Member:* Dubuque County, Iowa State (Member, Litigation Section; Member, Committees on: Uniform Jury Instructions, 1991-2000; Litigation Resources, Chair, 1991—), Illinois State (Member, Sections on: Civil Practice and Procedure; Tort and Insurance Law) and American (Member, Section on Litigation) Bar Associations; Iowa Defense Counsel Association (Member, Amicus Curiae Committee); American Board of Trial Advocates. Fellow, Iowa Academy of Trial Lawyers. ***PRACTICE AREAS:*** Litigation; Workers' Compensation. ***Email:*** lreddrick@kanenorbylaw.com

D. FLINT DRAKE, born Centerville, Iowa, April 14, 1966; admitted to bar, 1991, Iowa; 1998, Wisconsin. *Education:* University of Northern Iowa (B.A., with highest honors, 1988); University of Iowa (J.D., with distinction, 1991). *Member:* Dubuque County, Iowa State (Member, Corporation, Banking and Business Law Section) and American (Member: Business Law; Real Property, Probate and Trust Law Sections) Bar Associations. ***PRACTICE AREAS:*** Corporate/Commercial Law; Real Estate. ***Email:*** fdrake@kanenorbylaw.com

BRAD J. HEYING, born Dubuque, Iowa, September 15, 1966; admitted to bar, 1992, Iowa. *Education:* University of Northern Iowa (B.A., with highest honors, 1989); University of Iowa (J.D., with distinction, 1992). Certified Public Accountant, Iowa, 1989. *Member:* Dubuque County and Iowa State (Business Law Section) Bar Associations. ***PRACTICE AREAS:*** Corporate/Commercial Law; Probate; Estate Planning; Taxation. ***Email:*** bheying@kanenorbylaw.com

TODD L. STEVENSON, born Oskaloosa, Iowa, September 17, 1965; admitted to bar, 1990, Iowa; 1992, Illinois. *Education:* Buena Vista College (B.A., magna cum laude, 1987); University of Iowa (J.D., with distinction, 1990). *Member:* Dubuque County, Iowa State (Member, Sections on: Litigation; Environmental and Natural Resources Law), Illinois State and American (Member, Sections on: Tort and Insurance Practice; Natural Resources, Energy and Environmental Law) Bar Associations; Iowa Defense Counsel Association; Defense Research Institute. ***PRACTICE AREAS:*** Civil Litigation; Insurance Defense; Personal Injury; Commercial; Product Liability. ***Email:*** tstevenson@kanenorbylaw.com

MARYBETH PFEILER FLEMING, born Dubuque, Iowa, May 13, 1967; admitted to bar, 1995, Iowa. *Education:* St. Xavier College (B.A., 1991); University of Iowa (J.D., 1995). *Member:* Dubuque County and Iowa State Bar Associations; Iowa Trial Lawyers Association (Member, Workers' Compensation Section). ***PRACTICE AREAS:*** Personal Injury Law; Workers Compensation Law; Real Estate Law; Criminal Law. ***Email:*** mpfeiler@kanenorbylaw.com

KEVIN T. DEENY, born Dubuque, Iowa, June 29, 1976; admitted to bar, 2001, Iowa. *Education:* Luther College (B.A., 1998); University of Iowa (J.D., 2001). *Member:* Dubuque County, Iowa State and American Bar Associations. ***PRACTICE AREAS:*** General Practice. ***Email:*** kdeeny@kanenorbylaw.com

JOHN D. FREUND, born Waterloo, Iowa, May 25, 1978; admitted to bar, 2004, Iowa. *Education:* Loras College (B.A., maxima cum laude, 2000); University of Iowa (J.D., 2003). Delta Epsilon Sigma. *Member:* Dubuque County, Iowa State and American Bar Associations. ***LANGUAGES:*** Spanish. ***Email:*** jfreund@kanenorbylaw.com

OF COUNSEL

LOUIS P. PFEILER, born Holy Cross, Iowa, February 17, 1935; admitted to bar, 1964, Oregon; 1965, Iowa. *Education:* Loras College (B.A., magna cum laude, 1961); University of Notre Dame (J.D., 1964). Member, Notre Dame Law Review, 1963-1964. Law Clerk to U.S. District Judge John F. Kilkenny, 1964-1965. *Member:* Dubuque County (President, 1987-1988), Iowa State Bar Association; Iowa Trial Lawyers Association (Former Member, Board of Governors).

REPRESENTATIVE CLIENTS: A.Y. McDonald Manufacturing Co.; Alliant Energy Corporation; Alexis; Ambraco; Apex Concrete, L.L.C.; Atlantic Mutual Insurance Co.; Bituminous Insurance Companies; Capital Indemnity; CartéGraph Systems, Inc.; Chubb Group of Insurance Companies; City of Dubuque; ComElec Services, Inc.; Crawford and Company; Double L Group, Ltd.; Dubuque Bank & Trust Company; Dubuque Humane Society; Dubuque Internal Medicine, P.C.; East Dubuque Savings Bank; Environmental Management Services, Inc.; Farm Bureau Insurance; The Fischer Companies; Flexsteel Industries; HÆ Distributing Co.; Heartland Housing Initiative; Hills & Dales Child Development Center; Hospice of Dubuque; Illowa Communications, Inc.; McNamer Construction Systems; Medical Associates of Maquoketa, P.C.; Minnesota Mutual Life; Mutual Fire & Auto; Ohio Casualty Insurance Company; Peninsula Gaming Company, L.L.C.; Perfection Oil Company; Platinum Services, Inc.; Premier Bank; St. Paul Insurance Co.; Sisters of St. Francis of Dubuque; Sisters of the Presentation; Sisters of the Visitation; State Bank of Worthington; W. C. Stewart Construction, Inc.; Swiss Valley Ag Service, Inc.; Tschiggfrie Excavating Co.; Union Insurance Group; Woodward Communications, Inc.
REFERENCE: Dubuque Bank and Trust Company, Dubuque, Iowa.

O'CONNOR & THOMAS, P.C.

Established in 1840
DUBUQUE BUILDING
700 LOCUST STREET, SUITE 200
P.O. BOX 599
DUBUQUE, IOWA 52004-0599
Telephone: 563-557-8400
Facsimile: 563-556-1867
URL: http://www.octhomaslaw.com

Mailing Address: P.O. Box 599, Dubuque, IA 52004-0599

General Practice, Banking, Commercial, Corporate, Estate Planning, Family Law, Litigation, Personal Injury, Workers' Compensation, Probate, Product Liability, Real Estate and Taxation.

FIRM PROFILE: O'Connor & Thomas, P.C. was founded in 1840 and is the oldest law firm in Iowa. The firm offers a full range of legal services in Iowa, Illinois and Wisconsin. We at O'Connor & Thomas, P.C., have structured our firm to meet the broad range of legal expertise that is required by our clients in today's complicated society. The backgrounds of the firm's lawyers include not only impressive academic credentials, but also the extensive experience

(This Listing Continued)

(This Listing Continued)

O'CONNOR & THOMAS, P.C., Dubuque—Continued

required to meet the client's needs. O'Connor & Thomas, P.C., is proud to have continually maintained a reputation for skill, integrity and effectiveness in representing the interest of our clients.

JOHN C. O'CONNOR, born Dubuque, Iowa, January 28, 1949; admitted to bar, 1974, Iowa. *Education:* Loyola University of the South (B.B.A., 1971); Creighton University (J.D., 1974). Certified Public Accountant, Iowa, 1975. Chairman, Community Foundation of Greater Dubuque. Member, Board of Directors, Boys and Girls Club of Greater Dubuque. *Member:* Dubuque County, Iowa State (Member: Tax Committee, 1977-1982; Probate and Trust Law Council; Sections on: Business Law and Probate and Trust Law) and American (Member, Sections on: Real Property; Probate and Trust Law) Bar Associations; Iowa Society of Certified Public Accountants. Fellow, The American College of Trust and Estate Counsel. ***PRACTICE AREAS:*** Business Law; Probate; Estate Planning; Real Estate. ***Email:*** joconnor@octhomaslaw.com

BRENDAN T. QUANN, born Brooklyn, New York, June 22, 1941; admitted to bar, 1973, Iowa and U.S. District Court, Northern and Southern Districts of Iowa. *Education:* United States Military Academy (B.S., 1964); University of Iowa (J.D., 1973). Order of the Coif. Past President: West Point Society of the Prairies; Mississippi Valley Running Association. Member, Board of Trustees, Clarke College. *Member:* Dubuque County (Past President), Iowa State (Member, Sections on: Litigation, Health Law and Workers' Compensation Law) and American (Member, Sections on: Litigation, Labor and Employment Law and Health Law Forum) Bar Associations; Iowa Defense Counsel Association; The Iowa Association of Workers' Compensation Lawyers, Inc.; Selection Committee for Appointments to the United States Military Academy; The United States Naval Academy; United States Air Force Academy; Blair's ADR List; National Diocesan Attorneys Association. ***PRACTICE AREAS:*** Insurance Defense; Labor and Employment Law; Personal Injury; Trial Practice; Workers Compensation. ***Email:*** bquann@octhomaslaw.com

A. JOHN ARENZ, born Dubuque, Iowa, December 16, 1952; admitted to bar, 1978, Iowa; 1985, Wisconsin, U.S. District Court, Northern and Southern Districts of Iowa, U.S. District Court, Western District of Wisconsin and U.S. Supreme Court. *Education:* Marquette University (A.B., magna cum laude, 1975); Georgetown University (J.D., cum laude, 1978). Phi Beta Kappa. Member, Student Editorial Board, The Tax Lawyer, 1977-1978. *Member:* Dubuque County, Iowa State (Member, Section on Litigation) and American (Member, Sections on: Litigation; Tort and Insurance Practice) Bar Associations; State Bar of Wisconsin (Member, Section on Litigation); Defense Research Institute; Iowa Defense Counsel Association; Association of Trial Lawyers of Iowa (Associate Member); The Association of Trial Lawyers of America (Associate Member); The International Amusement and Leisure Defense Association; Iowa Title Guaranty Association; Iowa State Grievance Commission (Division Member). (Certified as a Civil Trial Advocate by the National Board of Trial Advocacy). ***PRACTICE AREAS:*** Insurance Defense; Personal Injury; Trial Practice; Workers' Compensation; Real Estate Law. ***Email:*** jarenz@octhomaslaw.com

CHAD C. LEITCH, born New Hampton, Iowa; admitted to bar, 1980, Iowa; 1981, Illinois and U.S. District Court, Northern District of Iowa. *Education:* Iowa State University (B.S., with honors, 1973); University of Iowa (J.D., with high distinction, 1979). Order of the Coif. *Member:* Dubuque County, Iowa State (Member, Sections on: Commercial and Bankruptcy Law; Business Law; Family and Juvenile Law; Real Estate and Title Law), Illinois State (Member, Sections on: Commercial Banking; Bankruptcy Law; Family Law) and American (Member, Family Law Section) Bar Associations. ***PRACTICE AREAS:*** Commercial Transactions; Creditor Rights; Bankruptcy; Real Estate Law; Family Law; Banking; Collections; Business Law; Labor Law. ***Email:*** cleitch@octhomaslaw.com

RICHARD K. WHITTY, born Belmond, Iowa; admitted to bar, 1980, Iowa. *Education:* Drake University, Phi Beta Kappa (B.A., summa cum laude, 1977); University of Iowa (J.D., with high distinction, 1980). Member, Iowa District 1A Judicial Nominating Commission, 2000—. *Member:* Dubuque County, Iowa State (Member, Sections on: Litigation; Workers' Compensation) and American (Member, Sections on: Litigation and Health Law Forum Committee) Bar Associations; Iowa Defense Counsel Association; Federation of Insurance and Corporate Counsel (Member, Section on: Medical Malpractice); Defense Research Institute; Dubuque Area Chamber of Commerce (Past President, Board of Directors, 1992-1997; Chairman, 1995-1996). ***PRACTICE AREAS:*** Civil Litigation; Insurance Defense; Personal Injury; Commercial Litigation; Professional Liability. ***Email:*** rwhitty@octhomaslaw.com

STEPHEN C. KRUMPE, born Hagerstown, Maryland; admitted to bar, 1985, Iowa; 1987, Wisconsin; 1997, Illinois. *Education:* Shepherd College (B.A., magna cum laude, 1978); University of Iowa (M.A., History, 1979); University of Iowa (J.D., with high distinction, 1984). Teaching-Research Fellowship, University of Iowa, 1978-1982. *Member:* Dubuque County, Iowa State (Member, Sections on: Labor and Employment Law and Litigation), Illinois State (Member, Sections on: Civil Practice and Procedure) and American (Member, Sections on: Litigation and Labor and Employment Law) Bar Associations; State Bar of Wisconsin (Member, Sections on: Litigation and General Practice); Iowa Defense Counsel Association; Civil Trial Counsel of Wisconsin. ***PRACTICE AREAS:*** Civil Litigation; Civil Appeals; Federal Practice; Labor Relations; Employment Litigation. ***Email:*** skrumpe@octhomaslaw.com

JAMES E. GOODMAN, JR., born Erie, Pennsylvania; admitted to bar, 1988, Iowa; 2001, Illinois; U.S. Tax Court. *Education:* Illinois State University (B.S., cum laude, 1985); University of Iowa (J.D., with distinction, 1988). Author/Presenter, Iowa State Bar Association Fall 1992 Traveling Seminar, "Many a Tax Tip, a Trust and Estate Attorney Should Not Skip," "Fiduciary Income Taxation and Withdrawal Powers," Vol. 3, No. 2, Trust and Estate Law Report, February 4, 1993; "Legal and Tax Consequences of Owning Property Jointly," Vol. 4, No. 4, Trust and Estate Law Report, August 5, 1994. President, Tri-State Estate Planning Council, 1993-1994. *Member:* Dubuque County, Iowa State (Member, Sections on: Probate and Trust Law), Illinois State and American (Member, Sections on: Real Property, Taxation and Young Lawyers Division) Bar Associations; Tri-State Estate Planning Council. ***PRACTICE AREAS:*** Estate Planning; Probate; Real Estate. ***Email:*** jgoodman@octhomaslaw.com

(This Listing Continued)

DAVIN C. CURTISS, born Silvis, Illinois; admitted to bar, 1995, Iowa; 1998, Illinois; 1999, Wisconsin; U.S. District Court, Northern and Southern Districts of Iowa and U.S. Bankruptcy Court. *Education:* Marquette University (B.A., summa cum laude, 1992); University of Iowa (J.D., with high distinction, 1995). Recipient, Award of Excellence for Student Scholarship, presented by the American Agricultural Law Association. Note and Comment Editor for the Journal of Corporation Law, 1994-1995. Author: "Fair Labor Standards Act and Child Labor in Agriculture", Journal of Corporation Law, 1995. *Member:* Dubuque County, Iowa State (Member, Sections on: General Practice, Litigation and Labor and Employment Law), Illinois State and American (Member, Sections on: General Practice, Litigation and Tort and Insurance Practice) Bar Associations; State Bar of Wisconsin. ***PRACTICE AREAS:*** Insurance Defense; Personal Injury; Trial Practice; Workers; Litigation; Workers Compensation. ***Email:*** dcurtiss@octhomaslaw.com

PAUL J. SIGWARTH, born Dubuque, Iowa, April 11, 1972; admitted to bar, 1997, Iowa; 1998, Wisconsin; U.S. District Court, Northern and Southern Districts of Iowa and Western District of Wisconsin. *Education:* University of Iowa (B.A., with distinction, 1994; J.D., with distinction, 1997). Case Editor, Moot Court Program (1996-1997), University of Iowa. Author: "It's My Privilege And I'll Assert It If I Want To: The Attorney-Client Privilege in Closely-Held Corporations," The Journal of Corporation Law, 1998. *Member:* Dubuque County, Iowa State (Member, Sections on: Litigation and General Practice) and American (Member, Sections on: Tort and Insurance Law and Litigation) Bar Associations; State Bar of Wisconsin (Member, Sections on: Litigation and General Practice). ***PRACTICE AREAS:*** General Practice; Litigation; Torts; Insurance Law; Business Law; Creditors Rights; Collections. ***Email:*** psigwarth@octhomaslaw.com

---

KERRIE L. LIEDTKE, born Spencer, Iowa; admitted to bar, 2001, Iowa; 2002, Wisconsin. *Education:* Wartburg College (B.A., magna cum laude, 1998); University of Iowa (J.D., 2001). Phi Delta Phi. Member, Society of Collegiate Journalists. Student Judge, Moot Court. *Member:* Dubuque (Co-Chair, Continuing Legal Education Committee, 2002), Iowa State and American Bar Associations; State Bar of Wisconsin. ***PRACTICE AREAS:*** General Practice; Business Law; Family Law. ***Email:*** kliedtke@octhomaslaw.com

PETER D. ARLING, born Dubuque, Iowa, December 12, 1977; admitted to bar, 2003, Iowa; 2004, Illinois; 2004, Minnesota; 2005, Wisconsin. *Education:* Loras College (B.A., Economics, magna cum laude, 2000); Creighton University School of Law (J.D., magna cum laude, 2003). President, International Moot Court Board, 2002-2003. *Member:* Dubuque County, Iowa State and American Bar Associations; State Bar of Wisconsin. ***PRACTICE AREAS:*** Business Law; Contracts; Corporate Law; Real Estate; Boundary Disputes; Litigation. ***Email:*** parling@octhomaslaw.com

JOSHUA P. WEIDEMANN, admitted to bar, 2004, Iowa. *Education:* University of Iowa (B.A., with Distinction, 2000; J.D., with High Distinction, 2004). Order of the Coif. *Member:* Dubuque County, Iowa State (Member, Probate Section) and American Bar Associations; Dubuque County Young Lawyers (Treasurer); Tri-State Estate Planning Council. ***PRACTICE AREAS:*** Probate; Business Law; Corporate Law; Trusts and Estates; Estate Planning; Creditors Rights; Taxation; Litigation; Real Estate.

CHRISTOPHER FRY, admitted to bar, 2004, Iowa. *Education:* Luther College (B.A., 2001); University of Iowa (J.D., 2004). *Member:* Iowa State, Dubuque County and American Bar Association. ***PRACTICE AREAS:*** Litigation; Insurance Defense; Personal Injury; Professional Liability; Business Law.

EMILY E. REINERS, born Waterloo, Iowa, November 15, 1979; admitted to bar, 2005, Iowa. *Education:* University of Northern Iowa (B.A., magna cum laude, 2002); Drake University (J.D., 2005).

OF COUNSEL

THOMAS S. COLLINS, born Cedar Rapids, Iowa; admitted to bar, 1998, Iowa. *Education:* University of Iowa (B.B.A., 1983; M.A., 1985; J.D., with high distinction, 1997). Certified Public Accountant, California and Iowa, 1986. Associate Professor, Business Law, Loras College. Adjunct Professor of Law, University of Iowa College of Law. *Member:* Dubuque County, Iowa State (Member, Sections on: Business Law; Real Property; Committees on: Limited Liability Company; Uniform Commercial Code) and American (Member, Sections on: Business Law; Labor and Employment Law) Bar Associations. ***PRACTICE AREAS:*** Business Law; Real Estate Law; Probate; Taxation. ***Email:*** tcollins@octhomaslaw.com

REPRESENTATIVE CLIENTS: *Corporate:* American Trust & Savings Bank; Dubuque Bank & Trust Company; US Bank, N.A.; East Dubuque Savings Bank; Citizens Finance Company; DuTrac Community Credit Union; Dupaco Community Credit Union; Wells Fargo Home Mortgage; Wells Fargo Financial; Crescent Electric Supply Co.; Klauer Mfg. Co.; Flexsteel Industries Inc.; Georgia-Pacific Corporation; Color-Box, LLC; Miller Electric Supply Co.; A.Y. McDonald Industries, Inc.; Barnstead Thermolyne Corporation; Morrison Bros. Company; Mercy Health Center; Medical Associates Clinic, P.C.; Medical Associates Health Plans; The Finley Hospital; Dubuque Racing Association, Ltd.; Lime Rock Springs; Noah's Ark Family Park, Inc.; Loras College; University of Dubuque; Clarke College; The Archdiocese of Dubuque; New Melleray Abbey; Wartburg Theological Seminary; Sisters of Charity; Sisters of St. Francis; Stonehill Franciscan Services; Stonehill Benevolent Foundation; Sinsinawa Dominicans Inc.; Our Lady of the Mississippi Abbey. *Insurance:* Acuity; Allstate Insurance Co.; CIGNA; Crawford & Company; Gallagher Bassett Insurance; General Casualty Cos.; Greatway Insurance; Great West Casualty Company; Grinnell Mutual Reinsurance Co.; The Hartford; Home Insurance Co.; Iowa Mutual Insurance Company; K&K Insurance Group; Metropolitan Life Insurance Co.; Metropolitan Property & Casualty Insurance; North Central Adjustment Company; Podiatry Insurance Company of America; Rockford Mutual Insurance Company; Rural Mutual Ins. Co.; Safeco Insurance; St. Paul Fire & Marine; SECURA Insurance; The Travelers Indemnity Company; U.S. Insurance Group.

SHUTTLEWORTH & INGERSOLL, P.L.C.

DUBUQUE, IOWA

(See Cedar Rapids)

Administrative Law, Agricultural Law, Alternative Dispute Resolution, Arbitration, Mediation, Antitrust, Unfair Trade, Bankruptcy, Banks and Banking, Biotechnology, Civil Litigation and Appellate Practice in all State and Federal Courts, Civil Rights, Commercial Law, Commercial Real Estate, Communications and Media, Computers and Software, Constitutional Law, Con-

(This Listing Continued)

struction Law, Contracts, Copyrights, Corporate Law, Debtor and Creditor, Disabilities, Education Law, Elder Law, Eminent Domain, Employee Benefits, Employment Law, Energy, Environmental Law, Estate Planning, General Practice, Health Care, Hospital Law, Insurance, Insurance Defense, Intellectual Property, Labor, Land Use, Medical Malpractice, Mergers, Acquisitions, and Divestitures, Municipal Law, Natural Resources, Nonprofit and Charitable Organizations, OSHA, Partnership Law, Patents, Personal Injury, Probate, Products Liability, Professional Liability, Real Estate, Securities, Tax Law, Technology and Science, Trademarks, Trusts and Estates, Utility Law, Wills, Workers Compensation, Zoning Law.

FITZGIBBONS LAW FIRM

A Partnership including a Professional Corporation

108 NORTH SEVENTH STREET
P.O. BOX 496
ESTHERVILLE, IOWA 51334
Telephone: 712-362-7215
Fax: 712-362-3526
Email: jfitz@fitzgibbonslawfirm.com

General Practice in all Courts. Trials and Appeals, Personal Injury, Litigation, Insurance, Banking, Corporation, Real Estate, Probate and School Law.

MEMBERS OF FIRM

LEO E. FITZGIBBONS (1915-2005)

FRANCIS FITZGIBBONS (1924-2004)

JOSEPH L. FITZGIBBONS, born Estherville, Iowa, June 16, 1954; admitted to bar, 1979, Iowa; 1984, U.S. Supreme Court. *Education:* Tulane University (B.A., 1976); University of Iowa (J.D., 1979). Listed in "Best Lawyers in America." Trustee, University of Iowa Law School Foundation, 1992-2004. District 3A Judicial Nominating Commission, 1998-2004; State of Iowa Judicial Nominating Commission, 2005—; Court Appointed Member, Merit Section Panel for U.S. Magistrate Judge, U.S. District Court, Northern District of Iowa, 1998. *Member:* Emmet County, Iowa State (Member: Iowa Civil Jury Instructions Committee, 1991-1993; Grievance Commission, 1992-2004; Board of Governors, 1999-2004) and American Bar Associations; The Iowa Trial Lawyers Association (Member, Board of Governors, 1986-1989); The Association of Trial Lawyers of America; Iowa Academy of Trial Lawyers; Iowa Defense Counsel Association. Fellow: American College of Trial Lawyers. ***Email:*** jfitz@fitzgibbonslawfirm.com

HAROLD W. WHITE, (P.C.), born Oak Ridge, Tennessee, September 9, 1946; admitted to bar, 1974, Iowa; 1983, U.S. Supreme Court. *Education:* Tennessee Technological University (B.S., 1970); University of South Dakota (M.A., 1970); University of Iowa (J.D. with distinction, 1974). Phi Alpha Delta. Author: Comment, "Advertising for the Discriminating Land Lord: The Media and Fair Housing Legislation," 58 Iowa L. Rev. 638, 1973. Assistant County Attorney, Lee County, Iowa, 1974. City Attorney, Arnolds Park, Iowa, 1982—; Member, Iowa State Board of Tax Review, 1991-1997; Commissioner, Iowa State Racing and Gaming Commission, 1997-1999. *Member:* Emmet County, Iowa State (Member, Committee on Commercial and Bankruptcy Law, 1984-1986) and American Bar Associations; Iowa Association of School Board Attorneys; Electric Cooperative Bar Association. ***Email:*** hwhite@fitzgibbonslawfirm.com

NED A. STOCKDALE, born Waterloo, Iowa, August 12, 1946; admitted to bar, 1975, Iowa; U.S. District Court, Northern and Southern District of Iowa; U.S. Court of Appeals, Eighth Circuit; U.S. Supreme Court. *Education:* Iowa State University (B.S., 1968); Drake University (J.D., 1975). Articles Editor, Drake Law Review, 1974-1975. *Member:* Iowa State and American Bar Associations; Iowa Defense Counsel Association; Iowa Academy of Trial Lawyers; The Iowa Trial Lawyers Association; The Association of Trial Lawyers of America. ***Email:*** nstock@fitzgibbonslawfirm.com

SCOT BAUERMEISTER, born Omaha, Nebraska, February 11, 1966; admitted to bar, 1991, Iowa; 1992, Arizona; U.S. District Court, District of Arizona and U.S. District Court, Northern and Southern Districts of Iowa. *Education:* Iowa State University (B.B.A., 1988); University of Iowa (J.D., 1991). City Attorney, Armstrong, Ringsted, Iowa, 1999—. *Member:* Iowa State and American Bar Associations; State Bar of Arizona; Defense Research Institute. ***Email:*** sbauer@fitzgibbonslawfirm.com

KEVIN R. SANDER, born Clinton, Iowa, July 30, 1975; admitted to bar, 2000, Iowa and U.S. District Court, Northern and Southern Districts of Iowa. *Education:* University of Iowa (B.A., 1997; J.D. with distinction, 2000). Note and Comment Editor, Journal of Corporation Law, 1999-2000. Author: "The Cold Shoulder of Occupational Disease Recovery, Ganske v. Spahn & Rose Lumber Co.," 25 J. Corp. L. 407 2000. *Member:* Iowa State and American Bar Associations. ***Email:*** ksander@fitzgibbonslawfirm.com

REPRESENTATIVE CLIENTS: Available Upon Request.

FORSYTH LAW OFFICE

121 NORTH SIXTH STREET
ESTHERVILLE, IOWA 51334
Telephone: 712-362-2637
Fax: 712-362-2638
Email: forlaw@rconnect.com

General Practice. Probate, Real Estate, Taxation, Personal Injury, Litigation and Municipal Law.

DAVID D. FORSYTH, born Estherville, Iowa, September 21, 1957; admitted to bar, 1990, Iowa. *Education:* Mankato State University (B.S., 1982); Drake University (J.D., 1988). Assistant City Attorney, City of Estherville, 1990. *Member:* Emmet County, Iowa State and American Bar Associations. ***Email:*** dforsyth@rconnect.com

HARRISON, MORELAND & WEBBER, P.C.

FAIRFIELD, IOWA

(See Ottumwa)

General Practice. Probate, Corporate, Real Estate, Health and Hospital, Labor and Employment and Insurance Law. Trials and Appeals.

JOHNSON, ERB, BICE, KRAMER, GOOD & MULHOLLAND, P.C.

Established in 1950

600 BOSTON CENTRE
809 CENTRAL AVENUE
P.O. BOX 1396
FORT DODGE, IOWA 50501-1396
Telephone: 515-573-2181
Fax: 515-573-2548
URL: http://www.lawyers.com/jebkgmlawfirm

Gowrie, Iowa Office: 1103 Market Street. Telephone: 515-352-3111. Fax: 515-352-3113.

General Practice Before all State and Federal Courts. Personal Injury, Corporation, Utility, Labor, Insurance, Real Estate and Probate Law. Trials and Appeals.

FIRM PROFILE: The firm traces its origin to its founder, Arthur H. Johnson, who commenced practicing law in 1948. In 1964, Mr. Johnson and the Burnquist Law Firm merged, becoming Johnson, Burnquist, Flattery and McCormick. Former partners in the firm have become both Iowa Supreme Court Justices and Iowa District Court Justices. Present partners in the firm have served as officers and board members of state and local bar associations as well as numerous community boards and organizations. The firm provides experienced attorneys at the shareholder level and well-trained and supervised associate attorneys and legal assistants.

DEAN P. ERB, born Des Moines, Iowa, March 16, 1940; admitted to bar, 1965, Iowa. *Education:* University of Iowa (B.B.A., 1962; LL.B., 1965). Phi Delta Phi. City Attorney: Gowrie, 1969; Callender, 1988. Attorney for Prairie Community School District, Area Education Agency #5, 1979. *Member:* Webster County (President, 1984-1985), Iowa State and American Bar Associations; Iowa Municipal Attorneys Association; Iowa Association of School Boards. (Gowrie Office)

THOMAS J. BICE, born Fort Dodge, Iowa, April 7, 1947; admitted to bar, 1972, Iowa and U.S. District Court, Northern District of Iowa; 1974, U.S. Court of Appeals, Eighth Circuit; 1975, U.S. District Court, Southern District of Iowa. *Education:* University of Iowa (B.A., 1969); Drake University (J.D., with honors, 1972). Order of the Coif; Delta Theta Phi. Editor-in-Chief, Drake Law Review, 1971-1972. Iowa Board of Law Examiners, 1999—. *Member:* Webster County (President, 1994-1995), Iowa State and American Bar Associations; Iowa Trial Lawyers Association; Iowa Academy of Trial Lawyers; American College of Trial Lawyers. ***PRACTICE AREAS:*** Civil Practice. ***Email:*** Thomas.Bice@JohnsonLawIA.com

JAMES L. KRAMER, born Fort Dodge, Iowa, February 22, 1948; admitted to bar, 1973, Iowa and U.S. District Court, Northern District of Iowa; 1974, U.S. Court of Appeals, Eighth Circuit; 1980, U.S. District Court, Southern District of Iowa; 1982, U.S. Supreme Court. *Education:* Stanford University (B.A., 1970); University of Minnesota (J.D., cum laude, 1973). Appointed to Iowa Supreme Court Advisory Committee on Rules of Criminal Procedure, 1976-1977, 1977-1981. *Member:* Webster County President, 1997-1998), Iowa State and American Bar Associations; Iowa Trial Lawyers Association; American Judicature Society; The Association of Trial Lawyers of America. ***PRACTICE AREAS:*** Appellate Practice; Banks and Banking; Commercial Law; Debtor and Creditor; Insurance. ***Email:*** James.Kramer@JohnsonLawIA.com

WILLIAM J. GOOD, born Ogden, Iowa, July 19, 1950; admitted to bar, 1977, Iowa; 1985, U.S. District Court, Northern District of Iowa; 1986, U.S. District Court, Southern District of Iowa. *Education:* Iowa State University (B.S., 1972); University of Iowa (J.D., with distinction, 1976). Phi Eta Sigma; Phi Kappa Phi; Gamma Sigma Delta. Certified Public Accountant, Iowa, 1976. *Member:* Webster County (President, 2003-2004), Iowa State and American Bar Associations. ***PRACTICE AREAS:*** Business Law; Probate; Real Estate; Trusts and Estates. ***Email:*** William.Good@JohnsonLawIA.com

NEVEN J. MULHOLLAND, born Fort Dodge, Iowa, August 17, 1953; admitted to bar, 1979, Iowa and U.S. District Court, Northern District of Iowa; 1983, U.S. District Court, Southern District of Iowa. *Education:* University of South Dakota (B.S., 1975); Creighton University (J.D., 1979). *Member:* Webster County, Iowa State and American Bar Associations; Iowa Trial Lawyers Association (President, 1999-2000; Board of Governors, 1989—); The Association of Trial Lawyers of America; Commercial Law League of America; Iowa Academy of Trial Lawyers; American Board of Trial Advocates. ***PRACTICE AREAS:*** Litigation; Medical Malpractice; Personal Injury; Workers' Compensation. ***Email:*** Neven.Mulholland@JohnsonLawIA.com

STUART J. COCHRANE, born Crookston, Minnesota, March 7, 1959; admitted to bar, 1985, Iowa; 1986, U.S. District Court, Northern and Southern Districts of Iowa. *Education:* University of Northern Iowa (B.A., 1982); University of Iowa (J.D., 1985). *Member:* Webster County, Iowa State and American Bar Associations; Iowa Trial Lawyers Association. ***PRACTICE AREAS:*** Civil Rights; Labor and Employment; Health Law. ***Email:*** Stu.Cochrane@JohnsonLawIA.com

ERIC J. EIDE, born Des Moines, Iowa, June 1, 1963; admitted to bar, 1988, Iowa; 1990, U.S. District Court, Northern and Southern Districts of Iowa. *Education:* Iowa State University (B.S., with highest honors, 1985); University of Iowa (J.D., with high distinction, 1988). Phi Kappa Phi; Order of the Coif. Semi-finalist, Jessup Moot Court National Competition. Attorney, Office of the General Counsel, U.S. Department of Agriculture, 1988-1990. *Member:* Webster County, Iowa State and American Bar Associations. ***PRACTICE AREAS:*** Commercial Law; Corporate Law; Environmental Law; Probate; Real Estate. ***Email:*** Eric.Eide@JohnsonLawIA.com

(This Listing Continued)

JOHNSON, ERB, BICE, KRAMER, GOOD & MULHOLLAND, P.C., Fort Dodge—Continued

ASSOCIATE

DARREN D. DRISCOLL, born Iowa City, Iowa, December 5, 1976; admitted to bar, 2003, Iowa. *Education:* University of Iowa (B.B.A., 1999; J.D., 2003). *Member:* Webster County, Iowa State and American Bar Associations. ***PRACTICE AREAS:*** Litigation. ***Email:*** darren.driscoll@johnsonlawia.com

OF COUNSEL

ARTHUR H. JOHNSON, born Fort Dodge, Iowa, March 15, 1921; admitted to bar, 1948, Iowa. *Education:* University of Iowa (B.A., 1946; J.D., 1948). Phi Delta Phi. Assistant County Attorney, 1949-1955. County Attorney, 1956-1960.

REPRESENTATIVE CLIENTS: NEW Cooperative, Inc.; First American Bank; First American Bank Group, Ltd.; First Federal Savings Bank; US Bank of Humboldt County; Farmland Mutual Insurance Co.; Trinity Regional Hospital; Iowa Commodities, Ltd.; City of Callender; Federated Insurance; Arrowhead Area Education Agency; Hamilton County Public Hospital; Trimark Physicians Group; Clarence Cooperative, Inc.; City of Humboldt; Heartland Bank; City of Gowrie; Fort Dodge Animal Health/Wyeth; United Bank of Iowa; Northern Country Cooperative; City of Otho; City of Somers; Cigna Property & Casualty Co.

KERSTEN BROWNLEE HENDRICKS, LLP

SNELL BUILDING
805 CENTRAL AVENUE, SEVENTH FLOOR
P.O. BOX 957
FORT DODGE, IOWA 50501
Telephone: 515-576-4127
Fax: 515-576-6340
Email: brownlee@frontiernet.net
URL: http://www.kerstenbrownleehendricks.com

General Practice. Personal Injury Law, Corporation, Insurance Defense, Workers Compensation, Bankruptcy, Banking, Probate and Estate Planning and Taxation Law. Trials.

MEMBERS OF FIRM

DON N. KERSTEN (1925-1998)

STEPHEN G. KERSTEN, born Des Moines, Iowa, August 29, 1953; admitted to bar, 1980, Iowa and U.S. District Court, Northern and Southern Districts of Iowa; 1990, U.S. Supreme Court. *Education:* Georgetown University (B.S., 1975); University of Iowa (M.S., 1977); Drake University (J.D., 1980). Part-Time Judicial Magistrate, 1992—. *Member:* Webster County, Iowa State and American Bar Associations; Iowa Defense Counsel Association (Board of Governors, 1996-2000); Iowa Academy of Trial Lawyers; Iowa Association of Workers Compensation Lawyers. ***PRACTICE AREAS:*** Insurance Defense; Personal Injury; Workers Compensation. ***Email:*** kerstn@frontiernet.net

MARK S. BROWNLEE, born Emmetsburg, Iowa, September 1, 1954; admitted to bar, 1979, Iowa; 1980, U.S. District Court, Northern and Southern Districts of Iowa. *Education:* Washington & Lee University and Iowa State University (B.S., 1976); University of Iowa (J.D., 1979). Law Clerk to the Second Judicial District of Iowa, 1979-1980. *Member:* Webster County and Iowa State (Member Litigation Section) Bar Associations; Iowa Defense Counsel Association (Co-Editor of "Defense Update," Board of Directors, 2000—; President Elect); Defense Research Institute; Iowa Academy of Trial Lawyers. ***PRACTICE AREAS:*** Insurance Defense; Personal Injury; Workers Compensation. ***Email:*** brownlee@frontiernet.net

STEVEN W. HENDRICKS, born Sioux City, Iowa, April 5, 1957; admitted to bar, 1982, Iowa and U.S. District Court, Northern and Southern Districts of Iowa. *Education:* University of Iowa (B.A., with honors and high distinction, 1979); Drake University (J.D., with honors, 1982). Order of the Coif; Phi Beta Kappa. *Member:* Webster County, Iowa State (Member: Legal Forms Committee, 1995-1999; Member, Probate and Trust Law Council, 1992-1994, 1996—; Chair, Probate and Trust Law Council, 1993-1994 and 1998-1999; Bridge the Gap Committee, Young Lawyers Section, 1983-1992; Board of Governors, 2000—) and American (Member: Section on Taxation; Committee on Attorneys in Small Law Offices, 1986-1989) Bar Associations. Fellow, American College of Trust and Estate Counsel. ***PRACTICE AREAS:*** Probate; Taxation; Estate Planning; Real Estate; Bankruptcy. ***Email:*** hendricks@frontiernet.net

REPRESENTATIVE CLIENTS: Allied Group; Kemper Group; Farm Bureau Mutual Insurance Co.; Employers Mutual Companies; Auto Owners Mutual Insurance Company; C.N.A.; Heritage Insurance Company; Mutual Fire & Auto.; American Family Insurance Co.; The Chubb Group; National Indemnity Co.; Farm & City Ins. Co.; Phico Ins. Co.; Continental Western Insurance Co.; K-Mart Corporation.
REFERENCE: Wells Fargo Bank.

BECKMAN AND HIRSCH

FORT MADISON, IOWA

(See Burlington)

Personal Injury, Appeals, Corporation, Taxation, Probate, Insurance, Real Estate, Criminal Defense, Commercial Litigation, Computer Law, Family Law, General Trial Practice in State and Federal Courts.

FEHSEKE & ESCHMAN LAW OFFICES

Established in 1944
1023 AVENUE G
FORT MADISON, IOWA 52627
Telephone: 319-372-7181
FAX: 319-372-7185
Email: info@fehsekelaw.com
URL: http://www.fehsekelaw.com

General Civil Practice including Trials and Appeals, Personal Injury, Probate, Real Estate, Workers Compensation Law, Maritime Law, Medical Malpractice, Products Liability, Trusts and Estates, Estate Planning, and Elder Law.

FIRM PROFILE: For over 60 years, three successful generations of the Fehseke family have been providing legal services in Fort Madison, Keokuk, Burlington, Mt. Pleasant, Muscatine, Davenport, Iowa City, Cedar Rapids, and Des Moines, Iowa, as well as in Quincy, Nauvoo, Niota, Carthage, and Dallas City, Illinois, to people from all walks of life and from all parts of the United States. The firm's founder, R. L. Fehseke, began practicing law in Ft. Madison in 1944. His son, R. L. Fehseke, Jr., and his grandchildren, Richard L. Fehseke III and Elaine Fehseke Eschman, continue his work.

MEMBERS OF FIRM

R. L. FEHSEKE (1918-1985)

R. L. FEHSEKE, JR., born Fort Madison, Iowa, August 17, 1944; admitted to bar, 1968, Iowa. *Education:* University of Iowa (B.A., 1966; J.D., 1968). Phi Beta Kappa; Order of the Coif; Phi Delta Phi. Managing Editor, Iowa Law Review, 1967-1968. *Member:* Lee County, Iowa State and American Bar Associations; Iowa Trial Lawyers Association; Iowa Academy of Trial Lawyers; The Association of Trial Lawyers of America. ***PRACTICE AREAS:*** Personal Injury; Probate; Trusts & Estates; Estate Planning; Medical Malpractice. ***Email:*** info@fehsekelaw.com

RICHARD L. FEHSEKE, III, born Burlington, Iowa, November 15, 1968; admitted to bar, 1994, Iowa; 2004, Illinois. *Education:* Vanderbilt University (B.A., cum laude, 1991); University of Iowa (J.D., with high distinction, 1994). Phi Sigma Alpha; Phi Delta Phi. Member, Iowa Law Review. *Member:* Lee County, Iowa State and Illinois State Bar Associations; Iowa Trial Lawyers Association; American Trial Lawyers Association. ***PRACTICE AREAS:*** Workers Compensation; Personal Injury Litigation; Real Estate; Probate; Estate Planning; Medical Malpractice; Trusts and Estates. ***Email:*** info@fehsekelaw.com

ELAINE FEHSEKE ESCHMAN, born Burlington, Iowa, April 12, 1972; admitted to bar, 1998, California; 1999, Iowa. *Education:* Vanderbilt University (B.A., magna cum laude, 1993); McGeorge School of Law (J.D., with distinction, 1998). Order of the Coif. Traynor Honor Society. Recipient, Annabel McGeorge Scholarship. *Member:* North Lee County (President, 2001—), Lee County, Iowa State and American Bar Associations; State Bar of California; Iowa Trial Lawyers Association. ***PRACTICE AREAS:*** Personal Injury; Products Liability; Medical Malpractice; Estate Planning; Trusts and Estates; Elder Law. ***Email:*** elaine@fehsekelaw.com

REPRESENTATIVE CLIENTS: Building Materials, Inc.; Jim Baier, Inc.; Lee County Abstract Company; Lee County Bank & Trust, N.A.; Millwright Services, Inc.; Hall Towing, Inc.; First Co, Inc.; Gaylord Construction, Inc.; Farmers Savings Bank; McWhirter Chevrolet-Buick, Inc.; Frank Baxter Construction; Burlington Basket Company. References: Fort Madison Bank & Trust Co.; Lee County Bank & Trust, N.A.

PETERS LAW FIRM, P.C.

Established in 1895
10 NORTH WALNUT
GLENWOOD, IOWA 51534
Telephone: 712-527-4877
FAX: 712-527-3418
URL: http://www.peterslawfirm.com

Council Bluffs, Iowa Office: 233 Pearl Street. P.O. Box 1078. Telephone: 712-328-3157. FAX: 712-328-9092.
Neola, Iowa Office: 401 Front Street, P.O. Box 282. Telephone: 712-485-2265.
South Omaha, Nebraska Office: 4828 South 24th Street, Suite 200, 68107. Telephone: 402-731-1711. Fax: 402-731-3363.

Personal Injury Litigation and Commercial Litigation. Insurance, Tax, Real Estate, Corporation, Probate and Bankruptcy Law.

JAMES A. THOMAS, born Council Bluffs, Iowa, April 14, 1942; admitted to bar, 1967, Iowa. *Education:* Morningside College (B.S., 1964); University of Iowa (J.D., 1967). Phi Delta Phi. Mills County Attorney, 1968-1972. *Member:* Mills County, Iowa State, Southwest Iowa (President, 1987-1988) and American Bar Associations.

MATTHEW G. WOODS, born Cedar Rapids, Iowa, November 11, 1966; admitted to bar, 1993, Iowa. *Education:* University of Iowa (B.B.A., 1989); Creighton University (J.D., 1993). *Member:* Mills County Bar Association (President, 2004); Iowa State and Southwest Iowa Bar Associations; Iowa Municipal Attorneys Association.

JUSTIN R. WYATT, born Loma Linda, California, July 5, 1975; admitted to bar, 2003, Iowa; 2004, Nebraska. *Education:* Creighton University (B.S., 1998; J.D., 2003). *Member:* Iowa State and Nebraska State Bar Associations. ***Email:*** justin@peterslawfirm.com

REPRESENTATIVE CLIENTS: Grinnell Mutual Re-Insurance Co.; Horace Mann Ins. Cos.; Kemper Group: Shelter Ins. Co.; State Farm Mutual Auto Ins.; United Fire & Casualty; The Cities McClelland, Glenwood, Underwood, Neola and Minden, IA; Iowa West Racing Assn.;

(This Listing Continued)

Mills County State Bank; Glenwood State Bank; 1st Community National Bank; Citizens Savings Bank; Peoples National Bank; Randolph State Bank; MidStates Bank; Ameristar Casino; North Pointe Insurance Co.
REFERENCE: Glenwood State Bank.

MALLOY LAW FIRM

PROFESSIONAL SERVICES BUILDING
503 MAIN STREET
P.O. BOX 128
GOLDFIELD, IOWA 50542
Telephone: 515-825-3181
Fax: 515-825-3898
Email: malloy@goldfieldaccess.net

West Des Moines, Iowa Office: 6935 Vista Drive, 50266. Telephone: 515-457-8501.

General Trial and Appellate Practice Before State and Federal Courts and Administrative Agencies, Agricultural, Corporate, Insurance, Personal Injury, Real Estate, Probate, Estate Planning Law.

ROBERT P. MALLOY, born Iowa City, Iowa, March 27, 1948; admitted to bar, 1974, Iowa and U.S. District Court, Northern and Southern Districts of Iowa; 1984, U.S. Tax Court and U.S. Court of Appeals, Eighth Circuit. *Education:* University of Iowa (B.A., 1971); Drake University (J.D., 1973). Author: "Estate Planning for the Farmer," Young Lawyers, Iowa Bar, 1975. Member and Speaker, "Rural Economic Developments in a Market Economy", U.S. Delegation to U.S.S.R., April 1991. Speaker, "Economic Development - 1990 Farm Act", Nat'l Telecast, January 10, 1991. President, 2B Judicial District of Iowa, 1984. City Attorney, City of Goldfield. Magistrate, Wright County, 1994-1997. *Member:* Wright County (President, 1985-1986), Iowa State (Chairman, Agricultural Law Section, 1999-2000) and American (Member, Sections on: Litigation, Real Estate and Probate; Chairman, 1999-2000 and Member, Agricultural Law Section; Vice-Chairman, Solo Practitioners Committee, Economics of Law Practice Section, 1982-1984; Chairman, Legislative Committee, 1990-1991) Bar Associations; Association of Trial Lawyers of Iowa; The Association of Trial Lawyers of America. [1st Lt., U.S. Army, 1974]. ***PRACTICE AREAS:*** Agricultural Law; Litigation; Corporate Law; Insurance Law; General Practice. ***Email:*** malloy@goldfieldaccess.net

ASSOCIATE

LYNN COLLINS SEABA, born Jackson, Mississippi, October 6, 1969; admitted to bar, 1996, Iowa and U.S. District Court, Northern District of Iowa. *Education:* University of Georgia (B.S.A., 1991); Drake University (J.D., 1996). *Member:* Wright County (President, 1999), Iowa State (Member, Agricultural Law Section) and American Bar Associations; Iowa Trial Lawyers Association. ***PRACTICE AREAS:*** General Practice; Agricultural Law; Criminal Law; Real Estate; Corporate Law. ***Email:*** lynnseaba@goldfieldaccess.net

REPRESENTATIVE CLIENTS: Security Savings Bank; Gold-Eagle Coop; Clarion Airmotive, Inc.; Goldfield Telephone Co.; Stratford Telephone Co.; Lehigh Telephone Co.; Grinnell Mutual Insurance Co.; Norway Rural Telephone Co.; Poky Feeders, Inc.; Anderson Seed; Ennis Truck Lines, Inc.; Murphy of Iowa, Inc.; Ennis Corporation; Boche & Company, Inc.; Hoffman-Rettig Foods, Inc.; Rettig Financial, Inc.; Stoecken Farms, Inc.; Rembrandt Enterprises, Inc.; Sparboe Companies; Oakridge Farms, Inc.; Clarion-Goldfield Schools; Goldfield Telecom; Clement Auto & Truck, Inc.; Meek Poultry, LLP.
REFERENCES: Security Savings Bank; First Citizens National Bank; Wells Fargo.

BEVERLY WILD LAW OFFICE, P.C.

Established in 1987
105 SOUTH FOURTH STREET
GUTHRIE CENTER, IOWA 50115
Telephone: 641-332-2900
Toll Free 888-554-3214
Fax: 641-332-2903
Email: wildlaw@netins.net
URL: http://www.lawyers.com/wild

Family, Divorce, Guardianships, Juvenile, Real Estate, Probate and Estate Planning and Criminal Law.

BEVERLY WILD, born Redfield, Iowa, February 19, 1943; admitted to bar, 1987, Iowa and U.S. District Court, Southern District of Iowa; 1995, U.S. District Court, Northern District of Iowa. *Education:* Drake University (B.S., 1984; J.D., 1987). Guthrie County Magistrate Nominating Commission, 1991-1997. District 5A Judicial Nominating Commission, 1996-1999. Judicial Hospitalization Referee, 1989—. City Attorney Adair Iowa, 1989—. City Attorney Redfield Iowa, 1989—. *Member:* Guthrie County and Iowa State Bar Associations; Iowa Municipal Attorneys Association. ***PRACTICE AREAS:*** General Practice; Municipal Law; Family Law; Guardianship; Juvenile Law; Criminal Law; Real Estate; Probate; Estate Planning. ***Email:*** wildlaw@netins.net

---

JOEL BAXTER, born Red Oak, Iowa, May 2, 1972; admitted to bar, 2003, Iowa. *Education:* Iowa State University (B.S., 1994); Drake University (J.D., 2002). ***PRACTICE AREAS:*** General Practice; Criminal Law; Municipal Law; Real Estate; Family Law; Divorce; Estate Planning; Guardianship; Juvenile Law; Probate. ***Email:*** wildlaw@netins.net

CHRISTINE L. SAND, born Jesup, Iowa, June 2, 1971; admitted to bar, 2003, Iowa. *Education:* Morningside College (B.A., magna cum laude, 1993); Drake University (J.D., with honors, 2003). *Member:* Polk County, Iowa State and American Bar Associations. ***Email:*** sandlaw@netins.net

HOBSON, CADY & CADY

Established in 1991
9 FIRST STREET S.W.
P.O. BOX 456
HAMPTON, IOWA 50441
Telephone: 641-456-2555
Fax: 641-456-3315
Email: cadyart@rconnect.com

General Practice in State and Federal Courts. Trials and Appeals. Insurance and Probate Law.

MEMBERS OF FIRM

A. J. HOBSON (1903-1972)

G. ARTHUR CADY, born Sioux Rapids, Iowa, August 29, 1926; admitted to bar, 1952, Iowa. *Education:* Buena Vista College and University of Iowa (B.A., 1950); Drake University (J.D., 1952). Order of the Coif. Board of Counsellors, Drake University, 1957-1960; 1970-1976. Franklin County Attorney, 1957-1963. Member, Hampton Community School Board, 1964-1969. *Member:* Franklin County (President, 1959), Iowa State (Member: Grievance Commission, 1989—; Council, Section of Probate and Trust Law, 1990-1992) and American Bar Associations; Iowa Academy of Trial Lawyers. ***REPORTED CASES:*** Iowa Grain vs. Farmers Feed Gv., 293 NW2d 22 (Iowa 1980); Hamilton vs. Wosepka 154 NW2d 164 (Iowa 1967). ***PRACTICE AREAS:*** Probate Law; Estate Planning; Business Law; Commercial Law. ***Email:*** cadyart@rconnect.com

G. A. CADY, III, born Des Moines, Iowa, August 30, 1952; admitted to bar, 1977, Iowa and U.S. District Court, Northern District of Iowa; 1981, U.S. Court of Appeals, Eighth Circuit. *Education:* Drake University (B.A., 1974; J.D., 1977). Omicron Delta Kappa. Franklin County Attorney, 1979-1982. Assistant Franklin County Attorney, 1983-1985 and County Attorney, 1985-1986. Iowa State Bar Association, Board of Governors, 1994-1999. Drake University Law School Board of Counselors, 1994-2001. *Member:* Franklin County (President, 1987-1989), Iowa State and American Bar Associations. ***REPORTED CASES:*** Beckman vs. Kitchen, 599 NW 3d 699 (Iowa 1999); DeCoster vs. Franklin County 497 Nw2d 849 (Iowa 1993); State v. Butler 415 NW2d 634 (Iowa 1987). ***PRACTICE AREAS:*** Personal Injury Litigation; Family Law; Probate and Estate Law. ***Email:*** cadyart@rconnect.com

A list of Representative Clients will be furnished upon request.
REFERENCES: First National Bank of Hampton.

SALVO, DEREN, SCHENCK & LAUTERBACH, P.C.

711 COURT STREET
P.O. BOX 509
HARLAN, IOWA 51537
Telephone: 712-755-3141
Fax: 712-755-3144
URL: http://www.sdsllaw.com

Earling, Iowa Office: 122 Main. Telephone: 712-747-6191.
Panama, Iowa Office: 100 Main. Telephone: 712-489-2424.
Walnut, Iowa Office: 301 Antique City Drive. Telephone: 712-784-3907.
Woodbine, Iowa Office: 414 Walker. Telephone: 712-647-3269.

General Practice, Commercial, Family, Negligence, Corporation, Real Estate, Tax and Probate Law. Trials, Civil and Criminal.

J. C. SALVO, born Council Bluffs, Iowa, December 10, 1947; admitted to bar, 1972, Iowa, Nebraska, U.S. District Court, District of Nebraska and U.S. District Court, Southern District of Iowa; 1980, U.S. Supreme Court. *Education:* Creighton University; Creighton University School of Law (J.D., 1972). *Member:* Iowa State (Member, Board of Governors, 1998-2002; President, 2005), Nebraska State and American Bar Associations; Iowa Trial Lawyers Association; The Association of Trial Lawyers of America. Fellow, Iowa Academy of Trial Lawyers (Member, Board of Governors; President, 1998). ***PRACTICE AREAS:*** Family Law; Personal Injury; Litigation. ***Email:*** jsalvo@sdsllaw.com

PATRICK T. DEREN, born Kenosha, Wisconsin, August 11, 1947; admitted to bar, 1975, Iowa; 1977, U.S. District Court, Southern District of Iowa and U.S. Tax Court. *Education:* Southern Illinois University (B.A., 1970); University of Tennessee (J.D., 1974); University of Florida (LL.M., 1978). *Member:* Iowa State Bar Association. ***PRACTICE AREAS:*** Probate; Taxation; Real Estate; Business Law. ***Email:*** pderen@sdsllaw.com

RICHARD C. SCHENCK, born Shenandoah, Iowa, June 30, 1953; admitted to bar, 1978, Iowa and U.S. District Court, Southern District of Iowa. *Education:* University of Iowa (B.A., with highest distinction, 1974; J.D., with honors, 1978). Phi Beta Kappa. *Member:* Iowa State Bar Association; Iowa Trial Lawyers Association. ***PRACTICE AREAS:*** Litigation; Commercial Law. ***Email:*** rschenck@sdsllaw.com

JOSEPH C. LAUTERBACH, born Minneapolis, Minnesota, December 2, 1953; admitted to bar, 1980, Iowa and U.S. District Court, Southern District of Iowa. *Education:* Cornell College (B.S.S., summa cum laude, 1977); University of Iowa (J.D., 1980). Phi Beta Kappa. City Attorney, Harlan, Iowa, 1992—. *Member:* Iowa State Bar Association. ***PRACTICE AREAS:*** Criminal Law; Collections; Litigation. ***Email:*** jlauterbach@sdsllaw.com

---

BRYAN D. SWAIN, born Shawnee, Kansas, September 9, 1975; admitted to bar, 2000, Iowa and U.S. District Court, Southern District of Iowa. *Education:* Truman State University (B.A., summa cum laude, 1997); University of Iowa (J.D., with highest distinction, 2000). Order of the Coif. Author: "Corporate Predecessor Liability for Defective Products," 25 Journal of Corporation Law 613 (2000). *Member:* Iowa State Bar Association.

(This Listing Continued)

SALVO, DEREN, SCHENCK & LAUTERBACH, P.C., Harlan—Continued

PRACTICE AREAS: Real Estate; Taxation; Appellate Practice. ***Email:*** bswain@sdsllaw.com

EELLS & TRONVOLD LAW OFFICES, P.L.C.

HIAWATHA, IOWA

(See Cedar Rapids)

General Practice with emphasis on Personal Injury, Litigation, Probate and Estate Planning, Trusts and Wills, Business Law and Mediation.

THADDEUS E. COSGROVE

102 NORTH MAIN
P.O. BOX 50
HOLSTEIN, IOWA 51025-0050
Telephone: 712-368-2616
Fax: 712-368-2389
Email: cosgrovelaw@netllc.net

Ida Grove, Iowa Office: 607 W Second Street, 51445. Telephone: 712-364-4138. Fax: 712-364-4445. Email: tcosgroveig@yahoo.com.

General Civil Trial Practice. Probate, Personal Injury, Insurance Defense and Corporate Law.

THADDEUS E. COSGROVE, born Sioux City, Iowa, February 27, 1959; admitted to bar, 1984, Iowa and U.S. District Court, Northern and Southern Districts of Iowa. *Education:* University of Iowa (B.A., 1981); Creighton University (J.D., cum laude, 1984). City Attorney: City of Holstein, 1991—; City of Cushing, 1997—. *Member:* Ida County (Past President, 1985-1986) and Iowa State Bar Associations; Iowa Trial Lawyers Association. ***PRACTICE AREAS:*** General Civil Practice; Trial Practice; Probate; Taxation.

REPRESENTATIVE CLIENTS: Great West Casualty Co.; Quad County Corn Processors Cooperative; Galva-Holstein Aq., LLC; Heritage Bank, N.A. (Holstein, Iowa); VT Industries, Inc. (Holstein, Iowa; Bryan, Texas; Shelbyville, Indiana; Rome, Georgia; Roseburg, .regon); City of Holstein; McGuire Auction Company, Inc.; American National Bank (Holstein, IA, Sac City, IA, Moville, IA, Pierson, IA, Galva, IA); GOMACO, Godberson - Smith Construction Co., United Bank of Iowa.

FORRISTAL & HENDERSON

103 NORTH HAMBURG STREET
P.O. BOX 160
HOLSTEIN, IOWA 51025
Telephone: 712-368-2646
Fax: 712-368-4588
Email: idaca@pionet.net
URL: http://www.forristallaw.com

Real Estate, Contracts, Family Law, Divorce, Estate Planning, Tax and Personal Injury Law.

MEMBERS OF FIRM

MATTHEW J. FORRISTAL, born Sioux City, Iowa, March 8, 1960; admitted to bar, 1985, Iowa and U.S. District Court, Northern District of Iowa. *Education:* Creighton University (B.S.B.A., 1982; J.D., 1985). *Member:* Woodbury County, Iowa State and American Bar Associations; Iowa Real Estate Association. ***PRACTICE AREAS:*** Taxation (20%, 250); Probate (15%, 20); Estate Planning (15%, 50); Real Estate (15%, 40).

KARLA J. HENDERSON, born Monmouth, Illinois, November 28, 1952; admitted to bar, 1987, Iowa and U.S. District Court, Northern District of Iowa. *Education:* Simpson College (B.A., 1974); University of Iowa (J.D., 1986); Iowa State University (M.P.A., 1987). *Member:* Linn County, Iowa State and American Bar Associations. ***PRACTICE AREAS:*** Criminal Law; Juvenile Law.

FORRISTAL & HENDERSON

IDA GROVE, IOWA

(See Holstein)

OUDERKIRK LAW FIRM

Established in 1951
108 SOUTH HOWARD STREET
P.O. BOX 156
INDIANOLA, IOWA 50125-0156
Telephone: 515-961-5315
Fax: 515-961-0304
Email: ouderkirklaw@aol.com
URL: http://www.lawyers.com/ouderkirk

Personal Injury, Family and Domestic Law, Probate, Workers Compensation, Real Estate.

MASON J. OUDERKIRK, born Des Moines, Iowa, February 1, 1953; admitted to bar, 1978, Iowa and U.S. District Court, Southern District of Iowa; 1989, U.S. Court of Appeals, Eighth Circuit. *Education:* Drake University (B.A., 1975; J.D., 1978). Iowa Real Estate Brokers License, 1974-2001. Iowa Real Estate Associates, Licensed, 1973. Member: Indianola Police Retirement Board, 1984-1989; Warren County Magistrate Appointing Commission, 2001—; Iowa 5A Judicial Nominating Commission, 2002—. *Member:* Warren County (Secretary/Treasurer, 1985-1989; Vice President, 1987-1988; President, 1989-1991), Iowa State and American Bar Associations; Iowa Trial Lawyers Association; Fifth Judicial Bar Association (Secretary/Treasurer, 1994-1995). ***PRACTICE AREAS:*** Personal Injury; Products Liability; Family and Domestic; Probate; Wills; Trusts and Estates; Guardianship; Conservatorship; Workers' Compensation; Real Estate. ***Email:*** ouderkirklaw@aol.com

OF COUNSEL

MASON G. OUDERKIRK, born Reynolds, Illinois, May 26, 1923; admitted to bar, 1951, Iowa. *Education:* Knox College; Drake University (B.A.; J.D., 1951). *Member:* Warren County and American Bar Associations. ***PRACTICE AREAS:*** Probate; Real Estate; Municipal Government.

J. KEITH RIGG

INDIANOLA, IOWA

(See Des Moines)

Criminal Trial Practice in Federal and State Courts. Civil Litigation.

WILSON, FOWLER & FUSCO

209 NORTH HOWARD STREET
P.O. BOX 197
INDIANOLA, IOWA 50125
Telephone: 515-961-5377
FAX: 515-961-2658
Email: wilsonfowler@yahoo.com
URL: http://www.lawyers.com/wilsonfowler

General Practice, Probate, Estate Planning, Real Estate, Tax, Criminal Law and Family Law.

MEMBERS OF FIRM

J. BERKLEY WILSON (1909-1993)

JAMES F. FOWLER, born Atlantic, Iowa, July 13, 1939; admitted to bar, 1965, Iowa and U.S. District Court, Southern District of Iowa; 1970, U.S. Court of Appeals, Eighth Circuit; 1977, U.S. Claims Court. *Education:* Simpson College; University of Iowa (B.A., 1961; LL.B., 1965). Lecturer, Criminal Procedure, Simpson College, 1973-1986. Assistant City Attorney, Des Moines, Iowa, 1967-1970. Managing Attorney, Legal Aid Society of Polk County, 1970-1973. *Member:* Warren County, Iowa State and American Bar Associations. ***Email:*** wilsonfowler@yahoo.com

LOUIS M. FUSCO, born New York, N.Y., November 11, 1949; admitted to bar, 1975, Iowa, U.S. District Court, Northern and Southern Districts of Iowa and U.S. Tax Court. *Education:* Simpson College (B.A., 1971); St. John's University (J.D., 1975). *Member:* Warren County (Secretary-Treasurer, 1977-1981; Vice President, 1990-1991; President, 1992-1993) and Iowa State Bar Associations; National Association of Criminal Defense Lawyers. ***Email:*** wilsonfowler@yahoo.com

REPRESENTATIVE CLIENTS AND REFERENCES: List Furnished upon Request.

BRADLEY & RILEY PC

Attorneys and Counselors
Established in 1981
TOWER PLACE
ONE SOUTH GILBERT STREET
IOWA CITY, IOWA 52240-3914
Telephone: 319-466-1511
Telecopier: 319-358-5560
URL: http://www.bradleyriley.com

Cedar Rapids, Iowa Office: 2007 First Avenue SE, 52406-2804. Telephone: 319-363-0101. Telecopier: 319-363-9824.

General Practice. Administrative, Antitrust, Arbitration, Banking, Bankruptcy, Civil Trial and Appellate Practice in all State and Federal Courts, Condominiums, Construction, Copyright, Corporate, E-Commerce, Employee Benefits, Environmental, Estate Planning, General Business, Government, Immigration, Insurance, Intellectual Property Labor and Employment Relations, Land Use, Mergers and Acquisitions, Municipal Bonds, Non-Profit, Pension and Profit Sharing, Personal Injury, Probate, Product Liability, Professional Liability, Real Estate, Securities, Taxation, Trademark and Trust Law.

DONALD G. THOMPSON, born Grand Island, Nebraska, July 1, 1949; admitted to bar, 1976, Nebraska, U.S. District Court, District of Nebraska and U.S. Court of Appeals, Eighth Circuit; 1983, Iowa and U.S. District Court, Northern and Southern Districts of Iowa; 1990, U.S. Supreme Court; 1992, U.S. District Court, Central District of Illinois; 1993, U.S. Court of Appeals, Seventh Circuit and U.S. Tax Court. *Education:* University of Nebraska at Lincoln (B.A., 1971; J.D., with distinction, 1976). Order of the Coif. Member, 1974-1975 and Competition Supervisor, 1975-1976, Allen Moot Court Board. Faculty Member: National Institute for Trial Advocacy, Mid-America Regional, 1984-1985, 1988-1991, 1994; Pacific Regional, 1990-1991; Southern California Regional, 1991; Deposition Program, Denver, 1990, 1992; Drake Legal Services Program, 2003. Past President, Dean Mason L. Ladd Inn of Court, 1991-1992. *Member:* Linn County, Iowa State (Chair, Federal Practice Committee, 1991-1995; Litigation Section Council, 1996-1999; Law Practice Management Section Council, 2000-2003), Nebraska State and American (Construction Industry Forum-Iowa Casenotes Editor of Construct, 2001—; Dispute Resolution, Law Practice Management, and Litigation Sections) Bar Associations; Iowa Trial Lawyers Association; The Association of Trial Lawyers of America; Defense Research Institute. ***PRACTICE AREAS:*** Civil Trials; Commercial Litigation; Construction Law; Appeals; Mediation; Arbitration. ***Email:*** dthompson@bradleyriley.com

PAUL D. BURNS, born Waterloo, Iowa, March 2, 1967; admitted to bar, 1993, Iowa; 1995, U.S. District Court, Southern and Northern Districts of Iowa. *Education:* University

(This Listing Continued)

of Northern Iowa (B.A., 1989); University of Iowa (J.D., with high distinction, 1993). Order of the Coif (1993). Articles Editor, Iowa Law Review, Vol. 78, 1992-1993. Law Clerk to the Hon. Harold D. Vietor, U.S. District Judge, Southern District of Iowa, 1993-1995. Contributor to: the Iowa section in the 50 State Survey of Payment Provisions in Construction Contacts, ABA Construction Lawyer Journal, Vol. 24 No. 4 (2004). Author: "Construction Contracting and Change Orders," Lorman Education Services (2004); "Overview of Mechanic's Lien Law in Iowa," Lorman Education Services (2003); "Licensing Issues in Design-Build," Lorman Education Services (2002); "Iowa Public Bidding Law," Lorman Education Services (2002); "Iowa Code Chapter 573" (Public Contracting), Lorman Education Services (2002); "State and Federal MBE/DBE Requirements," Lorman Education Services (2001). Co-author: "Computer Law" chapter in the Iowa Legal Research Guide (2003). Speaker, "Spoilation of Evidence: What Every Defense Lawyer Needs to Know," Iowa Defense Counsel Association Seminar (2005). *Member:* Linn County, Iowa State (Vice-Chair, Federal Practice Committee, 2005-2006; Chair, e-Commerce Section Council) and American Bar Associations (Litigation Section); Dean Mason Ladd Inn of Court. ***PRACTICE AREAS:*** Commercial Litigation. ***Email:*** pburns@bradleyriley.com

MICHAEL J. PUGH, born Pomona, California, July 16, 1965; admitted to bar, 1991, Illinois; 1992, U.S. District Court, Northern District of Illinois; 1994, Iowa. *Education:* University of Iowa (B.A., 1987); Indiana University (J.D., 1991). Co-Author: "Limited Liability Partnerships and Limited Liability Companies in Iowa,: 2001; "Limited Liability Companies in Iowa," 2002; "Iowa Land Use," 2003; "Zoning and Land Use in Iowa," 2004. President, Greater Iowa City Area Homebuilder's Association, 2005. Adjunct Lecturer, University of Iowa College of Business. Assistant State's Attorney, Cook County, Illinois, 1991-1994. Formerly with, Phelan, Tucker, Mullen, Walker, Tucker & Gelman, L.L.P., Iowa City, Iowa, 1994-2003. *Member:* Johnson County (Co-Chair, Title Standards/Real Estate Committee, 1999—), Iowa State (Member: Business Law Section Council, 2002—; Limited Liability Companies Subcommittee; Real Estate and Title Law Section; Probate and Trust Law Section) and American (Member: Forum on the Construction Industry; Business Law Section; Partnerships and Unincorporated Business Organizations Committee; Real Property, Probate and Trust Section) Bar Associations; Urban Land Institute. ***PRACTICE AREAS:*** Real Estate; Zoning, Planning and Land Use; Construction Law; Business Law; Banking Law; Wills; Trust Law. ***Email:*** mpugh@bradleyriley.com

---

SARAH E. SWARTZENDRUBER, born Iowa City, Iowa, April 30, 1976; admitted to bar, 2001, Iowa. *Education:* University of Iowa (B.A., 1997; J.D., with high distinction, 2001). Order of the Coif. Adjunct Lecturer, University of Iowa College of Business. Formerly with, Phelan, Tucker, Mullen, Walker, Tucker & Gelman, L.L.P., 2001-2003. Author: "Use of LLCs in Real Estate Transactions" as published in LLCs: Advising Small Business Start-Ups and Larger Companies by Lorman Business Center, Inc. (2005); "Restrictive Covenants and Common Interest Community Issues" as published in Current Land Development Issues in Iowa by Lorman Business Center, Inc. (2005). *Member:* Johnson County, Iowa State and American (Member: Business Law Section; Real Property, Probate and Trust Section) Bar Associations; Urban Land Institute. ***PRACTICE AREAS:*** Business Law; Real Estate; Contracts; Commercial Transactions; Construction Law; Zoning, Planning and Land Use. ***Email:*** sswartzendruber@bradleyriley.com

JOSEPH W. YOUNKER, born Decatur, Indiana; admitted to bar, 2005, Iowa. *Education:* Creighton University (B.A., 2001); University of Iowa College of Law (J.D., 2005).

AIMEE H. RHODES, born 1973; admitted to bar, 1999, Missouri. *Education:* Boston University (B.A., 1995); St. Louis University (J.D. 1999). ***PRACTICE AREAS:*** Taxation. ***Email:*** arhodes@bradleyriley.com

REPRESENTATIVE CLIENTS: Ahrens Concrete Company; Alliant Energy; APAC Customer Services, Inc.; Arlington Development, Inc.; Berthel Fisher & Company Financial Services, Inc.; Berthel Growth & Income Trust I; Bjornsen Investment Company; Blackford Farms, Inc.; Cardiologists, P.C.; Cedar Rapids Bank and Trust Company; Cellular Engineering Technologies, Inc.; Chubb Group of Insurance Companies; Collins Community Credit Union; Commercial Federal Bank; The Dexter Company; ESCO Electric Company; Fastek International, Ltd.; FOX 28 KFXA; Guaranty Bank and Trust Co.; Heartland Hotel Corp.; High Development Corp.; Highway Equipment Company; Hills Bank and Trust Company; Intuit, Inc.; Iowa Eye Center, P.C.; Iowa First Capital Fund, LP; Iowa Glass Depot, Inc.; Iowa Land and Building Co.; Investamerica Investment Advisors, Inc.; King's Material, Inc.; Kirkwood Community College; Knutson Construction Services Midwest, Inc.; K's Merchandise; Lil' Drug Store Products, Inc.; Linn Area Credit Union; Linn County OB-GYN, P.C.; Manpower Inc. of Cedar Rapids; Master Builders of Iowa (AGC Building Chapter of Iowa); Maxwell Construction, Inc.; McLeodUSA Incorporated; Merit Construction Company; MidAmerica Housing Partnership; Millhiser-Smith Insurance Agency, Inc.; MorAmerica Capital Corporation; Mount Mercy College; National Computer Systems, Inc.; Physicians Clinics of Iowa; Prime Ventures Development Inc.; Regency Homes of Eastern Iowa, L.C.; Roy J. Carver Charitable Trust; Telecommunications Income Fund IX, X & XI L.P.; United Fire & Casualty Co.; United Life Insurance Co.; University of Iowa Foundation; U.S. Bank, N.A.; Wells Fargo Bank, N.A.; Wholesale Feeds, Inc.; Worley Warehousing, Inc.; Woodward Communications, Inc.; Yellow Book.
REFERENCES: US Bank; Collins Community Credit Union.

BRAY & KLOCKAU, P.L.C.

402 SOUTH LINN STREET
IOWA CITY, IOWA 52240
Telephone: 319-338-7968
Fax: 319-354-4871
Email: brayklockau@bkfamilylaw.com
URL: http://www.lawyers.com/bray&klockau

Practice Limited to Domestic Relations, Family Law and Adoption Law.

DANIEL L. BRAY, born Bottineau, North Dakota, February 25, 1947; admitted to bar, 1973, Iowa; U.S. District Court, Northern and Southern Districts of Iowa. *Education:* University of Iowa (B.A., 1969; J.D., 1972). Author: *Iowa Matrimonial Law,* Butterworth Legal Publishers, 1994; "What is Equitable Distribution Anyway?" 2000; "The Effect of Bankruptcy on Domestic Relations," 1993; "The Preparation and Trial of Child Custody Cases: Back to Basics," 1993; "Iowa's Premarital Agreement Act," 1992; "Interface Between Family Law and Bankruptcy Law," 1992. Editor, ISBA Family Law Report, 1990-1994. Member, Iowa House of Representatives, 1971-1972. Chairman, Iowa Supreme Court Advisory Committee on Juvenile Rules of Procedure, 1975-1985. *Member:* Johnson County, Iowa State (Chair, Family Law Section, 2003-2005) and American (Member: Family Law Section; Publication Board of Family Law Section) Bar Associations. Fellow: American Academy of Matrimonial Lawyers. ***PRACTICE AREAS:*** Domestic Relations; Family Law.

(This Listing Continued)

LORI L. KLOCKAU, born Fort Madison, Iowa, December 26, 1953; admitted to bar, 1991, Iowa. *Education:* University of Iowa (B.S., 1980; M.A., with honors, 1982; J.D., 1991). Editor, ISBA Family Law Report, 1991-1994. Co-Editor, ISBA Family Law Section Newsletter, 2003-2005. Co-Author: "Promoting a Healthy Tomorrow Here for Children Adopted from Abroad," Contemporary Pediatrics Issue, February 2003. Author: "Adoption by Same-Sex Couples," October 21, 2004; "Adoption Law in Iowa," August 20, 2003; "Termination of Parental Rights and Iowa Adoption Law," October 9, 2002; "Making Visitation Fit the Child," June 20, 2002; "Alimony, Making the Payer's Case and Making the Recipient's Case," October 26, 2001; "Domestic Law in Iowa," September 14, 2001; "Adoption Primer," May 31, 2001; Adoption Law in Iowa Terminating Parental Rights - Laws You Need to Be Aware Of," March 29, 2001; "Adoption Law in Iowa," September, 14, 1999; "Adoption Law Update," October 16, 1998; "Tax Aspects of Divorce," May 30, 1997; "Adoption in Iowa," April 24, 1997; "The Basics of Spousal Support," June 18, 1997; "Tax Clauses in Divorce Settlements and Decrees," October 3-4, 1996; "Termination of Parental Rights and Adoption in Iowa," November 11, 1994; "The Bounds of Advocacy," October 8, 1993; "The Preparation and Trial of Child Custody Cases," June 1993. *Member:* Johnson County (Chair, Family Law Committee, 1993-1994), Iowa State (Member, Committee on Adoption) and American (Member, Family Law Section; Co-Chair, Adoption Committee) Bar Associations; American Academy of Adoption Attorneys. ***PRACTICE AREAS:*** Domestic Relations; Family Law; Adoption.

ASSOCIATES

CHAD A. KEPROS, born Cedar Rapids, Iowa, August 1, 1971; admitted to bar, 1996, Iowa. *Education:* Coe College (B.A., magna cum laude, 1993); University of Iowa (J.D., with high distinction, 1996). Co-Editor, ISBA Family Law Report, 2003-2005. Co-Editor, ISBA Family Law Report, 2003-2005. Author: "Organizing the Statement of the Case and Facts and the Appendix," 1998; "Support Master: Spitting Out More Than Numbers," 2002; "Web Resources for the Family Law Lawyer," 2003; "Strategies for the Family Law Appeal," 2003. *Member:* Johnson County, Iowa State (Member, Family Law Section, 1996—) and American (Member, Family Law Section, 1996—) Bar Associations. ***PRACTICE AREAS:*** Domestic Relations; Family Law.

KIMBERLY M. MURPHY, born Des Moines, Iowa, March 6, 1977; admitted to bar, 2004, Iowa. *Education:* Iowa State University (B.A., with honors, 1999); University of Iowa (J.D., 2004). *Member:* Johnson County, Iowa State (Member: Family Law Section; Young Lawyers Division; YLD Mock Trial Committee; YLD Domestic Abuse Committee) and American (Young Lawyers Section) Bar Associations. ***PRACTICE AREAS:*** Domestic Relations; Family Law.

MARTIN DIAZ LAW FIRM

Established in 1996

528 SOUTH CLINTON STREET
IOWA CITY, IOWA 52240
Telephone: 319-339-4350
Fax: 319-339-4426
URL: http://www.lawyers.com/diazlaw

Plaintiffs Personal Injury, Automobile Accidents and Injuries, Medical Malpractice, Civil Rights.

FIRM PROFILE: Martin Diaz Law Firm was established in 1996 serving clients throughout the state of Iowa with an emphasis in Johnson County. The firm engages in medical malpractice and personal injury practice. The firm has available effective, trained support personnel.

MARTIN A. DIAZ, born Cali, Colombia, September 28, 1958; admitted to bar, 1983, Minnesota; 1984; 1989, Iowa and U.S. Claims Court; 1990, U.S. District Court, Southern District of Iowa; 1991, U.S. District Court, Northern District of Iowa and U.S. Court of Appeals, Eighth Circuit; 1999, U.S. District Court, Central District of Illinois. *Education:* Creighton University (B.S.B.A., cum laude, 1980; J.D., cum laude, 1983); University of Oregon. Beta Gamma Sigma. Recipient, Superior Leadership Award, Creighton University Black Faculty and Administrators, 1983. *Member:* Johnson County and Iowa State Bar Associations; The Association of Trial Lawyers of America; Iowa Trial Lawyers Association; Iowa Academy of Trial Lawyers. ***LANGUAGES:*** Spanish.

EELLS & TRONVOLD LAW OFFICES, P.L.C.

IOWA CITY, IOWA
(See Cedar Rapids)

General Practice with emphasis on Personal Injury, Litigation, Probate and Estate Planning, Trusts and Wills, Business Law and Mediation.

DAVIS L. FOSTER

Established in 1994

703 SOUTH CLINTON
P.O. BOX 720
IOWA CITY, IOWA 52244
Telephone: 319-339-7727
Fax: 319-339-7712
Email: dfoster@fosterlaw.com
URL: http://www.davisfoster.com

Trials and Appeals in State and Federal Courts, Civil Litigation, Criminal Litigation, Personal Injury and Medical Malpractice Law.

(This Listing Continued)

DAVIS L. FOSTER, Iowa City—Continued

FIRM PROFILE: Foster Law Offices strives to meet the litigation needs of Eastern Iowa residents. Davis Foster maintains an extensive practice in Personal Injury and Trial Law. His practice includes all aspects of civil and criminal law trial matters. Mr. Davis' background and experience allows him to provide a full range of state and federal legal services commonly sought by Eastern Iowans.

DAVIS L. FOSTER, born Clarinda, Iowa, June 4, 1956; admitted to bar, 1981, Iowa; U.S. District Court, Northern and Southern Districts of Iowa. *Education:* University of Iowa (B.A., 1978; J.D., with distinction, 1981). *Member:* Johnson County, Iowa State and American Bar Associations; Iowa Trial Lawyers Association; The Association of Trial Lawyers of America. ***REPORTED CASES:*** Berg v. Des Moines General Hospital Co., 456 NW 2d 173 (Iowa 1990); Miller v. Component Homes, Inc., 356 NW 2d 213 (Iowa 1989). ***PRACTICE AREAS:*** Trial Practice; Personal Injury; Criminal Law.

GARTELOS, WAGNER & AMENT

IOWA CITY, IOWA

(See Waterloo)

General Trial Practice and Appeals. Corporation, Family, Insurance, Personal Injury, Real Estate, Probate, Estate Planning, Workers Compensation and Bankruptcy Law.

HAYEK, HAYEK, BROWN, MORELAND & HAYEK, L.L.P.

Established in 1926

120 1/2 EAST WASHINGTON STREET
IOWA CITY, IOWA 52240-3976
Telephone: 319-337-9606
Fax: 319-338-7376
URL: http://www.hhbmlaw.com
URL: http://www.lawyers.com/hhbm

General Practice, Real Estate, Municipal, Probate, Family Law, Trusts and Estates, Insurance, Criminal, Banking Law, Bankruptcy Law, Business and Corporate Law. Trials and Appeals in all Courts.

FIRM PROFILE: Hayek, Hayek, Brown, Moreland & Hayek, L.L.P. was founded in 1926 by Will J. Hayek. Having started with a local general practice, the firm now serves Eastern Iowa, particularly Johnson, Linn, Cedar, Iowa and Washington Counties, with a wide range of legal services.

MEMBERS OF THE FIRM

WILL J. HAYEK (1896-1982)

JOHN W. HAYEK, born Iowa City, Iowa, January 25, 1941; admitted to bar, 1966, Iowa; 1967, U.S. District Court, Southern District of Iowa; 1968, U.S. District Court, Northern District of Iowa; 1973, U.S. Court of Appeals, Eighth Circuit. *Education:* Harvard University (B.A., cum laude, 1963; J.D., 1966). Dean Mason Ladd American Inn of Court (Emeritus Master). First Assistant County Attorney, Johnson County, 1967-1970. City Attorney, Iowa City, 1974-1981. Special Counsel to City of Iowa City for Urban Renewal, 1970-1990. Member, Sixth Judicial District Nominating Commission, 1978-1983. Member, Iowa Supreme Court Family Court Committee, 1989. Chairperson, Sixth Judicial District Bench-Bar Liaison Committee, 1990-1995. Member, Sixth Judicial District Caseflow Management Committee, 1995-1996. *Member:* Johnson County (President, 1982-1983), Iowa State (Title Standards Committee, 1991-1998; Chair, Law Practice Management Section, 2001-2002) and American Bar Associations; Association of Trial Lawyers of Iowa; National Board of Trial Advocacy; Iowa Defense Counsel Association. Fellow, Iowa Academy of Trial Lawyers. ***PRACTICE AREAS:*** Litigation; Estate Planning Law; Domestic Relations Law; Real Estate Law; Family Law. ***Email:*** jhayek@hhbmlaw.com

DAVID E. BROWN, born Waukon, Iowa, January 6, 1949; admitted to bar, 1980, Iowa; 1981, U.S. District Court, Northern and Southern Districts of Iowa; 1988, U.S. Court of Appeals, Eighth Circuit; 1993, U.S. Supreme Court. *Education:* University of Iowa (B.A., 1971; J.D., 1974; M.A., 1978). Phi Beta Kappa. Assistant City Attorney, Iowa City, 1980-1987. City Attorney, City of Riverside, 1992-1993. *Member:* Johnson County and Iowa State Bar Associations; Iowa Defense Counsel Association. ***PRACTICE AREAS:*** Criminal Defense Law; Civil Defense Litigation; Domestic Relations Law. ***Email:*** dbrown@hhbmlaw.com

JOSEPH T. MORELAND, born Ottumwa, Iowa, April 29, 1970; admitted to bar, 1995, Iowa and U.S. District Court, Northern and Southern Districts of Iowa. *Education:* University of Notre Dame (B.A., 1992); University of Iowa College of Law (J.D., with distinction, 1994). Member, Journal of Corporate Law, 1993-1994. *Member:* Johnson County (Legal Aid Committee), Iowa State (Executive Council, Young Lawyers Division, 1998—; President, 2004-2005) and American Bar Associations; Iowa Association of Trial Lawyers; Association of Trial Lawyers of America; Iowa Defense Counsel Association. ***PRACTICE AREAS:*** Litigation; Real Estate Law; Criminal Defense; Domestic Relations Law. ***Email:*** moreland@hhbmlaw.com

MATTHEW J. HAYEK, born Iowa City, Iowa, December 5, 1969; admitted to bar, 1997, Georgia; 1999, Illinois and U.S. District Court, Northern District of Illinois; 2000, U.S. Court of Appeals, Seventh Circuit; 2001, Iowa; 2003, U.S. District Court, Northern and Southern Districts of Iowa. *Education:* University of Michigan (B.A., with honors, 1992; J.D., 1997). Recipient, Carl Gussin Memorial Prize. Editor, Michigan Journal of International Law. Volunteer, U.S. Peace Corps, Bolivia, 1992-1994. Chairperson: Iowa City Housing and Community Development Commission; Iowa City Scattered Site Housing Taskforce. *Member:* Johnson County and Iowa State (Member, Young Lawyers Division Executive Council) Bar Associations; Iowa Trial Lawyers Association; Iowa Defense Counsel Association; Dean Mason Ladd American Inn of Court. ***LANGUAGES:*** Spanish. ***PRACTICE AREAS:*** Litigation; Real Estate Law; Domestic Relations; Commercial Transactions; Banking Law. ***Email:*** mhayek@hhbmlaw.com

(This Listing Continued)

ASSOCIATE

ALISON W. SMITH, born Grinnell, Iowa, February 18, 1974; admitted to bar, 1999, Iowa and U.S. District Court, Southern District of Iowa; 2003, U.S. District Court, Northern District of Iowa. *Education:* University of Iowa (B.A., 1996; J.D. with distinction, 1998). Phi Alpha Delta. Clerk, Fifth Judicial District of Iowa, 1998-2000. Judicial Clerk, Iowa Court of Appeals, 2000-2003. Author: Chapter 3, *Iowa Legal Research Guide,* Drake University Law School, 2003. Member, National Debate Coaches Association, 1999—. Member, Planning and Zoning Commission, North Liberty, Iowa, 2003-2006. *Member:* Polk County, Johnson County and Iowa State (Member, Executive Council, 2000-2003 and Chair, State Fair Committee, 2001-2003, Young Lawyers Division; Member, Legal Heritage Committee, 2000-2003) Bar Associations; Iowa Organization of Women Attorneys; Dean Mason Ladd American Inn of Court. ***PRACTICE AREAS:*** Litigation; Domestic Relations; Appellate Practice; Criminal Defense; Civil Practice. ***Email:*** awsmith@hhbmlaw.com

OF COUNSEL

C. PETER HAYEK, born Iowa City, Iowa, October 26, 1944; admitted to bar, 1973, Iowa; 1974, U.S. District Court, Northern and Southern Districts of Iowa and U.S. Court of Appeals, Eighth Circuit; 1980, U.S. Tax Court. *Education:* Stanford University (B.A., 1966); University of Iowa (J.D., 1973). Iowa Judicial Magistrate, Johnson County, Iowa, 1973-1974. Chairperson, Johnson County Civil Service Commission, 1984—; Domestic Relations Mediator. Member, Johnson County Magistrate Appointing Commission, 1995. *Member:* Johnson County (President, 1996-1997), Iowa State (Member, Board of Governors, 1985-1988) and American Bar Associations. [Captain, USNR, active duty, 1966-1970]. ***PRACTICE AREAS:*** Real Estate Law; Domestic Relations; Probate Law; Commercial Transactions. ***Email:*** phayek@hhbmlaw.com

REPRESENTATIVE CLIENTS: Farmers & Merchants Savings Bank, Lone Tree, Iowa; City of Iowa City; River Products Co.; GRE Insurance Group; United Fire & Casualty Co.; Nationwide Insurance Co.; Continental Western Insurance Co.; American Bankers Insurance; American Family Insurance; Amerisure Company-MD; Austin Mutual Insurance; Connecticut Indemnity Company; Go America Auto Insurance; Orion Companies; Workmen's Auto Insurance Company; Iowa State Bank & Trust Company; Citi-Capital Commercial Corporation; General Growth Properties, Inc.; American Board of Pediatric Dentistry.
REFERENCES: Farmers & Merchants Savings Bank.

HAYES LORENZEN LAWYERS, PLC

PLAZA CENTRE ONE, SUITE 580
125 DUBUQUE STREET
IOWA CITY, IOWA 52244
Telephone: 319-887-3688
Fax: 319-887-3687
URL: http://www.lawyers.com/lorenzenlaw

Medical Malpractice.

JAMES P. HAYES, born Forest City, Iowa, August 4, 1938; admitted to bar, 1964, Iowa; 1996, U.S. District Court, Northern and Southern Districts of Iowa. *Education:* Loras College (B.A., 1960); University of Iowa (J.D., 1964). Phi Delta Phi. Deputy, State Public Safety Commissioner, 1964-1967. Director, Iowa Crime Commission, 1967-1968. *Member:* Johnson County (Secretary, 1969-1970; President, 1999-2000), Iowa State (Vice-Chair, Professionalism Committee, 1989-1990; Member, Litigation Section Council, 1990-1992) and American Bar Associations; Iowa Trial Lawyers Association (Member, Board of Governors, 1981-1987); The Association of Trial Lawyers of America. Fellow: Iowa Academy of Trial Lawyers (Board of Governors, 1991-1993; Vice President, 1993-1994; President, 1994-1995); American College of Trial Lawyers (State Chair, 2002-2004). ***PRACTICE AREAS:*** Medical Malpractice; Products Liability; Personal Injury. ***Email:*** jhayes@hlplc.com

KAREN A. LORENZEN, born Port Jefferson, New York, January 24, 1966; admitted to bar, 1993, Florida and U.S. District Court, Middle District of Florida; 1998, Iowa; 1999, U.S. District Court, Northern District of Iowa. *Education:* University of Iowa (B.S., with honors, 1988; J.D., with distinction, 1992). *Member:* Orange County, Johnson County and American Bar Associations; Iowa Trial Lawyers Association; The Association of Trial Lawyers of America. ***PRACTICE AREAS:*** Medical Malpractice; Personal Injury; Products Liability. ***Email:*** klorenzen@hlplc.com

IULIA ALBUL, born Chisianau, Moldoua, December 21, 1976; admitted to bar, 2003, Iowa. *Education:* The Academy of Economic Studies of Moldoua (B.A., 1999); University of Iowa College of Law (J.D., 2002). Johnson County, Iowa State and American Bar Associations; American Immigration Lawyers Association. ***LANGUAGES:*** Russian, Romanian, French, Spanish. ***Email:*** ialbul@hlplc.com

JACKSON & JACKSON P.L.C.

IOWA CITY, IOWA

(See Cedar Rapids)

Family Law, Adoptions, Child Custody, Child Support, Divorce, Domestic Violence, Visitation Rights, Real Estate, Probate, and Civil Trial Practice, Wills, Trusts, Estates.

JOHNSTON & NATHANSON, P.L.C.

Established in 1968

1902 BROADWAY
P.O. BOX 3400
IOWA CITY, IOWA 52244
Telephone: 319-354-1712
Fax: 319-354-7265
URL: http://www.jpnlaw.com
Email: jpnlaw@jpnlaw.com
URL: http://www.lawyers.com/johnstonnathanson

Cedar Rapids Office: 129 First Avenue, S.W., P.O. Box 74210. Telephone: 319-366-1000. Fax: 319-366-6973.

Personal Injury, Property Damage, Trial Practice, Corporation and Business, Debt and Bankruptcy, Estate Planning, Tax, Real Estate, Criminal, Domestic Relations, Workers Compensation, Business Litigation.

JOSEPH C. JOHNSTON, admitted to bar, 1968, Iowa. *Education:* University of Iowa (B.B.A., 1966; J.D., 1968).

JON R. PEARCE, admitted to bar, 1966, Iowa; 1981, California. *Education:* Minnesota State University, Mankato (B.A., 1963); Drake University (J.D., 1966).

DAVID BURBIDGE, admitted to bar, 1994, Minnesota; 1996, Iowa. *Education:* St. John's University (B.A., 1990); University of Minnesota (J.D., 1994).

CONSTANCE PESCHANG STANNARD, admitted to bar, 1985, Iowa. *Education:* MacMurray College (B.A., 1973); University of Iowa (J.D., 1985).

STEVEN G. KLESNER, admitted to bar, 1991, Iowa. *Education:* Central College (B.A., 1986); University of Iowa (J.D., 1990).

JACOB R. KOLLER, admitted to bar, 2003, Iowa. *Education:* Western Illinois University (B.A., 1999); University of Iowa (J.D., 2003).

KRUG LAW FIRM, P.L.C.

IOWA CITY, IOWA

(See Cedar Rapids)

General Civil Trial Practice emphasizing Insurance Defense, Labor and Employment Law (Management), Railroad/Transportation, Workers' Compensation, Mediation and Family Law.

LEFF LAW FIRM, LLP

Established in 1931

222 SOUTH LINN STREET
P.O. BOX 2447
IOWA CITY, IOWA 52244-2447
Telephone: 319-338-7551
FAX: 319-338-6902
Email: lhtw@qwest.net
URL: http://www.lawyers.com/lhts

General Practice. Real Estate, Corporate Law, Banks and Banking, Commercial Law, Insurance, Tax, Probate, Civil Litigation, Workers Compensation, Family Law and Trusts and Estates, Employment Law, Mediation, Arbitration, Divorce, Child Custody, Support and Adoptions.

MEMBERS OF FIRM

ARTHUR O. LEFF (1906-1989)

PHILIP A. LEFF, born Iowa City, Iowa, August 31, 1932; admitted to bar, 1959, Iowa. *Education:* University of Iowa (B.A., 1954; J.D., with Distinction, 1959). Phi Beta Kappa; Phi Delta Phi; Order of the Coif. Adjunct Professor, Title Examination and Real Estate Transactions, College of Law, University of Iowa, 1963—. *Member:* Johnson County (President, 1969-1970), Iowa State (Member, Title Standards Committee, 1990-1998) and American Bar Associations. [First Lieut., USAF, 1955-1958]. ***PRACTICE AREAS:*** Real Estate; Estate Planning; Probate; Corporate Law; Commercial Transactions; Business Law; Trusts and Estates. ***Email:*** lhtw@qwest.net

R. BRUCE HAUPERT, born Marshalltown, Iowa, August 20, 1939; admitted to bar, 1968, Iowa. *Education:* University of Iowa (B.S., 1962; J.D., 1968). Phi Delta Phi. Member, Board of Editors, Iowa Law Review, 1967-1968. U.S. Magistrate, 1971-1976. Member: Iowa Supreme Court Board of Professional Ethics and Conduct, 2001—; Advisory Committee on the Study of the Attorney Disciplinary System, 2001-2002. *Member:* Johnson County, (Chair, Johnson County Young Lawyers Section, 1970-1972; President, 1991-1992); Iowa State (Member, Committee on Title Standards, 1985-1988; Chair, Real Estate and Title Law Section, 1990-1991; Member, 1988-1997 and Chair, Iowa Supreme Court Grievance Commission, 1993-1997; Member, Board of Governors, 1998-2002) and American Bar Associations. [First Lieut., USAF, 1962-1965]. ***PRACTICE AREAS:*** Real Estate; Estate Planning; Business Law; Commercial Transactions; Corporate Law; Trusts and Estates. ***Email:*** bhlhtw@qwest.net

CHARLES T. TRAW, born Chicago, Illinois, May 13, 1941; admitted to bar, 1967, Iowa and Oregon. *Education:* University of Iowa (B.A., 1963; J.D., with highest distinction, 1967). Phi Delta Phi. Comments Editor, Iowa Law Review, 1966-1967. Certified Mediator: American Academy of ADR Attorneys; Chartered Institute of Arbitrators. *Member:* Johnson County, Iowa State (Member, Sections on: Alternative Dispute Resolution, Litigation Committee, Employment Law, Health Law, International Law), Federal and American Bar Associations; Association of Trial Lawyers of Iowa; The Association of Trial Lawyers of America; Iowa Defense Counsel Association; Defense Research Institute; Chartered Institute of Arbitrators. Fellow, Iowa Academy of Trial Lawyers. ***PRACTICE AREAS:*** Civil Litigation; Personal Injury; Business Litigation; Commercial Litigation; Mediation; Commercial Arbitration. ***Email:*** cttlhtw@qwest.net

RANDALL B. WILLMAN, born Hartford City, Indiana, February 10, 1957; admitted to bar, 1983, Iowa. *Education:* University of Iowa (B.A., 1979); University of Iowa (J.D., with high distinction, 1983). *Member:* Johnson County, Iowa State and American Bar Associations; Iowa Defense Counsel Association (Board of Directors, 2003—); Association of Trial Lawyers of Iowa. Master, Dean Mason Ladd Inn of Court (Board Member). ***PRACTICE AREAS:*** Civil Litigation; Personal Injury; Defense Litigation; Family Law. ***Email:*** rbwlhtw@qwest.net

STEVEN E. BALLARD, born Denver, Colorado, December 9, 1962; admitted to bar, 1990, Iowa. *Education:* Drake University (B.A., 1986); The University of Iowa College of Law (J.D., with distinction, 1989). Law Clerk to the Fifth Judicial District of Iowa, 1989-1991. *Member:* Johnson County, Iowa State and American Bar Associations; Iowa Trial Lawyers Association; The Association of Trial Lawyers of America; Iowa Municipal Attorneys Association. ***PRACTICE AREAS:*** Civil Litigation; Personal Injury; Municipal Law; Business Litigation; Commercial Litigation. ***Email:*** sballard_lhtw@qwest.net

MARK C. DANIELSON, born Fairfield, Iowa, May 13, 1964; admitted to bar, 1989, Iowa. *Education:* Iowa State University (B.S., 1986); University of Iowa School of Law (J.D., with distinction, 1989). *Member:* Johnson County, Iowa State (Member, Real Estate and Title Law Section, 1994-1998) and American Bar Associations. ***PRACTICE AREAS:*** Real Estate; Estate Planning; Probate; Commercial Transactions; Corporate Law; Business Law; Trusts and Estates. ***Email:*** mdanielson_lhtw@qwest.net

ASSOCIATES

PATRICK J. FORD, born Keosauqua, Iowa, July 6, 1968; admitted to bar, 2004, Iowa. *Education:* University of Iowa (B.A., 1998; J.D., with highest distinction, 2003). *Member:* Johnson County, Iowa State and American Bar Associations. ***PRACTICE AREAS:*** Real Estate; Corporate Law; Commercial Transactions; Municipal Law; Trusts and Estates.

JENNIFER K. WENDTGEISLER, born Sioux City, Iowa, January 15, 1975; admitted to bar, 2002, Iowa. *Education:* University of Iowa (B.A., 1997; J.D., 2002). Editor, Education of Tax Manual, Taxation Section, Iowa State Bar Association. *Member:* Johnson County, Iowa County (President, 2003-2004), Iowa State (Chair, Taxation Section, 2005-2006; Member, Real Estate Section) and American Bar Associations. ***LANGUAGES:*** American Sign Language. ***PRACTICE AREAS:*** Business Law; Commercial Real Estate; Corporate Law; Probate; Probate Taxation; Real Estate; Taxation; Trusts and Estates; Wills.

REPRESENTATIVE CLIENTS: The Proctor & Gamble Manufacturing Co.; City of University Heights, Iowa; University of Iowa; University of Iowa Hospitals and Clinics; Home Health Services, Inc.; Hawkeye State Bank; Brenton Bank; Allied Group Insurance; Chubb Group of Insurance Companies; Executive Risk Management Associates; State Farm Mutual Automobile Insurance Co; State Farm Fire and Casualty Co.; Iowa City Association of Realtors; Frantz Construction Co.; Hartwig Motors, Inc.

PAUL McANDREW LAW FIRM

IOWA CITY, IOWA

(See Coralville)

Workers' Compensation, Social Security.

MEARDON, SUEPPEL & DOWNER P.L.C.

Established in 1948

122 SOUTH LINN STREET
IOWA CITY, IOWA 52240
Telephone: 319-338-9222
Fax: 319-338-7250
URL: http://www.meardonlaw.com

General Practice.

WILLIAM L. MEARDON (1919-1997)

ROBERT N. DOWNER, born Newton, Iowa, July 15, 1939; admitted to bar, 1963, Iowa. *Education:* University of Iowa (B.A., 1961; J.D., 1963). Phi Delta Phi; Omicron Delta Kappa. Member, Board of Trustees, Iowa City Public Library, 1971-1975. Member, Iowa Supreme Court Commission on Continuing Legal Education, 1975-1983. *Member:* Johnson County (President, 1976), Iowa State (Member, 1983-1990 and Co-Chair, 1988-1990, Committee on Probate, Property and Trust Law; Chair, Probate and Trust Law Section, 1990-1993; Vice President, 1993-1994; President-Elect, 1994-1995; President, 1995—) and American (Member, Committee on Commercial Financial Services, Section on Business Law; Committee on Estate and Trust Litigation; Section on Real Property, Probate and Trust Law) Bar Associations. Fellow: American College of Trust and Estate Counsel; American Bar Foundation; Iowa State Bar Foundation.

JAMES D. McCARRAGHER, born Belvidere, Illinois, July 1, 1946; admitted to bar, 1971, Iowa. *Education:* University of Iowa (B.B.A., 1968; J.D., with distinction, 1971). Phi Delta Phi. Member, Board of Editors, Iowa Law Review, 1970-1971. Author: "The Commission Removal Plan: A Corrective Remedy For Judicial Misconduct in Iowa," 55 Iowa Law Review 1020, 1970; "Public Official and Actual Malice Standards: The Evolution of New York Times Co. v. Sullivan," 56 Iowa Law Review 393, 1970. *Member:* Johnson County, Iowa State and American Bar Associations; Iowa Trial Lawyers Association; The Association of Trial Lawyers of America.

MARK T. HAMER, born Omaha, Nebraska, June 7, 1947; admitted to bar, 1972, Iowa. *Education:* University of Iowa (B.A., 1969; J.D., with distinction, 1972). Phi Delta Phi; Delta Sigma Rho; Tau Kappa Alpha. Member, Industry Advisory Committee to the NASAA Franchise and Business Opportunity Committee, 1986-1989, 1992—. *Member:* Johnson County, Iowa State (Member: Trade Regulation Committee, 1988-1990; Trade Regulation Section Council, 1990-1992) and American Bar Associations.

(This Listing Continued)

MEARDON, SUEPPEL & DOWNER P.L.C., Iowa City—Continued

THOMAS D. HOBART, born Lake City, Iowa, January 1, 1947; admitted to bar, 1974, Iowa and U.S. District Court, Southern and Northern Districts of Iowa; 1988, U.S. Court of Appeals, Eighth Circuit. *Education:* University of Iowa (B.A., 1969; J.D., with highest distinctions, 1974). Phi Delta Phi; Order of the Coif. *Member:* Johnson County (President, 1993-1994), Iowa State and American Bar Associations; The Association of Trial Lawyers of America; The Iowa Trial Lawyers Association. Fellow, Iowa Academy of Trial Lawyers. [With USMC, 1969-1971]

MARGARET T. LAINSON, born Lake City, Iowa, January 20, 1939; admitted to bar, 1976, Iowa. *Education:* University of Iowa (B.A., with high honors, 1960; M.A., 1971; J.D., with distinction, 1976). Phi Beta Kappa; Alpha Lambda Delta. *Member:* Johnson County (Treasurer, 1986-1988), Iowa State (Member, Legal Forms Committee, 1988—; Vice Chair, Iowa Supreme Court Grievance Commission, 1993—; President, 1995—) and American Bar Associations. (Retired)

DOUGLAS D. RUPPERT, born Washington, Iowa, February 5, 1957; admitted to bar, 1982, Iowa. *Education:* University of Iowa (B.A., with high honors, 1979; J.D., with distinction, 1982). *Member:* Johnson County, Iowa State and American Bar Associations.

TIMOTHY J. KRUMM, born Newton, Iowa, December 29, 1960; admitted to bar, 1986, Iowa. *Education:* Cambridge University, Cambridge, England; St. Olaf College (B.A., 1983); University of Iowa (J.D., 1986). *Member:* Johnson County, Iowa State and American Bar Associations.

WILLIAM J. SUEPPEL, born Iowa City, Iowa, March 12, 1959; admitted to bar, 1985, Iowa. *Education:* St. Ambrose College (B.A., 1981); Hamline University (J.D., 1985). Assistant City Attorney, Waterloo, Iowa, 1985-1987. Assistant City Attorney, Iowa City, Iowa, 1987-1989. *Member:* Johnson County, Iowa State and American Bar Associations; Iowa Municipal Attorneys Association (Regional Vice President, 1988-1989); National Institute of Municipal Law Officers; Iowa Trial Lawyers Association.

CHARLES A. MEARDON, born Iowa City, Iowa, September 13, 1962; admitted to bar, 1989, Iowa. *Education:* University of Iowa (B.A., 1985; J.D., with high distinction, 1989). *Member:* Johnson County, Iowa State and American Bar Associations.

DENNIS J. MITCHELL, born Des Moines, Iowa, July 8, 1968; admitted to bar, 1995, Iowa. *Education:* Drake University (B.A., 1990; J.D., with honors, 1995). Member, Drake Law Review. Author: Note: "All Is Not Fair In War: The Need for a Permanent War Crimes Tribunal, 44 Drake Law Review, No. 3. *Member:* Johnson County, Iowa State and American Bar Associations. ***Email:*** dennism@msdnlaw.com

OF COUNSEL

WILLIAM F. SUEPPEL, born Iowa City, Iowa, September 23, 1929; admitted to bar, 1958, Iowa. *Education:* St. Ambrose College (B.A., 1950); North American College, Rome, Italy (S.T.B., 1953); University of Iowa (J.D., 1958). Phi Delta Phi; Order of the Coif. City Attorney, Iowa City, Iowa, 1961-1963. Safety Commissioner, State of Iowa, 1963-1965. *Member:* Johnson County (President, 1981), Iowa State (Chair, Government Practice Section, 1990) and American Bar Associations; National Institute of Municipal Law Officers. [U.S. Army, 1953-1955]

JEAN BARTLEY, born Perry, Iowa, April 11, 1927; admitted to bar, 1961, Iowa. *Education:* State University of Iowa (B.A., 1953; J.D., 1961). *Member:* Johnson County (President, 1980-1981), Iowa State (Member, Board of Governors, 1981-1985; Chair, CLE Committee, 1985—) and American Bar Associations. ***PRACTICE AREAS:*** Probate; Wills; Taxation-Estate & Gift Tax; Income Tax; Real Estate.

REPRESENTATIVE CLIENTS: United Technologies-Automotive; Hills Bancorporation; Hills Bank and Trust Co.; Perpetual Savings Bank; Metro Pavers, Inc.; League of Iowa Municipalities; Iowa Municipalities Workers Compensation Association; City of North Liberty; City of Muscatine; Lee County; Iowa Book and Supply Co.; Central States Theatre Corp.; Iowa City Ready Mix, Inc.; West Music Company, Inc.; McComas-Lacina Construction Co., Inc.; Selzer-Werderitsch Construction Co., Inc.; Economy Advertising Co.; City Carton Company, Inc.; Iowa Bridge and Culvert, Inc.; J.M. Swank Company, Inc.; Hawkeye Medical Supply, Inc.; Doyle Pacific Trade Co.; Iowa Management Systems, Inc. (Hardees); Diamond Dave's Taco Company, Inc.; Iowa City Apartment Assoc.; Hargrave-McEleney, Inc.; Toyota of Iowa City, Inc.; Carousel Motors, Inc.; ATI, Inc.; Lenoch and Cilek, Inc.; Iowa City Press Citizen; KRNA, Inc.

MELLON & SPIES

Established in 1976

102 S. CLINTON STREET, SUITE 411
IOWA CITY, IOWA 52240
Telephone: 319-337-4193
Fax: 319-337-2396

Family Law and Domestic Relations, State and Federal Criminal and Civil Trial and Appellate Practice.

MEMBERS OF FIRM

SHARON A. MELLON, born Ashtabula, Ohio, January 16, 1946; admitted to bar, 1974, Iowa. *Education:* University of Iowa (B.A., 1969; J.D., with distinction, 1974). *Member:* Johnson County (Vice President, 1987-1988; President, 1988-1989), Iowa State and American (Member, Family Law Section, 1981—) Bar Associations. ***PRACTICE AREAS:*** Family Law; Domestic Relations.

LEON F. SPIES, born Blue Grass, Iowa, October 8, 1950; admitted to bar, 1975, Iowa, U.S. District Court, Northern and Southern Districts of Iowa and U.S. Court of Appeals, Eighth Circuit; 1987, U.S. Supreme Court. *Education:* University of Iowa (B.B.A., with distinction, 1972; J.D., with distinction, 1975). Phi Eta Sigma; Omicron Delta Kappa. Judicial Magistrate, Sixth Judicial District of Iowa, 1978-1983. Instructor, Trial Advocacy, University of Iowa College of Law, 1996—. *Member:* Johnson County (Secretary, 1979-1981; Vice President, 2004-2005), Iowa State (Member, Criminal Law Litigation Section) and American (Member, Committees on: Ethics and Professionalism; Trial Evidence; Trial Practice; Criminal Law Litigation Section) Bar Associations. Fellow: American College of Trial Lawyers; Iowa Academy of Trial Lawyers; Association of Trial Lawyers of Iowa; The Association of Trial Lawyers of America; American Judicature Society; National Association of Criminal Defense Lawyers; American Inns of Court (Master; President, Dean Mason Ladd Inn, 1995-1996). ***PRACTICE AREAS:*** Criminal Law; Civil Trial; Appeals. ***Email:*** Spieslegal@aol.com

REFERENCE: Iowa State Bank & Trust Co.

PECK LAW OFFICE

403 IOWA STATE BANK BUILDING
102 SOUTH CLINTON STREET
IOWA CITY, IOWA 52240
Telephone: 319-351-2332
Fax: 319-358-8873
Email: sallipeck@aol.com
URL: http://www.pecklawoffice.com

Criminal Defense, Felonies, Sexual Abuse, Child Endangerment, Assault, Forgery, Theft, Misdemeanors, Drunk Driving, Family Law, Divorce, Custody, Support, Adoptions, Juvenile Law.

SALLY H. PECK, born Pittsfield, Massachusetts; admitted to bar, 1979, Indiana and U.S. District Court, Southern District of Indiana; 1982, Iowa and U.S. District Court, District of Iowa. *Education:* State University of New York at Cortland (B.A., 1965); Albany Law School; Indiana University (J.D., 1979). Phi Delta Phi. *Member:* Johnson County, Cedar County (Vice President, 1994-1998; President, 1998—), Iowa State, Indiana State and American Bar Associations.

PHELAN, TUCKER, MULLEN, WALKER, TUCKER & GELMAN, L.L.P.

321 EAST MARKET
P.O. BOX 2150
IOWA CITY, IOWA 52244
Telephone: 319-354-1104
Fax: 319-354-6962
URL: http://www.ptmlaw.com

General Civil Practice in State and Federal Courts. Trials, Appeals, Banking, Business Transactions, Contracts, Corporations and Business Entities, Probate and Estate Administration, Wills, Trusts and Estate Planning, Zoning, Land Use and Development, Criminal, Environmental, Exempt Organizations, Hospital and Health Care, Real Estate, Negligence, Workers Compensation, Defense, Tax Planning and Tax Return Preparation and Family Law.

FIRM PROFILE: The firm traces its beginning to 1907. Over the years it has matured into a general practice firm providing a broad mix of legal services to individuals, business entities and exempt organizations.

MEMBERS OF FIRM

LOUIS SHULMAN (1908-1982)

WILLIAM M. TUCKER (1922-2003)

CHARLES A. MULLEN (1937-2001)

BRUCE L. WALKER, born Des Moines, Iowa, July 18, 1946; admitted to bar, 1972, Iowa. *Education:* William Penn College; University of Iowa (B.A., 1968; J.D., with distinction, 1972). *Member:* Iowa State (Member, Uniform Jury Instructions) and American (Member, Trial Evidence Committee, 1982-1985) Bar Associations; Iowa Academy of Trial Lawyers; Iowa Association of Defense Counsel; Defense Research Institute; American Board of Trial Advocates; Association of Defense Trial Attorneys (State Chair, 1998—). ***PRACTICE AREAS:*** Negligence; Plaintiffs Trial Practice; Defense; Trial Practice; Workers Compensation. ***Email:*** walker@ptmlaw.com

RICHARD M. TUCKER, born Iowa City, Iowa, August 30, 1949; admitted to bar, 1975, Iowa. *Education:* Stanford University (B.A., with highest distinction, 1971); Georgetown University; University of Iowa (J.D., with distinction, 1975). *Member:* Johnson County, Iowa State and American Bar Associations; Iowa Association of Defense Counsel; Defense Research Institute; Iowa Academy of Trial Lawyers; American Health Lawyers Association. Fellow, American College of Trial Lawyers. ***PRACTICE AREAS:*** Defense Litigation; Medical Malpractice; Health Law. ***Email:*** tucker@ptmlaw.com

THOMAS H. GELMAN, born Iowa City, Iowa, March 20, 1953; admitted to bar, 1978, Iowa. *Education:* Harvard University (B.A., cum laude, 1975); University of Iowa (J.D., 1978). *Member:* Johnson County, Iowa State and American Bar Associations. ***PRACTICE AREAS:*** General Practice; Contracts; Wills; Trust Law; Estate Planning; Probate; Estate Administration; Real Estate; Corporate Law; Business Law; Business Transactions; Zoning, Planning and Land Use. ***Email:*** gelman@ptmlaw.com

GARY J. SCHMIT, born Hospers, Iowa, January 18, 1963; admitted to bar, 1988, Iowa. *Education:* Briar Cliff College (B.A., summa cum laude, 1985); University of Iowa (J.D., with distinction, 1988). Certified Public Accountant, Iowa, August 1986. *Member:* Johnson County, Iowa State and American Bar Associations. ***PRACTICE AREAS:*** Estate Planning; Probate; Taxation. ***Email:*** schmit@ptmlaw.com

MARGARET P. WINEGARDEN, born Oceanside, California, October 22, 1960; admitted to bar, 1987, Iowa. *Education:* University of Iowa (B.B.A., with highest distinction, 1983; J.D., with distinction, 1986). Assistant County Attorney, Johnson County, 1987-1989. *Member:* Johnson County, Iowa State and American Bar Associations; Iowa Association of Defense Counsel; Defense Research Institute. ***PRACTICE AREAS:*** Defense Litigation; Medical Malpractice Defense. ***Email:*** winegarden@ptmlaw.com

JOHN E. BEASLEY, born Iowa City, Iowa, March 8, 1961; admitted to bar, 1990, Iowa. *Education:* University of Iowa (B.A., 1987; J.D., 1989). Assistant County Attorney,

(This Listing Continued)

Johnson County, 1990-1991. *Member:* Johnson County, Iowa State and American Bar Associations. ***PRACTICE AREAS:*** Trial Practice; Criminal Law; Family Law; Real Estate; Land Use. ***Email:*** beasley@ptmlaw.com

DEAN D. CARRINGTON, born Iowa City, Iowa, February 1, 1958; admitted to bar, 1993, Iowa. *Education:* University of Iowa (B.B.A., 1981; M.A., 1983; J.D., with high distinction, 1993). Certified Public Accountant, Iowa, 1983. *Member:* Johnson County, Iowa State and American Bar Associations. ***PRACTICE AREAS:*** Estate Planning; Probate; Real Estate; Business Transactions. ***Email:*** carrington@ptmlaw.com

SUSAN J. FRYE, born Davenport, Iowa, August 11, 1951; admitted to bar, 1989, Iowa and U.S. District Court, Northern and Southern Districts of Iowa. *Education:* University of Iowa (B.S.N., 1973; J.D., 1989) Dean's List; University of Pennsylvania (M.S.N., 1979). Member: Office of the Governor, Iowa Alliance for Advanced Telecommunications Services. Former State Public Utilities Commissioner. Former Member, Johnson County Board of Health. *Member:* Johnson County, Scott County and Iowa State Bar Associations. ***PRACTICE AREAS:*** Environmental Law; Toxic Torts Litigation; Utility Law; Personal Injury; Medical Malpractice. ***Email:*** frye@ptmlaw.com

WILLIAM V. PHELAN, born Des Moines, Iowa, September 2, 1922; admitted to bar, 1949, Iowa. *Education:* University of Wisconsin; University of Notre Dame (J.D., 1949). Assistant Editor, Notre Dame Lawyer, 1948-1949. Co-Author: with Stephen F. Bright, "McCarty Iowa Probate," 3rd Edition, Lawyers Cooperative Publishing, 1993. Lecturer, College of Law, University of Iowa: Income, Estate and Gift Taxes; State and Local Taxation; Probate Practice; Estate Planning, 1956-1991. *Member:* Johnson County, Iowa State (Member, 1968-1982 and Chairman, 1975-1977, Committee on Taxation) and American Bar Associations. [Armed Forces, 1942-1945]. ***PRACTICE AREAS:*** Estate Planning; Probate; Banking Law; Health Care Litigation; Hospital Law; Tax Exempt Organizations. ***Email:*** phelan@ptmlaw.com

ASSOCIATES

DANIEL W. BOYLE, born Iowa City, Iowa, June 6, 1933; admitted to bar, 1960, Iowa. *Education:* University of Iowa (B.S.C., 1957; J.D., 1960). Phi Delta Phi. Police Judge, Iowa City, Iowa, 1963-1964. County Attorney, 1965-1966. *Member:* Johnson County (President, 1977), Iowa State and American Bar Associations. ***PRACTICE AREAS:*** Estate Planning; Probate; Real Estate; Taxation. ***Email:*** boyle@ptmlaw.com

POPE S. YAMADA, born Ann Arbor, Michigan; admitted to bar, 2003, Iowa. *Education:* Wesleyan University (B.A., 1996); University of Iowa College of Law (J.D., 2003). ***PRACTICE AREAS:*** Civil Litigation; Medical Malpractice; Intellectual Property. ***Email:*** yamada@ptmlaw.com

REPRESENTATIVE CLIENTS: ACT, Inc.; Farm Bureau Mutual Insurance Co.; Heartland Equipment Inc.; Iowa State Bank and Trust Co.; Mercy Hospital, Iowa City; University of Iowa Foundation.

DELL A. RICHARD

IOWA CITY, IOWA

(See Coralville)

Business Law, Commercial Real Estate, Corporate Law, Guardianships and Conservatorships, Leases and Leasing, Partnership Law, Probate, Real Estate Law, Trusts and Estates, Wills.

TOM RILEY LAW FIRM, P.L.C.

1210 HIGHWAY 6 WEST
IOWA CITY, IOWA 52246
Telephone: 319-351-4996
Fax: 319-351-7063
URL: http://www.tomrileylaw.com

Cedar Rapids Office: 4040 First Avenue, N.E., P.O. Box 998. Telephone: 319-363-4040. Fax: 319-363-9789.

Personal Injury, Medical Malpractice, Products Liability, Civil Litigation and corporate Litigation.

(For Complete Biographical Data on all Personnel, see Professional Biographies at Cedar Rapids, Iowa)

RUSH & NICHOLSON, PLC

IOWA CITY, IOWA

(See Cedar Rapids)

Personal Injury, Product Liability, Professional Liability, Labor and Employment, Workers Compensation.

SHUTTLEWORTH & INGERSOLL, P.L.C.

IOWA CITY, IOWA

(See Cedar Rapids)

Administrative Law, Agricultural Law, Alternative Dispute Resolution, Arbitration, Mediation, Antitrust, Unfair Trade, Bankruptcy, Banks and Banking, Biotechnology, Civil Litigation and Appellate Practice in all State and Federal Courts, Civil Rights, Commercial Law, Commercial Real Estate, Communications and Media, Computers and Software, Constitutional Law, Construction Law, Contracts, Copyrights, Corporate Law, Debtor and Creditor, Disabilities, Education Law, Elder Law, Eminent Domain, Employee Benefits, Employment Law, Energy, Environmental Law, Estate Planning, General Practice, Health Care, Hospital Law, Insurance, Insurance Defense, Intellectual Property, Labor, Land Use, Medical Malpractice, Mergers, Acquisitions, and Divestitures, Municipal Law, Natural Resources, Nonprofit and Charitable Organizations, OSHA, Partnership Law, Patents, Personal Injury, Probate, Products Liability,

(This Listing Continued)

Professional Liability, Real Estate, Securities, Tax Law, Technology and Science, Trademarks, Trusts and Estates, Utility Law, Wills, Workers Compensation, Zoning Law.

SIMMONS, PERRINE, ALBRIGHT & ELLWOOD, P.L.C.

Established in 1916

THIRD FLOOR TOWER PLACE
22 SOUTH LINN STREET
IOWA CITY, IOWA 52240
Telephone: 319-887-1368
Fax: 319-887-1372
URL: http://www.simmonsperrine.com

Cedar Rapids Office: 115 Third Street S.E., Suite 1200, 52401. Telephone: 319-366-7641. Telecopier: 319-366-1917.

General Practice. Trial and Appellate Practice, Commercial, Insurance, Personal Injury, Professional Malpractice, Workers' Compensation, Environmental, Labor, Employment, Banking, Bankruptcy, Antitrust and Unfair Competition, Construction and Products Liability, Corporation Practice, Tax, Probate, Estate Planning, Real Estate, Pension, Profit-Sharing and Employee Benefits, ERISA, Mergers and Acquisitions, International and Domestic Patent and Trademark Law and Domestic Copyright Law.

FIRM PROFILE: Simmons, Perrine, Albright & Ellwood, P.L.C. is a full service, eastern Iowa-based law firm providing high quality legal services and holding the performance of its lawyers to the highest ethical standards. We have a long history as a litigation firm in Iowa with extensive experience in federal and state courts, arbitration and mediation in Iowa and across the nation. Simmons, Perrine, Albright & Ellwood, P.L.C. has developed a comprehensive business practice consulting services. With skilled and experienced attorneys in nearly all fields of law, we serve individual and corporate clients from eastern Iowa and throughout the United States.

Our primary headquarters are in Cedar Rapids, Iowa. Our Iowa City office provides all of the services of our firm and a complete listing of all of the members of the firm as well as their biography information can be found in the Cedar Rapids Martindale-Hubbell listing.

GREGORY G. WILLIAMS, born San Diego, California, March 23, 1959; admitted to bar, 1985, Iowa and U.S. District Court, Northern and Southern Districts of Iowa; 1986, U.S. Court of Appeals for the Federal and Eighth Circuits; 2001, U.S. Supreme Court; registered to practice before U.S. Patent and Trademark Office. *Education:* University of Iowa (B.A. in Physics, 1982; J.D., 1985; M.B.A., 1997). Adjunct Instructor of Business Law, University of Iowa and Mount Mercy College. *Member:* Linn County, Johnson County and Iowa State Bar Associations; Iowa Intellectual Property Law Association (Member, Board of Governors, 1988-1991; President, 1999). ***PRACTICE AREAS:*** Patents; Trademark and Unfair Competition; Copyrights. ***Email:*** gwilliams@simmonsperrine.com

REPRESENTATIVE CLIENTS: D.C. Taylor Roofing Co.; Kleiman Construction Co.; Garling Construction Co.; N&N Sanitation Co.; Wells Fargo Bank, N.A.; City of Iowa City; Hills Bank & Trust; Commercial Federal Bank, N.A.; Alliant Energy Resources; Gazette Co.; Grain Processing Corp., a division of Varied Investments, Inc.; Kinze Manufacturing Co.; Crystal Group, Inc.; Diversified Software, Inc.; Amana Company, a Division of Goodman, Inc.; Cedar Memorial Funeral Home Co.; Croell Redi Mix Co.; Pickwick Manufacturing Co.; Grant Wood Area Education Agency; Herbert Hoover Presidential Library; Halls-Perrine Foundation; Greater Cedar Rapids Community Foundation; Raytheon Co.; Cryovac, Inc., a subsidiary of Sealed Air Corporation; Kent Feeds; Penford Products Co.; Weyerhaeuser paper Co.; Longview Fibre Co.; Howard R. Green Co.; Brown, Healey, Stone & Sauer Architects Co.; Varied Investments, Inc.; Norand Corp.; Firstar Bank, N.A.; Iowa Comprehensive Petroleum Underground Storage Tank Fund; Crawford and Company; Intermec Technologies Corp.; IES Utilities, Inc.
REPRESENTATIVE PATENT CLIENTS: Norand Mobile Data Systems; Rockwell International Corporation.
INSURANCE COMPANY CLIENTS: Design Professionals Insurance Co.; American States Insurance Co.; American International Group, Inc.; American International Underwriters; National Union Insurance Cos.; New Hampshire Insurance Group; Allstate Insurance Co.; Grinnell Mutual Reinsurance Co.; Hawkeye-Security Insurance Co.; Milwaukee Mutual Insurance Co.; The St. Paul Cos.; State Farm Fire & Casualty Company; Farmers Casualty Company Mutual; IMT Insurance Company; GAB Business Services; National Chiropractic Mutual Ins. Co.; Prudential Property & Casualty Insurance Company; Pharmacists Mutual Insurance Co.; Reliance Insurance Company; Pacific Employers Insurance Company.

(For complete biographical data on all personnel, see Professional Biographies at Cedar Rapids)

TERPSTRA, EPPING & WILLETT

IOWA CITY, IOWA

(See Cedar Rapids)

Creditors Rights, Real Estate, Civil Litigation, Bankruptcy Litigation, Commercial Transactions, Probate.

RANDY TRCA LAW FIRM

Established in 1981

1232 EAST BURLINGTON STREET
IOWA CITY, IOWA 52240-3212
Telephone: 319-354-8440
Fax: 319-354-8441
Email: RTLAWFIRM@prodigy.net
URL: http://www.randytrcalawoffice.com

Family Law, Personal Injury, Bankruptcy Law.

MEMBER OF FIRM

RANDY E. TRCA, born Mason City, Iowa, March 27, 1957; admitted to bar, 1981, Iowa; 1982, U.S. District Court, Southern and Northern Districts of Iowa. *Education:*

(This Listing Continued)

RANDY TRCA LAW FIRM, Iowa City—Continued

Northwest Missouri State University (B.S., History, 1978); University of Iowa (J.D., 1981; M.B.A., 1982). Lifetime Member, National Registry of Who's Who. Former Member, Iowa City Chamber of Commerce. *Member:* Johnson County, Iowa State and American Bar Associations. ***PRACTICE AREAS:*** Bankruptcy; Personal Injury; Family Law. ***Email:*** r.trca@mchsi.com

WOLFE LAW OFFICE

337 E. COLLEGE STREET
IOWA CITY, IOWA 52240
Telephone: 319-338-6529
Fax: 319-338-6531
Email: wolfelaw@aol.com
URL: http://www.lawyers.com/wolfejustice

Criminal Law, Family Law, Bankruptcy.

MEMBER OF FIRM

MARY LYNN WOLFE, born Washington, D.C., May 17, 1963; admitted to bar, 1992, Iowa; 1995, U.S. District Court, Southern District of Iowa. *Education:* University of Iowa (B.A., English, 1989; J.D., 1992). *Member:* Johnson County and Iowa State Bar Associations (Member: Criminal and Family Law Sections); Iowa Trial Lawyers Association (Member, Criminal Law Section Board); National Lawyers Guild; National Association of Criminal Defense Lawyers. ***PRACTICE AREAS:*** Criminal Defense; Domestic Relations; Personal Injury; Criminal Law. ***Email:*** wolfelaw@aol.com

LAW OFFICES OF JAMES P. HOFFMAN

Established in 1967
3550 270TH AVENUE
P.O. BOX 1087
KEOKUK, IOWA 52632-1087
Telephone: 319-524-4441
Fax: 319-524-1638
Email: jamesphoffman@aol.com

Personal Injury, Workers' Compensation Law and Corporate Law.

FIRM PROFILE: The firm's primary practice is plaintiff's workers compensation and plaintiff's personal injury.

JAMES P. HOFFMAN, born Waterloo, Iowa, September 7, 1943; admitted to bar, 1967, Iowa and U.S. Supreme Court; 1968, U.S. District Court, District of Iowa; 1971, U.S. District Court, District of Illinois and U.S. Tax Court. *Education:* University of Northern Iowa (B.A., in Psychoanalyst/ Hypnotist, 1966); University of Iowa (J.D., 1967). Attorney, Lee County, 1972-1974 and 1976-1978. President, Iowa Institute of Hypnosis, 1977-1992. Fellow, American Institute of Hypnosis, 1978—. Author: "The Trial Lawyer and the Use of Hypnosis," H. R. W., Ltd., 1980. *Member:* Lee County, Iowa State and American Bar Associations; Iowa Association of Workers Compensation; Illinois Trial Lawyers Association; Association of Trial Lawyers of Iowa; The Association of Trial Lawyers of America.

BERENSTEIN, MOORE, BERENSTEIN, HEFFERNAN & MOELLER, L.L.P.

LE MARS, IOWA

(See Sioux City)

General Civil and Trial Practice. Banking, Probate, Taxation, ERISA, Education Law, Employment Law, Trusts and Estates, Creditor's Rights, Real Estate, Corporation, Health and Hospital Law.

MURPHY, COLLINS & BIXENMAN, P.L.C.

Established in 1936
38 FIRST AVENUE, NORTHWEST
P.O. BOX 526
LE MARS, IOWA 51031-0526
Telephone: 712-546-8844
Telecopier: 712-546-8847
Email: murphlaw@lemarscomm.net

General Practice, Civil and Criminal Trials and Appeals, Personal Injury and Worker's Compensation, Products Liability, Commercial and Banking Law, Probate, Estate Planning, Real Estate, Family Law, Corporations, Agricultural and Municipal Law, School Law.

PATRICK N. MURPHY, born Wahoo, Nebraska, January 15, 1946; admitted to bar, 1973, Nebraska, Iowa and U.S. District Court, District of Nebraska; 1975, U.S. District Court, Northern District of Iowa; 1992, U.S. Supreme Court. *Education:* University of Nebraska (A.B., 1968); Creighton University (J.D., 1972). Phi Alpha Delta. Assistant Plymouth County Attorney, 1973-1995. Director, Le Mars Community Schools, 1996—. *Member:* Plymouth County (President, 1981-1983), Third Judicial District, Iowa State (Member, American Citizenship Committee, 1973—; Member, Grievance Commission, 1998—), Nebraska State and American Bar Associations; Iowa Trial Lawyers Association (Member, Board of Governors, 1993-1998); Nebraska Association of Trial Attorneys; The Association of Trial Lawyers of America. [U.S. Army, 1969-1971]. ***PRACTICE AREAS:*** Plaintiffs Personal Injury; Wrongful Death; Civil Litigation; Commercial Litigation; Real Estate; Family Law. ***Email:*** murphlaw@lemarscomm.net

W. E. (GENE) COLLINS, born Sioux City, Iowa, March 10, 1959; admitted to bar, 1993, Iowa and U.S. District Court, Northern District of Iowa. *Education:* Iowa State University (B.S., 1990); University of Nebraska (J.D., 1992). Assistant Plymouth County Attorney (1993-1995). *Member:* Plymouth County and Iowa State Bar Associations. ***LANGUAGES:*** Russian. ***PRACTICE AREAS:*** Probate; Estate Planning; Corporate Law; Real Estate; Family Law; General Practice; Plaintiffs Personal Injury. ***Email:*** murphlaw@lemarscomm.net

SCOTT L. BIXENMAN, born LeMars, Iowa, March 17, 1969; admitted to bar, 1996, Iowa; 2001, U.S. District Court, Northern District of Iowa. *Education:* Iowa State University (B.A., 1993); Drake University (J.D., with honors, 1996). Member, Delta Theta Phi. *Member:* Iowa State Bar Association; Iowa Trial Lawyers Association. [U.S. Army/Iowa Army National Guard, 1990-1999]. ***PRACTICE AREAS:*** Family Law; Personal Injury; Criminal Law; Workers Compensation; General Practice. ***Email:*** murphlaw@lemarscomm.net

MICHAEL P. MURPHY, born October 16, 1979; admitted to bar, 2005, Iowa. *Education:* Iowa State University (B.S., in Finance with Distinction, 2002); Drake University (J.D., with honors, 2005). Delta Theta Phi. Member, Drake Law Review. Author: "Tort Reform: Would a Non-Economic Damages Cap be Constitutional, and is One Necessary in Iowa?" 53 Drake Law Review 813, 2005. *Member:* Iowa State Bar Association; Iowa Trial Lawyers Association.

REPRESENTATIVE CLIENTS: American Bank, N.A.; American State Bank; Northwest Iowa Credit Union; Members Group Mortgage Services; Reardon Commodities, Inc.; Yamaha Golf & Equipment Company; Wiltgen Construction Company; Rowe's Millwright Service, Inc.; Midwest Equipment, Inc.; Sioux City Yamaha, Inc.; Prime Agency, LLC; City of Craig, Iowa; Clark Engineered Machine; Farmers Cooperative Company, Kingsley, Iowa; City of Merrill, Iowa; City of Westfield, Iowa; Farmers Cooperative Company, Hinton-Le Mars, Iowa; Farmers Exchange, Lake Park, Iowa; Farmers Coop Company, Paullina-Granville, Iowa.
REFERENCES: American Bank, N.A.; First National Bank; Primebank.

RAWLINGS, NIELAND, PROBASCO, KILLINGER, ELLWANGER, JACOBS & MOHRHAUSER

LE MARS, IOWA

(See Sioux City)

General Civil Practice. Appeals, Bankruptcy, Commercial Law and Litigation, Corporation, Creditors Rights, Employment, Estate Planning, Insurance, Medical-Legal, Personal Injury, Probate, Real Estate, Taxation, Trial Practice and Worker's Compensation.

SALVO, DEREN, SCHENCK & LAUTERBACH, P.C.

LOGAN, IOWA

(See Harlan)

General Practice. Commercial, Family, Negligence, Corporation, Real Estate, Tax and Probate Law. Trials, Civil and Criminal.

WHITE & JOHNSON, P.C.

MANCHESTER, IOWA

(See Cedar Rapids)

General Practice. Trials, Personal Injury, Insurance, Workers' Compensation, Tax, Corporate, Real Estate, Probate, Domestic Relations.

GAUKEL, NEVINS & WESTERGAARD

515 MAIN STREET
MAPLETON, IOWA 51034
Telephone: 712-881-2321
Fax: 712-882-2323

Anthon, Iowa Office: Main Street. Telephone: 712-373-5294.
Sloan, Iowa Office: Murray Insurance Building. Telephone: 712-428-3861.

General Practice. Probate, Real Estate, Personal Injury, Corporation, Estate Planning and Taxation Law. Trials and Appeals.

MEMBERS OF FIRM

JAMES F. GAUKEL, born Sioux City, Iowa, March 11, 1936; admitted to bar, 1962, Iowa. *Education:* College of St. Thomas (B.S., 1958); University of South Dakota (J.D., 1962). Phi Delta Phi. Monona County Attorney, 1964-1970. Referee, Juvenile Court for Monona, Crawford and Ida Counties, 1972-1978. *Member:* Monona County (President, 1963-1964), Iowa State (Member: Committee on Continuing Legal Education, 1968-1972; Committee on Probate, Real Estate and Trust Law, 1980-1982) Bar Associations. ***Email:*** jimg_gnw@yahoo.com

GAVIN R. NEVINS, born Onawa, Iowa, January 23, 1944; admitted to bar, 1969, Iowa. *Education:* University of Iowa and Northwestern University (P.A.P., 1970); University of Iowa (LL.B., 1969). Phi Delta Phi. Director, Division of Beer and Liquor Law Enforcement, State of Iowa, 1972-1974. *Member:* Iowa State and American Bar Associations. ***Email:*** gavinn_gnw@yahoo.com

JAMES R. WESTERGAARD, born Onawa, Iowa, November 26, 1952; admitted to bar, 1978, Iowa. *Education:* Morningside College (B.S., summa cum laude, 1975); Drake University (J.D., with honors, 1978). Order of the Coif. Managing Editor, Drake University

(This Listing Continued)

Law Review, 1977-1978. President and CEO, Valley Bank and Trust, Mapleton, Iowa, 2001—. *Member:* Iowa State Bar Association (Member, Real Estate and Title Law Section Council, 1990). **Email:** jimw_gnw@yahoo.com

REPRESENTATIVE CLIENTS: First State Bank of Mapleton; Mac's Chevrolet-Pontiac, Inc.; City of Mapleton; Valley Bank and Trust, Mapleton, Iowa; Heritage Bank, Anthon, Iowa; City of Blencoe.
REFERENCES: First State Bank of Mapleton, Mapleton, Iowa; Valley Bank and Trust, Mapleton, Iowa; Heritage Bank, Anthon, Iowa.

FUERSTE, CAREW, COYLE, JUERGENS & SUDMEIER, P.C.

MAQUOKETA, IOWA

(See Dubuque)

General Practice, including Construction Law, Corporate and Commercial, Discrimination, Education Law, Employment and Labor, Estate Planning, Trusts and Wills, Probate, Family Law, Insurance, Litigation, Personal Injury, Products Liability, Workers Compensation and Wrongful Death.

EELLS & TRONVOLD LAW OFFICES, P.L.C.

MARION, IOWA

(See Cedar Rapids)

General Practice with emphasis on Personal Injury, Litigation, Probate and Estate Planning, Trusts and Wills, Business Law and Mediation.

CARTWRIGHT, DRUKER & RYDEN

112 WEST CHURCH STREET
P.O. BOX 496
MARSHALLTOWN, IOWA 50158
Telephone: 641-752-5467
Fax: 641-752-4370

Insurance Defense and Insurance Law, Trials and Appeals. Corporation, Banking, Taxation, Labor, Real Estate and Probate Law, Personal Injury, Workers Compensation, Estate Planning and General Practice.

FIRM PROFILE: The firm is also listed in Martindale-Hubbell Bar Register of preeminent attorneys.

MEMBERS OF FIRM

H. G. CARTWRIGHT (1902-1982)

HARRY DRUKER (1907-2004)

REX J. RYDEN, born Des Moines, Iowa, February 5, 1930; admitted to bar, 1957, Iowa; 1958, New York. *Education:* University of Iowa (B.S., 1952; J.D., 1957). Order of the Coif; Phi Delta Phi; Omicron Delta Kappa. Editor-in-Chief, Iowa Law Review, 1956-1957. *Member:* Marshall County, Iowa State, New York State and American Bar Associations. ***PRACTICE AREAS:*** Business Law; Corporate Law; Education Law; Hospital Law; Labor and Employment; Probate; Real Estate; Taxation; Trusts and Estates. ***Email:*** rex@cdrlaw.com

JOHN B. GRIER, born Ottumwa, Iowa, September 18, 1938; admitted to bar, 1963, Iowa. *Education:* University of Iowa (B.Sc., 1960; J.D., with distinction, 1963). Assistant U.S. Attorney, Southern District of Iowa, 1970-1972. Member, Supreme Court Judicial Nominating Commission, 1988-1995. *Member:* Marshall County (President, 1984-1985), Iowa State and American Bar Associations; Federation of Defense and Corporate Counsel; Iowa Defense Counsel Association (President, 1992-1993); Iowa Academy of Trial Lawyers; International Association of Insurance Counsel; American Board of Trial Advocates. Fellow, American College of Trial Lawyers. ***PRACTICE AREAS:*** Insurance; Litigation; Negligence; Personal Injury; Products Liability. ***Email:*** jack@cdrlaw.com

JOHN F. VELDEY, born Fergus Falls, Minnesota, July 23, 1942; admitted to bar, 1967, Iowa. *Education:* State University of Iowa (B.A., 1966; J.D., 1967). Phi Delta Phi. *Member:* Marshall County, Iowa State and American Bar Associations. ***PRACTICE AREAS:*** Business Law; Corporate Law; Labor and Employment; Probate; Real Estate; Trusts and Estates. ***Email:*** john@cdrlaw.com

JOEL T. S. GREER, born Spencer, Iowa, February 26, 1953; admitted to bar, 1978, Iowa. *Education:* University of Iowa (B.A., with high distinction, 1975; J.D., 1978). Phi Beta Kappa; Omicron Delta Kappa. Barrister, Blackstone Inn of Court, 1989-1991. Co-Chair, Bench Bar Conference, 1990-1991. Iowa Supreme Court Grievance Commission, 1996—; Chair, 1999— District 2B Judicial Nominating Commission, 2000—; State Judicial Nominating Commission, 2001-2006. *Member:* Marshall County, Iowa State (Member, Executive Council, Young Lawyers Section, 1980-1985; Litigation Section Council, 1998—; Member, Public Relations Committee, 1995-2000 Chair, 2000; Board of Governors, 2000—) and American Bar Associations; Iowa Defense Counsel Association; Iowa Association of Workers Compensation Lawyers; Iowa Trial Lawyers Association (Member, Board of Governors, 1985-1992). Fellow: Iowa Academy of Trial Lawyers (Member, Board of Governors, 1995-2003; President, 2001-2002); American Academy of ADR Attorneys (Board of Directors, 1999-2002). ***PRACTICE AREAS:*** Personal Injury; Mediation; Adoption Law; Workers Compensation; Automobile Accidents and Injuries; Insurance Defense; Business Law; Medical Malpractice; Divorce; Products Liability. ***Email:*** joel@cdrlaw.com

SHARON SOORHOLTZ GREER, born Marshalltown, Iowa, December 3, 1955; admitted to bar, 1982, Iowa. *Education:* Iowa State University (B.S., with distinction, 1978); University of Iowa (J.D., 1982). Phi Delta Phi. Member, Board of Editors, Iowa Law Review, 1981-1982. Member, District 2-B Judicial Nominating Commission, 1991-1997. Supreme Court Commission on Continuing Legal Education, 1986-1995; Chair, 1990-1995. Chair, Supreme Court Iowa Rules of Professional Conduct Drafting Committee, 2001-2002. *Member:* Marshall County, Iowa State and American Bar Associations; Iowa Defense Counsel Association (President, 2004-2005); American Board of Trial Advocates; International Association of Defense Counsel. Fellow, Iowa Academy of Trial Lawyers. ***PRACTICE AREAS:*** Insurance; Insurance Defense; Civil Litigation; Personal Injury; Business Law. ***Email:*** sharon@cdrlaw.com

(This Listing Continued)

ASSOCIATE

MERRILL C. SWARTZ, born Estherville, Iowa, January 12, 1970; admitted to bar, 1995, Iowa. *Education:* Morningside College (B.A., summa cum laude, 1992); University of Iowa (J.D., with high distinction, 1995). Order of the Coif. Member, Moot Court Board, 1994-1995. *Member:* Marshall County, Iowa State (Litigation Section Council, 2002—) and American Bar Associations; Iowa Defense Counsel Association. ***PRACTICE AREAS:*** Civil Litigation; Insurance Defense; Insurance; Family Law; Personal Injury; Business Law; Divorce; Criminal Law; Animal Law. ***Email:*** merrill@cdrlaw.com

REPRESENTATIVE CLIENTS: Members First Community Credit Union; Lennox Employees' Credit Union; Marshalltown Company; Marshalltown Medical and Surgical Center; West Marshall, East Marshall, South Tama and Marshalltown Community School Districts; Merged Area VI Community College District; American Family Mutual Insurance Co.; United Fire & Casualty Co.; Atlanta Casualty Companies; State Farm Mutual Insurance Co.; IMT Insurance Co.; Farm Bureau Mutual Insurance Co.; Grinnell Mutual Reinsurance Co.; Secura Insurance; Allied Insurance Co., a division of Nationwide; McGregor Furniture Co. ; Board of Trustees, Marshalltown Water Works; Wolfe Clinic, P.C.; Racom, Corp.; Martha-Ellen Tye Foundation; Donco Industries; Handy Industries, L.L.C.; Cooper Manufacturing Co.; Gethmann Construction, Inc.; R.S. Stover Co.

MOORE, McKIBBEN, GOODMAN, LORENZ & ELLEFSON, LLP

Established in 1885

302 MASONIC TEMPLE BUILDING
P.O. BOX 618
MARSHALLTOWN, IOWA 50158
Telephone: 641-752-4271
Fax: 641-752-5266
Email: MWW@MTNIA.COM

General Practice. Trials in all State and Federal Courts. Banking, Corporation, Taxation, Probate, Real Estate, Personal Injury, Family Law, Bankruptcy and Commercial Law, Criminal.

FIRM PROFILE: Harrison, Brennecke, Moore, Smaha & McKibben was founded by B. F. Cummings in 1885, serving clients throughout Marshall, Tama, Grundy, Hardin, Story and surrounding counties. The firm engages in a general practice. The firm is also listed in the Martindale-Hubbell Bar Register of Preeminent Lawyers.

MEMBERS OF FIRM

G. A. MOTE (1874-1965)

ARLEY J. WILSON (1913-1982)

WILLIAM L. WELP (1920-1997)

LESLIE E. SMAHA (1943-2003)

JAMES R. MOORE, born Story City, Iowa, October 10, 1940; admitted to bar, 1966, Iowa and U.S. District Court, Southern and Northern Districts of Iowa. *Education:* Iowa State University (B.S., 1963); Drake University (J.D., 1966). Delta Theta Phi. Member, District 2B Judicial Nominating Commission, 1984-1990. *Member:* Marshall County (President, 1977-1978), Iowa State (Member: American Citizenship Committee, 1970-1974; Economics Committee, 1988-1990; Section, Council Law Practice Management, 1990-1992) and American Bar Associations. ***PRACTICE AREAS:*** Real Estate; Estate Planning; Probate; Taxation; Elder Law.

LARRY E. McKIBBEN, born Marshalltown, Iowa, January 5, 1947; admitted to bar, 1973, Iowa, U.S. District Court, Southern and Northern District of Iowa, U.S. Tax Court; U.S. Court of Appeals, Eighth Circuit. *Education:* University of Northern Iowa (B.A., 1970); University of Iowa (J.D., 1972). Phi Delta Phi. Author: "Granting Parole in Iowa: A Time for Change," Iowa Advocate, Vol. X, No. 3, Spring 1972. Member, The President's Youth Advisory Committee on the Selective Service System, 1969-1972. *Member:* Marshall County (President, 1986-1987) and Iowa State (Member: Executive Council, Young Lawyers Section, 1979-1982; Corporation and Business Law Committee, 1979-1981 and 1988; Agricultural Law Section Council, 1990-1992, 1996-1998) Bar Associations. ***PRACTICE AREAS:*** Business Law; Contracts; Corporate Law; Estate Planning; Probate; Taxation.

JAMES L. GOODMAN, born Marshalltown, Iowa, April 12, 1950; admitted to bar, 1981, Iowa, U.S. District Court, Southern and Northern Districts of Iowa, U.S. Court of Appeals, Eighth Circuit and U.S. Tax Court. *Education:* Iowa State University (B.S., 1973); Colorado State University (M.S.B.A., 1974); Drake University (J.D., 1980). *Member:* Marshall County (President, 1999-2000), Iowa State (Member, Sections on: Taxation; Commercial and Bankruptcy Law; Probate and Trust Law; Co-Chair, December Tax Schools, 1989-1990; Council Member, 1991-1993, 1994-1996 and 1998-2000, Vice-Chairman, 1991-1992, Chairman, 1992-1993, Tax Council) and American (Member, Taxation Section) Bar Associations; National Association of Accountants (Board Member, 1975-1978). ***PRACTICE AREAS:*** Taxation; Corporate Taxation; Probate; Estate Planning; Real Estate; Commercial Law; Bankruptcy.

WILLIAM J. LORENZ, born Independence, Iowa, August 19, 1952; admitted to bar, 1980, Iowa, U.S. District Court, Southern and Northern Districts of Iowa, U.S. Court of Appeals, Eighth Circuit and U.S. Supreme Court. *Education:* University of Northern Iowa (B.A., 1975); Drake University (J.D., 1980). City Attorney, Laurel, Iowa, 1987—. *Member:* Marshall County (President, 2000-2001; Chair, American Citizenship Committee, 1985-1999), Iowa State (Member, Criminal Law Committee, 1988-1990, CLE Chair, 1989-1990; Criminal Law Section Council, 1990-1992, 1994-1996, CLE Chair, 1990-1992; Section Chair, 1995-1996; Member, Real Estate and Litigation Sections; Annual Meeting Commit-

(This Listing Continued)

MOORE, McKIBBEN, GOODMAN, LORENZ & ELLEFSON, LLP, Marshalltown—Continued

tee, 1991-2000, 2002—; Co-Chair, 1998-1999; Exhibit Hall Chair, 1993-1996, 1999-2000; CLE Chair, 1995-1996; Judicial Nominating Commission, District 2B, 1993-1994; Member, Volunteer Lawyers Project Board of Directors, 1993-1998) and American (Member, Litigation Section) Bar Associations. Fellow, Iowa State Bar Foundation; Iowa Trial Lawyers Association; The Association of Trial Lawyers of America. ***PRACTICE AREAS:*** Real Estate Law; Civil Practice; Trial Practice; Commercial Law; Bankruptcy; Adoption Law; Automobile Accidents and Injuries; Debtor and Creditor; Products Liability; Taxation; Municipal Law.

JAMES C. ELLEFSON, born Boone, Iowa, December 26, 1951; admitted to bar, 1977, Iowa, U.S. District Court, Southern and Northern Districts of Iowa and U.S. Court of Appeals, D.C. and Eighth Circuit; 1983, U.S. Supreme Court; 1996, U.S. Tax Court. *Education:* Wartburg College (B.A., magna cum laude, 1974); Drake University (J.D., with honors, 1977). Member: Order of the Coif; Order of Barristers. Recipient, Community Service Award, Iowa State Bar Association, 2001. Staff Member, Drake Law Review, 1975-1977. Secretary, Drake Moot Court Board, 1976-1977. Clerk to Robert G. Allbee, Chief Judge, Iowa Court of Appeals and Justice, Iowa Supreme Court, 1977-1979. Member, District 2B Judicial Nominating Commission, 1984-1990. *Member:* Marshall County, Iowa State (Member, Board of Governors, 1984-1988; Litigation and Family Law Sections; Public Relations Committee, 1998-2004; Chair, 2000-2004) and American Bar Associations (Member, Litigation, Family Law and Dispute Resolution Sections); The Association of Trial Lawyers of America; Iowa Trial Lawyers Association; Iowa Academy of Trial Lawyers. Fellow, Iowa State Bar Foundation; Blackstone Inn of Court. ***PRACTICE AREAS:*** Personal Injury; Medical Malpractice; Family Law; Mediation; Automobile Accidents and Injuries; Child Custody; Child Support; Divorce; Products Liability; Legal Malpractice; Workers Compensation; Criminal Law.

DOUGLAS W. BEALS, born Iowa City, Iowa, August 29, 1961; admitted to bar, 1987, Iowa and U.S. District Court, Southern and Northern Districts of Iowa. *Education:* Buena Vista College (B.A., 1984); Creighton University (J.D., 1987). *Member:* Marshall County and Iowa State (Member, Sections on: Law Practice Management; Family Law; Probate) Bar Associations. ***PRACTICE AREAS:*** Criminal Law; Civil Practice; Trial Practice; Family Law; Taxation; Divorce; Child Custody; Child Support; Social Security; Probate.

MICHAEL R. HORN, born Monterey Park, California, May 14, 1966; admitted to bar, 1992, Iowa; U.S. District Court, Southern and Northern Districts of Iowa, U.S. Tax Court and U.S. Court of Appeals, Eighth Circuit. *Education:* University of Iowa (B.A., 1989); Drake University (J.D., 1992). *Member:* Marshall County and Iowa State (Member, Sections on: Agricultural Law; Taxation; Business Law, Commercial and Bankruptcy Law; Chair: December Tax School, 2002-2003) Bar Associations. ***PRACTICE AREAS:*** Corporate Law; Taxation; Business Law; Contracts; Bankruptcy; Landlord and Tenant Law; Social Security; Debtor and Creditor.

NORMA J. MEADE, born St. Nazaire, France, September 23, 1966; admitted to bar, 1997, Iowa; U.S. District Court, Northern and Southern Districts of Iowa. *Education:* Des Moines Area Community College (1989-1991); Marshalltown Community College (Certificate, Surgical Technology, 1986-1987); Iowa State University (B.A., 1993); Drake University (J.D., 1997). *Member:* Iowa State Bar Association. [Iowa National Guard, 1987-1993]. ***PRACTICE AREAS:*** Criminal Law; Civil Practice; Trial Practice; Family Law; Taxation; Divorce; Child Custody; Child Support; Driving While Intoxicated; Traffic Violations.

SEAN K. HEITMANN, born Marengo, Iowa, June 11, 1979; admitted to bar, 2003, Iowa. *Education:* Waldorf College (B.A., 2000); University of Iowa (J.D., 2003). *Member:* Marshall County, Iowa State and American Bar Associations.

OF COUNSEL

ROGER E. HARRISON, born Vinton, Iowa, April 3, 1932; admitted to bar, 1958, Iowa. *Education:* University of Iowa (B.S.C., 1956; J.D., 1958). Phi Delta Phi. *Member:* Marshall County (President, 1965-1966), Iowa State and American Bar Associations.

ALLEN E. BRENNECKE, born Marshalltown, Iowa, January 8, 1937; admitted to bar, 1961, Iowa, U.S. District Court, Southern and Northern Districts of Iowa, U.S. Court of Appeals, Seventh and Eighth Circuit and U.S. Supreme Court. *Education:* University of Iowa (B.B.A., 1959; J.D., 1961). Phi Delta Phi. Author: "Taxpayer's Undeveloped Muscle—The Refund Suit," 47 Notre Dame Lawyer, 304. Co-author: "Deferred Sale Contracts By Cash Basis Farmers," 65 American Bar Association Journal 832, 1979. Member, Board of Trustees, Iowa Law School Foundation, 1973-1986. Member, Board of Directors, National Judicial College, 1982-1988. Member, Martindale-Hubbell Legal Advisory Board, 1990—. *Member:* Marshall County (President, 1971-1972), Iowa State (President, Young Lawyers Section, 1970-1971; Member: Board of Governors, 1970-1971, 1988-1991; Vice President, 1988-1989; President Elect, 1989-1990; President 1990-1991; Taxation Committee, 1971-1988; Recipient, Award of Merit, 1987) and American (Member: Executive Council, Young Lawyers Section, 1970-1973; House of Delegates, 1971-1973, 1975—; Board of Governors, 1982-1986; Standing Committee on Resolutions, 1973-1974; Chair, Commission on Interest on Lawyers' Trust Accounts, 1986-1989; State Delegate, 1975-1982; Board of Editors, American Bar Association Journal, 1980-1982, 1984-1986, 1987-1996 and Chair, 1989-1995; Chairman, House of Delegates, 1984-1986) Bar Associations; American Arbitration Association (Panelist: Commercial Arbitration Panel, 1985—; Mediation Panel, 1995—). Fellow: Iowa State Bar Foundation; American Bar Foundation (Iowa Chairman, 1977-1982); American College of Trust and Estates Counsel (Iowa Chairman, 1977-1982; Member, Board of Regents, 1981-1982); American College of Tax Counsel. ***PRACTICE AREAS:*** Taxation; Estate Planning; Trusts and Estates; Corporate Law; Business Law; Labor Law.

REPRESENTATVE CLIENTS: Furnished Upon Request.

BROWN, KINSEY, FUNKHOUSER & LANDER, P.L.C.

Established in 1951
214 NORTH ADAMS
P.O. BOX 679
MASON CITY, IOWA 50402-0679
Telephone: 641-423-6223
Fax: 641-423-9995
URL: http://www.lawyers.com/brownkinseyfunkhouser

General Practice. Trials and Appeals. Corporation, Insurance, Workers' Compensation, Probate, Real Estate and Employment Law, Criminal Law, Personal Injury, Social Security Disability.

MEMBERS OF FIRM

DAVID E. FUNKHOUSER, born Fort Madison, Iowa, November 11, 1941; admitted to bar, 1967, Iowa. *Education:* University of Iowa (B.B.A., 1964; J.D., 1967). Listed in, The Best Lawyers in America, 1994—. Law Clerk, 1967-1968, Past Member, Iowa Supreme Court. Member: Commission on Continuing Legal Education, 1975-1982; Judicial Qualification Commission and Task Force on Equality in the Courts. *Member:* Iowa State Bar Association (President, 1988-1989, President-elect, 1987-1988, Vice President, 1986-1987, Board of Governors, 1982-1986; Past Chairman, Ways and Means, Scope and Correlation, Award of Merit Committees; Past Member, Uniform Court Instruction, Administrative Law, Bench-Bar Conference and Alternative Dispute Resolution Committees; Recipient, Award of Merit, 2002); American Bar Association; House of Delegate (Iowa State Delegate, 1996-2005; Board of Governors, 2005—). Fellow: American College of Trial Lawyers; Iowa Academy of Trial Lawyers (President, 1989); Iowa State Bar Foundation; American Bar Foundation. ***PRACTICE AREAS:*** Personal Injury; Trial Practice; Insurance Defense; Contested Wills; Mediation. ***Email:*** defunkhouser@iowabar.org

ROBERT S. KINSEY, III, born Highland Park, Illinois, December 31, 1944; admitted to bar, 1973, Iowa. *Education:* Grinnell College (B.A., 1967); University of Iowa (J.D., with distinction, 1973). *Member:* Cerro Gordo County, Iowa State (Member, Section on Workers Compensation, Section Chair, 1989-1991 and 2000-2001) and American Bar Associations; Association of Trial Lawyers of Iowa; Iowa Association of Workers' Compensation Attorneys (Board Member, 1979—; President, 1997-1998; Vice-President, 1996-1997; Secretary, 1995-1996; Treasurer, 1994-1995). ***PRACTICE AREAS:*** Workers' Compensation; Employment Law; Trials and Appeals. ***Email:*** rsklaw@iowabar.org

SCOTT D. BROWN, born Mason City, Iowa, June 6, 1956; admitted to bar, 1982, Iowa. *Education:* University of Iowa (B.A., 1978); Drake University (J.D., 1982). *Member:* Cerro Gordo County and Iowa State Bar Associations. Fellow, Iowa Academy of Trial Lawyers. ***Email:*** sdblaw@iowabar.org

JOHN P. LANDER, born Henry, Illinois, December 30, 1969; admitted to bar, 1995, Iowa and U.S. District Court, Northern and Southern Districts of Iowa and U.S. Court of Appeals, Eighth Circuit. *Education:* University of Illinois (B.A., 1992); Drake University (J.D., with high honors, 1995). Delta Theta Phi; Dean's List. Recipient, American Jurisprudence Awards, Contracts and Agency. *Member:* Cerro Gordo County Bar Association; Iowa State Bar Association (Member, Young Lawyers Division BTG Committee, 1995-2004); American Bar Association; Iowa Trial Lawyers Association. ***PRACTICE AREAS:*** Personal Injury; Criminal Defense; Civil Litigation.

ASSOCIATES

JACKIE D. ARMSTRONG, born Orlando, Florida, June 17, 1953; admitted to bar, 1978, Colorado; 1982, Michigan; 1983, Massachusetts; 1996, Iowa. *Education:* University of Michigan (B.A., with highest distinction, 1974; J.D., 1978). *Member:* Cerro Gordo County and Iowa State Bar Associations; Iowa Association of Workers' Compensation Attorneys; Iowa Organization of Women Attorneys (President, 2004-2005); Iowa Trial Lawyers Association; National Organization of Social Security Representatives. ***Email:*** jarmstrong@iowabar.org

KIM R. SNITKER, born Charles City, Iowa, April 28, 1970; admitted to bar, 2003, Iowa. *Education:* Mount Mercy College (B.A., 1992); University of Iowa (J.D., 2002). ***PRACTICE AREAS:*** General Practice. ***Email:*** ksnitker@iowabar.org

REPRESENTATIVE CLIENTS: The St. Paul Cos.; Home Insurance Co.; Countrywide Services, Inc.; American Home Assurance Co.; American International Adjusting Co.; American Underwriters Insurance Co.; United Fire & Casualty Co.; Underwriters Adjusting Co.; National Chiropractic Insurance Co.; New Hampshire Insurance Group; Metropolitan Life & Casualty; Continental Western Insurance Co.; American Family Insurance Co.

DE VRIES, PRICE & DAVENPORT

A PROFESSIONAL CORPORATION
Established in 1950
30 FOURTH STREET, N.W.
P.O. BOX 1953
MASON CITY, IOWA 50401
Telephone: 641-423-1173
Fax: 641-423-1731
Email: info@devrieslawfirm.com

General Practice. Trials and Appeals. Insurance Defense and Workers' Compensation.

WARREN L. DE VRIES, born Orange City, Iowa, May 28, 1925; admitted to bar, 1949, Iowa and U.S. Supreme Court. *Education:* Drake University (LL.B., 1949). *Member:* Fellow, Iowa Academy of Trial Lawyers. Fellow, American College of Trial Lawyers. (Retired)

C. BRADLEY PRICE, born Des Moines, Iowa, July 8, 1950; admitted to bar, 1982, Iowa. *Education:* University of Iowa (B.B.A., 1972; J.D., 1982). Member, Board of Editors,

(This Listing Continued)

Iowa Law Review, 1981-1982. Author: "Mistakenly Signed Reciprocal Wills: A Change in Tradition After In re Snide," 67 Iowa Law Review 205, 1981. President, District 2A Bar Association, 1994-1995. Member, Judicial Nominating Committee, Second Judicial District, 1994-2000. *Member:* Cerro Gordo County, Iowa State (Member, Litigation Section, Board of Governors, 1999—) and American Bar Associations (Member, Sections on: Litigation; Tort and Insurance Practice); Association of Trial Lawyers of Iowa; Defense Research Institute; Iowa Defense Counsel Association (Board of Directors, 1991-1994); Federation of Insurance and Corporate Counsel. Fellow, Iowa Academy of Trial Lawyers. ***PRACTICE AREAS:*** Insurance Defense; Litigation; General Practice; Agents and Brokers Liability; Professional Liability. ***Email:*** cbprice@devrieslawfirm.com

RUSTIN T. DAVENPORT, born Des Moines, Iowa, December 7, 1959; admitted to bar, 1985, Iowa. *Education:* Grand View College; Drake University (B.A., magna cum laude, 1982); University of Iowa (J.D., with distinction, 1985). Judicial Clerk: Iowa Second Judicial District, 1985-1986; Hon. David R. Hansen, U.S. District Court Judge, Northern District of Iowa, 1986-1988. *Member:* Cerro Gordo County, Iowa State (Executive Council, Young Lawyers Division, 1990-1995; Workers Compensation Section; Co-Chair, Workers Compensation Section, Newsletter Committee, 1992-1995) and American Bar Associations; Iowa Defense Counsel Association; Iowa Association of Workers' Compensation Lawyers, Inc. (Member, Board of Governors, 1998—). ***PRACTICE AREAS:*** Insurance Defense; Employment Defense; Workers Compensation; Civil Rights. ***Email:*** davenport@devrieslawfirm.com

REPRESENTATIVE CLIENTS: Allied Group; All National Insurance Co.; Allstate Insurance Co.; American Bankers Insurance Co.; Austin Mutual Insurance Co.; Auto Owners Insurance Co.; Bituminous Insurance Co.; Capitol Indemnity Co.; Chubb-Pacific Indemnity Group; CIGNA; Commercial Union Insurance Co.; The Continental Insurance Cos.; Continental Western Insurance Co.; Crawford & Company; Employers Mutuals of Wausau; Farm Bureau Mutual Insurance Co.; Farmers Casualty Co.; Federated Insurance; Frontier Insurance Co.; General Casualty Company of Wisconsin; Great West Insurance Co.; Grinnell Mutual Reinsurance Co.; Integrity Mutual Insurance Company; Iowa Mutual Insurance Co.; Milwaukee Mutual Insurance; Motor Club of Iowa AAA; Mutual Fire & Auto Insurance Co.; National Casualty Co.; National Insurance Co.; Northbrook Property and Casualty; Northwestern National Insurance Group; Partners Mutual Insurance Co.; PHICO Ins. Co.; Ranger Insurance; The Reliance Insurance Co.; Safeco Insurance; Security Insurance Group; Sedgwick James of Minnesota; Scottsdale Insurance; Steadfast Insurance; Travelers Insurance Group; Tri-States Ins. Co.; United Fire & Casualty Co.; Western Casualty & Surety Co.
REFERENCE: Bank of America.

FITZSIMMONS & VERVAECKE, LAW FIRM, PLC

5 NORTH FEDERAL AVENUE, SUITE 200
P.O. BOX 1661
MASON CITY, IOWA 50402-1661
Telephone: 641-422-0066
Toll Free: 1-877-476-9365
Fax: 641-422-0086
URL: http://www.fvinjurylaw.com

Trials and Appeals. Personal Injury and Workers Compensation Law.

JAMES T. FITZSIMMONS, born Vail, Iowa, September 20, 1966; admitted to bar, 1992, Iowa and Nebraska; 1993, U.S. District Court, Northern and Southern Districts of Iowa; 1998, U.S. Court of Appeals, Eighth Circuit. *Education:* Creighton University (B.A., 1989; J.D., 1992). Phi Alpha Delta. Vice-President, Student Bar Association. President, Moot Court Board. Appointed Attorney, Grievance Commission, Iowa Supreme Court, 2004—. *Member:* Cerro Gordo County (Secretary, 1994-1995), Iowa State (Member, Workers' Compensation Section Rules Committee, 1997-1998) and Nebraska State Bar Associations; Iowa Trial Lawyers Association (Member, Board of Governors, 1996—; CLE Committee, 1997—; CLE Chairperson, 2000-2004); The Association of Trial Lawyers of America (Member, Premises and Motor Vehicle Liability Section); Iowa Association of Workers' Compensation Lawyers (Member, Rules Committee, 2003—). ***PRACTICE AREAS:*** Trial Practice; Personal Injury; Workers Compensation. ***Email:*** fitz@netconx.net

MINDI M. VERVAECKE, born Galva, Iowa, August 10, 1971; admitted to bar, 1996, Minnesota; 1997, Iowa; 1998, U.S. Court of Appeals, Eighth Circuit; 1999, U.S. District Court, Northern District of Iowa; 2000, U.S. District Court, Southern District of Iowa. *Education:* University of Iowa (B.S., 1993; J.D., with distinction, 1996). Program Coordinator and Professor, Paralegal Program, Hamilton College, Mason City, Iowa, 1998-2004. Appointed: Iowa District 2A Judicial Nominating Commission, 2000—; Judicial Nominating Commission, Iowa Supreme Court, 2003—. *Member:* Cerro Gordo County (Treasurer, 1997-1998), Iowa State and Minnesota State Bar Associations; Iowa Trial Lawyers Association (Member: Board of Governors, 2000-2004; CLE Committee, 1998-2004; Vice-Chair, 2000-2001; Workers' Compensation Core Group, 2001—); The Association of Trial Lawyers of America (Member, Insurance Bad Faith Section). ***PRACTICE AREAS:*** Trial Practice; Personal Injury; Workers Compensation. ***Email:*** mindiv@netconx.net

---

COLIN C. MURPHY, born Omaha, Nebraska, March 4, 1969; admitted to bar, 1997, Pennsylvania; 1998, Iowa; 1999, U.S. District Court, Northern and Southern Districts of Iowa. *Education:* Grinnell College (B.A., 1991); Drake University (J.D., with honors, 1996). Member, Blackstone Inn of Court, 1995-1996. Research Editor, Drake Law Review, 1995-1996. *Member:* Cerro Gordo County (Treasurer, 1999-2000) and Iowa State (At Large Representative, Executive Council, Young Lawyers Division, 2003) Bar Associations; Iowa Trial Lawyers Association; The Association of Trial Lawyers of America. ***PRACTICE AREAS:*** Trial Practice; Personal Injury; Workers Compensation.

REFERENCE: First Citizens National Bank.

HOBSON, CADY & CADY

MASON CITY, IOWA

(See Hampton)

General Practice in State and Federal Courts. Trials and Appeals. Insurance and Probate Law.

LOCHER & MORRISON

103 E. STATE STREET
SUITE 721
MASON CITY, IOWA 50401
Telephone: 641-423-2432
Fax: 641-423-2433

General Practice. Corporation, Probate and Real Estate Law.

MEMBERS OF FIRM

HUGH H. SHEPARD (1876-1970)

ROBERT H. SHEPARD (1919-1989)

JAMES J. LOCHER, born Monticello, Iowa, September 17, 1946; admitted to bar, 1974, Iowa; 1975, U.S. District Court, Northern District of Iowa; 1979, U.S. District Court, Southern District of Iowa. *Education:* University of Notre Dame (B.A., 1968); Duke University (J.D., 1974). Clerk for Hon. Warren J. Rees, Iowa Supreme Court Justice, 1974-1975. *Member:* Cerro Gordo County, Iowa State (Member, Board of Governors, 1995-2000) and American Bar Associations. [With U.S. Army, 1969-1971]

WILLIAM T. MORRISON, born Mason City, Iowa, December 19, 1963; admitted to bar, 1989, Iowa; 1990, U.S. District Court, Northern District of Iowa. *Education:* University of Iowa (B.B.A., 1986; J.D., 1989). *Member:* Cerro Gordo County, Iowa State and American Bar Associations.

GENERAL COUNSEL FOR: Americo Industries, Ltd.; Brice Exploration Co.; Cashway Lumber Store, Inc. of Webster City; Cashway Lumber Store, Inc. of Marshalltown; Indianhead Farms, Inc.; MacNider & Co.; Mason City Hotel Corp.; Mason City Airport Commission; Mid-State Distributing Co.; North Iowa Land Co.
REFERENCES: Wells Fargo Bank Iowa, N.A.; First Citizen's National Bank.

McGUIRE LAW FIRM, P.C.

Established in 1970

101 SOUTH DELAWARE AVENUE
MASON CITY, IOWA 50401
Telephone: 641-424-1614
Fax: 641-424-1568
Email: jpmcguire@mcguirelawfirm.com
URL: http://www.mcguirelawfirm.com

Personal Injury Law, Medical Malpractice, Severe Burns, Water Heater Flammable Vapor Litigation, Products Liability, Railroad Litigation, Trial Practice.

JAMES P. McGUIRE, born Mason City, Iowa, October 8, 1942; admitted to bar, 1968, Iowa, Nebraska and U.S. District Court, Northern and Southern Districts of Iowa. *Education:* Creighton University (BS., 1965; J.D., 1968). Phi Alpha Delta. Assistant County Attorney, 1970-1975. *Member:* Cerro Gordo County (President, 1989), 2A District, Iowa State and Nebraska State Bar Associations; Iowa Trial Lawyers Association (Member, Board of Governors, 1980-1986); The Association of Trial Lawyers of America; Iowa Academy of Trial Lawyers (Member, Board of Governors, 2003—). ***PRACTICE AREAS:*** Personal Injury; Medical Malpractice; Severe Burns; Water Heater Flammable Vapor Litigation; Products Liability; Railroad Litigation; Trial Practice. ***Email:*** jpmcguire@mcguirelawfirm.com

SCHROEDER & ANDERSON

119 SECOND STREET N.W.
MASON CITY, IOWA 50401
Telephone: 641-423-4935
Fax: 641-424-4154
Email: rma@netconx.net

Affiliated with, Finley, Alt, Smith, Scharnberg, Craig, Hilmes & Gaffney, P.C.: 699 Walnut Street, 1900 Hubb Tower, Des Moines, Iowa, 50309. Telephone: 515-288-0145.

Health Care Law, Medical Malpractice Defense, General Practice, Probate, Real Estate and Family Law.

MEMBER OF FIRM

ROBERTA M. ANDERSON, born Mason City, Iowa, August 9, 1954; admitted to bar, 1981, Iowa; U.S. District Court, Northern and Southern Districts of Iowa. *Education:* University of Iowa (B.A., 1976; J.D., 1981). Phi Beta Kappa. Member, Grievance Commission, Iowa Supreme Court, 1989-1998. *Member:* Cerro Gordo County, 2A Judicial District (President, 1996), Iowa State (Past Member, Health Law Section Council) and American Bar Associations; Iowa Society of Health Care Attorneys (President, 1996); Iowa Defense Counsel Association; American Health Lawyers Association; Supreme Court Committee on Professional Conduct and Ethics. ***Email:*** rma@netconx.net

OF COUNSEL

WALTER C. SCHROEDER, born Davenport, Iowa, April 28, 1931; admitted to bar, 1957, Iowa; 1958, U.S. District Court, Northern District of Iowa; 1963, U.S. District Court, Southern District of Iowa. *Education:* University of Iowa (B.A., 1953; J.D., 1957). Chairman, Iowa Board of Bar Examiners, 1974-1982. *Member:* Iowa State Bar Association; American Health Lawyers Association (Charter Member). Fellow, Iowa Academy of Trial Lawyers. [First Lt., U.S. Army, 1953-1955]

REPRESENTATIVE CLIENTS: Trinity Health Services; Mercy Medical Center- North Iowa; Ellsworth Municipal Hospital; Franklin General Hospital; Hancock County Health Services; Regional Health Services of Howard County; Catholic Health Initiatives; Kossuth Regional Health Center; Mitchell County Regional Health Center; Palo Alto County Hospital; Mercy Medical Center-New Hampton.

WINSTON & BYRNE, LAWYERS

A PROFESSIONAL CORPORATION

Established in 1908

119 SECOND STREET, N.W.
MASON CITY, IOWA 50401
Telephone: 641-423-1913
Fax: 641-423-8998
Email: hwinston@netins.net
URL: http://www.winstonbyrne.com

General Practice. Trials and Appeals. Corporation Law. Civil Litigation, Real Estate, Probate, Estate Planning, Trusts, Wills, Family Law.

HAROLD R. WINSTON, born Atlantic, Iowa, February 7, 1932; admitted to bar, 1958, Iowa; 1960, U.S. District Court, Northern District of Iowa and U.S. Tax Court; 1962, U.S. District Court, Southern District of Iowa; 1969, U.S. Supreme Court; 1970, U.S. Court of Appeals, Eighth Circuit. *Education:* University of Iowa (B.A., 1954; J.D., 1958). Phi Delta Phi. *Member:* Cerro Gordo County (President, 1977), Second Judicial District, Iowa State (Member, State Bar Judiciary Committee, 1970-1973; Member, State Committee on Probate, Property and Trust Law, 1975-1979; Member, Board of Governors, 1979-1983; Iowa State Grievance Commission, 1983-1990) and American Bar Associations; American Judicature Society; The Association of Trial Lawyers of America. Fellow, American College of Trust and Estate Counsel. Fellow, American Bar Foundation. Fellow, Iowa State Bar Foundation. [First Lt., U.S. Air Force, 1955-1957]. ***PRACTICE AREAS:*** Probate; Estate Planning; Trusts and Wills; Corporate. ***Email:*** hwinston@netins.net

MICHAEL G. BYRNE, born Charles City, Iowa, September 20, 1954; admitted to bar, 1979, Iowa and U.S. District Court, Northern and Southern Districts of Iowa. *Education:* University of Iowa (B.A., with honors, 1976; J.D., 1979). Public Defender, Cerro Gordo County, 1983-1986. *Member:* Cerro Gordo County, Iowa State and American Bar Associations; Second Judicial District Bar Association; Association of Trial Lawyers of Iowa; The Association of Trial Lawyers of America; Iowa Trust Association. ***PRACTICE AREAS:*** Civil Litigation; Real Estate; Probate.

REPRESENTATIVE CLIENTS: Woodharbor Molding & Millworks, Inc.; Winkleman Farms, Inc.; Schmidt Family Farms, Inc.; Prostock, Inc.; Price Motors, Inc.; Mason City Warehouse Corporation; Marshall Heritage Farms, Inc.; Lewis Grain & Livestock Co.; LaJames College of Hairstyling; Lyndi, Ltd.; Home Lumber & Builders, Inc.; Davison Family Farm, Inc.; Creative Solutions Unlimited, Inc.; Carroll Sales Company, Inc.; Bertha Stebens Charitable Foundation; First Citizens Trust Company, N.A.
REFERENCE: First Citizens National Bank of Mason City, Iowa.

BECKMAN AND HIRSCH

MT. PLEASANT, IOWA

(See Burlington)

Personal Injury, Appeals, Corporation, Taxation, Probate, Insurance, Real Estate, Criminal Defense, Commercial Litigation, Computer Law, Family Law, General Trial Practice in State and Federal Courts.

McALLISTER LAW OFFICE

300 SOUTH JEFFERSON STREET
P.O. BOX 618
MT. PLEASANT, IOWA 52641
Telephone: 319-385-9524
Fax: 319-385-8921
Email: maclaw@iowatelecom.net

Real Estate, Probate, Estate Planning, Trusts and Wills, Corporate, Commercial Law and Abstract of Title and Escrow Services.

RANDE A. McALLISTER, born Mt. Pleasant, Iowa, December 26, 1945; admitted to bar, 1971, Iowa and U.S. District Court, Northern and Southern Districts of Iowa. *Education:* Iowa Wesleyan College (B.A., 1968); Washburn University (J.D., 1971). City Attorney, Mt. Pleasant, Iowa, 1974-1978. *Member:* Henry County, Iowa State and American Bar Associations.

REFERENCES: Pilot Grove Savings Bank, Pilot Grove, Iowa; Henry County Bank, Mt. Pleasure, Iwoa.

WHITFIELD & EDDY, P.L.C.

Established in 1928

110 N. JEFFERSON, SUITE 101
MT. PLEASANT, IOWA 52641-2016
Telephone: 319-385-9522
Fax: 319-385-3633
Email: info@whitfieldlaw.com
URL: http://www.whitfieldlaw.com

Des Moines, Iowa Office: 317 6th Avenue, Suite 1200, 50309-4195. Telephone: 515-288-6041. Fax: 515-246-1474. Email: info@whitfieldlaw.com. URL: http://www.whitfieldlaw.com.

Ankeny, Iowa Office: 213 North Ankeny Boulevard, Suite 100, 50021-1749. Telephone: 515-964-3633. Fax: 515-964-3692. Email: info@whitfieldlaw.com. URL: http://www.whitfieldlaw.com.

West Des Moines, Iowa Office: 3737 Woodland Avenue, Suite 400, 50266. Telephone: 515-558-0111. Fax: 515-222-0318. Email: info@whitfieldlaw.com. URL: http://www.whitfieldlaw.com.

(This Listing Continued)

General Practice including Trial and Appellate Practice and Business and Banking. Alternative Dispute Resolution, Antitrust and Trade Regulation, Arbitration, Bankruptcy, Banks and Banking, Business, Civil Rights, Commercial, Construction, Corporate, Criminal, Environmental, Family, Fidelity and Surety, Foreclosures, Health Care, Immigration and Naturalization, Insurance, Insurance Defense, Intellectual Property, Labor and Employment, Mediation, Municipal, Personal Injury, Probate, Products Liability, Professional Liability, Real Estate, Securities, Taxation, Transportation, Trust and Estates, Utility, Wills, Workers Compensation.

FIRM PROFILE: Please visit our web site for more detailed information on our practice areas, attorneys, locations and tradition of leadership in the legal community.

For a complete list of Representative Clients, see Des Moines, Iowa.

(For complete biographical data on all personnel, see Professional Biographies at Des Moines, Iowa)

WILLIAM J. BRIBRIESCO & ASSOCIATES

MUSCATINE, IOWA

(See Bettendorf)

Personal Injury, Workers Compensation, Products Liability, Business Law.

GOSMA, TARBOX & ASSOCIATES, P.L.C.

MUSCATINE, IOWA

(See Davenport)

General Civil Practice, including Business and Corporate Organization and Transactions, Banking, Real Estate, Estate Planning, Elder Law, Trust and Estate Administration, and Personal Injury, Business and Probate Litigation, Medical Malpractice, Business Enterprises, Slip and Fall, Personal Injury, Automobile Accidents, Wrongful Death, Buying and Selling, Zoning and Land Use, Construction, Asset Protection, Guardianships, Banking and Finance, Closely Held Business, Corporate, Franchise, Limited Liability, Small Business, Partnerships, Buying and Selling of Businesses, Creditors Rights, Contracts, Business Planning, Law Suites, Insurance, Commercial Leasing, Business Start-Ups.

McCARTHY, LAMMERS & HINES

MUSCATINE, IOWA

(See Davenport)

General Civil Practice. Trials, Personal Injury, Workers Compensation, Wills, Trusts, Probate, Criminal Law, Real Estate, Family Law, Divorce, Child Custody, Estate Planning, Bankruptcy, Juvenile.

STANLEY, LANDE & HUNTER

A PROFESSIONAL CORPORATION

301 IOWA AVENUE, SUITE 400
MUSCATINE, IOWA 52761
Telephone: 563-264-5000
Facsimile: 563-263-8775
Email: Contact.us@slhlaw.com
URL: http://www.slhlaw.com

Davenport, Iowa Office: 900 U.S. Bank Center, 201 West Second Street. Telephone: 563-324-1000. Facsimile: 563-326-6266.

Wilton, Iowa Office: 115 West Fourth, P.O. Box 481. Telephone: 563-732-4000. Facsimile: 563-732-2318.

Coralville, Iowa Office: 2201 East Grantview Drive, Suite 200. Telephone: 319-248-9000. Facsimile: 319-248-9001.

General Civil and Trial Practice. Corporation, Business, Banking, Taxation, Securities, Tax-Exempt Financing, Labor, Employment Discrimination, Administrative, Creditor Bankruptcy and Agricultural Law, Insurance Defense, Personal Injury and Property Damage Law, Pension and Profit-Sharing, Real Estate, Probate, Estate Planning and Charitable Trusts and Foundations Law.

ROGER L. LANDE, born Lake Mills, Iowa, November 7, 1936; admitted to bar, 1961, Iowa. *Education:* Iowa State University; University of Iowa (B.A., 1961); University of Iowa (J.D., with distinction, 1961). Member, Editorial Advisory Board, The Journal of Corporation Law, 1976-1999. Director, American Judicature Society, 1982-1986. Director, Iowa Law School Foundation, 1988-2000. Member, Iowa Board of Regents, 1996-2001. *Member:* Muscatine County (President, 1971-1972), Iowa State (Member: Executive Council, Young Lawyers Section, 1968-1973; Committee on Corporation and Business Law, 1970-1977; Board of Governors, 1977-1979; President, 1981-1982) and American Bar Associations. Fellow, American Bar Foundation; Member: Iowa Association of Business and Industry (Director, 1983-1993, Treasurer, 1989-1990, Vice Chairman, 1990-1991 and Chairman, 1991-1992). ***PRACTICE AREAS:*** Corporate Law; Business Acquisitions; Employment Law. ***Email:*** rlande@slhlaw.com

CHARLES R. COULTER, born Webster City, Iowa, June 10, 1940; admitted to bar, 1965, Iowa. *Education:* University of Iowa (B.A., 1962; J.D., with high distinction, 1965). Order of the Coif. *Member:* Muscatine County (President, 1975-1976), Iowa State (Member: Committee on Membership, 1973-1979; Committee on Bar Economics and Law Office Operations, 1979-1987, Chairman, 1981-1986) and American (Member, Section of Law Practice Management; Council Member, 1985-1988; Secretary, 1988-1989; Chair, 1991-1992; Coordinating Commission on Legal Technology, 1991-1997; Chair, 1994-1997; Standing Committee on Technology and Information Systems, 1997-1998) Bar As-

(This Listing Continued)

sociations. Fellow: American Bar Foundation; Iowa State Bar Foundation. ***PRACTICE AREAS:*** Corporate Law; Law Practice Management; Probate Law; Real Estate. ***Email:*** chuckcoulter@slhlaw.com

ROBERT L. LANDE, born Mason City, Iowa, April 17, 1947; admitted to bar, 1972, Washington; 1973, Iowa; 1977, Illinois; 1979, U.S. Supreme Court. *Education:* University of Iowa (B.S., 1969; J.D., with distinction, 1972). *Member:* Muscatine County (President, 1984-1985), Iowa State (Member, Trade Regulation, Corporate Counsel and Business Law Sections) and American Bar Associations. ***PRACTICE AREAS:*** Business Law; Banking Law; Commercial Law; Construction Law. ***Email:*** blande@slhlaw.com

DAVID J. MELOY, born Dubuque, Iowa, July 27, 1950; admitted to bar, 1975, Iowa; 1976, U.S. District Court, Southern District of Iowa; 1977, Illinois. *Education:* Iowa State University; University of Iowa (B.A., 1972; J.D., with high distinction, 1975). Order of the Coif; Phi Delta Phi. Law Clerk to Justice Harvey Uhlenhopp, Iowa Supreme Court, 1975-1976. *Member:* Muscatine County (President, 1990-1991) Iowa State and American Bar Associations. ***PRACTICE AREAS:*** Business Law; Environmental Law; Health Law. ***Email:*** dmeloy@slhlaw.com

JOAN U. AXEL, born Fargo, North Dakota, January 21, 1943; admitted to bar, 1982, Iowa. *Education:* Iowa State University (B.S., 1964); University of Iowa (J.D., 1982). Member, 1974-1978 and Chair, 1977-1978 Iowa State Lottery Commission 1986-1991. Member: Iowa Telecommunication and Technology Commission, 1994-2000; Muscatine County Board of Supervisors. Director, Iowa Law School Foundation, 2000—. Former Member: Supreme Court Grievance Commission; Supreme Court Commission on Rules of Civil Procedure. *Member:* Muscatine County, Iowa State (Member, Supreme Court Commission on Unauthorized Practice of Law, 1996—) and American Bar Associations; Iowa Bar Foundation. ***PRACTICE AREAS:*** Health Law; Real Estate; Estate Planning; Probate. ***Email:*** juaxel@slhlaw.com

ERIC J. THOMSEN, born Mason City, Iowa, March 19, 1953; admitted to bar, 1978, Iowa, Wisconsin and U.S. Tax Court. *Education:* Iowa State University (B.S., 1975); University of Iowa (J.D., with distinction, 1978). Certified Public Accountant, Iowa, 1982. Board Member: Luthern Homes Society; Muscatine Humane Society; Muscatine Community Endowment Foundation. *Member:* Muscatine County and Iowa State Bar Associations; American Institute of Certified Public Accountants; Iowa Society of Certified Public Accountants. (Probate, Estate Planning and Tax Department Chair). ***PRACTICE AREAS:*** Estate Planning; Individual Income Tax Planning; Business Tax Planning. ***Email:*** ethomsen@slhlaw.com

---

BRANDY DULCEAK, born Winfield, Illinois, October 1, 1972; admitted to bar, 2001, Iowa; 2002, Illinois. *Education:* University of Iowa (B.A., Communications, with honors, 1998; J.D., 2001). Recipient, National Association of Women Lawyers Award, 2001. Representative, Seventh District, I.O.W.A., 2001—. Chairperson, Membership Committee, I.O.W.A., 2002—. *Member:* Muscatine County (President, 2004—), Scott County, Iowa State (Member, 2001— and Member, Publicity Committee, 2001—, Young Lawyers Division) and American Bar Associations; Iowa Organization of Women Attorneys. ***PRACTICE AREAS:*** General Practice. ***Email:*** brandyd@slhlaw.com

JEAN E. DRAGON, born Chicago, Illinois, December 19, 1961; admitted to bar, 1995, Illinois; 2003, Iowa. *Education:* University of Dubuque (B.A., 1989); University of Iowa (J.D., with distinction, 1994). ***PRACTICE AREAS:*** General Practice. ***Email:*** jdragon@slhlaw.com

WES A. FOWLER, born Macomb, Illinois, January 10, 1976; admitted to bar, 2001, Iowa. *Education:* University of Iowa (B.A., Political Science, with distinction, 1998; J.D., 2001). *Member:* Iowa State and American Bar Associations. ***PRACTICE AREAS:*** General Practice. ***Email:*** wfowler@slhlaw.com

KENZA B. NELSON, born West Union, Iowa, December 12, 1979; admitted to bar, 2005, Iowa. *Education:* Wartburg College (B.A., English and Political Science, summa cum laude, 2002); University of Iowa (J.D., with high distinction, 2005). *Member:* Muscatine County, Iowa State and American Bar Associations. ***PRACTICE AREAS:*** General Practice. ***Email:*** knelson@slhlaw.com

REPRESENTATIVE CLIENTS: Bandag Incorporated; Carver Enterprise Group; Central Can Company; Central State Bank; Connoisseur Communications; Dovetail Development Group; Farm Bureau Mutual Insurance Co.; Farmers and Merchants Savings Bank (Lone Tree); First National Bank of Muscatine; General Motors Acceptance Corp.; Great American Insurance Co.; H.J. Heinz Company; HON INDUSTRIES, Inc. and its subsidiaries; IPSCO Steel Inc.; Liberty Trust & Savings Bank (Durant); Milwaukee Mutual Insurance Company; Monsanto Company; Tech Systems, Inc.; The Family Credit Union; The Stanley Foundation; The Travelers Group, Inc.; Stanley Consultants, Inc, and subsidiaries; Texaco, Inc.; Union Federal Savings and Loan Association of Kewanee, Illinois; Varied Investments, Inc. (Grain Processing Corporation, Kent Feeds, Inc.); West Liberty State Bank.
GENERAL COUNSEL FOR: HWH Corporation; John Keady's General Motors Superstore; Lujack's Northpark Auto Plaza; M.A. Ford Mfg. Co.; Royale International Beverage Co.; The State Bank of Annawan; BT Prime-Mover, Inc.; Tri State Companies, Inc.; Unity Health System; Wilton Industrial Development Corp.; Wilton Precision Steel; WTC Communications, Inc.

(For Complete Biographical Data on all Personnel, see Professional Biographies at Davenport, Iowa)

PETERS LAW FIRM, P.C.

Established in 1895

401 FRONT STREET
P.O. BOX 282
NEOLA, IOWA 51559
Telephone: 712-485-2265
URL: http://www.peterslawfirm.com

Council Bluffs, Iowa Office: 233 Pearl Street. P.O. Box 1078. Telephone: 712-328-3157. FAX: 712-328-9092.
Glenwood, Iowa Office: 10 North Walnut. Telephone: 712-527-4877. FAX: 712-527-3418.
South Omaha, Nebraska Office: 4828 South 24th Street, Suite 200, 68107. Telephone: 402-731-1711. Fax: 402-731-3363.

(This Listing Continued)

Personal Injury Litigation and Commercial Litigation. Insurance, Tax, Real Estate, Corporation, Probate and Bankruptcy Law.

REPRESENTATIVE CLIENTS: Grinnell Mutual Re-Insurance Co.; Horace Mann Ins. Cos.; Kemper Group: Shelter Ins. Co.; State Farm Mutual Auto Ins.; United Fire & Casualty; The Cities McClelland, Glenwood, Underwood, Neola and Minden, IA; Iowa West Racing Assn.; Mills County State Bank; Glenwood State Bank; 1st Community National Bank; Citizens Savings Bank; Peoples National Bank; Randolph State Bank; MidStates Bank; Ameristar Casino; North Pointe Insurance Co.; Edwards Archer Auto Plaza.
REFERENCE: Mid States Bank.

(For biographical data on all personnel, see Professional Biographies at Council Bluffs, Iowa)

CAHILL LAW OFFICES

Established in 1976

1015 FIFTH STREET
NEVADA, IOWA 50201
Telephone: 515-382-6571
Fax: 515-382-4338
URL: http://www.lawyers.com/cahilllawoffice

General Trial Practice. Probate, Court Practice, Municipal, Negligence, Real Estate and Insurance Law. Estate Planning, Trusts, Wills, Estates and Probate.

FIRM PROFILE: Cahill Law Office was originally founded by Donald L. Nelson in 1949 and the present lawyers have a combined experience of over 57 years practicing law. Serving clients throughout Central Iowa, with an emphasis in Story, Polk, Marshall, Boone and Webster counties.

MEMBERS OF FIRM

DONALD L. NELSON (1922-1984)

THOMAS J. CAHILL, born Louisville, Kentucky, June 25, 1944; admitted to bar, 1969, Iowa. *Education:* Iowa State University; University of Iowa (B.A., 1966; J.D., 1969). Phi Alpha Delta. Assistant County Attorney, Story County, 1973-1975. President, District 2B Bar Association, 1979-1981. Member, Judicial Nominating Committee, Second Judicial District, 1980-1986. *Member:* Story County (President, 1980-1982), Iowa State (Member, Board of Governors, 1988-1992) and American Bar Associations; Iowa Defense Counsel. ***PRACTICE AREAS:*** Probate; Estate Planning; Tax; Corporate; Commercial; Civil Trial. ***Email:*** tomcahilllaw@midiowa.net

JOSEPH R. CAHILL, born Fort Dodge, Iowa, October 12, 1951; admitted to bar, 1976, Iowa. *Education:* University of Iowa (B.A., 1973; J.D., 1976). Assistant Story County Attorney, 1979-1982. Story County Public Defender, 1982-1984. Member, Judicial Nominating Committee, Second Judicial District, 1986-1992. *Member:* Iowa State and American Bar Associations; National Association of Criminal Defense Attorneys. ***PRACTICE AREAS:*** Civil Litigation; Criminal; Family Law; Trials and Appeals. ***Email:*** Joecahilllaw@midiowa.net

GENERAL COUNSEL FOR: Community Bank; Hertz Farm Management Nevada, IA.; Story County Hospital.
REPRESENTATIVE CLIENTS: Colo Telephone Co.; State Bank & Trust, Nevada, Iowa; Iowa Mutual Insurance Co.; IMT Insurance Co.; Hertz Farm Management.

J. KEITH RIGG

NEVADA, IOWA

(See Des Moines)

Criminal Trial Practice in Federal and State Courts. Civil Litigation.

KENNEDY AND KENNEDY

KENNEDY LAW BUILDING
12 EAST MAIN STREET
P.O. BOX 406
NEW HAMPTON, IOWA 50659
Telephone: 641-394-3113
FAX: 641-394-5173
Email: kenndlaw@rconnect.com
URL: http://www.lawyers.com/kenndlaw

Lawler, Iowa Office: 411 East Grove. Telephone: 563-238-8761.

Probate, Real Estate, Criminal Law, Trial Practice.

MEMBERS OF FIRM

WILLIAM J. KENNEDY (1935-1979)

MICHAEL K. KENNEDY, born New Hampton, Iowa, October 30, 1939; admitted to bar, 1968, Iowa. *Education:* University of Notre Dame (B.A., 1961); Iowa University (J.D., 1968). Phi Delta Phi. Iowa State Representative, 1969-1983. *Member:* Iowa State Bar Association (Member, Board of Governors, 1981-1985). ***PRACTICE AREAS:*** Litigation; Probate; Real Estate.

KEVIN J. KENNEDY, born New Hampton, Iowa, December 30, 1948; admitted to bar, 1974, Iowa and U.S. District Court, Northern District of Iowa. *Education:* University of Notre Dame (A.B., 1971); University of Iowa (J.D., 1974). City Attorney, New Hampton, Iowa, 1986—. *Member:* Iowa State and American Bar Associations. ***PRACTICE AREAS:*** Litigation; Probate; Real Estate.

REPRESENTATIVE CLIENTS: First National Bank, New Hampton; City of New Hampton; Croell Redi-Mix, Inc.

CALDWELL, CALDWELL & CALDWELL, P.L.C.

Established in 1976

102 FIRST STREET NORTH
P.O. BOX 187
NEWTON, IOWA 50208
Telephone: 641-792-7235
Toll Free: 1-888-323-0654
Fax: 641-792-1721
URL: http://www.lawyeriowa.com
Email: caldwell1@iowatelecom.net
URL: http://www.lawyers.com/caldwell

General Practice in all Courts. Probate, Real Estate, Bankruptcy, Business Law, Employment, Special Education, Corporation and Taxation Law. Trials and Appeals. Family and Juvenile Law, Municipal.

FIRM PROFILE: Caldwell, Caldwell & Caldwell, P.L.C. was founded in 1976 by Gilbert R. Caldwell. Serving clients throughout Jasper, Polk, Marion, Poweshiek and surrounding counties. The firm engages in general practice with lawyers practicing in specific areas of law.

GILBERT R. CALDWELL (1921-1998)

GILBERT R. CALDWELL, III, born Newton, Iowa, June 14, 1952; admitted to bar, 1978, Iowa, U.S. District Court, Northern and Southern Districts of Iowa and U.S. Supreme Court. *Education:* Tulsa University (B.A., 1974; J.D., 1977). Presenter: Iowa State Bar Association Family Bar Section, Ethics, Drake University, 1993; Child Custody & Visitation in Iowa, NBI, 1997; Family Law, NBI, 1998; Family Law for Paralegals, Des Moines, 1995; Iowa State Bar Association "Hot Topics" Family Law Practice, June 1998; Iowa Association of Trial Lawyers, Family Law Seminar: Ethics, July 1998; Iowa State Bar Association Family Law, "From Birth to Dissolution", 1998; "Adoption Law," NBI Seminar, Iowa, 2003; Family Law in Iowa, August 25 & 26, 1998. Member, Iowa Supreme Court Select Committee to Review State Court Practices in Child Welfare Matters, 1998—, Co-Chair "Judicial Oversight of the Permanency Process Task Force," 1997. Iowa State Bar Association's Lawyers Professional Liability Insurance Company, 1999—. *Member:* Jasper County (President, 1990, 5A Judicial District, Bar President, 1991), Iowa State (Chairperson, Family and Juvenile Law Section, 1991-1992, 1998-1999; Chairman, Juvenile Law Committee, 1985; 5A Representative, Executive Council, Young Lawyers Division 1987-1989; Co-Chairman, Young Lawyers Division Membership and Minority Affairs Committee, 1988; Contributor: Young Lawyers Division and Juvenile Law Manual; Member, Family Law Resource Panel, Volunteer Lawyers Project, 1997—; Member, Family and Juvenile Law Section Council, 1997-2000) and American (Member: Executive Committee of the Juvenile Justice Committee, 1987-1990; Regional Coordinator for Child Advocacy and Protection Committee Juvenile Law Update, 1987-1990; Executive, Young Lawyers Division Committee, Child Advocacy and Protection Committee, 1988-1989; Vice-Chairperson, Family Law Committee, General Practice Section, 1991-1993) Bar Associations; Supreme Court Special Study Panel on Family Courts, 1990; Iowa Council for the Protection of Chemically Exposed Infants, 1991-2001; Iowa Trial Lawyers Association; The Association of Trial Lawyers of America; American Judicature Society; National Association of Counsel for Children (Prevent Child Abuse, Iowa Board of Directors, 2000-2003; Vice President, 2003; 5A Judicial Nominating Commission, 2002). ***REPORTED CASES:*** In Re the Marriage of Longman 619 N.W. 2d 369 (Iowa, 2000). ***PRACTICE AREAS:*** Litigation; Family Law. ***Email:*** caldwell3@iowatelecom.net

RANDAL B. CALDWELL, born Newton, Iowa, July 1, 1955; admitted to bar, 1979, Iowa, U.S. District Court, Southern District of Iowa and U.S. Supreme Court. *Education:* Central College (B.A., 1977); University of Iowa (J.D., with distinction, 1979). Contributor, Iowa Law Review, 1979. Co-Author: "The New Iowa Land Title Examination Standards," 34 Drake Law Review 3, 1985. Lecturer: "Conveyancing and Examination of Abstracts," 1987-1988 and "Basic Real Property," 1987-1988, Iowa State Bar Review School, Inc. Adjunct Instructor, Business Law, Upper Iowa University, 1992-1995. Member, 1995—; Chairman, 1997, Volunteer Lawyers Project Board of Directors. *Member:* Iowa State (Member: Iowa State Title Standards Committee, 1980-1989; Chairman, Real Property Committee, 1990-1991; Mason Ladd Legal Writing Award Committee, Young Lawyers Division, 1981-1987; Chairman, 1986; Council, Real Estate and Title Law Section, 1992-1993; Probate Committee Section Council, 1999—) and American (Member, Sections on: Real Property, Probate and Trust, 1999-2001; Legal Forms Committee, 1994—) Bar Associations; Title Guaranty Division, Iowa Finance Authority; Iowa Municipal Attorneys Association; Iowa Trust Association. ***PRACTICE AREAS:*** Trust Law; Business Law; Probate Law; Real Estate Law. ***Email:*** caldwell1@iowatelecom.net

REPRESENTATIVE CLIENTS: Farm Credit Services, Newton, Iowa; Jean and Murray Nelson Foundation; City of Prairie City, Iowa; City of Monroe, Iowa; City of Lambs Grove.
REFERENCE: Farm Credit Services, Newton, Iowa.

J. KEITH RIGG

NEWTON, IOWA

(See Des Moines)

Criminal Trial Practice in Federal and State Courts. Civil Litigation.

WALKER & BILLINGSLEY

208 NORTH SECOND AVENUE WEST
P.O. BOX 157
NEWTON, IOWA 50208
Telephone: 641-792-3595
Fax: 641-792-0289
URL: http://www.walklaw.com
Email: corey@walklaw.com
URL: http://www.lawyers.com/wkblaw

Des Moines, Iowa Office: 1000 73rd Street, Suite 24. Telephone: 515-440-2852. Fax: 515-440-6077.

(This Listing Continued)

Baxter, Iowa Office: 103 East State. Telephone: 641-227-3800.

General Practice, Personal Injury and Wrongful Death, Family Law and Domestic Relations (Divorce), Real Estate, Wills, Trusts, Estate Planning and Probate Law, Criminal Law, Taxation and Tax Returns, Litigation and Trial Law, Product Liability, Employment Law, Medical Malpractice, Workers' Compensation.

FIRM PROFILE: Walker & Billingsley is a seven lawyer firm with almost 100 years of combined experience and an emphasis in personal service. We handle a wide variety of cases throughout the State of Iowa and beyond. We have offices in Newton and Des Moines to better serve our clients. We meet our clients' needs by providing a "FREE Initial Consultation." Call 1-888-792-3595 to schedule your no obligation, no cost initial consultation. Also, we offer a "contingency fee" on injury cases such as automobile accidents, work injuries, falls, product liability, medical negligence and wrongful death. A "contingency fee" means there is no financial risk to you for attorney fees because we are not paid unless you make a recovery. We also have evening and weekend appointments available.

MEMBERS OF FIRM

LEE M. WALKER, admitted to bar, 1975, Iowa; U.S. District Court, Northern and Southern Districts of Iowa; U.S. Court of Appeals, 8th Circuit; U.S. Supreme Court; U.S. Tax Court. *Education:* Drake University (J.D., 1975). *Member:* Jasper County, Iowa State and American Bar Associations; Association of Trial Lawyers of Iowa; The Association of Trial Lawyers of America. ***PRACTICE AREAS:*** General Practice; Family Law; Divorce; Personal Injury; Real Estate; Wills; Estate Planning; Probate; Criminal Law; Taxation; Trial Practice. ***Email:*** lee@walklaw.com

JOHN E. BILLINGSLEY, admitted to bar, 1982, Iowa; U.S. District Court, Northern and Southern Districts of Iowa and District of Arizona; U.S. Court of Appeals, Eighth Circuit. *Education:* Drake University (J.D., 1981). *Member:* Jasper County, Iowa State and American Bar Associations; The Association of Trial Lawyers of Iowa. ***PRACTICE AREAS:*** General Practice; Criminal Law; Personal Injury; Trial Practice; Family Law. ***Email:*** john@walklaw.com

COREY J. L. WALKER, admitted to bar, 1997, Iowa; 1998, Minnesota; U.S. District Court, Northern and Southern Districts of Iowa; U.S. Court of Appeals, Eighth Circuit; U.S. Supreme Court. *Education:* Drake University (J.D., 1997). *Member:* Iowa State and American Bar Associations; Iowa Association of Trial Lawyers (Board Member, 2000—); The Association of Trial Lawyers of America. ***PRACTICE AREAS:*** Personal Injury; Workers' Compensation; Automobile Accidents and Injuries; Dog Bites; Slip and Fall; Products Liability; Trial Practice; Legal Malpractice; Medical Malpractice; Wrongful Death. ***Email:*** corey@walklaw.com

ASSOCIATES

KATHRYN "BETH" E. WALKER, admitted to bar, 2000, Iowa and Nebraska; U.S. District Court, Northern and Southern Districts of Iowa; U.S. Court of Appeals, Eighth Circuit. *Education:* Drake University (J.D., high honors, 2000). Delta Theta Phi; Order of the Coif. *Member:* Jasper County, Iowa State and American Bar Associations; Iowa Association of Trial Lawyers; The Association of Trial Lawyers of America. ***PRACTICE AREAS:*** General Practice; Criminal Law; Juvenile Law; Family Law; Divorce; Personal Injury; Real Estate; Wills; Estate Planning; Probate; Trial Practice. ***Email:*** beth@walklaw.com

ERIK D. BAIR, admitted to bar, 2001, Iowa. *Education:* Drake University (J.D., with honors, 2001). *Member:* Jasper County, Iowa State and American Bar Associations; The Iowa Trial Lawyers Association; The Association of Trial Lawyers of America. ***PRACTICE AREAS:*** General Practice; Criminal Law; Personal Injury; Family Law; Divorce; Trial Practice. ***Email:*** erik@walklaw.com

ERIC LONEY, admitted to bar, 2001, Iowa. *Education:* Drake Law School (J.D., with honors, 2001; Legislative Certificate, 2001). *Member:* Iowa State and American Bar Associations; Iowa Trial Lawyers Association (Member, Legislative Committee); The Association of Trial Lawyers of America; Polk County Lawyers Association. ***PRACTICE AREAS:*** General Practice; Workers Compensation; Personal Injury; Products Liability; Medical Malpractice; Slip and Fall; Trial Practice; Wrongful Death. ***Email:*** eric@walklaw.com

JANE ODLAND, born Osage, Iowa, November 14, 1955; admitted to bar, 2004, Iowa. *Education:* Iowa State University (B.S., Biology, 1977); Mercy Medical Center School of Medical Technology (MT, ASCP, 1980); University of Iowa (J.D., 2004). *Member:* Jasper County and Iowa State Bar Associations. ***PRACTICE AREAS:*** General Practice; Criminal Law; Juvenile Law; Family Law; Divorce; Taxation; Tax Preparation; Real Estate; Wills; Estates; Probate Law; Trial Practice. ***Email:*** jane@walklaw.com

---

THE POWELL LAW FIRM, P.C.

1424 SUNSET DRIVE
P.O. BOX 189
NORWALK, IOWA 50211
Telephone: 515-981-9150
Fax: 515-981-9220
Email: powelaw@aol.com
URL: http://www.lawyers.com/powelllawfirmpc

Mailing Address: P.O. Box 189, Norwalk, Iowa 50211

Business Law, Construction Law, Family Law, Personal Injury, Real Estate, Administrative Law, Appellate Practice, Commercial Law, Consumer Law, Contracts, Federal Practice, Government Contracts, Guardianship and Conservatorship, Litigation, Probate, Trusts and Estates, Wills, Elder Law, Child Custody, Child Support, Divorce, Criminal Defense, Automobile Accidents and Injuries, Commercial Real Estate, Residential Real Estate Sales, Zoning Planning and Land Use, Corporate Law, Franchise Law, Small Business Law, Business Organization.

(This Listing Continued)

FIRM PROFILE: The Powell Law Firm is dedicated to providing courteous, timely, and the highest quality legal services to our clients. Rod Powell has over thirty years of diverse national law practice experience, and has represented individuals, businesses, agencies and organizations, government entities, and multinational corporations in venues ranging from cases before administrative agencies to the U.S. Supreme Court. Mr. Powell and associate Katherine Daman are assisted in their practice by experienced legal assistants and other support staff. Achieving positive results for our clients is our highest priority.

ROD POWELL, born West Union, Iowa, January 20, 1947; admitted to bar, 1973, Iowa; 1978, Missouri; U.S. Supreme Court; U.S. Court of Appeals, Eighth Circuit; U.S. District Court, Southern and Northern Districts of Iowa; U.S. District Court, Eastern District of Missouri; U.S. Court of Military Appeals. *Education:* University of Iowa (B.A., 1969; J.D., 1972). Recipient: Iowa State Bar Association Pro Bono Award, 1999; Volunteer Lawyer Project Award from Legal Services Corporation of Iowa, 1999. National Business Institute Seminar Faculty: "Major Land Use Laws in Iowa," "Iowa land Use: Current Issues in Subdivision Annexation and Zoning Law," and "Boundary Law in Iowa." Author: "Major Land Use Laws in Iowa"; "Drugs and Alcohol in the Workplace"; "Miscellaneous Laws With Consumer Implications." Democratic Candidate for Congress, Fifth District of Iowa, 1990. National Board, Council on International Relations and United Nations Affairs, 1968-1971. Director, Des Moines United Nations Association. Professional Law Firm Host, Ukrainian Commercial Law Delegation, 2002. Iowa Council for International Understanding Community Connections Host for delegations from Moldova, Ukraine and Russia, 2001—. Lecturer: Grand View College, International Law and the United nations Charter, 2003; St. Louis University College of Law, Secured Transactions and Commercial Law, 1980; National Association of Attorneys General, The Truth-in-Lending Act and Deceptive Home Mortgage Practices, 1987. Chairman, Board of Housing Appeals, City of Ferguson, Missouri, 1986-1988. Chairman, Warren County Planning and Zoning Commission, 1989-1996. Staff Attorney, Consumer Law Department, 1977-1980. Managing Attorney, St. Louis County Office and Family Law Department, 1980-1988. Legal Services of Eastern Missouri, St. Louis, Missouri. Clinical Supervisor, St. Louis University and Washington University College of Law, St. Louis, Missouri, 1978-1988. *Member:* American Bar Association (Member, Sections on Business Law, General Practice, International Law, Real Property, Probate and Trust Law), Iowa State Bar Association (member, Sections on Business law, Commercial and Bankruptcy Law, International Law, Probate and Trust Law, Real Estate and Title Law and Trade Regulations); The Missouri Bar; Metropolitan St. Louis, Warren County and Polk County Bar Associations. [Capt. USAF, JAG, 1973-1977; Deputy Staff Judge Advocate, 1976-1977; Public Contract and Military Justice Law]. ***REPORTED CASES:*** State v. Wells, 629 N.W. 2d 346 (Iowa 2001); Ritz v. Wapello County Bd. of Supervisors, 595 N.W. 2d 786 (Iowa 1999); In Re. Marriage of Wessels, 542 N.W. 2d 486 (Iowa 1995); Verne R. Houghton Ins. Agency v. Orr Drywall Co., 470 N.W. 2d 39 (Iowa 1991); Blissenbach v. Provident Life and Accident Insurance Co., 689 S.W. 2d 707 (Mo. App. 1985); St. Louis Housing Authority v. Thompson, 657 S.W. 2d 390 (Mo. App. 1983); Simms v. Ford Motor Credit Company, 605 S.W. 2d 212 (Mo. App. 1980). ***Email:*** powelaw@aol.com

---

KATHERINE DAMAN, born Waterloo, Iowa, November 9, 1977; admitted to bar, 2004, Iowa. *Education:* Fayetteville State University, North Carolina (B.A., 2000); Drake University, Des Moines, Iowa (J.D., 2003). *Member:* Member: Warren County, Polk County and Iowa State Bar Associations; American Trial Lawyers Association. ***PRACTICE AREAS:*** Litigation; Dispute Resolution. ***Email:*** powelaw@aol.com

REPRESENTATIVE CLIENTS: Applied Agricultural Technologies, Inc.; Iowa Friends of Legal Services; Neal Appraisal Services; Turn-Reit Construction Services, Ltd.; Psychology Consultants; Vankie, Inc.; Movie Ad Media, Inc.; Great Plains Utility Engineering, Inc.; Organizational Solutions, Inc.; Jieng Community Association (Dinka) of the State of Iowa.

GAUKEL, NEVINS & WESTERGAARD

ONAWA, IOWA

(See Mapleton)

General Practice. Probate, Real Estate, Personal Injury, Corporation, Estate Planning and Taxation Law. Trials and Appeals.

KLAY, VELDHUIZEN, BINDNER, DE JONG & JACOBSMA, P.L.C.

121 ALBANY AVENUE, N.E.
P.O. BOX 405
ORANGE CITY, IOWA 51041
Telephone: 712-737-4851
Fax: 712-737-4853

Alton, Iowa Office: Mitchell Building, 306-10th Street, P.O. Box H, 51003-0908. Telephone: 712-756-4141, Fax: 712-756-4646.
Paullina, Iowa Office: 111 South Main Street, P.O. Box 617, 51046-0617. Telephone: 712-949-2142. Fax: 712-949-2140.

General Practice. Probate, Trusts and Estates, Real Estate, Taxation, Agricultural, Municipal, Corporate and Negligence Law. Trials and Appeals.

LOREN J. VELDHUIZEN, born Oskaloosa, Iowa, December 14, 1945; admitted to bar, 1971, Iowa and U.S. District Court, Northern District of Iowa; U.S. Supreme Court. *Education:* Calvin College (A.B., 1968); University of Iowa (J.D., with distinction, 1971). Member, Iowa Law Review, 1970. City Attorney, Orange City, 1975—. *Member:* Iowa State Bar Association; Iowa Trial Lawyers Association. ***Email:*** ljveldhuizen@klaylaw.com

ROGER D. BINDNER, born Alton, Iowa, June 13, 1939; admitted to bar, 1966, Iowa and U.S. District Court, Northern District of Iowa. *Education:* Drake University (B.A., 1963; J.D., 1966). *Member:* Iowa State Bar Association. ***Email:*** rdbindner@klaylaw.com

(This Listing Continued)

BRADLEY K. DE JONG, born Orange City, Iowa, December 19, 1956; admitted to bar, 1983, Iowa and U.S. District Court, Northern District of Iowa. *Education:* Northwestern College (B.A., 1979); Creighton University (J.D., 1983). *Member:* Iowa State Bar Association. ***Email:*** bkdejong@klaylaw.com

MICHAEL J. JACOBSMA, born Sheldon, Iowa, September 11, 1969; admitted to bar, 1997, Iowa and U.S. District Court, Northern and Southern Districts of Iowa; U.S. Supreme Court. *Education:* Northwestern College (B.A., 1992); Creighton University (J.D., 1996). ***Email:*** mjjacobsma@klaylaw.com

ORSBORN, BAUERLE, MILANI & GROTHE, L.L.P.

OSKALOOSA, IOWA

(See Ottumwa)

General Civil and Trial Practice in All Courts. Real Estate, Estate Planning and Probate Law, Personal Injury, Employment Litigation, Family Law, Products Liability and Insurance Defense.

BRECKENRIDGE & DUKER, PC

226 WEST MAIN STREET, SUITE 408
P.O. BOX 616
OTTUMWA, IOWA 52501-0616
Telephone: 641-684-6097
Fax: 641-684-0209
Email: bdpc@ottumwalaw.net
URL: http://www.ottumwalaw.net

General Practice, Civil and Criminal Trials and Appeals in all Courts, Corporation, Domestic Relations, Labor and Employment Relations, Insurance Defense, Products Liability, Probate, Personal Injury, Real Estate, Administrative, Government and School Law.

MEMBERS OF FIRM

ROBERT E. BRECKENRIDGE, II, born Ottumwa, Iowa, July 20, 1957; admitted to bar, 1982, Nebraska; 1990, U.S. Supreme Court; 1991, U.S. District Court, Eastern District of North Carolina and U.S. Court of Appeals, Fourth Circuit; 1993, Iowa. *Education:* University of Iowa (B.A., 1979); University of Nebraska (J.D., 1982); Judge Advocate General's School of the Army (LL.M., 1990). Member, University of Nebraska Law Review. *Member:* Wapello County, Eighth Judicial District, Nebraska State, Iowa State and American (Member, Sections on: Criminal Law; Family Law) Bar Associations; National Association of Criminal Defense Lawyers. [Maj., U.S.M.C., 1982-1993; Maj., U.S.M.C. Reserve, 1976-1982, 1993-1998]. ***Email:*** reb@ottumwalaw.net

KENNETH A. DUKER, born Kansas City, Missouri, August 30, 1967; admitted to bar, 1993, Iowa and Missouri. *Education:* Rockhurst University (B.A., with senior honors, 1989); University of Iowa (J.D., with high distinction, 1993). Phi Alpha Delta. Member, Multi-Jurisdiction Practice Committee, 2002-2003. Member, Journal of Corporation Law. *Member:* Wapello County, Eighth Judicial District, Iowa State (District Representative, Young Lawyers Division, 1996-1998; Member, Multi-Jurisdiction Practice Committee, 2002—) and American Bar Associations; The Missouri Bar. ***Email:*** kad@ottumwalaw.net

REPRESENTATIVE CLIENTS: Affinity Business Solutions, L.L.C.; Auto-Owners Mutual Insurance Company; Cardinal Community School District; Geico Casualty Insurance Company; Here and Now Company; Hickenbottom, Inc.; Lancaster Oil; Noel Insurance; Ottumwa Developments, Inc.; Ottumwa Manor; Ottumwa Tent & Awning; Ottumwa Housing Authority; Swallow Fabric Structures, L.L.C.; The Graphics Wizard, Inc.; U.S. Bank, N.A.; Vista Woods Care Center.

HARRISON, MORELAND & WEBBER, P.C.

Established in 1963
129 WEST FOURTH STREET
P.O. BOX 250
OTTUMWA, IOWA 52501
Telephone: 641-682-8326
Fax: 641-682-8329
Email: hmmw@hmmw.com

General Practice. Probate, Corporate, Real Estate, Health and Hospital, Labor and Employment and Insurance Law. Trials and Appeals.

FIRM PROFILE: The law firm began when John N. Moreland, a graduate of Notre Dame Law School, joined the law practice of Charles Bookin (1910-1965), a graduate of Drake Law School, in March of 1963. The firm of Bookin and Moreland was changed in 1965 to the Moreland Law Firm upon the death of Charles Bookin. Ottumwa native Timothy J. McKay joined John N. Moreland and the firm became McKay & Moreland, P.C. in 1982. John R. Webber III joined the firm in 1985 and the name was changed to McKay, Moreland & Webber, P.C. in 1989. Michael J. Moreland came to the firm in 1990 and became a shareholder in 1994. Gayla R. Harrison came to the firm and became a shareholder in 2001, and the name was changed to Harrison, McKay, Moreland & Webber, P.C. The firm offers extensive litigation services, both in the areas of insurance defense and plaintiff personal injury work, and offers a full range of real estate, employment and corporate related services.

JOHN R. WEBBER, III, born San Francisco, California, November 14, 1956; admitted to bar, 1982, Iowa, U.S. District Court, Northern and Southern Districts of Iowa, U.S. Tax Court, U.S. Claims Court and U.S. Court of Appeals, 8th Circuit; 1983, Missouri. *Education:* University of California at Los Angeles (B.A., 1979); Drake University (J.D., 1982). Member, 1992-1999, Vice Chairman, 1994-1998, President, 1999. Ottumwa Regional Health Center Board of Directors. *Member:* Wapello County, Iowa State and American

(This Listing Continued)

HARRISON, MORELAND & WEBBER, P.C., Ottumwa—Continued

(Member, Sections on: Corporation, Banking, Business, Health Law and Real Property, Probate and Trust Law) Bar Associations; The Missouri Bar; American Health Lawyers Association. ***Email:*** jwebber@hmmw.com

MICHAEL J. MORELAND, born Ottumwa, Iowa, December 9, 1962; admitted to bar, 1991, Iowa; U.S. Supreme Court; U.S. District Court, Northern and Southern Districts of Iowa. *Education:* Creighton University (B.S., 1985); University of Iowa (J.D., 1990). Pi Mu Epsilon; Phi Delta Phi. Member, University of Iowa Law Review, 1989-1990. Commissioner, Ottumwa City Planning and Zoning, 1990-1992. Representative, Iowa House of Representatives, 93rd District, 1993-1998. Assistant Minority Leader, 1995-1998. *Member:* Wapello County, Eighth Judicial District, Iowa State and American Bar Associations; Fellow, Iowa Academy of Trial Lawyers. ***Email:*** mmoreland@hmmw.com

GAYLA R. HARRISON, born Kirksville, Missouri, October 3, 1960; admitted to bar, 1986, Iowa; 1987, U.S. District Court, Northern and Southern Districts of Iowa and U.S. Court of Appeals, 8th Circuit. *Education:* Drake University (B.F.A., 1983; J.D., with honors, 1986). Law Clerk to Justice Arthur A. McGiverin, Iowa Supreme Court, 1986-1987. Co-Author: "Employment at Will in Iowa: A Journey Forward," 39 Drake Law Review 67, 1989-1990. *Member:* Wapello County, Iowa State (Member, Supreme Court Advisory Committee-Rules of Evidence, 1991-1996; Chair, Labor and Employment Law Section, 1999-2001) and American (Member, Sections on: Litigation; Labor and Employment Law) Bar Associations. ***PRACTICE AREAS:*** Employment Law. ***Email:*** gharrison@hmmw.com

---

SHANNON J. WOODS, born Clarinda, Iowa, January 13, 1978; admitted to bar, 2003, Iowa. *Education:* Buena Vista University (B.A., 2000); Drake Law School (J.D., 2003). Mediator, American Academy of Alternative Dispute Resolution Attorneys. *Member:* Wapello County, Iowa State and American Bar Associations. ***Email:*** swoods@hmmw.com

OF COUNSEL

JOHN N. MORELAND, born Mason City, Iowa, May 4, 1936; admitted to bar, 1961, Iowa. *Education:* University of Notre Dame (B.A., cum laude, 1958; J.D., 1961). Assistant County Attorney, 1961-1964. Alternate Judge, Municipal Court, City of Ottumwa, 1966-1970. Board Member and President, Ottumwa Catholic School System, 1967-1968; 1969-1970. President, Indian Hills Community College Foundation, 1999—. *Member:* Wapello County (Vice President, 1966-1967; President, 1968-1969), Eighth Judicial District, Iowa State and American Bar Associations. ***Email:*** jnmd1958@aol.com

REPRESENTATIVE CLIENTS: Ajinomoto Heartland, L.L.C.; Ajinomoto Food Ingredients L.L.C.; Al-Jon, Inc.; Dr. Pepper Seven-Up Bottling Group Midwest Division; Cameron Mutual; Carroll Lumber Co.; City of Agency; EMC Insurance Companies; Farm Bureau Mutual Insurance Company; Farm and City Insurance Co.; U.S. Bank; Golden Furrow; Great West Casualty Insurance Co.; Hartford Insurance; Indian Hills Community College; Interpower Corporation, Iowa Mutual Insurance Co.; Lumbermen's Underwriting Alliance; Musco Sports Lighting; Nationwide Mutual Insurance; Newell Rubbermaid, Inc.; Oskaloosa Food Products Corp.; Ottumwa Community School District; Ottumwa Good Samaritan Center; Ottumwa Pediatrics; Ottumwa Regional Health Center; Ottumwa School Employees Credit Union; Ottumwa Transit Authority; Pekin Insurance Company; State Farm Insurance Co.; United Fire & Casualty Co.; Wells Fargo Bank Iowa, N.A.; Wells Fargo Home Mortgage, Inc.; West Bend Mutual Insurance Co.; WINBCO Tank.

KEITH LAW FIRM

Established in 1995

1313 NORTH COURT

OTTUMWA, IOWA 52501

Telephone: 641-682-4377

Toll Free: 800-903-4377

Fax: 641-683-3472

General, Civil and Trial Practice in all Courts, Appellate Practice, Corporation, Insurance, Real Estate, Estate Planning and Probate, Personal Injury and Employment Discrimination Litigation.

KENNETH L. KEITH, born Cascade, Iowa, October 7, 1926; admitted to bar, 1952, Iowa. *Education:* State University of Iowa (B.S.C., 1949; J.D., 1952). Gamma Eta Gamma; Beta Gamma Sigma; Order of the Coif. Author: "Government Land Surveys and Related Problems," Iowa Law Review, 1952. Assistant Instructor, State University of Iowa Law School, 1952. *Member:* Wapello County, 8A District; Iowa State (Member: Committee on Public Relations, 1957-1967; Grievance Commission, 1969-1984; Board of Governors, 1984-1988), Federal and American Bar Associations; Iowa Defense Counsel Association (President, 1971-1972); Defense Research and Trial Lawyers Association. Fellow: American College of Trial Lawyers; American Board of Trial Advocates; Iowa Academy of Trial Lawyers. ***PRACTICE AREAS:*** General Trial Practice; Personal Injury Litigation; Products Liability Litigation; Insurance Defense Litigation; Employment Discrimination Litigation.

JONI KEITH, born Fontainebleau, France, October 29, 1956; admitted to bar, 1980, Iowa. *Education:* Ottumwa Heights College; Drake University (B.A. J., 1977; J.D., 1980). State of Iowa Scholar. Editor-in-Chief, Drake University Law School Gavel, 1979-1980. Former Council Member, Iowa Health Facilities, 1993-1999. Former Chairman and Director, Ottumwa Regional Health Center, 1985-1993. Former Member, Iowa Supreme Court Rules Advisory Council. Former Member, Iowa Board of Corrections, 1989-1993. *Member:* Wapello County, 8A District, Iowa State (Member, Membership Committee) Bar Associations; Iowa Certified Civil and Family Law Mediator, 1995. ***PRACTICE AREAS:*** Civil Rights; Law Enforcement; Labor and Employment; Estate Planning; Probate; Domestic Relations; Employment Discrimination Litigation.

LLOYD E. KEITH, born Ottumwa, Iowa, November 26, 1954; admitted to bar, 1980, Iowa. *Education:* Ottumwa Heights College (A.A., 1975), Phi Theta Kappa; Drake University (B.A., 1977; J.D., 1980). Judicial Magistrate, Part-time, 1999. *Member:* Wapello County (President, 1994), 8A District, Iowa State (Member, Litigation Council, 2004—)

(This Listing Continued)

Bar Associations; Iowa Defense Counsel Association (Member, Insurance Committee, 1989—). ***PRACTICE AREAS:*** General Trial Practice; Insurance Defense; Appellate Practice; Personal Injury.

REPRESENTATIVE CLIENTS: Bloomfield Foundry, Inc.; Drugtown; Hy-Vee, Inc.; K & L Corporation; M-W Livestock, Inc.; Productive Acres Manufacturing Co., Inc. (PAMCO); South Iowa Area Crime Commission; Winter Farms, Inc.

KIPLE, DENEFE, BEAVER, GARDNER & ZINGG, L.L.P.

Established in 1969

104 SOUTH COURT STREET

P.O. BOX 493

OTTUMWA, IOWA 52501

Telephone: 641-683-1626

Fax: 641-683-3597

Email: KIPLELAW@LISCO.COM

General Practice. Civil and Criminal Trials and Appeals, Probate, Real Estate, Labor, Insurance, Corporate, Personal Injury, Commercial, Workers Compensation, Municipal Law, Employment and Civil Rights Law.

MEMBERS OF FIRM

J. TERRENCE DENEFE, born Omaha, Nebraska, July 29, 1947; admitted to bar, 1973, Iowa and U.S. District Court, Northern and Southern Districts of Iowa. *Education:* Drake University (B.S.B.A., 1969; J.D., 1973). Assistant Wapello County Attorney, 1973-1976. *Member:* Wapello County (Secretary, 1973-1974; President, 1981-1982), Iowa State (Chairman, 1979-1984, and Member, 1978-1989, American Citizenship Committee), Eighth Judicial District (President, 1984-1986) Bar Associations; Iowa Trial Lawyers Association (Member, Board of Governors, 1996-2001); American Board of Trial Advocacy. Fellow, Iowa State Bar Foundation. ***Email:*** tdenefe@lisco.com

STEVEN GARDNER, born Ottumwa, Iowa, January 14, 1959; admitted to bar, 1984, Iowa and U.S. District Court, Southern District of Iowa. *Education:* University of Iowa (B.B.A., 1981); Drake University (J.D., with honors, 1984). Phi Alpha Delta. *Member:* Wapello County; Iowa State (Director, Young Lawyers Section, 1988-1990; Section Council, Criminal Law Section; Litigation Section; Labor and Employment Law); Eighth Judicial District and American Bar Associations. ***Email:*** sgardner@lisco.com

PAUL ZINGG, born Davenport, Iowa, December 19, 1962; admitted to bar, 1988, Iowa; 1989, U.S. District Court, Southern District of Iowa. *Education:* University of Iowa (B.A., 1985; J.D., with distinction, 1988). Special Prosecutor, Southeast Iowa Drug Task Force, 1996-1998. *Member:* Wapello County and Iowa State Bar Associations. ***Email:*** pzingg@lisco.com

OF COUNSEL

JEROME M. BEAVER, born Loyal, Wisconsin, March 25, 1940; admitted to bar, 1967, Iowa and U.S. District Court, Northern and Southern Districts of Iowa. *Education:* University of Dubuque (B.A., 1963); University of Iowa (J.D., with distinction, 1967). Phi Alpha Theta; Alpha Psi Omega. Member, Iowa Supreme Court Grievance Commission, 1996—. *Member:* Wapello County (President, 1978), Iowa State (Member: Legal Forms Committee, 1970-1981; Corporation and Business Law Committee, 1983-1990; Member of Council, Corporate, Banking and Business Law Section, 1990-1992; Sections on: Litigation; Probate and Trust; Business Law) and Eighth Judicial District Bar Associations; Iowa Trial Lawyers Association; Iowa Defense Counsel Association; Defense Research Institute. ***Email:*** jbeaver@lisco.com

GENERAL COUNSEL FOR: Winger Contracting Co.; Norris Asphalt Paving Co.; Wapello Rural Water Association, Inc.; Bud Heckart & Sons, Inc.; J.D. Carpenter Companies, Inc.; Elliott Oil, Inc.
REPRESENTATIVE CLIENTS: Farm Bureau Mutual Insurance Company; South Ottumwa Savings Bank; Libertyville Savings Bank; Central Valley Bank; Hedrick Savings Bank; Ottumwa McDonald's Restaurants; Tri-County Grain, Inc.; City of Eldon, Iowa; Douds Stone, Inc.; L & W Quarries, Inc.; Cobler Land & Cattle Co.; Cobler Farming Co.; Ottumwa Flying Service, Inc.; Tennyson Enterprises, Inc.; Warner Engineering Associates, Inc.; Southeast Iowa Neurological Associates, P.C.; Snowman Snowplow, Inc.; Regional Economic Development Investments, Inc.; Ideal Ready Mix Company, Inc.; J&J Steel, Inc.; Radiology Associates of Ottumwa, P.C.
REFERENCES: South Ottumwa Savings Bank; Hedrick Savings Bank.

ORSBORN, BAUERLE, MILANI & GROTHE, L.L.P.

Established in 1900

110 EAST THIRD

P.O. BOX 878

OTTUMWA, IOWA 52501

Telephone: 641-682-5447

Fax: 641-682-6940

Email: obmglaw@pcsia.net

URL: http://www.obmglaw.com

Centerville, Iowa Office: 105 West Van Buren, P. O. Box 518. Telephone: 641-856-3251. Fax: 641-856-5548.

General Civil and Trial Practice in All Courts. Real Estate, Estate Planning and Probate Law, Personal Injury, Employment Litigation, Family Law, Products Liability and Insurance Defense.

FIRM PROFILE: In the early 1900's, Merrill Gilmore began practice in Ottumwa. Wilbur Dull joined the firm in 1946. George A Milani joined Tom Fee in the practice of law in Centerville, Iowa, in 1928. The two firms merged in 1989 with offices in Ottumwa and Centerville. The firm has continuously engaged in the practice of law for more than a century. The firm offers a wide range of legal services throughout Southeastern Iowa.

(This Listing Continued)

MEMBERS OF FIRM

RICHARD C. BAUERLE, born Carroll, Iowa, June 2, 1931; admitted to bar, 1956, Iowa. *Education:* Iowa State University (B.S., 1953); University of Iowa (J.D., 1956). Tau Beta Pi; Phi Delta Phi. Board of Editors, Iowa Law Review, 1955-1956. *Member:* Wapello County (President, 1964-1965), Eighth Judicial District (President, 1966-1967), Iowa State (Member: Committee on Legal Education, 1962-1967; Executive Council, Junior Bar Section, 1961-1967; Professional Ethics and Conduct Committee, 1971-1983) and American Bar Associations; Iowa Defense Counsel Association (Member, Federal Practice Committee, Southern District of Iowa, 1981-1996); Defense Research Institute. ***PRACTICE AREAS:*** Products Liability; Trusts and Estates; Labor and Employment; Insurance Defense; Corporation Law. ***Email:*** dick@pcsia.net

ALLAN C. ORSBORN, born Emmetsburg, Iowa, March 15, 1951; admitted to bar, 1977, Iowa. *Education:* University of Iowa (B.S., 1973; J.D., with distinction, 1977). Phi Alpha Delta. *Member:* Wapello County, Eighth Judicial District, Iowa State (Member, Alternate Dispute Resolution Committee, 1988-1991) and American (Member, Litigation Section) Bar Associations; Iowa Trial Lawyers Association; American Board of Trial Advocacy. ***PRACTICE AREAS:*** Personal Injury; Domestic Relations; Insurance Defense; Criminal Defense; Trusts and Estates. ***Email:*** al@pcsia.net

GREGORY G. MILANI, born Centerville, Iowa, January 12, 1960; admitted to bar, 1987, Iowa. *Education:* Drake University (B.S., 1982; J.D., 1987). *Member:* Wapello County, Iowa State and American (Member, Sections on: General Practice; Law Office Management) Bar Associations; American Agricultural Law Association. ***PRACTICE AREAS:*** General Practice; Domestic Relations; Civil Trial Practice; Criminal Defense. ***Email:*** greg@pcsia.net

WILBUR R. DULL (1914-1994)

ASSOCIATE

RYAN J. MITCHELL, born Des Moines, Iowa, February 9, 1978; admitted to bar, 2003, Iowa. *Education:* Wartburg College (B.S., 2000); Drake University (J.D., 2003). *Member:* Wapello County and Iowa State Bar Associations. ***PRACTICE AREAS:*** General Practice; Civil Practice; Trial Practice. ***Email:*** ryan@pcsia.net

GENERAL COUNSEL FOR: McCune & Reed, Inc.; Answer Plus, Inc.; Ottumwa Medical Clinic, Inc.; Ottumwa Water Works.
REPRESENTATIVE CLIENTS: Central Valley Bank; Firstar Bank, Ottumwa; Le Mars Bank & Trust Co.; Grinnell Mutual Reinsurance Co.; Employers Mutual Cos.; Edward D. Jones & Co.; Allied Mutual Insurance Co.; Hormel Foods Corp.; MICO, Inc.; Purina Mills, Inc.; Grooms & Co. Construction; Indian Hills Community College, Centerville; Iowa Trust & Savings Bank, Centerville; United Fire & Casualty Co., Cedar Rapids, IA; Allied Group Insurance, Des Moines, IA.; Moore Hearing Clinic.

(For Additional Biographical Data on Other Personnel, see Professional Biographies at Centerville, Iowa).

BROWN, WINICK, GRAVES, GROSS, BASKERVILLE AND SCHOENEBAUM, P.L.C.

616 FRANKLIN PLACE
PELLA, IOWA 50219
Telephone: 641-628-4513
Fax: 641-628-8494
Email: bwg@ialawyers.com
URL: http://www.ialawyers.com

Des Moines, Iowa Office: 666 Grand Avenue, Suite 2000, 50309-2510.
West Des Moines, Iowa Office: Regency West 5, 4500 Westown Parkway, Suite 277, 50266-6717. Telephone: 515-242-2400. Fax: 515-242-2448.

FIRM PROFILE: Brown, Winick, Graves, Gross, Baskerville and Schoenebaum, P.L.C. is a major law firm with offices in Des Moines, West Des Moines, and Pella, Iowa. The firm originated as a tax law specialty firm in downtown Des Moines in 1951. Today the firm offers a broad range of legal services to clients throughout Iowa, regionally and nationally. The firm serves as counsel to a wide variety of service, manufacturing and commercial businesses and professionals. The firm's mission is to attract, retain and develop clients by providing effective and innovative solutions. We will provide a comprehensive range of legal services primarily to businesses, as well as to individuals in need of high quality legal services, inside and outside the State of Iowa.

(For complete biographical data on all firm personnel, see professional biographies at Des Moines, Iowa).

GREFE & SIDNEY, P.L.C.

810 WASHINGTON STREET
PELLA, IOWA 50219
Telephone: 641-628-4300
Fax: 515-245-4452
Email: grandfirm@grefesidney.com
URL: http://www.grefesidney.com

Des Moines, Iowa Office: 2222 Grand Avenue, P.O. Box 10434, 50306. Telephone: 515-245-4300. Telecopier: 515-245-4452.

General Civil and Trial Practice in all State and Federal Courts. Appellate Practice, Product Liability, Insurance, Negligence, Environmental, Toxic Torts, Professional Liability, Employment, Discrimination, Personal Injury, Workers Compensation, Real Estate, Probate and Estate Planning, Corporate Practice, Family Law, Commercial Litigation and Elder Law.

(This Listing Continued)

FIRM PROFILE: Grefe & Sidney, P.L.C. has established itself as a litigation firm in both defense and plaintiff's matters, as well as offering a business, corporate and tax division having a broad range of experience. The firm is listed in the Martindale-Hubbell Bar Register of Preeminent Lawyers.

(For complete biographical data on all personnel, see Professional Biographies at Des Moines, Iowa)

TRIPP, P.C.

Established in 2004
810 WASHINGTON STREET
PELLA, IOWA 50219-1525
Telephone: 641-628-9343
Toll Free: 800-368-1423
515-267-0110
Fax: 641-628-7252
URL: http://www.triplawfirm.com
URL: http://www.tripplaw.us

Social Security Law, General Practice.

TIMOTHY N. TRIPP, born Kalamazoo, Michigan, September 21, 1961; admitted to bar, 1990, New York; 1993, U.S. District Court, Southern and Eastern Districts of New York; 1996, Iowa; 1997, U.S. District Court, Southern and Northern Districts of Iowa; 2002, U.S. Court of Appeals, 8th Circuit. *Education:* Gordon College (1980-1982); University of Wisconsin-Madison (B.A., 1984); Brooklyn Law School (J.D., 1989). *Member:* Iowa State, New York State, Federal and American Bar Associations; National Organization of Social Security Claiment's Representatives (NOSSCR). ***REPORTED CASES:*** Hinders v. Barnhart, 349 F.Supp. 20 1218 (S.D. Iowa 2004); Downes v. Barnhart 289 F. Supp. 20 1072 (S.D. Iowa 2003); Roberts v. Barnhart, 283 F. Supp. 2d 1058 (S.D. Iowa 2003); Salk v. Barnhart, 234 F. Supp. 2d 1006 (S.D. Iowa 2002); Walker v. Barnhart, 302 F. Supp. 2d 1072 (S.D. Iowa 2003). ***PRACTICE AREAS:*** Social Security Law; General Practice. ***Email:*** ttripp@tripplaw.us

LEGAL SUPPORT PERSONNEL

KIMBERLY MEYER
TRACY TEACHART

SMITH, GRIGG, SHEA & KLINKER

A PROFESSIONAL CORPORATION
Established in 1906
120 SOUTH HAYES
P.O. BOX 98
PRIMGHAR, IOWA 51245
Telephone: 712-957-5465
Fax: 712-957-0121
Email: sgsk@tcaexpress.net

Sutherland, Iowa Office: Professional Building, 105 West Second Street, 51058. Telephone: 712-446-3650.

General Practice. Estate Planning, Probate, Personal Injury, Torts, Taxation and Mediation, Arbitration, Litigation and Real Estate, Family Law. Practice before State and Federal District and Appellate Courts and Administrative and Regulatory Agencies.

FIRM PROFILE: The firm and its predecessor partnerships have been practicing law since 1906 with offices in Primghar and Sutherland, Iowa. In addition to providing general practice services to clients in O'Brien County, the Firm has a long history of engaging in litigation. The litigation handled includes but is not limited to will contests, contract disputes, products liability, farm and auto accidents, and other torts for both plaintiffs and defendants, including litigation on behalf of insurance companies or their insureds.

RICHARD T. SMITH (1921-1990)

HAROLD R. GRIGG (1919-1997)

RONALD J. SHEA, born Primghar, Iowa, February 26, 1948; admitted to bar, 1973, Iowa, Nebraska and U.S. Court of Military Appeals; 1976, U.S. District Court, Northern District of Iowa. *Education:* Creighton University (B.A., 1970; J.D., 1972). *Member:* O'Brien County and Iowa State (Member, Board of Governors, 1984-1988) Bar Associations; Iowa Defense Counsel Association (Member, Board of Directors, 1989-1991); American Academy of Alternative Dispute Resolution Attorneys. [Capt., JAGC, U.S. Army, 1973-1976]. ***PRACTICE AREAS:*** Litigation; Probate; Real Estate; Taxation; Mediation; Arbitration; Estate Planning; Personal Injury; Torts. ***Email:*** rjshea@tcaexpress.net

WILLIAM K. KLINKER, born Blue Earth, Minnesota, January 6, 1959; admitted to bar, 1983, Iowa and U.S. District Court, Northern District of Iowa. *Education:* Augustana College (B.A., 1980); State University of Iowa (J.D., 1983). *Member:* O'Brien County and Iowa State (Member, Executive Council, Young Lawyers Division, 1988-1994; Grievance Commission, 2001—; Bench/Bar Conference Commission, 2001-2004) Bar Associations. ***PRACTICE AREAS:*** Litigation; Probate; Real Estate; Taxation; Estate Planning; Personal Injury; Torts; Family Law. ***Email:*** wklinker@tcaexpress.net

REPRESENTATIVE CLIENTS: First National Bank, Primghar, Iowa; Security State Bank, Sutherland, Iowa; State Farm Mutual Auto Insurance Co.; Grinnell Mutual Reinsurance Co.; Farm Bureau Mutual Insurance; Tri State Insurance Company of Minnesota; Iowa Mutual Insurance Group; Sheldon Livestock Sales, Inc.; Farmers Mutual Insurance Assoc.; Mutual Fire and Auto Insurance Co.; Producer's Coop of Gaza; Archer Coop of Archer; Vander Werff & Associates, Sanborn, Iowa.
REFERENCES: Security State Bank, Sutherland, Iowa; Ken Allers, United Fire & Casualty Insurance Co.; Mutual Fire and Auto Insurance Co., Cedar Rapids, Iowa; First National Bank, Primghar, Iowa; Grinnell Mutual Reinsurance Co.; Vander Werff & Associates, Sanborn, Iowa.

SWANSON LAW FIRM

Established in 1919

209 EAST COOLBAUGH STREET
P.O. BOX 78
RED OAK, IOWA 51566
Telephone: 712-623-2554
Fax: 712-623-3193
Email: swanlaw@heartland.net

Villisca, Iowa Office: Bickford Building. Telephone: 712-826-9562.

General Civil and Trial Practice in all Courts, Personal Injury and Negligence Litigation, Probate, Domestic Relations, Taxation, Real Estate.

FIRM PROFILE: Swanson Law Firm was founded by Ralph J. Swanson in 1919. Serving clients with a combined experience of over 100 years throughout Montgomery, Mills, Fremont, Cass, Page and Adams counties. The firm engages in a General Civil Practice, and has available effective, trained support personnel.

MEMBERS OF FIRM

RALPH J. SWANSON (1889-1968)

R. JOHN SWANSON, born Red Oak, Iowa, November 22, 1920; admitted to bar, 1948, Iowa. *Education:* Iowa State Teachers College; State University of Iowa (B.A., 1947); State University of Iowa (J.D., 1948). Phi Delta Phi (Legal). County Attorney, Montgomery County, 1951-1955. Member, State Judicial Nominating Commission, 1982-1985. *Member:* Montgomery County (Secretary, 1953-1959; President, 1980-1993), Southwest Iowa (President, 1976-1977), Iowa State and American Bar Associations.

MARK D. SWANSON, born Red Oak, Iowa, December 14, 1951; admitted to bar, 1978, Iowa; 1979, U.S. District Court, Southern District of Iowa. *Education:* Yale University (B.A., 1974); Boston University (J.D., 1977). County Attorney, Montgomery County, 1983-1990; Assistant County Attorney, Montgomery County, 1977-1982, 1991—. *Member:* Montgomery County, Southwest Iowa (President, 1994) and Iowa State Bar Associations; Iowa Trial Lawyers Association.

BRUCE E. SWANSON, born Red Oak, Iowa, December 31, 1957; admitted to bar, 1983, Iowa and Nebraska. *Education:* University of Iowa (B.S., with honors, 1980); Creighton University (J.D., 1983). Assistant Montgomery County Attorney, 1986-1990; County Attorney, 1991—. Deputy Pottawattamie County Public Defender, 1984-1986. *Member:* Southwest Iowa (President, 2003), Iowa State and Nebraska State Bar Associations.

GENERAL COUNSEL FOR: Audiological Services, Inc.; Lion Products Corp.; Hawkeye Ford, Inc.
LOCAL COUNSEL FOR: Farm Credit Service; Safetrans.
APPROVED ATTORNEYS FOR: Iowa Title Guaranty; Farmers Home Administration.
REFERENCES: Houghton State Bank, Red Oak, Iowa; US Bank, Red Oak, Iowa.

WAAGMEESTER & KRAMER, P.L.C.

Established in 1892

104 SOUTH MARSHALL STREET
P.O. BOX 630
ROCK RAPIDS, IOWA 51246-0630
Telephone: 712-472-3777
Fax: 712-472-3778
Email: waaglaw@rockrapids.net
URL: http://www.lawyers.com/waagmeester

Sioux Center, Iowa Office: 235 First Avenue N.E., 51250. Telephone: 712-722-3499. Facsimile: 712-722-2199.

General Practice including but not limited to Trial Law, Appellate Practice, Wills, Trusts, Estate Planning and Probate Law, Criminal Law, Family Law, Real Estate, Personal Injury, Worker's Compensation, Business Law and Contracts.

FIRM PROFILE: General practice firm serving primarily Northwestern Iowa, and Southeastern South Dakota. Established in 1892 by Simon Fisher (1861-1954), later joined in this law practice by his son, Earl H. Fisher (1908-1990), and thereafter by Donald G. DeWaay (1916-1992). This firm has been located in Rock Rapids, Iowa, for more than 100 years and provides general practice and litigation legal services.

SIMON FISHER (1861-1954)
EARL H. FISHER (1908-1990)
DON DeWAAY (1916-1992)

MEMBERS OF FIRM

RANDY L. WAAGMEESTER, born Rock Rapids, Iowa, June 19, 1953; admitted to bar, 1978, Iowa; 1985, South Dakota. *Education:* Buena Vista College (B.A., cum laude, 1975); Drake University (J.D., 1978). Lyon County Attorney and Assistant County Attorney, 1979-1986. *Member:* Lyon County and Sioux County, Iowa State (Board of Governors, 1983-1987, 2004—) and American (General Practice Section) Bar Associations; The State Bar of South Dakota; Iowa Trial Lawyers Association; Association of Trial Lawyers of America.

TIMOTHY J. KRAMER, born Edgerton, Minnesota, December 1, 1967; admitted to bar, 1993, Iowa; 1995, South Dakota; 1999, U.S. District Court, Northern District of Iowa. *Education:* Dordt College (B.A., 1990); University of South Dakota (J.D., 1993). *Member:* Lyon County, Sioux County and Iowa State Bar Associations; State Bar of South Dakota.

HESSEL R. ROORDA, born Sioux Center, Iowa, August 7, 1956; admitted to bar, 1981, Iowa. *Education:* Morningside College (B.A., summa cum laude, 1978); Creighton University (J.D., 1981); University of Denver (M.S.J.A., 1990). *Member:* Lyon County and Iowa State Bar Associations.

(This Listing Continued)

LEWIS S. HENDRICKS

Established in 1946

408 FIFTH STREET
P.O. BOX 111
ROCKWELL CITY, IOWA 50579
Telephone: 712-297-7567
Fax: 712-297-5407

Probate, Trust and Estate Planning.

LEWIS S. HENDRICKS, born September 30, 1919; admitted to bar, 1942, Iowa. *Education:* State University of Iowa (B.A., 1941; J.D., 1942). Phi Delta Phi. County Attorney, Calhoun County, Iowa, 1949-1955. Judicial Hospital Referee, 1976-1978. Member, Iowa Supreme Court Advisory Committee on Costs of Court-Appointed Counsel, 1985-1986. Member, Task Force on Quality of Life, 1993-1995. *Member:* Calhoun County, 16th Judicial District (Secretary, 1948-1949), Iowa State (Member, Committees on: Membership, 1951-1954; Public Relations, 1954-1956; Continuing Legal Education, 1956-1966; Member, 1968-1973 and Chairman, 1977-1987, Special Joint Committee on Methods of Appointment and Compensation for Court Appointed Counsel; Member: Board of Governors, 1972-1975; Probate, 1975-1977; Council, General Practice Section, 1990-1993) and American Bar Associations. Fellow: Iowa Academy of Trial Lawyers; American College of Trust and Estate Counsel. [Lieut. (j.g.) U.S. Naval Air Corps, 1942-1946; NSF, 1990]. ***PRACTICE AREAS:*** Probate; Estate Planning; Trusts; Real Estate; Taxation.

REFERENCE: United Bank of Iowa, Rockwell City, Iowa, formerly Alliance Bank and National Bank of Rockwell City.

LUNDBERG LAW FIRM, P.L.C.

SERGEANT BLUFF, IOWA

(See Sioux City)

General Practice including Personal Injury, Employment Law, Professional Liability and Commercial Law.

WOLFF, WHORLEY, DE HOOGH & SCHREURS

Established in 1935

SECURITY PROFESSIONAL PLAZA
934 THIRD AVENUE, SUITE 200
P.O. BOX 309
SHELDON, IOWA 51201
Telephone: 712-324-4385
FAX: 712-324-5106
URL: http://www.sheldon-law.com

General Practice, Personal Injury, Probate, Estate Planning, Real Estate, Corporate and Business Law, School, Banking and Taxation Law, Family, Workers' Compensation, Social Security Disability Claims, Municipal and Zoning, Trials and Appeals.

MEMBERS OF FIRM

PAUL WOLFF (1909-1987)

THOMAS J. WHORLEY, born Sheldon, Iowa, March 2, 1947; admitted to bar, 1972, Iowa; 1986, Minnesota. *Education:* University of South Dakota (B.A., 1969; J.D., 1972). Phi Delta Phi. Assistant Attorney General, State of Iowa, 1972-1973. City Attorney, City of Sheldon, 1974-1981. *Member:* O'Brien County (President, 1974-1977), Iowa State and Minnesota State Bar Associations; Iowa Trial Lawyers Association. **Email:** tomw@sheldon-law.com

JOHN F. DE HOOGH, born Ainsworth, Nebraska, December 21, 1944; admitted to bar, 1973, Mississippi; 1974, Iowa. *Education:* Western Washington State College (B.A., 1967); University of Mississippi (J.D., 1973). City Attorney, City of Sheldon, 1982—. *Member:* O'Brien County (President, 1980-1984) and Iowa State Bar Associations. ***Email:*** jackdh@sheldon-law.com

MICAH JOHN SCHREURS, born Sioux Center, Iowa, December 30, 1974; admitted to bar, 2000, Iowa; 2001, U.S. District Court, Northern District of Iowa. *Education:* Dordt College (B.A., 1997); University of Iowa (J.D., with high distinction, 2000). Order of the Coif. Law Clerk to Hon. Michael J. Streit, Iowa Court of Appeals, 2000-2001. Author: "VonFeldt v. Stifel Financial Corp: Clarifying the Scope of Delaware Indemnification Law," Journal of Corporation Law, Volume 25, p. 161 (Fall 1999). *Member:* O'Brien County and Iowa State Bar Association; Iowa Trial Lawyers Association. **Email:** micahs@sheldon-law.com

REPRESENTATIVE CLIENTS: Security State Bank of Sheldon, Iowa; Citizens State Bank of Sheldon, Iowa; Iowa State Bank, Sheldon, Iowa; George State Bank, George, Iowa; Farm Credit Services of Sheldon, Iowa; Sheldon Community School District; George-Little Rock Community School District; Sioux Central Community School District; Northwest Iowa Community College; Rosenboom Machine & Tool; Siebring Mfg. Co.; Otter Creek Ethanol LLC; Poppema-Sikma Construction; Midwest Farmers Cooperative; Northwest Iowa Health Center; City of Sheldon, Iowa.
REFERENCES: Citizens State Bank, Sheldon, Iowa; Security State Bank, Sheldon, Iowa; George State Bank, George, Iowa.

EDWARD E. (GENE) EATON

SHENANDOAH, IOWA

(See Sidney)

General Practice including but not limited to Commercial Law, Contracts, Corporate Law, Elder Law, Real Estate, Wills, Trusts, Estate Planning and Probate Law, Trial Law.

DEKOTER, THOLE & DAWSON, P.L.C.

Established in 1936
315 NINTH STREET
P.O. BOX 253
SIBLEY, IOWA 51249
Telephone: 712-754-4601
Fax: 712-754-2301
URL: http://www.lawyers.com/sibleylaw

General Practice, Trials, Insurance Defense, Products Liability, Personal Injury Litigation/ Workers Compensation, Estate Planning, Probate and Real Estate, Family Law, Corporate Business Law.

LOUIS L. CORCORAN (1912-1992)

DONALD E. SKIVER (1923-1989)

RICHARD D. ZITO (1944-1994)

DANIEL E. DEKOTER, born Orange City, Iowa, June 18, 1955; admitted to bar, 1980, Iowa. *Education:* Northwestern College and Calvin College (B.A., 1977); University of Iowa (J.D., with high honors, 1980). Author: Comment, "Resurrecting Claims Through Post-Judgment Appeal of Class Certification Denial," 64 Iowa Law Review 964, 1979. *Member:* Osceola County, Iowa State (Member, Legal Forms Committee, 1990-2000, Chair, 1997-2000) and American Bar Associations. ***PRACTICE AREAS:*** Products Liability; Personal Injury; Insurance Defense; Probate; Estate Planning. ***Email:*** dandekoter@sibleylaw.com

MICHAEL E. THOLE, born Sheldon, Iowa, November 27, 1952; admitted to bar, 1979, Nebraska; 1980, Iowa. *Education:* Southwest Minnesota State University; University of Iowa (B.B.A., 1974); Creighton University (J.D., 1979). County Attorney, Osceola County, 1983-1990; Assistant County Attorney, 1991-1995. Member, Grievance Commission, Supreme Court of Iowa, July 1996. *Member:* Osceola County, Iowa State and American Bar Associations. ***PRACTICE AREAS:*** Probate; Estate Planning; Real Estate. ***Email:*** mthole@sibleylaw.com

HAROLD D. DAWSON, born Des Moines, Iowa, September 29, 1955; admitted to bar, 1984, Iowa. *Education:* Arizona State University (B.S., 1978); University of Iowa (J.D., with distinction, 1984). Law Clerk, Fifth Judicial District of Iowa, 1984-1986. Assistant County Attorney, Osceola County, 1986-1990; County Attorney, 1991-1995. *Member:* Osceola County, Iowa State and American Bar Associations. ***PRACTICE AREAS:*** Workers Compensation; Personal Injury; Real Estate. ***Email:*** hdawson@sibleylaw.com

ASSOCIATE

NICOLE M. JENSEN-HARRIS, born Madison, South Dakota, May 4, 1976; admitted to bar, 2001, Iowa. *Education:* South Dakota State University (B.S., 1998); University of South Dakota (J.D., 2000). *Member:* Osceola County, Iowa State and American Bar Associations. ***PRACTICE AREAS:*** Real Estate; Personal Injury; Insurance Defense. ***Email:*** njharris@sibleylaw.com

REPRESENTATIVE CLIENTS: Sibley State Bank; The Conveyor Company; Village Northwest Unlimited; United Community Bank, Ocheyedan, Iowa; Melvin Savings Bank, Melvin, Iowa; Ashton State Bank; City of Harris; City of Ocheyedan; City of Melvin; City of Ashton; City of Little Rock; City of Sibley; St. Paul Fire and Marine Insurance Companies; Grinnell Mutual Reinsurance Co.; Co-operative Elevator Assn., Keith M. Merrick Company, Inc.; Dethmers Manufacturing Co.; Ranger All Season Corp.; Diversified Technologies, Inc.; Sudenga Industries, Inc.; Northwest Iowa Area Solid Waste Agency; Sibley-Ocheyedan Community School District; Osceola Community Hospital, Inc.; City of Sanborn; Iowa Mutual Insurance Co. of DeWitt, Iowa; Capitol Indemnity Corporation, Madison, Wisconsin; Sentry Insurance Companies; Creamery Credit Union; U.S. Liability Insurance Group; ZMI/Portec, Inc.; Society Insurance; Sanborn Savings Bank.
REFERENCES: Sibley State Bank, Sibley, Iowa; Dethmers Manufacturing Co., Boyden, Iowa; Keith M. Merrick Company, Inc., Sibley, Iowa.; Ashton State Bank, Ashton, Iowa; Sudenga Industries, Inc., George, Iowa.

EDWARD E. (GENE) EATON

Established in 1928
416 CLAY STREET
P.O. BOX 429
SIDNEY, IOWA 51652-0429
Telephone: 712-374-2641
Fax: 712-374-2642
Email: eatonlaw@iowatelecom.net

General Practice including but not limited to Commercial Law, Contracts, Corporate Law, Elder Law, Real Estate, Wills, Trusts, Estate Planning and Probate Law, Trial Law.

EDWARD E. (GENE) EATON, born Hamburg, Iowa, October 22, 1937; admitted to bar, 1962, Iowa. *Education:* Wentworth Military Academy; University of Iowa (B.A., 1960; J.D., 1962). Phi Alpha Delta. City Attorney, Tabor, Iowa, 1965-1978. City Attorney, Sidney, Iowa, 1994-2002. *Member:* Fremont County, Southwest Iowa (President, 1981-1982), Iowa State (Member, Board of Directors, Iowa Conference of Bar Association Presidents, 1969-1979; Member: Committee on Continuing Legal Education, 1972-1978. Membership Committee, 1970-1976) and American Bar Associations.

EDWARD E. EATON (1903-1978)

REPRESENTATIVE CLIENTS: First State Bank, Tabor, Iowa; Missouri Valley Drainage District; Benton-Washington Levee District; Walnut Creek Drainage District; Mickelwaite Drainage District.

BARON, SAR, GOODWIN, GILL & LOHR

750 PIERCE STREET
P.O. BOX 717
SIOUX CITY, IOWA 51102
Telephone: 712-277-1015
FAX: 712-277-3067

General Civil and Trial Practice in all Courts. Business, Commercial, Bankruptcy, Insurance, Workers Compensation, Banking, Corporation, Adoption, Labor Relations, Real Property, Probate Law, Administrative, Criminal and Domestic Relations Law.

MEMBERS OF FIRM

A. FRANK BARON, born Sioux City, Iowa, December 5, 1945; admitted to bar, 1971, Iowa; 1972, U.S. District Court, Northern District of Iowa; 1981, U.S. Court of Appeals, Eighth Circuit and U.S. District Court, Southern District of Iowa. *Education:* University of Iowa (B.A., 1968; J.D., with distinction, 1971). Omicron Delta Kappa; Phi Delta Phi; Order of the Coif. Author: "The Treatment of Jewish Law in American Decision," 9 Israel Law Review, 85, 1971. Law Clerk to Judge Martin D. Van Oosterhout, U.S. Court of Appeals for the 8th Circuit, 1971-1972. Member: Bankruptcy Rules Committee, Northern District, 1986—. *Member:* Woodbury County (Member, Ethics and Grievance Committee, 1978—; Chairman, 1981-1989, 1996—; President, 1993), Iowa State (Member, Commercial Law Committee, 1982-1990; Council Member, Commercial and Bankruptcy Law Section, 1990-1997) and American Bar Associations; Commercial Law League of America; American Bankruptcy Institute; President, Siouxland Estate Planning Council, 2000-2001. ***Email:*** afbaron@cableone.net

JEFFREY A. SAR, born Charles City, Iowa, 1949; admitted to bar, 1975, Iowa and South Dakota; 1976, U.S. Court of Appeals, Eighth and Eleventh Circuits; 2004, Nebraska; U.S. District Court, Northern District of Iowa; U.S. District Court, District of South Dakota. *Education:* Iowa State University (B.S., 1972); University of South Dakota (J.D., 1975). Phi Delta Phi. Author: "The Federal Advisory Committee Act: A Key to Washington's Back Door," 20 South Dakota Law Review 380, 1975. Member, Defense Research Institute. *Member:* Woodbury County, Iowa State (Member, Sections on: Litigation; Workers Compensation) and American (Member, Tort and Insurance Section) Bar Associations; State Bar of South Dakota; Iowa Defense Counsel Association. ***Email:*** jasar@cableone.net

F. LEE GOODWIN, born Sidney, Nebraska, March 11, 1949; admitted to bar, 1974, Iowa and Nebraska; 1975, U.S. District Court, Northern District of Iowa; 1976, U.S. District Court, District of Nebraska and U.S. Court of Appeals, Eighth Circuit; 1988, U.S. Supreme Court; 1989, U.S. Court of Appeals, Seventh Circuit. *Education:* University of Nebraska at Lincoln (B.S.B.A., 1971; J.D., 1974). Member, Supreme Court Advisory Committee on Iowa Criminal Rules. *Member:* Dakota County, Woodbury County (President, 1988), Iowa State (Member, Criminal Law and Family Law) and Nebraska State (Member, Criminal Law and Family Law) Bar Associations; Iowa Trial Lawyers Association. [1st Lt., US Army Reserve, 1971-1980]. ***Email:*** flgoodwin@cableone.net

DAVID L. GILL, born Carson City, Nevada, 1951; admitted to bar, 1976, Iowa and U.S. District Court, Southern and Northern Districts of Iowa; 1983, Nebraska. *Education:* Creighton University (B.S.B.A., 1973); University of Iowa (J.D., with distinction, 1976). Author: Recent Development "Forced Dividends-Cole Real Estate Corp. v. People Bank & Trust Company-A Minority Stockholder's Ability to Force a Dividend: The Necessary Elements," 1 The Journal of Corporation Law 420, 1975-1976. Business Administrator, The Journal of Corporation Law, 1975-1976. Assistant County Attorney, 1976-1978, and First Assistant County Attorney, 1979-1981, Woodbury County. *Member:* Woodbury County (President, 1999), Iowa State (Member, Sections on: Workers Compensation; Litigation; Criminal Law; Family Law; Probate) and Nebraska State Bar Associations. ***Email:*** dlgill@cableone.net

GREGORY N. LOHR, born Sioux City, Iowa, March 5, 1952; admitted to bar, 1980, Iowa, Nebraska and U.S. Court of Appeals, Eighth Circuit; U.S. District Court, Northern District of Iowa; U.S. District Court, Southern District of Iowa; U.S. District Court, District of Nebraska; 1982, U.S. Tax Court. *Education:* Briar Cliff College (B.A., 1975); Creighton University (J.D., 1980). *Member:* Woodbury County (Member, Fee Arbitration Committee, 1988—), Iowa State (Member, Real Estate and Title Law Section) and Nebraska State (Member, Real Property, Probate and Trust Section) Bar Associations. ***Email:*** gnlohr@cableone.net

REPRESENTATIVE CLIENTS: Citizens First National Bank; Citizens Bank; Pioneer Bank; St. Paul Insurance Company; Wausau Insurance Cos.; Horace Mann Insurance; City of Sloan; City of Whiting; Farmers Cereal Coop; Northwest Iowa Credit Bureau; Coldwell Banker Associated Brokers Realty, Inc.; Media/Professional Insurance; Security State Bank; Farmers Savings Bank; Premier Bank; Liberty Mutual Insurance; Victoria Insurance; Ag Services of America, Inc.; Randalls Formalwear; Farm Credit Services of the Midlands; AgriBank, FCB; Indian Hills Nursing and Rehab; Barkley Asphalt, Inc.
REFERENCES: Pioneer Bank; Bankers Multiple Line Insurance Co.

BERENSTEIN, MOORE, BERENSTEIN, HEFFERNAN & MOELLER, L.L.P.

Established in 1926
U.S. BANK BUILDING
501 PIERCE STREET, SUITE 300
P.O. BOX 3207
SIOUX CITY, IOWA 51102
Telephone: 712-252-0020
Fax: 712-252-0656
Email: BMBHM@berensteinlawfirm.com

General Civil and Trial Practice. Banking, Probate, Taxation, ERISA, Education Law, Employment Law, Trusts and Estates, Creditor's Rights, Real Estate, Corporation, Health and Hospital Law.

(This Listing Continued)

BERENSTEIN, MOORE, BERENSTEIN, HEFFERNAN & MOELLER, L.L.P., Sioux City—Continued

MEMBERS OF FIRM

MARVIN S. BERENSTEIN, born Des Moines, Iowa; admitted to bar, 1961, Iowa, U.S. District Court, Southern and Northern Districts of Iowa and U.S. Tax Court. *Education:* State University of Iowa (J.D., 1961). Iowa Attorney General's Staff, 1961; President, 1993-1995 and Member, 1989-1995, State of Iowa Board of Regents. Listed in *Best Lawyers in America,* Corporate Law, Taxation, Trusts and Estates. Recipient, Iowa State Bar Association Award of Merit, 1996. President: Iowa State Bar Association, 1980-1981; Young Lawyers Section, 1969-1970; Iowa State Bar Foundation, 1992-1993. Member: Federal Practice Committee; Federal Liaison Subcommittee, 1997—. *Member:* Iowa Society of Hospital Attorneys. Fellow: American College of Trust and Estate Counsel; Iowa State Bar Foundation; Iowa Society of Hospital Attorneys. ***Email:*** mberenstein@berensteinlawfirm.com

DAN A. MOORE, born Des Moines, Iowa; admitted to bar, 1977, Iowa, U.S. District Court, Northern District of Iowa and U.S. Tax Court. *Education:* Drake University (B.A., 1974; J.D., 1977). Phi Beta Kappa; Omicron Delta Epsilon. Co-Author: "The New Iowa Land Title Examination Standards," 34 Drake L. Rev. 589, 1984. President, Sioux City Lawyers Club, 1985. Member, 1981-1992, 1994— and Chairman, 1985-1988, City Planning and Zoning Commission, Sioux City, Iowa. Member: Board of Governors, 2000—, Committee on Title Standards, 1980-1989, 1996—, and Committee on Title Guaranty, 1988-1989, Real Estate and Title Law Section, 1990—, Chair, 1996-1997, Iowa State Bar Association. Listed in *The Best Lawyers in America,* Real Estate Category. *Member:* American Bar Association (Member, Real Property Section). ***Email:*** dmoore@berensteinlawfirm.com

CRAIG S. BERENSTEIN, born Iowa City, Iowa; admitted to bar, 1985, Iowa and U.S. District Court, Northern District of Iowa. *Education:* University of Iowa (B.A., with distinction, 1982; J.D., 1985). Phi Beta Kappa. Mayor, Sioux City, Iowa. Member: Corporation, Banking and Business Law Section, 1990-1994; Chair, Professional Corporation Committee, 1990-1994, Iowa State Bar Association. ***Email:*** cberenstein@berensteinlawfirm.com

MAUREEN BROWN HEFFERNAN, born Bethesda, Maryland; admitted to bar, 1985, Iowa and U.S. District Court, Northern and Southern Districts of Iowa. *Education:* University of Iowa (B.B.S., 1981; J.D., with distinction, 1985). Member, Sections on: Litigation and Employment Law, Iowa State Bar Association; Member, Sections on: Health Law and Labor and Employment Law, American Bar Association. *Member:* Iowa Society of Healthcare Attorneys; American Health Lawyers Association. ***Email:*** mheffernan@berensteinlawfirm.com

RICHARD H. MOELLER, born Mason City, Iowa; admitted to bar, 1985, Iowa and U.S. District Court, Northern District of Iowa; 1991, U.S. District Court, Southern District of Iowa; 1998, U.S. Court of Federal Claims; 1999, Nebraska; 2000, U.S. District Court, District of Nebraska. *Education:* Iowa State University (B.S., with distinction, 1982); University of Iowa (J.D., with distinction, 1985). Tau Beta Pi. *Member:* Iowa Council of School Board Attorneys (Executive Committee, 1998—). ***Email:*** rmoeller@berensteinlawfirm.com

JEFFREY A. JOHNSON, born Primghar, Iowa; admitted to bar, 1991, Iowa, Missouri, U.S. District Court, Northern and Southern Districts of Iowa and U.S. Tax Court; 1996, Nebraska. *Education:* Iowa State University (B.B.A.,1988); University of Missouri-Kansas City (J.D., 1991). Member, Section on: Taxation; Committees on: Taxation and Employee Benefits, Iowa State Bar Association. *Member:* Nebraska State Bar Association; The Missouri Bar. ***Email:*** jjohnson@berensteinlawfirm.com

ROBERT F. MEIS, born Sioux City, Iowa, January 15, 1958; admitted to bar, 1983, Iowa, Nebraska and U.S. District Court, Northern District of Iowa. *Education:* University of Iowa (B.B.A., with honors, 1980; J.D., with distinction, 1983). Beta Gamma Sigma. Co-Director of the Client Counseling Program, University of Iowa School of Law, 1983. *Member:* Woodbury County, Iowa State and American Bar Associations. ***PRACTICE AREAS:*** Probate; Estate Planning; Corporations; Real Estate.

MITCHELL A. HERIGSTAD, born Seattle, Washington; admitted to bar, 1994, Iowa, U.S. District Court, Southern District of Iowa and U.S. Tax Court; 1995, U.S. District Court, Northern District of Iowa. *Education:* College of St. Thomas (B.A., 1991); Drake University (J.D., 1994). Member, Sections on: Probate and Trust and E-Commerce, Iowa State Bar Association; Member, Intellectual Property Law Section, American Bar Association. ***Email:*** mherigstad@berensteinlawfirm.com

DAWN E. MASTALIR, born Iron Mountain, Michigan; admitted to bar, 1992, Iowa; 1997, U.S. District Court, Northern District of Iowa. *Education:* University of Nebraska (B.A., 1981); University of Iowa (J.D., with distinction, 1991). Finalist, Van Oosterhout Moot Court Competition, 1990. Member, National Moot Court Team, 1990. Best Respondent Brief, National Moot Court Regional Competition, 1990. Member, Litigation Section, Iowa State Bar Association. ***REPORTED CASES:*** Longstreth v. Tom Copple and MCI Telecommunications Corporation, 101 F.Supp.2nd 776 (N.D. Iowa, 2000), aff'd upon reh'g, 189 F.R.D. 401 (N.D. Iowa 1999). ***Email:*** dmastalir@berensteinlawfirm.com

KIMBERLY K. WOLFF, born Spencer, Iowa; admitted to bar, 1994, South Dakota; 1995, Iowa. *Education:* University of South Dakota (B.A., summa cum laude, 1991; J.D., 1994). Phi Beta Kappa. Co-Author: "The Section Survey on Use of Durable Powers of Attorney," Probate and Property, Jan/Feb 1996. Member: Probate and Trust Law Section, Iowa State Bar Association. *Member:* State Bar of South Dakota (Member, Real Property, Probate, and Trust Law Section). [CPT, SJA, ARNG, 1997—]. ***Email:*** kwolff@berensteinlawfirm.com

ASSOCIATE

KELLY K. SALKER, born Sioux City, Iowa; admitted to bar, 1997, Iowa. *Education:* Morningside College (B.S., cum laude, 1994); University of Iowa (J.D., 1997). Clerk to Honorable Terry L. Huitink, Iowa Court of Appeals, 1997-1998. ***Email:*** ksalker@berensteinlawfirm.com

All Attorneys are Members of the Woodbury County and Iowa State Bar Associations.

(This Listing Continued)

REPRESENTATIVE CLIENTS: Aalfs Mfg., Inc.; All Power, Inc.; Beef Products, Inc.; Briar Cliff University; Cardiovascular Associates; Canal Capital Corporation - Sioux City Stockyards; Dakota Dunes Development Co.; The Diocese of Sioux City; First American Bank; First National Bank; Firstar Bank, N.A.; Holtze Construction Co.; Irving F. Jensen Co.; Kind and Knox Co.; Mercy Health Services - Iowa Corp.; Mercy Medical Center - Sioux City; Metropolitan Life Insurance Co.; Mid-America Agri-Industries VEBA; Palmer Candy Company; Sears Roebuck; Servico, Inc. d/b/a Sioux City Hilton; Sioux City Community School District; Siouxland Foundation; Sioux Tools, Inc. - Snap-On Tools; Smithco Mfg., Inc.; C.W. Suter Services; TEC - Thompson Electric Co.; Terminal Grain Corp.; Trinity Health - Michigan; Waste Management of Sioux City; Wells Dairy & Blue Bunny Ice Cream; Wells Fargo Iowa, N.A.

BIKAKIS, ARNESON, KARPUK & HINDMAN

701 PIERCE STREET, SUITE 300
P.O. BOX 1678
SIOUX CITY, IOWA 51102-1678
Telephone: 712-277-1434
Fax: 712-255-8049
URL: http://www.bikakislaw.com

General Civil Trial Practice. Insurance, Personal Injury, Workers Compensation, Corporations, Probate, Real Estate, Employment, Estate Planning and Bankruptcy Law. Appeals.

MEMBERS OF FIRM

EMMANUEL S. BIKAKIS, born Sioux City, Iowa, March 3, 1936; admitted to bar, 1963, Iowa. *Education:* Iowa State University and Morningside College (B.S., 1958); University of South Dakota (J.D., 1963). Delta Theta Phi. *Member:* Woodbury County, Iowa State and American Bar Associations; Iowa Defense Counsel Association (Member: Board of Directors, 1985-1999); Iowa Association of Workers Compensation Lawyers; Defense Research Institute. ***PRACTICE AREAS:*** General Practice; Alternative Dispute Resolution; Business Law; Employment Law; Estate Planning; Insurance; Litigation; Personal Injury; Real Estate; Social Security Disability; Trial Law; Trusts and Estates; Wills and Probate; Workers Compensation. ***Email:*** ebikakis@iowabar.org

BRYAN J. ARNESON, born Faulkton, South Dakota, September 6, 1953; admitted to bar, 1978, Iowa; 1987, Nebraska. *Education:* University of South Dakota (B.S., magna cum laude, 1975); University of Iowa (J.D., with honors, 1978). Phi Delta Phi. City Solicitor, City of Sioux City, Iowa, 1980-1984. *Member:* Woodbury County, Iowa State and Nebraska State Bar Associations; Iowa Association of Trial Lawyers; The Association of Trial Lawyers of America; Iowa Defense Counsel Association; Defense Research Institute. ***PRACTICE AREAS:*** Personal Injury; Workers Compensation; Social Security Disability. ***Email:*** barneson@iowabar.org

THEODORE E. KARPUK, born Sioux City, Iowa, May 11, 1956; admitted to bar, 1981, Iowa; 2002, U.S. District Court, Northern District of Iowa. *Education:* Briar Cliff College (B.A., magna cum laude, 1978); University of Iowa (J.D., 1981). Phi Delta Phi. Law Clerk and Deputy Clerk, U.S. District Court, Northern District of Iowa, 1981-1983. *Member:* Woodbury County, Iowa State and American Bar Associations. ***PRACTICE AREAS:*** General Practice; Personal Injury; Workers Compensation; Probate; Real Estate; Estate Planning; Bankruptcy. ***Email:*** tkarpuk@iowabar.org

SCOTT A. HINDMAN, born Sioux City, Iowa, January 30, 1961; admitted to bar, 1986, Iowa and U.S. District Court, Northern District of Iowa; 1987, U.S. District Court, Southern District of Iowa; 1988, South Dakota; 1999, Nebraska. *Education:* Briar Cliff College (B.A., summa cum laude, 1983); University of Iowa (J.D., 1986). Contributing Author: *State-by-State Guide to Architect, Engineer and Contractor Licensing,* Aspen Law & Business, 1999. *Member:* Woodbury County, Iowa State, Nebraska State and American Bar Associations; State Bar of South Dakota; Iowa Defense Counsel Association; Defense Research Institute. ***PRACTICE AREAS:*** General Practice; Employment Law; Insurance Litigation; Personal Injury; Trial Practice. ***Email:*** shindman@iowabar.org

ASSOCIATE

TIMOTHY A. SCHERLE, born Council Bluffs, Iowa, July 23, 1958; admitted to bar, 1983, Iowa; 1999, Nebraska. *Education:* University of Iowa (B.A., 1980; J.D., with distinction, 1983). Phi Beta Kappa. *Member:* Iowa State Bar Association. Nebraska State Bar Association. ***PRACTICE AREAS:*** General Practice; Personal Injury; Workers Compensation; Trial Practice; Family Law; Bankruptcy; Real Estate. ***Email:*** scherleaw@aol.com

REPRESENTATIVE CLIENTS: Columbia Insurance Group; Farmers Insurance Group; General Casualty Co.; Siouxland Cardiovascular Surgeons, P.C.; United Fire & Casualty Insurance Co.; Farmers Casualty Insurance Co.; Mid-Plains Insurance Co.; Hyatt Legal Plans, Inc; Sedgwick CMS; Geico Insurance; St. Paul Travelers Insurance Co.; Farmland/Nationwide Agribusiness Insurance Co.; Millers First Insurance Co..
REFERENCE: Security National Bank of Sioux City.

LAW OFFICE OF DAVID J. BLAIR, P.C.

SIOUX CITY, IOWA

(See Cherokee)

ADR, Mediation, Arbitration.

CORBETT, ANDERSON, CORBETT, POULSON & VELLINGA

Established in 1896

400 SECURITY BUILDING
423 SIXTH STREET
P.O. BOX 3527
SIOUX CITY, IOWA 51102-3527
Telephone: 712-277-1261
Fax: 712-277-6631
Email: caclawfirm@corbettanderson.com
URL: http://www.corbettanderson.com

General Civil and Trial Practice in all Courts. Real Estate, Probate, Estate Planning, Corporation and Business, Banking, Bankruptcy and Commercial, Agricultural, Adoption, Health, Personal Injury, Workers Compensation, Social Security, Criminal, Employment, and Family Law.

MEMBERS OF FIRM

EDWARD M. CORBETT (1868-1940)

EDWARD V. CORBETT (1904-1973)

CARLTON M. CORBETT (1901-1976)

STANLEY M. CORBETT (1909-2004)

JOHN B. ANDERSON, born Sioux City, Iowa, August 4, 1936; admitted to bar, 1960, Iowa. *Education:* State University of Iowa (B.A., 1958; J.D., 1960). *Member:* Woodbury County (Secretary, 1976; Vice President, 1977; President, 1978), Iowa State (Member: Executive Council, Junior Bar Section, 1967-1968; Probate Section, 1970-1982, 1985—; Business Law Section, 1990—) and American Bar Associations; Sioux City Lawyers Club (President, 1965-1966); American College of Real Estate Lawyers. Fellow, American College of Trust and Estate Counsel. ***PRACTICE AREAS:*** Estate Planning; Probate; Real Estate; Business; Corporations. ***Email:*** janderson@corbettanderson.com

CHARLES L. CORBETT, born Sioux City, Iowa, March 10, 1947; admitted to bar, 1972, Iowa. *Education:* Grinnell College (B.A., 1969); University of Iowa (J.D., 1972). Phi Delta Phi. *Member:* Woodbury County (Treasurer, 1988; Secretary, 1989; Vice-President, 1990; President, 1991), Iowa State (Member, Real Estate and General Practice Sections) and American Bar Associations. ***PRACTICE AREAS:*** Real Estate; General Practice. ***Email:*** ccorbett@corbettanderson.com

JEFFREY L. POULSON, born Storm Lake, Iowa, December 22, 1951; admitted to bar, 1977, Iowa. *Education:* University of Wyoming (B.A., 1974); Drake University (J.D., 1977). *Member:* Iowa State and American Bar Associations. ***PRACTICE AREAS:*** Commercial; Bankruptcy; Agricultural; Real Estate; Litigation. ***Email:*** jpoulson@corbettanderson.com

RODNEY D. VELLINGA, born Orange City, Iowa, July 20, 1944; admitted to bar, 1972, Iowa; 2002, Nebraska. *Education:* Northwestern College and University of Iowa (B.A., 1967); University of Iowa (J.D., 1972). Assistant County Attorney, Woodbury County, 1972-1975. Magistrate, Woodbury County, 1975-1980. *Member:* Iowa State and American Bar Associations; Nebraska State Bar. ***PRACTICE AREAS:*** Workers Compensation; Criminal Law; Litigation; Social Security; Family Law. ***Email:*** rvellinga@corbettanderson.com

ASSOCIATES

DELAINE C. PETERSON, born Villisca, Iowa, July 28, 1936; admitted to bar, 1966, Iowa. *Education:* University of Iowa (B.B.A., 1963; J.D., 1966). *Member:* Woodbury County, Iowa State and American Bar Associations. ***PRACTICE AREAS:*** Estate Planning; Probate. ***Email:*** dpeterson@corbettanderson.com

MICHELE M. LEWON, born Sioux City, Iowa; admitted to bar, 2002, Iowa; 2003, Nebraska and South Dakota. *Education:* University of Nebraska-Lincoln (B.S., 1998; J.D., 2002). Phi Alpha Delta. Founding Member, Phi Alpha Delta Pre-Law Fraternity. Member: Moot Court Board; Order of the Barristers; National Moot Court Team. Chairperson, Moot Court Competition. Champion, Thomas Stinson Allen Moot Court Competition. *Member:* Woodbury County, Nebraska State and American Bar Associations; Iowa State Bar Association (Young Lawyers Division member; Mock Trial Committee, 2002-2004); State Bar of South Dakota; Student Bar Association(Executive President, 2001-2002). ***PRACTICE AREAS:*** Litigation; General Practice; Employment Law; Family Law. ***Email:*** mlewon@corbettanderson.com

ATTORNEYS FOR: American Popcorn Co.; First Federal Bank; St. Lukes Regional Medical Center of Sioux City; Charlie Zook Motors, Inc.; Pioneer Bank; Chris Hansen Construction Co., Inc.; Grandview Health Resources, Inc.; McHan Construction, Inc.; Rogers Farms; Graves Construction, Co.; Bomgaars Supply, Inc.; Boys and Girls Home and Family Services; Sioux City Brick and Tile Co.; Associated Sales; Rogers Electric Supply Co.; Goodwill Industries/Wall Street Mission.

CRARY, HUFF, INKSTER, SHEEHAN, RINGGENBERG, HARTNETT & STORM, P.C.

Established in 1896

614 PIERCE STREET
P.O. BOX 27
SIOUX CITY, IOWA 51102-0027
Telephone: 712-277-4561
Fax: 712-277-4605
Email: shuff@craryhuff.com
URL: http://www.craryhuff.com

South Sioux City, Nebraska Office: 1419 Dakota Avenue, 68776. Telephone: 402-494-2052.

(This Listing Continued)

Dakota Dunes, South Dakota Office: 600 Stevens Port Drive, Suite 300, 57049. Telephone: 605-232-3340.

General Practice, Agricultural, Banking, Bankruptcy, Business Formation, Business Transactions, Civil and Appellate Trial Practice, Civil Rights, Commercial, Commercial Collections, Construction, Contracts, Corporate, Criminal Law, Domestic, Education, Employer/Employee Relations, Employment Discrimination, Estate Planning, Family, Insurance, Insurance Defense Litigation, Medical Malpractice, Negligence, Personal Injury, Probate, Product Liability, Real Property, Reorganization, Taxation, Title, Workers Compensation, Wrongful Termination, Zoning, Planning and Land Use.

S. D. CRARY (1875-1969)

WALLACE W. HUFF (1910-1973)

RALPH W. CRARY (1898-1992)

BRUCE A. CRARY (1927-2001)

ROBERT J. CRARY (1917-2001)

STEWART A. HUFF, born Sioux City, Iowa, July 3, 1940; admitted to bar, 1965, Iowa; 1983, Nebraska; 2004, South Dakota. *Education:* Wentworth Military Academy; State University of Iowa (B.A., 1963; LL.B., 1965). ***PRACTICE AREAS:*** Business Organization; Business Transactions; Business Planning; Mergers and Acquisitions; Estate Planning; Real Estate Development; Managed Care; Managed Care Contracts. ***Email:*** shuff@craryhuff.com

SANDRA K. INKSTER EHRICH, born Sioux City, Iowa, January 8, 1947; admitted to bar, 1973, Nebraska; 1984, Iowa. *Education:* Doane College (B.A., magna cum laude, 1970); University of Nebraska (J.D., 1973). (Resident, South Sioux City, Nebraska Office). ***PRACTICE AREAS:*** Real Estate; Probate; Estate Planning; Corporate; Juvenile Law. ***Email:*** sehrich@craryhuff.com

ROSEMARY F. SHEEHAN, born Sioux City, Iowa, June 28, 1938; admitted to bar, 1977, Iowa; 1998, South Dakota. *Education:* Clarke College (B.A., magna cum laude, 1960); University of South Dakota (M.A., 1969; J.D., 1977). ***PRACTICE AREAS:*** Banking; Commercial Law; Business Law; Real Estate Development; Business Litigation; Estate Planning. ***Email:*** rsheehan@craryhuff.com

DENNIS R. RINGGENBERG, born Schaller, Iowa, December 23, 1952; admitted to bar, 1980, Iowa and Nebraska. *Education:* Morningside College; University of Northern Iowa (B.A., 1976); University of Nebraska at Lincoln (J.D., 1980). ***PRACTICE AREAS:*** Family Law. ***Email:*** dringgenberg@craryhuff.com

DANIEL L. HARTNETT, born Hubbard, Nebraska, February 22, 1956; admitted to bar, 1981, Iowa and Nebraska. *Education:* University of Nebraska (B.A., 1978; J.D., 1981). ***PRACTICE AREAS:*** Personal Injury; Insurance Defense; Business Litigation; Employment Litigation. ***Email:*** dhartnett@craryhuff.com

LARRY A. STORM, born Storm Lake, Iowa, November 22, 1948; admitted to bar, 1976, Minnesota; 1977, Iowa. *Education:* St. Olaf College (B.A., cum laude, 1971); William Mitchell College of Law (J.D., cum laude, 1976). ***PRACTICE AREAS:*** Estate Planning; Probate; Trust Law; Trust Administration; Real Estate. ***Email:*** lstorm@craryhuff.com

MICHAEL P. SCHMIEDT, born Sioux City, Iowa, February 25, 1963; admitted to bar, 1991, Nebraska; 1997, Iowa; 2004, South Dakota. *Education:* South Dakota State University; Wayne State College (B.S., 1985); University of Nebraska (J.D., 1991). (Resident, South Sioux City, Nebraska Office). ***PRACTICE AREAS:*** Criminal Law; Municipal Law; Insurance Defense; Personal Injury Litigation; Bankruptcy. ***Email:*** mschmiedt@craryhuff.com

DARRELL A. JESSE, born Madison, South Dakota, March 29, 1963; admitted to bar, 1989, South Dakota; 1995, Iowa. *Education:* University of South Dakota (B.S., Accounting, 1985; J.D., 1988). *Member:* Iowa State Bar Association; State Bar of South Dakota; Woodbury, Clay County and Union County Bar Associations. (Resident, Dakota Dunes, South Dakota Office). ***PRACTICE AREAS:*** Municipal Law; Real Estate; Corporate; Estate Planning; Business Law; Probate. ***Email:*** djesse@craryhuff.com

CODY M. McCULLOUGH, born Storm Lake, Iowa, February 17, 1970; admitted to bar, 1996, Iowa. *Education:* University of Iowa (B.A., honors and distinction, 1993); University of Iowa College of Law (J.D., high distinction, 1996). ***PRACTICE AREAS:*** Real Estate; Commercial Real Estate Development; Business Transactions; Business Law. ***Email:*** cmccullough@craryhuff.com

LAURA D. SCHMITT, born St. Louis, Missouri, March 2, 1967; admitted to bar, 1994, South Dakota; 1995, Iowa. *Education:* Morningside College (B.A., 1989); University of South Dakota (J.D., 1994). ***PRACTICE AREAS:*** Business Transactions; Business Law; Commercial Law. ***Email:*** lschmitt@craryhuff.com

MARCI L. ISEMINGER, born Le Mars, Iowa, June 6, 1963; admitted to bar, 1992, Colorado; 1995, U.S. Court of Appeals, Tenth Circuit; 1997, U.S. District Court, District of Colorado; 1999, Iowa; 2001, U.S. District Court, Northern District of Iowa; 2002, U.S. Court of Appeals, Eighth Circuit. *Education:* Iowa State University (B.B.A., 1985); University of Denver (J.D., 1991). ***PRACTICE AREAS:*** Insurance Defense; Business Litigation; Employment Litigation; Personal Injury. ***Email:*** miseminger@craryhuff.com

---

RYAN W. SNELL, born Hastings, Nebraska, October 11, 1968; admitted to bar, 2003, Iowa; 2004, South Dakota. *Education:* Iowa State University (B.A., 1991); University of South Dakota School of Law (J.D., 2003). Member: Sterling Honor Society; Order of Barristers. ***PRACTICE AREAS:*** Business Law; Business Transactions; Business Litigation. ***Email:*** rsnell@craryhuff.com

JONATHAN J. BLUM, born Sioux City, Iowa, July 23, 1978; admitted to bar, 2004, Iowa. *Education:* Morningside College (B.S., 2001); University of Iowa (J.D., 2004). Phi Delta Phi. ***PRACTICE AREAS:*** Litigation. ***Email:*** jblum@craryhuff.com

SABRINA L. LaFLEUR-SAYLER, born Sioux City, Iowa, September 18, 1977; admitted to bar, 2004, South Dakota. *Education:* Eastern New Mexico University (B.S., Corporate Communications, summa cum laude, 1999); University of South Dakota School of

(This Listing Continued)

CRARY, HUFF, INKSTER, SHEEHAN, RINGGENBERG, HARTNETT & STORM, P.C., Sioux City—Continued

Law (J.D., 2004). Member, Sterling Honor Society. *Member:* State Bar of South Dakota. (Resident, Dakota Dunes, South Dakota Office). ***PRACTICE AREAS:*** Domestic Relations; Litigation; Personal Injury; Business Law. ***Email:*** ssayler@craryhuff.com

GENERAL COUNSEL FOR: C & H Heavy Duty Specialists; Carlson Enterprises, Inc.; City of Jefferson, South Dakota; City of North Sioux City, South Dakota; City of Onawa, Iowa; Concrete Specialty, Inc.; Dakota Dunes Community Improvement District; Davenport Companies; Executive Copy Systems of Siouxland, Inc; First National Bank of Sioux Center; Heroes, Inc.; Interstates Construction Services, Inc.; Midstates Utility Trailer Sales, Inc.; Iowa-Nebraska State Bank; Kay Dee Feed Co.; Keizer Refrigeration; Keizer Trailer Sales; Morningside College; Nutra-Flo Co.; Office Systems Company; Pech Optical Corporation; Phillips Kiln Services, Ltd.; Plain States Distributing; Refrigerated Engineering; Schaller Telephone Company; Sioux City Explorers; Sioux Honey Assn.; The Boyle Companies; The Broyhill Company; The Health Club, Inc.; The Star Printing and Publishing Co.; Town of Homer, Nebraska; Village of Jackson, Nebraska.
REPRESENTATIVE CLIENTS: Alternative Continuum of Care LLC; American Family Insurance; American National Property & Casual Co.; Burke Engineering Sales Co.; City of South Sioux City, Nebraska; Custom Woodworks, Inc.; Davenport and Associates-Century 21; First National Bank of Akron, Iowa; First National Bank of Sioux City, Iowa; Halman Construction, Inc.; Hawkeye Distribution Inc.; Helvig Agricultural Services Co.; Interbake Foods; John Morrell & Co.; L & L Builders Co.; L & L Properties LC; Morton Buildings Inc.; Nelson Engineering & Construction Co.; Northpark Senior Living, LLC; Northwestern State Bank, Orange City, Iowa; Pender State Bank; Primebank; Security National Bank, Sioux City, Iowa; Security National Bank of South Dakota; Siouxland Chamber of Commerce; Siouxland Economic Development Corp.; Siouxland Medical Education Foundation; State Farm Fire and Casualty; The Harbor Group; The Warner Group; Unitrin Multi-Lines Insurance; Wells Fargo Financial Services; Western Iowa Cooperative Co.
REFERENCES: Security National Bank, Sioux City, Iowa; Iowa-Nebraska State Bank, South Sioux City, Nebraska.

WIL L. FORKER

Established in 1979

705 DOUGLAS STREET, SUITE 303
SIOUX CITY, IOWA 51101
Telephone: 712-252-1395
Fax: 712-252-4858
Email: forkerlaw@aol.com

Bankruptcy.

WIL L. FORKER, born Sioux City, Iowa, September 20, 1954; admitted to bar, 1979, Iowa; 1982, Nebraska. *Education:* Drake University (B.S., cum laude, 1975); Oregon State University Graduate School of Business; University of Iowa (J.D., with honors, 1979). Phi Delta Phi. Assistant Attorney, Woodbury County, 1979-1986; Attorney, Board of Supervisors, Woodbury County, 1986. *Member:* Woodbury County (President, 2005), Iowa State and Nebraska State Bar Associations; National Association of Bankruptcy Trustees. ***PRACTICE AREAS:*** Bankruptcy.

GILDEMEISTER & KEANE, L.L.P.

SUITE 702 TERRA CENTRE
600 FOURTH STREET
P.O. BOX 1379
SIOUX CITY, IOWA 51101
Telephone: 712-234-3088
Fax: 712-234-3077

General Practice. Insurance Defense, Personal Injury, Workers' Compensation, Real Estate, Corporate, Commercial Transactions and Family Law.

FIRM PROFILE: The firm which has achieved Martindale-Hubbell's highest rating for ethical standards and legal ability is dedicated to representing its clients in a manner befitting its rating.

G. DANIEL GILDEMEISTER, born Hull, Iowa, January 20, 1943; admitted to bar, 1968, Iowa; 1972, Arizona and U.S. District Court, Northern District of Iowa; 1979, U.S. Court of Appeals, 8th Circuit. *Education:* Coe College and University of Iowa (B.B.A., 1965); University of Iowa (J.D., 1968). Phi Delta Phi. *Member:* Woodbury County (President, 1984) and Iowa State Bar Associations; Iowa Defense Counsel Association; Defense Research Institute. [Capt., Judge Advocate Division, USAF, 1968-1972]. ***PRACTICE AREAS:*** General Liability Defense. ***Email:*** gdg@siouxcityattys.com

EDWARD J. KEANE, born Louisville, Kentucky, February 8, 1954; admitted to bar, 1979, Iowa and Nebraska; U.S. District Court, District of Iowa and U.S. Court of Appeals, Eighth Circuit. *Education:* Creighton University (B.S.B.A., 1976; J.D., 1979). *Member:* Woodbury County, Nebraska State, Iowa State and American Bar Associations; Association of Trial Lawyers of Iowa; The Association of Trial Lawyers of America. Fellow, Iowa Academy of Trial Lawyers. ***PRACTICE AREAS:*** Personal Injury; Workers Compensation. ***Email:*** ekeane3kid@aol.com

LEGAL SUPPORT PERSONNEL

LORI L. HERIGSTAD (Paralegal)

EILEEN M. HENZE (Paralegal)

REPRESENTATIVE CLIENTS: Farmland Insurance Company; Iowa Communities Assurance Pool; Acceptance Insurance Companies; First Mercury Insurance Company; Enviro Safe Air, Inc.; AAcme Technologies, Inc.; Ace Refrigeration Corporation; Morningside Dental Clinic, P.C.; Selective Petfood Services, Inc.; Remediation Specialists, Inc.; Mau Marine, Inc.

HEIDMAN, REDMOND, FREDREGILL, PATTERSON, PLAZA, DYKSTRA & PRAHL, L.L.P.

A Registered Limited Liability Partnership including Professional Corporations

Established in 1918

701 PIERCE STREET, SUITE 200
P.O. BOX 3086
SIOUX CITY, IOWA 51102
Telephone: 712-255-8838
Fax: 712-258-6714
Email: mail@heidmanlaw.com
URL: http://www.heidmanlaw.com

General Practice, Litigation and Transactional Law.

MEMBERS OF FIRM

JAMES W. REDMOND, born Sioux City, Iowa, June 17, 1947; admitted to bar, 1973, Wisconsin; 1974, Iowa; 1989, Nebraska; 2004, South Dakota. *Education:* Briar Cliff College (B.A., 1971); Marquette University (J.D., 1973). Member, National Moot Court Team, 1972-1973. Clerk for Justice Connor T. Hansen, Wisconsin Supreme Court, 1973-1974. *Member:* Woodbury County, Iowa State, Nebraska State and American Bar Associations; State Bar of South Dakota; Iowa Defense Counsel Association; The Association of Trial Lawyers of America. [With U.S. Army, 1966-1968]. ***PRACTICE AREAS:*** Construction Litigation; Commercial Liability; Professional Liability; Insurance Defense. ***Email:*** Jim.Redmond@heidmanlaw.com

ALAN E. FREDREGILL, (P.C.), born Adel, Iowa, March 19, 1948; admitted to bar, 1975, Iowa; 1984, Nebraska. *Education:* University of Iowa (B.B.A., 1970); Drake University (J.D., with honors, 1974). Order of the Coif. Staff Member, Drake Law Review, 1973-1974. *Member:* Woodbury County, Iowa State (President, 2002-2003; Member, Unauthorized Practice Committee, 1985-1995; Chairman, 1987-1989; Board of Governors, 1996-2003), Nebraska State and American (Member, Litigation Section) Bar Associations; Iowa Defense Counsel Association (President, 1990-1991); International Association of Defense Counsel; Defense Research Institute; American College of Trial Lawyers; Iowa Academy of Trial Lawyers; International Association of Arson Investigators; American Mock Trial Association Judges Hall of Fame (2002). ***PRACTICE AREAS:*** Personal Injury; Insurance Defense; Construction Law; Professional Liability; Arson and Insurance Fraud. ***Email:*** Alan.Fredregill@heidmanlaw.com

THOMAS M. PLAZA, born Cedar Rapids, Iowa, October 11, 1954; admitted to bar, 1979, Iowa. *Education:* University of Northern Iowa (B.A., with high honors, 1976); University of Iowa (J.D., with high honors, 1979). Member, Moot Court Board. Member, 1984— and Member, Board of Governors, 1989-2002, Iowa Association of Workers Compensation Lawyers. *Member:* Woodbury County, Iowa State and American Bar Associations; Nebraska State Bar Association. ***PRACTICE AREAS:*** Workers Compensation. ***Email:*** Thomas.Plaza@heidmanlaw.com

DANIEL D. DYKSTRA, born Paterson, New Jersey, October 29, 1955; admitted to bar, 1980, Iowa; 2004, South Dakota. *Education:* Dordt College (B.A., 1977); University of Iowa (J.D., with distinction, 1980). Managing Editor, Journal of Corporation Law, 1979-1980. *Member:* Woodbury County (Member, Probate Committee), Iowa State (Member, Legal Forms Committee; Chair, 1992-1994) and American Bar Associations; Estate Planning Council of Greater Siouxland; Planned Giving Council of Siouxland. ***PRACTICE AREAS:*** Business Law; Real Estate; Trusts and Estates; Probate; Corporate Law; Commercial Law. ***Email:*** Daniel.Dykstra@heidmanlaw.com

LANCE D. EHMCKE, born Cleghorn, Iowa, May 12, 1950; admitted to bar, 1980, Iowa; 1981, Nebraska. *Education:* Iowa State University (B.S., 1972); Drake University (J.D., 1980). Order of the Barristers. Staff Member, Drake Law Review, 1979-1980. Moot Court Board, 1979-1980. Author: "Insurance Solution or Tort Reform?—Iowa Joins the Nationwide Examination of Proposed Product Liability Legislation," 29 Drake Law Review, 113, 1980. Law Clerk to Hon. Ronald E. Longstaff, Southern District of Iowa, 1980-1981. *Member:* Woodbury County, Dakota County (President, 1991-1993), Iowa State, Nebraska State and American Bar Associations. Fellow, Nebraska State Bar Foundation. [Capt., S.C., USNR (Ret.), active duty, 1972-1977]. ***PRACTICE AREAS:*** Business Law; Real Estate; Trusts and Estates; Probate; Agricultural Law; Legislative Practice. ***Email:*** Lance.Ehmcke@heidmanlaw.com

CYNTHIA C. MOSER, born Belmond, Iowa, September 24, 1952; admitted to bar, 1977, Iowa and U.S. District Court, Southern District of Iowa; 1979, U.S. District Court, Northern District of Iowa. *Education:* Northwestern College (B.A., 1974); University of Iowa (J.D., with distinction, 1977). Law Clerk to Honorable W.C. Stuart, U.S. District Court Judge, Southern District of Iowa, 1977-1979. Commissioner, Iowa State Judicial Nominating Commission, 1999—. Listed in *The Best Lawyers in America,* Health Law Category. *Member:* Woodbury County, Iowa State (Member, Health Law Section, 2002—) and American Bar Associations; State Bar of South Dakota; Iowa Society of Healthcare Attorneys (President, 1993-1994); Task Force on HIPAA Preemption (2002—); American Health Lawyers Association. ***PRACTICE AREAS:*** Business Transactions; Health Law; Employment Law. ***Email:*** Cynthia.Moser@heidmanlaw.com

JOHN C. GRAY, born Fort Dodge, Iowa, January 3, 1955; admitted to bar, 1981, Iowa; 1989, Nebraska. *Education:* University of Iowa (B.A., 1978; J.D., 1981). Editor-in-Chief, Journal of Corporation Law, 1980-1981. Law Clerk to: the Hon. Donald P. Lay, Chief Judge of the Eighth Circuit Court of Appeals, 1981-1982; Hon. Louis W. Schultz, Justice of the Iowa Supreme Court, 1982-1983. *Member:* Woodbury County, Iowa State, Nebraska State and American Bar Associations; Iowa Defense Counsel. ***PRACTICE AREAS:*** Commercial Litigation; Personal Injury; Insurance; Federal Civil Practice; Insurance Defense; Professional Liability. ***Email:*** John.Gray@heidmanlaw.com

DANIEL B. SHUCK, born Ft. Belvoir, Virginia, February 27, 1960; admitted to bar, 1985, Iowa; 1992, Nebraska; 1996, Winnebago Tribal Court and U.S. District Court, Northern and Southern Districts of Iowa and District of Nebraska. *Education:* Creighton University (B.A., 1982); Drake University (J.D., 1985). Law Clerk to Hon. Maynard J.V. Hayden, Iowa Court of Appeals, 1986-1987. Assistant County Attorney, Black Hawk County, Iowa,

(This Listing Continued)

1987-1989. *Member:* Woodbury County, Iowa State, Nebraska State and American Bar Associations; Iowa Defense Counsel Association. ***PRACTICE AREAS:*** Civil Litigation; Toxic Tort; Complex Litigation; Insurance Defense; Personal Injury. ***Email:*** Dan.Shuck@heidmanlaw.com

RITA C. GRIMM, born Yankton, South Dakota, September 20, 1960; admitted to bar, 1985, Nebraska and U.S. District Court, District of Nebraska; 1991, Iowa; 1993, U.S. District Court, Northern District of Iowa. *Education:* Doane College (B.A., summa cum laude, 1982); University of Nebraska (J.D., 1985). Phi Alpha Theta. Member, Allen Moot Court Board. *Member:* Dakota County, Woodbury County, Iowa State (Member, Workers Compensation Section Council; Chair, 1995-1996), Nebraska State and American Bar Associations; Iowa Association of Workers Compensation Lawyers (Member, Board of Governors, 2002—); Iowa Association of Business and Industry Workers' Compensation Committee (Chair, 2000-2005). ***PRACTICE AREAS:*** Workers Compensation Appeals; Workers Compensation Defense; Workers Compensation Mediation; Workers Compensation Self Insurance; Workers Compensation Subrogation. ***Email:*** Rita.Grimm@heidmanlaw.com

PATRICK L. SEALEY, born Hastings, Nebraska, February 18, 1970; admitted to bar, 1995, Iowa, South Dakota and Nebraska. *Education:* University of Nebraska (B.A., with high distinction, 1992); University of Iowa (J.D., with distinction, 1995). Articles Editor, Journal of Corporation Law, 1994-1995. *Member:* Woodbury County, Iowa State (Member, District Representative, Young Lawyers Division, 1997-1999), Nebraska State, and American Bar Associations; State Bar of South Dakota; Iowa Defense Counsel Association; Nebraska Association of Trial Attorneys. ***PRACTICE AREAS:*** Insurance Defense; Insurance Civil Litigation; Commercial Litigation; Trial Practice; Personal Injury; Torts; Construction Law. ***Email:*** Patrick.Sealey@heidmanlaw.com

JEFF W. WRIGHT, born Sioux Center, Iowa, February 28, 1973; admitted to bar, 1998, Iowa and Nebraska. *Education:* Northwestern College (B.A., cum laude, 1995); University of Iowa (J.D., with distinction, 1998). *Member:* Woodbury County, Iowa State, Nebraska State and American Bar Associations; Iowa Defense Counsel Association. ***PRACTICE AREAS:*** Commercial Litigation; Personal Injury; Product Liability. ***Email:*** Jeff.Wright@heidmanlaw.com

ASSOCIATES

SARAH KUEHL KLEBER, born Dexter, Iowa, August 31, 1972; admitted to bar, 1998, Iowa and Nebraska; 1999, South Dakota. *Education:* Drake University (B.A., summa cum laude, 1995); Washington & Lee University (J.D., 1998). *Member:* Woodbury County, Iowa State (Member, Sections on: Employment Law; Workers Compensation), Nebraska State and American Bar Associations; State Bar of South Dakota. ***PRACTICE AREAS:*** Employment Law; Workers Compensation; Municipal Law. ***Email:*** Sarah.Kleber@heidmanlaw.com

ROSALYND J. KOOB, born Carroll, Iowa, September 30, 1975; admitted to bar, 2001, Iowa and Nebraska. *Education:* Briar Cliff College (B.A., magna cum laude, 1998); Creighton University (J.D., with distinction, 2001). Alpha Sigma Nu honoree; Moot Court Executive Board; Creighton Law Review Staff Member; Magistrar Phi Delta Phi. *Member:* Woodbury County, Iowa State, Nebraska State and American Bar Associations; Iowa Defense Counsel Association. ***PRACTICE AREAS:*** Commercial Litigation; Personal Injury; Insurance. ***Email:*** Roz.Koob@heidmanlaw.com

JOEL D. VOS, born Newton, Iowa, May 4, 1977; admitted to bar, 2002, Iowa; 2003, South Dakota. *Education:* Dordt College (B.A., Political Science, 1999); University of Iowa College of Law (J.D., with highest distinction, 2002). Managing Editor, Journal of Corporation Law, 2001-2002. *Member:* Woodbury County, Iowa State and American Bar Associations. ***PRACTICE AREAS:*** Business Law; Real Estate; Trusts and Estates. ***Email:*** Joel.Vos@heidmanlaw.com

JEANA L. GOOSMANN, born Karlstad, Minnesota, June 27, 1977; admitted to bar, 2002, Iowa; 2003, Nebraska and South Dakota. *Education:* University of Nebraska at Lincoln (B.S., Business, highest distinction, 1999); Creighton University School of Law (J.D., summa cum laude, 2002). Member: Moot Court; Mortar Board. Student Articles Editor of the Creighton Law Review, 2001-2002. Advanced Trial Practice Team, 2001-2002. Member, Client Counseling and Negotiations Board, 2000-2002. *Member:* Woodbury County, Iowa State, Nebraska State and American Bar Associations; State Bar of South Dakota; American Bankruptcy Institute; American Health Law Institute. ***PRACTICE AREAS:*** Business Law; Bankruptcy; Health Care. ***Email:*** Jeana.Goosmann@heidmanlaw.com

LISA A. PETERSON, born Sioux City, Iowa, January 22, 1977; admitted to bar, 2004, Iowa. *Education:* Central Missouri State University (B.A., English, 1999; M.A., 2001); Drake University (J.D., with honors, 2004). Articles Editor, Drake Journal of Agricultural Law, 2003-2004. Member, Moot Court Board, 2002-2004. *Member:* Woodbury County, Iowa State and American Bar Associations; State Bar of South Dakota. ***PRACTICE AREAS:*** Workers Compensation; Litigation. ***Email:*** lisa.peterson@heidmanlaw.com

OF COUNSEL

MARVIN F. HEIDMAN, born Des Moines, Iowa, March 28, 1938; admitted to bar, 1962, Iowa. *Education:* Iowa State University (B.S., 1960); Drake University (J.D., 1962). Editorial Notes Editor, Drake Law Review, 1961-1962. Listed in: The Best Lawyers in America (20 years). *Member:* Woodbury County (President, 1979-1980), Iowa State (Member: Committee on Litigation Legislation, 1975-1986; Supreme Court Advisory Committee on Rules, 1984-1988; Chairman, Litigation Section, 1992-1993) and American Bar Associations; Iowa Defense Counsel Association (President, 1979-1980; Member, Board of Directors, 1975-1993); Iowa Academy of Trial Lawyers (Member, Board of Directors, 1994-1998; President, 1999). Fellow, American College of Trial Lawyers. [Lieut., Law Specialist, U.S. Naval Reserve, active duty, 1962-1966]. ***Email:*** Marv.Heidman@heidmanlaw.com

JOHN W. GLEYSTEEN (1911-2000)

ROBERT R. EIDSMOE (Retired)

JACOB C. GLEYSTEEN (1883-1943)

H. CLIFFORD HARPER (1891-1959)

(This Listing Continued)

CHARLES T. PATTERSON, born Jacksonville, Illinois, August 30, 1950; admitted to bar, 1975, Iowa; 1986, Nebraska; 1994, South Dakota. *Education:* Southern Illinois University (B.S., 1972); Drake University (J.D., 1975). Member, Moot Court. *Member:* Woodbury County, Iowa State, Nebraska State and American (Member, Section on Corporation, Business and Banking Law) Bar Associations; State Bar of South Dakota; Iowa Defense Counsel Association; Iowa Association of Workers Compensation Lawyers; Iowa Academy of Trial Lawyers; International Association of Defense Counsel. ***PRACTICE AREAS:*** Litigation; Professional Liability; Agricultural Law. ***Email:*** Tom.Patterson@heidmanlaw.com

MARGARET M. PRAHL, born Lincoln, Nebraska, November 28, 1938; admitted to bar, 1981, Iowa; 1982, South Dakota; 1997, Nebraska. *Education:* University of Nebraska (B.A., 1960); University of South Dakota (J.D., with highest distinction, 1981). Sterling Honor Graduate, University of South Dakota. Editor-in-Chief, South Dakota Law Review, 1980-1981. Author: "Rezoning Dilemma; What May a Court do with an Invalid Zoning Classification?" 25 South Dakota Law Review, 181; "Anti-Trust Law, Zoning and Agreements to Zone; Delegation of Police Power After Lafayette v. Louisiana Power and Light," 25 South Dakota Law Review, 314, 1981. Member, Iowa Supreme Court Grievance Commission, 1989-1994. *Member:* Woodbury County, Iowa State (Member: Labor and Employment Section; Council, 1994-1997; CLE Committee, 1997-1998), Nebraska State and American (Member, Equal Employment Opportunity Committee) Bar Associations; State Bar of South Dakota; Iowa Municipal Attorneys Association; Iowa Organization of Women Attorneys; Defense Research Institute; Iowa Academy of Trial Lawyers. ***PRACTICE AREAS:*** Labor and Employment; Equal Employment Opportunity Law; Business Transactions; Civil Litigation; Trial Practice. ***Email:*** Margaret.Prahl@heidmanlaw.com

REPRESENTATIVE CLIENTS: Acuity Insurance Co.; Allied Insurance Group; American Family Insurance; American Foods Group; Argonaut Insurance Co.; Associated Aviation Underwriters; Atlantic Mutual Cos.; Auto Owners Insurance Co.; Braunger Food Service; Broadspire; Brower Construction Co.; Chubb Group of Insurance Cos.; City of Sergeant Bluff; ESIS; Continental Baking Co.; Continental Grain Co.; Crawford & Co.; CUNA Mortgage Corp.; Employers Reinsurance; Farm Bureau Insurance Co. of Nebraska; Farmers State Bank; Federated Mutual Insurance Co.; Fireman's Fund Insurance Co.; First State Bank of Ida Grove; Frank Audino Construction, Inc.; GAB Robins; Gelita USA; General Electric Co.; Grinnell Mutual Reinsurance Co.; Hardee's of Sioux City; Iowa Mutual Insurance Co.; Irving F. Jensen, Co.; J.I. Case Co.; John Deere Insurance Co.; John Hancock Mutual Life Insurance Co.; ITT Hartford Insurance Group; Liberty National Bank; Long Lines, Ltd.; Medical Protective Co.; Mercy Medical Center; Meridian Ins. Co.; Metropolitan Life Insurance Co.; Midlands Clinic P.C.; Midwest Community Credit Union; Midwest Medical Insurance Co.; New York Life Insurance Co.; PIC USA, Inc., P.L.C., Sygen; Pig Improvement Co.; Pioneer Bank; Primebank; Sioux City Urological Associates; Siouxland Surgery Center; Siouxland Community Health Center; PHO; State Farm Mutual Automobile Insurance Co.; State Farm Fire & Casualty; Terra International, Inc.; The Security National Bank of Sioux City; Travelers Insurance Co.; Tyson Foods, Inc.; United Fire & Casualty; Unitrin; VanBuskirk Construction Co.; Viking Insurance Co. of Wisconsin; Winnebago Tribe of Nebraska.

HELLIGE, FREY & ROE, R.L.L.P.

700 FRANCES BUILDING
505 FIFTH STREET
P.O. BOX 1828
SIOUX CITY, IOWA 51102
Telephone: 712-255-4444
Telecopier: 712-255-4465
Email: helligelaw@helligelaw.com

General and Trial Practice in Iowa, South Dakota and Nebraska State and Federal Courts.

MEMBERS OF FIRM

MICHAEL R. HELLIGE, born Fort Madison, Iowa, September 10, 1946; admitted to bar, 1971, Iowa, U.S. District Court, Northern and Southern Districts of Iowa and U.S. Court of Appeals, Eighth Circuit; 2000, Nebraska. *Education:* University of Iowa (B.A., with distinction, 1968; J.D., 1971). President, Woodbury County Bar Association, 1985. *Member:* Woodbury County, Dakota County, Iowa State and American Bar Associations; Iowa Academy of Trial Lawyers; Defense Counsel Association of Iowa. ***PRACTICE AREAS:*** Civil Litigation. ***Email:*** mikeh@helligelaw.com

MICHAEL J. FREY, born Sioux City, Iowa, April 4, 1965; admitted to bar, 1990, Iowa and U.S. Army Court of Military Review; 1992, U.S. District Court, Southern and Northern Districts of Iowa; 1996, Nebraska. *Education:* Fort Dodge Community College; Westmar College (B.A., 1987); Drake Law School (J.D., with honors, 1990). *Member:* Woodbury County, Dakota County and Iowa State (Member, Young Lawyers Division) Bar Associations; Iowa Defense Counsel Association. [Capt., U.S. Army Judge Advocate General's Corps, 1990-1992]. ***PRACTICE AREAS:*** Litigation. ***Email:*** mikef@helligelaw.com

KATHLEEN C. ROE, born Sioux City, Iowa, May 27, 1971; admitted to bar, 1999, Iowa and U.S. District Court, Northern District of Iowa; 2000, South Dakota and U.S. District Court, District of South Dakota. *Education:* Morningside College (B.A., 1994); Creighton University (J.D., 1998). *Member:* Woodbury County, South Dakota and Iowa State Bar Associations; Iowa Trial Lawyers Association; Iowa Defense Counsel Association. ***PRACTICE AREAS:*** Civil Litigation; Workers Compensation. ***Email:*** kathleenr@helligelaw.com

E. A. CHARLIE NICHOLS, born Memphis, Tennessee, August 2, 1979; admitted to bar, 2005, Iowa. *Education:* Morehouse College (B.A., 2001); University of Iowa City (J.D., 2004). *Member:* Woodbury County and Iowa State (Member, Young Lawyers Division) Bar Associations. ***PRACTICE AREAS:*** Workers Compensation; Civil Litigation. ***Email:*** charlien@helligelaw.com

LOCAL COUNSEL FOR: Allied Insurance Co.; American Family Insurance Group; American International Group; CIGNA; The Cincinnati Companies; Constitution State Service Company; Design Professionals Insurance Company; Employers Mutual Companies; Employers Reinsurance Corporation; Farm & City Insurance Company; Farmers Mutual of Nebraska; Ford Motor Company; GRE Insurance Group; Hartford; Hy-Vee Food Stores, Inc.; Liberty Mutual Insurance Company; MSI Insurance; Nationwide Insurance; Northwestern National Insurance Company; Preferred Risk Group; Prudential Insurance Company; St. Paul Insurance Company; The Travelers Group.

LUNDBERG LAW FIRM, P.L.C.

Established in 2002

906 TERRA CENTRE
600 4TH STREET
SIOUX CITY, IOWA 51101
Telephone: 712-234-3030
Fax: 712-234-3034
Email: paull@terracentre.net
URL: http://www.lundberglawfirm.com

General Practice including Personal Injury, Employment Law, Professional Liability and Commercial Law.

FIRM PROFILE: Solo trial practice of Paul D. Lundberg, a 1981 graduate of the University of Iowa College of Law. Mr. Lundberg is licensed to practice in Iowa, Nebraska and South Dakota and is admitted to practice before the United State Supreme Court. He is a member of the Iowa Academy of Trial Lawyers and the American Board of Trial Advocates.

PAUL D. LUNDBERG, born Harlan, Iowa, March 9, 1951; admitted to bar, 1981, Iowa, Nebraska, U.S. District Court, Northern District of Iowa and U.S. District Court, District of Nebraska; 1982, U.S. Court of Appeals, Eighth Circuit; 1997, U.S. Supreme Court; 2003, South Dakota. *Education:* University of Nebraska at Omaha (B.S., summa cum laude, 1978); University of Iowa (J.D., with high distinction, 1981). Phi Delta Phi; Order of the Coif. *Member:* Woodbury County (President, 2004), Dakota County, Iowa State, Nebraska State and American (Member, Litigation Section) Bar Associations; Iowa Academy of Trial Lawyers; American Board of Trial Advocates. ***REPORTED CASES:*** Lundell Manufacturing v. American Broadcasting Co., 98 F.3rd 351. ***PRACTICE AREAS:*** Civil Litigation; Personal Injury; Employment Law; Professional Liability; Commercial Law.

Languages: English.

REPRESENTATIVE CLIENTS: The Cincinnati Companies; Mobren Biological; Siouxland Orthopedics; Jones Eye Clinic; Safeco Insurance.

DENNIS J. MAHR

COMMERCE BUILDING, SUITE 334
520 NEBRASKA STREET
SIOUX CITY, IOWA 51101-1316
Telephone: 712-233-1623
Toll Free: 1-800-621-0783
Fax: 712-233-1625
Email: mahrlaw@cableone.net

Workers Compensation, Personal Injury and Social Security Disability Law for Plaintiffs and Claimants only.

DENNIS J. MAHR, born Iowa City, Iowa, December 12, 1950; admitted to bar, 1977, Iowa; 1978, Nebraska and U.S. Court of Appeals, Eighth Circuit; 1980, U.S. Supreme Court. *Education:* University of Iowa (B.G.S., 1974; M.A., 1976; J.D., 1976). *Member:* Woodbury County, Dakota County, Iowa State, Nebraska State (Chairman, Workers' Compensation Section, 1996-1997) and American Bar Associations; The Association of Trial Lawyers of America; National Organization of Social Security Claimants Representatives. ***REPORTED CASES:*** Citizens Against Lewis and Clark (Mowery) Landfill v. Pottawattamie County Bd. of Adjustment, 277 N.W. 2d 921 (Iowa 1979); State v. Webb, 309 N.W. 2d 404 (Iowa 1981); Myron v. Chicoine, 678 F.2d 727 (7th Cir. 1982); Norris v. Iowa Beef Processors, Inc., 402 N.W.2d 658 (Neb. 1987); Henriksen v. Younglove Const., 540 N.W.2d 254 (Iowa 1995); Weikamp v. Apfel, 116 F.Supp.2d 1056 (N.D. Iowa 2000); Marnell v. Barnhart, 253 F.Supp. 2d 254 (N.D. Iowa 2003); Mycogen Seeds v. Sands, 686 N.W. 2d 457 (Iowa 2004). ***PRACTICE AREAS:*** Workers Compensation; Personal Injury; Social Security Disability.

REFERENCE: Security National Bank, Sioux City, Iowa.

MAYNE & MADSEN

SUITE 405
PIONEER BANK BUILDING
701 PIERCE STREET
P.O. BOX 1347
SIOUX CITY, IOWA 51102-1347
Telephone: 712-252-3220
Fax: 712-252-1535
Email: jmayne@iowabar.org
URL: http://www.lawyers.com/maynemarks

Civil Trials and Appeals in all State and Federal Courts. Insurance, Commercial, Tort, Corporation, Estate Planning, Probate, Medical and Legal Malpractice.

MEMBERS OF FIRM

Wiley Mayne (Retired)
George F. Madsen (Retired)

JOHN D. MAYNE, born Sioux City, Iowa, November 20, 1947; admitted to bar, 1976, Iowa and U.S. District Court, Northern and Southern Districts of Iowa; U.S. District Court, District of Nebraska; U.S. Court of Appeals, Eighth Circuit; U.S. Supreme Court. *Education:* Harvard College (B.A., 1970); Drake University (J.D., with honors, 1976). Member, Iowa Supreme Court Advisory Committee on Rules of Civil Procedure, 1993-1995. Director, 1998-2001 and President, 2000-2001, Sioux City Community School District. *Member:* Iowa State (Member, 1979-1985 and Chairman, 1986-1988, Federal Practice Committee; Member, Board of Governors, 1988-1994); and American (Member, Litigation Section) Bar Associations; Iowa Defense Counsel Association; International Association of Defense Counsel (Member, Medical Malpractice Committee, 1993—). Fellow, Iowa Academy of Trial Lawyers; Fellow, Iowa State Bar Foundation. [Lt., USNR, active duty, 1970-1972]. ***PRACTICE AREAS:*** Litigation. ***Email:*** jmayne@iowabar.org

MISSY J. DENTON, born Syracuse, New York, July 5, 1970; admitted to bar, 1999, South Dakota; 2000, Iowa; U.S. District Court, Northern District of Iowa. *Education:* University of California at Davis, (B.A., magna cum laude, 1995); University of South Dakota School of Law (J.D., 1998). Phi Kappa Phi. Delta Theta Phi. *Member:* Iowa State (Member, Mock Trial Committee) and American Bar Associations; State Bar of South Dakota. ***Email:*** mdenton@iowabar.org

REPRESENTATIVE CLIENTS: American Empire Insurance Co.; American Home Insurance; American State Bank; American Telephone & Telegraph Co.; Amoco Oil Company; Atlanta Casualty Co.; Briar Cliff College; Capitol Indemnity Group; Central United Life Insurance Company; Chubb Insurance; Dakota County, Nebraska; Design Professionals Financial Corp.; First Federal Savings Bank of Siouxland; First Federal Savings Bank of Sioux City; First National Bank in Sioux City; Ford Motor Credit Company; Fremont Indemnity Company; Frontier Bank; Heritage Insurance; L & L Builders Co.; Podiatry Insurance Company of America; Ranger Insurance; Raytheon Corp.; Rudy Salem Employment Agency; Sara Lee Bakery Group; The Security National Bank of Sioux City, Iowa; The Security National Bank of South Dakota; Shell Chemical Company; Siouxland National Bank; Siouxland Oncology Hematology Associates; Utica Mutual Insurance Company; Valley Bank & Trust of Mapleton, Iowa; United Rentals, Inc.; Western Iowa Tech Community College.

RAWLINGS, NIELAND, PROBASCO, KILLINGER, ELLWANGER, JACOBS & MOHRHAUSER

Established in 1934

522 FOURTH STREET, SUITE 300
SIOUX CITY, IOWA 51101
Telephone: 712-277-2373
FAX: 712-277-3304
Email: rawlingsnieland.com

General Civil Practice. Appeals, Bankruptcy, Commercial Law and Litigation, Corporation, Creditors Rights, Employment, Estate Planning, Insurance, Medical-Legal, Personal Injury, Probate, Real Estate, Taxation, Trial Practice and Worker's Compensation.

JAMES W. KINDIG (1879-1950)
LOWELL C. KINDIG (1913-1992)
ROBERT E. BEEBE (1913-1988)
GENE A. PROBASCO (1931-1999)

MEMBERS OF FIRM

MAURICE B. NIELAND, born Carroll, Iowa, July 28, 1946; admitted to bar, 1970, Iowa, U.S. District Court, Northern District of Iowa and U.S. Court of Appeals, 8th Circuit; 1972, U.S. District Court, Southern District of Iowa; 1974, U.S. Supreme Court; 1997, U.S. Court of Appeals, 11th Circuit. *Education:* St. John's University; University of Iowa (B.A., 1968; J.D., with distinction, 1970). Phi Delta Phi. Managing Editor and Member, Board of Editors, Iowa Law Review, 1969-1970. Author: "Equality in the Selective Service System," 54 Iowa Law Review 21, December, 1968; "Subdivision Regulation in Iowa," 54 Iowa Law Review 1121, June, 1969. Assistant City Attorney, Sioux City, 1970-1971. President, Sioux City Lawyers Club, 1976. Member, State Judicial Selection Committee, 1993-1999. Member, Third Judicial District Judicial Selection Committee, 1982-1988. Member, 1976-1983 and Chairman, 1982-1983, Iowa State Board of Law Examiners. Trustee, University of Iowa Law School Foundation, 1990-2002. *Member:* Woodbury County, Iowa State and American Bar Associations; Iowa Academy of Trial Lawyers (Board of Governors, 1992-1998; President, 1996-1997); Iowa Defense Counsel Association; American College of Trial Lawyers (State Chairman, 2004—). ***Email:*** mnieland@rawlingsnieland.com

SAM S. KILLINGER, born Henderson, Iowa, September 5, 1940; admitted to bar, 1963, Iowa; 1974, U.S. District Court, Northern District of Iowa; 1983, U.S. Tax Court; 1984, U.S. Court of Appeals, 8th Circuit; 1991, U.S. District Court, Southern District of Iowa; 1999, U.S. Supreme Court. *Education:* State University of Iowa (B.A., 1962; LL.B., 1963). Phi Alpha Delta. *Member:* Woodbury County (President, 1992) and Iowa State (Member, Litigation Section; Board of Governors, 1994-1996) Bar Associations. ***Email:*** skillinger@rawlingsnieland.com

MICHAEL W. ELLWANGER, born Minneapolis, Minnesota, June 22, 1950; admitted to bar, 1975, Iowa; 1976, Nebraska, U.S. District Court, Northern and Southern Districts of Iowa; U.S. District Court, District of Nebraska, U.S. Co urt of Appeals, Eighth Circuit. *Education:* Morningside College (B.A., 1972); University of Iowa (J.D., 1975). Order of the Coif. Member, Moot Court Board. President, Sioux City Lawyers Club, 1981. Member, Board of Editors, Iowa Defense Counsel "Defense Update," 1988—. *Member:* Woodbury County (President, 2002), Dakota County, Iowa State (Member, Litigation and Health Law Sections) and Nebraska State Bar Associations; Iowa Defense Counsel Association (Board of Governors, 1991-2000; President, 2001-2002); Iowa Academy of Trial Lawyers. Fellow, American College of Trial Lawyers. ***Email:*** mellwanger@rawlingsnieland.com

MICHAEL P. JACOBS, born Sioux City, Iowa, February 10, 1954; admitted to bar, 1979, South Dakota, Iowa and U.S. District Court, Northern District of Iowa; 1981, U.S. District Court, District of South Dakota and U.S. Court of Appeals, 8th Circuit; 1986, U.S. Supreme Court; 1988, U.S. District Court, Southern District of Iowa. *Education:* Drake University; University of South Dakota (B.S. 1976; J.D., 1979). President, Sioux City Lawyers Club, 1984. *Member:* Woodbury County and Iowa State Bar Associations; State Bar of South Dakota; Iowa Defense Counsel Association. ***Email:*** mjacobs@rawlingsnieland.com

JEFFREY R. MOHRHAUSER, born Emmetsburg, Iowa, September 25, 1955; admitted to bar, 1981, Iowa, South Dakota, U.S. District Court, Northern District of Iowa and U.S. District Court, District of South Dakota; 1982, Nebraska; U.S. District Court, District of Nebraska. *Education:* University of Northern Iowa (B.A., 1978); University of South Dakota (J.D., 1981). Author: "Woodbury County Soil Conservation District v. Ortner: New Authority for Required Soil Conservation," 25 South Dakota Law Review 614, 1980. Member, Sioux Gateway Airport Board of Trustees, 1995-2001. *Member:* Woodbury County, Iowa State (Member: Business Law and Commercial and Bankruptcy Law Sec-

(This Listing Continued)

tions; Vice Chairperson, Ethics Committee, Business Law Section, 1994-1995), Nebraska State and American Bar Associations; State Bar of South Dakota; American Bankruptcy Institute. ***Email:*** jmohrhauser@rawlingsnieland.com

REBECCA A. NELSON, born Sioux City, Iowa, August 20, 1953; admitted to bar, 1995, Iowa and U.S. District Court, Northern District of Iowa; 1996, South Dakota; 1999, Nebraska and U.S. District Court, District of South Dakota; 2003, U.S. District Court, District of Nebraska. *Education:* Morningside College (B.S., summa cum laude, 1991); University of South Dakota (J.D., 1995). Treasurer and Vice President, Woodbury County, 2003. Member, Third Judicial District Nominating Commission, 2005—. *Member:* Woodbury County, Iowa State, Nebraska State and American Bar Associations; State Bar of South Dakota. ***Email:*** rnelson@rawlingsnieland.com

MATTHEW T. E. EARLY, born Fort Dodge, Iowa, July 23, 1966; admitted to bar, 1996, Iowa; 1997, U.S. District Court, Northern District of Iowa. *Education:* Iowa State University (B.A., 1990); University of Iowa (J.D., with distinction, 1995). *Member:* Woodbury County, Iowa State and American Bar Associations. ***Email:*** mearly@rawlingsnieland.com

ASSOCIATES

KARRIE R. HRUSKA, born Sioux Center, Iowa, April 12, 1974; admitted to bar, 1999, Iowa and U.S. District Court, Northern District of Iowa. *Education:* University of South Dakota (B.A., 1996); University of Iowa (J.D., 1999). Phi Delta Phi. Member, Stephenson Trial Advocacy Team, 1999. *Member:* Woodbury County and Iowa State Bar Associations. ***Email:*** khruska@rawlingsnieland.com

TODD A. IRGENS, born Sioux City, Iowa, January 9, 1971; admitted to bar, 2003, Iowa. *Education:* Morningside College (B.A., 2000); University of Iowa College of Law (J.D., 2003). ***PRACTICE AREAS:*** General Practice. ***Email:*** tirgens@rawlingsnieland.com

REPRESENTATIVE CLIENTS: Argosy Gaming Company; Adcraft, Inc.; Artisan Press, Inc.; Central Bank; Catholic Mutual Group; CNOS, P.C.; Chesterman Co.; CNA Insurance Co.; Continental Insurance Co.; Continental Western Insurance Co.; Diocese of Sioux City; Farm Bureau Mutual Insurance Company; Farmers Savings Bank of Remsen; Haco Engineering; Iowa Lamb Corporation; L.G. Everist, Inc.; Metal Specialists, Inc.; Minnesota Lawyers Mutual Insurance Co.; National Chiropractic Insurance Co.; NWIP, Inc.; Pathology Medical Services of Siouxland, P.C.; Premium Waters, Inc.; Regent Insurance Co.; St. Luke's Regional Medical Center; St. Paul Fire & Marine Insurance Co.; Sabre Communications Corp.; Siouxland Federal Credit Union; Siouxland Regional Cancer Center; Telco Triad Community Credit Union; Union National Bank, Correctionville; U.S. Insurance Group; Wells Fargo Equipment Finance, Inc; Wells Fargo Bank, N.A.; West Livestock Transportation, Inc.; Western Casualty and Surety Co.

ELIZABETH A. ROSENBAUM

SUITE 903, TERRA CENTRE
600 4TH STREET
SIOUX CITY, IOWA 51101
Telephone: 712-233-3632
Fax: 712-233-6101

Domestic Relations, Family Law, Adoptions, and Indian Child Welfare Act.

ELIZABETH A. ROSENBAUM, born Syracuse, New York, September 10, 1961; admitted to bar, 1989, Iowa, South Dakota, U.S. District Court, Northern District of Iowa, U.S. District Court, District of South Dakota and U.S. Court of Appeals, Eighth Circuit. *Education:* University of South Dakota (A.D.N., 1981; B.S., 1985; J.D., 1988). Registered Nurse: State of Iowa, 1981. *Member:* Woodbury County, Iowa State (Member, Family Law Section, Adoption Committee) and American (Member, Family Law Section, Adoption Committee) Bar Associations; State Bar of South Dakota (Member, Family Law Section).

IRENE A. SCHRUNK

TERRA CENTRE, SUITE 308
600 FOURTH STREET
SIOUX CITY, IOWA 51101
Telephone: 712-233-3625
Fax: 712-233-3675

Domestic Relations, Family Law, Divorce, Domestic Violence and Juvenile Law.

IRENE A. SCHRUNK, born Council Bluffs, Iowa, October 7, 1949; admitted to bar, 1978, Iowa, U.S. District Court, Northern District of Iowa, U.S. Court of Appeals, Eighth Circuit and U.S. District Court, District of Nebraska (inactive); 1979, Nebraska (inactive); 1988, U.S. District Court, Southern District of Iowa. *Education:* Creighton University (B.S.N., 1971); University of Iowa (J.D., with honors, 1978). Registered Nurse, Iowa, Nebraska and New Jersey. *Member:* Woodbury County, Iowa State (Member, Family Law Section) and Nebraska State Bar Associations. ***PRACTICE AREAS:*** Domestic Relations; Family Law; Divorce; Domestic Violence; Juvenile Law.

SMITH & McELWAIN

505 FIFTH, SUITE 530
P.O. BOX 1194
SIOUX CITY, IOWA 51102
Telephone: 712-255-8094
Fax: 712-255-3825
Email: smitmcel@aol.com
URL: http://www.smitmcel.com

Labor and Employment Law, Workers' Compensation Law.

(This Listing Continued)

MEMBERS OF FIRM

MACDONALD SMITH, born Sioux City, Iowa, February 23, 1948; admitted to bar, 1973, Iowa and U.S. District Court, Northern and Southern Districts of Iowa. *Education:* University of Notre Dame (A.B., 1970); University of Iowa (J.D., 1973). *Member:* Iowa State Bar Association. ***PRACTICE AREAS:*** Labor and Employment.

DENNIS M. McELWAIN, born Omaha, Nebraska, September 6, 1956; admitted to bar, 1983, Iowa; 1984, U.S. District Court, Northern District of Iowa; 1992, Nebraska. *Education:* University of Iowa (B.G.S., 1980; J.D., 1983). ***PRACTICE AREAS:*** Workers Compensation.

HARRY H. SMITH (1916-1999)

ASSOCIATE

JAY M. SMITH, born Sioux City, Iowa, 1978; admitted to bar, 2004, Iowa. *Education:* University of Notre Dame (B.A., magna cum laude, 2001); University of Iowa College of Law (J.D., 2004). ***Email:*** smitmcel@aol.com

REPRESENTATIVE CLIENTS: Iowa Federation of Labor; Iowa State Building & Construction Trades Council.
REFERENCE: Wells Fargo Bank, N.A.

TIEFENTHALER LAW OFFICE, P.C.

518 8TH STREET, SUITE D
SIOUX CITY, IOWA 51101
Telephone: 712-252-5080
Fax: 712-252-5087
Email: btief@hotmail.com
URL: http://www.tieflaw.com

Personal Injury, Workers' Compensation, Criminal Defense.

BOB TIEFENTHALER, born Sioux City, Iowa, May 4, 1969; admitted to bar, 1994, Iowa and U.S. District Court, Northern and Southern Districts of Iowa; 1995, South Dakota; 1996, Nebraska; U.S. District Court, District of South Dakota and U.S. District Court, District of Nebraska. *Education:* University of South Dakota (B.S., 1991; J.D., 1994). Iowa Trial Lawyers Criminal Law Core Group. *Member:* Woodbury County, Nebraska and Iowa State Bar Associations; The State Bar of South Dakota; Iowa Trial Lawyers Association; The American Trial Lawyers Association. ***PRACTICE AREAS:*** Personal Injury (35%); Workers Compensation (35%); Criminal Defense (30%). ***Email:*** btief@hotmail.com

VRIEZELAAR, TIGGES, EDGINGTON, BOTTARO, BODEN & ROSS, L.L.P.

421 NEBRASKA STREET
SIOUX CITY, IOWA 51101
Telephone: 712-252-3226
Fax: 712-252-4873
Email: vterbblaw@siouxcitylawyers.com
URL: http://www.siouxcitylawyers.net

Mailing Address: P.O. Box 1557, Sioux City, IA 51102

General Civil and Trial Practice in all Courts, ERISA, Corporate and Estate Planning, Probate, Taxation, Real Estate, Banking, Creditor's Rights, Employment, Personal Injury and Negligence Litigation (Plaintiff and Defense) and Workers' Compensation Law.

MEMBERS OF FIRM

KENT VRIEZELAAR, born Des Moines, Iowa, May 15, 1951; admitted to bar, 1976, Iowa, U.S. District Court, Northern District of Iowa and U.S. Tax Court; 1994, South Dakota, Nebraska and U.S. District Court, District of Nebraska; 1995, U.S. District Court, District of South Dakota. *Education:* University of Iowa (B.B.A., 1973; J.D., with honors, 1976). Beta Alpha Psi. Seminar Papers: Basic Retirement Planning: Simple IRAs/401K Plans/SEP IRAs, ISBA December Tax School, 2004 and Siouxland Estate Planning Council, 2005; Family Battles: the Real Post-Mortem Result, UILS/ISBA Spring Tax institute, 2004; Estate Planning Basics, ISBA YLD Summer Seminar, 2003; Job Creation and Worker Assistance Act, ISBA 2002 December Tax School; Changes in Tax Law, ISBA YLD Summer Seminar, 2002; Business Formation, ISBA Annual Meeting, 2001; 2001 Tax Act Retirement Planning Issues, ISBA 2001 December Tax School; The IRD Estate: Retirement Plans, IRAs, Stock Options Etc., UILS Probate Seminar, 1999; The IRD Estate: Retirement Plans, IRAs, Stock Options Etc., Estate Planning Council 1999; Choice of Entity: Income Tax Aspects, ISBA 1999 December Tax School; Choice of Business Entity in Iowa, YLD Summer Seminar, 1999; Taxpayer Relief Act of 1997, YLD Summer Seminar, 1998; 1998 Federal Income Tax Changes, Woodbury County Bar Association Annual CLE Seminar, 1998; ROTH IRAs & Related Topics, Lawyers Chautauqua, 1998; ROTH IRAs & Related Topics, ISBA/ILS 1998 Spring Tax Institute; ROTH IRA Update, ISBA 1998 December Tax School; Estate Planning With Retirement Benefits, Estate Planning Council, 1997; New IRAs, ISBA 1997 December Tax School; Ethical Considerations Regarding Retirement From or Realignment of Law Practices, YLD Summer Seminar 1996; Limited Liability Partnerships, Woodbury County Bar Association/Morningside College Seminar 1996; Pension Plan Distributions and the Estate Plan, ISBA 1996 December Tax School; Ethical and Tactical Problems When Leaving a Law Firm, Including Conflicts of Interest, ISBA 1996 Annual Meeting; Estate Planning For Retirement Benefits and the Marital Deduction, ISBA/ILS 1996 Spring Tax Institute; Cafeteria Plans, ISBA 1994 December Tax School; ERISA Rules for Divorce Cases: QDRO'S & QMSCO'S, 14th Annual Morningside College CLE Seminar, 1994; Retirement Plan Distributions, ISBA/Iowa Law School, 1994 Spring Tax Institute; Retirement Planning for Professionals, ISBA, 1993 December Tax School; Tax Changes in Deficit Reduction Bill, ISBA, Fall Traveling Seminar 1993; Federal and State Legislative Update, Morningside College, 1990 CLE; What Types of Employer Benefit Plans are Available, ISBA, Fall Traveling Seminar 1990; Section 89, ISBA, 1989 Summer Seminar; New Developments in Pensions and Employee Benefits, ISBA, Fall

(This Listing Continued)

VRIEZELAAR, TIGGES, EDGINGTON, BOTTARO, BODEN & ROSS, L.L.P., Sioux City—Continued

Traveling Seminar 1988; ISBA 1987 Tax School, Blue Ribbon Panel; ISBA Traveling Seminar 1987; Blame It on Rostenkowski: 1986 Tax Act Changes in Retirement and Employee Benefit Plans, ISBA, 1986 December Tax School; Retirement Plans and Employee Benefits, ISBA, 1986 Traveling Seminar; Tax Litigation, Sioux City Tax Group, Sioux City Tax Group 1986; 1984 Deficit Reduction Tax Act of 1984, ISBA, 1984 Traveling Seminar; Tax Shelter Problems: Bogus, Abusive and Leaky; The Economic Recovery Tax Act of 1981, ISBA, 1981 Traveling Seminar; Voluntary Corporate Dissolutions, O'Brien County Lawyers Chautauqua 1981; Maximum and Minimum Tax Changes, ISBA, 1979 Tax School; Investment Credit and Livestock Confinement Facilities, ISBA, 1977 Tax School. *Member:* Woodbury County (Grievance Committee, 1985-2005), Iowa State (Member: Taxation Committee, 1979-1990; Taxation Section, 1990—, Section Council, 1996-1999, 2002-2005, Employee Benefits Subcommittee, 1991—, Chair, 1991-1992 and 1998-1999; Legal Forms Committee, 1997—; Law Practice Management Section, 1991—, Section Council, 1993-1996, 1999-2002), Nebraska State and American (Member, Sections on: Litigation; Tax Law) Bar Associations; The State Bar of South Dakota. (Managing Partner). ***PRACTICE AREAS:*** Tax; ERISA; Corporate; Estate Planning; Business Litigation. ***Email:*** kvriezelaar@siouxcitylawyers.net

DALE C. TIGGES, born Carroll, Iowa, March 11, 1953; admitted to bar, 1980, Iowa, U.S. District Court, Northern District of Iowa and U.S. Tax Court. *Education:* University of South Dakota (B.S., 1975); Drake University (J.D., with honors, 1980). Order of Coif. Listed, Best Lawyers in America (Corporate, Mergers and Acquisitions Law). Member: Trade Regulation Committee, 1986-1989; Corporation and Business Law Committee, 1989-1990; Business Law Section, 1990—; Council, 1997-1999; Limited Liability Co. Committee, 1992-1996; Partnership Committee, 1996-1999; Nonprofit Corporations Committee, 2003-2004; Business Law Manual Committee, 2003-2004; Environmental and Natural Resources Section, 1990—, Iowa State Bar Association. ***PRACTICE AREAS:*** Corporate Law; Business Law; Trusts and Estates; Probate. ***Email:*** dtigges@siouxcitylawyers.net

RAY H. EDGINGTON, born Sioux City, Iowa, May 30, 1955; admitted to bar, 1981, Iowa and U.S. District Court, Northern District of Iowa; 1982, U.S. Tax Court; 1983, Nebraska. *Education:* Morningside College (B.A., 1977); University of Iowa (J.D., with high distinction, 1981). Member, Moot Court Board. Listed, Best Lawyers in America (Trusts and Estates). Chairman, Insurance Committee, 1989-1990; Member: Probate, Property and Trust Law Committee, 1988-1990, Probate and Trust Law Section, 1990—, Council, 1992; Taxation Section, 1993—, Estate Planning and Gift Tax Committee, 1995-1999, Iowa State Bar Association. Member, Iowa Supreme Court Commission on Unauthorized Practice of Law, 1990-1999. *Member:* Nebraska State Bar Association; Siouxland Estate Planning Council (President, 1997-1998). ***PRACTICE AREAS:*** Trusts and Estates; Probate; Real Estate; Taxation; Business Law. ***Email:*** redgington@siouxcitylawyers.net

TIMOTHY S. BOTTARO, born Buffalo, New York, September 20, 1958; admitted to bar, 1983, Iowa and U.S. District Court, Northern District of Iowa; 1984, U.S. Court of Appeals, Eighth Circuit. *Education:* Creighton University (B.A., 1981); University of Iowa (J.D., with distinction, 1983). Recipient, 1st Annual Iowa State Bar Association Community Service Award, 2000. First Vice-Chair, Moot Court Board. Chairman, Woodbury County Judicial Magistrate Appointing Commission, 1986-1991. Member, General Practice Law Section, Iowa State Bar Association. *Member:* Iowa Trial Lawyers Association; The Association of Trial Lawyers of America. ***PRACTICE AREAS:*** Personal Injury; Litigation; Insurance Litigation. ***Email:*** tbottaro@siouxcitylawyers.net

SUZAN E. BODEN, born Sac City, Iowa, January 12, 1955; admitted to bar, 1987, Iowa and U.S. District Court, Northern District of Iowa; 1988, South Dakota and U.S. District Court, District of South Dakota; 1994, U.S. Court of Appeals, Eighth Circuit. *Education:* University of Northern Iowa; Iowa State University (B.S., 1977); University of South Dakota (J.D., 1987). Phi Alpha Delta. Member: University of South Dakota Law Review, 1986; Client Counseling Board, 1985-1987. Client Counseling Team Winner, 1986. Medical Technologist, A.S.C.P., 1978-1986. Transportation Commissioner, State of Iowa, 2000-2008. *Member:* The Iowa State Bar Association; State Bar of South Dakota. ***PRACTICE AREAS:*** Workers Compensation; Litigation; Adoption. ***Email:*** sboden@siouxcitylawyers.net

RYAN C. ROSS, born Aurora, Nebraska, May 19, 1970; admitted to bar, 1995, South Dakota and U.S. District Court, District of South Dakota; 1996, Iowa; 1998, Nebraska; 1999, U.S. District Court, Northern District of Iowa. *Education:* Doane College (B.A., magna cum laude, 1992); Willamette University (J.D., 1995). Member, Moot Court Board, 1993-1995. Member: Sections on: Real Estate, 1999—, Probate, Property and Trust Law, 2001; YLD Elder Services Committee, 1999—. *Member:* The Iowa State Bar Association; The State Bar of South Dakota (Member, Gaming Law Committee, 1996-2004); Nebraska State Bar Association (Member, Real Estate, Probate and Trust Law Section, 2002—). ***PRACTICE AREAS:*** Real Estate; Business Law; Trusts and Estates; Probate; Collections. ***Email:*** rross@siouxcitylawyers.net

All Attorneys are members of the Woodbury County and Iowa State Bar Associations.

REPRESENTATIVE CLIENTS: Gateway, Inc.; Wells Fargo Bank Iowa, N.A.; Wells Fargo Bank South Dakota, N.A.; Milwaukee Insurance; Westfield Insurance; Progressive Insurance; CNA Excess and Select Insurance; Central Mutual Insurance; Essex Insurance; Cloverleaf Cold Storage Co.; Sioux City Foundry Co.; IBP, Inc.; Canal Capital Corporation-Sioux City Stockyards; Sioux-Preme Packing Co.; Wells Dairy & Blue Bunny Ice Cream Co.; West Iowa Telephone Co.; Hooper Telephone Co.; Argosy Gaming Corp.; Jetsun Aviation Centre; Diesel Specialities; Penncorp Financial; Russell's Ready Mix; Interstate Sanitation Co.; Weinrich Truck Line; Bekins Distribution Center; Catholic School Foundation of Diocese of Sioux City; City of Salix; Terminal Grain Corp./Big Soo Terminal; Louis-Dreyfus Holding Company, Inc.; AC & R, Inc.; Interstate Mechanical Corp.; Brown Commercial Construction Company; Executive Design, Inc.; MidlandsNet, Inc.; Mercedes-Benz Credit Corp.; Chrysler Financial Company; Woodbury County Deputy Sheriffs Association; Sioux City Conference Board; Case New Holland Credit, Inc.; Daimler Chrysler Services, N.A.; Firstclass Credit Union; Siouxland Economic Development Corporation.

CORNWALL, AVERY, BJORNSTAD & SCOTT

407 GRAND AVENUE
P.O. BOX 999
SPENCER, IOWA 51301
Telephone: 712-262-1630
Fax: 712-262-1211
URL: http://www.cabslaw.com

General Practice in all Courts. Corporation, Banking, Taxation, Probate and Insurance Law. Trials and Appeals.

MEMBERS OF FIRM

TOM W. CORNWALL, born Spencer, Iowa, February 13, 1927; admitted to bar, 1953, Iowa. *Education:* Dartmouth College (B.A., 1950); University of Iowa (J.D., 1953). Phi Delta Phi. *Member:* Clay County and Iowa State Bar Associations. ***PRACTICE AREAS:*** Estate Planning Law; Probate Law; Real Estate Law.

STEPHEN F. AVERY, born Spencer, Iowa, January 14, 1942; admitted to bar, 1966, Iowa; 1972, Florida. *Education:* University of Iowa (B.A., 1963; J.D., 1966). Phi Delta Phi. Clay County Attorney, 1971-1972. *Member:* Clay County, Iowa State (President, Young Lawyers Section, 1974-1975) and American (Member, Executive Council, Young Lawyers Section, 1974-1975) Bar Associations; Iowa Academy of Trial Lawyers. ***PRACTICE AREAS:*** Litigation. ***Email:*** steve@cabslaw.com

CHRISTOPHER A. BJORNSTAD, born Spencer, Iowa, February 6, 1948; admitted to bar, 1974, Iowa. *Education:* University of Iowa (B.A., with highest distinction, 1970; J.D., with distinction, 1974). Phi Beta Kappa; Omicron Delta Kappa. *Member:* Clay County, Iowa State and American Bar Associations. Fellow, American College of Trust and Estate Counsel; Iowa State Board of Tax Review. ***PRACTICE AREAS:*** Real Estate Law; Probate Law; Banking Law; Taxation Law; Corporation Law. ***Email:*** chris@cabslaw.com

DAVID A. SCOTT, born Mitchell, South Dakota, July 24, 1947; admitted to bar, 1972, Iowa. *Education:* University of South Dakota (B.A., 1969); University of Iowa (J.D., 1972). Omicron Delta Kappa; Pi Sigma Alpha; Phi Delta Phi. Law Clerk, Judge Edward McManus, United States District Court for the Northern District of Iowa, 1972. *Member:* Clay County, Iowa State (Member, Committee on Insurance, 1978-1982) and American Bar Associations; Association of Trial Lawyers of Iowa; Iowa Defense Counsel Association; The Iowa Association of Workers' Compensation Lawyers, Inc. ***PRACTICE AREAS:*** Litigation; Workers Compensation Law. ***Email:*** david@cabslaw.com

ATTORNEYS FOR: State Bank, Spencer, Iowa; Farmers Trust & Savings Bank, Spencer; Spencer Municipal Hospital; Northwest Federal Savings Bank; Spencer Community School District.

REPRESENTATIVE CLIENTS: Atlanta Casualty; Continental Casualty Co.; EMC Companies; General Casualty Insurance Company; Iowa Mutual Insurance Co.; IMT Insurance Company; Minnesota Mutual Fire and Casualty; St. Paul Companies; Travelers Ins. Co.; Home Insurance Co.

ZENOR, HOUCHINS & BORTH

Established in 1975
2000 HIGHWAY BOULEVARD
P.O. BOX 317
SPENCER, IOWA 51301
Telephone: 712-262-1187
Fax: 712-262-1189
Email: zenorlaw@ncn.net

General Trial and Appellate Practice including Personal Injury, Insurance, Labor, Tort, Probate, Corporate and Commercial Law.

FIRM PROFILE: Established in 1975, this 3-member firm provides a full range of services, including representation of plaintiffs and insurance companies, employment law, probate, real estate and commercial law.

MEMBERS OF FIRM

MICHAEL L. ZENOR, born Spencer, Iowa, April 20, 1949; admitted to bar, 1975, Iowa and U.S. District Court, Northern District of Iowa; U.S. District Court, Southern District of Iowa. *Education:* University of Iowa (B.A., 1971); University of Colorado; Drake University (J.D., 1975). County Attorney, Clay County, 1978-2005. *Member:* Iowa State and American Bar Associations; Iowa Trial Lawyers Association (Member, Board of Governors, 1992-1998). ***REPORTED CASES:*** Utica Mutual Insurance Co. v. Stockdale Agency, 50 F. Supp.2d 871; Christenson v. Ramaeker, 366 N.W.2d 905. ***PRACTICE AREAS:*** Personal Injury; Labor; Tort; Insurance; Probate; Corporate; Commercial Law. ***Email:*** zenorlaw@ncn.net

MICHAEL JAMES HOUCHINS, born Iowa City, Iowa, December 9, 1959; admitted to bar, 1987, Iowa. *Education:* University of Northern Iowa (B.A., 1984); Drake University (J.D., 1987). Assistant County Attorney, 1987-2005 and County Attorney, 2005—, Clay County. *Member:* Clay County, Iowa State and American Bar Associations; Iowa Trial Lawyers Association; American Trial Lawyers Association. ***REPORTED CASES:*** In re: Estate of Rutter, 633 N.W.2d 740. ***PRACTICE AREAS:*** Personal Injury; Labor; Tort; Probate; Corporate; Commercial Law. ***Email:*** mhouch@ncn.net

CHARLES K. BORTH, born Sleepy Eye, Minnesota, December 4, 1969; admitted to bar, 1995, Iowa. *Education:* Mankato State University (B.A., 1992); Drake University (J.D., with honors, 1995). Member, Drake Law Review, 1994-1995. Assistant County Attorney, Clay County, 1997—. *Member:* Iowa State Bar Association. ***PRACTICE AREAS:*** Criminal; Taxation; Family Law; Corporate; Business Planning. ***Email:*** cborth@ncn.net

REFERENCE: Farmers Trust & Savings Bank, Spencer, Iowa.

JAMES A. CLARITY, III

Established in 1976
1601 KEOKUK
P.O. BOX 469
SPIRIT LAKE, IOWA 51360
Telephone: 712-336-4611
Facsimile: 712-336-5072
Email: jaciii@rconnect.com
Email: jclarity@rconnect.com
URL: http://www.lawyers.com/jamesclarity

Civil Litigation and Criminal Defense in State and Federal Courts.

JAMES A. CLARITY, III, born Albert Lea, Minnesota, June 21, 1950; admitted to bar, 1976, Iowa and U.S. District Court, Northern and Southern Districts of Iowa; 1979, U.S. Court of Appeals, Eighth Circuit; 1980, U.S. Supreme Court; 1990, U.S. Claims Court. *Education:* Iowa State University (B.S., 1972); Creighton University (J.D., 1976). *Member:* Dickinson County, Iowa State (Member, Committee on Litigation Legislation, 1986-1990; Judicial Nominating Commissioner, Judicial District 3A, 1987-1992; Federal Practice Committee, 1992—) and American Bar Associations; The Federal Bar Association; Association of Trial Lawyers of Iowa (Member, Board of Governors, 1989-1992); The Association of Trial Lawyers of America (Member, Vaccine Litigation Group); National Board of Trial Advocacy (Diplomate); American Board of Trial Advocates (Associate). Fellow: Iowa Academy of Trial Lawyers. Certified as a Civil Trial Advocate by the National Board of Trial Advocacy. ***PRACTICE AREAS:*** Personal Injury; Products Liability; Professional Malpractice; Worker's Compensation; Criminal Defense.

REPRESENTATIVE CLIENTS: Cargill, Inc.; Armour Foods, Inc.; CONAGRA, Inc.; Home Insurance Company; Alexsis; Jaycox Implement, Inc.; Farmer Exchange Cooperatives; Iowa Great Lakes General Motors and Toyota; Iowa Community Assurance Pool; Pamida, Inc.
REFERENCES: Available Upon Request.

PHIL C. REDENBAUGH, P.C.

Established in 1975
111 WEST 6TH STREET
P.O. BOX 1284
STORM LAKE, IOWA 50588
Telephone: 712-732-1873
Fax: 712-732-4274

General Civil and Trial Practice. Personal Injury, Workers' Compensation and Real Estate, Insurance, Bad Faith.

PHIL C. REDENBAUGH, born Storm Lake, Iowa, October 19, 1941; admitted to bar, 1970, Iowa and U.S. District Court, Northern and Southern Districts of Iowa. *Education:* Buena Vista College (B.A., 1963); Drake University (J.D., 1970). Delta Theta Phi. Author, "Liability Considerations Concerning Insurance Agents & Brokers," Drake Insurance Law Annual, Drake Law Review. County Attorney, Buena Vista County, 1975-1978. *Member:* Buena Vista County (President, 1976) and Iowa State Bar Associations; Association of Trial Lawyers of Iowa (Member, Board of Governors, 1974-1980); The Association of Trial Lawyers of America; Iowa Defense Counsel; Iowa Academy of Trial Lawyers (Member, Board of Governors, 1998—; President, 2004); American College of Trial Lawyers. ***PRACTICE AREAS:*** General Practice; Personal Injury; Trial Practice. ***Email:*** redenlaw@iw.net

REPRESENTATIVE CLIENTS: Employers Mutual Casualty Co.; Rasmussen Ford Inc.; Farmers Casualty Mutual; IMT Insurance Co.; Hartford Insurance Co.; Great West Casualty Co.
REFERENCE: Citizens First National Bank.

ROTH LAW OFFICE

608 SENECA STREET
P.O. BOX 1126
STORM LAKE, IOWA 50588
Telephone: 712-732-4373
Fax: 712-732-4712
Email: rothlaw@iw.net
URL: http://www.lawyers.com/rothlaw

General Practice, Personal Injury, Social Security Disability, Trusts and Estates, Business Law, Wills, Probate.

STEVEN T. ROTH, born Storm Lake, Iowa, June 7, 1947; admitted to bar, 1972, Iowa; 1973, U.S. District Court, Northern District of Iowa; 1981, U.S. District Court, Southern District of Iowa. *Education:* University of South Dakota (B.S., 1969); Drake University (J.D., 1972). Order of the Coif. Member, District 3A Judicial Nominating Commission, 1994. *Member:* Buena Vista County and Iowa State (Member, Board of Governors, 1991—) Bar Associations; Association of Trial Lawyers of Iowa. [1st Lt., USAR, 1969-1978]. ***PRACTICE AREAS:*** General Practice; Personal Injury; Social Security Disability; Trusts and Estates; Business Law; Wills; Probate.

REFERENCES: Citizens First National Bank; Security Trust and Savings Bank.

FERNANDEZ LAW FIRM

2759 86TH STREET, SUITE 102
URBANDALE, IOWA 50322
Telephone: 515-254-1881
Fax: 515-254-1881
URL: http://www.fernandezlawiowa.com
Mailing Address: *P.O. Box 65344, West Des Moines, IA 50265*

Family Law, Bankruptcy, Personal Injury, Divorce, General Practice.

(This Listing Continued)

JOSEPH W. FERNANDEZ, born Middletown, New York; admitted to bar, 1994, Iowa; 1995, U.S. District Court, Southern and Northern Districts of Iowa. *Education:* Potsdam College of Arts and Sciences (B.A., 1985); University of Iowa College of Law (J.D., 1992). Sigma Tau Delta. Member: Chicano Hispanic Association for Legal Education, 1989-1992; Pace University Environmental Law National Moot Court Competitor. Law Clerk, Hon. Senior Judge Donald E. O'Brien, United States District Court for the Northern District of Iowa, 1993-1995. Previous Employment: Walker Law Firm P.C. (Representing the Iowa Attorney General in health care benefit reimbursement litigation against the Tobacco Industry). *Member:* Polk County and Iowa State (Co-Chairman and Member, Young Lawyers Division; Member: Women and Minorities Committee, 1996-2004; Co-Chairman, 1998-1999; State Fair Committee, 2004; Annual Meeting, 1998-2003; Litigation Section, 1996-2002) Bar Associations; Iowa Trial Lawyers Association; The Association of Trial Lawyers of America; American Inns of Court (Barrister, Blackstone Inns of Court, 1997—); Hispanic National Bar Association; National Employment Lawyers Association; Iowa National Elder Law Association. ***PRACTICE AREAS:*** Family Law; Bankruptcy; Personal Injury; Divorce; General Practice. ***Email:*** joe.fernandez@fernandezlawiowa.com

---

HOWE, CUNNINGHAM & LOWE, P.L.C.

2824 104TH STREET
URBANDALE, IOWA 50322
Telephone: 515-278-4200
Fax: 515-278-4655

General Practice including Trial and Appellate Practice in State and Federal Courts. Corporate, Transportation, Administrative, Insurance, Family, Divorce, Personal Injury, Estate Planning, Wills, Probate, Real Estate, and Creditor Law.

RICHARD D. HOWE, born Des Moines, Iowa, 1947; admitted to bar, 1973, Iowa; 1988, Nebraska. *Education:* Drake University (B.S., 1969; J.D., 1972). Executive Director, Iowa Reciprocity Board, 1972-1975. Commissioner, 1975-1976 and Board Chairman, 1977, Transportation Regulation Board, Iowa Department of Transportation. Vice-Chairman, Motor and Air Carrier Committee, National Association of Regulatory Utility Commissioners, 1977. Member, Governor's Task Force on Transportation, 1982. *Member:* Iowa State Bar Association. ***Email:*** howe@howelaw.net

MICHAEL J. CUNNINGHAM, born La Crosse, Wisconsin, 1951; admitted to bar, 1976, Iowa, Nebraska, U.S. District Court, Southern District of Iowa and U.S. District Court, District of Nebraska; 1978, U.S. District Court, Northern District of Iowa; 1988, U.S. Court of Appeals, Eighth Circuit. *Education:* Creighton University (B.A., 1973; J.D., 1976). *Member:* Polk County, Iowa State and Nebraska State Bar Associations. ***Email:*** cunningham@howelaw.net

CHIP LOWE, born Sioux City, Iowa, December 30, 1953; admitted to bar, 1979, South Dakota and North Dakota; 1983, Nebraska; 1988, Iowa. *Education:* University of Nebraska (B.A., 1976); University of South Dakota (J.D., 1979); University of Virginia (LL.M., 1987). Phi Beta Kappa. Editor-in-Chief, South Dakota Law Review, 1978-1979. Assistant Professor of Clinical Law, University of Nebraska Law School, 1983-1987. Visiting Associate Professor of Law, University of Arkansas-Little Rock Law School, 1987-1988. Author: "Alien Ownership of South Dakota Farmland— A Menace to the Family Farm?" 23 South Dakota Law Review 735, 1978; "Modern Sentencing Reform: A Preliminary Analysis of the Proposed Federal Sentencing Guidelines," 25 American Criminal Law Review 1, 1988. *Member:* Iowa State Bar Association. ***Email:*** lowe@howelaw.net

JEFFREY A. KELSO, born Wichita Falls, Texas, January 10, 1972; admitted to bar, 1997, Iowa; 2000, U.S. District Court, Northern and Southern Districts of Iowa. *Education:* Central College (B.A., 1994); Drake University Law School (J.D., 1997). Co-Author: "When Does the Clock Start Ticking? A Primer on Statutory and Contractual Time Limitation Issues in Uninsured and Underinsured Motorist Claim," 47 Drake Law Rev. 4 1999, republished 49 Defense Law Journal 3 (2000). *Member:* Iowa Trial Lawyers Association. ***Email:*** kelso@howelaw.net

REPRESENTATIVE CLIENTS: Iowa Motor Truck Association; Don Hummer Trucking Corp.; Mid Seven Transportation Co.; United Warehousing Corp.; National Interstate Truckers Assn.; Priority Express, Inc.; Wells Fargo Bank, N.A.; U.S. Bank; Beal Bank; GreenPoint Credit, L.L.C.; Vision Point Productions, Inc.; O'Callaghams, Inc.
REFERENCE: Wells Fargo Bank - Iowa.

WHITE & JOHNSON, P.C.

VINTON, IOWA

(See Cedar Rapids)

General Practice. Trials, Personal Injury, Insurance, Workers' Compensation, Tax, Corporate, Real Estate, Probate, Domestic Relations.

DAY MEEKER LAMPING & SCHLEGEL

112 SOUTH AVENUE B
P.O. BOX 929
WASHINGTON, IOWA 52353-0929
Telephone: 319-653-2147
Fax: 319-653-5181

General Practice. Insurance, Probate, Corporation and Tax Law. Trials and Appeals. No Small Collections.

MEMBERS OF FIRM

SCHUYLER W. LIVINGSTON (1872-1959)
LOUIS J. KEHOE (1896-1969)
ROBERT DAY (Retired)

(This Listing Continued)

DAY MEEKER LAMPING & SCHLEGEL, Washington—Continued

EVERETT MEEKER, born Gait, Iowa, April 13, 1925; admitted to bar, 1953, Iowa. *Education:* University of Iowa (B.S.C., 1950; J.D., 1953). Order of the Coif; Beta Gamma Sigma. *Member:* Washington County, Iowa State and American Bar Associations.

LESLIE D. LAMPING, born Mason City, Iowa, May 4, 1953; admitted to bar, 1981, Illinois; 1983, U.S. Tax Court; 1984, Iowa. *Education:* University of Illinois (B.A., 1974); John Marshall Law School (J.D., cum laude, 1981). *Member:* Washington County and Iowa State Bar Associations.

ROBERT G. SCHLEGEL, born Ottumwa, Iowa, October 24, 1953; admitted to bar, 1988, Iowa. *Education:* University of Iowa (B.F.A., 1981); McGeorge School of Law, University of the Pacific (J.D., 1988). Author: "Significant Developments in International Antitrust," Comparative Law Yearbook, Vol. 10, 1986. *Member:* Washington County, Iowa State and American Bar Associations.

ASSOCIATE

PATRICIA J. LIPSKI, born Independence, Iowa, October 28, 1975; admitted to bar, 2001, Iowa. *Education:* Loras College (B.A., 1998); University of Iowa (J.D., 2001). Delta Epsilon Sigma; Sigma Tau Delta; Phi Alpha Theta; Phi Delta Phi. *Member:* Washington County, Iowa State and American Bar Associations.

REFERENCE: Washington State Bank.

BALL, KIRK & HOLM, P.C.

3324 KIMBALL AVENUE
P.O. BOX 2696
WATERLOO, IOWA 50704
Telephone: 319-234-2638
Fax: 319-234-2237
Email: bkh@ballkirkholm.com
URL: http://www.ballkirkholm.com

General Civil Trial Practice in all courts. Personal Injury, Product Liability, Professional Negligence, Medical Malpractice, Corporate Law, Workers Compensation, Probate and Estate Planning, Real Estate and Tax Law, Family Law and General Practice.

WILLIAM C. BALL (Retired)

MAX E. KIRK, born Eldora, Iowa, December 5, 1947; admitted to bar, 1975, Iowa, U.S. District Court, Northern and Southern Districts of Iowa and U.S. Court of Appeals, Eighth Circuit. *Education:* Upper Iowa University (B.A., magna cum laude, 1970); University of Iowa (J.D., with distinction, 1975). Adjunct Professor, Business Law and Labor Relations, Upper Iowa University. *Member:* Black Hawk County, First Judicial District (President, 1995-1996; Member, Judicial Nominating Commission, 1988-1992) and Iowa State (Member, Board of Governors, 1995-2000) Bar Associations; The Association of Trial Lawyers of America; Iowa Trial Lawyers Association; American Board of Trial Advocates (Advocate); American College of Trial Lawyers. Fellow: Iowa Academy of Trial Lawyers. ***PRACTICE AREAS:*** Personal Injury; Professional Negligence. ***Email:*** bkh@ballkirkholm.com

H. DANIEL HOLM, JR., born Grundy Center, Iowa, April 7, 1955; admitted to bar, 1979, Iowa, U.S. District Court, Northern and Southern Districts of Iowa. *Education:* University of Northern Iowa (B.A., 1976); Drake University (J.D., 1979). Order of the Coif. Associate Case Notes Editor, Drake Law Review, 1978-1979. *Member:* Black Hawk County, Iowa State and American Bar Associations; Iowa Trial Lawyers Association (Governor at Large, 1986-1989; Parliamentarian, 1989-1990; Secretary, 1990; Vice-President for Legislation, 1991-1993; President Elect, 1993; President, 1994-1995; Member of the Year, 1987); The Association of Trial Lawyers of America; American Board of Trial Advocates (Associate). Fellow, Iowa Academy of Trial Lawyers. ***PRACTICE AREAS:*** Personal Injury; Professional Negligence. ***Email:*** bkh@ballkirkholm.com

DAVID W. STAMP, born Roseville, California, September 14, 1961; admitted to bar, 1986, Iowa; 1987, U.S. District Court, Northern and Southern Districts of Iowa. *Education:* University of Northern Iowa (B.A., with highest honors, 1983); University of Iowa (J.D., with distinction, 1986). Associate Editor, Journal of Corporation Law, 1985-1986; Trial Advocacy Board, 1985-1986. Adjunct Professor, Upper Iowa University, 1987-1992. *Member:* Black Hawk County, Iowa State (Member, Worker's Compensation Section; District Rep., Young Lawyers Division, 1994-1996) and American (Member, Section of Litigation) Bar Associations; Iowa Trial Lawyers Association (Governor at Large, 1997-2000; Workers' Compensation Core Group, 1997—); The Association of Trial Lawyers of America (Member, Breast Implant Litigation Group, 1997—); Workplace Injury Litigation Group, 1997—. ***PRACTICE AREAS:*** Personal Injury; Workers Compensation; Professional Negligence. ***Email:*** dstamp@ballkirkholm.com

MICHAEL W. BUCKNER, born Cedar Rapids, Iowa, January 15, 1946; admitted to bar, 1971, Iowa and U.S. District Court, Northern District of Iowa; 1985, U.S. Tax Court. *Education:* Bradley University (B.S., 1968); University of Iowa (J.D., 1971). Phi Alpha Delta. Assistant County Attorney, Black Hawk County, Iowa, 1973-1991. *Member:* Black Hawk County and Iowa State Bar Associations. ***PRACTICE AREAS:*** Estate Planning; Probate; Income Tax; Real Estate; Family Law; Personal Injury. ***Email:*** mbuckner@ballkirkholm.com

---

OBIE SADDLER, JR., born Port Huron, Michigan, March 30, 1970; admitted to bar, 1996, Iowa and U.S. District Court, Northern District of Iowa. *Education:* University of Iowa (B.S., 1993); University of Nebraska-Lincoln (J.D., 1996). Delta Theta Phi. *Member:* Black Hawk County (Secretary, 1998-2000) and Iowa State (District Representative, Young Lawyers Division, 1998-2000) Bar Associations; Iowa Trial Lawyers Association. ***PRACTICE AREAS:*** Personal Injury; Workers Compensation; Family Law. ***Email:*** osaddler@ballkirkholm.com

JEN BRIES, born Dubuque, Iowa, February 2, 1975; admitted to bar, 2000, Iowa, U.S. District Court, Northern and Southern Districts of Iowa. *Education:* University of Northern Iowa (B.A., 1997); Creighton University Law School (J.D., 2000). Phi Alph Delta (Marshall, 1998-1999, Justice, 1999-2000). Moot Court Board (Parliamentarian, 1999-2000). *Member:* Black Hawk County (Secretary, 2003-2004) and Iowa State Bar Associations (Young Lawyers Division, District Representative, 2004-2005, Secretary, 2004-2005); Association of Trial Lawyers of America; Iowa Trial Lawyers Association. ***PRACTICE AREAS:*** Professional Negligence; Family Law; Personal Injury. ***Email:*** jbries@ballkirkholm.com

A list of representative clients will be furnished on request.
REFERENCES: US Bank; Regions Bank, N.A. (Formerly Union Planters Bank, N.A.).

BEECHER, FIELD, WALKER, MORRIS, HOFFMAN & JOHNSON, P.C.

Established in 1918
SUITE 300 COURT SQUARE BUILDING
620 LAFAYETTE STREET
P.O. BOX 178
WATERLOO, IOWA 50704
Telephone: 319-234-1766
Telecopier: 319-234-1225
URL: http://www.beecherlaw.com

General Practice. Taxation, Real Estate, Probate, Estate Planning, Trust and Corporation Law, Bankruptcy, Personal Injury, Family Law, Banking, Environmental, Workers Compensation, Health Care, Employment Law, Social Security, Business Litigation, Consumer and Commercial Collections.

FIRM PROFILE: The firm was founded in 1918 by W. L. Beecher. The firm began its practice as a local, general and trial practice. The firm now provides services to Northeast Iowa and offers a wide range of legal services.

W. L. BEECHER (1891-1976)

JOHN W. RATHERT (Retired)

W. LOUIS BEECHER, born Dougherty, Iowa, September 17, 1921; admitted to bar, 1947, Iowa; 1956, U.S. Supreme Court. *Education:* University of Iowa (B.A., 1942; J.D., with Distinction, 1947). Phi Alpha Delta. *Member:* Black Hawk County (President, 1967-1968), Iowa State and American Bar Associations. ***PRACTICE AREAS:*** Corporate; Business; Probate; Real Estate; Estate Planning.

HUGH M. FIELD, born Milwaukee, Wisconsin, July 24, 1944; admitted to bar, 1969, Iowa. *Education:* Northwestern University (B.S., 1966); University of Iowa (J.D., 1969). Phi Delta Phi. Member, President's Council on Rural America, 1989-1992. Author: *Iowa Legal Forms-Corporation,* Butterworth Legal Publishers, 1982. City Attorney, City of Waterloo, 1986-1991. *Member:* Black Hawk County, Iowa State and American (Member, Health Law Section; Chair, 1995-1996) Bar Associations. ***PRACTICE AREAS:*** Corporate; Taxation; Health Care; Estate Planning; Business; Social Security. ***Email:*** hughfield@beecherlaw.com

JOHN R. WALKER, JR., born Iowa City, Iowa, March 14, 1948; admitted to bar, 1973, Iowa, U.S. District Court, Northern and Southern Districts of Iowa and U.S. Court of Appeals, Eighth Circuit. *Education:* St. Thomas College (B.A., 1970); Drake University (J.D., 1973). Editor, Gavel, 1972-1973. Assistant County Attorney, 1973-1975. *Member:* Black Hawk County and Iowa State Bar Associations. ***PRACTICE AREAS:*** Family Law; Personal Injury Litigation; Business Litigation; Worker's Compensation; Employment Law; ERISA Litigation. ***Email:*** jwalker@beecherlaw.com

RICHARD R. MORRIS, born Waterloo, Iowa, July 2, 1952; admitted to bar, 1977, Iowa. *Education:* University of Iowa (B.B.A., 1974; M.B.A., 1977; J.D., with distinction, 1977). Omicron Delta Kappa. *Member:* Black Hawk County, Iowa State and American Bar Associations. ***PRACTICE AREAS:*** Corporate; Real Estate; Bankruptcy; Probate; Wills; Estate Planning. ***Email:*** rmorris@beecherlaw.com

THERESA E. HOFFMAN, born Maquoketa, Iowa, November 11, 1958; admitted to bar, 1985, Iowa. *Education:* Loras College (B.A., 1981); University of Iowa (J.D., 1985). *Member:* Black Hawk County and Iowa State (Member, Probate Section) Bar Associations. ***PRACTICE AREAS:*** Probate; Business; Estate Planning; Trust Law; Wills; Corporate Law. ***Email:*** theresah@beecherlaw.com

ERIC W. JOHNSON, born Sioux City, Iowa, May 29, 1965; admitted to bar, 1991, Iowa. *Education:* University of Iowa (B.A., with distinction, 1988; M.B.A., 1991; J.D., with high distinction, 1991). Phi Beta Kappa, Mortar Board. Managing Editor, Iowa Law Review, 1991. *Member:* Black Hawk County, Iowa State and American Bar Associations. ***PRACTICE AREAS:*** Real Estate; Business; Debtor and Creditor; Bankruptcy; Commercial Collections; Wills; Estate Planning; Probate. ***Email:*** ewj@beecherlaw.com

KEVIN D. AHRENHOLZ, born West Point, New York, March 22, 1968; admitted to bar, 1993, Wisconsin; 1994, Iowa and U.S. District Court, Northern District of Iowa; 1995, U.S. Tax Court. *Education:* Wheaton College (B.A., 1990); Marquette University (J.D., 1993). Law Clerk to the Hon. J.L. Larson, Supreme Court of Iowa, 1993-1994. *Member:* Iowa State Bar Association; State Bar of Wisconsin; American Collectors Association (MAP Member; State Chair and PAC Chair); American Bankruptcy Institute. ***PRACTICE AREAS:*** Collections; Creditors Rights; Bankruptcy; Consumer Law; Commercial Law; Fiduciary Litigation. ***Email:*** ahrenholz@beecherlaw.com

---

D. RAYMOND WALTON, born Cedar Falls, Iowa, April 7, 1955; admitted to bar, 1982, Iowa; 2000, U.S. District Court, Northern District of Iowa. *Education:* University of Northern Iowa (B.A., 1977); University of Iowa (J.D., with distinction, 1982). *Member:* Black Hawk County and Iowa State Bar Associations. ***PRACTICE AREAS:*** Civil Litigation; Family Law; Probate; Estate Planning. ***Email:*** rwalton@beecherlaw.com

JOHN J. WOOD, born Cedar Falls, Iowa, June 1, 1968; admitted to bar, 1999, Iowa; 2000, U.S. District Court, Northern and Southern Districts of Iowa and U.S. Court of Ap-

(This Listing Continued)

peals, Eighth Circuit. *Education:* Iowa State University (B.B.A., 1990); Drake Law School (J.D., 1998). *Member:* Black Hawk County and Iowa State Bar Associations; Iowa Trial Lawyers Association; Association of Trial Lawyers of America. ***PRACTICE AREAS:*** Business Litigation; Employment Law; Family Law; Personal Injury. ***Email:*** johnjwood@beecherlaw.com

ADNAN MAHMUTAGIC, born Tuzla, Bosnia, Herzegovina, December 22, 1976; admitted to bar, 2003, Iowa. *Education:* Mount Mercy College (B.B.A., Accounting, 2000); Drake University Law School (J.D., 2002). *Member:* Iowa State Bar Association. ***LANGUAGES:*** Bosnian. ***PRACTICE AREAS:*** Workers Compensation; Personal Injury; Business Litigation. ***Email:*** adnan@beecherlaw.com

HEATHER A. PRENDERGAST, born New Bedford, Massachusetts, June 21, 1970; admitted to bar, 1995, Illinois; 1998, Missouri and U.S. District Court, Western District of Missouri; 1999, Kansas and U.S. District Court, District of Kansas; 2000, Iowa; U.S. Court of Appeals, Eighth Circuit. *Education:* University of Illinois (B.A., 1992); Western New England College (J.D., 1995). *Member:* Black Hawk County and Iowa State Bar Associations. ***PRACTICE AREAS:*** Real Estate; Wills; Probate; Litigation. ***Email:*** hprendergast@beecherlaw.com

ELIZABETH LEYTZE LOUNSBERRY, born Cedar Rapids, Iowa, February 7, 1968; admitted to bar, 1993, Iowa. *Education:* University of Iowa; Northwestern University (B.A., with honors, 1990); University of Iowa (J.D., 1993). *Member:* Black Hawk County and Iowa State Bar Associations. ***LANGUAGES:*** French.

GENERAL COUNSEL FOR: Alum-Line, Inc.; Bill Colwell Investment, Inc.; Crossroads Center, Inc.; Palace Clothiers, Inc.; Waterloo Mills Co.; Rydell Chevrolet, Inc.; Community Buick GMC; Community Motors Co., Inc.; B. Schultz Co.; Fahr Beverage, Inc.; Ron Weber and Associates of Iowa, Inc.; Kirk Gross Company; Windor, Inc.; Peoples Community Health Clinic, Inc.; Advanced Systems, Inc.; Bertch Cabinet Mfg.; Swicter Aircraft; The CBE Group, Inc.; Aerial Service, Inc.; Bloom Manufacturing; Basic Materials Corp.; Shawver Well; Mike Molstead Motors, Inc.; Next Generation Wireless; U.S. Bank.
REPRESENTATIVE CLIENTS: School Bus Sales Co.; Firstar Bank, National Association; Kies Electric Supply; Bearing Service Co.; The Equitable Life Assurance Society of the United States; Inc.; Warren Transport, Inc.; United Security Savings Bank; Farmers State Bank, Jesup; Peterson Contractors, Inc., Reinbeck; Mercy Hospital of Franciscan Sisters Oelwein; Baird Industries; Union Planters Bank, N.A.; Legacy Mortgage; Wayne Claassen Engineering and Surveying, Inc.; Covenant Medical Center Inc.; Jim Lind Standard.

CLARK, BUTLER, WALSH & HAMANN

Established in 1928

315 EAST 5TH STREET
P.O. BOX 596
WATERLOO, IOWA 50704
Telephone: 319-234-5701
Fax: 319-232-9579
Email: WLOOLAW@ATTGLOBAL.NET
URL: http://www.cbwh-law.com

General Practice. Trials and Appeals. Probate, Trust, Corporation, Real Estate, Banking, Surety, Dramshop, Subrogation and Insurance Law, Personal Injury, Workers Compensation.

MEMBERS OF FIRM

FRED G. CLARK (1894-1976)

FRED G. CLARK, JR. (1922-1984)

WALLACE W. BUTLER, born Sibley, Iowa, April 6, 1920; admitted to bar, 1948, Iowa. *Education:* University of Iowa (B.S.E.E., 1942; J.D., 1948). (Retired). ***PRACTICE AREAS:*** Probate; Real Estate Law.

CRAIG O. CLARK (1923-2004)

JAMES E. WALSH, JR., born Chicago, Illinois, October 10, 1949; admitted to bar, 1975, Illinois; 1976, Iowa; 1995, Wisconsin; 1996, Minnesota. *Education:* University of Illinois (B.A., 1971); Loyola University (J.D., 1975). City Attorney, Waterloo, Iowa, 1992—. *Member:* Black Hawk County, Iowa State and American Bar Associations; Defense Research and Trial Lawyers Association; Iowa Academy of Trial Lawyers. ***PRACTICE AREAS:*** Insurance Defense Law; Municipal Law; Banking Law; Health Care Law; Computer Law; Corporate Law. ***Email:*** wloolaw@attglobal.net

TIMOTHY W. HAMANN, born Waterloo, Iowa, November 15, 1954; admitted to bar, 1981, Iowa; 1997, Minnesota. *Education:* University of Iowa (B.B.A., with high honors, 1977; M.A., 1981; J.D., 1981). Phi Delta Phi. Instructor, Insurance Law, University of Northern Iowa, 1981—. Chartered Property and Casualty Underwriter. *Member:* Black Hawk County, Iowa State and American Bar Associations; Defense Research and Trial Lawyers Association; Iowa Defense Counsel Association; American Board of Trial Advocates; Iowa Academy of Trial Lawyers. ***PRACTICE AREAS:*** Insurance Defense Law; Products Liability Law; Environmental Law; Worker's Compensation Law; Commercial Law. ***Email:*** tim.hamann@cbwhlaw.com

CHRISTY R. LISS, born Atkinson, Nebraska, December 25, 1966; admitted to bar, 1992, Iowa. *Education:* University of Nebraska (B.A., magna cum laude, 1989); University of Iowa (J.D., with distinction, 1992). Mortar Board. *Member:* Black Hawk County, Iowa State and American Bar Associations. ***PRACTICE AREAS:*** Family Law; Insurance Defense; Juvenile Law. ***Email:*** christy.liss@cbwhlaw.com

CHRISTOPHER S. WENDLAND, born Sioux Falls, South Dakota, January 7, 1965; admitted to bar, 1995, Iowa. *Education:* Harvard University (A.B., cum laude, 1987); University of Iowa (J.D., with high distinction, 1995). Managing Editor, Iowa Law Review, 1994-1995. *Member:* Black Hawk County, Iowa State and American Bar Associations. ***PRACTICE AREAS:*** Business Law; Commercial Law; Real Estate Law; Wills and Probate; Estate Planning; Creditors Rights; Municipal Law. ***Email:*** chris.wendland@cbwhlaw.com

(This Listing Continued)

ASSOCIATES

JARED R. KNAPP, born Fairfield, Iowa, September 28, 1975; admitted to bar, 2001, Iowa. *Education:* Cornell College (B.A., 1998); University of Iowa (J.D., 2001). ***PRACTICE AREAS:*** Criminal Defense; Insurance Defense; Municipal Law. ***Email:*** wloolaw@attglobal.net

MATTHEW PITTENGER, born Sioux City, Iowa, August 13, 1972; admitted to bar, 2003, Iowa. *Education:* Morningside College (B.S., 1997); Drake University (J.D., 2002). *Member:* Iowa State Bar Association. ***PRACTICE AREAS:*** Criminal Law; Insurance Defense. ***Email:*** matt.pittenger@chwhlaw.com

LOCAL COUNSEL FOR: Aetna Life & Casualty Company; Agora Syndicate; Alliance Insurance Group; American Family Insurance Company; American Hardware Insurance Company; American States Insurance Company; Amerisure Insurance Group; Auto-Owners Insurance; Bankers Life Company; Bituminous Insurance Companies; Continental Insurance Company; Crawford & Company; Equitable Life Assurance Society of the United States; Farmers Insurance Group; Fireman's Fund Insurance Company; Fremont Indemnity; Gay & Taylor, Inc.; General American Insurance Company; General Motors Corporation; Government Employees Insurance Company; GRE Insurance Company; Great Central Insurance Company; Home Indemnity Company; Illinois National Insurance Company; I.M.T. Insurance Company; Iowa Mutual Insurance Company; John Deere Insurance Company; Milbank Insurance Company; Milwaukee Insurance Company; National States Insurance Company; Nationwide Insurance Company; New Hampshire Insurance Group; Northland Insurance Company; Old Republic Insurance Company; Pafco General Insurance Company; Partners Mutual Insurance Company; Pekin Insurance Company; Penn General Services Corporation; Phoenix of London Group; Preferred Risk Financial, Inc.; Prudential Insurance Company of America; Reliance Insurance Company; Royal Globe Insurance Companies; S.E.C.U.R.A.; Safeco Insurance; Scottsdale Insurance Company; Shand Morahan and Company; Shelter Insurance Company; State Farm Mutual Automobile Insurance Company; The Cincinnati Companies; Transamerican Insurance Group; U.S.F. and G Insurance; United Fire & Casualty Company; Universal Underwriter Insurance Company; Victoria Insurance Company; West Bend Mutual.
REPRESENTATIVE CLIENTS: Black Hawke Roof Co.; Community National Bank; Van 6 Miller and Associates; VGM Financial Services; City of Urbana; City of Waterloo.

L.J. COHRT LAW FIRM

3356 KIMBALL AVENUE
WATERLOO, IOWA 50702
Telephone: 319-233-0217
Fax: 319-287-6867
Email: ljcohrt@qwest.net

Civil Litigation, Medical Malpractice, Wills, Trusts and Estates, Probate, Real Estate, Employment Law.

LARRY J. COHRT, born Waterloo, Iowa, December 27, 1942; admitted to bar, 1969, Iowa and U.S. District Court, Northern District of Iowa; 1970, U.S. Court of Appeals, Eighth Circuit; 1978, U.S. District Court, Southern District of Iowa. *Education:* St. Olaf College (B.A., 1965); University of Iowa (J.D., with distinction, 1969). Phi Alpha Delta. Author: "Product Liability—Savings & Loan Associations —Liability for Defective Products Which It Financed," 53 Iowa Law Review 1378, 1968. *Member:* Black Hawk County (Treasurer, 1971-1972) and Iowa State Bar Associations; Defense Research Institute; Iowa Defense Counsel Association; Association of Defense Trial Attorneys; Association of Trial Lawyers of America.

DUTTON, BRAUN, STAACK & HELLMAN, P.L.C.

Established in 1919

3151 BROCKWAY ROAD
P.O. BOX 810
WATERLOO, IOWA 50704
Telephone: 319-234-4471
Fax: 319-234-8029
Email: dbsh@wloolaw.com

General Trial Practice in all Courts, Insurance, Personal Injury, Products Liability, Malpractice or Professional Negligence, Corporate, Workers Compensation and Labor Employment, Probate and Estate Planning, Real Estate.

DAVID J. DUTTON, born Aurora, Illinois, February 17, 1936; admitted to bar, 1960, Iowa, U.S. District Court, Northern and Southern Districts of Iowa, U.S. Court of Appeals, 8th Circuit. *Education:* University of Iowa (B.A., 1958; J.D., 1960). Phi Delta Phi. Listed in: Chambers USA, Leading Attorneys for Business Litigation, 2005; "The Best Lawyers in America" (Products Liability, Professional Malpractice, Automobile Collision, Business Litigation). County Attorney, Black Hawk County, 1969-1975. President, Iowa County Attorney's Association, 1975-1976. Member, Iowa Crime Commission, 1969-1974. Member, Supreme Court Committee on Rules of Criminal Procedure, 1978-1979. Member, Iowa Supreme Court Advisory Committee on Media Coverage of the Courts, 1979-1981, and Supreme Court Advisory Committee on Rules of Civil Procedure, 1989-1993. Member, State Bar Committee on Uniform Jury Instructions, 1982-1984. *Member:* Black Hawk County, Iowa State Bar Associations; Iowa Trial Lawyers Association; The Association of Trial Lawyers of America. Iowa Academy of Trial Lawyers (President, 1990-1991). Fellow: American College of Trial Lawyers (State Chairman, 1995-1996); American Board of Trial Advocates (President, Iowa Chapter, 1997-1998); Federation of Insurance and Corporate Counsel; Iowa Defense Counsel Association; Iowa State Bar Foundation. ***Email:*** duttond@wloolaw.com

ROBERT W. BRAUN, born Wichita Falls, Texas, August 30, 1938; admitted to bar, 1963, Iowa. *Education:* University of Iowa (B.B.A., 1960; J.D., 1963). Phi Delta Phi. Assistant County Attorney, Black Hawk County, Iowa, 1969-1975. *Member:* Black Hawk County, Iowa State (Chairman, Subcommittee for Development and Editor, Iowa Business Practice Manual published, 1994, Contributor, 2000, 2004; Member: Editorial Board, Iowa Business Practice Manual, 2005-2007; Grievance Commission, 2001-2007; Council Chair, Business Law Section, 1998-2000) and American (Member, Sections on: Real Property;

(This Listing Continued)

DUTTON, BRAUN, STAACK & HELLMAN, P.L.C., Waterloo—Continued

Probate; Trust Law; Business Law) Bar Associations; Iowa Association of Hospital Attorneys; Iowa Municipal Attorneys Association; Iowa State Bar Association Foundation. ***PRACTICE AREAS:*** Business Law. ***Email:*** braunr@wloolaw.com

THOMAS L. STAACK, born Waterloo, Iowa, April 5, 1946; admitted to bar, 1971, Iowa, U.S. Court of Appeals, Eighth Circuit, U.S. District Court, Northern and Southern Districts of Iowa, U.S. District Court, Eastern District of Wisconsin. *Education:* University of Iowa (B.A., 1968; J.D., 1971). Phi Delta Phi. Member, 1973—, and Chairman, 1979-1984, Waterloo Recreation Commission Chairman, 1979-1984. Mental Health Board, Black Hawk-Grundy County, Iowa, 1980-1985. Member, Iowa Supreme Court Grievance Commission. *Member:* Black Hawk County, Iowa State (Member: Litigation Section Alternative Dispute Resolution) Bar Associations; The Association of Trial Lawyers of America; Iowa Trial Lawyers Association (Member, Board of Governors); AIEG. Fellow, Iowa Academy of Trial Lawyers. American Board of Trial Advocates; Board of American Academy of ADR Attorneys; Qualified Neutral in Minnesota. ***Email:*** staackt@wloolaw.com

JAMES R. HELLMAN, born Waterloo, Iowa, January 4, 1950; admitted to bar, 1977, Iowa. *Education:* University of Northern Iowa; University of Iowa (B.A., 1974); University of Iowa (J.D., 1977). *Member:* Black Hawk County and Iowa State Bar Associations; Iowa Trial Lawyers Association; Iowa Defense Counsel Association; American Board of Trial Advocates. Fellow, Iowa Academy of Trial Lawyers. ***PRACTICE AREAS:*** Trial Law; Insurance. ***Email:*** hellmanj@wloolaw.com

MICHAEL A. McENROE, born Waterloo, Iowa, January 28, 1957; admitted to bar, 1982, Iowa. *Education:* Iowa State University (B.S., Industrial Administration, 1979); University of Iowa (J.D., 1982). *Member:* Black Hawk County, Iowa State Bar Associations; Iowa Defense Counsel Association; Iowa Trial Lawyers Association; The Association of Trial Lawyers of America; Iowa Association of Workers Compensation Lawyers, Inc. ***PRACTICE AREAS:*** Workers Compensation. ***Email:*** mcenroem@wloolaw.com

CHERYL L. WEBER, born Waterloo, Iowa, January 4, 1957; admitted to bar, 1983, Iowa. *Education:* Buena Vista College (B.A., 1979); University of Iowa (J.D., 1983). State Judicial Nominating Commission Member, 1990-1996. Supreme Court Advisory Committee on Rules of Evidence, 1997-2002; Chair Person, 2001-2002. *Member:* Black Hawk County (Vice President, 1996-1997; President, 1997-1998) Iowa State and American Bar Associations; Iowa Defense Council Association; Iowa Trial Lawyers Association; The Association of Trial Lawyers of America. Fellow, Iowa Academy of Trial Lawyers; American Board of Trial Advocates. ***Email:*** weberc@wloolaw.com

STEVEN K. DANIELS, born Atlantic, Iowa, July 20, 1958; admitted to bar, 1983, Iowa. *Education:* Drake University (B.A., 1980; J.D., 1983). Phi Beta Kappa. *Member:* Black Hawk County and Iowa State Bar Associations; Black Hawk County Estate Planning Council. ***PRACTICE AREAS:*** Wills; Trust Law; Estate Planning; Probate Law. ***Email:*** danielss@wloolaw.com

BRUCE L. BRALEY, born Grinnell, Iowa, October 30, 1957; admitted to bar, 1983, Iowa, U.S. District Court, Northern and Southern Districts of Iowa, U.S. District Court, District of North Dakota and U.S. Court of Appeals, Eighth Circuit. *Education:* Iowa State University (B.A., 1980); University of Iowa (J.D., 1983). Phi Delta Phi. Member: Iowa Supreme Court Commission on Planning for the Twenty-First Century, 1995-1996; Iowa Supreme Court Rules of Professional Conduct Drafting Committee, 2000-2002; Governor's Task Force on Consumer Privacy, 2000-2001; Iowa Legal Aid Board. *Member:* Black Hawk County (President, 1993-1994), Iowa State (Committee on Specialization, 1999—; Chair, YLD Professional Development Committee, 1991-1993; Litigation Section) Bar Associations; Iowa Trial Lawyers' Association (President, 2003-2004); The Association of Trial Lawyers of America (Newsletter Editor, Professional Negligence Section, 2003-2004); American Board of Trial Advocates (Associate). American College of Trial Lawyers; Iowa Academy of Trial Lawyers. Certified as a Civil Trial Advocate by the National Board of Trial Advocacy. ***Email:*** braleyb@wloolaw.com

JOHN J. HINES, born Monticello, Iowa, June 5, 1955; admitted to bar, 1980, Iowa. *Education:* Luther College (B.A., 1977); University of Iowa (J.D., 1980). Assistant Worth County Attorney, 1980-1982. Jones County Attorney, 1982-1986. *Member:* Black Hawk County and Iowa State Bar Associations; Iowa Trial Lawyers Association; The Association of Trial Lawyers of America; National Association of Criminal Defense Lawyers. ***Email:*** hinesj@wloolaw.com

JAMES F. KALKHOFF, born Carroll, Iowa, November 19, 1961; admitted to bar, 1987, Iowa; U.S. Court of Appeals, Eight Circuit; U.S. District Court, Northern and Southern Districts of Iowa. *Education:* Iowa State University (B.A., 1984); Drake University (J.D., 1987). Delta Theta Phi; Pi Sigma Alpha. *Member:* Black Hawk County, Iowa State Bar Associations; The Association of Trial Lawyers of America; Iowa Trial Lawyers Association. ***PRACTICE AREAS:*** Family Law; Personal Injury. ***Email:*** kalkhoffj@wloolaw.com

JAMES H. COOK, born Atlantic, Iowa, July 14, 1959; admitted to bar, 1987, California and U.S. District Court, Southern District of California; 1989, U.S. Court of Appeals, 9th Circuit; 1991, U.S. District Court, District of Arizona; 1998, Iowa; 1999, U.S. District Court, Northern and Southern Districts of Iowa and U.S. Court of Appeals, 8th Circuit. *Education:* University of Iowa (B.S., 1982; J.D., 1987). Phi Delta Phi; Phi Eta Sigma. Note and Comment Editor, 1985-1986; Senior Associate Editor, 1986-1987, Iowa Law Review. Author: Comment, "Seaman's Direct Buying Service, Inc. v. Standard Oil Co.: Tortious Breach of the Covenant of Good Faith and Fair Dealing in a Noninsurance Commercial Contract Case," 71 Iowa Law Review 893, 1986; Note, "The Legal Status of Physician Extenders in Iowa: Review, Speculations and Recommendations," 72 Iowa Law Review 215, 1986; Four Chapters of "Drinking/Driving Litigation: Criminal and Civil," Callaghan Publishing, 1985. *Member:* Black Hawk County and Iowa State Bar Associations; State Bar of California; Iowa Trial Lawyers Association; The Association of Trial Lawyers of America. ***REPORTED CASES:*** White v. Celotex Corp., 907 F.2d 104 (9th Cir. 1990). ***PRACTICE AREAS:*** Medical Malpractice; Personal Injury. ***Email:*** cookj@wloolaw.com

(This Listing Continued)

CAROLYN A. RAFFERTY, born Highland Park, Illinois, May 3, 1963; admitted to bar, 1988, Wisconsin and U.S. District Court, Eastern District of Wisconsin; 1992, Minnesota; 1995, Iowa. *Education:* University of St. Thomas (B.A., magna cum laude, 1985); University of Lancaster, England; Marquette University (J.D., 1988). Phi Delta Phi. St. Thomas Moore Scholar. Executive Editor, Marquette University Law Review, 1987-1988. Author: Note, 70 Marq. L Rev. 736, 1987; Comment, 71 Marq. L. Rev. 166, 1987. *Member:* Black Hawk County and Iowa State Bar Associations. ***Email:*** dbsh@wloolaw.com

CHAD A. SWANSON, born Waterloo, Iowa, February 16, 1970; admitted to bar, 1995, Iowa, U.S. District Court, Northern District of Iowa and U.S. Court of Appeals, Eighth Circuit. *Education:* University of Iowa (B.A., with distinction, 1992; J.D., with distinction, 1994). Phi Beta Kappa. Member, Iowa Law Review, 1993-1994. *Member:* Black Hawk County and Iowa State Bar Associations; Iowa Trial Lawyers Association; Association of Trial Lawyers of America. ***PRACTICE AREAS:*** Personal Injury. ***Email:*** swansonc@wloolaw.com

LYNN M. SMITH, born LaCrosse, Wisconsin, November 12, 1971; admitted to bar, 1997, Iowa and U.S. District Court, Northern and Southern Districts of Iowa; 1998, Minnesota. *Education:* Wartburg College (B.A., cum laude, 1994); Drake University Law School (J.D., with honors, 1997). Recipient: Civil Procedure II, Corpus Juris Secundum Award, 1995; Securities Law, Academic Achievement Award, 1996; Conflicts of Law, Academic Achievement Award, 1997. *Member:* Black Hawk County, Iowa State and Minnesota State Bar Associations. ***PRACTICE AREAS:*** Employment Law. ***Email:*** smithl@wloolaw.com

---

COREY R. LORENZEN, born Dysart, Iowa, February 22, 1977; admitted to bar, 2002, Iowa. *Education:* University of Northern Iowa (B.A., 1999); University of Iowa (J.D., 2002). *Member:* Blackhawk County and Iowa State Bar Associations. ***PRACTICE AREAS:*** Real Estate. ***Email:*** lorenzenc@wloolaw.com

MICHAEL R. YOUNG, born Waterloo, Iowa, July 7, 1976; admitted to bar, 2001, Illinois; 2002, Iowa, U.S. District Court Northern District of Illinois. *Education:* Texas Christian University (B.B.A., 1998); University of Iowa (J.D., 2001). *Member:* Black Hawk County, Iowa State and Illinois State Bar Associations. ***Email:*** youngm@wloolaw.com

ERIN P. LYONS, born Springfield, Illinois, October 25, 1976; admitted to bar, 2005, Iowa and U.S. District Court, Northern and Southern Districts of Iowa. *Education:* University of Iowa (B.A., 1999; J.D., with distinction, 2004). Author: "Give Me a Home Where the Buffalo Roam," Journal of Gender, Race & Justice, Volume 8, No. 3, Winter 2005. ***Email:*** lyonse@wloolaw.com

LOCAL COUNSEL FOR: CNA Insurance Cos.; Chubb Group of Insurance Cos.; Columbia Casualty Co.; American Express Property Casualty Cos.; Farm Bureau Mut. Co.; Principal Financial Group; LaPorte City, Iowa; The Harnack Co.; Crossroads Ford, Ltd.; Community National Bank; Friendship Village; Black Hawk County Solid Waste Management Commission; Heartland Inns of America, L.L.C.; Allen Memorial Hospital; John Deere; Tri/Mark, Inc.; Great West Casualty Company; American Express Property Casualty Companies; Decker Acquisition Corporation; Minkin Management, Inc.; Iowa Builders Retirement Plan; Fast Servers, Inc.
REFERENCES: Union Planters Bank of Waterloo; Community National Bank.

EELLS & TRONVOLD LAW OFFICES, P.L.C.

WATERLOO, IOWA

(See Cedar Rapids)

General Practice with emphasis on Personal Injury, Litigation, Probate and Estate Planning, Trusts and Wills, Business Law and Mediation.

GALLAGHER, LANGLAS & GALLAGHER, P.C.

Established in 1951

LAW BUILDING
405 EAST FIFTH STREET
P.O. BOX 2615
WATERLOO, IOWA 50704
Telephone: 319-233-6163
Fax: 319-233-6435

Personal Injury, Insurance Defense, Corporate Law, Negligence, Professional Malpractice, Real Estate, Municipal Law, Family Law, Labor and Employment Law, Workers Compensation, Probate, General Trial Practice in all Courts.

FIRM PROFILE: Founded in 1951, Gallagher, Langlas & Gallagher, P.C. has provided a wide range of legal services not only locally but statewide as well. The firm has an active practice before state and federal courts, as well as administrative boards. Though a general practice firm providing a broad sphere of legal services, Gallagher, Langlas & Gallagher, P.C. has a strong concentration in civil litigation, representing both plaintiffs and defendants.

EDWARD J. GALLAGHER, JR., born Waterloo, Iowa, December 6, 1925; admitted to bar, 1950, Iowa; 1958, U.S. Supreme Court and U.S. District Court, Northern and Southern Districts of Iowa. *Education:* Loras College (B.A., magna cum laude, 1948); Honorary Degree (LL.D., 1998); Georgetown University (J.D., 1950). Delta Theta Phi. Listed, Best Lawyers of America, (All Editions). City Attorney, Evansdale, Iowa, 1954-1958. Commander, Department of Iowa Amvets, 1954-1955. Member, Board of Trustees, National Amvet Service Foundation, 1955-1961; President, 1957-1961. City Solicitor, Waterloo, Iowa, 1966-1970. *Member:* Black Hawk County, First Judicial District and Iowa State (Chairman, Special Committee, Automobile Accident Reparations, 1972-1975; Member, Supreme Court Advisory Committee on Rules, 1980-1986) Bar Associations; The Association of Trial Lawyers of America (Iowa State Committeeman, 1966-1967; 1972-1973; Member, Board of Governors, 1977-1980); Iowa Trial Lawyers Association (Member, Board of Governors, 1971-1980); American Bar Foundation; American Board of Trial Advocates (National Representative, Iowa Chapter, 1989-1994). Fellow: Iowa Academy of Trial Lawyers (Member, Board of Governors, 1968-1992; Vice President, 1971-1972;

(This Listing Continued)

President, 1972-1973); American College of Trial Lawyers; International Society of Barristers; International Academy of Trial Lawyers (Member, Board of Directors, 1985-1991; 1993-1999). **PRACTICE AREAS:** Personal Injury; Business Law; Professional Negligence; Civil Litigation; Workers Compensation. **Email:** egallagher@glglaw.net

THOMAS W. LANGLAS, born Waterloo, Iowa, January 31, 1943; admitted to bar, 1967, Iowa; 1979, U.S. District Court, Northern District of Iowa; 1981, U.S. District Court, Southern District of Iowa. *Education:* University of St. Thomas (B.A., 1964); University of Iowa (J.D., 1967). Phi Alpha Delta. President, Iowa Student Bar Association, 1966-1967. Assistant City Solicitor, 1968-1976. Listed, Best Lawyers in America. Chairman, City of Waterloo Planning and Zoning Commission, 1988-2004. *Member:* First Judicial District, Black Hawk County, Iowa State (Chair, Family and Juvenile Law Section, 2000-2002) and American (Member, Family Law Section) Bar Associations; Iowa Trial Lawyers Association. Fellow: Iowa Academy of Trial Lawyers; American Academy of Matrimonial Lawyers. **PRACTICE AREAS:** Family Law; Civil Litigation; Personal Injury. **Email:** tlanglas@glglaw.net

EDWARD J. GALLAGHER, III, born Washington, D.C., October 16, 1949; admitted to bar, 1974, Iowa; 1975, U.S. District Court, Northern and Southern Districts of Iowa; 1980, U.S. Supreme Court. *Education:* University of St. Thomas (B.A., summa cum laude, 1971); Georgetown University (J.D., 1974). Delta Epsilon Sigma; Delta Theta Phi. Member, Staff and Editorial Board, American Criminal Law Review, 1973-1974. Dean, E.D. White Senate, Georgetown Law Center, 1973-1974. Co-author: Note, "Federal Decisions on the Constitutionality of Electronic Surveillance Legislation," 11 American Criminal Law Review 639, 1973. *Member:* Black Hawk County, First Judicial District, Iowa State (Member, Sections on: Litigation, Worker's Compensation, Labor and Employment Law, General Practice and Family Law) and American (Member, Sections of Individual Rights and Responsibilities, Insurance, Litigation, Negligence and Compensation Law, Law Office Management) Bar Associations; Iowa Trial Lawyers Association (Member, Board of Governors, 1983-2004; Executive Board, Member at Large, 1994-1995; Parliamentarian, 1995-1996; Secretary, 1996-1997; Vice-President, 1997-2000; President Elect, 2000-2001; President, 2001-2002); The Association of Trial Lawyers of America (State Delegate, 1993-1995; Member, Sections on: Employment Law, Civil Rights Law, Motor Vehicles Collision, Premises Liability); Iowa Academy of Trial Lawyers. **PRACTICE AREAS:** Civil Litigation; Personal Injury; Employment Law; Family Law. **Email:** ejgallagher@glglaw.net

GEORGE L. WEILEIN, born Waterloo, Iowa, December 14, 1955; admitted to bar, 1981, Iowa and U.S. District Court, Northern and Southern Districts of Iowa. *Education:* Loras College (B.A., magna cum laude, 1978); University of Iowa (J.D., with distinction, 1981). Delta Epsilon Sigma; Phi Alpha Theta; Phi Delta Phi; Delta Sigma (President, 1977-1978). Case Editor, Moot Court Board, 1980-1981. Recipient, American Jurisprudence Award in Conflict of Laws. Governor, Board of Governors of the Iowa State Bar Association, 2000—; Liaison from Board of Governors to Health Law Section of Iowa State Bar Association, 2000—. *Member:* Black Hawk County (Program Chairman, 1987-1988), Iowa State (Member, Iowa Jury Instructions Committee, 2003—; Member, Sections on: Health Law; Litigation) and American (Member, Sections on: Health Law; Litigation) Bar Associations; First Judicial District Bar Association. Fellow: Iowa Academy of Trial Lawyers. **PRACTICE AREAS:** Health Law; Hospital Liability; Civil Litigation; Professional Malpractice Law. **Email:** gweilein@glglaw.net

TIMOTHY C. BOLLER, born Waterloo, Iowa, July 17, 1956; admitted to bar, 1981, Iowa and U.S. District Court, Northern and Southern Districts of Iowa. *Education:* University of Iowa (B.A., with high distinction, 1978; J.D., with distinction, 1981). Phi Beta Kappa. Member, Board of Directors, 1983-1995 and Secretary, 1986-1991, Iowa State Bar Review School, Inc. Member, First Judicial District, Judicial Nomination Commission, 1998-2003. *Member:* Black Hawk County, First Judicial District and Iowa State (Member, Sections of Litigation and Labor Law) Bar Associations; Iowa Trial Lawyers Association; The Association of Trial Lawyers of America. **PRACTICE AREAS:** Civil Litigation; Professional Malpractice; Personal Injury; Labor and Employment Law. **Email:** tboller@glglaw.net

THOMAS C. VERHULST, born Yankton, South Dakota, March 28, 1963; admitted to bar, 1988, Iowa; U.S. District Court, Northern and Southern Districts of Iowa; 2003, U.S. Supreme Court. *Education:* Augustana College (B.A., 1985); University of Iowa (J.D., 1988). Phi Alpha Theta; Blue Key. Recipient: American Jurisprudence Book Awards, Trusts and Estates, Federal Courts; Roy and Lucille Dybvig Leadership Award. Author: "Demanding A Jury Trial In The Federal Court System: Federal Rules of Civil Procedure 38 and 39," Federation of Insurance and Corporate Counsel Quarterly, Vol. 37, No. 3, Spring, 1987; "Lost Chance of Survival Theory: Its Place in Medical Malpractice Litigation," Federation of Insurance and Corporate Counsel Quarterly, Vol. 38, No. 2, Winter, 1988. Member, Waterloo Rotary Club. *Member:* Black Hawk County (Secretary, 1992-1993) and Iowa State Bar Associations; Iowa Trial Lawyers Association. **PRACTICE AREAS:** Civil Litigation; Real Estate; Probate. **Email:** tverhulst@glglaw.net

DAVID A. ROTH, born Mason City, Iowa, May 10, 1963; admitted to bar, 1991, Iowa and U.S. District Court, Northern District of Iowa. *Education:* Iowa State University (B.L.S., 1988); Drake University (J.D., 1991). Delta Theta Phi. *Member:* Black Hawk County (Secretary, 1996-1997; Treasurer, 1998-2000), Iowa State and American (Member, Alternate Dispute Resolution, Litigation Sections) Bar Associations; Iowa Trial Lawyers Association. **PRACTICE AREAS:** Civil Litigation; Personal Injury; Criminal Law; Family Law. **Email:** droth@glglaw.net

LINDA A. HALL, born Kalamazoo, Michigan, February 10, 1960; admitted to bar, 1986, Iowa; 1998, U.S. District Court, Northern District of Iowa. *Education:* Ripon College (B.A., 1982); University of Tulsa (J.D., 1986). Assistant Black Hawk County Attorney, 1987-1998. Former Member: Iowa County Attorneys Association; American College of District Attorneys. *Member:* Black Hawk County and Iowa State Bar Associations; Iowa Trial Lawyers Association. **PRACTICE AREAS:** Personal Injury; Criminal Law; General Practice; Litigation; Family Law. **Email:** lhall@glglaw.net

(This Listing Continued)

LAURA E. RANGE, born Dubuque, Iowa, 1979; admitted to bar, 2005, Iowa. *Education:* University of Northern Iowa (B.A., summa cum laude, 2001); University of Iowa (J.D., 2005). *Member:* Black Hawk County and Iowa State Bar Associations. **Email:** lrange@glglaw.net

REPRESENTATIVE CLIENTS: A list will be furnished upon request.

GARTELOS, WAGNER & AMENT

3604 KIMBALL AVENUE
WATERLOO, IOWA 50702
Telephone: 319-234-3500
Fax: 319-234-0837
URL: http://www.gwalawoffice.com

General Trial Practice and Appeals. Corporation, Family, Insurance, Personal Injury, Real Estate, Probate, Estate Planning, Workers Compensation and Bankruptcy Law.

MEMBERS OF FIRM

PETER J. GARTELOS, born Moline, Illinois, January 12, 1943; admitted to bar, 1974, Iowa and U.S. District Court, Northern District of Iowa. *Education:* Northwestern University and Augustana College (B.A., 1966); Valparaiso University (J.D., 1973). Phi Alpha Delta. *Member:* Black Hawk County, Iowa State and American Bar Associations; Association of Trial Lawyers of Iowa; American Academy of ADR Attorneys (Director and Vice President). [With U.S. Army, 1969-1972]. **LANGUAGES:** Greek. **PRACTICE AREAS:** Insurance Defense (30%, 35); Personal Injury (30%, 25); Family Law (20%, 30); Real Estate (10%); Probate (10%).

JAMES L. WAGNER, born Waterloo, Iowa, February 21, 1950; admitted to bar, 1974, Iowa; 1975, U.S. District Court, Northern District of Iowa. *Education:* University of Iowa (B.A., Economics and Political Science, 1972; J.D., with distinction, 1974). President, Civitan Club, 1977-1978. Grand Knight, Knights of Columbus, 1985-1986. President, Sunrise Exchange Club, 1976-1977. *Member:* Black Hawk County, Iowa State and American Bar Associations. **REPORTED CASES:** Franzen v. Tweaten et. al (2002). **PRACTICE AREAS:** Real Estate; Estate Administration; Probate; Plaintiffs Personal Injury; Family Law.

TIMOTHY D. AMENT, born Dubuque, Iowa, October 4, 1962; admitted to bar, 1988, Iowa; 1989, U.S. District Court, Northern District of Iowa; 1992, U.S. District Court, Southern District of Iowa; 2002, U.S. Supreme Court. *Education:* Iowa State University; University of Northern Iowa (B.A., with highest honors, 1985); University of Iowa (J.D., with distinction, 1988). Phi Alpha Theta (President, 1984-1985). Recipient: Purple and Old Gold Award; Erma Plaehn Award. Iowa Teacher's Certification, 1985. *Member:* Black Hawk County and Iowa State (Treasurer, 2002-2004) Bar Associations; Iowa Trial Lawyers Association. **PRACTICE AREAS:** Personal Injury; Family Law; Workers Compensation; Contracts; Bankruptcy. **Email:** tament@gawaam.com

REPRESENTATIVE CLIENTS: Waterloo-Cedar Falls Board of Realtors; GRE America Insurance Group; Northwestern National Insurance Group; Iowa Metal Spinners, Inc.; Youngblut Contracting, Inc.; Youngblut Management, Inc.; Emergency Practice Services, Inc.; Gilbertville Locker, Inc.; Norwest Mortgage, Inc.
REFERENCES: Wells Fargo Bank; Pauline Company, Inc.; Society Insurance Company; Rice Insurance Company, Inc.

HOLMES & HOLMES

531 COMMERCIAL STREET, SUITE 612
WATERLOO, IOWA 50701
Telephone: 319-234-7506
Fax: 319-234-8277
Email: john@holmeslaw.us
URL: http://www.holmeslaw.us

Business Law, Closely Held Business Law, Buying and Selling of Businesses, Lawsuits, Contracts, Business Planning, Professional Liability.

MEMBER OF FIRM

WENDELL A. HOLMES (1916-2002)

JOHN W. HOLMES, born Washington, D.C., July 22, 1945; admitted to bar, 1974, Iowa; 1989, Nebraska; U.S. District Court, Northern and Southern Districts of Iowa, U.S. Court of Appeals, Eighth Circuit and U.S. Supreme Court. *Education:* University of Iowa (B.B.A., 1967; J.D., 1974). Phi Alpha Delta. Member, Board of Editors, Iowa Law Review, 1973-1974. City Attorney, City of Waterloo, Iowa, 1982-1983. *Member:* Black Hawk County (Secretary, 1976-1977), Iowa State and American Bar Associations; Iowa Trial Lawyers Association. [Lt., S.C., USNR, active duty, U.S. Navy, 1967-1971]. **LANGUAGES:** English. **REPORTED CASES:** Ratcliff v. Graether, 697 N.W.2d 119 (Iowa 2005) No. 03-1816; Immaculate Conception Corp. v. D.O.T., 656 N.W. 2d 513 (Iowa 1-23-2003) No. 174/01-1493, 1/2003; In Re the Marriage of Pagel, 2-273/01-1060 (Iowa App. 2002) No. 2-273/01-1060, 8/2002; Immaculate Corp. v. Dept. of Transp., 2-394/01-1493 (Iowa App. 6-19-2002) No. 2-394/01-1493, 6/2002; Pattison Bros. Ms. R. Trm. v. DC Clayton Cy., 630 N.W. 2d 783 (Iowa 2001) No. 69/99-0553, 7/2001; In Re Marriage of Volker, 00-0281 (Iowa App. 2000) No. 0-545/00-0281, 10/2000; Pflepsen v. Univ. of Osteopathic Medicine, 519 N.W. 2d 390 (Iowa 1994) No. 93-450, 1994; Farmers & Merch. Sav. v. Vandenberg Chev., 523 N.W. 2d 211 (Iowa 1994) No. 93-677, 7/1994; Linerty Manor v. Rinnels, 487 N.W. 2d 324 (Iowa 1992) No. 91-1352, 7/1992; Sage v. Johnson, 437 N.W. 2d 582 (Iowa 1989) No. 88-600, 3/1989; Rinkleff v. Knox, 375 N.W. 2d 262 (Iowa 1985) No. 84-1153, 10/1985; Sturtz v. Iowa Dept. of Revenue, 373 N.W. 2d 131 (Iowa 1985) No. 84-1890, 8/1985; Merged Area (Education) VII v. Bd. of Review, 326 N.W. 2d 310 (1982) No. 67103, 11/1982. **PRACTICE AREAS:** Business Law; Closely Held Business Law; Buying and Selling of Businesses; Contracts; Business Planning; Professional Liability. **Email:** john@holmeslaw.us

LAW OFFICES OF
C. KEVIN McCRINDLE

SUITE 500, FIRST NATIONAL BUILDING
607 SYCAMORE STREET
P.O. BOX 928
WATERLOO, IOWA 50704-0928
Telephone: 319-234-0535
Fax: 319-234-0320
Email: lawckm@mchsi.com

Hudson, Iowa Office: 326 4th Street. 50643. Telephone: 319-988-4315.

Agricultural Law, Business Planning, Real Estate, Probate, Estate Planning, Trusts and Estates, Taxation and Health Care.

C. KEVIN McCRINDLE, born Milwaukee, Wisconsin, January 6, 1950; admitted to bar, 1975, Iowa and U.S. Tax Court; 1983, Wisconsin. *Education:* St. Olaf College (B.A., 1972); Loyola University (J.D., 1975). Member, Law Journal, 1973-1975. Author, Case Comment, 6 Loy. U. of Chic. Law Rev. 688 (1974). *Member:* Black Hawk County, Iowa State (Member, Probate and Trust Law Section Council, 1994-1997, 2001— and Chair 2003-2004; Board of Governors, 2001-2003) and American (Member, Section of Taxation) Bar Associations; State Bar of Wisconsin; Black Hawk County Estate Planning Council. Fellow: American College of Trust and Estate Counsel.

ASSOCIATE

JOHN W. HARRIS, born New Hampton, Iowa, March 9, 1964; admitted to bar, 1996, Iowa. *Education:* Iowa State University (B.B.A., 1986; B.S., 1989); Hamline University (J.D., with honors, 1996). Member, Hamline Journal of Law and Policy. *Member:* Grundy County (President, 2000-2001), Black Hawk County and Iowa State Bar Associations. ***Email:*** john.harris@mchsi.com

McGUIRE LAW FIRM, P.C.

WATERLOO, IOWA

(See Mason City)

Personal Injury Law, Medical Malpractice, Severe Burns, Water Heater Flammable Vapor Litigation, Products Liability, Railroad Litigation, Trial Practice.

DAVID R. NAGLE

SUITE 704, 501 SYCAMORE STREET
P.O. BOX 792
WATERLOO, IOWA 50703
Telephone: 319-234-3623
Facsimile: 319-236-2228
Email: davenaglelaw@aol.com

Domestic Relations, Family Law, Personal Injury and Criminal Defense.

DAVID R. NAGLE, born Grinnell, Iowa, April 15, 1943; admitted to bar, 1968, Iowa. *Education:* University of Northern Iowa (B.A., 1965); University of Iowa (LL.B., 1968). Adjunct Professor, University of Northern Iowa, 1978-1981. Member, U.S. Congress, Third District, 1987-1993. Assistant County Attorney, Black Hawk County, Iowa, 1969-1970. City Attorney, Evansdale, Iowa, 1972-1974. Member, 1975-1980 and President, 1979, Black Hawk County Conservation Board. The Association of Trial Lawyers of America (1974-1993). *Member:* Black Hawk County and Iowa State Bar Associations; Association of Trial Lawyers of Iowa (Member, Board of Governors, 1980-1983); Iowa Academy of Trial Lawyers. ***PRACTICE AREAS:*** Civil Litigation; Criminal Litigation; Family Law; Commercial Law; Real Estate; Contracts.

REDFERN, MASON, DIETER, LARSEN & MOORE, P.L.C.

WATERLOO, IOWA

(See Cedar Falls)

Insurance, Litigation, Medical Malpractice and Product Liability, Wills, Trusts, Estate Planning and Probate Law, Taxation and Tax Returns, Labor Law, Employment Law, Commercial Law, Contracts, Elder Law, Mergers and Acquisitions, Trial Law, Workers' Compensation, Franchise Law, Municipal Law, Real Estate, Business Law, Corporate Law, Family Law, Public Utility Law, Civil Trial Practice in all Courts.

RUSH & NICHOLSON, PLC

WATERLOO, IOWA

(See Cedar Rapids)

Personal Injury, Product Liability, Professional Liability, Labor and Employment, Workers Compensation.

SHUTTLEWORTH & INGERSOLL, P.L.C.

WATERLOO, IOWA

(See Cedar Rapids)

Administrative Law, Agricultural Law, Alternative Dispute Resolution, Arbitration, Mediation, Antitrust, Unfair Trade, Bankruptcy, Banks and Banking, Biotechnology, Civil Litigation and Appellate Practice in all State and Federal Courts, Civil Rights, Commercial Law, Commercial Real Estate, Communications and Media, Computers and Software, Constitutional Law, Construction Law, Contracts, Copyrights, Corporate Law, Debtor and Creditor, Disabilities, Education Law, Elder Law, Eminent Domain, Employee Benefits, Employment Law, Energy, Environmental Law, Estate Planning, General Practice, Health Care, Hospital Law, Insurance, Insurance Defense, Intellectual Property, Labor, Land Use, Medical Malpractice, Mergers, Acquisitions, and Divestitures, Municipal Law, Natural Resources, Nonprofit and Charitable Organizations, OSHA, Partnership Law, Patents, Personal Injury, Probate, Products Liability, Professional Liability, Real Estate, Securities, Tax Law, Technology and Science, Trademarks, Trusts and Estates, Utility Law, Wills, Workers Compensation, Zoning Law.

SWISHER & COHRT, P.L.C.

Established in 1913

528 WEST 4TH STREET
P.O. BOX 1200
WATERLOO, IOWA 50704-1200
Telephone: 319-232-6555
FAX: 319-232-4835
Email: office@s-c-law.com
URL: http://www.swishercohrt.com

General Civil, Trial and Appellate Practice in all State and Federal Courts; Insurance; Insurance Defense; Corporation; Banks and Banking; Commercial; Labor and Employment (public and private sector); Workers Compensation; Probate; Wills; Trusts & Estates; Business; Civil Rights; Education; Municipal; Premises Liability; Products Liability Defense; Utility; Employee Benefits; Collections; Debtor-Creditor; Environmental; Leases and Leasing; Professional Liability; Media; Medical Malpractice; Franchise and Franchising; Contracts; Family; Estate Planning; Public Utility; Administrative; Real Estate; and Personal Injury Law; Torts.

FIRM PROFILE: Swisher & Cohrt is a full service law firm that prides itself in having lawyers who are good people who perform high quality legal work ethically, professionally and economically. Our practice area spans the state but is focused primarily in the eastern half of the state. We have a long history of doing insurance defense for many carriers both large and small and we have a strong history in the area of employment and labor relations. We have a large school law practice and represent many school districts throughout Northeast Iowa. We also take pride in our work in the area of probate and estate planning as well as other areas of general practice to meet the needs of our clientele.

STEVEN A. WEIDNER, born Waterloo, Iowa, September 6, 1940; admitted to bar, 1965, Iowa; 1966, U.S. Court of Military Appeals; 1969, U.S. District Court, Northern District of Iowa; 1970, U.S. Court of Appeals, Eighth Circuit; 1983, U.S. District Court, Southern District of Iowa. *Education:* University of Notre Dame (B.B.A., 1962; J.D., 1965). *Member:* Black Hawk County, First District and Iowa State Bar Associations; Iowa Council of School Board Attorneys. ***PRACTICE AREAS:*** Labor and Employment Law; Corporate Law; Real Estate; School Law; Business Law; Commercial Law; Probate; Estate Planning. ***Email:*** weidner@s-c-law.com

STEPHEN J. POWELL, born Highland Park, Illinois, August 7, 1950; admitted to bar, 1975, Iowa, U.S. District Court, Northern District of Iowa and U.S. Court of Appeals, Eighth Circuit; 1983, U.S. District Court, Southern District of Iowa. *Education:* University of Northern Colorado (B.A., 1972); Drake University (J.D., with honors, 1974). Member, Drake Law Review, 1973-1974. *Member:* Black Hawk County and Iowa State Bar Associations; Iowa Defense Counsel Association; Defense Research Institute; Association of Defense Trial Attorneys; Iowa Academy of Trial Lawyers; American Board of Trial Advocates; International Association of Defense Counsel. ***PRACTICE AREAS:*** Insurance Defense; Personal Injury; Medical Malpractice; Labor and Employment. ***Email:*** powell@s-c-law.com

JIM D. DeKOSTER, born Camp LeJeune, North Carolina, January 13, 1945; admitted to bar, 1970, Iowa; 1977, U.S. Court of Appeals, Eighth Circuit and U.S. District Court, Northern District of Iowa; 1980, U.S. District Court, Southern District of Iowa; 1983, U.S. Supreme Court. *Education:* Iowa State University (B.S., 1967); University of Iowa (J.D., with distinction, 1970). Phi Alpha Delta; Phi Eta Sigma. *Member:* Black Hawk County, First Judicial District (Nominating Commission, 1988-1994) and Iowa State (Member, Committee on Administrative Law, 1983-1987) Bar Associations. [Lt., USNR, JAGC, 1970-1976]. ***PRACTICE AREAS:*** General Practice; Appellate Practice; Civil Rights; Education Law; Employment; Insurance Defense Law. ***Email:*** dekoster@s-c-law.com

SAMUEL C. ANDERSON, born Centerville, Iowa, August 13, 1959; admitted to bar, 1984, Iowa and U.S. District Court, Northern and Southern Districts of Iowa. *Education:* University of Iowa (B.A., 1981); Drake University Law School (J.D., 1984). Phi Beta Kappa. Recipient: 1984 H.G. Cartwright Award. Member, 1982-1984 and Note Editor, 1983-1984, Drake Law Review. Author: Casenote, 32 Drake Law Review 531 (1983); Note, 32 Drake Law Review 785 (1983). *Member:* Black Hawk County and Iowa State Bar Associations (Executive Council of Young Lawyer's Division, 1988-1994); Defense Research Institute; Iowa Defense Counsel Association; Association of Defense Trial Attorneys; Iowa Academy of Trial Lawyers. ***PRACTICE AREAS:*** General Practice; Civil Litigation; Workers Compensation; Insurance Defense; Personal Injury. ***Email:*** sanderson@s-c-law.com

KEVIN R. ROGERS, born St. Paul, Minnesota, September 8, 1958; admitted to bar, 1987, Iowa and U.S. District Court, Northern and Southern Districts of Iowa. *Education:* University of Iowa (B.A., 1984); Drake University Law School (J.D., with honors, 1987). Member, Drake Law Review, 1985-1987. Author: Note, 35 Drake Law Review 611 (1987); Casenote, 36 Drake Law Review 201 (1987). *Member:* Black Hawk County and Iowa State Bar Associations; Defense Research Institute; Iowa Defense Counsel Association; Iowa Association of Workers Compensation Lawyers, Inc. (Member, Board of Governors, 2004). ***PRACTICE AREAS:*** Workers Compensation; Personal Injury; School Law; Labor and Employment Law. ***Email:*** rogers@s-c-law.com

BETH E. HANSEN, born Omaha, Nebraska, June 18, 1951; admitted to bar, 1991, Iowa and U.S. District Court, Northern and Southern Districts of Iowa; U.S. Court of Appeals, Eighth Circuit; U.S. Supreme Court. *Education:* University of Iowa (B.A., 1973);

(This Listing Continued)

Creighton University (J.D., cum laude, 1991). *Member:* Black Hawk County (Past President) and Iowa State Bar Associations; Iowa Defense Counsel Association; Defense Research Institute; Association of Defense Trial Attorneys; Iowa Council of School Board Attorneys. ***PRACTICE AREAS:*** Insurance Defence; Labor and Employment Law. ***Email:*** hansen@s-c-law.com

MARK F. CONWAY, born Scott Air Force Base, St. Louis, Illinois, January 15, 1960; admitted to bar, 1991, Iowa and U.S. District Court, Northern and Southern Districts of Iowa; U.S. Court of Appeals, Eighth Circuit. *Education:* Buena Vista College (B.A., 1982); University of South Dakota (J.D., 1991). Managing Editor, South Dakota Law Review, 1990-1991. *Member:* Black Hawk County, Iowa State (Member, Commercial & Bankruptcy Law Section Council, 1994—) and American Bar Associations. ***PRACTICE AREAS:*** Business Law; Corporate Law; Estate Planning; Probate; Banking. ***Email:*** conway@s-c-law.com

NATALIE WILLIAMS BURRIS, born Omaha, Nebraska, March 25, 1969; admitted to bar, 1994, Iowa and U.S. District Court, Northern and Southern Districts of Iowa. *Education:* University of Northern Iowa (B.A., 1991); University of Iowa (J.D., with distinction, 1994). Author, Comment, "Updated Guidelines for Juvenile Curfews: City of Maquoketa v. Russell," 79 Iowa Law Review 465, 1994. *Member:* Black Hawk County and Iowa State Bar Associations. ***PRACTICE AREAS:*** Insurance Defense; Civil Litigation; Probate; Wills; Adoption Law. ***Email:*** burris@s-c-law.com

AARON R. BIXBY, born Clarksville, Iowa, September 19, 1969; admitted to bar, 1995, Iowa; 1996, U.S. District Court, Northern and Southern Districts of Iowa. *Education:* Iowa State University (B.S., 1992); University of Iowa (J.D., with distinction, 1995). *Member:* Black Hawk County (Secretary, 2004-2005) and Iowa State Bar Associations. ***PRACTICE AREAS:*** Real Estate; Probate; Estate Planning; Wills; Family Law. ***Email:*** bixby@s-c-law.com

---

MEGAN S. FEREDAY, born Akron, Ohio, March 6, 1974; admitted to bar, 2000, Wisconsin and U.S. District Court, Eastern District of Wisconsin; 2002, Iowa. *Education:* University of Notre Dame (B.A., 1996); Marquette University (J.D., 2000). Formerly with Office of the State Public Defender, Milwaukee, Wisconsin, 2000-2001. *Member:* Black Hawk County and American Bar Associations; State Bar of Wisconsin. ***PRACTICE AREAS:*** Insurance Defense; Civil Litigation; Criminal Law; Estate Planning. ***Email:*** fereday@s-c-law.com

FIRM IS COUNSEL FOR: Area Education Agency 267; Benton Mutual Insurance Assn.; Black Hawk Economic Development, Inc.; Community Foundation of Waterloo and Northeast Iowa; Exceptional Persons, Inc.; Family YMCA of Black Hawk County; First Security State Bank; Hawkeye Community College; Koehring Corp.; Mid American Energy Co.; MidwestOne Bank & Trust; Professional Office Services, Inc.; State Bank of Lawler; The Powers Manufacturing Company; Viking Pump Division, IDEX Corp.; Waterloo Community School District; Waterloo Industrial Development Association; Waterloo Industries Inc.; Waterloo Water Works.

FIRM IS LOCAL COUNSEL FOR: Acuity; Allied Insurance Group; American Family Insurance; Austin Mutual Insurance Co.; Church Mutual Insurance; Eagle Ottawa, LLC; Country Insurance & Financial Services; Deere & Company; Eagle Ottawa, LLC; EMC Insurance; Farm & City Insurance; Gallagher-Bassett; Guaranty National Companies; Hawkeye-Security Insurance; Indiana Insurance; Liberty Mutual Group; MSI Insurance; Nationwide Insurance Group; Orion Auto Insurance; PIC Wisconsin Insurance; Regions Bank; Royal & SunAlliance; Sentry Insurance; Society Insurance; Terex Cranes, Inc.; United Fire & Casualty Co.; United States Fire Insurance Co.; Unitrin Insurance Group; Universal Underwriters Group; Viking Insurance; Wausau Insurance; West Bend Mutual Insurance; Western Reserve Group; Western World Insurance.

YAGLA, McCOY & RILEY, P.L.C.

Established in 1970

LINCOLN PARK BUILDING
327 EAST FOURTH STREET, SUITE 300
P.O. BOX 960
WATERLOO, IOWA 50704-0960
Telephone: 319-234-4631
Fax: 319-234-8346
Email: gyagla@ymrlaw.com

Insurance Defense, Corporate, Trust, Business and Administrative Law. Personal Injury, Insurance, Real Estate, General Trial Practice..

MEMBERS OF FIRM

JAMES H. YAGLA (1937-1985)

GENE R. YAGLA, born Waterloo, Iowa, May 5, 1946; admitted to bar, 1974, Iowa; U.S. District Court, Northern District of Iowa. *Education:* University of Northern Iowa (B.A., summa cum laude, 1971); University of Iowa (J.D., with honors, 1974). Member and Former President, Waterloo Board of Park Commissioners. *Member:* Iowa State Bar Association; Iowa Defense Counsel Association. [With U.S. Navy, 1964-1968]. ***PRACTICE AREAS:*** Insurance Defense; Bodily Injury and Property Damage - Defendant; Bodily Injury and Property Damage - Plaintiff; Litigation. ***Email:*** gyagla@ymrlaw.com

JOHN T. McCOY, born Texarkana, Arkansas, February 15, 1950; admitted to bar, 1977, Iowa and U.S. District Court, Northern and Southern Districts. *Education:* University of Notre Dame (B.A., 1972); University of Iowa (J.D., with honors, 1977). Executive Editor, The Journal of Corporation Law, 1976-1977. Author: "Securities Regulation—Section 16(b), The Family and Control," 2 Journal of Corporation Law 188, 1976. *Member:* Black Hawk (President, 1988-1989), Iowa State and American Bar Associations; Iowa Defense Counsel Association; Defense Research Institute; Iowa Municipal Attorneys Association. ***PRACTICE AREAS:*** Insurance Defense; Bodily Injury and Property Damage - Defendant; Bodily Injury and Property Damage - Plaintiff; Litigation. ***Email:*** jmccoy@ymrlaw.com

DAVID RILEY, born Waterloo, Iowa, October 28, 1954; admitted to bar, 1979, Iowa; 1981, U.S. District Court, Northern District of Iowa. *Education:* University of Iowa (B.A., with high distinction, 1975; J.D., with distinction, 1979). *Member:* Black Hawk County Bar Association; Iowa Defense Counsel Association (Member and Director). ***PRACTICE AREAS:*** Insurance Defense; Bodily Injury and Property Damage - Defendant; Bodily Injury and Property Damage - Plaintiff; Litigation. ***Email:*** driley@ymrlaw.com

(This Listing Continued)

KARLA J. SHEA, born Cherokee, Iowa, June 30, 1965; admitted to bar, 1991, Iowa and U.S. District Court, Northern District of Iowa. *Education:* Iowa State University (B.A., 1987); Drake University (J.D., 1991). *Member:* Black Hawk County and Iowa State Bar Associations; Iowa Defense Council Association. ***PRACTICE AREAS:*** Insurance Defense; Bodily Injury and Property Damage - Defendant; Bodily Injury and Property Damage - Plaintiff; Litigation; Family Law. ***Email:*** kshea@ymrlaw.com

HENRY J. BEVEL III, born Frankfort, Kentucky, March 3, 1959; admitted to bar, 1988, Iowa and U.S. District Court, Northern District of Iowa. *Education:* Kentucky State University (B.A, magna cum laude, 1981); University of Kentucky (J.D., 1984). Alpha Kappa Mu. Assistant Public Defender, 1989-1991 and Assistant County Attorney, 1991-1993, Black Hawk County, Iowa. *Member:* Black Hawk County, Iowa State and American Bar Associations; Iowa Defense Counsel Association; American Board of Trial Advocates. ***PRACTICE AREAS:*** Insurance Defense; Bodily Injury and Property Damage - Defendant; Bodily Injury and Property Damage - Plaintiff; Litigation. ***Email:*** hjbevel@ymrlaw.com

REPRESENTATIVE CLIENTS: American Family Ins. Co.; American National Property & Casualty Ins.Co.; Continental Western Ins. Co.; Grinnell Mutual Ins. Co.; Iowa Mutual Ins. Co.; Mutual Fire Ins. Co.; Progressive Ins. Co.; Scottsdale Ins. Co.; State Farm Ins. Co.; TIGF Specialty Ins.; United Fire Ins. Co.; West Bend Ins. Co.; Windsor Group Ins.

McDONALD, BROWN & FAGEN

WAUKEE, IOWA

(See Dallas Center)

General Practice, including: Real Estate, Wills, Trusts, Estate Planning, and Probate, Business and Commercial, Taxation Law and Tax Returns, Family Law, Litigation and Appeals, Debtor and Creditor, Municipal and School Law.

ENGELBRECHT, ACKERMAN & HASSMAN

Established in 1895

123 FIRST STREET, S.E.
P.O. BOX 59
WAVERLY, IOWA 50677
Telephone: 319-352-1148
FAX: 319-352-5603

Clarksville, Iowa Office: 101 South Main Street. Telephone: 319-278-4402.
Tripoli, Iowa Office: 207 South Main Street. Telephone: 319-882-3203.
Readlyn, Iowa Office: 307 Main Street. Telephone: 319-279-3185.

General Civil and Trial Practice in State and Federal Courts. Real Estate, Probate, Negligence and Corporation Law. Trials and Appeals. Corporation, Estate Planning, Insurance, Personal Injury, Workers Compensation and Administrative Law.

MEMBERS OF FIRM

WM. H. ENGELBRECHT, born Waverly, Iowa, March 25, 1927; admitted to bar, 1951, Iowa; 1954, U.S. District Court, Northern District of Iowa; 1992, U.S. Supreme Court. *Education:* Wartburg College; Drake University (J.D., 1951). Delta Theta Phi. Recipient, 1989 Award of Merit, Iowa State Bar Association. Iowa State Delegate, House of Delegates of American Bar Association, 1986-1992. Member, Church Council, Evangelical Lutheran Church in America, 1991-1997. *Member:* Bremer County, Iowa State (Member, Board of Governors, 1978-1984; President, 1983-1984) and American Bar Associations; American College of Trust and Estate Counsel. [With U.S. Navy, 1944-1946]

IVAN J. ACKERMAN, born Allison, Iowa, January 23, 1939; admitted to bar, 1963, Iowa and U.S. District Court, Northern District of Iowa. *Education:* University of Iowa (B.A., with high distinction, 1961; J.D., with distinction, 1963). Order of the Coif; Phi Beta Kappa. Mayor, City of Waverly, 1998—. *Member:* Bremer County, Iowa State (Chairman, Iowa Law Pac, 1999-2003) and American Bar Associations. ***Email:*** ike@wlpnet.net

GAYLEN V. HASSMAN, born Cedar Falls, Iowa, April 20, 1945; admitted to bar, 1974, Iowa. *Education:* University of Northern Iowa (B.A., with highest honors, 1971); University of Iowa (J.D., with distinction, 1974). *Member:* Bremer County, Second Judicial District and Iowa State Bar Associations; Association of Trial Lawyers of Iowa; Christian Legal Society; The Association of Trial Lawyers of America. [With U.S. Army, 1965-1968]

DAVID M. ENGELBRECHT, born Waverly, Iowa, September 6, 1958; admitted to bar, 1982, Iowa; 1992, U.S. Supreme Court. *Education:* Wartburg College (B.A., 1979); Drake University (J.D., 1982). *Member:* Bremer County, Second Judicial District and Iowa State (Chairman, Commercial and Bankruptcy Section, 1990-1991) Bar Associations; Iowa Trial Lawyers Association.

KERSTEN BROWNLEE HENDRICKS, LLP

WEBSTER CITY, IOWA

(See Fort Dodge)

General Practice. Personal Injury Law, Corporation, Insurance Defense, Workers Compensation, Bankruptcy, Banking, Probate and Estate Planning and Taxation Law. Trials.

ANDERSON & TULLY

A PROFESSIONAL CORPORATION

Established in 1973

700 WEST TOWERS

1200 VALLEY WEST DRIVE

WEST DES MOINES, IOWA 50266-1908

Telephone: 515-225-4844

Facsimile: 515-225-7549

Email: lawfirm@andersontullylaw.com

URL: http://www.andersontullylaw.com

General Civil and Trial Practice in State and Federal Courts. Corporation, Securities, Estate Planning, Trusts, Probate, Real Estate, Insurance, Personal Injury, Workers Compensation and Administrative Law.

FREDERICK B. ANDERSON, born Duluth, Minnesota, February 4, 1952; admitted to bar, 1977, Iowa; 1982, U.S. Supreme Court. *Education:* University of Minnesota (B.A., with honors, 1974); Drake University (J.D., with honors, 1977). Order of the Coif. Member, Drake University Law Review, 1976-1977. Associate Editor, Legal Research Service, 1975-1977. *Member:* Association of Trial Lawyers of Iowa; American Board of Trial Advocates; Iowa Academy of Trial Lawyers. ***Email:*** anderson@andersontullylaw.com

ROBERT G. TULLY, born Dubuque, Iowa, September 7, 1955; admitted to bar, 1981, Iowa, U.S. District Courts, Southern and Northern Districts of Iowa and U.S. Court of Appeals, Eighth Circuit; U.S. Supreme Court. *Education:* University of Notre Dame (B.A., 1977); Drake University (J.D., 1981); University of Notre Dame, London, England. Phi Alpha Delta. Order of Barristers. Adjunct Professor, Trial Advocacy, Drake University Law School, 1997. Democratic Candidate for Congress, Second District of Iowa, 1998. Chair, Iowa Democratic Party, 1999-2001. *Member:* Polk County (Board of Directors, 1992-1996), Iowa State (Member, Uniform Jury Instruction Committee) and American Bar Associations; Iowa Trial Lawyers Association (President, 1992-1993; Member, Board of Governors, 1983—; Co-Chair, Continuing Legal Education Committee, 1994-1996); The Association of Trial Lawyers of America (Member, Board of Governors, 1992-2004; State Delegate, 1988-1992; Member, Key Person Committee, 1992-2004). Fellow: Iowa Academy of Trial Lawyers; Blackstone Inn of Court; American Board of Trial Advocates. ***PRACTICE AREAS:*** Litigation; Personal Injury; Trial Law. ***Email:*** tully@andersontullylaw.com

BARNHILL & ASSOCIATES, P.C.

Established in 1991

2100 WESTOWN PARKWAY, SUITE 210

WEST DES MOINES, IOWA 50265

Telephone: 515-223-7230

Facsimile: 515-223-7234

Email: dalfrey@barnhillpclaw.net

URL: http://www.barnhillpc.com

Construction Law, Government Contracts, Public Construction, Business Law, Contracts, Real Estate, Architectural Copyrights, Corporate Law and Litigation, Eminent Domain, Intellectual Property, Labor and Employment Law, Civil Practice, Class Actions, Construction Litigation, Highways, Commercial Law, Litigation, Trusts and Estates Litigation, Zoning, Planning and Land Use, Unfair Competition, Trade Secrets, Collections, Public Bids and Bidding, Tax Litigation, Business Litigation, Shareholder and Business Valuation Litigation, Trademark and Copyright Litigation.

KATHRYN SCHWEIKER BARNHILL, born Des Moines, Iowa; admitted to bar, 1989, Iowa, U.S. Tax Court, U.S. District Court, Northern and Southern Districts of Iowa and U.S. Court of Appeals, 8th Circuit. *Education:* Drake University (B.A., 1970; M.B.A., 1989; J.D., with honors, 1989). Phi Alpha Delta; Order of the Coif. Member, Board of Directors, Iowans for Right to Work. *Member:* Polk County and Iowa State Bar Associations; American Bar Association (Member: Business Law Section; Real Property and Probate Section; Construction Committee, Litigation Section; Environmental Law Committee); Homebuilder's Association of Greater Des Moines (Builder Member; Board of Directors); Associated Builders and Contractors (Board of Directors); Homebuilder's Association of Iowa; Associated General Contractors;. ***LANGUAGES:*** German. ***REPORTED CASES:*** Gerst v. Marshall, 549 NW2d 810 (IA 1996); Iowa Comprehensive Petroleum v. Mobil Oil, 606 NW 2d 359 (IA 2000); In re marriage of Rietz, 585 NW 2d 226 (IA 1998); Temm v. Clement, 574 NW 2d 368 (IA App. 1997); Garden Gate v. Northstar Mfg., 526 NW 2d.305 (IA 1995). ***PRACTICE AREAS:*** Construction Law; Government Contracts; Business Law; Corporate Law and Litigation; Contracts; Construction Litigation; Class Actions; Architectural Copyrights; Highways; Litigation; Trusts and Estates Litigation; Zoning, Planning and Land Use; Environmental; Civil Practice; Real Estate; Commercial Litigation; Tax Litigation; Shareholders Law; Corporate Litigation; Business Valuation; Business Associations Law; Business Development; Business Dissolutions; Commercial Law; Corporate Law; Closely Held Corporations; Corporate Commercial Law; Corporate Contracts; Corporate Dissolutions; Corporate Fiduciary Law; Condominium Development; Land Development. ***Email:*** kathrynbarnhill@barnhillpclaw.net

---

STEVE R. NEWLANDER, admitted to bar, 2004, Iowa; 2005, Arizona. *Education:* Southern Illinois University (B.S., Mechanical Engineering, 1985); University of Nevada Las Vegas (M.B.A., 1996); Drake University Law School (J.D., 2003). Legal Intern, MidAmerican Energy Company, 2001-2003. *Member:* Iowa and American Bar Associations; Energy Bar Association. ***PRACTICE AREAS:*** Construction Law; Architectural Law; Construction and Design Law; Construction and Surety Law; Construction Arbitration; Construction Claims; Construction Contracts; Construction Defects; Copyrights; Copyright Infringement; Copyright Licensing; Copyright Litigation; Copyright Prosecution; Copyright Protection; Copyright Registration; Intellectual Property; Industrial Property; Industrial Models and Designs; Industrial Property Rights; Intellectual Property Arbitration; Government Contracts; Bid Protests; Federal Contracts; Government Construction Contracts; Government Contract Arbitration; Government Contract Cost Accounting; Trademarks; Internet Trademarks; Lanham Act; Trade Dress; Trade Names; Trademark Arbitration; Trademark Infringement; Trademark Licensing; Utility Law; Electric Cooperatives Law; Electric Utilities; Electric Utility Finance; Electric Utility Regulation; Electric Utility Restructuring; Gas Utilities; Gas Utility Regulation; Public Utility Finance; Public Utility Law. ***Email:*** snewlander@barnhillpclaw.net

DEBORAH LEPES, born Pittsburgh, Pennsylvania, February 9, 1973; admitted to bar, 2001, Massachusetts; 2004, Iowa. *Education:* University of Rochester (B.A., Psychology, 1995); Boston College Law School (J.D., 2000). ***PRACTICE AREAS:*** Construction Law; Labor and Employment; Government Contracts; Highways Litigation; Construction Defects; Construction Insurance; Construction Insurance Defense; Construction Liens; Construction Litigation; Mechanics Liens; Bid Protests; Commercial Litigation; Litigation; Civil Litigation; Complex Litigation; Defense Litigation; Federal Civil Litigation; Federal Litigation; Trial Practice.

REPRESENTATIVE CLIENTS: Rottlund Homes of Iowa; Jerry's Homes Inc.; Gethmann Construction, Inc.; Badding Construction; Eco-Tech ,Inc.; Concrete Supply; HPC, LLC; Qualite Sports Lighting, Inc.; Armada/Hoffler; Dahl Heating & A/C; Shriver Construction; Allied Engineering; Trojan Energy Systems; Kohler Plumbing; Edward Jones; Artistic Waste Services, Inc.; Simplex/Grinnell, Inc.; Meisner Electric, Inc..

BROWN, WINICK, GRAVES, GROSS, BASKERVILLE AND SCHOENEBAUM, P.L.C.

REGENCY WEST 5

4500 WESTOWN PARKWAY, SUITE 277

WEST DES MOINES, IOWA 50266-6717

Telephone: 515-242-2400

Fax: 515-242-2448

Email: bwg@ialawyers.com

URL: http://www.ialawyers.com

Des Moines, Iowa Office: 666 Grand Avenue, Suite 2000, 50309-2510.
Pella, Iowa Office: 616 Franklin Place, 50219. Telephone: 641-628-4513. Fax: 641-628-8494.

FIRM PROFILE: Brown, Winick, Graves, Gross, Baskerville and Schoenebaum, P.L.C. is a major law firm with offices in Des Moines, West Des Moines, and Pella, Iowa. The firm originated as a tax law specialty firm in downtown Des Moines in 1951. Today the firm offers a broad range of legal services to clients throughout Iowa, regionally and nationally. The firm serves as counsel to a wide variety of service, manufacturing and commercial businesses and professionals. The firm's mission is to attract, retain and develop clients by providing effective and innovative solutions. We will provide a comprehensive range of legal services primarily to businesses, as well as to individuals in need of high quality legal services, inside and outside the State of Iowa.

(For complete biographical data on all firm personnel, see professional biographies at Des Moines, Iowa).

CUTLER LAW FIRM, P.C.

1307 50TH STREET

WEST DES MOINES, IOWA 50266

Telephone: 515-223-6600

FAX: 515-223-6787

Email: mkb@cutlerfirm.com

URL: http://www.lawyers.com/cutlerfirm

FIRM PROFILE: General Practice including but not limited to Personal Injury, Trial Law, Worker's Compensation, Professional Liability and Product Liability.

CHARLES E. CUTLER, born Des Moines, Iowa, April 2, 1956; admitted to bar, 1981, Iowa. *Education:* St. Olaf College; University of Iowa (B.S., 1978; J.D., 1981). *Member:* Polk County, Iowa State (Member, Alternative Dispute Resolution Committee, 1987-1988, Litigation Section and Workers' Compensation Section) and American (Member, Tort and Insurance Sections) Bar Associations; Iowa Association of Workers' Compensation Lawyers (Board of Governors, 1999—); Defense Research Institute; Iowa Defense Counsel Association (Chair, Workers' Compensation Committee, 2001-2003); Iowa Workers' Compensation Commissioner's Advisory Committee, 1996-1998. ***Email:*** ccutler@cutlerfirm.com

BRUCE E. JOHNSON, born Des Moines, Iowa, May 13, 1947; admitted to bar, 1973, Iowa; 1974, U.S. Court of Appeals, Eighth Circuit; 1975, U.S. District Court, Southern District of Iowa; 1977, U.S. District Court, Northern District of Iowa; 1981, U.S. Supreme Court; 1995, U.S. District Court, District of Nebraska; 1998, Federal Circuit. *Education:* Morningside College, University of Iowa (B.A., 1969); University of Iowa (J.D., with high distinction, 1973). Order of the Coif. Recipient, Merrit Law Scholarship. *Member:* Polk County and Iowa State Bar Associations; National Association of Railroad Trial Counsel; Iowa Defense Counsel Association; Defense Research Institute. ***PRACTICE AREAS:*** Trial Practice; Appeals. ***Email:*** bej@cutlerfirm.com

M. KATHLEEN BROWN, born Sioux City, Iowa, May 4, 1973; admitted to bar, 1999, Iowa. *Education:* Saint Mary's College of Notre Dame (B.A., 1995); Drake University (J.D., with honors, 1999). *Member:* Polk County, Iowa State (Member, Sections on: Family and Juvenile Law, Labor and Employment Law, Workers' Compensation Law) and American Bar Associations; Iowa Association of Workers' Compensation Lawyers. ***Email:*** mkb@cutlerfirm.com

(This Listing Continued)

JACK H. PENNINGTON, born Ankeny, Iowa, January 6, 1978; admitted to bar, 2003, Iowa. *Education:* University of Iowa (B.A., 2000); Creighton University (J.D., 2003; M.S., 2003). *Member:* Polk County, Iowa State and American Bar Associations. ***Email:*** jhp@cutlerfirm.com

REPRESENTATIVE CLIENTS: Frito-Lay; Qwest, R.R. Donnelley; Fort Dodge Animal Health; Seedorff Masonry, Inc.; Cigna/ACE USA; Bituminous Insurance Companies; Cannon Cochran Management Services; Gallagher Bassett Services; Zurich North America; CNA/RSKCo.; Iowa Mutual Insurance Company; Sedgwick CMS; Risk Administration Services; Union Pacific Railroad Company; Duetsche Bank Securities, Inc.

DAVIS, BROWN, KOEHN, SHORS & ROBERTS, P.C.

4201 WESTOWN PARKWAY, SUITE 300
WEST DES MOINES, IOWA 50266
Telephone: 515-288-2500
Fax: 515-246-7997

Des Moines, Iowa Office: The Financial Center, 666 Walnut Street, Suite 2500, 50309-3993. Telephone: 515-288-2500. Facsimile: 515-243-0654.

Administrative, Agricultural, Alternative Dispute Resolution, Antitrust and Trade Regulation, Appellate Practice, Bankruptcy, Banks and Banking, Biotechnology, Business Law, Civil, Class Actions, Commercial, Commercial Real Estate, Communications and Media, Complex and Multi-District Litigation, Computers and Software, Constitutional, Construction, Consumer, Contracts, Copyrights, Corporate, Debtor and Creditor, Education, Employee Benefits, Energy, Environmental, Equipment Finance and Leasing, Family, Finance, Franchises and Franchising, Government, Government Contracts, Guardianship and Conservatorship, Health Care, Hospital Law, Human and Civil Rights, Immigration and Naturalization, Insurance, Insurance Defense, Intellectual Property, International Law, International Trade, Labor and Employment, Leases and Leasing, Legal Ethics and Professional Responsibility, Libel, Slander and Defamation, Litigation, Media Law, Medical Malpractice, Mergers, Acquisitions and Divestitures, Municipal Law, Natural Resources, Nonprofit and Charitable Organizations, Partnership, Patents, Personal Injury, Probate. Products Liability, Professional Liability, Property, Public Finance, Real Estate, Regulatory, Securities, Taxation, Technology and Science, Torts, Trade and Professional Associations, Trade Secrets, Trademarks, Transportation, Trusts and Estates, Utilities, Wills, Workers Compensation, Zoning, Planning and Land Use.

(For Complete biographical data on firm personnel please see biographical listing at Des Moines, Iowa)

GONZALEZ, SAGGIO & HARLAN, L.L.P.

1501 42ND STREET, SUITE 465
WEST DES MOINES, IOWA 50266
Telephone: 515-453-8509
Fax: 515-267-1408
Email: main@gshllp.com
URL: http://www.gshllp.com

Milwaukee, Wisconsin Office: 225 East Michigan, 4th Floor, 53202. Telephone: 414-277-8500. Fax: 414-277-8521.
Indianapolis, Indiana Office: 201 North Illinois Street, Suite 1900, 46204. Telephone: 317-686-9800. Fax: 317-686-9821.
Cincinnati, Ohio Office: Carew Tower, 441 Vine Street, Suite 3615, 45202. Telephone: 513-651-3456. Fax: 513-651-3446.
Chicago, Illinois Office: 208 LaSalle Street, Suite 1460, 60604. Telephone: 312-236-0475. Facsimile: 312-236-1750.

Business and Corporate Law, Civil Litigation, Insurance Defense Law, Equal Opportunities and Employment, School Law, Municipal Finance, Business and Commercial Litigation, Real Estate, Construction, Condemnation Law, Environmental, Taxation, Utilities Law, Trials and Appeals, Government Relations.

FIRM PROFILE: Gonzalez, Saggio & Harlan, L.L.P. is one of the fastest growing law firms in the Midwest. This growth is a reflection of the firm's devotion to quality, efficiency and frank communication in servicing client needs. Furthermore, as a minority-owned law firm, we believe that our diverse backgrounds add value to those clients wanting to better serve a changing and dynamic environment.

KERRIE M. MURPHY, born Watertown, South Dakota, May 16, 1964; admitted to bar, 1991, Iowa; 1992, U.S. District Court, Northern District of Iowa; 1993, U.S. District Court, Southern District of Iowa. *Education:* University of Iowa (B.A., 1986); Drake University (J.D., 1991). *Member:* Iowa State Bar Association (Member, Women and Minority Committee); Polk County Women Attorneys; Iowa Organization of Women Attorneys; Society for Human Resources Management, Central Iowa Chapter; Blackstone Inn of Court. ***PRACTICE AREAS:*** Defense Litigation; Workers Compensation; Employment Law. ***Email:*** kerrie_plummer@gshllp.com

LORA L. McCOLLOM, born Des Moines, Iowa, July 12, 1968; admitted to bar, 1993, Iowa; 1994, U.S. District Court, Southern District of Iowa; 1995, U.S. District Court, Northern District of Iowa; 2003, U.S. Court of Appeals, Eighth Circuit. *Education:* Creighton University (B.A., 1990; J.D., 1993). Member: Blackstone Inn of Court, Polk County Women Attorneys; American Academy of ADR Attorneys. *Member:* Polk County, Iowa State and American Bar Associations. ***PRACTICE AREAS:*** Litigation; Family Law; Employment Law. ***Email:*** lora_mccollom@gshllp.com

REPRESENTATIVE CLIENTS: Accenture; Alliant Energy; Bear, Stears & Co.; Chubb Insurance Company; City of Milwaukee; CNH Global N.V.; Darden Restaurants, Inc.; Denny's; Eastman Kodak Company; E.I. du Pont de Nemours and Company; Family Dollar Stores, Inc.; Forest County Potawatomi Community; Harley-Davidson Motor Company; Kohl's Corporation; Luxottica Group; Menard, Inc.; Midwest Airlines; PepsiAmericas, Inc.; Starwood Hotels & Resorts Worldwide, Inc.; State of Wisconsin; Target Corporation; Time Warner Cable; We Energies; Wisconsin Housing and Economic Development Authority (WHEDA); Zale Corporation.

(For complete biographical data on all personnel, see Professional Biographies at Milwaukee, Wisconsin)

HUDSON, MALLANEY & SHINDLER, P.C.

5015 GRAND RIDGE DRIVE, SUITE 100
WEST DES MOINES, IOWA 50265
Telephone: 515-223-4567
Fax: 515-223-8887
Email: lawyers@hudsonlaw.net
URL: http://www.hudsonlaw.net

General Civil Trial, Civil, Criminal, Commercial Litigation and Appellate Practice in all Courts, Commercial, Corporation, Family Law, Mediation, Workers Compensation, Real Estate, Taxation, Personal Injury, Bankruptcy, Probate, Administrative Law and Employment Law.

ROGER J. HUDSON, born Des Moines, Iowa, February 13, 1943; admitted to bar, 1972, Iowa. *Education:* Drake University (B.A., 1969; J.D., 1972). Delta Theta Phi. Lecturer of Law, Trial Practice: Negotiation and Settlement, Drake University Law School, 1983-1985. Member, Board of Counselors, Drake University Law School, 1976-1985. *Member:* Polk County (Secretary, 1988-1989), Iowa State and American Bar Associations; Association of Trial Lawyers of Iowa; The Association of Trial Lawyers of America. ***PRACTICE AREAS:*** Family Law; Personal Injury; Employment Law; Real Estate; Workers Compensation. ***Email:*** RHudson@hudsonlaw.net

MICHAEL P. MALLANEY, born Kankakee, Illinois, December 17, 1949; admitted to bar, 1980, Iowa; U.S. District Court, Southern and Northern Districts of Iowa; U.S. Court of Appeals, Eighth Circuit. *Education:* Eastern Illinois University (B.S., 1972; M.A., 1975); Drake University (J.D., with honors, 1979). Phi Alpha Delta. Recipient, American Jurisprudence Awards in Agency Partnership and Administrative Law. Member, Drake Law Review, 1978-1979. Author: Casenote, Drake Law Review, Vol. 27, No. 4, 1978. Law Clerk to Bankruptcy Judge Richard F. Stageman, U.S. Bankruptcy Court, Southern District of Iowa, 1980-1982. *Member:* Polk County, Iowa State and American Bar Associations. ***PRACTICE AREAS:*** Bankruptcy; Commercial Litigation. ***Email:*** MPMallaney@hudsonlaw.net

STEVEN H. SHINDLER, born Yankton, South Dakota, November 26, 1954; admitted to bar, 1983, Missouri; 1984, Nebraska and Iowa. *Education:* Drake University (B.A., 1977); California Western School of Law (J.D., 1982). Order of Barristers. Author: "The Speed of Trial Timeclock," Criminal Law Techniques, Matthew Bender, 1992. Legal Counsel, Jackson County, Kansas City, Missouri, 1983. Executive Assistant to Chief Justice W.W. Reynoldson, Iowa Supreme Court, 1983-1984. *Member:* Polk County, Iowa State, Nebraska State and American Bar Associations; The Missouri Bar. ***PRACTICE AREAS:*** Family Law; Personal Injury. ***Email:*** Shin@hudsonlaw.net

R. J. HUDSON, II, born Des Moines, Iowa, May 6, 1966; admitted to bar, 1993, Iowa and U.S. District Court, Northern and Southern Districts of Iowa; 1994, U.S. Court of Appeals, Eighth Circuit. *Education:* University of Iowa (B.S., 1988); Drake University (J.D., with honors, 1993). Delta Theta Phi. Barrister: American Inns of Court; Blackstone Inn of Court. *Member:* Polk County, Iowa State and American Bar Associations; Iowa Trial Lawyers Association; The Association of Trial Lawyers of America; National Association of Criminal Defense Lawyers. ***PRACTICE AREAS:*** Criminal Law; Family Law; Personal Injury. ***Email:*** RHuds@hudsonlaw.net

J. BARTON GOPLERUD, born Iowa City, Iowa, October 9, 1958; admitted to bar, 1990, Iowa and U.S. District Court, Northern and Southern Districts of Iowa. *Education:* University of Iowa (B.A., 1982); Drake University (J.D., 1990). Order of the Coif; Order of the Barristers. Editor, Drake Law Review. Author: "Liability of Schools and Coaches: The Current Status of Sovereign Immunity and Assumption of the Risk," 39 Drake Law Review 759. Adjunct Professor of Law, Drake Law School, 1993-present. Legal Negotiations, Pre-Trial Advocacy, Mediation. *Member:* Iowa State and American Bar Associations; The Association of Trial Lawyers of America; Iowa Trial Lawyers Association. ***PRACTICE AREAS:*** Personal Injury; Insurance; Mediation. ***Email:*** JBGoplerud@hudsonlaw.net

ANDREW B. HOWIE, born Elgin, Illinois, April 26, 1971; admitted to bar, 1996, Iowa and U.S. District Court, Northern and Southern Districts of Iowa; U.S. Court of Appeals, Eighth Circuit; 1999, U.S. Supreme Court. *Education:* Wartburg College (B.A., 1993); University of Iowa (J.D., with distinction, 1996). Member, Moot Court Board. Law Clerk, Iowa Judicial District 8(B), 1996-1997. *Member:* Polk County, Iowa State and American Bar Associations. ***PRACTICE AREAS:*** Family Law; Commercial Litigation; Appellate Practice. ***Email:*** AHowie@hudsonlaw.net

RYAN EDWARD WEESE, born Mason City, Iowa, May 2, 1976; admitted to bar, 2001, Iowa, U.S. District Court, Northern and Southern Districts of Iowa and U.S Court of Appeals. *Education:* Drake University (B.S.A., magna cum laude, 1998; J.D., 2001). Delta Theta Phi. *Member:* Polk County, Iowa State and American Bar Associations; Iowa Trial Lawyers Association; American Trial lawyers Association. ***PRACTICE AREAS:*** Family Law; Bankruptcy; Criminal Defense; Employment Law. ***Email:*** rweese@hudsonlaw.net

BRYAN S. WITHERWAX, born Pawtucket, Rhode Island, May 6, 1971; admitted to bar, 2004, Iowa. *Education:* University of Iowa (B.S., 1993); Iowa State University (M.S., 2001); Drake University (J.D., 2003). ***PRACTICE AREAS:*** Business Organization; Business Development; Real Estate Transfers; Estate Planning; Probate; Bankruptcy. ***Email:*** bwitherwax@hudsonlaw.net

OF COUNSEL

RAY A. FENTON, born Buckingham, Iowa, August 13, 1930; admitted to bar, 1957, Iowa. *Education:* Ohio State; Drake University (LL.B., 1957). Polk County Attorney, 1965-

(This Listing Continued)

HUDSON, MALLANEY & SHINDLER, P.C., West Des Moines—Continued

1977. Iowa District Court Judge, 1977-1998. [Sgt., U.S. Air Force, 1949-1952]. ***PRACTICE AREAS:*** Mediation; General Trial; Criminal Law. ***Email:*** RFenton@hudsonlaw.net

REPRESENTATIVE CLIENTS: Ryko Manufacturing Co.; Kent Packaging & Paper, Inc.; System Parking, Inc.; Teikyo University Foundation; Firstar Bank Iowa, N.A.; Iowa League Corporate Central Union; P.J. Iowa, Inc.; Papa John's Pizza; Secure Care, Inc.; Stewart Title Guaranty, Inc.; Safetrans; Des Moines Chrysler/Plymouth; First Financial Bank, fsb; Champion Crane Services, Inc.; Public Mini-Storage, Ltd; Mid-Plains Insurance Co.

KREAMER LAW FIRM, P.C.

Established in 2005

6600 WESTOWN PARKWAY, SUITE 260
WEST DES MOINES, IOWA 50266
Telephone: 515-727-0900
Fax: 515-727-0939
Email: sikjdcpa@kreamerlaw.com
URL: http://www.kreamerlaw.com

Business Law, Corporate, Mergers and Acquisitions, Estate Planning, Wills, Trusts and Estates, Probate.

SAMUEL I. KREAMER, C.P.A., born Des Moines, Iowa, July 28, 1956; admitted to bar, 1981, Iowa; U.S. District Court, Southern District of Iowa; U.S. Tax Court; U.S. Court of Appeals, 8th Circuit; 1995, U.S. District Court, Northern District of Iowa. *Education:* University of Southern California (B.S., 1978); Drake University (J.D., 1981). Certified Public Accountant, Iowa, 1980. Commissioner, West Des Moines Planning and Zoning Commission, 1998—. *Member:* Polk County and Iowa (Member, Sections on: Business Law; Probate and Trust Law) Bar Associations; Iowa Society of Certified Public Accountants. ***PRACTICE AREAS:*** Business Law; Estate Planning; Wills; Probate; Corporate Law; Mergers and Acquisitions; Trusts and Estates. ***Email:*** sikjdcpa@kreamerlaw.com

DAVID J. HELLSTERN, born Mechanicsville, Iowa, February, 1978; admitted to bar, 2005, Iowa. *Education:* University of Iowa (B.B.A., 2000); Drake University Law School (J.D., 2004). *Member:* Polk County and Iowa State Bar Associations; American Bar Association. ***Email:*** dhellstern@kreamerlaw.com

LAMARCA & LANDRY, P.C.

WEST DES MOINES, IOWA

(See Des Moines)

Trial Practice in State and Federal Courts. Aviation Law, Commercial Litigation, Personal Injury, Wrongful Death, Medical Malpractice, Legal Malpractice, Workers Compensation, Products Liability.

LEITNER LAW OFFICE

WEST TOWERS
SUITE 302
1200 VALLEY WEST DRIVE
WEST DES MOINES, IOWA 50266
Telephone: 515-252-0777
Fax: 515-252-0798
Email: dleitnerlaw@cs.com
URL: http://www.leitnerlawfirm.com

General Civil Trial Practice. Insurance and Personal Injury Law.

DAVID L. LEITNER, born Brooklyn, New York, February 20, 1956; admitted to bar, 1979, Iowa, U.S. District Court, Northern and Southern Districts of Iowa and U.S. Court of Appeals, Seventh Circuit; 1980, U.S. District Court, Central District of Illinois and U.S. Court of Appeals, Eighth Circuit; 1994, U.S. Supreme Court; 2000, Nebraska. *Education:* State University of New York, College at Brockport; State University of New York at Stony Brook (B.A., History, 1976); University of Iowa College of Law (J.D., 1979). Chartered Property Casualty Underwriter (CPCU) 1987. Editor, Tort and Insurance Law Journal, 1989-1993. Author: "Maintaining a Case Processing System," in Iowa Advanced Litigation Skills for Paralegals, Published by HalfMoon (2001); Law and Practice of Insurance Coverage, (Editor) published by West Publishing Company (2000); "Interpretation of Insurance Policies," Presented at the Annual Meeting of the American Bar Association, Atlanta, Georgia, August 7, 1999; Attorney's Guide to Juris, Published by American Bar Association (1999); Attorney's Guide to CaseMap, Published by American Bar Association (1999); Employment Discrimination Litigation, Published by American Bar Association (1999); Insurance Coverage Law in Iowa, Published by National Business Institute (1997); Tobacco Litigation and Insurance (Editor), Published by American Bar Association (1997); Liability Issues in Managed Care (Editor), Publishes by American Bar Association (1997); Recurring Issues in Insurance Disputes, Published by American Bar Association (1996); Bad Faith Litigation in Iowa, Published by National Business Institute (1995); Truck Accident Litigation and Insurance (Editor), Published by Americna Bar Association (1994); "Underinsured Motorist Coverage," in No Fault and Uninsured Motorist Automobile Insurance, Published by Matthew Bender and Company (1992); "Insurance Coverage 1989," F.I.C.C. Update (August, 1989); "Enforcing the Consumer's Reasonable Expectations in Interpreting Insurance Contracts: A Doctrine in Search of Coherent Definition," 38 Federation of Insurance and Corporate Counsel Quarterly (1988); "Pedestrians," in Automobile Accident Law and Practice, Published by Matthew Bender and Company (1988); "A Constitutional Assessment of Current Punitive Damages Law and Practice," presented at the Annual Meeting of the Tort and Insurance Practice Section of the American Bar Association, Washington, D.C., May 15, 1987. Reprinted at 38 Federation of Insurance and Corporate Counsel Quarterly 119-136 (1988); "Punitive Damages and First Party Automobile Liability Insurance Coverages," 54 Defense Counsel Journal 112-119 (1987); "Negligent Entrustment of a Motor Vehicle and the Homeowner's Policy," 35 Federation of Insurance Counsel Quarterly 335-350 (1985); "Laetrile and the Law," 5 Oklahoma City University Law Review 11-35 (1979); "Belligerent Recognition in International Law: Eritrea: A Case Study," 13 Towson State Journal of International Affairs 77-96 (1979). Listed in: Who's Who in American Law; Who's Who in Emerging Leaders in America; Who's Who in the Midwest; Who's Who in America; Who's Who in The World. *Member:* Iowa State, Nebraska State and American (Member, Tort, Trial and Insurance Practice Section) Bar Associations; Iowa Trial Lawyers Association; Association of Trial Lawyers of America. ***PRACTICE AREAS:*** Personal Injury; Legal Malpractice; Trusts and Estates; Civil Litigation; Business Litigation; Automobile Accidents and Injuries; Real Estate.

MARCUCCI & CONGER, P.L.C.

701 WEST TOWERS
1200 VALLEY WEST DRIVE
WEST DES MOINES, IOWA 50266
Telephone: 515-440-2400
Fax: 515-440-2408

General Civil Trial Practice, Commercial Litigation, Negligence, Personal Injury.

LAWRENCE L. MARCUCCI, born Chicago, Illinois, March 1, 1950; admitted to bar, 1975, Iowa and U.S. District Court, Northern and Southern Districts of Iowa; 1976, U.S. Court of Appeals, Eighth Circuit; 1981, U.S. Court of Appeals, Ninth Circuit; 1983, U.S. Tax Court, U.S. District Court, District of Arizona, U.S. District Court, Eastern District of Wisconsin, U.S. District Court, Eastern District of Michigan and U.S. District Court, District of Nebraska; 1994, U.S. Court of Appeals, Seventh Circuit. *Education:* College of the Holy Cross (A.B., 1972); Drake University (J.D., 1975). Member, Board of Trustees of Legal Aid Society of Polk County, 1986—. *Member:* Polk County (President, 1989-1990), Iowa State (Member: Board of Governors, 1990-1992; Section on Litigation and Corporation Law) and American (Member, Sections on: Litigation; Corporation, Banking and Business Law) Bar Associations; Association of Trial Lawyers of Iowa (Member, Board of Governors, 1983-1989; Chairman, Business Torts Committee, 1989-1991). ***PRACTICE AREAS:*** Civil Trial Practice. ***Email:*** lmarcucci@mandc-law.com

JOHN C. CONGER, born Des Moines, Iowa, August 3, 1953; admitted to bar, 1979, Iowa; 1981, U.S. District Court, Southern District of Iowa; 1984, U.S. District Court, Northern District of Iowa and U.S. Court of Appeals, Eighth Circuit; 1994, U.S. Court of Federal Claims. *Education:* University of Iowa (B.S., 1975); Drake University (J.D., 1979). Law Clerk, U.S. District Court, Southern District of Iowa, 1979-1981. *Member:* Polk County, Iowa State and American Bar Associations; Association of Trial Lawyers of Iowa; The Association of Trial Lawyers of America. ***PRACTICE AREAS:*** Civil Trial Practice. ***Email:*** jconger@mandc-law.com

MCCARTHY & HAMROCK, P.C.

1200 VALLEY WEST DRIVE, SUITE 400
WEST DES MOINES, IOWA 50266
Telephone: 515-279-9700
Fax: 515-279-8355
Email: tim@mccarthyandhamrock.com
Email: aaron@mccarthyhamrock.com
URL: http://www.mccarthyhamrock.com

Criminal Law, Personal Injury, Driving While Intoxicated, Drug Crimes, Juvenile Criminal Law, Parole and Probation, Traffic Violations, Automobile Accidents, Slip and Fall, Wrongful Death.

TIMOTHY McCARTHY II, born Cedar Rapids, Iowa, July 8, 1958; admitted to bar, 1983, Iowa; 1986, U.S. District Court, Northern and Southern Districts of Iowa; 1987, U.S. Court of Appeals, Eighth Circuit; 1996, U.S. Supreme Court. *Education:* University of Kansas; Drake University (B.A., 1980; J.D., 1983). Phi Alpha Delta. Faculty Member Drake University Law School Trial Advocacy Institute. *Member:* Polk County, Iowa State and American Bar Associations; National Association of Criminal Defense Lawyers; NORML Legal Committee; Iowa Association of Criminal Defense Lawyers. ***PRACTICE AREAS:*** Criminal Law; Federal Criminal Law. ***Email:*** tim@mccarthyandhamrock.com

AARON D. HAMROCK, born Kansas City, Missouri, 1970; admitted to bar, 1995, Iowa, U.S. District Court, Southern and Northern Districts of Iowa and Iowa Supreme Court; 2000, U.S. Court of Appeals, Eighth Circuit. *Education:* Central College (B.A., 1992); Drake University (J.D., 1994). *Member:* Polk County and American (Member, Litigation Section) Bar Associations; Iowa Trial Lawyers Association; National Association of Criminal Defense Lawyers. ***PRACTICE AREAS:*** Criminal Law; Personal Injury. ***Email:*** aaron@mccarthyandhamrock.com

MCENROE, GOTSDINER, BREWER, BURDETTE & STEINBACH, P.C.

WESTOWN BUSINESS CENTER I
1701 48TH STREET, SUITE 100
WEST DES MOINES, IOWA 50266-6723
Telephone: 515-267-9000
FAX: 515-267-8100

General Practice. Corporate, Real Estate, Bankruptcy, Commercial Collection, Personal Injury, Criminal, Probate, Domestic Relations, Transportation and Products Liability Law. Litigation in all Courts.

(This Listing Continued)

WILLIAM G. BREWER, born Dubuque, Iowa, May 12, 1957; admitted to bar, 1982, Iowa; 1985, U.S. District Court, Southern District of Iowa; 1987, U.S. Court of Appeals, Eighth Circuit; 1989, U.S. District Court, Northern District of Iowa. *Education:* University of Iowa (B.B.A., 1979); Drake University (J.D., 1982). Panel Attorney, Federal Criminal Justice Act. Assistant County Attorney, Des Moines, 1983-1985. *Member:* Polk County, Iowa State and American Bar Associations; Iowa Trial Lawyers Association; American Trial Lawyers Association. ***Email:*** brewer@mcenroelaw.com

MICHAEL J. BURDETTE, born Waterloo, Iowa, April 24, 1949; admitted to bar, 1975, Iowa; 1980, U.S. District Court, Southern District of Iowa; 1991, U.S. Court of Appeals, Eighth Circuit. *Education:* Iowa State University (B.S., 1971); University of Arkansas (J.D., 1974). Delta Theta Phi. Adjunct Lecturer in Business Law, Simpson College, Indianola, Iowa, 1986-1987. Director, Wage and Work Place Standards Division, Iowa Bureau of Labor, 1976-1982. Corporations Division Director and Legal Counsel, Iowa Secretary of State, 1982-1987. Panel Attorney, Federal Criminal Justice Court. *Member:* Polk County, Warren County and Iowa State (Co-Chair, Fall Traveling Seminar Committee) Bar Associations; National Association of Criminal Defense Lawyers; Iowa Association of Criminal Defense Lawyers; Mentor Iowa (Member, Board of Directors). ***Email:*** mburdette@mcenroelaw.com

MURRAY B. GOTSDINER, born Des Moines, Iowa, January 2, 1953; admitted to bar, 1980, Iowa and U.S. District Court, Northern and Southern Districts of Iowa; 1982, U.S. Court of Appeals, Eighth Circuit; 1983, U.S. Supreme Court; 1989, Texas. *Education:* Drake University (B.A., 1975; J.D., 1979). Phi Alpha Delta. *Member:* Polk County and Iowa State (Member, Sections on: Business Law, Commercial and Bankruptcy Law; Trade Regulations; Real Estate and Title Law) Bar Associations; State Bar of Texas (Member, Sections on: Business Law; Consumer Law). ***Email:*** mgotsdiner@mcenroelaw.com

MICHAEL L. McENROE, born Fort Dodge, Iowa, July 31, 1951; admitted to bar, 1976, Illinois; 1977, Iowa and U.S. District Court, Northern District of Iowa; 1988, U.S. District Court, Southern District of Iowa; 1992, U.S. Supreme Court. *Education:* Loras College (B.A., magna cum laude, 1973); Creighton University (J.D., 1976). Delta Epsilon Sigma. Judicial Magistrate, Kossuth County, 1981-1989. Faculty Member, NBI Real Estate Law Seminar, 1991. *Member:* Polk County, Illinois State and Iowa State (Member: Agricultural Law Committee, 1986-1990; Executive Council, Young Lawyers Section, 1986-1988; General Practice Section, 2000-2003; Litigation Section; Real Estate and Title Law Section; Probate and Trust Law Section) Bar Associations; Iowa Trial Lawyers Association; Blackstone Inn of Court. ***Email:*** mmcenroe@mcenroelaw.com

FRANK STEINBACH, III, born Des Moines, Iowa, March 16, 1964; admitted to bar, 1989, Iowa and U.S. District Court, Southern District of Iowa; 1991, U.S. Court of Appeals, Eighth Circuit and U.S. Supreme Court. *Education:* Iowa State University (B.S., 1986); Drake University (J.D., 1989). *Member:* Polk County, Dallas County and Iowa State (Member, Sections on: Criminal; Family; Juvenile) Bar Associations. ***Email:*** FSteinbach@mcenroelaw.com

---

PATRICK A. HENRICHSEN, born Neligh, Nebraska, August 22, 1970; admitted to bar, 2000, Iowa; 2001, U.S. District Court, Northern and Southern Districts of Iowa, U.S. Court of Appeals, Eighth Circuit and U.S. Tax Court. *Education:* Iowa State University (B.B.A., Accounting, 1993); University of Iowa (J.D., 2000). Certified Public Accountant, Iowa, 2000. Charter Property and Casualty Underwriter, 1997. *Member:* Iowa State Bar Association; Iowa State Bar Review School, Inc. (Treasurer); Iowa Society of Certified Public Accountants. ***Email:*** PHenrichsen@mcenroelaw.com

WILLIAM J. SCHADLE, born Dubuque, Iowa, August 4, 1932; admitted to bar, 1984, Iowa. *Education:* University of Iowa (B.A., 1959); Drake University (J.D., 1984). *Member:* Iowa State Bar Association. [U.S. Navy, 1952-1956]. ***PRACTICE AREAS:*** General Practice.

REPRESENTATIVE CLIENTS: Great Plains Transportation Services Inc.; Algona Realty; Gateway Management Associates; Iowa Professional Firefighters; Aqua-Tech Energy Corp.; A-Tec Recycling; All Lines of Iowa Insurance Agency; Industrial Refrigeration Services, Inc.; Palmer Mortgage Group, Inc.; Shaw Industries, Inc.; Merit Resources, Inc.; Independent Mortgage, L.C.; Essential Mortgage Inc.; Active Alarm Services, Inc.; Vodaci Technologies, Inc.; Anubus Technologies, Inc.; Circle Wind Corp.; BALS Eateries, Inc. d/b/a The Hungry Hobo; D & L Medical Supplies, Inc.; McIntire Electric, Inc.; Hockmuth Concrete Services, Inc.; The Coffee Merchant, Inc.; Group Pizza, Inc. d/b/a Felix & Oscars; Gold Key Mortgage; Arthur Andrews Properties LLC; Westbank; Steven R. Gates & Associates Ltd.; Reynolds General Construction, Inc.
REFERENCES: Bankers Trust Company; Westbank.

MORAIN & PUGH, P.L.C.

Established in 1943

5400 UNIVERSITY AVENUE
WEST DES MOINES, IOWA 50266
Telephone: 515-225-5410
Fax: 515-225-4686

General Practice, Corporation, Insurance, Administrative, Probate, Real Estate, Litigation and Appeals in Federal and State Courts.

STEPHEN M. MORAIN, born Jefferson, Iowa, September 12, 1945; admitted to bar, 1971, Iowa. *Education:* University of Iowa (B.A., 1968; J.D., with distinction, 1971). Omicron Delta Kappa, Phi Delta Phi. Articles Editor, Iowa Law Review, 1970-1971. General Counsel, Iowa Farm Bureau Federation and Affiliated Companies, 1982—. Assistant Commerce Counsel, Iowa State Commerce Commission, 1971. Chair, Iowa Life and Health Insurance Guarantee Association, 1998—. *Member:* Polk County, Iowa State (Member, Committee on Bar Review, Young Lawyers Section, 1976-1980; Secretary, 1977-1978; Chair, 1978-1979; Member, Executive Council, 1978-1981; Chair, Corporate Counsel Section, 1992-1994; Committee on Agricultural Law, 1984-1987, 1991-1995; Committee on Corporations and Business Law, 1988-1992) and American Bar Associations; Iowa Defense Counsel Association; Association of Corporate Counsel; Association of Life Insurance Counsel; American Council of Life Insurance (Member, Legal Section). ***Email:*** smorain@fbfs.com

(This Listing Continued)

JAMES A. PUGH, born Davenport, Iowa, April 21, 1952; admitted to bar, 1977, Iowa. *Education:* Iowa State University (B.S., 1974); Creighton University (J.D., 1977). Assistant General Counsel, Iowa Farm Bureau Federation and Affiliated Companies, 1983—. *Member:* Polk County, Iowa State and American Bar Associations; Iowa Defense Counsel Association (Member, Board of Directors, 1993—; Treasurer, 1996-2003); International Association of Arson Investigators; Defense Research Institute. ***Email:*** jpugh@fbfs.com

ROBERT A. SIMONS, born Sioux Falls, South Dakota, December 24, 1945; admitted to bar, 1973, Iowa. *Education:* Augustana College (B.A., 1967); University of Minnesota (J.D., 1972). Assistant General Counsel, Securities, Iowa Farm Bureau Federation and Affiliated Companies, 1994—. *Member:* Polk County, Iowa State and American (Member, Section of Business Law) Bar Associations; Association of Corporate Counsel (Member, Board of Directors, 1998— and President, 2000-2004, Iowa Chapter). ***Email:*** bsimons@fbfs.com

DAVID A. McNEILL, born Iowa Falls, Iowa, September 14, 1954; admitted to bar, 1985, Iowa and Missouri. *Education:* Simpson College (B.A., 1979); Drake University (J.D., with honors, 1985). Author: Note, 33 Drake Law Review 929, 1983-1984; Casenote, 33 Drake Law Review 727, 1983-1984. Chartered Life Underwriter (CLU). Assistant General Counsel, Iowa Farm Bureau Federation and Affiliated Companies, 1989—. *Member:* Polk County, Iowa State and American Bar Associations; The Missouri Bar; Association of Corporate Counsel. ***Email:*** dmcneill@fbfs.com

ANGELA T. ALTHOFF, born Washington, D.C., June 26, 1961; admitted to bar, 1987, Iowa. *Education:* University of Iowa (B.A., 1983); Drake University (J.D., 1987). Order of the Barristers. Recipient: International Academy of Trial Attorneys Outstanding Trial Attorney Award. Senior Counsel, Iowa Farm Bureau Federation and Affiliated Companies, 1989—. Adjunct Professor, Drake Law School. Member, Workers' Compensation Advisory Committee. *Member:* Polk County, Iowa State and American Bar Associations; Iowa Defense Counsel Association. Fellow, Iowa State Bar Foundation. ***Email:*** aalthoff@fbfs.com

LORI K. GEADELMANN, born Des Moines, Iowa, December 17, 1965; admitted to bar, 1993, Iowa. *Education:* Iowa State University (B.A., with distinction, 1988); Drake University (J.D., with honors, 1993). Phi Kappa Phi; Kappa Tau Alpha; Order of the Coif. Associate Editor, Drake Law Review, 1992-1993. Chartered Life Underwriter (CLU). Senior Counsel, Iowa Farm Bureau Federation and Affiliated Companies, 1993—. *Member:* Polk County, Iowa State and American Bar Associations; Association of Corporate Counsel. ***Email:*** lgeadelmann@fbfs.com

EDWARD G. PARKER, born Des Moines, Iowa, January 22, 1959; admitted to bar, 1993, Iowa and U.S. District Court, Northern and Southern Districts of Iowa. *Education:* University of Northern Iowa (B.S., highest honors, 1990); University of Iowa College of Law (J.D., high distinction, 1993). Order of the Coif. Member, Iowa House of Representatives, 1983-1988. Senior Counsel, Iowa Farm Bureau Federation and Affiliated Companies, 1994—. *Member:* Polk County, Iowa State and American Bar Associations; Iowa Defense Counsel Association. ***Email:*** eparker@fbfs.com

PAUL S. SWINTON, born Montrose, Pennsylvania, February 22, 1961; admitted to bar, 1995, Iowa and U.S. District Court, Northern and Southern Districts of Iowa. *Education:* University of Northern Iowa (B.A., 1992); Drake University (J.D., with honors, 1995). Articles Editor, Drake Law Review, 1994-1995. Author: "Iowa Stamps on Drugs: A Constitutional Analysis of Iowa Code Chapter 453B," 44 Drake Law Review 81. Counsel, Iowa Farm Bureau Federation and Affiliated Companies, 1997—. *Member:* Polk County, Iowa State and American Bar Associations; Iowa Defense Counsel Association. ***Email:*** pswinton@fbfs.com

JENNIFER S. MOORMAN, born Marshalltown, Iowa, September 29, 1969; admitted to bar, 1997, Missouri; 1998, Kansas; 1999, Iowa. *Education:* Iowa State University (B.A., with distinction, 1991); University of Iowa (J.D., with highest distinction, 1997). Order of the Coif. Recipient, West Publishing Company Award for Outstanding Academic Achievement. Author: "Finders Weepers, Losers Weepers? Benjamin v. Lindner Aviation," 82 Iowa Law Review, Issue 2 (January 1997). Associate Counsel, Iowa Farm Bureau Federation and Affiliated Companies, 1998—. *Member:* Polk County, Iowa State, Kansas and American Bar Associations; The Missouri Bar. ***Email:*** jmoorman@fbfs.com

MICHELLE F. INGLE, born Perth Amboy, New Jersey, September 25, 1969; admitted to bar, 1994, South Carolina; 2003, Iowa. *Education:* Wake Forest University (B.A., magna cum laude, 1991); Wake Forest University School of Law (J.D., 1994). Recipient, The Bureau of National Affairs Law Student Award. Associate Counsel, Iowa Farm Bureau Federation and Affiliated Companies, 2003—. *Member:* Polk County, Iowa State and American Bar Associations. ***Email:*** mingle@fbfs.com

OF COUNSEL

THOMAS E. BURLINGAME, born Clinton, Iowa, January 22, 1945; admitted to bar, 1975, Iowa. *Education:* University of Iowa (B.B.A., 1972; J.D., with distinction, 1975). Notes and Comments Editor, Iowa Law Review, 1974-1975. Associate General Counsel, Iowa Farm Bureau Federation and Affiliated Companies, 1982-2003. *Member:* Polk County, Iowa State and American Bar Associations.

JAMES E. McCARTHY, born Washington, Iowa, June 30, 1949; admitted to bar, 1976, Iowa and Nebraska. *Education:* University of Notre Dame (B.B.A., 1972); Creighton University (J.D., 1976). Author, Casenote, 9 Creighton Law Review 544, 1976. *Member:* Polk County, Iowa State, Nebraska State and American Bar Associations. ***Email:*** jmccarthy@fbfs.com

GENERAL COUNSEL FOR: Iowa Farm Bureau Federation; FBL Financial Group, Inc.; Farm Bureau Life Insurance Co.; Farm Bureau Mutual Insurance Co.; Western Agricultural Insurance Co.; EquiTrust Life Insurance Co.; KFB Insurance Company, Inc.
REPRESENTATIVE CLIENTS: Iowa FS Companies; EquiTrust Mutual Funds; EquiTrust Investment Management Services, Inc.
REFERENCES: Firstar Bank, Des Moines, Iowa; Bank of America, Des Moines, Iowa.

PEARSON VAN HOUTEN PLC

Established in 2003

1415 28TH STREET, SUITE 160
WEST DES MOINES, IOWA 50266
Telephone: 515-327-0101
Fax: 515-327-8514
URL: http://www.pvhlaw.com
URL: http://www.pearsonvanhouten.com

Business Law, Banking Law, Probate, Estate Planning, Taxation, Trusts and Estates, Wills, Employee Benefits, Real Estate, Elder Law.

PHYLLIS E. PEARSON, born Cedar Rapids, Iowa, December 11, 1947; admitted to bar, 1979, Iowa. *Education:* Iowa State University (B.S., 1969); Drake University (J.D., 1979). Order of the Coif. Staff Member, Drake Law Review, 1977-1979. Member, Supreme Court of Iowa Client Security and Attorney Disciplinary Commission, 1985-1994, Chair, 1991-1994. *Member:* Polk County, Iowa State (Chair, Counsel of Business Law Section, 1992-1993) and American (Member, Business Law Section) Bar Associations. ***PRACTICE AREAS:*** Business Law; Banking Law; Probate; Estate Planning; Elder Law. ***Email:*** pearson@pvhlaw.com

MARGARET D. VAN HOUTEN, born Lancaster, Wisconsin, July 18, 1953; admitted to bar, 1979, Iowa; 1981, Tennessee; 1984, U.S. Tax Court; 1985, U.S. District Court, Northern and Southern Districts of Iowa. *Education:* Iowa State University (B.A., 1975); University of Iowa (J.D., with distinction, 1979); New York University (LL.M. in Taxation, 1984). Phi Beta Kappa. Adjunct Professor of Law, Drake University, 1995-1996. Member, 1990-1999 and Chair, 1994-1996, Iowa Supreme Court Commission on the Unauthorized Practice of Law. *Member:* Polk County, Iowa State (Council Member, Taxation Section, 1990-1993, 1997-2000, 2002—; Chair, Employee Benefits Committee, 1993-1994; Member, Probate and Trust Law Section) and American (Member, Employee Benefits Committee, Taxation Section, 1990—) Bar Associations. Fellow, American College of Trust and Estate Counsel (Iowa State Chair, 2005—; Member: Technology Committee, 1996—; Estate and Gift Tax Committee, 2002—). ***PRACTICE AREAS:*** Taxation; Estate Planning; Trusts and Estates; Employee Benefits. ***Email:*** vanhouten@pvhlaw.com

JOAN D. TROUT, born Sigourney, Iowa, January 6, 1967; admitted to bar, 1992, Iowa. *Education:* University of Iowa (B.B.A., 1989; J.D., 1992). Associate Editor, Journal of Corporation Law, 1991-1992. Author: "The Non-Presumption After Curtin Matheson, Journal of Corporation Law, 1991. Co-Author: "Life insurance Trusts in the Estate Plan, Drake Law Review, 1995. *Member:* Polk County, Iowa State (Member, Corporate Counsel Section) and American Bar Associations. ***PRACTICE AREAS:*** Business Law; Real Estate. ***Email:*** trout@pvhlaw.com

---

RYAN D. HERVEY, born Des Moines, Iowa, October 5, 1977; admitted to bar, 2004, Iowa. *Education:* Simpson College (B.A., 2001); Drake University (J.D., with honors, 2004). ***PRACTICE AREAS:*** Business Law; Taxation; Estate Planning. ***Email:*** hervey@pvhlaw.com

REPRESENTATIVE CLIENTS: Aegon USA Charitable Foundation, Inc.; Applied Mechanical Products, Inc.; Artistic Manufacturing Corp.; Asset Protection Agency, Inc.; Bear Linear LLC; Big Sky Life, Inc.; Brown's Shoe Fit Co.; Chrysalis Foundation; Communication Development Co.; Jody Currie Dance Studio, Inc.; Design 4U Consulting, LLC; Diagnostic Imaging of Iowa, Inc.; Earl May Seed & Nursery, LLC; Barbara E. Evans, M.D., P.C.; Farmers Savings Bank - Keota; Fogg, Nims & Co., LLP; North Bay Reinsurance, Ltd.; Plasti-Pak, L.C.; Star Equipment, Ltd.; Superiorgas Energy, LLC; Two Rivers Martial Arts, Inc.; Freedom Financial Bank; Blue Willis by Kathy, Inc.; Action Print; Aging Resources of Central Iowa.

SULLIVAN & WARD, P.C.

6601 WESTOWN PARKWAY, SUITE 200
WEST DES MOINES, IOWA 50266
Telephone: 515-244-3500
Telecopier: 515-244-3599
Email: swpc@sullivan-ward.com
URL: http://www.sullivan-ward.com

General Civil Practice. Corporation, Public Utility, Labor, Environmental, OSHA, Real Estate, Probate, Taxation, Insurance and Administrative Law. Trials in all Courts, Family Law, Mediation and Arbitration.

FIRM PROFILE: Sullivan & Ward, P.C. is listed in Martindale-Hubbell Bar Register of Preeminent Lawyers.

JOHN T. WARD, born Knoxville, Iowa, October 19, 1940; admitted to bar, 1964, Iowa and U.S. District Court, Southern District of Iowa; 1967, U.S. District Court, Northern District of Iowa and U.S. Supreme Court. *Education:* Drake University (B.A., 1962; J.D., 1964). Phi Alpha Delta. Member, Drake Law Review, 1963-1964. Member, Board of Directors, 1976-1982 and President, 1979-1981, West Des Moines Community School District. *Member:* Polk County, Iowa State and American Bar Associations. ***Email:*** jward@sullivan-ward.com

HARLAN (BUD) HOCKENBERG, born Des Moines, Iowa, 1927; admitted to bar, 1952, Iowa; 1968, District of Columbia. *Education:* University of Iowa (B.A., 1949; J.D., 1952). Omicron Delta Kappa; Delta Sigma Rho. Member, Board of Editors, Iowa Law Review, 1952. Member: United States Holocaust Memorial Council, 2003—; The President's Commission on White House Fellowships, 1988-1993. *Member:* Polk County, Iowa State and American Bar Associations. ***Email:*** hhockenberg@sullivan-ward.com

MICHAEL P. JOYNT, born Des Moines, Iowa, October 16, 1941; admitted to bar, 1971, Iowa, U.S. District Court, Southern and Northern Districts of Iowa; 1975, U.S. Supreme Court and U.S. Court of Military Appeals. *Education:* University of Iowa (B.A., 1963); Drake University (J.D., 1971). Order of the Coif; Phi Alpha Delta. *Member:* Polk County, Iowa State and American Bar Associations. ***Email:*** mjoynt@sullivan-ward.com

(This Listing Continued)

LOUIS R. HOCKENBERG, born Des Moines, Iowa, August 23, 1948; admitted to bar, 1973, Iowa and U.S. District Court, Southern District of Iowa; 1974, U.S. District Court, Northern District of Iowa; U.S. Tax Court. *Education:* University of Iowa (B.A., 1966); Drake University (J.D., 1973). *Member:* Polk County, Iowa State (Member, Committee on Probate, Property and Trust Law, 1978—; Member, Special Committee on Iowa Property Law, 1980) and American (Member, Sections on: Real Property, Probate and Trust Law; Taxation) Bar Associations. ***Email:*** lhockenberg@sullivan-ward.com

RICHARD R. CHABOT, born Duluth, Minnesota, August 23, 1937; admitted to bar, 1964, Iowa and Minnesota; U.S. District Court, Northern and Southern Districts of Iowa; U.S. Court of Appeals, Eighth Circuit. *Education:* Marquette University (B.S., 1959); University of Minnesota (J.D., 1964). *Member:* Polk County, Iowa State and American Bar Associations. ***Email:*** rchabot@sullivan-ward.com

ROBERT M. HOLLIDAY, born Little Rock, Arkansas, September 1, 1943; admitted to bar, 1968, Iowa; 1970, U.S. District Court, Southern District of Iowa; 1978, U.S. Tax Court; 1981, U.S. District Court, Northern District of Iowa; 1984, U.S. Supreme Court. *Education:* Drake University (B.A., 1965; J.D., 1968). Phi Alpha Delta. Law Clerk to Honorable Bruce M. Snell, Justice Iowa Supreme Court, 1968-1969. President, Polk County Junior Bar Association, 1977-1978. Member, Drake University Law School Board of Counselors, 1992—. *Member:* Polk County (Member, Committee on Professional Ethics and Conduct, 1985-1991; Bench-Bar Committee, 1991-1994), Iowa State (Member, Committee on Legal Education and Admission to the Bar, 1977; Ethics Committee, Litigation Section, 1991-1994) and American Bar Associations; C. Edwin Moore Inns of Court (Master of the Bench); Association of Trial Lawyers of Iowa; Iowa Academy of Trial Lawyers; The Association of Trial Lawyers of America. ***Email:*** bholliday@sullivan-ward.com

MARK LANDA, born Ely, Minnesota, March 19, 1954; admitted to bar, 1981, Iowa and North Dakota. *Education:* Vermillion Community College (A.A., 1974); College of St. Thomas (B.A., magna cum laude, 1976); Drake University (J.D., 1980). Delta Epsilon Sigma. *Member:* Polk County, Iowa State and American Bar Associations. ***Email:*** mlanda@sullivan-ward.com

JOHN V. DONNELLY, born Chariton, Iowa, April 25, 1940; admitted to bar, 1965, Iowa, U.S. Tax Court and U.S. Claims Court; 1977, U.S. Supreme Court. *Education:* Harvard University (A.B., cum laude, 1962); University of Michigan (LL.B., 1965). *Member:* Polk County, Iowa State and American Bar Associations. ***Email:*** jdonnelly@sullivan-ward.com

DENNIS L. PUCKETT, born Wadena, Minnesota, March 20, 1966; admitted to bar, 1991, Iowa. *Education:* University of Kansas (B.S., 1988); Drake University (J.D., with honors, 1991). President, Student Division of Iowa Trial Lawyers Association, 1990-1991. *Member:* Polk County, Iowa State and American Bar Associations; Association of Iowa Trial Lawyers; Co-op Bar Association. ***Email:*** dpuckett@sullivan-ward.com

LAWRENCE P. McLELLAN, born Jefferson, Iowa, September 5, 1957; admitted to bar, 1983, Iowa; U.S. District Court, Northern and Southern Districts of Iowa; U.S. Court of Appeals, Eighth Circuit; U.S. Supreme Court. *Education:* Drake University (B.A., summa cum laude, 1979; J.D., with honors, 1983). Phi Beta Kappa. Articles Editor, Drake Law Review, 1982-1983. Judicial Law Clerk for U.S. District Court Judge R. E. Longstaff, Southern District of Iowa, formerly U.S. Magistrate, 1983-1984. Board Certified Mediator by the American Academy of Alternative Dispute Resolution Attorneys. *Member:* Polk County, Iowa State and American Bar Associations; American Trial Lawyers Association; Iowa Trial Lawyers Association; Defense Research Institute. ***PRACTICE AREAS:*** Commercial Litigation; Environmental Law; Alternative Dispute Resolution; Personal Injury; Employment Law; Insurance. ***Email:*** lmclellan@sullivan-ward.com

MATTHEW D. GARDNER, born Centerville, Iowa, August 23, 1969; admitted to bar, 1997, Iowa. *Education:* Iowa State University (B.A., 1992); Drake Law School (J.D., with honors, 1997). *Member:* Polk County, Iowa State (Chairperson, Services to the Elderly Committee, Young Lawyers Division, 2002-2004) and American Bar Associations. ***Email:*** mgardner@sullivan-ward.com

RUSH NIGUT, born Wurzburg, Germany, 1968; admitted to bar, 1994, Iowa and U.S. District Court, Northern and Southern Districts of Iowa. *Education:* Simpson College (B.A., 1991); Drake University (J.D., 1994). Member: Des Moines Leadership Institute; Corporate Development Committee, Simpson College. *Member:* Polk County, Iowa State and American Bar Associations. ***PRACTICE AREAS:*** Business Law; Corporate Law; Electronic Commerce. ***Email:*** rnigut@sullivan-ward.com

OF COUNSEL

LAWRENCE F. SCALISE, born Des Moines, Iowa, April 25, 1933; admitted to bar, 1958, Iowa and U.S. District Court, Northern and Southern Districts of Iowa; U.S. Court of Appeals, 8th Circuit; U.S. District Court, Northern District of California and U.S. Supreme Court. *Education:* University of Iowa (B.A., 1955; LL.B., 1958). Phi Delta Phi. Assistant County Attorney, Polk County, Iowa, 1959-1961. Director, Law Enforcement Division, Iowa Liquor Control Commission, 1963. Attorney General of Iowa, 1965-1967. Vice-Chairman, Campaign Finance Disclosure Commission, 1974-1977. Chairman, Iowa State Racing Commission, 1983-1988. Deputy, Independent Counsel, Office of Independent Counsel in re: Cisneros matters, Washington, D.C., September, 1995-2001. *Member:* Iowa State and American Bar Associations; Iowa Academy of Trial Lawyers; Blackstone Inn of Court (Master of the Bench, 1989—). Fellow: American Academy of Trial Lawyers. ***Email:*** lscalise@sullivan-ward.com

JILL MATAYA CORRY, born Ames, Iowa, July 7, 1968; admitted to bar, 1994, Iowa. *Education:* Drake University (B.A., magna cum laude, 1990); University of Iowa (J.D., with high distinction, 1994). Pi Sigma Alpha. *Member:* Polk County, Iowa State and American Bar Associations; American Health Lawyers Association. ***Email:*** jcorry@sullivan-ward.com

---

JENNIFER JASKOLKA-BROWN, born New York, N.Y., 1973; admitted to bar, 1999, Iowa and Nebraska; U.S. District Court, Northern and Southern Districts of Iowa and U.S. Court of Appeals, Eighth Circuit. *Education:* University of Nebraska (J.D., 1999). Member, Board of Directors: Ballet Theatre of Des Moines; Greater Des Moines Partner-

(This Listing Continued)

ship Young Professionals Connection. *Member:* Polk County, Iowa State (Member, Young Lawyers Division) and American Bar Associations; Iowa Trial Lawyers Association; American Immigration Lawyers Association. ***PRACTICE AREAS:*** Litigation; Family Law. ***Email:*** jaskolka@sullivan-ward.com

KYLE A. KRUIDENIER, born Des Moines, Iowa, 1971; admitted to bar, 2004, Iowa. *Education:* University of Iowa (B.S., 1994); Drake University (J.D., 2004). *Member:* Polk County, Iowa State and American Bar Associations. ***Email:*** kkruidenier@sullivan-ward.com

GENERAL COUNSEL FOR: Iowa Association of Electric Cooperatives; Central Iowa Power Cooperative; Corn Belt Power Cooperative; Northwest Iowa Power Cooperative; Iowa Network Services; Iowa Rural Water Assn.
REPRESENTATIVE CLIENTS: National Rural Utilities Cooperative Finance Corp.; First Union Mortgage Corporation; Quality Wine Company, Inc.; Greenfield Plaza/Hills of Coventry Sanitary District; Commercial Federal Bank; EarthWeb, Inc.; Meredith Corporation; Federated Rural Electric Insurance Co.; Iowa Wireless Services, L.P.; Iowa Telecommunications Services, Inc; Maurices, Inc.; Strategic America.

TURNER LAW OFFICES

1200 GRAND AVENUE
WEST DES MOINES, IOWA 50265
Telephone: 515-245-9509
Fax: 515-245-9519
Email: attorneys@turnerlaw.com

General Civil and Trial Practice in all State and Federal Courts. Litigation, Corporate and Business, Insurance, Labor and Employment, Construction, Personal Injury, Real Estate, Wills and Probate, Trusts and Estates.

ERIC F. TURNER, born Corning, Iowa, October 24, 1955; admitted to bar, 1981, Iowa. *Education:* Drake University (B.S.B.A., summa cum laude, 1978); University of Iowa (J.D. with high distinction, 1981). Beta Gamma Sigma; Omicron Delta Kappa. *Member:* Polk County (Vice-President, Board of Directors), Iowa State and American (Member: General Practice; Litigation; Business Law; Real Property and Probate Sections) Bar Associations; Iowa Defense Counsel Association; Master, C. Edwin Moore American Inn of Court. ***PRACTICE AREAS:*** Civil Litigation; Corporate; Business; Labor and Employment; Construction; Real Estate; Trusts and Estates; Insurance.

REPRESENTATIVE CLIENTS: West Des Moines State Bank; Nebraska State Bank of Omaha; J.B. Hunt Transport, Inc.; St. Paul Surety Cos.; Anixter, Inc.; Dewey Ford, Inc.; Electronic Engineering Co.; Olsten Corp.; Mediacom; The Graham Group; Kin Properties, Inc.

WASKER, DORR, WIMMER & MARCOUILLER, P.C.

THREE FOUNTAINS OFFICE PARK
HIGHLAND BUILDING
4201 WESTOWN PARKWAY, SUITE 250
WEST DES MOINES, IOWA 50266-6720
Telephone: 515-283-1801
Facsimile: 515-283-1802
Email: lawfirm@wdwm.net
URL: http://www.lawyers.com/waskerdorrwimmermarcouiller

General Civil and Trial Practice, Real Estate, Government Relations, Corporation, Public Utility, Labor, Probate, Estate Planning, Taxation, Insurance and Administrative Law.

CHARLES F. WASKER, born Everett, Massachusetts, February 4, 1926; admitted to bar, 1952, Iowa and U.S. District Court, Southern District of Iowa; 1955, U.S. District Court, Northern District of Iowa. *Education:* Drake University (B.A., 1951; J.D., 1952). Phi Alpha Delta. Director, Federal Home Bank of Des Moines, 1982-1986. *Member:* Polk County (President, 1979-1980), Iowa State (Member, Board of Governors, 1980-1984) and American (Member, Section on Real Property, Probate and Trust Law) Bar Associations. ***PRACTICE AREAS:*** Government Relations. ***Email:*** cwasker@wdwm.net

FRED L. DORR, born Cherokee, Iowa, November 30, 1947; admitted to bar, 1976, Iowa, U.S. District Court, Northern and Southern Districts of Iowa, U.S. Court of Appeals, Eighth Circuit and U.S. Supreme Court. *Education:* Northwestern University (B.S., 1970); Drake University (J.D., 1975). Order of the Barristers. Member, Drake University National Moot Court Team, 1975. Author: Case Note, 24 Drake Law Review 704, 1975. Member, Board of Directors: West Des Moines Community School District, 1989-1995; President, 1992-1993. *Member:* Polk County, Iowa State and American (Member, Litigation Section) Bar Associations; The Iowa Defense Counsel Association; Iowa Trial Lawyers Association. ***PRACTICE AREAS:*** Civil Litigation; Utility Law. ***Email:*** fdorr@wdwm.net

WILLIAM J. WIMMER, born Creston, Iowa, November 8, 1949; admitted to bar, 1976, Iowa and U.S. District Court, Northern and Southern Districts of Iowa. *Education:* Northwest Missouri State University (B.S., 1971); Cumberland School of Law of Samford University (J.D., 1976). Phi Delta Phi. *Member:* Polk County, Iowa State and American Bar Associations; The Association of Trial Lawyers of America; Iowa Trial Lawyers Association. ***PRACTICE AREAS:*** Government Relations. ***Email:*** bwimmer@wdwm.net

D. MARK MARCOUILLER, born Green Bay, Wisconsin, September 5, 1954; admitted to bar, 1979, Iowa and U.S. District Court, Northern and Southern Districts of Iowa. *Education:* Drake University (B.S.B.A., 1976; M.B.A., 1978; J.D., 1979). Phi Alpha Delta. *Member:* Polk County, Iowa State and American (Member, Real Estate and Title Law Sections) Bar Associations. ***PRACTICE AREAS:*** Real Estate; Corporate Law. ***Email:*** mmarcouiller@wdwm.net

MATTHEW D. KERN, born Des Moines, Iowa, December 22, 1967; admitted to bar, 1993, Iowa. *Education:* University of Northern Iowa (B.A., 1990); Drake University (J.D., with honors, 1993). Member, Moot Court Board, 1991-1992. *Member:* Polk County, Iowa State and American Bar Associations. ***PRACTICE AREAS:*** Real Estate; General Practice. ***Email:*** mkern@wdwm.net

(This Listing Continued)

MARK R. ADAMS, born Iowa City, Iowa, October 30, 1952; admitted to bar, 1977, Iowa, U.S. District Court, Northern and Southern Districts of Iowa and U.S. Tax Court. *Education:* University of Northern Iowa (B.A., 1974); Drake University (J.D., 1977). *Member:* Polk County, Iowa State and American Bar Associations. ***PRACTICE AREAS:*** Insurance; Corporate Law; Real Estate; Probate; Estate Planning; General Practice. ***Email:*** madams@wdwm.net

DAVID C. PULLIAM, born Des Moines, Iowa, November 16, 1969; admitted to bar, 1995, Iowa; 1996, U.S. District Court, Northern District of Iowa. *Education:* Iowa State University (B.A., with distinction, 1992); University of Iowa (J.D., with distinction, 1995). Phi Beta Kappa; Phi Kappa Phi. Member, Iowa Law Review. *Member:* Polk County, Iowa State and American Bar Associations. ***PRACTICE AREAS:*** Real Estate; General Practice. ***Email:*** dcpulliam@wdwm.net

MATTHEW M. HURN, born Cedar Rapids, Iowa, October 13, 1969; admitted to bar, 1998, Iowa and U.S. District Court, Southern District of Iowa. *Education:* Simpson College (B.A., 1992); Drake University (J.D., with honors, 1998). *Member:* Polk County and Iowa State Bar Associations. ***PRACTICE AREAS:*** Real Estate; General Practice. ***Email:*** mhurn@wdwm.net

CRAIG R. SCHOENFELD, born Galesburg, Illinois, August 19, 1968; admitted to bar, 1994, Iowa. *Education:* University of Wisconsin-Stevens Point (B.A., 1991); Drake University (M.A., 1994; J.D., 1994). Delta Theta Phi. *Member:* Polk County and Iowa State Bar Associations. ***PRACTICE AREAS:*** Government Relations. ***Email:*** cschoenfeld@wdwm.net

CHARLES HENDRICKS, born Hayward, Wisconsin, April 30, 1972; admitted to bar, 1999, Iowa; 2001, Minnesota, U.S. District Court, Northern and Southern Districts of Iowa and U.S. Court of Appeals, Eighth Circuit. *Education:* University of Wisconsin at Eau Claire (B.B.A., 1995); Drake University (J.D., with honors, 1999). Author: "Offering Tort Victims Some Solace - Why States Should Incorporate a 20% Set - Aside into Their Versions of Article 9," 104 Comm. L.J. 265 (1999); "100 Years of Double Jeopardy Erosion - Criminal Collateral Estoppel Made Extinct," 48 Drake L. Rev. 379 (2000). ***PRACTICE AREAS:*** Litigation. ***Email:*** chendricks@wdwm.net

RETIRED

RUSSELL H. LAIRD, born 1927; admitted to bar, 1952, Iowa. *Education:* University of Nebraska at Lincoln (B.S.; LL.B.).

GENERAL COUNSEL FOR: Homebuilders Association of Iowa.
REPRESENTATIVE CLIENTS: Governor Thomas J. Vilsack; AFLAC; Bank of America; Biermann Electric Co.; Cedar Rapids Physician-Hospital Organization; Chesapeake Display & Packaging Co.; Cigar Association of America, Inc.; Crystal Distribution Services, Inc.; Dubuque Greyhound Park & Casino; Enterprise Rent-A-Car; Federated Rural Electric Insurance Corp.; First Health Services Corporation; First Horizon Home Mortgage; First National Acceptance Co.; Forrest & Associates, Inc.; Gold Key Mortgage; Hawkeye Mortgage; Homesteaders Life Co.; Hy-Vee, Inc.; Iowa Beverage Association; Iowa Court Reporters Association; Iowa Environmental & Education Project; Iowa Judges Association; Iowa Lumber Association; Iowa Mortgage Association; Iowa Mortgage Professionals; Iowa Network Services, Inc.; Iowa Pharmacy Association; Iowa Retired School Personnel Association; Iowa Trial Lawyers Association; Iowa Wholesale Distributors Association; Liberty Bank; Merit Resources, Inc.; MetaBank; Metropolitan Transit Authority; Mid-Iowa Mortgage; Mortgage Financial Group; National Hairdressers & Cosmetologists Association of Iowa; Nationwide Home Mortgage; North West Rural Electric Cooperative; Old Standard Life Assurance Co.; One Source Mortgage; Pella Cooperative Electric Association; Pinnacle Mortgage; Principal Residential Mortgage, Inc.; The Proctor & Gamble Co.; R.J. Reynolds Tobacco Co.; Scottish Rite Park; Stivers Lincoln Mercury, Inc.; T.I.P. Rural Electric Cooperative; Wells Fargo Home Mortgage; Xerox Corp.
REFERENCES: Wells Fargo Bank; Commercial Federal Bank; MetaBank.

STANLEY, LANDE & HUNTER

A PROFESSIONAL CORPORATION
115 WEST FOURTH
P.O. BOX 481
WILTON, IOWA 52778
Telephone: 563-732-4000
Facsimile: 563-732-2318
Email: Contact.us@slhlaw.com
URL: http://www.slhlaw.com

Muscatine, Iowa Office: 301 Iowa Avenue, Suite 400. Telephone: 563-264-5000. Facsimile: 563-263-8775.

Davenport, Iowa Office: 900 U.S. Bank Center, 201 West Second Street. Telephone: 563-324-1000. Facsimile: 563-326-6266.

Coralville, Iowa Office: 2201 East Grantview Drive, Suite 200. Telephone: 319-248-9000. Facsimile: 319-248-9001.

General Civil and Trial Practice. Corporation, Business, Banking, Taxation, Securities, Tax-Exempt Financing, Labor, Employment Discrimination, Administrative, Creditor Bankruptcy and Agricultural Law, Insurance Defense, Personal Injury and Property Damage Law, Pension and Profit-Sharing, Real Estate, Probate, Estate Planning and Charitable Trusts and Foundations Law.

(For Complete Biographical Data on all Personnel, see Professional Biographies at Davenport, Iowa)

JORDAN, OLIVER & WALTERS, P.C.

Established in 1932
FARMERS & MERCHANTS BANK BUILDING
P.O. BOX 230
WINTERSET, IOWA 50273
Telephone: 515-462-3731
Fax: 515-462-3734

Elder Law, General Practice, Personal Injury, Real Estate, Taxation, Trusts and Estates, Wills and Probate, Family Law, Insurance.

(This Listing Continued)

JORDAN, OLIVER & WALTERS, P.C., Winterset—Continued

FIRM PROFILE: The firm and its predecessors have been practicing law in Winterset since 1932. All lawyers have law degrees from Iowa.

SHIRLEY A. WEBSTER (1909-1989)

LEWIS H. JORDAN, born Spencer, Iowa, April 12, 1930; admitted to bar, 1958, Iowa; 1962, U.S. District Court, Southern District of Iowa; 1970, U.S. Tax Court. *Education:* State University of Iowa (B.A., 1957; J.D., 1958). County Attorney, 1963-1967. *Member:* Madison County, Fifth Judicial District (Secretary, 1963-1964; President, 1969-1970), Iowa State (Member: Judicial Administration Committee, 1972-1973; Executive Council, Junior Bar Section, 1963-1966; Special Committee on Criminal Law, 1964-1972; Membership Committee, 1974-1986; Special Committee on Title Insurance, 1980-1985; Board of Governors, 1985-1987) and American Bar Associations; Iowa Academy of Trial Lawyers; The Association of Trial Lawyers of America. Fellow, Iowa State Bar Foundation. [With U.S.N., 1951-1954]. ***PRACTICE AREAS:*** Elder Law; General Practice; Real Estate; Taxation; Trusts and Estates; Wills; Probate. ***Email:*** lew@jowlaw.com

JERROLD B. OLIVER, born Sioux City, Iowa, January 13, 1943; admitted to bar, 1967, Iowa; 1968, U.S. District Court, Southern District of Iowa; 1970, U.S. Tax Court. *Education:* University of Iowa (B.A., 1966; J.D., 1967). Delta Theta Phi. City Attorney, 1968-1972. County Attorney, Madison County, 1973-1978. *Member:* Madison County, District 5A(Secretary, 1969-1970; President, 1999-2000), Iowa State (Member: Executive Council, Young Lawyers Section, 1970-1976; Taxation Committee, 1972-1990, Co-Chairperson, 1988-1990; Member: Special Committee on Legal Assistants, 1974-1976; Legal Forms Committee, 1990—; Chairperson, 2000-2005; Council Tax Section, 1992-1993; *(This Listing Continued)* Technology Committee, 1997—) and American Bar Associations. American College of Trust and Estate Counsel. Fellow, Iowa State Bar Foundation. ***PRACTICE AREAS:*** Elder Law; General Practice; Real Estate; Taxation; Trusts and Estates; Wills; Probate. ***Email:*** jbo@jowlaw.com

G. STEPHEN WALTERS, born Sioux City, Iowa, February 7, 1948; admitted to bar, 1973, Iowa; 1974, U.S. District Court, Southern District of Iowa and U.S. Tax Court; 1981, U.S. District Court, Northern District of Iowa and U.S. Court of Appeals, Eighth Circuit. *Education:* Iowa State University (B.S., 1970); University of Iowa (J.D., 1973). Phi Alpha Delta. Note and Comment Editor, Iowa Law Review, 1972-1973. Winterset City Attorney, 1975-1976. *Member:* Madison County, District 5A (President, 1993-1994; Secretary-Treasurer, 1981-1982 and 2000-2001), Iowa State (Member, Committees on: Specialization, 1986-1990; Membership, 1986-1987) and American Bar Associations; Association of Trial Lawyers of Iowa; Iowa Defense Counsel Association. Fellow, Iowa State Bar Foundation. ***PRACTICE AREAS:*** Elder Law; General Practice; Real Estate; Taxation; Trusts and Estates; Wills; Probate; Family Law; Insurance. ***Email:*** kim@jowlaw.com

A list of Representative Clients will be furnished upon request.
REFERENCE: Farmers & Merchants State Bank, Winterset, Iowa.

J. KEITH RIGG

WINTERSET, IOWA

(See Des Moines)

Criminal Trial Practice in Federal and State Courts. Civil Litigation.

ATTENTION:

Expert Witnesses, Investigators, Court Reporters, Process Servers and other Legal Service Providers…

Are you looking for targeted ways to reach attorneys?

Go to the Experts & Services Section at **martindale.com/resources** or call **1-800-526-4902**, ext. **8010**

Martindale-Hubbell® Experts & Services Section

Martindale-Hubbell, through its Experts & Services Section, offers a wide variety of advertising options that provide you maximum reach into the legal market:

Online: Our exclusive Experts & Services Section, available at *martindale.com/resources*, is an excellent way to increase your visibility to prospective legal clients. You benefit from the connection to *martindale.com*®—which is searched more than 2.5 million times each month. And, through advertising alliances with Internet leaders such as MSN and Google, we have dramatically increased the number of visitors to—and visibility of—the Experts & Services Section.

A paid listing in the Law Directory also gets you listed online via LexisNexis®, used by 2.7 million legal and business users worldwide.

The Martindale-Hubbell Law Directory: Promoting your business in the **Law Directory**—an indispensable resource used by over 90% of the legal community—is a time-proven way to market your services. Each Law Directory volume contains a section devoted to the promotion of services to the legal market—from Court Reporters to Expert Witnesses to Software Companies to Investigators—organized by city/state and category. Your listing will also be featured on the Martindale-Hubbell CD-ROM, which boasts a networked user base of over 100,000.

The Martindale-Hubbell Directory of Experts & Legal Services (Buyer's Guide): This handy, single-volume desktop directory gives users one-stop, national access to all the advertisers covered in each of the Law Directory's individual volumes. You can complement your representation in the Experts & Services Section by purchasing Enhanced Listings and Display Ads in the **Directory of Experts & Legal Services.**

For more information on how advertising your services can help grow your business, contact us at:
1-800-526-4902, ext. **8010**

Martindale-Hubbell
The Primary Source for Information on the Worldwide Legal Profession

Martindale-Hubbell has been serving the legal profession for over 135 years and is widely acknowledged as the premier source of information on attorneys and law firms worldwide. With a circulation base that encompasses lawyers, law firms and corporate counsel across town and around the world, the Martindale-Hubbell Law Directory offers you an unparalleled opportunity to reach this key and influential market that regularly requires the services and products you provide.

Because no other legal resource is referred to as often or trusted as much, Martindale-Hubbell remains the best way to reach a global network of legal professionals. Depending on your marketing objectives and budget, you can choose from a number of advertising options, from Print Ads in the *Experts & Services Section* and the Directory of Experts & Legal Services to Logos, Cross References and Banner Ads. Plus, your advertising investment benefits from our vast circulation network to lawyers and firms via print and electronic formats.

LexisNexis®
Martindale-Hubbell®

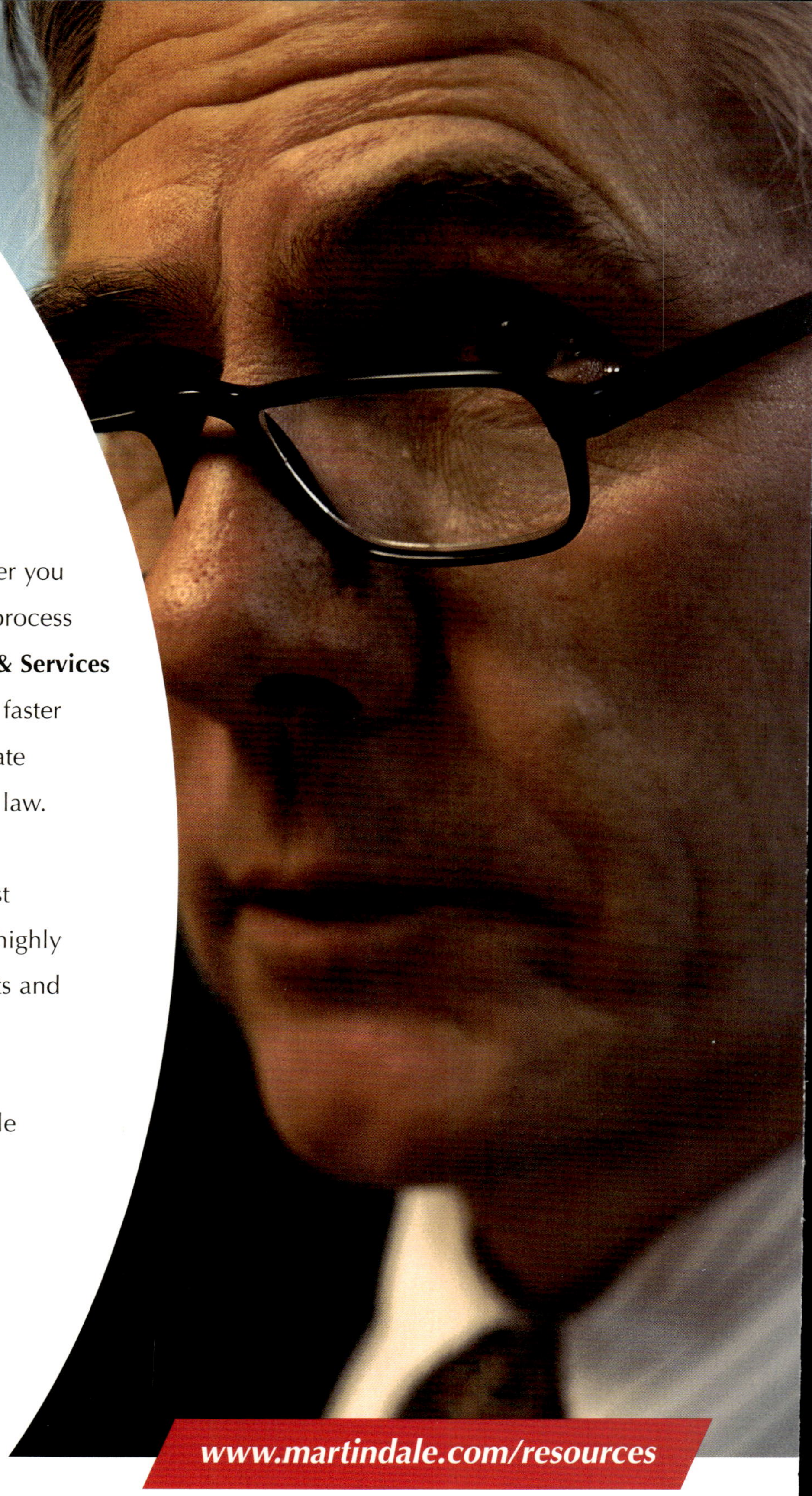
www.martindale.com/resources

EXPERTS & SERVICES SECTION

IDAHO, ILLINOIS INDIANA, IOWA

The Experts & Services Section provides information on businesses and professionals serving the legal community. This section is arranged alphabetically by state, city, or town, category of service provided and company name.

The Advertiser Index is listed alphabetically by category then within each category alphabetically by state, city and company name. Whether you are looking for a court reporter in your own jurisdiction or an expert witness in another state, the Experts & Services Section is your direct link to legal and non-legal services.

For additional categories/states go to the Martindale-Hubbell Experts & Services Section via the Internet at www.martindale.com/resources where you can quickly find thousands of experts and service providers.

To advertise in this section please call 800-526-4902, ext. 8010.

Experts & Services
Advertiser Index

COURT REPORTERS

IDAHO

BOISE .... HEDRICK COURT REPORTING
M&M COURT REPORTING SERVICE, INC.

ILLINOIS

BELLEVILLE .... GORE, PERRY, GATEWAY & LIPA REPORTING CO.
RANKIN REPORTING & LEGAL VIDEO, INC.

CHICAGO .... 1-2-3 REPORTING SERVICE A DIVISION OF CERTIFIED REPORTING COMPANY
ADVANTAGE REPORTING SERVICE
AREA COURT REPORTERS
BENEDIA CERTIFIED COURT REPORTING SERVICE
CENTRAL REPORTERS ASSOCIATED
DIANE HROMEK'S COURT REPORTERS, INC.
DOERNER & GOLDBERG INC.
LEGALINK CORPORATE
PATTI BLAIR COURT REPORTERS, P.C.
SULLIVAN REPORTING COMPANY
VICTORIA COURT REPORTING SERVICE, INC.
WICHMANN REPORTING SERVICE
WINKLER AND CHIMNIAK, INC.

DECATUR .... ANCHOR COURT REPORTING

EDWARDSVILLE .... GORE, PERRY, GATEWAY & LIPA REPORTING CO.
RANKIN REPORTING & LEGAL VIDEO, INC.

JOLIET .... ADVANTAGE REPORTING SERVICE
GEORGE E. RYDMAN & ASSOCIATES, LTD.

NAPERVILLE .... AREA COURT REPORTERS

NASHVILLE .... RANKIN REPORTING & LEGAL VIDEO, INC.

PEORIA .... ADVANTAGE REPORTING SERVICE

ROCKFORD .... LAUNIUS REPORTING SERVICE
MIDWEST PROFESSIONAL REPORTING, INC.

SCHAUMBERG .... AREA COURT REPORTERS

SPRINGFIELD .... ADVANTAGE REPORTING SERVICE

WHEATON .... COUNTY COURT REPORTERS, INC.

INDIANA

FORT WAYNE .... SUMMIT CITY REPORTING, INC.

HAMMOND .... 1-2-3 REPORTING SERVICE A DIVISION OF CERTIFIED REPORTING COMPANY

INDIANAPOLIS .... 1-2-3 REPORTING SERVICE A DIVISION OF CERTIFIED REPORTING COMPANY
ASSOCIATED REPORTING, INC.
CONNOR+ASSOCIATES
STEWART RICHARDSON & ASSOCIATES

SOUTH BEND .... MIDWEST REPORTING
OLMSTED & ASSOCIATES LTD.

VALPARAISO .... SEIDEL & SASSE COURT REPORTERS, INC.

IOWA

CEDAR RAPIDS .... KOOL & NYGREN, INC.

DES MOINES .... HUNEY - VAUGHN COURT REPORTERS, LTD.
LAUNSPACH, LEWIS, BURNS & KLUENDER, INC.

CRIMINAL BACKGROUND CHECKS

ILLINOIS
CHICAGO .... PEOPLESEARCH

INDIANA
INDIANAPOLIS .... INTERNATIONAL INVESTIGATORS, INC.

CRIMINAL DEFENSE

INDIANA
INDIANAPOLIS .... INTERNATIONAL INVESTIGATORS, INC.

CRIMINAL INVESTIGATIONS

INDIANA
INDIANAPOLIS .... INTERNATIONAL INVESTIGATORS, INC.

DEPOSITIONS - VIDEO & AUDIO

ILLINOIS
CHICAGO .... LEGAL VIDEO INTERNATIONAL

DOCUMENT RESEARCH, RETRIEVAL & FILING

IDAHO
JEROME .... AARDVARK LEGAL SUPPORT SERVICE

ILLINOIS
CHICAGO .... PEOPLESEARCH

DOMESTIC/SPOUSAL COMPUTER INVESTIGATION

INDIANA
INDIANAPOLIS .... INTERNATIONAL INVESTIGATORS, INC.

DUE DILIGENCE INVESTIGATIONS

INDIANA
INDIANAPOLIS .... INTERNATIONAL INVESTIGATORS, INC.

ECONOMIC AND STATISTICAL CONSULTING SERVICES

ILLINOIS
CHICAGO .... LEXECON

ELECTRONIC COUNTERMEASURES

INDIANA
INDIANAPOLIS .... INTERNATIONAL INVESTIGATORS, INC.

ELECTRONIC FILING

ILLINOIS
CHICAGO .... LEXISNEXIS ® FILE & SERVE

ENGINEERING & SCIENTIFIC CONSULTING SERVICES

ILLINOIS
CHICAGO .... CTLGROUP

EXPERT WITNESS

ACCIDENT INVESTIGATION & RECONSTRUCTION

ILLINOIS
CHICAGO .... PACKER ENGINEERING, INC.

ACCIDENTS/FIRES/PRODUCT LIABILITY

ILLINOIS
CHICAGO .... JOHN MICHAEL AGOSTI

EXPERT WITNESS - ACCIDENTS/FIRES/PRODUCT LIABILITY - Continued

INDIANA

INDIANAPOLIS .... JOHN MICHAEL AGOSTI

ACTUARY

ILLINOIS

CHICAGO .... WILLIAM C. CUTLIP CONSULTING

ARCHITECTS

ILLINOIS

CHICAGO .... WISS, JANNEY, ELSTNER ASSOCIATES, INC.

BANKING

FINANCE

ILLINOIS

CHICAGO .... TAVAKOLI STRUCTURED FINANCE, INC.

BUSINESS VALUATION

ILLINOIS

CHICAGO .... LEXECON

COATINGS/PAINT

ILLINOIS

CHICAGO .... WISS, JANNEY, ELSTNER ASSOCIATES, INC.

COMMODITY FUTURES

ILLINOIS

CHICAGO .... PETER J. PFEFFER

CONSTRUCTION

ILLINOIS

CHICAGO .... CTLGROUP

BUILDING CODES

ILLINOIS

CHICAGO .... ROLF JENSEN & ASSOCIATES, INC.

DRUGS/ALCOHOL/TOXICOLOGY

ILLINOIS

CHICAGO .... PHARMACONSULTANTS INC.

ECONOMICS/ECONOMISTS

ILLINOIS

CHICAGO .... LEXECON

ECONOMICS/STATISTICS

ILLINOIS

CHICAGO .... LEXECON

ENGINEERS/ENGINEERING

ILLINOIS

CHICAGO .... PACKER ENGINEERING, INC.
SAFETY CONSULTING ENGINEERS, INC.
WISS, JANNEY, ELSTNER ASSOCIATES, INC.

CIVIL/MECHANICAL/STRUCTURAL

ILLINOIS

CHICAGO .... CTLGROUP
WISS, JANNEY, ELSTNER ASSOCIATES, INC.

FIRE PROTECTION

ILLINOIS

CHICAGO .... ROLF JENSEN & ASSOCIATES, INC.

FORENSIC ENGINEERING

ILLINOIS

CHICAGO .... CTLGROUP
WISS, JANNEY, ELSTNER ASSOCIATES, INC.

FAILURE ANALYSIS

ILLINOIS

CHICAGO .... CTLGROUP
WISS, JANNEY, ELSTNER ASSOCIATES, INC.

FIRE

ILLINOIS

CHICAGO .... JOHN MICHAEL AGOSTI
VARLEY-CAMPBELL & ASSOCIATES, INC.

INDIANA

INDIANAPOLIS .... JOHN MICHAEL AGOSTI

PROTECTION, INVESTIGATION

ILLINOIS

CHICAGO .... JOHN MICHAEL AGOSTI

INDIANA

INDIANAPOLIS .... JOHN MICHAEL AGOSTI

RECONSTRUCTION

ILLINOIS

CHICAGO .... JOHN MICHAEL AGOSTI

INDIANA

INDIANAPOLIS .... JOHN MICHAEL AGOSTI

FIRE CAUSE & ORIGIN

ILLINOIS

CHICAGO .... JOHN MICHAEL AGOSTI

INDIANA

INDIANAPOLIS .... JOHN MICHAEL AGOSTI

FIRE/CONSULTING

ILLINOIS

CHICAGO .... JOHN MICHAEL AGOSTI

INDIANA

INDIANAPOLIS .... JOHN MICHAEL AGOSTI

FORENSIC ACCOUNTING

IDAHO

BOISE .... COOPER NORMAN CERTIFIED PUBLIC ACCOUNTANTS

INDIANA

WHITELAND .... LOPSHIRE & COMPANY

FORENSIC CASE MANAGEMENT

ILLINOIS

CHICAGO .... HESS, KARFOMENOS & ASSOCIATES, LLC

INSURANCE

LIFE, DISABILITY & LONG TERM CARE

ILLINOIS

CHICAGO .... PATRICK F. BRAUN, CLU, LUTCF, FIC

INSURANCE / REINSURANCE

ILLINOIS

CHICAGO .... WILLIAM C. CUTLIP CONSULTING

INTELLECTUAL PROPERTY

MANUFACTURED PRODUCTS

INDIANA

INDIANAPOLIS .... ADVANCED SURFACE MICROSCOPY, INC.

INTELLECTUAL PROPERTY/INFRINGEMENT DAMAGES

ILLINOIS

CHICAGO .... LEXECON

LITIGATION SUPPORT

ILLINOIS

CHICAGO .... LEXECON
WILLIAM C. CUTLIP CONSULTING

EXPERT WITNESS - Continued

PATENT INFRINGEMENT

ILLINOIS

CHICAGO .... LEXECON

PLASTICS PROCESSING AND PRODUCTS

ILLINOIS

CHICAGO .... BOTTOM LINE CONSULTING, INC.

ROOFING & WATERPROOFING

ILLINOIS

CHICAGO .... WISS, JANNEY, ELSTNER ASSOCIATES, INC.

SECURITIES LAW

ILLINOIS

CHICAGO .... LEXECON

SECURITIES/LITIGATION SUPPORT

ILLINOIS

CHICAGO .... PETER J. PFEFFER
TAVAKOLI STRUCTURED FINANCE, INC.

TELECOMMUNICATIONS

ILLINOIS

CHICAGO .... LEXECON

UTILITIES

ILLINOIS

CHICAGO .... LEXECON

VEHICLE FIRES AND COLLISION

ILLINOIS

CHICAGO .... JOHN MICHAEL AGOSTI

INDIANA

INDIANAPOLIS .... JOHN MICHAEL AGOSTI

EXPERT WITNESS REFERRAL SERVICES

ILLINOIS

CHICAGO .... TASA

FAILURE ANALYSIS/TESTING SERVICES

ILLINOIS

CHICAGO .... WISS, JANNEY, ELSTNER ASSOCIATES, INC.

FIRE INVESTIGATORS

ILLINOIS

CHICAGO .... JOHN MICHAEL AGOSTI

INDIANA

INDIANAPOLIS .... JOHN MICHAEL AGOSTI

FORENSIC ENGINEERS

ILLINOIS

CHICAGO .... CTLGROUP
WISS, JANNEY, ELSTNER ASSOCIATES, INC.

GENEALOGICAL SERVICES

ILLINOIS

CHICAGO .... HOERNER BANK
LANDEX RESEARCH, INC.

GENERAL INVESTIGATORS

INDIANA

INDIANAPOLIS .... INTERNATIONAL INVESTIGATORS, INC.

HEALTHCARE FINANCE & REIMBURSEMENT
ILLINOIS
CHICAGO .... AHERN & ASSOCIATES

HEIR TRACERS
ILLINOIS
CHICAGO .... HOERNER BANK
LANDEX RESEARCH, INC.
PEOPLESEARCH

INTERPRETERS & TRANSLATORS
ILLINOIS
CHICAGO .... 1ST METROPOLITAN TRANSLATION SERVICES, INC.

LAWYER SEARCH & PLACEMENT CONSULTANTS
ILLINOIS
CHICAGO .... MCCORMACK SCHREIBER LEGAL SEARCH
TECH LAW RECRUITING, INC.

LEGAL ASSOCIATIONS
ILLINOIS
CHICAGO .... ASSOCIATION OF LEGAL ADMINISTRATORS

LEGAL PUBLICATIONS
ILLINOIS
CHICAGO .... ASSOCIATION OF LEGAL ADMINISTRATORS

LIFE CARE PLANNING
ILLINOIS
CHICAGO .... HESS, KARFOMENOS & ASSOCIATES, LLC
ROBERT H. JACKSON & ASSOCIATES, INC.

LITIGATION CONSULTING
ILLINOIS
CHICAGO .... WILLIAM C. CUTLIP CONSULTING

LITIGATION SUPPORT SERVICES
IDAHO
BOISE .... COOPER NORMAN CERTIFIED PUBLIC ACCOUNTANTS

LITIGATION/LAWSUIT FUNDING
ILLINOIS
CHICAGO .... BEACON LEGAL FINANCE, LLC

MEDICAL CASE REVIEW & PREPARATION/TRIAL CONSULTING
ILLINOIS
CHICAGO .... HESS, KARFOMENOS & ASSOCIATES, LLC

MEDICAL EXPERT WITNESS
CARDIOLOGY
ILLINOIS
CHICAGO .... MARTIN MEDICAL CONSULTING, INC.
PHARMACY & PHARMACOLOGY
ILLINOIS
CHICAGO .... PHARMACONSULTANTS INC.
SOCIAL SERVICES
ILLINOIS
CHICAGO .... EVAN M. PETERSON, LCSW

MEDICAL EXPERT WITNESS REFERRAL SERVICES
ILLINOIS
CHICAGO .... TASAMED

METALLURGY & MATERIALS SCIENCE ENGINEERING
INDIANA
INDIANAPOLIS .... ADVANCED SURFACE MICROSCOPY, INC.

MISSING PERSONS
INDIANA
INDIANAPOLIS .... INTERNATIONAL INVESTIGATORS, INC.

NURSING CONSULTANTS
ILLINOIS
CHICAGO .... TANNER ASSOCIATES MEDICAL/LEGAL CONSULTING

PROCESS SERVERS & DOCUMENT DELIVERY SERVICES
IDAHO
JEROME .... AARDVARK LEGAL SUPPORT SERVICE
ILLINOIS
CHICAGO .... BORG PROCESS SERVERS INC.
IT'S YOUR SERVE - IYS
INDIANA
INDIANAPOLIS .... INTERNATIONAL INVESTIGATORS, INC.

SKIP TRACERS
INDIANA
INDIANAPOLIS .... INTERNATIONAL INVESTIGATORS, INC.

TSCM/TECHNICAL SURVEILLANCE COUNTERMEASURES
INDIANA
INDIANAPOLIS .... INTERNATIONAL INVESTIGATORS, INC.

TITLE INSURANCE
ILLINOIS
CHICAGO .... CHICAGO TITLE INSURANCE COMPANY

TRADE SECRETS THEFT INVESTIGATION
INDIANA
INDIANAPOLIS .... INTERNATIONAL INVESTIGATORS, INC.

TRANSCRIPTION SERVICES
IDAHO
BOISE .... HEDRICK COURT REPORTING
ILLINOIS
CHICAGO .... ADEPT TRANSCRIPTION SERVICES

VIDEO TAPE SERVICES
IDAHO
BOISE .... HEDRICK COURT REPORTING
ILLINOIS
CHICAGO .... BENEDIA CERTIFIED COURT REPORTING SERVICE
INDIANA
INDIANAPOLIS .... LEGAL VIDEO SERVICES, INC.

SOUTH BEND .... OLMSTED & ASSOCIATES LTD.

WHITE COLLAR CRIMINAL/FRAUD INVESTIGATION

INDIANA

INDIANAPOLIS .... INTERNATIONAL INVESTIGATORS, INC.

WORKERS COMPENSATION

INDIANA

INDIANAPOLIS .... INTERNATIONAL INVESTIGATORS, INC.

BOISE,* 125,738, *Ada Co.*

COURT REPORTERS

Hedrick
COURT REPORTING

Idaho's Full-Service Court Reporting Professionals

Serving ALL of Idaho, Eastern Oregon and Eastern Washington

Services Include:

- Technical Depositions
- Both Governmental & private sector specialists
- Easy access deposition suite
- Telephone conference depositions
- Quick turnaround of depositions
- ASCII Disks
- Condensed Transcripts with complete work index at NO COST
- Video taping
- E-mail & faxing of transcripts
- Daily transcripts
- Meetings, hearings, conferences & workshops

"Serving The Legal Community Since 1978"

Idaho Certified Shorthand Reporters
Registered Professional Reporters
Members of National & State Court Reporters Associations

Hedrick Court Reporting
1655 Fairview Ave.
Suite 201
Boise, Idaho 83702
Telephone: (208) 336-9208
Fax: (208) 388-3853
Email: wallyhedrick@aol.com

Celebrating Our 27th Year of Service to our Clients

Call us, we are ready to help you!!!

M &M

Court Reporting Service, Inc.
Website: www.m-mservice.com

(This Listing Continued)

Since 1970, M&M Court Reporting Service has provided quality litigation services to the Idaho legal community. M&M covers all of Idaho, Eastern Oregon, and Spokane, Washington. Our main offices are in Boise and Coeur d'Alene, with branch offices in Twin Falls and Pocatello, Idaho, Ontario, Oregon, and Spokane. If you need to take depositions in an outlying area, we can find a facility for you to use. We can help with scheduling out-of-state reporters as well. Just call us.

M&M continues to be a leader in technology, offering exhibit scanning and electronic presentations. M&M's dedication to our clients includes providing software and training to keep clients on the leading edge of litigation technology. M&M sponsors lunches during which real-time reporting, database preparation and usage, video sync programs, and trial presentation are demonstrated.

SERVICES

- Real-time Reporting
- Internet Reporting
- Daily Copy
- Locating Reporters in Outside Areas
- CART (Captioning)
- Drag-n-Drop Jury Instruction Program
- Work Comp Decisions on CD
- Video / Transcript Synchronization
- Software Vendors / Software Support
- Trial Presentations / Consulting
- Database Construction / Data Entry
- Document Imaging / CD Archival
- PowerPoint Presentations

SCHEDULING DEPOSITIONS

Southern Idaho / Eastern OR
Boise Office
Telephone: 208 / 345-9611
Toll Free: 1-800-234-9611
Fax: 208 / 345-8800
Email: m-and-m@qwest.net

Northern Idaho / Spokane, WA
Coeur d'Alene Office
Telephone: 208 / 765-1700
Toll Free: 1-800-879-1700
Fax: 208 / 765-8097
Email: csmith@mmcourt.com

EXPERT WITNESS
FORENSIC ACCOUNTING

Cooper Norman
CERTIFIED PUBLIC ACCOUNTANTS
A PROFESSIONAL LIMITED LIABILITY COMPANY

"Not Your Average Bean Counters"

Boise
(208) 336-0800

Twin Falls
(208) 733-6581

Idaho Falls
(208) 523-0862

(This Listing Continued)

EXPERT WITNESS
FORENSIC ACCOUNTING (cont'd)

Cooper Norman Certified Public Accountants (cont'd)

We Specialize In

- **Divorce**
- **Expert Testimony**
- **Wrongful Death**
- **Mergers and Acquisitions**
- **Buy-Sell Agreements**
- **Employee Benefit Plans**
- **Estate and Gift Tax Return**
- **Economic Loss**
- **Divestitures**
- **Business Valuations**
- **Wrongful Termination**
- **Purchase / Sale of Stock**
- **Sale of Business**
- **Employee Stock Ownership Plans**
- **Shareholder Disputes**
- **Eminent Domain**
- **Litigation**

www.coopernorman.com

LITIGATION SUPPORT SERVICES

Cooper Norman
Certified Public Accountants

Boise
(208) 336-0800

Twin Falls
(208) 733-6581

Idaho Falls
(208) 523-0862

LITIGATION SUPPORT SERVICES

Cooper Norman
CERTIFIED PUBLIC ACCOUNTANTS
A PROFESSIONAL LIMITED LIABILITY COMPANY

"Not Your Average Bean Counters"

Boise	Twin Falls	Idaho Falls
(208) 336-0800	(208) 733-6581	(208) 523-0862

We Specialize In

- **Divorce**
- **Expert Testimony**
- **Wrongful Death**
- **Mergers and Acquisitions**
- **Buy-Sell Agreements**
- **Employee Benefit Plans**
- **Estate and Gift Tax Return**
- **Economic Loss**
- **Divestitures**
- **Business Valuations**
- **Wrongful Termination**
- **Purchase / Sale of Stock**
- **Sale of Business**
- **Employee Stock Ownership Plans**
- **Shareholder Disputes**
- **Eminent Domain**
- **Litigation**

www.coopernorman.com

(This Listing Continued)

LITIGATION SUPPORT SERVICES

Cooper Norman
Certified Public Accountants

Boise
(208) 336-0800

Twin Falls
(208) 733-6581

Idaho Falls
(208) 523-0862

TRANSCRIPTION SERVICES

Hedrick
COURT REPORTING

Idaho's Full-Service Court Reporting Professionals

Serving ALL of Idaho, Eastern Oregon and Eastern Washington

Services Include:

- Technical Depositions
- Both Governmental & private sector specialists
- Easy access deposition suite
- Telephone conference depositions
- Quick turnaround of depositions
- ASCII Disks
- Condensed Transcripts with complete work index at NO COST
- Video taping
- E-mail & faxing of transcripts
- Daily transcripts
- Meetings, hearings, conferences & workshops

"Serving The Legal Community Since 1978"

Idaho Certified Shorthand Reporters
Registered Professional Reporters
Members of National & State Court Reporters Associations

Hedrick Court Reporting

1655 Fairview Ave.
Suite 201
Boise, Idaho 83702
Telephone: (208) 336-9208
Fax: (208) 388-3853
Email: wallyhedrick@aol.com

Celebrating Our 27th Year of Service to our Clients

Call us, we are ready to help you!!!

VIDEO TAPE SERVICES

Hedrick
COURT REPORTING

Idaho's Full-Service Court Reporting Professionals

Serving ALL of Idaho, Eastern Oregon and Eastern Washington

Services Include:

- Technical Depositions
- Both Governmental & private sector specialists
- Easy access deposition suite
- Telephone conference depositions
- Quick turnaround of depositions
- ASCII Disks
- Condensed Transcripts with complete work index at NO COST
- Video taping
- E-mail & faxing of transcripts
- Daily transcripts
- Meetings, hearings, conferences & workshops

"Serving The Legal Community Since 1978"

Idaho Certified Shorthand Reporters
Registered Professional Reporters
Members of National & State Court Reporters Associations

Hedrick Court Reporting

1655 Fairview Ave.
Suite 201
Boise, Idaho 83702
Telephone: (208) 336-9208
Fax: (208) 388-3853
Email: wallyhedrick@aol.com

Celebrating Our 27th Year of Service to our Clients

Call us, we are ready to help you!!!

JEROME,* 6,529, *Jerome Co.*

DOCUMENT RESEARCH, RETRIEVAL & FILING

Aardvark Legal Support Service

132 West Main
Jerome, Idaho 83338
Home Office: 208-644-1444
Toll Free: 877-324-2026
Fax: 208-324-4620
Email: info@aardvarkllc.com

(This Listing Continued)

Founded in 2000, Aardvark Legal Support Service is an attorney service bureau located in the heart of Idaho, providing services throughout the United States and Canada. As a company we have been fortunate to engage a group of dedicated and knowledgeable individuals, who combine the latest technology with personalized service, thereby delivering to the client a professional service with a personal touch. Our team approach provides clients with exceptional services at affordable fees while preserving customer satisfaction.

We provide complete service of process of all documents such as summons & complaints, small claims, cross-complaints, and personal subpoenas, as well as skip tracing/locates, court records searches and court filings. We utilize only professional process servers to effect service of process, which ensures that your work is completed professionally and accurately the first time.

We Serve the STATE OF IDAHO

We Also Offer These Services:

- Process Service (Rush Service Available)
- Investigations
- Real Estate Postings
- Locate/Skip Tracing
- Records Searches
- Court Filings
- Traveling Notary

Member: National Association of Professional Process Servers
United States Process Servers Association
International Process Servers Association

PROCESS SERVERS & DOCUMENT DELIVERY SERVICES

Aardvark Legal Support Service

132 West Main
Jerome, Idaho 83338
Home Office: 208-644-1444
Toll Free: 877-324-2026
Fax: 208-324-4620
Email: info@aardvarkllc.com

Founded in 2000, Aardvark Legal Support Service is an attorney service bureau located in the heart of Idaho, providing services throughout the United States and Canada. As a company we have been fortunate to engage a group of dedicated and knowledgeable individuals, who combine the latest technology with personalized service, thereby delivering to the client a professional service with a personal touch. Our team approach provides clients with exceptional services at affordable fees while preserving customer satisfaction.

We provide complete service of process of all documents such as summons & complaints, small claims, cross-complaints, and personal subpoenas, as well as skip tracing/locates, court records searches and court filings. We utilize only professional process servers to effect service of process, which ensures that your work is completed professionally and accurately the first time.

(This Listing Continued)

PROCESS SERVERS & DOCUMENT DELIVERY SERVICES (cont'd)

Aardvark Legal Support Service (cont'd)

We Serve the STATE OF IDAHO

We Also Offer These Services:

- Process Service (Rush Service Available)
- Investigations
- Real Estate Postings
- Locate/Skip Tracing
- Records Searches
- Court Filings
- Traveling Notary

Member: National Association of Professional Process Servers
United States Process Servers Association
International Process Servers Association

BELLEVILLE,* 42,785, *St. Clair Co.*

COURT REPORTERS

Reporting Company

Gore, Perry, Gateway & Lipa Reporting Co.

A Full Service Reporting Firm Serving
Eastern Missouri and Southern Illinois

Established 1933

515 Olive Street
Suite 700
St. Louis, MO 63101

1-800-878-6750 (314) 241-6750
Fax (314) 241-5070
Email: gpgl@sbcglobal.net

Ronald A. Gore, CM, RPR, CSR (MO, IL)
Robert Perry, CSR (MO, IL)

Certificates of Merit
Certified Shorthand Reporters
Certified Court Reporters
Registered Professional Reporters

- Medical/Technical/Chemical
- Video
- Conference Rooms
- ASCII/Discovery ZX/WordPerfect
- Min-U-Script/Word Index
- Arbitrations
- Process Service
- Conventions
- Hotel Referrals
- Videoconference

RANKIN REPORTING & LEGAL VIDEO, INC.

Serving the Legal Community since 1966

Rankin Certified Court Reporters are licensed in both Missouri and Illinois. Their superior skills meet the demands of the most complex litigation projects including examinations under oath, depositions, arbitrations, administrative hearings and trials. Your needs receive our undivided attention.

Certified Realtime Reporters	Registered Professional Reporters
Registered Diplomate	Certified Shorthand Reporters
Reporters	Certified Court Reporters
Registered Merit Reporters	Certified Legal Video Specialist

TRANSCRIPT DELIVERY IN ACCORDANCE WITH YOUR REQUEST

(This Listing Continued)

COMPETITIVE RATES

- LiveNote, web site transcript repository
- Deposition Specialists: Scientific/Technical/Medical
- Hearings and Arbitrations
- Compressed Transcripts/Word Index
- Realtime Reporting
- Text/Video Sync
- Complimentary Deposition Suites
- Video: taping, editing, presentation, conferencing
- Covering all of eastern Missouri and southern Illinois
- E-Transcript/E-Binder

Telephone: 1-314-231-2202 www.rankinreporting.com

Fax: 1-314-231-7432 email: traci@rankinreporting.com

1015 Locust Street - Suite 911
St. Louis, Missouri 63101-1329
Call us Toll Free at 1-800-285-2115

CHICAGO, 2,783,726, *Cook Co.*

ACTUARIAL ANALYSIS

WILLIAM C. CUTLIP CONSULTING

William C. Cutlip
FSA, MAAA, FCA, CLU, ChFC, CPCU

Web Site: www.cutlipconsulting.com

3048 Woods Edge Way	8021 Wildomar Drive
Madison, WI 53711	Tucson, AZ 85743
Phone: (608) 443-0669	Phone: (520) 572-8833
Fax: (608) 443-0668	Fax: (520) 579-6688

Cell: (520) 247-6592

Areas of Expertise: Expert Witness / Forensics / Litigation Support / Arbitrations

Financial Evaluation for:

- damages
- investment
- merger & acquisition
- structured settlements
- grievances
- equitable distribution

Legal Ammunition for:

- pre-filing evaluation
- case strength
- surprise reduction
- strategy support
- opposition analysis
- scientifically supported evaluation

Professional Profile:
Educated at Massachusetts Institute of Technology and Oklahoma State University, William C. Cutlip has over 40 years of industry experience and specializes in risk evaluation and expert witness work for attorneys, product development for insurance companies, and business consulting.

(This Listing Continued)

ACTUARIAL ANALYSIS (cont'd)

William C. Cutlip Consulting (cont'd)

Professional Qualifications:

Fellow, Society of Actuaries (FSA)
Member, American Academy of Actuaries (MAAA)
Fellow, Conference of Consulting Actuaries (FCA)
Chartered Life Underwriter (CLU)
Chartered Financial Consultant (ChFC)
Member, International Association of Consulting Actuaries

Cases/Clients: Plaintiff and Defense

Geographical Area: No Limitation

E-mail Contact: cutlipconsulting@cs.com

ADMIRALTY & MARITIME EXPERT & CONSULTANT

WORK DONE IN ALL STATES

DAVID E. COLE
COMMANDER, U.S.C.G. (RET.)
20 YEARS OF SERVICE

MARITIME - ADMIRALTY SERVICES
CONSULTANT AND EXPERT WITNESS
ESTABLISHED 1989

TEXAS OFFICE
PHONE: 1-817-571-7731
LOUISIANA OFFICE
PHONE: 1-504-340-8942
WWW.DAVIDECOLE.COM
COLEBIGSHIP@AOL.COM

AREAS OF EXPERTISE

(BOTH PLAINTIFF AND DEFENDANT)
PERSONAL INJURY AND DEATH
GROUNDINGS AND DETERMINATION OF NAVIGABLE WATERS
PERMITTING AND BRIDGES
VESSEL ACCESS AND REGULATORY ANALYSIS
COLLISIONS AND ALLISONS
JONES ACT AND LONGSHORE
NAVIGATION AND SEAMANSHIP
GENERAL MARITIME SAFETY AND OFFSHORE
VESSEL OPERATION AND MANNING

(This Listing Continued)

SERVICES

LITIGATION SUPPORT
NAVIGATION ANALYSIS
VESSEL INSPECTIONS
COLLISION ANALYSIS
DEPOSITION APPEARANCES
RESEARCH
REPORTS
AGENCY LIAISON
TRIAL APPEARANCES
(QUALIFIED TO TESTIFY IN FEDERAL AND STATE COURTS)

ALL TYPES OF VESSELS

RECREATIONAL BOATS AND PERSONAL WATERCRAFT
TOWING VESSELS AND TUG BOATS
CHARTER VESSELS AND TANK SHIPS
PASSENGER AND CARGO VESSELS
BARGES AND FISHING VESSELS
CREW AND SUPPLY BOATS

PROFESSIONAL EXPERIENCE

DAVID E. COLE, CONSULTANT, SINCE 1989 NEW ORLEANS, LOUISIANA AREA
LATHAM & ASSOCIATES, 1988-1989, NEW ORLEANS, LOUISIANA AREA
8th USCG DISTRICT, 1986-1987, NEW ORLEANS, LOUISIANA
USCG MARINE INSPECTION OFFICE, 1982-1986, NEW ORLEANS, LOUISIANA
SECOND USCG DISTRICT, 1979-1982, ST. LOUIS, MISSOURI
USCG MARINE SAFETY OFFICE, 1976-1978, HUNTINGTON, WEST VIRGINIA
USCG MARINE INSPECTION, 1972-1975, NEW YORK, NEW YORK
USCGC KLAMATH, 1970-1972, SEATTLE, WASHINGTON
USCG MARINE INSPECTION OFFICE, 1967-1970, SEATTLE, WASHINGTON

EDUCATION

JURIS DOCTOR, LOYOLA UNIVERSITY OF N.O. L.A. 1987
BACHELOR OF SCIENCE, STATE UNIVERSITY OF NEW YORK, MARITIME COLLEGE (FORT SCHUYLER)
EXTENSIVE GRADUATE WORK IN TRANSPORTATION MANAGEMENT, STATE UNIVERSITY OF NEW YORK
NUMEROUS COURSES IN SHIPYARD AND SHIP BOARD SAFETY, NATIONWIDE
UNIVERSITY OF SOUTHWEST LOUISIANA, OFFSHORE OIL TECHNOLOGY
TULANE ADMIRALTY LAW INSTITUTE
AMERICAN WATERWAYS OPERATORS INDUSTRY TRAINING
DALE CARNEGIE COURSE IN EFFECTIVE SPEAKING

MEMBERSHIPS

AMERICAN BAR ASSOCIATION
NEW ORLEANS BAR ASSOCIATION
LOUISIANA TRIAL LAWYERS ASSOCIATION
BOAT/U.S. TECHNICAL INFORMATION EXCHANGE FOR MARINE PROFESSIONALS
MARITIME LAW ASSOCIATION OF THE UNITED STATES
LOUISIANA BAR ASSOCIATION
ASSOCIATION OF TRIAL LAWYERS OF AMERICA
AMERICAN BOAT AND YACHT COUNCIL
NATIONAL FIRE PROTECTION ASSOCIATION
SOUTHEASTERN ADMIRALTY LAW INSTITUTE
PROPELLER CLUB

ARBITRATION & MEDIATION SERVICES

ADR SYSTEMS OF AMERICA

123 Madison Street
22nd Floor
Chicago, IL 60602

Phone: (312) 960-2260
Fax: (312) 960-2268

Toll Free: 1-800-423-7010

Email: mbecker@adrsystems.net
Website: www.adrsystems.com

ADR Systems of America has been providing an alternative means of dispute resolution since October of 1994. The number of private cases heard is quickly approaching 8000.

ADR Systems of America is the only ADR service that exclusively utilizes the assistance of retired judges for its **personal injury division**. Our distinguished panel of retired judges is trained for the purpose of providing arbitration and mediation hearings.

In our **commercial division**, we use the assistance of retired judges as well as some of the country's most respected attorneys/experts for arbitration and mediation. ADR systems of America maintains its corporate office in Chicago, Illinois but provides ADR services in many locations across the United States.

ADR Systems is now providing arbitrations and mediations for complex commercial disputes.
Please see our website for our streamlined Rules of Arbitration.

ADR Services

- ADR Procedures
- Case Coordination
- Training Seminars
- Case Consulting

ADR Procedures
ADR Systems provides a wide variety of Dispute Resolution procedures which can be tailored to meet your specific needs.

- Binding Arbitration
- Mediation
- Binding Mediation
- Med/Arb
- Appellate Insights
- Tele/mediation
- Paper Arbitrations

Our goal is to provide clients with prompt and professional service...to supply a forum to resolve disputes in an impartial manner...to be large enough to handle all your needs but small enough to give you the individual attention you require.

JAMS

THE RESOLUTION EXPERTS

www.jamsadr.com
1-800-352-JAMS

JAMS, The Resolution Experts, offers its domestic and international clients an exclusive panel of justices, judges and attorneys with proven track records for resolving the most complex and high stakes cases. With over 20 offices nationwide, JAMS and its 200 full-time neutrals are responsible for resolving thousands of cases in the United States and abroad.

The JAMS difference lies in its expert neutrals and highly trained case managers. JAMS selects the world's top judges and attorneys based on their experience, reputation and proven ability to adjudicate cases and settle large and complex disputes. JAMS has neutrals with experience in all case types, and with specialized knowledge in individual practice areas such as employment, construction, real estate, environmental, intellectual property, bankruptcy and insurance coverage. In addition, JAMS case managers excel at getting parties to agree on a neutral, procedure, location, and date - all with a unified agenda of gaining resolution to disputes.

While JAMS neutrals are especially adept at resolving complex, multi-party, and difficult disputes, JAMS offers a full scope of ADR services and can resolve disputes in any price category. Some of the ADR services JAMS provides include: mediation, arbitration, special mastering, neutral fact finding, private jury trials, settlements conferences, ADR training and class action settlement adjudication.

JAMS is united in providing world-class resolution services. The various ADR processes employed by JAMS have proven their merit in case after case.

JAMS can be reached at its Chicago, IL resolution center:

222 S. Riverside Plaza
Suite 1850
Chicago, IL 60606
(312) 655-0555
Fax (312) 655-0644

ATTORNEY SERVICES

BPSI
Borg Process Servers Inc.

serving the legal profession since 1973,
throughout Canada & U.S.A.

5511 Steeles Ave. W., #208
Toronto, Ontario CANADA M9L 1S7
Email: Admin@borgps.com
Website: www.borgps.com

(This Listing Continued)

ATTORNEY SERVICES (cont'd)

Borg Process Servers Inc. (cont'd)

Specialists in:

- Process Serving
- Court Processing & Searching
- Business, Personal and Ministry of Transportation Searches

Office hours 7:30a.m. to 6:00p.m. Eastern Time

1-800-567-2674 (BORG)
Fax 416-746-2329

BAR ASSOCIATIONS

Association of Legal Administrators

75 Tri-State International Suite 222
Lincolnshire, IL 60069-4435
Telephone: (847) 267-1252
Fax: (847) 267-1329
www.alanet.org

The Association of Legal Administrators (ALA), founded in 1971, provides educational opportunities and services to law office administrators who manage such areas as finance, human resources, systems and technology, facilities, marketing and practice development. ALA has more than 9,000 members in 27 countries. The Association's mission is to "promote and enhance the competence and professionalism of legal administrators and all members of the management team."

ALA's Web site - at *www.alanet.org* - provides the legal community with information about ALA's educational programs and member services, print and online management resources, online educational opportunities and jobs available in legal management, and links to more than 250 law-related resources and organizations.

ALA's Annual Educational Conference and Exposition features more than 100 expert speakers, including law office managers, attorneys and management professors, and the latest products and services from more than 250 vendors.

ALA also offers an opportunity for legal administrators to add to their credentials by becoming a Certified Legal Manager (CLM)℠. The voluntary CLM℠ certification program allows a qualified legal administrator to demonstrate, through an examination process, a mastery of core areas of knowledge identified as essential to the effective performance of a principal administrator. Examinations are administered each autumn and then each spring during the Annual Educational Conference and Exposition.

(This Listing Continued)

Each fall, ALA sponsors the Corporate/Government Fall Forum, the Large Firm Principal Administrator Retreat and the Intellectual Property Retreat. These events address the unique needs of managers from these types of law practices. ALA's Regions also host individual Conferences each autumn, and ALA's chapters conduct many seminars and retreats at the local level.

The latest developments in law office management are covered in *Legal Management,* ALA's journal. ALA offers many other publications, audiotapes and videotapes on such subjects as communication and general management, human resources, office systems, finance and client development.

Regular membership in ALA is open to any full-time administrator or support manager who is employed in a private law firm, corporate, government or university legal department, or charitable legal agency. Associate membership is available to some categories of individuals. Membership is not open to vendors or consultants.

BUILDING EVALUATION - DUE DILIGENCE

Wiss, Janney, Elstner Associates, Inc.

Engineers, Architects, Materials Scientists
330 Pfingsten Road
Northbrook, IL 60062
Offices nationwide

Phone	800/345-3199
Fax	847/291-9599
Internet	www.wje.com
Contact	Gary Klein, EVP

WJE is a professional firm providing practical, innovative, and technically sound solutions to structural, architectural, and materials problems. During our 49-year history, we have successfully completed more than 60,000 projects involving virtually every type of construction material, structural system, and architectural component.

WJE's staff of forensic consultants have extensive field and laboratory experience providing investigative, testing, and assessment services for building materials; design / construction deficiencies and practices; and building code compliance.

Specialized services include:

- Structural and Architectural Assessments
- Failure Investigation and Analysis
- Repair / Rehabilitation Design
- Construction Materials Evaluation / Testing
- Computerized Failure Simulations
- Courtroom Exhibits / Models
- Due Diligence / Prepurchase Surveys
- Expert Witness Testimony
- Litigation Support

Many of WJE's staff of more than 280 engineers, architects, and materials scientists are nationally recognized experts. WJE maintains offices across the country with professional engineering or architectural registration in every state.

CLASS ACTION NOTICE

A.B. Data, Ltd.

4057 N. Wilson Drive
Milwaukee, WI 53211
Phone: 414-963-6440
Fax: 414-963-7950

A.B. Data, Ltd., founded in 1980, is an international firm that offers class action, bankruptcy and complex litigation support services, with offices in Milwaukee, Wisconsin, Washington, D.C., and Tel Aviv. A.B. Data's international reputation of key role playing in complex settlements, along with its strong, focused management, provides the very best approach and the most cost-effective manner to execute a creative plan in partnership with each client that achieves efficient and effective results in cases with the most exacting specifications.

A.B. Data provides a complete range of class action support services to achieve judicial finality by implementing proper notice, claims and settlement administration, telephony, web, data, documents, print and mail, and fund disbursement services. Through the investment in hardware and skilled specialists, A.B. Data helps attorneys focus on law without the distraction of collateral functions.

With over 320 employees in its class action and bankruptcy services, consulting, data, print and mail processing business, A.B. Data has responded to class actions with over 900 additional notice and investigative staff members. More than a million documents were scanned and processed to a searchable database, and more than 150,000 disadvantaged claimants personally assisted with claims completion.

A.B. Data has effectively handled hundreds of thousands of claims, and communicated with over two million potential class members who spoke more than 80 languages, lived in 109 countries and were mostly 65 and older.

(This Listing Continued)

The Data Services Division offers the highest level of security and is able to produce one million personalized mail pieces every 24 hours. A.B. Data's 180,000 sq. ft. Mail Distribution Center, with its own on-site USPS postal sub-station, is one of the nation's largest and most advanced facilities, capable of mailing four million pieces a day and has been entrusted to MICR print and mail 70,000 checks a week totaling a billion dollars annually.

CLASS ACTION SETTLEMENT ADMINISTRATION

A.B. Data, Ltd.

4057 N. Wilson Drive
Milwaukee, WI 53211
Phone: 414-963-6440
Fax: 414-963-7950

A.B. Data, Ltd., founded in 1980, is an international firm that offers class action, bankruptcy and complex litigation support services, with offices in Milwaukee, Wisconsin, Washington, D.C., and Tel Aviv. A.B. Data's international reputation of key role playing in complex settlements, along with its strong, focused management, provides the very best approach and the most cost-effective manner to execute a creative plan in partnership with each client that achieves efficient and effective results in cases with the most exacting specifications.

(This Listing Continued)

A.B. Data provides a complete range of class action support services to achieve judicial finality by implementing proper notice, claims and settlement administration, telephony, web, data, documents, print and mail, and fund disbursement services. Through the investment in hardware and skilled specialists, A.B. Data helps attorneys focus on law without the distraction of collateral functions.

With over 320 employees in its class action and bankruptcy services, consulting, data, print and mail processing business, A.B. Data has responded to class actions with over 900 additional notice and investigative staff members. More than a million documents were scanned and processed to a searchable database, and more than 150,000 disadvantaged claimants personally assisted with claims completion.

A.B. Data has effectively handled hundreds of thousands of claims, and communicated with over two million potential class members who spoke more than 80 languages, lived in 109 countries and were mostly 65 and older.

The Data Services Division offers the highest level of security and is able to produce one million personalized mail pieces every 24 hours. A.B. Data's 180,000 sq. ft. Mail Distribution Center, with its own on-site USPS postal sub-station, is one of the nation's largest and most advanced facilities, capable of mailing four million pieces a day and has been entrusted to MICR print and mail 70,000 checks a week totaling a billion dollars annually.

GCG

The Garden City Group, Inc.

As specialists in legal administration services, The Garden City Group, Inc. (GCG) provides comprehensive solutions to: administer class actions, design legal notice programs, and manage chapter 11 claims administrations. We are a respected resource for plaintiff and defense counsel as well as corporations who seek our expert consultation to address a variety of legal service issues and challenges. GCG is a technology-driven organization led by a multi-disciplinary team comprised of experts from IT, management, and law. We welcome an opportunity to learn more about your needs and how we can address them through our class action service division.

GCG Class Action Services is a neutral resource trusted by all counsel to administer consumer, employee-related, human rights, mass tort, antitrust, insurance, chapter 11, product, and securities class actions.

We offer a variety of synergistic services to develop, manage, and execute all stages of integrated class action settlement plans

- from first contact through closure
- from database management through design and production
- from notification through authentication
- from claims processing through storage and distribution

Need greater productivity at reduced cost?
Working with limited in-house resources or expertise in class action?
Consider outsourcing your settlement functions
to GCG Class Action Services.
We're a cost-effective outsourcing solution for the settlement function.

(This Listing Continued)

CLASS ACTION SETTLEMENT ADMINISTRATION (cont'd)

The Garden City Group, Inc. (cont'd)

Notable Cases

American Family Publishers (AFP) Business Practices Settlement
Auction Houses Antitrust Litigation
Baxter Healthcare Corp Gammagard® Products Liability Settlement
General Motors Brake Litigation
Johnson & Johnson Acuvue® Settlement
Lucent Technologies Settlement
Manville Personal Injury Settlement
Merrill Lynch Securities Litigation Settlement
Non-Starlink Corn Products Liability Litigation
Philip Morris Securities Settlement
Sears Reaffirmation Settlement
USAA Diminished Value Settlement
Visa/Mastercard Debit Card Antitrust Litigation
Western Union Money Transfer Litigation
WorldCom Inc. Securities Litigation

The Garden City Group, Inc.

105 Maxess Road
Melville, New York 11747
Phone: (631) 470-5000 – Fax: (631) 470-5100
Toll Free: 1-800-327-3664
www.gardencitygroup.com

CONSTRUCTION CONSULTANTS

CTLGROUP

5400 OLD ORCHARD ROAD
Skokie, IL 60077-1030
Telephone: 800.522.2285
Fax: 847.965.6541
Web Site: www.CTLGroup.com
Email: JGarrett@CTLGroup.com

CTLGroup is an internationally recognized consulting engineering firm with an 85-year history of offering professional structural engineering, testing and research services. CTLGroup's staff of 140 professionals offers a unique combination of structural investigative services, structural engineering analysis and design services, construction materials testing and research, and structural diagnostics testing and laboratory services. Our expertise includes:

- Consulting engineering
- Condition and damage assessments
- Structural failure investigations and root cause determinations
- Nondestructive testing and in-situ evaluations
- Building material failure analyses and remediation
- Structural system failure analyses and remediation
- Laboratory material testing and evaluation
- Laboratory structural component testing and evaluation
- Real-time in-situ structural health monitoring
- Design and construction standard of care issues
- Litigation and legal support, including
  - Expert Testimony
  - Demonstrative evidence

Wiss, Janney, Elstner Associates, Inc.

Engineers, Architects, Materials Scientists
330 Pfingsten Road
Northbrook, IL 60062
Offices nationwide

Phone	800/345-3199
Fax	847/291-9599
Internet	www.wje.com
Contact	Gary Klein, EVP

WJE is a professional firm providing practical, innovative, and technically sound solutions to structural, architectural, and materials problems. During our 49-year history, we have successfully completed more than 60,000 projects involving virtually every type of construction material, structural system, and architectural component.

WJE's staff of forensic consultants have extensive field and laboratory experience providing investigative, testing, and assessment services for building materials; design / construction deficiencies and practices; and building code compliance.

Specialized services include:

- Structural and Architectural Assessments
- Failure Investigation and Analysis
- Repair / Rehabilitation Design
- Construction Materials Evaluation / Testing
- Computerized Failure Simulations
- Courtroom Exhibits / Models
- Due Diligence / Prepurchase Surveys
- Expert Witness Testimony
- Litigation Support

Many of WJE's staff of more than 280 engineers, architects, and materials scientists are nationally recognized experts. WJE maintains offices across the country with professional engineering or architectural registration in every state.

CONSTRUCTION CONSULTANTS-STRUCTURAL DAMAGE

CTLGROUP

5400 OLD ORCHARD ROAD
Skokie, IL 60077-1030
Telephone: 800.522.2285
Fax: 847.965.6541
Web Site: www.CTLGroup.com
Email: JGarrett@CTLGroup.com

CTLGroup is an internationally recognized consulting engineering firm with an 85-year history of offering professional structural engineering, testing and research services. CTLGroup's staff of 140 professionals offers a unique combination of structural investigative services, structural engineering analysis and design services, construction materials testing and research, and structural diagnostics testing and laboratory services. Our expertise includes:

(This Listing Continued)

- Consulting engineering
- Condition and damage assessments
- Structural failure investigations and root cause determinations
- Nondestructive testing and in-situ evaluations
- Building material failure analyses and remediation
- Structural system failure analyses and remediation
- Laboratory material testing and evaluation
- Laboratory structural component testing and evaluation
- Real-time in-situ structural health monitoring
- Design and construction standard of care issues
- Litigation and legal support, including
  - Expert Testimony
  - Demonstrative evidence

Wiss, Janney, Elstner Associates, Inc.

Engineers, Architects, Materials Scientists
330 Pfingsten Road
Northbrook, IL 60062
Offices nationwide

Phone	800/345-3199
Fax	847/291-9599
Internet	www.wje.com
Contact	Gary Klein, EVP

WJE is a professional firm providing practical, innovative, and technically scund solutions to structural, architectural, and materials problems. During our 49-year history, we have successfully completed more than 60,000 projects involving virtually every type of construction material, structural system, and architectural component.

WJE's staff of forensic consultants have extensive field and laboratory experience providing investigative, testing, and assessment services for building materials; design / construction deficiencies and practices; and building code compliance.

Specialized services include:

- Structural and Architectural Assessments
- Failure Investigation and Analysis
- Repair / Rehabilitation Design
- Construction Materials Evaluation / Testing
- Computerized Failure Simulations
- Courtroom Exhibits / Models
- Due Diligence / Prepurchase Surveys
- Expert Witness Testimony
- Litigation Support

Many of WJE's staff of more than 280 engineers, architects, and materials scientists are nationally recognized experts. WJE maintains offices across the country with professional engineering or architectural registration in every state.

COURT REPORTERS

1-2-3

1-800-682-5201

For Chicago Depositions
1-2-3 Reporting Service
a division of Certified Reporting Company
11 East Adams Street
Suite 1108
Chicago, Illinois 60603-5603

24 HOUR PHONE: 800-682-5201
Email: certifiedreportingco@prodigy.net
www.certifiedreportingco.com

COURT REPORTER OWNED AND COURT REPORTER MANAGED

- Only Experienced Certified and RPR Shorthand Reporters
- Realtime Reporters Upon Request
- Technical, Malpractice, Product Liability and Patent Depositions
- Computer-Aided Transcription
- Daily and Expedited Delivery on Transcripts
- Min-U-Script® Condensed Transcripts and Master Indexes Available
- Complete Litigation Support Available
- ASCII and Discovery ZX Diskettes Available Compatible with Any DOS-Based System
- Key Word Indexing and Proximity Search
- Complimentary Deposition Suites Available
- Video Depositions by Certified Technicians/Attorney Including "Day In The Life" Record and Accident Scene Videos
- Subpoena Services Available
- Timestamping of Depositions

MEMBER OF:
NATIONAL COURT REPORTERS ASSOCIATION
ILLINOIS STATE REPORTERS ASSOCIATION
CHICAGO METROPOLITAN REPORTERS ASSOCIATION

References upon request.

SEE OUR AD ON PAGE IL8S

ADVANTAGE REPORTING SERVICE

Statewide Services
Certified Shorthand and Registered Professional Reporters

Realtime Reporting
Complimentary Deposition Suites
Certified Videotaped Depositions
Condensed Transcripts/Index
E-Transcripts
ASCII/IBM Compatible Discs
Daily and Expedited Service
Technical/Medical Expertise
All Phases of Reporting

1000 Essington Road
Lincolnshire Business Center
Joliet, IL 60435

1-800-347-3124

ADVANTAGE REPORTING SERVICE

Statewide Services
Certified Shorthand and Registered Professional Reporters

Member: National Court Reporters' Association
Illinois Shorthand Reporters' Association

- Realtime Reporting
- Complimentary Deposition Suites
- Certified Videotaped Depositions
- Condensed Transcripts/Index
- ASCII/IBM Compatible Disks
- E-transcripts
- Daily and Expedited Service
- Technical/Medical Expertise
- All Phases of Reporting

(800) 347-3124
FAX: (800) 690-3376

401 North Michigan Avenue
Suite 1200-#24
Chicago, IL 60611

SEE OUR AD ON PAGE IL9S

CENTRAL REPORTERS ASSOCIATED

29 E. Madison Street
Suite 1826
Chicago, Illinois 60606

(312) 630-2007
Fax (312) 630-2015
Toll Free (877) 630-7533
E-mail CRA2007@aol.com

Conveniently located in downtown Chicago

Highly-qualified, experienced **Certified Shorthand Reporters** serving the Chicago Metropolitan area, Cook, Lake & Dupage Counties.

- Conference Facilities on site.
- Condensed transcripts with indexing.
- Encripted email transcripts with Etrans.
- Videotaping, Reproduction and RealTime reporting available upon request.

MEMBERS:
National Court Reporters Association
Illinois Shorthand Reporters Association

Proudly serving the legal profession for over 25 years.

AREA COURT REPORTERS

24-HOUR PHONE: (800) 224-1568
(847) 352-8059
FAX: (847) 870-7971

COMPUTERIZED TRANSCRIPTION

ASCII FORMATTED DISKETTES

CONDENSED TRANSCRIPTS

KEY WORD INDEXING

COMPLETE VIDEOTAPE SERVICES

Conference rooms at O'HARE INTERNATIONAL AIRPORT and in Schaumburg

Depositions * Arbitrations * Court Hearings
Conventions * Meetings

Subpoena and Notice Services

Serving Chicago and all suburban areas

Established 1978

335 Wingate Drive
Schaumburg, Illinois 60193

COURT REPORTERS (cont'd)

BENEDIA
CERTIFIED COURT REPORTING SERVICE

Servicing
Chicago Phoenix
Chicago Headquarters
175 E. Delaware St.
Suite 6105
Chicago, IL 60611
Phone: (312) 482-8990 Fax: (312) 482-8992
Toll Free: (877) 482-8990
E-mail: phil@benedia.com
Website: www.benedia.com

SERVICES

- Trials
- Motions
- Hearings
- Prove-ups
- Conventions
- Arbitrations
- Board Meetings
- Depositions
- Statements
- Online Repository
- Telephone Depositions
- Real-time Reporting
- Transcripts from Audio Tape
- Video Tape Services
- Electronic Reporting
- Video Conferencing
- Translations & Interpreters
- E-mailing of Transcripts
- Keyword Indexing
- Examinations Under Oath
- Conference Room

NOTABLE FEATURES

Most notable for our state of the art equipment, which helps us to handle some of the most complex cases. Our "Online Repository" gives you access to all your cases, invoices and transcripts 24 hours a day, 7 days a week.
Log on Anywhere.

WE MAKE YOUR JOB EASIER!

If you are searching for a court reporting agency with sound ethics, and integrity...who delivers accurate and prompt service...who meets your needs...then look no further!

Central Reporters Associated

29 E. Madison St.
Suite 1826
Chicago, Illinois 60606
(312) 630-2007
Fax (312) 630-2015
Toll Free (877) 630-7333
E-mail CRA2007@aol.com

Conveniently located in downtown Chicago.

Highly-qualified, experienced Certified Shorthand Reporters serving the Chicago Metropolitan area, Cook, Lake and Dupage Counties.

- Conference facilities on site.
- Condensed transcripts with indexing.
- Encrypted email transcripts with ETRANS.
- Litigation support diskettes.
- Videotaping, Reproduction and RealTime reporting available upon request

MEMBERS:
National Court Reporters Association
Illinois Shorthand Reporters Association

Proudly serving the legal profession for over 25 years.

(This Listing Continued)

SEE OUR AD ON PAGE IL9S

Dear Attorneys and Support Staff,

Diane Hromek's Court Reporters, Inc., is happy to serve your court reporting needs in Chicago and Western Suburbs. Additionally, from December through June each year, we are also available in SW Florida.

Please consider us for depositions and arbitrations at least 4 plus hours in duration daily, where at least an original and one copy of the transcript will be required. Multi-day depositions are appreciated, too!

Areas of specialty are: Aviation, Real Estate, Product Liability, Personal Injury, Environmental, Construction, Human Relations, Securities.

EXPERIENCE, reporting since 1968, and TECHNOLOGY and PRIDE in producing outstanding QUALITY as well as CAREFUL handling of exhibits and witness signatures.

You can REST knowing an honest job of reporting will be done, especially with our ability to sync the written word to the spoken word through our computer technology.

We offer: RealLegal E-tran; Ascii, CD, Realtime, AudioSync, TimeSync, Videography.

FREE CONFERENCE ROOMS:

in Downers Grove, Oak Brook, Wheeling, Palatine, West Chicago. Conference rooms with a charge are at O'Hare, Midway Airports.

Thank you!

Diane Hromek

Diane Hromek's Court Reporters, Inc.
1202 N. 75th Street
Downers Grove, IL 60516
1-800-556-5554
Fax: 630-910-6070
e-mail: dianehromek@cs.com
website: chicagocourtreporters.com

Better in every case.

Doerner&Goldberg, Inc.

Deposition and Litigation Support Services

Headquarters:
5 Becker Farm Rd., 4th Floor
Roseland, NJ 07068
800-525-9915 or 973-740-1100
Fax: 973-716-9572

Additional Office:
2 Penn Plaza
Suite 1500
New York, NY 10121
800-525-9915

email: info@doernergoldberg.com
Web site: www.doernergoldberg.com

Services:
Internet Depositions
Real-time Depositions
e-mailed Delivery
Encryption of Depositions
Condensed Depositions
Videography-Analog or Digital
Video and Text Synchronization Conversions
Global Video teleconferencing
Repository
Translators/Interpreters
Electronically Hyperlinked Word Indices
Premium Package of Value-Added Services
No Travel Charges
Free LiveNote RT Training
Free e-transcript
Free Technology Seminars
Free Real-time Training

Notable Features: reallegal.com e-transcript™, court/deposition reporting,

Internet depositions, repository, legal videography, realtime reporters, video conferencing, compressed transcripts, video text synchronization, electronic (e-mail or ftp) delivery of transcripts, expedited, next day or same day service

Professional Qualifications: Our court reporters and litigation support staff adhere to the highest professional standards for proficiency and integrity. D&G is proud to have some of the nation's top reporters that have captured depositions around the country and around the world.

Professional Experience: In 1970, Doerner & Goldberg was founded based on one simple principle, "nothing beats experienced reporters who know the language of your practice." No matter what venue, we cover your depositions.

LEGALINK®

A **WORD**WAVE COMPANY

Serving the state of Illinois and 400 other locations across the globe

(This Listing Continued)

LegaLink Chicago
230 W. Monroe Street
Suite 1500
Chicago, IL 60606
(tel) 312.263.3524
(tel) 800.868.0061
(fax) 312.263.3544
info.chicago@legalink.com
www.legalink.com

LegaLink is the Global Leader in Court Reporting, Legal Videography, and Trial Services

Whether your deposition needs are across town or around the globe, one call to LegaLink and you can arrange for the following services anywhere, anytime:

- Experienced Court Reporters
- Certified Legal Video Specialist (CLVS)
- Interactive Realtime Depositions and Realtime over the Internet
- Exhibits Linked to the Transcript
- Compressed Transcript/Word Indexing
- Secure Electronic Transcript Delivery via E-Transcript™ Software
- Videoconferencing
- Video/Text Synchronization
- Video Editing
- Complete Trial Preparation and Presentation Services
- Worldwide Scheduling
- Spacious Deposition Suites

Patti Blair Court Reporters, P.C.

Member of
National Shorthand Reporters Association (N.S.R.A.)
Illinois Shorthand Reporters Association (I.S.R.A.)
Women's Business Enterprise (WBE)

Serving the Legal Profession for over 30 years.

Highly qualified Certified Shorthand Reporters offering the following court reporting services:

- **SPECIALIZING IN MEDICAL & TECHNICAL DEPOSITIONS**
- **FULL RANGE OF COMPUTER AIDED TRANSCRIPTIONS**
- **ASCII DISK FOR LITIGATION SUPPORT PROGRAMS**
- **CONDENSED TRANSCRIPT & KEYWORD INDEXING**
- **REAL TIME CAPABILITY**
- **TELECOMMUNICATION SERVICES**
- **VIDEO DEPOSITION SERVICES**
- **CONFERENCE ROOM**
- **SERVING GREATER METROPOLITAN CHICAGO & SUBURBS**

(312) 782-8376
FAX (312) 782-8377
105 W. Adams St., 25th Floor * Chicago, Illinois 60603

President
Patricia A. Blair

Manager of Operations
Robin Wagman

COURT REPORTERS (cont'd)

Sullivan Reporting Company

35 Certified Court Reporters
Two North La Salle Street -- Suite 1780
Chicago, IL 60602

Phone: (312) 782-4705
Fax: (312) 782-7471

FULL SERVICE AGENCY SERVING CHICAGO
AND SURROUNDING SUBURBS
depositions trials conventions arbitrations

Specializing in:
MEDICAL/TECHNICAL TESTIMONY

We offer:
IBM compatible litigation support - ASCII
Condensed transcripts with word indexes
A full range of delivery options including
Realtime Reporting
Video service & Interpreter referrals
Complimentary conference room downtown

Victoria Court Reporting Service, Inc.

ANYWHERE. ANYTIME.

Victoria E. Rock
President/CEO
29 South LaSalle Street
Suite 200
Chicago, Illinois 60603-1502
Phone: 800.827.7708
Fax: 800.841.6647
Email: Victoria@VictoriaRptg.com
www.VictoriaRptg.com

Victoria Court Reporting Service, Inc. (VCRS), headquartered in Chicago, Illinois, partners the latest communications technology with exceptional customer service to give you the competitive edge.

Established by Victoria E. Rock in 1981, VCRS is known as an innovator in technology integration and utilization. By seamlessly combining the latest litigation support technology with an extensive network of reporting affiliates and business advisors, VCRS is able to provide a wide range of services to clients throughout the nation and the world.

Our experienced customer service team is dedicated to ongoing client and technology support to make sure that you get the most from our tools and therefore make the most of your time. From standard court reporting and transcription to the latest technology, let VCRS be your single source for litigation support anywhere, anytime.

(This Listing Continued)

- **National and International Court Reporting** for depositions, court proceedings, meetings, conventions, focus groups, and interviews
- **Realtime and Internet Realtime** using LiveNote, Summation, Binder, or CaseView
- **Online Scheduling and Document Repository** for easy access anywhere, anytime
- **Transcripts with Linked Exhibits** on CD-ROM to save time and space
- **Videoconferencing Services and Facilities** throughout the world
- **Audio Taping, Videography, and Video Synchronization** for dynamic presentations
- VCRS is WBE/FBE certified

For scheduling or additional information, please contact Pam Zallis, Director of Client Relations

Phone 800.827.7708

Email pzallis@VictoriaRptg.com

WICHMANN REPORTING SERVICE

Certified Court Reporters
Registered Professional Reporters

Suite 920
79 West Monroe Street
Chicago, Illinois 60603

Telephone: 312-368-1228 or 1-800-803-7900
FAX: 312-368-1448
Email: BWichmann@Prodigy.net

We combine our wide-ranging experience in reporting complex litigation and technical matters with our commitment to provide accurate transcripts and litigation support services and products as quickly as necessary.

- PROMPT DELIVERY
  Daily/expedited as requested
- IBM-COMPATIBLE DISKETTES
  ASCII, Discovery ZX and others as required
- REAL TIME
  LiveNote, CaseView, Summation
- CONFERENCE ROOM
- PROFESSIONAL VIDEOTAPING
- EXHIBIT DUPLICATION FACILITIES ON PREMISES

Members:
National Court Reporters Association
Illinois Shorthand Reporters Association

WINKLER AND CHIMNIAK, INC.

CERTIFIED SHORTHAND REPORTERS

200 North Dearborn Street
Suite 2503
Chicago, Illinois 60601-1616

(This Listing Continued)

24-hour scheduling
Phone: (312) 236-1661
Fax: (312) 236-1675
Internet: www.winkchim.com

SERVING NORTHERN ILLINOIS, SOUTHERN, WISCONSIN, NORTHWEST INDIANA SINCE 1992

Depositions, Arbitrations, Conferences, Meetings
Daily Copy and Immediate Copy
Realtime Transcript, On-Site & Via Internet
Certified Videography, single & multi camera
Video/Text Synchronization
Transcript Repository
Conference Room
E-Transcript
Interpreters
Document Conversion-OCR, PDF
Legal Coding
Enterprise Content Management
Electronic Data Discovery

PROFESSIONAL SERVICE WITH A PERSONAL TOUCH

CRIMINAL BACKGROUND CHECKS

PeopleSearch

Nationwide Investigative Information Service

PHONE: 847-360-0360
FAX: 847-623-3501

Information Services...About People for People

PeopleSearch is a nationwide investigative information service with field agents working across the nation retrieving information from every county courthouse and United States Federal District Court in the country. Our innovative services provide employers, owners and individuals with complete background information about applicants for any position.

Joanne Layne, founder of PeopleSearch, is a research specialist with more than twenty-five years experience in courthouse and genealogical research and more than nine years experience in researching criminal background checks. Layne was trained at the National Archives in Washington, D.C. and at Samford University in Birmingham, AL. She is a Certified Confidential Adoption Intermediary for the State of Illinois.

Services:

- Background Checks
- Employment Screenings
- Tenant Approvals
- Skip Tracing
- Computer/Paper Trails
- Locating Missing Persons
- Witnesses in Court Cases
- Missing or Unknown Heirs
- Lost Loves
- School, Family or Military Reunions

DEPOSITIONS - VIDEO & AUDIO

Legal Video International

Video Depositions - Day in the Life Documentaries
Expert Witness Presentations
Settlement Videos - Transcript Synchronization
DVD Authoring - Video Editing

Legal Video International has grown out of more than three decades of experience in international photojournalism and documentary film making. We bring the same demanding standards of professionalism, and accuracy to our client's legal video needs as we bring to broadcast production. We are used to operating on tight deadlines often in hostile environments, while producing high quality results.

Our reliance on cutting edge digital technology makes it possible for us to operate as effectively on location or in our studios. Because we regard our clients as individuals, we are able to adapt to the special demands of each assignment. Be it a translated deposition in a remote location or a sight inspection in the bowels of a ship or quick turn around on-location DVD production, we are ready with a solution.

LVI owner and lead videographer, **John Giannini**, will be happy to help with all your legal video needs. Please contact him at:

Legal Video International
1330 South Harvard Avenue
Arlington Heights, IL 60005
USA
Toll-free in the USA 1 (847) LVI-DEPS (584-3377)
International call: +1 (847) 912-3987
FAX: 1 (847) 577-0957

Email: info@legalvideointl.com
URL: http://www.legalvideointl.com

DOCUMENT RESEARCH, RETRIEVAL & FILING

PeopleSearch

Nationwide Investigative Information Service

PHONE: 847-360-0360
FAX: 847-623-3501

Information Services...About People for People

PeopleSearch is a nationwide investigative information service with field agents working across the nation retrieving information from every county courthouse and United States Federal District Court in the country. Our innovative services provide employers, owners and individuals with complete background information about applicants for any position.

Joanne Layne, founder of PeopleSearch, is a research specialist with more than twenty-five years experience in courthouse and genealogical research and more than nine years experience in researching criminal background checks. Layne was trained at the National Archives in Washington, D.C. and at Samford University in Birmingham, AL. She is a Certified Confidential Adoption Intermediary for the State of Illinois.

(This Listing Continued)

DOCUMENT RESEARCH, RETRIEVAL & FILING (cond'd)

PeopleSearch (cont'd)

Services:

- Background Checks
- Employment Screenings
- Tenant Approvals
- Skip Tracing
- Computer/Paper Trails
- Locating Missing Persons
- Witnesses in Court Cases
- Missing or Unknown Heirs
- Lost Loves
- School, Family or Military Reunions

ECONOMIC AND STATISTICAL CONSULTING SERVICES

Lexecon

www.lexecon.com

332 South Michigan Avenue
Chicago, Illinois 60604
312-322-0200

20 University Road
Cambridge, Massachusetts 02138
617-520-0200

A consulting firm offering a full range of litigation support services, including economic, financial and statistical analysis, and assistance in the selection and preparation of testifying experts. Lexecon has extensive experience in complex litigation involving antitrust, securities, regulatory design, intellectual property, employment discrimination, contract damages and valuation. It also offers business consulting services and public policy counsel.

Members of the firm have extensive experience in financial, energy, technology, insurance, health care, telecommunications, consumer products, transportation and manufacturing industries.

M&A Analysis

Securities

Regulatory Design

Statistical Analyses and Damages Estimation

Assistance in the Selection and Preparation of Economic, Accounting and Other Expert Witnesses

Lexecon Professionals: Dennis W. Carlton, Daniel R. Fischel, Joseph P. Kalt, Rachelle F. Alcain, Charles W. Augustine, Gustavo E. Bamberger, Catherine Barron, Margaret M. Bennett, Nancy Bonn, John Robert Broxson, Amy Bertin Candell, Joseph Cavicchi, Carolyn Y. Chong, Irfan Ciputra, Charles C. Cox, James M. Coyne, Helena Croce, Deborah L. Dobrusin, James Donovan, Ronald A. Dye, Laona A. Fleischer, Fredrick A. Flyer, Rajiv B. Gokhale, Kenneth W. Grant II, David B. Gross, Timothy R. Guimond, Alan S. Frankel, Austan Goolsbee, Robert S. Hamada, Seth A. Hamstead, Kevin D. Hartt, Prescott C. Hartshorne, James J. Heckman, Eric Henson, Scott T. Jones, Michael A. Keable, Kenneth W. Kipp, Randall S. Kroszner, Elisabeth M. Landes,

(This Listing Continued)

Andrew Y. Lemon, H. Neal Lenhoff, Youngsik Lim, Colleen P. Loughlin, William J. Lynk, Stephen Makowka, Jessica P. Mandel, Ronnie A. Martin, Glen Meyers, Erich Muehlegger, Avisheh Mohsenin, Lynette R. Neumann, Cathy M. Niden, Joshua H. Nixt, Eugene Orlov, David G. Ownby, Gregory J. Pelnar, Hans-Jürgen Petersen, Steven R. Peterson, Wendy L. Petropoulos, Tomas J. Philipson, Jonathan S. Polonsky, Kirupakaran C. Ramaiah, Bradley N. Reiff, David Reishus, David J. Ross, Rahul Sekhar, Allan L. Shampine, Philip R. Sharp, Hal S. Sider, Heather R. Spang, Kristin D. Stanton, Collin K. Starkweather, Thomas A. Stemwedel, Kenneth M. Stern, Daniel W. Stone, David Strahlberg, Alan O. Sykes, Jeffrey D. Tranen, Laurel C. Van Allen, Eugenia Vinogradsky, Elizabeth A. Wall, Patrick Wang, Yili Wang, Vincent A. Warther, Anne Marie Yale, Deborah W. Zimmermann.

Representative Clients: Arnold & Porter; Baker Botts; Baker & Hostetler; Bell Boyd & Lloyd; Boies, Schiller & Flexner; Covington & Burling; Cravath, Swaine & Moore; Davis Polk & Wardwell; Fish & Neave; Fried, Frank, Harris, Shriver & Jacobson; Freeman, Freeman & Salzman; Fulbright & Jaworski; Gardner, Carton & Douglas; Heller Ehrman White & McAuliffe; Jenner & Block; Katten Muchin Zavis Rosenman; Kirkland & Ellis; Latham & Watkins; Mayer, Brown Rowe & Maw; Morgan, Lewis & Bockius; Morrison & Foerster; Paul, Weiss, Rifkind, Wharton & Garrison; Shearman & Sterling; Sullivan & Cromwell; Skadden, Arps, Slate, Meagher & Flom; Steptoe & Johnson; Wachtell, Lipton, Rosen & Katz; Weil, Gotshal & Manges; Wilmer Cutler Pickering Hale & Dorr; federal & state government agencies.

ELECTRONIC FILING

LexisNexis® *File & Serve*

LexisNexis® File & Serve is an Internet-based service that provides law firms and courts with the ability to **improve litigation management** and **gain more direct control over filing and service activity.**

Over 50,000 attorneys, legal professionals, and court staff are registered with LexisNexis File & Serve, and 6 million legal documents are electronically filed and served annually in state courts around the country.

No electronic court filing in your jurisdiction yet? If you're involved in complex litigation or other cases with multiple parties, start with an e-service project and improve management of service of discovery and other document exchange.

Safer and more reliable delivery

- Online delivery
- Service list management
- Extended deadlines
- Judicial grade security

Better Case Monitoring

- Automated Alerts
- Online document access
- Proof-of-service and filing receipts
- Litigation and docket reports

Improve Client Billing and Cost Management

- Online fee payment and monthly billing
- Client/matter coding
- Reduced the reliance on runners, U.S. Mail and photocopiers

We have electronic filing and/or electronic service projects in 22 states. Please visit us at www.lexisnexis.com/fileandserve or call 800-869-1910 and learn how you can participate in an existing e-filing project or start an e-service project for your litigation.

LexisNexis
LexisNexis® File & Serve
13427 NE 16th Street
Bellevue, WA 98005

ENGINEERING & SCIENTIFIC CONSULTING SERVICES

CTLGROUP

5400 OLD ORCHARD ROAD
Skokie, IL 60077-1030
Telephone: 800.522.2285
Fax: 847.965.6541
Web Site: www.CTLGroup.com
Email: JGarrett@CTLGroup.com

CTLGroup is an internationally recognized consulting engineering firm with an 85-year history of offering professional structural engineering, testing and research services. CTLGroup's staff of 140 professionals offers a unique combination of structural investigative services, structural engineering analysis and design services, construction materials testing and research, and structural diagnostics testing and laboratory services. Our expertise includes:

- Consulting engineering
- Condition and damage assessments
- Structural failure investigations and root cause determinations
- Nondestructive testing and in-situ evaluations
- Building material failure analyses and remediation
- Structural system failure analyses and remediation
- Laboratory material testing and evaluation
- Laboratory structural component testing and evaluation
- Real-time in-situ structural health monitoring
- Design and construction standard of care issues
- Litigation and legal support, including
  - Expert Testimony
  - Demonstrative evidence

EXPERT WITNESS
ACCIDENT INVESTIGATION & RECONSTRUCTION

PACKER ENGINEERING, INC.

1950 North Washington Street
Naperville, Illinois 60563

Phone: 630-505-5722
Toll-free: 888-722-5372
Fax: 630-505-1986
Web site: www.packereng.com
Email: peinfo@packereng.com

Packer Engineering's scientists, engineers and technologists have strong academic credentials as well as vital industrial experience. Our work applies a scientific methodology to the principles of engineering to obtain the correct answer to the questions we are asked and the problems we are presented.

Our multidisciplinary staff includes engineers and technicians in the following disciplines and support services.

(This Listing Continued)

Disciplines:
- Aviation/Aerospace
- Biomedical/Biomechanical
- Chemical, Fire and Explosion
- Civil/Structural
- Construction Technology
- Electrical/Electronics
- Firearms Technology
- Human Factors/Ergonomics
- Intellectual Property
- Machinery/Equipment
- Materials/Metallurgy
- Process Industries
- Transportation

Support Services:

- Laboratory
- Library
- Project Coordination
- Visualization

For more than four decades, insurers and the attorneys that represent them have chosen Packer Engineering's consulting and technical services for the breadth of our experience, the depth of our expertise and the value that comes from timely and economical project management.

The nature of our work and the projects we have been assigned cross into both litigation services and insurance investigation:

LITIGATION
For over 43 years, attorneys have chosen Packer Engineering to provide technical expertise and comprehensive, timely and understandable engineering consulting on a wide array of disputes and legal actions. Our services include accident investigation and reconstruction, failure analysis, product safety and liability studies, design analysis, custom testing, intellectual property & pretrial and courtroom testimony. Other litigation support services include the design and production of demonstrative evidence, physical models and exhibits, dynamic simulations and engineering animations.
- System Failure Analysis and Recovery Consulting
- Product Liability
- Failure Analysis
- Cause and Origin Investigations
- Warnings and Guards
- Warranties and Guarantees
- Vehicular and Transportation Equipment
- Residential, Workplace and Construction Site Accidents
- Premise Liabilities
- Intellectual Property and Patents
- Personal Injury

INSURANCE
When it comes to investigating insurance claims, Packer Engineering provides a wide range of services which enable insurers to validate claims, assess damages and effectively manage losses. Our experience includes assignments involving both property and casualty claims. We offer a comprehensive package of services from accident site investigations and inspections through litigation services.

If you have an immediate need and would like to speak with one of our staff, please call toll-free at **888-722-5372** or click on our website hot link and leave us a message at www.packereng.com or email us at peinfo@packereng.com

Packer Engineering, Inc. is a wholly-owned subsidiary of The Packer Group, Inc., a corporation of technology-driven service and product companies serving the diversity of industry and commerce.

EXPERT WITNESS
ACCIDENTS/FIRES/PRODUCT LIABILITY

JOHN MICHAEL AGOSTI

Fire Analyst and Consultant

23808 North Overhill
Lake Zurich, Illinois 60047
Phone: 847-682-6793
E-mail: johnagosti@earthlink.net
Web: www.arsonexpert.com

As a member of the Skokie, Illinois Fire Department for twenty-eight years, Mr. Agosti progressed from a Firefighter/Paramedic to the position of Deputy Fire Chief. Mr. Agosti has responded to hundreds of major fire and crime scenes and has testified in court on the conclusions of his investigations. His investigations have led to successful criminal indictments and convictions. Mr. Agosti's fire department responsibilities included the review of all construction plans for compliance to fire and building codes. His expertise in building construction and fire spread, lends a unique blend to his fire investigation capabilities.

In addition to his fire department exposure to hundreds of fire investigations, Mr. Agosti has extensive experience in the private sector also. Over the past 11 years Mr. Agosti has conducted over eight hundred fire investigations as a private fire cause and origin analyst.

Practice areas include:

Fire and Explosions:
Arson defense/prosecution; gas explosions; vehicular fires; structure fires; fire deaths/injuries.

Building and Fire Codes:
Fire/Building code violation; Life Safety Code violations; smoke detector issues; fire prevention analysis.

Fire Department Practices:
Fire department operations/practices/management; firefighter deaths/injuries/safety.

Mr. Agosti has an Associates Degree in Fire Science and Technology. He is also certified as a Fire and Arson Investigator.

PROJECT EXPERIENCE

Fire and building code analysis
Automobile accident reconstruction
Gas leak surveys
Distribution gas pipe ruptures and leaks
Investigation of fire fatalities and electrocutions
Investigation of bombings
Investigation for cause and origin of fires and explosions

PROFESSIONAL SOCIETIES

National Fire Protection Association
Fire Marshals Association of North America
International Association of Fire Chiefs
Building Officials/Code Administrators International
Fire Investigators Strike Force
Illinois Fire Inspectors Association
International Association of Arson Investigators

EXPERT WITNESS
ACTUARY

WILLIAM C. CUTLIP CONSULTING

William C. Cutlip
FSA, MAAA, FCA, CLU, ChFC, CPCU

Web Site: www.cutlipconsulting.com

3048 Woods Edge Way
Madison, WI 53711
Phone: (608) 443-0669
Fax: (608) 443-0668

8021 Wildomar Drive
Tucson, AZ 85743
Phone: (520) 572-8833
Fax: (520) 579-6688

Cell: (520) 247-6592

Areas of Expertise: Expert Witness / Forensics / Litigation Support / Arbitrations

Financial Evaluation for:

- damages
- investment
- merger & acquisition
- structured settlements
- grievances
- equitable distribution

Legal Ammunition for:

- pre-filing evaluation
- case strength
- surprise reduction
- strategy support
- opposition analysis
- scientifically supported evaluation

Professional Profile:

Educated at Massachusetts Institute of Technology and Oklahoma State University, William C. Cutlip has over 40 years of industry experience and specializes in risk evaluation and expert witness work for attorneys, product development for insurance companies, and business consulting.

Professional Qualifications:

Fellow, Society of Actuaries (FSA)
Member, American Academy of Actuaries (MAAA)
Fellow, Conference of Consulting Actuaries (FCA)
Chartered Life Underwriter (CLU)
Chartered Financial Consultant (ChFC)
Member, International Association of Consulting Actuaries

Cases/Clients: Plaintiff and Defense

Geographical Area: No Limitation

E-mail Contact: cutlipconsulting@cs.com

EXPERT WITNESS
ARCHITECTS

Wiss, Janney, Elstner Associates, Inc.

Engineers, Architects, Materials Scientists
330 Pfingsten Road
Northbrook, IL 60062
Offices nationwide

Phone	800/345-3199
Fax	847/291-9599
Internet	www.wje.com
Contact	Gary Klein, EVP

WJE is a professional firm providing practical, innovative, and technically sound solutions to structural, architectural, and materials problems. During our 49-year history, we have successfully completed more than 60,000 projects involving virtually every type of construction material, structural system, and architectural component.

WJE's staff of forensic consultants have extensive field and laboratory experience providing investigative, testing, and assessment services for building materials; design / construction deficiencies and practices; and building code compliance.

Specialized services include:

- Structural and Architectural Assessments
- Failure Investigation and Analysis
- Repair / Rehabilitation Design
- Construction Materials Evaluation / Testing
- Computerized Failure Simulations
- Courtroom Exhibits / Models
- Due Diligence / Prepurchase Surveys
- Expert Witness Testimony
- Litigation Support

Many of WJE's staff of more than 280 engineers, architects, and materials scientists are nationally recognized experts. WJE maintains offices across the country with professional engineering or architectural registration in every state.

EXPERT WITNESS
BANKING
FINANCE

TAVAKOLI STRUCTURED FINANCE, INC.

360 E. Randolph St., Suite 3007
Chicago, Illinois 60601
(312) 540-0243
Email: jt@tavakolistructuredfinance.com
Web site: www.tavakolistructuredfinance.com

(This Listing Continued)

Janet Tavakoli is the president of Tavakoli Structured Finance, Inc., an independent consulting firm, specializing in maximizing value in structured finance. Structured financial products include derivatives, credit derivatives, credit default swaps, total return swaps, interest rate swaps, options, swaptions, collateralized debt obligations, mortgage backed securities, hedge funds, special purpose entities, bonds, emerging markets, equities, and the instruments of the capital markets.

Ms. Tavakoli has over 18 years of Wall Street experience at major financial institutions in New York and London. She earned her B.S. in Chemical Engineering from the Illinois Institute of Technology. She has an MBA from the University of Chicago, and was an adjunct professor of finance at the University of Chicago's Graduate School of Business where she taught Derivatives.

She has been registered and licensed with the SFA, NASD, ASE, CBOE, NYSE, PSE, and the NFA and has passed the series 7, 63, and 3 qualifying exams from 1985-2002.

Janet Tavakoli is the author of the global best selling books in their respective fields: *Credit Derivatives & Synthetic Structures* 2nd Edition, John Wiley & Sons, 2001, and *Collateralized Debt Obligations and Structured Finance: New Developments in Cash and Synthetic Securitization*, John Wiley & Sons 2003. Other topics include: Enron, hedge funds, Freddie Mac, Fannie Mae, and Parmalat.

EXPERT WITNESS
BUSINESS VALUATION

Lexecon

www.lexecon.com

332 South Michigan Avenue	20 University Road
Chicago, Illinois 60604	Cambridge, Massachusetts 02138
312-322-0200	617-520-0200

A consulting firm offering a full range of litigation support services, including economic, financial and statistical analysis, and assistance in the selection and preparation of testifying experts. Lexecon has extensive experience in complex litigation involving antitrust, securities, regulatory design, intellectual property, employment discrimination, contract damages and valuation. It also offers business consulting services and public policy counsel.

Members of the firm have extensive experience in financial, energy, technology, insurance, health care, telecommunications, consumer products, transportation and manufacturing industries.

M&A Analysis
Securities
Regulatory Design
Statistical Analyses and Damages Estimation
Assistance in the Selection and Preparation of Economic, Accounting and Other Expert Witnesses

Lexecon Professionals: Dennis W. Carlton, Daniel R. Fischel, Joseph P. Kalt, Rachelle F. Alcain, Charles W. Augustine, Gustavo E. Bamberger, Catherine Barron, Margaret M. Bennett, Nancy Bonn, John Robert Broxson, Amy Bertin Candell, Joseph Cavicchi, Carolyn Y. Chong, Irfan Ciputra, Charles C. Cox, James M. Coyne, Helena Croce, Deborah L. Dobrusin, James Donovan, Ronald A. Dye, Laona A. Fleischer, Fredrick A. Flyer, Rajiv B. Gokhale, Kenneth W. Grant II, David B. Gross, Timothy R. Guimond, Alan S. Frankel, Austan Goolsbee, Robert S. Hamada, Seth A. Hamstead, Kevin D. Hartt, Prescott C. Hartshorne, James J. Heckman, Eric Henson, Scott T. Jones, Michael A. Keable,

(This Listing Continued)

EXPERT WITNESS
BUSINESS VALUATION (cont'd)

Lexecon (cont'd)

Kenneth W. Kipp, Randall S. Kroszner, Elisabeth M. Landes, Andrew Y. Lemon, H. Neal Lenhoff, Youngsik Lim, Colleen P. Loughlin, William J. Lynk, Stephen Makowka, Jessica P. Mandel, Ronnie A. Martin, Glen Meyers, Erich Muehlegger, Avisheh Mohsenin, Lynette R. Neumann, Cathy M. Niden, Joshua H. Nixt, Eugene Orlov, David G. Ownby, Gregory J. Pelnar, Hans-Jürgen Petersen, Steven R. Peterson, Wendy L. Petropoulos, Tomas J. Philipson, Jonathan S. Polonsky, Kirupakaran C. Ramaiah, Bradley N. Reiff, David Reishus, David J. Ross, Rahul Sekhar, Allan L. Shampine, Philip R. Sharp, Hal S. Sider, Heather R. Spang, Kristin D. Stanton, Collin K. Starkweather, Thomas A. Stemwedel, Kenneth M. Stern, Daniel W. Stone, David Strahlberg, Alan O. Sykes, Jeffrey D. Tranen, Laurel C. Van Allen, Eugenia Vinogradsky, Elizabeth A. Wall, Patrick Wang, Yili Wang, Vincent A. Warther, Anne Marie Yale, Deborah W. Zimmermann.

Representative Clients: Arnold & Porter; Baker Botts; Baker & Hostetler; Bell Boyd & Lloyd; Boies, Schiller & Flexner; Covington & Burling; Cravath, Swaine & Moore; Davis Polk & Wardwell; Fish & Neave; Fried, Frank, Harris, Shriver & Jacobson; Freeman, Freeman & Salzman; Fulbright & Jaworski; Gardner, Carton & Douglas; Heller Ehrman White & McAuliffe; Jenner & Block; Katten Muchin Zavis Rosenman; Kirkland & Ellis; Latham & Watkins; Mayer, Brown Rowe & Maw; Morgan, Lewis & Bockius; Morrison & Foerster; Paul, Weiss, Rifkind, Wharton & Garrison; Shearman & Sterling; Sullivan & Cromwell; Skadden, Arps, Slate, Meagher & Flom; Steptoe & Johnson; Wachtell, Lipton, Rosen & Katz; Weil, Gotshal & Manges; Wilmer Cutler Pickering Hale & Dorr; federal & state government agencies.

EXPERT WITNESS
COATINGS/PAINT

Wiss, Janney, Elstner Associates, Inc.

Engineers, Architects, Materials Scientists
330 Pfingsten Road
Northbrook, IL 60062
Offices nationwide

Phone	800/345-3199
Fax	847/291-9599
Internet	www.wje.com
Contact	Gary Klein, EVP

WJE is a professional firm providing practical, innovative, and technically sound solutions to structural, architectural, and materials problems. During our 49-year history, we have successfully completed more than 60,000 projects involving virtually every type of construction material, structural system, and architectural component.

WJE's staff of forensic consultants have extensive field and laboratory experience providing investigative, testing, and assessment services for building materials; design / construction deficiencies and practices; and building code compliance.

Specialized services include:
- Structural and Architectural Assessments
- Failure Investigation and Analysis
- Repair / Rehabilitation Design
- Construction Materials Evaluation / Testing
- Computerized Failure Simulations
- Courtroom Exhibits / Models
- Due Diligence / Prepurchase Surveys
- Expert Witness Testimony
- Litigation Support

Many of WJE's staff of more than 280 engineers, architects, and materials scientists are nationally recognized experts. WJE maintains offices across the country with professional engineering or architectural registration in every state.

EXPERT WITNESS
COMMODITY FUTURES

Peter J. Pfeffer

605 Woodhaven Dr.

Mundelein (metro Chicago), IL, 60060
ph: 847-837-0791 fax: 847-970-6383
e-mail: barlowe@interaccess.com
url: http://www.walshpfeffer.com

Services: Dispute mediation, Case Evaluation, Written Opinions, Testimony, Portfolio evaluation, Damage Calculation, Turn-over analysis, Suitability, Registered Employee vs. brokerage firm disputes, supervision analysis, Industry Rules & practices. Financial Suicide, Annuities and Variable Annuities.

Profile: Securities Fraud Examiner; Expertise in all facets of investment and trading in securities and derivatives; Defense & Plaintiff, Domestic & Foreign.

States: ALL

Professional Qualifications: Registrations: S-3 (Commodity Futures), S-7 (General Securities), S-8 (Sales Supervision), S8BM (NYSE Branch Office Manager), S-24 (Securities Principal), S-52 (Municipal), S-63 (State's Blue Sky), all granted 1969 thru 1980.

Professional Experience: Registered Rep. Branch office Manager, Principal, Regional Manager, Executive Vice President (National Securities Firm), Chairman (Trust Company). For details, see website http://firms.findlaw.com/Pfeffer.

Licenses: See website

Professional Affiliations: : See website

Education: University of Wisconsin-Economics

Cases: Arbitrator or Expert testimony: AAA, NASD, Exchanges, NFA, Appellate Panelist, Federal Reparations Proceedings; Federal and State jury and bench trials since late '70's.

Publications: Investment/trading research, Compliance and operations manuals.

(This Listing Continued)

Teaching: Trained over 500 securities and derivative brokers. Guest lecturer on Capital formation and central markets. Instructed key employees of major Japanese and Korean financial Institutions in year-long course in trading of capital and derivative markets-real-time trading of employer-funded accounts.

Contact: Peter J. Pfeffer

References: Available from attorneys of prior cases.

Areas of Expertise: securities fraud, day trading, securities arbitration, churning, currency trading, derivatives, futures, NASD regulations, securities arbitration, investment fraud, stock market, commodities, damage calculations, employee disputes, investments, options, securities regulations, mediation practice.

EXPERT WITNESS
CONSTRUCTION

CTLGROUP

5400 OLD ORCHARD ROAD
Skokie, IL 60077-1030
Telephone: 800.522.2285
Fax: 847.965.6541
Web Site: www.CTLGroup.com
Email: JGarrett@CTLGroup.com

CTLGroup is an internationally recognized consulting engineering firm with an 85-year history of offering professional structural engineering, testing and research services. CTLGroup's staff of 140 professionals offers a unique combination of structural investigative services, structural engineering analysis and design services, construction materials testing and research, and structural diagnostics testing and laboratory services. Our expertise includes:

- Consulting engineering
- Condition and damage assessments
- Structural failure investigations and root cause determinations
- Nondestructive testing and in-situ evaluations
- Building material failure analyses and remediation
- Structural system failure analyses and remediation
- Laboratory material testing and evaluation
- Laboratory structural component testing and evaluation
- Real-time in-situ structural health monitoring
- Design and construction standard of care issues
- Litigation and legal support, including
    - Expert Testimony
    - Demonstrative evidence

EXPERT WITNESS
CONSTRUCTION
BUILDING CODES

ROLF JENSEN & ASSOCIATES, INC.

600 West Fulton, Suite 500
Chicago, Illinois 60661
Tel: 312-879-7200
Fax: 312-879-7210

www.rjainc.com

Rolf Jensen & Associates Inc. has over thirty-five years of experience providing fire protection engineering services to the legal community. From conducting fire investigations and loss prevention site surveys to serving as expert witnesses, RJA has an excellent reputation for providing thorough investigations and research.

RJA employs more than 150 professionals, many of which hold advanced degrees in a variety of engineering disciplines, including fire protection, mechanical, electrical and civil. RJA's engineering professionals are registered fire protection engineers in almost all of the 50 states.

RJA provides clients throughout the world with effective solutions to their life safety and fire protection challenges through engineering, performance-based design and construction management. We accomplish our mission in an atmosphere of professional integrity, adhering to the principles of client focus, industry leadership, innovation, technological advancement, and respect for both the team and the individual.

Areas of Expertise

- Fire Protection Engineering Code Consulting
- Fire Protection Engineering Systems Design
- Forensic Fire Modeling
- Building Code Compliance
- Fire Investigation
- Construction Claim Dispute Resolution
- Failure Analysis of Systems and Components
- ADA Compliance

Associations

- National Fire Protection Association
- Society of Fire Protection Engineers
- Risk & Insurance Management Society

Offices in:
Atlanta, Baltimore, Boston, Dallas, Denver, Houston, Las Vegas, Los Angeles, New York, Orlando, Phoenix, Raleigh, San Diego, San Francisco, Shanghai and Washington, DC

EXPERT WITNESS
DRUGS/ALCOHOL/TOXICOLOGY

PHARMACONSULTANTS INC.

1935 S. PLUM GROVE ROAD
PMB 255
PALATINE, IL 60067

(This Listing Continued)

EXPERT WITNESS
DRUGS/ALCOHOL/TOXICOLOGY (cont'd)

PHARMACONSULTANTS INC. (cont'd)

800-872-9326
847-991-4433
FAX 847-991-4584
VM/PAGER 847-769-2843

Email: jodonn1935@aol.com
www.pharmaconsultantinc.com
www.rushu.rush.edu/pharm/dept/fac/jodonnell/

DR. JAMES O'DONNELL
PHARMACOLOGIST PHARMACIST NUTRITIONIST
DIPLOMATE - AMERICAN BOARD OF CLINICAL PHARMACOLOGY
DIPLOMATE - BOARD OF NUTRITIONAL SPECIALTIES
FOUNDING EDITOR JOURNAL OF PHARMACY PRACTICE
REGISTERED PHARMACIST
FELLOW-AMERICAN COLLEGE OF CLINICAL PHARMACOLOGY

Dr. O'Donnell is both a consultant and expert witness in pharmacology, drug product liability/warnings, drug injury, pharmacy malpractice, nutrition and dietary supplement matters, and alcohol toxicity. He has served nationwide for both the plaintiff and defense. He received his Bachelor of Science from the University of Illinois College of Pharmacy, his Masters in Nutrition from Rush University and his Doctor of Pharmacy from the University of Michigan. He is a fellow of the American College of Nutrition. He is an associate professor of Pharmacology at the Rush Medical College. He is the editor of Drug Injury: Liability, Analysis, and Prevention.

MEMBERSHIPS:
American College of Clinical Pharmacology
American College of Clinical Pharmacy
American Academy of Clinical Toxicology
American Pharmaceutical Association
American College of Nutrition
American Society of Pharmacy Law
American College of Legal Medicine

EXPERT WITNESS
ECONOMICS/ECONOMISTS

Lexecon

www.lexecon.com

332 South Michigan Avenue
Chicago, Illinois 60604
312-322-0200

20 University Road
Cambridge, Massachusetts 02138
617-520-0200

A consulting firm offering a full range of litigation support services, including economic, financial and statistical analysis, and assistance in the selection and preparation of testifying experts. Lexecon has extensive experience in complex litigation involving antitrust, securities, regulatory design, intellectual property, employment discrimination, contract damages and valuation. It also offers business consulting services and public policy counsel.

(This Listing Continued)

Members of the firm have extensive experience in financial, energy, technology, insurance, health care, telecommunications, consumer products, transportation and manufacturing industries.

M&A Analysis
Securities
Regulatory Design
Statistical Analyses and Damages Estimation
Assistance in the Selection and Preparation of Economic, Accounting and Other Expert Witnesses

Lexecon Professionals: Dennis W. Carlton, Daniel R. Fischel, Joseph P. Kalt, Rachelle F. Alcain, Charles W. Augustine, Gustavo E. Bamberger, Catherine Barron, Margaret M. Bennett, Nancy Bonn, John Robert Broxson, Amy Bertin Candell, Joseph Cavicchi, Carolyn Y. Chong, Irfan Ciputra, Charles C. Cox, James M. Coyne, Helena Croce, Deborah L. Dobrusin, James Donovan, Ronald A. Dye, Laona A. Fleischer, Fredrick A. Flyer, Rajiv B. Gokhale, Kenneth W. Grant II, David B. Gross, Timothy R. Guimond, Alan S. Frankel, Austan Goolsbee, Robert S. Hamada, Seth A. Hamstead, Kevin D. Hartt, Prescott C. Hartshorne, James J. Heckman, Eric Henson, Scott T. Jones, Michael A. Keable, Kenneth W. Kipp, Randall S. Kroszner, Elisabeth M. Landes, Andrew Y. Lemon, H. Neal Lenhoff, Youngsik Lim, Colleen P. Loughlin, William J. Lynk, Stephen Makowka, Jessica P. Mandel, Ronnie A. Martin, Glen Meyers, Erich Muehlegger, Avisheh Mohsenin, Lynette R. Neumann, Cathy M. Niden, Joshua H. Nixt, Eugene Orlov, David G. Ownby, Gregory J. Pelnar, Hans-Jürgen Petersen, Steven R. Peterson, Wendy L. Petropoulos, Tomas J. Philipson, Jonathan S. Polonsky, Kirupakaran C. Ramaiah, Bradley N. Reiff, David Reishus, David J. Ross, Rahul Sekhar, Allan L. Shampine, Philip R. Sharp, Hal S. Sider, Heather R. Spang, Kristin D. Stanton, Collin K. Starkweather, Thomas A. Stemwedel, Kenneth M. Stern, Daniel W. Stone, David Strahlberg, Alan O. Sykes, Jeffrey D. Tranen, Laurel C. Van Allen, Eugenia Vinogradsky, Elizabeth A. Wall, Patrick Wang, Yili Wang, Vincent A. Warther, Anne Marie Yale, Deborah W. Zimmermann.

Representative Clients: Arnold & Porter; Baker Botts; Baker & Hostetler; Bell Boyd & Lloyd; Boies, Schiller & Flexner; Covington & Burling; Cravath, Swaine & Moore; Davis Polk & Wardwell; Fish & Neave; Fried, Frank, Harris, Shriver & Jacobson; Freeman, Freeman & Salzman; Fulbright & Jaworski; Gardner, Carton & Douglas; Heller Ehrman White & McAuliffe; Jenner & Block; Katten Muchin Zavis Rosenman; Kirkland & Ellis; Latham & Watkins; Mayer, Brown Rowe & Maw; Morgan, Lewis & Bockius; Morrison & Foerster; Paul, Weiss, Rifkind, Wharton & Garrison; Shearman & Sterling; Sullivan & Cromwell; Skadden, Arps, Slate, Meagher & Flom; Steptoe & Johnson; Wachtell, Lipton, Rosen & Katz; Weil, Gotshal & Manges; Wilmer Cutler Pickering Hale & Dorr; federal & state government agencies.

EXPERT WITNESS
ECONOMICS/STATISTICS

Lexecon

www.lexecon.com

332 South Michigan Avenue
Chicago, Illinois 60604
312-322-0200

20 University Road
Cambridge, Massachusetts 02138
617-520-0200

A consulting firm offering a full range of litigation support services, including economic, financial and statistical analysis, and assistance in the selection and preparation of testifying experts. Lexecon has extensive experience in complex litigation involving antitrust, securities, regulatory design, intellectual property, employment discrimination, contract damages and valuation. It also offers business consulting services and public policy counsel.

(This Listing Continued)

Members of the firm have extensive experience in financial, energy, technology, insurance, health care, telecommunications, consumer products, transportation and manufacturing industries.

M&A Analysis

Securities

Regulatory Design

Statistical Analyses and Damages Estimation

Assistance in the Selection and Preparation of Economic, Accounting and Other Expert Witnesses

Lexecon Professionals: Dennis W. Carlton, Daniel R. Fischel, Joseph P. Kalt, Rachelle F. Alcain, Charles W. Augustine, Gustavo E. Bamberger, Catherine Barron, Margaret M. Bennett, Nancy Bonn, John Robert Broxson, Amy Bertin Candell, Joseph Cavicchi, Carolyn Y. Chong, Irfan Ciputra, Charles C. Cox, James M. Coyne, Helena Croce, Deborah L. Dobrusin, James Donovan, Ronald A. Dye, Laona A. Fleischer, Fredrick A. Flyer, Rajiv B. Gokhale, Kenneth W. Grant II, David B. Gross, Timothy R. Guimond, Alan S. Frankel, Austan Goolsbee, Robert S. Hamada, Seth A. Hamstead, Kevin D. Hartt, Prescott C. Hartshorne, James J. Heckman, Eric Henson, Scott T. Jones, Michael A. Keable, Kenneth W. Kipp, Randall S. Kroszner, Elisabeth M. Landes, Andrew Y. Lemon, H. Neal Lenhoff, Youngsik Lim, Colleen P. Loughlin, William J. Lynk, Stephen Makowka, Jessica P. Mandel, Ronnie A. Martin, Glen Meyers, Erich Muehlegger, Avisheh Mohsenin, Lynette R. Neumann, Cathy M. Niden, Joshua H. Nixt, Eugene Orlov, David G. Ownby, Gregory J. Pelnar, Hans-Jürgen Petersen, Steven R. Peterson, Wendy L. Petropoulos, Tomas J. Philipson, Jonathan S. Polonsky, Kirupakaran C. Ramaiah, Bradley N. Reiff, David Reishus, David J. Ross, Rahul Sekhar, Allan L. Shampine, Philip R. Sharp, Hal S. Sider, Heather R. Spang, Kristin D. Stanton, Collin K. Starkweather, Thomas A. Stemwedel, Kenneth M. Stern, Daniel W. Stone, David Strahlberg, Alan O. Sykes, Jeffrey D. Tranen, Laurel C. Van Allen, Eugenia Vinogradsky, Elizabeth A. Wall, Patrick Wang, Yili Wang, Vincent A. Warther, Anne Marie Yale, Deborah W. Zimmermann.

Representative Clients: Arnold & Porter; Baker Botts; Baker & Hostetler; Bell Boyd & Lloyd; Boies, Schiller & Flexner; Covington & Burling; Cravath, Swaine & Moore; Davis Polk & Wardwell; Fish & Neave; Fried, Frank, Harris, Shriver & Jacobson; Freeman, Freeman & Salzman; Fulbright & Jaworski; Gardner, Carton & Douglas; Heller Ehrman White & McAuliffe; Jenner & Block; Katten Muchin Zavis Rosenman; Kirkland & Ellis; Latham & Watkins; Mayer, Brown Rowe & Maw; Morgan, Lewis & Bockius; Morrison & Foerster; Paul, Weiss, Rifkind, Wharton & Garrison; Shearman & Sterling; Sullivan & Cromwell; Skadden, Arps, Slate, Meagher & Flom; Steptoe & Johnson; Wachtell, Lipton, Rosen & Katz; Weil, Gotshal & Manges; Wilmer Cutler Pickering Hale & Dorr; federal & state government agencies.

EXPERT WITNESS
ENGINEERS/ENGINEERING

WJE ENGINEERS ARCHITECTS MATERIALS SCIENTISTS

Wiss, Janney, Elstner Associates, Inc.

330 Pfingsten Road
Northbrook, IL 60062
Offices Nationwide
Phone 800/345-3199
Fax 847/291-9599
Internet www.wje.com

WJE is a professional firm providing practical, innovative, and technically sound solutions to structural, architectural, and materials problems. During our 49-year history, we have successfully completed more than 60,000 projects involving virtually every type of construction material, structural system, and architectural component.

WJE's staff of forensic consultants have extensive field and laboratory experience providing investigation, evaluation, testing, and assessment services for building materials; design/construction deficiencies and practices; and building code compliance.

Specialized services include:

- Structural and Architectural Assessments
- Failure Investigation and Analysis
- Repair/Rehabilitation Design
- Construction Materials Evaluation/Testing
- Computerized Failure Simulations
- Courtroom Exhibits/Models
- Due Diligence/Prepurchase Surveys
- Expert Witness Testimony
- Litigation Support

Many of WJE's staff of more than 280 engineers, architects, and materials scientists are nationally recognized experts. WJE maintains 20 offices across the country with professional engineering or architectural registration in every state.

PACKER ENGINEERING, INC.

1950 North Washington Street
Naperville, Illinois 60563

Phone: 630-505-5722
Toll-free: 888-722-5372
Fax: 630-505-1986
Web site: www.packereng.com
Email: peinfo@packereng.com

Packer Engineering's scientists, engineers and technologists have strong academic credentials as well as vital industrial experience. Our work applies a scientific methodology to the principles of engineering to obtain the correct answer to the questions we are asked and the problems we are presented.

Our multidisciplinary staff includes engineers and technicians in the following disciplines and support services.

Disciplines:

(This Listing Continued)

EXPERT WITNESS
ENGINEERS/ENGINEERING (cont'd)

Packer Engineering, Inc. (cont'd)

- Aviation/Aerospace
- Biomedical/Biomechanical
- Chemical, Fire and Explosion
- Civil/Structural
- Construction Technology
- Electrical/Electronics
- Firearms Technology
- Human Factors/Ergonomics
- Intellectual Property
- Machinery/Equipment
- Materials/Metallurgy
- Process Industries
- Transportation

Support Services:

- Laboratory
- Library
- Project Coordination
- Visualization

For more than four decades, insurers and the attorneys that represent them have chosen Packer Engineering's consulting and technical services for the breadth of our experience, the depth of our expertise and the value that comes from timely and economical project management.

The nature of our work and the projects we have been assigned cross into both litigation services and insurance investigation:

LITIGATION

For over 43 years, attorneys have chosen Packer Engineering to provide technical expertise and comprehensive, timely and understandable engineering consulting on a wide array of disputes and legal actions. Our services include accident investigation and reconstruction, failure analysis, product safety and liability studies, design analysis, custom testing, intellectual property & pretrial and courtroom testimony. Other litigation support services include the design and production of demonstrative evidence, physical models and exhibits, dynamic simulations and engineering animations.

- System Failure Analysis and Recovery Consulting
- Product Liability
- Failure Analysis
- Cause and Origin Investigations
- Warnings and Guards
- Warranties and Guarantees
- Vehicular and Transportation Equipment
- Residential, Workplace and Construction Site Accidents
- Premise Liabilities
- Intellectual Property and Patents
- Personal Injury

INSURANCE

When it comes to investigating insurance claims, Packer Engineering provides a wide range of services which enable insurers to validate claims, assess damages and effectively manage losses. Our experience includes assignments involving both property and casualty claims. We offer a comprehensive package of services from accident site investigations and inspections through litigation services.

If you have an immediate need and would like to speak with one of our staff, please call toll-free at **888-722-5372** or click on our website hot link and leave us a message at www.packereng.com or email us at peinfo@packereng.com

Packer Engineering, Inc. is a wholly-owned subsidiary of The Packer Group, Inc., a corporation of technology-driven service and product companies serving the diversity of industry and commerce.

Safety Consulting Engineers, Inc.

2131 Hammond Drive
Schaumburg, IL 60173
Phone: 847-925-8100
Fax: 847-925-8120
Email: sceinc@sceinc.com
Website: www.sceinc.com

"Making The World a Safer Place"

C. James Dahn, President

Degrees/Licenses:
B.S. Aeronautical Engineering

Specialties:
Consulting, research & testing for fire and explosion hazards involving chemical, propellant, pyrotechnic and explosives manufacturing. Testing includes dust explosibility, electrostatics, thermal stability and mechanical sensitivity. Outdoor test site available fore large-scale processing and testing.

Wiss, Janney, Elstner Associates, Inc.

Engineers, Architects, Materials Scientists
330 Pfingsten Road
Northbrook, IL 60062
Offices nationwide

Phone	800/345-3199
Fax	847/291-9599
Internet	www.wje.com
Contact	Gary Klein, EVP

WJE is a professional firm providing practical, innovative, and technically sound solutions to structural, architectural, and materials problems. During our 49-year history, we have successfully completed more than 60,000 projects involving virtually every type of construction material, structural system, and architectural component.

WJE's staff of forensic consultants have extensive field and laboratory experience providing investigative, testing, and assessment services for building materials; design / construction deficiencies and practices; and building code compliance.

Specialized services include:

- Structural and Architectural Assessments
- Failure Investigation and Analysis
- Repair / Rehabilitation Design
- Construction Materials Evaluation / Testing
- Computerized Failure Simulations
- Courtroom Exhibits / Models
- Due Diligence / Prepurchase Surveys
- Expert Witness Testimony
- Litigation Support

Many of WJE's staff of more than 280 engineers, architects, and materials scientists are nationally recognized experts. WJE maintains offices across the country with professional engineering or architectural registration in every state.

SEE OUR AD ON PAGE IL21S

EXPERT WITNESS
ENGINEERS/ENGINEERING
CIVIL/MECHANICAL/STRUCTURAL

CTLGROUP

5400 OLD ORCHARD ROAD
Skokie, IL 60077-1030
Telephone: 800.522.2285
Fax: 847.965.6541
Web Site: www.CTLGroup.com
Email: JGarrett@CTLGroup.com

CTLGroup is an internationally recognized consulting engineering firm with an 85-year history of offering professional structural engineering, testing and research services. CTLGroup's staff of 140 professionals offers a unique combination of structural investigative services, structural engineering analysis and design services, construction materials testing and research, and structural diagnostics testing and laboratory services. Our expertise includes:

- Consulting engineering
- Condition and damage assessments
- Structural failure investigations and root cause determinations
- Nondestructive testing and in-situ evaluations
- Building material failure analyses and remediation
- Structural system failure analyses and remediation
- Laboratory material testing and evaluation
- Laboratory structural component testing and evaluation
- Real-time in-situ structural health monitoring
- Design and construction standard of care issues
- Litigation and legal support, including
  - Expert Testimony
  - Demonstrative evidence

Wiss, Janney, Elstner Associates, Inc.

Engineers, Architects, Materials Scientists
330 Pfingsten Road
Northbrook, IL 60062
Offices nationwide

Phone	800/345-3199
Fax	847/291-9599
Internet	www.wje.com
Contact	Gary Klein, EVP

WJE is a professional firm providing practical, innovative, and technically sound solutions to structural, architectural, and materials problems. During our 49-year history, we have successfully completed more than 60,000 projects involving virtually every type of construction material, structural system, and architectural component.

WJE's staff of forensic consultants have extensive field and laboratory experience providing investigative, testing, and assessment services for building materials; design / construction deficiencies and practices; and building code compliance.

(This Listing Continued)

Specialized services include:

- Structural and Architectural Assessments
- Failure Investigation and Analysis
- Repair / Rehabilitation Design
- Construction Materials Evaluation / Testing
- Computerized Failure Simulations
- Courtroom Exhibits / Models
- Due Diligence / Prepurchase Surveys
- Expert Witness Testimony
- Litigation Support

Many of WJE's staff of more than 280 engineers, architects, and materials scientists are nationally recognized experts. WJE maintains offices across the country with professional engineering or architectural registration in every state.

EXPERT WITNESS
ENGINEERS/ENGINEERING
FIRE PROTECTION

ROLF JENSEN & ASSOCIATES, INC.

600 West Fulton, Suite 500
Chicago, Illinois 60661
Tel: 312-879-7200
Fax: 312-879-7210

www.rjainc.com

Rolf Jensen & Associates Inc. has over thirty-five years of experience providing fire protection engineering services to the legal community. From conducting fire investigations and loss prevention site surveys to serving as expert witnesses, RJA has an excellent reputation for providing thorough investigations and research.

RJA employs more than 150 professionals, many of which hold advanced degrees in a variety of engineering disciplines, including fire protection, mechanical, electrical and civil. RJA's engineering professionals are registered fire protection engineers in almost all of the 50 states.

RJA provides clients throughout the world with effective solutions to their life safety and fire protection challenges through engineering, performance-based design and construction management. We accomplish our mission in an atmosphere of professional integrity, adhering to the principles of client focus, industry leadership, innovation, technological advancement, and respect for both the team and the individual.

Areas of Expertise

- Fire Protection Engineering Code Consulting
- Fire Protection Engineering Systems Design
- Forensic Fire Modeling
- Building Code Compliance
- Fire Investigation
- Construction Claim Dispute Resolution
- Failure Analysis of Systems and Components
- ADA Compliance

Associations

- National Fire Protection Association
- Society of Fire Protection Engineers
- Risk & Insurance Management Society

Offices in:
Atlanta, Baltimore, Boston, Dallas, Denver, Houston, Las Vegas, Los Angeles, New York, Orlando, Phoenix, Raleigh, San Diego, San Francisco, Shanghai and Washington, DC

EXPERT WITNESS
ENGINEERS/ENGINEERING
FORENSIC ENGINEERING

CTLGROUP

5400 OLD ORCHARD ROAD
Skokie, IL 60077-1030
Telephone: 800.522.2285
Fax: 847.965.6541
Web Site: www.CTLGroup.com
Email: JGarrett@CTLGroup.com

CTLGroup is an internationally recognized consulting engineering firm with an 85-year history of offering professional structural engineering, testing and research services. CTLGroup's staff of 140 professionals offers a unique combination of structural investigative services, structural engineering analysis and design services, construction materials testing and research, and structural diagnostics testing and laboratory services. Our expertise includes:

- Consulting engineering
- Condition and damage assessments
- Structural failure investigations and root cause determinations
- Nondestructive testing and in-situ evaluations
- Building material failure analyses and remediation
- Structural system failure analyses and remediation
- Laboratory material testing and evaluation
- Laboratory structural component testing and evaluation
- Real-time in-situ structural health monitoring
- Design and construction standard of care issues
- Litigation and legal support, including
  - Expert Testimony
  - Demonstrative evidence

Wiss, Janney, Elstner Associates, Inc.
Engineers, Architects, Materials Scientists
330 Pfingsten Road
Northbrook, IL 60062
Offices nationwide

Phone	800/345-3199
Fax	847/291-9599
Internet	www.wje.com
Contact	Gary Klein, EVP

WJE is a professional firm providing practical, innovative, and technically sound solutions to structural, architectural, and materials problems. During our 49-year history, we have successfully completed more than 60,000 projects involving virtually every type of construction material, structural system, and architectural component.

WJE's staff of forensic consultants have extensive field and laboratory experience providing investigative, testing, and assessment services for building materials; design / construction deficiencies and practices; and building code compliance.

(This Listing Continued)

Specialized services include:
- Structural and Architectural Assessments
- Failure Investigation and Analysis
- Repair / Rehabilitation Design
- Construction Materials Evaluation / Testing
- Computerized Failure Simulations
- Courtroom Exhibits / Models
- Due Diligence / Prepurchase Surveys
- Expert Witness Testimony
- Litigation Support

Many of WJE's staff of more than 280 engineers, architects, and materials scientists are nationally recognized experts. WJE maintains offices across the country with professional engineering or architectural registration in every state.

EXPERT WITNESS
FAILURE ANALYSIS

CTLGROUP

5400 OLD ORCHARD ROAD
Skokie, IL 60077-1030
Telephone: 800.522.2285
Fax: 847.965.6541
Web Site: www.CTLGroup.com
Email: JGarrett@CTLGroup.com

CTLGroup is an internationally recognized consulting engineering firm with an 85-year history of offering professional structural engineering, testing and research services. CTLGroup's staff of 140 professionals offers a unique combination of structural investigative services, structural engineering analysis and design services, construction materials testing and research, and structural diagnostics testing and laboratory services. Our expertise includes:

- Consulting engineering
- Condition and damage assessments
- Structural failure investigations and root cause determinations
- Nondestructive testing and in-situ evaluations
- Building material failure analyses and remediation
- Structural system failure analyses and remediation
- Laboratory material testing and evaluation
- Laboratory structural component testing and evaluation
- Real-time in-situ structural health monitoring
- Design and construction standard of care issues
- Litigation and legal support, including
  - Expert Testimony
  - Demonstrative evidence

Wiss, Janney, Elstner Associates, Inc.
Engineers, Architects, Materials Scientists
330 Pfingsten Road
Northbrook, IL 60062
Offices nationwide

Phone	800/345-3199
Fax	847/291-9599
Internet	www.wje.com
Contact	Gary Klein, EVP

(This Listing Continued)

WJE is a professional firm providing practical, innovative, and technically sound solutions to structural, architectural, and materials problems. During our 49-year history, we have successfully completed more than 60,000 projects involving virtually every type of construction material, structural system, and architectural component.

WJE's staff of forensic consultants have extensive field and laboratory experience providing investigative, testing, and assessment services for building materials; design / construction deficiencies and practices; and building code compliance.

Specialized services include:

- Structural and Architectural Assessments
- Failure Investigation and Analysis
- Repair / Rehabilitation Design
- Construction Materials Evaluation / Testing
- Computerized Failure Simulations
- Courtroom Exhibits / Models
- Due Diligence / Prepurchase Surveys
- Expert Witness Testimony
- Litigation Support

Many of WJE's staff of more than 280 engineers, architects, and materials scientists are nationally recognized experts. WJE maintains offices across the country with professional engineering or architectural registration in every state.

EXPERT WITNESS
FIRE

JOHN MICHAEL AGOSTI

Fire Analyst and Consultant
23808 North Overhill
Lake Zurich, Illinois 60047
Phone: 847-682-6793
E-mail: johnagosti@earthlink.net
Web: www.arsonexpert.com

As a member of the Skokie, Illinois Fire Department for twenty-eight years, Mr. Agosti progressed from a Firefighter/Paramedic to the position of Deputy Fire Chief. Mr. Agosti has responded to hundreds of major fire and crime scenes and has testified in court on the conclusions of his investigations. His investigations have led to successful criminal indictments and convictions. Mr. Agosti's fire department responsibilities included the review of all construction plans for compliance to fire and building codes. His expertise in building construction and fire spread, lends a unique blend to his fire investigation capabilities.
In addition to his fire department exposure to hundreds of fire investigations, Mr. Agosti has extensive experience in the private sector also. Over the past 11 years Mr. Agosti has conducted over eight hundred fire investigations as a private fire cause and origin analyst.

(This Listing Continued)

Practice areas include:

Fire and Explosions:
Arson defense/prosecution; gas explosions;
vehicular fires; structure fires; fire deaths/injuries.

Building and Fire Codes:
Fire/Building code violation; Life Safety Code violations;
smoke detector issues; fire prevention analysis.

Fire Department Practices:
Fire department operations/practices/management;
firefighter deaths/injuries/safety.

Mr. Agosti has an Associates Degree in Fire Science and Technology. He is also certified as a Fire and Arson Investigator.

PROJECT EXPERIENCE

Fire and building code analysis
Automobile accident reconstruction
Gas leak surveys
Distribution gas pipe ruptures and leaks
Investigation of fire fatalities and electrocutions
Investigation of bombings
Investigation for cause and origin of fires and explosions

PROFESSIONAL SOCIETIES

National Fire Protection Association
Fire Marshals Association of North America
International Association of Fire Chiefs
Building Officials/Code Administrators International
Fire Investigators Strike Force
Illinois Fire Inspectors Association
International Association of Arson Investigators

VARLEY-CAMPBELL & ASSOCIATES, INC.

Consulting Fire Protection Engineers
2625 Butterfield Road
Suite 138S
Oak Brook, Illinois 60523
telephone: 630-573-7730 *fax*: 630-574-8026
www.varley-campbell.com

Varley-Campbell & Associates offer a single source of professional capabilities in the specialized discipline of fire protection engineering. The firm applies recognized engineering techniques to the analysis of diverse fire events, from the inappropriate release of a sprinkler system to multi-fatality fires. Our services include fire and explosion investigation, event reconstruction, analysis and expert witness services. Advanced technical support is provided through fire modeling, fire testing and the analysis of test data.

The engineers of Varley-Campbell have extensive experience in all aspects of fire protection engineering, from system design and evaluation to code consulting and life safety issues. They are Members in the Society of Fire Protection Engineers and are actively involved in the standards making process. They regularly provide consulting services related to system failures, event reconstruction and engineering analysis of fire incidents.

Thomas H. Miller P.E. has over 25 years of experience in the investigation and analysis of fire system failures, fires and explosions. Mr. Miller has provided these services to a variety of clients, including insurance, legal and government clients. As lead investigator, he has published several major fire investigation studies for the United States Fire Administration. Mr. Miller has been qualified as an expert witness in state and federal courts.

Mr. Miller is an author, educator and volunteer firefighter. He is actively involved in the National Fire Protection Association and currently serves on the automatic sprinkler system standard committee. He is a Member of the Society of Fire Protection Engineers and National Society of Professional Engineers.

EXPERT WITNESS
FIRE
PROTECTION, INVESTIGATION

JOHN MICHAEL AGOSTI

Fire Analyst and Consultant

23808 North Overhill
Lake Zurich, Illinois 60047
Phone: 847-682-6793
E-mail: johnagosti@earthlink.net
Web: www.arsonexpert.com

As a member of the Skokie, Illinois Fire Department for twenty-eight years, Mr. Agosti progressed from a Firefighter/Paramedic to the position of Deputy Fire Chief. Mr. Agosti has responded to hundreds of major fire and crime scenes and has testified in court on the conclusions of his investigations. His investigations have led to successful criminal indictments and convictions. Mr. Agosti's fire department responsibilities included the review of all construction plans for compliance to fire and building codes. His expertise in building construction and fire spread, lends a unique blend to his fire investigation capabilities.

In addition to his fire department exposure to hundreds of fire investigations, Mr. Agosti has extensive experience in the private sector also. Over the past 11 years Mr. Agosti has conducted over eight hundred fire investigations as a private fire cause and origin analyst.

Practice areas include:

Fire and Explosions:
Arson defense/prosecution; gas explosions; vehicular fires; structure fires; fire deaths/injuries.

Building and Fire Codes:
Fire/Building code violation; Life Safety Code violations; smoke detector issues; fire prevention analysis.

Fire Department Practices:
Fire department operations/practices/management; firefighter deaths/injuries/safety.

Mr. Agosti has an Associates Degree in Fire Science and Technology. He is also certified as a Fire and Arson Investigator.

PROJECT EXPERIENCE

Fire and building code analysis
Automobile accident reconstruction
Gas leak surveys
Distribution gas pipe ruptures and leaks
Investigation of fire fatalities and electrocutions
Investigation of bombings
Investigation for cause and origin of fires and explosions

PROFESSIONAL SOCIETIES

National Fire Protection Association
Fire Marshals Association of North America
International Association of Fire Chiefs
Building Officials/Code Administrators International
Fire Investigators Strike Force
Illinois Fire Inspectors Association
International Association of Arson Investigators

EXPERT WITNESS
FIRE
RECONSTRUCTION

JOHN MICHAEL AGOSTI

Fire Analyst and Consultant

23808 North Overhill
Lake Zurich, Illinois 60047
Phone: 847-682-6793
E-mail: johnagosti@earthlink.net
Web: www.arsonexpert.com

As a member of the Skokie, Illinois Fire Department for twenty-eight years, Mr. Agosti progressed from a Firefighter/Paramedic to the position of Deputy Fire Chief. Mr. Agosti has responded to hundreds of major fire and crime scenes and has testified in court on the conclusions of his investigations. His investigations have led to successful criminal indictments and convictions. Mr. Agosti's fire department responsibilities included the review of all construction plans for compliance to fire and building codes. His expertise in building construction and fire spread, lends a unique blend to his fire investigation capabilities.

In addition to his fire department exposure to hundreds of fire investigations, Mr. Agosti has extensive experience in the private sector also. Over the past 11 years Mr. Agosti has conducted over eight hundred fire investigations as a private fire cause and origin analyst.

Practice areas include:

Fire and Explosions:
Arson defense/prosecution; gas explosions; vehicular fires; structure fires; fire deaths/injuries.

Building and Fire Codes:
Fire/Building code violation; Life Safety Code violations; smoke detector issues; fire prevention analysis.

Fire Department Practices:
Fire department operations/practices/management; firefighter deaths/injuries/safety.

Mr. Agosti has an Associates Degree in Fire Science and Technology. He is also certified as a Fire and Arson Investigator.

PROJECT EXPERIENCE

Fire and building code analysis
Automobile accident reconstruction
Gas leak surveys
Distribution gas pipe ruptures and leaks
Investigation of fire fatalities and electrocutions
Investigation of bombings
Investigation for cause and origin of fires and explosions

PROFESSIONAL SOCIETIES

National Fire Protection Association
Fire Marshals Association of North America
International Association of Fire Chiefs
Building Officials/Code Administrators International
Fire Investigators Strike Force
Illinois Fire Inspectors Association
International Association of Arson Investigators

EXPERT WITNESS
FIRE CAUSE & ORIGIN

JOHN MICHAEL AGOSTI & ASSOCIATES
FIREINVESTIGATIONS
johnagosti@earthlink.net

JOHN MICHAEL AGOSTI
Fire Analyst and Consultant
23808 North Overhill
Lake Zurich, Illinois 60047
Phone: 847-682-6793
E-mail: johnagosti@earthlink.net
Web: www.arsonexpert.com

As a member of the Skokie, Illinois Fire Department for twenty-eight years, Mr. Agosti progressed from a Firefighter/Paramedic to the position of Deputy Fire Chief. Mr. Agosti has responded to hundreds of major fire and crime scenes and has testified in court on the conclusions of his investigations. His investigations have led to successful criminal indictments and convictions. Mr. Agosti's fire department responsibilities included the review of all construction plans for compliance to fire and building codes. His expertise in building construction and fire spread, lends a unique blend to his fire investigation capabilities.

In addition to his fire department exposure to hundreds of fire investigations, Mr. Agosti has extensive experience in the private sector also. Over the past 11 years Mr. Agosti has conducted over eight hundred fire investigations as a private fire cause and origin analyst.

Practice areas include:

- Fire and Explosions:
  - Arson defense/prosecution; gas explosions; vehicular fires; structure fires; fire deaths/injuries.
- Building and Fire Codes:
  - Fire/Building code violation; Life Safety Code violations; smoke detector issues; fire prevention analysis.
- Fire Department Practices:
  - Fire department operations/practices/management; firefighter deaths/injuries/safety.

Mr. Agosti has an Associates Degree in Fire Science and Technology. He is also certified as a Fire and Arson Investigator.

PROJECT EXPERIENCE

Fire and building code analysis
Automobile accident reconstruction
Gas leak surveys
Distribution gas pipe ruptures and leaks
Investigation of fire fatalities and electrocutions
Investigation of bombings
Investigation for cause and origin of fires and explosions

PROFESSIONAL SOCIETIES

National Fire Protection Association
Fire Marshals Association of North America
International Association of Fire Chiefs
Building Officials/Code Administrators International
Fire Investigators Strike Force
Illinois Fire Inspectors Association
International Association of Arson Investigators

EXPERT WITNESS
FIRE/CONSULTING

JOHN MICHAEL AGOSTI & ASSOCIATES
FIREINVESTIGATIONS
johnagosti@earthlink.net

JOHN MICHAEL AGOSTI
Fire Analyst and Consultant
23808 North Overhill
Lake Zurich, Illinois 60047
Phone: 847-682-6793
E-mail: johnagosti@earthlink.net
Web: www.arsonexpert.com

As a member of the Skokie, Illinois Fire Department for twenty-eight years, Mr. Agosti progressed from a Firefighter/Paramedic to the position of Deputy Fire Chief. Mr. Agosti has responded to hundreds of major fire and crime scenes and has testified in court on the conclusions of his investigations. His investigations have led to successful criminal indictments and convictions. Mr. Agosti's fire department responsibilities included the review of all construction plans for compliance to fire and building codes. His expertise in building construction and fire spread, lends a unique blend to his fire investigation capabilities.

In addition to his fire department exposure to hundreds of fire investigations, Mr. Agosti has extensive experience in the private sector also. Over the past 11 years Mr. Agosti has conducted over eight hundred fire investigations as a private fire cause and origin analyst.

Practice areas include:

- Fire and Explosions:
  - Arson defense/prosecution; gas explosions; vehicular fires; structure fires; fire deaths/injuries.
- Building and Fire Codes:
  - Fire/Building code violation; Life Safety Code violations; smoke detector issues; fire prevention analysis.
- Fire Department Practices:
  - Fire department operations/practices/management; firefighter deaths/injuries/safety.

Mr. Agosti has an Associates Degree in Fire Science and Technology. He is also certified as a Fire and Arson Investigator.

PROJECT EXPERIENCE

Fire and building code analysis
Automobile accident reconstruction
Gas leak surveys
Distribution gas pipe ruptures and leaks
Investigation of fire fatalities and electrocutions
Investigation of bombings
Investigation for cause and origin of fires and explosions

PROFESSIONAL SOCIETIES

National Fire Protection Association
Fire Marshals Association of North America
International Association of Fire Chiefs
Building Officials/Code Administrators International
Fire Investigators Strike Force
Illinois Fire Inspectors Association
International Association of Arson Investigators

EXPERT WITNESS
FORENSIC CASE MANAGEMENT

Hess, Karfomenos & Associates, LLC
54722 Country Road 8
Middlebury, IN 46540
Toll Free: 866-219-2273
Phone: 574-825-9000
Fax: 574-825-3355
Email: hkamedlegal@starband.net
www.hkamedlegal.com

Medical and Forensic Case Management, Life Care Planning, Medicare Set-Aside Allocations, and Medical-Legal File Analysis/Review, these are the focused specialties of the staff of *Hess, Karfomenos & Associates, LLC.*

Professional Forensic Case Management ensures your client is afforded the highest quality of care and treatment, coordinated by a licensed professional nurse who is nationally certified as a medical case manager. Our staff has extensive experience in managing the medical care of Worker's Compensation, Group Health and Catastrophic Injury cases as well as negotiating costs and coordinating ancillary services. The benefit to you and your client? *You are afforded access to the finest medical and professional practitioners available nationwide and the knowledge that expedient and appropriate medical care, is being delivered-allowing you to focus on the intricacies of the litigation process.*

Collectively our firm's nurses bring over 100 years of nursing experience and over 40 years of case managers through CMSA, CCMC and also state case management endorsement by several state governments. Workers's Compensation, Group Health, LTD/STD and catastrophic case management are our specialities.

We at Hess, Karfomenos & Associates, LLC, welcome the opportunity to assist you in your practice.

"Let our expertise enhance your successes."

Members: American Association of Nurse Life Care Planners, American Association of Legal Nurse Consultants, Indianapolis Chapter-American Association of Legal Nurse Consultants, Academy of Certified Case Managers, American Nurses Association, Indian State Nurses Association, Emergency Nurses Association, Case Management Society of America, International Association of Rehabilitation Providers, Tri-State Case Managers Association, International Academy of Life Care Planners and the Indiana Bar Association.

Professional Nursing Licenses: Indiana, Michigan, Tennessee and Texas

National Certifications: Certified Case Managers (CCM)
Certified Nurse Life Care Planners (CNLCP)

State Certifications/Case Management: TN, OH and KY
Certified Provider/Life Care Planning/Case Management-Ohio BWC

EXPERT WITNESS
INSURANCE
LIFE, DISABILITY & LONG TERM CARE

Patrick F. Braun, CLU, LUTCF, FIC

P.O. Box 628
Whitewater, WI 53190
Cell: (262) 893-6675
Home: (262) 473-1850
E-mail: patrickbraun@idcnet.com

33 Years in the Life Insurance business
Expert Witness Experience in both State & Federal cases
Management for 29 years
Senior Management (Officer Level) 12 years
Chartered Life Underwriter (CLU)
Graduate - Life Underwriter Training Fellow (LUTCF)
Graduate - Fraternal Insurance Counselor (FIC)
Former school Teacher and Principal
Knowledge in a broad range of management and life insurance subjects

Specific areas of advanced knowledge:

- How Life Insurance Works.
- The Sale of Life Insurance.
- Underwriting of Policies.
- Business Life Insurance.
- Programming Techniques (How much Life Insurance is needed).
- Quality Management Concepts.
- Hiring Practices.
- Termination Practices.
- Supervision of Agents & Field Managers.
- Employee Vs. Independent Contractors as related to Life Insurance producers.
- Instructor of Ethics as related to the Sale of Life Insurance - LUTC Instructor.

Interpersonal Attributes:

- Excellent Communication Skills, both Oral & Written.
- Coaching Skills.
- Ability to Break Complicated Subject into Simple Concepts & Teach these Concepts in a Friendly, Non-Threatening Manner.
- Ability to Quickly Relate to all Personality types. Expert in Building Relationships.
- Professional Looking & Sounding while also Appearing Warm & Trustworthy.

EXPERT WITNESS
INSURANCE / REINSURANCE

WILLIAM C. CUTLIP CONSULTING

William C. Cutlip
FSA, MAAA, FCA, CLU, ChFC, CPCU

Web Site: www.cutlipconsulting.com

(This Listing Continued)

3048 Woods Edge Way
Madison, WI 53711
Phone: (608) 443-0669
Fax: (608) 443-0668

8021 Wildomar Drive
Tucson, AZ 85743
Phone: (520) 572-8833
Fax: (520) 579-6688

Cell: (520) 247-6592

Areas of Expertise: Expert Witness / Forensics / Litigation Support / Arbitrations

Financial Evaluation for:

- damages
- investment
- merger & acquisition
- structured settlements
- grievances
- equitable distribution

Legal Ammunition for:

- pre-filing evaluation
- case strength
- surprise reduction
- strategy support
- opposition analysis
- scientifically supported evaluation

Professional Profile:

Educated at Massachusetts Institute of Technology and Oklahoma State University, William C. Cutlip has over 40 years of industry experience and specializes in risk evaluation and expert witness work for attorneys, product development for insurance companies, and business consulting.

Professional Qualifications:

Fellow, Society of Actuaries (FSA)
Member, American Academy of Actuaries (MAAA)
Fellow, Conference of Consulting Actuaries (FCA)
Chartered Life Underwriter (CLU)
Chartered Financial Consultant (ChFC)
Member, International Association of Consulting Actuaries

Cases/Clients: Plaintiff and Defense

Geographical Area: No Limitation

E-mail Contact: cutlipconsulting@cs.com

EXPERT WITNESS
INTELLECTUAL PROPERTY/INFRINGEMENT DAMAGES

Lexecon

www.lexecon.com

332 South Michigan Avenue
Chicago, Illinois 60604
312-322-0200

20 University Road
Cambridge, Massachusetts 02138
617-520-0200

A consulting firm offering a full range of litigation support services, including economic, financial and statistical analysis, and assistance in the selection and preparation of testifying experts. Lexecon has extensive experience in complex litigation involving antitrust, securities, regulatory design, intellectual property, employment discrimination, contract damages and valuation. It also offers business consulting services and public policy counsel.

(This Listing Continued)

Members of the firm have extensive experience in financial, energy, technology, insurance, health care, telecommunications, consumer products, transportation and manufacturing industries.

M&A Analysis
Securities
Regulatory Design
Statistical Analyses and Damages Estimation
Assistance in the Selection and Preparation of Economic, Accounting and Other Expert Witnesses

Lexecon Professionals: Dennis W. Carlton, Daniel R. Fischel, Joseph P. Kalt, Rachelle F. Alcain, Charles W. Augustine, Gustavo E. Bamberger, Catherine Barron, Margaret M. Bennett, Nancy Bonn, John Robert Broxson, Amy Bertin Candell, Joseph Cavicchi, Carolyn Y. Chong, Irfan Ciputra, Charles C. Cox, James M. Coyne, Helena Croce, Deborah L. Dobrusin, James Donovan, Ronald A. Dye, Laona A. Fleischer, Fredrick A. Flyer, Rajiv B. Gokhale, Kenneth W. Grant II, David B. Gross, Timothy R. Guimond, Alan S. Frankel, Austan Goolsbee, Robert S. Hamada, Seth A. Hamstead, Kevin D. Hartt, Prescott C. Hartshorne, James J. Heckman, Eric Henson, Scott T. Jones, Michael A. Keable, Kenneth W. Kipp, Randall S. Kroszner, Elisabeth M. Landes, Andrew Y. Lemon, H. Neal Lenhoff, Youngsik Lim, Colleen P. Loughlin, William J. Lynk, Stephen Makowka, Jessica P. Mandel, Ronnie A. Martin, Glen Meyers, Erich Muehlegger, Avisheh Mohsenin, Lynette R. Neumann, Cathy M. Niden, Joshua H. Nixt, Eugene Orlov, David G. Ownby, Gregory J. Pelnar, Hans-Jürgen Petersen, Steven R. Peterson, Wendy L. Petropoulos, Tomas J. Philipson, Jonathan S. Polonsky, Kirupakaran C. Ramaiah, Bradley N. Reiff, David Reishus, David J. Ross, Rahul Sekhar, Allan L. Shampine, Philip R. Sharp, Hal S. Sider, Heather R. Spang, Kristin D. Stanton, Collin K. Starkweather, Thomas A. Stemwedel, Kenneth M. Stern, Daniel W. Stone, David Strahlberg, Alan O. Sykes, Jeffrey D. Tranen, Laurel C. Van Allen, Eugenia Vinogradsky, Elizabeth A. Wall, Patrick Wang, Yili Wang, Vincent A. Warther, Anne Marie Yale, Deborah W. Zimmermann.

Representative Clients: Arnold & Porter; Baker Botts; Baker & Hostetler; Bell Boyd & Lloyd; Boies, Schiller & Flexner; Covington & Burling; Cravath, Swaine & Moore; Davis Polk & Wardwell; Fish & Neave; Fried, Frank, Harris, Shriver & Jacobson; Freeman, Freeman & Salzman; Fulbright & Jaworski; Gardner, Carton & Douglas; Heller Ehrman White & McAuliffe; Jenner & Block; Katten Muchin Zavis Rosenman; Kirkland & Ellis; Latham & Watkins; Mayer, Brown Rowe & Maw; Morgan, Lewis & Bockius; Morrison & Foerster; Paul, Weiss, Rifkind, Wharton & Garrison; Shearman & Sterling; Sullivan & Cromwell; Skadden, Arps, Slate, Meagher & Flom; Steptoe & Johnson; Wachtell, Lipton, Rosen & Katz; Weil, Gotshal & Manges; Wilmer Cutler Pickering Hale & Dorr; federal & state government agencies.

EXPERT WITNESS
LITIGATION SUPPORT

Lexecon

www.lexecon.com

332 South Michigan Avenue
Chicago, Illinois 60604
312-322-0200

20 University Road
Cambridge, Massachusetts 02138
617-520-0200

A consulting firm offering a full range of litigation support services, including economic, financial and statistical analysis, and assistance in the selection and preparation of testifying experts. Lexecon has extensive experience in complex litigation involving antitrust, securities, regulatory design, intellectual property, employment discrimination, contract damages and valuation. It also offers business consulting services and public policy counsel.

(This Listing Continued)

EXPERT WITNESS
LITIGATION SUPPORT (cont'd)

Lexecon (cont'd)

Members of the firm have extensive experience in financial, energy, technology, insurance, health care, telecommunications, consumer products, transportation and manufacturing industries.

M&A Analysis
Securities
Regulatory Design
Statistical Analyses and Damages Estimation
Assistance in the Selection and Preparation of Economic, Accounting and Other Expert Witnesses

Lexecon Professionals: Dennis W. Carlton, Daniel R. Fischel, Joseph P. Kalt, Rachelle F. Alcain, Charles W. Augustine, Gustavo E. Bamberger, Catherine Barron, Margaret M. Bennett, Nancy Bonn, John Robert Broxson, Amy Bertin Candell, Joseph Cavicchi, Carolyn Y. Chong, Irfan Ciputra, Charles C. Cox, James M. Coyne, Helena Croce, Deborah L. Dobrusin, James Donovan, Ronald A. Dye, Laona A. Fleischer, Fredrick A. Flyer, Rajiv B. Gokhale, Kenneth W. Grant II, David B. Gross, Timothy R. Guimond, Alan S. Frankel, Austan Goolsbee, Robert S. Hamada, Seth A. Hamstead, Kevin D. Hartt, Prescott C. Hartshorne, James J. Heckman, Eric Henson, Scott T. Jones, Michael A. Keable, Kenneth W. Kipp, Randall S. Kroszner, Elisabeth M. Landes, Andrew Y. Lemon, H. Neal Lenhoff, Youngsik Lim, Colleen P. Loughlin, William J. Lynk, Stephen Makowka, Jessica P. Mandel, Ronnie A. Martin, Glen Meyers, Erich Muehlegger, Avisheh Mohsenin, Lynette R. Neumann, Cathy M. Niden, Joshua H. Nixt, Eugene Orlov, David G. Ownby, Gregory J. Pelnar, Hans-Jürgen Petersen, Steven R. Peterson, Wendy L. Petropoulos, Tomas J. Philipson, Jonathan S. Polonsky, Kirupakaran C. Ramaiah, Bradley N. Reiff, David Reishus, David J. Ross, Rahul Sekhar, Allan L. Shampine, Philip R. Sharp, Hal S. Sider, Heather R. Spang, Kristin D. Stanton, Collin K. Starkweather, Thomas A. Stemwedel, Kenneth M. Stern, Daniel W. Stone, David Strahlberg, Alan O. Sykes, Jeffrey D. Tranen, Laurel C. Van Allen, Eugenia Vinogradsky, Elizabeth A. Wall, Patrick Wang, Yili Wang, Vincent A. Warther, Anne Marie Yale, Deborah W. Zimmermann.

Representative Clients: Arnold & Porter; Baker Botts; Baker & Hostetler; Bell Boyd & Lloyd; Boies, Schiller & Flexner; Covington & Burling; Cravath, Swaine & Moore; Davis Polk & Wardwell; Fish & Neave; Fried, Frank, Harris, Shriver & Jacobson; Freeman, Freeman & Salzman; Fulbright & Jaworski; Gardner, Carton & Douglas; Heller Ehrman White & McAuliffe; Jenner & Block; Katten Muchin Zavis Rosenman; Kirkland & Ellis; Latham & Watkins; Mayer, Brown Rowe & Maw; Morgan, Lewis & Bockius; Morrison & Foerster; Paul, Weiss, Rifkind, Wharton & Garrison; Shearman & Sterling; Sullivan & Cromwell; Skadden, Arps, Slate, Meagher & Flom; Steptoe & Johnson; Wachtell, Lipton, Rosen & Katz; Weil, Gotshal & Manges; Wilmer Cutler Pickering Hale & Dorr; federal & state government agencies.

WILLIAM C. CUTLIP CONSULTING

William C. Cutlip
FSA, MAAA, FCA, CLU, ChFC, CPCU

Web Site: www.cutlipconsulting.com

3048 Woods Edge Way
Madison, WI 53711
Phone: (608) 443-0669
Fax: (608) 443-0668

8021 Wildomar Drive
Tucson, AZ 85743
Phone: (520) 572-8833
Fax: (520) 579-6688

Cell: (520) 247-6592

(This Listing Continued)

Areas of Expertise: Expert Witness / Forensics / Litigation Support / Arbitrations

Financial Evaluation for:
- damages
- investment
- merger & acquisition
- structured settlements
- grievances
- equitable distribution

Legal Ammunition for:
- pre-filing evaluation
- case strength
- surprise reduction
- strategy support
- opposition analysis
- scientifically supported evaluation

Professional Profile:
Educated at Massachusetts Institute of Technology and Oklahoma State University, William C. Cutlip has over 40 years of industry experience and specializes in risk evaluation and expert witness work for attorneys, product development for insurance companies, and business consulting.

Professional Qualifications:
Fellow, Society of Actuaries (FSA)
Member, American Academy of Actuaries (MAAA)
Fellow, Conference of Consulting Actuaries (FCA)
Chartered Life Underwriter (CLU)
Chartered Financial Consultant (ChFC)
Member, International Association of Consulting Actuaries

Cases/Clients: Plaintiff and Defense

Geographical Area: No Limitation

E-mail Contact: cutlipconsulting@cs.com

EXPERT WITNESS
PATENT INFRINGEMENT

Lexecon
www.lexecon.com

332 South Michigan Avenue
Chicago, Illinois 60604
312-322-0200

20 University Road
Cambridge, Massachusetts 02138
617-520-0200

A consulting firm offering a full range of litigation support services, including economic, financial and statistical analysis, and assistance in the selection and preparation of testifying experts. Lexecon has extensive experience in complex litigation involving antitrust, securities, regulatory design, intellectual property, employment discrimination, contract damages and valuation. It also offers business consulting services and public policy counsel.

Members of the firm have extensive experience in financial, energy, technology, insurance, health care, telecommunications, consumer products, transportation and manufacturing industries.

M&A Analysis
Securities
Regulatory Design
Statistical Analyses and Damages Estimation

(This Listing Continued)

Assistance in the Selection and Preparation of Economic, Accounting and Other Expert Witnesses

Lexecon Professionals: Dennis W. Carlton, Daniel R. Fischel, Joseph P. Kalt, Rachelle F. Alcain, Charles W. Augustine, Gustavo E. Bamberger, Catherine Barron, Margaret M. Bennett, Nancy Bonn, John Robert Broxson, Amy Bertin Candell, Joseph Cavicchi, Carolyn Y. Chong, Irfan Ciputra, Charles C. Cox, James M. Coyne, Helena Croce, Deborah L. Dobrusin, James Donovan, Ronald A. Dye, Laona A. Fleischer, Fredrick A. Flyer, Rajiv B. Gokhale, Kenneth W. Grant II, David B. Gross, Timothy R. Guimond, Alan S. Frankel, Austan Goolsbee, Robert S. Hamada, Seth A. Hamstead, Kevin D. Hartt, Prescott C. Hartshorne, James J. Heckman, Eric Henson, Scott T. Jones, Michael A. Keable, Kenneth W. Kipp, Randall S. Kroszner, Elisabeth M. Landes, Andrew Y. Lemon, H. Neal Lenhoff, Youngsik Lim, Colleen P. Loughlin, William J. Lynk, Stephen Makowka, Jessica P. Mandel, Ronnie A. Martin, Glen Meyers, Erich Muehlegger, Avisheh Mohsenin, Lynette R. Neumann, Cathy M. Niden, Joshua H. Nixt, Eugene Orlov, David G. Ownby, Gregory J. Pelnar, Hans-Jürgen Petersen, Steven R. Peterson, Wendy L. Petropoulos, Tomas J. Philipson, Jonathan S. Polonsky, Kirupakaran C. Ramaiah, Bradley N. Reiff, David Reishus, David J. Ross, Rahul Sekhar, Allan L. Shampine, Philip R. Sharp, Hal S. Sider, Heather R. Spang, Kristin D. Stanton, Collin K. Starkweather, Thomas A. Stemwedel, Kenneth M. Stern, Daniel W. Stone, David Strahlberg, Alan O. Sykes, Jeffrey D. Tranen, Laurel C. Van Allen, Eugenia Vinogradsky, Elizabeth A. Wall, Patrick Wang, Yili Wang, Vincent A. Warther, Anne Marie Yale, Deborah W. Zimmermann.

Representative Clients: Arnold & Porter; Baker Botts; Baker & Hostetler; Bell Boyd & Lloyd; Boies, Schiller & Flexner; Covington & Burling; Cravath, Swaine & Moore; Davis Polk & Wardwell; Fish & Neave; Fried, Frank, Harris, Shriver & Jacobson; Freeman, Freeman & Salzman; Fulbright & Jaworski; Gardner, Carton & Douglas; Heller Ehrman White & McAuliffe; Jenner & Block; Katten Muchin Zavis Rosenman; Kirkland & Ellis; Latham & Watkins; Mayer, Brown Rowe & Maw; Morgan, Lewis & Bockius; Morrison & Foerster; Paul, Weiss, Rifkind, Wharton & Garrison; Shearman & Sterling; Sullivan & Cromwell; Skadden, Arps, Slate, Meagher & Flom; Steptoe & Johnson; Wachtell, Lipton, Rosen & Katz; Weil, Gotshal & Manges; Wilmer Cutler Pickering Hale & Dorr; federal & state government agencies.

EXPERT WITNESS
Plastics Processing and Products

Bottom Line Consulting, Inc.

27248 Twin Pond Road
Lake Barrington, IL 60010
Phone: 847-381-0597
Fax: 847-381-0598
Email: blcjhf@aol.com

John Fearncombe, President

BIOGRAPHICAL INFORMATION:
John Fearncombe founded Bottom Line Consulting, Inc. in 1987 to add value to clients in the plastics and recycling industries. He is a practical Chemical Engineer/MBA with exceptional ability to understand and explain complex plastic chemistry, technology, and processing issues. His experiences encompass all major thermoplastics, compounds and blends, additives, processing, testing and specifications, and technologies.

Years in Business:
18 years at Bottom Line Consulting, Inc., 36 years total in plastics industry

Prior to 1987, Mr. Fearncombe had 18 years of industrial experience at two major resin companies: BASF Corporation and Northern Petrochemicals Company (now Equistar Chemicals). He held various management and technical positions in new business development, technology selection and

(This Listing Continued)

plant expansions, plant operations, startups, and troubleshooting. This combination of in-plant and management experiences forms the basis for the practical consulting advice each client receives.

Education Background:
Wayne State University - Detroit, MI
B.S. Degree in Chemical Engineering
M.B.A. in Finance

LIST OF SERVICES:
Expert witness and due diligence
Trouble-shooting product performance problems
Establishing process conditions that minimize resin degradation
Developing custom formulations to maximize long-term part performance
Implementing new technology for competitive market/cost advantages
Fast-tracking the commercialization of quality recycled-content products

MISSION STATEMENT: To add value to each client's bottom line

EXPERT WITNESS
ROOFING & WATERPROOFING

Wiss, Janney, Elstner Associates, Inc.

Engineers, Architects, Materials Scientists
330 Pfingsten Road
Northbrook, IL 60062
Offices nationwide

Phone	800/345-3199
Fax	847/291-9599
Internet	www.wje.com
Contact	Gary Klein, EVP

WJE is a professional firm providing practical, innovative, and technically sound solutions to structural, architectural, and materials problems. During our 49-year history, we have successfully completed more than 60,000 projects involving virtually every type of construction material, structural system, and architectural component.

WJE's staff of forensic consultants have extensive field and laboratory experience providing investigative, testing, and assessment services for building materials; design / construction deficiencies and practices; and building code compliance.

Specialized services include:
- Structural and Architectural Assessments
- Failure Investigation and Analysis
- Repair / Rehabilitation Design
- Construction Materials Evaluation / Testing
- Computerized Failure Simulations
- Courtroom Exhibits / Models
- Due Diligence / Prepurchase Surveys
- Expert Witness Testimony
- Litigation Support

Many of WJE's staff of more than 280 engineers, architects, and materials scientists are nationally recognized experts. WJE maintains offices across the country with professional engineering or architectural registration in every state.

EXPERT WITNESS
SECURITIES LAW

Lexecon

www.lexecon.com

332 South Michigan Avenue
Chicago, Illinois 60604
312-322-0200

20 University Road
Cambridge, Massachusetts 02138
617-520-0200

A consulting firm offering a full range of litigation support services, including economic, financial and statistical analysis, and assistance in the selection and preparation of testifying experts. Lexecon has extensive experience in complex litigation involving antitrust, securities, regulatory design, intellectual property, employment discrimination, contract damages and valuation. It also offers business consulting services and public policy counsel.

Members of the firm have extensive experience in financial, energy, technology, insurance, health care, telecommunications, consumer products, transportation and manufacturing industries.

M&A Analysis

Securities

Regulatory Design

Statistical Analyses and Damages Estimation

Assistance in the Selection and Preparation of Economic, Accounting and Other Expert Witnesses

Lexecon Professionals: Dennis W. Carlton, Daniel R. Fischel, Joseph P. Kalt, Rachelle F. Alcain, Charles W. Augustine, Gustavo E. Bamberger, Catherine Barron, Margaret M. Bennett, Nancy Bonn, John Robert Broxson, Amy Bertin Candell, Joseph Cavicchi, Carolyn Y. Chong, Irfan Ciputra, Charles C. Cox, James M. Coyne, Helena Croce, Deborah L. Dobrusin, James Donovan, Ronald A. Dye, Laona A. Fleischer, Fredrick A. Flyer, Rajiv B. Gokhale, Kenneth W. Grant II, David B. Gross, Timothy R. Guimond, Alan S. Frankel, Austan Goolsbee, Robert S. Hamada, Seth A. Hamstead, Kevin D. Hartt, Prescott C. Hartshorne, James J. Heckman, Eric Henson, Scott T. Jones, Michael A. Keable, Kenneth W. Kipp, Randall S. Kroszner, Elisabeth M. Landes, Andrew Y. Lemon, H. Neal Lenhoff, Youngsik Lim, Colleen P. Loughlin, William J. Lynk, Stephen Makowka, Jessica P. Mandel, Ronnie A. Martin, Glen Meyers, Erich Muehlegger, Avisheh Mohsenin, Lynette R. Neumann, Cathy M. Niden, Joshua H. Nixt, Eugene Orlov, David G. Ownby, Gregory J. Pelnar, Hans-Jürgen Petersen, Steven R. Peterson, Wendy L. Petropoulos, Tomas J. Philipson, Jonathan S. Polonsky, Kirupakaran C. Ramaiah, Bradley N. Reiff, David Reishus, David J. Ross, Rahul Sekhar, Allan L. Shampine, Philip R. Sharp, Hal S. Sider, Heather R. Spang, Kristin D. Stanton, Collin K. Starkweather, Thomas A. Stemwedel, Kenneth M. Stern, Daniel W. Stone, David Strahlberg, Alan O. Sykes, Jeffrey D. Tranen, Laurel C. Van Allen, Eugenia Vinogradsky, Elizabeth A. Wall, Patrick Wang, Yili Wang, Vincent A. Warther, Anne Marie Yale, Deborah W. Zimmermann.

Representative Clients: Arnold & Porter; Baker Botts; Baker & Hostetler; Bell Boyd & Lloyd; Boies, Schiller & Flexner; Covington & Burling; Cravath, Swaine & Moore; Davis Polk & Wardwell; Fish & Neave; Fried, Frank, Harris, Shriver & Jacobson; Freeman, Freeman & Salzman; Fulbright & Jaworski; Gardner, Carton & Douglas; Heller Ehrman White & McAuliffe; Jenner & Block; Katten Muchin Zavis Rosenman; Kirkland & Ellis; Latham & Watkins; Mayer, Brown Rowe & Maw; Morgan, Lewis & Bockius; Morrison & Foerster; Paul, Weiss, Rifkind, Wharton & Garrison; Shearman & Sterling; Sullivan & Cromwell; Skadden, Arps, Slate, Meagher & Flom; Steptoe & Johnson; Wachtell, Lipton, Rosen & Katz; Weil, Gotshal & Manges; Wilmer Cutler Pickering Hale & Dorr; federal & state government agencies.

EXPERT WITNESS
SECURITIES/LITIGATION SUPPORT

Peter J. Pfeffer

605 Woodhaven Dr.

Mundelein (metro Chicago), IL, 60060
ph: 847-837-0791 fax: 847-970-6383
e-mail: barlowe@interaccess.com
url: http://www.walshpfeffer.com

Services: Dispute mediation, Case Evaluation, Written Opinions, Testimony, Portfolio evaluation, Damage Calculation, Turn-over analysis, Suitability, Registered Employee vs. brokerage firm disputes, supervision analysis, Industry Rules & practices. Financial Suicide, Annuities and Variable Annuities.

Profile: Securities Fraud Examiner; Expertise in all facets of investment and trading in securities and derivatives; Defense & Plaintiff, Domestic & Foreign.

States: ALL

Professional Qualifications: Registrations: S-3 (Commodity Futures), S-7 (General Securities), S-8 (Sales Supervision), S8BM (NYSE Branch Office Manager), S-24 (Securities Principal), S-52 (Municipal), S-63 (State's Blue Sky), all granted 1969 thru 1980.

Professional Experience: Registered Rep. Branch office Manager, Principal, Regional Manager, Executive Vice President (National Securities Firm), Chairman (Trust Company). For details, see website http://firms.findlaw.com/Pfeffer.

Licenses: See website

Professional Affiliations: : See website

Education: University of Wisconsin-Economics

Cases: Arbitrator or Expert testimony: AAA, NASD, Exchanges, NFA, Appellate Panelist, Federal Reparations Proceedings; Federal and State jury and bench trials since late '70's.

Publications: Investment/trading research, Compliance and operations manuals.

Teaching: Trained over 500 securities and derivative brokers. Guest lecturer on Capital formation and central markets. Instructed key employees of major Japanese and Korean financial Institutions in year-long course in trading of capital and derivative markets-real-time trading of employer-funded accounts.

Contact: Peter J. Pfeffer

References: Available from attorneys of prior cases.

Areas of Expertise: securities fraud, day trading, securities arbitration, churning, currency trading, derivatives, futures, NASD regulations, securities arbitration, investment fraud, stock market, commodities, damage calculations, employee disputes, investments, options, securities regulations, mediation practice.

TAVAKOLI STRUCTURED FINANCE, INC.

360 E. Randolph St., Suite 3007
Chicago, Illinois 60601
(312) 540-0243
Email: jt@tavakolistructuredfinance.com
Web site: www.tavakolistructuredfinance.com

Janet Tavakoli is the president of Tavakoli Structured Finance, Inc., an independent consulting firm, specializing in maximizing value in structured finance. Structured financial products include derivatives, credit derivatives, credit default swaps, total return swaps, interest rate swaps, options, swaptions, collateralized debt obligations, mortgage backed securities, hedge funds, special purpose entities, bonds, emerging markets, equities, and the instruments of the capital markets.

Ms. Tavakoli has over 18 years of Wall Street experience at major financial institutions in New York and London. She earned her B.S. in Chemical Engineering from the Illinois Institute of Technology. She has an MBA from the University of Chicago, and was an adjunct professor of finance at the University of Chicago's Graduate School of Business where she taught Derivatives.

She has been registered and licensed with the SFA, NASD, ASE, CBOE, NYSE, PSE, and the NFA and has passed the series 7, 63, and 3 qualifying exams from 1985-2002.

Janet Tavakoli is the author of the global best selling books in their respective fields: *Credit Derivatives & Synthetic Structures* 2nd Edition, John Wiley & Sons, 2001, and *Collateralized Debt Obligations and Structured Finance: New Developments in Cash and Synthetic Securitization*, John Wiley & Sons 2003. Other topics include: Enron, hedge funds, Freddie Mac, Fannie Mae, and Parmalat.

EXPERT WITNESS
TELECOMMUNICATIONS

Lexecon

www.lexecon.com

332 South Michigan Avenue
Chicago, Illinois 60604
312-322-0200

20 University Road
Cambridge, Massachusetts 02138
617-520-0200

A consulting firm offering a full range of litigation support services, including economic, financial and statistical analysis, and assistance in the selection and preparation of testifying experts. Lexecon has extensive experience in complex litigation involving antitrust, securities, regulatory design, intellectual property, employment discrimination, contract damages and valuation. It also offers business consulting services and public policy counsel.

Members of the firm have extensive experience in financial, energy, technology, insurance, health care, telecommunications, consumer products, transportation and manufacturing industries.

M&A Analysis

Securities

(This Listing Continued)

Regulatory Design

Statistical Analyses and Damages Estimation

Assistance in the Selection and Preparation of Economic, Accounting and Other Expert Witnesses

Lexecon Professionals: Dennis W. Carlton, Daniel R. Fischel, Joseph P. Kalt, Rachelle F. Alcain, Charles W. Augustine, Gustavo E. Bamberger, Catherine Barron, Margaret M. Bennett, Nancy Bonn, John Robert Broxson, Amy Bertin Candell, Joseph Cavicchi, Carolyn Y. Chong, Irfan Ciputra, Charles C. Cox, James M. Coyne, Helena Croce, Deborah L. Dobrusin, James Donovan, Ronald A. Dye, Laona A. Fleischer, Fredrick A. Flyer, Rajiv B. Gokhale, Kenneth W. Grant II, David B. Gross, Timothy R. Guimond, Alan S. Frankel, Austan Goolsbee, Robert S. Hamada, Seth A. Hamstead, Kevin D. Hartt, Prescott C. Hartshorne, James J. Heckman, Eric Henson, Scott T. Jones, Michael A. Keable, Kenneth W. Kipp, Randall S. Kroszner, Elisabeth M. Landes, Andrew Y. Lemon, H. Neal Lenhoff, Youngsik Lim, Colleen P. Loughlin, William J. Lynk, Stephen Makowka, Jessica P. Mandel, Ronnie A. Martin, Glen Meyers, Erich Muehlegger, Avisheh Mohsenin, Lynette R. Neumann, Cathy M. Niden, Joshua H. Nixt, Eugene Orlov, David G. Ownby, Gregory J. Pelnar, Hans-Jürgen Petersen, Steven R. Peterson, Wendy L. Petropoulos, Tomas J. Philipson, Jonathan S. Polonsky, Kirupakaran C. Ramaiah, Bradley N. Reiff, David Reishus, David J. Ross, Rahul Sekhar, Allan L. Shampine, Philip R. Sharp, Hal S. Sider, Heather R. Spang, Kristin D. Stanton, Collin K. Starkweather, Thomas A. Stemwedel, Kenneth M. Stern, Daniel W. Stone, David Strahlberg, Alan O. Sykes, Jeffrey D. Tranen, Laurel C. Van Allen, Eugenia Vinogradsky, Elizabeth A. Wall, Patrick Wang, Yili Wang, Vincent A. Warther, Anne Marie Yale, Deborah W. Zimmermann.

Representative Clients: Arnold & Porter; Baker Botts; Baker & Hostetler; Bell Boyd & Lloyd; Boies, Schiller & Flexner; Covington & Burling; Cravath, Swaine & Moore; Davis Polk & Wardwell; Fish & Neave; Fried, Frank, Harris, Shriver & Jacobson; Freeman, Freeman & Salzman; Fulbright & Jaworski; Gardner, Carton & Douglas; Heller Ehrman White & McAuliffe; Jenner & Block; Katten Muchin Zavis Rosenman; Kirkland & Ellis; Latham & Watkins; Mayer, Brown Rowe & Maw; Morgan, Lewis & Bockius; Morrison & Foerster; Paul, Weiss, Rifkind, Wharton & Garrison; Shearman & Sterling; Sullivan & Cromwell; Skadden, Arps, Slate, Meagher & Flom; Steptoe & Johnson; Wachtell, Lipton, Rosen & Katz; Weil, Gotshal & Manges; Wilmer Cutler Pickering Hale & Dorr; federal & state government agencies.

EXPERT WITNESS
UTILITIES

Lexecon

www.lexecon.com

332 South Michigan Avenue
Chicago, Illinois 60604
312-322-0200

20 University Road
Cambridge, Massachusetts 02138
617-520-0200

A consulting firm offering a full range of litigation support services, including economic, financial and statistical analysis, and assistance in the selection and preparation of testifying experts. Lexecon has extensive experience in complex litigation involving antitrust, securities, regulatory design, intellectual property, employment discrimination, contract damages and valuation. It also offers business consulting services and public policy counsel.

Members of the firm have extensive experience in financial, energy, technology, insurance, health care, telecommunications, consumer products, transportation and manufacturing industries.

M&A Analysis

Securities

(This Listing Continued)

EXPERT WITNESS
UTILITIES (cont'd)

Lexecon (cont'd)

Regulatory Design

Statistical Analyses and Damages Estimation

Assistance in the Selection and Preparation of Economic, Accounting and Other Expert Witnesses

Lexecon Professionals: Dennis W. Carlton, Daniel R. Fischel, Joseph P. Kalt, Rachelle F. Alcain, Charles W. Augustine, Gustavo E. Bamberger, Catherine Barron, Margaret M. Bennett, Nancy Bonn, John Robert Broxson, Amy Bertin Candell, Joseph Cavicchi, Carolyn Y. Chong, Irfan Ciputra, Charles C. Cox, James M. Coyne, Helena Croce, Deborah L. Dobrusin, James Donovan, Ronald A. Dye, Laona A. Fleischer, Fredrick A. Flyer, Rajiv B. Gokhale, Kenneth W. Grant II, David B. Gross, Timothy R. Guimond, Alan S. Frankel, Austan Goolsbee, Robert S. Hamada, Seth A. Hamstead, Kevin D. Hartt, Prescott C. Hartshorne, James J. Heckman, Eric Henson, Scott T. Jones, Michael A. Keable, Kenneth W. Kipp, Randall S. Kroszner, Elisabeth M. Landes, Andrew Y. Lemon, H. Neal Lenhoff, Youngsik Lim, Colleen P. Loughlin, William J. Lynk, Stephen Makowka, Jessica P. Mandel, Ronnie A. Martin, Glen Meyers, Erich Muehlegger, Avisheh Mohsenin, Lynette R. Neumann, Cathy M. Niden, Joshua H. Nixt, Eugene Orlov, David G. Ownby, Gregory J. Pelnar, Hans-Jürgen Petersen, Steven R. Peterson, Wendy L. Petropoulos, Tomas J. Philipson, Jonathan S. Polonsky, Kirupakaran C. Ramaiah, Bradley N. Reiff, David Reishus, David J. Ross, Rahul Sekhar, Allan L. Shampine, Philip R. Sharp, Hal S. Sider, Heather R. Spang, Kristin D. Stanton, Collin K. Starkweather, Thomas A. Stemwedel, Kenneth M. Stern, Daniel W. Stone, David Strahlberg, Alan O. Sykes, Jeffrey D. Tranen, Laurel C. Van Allen, Eugenia Vinogradsky, Elizabeth A. Wall, Patrick Wang, Yili Wang, Vincent A. Warther, Anne Marie Yale, Deborah W. Zimmermann.

Representative Clients: Arnold & Porter; Baker Botts; Baker & Hostetler; Bell Boyd & Lloyd; Boies, Schiller & Flexner; Covington & Burling; Cravath, Swaine & Moore; Davis Polk & Wardwell; Fish & Neave; Fried, Frank, Harris, Shriver & Jacobson; Freeman, Freeman & Salzman; Fulbright & Jaworski; Gardner, Carton & Douglas; Heller Ehrman White & McAuliffe; Jenner & Block; Katten Muchin Zavis Rosenman; Kirkland & Ellis; Latham & Watkins; Mayer, Brown Rowe & Maw; Morgan, Lewis & Bockius; Morrison & Foerster; Paul, Weiss, Rifkind, Wharton & Garrison; Shearman & Sterling; Sullivan & Cromwell; Skadden, Arps, Slate, Meagher & Flom; Steptoe & Johnson; Wachtell, Lipton, Rosen & Katz; Weil, Gotshal & Manges; Wilmer Cutler Pickering Hale & Dorr; federal & state government agencies.

EXPERT WITNESS
VEHICLE FIRES AND COLLISION

JOHN MICHAEL AGOSTI

Fire Analyst and Consultant

23808 North Overhill
Lake Zurich, Illinois 60047
Phone: 847-682-6793
E-mail: johnagosti@earthlink.net
Web: www.arsonexpert.com

(This Listing Continued)

As a member of the Skokie, Illinois Fire Department for twenty-eight years, Mr. Agosti progressed from a Firefighter/Paramedic to the position of Deputy Fire Chief. Mr. Agosti has responded to hundreds of major fire and crime scenes and has testified in court on the conclusions of his investigations. His investigations have led to successful criminal indictments and convictions. Mr. Agosti's fire department responsibilities included the review of all construction plans for compliance to fire and building codes. His expertise in building construction and fire spread, lends a unique blend to his fire investigation capabilities.

In addition to his fire department exposure to hundreds of fire investigations, Mr. Agosti has extensive experience in the private sector also. Over the past 11 years Mr. Agosti has conducted over eight hundred fire investigations as a private fire cause and origin analyst.

Practice areas include:

- Fire and Explosions:
  - Arson defense/prosecution; gas explosions; vehicular fires; structure fires; fire deaths/injuries.
- Building and Fire Codes:
  - Fire/Building code violation; Life Safety Code violations; smoke detector issues; fire prevention analysis.
- Fire Department Practices:
  - Fire department operations/practices/management; firefighter deaths/injuries/safety.

Mr. Agosti has an Associates Degree in Fire Science and Technology. He is also certified as a Fire and Arson Investigator.

PROJECT EXPERIENCE

Fire and building code analysis
Automobile accident reconstruction
Gas leak surveys
Distribution gas pipe ruptures and leaks
Investigation of fire fatalities and electrocutions
Investigation of bombings
Investigation for cause and origin of fires and explosions

PROFESSIONAL SOCIETIES

National Fire Protection Association
Fire Marshals Association of North America
International Association of Fire Chiefs
Building Officials/Code Administrators International
Fire Investigators Strike Force
Illinois Fire Inspectors Association
International Association of Arson Investigators

EXPERT WITNESS REFERRAL SERVICES

TASA
SINCE 1961

TECHNICAL ADVISORY SERVICE FOR ATTORNEYS

Headquarters: 1166 DeKalb Pike, Blue Bell, PA 19422-1853
U.S. and Canada: 800-523-2319 Fax: 800-329-8272
United Kingdom: 0800-89-1292
experts@tasanet.com • www.tasanet.com

THE BEST SOURCE FOR EXPERTS WORLDWIDE®

North America's Largest And Most Experienced Expert Referral Service® is the leading source of Consulting Experts, Testifying Experts, and ADR Specialists for attorneys and insurance firms.

(This Listing Continued)

TASA SAVES YOU TIME, EFFORT AND MONEY

- Thousands of independent experts
- Over 10,000 categories, including medical and ADR
- Over 200,000 clients • over 44 years' experience
- For cases of all kinds and sizes; plaintiff or defense
- Competitive fees • Exceptional service

NO CHARGE FOR REFERRALS

A small sample of expertise available through TASA:

AGRICULTURE: chemicals, machinery, explosions, crops, feed, forestry, food processing, farming accidents.

AUTOMOTIVE/TRANSPORTATION: accident reconstruction, seat belts, vehicle/road design, trucks, railroads, aviation, motorcycles.

BUSINESS/FINANCE/ECONOMICS: banking, securities, insurance, economic valuation, appraisals, real estate, franchising.

COMPUTERS AND ELECTRONICS: computer hardware, printers software, languages, security, networking, viruses, hacking, simulation; embedded systems; telecommunications; wiring, cable.

CONSTRUCTION/ARCHITECTURE: building design, maintenance, structural integrity, HVAC, plumbing; bridges, equipment, codes.

CRIMINOLOGY/POLICE PROCEDURES: document examination, fingerprinting, ballistics, prisons, tape analysis, DNA, firearms.

ELEVATORS/LIFTS: cranes, controls, design and safety, escalators.

ENVIRONMENT: water, air & noise pollution; hazardous waste, asbestos, ecology, toxic mold and mildew, erosion, lead.

FALLS: lighting, surfaces, ladders, scaffolding, weather, shoes, safety.

FIRES: explosions, arson, flammable clothing, codes, alarms.

MACHINERY: design/safety; industrial, agricultural, appliances, OSHA.

MARITIME: seamanship, cargo handling, ship/boat design, accident reconstruction, navigational aids, fishing, oil spills.

MEDICAL/HEALTH CARE: issues relating to medical personnel, institutions and procedures, over 900 medical specialties through the TASAmed division.

MATERIALS: metals, polymers, glass, wood; textiles.

INTELLECTUAL PROPERTY: patents/copyrights/trademarks, secrets, etc.

PERSONNEL/LABOR: wages & hours, discrimination, workplace safety, ADA issues, sexual harassment.

PHARMACEUTICALS/TOXICOLOGY: drugs, food poisoning, labels & warnings, cosmetics, coatings, packaging, delivery systems.

SAFETY AND SECURITY: Aviation, Building & Homeland Security; Emergency Systems; Terrorism; Risk Analysis

SPORTS/RECREATION: equipment, supervision, facilities, pools.

Call for TASA's free Expertise Directory & Guide.

800-523-2319

FAILURE ANALYSIS/TESTING SERVICES

Wiss, Janney, Elstner Associates, Inc.

Engineers, Architects, Materials Scientists
330 Pfingsten Road
Northbrook, IL 60062
Offices nationwide

Phone	800/345-3199
Fax	847/291-9599
Internet	www.wje.com
Contact	Gary Klein, EVP

(This Listing Continued)

WJE is a professional firm providing practical, innovative, and technically sound solutions to structural, architectural, and materials problems. During our 49-year history, we have successfully completed more than 60,000 projects involving virtually every type of construction material, structural system, and architectural component.

WJE's staff of forensic consultants have extensive field and laboratory experience providing investigative, testing, and assessment services for building materials; design / construction deficiencies and practices; and building code compliance.

Specialized services include:

- Structural and Architectural Assessments
- Failure Investigation and Analysis
- Repair / Rehabilitation Design
- Construction Materials Evaluation / Testing
- Computerized Failure Simulations
- Courtroom Exhibits / Models
- Due Diligence / Prepurchase Surveys
- Expert Witness Testimony
- Litigation Support

Many of WJE's staff of more than 280 engineers, architects, and materials scientists are nationally recognized experts. WJE maintains offices across the country with professional engineering or architectural registration in every state.

FIRE INVESTIGATORS

JOHN MICHAEL AGOSTI

Fire Analyst and Consultant

23808 North Overhill
Lake Zurich, Illinois 60047
Phone: 847-682-6793
E-mail: johnagosti@earthlink.net
Web: www.arsonexpert.com

As a member of the Skokie, Illinois Fire Department for twenty-eight years, Mr. Agosti progressed from a Firefighter/Paramedic to the position of Deputy Fire Chief. Mr. Agosti has responded to hundreds of major fire and crime scenes and has testified in court on the conclusions of his investigations. His investigations have led to successful criminal indictments and convictions. Mr. Agosti's fire department responsibilities included the review of all construction plans for compliance to fire and building codes. His expertise in building construction and fire spread, lends a unique blend to his fire investigation capabilities.

In addition to his fire department exposure to hundreds of fire investigations, Mr. Agosti has extensive experience in the private sector also. Over the past 11 years Mr. Agosti has conducted over eight hundred fire investigations as a private fire cause and origin analyst.

Practice areas include:

Fire and Explosions:
Arson defense/prosecution; gas explosions; vehicular fires; structure fires; fire deaths/injuries.

Building and Fire Codes:
Fire/Building code violation; Life Safety Code violations; smoke detector issues; fire prevention analysis.

(This Listing Continued)

FIRE INVESTIGATORS (cont'd)

John Michael Agosti (cont'd)

Fire Department Practices:
Fire department operations/practices/management; firefighter deaths/injuries/safety.

Mr. Agosti has an Associates Degree in Fire Science and Technology. He is also certified as a Fire and Arson Investigator.

PROJECT EXPERIENCE

Fire and building code analysis
Automobile accident reconstruction
Gas leak surveys
Distribution gas pipe ruptures and leaks
Investigation of fire fatalities and electrocutions
Investigation of bombings
Investigation for cause and origin of fires and explosions

PROFESSIONAL SOCIETIES

National Fire Protection Association
Fire Marshals Association of North America
International Association of Fire Chiefs
Building Officials/Code Administrators International
Fire Investigators Strike Force
Illinois Fire Inspectors Association
International Association of Arson Investigators

FORENSIC ENGINEERS

CTLGROUP

5400 OLD ORCHARD ROAD
Skokie, IL 60077-1030
Telephone: 800.522.2285
Fax: 847.965.6541
Web Site: www.CTLGroup.com
Email: JGarrett@CTLGroup.com

CTLGroup is an internationally recognized consulting engineering firm with an 85-year history of offering professional structural engineering, testing and research services. CTLGroup's staff of 140 professionals offers a unique combination of structural investigative services, structural engineering analysis and design services, construction materials testing and research, and structural diagnostics testing and laboratory services. Our expertise includes:

- Consulting engineering
- Condition and damage assessments
- Structural failure investigations and root cause determinations
- Nondestructive testing and in-situ evaluations
- Building material failure analyses and remediation
- Structural system failure analyses and remediation
- Laboratory material testing and evaluation
- Laboratory structural component testing and evaluation
- Real-time in-situ structural health monitoring
- Design and construction standard of care issues
- Litigation and legal support, including
    - Expert Testimony
    - Demonstrative evidence

Wiss, Janney, Elstner Associates, Inc.

Engineers, Architects, Materials Scientists
330 Pfingsten Road
Northbrook, IL 60062
Offices nationwide

Phone	800/345-3199
Fax	847/291-9599
Internet	www.wje.com
Contact	Gary Klein, EVP

WJE is a professional firm providing practical, innovative, and technically sound solutions to structural, architectural, and materials problems. During our 49-year history, we have successfully completed more than 60,000 projects involving virtually every type of construction material, structural system, and architectural component.

WJE's staff of forensic consultants have extensive field and laboratory experience providing investigative, testing, and assessment services for building materials; design / construction deficiencies and practices; and building code compliance.

Specialized services include:

- Structural and Architectural Assessments
- Failure Investigation and Analysis
- Repair / Rehabilitation Design
- Construction Materials Evaluation / Testing
- Computerized Failure Simulations
- Courtroom Exhibits / Models
- Due Diligence / Prepurchase Surveys
- Expert Witness Testimony
- Litigation Support

Many of WJE's staff of more than 280 engineers, architects, and materials scientists are nationally recognized experts. WJE maintains offices across the country with professional engineering or architectural registration in every state.

GENEALOGICAL SERVICES

SEIT 1849

HOERNER BANK
AKTIENGESELLSCHAFT

GENEALOGICAL RESEARCH
HOERNER BANK
A BANK LICENSED IN GERMANY

- The oldest established and one of the largest firms specializing in genealogical research
- Location of missing heirs and searches for persons who are entitled to assets of all description
- Services rendered to surrogate courts, personal representatives of estates, heirs, beneficiaries and persons entitled to assets of missing persons
- Services include searches for unknown or missing heirs, required research to locate and collect assets world-wide
- Highly qualified research staff consisting of licensed lawyers, accountants and specialists in genealogical research, all experts in world-wide research
- Translations and services with respect to all European languages
- Supervision, advice and facilitation of real estate sales, collections, transfer of bank accounts and securities
- Preparation of legal documents, initiating and completing legal proceedings affecting missing persons world-wide
- All other traditional banking business
- Contingent fees or fees as otherwise agreed to by parties

(This Listing Continued)

Challenge Our Efficiency
HOERNER BANK AKTIENGESELLSCHAFT
FOREIGN ESTATES DEPARTMENT
74072 Heilbronn, Oststrasse 77
Germany
Tel: 011 49-7131 / 93 22-255 Fax: 011 49-7131 / 93 22-299
reichert@hoernerbank.de www.hoernerbank.de

Landex Research, Inc.

2 North LaSalle Street
Chicago, Illinois 60602
Phone: 312-726-6778
Fax: 312-726-6990

MISSING AND UNKNOWN
HEIRS LOCATED
WITH NO EXPENSE TO THE ESTATE

Since 1956, Landex Research, Inc. has been locating missing and unknown heirs around the world. We provide genealogical charts and document proof of heirship. The search to identify and locate missing or unknown heirs is conducted by Landex Research, Inc. solely at its own expense.

Domestic & International Service for:

- Courts
- Lawyers
- Trust Officers
- Administrators
- Executors

HEALTHCARE FINANCE & REIMBURSEMENT

Ahern & Associates

841 C South Racine Avenue
Chicago, IL 60607
312-997-2177

1050 17th Street, Suite 600
Washington, DC 20036
202-776-7185

AhernConsulting@aol.com
www.ahernconsulting.com
Offices in Chicago, Illinois & Washington, DC
Healthcare Finance & Reimbursement Experts

Healthcare Finance Expert Witness - We provide necessary litigation support in the areas of economic damages, regulatory matters, impact of market and business dynamics on a given entity. Jack Ahern, our principal, is both a consultant and an Asst. Professor of Healthcare Finance at Rush University Medical Center. He publishes nationally on healthcare finance issues and frequently has been called upon to testify before a variety of tribunals. Most recently he testified regarding Tenet Healthcare and its charging practices.

(This Listing Continued)

Issues upon which testimony has been provided include:

- Physician Payment
- Graduate Medical Education Reimbursement (payment for hospital residents)
- Medicare cost report preparation
- Joint Venture status
- Hospital Pricing / Chargemaster development
- Facility billing practices
- HMO contracting
- Hospital billing for pharmaceuticals
- Hospital DRG Outlier payment
- Skilled Nursing Reimbursement
- Renal Dialysis Reimbursement

Testimony has been used in proceedings before the following tribunals:

- United States District Court for Northern Illinois
- United States District Court, Western District of Michigan
- Provider Reimbursement Review Board (PRRB), (United States Department of Health and Human Services, Centers for Medicare and Medicaid Services) Baltimore, Maryland
- Arbitration Board appointed by the American Health Lawyers Association, Ft. Lauderdale, Florida

Reimbursement - Recently we have been consulted in several high profile healthcare reimbursement related legal disputes. Our reimbursement expertise ranges from billing practices to contract negotiation. We specialize in Medicare payment policies and cost reporting issues. We have provided advice on facility valuation and guidance on reimbursement issues to several major international accounting firms.

Renal Dialysis - We have in-depth knowledge and expertise in reimbursement issues associated with dialysis facilities and nephrology practices. We are nationally recognized in the field of renal cost reporting, payment analysis and exception request preparation.

Operations - Our operational work has extended to Strategic planning, Management and Staff training. We have also provided third party guidance to assist with financial software selection.

Since 1989, we have succeeded in advancing the financial goals of over 50 healthcare providers nationwide, including physician groups, clinics and hospitals.

About Jack Ahern

As an experienced consultant and financial manager he brings to the table over 18 years of experience in healthcare finance working with over a hundred healthcare entities ranging from single physician practices to large academic medical centers. His expertise ranges from issues pertaining to physician and hospital billing practices to administrative and strategic planning challenges faced by healthcare providers. Early in his career he gained considerable expertise in renal dialysis reimbursement and continues to work with renal providers throughout the nation. Quite often his projects have been intimately intermingled with regulatory issues.

Jack has worked both as a consultant as well as a Director of Financial Systems at Rush Medical Center, a large academic medical center. Several of his achievements in reimbursement have been nationally recognized. At this point in his career, he carries out the dual role of consulting as well as teaching Healthcare Finance at Rush University Medical Center in Chicago. He has assisted several of the big five accounting firms in issues pertaining to the valuation of healthcare practices and Medicare reimbursement.

Education

UNIVERSITY OF CHICAGO, GRADUATE SCHOOL OF BUSINESS 2002
Master of Business Administration,
Concentrations:
Finance, Accounting, Strategic Management, Managerial and Organizational Behavior

Vice President, Professional Finance Club

DALHOUSIE UNIVERSITY
Bachelor of Mechanical Engineering 1993
Bachelor of Science in Chemistry 1988

HEIR TRACERS

SEIT 1849

HOERNER BANK

AKTIENGESELLSCHAFT

GENEALOGICAL RESEARCH

HOERNER BANK
A BANK LICENSED IN GERMANY

- The oldest established and one of the largest firms specializing in genealogical research
- Location of missing heirs and searches for persons who are entitled to assets of all description
- Services rendered to surrogate courts, personal representatives of estates, heirs, beneficiaries and persons entitled to assets of missing persons
- Services include searches for unknown or missing heirs, required research to locate and collect assets world-wide
- Highly qualified research staff consisting of licensed lawyers, accountants and specialists in genealogical research, all experts in world-wide research
- Translations and services with respect to all European languages
- Supervision, advice and facilitation of real estate sales, collections, transfer of bank accounts and securities
- Preparation of legal documents, initiating and completing legal proceedings affecting missing persons world-wide
- All other traditional banking business
- Contingent fees or fees as otherwise agreed to by parties

Challenge Our Efficiency
HOERNER BANK AKTIENGESELLSCHAFT
FOREIGN ESTATES DEPARTMENT
74072 Heilbronn, Oststrasse 77
Germany

Tel: 011 49-7131 / 93 22-255
reichert@hoernerbank.de

Fax: 011 49-7131 / 93 22-299
www.hoernerbank.de

Landex Research, Inc.
2 North LaSalle Street
Chicago, Illinois 60602
Phone: 312-726-6778
Fax: 312-726-6990

TOLL FREE: **800-844-6778**

Email: info@landexresearch.com
Web Site: www.landexresearch.com

(This Listing Continued)

MISSING AND UNKNOWN
HEIRS LOCATED
WITH NO EXPENSE TO THE ESTATE

Since 1956, Landex Research, Inc. has been locating missing and unknown heirs around the world. We provide genealogical charts and documented proof of heirship. The search to identify and locate missing or unknown heirs is conducted by Landex Research, Inc. solely at its own expense.

Domestic & International Service for:

- Courts
- Lawyers
- Trust Officers
- Administrators
- Executors

SEE OUR AD ON PAGE IL39S

PeopleSearch

Nationwide Investigative Information Service

PHONE: 847-360-0360
FAX: 847-623-3501

Information Services...About People for People

PeopleSearch is a nationwide investigative information service with field agents working across the nation retrieving information from every county courthouse and United States Federal District Court in the country. Our innovative services provide employers, owners and individuals with complete background information about applicants for any position.

Joanne Layne, founder of PeopleSearch, is a research specialist with more than twenty-five years experience in courthouse and genealogical research and more than nine years experience in researching criminal background checks. Layne was trained at the National Archives in Washington, D.C. and at Samford University in Birmingham, AL. She is a Certified Confidential Adoption Intermediary for the State of Illinois.

Services:

- Background Checks
- Employment Screenings
- Tenant Approvals
- Skip Tracing
- Computer/Paper Trails
- Locating Missing Persons
- Witnesses in Court Cases
- Missing or Unknown Heirs
- Lost Loves
- School, Family or Military Reunions

FAST ... EASY ... FLEXIBLE ...

The Martindale-Hubbell® Law Directory on CD-ROM™

Get instant access to information on legal professionals in the U.S., Canada, and the international community with the **Martindale-Hubbell Law Directory on CD-ROM.™** Easy-to-use menus, pop-up screens, and flexible search criteria help you zero in on any of over 1,000,000 lawyers and law firms.
The possibilities are endless!

For more information
call **1-800-526-4902. ext. 8005**

LexisNexis®
Martindale-Hubbell®

MISSING AND UNKNOWN HEIRS LOCATED WITH NO EXPENSE TO THE ESTATE

For over 45 years, Landex Research, Inc. has been locating missing and unknown heirs around the world. We provide genealogical charts and documented proof of heirship. The search to identify and locate missing or unknown heirs is conducted by Landex Research, Inc. solely at its own expense.

LANDEX
PROBATE RESEARCH

Domestic & International Service for:

- Courts
- Lawyers
- Trust Officers
- Administrators
- Executors

Landex Research, Inc.

Two North LaSalle Street, Chicago, Illinois 60602
Telephone: 800-844-6778 Fax: 312-726-6990
Email: info@landexresearch.com
Web Site: www.landexresearch.com

INTERPRETERS & TRANSLATORS

LAWYER SEARCH & PLACEMENT CONSULTANTS

(This Listing Continued)

LEGAL ASSOCIATIONS

Association of Legal Administrators

75 Tri-State International Suite 222
Lincolnshire, IL 60069-4435
Telephone: (847) 267-1252
Fax: (847) 267-1329
www.alanet.org

The Association of Legal Administrators (ALA), founded in 1971, provides educational opportunities and services to law office administrators who manage such areas as finance, human resources, systems and technology, facilities, marketing and practice development. ALA has more than 9,000 members in 27 countries. The Association's mission is to "promote and enhance the competence and professionalism of legal administrators and all members of the management team."

ALA's Web site - at *www.alanet.org* - provides the legal community with information about ALA's educational programs and member services, print and online management resources, online educational opportunities and jobs available in legal management, and links to more than 250 law-related resources and organizations.

ALA's Annual Educational Conference and Exposition features more than 100 expert speakers, including law office managers, attorneys and management professors, and the latest products and services from more than 250 vendors.

ALA also offers an opportunity for legal administrators to add to their credentials by becoming a Certified Legal Manager (CLM)℠. The voluntary CLM℠ certification program allows a qualified legal administrator to demonstrate, through an examination process, a mastery of core areas of knowledge identified as essential to the effective performance of a principal administrator. Examinations are administered each autumn and then each spring during the Annual Educational Conference and Exposition.

Each fall, ALA sponsors the Corporate/Government Fall Forum, the Large Firm Principal Administrator Retreat and the Intellectual Property Retreat. These events address the unique needs of managers from these types of law practices. ALA's Regions also host individual Conferences each autumn, and ALA's chapters conduct many seminars and retreats at the local level.

The latest developments in law office management are covered in *Legal Management,* ALA's journal. ALA offers many other publications, audiotapes and videotapes on such subjects as communication and general management, human resources, office systems, finance and client development.

Regular membership in ALA is open to any full-time administrator or support manager who is employed in a private law firm, corporate, government or university legal department, or charitable legal agency. Associate membership is available to some categories of individuals. Membership is not open to vendors or consultants.

LEGAL PUBLICATIONS

Association of Legal Administrators

75 Tri-State International Suite 222
Lincolnshire, IL 60069-4435
Telephone: (847) 267-1252
Fax: (847) 267-1329
www.alanet.org

The Association of Legal Administrators (ALA), founded in 1971, provides educational opportunities and services to law office administrators who manage such areas as finance, human resources, systems and technology, facilities, marketing and practice development. ALA has more than 9,000 members in 27 countries. The Association's mission is to "promote and enhance the competence and professionalism of legal administrators and all members of the management team."

ALA's Web site - at *www.alanet.org* - provides the legal community with information about ALA's educational programs and member services, print and online management resources, online educational opportunities and jobs available in legal management, and links to more than 250 law-related resources and organizations.

ALA's Annual Educational Conference and Exposition features more than 100 expert speakers, including law office managers, attorneys and management professors, and the latest products and services from more than 250 vendors.

ALA also offers an opportunity for legal administrators to add to their credentials by becoming a Certified Legal Manager (CLM)℠. The voluntary CLM℠ certification program allows a qualified legal administrator to demonstrate, through an examination process, a mastery of core areas of knowledge identified as essential to the effective performance of a principal administrator. Examinations are administered each autumn and then each spring during the Annual Educational Conference and Exposition.

Each fall, ALA sponsors the Corporate/Government Fall Forum, the Large Firm Principal Administrator Retreat and the Intellectual Property Retreat. These events address the unique needs of managers from these types of law practices. ALA's Regions also host individual Conferences each autumn, and ALA's chapters conduct many seminars and retreats at the local level.

The latest developments in law office management are covered in *Legal Management,* ALA's journal. ALA offers many other publications, audiotapes and videotapes on such subjects as communication and general management, human resources, office systems, finance and client development.

Regular membership in ALA is open to any full-time administrator or support manager who is employed in a private law firm, corporate, government or university legal department, or charitable legal agency. Associate membership is available to some categories of individuals. Membership is not open to vendors or consultants.

LIFE CARE PLANNING

Hess, Karfomenos & Associates, LLC
54722 Country Road 8
Middlebury, IN 46540
Toll Free: 866-219-2273
Phone: 574-825-9000
Fax: 574-825-3355
Email: hkamedlegal@starband.net
www.hkamedlegal.com

Medical and Forensic Case Management, Life Care Planning, Medicare Set-Aside Allocations, and Medical-Legal File Analysis/Review, these are the focused specialties of the staff of Hess, Karfomenos & Associates, LLC.

A well researched and prepared settlement package can mean the difference between settlement or having to file suit and subsequently litigating a case. Our professional staff can enhance your position by means of ***Medical/Legal File Review & Analysis***. Allow us to do the medical review and research on your files. We provide extensive professional background and expertise in: mechanism of injury, critical care and surgical issues, occupational injuries, trauma, rehabilitation, catastrophic injuries, coding/costing as well as chronic diseases. Our services will enhance your position by means of the skills and expertise of professionally licensed, nationally certified and registered nurse/forensic experts. These services bring value and benefit to any litigant.

Damage and Disability Analysis/Life Care Planning is one of the functions of the ***Certified Nurse Life Care Planner***. Hess, Karfomenos & Associates LLC will assist you in building an Expert Damages Team. Our goal is to assure the disciplines necessary to evaluate the client and present an objective analysis. We apply a scientific and systematic approach to servicing your needs.

The Certified Nurse Life Care Planner will initially review the case, contact and interview all the current providers and coordinate any additional specialty evaluations needed for a complete disability analysis and future needs projection. A team of medical professionals is then selectively assembled to assess and evaluate the current and future medical needs of your client, to provide a complete and thorough customized projection forming the backbone of the Life Care Plan.

The Team-
Consisting of Physicians: Psychiatrist, Psychologist/NeuroPsychologist (to name a few specialities), Vocational & Rehabilitation Specialist, Physical and Occupational Therapists and the Nurse Life Care Planner conduct individual client interviews and testing.

All findings and opinions are shared, ultimately culminating in a review by an Economist of Accountant. This provides discussion related to the multiplicity of economic issues impacting the case and ensures that he damage testimony of the experts is presented in an accurate, consistent and qualified manner.

The ultimate outcome is **ONE COMPREHENSIVE REPORT** that provides a consistent, professionally prepared and validated, presentation of damages. We recognize the demands of a busy law practice and understand the need to control costs.

We at ***Hess, Karfomenos & Associates LLC,*** welcome the opportunity to assist you in your practice.

"Let our expertise enhance your successes."

(This Listing Continued)

Members: American Association of Nurse Life Care Planners, American Association of Legal Nurse Consultants, Indianapolis Chapter-American Association of Legal Nurse Consultants, Academy of Certified Case Managers, American Nurses Association, Indiana State Nurses Association, Emergency Nurses Association, Case Management Society of America, International Association of Rehabilitation Providers, Tri-State Case Managers Association, International Academy of Life Care Planners and the Indiana Bar Association.

Professional Nursing Licenses: Indiana, Michigan, Tennessee and Texas

National Certifications: Certified Case Managers (CCM)
Certified Nurse Life Care Planners (CNLCP)

State Certifications/Case Management: TN, OH and KY
Certified Provider/Life Care Planning/Case Management-Ohio BWC

PERSONAL EXPERIENCE PROVEN STRATEGIES REAL LIFE SOLUTIONS

Robert H. Jackson & Associates, Inc.
P.O. Box 3187
Oak Brook, Illinois 60522
Phone: 630-960-5588
Fax: 630-960-5850
admin@rhjaconsulting.com
www.rhjaconsulting.com

Robert H. Jackson & Associates, Inc. is a rehabilitation consulting and case management firm specializing in catastrophic injury. A spinal cord injury survivor since 1968, Robert Jackson has a long history of providing insight and strategy assistance in catastrophic injury cases nationwide.

Services:
- Catastrophic Injury Consulting
- Mediation Preparation
- Litigation Support
- Expert Testimony
- Life Care Planning
- Research and Strategy Planning
- Cost Analysis
- Medical Record Review
- Rehabilitation Case Management

Injury Experience (Adult & Pediatric):
- Spinal Cord Injury
- Brain Injury
- Neurological Disorders
- Burn/Electrical Burn
- Amputation
- Orthopedic Injury

Curriculum vitae, testimony history, references and additional information available upon request.

LITIGATION CONSULTING

WILLIAM C. CUTLIP CONSULTING

William C. Cutlip
FSA, MAAA, FCA, CLU, ChFC, CPCU
Web Site: www.cutlipconsulting.com

(This Listing Continued)

3048 Woods Edge Way
Madison, WI 53711
Phone: (608) 443-0669
Fax: (608) 443-0668

8021 Wildomar Drive
Tucson, AZ 85743
Phone: (520) 572-8833
Fax: (520) 579-6688
Cell: (520) 247-6592

Areas of Expertise: Expert Witness / Forensics / Litigation Support / Arbitrations

Financial Evaluation for:

- damages
- investment
- merger & acquisition
- structured settlements
- grievances
- equitable distribution

Legal Ammunition for:

- pre-filing evaluation
- case strength
- surprise reduction
- strategy support
- opposition analysis
- scientifically supported evaluation

Professional Profile:

Educated at Massachusetts Institute of Technology and Oklahoma State University, William C. Cutlip has over 40 years of industry experience and specializes in risk evaluation and expert witness work for attorneys, product development for insurance companies, and business consulting.

Professional Qualifications:

Fellow, Society of Actuaries (FSA)
Member, American Academy of Actuaries (MAAA)
Fellow, Conference of Consulting Actuaries (FCA)
Chartered Life Underwriter (CLU)
Chartered Financial Consultant (ChFC)
Member, International Association of Consulting Actuaries

Cases/Clients: Plaintiff and Defense
Geographical Area: No Limitation
E-mail Contact: cutlipconsulting@cs.com

LITIGATION/LAWSUIT FUNDING

BEACON LEGAL FINANCE

Beacon Legal Finance provides funding to plaintiff law firms and their clients.

LAW FIRM FUNDING BENEFITS

- Borrow $25K to $5MM. Institutional funding provides deep, market-priced capital resources.
- Avoid fee-splitting with another law firm, allowing you to maintain full control and reward of the fees from the case.
- Funding secured by law firm receivables, not personal assets.
- Interest or fees charged may be charged as case expenses, thus may be returned from plaintiff's proceeds to the law practice, provided that the retainer agreement permits such costs to be treated as case expenses advanced and reimbursed.
- Interest or fees charged for the loan may be tax-deductible.
- Lowering the loan's cost makes it more affordable to obtain financing to help make the best cases more powerful for market-level settlement.
-

(This Listing Continued)

PLAINTIFF FUNDING BENEFITS

- Beacon makes cash advances against a portion of future potential case settlement value. If the case does not win or settle, the plaintiff may owe Beacon nothing in return. Beacon has "no recourse to come after plaintiff or law firm assets" if the case does not win or settle.
- Beacon's pricing is a low average monthly rate of only 2.9%.
- Beacon charges no additional fees.
- Institutional funding provides low cost of capital.
- Beacon Legal Finance is licensed as a lender by the State of Illinois Department of Financial Institutions, and follows disclosure requirements issued by the Office of the Attorney General of the State of New York.

Beacon Legal Finance, LLC

820 North Orleans St., Suite 216
Chicago, IL 60610
Toll Free: 888-723-2266
Fax: 312-787-2728
E-mail: acctmgr@beaconlegal.com
www.beaconlegal.com

MEDICAL CASE REVIEW & PREPARATION/TRIAL CONSULTING

HK&A

Hess, Karfomenos & Associates, LLC

54722 Country Road 8
Middlebury, IN 46540
Toll Free: 866-219-2273
Phone: 574-825-9000
Fax: 574-825-3355
Email: hkamedlegal@starband.net
www.hkamedlegal.com

Medical and Forensic Case Management, Life Care Planning, Medicare Set-Aside Allocations, and Medical-Legal File Analysis/Review, these are the focused specialties of the staff of *Hess, Karfomenos & Associates, LLC.*

Professional Forensic Case Management ensures your client is afforded the highest quality of care and treatment, coordinated by a licensed professional nurse who is nationally certified as a medical case manager. Our staff has extensive experience in managing the medical care of Worker's compensation, Group Health and Catastrophic Injury cases as well as negotiating costs and coordinating ancillary services. The benefit to you and your client? *You are afforded access to the finest medical and professional practitioners available nationwide and the knowledge that expedient and appropriate medical care, is being delivered-allowing you to focus on the intricacies of the litigation process.*

Coordination of Independent Medical Exams (IME), Medical Peer reviews (including Chiropractic), Second Opinions and Consults are strategic interventions. PEER Reviews are generated through a national network of specialized physicians. Make sure your client is seen by *the most appropriate provider,* at the *most appropriate time* and that the *most appropriate medical issues* are addressed.

Communication with healthcare providers is essential to your success-*Hess, Karfomenos & Associates LLC*, is the professional interpretation, between you and the medical treatment team. We will deliver records, films and even accompany your client to these exams, if appropriate.

(This Listing Continued)

MEDICAL CASE REVIEW & PREPARATION/TRIAL CONSULTING (cont'd)

Hess, Karfomenos & Associates, LLC (cont'd)

A well researched and prepared settlement package can mean the difference between settlement or having to file suit and subsequently litigating a case. Our professional staff can enhance your position by means of ***Medical/Legal File Review & Analysis.*** Allow us to do the medical review and research on your files. We provide extensive professional background and expertise in: mechanism of injury, critical care and surgical issues, occupational injuries, trauma, rehabilitation, catastrophic injuries, coding/costing as well as chronic diseases. Our services will enhance your position by means of the skills and expertise of professionally licensed, nationally certified and registered nurse/forensic experts. These services bring value and benefit to any litigant.

Damage and Disability Analysis/Life Care Planning is one of the functions of the **Certified Nurse Life Care Planner.** *Hess, Karfomenos & Associates LLC* will assist you in building an Expert Damages Team. Our goal is to assure the disciplines necessary to evaluate the client and present an objective analysis. We apply a scientific and systematic approach to servicing your needs.

All findings and opinions are shared, ultimately culminating in a review by an Economist or Accountant. This provides discussion related to the multiplicity of economic issues impacting the case and ensures that the damage testimony of the experts is presented in an accurate, consistent and qualified manner.

The ultimate outcome is ***ONE COMPREHENSIVE REPORT*** that provides a consistent, professionally prepared and validated, presentation of damages. We recognize the demands of a busy law practice and understand the need to control costs.

We at ***Hess, Karfomenos & Associates LLC,*** welcome the opportunity to assist you in your practice.

"Let our expertise enhance your successes."

Members: American Association of Nurse Life Care Planners, American Association of Legal Nurse Consultants, Indianapolis Chapter-American Association of Legal Nurse Consultants, Academy of Certified Case Managers, American Nurses Association, Indiana State Nurses Association, Emergency Nurses Association , Case Management Society of America, International Association of Rehabilitation Providers, Tri-State Case Managers Association, International Academy of Life Care Planners and the Indiana Bar Association.

Professional Nursing Licenses: Indiana, Michigan, Tennessee and Texas

National Certifications: Certified Case Managers (CCM)
Certified Nurse Life Care Planners (CNLCP)

State Certifications/Case Management: TN, OH and KY
Certified Provider/Life Care Planning/Case Management-Ohio BWC

MEDICAL EXPERT WITNESS
CARDIOLOGY

Martin Medical Consulting, Inc.

2901 Old Jacksonville Rd.
Springfield, IL 62702
United States of America

Contact: Dr. Randolph Martin
Tel: 217-546-0750, Fax: 217-546-0894

Email: martinmd@insightbb.com

Medical Expert in Clinical Cardiology. Available for defense or plaintiff work. Wrongful death, misdiagnosis, specializes in acute coronary syndromes: unstable angina, myocardial infarct (MI), malignant arrythmias - (Sudden Cardiac Death).

Services
- Review medical records and medical literature.
- Prepare reports from medical records, literature (including journals, articles, publications).
- Deposition.
- Expert Witness at trial.

Licenses
Illinois (active)

Professional Experience
Dr. Martin has been with a large medical group practice (150+ Physicians) in Illinois from 1989-2004. Now in Private Practice.

He has vast experience in the following areas:

All non-invasive testing including: Stress Testing, Electrocardiogram Interpretation, Echocardiography Interpretation, Dobutamine Stress Echo, Holter Monitor Interpretation, and Pacemaker/Defibrillator (AICD) Interrogation.

All invasive and interventional cardiovascular procedures including: Percutaneous Transluminal Angioplasty (PTCA), Coronary Stenting (including atherectomy and rotablator) Pacemaker and Defibrillator (AICD) placement, and management.

Teaching Experience:
Volunteer Staff at SIU School of Medicine

Legal Experience
Involvement in previous legal cases include the following areas:
Pacing and Rhythm Disturbances.
Management of Acute Myocardial Infarcation.
Death due to Central Line Placement and intra-aortic balloon placement.
Death from cardiac cause in work related injuries.
Misdiagnosis of Cardiovascular Illness.
Preoperative Clearance (Defense work).

(This Listing Continued)

Member of the American Medical Association
Fellow of the American College of Cardiology
Professor of Clinical Medicine -
Southern Illinois University School of Medicine

Qualifications
Non Invasive Cardiology:
Over five thousand stress tests administered.
Over ten thousand echocardiograms interpreted
Over twenty five thousand EKG's interpreted

Invasive/Interventional Cardiology:
Over six thousand Cardiac Catherizations
Hundreds of carotid, renal and peripheral angiograms
Over one thousand coronary angioplasties and stents

Never been sued for Malpractice in Cardiology

Education
The Albany Medical College of Union University: M.D. in 1982
Cornell Cooperating Hospitals (North Shore University)
Medical Resident 1982-1985
Fellow in Cardiology 1985-1987

MEDICAL EXPERT WITNESS
PHARMACY & PHARMACOLOGY

PHARMACONSULTANTS INC.

1935 S. PLUM GROVE ROAD
PMB 255
PALATINE, IL 60067

800-872-9326
847-991-4433
FAX 847-991-4584
VM/PAGER 847-769-2843

Email: jodonn1935@aol.com
www.pharmaconsultantinc.com
www.rushu.rush.edu/pharm/dept/fac/jodonnell/

DR. JAMES O'DONNELL
PHARMACOLOGIST PHARMACIST NUTRITIONIST
DIPLOMATE - AMERICAN BOARD OF CLINICAL PHARMACOLOGY
DIPLOMATE - BOARD OF NUTRITIONAL SPECIALTIES
FOUNDING EDITOR JOURNAL OF PHARMACY PRACTICE
REGISTERED PHARMACIST
FELLOW-AMERICAN COLLEGE OF CLINICAL PHARMACOLOGY

Dr. O'Donnell is both a consultant and expert witness in pharmacology, drug product liability/warnings, drug injury, pharmacy malpractice, nutrition and dietary supplement matters, and alcohol toxicity. He has served nationwide for both the plaintiff and defense. He received his Bachelor of Science from the University of Illinois College of Pharmacy, his Masters in Nutrition from Rush University and his Doctor of Pharmacy from the University of Michigan. He is a fellow of the American College of Nutrition. He is an associate professor of Pharmacology at the Rush Medical College. He is the editor of Drug Injury: Liability, Analysis, and Prevention.

MEMBERSHIPS:
American College of Clinical Pharmacology
American College of Clinical Pharmacy
American Academy of Clinical Toxicology
American Pharmaceutical Association
American College of Nutrition
American Society of Pharmacy Law
American College of Legal Medicine

MEDICAL EXPERT WITNESS
SOCIAL SERVICES

Evan M. Peterson, LCSW
60 W. Terra Cotta Ave # 227
Crystal Lake, Illinois 60014
Telephone: 815-356-9630
Fax: 815-356-9828
Email: evan@askdove.com
URL: http://www.evanmpeterson.com

Evan M. Peterson has an extensive background in social services, providing expert opinions and testimony. Mr. Peterson has worked in criminal, juvenile, and civil proceedings and his experience includes State and Federal Court. He has been an expert in over 100 cases.

Mr. Peterson will consider retainer in cases related to the following areas of expertise:
- Child Abuse and neglect investigations
- Critical Incident Stress Debriefing
- Drug and alcohol treatment
- Employee Assistance Programs
- Hotline/crisis management of mental health and substance abuse concerns
- Head Start
- Impaired professionals
- Mental health & developmental disabilities confidentiality
- Outpatient psychotherapy provided by Master's level clinicians
- Residential care of emotionally disturbed adolescents and adults
- Reasonable suspicion of drug or alcohol use
- Social service standards of care
- Social work
- Substance abuse
- USDOT Safety Regulations regarding drugs and alcohol

Mr. Peterson received an MA in Social Service Administration from the University of Chicago and a BA in Philosophy, Summa Cum Laude, from North Park University. He is an Illinois Licensed Clinical Social Worker, a Michigan Licensed Master's Social Worker, a certified Disaster Mental Health Technician for the American Red Cross, and qualified Substance Abuse Professional under US Department of Transportation regulations.

Mr. Peterson is a former Cook County, Illinois, Juvenile Probation Officer. As Vice President of Dovetail, Inc., he provides risk management consultation, training, coordination of fitness for duty evaluations, employee assistance program counseling, critical incident debriefing, substance abuse and mental health assessments for municipalities, law enforcement, human services and professional associations, insurance companies, manufacturing and transportation employers, and utilities.

Additional information of Evan M. Peterson's background, areas of practice, expertise, and professional philosophy can be found at http://www.evanmpeterson.com. Users of handheld devices with tiny browsers may find http://www.evanmpeterson.com/text more friendly to your gadget.

MEDICAL EXPERT WITNESS REFERRAL SERVICES

TASA med

A Division of The TASA Group, Inc.
Your First Source for Medical and Health Care Specialists
1166 DeKalb Pike
Blue Bell, PA 19422-1953
U.S. and Canada: 800-659-8464 Fax: 800-850-8272
United Kingdom: 0800-89-1292
www.tasamed.net tasamed@tasanet.com

Advantages: **Find your Medical Expert with one call or click.** We've done the legwork to save you and your staff hours of search time, effort, and expense. There is **NO CHARGE** for our customized searches, referral, resumes, and your initial screening interviews with candidates until you designate or engage an expert. TASAmed is consistently the best way to locate the finest testifying and consulting experts in every health care category.

Experience: **No other referral service has more experience.** We successfully refer thousands of experienced medical experts, expert witnesses, and consultants every year, and it's likely we have referred experts for matters like yours, many times. More than 1/3 of our staff have 10 or more years of referral experience - an exceptional record that benefits you with every call. TASAmed is a division of The TASA Group, North America's largest and most experienced EXPERT REFERRAL SERVICE ®.

Scope of Expertise: **Unlimited.** Our network includes distinguished experts and consultants in virtually every facet of health care - **more than 900 categories.** Specialists are available to review records, advise on case merits, explain technical terms, conduct IMEs, prepare reports, and testify.

Sample Categories:

Anesthesiology	Neonatology
Cardiology	Nephrology
Closed Head Injury	Neurology
Cosmetic Surgery	Neurosurgery
Critical Care Nursing	Nursing
Elder Abuse	Obstetrics
Emergency Care	Occupational Medicine
Environmental Medicine	Oncology
Epidemiology	Ophthalmology
Forensic Pathology	Orthopedics
Forensic Toxicology	Pain Management
General Dentistry	Pediatrics
Gerontology	Plastic Surgery
Gynecology	Psychiatry
IMEs	Radiology
Immunology	Serology
Laser Surgery	Sports Medicine
Malpractice	Surgery
Midwifery	and much more

Service Area: **Global.** With our vast resources, we can provide the medical experts you need in virtually any location and at any stage in your case.

(This Listing Continued)

Experts: **They are respected authorities,** valued for their knowledge, experience, and integrity. Most of the distinguished men and women on our medical roster work full-time in medical practices, universities, or in industry. All are independent contractors.

Fees: **Our fees are competitive and fair,** particularly when you consider the value of your time, the effort you save with just one call to TASAmed, and the influence that a carefully-chosen medical expert can have on the outcome of your case. There is **NO CHARGE** for our customized searches, referral, resumes, and your initial screening interviews with candidates until you designate or engage an expert.

Reputation: **TASAmed is known for integrity,** high standards, and excellent service. We are neutral, serve either plaintiff or defendant, do not work on a contingent fee basis, and have no financial stake in the outcome of a case.

Clients: **The TASA Group has served hundreds of thousands of clients** in law and insurance firms, the business sector, and government agencies in more than 44 years. Most clients use us again and again, demonstrating their high level of satisfaction with our services.

NURSING CONSULTANTS

Tanner Associates

MEDICAL / LEGAL CONSULTING

5 South 428 Glenoban Drive
Naperville, Illinois 60563
Phone: (630) 983-4497
Fax: (630) 983-4496
catherine.tanner@sbcglobal.net

Are you frustrated by spending precious time and money wading through medical records that appear to be in a foreign language, while trying to determine whether your client received appropriate medical care?

If so, get help from experts who know the inner-workings, secret handshakes and passwords of the health care system!

Tanner Associates will:

- **Save you time**
- **Save you money**
- **Help you make your best case**

- **WE QUICKLY ESTABLISH CASE MERIT.**
  We will screen the medical records to determine if all standards of care were adhered to.

- **PROVIDE YOU WITH EITHER A COMPREHENSIVE OR BRIEF REPORT.**
  All medical jargon is clearly defined for you. We organize and review all documents and present you with a chronology of all pertinent occurrences and individuals involved.

- **PERFORM A THOROUGH SEARCH OF THE RELEVANT MEDICAL LITERATURE.**
  We will research articles, standards and guidelines related to your case, and provide you with summarized copies.

(This Listing Continued)

- **LOCATE CASE-SUPPORTING TESTIFYING EXPERTS.** We have a nationwide network of medical and nursing specialists to choose from, and can help you prepare the expert for deposition or trial.

Catherine S. Tanner, RN, BSN, CLNC, the founder of Tanner Associates Medical / Legal Consulting, has over 15 years of professional nursing experience in critical care, medical, surgical, ER, OB/BYN, nursery, recovery room, cardiac cath lab, outpatient surgery, and JCAHO survey preparation. She has an extensive network of medical and nursing specialists on call, who can provide consulting and testifying services.

Catherine welcomes your inquiries.

PROCESS SERVERS & DOCUMENT DELIVERY SERVICES

BPSI

Borg Process Servers Inc.

serving the legal profession since 1973,
throughout Canada & U.S.A.

5511 Steeles Ave. W., #208
Toronto, Ontario CANADA M9L 1S7
Email: Admin@borgps.com
Website: www.borgps.com

Specialists in:

- Process Serving
- Court Processing & Searching
- Business, Personal and Ministry of Transportation Searches

Office hours 7:30a.m. to 6:00p.m. Eastern Time

1-800-567-2674 (BORG)
Fax 416-746-2329

It's Your Serve - IYS

134 N. LaSalle St. #1200
Chicago, IL 60602
PHONE 312-855-0303
FAX 312-855-0306
EMAIL info@iys.us
WEB www.iys.us

IT'S YOUR SERVE

Chicago's Premier Process & Clerking Service

(This Listing Continued)

Our professionalism and superior service has made us known as the Midwest's #1 Process Server with an ever growing family of over 3,000 Chicagoland customers including Chicago's top law firms. Our reputation as the ***premier process server in Illinois*** has spread to an extensive network of clients coast to coast, numbering in the thousands, including Alaska, Hawaii, and parts of Canada and Mexico.

Rush Fillings and Process Service - RUSH service is our speciality, with Guaranteed 24-hour turnaround on rush process service and same day fillings outside the Chicago Loop when your assignment is received by 12 noon.

Real Time Serve Status - Upon execution of a serve, details are reported into our central office and immediately entered into our web-based online tracking system. This gives you the ability to immediately view real time results, on-line.

- **Process Service**
- **Clerking Service**
- **Skip Tracing**
- **Notary Service**
- **Out of State Process Service**

- **Flat Fees** *On Standard Assignments*
- **24 Hr. Availability 7 days a Week**
- **Free Pick-Up & Delivery** *To Chicago Loop Clients*
- **Licensed Private Detective** License #117-000885
- **WBE Certified**

312-855-0303

TITLE INSURANCE

Chicago Title Insurance Company

171 North Clark Street
Chicago, Illinois 60601-3294
Telephone: 312-223-2402
Fax: 312-223-2658

Chicago Title Insurance Company (CTIC) provides title insurance and related real estate services across the United States, Puerto Rico, Canada and Mexico through its geographically diverse network of offices and agents.

Together with its partner companies, Fidelity National Title Insurance (FNTI), Security Union Title Insurance Co. (SUTIC), Ticor Title Insurance Co.(TTIC) Chicago Title is part of the nation's largest title insurance family of companies. Other real estate related products and services offered include property inspection, escrow collection, credit reporting, attorney services, reconveyances, recordings and flood certification.

The organization's national commercial group provides one-stop shopping for customers engaged in multi-state, multi-site transactions. It operates through strategically located offices staffed with local and national professionals who have the skills, resources and authority to facilitate your transactions effectively, efficiently, economically and promptly.

Corporate officers include William P. Foley, II, Chairman of the Board and Chief Executive Officer; Frank P. Willey, Vice Chairman; Randy Quirk, President and Chief Operating Officer; Alan L. Stinson, Executive Vice President, Chief Financial Officer and Treasurer; Peter Sadowski, Executive Vice President and General Counsel and Christopher Abbinante, Executive Vice President and Division Manager.

For additional information, please visit our web site: www.ctic.com

TRANSCRIPTION SERVICES

ADEPT TRANSCRIPTION SERVICES

659 Cornflower Way
Perris, CA 92571
email: amuriel1@verizon.net

Over 20 Years of Experience

TRANSCRIBING

- Legal
- Special Projects
- Investigative Reports
- Much More

(800) 291-2876

VIDEO TAPE SERVICES

BENEDIA

CERTIFIED COURT REPORTING SERVICE

Servicing
Chicago Phoenix
Chicago Headquarters
175 E. Delaware St.
Suite 6105
Chicago, IL 60611
Phone: (312) 482-8990 Fax: (312) 482-8992
Toll Free: (877) 482-8990
E-mail: phil@benedia.com
Website: www.benedia.com

SERVICES

- Trials
- Motions
- Hearings
- Prove-ups
- Conventions
- Arbitrations
- Board Meetings
- Depositions
- Statements
- Online Repository
- Telephone Depositions
- Real-time Reporting
- Transcripts from Audio Tape
- Video Tape Services
- Electronic Reporting
- Video Conferencing
- Translations & Interpreters
- E-mailing of Transcripts
- Keyword Indexing
- Examinations Under Oath
- Conference Room

NOTABLE FEATURES

Most notable for our state of the art equipment, which helps us to handle some of the most complex cases. Our "Online Repository" gives you access to all your cases, invoices and transcripts 24 hours a day, 7 days a week.
Log on Anywhere.

WE MAKE YOUR JOB EASIER!

If you are searching for a court reporting agency with sound ethics, and integrity...who delivers accurate and prompt service...who meets your needs...then look no further!

DECATUR,* 83,885, *Macon Co.*

COURT REPORTERS

ANCHOR COURT REPORTING

P. O. Box 25471
Decatur, IL 62521

(800) 774-8374
(217) 428-0946

Fax: (217) 876-1449
e-mail: nhubert@insightbb.com

Serving Central Illinois area:
Bloomington, Champaign, Decatur, Normal, Springfield.

Certified Court Reporters
Registered Professional Reporters

Arbitrations
Medical/Technical Expertise
Compressed Transcripts/Word Index
ASCII/IBM Compatible Disks
Complimentary Conference Room
Video

Member:
National Court Reporters Association
Illinois Shorthand Reporters Association

COMPETITIVE RATES
No travel or mileage charge

EDWARDSVILLE,* 14,579, *Madison Co.*

COURT REPORTERS

GORE PERRY & GATEWAY LIPA
Reporting Company

Gore, Perry, Gateway & Lipa Reporting Co.

A Full Service Reporting Firm Serving
Eastern Missouri and Southern Illinois

Established 1933

515 Olive Street
Suite 700
St. Louis, MO 63101

1-800-878-6750 (314) 241-6750
Fax (314) 241-5070
Email: gpgl@sbcglobal.net

Ronald A. Gore, CM, RPR, CSR (MO, IL)
Robert Perry, CSR (MO, IL)

Certificates of Merit
Certified Shorthand Reporters
Certified Court Reporters
Registered Professional Reporters

- Medical/Technical/Chemical
- Video
- Conference Rooms
- ASCII/Discovery ZX/WordPerfect
- Min-U-Script/Word Index
- Arbitrations
- Process Service
- Conventions
- Hotel Referrals
- Videoconference

RANKIN REPORTING & LEGAL VIDEO, INC.

Serving the Legal Community since 1966

Rankin Certified Court Reporters are licensed in both Missouri and Illinois. Their superior skills meet the demands of the most complex litigation projects including examinations under oath, depositions, arbitrations, administrative hearings and trials. Your needs receive our undivided attention.

Certified Realtime Reporters	Registered Professional Reporters
Registered Diplomate	Certified Shorthand Reporters
Reporters	Certified Court Reporters
Registered Merit Reporters	Certified Legal Video Specialist

TRANSCRIPT DELIVERY IN ACCORDANCE WITH YOUR REQUEST

COMPETITIVE RATES

(This Listing Continued)

- LiveNote, web site transcript repository
- Deposition Specialists: Scientific/Technical/Medical
- Hearings and Arbitrations
- Compressed Transcripts/Word Index
- Realtime Reporting
- Text/Video Sync
- Complimentary Deposition Suites
- Video: taping, editing, presentation, conferencing
- Covering all of eastern Missouri and southern Illinois
- E-Transcript/E-Binder

Telephone: 1-314-231-2202 www.rankinreporting.com

Fax: 1-314-231-7432 email: traci@rankinreporting.com

1015 Locust Street - Suite 911
St. Louis, Missouri 63101-1329
Call us Toll Free at 1-800-285-2115

JOLIET,* 76,836, *Will Co.*

COURT REPORTERS

ADVANTAGE REPORTING SERVICE

Statewide Services
Certified Shorthand and Registered Professional Reporters

Member: National Court Reporters' Association
Illinois Shorthand Reporters' Association

- Realtime Reporting
- Complimentary Deposition Suites
- Certified Videotaped Depositions
- Condensed Transcripts/Index
- ASCII/IBM Compatible Disks
- E-transcripts
- Daily and Expedited Service
- Technical/Medical Expertise
- All Phases of Reporting

(800) 347-3124
FAX: (800) 690-3376

1000 Essington Road
Lincolnshire Business Center
Joliet, IL 60435

GEORGE E. RYDMAN & ASSOCIATES, LTD.

Certified Court Reporters and Video

Our 30th Year of Reporting Excellence

Joliet, Morris, Naperville, Ottawa and surrounding locales

(This Listing Continued)

COURT REPORTERS (cont'd)

George E. Rydman & Associates, Ltd. (cont'd)

Complimentary Deposition Suites Video Depositions
Teleconference Depositions ASCII Diskettes Immediate, Daily & Expedited Transcripts
Condensed and Indexed Transcripts
Directly Across From Will County Courthouse

Confidence, Quality and Service

A FULL SERVICE REPORTING COMPANY

15 W. Jefferson Street Joliet, Illinois 60432
800-608-5523 815-727-4363 FAX 815-727-7186

NAPERVILLE, 85,351, *Du Page Co.*

COURT REPORTERS

AREA COURT REPORTERS

Certified Shorthand Reporters

Tel. 800-224-1568
Fax 847-870-7971

Serving Naperville, Oak Brook, Aurora, and all of DuPage County

Legal Videotape Services

Subpoena Service

Deposition Suites

- Medical and Technical Specialists
- Depositions
- Arbitrations/Hearings
- Condensed Transcripts
- Key word Indexing
- ASCII disks

3617 E. Ogden Ave.
Naperville, Illinois 60540

NASHVILLE,* 3,202, *Washington Co.*

COURT REPORTERS

RANKIN REPORTING & LEGAL VIDEO, INC.

Serving the Legal Community since 1966

Rankin Certified Court Reporters are licensed in both Missouri and Illinois. Their superior skills meet the demands of the most complex litigation projects including examinations under oath, depositions, arbitrations, administrative hearings and trials. Your needs receive our undivided attention.

(This Listing Continued)

Certified Realtime Reporters | Registered Professional Reporters
Registered Diplomate | Certified Shorthand Reporters
Reporters | Certified Court Reporters
Registered Merit Reporters | Certified Legal Video Specialist

TRANSCRIPT DELIVERY IN ACCORDANCE WITH YOUR REQUEST

COMPETITIVE RATES

- LiveNote, web site transcript repository
- Deposition Specialists: Scientific/Technical/Medical
- Hearings and Arbitrations
- Compressed Transcripts/Word Index
- Realtime Reporting
- Text/Video Sync
- Complimentary Deposition Suites
- Video: taping, editing, presentation, conferencing
- Covering all of eastern Missouri and southern Illinois
- E-Transcript/E-Binder

Telephone: 1-314-231-2202 www.rankinreporting.com

Fax: 1-314-231-7432 email: traci@rankinreporting.com

1015 Locust Street - Suite 911
St. Louis, Missouri 63101-1329
Call us Toll Free at 1-800-285-2115

PEORIA,* 113,504, *Peoria Co.*

COURT REPORTERS

ADVANTAGE REPORTING SERVICE

Statewide Services
Certified Shorthand and Registered Professional Reporters

We are the DepoNet® court reporting firm selected by legal professionals in our area.

Member: National Court Reporters' Association
Illinois Shorthand Reporters' Association

- Realtime Reporting
- Complimentary Deposition Suites
- Certified Videotaped Depositions
- Condensed Transcripts/Index
- ASCII/IBM Compatible Disks
- E-transcripts
- Daily and Expedited Service
- Technical/Medical Expertise
- Full Service Agency

(800) 347-3124
(309) 673-1881
FAX: (800) 690-3376

(This Listing Continued)

110 S.W. Jefferson
Suite 430
Peoria, IL 61602

1-800-DEPONET

The reliable source for quality-assured legal support services worldwide.

ROCKFORD,* 139,426, *Winnebago Co.*

COURT REPORTERS

LAUNIUS REPORTING SERVICE

Certified and Registered Professional Reporters
P.O. Box 5483
Rockford, Illinois 61125-0483

Telephone: (815) 397-3933
Facsimile: (815) 433-1109

Serving all of Northern and Central Illinois

- Medical and Technical Specialists
- Computer-Assisted Transcription
- Standard Two-Week Delivery
- Expedited, Daily & Immediate Transcripts
- IBM-Compatible/ASCII Diskettes
- Complimentary Conference/Deposition Suites
- Videotaped Deposition Services

Memberships:
National Court Reporters Association
Illinois Court Reporters Association

References upon request.

MIDWEST PROFESSIONAL REPORTING, INC.
(815) 968-0015

916 North Church Street • Rockford, IL 61103
Fax# (815) 968-0234 • Email: MPREPORT@AOL.COM

"DEDICATED TO THE HIGHEST STANDARDS OF TRANSCRIPT QUALITY AND AN UNCOMPROMISING COMMITMENT TO CLIENT SATISFACTION"

Established 1983

The area's largest reporting agency providing service to twelve counties of Northern Illinois and Southern Wisconsin WITHOUT TRAVEL CHARGES.

Professional Services

(This Listing Continued)

- REPORTING DEPOSITIONS - HEARINGS - TRIALS - ARBITRATIONS
- ALL REPORTERS ARE STATE CERTIFIED
- SPECIALISTS IN MEDICAL, EXPERT AND TECHNICAL TESTIMONY
- COMPLIMENTARY DEPOSITION SUITE AND PARKING
- COMPUTER AIDED TRANSCRIPTION
- COMPRESSED TRANSCRIPTS AVAILABLE
- ASCII / AMICUS DISK CONVERSION
- KEY / MULTI - WORD INDEXING
- DIGITAL EXHIBIT REPRODUCTION
- VIDEO SERVICES AVAILABLE
- DAILY COPY AND EXPEDITED SERVICE

The area's largest staff on duty to accommodate last minute scheduling with evening and weekend service provided at
NO ADDITIONAL CHARGE.
Our convenient downtown location is minutes away from the Winnebago County courthouse, The Greater Rockford Airport and Interstate 90.
ACCREDITATION:
REGISTERED MERIT REPORTERS
REGISTERED PROFESSIONAL REPORTERS
CERTIFIED SHORTHAND REPORTERS
NOTARIES PUBLIC
MEMBER:
National Court Reporters Association
Illinois Court Reporters Association

SCHAUMBURG, 68,586, *Cook & Du Page Cos.*

COURT REPORTERS

AREA COURT REPORTERS

CONFERENCE ROOMS AVAILABLE at O'Hare Airport and Schaumburg

(800) 224-1568

Fax: 847-870-7971

FULLY COMPUTERIZED

VIDEOTAPE SERVICES

SUBPOENA SERVICES AVAILABLE

Established 1978

335 Wingate Drive
Schaumburg, Illinois 60193

SPRINGFIELD,* 105,227, *Sangamon Co.*

COURT REPORTERS

ADVANTAGE REPORTING SERVICE

Statewide Services
Certified Shorthand and Registered Professional Reporters

We are the DepoNet® court reporting firm selected by legal professionals in our area.

Member: National Court Reporters' Association
Illinois Shorthand Reporters' Association

- Realtime Reporting
- Complimentary Deposition Suites
- Certified Videotaped Depositions
- Condensed Transcripts/Index
- ASCII/IBM Compatible Disks
- E-transcripts
- Daily and Expedited Service
- Technical/Medical Expertise
- All Phases of Reporting

(800) 347-3124
(217) 789-2744
FAX: (800) 690-3376
Capitol Place Office Suites
118 West Edwards Street
Suite 100
Springfield, IL 62704

1-800-DEPONET

The reliable source for quality-assured legal support services worldwide.

WHEATON,* 51,464, *Du Page Co.*

COURT REPORTERS

COUNTY COURT REPORTERS, INC.

600 S. COUNTY FARM RD., SUITE 200
WHEATON, IL 60187
TEL: 630-653-1622 FAX: 630-653-4119
E-MAIL: CCR600@AMERITECH.NET

MEMBER:

- ILLINOIS CERTIFIED SHORTHAND REPORTERS
- NATIONAL COURT REPORTERS ASSOCIATION
- DUPAGE COUNTY BAR ASSOCIATION
- NATIONAL ASSOCIATION OF LEGAL SECRETARIES
- NATIONAL ASSOCIATION FOR FEMALE EXECUTIVES
- NATIONAL WOMEN BUSINESS OWNERS CORPORATION

(This Listing Continued)

PARTICIPATIONS:

- ILLINOIS COOPERATIVE EDUCATION PROGRAM
- DUPAGE COUNTY ASSOCIATION OF FEMALE LAWYERS
- WHEATON CHAMBER OF COMMERCE

30 EXPERIENCED REPORTERS
COMPLIMENTARY DEPOSITION SUITES IN WHEATON AND GENEVA
CERTIFIED VIDEOTAPED DEPOSITIONS
FREE CONDENSED TRANSCRIPTS (UPON REQUEST)
FREE WORD INDEX PROVIDED WITH EACH TRANSCRIPT
FREE ASCII/IBM COMPATIBLE DISKS
DAILY AND EXPEDITED SERVICE
TECHNICAL/MEDICAL EXPERTISE
REAL TIME
TRANSCRIPTS AVAILABLE VIA E-MAIL OR PDF FORMAT
AFTER HOURS PAGING AND EMERGENCY PHONE NUMBER

1 BLOCK FROM THE DUPAGE COUNTY COURTHOUSE

FORT WAYNE,* 173,072, *Allen Co.*

COURT REPORTERS

SUMMIT CITY REPORTING, INC.
Certified Stenographic Reporters

SERVING ALL OF INDIANA AND WESTERN OHIO

3492-B Stellhorn Road
Fort Wayne, Indiana 46815

800-977-DEPO
260-486-3954
Fax: 260-485-2596
email: ginger_summitcityreporting@verizon.net
www.summitcityreporting.com

- Complete Reporting Service
- Computer - Aided Transcription
- Standard 8-Day Turnaround
- Realtime Reporting
- In-House Commercial Quality Video
- Daily, Expedited Transcripts
- National and State Certifications
- E-Transcript ™
- Downtown Conference Rooms
- Statewide Deposition Service

MEMBER
National Court Reporters Association

800-977-DEPO

HAMMOND, 84,236, *Lake Co.*

COURT REPORTERS

1-2-3
1-800-682-5201

1-2-3 Reporting Service
a division of Certified Reporting Company

24 HOUR PHONE: 800-682-5201
E-mail: 123reporting@prodigy.net
www.123reporting.com

COURT REPORTER OWNED AND COURT REPORTER MANAGED

- Only Experienced Certified and RPR Shorthand Reporters
- Realtime Reporters Upon Request
- Technical, Malpractice, Product Liability and Patent Depositions

(This Listing Continued)

- Computer-Aided Transcription
- Daily and Expedited Delivery on Transcripts
- Min-U-Script® Condensed Transcripts and Master Indexes Available
- Complete Litigation Support Available
- ASCII and Discovery ZX Diskettes Available Compatible with Any DOS-Based System
- Key Word Indexing and Proximity Search
- Complimentary Deposition Suites Available
- Video Depositions by Certified Technicians/Attorney Including "Day In The Life" Record and Accident Scene Videos
- Subpoena Services Available
- Timestamping of Depositions

MEMBER OF:
NATIONAL COURT REPORTERS ASSOCIATION
ILLINOIS STATE REPORTERS ASSOCIATION
CHICAGO METROPOLITAN REPORTERS ASSOCIATION

References upon request.

INDIANAPOLIS,* 731,327, *Marion Co.*

CORPORATE INVESTIGATORS

International Investigators, Inc.
Forensic Accounting and Fraud Audits
CPA's and CFE's
3216 North Pennsylvania Street
Indianapolis, IN 46205-3414
Tele. (317) 925-1496 1-800-403-8111 Fax (317) 926-1177
(Email) info@iiiweb.net and timwilcox@iiiweb.net
Web Site Address: www.internationalinvestigators.com

C. Tim Wilcox, President

Stanley R. Large, Senior Investigator

Brenda McGinley
Investigations Coordinator

Russell L. Ferguson
Technical Consultant

Jennifer J. Lambert
Sr. Investigative Consultant

International Investigators, Inc. is licensed and insured, with over 45 years of experience. Formed in 1960 by former FBI Agents. Investigative capabilities throughout North America and over 70 countries.

We provide State of the Art computer investigations, with access to over 6,000 computer data bases, and have investigative and intelligence capability worldwide. We provide comprehensive investigations for the legal community, to include:

(This Listing Continued)

CORPORATE INVESTIGATORS (cont'd)

International Investigators, Inc. (cont'd)

Asset & Financial Investigations - Develop individual and/or corporate net worth and locate hidden assets.
Liability Investigations - Investigation of accidents.
Accident Reconstruction - Accident scene investigation - NOT an engineering service.
Litigation - Background profiles on corporations and individuals involved in litigated matters.
Due Diligence - In-depth look at all aspects of corporations and significant individuals.
Criminal Defense - Investigation of potential witnesses and review of evidence.
Forensic Laboratory Services & Crime Scene Analysis
Electronic Eavesdropping Countermeasures Sweeps-(TSCM)
Jury Panel - Background information on jury members.
Workers' Compensation - Background profile and investigation of circumstances of the accident, as well as the claimant's work and claim history. Discreet surveillance of claimant's activities.
Locates & Skip Tracing
Statements Recorded, Audio, Video or Both
Handwriting & Document Examinations
Legal Testimony
Child Custody - Determination of welfare of children and location of missing children.
Contested Wills, Estate Research, Location of Assets
Domestic - Background and financial asset investigations, as well as surveillance of individuals.

Surveillance - Utilize State of the Art video camcorders and 35mm equipment, to include ultra-discreet equipment and high-tech techniques. Unobtrusive vans with concealed periscopes.
GPS - Cellular Vehicle Tracking.
Polygraph or PSE Examinations - Pre-stipulated or stipulated tests.
Subpoena Services - Service of legal documents. U.S. and worldwide.
Environmental, Toxic Contamination, Spills Investigation of Negligent or Responsible Parties.
Computer Security - Highest Level
  Assessment - Security Review of Infrastructure, Systems, Policies & Procedures
  Perimeter - External Penetration and Vulnerability Testing - Hacking
  Monitoring - 24-7 Managed Internet Firewall Monitoring Services
  Intrusion - 24-7 Managed Intrusion Detection System (IDS) Monitoring Services

Members:
National Association of Legal Investigators
World Association of Detectives
American Society for Industrial Security
Society of Competitive Intelligence Professionals
Council of International Investigators
National Association of Professional Process Servers
World Investigative Network

COURT REPORTERS

1-2-3
1-800-682-5201

1-2-3 Reporting Service
a division of Certified Reporting Company

24 HOUR PHONE: 800-682-5201
E-mail: 123reporting@prodigy.net
www.123reporting.com

COURT REPORTER OWNED AND COURT REPORTER MANAGED

- Only Experienced Certified and RPR Shorthand Reporters
- Realtime Reporters Upon Request
- Technical, Malpractice, Product Liability and Patent Depositions
- Computer-Aided Transcription
- Daily and Expedited Delivery on Transcripts
- Min-U-Script® Condensed Transcripts and Master Indexes Available
- Complete Litigation Support Available
- ASCII and Discovery ZX Diskettes Available Compatible with Any DOS-Based System
- Key Word Indexing and Proximity Search
- Complimentary Deposition Suites Available
- Video Depositions by Certified Technicians/Attorney Including "Day In The Life" Record and Accident Scene Videos
- Subpoena Services Available
- Timestamping of Depositions

MEMBER OF:
NATIONAL COURT REPORTERS ASSOCIATION
ILLINOIS STATE REPORTERS ASSOCIATION
CHICAGO METROPOLITAN REPORTERS ASSOCIATION

References upon request.

ASSOCIATED REPORTING, INC.
Certified and Registered Professional Reporters

251 East Ohio Street
Suite 940
Indianapolis, Indiana 46204

Telephone: 317-631-0940
FAX: 317-231-6601

(This Listing Continued)

Complete Reporting Service - Litigation Support, Realtime,
Computer Aided Transcription - Compressed Transcripts
ASCII - Daily Copy Services
Video Tape Services - Sworn Statements
Four Conference Rooms Available - Arbitrations
Serving the entire State of Indiana

Member: Indiana Shorthand Reporters Association
National Court Reporters Association

1-800-DEPONET

The reliable source for quality-assured legal support services worldwide.

Connor+Associates

Reporting+Videoconferencing

1650 One American Square
Box 82020
Indianapolis, Indiana 46282
Telephone: 317-236-6022
800-554-3376
Fax: 317-236-6015
Email address: info@connorreporting.com
www.connorreporting.com

CENTRALLY LOCATED IN THE HEART OF THE DOWNTOWN BUSINESS DISTRICT

On-Line Scheduling
Complete Reporting Service
All Certified/RMR Reporters
Realtime Reporting
Condensed Transcripts
Videotape Services
Videoconferencing
CD Bundles & Document Imaging
Instant and Daily Copy Services
E-Transcript
LiveNote™
Conference Room Available
Available for Statewide and National Travel

Reference: Local Bench and Bar

Member Indiana Shorthand Reporters Association
Member National Court Reporters Association

Stewart Richardson & Associates

211 N. Pennsylvania
2425 One Indiana Square
Indianapolis, IN 46204

Toll Free: 1.800.869.0873
Local Phone: 317.237.3773
Fax: 317.237.3767

(This Listing Continued)

Since 1976, Stewart Richardson & Associates has built its court reporting reputation on providing exemplary service, dedication to detail, and cutting-edge technology. Located in downtown Indianapolis, minutes from the airport, Stewart-Richardson's offices offer a comfortable, yet professional environment; and our large conference rooms can easily accommodate 25 people.

Our staff of Certified Realtime Reporters deliver timely, accurate transcripts under even the most demanding circumstances, and our state-of-the-art litigation support services enable attorneys to succeed in today's legal environment.

SERVICES

Stewart Richardson offers a wide range of services, including the latest in litigation technology. Our staff of friendly, knowledgeable people can show you the way. Whether you need a realtime reporter, expedited service, e-Transcripts, or scanned exhibits, we can help. Our secure online document repository allows access to your transcripts 24 hours a day.

- Certified Realtime Reporters using LiveNote™, Case View™, Summation™, or Legal Assistant™
- Expedited/daily copy service
- Deposition Suites
- e-Transcripts™
- Digitally videotaped depositions in DVD or VHS format
- Video conferencing
- Online document repository
- High-volume case management
- Expertise in complex litigation
- Access to a nationwide reporter network
- Competitive Rates

VIDEO CONFERENCING

Want to be more productive? Tired of airline delays and expense? Video conferencing is the answer, saving you both time and money. Our courteous staff can make all the necessary arrangements. With memberships in all the major video conferencing, networks, we can arrange locations in most of the United States and the world. All you need to do is show up.

Our services include document cameras, scan converters, VCRs, projectors, photocopying, and a knowledgeable staff. Our large conference room can easily accommodate 25 people.

CRIMINAL BACKGROUND CHECKS

International Investigators, Inc.

Forensic Accounting and Fraud Audits
CPA's and CFE's
3216 North Pennsylvania Street
Indianapolis, IN 46205-3414
Tele. (317) 925-1496 1-800-403-8111 Fax (317) 926-1177
(Email) info@iiiweb.net and timwilcox@iiiweb.net
Web Site Address: www.internationalinvestigators.com

C. Tim Wilcox, President
Stanley R. Large, Senior Investigator

Brenda McGinley
Investigations Coordinator

Russell L. Ferguson
Technical Consultant

Jennifer J. Lambert
Sr. Investigative Consultant

(This Listing Continued)

CRIMINAL BACKGROUND CHECKS (cont'd)

International Investigators, Inc. (cont'd)

International Investigators, Inc. is licensed and insured, with over 45 years of experience. Formed in 1960 by former FBI Agents. Investigative capabilities throughout North America and over 70 countries.

We provide State of the Art computer investigations, with access to over 6,000 computer data bases, and have investigative and intelligence capability worldwide. We provide comprehensive investigations for the legal community, to include:

Asset & Financial Investigations - Develop individual and/or corporate net worth and locate hidden assets.
Liability Investigations - Investigation of accidents.
Accident Reconstruction - Accident scene investigation - NOT an engineering service.
Litigation - Background profiles on corporations and individuals involved in litigated matters.
Due Diligence - In-depth look at all aspects of corporations and significant individuals.
Criminal Defense - Investigation of potential witnesses and review of evidence.
Forensic Laboratory Services & Crime Scene Analysis
Electronic Eavesdropping Countermeasures Sweeps-(TSCM)
Jury Panel - Background information on jury members.
Workers' Compensation - Background profile and investigation of circumstances of the accident, as well as the claimant's work and claim history. Discreet surveillance of claimant's activities.
Locates & Skip Tracing
Statements Recorded, Audio, Video or Both
Handwriting & Document Examinations
Legal Testimony
Child Custody - Determination of welfare of children and location of missing children.
Contested Wills, Estate Research, Location of Assets
Domestic - Background and financial asset investigations, as well as surveillance of individuals.

Surveillance - Utilize State of the Art video camcorders and 35mm equipment, to include ultra-discreet equipment and high-tech techniques. Unobtrusive vans with concealed periscopes.
GPS - Cellular Vehicle Tracking.
Polygraph or PSE Examinations - Pre-stipulated or stipulated tests.
Subpoena Services - Service of legal documents. U.S. and worldwide.
Environmental, Toxic Contamination, Spills Investigation of Negligent or Responsible Parties.
Computer Security - Highest Level
- **Assessment** - Security Review of Infrastructure, Systems, Policies & Procedures
- **Perimeter** - External Penetration and Vulnerability Testing - Hacking
- **Monitoring** - 24-7 Managed Internet Firewall Monitoring Services
- **Intrusion** - 24-7 Managed Intrusion Detection System (IDS) Monitoring Services

Members:
National Association of Legal Investigators
World Association of Detectives
American Society for Industrial Security
Society of Competitive Intelligence Professionals
Council of International Investigators
National Association of Professional Process Servers
World Investigative Network

CRIMINAL DEFENSE

International Investigators, Inc.

Forensic Accounting and Fraud Audits
CPA's and CFE's
3216 North Pennsylvania Street
Indianapolis, IN 46205-3414
Tele. (317) 925-1496 1-800-403-8111 Fax (317) 926-1177
(Email) info@iiiweb.net and timwilcox@iiiweb.net
Web Site Address: www.internationalinvestigators.com

C. Tim Wilcox, President — Stanley R. Large, Senior Investigator

Brenda McGinley
Investigations Coordinator

Russell L. Ferguson, Technical Consultant — Jennifer J. Lambert, Sr. Investigative Consultant

International Investigators, Inc. is licensed and insured, with over 45 years of experience. Formed in 1960 by former FBI Agents. Investigative capabilities throughout North America and over 70 countries.

We provide State of the Art computer investigations, with access to over 6,000 computer data bases, and have investigative and intelligence capability worldwide. We provide comprehensive investigations for the legal community, to include:

Asset & Financial Investigations - Develop individual and/or corporate net worth and locate hidden assets.
Liability Investigations - Investigation of accidents.
Accident Reconstruction - Accident scene investigation - NOT an engineering service.
Litigation - Background profiles on corporations and individuals involved in litigated matters.
Due Diligence - In-depth look at all aspects of corporations and significant individuals.
Criminal Defense - Investigation of potential witnesses and review of evidence.
Forensic Laboratory Services & Crime Scene Analysis
Electronic Eavesdropping Countermeasures Sweeps-(TSCM)
Jury Panel - Background information on jury members.
Workers' Compensation - Background profile and investigation of circumstances of the accident, as well as the claimant's work and claim history. Discreet surveillance of claimant's activities.
Locates & Skip Tracing
Statements Recorded, Audio, Video or Both
Handwriting & Document Examinations
Legal Testimony
Child Custody - Determination of welfare of children and location of missing children.
Contested Wills, Estate Research, Location of Assets
Domestic - Background and financial asset investigations, as well as surveillance of individuals.

Surveillance - Utilize State of the Art video camcorders and 35mm equipment, to include ultra-discreet equipment and high-tech techniques. Unobtrusive vans with concealed periscopes.
GPS - Cellular Vehicle Tracking.
Polygraph or PSE Examinations - Pre-stipulated or stipulated tests.
Subpoena Services - Service of legal documents. U.S. and worldwide.
Environmental, Toxic Contamination, Spills Investigation of Negligent or Responsible Parties.
Computer Security - Highest Level
- **Assessment** - Security Review of Infrastructure, Systems, Policies & Procedures
- **Perimeter** - External Penetration and Vulnerability Testing - Hacking
- **Monitoring** - 24-7 Managed Internet Firewall Monitoring Services
- **Intrusion** - 24-7 Managed Intrusion Detection System (IDS) Monitoring Services

(This Listing Continued)

Members: National Association of Legal Investigators
World Association of Detectives
American Society for Industrial Security
Society of Competitive Intelligence Professionals
Council of International Investigators
National Association of Professional Process Servers
World Investigative Network

CRIMINAL INVESTIGATIONS

International Investigators, Inc.

Forensic Accounting and Fraud Audits
CPA's and CFE's
3216 North Pennsylvania Street
Indianapolis, IN 46205-3414
Tele. (317) 925-1496 1-800-403-8111 Fax (317) 926-1177
(Email) info@iiiweb.net and timwilcox@iiiweb.net
Web Site Address: www.internationalinvestigators.com

C. Tim Wilcox, President
Stanley R. Large, Senior Investigator
Brenda McGinley, Investigations Coordinator
Russell L. Ferguson, Technical Consultant
Jennifer J. Lambert, Sr. Investigative Consultant

International Investigators, Inc. is licensed and insured, with over 45 years of experience. Formed in 1960 by former FBI Agents. Investigative capabilities throughout North America and over 70 countries.

We provide State of the Art computer investigations, with access to over 6,000 computer data bases, and have investigative and intelligence capability worldwide. We provide comprehensive investigations for the legal community, to include:

Asset & Financial Investigations - Develop individual and/or corporate net worth and locate hidden assets.
Liability Investigations - Investigation of accidents.
Accident Reconstruction - Accident scene investigation - NOT an engineering service.
Litigation - Background profiles on corporations and individuals involved in litigated matters.
Due Diligence - In-depth look at all aspects of corporations and significant individuals.
Criminal Defense - Investigation of potential witnesses and review of evidence.
Forensic Laboratory Services & Crime Scene Analysis
Electronic Eavesdropping Countermeasures Sweeps-(TSCM)
Jury Panel - Background information on jury members.
Workers' Compensation - Background profile and investigation of circumstances of the accident, as well as the claimant's work and claim history. Discreet surveillance of claimant's activities.
Locates & Skip Tracing
Statements Recorded, Audio, Video or Both
Handwriting & Document Examinations
Legal Testimony
Child Custody - Determination of welfare of children and location of missing children.
Contested Wills, Estate Research, Location of Assets
Domestic - Background and financial asset investigations, as well as surveillance of individuals.

(This Listing Continued)

Surveillance - Utilize State of the Art video camcorders and 35mm equipment, to include ultra-discreet equipment and high-tech techniques. Unobtrusive vans with concealed periscopes.
GPS - Cellular Vehicle Tracking.
Polygraph or PSE Examinations - Pre-stipulated or stipulated tests.
Subpoena Services - Service of legal documents. U.S. and worldwide.
Environmental, Toxic Contamination, Spills Investigation of Negligent or Responsible Parties.
Computer Security - Highest Level
Assessment - Security Review of Infrastructure, Systems, Policies & Procedures
Perimeter - External Penetration and Vulnerability Testing - Hacking
Monitoring - 24-7 Managed Internet Firewall Monitoring Services
Intrusion - 24-7 Managed Intrusion Detection System (IDS) Monitoring Services

Members: National Association of Legal Investigators
World Association of Detectives
American Society for Industrial Security
Society of Competitive Intelligence Professionals
Council of International Investigators
National Association of Professional Process Servers
World Investigative Network

DOMESTIC/SPOUSAL COMPUTER INVESTIGATION

International Investigators, Inc.

Forensic Accounting and Fraud Audits
CPA's and CFE's
3216 North Pennsylvania Street
Indianapolis, IN 46205-3414
Tele. (317) 925-1496 1-800-403-8111 Fax (317) 926-1177
(Email) info@iiiweb.net and timwilcox@iiiweb.net
Web Site Address: www.internationalinvestigators.com

C. Tim Wilcox, President
Stanley R. Large, Senior Investigator
Brenda McGinley, Investigations Coordinator
Russell L. Ferguson, Technical Consultant
Jennifer J. Lambert, Sr. Investigative Consultant

International Investigators, Inc. is licensed and insured, with over 45 years of experience. Formed in 1960 by former FBI Agents. Investigative capabilities throughout North America and over 70 countries.

We provide State of the Art computer investigations, with access to over 6,000 computer data bases, and have investigative and intelligence capability worldwide. We provide comprehensive investigations for the legal community, to include:

Asset & Financial Investigations - Develop individual and/or corporate net worth and locate hidden assets.
Liability Investigations - Investigation of accidents.
Accident Reconstruction - Accident scene investigation - NOT an engineering service.
Litigation - Background profiles on corporations and individuals involved in litigated matters.
Due Diligence - In-depth look at all aspects of corporations and significant individuals.
Criminal Defense - Investigation of potential witnesses and review of evidence.
Forensic Laboratory Services & Crime Scene Analysis
Electronic Eavesdropping Countermeasures Sweeps-(TSCM)

(This Listing Continued)

DOMESTIC/SPOUSAL COMPUTER INVESTIGATION (cont'd)

International Investigators, Inc. (cont'd)

Jury Panel - Background information on jury members.
Workers' Compensation - Background profile and investigation of circumstances of the accident, as well as the claimant's work and claim history. Discreet surveillance of claimant's activities.
Locates & Skip Tracing
Statements Recorded, Audio, Video or Both
Handwriting & Document Examinations
Legal Testimony
Child Custody - Determination of welfare of children and location of missing children.
Contested Wills, Estate Research, Location of Assets
Domestic - Background and financial asset investigations, as well as surveillance of individuals.
Surveillance - Utilize State of the Art video camcorders and 35mm equipment, to include ultra-discreet equipment and high-tech techniques. Unobtrusive vans with concealed periscopes.
GPS - Cellular Vehicle Tracking.
Polygraph or PSE Examinations - Pre-stipulated or stipulated tests.
Subpoena Services - Service of legal documents. U.S. and worldwide.
Environmental, Toxic Contamination, Spills Investigation of Negligent or Responsible Parties.
Computer Security - Highest Level
Assessment - Security Review of Infrastructure, Systems, Policies & Procedures
Perimeter - External Penetration and Vulnerability Testing - Hacking
Monitoring - 24-7 Managed Internet Firewall Monitoring Services
Intrusion - 24-7 Managed Intrusion Detection System (IDS) Monitoring Services

Members: National Association of Legal Investigators
World Association of Detectives
American Society for Industrial Security
Society of Competitive Intelligence Professionals
Council of International Investigators
National Association of Professional Process Servers
World Investigative Network

DUE DILIGENCE INVESTIGATIONS

International Investigators, Inc.

Forensic Accounting and Fraud Audits
CPA's and CFE's
3216 North Pennsylvania Street
Indianapolis, IN 46205-3414
Tele. (317) 925-1496 1-800-403-8111 Fax (317) 926-1177
(Email) info@iiiweb.net and timwilcox@iiiweb.net
Web Site Address: www.internationalinvestigators.com

C. Tim Wilcox, President
Stanley R. Large, Senior Investigator
Brenda McGinley, Investigations Coordinator
Russell L. Ferguson, Technical Consultant
Jennifer J. Lambert, Sr. Investigative Consultant

International Investigators, Inc. is licensed and insured, with over 45 years of experience. Formed in 1960 by former FBI Agents. Investigative capabilities throughout North America and over 70 countries.

We provide State of the Art computer investigations, with access to over 6,000 computer data bases, and have investigative and intelligence capability worldwide. We provide comprehensive investigations for the legal community, to include:

Asset & Financial Investigations - Develop individual and/or corporate net worth and locate hidden assets.
Liability Investigations - Investigation of accidents.
Accident Reconstruction - Accident scene investigation - NOT an engineering service.
Litigation - Background profiles on corporations and individuals involved in litigated matters.
Due Diligence - In-depth look at all aspects of corporations and significant individuals.
Criminal Defense - Investigation of potential witnesses and review of evidence.
Forensic Laboratory Services & Crime Scene Analysis
Electronic Eavesdropping Countermeasures Sweeps-(TSCM)
Jury Panel - Background information on jury members.
Workers' Compensation - Background profile and investigation of circumstances of the accident, as well as the claimant's work and claim history. Discreet surveillance of claimant's activities.
Locates & Skip Tracing
Statements Recorded, Audio, Video or Both
Handwriting & Document Examinations
Legal Testimony
Child Custody - Determination of welfare of children and location of missing children.
Contested Wills, Estate Research, Location of Assets
Domestic - Background and financial asset investigations, as well as surveillance of individuals.
Surveillance - Utilize State of the Art video camcorders and 35mm equipment, to include ultra-discreet equipment and high-tech techniques. Unobtrusive vans with concealed periscopes.
GPS - Cellular Vehicle Tracking.
Polygraph or PSE Examinations - Pre-stipulated or stipulated tests.
Subpoena Services - Service of legal documents. U.S. and worldwide.
Environmental, Toxic Contamination, Spills Investigation of Negligent or Responsible Parties.
Computer Security - Highest Level
Assessment - Security Review of Infrastructure, Systems, Policies & Procedures
Perimeter - External Penetration and Vulnerability Testing - Hacking
Monitoring - 24-7 Managed Internet Firewall Monitoring Services
Intrusion - 24-7 Managed Intrusion Detection System (IDS) Monitoring Services

Members: National Association of Legal Investigators
World Association of Detectives
American Society for Industrial Security
Society of Competitive Intelligence Professionals
Council of International Investigators
National Association of Professional Process Servers
World Investigative Network

(This Listing Continued)

ELECTRONIC COUNTERMEASURES

International Investigators, Inc.

Forensic Accounting and Fraud Audits
CPA's and CFE's
3216 North Pennsylvania Street
Indianapolis, IN 46205-3414
Tele. (317) 925-1496   1-800-403-8111   Fax (317) 926-1177
(Email) info@iiiweb.net and timwilcox@iiiweb.net
Web Site Address: www.internationalinvestigators.com

C. Tim Wilcox, President   Stanley R. Large, Senior Investigator

Brenda McGinley
Investigations Coordinator

Russell L. Ferguson
Technical Consultant

Jennifer J. Lambert
Sr. Investigative Consultant

International Investigators, Inc. is licensed and insured, with over 45 years of experience. Formed in 1960 by former FBI Agents. Investigative capabilities throughout North America and over 70 countries.

We provide State of the Art computer investigations, with access to over 6,000 computer data bases, and have investigative and intelligence capability worldwide. We provide comprehensive investigations for the legal community, to include:

Asset & Financial Investigations - Develop individual and/or corporate net worth and locate hidden assets.
Liability Investigations - Investigation of accidents.
Accident Reconstruction - Accident scene investigation - NOT an engineering service.
Litigation - Background profiles on corporations and individuals involved in litigated matters.
Due Diligence - In-depth look at all aspects of corporations and significant individuals.
Criminal Defense - Investigation of potential witnesses and review of evidence.
Forensic Laboratory Services & Crime Scene Analysis
Electronic Eavesdropping Countermeasures Sweeps-(TSCM)
Jury Panel - Background information on jury members.
Workers' Compensation - Background profile and investigation of circumstances of the accident, as well as the claimant's work and claim history. Discreet surveillance of claimant's activities.
Locates & Skip Tracing
Statements Recorded, Audio, Video or Both
Handwriting & Document Examinations
Legal Testimony
Child Custody - Determination of welfare of children and location of missing children.
Contested Wills, Estate Research, Location of Assets
Domestic - Background and financial asset investigations, as well as surveillance of individuals.
Surveillance - Utilize State of the Art video camcorders and 35mm equipment, to include ultra-discreet equipment and high-tech techniques. Unobtrusive vans with concealed periscopes.
GPS - Cellular Vehicle Tracking.
Polygraph or PSE Examinations - Pre-stipulated or stipulated tests.
Subpoena Services - Service of legal documents. U.S. and worldwide.
Environmental, Toxic Contamination, Spills Investigation of Negligent or Responsible Parties.
Computer Security - Highest Level
- **Assessment** - Security Review of Infrastructure, Systems, Policies & Procedures
- **Perimeter** - External Penetration and Vulnerability Testing - Hacking
- **Monitoring** - 24-7 Managed Internet Firewall Monitoring Services
- **Intrusion** - 24-7 Managed Intrusion Detection System (IDS) Monitoring Services

(This Listing Continued)

Members: National Association of Legal Investigators
World Association of Detectives
American Society for Industrial Security
Society of Competitive Intelligence Professionals
Council of International Investigators
National Association of Professional Process Servers
World Investigative Network

EXPERT WITNESS
ACCIDENTS/FIRES/PRODUCT LIABILITY

JOHN MICHAEL AGOSTI

Fire Analyst and Consultant
23808 North Overhill
Lake Zurich, Illinois 60047
Phone: 847-682-6793
E-mail: johnagosti@earthlink.net
Web: www.arsonexpert.com

As a member of the Skokie, Illinois Fire Department for twenty-eight years, Mr. Agosti progressed from a Firefighter/Paramedic to the position of Deputy Fire Chief. Mr. Agosti has responded to hundreds of major fire and crime scenes and has testified in court on the conclusions of his investigations. His investigations have led to successful criminal indictments and convictions. Mr. Agosti's fire department responsibilities included the review of all construction plans for compliance to fire and building codes. His expertise in building construction and fire spread, lends a unique blend to his fire investigation capabilities.

In addition to his fire department exposure to hundreds of fire investigations, Mr. Agosti has extensive experience in the private sector also. Over the past 11 years Mr. Agosti has conducted over eight hundred fire investigations as a private fire cause and origin analyst.

Practice areas include:

Fire and Explosions:
Arson defense/prosecution; gas explosions;
vehicular fires; structure fires; fire deaths/injuries.

Building and Fire Codes:
Fire/Building code violation; Life Safety Code violations;
smoke detector issues; fire prevention analysis.

Fire Department Practices:
Fire department operations/practices/management;
firefighter deaths/injuries/safety.

(This Listing Continued)

EXPERT WITNESS
ACCIDENTS/FIRES/PRODUCT LIABILITY (cont'd)

John Michael Agosti (cont'd)

Mr. Agosti has an Associates Degree in Fire Science and Technology. He is also certified as a Fire and Arson Investigator.

PROJECT EXPERIENCE

Fire and building code analysis
Automobile accident reconstruction
Gas leak surveys
Distribution gas pipe ruptures and leaks
Investigation of fire fatalities and electrocutions
Investigation of bombings
Investigation for cause and origin of fires and explosions

PROFESSIONAL SOCIETIES

National Fire Protection Association
Fire Marshals Association of North America
International Association of Fire Chiefs
Building Officials/Code Administrators International
Fire Investigators Strike Force
Illinois Fire Inspectors Association
International Association of Arson Investigators

EXPERT WITNESS
FIRE

JOHN MICHAEL AGOSTI

Fire Analyst and Consultant

23808 North Overhill
Lake Zurich, Illinois 60047
Phone: 847-682-6793
E-mail: johnagosti@earthlink.net
Web: www.arsonexpert.com

As a member of the Skokie, Illinois Fire Department for twenty-eight years, Mr. Agosti progressed from a Firefighter/Paramedic to the position of Deputy Fire Chief. Mr. Agosti has responded to hundreds of major fire and crime scenes and has testified in court on the conclusions of his investigations. His investigations have led to successful criminal indictments and convictions. Mr. Agosti's fire department responsibilities included the review of all construction plans for compliance to fire and building codes. His expertise in building construction and fire spread, lends a unique blend to his fire investigation capabilities.

In addition to his fire department exposure to hundreds of fire investigations, Mr. Agosti has extensive experience in the private sector also. Over the past 11 years Mr. Agosti has conducted over eight hundred fire investigations as a private fire cause and origin analyst.

Practice areas include:

Fire and Explosions:

(This Listing Continued)

Arson defense/prosecution; gas explosions; vehicular fires; structure fires; fire deaths/injuries.

Building and Fire Codes:

Fire/Building code violation; Life Safety Code violations; smoke detector issues; fire prevention analysis.

Fire Department Practices:

Fire department operations/practices/management; firefighter deaths/injuries/safety.

Mr. Agosti has an Associates Degree in Fire Science and Technology. He is also certified as a Fire and Arson Investigator.

PROJECT EXPERIENCE

Fire and building code analysis
Automobile accident reconstruction
Gas leak surveys
Distribution gas pipe ruptures and leaks
Investigation of fire fatalities and electrocutions
Investigation of bombings
Investigation for cause and origin of fires and explosions

PROFESSIONAL SOCIETIES

National Fire Protection Association
Fire Marshals Association of North America
International Association of Fire Chiefs
Building Officials/Code Administrators International
Fire Investigators Strike Force
Illinois Fire Inspectors Association
International Association of Arson Investigators

EXPERT WITNESS
FIRE
PROTECTION, INVESTIGATION

JOHN MICHAEL AGOSTI

Fire Analyst and Consultant

23808 North Overhill
Lake Zurich, Illinois 60047
Phone: 847-682-6793
E-mail: johnagosti@earthlink.net
Web: www.arsonexpert.com

As a member of the Skokie, Illinois Fire Department for twenty-eight years, Mr. Agosti progressed from a Firefighter/Paramedic to the position of Deputy Fire Chief. Mr. Agosti has responded to hundreds of major fire and crime scenes and has testified in court on the conclusions of his investigations. His investigations have led to successful criminal indictments and convictions. Mr. Agosti's fire department responsibilities included the review of all construction plans for compliance to fire and building codes. His expertise in building construction and fire spread, lends a unique blend to his fire investigation capabilities.

In addition to his fire department exposure to hundreds of fire investigations, Mr. Agosti has extensive experience in the private sector also. Over the past 11 years Mr. Agosti has conducted over eight hundred fire investigations as a private fire cause and origin analyst.

(This Listing Continued)

Practice areas include:

Fire and Explosions:
- Arson defense/prosecution; gas explosions; vehicular fires; structure fires; fire deaths/injuries.

Building and Fire Codes:
- Fire/Building code violation; Life Safety Code violations; smoke detector issues; fire prevention analysis.

Fire Department Practices:
- Fire department operations/practices/management; firefighter deaths/injuries/safety.

Mr. Agosti has an Associates Degree in Fire Science and Technology. He is also certified as a Fire and Arson Investigator.

PROJECT EXPERIENCE

Fire and building code analysis
Automobile accident reconstruction
Gas leak surveys
Distribution gas pipe ruptures and leaks
Investigation of fire fatalities and electrocutions
Investigation of bombings
Investigation for cause and origin of fires and explosions

PROFESSIONAL SOCIETIES

National Fire Protection Association
Fire Marshals Association of North America
International Association of Fire Chiefs
Building Officials/Code Administrators International
Fire Investigators Strike Force
Illinois Fire Inspectors Association
International Association of Arson Investigators

EXPERT WITNESS
FIRE RECONSTRUCTION

JOHN MICHAEL AGOSTI
Fire Analyst and Consultant

23808 North Overhill
Lake Zurich, Illinois 60047
Phone: 847-682-6793
E-mail: johnagosti@earthlink.net
Web: www.arsonexpert.com

As a member of the Skokie, Illinois Fire Department for twenty-eight years, Mr. Agosti progressed from a Firefighter/Paramedic to the position of Deputy Fire Chief. Mr. Agosti has responded to hundreds of major fire and crime scenes and has testified in court on the conclusions of his investigations. His investigations have led to successful criminal indictments and convictions. Mr. Agosti's fire department responsibilities included the review of all construction plans for compliance to fire and building codes. His expertise in building construction and fire spread, lends a unique blend to his fire investigation capabilities.

In addition to his fire department exposure to hundreds of fire investigations, Mr. Agosti has extensive experience in the private sector also. Over the past 11 years Mr. Agosti has conducted over eight hundred fire investigations as a private fire cause and origin analyst.

(This Listing Continued)

Practice areas include:

Fire and Explosions:
- Arson defense/prosecution; gas explosions; vehicular fires; structure fires; fire deaths/injuries.

Building and Fire Codes:
- Fire/Building code violation; Life Safety Code violations; smoke detector issues; fire prevention analysis.

Fire Department Practices:
- Fire department operations/practices/management; firefighter deaths/injuries/safety.

Mr. Agosti has an Associates Degree in Fire Science and Technology. He is also certified as a Fire and Arson Investigator.

PROJECT EXPERIENCE

Fire and building code analysis
Automobile accident reconstruction
Gas leak surveys
Distribution gas pipe ruptures and leaks
Investigation of fire fatalities and electrocutions
Investigation of bombings
Investigation for cause and origin of fires and explosions

PROFESSIONAL SOCIETIES

National Fire Protection Association
Fire Marshals Association of North America
International Association of Fire Chiefs
Building Officials/Code Administrators International
Fire Investigators Strike Force
Illinois Fire Inspectors Association
International Association of Arson Investigators

EXPERT WITNESS
FIRE CAUSE & ORIGIN

JOHN MICHAEL AGOSTI
Fire Analyst and Consultant

23808 North Overhill
Lake Zurich, Illinois 60047
Phone: 847-682-6793
E-mail: johnagosti@earthlink.net
Web: www.arsonexpert.com

As a member of the Skokie, Illinois Fire Department for twenty-eight years, Mr. Agosti progressed from a Firefighter/Paramedic to the position of Deputy Fire Chief. Mr. Agosti has responded to hundreds of major fire and crime scenes and has testified in court on the conclusions of his investigations. His investigations have led to successful criminal indictments and convictions. Mr. Agosti's fire department responsibilities included the review of all construction plans for compliance to fire and building codes. His expertise in building construction and fire spread, lends a unique blend to his fire investigation capabilities.

In addition to his fire department exposure to hundreds of fire investigations, Mr. Agosti has extensive experience in the private sector also. Over the past 11 years Mr. Agosti has conducted over eight hundred fire investigations as a private fire cause and origin analyst.

(This Listing Continued)

EXPERT WITNESS
FIRE CAUSE & ORIGIN (cont'd)

John Michael Agosti (cont'd)

Practice areas include:

Fire and Explosions:
Arson defense/prosecution; gas explosions;
vehicular fires; structure fires; fire deaths/injuries.

Building and Fire Codes:
Fire/Building code violation; Life Safety Code violations;
smoke detector issues; fire prevention analysis.

Fire Department Practices:
Fire department operations/practices/management;
firefighter deaths/injuries/safety.

Mr. Agosti has an Associates Degree in Fire Science and Technology.
He is also certified as a Fire and Arson Investigator.

PROJECT EXPERIENCE

Fire and building code analysis
Automobile accident reconstruction
Gas leak surveys
Distribution gas pipe ruptures and leaks
Investigation of fire fatalities and electrocutions
Investigation of bombings
Investigation for cause and origin of fires and explosions

PROFESSIONAL SOCIETIES

National Fire Protection Association
Fire Marshals Association of North America
International Association of Fire Chiefs
Building Officials/Code Administrators International
Fire Investigators Strike Force
Illinois Fire Inspectors Association
International Association of Arson Investigators

EXPERT WITNESS
FIRE/CONSULTING

JOHN MICHAEL AGOSTI

Fire Analyst and Consultant
23808 North Overhill
Lake Zurich, Illinois 60047
Phone: 847-682-6793
E-mail: johnagosti@earthlink.net
Web: www.arsonexpert.com

As a member of the Skokie, Illinois Fire Department for twenty-eight years, Mr. Agosti progressed from a Firefighter/Paramedic to the position of Deputy Fire Chief. Mr. Agosti has responded to hundreds of major fire and crime scenes and has testified in court on the conclusions of his investigations. His investigations have led to successful criminal indictments and convictions. Mr. Agosti's fire department responsibilities included the review of all construction plans for compliance to fire and building codes. His expertise in building construction and fire spread, lends a unique blend to his fire investigation capabilities.

(This Listing Continued)

In addition to his fire department exposure to hundreds of fire investigations, Mr. Agosti has extensive experience in the private sector also. Over the past 11 years Mr. Agosti has conducted over eight hundred fire investigations as a private fire cause and origin analyst.

Practice areas include:

Fire and Explosions:
Arson defense/prosecution; gas explosions;
vehicular fires; structure fires; fire deaths/injuries.

Building and Fire Codes:
Fire/Building code violation; Life Safety Code violations;
smoke detector issues; fire prevention analysis.

Fire Department Practices:
Fire department operations/practices/management;
firefighter deaths/injuries/safety.

Mr. Agosti has an Associates Degree in Fire Science and Technology.
He is also certified as a Fire and Arson Investigator.

PROJECT EXPERIENCE

Fire and building code analysis
Automobile accident reconstruction
Gas leak surveys
Distribution gas pipe ruptures and leaks
Investigation of fire fatalities and electrocutions
Investigation of bombings
Investigation for cause and origin of fires and explosions

PROFESSIONAL SOCIETIES

National Fire Protection Association
Fire Marshals Association of North America
International Association of Fire Chiefs
Building Officials/Code Administrators International
Fire Investigators Strike Force
Illinois Fire Inspectors Association
International Association of Arson Investigators

EXPERT WITNESS
INTELLECTUAL PROPERTY
MANUFACTURED PRODUCTS

Advanced Surface Microscopy, Inc.

3250 N. Post Road, Suite 120
Indianapolis, IN 46226 USA
Phone: +1-317-895-5630
Fax: +1-317-895-5652
www.asmicro.com
info@asmicro.com

TOLL FREE: 1-800-374-8557 (US & Canada)

Advanced Surface Microscopy, Inc. is an independent analytical testing and research laboratory, specializing in materials and device analysis using Atomic Force Microscopy (AFM) and related techniques (MFM, EFM).

Any surface you can touch is a potential target for analysis. Since 1990, we've completed more than 1000 analytical projects for over 200 customers, examining more than 100 types of materials and devices, including:

- pharmaceutical materials
- optical discs (CD, DVD, HD-DVD, Blu-Ray)
- magnetic disks and recording heads
- DNA and other biopolymers
- semiconductors, electronics
- paper, polymers and much more.

(This Listing Continued)

Don Chernoff, Ph.D., has provided expert consulting, analysis and testimony in numerous intellectual property matters, where infringement of structural, composition and process patents was revealed by microscopic examination of the material or device. We look at the structure to see what it is (for comparison with a designed structure) and to see what it says about the process that formed the structure. Some work uses our unique capability of making calibrated images and ultra-precise measurements.

We use simple, concise language to express how AFM works and what the pictures show, drawing appropriate analogies to everyday experiences. We are skilled at organizing data and presenting images that accurately support and illustrate our conclusions.

Wondering whether we can help win your case? Contact us or read more on our website.

EXPERT WITNESS
VEHICLE FIRES AND COLLISION

JOHN MICHAEL AGOSTI & ASSOCIATES
FIRE INVESTIGATIONS
johnagosti@earthlink.net

JOHN MICHAEL AGOSTI

Fire Analyst and Consultant

23808 North Overhill
Lake Zurich, Illinois 60047
Phone: 847-682-6793
E-mail: johnagosti@earthlink.net
Web: www.arsonexpert.com

As a member of the Skokie, Illinois Fire Department for twenty-eight years, Mr. Agosti progressed from a Firefighter/Paramedic to the position of Deputy Fire Chief. Mr. Agosti has responded to hundreds of major fire and crime scenes and has testified in court on the conclusions of his investigations. His investigations have led to successful criminal indictments and convictions. Mr. Agosti's fire department responsibilities included the review of all construction plans for compliance to fire and building codes. His expertise in building construction and fire spread, lends a unique blend to his fire investigation capabilities.

In addition to his fire department exposure to hundreds of fire investigations, Mr. Agosti has extensive experience in the private sector also. Over the past 11 years Mr. Agosti has conducted over eight hundred fire investigations as a private fire cause and origin analyst.

Practice areas include:

- Fire and Explosions:
  - Arson defense/prosecution; gas explosions; vehicular fires; structure fires; fire deaths/injuries.
- Building and Fire Codes:
  - Fire/Building code violation; Life Safety Code violations; smoke detector issues; fire prevention analysis.
- Fire Department Practices:
  - Fire department operations/practices/management; firefighter deaths/injuries/safety.

Mr. Agosti has an Associates Degree in Fire Science and Technology. He is also certified as a Fire and Arson Investigator.

PROJECT EXPERIENCE

Fire and building code analysis
Automobile accident reconstruction
Gas leak surveys
Distribution gas pipe ruptures and leaks
Investigation of fire fatalities and electrocutions
Investigation of bombings
Investigation for cause and origin of fires and explosions

(This Listing Continued)

PROFESSIONAL SOCIETIES

National Fire Protection Association
Fire Marshals Association of North America
International Association of Fire Chiefs
Building Officials/Code Administrators International
Fire Investigators Strike Force
Illinois Fire Inspectors Association
International Association of Arson Investigators

FIRE INVESTIGATORS

JOHN MICHAEL AGOSTI & ASSOCIATES
FIRE INVESTIGATIONS
johnagosti@earthlink.net

JOHN MICHAEL AGOSTI

Fire Analyst and Consultant

23808 North Overhill
Lake Zurich, Illinois 60047
Phone: 847-682-6793
E-mail: johnagosti@earthlink.net
Web: www.arsonexpert.com

As a member of the Skokie, Illinois Fire Department for twenty-eight years, Mr. Agosti progressed from a Firefighter/Paramedic to the position of Deputy Fire Chief. Mr. Agosti has responded to hundreds of major fire and crime scenes and has testified in court on the conclusions of his investigations. His investigations have led to successful criminal indictments and convictions. Mr. Agosti's fire department responsibilities included the review of all construction plans for compliance to fire and building codes. His expertise in building construction and fire spread, lends a unique blend to his fire investigation capabilities.

In addition to his fire department exposure to hundreds of fire investigations, Mr. Agosti has extensive experience in the private sector also. Over the past 11 years Mr. Agosti has conducted over eight hundred fire investigations as a private fire cause and origin analyst.

Practice areas include:

- Fire and Explosions:
  - Arson defense/prosecution; gas explosions; vehicular fires; structure fires; fire deaths/injuries.
- Building and Fire Codes:
  - Fire/Building code violation; Life Safety Code violations; smoke detector issues; fire prevention analysis.
- Fire Department Practices:
  - Fire department operations/practices/management; firefighter deaths/injuries/safety.

Mr. Agosti has an Associates Degree in Fire Science and Technology. He is also certified as a Fire and Arson Investigator.

PROJECT EXPERIENCE

Fire and building code analysis
Automobile accident reconstruction
Gas leak surveys
Distribution gas pipe ruptures and leaks
Investigation of fire fatalities and electrocutions
Investigation of bombings
Investigation for cause and origin of fires and explosions

PROFESSIONAL SOCIETIES

National Fire Protection Association
Fire Marshals Association of North America
International Association of Fire Chiefs
Building Officials/Code Administrators International
Fire Investigators Strike Force
Illinois Fire Inspectors Association
International Association of Arson Investigators

GENERAL INVESTIGATORS

International Investigators, Inc.

Forensic Accounting and Fraud Audits
CPA's and CFE's
3216 North Pennsylvania Street
Indianapolis, IN 46205-3414
Tele. (317) 925-1496 1-800-403-8111 Fax (317) 926-1177
(Email) info@iiiweb.net and timwilcox@iiiweb.net
Web Site Address: www.internationalinvestigators.com

C. Tim Wilcox, President Stanley R. Large, Senior Investigator

Brenda McGinley
Investigations Coordinator

Russell L. Ferguson
Technical Consultant

Jennifer J. Lambert
Sr. Investigative Consultant

International Investigators, Inc. is licensed and insured, with over 45 years of experience. Formed in 1960 by former FBI Agents. Investigative capabilities throughout North America and over 70 countries.

We provide State of the Art computer investigations, with access to over 6,000 computer data bases, and have investigative and intelligence capability worldwide. We provide comprehensive investigations for the legal community, to include:

Asset & Financial Investigations - Develop individual and/or corporate net worth and locate hidden assets.
Liability Investigations - Investigation of accidents.
Accident Reconstruction - Accident scene investigation - NOT an engineering service.
Litigation - Background profiles on corporations and individuals involved in litigated matters.
Due Diligence - In-depth look at all aspects of corporations and significant individuals.
Criminal Defense - Investigation of potential witnesses and review of evidence.
Forensic Laboratory Services & Crime Scene Analysis
Electronic Eavesdropping Countermeasures Sweeps-(TSCM)
Jury Panel - Background information on jury members.
Workers' Compensation - Background profile and investigation of circumstances of the accident, as well as the claimant's work and claim history. Discreet surveillance of claimant's activities.
Locates & Skip Tracing
Statements Recorded, Audio, Video or Both
Handwriting & Document Examinations
Legal Testimony
Child Custody - Determination of welfare of children and location of missing children.
Contested Wills, Estate Research, Location of Assets
Domestic - Background and financial asset investigations, as well as surveillance of individuals.

Surveillance - Utilize State of the Art video camcorders and 35mm equipment, to include ultra-discreet equipment and high-tech techniques. Unobtrusive vans with concealed periscopes.
GPS - Cellular Vehicle Tracking.
Polygraph or PSE Examinations - Pre-stipulated or stipulated tests.
Subpoena Services - Service of legal documents. U.S. and worldwide.
Environmental, Toxic Contamination, Spills Investigation of Negligent or Responsible Parties.
Computer Security - Highest Level
Assessment - Security Review of Infrastructure, Systems, Policies & Procedures
Perimeter - External Penetration and Vulnerability Testing - Hacking
Monitoring - 24-7 Managed Internet Firewall Monitoring Services
Intrusion - 24-7 Managed Intrusion Detection System (IDS) Monitoring Services

(This Listing Continued)

Members: National Association of Legal Investigators
World Association of Detectives
American Society for Industrial Security
Society of Competitive Intelligence Professionals
Council of International Investigators
National Association of Professional Process Servers
World Investigative Network

METALLURGY & MATERIALS SCIENCE ENGINEERING

Advanced Surface Microscopy, Inc.

3250 N. Post Road, Suite 120
Indianapolis, IN 46226 USA
Phone: +1-317-895-5630
Fax: +1-317-895-5652
www.asmicro.com
info@asmicro.com

TOLL FREE: 1-800-374-8557 (US & Canada)

Advanced Surface Microscopy, Inc. is an independent analytical testing and research laboratory, specializing in materials and device analysis using Atomic Force Microscopy (AFM) and related techniques (MFM, EFM).

Any surface you can touch is a potential target for analysis. Since 1990, we've completed more than 1000 analytical projects for over 200 customers, examining more than 100 types of materials and devices, including:

- pharmaceutical materials
- optical discs (CD, DVD, HD-DVD, Blu-Ray)
- magnetic disks and recording heads
- DNA and other biopolymers
- semiconductors, electronics
- paper, polymers and much more.

Don Chernoff, Ph.D., has provided expert consulting, analysis and testimony in numerous intellectual property matters, where infringement of structural, composition and process patents was revealed by microscopic examination of the material or device. We look at the structure to see what it is (for comparison with a designed structure) and to see what it says about the process that formed the structure. Some work uses our unique capability of making calibrated images and ultra-precise measurements.

We use simple, concise language to express how AFM works and what the pictures show, drawing appropriate analogies to everyday experiences. We are skilled at organizing data and presenting images that accurately support and illustrate our conclusions.

Wondering whether we can help win your case? Contact us or read more on our website.

MISSING PERSONS

International Investigators, Inc.

Forensic Accounting and Fraud Audits
CPA's and CFE's
3216 North Pennsylvania Street
Indianapolis, IN 46205-3414
Tele. (317) 925-1496 1-800-403-8111 Fax (317) 926-1177
(Email) info@iiiweb.net and timwilcox@iiiweb.net
Web Site Address: www.internationalinvestigators.com

(This Listing Continued)

C. Tim Wilcox, President | Stanley R. Large, Senior Investigator

Brenda McGinley
Investigations Coordinator

Russell L. Ferguson, Technical Consultant | Jennifer J. Lambert, Sr. Investigative Consultant

International Investigators, Inc. is licensed and insured, with over 45 years of experience. Formed in 1960 by former FBI Agents. Investigative capabilities throughout North America and over 70 countries.

We provide State of the Art computer investigations, with access to over 6,000 computer data bases, and have investigative and intelligence capability worldwide. We provide comprehensive investigations for the legal community, to include:

Asset & Financial Investigations - Develop individual and/or corporate net worth and locate hidden assets.
Liability Investigations - Investigation of accidents.
Accident Reconstruction - Accident scene investigation - NOT an engineering service.
Litigation - Background profiles on corporations and individuals involved in litigated matters.
Due Diligence - In-depth look at all aspects of corporations and significant individuals.
Criminal Defense - Investigation of potential witnesses and review of evidence.
Forensic Laboratory Services & Crime Scene Analysis
Electronic Eavesdropping Countermeasures Sweeps-(TSCM)
Jury Panel - Background information on jury members.
Workers' Compensation - Background profile and investigation of circumstances of the accident, as well as the claimant's work and claim history. Discreet surveillance of claimant's activities.
Locates & Skip Tracing
Statements Recorded, Audio, Video or Both
Handwriting & Document Examinations
Legal Testimony
Child Custody - Determination of welfare of children and location of missing children.
Contested Wills, Estate Research, Location of Assets
Domestic - Background and financial asset investigations, as well as surveillance of individuals.

Surveillance - Utilize State of the Art video camcorders and 35mm equipment, to include ultra-discreet equipment and high-tech techniques. Unobtrusive vans with concealed periscopes.
GPS - Cellular Vehicle Tracking.
Polygraph or PSE Examinations - Pre-stipulated or stipulated tests.
Subpoena Services - Service of legal documents. U.S. and worldwide.
Environmental, Toxic Contamination, Spills Investigation of Negligent or Responsible Parties.
Computer Security - Highest Level
- **Assessment** - Security Review of Infrastructure, Systems, Policies & Procedures
- **Perimeter** - External Penetration and Vulnerability Testing - Hacking
- **Monitoring** - 24-7 Managed Internet Firewall Monitoring Services
- **Intrusion** - 24-7 Managed Intrusion Detection System (IDS) Monitoring Services

Members:
- National Association of Legal Investigators
- World Association of Detectives
- American Society for Industrial Security
- Society of Competitive Intelligence Professionals
- Council of International Investigators
- National Association of Professional Process Servers
- World Investigative Network

PROCESS SERVERS & DOCUMENT DELIVERY SERVICES

International Investigators, Inc.

Forensic Accounting and Fraud Audits
CPA's and CFE's
3216 North Pennsylvania Street
Indianapolis, IN 46205-3414
Tele. (317) 925-1496 1-800-403-8111 Fax (317) 926-1177
(Email) info@iiiweb.net and timwilcox@iiiweb.net
Web Site Address: www.internationalinvestigators.com

C. Tim Wilcox, President | Stanley R. Large, Senior Investigator

Brenda McGinley
Investigations Coordinator

Russell L. Ferguson, Technical Consultant | Jennifer J. Lambert, Sr. Investigative Consultant

International Investigators, Inc. is licensed and insured, with over 45 years of experience. Formed in 1960 by former FBI Agents. Investigative capabilities throughout North America and over 70 countries.

We provide State of the Art computer investigations, with access to over 6,000 computer data bases, and have investigative and intelligence capability worldwide. We provide comprehensive investigations for the legal community, to include:

Asset & Financial Investigations - Develop individual and/or corporate net worth and locate hidden assets.
Liability Investigations - Investigation of accidents.
Accident Reconstruction - Accident scene investigation - NOT an engineering service.
Litigation - Background profiles on corporations and individuals involved in litigated matters.
Due Diligence - In-depth look at all aspects of corporations and significant individuals.
Criminal Defense - Investigation of potential witnesses and review of evidence.
Forensic Laboratory Services & Crime Scene Analysis
Electronic Eavesdropping Countermeasures Sweeps-(TSCM)
Jury Panel - Background information on jury members.
Workers' Compensation - Background profile and investigation of circumstances of the accident, as well as the claimant's work and claim history. Discreet surveillance of claimant's activities.
Locates & Skip Tracing
Statements Recorded, Audio, Video or Both
Handwriting & Document Examinations
Legal Testimony
Child Custody - Determination of welfare of children and location of missing children.
Contested Wills, Estate Research, Location of Assets
Domestic - Background and financial asset investigations, as well as surveillance of individuals.

Surveillance - Utilize State of the Art video camcorders and 35mm equipment, to include ultra-discreet equipment and high-tech techniques. Unobtrusive vans with concealed periscopes.
GPS - Cellular Vehicle Tracking.
Polygraph or PSE Examinations - Pre-stipulated or stipulated tests.
Subpoena Services - Service of legal documents. U.S. and worldwide.
Environmental, Toxic Contamination, Spills Investigation of Negligent or Responsible Parties.
Computer Security - Highest Level
- **Assessment** - Security Review of Infrastructure, Systems, Policies & Procedures
- **Perimeter** - External Penetration and Vulnerability Testing - Hacking
- **Monitoring** - 24-7 Managed Internet Firewall Monitoring Services
- **Intrusion** - 24-7 Managed Intrusion Detection System (IDS) Monitoring Services

(This Listing Continued)

PROCESS SERVERS & DOCUMENT DELIVERY SERVICES (cont'd)

International Investigators, Inc. (cont'd)

Members: National Association of Legal Investigators
World Association of Detectives
American Society for Industrial Security
Society of Competitive Intelligence Professionals
Council of International Investigators
National Association of Professional Process Servers
World Investigative Network

SKIP TRACERS

International Investigators, Inc.

Forensic Accounting and Fraud Audits
CPA's and CFE's
3216 North Pennsylvania Street
Indianapolis, IN 46205-3414
Tele. (317) 925-1496 1-800-403-8111 Fax (317) 926-1177
(Email) info@iiiweb.net and timwilcox@iiiweb.net
Web Site Address: www.internationalinvestigators.com

C. Tim Wilcox, President Stanley R. Large, Senior Investigator

Brenda McGinley
Investigations Coordinator

Russell L. Ferguson Jennifer J. Lambert
Technical Consultant Sr. Investigative Consultant

International Investigators, Inc. is licensed and insured, with over 45 years of experience. Formed in 1960 by former FBI Agents. Investigative capabilities throughout North America and over 70 countries.

We provide State of the Art computer investigations, with access to over 6,000 computer data bases, and have investigative and intelligence capability worldwide. We provide comprehensive investigations for the legal community, to include:

Asset & Financial Investigations - Develop individual and/or corporate net worth and locate hidden assets.
Liability Investigations - Investigation of accidents.
Accident Reconstruction - Accident scene investigation - NOT an engineering service.
Litigation - Background profiles on corporations and individuals involved in litigated matters.
Due Diligence - In-depth look at all aspects of corporations and significant individuals.
Criminal Defense - Investigation of potential witnesses and review of evidence. **Forensic Laboratory Services & Crime Scene Analysis**
Electronic Eavesdropping Countermeasures Sweeps-(TSCM)
Jury Panel - Background information on jury members.

(This Listing Continued)

Workers' Compensation - Background profile and investigation of circumstances of the accident, as well as the claimant's work and claim history. Discreet surveillance of claimant's activities.
Locates & Skip Tracing
Statements Recorded, Audio, Video or Both
Handwriting & Document Examinations
Legal Testimony
Child Custody - Determination of welfare of children and location of missing children.
Contested Wills, Estate Research, Location of Assets
Domestic - Background and financial asset investigations, as well as surveillance of individuals.

Surveillance - Utilize State of the Art video camcorders and 35mm equipment, to include ultra-discreet equipment and high-tech techniques. Unobtrusive vans with concealed periscopes.
GPS - Cellular Vehicle Tracking.
Polygraph or PSE Examinations - Pre-stipulated or stipulated tests.
Subpoena Services - Service of legal documents. U.S. and worldwide.
Environmental, Toxic Contamination, Spills Investigation of Negligent or Responsible Parties.
Computer Security - Highest Level
Assessment - Security Review of Infrastructure, Systems, Policies & Procedures
Perimeter - External Penetration and Vulnerability Testing - Hacking
Monitoring - 24-7 Managed Internet Firewall Monitoring Services
Intrusion - 24-7 Managed Intrusion Detection System (IDS) Monitoring Services

Members: National Association of Legal Investigators
World Association of Detectives
American Society for Industrial Security
Society of Competitive Intelligence Professionals
Council of International Investigators
National Association of Professional Process Servers
World Investigative Network

TRADE SECRETS THEFT INVESTIGATION

International Investigators, Inc.

Forensic Accounting and Fraud Audits
CPA's and CFE's
3216 North Pennsylvania Street
Indianapolis, IN 46205-3414
Tele. (317) 925-1496 1-800-403-8111 Fax (317) 926-1177
(Email) info@iiiweb.net and timwilcox@iiiweb.net
Web Site Address: www.internationalinvestigators.com

C. Tim Wilcox, President Stanley R. Large, Senior Investigator

Brenda McGinley
Investigations Coordinator

Russell L. Ferguson Jennifer J. Lambert
Technical Consultant Sr. Investigative Consultant

International Investigators, Inc. is licensed and insured, with over 45 years of experience. Formed in 1960 by former FBI Agents. Investigative capabilities throughout North America and over 70 countries.

We provide State of the Art computer investigations, with access to over 6,000 computer data bases, and have investigative and intelligence capability worldwide. We provide comprehensive investigations for the legal community, to include:

(This Listing Continued)

Asset & Financial Investigations - Develop individual and/or corporate net worth and locate hidden assets.
Liability Investigations - Investigation of accidents.
Accident Reconstruction - Accident scene investigation - NOT an engineering service.
Litigation - Background profiles on corporations and individuals involved in litigated matters.
Due Diligence - In-depth look at all aspects of corporations and significant individuals.
Criminal Defense - Investigation of potential witnesses and review of evidence.
Forensic Laboratory Services & Crime Scene Analysis
Electronic Eavesdropping Countermeasures Sweeps-(TSCM)
Jury Panel - Background information on jury members.
Workers' Compensation - Background profile and investigation of circumstances of the accident, as well as the claimant's work and claim history. Discreet surveillance of claimant's activities.
Locates & Skip Tracing
Statements Recorded, Audio, Video or Both
Handwriting & Document Examinations
Legal Testimony
Child Custody - Determination of welfare of children and location of missing children.
Contested Wills, Estate Research, Location of Assets
Domestic - Background and financial asset investigations, as well as surveillance of individuals.

Surveillance - Utilize State of the Art video camcorders and 35mm equipment, to include ultra-discreet equipment and high-tech techniques. Unobtrusive vans with concealed periscopes.
GPS - Cellular Vehicle Tracking.
Polygraph or PSE Examinations - Pre-stipulated or stipulated tests.
Subpoena Services - Service of legal documents. U.S. and worldwide.
Environmental, Toxic Contamination, Spills Investigation of Negligent or Responsible Parties.
Computer Security - Highest Level
Assessment - Security Review of Infrastructure, Systems, Policies & Procedures
Perimeter - External Penetration and Vulnerability Testing - Hacking
Monitoring - 24-7 Managed Internet Firewall Monitoring Services
Intrusion - 24-7 Managed Intrusion Detection System (IDS) Monitoring Services

Members: National Association of Legal Investigators
World Association of Detectives
American Society for Industrial Security
Society of Competitive Intelligence Professionals
Council of International Investigators
National Association of Professional Process Servers
World Investigative Network

TSCM/TECHNICAL SURVEILLANCE COUNTERMEASURES

International Investigators, Inc.

Forensic Accounting and Fraud Audits
CPA's and CFE's
3216 North Pennsylvania Street
Indianapolis, IN 46205-3414
Tele. (317) 925-1496 1-800-403-8111 Fax (317) 926-1177
(Email) info@iiiweb.net and timwilcox@iiiweb.net
Web Site Address: www.internationalinvestigators.com

C. Tim Wilcox, President — Stanley R. Large, Senior Investigator

Brenda McGinley
Investigations Coordinator

(This Listing Continued)

Russell L. Ferguson
Technical Consultant

Jennifer J. Lambert
Sr. Investigative Consultant

International Investigators, Inc. is licensed and insured, with over 45 years of experience. Formed in 1960 by former FBI Agents. Investigative capabilities throughout North America and over 70 countries.

We provide State of the Art computer investigations, with access to over 6,000 computer data bases, and have investigative and intelligence capability worldwide. We provide comprehensive investigations for the legal community, to include:

Asset & Financial Investigations - Develop individual and/or corporate net worth and locate hidden assets.
Liability Investigations - Investigation of accidents.
Accident Reconstruction - Accident scene investigation - NOT an engineering service.
Litigation - Background profiles on corporations and individuals involved in litigated matters.
Due Diligence - In-depth look at all aspects of corporations and significant individuals.
Criminal Defense - Investigation of potential witnesses and review of evidence.
Forensic Laboratory Services & Crime Scene Analysis
Electronic Eavesdropping Countermeasures Sweeps-(TSCM)
Jury Panel - Background information on jury members.
Workers' Compensation - Background profile and investigation of circumstances of the accident, as well as the claimant's work and claim history. Discreet surveillance of claimant's activities.
Locates & Skip Tracing
Statements Recorded, Audio, Video or Both
Handwriting & Document Examinations
Legal Testimony
Child Custody - Determination of welfare of children and location of missing children.
Contested Wills, Estate Research, Location of Assets
Domestic - Background and financial asset investigations, as well as surveillance of individuals.

Surveillance - Utilize State of the Art video camcorders and 35mm equipment, to include ultra-discreet equipment and high-tech techniques. Unobtrusive vans with concealed periscopes.
GPS - Cellular Vehicle Tracking.
Polygraph or PSE Examinations - Pre-stipulated or stipulated tests.
Subpoena Services - Service of legal documents. U.S. and worldwide.
Environmental, Toxic Contamination, Spills Investigation of Negligent or Responsible Parties.
Computer Security - Highest Level
Assessment - Security Review of Infrastructure, Systems, Policies & Procedures
Perimeter - External Penetration and Vulnerability Testing - Hacking
Monitoring - 24-7 Managed Internet Firewall Monitoring Services
Intrusion - 24-7 Managed Intrusion Detection System (IDS) Monitoring Services

Members: National Association of Legal Investigators
World Association of Detectives
American Society for Industrial Security
Society of Competitive Intelligence Professionals
Council of International Investigators
National Association of Professional Process Servers
World Investigative Network

(This Listing Continued)

(This Listing Continued)

We provide State of the Art computer investigations, with access to over 6,000 computer data bases, and have investigative and intelligence capability worldwide. We provide comprehensive investigations for the legal community, to include:

Asset & Financial Investigations - Develop individual and/or corporate net worth and locate hidden assets.
Liability Investigations - Investigation of accidents.
Accident Reconstruction - Accident scene investigation - NOT an engineering service.
Litigation - Background profiles on corporations and individuals involved in litigated matters.
Due Diligence - In-depth look at all aspects of corporations and significant individuals.
Criminal Defense - Investigation of potential witnesses and review of evidence.
Forensic Laboratory Services & Crime Scene Analysis
Electronic Eavesdropping Countermeasures Sweeps-(TSCM)
Jury Panel - Background information on jury members.
Workers' Compensation - Background profile and investigation of circumstances of the accident, as well as the claimant's work and claim history. Discreet surveillance of claimant's activities.
Locates & Skip Tracing
Statements Recorded, Audio, Video or Both
Handwriting & Document Examinations
Legal Testimony
Child Custody - Determination of welfare of children and location of missing children.
Contested Wills, Estate Research, Location of Assets
Domestic - Background and financial asset investigations, as well as surveillance of individuals.

Surveillance - Utilize State of the Art video camcorders and 35mm equipment, to include ultra-discreet equipment and high-tech techniques. Unobtrusive vans with concealed periscopes.
GPS - Cellular Vehicle Tracking.
Polygraph or PSE Examinations - Pre-stipulated or stipulated tests.
Subpoena Services - Service of legal documents. U.S. and worldwide.
Environmental, Toxic Contamination, Spills Investigation of Negligent or Responsible Parties.
Computer Security - Highest Level
Assessment - Security Review of Infrastructure, Systems, Policies & Procedures
Perimeter - External Penetration and Vulnerability Testing - Hacking
Monitoring - 24-7 Managed Internet Firewall Monitoring Services
Intrusion - 24-7 Managed Intrusion Detection System (IDS) Monitoring Services

Members: National Association of Legal Investigators
World Association of Detectives
American Society for Industrial Security
Society of Competitive Intelligence Professionals
Council of International Investigators
National Association of Professional Process Servers
World Investigative Network

SOUTH BEND,* 105,511, *St. Joseph Co.*

COURT REPORTERS

MIDWEST PROFESSIONAL REPORTING, INC.
(815) 968-0015

SERVING ALL OF NORTHERN INDIANA & SOUTHERN MICHIGAN

300 No. Michigan Street
South Bend, Indiana 46601

(800) 270-3121
(574) 255-3121
FAX: (574) 258-5939

17 Certified Shorthand Reporters
Depositions Hearings Arbitrations

In our commitment to excellence we provide:

- DAILY COPY
- DEPOSITION SUITES
- EXPEDITED DELIVERY
- ALPHA INDEXING
- LITIGATION SUPPORT
- ASCII FORMATS
- MINI TRANSCRIPTS
- VIDEOCONFERENCING
- VIDEOTAPING
- REALTIME REPORTERS

Member
National Court Reporters Association
Indiana Shorthand Reporters Association

(800) 270-3121

OLMSTED & ASSOCIATES Ltd.

Charles A. Olmsted, C.S.R., R.P.R., C.M.

SOUTH BEND OFFICE800-439-4478574-256-5400FAX 574-256-5800

e-mail: olmsted800@aol.com

Certified Shorthand ReportersDEPOSITIONS - HEARINGS - ARBITRATIONSVIDEO TAPING

Serving all of Northern Indiana and Southwestern Michigan

Including - but not limited to - such cities as:

(This Listing Continued)

COURT REPORTERS (cont'd)

Olmsted & Associates Ltd. (cont'd)

Angola	LaGrange
Auburn	LaPorte
Benton Harbor	Merrillville
Berrien Springs	Michigan City
Cassopolis	New Buffalo
Columbia City	Niles
Crown Point	Peru
Edwardsburg	Plymouth
Elkhart	Portage
Fort Wayne	South Bend
Goshen	St. Joseph, MI
Huntington	Valparaiso
Knox	Wabash

Warsaw

We have over 40 years of experience and offer the following:

- Video-Conference
- Conference Rooms Available
- Daily Copy Specialist
- Teleconference
- E-Transcript
- CD/Diskettes
- Patent/Trademark/Copyright Matters
- Subpoena Service
- Video Taping
- Transcript/Video-Synching
- Document Scanning and Archiving
- Exhibits/Transcripts Hyperlinked

...Anywhere the Spoken Word is Preserved

Special Commissioner-United States District Court
Quality Verbatim Court Reporting Services.
Certificate of Merit Reporter
Notary Publics

MEMBER
National Court Reporters Association
Indiana Shorthand Reporters Association
Michigan Shorthand Reporters Association
United States Court Reporters Association

800-439-4478

VIDEO TAPE SERVICES

OLMSTED & ASSOCIATES Ltd.

Charles A. Olmsted, C.S.R., R.P.R., C.M.

SOUTH BEND OFFICE
800-439-4478
574-256-5400
FAX 574-256-5800

e-mail: olmsted800@aol.com

Certified Shorthand Reporters
DEPOSITIONS - HEARINGS - ARBITRATIONS
VIDEO TAPING

(This Listing Continued)

Serving all of Northern Indiana and Southwestern Michigan

Including - but not limited to - such cities as:

Angola	LaGrange
Auburn	LaPorte
Benton Harbor	Merrillville
Berrien Springs	Michigan City
Cassopolis	New Buffalo
Columbia City	Niles
Crown Point	Peru
Edwardsburg	Plymouth
Elkhart	Portage
Fort Wayne	South Bend
Goshen	St. Joseph, MI
Huntington	Valparaiso
Knox	Wabash

Warsaw

We have over 40 years of experience and offer the following:

- Video-Conference
- Conference Rooms Available
- Daily Copy Specialist
- Teleconference
- E-Transcript
- CD/Diskettes
- Patent/Trademark/Copyright Matters
- Subpoena Service
- Video Taping
- Transcript/Video-Synching
- Document Scanning and Archiving
- Exhibits/Transcripts Hyperlinked

...Anywhere the Spoken Word is Preserved

Special Commissioner-United States District Court
Quality Verbatim Court Reporting Services.
Certificate of Merit Reporter
Notary Publics

MEMBER
National Court Reporters Association
Indiana Shorthand Reporters Association
Michigan Shorthand Reporters Association
United States Court Reporters Association

800-439-4478

VALPARAISO,* 24,414, *Porter Co.*

COURT REPORTERS

SEIDEL & SASSE COURT REPORTERS, INC.

150 W. Lincolnway, Suite 1005
Valparaiso, IN 46383
800-219-0600
219-462-3201 Fax
reporters@seidelsasse.com

Kathryn M. Seidel and Drea Sasse founded Seidel & Sasse Court Reporters, Inc. in 1996. Both have been working reporters for 25 years, and they continue to report as well as oversee their agency in order to maintain the high standards that their clients have come to expect.

(This Listing Continued)

All of their reporters are certified, professional and committed to providing superior transcripts in a timely fashion at a reasonable rate. Their experience, accuracy, reliability and integrity have earned them a reputation of excellence in the court reporting field.

SERVICES

- Deposition/Arbitration Reporting
- Expertise in Technical/Medical Testimony
- Daily/Expedited Transcripts
- RealLegal E-Transcripts/ASCIIs
- Realtime Reporting
- Video Deps/Video Conferencing
- Huge Conference Rooms
- Keyword Indexing provided with all transcripts

Serving Northwest Indiana and Chicagoland areas

WHITELAND, 3,958, *Johnson*

EXPERT WITNESS
FORENSIC ACCOUNTING

LOPSHIRE & COMPANY
Fraud and Forensic Specialist
www.lcforensic.com

Larry Lopshire
"I'll even fly myself to get to the scene!"

410 U.S. 31 North
Whiteland, Indiana 46194
P: (317) 535-5588
F: (317) 535-0808
larry@lcforensic.com

Lopshire & Company is a certified public accounting firm with extensive knowledge and experience in investigation, analysis, and consulting experience. Since 1990, Lopshire & Company has been combining its litigation and fiscal examination to meet the needs of its clients.

Services Offered
General Forensic Accounting
Fraud Investigation
Litigation Support

Certifications and Memberships
Certified Fraud Examiner, Association of Certified Fraud Examiners
Featured Associate Member, Association of Certified Fraud Examiners - 1998/1999
Recognized by National Association of Forensic Accountants
American Institute of Certified Public Accountants
Indiana Association of Certified Public Accountants

CEDAR RAPIDS,* 108,751, *Linn Co.*

COURT REPORTERS

KOOL & NYGREN, INC.
CERTIFIED SHORTHAND REPORTERS
CERTIFIED LEGAL VIDEO SPECIALIST
422 2nd Avenue S.E.
Cedar Rapids, Iowa 52401
(319) 362-2200
FAX (319) 399-1617

*** 1-800-332-2225 ***

Norman L. Kool, CSR, CM
Wesley E. Nygren, CSR, CM, CLVS
Sharon Clark, Office Coordinator
Certified Staff Reporters
ALSO SERVING IOWA CITY AND UNIVERSITY OF IOWA HOSPITALS
VIDEOCONFERENCING

Complimentary Conference Room
Videotaping Services
Computer Assisted Transcription
Litigation Support
ASCII
Discovery ZX
Photocopying

ESTABLISHED 1974
Reference: The Bench and Bar of Linn and Johnson Counties in Iowa

DES MOINES,* 193,187, *Polk Co.*

COURT REPORTERS

HUNEY - VAUGHN COURT REPORTERS, LTD.

604 Locust - Suite 307
Des Moines, Iowa 50309
(Offices Also In Davenport and Council Bluffs, Iowa)

George R. Huney, Principal
Mervin E. Vaughn, Principal

Staff of 15 Certified Reporters
9 Member Support Staff

(This Listing Continued)

CERTIFIED SHORTHAND REPORTERS

Telephone: 515-288-4910
Wats: 1-800-383-4911
Fax: 515-237-4096

Certified by State Examining Board
Video Teleconference Center
CaseView/Real-Time Reporting
Condensed Transcript
Complete Deposition Service
Full Service Copy Center
Full Color Copy/Exhibit Reproduction
Poster Prints/Legal Exhibits
Deposition Rooms Available
References: The Bench and Bar, Polk County, Iowa

1-800-383-4911

schedule@huneyvaughn.com

LAUNSPACH, LEWIS, BURNS & KLUENDER, INC.
Certified Shorthand Reporters

206 Sixth Avenue
1100 Midland Building
Des Moines, IA 50309-4002
515-282-7884 Fax 515-282-2917
1-800-872-6464

- Conference Room
- Condensed Transcripts
- E-Transcript
- Daily Copy and Expedited Delivery
- Real-time Reporting
- Videotape Services
- Experienced Registered Professional Reporters

Email: info@llbk.com

IOWA CITY,* 59,738, *Johnson Co.*